THE OFFICIAL ENCYCLOPEDIA OF THE NATIONAL HOCKEY LEAGUE®

TOTAL HOCKEY

SECOND EDITION

DAN DIAMOND
EDITOR

RALPH DINGER
JAMES DUPLACEY
ERIC ZWEIG
MANAGING EDITORS

GARY MEAGHER
SENIOR CONTRIBUTING EDITOR

IGOR KUPERMAN
INTERNATIONAL EDITOR

JOHN PASTERNAK
DATA MANAGER

ERNIE FITZSIMMONS
CONSULTING STATISTICIAN

PAUL BONTJE
ASSISTANT EDITOR

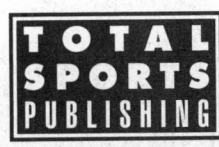

TOTAL SPORTS PUBLISHING

For everyone who cares for the game

and for Maurice "Rocket" Richard

For information about permission to reproduce selections from this book, please write to:
Permissions, Total Sports Publishing,
100 Enterprise Drive, Kingston, New York 12401.

Official publication of the National Hockey League

ISBN: 1-892129-85-X

Library of Congress Card Number: 00-107051

Printed in Canada by vistainfo, Scarborough, Ontario

10 9 8 7 6 5 4 3 2 1

TOTAL HOCKEY

CONTENTS

I ORIGINS

II THE STATE OF THE GAME

III THE NATIONAL HOCKEY LEAGUE

IV JUNIOR AND OTHER PRO HOCKEY

V THE INTERNATIONAL GAME

VI OTHER FACETS OF THE GAME

VII STATISTICAL AND BIOGRAPHICAL REGISTERS

OFFICE OF THE COMMISSIONER

Welcome to *Total Hockey*, the Official Encyclopedia of the National Hockey League. This is the second edition. When first published in 1998, *Total Hockey* was acclaimed by the hockey world, immediately becoming both a bestseller and the game's ultimate source of information.

In the two years since, *Total Hockey* has grown with the game in all directions. As we enter a new century, stories about hockey's origins take us back to the earliest days of the sport, putting us on the ice and in the seats at the turn of the previous century. You will find a three-story tribute to the late Maurice "Rocket" Richard. Extensive coverage on the state of today's game deals with everything from elite player development to pickup hockey in Canada, the United States and Europe.

Total Hockey's coverage of the NHL includes histories of every franchise from the oldest, the Montreal Canadiens, to the newest, the Columbus Blue Jackets and Minnesota Wild. There are summaries of every season, stories from some of today's top stars describing the different routes they took to reach the NHL, and a complete listing of 7,221 draft choices.

There are hypothetical Olympic rosters for each major hockey country for the 2002 Winter Games in Salt Lake City and country-by-country profiles of hockey everywhere the game is played. How many teams are there in New Zealand? How are the playoffs organized in Norway? The answers are here.

And there is more. There are stories about arenas, sticks and goalie masks, and about hockey on television and in the movies, in video games and on the Internet. A huge list of hockey books and a study of the fine art of the hockey cliché are also included. It is quite an array.

Any sport's encyclopedia is judged by the quality of its player register, and it is here that *Total Hockey* really shines. There is complete career coverage of every player ever to appear in an NHL game, from midget hockey to junior, senior, minor pro and European leagues. The editors have corresponded with hundreds of historians and statisticians from around the world to make *Total Hockey*'s player panels hockey's gold standard for information. There are tens of thousands of lines of statistics here that have never been published before.

Total Hockey is a remarkable record of the past, present and future for the NHL and the world of hockey.

Read on and enjoy.

Gary B. Bettman

Gary B. Bettman
Commissioner

Introduction

WELCOME TO THE SECOND EDITION of *Total Hockey*, the official encyclopedia of the National Hockey League. It is a book that builds upon the achievements of its predecessor and is a result of the success of that first edition. When we set out to create a definitive hockey encyclopedia in the late stages of the previous century, we did so knowing that the judgment of the marketplace would rule. Would people care enough about the nuances and historical record of hockey to buy a 2,000-page encyclopedia? It turned out they would and did. Positive reviews led to strong sales and to a buzz throughout hockey communities around the world. From the day of publication in October, 1998, we received the first of what eventually would grow into thousands of e-mails, faxes and letters packed with suggestions for features, additional lines of statistics and some sharp-eyed proofreading. The result is this second edition, which, with its many new stories and vastly expanded statistical registers, covers hockey in both breadth and depth.

One thing hasn't changed: *Total Hockey* celebrates the history of the sport, pays close attention to how today's hockey works and, above all, respects the game and the accomplishments of the men (and women) who play it.

The book is divided into seven sections:

- Section I deals with the origins of the game and its earliest days.
- Section II examines the state of the game in four spheres: Canada, the United States, Europe and women's hockey.
- Section III tells the story of the National Hockey League from its founding in 1917 to the 30-team circuit of 2000–01.
- Section IV reports on junior and minor pro hockey in North America, with an emphasis on little-known and forgotten teams.
- Section V looks at international hockey, the Olympics and European national leagues.
- Section VI covers hockey's many other facets, including fan clubs, books, television, goalie masks, the Internet, oddities and families.
- Section VII presents complete registers for players, goaltenders and coaches. Selected biographies are found here as well.

A bit of a whirlwind tour . . .

"Being a Hockey Fan in 1900" by Howard Mickoski *(page 25)* takes you into the stands at a typical game at the turn of the last century. Dress warmly and stay alert!

"Common Ice" by Aidan O'Hara *(page 30)* describes hockey's origins in Boston.

Ken Dryden's "Open Ice: Canada's Hockey Summit" *(page 57)* comes from opening remarks delivered by the president of the Toronto Maple Leafs at a national hockey conference and examines the history of hockey in Canada.

"They Play How Many Periods?" *(page 87)* by Steve Cherwonak of the Western Professional Hockey League describes the pleasure and the challenge of introducing minor pro hockey to places with little hockey history.

"Adventures in the B Pool" *(page 108)* follows British hockey writer Stewart Roberts on the road with Great Britain's national hockey team.

Total Hockey reflects on the superb career of the late Maurice "Rocket" Richard through three stories that begin on page 153. All are reprinted from period sources. Herbert Warren Wind's "Fire on the Ice" ran in *Sports Illustrated,* December 6, 1954, and is a complete personality profile of Richard. Sidney Katz's excellent story, "The Richard Hockey Riot," ran in *Maclean's* magazine, September 17, 1955. "Richard Inspires Thunderous Applause" by Ingrid Peritz and Tu Thanh Ha from *The Globe and Mail* describes the moving state funeral accorded the Rocket on May 31, 2000.

"I Did It My Way" by Chris Tredree *(page 166)* uses in-depth interviews with five NHL players to illustrate the multitude of ways to reach the National Hockey League, from that of consensus number-one draft choice Mats Sundin to the route traveled by 171st pick Luc Robitaille.

"Keepers of the Stanley Cup" *(page 355)* presents the 1947 agreement between the trustees of the Stanley Cup and the National Hockey League formalizing the relationship whereby the NHL presents the glittering silver trophy to its playoff champion each spring.

"The Memorial Cup" by Gregg Drinnan and Eric Zweig provides a year-by-year summary of the annual competition for the ultimate prize in junior hockey.

"Team Building for the 2002 Olympics" *(page 468)* brings together the work of eight writers from around the hockey world. Theories of constructing a successful team for the Salt Lake City Olympics are discussed and hypothetical rosters are named for Canada, the Czech Republic, Finland, Russia, Slovakia, Sweden and the United States.

The "Introduction to the Player Registers" *(page 610)* and the explanatory page that precedes the Pre-Expansion Player, Modern Player and Goaltender registers. *(pages 646, 832 and 1782)* list numerous additions and refinements incorporated in this edition. The registers themselves contain the complete statistical record of every forward, defenseman and goaltender to see action in an NHL regular-season or playoff game. Data panels beginning on page 616 cover the careers of notable North American and European non-NHLers.

Hundreds of people contributed to *Total Hockey*. They are profiled or acknowledged beginning on page 1970.

Contact information appears on page 1974.

The editors welcome your comments, suggestions and corrections. All of them make *Total Hockey* better.

Dan Diamond
July, 2000

I

Origins of Hockey

Members of the Stanley Cup challengers from Dawson City, Yukon, pose in front of Dey's Rink in Ottawa on January 14, 1905. Top row, (left to right): Hector Smith, George Kennedy, Lorne Hannay, Jim Johnstone and Norm Watt. Bottom row, (left to right): Albert Forrest, Joe Boyle and Randy McLellan.
Yukon Archives photo

STANLEY CUP WINNERS PRIOR TO THE FORMATION OF THE NHL 1893 TO 1917

Year	Winner	Coach	Finalist	Coach
1917	Seattle Metropolitans	Pete Muldoon	Montreal Canadiens	Newsy Lalonde
1916	Montreal Canadiens	Newsy Lalonde	Portland Rosebuds	E.H. Savage (manager)
1915	Vancouver Millionaires	Frank Patrick	Ottawa Senators	Frank Shaughnessy (manager)
1914	Toronto Blueshirts	Scotty Davidson	Victoria Cougars	Lester Patrick
			Montreal Canadiens	Jimmy Gardner
1913	Quebec Bulldogs	Joe Malone (captain)	Sydney Miners	—
1912	Quebec Bulldogs	Mike Quinn	Moncton Victories	—
1911	Ottawa Senators	Bruce Stuart (captain)	Port Arthur Bearcats	—
			Galt	—
1910	Montreal Wanderers	Pud Glass (captain)	Berlin Union Jacks	—
	Ottawa Senators	Bruce Stuart (captain)	Edmonton Eskimos	—
			Galt	—
1909	Ottawa Senators	Bruce Stuart (captain)	(no challengers)	
1908	Montreal Wanderers	Cecil Blachford	Edmonton Eskimos	—
			Toronto Trolley Leaguers	—
			Winnipeg Maple Leafs	—
			Ottawa Victorias	—
1907	Montreal Wanderers	Cecil Blachford	Kenora Thistles	—
	Kenora Thistles	Tommy Phillips (captain)	Montreal Wanderers	—
1906	Montreal Wanderers	Cecil Blachford (captain)	New Glascow Cubs	—
			Ottawa Silver Seven	—
	Ottawa Silver Seven	A.T. Smith (manager)	Montreal Wanderers	—
			Smiths Falls	—
			Queen's University	—
1905	Ottawa Silver Seven	A.T. Smith (manager)	Rat Portage Thistles	—
			Dawson City Nuggets	—
1904	Ottawa Silver Seven	A.T. Smith (manager)	Brandon Wheat Kings	—
			Montreal Wanderers	—
			Toronto Marlboros	—
			Winnipeg Rowing Club	—
1903	Ottawa Silver Seven	A.T. Smith (manager)	Rat Portage Thistles	—
			Montreal Victorias	—
	Montreal AAA	Clare McKerrow	Winnipeg Victorias	—
1902	Montreal AAA	Clare McKerrow	Winnipeg Victorias	—
	Winnipeg Victorias	—	Toronto Wellingtons	—
1901	Winnipeg Victorias	Dan Bain (captain)	Montreal Shamrocks	—
1900	Montreal Shamrocks	Harry Trihey (captain)	Halifax Crescents	—
			Winnipeg Victorias	—
1899	Montreal Shamrocks	Harry Trihey (captain)	Queen's University	—
	Montreal Victorias	—	Winnipeg Victorias	—
1898	Montreal Victorias	Frank Richardson (mgr.)	(no challengers)	
1897	Montreal Victorias	Mike Grant (captain)	Ottawa Capitals	—
1896	Montreal Victorias	Mike Grant (captain)	Winnipeg Victorias	—
	Winnipeg Victorias	Jack Armytage (manager)	Montreal Victorias	—
1895	Montreal Victorias	Mike Grant (captain)	(no challengers)	
1894	Montreal AAA	—	Ottawa Generals	—
1893	Montreal AAA	—	(no challengers)	

* Indicates captain. Early teams were frequently run by their captain.

** Victoria defeated Quebec in challenge series. No official recognition.

NATIONAL HOCKEY ASSOCIATION CHAMPIONS

1910 Montreal Wanderers
1911 Ottawa Senators
1912 Quebec Bulldogs
1913 Quebec Bulldogs
1914 Toronto Blueshirts
1915 Ottawa Senators
1916 Montreal Canadiens
1917 Montreal Canadiens

PACIFIC COAST HOCKEY ASSOCIATION CHAMPIONS

1913 New Westminster Royals
1913 Victoria Aristocrats
1914 Victoria Aristocrats
1915 Vancouver Millionaires
1916 Portland Rosebuds
1917 Seattle Metropolitans
1918 Vancouver Millionaires
1919 Seattle Metropolitans
1920 Seattle Metropolitans
1921 Vancouver Millionaires
1922 Vancouver Millionaires
1923 Vancouver Maroons
1924 Vancouver Maroons

WESTERN CANADA HOCKEY LEAGUE CHAMPIONS

1922 Regina Capitals
1923 Edmonton Eskimos
1924 Calgary Tigers
1925 Victoria Cougars

WESTERN HOCKEY LEAGUE CHAMPIONS

1926 Victoria Cougars

CHAPTER 1

The Origins of "Hockey"

Behind the Dictionary Definition

Gerald Owen

EXAMINING THE ORIGIN OF THE WORD "HOCKEY" and the origin of the sport itself can make for a fascinating experience.

In the Germanic languages, there is a very old root word: *hok* or *hak*. This root goes back even further, to the Indo-European *keg*. The meaning—a bent or curved piece of wood or metal—is still evident in the English word "hook." From the wider language family, Russian has the word *kogot*, meaning "iron claw" or "hook."

Though French mainly comes from Latin, France is named after a Germanic people, the Franks, and there are a great many words of Frankish origin in the modern language. *Hoquet* is an old French word that comes from the same root as hook: it means "curved stick" or, more specifically, "shepherd's crook."

It is possible *hoquet* could merely be a cousin, not a grandfather, of the word "hockey," which could just as well come from Old English, one of the Scandinavian languages or even Dutch—all Germanic languages that draw upon the same *hok-* or *hak-* root. However, an enormous number of French words passed into English and lowland Scots because of the Norman Conquest. This may or may not explain the earliest recorded appearance of "hockey sticks" in English.

On November 5, 1785, William Cowper, one of the leading 18th-century English poets, said in a letter, "The boys at Olney [a market town in Buckinghamshire where he lived for 19 years] have likewise a very entertaining sport, which commences annually upon this day; they call it Hockey; and it consists in dashing each other with mud, and the windows also." This, too, is rather mysterious: Cowper does not actually mention sticks or balls, but surely mere mud-throwing would have been too chaotic to form a regular game, with a season.

By the 1830s and 1840s, *hockey* or *hawkey* suddenly starts to appear quite often in the whole English-speaking world, with reasonably clear meanings. In my opinion, the quotations strongly suggest that the word meant primarily "curved or bent stick" and only secondarily "a game played with a curved or bent stick." In 1857, an English source (*Chambers' Information for the People,* Vol. II, page 703) says of sports and games in a clear, downright fashion, "Shinty in Scotland, Hockey in England, and Hurling in Ireland seem to be very much the same out-of-door sport." Previously, a traveler in India in 1842 had explained polo in this striking way: "At Shighur I first saw the game of the Chaughan … It is in fact hockey on horseback … The ball is called in Tibiti pulu." (Godfrey Vigne, *Travels in Kashmir, Ladak, Iskardo*, Vol. II, page 289.) The writer speaks of the game "hockey" as if it was already well-known—feeling free to use the term to liken something to it. For us in North America, and in Canada in particular, it is hard to think of hockey as meaning field hockey—or rather as a wide range of local games with various rules, played on a field and perhaps sometimes on ice. But in the 18th and early 19th centuries, there were not yet two distinct games, internationally known and standardized. Then, it was simply the curved or bent stick that conferred its name on a set of games.

As early as 1838, William Holloway, in *A Dictionary of Provincialisms*, gives Hawkey as a word from the western part of the English county of Sussex: "The name of a game played by several boys on each side with sticks, called hawkey-bats, and a ball." Thackeray, in his novel *Pendennis* (chapter 3), mentions a "hockey-stick" as something with which one schoolboy might hit another. The book came out in 1849, but the school passages were influenced by his own memories from the 1820s. In 1839, an American writer, Jacob Abbott, has a chapter called "The Hawkies" in his book *Caleb in Town*: "Now, a hawkey is a small, round stick, about as long as a man's cane, with a crook in the lower end, so that a boy can hit balls and little stones with it, when lying upon the ground. A good hawkey is a great prize to a Boston boy." Two more New England quotations from the 1860s reflect earlier memories from youth, one a Harvard reminiscence: "I remember him as yesterday, full of fun and courage, with his hockey in hand." The other, from *Little Women*, Book I, Chapter 8, at least has to do with ice—but here a boy is rescuing, by means of a stick, a girl who has ventured out onto the ice: "Laurie lying flat [on the ice] held Amy up by his arm and hockey." Similarly, Dr. A. J. Young of Dalhousie University, in *A Sport History of Nova Scotia*, Vol. II, page 12, says, "The initial use of the word 'hockey' came in early Nova Scotian newspapers which would refer to the boys and men playing with their 'hockies.' "

J.W. "Bill" Fitsell, of the Society for International Hockey Research and the *Kingston Whig-Standard*, has uncovered an earlier Canadian reference than the dictionaries I have consulted. This reference is to an army officer playing "hockey on the ice" in Kingston, Ontario, in 1843, followed by similar English references from 1846 and 1853. When he says this was field hockey, I take it he means that the players did not wear skates or use a puck. His earlier references from 1829 to "idlers with skates on feet and hurly in hand" playing "break shins" in Nova Scotia seem to establish Nova Scotian priority for the roots of the game of hockey—but not yet under that name—especially when combined with a still earlier mention of hurley on ice at Windsor, Nova Scotia, in 1810. Thomas Chandler Haliburton (best known for his satirical novel *The Clockmaker* and its character Sam Slick), writing about his boyhood in Nova Scotia, mentions playing hurley on the ice a few years after his birth in 1796. This was in an English magazine called *Attaché* from 1844, a reference provided by C. Bruce Fergusson, a Nova Scotia archivist, to Dr. Young, who has similar quotations about hurley on ice from 1831 and 1833 and later ones referring back to the 1820s, 1830s and 1840s. The *Boston Evening Gazette* reported of Nova Scotia in 1859 that "ricket" was played on ice: "Each ricketer is provided with a hurley (or hockey as it is termed here)."

Perhaps the most intriguing quotation I came across—though hardly of significance to the word's history—is from the next decade. Elisha Kent Kane was an American physician and explorer who took part in two expeditions to the Arctic to search for the ill-fated Sir John Franklin. He led the second one, passing through Smith's Sound between Baffin Island and Greenland into what is now called the Kane Basin, and spent two winters in those parts, from 1853 to 1855. In 1865, another writer (Sir John Lubbock, *Prehistoric Times, As Illustrated by Ancient Remains*, and the *Manners and Customs of Modern Savages*, xiv, 1869, page 498) said: "Kane saw the children in Smith's sound playing hockey on the ice." It is not clear if this reference comes from Kane's own book, *The Second Grinnell Expedition* (1856). It is clear, however, that these are Inuit children playing a game like hockey. And according to Dr. Young, oral history reports that the Micmac played hockey in the early days of Nova Scotia.

It is obvious from references quoted by Dr. Young that by the 1860s the word "hockey" had attached itself to the game on ice, as in "a match game called hockey" (*Halifax Reporter*, February 10, 1867). Dictionary references for "ice hockey" are not usually this early, but do point to Canada.

So the history, or prehistory, of hockey in what is now Canada may be much older than we sometimes think. Let me restate all this in relation to what Dr. Garth Vaughan says about the origins of the word hockey in *The Puck Starts Here*, his book about the origins of hockey in Windsor, Nova Scotia. He is right that hockey is an old English word. His suggestion that the word is connected to things called hock-carts or to a harvest-home festival called hockey in August or September seems unlikely to me—though perhaps the poet Cowper's letter, dated on another festival, Guy Fawkes Day, is a clue in favor of some such link.

Dr. Vaughan quite reasonably says, "It is quite possible that the English family name 'Hockey' was influential in changing the name of the game"—from hurley to hockey, that is. There is evidence of Hockeys in early Nova Scotia, and there is some tradition that the game was named after one of them, a Colonel Hockey. That tradition sounds like an exaggeration; the association of curved or bent sticks with the word hockey is too widespread in the English-speaking world for one man's name to have been decisive, even in the province that played a decisive part in the early history of the game. But yes, the surname could well have been an influence—a pun-like coincidence that may have delighted people if Colonel Hockey himself played, or watched, hurley/bandy/shinty/randy/ricket/wicket/break-shins/hockey.

The association of "hurling" and hockey sticks does go back at least to Galway, in Connaught on the west coast of Ireland in the reign of Henry VIII—strangely solitary though that piece of evidence is.

As for *hoquet*, Dr. Vaughan is again right when he says in his book that early 19th-century Nova Scotians could hardly have named the game after an archaic French word, especially as the Acadians had already been deported. But I don't think that any scholar has alleged a direct derivation from French in the 19th century. Some, like Dr. Vaughan, doubt that there is any such connection at all.

To me, it seems likely that hockey does belong to the same family as hook, hackle, hake, hoquet, and many other words in Germanic or partly Germanic languages. Still, word historians have not fared very well with game names. Bandy, shinty, shinny, ricket, hockey—many such words may be untraceable, being as hard to make sense of as nicknames that originate in chance associations or private jokes. But it's striking that cricket is another game word apparently derived from the same root as crook—much the same idea as "hook". Linguists and lexicographers (dictionary-makers, that is) approach words differently from those who care about the history of a particular subject, such as a sport. They are interested in how sounds and meanings change, and they collect specimens—quotations—from wherever they can. Sometimes they come upon evidence in places where others might not look, so I hope that people interested in the history of hockey will enjoy this essay.

CHAPTER 2

The Rise and Fall of Ice Polo

The Roots of Hockey

Bill Fitsell

The game of hockey, though much in vogue on the ice in New England and other parts of the United States, is not much known here. In consequence the game of last evening (Montreal Football Club versus Victoria Skating Rink) was looked forward to with great interest.

– *Montreal Gazette*, March 4, 1875.

FOR THOSE WHO CLAIM THAT ICE HOCKEY is a truly Canadian game by creation and practice, this statement—printed the morning after what is generally considered to be the first game of the "modern" sport of hockey was played in Montreal—is somewhat startling. Almost shocking. Could it be possible that hockey originated in the United States of America?

There are other indications that this might be so. For instance, Robert W. Henderson's *Ball, Bat and Bishop* reported in 1786 that hockey was played in Stoney Brook (now Princeton, New Jersey) in the winter of 1786 shortly after the American Revolution. British troops, before fleeing New York in 1783, are reported to have played another stick-ball game, the Irish field game of hurley, on skates and on ice.

There are two prominent newspaper references to hockey being played in New England during the following century, including this one unearthed on a 1991 visit to North Carolina and Williamsburg, Virginia:

Boys in the middle and northern colonies played bandy on ice and called it shinny [in 1802]. They made their own rules and used any kind of puck—barrel bung, knob of wood and the like.

– *Colonial Virginians at Play*, Jane Carson, 1965.

(*Norfolk Herald*, Nov. 13, 1802.)

Then there is the journal of Henry David Thoreau, prominent American naturalist, which notes on April 24, 1854, that "Hawkie like the game of ball was played all over the State of Massachusetts." There are other literary references to the game and the main implement of the New England game under various spellings (see Chapter 1 – The Origins of "Hockey").

Clearly, New Englanders were engaged in some sort of ice sport at this time, but then so too were the citizens of Canada's east coast. This is hardly surprising when one considers that Maritime Canadians would often visit "The Boston States" (and vice versa) and that there had been a free flow or exchange of people and goods along the eastern seaboard since the day of the sailing ship. But what might be called hockey then would bear only the simplest resemblance to what we would recognize as hockey today.

New Brunswick, like other provinces, had its recreational ice games mostly played by youth. Recorded descriptions usually depended on the experience or home country of the viewers. (Ireland: hurling; Scotland: shinty; England: bandy or field hockey). For instance, John J. Rowan, an English immigrant, skating on a bay near Bathurst in 1876, spotted a young French boy in a fur cap and homespun, man-size trousers who led him on a merry chase over the ice until they approached a group of boys playing a game he called "hockey" but could more accurately be described as "shinny."

Putting the crooked end of his stick to the ice, and seizing it with both hands, he bent down; then with a shout, plunged into the thickest of the fray. In [seconds] he was out again at the other side of the crowd, zig-zagging like a jack snipe, shoving the ball before him, and pursued by at least 20 youths.

— *The Emigrant and Sportsman in Canada*, Edward Stanford, London, 1876.

Still, if a game called hockey was popular in New England, there should be no trouble in corroborating the statement of the *Montreal Gazette*. However, a cursory search in libraries in Boston and Albany, New York, revealed little more than a pen and ink sketch of a skating scene in New England. Further research led to a reference to a game called roller polo being played in New England and its spread to New York state and the province of Ontario. In fact, in the first game of organized hockey reported in Kingston, Ontario, in 1886, roller polo sticks were borrowed by Queen's and Royal Military colleges from the new roller rink. Delving into the cross-border travels of the hockey teams of Queen's at Kingston in the mid-1890s produced references to ice polo being played in Pittsburgh, Pennsylvania; Washington, D.C.; and Baltimore, Maryland.

These findings posed several questions: What are the origins of roller polo? When was the game first played on ice? and Why did ice polo succumb to Canadian ice hockey?

The first query proved easy to answer. Roller polo could be traced from the introduction of roller skates and the game of polo—"hockey on horseback"—in the late 1800s. Polo, with equestrians wielding mallets, came to North America via India and England in the 1870s. It was introduced (indoors) at New York in 1876 and (outdoors) at Halifax, Nova Scotia, in 1878. American James Plimpton, the father of the modern roller skate, had introduced the four-wheel variety at Newport, Rhode Island, in 1866. Polo players in this exclusive community of prominent socialites developed roller polo, according to the *Great American Sports Book*. They played five or six a side on an indoor floor 40 feet wide and 80 feet long, using narrow-bladed, four-foot sticks and a ball.

Roller polo was first played by regular clubs in 1878, says *Henley's Official Polo Guide*, 1885, which states: "Roller polo rapidly increased in public form, until now every good roller skating rink has a well organized club."

From Newport, roller polo spread to "The Ivy League" which included such prestigious east coast universities as Brown, Harvard, Princeton and Yale—all of which soon became prominent in the late 19th century games of ice polo and played a prominent role in the transition to, or introduction of, Canadian hockey.

Meanwhile, roller polo was popular enough to be illustrated in *Harper's Weekly* magazine (September 4, 1883). The new American game attracted attention in the Canadian press. The *Toronto Mail* reported that in 1883, polo was flourishing in the New England towns of Lynn, Gloucester, Waltham, Chelsea, Salem and Fall River. "Every town has its rink. Boston has a dozen." By the mid-1880s, roller skating had spread to Ontario (Chatham, Toronto, Ottawa and Kingston) and regular roller polo matches were played and reported in the press. The Massachusetts Polo League, organized September 15, 1884, adopted a goal made of wire netting and a 42-inch, half-circle goal crease. The number of players was restricted to six "which will allow greater opportunities for skillful play and afford greater attractiveness to audiences."

So, where was the game of roller polo transferred from hardwood floor to the frozen ice of the outdoor pond or the indoor skating rink? Naturally, one would assume that it was in New England. However, it was in the province of New Brunswick, where roller skating was introduced to the Maritimes, that ice polo made its Canadian, if not its North American and worldwide, debut.

The grand opening of the Saint John Roller Rink was held in August 1884 with champion, trick, fancy and acrobatic skaters. Three months later, the Frontiers of Calais, Maine, played a very exciting roller polo match against the members of the Saint John Polo Club (*The Daily Sun*, December 8, 1884). The next month—January 1885—the Saint John team traveled to Halifax to play the Wanderers, who had just introduced the new game of indoor hockey to the Nova Scotia capital. While the indoor hockey match was barely mentioned in the Halifax papers, a roller polo match between Halifax and Calais was reported in great detail.

Later, when the Saint John roller poloists were off on a tour of Maine, a new version of the roller game made its debut at the Lansdowne ice rink next door to the Saint John roller rink. As reported in Brian Flood's fascinating 1885 book, *Saint John—A Sporting Tradition*, seven teams registered in the Lansdowne polo league. Carleton, Wellington, City, Long Reach, Lansdowne, Bluenoses and the Maliseet Indians all participated in ice polo matches during a five-day "Grand Winter Carnival."

While skating races for women and a practice game of lacrosse on ice were featured novelties, an ice polo game between the noted speed skaters of Long Reach and the Maliseet Indians drew the most comments: "It was a well contested game and caused much laughter. The Long Reach players being hardly able to stand up when they struck the ball. The Indians won, 3–2." according to *The Daily Sun*, January 25, 1885.

Said Flood:

In those days Indians would travel up from their homes in the Passamaquoddy Bay area to compete in these contests [that] matched the raw strength of the Indians against the speed of the Saint John men. More often than not, white men scored three goals first. The Passamaquoddy Indians were not the best of polo players but could play lacrosse superbly.

Robert Leavitt of the Micmac-Maliseet Institute at the University of New Brunswick in Fredericton confirmed in 1987 that the Passamaquoddy Indians of Point Pleasant, Maine, had played polo on the ice and quoted 70-year-old David A. Francis who recalled playing polo "all day Sunday" on the ice as a boy.

They used a cloth ball and set up two rocks, five feet apart, for each goal. The goals were defended by a goal-tender and goal-cover, who protected the goal-tender. The players wore no skates. Any number could play but the more players, the longer the game since the goals were better defended. The first team to score three points won. [This was an early lacrosse rule that was followed in the early Halifax and Montreal hockey games.]

The lineup of a Halifax ice polo team that faced the Abenaquis of Passamaquoddy reflected the player positions of roller polo and these names popped up in reports of early hockey games in the Maritimes. They were a mixture of different international positional descriptions. The goalkeeper, who stood in front of two poles about eight feet apart with small red flags on top, was goal tend or goal coverer. The defencemen carried the names of lacrosse defenders—point and cover point.

In the various five-, six- and seven-man ice games, there were also halfbacks, a football term which was used in the original nine-man Montreal game of hockey played indoors. Some halfbacks in five-man polo were regarded as first defense. The forwards in roller and ice polo were designated as rushers—first and second—a term used for offensive linemen in early American football.

The American roller polo game, as adapted to ice rinks, was an easy fit with the variety of other ice sports that had been played in the Maritimes throughout the 1800s. Polo was a free wheeling game with no offsides. So was lacrosse. Forward passing was permitted in polo, just as it was in lacrosse and in the Halifax-area ice games played under the various names of wicket, ricket and hurley. All of these games involved a ball, though the narrow polo stick contrasted in shape with the round-handled, broad-bladed hurley stick.

So, why didn't the five- or six-man game of ice polo prevail in the Maritimes?

Almost a decade earlier, another game—called hockey—had been developing in Montreal. It started with nine players but was soon reduced to seven. Hockey was a strictly onside game, meaning there was no passing to a man ahead. Lateral or back passes were acceptable because the Montreal game was based on rugby-football rules. Anyone ahead of the ball, as in today's rugger or rugby game, is offside (out of play) and subject to a penalty and/or stoppage in play.

The Montreal hockey rules were reprinted in the Halifax newspaper in 1886, but the Nova Scotians stuck with their own version of the ice game. Halifax and Dartmouth games were played with the same seven men as in Montreal, but included two halfbacks, three rushers and a home—a term used in lacrosse for the attacker who positioned himself in front of the opponent's goal. The object of pursuit was a cube not yet publicly called a puck and quite often identified in newspapers as a ball.

Seven-man hockey had become quite popular in Dartmouth with the opening of a new skating rink in 1884. By 1888, there were a half-dozen teams in the Halifax-Dartmouth area. In 1889, the Montreal and Halifax versions of hockey clashed for the first time when the Dartmouth Chebuctos became the first Nova Scotian club to invade the province of Quebec. Dartmouth proved much inferior in both versions of the sport against the Montreal AAA, the Crystals and Quebec City, losing four games by a combined score of 23–3.

> *It is easier for the local men (skilled in lacrosse) to fall into Halifax rules which are simpler than ours than vice versa. But not withstanding, the odds were against them, Chebuctos made a very plucky stand.*
>
> – *Montreal Witness/Halifax Recorder*, March 4, 1889.

After that history-making series, the Nova Scotians dropped their forward passing game with goals marked by stones and facing the sides of the rink and adopted the Montreal version with its goal posts and strict onside regulations. Saint John, New Brunswick, adopted the Quebec game in 1892 when bankers transferred from Montreal arrived in the city, where previously only hurley, ice polo or shinny had been played. The same story is true in Newfoundland.

While roller polo continued to be played in New Brunswick, ice polo seems to have disappeared from the indoor rinks of Canada's Maritime provinces. However, in the New England states, the ice game was "dear to the heart of the small boy who plays on the frozen pond or in the streets of the crowded city" (R. Tait McKenzie, *Dominion Illustrated Monthly*, 1893).

St. Paul's School, Concord, New Hampshire (founded 1855), played an early ice game, and by 1876 had noted the popularity of playing "hockey on the ice," restructured it and created their own rules using hockeys and a block. Pictures taken in 1905 show students on Turkey Pond using traditional straight blade hockey sticks and narrow, curved polo sticks that look like inverted walking canes (*International Journal of History of Sport*, Vol. 14, No. 1, 1997). Brown University in Providence, Rhode Island, was reported to have played ice polo as early as 1890 (*Skates, Sticks and Men*). In 1891, the *Montreal Gazette* reported an ice polo tournament on Spy Pond featuring teams from Harvard, Cambridge, Stoneham and three secondary schools from the Boston area.

By 1892, the ice polo game had moved to Duluth on the Minnesota-Wisconsin border, where the positions were designated as point, rush, backer and goal. By the following year, it had spread to St. Paul, Minnesota. The game remained strong in New England, where the Harvard Ice Polo Association was formed. Games were played annually against Brown.

Although ice polo had begun in Saint John, New Brunswick, in 1885, and Burlington, Vermont, roller poloists are known to have played ice hockey against Montreal teams in 1886, the first serious clash of the two games did not occur until a decade later.

During the Christmas holidays of 1894–95, a group of New England ice polo players organized a tour of Toronto, Ottawa, Kingston and Montreal. Noted tennis stars and football players, the visitors from Brown, Columbia, Boston Tech, Harvard and Yale universities played eight games against hockey teams, half under each other's rules. Six of the American polo rules differed from those of Canadian hockey. Number Three stated: "No player except the goalkeeper is allowed within a radius of three feet in front of the goal line to be marked on the ice. If the goalkeeper leaves his position, another player may take his place from time to time" (*Toronto Star*, December 27, 1894). Rule Six declared: "Offside [forward passing] is allowed but any unwarranted interference by one player with another is forbidden." *The Toronto Mail* (December 4, 1894) pointed out before the tour that interference is allowed to "a certain extent as in American football," but stressed: "A great point in the [polo] game is to manipulate the ball by hopping it on the ice so as to elude an opponent."

The U.S. collegians won two games or innings under polo rules during the series but could only manage to tie the other two. They lost all four games under hockey rules and were outscored 32–2. A polo team from Chicago toured Western Ontario during the winter of 1895 and fared no better. They were strong individual skaters but were found lacking in combination play.

In January 1896, Queen's University touring seniors arranged a series of games in Pittsburgh "to teach our American cousins how to play hockey." The champion Kingston team played half under ice polo rules and half under Ontario Hockey Association regulations and won handily. Within a week, the Pittsburghers had adopted the Canadian hockey stick (but retained the ball instead of the puck) and subsequently switched to the onside Canadian game. The freewheeling ice polo game died, just as it had in Canada's Maritime provinces and just as it would throughout the rest of the United States—replaced by the Canadian sport of hockey.

CHAPTER 3

Before *The Trail of the Stanley Cup*

The Amateur Hockey Association of Canada 1886 to 1892 inclusive

Paul Kitchen

THE NATIONAL HOCKEY LEAGUE can trace its lineage back to December 8, 1886, when the Amateur Hockey Association of Canada was founded in Montreal. The AHAC was the first formally organized hockey league. It had member clubs, a statement of objectives, a set of officers, a set of rules, and an operating code that established the manner in which the Association championship would be contested.

In its early years, the Association vacillated on whether it should operate according to a challenge system or a series system. According to the challenge system, there was no prescribed schedule of games among all the teams. Rather, the only official matches were those in which the champions were challenged by a member club. The championship could thus change hands from week to week. Other matches among member clubs were "friendlies," or exhibitions. The series system meant a regular schedule drawn up in advance. The club with the most wins at the end of the season became the champion. The series system was tried out for the first time in 1888 but abandoned until 1893 when it became the standard method of operation. The challenge system was used in 1887, and from 1889 through 1892. The Stanley Cup itself remained a challenge trophy for many years, with challenges coming to the defenders from the champions of other leagues.

Charles Coleman's monumental work *The Trail of the Stanley Cup*, Volume I, is a majestic record of the results, players and goal scorers of games in all leagues yielding a champion that contested the Stanley Cup from 1893 to 1926. Referring to the earlier days of the Amateur Hockey Association of Canada, Mr. Coleman points out that "incomplete records are available." The compilation here presented attempts, as much as possible, to fill in the void between the start of it all in 1886 and what was to become the first Stanley Cup season. In honor of Mr. Coleman's achievement, this record tries to follow the same format and style as the original. This work is not intended as a history of the first years of the AHAC, but as a factual framework that will aid and encourage hockey historians in interpreting that period and telling the full story. It is dedicated to the memory of Charles L. Coleman.

This compilation is based on newspaper accounts, but includes some information from other published sources and from the manuscript records of the Montreal Amateur Athletic Association. Since the quality of hockey reporting varied greatly in accuracy and detail, many different newspapers had to be consulted. Most of the information required to present a comprehensive picture of the earliest days of the Amateur Hockey Association of Canada (AHAC) has been pieced together; but, unfortunately, some data remain missing. For example, no scorer is credited for 24 of the 245 goals in the 45 official AHAC matches played between 1887 and 1892. Were those goals ever recorded? As fate would have it, all ten goal-getters went unidentified in one of the highest scoring matches ever (an 8–2 victory by the Montreal Amateur Athletic Association over the Crystals), which occurred on the night of the Canadian federal general election, March 5, 1891. The big interest of newspapers the next day was politics, not matters sporting, and the various accounts of the match were brief.

Except for gaps in scorer identifications, the record here produced is reasonably complete: all games, all dates, all results, all locations, all players. In addition, a clear distinction has been made (and one that not all newspapers or teams themselves fully understood) between official AHAC matches counting in one way or another toward the championships and other matches that did not. These latter matches included carnival tournaments and practice games (sometimes referred to as exhibition or friendly games).

The anchor for this compilation was the *Montreal Gazette*, for it took the earliest and most consistent interest in the newly emerging game and association. That paper, more than any other at the time, made a point of reporting games, usually with lineups and descriptions of the play. Nevertheless, there were errors and omissions in these accounts: occasional failure to record the name of a goal scorer, frequent omission of players' initials (the use of full first names was infrequent in newspapers), and variations in the spelling of names. Where, for any match, the *Gazette* account was not completely satisfactory, or was suspect, other newspapers were appealed to. The best alternative source was the *Montreal Herald*. For matches played outside of Montreal, that is, in Ottawa and Quebec, the hometown papers were consulted. Thus, sources yielding some relevant information (sometimes no more than confirmation of a result) were: *Montreal Gazette*, *Montreal Herald*, *Montreal Star*, *Montreal Witness*, *Ottawa Citizen*, *Ottawa Journal*, *Quebec Mercury*. In desperation, and with faint hope, some issues of the following newspapers were also looked at: *Montreal La Presse*, *Toronto Globe and Mail*, and *Manitoba Free Press*.

The core of the searching was a day-by-day examination of all issues of the *Gazette* from November 1st to March 31st of each season from 1886 to 1892. The main reason for daily scanning was that schedules were not published in advance. Key information about the Association was provided in the published reports of its annual meetings, held in November or early December. As well, useful follow-up stories on the season completed could sometimes be found in late March. In a few instances, an educated guess had to be made about the identity of a goal scorer. This happened when newspapers were at odds about the player "doing the needful," as reporters were fond of saying. There was also occasional confusion over the respective positions of two players having the same surname.

Here are some additional details on the compilation process.

1. Where, over one or more seasons, minor variances occur in what is judged to be the name of the same player, these have been reconciled by selecting the most commonly cited form (e.g., Findlay over Finley); or by using the name spelling found in other published reference sources such as the *Montreal City Directory* (e.g., Laing over Lang).
2. Where two quite similar names appear in the lineups over a season for the same team, though never together in the same lineup, and there is no apparent reason to conclude a spelling error had occurred, the names are treated as being those of two different players (e.g., J. McDonald, J. McDonnell).
3. Where, in any lineup, a name is printed without an initial, but the same name is accompanied by an initial in other games or seasons for the same or successor team, that initial is deemed to apply where it is missing.
4. Dual initials are applied where it is necessary to distinguish two or more players on the same team having the same surname (e.g., A.D., A.E., and H.E. Scott). Dual initials are also used where players are customarily known by two initials (e.g., P.D. Ross, T.L. Paton, J.A. Stewart).

Corrections and additions would be most welcome. A word of caution, however, is offered to hockey researchers. A piece of information taken from a single newspaper and which does not correspond with what appears here may not necessarily represent an error in this compilation since, as mentioned above, newspaper reports were frequently inconsistent.

This compilation attempts to replicate the style and format of Charles Coleman's *The Trail of the Stanley Cup, Volume I,* published by the National Hockey League in 1966. In one minor departure from *The Trail of the Stanley Cup* convention, "MAAA" is used in place of "Montreal" to identify the hockey club of the Montreal Amateur Athletic Association. This removes any ambiguity that might arise from the fact that over the years most teams in the Association were Montreal-based: McGill, Victorias, Crystals, Dominions and Shamrocks. In fact, both "MAAA" and "Montreal Hockey Club" are correct appellations and were used interchangeably by the press, the AHAC and MAAA itself.

Rules of the Amateur Hockey Association of Canada

(adopted at the founding meeting, December 8, 1886)

1. *The captains of contesting teams shall agree upon two umpires (one to be stationed at each goal) and a referee.*
2. *All questions as to games shall be settled by the umpires and their decision shall be final.* [Editor's note: "Games" in this time period meant goals scored.]
3. *All disputes on the ice shall be settled by the referee, and his decision shall be final.*
4. *The game shall be commenced and renewed by a bully [a face-off] in the centre of the rink.* [In the early days of hockey, "the game" referred to the time played until a goal was scored.] *Goals, six feet wide and four feet high, which shall be changed after each game* [goal scored], *unless otherwise agreed.*
5. *When a player hits the puck, anyone of the same side who at such moment of hitting is nearer the opponent's goal line is out of play, and may not touch the puck himself, or in any way whatever prevent any other player from doing so until the puck has been played. A player must always be on his side of the [puck].*
6. *The puck may be stopped, but not carried or knocked on, by any part of the body. No player shall raise his stick above his shoulder. Charging from behind, tripping, collaring, kicking or shinning shall not be allowed, and any player after having been twice warned by the referee, it shall become his duty to rule the player off the ice for that match.*
7. *When the puck gets off the ice behind the goals it shall be taken by the referee at five yards at right angles from the goal line and there faced.*
8. *The goal keeper must not, during play, lie, kneel or sit upon the ice, but must maintain a standing position.*
9. *Hockey sticks shall not be more than three inches wide at any part.*
10. *Goal shall be scored when the puck shall have passed between the goal posts and below the top and passed from in front below an imaginary line across the top of the posts.*
11. *The puck must be made of vulcanized rubber, one inch thick all through, and three inches in diameter.*
12. *A team shall be composed of seven players, who shall be bona fide members of the club they represent. No player shall be allowed to play on more than one team during a season except in a case of bona fide change of residence.*
13. *Two half-hours with an intermission of ten minutes between will be time allowed for the matches. A match will be decided by the team winning the greatest number of games [scoring the most goals] during that time. In case of a tie after playing the specified two half hours, play will continue until one side secures a game [scores a goal], unless otherwise agreed upon between the captains before the match.*
14. *No change of players must be made after a match has commenced except for reason of accidents or injury during the game.*
15. *Should any player be injured during a match and compelled to leave the field his side shall have the option of putting on a spare man from the reserve to equalize the teams; in the event of any dispute between the captains as to the injured player's fitness to continue the game the matter shall at once be decided by the referee.*
16. *Should a game be temporarily stopped by the infringement of any of the rules the puck shall be brought back and a bully [face-off] shall take place.*

1887

The Amateur Hockey Association of Canada came into being on the evening of December 8, 1886, when representatives of interested clubs met at the Victoria Skating Rink in Montreal. Delegates present were: J.G. Monk, J. Arnton and J. Muir of the Victoria Hockey Club; T.D. Green and Hamilton of Ottawa; C.H. MacNutt, Holden and Wylde of McGill College; E. Sheppard and W. Barlow of the Montreal Amateur Athletic Association; and R. Laing and McCaffrey of the Crystal Hockey Club. The Quebec Hockey Club had been invited to send a representative but did not do so.

The officers elected for the 1887 season were:

President ......T.D. Green, Ottawa
1st Vice-Pres. J. Arnton, Victorias
2nd Vice-Pres. R. Laing, Crystals
Sec.-Treasurer E. Stevenson, Victorias
Council .........J.A. Stewart, Crystals
..................J.G. Monk, Victorias
..................H.A. Budden, McGill
..................E. Sheppard, MAAA
..................P. Myles, Ottawa

Crystals representative J.A. Stewart had defected to the MAAA club, having been admitted to membership one month to the day before the AHAC annual meeting at which he represented his former team.

It was agreed that the season should be from the 1st of January to the 15th of March, and that, with few alterations, the rules of the previous season should be applied. The object of the Association was "to improve, foster and perpetuate the game of hockey in Canada; protect it from professionalism, and to promote the cultivation of kindly feeling among the members of the hockey clubs."

The Association decided to operate on a challenge system. According to the AHAC code: "the club holding the championship trophy will accept all challenges in the order of their reception and shall be obliged to play all such championship matches with an intermission of not more than seven days between each match." All challenges were to be sent by registered post to the secretary of the club being challenged. A club holding the championship was, on being defeated, required to deliver the championship trophy to their victors within one week of defeat.

At the start, there was no trophy as the Association had little funds for the purchase of one. With the assistance, however, of the Victoria Rink, which contributed $50, the directors did acquire a handsome trophy emblematic of the championship. The owner of the Crystal Rink, one of the Association's venues, refused to make a contribution.

The Crystals were considered the reigning champions, having defeated Quebec the previous season in what amounted to an unofficial championship match. The AHAC championship was therefore theirs to defend. The Montreal hockey season got underway with a practice match when MAAA defeated Victorias 4–0 on January 6.

The official season opened on January 7 when the Crystals defeated McGill 3–1 at the Crystal Rink in the AHAC's first challenge match. The following week, the Crystals accepted the challenge of the Victorias. Playing at the Crystal Rink, the challengers handily defeated the champions 4–0 and took possession of the title. The Victorias successfully defended it over the following five matches before losing to the Crystals in the last contest of the season.

The Ottawa club were quite upset about their challenge not being accepted until January 27. They had sent it in by post in December with the hope of having an early match and, in the event of victory, with the anticipation of playing host to one or more additional championship contests at Ottawa's Dey's Rink.

In the final championship match of the season on March 11th at the Victoria Rink, S. McQuisten, with two goals, and D. Brown, with one, "did the needful" to secure victory for the Crystals, while J. Arnton replied with both Victoria goals. The Victorias protested the match over one of their goals being disallowed, but their complaint came to nothing.

The 1887 season also saw the resumption of the Montreal Winter Carnival, following the cancellation of the 1886 event because of a smallpox epidemic. The carnival always featured a hockey tournament and 1887 was no exception. Scheduling problems in the rinks, however, forced organizers to hold the tournament several days after the conclusion of the carnival. This caused confusion as to the status of the matches in the minds of many people who failed to see the connection of these games with a carnival that was long over. Newspapers shared the confusion, as did the MAAA club. Several years later in a public statement, the MAAA perpetuated its misconception that the 1887 season had been played under the series system (as opposed to the challenge system) and that the carnival tournament was included in the championship schedule. In the "carnival" tournament, MAAA defeated the Crystals 1–0 on February 21 and the Victorias defeated McGill 5–1 on February 23. The *Gazette*, in one of its references to the McGill game, mistakenly said it was a friendly. In the carnival's championship game, MAAA defeated the Victorias 1–0 on February 25. Members of the winning team received carnival diamond pins for their labors.

AHAC Challenge System

Date	Winner	Loser
Jan. 7th	Crystals (3) at Crystal Rink	McGill (1)
Jan. 14th	Victorias (4) at Crystal Rink	Crystals (0)
Jan. 21st	Victorias (5) at Victoria Rink	MAAA (2)
Jan. 27th	Victorias (5) at Victoria Rink	Ottawa (1)
Feb. 4th	Victorias (3) at Victoria Rink	Crystals (0)
Feb. 24th	Victorias (2) at Victoria Rink	Crystals (1)
Mar. 11th	Crystals (3) at Victoria Rink	Victorias (2)

Goalkeeper Averages

Name	Club	GP	GA	SO	Avg.
Arnton, T.	Victorias	6	7	2	1.2
Norris, W.	Crystals	3	7		2.3
Boon, G.	Crystals	2	5		2.5
Shanks	McGill	1	3		3.0
Hutchison, W.	MAAA	1	5		5.0
Low, A.	Ottawa	1	5		5.0

Scoring Summary

Name	Club	GP	G
Arnton, J.	Victorias	4	4
Craven, J.	Victorias	6	4
Campbell, J.	Victorias	6	3
McQuisten, S.	Crystals	3	3
Swift, D.	Victorias	1	3
Swift, L.	Victorias	1	3
Shearer, A.	Victorias	6	2
Swift, A.	Victorias	2	2
Brown, D.	Crystals	2	1
Currier, C.	Ottawa	1	1
Dowd, F.	Crystals	3	1
Hodgson, W.	MAAA	1	1
Laing, R.	Crystals	4	1
Lucas, D.	McGill	1	1
McGoldrick, J.	Crystals	4	1
Barlow, E.	Victorias	5	0
Baxter, F.	Victorias	1	0
Budden, H.	McGill	1	0
Cameron, A.	MAAA	1	0
Dey, E.	Ottawa	1	0
Drysdale, W.	Crystals	1	0
Ellard, C.	Crystals	3	0
Elliott, D.	Crystals	1	0
Findlay, J.	MAAA	1	0
Greene, T.D.	Ottawa	1	0
Hamilton, D.	McGill	1	0
Hamilton, W.	McGill	1	0
Howe, S.	Ottawa	1	0
Kerr, J.	Ottawa	1	0
Kinghorn, J.	Victorias	1	0
Kirby, H.S.	Ottawa	1	0
Lee, S.	Crystals	2	0
McDonald, J	Crystals	5	0
McIntyre, A.	MAAA	1	0
McIntyre, D.	MAAA	1	0
McVeity, F.	Ottawa	1	0
Meigher, F.	McGill	1	0
Muir, J.	Victorias	5	0
Myles, P.	Ottawa	1	0
Norris, W.	Crystals	2	0
Stewart, J.A.	MAAA	1	0
Virtue, J.	MAAA	1	1
Warden	McGill	1	0

Note: No player credited for second MAAA goal, Jan. 21. Vics player put it through own goal.

MONTREAL CRYSTALS

AHAC Champions

Boon, G.	—	goal
Brown, D.*	—	forward
Dowd, F.	—	forward
Drysdale, W.*	—	forward
Ellard, C.*	—	cover point
Elliott, D.*	—	forward
Laing, R.	—	point, forward
McDonald, J.*	—	forward, point
McGoldrick, J.	—	forward
McQuisten, S.*	—	forward
Norris, W.*	—	goal

* Appeared in final championship match.

1888

The Amateur Hockey Association of Canada held its first annual meeting on November 9, 1887, at the Victoria Rink in Montreal. There was a good attendance of delegates.

The officers elected for the ensuing season were:

President ......J.J. Arnton, Victorias
1st Vice-Pres. J.A. Stewart, MAAA
2nd Vice-Pres. H.A. Budden, McGill
Sec.-Treasurer W.E. Stevenson, Victorias
Council .........A.L. Shanks, McGill
.................D.A. Elliott, Crystals
.................A. Shearer, Victorias
.................L. Barlow, MAAA

The Association's financial statement for the year revealed receipts of $100 and expenditures of $94.91, including $75 for a championship trophy, leaving a balance of $5.09. The meeting discussed but did not act upon a suggestion that the Association establish a junior championship series. The meeting also discussed the format for the scheduling of championship matches. The secretary-treasurer advised that under the challenge system in effect the previous year, the club holding the championship were at a disadvantage since they were required to meet all comers every seven days and were thus apt to become "stale." It was unanimously resolved to adopt the series system for the ensuing season.

The Council met on December 13 to fix the schedule. The four clubs (MAAA, Crystals, Victorias and McGill) were to play each opponent twice, making a six-game regular season. In exhibition play, the Victorias defeated MAAA 2–0 on December 28; the Crystals defeated McGill 6–0 on January 6 and then defeated the Victorias 2–1 on January 7.

The MAAA got off to a good start, winning the official season's opening game 4–1 over the Crystals. The MAAA went on to win four more games over the regular schedule, losing only to the Victorias. The latter team, however, had an equal record, thus forcing a deciding playoff match. Meanwhile, the McGill team demonstrated its inability to compete at the senior level, losing all six games and being outscored 40–4.

A special meeting of the AHAC Council was convened on March 13 to decide the date and place for playing off the MAAA/Victorias tie. Two options were discussed: to play the championship match on March 15 at the Crystal Rink (home of the MAAA) or on March 17 at the Victoria Rink (home of the Victorias). Since two of the Victoria players were injured and would not be ready until the 17, the AHAC secretary-treasurer suggested the latter date. A vote was taken, resulting in a tie, leaving the casting vote to the chairman of that night's meeting, J.A. Stewart of the MAAA, who was also a player on the team. Stewart voted for the earlier date at his own team's rink. This action generated considerable criticism in the press on two grounds. Newspapers considered it unsportsmanlike to deny Victorias the chance to play with their best team. Also, the press could not understand why, for such an important and popular attraction, the match should have to be played in a building with a small seating capacity when the larger and more comfortable Victoria Rink would be available two nights later.

Playing without the injured Arnton and Ashe in the match to decide the title, the Victorias could manage only one goal, that by their stellar cover point J. Campbell, and suffered defeat. A. and W. Hodgson scored the two MAAA goals.

In his first season of AHAC play, MAAA goalkeeper T.L. (Tom) Paton gave every indication he would be a splendid barrier to the opposition in years to come, yielding only seven goals in his seven games.

The Ottawa Hockey Club were presumed to have withdrawn from AHAC membership in 1888 as they sent no representatives to meetings and failed to pay their dues.

AHAC Series System

Jan. 13th	MAAA	(4)	Crystals	(1)
	at Crystal Rink			
Jan. 18th	Victorias	(8)	McGill	(1)
	at Victoria Rink			
Jan. 23rd	MAAA	(5)	McGill	(0)
	at Crystal Rink			
Jan. 27th	Victorias	(3)	Crystals	(1)
	at Crystal Rink			
Feb. 3rd	Victorias	(3)	MAAA	(1)
	at Victoria Rink			
Feb. 10th	Crystals	(4)	McGill	(1)
	at Crystal Rink			
Feb. 15th	MAAA	(3)	Crystals	(1)
	at Crystal Rink			
Feb. 22nd	Victorias	(6)	McGill	(2)
	at Crystal Rink			
Feb. 27th	MAAA	(2)	Victorias	(1)
	at Crystal Rink			
Mar. 2nd	MAAA	(8)	McGill	(0)
	at Crystal Rink			
Mar. 7th	Victorias	(3)	Crystals	(2)
	at Victoria Rink			
Mar. 12th	Crystals	(9)	McGill	(0)
	at Crystal Rink			

Final Standings

Team	W	L	GF	GF
MAAA	5	1	23	6
Victorias	5	1	24	9
Crystals	2	4	18	14
McGill	0	6	4	40

Playoff for Championship

Mar. 15th MAAA (2) Victorias (1)
at Crystal Rink

Goalkeeper Averages

includes playoff

Name	Club	GP	GA	SO	Avg.
Paton, T.L.	MAAA	7	7	2	1.0
Scanlan, R.	Crystals	1	1		1.0
Crathern, J.	Victorias	5	7		1.4
Arnton, T.	Victorias	2	4		2.0
Virtue, W.	Crystals	4	9	1	2.3
Norris, W.	Crystals	1	4		4.0
Shanks, A.	McGill	6	40		6.7

Scoring Summary

includes playoff

Name	Club	GP	G
Arnton, J.	Victorias	4	4
Campbell, J.	Victorias	7	8
Elliott, D.	Crystals	6	8
Virtue, J.	MAAA	7	8
Hodgson, W.	MAAA	4	6
Ashe, F.	Victorias	5	5
Hodgson, A.	MAAA	7	5
Kinghorn, J.	Victorias	7	5
Lee, S.	Crystals	4	4
Shearer, A.	Victorias	7	4
Drysdale, W.	Crystals	2	3
Low, G.S.	MAAA	7	3
Barlow, E.	Victorias	7	2
Findlay, J.	MAAA	4	2
Lucas, W.V.	McGill	4	2
McQuisten, S.	Crystals	5	2
Fry, F.	McGill	5	1
Harris, J.	Victorias	4	1
Jamieson, W.	McGill	6	1
McCabe, H.	Crystals	4	1
McNaughton, A.	MAAA	1	1
Arnton, J.	Victorias	2	0
Brown, D.	Crystals	2	0
Cameron, A.	MAAA	5	0
Ellard, C.	Crystals	2	0
Hamilton, W.	McGill	4	0
Holden, D.	McGill	3	0
Lucas, F.M.	McGill	6	0
McDonald, J.	Crystals	2	0
McDonnell, J.	Crystals	4	0
Nichol	Victorias	1	0
Norris, W.	Crystals	5	0
Stewart, J.A.	MAAA	7	0
Walsh, R.N.	McGill	2	0
Walsh, T.N.	McGill	6	0
Wadd, J.	Victorias	2	0

MAAA

AHAC Champions

Cameron, A.*	—	cover point
Findlay, J.	—	forward
Hodgson, A.*	—	forward, cover point
Hodgson, W.*	—	forward
Low, G.S.*	—	forward
McNaughton, A.	—	cover point
Paton, T.L.*	—	goal
Stewart, J.A.*	—	point
Virtue, J.*	—	forward

* Appeared in final championship match.

1889

The Amateur Hockey Association of Canada held its second annual meeting at the Victoria Rink in Montreal on November 16, 1888. The Victoria, McGill, Crystal and MAAA clubs were well represented.

The officers elected for the forthcoming season were:

President	J.A. Stewart
1st Vice-Pres.	A. Shearer
2nd Vice-Pres.	D.B. Holden
Sec.-Treasurer	A. Hodgson
Council	H. Kinghorn, McGill
	S. Lee, Crystals
	T. Arnton, Victorias
	A.G. Higginson, MAAA

The secretary-treasurer said the Association's finances were in a "flourishing condition," showing a credit balance of $32.51.

The first major item of business was the amendment of rule 16, to read: "Should a game be temporarily stopped by an infringement of any of the rules, the captain of the opposite side may claim that the puck be taken back and a bully take place where it was last played before the said infringement occurred." The amendment made the rule more specific as to where the bully should take place; but it also allowed the team being infringed against the choice of having the puck taken back to the point of infringement or having it set in motion at the point where the play was stopped.

A more important matter had to do with the scheduling of matches. The retiring secretary-treasurer cautioned the Council that while the series system employed the previous year was an "unqualified success," it did have the disadvantage of debarring clubs from outside Montreal. Since most clubs were Montreal-based, most of the matches would have to be played in the metropolis, thus putting visiting clubs to heavy traveling expenses and discouraging participation. The meeting resolved to abolish the series system and to decide the championship by returning to the old challenge system. It was expected that this system would arouse the interest of the Ottawa, Quebec and Toronto clubs. Quebec did return to the fold in 1889 but Ottawa did not re-enter until 1891. Toronto remained unheard from.

The most noticeable effect of the decision to return to the challenge system was the sharp reduction in the number of official matches from 13 over a two-month period in 1888 to only four over less than a month-and-a-half in 1889. This resulted in far less attention being given to senior hockey in the newspapers and went against the Association's stated objective of fostering and perpetuating the game of hockey in Canada.

The senior hockey season began on December 15 when MAAA defeated the Victorias 3–1 in a friendly match opening the Victoria Rink for the new season. In further exhibition play, the Crystals defeated McGill 8–4 on January 11; MAAA defeated the Crystals 2–1 on January 18; the Victorias defeated the Crystals 5–2 on January 31; MAAA defeated the visiting Dartmouth Chebuctos 6–1 on February 25; and the Crystals defeated the same Maritimers 4–1 two nights later.

Though the Crystals had lost their final two exhibition games, they rebounded in the first official match, defeating MAAA 3–2 on February 2 at the Crystal rink. This meant that after only one game they had become champions. It was a hard-fought tussle, requiring overtime to decide the outcome. Not only was the game late finishing, it was late starting. Scheduled to begin at 4:30 p.m., the match was delayed for an hour because no referee could be found until Mr. F. Crathern agreed to preside, much to the relief of the large audience, "among which was a fair sprinkling of ladies."

The intervention of the Winter Carnival forced a delay in official AHAC matches and it was not until March 1 that the challenge series resumed. The Crystals relinquished their championship to MAAA who then won the two concluding games against Quebec and the Victorias to hold the honors at season's end. The Association gave medals, at a total cost of $40, to MAAA team members in recognition of their having won the greatest number of championship matches during the season.

The carnival series, held between February 4 and February 18, was significant in one historical respect. It marked the first exposure of the recently appointed Governor-General, Lord Stanley of Preston, to the game of hockey. He had come to the carnival to experience the full flavor of Canadian winter culture and was immediately taken with the game. And the city of Montreal was thrilled to have him. He arrived at the Victoria Rink at precisely 9:05 p.m. on February 4 and proceeded straight to the directors' gallery for a good view of the MAAA match against the Victorias, already in progress. A trumpet heralded his entrance. The players stopped the game and lined up at center ice while the band played "God Save the Queen." Captain J. Arnton of the Victorias called for three cheers for His Excellency, to which the players hastily responded. The spectators joined the general enthusiasm. His Excellency pronounced his great delight with the game of hockey and the expertness of the players. Little did the players know that within a few short years, Lord Stanley would give tangible evidence that he liked what he saw that night.

The results of the 1889 Montreal Winter Carnival hockey tournament were: Victorias (2), MAAA (1) on February 4; Crystals (7), McGill (3) on February 9; and Victorias (3), Crystals (2) on February 18. Newspapers ambiguously called the tournament a "championship series." The carnival committee presented medals to the winning Victoria side.

AHAC Challenge System

Feb. 2nd	Crystal (3) at Crystal Rink	MAAA (2)
Mar. 1st	MAAA (4) at Crystal Rink	Crystals (0)
Mar. 7th	MAAA (3) at Crystal Rink	Quebec (2)
Mar. 12th	MAAA (6) at Crystal Rink	Victorias (1)

Goalkeeper Averages

Name	Club	GP	GA	SO	Avg.
Paton, T.L.	MAAA	4	6	1	1.5
Norris, W.	Crystals	1	2		2.0
Laurie, A.	Quebec	1	3		3.0
Scanlan, R.	Crystals	1	4		4.0
Jones, R.	Victorias	1	6		6.0

Scoring Summary

Name	Club	GP	G
McNaughton, A.	MAAA	4	5
Findlay, J.	MAAA	4	4
Hodgson, A.	MAAA	4	4
Low, G.S.	MAAA	3	2
Barlow, E.	Victorias	1	1
Brown, D.	Crystals	2	1
Davidson, R.	Quebec	1	1
Lee, S.	Crystals	2	1
McDonald, J.	Crystals	2	1
Scott, A.	Quebec	1	1
Arnton, J.	Victorias	1	0
Barlow, F.	MAAA	1	0
Bignell, H.	Quebec	1	0
Cameron, A.	MAAA	4	0
Campbell, J.	Victorias	1	0
Ellard, C.	Crystals	2	0
Elliott, D.	Victorias	1	0
Holme, W.	Quebec	1	0
McCabe, H.	Crystals	1	0

McQuisten, S.	Crystals	1	0
Norris, W.	Crystals	2	0
Scott, F.	Victorias	1	0
Scott, H.	Quebec	1	0
Stewart, J.A.	MAAA	4	0
Swift, A.	Quebec	1	0
Virtue, J.	Victorias	1	0

MAAA
AHAC Champions

Barlow, F.	—	forward
Cameron, A.*	—	cover point
Findlay, J.*	—	forward
Hodgson, A.*	—	forward
Low, G.S.*	—	forward
McNaughton, A.	—	forward
Paton, T.L.*	—	goal
Stewart, J.A.*	—	point

* Appeared in final championship match.

1890

The Amateur Hockey Association of Canada held its third annual meeting on November 22, 1889, in the rooms of the Montreal Amateur Athletic Association.

The election of officers resulted as follows:

President ......J.A. Stewart, MAAA
1st Vice-Pres. H. Kinghorn, McGill
2nd Vice-Pres. W.G. Cameron, Victorias
Sec.-Treasurer J.A. Findlay, MAAA
Council .........A.E. McNaughton, MAAA
..................W.E. Stevenson, Victorias
..................D.B. Holden, McGill
..................J. McDonald, Crystals
..................R. Davidson, Quebec

The secretary-treasurer reported a balance of $29.29 to be carried forward to the coming season. There was little business to conduct, the main decisions being to admit Quebec as a regular member, and to allow the Crystals to change their name to the Dominions.

As was the custom prior to the beginning of each season, member clubs conducted their own annual meetings to select officers for the coming year. The most notable of these appointments was that of H. Montagu Allan of the Allan Line Shipping Company as honorary president of the Victoria Hockey Club.

The season began with a friendly match on January 3 when MAAA defeated the Victorias 5–4. Noteworthy was the fact that this game marked a change in venue from the Victoria Rink to the Dominion Rink. Formerly unsuitable for senior play, the rink was now refurbished. The rows of pillars running down its centre were gone; the ice surface was enlarged to 170 feet by 60 feet and was surrounded by a solid wooden fence four feet high. This innovation captured the attention of the *Montreal Gazette*, which told its readers that the fence "not only prevents the players breaking their shins over the edge of the rink but keeps the spectators from crowding on the ice during the game." The only criticism of the rink was that the goal posts were not frozen firmly into the ice. The umpires remonstrated at the way the posts shifted about and grew perceptibly closer during the more exciting moments.

Other exhibition matches were: Victorias (11), McGill (4) on January 13; Dominions (4), McGill (1) on January 24; MAAA (5), Victorias (1) on January 28; and Victorias (3), Ottawa (1) on February 25 at the new Rideau Rink in the capital. In non-Association play on February 19, a select team of Montrealers led by Montagu Allan whipped a club from Ottawa 9–3 at the Victoria Rink. In the Ottawa lineup were Hon. E. Stanley and Hon. A. Stanley.

MAAA forward "Bunny" Low broke his thumb in the opening game of the challenge series when his team defeated Quebec 5–1 and was out for the season. He was capably replaced by Sam Lee. The MAAA dominated the season, winning all seven championship matches. Since this was their third consecutive title, they took permanent possession of the AHAC trophy. The Association also presented team members with medals for again winning the greatest number of games.

AHAC Challenge System

Jan. 7th	MAAA (5) at Dominion Rink	Quebec (1)
Jan. 17th	MAAA (4) at Dominion Rink	Victorias (2)
Jan. 31st	MAAA (6) at Dominion Rink	Dominions (4)
Feb. 11th	MAAA (6) at Dominion Rink	Dominions (2)
Feb. 18th	MAAA (2) at Dominion Rink	Victorias (1)
Feb. 25th	MAAA (3) at Crystal Rink	Dominions(2)
Mar. 4th	MAAA (2) at Crystal Rink	Victorias (1)

Goalkeeper Averages

Name	Club	GP	GA	SO	Avg.
Paton, T.L.	MAAA	7	13		1.9
Jones, R.	Victorias	3	8		2.7
Fyfe, J.	Dominions	1	3		3.0
Laurie, A.	Quebec	1	5		5.0
Scanlan, R.	Dominions	2	12		6.0

Scoring Summary

Name	Club	GP	G
McNaughton, A.	MAAA	7	12
Findlay, J.	MAAA	7	6
Brown, D.	Dominions	3	4
Kingan, A.	MAAA	2	3
Cameron, A.	MAAA	6	2
Lee, S.	MAAA	4	2
Ritchie, A.	Dominions	3	2
Arnton, J.	Victorias	2	1
Barlow, E.	Victorias	3	1
Campbell, J.	Victorias	3	1
Clapperton, A.	Dominions	3	1
Elliott, R.A.	MAAA	7	1
Laing, R.	Dominions	3	1
Low, G.S.	MAAA	1	1
Scott, A.	Quebec	1	1
Crathern, J.	Victorias	1	0
Davidson, R.	Quebec	1	0
Fairbanks, F.	Victorias	1	0
Kinghorn, J.	Victorias	1	0
Laing, W.	Dominions	3	0
Laurier, A.	Quebec	1	0
McDonald, J.	Dominions	2	0
McDonnell, J.	Dominions	1	0
McQuisten, S.	Victorias	2	0
Norris, W.	Victorias	2	0
Paton, R.	Quebec	1	0
Scott, H.	Quebec	1	0
Stewart, J.A.	MAAA	7	0
Warden, W.	Victorias	3	0
Watson, D.	Quebec	1	0

Note: Scorer not identified for one MAAA goal, February 11th; and Victoria goal, February 18th.

MAAA
AHAC Champions

Cameron, A.	—	cover point
Elliott, R.A.*	—	forward
Findlay, J.*	—	forward
Kingan, A.*	—	forward
Lee, S.*	—	forward
Low, G.S.	—	forward
McNaughton, A*	—	forward
Paton, T.L.*	—	goal
Stewart, J.A.*	—	point

* Appeared in final championship match.

1891

The Amateur Hockey Association of Canada held its fourth annual meeting in the rooms of the Montreal Amateur Athletic Association on November 28, 1890. Delegates from the Victoria, MAAA, McGill, Crescent, Quebec and Ottawa clubs attended.

The secretary-treasurer showed a balance of nearly $50.

Officers were elected as follows:

President ......J.A. Stewart
1st Vice-Pres. E.C. Grant
2nd Vice-Pres. J. McDonnell
Sec.-Treasurer J.A. Findlay
Council ....J. Russell, McGill
..................A.E. McNaughton, MAAA
..................J.C. Crathern, Victorias
..................P.D. Ross, Ottawa
..................P.S. McCaffrey, Crescents
..................Davidson, Quebec

The meeting referred an application from the Shamrock Hockey Club to the Council. The delegates embarked on a lengthy discussion of the relative merits of the challenge and series systems before again choosing the former. Any other course, reasoned the Association, would squeeze out teams from beyond the metropolis. The meeting decided that the Association should ask the different rinks to come up with a challenge trophy to be won three consecutive years by a team and then retained. Any team defaulting a game without good reason was to be disqualified from further championship competition that season. The meeting also discussed establishing an intermediate championship series but came to no resolution.

The season got underway with a practice match on December 19, McGill defeating MAAA 3–1. Other practice (or friendly) matches were: Crescents (2), MAAA (1) on January 2; Ottawa (3), McGill (2) at Ottawa on January 17; Victorias (3), Crescents (1) on January 29; Ottawa (1), Victorias (0) at Ottawa on January 31; and Victorias (6), McGill (5) on February 9.

The Association's decision to adopt a policy on a team defaulting proved prescient, for what was supposed to have been the first challenge match of the season on January 7 was canceled because Quebec failed to show up for its contest against MAAA. In conformity with the new policy, Quebec was prohibited from issuing any further challenges that season.

In the first official match, MAAA picked up where they had left off the previous season, defeating the Victorias 4–1. An unknown substitute, Haviland Routh, made his AHAC debut, replacing the MAAA's Alex Kingan in the second half. It was the only action the young forward would see that season. Two years later he would become the Association's leading scorer.

The Shamrocks played their maiden match in the AHAC on January 28, falling to the mighty MAAA 4–1. Complaining that there was not much "genuine hockey" played that night, the *Gazette* said "there was more body-checking and foul play than there was any necessity for."

In an historic match on February 21, MAAA faced the Ottawa Hockey Club for the first time ever. It was Saturday night hockey at its best in the Crystal Rink and though the visitors from the capital gave a good account of themselves they could not crack the armor of MAAA goalkeeper Tom Paton. MAAA won the contest 3–0. The first goal came out of a confused heap of players, with neither Kingan or Findlay knowing which of them gave the puck its final tap. The *Ottawa Journal* said the goal was "an unlucky accident which would not happen again in fifty matches." Responding to the shouts of the crowd "go it Bunny," G.S. Low did just that, rushing up the ice and putting the puck through. Ottawa thought neither of the goals should have counted, but there was no disputing Low's second goal, thus assuring the MAAA of victory in everyone's book. Both sides were well pleased with the match and good feelings prevailed. According to the *Journal*, the Montreal passing was a revelation to the Ottawas, while the Montrealers thought the Ottawas had played the fastest forward game they had seen that season. After the match the teams repaired to the Fencing Room of the Montreal Amateur Athletic Association where the home team entertained the Ottawas at dinner.

MAAA closed out the season with two more victories to retain the championship.

AHAC Challenge System

Jan. 7th	MAAA by default over Quebec			
Jan. 19th	MAAA	(4)	Victorias	(1)
	at Crystal Rink			
Jan. 28th	MAAA	(4)	Shamrocks	(1)
	at Crystal Rink			
Feb. 4th	MAAA	(2)	Crescents	(1)
	at Crystal Rink			
Feb. 12th	MAAA	(2)	Victorias	(1)
	at Crystal Rink			
Feb. 21st	MAAA	(3)	Ottawa	(0)
	at Crystal Rink			
Feb. 27th	MAAA	(5)	Shamrocks	(1)
	at Crystal Rink			
Mar. 5th	MAAA	(8)	Crescents	(2)
	at Crystal Rink			

Goalkeeper Averages

Name	Club	GP	GA	SO	Avg.
McNaughton, A.	MAAA	1	1		1.0
Paton, T.L.	MAAA	6	6	1	1.0
Clapperton, A.	Crescents	1	2		2.0
Jones, R.	Victorias	2	6		3.0
Morel, A.	Ottawa	1	3		3.0
McKenna, J.	Shamrocks	2	9		4.5
Fyfe, J.	Crescents	1	8		8.0

Scoring Summary

Name Club GP G

Name	Club	GP	G
Kingan, A.	MAAA	7	5
Low, G.S.	MAAA	6	4
McNaughton, A.	MAAA	6	3
Cafferty, T.	Shamrocks	2	1
Cameron, A.	MAAA	6	1
Kinghorn, J.	Victorias	1	1
Lee, S.	MAAA	1	1
McQuisten, S.	Crescents	2	1
Warden, W.	Victorias	2	1
Ashe, F.	Victorias	1	0
Barlow, E.	Victorias	2	0
Barlow, W.	Victorias	1	0
Barry, J.	Victorias	2	0
Boon, S.	Crescents	1	0
Brown, D.	Crescents	2	0
Cooke, J.	Shamrocks	1	0
Dwyer, J.	Shamrocks	1	0
Dwyer, T.	Shamrocks	2	0
Elliott, R.A.	MAAA	5	0
Fairbairn, W.	Shamrocks	2	0
Findlay, J.	MAAA	3	0
Fyfe, J.	Crescents	1	0
Irving, A.	MAAA	2	0
Jamieson, W.	Victorias	1	0
Kerr, J.	Ottawa	1	0
Kirby, C.	Ottawa	1	0
Kirby, H.	Ottawa	1	0
Laing, R.	Crescents	2	0
Laing, W.	Crescents	1	0
Lavery, A.	Shamrocks	2	0
McDonnell, J.	Crescents	2	0
Price, J.	Shamrocks	2	0
Ritchie, A.	Crescents	1	0
Ross, P.D.	Ottawa	1	0
Routh, H.	MAAA	1	0
Shearer, A.	Victorias	2	0
Smith, C.	Ottawa	1	0
Stewart, J.A.	MAAA	7	0
Tansey, M.	Shamrocks	1	0
Young, W.C.	Ottawa	1	0

Note: Scorers not identified for one MAAA goal, February 4th; all six goals, MAAA and Shamrocks, February 27th; all ten goals, MAAA and Crescents, March 5th. (Total: 17)

MAAA
AHAC Champions

Cameron, A.*	—	cover point, forward
Elliott, R.A.	—	cover point, forward
Findlay, J.	—	forward
Irving, A.*	—	forward
Kingan, A.*	—	forward
Lee, S.	—	forward
Low, G.S.*	—	forward
McNaughton, A.*	—	forward, goal
Paton, T.L.*	—	goal
Routh, H.	—	forward
Stewart, J.A.*	—	point

* Appeared in final championship match.

1892

The Amateur Hockey Association of Canada held its fifth annual meeting in the Montreal Amateur Athletic Association rooms on December 2, 1891. Attending the meeting were representatives of the MAAA, Victoria, Shamrock, Britannia, Crescent, Sherbrooke and Ottawa clubs.

The following officers were elected:

President ……	J.A. Stewart
1st Vice-Pres.	F.M.S. Jenkins
2nd Vice-Pres.	G. Carpenter
Sec.-Treasurer	J. Findlay
Council ………	A. Laurie
………………	B.B. Stevenson
………………	J. Crathern
………………	Kelly
………………	H. Ash

After much discussion, the Association decided to retain the challenge system for deciding the championship. J. Crathern and J. Findlay were appointed to a committee to arrange for a championship cup.

In AHAC friendly matches, Quebec

defeated Sherbrooke 14–1 on January 26; the Shamrocks defeated MAAA 2–1 on January 29; Sherbrooke defeated the Victorias 6–5 on January 30; the Victorias defeated MAAA 8–4 on February 2; MAAA and Britannia played to a 2–2 draw on February 3; and MAAA defeated the Shamrocks 4–1 on February 5.

The official season started on January 8 when MAAA accepted the Ottawa challenge at the Crystal Rink. It would prove to be the only championship match played in Montreal that season. Ottawa surprised everyone by defeating the seemingly invincible MAAA 4–3, though overtime was required to settle matters after MAAA tied the game with moments to play. Ottawa had the best of it and finally won on a "neat" goal by J. Kerr. The Ottawas were now the champions and the first team from outside Montreal to hold that distinction. With the title theirs to defend, they would now enjoy the advantage of meeting any challenger in the familiar surroundings of the Rideau Rink in Ottawa.

One of the largest crowds to witness a hockey contest in the capital turned out on January 15 to see the first AHAC championship match to be played there, with the Shamrocks as the visitors. The struggle was said to be by no means as one-sided as the score indicated but, nevertheless, the champions prevailed 8–3 and looked forward to their next defence. That came six days later when MAAA arrived to settle accounts, but it was not to be. The Montreal club entered the game under a severe handicap—their regular goalkeeper, Tom Paton, was not in uniform and his place was to be taken by the club's secretary-treasurer Harry Shaw. Shaw's only previous experience in the AHAC had come two years earlier when, as a last-minute replacement, he played goal for the Victorias in a friendly match against his own MAAA club. On that occasion, his erstwhile colleagues showed no mercy on their administrator, putting the puck through five times. The Ottawa fixture was strictly no contest as the locals scored ten times on the hapless substitute while MAAA could manage only two on Ottawa's A. Morel.

In their next three matches at the Rideau Rink, the Ottawas withstood two challenges from Quebec and another from the MAAA. In the first of those three, Quebec's Herb Scott played with a pink handkerchief around his head. The final championship match of the season was slated for the Rideau Rink on March 7 when MAAA would yet again be the challengers. Coming into that contest, Ottawa had won all six of its AHAC matches while MAAA had lost their three, all against Ottawa. A contingent of 200 Montreal supporters, including some of the city's leading sporting men, went up to Ottawa on a Canada Atlantic Railway special. They were not disappointed as A. Hodgson scored the game's only goal to bring the championship back to Montreal. People were startled by the turn of events and the *Montreal Gazette* proclaimed Ottawa supporters to be soreheads. But in a letter to the editor, a reader questioned the fairness of the system, pointing out that Ottawa had lost only one game all season while MAAA had won only one. In its reply, the *Gazette* defended the legitimacy of the title going to the Montreal club, saying "the Ottawas now get back some of their own medicine," and concluding with the barb that Ottawa "wanted a challenge system and they got it."

At a dinner honoring the Ottawa Hockey Club in the Russell House hotel on March 18, an aide to Canada's Governor-General, Lord Stanley of Preston, announced the intention of His Excellency to donate a challenge cup to be held each year by the champion hockey team in the Dominion.

AHAC Challenge System

Date	Team	Score	Team	Score
Jan. 8th	Ottawa	(4)	MAAA	(3)
	at Crystal Rink			
Jan. 15th	Ottawa	(8)	Shamrocks	(3)
	at Rideau Rink			
Jan. 21st	Ottawa	(10)	MAAA	(2)
	at Rideau Rink			
Jan. 28th	Ottawa	(4)	Quebec	(3)
	at Rideau Rink			
Feb. 11th	Ottawa	(3)	MAAA	(1)
	at Rideau Rink			
Feb. 18th	Ottawa	(2)	Quebec	(0)
	at Rideau Rink			
Mar. 7th	MAAA	(1)	Ottawa	(0)
	at Rideau Rink			

Goalkeeper Averages

Name	Club	GP	GA	SO	Avg.
Morel, A.	Ottawa	7	13	1	1.9
Paton, T.L.	MAAA	3	7	1	2.3
Patten, H.	Quebec	2	6		3.0
McKenna, J.	Shamrocks	1	8		8.0
Shaw, H.	MAAA	1	10		10.0

Scoring Summary +

Name	Club	GP	G
Bradley, R.	Ottawa	7	12
Kirby, C.	Ottawa	7	5
Kerr, J.	Ottawa	7	4
Kirby, H.	Ottawa	6	4
Russell, B.	Ottawa	7	3
Murray, W.	Shamrocks	1	2
Scott, H.E.	Quebec	1	2
Barlow, W.	MAAA	2	1
Brown, D.	Shamrocks	1	1
Elliott, R.A..	MAAA	1	1
Hodgson, A.	MAAA	1	1
Kingan, A.	MAAA	3	1
Lee, S.	MAAA	2	1
Low, G.S.	MAAA	4	1
Barry, J.	MAAA	2	0
Bignell, H.	Quebec	2	0
Cameron, A.	MAAA	1	0
Davidson, R.	Quebec	2	0
Dwyer, T.	Shamrocks	1	0
Irving, A.	MAAA	3	0
Jenkins, F.M.S.	Ottawa	2	0
Laing, W.	Shamrocks	1	0
McDonald, J.	Shamrocks	1	0
McNaughton, A.	MAAA	1	0
McQuisten, S.	Shamrocks	1	0
Routh, H.	MAAA	1	0
Scott, A.D.	Quebec	2	0
Scott, A.E.	Quebec	2	0
Smith, C.	Quebec	1	0
Stewart, J.A.	MAAA	3	0
Watson, D.	Quebec	2	0
Young, W.C.	Ottawa	7	0

+ Scorers not identified for: one MAAA goal, January 8; three Ottawa goals, January 15; one Quebec goal, January 28.

MAAA
AHAC Champions

Name		Position
Barlow, W.	—	forward, point
Barry, J.	—	cover point
Cameron, A.*	—	cover point
Elliott, R.A.	—	forward
Hodgson, A.*	—	forward
Irving, A.	—	forward
Kingan, A.*	—	forward
Lee, S.	—	forward
Low, G.S.*	—	forward
McNaughton, A.*	—	forward
Paton, T.L.*	—	goal
Routh, H.	—	cover point
Stewart, J.A.*	—	point
Shaw, H.	—	goal

*Appeared in final championship match.

CHAPTER 4

McGill University

The Missing Link to the Birthplace of Hockey

Earl Zukerman

TITLE TO THE "BIRTHPLACE OF HOCKEY" has been a hotly disputed topic since the 1930s, with historians debating whether hockey began in Montreal, Kingston or in the Halifax-Windsor region of Nova Scotia. In recent years, Kingston historians have conceded that their early form of the game was indeed "shinny," which is different and distinct from "hockey." The Maritime claim however, has steadfastly refused to accept the argument presented by the Montreal case, which involves a number of students at McGill University.

One thing is clear—hockey was not invented overnight. The game evolved over a long period of time. It is apparent that rudimentary forms of hockey, such as shinny, were played in Nova Scotia prior to the first organized hockey game in Montreal. However, if one accepts the premise that shinny is synonymous with hockey, then one also must throw out any claims to hockey's birthplace being in Canada, as there is much documentation of shinny-like games in Europe which predate all Nova Scotian references.

Shinny indeed may have been a precursor to the game of hockey, but shinny undoubtedly evolved from other stick and ball games like polo and field hockey, which date to Europe in the dark ages. In the fifth century B.C., the Greeks had a game that was played with crooked sticks and a ball. A crude form of this sport also was played in ancient Rome and spread to Asia, but never assumed any importance as a competitive sport until adopted by the European countries. When Europe took up field hockey, it made specific rules that disassociated it completely from other similar games.

In its many variations, "hockey-like" games were known to most northern people in Europe and Asia. In Scotland, their version was called "Shinty." In Ireland, they played "Hurley." Another similar game, called "Bandy," was played for centuries in northern Europe. All these outdoor games were similar to hockey and forms of these games were played on frozen ponds and lakes during the winter.

Forms of the game most commonly known as shinny, hurling, hurtling or hurley were brought to North America when Irish, English, French and Scots immigrated. They brought with them all these versions of the sport, which eventually was thrown into a melting pot and came out as hockey. The sport of hockey also would adopt rules from field hockey, lacrosse and rugby football.

Hockey indeed may have had its seed planted in Nova Scotia in various forms of shinny and hurley, but the evidence is overwhelming that the sport was harvested in Montreal. Those who support the Windsor-Halifax claim to hockey's beginnings argue that earlier forms of the sport are proof that hockey was first played in the Maritimes. The game in Canada clearly has its roots in Nova Scotia of the early 1800s, when the Mi'kmaq on-ice folk game of "Oochamukunutk" (Mi'kmaq Natives also played an early form of lacrosse known as "Baggataway") was blended with the games transplanted from the British Isles. The similar ice games of ricket and hurley were documented in Nova Scotia by an article in the *Boston Evening Gazette* on November 5, 1859. But are these games hockey?

To argue the issue logically, one first must define what constitutes the game of hockey. *Webster's New World Dictionary* defines a game as "any specific amusement or sport involving competition under specific rules: as football and chess are games." To use a simple metaphor, Montreal is debating that hockey has a distinct shape, much like an apple has a shape. But the Windsor-Halifax proponents counter-punch that the word "hockey" can be interchanged with "shinny" or "hurley," both early forms of hockey. That's like saying that an apple seed is the same as an apple. Certainly you cannot have an apple without first having a seed, but is a seed an apple? Is shinny or hurley on ice the same as hockey on ice?

On Dec. 1, 1877, the *McGill University Gazette* had the following entry:

> *"Many fancy that hockey and 'shinney' are synonymous. Never was a greater mistake made. Hockey is like 'shinney' in being played with a peculiar stick and block—in that respect alone. The rules of the Halifax Hockey Club, as they are called, are modeled after football rules. 'Offside' is strictly kept. Charging in any way from behind is allowed, and so on."*

This excerpt clearly makes a distinction between the two sports. This is also the first reference to the so-called "Halifax Rules," although there was no printed set of these rules until decades later, when James Power of the *Halifax Herald* supposedly listed them in 1937. According to the *McGill University Gazette* reference, the Nova Scotian game featured an offside rule. But other references to the Halifax rules indicated that the game allowed forward passing, something not used in the Montreal game until bluelines were introduced to the NHL in 1918–19. The Halifax game also featured goals that were facing the sides of the rink rather than the opposite end. This quirk allowed players to score from either side of the goal line!

In 1943, Professor Emanuel M. Orlick, an assistant director of physical education at McGill, wrote a series of articles on the origins of hockey for both the *Montreal Gazette* and *The McGill News*. Aided by the research of McGill professors F.M. Van Wagner and A.S. Lamb, Orlick used documented evidence and concluded that McGill students formed the first organized team, were responsible for the introduction of codified rules, a flat circular puck, the use of goaltenders and regulated goal areas, hockey officials and team uniforms, among other things.

Orlick, in his well-researched article entitled "McGill Contributions to the Origin of Ice Hockey," hit the hammer on the nail when he wrote: "The question is not when the games of field hockey, hoquet, hurley or shinney started, but rather, when and where did hurley or shinney develop into the game of Ice Hockey as we know it today?"

The first-hand evidence, which includes numerous old letters and newspaper accounts found at the McGill Archives, clearly indicates that McGill students have been instrumental in the evolution of "modern-day" hockey.

James George Aylwin Creighton, a native of Halifax who moved to Montreal in 1872 and graduated from McGill law school in 1880, is said to have drafted some informal rules for *"ice hockey"* in 1873 after he and other friends, including McGill student Henry Joseph, tried to play lacrosse on skates in the Victoria Skating Rink. Creighton eventually captained one of the teams that played in the world's first public display of an ice hockey game played indoors. The contest was played on March 3, 1875, at the Victoria Skating Rink, located in the part of Montreal that is bordered by three streets: Drummond, De Maisonneuve and Dorchester (now Rene Levesque Boulevard).

The boundaries of the three streets limited the dimensions of the arena ice surface to approximately 200 feet by 85 feet and forever changed the game. The smaller indoor playing surface necessitated limiting the number of players on each team. Prior to then, games of shinny were played on wide-open frozen lakes and rivers with dozens, even hundreds, of participants.

Pre- and post-event articles about the 1875 game were published in the *Montreal Gazette*. The contest was divided into two halves and played with nine men per side. At least nine of the 18 players were believed to be McGill students. One team was composed of Creighton (captain), Joseph, Esdaile, Henshaw, Chapman, Powell, Clouston and the Campbell brothers. The players on the other side were Torrance (captain), Meagher, Potter, Goff, Barnston, Gardner, Griffin, Jarvis and Whiting.

The 1875 game introduced standardized goals, positions (including goalkeepers), referees, goal judges and playing uniforms. The indoor game also necessitated the change from a lacrosse ball to a flat wooden disk to reduce the chance of injury to spectators and glass windows! The word "puck" was first used by a newspaper in an 1876 account of a game reported in the *Montreal Gazette*. It is believed to derive from the Scottish and Gaelic word "puc." This definition is explained in a book entitled *English as We Speak It in Ireland* by P.W. Joyce. The book, published by Longmans, Green and Co. in 1910, contains the following reference on page 308:

> *"Puck: a blow. 'He gave him a puck of a stick on the head. More commonly applied to a punch or blow of the horns of a cow or goat! The cow gave him a puck (or pucked him) with her horns and knocked him down. The blow given by a hurler to the ball with his caman or hurley is always called a puck. Irish poc, same sound and meaning."*

The origin of the name "hockey" also is interesting. One theory is that ancient France gave its "ball and stick game" the modern-day name of "*hoquet*" (pronounced ho-kay). The word meant "shepherd's crook" and was applied to the game because it was played with a hooked stick. Some historians say that England took the pronunciation and spelled it "hockey," i.e., field hockey. (For more on the origins of the word hockey see Gerald Owen's article The Origins of "Hockey" on page 3 of this edition of *Total Hockey*.)

Rules Published and First Team Organized in 1877

The *McGill University Gazette*, dated February 1, 1877, reported that McGill students had formed an organized ice hockey club. There is no evidence of another hockey team being organized formally prior to the McGill club. Archibald Dunbar Taylor was elected as McGill's team president, Harry Abbott the team captain, R.J. Howard, secretary and treasurer. Fred Torrence and Lorne Campbell (goalie) also were elected to the executive. Other members of the team were Nelson, W. Redpath, Coverhill and Dawson.

The publication reported that the first of three contests with the "Victorias" was a 2–1 victory for McGill on January 31, 1877. The Victorias were then an unofficial team, composed of an amalgamation of players from the Montreal Lacrosse Club, the Montreal Football Club and other members of the Victoria Rink. McGill lost its second game 1–0 on March 19, 1877, but bounced back with a win against the Victorias in the third contest.

The rules of ice hockey first were published in the *Montreal Gazette* on February 27, 1877, only a few weeks after the McGill hockey club played its first official game. Although there is no hard evidence, it is theorized that Creighton, who worked for the newspaper around that time, submitted the rules [below]. Except for the use of the word "ice" in Rule 5, these rules were identical to the field hockey rules created in England in 1875. Note that the word "Bully" refers to a face-off and the word "game" usually refers to a "goal."

1. *The game shall be commenced and renewed by a Bully in the centre of the ground. Goals shall be changed after each game.*
2. *When a player hits the ball, any one of the same side who at such moment of hitting is nearer to the opponents' goal line is out of play, and may not touch the ball himself, or in any way whatever prevent any other player from doing so, until the ball has been played. A player must always be on his own side of the ball.*
3. *The ball may be stopped, but not carried or knocked on by any part of the body. No player shall raise his stick above his shoulder. Charging from behind, tripping, collaring, kicking or shinning shall not be allowed.*
4. *When the ball is hit behind the goal line by the attacking side, it shall be brought out straight 15 yards, and started again by a Bully; but, if hit behind by any one of the side whose goal line it is, a player of the opposite side shall hit it out from within one yard of the nearest corner, no player of the attacking side at that time shall be within 20 yards of the goal line, and the defenders, with the exception of the goal-keeper, must be behind their goal line.*
5. *When the ball goes off at the side, a player of the opposite side to that which hit it out shall roll it out from the point on the boundary line at which it went off at right angles with the boundary line, and it shall not be in play until it has touched the ice, and the player rolling it in*

shall not play it until it has been played by another player, every player being then behind the ball.
6. *On the infringement of any of the above rules, the ball shall be brought back and a Bully shall take place.*
7. *All disputes shall be settled by the Umpires, or in the event of their disagreement, by the Referee.*

Sometime between 1877 and 1886 the rules underwent radical changes and it appears McGill students were involved in making the newer rules distinct from the adopted "field hockey" rules of 1877.

In 1908, McGill graduate Richard F. Smith told *The Montreal Star* he and two friends had drafted the rules to hockey in September, 1878. Smith claims that he then submitted the rules of hockey to a group of fellow students on September 17, 1879. Smith explained he borrowed some rules from field hockey, designed a few of his own and then mixed in some rugby football rules. But in an unrelated letter, McGill graduate William Fleet Robertson reported that he came upon a game of field hockey on a visit to England in 1879, and upon his return to studies in the winter, helped better organize the sport at McGill.

However, W.L. (Chick) Murray, another McGill graduate, claims it was he who drafted the first official set of rules to ice hockey, then known as "Shinny on Your Own Side," on November 10, 1879. Murray says the next day he discussed the rules with classmate R.F. Smith. On November 12, 1879, Murray, Smith and Robertson revised the rules and agreed Smith would write them down. They indicated the first game under these new rules was played—with a square puck cut by Smith from a rubber ball—on the ice of the St. Lawrence River in December, 1879. Original rules called for nine players on each side, but over 30 participated in that first game. The rules stipulated the stick could not be lifted higher than the knee, which Smith later amended to make the hips the limit. Smith and Robertson, both football players at McGill, incorporated football's onside pass into the hockey rules. (Offsides remained constant in hockey for 40 years until Frank and Lester Patrick, both former McGill students, the code for the first time, revolutionizing the game with forward passing rules as a box-office attraction in their Pacific Coast Hockey Association.)

More fuel was added to the fire regarding the game's early rules in 1899, when former McGill player Arthur Farrell authored the first book on the subject of hockey *(Hockey: Canada's Royal Winter Game)*. Farrell wrote that no rules were known prior to 1880, which, of course, was incorrect; the *Montreal Gazette* had published hockey rules in 1877.

During the winter of 1879–80, several McGill class teams played against each other, but none took the sport seriously enough to keep track of wins and losses. Usually they started with nine players aside but, due to fatigue, often had fewer players by game's end. The original playing time was two hours but as the game became more popular, each side would have substitutes and the time limit was extended to three hours.

First Hockey Team Photo in 1881

On February 21, 1881, the McGill hockey club posed at the Crystal Palace Skating Rink for what is believed to be the first official photograph of a hockey team. Pictured in the William Notman photo were: Albert Peter Low, W.W. Weeks, P.L. Foster, T. Drummond, R.C. Smith, John Alexander Kinlock, Frederick Hague, F.W. Skaife, John J. Collins, W.L. Murray and referee Frank Weir.

Upon graduation, A.P. Low and a few of his classmates moved to Ottawa and apparently introduced the game there. A few years earlier, Edward Thornton Taylor, who had graduated from McGill in 1878, had gone on to Royal Military College in Kingston, where he reportedly introduced the game to that city.

The World's First Hockey Championship

In 1883, the world's first hockey championship, a three-team tourney, was contested on the St. Lawrence River at the Montreal Winter Carnival. The teams played with a square wooden puck and the sticks used were much the same as those used today in field hockey. A significant rule change to seven players per side was made at the last minute by the rules committee, as the Quebec City entry was only able to field a seven-man team.

McGill defeated the Victorias, 1–0, and tied Quebec, 2–2, to win the silver Birks Cup, sometimes referred to as the Bedouin Cup, then valued at $750. Each member of the winning team also received a silver clasp. The Birks Cup can be found today at McGill's McCord Museum of Canadian History. Names of the first official championship team, along with referee N.T. Rielle, were engraved on the cup, a tradition later maintained on the Stanley Cup. Those engraved on the first Birks Cup included A.P. Low (goalie), J.M. Elder (point) and P.D. Green (cover point), plus forwards Richard W. Smith, W.L. Murray, J.A. Kinlock (captain) and P.L. Foster.

In 1884, the Montreal Winter Carnival tournament, played outdoors on the McGill campus rink, was expanded to five teams, including four from Montreal (McGill, Victorias, Wanderers, Crystals) and the Ottawa Hockey Club. Similar to the previous year, the Carnival rules committee arbitrarily reduced team sizes from nine to seven. Though this move was criticized in the *McGill University Gazette*, seven players per side would soon become the standard. The Victorias, led by McGill graduate R.F. Smith, won the mythical "Canadian championship" on February 21, 1884, after defeating Ottawa. In 1885, Smith helped found the Montreal Amateur Athletic Association team and entered them into the Winter Carnival tournament, which was played indoors at the Crystal Rink. The Winter Carnival hockey championship featured the MAAA, McGill, Crystals, Victorias, the Montreal Football Club and Ottawa. The MAAA defeated McGill, 1–0, in the semifinals and beat Ottawa in the finals.

It was with this set of games over three years at the Montreal Winter Carnival that hockey began to come into its own. In a letter to the editor of the *McGill University Gazette* on March 31, 1886, McGill team captain Arthur Weir presented his team's year-end report. He wrote in part: "With the other city clubs, we entered the matches for the Championship of Montreal, and sent our delegate to the committee for revising the rules. Our rules were adopted almost without exception…"

On December 8, 1886, the first official hockey league, the Amateur Hockey Association of Canada, was founded in Montreal. The Dominion Hockey Association, as it also was known, was divided into senior and junior sections, the latter consisting of the more recent members until their play merited promotion to the senior ranking. As these matches were under the jurisdiction of the Dominion Hockey Association, the winner of the senior group was declared Canadian champion.

There were five original senior members: McGill, MAAA, Montreal Victorias, Ottawa and the Montreal Crystals. The first league game was a 3–1 decision for the Crystals over McGill at the Crystal Rink on January 7, 1887. The Victorias soon captured the league championship, but subsequently abdicated the title to the Crystals in March. The Victorias later challenged the Crystals and won the mythical "Canadian championship."

The McGill rules that were adopted by the Dominion Hockey Association were published in the *Montreal Gazette* on December 23, 1886. Unlike the 1877 published rules, the 1886 version is remarkably similar, although less detailed, to the rules of the game today. The rule that specifies the size and composition of the "vulcanized" puck, is still the same more than a century later! (The rules and history of the Amateur Hockey Association of Canada can be found on page 9 of this book.)

McGILL PROMINENT IN HOCKEY INTO THE 20TH CENTURY

Two decades after McGill met Harvard in the first international intercollegiate football game (1874) and hockey had moved indoors in Montreal (1875), the two schools were reported to have locked horns in a hockey game at the Victoria Rink on February 23, 1894. A newspaper made reference to McGill winning 14–1 in a contest that marked the first "international" game. However, Harvard does not have this game in its modern-day records.

On February 2, 1895, Queen's defeated McGill, 6–5, in Kingston, beginning what is the second-longest existing active rivalry in hockey after the Queen's-RMC rivalry that began in 1886. On February 20, 1899, McGill defeated the Toronto Varsity Blues, 8–4, in Montreal, beginning another rivalry still active more than a century later.

In 1900–01, Lester Patrick and H.L. "Billy" Gilmour, both future McGill team captains and Hockey Hall of Fame members, made their debut in a McGill uniform. A new intercollegiate league was proposed after a meeting in 1901 with McGill, Queen's, Toronto, Royal Military College, Osgoode Hall, Ottawa College and Trinity University. In exhibition matches, McGill lost, 8–6, at Toronto on February 13, 1902, and subsequently lost, 5–3, at Queen's two days later. In that game, the first half was played under "Quebec rules" while the second half was played under "Ontario rules."

The world's first university hockey league—the Canadian Intercollegiate Hockey Union—became a reality on January 7, 1903, when McGill, Queen's and the University of Toronto officially formed the conference. McGill lost their league opener, 7–0, versus Queen's on January 23, but won the CIHU's first-ever "Queen's Cup" championship after Toronto defeated Queen's and McGill subsequently defeated the Varsity Blues, 9–7, on January 30, 1903.

McGill won the Queen's Cup again in 1904–05 by winning the CIHU title with a 3–1 record. Lester Patrick made a return to the McGill lineup and joined his brother Frank. That season, Dunny McCallum established a McGill single-game scoring record that still stands by notching eight goals in a 14–2 home-ice win versus Toronto on February 10, 1905.

McGill has had a profound and ongoing impact on the development of hockey. Students from the university in Montreal helped pioneer the game and left a discernable trail of breadcrumbs in their wake as proof of their pivotal role. In the first few decades after they helped to organize the game, 12 members of the McGill hockey club went on to be inducted into the Hockey Hall of Fame. Thirteen of McGill's hockey team members combined to win a total of 34 Stanley Cup titles.

If one's definition of hockey begins with the introduction of such sports as hurley or shinny, then the game is definitely not Canadian. Those games clearly evolved from European influences. However, if one defines the game of hockey with the advent of standardized written rules, a limit to the number of players, regulated ice dimensions, a basic formal structure with organized clubs, team jerseys, referees and regulation goal areas, then the game truly originated with the input of McGill University students in Montreal during the mid-1870s.

Bill Fitsell, past-president of the Society of International Hockey Research, summed it up best when he wrote the following passage in his book *Hockey's Captains, Colonels & Kings*: "In brief, the game was conceived in Halifax, but born in Montreal and grew to a strapping youngster in those two cities and later in Quebec City and Ottawa."

CHAPTER 5

They Refused the Stanley Cup

Anatomy of a Controversy

Paul Kitchen

JUST AS THE GATHERING of well-established merchants, entrepreneurs, commission agents, rising young bank clerks and business administrators was settling into their seats in the gymnasium at the appointed hour of nine o'clock on the evening of May 15, 1893, their president called to order the 12th annual meeting of the Montreal Amateur Athletic Association.

After the short but necessary preliminary task of reading the published notice of meeting, the president went straight to the agenda's highlight—the presentation, for the first time, of the Stanley hockey championship cup. Ushered ceremoniously by one of the Association's past presidents, a distinguished looking gentleman from Ottawa approached the front of the room carrying a magnificent mahogany box enclosing the bowl-shaped silver trophy. As one of the cup's two trustees, it was his duty to present the prize to the MAAA in recognition of their senior team's championship of the Amateur Hockey Association of Canada. A hearty round of applause followed the genteel exchange of pleasantries between the trustee and the grateful MAAA president, who received the Cup with all the grace and dignity one would expect from the head of the city's most prestigious athletic organization. Newspapers the next day reported the occasion in glowing terms.

The smooth orchestration of events had worked perfectly. The public would have no idea of the turmoil that wracked the Association. They would know nothing about petty omissions, petulant assertions in internal letters, or demands that the trophy not be accepted. The MAAA's pristine public image, carefully cultivated by successive secretaries and boards of directors, would be preserved.

The innermost thoughts dictating the actions of the story's chief antagonist, the president of the Montreal Hockey Club, in refusing the Cup will never be known to us. But elements of the story can be pieced together through an examination of the records of the MAAA and the Montreal Hockey Club connected to it.

To understand the backdrop to the Stanley Cup controversy, it is necessary to begin with the creation of the Montreal Amateur Athletic Association itself in 1881. On June 20 of that year, the Legislature of Quebec gave final approval to an act of incorporation bringing together into one new organization three existing athletic bodies: the Montreal Lacrosse, Snow Shoe and Bicycle Clubs. They surrendered their individual autonomy in order that a larger umbrella organization might look after the affairs of the three associations more effectively and with the idea that pooled resources would allow the activities of all three to flourish. Provision was made for other clubs to join, and by 1885 both the Montreal Football Club and the Tuque Bleue Toboggan Club had done so. The presidents of these affiliated clubs, along with additional representatives elected by the clubs, made up the MAAA's board of directors.

The original constitution of the Association stated its objectives to be "the encouragement of athletic sports, the promotion of physical and mental culture, and the providing of rational amusements for its members." Sportsmen in the comfortable middle and upper classes placed great value on the concept of amateurism and generally disdained the motive of monetary gain from athletic participation that was creeping into many sports such as foot racing, rowing, wrestling and lacrosse. To them, professionalism—with which rigged outcomes and under-the-table payments were frequently associated—tarnished sport's honorable objectives of discipline, team loyalty, fair play and proper sporting conduct. The joy of physical activity, gentlemanly competition and sport for sport's sake should be reward enough, thought the MAAA. Wishing to attract members who shared those values and to bar others who did not, the newly founded organization adopted a rigidly idealistic definition of an amateur athlete. "An amateur," proclaimed the constitution, "is any person who has never competed in any open competition, or for a stake, or for public money, or under a false name; or with a professional, for a prize or where gate money is charged; and who has never at any period of his life taught or assisted in the pursuit of athletic exercises as a means of a livelihood." (An astute business decision taken by the board in 1886 saw the prohibition against gate money removed from the Association's revised constitution. It was one thing for the MAAA's members to be simon-pure amateurs and quite another for the Association to miss out on the revenue potential afforded by admission charges to its competitive events.)

Admittance to the ranks of the MAAA was privileged. To gain entry, a prospective member had to be elected by the board. Lists of applicants, called "propositions" and duly nominated and seconded by existing members, would be brought to board meetings. For each list, a "Committee of Enquiry" would be formed to scrutinize the applications and recommend whether the prospects were worthy or not. At a following meeting, the board would vote. The MAAA drew its membership very largely from the business and mercantile population of English Montreal residing in the sprawling St. Antoine ward which stretched out from the east slope of Mount Royal. The wealthy enclave of Westmount, reaching up the mountain on the south, was also well represented. Though the Association catered to the middle and upper-middle classes, it did not attract the true economic and political elite who favored even more exclusive association in the tandem and hunt clubs of the day.

Typical of the members who at one time or another served on the MAAA board before the turn of the last century were founding members William L. Maltby, president of a roofing cement company who resided at the luxurious

Windsor Hotel, and Thomas L. Paton, a manufacturer's agent who enjoyed a summer residence at Valois. Both would figure in the Stanley Cup controversy. Another prominent early director was James G. Ross, an accountant in the firm of P.S. Ross and Sons who lived in Westmount and summered at Lakeside. Ross, who remained an MAAA member for many years, and who also had a role in the Cup dispute, later distinguished himself overseas in the Great War, becoming Paymaster in Chief on the Canadian Expeditionary Force.

By 1884 the directors had reason to be optimistic about the future of the Montreal Amateur Athletic Association. The debt on the gymnasium building, acquired at the outset as a headquarters, was well on the way to being paid off, membership was growing and the affiliated clubs were thriving. As such, at a board meeting in late November, when director Tom Paton sought permission to call a meeting for the purpose of forming a hockey club within the Association, the directors were in a frame of mind to consider new ideas and swiftly approved Paton's request. Paton was an ardent skater and a hockey enthusiast and was well aware of the impact the new sport was beginning to have on the winter recreational scene. He acted quickly and within four days the "Montreal Hockey Club," as the name was recorded in the minutes of the board's next meeting, was a reality.

Soon to be familiarly known as the MAAA, the hockey club started practicing at the Crystal Rink almost immediately and soon felt confident enough to enter the hockey tournament at the third annual Montreal Winter Carnival in February 1885. Astonishingly, the newly assembled MAAA team won the tournament and proudly presented a handsome trophy to the directors, who promptly ordered that it be put on display in the Association's rooms. So began a mutually rewarding relationship between a constituent club of the Association and the Association's board of directors. The club received numerous encouragements and financial considerations over the next nine years and the board basked in the glory the hockey players brought to the Association.

Characteristic of an organization with a mercantile and professional membership base, the board of directors operated the affairs of the Association in a business-like manner. They were diligent about meetings, assembling each week to review the Association's activities. This enabled them to look into every imaginable administrative detail, which they relished doing. On one occasion they resolved to subscribe to the *Ottawa Journal* for the library's reading room. On another, they decided to buy a blanket for the horse earlier acquired for work on the grounds. Subsequently, when they found the animal too spirited, they formed a sub-committee to deal with the problem and instructed it to make whatever changes were necessary in obtaining a horse better fitted to the task. It was therefore completely consistent with its managerial style for the board to stay closely in touch with the hockey club's progress.

Over the first nine years of its existence, right up to the first presentation of the Stanley Cup, the Montreal Hockey Club enjoyed the almost paternalistic support of the board of directors. There were two reasons for this. First, the hockey club was a creature of the board itself. Unlike the affiliated clubs, such as the Lacrosse, Snow Shoe and Bicycle Clubs, which had had an independent identity prior to their affiliation with the MAAA, the hockey club was born of the MAAA. Moreover, unlike an affiliated club where a member was permitted to belong to it alone and was not required to take out a full membership in the MAAA, all members of the hockey club were required to carry full MAAA membership cards. For descriptive purposes, the Montreal Hockey Club was identified organizationally as a "connected club."

The second reason for the board's attentiveness to the club was not structural but personal, in the name of Thomas L. Paton. Tom Paton was the MAAA's strongest proponent. He was a founding member of the body and one of its most tireless workers, primarily in his capacity as a director for 13 of the Association's first 14 years. As well as being the founder of the hockey club, he was also for years a leading player on the senior team, including the one that brought the Association its first Stanley Cup title. Thus, not only did the hockey club have the inherent support of the board, it had the immediate benefit of one of the board's most powerful directors being a member of, and advocate for, the club.

Time and time again, the board, and Tom Paton as a director, lent moral support, extended courtesies, and provided funding to the club. On numerous occasions, the board acknowledged upcoming important matches and let it be known that the presence of MAAA members at these contests would be appreciated. In an unprecedented move on March 7, 1892, the board, which was rigorous in maintaining its meeting schedule, postponed a meeting for one day to accommodate attendance at a match. The board routinely made rooms available for hockey club meetings and the club unfailingly responded with thank-you letters. Once, at the request of Tom Paton, the board granted freedom of the Association to the visiting members of the Chebucto Hockey Club of Dartmouth, Nova Scotia. On another occasion, when it was anticipated the Ottawa Hockey Team would be in town for a Saturday match, the directors granted a sum of $15 to Paton "on behalf of our hockey team" so that the Ottawa club might be entertained with a dinner in the Fencing Room after the match. Yet another significant gesture was the Board's allowance of the Association's winged wheel insignia, which the team wore on its uniform, in newspaper ads the club placed to promote matches.

The board's financial assistance took the form of both grants and loans. In the early days, the board simply assumed the hockey club's expenses, typically for rink rentals, team memberships in the rink, and travel costs for matches in Quebec and Ottawa. Later, as hockey became an increasingly attractive spectator sport, and thanks to the board's foresight in allowing gate charges for amateur matches, the MAAA senior and intermediate teams were able to meet most of their expenses through the admission revenues they shared with rink owners. This meant that the hockey club required only loans to finance its operations, which the board granted knowing that gate receipts would be sufficient to repay these advances.

For its part, the hockey club reciprocated the goodwill. It presented its first trophy to the board and handed over team photographs as a matter of course. When the club applied a $50 appropriation from the directors to the rental of ice time two nights a week at the Crystal Rink in 1887, it made sure the rink would also be available to the whole MAAA membership. At the conclusion of the 1893 season, the club presented the board with cheques totaling $162.72 "in recognition of past financial assistance received by the MHC."

Through these gestures, courtesies and cooperative acts,

a strong bond had been built up between the MAAA board and one of its prized clubs.

A meeting at the Victoria Skating Rink in Montreal in December 1886 proved to be a pivotal moment in hockey's organizational development, for it was then and there that representatives of the Montreal Hockey Club, the Victorias, the Crystals, the McGill College club, and the Ottawa Hockey Club formed the Amateur Hockey Association of Canada. (Though not present at the gathering, the Quebec club soon entered the fold and McGill eventually dropped out.) Until that time, there was no league, as such, where teams played a regular pre-determined schedule. Competition was in the form of ad hoc tournaments and series, in which the MAAA club had done very well. Now there would be a more systematic scheduling of games from the beginning of January until the middle of March. The meeting approved a set of playing rules and agreed on the Hockey Association's objective, which was "to improve, foster and perpetuate the game of hockey in Canada; protect it from professionalism, and to promote the cultivation of kindly feeling among the members of the hockey clubs." The MAAA dominated, winning six championships in the league's first seven years. It was the sixth championship, in 1893, that would lead to Stanley Cup troubles.

That season started badly for the MAAA when they lost their opening match against Ottawa. Thereafter they performed flawlessly, winning their remaining seven games, including a second match with Ottawa. The victory assured the MAAA of a first-place finish, giving them one more win than the runners-up from the capital. Tom Paton allowed the fewest goals of any netminder while teammate Haviland Routh led the league with 12 goals scored.

The year before in Ottawa, at a banquet tendered to the Ottawa Hockey Club in honor of its success that season, the Governor-General of Canada let it be known, through a speech by his aide-de-camp, that he wished to donate a "challenge cup which should be held year to year by the champion hockey team in the Dominion." Sir Frederick Arthur Stanley had begun his duties in the summer of 1888 and had seen his first game of hockey at the Montreal Winter Carnival the following February. He immediately became an enthusiast, often attended matches in Ottawa, and rejoiced in the fact that his sons had taken up the sport.

Before returning to England in 1893 at the conclusion of his term, Lord Stanley appointed two trustees, Philip Dansken Ross and Dr. John Sweetland, to administer the trophy he was in the process of acquiring. Both were prominent Ottawa citizens and frequent visitors to the Governor-General's residence at Rideau Hall. Ross, at 35 years of age, was the owner and publisher of the *Ottawa Journal* and an avid sportsman who had played for the Ottawa Hockey Club. At the time of his appointment, he was, in fact, president of the club. It seemed to trouble neither Ross nor Lord Stanley that the senior official of a team competing annually for the Canadian championship should also be one of those responsible for its administration. (In reality, Ross distinguished himself in his role, skillfully managing many contentious issues, especially in the early years, over an astounding 56-year custodianship.)

John Sweetland, the older of the trustees at 58, was a fixture among the city's social elite and the highly respected Sheriff of Ottawa. By profession he was a medical doctor who had served as president of the Ottawa Medical Chirurgical Society and as Ontario secretary of the Canada Medical Association. He had been president of the Ottawa Poor Relief Society and was a founding director of the Ottawa Ladies' College. Together, Ross and Sweetland made for a nice balance of youth and experience and were an admirably suited team to administer Lord Stanley's trophy.

Thus, by the spring of 1893 the Stanley Cup's administrative personnel were in place and the final details for the trophy's presentation were being arranged. On a Saturday in late April, Ross met the Governor-General's aide-de-camp, Lord Kilcoursie, over lunch at the Rideau Club and then spent Sunday morning drafting, as he phrased it in his diary, the "Hockey Cup rules." After breakfast the following Sunday, Ross went over to Dr. Sweetland's home to take his first look at the Stanley Cup which had only a few days earlier arrived from England.

A week later, both Ross's *Ottawa Journal* and the *Montreal Gazette* announced His Excellency's gift of the trophy. The article explained that the Cup would be presented to the Montreal Amateur Athletic Association "whose team defeated all comers during the late season, including the champions of the Ontario association." That team was the same Ottawa club that participated as well in the AHAC and it was by virtue of the MAAA victory over the Ottawas in regular AHAC play that, as the trustees saw it, entitled the Montreal club to the Stanley Cup. Among the terms under which the Cup was to be awarded was one stating that the winning team was to assume responsibility for engraving on the trophy its name and the year in which the team had won it. In parentheses, the article said "in the first instance the MAAA will find the Cup already engraved for them." The inscription read "Montreal AAA 1893."

Around the same time, Lord Kilcoursie sent a telegram to the MAAA asking for the date of its annual meeting when the Hockey Challenge trophy might be presented. With this confirmed, Ross wrote to advise that Sheriff Sweetland would be going to the meeting to present the cup. By then, Association secretary W.S. Weldon, on the instructions of president James A. Taylor, had notified Montreal Hockey Club president James Stewart (who also played on the team) to be present to receive the trophy. It was going to be a grand occasion and to emphasize the board's pride in the team's accomplishment, engraved gold rings would be presented to the players. The press had been notified and everything was set.

And then came the astounding news from the secretary and the president of the hockey club. They did not wish anyone to receive the trophy on behalf of the club until, as recorded in the MAAA board minutes, "the proper representatives of said club had an opportunity of learning the conditions upon which said trophy was to be held." In the letter dropping this bombshell, the hockey club also asked the board to communicate their position to the trustees. Taylor refused both demands and decided the ceremony should go ahead with himself as Association president receiving the Cup on behalf of the team.

At a meeting of the board held only one hour before the scheduled start of the annual general meeting, directors ratified Taylor's position in a formal motion moved by Gordon Kingan, the brother of Alex B. Kingan, a member of the championship team. Also present at that meeting was another board member whose link with the hockey club was even more direct—Tom Paton, the MAAA goalkeeper. What, if anything, he had to say about the matter and whether or how he voted on the motion is not recorded but he was clearly in an uncomfortable position. On the one hand, he must have felt some duty to support, or at least not oppose, the position of hockey club president James Stewart. On the other hand, he was less than an hour away from what had promised to be a warmly satisfying personal experience. He was, after all, the board member who less than nine years earlier had obtained permission to form a hockey club and now that club, but for Stewart's intervention, would have been readying itself to claim the new Dominion championship trophy. Furthermore Paton was a dedicated organization man, committed to the Association. Moreover, in a separate presentation, he was about to be officially honored at the annual meeting for that very dedication. It is possible but unlikely that he agreed with Stewart's insistence that the Stanley Cup be refused.

And so the board meeting ended and the annual meeting began, with Sheriff Sweetland presenting the Stanley Cup not to Montreal Hockey Club president James Stewart but to MAAA president James Taylor. Next, according to the *Gazette* and the *Daily Herald*, came the presentation of the souvenir rings to the members of the Montreal Hockey Club, followed by the presentation of a Heintzman piano to Tom Paton for his many services to the Association. There was no hint whatsoever in newspaper coverage of the event that dissension lurked just behind the happy facade.

What is not clear from official records and newspaper accounts is who among the hockey team members were actually present that night. Did some of them boycott the ring presentation ceremony? The minutes of the annual meeting note discreetly that the Stanley Cup was presented to Taylor "owing to the unavoidable absence of Mr. Stewart the president of the Mtl. Hockey Club." Paton was surely there to receive his piano but, curiously, the minutes do not record his name in the list of directors in attendance. (Several months later in an article dealing with the conditions for holding the Stanley Cup, the *Gazette* recalled that at the initial presentation "none of the officials of the Montreal Hockey Club … were present.")

With the hastily contrived ceremony over, the annual meeting complete, and the Association's shining public image intact, the directors could now turn their attention to the summer's program of field sports under their newly elected president, Tom Paton. And the small problem of symbolic possession of the Stanley Cup could easily be forgotten. The MAAA winged wheel was still on the Montreal Hockey Club's sweater, the MAAA name was on the trophy and the trophy was on a shelf in the MAAA rooms. Everything was just as it would have been had the hockey club itself accepted the cup.

But Paton, as the main conduit between the board and the hockey club, could not let the matter drop. At a board meeting in late November he re-introduced the subject, noting that his presidential predecessor James Taylor had contemplated returning the Cup to the trustees since the club would not accept it. Paton asked the directors for an expression of opinion and after a long discussion they concluded that "such action would tend to lower the name of this association in the eyes of the general public." Instead, they formed a sub-committee to meet with the hockey club to find out why it was refusing the trophy. After a meeting with representatives of the hockey club committee, including playing president Stewart, the MAAA sub-committee reported back to the directors with the information that the hockey club committee felt slighted in as much as it had not been communicated with directly by the Stanley Cup trustees when the trophy was presented. Further, the hockey club representatives wanted it understood they spoke for the entire hockey club and, as recorded in the MAAA minutes, would not agree to any propositions "whereby any petty omissions might be overlooked, and the Cup accepted by them." It is unclear who used the word "petty" to describe the so-called omissions, the MAAA sub-committee in interpreting the hockey club's attitude, or the club itself. It was crystal clear that the Montreal Hockey Club had dug in its heels.

The directors decided to take a week to think about what they had just heard but in the meantime, on a motion moved by Gordon Kingan, they asked Secretary Weldon to instruct the hockey club to have a meeting of all its members to confirm the position their three spokesmen had taken in rejecting the trophy. The club had a membership of about thirty, from which the players on the senior and intermediate teams were drawn. This was the second time that Kingan, the brother of the senior hockey team's Kingan, had raised a suspicion that the club's leaders were not necessarily representing the wishes of the membership but had their own agenda. The hockey club executive immediately dismissed the demand, saying the matter had been thoroughly discussed and that it was not necessary to call a meeting of the club.

In the midst of these increasingly tense communications, the hockey club had a request of its own. As if relations between the board and the club were perfectly fine, it serenely asked for the loan of $175 against future gate receipts to look after the season's start-up expenses. The directors had always routinely approved such advances, but this time, their patience sorely tried by the club's intransigence on the other matter, the directors balked. They resolved that "the request be laid on the table," a term used in parliamentary procedure when an issue is put aside so as to attend to more important business. Nevertheless, the board did deal with the financial request at its next meeting. It rejected a motion to further postpone consideration and then flatly rejected the loan. It was the first time the board had ever denied any kind of assistance to the Montreal Hockey Club.

Clearly, the directors were taken aback by the gall of the hockey club in expecting unquestioned cooperation from the board while at the same time standing in the way of an amicable solution to what really was a petty complaint. At the same meeting in which the funding was denied, the board responded to the hockey club's refusal to consult the membership on the handling of the Stanley Cup by deciding to hold the trophy in trust pending direction from the trustees. Sadly, the positive relationship between the board and the club, carefully nurtured over many years, had dissolved into bitterness.

Having heard that the MAAA board intended to seek instructions from the Stanley Cup trustees, the hockey club decided to make a pre-emptive strike of its own and sent off a letter to Sheriff Sweetland. Pointedly, the letter stated that the club had not received the trophy and "would like to know to whom to apply for same." It was a stunning bit of duplicity for the club's executive, which had bluntly and repeatedly rejected the board's attempts to hand the Cup over, to now ask Sweetland how they could get it.

In addition to Tom Paton, there was another member of the MAAA board who had a special interest in the dispute. That was James G. Ross, brother of Cup trustee Philip Ross. It is difficult to imagine that James, who was close to his brother and frequently socialized with him, would not have disclosed the facts to the trustee. It was not long before trustee Ross replied to the hockey club's letter to Sweetland. Admitting the possibility that the trustees may have misunderstood the relationship between the MAAA and the club, he said they would be glad to receive suggestions "to aid in the proper execution of Lord Stanley's wish to present this Cup to the champions of the Dominion."

Several weeks later, in February 1894, P.D. Ross went to Montreal to attend a meeting of the Amateur Hockey Association of Canada. The purpose was to discuss the terms under which the Stanley Cup would be competed for in the future. But the controversy was still very much on the mind of P.D. Ross. His diary reveals that the next morning he met with Montreal Hockey Club president James Stewart, and that evening attended a hockey match with his brother "Jim" of the MAAA board. It appears that these *tête-à-têtes* brought resolution, for three days later, letters signed by Sweetland and Ross went out to the MAAA and the hockey club confirming arrangements for the transfer of the Cup. The letter to Stewart acknowledged an "accidental misunderstanding" and assured him the MAAA would comply. The letter noted that it was to be held "until this year's championship has been decided." With that letter, Ross and Sweetland enclosed another addressed to MAAA Secretary-Treasurer W.S. Weldon. This was the instrument the hockey club was to use in requesting the Cup. It said that the MAAA directors "are hereby requested and authorized to deliver the Stanley hockey challenge cup, which they have kindly had in their care, to the order of Mr. J.A. Stewart, president of the Montreal Hockey Club."

Sweetland and Ross also wrote directly to Weldon. That letter served two purposes. One was as a courtesy to the Association to inform the directors of what the arrangements were and to thank the Association for its care of the Cup. The other purpose was to assure the directors that the hockey club would indeed accept it from them. Ross and Sweetland most certainly knew of the club's past obstinacy in that regard and the assurance was a subtle communication that the trustees understood the directors' dilemma.

It seemed the matter was all but concluded but there were still different interpretations over the meaning of "deliver" in the Sweetland and Ross correspondence. To the hockey club it meant that the MAAA was to physically bring the trophy to the club, and club president Stewart put it that way in his letter to Weldon. To the MAAA directors, "deliver" was to be read in the context of "to the order of J.A. Stewart." They saw the Sweetland and Ross letter as a requisition. If the club wanted the trophy, its representative could bring the requisition to the directors and "take the cup." It could not be taken far, though, since the only place the hockey club could rest it was in the MAAA's rooms.

Sometime between March 5 and March 15, 1894, the Stanley Cup came into the hands of the Montreal Hockey Club. How the transfer actually took place is not recorded. On March 22, the club defeated Ottawa in the championship game of that season and retained the trophy. Goalkeeper Tom Paton was no longer on the team and club president James Stewart played in only four games.

At its meeting of April 22, the hockey club committee instructed the secretary to send the Cup out for engraving. When it came back, the answer to the club's unhappiness, never revealed in the minutes of either the MAAA board or the hockey club committee, was right there on the trophy. The inscription read "Montreal 1894." The club had made the point that it had not wished to be publicly identified in the first place as the MAAA team but as the Montreal team.

There were residual hard feelings. When, in April of that year, the secretary of the hockey club asked if its report for the year was wanted for the MAAA annual report, the annoyed MAAA board said it was not, because of its understanding that the hockey club had decided it was not connected in any way with the Association. The club denied that it had ever seceded, and indeed had continued to avail itself of the Association's benefits. Later, when MAAA director Gordon Kingan, possibly as a gesture to reconcile the club and the board, sought a constitutional amendment which would grant "department" status to the club, club president James Stewart worked successfully to have the amendment defeated.

Was there a sense of dissatisfaction within the hockey club that its organizational standing in the Association was not as high as that of the founding clubs, those with "affiliated" status? If so, that view was clearly without merit. In all its years of existence, the club received nothing but the full support and encouragement of the Association and never, until the period of the dispute, was any request of any kind ever denied the club. A year after the Stanley Cup crisis, the club did seek affiliated status but there is no evidence that the absence of this designation was related to the Cup controversy. In any event, the application was misguided. As former president William Maltby pointed out, the hockey club was founded and supported by the members of the Association and was "part and parcel of the Association." In denying the application, the board said it "could not affiliate a club, all of whose members were already members of our Association."

The Montreal Hockey Club's stance in considering itself a club of the Montreal Amateur Athletic Association and enjoying all the privileges that connection entailed while at the same time objecting to the MAAA name being on the trophy, was poorly thought out. As such, the responsibility for the Stanley Cup fiasco rests squarely on the shoulders of the hockey club and its executive. The club was adamant in its stated position, which was that it felt slighted the trustees of the Stanley Cup had not at the beginning communicated directly with its officials as to the conditions under which the trophy would be held but instead had dealt directly with the MAAA board. But since the Montreal Hockey Club was well known as an MAAA team, it is understandable that the trustees would discuss arrangements for the presentation of the trophy with the MAAA secretary and would put the MAAA inscription on it. Furthermore, it had always been the stated intention of the MAAA for the hockey club's president to be the official recipient of the Cup at the annual meeting. Not until later, when the club had the opportunity to supervise the engraving of its second championship, did the sensitivity about its identity become explicit. Beforehand, even if it is conceded that there was an omission by the trustees in not making direct contact with the hockey club, it was too trivial for the issue that was made of it. The reaction of the Montreal Hockey Club was disruptive and had the potential to embarrass the Association in front of the former Governor-General's representatives and in the eyes of the public. They were not the actions of gentlemen, the attributes of which appellation were at the heart of the MAAA's sporting philosophy.

CHAPTER 6

Being a Hockey Fan in 1900

A Chilly Rink Through a Smoky Haze

Howard "Howdie" Mickoski

AH, TO BE A SPORTS FAN with access to a time machine. Which great sporting moments would you want to experience? A gladiatorial contest in ancient Rome? Ruth and Gehrig slugging home runs at Yankee Stadium in 1927? The first Kentucky Derby?

Given the choice, I would want to be a part of the amazing excitement of attending a championship-level hockey game at the turn of the 20th century. In the year 2000, hockey fans are more like patrons attending a concert or movie. Modern buildings offer comfortable seats in a climate controlled environment, lots of concessions and plenty of activities while we sit and watch the action. But in 1900, fans were not just watching, they were part of the action.

As the sport of hockey grew like wildfire across Canada and the northern United States in the latter part of the 19th century, spectators began to overflow the small seating capacities of the game's earliest indoor rinks. Rink owners were quick to realize that more money could be made from hockey than from pleasure skating (the reason most of the rinks had been built in the first place) and they began to build new, larger arenas specifically for hockey. In 1898, the largest rink in the world opened at Wood Avenue and St. Catherine Street in Montreal. The Westmount Arena could hold close to 7,000 fans and was often filled to capacity. The rink boasted buffet and smoking rooms, and offered blankets for rent to those who felt the rink drafty. The seats inside the Westmount Arena were marked, meaning that, for the first time, reserved tickets could be purchased in a warm, heated lobby.

Early hockey games of the 1880s had been more like social events than rugged contests. Fans came as they might to a theater for a play; to mingle with friends and watch the production. Buffet tables were often produced at half time so that players and fans could enjoy a feast before the players returned to action for the second half. Hockey uniforms at this time were very simple. Usually a player's uniform consisted of a turtleneck sweater with football pants and knee high socks. (Since most players played football in the fall, they simply used the same pants for hockey.) With so few people involved in early hockey games, there was little need for decidedly different sweaters, as the players and fans all knew each other. The casual atmosphere on the ice and in the stands began to change when more and more people started to attend the matches. As money became more prevalent, games began to get more cutthroat and city rivalries began to emerge. No longer was a hockey game a mere social outing.

By the turn of the 20th century, fans might come from anywhere to attend a game. Most lived close by and walked to the arena. Others might bundle their friends and come by toboggan, each perhaps taking a turn pulling the others along. Those who had a greater distance to travel would arrive by horse and carriage. Soon, every city had its own special hockey trains to take supporters of the local team to visiting rinks for road games. Advertisements could always be found in the local papers on the day of a hockey match, such as this one in the *Galt Daily Reporter* on January 15, 1909: "The best Professional game of the season—Galt vs. Brantford. Special trains leave Galt tomorrow night at 6:45 via GTR [Grand Trunk Railroad] returning from Brantford at 11:30. The fare is 85 cents." Author Scott Young commented in his book *One Hundred Years of Dropping the Puck* that the railway coaches were old and could no longer be used for regular travel, but they "were fine for the party atmosphere of a hockey special. Cigar smoke was everywhere. Bottles were passed around, often even to the uniformed conductor."

Hockey now had many new indoor arenas, but the temperature inside the rink was usually the same as the temperature outside. Since all rinks in Canada at the turn of the century relied on natural ice, games could only be scheduled between January and mid-March when the weather was coldest. In fact, teams usually did not even assemble for their first practice until after Christmas. The vast majority of games were played on the weekend because the players had regular jobs.

Fans who attended turn-of-the-century hockey games came dressed in large coats, boots and gloves, much like a modern hockey parent at a 6 a.m. practice. Unlike those modern parents, they might also use baked potatoes as hand warmers or rest their booted feet on bricks they'd heated in the oven at home. Cyclone Taylor later commented that "the fans of those days were an amazingly hearty lot, and they had to be."

Fans could get hot coffee during intermissions (it was brewed under the stands during the game), but many chose other forms of liquid refreshment to take off the chill. The best alcohol could be purchased for less than a dollar a bottle. The cold weather encouraged people to have a few in order to stay warm.

Besides alcohol, smoking was another vice of the hockey fan. Playing in indoor arenas without proper ventilation, tobacco consumption could sometimes led to problems. On January 5, 1910, a reporter for the *Montreal Gazette* covered the first game played by the city's newest team, the Canadiens. In his write-up the following day, he told of a heavy mist over the ice because of all the smoke. The story even claimed the smoke was so thick that it was difficult to distinguish the players by the second half.

Hockey fans at the turn of the century were a unique group. In Berlin (now Kitchener), Ontario, most of the cheering was done in German. In Brantford, fans came to the game with horns, megaphones and other noise devices. Fans in Ottawa were known to bring salt, to slow up the ice against fast-skating opponents. Those who could not get into a championship game would often gather at local hotels to hear the telegraph reports. Some used the new invention of the telephone to call operators and find out the score of out-of-town games. The following day's newspaper would often print the telegraph report, which was, in effect, a play-by-play account of the game.

If a modern fan had access to a time machine, the game that he would see on the ice at the beginning of the 20th century would be even more different to him than the appearance of the fans in the stands. Since 1886, a hockey team had officially consisted of seven players: goalie, point, cover point (now the two defensemen), three forwards and a rover (usually the team's best player who alternated on the rush and on defense). There was no substitution in these days. Players played the entire game; the defense stayed in the defensive end, and the forwards in the other. They were usually too tired to skate any farther. When a player was injured, the other team was required by gentleman's agreement to drop one of its own. Only for a match penalty would a team play with fewer skaters than its opponent.

Games in hockey's early days lasted 60 minutes, played in two 30-minute halves with a 10-minute break in between. The referee timed the game himself on his watch like a modern soccer referee. Without stop-time, games could conclude exactly one hour and 10 minutes after they started. Imagine an 8 o'clock game today that ended at 9:10.

Because games could be so perfectly timed, hockey owners were able to use special promotions with other events in the community. The hockey team in Galt in 1909 offered such a promotion: "The Opera House management and the manager of the Pro Hockey Team have got together and evolved a plan whereby citizens will be able to see both the game between Guelph and Galt, and the *Gay Musician* on Monday night. The hockey game will start at 7:30 sharp and will be through at 8:30 [the intermission for this game had been eliminated]. The curtain will rise at 8:35 so that the public can see both attractions."

Most referees in hockey's early days were players from teams that were not taking part on that particular night. Very few men were strictly referees, unless their playing careers had ended. Early officials wore suits and derby hats when officiating games. Assistants similar to today's linesmen, called umpires or the judge of play, worked with the referee during the game. These men were usually locals, as were the goal judges who would come right out of the crowd prior to the game. The referee had the option of sending these men back to the stands and choosing new ones at any time. Goal judges waved a hankie or rang a bell to signify that a team had scored. The job was extremely difficult in the early years of hockey because the goal consisted of nothing more than two posts in the ice. Goal judges spent more time dodging pucks than determining if goals were scored, until nets were added to the posts in 1899.

Due to the influence of rugby, when the rules for hockey were first written down in Montreal in the 1870s, early players were not allowed to pass the puck forward. (This would not change until the 1910s.) The puck could only be advanced by skating and stickhandling. Lateral and back passes were allowed, and a few players could perform the difficult maneuver of passing the puck forward, then catching up to it by the time his teammate had received it, thus qualifying the pass as a lateral. The small rinks limited the amount of available ice space and put attackers within easy reach of the poke check, the common defensive practice of the day. To clear the puck from their own end, teams often resorted to the lift, which would see the point or cover point lift the puck high into the air and down to the other end of the rink. That team's forwards would then scramble to retrieve the puck once it had been played by a member of the opposing team or if it had been cleared all the way past them. By 1900, the Montreal Shamrocks were no longer using the lift, choosing to concentrate on stickhandling and skating, a tactic which most other teams began to copy.

An early rule in hockey had forbidden a shooter to lift the puck off the ice. Similar to the rules people might impose today on a game of outdoor shinny, the ban against raised shots was designed to protect goalies who played without any special equipment. In order to allow goals to be scored, goalies were forbidden to fall to the ice to make a save. Goalies who did fall to the ice were not usually penalized, but fined. This system worked well until the rule of lifting the puck began to fall by the wayside in games played in Winnipeg during the 1890s. Goalies there soon resorted to wearing cricket pads. Although this practice caught on quickly, goalies were still not allowed to fall to the ice for some time, making goaltending a difficult chore. Games in hockey's early years were high scoring, and this rule was one of the main reasons. The Colored Hockey League of the Maritimes in 1900 was the first league to allow goalies to fall to the ice to make saves. Other leagues wouldn't follow suit for another decade or more.

No players in hockey's early years used much equipment. The main concern was to protect the head from the elements rather than from serious injury. The first head or facial protection for a player came when Dan Bain of Winnipeg wore a mask for a Stanley Cup game in 1901. Simple leather gloves had begun to appear by 1900, and were referred to as "gauntlets." Tube skates, the precursor of all modern hockey skates, began to come into vogue around this time, likely perfected by Jack McCulloch of the Winnipeg Victorias. The tube skate provided players with better control on the ice, and made turning much easier.

Despite limited protective equipment, the key component of early hockey was the fact that the game was rough and mean. In 1910, Art Farrell, future Hall of Famer and one of hockey's earliest writers, claimed that hockey was "a game for men. It needs strong, full-blooded men. Weaklings can not play in it, and the timid have no place for it."

Many players in the early era felt that the best way to slow down an opposition rush was to crash a stick over the head of the puck carrier. Originally, all infractions of hockey rules resulted in the player receiving a warning from the referee. After a number of warnings, usually three, the player could be ejected. In 1904, players began to miss a designated amount of playing time depending upon the foul. The amount of time varied by league.

Off-ice, rivalries between teams were played out in the stands. Everything from lemons to boots to chairs was heaved onto the ice. Many referees were unhappy when the change was made from the cowbell to the whistle, as they had used the cowbell to quell angry fans by smashing them over the head.

Needless to say, an early-era hockey game would have been quite an experience. So next time you sit in a modern arena, eating nachos or sipping wine, think of the fan at the turn of the century, huddled in a blanket and ready to lean over and punch an opponent. Now who brought the Scotch?

CHAPTER 7

The History of Hockey in Toronto

From Granite Club to Air Canada Centre

Leonard Kotylo

ALTHOUGH THE FIRST KNOWN RULES OF HOCKEY were created in Montreal for the first formal game in 1875, it took a further 13 years before the first recorded Toronto hockey game was played in 1888. Tom L. Paton, goaltender for the Montreal Amateur Athletic Association, is said to have been the person who started hockey in Toronto.

Apparently, while on a visit to the city, Paton discovered that people in Toronto were not familiar with the sport. He telegraphed to Montreal for hockey sticks and a puck, which arrived by train the next day. Paton then gathered a group of 10 players who engaged in scrimmages on the ice of the Granite Curling Club at 555 Church Street, where the first recorded Toronto hockey game took place on February 16, 1888. The Granite Curling Club beat the Caledonians Curling Club by a score of 4–1.

The major event that would shape Toronto hockey history was the visit of the Ottawa Rideau Rebels hockey team to the city in the spring of 1890. The team comprised Ottawa parliamentarians and government workers, and included two sons of Lord Stanley (Canada's Governor-General) along with James G.A. Creighton, the person said to have been the creator of hockey's first rules in 1875.

The Rideau team played games against the Granites and the Victoria Athletic Club. After those events, Arthur Stanley suggested the formation of an Ontario hockey league. This led to the organization of the Ontario Hockey Association in the fall of 1890. The new league featured six Toronto athletic clubs—Granites, Victorias, St. George's, the Athletic Lacrosse Club, the Royal School of Infantry and Osgoode Hall—among the 13 founding members. The first Toronto championship team for the Province of Ontario was the 1894 Osgoode Senior team.

Once planted in Toronto, the hockey concept spread. Financiers were said to have been playing in a league from 1889 with teams from the Dominion Bank, the Commerce Bank and the Imperial Bank. Women from the Granite Club took to the ice with sticks and puck. The University of Toronto started a hockey team in 1891 in response to a challenge from McGill University, though the match did not materialize until 1894. A university league including Toronto, McGill, and Queen's University in Kingston was started in January, 1903. The Toronto Junior Hockey League was formed in 1893 for local teams including Upper Canada College, Trinity, Varsity, Victorias and the Granites. The OHA continued to grow and instituted junior (1895) and intermediate (1896) categories to expand opportunities for younger players. Toronto teams played on curling rinks at the Granite Club and at the Caledonians Club (which later became the site of the Mutual Street Arena). There was also the tiny Trinity rink and a covered facility, the Victoria rink at 277 Huron Street, which had hosted a Rideau Rebels game with the St. George's club in the spring of 1890.

Though hockey had only been established in Winnipeg in 1890, Winnipeg teams had already won the Stanley Cup in 1896 and 1901 by the time a Toronto team traveled to the western metropolis for the city's first Stanley Cup challenge in 1902. The 1902 Stanley Cup challenge of the Toronto Wellingtons, three time senior OHA champions, marked the city's entry into the upper echelon of hockey. It had taken Toronto 27 years to reach that point.

In 1904 the Toronto Marlboros challenged the Ottawa Silver Seven for the Stanley Cup. However, a whole new level of hockey was attained in 1903–04 when the University of Toronto became the first Toronto team to play against a professional club. The team from Sault Ste. Marie, Michigan, was soon to be part of the International Hockey League, the game's first fully professional league.

The folding of the International Hockey League in 1907 made its professional players widely available to other teams, and soon Buck Irving used some of them to begin the Ontario Professional Hockey League—Canada's first openly pay-for-play organization. Because the league included teams in Toronto, Guelph, Brantford and Berlin (later Kitchener)—all communities which could be reached by connecting electric railway lines—it soon became known as the "Trolley League." The Toronto franchise won the first league title in 1908. Newsy Lalonde, the team's top player, won the scoring championship. Toronto challenged the Montreal Wanderers for the Stanley Cup, but narrowly lost 6–4 in the one-game matchup. Toronto placed fourth in 1908–09 OPHL standings and then disbanded. The "Trolley League" followed by 1911. But the formation of the National Hockey Association for the 1909–10 season soon permitted a new forum for Toronto pro teams.

Following the 1910–11 season of the NHA, Toronto sportsmen purchased two disbanded franchises from league founder Ambrose O'Brien: the Renfrew Millionaires and the original Montreal Canadiens. Scheduled to enter the NHL in 1911–12, delays in the construction of eastern Canada's first artificial ice rink—the Arena Gardens on Mutual Street—saw the Toronto Tecumsehs and Toronto Blueshirts actually begin operating in 1912–13. The Tecumsehs struggled and would later become the Ontarios, then the Shamrocks. The Blueshirts flourished and became the first Toronto team to win the Stanley Cup in their second season of 1913–14. Among the roster were future Hockey Hall of Famers Jack Walker, Frank Foyston, Harry Cameron and Scotty Davidson. Unfortunately, the Pacific Coast Hockey Association pillaged Toronto's champions for its new Seattle franchise in 1915–16.

By this time, Eddie Livingstone had assumed ownership of both of Toronto's professional franchises—a situation that did not sit well with other NHA owners who demanded he sell one of the teams. However, after Seattle raided his roster, Livingstone chose to fold the Toronto Shamrocks and use its players to re-stock the depleted Blueshirts. Trouble was thus avoided—for the time being.

The advent of World War I brought the creation of military teams, which played in various leagues until they were assigned overseas. The 228th Battalion of Toronto participated in the NHA along with the Blueshirts in 1916–17. When the 228th Battalion was ordered overseas on February 9, 1917, it precipitated a new crisis in the NHA.

The National Hockey Association felt it needed two Toronto teams to make road trips from Ottawa, Montreal and Quebec City financially viable. On February 11, 1917, the NHA convened a meeting in Montreal, and, in the absence of Eddie Livingstone, wrote his lone Toronto team out of the remaining schedule and distributed his players among the rest of the teams. Thereafter, Toronto was directly responsible for the creation of the National Hockey League. Determined to continue to exclude the argumentative Eddie Livingstone, NHA owners formed a new league, the NHL, and left Toronto as the only team in the NHA.

Ironically, Eddie Livingstone's team was able to participate in the NHL in 1917–18 without him. He had leased his players and equipment to the Arena Gardens of Toronto Limited and his former Blueshirts won the Stanley Cup as the Toronto Arenas. In 1920 the Toronto St. Patricks, formerly an amateur sports organization, bought the Arenas for $7,000. The St. Pats won the Stanley Cup in 1922.

Meanwhile, the conclusion of World War I led to the creation of a new nationwide trophy for Canada's junior hockey teams. The Memorial Cup was first won by the University of Toronto Schools high school team in 1919. The next year, the Toronto Canoe Club was victorious. This hand-picked team of junior superstars included three future Hall of Fame players: Lionel Conacher, Canada's athlete of the first half of the 20th century, Roy Worters, future New York Americans goaltender and perhaps the best netminder to come out of Toronto, and Billy Burch, another future New York American who was born in Yonkers, New York.

In addition to its other post-War successes, Toronto also had the best collection of senior amateur hockey players in the OHA and in the country during the early 1920s. The Toronto Granite Club team, with superstar Harry Watson and future Montreal Maroons stars Dunc Munro and Hooley Smith, won the Allan Cup in 1922 and 1923. Beattie Ramsay, a future Maple Leafs player and hockey coach at Princeton, had also won the Allan Cup with the University of Toronto in 1921 before playing for the Granites' championship club of 1923. These players became the best in the world when the Granite Club won the Olympic gold medal in Chamonix, France, in 1924. (Toronto teams would continue to participate internationally. The Varsity Grads captured the Olympics in St. Moritz, Switzerland, in 1928, and the Toronto CCMs won the first World Championship held independently of the Olympics in 1930. The University of Toronto formed an intercollegiate league with American universities Harvard, Yale, Dartmouth and Princeton in 1936.)

In 1922, the Canadian Amateur Hockey Association had 6,726 participants. The OHA alone had 164 teams comprising about 4,000 players. By 1922–23, there were about 8,300 players of all ages and genders comprising about 600 teams in Toronto amateur hockey associations. The Inter-Church League had 128 teams and the Toronto Hockey League had over 100 teams. A youth league originally formed as the Beaches Hockey League with 99 players in 1911 would grow to become the Metropolitan Toronto Hockey League, and still continues to operate as the largest hockey league in Canada under the name of the Greater Toronto Hockey League. Nels Stewart, who scored 324 career NHL goals, was a famous early graduate.

Public school hockey had been played in Toronto since 1916, and area high schools had teams that participated in the OHA and generated players for the NHL. Baldy Cotton of the Toronto Maple Leafs had played for Jarvis Collegiate. De La Salle high school produced both Red Green of the New York Americans and Babe Dye, a 200-goal scorer with Toronto and Chicago.

Women in Toronto had gained entry to hockey as members of the city's hockey playing institutions. These included women of the Granite Club (1890s), University of Toronto colleges (1901) and Toronto Wellingtons (1907). By 1921, two ladies leagues were part of the Toronto Hockey League. Bobbie Rosenfeld, Canada's female athlete of the half-century and an Olympic gold medal sprinter in 1928, played for the North Toronto Ladies team in 1923. She was elected as secretary-treasurer of the Ladies' Ontario Hockey Association in 1924, and played for the Ontario champion Toronto Patterson Pats of 1926, 1929, and 1930. Women's hockey was only attenuated by the start of World War II and by a shift of sponsorship money to men's hockey.

By 1925, three indoor artificial ice rinks were operating in Toronto: the Mutual Street Arena Gardens, Ravina Gardens and the University of Toronto's Varsity Arena. But Toronto's hockey landscape changed forever in February, 1927 when Conn Smythe purchased the Toronto St. Pats. He immediately renamed the team the Toronto Maple Leafs, then built Maple Leaf Gardens at the corner of Church and Carlton Streets in 1931. Foster Hewitt's radio broadcasts from the gondola of the Gardens would spread the image of the Leafs and their arena all across Canada, but in the beginning Conn Smythe's team did not have Toronto's pro hockey scene to itself.

In 1928, Toronto had a hockey team called the Millionaires. It was eponymously named after a trait of its owner, multi-millionaire Ted Oke, who operated his team in the Can-Pro League and the International League. Oke needed his millions to defray operating costs since attendance numbered in the hundreds at the Mutual Street Arena. The Toronto Ravinas, operated by Frank Selke out of the Ravina Gardens, had played in the Can-Pro League in 1927–28 with similar results. By 1930, professional hockey was left exclusively to the Maple Leafs.

While the Leafs became the only pro game in town, the decade of the 1930s produced two dramatic changes in the manner in which men's amateur hockey teams were organized. Previously, athletic clubs and interested social groups had created teams. Rowing clubs such as the Parkdale Canoe Club and the Argonaut Rowing Club had maintained teams as winter fitness conditioning for their rowers. However, when the OHA relaxed its rule against commercial sponsorship in 1930, companies and commercial organizations undertook the funding of teams. Secondly, the practice whereby the Toronto Maple Leafs had begun assisting junior hockey teams with ice facilities, equipment and players became extended to the entire NHL.

In exchange for their gifts in Toronto, the Leafs were able to draw on the city's amateur players for their professional team. After the Toronto Marlboros won the Memorial Cup in 1929 the Leafs procured star players Red Horner, Busher Jackson and Charlie Conacher who helped them win the Stanley Cup for the first time in 1932. Henceforth, the success of teams like the Toronto Goodyears senior squad, the Toronto Marlboros juniors, and the St. Michael's College Majors (who went undefeated en route to winning the Memorial Cup in 1934) was due to Leaf importation of players to stock the teams. The Maple Leafs recruited youngsters for these teams, and they groomed them for the NHL.

Sponsorship either by NHL teams or commercial businesses had become the means to operate amateur teams. As the range of potential team owners expanded, the need for an underlying athletic club organization was removed and these clubs withdrew. The Second World War accelerated the demise of such teams. The war effort stripped athletic clubs of their players and, even with the reintroduction of military teams as participants, OHA teams dropped from 193 in 1939 to 86 by 1944.

The return of players at war's end led to a strengthening of Toronto teams. The Maple Leafs won four Stanley Cup titles between 1947 and 1951. The Toronto Marlboros Seniors won the OHA in 1949 and 1950, adding an Allan Cup championship the second year. But on the world stage, the Toronto East York Lyndhursts Senior B team caused a national hockey crisis. They lost to the Soviet national team at the World Championships in 1954. Thereafter, international success could not be taken for granted. Three years later, when Russian hockey invaded Canada, the first game was played at Toronto's Maple Leaf Gardens on November 22, 1957, between the Whitby Dunlops and the Moscow Selects. The Dunlops won 7–2.

Locally, Toronto high schools continued to produce notable hockey people. On De La Salle's 1944 Junior B champions was Sid Smith, who went on to score 186 NHL goals for the Toronto Maple Leafs and later played for the world champion Whitby Dunlops. A teammate of Smith's at De La Salle was goaltender John MacInnes, who later coached the Michigan Tech University hockey team to over 500 wins and three NCAA championships. Malvern Collegiate produced Jack Kent Cooke, who later owned the Toronto Maple Leafs baseball club, the Los Angeles Kings hockey club and the Washington Redskins football team.

The University of Toronto also proved to be a breeding ground for future hockey owners. Conn Smythe had played for the 1915 Varsity Junior Ontario champions and coached the Varsity from 1923 to 1926. His son Stafford also played for Varsity. Future NHL coaches Dave Chambers (Quebec Nordiques), Harry Neale (Vancouver Canucks), Tom Watt (Winnipeg Jets) and Mike Keenan (Philadelphia Flyers) are Varsity player alumni.

On the ice, University of Toronto teams have excelled. The Varsity Blues won 41 Queen's Cup titles as intercollegiate champions between 1906 and 1993. When Canadian university hockey introduced a national championship in 1963, Varsity won 10 titles, including five in a row from 1969 to 1973. Only the programs at McGill University and the University of Alberta can rival Toronto. The city saw the academic scene expanded with the formation of York University and Ryerson. York won national championships in 1985, 1988 and 1989.

In the professional game, Toronto thrived both at the box office and on the ice. After their initial Stanley Cup victory in 1932, the Maple Leafs reached the finals again on six occasions over the next nine years. In the 10 seasons from 1942 to 1951 they won the Cup six times. Under the direction of Punch Imlach, a former local player with the Young Rangers and Toronto Goodyears, Toronto won the Stanley Cup four more times between 1962 and 1967. However, aging players, NHL expansion, the abolition of the junior sponsorship program, and the creation of the World Hockey Association deleted their talent pool in the 1970s.

The Toronto Toros of the WHA became the first professional competition for the Maple Leafs in 43 years when the team arrived from Ottawa in 1973. The Toros were owned by John F. Bassett Jr., son of John Bassett, a former part-owner of the Leafs. Bassett Jr. understood that he had to produce publicity in order to bring attention to his team. He arranged for the defection from Czechoslovakia of European superstar Vaclav Nedomansky and Richard Farda, and also proceeded to sign a trio of popular former Leafs: Frank Mahovlich, 1972 Summit Series hero Paul Henderson, and Billy Harris (as coach). However, Bassett's biggest problem was that he did not have a satisfactory arena. The first year he used Varsity Arena, which only seated 4,760. He then paid exorbitant rent for Maple Leaf Gardens. After a poor second-year performance, his team moved to Birmingham, Alabama, and became the Bulls.

Other teams also left Toronto as television changed the sports market place. Except for the North York-Marlboro team of 1966 to 1968, Senior A hockey had withdrawn from Toronto in 1951. St. Michael's discontinued its Junior A hockey program shortly after its Memorial Cup title in 1961. The Toronto Marlboros juniors moved to Hamilton in 1989. The market was left to the Toronto Maple Leafs—and to women and children.

Youth and adult recreational hockey have proliferated in recent years. The Greater Toronto Hockey League had 32,332 players in 1998. A further 17,123 boys played high school hockey. Women's hockey has expanded throughout the country. In 1988 there were just 7,300 girls and women playing in leagues. By 1999 there were 37,748. Toronto teams have participated in this growth in the National Women's Hockey League and the Central Ontario Women's Hockey League. In high school hockey, 13,526 girls were playing in the Toronto area by 1998.

In the 112-year history of hockey in Toronto, the game has undergone a social transformation. Defined ethnic groups, athletic clubs and churches have all receded from operating teams. Adults have withdrawn from full-contact leagues. Major sponsors have moved towards funding tournaments and arenas such as the new Air Canada Centre. Organizations such as the OHA and the Greater Toronto Hockey League, which depend extensively on volunteer participation for their operation, maintain youth and junior hockey. Yet certain aspects continue. The University of Toronto and Upper Canada College have maintained teams since the 19th century. St. Michael's College reintroduced its team and restored junior hockey competition in the Toronto area, which now also has teams in Mississauga and Brampton. Minor professional hockey also is returning in the form of the Toronto Roadrunners, an International Hockey League franchise that proposes to play in a newly renovated arena at the Coliseum on the grounds of the Canadian National Exhibition just west of the city's downtown.

It is variety in the ebb and flow of hockey development—and the Toronto Maple Leaf—that are the constants in Toronto's hockey history.

CHAPTER 8

Common Ice

The Culture of Ice Hockey in Greater Boston

by Aidan O'Hara

In December, 1859, an article entitled "Winter Sports in Nova Scotia" appeared in the *Boston Evening Gazette*. It told of the great skating ability of Nova Scotians and described an ice game that was an early form of hockey. The editor added a note to the article saying that he had sent to Nova Scotia for a set of sticks so that Bostonian skaters could give the game a try. By 1876, a municipal report published by the city's recreation department noted that a Jamaica Plain pond was "a favorite resort of skaters in winter." This initial growth of both skating and hockey was a phenomenon that not only laid the foundation for hockey as a wintertime tradition in Boston but marked the creation of a hockey culture unique to the area.

Much of the early development of hockey in "The Hub City" centers around Harvard University, which first officially took up the game on January 19, 1898, with a match against Brown at flooded Franklin Park in Boston. (By 1903 the university had a pair of outdoor rinks in the new Harvard Stadium.) A game with arch-rival Yale was first played in 1900, with Princeton joining the schedule in 1901–02. Dartmouth came on board in 1906. By 1913, hockey was one of five "major" varsity sports at Harvard and was now receiving the financial support it needed to put down roots. The university had become the premier hockey institution in the Boston area, and it helped establish Boston as one of the first American hockey towns.

College hockey became increasingly popular after World War I, and the Harvard University Athletic Association (HAA) provides outstanding evidence of the strong hockey foundation in the Boston area. But because hockey rose to prominence through the university game, its early popularity in the city was almost exclusively the domain of the upper class. The Harvard ice hockey program became a community organization through recruitment and marketing initiatives, but it primarily drew its student athletes from greater Boston prep schools like Milton Academy, Exeter and Nobles & Greenough as well as from other wealthier public school districts in Newton, Boston and Cambridge. The HAA would include these schools on its freshman and second varsity schedules, and it was not uncommon for a young Harvard player to lace up his skates against teammates from his former high school. This created a strong network of players and families who fueled and perpetuated the wintertime tradition of hockey. By the 1920s this growing hockey culture began to touch the hearts and souls of all Bostonians.

The Golden Age of Sport, which fueled the rise of baseball and college football in America, also gave rise to the commercial success of hockey, and as this era created more leisure time pursuits for the upper and middle classes, it becomes evident that it also allowed hockey to find popularity and financial support among the working classes of Boston. For example, in 1920, the City of Boston's Forty-fifth Annual Report by the Park Department noted that ice skating was "enjoyed more this year than for a great many years …. From eight to ten thousand people enjoying these sports evenings and Sundays – [they] are being allowed on Sunday for the first time in seven years [sic.]" Sunday sports provide key evidence that hockey was growing across class lines, as cultural historians target evenings and Sundays as ideal times of leisure for the working class. Whereas the upper classes could partake in afternoon baseball games at Fenway Park, the working class was limited by the hours of the working day. Sundays became more a time for recreation with family and friends than a day of worship for the working class.

Throughout the rest of the 1920s the Department of Parks recorded annual attendance at public ponds and lakes to be 500,000 to 700,000 (depending on the number of "skating days") each winter. On December 24, 1924, the *Boston Globe* ran a headline stating: "Skaters Throng Ice of this City in Best Saturday Yet for Sports. All Sizes and Ages Vie at Jamaica Pond, Franklin Field, and Other Surfaces in Boston." The article further reported on many "impromptu hockey matches." Throughout the city the hockey culture was now being played out on public ponds where people could participate and watch hockey without a prep school background.

The National Hockey League was six years old when it began to look to the United States for possible expansion teams. Hockey promoters were eager to make a profit in America where the Golden Age of Sport had already made lucrative legends out of athletes like Babe Ruth and Jack Dempsey. The strong and dynamic hockey culture of Boston made it an ideal fit for the NHL, and the Board of Governors passed over applications from New York, Philadelphia and Pittsburgh to offer Boston the first American franchise on August 31, 1924. The evolution of Boston hockey was in full bloom.

Charles F. Adams, a local grocer and businessman, bought the franchise and named himself president of the Boston Bruins Professional Hockey Club. As owner, his first act was to hire early hockey legend Art Ross. Adams came across Ross while on a trip to Montreal to observe the 1924 Stanley Cup finals. He was later quoted as saying Ross "is a thorough sportsman, a gentleman, a prosperous Montreal merchant, and, above all, is thoroughly grounded in all phases of hockey. Boston fans will like Ross."

Though an avid hockey fan, Charles Adams's first priority was to run a financially successful sports franchise. As hockey was now becoming of interest to people of all classes in Boston, the Bruins owner seized the opportunity to market his team to all segments of society. Monday night became "Hockey Night" in Boston. Games were scheduled at the Boston Arena at 8:15 in order to accommodate the after-work crowd, and the price of admission included a postgame skate on the Arena ice. The targeting of working class fans is clearly apparent in the Bruins' early game programs. For example, notes in the 1926 game program point out that "Lionel Hitchman is a salesman in the offseason … Jimmy Herberts is a mariner … William Stuart is an automobile salesman … and E. Archie Briden is an electrical engineer." The 1927 program refers to Eddie Shore as "The Red Grange of Hockey," but points out that he also "sells automobiles when he isn't shoveling a million tons of coal into a locomotive." Soon the *Boston Globe* would take to calling Shore "The Babe Ruth of Hockey," as the man who personified the rough-and-tumble game came to be the top ambassador of hockey in Boston. Caricatures frequently appeared in the newspapers with such captions as "When Eddie tosses 'em, they stay tossed." While in truth Shore was a lonely, often bitter man, the public saw him as a working class hero they could emulate. He was active in the local community and was often seen on the ponds of Boston teaching hockey skills to children and their families.

As cultural historians have noted, promoters in the Golden Age liked to portray their athletes as icons and heroes. Charles Adams packaged his players as working class heroes because more and more it was the working class that was filling up a larger part of the stands. He also acknowledged women as an important part of the Bruins' fan base. In an article in the 1931 game program entitled "President C.F. Adams Lauds Women Fans" he said, "women never become critical of their favorites, and in hockey the favorites are all the members of the home team. The man is loyal, but rarely as blindly so as the woman. He admits that his team may have some faults. With a woman, the home team is perfect." In a further comment on the passion of Boston's women spectators, Adams noted: "That's her only display of emotion. It's her only outlet."

The evolution of Boston hockey reached a new level on the evening of November 20, 1928. That night the Bruins played their first game in their new home, the Boston Madison Square Garden. The arena (which was almost immediately dubbed the Boston Garden) had actually opened four nights before with a featherweight fight between Honey Boy Finnegan and Andre Routis, but the Bruins debut would be its first real test. Charles Adams asked that the fans arrive early, though there would be no opening festivities. Newspapers commented that the Bruins president did "not believe fans care for any preliminaries and believe there will be enough thrills and frills once the game gets under way."

The game was not scheduled to start until 8:15, but by 7 o'clock pandemonium reigned outside the Garden. Hoping to attract any and every fan that wanted to see hockey, Adams was selling the last 1,500 seats—the cheap seats—for just 50 cents. The result was a lineup hundreds of people long that stretched down to the Warren Bridge. Ticket scalping was rampant. Police estimated that 2,000 people sought tickets through illegal sale, at up to three times the price. Scalpers dressed as newspaper boys and attempted to hide their transactions in the newspapers they sold. When the doors finally opened, over 16,000 people attempted to fill a 14,500-capacity building. *Boston Globe* hockey columnist John J. Hallahan commented that "almost every hockey fan in greater Boston and those from the suburban cities [was] present … Boston went hockey mad."

In contrast to the black-tie affair that had opened New York's new Madison Square Garden three years earlier, the Boston opening sparked a near-riot by fans spirited by the desire to cheer and carry their Bruins club. As the 1928–29 season progressed, the new hockey facility also proved to be a bonanza for Harvard University. The hockey team moved both its games and practices from the Arena to the Garden, which was no cheap venture as contracts with the Boston Arena and Madison Square Garden show that rink time averaged about $200 a day. The investment proved successful as rivalries exploded between Harvard and teams like Yale and Princeton. The popularity of these games in the new rink meant tickets had to be sold by lottery and ensured that the Boston Garden was filled to capacity. The HAA took home 15 to 20 percent of the gate receipts.

An extremely successful 1928–29 hockey season ended with the Bruins defeating the New York Rangers to win their first Stanley Cup championship. Hockey was now permanently woven into Boston's fabric. Newspapers reported that "the rush seat line started at 1:30 p.m., seven hours before game time" for game one of the Stanley Cup series. Charles Adams continued his "cheap seat" policy and 1,500 tickets were sold for 50 cents apiece. Games were also heard over the radio on stations WLOE and WBZ.

Two months into their Stanley Cup season, the Boston Bruins had signed George Owen to a contract. (Owen had been negotiating with Conn Smythe of the Toronto Maple Leafs, and the fact that the Bruins were able to sign him fueled a long-running feud between Smythe and Art Ross.) Owen made his NHL debut on January 8, 1929, and helped the Bruins down the Maple Leafs 5–2.

Though he was born in Hamilton, Ontario, Owen had been raised in Boston and his hockey career paralleled the sport's growth in the city. He was a product of the Newton High School hockey program who went on to legendary success at Harvard. Owen captained the freshman hockey team in 1919–20 and later served two seasons as captain of the varsity squad—a rare feat at Harvard. His four years at the University became known as "The Owen Era." While working in the bond business after school, he continued to play hockey in a closely followed career in the amateur ranks with such local teams as the Boston Athletic Association and the University Club. Upon his decision to enter the professional ranks and join the Bruins, the *Boston Globe* printed a four-part memoir by Owen entitled "Why I Turned Pro." He was by far the most famous local player Boston had seen, and his decision to communicate his thoughts with the people of the city only added to his image as a local ambassador for the game of hockey.

The addition of George Owen—the first American, let alone Bostonian—to the Bruins roster made the Stanley Cup season of 1928–29 even more special to fans of the team. He was a product of both the culture of Boston and the culture of hockey, and his fame broke through class boundaries to reach the entire city.

It is apparent that hockey had done the same thing.

CHAPTER 9

Early Pro Leagues

The First Days of Play-for-Pay Hockey

Ernie Fitzsimmons

MOST HOCKEY HISTORIANS consider the International Hockey League that operated from 1904 to 1907 to be the very first fully professional hockey league. The truth is, the IHL was beaten to the punch by a full two years by the Western Pennsylvania Hockey League (WPHL), which operated as a city circuit in Pittsburgh.

Pittsburgh was blessed with artificial ice by the turn of the 20th century. This fact helped to lure players from Canada because they could start to play hockey in Pittsburgh earlier than they could at home. Though the game was supposed to be strictly amateur at this time, many "hockeyists" jumped at the chance to play for pay in Pittsburgh. By 1901–02 the WPHL (which had already been in operation for a few years) was now made up almost entirely of paid players from Canada. The third place team in the three-team loop that year was the Bankers, a group that included goalie Frank Richardson from Montreal, Dunc Taylor and Cecil Henderson from Port Arthur, and a budding star in Lorne Campbell of Ottawa via Montreal. The Pittsburgh Athletic Club (PAC) finished second with a roster that was nearly all from Kingston, Ontario. George "Pinky" Lamb was in goal with Bill Hamilton, Bill Shields, Herb Reynor and Jigger Robinson augmented by future Hall of Famer Alf Smith of Ottawa. Art Sixsmith came in from Ottawa to organize the first-place Keystones. His best move was to import goaltender Riley Hern from Stratford, Ontario. Other soon-to-be-well-known players included Bert Morrison, Ernie Westcott and a young player named Harry Peel from London, Ontario.

Despite the fact that the players in the WPHL were being paid, the league was supposed to be amateur and its teams played exhibition games against amateur clubs like Yale University, Philadelphia, Kingston, Cleveland and Queen's University. Despite the strict amateur code of this era, none of the players on these teams was ever suspended for playing against the Pittsburgh teams. The same was not true for Harry Peel of the Keystones who, on his return to Canada, foolishly admitted to Ontario Hockey Association officials that he had accepted $30 per game to play in Pittsburgh. As an ex-pro, Peel was immediately suspended—a decision that was upheld on December 10, 1903, and again on November 30, 1904. Peel gave up on his playing career but was a long-time referee in Ontario.

During the 14-game 1901–02 campaign, the Keystones had all-stars in Riley Hern, Peel (who had four goals and four assists for eight points), Art Sixsmith (12–2–14) and Bert Morrison (10–4–14). PAC had co-leading scorers in Herb Reynor (13–7–20) and Alf Smith (11–9–20), while Billy Shields (10–3–13) and penalty leader Jerry Curtin (23 minutes) of Hamilton were strong performers. The Bankers drew up the bottom of the standings with only four wins during the season, but Lorne Campbell (6–6–12), Thomas Howard (10–2–12) and Dunc Taylor (7–1–8) were dangerous.

By 1902–03, all pretense of amateurism was given up and the WPHL became a full-fledged professional league with the Victorias joining the others to make a four-team circuit that played a 14-game schedule. The Bankers rebounded to finish first in the standings this year as Lorne Campbell (14–8–22) became a star. The team had also imported fellow Ottawa natives Jack Roberts (14–3–17) and Hod Stuart (7–8–15)—a future Hall of Famer like his brother Bruce. Charlie Liffiton (8–9–17) was talked into turning pro and leaving the Montreal AAA for Pittsburgh in early January. Frank Richardson led the league with a 1.23 goals-against average and had five shutouts.

PAC was second in the WPHL standings in 1902–03 while still using a mostly Kingston lineup. They did add rugged George McCarron (14–5–19) from Quebec, who led the league with 47 penalty minutes. Jigger Robinson chipped in with 10 goals and five assists. Bill Shields (6–8–14) and Bill Hamilton (0–6–6) were still strong, but Herb Reynor dropped well off his pace as scoring leader in 1901–02 and collected just four goals and two assists in 11 games. The Victorias finished third but Art Sixsmith, who had jumped from the Keystones, introduced old Ottawa buddies Bruce Stuart (16–6–22), Harold "Chick" Henry (11–4–15), Charlie "Baldy" Spittall (2–4–6), his brother Garnet Sixsmith (8–2–10) and Bill "Peg" Duval to professional hockey.

The Keystones dropped from first place to last in 1902–03 despite having retained future Hall of Fame goalie Riley Hern (who had just one win and 10 losses). They had lost Art Sixsmith, Bert Morrison and others, and while Dunc Taylor (6–1–7) came over from the Bankers, most of the club's new imports didn't pan out. Future star Fred Lake played just five games before jumping to Portage Lakes.

At the same time as the WPHL was flourishing in Pittsburgh, Doctor John Liddell "Jack" Gibson was operating a team of professional imports in Houghton, Michigan. Known as Portage Lakes, Gibson's boys ran up a perfect record of 12–0 in exhibition games (they did not yet have a league to play in) with a roster that included Joseph "Chief" Jones in goal and Gibson and Jack Baker on defense. Up front they had scoring leader Joe Stevens (34 goals in 12 games), Herman Meinke, Bobby Rowe, Ernie Westcott and Fred Lake, who scored eight goals in just two games after leaving the Keystones.

In what was widely advertised as the battle for the professional hockey championship of the United States, Portage Lakes faced the Bankers in a series that followed the 1902–03 WPHL season. Though the Bankers were augmented with Bill Shields and Bill Hamilton of PAC, Portage Lakes won the series two games to one with one game tied. The Pittsburgh team did outscore their Michigan peninsula rivals 11–6 in the series thanks to one eight-goal outburst and Lorne Campbell (4–1–5) was the leading scorer. Charlie Liffiton had three goals for the Bankers, while Joe Stevens and 17-year-old Bobby Rowe clicked twice for Portage Lakes.

The status quo prevailed in 1903–04 when the WPHL was back with four teams, but the Portage Lakes team was having more difficulty finding decent opponents. Sault Ste. Marie, Michigan (American Soo) and Sault Ste. Marie, Ontario (Canadian Soo) were lured into professional competition against Portage Lakes, while the Keystones and PAC played exhibitions against them. Both Pittsburgh teams lost a pair of games to Doc Gibson's team.

In their second year of existence, the Victorias surged to first place in the WPHL under the tutelage of playing-manager Art Sixsmith (16–8–24). He recruited more Ottawa friends in goalie Jim MacKay (10 wins and two losses) and Ed Roberts (23–5–28), who led the league in goals. Garnet Sixsmith (10–4–14) and Chick Henry (6–6–12) were the other forwards, while Baldy Spittall and Peg Duval spearheaded the rock-ribbed defense.

The Bankers yielded first place by dropping their last three games to the Victorias. Lorne Campbell (21–8–29) was the league's top scorer, but only Jack Roberts (8–6–14) gave him much scoring support. Rugged Charlie Ross led the league with 30 penalty minutes and competent wing Alwyn Kent was introduced from Ottawa. PAC manager Charlie Miller had a rough time winning despite decent scoring from Jigger Robinson (14–8–22) and Dunc Taylor (15–6–21), the latter coming over during the season when the Keystones folded. Another Kingston boy, Dick Wilson, contributed 15 goals and six assists. Tough guy George McCarron fell way off in scoring and bashing Bill Hamilton was banned from the league for rough play and joined American Soo. Promising wing Jack Fenwick contracted typhoid fever and died in March.

The Keystones didn't play too badly, posting two wins and four losses, but were unable to continue and withdrew from the league on January 17, 1904. Leading scorer Dunc Taylor was grabbed by PAC, who also picked up Thomas "Rube" Melville. Stanley Willett joined the Victorias, while Rossie Fields signed on with the Bankers. As an interesting aside to the 1903–04 season, Kingston had lost so many players to the WPHL that the city was unable to ice a team in the Senior OHA for the first time. Famous Canadian referee Roy Schooley was brought in as a referee by the WPHL and stayed in Pittsburgh as a hockey executive for many years.

Portage Lakes had lured Bert Morrison, Bruce Stuart, Bill Shields, Hod Stuart and goalie Riley Hern away from their Pittsburgh teams in 1903–04 and dropped many of their best players from the 1902–03 squad. The new roster rolled to a 13–1 exhibition record (losing one to American Soo) and outscored opponents 168–21. Morrison blasted in 68 goals, followed by Bruce Stuart (44), Shields (21) and Hod Stuart (13). In a challenge series they outscored the Pittsburgh Bankers 29–12 (though some sources indicate 28–12) in two games, then proceeded to sweep American Soo in four straight playoff games. In the final for the U.S. pro championship Portage Lakes topped the Pittsburgh Victorias two games to one with all tilts held in Pittsburgh.

In the final games to be played that year, the Montreal Wanderers (soon to be a powerhouse in Canadian hockey) lost two straight games (8–4 and 9–2) at Portage Lakes in what was billed as the World Championship series. After their losses in Houghton the Wanderers tackled the WPHL champion Pittsburgh Victorias and were again beaten, this time two games to one. In 11 playoff games Bruce Stuart led Portage Lakes with 31 goals, while Bert Morrison scored 26. Top performers on the Victorias were Ed Roberts with seven goals and two assists in five games and captain Art Sixsmith (5–3–8).

After the success of the two series against the Montreal Wanderers, a decision was made to bring together the two regions of professional hockey with the formation of the International Hockey League. The IHL would boast one team in Pittsburgh, as well as Michigan teams in Houghton (Portage Lakes), Calumet and Sault Ste. Marie, plus the Canadian Soo. Fifteen of the 35 regular players in the inaugural IHL season of 1904–05 had gotten their pro start in the WPHL.

The International Hockey League lasted through the 1906–07 campaign, but when plans for the 1907–08 season fell through due to an economic slump in Michigan's copper mining region, the Western Pennsylvania Hockey League decided to start up again. The Bankers were back with Art Sixsmith at the helm, while Charlie Miller re-organized PAC. Frank Dahaney started a new team called Lyceum who finished just behind the Bankers in the battle for first place. Richard Guy formed a team called the Pirates who finished just ahead of PAC.

The Bankers' only connection with the old WPHL in 1907–08 was playing-manager Art Sixsmith. The rest of the roster included top pros like Fred Povey and goalie James Donnelly from Montreal, along with Cliff Bennest of Winnipeg, who had been lined up by the IHL. When Harry Smith (brother of Alf) was suspended for rough play by the pro league in Manitoba he signed with the Bankers on January 5, 1908, and led the league with 44 goals. Unlike the Bankers, PAC went back to old WPHL players in goalie Frank Richardson, Garnet Sixsmith, Jigger Robinson and Herb Reynor, but augmented them with Albert "Dubbie" Kerr (15 goals) of Brockville, Theophile "Tuff" Bellefeuille and Grindy Forrester.

For their first season Lyceum put together a team that was virtually unknown to Pittsburgh fans. Future Hall of Famer Tommy Smith (32 goals) was joined by former IHL players like Jim Mallen (24 goals), Art Throop, Pete Charlton, Alfred "Cap" McDonald and James "Stoke" Doran. On December 23, 1907, they signed goalie Tom Ross to replace Mark Tooze.

The Pirates started with old WPHL goalie Jim MacKay and forward Dunc Taylor, but brought in starry players like Ed Robitaille (11goals), Ray Robinson, Harry McRobie, Edgar Dey and Charlie Masson. In what must have been the first trade of pro hockey players, the Pirates dealt MacKay, Dey and Taylor to the Bankers on January 28, 1908, in exchange for Joseph Donnelly, Cliff Bennest and a player named McGuire. The deal was a result of a player revolt after the Pirates released Dey on January 23. During the season players from around the league (like Ed Robitaille, Jack Marks, Grindy Forrester and Art Leader) all jumped to teams in Canada.

The Bankers' trade for MacKay and company paid off in spades as they recorded eight wins and two ties in 12 games after the deal. Taylor had 13 goals and Dey added seven. There was no playoff for the U.S. title this year as there were no other pro leagues, but the so-called World Series was revived when the Stanley Cup champion Montreal Wanderers came in and beat the Bankers two games to one while outscoring them 17–11. Tommy Smith joined the Bankers for the series and both he and brother Harry scored three goals against the Wanderers. It was pretty obvious that the quality of play in the new WPHL was close to that of the old IHL, but many doubts existed as to whether a city league could afford to continue paying such big salaries.

Whatever the worries, the WPHL came back with four teams again in 1908–09. Art Sixsmith was still in charge of the Bankers; Lorne Campbell came back from a year in the Manitoba Pro league to guide PAC; Jim MacKay took charge of Lyceum; and old star Alf Smith was brought in to look after the new Duquesne Athletic Club (DAC).

Things looked promising for the league at the beginning of the season (November 12, 1908) as the Bankers had Harry Smith back to join Art Sixsmith, Dunc Taylor, imported stars Erskine "Skene" Ronan and Stoke Doran, plus the locally developed Dutch Koch. Alf Smith had Harry McRobie and Ray Robinson over from the defunct Pirates along with imports like Tommy Westwick, Joe Dennison and Horace Gaul (all of Ottawa), and goalie Art Brooks. After a slow start DAC replaced Brooks with Hugh Liddell of Cornwall. PAC had Frank Richardson in goal along with Lorne Campbell, Dubbie Kerr, Fred Lake and Fred "Cyclone" Taylor. The team looked like a powerhouse. Lyceum had MacKay in goal and scoring machine Tommy Smith up front to join Jimmy Mallen, Garnet Sixsmith, Art Throop, Fred Povey and old Maritimes star Jack D. McDonald.

Perhaps the Western Pennsylvania Hockey League should have seen the writing on the wall when Alf Smith got fired as manager of DAC for rough play. He resurfaced with Bankers for three games but was soon on his way back home. The real fly in the ointment, however, was the fact that there were now several pro leagues operating in Canada. As soon as it got cold enough to put ice into Canadian rinks a mass exodus of players began. The Bankers lost Stoke Doran, Skene Ronan and Harry Smith, while DAC missed Horace Gaul. PAC had to replace Con Corbeau, Fred Lake, Cyclone Taylor and Bill "Lady" Taylor at various times. Lyceum saw Fred Povey, Tommy Smith and Art Throop jump ship for higher salaries.

There were no agreements between leagues about players rights and so any player could move freely when he wished. Still, WPHL officials were dumbfounded by the defections. They felt that they had provided an opportunity for these players and the least they could do was to play out the season. Instead of folding the league it was decided that Lyceum would withdraw on December 23 and that the remaining players would be split among the other three teams. The Bankers edged DAC by one point in a 15-game schedule. Ogal Mallen, who played with Lyceum and DAC, won the scoring title with 21 goals in 12 games. He was followed by Art Sixsmith with 17 tallies in 15 outings. Showing just how good they were, brothers Tommy and Harry Smith were third and fourth in scoring despite having played just six and seven games respectively. Tommy scored 15 times while Harry netted 14 goals. The conclusion of the abbreviated 1908–09 season marked the end of pro hockey for many years in Pittsburgh, though local teams were often suspected of paying their players as some very good amateur teams graced the ice in that fair city.

While professional hockey had been flourishing in Pittsburgh, another relatively unknown loop was starting up in northwestern Ontario because of disenchantment with the OHA. Officials in Port Arthur and Fort William were constantly upset by rulings from Toronto about such things as the final date for registering new players. After operating as an outlaw group for awhile, hockey officials in those two cities decided to start their own pro league called the New Ontario Hockey League (NOHL) in 1907–08. The teams in the league that first season were the Fort William Wanderers, Port Arthur Lake City, the Port Arthur Thunder Bays and the Fort William Arenas. A league residency rule stated that a player must be in town for 20 days before he could play.

The Fort William Arenas folded after just five games and many of their players were absorbed by other teams. Lake City had the league scoring leader in former Canadian Soo player Frank Clifton (18 goals in eight games). He had help from Willard MacGregor, Frank Tremblay and future Hall of Famer Jack Walker. Thunder Bays manager George Nichols had all-star goalie Jack Hanley, along with a homebrew crew that included Harry Servais, Russell Meikle, Harry Ruttan and former WPHL player Cecil Henderson.

The Wanderers, under manager William Sweet, walked away with NOHL honors with an 8–3 record during the inaugural season. The team was led by future Montreal Canadiens player Harry Scott (18 goals in 10 games). Other stars on the team were goalie Harold Rochon, Doug Stewart (13 goals), Charlie Lightfoot, Scotty Fraser and Paddy McDonough. The champion Wanderers played off with an all-star team from the rest of the league and edged them 17–16 after four games. No Stanley Cup or other outside challenges were accepted in that inaugural season.

By 1908–09 pro hockey was booming in Canada with the Eastern Canada Hockey Association, the Ontario Professional Hockey League, Temiskaming Pro, Manitoba, Edmonton and Federal leagues all competing for players. While the intense competition would kill the WPHL, the NOHL was able to stick with the players they had from the previous year. A few outsiders even came in, the most prominent being huge Harry Mummery who signed on with the new Fort William Forts. The Forts also brought in former IHL player Ed Schaeffer. Goaltender Herman Zeigler joined the Wanderers. The top local player developed this season was Ran McDonald, who would later play for several years in the Pacific Coast Hockey Association.

The Port Arthur Hockey Club replaced Lake City for the 1908–09 season and was a distant last while giving up way too many goals. Their best players were Willard McGregor (11 goals), Jack Walker, Soo import George Axelson and George Grant. The Fort William Forts were a new team but had all-stars in Mummery, Schaeffer and Harry Scott (21 goals), while Doug Stewart (15 goals), Ran McDonald and Ed Longfellow were solid, as was local goalie Fred Dulmage. The Wanderers had big holes to fill with the loss of goalie Harold Rochon, Harry Scott and Doug Stewart. Ziegler was a big help in goal and led the league with a 3.29 average behind the strong defense of Paddy McDonough and Ted Jackson. David Bole led the scoring (16 goals), followed by Scotty Fraser (13) and Charlie McGimsie (5).

The defending champion Wanderers fell to third place behind the Forts and Thunder Bays who still had the top goalie in Jack Hanley, along with repeat scoring leader Frank Clifton (23 goals). Russell Meikle (15 goals) and Frank Tremblay were solid up front, while Cecil Henderson and Martin McGuire minded to matters in their own end. The Thunder Bays had finished only one point ahead of the Forts during the regular season, but in the playoffs they cruised past them by a 12–3 margin in a two-game, total-goals affair. Frank Clifton starred with seven goals in the two games.

By the time the 1909–10 season rolled around there was no more pro hockey in the Temiskaming, Manitoba, and Federal leagues, and the Edmonton league played only a few games. The National Hockey Association (forerunner of the NHL) was newly formed, while the OPHL still operated. So, too, did the NOHL.

Port Arthur was again known as Lake City in 1909–10 and jumped into first place under the guidance of player-manager Paddy McDonough. He grabbed goalie Herman Ziegler from the Wanderers, while developing star Jack Walker improved to third place in the scoring race (21 goals), just ahead of linemate George Grant (18). Doug Stewart (13 goals) and Willard McGregor (10) were important contributors. The Thunder Bays again challenged for the top with super scorer Frank Clifton repeating his 23-goal performance in only 13 games to lead the league. Ed Carpenter was introduced to Port Arthur fans and helped veteran Cecil Henderson to protect goalie Jack Hanley. Russell Meikle (17 goals), Frank Tremblay (12) and Harry Servais were mainstays up front.

The Forts fell off their pace of the previous season despite new additions like former IHL player Jack Ward (21 goals), Bob Genge and Russ Phillips (brother of Hall of Famer Tommy Phillips). Ran McDonald (12 goals) and Harry Scott (10) were back along with Scotty Fraser, but they never got in sync. Local goalie Stanley Bliss played for the North Stars, who replaced the Wanderers for the 1909–10 season. Joel Rochon (17 goals) and Edge Wilson (11) were the big gunners under playing-manager George Rochon, while Charlie Lightfoot and Bert Cameron were members of the supporting cast. There were no playoffs in the NOHL this year, nor were there any outside challenges.

Two new pro leagues, the Maritime Professional Hockey League and the Eastern Ontario Professional League, were on the prowl for players in 1910–11 but the NOHL decided to expand and added the Schreiber Colts to the fold. The Lake City team, under Paddy McDonough, was able to keep most of its players and rolled to a perfect 15–0 record. They still had Herman Ziegler in goal and grabbed Ed Carpenter from the Thunder Bays to join McDonough on the defense. Up front they still had Jack Walker (24 goals) and Willard McGregor (17). They imported center Mike O'Leary from Ottawa and he led the league with 29 goals. To help matters, local wing Wes Wellington developed into a regular.

The Forts brought in Bill McGimsie as manager in 1910–11, but the loss of star players Harry Scott (to the Maritime Pro league) and Ran McDonald (to the North Stars) was too much to overcome and they finished second. Jack Ward was back and tied for the scoring lead with 29 tallies. Bob Genge became a star at rover with 15 goals, while veteran Ed Roberts was brought in from Ottawa to play defense with Jim Green. Fred Dulmage was solid in goal but a lack of scoring depth from wings Scotty Fraser and Bill Cotter didn't help.

The Thunder Bays had lost Ed Carpenter to Lake City and Frank Tremblay moved to the North Stars. They still had goalie Jack Hanley and Cecil Henderson on defense, but star scorer Frank Clifton missed six of the 15 games and fell off to 11 goals. Russell Meikle (10 goals) and Harry Servais (4) also had off seasons. Former Temiskaming player Joseph Woods played left wing and local boy Alex "Duke" Wellington had nine goals in five games to give promise of things to come.

The North Stars hired Rosie Helmer as manager part way through the 1910–11 season. They had most of the same cast back and added Frank Tremblay from the Thunder Bays. Ran McDonald returned from a stint in the British Columbia Boundary League in late January. Joel Rochon (12 goals) and Edge Wilson (11) were their best players, while McDonald had six goals in seven games. Schreiber stuck mostly with local players and finished 1–15. Their best scorers were Jack Rattray (seven goals) and Eastman (8). Part way through the season they imported former Pittsburgh pro Bill Simon to play defense.

The Stanley Cup trustees finally gave the NOHL a shot at the prized trophy this year, but first the champion Port Arthur Lake City team had to play off against a team from Prince Albert, Saskatchewan. Lake City beat Prince Albert 6–3 in both games (played in Winnipeg) but were ripped 13–4 by Ottawa in a Stanley Cup challenge. Wes Wellington had seven goals in the three playoff games, while Jack Walker and Willard McGregor had three each.

The 1911–12 season presented the biggest obstacle yet for the NOHL when brothers Frank and Lester Patrick introduced their new rival major league, the Pacific Coast Hockey Association. While the PCHA battled the NHA for top players, Saskatchewan, the Maritimes and the British Columbia Boundary League were also on the prowl for players. Paddy McDonough, Douglas "Dad" Stewart, Harry Mummery and Herman Ziegler were former NOHL players who had jumped to the Saskatchewan league. Ran McDonald was with New Westminster of the PCHA.

With the player losses, the NOHL dropped back to three teams (Port Arthur Lake City, Fort William North Stars and Schreiber Colts). Schreiber lost its first three games badly before the team signed roving mercenary Harry Smith from Temiskaming in early January. Smith did what he so often did, that is, lead the loop in goals with 32 in only 13 games. The most any other player on the team had was seven, but captain Jim Green at cover point (defense) and Ellard White at rover played well. The Colts split their last six games and import goalie Bill Kerr of Brockville starred, despite a 5.33 goals against average. Still, the Colts finished last.

The Fort William North Stars added star goalie Jack Hanley and it was a dog fight with Port Arthur all season. Point man Bob Genge had nine goals while helping George Rochon on defense. Jack Ward (17 goals) continued to score and had lots of help from Joel Rochon (9), Russell Meikle (8) and Scotty Fraser.

Lake City had lost goalie Herman Ziegler and Paddy McDonough to Saskatoon but replaced them with goalie Harold Rochon and a young defenseman named Harry Cameron. Mike O'Leary (27 goals) again led the offense along with Jack Walker (18), Wes Wellington (15) and Willard McGregor (12). Cameron, a future Hall of Famer, had eight goals on defense with Ed Carpenter. Lake City introduced Frank Nighbor, another future Hall of Famer, to the pro game this year. He played just four games and tallied once. The Port Arthur team was in first place when Fort William refused to play a game under referee R. A. Lockerby and the game was awarded to Port Arthur. The

North Stars were kicked out of the league for their action, which ultimately was the death knell for the whole operation.

The Stanley Cup trustees had accepted another challenge from the NOHL and the champion Lake City team was again off to Winnipeg, this time to meet the Saskatoon Wholesalers. The Wholesalers were really a combination of two Saskatoon teams who joined forces right at the end of the season, but it didn't matter as Lake City came out on top 12–6 in the total-goals series. However, because of the expense involved and the fact that they had been beaten so badly the year before, Port Arthur declined the opportunity to face the Quebec Bulldogs for the Stanley Cup.

The New Ontario Hockey League had run its course, but if success can be measured by the number of players who moved on to the two so-called major leagues (the NHA and the PCHA), then the NOHL was indeed a success. The following players all went on to star after their NOHL days:

Jack Walker—Member of Hockey Hall of Fame… Went from the NOHL to play in the major leagues for 16 years with Seattle, Victoria and Detroit (then had five more minor pro seasons while playing to age 46)… On three Stanley Cup winners… Finished in top 10 in points seven times and earned five PCHA all-star berths.

Harry Cameron—Member of Hockey Hall of Fame… Played in the majors for 14 more seasons and had six minor pro years to the age of 43… Won three Stanley Cup titles… Was a rushing defenseman before it was fashionable and was fifth in points in the NHL with Toronto St. Pats in 1920–21 and 1921–22… Had 17 goals in 21 games in 1917–18.

Harry Mummery—Massive blueliner went on to play 11 seasons in the NHA/NHL… Won the Stanley Cup in Quebec and Toronto… Wore a 12' x 18" rubber band around his waist during games to try and keep his weight down.

Harry Scott—Left the NOHL after three strong years and played three more seasons in the Maritime Professional Hockey League… Set a Maritime Pro record with 54 goals in 18 game in 1911–12… Played two seasons in the NHA with the Toronto Ontarios and Montreal Canadiens until 1914–15… Was a long-time referee in Western Canada and a sports editor in Calgary.

Ed Carpenter—Went to the Maritime Pro league for two years after the NOHL then had three major league seasons in the NHA and PCHA until missing two years to War duties… Back for two more NHL seasons… Won the Stanley Cup with the Seattle Metropolitans… Came back to Port Arthur to coach in the 1920s.

Ranald "Ran" McDonald—Rugged wing was a four-time all-star in eight PCHA seasons… The only player to play for all six PCHA teams… Was on a Stanley Cup finalist his last two seasons

Bob Genge—Huge 6'4" blueliner went to Swift Current of the Saskatchewan Pro league in 1912–13 but soon was signed and played eight years in the PCHA… Was a second-team all-star in 1916.

George Rochon—Moved to New Westminster (PCHA) from the NOHL in 1912–13 and had two fine seasons before a career ending knee injury in 1913–14.

Joel Rochon—Brother of George played in the B.C. Boundary League and Saskatchewan Pro leagues for several years… Got a trial with Montreal Canadiens (NHA) in 1916–17 even though he was retired in Calgary.

Alex "Duke" Wellington—Went to the Maritime Pro league in 1912–13… Played in amateur hockey in Cleveland, St. Paul, Pittsburgh and New York, although always under a cloud that he may have been paid to play… Got into one NHL game with Quebec in 1919–20.

Mike O'Leary—Signed with Toronto in 1912–13 but ended up playing two years with the Halifax Socials (MPHL) before earning a Montreal Wanderers (NHA) trial in 1914–15… Continued playing in the B.C. Boundary League and the Alberta Big 4 semi-pro league into the 1920s.

Willard McGregor—Was aging when the NOHL ceased operations in 1912 but still played two more years in the Maritime Pro league with Moncton and New Glasgow… Had a tryout with Toronto Blueshirts (NHA) in 1912–13 and with Portland (PCHA) in 1914–15.

We still don't know everything about hockey in the 1900s and 1910s but it is one of the most interesting eras in history to study. Without these early pioneers who knows what pro hockey would look like today?

CHAPTER 10

Dawson's Stanley Cup Challenge

From the Gold Rush to the Search for Silver

Don Reddick

IN THE EARLY DAYS OF STANLEY CUP COMPETITION a team could win the championship in two different ways: first, by winning the league in which the defending Cup champion currently played, as the Montreal Victorias did in 1895; and secondly, by issuing a written challenge to the current Cup holder and then defeating them, a feat first accomplished by the Winnipeg Victorias in 1896.

In the first instance, there was little more for Stanley Cup trustees John Sweetland and P.D. Ross to do than watch. The second, however, became their domain, where any and all decisions rendered were irrevocable. The trustees took their responsibility seriously, formulating a system where only challenges from champions of recognized senior leagues were even considered. And it was this rule that guided the initial rustling of interest in the far-off settlement of Dawson City, in the Yukon Territory.

JACK EILBECK AT THE HELM

Six or seven thousand individuals inhabited Dawson in 1903, with another 20,000 or so working the neighboring gold fields. Athletics were a popular distraction from the harsh living and working conditions, with organized leagues playing indoor and outdoor baseball, curling, lacrosse and ice hockey. As early as 1901, four rinks were set up out on the Yukon River's ice.

Because of cold, wind, and snow, the Dawson Amateur Athletic Association built the first enclosed hockey rink west of Winnipeg during the fall of 1902. That winter a four-team hockey league was formed. It consisted of the Eagles (boasting the prowess of one George "Old Sureshot" Kennedy), the Mounties (led by strong-skating Jimmy Johnstone), Joe Boyle's Dawson Amateur Athletic Association team, the DAAA (which included Boyle's sidekick Archie Martin and two Forrest brothers), and lastly the powerhouse Civil Service team, under the watchful eye of Jack Eilbeck and featuring such stars as Captain Lionel Bennett, Randy McLennan and Norman Watt. Of the dozens of individuals who participated in the evolution of the Dawson City Klondikers, it was probably the forgotten Jack Eilbeck who played the most prominent role.

Sheriff Eilbeck, described in the *Dawson Daily News* as "not only president, but also financial backer, chief rooter and mascot" of the Civil Service athletic club, was from Kingston, Ontario. He was an aging athlete "famed in the Yukon as a star baseball player" who boasted of playing against Albert Spalding in the 1870s. He spared no effort in building up the Civil Service teams, and rumors of bribes, payoffs, and the awarding of government jobs to good athletes simmered and sometimes flared, garnering outraged headlines in the local newspapers. One of the more interesting incidents was Eilbeck's attempt to lure Sureshot Kennedy from the Idyll Hour's baseball team to the Civil Service in June, 1903, promising a $7.50-a-day government job and a spot on the Civil Service's hockey tour the following winter.

This is one of the first indications that a hockey tour was being discussed, and though there is no written account of exactly how the challenge evolved, it is easy to understand why the topic was being discussed. Athletic touring was common in the days before far-flung, organized leagues. Barnstorming was a way for athletes to gain some money, as well as a little adventure, in the days of amateur sports. An all-Indian hockey team from Calgary was preparing to tour, and Joe Boyle had toured the continent with Australian boxer Frank Slavin, "the Sydney Slasher." Two of the Civil Service hockey players, Randy McLennan and E.C. Senkler, had touring experience. McLennan's Queen's University team toured the U.S. in 1894, winning 30 consecutive games and allowing only one goal against. Senkler (a goalie) had toured England several years earlier with the Canadian association football (soccer) team. It was within this atmosphere that the idea for a hockey tour developed.

Wherever the notion originated, Eilbeck ran with it. He went outside in the spring of 1903, presumably to Ottawa, "promoting the hockey idea." And it was during this trip that the inclusion of a Stanley Cup challenge evolved—and was initially frowned upon. (Dawson's league was not recognized as a legitimate senior league, and the Civil Service team was therefore not qualified for competition.) In response to this rebuff, Eilbeck countered with the proposal that an all-star team, drawn from all four Dawson clubs, could represent the Klondike. This engendered a more favorable response, and Eilbeck returned to Dawson City with a more plausible plan for challenging for the Cup.

During the following year Eilbeck wrote numerous letters to prospective opponents across Canada, eliciting interest from teams across the Dominion from Brandon, Manitoba, to Sydney, Nova Scotia. He also wrote the CPR for particulars on securing a train car for the trip, determining how much it would cost to transport and feed the team on their four-month-long journey. The *Dawson Daily News* reported that "the replies are satisfactory. They show that the trip will not cost the barrel of money many people expected." It is unknown who wrote the official challenge, directed at the powerhouse defending champion Ottawa Silver Seven, and delivered it to the Cup trustees, but it almost certainly was Eilbeck. And so it must have been more than heartbreaking when on September 3, 1904—just six days before Philip Ross officially acknowledged receipt of the Dawson challenge—Sheriff Jack Eilbeck was dismissed from his presidency of the Civil Service athletic club because of one final, inexcusable attempt to influence the championship of the Dawson baseball league. Eilbeck would soon leave the Klondike for California, and instead of standing on the bench in Dey's Arena behind the team he had fostered, he would lie in a San Francisco hospital during the games, recovering from a broken leg amid the tremors of a soon to be ruined city.

Joe Boyle and Weldy Young Take the Reins

Joe Boyle, who had played on Eilbeck's curling team, became more prominent in the Cup challenge, likely because he was outside the Klondike tending business in Detroit and Ottawa, and therefore in a position to petition the Cup trustees personally. Known far and wide as a very tough, charming individual, Boyle must have been persuasive, and though the games would not be officially sanctioned until December 10, Ross and Sweetland conveyed to Boyle that Dawson was in.

On October 27 the *Dawson Daily News* reported that the hockey players were petitioning Ottawa for a postponement of the games, originally to be completed by January 10, so that they could participate in elections scheduled for December 16. Meanwhile, on November 12, the hockey club assembled to establish a committee to select the team's players. The DAAA rink opened on the following Tuesday, and on Wednesday the Klondikers held their first practice, announcing that the players would work out on the ice every night until they left.

With more than 20 players trying out, it was decided to hold four scrimmage games to determine the final team. One of the men entrusted with the decisions, and expected to play himself, was former Ottawa star Weldy Young.

Young had played seven tumultuous seasons for Ottawa, six of them with the famous Harvey Pulford as his defense partner. In 1894, he played in a losing cause against Montreal in the first Stanley Cup game ever played. Having been charged with brutality in a game in Quebec in 1895, and later charging into the stands in Dey's Arena to assault a fan in 1898, Young left a checkered, notorious past when he decided that gold was more valuable than silver after the 1899 season. Had he chosen to stay in the Canadian capital, his hockey-playing legacy might have been considerably more illustrious. The Ottawas verged on dominating senior hockey and the Stanley Cup. Had he remained, Young almost certainly would be in the Hall of Fame today alongside his partner Pulford and five other members of what became known as the Ottawa Silver Seven: Alf Smith, Bouse Hutton, Frank McGee, Harry Westwick and Billy Gilmour.

Young had not played in the Dawson league the previous season, having spent the winter working his claim on Lower Dominion Creek. But, enjoying an elevated status as a former senior league player, and despite the fact he was well into his 30s, he was expected not only to lead the Dawson team, but help in its direction. Facing his former teammates must have been an exciting possibility, but Young soon faced a dilemma.

When the Stanley Cup trustees agreed to delay the start of the Stanley Cup series, the first game was pushed back to Friday, January 13. In a passage soon to be prophetic, the Dawson newspaper stated, "had the original dates been carried out it would have meant that the visitors would have had to go onto the ice immediately on their arrival after a 4,000-mile trip and they would naturally have been severely handicapped. With the change of dates the team will have a week to practice before their initial effort to lift the Stanley Cup." However, for Weldy Young this short delay was devastating news. His new Civil Service job required him to assist in the election returns, which would prevent him from departing with the team. Uncertain as to what he would do, Young continued supervising the practice sessions and scrimmages and was elected captain of the team by a vote of the players on November 20.

The All-Klondike team was selected in early December. Chosen to play alongside Weldy Young were: Captain Lionel Bennett of the Civil Service, "formerly of Nova Scotia and a star;" Norman Watt of Aylmer, Quebec, "left wing, a fast, scientific player, quick on his feet and a good combination player;" Dr. Randy McLennan, "with all the craftiness of the veteran and a hard player." He was a graduate of Queen's University and veteran of one Stanley Cup game, a loss to Montreal in 1895; George Kennedy, "or 'Old Sureshot' as he is called, who received his first lessons in hockey at Winnipeg and played on a number of teams in that city and also for Rat Portage, Selkirk and similar places, and is one of the Civil Service stars."

Also selected were Hector Smith, from Kennedy's hometown of Selkirk, Manitoba, Jimmy Johnstone of Ottawa, and, despite never having played goal before, Albert Forrest, formerly of Three Rivers, Quebec.

The *Dawson Daily News* proclaimed that "the boys are in much need of financing and are working like beavers to get it." Meanwhile, practice games with the gate money added to the tour kitty, with teams drawn from rejected players. These games were not without some rancor. Some of the cut players were already arranging new teams to compete for the Cup after it was brought back to Dawson. But as time grew short, two calamities befell the team.

Weldy Young, after agonizing for weeks, decided he could not leave his Civil Service job, and suddenly the team was without its star player-coach. The blow was compounded when Captain Bennett also declined the tour. His wife had been severely injured the previous winter when she was dragged 60 feet by a runaway sleigh in front of the Northern Hotel at the corner of 3rd and Queen, and he decided he could not leave her alone in Dawson. It was then decided to arrange for the addition of both Lorne Hannay, "formerly of the Yukon," and now living in Brandon, Manitoba, and Archie Martin, one of Joe Boyle's best friends but better known as a lacrosse player, to the team.

Hannay was from the Maritimes and had played in Brandon's Stanley Cup challenge to the Silver Seven the previous March, scoring two goals. He had seen first hand Ottawa's fearsome stars Frank McGee and Alf Smith score 13 of 15 goals against Brandon in the two-game series. It seems the Klondikers felt he was eligible simply because he had once been in the Yukon. And so the team was set: Smith, Kennedy, Watt and McLennan the forwards, Hannay and Johnstone the defense, Albert Forrest the goalie, with Archie Martin as spare.

On December 14, 1904, Frank Slavin, Boyle's old pugilist partner, arrived off the trail from Whitehorse suffering from appendicitis and with bad news: there was little snow. The team members appear to have differed in their view on how to proceed. Martin, Kennedy and Smith, hoping for snow, would leave with dog teams. The rest of the players would depart on bicycles the following day. Newspapers of the time reported, "If the snow is well packed the time will be much better than otherwise. If much light snow is encountered the lads will have the experience of pushing their wheels through the accumulation until good stretches can be found..."

It was 10 degrees below zero Fahrenheit on Sunday

morning, December 18, 1904, when Martin, Kennedy and Smith assembled on the streets of Dawson City. And with their first steps toward the wilderness, amidst the cheers and well-wishes of their other teammates, friends, and families, the odyssey had begun.

THE JOURNEY

The travel plans were daunting. The team would bicycle and dog sled the new overland route to Whitehorse. There they would board the Whitehorse-White Pass Railway for the short trip to Skagway, where they would board the *Amur*. Down the Alaskan panhandle they would steam to Vancouver, where a Pullman coach awaited to carry them across half a continent. This would place the team in Ottawa with a week to spare, giving them time to recuperate from their arduous journey.

The enthusiasm of the Stanley Cup challengers was quickly tested. Albert Forrest's bicycle broke down at Yukon Crossing. There was no snow for the dog teams. Struggling most of the way on foot, the Klondikers staggered through the Yukon wilderness, arriving in Whitehorse ten days later. Randy McLennan wired back to Dawson, "We are very tired, but we are on schedule." But no schedule could survive the surprise snowstorm that descended that evening. The players awoke to reports that 17 snowslides had shut down the railway. Frantic that their ship would leave without them, they received assurances that it would wait. But when the team finally arrived in Skagway, they found that the *Amur* had departed an hour earlier, when the captain, no doubt with a schedule of his own to keep, had given up on them.

The team languished three days awaiting the next steamer south. To their further chagrin they were informed that they would arrive not in Vancouver but Seattle, necessitating a scramble back north to their original destination, costing them another day. It must have been with vast relief that they finally settled into their Pullman coach, the worst of their travails behind them.

The team picked up Lorne Hannay in Winnipeg, but realizing their schedule was shattered, they asked Joe Boyle, awaiting them in Ottawa, to again delay the games. Surely reason and fair play dictated another delay. Who could expect them, after their grueling odyssey, to step off the train and immediately play the champions? But on January 11, 1905, celebrating their long-awaited arrival in Ottawa as well as Albert Forrest's 19th birthday, the players were stunned to learn that Boyle had waited until the last moment to ask for a delay, and had been denied. To add to their woes, the Silver Seven had officially protested the series due to the addition of Hannay. Even if they were to beat the champs, they were not assured of winning the Stanley Cup. Without their two best players, exhausted from their 25-day ordeal, and with only one day in which to rest, the Klondikers prepared to face the greatest hockey team ever assembled.

THE GAMES BEGIN

Before a sold-out crowd that included Governor-General Earl Grey, the talent gap between the two squads was quickly apparent. Ottawa defeated Dawson 9-2. Boyle remained optimistic: "… it was a great game, and the score is no criteria of it …." But the truth lay more in this observation by the *Ottawa Citizen*: "… the Dawson team … were clearly outclassed last evening … the form they showed was of the most mediocre kind."

Dawson had to regroup fast. Boyle assured newspaper reporters and anyone else who would listen that they would win the second game, and then, with Weldy Young back in the lineup, take the Cup in the third. Young, upon hearing of the team's delay in Whitehorse, had promptly fudged his election returns and fled Dawson, desperately trying to catch up.

But despite Boyle's boast, the second game was nothing less than a debacle for the Klondikers. Best remembered for the 14 goals Frank McGee scored—he also netted two more that were called back for offsides—the game also established a mark for goals allowed in a Cup match. The northerners were so humiliated that play was called early, the final score 23–2. This time the newspapers were brutal in their evaluation of the Dawson gang: "…the worst consignment of hockey junk ever to come over the metals of the CPR. The visitors couldn't shoot, couldn't skate, in fact they had about as much chance to lift the cup as the liberals had of beating Ed Dunlop in North Renfrew." But Dawson had little time to lament their loss. Their barnstorming tour had only just begun.

THE TOUR

Following the debacle in Ottawa, the team rode the rails east. Beginning in Amherst, Nova Scotia, on January 23, the Klondikers played on 12 consecutive nights, crisscrossing the Maritime provinces each day by rail for the evening's contest. To put this feat of endurance in perspective, remember that these players were all "60-minute men" as the rules of the day allowed no substitutions save for injury. When compared to today's standard of using four forward lines in a game, the Klondikers' hockey marathon could almost be considered the equivalent of playing 48 hockey games in 12 days!

Leaving the Maritimes, the team rode a four-game winning streak into Forrest's hometown of Three Rivers (Trois Rivières), Quebec, only to be drubbed by the locals, 7–2. Turning west, they played in Montreal, were routed by Queen's University, and visited Brockville, Ontario, before descending on Pittsburgh to play the "declared professionals." It was by design that Pittsburgh was on the back end of the tour, as the controversy over professionalism was such that had they played there earlier, many of their opponents would have refused to play them at all for risk of tarnishing their amateur standing. Charges were now leveled that the Klondikers were themselves professionals, raking in a fortune on their trip.

From Pittsburgh, the team headed north for the final leg of the tour. They defeated Port Arthur 8–4 before losing 8–1 to the powerhouse Winnipeg Vics. On March 21, 1905, the weather turning against them, they routed Brandon 8–1 in a game marred by rough play. Exhausted, homesick, their bodies beaten, the players agreed to cancel the remaining games. The record of the Dawson City team stood at 11 wins and 13 losses.

On April 5, Norman Watt, George Kennedy, Jimmy Johnstone, Randy McLennan and Albert Forrest arrived in Whitehorse, and announced they would walk the remaining 400 miles to Dawson. Forrest was the first to arrive, receiving a hero's welcome. One by one the others followed, ready to resume the quiet, nondescript lives they had abandoned almost four months earlier. Never fully realizing it during their lifetimes, these Dawson men had created a hockey legend.

CHAPTER 11

Hockey's Famous Shamrock

The Story of Harry Trihey

John Jason Wilson

DURING THE YEARS LEADING UP TO WORLD WAR I, hockey players at the senior level in Canada enjoyed a certain degree of celebrity. However, their celebrity was no greater than Canada's key military figures of the age. In fact, in many cases, the military was an inevitable graduation from playing hockey when war did finally break out in 1914. It follows that the Canadian Expeditionary Forces (CEF) received great support from the hockey world during the Great War. Many players of that time, as well as several retired ones, volunteered and served their country proudly. Hockey heroes like Frank McGee and Allan "Scotty" Davidson lost their lives representing Canada in the European theater of war. Several other notable players also joined Canada's fighting ranks, though perhaps one of the most compelling stories is of one hockey star who was never given the chance to fulfill his service to Canada.

History suggests that the genesis of a Canadian identity was first formed during the Great War (1914–18). Indeed, Canada's participation in World War I was crucial to the war's outcome, but more profound was the effect the war had on Canadians. Tales of honor and glory at Vimy Ridge combined with a nation's respectful mourning of the over 155,000 wounded and 60,000 dead did much to allow a Canadian identity to blossom.

Prior to 1914, patriotic fervor in Canada was divided between the new world and the old. Many people during this period, sometimes even third- and fourth-generation Canadians, held fast to the traditions of the homeland from where they or their ancestors had emigrated while exploring the new idea of what exactly it meant to be Canadian. The Irish-Canadian pocket was no exception. As a population in a foreign land, the displaced Irish and later their children would embrace their new home in Canada. They enjoyed greater religious freedom than they had ever known, improved possibilities of prosperity, success in business and commerce, open participation in Canadian social and political realms, and of course, hockey.

The Trihey family had come to Canada in the 1700s. Harry Trihey was born in Montreal on Christmas Day, 1877. A true leader, his self-discipline and commitment to his community are evident in the countless organizations in Montreal that Trihey became involved with throughout his life. He was considered by those who knew him well to be a very serious man.

Trihey attended the Jesuit college of St. Mary's and not only starred in hockey, but also excelled at lacrosse and rugby football. St. Mary's College was a prep school for McGill University. It was a small school and often had as few as 10 graduating students a year. Harry Trihey studied law at McGill and later enjoyed a long and distinguished career at the bar. However, it was his days as a hockey star that gave him his greatest celebrity—and his days in the military that gave him his greatest regrets.

Trihey grew up in the Westmount area of Montreal and honed his hockey skills on a pond that today is the North Shamrock Avenue Market. It was at St. Mary's that Trihey began playing with Arthur Farrell and Dr. Jack Brannen. Farrell would write the first book about hockey (*Hockey: Canada's Royal Winter Game*) in 1898. Brannen is best remembered for penning hockey's first instructional book in 1906, entitled *Spalding's First Standard Guide to Hockey*. Trihey, too, would leave an indelible mark on the game he loved.

Playing for Father Bernard Devlin's St. Mary's hockey team of 1893, the combination of Trihey, Farrell and Brannen soon began to revolutionize the tempo of the game. At a time when hockey was still an onside game (like rugby where no forward passes were allowed), the Irish trio relied on a new method of completing quick, successive and parallel passes. This approach left the fourth forward, the rover, to freelance about the play and negotiate a potential scoring position. The rapid passes on their own were enough to create scoring chances and both of Trihey's teams, St. Mary's and later the Montreal Shamrocks, found great success with this method.

Trihey is not only known to be the first to organize this style of attack, but several hockey historians have also credited him with another important innovation: he was the first to encourage the defensemen of his side to carry the puck rather than simply lob it through the air and into the opposition's corner, as was the standard procedure for defensemen of this early hockey age.

Trihey was a superb stickhandler and developed a flipshot that fooled many goaltenders. He also spliced an extra piece of wood into the blade of his stick, which gave additional power to his already strong shot. The strength of Trihey's shot did not always serve him well. On one occasion, the Shamrocks were playing the Wanderers in a friendly game in Halifax. New wire netting had been added to the back of the goals to keep the puck in the net. Trihey's shots were so powerful in this particular game that the puck bounced off the wire netting and came back out of the net so quickly that the umpire would rule no goal. It follows that the Shamrock players were not fans of the introduction of nets to hockey.

When Trihey, Farrell and Brannen left St. Mary's to become members of the Montreal Shamrocks Hockey Club, their place of honor in hockey history—and in the hearts of the Irish of Montreal—awaited them. Harry Trihey joined the Shamrocks in 1897. Soon, in addition to the St. Mary's trio, the Shamrocks' seven included the two Franks—defensemen Frank Wall and Frank Tansey—rover Fred

Scanlon and sturdy goaltender Joe McKenna who was reputed to be a poor skater but possessed the eye of an eagle. By 1899, the Shamrocks outclassed the Montreal Victorias to finish first in the Canadian Amateur Hockey League. By defeating the defending champions for the title in their own league, the Shamrocks became the first and only Irish-Canadian team to win the Stanley Cup. Wearing gray uniforms with green trim, their support from the sizeable Irish population of Montreal was immense.

Though Trihey may not have had the scoring prowess of the legendary Frank McGee, he did have a knack for figuring in important games. On February 4, 1899, Trihey managed 10 goals in a 13–4 victory over Quebec. The output that evening still represents the highest regular-season total ever recorded in a league that competes for the Stanley Cup. However, it was his play in Stanley Cup challenges that awarded Trihey immortality in the history of hockey.

Playing against Queen's University in 1899, Trihey scored a hat trick in a 6-2 victory in a one-game series. In the next Stanley Cup challenge, the first of the 20th century, the Shamrocks defended their claim to the Cup against the Winnipeg Victorias. They took to the ice at the Westmount Arena in a three-game series. The Victorias, or the "Buffalos" (a nickname that reflected the buffalo embroidered on their sweaters), preferred to have their defensemen dump the puck into their opponents' end with the hope that their forwards would outskate the other team and create a scoring opportunity. The Shamrocks relied on the combination passing style of their forwards and on the puck-carrying skill of their defensemen, a system, as aforementioned, designed by Harry Trihey.

The contrasting styles of the two teams, and the fact that Montreal was hosting a team from far off Winnipeg, gave even greater importance to an event that was becoming the premier attraction on the Canadian sporting calendar. Sportswriters from across the country were in attendance, as was a reporter from the *New York World*. Telegraph operators from the Canadian Pacific Railway and the Great North Western Telegraph reported the game so people across the country could retrieve up-to-the-minute reports from the local train station.

The three Shamrock-Victoria games were sold out. Crowds of over 7,000 attended each game. Scalpers are said to have received as much as six dollars for a 50-cent ticket. Winnipeg won the opening match, 4–3, and was leading the second game, 2–1, with only minutes remaining. Harry Trihey tied the game and then scored the winner with just half a minute left.

On February 16, 1900, another jam-packed arena watched the most exciting finish to a Stanley Cup challenge there had ever been. With the score tied, 4–4, once again it was Trihey who provided terrific drama by netting the winner with just 30 seconds remaining. The Shamrocks were carried off the ice and into the dressing room by their fans and Trihey was presented with a bouquet of violets.

Trihey spent another year as a player-coach with the Shamrocks, but they lost the Stanley Cup to that same Winnipeg squad in 1901. Trihey retired after the Victorias had exacted their revenge, but he remained closely affiliated with the sport, refereeing many league and Stanley Cup games and later becoming an advisor to the Montreal Wanderers. He also served as secretary-treasurer of the Canadian Amateur Hockey League and later as its president. It was as president that Harry Trihey led the amateur league through its disputes with the Federal League concerning the idea of professionalism and its infiltration into the sport of hockey.

Following his hockey career Trihey went into practice in the Montreal legal firm Trihey and Bercovitch, then Trihey, Coonan and Plimsoll, and later still Trihey and McManamy. In 1914, Trihey was named King's Counsel. Yet hockey fans and the Irish population of Montreal would long remember Trihey's incredible display in the 1900 series against Winnipeg. When war broke out, the born leader would call upon the community that had revered his hockey heroics and made him into an Irish-Canadian icon.

Irish-Canadians of Montreal had followed the affairs of Ireland during that country's turbulent beginning to the 20th century. In an age long before television, radio or the internet, Irish-Canadians would have read in local newspapers about Ireland's conscription crisis during the First World War. A crisis that was compounded by the fact that Irish nationalists during this period were aiming to establish independence from Britain. Many Irish people, feeling that they had long suffered at the hands of the British, were not enthused with the prospect of fighting alongside Britain in World War I.

Then came the famous Easter Rising. Patrick Pearse for the Irish Volunteers and James Connolly for the Irish Citizen Army, along with approximately 1,000 men, seized Dublin's Post Office and other buildings in the city on Easter Monday, April 24, 1916. Four days later, after Pearse and Connolly had proclaimed an Irish Republic, the British Army bombarded their holdings sufficiently enough to procure a surrender. The Rising in itself was important, but not nearly as explosive as its consequences. Despite a public outcry, 15 rebels were executed. The panic that ensued brought Irish officials to impose martial law. Public opinion in Ireland swayed overwhelminglt toward the nationalist political party, Sinn Fein. Consequently Irish support for Britain's war struggle became negligible.

Remarkably, several prominent Irish-Canadians including the Honourable C.J. Doherty (Canada's Minister of Justice) and hockey-hero-turned-lawyer Harry Trihey had designs to form an exclusive Irish-Canadian army regiment to represent the Irish-Canadian community in Montreal. One month following the outbreak of war in Europe, a 12-man committee, including Trihey, gathered to organize an Irish regiment for the Canadian Military. The man whose talent and sense of duty had led the Shamrocks to the Stanley Cup in 1900, was now, in August, 1914, going to guide the first Irish-Canadian militia regiment in the CEF—Harry Trihey was named the commanding officer of the 199th Battalion, the Irish Canadian Rangers.

One might ask how the organizers of the new Irish-Canadian Rangers were able to secure enough recruits to form their regiment given the delicate political questions involved? Firstly, the prevailing sentiment for dispossessed peoples around the world at this time was that "small nations must be free." Many Irish in both Ireland and Canada embraced this notion and hoped that if the Irish, in good faith, fought alongside the British to rid the world of tyranny, surely one outcome of the war would be Irish independence from Britain. However, it would still take some convincing for many Irish to rationalize fighting alongside the British.

Enter Harry Trihey.

Trihey's oratory skills had so impressed the Canadian

authorities that they had entrusted him with the leadership of the Irish Canadian Rangers. These same skills, along with the celebrity that came with being a former hockey star, aided Trihey in finding funds for the Rangers, as private Irish-Canadian citizens soon managed to raise $40,000 to begin the recruiting process.

If fighting for the freedom of small nations was one reason Irish-Canadians had joined Trihey and company, another, perhaps more important one, was that Irish-Canadians felt the need to be represented at the Great War. Likely not fully aware of the horrors of trench warfare, few wanted to miss the big dance. Furthermore, if English, Scottish and French-Canadians had regimental representation at the front in the form of the Royal Montrealers, the Black Watch and the Van Doos, the popular feeling was that so should Irish-Canadians. Suitably, the Rangers' uniforms would feature a Shamrock on the cap and a harp on the collar.

The only condition laid forth by Trihey and the organizers of the 199th was that to become a Ranger, one must be of Irish descent. "There will be no religious or other lines drawn, but the regiment will be purely Irish-Canadian in the best sense of the word." The Rangers would have two chaplains, one Methodist and one Catholic. The latter denomination had greater representation in the Rangers but the very fact that there were Irish Protestants and Catholics training together impressed and intrigued many important people including Prime Minister Robert Borden.

By St. Patrick's Day 1916, Harry Trihey, K.C., along with his enthusiastic, if inexperienced band of Irish-Canadian soldiers, had captured the hearts of the Irish community in Montreal. While the bid for home rule was beating in the hearts of Irish nationalists in Ireland, Montreal's Irish could boast a regiment that exemplified the possibilities of a United Ireland—Catholics and Protestants, each with their own regimental chaplain, serving side by side. Fitting was the Rangers' battalion motto—*Quis Separabit*, "Who Shall Separate Us?"

The growing popularity of the regiment caught the eye of the Duchess of Connaught. Louise Margaret, the wife of the Governor-General, Prince Arthur the Duke of Connaught, embroidered the unit's camp flag and lent her name to the battalion. Henceforth, the regiment became known as The Duchess of Connaught's Own Irish Canadian Rangers.

The Rangers were originally designed as a militia for home service only. However, that status changed in 1916. Recruiting had been swift, but Rangers' officers were largely inexperienced, except for the Adjutant Major John Long and Lieutenant Colonel Trihey who had attended officer's school in Halifax. But military inexperience and unresolved political questions in Ireland were not the only problems facing the 199th Battalion as they prepared for service overseas. Another concern was the health of the recruits.

Poor health in men who sought to serve their country was not exclusively an Irish-Canadian problem, rather it was a fact that permeated most working class communities in Canada's urban centers at this time. After three months of recruiting, the Rangers had rejected 1,000 men because they failed their medicals. Later still, only one of four recruits were deemed healthy enough for service. In November, 1916, the Canadian Military's Inspector General had these poor remarks following the regiment's inspection: "On the whole the unit is only fit for [checkers] and will require a lot of work to make them fit at that."

So how then, given their military inexperience and failure to achieve respectability in the eyes of the Inspector General, did the Rangers make it overseas? One most obvious reason is that in 1916, given the loss of life, the growing conscription crisis and the dwindling numbers of able-bodied men in Canada, a lack of military experience certainly would have been overlooked when men readily offered their services. Secondly, the Irish-Canadian Battalion was heaven sent as far as the British authorities were concerned; here were Catholic and Protestant Irish-Canadians, working hand in hand toward the British war effort. Andrew Bonar-Law, Britain's Colonial Secretary, hoped to bottle this commitment and have the people of Ireland witness the remarkable Canadian regiment. Not only did Bonar-Law wish that the Rangers, in some small way, might help recruitment in Ireland, but perhaps more importantly, quell any pro-German sentiment that cast shadows there. A Rangers journey overseas would make way for the political power-play Bonar-Law had envisioned when first he learned of the regiment.

However, Trihey and the rest of the Rangers were unaware of Bonar-Law's ulterior interest in the regiment. As far as Trihey knew, when the regiment headed overseas, the unit would remain intact to fight just as other hyphenated-Canadian regiments like the Van Doos or the Black Watch had. In fact, Trihey had been personally assured by the Canadian government at recruiting rallies and fundraising events that his Irish-Canadian regiment would stay and fight together.

The Irish Canadian Rangers left for England from Halifax harbor on the S.S. Olympic on December 21, 1916. Colonel Trihey would have done well to heed the omen of the news he received before he embarked for England when he learned that a fire had destroyed his home in Westmount only moments after he had left Montreal. Fortunately, Mary Elizabeth Mullin (his wife since 1908) and their three children, Elizabeth, Patrick and Harry Jr., were spared.

The Irish-Canadian troops arrived in England on December 26, 1916, one day after Harry Trihey's 39th birthday. Only eight days later, on January 3, 1917, Trihey was informed that the Rangers were going to be separated and that the soldiers of the regiment would be sent to other existing English-speaking regiments. He resigned as Commanding Officer of the Duchess of Connaught's Own Irish Canadian Rangers on January 9, 1917. Not only was Trihey cheated out of leading his team to victory one more time, Providence would also cheat him out of serving in the First World War at all. The officers of the Rangers regiment were not going to be used and would instead be dispersed throughout the British Army like the regiment's soldiers. Even if Trihey had wanted to fight as a regular soldier in another regiment, his age, which was above the subaltern maximum, prohibited him from doing so. He had no choice but to return to his fire-gutted home in Canada.

Meanwhile, before breaking them up, the British government planned a tour for the Rangers that would see them parade through various Irish cities to show the people that the good Irishmen of Canada had put their religious and class differences aside when it came to answering the call to arms. Now without their leader, the Rangers were paraded through the streets of Dublin, Cork, Armagh, Belfast and Limerick in an attempt to bolster Irish recruiting. They never saw active duty as a unit and were separated and dispersed throughout the British and Colonial English-speaking regiments. The Rangers were officially disbanded on May 23, 1917.

In all probability, Harry Trihey would have been held suspect by many members of the Irish community upon his premature return to Montreal. After all, he was the middle man between the soldiers and the government and the main advocate of the Irish-Canadian regiment from the beginning. As a man of uncompromising character, to be held in suspicion must have been torturous for Trihey. Though he was subject to a "gag" rule when he returned to Canada, the situation was only remedied by the composition and publication of his side of the Rangers' story in an open letter to the *New York Post*—despite the danger this involved.

Trihey's emotive letter to the *Post* did not disguise his feelings about the disbandment of his regiment. His betrayal challenged the whole idea of the formation of the Rangers and Trihey let readers know how the Irish-Canadian soldier felt:

> *He realizes what he formerly heard, but did not appreciate that Ireland is under martial law and is occupied by an English army. He reads in the press that English soldiers in Dublin and Cork, with rifle and with machine gun fight those of his kinsmen who believe Ireland to be a small nation worthy of freedom. He wonders if the conscripting of 100,000 more Canadians would still be necessary if the 100,000 men comprising the English army in Ireland were sent to fight in France. He also wonders where Canadians now may best maintain the war purpose vital to Canada, small nations must be free.*

Perhaps in an attempt to temper this confession, Trihey adds, "If conscription becomes law, of course Irish-Canadians will loyally observe the law, for they are Canadians."

Trihey's letter was succinct, direct, but fair—much fairer than those who had broken their promise to the Irish regiment. Moreover, Bonar-Law's request of Prime Minister Borden to present the Rangers to the people of Ireland is a fact made even worse when one considers that this request came on October 30, 1916, two months before the Battalion had even left for England. The writing was on the wall for the disbandment of the Irish-Canadian regiment before they even set sail for war. All along, their Commanding Officer was kept in the dark and not informed until his arrival in England.

Perhaps Trihey did not expect his letter to the *Post* to be reprinted in the *Montreal Gazette*. When it was, Canadian military authorities came extremely close to taking legal action against him on the grounds that the letter had contravened the King's Regulations and Orders. Trihey was spared any official punishment with the help of fellow Irish-Canadian and Minister of Justice C.J. Doherty.

Despite his disappointment in his military experience, Trihey carried on, as an anonymous source assures us. "This flagrant betrayal of trust and the subsequent silencing of the true facts could have broken a man of lesser calibre. Not so with Harry Trihey. He returned to civilian life where he subsequently carved a memorable name for himself." Trihey thrived as a prominent Montreal lawyer for many years following the war and got involved with several charitable and philanthropic organizations. He and his wife remained in Montreal where their children gave them eight grandchildren. While war raged in Europe for the second time in the 20th century, Colonel Harry J. Trihey succumbed to stomach cancer in the city of Montreal on December 9, 1942.

Harry Trihey's innovations in the game he loved are so fundamental that even today, one wonders if hockey would have been the same without him. He was inducted into the Hall of Fame in 1950. Perhaps his one regret in life was the premature disbandment of the Irish Canadian Rangers, a regiment he had worked so hard to raise.

CHAPTER 12

Montreal Senior Leagues to 1918

Amateur Hockey in the Era of Professionals

Dave Clamen

Although Montreal already had a long history as the home of hockey, several factors combined around 1910 to lead to an explosion of the game at the local senior amateur level. At the time, the city was home to five professional teams as the Canadian Hockey Association and the National Hockey Association each tried to stake their claim as the country's dominant professional league. When the NHA won the power struggle, the city was soon left with only the Canadiens and the Wanderers among the pro ranks and there was room for the amateur game to thrive.

Meanwhile, as professional hockey was coming to dominate Stanley Cup competition, Sir H. Montagu Allan of Montreal donated a trophy to recognize the best amateur team in Canada. This gave senior hockey teams a national trophy that was theirs alone, and one for which all Canadian amateur teams could compete. In 1908, the Ottawa Cliffsides of the Interprovincial League were proclaimed the Allan Cup's first champions, only to be defeated by the Intercollegiate champions from Queen's University in the first actual competition in 1909.

The second competition for the Allan Cup in 1910 involved teams from the four major amateur leagues: Intercollegiate, Interprovincial, the St. Lawrence and the Ontario Hockey Association. St. Michael's College of the OHA emerged as the victor in a series of games played between the league champions in Kingston and Toronto. Although no Montreal team had won its league, several, including the Victorias, AAA, McGill and Westmount, had been involved in senior amateur play that year.

It was anticipated that a similar format would be followed in 1911, but instead the Allan Cup trustees ordered St. Michael's to honor a challenge from the Manitoba champions. When St. Michael's, then in the middle of the OHA season, refused, the trustees simply awarded the Cup to the Winnipeg Victorias. The OHA and the other eastern teams refused to recognize this move, which effectively isolated the Allan Cup out west. For the next few years, the western teams played off against each other for the Cup with only the occasional challenge coming from the east. Until 1917, the Allan Cup remained west of Lake Superior while eastern teams largely ignored it. The beginning of World War I had worsened the situation.

With so many men overseas in the Canadian army, and so many resources needed at home to produce munitions, travel during the Great War was restricted to essential services. Hockey teams that had begun to make trips between eastern and western Canada found themselves forced to seek competition closer to home. In Montreal, this led to the expansion of local city leagues. The Interprovincial League covering Quebec and eastern Ontario tried to compete in Montreal, but Montrealers (both players and fans) were far more interested in local competition than national contests.

One reason for Montreal's isolationist view was the physical setting of the city itself. There was (and is) a lack of large towns nearby, and, being on an island, Montreal tended to consider itself apart from the surrounding countryside, anyway. The island itself is broken into sections by Mount Royal, a number of cliffs, the Lachine Canal and a plethora of railroad tracks. These physical barriers helped enforce a very strict ethnic division of the city. Each neighborhood was mostly made up of one group—French, English, Scottish and Irish being predominant. The local hockey teams of Montreal, therefore, were often made up of one single ethnic group. The French papers followed the fortunes of Laval and National, while the English papers wrote about the Garnets, McGill, the AAA and the Shamrocks.

Beginning in 1910–11, the City League in Montreal had six teams all playing games at the Jubilee Rink. The Garnets won the Jubilee Cup that year and defended it against the District League champions, Baillegeron Buffet. Then began a tradition of allowing outside teams to challenge for what was, essentially, a Montreal trophy. Vankleek Hill (Ottawa district champions) and the Kingston Granites, who had won the Kingston City League, were both defeated by the Garnets in a pair of unsuccessful tries for the Jubilee Cup. Meanwhile, the two teams from Montreal that competed in the Interprovincial League (the Victorias and the AAA) were so weak that the Ottawa clubs protested.

Though the Victorias and the AAA had dominated the first decade of Stanley Cup play before professional teams took over, they no longer appeared capable of keeping up in the increasingly competitive world of amateur hockey. The Montreal Amateur Athletic Association was a merger of various sports clubs (such as hockey, rugby, snowshoeing, and cycling). There were many good hockey players among these athletes, but with more choices open to them they would often play for other teams while maintaining their membership in the MAAA mainly for social or prestige purposes. Similarly, the Victorias were mostly upper crust Anglos who had a small following in Montreal and a difficult time maintaining interest in intra-city matches against teams seen to be beneath them socially. In 1911–12, a new division of the Interprovincial League was formed to separate the Ottawa and Montreal teams, but it was of little avail. The champions of the Montreal division were embarrassed in the playoffs against the Ottawa team.

In addition to weak Montreal representation, the Interprovincial League had to contend with tight schedules for Allan Cup challenges. Since there was little artificial ice available, a champion had to be declared by mid-March at the latest in order to allow for games in Winnipeg on natural ice. This deadline was rarely met, so the Interprovincial champions only challenged once for the Allan Cup. Without this *raison d'etre*, the league could not survive in Montreal.

With the Interprovincial generating little interest by 1911–12, the emphasis on local leagues in Montreal intensified. In a tight race the Garnets again emerged as the winners in the City League. They defended the Jubilee Cup against a team from Shawinigan and then against Allis-Chalmers-Bullock, the champions of Montreal's Manufacturers League. That season also saw a new league, the Montreal Hockey Association, start up to challenge the established teams of the City League. In 1912–13, the Montreal and City leagues merged. In a bid to capitalize on their newfound popularity, the lease with the Jubilee Rink was dropped in midseason and games were moved to the newer and larger Montreal Arena. The Jubilee Cup was replaced by the Art Ross Trophy (named after the president of the local hockey association, not the future Hall of Fame hockey pioneer).

Games in the revamped City League were now played as doubleheaders or even tripleheaders in the Montreal Arena on weekday evenings. Right from the start, these games were a huge success as over 2,500 fans attended the first tripleheader. They saw the Stars edge the Shamrocks 2–1 in game one, then watched a 1–1 first-half tie turn into a 4–1 Garnets victory over Champetre. The final game was a 2–2 tie at the end of the first half before Hochelaga scored seven unanswered goals in the second. To increase interest throughout the season, the Arena would offer telegraphic reports of out-of-town NHA games.

Champetre went on to win the 1912–13 City League title but lost the Art Ross Trophy to Dominion Bridge of the Manufacturers League in a major upset. Dominion then defended it successfully against the Quebec City Crescents. Meanwhile, the Interprovincial League expanded to no fewer than five divisions. The league champion was Grand Mere of the Eastern Division who had no time for an Allan Cup challenge after a lengthy playoff. Once again this season, Montreal teams had proved to be the weakness of the Interprovincial.

The 1913–14 season saw the first year of six-man hockey at this level of competition. It also saw the end of Montreal's participation in the Interprovincial League. Fed up with perpetually losing, the Victorias and AAA joined the City League as the Interprovincial reduced in size to a sole Eastern Division. Grand Mere won the league title (as usual) and then defeated the Victorias, who had won the Montreal City championship. Despite the loss, the Victorias went on to defeat Dominion Bridge and the Quebec City Emmets in competition for the Art Ross Trophy. Grand Mere advanced to play for the Allan Cup but was defeated by the Regina Victorias in what proved to be the last gasp for the Interprovincial League before it disappeared during World War I.

When the Interprovincial died in 1914–15, senior leagues based in Ottawa, Quebec City and Montreal filled the void. In Montreal, the established City League playing out of Montreal Arena now faced the new Montreal League based in the Jubilee Rink. Both circuits had their own supporters and both thrived. The Stars won the Montreal League, and then defeated the City League champion AAA club to win the Art Ross Trophy only to lose it to Aberdeen (the Ottawa champions). However, a protest over ineligible players was upheld and the Stars retained the Trophy. They then defeated the Laurentides (champions of the Quebec City league), but wartime travel restrictions kept any eastern team from traveling west for the Allan Cup.

As they became increasingly isolated from other teams in the rest of Canada, the Montreal teams turned to the United States for competition. This decision led to the most famous moment in the history of Art Ross Trophy competition—the challenge of the New York St. Nicholas team, led by the legendary Hobey Baker, in December, 1915.

In front of "the biggest crowd that ever attended an amateur hockey match in Montreal," Baker dazzled the fans. With two goals and three assists, he led St. Nicholas to a 6–2 victory over the defending champion Stars in the opener of the three-game set. Montreal observers lauded the foreign world-class hockey player; George Kennedy, owner of the Canadiens, made a pro offer to Baker on the spot.

The second game between the Stars and St. Nick's was played to a 2–2 draw in New York. On a smaller rink, the seven-man teams dictated by American rules ironically gave the advantage to the visiting Montreal side by limiting Baker's freedom of movement. Also, having been forewarned, the Stars chose to assign Harry Bell to shadow Baker and he was held to just one goal. The Stars went on to win the third game, 2–1, which meant that as defending champions they were entitled to retain their trophy even though the set of games had ended in a tie. This series has been called the historical zenith of American hockey. It was a big boost to the Montreal amateur game as well.

Buoyed by the success of the New York series, and by the recent games played by NHA teams in the United States, the Ottawa and Montreal hockey leagues started sending teams across the border to play exhibitions in Pittsburgh and Cleveland. This led to a direct split with the Canadian Amateur Hockey Association.

The Ontario Hockey Association had been badly burned by the recruiting methods of the Cleveland team and had lost some good players to them. In retaliation, the OHA alleged that the team was made up of paid professionals—a deadly accusation in this era. The national body, egged on by the OHA, backed this claim. As a result, any of the Montreal and Ottawa players who played against the Americans would be suspended by the CAHA—as would anybody who subsequently played against any suspended players. This decision kept these leagues out of the Allan Cup picture, but the OHA, which was the main instigator behind the threat of suspensions, could not take full advantage of the absence of competition from Ottawa and Montreal. Their champion, the Toronto Riversides, was unable to challenge for the Allan Cup because of lack of time to go out west.

Meanwhile, Montreal and Ottawa chose to continue going it alone without the rest of the country. Lachine won the Montreal League in 1915–16, and though they could manage no more than a tie in Art Ross Trophy play against the City League champion AAA, Lachine was entitled to claim the prize. (They were considered defending champions because the Stars of the Montreal League were the previous year's winner.) Lachine then defeated New Edinburgh, who were the Ottawa champs. Future Hockey Hall of Famer Moose Goheen then led his St. Paul, Minnesota, team to victory over Lachine in another international challenge for the Art Ross Trophy. However, St. Paul's use of ineligible players kept the trophy in Lachine's hands once again. In an ironic move, the OHA had cooperated in confirming that St. Paul was using suspended players. One player named Mohan had been suspended by the

OHA for playing in the Maritime Professional League and had lied about his reinstatement. Two others—Bonney and Wellington—had played with Pittsburgh of the International (Professional) Hockey League and were therefore also ineligible for amateur play. But Montreal could not keep the Art Ross Trophy forever. The Quebec City Sons of Ireland defeated Lachine and an out-of-town team finally took possession of the trophy.

In 1916–17, there were close races in what were now the three "major leagues" in Montreal. Loyola won the City League over McGill, the Stars nosed out *La Casquette* for the Montreal League title, and Canadian Vickers beat out Lyalls for honors in the Munitions League. All three champions made the pilgrimage to Quebec City only to be beaten out for the Art Ross Trophy by the Sons of Ireland. The Sons were so busy that they had to defer a challenge from the Royal Canadiens of Ottawa until the following January.

The 1917–18 season proved to be another exciting one—perhaps too exciting in some cases. In the Montreal League, one player (Davins) was suspended for two weeks after jumping onto the ice from the penalty box and hitting an opponent. In some later games big policemen were stationed at the rink to prevent spectators and players on the bench from jumping on the ice to join in the fights.

The City League season ended in a two-way tie between McGill and Loyola. A record crowd of more than 2,500 turned out to see what was hoped to be an exciting playoff between the two leaders. McGill, however, had little sense of excitement and walloped Loyola, 14–1. Meanwhile, three of six teams had finished tied for first place at the conclusion of the regular season in the Montreal League. In a playoff arranged to break the deadlock, Ste. Anne beat Lyalls, 2–1, in a hard-fought semifinal game. The final was equally close—a 4–3 win for Hochelaga.

As champions of the Montreal League, Hochelaga made the trip to Quebec City to try and bring back the Art Ross Trophy. They succeeded, blanking the Sons of Ireland, 4–0. In subsequent challenges, neither McGill nor the Ottawa champion Imperial Munitions could take the trophy away from Hochelaga. The Montreal champs then went off to Pittsburgh to play for the Fellows International Challenge Trophy, which they lost in a three-game series.

The 1917–18 hockey season proved to be the end of an era in the amateur game. Montreal's isolation from the rest of Canada concluded after World War I when the CAHA moved to regularize the competition for the Allan Cup. In the East, five regions were set up—Quebec, Ottawa, Northern Ontario, Ontario and Intercollegiate. Each season there would be a regular setup of playoffs to decide an eastern champion who would then play the western champion at a pre-determined location. Teams from Montreal would have limited success on the national stage in the 1920s and 1930s. Only four times would a local club reach the national finals, with the sole Allan Cup title coming when the Montreal AAA beat Port Arthur in 1930. But senior amateur hockey in Quebec would continue to go strong, with its roots in the exciting competitions of the 1910s.

Montreal Senior Leagues, Standings and Playoff Results 1908–09 to 1917–18

1908-09

Interprovincial	W	L	T	GF	GA
Ottawa Cliffsides	5	1	0	-	-
Montreal Victorias	4	2	0	-	-
Montreal AAA	3	3	0	-	-
Toronto Athletic Club	0	6	0	-	-

Intercollegiate	W	L	T	GF	GA
Queen's University	-	-	-	-	-
McGill University	-	-	-	-	-
University of Toronto	-	-	-	-	-
Laval University (Montreal)	-	-	-	-	-

Allan Cup final
Queen's 5, Ottawa 4

1909-10

Interprovincial	W	L	T	GF	GA
Ottawa Cliffsides	4	2	0	-	-
Montreal Victorias	4	2	0	-	-
Toronto Athletic Club	3	3	0	-	-
Montreal AAA	1	5	0	-	-

St. Lawrence	W	L	T	GF	GA
Westmount	4	2	0	-	-
Sherbrooke	4	2	0	-	-
Trois Rivieres	3	3	0	-	-
Grand Mere	1	5	0	-	-

1910-11

Interprovincial Central	W	L	T	GF	GA
New Edinburgh	5	1	0	-	-
Ottawa Cliffsides	5	1	0	-	-
Montreal AAA	2	4	0	-	-
Montreal Victorias	0	6	0	-	-

Division Final: New Edinburgh 7, Cliffsides 4

Interprovincial Eastern	W	L	T	GF	GA
Grand Mere	4	2	0	54	36
Trois Rivieres	3	3	0	48	46
Westmount	3	3	0	23	40
Sherbrooke	2	4	0	41	44

Division Final: Grand Mere 18, Trois Rivieres 10
(Note: most playoffs are two-game, total-goals)

League Final: New Edinburgh 16, Grand Mere 9

(Montreal) City	W	L	T	GF	GA
Garnets	9	1	0	57	24
Nationals	9	1	0	47	18
Stars	4	6	0	27	35
Baillegeron Express	3	5	2	27	31
Astor	2	7	1	13	42
Cercle St. Jacques	1	8	1	16	39

Final: Garnets 13, Nationals 4

Jubilee Cup games
Garnets 4, Baillegeron Buffet 2
Garnets 6, Vankleek Hill 5
Garnets 5, Kingston Granites 0

1911-12

Interprovincial Central	W	L	T	GF	GA
New Edinburgh	9	0	0	-	-
Stewarton	8	2	0	-	-
Montreal National	3	10	0	-	-
Renfrew	1	9	0	-	-

Interprovincial Eastern	W	L	T	GF	GA
Grand Mere	6	1	0	-	-
Trois Rivieres	4	3	0	-	-
Sherbrooke	3	4	1	-	-
Westmount	3	4	1	-	-
Montreal St. Patrick's	1	5	0	-	-

Interprovincial Montreal	W	L	T	GF	GA
Montreal Victorias	4	1	0	-	-
Montreal AAA	3	2	0	-	-
Montreal Shamrocks	2	3	0	-	-
Brockville	0	3	0	-	-

Semifinal: New Edinburgh 12, Grand Mere 10
Final: New Edinburgh 34, Montreal Victorias 10

(Montreal) City	W	L	T	GF	GA
Garnets	9	0	1	59	12
Stars	7	2	1	40	24
Baillegeron	5	5	0	41	39
St. Jacques	5	5	0	31	35
Nationals	2	8	0	20	52
Astor	1	9	0	14	45

(Montreal) Manufacturers	W	L	T	GF	GA
Allis-Chalmers-Bullock	6	0	4	-	-
Grand Trunk Railroad	7	2	1	-	-
Dominion Bridge	5	5	0	-	-
Canadian Pacific Railroad	4	4	2	-	-
Bell Telephone	3	6	1	-	-
Mtl. Light Heat & Power	1	9	0	-	-

Jubilee Cup games
Garnets 6, Shawinigan Falls 5
Garnets 12, Allis-Chalmers-Bullock 1

1912-13

Interprovincial Ottawa Valley	W	L	T	GF	GA
Renfrew	-	-	-	-	-
Pembroke	-	-	-	-	-
Almonte	-	-	-	-	-
Carleton Place	-	-	-	-	-

Interprovincial Central	W	L	T	GF	GA
New Edinburgh	6	2	0	-	-
Ottawa College	4	4	0	-	-
Stewarton	2	6	0	-	-

Interprovincial West	W	L	T	GF	GA
Smiths Falls	-	-	-	-	-
Brockville	-	-	-	-	-
Perth	-	-	-	-	-

Interprovincial Montreal	W	L	T	GF	GA
Montreal AAA	5	1	0	-	-
Shawinigan Falls	2	2	0	-	-
Quebec St. Patrick's	2	4	0	-	-
Montreal Victorias	1	3	0	-	-

Interprovincial St. Lawrence	W	L	T	GF	GA
Grand Mere	8	0	0	-	-

Quarterfinal: New Edinburgh 4, Renfrew 0
Semifinal: New Edinburgh 5, Brockville 2
Semifinal: Grand Mere 23, Montreal AAA 2
Final: Grand Mere 7, New Edinburgh 4

(Montreal) City	W	L	T	GF	GA
Hochelaga	8	2	0	-	-
Champetre	7	1	2	-	-
Garnets	6	4	0	-	-
St. Jacques	4	6	0	-	-
Shamrocks	2	8	0	-	-
Stars	2	8	0	-	-

(Montreal) Manufacturers	W	L	T	GF	GA
Dominion Bridge	7	1	1	-	-
CPR	5	2	2	-	-
Grand Trunk Railroad	4	3	2	-	-
Mtl. Light Heat & Power	2	3	4	-	-
Allis-Chalmers-Bullock	2	6	0	-	-
Bell Telephone	1	7	1	-	-

Art Ross Trophy games
Dominion Bridge 3, Champetre 2
Dominion Bridge 2, Quebec City Crescents 1

1913-14

Interprovincial East	W	L	T	GF	GA
Grand Mere	-	-	-	-	-
Shawinigan Falls	-	-	-	-	-
Sherbrooke	-	-	-	-	-
Quebec Laurentides	-	-	-	-	-
Quebec St. Patrick's	-	-	-	-	-

(Montreal) City	W	L	T	GF	GA
Victorias	8	2	0	-	-
Montreal AAA	6	3	1	-	-
Champetre	5	5	0	-	-
Shamrocks	4	5	1	-	-
Hochelaga	3	7	0	-	-
Garnets	3	7	0	-	-

Final: Grand Mere 9, Montreal Victorias 1

Allan Cup final
Regina Victorias 10, Grand Mere 5

Art Ross Trophy games
Montreal Victorias 3, Dominion Bridge 1
Montreal Victorias 22, Quebec City Emmetts 9

1914-15

Montreal	W	L	T	GF	GA
Stars	8	2	0	-	-
Garnets	7	2	1	-	-
All-Montreal	5	4	1	-	-
Hochelaga	5	5	0	-	-
St. Zotique	2	8	0	-	-
La Casquette	2	8	0	-	-

Semifinal: Garnets 3 All-Montreal 2
Final: Stars 8 Garnets 1

(Montreal) City	W	L	T	GF	GA
Montreal AAA	8	1	1	-	-
Victorias	6	2	2	-	-
Nationals	6	2	2	-	-
Laval University (Montreal)	4	6	0	-	-
McGill University	2	7	1	-	-
Shamrocks	1	9	0	-	-

Art Ross Trophy games
Stars 3, Montreal AAA 1
Ottawa Aberdeen 6, Stars 3
(protested due to ineligible players)
Stars 3, Quebec City Laurentides 2

St. Nicholas 6, Stars 2
Stars 2, St. Nicholas 2
Stars 2, St. Nichols 1 (Stars retain trophy)
[Series played in December, 1915]

1915-16

(Montreal) City	W	L	T	GF	GA
Montreal AAA	8	2	0	35	16
Laval University (Montreal)	7	1	2	36	15
Victorias	7	2	1	29	17
Shamrocks	2	5	3	17	28
McGill University	1	7	2	16	39
Nationals	1	9	0	17	35

Final: AAA 3, Laval 1

Montreal	W	L	T	GF	GA
Lachine	7	2	1	27	13
La Casquette	6	4	0	26	14
Stars	6	4	0	29	24
All-Montreal	4	5	1	23	26
Ste. Anne	3	6	1	15	21
St. Thomas D'Aquinas	2	7	1	10	32

Art Ross Trophy games
Lachine 2, Montreal AAA 2 (Lachine retains trophy)
Lachine 3, Ottawa New Edinburgh 2
St. Paul 7, Lachine 6
(protested due to ineligible players)
Quebec Sons of Ireland 6, Lachine 1

1916-17

(Montreal) City	W	L	T	GF	GA
Loyola College	7	2	1	26	16
McGill University	6	3	1	28	19
Laval University (Montreal)	4	4	2	26	22
Nationals	4	5	1	19	29
Shamrocks	4	6	0	19	22
244th Battalion	2	7	1	28	38

Montreal	W	L	T	GF	GA
Stars	7	1	1	25	15
La Casquette	6	3	0	18	14
Ste. Anne	2	6	1	13	23
Garnets	2	7	0	17	21

Munitions	W	L	T	GF	GA
Canadian Vickers	7	1	2	31	6
Lyalls	7	2	1	40	10
Canadian Cement	6	3	1	23	16
Dominion Bridge	5	3	2	33	14
Canadian Car	2	8	0	15	43
Canadian Explosives	0	10	0	7	60

Art Ross Trophy games
Sons of Ireland 2, Stars 1
Sons of Ireland 1, Loyola 0
Sons of Ireland 3, Canadian Vickers 0
Sons of Ireland 3, Ottawa Royal Canadiens 3
(Sons of Ireland retain trophy)
[Game played in January, 1918]

1917-18

(Montreal) City	W	L	T	GF	GA
Loyola College	7	1	2	46	31
McGill University	7	1	2	31	12
Shamrocks	5	4	1	29	24
Laval University (Montreal)	4	6	0	24	31
Nationals	3	7	0	16	38
Canadian Vickers	1	8	1	12	32

Final: McGill 14, Loyola 1

Montreal	W	L	T	GF	GA
Hochelaga	7	3	0	58	51
Lyalls	7	3	0	43	25
Ste. Anne	7	3	0	43	31
Garnets	6	4	0	28	24
Stars	3	7	0	37	51
La Casquette	0	10	0	31	68

Semifinal: Ste. Anne 2, Lyalls 1
Final: Hochelaga 4, Ste. Anne 3

Art Ross Trophy games
Hochelaga 4, Quebec City Sons of Ireland 0
Hochelaga 4, Ottawa Imperial Munitions 3
Hochelaga 7, McGill University 3

CHAPTER 13

The Death of Frank McGee

The Unfortunate Fate of One of Hockey's Greatest Stars

Don Reddick

Accounts of "One-Eyed" Frank McGee have long described his legendary career. They tell of his remarkable scoring ability, and the fact that he played only four seasons before abruptly retiring after the famed Ottawa Silver Seven lost the Stanley Cup to the Montreal Wanderers in 1906. Invariably these articles end the same way: "McGee joined the Canadian Expeditionary Force and gave his life overseas."

Gave his life overseas…

Expressed almost as an afterthought, it is a haunting, unexplored line.

Frank McGee was the sixth of eight children born to Elizabeth and John McGee, an Irish Roman Catholic family well known at the turn of the last century not only because John was Head of the Privy Council, but also because he was the half-brother of famous orator and assassinated Father of Confederation, Thomas D'Arcy McGee.

The Irish rebel's nephew grew up skating on the frozen Rideau Canal in Ottawa before joining the St. Mary's Aberdeens hockey team. On March 21, 1900, Frank McGee was playing with Ottawa's Canadian Pacific Railway intermediate hockey team against a side from nearby Hawkesbury. The game was a benefit for the Canadian Patriotic Fund to raise money for the families of Canadian soldiers serving in the Boer War. That night, McGee was struck in the eye when the puck was lifted too high. By May 5, the *Ottawa Citizen* reported that the injured eye would never "be perfect."

Despite his injury, McGee brought his services to Ottawa's senior hockey squad as a 19-year-old. At 5'6" and 140 pounds, McGee's main strength was his scoring prowess. Even casual hockey fans can recognize his remarkable statistics. In only 23 regular-season games for Ottawa between 1903 and 1906, McGee scored 71 goals for an average of better than three per outing. In 22 playoff games, he scored 63 times. After helping Ottawa to win the Stanley Cup in his rookie season, McGee and the Senators successfully defended it nine more times into 1906. His greatest moment—and the one that secured his legendary status—came on January 16, 1905, when he scored 14 goals in a Stanley Cup game against Dawson City. Yet he was also adept at the extreme physical dimension of the game. "McGee several times hit Thistle players over the head with his stick," reported the *Toronto Globe* during a Stanley Cup series with Rat Portage (Kenora) later that year.

McGee had missed the first game of the Thistles series due to a broken wrist, but he was rushed back into the lineup after the Silver Seven suffered a 9–3 setback. In a clever and successful attempt to fool his opponents, McGee used an obtrusive metal brace on what was in fact his healthy wrist and wore only a small concealed cloth bandage on the one that was broken. With the Thistles attacking what was actually his good side, McGee scored a hat trick in each of the next two games, netting the game winner in the second as Ottawa rallied to take the best-of-three series.

It may appear that McGee's retirement from hockey at the age of 24 was premature after only four seasons. But McGee's reputation as the game's greatest scorer had made him an obvious target . The sport had cost him the sight in one eye, several broken bones and countless scars. Thus when his civil servant job in the Interior Department of the Canadian Government promised him a $1,500 *raise* at a time when this figure itself would have represented a healthy salary, McGee hung up his skates for good.

Frank McGee did not lose his sporting enthusiasm after he left hockey. He continued playing rugby and was also an amateur golf champion. However, his greatest battle lay 10 years beyond his retirement from the sport that had made him famous.

Serving King and Country

Military Service was an accepted part of McGee life. Uncle James McGee of New York City fought under Thomas Francis Meagher in the famous Irish Brigade during the American Civil War. Older brother Charles served with the Canadian Expeditionary Force in South Africa during the Boer War and returned a hero. At the turn of the last century, in a society where military officers held much of the admiration and respect athletes now enjoy, it would not be unusual for the McGee brothers to join the Canadian Militia, and they did so.

In August, 1914, Canada entered the Great War. As members of the Non-Permanent Active Militia of Canada, both McGee brothers were mobilized for active service, Charles with the 11th and Frank with the 43rd Regiment. Charles was appointed Captain at Valcartier on September 25, sailing shortly thereafter with the first of the Canadian contingent from Quebec City aboard the SS Royal. On November 10, 1914, Frank McGee was transferred to the Canadian Overseas Expeditionary Force. The next day at Kingston, Ontario, he was appointed Temporary Lieutenant, 21st Battalion.

One of the enduring myths of the McGee legend, handed down through his family, is of his tricking the Medical Board about his eyesight. When asked to read a wall chart to test his eyesight, Frank allegedly covered his left eye with his left hand, and then, when asked to read from his left eye, raised his right hand, but covered the same left eye. This explanation is plausible, but unlikely. McGee was famous. He was also the son of one of the most prominent politicians in Canada. Given the "pull" of politicians and the society in which the McGees lived, along with a worldwide naiveté about what was actually about to occur in

Europe, it seems more likely that John McGee's influence is what enabled Frank to enter the service. Investigation of McGee's military record does produce one interesting piece of evidence, albeit circumstantial. But as Henry Thoreau once said, "Circumstantial evidence can be quite convincing—as when a trout is found in the milk."

This trout lay deep in the National Archives in Ottawa. Frank McGee's Medical History, Army Form B 178, contains a series of questions all answered by attending Medical Officer Captain K.E. Cooke, with one glaring exception. McGee is listed as 32 years old, 5'6" and 165 pounds. He has two vaccination marks on his right shoulder, and an appendectomy scar. To the right of "R.E.- V =" (Right Eye Vision) is handwritten, "Good," while next to "L.E.- V =" *nothing is written*! It is the only question left blank. Was it merely an oversight, or did Captain Cooke, obliged by the murky responsibilities of political pressure, retain one last vestige of medical integrity by leaving it blank instead of lying? Of course we will never know. What we do know is that Francis Clarence McGee was admitted into the Canadian Army.

CASUALTIES OF WAR

Lieutenant Frank McGee embarked for England with the 21st Battalion on May 5, 1915. One month after he left Canada, the "one-eyed" former hockey star, remarkably, became qualified in machine gunnery. Around the same time, the McGee family was faced with its first tragedy of the war. Captain Charles Edward McGee was killed in action in the Orchard at Festubert on May 26, 1915. On September 14, after a tedious summer in rainy England and no doubt harboring the burden of his brother's death, Frank and the 21st proceeded to France, where Canadian units were slowly being integrated into the trenches.

There can be no understating the mental and physical rigor of trench warfare. The experience ranged from mere discomfort in rain-soaked, rat-infested ditches to the virtual hell on earth of places like Ypres where body parts were "embedded in the walls of trenches... just as they had been shoveled out of the way by work crews," amidst the stench of putrefaction "so disgusting that it almost gives a certain charm to gas shells."

After just two months, Frank McGee was wounded at Dickebusch on December 17. A report states that "this Officer, whilst in action and handling a gun in an armored car, which was blown up by the bursting of a H. E. shell into a ditch six feet deep, and into this he fell striking his right knee against some part of the car and received a small puncture wound of superficial tissues just inside the patella. Synovitis was caused by the blow, and the knee became much swollen."

McGee was invalided to England on December 28, 1916. His knee would never fully recover from the synovitis, thus, his days as a gunner were over. There are no fewer than seven medical reports ensuring that he was unable to march, rendering him unfit for general service. Frank McGee's medical sabbatical finally ended on July 7, 1916, when it was determined he was now "Fit for General Service (Without Marching)." It was the very same day younger brother Walter, who had enlisted and hastily married his sweetheart Frances McCool of Pembroke, was transferred to the 77th Battalion, which was then preparing to cross the English Channel into France. Frank McGee returned once again to his 21st Battalion on August 29, 1916. Two days later he was "Taken on strength," rejoining his comrades on September 5, just in time to participate in Canada's first involvement at the battle of the Somme.

McGee, without sight in one eye and with limited mobility, had managed to secure an active position as a motorcycle dispatch rider. He could have chosen a safe clerical position instead. In fact, in a letter dated September 4, 1916, and received by his oldest brother D'Arcy McGee in Ottawa, Frank claimed that he had been offered a post at Le Havre, but had refused so that he could rejoin his mates at the front.

THE BATTLE OF THE SOMME

The battle of the Somme was a response to Germany's onslaught at Verdun. In order to relieve that holocaust, 13 divisions went over the top on July 1, 1916. On that day, mostly within the first 10 minutes, 60,000 casualties were inflicted upon Lord Kitchener's army, including 21,000 deaths. For the next two and a half months, the attack stalled into yet another war of attrition with an average "wastage" of almost 7,000 casualties per day. Fearing the coming of winter, the Allies decided on one last "Big Push," scheduling it for September 15.

In early September the Canadians relieved the Australians from their trenches criss-crossing the long, sloping ridge at Pozieres. This area had seen some of the worst carnage in the war. The English had failed to gain the ridge during July and gave way to the Anzac Divisions, who were anxious to restore their pride and honor after their humiliation at Gallipoli. The Australians accomplished what the English could not, but the cost was 20,000 casualties, forever linking their name with that place in the annals of warfare. "Pozieres was the last word in frightfulness," recounts Philip Gibbs in his book *Now It Can Be Told*. "Many of their [Australian] wounded told me that it had broken their nerve. They would never fight again without a sense of horror." It was into this web of earthworks that the 4th Canadian Infantry Brigade, including the 18th, 20th, and 21st Divisions, entered on the night of September 14, 1916. At dawn they would go over the top and enter what has become known as the Battle of Flers-Courcelette.

Standing at what has long since been the Courcelette British Cemetery, resting at what was approximately the Canadian jumping-off trenches, the most striking feature of the long, rolling landscape is its complete openness. Attacking entrenched machine gun positions from here was nothing short of suicidal, but the Canadians did so, attaining all their objectives for the battle, particularly the capturing of the ruined structure of a former beet processing plant, referred to as the Sugar Factory. Thomas Trembley of the 22nd Quebec Regiment (the Van Doos) wrote of the mission: "If hell is as bad as what I have seen at Courcelette, I would not wish my worst enemy to go there." Said a German soldier of the 17th Bavarian Regiment: "You can no longer call it war. It is mere murder."

The next day, at Mouquet Farm just west of Courcelette, Private John Chipman Kerr of Edmonton led a charge, and "although his finger was blown off, he raced along trenches shooting down enemy bombers from traverse to traverse. This was the last straw for the Germans, 62 of which surrendered, Kerr delivering them to a support trench, then returned to action." He was awarded the Victoria Cross for his actions on September 16, 1916—the day Frank McGee died.

Frank McGee is not among the register of names of those interred at the Courcelette British Cemetery, though 1,177 of the more than 2,000 graves contain unknown soldiers. Fallen officers of this battle were removed and interred at the Bapaume Post Military Cemetery outside of Albert, but he does not lie there, either. The registers of other cemeteries in the area, the Regina Trench Cemetery at Courcelette, the 2nd Canadian Cemetery, and the Pozieres British Cemetery, reveal nothing about how or where Frank McGee fell, but microfilm in the National Archives in Ottawa reveals a stunning find.

The War Diaries are written day-to-day accounts for each Division. In the 21st's diary the course of their part in the battle of the Somme is recorded: how tanks were used for the first time, how the boys "jumped the bags" and engaged in a horrific hand-to-hand struggle in attaining their objectives and then repulsed wave after wave of German counterattacks before enduring intense shelling. The discovery is a specific mention of Frank McGee on the day he died.

"At 11:00 a.m. 16th, Lieut. McGee reported to Battalion H.Q. with 50 O.R. who had been engaged on various other duties and proceeded from there to Sugar Factory line."

To have him mentioned in dispatches on the day he died is nothing short of miraculous. It locates him at the Sugar Factory about noontime, and suggests other details of his last hours. Almost certainly he did not participate in the assault on the previous day, his knee discouraging that. One wonders if McGee had stood at the high ridge of Pozieres and looked down at the Sugar Factory and the village of Courcelette and saw what lay ahead for the Canadian soldiers. Perhaps he had shared a rum tot with the men who now occupied the trenches at the Sugar Factory line that, only hours before, had been held by the Germans. Once the 21st had lost most if its officers in the advance, however, McGee was needed up front bad knee or not.

He would have ridden his motorcycle to Battalion headquarters on the morning of September 16, 1916. Later, sometime after noon, during a German counterattack at the Battle of Flers-Courcelette, Frank Clarence McGee passed from this world, leaving his legacy of courage and academic sense of duty to his team and country.

But what happened?

Killing Frank McGee

In a file at the National Archives are the words: "Body unrecovered for burial."

After the Great War ended, it took years to locate and bury the dead on the Somme battlefield. Over 700 bodies were discovered in 1935 alone. On memorials in France are listed over 220,000 men with no known grave; in the cemeteries are buried only 110,000 unknown soldiers. Considering the pains to which officers were located and removed from the field of battle while those serving under them were left, it is apparent that Frank McGee has died in the most feared manner possible to a Great War participant—by shellfire. Not only was he killed, he disappeared, suggesting, in a final, brutal analysis, that Frank McGee's body was utterly destroyed.

Probably the best insight into his last moments on earth can be gained from this Frenchman's description of shellfire: "When one heard the whistle in the distance, one's whole body contracted to resist the vibrations of explosion, even the most solid nerves cannot resist for long, the moment arrives when blood mounts to the head and where nerves, exhausted, become incapable of reacting. Finally one gives in to it, has no longer strength to even cover oneself and scarcely strength to pray to God—to be killed by a bullet is nothing, to be dismembered, torn to pieces, reduced to pulp is fear flesh cannot support—it is the greatest possible suffering."

The front page of the *Ottawa Citizen* exploded with casualty lists following the advance of the 15th. On Friday a rumor of Frank's death was answered by brother D'Arcy, who referred to Frank's letter of the 4th. "As far as we know," he told the *Citizen*, "Frank is alive and well." The next day, however, saw the rumor confirmed when a member of the Militia Department paid yet another visit to 185 Daley Avenue. The newspapers conveyed the ensuing shock: "... once again there has been brought home with gripping grief and pain the grim reality of the present conflict of nations. It is doubtful if the loss of any one of the splendid young Ottawans who have fallen at the front since the outbreak of war has occasioned such keen regret as that of the late Lt. Frank McGee... Frank McGee dead? Thousands of Ottawans knew him. Few seemed able to believe that he too had given up his life in the struggle for freedom..."

Frank's death did not end the pain of the McGee family. On November 18, barely 1,000 yards from the Sugar Factory, younger brother Walter McGee received a gun shot wound through his left shoulder while assaulting Desire Trench. Walter was awarded the Military Cross for his conduct that day, the citation stating: "For conspicuous gallantry in action. Although wounded he continued to lead his men with great courage, and remained in the front line until his battalion was relieved some 30 hours later."

The youngest McGee brother survived the war and returned to Ottawa on compassionate grounds in 1919, to walk the forever changed streets of his beloved Sandy Hill district. Some eighty years later, Walter McGee's son sits in his Spadina Road apartment in Toronto. Asked what his father told him of the war, Frank McGee's nephew and namesake shrugs and says, "He would never talk of it."

The legend of Frank McGee is now complete. Far from unique, his was a fate shared by millions of unfortunates born in the wrong place, and at the wrong time.

CHAPTER 14

The Pacific Coast Hockey Association

Innovative Pioneer League Took Top Hockey West

Ron Boileau and Philip Wolf

IT BEGAN AS A SIMPLE FAMILY DISCUSSION in Nelson, British Columbia, in 1911. What emerged from that meeting would essentially take hockey from a pastime played on frozen ponds to a true profession featuring mammoth arenas in major markets. The Pacific Coast Hockey Association would force the game to develop faster than anybody thought it could.

Although it began by using a seven-man game in an era in which the rover was already being phased out, the Pacific Coast Hockey Association would pioneer many of the modern rules of hockey and distinguish itself for its numerous innovations during its 15-year run. From the PCHA emerged such ideas as allowing the forward pass, installing numbers on players' sweaters, allowing goaltenders to leave their feet to make saves, the introduction of blue lines and the goal crease, the awarding of assists, delayed penalties and the penalty shot. The league also introduced the forebearers of today's current NHL farm system, created the playoffs, and was the first Canadian league to award a franchise to a city in the United States. Some 180 players suited up in the PCHA during its existence, with 33 of them now in the Hockey Hall of Fame. At the end of its 15-year existence, the entire league was sold to eastern interests in New York, Detroit and Chicago—fueling the first big expansion of the NHL into the United States.

Three Patricks, father Joseph—a lumber baron—and his sons Lester, 27, and Frank, 25, sat in their comfortable Nelson home in the spring of 1911, wondering what to do with their family fortune of just under $340,000. Both Lester and Frank were already accomplished hockey players—Lester having captained the Montreal Wanderers to a pair of Stanley Cup championships. The brothers were later teammates with the 1909–10 Renfrew Millionaires of the National Hockey Association—at the time the top professional circuit in hockey.

While Lester, one of the most innovative and shrewd individuals in the history of the game, was and is the more famous of the two Patrick brothers, both made enormous contributions to the evolution of pro hockey. It is Frank, however, who is considered to be the main architect behind the PCHA.

At the fateful meeting with his father and brother, Frank detailed his dream for a professional hockey league on the Pacific Coast. At the time, the game was virtually unknown west of the Rocky Mountains, and climate conditions would mandate the use of costly artificial ice rinks—of which there were only eight in the world, and none in Canada. Though Lester had always dreamed of managing his own team and operating his own league, he doubted the merits of gambling away the family fortune in such a manner, and voted against Frank's notion.

The decision fell to father Joseph, who voted to pursue the venture—earning himself an often overlooked place in hockey history as one of the patriarchs of the modern game.

On December 7, 1911, brothers Frank and Lester Patrick announced the formation of the Pacific Coast Hockey Association, adopting a constitution similar to that of the NHA. Three franchises were granted, with the Vancouver Millionaires, the New Westminster Royals and the Victoria Senators (soon to be known as the Aristocrats) taking to the ice for the initial PCHA season. In selling the game to a brand new audience, it was hoped that the upper crust monikers would lend a touch of class.

In addition to serving as president of the PCHA for many years, Frank Patrick was also a star defenseman, coach, manager and owner of the Vancouver franchise. Lester operated the Victoria club and played every position from defense to rover to goalie when the challenge arose. The showcase for the PCHA was the majestic Denman Street Arena in Vancouver, which the Patrick family fortune financed to the tune of a then-astonishing $175,000. Though Vancouver's population was only 100,000 at the time, the arena could hold 10,500—a building capacity surpassed only by Madison Square Garden in New York. Victoria's Willow Street Arena was built for $110,000 and had a capacity of 4,000 fans. The New Westminster franchise would play all of its home games in Vancouver during the inaugural 1911–12 season while its own Royal City Arena was under construction.

In addition to getting the arenas constructed, a major concern for the PCHA was finding high-calibre players. The solution proved simple—raid the rosters of the talent-rich NHA.

With their connections from years of playing back east, the Patricks were able to entice a wide variety of players to the PCHA. Frank Patrick's crew was headed by former Montreal Canadiens star Newsy Lalonde, while Lester's roster was comprised entirely of ex-NHA stars—including Bobby Rowe and goalie Bert Lindsay, the father of Hall of Famer Ted Lindsay and the first netminder ever to be credited with an assist. Rowe, Lindsay and Lalonde had all played with the Patricks in Renfrew. Making his debut for New Westminster was Ernie "Moose" Johnson, a former teammate of Lester's with the Wanderers and a player who would become a fan favorite out west until his retirement in 1922.

The first game in the history of the PCHA took place in Victoria on January 2, 1912. A crowd of 2,500 fans watched the host side fall to the New Westminster Royals 8–3.

"With all due reverence for cricket, we think hockey is a trifle faster," gushed the *Victoria Times* after the match. The newspaper had explained the game and its rules in great detail for its eager readers. "For genuine thrills, hockey has every other game faded to a shadow. It is the swiftest exhibition of skill in the sporting world."

A love affair on the West Coast was born.

The Royals won the inaugural league title with a 9–6 record, thanks in large part to high-scoring Harry Hyland, who potted 26 goals. Lalonde, in his only PCHA season, led the circuit in scoring with 27 goals. Other highlights included Frank Patrick scoring six times (still a major league record for defensemen) in a 10–6 win over the Royals on March 5. At season's end, over 20,000 fans watched a three-game series between the NHA all-stars and a team of the PCHA's best. The westerners easily won the first two games by wide margins before falling 6–5 in the final contest.

The 1912–13 hockey season began with a suggestion from Frank Patrick that the Stanley Cup be challenged for in a best-of-three or best-of-five-game series rather than the two-game, total-goals format of the time. However, Cup trustees still refused to recognize the PCHA or allow its teams to challenge for the prized trophy.

On the ice, the league took a major step towards credibility when another former Renfrew teammate made his West Coast debut. Fred "Cyclone" Taylor joined the Vancouver Millionaires for the league's second season.

"Taylor made the big hit with the crowd," wrote one local sports writer after watching him play. "Whenever he took hold of the puck the fans stood up in noisy expectancy and it was seldom that the Listowel wonder failed to turn something that made the crowd shriek with joy."

The seeds for future growth in the western game were sown later in the year when New Westminster, still plagued by construction problems on its own arena, played its final two games of the season in Calgary and Regina.

Victoria (now under its new team name) captured the PCHA title with a 10–5 record in 1912–13. The Aristocrats' Tom Dunderdale won the scoring title with 24 goals. "Silent" Jack Ullrich, the only known deaf-mute player in pro hockey history, scored two goals during the season. Both were overtime winners.

The 1913–14 season marked the year that Frank Patrick made his debut as PCHA president (taking the reins from C.E. Doherty, who had succeeded initial president W.P. Irving). On November 14, 1913, trustee William Foran finally gave his approval for the PCHA to challenge for the Stanley Cup—beginning a string of 13 years in which the western and eastern champions would meet to decide hockey supremacy. Because of the distances involved, all games in a given year would be played in one location, the site alternating yearly between the champions of the east and west. The differing set of rules would be switched from game to game.

The rules of hockey as they were played in the West would continue to differ from those in the East as the Patricks were intent on fine-tuning their sport. They had already allowed goalies to leave their feet to make a save, but the change that would truly revolutionize the game had its roots in a conversation between Frank Patrick and Cyclone Taylor on a boat one night in Victoria. With seas too rough to sleep, the pair came up with a system designed to limit the number of play stoppages due to offsides. The result was that the PCHA would use a pair of blue lines to divide the ice into three zones. Forward passing would be allowed in the center zone.

With forward passing now a part of hockey for the first time, the PCHA would begin to credit a player with an assist if he helped to set up a goal. Other innovations that year saw substitution of players allowed at any time, no players allowed within five feet of those taking a face-off, separate dressing rooms for officials, and a dark line (forerunner of the goal line) drawn between the goal posts to assist the goal judge. Players were also permitted to kick the puck—though not into the goal.

Victoria lost Lester Patrick to a broken arm in the preseason, but rallied behind its coach and defenseman to claim the league title for the second year in a row. Taylor won the league scoring title with 18 goals and 14 assists for Vancouver, while Dunderdale scored in all 16 of Victoria's games.

Though no formal challenge was issued, Victoria traveled to Toronto to face the Blueshirts for the Stanley Cup. Had Victoria won the series, there might have been quite a wrangle with the Stanley Cup trustees; but the Aristocrats lost in three straight games. The Cup winners each received $446, while Victoria players each got $264.

Despite the setback, the Patricks continued to tinker with the game. They installed a rule prohibiting bodychecking within 10 feet of the boards and also established a minor league farm system (the Boundary Hockey League) with teams in the British Columbia towns of Grand Forks, Greenwood and Phoenix—now a ghost town. However, as a chilling harbinger of things to come for today's Canadian hockey fans, the New Westminster franchise was transferred to Portland, Oregon, for the 1914–15 season. The Royals became known as the Rosebuds; Portland being "The Rose City."

On the ice, rookie sensation Mickey MacKay of Vancouver scored a league-leading 33 goals, but missed the scoring title in the final game by one point to teammate Cyclone Taylor. The Millionaires enjoyed their finest season, winning 13 of 17 games and then sweeping the Ottawa Senators 6–2, 8–3 and 12–3 for the Stanley Cup championship, the first for the PCHA. The Millionaires roster sported seven future Hall of Famers: Taylor, MacKay, Frank Nighbor, Barney Stanley, Si Griffis, Frank Patrick and goalie Hugh Lehman. The squad is generally regarded as the best in the 15-year history of the league.

Growth continued the following season with the addition of the Seattle Metropolitans—so named, reported the *Seattle Post-Intelligencer*, because "it would be quite in keeping with the high-brow cognomens of the Vancouver and Victoria clubs; quite in keeping with the dignity of the great city the club will represent …; and a fair compliment to the Metropolitan Building Company, whose enterprise in the erection of the Seattle Arena had made possible the entrance of the city into this distinguished sport company."

To ensure that Seattle would have a strong team, the Mets were stocked with players from Toronto, including netminder Harry "Hap" Holmes and star forwards Jack Walker and Frank Foyston. In retaliation for the raid on the Blueshirts, the NHA declared all PCHA players to be free agents and lured several of them back east. The costliest loss was Frank Nighbor, who left Vancouver for Ottawa. The Millionaires slipped to second place in the PCHA standings in 1915–16 despite Cyclone Taylor's third straight scoring title, and Portland made history by winning the league title and becoming the first American-based team to challenge for the Stanley Cup. They lost three games to two to the Montreal Canadiens, who won the first of what would be a record 24 titles.

With the Canadian government expropriating the Willows Arena for military purposes associated with World War I, the Aristocrats were transferred to Spokane, Washington, for the 1916–17 season. Vancouver was now the league's sole Canadian franchise, though the PCHA would return to Victoria in 1918–19 when the Portland franchise moved back north of the border.

Another marquee player arrived on the scene in 1916–17. Former Winnipeg amateur star Dick Irvin scored 35 goals for Portland. Gordon Roberts of Vancouver led all goal scorers with 43, while Bernie Morris of the Metropolitans set a league record with 54 points. Seattle then became the first U.S.-based team to win the Stanley Cup, beating the visiting Montreal Canadiens three games to one. Morris scored 14 times in the series, including six goals in a 9–1 victory in the finalé.

Despite the success in Seattle, the franchise in Spokane proved to be a total disaster. The team, known as the Canaries for its yellow uniforms, folded after just one season. Undaunted, president Patrick had his innovators cap back on for the 1917–18 season. He introduced the delayed penalty system (meaning a team would never have to play more than two-men short) and implemented a playoff series. Hockey leagues had previously used playoffs only to break ties for top spot at season's end. The PCHA would now have its first-place team met the runner-up in a post-season series in the belief that it was not right to punish a second-place team that might be coming on strong after a slow start due to injuries or other circumstances. The first PCHA playoff saw second-place Vancouver knock off first-place Seattle 3–2 in a two-game, total-goals series.

The win by the Millionaires qualified Vancouver to travel to Toronto to play the Arenas of the newly formed National Hockey League. The series marked the first time the forward pass was used in the East (in games two and four under western rules). Vancouver won both of those games but lost the other three games and the series.

On February 26, 1919, Cully Wilson of Seattle cross-checked Millionaires star Mickey MacKay in the jaw, resulting in a compound fracture. MacKay missed the balance of the 1918–19 schedule and refused to play in the PCHA the following season. Wilson became one of the first to feel the wrath of organized hockey for his deliberate attempt to injure an opponent. Wilson was fined $500 and was banished from the PCHA for the entire 1919–20 season (though he did make his way east and wind up playing in the NHL).

Meanwhile, Seattle beat Vancouver in a playoff to win the 1918–19 PCHA title, and once again hosted the Montreal Canadiens for the Stanley Cup. But there would be no champion declared for the 1918–19 season. The Spanish Influenza epidemic, which had swept the world in the fall of 1918 and killed tens of millions of people, infected several Montreal and Seattle hockey players, and the Stanley Cup series was abandoned. Montreal's Joe Hall died in a Seattle hospital on April 5, 1919.

Seattle returned to battle for the Stanley Cup again in 1920, but the 1919–20 season had not been without problems of its own. The three league teams (Seattle, Vancouver and Victoria) were so evenly matched (only two wins separated first-place Seattle and third-place Victoria) that allegations of match fixing arose. Frank Patrick was so incensed by the talk that he offered a reward of $1,000 to anyone with proof leading to the conviction of those making such slanderous statements. Seattle qualified for the Stanley Cup finals by defeating Vancouver in the playoffs, but the Mets were defeated by the Ottawa Senators.

With age slowing down Cyclone Taylor, the PCHA was on the hunt for a new marquee player. One would emerge for the 1920–21 season when Lester Patrick signed Winnipeg sensation Frank Fredrickson to a contract. The long-time senior hockey standout had recently led the Winnipeg Falcons to the Olympic gold medal. While Taylor scored the last five goals of his career during the 1920–21 season, the rookie in Victoria led the PCHA with 32 points in 20 games. Still, it was Vancouver that earned the right to battle Ottawa for the Stanley Cup. The 1921 series was a huge box office hit. The five games in Vancouver drew more than 50,000 fans who were ultimately disappointed by an Ottawa victory.

Further innovations came in 1921–22 when the PCHA introduced the penalty shot. Frank Patrick, frustrated by an abundance of deliberate fouls on players with good scoring opportunities, decided to award the free shot.

"The rule is a good one and finds favor with the fans," wrote the *Vancouver Province* on December 6, 1921, detailing hockey's first penalty shot (Vancouver's Hugh Lehman stopped Jack Walker of the Mets). "It will have a good effect in discouraging the tripping practice so common in the past."

To incorporate the penalty shot into the game, three spots were painted on the ice about 35 feet in front of the net. The puck was placed on the dot of the shooter's choice and he had to shoot from there. Many players skated full speed at the puck, which sometimes resulted in their missing it completely when they swung their stick. The first tally on a penalty shot came on December 12, 1921, when Tom Dunderdale scored on Lehman. Only seven of 21 shots that year resulted in goals. Just 23 of 98 attempts wound up in the net over the league's history.

Vancouver won the league crown again in 1921–22, but the PCHA champs were no longer automatic representatives for the West in the Stanley Cup finals. A new league had come into existence on the Canadian prairies, and to qualify for the Stanley Cup the Millionaires had to face the Western Canada Hockey League champion Regina Capitals in a two-game series. Regina won the opener 2–1 before more than 10,000 fans in Vancouver. One-time Portland star Dick Irvin netted the winner. Art Duncan scored a hat trick before a much smaller full house in Regina for game two as Vancouver won, 4–0, to take the total-goal series 5–2. Frank Patrick inserted brother Lester behind the bench for the Stanley Cup finals, but Vancouver still fell to Babe Dye and the powerful Toronto St. Patricks in five games.

Further changes were on the horizon for the PCHA as the 1922–23 season marked the end of seven-man hockey on the West Coast. The league finally abandoned the position of rover in order to play an interlocking schedule with the Western Canada Hockey League, which used six-man rules. (Also, the NHL was tired of alternating between the six-man eastern game and seven-man PCHA style in the Stanley Cup finals.) PCHA teams went 15–8–1 in the first year of interlocking western play, with Vancouver (now called the Maroons) winning the league's regular-season title by edging Victoria 33 points to 32. Victoria's Frank Fredrickson led the circuit with 39 goals.

Vancouver beat Victoria again in the league playoff series and took on the Ottawa Senators in what was essentially the first Stanley Cup semifinal. Punch Broadbent led the Sens to a four-game series win. Ottawa then proceeded to sweep the WCHL champion Edmonton Eskimos in two straight games in the best-of-three Stanley Cup final.

The 1923–24 campaign proved to be the final season for

the original PCHA. As usual, there were a variety of rule changes, including a restriction on goalie pads to a maximum width of 12 inches apiece. Teams from the WCHL won 29 of 48 interlocking contests this year, leaving the PCHA regular-season champion Seattle Metropolitans with a record of just 14 wins and 16 losses, but one point ahead of Vancouver. However, Frank Boucher's goal 14 minutes into overtime in game two of the league final (game one was a 2–2 draw) gave Vancouver the league crown. The Maroons then met the WCHL champion Calgary Tigers, with the winner to earn a bye into the Stanley Cup finals. The series between Vancouver and Calgary would be played while the two teams traveled east to Montreal.

More than 10,000 fans attended game one in Vancouver, with 2,000 more gathering in front of the newspaper office in Calgary to listen to a direct-wire megaphone service. The Maroons produced a 3–1 win. The infamous Cully Wilson scored three times when Calgary won game two on home ice before 5,000 fans. Game three was played in Winnipeg, and the Tigers wrapped up the series with a 3–1 victory. Upon arrival in Montreal, Vancouver played the powerful Canadiens, who won two straight games. The Canadiens then dispatched Calgary just as easily in the Stanley Cup finals.

Prior to the 1924–25 season, the ice was removed from the Seattle Arena (it was being converted into a parking garage). The Metropolitans were no more. The Patrick brothers had no choice but to formally join ranks with the Western Canada Hockey League. The addition of Vancouver and Victoria (called the Cougars since 1923–24) swelled the league's ranks to six teams, matching the number of franchises in the NHL as that league had expanded into Boston and added a second team in Montreal. A future Bruins superstar entered the pro game when the Regina Capitals introduced WCHL fans to a 22-year-old named Eddie Shore. The rookie was used as a forward that season.

Lester Patrick continued his innovative ways in the WCHL. He became the first coach to employ a true team concept with second-line players that were as good as his first. Previously, it had been customary for starters to play the entire game, with substitutes used infrequently and often only in the case of injuries. But Patrick, behind the bench of the Cougars—who beat Calgary to earn the right to meet the Canadiens in the Stanley Cup finals—felt that if he mixed up his lines, including the odd change on the fly, his club could beat the speedy Habs.

The Stanley Cup series took place in Victoria, and "the Westerners simply skated the Canadiens dizzy," reported one Montreal paper. "The blazing speed of [Howie] Morenz was negated and they just could not handle the Cougars' non-stop attack." Victoria won the series three games to one and became the last non-NHL team to win the Stanley Cup.

Lester Patrick's Cougars (with the 42-year-old "Silver Fox" returning for a full season on defense) first slipped past Bill Cook, Newsy Lalonde and the Saskatoon Crescents, then the Edmonton Eskimos in playoff action to win the Western title again in 1925–26. Victoria then fell to the Montreal Maroons in a series that ended on April 6, 1926, and marked the last time a non-NHL team was involved in a Stanley Cup playoff game.

Economics came to dominate the hockey landscape in the late 1920s. With a smaller population base out west, the cash-strapped WCHL—which had dropped the word "Canada" from its title and become the Western Hockey League when Regina relocated to Portland for the 1925–26 season—simply could not match salaries with the powerful NHL. Though both the PCHA and the WCHL/WHL had now run their course, Frank Patrick's impact on the game was not yet finished.

With the NHL planning a full-scale assault on major American markets, Patrick engineered the largest transaction in hockey history. He sold virtually the entire Western Hockey League to the NHL for a total of $272,000. The Chicago Black Hawks purchased the Portland franchise. Detroit bought the Stanley Cup finalist Victoria squad and named its team the Cougars. Players such as Bill and Bun Cook joined Frank Boucher with the New York Rangers. Boston acquired Eddie Shore and Harry Oliver. Herb Gardiner and George Hainsworth joined the Canadiens, while Calgary's Red Dutton (a future NHL president) ended up with the Montreal Maroons.

The Patrick brothers also moved on to the NHL. Lester headed up the New York Rangers and became a key factor in hockey's success in the city. He remained with the team until 1947. Frank, the architect of the old PCHA, made his NHL entrance as managing director of the league in 1933–34. A year later, he joined the Boston Bruins as coach. He also had a brief stint as the business manager of the Montreal Canadiens.

While their grand vision of hockey in Western Canada succumbed to the inevitable pitfalls of the game's economics, the legacy of innovation left by the Patrick brothers and the PCHA continues to play a large role in the modern game of hockey.

II

The State of the Game

An artist's rendering of the interior of the Excel Energy Center, home of the Minnesota Wild. The Wild and the Columbus Blue Jackets are the newest members of the National Hockey League, beginning play in 2000–2001.
Minnesota Wild image

NHL ATTENDANCE

1960–61 TO 1999–2000

	Regular Season		Playoffs		Total
Season	Games	Attendance	Games	Attendance	Attendance
1960-61	210	2,317,142	17	242,000	2,559,142
1961-62	210	2,435,424	18	277,000	2,712,424
1962-63	210	2,590,574	16	220,906	2,811,480
1963-64	210	2,732,642	21	309,149	3,041,791
1964-65	210	2,822,635	20	303,859	3,126,494
1965-66	210	2,941,164	16	249,000	3,190,184
1966-67	210	3,084,759	16	248,336	3,333,095
1967-68 [1]	444	4,938,043	40	495,089	5,433,132
1968-69	456	5,550,613	33	431,739	5,982,352
1969-70	456	5,992,065	34	461,694	6,453,759
1970-71 [2]	546	7,257,677	43	707,633	7,965,310
1971-72	546	7,609,368	36	582,666	8,192,034
1972-73 [3]	624	8,575,651	38	624,637	9,200,288
1973-74	624	8,640,978	38	600,442	9,241,420
1974-75 [4]	720	9,521,536	51	784,181	10,305,717
1975-76	720	9,103,761	48	726,279	9,830,040
1976-77	720	8,563,890	44	646,279	9,210,169
1977-78	720	8,526,564	45	686,634	9,213,198
1978-79	680	7,758,053	45	694,521	8,452,574
1979-80 [5]	840	10,533,623	63	976,699	11,510,322
1980-81	840	10,726,198	68	966,390	11,692,588
1981-82	840	10,710,894	71	1,058,948	11,769,842
1982-83	840	11,020,610	66	1,088,222	12,028,832
1983-84	840	11,359,386	70	1,107,400	12,466,786
1984-85	840	11,633,730	70	1,107,500	12,741,230
1985-86	840	11,621,000	72	1,152,503	12,773,503
1986-87	840	11,855,880	87	1,383,967	13,239,847
1987-88	840	12,117,512	83	1,336,901	13,454,413
1988-89	840	12,417,969	83	1,327,214	13,745,183
1989-90	840	12,579,651	85	1,355,593	13,935,244
1990-91	840	12,343,897	92	1,442,203	13,786,100
1991-92 [6]	880	12,769,676	86	1,327,920	14,097,596
1992-93 [7]	[8] 1,008	14,158,177	83	1,346,034	15,504,211
1993-94 [9]	[10] 1,092	16,105,604	90	1,440,095	17,545,699
1994-95	[11] 624	9,233,884	81	1,329,130	10,563,014
1995-96	1,066	17,041,614	86	1,540,140	18,581,754
1996-97	1,066	17,640,529	82	1,494,878	19,135,407
1997-98	1,066	17,264,678	82	1,507,416	18,772,094
1998-99 [12]	1,107	18,001,741	86	1,509,411	19,511,152
1999-2000 [13]	1148	18,800,139	83	1,524,629	20,324,768

1 First expansion: Los Angeles, Pittsburgh, California (Cleveland),Philadelphia, St. Louis and Minnesota (Dallas)
2 Second expansion: Buffalo and Vancouver
3 Third expansion: Atlanta (Calgary) and New York Islanders
4 Fourth expansion: Kansas City (Colorado, New Jersey) and Washington
5 Fifth expansion: Edmonton, Hartford, Quebec (Colorado) and Winnipeg
5 Sixth expansion: San Jose
7 Seventh expansion: Ottawa and Tampa Bay
8 Includes 24 neutral site games
9 Eighth expansion: Anaheim and Florida
10 Includes 26 neutral site games
11 Lockout resulted in cancellation of 468 regular-season games
12 Ninth expansion: Nashville
13 Tenth expansion: Atlanta

CHAPTER 15

Canadian Hockey

The State of the Game

OPEN ICE: CANADA'S HOCKEY SUMMIT

Ken Dryden

This essay is based on remarks delivered at the opening of a conference called "Open Ice" that took place in Toronto August 25-27, 1999. The event brought together concerned individuals from all strata of organized hockey in Canada. Their purpose was to take stock of the state of the game in the country where it began, to exchange what sometimes proved to be very strongly held opinions and to open new channels of communication across the length and breadth of Canadian hockey. These goals contribute to a process that has at its heart a larger purpose: to propose some next steps and directions for the game as it enters its third century.

THE END OF ONE CENTURY and the beginning of another offers a wonderful excuse to look back as a way of looking ahead, to see where we've been to help us see where we are going. One hundred years ago, there may have been people like us who, at the start of the 20th century, were wondering what hockey's future would be like. Hockey was almost entirely Canadian then with just a few players in the northern United States and some Norwegians, Russians and Swedes (Finland was part of Sweden then) playing "bandy"—field hockey on ice. In Canada, there weren't more than a thousand players. A few women played as well, but that would soon change; mostly hockey was for young men, not even for kids or oldtimers.

They played outdoors with few exceptions, and always on natural ice. So, only some parts of the country were able to play, and only if the weather wasn't too good, or too bad—cold was good, too cold wasn't—and then only for a few months of the year. Little could be organized or scheduled. If you were going to play, it had to be "pick up"—putting together whoever was around under whatever conditions you were willing to put up with, playing whatever variation of hockey you could dream up. So, more often rinks were frozen-over roadways and pucks were "road apples" or slices from a tree branch of the correct diameter.

Almost no one watched, for who wanted to stand around in the cold? The players kept warm by moving—seven players to a side, a rover included, with everyone on the ice at the same time. There were no substitutions. As a player, you had to pace yourself—circle, look for an opening, burst into action; circle, rest. The rink was small. There were no Zambonis—the snow on the ice got deeper and heavier as the game went on. There were two periods, each thirty minutes long. Long, flat skate blades wobbled because they were strapped onto boots. This made turning difficult, so the game moved back and forth in straight lines. Sticks were short, thick and unbendable like those used in field hockey. Shots were wristed and slow, which was a good thing, because goalies wore almost no equipment, save for leg guards borrowed from the wicketkeeper in cricket and a thick pair of gloves designed to keep out the cold, not the pain. Masks? For what? And if goalies were dumb enough to fall on the ice to make a save, they were penalized because lying down and getting hit by the puck because opposing shooters couldn't raise it was not considered a skill. It wasn't "cricket." It wasn't even hockey! It was simply not done. Two minutes.

But besides the equipment, the lack of substitutions and the outdoor nature of the game and the weather, what shaped hockey most in 1900 was one fundamental rule: no forward passing. A puck could be advanced *only* by the puck carrier. Just as in rugby, a pass could go *only* to a teammate who was behind you. This made stickhandling the main weapon used by players on offense while, for the defense—with an opponent's head down and no one ahead to pass to—the main weapon was bodychecking.

That was the game in 1900. So, as those hockey officials got together, what would they have imagined for the 20th century ahead? Arenas that would be covered? Sure, some already existed. But with 20,000 people inside them, with music and mascots, artificial ice, Zambonis and videoboards at a time when the automobile was unproven and radio and computers not invented? No way. Better equipment? Sure. Fewer than seven players on the ice at one time? Maybe. But a season that lasted nine months of the year? One hundred-plus games including exhibitions and playoffs? A game where after 45 seconds, players were replaced and rested? Not a chance. Where forward passing was permitted? NEVER! Not even close. Some things you can tinker with; some are sacred. A game with forward passing simply would not be hockey.

It took 30 years for the unthinkable to occur and it only happened because coaches, as coaches do, learned and adapted. Defenses stacked up and nobody could score. (George Hainsworth's 22 shutouts in 44 games were no anomaly: in the NHL in 1928–29, both teams, together, scored *fewer* than two goals a game.) By that time, the NHL was established as the sport's leading professional league, fans were paying money to watch games, the league had expanded to the United States for the first time and radio was beginning to create heroes and send descriptions of their exploits to millions across the country. By 1930, hockey was becoming a Canadian passion.

Other countries were starting to play too but not very

well. Once, Canada had been the only hockey-playing country. Now we weren't alone; we were the best, which was much better. World Hockey Championships, putting their best against our second or third rate, were a license for slaughter. In the 1924 Winter Olympics, it was Canada 22, Sweden 0. For Canadians, it was wonderful.

The following years saw the introduction of the red line, great stars such as Morenz and Shore, Depression and wartime hockey, the NHL finally shrinking to six teams—the Original Six we call them now (Toronto, Montreal, Boston, Chicago, Detroit, and the Rangers) which were original only if you started to follow the game after 1942.

After the Second World War ended, with Europe battered, the future moved to North America. Our economy boomed and people had money in their pockets. Lives put on hold for the Depression and the war were ready to be lived. For themselves, people bought homes, cars and refrigerators; for their communities, schools and playgrounds. All across the country, to commemorate the soldiers' sacrifice, they put up Memorial Arenas. *Indoor arenas!* Most with natural ice, but now with walls and a roof to keep out the worst of winter and the best of fall and spring. Now, hockey seasons could be longer. Now, kids had a chance to play.

In the 1950s, minor hockey in Canada took off. In 1930, fewer that 14,000 kids played. In 1957, almost 100,000. But old habits die slowly, especially those that are fun. So the tradition of "pick up" hockey on streets and in backyards continued, even as the game became organized and moved indoors. The season grew longer, pushing at the edges of football in the fall and baseball in the spring. Organized games meant equipment to buy and ice time to rent. More parents had to get involved, coaching, transporting, paying and watching. The catch phrase of the day was, "Take your boy to the rink, don't send him." Almost all of Canada's best male athletes chose hockey. Maple Leaf Gardens and the Montreal Forum were full. To millions, Saturday night was "Hockey Night In Canada" on television; a ritual that had begun on radio continued and grew.

The NHL had two great stars—Rocket Richard and Gordie Howe—and two great stars in the making—Bobby Hull and Frank Mahovlich. But the style of the game hadn't changed much since the 1930s. Forwards and defensemen still played in shifts that averaged more than two minutes in length. Offenses still moved up the ice in straight lines—"three abreast," as Foster Hewitt used to say. Defenses—wing on wing—moved back the same way. Goalies stayed on their feet because it was said that this was the best way to stop pucks, but the real reason was to protect their unguarded faces by keeping their heads above the crossbar. Jacques Plante of the Canadiens put on a mask and enjoyed success but few other NHL goaltenders followed suit.

These were the golden years of Canada and Canadian hockey—a time of high performance and high promise. Today was great, tomorrow would be better.

In the late 1950s, a young girl cut her hair short, called herself Abby and joined a boys' team in Toronto until the boys found out, ending the hockey career of Abigail Hoffman, future Olympic runner. Hockey in the 1950s was for kids, but not, apparently, for kids who were girls.

One more thing: appearing for the first time on the edges of our radar screens, just visible and still irrelevant, were the Soviets.

The 1960s began well: the slapshot, the banana blade, a game of power and speed and, later in the decade, Bobby Orr. Television was transforming sports. It brought into every home events that were staged in only a few cities, creating an appetite for the live product in other locales. The United States was growing west and south. For emerging new cities, true big league status required having big league teams. Baseball had moved west in the late 1950s. Until 1967, the NHL was a cozy, regional league, its cities an overnight train ride apart north and south, east and west. Civic pride, new money, personal ambition and the fear of rival leagues drove sports to expand; the airplane allowed it to happen.

The old six-team NHL—the Original Six—suddenly doubled with the addition of half a dozen new clubs. The NHL's quality of play, which since the war had been getting better and better, suddenly hit a snag. Nobody asked Canadians if they wanted to see six new bad teams join the NHL. It was money; it was Americans. Whose game was this anyway? Until now, nobody ever had to ask.

And the Soviet blip on the radar screen? It was getting bigger. By the end of the 1960s, the Soviets had buried the amateur world. Only the NHL was left.

On the home front, to commemorate our past and to express our belief in the future, "Centennial Arenas" went up across the country. Debates about the game focused mostly on the impact of television and how it was killing the great town-versus-town rivalries of senior hockey, and on a junior hockey system that encouraged high school drop-outs. There wasn't much talk about style of play or player development. We were the best, so it must be that we did things the best way.

1972...

...It was the most important hockey year of the century.

In 1972, the World Hockey Association began. Bobby Hull left Chicago, joined the new league and became the game's first million dollar player. Hockey players had always seemed like the guy next door. Now, they were in a salary neighborhood all their own and they could never go back. The "Age of Money, Part One" had begun.

But more than that, 1972 was "The Summit Series," the NHL's and Canada's best professional players (except for Bobby Hull who had joined the rival WHA) against the World and Olympic champion Soviet national team. It was Canadian hockey's chance to show the world what we had never had to show before—that we were the best. The series began as celebration in the making. Then, instead, it lurched to disaster, then rebirth and, finally, to celebration—with 34 seconds to spare. What a ride it was: four wins by Canada, three of which came in Moscow on late goals by Paul Henderson, three wins by the Soviets and one game tied.

Though we had won, we would never feel the same about ourselves and our game again. We had been the best. It was an understanding we had earned and repeated to ourselves from birth: our way was the best way. Now, however, our way still may have been the best, but, clearly, there was another way, too.

There was such anger in Canada: at our fat, overpaid, arrogant pros; at the NHL for making them that way; at our own national selves, getting caught from behind.

In 1972, we lost our confidence.

The divide between the NHL and minor hockey in Canada widened. There had been strong criticism of the

NHL and its player development system, notably from former Canadian national team coach Father David Bauer and from the Canadian Amateur Hockey Association, and now those critics had the ammunition they were missing. Because there was clearly *one* other way—the Soviet system—and maybe there were *lots* of other ways. Why *does* our game move in straight lines, forward and back? Our skate blades aren't long, flat and strapped onto boots any longer; they haven't been for decades. Why *does* our game focus on the puck carrier, the way it needed to before forward passing was allowed, the other five skaters waiting, unthreatening and non-creative? Why *don't* we pass more and better? And though we have more arenas than anyone else, is there something important we miss about off-ice training? Why *do* we play so many games and practice so little? Because parents like to watch games and go to tournaments? Because coaches don't have enough drills to keep a practice moving? Because parents and coaches think kids prefer games? If we are what we eat, do we become what we practice, or play?

What about the body contact in our game, the stickwork, hitting and fighting? Is it spontaneous and natural, or is it just us? Does it get in the way of developing other skills? You don't put a kid in the water with sharks when he's learning to swim. Then he can't focus on swimming. Then he'll just learn to tread water and watch out for the sharks. Are we creating generations of "water treaders?" Why do *they* look more skilful than *we* do? Why do *they* look the way we remember *we* looked many years ago? What happened to us as a hockey nation, as a people? A barrage of studies and reports followed—a barrage that has never stopped, more than a quarter of a century later.

As for the NHL, some coaches and players learned and adapted; the league, preoccupied with its battle with the WHA and the rise of intimidation hockey in Boston and Philadelphia, carried on as if nothing had happened.

For a few years, things began to feel less urgent. We won the Canada Cup in 1976. In games between Soviet club teams and the NHL, the Soviets won more often, but not against our best teams. Then, in 1979, came the Challenge Cup.

If 1972 is the most important year of the hockey century, then 1929—the year of the forward pass—and 1979 are tied for second. The WHA died in 1979 when four of its teams joined the NHL. Now, there were six Canadian teams and, a year later, seven when Atlanta moved to Calgary. One-third of the league was based in Canada, just as it had been during the glory years of the Original Six. And now with the demise of the WHA, the competitive force that had driven salaries higher was gone.

In New York, a one-time event took the place of the NHL All-Star Game in February, 1979. The Challenge Cup was a best-of-three series between the NHL All-Stars, including European and American players, against the Soviet Nationals. The NHLers won the first game, the Soviets the second and the third, with the score of the last game a resounding 6–0! It was a midseason competition, so there could be no excuses for poor conditioning. There was no ambush from overconfidence as in 1972. The games were in North America on an NHL-sized rink. We were left with no place to hide; we had been pushed off the top of the competitive mountain. They were the best, and they had numbers, climate, hard work and a hockey system on their side to win in the future. Sure, a year later they lost Olympic gold in Lake Placid—to a team of American collegians, no less—but even a blind squirrel finds an acorn sometimes. Even the most loyal supporter of Team USA recognized the American win as a miraculous and inspired upset of a superior opponent. When it counted again, at the Canada Cup in 1981, the Soviets won again—8–1 over Canada in the final game.

But 1979 was a watershed year for a third reason—in October, Wayne Gretzky entered the NHL. With his Edmonton Oiler teammates, he would open up the game. For Gretzky, the greatest goal scorer in NHL history, was really, first of all and best of all, a playmaker. But passing required a reason to pass and someone to pass to, and Gretzky pushed his teammates to skate, think ahead, create and find open ice in order to be in position to receive one of his on-the-tape passes. Playing this way, they had to become better players, and they did. Because open ice is rarely found at the end of a straight ahead dash up the ice, but across the width of the ice where there is more space, that's where they went.

The old pre-forward passing patterns, with their rugby roots, were finally dead.

It had taken 50 years.

Gretzky also changed the focus of our play. A passing game made the player without the puck more important than the player with it. He was quicker, more creative and maneuverable. He was the more dangerous one. So, being able to "play away from the puck," offensively and defensively, became a coach's mantra. The game picked up speed. Lots more goals went in and, for awhile, things went excitingly out of control. Then, as always, coaches adapted. Along came "the trap," space in the center zone disappeared, defenders were suddenly close enough to hook and hold, and the game slowed down again. Today, scoring champions have lower point totals than in the pre-Gretzky years. And in a low-scoring game, it is the goalie who becomes the most important player. Gretzky not only triggered the opening up of the game but—action and reaction—triggered its shut down, too. He remains one of hockey's great influences of the last 20 years.

Another important influence on the game has been changes in the way Canadians live. With greater wealth, new technologies and new opportunities, there are many more things for Canadian kids and parents to do. More activities to get involved in—music, computers, part-time jobs, other sports—more sources of entertainment—more TV channels, CD-ROMs, the Internet. Even the busiest kids don't *all* choose sports. The best male athletes don't *all* choose hockey. Hockey doesn't hold the same monopoly it once had and never will again.

In the 1980s and 1990s, we've also seen the rise of women's and oldtimers' hockey. If this is such a good game, women and oldtimers have said for years, what do gender and age matter? Why can't I play, too? In 1980, about 5,000 women played hockey; today, almost 40,000 do. As for the oldtimers, from only a few, the number has exploded to one almost uncountable—more than 500,000 by some estimates. Arena operators, facing flat numbers in boys' hockey, now had what they were looking for: two new categories of hockey to soak up hours of ice rental. A flurry of privately built, multi-sheet arenas were constructed in the late 1990s to satisfy these new markets.

The other two great influences on Canadian hockey in the 1980s and 1990s were money and Europeans in the NHL.

In the area of money, Gretzky had a big effect as well. In 1979-80, the NHL's average salary, using U.S. dollars, was $108,000 (Cdn$157,000). In 1999-2000, it was $1,356,380 (Cdn$1,966,606). When the WHA disappeared in 1979, with no free agency, player salaries should have gone down and, factoring in inflation, they did a little. But Gretzky overcame that. How do you decide what to pay someone like him? You pay him more than anybody else, of course, but nothing is forcing you to pay him *that* much more. Where's he going to go? What's he going to do? Except that he's so much better than anybody else, it seems unconscionable if you don't. Plus, with the NHL looking to become more important in the United States, Gretzky was unimaginable good news: a star on the order of magnitude of Magic Johnson or Michael Jordan and a nice guy, too. The bad news for NHL owners was that money had become the important measure of superstardom and, for him to be taken as seriously as superstars in other sports, he had to be paid like them. His salary soared. He was the understandable exception. Then, along came Mario Lemieux, a player of such talent that he was nearly comparable to Gretzky. Then, Mark Messier emerged as a complete player, nearly comparable to Lemieux. A salary bridge was built to connect the unconnectable Gretzky to the rest. Salaries took off across the board. Plus, after a players' strike in 1992 and an owners' lockout in 1994-95, meaningful free agency and salary arbitration became business realities in the NHL of the mid-1990s. The salary escalator continued with no one really sure where we'd find the top floor.

These salaries created giant waves across the system. A generation of arenas became obsolete. More seats and more corporate boxes were needed; the Montreal Forum and Maple Leaf Gardens were soon history. Owners, players, corporate sponsors, kids and parents realized that more money could be made from this game. But to get it, more of everything would be demanded of them. Franchises cost more money to buy. Owners needed partners and banks to help them pay the price. Teams became less personal, more corporate. Parents dreamed harder for their kids, committing more—more time, more money, more emotional energy—and, in turn, demanding more from them and their coaches. The atmosphere of minor hockey changed.

Money came to affect competition. Before free agency, money in sports was like money in the old Soviet Union—it didn't matter because there was nothing to buy. Now there was. Teams came to be described as "big market" or "small market." Small market might show competitive promise; but year-in, year-out, big market almost always wins. What happens to a city's fans when their team can't win? When despite the near-infinite capacity of fans to dream and despite the inalienable law of sports—that there's *always* a way to win and *always* a way to lose—*there is just no way*. Like the Montreal Expos. What then? What would hockey feel like if that happened?

Money has also come to affect where the future seems to be. The Quebec Nordiques and Winnipeg Jets moved south. Other Canadian teams are vulnerable. What will hockey in Canada be like if other teams leave, too?

Money has had its effect on junior hockey as well. More franchises have been awarded and new, bigger community arenas have gone up; more money can be made. Players have been brought in from the U.S. and Europe to augment the Canadian talent pool. It's all necessary to feed the business and who can fight back? But what effect does this have on young players, on minor hockey, on player development and on Canada's future in the game?

As for the Europeans, in 1970, there was not one European player in the NHL; in 1990, there were 69; now there are 160, 24% of the NHL's players. Expansion, the 1972 series and the WHA started NHL teams on the road to recruiting Europeans; the fall of the Iron Curtain did the rest. The NHL has become the only truly global league in pro sports, employing all the world's best players. The dream of today's young hockey players in Stockholm, St. Petersburg, Helsinki, Bratislava, Prague, St. Paul and Saskatoon is the same: not to play on a national or Olympic team, but to play in the NHL.

The impact of European players is growing. Borje Salming was the only European named to an NHL All-Star team in the 1970s. Jari Kurri and four others were named in the 1980s. In 1996–97, of the six First Team All-Stars, three were European; a year later, it was four; last season, four as well. In those same years since 1996–97, of the NHL's top ten scorers, four, six and five of the players were Europeans. As for the winners of the four major NHL trophies—Hart, Ross, Vezina and Norris—last year, three of four were won by Europeans. Is this historical accident, or is it a trend? In the 1999 Entry Draft, players from 10 countries, including Belarus, Ukraine and Switzerland, were taken in the first round. Over the nine rounds of the draft, players were selected from 16 countries.

In 2000, hockey is no longer just a Canadian game.

What is the message here?

Canadians remain the clear majority in the NHL, but their percentage is falling. Beyond numbers, what roles do Canadian players play on their teams? What skills do they bring with them from minor hockey? Do they play more often on the first line, or the third? On the power play? Do they kill penalties? How important are they to their teams? And is this changing? If so, how? If so, why? If so, what can we do?

What is the future?

It has been a remarkable journey. We are nowhere near where we could have imagined ourselves being 100 years ago. Yet indisputably, our game is far better to play and watch and follow in almost every way. Just imagine the unrelenting boredom of a game without forward passing on slow, heavy ice. One hundred years from now, hockey observers will look back on a century of change and the unimaginably different game of 2000. What will be the "forward pass" of *our* future, the one fundamental and unthinkable change that changes everything? Will it be four skaters instead of five? Or three? Man-to-man defenses? Bigger nets? And will Canada still be the world's number-one hockey country? We got to where we are today by being the first and by having the most—most minor hockey players, most coaches, most rinks. But being first doesn't matter much now, and numbers may not either.

Individual passion, hard work and developing our players the best way possible may matter more. On the ice, because the NHL has become the dream of all the world's players, styles of play are converging. But the ways of developing players to play this hybrid style are not. We play many more games. Others practice a lot more often. Which way will win the future?

As Canadians, we don't know how much the feeling we

have for this game comes from our dominance of it—from the number of Canadians in the NHL, from the number of Canadian stars, from Canadian teams winning the Stanley Cup. We've never had to know. If, in the future, we aren't so dominant, if fewer kids play, will hockey remain a Canadian passion?

We got here without a road map; without anyone to guide and direct us. This has frustrated us at times, especially since 1972 when we have seen others gain on us. We want to know where to go; we want someone to help us get there. Why do we just talk? Why do we say the same things, make the same recommendations and nothing gets done? Maybe because, so immersed in the game for so long, we talk to each other in conclusions: the practice to game ratio should be *x to y*; the age body contact should be allowed is *z*. We put aside all the reasons that got us here. But a conclusion without a reason is like a punch line without its story: no punch, no power, no possibility of common ground and no action. A "how" needs a "why" for its energy and will. Too often we have stopped at the "whats" and nothing gets done. But you tell me your "why" and I'll tell you mine, and maybe together we can discover the "how." The value of "whys" is that they represent ways to get to "hows."

While it seems that things have moved too slowly when they have moved at all and that we lack the nerve to change, the single dominant feature of this century has been change. This change usually has not come first from institutions or from those who govern the game, but from individuals—players, coaches, owners—from the human need to do something you couldn't do yesterday, to get a competitive edge on your opponent or to get rich. Then others, seeing the difference and competing for the same rewards, pick up on anything that might bring success. The result: a system changes.

It may be that the best an institution can do is to encourage and not to discourage. It may be that the job of the "hockey system" in all its forms is to acknowledge its role as the conscience of the game, giving it the moral authority to shape change. It may be that how we do in the next hundred years will have to do most with our ability to make change happen and accommodate it when it does.

It may be that how we do on the ice will have everything to do with how we do off it.

THE FREEDOM OF THE FIRST NATIONS OF HOCKEY

Jari Sarkka

FOR SIX MONTHS DURING THE WINTER OF 1997–98, on the Summer Beaver Native reserve in northern Ontario—on outdoor ice, on days and nights of -30°C—I had the privilege and pleasure of seeing hockey played in a way that I had not seen it played since I was a boy on the outdoor rinks of Toronto during the 1960s. The play was artistic, free-form, and lightning-fast. For the most part, it was heedless of the number of goals scored or the length or outcome of impromptu games that began when school ended during the mid-afternoon and sometimes continued into the darkness for four or five hours.

The games invariably were marked by laughter and kibitzing and, perhaps more importantly, by mutual respect among players who ranged in age from school children to highly skilled young men in their early and mid-20s.

For warmth, we built bonfires of spruce fall and birch in the snowbanks alongside the boards, and it is worth noting, at least symbolically, that games often took place under vast displays of stars or of mercurial northern lights. On snowy nights, games would stop periodically, and kids pushing 4' x 8' sheets of plywood—the Summer Beaver version of the Zamboni—would power up and down the rink, side by side, clearing the ice in a matter of minutes, while others used shovels to toss the accumulated piles over the boards.

Then the game would go on.

It has occurred to me many times since, that if what I witnessed that winter somehow could be extracted, it could be used almost as a prescription for the well-documented difficulties that have befallen a minor hockey system in which I now coach in Thunder Bay, Ontario, and in which my sons, Ben and Jari, have played for several years. It is a system I have studied and written about as I work toward my M.A. in Education at Lakehead University.

My year at Summer Beaver began with the signing of a contract with the Nibinimik Education Centre. I was to teach a variety of subjects to ninth- and tenth-grade Ojibwa and Cree students. The Summer Beaver Reserve is located 600 kilometers (360 miles) north of Thunder Bay, is accessible only by air, and is home to some 400 Native residents, most of whom speak English as a second language. While the local school is a modern brick structure with a range of amenities, the teachers' quarters are a rustic collection of log cabins on the shores of Nibinimik Lake. In accordance with the local teaching contracts, each cabin is supplied with a small portable potty, 10 cords of split firewood a year, and a weekly supply of fresh water, brought by the school custodian, Lawson Yellowhead, whose son, Sandy, is the Band Chief, and whose grandson, Lias, is the school's Native Language teacher.

I arrived at the settlement by float plane the day before school began, and met Lias Yellowhead at an introductory fish fry that evening. His T-shirt was emblazoned with the logo of the Toronto Maple Leafs and the command 'Respect the Opposition!' (only later did I notice that the back of the shirt bore the less forgiving injunction 'Then Crush Them!') We hit it off, as two old Leaf fans might—to a degree that, within minutes, Lias had recruited me not just to help with the hockey program that winter but to serve as a kind of all-purpose manager and coach of the boys' peewee Wildcats, the boys' bantam Cougars, the men's Wolves, and the young women's Native Stars.

"Where's the arena?" I asked him later that evening. He responded with a knowing smile and a question about my background in hockey.

Several days would pass before I was directed to that "arena," a roofless enclosure of plywood boards situated on a patch of low-lying marsh for easy flooding. The boards were flanked by roofed benches and a number of posts on which light bulbs eventually would be mounted. While winter comes early in these parts, a skating surface could not be laid down until the daylight hours were frosty enough to preserve ice made on nights that mostly were well below freezing by the middle of October.

In the meantime, in anticipation of that day, I went about organizing the teams with the help of Lias and his younger brother Ricky, the captain and star of the Summer Beaver Wolves. We spent endless hours in the gym with the kids, playing floor hockey, volleyball, and dodge ball. We went on hikes and runs—did push-ups and knee-bends and reflex training. As the days shortened precipitously, talk in the community was all hockey: about the upcoming season, the annual out-of-town tournaments, the beginning of the NHL schedule; everybody had a favorite pro team.

I do not believe it dishonors anyone to note that Summer Beaver is so passionate about hockey it has come to view the game as a kind of "traditional" cultural activity, in some case almost a spiritual activity, on the level of hunting, fishing and trapping. School lets out for a week during moose hunting season, and another week or two for the year's main hockey tournaments. The dark side of this obsession is that, for the young people, whose desire to start skating is nearly frantic by late fall, the weeks leading up to freeze-up are among the most emotionally difficult of the year. To alleviate impatience as the days shortened and the weeks passed, I increased the exercise regimen. But boredom and frustration were never far off. For reasons that were not clear to me, no one made any attempt to begin flooding the rink even as the temperatures dropped deep into the minus range in early and mid-November. I assumed this was to get past any possibility of a late warm spell—what we white men refer to as "Indian summer."

Because it is little understood further south, I should say that, in a far northern community, the darkness at this time of year can be close to overwhelming. By mid-November, the days have shortened to the point where the school day, for instance, both begins and ends in pitch blackness. Often as I walked home in the late afternoon, I would hear someone call "Hi, Jari!" but did not have a clue as to who had greeted me or even the direction from which the voices had come.

Darkness descended in another way on Summer Beaver on the weekend of November 15 and 16, when the assistant captain of the Wolves, 22-year-old Dwayne Sugarhead, hung himself in the family home. My perspective is incomplete, but at the time I could not help speculating on what might have happened had the hockey season begun just a couple of weeks earlier, giving this capable young athlete the impetus he might have needed to keep going.

If there was redemption, its initial stroke came on the afternoon of November 29, when it seemed almost the entire able-bodied community donned skates and, in accordance with historic community tradition, took to the newly frozen lake to inaugurate not just the hockey season but, it seemed, the winter itself. For several hours, a vast game of shinny moved up and down the lake, with as many as 50 players a side, limited only by distant shorelines. Each team's aim was simply to keep possession of the puck while the opposing team tried to take it away. At times, a single player would break free and skate a kilometer or more up the lake, swooping and teasing as the others followed in a scattered parade. Shouts and laughter echoed up the hill off the lake.

As I stood watching, the local telephone technician, George Wabasse, came along and told me his first exposure to hockey as a boy had come during this annual ritual, and that his skills as a puck handler had been honed on exactly the type of play we were witnessing. He told me that, occasionally in the old days, during the week or so of grace between the freezing of the water and the first heavy snowfall, he and others would play so heedlessly that, at sunset, they'd find themselves miles off at the north end of the lake, with only the lights of the community to guide them home.

Like many of Summer Beaver's better hockey players, George did not play formalized hockey until he was 14 or 15—but nonetheless developed sufficient skills that, like others in the community, he was offered the opportunity to play at a higher level in the southern junior leagues. But he chose to stay at Summer Beaver, where he now was one of the mainstays of the local Wolves.

"Well," he said finally, "I gotta go," and with his large brown skates slung over his shoulder, he walked down to the lake to join his daughter Jolene who was already part of the game.

By mid-December the lake was solid enough to land incoming aircraft—which meant that, by agreement with Goldbelt Airways, skating was prohibited as a safety measure.

Fortunately, through the hard work of the men's hockey team, the "arena" was now ready, and the somewhat restricted version of the game for which we had pined so long began in earnest. With the scrimmages and practices and pickup games—and with the anticipation of upcoming tournaments—the mood of the community shifted. Parents of the players held "bush" parties and cookouts by the rink, feasting on moose stew, pickerel filets, hot dogs. They watched the kids intensely, laughing and commenting on the play but, unlike their more stereotypical counterparts in the larger centers, applying no pressure, voicing no ill will, and tending to see as much value in a lesser player's participation as in that of a more-talented boy or girl.

On the ice, the kids could go for hours simply testing their speed and puckhandling and passing. Even during scrub games, they often created plays of such intricacy (how many times that winter did I see a four- or five-way passing play result in a slam-dunk goal?) that I was reminded of the European and Soviet players who first showed their talents in North America during the mid- and late 1960s. With endless hours available to them for shooting practice, the older boys could shoot bullets into any part of the net. It has occurred to me since that their skills with a stick and puck were a function not just of practice, however, but of the same brilliant hand-eye coordination that made them such capable marksmen and hunters.

Interspersed among the hours of shinny, we held more formalized practices, often dividing up the teams for full-equipment scrimmages. Play was often rough and tumble, and yet even the smallest boys never seemed to show any fear. They didn't have to; they weren't threatened. From the age of 11 or 12, they could bodycheck, and could take a check, without retaliating. Stickwork and taunting and hitting from behind were simply not a part of the action.

By January, I had focused my coaching mainly on the boys' peewee and bantam teams. (Wolves captain Ricky Yellowhead had taken charge of the young women's team.) Our two main tournaments were to take place in March, the first at Kasabonika, the second at Wunnumin Lake, and these became the focus of our workouts.

One of my main concerns was always that I might tamper too much with the kids' intuitions and openness and simple joy in the game, which seemed to work so well for them. But would they work at the tournaments? I didn't know. Perhaps a little more structure might be beneficial. One night, in an attempt to show them a power-play strategy, I positioned each of them for a face-off in the opposing team's end, told them what they should do when the puck was dropped, and told my top centerman, Eli Wabasse, that he should take the face-off on his backhand, draw it directly to the wing stationed behind him, and then move to the net, as the shot came in. I dropped the puck, but he was unable to control it. We tried again, then again, and again, each time with the same result. Out of respect, Eli resisted challenging me. But eventually he said calmly, "Jari, this is how we do it." Like most of the Summer Beaver Players, Eli is a right-hand shot. And when I dropped the puck again, he pivoted instantly to his left, took the face-off on his forehand and slid the puck to defenceman Laighton Oskineegish. Laighton slid it immediately to the other point, where Gershom Beaver took a quick hard slapshot. In the meantime, Eli had blocked the opposing center, and his wings had gone to the net for a rebound that never came, because the puck had sailed directly into the top corner of the twine. Eli looked at me, smiled, and said, "Just like that."

On another night, out of an awareness that some of them might be tensing as the tournament approached—and perhaps an increased awareness of my own humble place in the grand scheme—I gathered them around the bonfire by the rink and urged them to look upwards at the sparks as they disappeared into the night sky. "They're free," I told them. "They have no plan, they don't need one."

"Just like us," one of them laughed.

"Exactly," I smiled. "We're just going to go to Kasabonika and play our game and have fun."

The player contracts for the Summer Beaver teams that year were a model of practical simplicity—and a kind of touchstone for the privations and difficulties of life in the community. The first clause stipulated that for "services during the 1997–98 season," the "undersigned" would be paid his or her salary in "pop and chips." A joking matter, but one that acknowledges the obvious: that in an isolated community, small treats and awards take on exaggerated significance (a case of pop at Summer Beaver retails for nearly $30). The team rules, as listed in the contract, included "No drugs or alcohol," "No sniffing gas (or anything else)," "No break-ins," "No fighting," "Don't drive fast," "Listen good to your parents or guardians," "No writing on walls," and "Don't watch too much movies."

We made the 40-minute flight north to Kasibonika in a Cessna Caravan Turbine, which made three or four trips in order to get us all there. Our equipment was rammed into the belly pods beneath the plane. Numerous elders and parents, and especially my fellow teacher Lias Yellowhead, had worked many weeks to make sure every organizational detail was taken care of and the money was in place to pay for the flights and expenses.

We were perhaps 40 in all, including coaches, elders, parents, and some 25 peewee and bantam players. I was billeted with half a dozen boys and my assistant coaches, Marty Moonias and Michael Sugarhead, in the basement of a home owned by a local band member, Randy Anderson. The rest had other basement floors on which to unroll their mattresses and sleeping bags. But we all ate together—heaps of moosemeat stew, smoked whitefish, bannock, Klik canned ham, all the meals prepared by the mothers of three of our players, Annie Oskineegish, Victoria Neshnapaise and Emily Beaver.

One of the most perplexing challenges we faced in the tournament was that, this year for the first time, the bantams were required to wear full face shields, and the plastic ones we had brought along tended to fog heavily in the frigid arena. So, at the last minute, the organizers kindly lent each of our players a helmet with a wire cage. So there we were, sorting them in the dressing room prior to the first game, trying to find helmets that fit, a sometimes laughable procedure that kept us loose as the minutes ticked down.

Just before we took to the ice, one of the community's most respected elders, Mike Wabasse, came into the dressing room. As always, this was our signal to form a circle, placing our arms over one another's shoulders as Mike offered a prayer for the well-being, safety and prosperity of the players on both teams.

Playing as freely and unburdened as we had ever played back in Summer Beaver, we won that first game. And then another. And another. One by one, we knocked off the teams: the Big Trout Lake Posse, the Sandy Lake Hawks, Wunnumin Lake River Rats, Kingfisher Lake Flyers, Sachigo Lake Penguins, Bearskin Lake Eagles, Kasabonika Snipers. Our peewees kept pace with their own string of victories.

To this day, our big bright championship trophies—not to mention trophies for the top coaches in the tournament—stand in the school display case at Summer Beaver.

Now, it is March, 2000 at the Norwest Arena in Thunder Bay, and I am helping to coach the Volunteer Pool Bearcat Atom AA hockey team, on which my 11-year-old son Jari is a player. A disappointing tournament game has just ended, and our dejected kids are shuffling back into the dressing room, losers on the all-important scoreboard. We had been leading 4–1 during the final period, against a team we had lost to half a dozen times during the season. We had begun the third period in the way we had begun the game, with a kind of coach's litany of directives: play your position, cover your man, pass this way, shoot that way, backcheck, forecheck, work hard, think one shift at a time, win your shift, get off after 45 seconds, dump the puck in, chase it, use the trap, cycle the puck, don't take chances. Just play like we tell you and we'll win… and, oh, by the way, boys, go out and have fun.

In the stands, the parents had seemed hungrier for the victory than the boys themselves. They had hollered, harassed and chanted. Under the pressure to win and to avoid mistakes—and in the light of their parents' fierce hopes—our kids' sticks had seemed to grow heavy in their hands as the game wore on. And their resources had crumbled as our opponents found strength. Expectations had been high, and they had not been met.

If anything could be salvaged from the emotional debris in the dressing room afterwards, it came when the coach brought in a big brown box and set it on the dressing room floor. The boys stared—then came the inevitable. What's in the box? Open it up! And we did, revealing Hasbro "action figures," likenesses of NHL hockey players, one for each player who had participated in the tournament. Within seconds, every boy had one and gleefully had torn it from its box, in some cases against a parent's advice that the figures would be "worth more" with the box intact. The kids knew what they were worth—and proceeded to play with them, and trade them, the disappointments of the game temporarily forgotten.

A few nights later, at a time when my sons should have been asleep, I stopped at their bedroom door as they played a vigorous imaginary hockey game with those same action figures. They had set up on the bed sheet, with a pair of toy nets and a little Zamboni purchased from the souvenir shop during a recent visit to Air Canada Centre in Toronto. "He passes the puck to Gretzky, then slips it over to Amonte," gasped Ben. "He winds up, he shoots… SCORES between Martin Brodeur's legs! … Now here's Thornton. Oh, what a move on Gretzky!" Now my older son, Jari, was in on the action, laughing, cajoling, both boys delighting in their fantasies, responsive only to their instincts and imagination.

I am a long way from Summer Beaver and Kasabonika these days. But that night as I stood watching my boys, with the beauty of unencumbered play on my mind, I couldn't help thinking of the outdoor rink… the snow, the lake, the teams and tournaments… and of course the bonfires and the unburdened faces of the kids gazing upwards as a fountain of sparks rose and disappeared into the night sky.

Oldtimers' Hockey

Ted Barris

In the winter of 1964, a group of doctors, lawyers and civil servants interested in playing pickup hockey began renting the arena at St. Mary's University in Halifax regularly on Saturday afternoons. In 1966, a bunch of University of British Columbia business graduates started playing shinny on Wednesday nights in Vancouver. About the same time, a corps of inveterate hockey enthusiasts began gathering at the arena in Pointe-Claire, Quebec, on Sunday nights. Nobody seemed interested in renting the ice after 7 o'clock in the evening, so this ad hoc group of over-35-year-olds, calling themselves the Pointe-Claire Oldtimers' Hockey Club, started a six-team league of friendly competition.

In fact, it was Pointe-Claire defenseman and club organizer Bill Wilkinson who decided not to call it "hockey for seniors" and who coined the phrase "oldtimers' hockey." In addition to Sunday night hockey, in 1970 Wilkinson and the Pointe-Claire club inaugurated their own International Oldtimers' Invitational Tournament. Each year teams from Quebec, Ontario and the northern United States traveled to the Pointe-Claire area (near Montreal) to compete in a weekend tournament and to use up much of the ice time that nobody else wanted.

What these men's groups, and hundreds more like them, discovered almost simultaneously in Canada was that men born during or just after the Second World War were now approaching middle age. As kids, they had played hockey in the street, in driveways, on frozen ponds and creeks, and some organized house league and rep hockey. Some had even gone as far as semi-pro. But by about the age of 20 they had quit or been forced to quit because, unless they were destined for the NHL or amateur coaching, the game had no place for them. Marriage, jobs and families became the priorities in their lives, while sticks, skates and aging hockey equipment were discarded and forgotten.

But the coming of oldtimers' hockey "opened up a brand new world for these guys," says Gerry "Tubby" Aherne, one-time backup goalie for the Toronto Maple Leafs. "Suddenly, their boyhood game, the game they'd grown up with, was theirs to play again. And it didn't matter how good or bad you were, whether you played all the time as a kid or for the first time as a 35-year-old, there was a competitive division in oldtimers for you."

What is "oldtimers' hockey?" It's the recreational side of the game that has evolved from street and pond hockey. It's adults picking up the hockey traditions and styles they enjoyed—or wish they had enjoyed—as youths. It's shinny, a little slower. It's house league play for the adult camaraderie. It's tournament competition, without the do-or-die pressure of the seventh game of the Stanley Cup finals. It's the most common form of hockey being played—in neighborhood arenas, on the frozen canal, at outdoor rinks, or even sometimes on the manicured ice surfaces of a Gardens, Forum, Stadium, Arena or Coliseum.

One of the alumni from those early tourneys in Pointe-Claire was a schoolteacher from Ennismore, just north of Peterborough, Ontario. In March, 1974, John Gouett teamed up with Gerry Aherne and organized a St. Michael's College oldtimers' hockey team to stage a barnstorming tour of Canada's western provinces. "During the spring break we played eight games in 10 days," Gouett recalled, "And while we were out there we asked everybody what they thought of oldtimer hockey and if they would come to a national tournament if we organized one."

The western trip attracted numerous teams, plenty of small-town crowds and press, but most of all a positive response to their blue-sky idea of a national oldtimers' hockey association and tournament. That summer, Gouett quit teaching, assigned the family house and personal assets to guarantee a $15,000 line of credit, and formed the Canadian Oldtimers' Hockey Association. He and Aherne got a $4,500 grant from Recreation Canada. They booked hotels and ice time, landed a few sponsors and arm-twisted enough players to make this national dream come true.

The result? At 8 o'clock in the morning, on Friday, February 21, 1975, five referees dropped pucks at center ice in five different arenas in the Peterborough area, inaugurating the first national oldtimers' hockey tournament staged in Canada. Fifty-six teams (over 1,200 players) had arrived to play in four divisions based on age and players' hockey backgrounds. And while referee-in-chief Jim Orr managed to keep the games relatively safe (based essentially on a no body-contact rule), friendly and running on time, Aherne and Gouett had enough trophies, team photo sessions and postgame coolers of beer on hand to keep everybody happy.

Spectators flocked to the five arenas. Along with several hometown heroes to cheer for, such as 1950s Peterborough Petes stalwarts George Montague and Larry Babcock, there were plenty of bona fide former hockey stars to see again. The Grande Prairie Oldtimers, with an average age of 45, featured Garry "Duke" Edmundson, who had played for the 1951 Stanley Cup champion Montreal Canadiens. A Stanley Cup alumnus with the Detroit Red Wings, Marcel Pronovost arrived with the Toronto St. Michael's Oldtimers, while long-time Chicago Black Hawks right wing Chico Maki (then 35) appeared with the Simcoe Oldtimers. And the Yorkton Oldtime Terriers (from Saskatchewan) had no fewer than six former pros, including 1940s veteran Metro Prystai, who had played on a line with Gordie Howe and Ted Lindsay.

That First Annual National Oldtimers' Hockey Tournament did more than fill a few arenas with fans, bellies with beer and hearts with nostalgia. It launched the fledgling COHA, which soon moved its office to Ottawa to officially become part of Fitness Canada; by 1980 it had 300 registered teams and by 1990 it had 3,000. It attracted sponsorship for the staging of annual tournaments in Canada, the U.S. and Europe. It gave writer/publisher Dave Tatham the grist for a monthly publication—*Canadian Oldtimers' Hockey News*. But most important of all it demonstrated to adult men and women the universal appeal of returning to the game of their youth—playing hockey just for the fun of it.

Like the youthful rites of passage into the game—frozen toes, the Saturday morning practice and your goal written up in the weekly newspaper—oldtimers' hockey is attracting more adults than ever before. Adult recreational hockey (there are now more than 80,000 players registered in Canada) has become so widespread in North America that it's fair to say at any time of day or night somewhere in Canada or the U.S. a puck is sliding across the ice in an oldtimers' hockey game. Wherever the game was reintroduced to adults it found a natural home. One of those locations was a rink in Saskatoon's north end. In the fall of 1977 a Saturday afternoon meeting was called at the change shack adjacent to River Heights Elementary School. About 40 men ranging in age from their late-20s to their mid-40s gathered to talk about starting up an oldtimers' hockey team. A ready-mix concrete company sponsored the team with a set of sweaters and the River Heights Mixers oldtimers' hockey club was born.

Every Monday morning, at about the time the inhabitants of most London, Ontario offices are brewing their first cup of liquid inspiration, two of the six teams known as the Huff n' Puffs are taking to the ice at the Earl Nichols Arena on the south side of the city. The idea of an adult hockey scrimmage for retirees came from Al Finch and Ted Froats, who had a number of ex-air force buddies in southwestern Ontario. At first they rented the ice for an hour. As their numbers swelled, they paid for time at another arena. Today, Huff n' Puffs Hockey has attracted about 100 skaters and a handful of goalies who show up three times a week year round. None of the players is younger than 55 and most are in their 60s and 70s.

In the mid-1960s when the B.C. lower mainland had only three indoor hockey arenas to speak of and two hometown heroes to look up to (the legendary Fred "Cyclone" Taylor and Montreal Canadiens tough guy John Ferguson), organized adult hockey was nearly non-existent. About 1966, a handful of hockey-hungry grad students at UBC approached the management at the newly built Thunderbird Winter Sports Complex for some ice time. They got Wednesday nights at 8 o'clock.

"It was pure shinny," remembers Keith Morrison. "Guys went out there, split into two more-or-less-even teams, went at it for an hour and a half, no referees, no whistles, just non-stop hockey." A decade later, with the phrase "oldtimers' hockey" steadily creeping into the hockey lexicon, Morrison and company were ready to establish a formal association. The ex-shinny players responded to a newspaper ad promoting the first Oldtimer Invitational tournament in nearby Port Coquitlam. They fit almost all the criteria. They were all over 35. They had adapted to no-slapshot, non-contact hockey. The trouble was, they had no name and no uniforms. Morrison's first *Hockey Newsletter* documents the solution: "After 11 years of deliberation and procrastination, a Uniform Committee was struck. As usual [we] knew someone who could 'get us a deal,' which turned out to be the Atlanta Flames road uniform. Turning the Atlanta flaming 'A' upside down gave us the flaming 'V' crest. And a new name—the Vancouver Flames. Cost $20."

On summer evenings in July and August, die-hard hockey players, some clad in shorts and T-shirts, others in business clothes, leave the warm evening air for the chill of an arena in Brossard, Quebec, across the Champlain Bridge from Montreal on the south shore of the St. Lawrence River. These 20-odd players chase pucks at Les 4 Glaces as members of various oldtimers' teams—the Rusty Blades, SWAT (Senior Westmount All-Star Team), the Montreal Old Puckers and even some from one of the original oldtimers' organizations in Montreal, the Fakawie Hockey League—all summer long.

"People think we're crazy to play hockey in the summertime," says Brook Ellis, who's been playing hockey since the days he was a high school student in the Toronto area in the 1950s. "I tell them summer hockey is a wonderful thing. When it's hot outside, it's great to walk into a nice cool rink, work up a sweat, then afterwards, when you're good and thirsty, have a cool drink. There isn't a game like it in the world. I feel sorry for the Americans who've only played baseball. They grow old and can't do it anymore. Canadian kids grow up into old men like us and can continue to play our game."

In the final days of the 1970 minor hockey season in east end Toronto, the tension of the bantam hockey playoffs got to the coaches of the two finalists. Dave Bayford and Bill Loreti were actually close friends, but in the excitement and pressure of the game the two coaches actually got into a fight in the penalty box. Following that game, they quit minor hockey forever, deciding instead to teach visually impaired or blind youngsters how to play hockey. The result was a team of young men—called the Ice Owls—80 percent of whose members are legally blind. Since 1972, the group has played regular games on Sunday mornings, competing in blind-players' tournaments across Canada and even in exhibition matches against NHL oldtimers and against sighted players in Helsinki, Leningrad and Kiev.

The evolution of the Ice Owls' hockey puck is a study in ingenuity. First they tried a tin can, then a tin can with marbles or ball bearings inside, a wooden puck and one with a chain attached to it. Another prototype used an empty plastic computer tape case rigged with a buzzer inside. It worked until snow and ice gummed up the buzzer or until the wear and tear shattered the plastic case. Ultimately, the blind oldtimers' team came up with a plastic wheel from a push-toy. They drilled a hole through to the hollow center of the wheel and inserted several steel piano tuning pegs; the combination of the hard plastic wheel clattering across the ice and the tuning pins rattling inside gave the Ice Owls a relatively lightweight, durable puck they could hear above any arena din.

On several occasions over the years, the Ice Owls oldtimers have played another oldtimers' institution—the Flying Fathers. In the early 1960s, North Bay broadcaster Terry Spearin got talking to local parish priest Brian McKee about the possibility of staging an adult hockey game to raise funds for the Catholic Youth Organization in town. On February 20, 1964, the 5,000-seat North Bay Memorial Gardens was nearly sold out to watch the broadcast team—the Statics—take on a number of ex-seminarians and priests from Sudbury, Sault Ste. Marie and Timmins, including Father Les Costello, who had played on the Toronto Maple Leafs Stanley Cup-winning team in 1948. During the lead up to the game, someone coined the phrase "The Flying Fathers." It stuck.

As their reputation for playing good oldtimer hockey spread, the priests—playing these fun-matches on their own vacation time—adopted a seemingly never-ending repertoire of hockey shtick to spice up each game. They taunted referees with an assortment of cream pies and buckets of water. They confused their opposition by conducting pseudo-religious ordinations and blessings on the ice. For a time, they dressed up a member of their team in a nun's habit as Sister Mary Shooter and even brought a draft horse named Penance onto the ice in goalie pads to play net. Like the Harlem Globetrotters on ice, the Flying Fathers oldtimers' team has become one of the most sought-after fund-raising phenomena in the world.

In their first 30 years of "playing and praying for a better world," the Flying Fathers accumulated many firsts as oldtimers, hockey players and ambassadors for Canada and the priesthood. They played nearly 1,000 games for charity and won nearly all of them. Their record is five games in one day. During one trip across Canada and the U.S., they played 16 games in 15 cities in 20 days, traveling 14,000 miles. The largest crowd they drew was 15,396 at Vancouver's Pacific Coliseum. A single game at the Montreal Forum in 1984 raised $50,000 for the Shriners Hospital. During a charity game at Maple Leaf Gardens in 1985, nearly 14,000 spectators watched the Flying Fathers play the Maple Leaf alumni. Leaf owner Harold Ballard turned over all gate receipts and proceeds from concessions that day, raising $240,000 for cancer research.

Each year between October and May, in addition to the thousands of oldtimers' house-league games, once-a-week senior recreational games, shinny matches and pickup sessions across the continent, the calendar is full of weekend tourneys. Some are local. Many are national tournaments, sponsored by the Canadian Adult Recreational Hockey Association (formerly the COHA), including the Hub City in Saskatoon, the McMurtry Cup in Toronto, and the Monctonian. For those looking offshore, there are annual tour-and-play packages to Florida, Arizona, Nevada, Hawaii and Europe.

It's generally agreed by most oldtimers' hockey players, however, that the annual Snoopy's Senior World Hockey Tournament, organized by the late "Peanuts" cartoonist Charles M. Schulz, has been the mecca of oldtimers' hockey. Staged in mid-July in Santa Rosa (north of San Francisco), competition to get into the tourney is tough; of the 300 to 400 teams that apply to play, only 50 to 60 get in. All games take place at Redwood Empire Ice Arena, built in 1969 by Schulz for his figure-skating daughter and hockey-crazed sons.

"We used to sneak onto the St. Paul Academy rink and play under the light of the moon," cartoonist Schulz said in 1993 about his childhood passion for hockey in Minnesota during the 1930s. "Nobody had pads. We used copies of National Geographic for shin pads."

And when there was nobody else around to play shinny with him, Schulz's mother would agree to play goal while he practiced his shot. In 1974, he launched Snoopy's Senior World Hockey Tournament at his own expense. Neither relentless press deadlines for his Peanuts cartoons nor quadruple heart bypass surgery in his later years prevented him from playing regularly for his Santa Rosa Diamond Icers. At age 77, Schulz died in his sleep in February, 2000, following a three-month battle with colon cancer; most agree the tournament should continue in his memory.

Among the legendary teams that regularly came to play against Schulz's Diamond Icers, the Mandai Memorials from Japan are a study in oldtimers' hockey dedication. In 1933, while Japanese colonial armies occupied northern China, a 24-year-old Japanese medical student named Toshihiko Shoji was training at the Manchurian Medical College. That autumn, as creeks and ponds froze, Shoji gathered a handful of his colleagues together. He described a winter game he had first seen during the 1920s, when an ice hockey team—the Battleford Millers—had visited Japan from western Canada to play exhibition games.

"We heated willow branches and bent them like field hockey sticks," explained Dr. Shoji. "And we used a small tennis ball for a puck. We used the rules explained in a hockey history book by the Spalding company." The Mandai hockey club was born. In 1975, long after those games in Manchuria had faded from memory, Dr. Shoji heard about the oldtimers' concept and formed the Mandai Memorial Ice Hockey Club with Japanese doctors in their 50s and 60s.

Until they got their skating legs back, Dr. Shoji and his teammates chose the opposition carefully. At first, they played inexperienced women's teams. Then, at the invitation of the Port Coquitlam Ambassadors, they headed to Canada in 1978. "Of course, we lost," said Shoji. But in 1981, the Memorials came to the Snoopy Tournament in the 60-plus division. "I think we have won only two or three games ever in this tournament," the doctor admitted shortly before his death in 1995, "but coming to Santa Rosa each year is a kind of medicine for each of us. It's motivation to keep in good health, to practice and think young."

Pickup Hockey

Mike Kaiser

I play hockey all year round, but I don't play in a league. I don't use referees, I don't have standings or playoffs and I don't keep score. I play pickup hockey. I've played hockey since I was six years old, but I'll never go back to a league. Here's how I became a full-time pickup player.

It was mid-April. We had just played the last hockey game of the season, losing in the semifinal. If we had won, we would only have played one more game for the championship. Our season had started in October and finished in April. Seven months with hockey, five months without. Five months off was too long for me and my hockey-loving teammates. As the organizer, it fell to me to find us some more.

The obvious answer was to join a summer league, which would give us more of the same. But I wanted to try something different, because too little hockey was only part of the problem. The other problem was the kind of hockey we were playing.

The league games were too often chippy, penalty-filled matches. Lots of penalties meant fewer shifts. Fewer shifts meant only five or six minutes of actual ice time for a two- to three-hour evening commitment. The only way to justify that was to win. And if you only play to win, then hockey isn't fun anymore.

I had a better idea. Two years earlier I had finished college, where it could be said that I majored in hockey and minored in an education. Though we didn't play many games, we practiced a lot. Most of our practices were taken up with scrimmages, which were almost as much fun as our regular games. What if I could put together an hour of scrimmaging with my buddies that had the same intensity and pace of our league games?

I rented an hour of ice at a centrally located arena, signed on the players from my team and some of their friends, and began our first organized pickup game that summer. Nineteen years later, I not only continue to organize that same hour, I've added two more so that I can play all year round. Here's how I put together a successful game of pickup.

I realized early on that what I would be doing was providing a service—a service that I had to "sell" to the players I needed to join me. And my goal was to keep it going year after year. The service that I had to sell was a competitive, fast-paced game, cleanly played and well policed, always with two goalies and with two lines of skaters, paid in advance. That's the kind of game I wanted to play. I hoped my buddies would want the same.

First we needed a place to play. This is the easiest part, for in a hockey-playing country there is no shortage of arenas. First rule of a successful pickup game: any place is a good place to play if you and your buddies can get there. It helps to have a big ice surface rather than a small one and spacious dressing rooms rather than cramped ones.

Next we needed to choose a time. I wanted an hour in prime time because I thought it would be easier to sell. Though adults are playing hockey in the wee hours of the morning all over the world, I didn't want to be one of them. I lucked into what I thought was the perfect hour: 9 p.m. on a Wednesday. I was surprised to discover the reactions when I began canvassing for recruits: "Wednesday's bad for me, how about Tuesday?" or "Wednesday at 9 p.m. isn't good for me, can't you make it 7 p.m.?" or "why can't we play on the weekend?" etc. Hence the second rule of pickup hockey: any hour is a good hour if you can sell it to your players. Maybe you know 20 guys who would love to play at 2 a.m. on a Tuesday and not one who can play at 3:30 p.m. on a Sunday afternoon. If so, you have a 2 a.m. hour you can sell. Fortunately for me, I was able to sell my 9 p.m. hour.

Once you've got a time and a place, you have to sign up the players. I wanted two full lines so I needed to sign up 19 players (me being the 20th). Unless you have a large extended family, you're going to have to do some recruiting, which must lead to you asking yourself just who it is you are going to recruit. If you're already playing on a team, you can ask your fellow players who in turn can ask their buddies. What you are looking for with these recruits are players of a similar skating level who buy into your idea of the game. You need a bench mark for that skating level, which will be your skating level—assuming that as organizer you also play. This brings us to the next crucial rule of a good pickup game: the difference between your most skilled player and your least skilled player must be kept to a minimum. Otherwise, here's the problem: if a player can't keep up, then the game will suffer and you will lose players. On the other hand, if somebody is too good, chances are that player will hog both the puck and the ice. The game will suffer and you will lose players.

How do you know you have your 19 committed players? A verbal agreement? A handshake? No. They are committed when they pay the fee. We've all been in dressing rooms where the beleaguered organizer, having scrambled around after the game trying to collect money for the hour, fell short and had to make up the difference himself. And then there was a buddy of mine who rented an hour of ice and avoided the money problem by standing outside the rink and not letting us pass until we coughed up the dough, a smile on his face all the while. The lesson I learned is the next rule of successful pickup: get the money up front before the pickup season begins.

We know how much the hour is costing us, so what do we charge per player? To some extent, how many players you want will affect how much you charge them. But if you think the fee you should charge is your ice cost divided by the number of recruited players then you are going to lose money and you will be out of the pickup business fast. Why? Because if one of your regulars incurs a season-ending injury or has to move out of town, you must provide a refund for the missed skates. (This way you'll acquire a rep for being fair, which will pay great dividends for future recruiting.) Adding a few dollars to the cost for each player will build in some insurance. The extra couple of bucks will mean little to the players, but it will mean a lot to you if you have to give back hundreds of dollars you don't have.

How much of a fee is the right fee? In my first year, I had two responses to my fee: one buddy asked me all the cost questions—how much per hour, how many guys playing—figured out exactly how much money was changing hands and concluded that he was getting more or less fair value for the price. Another buddy simply said to me "you better be making a buck on this." If you are providing a well-run game, cover the costs and your time, and build in some insurance money so you won't end up out of pocket.

When I polled my regulars, asking them what they thought made for a good pickup game, there were many varied responses, but on one point they all agreed: there must be two goalies. The answer to the eternal pickup player game-night question, "do we have two goalies?" must always be "yes." It's not fair that so much emphasis should be placed on two players out of 22, but it is an incontestable fact. There must be two goalies. Pickup players know their priorities. If one stormy winter's night, when the roads are almost impassible and only four of your players show for the skate, if two of those four are the goalies, I guarantee you the other two will be happy hockey players.

There is no question that as an organizer you will make or break your reputation over goalies. Find two regular goalies who commit to the skate. Have more goalies on call if your regulars can't make it. Finally, if all else fails, use a reliable goalie rental service. There is nothing worse than having a full turnout, promising a wickedly fast game, and having only one goalie show. As the organizer, there is no "I've done all I can" answer to the look on 19 skaters' faces when you tell them there is no second goalie (if you don't even have one, resign and take up cards). Whether it takes two calls or 20 (I've done both), you must have two goalies. Anything less is total failure on your part. But there is an upside. Once you have a rep for always having two goalies, the players will beat a path to your game.

You've got the players and their money. You've got a goalie list the size of which would impress the editors of *Total Hockey*. All your preliminary work has been done. It's game night. Now comes the last part, the best part, the toughest part: managing the game itself. Keep the rules simple, but enforce them aggressively. Soon everyone will know what you want, and they'll either embrace the game or leave.

Don't keep score. Most of the players will, but don't make it official. Once winning the pickup game means too much, the chippy play will follow. Whenever someone asks you the score, tell them you don't know.

No bodychecking, but allow for contact. After all we are playing hockey. Make sure your players know the difference between the two. Remember, we want a game as close to the real thing as possible.

Don't water down the game with no slap shot rules or no equipment rules. Most arenas nowadays demand helmets.

Absolutely no stick fouls. It's very simple. You don't take a stick to your buddy. Almost without exception, the newcomers to our game tell me what a pleasure it is to break in on goal and not be two-handed across the arms, or cross-checked in front of the net, or slashed.

Have a face-off at center ice after every goal. I never liked the players coming out of their end after a goal, everyone moving at full speed while the team that just scored is standing still at center. Facing off allows for changes and gives your pickup that game feel.

The organizer makes the teams. Every night. This is very important. None of this toss the sticks in a pile at center ice, or everyone in this room wear white and everyone in this room wear colored. For the well organized pickup game, this just won't do. You make the teams based on your knowledge of the players and what has happened from week to week. Next rule of pickup: change the teams weekly to avoid feuding and to encourage socializing. If two players had a bit of a tiff last week, put them on the same team this week. It's easier to keep a clean game if the players know tonight's adversary is next week's linemate. Changing the teams also makes for a different game every night, keeping the games fresh and unpredictable. You'll like playing with and against everybody who participates. This way, you'll get to know the players better and be able to manage them better.

You have to stay on top of incidents and deal with problems the same night or the next game night. For your pickup game to be a success, you must gain a reputation for being tough but fair. There are little problems and big problems. The little ones will lose you players; the big ones will get someone hurt. You want neither to happen.

Puck hogs and ice hogs are the two main little problems that get everyone upset and start people complaining. Remind these players right away to move the puck and change frequently. Let it go, and the other players will go. It's as simple as that. Usually peer pressure works with players who have acquired these bad habits at other pickup games, not yours. If they don't improve, you have to refund their money and wish them well.

Stick work and fighting are the big problems that have no place in any pickup game. You must realize that all your players want to get up the next morning and go to work. Any incident where it looks like someone is trying to hurt somebody must be dealt with harshly. I have been lucky in that I have had only a few incidents and those were many years ago. But you have to make the call, return the money, and tell them it just isn't working out. I'm not depriving anyone of playing hockey. There are lots of games out there. I'm just looking out for my own game.

When, after a few years or less, you've done all these things and you get it right and you've got the game you want, then the magic begins. Players call you asking to join your game and the regulars police themselves and the newcomers without you having to do anything. Collecting the money gets easier and the game gets better. One of my regulars sums it up best:

"Pay your money, play hard, be good and you'll have a place to play the rest of your life. But just make sure there are two goalies."

CONFESSIONS OF A HOCKEY COLLECTOR

Martin Wright

The first time I was introduced to hockey was in the fall of 1967. I was seven years old and watched on television from my childhood home in Mississauga, Ontario. From that very first time I was hooked. Hockey was my game and the defending Stanley Cup-champion Toronto Maple Leafs were my team.

At nine, I began collecting hockey cards with the guys at school. Every year after that, it became a ritual for my father to drive me downtown for the Leafs open practice at Maple Leaf Gardens. Three decades later, my fascination with the hockey team, past and present, has only intensified. I have become a much more serious collector of hockey memorabilia, meeting with past heroes at autograph sessions and commemorating these get-togethers with photographs (which I often have signed for me at subsequent shows). Recently, I have taken my hobby to a new level: collecting addresses and phone numbers of former hockey players and pursuing a personal connection between my heroes and me.

To meet with these men is to be transported to another era. That's the real thrill; to sit down and discuss what it was like to play hockey in days gone by. To find out who the players roomed with on the road, who their linemates were or who their defense partner was. To hear the stories you will never find in any book or newspaper. The players become like a sort of time machine, taking you back to the days when these ice gladiators waged war on one another. Grudges were very real, and were connected from game to game because the teams faced-off against each other so many times in a season. Some of these grudges still hold true. Just ask Cal Gardner or Ken Reardon.

I recently attended an autograph session and began talking with fellow enthusiasts. One gentleman claimed to have the address and phone number of many former Leafs players. He sent me a copy of his list by mail and I have methodically called every Leaf on it—from Gary Aldcorn to Johnny Wilson. Most responded positively. But, to me, the most exciting experiences transpire when finding "lost" players—those who seem to have disappeared for one reason or another. Recently, using new phone directories and the Internet and working with friends Peter Bertkowski and John Storrison (John was the one who sent me the list), I've been able to locate two such players: Harry Taylor and Earl "Spider" Balfour. To finally speak with them, to catch up on old times and find out what happened, these are the most satisfying accomplishments. We still are searching for others.

What follows are just a few of my many personal accounts with members of the Toronto Maple Leafs, either on the phone or in person. Through them I have been able to enhance my enjoyment of the game and appreciate what it was like as far back as the 1920s.

Venture back to a time when ice for the icebox was delivered by horse and wagon, a time when Foster Hewitt was the voice of hockey, a time when the Toronto Maple Leafs were just beginning to establish themselves as a force to be reckoned with. It is 1929, and a 22-year-old rookie named Gord Brydson is rooming with another young Leafs prospect named Joe Primeau. Primeau would go on to a

Hall of Fame career, but Brydson would spend just eight games in a Maple Leafs uniform. He told me that he didn't like the money Conn Smythe was offering and chose to ply his trade in the minor leagues where he played under Babe Dye in Chicago.

When I met Brydson in October, 1999, he was a spry 92-year-old. The oldest living member of the Toronto Maple Leafs sat with me in his living room and we talked together for an hour. He signed my photo and pucks and gave me a booklet on the celebration of his 80th birthday from the Mississauga Golf Club (he had become the club pro upon his retirement from hockey). The booklet revealed many interesting tidbits of his life, including a quote from golf legend Sam Snead in which he said that Brydson had the softest hands in golf. Little known for his accomplishments in hockey, Brydson is the oldest living winner of the Canadian Open golf tournament.

In the fall of 1999, Hank Goldup invited me to meet him at the rehab center where he was going to be recuperating after surgery to replace his right knee. One of just six remaining members of the 1942 Comeback Kids (the others are Lorne Carr, Pete Langelle, Wally Stanowski, Don Metz and Gaye Stewart), Goldup was wearing a vintage Leafs jersey when I met him in his hospital room. Although this initial meeting was brief, we have since met two more times at his home and he has given me a photo taken at the Leafs training camp in St. Catharines, Ontario, in 1939.

Recently I met with Paul Masnick who played with the Maple Leafs in 1957–58, but was a member of the Canadiens when Bill Barilko scored the Stanley Cup-winning goal for Toronto against Montreal in 1951. He looks much younger than his 68 years and still wears his hair in the same crewcut style of his playing days. His apartment is neatly furnished and elegantly decorated with a number of paintings. We sat in a glass-enclosed office and he proceeded to show me pictures from his hockey days while telling me stories about the 1951 Stanley Cup finals.

"The players had just returned to the dressing room," Masnick said, "when Dick Irvin stormed in and exclaimed, 'You know, some of you guys won't be here next year.' And as fast as that he made his exit."

Brit Selby was six years old when Bill Barilko scored his famous goal. We met in his Toronto high school history classroom. Today Selby is a fit 54-year-old teacher with short-cropped graying hair. He offered me a seat at the front of the classroom, but I preferred an empty chair in the back corner. I spread out my wares as he sat down beside me and felt 32 pairs of eyes following our every move. Most had no idea of his career before teaching and were soon gathered around us wanting to know what the fuss was about. "Why would you want Mr. Selby's autograph?" one student asked.

"He was NHL rookie of the year in 1966," I explained. I could see that Brit was uncomfortable with the fuss, and in the voice of authority that only a teacher can possess, he asked the students if they still had any homework to do.

After autographing some photos, Mr. Selby returned to the front of the class to continue discussing the beginning of Canada's involvement in World War II. After 10 minutes of classroom talk he looked at me and announced, "Martin, you're free to go."

I nodded and got up, feeling 25 years younger.

CANADIAN UNIVERSITY HOCKEY

Steve Knowles

ONCE CALLED CANADA'S BEST-KEPT SECRET, collegiate hockey no longer takes a back seat in the country's hockey community. The Canadian Interuniversity Athletic Union continues a rich tradition of hockey excellence that dates back to 1877 when McGill University of Montreal formed the first organized hockey club. In 1886 Queen's University and the Royal Military College of Canada ushered in intercollegiate hockey when they played the first organized game in Kingston, Ontario. Since then Canadian university teams have competed for the Stanley Cup, Allan Cup and Memorial Cup. Canadian college players have skated in the NHL and on the international stage at the Olympics, World Championships and World Student Games.

THE EARLY YEARS

Although the precise origins of the game of hockey remain strongly debated by historians, what can be proven is that the game of ice hockey evolved in Canada, and that the first recorded game to be played indoors took place in Montreal at the Victoria Skating Rink on March 3, 1875. That historic contest had its first connection with Canadian universities as the two teams of nine players contained several students from McGill University. Serving as captain of one of the teams was James George Aylwin Creighton, who drafted the first rules for ice hockey after he and other friends, including fellow McGill classmate Henry Joseph, tried to play lacrosse on skates at the Victoria Rink. Creighton's team was victorious in this first game by a 2–1 score.

In 1877 McGill became the first university in the world to ice an intercollegiate team. *The McGill University Gazette* of February 1, 1877, reported that McGill students officially formed an organized ice hockey club and played its first game against the Montreal Victorias. McGill's first officially organized game was a 2–1 victory over the Victorias on January 31, 1877. In its first season of hockey, McGill would finish with a 2–1 record in three games against the Victorias.

The roster of McGill's first ice hockey team consisted of Archibald Dunbar Taylor, who was elected the team president, Harry Abbott (team captain), R.J. Howard, Fred Torrence, Lorne Campbell (goalie), W. Redpath, Nelson, Coverhill and Dawson. This group of students was the first in a long line of student-athletes who have represented McGill in an intercollegiate hockey program that continues to this day.

In 1883 the Montreal Winter Carnival hosted the first ice hockey tournament. Three teams were featured in the competition as McGill was joined by the Montreal Victorias and a team from Quebec City. McGill defeated the Victorias 1–0 and then tied Quebec 2–2 to win the world's first official hockey championship. On December 8, 1886, the first official hockey league, the Amateur Hockey Association of Canada, was formed in Montreal. McGill was one of five charter members of the AHA's senior division, which also included the Montreal Amateur Athletic Association, the Montreal Victorias, the Ottawa Hockey Club and the Montreal Crystals. The first game played in league history took place on January 7, 1887, as the Crystals earned a 3–1 victory over McGill.

While McGill was an integral part of the development of hockey and its rules in the Montreal area, graduates of the school also helped to organize and develop the game in other locations. One McGill grad, Edward Thornton Taylor, went to Kingston, Ontario, and introduced the game to the cadets at the Royal Military College of Canada in 1877.

Kingston was a hotbed of hockey as early as 1855 when a form of the game was played on the frozen harbor by British soldiers stationed in the area. Along with the cadets at RMC, Kingston was also home to Queen's University and this proximity saw the schools become arch-rivals. The rivalry began with football and in 1886 the RMC cadets challenged Queen's to a game of hockey—the first organized intercollegiate game in history.

A community skating rink just off shore from the Fort Frontenac barracks was the site of the game. The rink featured a large wooden bandstand right in the middle of the ice, which prevented the opposing goalies from seeing one another. Despite this obstacle, the game was played in a spirited manner. Lennox Irving, captain of the Queen's squad, became the first player to score a goal in intercollegiate play as he netted the winner in a 1–0 victory. A Queen's account says the winning goal was scored by Irving, "an excellent skater," who "swept up to the RMC goal, bounced the puck off the goalie's shoulder, struck the rebounding puck in midair, and knocked it into the goal for the game." The next season RMC gained revenge with a 4–0 victory over Queen's and the collegiate game was on its way in Canada.

Ten seasons after playing the first intercollegiate game, Queen's recorded another first as the Golden Gaels became the first, and only, collegiate team to challenge for the Stanley Cup. In 1895 Queen's made its first of three challenges for Lord Stanley's Cup when they faced off against the Montreal Amateur Athletic Association on March 9, 1895. Montreal AAA won the challenge, defeating Queen's 5–1. Queen's would also challenge for the Cup in 1899 and 1906. In March 1899 the Golden Gaels lost 6–2 to the Montreal Shamrocks and in 1906 they dropped two games to the Ottawa Silver Seven by scores of 16–7 and 12–7 on February 27 and 28. For Queen's, it was their final attempt at winning the Stanley Cup and it marked the last time that a collegiate team would compete for hockey's most illustrious trophy. Although Queen's failed to win the Stanley Cup, it did capture the 1909 Allan Cup as Canada's senior amateur champions.

Marty Walsh was a member of the Queen's team during the Golden Gaels' Stanley Cup challenge in 1906 and although he did not win the prized trophy for his university, the high-scoring center would later sip champagne from the Cup. Walsh won the Stanley Cup for the first time with the Ottawa Senators in 1908–09 and he was a member of the Ottawa team that successfully defended the Cup against challengers from Galt and Edmonton early in the 1909–10 season. After Ottawa let the Cup slip away later that season, Walsh netted a career-high 10 goals against Port Arthur in a Stanley Cup challenge on March 16, 1911, as he fell four goals shy of the Cup record for goals in a game set by Frank McGee of the Ottawa Silver Seven in 1905. In total, Walsh scored 25 goals in eight Stanley Cup playoff games and was a scoring leader in both the Eastern Canada Hockey Association and the National Hockey Association. He was elected to the Hockey Hall of Fame in 1962.

During the final decade of the 19th century, McGill hockey enjoyed one of its most historic eras as four players who went on to become Honoured Members of the Hockey Hall of Fame skated for the Montreal school. Charles Graham Drinkwater was a member of McGill's hockey team from 1894 to 1898, while Fred Scanlan, Arthur F. Farrell and Harry J. Trihey played at the school from 1898 to 1900. This quartet of McGill stars, along with Jack Brannen, who also skated for McGill from 1898 to 1900, would combine to win 12 Stanley Cup championships. Three of the McGill skaters—Trihey, Scanlan and Farrell—formed one of the greatest forward lines in early hockey history and helped the Montreal Shamrocks win consecutive Stanley Cup titles in 1899 and 1900. Trihey, the captain of both Shamrock championship teams, netted a hat trick and Farrell scored twice in Montreal's 6–2 win over Queen's in 1899. Three more future members of the Hockey Hall of Fame would join McGill in the 1900s as Lester Patrick and Billy Gilmour made their debut in a McGill uniform in 1900–01. They would be followed by Patrick's younger brother, Frank, in 1904.

The Next Step

As the game of hockey became more popular and gained increased recognition throughout Canada, the intercollegiate version of the sport also continued to grow. Ever since the first game between Queen's and RMC in 1886, universities had been adopting the sport as part of their athletic programs with teams taking to the ice throughout the Maritimes, Ontario and Quebec. These teams played at a variety of levels of competition ranging from intramural to senior leagues, including the Stanley Cup challenges of Queen's University. There were some intercollegiate games played during this time, but there was no official league for college teams.

Included among the early intercollegiate games were three of major significance. Two decades after McGill met Harvard University in the first international collegiate football game, the schools met on the ice at Victoria Rink in Montreal on February 23, 1894. McGill would win the game 14–1 in what is believed to be the first collegiate hockey game to be played between teams from Canada and the United States. Another cross-border matchup took place in December 1895 when Queen's made a trip to New York and defeated the Yale University Elis 3–0. What would prove to be another durable collegiate hockey rivalry began on February 2, 1895, when Queen's skated to a 6–5 victory over McGill in Kingston.

In 1901 an intercollegiate league was proposed after a meeting with several teams in Quebec and Ontario. The Canadian Intercollegiate Hockey Union became a reality on January 7, 1903, when McGill, Queen's and the University of Toronto Varsity Blues officially formed Canada's first collegiate hockey league. The first season saw the CIHU take a small step as only three games were played. McGill won the inaugural "Queen's Cup," which was presented by Queen's University in the first season. The Queen's Cup, which is currently awarded to the champion of the Ontario University Athletics conference, is the second oldest trophy competed for in Canadian intercollegiate history.

McGill and Queen's would both win two of the first four CIHU championships before Toronto captured the title in 1906–07. It was the first championship for the Varsity Blues since Toronto began its hockey team on January 15, 1891 and the beginning of one of the most successful programs in the country. During their storied history, the Varsity Blues have won the Queen's Cup a total of 41 times, including 10 consecutive seasons from 1919–20 to 1928–29 and eight more from 1965–66 to 1972–73.

As with McGill, Toronto's early years saw several of hockey's eventual elite involved with the Varsity Blues. Hall of Famer Conn Smythe was the captain of the 1915 Varsity Blues, which won the Ontario junior championship. He coached Toronto from 1923 to 1926 and led the Blues to the 1927 Allan Cup. This victory was the third Allan Cup title for the school as the varsity team had first won the trophy in 1921 after the Toronto Dentals had been victorious in 1917.

The 1927 victory earned Toronto the right to represent Canada at the 1928 Olympic Games in St. Moritz, Switzerland. The Varsity Grads won the gold medal with a 3–0 record at the second Winter Olympic Games, outscoring the opposition 38–0.

Smythe is only one of several prominent coaches in University of Toronto history. The list also includes former Canadian Prime Minister Lester Pearson (1926 to 1928), Maple Leaf Ace Bailey (1935 to 1940, 1945 to 1949), Judge Joseph Kane (1962 to 1965), Tom Watt (1966 to 1979, 1985) and Mike Keenan (1984).

The First World War halted intercollegiate play for four seasons from 1915–16 to 1918–19, but the CIHU returned to action in 1919–20. Over the next 21 seasons, from 1919–20 to 1939–40, the CIHU fluctuated in size from a low of two teams in the years following the 1929 stock market crash to four teams. During this span the original three members of the league were joined at various times by teams from the University of Montreal, the University of Western Ontario and Laval University.

In 1936–37, one of the most unique arrangements in intercollegiate sport occurred. That season saw the formation of the International Intercollegiate Hockey League, which brought together teams from the CIHU and the U.S.-based Ivy League. McGill, Toronto, Queen's and Montreal were joined by Harvard, Yale, Princeton and Dartmouth to form an eight-team league that played a 10-game schedule. McGill won the first three IIHL titles as they compiled a record of 28–2 from 1936–37 to 1938–39.

In 1939–40 league membership fell to seven teams as Montreal withdrew from the circuit. Toronto went undefeated with an 8–0–0 record to capture the final championship in IIHL history before the league ceased operations due to World War II.

With the end of World War II, intercollegiate hockey resumed play across Canada. In Ontario and Quebec, the CIHU faded from the scene but was replaced by the four-team Senior Intercollegiate Hockey League, which included McGill, Toronto, Queen's and Laval.

While intercollegiate hockey was evolving in Ontario and Quebec, the sport was also enjoying success on the campuses of universities in Atlantic and Western Canada. In the Maritimes, hockey had been played at universities since the late 19th century with competition between Dalhousie, St. Francis Xavier, King's College and Acadia in Nova Scotia and the University of New Brunswick and Mount Allison University in New Brunswick. These schools formed the Maritimes Intercollegiate Athletic Association in 1910 and competed in a variety of sports including hockey, rugby, track, tennis and basketball.

Following the First World War, the MIAA expanded to a total membership of 10 schools and in 1968 the conference became the Atlantic Intercollegiate Athletic Association with the addition of Memorial University of Newfoundland. In April, 1974, the AIAA once again changed its name, becoming the Atlantic Universities Athletic Association. A further name change occurred in 1999 as the AUAA, in a move to bring more recognition to intercollegiate sports, opted for the title Atlantic University Sports.

St. Francis Xavier University, from Antigonish, Nova Scotia, was an early powerhouse in the MIAA as the X-Men captured 17 of 32 championships from 1928–29 to 1961–62, including 14 of the 18 titles contested from 1940–41 to 1958–59. The 1950s belonged to the X-Men as they won every title from 1950 to 1959, with the exception of 1952–53 when no conference champion was declared because of the collapse of the arena that was hosting the MIAA championship. Also prominent on the East Coast was Mount Allison University, winners of six of nine MIAA championships from 1930–31 to 1938–39. The Mounties won three consecutive titles from 1931 to 1933, one in 1935 and two more in 1938 and 1939.

Western Canada was also home to intercollegiate hockey with teams in each of the four western provinces. The University of Alberta Golden Bears began play during the 1908–09 season as a member of the Edmonton Collegiate League. In Manitoba, the University of Manitoba Bisons were members of the local Winnipeg hockey league, while in Saskatoon the University of Saskatchewan Huskies were formed in the early 1910s. At Vancouver, the University of British Columbia has iced a hockey team since 1915–16.

The early years of all four western schools saw the hockey teams compete in local city leagues as well as provincial senior and intermediate leagues as there was no formal intercollegiate league. However, several of the teams played exhibition games against each other.

The first such game occurred on February 27, 1911, when Alberta visited Saskatoon and defeated Saskatchewan 16–0 as Roy Goodridge scored a Golden Bears team-record eight goals. This record still stands.

In the fall of 1919 intercollegiate athletics in the west took a monumental step forward as Alberta, Manitoba and Saskatchewan met at the Hotel MacDonald in Edmonton to form an athletic conference for the western universities. The Western Canada Intercollegiate Athletic Union was the product of this meeting and in January, 1920 the first hockey game was played. Manitoba won the first WCIAU title as the Bisons won three of their four games to finish two points ahead of second-place Alberta.

In the early 1920s three western schools enjoyed particular success. In 1920–21 the UBC Thunderbirds won the Savage Cup as British Columbia Senior A champions and earned the right to move on to the Allan Cup playoffs. (The Thunderbirds were unable to skate for the Allan Cup as the school's final exams schedule conflicted with the playoff schedule.) The University of Manitoba won the 1923 Memorial Cup and captured the Manitoba Amateur Hockey Association junior championship in 1922, 1923 and 1925. Saskatchewan reached the Allan Cup finals in 1923 after having won the Saskatchewan and Western Canadian senior titles. Other Canadian universities to advance in the Memorial Cup playoffs included Quebec's Loyola College in 1920 and McGill in 1923.

In 1922, Dr. J. Halpenny of the University of Saskatchewan donated a trophy to the WCIAU to be awarded to the annual champion. The Halpenny Trophy was competed for on an annual basis until 1950, with the exception of several seasons during the 1930s and early 1940s, when competition was halted due to the Depression and World War II. In March, 1950 the Halpenny Trophy was retired in the permanent possession of Alberta after the Golden Bears won the trophy for the 17th consecutive season. The Halpenny Trophy was replaced by the W.G. Hardy Trophy in 1950–51.

The Hardy Trophy was named after Dr. W. George Hardy, a professor of Classics at the University of Alberta, who coached the Golden Bears from 1924 to 1928. Hardy was renowned for both his academic and athletic endeavors and served as president of the Alberta Amateur Hockey Association from 1931 to 1933, the Canadian Amateur Hockey Association from 1938 to 1939 and the International Ice Hockey Federation from 1948 to 1951.

The Canadian Interuniversity Athletic Union

In 1961 the Canadian Intercollegiate Athletic Union was formed as the governing body for intercollegiate sport in Canada. The CIAU, which would change its name to the present Canadian Interuniversity Athletic Union in 1978, began with five regional conferences: the Maritime Intercollegiate Athletic Association, Ottawa-St. Lawrence Intercollegiate Athletic Association, the Ontario-Quebec Athletic Association, Ontario Intercollegiate Athletic Association and the Western Canadian Intercollegiate Athletic Association.

Through the years the CIAU has grown and this growth has resulted in several different alignments in the various conferences across the country. In the Maritimes, the AUAA has grown from six teams to as many as 10, and currently has eight teams playing in two divisions. Intercollegiate hockey in Quebec saw the Ontario-Quebec Association thrive for a decade as the conference ranged in size from four to nine teams. In 1970–71 the OQAA became the Quebec University Athletic Association and eight schools competed for the conference title. In the early 1980s a trend developed that saw several QUAA schools drop their hockey programs due to budget constraints and by 1986–87 the conference was down to only four teams. In 1987 the *Université du Québec à Chicoutimi* dropped its hockey program, leaving McGill, Concordia and *Québec à Trois-Rivières* as the only remaining Quebec universities with an active hockey program. The three surviving members of the QUAA then joined the Ontario Universities Athletic Association in time for the 1987–88 season, where they remain today.

Following the 1999–2000 season, officials from the *Université de Sherbrooke* made it known that they were looking to reinstate the men's hockey program and begin a women's program in time for the 2000–01 season. The *Vert & Or* had been a member of the QUAA until the late 1970s. With the possible return of Sherbrooke to the intercollegiate arena the future may also see the return of a separate conference of Quebec schools as a part of CIAU hockey.

In Ontario, collegiate hockey continued to flourish with as many as 16 teams competing for the conference title. The conference has seen several changes to its membership and make-up over the years and most recently had 16 teams competing in four four-team divisions.

At the conclusion of the 1999–2000 season, the University of Laurentian decided to reduce the number of its intercollegiate athletic teams with the Voyageurs hockey team being one of the programs that was discontinued. With Laurentian's withdrawal the OUA hockey roster stands at 15 teams entering the 2000–01 season. The OUA may see further changes in the near future as Lakehead University is looking to join the conference. The Thunderwolves were former members of the Great Plains Athletic Conference before discontinuing the hockey program following the 1984–85 season.

College hockey in the western provinces saw the original WCIAU move from its three charter members—Alberta, Manitoba and Saskatchewan—to a two-team league for several years in the 1930s and 1940s. In 1956–57 the conference expanded to four teams with the addition of the Brandon College Caps. Brandon played two seasons in the WCIAU before withdrawing, but the Caps were replaced by the University of British Columbia Thunderbirds in 1961–62.

The WCIAU became the Western Canadian Intercollegiate Athletic Association in 1962–63 and the conference membership grew to eight teams by 1970–71 as the University of Calgary joined in 1964–65 and was followed by the University of Winnipeg in 1968–69, the University of Victoria in 1969–70 and the return of Brandon to the fold that same season. From 1969–70 to 1971–72, the WCIAU remained an eight-team conference, but in 1972–73 it separated into two new leagues. Alberta, Saskatchewan, Calgary, UBC and Victoria formed the Canada West University Athletic Association while Brandon, Manitoba and Winnipeg began the Great Plains Athletic Conference.

Victoria would drop its hockey program in 1973–74 after suffering through four seasons with an overall record of 3–75–0. The Vikings' departure left the CWUAA with four teams for the next 11 seasons until 1984–85 when the University of Lethbridge Pronghorns joined the association. While the CWUAA remained stable, GPAC was growing as Lakehead University began play in 1972–73 and won the conference's first title that season. GPAC upped its membership to five teams in 1976–77 with the addition of the University of Regina Cougars. Winnipeg and Lakehead shelved their hockey programs in the mid-1980s, leaving GPAC membership at three with only Brandon, Manitoba and Regina icing squads. In 1985–86 the CWUAA and remaining GPAC teams merged to form an eight-team conference under the banner of the CWUAA.

The University Cup

With the formation of the CIAU in 1961 as the governing body of intercollegiate athletics in Canada, the concept of national championships became a reality. The 1962–63 season saw the first CIAU championships held in hockey and basketball. The annual CIAU hockey champion has been awarded the University Cup since the first national championship was played. Queen's University and the Royal Military College of Canada—the two schools that participated in the first intercollegiate game in history—donated the University Cup to the CIAU in recognition of the contribution made to the game of hockey by outstanding university players.

During the course of its history, the format of the

University Cup playoffs has varied. The first two tournaments in 1962–63 and 1963–64 were co-hosted by Queen's and the Royal Military College and featured four teams playing two semifinal games that led to a championship and consolation final. Since then the tournament has varied from four- to six-team fields featuring conference champions, host and wild card teams, to progressive best-of-three regional series between conference champions. The championship tournament has been contested in sites across Canada from Edmonton and Calgary in the west to Moncton and Charlottetown in the east. For 10 seasons, from 1987–88 to 1996–97, the University of Toronto was host to the national tournament. Games were played at the school's Varsity Arena, though from 1992–93 to 1996–97 Maple Leaf Gardens served as the site of the CIAU championship game. In 1997–98 the tournament returned to the west as the University of Saskatchewan earned the right to host the final for three seasons (1997–98 to 1999–2000) at Saskatchewan Place in Saskatoon.

Through 2000 a total of 13 teams have won the University Cup. The McMaster University Marlins, in their only tournament appearance, won the inaugural championship in 1963 with a 3–2 victory over the UBC Thunderbirds. Joining McMaster as CIAU champions are the Toronto Varsity Blues and Alberta Golden Bears, who share the CIAU record with 10 titles, the Moncton *Aigles Bleus* (4), the York Yeomen (3), the Acadia Axemen (2), the Trois-Rivieres *Patriotes* (2) and the Guelph Gryphons, Lethbridge Pronghorns, Manitoba Bisons, New Brunswick Varsity Reds, Saskatchewan Huskies and Waterloo Warriors who have each won the University Cup once.

Toronto, under the guidance of Tom Watt (CIAU coach of the year in 1971 and the National Hockey League coach of the year with the Winnipeg Jets in 1981–82) won its first University Cup title in 1965–66. It was the first of Toronto's 10 titles and it began an unprecedented streak of success for the Varsity Blues as they would win seven University Cup competitions in a span of eight seasons from 1965–66 to 1972–73, including five straight from 1968–69 to 1972–73. The final four championships in Toronto's amazing streak came against the same opponent. From 1969–70 through 1972–73 the Varsity Blues would face the Saint Mary's University Huskies of the AUAA for the national crown. Saint Mary's, from Halifax, Nova Scotia, was coached by Bob Boucher, who would guide the Huskies to the AUAA championship eight times in nine seasons from 1968–69 to 1976–77. Toronto recorded one-goal victories in three of its four games with Huskies as the Varsity Blues won 3–2 in 1970 and 1973 and 5–4 in 1971. Back-to-back titles in 1975–76 and 1976–77 gave the Varsity Blues their eighth and ninth University Cup victories under Watt and Toronto won its 10th national championship in 1983–84 as Mike Keenan guided the team to a 9–1 victory over the Concordia Stingers.

Matching the success of the Varsity Blues is the Alberta Golden Bears. The Edmonton-based school has made a record 25 appearances at the University Cup tournament, reaching the championship game on 13 occasions and winning the University Cup honors 10 times, including once in each of the five decades of trophy competition. Alberta won its first title in 1963–64 and earned its second four years later with an exciting last-minute victory over Loyola College. Before a University Cup-record crowd of 12,000 at the Montreal Forum, Ron Cebryk netted the game-winning goal with only 17 seconds remaining to give the Golden Bears a 5–4 win over the hometown Warriors and the 1967–68 University Cup. For Alberta Golden Bears head coach Clare Drake the national title was his second of the season. Drake, who ended his 28 seasons behind the Alberta bench as the winningest coach in North American intercollegiate hockey with a record of 697–296–37, had earlier guided the Golden Bears football team to the 1967 Vanier Cup—the Canadian college football championship. It is the only time in CIAU history that one coach has won national championships in two sports during the same season.

For four seasons from 1976–77 to 1979–80, the Golden Bears were the dominant team in the CIAU as they appeared in four consecutive University Cup finals, winning three consecutively from 1977–78 to 1979–80. Alberta would win again in 1985–86 and capture their eighth title in 1991–92. Titles number nine and ten came in consecutive seasons as Alberta claimed the 1999 and 2000 University Cup championships in Saskatoon. Under the guidance of head coach Rob Daum, the Golden Bears defeated *les Aigles Bleus de l'Université de Moncton* 6–2 in 1999 as forward Cam Danyluk scored three times to earn tournament MVP honors. In 2000 the Golden Bears equaled Toronto's 10 University Cup championships as Russ Hewson, the Sullivan Trophy winner as the CIAU's outstanding player, capped an outstanding season by scoring the game-winning goal at 8:18 of the second overtime period to give Alberta a 5–4 victory over the University of New Brunswick Varsity Reds. The win ended New Brunswick's 10-game overtime winning streak that had stretched from October 13, 1999, to March 25, 2000. The streak included six playoff victories, four of which went into double overtime.

The consecutive championships for Alberta in 1999 and 2000 marked the first time since 1987–88 and 1988–89 that a team had repeated as University Cup champions. Both Alberta victories came at Saskatchewan Place in Saskatoon, where the tournament organizing committee and the University of Saskatchewan's athletic department helped set attendance records for three straight years. The 2000 tournament drew a total of 40,956 fans to Saskatchewan Place for an average of 5,851 per game for the seven-game schedule. Saskatchewan had set the previous CIAU attendance record of 37,184 (5,312 average) in 1999, while the third highest single tournament attendance record came in 1998 during the first season at Saskatchewan Place with 37,121 (5,303 average). On March 25, 2000, the host Saskatchewan Huskies dropped a dramatic 5–4 double overtime decision to New Brunswick before a crowd of 10,152—the largest single-game crowd during the tournament's three-years in Saskatoon and the biggest attendance figure since 12,000 fans had showed up in Montreal in 1968.

Over the years, several teams have enjoyed success at the conference level but have not been able to capture the University Cup. As noted earlier, Saint Mary's lost four consecutive national finals to Toronto in the early 1970s. The Huskies disappointment can be matched by the Concordia Stingers, Calgary Dinosaurs and St. Francis Xavier X-Men.

Concordia was the dominant team in the Quebec Universities Athletic Association from the mid-1970s to the mid-1980s when Trois-Rivieres emerged as one of Canada's premier teams. Leading the way for Concordia was head coach Paul Arsenault who won 17 conference championships during his 22-season career. With Arsenault behind the bench, the Stingers made nine appearances in the University Cup tournament and reached the championship twice, losing to Saskatchewan in 1983 and Toronto in 1984. Calgary and St. Francis Xavier have made 10 and six visits respectively to the tournament without a title as both schools have yet to reach the championship final.

For the Saskatchewan Huskies and Guelph Gryphons, the disappointment of several missed chances was finally washed away with a victory. Dave King, later the longtime coach of the Canadian Olympic team and an NHL head coach with the Calgary Flames and Columbus Blue Jackets, was with his alma mater in Saskatoon in 1979–80 and the former Huskies forward built Saskatchewan into a force in the CWUAA. Under King, the Huskies won three consecutive Canada West conference titles from 1980–81 to 1982–83 and advanced to the University Cup championship game in each season. The Huskies suffered disappointing losses to Moncton in the title game in their first two appearances before winning the 1982–83 national crown with a 6–2 victory over Concordia.

For Guelph, the road to the top was a long one as the Gryphons finally earned the University Cup in 1996–97 in their seventh appearance. Guelph made its first journey to the national tournament in 1975–76 as OUAA champions and advanced to the title game before losing 7–2 to Toronto. Guelph would not return to the final game for 18 seasons, but when they did the Gryphons would play in four consecutive championship games from 1993–94 to 1996–97. The Gryphons lost 5–2 to Lethbridge in 1994 and 5–1 against Moncton in 1995 before winning the Cup in 1997. Coach Marlin Muylaert was the driving force behind Guelph's success in the 1990s. In his first season at Guelph, Muylaert and the Gryphons missed the postseason but it would be the only time that Guelph would fail to qualify for the playoffs under Muylaert (who is married to former 1984 Canadian Olympic swimming gold medalist Anne Ottenbrite). From 1989–90 to their championship season of 1996–97, the Gryphons would qualify for the playoffs eight times, win two OUAA conference titles, qualify for the University Cup tournament three times and win the CIAU title once.

The CIAU and the NHL

From hockey's beginning, players from Canadian universities have played a vital role in the development and expansion of the sport. In the early years, students from McGill, Queen's and Toronto helped to formulate hockey rules and develop the sport's equipment. Today, players from CIAU teams are skating for NHL teams as well as teams at other levels of professional hockey in North America and Europe. Although not known as a pipeline to the National Hockey League, the CIAU has sent its share of players, coaches and administrators to the pro ranks.

In addition to such famed hockey men as Conn Smythe and Frank and Lester Patrick, another former Canadian university student to have a direct impact on the NHL was Clarence Campbell. Campbell was a Rhodes Scholar from the University of Alberta who began his hockey career as an administrator and referee in local hockey leagues in Edmonton prior to World War II. He succeeded Red Dutton as president of the NHL in 1946 and during his 31 years as NHL president, Campbell helped to establish the NHL Pension Society in 1946 and spearheaded the league's expansion from six to 12 teams in 1967–68. The longest serving president in NHL history, he was elected to the Hockey Hall of Fame in 1966.

Another former Canadian university student would become most influential in the growth of the Stanley Cup into hockey's most prized trophy. When Lord Stanley of Preston donated the trophy named after him to Canadian hockey in 1893, one of the trustees he appointed to insure the integrity of the Cup was Philip Dansken Ross of Ottawa. The former McGill hockey and football star played an integral role in decisions concerning the Stanley Cup and its evolvement into the oldest trophy in North American professional sport. Elected to the Hall of Fame in 1976, Ross served as trustee of the Stanley Cup for 56 years until his death in 1949.

In addition to the administration of the Stanley Cup, players from the CIAU have been members of Cup-winning teams. Only 54 players in the history of the Stanley Cup have won five or more championships since the trophy was first awarded in 1893. Among those five-time Stanley Cup champions is Randy Gregg. A defenseman with the University of Alberta, Gregg was a member of two CIAU national championship teams with the Golden Bears and was the 1979 recipient of the Senator Joseph A. Sullivan Trophy as the nation's most outstanding player. After graduating from Alberta with his degree in Medicine, Gregg was captain of the 1980 Canadian Olympic team and then played two seasons in Japan before joining the Edmonton Oilers, where he was a member of five Stanley Cup championship teams playing alongside the likes of Wayne Gretzky, Mark Messier, Kevin Lowe, Jari Kurri, Grant Fuhr and Paul Coffey.

McGill is the home of 13 players to have won the Stanley Cup, though many of these players did so before the formation of the NHL. Among McGill's NHLers is goaltender Jack Gelineau, winner of the Calder Trophy as rookie of the year. Gelineau won the award in 1949–50 after recording three shutouts and a 3.28 goals-against average in 67 games. Joining Gelineau on the NHL's honor roll is Al MacAdam, a University of Prince Edward Island Panther before embarking on an NHL career that would see him play 12 seasons with Philadelphia, Calgary, Cleveland, Minnesota and Vancouver. In 1979–80 he led the Minnesota North Stars in scoring and was the winner of the Bill Masterton Trophy, which is awarded annually to the NHL player who best exemplifies perseverance, sportsmanship and dedication to hockey.

One of the first collegians from western Canada to make the NHL was Alberta defenseman Dave MacKay who played one season with the Chicago Black Hawks in 1940–41. After his rookie season in "the Windy City," MacKay cut short his NHL career, and, like many Canadians, joined the war effort, serving three years with the Canadian Army Engineers.

The 1990s have seen several CIAU graduates in the NHL. Steve Rucchin of the University of Western Ontario Mustangs has played six seasons with the Mighty Ducks of Anaheim and the former all-Canadian has centered two of the NHL's superstars—Teemu Selanne and Paul Kariya. In 1999, former Alberta Golden Bear defenseman Brent Severyn capped an eight-year NHL career with Quebec, Florida, New York Islanders, Colorado, Anaheim and Dallas by helping the Stars win the Stanley Cup championship. Following his NHL career, Severyn, who was the MVP of the prestigious Viking Cup Tournament in 1988, went to Germany where he won the Deutsche Eishockey

Liga championship with Munich.

Joining Rucchin and Severyn on NHL rosters were Alberta defensemen Cory Cross of the Toronto Maple Leafs and Ian Herbers of the New York Islanders, UBC's Dan Smith (Colorado) and Trois-Rivieres' Eric Messier (Colorado) and forwards Mike Kennedy (UBC) of Dallas, Stu Grimson (Manitoba) of Anaheim and P.J. Stock (St. Francis Xavier) of the New York Rangers. These players continue a line of CIAU student-athletes who have made their way to the NHL, following in the skate strides of players such as Bob Berry.

Berry played eight seasons in the NHL from 1968–69 to 1976–77 with the Montreal Canadiens and Los Angeles Kings after an outstanding career as an all-star forward with the Sir George Williams University Georgians of the Ottawa-St. Lawrence Athletic Association in the mid-1960s. Following his playing career, Berry served as head coach of Los Angeles, Montreal, Pittsburgh and St. Louis and was the runner-up for the Jack Adams Award as the NHL's coach of the year with the Kings in 1980–81.

Other Canadian university players who have gone on to the NHL include former goaltenders Ken Lockett of Guelph (Vancouver Canucks), Toronto's Gary Inness (Pittsburgh, Philadelphia, Washington), UBC's Ken Broderick (Minnesota, Boston), Ross McKay (Hartford) of Saskatchewan, Bernie Wolfe (Washington) of Sir George Williams and Jim Corsi (Edmonton) of Loyola and Concordia. Larry Carriere, a stalwart defenseman with Loyola College in Montreal, was drafted by the Buffalo Sabres 25th overall in the 1972 NHL Amateur Draft and played seven seasons with five NHL teams. He is now the assistant to the Sabres general manager. Another blueliner of note was Bob Murdoch of the Waterloo Warriors. An OUAA all-star, Murdoch won the Stanley Cup with Montreal in 1971 and 1973 during a 12-year NHL career. He would go on to coach in the NHL with Chicago and Winnipeg.

The most prolific CIAU scorer to play in the NHL was Manitoba's Mike Ridley. The CIAU's outstanding player and freshman of the year in 1983–84, Ridley led the Bisons to two GPAC titles during his collegiate career before turning pro with the New York Rangers in the 1985–86 season. Scoring 22 goals and 65 points in his rookie season, Ridley was named to the NHL's All-Rookie Team that season. During a 12-year NHL career from 1985–86 to 1996–97, Ridley would score 292 goals and 466 assists for 758 points in 866 career games.

The CIAU can also be found behind the bench in the NHL as there have been a host of former Canadian university coaches in the league, including two winners of the Jack Adams Award. Mike Keenan, who guided the Toronto Varsity Blues to the 1984 CIAU title, has coached five NHL teams including one Stanley Cup champion and three Cup finalists. The Jack Adams Award winner in 1984–85 with Philadelphia, Keenan took the Flyers to the Stanley Cup finals in 1985 and 1987 and the Chicago Blackhawks in 1992 before winning the Stanley Cup with the New York Rangers in 1994. Keenan's career has also seen him guide Team Canada to Canada Cup championships in 1987 and 1991 and the Rochester Americans to the 1983 American Hockey League Calder Cup title.

The other CIAU coach to be named the NHL coach of the year is Tom Watt. Like Keenan, Watt was coach of the University of Toronto before turning pro and led the Varsity Blues to what was then a CIAU-record nine University Cup championships while compiling a career coaching record of 410–102–34 in 15 seasons. Watt won the Jack Adams Award in 1981–82 with the Winnipeg Jets. He would also coach Vancouver and Toronto during his career and was an assistant coach with Vancouver and Calgary, helping the Flames win the Stanley Cup in 1988–89.

Joining Keenan and Watt among the NHL coaching ranks was Doug MacLean of the Florida Panthers. The former UPEI player and New Brunswick Varsity Reds head coach guided the Panthers to the 1996 Stanley Cup finals and was a finalist for the Jack Adams Award that season. Relieved of his coaching duties midway through the 1997–98 season, MacLean is currently the general manager of the NHL expansion Columbus Blue Jackets. Also behind the bench for NHL teams have been Pierre Page (Dalhousie) with the Mighty Ducks of Anaheim, Montreal assistant coach Clement Jodoin (Trois-Rivieres), New York Rangers assistant Bill Moores (Alberta), New York Islanders and Phoenix Coyotes assistant Wayne Fleming (Manitoba) and Vancouver assistant Terry Bangen (McGill). Clare Drake (Alberta), Harry Neale (Toronto), Gary Green (Guelph), Jean Perron (Moncton), George Kingston (Calgary), Dave Chambers (Saskatchewan, Guelph and York), Ron Smith (York), Conn Smythe (Toronto), Art Ross (McGill), George Burnett (McGill), Doug Carpenter (MacDonald College), Kevin Primeau (Alberta) and Charles Thiffault (Sherbrooke) are others to become head or assistant coaches in the NHL after playing and/or coaching in the CIAU.

NHL front offices have also had their fair share of former CIAU coaches and players in important roles. John Blackwell, a former student trainer with Alberta served as the Philadelphia Flyers assistant general manager for nine seasons from 1990–91 to 1998–99. Blackwell spent four seasons with Alberta in the late 1960s and early 1970s before joining the Edmonton Oilers in 1972–73 while they were a member of the World Hockey Association. He would spend 18 seasons with Edmonton in various roles in the front office and contribute to the Oilers' five Stanley Cup titles during his 27 seasons in professional hockey. Former Regina Cougars head coach Al Murray has served as the Los Angeles Kings' director of amateur scouting since 1988–89. Jim Nill, a former forward with the Calgary Dinosaurs, enjoyed a nine-year NHL career playing with Boston, Vancouver, St. Louis, Winnipeg and Detroit. Following his playing career, Nill became a scout with the Ottawa Senators for three seasons before joining the Red Wings organization in the summer of 1994. With the Red Wings, Nill served as a scout and the team's director of player development before being named assistant general manager in 1998–99. He was also in the running for the job as general manager of the Calgary Flames following the 1999–2000 season.

As the NHL expands to 30 teams in 2000–2001 with the addition of the Minnesota Wild and Columbus Blue Jackets, the opportunities for CIAU players to advance to the professional ranks are increasing and the players are coming under greater scrutiny by NHL scouting staffs. One of the more sought-after CIAU players has been Mathieu Darche of McGill University. The Redmen captain became the tenth McGill player to sign with an NHL team as he was inked to an NHL contract by Columbus on May 5, 2000, after finishing an outstanding career with McGill. The CIAU all-Canadian left wing had been courted by a dozen

NHL teams, including his hometown Montreal Canadiens, St. Louis and New Jersey during the 1999–2000 season as he scored 33 goals and 82 points in only 38 games to lead the nation in scoring. A three-time McGill MVP, Darche was a finalist for the Sullivan Trophy in 2000 and was the winner of the TSN-Randy Gregg Award, presented to the CIAU player who best combines hockey with academics and citizenship. Success runs in the Darche family, as Mathieu's older brother, Jean-Philippe, signed a contract with the National Football League's Seattle Seahawks on the same day.

On the World Stage

As well as its contribution to the NHL, the CIAU has made a significant contribution to Canada's role on the world hockey stage.

In August, 1962, Father David Bauer unveiled a plan to establish a Canadian national hockey team that would represent the country at the Olympics and World Championships. The Canadian Amateur Hockey Association accepted the plan and Bauer put together a group of top CIAU and senior players who would prepare for international competition in Vancouver at the University of British Columbia. Prior to the national program, Bauer, the brother of NHL star Bobby Bauer, had guided the Toronto St. Michael's junior team to the 1961 Memorial Cup title. Bauer's success would carry over to Canada's national program as he officially began his role as coach on August 21, 1963.

In its first major competition, the Canadian national team, which had four members of the 1962–63 CIAU finalist UBC Thunderbirds on the roster, placed fourth at the 1964 Winter Olympics in Innsbruck, Austria, with a 5–2–0 record. Canada's only losses were to the gold medal-winning Russians and the Czechs, who won the bronze medal. Bauer, who was elected to the Hockey Hall of Fame in 1989, would continue with the national program through the 1968 Winter Olympics, winning a bronze medal at the World Championships in 1966 and 1967 and at the Grenoble Olympic Games. On the Canadian roster in 1968 were Ken Broderick, Barry MacKenzie and Terry O'Malley of UBC, Herb Pinder of Manitoba and Toronto's Steve Monteith.

Following the 1968 Olympic Games, Canada withdrew from international play over the issue of professionalism and it would not be until 1980 that Canadians would once again skate at the Olympic Games. Prominent behind Canada's return to the Olympic stage was Father Bauer. Serving as the managing director, Bauer brought together a team composed mainly of CIAU players and selected Clare Drake (Alberta), Tom Watt (Toronto) and Lorne Davis to serve as co-coaches. Between Drake and Watt, the two had combined to win 13 of 14 CIAU titles between 1966 and 1979.

Based in Calgary, the 1980 Canadian Olympic team included 15 CIAU players: Randy Gregg, who was selected captain, John Devaney, Don Spring, Kevin Primeau and Dave Hindmarch of Alberta; Warren Anderson, Joe Grant, Dan D'Alvise, Stelio Zupancich, Cary Farelli and Shane Pearsall of Toronto; UBC's Terry O'Malley and Ron Paterson; Paul MacLean of the Dalhousie Tigers and Jim Nill of Calgary. For O'Malley, it was his third Olympic appearance having previously represented Canada in 1964 and 1968. In its return to the Olympics, Canada would finish sixth at Lake Placid, New York.

Following the 1980 Olympics, Hockey Canada decided to continue Bauer's national program on a full-time basis with the team headquartered in Calgary. Dave King of the University of Saskatchewan was named the head coach of Team Canada and the 1980 CIAU coach of the year would guide the team at three Olympics. Under King, Canada finished fourth at both the 1984 Games at Sarajevo, Yugoslavia, and at Calgary in 1988 before winning a silver medal at Albertville, France, in 1992. He would also coach Canada at four World Championship tournaments and participate in a gold medal win for Canada at the World Junior Championships in 1982. He added a bronze in 1983.

During King's tenure with Team Canada, he had several CIAU players as members of the Olympic team. In 1984 Warren Anderson and Darren Lowe (Toronto), Robin Bartel (Saskatchewan) and Vaughn Karpan (Manitoba) wore the maple leaf, while George Kingston (Calgary) and Jean Perron (Moncton) served as King's assistants. Moncton's Claude Vilgrain was a member of the 1988 team and was joined by Karpan and Gregg. For both Gregg and Karpan, it marked their second stint with the Olympic program.

There were no CIAU players on Team Canada at the 1992 Olympics in Albertville, but the 1994 team in Lillehammer, Norway, had Saskatchewan defenseman Ken Lovsin on the roster. UQTR head coach Dany Dube was an assistant to head coach Tom Renney and George Kingston served in management as the team's director of hockey operations.

Besides the players on the Canadian Olympic team, there have been several players from the CIAU representing other countries at the Olympics and World Championships. Ron Fischer of Calgary (1988, 1992) and Rick Amann of UBC (1992, 1994) were both members of Germany's Olympic team, while Regina's Rick Nasheim skated for Austria in 1994 and 1998. A trio of Calgary Dinosaurs represented the CIAU at the 1998 games in Nagano, Japan. Defenseman Chad Biafore skated for Italy and Matt Kabayama and Steve Tsujuira were members of the host Japanese Olympic team.

Even prior to Father Bauer's national program, Canadian university athletes had often represented their country internationally. In 1928 the University of Toronto Grads won the Olympic gold medal at St. Moritz, Switzerland. One member of the team was Dr. Joseph A. Sullivan. Playing goal for Canada, Sullivan earned two shutouts to backstop the Grads to an undefeated record. Following the Games, Sullivan would go on to serve in Canada's senate and the trophy awarded to the CIAU's outstanding player is named in his honour.

The CIAU has also represented Canada at the World Student Games six times since 1968. That season the Toronto Varsity Blues won a bronze medal for Canada at Innsbruck and in 1972 a CIAU all-star team won silver at Lake Placid. In 1980 the Alberta Golden Bears won the gold medal in Jaca, Spain, and later earned a bronze medal in 1987 in Strbske Pleso, Czechoslovakia. In its last two appearances at the World Student Games Canada has won bronze medals. January, 1997 saw an all-star team from the CWUAA win bronze in South Korea, while an OUA all-star squad finished in third place at the 1999 games in Slovakia with a 5–1 victory over Russia in the bronze medal game. The CIAU's next appearance on the world stage will come in February 2001 as an all-star team from Atlantic

University Sports will be Canada's representative in Zakopane, Poland.

Since 1997 the CIAU and NCAA have competed in an annual cross-border challenge series. Named the World University Hockey Challenge, and since re-named the North American College Hockey Championships, the series pits an all-star team from Canada against an all-star team from American schools. The first two seasons saw the challenge played at Joe Louis Arena in Detroit where the teams split the series. In an exciting overtime victory, the CIAU took the inaugural game 6–5 in 1997 as Guelph Gryphons defenseman J.P. Davis tied the game with only 0.9 seconds left in regulation and Greg Clancy of Acadia University netted the winner just 1:49 into overtime. The NCAA evened the series with a 3–1 win in 1998.

In 1999 the series expanded to a two-game affair with one game played in the United States and the second in Canada. Alberta head coach Rob Daum guided the CIAU to a sweep of the 1999 series with a 4–2 win at Detroit and a 5–4 overtime shootout victory at the Air Canada Centre in Toronto. The NCAA rallied to tie the series in 2000 with 6–2 and 5–4 (overtime) wins in Detroit and Hamilton. The championship has brought further recognition to both the CIAU and NCAA with many NHL general managers and scouts in attendance.

Over the years CIAU student-athletes and coaches have also represented Canada at international tournaments such as the Canada Cup, Spengler Cup, Izvestia Cup, the World Championships and the World Junior Championships. In the process they have helped to carry on the rich tradition of Canadian intercollegiate hockey.

CIAU Women's Hockey

February 26, 1998, was an historic date for Canadian intercollegiate sport as the puck was dropped at the very first CIAU women's ice hockey championship. Although women's hockey had been a varsity sport for more than 25 years in Ontario and 20 years in Quebec, there had been no national championship sanctioned by the CIAU. With the popularity of women's hockey exploding at all levels since 1990 many universities were adding hockey to the roster of women's varsity sports and with the increase in teams, the CIAU officially sanctioned women's hockey as a championship sport in the summer of 1997.

The first championship tournament was awarded to the Concordia University Stingers and was held in Montreal. Six teams qualified for the championship event as the host Stingers were joined by the Alberta Pandas, Guelph Gryphons, Toronto Varsity Blues, Saint Mary's Huskies and Trois-Rivieres *Patriotes*. Nicky Walder made history as the Trois-Rivieres right wing scored the first ever goal in CIAU women's hockey championship history with the game-winner at 4:29 of the second period as the Patriotes skated to a 2–0 win over Guelph.

Concordia and Toronto met in the first championship final with the Stingers claiming the first "Golden Path" Trophy as CIAU champions with a 4–1 victory over the Varsity Blues. Defenseman Marie Claude Pelletier scored the game-winning goal 3:26 into the third period. The Stingers would successfully defend their championship in 1999 as Concordia blanked Alberta 2–0.

Alberta returned to the CIAU championship tournament in 2000, making its third consecutive appearance after winning the Canada West conference championship for the third time. With 14 players returning from its silver medal performance of 1999, the Pandas were looking to break Concordia's run as national champions. After defeating the Guelph Gryphons 4–2 in their opening game, the Pandas faced off against Concordia in the semifinals with the winner advancing to the final. The second ranked Pandas battled through regulation play tied at 2–2 and the teams remained tied following a scoreless 10 minutes of overtime. The teams then went to a shootout to determine a winner and the Pandas emerged victorious, outscoring the Stingers 3–2. Lori Shupak and CIAU rookie of the year Danielle Bourgeois then scored for Alberta in the final to give the Pandas a 2–0 win over the McGill University Martlets and their first national championship. With the victory the University of Alberta became the first Canadian school to win national championships in both men's and women's hockey in the same season. McGill goaltender Kim St. Pierre earned MVP honors at the women's tournament. The Canadian national team member allowed only two goals on 106 shots in the Martlets' three games, including 41 shots in the final.

Women's hockey at the collegiate level in Canada has been strongest in Ontario and Quebec. Ontario has had a conference schedule and championship since 1971–72 and Quebec since 1980–81, while both Canada West and the Atlantic conferences have only been active since 1997–98. The most dominant team in women's hockey in the CIAU has been the Concordia Stingers. Beginning 33 years ago as a club team that participated in a Montreal women's league, the Stingers have won 18 conference championships in addition to the first two CIAU titles.

Les Lawton, "The Dean of Women's Hockey," has been behind the Concordia bench for 17 seasons and has helped produce 13 national team members since 1992 as well as three CIAU outstanding player awards. Each of the outstanding player awards has been won by Corinne Swirsky, as the Stingers forward has won the Brodrick Trophy in each of its first three years since 1998. A native of Thompson, Manitoba, Swirsky is one of only four athletes in CIAU history to be named their sport's most valuable player three times. In 1999–2000, Swirsky led the CIAU in scoring for the second consecutive season by collecting 43 points in only 10 conference games. A three-time all-Canadian and four-time QSSF MVP, Swirsky is a member of Canada's Under-22 national team and was featured in *Chatelaine* magazine as one of 15 women who will lead Canada into the 21st century.

CIAU Men's Champions

Year	Champion	Year	Champion
1963	McMaster Marlins	1964	Alberta Golden Bears
1965	Manitoba Bisons	1966	Toronto Varsity Blues
1967	Toronto Varsity Blues	1968	Alberta Golden Bears
1969	Toronto Varsity Blues	1970	Toronto Varsity Blues
1971	Toronto Varsity Blues	1972	Toronto Varsity Blues
1973	Toronto Varsity Blues	1974	Waterloo Warriors
1975	Alberta Golden Bears	1976	Toronto Varsity Blues
1977	Toronto Varsity Blues	1978	Alberta Golden Bears
1979	Alberta Golden Bears	1980	Alberta Golden Bears
1981	Moncton Aigles Bleus	1982	Moncton Aigles Bleus
1983	Saskatchewan Huskies	1984	Toronto Varsity Blues
1985	York Yeomen	1986	Alberta Golden Bears

CIAU MEN'S CHAMPIONS *continued*

1987 Trois-Rivieres Patriotes	1988 York Yeomen
1989 York Yeomen	1990 Moncton Aigles Bleus
1991 Trois-Rivieres Patriotes	1992 Alberta Golden Bears
1993 Acadia Axemen	1994 Lethbridge Pronghorns
1995 Moncton Aigles Bleus	1996 Acadia Axemen
1997 Guelph Gryphons	1998 New Brunswick Varsity Reds
1999 Alberta Golden Bears	2000 Alberta Golden Bears

CIAU WOMEN'S CHAMPIONS

1998 Concordia Stingers	1999 Concordia Stingers
2000 Alberta Pandas	

CANADIAN COLLEGES ATHLETIC ASSOCIATION HOCKEY

Brian Stein

FOR OVER A QUARTER OF A CENTURY, the Canadian Colleges Athletic Association (CCAA) has been the national governing body for college sports in Canada. Like the National Collegiate Athletic Association (NCAA) and the Canadian Interuniversity Athletic Union (CIAU), the CCAA offers numerous hockey opportunities in an educational environment.

PROVINCIAL RIVALRY

The creation of organized conferences for colleges occurred much later than it did for universities in Canada. Prior to conference play, some colleges competed against one another and also against university teams, while others fielded teams in local leagues. Between 1961 and 1971, institutes in seven provinces established conferences to develop sport, fitness, and recreational opportunities at the college level.

By 1965, college hockey in Quebec was in its 25th year and encompassed the junior, juvenile, intermediate and senior ranks. Off the ice, the *Federation des Associations Sportives Collegiales du Quebec* (FASCQ) began to formalize college sport in the province under one sanctioning body. In 1988, reorganization brought FASCQ under the umbrella of *Federation Quebecoise du Sport Etudiant*/Quebec Student Sports Federation (FQSE/QSSF). Over the years, a three-tier configuration emerged with AAA, AA, and A college leagues.

The AAA College League, in existence from 1979 through 1988, had as many as eight teams and as few as four. Original members included *les Titans de Limoilou*, *les Condors de Saint-Georges*, *les Filons de la Region de l'Amiante*, and *les Cheminots de Saint-Jerome*. The league produced Quebec's best showings at the CCAA Championships with *les Laureats du Cegep de Saint-Hyacinthe* (1983-1984) and *les Patriotes du Cegep de Saint-Laurent* (1987) winning national titles.

Now in its fourth decade, the AA College League has had as many as 18 members. Currently, five teams compete for league supremacy—*le College Lafleche*, *les Gaillards de Jonquiere*, *les Patriotes de Saint-Laurent*, *les Faucons de Levis-Lauzon*, and *les Cougars de Lennoxville*. The A College League operated for four seasons between 1986 and 1990 with five different teams participating.

Out west in Alberta, a mandate to regulate and promote athletic activities within the province resulted in the creation of the Western Inter-College Conference in 1964. By 1969 the WICC had evolved into the Alberta Colleges Athletic Conference (ACAC). The first conference hockey game occurred on January 15, 1966, when the Northern Alberta Institute of Technology (NAIT) downed Camrose Lutheran College, 7–1. Mount Royal Junior College (now Mount Royal College) and the Southern Alberta Institute of Technology (SAIT) also competed in the first season. By the 1971–72 campaign, only three colleges engaged in conference hockey. Presently, the league is composed of eight teams in two provinces (Alberta and Saskatchewan). Over the years, five members have fielded teams for at least 30 seasons and ACAC representatives have won more CCAA titles (16) than all other conferences combined. Four of these teams—the NAIT Ooks from Edmonton, the Mount Royal College Cougars from Calgary, the Red Deer College Kings from Red Deer, and the SAIT Trojans from Calgary—have won multiple gold medals at the national level.

Founded in May, 1967, the Nova Scotia College Conference (NSCC) is now known as the Atlantic Conference Athletic Association (ACAA) due to growth beyond provincial boundaries. A total of 10 colleges fielded teams in the conference between 1967 and 1987. Formerly known as Xavier College and Saint-Francis Xavier University-Sydney Campus, the (University) College of Cape Breton dominated the conference by winning 15 league titles and making an unprecedented 11 national tournament appearances. In addition, the Capers captured seven Cape Breton Senior League championships and two Nova Scotia Senior A championships.

Less than a month after the NSCC's establishment, the Ontario Colleges Athletic Association (OCAA) came into being. Northern College (Kirkland Lake), St. Clair College (Windsor), Fanshawe College (London), George Brown College (Toronto), Centennial College (Scarborough), Mohawk College (Hamilton) and Algonquin College (Nepean) fielded teams in the inaugural season of 1967–68. By the early 1970s, the league had expanded to 22 teams in four divisions. Currently, there are six teams in the conference. The OCAA has been represented at each one of the CCAA Championships, but only the St. Clair College Saints (1976) and the Cambrian College Golden Shield (1997) have brought home national titles. Beginning with the 1985–86 season, the Humber College Hawks from Etobicoke, with Dana Shutt at the helm, won five consecutive conference championships and acquired three silver medals at the nationals.

Following the introduction of exhibition play in 1968, the institutes of the Manitoba Colleges Athletic Association organized championships in 1970–71. Between 1970 and 1986, Red River Community College (Winnipeg), Assiniboine Community College (Brandon) and Keewatin Community College (The Pas) were conference pillars and often competed in other leagues. In addition to winning 12 MCAA titles, Red River also became champions of the Manitoba Intermediate B Hockey League. Assiniboine won titles in the Brandon Commercial League and the Manitoba Southwest Hockey League as well as three conference championships. In 1983, the three teams became charter members of the Midwest International College Hockey League (MICHL).

From 1969 through 1990, the Prairie Athletic Conference

(PAC) sanctioned hockey in Saskatchewan. The Saskatchewan Technical Institute (now SIAST Palliser) from Moose Jaw, Kelsey Institute (now SIAST Kelsey) from Saskatoon and Briercrest Bible Institute (now Briercrest Bible College) from Caronport were the mainstays of the conference with Kelsey winning 12 PAC championships. As many as six teams and as few as three competed in the conference over the years with the University of Regina, Athol Murray College of Notre Dame, Canadian Bible College and Canadian Forces Base Moose Jaw all participating.

In 1985, the PAC teams from Saskatchewan joined the Midwest International College Hockey League, which already included post secondary institutes from Manitoba and North Dakota. The MICHL received substantial support from the NHL's Winnipeg Jets who donated the championship trophy (the Jets Cup) and allowed Tim Watters to serve as honorary league president. At its peak during the 1985–86 season, the league included the Kelsey Institute Amaruks, the Saskatchewan Technical Institute Beavers, the Briercrest Bible College Clippers, the Athol Murray College of Notre Dame Hounds, the Assiniboine Community College Cougars, the Keewatin Community College Badgers, the Red River Community College Rebels and the North Dakota State University-Bottineau Lumberjacks. A season later, the league dwindled down to four teams as Notre Dame moved to another league and athletic programs were cut in Manitoba. For the 1989–90 season, the Saskatchewan colleges joined forces for a last hurrah under the PAC banner before cutbacks took a further toll. Today, the Hounds are in the Saskatchewan Junior Hockey League while the Clippers are in the ACAC.

Established in 1970, the Totem Conference Athletic Association (TCAA) changed its name to the British Columbia Colleges' Athletic Association (BCCAA) in 1986. League play in Canada's westernmost province existed between 1971 and 1979 and 1983 and 1989. Of the 10 institutes to participate in the conference, the Cariboo College Chiefs were the most successful, winning 12 of 15 league titles. After Cliff Russell guided the Chiefs to three TCAA titles in the early 1970s, Terry Bangen coached Cariboo to nine conference championships and five consecutive appearances at the CCAA Championships between 1976 and 1988.

Prior to the existence of the TCAA, the Pacific Intercollegiate Hockey League (PIHL) brought together college and university teams from British Columbia, Washington and Alaska. PIHL competitors from B.C. included Cariboo College in Kamloops, the British Columbia Institute of Technology (BCIT) from Burnaby, Malaspina College of Nanaimo, New Caledonia College of Prince George, Selkirk College in Castlegar, Simon Fraser University in Burnaby and a University of British Columbia junior varsity squad from Vancouver. Gonzaga University in Spokane, the University of Seattle and Alaska Methodist University from Anchorage added an international flavor to the league.

With the development of conferences, the college game also acquired unique characteristics. The OCAA became one of the first Canadian leagues to experiment with the elimination of the two-line offside and the rule has been adopted throughout the CCAA. For the most part, the CCAA and its conferences follow the rules of the Canadian Hockey Association.

NATIONAL GLORY

Interprovincial competition between Canadian colleges began in 1971 when the provincial conferences of British Columbia, Alberta, Saskatchewan, and Manitoba founded the 4-West Championships. The provincial conferences of Quebec and Ontario initiated similar competitions in 1972. Following the success of these competitions, the Canadian Colleges Athletic Association was formally established in 1973. Two years later the CCAA awarded the first CCAA national hockey championship tournament to Sydney, Nova Scotia.

On March 21, 1975, at the Sydney Arena, the 1974–75 champions of the 4-West, OCAA, FASCQ and NSCC laced their skates with the opportunity to advance to the championship final or proceed to the bronze medal game the following day. Of the four, none had faced the obstacles of the Camrose Lutheran College Vikings (now Augustana University College) from Camrose, Alberta. While some CCAA members had enrollments approaching 10,000, Camrose College had a student body of 390. A local scribe pegged the Vikings as the ACAC's fourth best at the season's start only to see Joe Voytechek coach the team to their first ACAC and 4-West titles. Camrose then doubled the hometown College of Cape Breton Capers 6–3 to advance against the favored St. Clair College Saints who had five OCAA titles in the conference's first eight seasons. The underdog Vikings jumped out to a 3–0 lead in the first and extended the advantage to 4–0 in the second before the Saints cut the margin to 4–2. In the third, Camrose added two more goals to score a 6–2 win and become the inaugural winners of the CCAA Championship Bowl.

During the Christmas break of their championship season, the Vikings made a memorable trip to Europe, playing games in Sweden, Denmark and Norway. The reception that the Camrose squad received set the stage for a return trip to Europe five years later. On a train to the Soviet Union, team officials tossed around the idea of hosting the clubs they played against. Since its humble beginnings, the Viking Cup has evolved into a biennial event featuring national teams from Europe and North America as well as all-star teams from the Canadian Junior A Hockey League.

Though Camrose College hosted the second CCAA Championships in 1976, the Vikings were not back to defend their crown and the absence of the host team was felt as the champions of the 4-West, OCAA, FASCQ and NSCC gathered. The St. Clair College Saints, the College of Cape Breton Capers, the Selkirk College Saints and *les Faucons de Levis-Lauzon* competed. The semifinals unfolded with St. Clair downing Cape Breton, 10–4, and Selkirk shading Levis-Lauzon, 7–6, in overtime. St. Clair capped off an undefeated season with a national title as Tim Ornstead netted three goals in an 11–2 triumph over Selkirk.

The 1977 CCAA Championships at Oakville, Ontario, became a five-team, five-game affair when a host entry supplemented the four champion berths. The extra game saw the hosts square off against the fourth seed with the winner going into the semifinals. With strong support, the host Sheridan College Bruins advanced to the final by edging the Dawson College Blues, 3–2, and the College of Cape Breton Capers, 4–3, only to fall to the 4-West champion Red Deer College Kings, 5–1.

Further changes were made to the format of the CCAA Championships in Montreal in 1978. A wild card team entered the mix, expanded the tournament to six schools. Two of the qualifiers received a bye into the semifinals. After winning consecutive 4-West titles, Red Deer College outscored the Centennial College Colts, 7–4, to move within a victory of repeating as national champions. Meanwhile, the College of Cape Breton ended the gold medal aspirations of *les Titans d'Andre-Laurendeau* with an 11–6 victory and the Humber College Hawks with a 7–6 win. Following 60 minutes of the championship final, the Capers and the Kings were deadlocked at 3–3. In the full 10-minute overtime, the teams exchanged markers before Cape Breton's Kevin MacRae intercepted an errant pass and netted a shorthand goal at 9:44 to capture the hardware the Capers had donated four years earlier. The Sydney squad was coached by Dr. Carl "Bucky" Buchanan, who led Cape Breton to the greatest of its many successes over the years, including four of its five medal-winning performances at the national level—one gold, one silver and two bronze.

Having been unseated as champions by Cape Breton, the Red Deer College Kings then made the most of a wild card berth at the 1979 CCAA Championships in Saint-Georges de Beauce, Quebec. They blanked *les Patriotes de Saint-Laurent,* 6–0, and then edged the Capers, 5–4. In the gold medal game, the Kings scored an 11–4 victory over the 4-West champion SAIT Trojans to become the first multiple winner of national titles.

The 1980 Championships at Red Deer, Alberta, took on yet another new look as four of five conference champions and a host entry competed. In preliminary action, the 4-West/ACAC champion Red Deer College Kings defeated the College of Cape Breton Capers, 12–2, while the SAIT Trojans outscored the Briercrest Bible Institute Clippers 11–6 and the Seneca College Braves, 9–1, to set the stage for a second consecutive all-Alberta final. Alvin Szott scored five goals, including one on a penalty shot, as the Kings rolled to a 14–1 win. Under the coaching of Allan Ferchuk, now president of the CCAA, Red Deer had won three national championships in four years and had come within an overtime tally of winning four consecutive titles.

With the demise of the 4-West Championships, the 1981 CCAA Championships at Kitchener, Ontario, reverted to a four-team affair with three regional representatives and the host Conestoga College Condors. Interconference qualifiers resulted in the SAIT Trojans (Alberta-Saskatchewan), the Humber College Hawks (Manitoba-Ontario) and the College of Cape Breton Capers (Quebec-Nova Scotia) advancing. In semifinal play, the Trojans doubled the Condors, 4–2, while the Capers defeated the Hawks 7–5. After two silvers, SAIT captured gold with a, 7–4, victory over Cape Breton.

The 1982 CCAA Championships at Calgary also featured three regional representatives and a host entry. The NAIT Ooks received the host berth when the ACAC champion SAIT Trojans advanced from the Alberta-Saskatchewan qualifier. Because the FASCQ playoffs were still under way, the fifth place *les Titans du College de Limoilou* received the call to represent Canada's largest province and moved on to the nationals after winning the Quebec-Nova Scotia qualifier. *Les Titans* dropped a 10–3 decision to the Ooks, while the Seneca College Braves upset the Trojans, 4–3, to set the championship final pairing. With Ken Hodge stopping 43 shots, NAIT blanked Seneca, 3–0.

The 1983 CCAA Championships at North York, Ontario, expanded to seven teams with six conference champions and a host entry participating. The conference of the defending national champions (ACAC) received a first-round bye while the remaining teams required a win to advance into the semifinals. Saint-Hyacinthe doubled the Kelsey Institute Amaruks 4–2 and outscored Assiniboine Community College 14–8 only to battle five time finalists Red Deer College for gold. *Les Laureats* defeated the Kings, 4–1, to become the first team to win the CCAA Championship Bowl in their inaugural season.

Seven conference champions and a host entry took part in the 1984 CCAA Championships at Saint-Hyacinthe, Quebec. The expanded tournament featured quarterfinals, semifinals and a championship final. Coach Clement Jodoin's defending champions from Saint-Hyacinthe became only the second team to win back to back titles with a 12–2 victory over the Cariboo College Chiefs, an 8–2 win over the College of Cape Breton Capers and a 10–2 triumph over *les Condors de Saint-Georges.*

The NAIT Ooks were the focus of attention at the 1985 CCAA Championships in Moose Jaw, Saskatchewan. Not only did NAIT sport a perfect record in the regular season (25–0–0) and in the playoffs (5–0–0), but the Ooks had also posted a 5–3 victory over the eventual Canadian university champion York Yeomen at the Altjahres Cup in Adelboden, Switzerland. At the CCAA tourney, the Ooks downed the Cariboo College Chiefs, 8–2, the Seneca College Braves, 5–2, and *les Vulkins de Victoriaville,* 9–2, to become the first team from the ACAC to go unbeaten in the regular season, the league playoffs, and the national championships.

NAIT's undefeated streak against ACAC competition ran to 50 games before they were defeated during the 1985–86 campaign, but the Ooks entered the 1986 CCAA Championships at Kamloops, British Columbia, as consecutive champions of the Viking Cup International Hockey Tournament. After scoring a 13–0 win over the Douglas College Royals and a 7–3 victory over Red River Community College, NAIT overcame two-goal deficits on three occasions to record an 8–6 triumph over the Humber College Hawks and retain the national title.

The 1987 CCAA Championships at Camrose, Alberta, was reduced to a seven-team affair with the demise of the MCAA. The necessary change in format saw one three-team pool determine two semifinalists through round-robin play while a four-team pool decided the other two semifinalists through single elimination. The possibility of an all Alberta final ended when *Cegep de Saint-Laurent* doubled the NAIT Ooks, 4–2, and the Humber College Hawks edged Camrose Lutheran College, 7–6, in the semifinals. Mario Thyer tallied twice in the tournament finalé to pace *les Patriotes* in a 4–1 win over the Hawks.

With no representative from Nova Scotia, the 1988 CCAA Championships at Levis, Quebec, saw six teams going for gold. The participants were divided into three-team pools with the top two teams from each advancing to the semifinals. The Mount Royal College Cougars then defeated the Humber College Hawks, 5–3, and *le Bleu-Blanc-Rouge du College Francais* downed *les Faucons du Cegep de Levis-Lauzon,* 12–3. Mike Cormack scored 11 minutes into the second overtime of the championship final to give Mount Royal College a 7–6 victory in the title game.

The folding of Quebec's AAA College League resulted in the defending national champions from Mount Royal College drawing a wild-card entry into the six-team 1989 CCAA Championships in Edmonton. Following the elimination of Mount Royal and BCIT in round-robin pool play, the NAIT Ooks outscored the SIAST Palliser Campus Beavers 12–4, while the Red Deer College Kings tripled the Humber College Hawks 6–2 in the semifinals. The Hawks then defeated the Beavers, 11–2, in the last bronze medal game to be played to date at the CCAA Championships. In the title game, Scott Melnyk completed the hat trick to rally the Ooks for a 5–4 come-from-behind victory over the Kings in their fourth championship triumph.

The collapse of college hockey in British Columbia led to changes at the national level in 1989–90. The NAIT Ooks swept the PAC champion SIAST Kelsey Campus Amaruks in a best-of-three qualifier to earn the right to play the OCAA champion Humber College Hawks in the two-team 1990 CCAA Championships at Etobicoke, Ontario. In the best-of-three series, NAIT triumphed, 2–1, in triple overtime but then lost 2–1 to Humber to set the stage for a dramatic deciding game. Mark Hilton scored in the second overtime to lift the Ooks to a 4–3 victory over the Hawks.

For the next five seasons, the CCAA Championships were not held due to economic difficulties. When the event resumed in 1996 in Kitchener, Ontario, the NAIT Ooks were again victorious, sweeping Cambrian College with 7–5 and 6–2 victories.

The host entry was reinstated for the 1997 CCAA Championships, which were again held in Kitchener. In the round-robin portion, the ACAC champion SAIT Trojans defeated the OCAA champion Cambrian College Golden Shield 5–2 and the host Conestoga College Condors, 6–1. The Golden Shield shaded the Condors, 3–1, to reach the finals where they got their revenge against SAIT with a 3–2 victory in the gold medal match.

The 1998 CCAA Championships in Sudbury, Ontario, were hosted by the defending champs from Cambrian College. The Golden Shield advanced to the finals despite a loss to the Mount Royal College Cougars (who also beat the OCAA champion Seneca College Braves, 9–3, in preliminary action). In the finalé, Mike Pozzo's backhand shot at 4:56 of the first overtime gave the Cougars a 4–3 victory over the Golden Shield. Mount Royal College continued its reign at the 1999 CCAA Championships in Kitchener. After defeating Cambrian College, 12–4, and the Conestoga College Condors, 6–2, in the round robin, Jason Fricker recorded the shutout in the championship game as the Cougars blanked the host Condors, 6–0. A common thread between Mount Royal's three national titles is Scott Atkinson, who was an assistant coach in 1988 and head coach in 1998 and 1999.

The 2000 CCAA Championships in North York featured the Seneca College Sting, the SAIT Trojans and the Sir Sandford Fleming College Knights (who acquired the host berth when Seneca won the OCAA championship). The ACAC champion Trojans outscored the Sting, 9–3, and the Knights, 7–1, in round-robin play. SAIT then became the fifth CCAA member to win multiple national championships with a 16–2 romp over Sir Sandford Fleming. Though 19 seasons separated the SAIT championship teams of Bob Moore and Ken Babey, both coaches had directed their squads to two silver medals at nationals before winning gold.

International Prestige

The CCAA's influence extends from minor hockey to the pros within and beyond Canada's borders. Many former CCAA coaches have been part of NHL coaching staffs, including Terry Bangen (Vancouver), Ray Bennett (Los Angeles), Mike Johnston (Vancouver), Clement Jodoin (Pittsburgh, Quebec, Montreal), Jacques Martin (St. Louis, Chicago, Quebec, Colorado, Ottawa), Perry Pearn (Winnipeg, Ottawa) and Drew Remenda (San Jose). Other CCAA coaches, such as Alain Chainey and John Phelan, are involved in the NHL's scouting community.

CCAA players who have donned skates in the NHL include Brett Callighen of Centennial College (Edmonton), Dean Clark of NAIT (Edmonton), Mike Heidt of Mount Royal College (Los Angeles), Joe Juneau of *Cegep de Levis-Lauzon* (Boston, Washington, Buffalo, Ottawa, Phoenix), Ken Lovsin (Washington) and Mitch Molloy (Buffalo) of Camrose Lutheran College, Del Hall (California) and Dan Newman (New York Rangers, Montreal, Edmonton) of St. Clair College and Vincent Riendeau of *College de Sherbrooke* (Montreal, St. Louis, Detroit, Boston).

The CCAA also has strong ties to international hockey. Mike Babcock, Terry Bangen, Ray Bennett, Dean Clark, Dale Henwood, Mike Johnston, Perry Pearn and Drew Remenda have guided Canadian teams at events ranging from the World Junior Championships to the Olympics. The number of former CCAA players to play for Canada's national team is in the double digits. In addition, members of the Canadian Olympic teams from the CCAA include Joe Juneau, Ken Lovsin and Serge Roy of *Cegep de Saint-Hyacinthe*. Three players from Mount Royal College have also participated in the Olympics for other countries: Matt Kabayama (Japan), Chad Biafore (Italy) and Mike Heidt (Germany).

CCAA Champions

The CCAA Championship Bowl was donated by the College of Cape Breton in 1975 when they hosted the first Canadian College Athletic Association (CCAA) National Hockey Championships. In 1996, the award was renamed as the Al Bohonous CCAA Championship Bowl in memory of the former Mount Royal College athletic director.

Season	Champions	Runner-up
1974–75	Camrose Lutheran College Vikings	St. Clair College Saints
1975–76	St. Clair College Saints	Selkirk College Saints
1976–77	Red Deer College Kings	Sheridan College Bruins
1977–78	College of Cape Breton Capers	Red Deer College Kings
1978–79	Red Deer College Kings	SAIT Trojans
1979–80	Red Deer College Kings	SAIT Trojans
1980–81	SAIT Trojans	College of Cape Breton Capers
1981–82	NAIT Ooks	Seneca College Braves
1982–83	Les Laureats de Saint-Hyacinthe	Red Deer College Kings
1983–84	Les Laureats de Saint-Hyacinthe	Les Condors de Saint-Georges
1984–85	NAIT Ooks	Les Vulkins de Victoriaville
1985–86	NAIT Ooks	Humber College Hawks
1986–87	Les Patriotes de Saint-Laurent	Humber College Hawks
1987–88	Mount Royal College Cougars	Le Bleu-Blanc-Rouge du College Francais
1988–89	NAIT Ooks	Red Deer College Kings
1989–90	NAIT Ooks	Humber College Hawks
1990–1995	No CCAA hockey championship	
1995–96	NAIT Ooks	Cambrian College Golden Shield
1996–97	Cambrian College Golden Shield	SAIT Trojans
1997–98	Mount Royal College Cougars	Cambrian College Golden Shield
1998–99	Mount Royal College Cougars	Conestoga College Condors
1999–2000	SAIT Trojans	Sir Sandford Fleming College Knights

DEVELOPING HOCKEY SKILLS IN CANADA

Brian O'Byrne

HOCKEY, LIKE ALL COMPETITIVE SPORTS, is driven by enthusiasm and emotion from top to bottom. From house league to the NHL, from volunteer coach to Hart Trophy winner, people are there because they love the game and care about it.

Minor hockey and player development in Canada—for all the criticism levelled against it—is driven by this same passion and love of hockey. So why does Canada's development system sometimes seem off track?

When Canadian hockey had no equal and there were only 120 jobs in the NHL, player evaluation and development didn't matter as enough supremely talented players made it through to keep the pipeline full as it wended its way from minor hockey through junior to the pros.

Before World War II, minor hockey was a much more casual proposition than it is today. Most leagues were organized by churches, settlement houses or ethnic social clubs, but hockey for kids coalesced around neighborhood outdoor rinks where a winter-long crazy quilt of organized games, pickup and shinny ran until nightfall or until the lights were turned out. Players logged limitless hours on the ice, learning from each other and from endless noodling with the puck.

In the 1950s, as Canadian suburbs sprawled and new families came of age for hockey, communities began to offer hockey programs open to all. The best players from these "house leagues" were soon named to all-star teams that played other all-star teams, creating an elite tier of minor hockey.

Even today, it is the house-league system that drives minor hockey. It is Canada's great strength in minor hockey: a decent low-pressure hockey experience available to anyone who wants it. Other hockey countries base their system on streaming players and focusing on the elite. Canada offers a mass experience.

Hockey for the best players—the top 20 percent in any age group—presents an entirely different set of issues. At the heart of the issue is a simple question: Why aren't we developing more skilled players?

In the European model, a system is in place that trains players to be good through detailed expectations, measurement and testing. These programs extend off the ice as well and cover all aspects of skill development, training, nutrition, psychology and fitness. The best players are the ones who master the curriculum and pass the tests and they are the ones streamed up and forward.

In Canadian hockey, there aren't any formal measurements. Instead, an intuitive yardstick is used that measures the elusive quality of "being good" which, in Canadian minor hockey, seems to mean a combination of size and being able to skate reasonably well. We perceive hockey as a robust, physical game that rewards aggression. The European perception starts with speed, agility and finesse. Both systems try to create hockey environments that allow players who conform to these perceptions to shine.

Canadian hockey players are also felt to lead the world in a combination of grit and toughness that is known as "heart." Fans of Canadian teams in international hockey—and even the Canadian players and coaches themselves—believe that having more heart provides an important edge, one that enables their teams to come together, refuse to lose and find a way to win. Eight gold medals at the World Junior Championships from 1988 to 1997 supported the theory that Canada's heart advantage could carry the day, but more recent events have demonstrated that other nations can play with heart and that a combination of skill and heart has the best chance to succeed.

Top young players in Canada participate in a system that is for all intents, minor professional hockey without salaries. Just like the pro game, elite minor or junior hockey is based on a huge number of games played and a constant expectation to win. This setup is incompatible with developing the skills of our best young players. NHL scouts and general managers have figured this out. Professional hockey now picks its talent from an international pool that provides many players developed in other systems. Today, NHL teams pick skills first and the very best European players have had their skills developed.

A strange byproduct of Canadian minor hockey is that players from small communities that don't have enough all-star players to fill out a true "AAA" roster often arrive as more complete players than urban superstars who've been trapped in a win-at-all-costs AAA systems. Stars on small-town teams have had a chance to stand out, exploit their abilities, take chances and improve rapidly. The system played by many AAA teams might win games, but does so at the expense of player development.

The volunteers and paid staff who manage Canadian minor hockey have to make some choices regarding player development. Skills are rarely developed in games and never developed sitting on the bench. It's the quality of time spent that counts. Playing 80 to 100 games in a season doesn't necessarily make a player better. Focused practices and drills to develop skills do.

A vibrant training environment isn't easy to put in place, but the rewards for doing so are tremendous. Canada, despite producing the majority of the world's players for a century, has produced few of the game's greatest teachers. We have to commit the resources to develop more teachers of hockey skills.

We have to reassess the game from the players' point of view, removing the focus on winning. Teaching skills is a very different coaching job than managing people or changing players from behind the bench. In the European model, a team's training staff is much higher on the food chain than their North American equivalents. Running an effective practice is a difficult job that terrifies many volunteer coaches. It takes lots of preparation to be effective. Coaches must work in environments that encourage this effort.

A commitment to improved skills requires recognized standards and opportunities to measure progress by testing. Programs—both formal and informal—are required to enable young players to work on the skills necessary to meet these standards.

A fundamental change is required in minor hockey in that formal recognition must be given to the principle that the game is based on skills instead of physical play. The game of hockey can be intimidating if the rules don't adequately restrict physical or rough play. Thousands of talented kids have quit hockey because of this in the past, yet skilled players have the ability to protect themselves, slip a check and start a counterattack. For all the protection that he received from his teammates, it was Wayne Gretzky's skill that allowed him to rewrite the NHL record book while rarely getting hit.

There is a simple way to test the assumption that skills development programs yield results. In AAA leagues across Canada, recruit two teams and have them play half the number of games as their opponents. Award four points for a win and two for a tie so that they can remain competitive in the standings. Use the time freed up by a shorter schedule to run intensive skill development practices. By the season's end, it's likely that the teams who've played less and practiced more will be markedly more competitive in their leagues. Players will be more skilled and have more fun.

Modification to the rules also must be undertaken to discourage the slow-moving dump-it-in, chip-it-out systems so many teams play.

Canadians must clarify their thinking, and not confuse minor hockey—which is the only opportunity for skill development that most players will receive—with the pro game beamed into our homes on TV night after night. They should be regarded as utterly different games, from their rules to the attitudes that govern play. As long as pro hockey standards and expectations are applied in minor hockey, Canadians will have to live with the results returned from international competitions and from the NHL Entry Draft.

NCAA Champions

1948 Michigan Wolverines
1949 Boston College Eagles
1950 Colorado College Tigers
1951 Michigan Wolverines
1952 Michigan Wolverines
1953 Michigan Wolverines
1954 RPI Engineers
1955 Michigan Wolverines
1956 Michigan Wolverines
1957 Colorado College Tigers
1958 Denver Pioneers
1959 North Dakota Fighting Sioux
1960 Denver Pioneers
1961 Denver Pioneers
1962 Michigan Tech Huskies
1963 North Dakota Fighting Sioux
1964 Michigan Wolverines
1965 Michigan Tech Huskies
1966 Michigan State Spartans
1967 Cornell Big Red
1968 Denver Pioneers
1969 Denver Pioneers
1970 Cornell Big Red
1971 Boston University Terriers
1972 Boston University Terriers
1973 Wisconsin Badgers
1974 Minnesota Golden Gophers
1975 Michigan Tech Huskies
1976 Minnesota Golden Gophers
1977 Wisconsin Badgers
1978 Boston University Terriers
1979 Minnesota Golden Gophers
1980 North Dakota Fighting Sioux
1981 Wisconsin Badgers
1982 North Dakota Fighting Sioux
1983 Wisconsin Badgers
1984 Bowling Green Falcons
1985 RPI Engineers
1986 Michigan State Spartans
1987 North Dakota Fighting Sioux
1988 Lake Superior Lakers
1989 Harvard Crimson
1990 Wisconsin Badgers
1991 Northern Michigan U. Wildcats
1992 Lake Superior Lakers
1993 University of Maine Black Bears
1994 Lake Superior Lakers
1995 Boston University Terriers
1996 Michigan Wolverines
1997 North Dakota Fighting Sioux
1998 Michigan Wolverines
1999 University of Maine Black Bears
2000 North Dakota Fighting Sioux

Hobey Baker Award Winners

NCAA Most Valuable Player

Year	Hobey Winner	Position	School
2000	Michael Mottau	Defense	Boston College
1999	Jason Krog	Center	New Hampshire
1998	Chris Drury	Center	Boston University
1997	Brendan Morrison	Center	Michigan
1996	Brian Bonin	Center	Minnesota
1995	Brian Holzinger	Center	Bowling Green
1994	Chris Marinucci	Forward	Minn-Duluth
1993	Paul Kariya	Forward	Maine
1992	Scott Pellerin	Forward	Maine
1991	Dave Emma	Forward	Boston College
1990	Kip Miller	Forward	Michigan State
1989	Lane MacDonald	Forward	Harvard
1988	Robb Stauber	Goalie	Minnesota
1987	Tony Hrkac	Forward	North Dakota
1986	Scott Fusco	Forward	Harvard
1985	Bill Watson	Forward	Minn-Duluth
1984	Tom Kurvers	Defense	Minn-Duluth
1983	Mark Fusco	Defense	Harvard
1982	George McPhee	Forward	Bowling Green
1981	Neal Broten	Forward	Minnesot

CHAPTER 16

American Hockey

The State of the Game

Hockey in America

Kevin Allen

As National Hockey League vice president of media relations Frank Brown considers how to describe hockey's growth in the United States, he turns to a map in his office to find the most direct route. Each significant junior team and every pro team is highlighted on this colorful geographic rendering of North America. The Western Pro League franchises are yellow. The American Hockey League teams are orange. Each league has its own hue. As Brown stares at his map, he sees America's remarkable growth in a rainbow of colors.

"This map tells a remarkable story," Brown said. "The story is that from the Monroe Moccasins of the Western Pro League, to the Cedar Rapids Rough Riders of the United States Hockey League, to the Fresno Falcons [of the West Coast Hockey League] there isn't a lot of empty space."

Over the last decade, the interest in hockey has spiked dramatically in all regions of the United States. Once considered a game of only regional interest, hockey has become a trendy national pastime. Participation is up, television ratings are up, merchandise sales are up, and— most importantly—awareness is up. Most areas in the country have been exposed to hockey in some manner, whether it is through the 98 professional minor league teams, 54 NCAA teams, or the NHL's expanded national footprint. Then there's the American youth hockey explosion. In 1990–91, USA Hockey registered a total of 195,125 players and 10,316 officials. It didn't even bother to count the coaches. In 1998–99, USA Hockey registered 421,399 players, 53,638 coaches and 21,491 officials. Adult recreational level hockey doubled in size during the decade—with the number of teams increasing from 28,709 to 63,874 heading into the 1999–2000 season. Even Hawaii had 222 youth teams and 133 adult men's recreational teams in 1999. Florida has 1,614 adult men's teams and 6,286 youth teams.

Beyond participation, recognition of hockey is up coast-to-coast. "When I pick up my kids at school I see tons of kids wearing hockey jackets, or NHL jerseys, or shirts from their local hockey association," said Central Collegiate Hockey Association commissioner Tom Anastos. "When I was a kid, that was so uncommon. It would have been incredible to see more than a couple of kids wearing that stuff."

Here are the factors contributing to hockey's growth in the United States:

Lake Placid Fever: Those youngsters who became interested in hockey because of the USA's gold medal triumph at the 1980 Winter Olympic Games in Lake Placid are now the parents of a new generation of players. (Highly prized 2000 NHL draft prospect Brooks Orpik of Boston College was named after 1980 U.S. coach Herb Brooks.)

Gretzky's migration: When Wayne Gretzky was traded from the Edmonton Oilers to the Los Angeles Kings, the view of hockey in America was altered forever. He gave the sport credibility every time his face was featured on a national commercial. He gave the sport broader exposure and softened the game's image, particularly among those who perceived hockey to be nothing more than scheduled mayhem. After Gretzky came to Los Angeles, even people who couldn't name one NHL team knew Gretzky was the game's top player. His move to the United States made hockey more appealing to Madison Avenue. It's widely held that the NHL's growth in America wouldn't have happened so quickly had then Kings owner Bruce McNall not hatched his wild idea of trading for Gretzky.

Following the sun: In 1990, the NHL had 21 teams and 14 were in America. In 2000-2001, the NHL will have 30 teams and 24 will be American based. In the past decade, the NHL has expanded to southern and northern Florida, San Jose, Anaheim, Nashville and Atlanta, and shuffled teams (two of them Canadian) to Phoenix, Dallas and Colorado. Each of those teams has spawned rapidly growing youth hockey organizations. "I think some day we are going to see NHL players coming out of Florida," Panthers president Bill Torrey says. "They skate all the time on in-line skates when they aren't on the ice. We started with 300 or 400 in our street program. Now we have 15,000."

In-line skating craze: Youngsters, particularly in the sun-belt areas, have been introduced to the concept of hockey through in-line skating. It's too early to tell whether this will have a lasting carry-over into ice hockey, but it has stirred some interest. "Another great thing about hockey is that it is the only sport that translates into other mediums," Brown says. "You can play it on foot in your driveway, as many of our pros have. You can play in rollers in the schoolyard or in the street. And you can play it on ice skates. In football, baseball and basketball that doesn't happen. You play it on foot, period."

USA Hockey boasts about 70,000 registered in-line players. "I think that helps a great deal in bringing the game to places where they have no rinks," says USA Hockey executive director Doug Palazzari.

Construction zone: When baby boomers were growing up in America, hockey was restricted to northern climates because that's where outdoor rinks could freeze in the winter. Even into the 1980s there was a shortage of indoor rinks. But the steady increase in the number of indoor rinks, particularly in sun-belt areas, has helped fuel growth.

"Frankly we have to fight to keep up with the demand," said Chuck Menke, USA Hockey's director of media relations. "And we aren't keeping up yet. That's one of the biggest issues in the game today. With the increased expansion, ice time is still at a premium—particularly in warmer climates. As this sport continues to grow, we just need more and more rinks."

Most of today's arenas are going up with multiple ice sheets to help ease the difficulty. Private ownership has replaced municipal funding for most ice facilities.

Major impact from minor leagues: U.S. interest in minor-league hockey has been tornado-like in its intensity—swirling, at times, out of control. For example, when the East Coast Hockey League was launched in 1988–89, the league had five teams and the expansion fee was $25,000. Today the league has 28 teams and plans to expand to 31 teams within three years. The expansion fee is $2 million. Eighteen of the ECHL's 28 teams are located in the Sun Belt. States with teams include Alabama, North and South Carolina, Florida, Georgia, Louisiana, Mississippi and Arkansas. How rabid can the fans be below the Mason-Dixon line? The Florida Everblades, located near Naples, were in their second year in 1999–2000 and sold out their final 27 regular-season games in a building that seats 7,181.

Not just a man's world: Women's hockey is considered by many to be the fastest growing sport in America. At the start of the 1990s about 6,335 females of all ages were registered in the USA Hockey program. Today, almost 40,000 are playing the sport. Women's college hockey also has known noteworthy growth over the last three or four years. Awareness of women's hockey was aided significantly by Team USA capturing the gold medal at the 1998 Winter Olympics in Nagano. The triumph was considered significant enough that the team was put on a Wheaties box. While her contributions are modest compared to those of Wayne Gretzky, U.S. standout Cammi Granato, sister of NHL player Tony Granato, has enjoyed a national exposure that has aided the growth of the sport in the United States.

All of these factors have contributed to USA Hockey enjoying steady growth for about 15 years, according to Doug Palazzari. The growth rate has been at about five percent per year in recent years. "As an organization we had a vision and preparedness for this growth spurt," said Palazzari, a Minnesotan who played in the NHL. That's an important issue because USA Hockey was not prepared to take advantage of the exposure generated by the 1980 Olympic team. Today, when a community wants to launch a youth hockey program, USA Hockey is ready to assist with every aspect from providing insurance to offering suggestions on how to finance an arena.

"I don't think anything is slowing us down," Palazzari said. "But if anything will slow us, it will be rinks and cost. Every high school has a gymnasium, and if you need a baseball, soccer, or football field, public money will build it. But only a few northern cities will consider a hockey rink. And the cost of hockey for the players certainly is an issue."

Undeniably hockey enjoys a much higher level of sophistication than it had 10 or 20 years ago. Even junior teams now are run with a pro mentality. "The money tied to the sport is far more significant, and not just at the NHL level," said Tom Anastos, who was commissioner of the North American (junior) Hockey League before taking the CCHA position. "When I played at the highest level of youth hockey—which was junior hockey—it was all localized. You lived at home and went to the game with your parents. Only your family, your girlfriend and some of your friends came to watch. You didn't move away from home like they do today. An operating budget was probably about $50,000 and that would have been a very well-financed team. Today teams are running around with budgets of $500,000."

USA Hockey now offers an Under-18 national development program in Ann Arbor, Michigan, for the most gifted and talented players. The theory is that just as America's top musicians, dancers and actresses might attend a fine arts academy to hone their talents, a prime hockey athlete should have an opportunity to be in an environment where he can hone his talents. Players spend as much time in the weight room and on the practice ice as they do competing in games. The idea was to create better elite players, and to improve the USA's competitiveness in international arenas. Jeff Jackson, the original director of the program, was fired after the 1999–2000 season primarily because the team had failed to make an impact in international competition. But the program has produced such top-echelon NHL prospects as David Tanabe of the Carolina Hurricanes. Tanabe went from the national team program to the University of Wisconsin for one year before jumping directly to the NHL in 1999. All of Jackson's 2000 national team graduates received college scholarships to play hockey.

It's difficult to solve the riddle of whether the chicken or egg came first in the American hockey race to become mainstream. NHL expansion has created new pockets of hockey interest, but the younger players created by those teams could end up being missionaries for the spread of hockey to other areas.

"I always remind folks that Michael Jordan's interest in basketball didn't start when he got to the University of North Carolina," Anastos said. "He was probably playing all the time and in many different places when he was young. That's what has to happen with hockey. You need the kids who want to play street hockey when they aren't playing ice hockey."

In another decade, the expectation is that players from the non-traditional markets of Texas, Florida and Nashville could end up in the NHL draft. "Washington's Jeff Halpern is already an example of a player coming from what has to be described as an under-recognized or under-rated hockey area," Brown said. Halpern grew up in the North Virginia/Maryland area, and was overlooked in his draft year. His hometown team ended up signing him as a free agent after a standout college career.

"There is always missionary work to do," Brown said. "But it's not just the National Hockey League doing the work. The minor leagues are so popular. When I think about hockey's growth, I think about coaching programs, officiating programs and all the people who love minor league hockey. I think of people of all ages who play recreationally—the people who jam the rinks from 8 a.m. until 7:30 the next morning pleading for ice time. That's what I see."

Hockey's face continues to be re-molded each year. Anastos, a former standout college player at Michigan State, remembers playing in anonymity when he was a teenager, even though he was performing at the highest levels of U.S. junior hockey. Youth hockey wasn't on anyone's radar in those days, even in a hockey-friendly Michigan climate. None of his classmates had any concept of what junior hockey was all about.

"Hockey had such a low profile that my peers had no idea that I was even a decent athlete," Anastos said. "On the night before my high school commencement I was drafted (in 1981) by the Montreal Canadiens. It was in the newspapers that morning. My teachers and classmates were blown away. Here was this guy who was drafted by the pros and they didn't even know I was an athlete."

Two decades later, Anastos still lives in suburban Detroit. Now that region is referred to as "Hockeytown."

THEY PLAY HOW MANY PERIODS?

THE NEW MINOR LEAGUES

Steve Cherwonak

THE WESTERN PROFESSIONAL HOCKEY LEAGUE enters its fifth professional season in October, 2000. The league boasts 15 member teams in five southwestern states, each with a loyal base of committed fans dedicated to supporting professional ice hockey in their market.

Former Western Professional Hockey League president Rick Kozuback took the concept of ice hockey in non-traditional areas and developed it beyond the point that many thought possible. However, the term "non-traditional" may not be enough to fully explain some of the challenges and obstacles that Kozuback and his staff faced during the long process of establishing a minor professional hockey league in Texas, New Mexico, Mississippi, Arkansas and Louisiana.

October 16, 1996. The Western Professional Hockey League played its first game. Over 6,000 curious spectators at the Bell County Exposition Center in Belton welcomed their hometown Central Texas Stampede to the ice. Just 22 seconds into that first game, Stampede forward Troy Frederick made history by scoring the first WPHL goal with a puck that now sits in a place of honor on Kozuback's wall. After two periods of physical play, the buzzer sounded and something odd occured. Nearly 2,000 fans applauded heartily and headed for the exits.

Were they unhappy with the level of play? Was the music too loud? Possibly the arena was too cold?

As it turns out, the fans simply didn't understand that ice hockey required a third period. After some feverish on-the-job training by Kozuback and WPHL and Stampede staff members, order was quickly restored and the fans settled back into their seats for the third period. They were eventually rewarded for their support by witnessing another WPHL first, a shootout victory by their newfound heroes.

A few short days later, the New Mexico Scorpions played a home game and were rewarded by an exceptional individual effort. A Scorpions player had managed to score three goals and several knowledgeable hockey fans took the opportunity to pay tribute to the hat trick by heaving their headgear onto the ice. Unfortunately, this time-honored tradition of hockey celebration had not been properly explained to the security staff, which had been strongly advised that fans were not allowed to throw anything on the ice. Those who tossed their hats were quickly detained by the security crew. Again, a quick training session was required to explain the nuances of the tradition. The fans were allowed to return to their seats.

Since those early days, the Western Professional Hockey League has made a very strong commitment not only to provide an enjoyable and affordable entertainment option, but to educating fans through advertising campaigns and "Hockey 101" clinics. Coaches and administrative staffs have spent, and continue to devote, a great deal of time and energy to explaining such terms as icing and face-off, and the exact purpose of that extremely well-padded player in front of the net. While professional hockey may well be the most enjoyable of all spectator sports, assisting fans to develop their knowledge base and understanding of the game remains a chief priority.

Certainly the Western Professional Hockey League can't take all the credit for the growth of hockey in non-traditional areas. The East Coast Hockey League has developed a reputation as an excellent organization in its 10-plus seasons to date, and the Central, United and West Coast Hockey Leagues have all significantly added to the minor professional hockey landscape long established by the American and International Hockey Leagues. But the most significant events leading to the inception of the WPHL, and the growth of minor professional hockey in general, are National Hockey League related. First, in 1988, the game's greatest player, Wayne Gretzky, was traded to the Los Angeles Kings in a move that shocked the entire nation of Canada, but increased awareness of professional hockey to newfound levels in the United States. In almost overnight fashion, the National Hockey League increased its somewhat regional following and became a full-fledged member of America's professional sports elite, along with the National Football League, the National Basketball Association and Major League Baseball. Gretzky, the game's greatest player and ambassador, was also largely responsible for the National Hockey League's expansion deep into previously unheard of markets, giving the NHL a clearly identifiable superstar to promote the "coolest game on ice."

The San Jose Sharks began the pilgrimage south in the 1991–92 season, followed quickly by the Mighty Ducks of Anaheim (1993–94), the Florida Panthers (1993–94), the Colorado Avalanche (1995–96) and the Phoenix Coyotes (1996–97). Also, in 1993–94, the North Stars left Minnesota, long considered the heartland of American hockey, and arrived in Dallas, Texas. They brought the Stanley Cup to football country five seasons later. Who would have thought back in the late 1980s that under a decade later there would be more professional hockey teams in the state of Texas than in all of Canada?

In the mid 1990s, a motivated group of businessmen led by soon to be WPHL President Rick Kozuback and business associates James Treliving, George Melville and Nigel King, considered a plan to start their own professional hockey organization. Treliving had nearly purchased an East Coast Hockey League franchise in the late 1980s, but had relented. After lengthy discussion, his group decided to fund a feasibility study to determine if minor professional hockey was viable in previously untamed southwestern markets. Kozuback and WPHL vice president Brad Treliving (a league investor and former professional player) began the lengthy process of traveling from city to city, speaking with arena managers, civic officials and potential investors.

Despite the growth of professional hockey in recent years, selling the concept of a minor professional hockey league to these individuals may have been Kozuback's most monumental task. The challenge was to convince city officials, building managers and potential franchisees that professional hockey could thrive in their market. As Kozuback began to develop support, the concept of a southwestern hockey league started to become a reality. After close to two years of traveling and preparation, the Western Professional Hockey League was officially introduced on January 18, 1996, in Austin, Texas—a city soon to become home to the Austin Ice Bats, a charter member of the WPHL.

While establishing hockey in new markets, the WPHL was allowed some flexibility in creating team names and logos. While names such as the Maple Leafs, Rangers, Bruins and Canadiens have strong, established historic ties to their communities, the WPHL focused on targeting unique names and logos that met specific criteria. First, the WPHL wanted to ensure that there was a local tie to the community or region. Second, the name and logo must lend itself well to the use of a mascot. Third, the name and image should be appealing to sports fans across many different demographics. That philosophy has led to the creation of teams such as the El Paso Buzzards, the Fort Worth Brahmas, the Odessa Jackalopes and the Bossier-Shreveport Mudbugs, among others.

While chiefly located in Texas (nine of 15 teams scheduled to play the 2000–2001 season reside in the Lone Star State), the WPHL is made up of several different demographics. Attend a game in El Paso and you will notice a distinct Latin flair, often combining professional hockey with boisterous mariachi bands and tortillas that are tossed onto the ice to celebrate a goal. Games in West Texas are often enjoyed by guests wearing cowboy boots and 10-gallon hats, while the Mardi Gras theme rings true throughout Lake Charles, Louisiana—home of the Ice Pirates.

When attending hockey games in Canada, it is very clear that Canadians have a strong passion and knowledge for the game. Many Canadian hockey fans take an analytical approach when attending games, noting the particulars of special-teams play or offensive and defensive systems. Such an approach is significantly different from that of the typical hockey fan in the chosen markets of the WPHL. These fans may not yet understand all the rules, regulations and strategies involved in the game of hockey, but they want to be entertained. Loud music, interactive on-ice promotions and a strong bond with the team and players are what keep WPHL fans supportive of the sport.

With the majority of fans not having any preconceived notion of what is, and what is not, typical at a professional hockey game, member teams were encouraged to be creative and off-the-wall when entertaining guests. That concept has led to such wild and zany promotions as the "Win Your Own Funeral" in Austin, where one fan was driven off the ice in a hearse after winning the grand prize—his own casket and burial plot. The Lake Charles Ice Pirates had their own unique "Snip and Trip" promotion, sponsored by a local doctor, which gave the winner a vasectomy and a vacation. Season ticket holders in Corpus Christi who got their orders in early for the 2000–2001 season received an official invitation to the IceRays' version of "The Royal Wedding." Power forward and local cult hero Geoff Bumstead married his native Texan girlfriend on July 1, 2000, in front of more than 1,000 of the team's biggest supporters.

Demands on their time make it difficult for NHL players to interact with their fans, but the WPHL encourages member teams and players to strengthen the bond with fans as much as possible. Programs such as postgame skating lessons with the players or the very successful "Grades for Blades" program, which rewards students for school attendance, help to accomplish that objective. It may be extremely difficult to shake hands with, or receive an autograph from, an NHL player, but WPHL fans receive tremendous access to the league's biggest asset, its players.

As the WPHL continues to grow, an increased focus on developing youth hockey programs will be established, encouraging young athletes not only to enjoy professional hockey as a spectator, but as a competitor. Youth hockey has shown significant development in many WPHL cities, with five-year-old children learning the game and developing the motor skills to skate and handle the puck. It may not be long before some of the strapping, athletic teenagers who previously dreamt of playing tight end for the Dallas Cowboys switch their allegiances and pursue the goal of playing left wing for the Dallas Stars.

There is no question that one of the main reasons that the southwestern region was targeted to develop professional hockey was the traditionally strong fan support shown towards other sports. The Cowboys are "America's Team," and the state of Texas supports two Major League baseball teams and three National Basketball Association franchises. Perhaps an even more important factor was the strong support shown to collegiate and high school athletics. The rivalries already established in these sports made some of the WPHL's franchise location choices simple. The cities of El Paso, Texas, and Albuquerque, New Mexico, have waged sporting battles for several decades, and it didn't take long to realize that the same animosity would occur when the WPHL's Buzzards and Scorpions meet. Another tremendous rivalry takes place in West Texas, where the Odessa Jackalopes and San Angelo Outlaws, two teams separated by a less-than-two-hour drive, have staged their own private feud. Busloads of supporters regularly make the journey to road games, in large part due to the strong rivalry already in place amongst high school football teams.

The newest addition to the WPHL is the Lubbock Cotton Kings, who led the league with an average attendance of nearly 5,500 fans per game in their inaugural season of 1999–2000. This success didn't happen overnight, as the team had nearly a year to prepare for its first season. This preparation time was well spent, developing interactive community programs and youth hockey clinics designed to gain support for the newest game in town. With a competitive team and a business plan based on customer service, the Cotton Kings have set the stage for long-term prosperity.

Having now established its viability in the Southwest, a new direction is being taken as the Western Professional Hockey League enters its fifth season. A stronger emphasis is being placed on arena construction with an eye toward developing even newer markets for professional hockey. Southwestern cities will continue to be targeted as potential sites, with arenas projected to be in the 6,000- to 8,000-seat range and designed as multipurpose venues to attract additional events besides WPHL games. This new direction will allow the league to continue to develop fans in new markets and provide job opportunities for the many players, coaches and administrators that pursue professional hockey as a career.

The future looks bright for the Western Professional Hockey League, and minor professional hockey in general. The focus will remain on providing an exceptional level of customer service while educating new fans on the most thrilling of all spectator sports. Now how many periods do they play again?

THE U.S. NATIONAL TEAM DEVELOPMENT PROGRAM

Jenny Wiedeke

WITH 46 OF THE NATION'S top young hockey players and a first-rate schedule, the National Team Development Program (NTDP), based in Ann Arbor, Michigan, has become known as the hockey hothouse for up-and-coming American players. The program, which has completed three full seasons, was formally introduced to the Ann Arbor community in March, 1997. Since then, the team has brought home first-place finishes at both the Three Nations and Five Nations tournaments and participated in more than 30 international contests. Perhaps the most dramatic effect of the NTDP could be seen at the 2000 World Junior Championships where the American squad, made up primarily of NTDP graduates, finished in fourth place—a marked improvement from the previous year's seventh-place finish.

The concept behind the NTDP is simple: bring together the top 16- and 17-year-old players from all over the nation to train year-round in a setting that promotes growth, both on the ice and off it. The program was the inspiration of former national coach Jeff Jackson.

"I think it is really important for the future of American hockey to give top players an opportunity like the NTDP to train in a year-round competitive atmosphere," Jackson says. "Not only do the players improve on the ice, but they get a sense of national pride and realize what an honor it is to wear the USA crest on their jersey."

Selected players are found by a team of scouts in different regions and at USA Hockey's Select Festivals, which are held during the summer. Players come to an annual tryout camp and then earn an invitation to train with the only standing U.S. national hockey team for nine months at the Ann Arbor Ice Cube.

Once in Ann Arbor, players are split into two teams; an Under-17 team, which competes in the North American Hockey League (NAHL), and an Under-18 team that plays in the United States Hockey League (USHL). Both leagues offer a competitive schedule featuring more than 60 games per season and older competition to help accelerate the development of the younger Team USA players. In addition, the Under-17 team hosts one or two international series each season, and the Under-18 team travels to a minimum of three international tournaments. All in all, the schedule offers far more competition than the average 17-year-old is exposed to and gives NTDP players the tools necessary to succeed in their future hockey careers.

Jackson explains the NTDP by saying, "It is similar to what Canada did with its national team program, but we have decided to take it to a younger level and have an impact on 16- and 17-year-old players. When they move on to junior hockey, or into college, instead of being a third or fourth-liner, these kids will be able to step in and have an impact."

Unlike most competitive athletic teams, the success of the NTDP is not gauged on wins and losses. Instead, the focus is on the development of skills and on acquiring experience. However, as the program has evolved, the NTDP players have found themselves able to compete—even against the 20-year-olds in the NAHL and USHL. During the 1999–2000 season the Under-17 team qualified for the playoffs for the second time in the program's three-year history, while the Under-18 team topped its division in the USHL and finished second overall in the regular-season standings by only two points.

National Team Development Program players hail from all over the United States. Last season, 15 states were represented in the program, with players coming from as far away as Alaska and as close as Brighton, Michigan. While in Ann Arbor, the players stay with host families and attend one of two public high schools. Still, adjusting to life in Ann Arbor is a surprise for many players.

"I went to my first day at Pioneer High School and was shocked," said former U.S. forward Jon Waibel. "There were more people in the school than in my entire hometown."

Waibel was one of three players on the 1999–2000 squad from the tiny town of Baudette (population 1,000) and one of 11 players from Minnesota. He soon got over his culture shock and served as the captain of the Under-18 team last season while collecting 20 goals and 24 assists. He will attend the University of Minnesota in 2000–01.

Waibel is not unlike most NTDP players who come to Ann Arbor for their junior and senior years of high school and leave with a scholarship to play for a Division I college hockey program. In the first year graduates of the program were eligible to enter college, 18 players signed national letters of intent with Division I college programs. In 1998–99, 17 players moved into the college ranks. This past year, 19 players signed to play with college squads. Not only are NTDP graduates making the decision to go to school, they are choosing some of the most successful college hockey programs and rigorous academic institutions in the nation. Quinn Fylling, a forward on the 1999–2000 squad, will play for the national champions from North Dakota next year. Two former NTDP players were on the University of Maine team that won the 1999 national championship, while four players were on the 1999–2000 Wisconsin team that reached the "Frozen Four" NCAA championship. Overall, the University of Notre Dame boasts the most NTDP graduates with eight players, including U.S. national junior team members Brett Henning and Connor Dunlop. Rob Globke, a forward on the 1999–2000 squad, will soon join the Fighting Irish. Globke finished last season with a hat trick against Belarus at the World Under-18 Championship and led the American team with four goals overall.

The World Under-18 Championship is just one of several international competitions in which NTDP players participate during their two years in Ann Arbor. The team plays in the annual Three Nations Tournament in November and the Five Nations Tournament in February. The last two years, the team has finished no lower than second at both these annual competitions. The Under-17 team hosts a Swiss team each year in November and plays in the World Under-17 Challenge. Last season, the Under-17 team earned a fourth-place finish at the Challenge.

The early international experience gained by NTDP players prepares them for future competition and helps to make them a dominant force. A prime example of this phenomenon came at the 2000 Viking Cup in Camrose, Alberta. The U.S. squad had two NTDP alumni: Todd Jackson, who finished the tournament leading the American team with seven goals, and J.D. Forrest, who was the top-scoring defenseman with seven points.

As Jeff Jackson indicated, NTDP graduates often become standouts on their college squads, as well. During the 1999–2000 season, 14 former NTDP players earned college accolades. Former NTDP goaltender Rick DiPietro was named the Hockey East rookie of the year and was named the top goaltender at the 2000 World Junior Championship. Inaugural season members Doug Janik and Barrett Heisten earned honorable mention in the Hockey East, while Jordan Leopold was one of only six repeat selections on the Western Collegiate Hockey Association all-Conference team. Brian Fahey was named to the all-rookie team in the WCHA, Andy Hilbert earned similar honors in the Central Collegiate Hockey Association, and Freddy Meyer completed the trio of all-rookie selections in the Hockey East. Meyer's accomplishment was especially impressive considering the fact that he graduated from the NTDP a semester early and was a member of the University of Boston team for only half of the season.

"I definitely owe a lot to USA Hockey and the NTDP," Meyer said. "What I learned on and off the ice will stay with me through my hockey career."

Other players echo Meyer's sentiments.

"The NTDP was a huge stepping stone for my hockey career," says defenseman Neil Komadoski. "It provided me with the best on-ice instruction and helped me get stronger off the ice. Without the NTDP, I wouldn't be headed in the direction that I am today." Komadoski, the son of former St. Louis Blues player Neil Komadoski, will play for Notre Dame in 2000–01.

Komadoski is one of a handful of players that comes to the NTDP with a strong hockey lineage. Joe Goodenow, son of NHL Players' Association boss Bob Goodenow, played in the program's inaugural season and now plays at Michigan State. Pat Murphy, son of NHL vice president of hockey operations Mike Murphy, will play on the Under-18 team next year after completing his first season with the Under-17 team.

After college, several NTDP graduates are ready to take the next natural step in the hockey progression. Toward this end, the 1999 NHL Entry Draft proved a crucial step for the program. It helped place American-born hockey players at the top level of hockey competition, which is the NTDP's ultimate goal. Overall, 14 graduates of the program's inaugural season went to NHL teams in 1999. Of that group, eight were selected in the first three rounds, including two in the first round and four in the second. Defenseman Dave Tanabe was the top pick from the NTDP. The Carolina Hurricanes drafted the native of White Bear Lake, Minnesota, with the 16th overall pick. Tanabe is now a steady player in a Carolina uniform. When he scored his first NHL goal on October 11, 1999, he became the first NTDP graduate to score in the NHL. The other 1999 first-round selection from the NTDP was Barrett Heisten, an Anchorage, Alaska, native who went to the Stanley Cup finalist Buffalo Sabres as the 20th selection. Heisten scored two goals and assisted on one other for the 2000 U.S. national junior team.

It was a positive year for NTDP graduates at the 1999 draft, and for American hockey as a whole. Over 20 percent of the first 100 picks were Americans, compared to 16 percent in 1998. Of the 19 American players taken in the first three rounds, 42 percent were NTDP graduates. NTDP alumni also accounted for more than half of the 27 American-born college players drafted that year. That's a lot of numbers all supporting the same conclusion: the National Team Development Program is having a dramatic effect on the American presence in the NHL. And the extent of success of the NTDP has yet to be fully seen. With many of its graduates still in the college ranks, its full effect on professional hockey is still to come.

By choosing "The Cube" as its training facility, the NTDP helped to extend the focus of hockey in the metro Detroit area. "Ann Arbor is an ideal location for us, not just because of its central location in the country, but also because it is so accessible to so many levels of competitive hockey," said Jackson. Ann Arbor has become a hotbed of talent in the hockey world, as the NTDP continues to bring in highly regarded athletes from around the country.

The job of charting the future success of the program falls upon Mike Eaves, who was named the new U.S. National Development coach on May 18, 2000. A former NHL player with coaching experience at the youth, college, international and professional levels, Eaves will serve as head coach of the Under-18 team and oversee the entire program. "The USA Hockey National Development Team Program has grown immensely since it was started four years ago," says Eaves. "Coming in now, I'm excited about the opportunity to help bring it to the next level."

U.S. NATIONAL TEAM DEVELOPMENT PROGRAM GRADUATES SELECTED IN THE 1999 NHL ENTRY DRAFT

Round	Rank	NHL Team	Name	1998–99 Team
1	16	Carolina	Dave Tanabe	Wisconsin
1	20	Buffalo	Barrett Heisten	Maine
2	44	Anaheim	Jordan Leopold	Minnesota
2	52	Nashville	Adam Hall	Michigan State
2	54	Nashville	Andrew Hutchinson	Michigan State
2	55	Buffalo	Doug Janik	Maine
3	81	Edmonton	Adam Hauser	Minnesota
3	90	NY Rangers	Pat Aufiero	Boston University
4	111	San Jose	Willie Levesque	Northeastern
5	135	Calgary	Matt Doman	Wisconsin
5	142	Colorado	Will Magnuson	Lake Superior
6	175	Washington	Kyle Clark	Harvard
6	176	Pittsburgh	Doug Meyer	Minnesota
9	255	NY Islanders	Brett Henning	Notre Dame

U.S. NATIONAL TEAM DEVELOPMENT PROGRAM GRADUATES SELECTED IN THE 2000 NHL ENTRY DRAFT

Round	Rank	NHL Team	Name	1999-2000 Team
1	1	N.Y. Islanders	Rick DiPietro	Boston University
1	13	Montreal	Ron Hainsey	Umass-Lowell
2	35	Edmonton	Brad Winchester	Wisconsin
2	37	Boston	Andy Hilbert	Michigan
2	51	Toronto	Kris Vernarsky	Plymouth (OHL)
4	103	Boston	Brett Nowak	Harvard
4	119	Colorado	Brian Fahey	Wisconsin
5	153	Anaheim	Bill Cass	Boston College
5	159	Colorado	John Michael Liles	Michigan State
6	181	Carolina	Justin Forrest	NTDP
6	185	Pittsburgh	Patrick Foley	New Hampshire
7	210	Philadelphia	John Eichelberger	Green Bay (USHL)
7	211	Edmonton	Joe Cullen	Colorado College
8	244	Atlanta	Eric Bowen	Portland (WHL)
8	251	Detroit	Todd Jackson	NTDP
9	276	Carolina	Troy Ferguson	Michigan State

U.S. NATIONAL TEAM DEVELOPMENT PROGRAM COLLEGE SIGNINGS

as of May 14, 2000

* indicates player on current roster with verbal or written commitment

** indicates junior on current roster making verbal commitment

School/Name	Pos.	Hometown	Last Year with NTDP
Boston College			
Bill Cass	D	Hingham, Mass.	1998–99
Justin Forrest*	D	Auburn, N.Y.	1999–00
Boston University			
Pat Aufiero	D	Winchester, Mass.	1997–98
Rick DiPietro	G	Winthrop, Mass.	1998–99
John Sabo	F	Summit, N.J.	1998–99
Freddy Meyer*	D	Sanbornville, N.H.	1999–00
Justin Maiser**	F	Edina, Minn.	1999–00
Brian McConnell**	F	Norfolk, Mass.	2000–01
Colby			
James Laliberty	F	Waterville, Maine	1997–98
Colorado College			
Joe Cullen	F	Moorhead, Minn.	1998–99
Cornell University			
Chris Gartman	G	Baldwin, N.Y.	1998–99
Harvard University			
Kyle Clark	F	Essex, Vt.	1997–98
Dennis Packard*	F	Kingston, Pa.	1999–00
Ken Smith*	D	Stoneham, Mass.	1999–00
Lake Superior State			
Will Magnuson	D	Anchorage, Alaska	1997–98
University of Maine			
Barrett Heisten	F	Anchorage, Alaska	1997–98
Doug Janik	D	Agawam, Mass.	1997–98
James Laliberty	F	Waterville, Maine	1997–98
Todd Jackson*	F	Cortland, N.Y.	1999–00
Miami Ohio			
David Bowen	G	Bloomfield Hills, Mich	1997–98
Joe Pomaranski**	D	Gurnee, Ill.	2000–01
University of Michigan			
Andy Hilbert	F	Howell, Mich.	1998–99
Michael Komisarek*	F	Islip Terrace, N.Y.	1999–00
Dwight Helmnen**	F	Brighton, Mich.	2000–01
Michigan State			
Joe Goodenow	F	Toronto, Ontario	1997–98
Adam Hall	F	Kalamazoo, Mich.	1997–98
Andrew Hutchinson	D	Rochester Hills, Mich.	1997–98
Jon Insana	D	New Baltimore, Mich.	1997–98
Troy Ferguson	F	Seattle, Wash.	1998–99
John-Michael Liles	D	Zionsville, Ind.	1998–99
Joey Hope*	D	Anchorage, Alaska	1999–00
Michigan Tech University			
Bryan Perez*	F	Blaine, Minn.	1999–00
John Snowden*	F	Snohomish, Wash.	1999–00
University of Minnesota			
Adam Hauser	G	Bovey, Minn.	1997–98
Jordan Leopold	D	Golden Valley, Minn.	1997–98
Doug Meyer	F	Bloomington, Minn.	1997–98
Shawn Roed	F	White Bear Lake, Minn.	1997–98
Jon Waibel*	F	Baudette, Minn.	1999–00
Minnesota State/Mankato			
Cole Bassett*	F	Oakdale, Minn.	1999–00
New Hampshire			
Pat Foley	F	Milton, Mass.	1998–99
North Dakota			
Quinn Fylling*	F	Minot, N.D.	1999–00
Niagara			
Rob Bonk*	G	Hartland, Mich.	1999–00
Northeastern			
Willie Levesque	F	Vineyard Haven, Mass.	1997–98
Notre Dame			
Michael Chin	F	Urbana, Ill.	1997–98
Brett Henning	F	Buffalo Grove, Ill.	1997–98
Connor Dunlop	F	St. Louis, Mo.	1998–99
Paul Harris	D	Ridgefield, Conn.	1998–99
John Wroblewski	F	Neenah, Wis.	1998–99
Rob Globke*	F	West Bloomfield, Mich.	2000–01
Neil Komadoski*	D	Chesterfield, Mo.	1999–00
Brett Lebda*	D	Buffalo Grove, Ill.	1999–00
Derek Smith**	D	Marysville, Mich.	2000–01
Ohio State University			
Scott Titus	D	E. Grand Rapids, Mich.	1997–98
R.J. Umberger*	F	Pittsburgh, Pa.	1999–00
David Steckel*	F	West Bend, Wis.	1999–00
Princeton University			
Matt Maglione*	D	Fayetteville, N.Y.	1999–00
St. Cloud State			
Chris Purslow	F	Greenlawn, N.Y.	1998–99
Jim McNamara*	D	Macomb, Mich.	1999–00
U. Mass-Lowell			
Ron Hainsey	D	Bolton, Conn.	1998–99
Wayne State			
Nick Schrader	F	Blissfield, Mich.	1997–98
University of Wisconsin			
Matt Doman	F	Sartell, Minn.	1997–98
John Eichelberger	F	Glencoe, Ill.	1997–98
Dave Tanabe	D	White Bear Lake, Minn.	1997–98
Brian Fahey	D	Glenview, Ill.	1998–99
Brad Winchester	F	Madison, Wis.	1998–99
Jason Reimers	D	Cottage Grove, Ill.	1998–99

U.S. TIER I JUNIOR HOCKEY

Jim Leitner

LIFE COULDN'T GET ANY BETTER for Ed Hill as he and his Green Bay Gamblers teammates took turns skating around the Nelson Center in Springfield, Illinois, with the Gold Cup held high above their sweaty heads.

It was one of those rare moments in life, when the feelings of exhaustion and relief are overcome by adrenaline and excitement, and your body just goes numb for a while. For 80 games, the Gamblers had battled and bonded before reaching the pinnacle, a 2–0 victory over the Detroit Compuware Ambassadors in the championship game of USA Hockey's 1997 National Junior A tournament.

"It was such a long season, from August to the middle of May, and you're so tired and so glad that it's all over, and you feel just about every emotion you can imagine," said Hill, a second-round draft pick of the Nashville Predators and the 61st player taken overall in the 1999 NHL Entry Draft. "It was such an unbelievable rush, and something I'll never forget. It was a lot like when I heard my name called at the [NHL] draft. It's hard to explain, but it's almost what you would call an out-of-body experience."

Hill got to feel the rush as a 16-year-old rookie in the United States Hockey League, playing in front of more than 3,000 fans a night in a rustic arena located a long slapshot away from historic Lambeau Field—home of the Green Bay Packers. It gave the native of Newburyport, Massachusetts, a tremendous sense of accomplishment, but it also left him craving more from his hockey career. After spending one more season in the USHL, he decided he needed a new challenge to fulfill his dream of playing in the NHL.

Hill, a 6'2", 215-pound defenseman, took his game to the Barrie Colts, a member of the prestigious Ontario Hockey League, a Canadian major junior league renowned for preparing players for the NHL.

"Green Bay was great," Hill said. "My housing parents were great, the fans were great, the organization was great. But I was going to be a senior [in high school], I'd already played in the league the two years, and I honestly felt as though I was ready to move on to the next level after my first year there. College would have been a great step up for me, but I was still only a senior. I felt as though I had to go somewhere else to get better.

"Playing in all-star games with guys from other teams, you get a feel for what other places are like. And from what I've gathered, Barrie is one of the best organizations in major junior. We've got the best ownership in the league, and everything's set up in a professional environment. You get a taste of what it's going to be like at the next level. So this was definitely the right move for my career."

Much like Hill after his second season in Green Bay, USA Hockey wants to take its game to the next level.

For the better part of the decade of the 1990s, USA Hockey's Junior Council and four separate subcommittees have worked on developing a league one step beyond Tier II, currently the highest level of amateur hockey available in the United States to players under the age of 20. This proposed super-league, or "mini-NHL," while still some years away, would assemble the country's best juniors on six to 12 teams with an eye toward developing its players for college, international and professional hockey. Teams would pick up more of the tab for players than they currently do without jeopardizing amateur status or NCAA eligibility and would attract more National Hockey League scouts.

"This is something that would really benefit the top-end players in the United States," said Dave Hakstol, head coach of the USHL's Sioux City Musketeers. "Right now, we have a lot of top-end players who are leaving the country to go play hockey in Canada. They should have the option to stay here in the United States with the same benefits. If we do have a Tier I league, they'd have the same development benefits and opportunities to be scouted as they would in Canada. Plus, they'd have better opportunities within the NCAA. It's like they would be getting the best of both worlds."

The 14-team USHL has built its reputation on preparing its players for the college ranks. It perennially accounts for more than half of the roughly 150 players who parlay Tier II careers into scholarships to NCAA institutions. The North American Hockey League and America West League account for the other 17 Tier II teams in the United States.

Tier II teams sell their college-placement success rates to recruits, but it's the ones who get away who concern USA Hockey. Each season, roughly 25 to 30 players opt for the professional atmosphere of the one of three members of the Canadian Hockey League—the Western Hockey League, the Ontario Hockey League and the Quebec Major Junior Hockey League. Another 25 to 30 Americans accept roster spots with Canadian Tier II or Junior B teams. USA Hockey doesn't want the future Mike Modanos or Jeremy Roenicks or David Legwands of American hockey to feel they have to leave the country to become a high NHL draft pick.

"The way the Tier II teams have pumped out scholarships is not a success rate to be taken lightly," said David Tyler, a Waterloo, Iowa-based attorney and USA Hockey's Junior Council chairman. "If we were to have six or eight teams replace the 31 we have now, then we've done a disservice to the kids. There definitely would still be a place for Tier II as a developmental option. What we're trying to do is enhance or improve upon that record of success without taking away opportunities for kids. There is a recognition within junior hockey that there is a need for an advanced level of hockey like this."

USA Hockey saw that first-hand with its National Team Development Program, which gathered the country's best Under-18 and Under-17 players in Ann Arbor, Michigan, and placed them on two teams that competed in the USHL and NAHL and also play in international age-group tournaments. With world-class training facilities and coaches—not to mention a strict academic setting—the NTDP sent 36 players to Division I college programs in its first two seasons after being introduced amid plenty of skepticism from the American hockey public in the spring of 1997. The NTDP also had 14 players selected in the NHL draft in 1999, the first year its players became draft-eligible. The Carolina Hurricanes selected David Tanabe and the Buffalo Sabres took Barrett Heisten in the first round. Four other NTDP products went in the second round.

Tier I hockey, in essence, will become a fan-based league of teams structured by high standards and strict regulations. Under USA Hockey legislation, the Tier I teams will play in venues with seating capacities of no less than 2,500 in an effort to draw a minimum of 60,000 fans per season. The ice surface will be no smaller than 200-by-85 feet, and the team will have to provide professional-quality accommodations for its players and training staffs at home and on the road during a season that would include a minimum of 48 regular-season games, plus a three-round playoff.

Teams will be responsible for all of the players' equipment, including sticks and skates, and must arrange and pay for suitable room and board, as well as all costs related to team travel. Teams will also provide academic counseling and tutoring. Basically, they will provide as much as NCAA eligibility rules allow.

That's been the gray matter in the junior hockey equation. The NCAA has thrown its whole eligibility stance out of whack by raising the possibility of allowing players whose professional careers didn't pan out the opportunity to attend member institutions and play college sports. That plays right into the hands of the major junior player whose hands or feet weren't quite quick enough for NHL scouts.

"So much right now is dependent on the NCAA," said Tom Carroll, an assistant coach at the University of Notre Dame from 1985 to 1999 before taking over the head coaching position with Des Moines of the USHL. "If they relax the restrictions on major junior players and allow them to maintain their college eligibility, then the USHL really has to make the move up to Tier I to maintain the niche it has made for itself over the past 20 years as being the top league in the country for moving kids on to college.

"I can see why the NCAA would do that, because there is so much red tape and questions about the eligibility of kids who used to play in pro leagues or tournaments. They probably deal with those issues moreso in basketball or tennis or soccer than hockey, but it's still a major issue."

The USHL has kept a close eye on USA Hockey's work on the Tier I proposal, and has postured itself as the league most likely to make the step up. The majority of the teams in the USHL already have solid marketing staffs—eight surpassed the proposed attendance requirements during the 1999–2000 season and a ninth missed by less than 2,000 fans—they employ high-quality coaching and training staffs and have placed an emphasis on off-ice training and nutrition. With a few adjustments—paying the players' equipment and housing costs and adopting USA Hockey's player procurement rules—most of the USHL's teams would qualify for Tier I status.

USA Hockey's Tier I proposal specifies each team to carry eight Under-18 players and three Under-17 players on its 22-man roster. (Current Tier II teams have no age-group requirements.) Teams will be allowed two non-citizen players—excluding goaltenders—which is similar to current operating practices.

"The timetable for this is going to be dictated by USA Hockey, and the teams, leagues, owners and entrepreneurs who are going to make this happen," said USHL commissioner Gino Gasparini, a former national championship coach at perennial NCAA Division I powerhouse North Dakota. "The big thing for us as a league and me as a commissioner is to be prepared for it when it comes, and I think we are. I think it's in the best interest of the game and the prospects of tomorrow. There are a lot of blueprints out there for how this can be done, but my feeling is, 'If this can be done anywhere in the world, the USHL can do it better than anybody else.'

"I think a lot of that comes from the fact that the USHL has 20 years of tradition, and that in the last four or five years we've made tremendous progress in our presence in the hockey world. Our growth has been phenomenal. Moving to a Tier I league would just be the next step for us," Gasparini said.

In 1999–2000, the USHL became the first junior league in the United States to surpass one million in attendance, attracting 1,038,721 fans to 380 openings for an average of 2,733 per contest. Omaha led the league with an average of 5,615 fans to 30 home dates, while Lincoln, Sioux Falls, Cedar Rapids and Des Moines surpassed the 100,000-fan plateau. All but three teams drew at least 1,000 fans per game. By comparison, the Canadian Hockey League averaged 3,455 fans to 1,904 games.

The USHL's attendance numbers have increased significantly since Gasparini took over in 1995–96, when the league drew 551,925 fans (an average of 2,057 per game). The difference? The USHL has placed an increased emphasis on marketing, and it has expanded and relocated into larger communities in the Midwest.

"The fans in the USHL are the best," says Lincoln forward Preston Callander, a native of Regina, Saskatchewan. "Playing in front of crowds of 5,000 every night is pretty sweet and gets the players fired up. The whole league has a great atmosphere, and it's fun to be playing here."

The USHL doesn't pump out first-round draft picks quite like the Canadian Hockey League, but it's not too far behind in atmosphere and skill level. And the word is starting to spread.

Rob Sandrock figured his Junior hockey career had come to an end when the Kelowna Rockets released him midway through his fourth and final season of eligibility in the Western Hockey League. The 6', 195-pound defenseman from Williams Lake, British Columbia, had started thinking about joining the real-world workforce when the phone rang.

It was Mike Hastings, the head coach of a Tier II team in Nebraska. Hastings hadn't seen Sandrock play, but decided to offer him a roster spot with the Omaha Lancers based on the recommendation from the father of a former player.

"At the time, I thought that being out of the WHL was about it for me in hockey, and I really didn't think about moving on in the game," said Sandrock, who also played for the Spokane Chiefs, Swift Current Broncos and Medicine Hat Tigers during his major junior career. "I was upset about being released, and that was really the major factor in me not wanting to play the game any more.

"Then, I guess, I thought about the pros and cons. I really still wanted to play hockey, and I guess I wasn't ready to work for the rest of my life," Sandrock said. "My buddy Neil Breen played in Omaha and liked it, and my mom really didn't want me to give it up. So I decided to give it a try."

From the moment Sandrock arrived in Omaha midway through the 1998–99 season, his eyes were opened to a whole new world—one that compared favorably to the hockey he had become accustomed to in three-plus years spent riding buses through Western Canada.

From Thunder Bay, Ontario, to Des Moines, Iowa; from Green Bay, Wisconsin, to Lincoln, Nebraska, Sandrock played in front of large, raucous crowds and against players hoping to become the American college hockey stars of the future. He enjoyed playing hockey again, and his 11 goals and 16 assists in 26 regular-season and playoff games helped the Lancers advance to the semifinals of the national Junior A championships.

"The year I played in Omaha, I think we would have done pretty well if we would have been playing in the WHL," said Sandrock, who was ineligible for college hockey because of his time in major junior and who was using his time in Omaha as an audition for a minor pro career he began in 1999–2000 with San Angelo of the Western Professional Hockey League. "The speed of the game was about the same, and there were a lot of talented players in both leagues. The fans, the way the organizations are run, it's just about the same.

"Physically, the only difference was guys in the WHL were about 6'1" on average, and guys in the USHL were maybe 5'10", and they were just as fast. But I guess the biggest difference between the two is the mindset. In major junior, everything you do is geared toward making it in the NHL. In Omaha, it's all about getting yourself prepared to go to college. If you don't keep your grades up, you don't play."

While the USHL might have the inside track for a move up to Tier I, David Tyler said USA Hockey has other options. He has listened to business proposals from interested parties in major suburban markets like Detroit, Chicago and St. Louis, as well as other medium-sized cities in the Midwest. Another option could include elevating select franchises from current Tier II leagues to form a super-league. The playing surface would then become a little more level for the Tier II teams that now struggle to compete with the larger-market franchises.

"Anything that can be handled by bus is within the realm of possibility," Tyler said. "Once you start getting into flying players to games, I think you'd be looking at more of a struggle for survival financially. And when you're talking about high school kids having extensive travel, you're taking them away from their studies, which would pretty much defeat the purpose of the league in the first place.

"We realize there's a chance that Tier I might not get off the ground, but the one thing we have done is stretched the junior program, and any time you can do that, it's a positive. I think a lot of people have evaluated their programs and elevated their organizations because we've brought this issue to the forefront. And that's good for hockey and the American hockey player."

And the elite players in the United States like Ed Hill could enjoy the best of both worlds without having to leave the country.

NCAA HOCKEY HISTORY

Kevin Allen

ONE OF THE CHARMING ASPECTS of U.S. college hockey is that it has resisted the urge to become fully grown up. In a sports world dominated by marketing, logos and corporate sponsorship, there's still an endearing rah-rah quality that won't go away. The college game doesn't depart from the pros just because there's no red line and players wear full-face shields. College hockey is as much about painted faces, outrageous student bodies, colorful mascots, bare-chested fans, vulgar chanting and lively bands as it is about goals and assists. About 43 percent of the players in U.S. college hockey are in fact Canadian, but the zaniness is uniquely American.

"College hockey isn't just about the guys going on to the pros from the big schools," says Hockey East commissioner Joe Bertagna. "It's a lot of little venues where it's the only game in town."

College hockey is a 10-hour bus ride to take on Lake Superior State College in a packed house in Sault Ste. Marie, Michigan. College hockey is North Dakota band members leaning over the plexiglass and almost nailing the other team's players with enthusiastic trombone slides. College hockey is Bowling Green holding a "Ron Mason look-alike contest" when the Falcons' former coach returned to his old home rink employed as the coach of Michigan State. College hockey is fans in every college arena screaming "Sieve! Sieve!" every time an opposing goaltender lets in a goal.

These kinds of hijinks have been going on forever in college hockey, probably since the first documented game was played in Baltimore between Johns Hopkins and Yale on February 3, 1896. The *Baltimore Sun* carried a report of this game that said it drew "the largest crowd of the season," from which we might easily extrapolate that others were played before then.

Rivalries are steeped in tradition and history. The one between Harvard and Brown began in January 1898; no two schools have faced each other more often than Harvard and Yale, with 201 meetings dating back to just before the turn of the century as of 1998–99. Competition was keen even from the beginning. In 1897, the University of Maryland hired three high-priced attorneys to fight a court challenge to its McNaughton Cup championship when the losing team claimed a referee had allowed a goal that appeared to be "too high."

Early in the 20th century, college hockey was well received in the east and most of the top games were played to large, loud, boisterous crowds. By the 1930s, it enjoyed a high level of popularity, particularly in the Boston area, where a Harvard–Yale game could draw 14,000. Hockey also spread to the West Coast, where USC, UCLA and Loyola also had club teams. But college hockey as we recognize it today didn't really begin until World War II ended.

The Eddie Jeremiah-coached Dartmouth squad was modern college hockey's first juggernaut squad. In the early 1940s, no other team could match Dartmouth. They won 46 consecutive games at one stretch, showing virtually no hint of vulnerability until the University of Michigan defeated them for the championship at the first NCAA tournament in 1948. The next year, Dartmouth fell to Boston College in the NCAA finals. Given how strong its program was in that era, no one would have believed that Dartmouth wouldn't return to the Final Four again until 1979. The main architect of the early success, Jeremiah was a principled man who was always trying to tidy up the NCAA rules to make the competition as fair as it could be. "He is to college hockey what Ted Williams was to baseball," said another great coach, Snooks Kelley, in 1966. "Being on Jerry's team was like being with a Broadway musical and it was a long run," said former player Jim Malone when Jeremiah retired in 1967.

The introduction of the NCAA championship clearly changed the landscape of college hockey. With a Holy Grail to pursue, western teams began to recruit older Canadians (much to the chagrin of the coaches in the east who thought this gave Western schools an unfair advantage). Teams from the west won 18 of the first 20 titles, with coach Vic Heylinger's Michigan team winning six more (1951, 1952, 1953, 1955, 1956 and 1964) after the initial victory in 1948, while Denver won five (1958, 1960, 1961, 1968 and 1969). The rules were so lax that Wally Maxwell was allowed to play for Michigan in the 1957 NCAA tournament even though he had played two games for the NHL's Toronto Maple Leafs four years earlier. Colorado College had a 36-

year-old player named Jack Smith. U.S. college hockey became the final destination for Canadians who had no further options in the pros or in Canada. "Tony Frasca was 30 when he was coaching at Colorado College and he had players who were older than he was," noted former Colorado College player Art Berglund. "Only the real talented Americans got a chance to play at some schools."

Not every coach in the west believed in using Canadian players. Minnesota's John Mariucci (one of the few Americans to play in the NHL in the 1940s) began to lobby for reforming the rules and increasing the use of American-born players. "John wasn't anti-Canadian," recalls one of his players, 1980 Olympic coach Herb Brooks. "He was pro-American."

Incensed one night when his players were manhandled by Denver's older Canadian players, Mariucci vowed he would never play Denver again and in 1958 he called in some of his friendship markers to convince officials at Minnesota, Michigan State, the University of Michigan and Michigan Tech to leave the Western Intercollegiate Hockey League. The top college teams in the West re-formed as the Western Collegiate Hockey Association in 1959. It would be quite a few years before Mariucci was comfortable playing Denver. When he was forced to do so at the NCAA tournament in 1961, he had Lou Nanne, a naturalized American player, carry a sign that read, "We fry Canadian bacon."

While Mariucci was lobbying for reform in the West, equally colorful characters were changing the game in the East. Cornell's Ned Harkness was a feisty coach who didn't like losing and didn't think much of the west's dominance in the NCAA finals. Boston University's Jack Kelley was another fire-breathing coach with little patience (and less humor) for losing.

Everyone who knows Kelley seems to have a story about his competitiveness and intense rivalry with Boston College and its long-time coach, Snooks Kelley. One that has stood the test of time concerns a chair turned to kindling. In 1972, the college hockey community knew Jack Kelley was planning to quit at Boston University and each of his opponents decided to give him a gift. The Boston College officials made the mistake of presenting Kelley with a BC chair—before the BC–BU game. Legend has it that Jack Kelley broke the chair into pieces when his team lost in what coincidentally was Snooks Kelley's 500th career win. Jack Kelley himself says the tale has been exaggerated over time. "All I can tell you is that I've never seen that chair in our house or in his office," says his son, Mark, a scout with the Pittsburgh Penguins. Jack Parker was Jack Kelley's assistant. As he remembers the situation, "Oh, he threw it, and was kicking it. I'm not saying he broke it."

Under Harkness and Kelley, Cornell and Boston University were at last able to break the chains of the west's domination. In 1967, Cornell won the NCAA title and BU finished second, the first time a team from the east had won since Rensselaer Polytechnic in 1954. Cornell won again in 1970 while Boston University won consecutive titles in 1971 and 1972. The name most associated with hockey at Cornell in that era is Hall of Famer Ken Dryden, who played goal for Cornell before signing with the Montreal Canadiens. Dryden, now president of the Maple Leafs, was one of the most advanced, technically sound goaltenders in NCAA history, but the most celebrated Cornell team of that era is the 1969–70 squad, the only Division I team in college hockey history to record a perfect season en route to an NCAA championship.

The Big Red was 29–0 that season; the closest they came to a loss was in the Eastern Collegiate Athletic Conference Game when John Hughes scored with 14 seconds left to leave Cornell 3–2 up against Clarkson. "Most people would be willing to bet that Ken Dryden was the goaltender on that team," says Joe Bertagna, a former Harvard goaltender and current Hockey East commissioner, "but he wasn't." The 6'4", 210-pound Dryden graduated the season before and Cornell's new goaltender, Brian Cropper, was 5'5" and barely weighed 125 pounds with a pocketful of change.

Most coaches figured that Cornell's years of dominance would be over when Dryden left, but they hadn't counted on the star player of the 1969–70 team. Dan Lodboa was a rocket-fueled speedster with a nifty scoring touch who was much chagrined when Harkness switched him from left wing to defense, but he ended up being the country's best puck-carrying defenseman. He scored 24 goals in the season and netted three third-period goals to help Cornell beat Clarkson 6–4 in the 1970 NCAA championship game. "He was my Bobby Orr," said Harkness years later. "Boa was the greatest hockey player I ever coached, the greatest college player I ever saw."

Over the past 30 years, only the 1992–93 Maine team has come close to matching Cornell's feat of the perfect season when the Black Bears went 42–1–2 and Paul Kariya won the Hobey Baker Award as college player of the year. "He dominated college hockey like Michael Jordan dominated basketball," says Maine coach Shawn Walsh. "He was electrifying." The goalies on that team were Garth Snow, now with the Vancouver Canucks, and Mike Dunham, now with the Nashville Predators. The Black Bears beat Lake Superior State for the national championship that year, and in 1994–95 they defeated Michigan in what is considered one of the greatest games in NCAA hockey history. It was also the longest game in NCAA history. Dan Shermerhorn scored 28 seconds into the third overtime to give the Black Bears a 4–3 win in the semifinals. With end-to-end action throughout the game, Maine goaltender Blair Allison and Michigan's Marty Turco combined for 99 saves. "It was an unbelievable game," Walsh says. "It was hard to call anyone a loser in that game." Indeed, Turco's disappointment would be eased by winning NCAA titles in 1996 and 1998.

The other game that makes anyone's list of top games in NCAA history is Bowling Green's 5–4 win over Minnesota-Duluth in the 1984 NCAA championship game. That contest lasted 97 minutes and 11 seconds before Gino Cavallini scored for Bowling Green's victory (Cavallini eventually played in the NHL with Calgary, St. Louis and Quebec.) "That game was like fighters cold-cocking each other. No one would go down," said writer Mike Prisuta, who covered the game.

But college hockey history is rich in great players, colorful coaches and legendary stories, none more telling than the tale of the snow-covered Beanpot Tournament of 1978.

The Beanpot Tournament (which began in December of 1952) brings together teams from Harvard, Boston University, Boston College and Northeastern for an annual tournament to crown the city champions. Next to a national championship, winning this may mean more to these players than anything else they accomplish in hockey. Students and fans also take it quite seriously, which explains what happened during the blizzard of 1978.

As the games were being played in the Boston Garden, the snow kept coming down. In the middle of the second game, the announcer on the public address suggested that those in attendance go home because the city was being hammered by the worst blizzard in its history. But a good many didn't want to go home and spent the night in the Garden, foraging for leftover popcorn and overcooked hot dogs. People were sacked out all over the building.

In 1962, University of Michigan player Red Berenson earned a rough ride by becoming the first player in that era to jump directly from college hockey to the pros. Berenson played for the Montreal Canadiens the night after he played for the Wolverines in an NCAA consolation game.

Berenson says his NHL peers looked at him as if he had sprouted three heads. "I was considered an intellectual geek." And indeed he returned to his roots as Michigan's head coach since 1984–85.

Since Berenson's debut, college players' foothold in the NHL has strengthened each year and they are now in abundant supply. Among the NHL's leading scorers in 1999–2000 are former college players Paul Kariya, Tony Amonte (Boston University) and John LeClair (Vermont). Other top collegians include 1999 Calder Trophy winner Chris Drury (Boston U), Adam Oates (RPI), Rod Brind'Amour (Michigan State), Brett Hull (Minnesota-Duluth), Doug Weight (Lake Superior State), Joe Nieuwendyk (Cornell), Keith Tkachuk (Boston University) and Ed Belfour (North Dakota).

Coaches have played a major role in developing the game. We have touched on the pivotal roles played by Eddie Jeremiah in the east and John Mariucci in the west, but college hockey never had a better promoter than Wisconsin coach Bob Johnson, who became known simply as "Badger Bob." Johnson took his players to shopping malls in full gear and had them give talks on the use of equipment. And he promoted the game even more with what he could do on the ice, leading Wisconsin to NCAA titles in 1973, 1977 and 1981. "No man was ever more enthusiastic about hockey than Bob Johnson," says Art Berglund.

Still, the NHL resisted hiring college coaches (particularly after Harkness was given a try and proved a bust with the Detroit Red Wings in the 1970s) until former Minnesota and U.S. Olympic coach Herb Brooks was hired by the New York Rangers in 1981. In 1982, his long-time rival Johnson was named coach of the Calgary Flames.

The Minnesota Gophers program remains one of the most successful in college hockey. They have made 24 NCAA tournament appearances, including 13 in a row from 1983-84 through 1996-97. What makes the program unique is that it relies almost exclusively on Minnesota-bred players. In fact, the 2000-2001 Gophers will include the first non-Minnesotan to wear the Maroon and Gold since 1987. Minnesota, Boston University and Michigan have made a combined 72 NCAA tournament appearances and have totaled 29 appearances in the national championship game. Michigan (which won the first NCAA title in 1948) won its NCAA-record ninth championship in 1998. Boston University holds the record for NCAA tournament appearances with 25, many of them with Jack Parker behind the bench. He replaced Jack Kelley in 1973 and has notched more than 600 wins through the 1999-2000 season. He's fourth on the all-time list but still more than 200 wins short of Michigan State's Ron Mason, who holds the college record of 864 heading into the 2000-01 season.

College hockey has tremendous respect for its history. The Boston University–Boston College rivalry is as fresh today as it was when Jack Kelley and Snooks Kelly were behind the two benches. Bragging rights are still extremely important in college hockey. "What makes a difference in college hockey is the fans and school spirit aspect," observed Mike Prisuta. "BU in the east and Michigan in the west are famous for their choreographed cheers for each situation in a game. And they all know what to do. It can be very intimidating."

Imagine what the players thought the night Goldy the Gopher recorded a huge takedown of Bucky the Badger in the pregame hoopla surrounding a Minnesota–Wisconsin game. North Dakota fans may have crossed the line at one game when they threw a dead gopher on the ice, just to let Minnesota know what their players would look like when North Dakota reduced them to road kill. College hockey arenas are one of the few venues where you can catch a 60-year-old, bespectacled history professor taking part in the organized public chanting of expletives perhaps best deleted when he doesn't like a high-sticking call. Through the years at Harvard, in the rare moments when the hockey squad is struggling, the famously well-heeled and supposedly intellectually superior student body has chanted, "That's all right, that's OK, you're going to work for us someday." Bertagna didn't enjoy that one much when he played. He preferred Harvard's reaction to the rumors Ned Harkness was enrolling Canadian players in Cornell's agriculture program. When players from Cornell arrived at the Harvard arena, they were greeted by signs that read, "Welcome Canada's future farmers," or "Hey, Cornell, if you're here, who's milking the cows?"

No one is sure what school's fans started playing a major role first. It is thought to have been more pronounced in the east before it became fashionable in the west. "Some people make the case that the wise guy cheers might have some sort of Ivy League band history. They have an irreverence," Bertagna says. But it's all in good fun, and most coaches wouldn't want the game to lose the edge that it gets from fans' antics. Even goaltenders, who usually take the brunt of fan zaniness, don't seem to mind. Everyone who loves the game has their fond memories: the Boston University band playing the Peter Gunn theme a good many years ago now; Wisconsin's repeated rendition of the Budweiser song, the closest the game has yet come to an overall theme song. Players know they have played a real away game when they leave Badgerland with their ears ringing to it. They all preserve the closeness of the fraternity—even if the sport hasn't grown like it could.

"What's interesting is our uniqueness is also what holds us back," Bertagna explains. "We have [big schools like] Michigan and Ohio State … but a big part of who we are is Saturday night in Potsdam, New York, or Saturday night in Sault Ste. Marie [Lake Superior] or Houghton [Michigan Tech]. Houston Field House in Troy, New York, [RPI] and Gutterson [Arena] in Burlington [Vermont]. These are great storied places that are a big part of our tradition. We have some unusually small schools where we are the only game in town."

As television expresses more interest, there is a concern that the small college teams will be squeezed out, especially if bigger schools embrace the sport. "Unfortunately, the world is changing, and we have a dilemma," Bertagna concludes. "How do we advance our game without it being done at the expense of our game?"

NCAA Hockey Today

Patrick Lethert

College hockey is a paradox. In many ways, it is a niche sport. As the National Hockey League expands into the Sun Belt, college hockey remains the possession of those who shovel snow. Rabid college hockey fans will drive hours in January cold to watch their team compete in a 2,000-seat arena. College hockey is growing. Hundreds of games are now televised every year. Top college players are drafted—and well paid—by NHL teams. But despite growing popularity, college hockey has remained true to its roots. As the number of teams and amount of exposure increases, the game retains its collegiate atmosphere. College hockey is a major sport in which it is not absurd to imagine the University of Michigan facing Dartmouth College for the national championship before 20,000 fans.

American college hockey has its roots in four primary geographic pockets: New England, New York state, the upper Midwest and Colorado. These areas were home to the finest teams in the nation over the second half of the 20th century. Boston, the hub of New England college hockey, is home to four Division I hockey programs. Three of them—Boston College, Boston University and Harvard—have won the NCAA title. New York state is home to former national champions Rensselaer Polytechnic Institute and Cornell, as well as perennial powers Clarkson and St. Lawrence. The upper Midwest is home to Minnesota, Michigan, Michigan State, North Dakota and Wisconsin. These five programs have combined for 25 NCAA titles since 1948. Finally, Colorado College and the University of Denver have brought seven national titles to the Rocky Mountain State.

After early development in the east, college hockey expanded into the Midwest and West with great success. In fact, of the first 10 NCAA hockey tournaments, the University of Michigan won six titles (including the first in 1948) while Colorado College won two. Colorado College had hosted the event for each of the first 10 seasons. Today, the NCAA Frozen Four—the name given to the semifinals and finals of the national championship tournament—is televised nationally. Championship venues are no longer small auditoriums, but major arenas such as Detroit's Joe Louis Arena, Milwaukee's Bradley Center and FleetCenter in Boston. Despite using much larger buildings than in the past, the NCAA has had to resort to a lottery to allocate Frozen Four tickets. There are Internet sites devoted specifically to college hockey that receive thousands of visits every day. Yet, old rivalries still run deep, fans still roar well-rehearsed chants at opposing players, and colleges with 2,000 students can still compete for national titles with universities 10 times their size.

Ironically, the best-remembered game involving college hockey players was not part of the NCAA tournament. It wasn't even a college hockey game. In 1980, University of Minnesota coach Herb Brooks led a team of 20 American college players and alumni to the stunning "Miracle on Ice" victory over the Soviet juggernaut. The 20 players on Brooks's team represented Boston University (4), Bowling Green (2), Minnesota (9), Minnesota-Duluth (2), North Dakota (1), and Wisconsin (2). The Olympic gold brought the spotlight on this group of college players, several of whom went on to long NHL careers.

Through the 1980s and 1990s, the universe of NCAA Division I Ice Hockey was clearly divided into East and West. Although the West stretched to Alaska, the dividing line between the two regions was in Ohio. There were two conferences to the East and two conferences to the West. In the East, the Eastern College Athletic Conference (ECAC) now consists of 12 teams (Brown, Clarkson, Colgate, Cornell, Dartmouth, Harvard, Princeton, Rensselaer, St. Lawrence, Union College, Vermont and Yale). The Hockey East Association (HE) has nine teams (Boston College, Boston University, Maine, Massachusetts-Amherst, Massachusetts-Lowell, New Hampshire, Merrimack, Northeastern and Providence). In the West, the Central Collegiate Hockey Association (CCHA) is now 12 teams strong (Alaska-Fairbanks, Bowling Green, Ferris State, Lake Superior State, Miami (Ohio), Michigan, Michigan State, Nebraska-Omaha, Northern Michigan, Notre Dame, Ohio State and Western Michigan). The Western Collegiate Hockey Association (WCHA) has 10 members (Alaska-Anchorage, Colorado College, Denver, Michigan Tech, Minnesota, Minnesota-Duluth, Minnesota State-Mankato, North Dakota, St. Cloud State and Wisconsin).

Beginning in 1999–2000, the ranks of Division I Independents (teams not affiliated with a conference) were eliminated as College Hockey America was formed. The seven schools in CHA (Air Force, Alabama-Huntsville, Army, Bemidji State, Findlay, Niagara and Wayne State) are not located near one another, but the conference has allowed all of the schools to schedule a full slate of Division I games. A third Eastern conference was also added in 1999, as the Metro Atlantic Athletic Conference's (MAAC) 10 schools joined Division I (American-International, Bentley, Canisius, Connecticut, Fairfield, Holy Cross, Iona, Mercyhurst, Quinnipiac and Sacred Heart).

The college hockey regular season stretches from mid-October to the beginning of March. With the notable exception of Hockey East, where the nine schools are closely situated, most college hockey games are played in two-game series on Friday and Saturday nights. In most conferences, these series consist of consecutive games against the same opponent and can become very intense. In the ECAC, teams are paired as travel partners and a home series consists of playing each of two visiting teams on successive nights. Most teams play 32 to 40 regular-season games. The regular-season champion of each of the four "established" conferences automatically receives one of the 12 berths in the NCAA tournament.

At the conclusion of the regular season, each conference conducts its own playoffs. In most cases, the first rounds are held at the site of the higher seeded team, with the semifinals and finals moved to a single location. Some of these locations rotate while others are held annually at a single major venue. The champion of the Hockey East playoffs is crowned annually at Boston's FleetCenter, while the CCHA playoffs lead teams on "The Road to the Joe" (as in Joe Louis Arena). The playoff winners of all six conferences receive NCAA bids. Thus, as many as 10 NCAA bids can be gained by winning conference titles. However, if regular-season champions also win conference tournaments the number of at-large berths for the NCAA tournament will be increased.

At-large NCAA tournament bids are awarded by a system known as Pairwise Rankings. The Pairwise system is completely objective in determining the tournament field;

however, a committee does oversee the seeding of teams that qualify for the tournament. To qualify for Pairwise consideration, a team must have a record of .500 or better. Each "Team Under Consideration" is then scored in five categories relative to every other team at or above .500. Thus, each Team Under Consideration essentially "plays" each of the others for one Pairwise point. The five criteria considered for the Pairwise Rankings are: head-to-head record, record against other Teams Under Consideration, record against common opponents, record in the last 16 games, and Ratings Percentage Index which is based upon winning percentage and strength of schedule. Each category awards one point to the winner, with the exception of head-to-head wins, which each count as one point. A sample Pairwise comparison might look like this:

MINNESOTA	CRITERIA	WISCONSIN
.604	RPI	.593
10–6	Common Opponents	8–8
14–4	Teams Under Consideration	10–5
11–5	Last 16 Games	12–4
2	**Head to Head**	**2**
5	Points	3

In the above comparison, Minnesota receives a point for having a higher RPI, one for a better record against teams that each has played, one for a better record against other Teams Under Consideration, and two points for two wins over Wisconsin. Wisconsin receives one point for having fared better in its last 16 games and two points for two head-to-head wins over Minnesota. After all points are awarded, Minnesota wins the comparison 5–3 and receives one Pairwise point. After every team over .500 is compared with every over in this way, the teams are ranked by the number of comparisons that they win.

The Pairwise Rankings are a source of great interest to college hockey fans throughout the season. First, because the system used by the committee is known, fans can be nearly certain of where their team stands in relation to an at-large NCAA berth at any time. Second, the Pairwise Rankings can prove a fragile ecosystem. For instance, in the example above, if Minnesota has four wins against North Dakota, but North Dakota falls below .500, Minnesota's record against Teams Under Consideration suddenly falls from 14–4 to 10–4. If Minnesota is 0–2 against Michigan and Wisconsin defeats Michigan in their first two meetings of the season, the two teams both would have 10–8 records against common opponents. Seemingly small changes can affect many teams. The complex system has its detractors, but it is objective and avoids many of the political allegations that accompany selections made by committees in other sports.

Currently, the NCAA Tournament field includes 12 teams. As noted, between six and 10 of the entrants earn bids by winning their conference's regular-season title or postseason playoffs. At the conclusion of the playoff tournaments, the remaining berths are awarded to the teams with the best Pairwise rankings. The final berths are actually determined by a slightly modified system in which the "bubble teams" are compared to each other rather than the field at large. The 12 teams that qualify for the NCAA tournament are then seeded into two regional fields. The top two seeds in each region receive first-round byes while teams five through 12 compete for the right to play the top four teams the following day. The four semifinalists then move to one location for the Frozen Four—so named to give it a separate identity from its basketball counterpart. This event has been staged in cities associated with college hockey such as Boston, Detroit, St. Paul and Albany, as well as in cities without a college hockey presence such as Cincinnati and Anaheim. The Frozen Four crowns the Men's Division I national champion.

As college football has its Heisman Trophy, college hockey bestows the Hobey Baker Award on its finest player. "The Hobey," named for the legendary Princeton star of the 1910s and presented by the Decathlon Club of Bloomington, Minnesota, is awarded based on voting by college coaches, media, and the public. Such public input is rare in sports award voting, but fans are encouraged to participate on the internet at U.S. College Hockey Online. The entire fan vote at USCHO is essentially given the weight of one ballot. Minnesota's Neal Broten was the first Hobey Baker recipient in 1981. Other winners have included players with long, or accomplished National Hockey League careers such as Maine's Paul Kariya, Bowling Green's Brian Holzinger and Tom Kurvers of Minnesota-Duluth, but there have also been Hobey winners whose outstanding college careers did not lead to NHL success.

Prior to the 1970s, well over 90 percent of the NHL players were Canadian-born and trained in Canada's major junior leagues. College hockey players only occasionally reached the NHL, and even then these superstars of the college game tended to become role players. Far more common were the former college all-Americans who saw little NHL duty and spent most of their professional careers in the minor leagues or in Europe. College players tended to have cultural differences with the vast majority of their NHL teammates whose formal education had often ended when they chose junior hockey in their mid-teens. In the 1960s and 1970s, the small minority of all-star caliber NCAA alums playing in the NHL included Michigan center Red Berenson and Cornell goaltender Ken Dryden.

In the past 20 years, several factors have increased the presence of NHL caliber prospects in college hockey. First, the 1980 U.S. Olympic victory made celebrities of many former college hockey players. Second, the number of NHL teams has increased from six in 1967 to 30 for the 2000–2001 season. Third, rather than simply being role players, the NCAA alums in the NHL today have become some of the game's biggest stars. During the 1999–2000 season over 170 NCAA alumni saw action in the NHL.

If the 1980 Olympics were U.S. collegiate hockey's graduation to the big time, the 1996 World Cup was its lifetime achievement award. In 1996, Team USA won the World Cup of Hockey with a team made up primarily of NHL players who were college hockey alumni. Perhaps as significant as the U.S. victory was the fact that the World Cup title was not considered a major upset like the 1980 Olympic title had been. Clearly the top U.S. college alums were stars of the same magnitude as players who cut their teeth in Canada or Europe. A short list of NCAA alums who have represented the United States in recent international events includes Joel Otto (Bemidji State), Tony Amonte (Boston University), Brian Rolston (Lake Superior State), Brian Leetch (Boston College), John LeClair (Vermont), Brett Hull (Minnesota-Duluth), Chris Chelios (Wisconsin), Keith Tkachuk (Boston U.), Bryan Smolinski (Michigan State), Mike Richter (Wisconsin) and Todd Marchant (Clarkson). Team Canada members who chose U.S. college hockey as their path to the NHL have included Paul Kariya (Maine), Joe Nieuwendyk (Cornell), Curtis Joseph (Wisconsin), Rob Blake (Bowling Green) and Rod Brind'Amour (Michigan State).

Unlike NCAA football and basketball players, recruits to college hockey are virtually always unknown to anyone but recruiters and hard-core fans. Football and basketball recruits are well publicized by television and print journalists and often are already stars when they walk onto campus as freshmen, but college hockey recruits come from much less heralded places. Key recruiting leagues for NCAA hockey teams are Provincial Junior A leagues in Canada and developmental leagues such as the United States Hockey League, the North American Hockey League and the Eastern Junior Hockey League. USHL, NAHL and EJHL teams are stocked primarily with players who have completed high school and are seeking a Division I scholarship. Many NCAA players also come directly from prep school hockey programs in the northeast, Minnesota high school hockey and the United States Development Team. In 1998–99, the largest numbers of Division I players came from the Canadian province of Ontario and from Minnesota.

In addition to the marquee programs in Division I, there are a significant number of smaller colleges that compete in varsity hockey at the Division II and III levels. Geographically, the lower divisions mirror Division I with two key exceptions: there are no Division II or III programs west of Minnesota, and there are very few Division II or III programs between New York and Wisconsin. In the East, there are five college hockey conferences in the lower divisions. Four of these conferences are constituents of the ECAC. The fifth, SUNYAC, is comprised of the various campuses of the State University of New York. In the Midwest, the Minnesota Intercollegiate Athletic Conference, the Northern Collegiate Hockey Association and the Midwest Collegiate Hockey Association cover Illinois, Wisconsin and Minnesota. In addition to Division II and III, there are over 100 colleges and universities that sponsor club teams that compete under the American Collegiate Hockey Association.

The success of Division II and III college hockey has produced both Division I programs and NHL alumni. Some former Division II and III champions that now compete at the Division I level include: Merrimack, Minnesota State-Mankato (then Mankato State), Lowell, Alabama-Huntsville, Bemidji State and the members of the MAAC conference. Division II/III alumni who have skated in the NHL include Gary Sargent, Joel Otto and Jim McElmury (all of Bemidji State), Hubie McDonough (St. Anselm), Todd Krygier (Connecticut), Dave Forbes (American-International), Craig MacTavish and Mark Kumpel (Lowell), Guy Hebert (Hamilton), Ralph Barahona (Wisconsin-Stevens Point) and Alex Hicks (Wisconsin-Eau Claire).

Eighteen years after "The Miracle on Ice," the dazzling gold medal performance by the United States women's hockey team in 1998 put that team on Wheaties boxes and women's college hockey on the map.

Without professional stars to represent them, the United States and Canada won gold and silver medals respectively at Nagano by using teams made up of primarily college-aged players. The excitement created by the American gold medal victory jump-started growth of women's college hockey in the U.S. In 1997, only 12 Division I programs existed, none of which played west of New York state. The *de facto* national champion was the winner of the ECAC. In 1998, the University of Minnesota became the first "western" women's team. In 1999–2000, the WCHA began sponsoring women's hockey and the number of Division I programs increased to 20: 13 in the ECAC and seven in the WCHA.

From 1998 through 2000, the champion of U.S. women's college hockey was determined by a tournament sponsored by the American Women's College Hockey Alliance, an arm of USA Hockey. Not surprisingly, schools with rich hockey histories field many of the top women's teams. The winners of the first three AWCHA tournaments were New Hampshire, Harvard and Minnesota.

The top player in women's college hockey receives the Patty Kazmaier Memorial Award. The award is named in honor of the former Princeton athlete who starred on the hockey team from 1981–82 through 1985–86 before passing away from a rare blood disease in 1990 at the age of 28. (Patty's father Richard was a former Heisman Trophy winner at Princeton.) In its first three years, the winners of "The Patty" have been A.J. Mleczko (Harvard), Brandy Fisher (New Hampshire) and Alison Brewer (Brown). The award is presented annually by the USA Hockey Foundation.

The future is now for women's ice hockey. The number of young girls playing hockey continues to grow, as does the number of varsity teams. In 2000–2001, the American Collegiate Hockey Association will add a woman's division, allowing for championship play for more participants at varying levels of ability. Beginning in 2001, the NCAA will sponsor a national tournament for women's ice hockey.

MINNESOTA'S HOLY WEEK

Patrick Lethert

Minneapolis-St. Paul magazine once published a quiz to help Minnesota newcomers assess their transition to life in the state. One question asked for another name for the Minnesota State High School Hockey Tournament. The answer: Holy Week. The author's humorous attempt to warn outsiders how seriously Minnesotans take their hockey overstated the importance of the event—but not by much. The Minnesota State High School Hockey Tournament is perhaps the state's most celebrated annual event and is the source of some of its most colorful legends.

Minnesota high schools have been playing hockey in some form since at least the 1890s. By the 1920s, high school hockey was flourishing in St. Paul, Minneapolis and in northern Minnesota. Because there were few artificial ice rinks in existence, almost all games were played outdoors. The best teams were often those with the best access to a lake to skate on. By 1944, St. Paul City Conference hockey games were drawing so well that city athletic director Gene Aldrich proposed a state tournament to crown a formal hockey champion. After obtaining private financial backing, Aldrich organized the first statewide high school hockey tournament in the United States in March, 1945.

The inaugural Minnesota State High School Hockey Tournament was held at the St. Paul Auditorium in downtown St. Paul. A total of 8,434 fans turned out to watch 11 games that culminated with Eveleth's 4–3 victory over Thief River Falls. Testament to the superiority of those two teams was the fact that their semifinal victories came by scores of 12–0 and 10–0, respectively. Testament to the foresight of Gene Aldrich was the fact that the event would eventually outgrow the St. Paul Auditorium and the Metropolitan Sports Center before settling into the 17,000-seat St. Paul Civic Center.

Since the beginning, every state tournament has included eight schools, winners of the eight regional tournaments. While the regional boundaries have been redrawn from time to time, a typical field throughout much of the tournament's history included five teams from the Minneapolis-St. Paul metropolitan area and three from "out state." At least two of these "out state" teams have always come from northern Minnesota. Because the northern teams generally represent small towns, the state's hockey fans tend to embrace them as underdogs. Most Twin Cities fans whose team is not in the tournament find themselves pulling for the boys from the frozen tundra. In the earliest years of the tournament, these northern towns dominated.

The first dynasty in Minnesota high school hockey was Eveleth. This small town, located in what was once Minnesota's "Iron Range," was the home of Hall of Fame goaltender Frank Brimsek and of John Mariucci—the godfather of Minnesota hockey. From 1945 to 1956, Eveleth qualified for all 12 tournaments, was the state's undefeated state champion five times, finished second twice, and took third place three times. Although several star players led Eveleth, the two most notable products of this era were Willard Ikola and John Mayasich. Ikola was a goaltender who went on to the University of Michigan and later coached a Minnesota high school hockey dynasty at Edina. Mayasich went on to become the all-time leading scorer at the University of Minnesota and a two-time U.S. Olympian. He still holds 10 state high school tournament records including most career points (46 in 12 games over 4 years), most goals (36), consecutive games scoring a goal (12), goals and points in one tournament (15, 18) and goals and points in one game (seven and eight).

But Eveleth was not the only northern town to bring dominant hockey teams down to the Twin Cities during the first quarter-century of the tournament. International Falls, located on the Canadian border—and the inspiration for Rocky and Bullwinkle's home town of Frostbite Falls—won state titles in 1957, 1962, 1964, 1965 (26–0), 1966 (26–0) and 1972. Roseau, another town located just minutes from Canada, won the tournament in 1946, 1958, 1959 (30–0), 1961 and later in 1990. The last of the northern dynasties was the Iron Range town of Grand Rapids, which won titles in 1975, 1976 and 1980. Clad in orange and black, the Grand Rapids "Halloween Machine" was led during this era by future NHLers Bill Baker, Jon Casey and Scot Kleinendorst.

By the 1980s, the balance of power had shifted from the small towns of the north to the suburban schools located near Minneapolis and St. Paul. The rink rats who honed their games over long hours on the lake or at the local outdoor rink had given way to players who learned the game at summer hockey camps and had played almost exclusively on indoor ice. The dominance of the larger suburban schools caused the state high school league to end the one-class tournament format in 1992. The tournament now consists of Class AA (large schools) and Class A (smaller schools). Some small schools, notably Roseau (a town of 2,700 which boasts a record 29 Tournament appearances), "play up" to Class AA. In 1999, Roseau conjured up memories of days gone by with a dramatic march to the Class AA championship.

Perhaps the most successful suburban school in the state tournament has come from the upscale community of Edina. Edina won state championships in 1969, 1971, 1974, 1978, 1979, 1982, 1984, 1988 and 1997. Hornet alumni have included NHLers Bill Nyrop, Craig Norwich, Ben Hankinson, Dan Plante, current Carolina Hurricane Paul Ranheim and dozens of NCAA Division I players.

Hill-Murray, South St. Paul and Bloomington-Jefferson are other suburban programs that have had great success in the state tournament. Hill-Murray, ineligible until 1975 because it's a private Catholic school, has accumulated 17 tournament appearances, two state titles and five runner-up finishes. Hill-Murray's NHL alumni include Dave Langevin, Chris Pryor, Steve Janaszak and current NHLers Craig Johnson (Los Angeles) and David Tanabe (Carolina). South St. Paul has made 27 state tournament appearances and boasts former NCAA all-American Doug Woog and NHL All-Star defenseman Phil Housley as alumni. Jefferson High School of Bloomington has been perhaps the most dominant team of the 1990s, winning state titles in 1989, 1992, 1993 and 1994. The 1993 and 1994 Jefferson teams iced eight and nine future Division I college players respectively. Members of those teams included NHLers Mark Parrish (NY Islanders), Mike Crowley (Anaheim) and Ben Clymer (Tampa Bay).

The Minnesota State High School Hockey Tournament has long been the anchor of Minnesota's winter high school sports season. After all eyes focus on the sectional qualifiers, the spotlight turns to St. Paul for tournament week. First-round games begin at noon on both Wednesday and

Thursday and it's not uncommon to see offices and classrooms throughout the state take those afternoons off. Both of the Twin Cities' metropolitan newspapers offer special sections introducing the teams and matchups for the weekend. All championship-round games are broadcast live throughout the state on radio and television. The TV rights to the tourney have generated over $500,000 annually as stations bid for the opportunity to air the games. Annual attendance tops 100,000 over a long weekend with the record set in 1992 when 117,563 fans attended. As the event has moved to larger and larger venues, more spectators have been accommodated but there remains a substantial season ticket waiting list.

With the attention of the entire state (as well as college hockey recruiters and scouts from numerous NHL teams) on them, some players have used the spotlight to grab a place in Minnesota history. The legend of John Mayasich began in 1951, when he tallied 15 goals in three games to lead Eveleth to the state title. Future U.S. Olympian and University of Minnesota player and coach Doug Woog tallied goals in 10 of 12 games over four appearances for South St. Paul. Future St. Louis Blue Joe Micheletti scored seven goals in three games to bring Hibbing the state title in 1973. Future WHA and NHL player Mike Antonovich of Greenway-Coleraine did the same in 1967. In 1978, Roseau came south featuring a first line of three future NHLers: Neal Broten, Aaron Broten and Bryan "Butsy" Erickson. The line put on a tremendous offensive show but the Rams were unable to bring home a championship—proving just how difficult it is to win a Minnesota high school hockey title. More recently, Duluth East's Dave Spehar, also a future Minnesota Gopher, scored hat tricks in all three tournament games to lead the Greyhounds to the 1995 championship.

Fans of the tournament often speak of spectacular games in which young men have battled beyond regulation time for a place in history. The longest of these thrillers went 11 overtime periods (five minutes each) before Minneapolis South defeated perennial power Thief River Falls in 1955. The latter overtime periods of that contest had to be played between periods of the next game. In 1970, goaltender Brad Shelstad of Minneapolis Southwest carried a shutout into overtime of the championship game before his teammates finally tallied for a 1–0 win over defending champion Edina. Shelstad's save on Hornet sniper Bobby Krieger's breakaway in the final minute of the third period sparked the Indians to the only championship ever won by a Minneapolis city school. In 1978, Edina defeated the Brotens and Roseau in the semifinal before taking a double-overtime classic from Iron Range powerhouse Grand Rapids despite being outshot, 52–23.

Perhaps the most memorable game in state tournament history came in 1969, the year that the tournament moved from the St. Paul Auditorium to the 15,000-seat Met Center. Warroad, another small northern town, upset its way into the title game. The Warriors were led by a smooth skating defenseman named Henry Boucha whose shot had bent goal pipes. Boucha had both talent and stamina, resting for only 24 seconds of Warroad's first two games. The other finalist that year was future powerhouse Edina, but most of the state, and 90 percent of the packed Met Center, was passionately supporting Warroad.

With Edina leading 3–2 in the second period, Boucha was driven into the boards by a Hornet defenseman. He fell to the ice with a concussion and was taken straight to the hospital. With Boucha gone, Warroad fell behind 4–2 before mounting a furious rally to tie the score 4–4 and send the crowd into a frenzy. Although Edina went on to win the game in overtime, Boucha and Warroad had written their name in state legend.

The most recent overtime classic at the high school tournament came in 1996 as defending champion Duluth East battled Apple Valley in a semifinal game. After ending regulation time at 4–4, the teams slugged it out for five extra periods (ranging in time from eight to 15 minutes) before Apple Valley's Aaron Dwyer finally scored to give the Eagles a win well after 1 o'clock in the morning. Among the participants in that game were no fewer than seven future Division I college hockey players including Dwyer, Dave Spehar and Apple Valley goaltender Karl Goehring (who would backstop the University of North Dakota to the 2000 NCAA championship). The words of Duluth East's coach Mike Randolph summed up the Apple Valley game and the Minnesota State High School Hockey Tournament: "This was high school hockey at its best." Despite fatigue, Apple Valley went on to beat Edina, 3–2, the next night and claim its first state title.

After several years of development, Minnesota became the first state to sanction a varsity girls' hockey program when 24 teams dropped the puck for the 1994–95 season. That winter, four teams advanced to the first girls' state tournament. There was a distinctly suburban flavor, as the participants (eventual state champion Apple Valley, South St. Paul, Stillwater and Henry Sibley of West St. Paul) were all located within 30 minutes of St. Paul. The games were held at Aldrich Arena, which was named for Gene Aldrich, the father of the original Minnesota State High School Hockey Tournament back in 1945. A crowd of 4,085 fans turned out for the first session. By 1998, over 13,000 fans attended the eight-team tournament and the championship game was televised. With 112 hockey teams having competed in 1999–2000, it's quite likely that the girls will begin creating Minnesota hockey memories too.

CHAPTER 17

European Hockey

The State of the Game

The International Ice Hockey Federation

Janne Stark

The International Ice Hockey Federation was formed in Paris in May, 1908 when French journalist Louis Magnus invited delegates from six countries, Belgium, France, Great Britain, Switzerland, Germany and Russia, to discuss the future of the new game. Germany and Russia declined the invitation, but the others established the *Ligue Internationale de Hockey sur Glace* (LIHG) and chose Magnus as the first president. This meeting is considered to be the First Congress of the International Ice Hockey Federation, the name the organization adopted in 1912.

From four countries in the beginning, IIHF membership now numbers almost 60 nations around the globe. But what is the state of the IIHF in the new millennium?

Financially, the IIHF appears sound. Solid agreements with strong partners have set a stable foundation for the Swiss-based federation, led by president Rene Fasel and general secretary Jan-Ake Edvinsson. The main agreement is with German-based CWL, a company that provides television and radio contracts, advertisement and many other services. CWL has negotiated tremendous deals with Skoda Auto and Nike, for example. The only concern with the German company in recent years has been the fear that the market in Germany would lose interest in hockey because the German team had fallen from the ranks of the World Championship A Pool. These concerns have been alleviated now that Germany has qualified to return to the A Pool in 2001. It is important that the A Pool World Championships remain strong because the IIHF uses the revenues from this tournament and the Olympic Games to finance all its other tournaments. In 1998, the IIHF rendered a net profit of 5.5 million Swiss francs (approximately $3.6 million U.S.) from the Nagano Olympics.

Looking ahead, the IIHF will continue to stage the World Championships every year and the Olympic Games every fourth year. This is a necessity financially, but, strictly in hockey terms, is perhaps not the best situation. Obviously, the biggest concern regarding the World Championships is that the best players are not available to take part. Like Canada and the United States, so many European countries now see their best players skating in the NHL and competing for the Stanley Cup instead of for international honors. It might be best if the IIHF decided to stage the World Championships every four years like the Olympics and worked out a deal with the NHL so that the best players could compete. A scenario such as this would see the following tournament structure: 2002 Olympic Games, 2004 World Championships, 2006 Olympic Games, 2008 World Championships, etc. This is, of course, wishful thinking, but it is a tempting proposition.

On the ice, some problems began to show in the IIHF in 1999–2000. The season ended with the collapse of the European Hockey League, a tournament structure that had included teams from countries all over Europe. A lack of interest, mainly from Swedish teams and their sponsors, led to the collapse. However, the IIHF and most of the teams that took part were losing money on the EHL and it was probably a wise financial decision to let it go.

Though staging tournaments is its most obvious function, the IIHF does much more for world hockey. Annual seminars are held for coaches, referees and linesmen and have resulted in the publication of two manuals: one on coaching development and one for referees. Last season, the first global educational programs for coaches, referees and linesmen were held. Trained IIHF instructors, together with national association instructors, paved the way for over 400 member associations to take responsibility for developing the sport within their countries by using their own people. The first IIHF hockey development camp took place in Nymburk in the Czech Republic in 1999 and was an overwhelming success. Over 200 participants from 41 countries received both practical experience and theoretical information during the seven-day event. The partnership-for-progress working arrangement, created less than four years ago, is starting to pay dividends all around world.

One other important aspect of the IIHF is the control of the transfer market. Last season, the federation processed more than 2,500 player transfers as the international player transfer program, developed together with the NHL, continues to grow. In an attempt to make the program even more efficient, the federation is developing a system to be used on the Internet.

The IIHF also works together with the Hockey Hall of Fame in Toronto, where a permanent exhibit on international hockey was opened in 1998. Remembering the roots of the international game is a very important part of the sport, but a growing aspect of the game today is in-line activities. Two years ago, the IIHF undertook the responsibility of educating instructors so that they were able to instruct coaches, referees and off-rink officials in their national associations. A program has been developed to provide the associations with information on how to form in-line leagues and grassroots programs. Leading the way in this endeavor is Allan Matthews of the Canadian Hockey Association.

The International Ice Hockey Federation has entered the 21st century feeling healthy and prosperous, but president Rene Fasel does have some concerns. He believes that the sport needs more exposure in countries like Austria, Germany, Great Britain, Switzerland, Italy and France. Soccer has long been considered the national pastime in these countries and the IIHF will face big challenges in trying to make significant inroads for the game of hockey.

THE BUSINESS OF EUROPEAN HOCKEY

Ulf Jansson

PLAYER SALARIES IN THE NHL have always been higher than those of European clubs. Smaller arenas, shorter schedules and the absence of large television rights fees all contribute to this disparity. For comparison, a club in Sweden's Elite League, Brynas IF Gavle, for example, has a salary budget of approximately $1.6 million per season. (All sums in U.S. dollars.) This payroll covers three goalies, nine defensemen and 13 forwards. In the NHL, Swedish native Peter Forsberg of the Colorado Avalanche earns a comparable sum in about two months.

The total player payroll for clubs in the Swedish Elite League ranges between $1.2 and $3.2 million. Djurgarden, the 1999–2000 champions, falls somewhere in the middle. It is difficult to compare club budgets because conditions vary. Djurgarden, for example, pays $1.6 million in arena rental each year to play in the new Globen arena in Stockholm.

The average player salary in the Swedish Elite League is about $5,600 per month. From this sum, a player is responsible for personal expenses while being taxed at a rate as high as 50 percent. The highest paid player in Sweden (Norwegian Espen Knutsen) earned about $280,000 playing for Djurgarden last season before signing with the NHL's expansion Columbus Blue Jackets for 2000–01. Knutsen finished second in scoring in the Elite League in 1999–2000, behind another import player from Finland, Juha Riihijarvi of Malmo.

Another Finn, veteran national team goaltender Jarmo Myllys, earned about $200,000 playing for Lulea, but that amount has been reduced as the club, with millions of dollars in debt, could no longer afford this salary. The team's two stars from the Czech Republic, Jiri Kuzera and Martin Hostak, each earn about $110,000 a year. Import players like these play a significant role in Swedish hockey. In 1999–2000, Sweden was a net exporter of hockey talent: 181 import players skated for Swedish clubs while 246 players from Sweden played elsewhere.

Player salaries in Finland are approximately 20 percent higher than those in Sweden. Jokerit Helsinki's roster includes a league-high eight players whose rights are owned by NHL clubs. Jokerit's owner, Hjallis Harkimo, is also majority owner of the country's largest rink, the Hartwall Arena. With a capacity of 13,290, and with ticket prices increasing, Jokerit can afford to pay higher salaries. Like Sweden, Finland is a net exporter of hockey talent: 104 imports play in Finnish leagues while 248 players are employed outside the country.

The average player in the German league earns about $90,000 a year but players in Germany do not pay income tax. Imports, of which there were a European high of 830 in 1999–2000, can earn up to $150,000 for a one-year contract. Ten of 15 teams in the Deutsche Eishockey Liga have Canadian coaches. (Three teams have German coaches, one is Czech and one is Swedish.) Dave King recently left Adler Mannheim to assume the head coaching job with Columbus.

The majority of imports in German hockey are Canadian. The number of foreign players on each club has recently been reduced from 18 to 16. If a team does not have 16 foreigners on its roster at the start of the season, it can carry no more than 14 during the year. These new restrictions have reduced the number of jobs available to international players. As a result, negotiations between clubs and agents representing foreign clients have become much tougher.

In Switzerland, five imports are allowed on each club's roster, though only three are allowed to dress for any one game. As in Germany, player salaries are tax free. Top players from abroad earn approximately $220,000 a year. Leading Swiss-born players earn about $130,000 while the Swiss National League's average salary is about $85,000. Regular season champions Lugano, sponsored by travel agent-king Geomanlegazza, is traditionally the richest club. The status of the others varies. Kloten was in financial trouble this past year but was saved by a new sponsorship agreement with Swiss Air.

Player movement from country to country in Europe has increased steadily since the "Bosman Decision," a landmark ruling by a European court that dealt with a soccer player but had implications for all professional athletes who are citizens of countries within the European Union. The court determined that once an athlete's contract has expired, he has the right to play anywhere he chooses within Europe. The court also stipulated that the club that acquires him is under no obligation to provide compensation to his former team. Throughout European sports, this has resulted in a freer movement of players from league to league and country to country.

In hockey, Germany and Switzerland have prospered most in this era of liberalized player movement and have had the highest level of success importing players to upgrade their club teams. Imported players have also found plenty of work in Great Britain (33 exports, 238 imports). In Sweden, Russia and Finland, the overall quality of league play would appear to have declined because of the number of players that have left their countries to play abroad. The Czech Republic, with its growing economy, has had some success keeping its stars though many other players have departed. The number of Czech players leaving to play elsewhere is a European high 314. Only 68 imports appeared in the Czech Republic in 1999–2000. Slovakia exhibits comparable numbers: 182 exports, 39 imports.

In the Czech Republic, Robert Reichel was making $300,000 in Litvinov last season while David Vyborny made about the same with Sparta Praha. The average salary in the Czech league is about $30,000 a year, but, in comparison to other European countries, the cost of living there is low. Players also receive many perks, such as free apartments, free cars and discount shopping. The stars of sport have always been a privileged class in Eastern Europe and some of this is still true in the Czech Republic and Slovakia.

In Russia, the richest teams are now in the Urals and the far East, where leading industrial companies often sponsor clubs. Ak Bars Kazan, for example, pays up to $100,000 a year for some stars and between $30,000 to $40,000 for average players. But in Moscow, where the most successful teams previously were based, there are many young players glad to play for $12,000 a year. The average salary for Moscow Dynamo is approximately $30,000 a year but Moscow's other major clubs—CSKA (Central Red Army), Soviet Wings and Spartak—are currently facing financial hardship despite past glories.

Throughout Europe, most clubs cannot remain economically viable on ticket sales alone. This is instantly apparent at any European game as every available surface is covered with sponsors' logos. Players' uniforms, the ice surface, rinkboards and numerous banners combine to make a commercial crazy-quilt of color. Every opportunity to maximize advertising, marketing rights and sponsorships is being exploited to help relieve the financial challenges that many clubs and leagues continue to face.

Russian Hockey: Is the Game's Cold War Finally Over?

Igor Kuperman

YOU ALWAYS WANT TO KNOW what your main rival is doing. In life. In politics. In sports. In hockey, in particular. For decades, Canadians kept their eyes on Russian hockey. But the Russian game has been in a deep crisis since the beginning of the 1990s. The World Championships and Olympic triumphs are long gone. More recently, the concerns have been is the Russian Bear still alive? Who is leaving for the NHL next? Is the level of play in the Russian league still high?

Hockey players were among the first people to experience the impact of the dissolution of the Soviet Union. The country's team that won the World Junior Championship in 1991–92 entered the competition as the USSR but closed it as a team representing the Commonwealth of Independent States. Though they won the tournament, the players were never again to hear the sounds of the Soviet anthem.

Internally, Russian hockey started to change at the end of the 1990s. In 1996, the Russian Hockey League (RHL) was formed, replacing the former Inter-State Hockey League which had included the clubs from former Soviet Republics. However, this new league did not always consider the wishes and requirements of the Russian Hockey Federation, and this led to conflict. The conflict was finally resolved in typical Russian fashion. A decision of the government in 1999 decreed that the sports federations would be responsible for the development of individual sports in the country. Based on this decree, Hockey Federation president Alexander Steblin ruled that the RHL be closed down. The new Professional Hockey League (PHL) took over. It included 43 teams: 20 in the Superleague plus a 23-team First League.

Participation in the PHL costs the teams money in membership fees. In addition, each team needs about $3 million a year to cover salaries, transportation, medical care, supplies, performance bonuses, ice and arena rental, etc. Many teams are struggling just to survive, but some go all-out to win. For example, Severstal Cherepovets spent $250,000 in transfer fees to acquire 16 new players in 1999–2000. By Russian hockey standards, this is an incredible sum.

Since 1998–99, a rule has been in place in Russian hockey that allows teams to lend out players who can't earn a spot in their lineup to other clubs. The original team still pays their players' salaries, but has the right to recall them at any time. Also interesting is the fact that Russia must be the only country where teams have to pay television networks to show their games and not the other way round. PHL president Nikolai Uryupin is trying to change this, but so far he's been unsuccessful.

With the democratic changes the country has been going through, Russian hockey clubs now have the chance to invite foreign players to join them. Remarkably, Canadian players—historically Russia's main rivals—are the focal point of interest for Russian hockey clubs.

Inviting foreigners makes economic sense for the Russian clubs since the transfer of Canadians costs about 30 times less than the transfer of a Russian player. The Canadian players also stand to gain. For example, Canadians dressing for Molot-Prikamje Perm make $50,000 U.S. per year while getting an apartment for free and paying no taxes. Alexander Tyzhnykh, a former Russian goalie who played for the Central Red Army club in Moscow and used to be Vladislav Tretiak's backup, is now an agent who is the main supplier of Canadian players to clubs in Russia.

American-born Tod Hartje was the first North American to make the trek behind the Iron Curtain. He played in what used to be the Soviet Union, spending the full 1990–91 season with the Sokol team in Kiev. He would later write a book about his experience. Russ Romaniuk and Pat Elynuik came to Dynamo Moscow from the Winnipeg Jets in 1991. They took part in the team's training camp, but while they were in Moscow the communists staged an uprising.

At the beginning of the 1999–2000 Russian hockey season, there were eight Canadians in the league. Six of them finished the year in Russia. Former NHL goalie Vincent Riendeau played for Lada. Defencemen Cory Murphy and Steve Wilson, both former members of Chesapeake in the East Coast Hockey League, played for Molot-Prikamje Perm. Defenceman Chris Coveny, from Peoria of the ECHL, played for Avangard Omsk. Goalie Andre Racicot, who used to play for the Montreal Canadiens, dressed for Neftekhimik, while netminder Steve Plouffe played for Amur Khabarovsk. The two Canadians who didn't finish out the season were Steve Zoryk and Shawn Allard. Zoryk, who came to Avangard from South Carolina in the ECHL, was dismissed after he took part in a drunken brawl in a night club. Allard, formerly of Wheeling in the ECHL, had played for Amur before being sent home when his skills were found lacking.

Riendeau had played for Lada in 1998–99 and liked it so much that he decided to return to Russia. He pushed the club's former number-one goalie, Sergei Nikolayev, into a backup position in 1999–2000. On the other hand, Racicot, who won a Stanley Cup ring with the Montreal Canadiens in 1993, had difficulty adjusting to Russian food. He did eventually get used to it and began to join his Russian teammates for their favorite meat-and-potatoes feasts.

Canadians are not the only foreigners playing in Russia. Since the fall of the Soviet Union, players from its former republics have all become foreigners. Belarussian Oleg Mikulchik and brothers Yevgeny and Alexander Koreshkov from Kazakhstan played for Metallurg Magnitogorsk. Belarussian Alexei Kalyuzhny dressed for Dynamo Moscow. Russian teams are happy to accept good players no matter where they come from, but there are now so many foreigners that the Russian hockey federation had to impose a limit. No more than three players without Russian passports are allowed to be in a team's lineup in any given game. Russian officials say they learned their lesson from Germany, where the league is full of foreign players but the national team has been relegated to the B Pool of the World Championships because local players get no chance to develop.

The decision to limit the number of foreigners sparked an unexpected reaction, as a founding conference of the Interregional professional union of Russian hockey players took place in Magnitogorsk in mid-February, 2000. Most of the Superleague and First League teams were represented. There were 10 representatives from former republics of the USSR—including seven from Kazakhstan—on the Metallurg Magnitogorsk roster. They were the main victims of the federation decision not to permit more than three non-Russian players on each team.

"Our local club suffers from spiteful decisions made by Russian hockey leaders," said Metallurg forward Mikhail Borodulin, the president-elect of the new union. "The Interregional professional union's main objective is to defend players' rights against the Russian hockey federation, as well against as individual league and club managers." The new organization will also help players negotiate contracts.

"We haven't got agents yet," Borodulin said. "But we will try to fill the void. When needed, we will send lawyers to help players negotiate their deals. This assistance will be free of charge."

Though there is still inner turmoil, successes at the last few World Junior Championships have proven that the rumors of Russian hockey's demise have been premature. The complicated economic situation in the country does not help Russian players, but much of the hockey infrastructure has remained and the coaches are still working hard. And there is no shortage of talent, either. After all, four players from the 1998–99 Russian junior national team are already in the NHL: Roman Lyashenko (Dallas), Artem Chubarov (Vancouver), Vitali Vishnevsky (Anaheim) and Maxim Afinogenov (Buffalo). Two more players from that team—Maxim Balmochnykh (Anaheim) and Petr Schastlivy (Ottawa)—played on NHL farm teams in 1999–2000.

Despite reports to the contrary, it would appear that the Russian bear is still alive and kicking.

CZECH AND SLOVAK HOCKEY

Pavel Barta

WHEN THE CZECH REPUBLIC FACED SLOVAKIA in the 2000 World Championships final, the dreams of many people in both countries came true. The media had trumpeted "The Battle of the Slavs," but almost everybody had expected a different Slavic showdown in St. Petersburg. However, Russia, with a roster sprinkled with some of hockey's biggest names—including NHL goal-scoring leader Pavel Bure and holdout Alexei Yashin—crashed out of the tournament after the qualifying round en route to a stunning 11th-place finish.

Since the former Czechoslovakia split up on December 31, 1992, the Czech Republic, with only 10.5 million citizens and some 50,000 registered players, has established itself as a global hockey power. In the past eight World Championships, the Czechs have reached the medal podium six times and won the title on three occasions: 1996, 1999 and 2000. They are the only country to emerge with a medal at the last five consecutive championships. When the gold medal performance at the Nagano Olympics is added to the streak of World Championship success, the Czechs have certainly established themselves as international hockey's current dynasty.

Slovakia, a country with just 12,000 registered players (and only eight indoor rinks) among a population of five million people, has been slower to carve out its place on the international scene. The Czech Republic was considered the successor to Czechoslovakia in the international hockey hierarchy, while the Slovaks had to earn their participation in the A Pool. They made it up from the C Pool in just three years, the shortest time possible. However, Slovakia's best finish in a major championship prior to 2000 was a sixth-place ranking at the 1994 Olympics in Lillehammer, Norway—the first big tournament in which Slovakia participated as an independent country.

Over the years, there were only 11 Slovakia-born players, including national hero Peter Stastny, and one Slovak coach, who were members of the teams that won six World Championships for Czechoslovakia between 1947 and 1985. Two other gold medalists—forward Vaclav Nedomansky and goaltender Jiri Holecek—played for Elite League teams based in the eastern part of the old federation. Back then, though, these teams were considered Czech. Only three Slovak clubs ever won the old federal league: Slovan Bratislava in 1979, VSZ Kosice in 1986 and 1988, and Dukla Trencin in 1992. Since the country split up, the Slovaks had never beaten the Czechs at the major tournament as they prepared for the 2000 World Championships. In winning 16 of the 18 games the teams had played (including a 4–0 record in previous World Championships), the Czechs had certainly gained the respect of the Slovaks. Perhaps the Slovaks gave them too much respect.

During the 2000 tournament, many people felt that the Slovaks could beat anybody. With one exception. The Czechs had not lost a gold medal game since the playoff system was introduced at the international level in 1992. They would hardly stand for any defeat in the finals, but they could not even begin to imagine losing to the Slovaks. The semifinal match between Finland and Slovakia was played before the other game between the Czechs and Canada. "When the Slovaks advanced, they were celebrating in front of our locker room. We knew we must reach the finals too and knock them down a little," said forward David Vyborny. "Why should it finish? And why right now?" added head coach Josef Augusta when asked about the Czech unbeaten streak prior to the deciding game with Slovakia. Politics, perhaps, but the extreme emotions generated between Czech and Slovak hockey players can best be described as a family rivalry—the big brother versus the little brother.

The 2000 World Championship tournament was littered with upsets, warning that the gaping gulf between hockey's have and have-nots was closing. Norway, Latvia, Belarus, Switzerland and Slovakia all proved to be major hurdles for the top hockey nations, though the mighty Czechs beat Slovakia 5–3 in the gold medal final to claim their second consecutive title. The Czech Republic became the first country to win consecutive championships since Sweden in 1991 and 1992.

A three-goal explosion by the Czechs in the opening period made sure that there would be no Hollywood happy ending to Slovakia's storybook journey to its first major final. Still, by gaining the silver, Slovakia became the first country that is not considered one of the top six hockey powers (Canada, the Czech Republic, Finland, Russia, Sweden and the United States) to win a medal at the senior World Championship tournament in 47 years.

People who had been paying attention to what was happening in the previous years could see that the rise of one of hockey's dwarfs was imminent. Slovakia had strived to reach the upper level for several years, and was now there. The first sign of better times for them was the bronze medal at the 1999 Under-20 World Junior Championships. Until winning the World Junior title in 2000, the Czechs had not gained anything at this level since 1993, when the Czechoslovakian junior national team had finished third. Czechs David Vyborny and Frantisek Kaberle and Slovak Richard Kapus were members of that team. After New Year's Day 1993 (the tournament had begun over Christmas), these players represented a country that no longer existed. They heard the anthem of the International Ice Hockey Federation after winning games. Seven years later, they faced-off as opponents in the World Championships final.

Europe's history is not exactly filled with positive examples of countries that have separated along nationalist lines. Problems in the Balkans still flare up every year or two, the former Soviet republics squabble on a regular basis, and even in Germany, where it was a case of reunification and not separation, there is still some social tension between the rich West and the poor East. The Czechs and Slovaks are an exception. The breakup of the former Czechoslovakia into two independent states does not seem to have created much enmity between the people.

Part of the reason that there has been so little animosity between the two new countries may be found in the case of such people as Miroslav Hlinka. His father was a Czech who moved to the eastern part of the former country and married a Slovak woman. Miroslav was born in Slovakia, but when he skated for Sparta Prague in the Czech Elite League, he demanded Czech citizenship and later wore the Czech national team sweater in some games. He almost earned a spot in the lineup for the Czech Republic at the 1999 World Championships. After returning to his homeland, he became Slovak again and represented his country at the 2000 tournament.

A large number of players on the Czech and Slovak teams know each other fairly well. Some of them are friends. Some are relatives. Miroslav Hlinka's cousin Jaroslav, a former linemate in Sparta Prague, played on the Czech squad during the 1999 Baltika Cup in Moscow. "Before and after the game we are friends and joke," they say. "But during the games it is more like a war." Given what was happening elsewhere in Europe, it is nice to know that this is the only type of war waged between the Czechs and Slovaks.

When Czechoslovakia and its hockey association split into two separate countries and entities, the federal hockey league finished up what would be its final campaign in 1992–93. There have since been attempts to create a Czech-Slovak league, but the Czechs have not been too enthusiastic about any such plan. The Slovaks are fighting an uphill battle in their effort to compete with the Czechs in hockey, though there will be a Czech-Slovak handball league starting in the 2000–2001 season.

One of the arguments against a joint hockey league is that the competition in the current Czech league is considered much more balanced and strong than that in Slovakia. Czech hockey representatives feel there would be no benefit to them in a common league. In addition to the sporting side of the argument, there is also the matter of money. Even the poorest Czech clubs are still richer than most of the Slovak teams.

"Our competition isn't as fierce because we don't have as many good players," says defenseman Stanislav Jasecko, who dressed with HC Ceske Budejovice and became one of two dozen Slovak players employed by Czech Elite League clubs in the 1999–2000 season. "We've got three or four strong teams that are expected to beat all of the weak sisters. If you want to grow and improve, you cross the border to the Czech Republic. Each game there is tough and important and that helps your motivation. And the fact that money isn't bad doesn't hurt either."

Nine of 14 Czech teams employed Slovak players in 1999–2000, with three teams using the services of four Slovaks each. The problem is, only three foreigners can be on the roster of a Czech league team at any given time. Of course, it does help that there is a rule stipulating that a foreign player is not considered an import as soon as he has lived three years in the Czech Republic—even if that player retains his original citizenship. There used to be times, before the Second World War, when poor Slovak tradesmen would travel to the Czech part of the republic in search of odd jobs and some money. These days, Slovak hockey players are making the same trek—and for the same reasons. To be fair, some Czechs have been going in the opposite direction too, though mostly after their careers have begun the inevitable decline. Others were simply not deemed good enough by any Czech club.

The number of registered hockey players has increased by 20 percent in the Czech Republic in the last four years. Much of this increase is made up of young players. This is partly a reflection of international success, and partly a response to the success of such Czech NHLers as Jaromir Jagr and Dominik Hasek. Elite-level Czech clubs usually support high-quality junior teams to lean on in times of need, but they still need more mature players too. Some of the Czech teams can't afford to pay for expensive stars, and there are not too many good and experienced import players whose signing would not break the bank.That's where the Slovaks come in.

In general, Slovak hockey players feel isolated and are looking for a way out. They would dearly love to join the Euro Hockey Tour, a four-tournament event that includes teams from the Czech Republic, Finland, Russia and Sweden. But there is little chance that the top European hockey powers will add any new members in the near future. If they do, they will likely be looking only to add "wild card" participants for some of the tournaments, and not on a regular basis. Understandably, the Slovaks feel they can't really gauge the skill of their best players when playing against lesser lights. During the 1999–2000 season, their national team played only four games against the world's elite (the Czechs). As they showed at the World Championships in St. Petersburg, they can compete with the best teams, but crossing the border or going to North America (or anywhere else in the hockey world) will remain one of the few ways for the Slovak players to improve.

THE STATE OF SWEDISH HOCKEY

Janne Stark

THERE ARE MANY THINGS TO CONSIDER when examining the state of hockey in Sweden. Some of them are good, but a lot of them are not.

First, the good things.

Hockey is still the most popular winter sport in Sweden and, considering that there are over 280 indoor ice rinks in the country, the sport should continue to grow in the future. The number of registered players in Sweden has already increased by almost 35 percent over the past 10 seasons. This makes for a solid foundation to a youth program that is considered the best in the world. Average attendance for games in the country's top league (Elitserien) is increasing slowly, but steadily, and the interest from the media is better than ever. Internationally, Sweden has won the World Championships three times and the Olympic gold medal once during the past 10 seasons. Only the Czech Republic can match those numbers.

So what is bad about Swedish hockey?

For one thing, Sweden has slipped on the international scene in recent years. The Swedish team was beaten in the quarterfinals at the 2000 World Championships in St. Petersburg, Russia, and finished seventh. This was the worst performance by a Swedish national team since 1937. Not only did general manager Peter Wallin lose his job, but the management system of the past two seasons (one general manager and revolving coaches from tournament to tournament) has been scrapped. For the next two years at least, former superstar player and now ex-NHL executive Anders Hedberg will not only be responsible for the Swedish national team but for all of the country's national teams from the level of boys to juniors to the top. Hedberg is going to act as the director of all players in Swedish hockey. It will be a tough assignment, but with his experience there is no doubt whatsoever that he will be able to cope.

As for coaching, Hardy Nilsson will take over the national team in 2000–2001. At first, he will also continue to coach his Djurgarden club (national champions in 1999–2000), since he is under contract there until the spring of 2001. Nilsson and Hedberg are seen as a dynamic duo with new and different ideas that will lead the Three Crowns into the future.

A key problem in Swedish hockey appears to be the drop-off in talent that occurs between the youth and junior levels. This can be illustrated through recent international results. At the last eight international championships for 18-year-olds, Sweden has earned a medal in every tournament: three gold medals, two silver and three bronze. However, the record for 20-year-olds at the World Junior Championships during this same time period is just three silver medals and one bronze. Even more frustrating, Sweden has not earned a single medal at the last four tournaments.

Why are we seeing this drop-off?

One major reason is that teams in the Elite League seldom show confidence in the country's young players. Instead, these teams tend to import older foreign players. As a result, young Swedish players do not get enough opportunities on the senior level. In the long run, this will diminish the level of Swedish national teams.

Money is another reason for the drop-off in talent in Sweden. The best young hockey players are drafted by the NHL teams and disappear to North America. This is, of course, the main goal for many players and nothing is going to stop them from going when the money they can earn is so good. Added to the problem of losing talent to the NHL is the problem of losing talent to other European leagues. Because wages for hockey players are much better in countries like Germany and Switzerland, many more Swedish players between the ages of 20 and 30 are leaving home.

Sadly, Sweden finds itself with a hockey system that is capable of developing skilled young players but one that cannot (or will not, or cannot afford) to take care of these players once they reach the age of 19 to 21.

Monetary problems in Swedish hockey not only affect the country's players but also its top teams. Many clubs are having a tough time making ends meet. Vasteras, for example, who faced relegation from the Elite League after a dismal showing in 1999–2000, went bankrupt after the season. Financial concerns plague a great many Swedish hockey teams, who have professional players but amateurs in the front office. Since Swedish clubs (unlike NHL teams) are not only responsible for their own team but for a number of youth teams as well, there is often a lot of conflict between the professionals that take care of the elite team and the volunteers that run the junior teams.

The difficult economic situation in Swedish hockey has forced the national federation and the league association to take tough measures. Over the next three seasons, clubs in the Elite League will have to show a positive balance in their financial ledgers or face expulsion from the league. This is a tough decision but a necessary one. It will force the clubs to take economic responsibility in a sensible way.

ADVENTURES IN THE B POOL

Stewart Roberts

I HAVE BEEN FOLLOWING GREAT BRITAIN'S FORTUNES in the World Championships for almost 30 years. It's not the most glamorous of assignments for a hockey writer. In all that time Britain has only once, in 1994, aspired to the heights of Pool A.

Not quite where elephants go to die, the lower championship pools, B and C, are qualifying rounds through which the 57 member nations of the International Ice Hockey Federation must qualify in order to reach the A Pool, the "real" World Championships. Conversely, teams can be relegated along the usual lines of European sports leagues. These extra pools have been in existence on an annual basis since 1961, though there were occasions before that when they were added after the championships became over-subscribed.

Each group is held in a different country to widen interest in both the championships and the sport. As the lower pools are usually run at a loss, the host nation receives a subsidy from the IIHF to cover the costs of running the tournament, taken from the proceeds of the A Pool, which invariably turns a profit.

While Pool A is normally held in prominent western nations like Sweden, Finland, Italy or Germany among teams with at least a smattering of NHL players, the lesser groups are more likely to be awarded to some obscure place in eastern Europe or to a small country like Denmark or The Netherlands. In recent years, I have explored the delights of Slovakia, Slovenia and Poland, watching players who are famous only in their own country. I'm being rather unkind, though, because some of the most memorable games I've seen have been played in front of fervent patriots from the newly created eastern republics. In such cities, there is a crackling atmosphere whenever the home boys skate out.

One of the high points of my hockey travels was watching half the good-natured crowd of 7,000 that was packed into the Ljubljana arena unfurl their giant Green Dragon national flag along the whole of one side, cheering and jumping up and down throughout the game, while chanting "if you don't jump high, you're not a Slovenian."

You will need an up-to-date map to find Slovenia, by the way. It's a new country which until the early 1990s was part of Yugoslavia. Ljubljana is the capital. A lot of these places blossomed into minor hockey powers during the last decade. Of course, arenas in cities like Ljubljana aren't exactly Madison Square Garden, a point in their favor purists would say.

The sight lines are invariably excellent for the fans and there's usually plenty of standing room. Standing at sports events is very much a European thing. Outdoor arenas have mostly disappeared, though they were a regular feature until the 1970s. Most of the venues are home to a club side for the rest of the season and it's surprising how often I'm told that the national team attracts larger crowds than the local club. As Canadian and American national teams rarely draw bigger followings than the nearest NHL side, this helps to explain why the lower pools have never been held in North America.

The Pool B teams are a varied bunch. Some are Pool A nations who have hit hard times. Some, like Britain, have never known much else since World War II. Others, like the former Russian republics, are rising fast. Watch out Canada, countries like Kazakhstan and Estonia are coming soon to a rink near you.

These teams are refreshing to watch, as most are staffed with players who were born and bred in the country they are representing. This may seem obvious, but more mobile players and the breaking down of nationalities hastened by the liberal laws of the European Union make this increasingly uncommon.

These laws reflect the view that a citizen of any member nation of the European Union is a citizen of all of them: a Swede can play league hockey in Britain as a citizen of Europe as freely as a Texan can play in Chicago as a citizen of the USA. That may be perfectly normal in the United States but it's taking some getting used to in multicultural, multilingual Europe.

Due to their strong European ancestry, North Americans—especially Canadians—can easily obtain passports proving they are "Europeans." This law has been taken advantage of in Germany and my own country to such an extent that both nations pack their elite leagues almost entirely with non-Germans and non-Britons.

Because so many players are brought in from elsewhere, the selection of British and German national teams is a problem. It is also an important factor in why both these major Western countries have been laboring in Pool B rather than Pool A. Both have strong pro leagues but weak national squads, with Germany relying on youngsters and Britain dependent on dual-national British-Canadians, mostly from the North American minor leagues.

Ironically, the main reason Pool A twice has expanded in the past decade was to give every possible opportunity to wealthy countries like these to move up and thus enable the IIHF to attract more lucrative TV and advertising contracts. In a further irony, Germany, which has perhaps the largest and most passionate hockey following in Europe, will be in Pool A in 2001 regardless of where they finished in Pool B in 2000. The Pool A games will be held in Germany in 2001, so their squad has an automatic entry as the host.

It may be hard to believe, but Britain has acted like the NHL when it comes to world championships—prizing league success more highly than it does world championship glory basically because it is more lucrative. When the British League playoffs clashed with the World Championships in 1995, Britain's nationals almost ended up being relegated to Pool C. Three British players, including our skipper, missed two championship games in Bratislava, Slovakia, because they flew back to London for the playoff finals weekend at Wembley and then returned to Bratislava on the Monday.

Behavior like this plays into the hands of the smaller countries who take great pride in their national team. They have other advantages: they play comparatively few league games and so have more time for national team training, following the example of the hugely successful Soviet Union/CSKA Moscow system; their club sides play a similar style which makes the moulding of a national squad simpler; and in the poorer eastern parts, there is always the dream that an NHL scout might have secreted himself away in the championship crowd to whisk them off to the untold riches of North America. Europe's top talent, as we know, is quickly creamed off by the North American leagues. If any of them return to play for their country, it's only because their team has failed to make the playoffs, just as in Pool A. I recall seeing only New York Islanders wing Mariusz Czerkawski with Poland and Latvian goalie Arturs Irbe of the San Jose Sharks play in Pool B.

Funding for national teams is relatively easy for those former Communist countries whose governments still see sport as a way of proving the nation's manhood, although the support is nowhere near the level they used to enjoy in the heyday of the Soviet Union.

Britain, as I said, enjoys none of these advantages. One of the very few points in our favor is the team's 300-strong fan club, or as we call it, supporters' club. Invariably, the British fans are among the noisiest ones in Pool B, being out-shouted only by the Germans and, of course, the home side's patriots.

Most countries bring just a handful of traveling fans. I fondly recall the Latvian enthusiasts in 1996 who drove 1,000 miles through northern Poland and Germany to Eindhoven in the Netherlands to root for their countrymen. Few teams have to put up with the officiating the Brits have to endure. The B and C Pools are full of teams playing the fluent, fast skating and slick passing "European" style game. Britain, on the other hand, prefers the hard, physical, drive-for-the-net North American style which is greatly preferred by the fans (our links with our North American "cousins" remain strong). So the Brits inevitably spend a fair proportion of their game shorthanded, much like any North American side does when it plays in Europe. Britain's excuse when we lose is almost always "we took too many penalties," the inference being that it was the referee's fault rather than the team's.

Britain's championship decider against hosts Denmark in 1999 is a good example. The contest was marred by an endless stream of players from both sides into the sin bin. Not only did this render the contest almost unwatchable, it also incensed a couple of our players so much that they declined to enter the next international tournament.

Britain's promotion in 1993 to Pool A for the first time since 1962 was also controversial. Britain, under Nipigon, Ontario-born coach Alex Dampier, won all seven Pool B games that year with the most crucial victory coming against host Poland in the opening game. With the score 3–3, Britain was hurling rubber at Polish keeper Batkiewicz on a power-play, to no avail. Then Dampier had a brainwave and called for a stick measurement on the opposition. He won the call and Tim Cranston scored the winner on a two-man advantage. Britain never looked back after that.

This is not an uncommon call in North American hockey, of course. Indeed, that same year Jacques Demers of Montreal virtually won game two of the Stanley Cup finals after successfully catching Marty McSorley of Los Angeles with a questionable stick. But it is considered distinctly unsporting in European circles.

Britain's 1993 triumph was a Pyrrhic one for the 13 native British players on our 23-man squad. With the new European nations coming up fast (of the seven new countries in Pools A and B in 1999, four had been in Pool C six years earlier and the other three had not even entered), Britain felt it essential to bring in British-Canadian reinforcements.

By the time of the 1999 championships there were only eight players on the roster, including the backup netminder, who had learned their hockey in the British Isles. Despite this, Britain has yet to return to Pool A, missing it by a hairsbreadth in 1999 after going through an agonizingly close four-game qualifying round.

Actually, this essay is something of a history lesson because after 40 years, Pools B and C will be replaced in 2001. A new 12-nation Division I will be created, divided on merit and geography into two six-team groups. The division will be composed of the top four teams from C, the bottom one or two from A and those remaining in B. We'll have to wait and see whether this new system will ease Britain's path to Pool A glory. They have toyed with the idea of "doing a Germany" and applying to host Pool A in 2004 (the 1992 Pool C in Hull, Yorkshire, was the last one we staged) but this plan has yet to be confirmed. It the meantime, for me, it looks like a few more years of admiring jumping Slovenians!

CHAPTER 18

Women's Hockey

The State of the Game

Glynis Peters

FOR THE SIXTH TIME IN A DECADE, and the third time in Canada, the Canadian national anthem was played after the gold medal game of the Women's World Championships. From fluorescent, and some would say insulting, bright pink uniforms in 1990 to an almost fully sponsored machine in 2000, the Canadian women's team has seen more changes to its game in one decade than in the previous 125-year history of the sport.

Back in 1990, none of the teams involved in the first official Women's World Championships could claim to have a strong development system, let alone a high-performance program for their sport. National organizations focused entirely on men's hockey were suddenly asked to select a national women's team and they scrambled to ice 20 players. In Canada, Angela James, already the Wayne Gretzky of women's ice hockey, was left off the first list of players. This shock to the world of women's hockey was remedied before the event, but it served as a wake-up call for national organizations that a whole women's network existed and that it was time to learn who was out there and how to evaluate them.

The 1992 World Championships in Finland was poorly attended by fans and media. Without the loyal families of the U.S. and Canadian players, there would have been virtually no atmosphere at all in the Tampere arena when Canada won for the second time in a row. The lack of support was disappointing in light of the fact that the International Olympic Committee had actually sent two observers to examine the viability of women's ice hockey as an Olympic sport. Word of this spread quickly and while everyone dared to dream, no one really imagined that women's Olympic hockey would become a reality for another 20 years. Minutes from IOC Sport committee meetings show a lack of support for the addition of women's hockey, even by a Canadian representative (who didn't support curling either). But with only one team sport in the Games and growing pressure on the IOC to increase the number of women participants, plus the staggering of the Summer Games and Winter Games every two years leaving room to expand the winter program, it seemed the planets were lining up to make a dream into reality much quicker than anyone would ever have imagined.

The Canadian Hockey Association had realized the potential of the game after 1990 and hired an individual to oversee the entire women's program full-time. Player and coach selection had evolved significantly by the 1992 World Championship, with formal coaching applications and interviews in Canada for three positions. (Canada made a commitment to developing women coaches and officials through strong affirmative action programs. Team USA followed their lead initially, but that was to change.) In 1993 Canada arranged the first Under-18 series against an Under-20 American team. The Canadian players were all local Ottawa stars and were led by local coaches. This series marked the debut of Jayna Hefford who, at the time, was living outside any major Canadian center and scoring goals unnoticed by the CHA. The Under-18 event, along with a strong performance at the Canada Winter Games, put Hefford's career on track but it was obvious that women's hockey was a long way from any comprehensive scouting system.

When the International Ice Hockey Federation created a Women's Committee, headed by USA Hockey president Walter Bush, one of its first tasks was to collect data. A questionnaire first distributed in 1994 showed that the number of participants was growing steadily in North America, but that no real progress was being made elsewhere in the world. (The year 2000 questionnaire shows 50,000 girls and women registered worldwide, while 500,000 boys and men are registered in Canada alone.)

The Women's World Championships returned to North America in 1994 when Lake Placid hosted, and it was clear that the countries destined to finish in the top three each year—Canada, the USA and Finland—would be the only ones stepping forward to host the event in the near future. Other countries already were reviewing their commitment to the women's game and, in the case of Denmark, had started to cut budgets. The Lake Placid tournament saw Canada finish first again, and while the final game was televised in Canada on The Sports Network, it was tape-delayed.

At this time female players were beginning specialized training, but many still played on teams that might practice only once a week or sometimes not at all. The winds of change started to blow when confirmation arrived that women's hockey had been accepted for the 1998 Winter Olympics. The IIHF decided to use the World Championships to establish seeding for Nagano and shifted the next event, scheduled for 1996, to 1997. By then many countries ran "high-performance" programs, athletes had begun training off-ice and, in Canada, women's university hockey was being revived.

With the upcoming Olympic Games as a promotional tool, the 1997 World Championships was a huge media success. It launched Team USA and Team Canada on their paths to Nagano, but Russia's non-qualification put their program in serious jeopardy, held together only by one or two zealots.

With the Olympics on the horizon, had the game itself changed? On the ice, women's hockey was certainly getting faster. Players were becoming stronger and perhaps more physical and they were showing the effects of better coaching. Preparation, however, was still limited to just a few camps a year and two international events, the new Three Nations Cup having been added to the program. In Canada, players were gravitating to Montreal and Toronto with their long-established leagues or to Calgary where a training center for elite female hockey players had been started at the Olympic Oval. The USA depended upon the college system, with a relatively short season and uneven coaching standards. Obviously the elements of a truly Olympic high-performance program were still not in place but after only seven years of international competition to drive it, women's hockey was at least evolving in that direction.

Every country involved in the 1998 Olympic Games invested time and money in preparation for their team, but the support of national federations varied drastically. Not surprisingly, Canada and the USA led the way with close to full-time programs. Rumors abounded concerning a professional women's hockey league, players were signing sponsorship contracts and young girls were collecting hockey cards and posters of their favorite female players. Much has already been written about the impact of Nagano and the U.S. Olympic victory, and more ink will run in the future every time women's hockey takes another step forward and its short international history is revisited. But what will be written after 2002? After 2006? Or 2010? Will the next 10 years see more dramatic changes?

The first steps into the future were taken at the "Millennium" World Championships in Mississauga, Ontario—an event that served as an Olympic qualifier for the 2002 Salt Lake City Games. The 2000 tournament was a big success. The final game was sold out well in advance, more games than ever were televised and the final was carried live for the first time. Even games in smaller centers between China and Sweden drew 3,000 spectators, mostly teams of young players eager to see any women's hockey they could. After all, even a devoted fan or parent who could claim to have seen every Canadian women's national team game would have seen less than 60 in 10 years.

The Canadian team, which had rebounded from its Olympic setback to beat the U.S. at the 1999 World Championships, won again in 2000. Of the thrilling 3–2 victory in the finals, even Team USA coach Ben Smith had to admit that "from a screenwriter's point of view it was the perfect event. There were two of the best teams in the sport laying it on the line in a beautiful building in front of a hometown crowd and with the home team making a dramatic come back to win in overtime."

The top six teams in Mississauga—Canada, the United States, Finland, Sweden, Russia and China—all earned a spot at the 2002 Olympics. (Further qualifying to fill out the eight-team field will take place in February, 2001.) That Canada and the Americans again emerged as the top two nations was far from unexpected, but there were some surprising revelations during the tournament. Finland, a distant third in all previous championships, led the USA, 3–1, in their final pool game, taking the States by surprise and forcing a come-from-behind victory. Canada, too, struggled against the Finns. The tournament upset may have been Russia's victory over China, though the history of men's hockey in the former Soviet Union leaves anyone involved in the game wary and respectful of the potential behind any Russian team. China appears to be a team in decline, with an unchanged roster and diminished performance. Injuries to several top players revealed Sweden's lack of depth.

Despite the inroads made by women's hockey in recent years, the vast majority of North Americans have never seen women play the game at a high level. Devotees of the sport are thirsty for more exposure. This led to last season's creation of the National Women's Hockey League in Canada. Four teams based in the Toronto area, three in Montreal and one in Ottawa provide the best competition in the world for the players involved. The Brampton Thunder attracts between 300 and 500 fans at home games. Canada's Women's Television Network has committed to broadcasting several NWHL games in 2000–01. But the 2000 World Championships was still not televised in the USA. There's little doubt, however, that the 2002 Winter Olympics in Salt Lake City will be the catalyst for greater media interest.

In the States, players out of college continue to struggle for a place to play. There is no league to provide similar competition to that available in Canada and, leading up to the 2000 World Championships, marquee players like Cammi Granato, Karen Bye and other members of Team USA had no choice but to centralize in the Boston area and train together. Could they go one step further and create a team to compete in the fledgling NWHL?

Analysts of the Women's National Basketball Association believe the creation and success of that league is linked directly to NBA support. When asked his opinion on women's professional hockey, Ben Smith replies "I'm a history major, not an economics major. Sometime, someone will try to invest their time, effort and money into such a venture and at some point it might be successful. But it is not needed."

Today in women's hockey the stakes are higher and the goals more lofty, but is the support there for players to put their lives on hold for an Olympic dream? In Canada and the USA, players receive some financial support as national team athletes and a few have sponsorship contracts. However, they are caught in the gap between an amateur Olympic athlete and a professional, neither fully one or the other.

The elements of a high-performance program are development opportunities for players, training and opportunities for coaches, and competition. In all of these areas, women's hockey has made great strides since 1990 but much remains to be done. The Olympic exposure has created a goal that attracts young players to the game and encourages parental support. Canada's development of an Under-22 program has spurred other countries to follow suit and a junior age World Championships has been discussed by the IIHF. Coaches have growing opportunities for training in the men's program and attempts are being made to offer specialty clinics focused on the women's game.

There is a growing sense of professionalism at the higher levels of coaching, particularly in the college and university ranks. Several Canadian coaches have been drawn to one of the many new programs which are being added in Division I, II and III schools throughout the United States. Among them is Melody Davidson, head coach of the 2000 Canadian women's national team. However, Davidson points out that she is an exception. "While demands on national team players and coaches for training and competition are increasing," she says, "opportunities to earn a living at the game they love, and have devoted their lives to, aren't increasing at the same rate."

The women's international program has grown from one event—the World Championships—to include such tournaments as the Three Nations Cup, a Pool B World Championships and, in North America, the TSN Challenge for Team Canada and Team USA. More players, more events, more media and more marketing all auger well for the future of the women's game, but it's still evolving. The next decade will need the continued support and direction of those who have maintained the high level of sportsmanship that integrates fun, enthusiasm and a passion for the sport wherever girls and women put on their skates.

WOMEN'S CHAMPIONSHIP TOURNAMENT SUMMARIES

WOMEN'S WORLD CHAMPIONSHIPS

THE FIRST OFFICIAL IIHF Women's World Hockey Championships were held in 1990, three years after an unofficial women's world tournament had been held for the first time. Additional championship events were held in 1992, 1994 and 1997. After making its debut as an Olympic sport in Nagano, the tournament has been held each year since 1999.

Beginning in 1999, separate A and B Pool competitions were held. The World B Pool replaced separate European Championships that had been held in 1989, 1991, 1993, 1995 and 1996.

The eight nations participating at the Women's World Championships A Pool are split into two divisions with a round robin played within each group. After the round robin, the top two teams in both groups advance to one-game semifinals. Semifinals winners play for the overall championship while the losers play off for third place. The teams finishing third and fourth in the two round-robin groups use the same playoff format to decide fifth through eighth place.

Brief summaries of each IIHF Women's World Championship event follow below.

1987 (UNOFFICIAL)

The first Women's World Championships were held in Toronto from April 21 to April 26, 1987. It was not recognized as an official tournament by the International Ice Hockey Federation. Teams from Canada, the United States, Sweden, Switzerland, Japan and Holland were on hand, as well as a team representing the Canadian province of Ontario.

Though the Ontario team beat the United States in the semifinals before losing 4–0 to Canada in the title game, the provincial team was not assigned a ranking in the final standings, meaning that the United States was considered to be the second-place finisher after defeating Sweden 5–0 in what otherwise would have been the bronze medal game. Sweden was ranked third. Canada ran up a perfect record of 6–0 in winning the event.

1990

The first official Women's World Championships were held in Ottawa from March 19 to 25, 1990. Eight nations were present at the tournament, with Canada, Sweden, West Germany and Japan playing in Group A while the United States, Finland, Switzerland and Norway comprised Group B. In the round-robin schedule, Canada beat Sweden 15–1, West Germany 17–0 and Japan 18–0 to top its group while the United States edged Finland 5–4 and crushed Switzerland 16–3 and Norway 17–0 to win Group B.

In the playoffs, teams from Group A crossed over to meet teams from Group B with a separate series of games to determine the medal winners and to round out the standings of the teams ranking five through eight. Canada narrowly defeated Finland 5–4 to advance to the gold medal game, while the Americans crushed Sweden 10–3. In the bronze medal game, Finland beat Sweden 6–3. The championship was won by Canada, who defeated the United States 5–2.

Among those leading the gold medal-winning Canadians were Angela James (11 goals) and Heather Ginzel (seven goals and five assists). Goaltenders Denis Caron (2.08 goals-against average in three games) and Cathy Phillips (1.15 in four) also starred. American Cindy Curley enjoyed the best individual performance of the tournament with 11 goals and 12 assists. Cammi Granato added nine goals to the U.S. total.

1992

China and Denmark each made their Women's World Championship debut in the tournament held in Tampere, Finland from April 20 to April 26, 1992. The two new countries played with Canada and Sweden in Group A, while Group B was made up of the United States, Finland, Switzerland and Norway as it had been in 1990. Once again the Canadians proved to be easily the best in their group, defeating Sweden 6–1, China 8–0 and Denmark 10–0. The United States, challenged only by Finland, edged the Finns 5–3, and crushed Norway 9–1 and the Swiss 13–0 to top Group B. In the semifinals, Canada beat Finland and the United States topped Sweden to set up another Canadian–American finals. This time Canada crushed the United States 8–0 to retain the World Championship, while Finland beat Sweden 5–4 to claim the bronze medal.

The 1992 Women's World Championships introduced Manon Rheaume to international play. The Canadian netminder was named to the tournament all-star team after allowing just two goals in the three games she played, although Sweden's Annica Ahlen was named best goalie at the event. Cammi Granato of the United States was named best forward after scoring eight goals in six games, while Canada's Geraldine Heaney was named best defenseman. Heaney was joined by American Ellen Weinberg as the all-star defensemen, while Granato, Canada's Angela James and Finland's Riikka Nieminen were the all-star forwards.

1994

Lake Placid, New York, was the sight of the 1994 Women's World Championships, but there would be no "Miracle on Ice" for the United States squad, who would lose only one game at the tournament again—the gold medal game against Team Canada.

As in past years, Canada breezed to the top of Group A with a 7–1 win over China, an 8–2 win over Sweden and a 12–0 whitewash of Norway. The Americans edged Finland 2–1, downed Switzerland 6–0 and crushed Germany 16–0 to finish atop Group B. When the teams crossed over to play the semifinals, Canada downed Finland 4–1, while the Americans humbled China 14–3. Finland then claimed its third bronze medal with an 8–1 drubbing of China. Canada downed the United States 6–3 to remain the World Champions.

As in 1992, Canada's Manon Rheaume was named the goaltender on the tournament all-star team without being named best goalie. This year, the honor went to Erin Whitten of the United States. Best defenseman was once again Geraldine Heaney of Canada, while best forward was Riikka Nieminen. The flashy Finn had four goals and nine assists for 13 points in five games. Canada's Danielle Goyette led the tournament with nine goals and joined Nieminen as a forward on the all-star team along with American Karen Bye. Rounding out the all-star team were Canada's Therese Brisson and Kelly O'Leary of the United States, who were chosen for the defense.

1997

Russia made its debut at the Women's World Championships in 1997 and finished sixth among the eight teams taking part at the tournament played in six cities across southwestern Ontario. Russia tied Switzerland 3–3 for its only point in three games during the round-robin portion of the tournament, then beat Norway 2–1 in the playoffs before losing 3–1 to Sweden in the game to decide fifth and sixth place. Switzerland and Norway ranked seventh and eighth respectively.

For the fourth time in the four official Women's World Championships, Canada ran up a perfect record at the tournament to take the title. This year, however, it took overtime to defeat the Americans 4–3 in the gold medal game. Nancy Drolet scored the game winner for Canada to cap a three-goal performance. Canada had reached the gold medal game by defeating China 7–1, Russia 9–1 and Switzerland 6–0 to win Group A, then edging Finland 2–1 in the semifinals. The United States won Group B with wins of 10–0 over Sweden and 7–0 over Norway, but only managed a 3–3 tie with Finland before blanking China 6–0 in the semifinals. Finland shut out China 3–0 to win its fourth straight bronze medal at the Women's World Championships.

Among the top performers at the 1997 Women's World

Championships were Finland's Riikka Nieminen (five goals and five assists), Canada's Hayley Wickenheiser (four goals and five assists) and Cammie Granato of the United States (five goals and three assists). All three were named all-star forwards at the event.

Canada's Cassie Campbell had two goals and six assists and earned a selection as an all-star defenseman, as did Kelly O'Leary of the United States. Rounding out the all-star team was goaltender Patricia Sautter of Switzerland.

1999

The Women's World Championship was split into A and B pools for the first time in 1999, with eight nations competing in each. The A Pool was played in Espoo and Vantaa, Finland, from March 8 to 14 and consisted of Canada, Finland, Germany and Switzerland in one group. The USA, Sweden, China and Russia made up the second group. The B Pool was played the last week of March in France and was won by Japan. Other competing nations were Norway, France, the Czech Republic, Latvia, Denmark, Slovakia, and the Netherlands. By winning the B Pool, Japan returned to the A Pool at the 2000 tournament in Canada. Switzerland was relegated to the B Pool.

Despite having lost to the United States at the 1998 Winter Olympics, Canada never had lost a game at the Women's World Championship and carried a veteran team into the 1999 event. Back were stars such as Cassie Campbell, Nancy Drolet, and France St-Louis, and they led Canada to 10–0, 13–0 and 1–0 victories over Switzerland, Germany and Finland, respectively. American stars Cammi Granato, Karen Bye and Tara Mounsey paced the USA to 10–2, 11–0 and 6–0 victories over Russia, Sweden and China.

Finland and Sweden joined Canada and the United States in the medal round with the U.S. crossing over to beat the Finns, 3–1, while the Canadian team downed the Swedes, 4–1. Finland, led by Petra Vaarakallio and Sari Fisk, then downed Sweden, 8–2, to win the bronze medal for the sixth time, including the Olympics.

As always at the Women's World Championship, the gold medal-game was a battle between Canada and the United States. The Americans got on the scoreboard first on a goal by Jenny Schmidgall midway through the second period. Caroline Ouellette tied the score for Canada, and third-period goals by Danielle Goyette and Geraldine Heaney gave the Canadians a 3–1 victory.

Canadian goalie Sami Jo Small made 26 saves in the gold-medal game. She was named the tournament's best goalie and earned a spot on the all-star team. All-star defensemen were American Sue Merz and Finland's Kirsi Hanninen, who was also named the best defenseman. Canadian forwards Jayna Hefford and Hayley Wickenheiser were named to the all-star team along with Jenny Schmidgall, who was named the best forward at the tournament after leading the World Championships with five goals and seven assists in five games.

2000

Canada maintained its perfect record at the Women's World Championship in the year 2000, but, just as in 1997 when the country last hosted the tournament, it took an overtime goal in the final game to ice the gold medal. The hero once again was Nancy Drolet, who found net for the first time in the tournament at 6:50 of overtime as Team Canada downed the United States, 3–2.

The Canadians opened the tournament with a 9–0 win over Japan followed by an 8–1 win over China. Next came a 4–0 win over Sweden as Canada finished up the preliminary round undefeated. The Americans were even more dominant in their first two games, breezing to a 16–1 win over Germany and a 15–0 trouncing of Russia, but had to survive a scare against Finland in game three. Two goals from Katja Riipi had the Finns up, 3–1, before the Americans rallied. Veteran Cammi Granato scored the tying goal and Stephanie O'Sullivan netted the winner on a breakaway with 3:26 to play. Canada also had a tough time with the Finns in the first game of the medal round, but two goals from Danielle Goyette sparked the team to a 3–2 victory. A pair of goals from Karen Bye led the U.S. to a 7–1 victory over Sweden, and once again it was Canada and the United States in the gold medal game.

After a scoreless first period, the Americans seemed to take control when they outshot Canada, 15–3, in the second period and went ahead, 2–0. But, Canada's exceptional depth allowed the team to come back. Jayna Hefford scored twice in the third period, the first on a spectacular end-to-end rush, and set the stage for Drolet's winner as the U.S. had to settle for silver once again. Finland's 7–1 victory over Sweden earlier in the day meant they claimed the bronze as usual. Canada's Sami Jo Small was named best goalie at the tournament for the second year in a row. Honors as best forward and best defenseman went to Katja Riipi of Finland and Angela Ruggiero of the United States, respectively.

The top six teams at the 2000 tournament all earned a spot in the 2002 Winter Olympics. Germany and Japan (which face relegation to the B Pool) will play off against B Pool champion Kazakhstan and runners-up Switzerland in February, 2001, to fill out the eight-team Olympic lineup.

Women's Olympics 1998

Women's hockey made its debut at the Olympics Games in Nagano in 1998. Qualification for the event began at the Women's World Championships in 1997. The top five countries from the 1997 event qualified for the Olympics along with the host country, resulting in a six-team field comprising Canada, the United States, Finland, Sweden, China and Japan. As winners of every previous Women's World Championship (1990, 1992, 1994 and 1997) Canada was expected to bring home the first women's Olympic gold medal, but the tide clearly was turning in the months leading up to the tournament. A 13-game pre-Olympic series between the sport's two powers saw the Americans post a 6–7–0 record, but the United States defeated Canada handily at the 3-Nations Cup in Lake Placid prior to Christmas 1997 and seemed to be getting stronger as the Olympics approached.

Having won all of the medals available at the previous World Championships, Canada, the United States and Finland were clearly the class of the Women's Olympic tournament and proved it in their opening games as Canada beat Japan 13–0, the U.S. beat China 5–0 and Finland beat Sweden 6–0. Canada, however, struggled through its next three games, managing only a 2–0 win over China, a 5–3 win over Sweden and a 4–2 win over Finland, while the Americans ran up victories of 7–1, 4–2 and 10–0 over Sweden, Finland and Japan. Leslie Reddon was struggling in goal for the Canadians, though Manon Rheaume was proving solid. However, the two were not providing the type of clutch goaltending the Americans were receiving from their netminding duo of Sarah Tueting and Sara Decosta. This point was made clear when the Canadians and Americans met to close out the preliminary round. Reddon allowed the U.S. to score six goals in a span of 11:53 late in the third period as the Americans turned a 4–1 deficit into a 7–4 victory and finished with a perfect 5–0 record. Canada was 4–1 but would have its chance for revenge in the gold medal game.

Meanwhile, Finland had proven to be the best of the rest, adding an 11–1 win over Japan and a 6–1 win over China to its 6–0 win over Sweden to finish the preliminary round with a record of 3–2. China, who had defeated Japan and Sweden by scores of 6–1 and 3–1, provided the opposition for Finland in the bronze medal game. The Finns were 4–1 winners behind a goal and an assist from Rikka Nieminen, who led the tournament in scoring with 12 points on seven goals and five assists.

Sarah Tueting and Manon Rheaume provided solid goaltending for their respective countries in the gold medal clash between the United States and Canada, but Tueting proved to be just a little bit better as the Americans carried a 2–0 lead into the game's final minutes. Danielle Goyette (who was the tournament's leading goal scorer with nine goals despite the death of her father shortly before the Olympics) put Canada on the scoreboard at 15:59 of the third period, but an empty-net goal at 19:52 sealed Canada's fate. While American captain Cammie Granato led her teammates in celebration, the Canadian women could not conceal the disappointment they felt in taking home a silver medal from the most important tournament of their lives.

WOMEN'S CHAMPIONSHIP EVENTS STANDINGS AND LEADING SCORERS

OLYMPIC GAMES

Nagano, Japan • 1998 • Women

Rank	Team	GP	W	L	T	GF	GA	Pts
1	USA	5	5	0	0	33	7	10
2	Canada	5	4	1	0	28	12	8
3	Finland	5	3	2	0	27	10	6
4	China	5	2	3	0	10	15	4
5	Sweden	5	1	4	0	10	21	2
6	Japan	5	0	5	0	2	45	0

Bronze Medal game Finland 4 China 1
Gold Medal game USA 3 Canada 1

1998 Scoring Leaders

Player	Team	GP	G	A	PTS	PIM
Rikka Nieminen	Finland	6	7	5	12	4
Danielle Goyette	Canada	6	8	1	9	10
Karyn Bye	USA	6	5	3	8	4
Cammi Granato	USA	6	4	4	8	0
Katie King	USA	6	4	4	8	2
Gretchen Ulion	USA	6	3	5	8	4
H. Wickenheiser	Canada	6	2	6	8	4
Therese Brisson	Canada	6	5	2	7	6
Kirsi Hanninen	Finland	6	4	3	7	6
Laurie Baker	USA	6	4	3	7	6

WOMEN'S WORLD CHAMPIONSHIPS

1987 (UNOFFICIAL)

Rank	Team	GP	W	L	T	GF	GA	Pts
1	Canada	6	6	0	0	51		12
2	USA	6	5	1	0	61		10
3	Sweden	6	3	3	0	16		6
4	Switzerland	6	2	4	0	12		4
5	Japan	6	1	5	0	9		2
6	Holland	6	0	6	0	6		0

1990

Rank	Team	GP	W	L	T	GF	GA	Pts
1	Canada	5	5	0	0	61	8	10
2	USA	5	4	1	0	50	15	8
3	Finland	5	3	2	0	35	15	6
4	Sweden	5	2	3	0	25	35	4
5	Switzerland	5	3	2	0	23	39	6
6	Norway	5	1	4	0	16	45	2
7	W. Germany	5	2	3	0	16	33	4
8	Japan	5	0	5	0	11	47	0

1992

Rank	Team	GP	W	L	T	GF	GA	Pts
1	Canada	4	4	0	0	32	1	8
2	USA	4	3	1	0	27	12	6
3	Finland	4	3	1	0	32	13	6
4	Sweden	4	2	2	0	15	14	4
5	China	5	3	2	0	11	18	6
6	Norway	5	2	3	0	11	23	4
7	Denmark	5	1	4	0	7	24	2
8	Switzerland	5	0	5	0	6	36	0

1994

Rank	Team	GP	W	L	T	GF	GA	Pts
1	Canada	5	5	0	0	37	7	10
2	USA	5	4	1	0	41	10	8
3	Finland	5	3	2	0	40	8	6
4	China	5	1	3	1	17	34	3
5	Sweden	5	3	1	1	22	17	7
6	Norway	5	1	4	0	12	33	2
7	Switzerland	5	2	3	0	10	30	4
8	Germany	5	0	5	0	6	46	0

1997

Rank	Team	GP	W	L	T	GF	GA	Pts
1	Canada	5	5	0	0	28	6	10
2	USA	5	3	1	1	29	7	7
3	Finland	5	3	1	1	22	5	7
4	China	5	2	3	0	18	21	4
5	Sweden	5	2	2	1	12	19	5
6	Russia	5	1	3	1	9	22	3
7	Switzerland	5	1	3	1	8	27	3
8	Norway	5	0	4	1	3	22	1

1999 – A

Rank	Team	GP	W	L	T	GF	GA	Pts
1	Canada	5	5	0	0	31	2	10
2	USA	5	4	1	0	31	6	8
3	Finland	5	3	2	0	25	6	6
4	Sweden	5	2	3	0	13	24	4
5	China	5	3	2	0	11	14	6
6	Russia	5	1	4	0	11	26	2
7	Germany	5	2	3	0	10	32	4
8	Switzerland	5	0	5	0	6	28	0

1999 – B

Rank	Team	GP	W	L	T	GF	GA	Pts
9	Japan	5	5	0	0	25	4	10
10	Norway	5	2	3	0	9	17	4
11	France	5	3	1	1	21	10	7
12	Czech Republic	5	2	2	1	19	11	5
13	Latvia	5	3	2	0	18	12	6
14	Denmark	5	2	3	0	16	17	4
15	Slovakia	5	2	3	0	14	23	4
16	Holland	5	0	5	0	11	39	0

2000 – A

Rank	Team	GP	W	L	T	GF	GA	Pts
1	Canada	5	5	0	0	27	5	10
2	USA	5	4	1	0	44	8	8
3	Finland	5	3	2	0	23	10	6
4	Sweden	5	1	3	1	13	19	3
5	Russia	5	3	2	0	20	28	6
6	China	5	2	2	1	8	13	5
7	Germany	5	1	4	0	7	32	2
8	Japan	5	0	5	0	6	33	0

2000 – B

Rank	Team	GP	W	L	T	GF	GA	Pts
9	Kazakhstan	5	5	0	0	13	4	10
10	Switzerland	5	3	1	1	16	6	7
11	Norway	5	3	1	1	19	7	7
12	Denmark	5	1	3	1	8	12	3
13	France	5	2	1	2	16	13	6
14	Latvia	5	1	2	2	7	13	4
15	Czech Republic	5	1	3	1	13	12	3
16	Italy	5	0	5	0	4	29	0

Men's Olympic results on page 493

WOMEN'S EUROPEAN CHAMPIONSHIPS

1989

Rank	Team	GP	W	L	T	GF	GA	Pts
1	Finland	3	3	0	0	56	0	6
2	Sweden	3	3	0	0	24	3	6
3	West Germany	3	2	1	0	17	5	4
4	Norway	3	2	1	1	18	6	3
5	Switzerland	3	2	1	1	24	15	3
6	Denmark	3	1	2	0	6	19	2
7	Czechoslovakia	3	0	3	0	0	55	0
8	Netherlands	3	0	3	0	1	43	0

1991

Rank	Team	GP	W	L	T	GF	GA	Pts
1	Finland	5	5	0	0	73	1	10
2	Sweden	5	4	1	0	54	4	8
3	Denmark	5	4	1	0	13	15	8
4	Norway	5	3	2	0	32	15	6
5	Switzerland	5	3	2	0	30	22	6
6	Germany	5	2	3	0	20	20	4
7	France	5	2	3	0	6	54	4
8	Czechoslovakia	5	0	4	1	4	31	1
9	Great Britain	5	1	3	1	5	28	3
10	Netherlands	5	0	5	0	2	49	0

1993 – A

Rank	Team	GP	W	L	T	GF	GA	Pts
1	Finland	3	3	0	0	33	6	6
2	Sweden	3	2	1	0	18	11	4
3	Norway	3	2	1	0	14	13	4
4	Germany	3	1	2	0	12	20	2
5	Switzerland	3	1	2	0	7	23	2
6	Denmark	3	0	3	0	5	16	0

1993 – B

Rank	Team	GP	W	L	T	GF	GA	Pts
7	Latvia	5	3	1	0	10	5	6
8	Czech Republic	5	2	1	1	8	6	5
9	France	5	2	2	0	13	9	4
10	Great Britain	5	1	2	1	4	11	3
11	Ukraine	5	1	3	0	1	5	2

1995 – A

Rank	Team	GP	W	L	T	GF	GA	Pts
1	Finland	5	5	0	0	61	2	10
2	Sweden	5	4	1	0	27	10	8
3	Switzerland	5	3	2	0	11	20	6
4	Norway	5	2	3	0	7	20	4
5	Germany	5	1	4	0	11	35	2
6	Latvia	5	0	5	0	5	35	0

1995 – B

Rank	Team	GP	W	L	T	GF	GA	Pts
1	Russia	3	3	0	0	37	1	6
2	Denmark	3	3	0	0	23	2	6
3	Czech Republic	3	2	1	0	15	11	4
4	Slovakia	3	1	1	1	9	8	3
5	France	3	1	2	0	9	23	2
6	Netherlands	3	1	1	1	11	12	3
7	Great Britain	3	0	3	0	4	25	0
8	Ukraine	3	0	3	0	2	28	0

1996 – A

Rank	Team	GP	W	L	T	GF	GA	Pts
1	Sweden	5	4	0	1	20	11	9
2	Russia	5	4	1	0	17	15	8
3	Finland	5	3	2	0	24	5	6
4	Norway	5	2	3	0	14	21	4
5	Switzerland	5	1	4	0	11	21	2
6	Germany	5	0	4	1	7	20	1

1996 – B

Rank	Team	GP	W	L	T	GF	GA	Pts
7	Denmark	4	4	0	0	16	4	8
8	Latvia	4	3	1	0	11	7	6
9	Czech Republic	4	2	1	1	19	12	5
10	Slovakia	4	2	2	0	11	12	4
11	France	4	2	2	0	16	15	4
12	Netherlands	4	1	2	1	15	15	3
13	Kazakhstan	4	1	3	0	10	15	2
14	Great Britain	4	0	4	0	6	24	0

WOMEN'S PACIFIC CHAMPIONSHIPS

1995

Rank	Team	GP	W	L	T	GF	GA	Pts
1	USA	5	4	1	0	35	6	8
2	Canada	5	4	1	0	28	9	8
3	China	5	2	3	0	13	16	4
4	Japan	5	0	5	0	1	46	0

1996

Rank	Team	GP	W	L	T	GF	GA	Pts
1	Canada	5	5	0	0	38	3	10
2	USA	5	3	2	0	30	9	6
3	China	5	2	3	0	11	12	4
4	Japan	5	0	5	0	2	57	0

WOMEN'S HOCKEY BIOGRAPHICAL REGISTER

CANADA

JENNIFER BOTTERILL became a member of Canada's national women's team in 1997–98 and played at the Nagano Olympics. She has since been a member of gold medal-winning teams at both the 1999 and 2000 Women's World Championships and ranks as one of the team's top playmakers. Botterill was named an Ivy League all-star and rookie of the year after helping Harvard win the United States National Women's Hockey Championship in 1998–99. Brother Jason is an NHL player who won three gold medals with Canada's national junior team. Father Cal Botterill is a noted sports psychologist who was worked with NHL teams and Canadian national teams.

CASSIE CAMPBELL was Canada's top-scoring defenseman at the 1997 Women's World Championships, with two goals and six assists for the gold medal winners, and was named to the tournament all-star team. She was also a member of Canada's Women's World Championship team in 1994. After Canada's silver medal performance at the 1998 Nagano Olympics, Campbell was converted to forward and helped Canada win World Championships again that year and in 2000. She was named the top forward at the 2000 Canadian National Championship. Campbell was the sportswoman of the year at Guelph University in 1996.

NANCY DROLET scored three goals, including the game winner in overtime, when Canada beat the United States in the gold medal game at the 1997 Women's World Championships. In 1999, she was second on the Canadian team with four goals in five games as Canada again claimed the world title. She scored the overtime winner again in 2000 when Canada edged the United States 3-2 in the championship game. Drolet was also a member of Canada's championship teams in 1994 and 1992, and represented her country at the Pacific Rim Championship in 1996. Drolet played on the Canadian team that won a silver medal at the 1998 Olympic Games in Nagano. She is an all-round athlete and a top-class softball player.

DANIELLE GOYETTE overcame the death of her father shortly before the 1998 Olympics to be Canada's leading scorer with nine points in Nagano. She led the tournament with eight goals and had the lone Canadian goal in the gold medal game. A great skater with an accurate shot, Goyette scored the winning goal in a 3–1 victory over the Americans in the finals of the 1999 Women's World Championships and scored several key goals during the 2000 tournament. Previously, she had led Canada in scoring with 10 points (three goals and seven assists) at the 1992 Women's World Championships, and was an all-star at the 1994 tournament when she again led Canada with nine goals and 12 points. Goyette was also a member of a World Champion squad in 1997. She represented Canada at the Pacific Rim Championship in both 1995 and 1996, scoring the winning goal in a shootout with the Americans at the 1995 event. Goyette is part owner of a women's sporting goods store in Calgary.

GERALDINE HEANEY, the best offensive defenseman on Canada's team, was a member of the World Championship squads in 1990, 1992, 1994, 1997, 1999 and 2000. In both 1992 and 1994 she was named best defenseman at the Women's World Championships, an honor that she also garnered at the Pacific Rim Championship in 1996. She scored the clinching goal in a 3–1 victory over the Americans in the gold medal game at the 1999 Women's World Championships. Heaney collected six points to rank fourth in scoring for the Canadian team at the Winter Olympics in Nagano in 1998. She ranked seventh in scoring during the 1999–2000 inaugural season of the Women's National Hockey League.

A fitness fanatic and an all-around athlete, Heaney is considered one of the top female in-line hockey players in the world. She has also been invited to try out for Northern Ireland's national women's Gaelic football team.

JAYNA HEFFORD first began to attract attention as a member of Team Ontario's gold medalists at the 1995 Canada Winter Games. She has since become a fixture on Team Canada, starring at the Three Nations Cup in both 1997 and 1998. In 1999 Hefford ranked first on Canada, and second overall behind Jenny Schmidgall of the United States, with 11 points (five goals, six assists) at the Women's World Championships and was named to the all-star team. Her two third-period goals in the final of the 2000 tournament sparked Canada's rally for a 3–2 victory over the United States.

ANGELA JAMES is a legendary name in Canadian women's hockey. The decision to leave her off the roster of the 1998 Olympic team was as controversial as the decision to leave Mark Messier off the men's team. James had been a member of Canada's champion teams at each of the previous four Women's World Championships.

James was Canada's leading scorer with 11 goals at the 1990 Women's World Championships and was an all-star forward at the 1992 event. She had also been a top Canadian scoring threat at the 1994 and 1997 World tournaments, and represented her country at the Pacific Rim Championship in 1996. Though no longer a member of the national team, she played in the Women's National Hockey League during the inaugural season of 1999–2000. James is also a top referee and coached Team Ontario at the 1999 Canada Winter Games.

KAREN NYSTROM is a speedy right wing with a hard, accurate shot. She was a member of Canada's Women's World Championship teams in 1992, 1994 and 1997. She also played for Canada at the Nagano Olympics in 1998. She was the top scorer in the Central Ontario Hockey League three times.

An excellent soccer player in addition to her hockey skills, Nystrom was her high school's MVP in both sports from grade 9 through grade 13. She is also a five-time Ontario Cup winner in soccer.

LESLEY REDDON played on Ontario championship teams in each of her four seasons at the University of Toronto, and was the first woman to play on the men's hockey team at the University of New Brunswick. She was the top goalie on the 1997 Canadian Women's World Championship team after sharing the job with Manon Rheaume in 1994. Reddon and Rheaume again shared netminding duties for Canada in Nagano in 1998.

MANON RHEAUME is perhaps the most famous female hockey player in the world. Rheaume was the first woman to play with an NHL team when she saw action in a 1992 preseason game for the Tampa Bay Lightning. She has since played for a variety of men's minor-league teams.

Rheaume first appeared with Canada's national women's team in 1992. She was named to the all-star team when Canada won the Women's World Championship in 1992 and 1994, but was cut from the team prior to the 1997 World Championships. An aggressive goaltender who can handle the puck well, Rheaume regained her spot on the national team and played well at the 1998 Olympics. Married after the Nagano Games, she took time off from hockey to have a child and now has a son named Dylan. She announced her retirement from hockey in the summer of 2000.

FRANCE ST-LOUIS was the oldest player on Canada's women's team at the 1998 Nagano Olympics. Then 39 years old, St-Louis was a veteran of Canada's Women's World Championship teams of 1990, 1992, 1994 and 1997. She retired from the national team a champion after playing for Team Canada again in 1999, though she was still active in the National Women's Hockey League during its inaugural season of 1999–2000 and led the league in power-play goals at the age of 41. St-Louis was the top scorer in the Quebec Senior Hockey League as a 38-year-old in 1996–97, but is noted as an outstanding defensive center who excelled at winning face-offs. She was Quebec's female athlete of the decade in hockey and lacrosse for 1980 to 1990, and the athlete of the year in 1986. St-Louis now serves as president of the Women's Ice Hockey Program in the province of Quebec

SAMI-JO SMALL was named top goalie and earned a spot on the tournament all-star team at the 1999 Women's World Championships. She made 26 saves in the 3–1 gold medal victory over the United States, with the one goal in that game being the only one she allowed in three games at the tournament. Small was named best goalie when Canada won the World Championship again in 2000.

VICKY SUNOHARA was a star player with Northeastern University and represented Canada at the first official Women's World Championships in 1990, collecting six goals and three assists in five games. She did not play with the national team again until 1997. Sunohara was a member of the Canadian women's team at the 1998 Olympics, where she attracted much attention because her grandparents were born in Nagano. She also played for Canada's Women's World Championship team in 1999 and 2000.

HAYLEY WICKENHEISER is a physically dominant player who is also an excellent passer. The 19-year-old Wickenheiser's six assists led the women's Olympic tournament in Nagano in 1998. Her eight points ranked her second on her team, one point behind Danielle Goyette, and tied her for third at the Olympics. The Philadelphia Flyers offered her an invitation to work out at the team's rookie camp in 1998.

Wickenheiser first joined the Canadian women's national team as a 15-year-old in 1994 and was part of championship wins in both 1994 and 1997. Her four goals and five assists at the 1997 tournament ranked second in scoring and earned her a spot on the all-star team. She was an all-star when Canada won the World Championship again in 1999. Wickenheiser's eight points (three goals, five assists) in five games tied her for second spot on the Canadian team and fifth at the tournament. She helped Canada win the World Championship again in 2000, playing in the final game against the United States despite a serious shoulder injury, and then went straight to a national softball competition in Australia. She has also represented Canada in hockey at the Pacific Rim Championship in 1995 and 1996.

Growing up in Shaunavon, Saskatchewan, Wickenheiser consistently rated as the best player on boys teams in older age groups. As a 12-year-old in 1991, she scored the winning goal in the gold medal game in the 17-and-under girls division at the Canada Summer Games. Four years later she was a pitcher and shortstop with Canada's team at the 1995 World Junior Softball Championship In 2000, she played at the Sydney Olympics with the Canadian women's softball team. She is the fourth cousin of former NHL player Doug Wickenheiser.

STACY WILSON is now an assistant coach at the University of Minnesota-Duluth. She is a veteran of Canada's Women's World Championship teams in 1990, 1992, 1994 and 1997. Wilson served as a team captain with tremendous leadership skills. In the national championship in 1997, Wilson had a medal she received as MVP of a game cut into 20 pieces in order to share it with her teammates. Her five assists at the Olympics in 1998 ranked her second on the Canadian team behind Hayley Wickenheiser and tied her for second overall in the tournament, though Canada had to settle for a silver medal behind the United States.

CHINA

HONG DANG was a member of the team from China that finished fifth at the Women's World Championships in 1992. She also played for the Chinese teams that finished fourth at the world event behind Canada, the United States and Finland in 1994 and 1997. Dang represented China at the Nagano Olympics in 1998 as a member of the team that finished fourth once again behind the U.S., Canada and Finland.

HONG GUO was a member of the Chinese national team at the Women's World Championships in 1992, 1994, 1999 and 2000. She emerged as one of the top goaltenders in women's hockey at the Pacific Rim Championship, helping China earn a bronze medal in 1995 and being named the best goalie at the event when China earned another bronze medal in 1996. Her stellar goaltending at the Nagano Olympics led China to the bronze medal game against Finland, though the Chinese team had to settle for fourth place after a 4–1 loss to the Finns.

WEI GUO scored three goals for China at the Nagano Olympics in 1998, tying for the lead on a team that finished fourth behind the United States, Canada and Finland. Guo had previously been a member of the Chinese teams that finished fourth behind Canada, the U.S. and Finland at the Women's World Championships in 1994 and 1997. She first played at the world tourney in 1992, when China finished fifth.

HONGMEI LIU had two goals and three assists in five games to tie for top spot in scoring on the Chinese team at the Nagano Olympics in 1998. China finished fourth at that tournament behind the United States, Canada and China. She was the team's top scorer with seven points again at the Women's World Championships in 1999, but China fell into fifth place. Her five goals ranked among the tournament leaders in 2000, though the Chinese team could only manage a sixth-place finish.

Liu first appeared on the international arena at the Women's World Championships in 1992, and had eight goals and three assists to lead China to a fourth-place finish at the world tourney in 1994. China again finished fourth in 1997. Liu was a member of the Chinese team that earned a bronze medal behind the United States and Canada at the Pacific Rim Championship in 1995.

FINLAND

SARI FISK played for Finland when the team won the European Women's Championships in 1991, collecting 10 goals and two assists for a Finnish team that outscored its opposition 71–0. In 1992, she won a bronze medal with Finland at the Women's World Championships and would win bronze again in 1994, 1997, 1999 and 2000. Her four goals and five assists in 1999 ranked her among the tournament leaders. Fisk was third on the team in scoring with six points (two goals and four assists) in six games when Finland earned a bronze medal at the Nagano Olympics in 1998. She was also a member of the Finnish team that won the European Women's Championships in 1995.

KIRSI HANNINEN was an all-star defenseman at the 1999 Women's World Championships. Her five goals and five assists tied her for the Finnish lead with 10 points and ranked her tied for third in the tourney. Hanninen helped Finland finish in third place again in 1999, just as she would in 2000.

MARIANNE IHALAINEN was a member of the teams from Finland that won the bronze medal at the Women's World Championships in 1990, 1992, 1994 and 1997. She was also a member of the Finnish team that claimed the bronze medal at the 1998 Nagano Olympics. She returned to the national team and earned yet another bronze medal in 2000.

SARI KROOKS was a member of the Finnish team that came in third behind Canada and the United States at the Women's World Championships in 1990, 1992, 1994, 1997 and 1999. She played with the Olympic team from Finland that recorded a third-place finish behind the United States and Canada at the Nagano Olympics in 1998. Krooks also played for the Finnish teams that won the European Women's Championships in 1989 and 1995. She was named to the tournament all-star team in 1995 after collecting six goals and eight assists in five games.

MARIKA LEHTIMAKI is a veteran of women's hockey in Finland, helping the Finnish team win the European Women's Championship in 1993, 1995 and 1996. She also played for third-place teams from Finland at the Women's World Championships in 1990, 1992 and 1994. Though she missed the world tournament in 1997, Lehtimaki was again a member of the Finnish team when Finland earned a bronze medal at the Nagano Olympics in 1998.

RIIKKA NIEMINEN is one of the top offensive talents in women's hockey. Nieminen led the Olympic tournament in scoring with 12 points, and was second behind Canada's Danielle Goyette with seven goals, in Nagano in 1998. Nieminen led Finland to a bronze medal that year after having played with Finnish teams that had placed third at the Women's World Championships in 1990, 1992, 1994 and 1997. She was named a tournament all-star in 1992, 1994 and 1997, and was also named the best forward in 1994 after collecting 13 points (four goals and nine assists) in five games. Nieminen had nine goals and 14 assists in five games in 1995 when she led Finland to a gold medal in the European Women's Championships. She had also earned gold at the European event in 1989.

TUULA PUPUTTI joined the Finnish national team in 1993. Her goaltending helped Finland win gold medals at the European Women's Championships in 1993 and 1995, and bronze medals at the Women's World Championships in 1997, 1999 and 2000. Puputti posted a 1.55 goals-against average in five games when Finland earned a bronze medal at the 1998 Nagano Olympics.

KATJA RIIPI stepped into the gap left by injuries to Riikka Nieminen when she asserted herself as Finland's top scorer with seven goals at the 2000 Women's World Championships. Her hat trick in the bronze medal game led Finland to a 7–1 rout of Sweden. A member of the national team since 1995, Riipi also earned bronze medals with the Finnish team at the Women's World Championships in 1997 and 1999 and at the Nagano Olympics in 1998.

GERMANY

MAREN VALENTI played for West Germany at the first official Women's World Championships in 1990. She had three goals and two assists on a low-scoring team that finished in fourth place at the European Women's Championships in 1993. In 1994, 1999 and 2000 she again played for the German team at the Women's World Championships. She led the team in scoring with two goals and three assists in five games at the 2000 tournament. In 1995 she had four goals and three assists on a German team that scored only 11 goals at the European Women's Championships.

RUSSIA

YEKATERINA PASHKEVICH collected five goals and 14 assists in just four games for Russia while playing in the B Pool of the European Women's Championships in 1995. In 1996, she had six goals in five games and was a tournament all-star as Russia earned a silver medal behind Sweden in the A Pool of the European Women's Championships. The performance earned Russia a spot in the 1997 Women's World Championships, where Pashkevich collected three goals for a Russian team that finished sixth. She led the Russian team with four goals at the 1999 Women's World Championships and ranked among the tournament leaders with six goals in 2000.

TATJANA TSAREVA had eight goals and four assists in just four games for Russia in the B Pool of the European Women's Championships in 1995. In 1997, she was a member of the first Russian team to make an appearance at the Women's World Championships. She led Russia with six points (two goals, four assists) in a sixth-place finish at the 1999 tournament and was a member of the team that finished fifth in 2000.

SWEDEN

LOTTA ALMBLAD was a member of the Swedish national women's team at the Women's World Championships in 1992, 1994, 1997, 1999 and 2000. She also represented Sweden at the Nagano Olympics in 1998. Almblad was a member of the Swedish team that ranked second to Finland at the 1995 European Women's Championships, and played for the team that won the European tournament in 1996.

GUNILLA ANDERSSON has represented Sweden at the Women's World Championships in 1992, 1994, 1997, 1999 and 2000. She also played at the Nagano Olympics in 1998. Anderson was named the best defenseman when Sweden finished second behind Finland at the 1995 European Women's Championships.

KRISTINA BERGSTRAND represented Sweden at the European Women's Championships in 1989 and 1991. In 1991 she was named to the tournament all-star team and was also picked as the best forward after tallying eight goals and 12 assists in just five games. Sweden finished second behind Finland that year. Bergstrand has also represented Sweden at the Women's World Championships in 1990, 1992, 1994, 1997 and 2000. The Swedish veteran also played at the Nagano Olympics in 1998.

CAMILLA KEMPE played for Sweden at the Women's World Championships in 1990, 1992, 1994 and 1997, collecting five goals in five games at the event in both 1990 and 1992. She was also a member of the Swedish team that came in second behind Finland at the European Women's Championships in 1993.

USA

LISA BROWN-MILLER was the only married member of the gold medal-winning United States national women's team at the Nagano Olympics in 1998. She was married in August 1995 and left the next day for the U.S. National Women's Team training camp. In 1996, she gave up her job as head coach of the women's team at Princeton University in order to train full time for the national team.

Brown-Miller was considered one of the American team's strongest players and was a determined forechecker who anchored the team's penalty-killing unit. In addition to her Olympic experience, she played with the U.S. team that finished second behind Canada at the Women's World Championships in 1990, 1992, 1994 and 1997. She also took part in the Pacific Rim Championship in 1995.

KARYN BYE was the United States' top scorer with five goals in six games on the gold medal-winning women's team at the 1998 Nagano Olympics. She is considered to have one of the hardest shots in women's hockey and is a good skater with excellent puck control who has averaged a goal per game in international competition. Her five goals at the Women's World Championships in 1999 tied for top spot in the tournament as the Americans settled for the silver medal behind Team Canada. Her eight goals in 2000 led the tournament and her 10 points ranked third as Team USA finished second once again.

Bye played high school hockey on the boys team in River Falls, Wisconsin before going on to play women's university hockey at New Hampshire. As a member of the United States national women's team, she has also appeared at the Women's World Championships in 1992, 1994, and 1997, where the Americans finished second behind Canada every year. Bye was named to the tournament all-star team in 1994. She has also represented the United States at the Pacific Rim Championship in 1995 and 1996.

COLLEEN COYNE, the top defensive defenseman on the United States national women's team, helped the U.S. record the lowest team goals-against average (1.33) en route to winning the gold medal over Canada at the Nagano Olympics in 1998. Coyne had previously been a member of the U.S. teams that had lost the Women's World Championship to Canada in 1992, 1994 and 1997. She was an assistant coach with Team USA at the 2000 tournament.

In addition to her international experience, Coyne starred in women's university hockey at New Hampshire. She was also an all-American in lacrosse in 1989 and was the assistant coach with the women's hockey team in 1993–94 while continuing her studies.

SARA DECOSTA picked up victories in all three preliminary round games at the 1998 Nagano Olympics as the United States went on to claim the gold medal. Previously, she had a shutout against Canada in a 3–0 U.S. victory in the final game of the 1997 Three Nations Cup. That game marked the first time the Americans had defeated Canada in a tournament and the first time that Canada had been kept off the scoreboard in an international game.

A star at Providence College, Decosta was one of four finalists for the Patty Kazmaier Memorial Award, presented annually to the top U.S. women's varsity hockey player, as a junior in 1999–2000. She also played for the U.S. team that finished second behind Canada at the 2000 Women's World Championships.

CAMMI GRANATO is the only American player to have appeared in each of the first six Women's World Championships. Granato's 36 goals and 59 points in 30 games make her the leading scorer in the history of the tournament through 2000. After losing to Canada in 1990, 1992, 1994 and 1997, Granato was captain of the United States team that earned a gold medal victory at the 1998 Olympic Games in Nagano. Her four goals and four assists at the Olympics ranked her in a four-way tie for top spot on the American squad. Her eight points in 1999 ranked her among the tournament leaders when the Americans once again had to settle for a silver medal behind Canada at the Women's World Championships. She ranked among the leaders with six goals when the Americans recorded yet another second-place finish in 2000.

The brother of NHL player Tony Granato, Cammie Granato has done more than any other player to popularize women's hockey in the United States. She has been named both the best forward and a member of the tournament all-star team at the Women's World Championships in 1992 and 1997 and has also represented the United States at the Pacific Rim Championship in 1995 and 1996. She is the all-time leading scorer in women's hockey at Providence College.

SHELLEY LOONEY was one of the American team's top scorers with four goals in six games as the United States won the gold medal in women's hockey at the 1998 Nagano Olympics. Her goal at 10:57 of the second period in the gold medal game against Canada gave the Americans a 2–0 lead and proved to be the game winner in a 3–1 victory.

A tough competitor and all-around player who is solid both offensively and defensively, Looney suffered a broken jaw at the Women's World Championships in 1997 after blocking a shot in overtime in the gold medal game eventually won by Canada. Previously, Looney had played for the U.S. team that was beaten by Canada for the World Championship in 1992 and 1994. She was also on the American team that lost to Canada again in 1999 and 2000. Looney has also represented her country at the Pacific Rim Championship in 1995.

SUE MERZ is a veteran of the American women's team, having appeared at the Women's World Championships in 1990, 1992, 1994, 1999 and 2000. She was an all-star defenseman at the 1999 tournament. In 1998, she assisted on the first goal against Canada in the gold medal game at the Nagano Olympics. Merz had also represented the United States at the Pacific Rim Championship (1995 and 1996) and at the Three Nations Cup (1996 and 1998). She played collegiate hockey at the University of New Hampshire (1990 to 1994). Previously, Merz was a member of the Connecticut Polar Bears for three seasons, leading the team to the 1990 USA Hockey Girls' Midget National Championship. She also played overseas for SC Lyss of the Swiss National League.

TARA MOUNSEY was the third-youngest player on the United States national women's team at the 1998 Nagano Olympics, but the 19-year-old was considered the team's top defenseman and possibly the best all-around talent. A slick skater with a booming shot, Mounsey's six points (two goals and four assists) in six games topped all American defenseman at the Olympics and ranked her sixth overall in scoring for the gold medal winners.

Dubbed "the Bobby Orr of Women's Hockey," Mounsey starred on a boys high school team in Concord, New Hampshire, before going on to play women's hockey at Brown University. In addition to the Olympics, she has represented the United States at the Women's World Championships in 1997 and 1999.

STEPHANIE O'SULLIVAN ranked second in scoring behind American teammate Krissy Wendell at the 2000 Women's World Championships. O'Sullivan's 12 points were just one back of Wendell and her five goals and seven assists also ranked among the tournament leaders. She scored the winning goal when the U.S. rallied to beat Finland 4–3 in the final game of the preliminary round. In addition to the silver medal O'Sullivan earned at the 2000 tournament, she has been part of American teams that have finished as the runner-up behind Canada at the 1994, 1997 and 1999 Women's World Championships. She competed with the American team during the 1997–98 pre-Olympic tournament, but was not part of the team that won gold at Nagano.

O'Sullivan played university hockey at Providence College, where her 253 points (126 goals, 127 assists) rank second on the Friars' all-time scoring list behind Cammie Granato. Brother Chris O'Sullivan is a player in the NHL.

JENNY SCHMIDGALL was the leading scorer at the 1999 Women's World Championships with 12 points on five goals and seven assists. She scored the U.S. team's only goal in a 3–1 loss to Canada in the gold medal game. Her offensive performance not only saw her earn a spot on the tournament all-star team, she also was named the best forward. Schmidgall was a member of the American team that earned a silver medal again in 2000. In 1998, she played for the U.S. team that beat Canada for the gold medal at the Nagano Olympics.

After spending her freshman season at the University of Minnesota, Schmidgall transferred to Minnesota-Duluth for the 1999–2000 season and led the nation in scoring with 88 points (39 goals, 49 assists) in 30 games and was a finalist for the Patty Kazmaier Memorial Award, presented annually to the top U.S. women's varsity hockey player.

BEN SMITH was named the first full-time head coach of the U.S. women's national team on June 3, 1996. In 1997, he led the women's team to yet another silver medal behind Canada at the Women's World Championships, but in 1998 he coached the American team to a gold medal victory at the Nagano Olympics. Since then, the U.S. has had to settle for silver again behind Canada at the 1999 and 2000 Women's World Championships. In international men's hockey, Smith served as an assistant coach for the U.S. national junior team from 1985 to 1987, for the men's national team in 1987 and 1990 and for the 1988 U.S. Olympic team. Smith's most recent men's assignment came in 1998 when he helped the U.S. qualify for the A Pool of the 1999 World Championships.

A graduate of Harvard University in 1968, Smith worked as an assistant coach at the University of Massachusetts-Amherst and at Yale before spending nine seasons (1981 to 1990) as the top assistant at Boston University. In 1991, he began a five-year stint as head coach at Northeastern University.

SARAH TUETING compiled a 1.15 goals-against average and a .937 save percentage to lead all goaltenders at the 1998 Nagano Olympics. She stopped 21 of 22 shots to lead the U.S. to a 3–1 victory over Canada in the gold medal game. Tueting made her first appearance on an elite-level U.S. women's team at the 1996 Three Nations Cup. She has also represented the United States at the Women's World Championships in 1997 and 2000. She was named Ivy League rookie of the year with Dartmouth College in 1994–95 and also played in the school's symphony orchestra.

KRISSY WENDELL was still a senior in high school when she led the 2000 Women's World Championships in scoring with two goals and 11 assists. She had a goal and four assists when the U.S. trounced Russia 15–0 during the preliminary round. The Americans earned a silver medal behind Canada that year, just as they had when Wendell made her national team debut at the 1999 tournament. In 1998, she had been a member of the U.S. select team that placed second at the Three Nations Cup.

Wendell tallied 166 points in just 27 games for her Park Center High School team in 1999–2000, scoring 110 goals to break the record of 109 she had set the year before and leading the Pirates to the state championship. As a member of the Park Center boys team in 1997–98, Wendell had 12 goals and eight assists in 10 games before an injury cut short her season. In 1994, she became the first girl to start in the Little League World Series. Her brother Erik was drafted by the Washington Capitals in 1998.

ERIN WHITTEN began playing with the Toledo Storm of the East Coast Hockey League 14 months after Canadian goaltender Manon Rheaume broke the gender barrier by appearing in a 1992 Tampa Bay Lightning NHL exhibition game. On October 30, 1993, Whitten became the first female goaltender to record a victory in a professional game.

A high school star on the boys team in her hometown of Glens Falls, New York, Whitten developed into an elite goaltender during four seasons of women's university hockey at New Hampshire. She was the top goaltender on the United States national women's team, appearing at the Women's World Championships in 1992, 1994, 1997 and 1999, where the team finished second behind Canada every year. In 1994, Whitten was named the best goalie at the tournament.

III

The National Hockey League

The puck stops here! A hard shot ended up lodged between the bars of rookie goaltender Brian Boucher's mask in a game between the Philadelphia Flyers and New Jersey Devils during the 2000 Eastern Conference Finals. Boucher was able to stay in the game, wearing a spare mask as this one was repaired.
NHL Images photo

STANLEY CUP WINNERS SINCE THE FORMATION OF THE NHL IN 1917

YEAR	W–L IN FINALS	WINNER	COACH	FINALIST	COACH
2000	4–2	New Jersey	Larry Robinson	Dallas	Ken Hitchcock
1999	4–2	Dallas	Ken Hitchcock	Buffalo	Lindy Ruff
1998	4–0	Detroit	Scotty Bowman	Washington	Ron Wilson
1997	4–0	Detroit	Scotty Bowman	Philadelphia	Terry Murray
1996	4–0	Colorado	Marc Crawford	Florida	Doug MacLean
1995	4–0	New Jersey	Jacques Lemaire	Detroit	Scotty Bowman
1994	4–3	NY Rangers	Mike Keenan	Vancouver	Pat Quinn
1993	4–1	Montreal	Jacques Demers	Los Angeles	Barry Melrose
1992	4–0	Pittsburgh	Scotty Bowman	Chicago	Mike Keenan
1991	4–2	Pittsburgh	Bob Johnson	Minnesota	Bob Gainey
1990	4–1	Edmonton	John Muckler	Boston	Mike Milbury
1989	4–2	Calgary	Terry Crisp	Montreal	Pat Burns
1988	4–0	Edmonton	Glen Sather	Boston	Terry O'Reilly
1987	4–3	Edmonton	Glen Sather	Philadelphia	Mike Keenan
1986	4–1	Montreal	Jean Perron	Calgary	Bob Johnson
1985	4–1	Edmonton	Glen Sather	Philadelphia	Mike Keenan
1984	4–1	Edmonton	Glen Sather	NY Islanders	Al Arbour
1983	4–0	NY Islanders	Al Arbour	Edmonton	Glen Sather
1982	4–0	NY Islanders	Al Arbour	Vancouver	Roger Neilson
1981	4–1	NY Islanders	Al Arbour	Minnesota	Glen Sonmor
1980	4–2	NY Islanders	Al Arbour	Philadelphia	Pat Quinn
1979	4–1	Montreal	Scotty Bowman	NY Rangers	Fred Shero
1978	4–2	Montreal	Scotty Bowman	Boston	Don Cherry
1977	4–0	Montreal	Scotty Bowman	Boston	Don Cherry
1976	4–0	Montreal	Scotty Bowman	Philadelphia	Fred Shero
1975	4–2	Philadelphia	Fred Shero	Buffalo	Floyd Smith
1974	4–2	Philadelphia	Fred Shero	Boston	Bep Guidolin
1973	4–2	Montreal	Scotty Bowman	Chicago	Billy Reay
1972	4–2	Boston	Tom Johnson	NY Rangers	Emile Francis
1971	4–3	Montreal	Al MacNeil	Chicago	Billy Reay
1970	4–0	Boston	Harry Sinden	St. Louis	Scotty Bowman
1969	4–0	Montreal	Claude Ruel	St. Louis	Scotty Bowman
1968	4–0	Montreal	Toe Blake	St. Louis	Scotty Bowman
1967	4–2	Toronto	Punch Imlach	Montreal	Toe Blake
1966	4–2	Montreal	Toe Blake	Detroit	Sid Abel
1965	4–3	Montreal	Toe Blake	Chicago	Billy Reay
1964	4–3	Toronto	Punch Imlach	Detroit	Sid Abel
1963	4–1	Toronto	Punch Imlach	Detroit	Sid Abel
1962	4–2	Toronto	Punch Imlach	Chicago	Rudy Pilous
1961	4–2	Chicago	Rudy Pilous	Detroit	Sid Abel
1960	4–3	Montreal	Toe Blake	Toronto	Punch Imlach
1959	4–1	Montreal	Toe Blake	Toronto	Punch Imlach
1958	4–2	Montreal	Toe Blake	Boston	Milt Schmidt
1957	4–1	Montreal	Toe Blake	Boston	Milt Schmidt
1956	4–1	Montreal	Toe Blake	Detroit	Jimmy Skinner
1955	4–3	Detroit	Jimmy Skinner	Montreal	Dick Irvin
1954	4–3	Detroit	Tommy Ivan	Montreal	Dick Irvin
1953	4–1	Montreal	Dick Irvin	Boston	Lynn Patrick
1952	4–0	Detroit	Tommy Ivan	Montreal	Dick Irvin
1951	4–1	Toronto	Joe Primeau	Montreal	Dick Irvin
1950	4–3	Detroit	Tommy Ivan	NY Rangers	Lynn Patrick
1949	4–0	Toronto	Hap Day	Detroit	Tommy Ivan
1948	4–0	Toronto	Hap Day	Detroit	Tommy Ivan
1947	4–2	Toronto	Hap Day	Montreal	Dick Irvin
1946	4–1	Montreal	Dick Irvin	Boston	Dit Clapper
1945	4–3	Toronto	Hap Day	Detroit	Jack Adams
1944	4–0	Montreal	Dick Irvin	Chicago	Paul Thompson
1943	4–0	Detroit	Jack Adams	Boston	Art Ross
1942	4–3	Toronto	Hap Day	Detroit	Jack Adams
1941	4–0	Boston	Cooney Weiland	Detroit	Ebbie Goodfellow
1940	4–2	NY Rangers	Frank Boucher	Toronto	Dick Irvin
1939	4–1	Boston	Art Ross	Toronto	Dick Irvin
1938	3–1	Chicago	Bill Stewart	Toronto	Dick Irvin
1937	3–2	Detroit	Jack Adams	NY Rangers	Lester Patrick
1936	3–1	Detroit	Jack Adams	Toronto	Dick Irvin
1935	3–0	Mtl. Maroons	Tommy Gorman	Toronto	Dick Irvin
1934	3–1	Chicago	Tommy Gorman	Detroit	Herbie Lewis
1933	3–1	NY Rangers	Lester Patrick	Toronto	Dick Irvin
1932	3–0	Toronto	Dick Irvin	NY Rangers	Lester Patrick
1931	3–2	Montreal	Cecil Hart	Chicago	Dick Irvin
1930	2–0	Montreal	Cecil Hart	Boston	Art Ross
1929	2–0	Boston	Cy Denneny	NY Rangers	Lester Patrick
1928	3–2	NY Rangers	Lester Patrick	Mtl. Maroons	Eddie Gerard
1927	2–0–2	Ottawa	Dave Gill	Boston	Art Ross
	The National Hockey League assumed control of Stanley Cup competition after 1926.				
1926	3–1	Mtl. Maroons	Eddie Gerard	Victoria	Lester Patrick
1925	3–1	Victoria	Lester Patrick	Montreal	Leo Dandurand
1924	2–0	Montreal	Leo Dandurand	Cgy. Tigers	
	2–0			Van. Maroons	
1923	2–0	Ottawa	Pete Green	Edm. Eskimos	
	3–1			Van. Maroons	
1922	3–2	Tor. St. Pats	Eddie Powers	Van. Millionaires	Frank Patrick
1921	3–2	Ottawa	Pete Green	Van. Millionaires	Frank Patrick
1920	3–2	Ottawa	Pete Green	Seattle	
1919	2–2–1	No decision – series between Montreal and Seattle cancelled due to influenza epidemic			
1918	3–2	Tor. Arenas	Dick Carroll	Van. Millionaires	Frank Patrick

CHAPTER 19

A Short History of the National Hockey League

The Founding of a New League

Brian McFarlane

There might never have been a National Hockey League had it not been for a number of quarrels and disputes between owners of teams in the National Hockey Association, the circuit that came just before the NHL. Such disagreements were particularly vitriolic during the 1916–17 season, in the unique situations of wartime.

In 1916, the NHA was comprised of six teams: Montreal Canadiens, Montreal Wanderers, Ottawa Senators, Quebec Bulldogs, the Torontos (often referred to as the Blueshirts or the Arenas) and a team of enlisted men, soldiers on skates representing the 228th Battalion, stationed in Toronto. Because of the war and a shortage of skilled players, Ottawa sought to withdraw from the league but was persuaded to stay on under new management. Sam Lichtenhein, manager of the Wanderers, came up with the patriotic idea that the Montreal club would sign only married men and munitions workers. But perhaps the biggest source of dispute was the team wearing khaki.

When the 228th Battalion recruited Gordon "Duke" Keats, one of his best players, Eddie Livingstone, owner of the Toronto team, protested so vehemently the Battalion commander allowed Keats to play for Toronto in his off-duty hours. But then most of the players in the league became angry when Livingstone refused to release Ottawa native Cy Denneny to his hometown, where he'd taken a job. Livingstone wanted the exorbitant sum of $1,800 and refused offers to trade for Denneny's release. Because of Livingstone's stance, a number of players talked about forming a union, or at least an association, though nothing came of it then. Eventually, Livingstone accepted $750 and goaltender Sammy Hebert for Denneny. Still, things could get worse: In less than a year, Livingstone was involved in a bitter battle with his fellow owners, threatened to start a new league, initiated lawsuits and injunctions and even claimed that Denneny's rights still belonged to him.

The boys in the 228th were a major attraction. Their khaki uniforms may have come across as what we'd call these days a fashion statement, but there was more to them than patriotic sentiment on ice. In their opening game, they scored no less than 10 goals to beat Ottawa 10–7. In a return match in Ottawa, Howard McNamara (arguably the Battalion's most temperamental player) took two major penalties—including one for attacking the referee with his fists. He may have been somewhat surprised to receive a few solid punches in return from the no-nonsense Cooper Smeaton. But that was only a start. On February 3, 1917, in Quebec, the soldiers arrived late from Toronto, missed their pregame meal and were perchance in a foul mood. They took the Quebec players on at the outset and were pelted with bottles, programs and other debris from the stands. Police had to escort the visiting team to their dressing room, but an angry mob was waiting for them after the game and they did not reach the train station unscathed.

The 228th Battalion's stay in pro hockey, however eventful, was brief. Knowing that their future in hockey was unpredictable, the Battalion had taken out a $3,000 bond with the Ocean Accident and Guarantee Company against the possibility of their being called overseas prior to the end of the schedule. By January 27, 1917, the 228th had completed the first half of the NHA's split season with a 6–4 record (the Canadiens won the first half with a 7–3 mark), but on February 10 the club withdrew from the NHA because the Battalion was ordered to ship out. The following day, the league owners met and a shouting match resulted when Eddie Livingstone insisted on a revamping of the schedule. Before the meeting ended, Livingstone's team in Toronto had been dropped from the league and his players divided among the clubs that were left. Livingstone stormed out of the meeting an irate owner and former franchise holder.

The second half of the NHA's split season saw Ottawa emerge victorious and meet Montreal in a two-game total-goals playoff. After the Canadiens won the first game 5–2, huge crowds, with mounted police maintaining order, waited outside the arena in Ottawa, hoping for a chance to buy tickets for the second. Local recruiting officers worked up and down the line, trying to persuade able-bodied youth to sign up for military service. Not a single one chose to forgo watching hockey for a more serious life in the army and Ottawa won, but by only 4–2.

On the strength of its one-goal advantage, Montreal qualified to go west to meet Seattle, current champions of the Pacific Coast Hockey Association, for the Stanley Cup. On the coast, Seattle's Bernie Morris was sensational, scoring 14 goals against the Canadiens in the four-game series, which was won by Seattle three games to one. Game two was especially intense. A Seattle sportswriter wrote: "Harry Mummery threw himself into Jack Walker with such force that the frail forward of the Seattle team had to be stretched out and carried off the ice. Mummery and Rickey swung their sticks on one another's heads so hard that the raps could be heard up in the gods. Then Rickey and Couture staged a bout that would have furnished a lively reel for the movies." And to cap the climax of the most exciting scenes ever enacted in the Seattle Arena, Newsy Lalonde swatted referee George Irvine across the face, whereupon judge of play Mickey Ion pitched into Lalonde and chased him off the ice, adding a fine of $25.

Thus ended the last season of play in the NHA. But if the eastern league owners thought they were in for a peaceful offseason, they were badly mistaken. Eddie Livingstone was still fuming, and he certainly wasn't just going away.

Even before the Stanley Cup was decided in 1917, Livingstone was demanding the expulsion of the Wanderers from the NHA, charging the team with attempting to lure two of his Toronto players to Montreal. Then he demanded $20,000 as his share of the Toronto Arena's profits for the 1916–17 season. When Arena officials offered him $6,000, he scoffed at the sum. He even railed against the team for providing the players with jackets.

Factions were forming and this small, local war escalating. Charlie Querrie, a highly respected sportsman and manager of the Toronto Arena, was approached by his friend Percy Quinn, a Toronto man who had purchased the Quebec franchise in the NHA. Quinn wanted to know if he could rent the Arena if he were to move. "Not on your life," Querrie answered. "If the Quebec team moves here, it will not get ice as long as you have any dealings at all with Mr. Livingstone."

Well heated, the climate of controversy between the Quinn–Livingstone side and the rest of the owners simmered all summer and boiled up again in the fall when Quinn and Livingstone announced the formation of a rival league, the Canadian Hockey Association. Quinn boasted that he had the exclusive rights to the ice in Ottawa and expected one or two clubs from that city to join his league. "That is absolutely false," declared E.P. Dey, owner of the Ottawa rink. "Mr.Quinn held an option on the ice here but his option expired some time ago. He sent us $25 and his cheque has been returned to him." The CHA also claimed to have an option on Montreal's Jubilee Rink, an arena affiliated with the Canadiens, then owned by George Kennedy. Kennedy wasn't worried, even when Livingstone's people made a night-time entry, turned on the hose and began making ice for the coming season. "If I can't get ice in Montreal, the Canadiens will play all their home games in Ottawa," he said. "The Ottawa rink seats twice as many fans as the Jubilee and I'll make twice as much money." But then Kennedy held strong opinions about Livingstone's plans for a rival league. "The new league is a joke, a scream. Just imagine anyone so foolish as to try to operate two teams in Ottawa. And to make jumps between Hamilton and Quebec. The latter is dead and the rink in Hamilton is not big enough. The NHA will be in operation again. Don't worry about that."

In Toronto, Eddie Livingstone talked of negotiating for the use of the Riverdale rink for his CHA team. The *Toronto Telegram* scoffed: "The Riverdale rink is a box. The attempt to rent it is like a drowning man grasping for something to hold him up. It is too narrow and brilliant play will be prevented by this condition." And when Livingstone repeated that he had control of Toronto's top players, team captain Ken Randall had a comeback. "Livingstone didn't pay me in 1916 and 1917. How can a contract still hold me?" Meanwhile, Percy Quinn applied for an injunction to prevent the Ottawa club from playing in the NHA, claiming once more that he had a prior arrangement to lease the ice in Ottawa.

While Livingstone's threat of a rival league appeared to be little more than empty rhetoric, talk of change was certainly in the air. There was much speculation after a meeting in Montreal on November 3 that the other NHA owners were planning to organize a new league, but six days later president Frank Robinson and secretary Frank Calder denied there were any changes planned. However, rumors of a new league again surfaced after another NHA meeting on November 10.

On that day, the governors of the NHA held a brief meeting in Montreal and afterwards announced that the league would suspend operations for the upcoming season, citing it as "unfeasible" with the scarcity of pro players due to the war. What people didn't know was that shortly after the NHA meeting adjourned, the owners of the Ottawa and Quebec franchises and the two Montreal clubs—the Canadiens and the Wanderers—gathered to hold a second meeting, welcoming a group representing the Toronto Arena Company.

Soon, the real reason for the suspension of the NHA would become public knowledge. It had less to do with a player shortage and more to do with getting rid of bombastic Toronto owner Eddie Livingstone. An earlier report in a Toronto newspaper had suggested there was "renewed determination on the part of the Ottawa, Montreal and Quebec clubs not to tolerate the Toronto club any longer."

A story in the November 12, 1917, edition of the *Toronto Globe* suggested that there was "something doing in pro hockey," amidst rumors of a new league being founded with Frank Calder, who had been secretary of the NHA, serving as president. On November 17, it was announced that Quebec had dropped out of the NHA but that the league would continue to operate with the Wanderers, Canadiens, Ottawa, and Toronto.

Five days later NHA owners met again in Montreal, but no official report of their discussions was released. The November 22 meeting was adjourned until November 24 but was not actually held until November 26 at Montreal's Windsor Hotel. On that day it was formally announced that there would be a new hockey league—the National Hockey League. As expected, Calder was named president. The loop consisted of five teams—Quebec, Ottawa, the two Montreal clubs and a new Toronto franchise. "A syndicate of Toronto sportsmen purchased the team," Calder stated. The club had been bought by the owners of the Toronto Arena and would be operated by Charles Querrie. "The new owners were thoroughly acceptable" to the other clubs of the league said Calder. Other team owners weren't as polite about the change as their league's new president. "He was always arguing about everything," Ottawa's Tommy Gorman said of Livingstone. "Without him, we can get down to the business of making money."

Eddie Livingstone had been left out of the picture by his former fellow owners, but any fears that he might actually form a league of his own were all but put to rest when George Kennedy produced a signed lease for the use of the Jubilee Rink. The new hockey season was already fast approaching, and while there was still some litigation pending, the club owners felt optimistic about the future of the new league. "We ought to pass Eddie Livingstone a vote of thanks for solidifying our league," laughed George Kennedy when the meetings were over.

But Livingstone and Quinn weren't quite finished. They tried to obtain an injunction against the NHL to prevent the opening games of the new season from taking place. They notified the Ottawa Senators that the team had no rights to Hap Holmes, Alf Skinner, Jack Adams, Ken Randall, Gordon Meeking or Cy Denneny (for whom, as noted above, Livingstone received cash and a goaltender a few months earlier). Livingstone further claimed rights to several NHL players and warned them not to set foot on NHL ice. Quinn continued to insist he had a lease on the Ottawa ice and any team that played on it was doing so illegally.

In the middle of all of this strife, amid rumors of lawsuits, injunctions, threats and intimidation tactics, one veteran player showed a keen sense of humour. Having read in the papers that Percy Quinn had forbidden him from playing in the season opener, "Bad" Joe Hall wired Quinn and asked innocently: "I have read the papers. Am I permitted to play? I have no contract."

Not recognizing the sarcasm, Quinn wired back, "I regret you cannot play under any circumstances." Hall chuckled and went out and played. The next day he received another wire from Quinn. "You have been fined $200 for playing." Hall's reply was reported to be unprintable. Even in telegraphic form, the contents were said to be "hot enough to start a small fire without a match."

Under its new ownership, the Toronto Arenas (the name would not become official until the following year) won the first NHL championship and hosted the Vancouver Millionaires in the 1918 Stanley Cup playoffs, a best-of-five affair. In the final game, a goal by Corbett Denneny proved to be the winner in a 2–1 Toronto victory. Eddie Livingstone and Percy Quinn were left on the sidelines, maybe wondering what might have been. Stubborn, ambitious, confrontational characters, they could have easily played major roles when the new league was formed and become NHL pioneers had they not chosen to argue, scrap, threaten and litigate until other owners had just had enough. Today, their names are all but forgotten in the often told stories of NHL history.

SETTING THE FOUNDATION 1917–18 TO 1925–26

Bob Duff

RAPID GROWTH IN LEAGUE SIZE. Major expansion into the United States and grave Canadian fears that the Americans were "stealing our game." Contract holdouts. Soaring salaries. A players' strike that disrupts the Stanley Cup playoffs. Anti-defense rules designed to increase scoring. The first decade of the National Hockey League really wasn't all that different from the modern era.

Professional hockey was in dire straits as the governors of the National Hockey Association were set to gather in November 1917. The Great War raged in Europe and many of the game's top stars had traded in their skates and sticks for boots and rifles. "Pro Hockey on Last Legs" screamed the headline in the *Toronto Globe* on November 6, 1917, as the dearth of available hockey talent seemed ready to bring about the demise of the NHA, a league that had been in existence since 1909.

"The public want first-class hockey and unless we can furnish it for them, we will reserve the ice for skating purposes only," said E.D. Sheppard, president of the Montreal Arena Company, suggesting that pro hockey might not be part of the winter scenery that year.

With so many good young men heading off to war, the ranks of the NHA had dwindled to the old and infirm and the professional game had lost much of its fan support. "Futile attempts have been made to get amateur stars to become professionals to replace the worn-out oldtimers who have been playing on the NHA teams for year," noted the *Globe*. "Fast, young amateur stars have stolen the patronage from the pros."

Reorganizing the NHA into the National Hockey League may have cured some problems, but the infant league still had concerns. Immediately, the Quebec franchise took a leave of absence, reducing the NHL to a four-team outfit. Furthermore it became apparent that the change of name wasn't fooling anyone as far as the quality of the product was concerned. When the NHL's first season opened on December 19, 1917, only 700 fans were on hand at Montreal's Westmount Arena—even though soldiers in uniform were admitted free of charge.

The Wanderers outscored Toronto 10–9 for the one and only victory of their brief NHL history. The Westmount Arena burnt to the ground January 2, 1918. Both the Wanderers and the Montreal Canadiens lost everything. The Canadiens scrounged up some new gear and moved into the tiny, 3,250-seat Jubilee Arena, but the Wanderers, citing operating losses of $30,000, elected to fold their franchise.

While teams were going down, NHL goaltenders couldn't —but that didn't stop them. League rules prohibited goalies from leaving their feet to make a save, but, as Ottawa's Clint Benedict pointed out "you could make it look like an accident" and get away with it. "The Praying Goaltender," as Benedict was known because he spent so much time on his knees, led to the league's first rule change. On January 9, 1918, Calder announced that goaltenders would be allowed to leave their feet to make a stop.

Announcing the rule change, Calder said of NHL netminders: "As far as I'm concerned, they can stand on their head if they choose to," coining a phrase still used by hockey people today.

Modern-day hockey fans wouldn't have recognized the NHL game in its infancy. Forward passing was not allowed, making stickhandling and skating required elements for success. There were no zones on the ice, players were not allowed to kick the puck and immediate substitution was allowed in the event of a penalty, no matter how severe. Minor penalties were three minutes in length and goaltenders would serve their own penalties, meaning a forward or defenseman would have to take over in net for the duration of the sentence.

The winner of the NHL would meet the champions of the Pacific Coast Hockey Association, a loop run on the West Coast by the Patrick brothers, Frank and Lester, for the Stanley Cup. A third major league, the Western Canada Hockey League, formed on the Canadian prairies in 1921, also joined the competition for Lord Stanley's mug.

Rules varied from league to league. The Pacific league still played seven-player hockey, employing a rover, a position the NHA had dropped in 1911. Rules would be enforced on an alternating basis in Stanley Cup play, with the league having home-ice advantage playing the extra game under its rules.

Many PCHA rules were eventually adopted by the NHL, such as forward passing, dividing the rink into zones, playing short-handed while penalized and allowing players to kick the puck. The PCHA brought in the penalty shot in 1921, something the NHL did not do until the mid-1930s. The first time NHL fans got a look at the so-called free shot was in game two of the 1922 Stanley Cup finals when

Toronto's Babe Dye fired his penalty shot over the net.

The PCHA was also considered more of a finesse and skating league than the NHL, which was known for its vicious brand of hockey. Seattle's Cully Wilson, banned from the PCHA in 1919 after a violent stick attack on Vancouver's Mickey Mackay, immediately signed with Hamilton of the NHL and proceeded to lead the league in penalty minutes in 1919–20.

Survival of the fittest was the name of the game in the early NHL and even the league's best players—stars like Newsy Lalonde, Punch Broadbent, Nels Stewart and Reg Noble—were as adept at applying the hickory as they were at using their sticks to direct the puck towards the goal.

Early NHL hockey wasn't the glamour game it is today. Harry Cameron, the highest-paid player on Toronto's 1918 Stanley Cup winner, earned $900. Joe Malone, who scored an amazing 44 goals in 20 games in 1917–18 (a league mark which would stand until 1944–45) became a part-time player in the 1918–19 season, playing just nine games for the Canadiens. "I had hooked on to a good job in Quebec City which promised a secure future, something hockey in those days couldn't," said Malone, who played only in Montreal's home games that season.

Paul Jacobs, a promising amateur defenseman signed by Toronto in 1918, quit the team after one game when he received a job offer in Montreal. Out west, PCHA stars Frank Foyston and Frank Fredrickson both left hockey briefly to enter private business—Foyston was a butcher and Fredrickson ran a music shop.

Low salaries meant convincing top amateurs to turn pro was nearly impossible, since the majority of them were well-educated and knew the real world offered the better future prospects than the ice rink. Besides, the best amateurs, or "Simon Pures," as they were called, were being paid quite handsomely—under the table, naturally—to remain with their teams.

The Canadiens and Senators were the dominant franchises in the league's first decade. Between them, they were the NHL representatives in six of the first nine Stanley Cup series. The Habs had won the Stanley Cup in 1916 and reached the finals in 1917, prior to the formation of the NHL. In 1919 they played in the ill-fated series in which no decision was reached.

The Spanish influenza epidemic worked its way through North America and it had already touched the NHL before Montreal headed west to play Seattle, the Pacific Coast champions.

The virus claimed the life of Ottawa defenseman Hamby Shore prior to the start of the season. By early 1919, the majority of the roster of Victoria's PCHA franchise was laid up with flu.

As the 1919 final wore on, five Montreal players became stricken with the illness. After five games, with the series deadlocked at 2–2–1 (including a 100-minute scoreless draw in game four), the Canadiens were so ill they couldn't ice a team. The Stanley Cup trustees offered the title to Seattle by default, but they refused to accept and the series was halted without a winner being declared. Canadiens defenseman Joe Hall never recovered from his illness and died April 5 in a Seattle hospital. Canadiens owner George Kennedy also never fully regained his health and died in the autumn of 1920.

Montreal had vanquished Ottawa in the league finals en route to Seattle, but the Senators were about to go to the top of the class. Goalie Benedict, defenseman Eddie Gerard, center Frank Nighbor and left wing Cy Denneny were already in place when the NHL was formed.

Rugged defenseman Sprague Cleghorn, considered the toughest NHLer of the era, was signed prior to the 1918–19 campaign. Completing the lineup of six starters was right wing Punch Broadbent, who returned to NHL play early in 1919 after serving in combat in World War I, where he was decorated for bravery.

Commencing with the 1919–20 season, Ottawa would take home the Stanley Cup three times in four seasons. So deep in talent were the Senators that during the 1921–22 season, rookie King Clancy and Frank Boucher, both future Hall of Famers, rarely got off the bench. The Senators swept both halves of the NHL's split season in 1919–20 and whipped Seattle in the Stanley Cup finals. When Ottawa opened up with five straight wins to start the 1920–21 campaign, the rest of the NHL screamed foul.

At issue was the Senators' defensive system. Simply explained, the Senators, once they secured a lead, would keep a forward and two defensemen in their own zone of the rink at all times. On the surface, other NHL clubs insisted this style of hockey would be the ruination of the game, but they also realized the effectiveness of Ottawa's system and began employing it. As scoring dwindled, the NHL decided to act and in 1924 adopted the anti-defense rule, which made it illegal for more than two defending players, other than the goaltender, to be in the defensive zone when the puck was not. "I think the fans want to see more scoring," Calder said in introducing the new regulation.

While some teams were thriving, the NHL was still seeking over-all stability. The Toronto Arenas folded in February 1919, and a new ownership group renamed the team the St. Patricks in 1919–20. Toronto entrepreneur Percy Quinn acquired an option on the dormant Quebec franchise in 1917–18, but when the league told him he couldn't move the club to Toronto, he tried to form his own league, the Canadian Hockey Association. He worked closely with Eddie Livingstone, but the new circuit never got off the ground.

Quebec finally rejoined the NHL in 1919. Its lone highlight came January 31, 1920, when Joe Malone potted seven goals against Toronto, an NHL record still on the books today. Malone had an eighth goal disallowed. After the season, the Quebec franchise was sold to Hamilton interests.

Calder felt it was necessary for the other clubs to ensure Hamilton could ice a competitive club. Toronto had loaned Dye to the Tigers prior to the season, but when he sniped two goals in Hamilton's 5–0 opening-night win over the Canadiens, they quickly recalled him. Citing a need to bring more balance into the league, on December 30, 1920, the NHL announced that both Broadbent and Cleghorn had been taken from the Senators and awarded to Hamilton. Senators' management felt they were being unfairly singled out and the issue became further muddled when both Broadbent and Cleghorn refused to report. By the end of the season, both players were back in Canada's capital city, helping Ottawa win the Cup again.

Meanwhile, the Canadiens were foundering. Manager Leo Dandurand, who was part of a group that purchased the club for $11,000 from Kennedy's estate, sought reasons for the decline and early in the 1920–21 season, banned his players from driving their motor cars, feeling that it was causing their arm and leg muscles to cramp. The actual concern was dental in nature—Montreal's lineup was long in the tooth. While veteran Georges Vezina was still spectacular in goal, the forward unit of Lalonde, Didier Pitre and Louis Berlinquette had seen its best days.

The fans began to turn on Lalonde, who lost his job as the starting center to Odie Cleghorn in 1921 and quit the team in disgust. Lalonde returned to finish the 1921–22 campaign, but after the season Dandurand traded him to Saskatoon of the WCHL for $35,000 and the rights to an amateur named Aurel Joliat.

Sprague Cleghorn had been acquired and teamed with Billy Coutu to give the Habs the toughest defense pair in the NHL. Two other speedy amateurs, Howie Morenz and Billy Boucher, joined Joliat up front and the rebuilt Canadiens were Stanley Cup champions in 1924 and finalists in 1925—the season Victoria became the last team from outside the NHL to win the Stanley Cup. On-ice success was buoyed by the opening of two new facilities that served as home to the Montreal Canadiens—the Mount Royal Arena in January 1920, and the $1 million Forum in November, 1924. The Forum was actually built to house a new Montreal franchise, the Maroons, who entered the NHL in 1924.

Maroons owner James Strachan paid $15,000 for his franchise—$11,000 of which was paid to the Canadiens for infringing on their territorial rights. Dandurand saw a natural intra-city rivalry quickly developing and he was right. The Maroons helped heat things up by icing a roster of English-speaking players from Ontario—the perfect foil to the Canadiens French-Canadian base. Strachan quickly assembled an outstanding team, purchasing veterans Benedict, Broadbent and Noble, while signing talented amateurs Stewart, Dunc Munro and Babe Siebert. It didn't hurt the rivalry when the Maroons won the Cup in 1925–26, their second season in the league.

The Hamilton Tigers, after four straight seasons out of the playoffs, finished first in 1924–25, but all was not joyous in Canada's Steel City. The NHL schedule had expanded from 24 to 30 games and while many teams had increased their salary structure, Hamilton was not one of them. Led by captain Shorty Green and goalie Jake Forbes—who sat out the entire 1921–22 season in a contract dispute with Toronto—the club staged a walkout prior to the NHL final against the Canadiens, refusing to play unless each player was paid a $200 bonus. When the striking players refused to budge, Calder suspended the entire team, awarding the title to the Habs.

The NHL readied for its ninth season in the fall of 1925. Through it all, there had been one constant—Canadiens goaltender Georges Vezina. The ironman of the league, Vezina had never missed a game, He was the only original NHLer who could make this boast. In fact, he'd never missed a game in 16 years with the Habs. "His history in hockey is the history of the pro end of the sport since its inception," Dandurand said of Vezina.

At the Canadiens' training camp, Vezina was bedridden with a severe cold. Despite a temperature of 102, he took to the ice for Montreal's season opener. He was unable to continue after the first period and gave way to backup Alphonse Lacroix. A few days later it was revealed that Vezina was suffering from tuberculosis. He had lost 35 pounds in six weeks.

The Canadiens had a game the day that Vezina found out about his illness and he didn't want to upset them, so he asked that no one be told until he had returned to his home in Chicoutimi, Quebec. When Vezina arrived at the Forum that morning, trainer Eddie Dufour assumed he was there to play goal and laid out Vezina's gear in his stall. Vezina sat quietly with his equipment, tears rolling down his cheeks. Then he took the jersey he had worn in the 1924 Stanley Cup finals and left, never to return. Vezina died March 27, 1926. A testament to his talent was evidenced by the fact that the Canadiens, who had reached the Stanley Cup finals the two previous seasons, finished last in the NHL in 1925–26.

"He was as loveable as he was athletic and I cannot say any more than that," Dandurand stated, paying tribute to his long-time goalie.

Perhaps it was fitting that Lacroix, the goaltender for the 1924 U.S. Olympic team, replaced Vezina, since many Canadians were convinced that their game was being taken over by Americans. NHL growth also extended south of the 49th parallel for the first time in 1924, when the Boston Bruins joined the league.

The NHL had hoped to add teams in Boston and New York for the 1924–25 season, but Tex Rickard, who owned Madison Square Garden, had not yet been convinced to include an ice-making facility in his new building. Rickard apparently changed his mind after an invitation to Montreal to watch the Canadiens play during the 1924–25 season. He is said to have been so impressed by Howie Morenz that he finally agreed to install ice at the Garden provided that Morenz would be on hand for the first game there. Bootlegger "Big Bill" Dwyer purchased New York City's first NHL team for the 1925–26 season and the Americans played out of Rickard's 18,000-seat venue. Morenz led Montreal into Madison Square Garden on December 15, 1925, and scored a goal in the Canadiens' 3–1 win over the Americans in a game played before the Who's Who of New York society.

The New York Americans entered the NHL at the expense of the Hamilton Tigers. Dwyer had purchased the roster of the striking team for $75,000 and Hamilton lost its NHL franchise. Each of the players had to pay a $200 fine and write a letter of apology to Calder before they could resume their careers.

The Pittsburgh Pirates also entered the NHL for the 1925–26 season. With Odie Cleghorn as player-manager, the Pirates made the playoffs in their first season. Cleghorn helped revolutionize the way the game was played by alternating three set forward lines.

Boston, which had struggled to draw fans in its first season, saw such a turnaround in 1925–26 that it announced plans to expand the size of its arena. New rinks were being built in Chicago, Newark and Jersey City. Ottawa president Frank Ahearn rejected a $100,000 bid for his franchise from the Jersey City group. Detroit, Chicago, Buffalo and a second New York group were also pursuing NHL franchises. Hockey was so popular at Madison Square Garden that Tex Rickard, a man who gained a worldwide reputation as a fight promoter, found the new game to be a gold mine.

"I can make bigger money with less worry and fewer risks out of hockey than I have been getting out of boxing," Rickard said, pointing to the large throngs attending Americans games, which often filled the rink.

There were rumors that a separate U.S. pro league was being organized, which would have two teams in New

York, as well as franchises in Boston, Pittsburgh, Chicago, Detroit, Buffalo, Los Angeles, San Francisco, Seattle and Portland, Oregon. Eddie Livingstone, spurned by the NHL in 1917, was also trying to put together a rival pro league based in the U.S. "Hockey will sweep the United States from coast to coast within five years," predicted the *Toronto Globe* in a 1925 editorial.

Tom Duggan, managing director of the Americans franchise, scoffed at suggestions that America was usurping the Canadian game. "Stories in Canadian papers about the alleged Americanization of hockey are absurd," Duggan said. "The Canadian clubs are essential drawing cards and the New York club has no intention of ever cutting away from them."

The NHL was now attracting the top amateurs and playing in major centers. Salaries had grown with the league. Pittsburgh signed defenseman Lionel Conacher to a three-year deal at $7,500 a year. Other top earners included Dunc Munro ($7,000), Joe Simpson ($6,000) and Billy Burch ($6,500) of the Amerks and Toronto's Hap Day ($6,000). The NHL installed $35,000 salary caps on each club. Dandurand, who had purchased the Canadiens for $11,000 in 1921, insured the franchise for $150,000 in 1925.

Out west, things were headed in the other direction. The PCHA and WCHL had merged in 1924 and the owners of small-market teams situated on the Canadian prairies could see the handwriting on the wall. "It is a regrettable situation so far as the smaller Canadian centers are concerned," Calgary Tigers owner Lloyd Turner said. "In the larger American cities, they are prepared to pay higher prices. It is a situation that I felt would arise as soon as the United States cities took up hockey."

Big changes had already been undertaken and more were just around the corner. The NHL had opened on Broadway and it was a hit.

THE ESTABLISHMENT YEARS 1926–27 TO 1941–42

Eric Zweig

THE STANLEY CUP became the exclusive property of the NHL for the 1926–27 season. Nothing better symbolized the importance of this era to the future of the NHL. Not only did the years between 1926–27 and 1941–42 see the game populated by some of the most colorful personalities in hockey history, it also introduced new rules and new franchises that would begin to define the modern NHL.

The 1920s have been called "The Golden Age of Sports" and with good reason. The Great War was over and gone with it was much of the rigid class structure that had existed before. A new generation of North Americans was in the mood to celebrate and the "Roaring Twenties" would be a time of great excess, with the pursuit of leisure taking on an importance it had not been allowed in the past. Music was jazzier, movies began to talk, and the popularity of sports exploded. Babe Ruth hit home runs farther and more often than anyone had ever seen. Red Grange tore up the gridiron at the University of Illinois, then gave the fledgling National Football League an air of respectability when he signed with the Chicago Bears. Jack Dempsey was boxing's heavyweight champion until losing to Gene Tunney. Golf had Bobby Jones. Tennis had Bill Tilden and Helen Wills Moody. Even swimming had superstars in Johnny Weissmuller and Gertrude Ederle (who became the first woman to swim the English Channel in 1926). It was during this period of unprecedented sports popularity that the NHL grew from a tiny all-Canadian circuit into a major North American league.

When the NHL began play in 1917–18, it only had teams in Toronto, Ottawa, and Montreal and shared the Stanley Cup (and professional hockey supremacy) with the Pacific Coast Hockey Association. By 1921–22, the NHL was also in Hamilton and the Stanley Cup had become a three-league affair with the creation of the Western Canada Hockey League. The NHL had the advantage of the larger population base in the east, but the PCHA and WCHL compensated by banding together to play an interlocking schedule in 1922–23. The two leagues merged into one six-team circuit in 1924–25. The NHL also expanded to six teams that year, adding a second team in Montreal and making its first foray into the United States with the admission of the Boston Bruins. The New York Americans and Pittsburgh Pirates joined the league one year later.

NHL hockey was a big hit in the Big Apple and the New York Americans drew more fans in their first season than any four teams of the Western Canada Hockey League combined. The Pittsburgh Pirates had also been a success in 1925–26, reaching the playoffs in their first season. In just their second season, the Boston Bruins had demonstrated they were an emerging power and the Montreal Maroons were Stanley Cup champions while playing to sellout crowds in the 10,000-seat Montreal Forum. (The Canadiens did not become full-time Forum tenants until 1926–27.)

Having survived the instability of its early years, the NHL was now a financial success and potential owners were lining up to obtain teams in Chicago and Detroit for 1926–27. Tex Rickard also wanted his own New York franchise for Madison Square Garden. The sudden prosperity of the NHL was not lost on the owners of the Western Hockey League. With the NHL adding three more franchises, brothers Frank and Lester Patrick decided it was time to close up shop in the west. As Frank Patrick would later recall: "With our top salary range of about $4,000 we were already squeezing our population draw to its limits. [NHL players were now making close to $10,000] and there was no way we could keep good hockey players in the West beyond maybe one more season." Rather than cut their losses and operate as long as possible by selling off stars to the NHL, "which would reduce our league to minor status," Patrick convinced five of the six WHL owners to entrust their players to him. "My plan," he recalled, "was to merge the five rosters into three strong teams and then sell the teams intact for $100,000 each."

Patrick's sale did not go entirely as planned, but he was more or less able to sell the roster of the Portland Rosebuds to the new owner of the Chicago Black Hawks and stock Detroit's new NHL team with players from the Victoria Cougars. (Detroit would be known as the Cougars for its first four seasons, before becoming the Falcons, and then the Red Wings in 1932–33.) The new team in New York was not willing to buy in bulk. Conn Smythe had already been hired to assemble the team (dubbed Tex's Rangers by the press as a play on words for Rickard and the famed Texas lawmen). The Rangers did purchase such WHL stars as Frank Boucher and Bill and Bun Cook and would later land Lester Patrick to replace Conn Smythe as coach and general manager. (Smythe would soon resurface in the NHL after buying the Toronto St. Pats and changing the name to Maple Leafs.) The Boston Bruins purchased $50,000 worth of WHL talent, including Eddie Shore, while other deals for individual WHL players created rights-of-ownership disputes, which eventually forced the NHL to sort out distribution. That done, the NHL emerged as hockey's only major professional league and the exclusive holder of the Stanley Cup.

The newly expanded 10-team NHL split into two five-team divisions. The Boston Bruins, Pittsburgh Pirates, New York Rangers, Chicago Black Hawks and Detroit Cougars played in the American Division, while the Montreal Canadiens, Montreal Maroons, Ottawa Senators, Toronto St. Pats/Maple Leafs and New York Americans played in the Canadian Division. Both Detroit and Chicago were expected to have new arenas ready as part of their inclusion in the NHL, but experienced delays. The Red Wings actually played their first season across the border in Windsor, Ontario before moving into the Olympia in 1927–28. The 1928–29 season saw the Bruins move into the Boston Garden. As for the Black Hawks, Chicago Stadium would not be ready until December 1929.

With the best available players now in one league, competition in the NHL was better than ever. Every man who finished among the top 10 in scoring in 1926–27 would later be elected to the Hockey Hall of Fame though the close competition ensured that over-all scoring was lower than ever with an average of only 3.80 goals-per-game. In an effort to increase offense, forward passing, which had been permitted since 1918–19, but only in the neutral zone between the two blue lines, was expanded to include the defensive zone. Still, goal-scoring fell to 3.67 goals-per-game in 1927–28. In 1928–29, scoring reached an all-time low with just 2.80 goals-per-game. This was the year in which George Hainsworth registered 22 shutouts in 44 games while posting a 0.92 goals-against average. Eight of the NHL's top 10 goaltenders had at least 10 shutouts that year and all 10 had averages below 2.00. Netminders like Boston's Tiny Thompson, Chicago's Chuck Gardiner, and Roy Worters of the New York Americans would continue to be among the best in the league for years.

In an effort to increase offense, the NHL finally authorized forward passing in all three zones in 1929–30. The only restriction was that the puck could not be passed across the blue line. However, there was nothing to prevent a player from parking himself in front of the opposing goal and waiting for a teammate to bring the puck across the blue line before feeding it to him. Players like Nels Stewart and Cooney Weiland employed this tactic to pile up goals, but the NHL soon realized the error of its ways. With scoring up a whopping four goals-per-game (to 6.91) through the first quarter of the season, the passing rules were amended to state that no player would be permitted to cross the blue line ahead of the puck. It was the birth of the modern offside rule and restored a more competitive balance between offense and defense in the NHL.

Forward passing is the greatest legacy to the rules of the game introduced during this time period, but over the next 10 seasons the NHL developed many other rules and innovations that are still part of the game. Though there is no record of a team ever trying to use two goaltenders at once, a rule was instituted for 1931–32 stating that teams could only have one goaltender on the ice at one time. In 1933–34, the NHL ruled that a visible time clock was required in every arena. Penalty shots were instituted in 1934–35. Rules governing icing the puck were put in place in 1937–38. Flooding the ice between periods became mandatory in 1940–41 and the system of one referee and two linesmen to officiate games was instituted in 1941–42.

In addition to creating more offense, forward passing changed hockey from a game of individual rushes to one that focused on combination play. As a result, the 1930s became a time of great lines. Boston's Dynamite Line of Cooney Weiland, Dit Clapper and Dutch Gainor helped the Bruins follow up their first Stanley Cup victory in 1928–29 with a record of 38–5–1 in 1929–30 for an .875 winning percentage that remains the best in NHL history. Weiland led the NHL with 43 goals and 73 points in 44 games in 1929–30, but the Hart Trophy went to the Maroons' Nels Stewart. Stewart was triggerman for the powerful S-Line with Babe Seibert and Hooley Smith. The Toronto Maple Leafs unveiled the Kid Line of Busher Jackson, Joe Primeau, and Charlie Conacher in 1929–30. In 1931–32, they finished first, second, and fourth in the NHL scoring race and led the Maple Leafs to the Stanley Cup. Later, the Bruins featured the Kraut Line of Milt Schmidt, Bobby Bauer and Woody Dumart and won the Stanley Cup in 1939 and 1941.

The first of the NHL's great lines was the New York Rangers trio of Bill Cook, Frank Boucher, and Bun Cook. Teamed up for the Rangers' first season, the elegant Boucher became the game's best passer and winner of the Lady Byng Trophy seven times in eight years between 1927–28 and 1934–35. Bill Cook was rivaled only by Charlie Conacher as the NHL's most dangerous scorer. Together with Bun Cook, they devised passing patterns that revolutionized offensive play and helped the Rangers win the Stanley Cup in 1928 and 1933. Boucher coached the team to a third Stanley Cup triumph in 1940. But even in an era that emphasized teamwork, two individuals stand out from the others: Eddie Shore and Howie Morenz.

Known as "The Stratford Streak," Morenz brought a combination of speed and skill to the NHL that was unsurpassed. He led the league in scoring in 1927–28 and in 1930–31, adding the Hart Trophy in both of those years and winning it again in 1931–32. Morenz also led the Canadiens to consecutive Stanley Cup victories in 1930 and 1931 (after having won it previously in 1924). Above all, Morenz was the player fans of his era wanted to see. His appearance in the NHL's new American cities virtually guaranteed a sellout and he became known as "The Babe Ruth of Hockey" for his box-office appeal. The funeral following his unexpected death on March 8, 1937, attracted more than 10,000 people to the Montreal Forum, while thousands more lined the route of the funeral cortege.

Like Morenz, Eddie Shore put fans in the stands. In a rough-and-tumble era, he took a backseat to no one, with a combination of skill and bravado that was matched by an explosive temper. When he took off on a rush, he would literally knock down opponents who got in his way. Shore was left scarred and toothless from his many on-ice battles, and nearly saw his career terminated after his hit from behind fractured Ace Bailey's skull in December 1933. But he was no mere goon. Shore was named an All-Star eight years in a row (including seven selections to the NHL First All-Star Team) between 1930–31 and 1938–39 and is still the only defenseman to win the Hart Trophy four times. He was a key contributor to Boston's first Stanley Cup victory in 1929 and was still going strong when the Bruins won again 10 years later.

While Morenz, Shore, and others kept fans entertained with their on-ice exploits, the time period of 1926–27 to 1941–42 was also graced with larger-than-life personalities behind the scenes. Black Hawks owner Major Frederic McLaughlin fired coaches like a 1930s George Steinbrenner and watched his Chicago team win the Stanley Cup in 1934 and 1938. Jack Adams was hired to head up Detroit's hockey operations in 1927–28 and built the club into consecutive Stanley Cup champions in 1936 and 1937. (He later built the Red Wings' great dynasty of 1949 to 1955.) However, it was Art Ross of the Bruins and Lester Patrick of the Rangers who were probably more responsible than anyone else for the success of NHL hockey in the United States.

Lifelong friends who had grown up together in Montreal and been star players themselves, Ross and Patrick did more than just build championship teams in Boston and New York—they made the Canadian game a part of the American sporting scene. Patrick was particularly adept at handling the influential New York press. "The Silver Fox," as he became known, would speak to the writers one-on-one or summon them in groups for seminars in which he would skillfully explain the intricacies of the game. By successfully courting the press, Patrick and his players were soon Manhattan celebrities while famous fans such as Babe Ruth and Lou Gehrig, mayor Jimmy Walker, movie stars Humphrey Bogart and George Raft, bandleader Cab Calloway, and a parade of Broadway's best and most recognizable faces made Madison Square Garden the place to be and be seen throughout the era.

In Canada, hockey did not require the hype it needed to survive in the United States and yet strong leadership certainly didn't hurt. When Conn Smythe put together a group to purchase the Toronto St. Pats on February 14, 1927, the Stanley Cup champions of 1922 were clearly a team in decline. The newly renamed Maple Leafs finished last in the Canadian Division in 1926–27 and would miss the playoffs again in 1927–28.

Though many on the team's board of directors disagreed, Smythe believed putting the team's games on the radio would help attract fans and Foster Hewitt's broadcasts did exactly that. Soon, all 8,000 seats at the Mutual Street Arena were being filled. In Montreal, Maroons and Canadiens games began to be broadcast as well, while in Toronto, Smythe dreamed of a bigger and better home for his hockey team. Maple Leafs Gardens was built in five months during the height of the Great Depression and opened on November 12, 1931. Though the Maple Leafs would lose 2–1 to Chicago that night, they would finish the 1931–32 season as Stanley Cup champions. By January 1933, Hewitt's broadcasts from Maple Leaf Gardens were being carried on 20 radio stations across Canada. The nation's population was less than 10 million at the time. Audiences were estimated at almost one million per game.

While the Maple Leafs flourished despite the Depression, the same could not be said for all of the NHL's 10 teams. In 1927, the Senators won their fourth Stanley Cup title in six years, but U.S. expansion had left Ottawa with the league's smallest market, just 150,000 people. Unable to compete financially, the team began trading and selling stars, including King Clancy to the Toronto Maple Leafs for a record $35,000 on October 11, 1930.

Meanwhile, Pittsburgh's steel industry had been hit hard by the stock market crash in 1929 and the Pirates were also forced to peddle their star players. In 1930–31, the team relocated to become the Philadelphia Quakers. Both Ottawa and the Pittsburgh–Philadelphia franchise suspended operations prior to the 1931–32 season. The Senators returned to the NHL in 1932–33, but further poor performances both on the ice and at the box office doomed the club. The Senators moved south and became the St. Louis Eagles in 1934–35, but folded at year-end.

The 1934–35 season saw the Montreal Maroons win the Stanley Cup, but as in Ottawa, success did not mean financial stability. Both the Canadiens and the Maroons were struggling to attract fans during the Great Depression and with the prospects of war in Europe on the horizon, the Maroons management withdrew its team from the league following a dismal 1937–38 season. With three teams gone, the NHL ended its divisional format and operated as one seven-team league in 1938–39. However, there was still one more problem franchise.

The New York Americans had preceded the Rangers into the NHL by one season, but as mere tenants at Madison Square Garden they never had the same economic advantages of the Rangers. Neither did they enjoy similar on-ice success, nor the same starry fan base. Years of financial instability and bailouts by the league turned the Americans into a virtual farm club, providing young talent to other NHL clubs and a rest home for veterans past their prime. The franchise hit bottom in 1940–41 with a last-place record of 8–29–11. Hoping to forge a new identity, the club became the Brooklyn Americans in 1941–42. After missing the playoffs again, operations were suspended for the duration of World War II. The franchise was never reactivated.

From the heady optimism of the Roaring Twenties, through the bleak years of the Great Depression, to the uncertainty of World War II, the NHL had gone through more changes in 16 seasons than it would again until 1967 and the years beyond. But the 'Original Six' teams that survived this era would carry the NHL into a new period of unprecedented stability and pave the way for the expansion that would follow.

The "Original Six" 1942–43 to 1966–67

Douglas Hunter

The era of the NHL's "Original Six," which ran from 1942–43 until 1966–67, has been called the golden age of professional hockey. The six teams—the Boston Bruins, Chicago Black Hawks, Detroit Red Wings, Toronto Maple Leafs, New York Rangers and Montreal Canadiens—that battled among themselves for Stanley Cup supremacy for 25 years were "original" in the sense that they preceded the expansion teams of 1967–68. But the "Original Six" were original in more ways than that. It's easy to view the league in those days before expansion, glowing pucks, multi-million-dollar player contracts and ever-increasing dominance by European and American players as a static, almost prosaic enterprise. But although the league's membership was static, the game would change considerably during this quarter century. With successive waves of new talent entering the NHL during and after the Second World War, playing a faster-breaking game made possible by the introduction of the center red line and the two-line offside in 1943–44, the "Original Six" were original in many ways. These were the years that ushered in firewagon hockey, the slapshot and the functional goaltender's mask. The NHL was defining itself, creating a modern game and modern heroes.

The league was an exclusive enterprise in those days. Only about 100 players had steady jobs, and it was hardest of all to break in as a goaltender—until 1965–66 teams carried only one. And with the advent of the 70-game schedule in 1949–50, teams faced each other 14 times during the regular season. This familiarity between teams—impossible to imagine today, when a team might face a non-conference rival only once in a season—for the most part bred contempt. Grudges were honed and vengeance regularly sought. Many players enjoyed long careers—15 or even 20 seasons—so feuds would be carried on over several seasons. Partly in response to gambling scandals that had dogged many sports, hockey included, Clarence Campbell introduced a rule after being named league president in 1946 banning fraternization between players on rival teams. The idea was to eliminate opportunities for game-fixing and to ensure public confidence that NHL rivalries were legitimate. It's doubtful such a rule would have been necessary. Although NHLers respected each other, and some inevitably were friends through playing for the same team in the past, the law of supply and demand did more than any league edict could to promote antagonism.

Observers who denounce today's game and harken back to a more stylish, gentlemanly era of play forget (or perhaps never noticed) just how vicious the NHL could be in those postwar years. Stick-swinging incidents and bench-clearing brawls were routine. On-ice officials were punched out. On September 28, 1946, the newly arrived Campbell defined hockey as "a game of speed and fierce bodily contact. If these go out, hockey will vanish." However, the game would become so violent at all levels that many fans feared for its survival.

The game was also the center of a number of controversies. Educators were alarmed by the influence the game had on the (lack of) dedication young athletes gave their studies. After the war, the NHL and its affiliated minor pro loops—which were growing in number and size—had a voracious appetite for new talent. Even the British professional ice hockey league was sending scouts into the Canadian hinterlands to find players. With so few jobs available in the NHL, it was felt, with no small amount of justification, that boys were being lured by dreams of professional glory into dead-end playing careers that would leave them with nothing to fall back on. Some officials in the Canadian amateur system also resented the way professional hockey had come to completely dominate their game, sponsoring clubs, paying de facto salaries to junior and senior players, and securing rights to players as young as 16.

The Canadian Amateur Hockey Association was in a sometimes-uneasy alliance with the National Hockey League, becoming its main source of talent in exchange for annual block payments. Before the Second World War, Americans could be found in the league in reasonable numbers. Two of the greatest goaltenders—Frank Brimsek in Boston, Mike Karakas in Chicago—were Minnesotans, and the Black Hawks had eight Americans in the lineup when they won the 1937–38 Stanley Cup. By the 1960s, the only American-born player with an NHL starting job was Tommy Williams of the Bruins. (The most notable American player of the era, Red Berenson, was born in Regina, Saskatchewan, although he was raised in the United States and played hockey at the University of Michigan before joining the Montreal Canadiens.) Americans would return to the game in large numbers beginning in the 1970s, but for many years the league was over 95 percent Canadian.

Many of those players hailed far from the major urban centers—from the Prairie provinces, or the mining towns of Quebec and Northern Ontario. They were scouted and signed as teens and fed into the development system at the junior level. Once their signature was on a C-form—a promise of professional services that allowed a professional club to call them up within one year—they were literally the property of a team for life. Players' rights remained with their teams even after retirement: an ex-player couldn't accept a coaching job with another club unless the arrangement was approved by the last team he played for. An NHL players association had been contemplated in 1946–47 but was abandoned when the league created a pension plan for its players. Another effort to organize, in 1957–58, was crushed by the owners. It would be 1967 before the players organized, and the resulting NHL Players' Association wasn't formally certified as a union until 1976. So, a player's career was subject completely to the whims of the team owners, and he could be promoted, demoted, traded, buried in the minor leagues, and paid whatever salary the owner deemed appropriate—all without recourse. Players lived in constant fear of losing their jobs, whether through injury, fading skills or by running afoul of management.

With a very few notable exceptions—such as Jean Beliveau, whom the Canadiens were desperate to sign and who ended an extended courtship by signing a five-year, $105,000 contract in 1953—NHLers for the most part earned only modest wages. In 1957, as part of the move to head off the players association, the minimum salary was set at $7,500. A journeyman player in the early 1960s made $10,000 to $15,000—about the same as a high-school principal or a police chief. And it was sometimes possible to make more money as a star in a minor league than as a marginal player in the NHL. At the close of World War II, former Chicago Black Hawk Bob Carse, who had nearly died as a German prisoner of war, weighed an offer from the American Hockey League's Cleveland Barons against a job selling insurance in Edmonton, Alberta. The Barons lured him back to the game with a two-year, $11,000 contract. At the time Carse was earning more in Cleveland than Gordie Howe was making in his first years as a Detroit Red Wing.

Still, while the structure could not compare to today's multi-million-dollar standards, it paid a far sight better than the vast majority of jobs, perhaps explaining why so many were prepared to abandon their education and a safer white-collar career for a chance to earn their living playing a vicious game. In the late 1940s, the best-paid laborers in Ontario were miners, who could make about $40 a week. For a teenager from one of those mining towns who was being offered $200 a week to play for an NHL club's amateur development team in the U.S., the math was elementary: five times as much money as his father made in a year, for only six months of work. And even during those six months, he would be "working" no more than a few hours a day.

Compared to hacking away at a vein of nickel or gold deep below the earth's surface, professional hockey seemed like a paid holiday. Of course, the odds against making this "easy" money were extremely long. Even a top-flight junior team could expect to send only a handful of players each season on to the NHL. For instance, the Montreal Royals won Canadian junior hockey's national championship (the Memorial Cup) in 1949. Only one member of that team, Dickie Moore, went on to an NHL career.

Despite the bountiful supply of talent available and the minimal demand for players, competition in the Original Six was frequently lopsided. The New York Rangers, winners of the 1940 Stanley Cup, lost their momentum in wartime and did not recover fully until after the 1967 expansion. They missed the playoffs 18 times in 24 years between 1942 and 1966. Their next Stanley Cup win didn't come until 1993–94. The Chicago Black Hawks turned in nine last-place finishes between 1946–47 and 1956–57. The Bruins, like the Rangers, were hobbled by wartime. A top team in the 1930s, and winners of the Cup in 1939 and 1941, the Bruins' limited player development resources prevented them from being consistent. But Boston management made the most of what they had and they built a sometimes-competitive club that played in (and lost) the Stanley Cup finals in 1943, 1946, 1953, 1957 and 1958.

The Toronto Maple Leafs were the dominant playoff team of the 1940s, winning the Stanley Cup four times in five seasons between 1946–47 and 1950–51. Coached by former captain Hap Day, these Leafs played a rugged two-way game and enjoyed superb goaltending in the clutch from Walter "Turk" Broda. But the team lost its way for most of the 1950s, bottoming out with a last-place finish in 1957–58. His hockey senses dulling, general manager Conn Smythe—who had fronted the purchase of the Toronto St. Patricks in 1927 and turned them into the Maple Leafs—made a series of debilitating trades, sacrificing scoring power just as the league's best teams were mounting powerful offenses.

The Detroit Red Wings and the Montreal Canadiens were the class of the league through the 1950s. The Red Wings, under coach/general manager Jack Adams, had come to the fore during the war years, appearing in the finals six times during the decade and winning the Cup in 1943. Adams relinquished the coaching duties to Tommy Ivan in 1947, and together they created one of the most dynamic teams in NHL history. Their goaltender, Terry Sawchuk, who arrived to stay in 1950–51, may have been the greatest the game has ever seen. The defense featured the likes of Red Kelly, Marcel Pronovost and Bob Goldham, while their offensive stars comprised the famed and feared Production Line of Ted Lindsay, Gordie Howe and Sid Abel. The Red Wings defeated the upstart Rangers in double-overtime of the seventh game to win the 1949–50 Cup. Detroit won seven straight regular season titles from 1948–49 to 1954–55, appeared in seven finals between 1948 and 1956, and won the Stanley Cup four times.

At the outset of the Original Six era, Detroit's main rival was Toronto. The Leafs and Red Wings had tangled in seven-game finals in 1942 and 1945, both of which the Leafs won. But as the 1950s dawned, the league's main rivalry involved Detroit and Montreal. The Canadiens appeared in 10 consecutive finals from 1950–51 to 1959–60, and in the first half of the decade their blood feud with the Red Wings was unparalleled. The Red Wings defeated the Canadiens in 1952 in a four-game sweep as Detroit moved through the two playoff rounds without a single loss. After pausing in 1952–53 to give the Bruins a run at Montreal (in a series the Canadiens won in five), the Wings hooked up with the Habs in the next three finals. Detroit won the first two engagements, both of which went the full seven games. When Montreal won the third encounter in five in 1955–56, Detroit's reign was over, while the Canadiens had won the first of five consecutive Stanley Cup titles—a league record—winning 40 of 49 playoff games along the way.

The Canadiens team that came to dominate in the 1950s was a product of remarkable talent spotting. Few of their players had been acquired through trades; the team had signed the vast majority of its players as young amateurs and brought them along in the development system built by Frank Selke, Sr., who had joined the Habs as general manager in 1946 after a lengthy term in the Maple Leafs front office. Selke's system was not limited to francophone Quebec; it stretched across the country and featured such junior teams as Manitoba's St. Boniface Canadiens and Saskatchewan's Regina Pats. Selke's talent pipeline fed a steady stream of new recruits into the Canadiens lineup, which was coached by Dick Irvin from 1940 until 1955.

Irvin's main star was Maurice "Rocket" Richard, who first played for Montreal in 1942–43. His ferocious temper regularly got him into trouble with officials, and it was his outburst during a game in Boston on March 13, 1955, that became more famous than any goal he scored. In the midst of a brawl with Bruins defenseman Hal Laycoe, in which he broke a stick over Laycoe's back, Richard landed two punches in the face of a linesman. Clarence Campbell suspended him for the rest of the season and the playoffs. When Campbell appeared at the Montreal Forum to watch the Canadiens—sans Richard—play the Red Wings on March 17, the fans rioted and went on a destructive tear through Montreal.

After the Canadiens lost the 1955 finals to Detroit, Selke replaced Irvin with Toe Blake. The former Canadiens captain had had his career ended by a bad ankle fracture in January 1948; until then, he had been part of the great Punch Line with Richard and Elmer Lach. Selke figured Blake could do a better job of reining in the Rocket's volcanic temperament. The result was the streak of five consecutive Cup wins, and eight in the 13 seasons Blake ran the Canadiens bench.

Montreal had so many wonderful players in the 1950s that it seems remiss not to list them all. But among the standouts were goaltender Jacques Plante, who won six Vezina Trophy titles with the Canadiens and introduced the modern fiberglass mask to the game in November 1959; center Jean Beliveau, a superstar for the ages who assumed the captaincy when Maurice Richard retired after the 1959–60 Cup win; the Rocket's younger brother, Henri the "Pocket Rocket," who came to the team in 1955, succeeded Beliveau as captain, and retired in 1975 with 11 Cup wins, more than any other player in NHL history; scoring stars Dickie Moore and Bernie "Boom Boom" Geoffrion, who brought the first fully developed slap shot to the NHL in 1950–51; and defenseman Doug Harvey, a seven-time Norris Trophy winner.

In 1958–59, Montreal encountered a relatively new Stanley Cup opponent, the Toronto Maple Leafs, who hadn't been in a final since defeating the Habs in 1951.

George "Punch" Imlach had just taken over as coach and general manager, and the Leafs squeaked into the final playoff spot by a single point over the Rangers, then took seven games to upset the Bruins and make the finals. Though they lost to the Canadiens in five games, Toronto was back again to face Montreal in the 1959–60 finals. This time the Canadiens swept the Leafs, but a changing of the guard was taking place within the NHL: Montreal would be shut out of the next four finals, while Toronto and Chicago were ascendant.

In the early 1950s, player transactions were initiated by the league's other teams to keep the Hawks viable. Suddenly, in the late 1950s, Chicago emerged as a contender. The Black Hawks had benefited from the union-busting tactics of owners in Detroit and Toronto, who in 1957–58 shipped their principal players' association organizers to Chicago—where there was little chance of earning playoff bonus money—as punishment. Collecting Tod Sloan and Jim Thomson from the Maple Leafs, and Ted Lindsay and Glenn Hall from the Wings, Chicago had a foundation on which to build a champion. Its junior operations contributed stars like Bobby Hull and Stan Mikita, and a team that had missed the playoffs for the 11th time in 12 seasons in 1957–58 recovered so rapidly that it won the Stanley Cup in 1961.

Thus began the NHL's most competitive era. Every season from 1962–63 to 1966–67, the four playoff qualifiers had winning records, a circumstance not seen since 1953–54. In 1962–63, the most closely contested season in league history, only five points separated first-place Toronto from fourth-place Detroit. In these years, the playoffs were a toss-up between four evenly matched teams: Montreal, Detroit, Chicago and Toronto. Unfortunately, some of the success of these teams was built on the misery of the Bruins and the Rangers, both of whom had faded badly in the late 1950s.

The Maple Leafs prevailed in the playoff battles of the early 1960s, winning three straight Cup championships from 1962 to 1964 before giving way to a resurgent Canadiens team that emerged victorious four times over the next five seasons, a streak interrupted only by an aging Toronto team's last golden hurrah in 1967.

The Maple Leaf teams of the 1960s were the first truly engineered dynasty. Manager Punch Imlach retained established team veterans like Tim Horton, Ron Stewart and George Armstrong, and added such new talents from the farm system as Carl Brewer, Bob Baun, Dick Duff, Bob Nevin, Bob Pulford, Billy Harris and Ron Ellis. Then he stirred in veterans from other teams—Bert Olmstead from Montreal; Allan Stanley from Boston; Red Kelly, Al Arbour, Terry Sawchuk, Larry Hillman and Marcel Pronovost from Detroit; Ed Litzenberger from Chicago; and Andy Bathgate and Don McKenney from New York. It was a concoction that bore no resemblance to the carefully scouted and nurtured lineups of Detroit and Montreal in the 1950s, but it brought results.

The Black Hawks, despite a lineup chock full of all-stars, could not convert their regular season accomplishments into playoff success. They won in 1960–61—before the team's top players had fully developed into mature NHL stars—but would only return to the finals once, in 1965, losing to Montreal in seven games. Meanwhile, the Red Wings, a relentless checking outfit in the 1960s, reached the finals three times in four years and lost on every occasion.

The last Stanley Cup of the Original Six era was contested by the Leafs and the Canadiens. Chicago had run away with the regular season, winning their first league title, and claimed five of the six berths on the First All-Star Team. But Imlach's aging Leafs ground them down in six before doing the same to Montreal in the finals.

The league doubled in size for the 1967–68 season, and many good players who had been languishing in the minors surfaced for air. In 1969, the league's old recruitment and development system went by the wayside as the expanded league held its first universal Amateur Draft. Three years later, the NHL had a full-blown rival in the World Hockey Association, and the NHL's Canadian stars battled to maintain their country's global bragging rights in the sport as they tangled with the Soviet Union in an eight-game exhibition. A scant five years after its passing, the Original Six seemed like something out of ancient history.

To this day the players who had excelled during the NHL's second quarter century from 1942 to 1967 are remembered with a particular reverence and affection.

PUSHING THE BOUNDARIES 1967–68 TO 1978–79

Jeff Z. Klein and Karl-Eric Reif

A DECADE HAS BEEN REDISCOVERED. Someone opened a hockey time capsule full of 1970s memorabilia, and suddenly an era that until recently had been remembered only as a cultureless wasteland of bad clothes and bad hair is being recalled with nostalgic affection.

What artifacts were buried in that box? Let's take a quick look—ah! An equipment bag from the Kansas City Scouts … a stained Flyers sweater … Inge Hammarstrom's passport … a season ticket order-form from the Miami Screaming Eagles … a Canadiens Stanley Cup banner … a pair of white skates and Henry Boucha's headband!

These artifacts come from an era that was curious, tumultuous, in some ways disastrous and sometimes a hugely entertaining time for hockey. It's all there: expansion, the Broad Street Bullies, the arrival of European players, the WHA, the elegance and excellence of Montreal's 1970s Cup dynasty, and yes, strange uniforms, long hair and sideburns.

In a larger sense, the 1970s really includes the first three seasons of the expansion era, starting in 1967–68. For a quarter century the NHL had been an insular six-team loop, during which time Detroit owner Jim Norris also had an interest either in the Chicago, Boston, and New York franchises or their arenas. Stability reigned: from 1949 through 1966, Montreal never missed the playoffs, Detroit missed only twice, and Toronto just three times, while neither Chicago, Boston nor New York ever won a regular-season title in that span and combined to finish higher than third only six times.

By the mid-1960s, the prospect of substantial profits and the threat of a new major hockey league combined to convince the NHL's club owners to take a great leap forward, doubling in size by adding six new teams. A lot of politicking and networking determined which cities would be awarded new franchises; thus were created the St. Louis Blues, Pittsburgh Penguins, Minnesota North Stars, Los Angeles Kings, Oakland Seals and Philadelphia Flyers. The league split into two divisions, the established teams in the East and the expansion teams lumped together in the West, ensuring playoff participation and playoff dollars for the expansion sides.

A surprising amount of talent was available in that first expansion; plenty of NHL-worthy players who'd languished in the minors simply because they'd never gotten a real shot in the tiny six-team league, journeymen who blossomed in a bigger role on an expansion team, and an especially rich harvest of youngsters who could now step into the NHL right out of junior hockey. Expansion also extended the careers of many players to unprecedented lengths; with more NHL roster spots than established NHL talent, players just kept on playing through their thirties and sometimes past 40. It was strange to be an adult fan and see guys out on the ice older than your dad, but it provided a sense of history, a lovingly prolonged view of the torch being passed from one era to the next, and it made the expansion era unique.

The "Original Six" era closed and the expansion age opened with appropriate symmetry. Toronto closed the six-team chapter with a Stanley Cup victory in Canada's centennial year, and Montreal won the first Cup in hockey's new age. The Canadiens were rapidly aging in places—Jean Beliveau and Henri Richard were key centermen, and the venerable Gump Worsley split time in goal—and youthful in others, but blended well enough to win the Cup the first two years of the expansion era. Brilliant general manager. Sam Pollock moved veterans in and out with dazzling acumen to keep the team fresh and strong. The younger athletes—Jacques Lemaire, Yvan Cournoyer, Peter Mahovlich, goalie Ken Dryden—moved to the forefront as the Habs took the Cup again in 1971 and 1973. But the best was yet to come, as Montreal would stake out a Cup dynasty and establish themselves as the team of the 1970s.

There was room for only one team to dominate as the Canadiens did. And as the decade played out and each expansion side improved, the other clubs from the six-team era found the going tougher.

Boston, NHL doormats since the 1940s, turned the franchise's fortunes around with just two moves as expansion dawned: signing junior sensation Bobby Orr, and stealing Phil Esposito from Chicago in a still-infamous six-player trade. Both proceeded to rewrite the record book: Espo with some of the greatest goals-scoring seasons in history, Orr revolutionizing the way defense was played en route to becoming the best defenseman—some would simply say the best—ever to play the game. Together they galvanized the team that earned a reputation as "The Big Bad Bruins," a sneering, black-garbed, provoked-at-a-glance hit squad of a hockey team that seemed to run up seven or eight goals every night and beat the tar out of the opposition while they were at it. Boston won the Cup in 1970 and 1972, yet left the feeling there should have been more despite a remarkable string of consecutive postseason participation, including appearances in the 1974, 1977 and 1978 finals.

New York had last won it all in 1940 and since then had been even weaker than Boston. But like the Bruins the Rangers began building when expansion arrived, and by the early 1970s had assembled a swift, clean, skillful side able to contend for the Cup. Those Ranger teams reeked of style and featured the slick forward line of Jean Ratelle, Rod Gilbert and Vic Hadfield, centers like Walt Tkaczuk and Bobby Rousseau, young defenseman Brad Park (the poor man's Orr) and the great goaltending of Eddie Giacomin and Gilles Villemeure. This talent base enabled the team to reach the finals in 1972. But the Rangers always lacked some physical element, some critical mass for combustion. They faded in the mid-1970s, were rebuilt with the acquisition of Phil Esposito and WHA superstars Ulf Nilsson and Anders Hedberg, and returned to the finals in 1979. But this edition of the team—the "Ooh-la-la" Rangers of the Ron Duguay-Don Murdoch-Ron Greschner years—had the bad timing to face the Montreal dynasty, and New York fans would have to wait until 1994.

Although they were snookered in the Esposito deal, Chicago still had superstars like Bobby Hull and Stan Mikita leading a team that had been strong through the 1960s. They wound up last among the old guard in the East in 1968–69 despite finishing over .500, but rebounded to win the division in 1969–70, and got a further boost when the NHL added two more expansion teams in 1970 and moved the Black Hawks in with the *arrivistes* of the West. With Bill White, Pat Stapleton, and Keith Magnuson leading a superb blue line corps and Tony Esposito in the nets, Chicago won the division in a cakewalk for the next three years, and twice went through to the finals. Both times, however, they fell to Montreal, first in a seven-game thriller in 1971, and then in a crazy-quilt comedy-of-errors finals of 1973. Then the prospect of healthy pay raises drove Hull and other key players into the beckoning arms of the World Hockey Association. Mikita and Esposito were still plugging away as the decade drew to a close, but weren't part of a contender in the latter half of the 1970s.

In Toronto, Maple Leaf owner Harold Ballard spent the decade embarrassing English-speaking Canada's favorite team with front-office chaos and boorish comments. In spite of him, the Leafs made the transition from the Dave Keon-Norm Ullman-George Armstrong era to the Darryl Sittler-Lanny McDonald-Borje Salming years without too many low spots, and often provided plenty of entertainment in the playoffs. The "Pyramid Power" series against Philadelphia and the 1978 seventh-game overtime series against the Islanders were particularly memorable as was Keon's joining the league-wide fashion trend, switching from his traditional crewcut to a pompadour with long sideburns. Although the "Buds" reached the semifinals only once in all that time, still harder times lay ahead for the franchise and its loyal fans in the 1980s.

Ironically, none of the Original Six fell further in the age of expansion than did Detroit. Led by veterans Gordie Howe and Alex Delvecchio, the Red Wings were still a respectable side as expansion dawned. But the club's front office soon made a habit of alienating their best players. Howe retired, then joined the WHA, and young phenom Marcel Dionne escaped to Los Angeles. Mickey Redmond was lost to a career-ending injury. These developments left a journeyman cast, forcing goalie Jim Rutherford to face more rubber than probably any netminder of the 1970s. Detroit qualified for postseason play only twice from 1967 to 1983, and wouldn't contend until the late 1980s.

So for hockey's old guard in expansion's first decade-plus, Montreal thrived spectacularly, Boston found some glory and just missed more, and New York and Chicago fell just short in their brush with greatness. Even Toronto had its little moments and only Detroit withered away. The new teams were frequently more exciting than their established brethren, and often more colorful.

The addition of six new franchises—California/Oakland, Los Angeles, Minnesota, Philadelphia, Pittsburgh and St. Louis—doubled the league's membership.

St. Louis, the city where the original Ottawa Senators went to die in the 1934–35 season, was the best of the expansion clubs in the late 1960s. General manager Lynn Patrick assembled a team of past-their-prime but extremely savvy veterans, starting with Hall of Famer Glenn Hall in goal. The Blues just missed the first West Division title, took it in 1969 and 1970, and went to the Stanley Cup finals in each of those first three expansion years, where they were dispatched in four straight games on each occasion by the NHL's old guard. Castoffs like centermen Red Berenson and Garry Unger became stars in St. Louis, three Plager brothers patrolled their blue line, Ernie Wakely, Eddie Staniowski and Jacques Caron shone briefly in goal, and stylish workers like Frank St. Marseille and Gary Sabourin defined the team's identity. St. Louis remained competitive though the first half of the decade, then decayed in the late 1970s, but the emergence of youngsters like Bernie Federko spelled hope for the 1980s in St. Louis.

Pittsburgh was another expansion city with plenty of hockey in its history. It had been home to an NHL club in an earlier era. The city also had been a charter member of the old International (Pro) Hockey League in 1904, was home to the NHL's Pirates in the 1920s and, with the Hornets, hosted a successful AHL franchise. The newly established NHL Penguins struggled until the mid-1970s. Players seemed to toil there forever, clad in those powder blue sweaters with the industrial-league look. Logging time in the Civic Arena were Ken Schinkel, Bryan Hextall Jr., Jean Pronovost, Syl Apps Jr., Lowell MacDonald, Ron Schock, Nick Harbaruk, Greg Polis, Val Fonteyne and fine goalies such as Les Binkley and Denis Herron who were bombarded with rubber nightly. The Penguins' first successful season, an 89-point effort in 1974–75, was the first of three consecutive campaigns over .500 as Greg Malone and Rick Kehoe improved the club. Still, the Pens finished more than two games over .500 just twice and won only three playoff series in their first dozen seasons. As the 1980s dawned, Mario Lemieux was still five years away.

The North Stars, set down in the high school and college hockey hotbed of Minnesota, were an entertaining side with plenty of color, and busy in the expansion playoff mix early on. The North Stars were loaded with veterans like Dean Prentice, Doug Mohns, Ted Harris, Ted Hampson, Bob Nevin, and Charlie Burns and his turban-shaped helmet, not to mention the venerable Gump Worsley, who along with Cesare Maniago gave the early Stars solid goaltending. J.P. Parise and Bill Goldsworthy were notable forwards, but Minnesota failed to build a contender and the Stars faded badly by the mid-1970s. They won only two playoff series until they absorbed the foundering Cleveland Barons in 1978; that influx of talent allowed them to shine briefly in the early 1980s.

Los Angeles had a history in the minors since the 1940s, but really got an expansion nod as a media center with a huge population. Expatriate Canadian Jack Kent Cooke, the team's eccentric owner, thought he had a built-in fan base for hockey with word that 300,000 ex-Canadians lived in metropolitan Los Angeles. "I found out why they moved," he said later. "They hated hockey." Unless you had a real passion for purple-and-gold—or at least Vic Venasky—the Kings had little to offer until the mid-1970s, when little Rogie Vachon from Montreal took over in goal, and Butch Goring and Juha Widing emerged as solid pivots. The Kings then acquired future Hall of Famer Marcel Dionne from Detroit and though the Kings won little in the 1970s, as the 1980s neared, they were an exciting team to watch.

Then there were the Seals, a team that seemed to have been born under an unfortunate star. No matter what they did, it turned sour or, just as often, hilarious. Disdaining the Amateur Draft, the Seals traded away their picks for journeymen. That strategy got them a second-place finish in their second season, but soon proved calamitous. A few worthy old-timers quickly came and went, but for the most part a parade of characters now fondly remembered only as answers to trivia questions filled the Seals bench, while their traded draft choices became superstars for other teams. The California Seals became the Oakland Seals and then the California Golden Seals when flamboyant baseball owner Charlie O. Finley bought the team and changed their yellow-and-aqua uniforms to green-and-gold with unforgettable white skates. But by any name and in any colors, the Seals finished last year after year, and there was nothing anyone from Joey Johnston and Carol Vadnais to Ivan Boldirev and Gilles Meloche to Len Frig and Morris Mott could do about it. The team moved to Cleveland in 1976, became the Barons, and spent two more years in the cellar before finally closing up shop and merging its roster with that of the struggling Minnesota North Stars.

The Philadelphia Flyers, though, were a book unto themselves—the most successful of the first wave of expansion while at the same time the most infamous. A decent side in their first few NHL campaigns, the Flyers opted to get much tougher. The Flyers took up where the Big Bad Bruins of the early 1970s had left off. Because of Philadelphia's success on the ice, some teams adopted elements of the Flyers' aggressive style.

Alongside their tough guys and plumbers, the Flyers had an elegant forward in Rick MacLeish as well as an effective first line in Bill Barber, Bobby Clarke and Reggie Leach. They were backstopped by the affable and spectacular Bernie Parent, one of the best goaltenders of the 1970s. The Flyers were wildly successful, winning four straight division titles and consecutive Stanley Cup championships in 1974 and 1975.

The NHL added two more new teams in 1970. Former Maple Leaf major-domo Punch Imlach quickly built an exciting, contending side in Buffalo, with acrobatic little Roger Crozier in net and one of the most spectacular young forward lines of the era, the French Connection of Gilbert Perreault, Rick Martin and Rene Robert, up front. Along with superb checking forwards like Craig Ramsay and Don Luce and fine defensemen like Jim Schoenfeld and Bill Hajt, the Sabres reached the finals in just their fifth year of existence. While Buffalo remained among the league's best and most entertaining regular-season teams through the 1970s, the team had little playoff success.

Vancouver, on the other hand, was often as bland as its blue-and-green uniforms. Nifty little forwards like Andre Boudrias and Don Lever helped the Canucks win a division title in 1975, but Vancouver missed the playoffs in six of its first eight seasons and did not win a single playoff series in the 1970s. Goalie Dunc Wilson, though, may have set an NHL record for the largest muttonchops.

Hockey in North America had certainly gotten bigger, but not necessarily better. In Europe and the Soviet Union, however, the game had both legitimacy and a style all its own. The Soviets earned the gold medal in every World Championship and Olympic tournament from 1963 to 1971. That Soviet hegemony stuck in Canada's collective craw, but the common wisdom over here was that the Soviets beat us in the Olympics because they were amateurs in name only, that our professionals would skate them dizzy if they ever met up. Hockey Canada arranged an eight-game Summit Series in 1972 between Canada's top NHL players and the Soviet Nationals to settle the issue, igniting a flag-waving, chest-thumping nationalistic fervor on these shores. Every hockey pundit in North America felt the NHLers would win in a cakewalk.

It began with embarrassing ease, as the NHL stars sprinted out to a 2–0 lead in game one in Montreal. Then everything went awry. The cream of the NHL staggered off goggle-eyed at game's end after the Soviets put on a skills exhibition and breezed to a 7–3 victory. Team Canada managed a win and a tie in the four games on Canadian ice, and the whole tournament was made a microcosm of the Cold War: their way of life against ours. In the end, the NHL players hacked their way to three heart-stopping victories in Moscow to close the series as narrow winners.

The Summit Series was a defining moment not only for North American hockey but for the Canadian identity; more than 25 years later this tournament is still constantly revisited, victory and defeat rolled into one, revered and reviewed, dissected and debated game by game and shot by shot. Paul Henderson's winning goal and the celebrations it touched off obscured the real point: the cloistered, self-absorbed North American version of the game had stagnated, and the game outside North America, so different, was now every bit as good.

Top Soviet club teams made the first of several midseason tours in 1975–76. Central Red Army and Montreal played to a memorable 3–3 tie on New Year's Eve, 1975. Four European national teams joined Canadian and American NHL stars in an inaugural Canada Cup tournament in September of 1976 with Canada defeating Czechoslovakia in the final.

EuroSoviet hockey was a revelation with its swirling, cycling, criss-crossing patterns of attack and emphasis on skating and passing, the very antithesis of the straight up-and-down-the-lanes North American style in which hitting, shooting and jamming the net were supreme. The Soviets couldn't leave their country to play here, but word circulated that there were many good players in Sweden, and the Leafs lured Inge Hammarstrom and Borje Salming to the Maple Leafs. Hammarstrom was adequate as an NHLer, but Salming proved to be a gem who was as smooth, skillful, smart and tough as any NHL defenseman.

The rival World Hockey Association began play in 1972–73, and from its inception, welcomed players from Europe. The WHA, organized by American Basketball Association entrepreneurs Gary Davidson and Dennis Murphy, set up shop with teams in a dozen towns. Six were cities bypassed by the NHL—Edmonton, Winnipeg, Quebec, Ottawa, Cleveland and Houston—and six went head-to-head with NHL teams in the bigger media centers or more hockey-crazed regions—New York, Los Angeles, Chicago, Philadelphia, Minnesota and New England. Some of the NHL's biggest stars jumped to WHA teams. Bobby Hull gave the new league credibility as did Frank Mahovlich, Paul Henderson, J.C. Tremblay, Dave Keon, Jacques Plante, Gordie Howe and others. While the WHA's on-ice product was not, at first, NHL quality, it soon wasn't far off, complete with its own garish uniforms and, on occasion, white skates.

Along with a horde of minor-leaguers, numerous NHLers flocked to the rebel circuit, lifting its quality, lowering the NHL's, and hiking the average player salary in both leagues. Some second-line NHLers like Andre Lacroix and Marc Tardif became superstars in the new league, but established NHL stars who jumped did not outshine them. Parity was further indicated by young WHA talents who later joined the NHL and remained stars there including Anders Hedberg, Ulf Nilsson, Mark Messier, Mike Gartner, Mark Howe and, of course, Wayne Gretzky.

The Winnipeg Jets won WHA championships with an electrifying, largely European roster and NHL scouts began to scour Scandinavia and Czechoslovakia for talent. By the second half of the 1970s, North American teams eagerly, if at first ineptly, began to copy the EuroSoviet offensive style. North American defense, on the other hand, diluted by expansion and the clutch-and-grab tactics in vogue in the early part of the decade, took longer to adapt.

The WHA operated on a financial tightrope for seven seasons before it went out of business in 1979. The only four teams that remained in constant operation through all seven WHA seasons—Edmonton, Quebec, Winnipeg, and New England (Hartford)—joined the NHL, albeit stripped of all but four players each.

The NHL's major reaction to the WHA was a desperate scramble to mint more NHL franchises. In a preemptive strike to head off the rebel loop's planting teams in cities in which neither league yet had a foothold, the NHL put the Flames in Atlanta and the Islanders in New York's Long Island suburbs in 1972, and then begat the Washington Capitals and Kansas City Scouts in 1974.

With as many 32 teams in the NHL and WHA combined and slim pickings available in expansion drafts, these new clubs weren't competitive. In addition, poor crowds forced several NHL franchises to relocate: Oakland moved to Cleveland, Kansas City decamped for Colorado, and Minnesota stayed afloat only because Cleveland failed. The novelty would soon wear off in Atlanta, as well, and Colorado would relocate to New Jersey.

One team rose above the thuggery that threatened to drag the game down in the 1970s. The Montreal Canadiens returned as conquering heroes in 1976, paragons of the best hockey had to offer. Many of the players who were part of great Montreal teams in the early 1970s were still in place, but in addition to this talent base, Guy Lafleur had blossomed into the game's most electrifying scorer, Steve Shutt proved a capable sniper on the opposite wing, checking forward Bob Gainey turned into a force of nature at playoff time, and Serge Savard, Larry Robinson, and Guy Lapointe—the "Big Three" on defense—were numbered among the best rearguards in the game.

In 1975–76, Montreal breezed through the regular season and early playoff rounds to face the defending Cup champion Flyers in the finals. In this showdown of hockey philosophies, the Canadiens swept Philadelphia aside in four straight games.

Montreal rarely took a night off for the rest of the decade. In the 1976–77 season, the Canadiens won a record 60 games and repeated in the finals with a four-game sweep of Boston. Another regular-season cakewalk followed in

1977–78, capped with another Cup victory over the Bruins. And the Canadiens topped their 115-point regular season in 1978–79 with a fourth consecutive Cup win, dashing the Rangers four games to one. The decade of the Seals and Scouts, of Peter Puck, of Fighting Saints and Golden Blades, of Hound Dog, the Hammer and the Moose, of Hockey Sock Rock, of white skates and giant sideburns ended with hockey artistry ascendant. The Islanders and Oilers—dynasties that followed the Canadiens—both used aspects of the Canadiens' system as models for their own.

99 AND 66
1979–80 TO 1991–92

Gary Mason

IT WOULD BE ONE OF HOCKEY'S MOST EXCITING ERAS. While the upstart World Hockey Association would draw its last breath, the National Hockey League would flourish on the ice in the 1980s and early 1990s, evolving into an international super-league employing great players from around the world. This period also would produce the games' last two dynasty teams—the New York Islanders and Edmonton Oilers—and would provide the setting for two of the game's greatest players to perform their magic—Wayne Gretzky and Mario Lemieux.

Off-ice, the era would be defined by the relationship between three men: chairman of the NHL's Board of Governors and owner of the Chicago Blackhawks Bill Wirtz, league president John Ziegler and Players' Association executive director Alan Eagleson. Through the WHA years as salaries soared, labor and management needed to work together creatively to ensure franchise stability and preserve players' jobs in the NHL. The triumvirate of Wirtz, Ziegler and Eagleson allowed this to happen but, by 1990 many players would become increasingly uncomfortable with this relationship. By October of 1992 Eagleson and Ziegler would be replaced and Wirtz's tenure as chairman of the Board of Governors ended.

The WHA had started in 1972. For seven years it challenged the NHL in cities across North America, signing some of the game's biggest names, most notably Bobby Hull, while allowing future stars like Gretzky and Mark Messier to make their professional debuts as teenagers. But the league's shaky financial foundation eventually collapsed and, in 1979, the NHL expanded into four WHA markets—Edmonton, Quebec, Hartford and Winnipeg. Before Edmonton joined the NHL, and was still operating in the WHA, the team purchased Gretzky, who first had played with the Indianapolis Racers. Before Edmonton joined the NHL, it had to be assured it wouldn't lose the rights to Gretzky.

Meantime, another former expansion franchise, the New York Islanders, had quietly built an outstanding hockey team under the guidance of general manager Bill Torrey, coach Al Arbour and a gifted scouting staff.

The team revolved around its captain, All-Star defenseman Denis Potvin, forwards Bryan Trottier and Mike Bossy and goaltender Billy Smith. Like any great hockey team, the Islanders also had a talented supporting cast that included players like Clark Gillies, Bob Nystrom and Butch Goring. The Islanders were never flashy, they played a tough, disciplined game and made few mistakes. Their coach, Al Arbour, was a man of few expressions who rarely got flustered in the heat of battle. Arbour's composure under fire rubbed off on his team. Before retiring, Arbour would compile one of the most impressive coaching records in hockey.

The team's undisputed leader was also one of the finest defensemen in the game. Denis Potvin would go on to have a distinguished NHL career, breaking Bobby Orr's all-time scoring records for defensemen and becoming the first blueliner in the league to top 300 goals.

In 1979-80, their eighth NHL season, the Islanders became the second expansion team to win the Stanley Cup. Two players, Smith and Nystrom, had been with the team since its inception in 1972. The team would go on to win the Cup the next three years as well, becoming only the second NHL franchise in history to win four championships in a row. The Islanders would beat the Edmonton Oilers in four games to win their fourth Cup. The Oilers, however, would learn from their defeat.

Edmonton general manager Glen Sather, coach of the Oilers at the time, remembers walking by the Islander dressing room after the final game.

"They all had ice packs on," Sather recalled. "None of our guys were beat up like that. We just didn't know how hard we had to go to win. To be a Stanley Cup champion." They would learn.

Sather was building a different team from the conservative style of the Islanders. Sather had gone to Europe when he was coaching the Oilers in the WHA. He went to Finland and Sweden and he watched how midget hockey teams there practiced. He liked what he saw.

"They were teaching kids the fundamentals of the game," Sather recalled. "But they were also teaching them about switching lanes and creating open ice. " He saw defensemen jumping up into the play. It was a style that demanded creativeness and Sather knew he had one of the most creative players in the game—a slender kid from Brantford, Ontario, named Wayne Gretzky.

"I knew he was probably the most creative player who had skated in the NHL. He had tremendous peripheral vision," said Sather.

To emulate what he had seen in Europe, Sather needed players who could skate. And that's who he went after. Soon, the Oilers would have the likes of Jari Kurri, Glenn Anderson and Paul Coffey joining Gretzky and Mark Messier, a tough-as-nails forward with blazing speed. The team also found a great goaltender in Grant Fuhr. And they would need him. The Oilers had a high-octane offense. Defense was something they didn't pay as much attention to. The Oilers' European-style of play, which highlighted European players like Kurri, Esa Tikkanen, Jaroslav Pouzar, Reijo Ruotsalainen and others, opened up the eyes of other NHL teams to the talent pool that existed overseas.

While great players like Toronto's Borje Salming had earlier proved that Europeans could not only play but thrive in the NHL, it would be the success of the Oilers and, earlier, the WHA's Winnipeg Jets that would up the stock of European players.

"The European players were highly skilled," said Sather. "And just as tough as we were." On May 19, 1984, in only their fifth NHL season, the Oilers captured the Stanley Cup for the first time. Edmonton defeated the defending champion Islanders 5–2 in game five to clinch the series. The torch had been passed from one dynasty to another. And the Oilers would dominate the rest of the decade.

"Our skill level was probably the biggest thing that made us so tough," Mark Messier remembered of those Oiler teams. "We forced all the teams to find better skilled players to be able to compete. Consequently, the ability and skill level of the entire league rose." Messier says the foundation of the Oilers was a special group of players that could play the game on anyone's terms.

"I think that was the biggest facet of that team," Messier said. "If you wanted to play it in the alley we could play it there. If you wanted to play it in the streets, we could play a fast, wide-open game. If you wanted tight-checking, we could beat you there. We could beat you at any game." Harry Neale, former NHL coach and general manager, had the unenviable task of facing the Oilers in the league's Smythe Division. He was coach of the Vancouver Canucks.

"They forced other teams, certainly in our division, into coping with their style," said Neale. "You weren't going to beat them if you were a slow-footed, checking team." Neale said the Oilers were especially deadly when teams were four on four. With Gretzky and Kurri on the ice and Paul Coffey on defense, Neale said, they could make the other team's four players look like minor-leaguers. Neale said when the league, in 1985, changed the rule concerning coincidental minors so teams would remain five aside and would no longer play with only four players, he referred to it as the Edmonton Oiler rule.

"I always said they changed the rule because the Oilers were scoring so many goals in four-on-four situations," Neale observed.

The key to the Oilers, however, was the incomparable talents of its captain, Wayne Gretzky.

"Gretzky terrified you," said Neale.

Gretzky's coach agreed.

"Wayne was really the main piece of the whole puzzle," said Sather. "He was such a great player he made the players around him better and they all developed from his confidence and the way he could play the game." Sather said it all started from practice. "Wayne never had a bad practice in 11 years." Gretzky would make his mark in the NHL right from the start. On a February night in 1980, he would tie the NHL record for most assists in one game with seven. His legend would grow from there. Gretzky, of course, would shatter and own endless NHL records.

As prolific a scorer as he was, Gretzky's greatest asset was his ability to set up others. He did things with the puck defenders never saw before. He would park himself behind an opponent's net and the moment a defender made a move, Gretzky seemed to find a teammate who was open. His position behind the net would become known as "Gretzky's office." He was a rare player who could take over a game himself. He was often double-shifted by his coach and would play half the game. He was never the fastest player but he never had to be, so shifty were his moves.

The Oilers would win a second Cup in 1985, beating the Philadelphia Flyers in five games. Gretzky would win the Conn Smythe Trophy as the most valuable playoff performer. The Oilers looked like they might own the Cup forever. But they would falter the following year, enabling the Montreal Canadiens to win their 23rd Stanley Cup title behind the brilliant goaltending of a 20-year-old from Quebec named Patrick Roy. It would be the stunning debut of one of the game's great pressure goaltenders.

But the Oilers would reclaim hockey's greatest prize the next two seasons, beating the Flyers again in 1987 and the Boston Bruins the following year.

However, cracks were beginning to show in the great Oiler dynasty. The team's enormous success had driven up the value of its star players. Oilers owner Peter Pocklington was beginning to feel squeezed financially as the costs of doing business in the league began to soar. In November 1987, the Oilers traded Paul Coffey to the Pittsburgh Penguins in a seven-player deal. It would set the stage for the most shocking trade in NHL history the following year.

On August 9, 1988, a sobbing Wayne Gretzky announced he was being traded to the Los Angeles Kings. Two other Oilers, Mike Krushelnyski and Marty McSorley would join him. In return, the Oilers got Jimmy Carson and Martin Gelinas plus L.A.'s first round picks in 1989, 1991 and 1993. Plus $15 million.

The move shocked a nation. Gretzky was a national hero in Canada and the thought of losing such a treasure seemed like heresy. Pocklington was vilified in his own city. Fans wanted to blame anybody, including Gretzky's new wife, actress Janet Jones, for luring him to the bright lights of Hollywood.

The trade would have profound ramifications on the NHL. First, Gretzky would become a glamorous spokesman for the game in the United States where someone of his stature was needed to sell the game. Almost overnight, Gretzky made hockey cool in sunny California. Some of Hollywood's biggest stars came to see him play.

There is little question that Gretzky's move precipitated the eventual expansion of the NHL game into several U.S. markets. In California, where Gretzky landed, franchises would later spring up in San Jose and Anaheim.

Beyond the impact Gretzky would have in the U.S., the trade would forever change the landscape of team-player relations. If Wayne Gretzky could be traded, then anyone could be traded.

"Once Wayne Gretzky got traded it changed everything," said Harry Neale. "Before you traded to make your team better. Now, teams were trading for economic reasons. And that's what the trade really highlighted; how the economics of hockey were changing." Once in L.A., Gretzky was told by the Kings' flamboyant owner Bruce McNall to write his own cheque. Gretzky would get close to $2 million a year, plus bonuses. It would set a new standard by which other players would want to be paid.

The Oilers would feel Gretzky's absence immediately. While still a strong team, The Great One's departure would be too much to handle the following season. The Calgary Flames would capture the Cup in 1989 and one of hockey's most enduring personalities, Lanny McDonald, would sip from the silver chalice for the first time in a long and distinguished career.

The Oilers, however, would bounce back and grab glory one more time. It would be their most unlikely Cup victory and perhaps, in many ways, the most gratifying. In 1990, Mark Messier, now wearing the captain's "C" would lead his team to the Cup, beating the Boston Bruins in five games. It would be the final curtain call for one of the game's greatest dynasties. The economics of hockey would eventually force the Oilers to lose Messier, Anderson, Kurri and Fuhr. Only the team photos outside the Edmonton dressing room would remain to remind future players of the past greatness that once occupied the room.

The Oilers, despite finishing below .500 in their first two seasons in the NHL, would accumulate the best overall record during the years 1979–80 to 1988–89. The Oilers racked up 996 points and a .623 winning percentage, just fractionally ahead of the Philadelphia Flyers.

While Gretzky would get most of the spotlight in the 1980s, he would eventually share center-stage with an emerging superstar in Pittsburgh.

Mario Lemieux became Pittsburgh's first pick, the top choice overall, in the 1984 Entry Draft. The lanky and stylish centre from the Laval Voisins of the Quebec Major Junior Hockey League had been touted by everyone as a sure-fire franchise player. He didn't disappoint.

In his first season, Lemieux reached the 100-point plateau. In 1987-88, he would stop Gretzky's string of eight consecutive MVP awards by winning the Hart Trophy. Pittsburgh's number 66 would also top Gretzky in the race for the Art Ross Trophy, finishing with 168 points, 19 more than number 99.

Lemieux and Gretzky weren't always on opposite sides of the ice. In 1987, the two joined forces for their country in the Canada Cup tournament. As expected, Canada and the Soviet Union met in the final. The teams had split the first two games of the three-game series by identical scores of 6–5. In game three, the score was tied 5–5 in the dying minutes of regulation time when Gretzky broke down the left side of the ice with Lemieux trailing. Number 99 would wait until the last possible instant, drawing the Russian defenders toward him, before dropping a pass to Lemieux who snapped a shot to the top corner of the net, allowing Canada to win by the now-familiar score of 6–5. It may have been the second-greatest moment in the history of Canada and Russia's hockey rivalry, falling only in the shadow of Paul Henderson's goal in 1972.

Many felt Lemieux's game winner ignited him, pushed him to reach greater heights in hockey. If there was one frustration with Lemieux, it was that he didn't seem to possess the same passion for the game as Gretzky. But his skills were undeniably magnificent, enabling him to lead the Penguins to consecutive Stanley Cup triumphs in 1991 and 1992.

Several tournaments and exhibition series with teams from the Soviet Union and other European hockey powers took place in the 1980s utilizing a variety of formats. The second edition of the six-nation Canada Cup was played in 1981, with the Soviets defeating Canada 8–1 in the championship game. Additional Canada Cup tournaments were played in 1984, 1987 (described above) and 1991 with Team Canada winning all three. Significantly, by 1991 Canada's final series opponent was not the Soviet Union but the United States.

Soviet teams and NHL clubs would stage a number of meetings throughout the 1980s. Central Red Army and Dynamo Moscow came over to play NHL teams in the 1979–80 season. The NHL teams won four of the nine games. In 1982–83, a Soviet all-star team played six NHL clubs, losing only to Edmonton and Calgary. The Central Red Army and Dynamo Moscow returned in 1985–86 and won eight out of 10 meetings with NHL teams.

Rendez-Vous 87 was played at Le Colisee in Quebec City, pitting the NHL All-Stars against the Soviet Nationals. The NHLers took the first game 4–3 but the Soviets won the second 5–3 with Valeri Kamensky starring for the Soviets. Additional Super Series were staged in 1988–89, 1989–90 and 1990–91. Fifty-six games were played in all, with NHL teams winning 21 and Soviet clubs 29. Six games were tied.

NHL clubs also paid preseason visits to the Soviet Union. The Calgary Flames and Washington Capitals each played four Soviet opponents in September 1989. The Minnesota North Stars and Montreal Canadiens played a similar schedule of games one year later.

The NHL would undergo a noticeable change in the demographic makeup of its players in the 1980s. The percentage of Canadian-born players, 82.1 percent in 1979–80, slipped to 75.5 percent by decade's end. The difference was made up in almost equal numbers by U.S.-born and European players. The decade also saw a dramatic increase in U.S. college and U.S. high school players selected in the annual NHL Entry Draft. Interest in U.S. hockey increased, particularly, after that country's upset gold medal at the 1980 Winter Olympics in Lake Placid. Several players on the team would have distinguished NHL careers. More importantly, the high-profile victory had a huge impact on the number of American children playing the game.

Soviet journeyman Sergei Priakhin became the first product of the Soviet hockey system permitted to join an NHL club when he signed a contract with the Calgary Flames in 1988–89. Beginning in 1989–90, top Soviet players like Sergei Makarov, Alexander Mogilny and Viacheslav Fetisov appeared in the NHL with many others to follow.

Several rule changes were introduced throughout the 1980s. By decade's end the league responded to growing concern about players being checked into the boards in an unsafe manner. The league ruled that any player who received a major penalty for boarding that resulted in an injury to the head or face of an opponent, also received an automatic game misconduct. Any player who incurred a total of two game misconduct penalties for boarding would be suspended for one game.

In 1982, rosters were expanded to 18 skaters plus two goaltenders from 17 skaters and two goaltenders. In 1983, a five-minute sudden-death overtime period was instituted.

Overall and average attendance at National Hockey League games rose to record levels throughout the 1980s. In 1979–80, the average league attendance was 12,747. By the end of the decade, average attendance had climbed to 14,908.

Though there were two franchise moves (Atlanta to Calgary in 1980 and Colorado to New Jersey in 1982), the 1980s would be a period of consolidation for the NHL. But by the beginning of the 1990s, the league was poised for change. An additional team was added in 1991–92 when San Jose entered the league. Ottawa and Tampa Bay joined as expansion franchises in 1992–93 with Florida and Anaheim making the NHL into a 26-team circuit the following season.

Off the ice, criticism of NHL president John Ziegler's management style mounted. During the 1988 playoffs New Jersey Devils coach Jim Schoenfeld was suspended for clashing with referee Don Koharski ("have another donut, you fat pig!) after a game. When the Devils obtained a temporary restraining order to overturn Schoenfeld's suspension, the referee and linesmen scheduled to work the next game refused to take the ice. The league found substitute officials and, after a lengthy delay the game was played that same Sunday evening.

The substitute referee had his own striped shirt but the new linesmen were forced to work the first period in oversized yellow practice jerseys. The officials did a good job, but after this "mini-crisis" media coverage came to revolve around the fact that Ziegler was not available to help resolve the issue. When added to an existing perception that he was aloof, this unfortunate incident—known as "Yellow Sunday"—strengthened growing opposition to Ziegler's regime among some members of the league's Board of Governors.

Fundamental changes also were under way at the NHL Players' Association which, since its inception, had been dominated by the personality and actions of its executive director Alan Eagleson. By the end of the 1980s many players had come to believe that Eagleson was too close to NHL club owners and accordingly was not acting in the players' best interests.

His involvements as an individual player agent and as the organizer of the Canada Cup international tournament placed him in what many felt were unacceptable conflicts of interest. These fears would later be realized when Eagleson was convicted on fraud charges in Boston and Toronto courtrooms in January 1998.

In September 1990, a Michigan lawyer and player agent by the name of Bob Goodenow was brought aboard the NHLPA and after a two-year transition period, took over as Executive Director on January 1, 1992. His mandate was to revamp the operation.

"There was an association in name but not in operation," Goodenow said recently.

It wouldn't take long for NHL owners to realize they were now dealing with a new NHL Players' Association that was run along completely different lines than the one Eagleson had been operating.

In April 1992, just four months after assuming control, Goodenow led the first league-wide players' strike in NHL history. As what would have been the final days of the regular season ticked by, the strike threatened the Stanley Cup playoffs.

The labor dispute lasted 10 days before a settlement was reached. The players acquired some improved free agency provisions and greater control over licensing of their likenesses. The players had served notice they were to be taken seriously by the owners.

"That was a major moment," said Goodenow. "The players were committed to getting the respect of the owners which they didn't feel they had before. I don't think the owners took the players seriously and it wasn't until the strike that they understood the players were serious." Goodenow would lead the players in other battles. It was clear that the NHL was much different than it was in 1979–80.

John Ziegler was replaced as league president by Gil Stein in 1992. A new office of the commissioner would soon be created with Gary Bettman elected to lead the NHL into a new era.

The World's Best 1992–93 to 1999-2000

Cammy Clark

Welcome to the new era of the NHL, when Russians became regulars, salaries skyrocketed, fabled arenas made way for state-of-the-art stadiums with luxury boxes, pucks were changed to blue dots on TV, two Canadian teams relocated, "zero tolerance" became a catch phrase, NHL players went to the Winter Olympics en masse, Brett Hull learned to backcheck and Wayne Gretzky no longer was the only hockey player people recognized south of the Mason-Dixon Line.

The new era unofficially began in 1992. A leadership overhaul took place to make way for people who believed that hockey's status quo needed changing.

The NHL Players' Association was the first to change. Gone was longtime executive director Alan Eagleson, whose place was taken by strong-willed Bob Goodenow. The players went on strike for the first time in NHL history in the spring of 1992.

Longtime NHL president John Ziegler was replaced on an interim basis by Gil Stein, the NHL's vice president and general counsel. Stein believed the league could be a much bigger force on the North American sports scene with greater marketing efforts. He also pushed for the NHL to go to the Winter Olympics. Stein desperately wanted to become the first commissioner of the NHL but was seen to be part of the old regime. It was time for new blood and, after considering several candidates, the NHL's Board of Governors elected NBA senior vice president Gary Bettman to steer the league through what would prove a major growth spurt.

"He's exactly what we needed," longtime Boston Bruins executive Harry Sinden told the *Boston Globe* in 1996. "We couldn't have had a better person at the right time, in the right place. We got someone with energy, with knowledge, a guy who is current, upscale, vibrant—and someone who wasn't locked into our stupid traditions."

Gone were the days of croquet matches in period costumes after Board of Governors meetings in Florida.

"When Gary came in, he was all business," former Tampa Bay Lightning governor David LeFevre said. "He was organized and right from the beginning everyone knew he was running the show."

Bettman, who had been a top executive at the NBA during its tremendous growth period of the 1980s, did not take the job until he had assurances from the league he would have power to make decisions on his own. The Board of Governors gave him the authority. Cumbersome league committees were eliminated as most of the business of the NHL was conducted out of league offices.

The NHL was "sort of sleepy in marketing themselves," said Tony Ponturo, vice president of corporate media and sports marketing for Anheuser-Busch. "We got excited about the new attitude of Bettman and his people. They offered all the ingredients in the pot, with the potential for big growth for a reasonable price."

Brett Hull, in his pre-backchecking days, described the NHL's previous efforts to sell the game by evoking the name of the game's top player: "Until now, the league's idea of marketing was Wayne, Wayne and more Wayne."

Increased exposure for the NHL was part of the rationale behind the granting of expansion franchises that took place before Bettman took over in 1993. Two new franchises—the Tampa Bay Lightning and Ottawa Senators—began play in the fall of 1992. Tampa represented a new market for the NHL. Ottawa marked the return of the league to a city where it last had a team in 1933–34. Two other expansion franchises had been awarded one day before Bettman was elected: the Disney-owned Mighty Ducks of Anaheim and the Blockbuster Entertainment-owned Florida Panthers.

The addition of four franchises in important markets helped the NHL land its first U.S. network television contract in 20 years, with FOX-TV. The NHL also had heavy commitments on cable with ESPN and ESPN2. More games on more television outlets greatly increased viewers' options. At the same time, the NHL's presence on Hockey Night in Canada increased.

"Bettman has advanced the league 10 years in the year and a half he's been here," Edmonton Oilers owner Peter Pocklington said in 1994. "He's brought energy, vision, leadership and a sense of how to make the business work."

Bettman took his share of criticism during the NHL's lockout of its players that resulted in the 1994–95 regular season being reduced to 48 games. The lockout came at a time when the New York Rangers, playing in the number one media market, had won their first Stanley Cup since 1940 with a thrilling seven-game final series win over the Vancouver Canucks. Any audience-building momentum created by the Rangers victory was halted in its tracks when the NHL shut its doors on October 1, 1994. Play was suspended for 103 days while the players and owners haggled over a new collective bargaining agreement.

Christmas, 1994, came and went with NHL players scattered throughout Europe. With the season on the verge of being canceled in January, Harry Sinden stated that the NHL's most recent proposal was, "our final, final, final, final, final offer."

After 11th-hour marathon negotiating sessions, a deal was struck as the players and owners approved a new Collective Bargaining Agreement. One of the owners who opposed the deal was Marcel Aubut of the Quebec Nordiques whose franchise, in essence, had been handed a death sentence.

"I recognize that the majority of the industry can live with the agreement that was negotiated, but it is difficult to accept for a small market such as Quebec," he said.

"It would have been bad if we had lost a season," Bettman said. "I'm not happy we lost half a season. But we had to make a deal that was sensible." As it was, when play resumed on January 20, 1995, 468 games were lopped from the original 1994–95 regular-season schedule.

Expansion was the key to the overall growth of the NHL in the 1990s. Phil Esposito was part of the first new expansion wave in the early 1990s, convincing the Board of Governors to grant an expansion franchise for the virgin hockey territory of Tampa Bay by promising what he knew the Board wanted to hear.

"Everybody thought I was nuts," Esposito said, but he set out to make believers of those who thought hockey would have as much chance in Florida as a female would of playing goal in the NHL. (Esposito tried this, too. Goaltender Manon Rheaume garnered plenty of publicity for the Lightning when she played one period in an exhibition game, but her real impact was in raising the profile of women's hockey.)

The Tampa Bay Hockey Group staged a preseason game in St. Petersburg between the Pittsburgh Penguins and Los Angeles Kings in ThunderDome, a stadium built for a non-existent baseball team. An NHL record 25,581 people showed up.

"It would be good exposure for the league to play in Florida," said Wayne Gretzky, who played in that game for the Kings.

Hockey would show it could survive in Florida. The Lightning drew record crowds of 20,000-plus during their days in ThunderDome. The Florida Panthers, who joined the league in 1993–94, went on a storybook run to the Stanley Cup finals in only their third season.

But it became inevitable that some franchises in the smallest markets would be forced to relocate. Economics, and the absence of a local ownership group that would keep the team in place, forced the sale of the Quebec Nordiques to the Ascent Entertainment Group. Renamed and refinanced, the old Nordiques won the Stanley Cup in their first season as the Colorado Avalanche in Denver. Winnipeg, despite a grassroots "Save the Jets" campaign, lost its team a year after Quebec. New owners relocated the franchise to Arizona, where it became the Phoenix Coyotes.

The Nordiques and Jets are former WHA teams—as are the Hartford Whalers who, in 1997–98, relocated to another exotic hockey market, North Carolina. Renamed the Carolina Hurricanes, they began play in Greensboro until a new arena was ready in Raleigh in October, 1999.

The NHL, which had 21 teams as recently as 1991, now has 30. The Nashville Predators began play in 1998–99 and proved a big hit with fans. The Predators drew 664,000 fans during their inaugural season for an average attendance of 16,202 (94% of capacity). Atlanta, home to the Flames before their move to Calgary in 1980, was even more enthusiastic in welcoming the Thrashers to the NHL for the 1999–2000 season. A capacity crowd of 18,545 filled the new Philips Arena for the team's first regular-season game on October 2, 1999. By season's end, the Thrashers had become the first NHL expansion team to average better than 17,000 fans per game. The NHL's two newest teams will be taking aim at those numbers when they begin play in 2000–2001. Minneapolis-St. Paul, which lost its team in 1993 when the North Stars moved to Dallas, now have a new team known as the Minnesota Wild. They enter the NHL alongside the Columbus (Ohio) Blue Jackets.

The rapid growth of the NHL has been fueled, in no small part, by the greater access to foreign hockey markets. "We can expand because of the Europeans," said former Mighty Ducks of Anaheim coach Pierre Page. "We've gone from a redneck league to an international one."

The league for years has had a sprinkling of players from Sweden, the Czech Republic and Finland, but the real influx didn't begin until the early 1990s, when players from Eastern Europe could come to North America without having to defect.

Dave King was coach of the Calgary Flames when he said, "No one would argue that our game hasn't been improved by the Europeans. A person seeing his first game will invariably pick out a European player if you asked him to choose the best player in the game. That's because their skills are refined at such an early age."

The NHL has gone so international that the 48th All-Star Game in 1998 introduced a new format: North America versus The World. In the Mighty Ducks dressing room alone that season, six languages were spoken: English, French, Russian, Finnish, Swedish and Czech. "No other job you'd see that unless you were a U.N. ambassador," Ducks goalie Guy Hebert said.

In the first "Dream Team" Olympic tournament, the 1998 Winter Games at Nagano, Japan, the two favored teams went home without a medal. Canada and the United States, were off the podium as the Czechs beat the Russians in the gold medal game and the Finns took the bronze.

Many branded the venture a disaster but Teemu Selanne said, "It was something unbelievable. I still think it was worth it. We've got to grow this game. The Olympics were good for hockey." The NHL and the International Ice Hockey Federation have agreed to terms on the league's participation at the 2002 Winter Olympic Games in Salt Lake City.

The NHL's top scorer every season since 1997–98 has been a Czech (Jaromir Jagr). Goal-scoring leaders since 1997–98 have included a Finn (Teemu Selanne), a Slovak (Peter Bondra) and a Russian (Pavel Bure). In 1997–98, nearly a quarter of the NHL players (22.5 percent) came from outside North America, representing 16 countries. By the start of the 1999–2000 season, 28 percent of the NHL (183 players) was from Europe. There were 50 players in the NHL from the Czech Republic alone. When Wayne Gretzky announced his retirement late in the 1998–99 season, his New York Rangers (Gretzky had moved from L.A. to New York—with a brief stop in St. Louis—in 1996), were beaten by Jaromir Jagr's Pittsburgh Penguins in "The Great One's" final game. Jagr scored the winning goal in overtime that afternoon and Gretzky spoke of the torch being passed.

Speculation that Gretzky might be ready to call it a career had begun quietly when he was injured in February, 1999. Then, on April 10, 1999, analyst John Davidson told a *Hockey Night in Canada* audience that there was an 80% chance his good friend Wayne was going to retire.

Over the next few days, Gretzky himself announced he had all but made up his mind. Many, including Wayne's wife Janet, hoped to convince him to stay on for one more year, but by the evening of Thursday, April 15, it appeared that Gretzky was about to play his last NHL game in Canada. Ottawa fans gave him a resounding send-off following a 2–2 tie between the Senators and the Rangers. In a lengthy press conference after the game, Gretzky confirmed that he would meet one last time with the New York brass, but that it would "take a miracle" for him to change his mind.

The meeting was held on Friday morning. Friday afternoon, Wayne Gretzky announced he was done. Since the Rangers had failed to make the playoffs, the regular-season finalé on Sunday afternoon, April 18, would be his final game in the National Hockey League.

Gretzky insisted that he was at peace with his decision and that his retirement should be treated as a celebration, "a moving on, not a passing on." The fans at Madison Square Garden—plus the millions watching on television in Canada—certainly treated it that way. From the special ceremonies before the game (which included the announcement from Commissioner Bettman that the number 99 would never again be worn by an NHL player), to the video greetings (from the likes of Gordie Howe and Michael Jordan) which were displayed on the scoreboard throughout, to the rousing ovations at its conclusion, the game was a celebration of the greatest ambassador hockey has ever known. Two months after his final game, the Hockey Hall of Fame announced that the three-year waiting period would be waived and that number 99 would be inducted in 1999. Gretzky was the 10th player to receive fast-track admittance into the Hall of Fame, and will be the last to be accorded this honor.

When Gretzky entered the NHL in 1979–80, the average salary in the league was $108,000. Over the next 10 years, that number doubled to $232,000. By 1996–97, there were 186 players making a million dollars or more. The major reason for the escalation is "salary disclosure," according to Goodenow. "At the end of the day, the objective of everyone who plays is to get paid in a way that reflects their value to the overall enterprise," Goodeneow said. In 1997–98, the average NHL salary topped $1 million for the first time. By 1999–2000, even with Gretzky out of the game, the average salary in the NHL had climbed over $1.3 million.

Much of the money found to pay these increased salaries has come from revenues generated in large new arenas with luxurious skyboxes and corporate names. Buffalo's Memorial Auditorium, the St. Louis Arena, Pacific Coliseum, Capital Centre, Philadelphia Spectrum and the Great Western Forum no longer host NHL teams. Such legendary buildings as Chicago Stadium and Boston Garden, rats and all, disappeared from the hockey landscape in the 1990s. The Montreal Forum, once known as the mecca of hockey, no longer is home to the game's most successful franchise. The last of the NHL's "Original Six" buildings, Maple Leaf Gardens, closed its doors to the NHL on February 13, 1999. One week later, Toronto hosted Montreal at the Air Canada Centre.

The game on the ice also began to change in the late 1990s. In 1998–99, the NHL implemented a two-referee system, with each team to play 20 games with a pair of referees and two linesmen. The two-referee system was increased to 50 games per team in 1999–2000. The 1999–2000 season also saw the introduction of four-on-four overtime in a successful attempt to see more games finish with a winner and a loser. Each team was awarded a point when the score was deadlocked after 60 minutes, with the team that scored in overtime receiving an additional point for the victory.

The 1999–2000 NHL season also marked the beginning of a five-year television deal with ABC and an expanded deal with ESPN and ESPN2 that would see the cable networks air nearly 200 games per year. ABC, which had last covered the NHL in 1993–94, began its new NHL coverage with the 50th NHL All-Star Game from Toronto in February, 2000, and continued with regular weekend broadcasts throughout the rest of the season. Though regular-season ratings remained essentially even with those seen on FOX, the numbers rose during the Stanley Cup finals. In fact, the triple-overtime game-five matchup between New Jersey and Dallas attracted the largest U.S. television ratings for the NHL in 20 years.

The NHL doesn't expect to overtake the NBA, NFL or Major League Baseball anytime soon. But it is the most aggressive in going after new fans. During the Bettman era, the NHL embarked on grassroots marketing efforts to reach boys and girls, aged six to 16, through street hockey and in-line hockey programs.

"We just want to be as good as we can be," Bettman said. "We're the league where the kids take the parents and not the parents taking the kids. And we have a lot of room for growth."

Though the NHL experienced unprecedented growth during the 1990s, there are challenges in the new century—particularly among the league's Canadian fans. The fate of Canada's NHL teams was very much in the news during the 1999–2000 season when Ottawa Senators owner Rod Bryden declared that, in the absence of tax concessions similar to those received by almost every American NHL team, there was no way for the Senators to make a go of it in Ottawa. He would be forced to move the team to the United States.

The five other Canadian teams, all of whom had been trying to negotiate separate concessions from their provincial and municipal governments, joined in Ottawa's federal lobbying effort. On January 18, 2000, the Canadian government announced a subsidy plan, only to revoke it two days later. Calgary fans rallied to purchase 14,000 season tickets in the summer of 2000, in order to ensure the franchise's survival. That same summer, the Montreal Canadiens were put up for sale.

Problems of economy have been most severe in Canada in recent years, but American teams have not been immune. The Pittsburgh Penguins went into bankruptcy during the 1998–99 season. There were rumors the team might move to Portland until former Penguins superstar Mario Lemieux was able to put together an ownership group to keep the team in Pittsburgh. The city of Portland came up again in speculation when owner Richard Burke decided to sell the Phoenix Coyotes during the 1999–2000 season. Steve Ellman's purchase of the team, for $87 million, means the Coyotes will continue to roam the desert, but the deal was not finalized until the last moments. Joining Ellman as a minority owner is Wayne Gretzky, who is expected to take an active role in the team's hockey operations.

With Gretzky and Lemieux part of NHL ownership, it is hoped that a better relationship can be forged between the league and its Players' Association. With all the advancements the game has made in recent years, a less acrimonious relationship when the two sides sit down to renegotiate the Collective Bargaining Agreement in 2004 just might be the biggest advancement of all.

But who will be hockey's biggest stars by the time we reach 2004? Perhaps such players as Joe Thornton and Vincent Lecavalier, first overall selections in the NHL entry drafts of 1997 and 1998 who began to come into their own in 1999–2000. Perhaps Colorado teammates Chris Drury (the Calder Trophy winner) and Milan Hejduk (the top rookie scorer), who burst on the scene with such success in 1998–99 and were both even better in 1999–2000. Brian Boucher posted an NHL-best 1.91 goals-against average in 1999–2000 and was the first rookie netminder to finish below 2.00 since Terry Sawchuk and Al Rollins in 1950–51.

And then there were the Stanley Cup champion New Jersey Devils, who featured a quartet of outstanding rookies in key roles: two-way center John Madden, who led the NHL with six shorthand goals; rock-solid defenseman Colin White; Brian Rafalski, an American who spent four seasons in Europe; and Calder Trophy winner Scott Gomez. Born in Alaska to a Mexican father and a Colombian mother, Gomez is the first Hispanic player in NHL history. Newcomers to watch in 2000–2001 include Daniel and Henrik Sedin, twin brothers from Sweden who were selected second and third, respectively, by the Vancouver Canucks in the 1999 Entry Draft, and Rick DiPietro, who became the first goalie to be taken first overall when the New York Islanders selected him in 2000.

NHL FINAL STANDINGS AND TOP 10 SCORERS

1917–18 TO 1999–2000

** – Stanley Cup winner*

1917-18

Team	GP	W	L	T	GF	GA	PTS
Montreal	22	13	9	0	115	84	26
*Toronto	22	13	9	0	108	109	26
Ottawa	22	9	13	0	102	114	18
**Mtl. Wanderers	6	1	5	0	17	35	2

** Montreal Arena burned down and Wanderers forced to withdraw. Canadiens and Toronto each counted a win for defaulted games.

Leading Scorers

Player	Club	GP	G	A	PTS	PIM
Malone, Joe	Montreal	20	44	4	48	30
Denneny, Cy	Ottawa	20	36	10	46	80
Noble, Reg	Toronto	20	30	10	40	35
Lalonde, Newsy	Montreal	14	23	7	30	51
Denneny, Corbett	Toronto	21	20	9	29	14
Cameron, Harry	Toronto	21	17	10	27	28
Pitre, Didier	Montreal	20	17	6	23	29
Gerard, Eddie	Ottawa	20	13	7	20	26
Darragh, Jack	Ottawa	18	14	5	19	26
Nighbor, Frank	Ottawa	10	11	8	19	6
Meeking, Harry	Toronto	21	10	9	19	28

1918-19

Team	GP	W	L	T	GF	GA	PTS
Ottawa	18	12	6	0	71	53	24
Montreal	18	10	8	0	88	78	20
Toronto	18	5	13	0	64	92	10

Leading Scorers

Player	Club	GP	G	A	PTS	PIM
Lalonde, Newsy	Montreal	17	22	10	32	40
Cleghorn, Odie	Montreal	17	22	6	28	22
Nighbor, Frank	Ottawa	18	19	9	28	27
Denneny, Cy	Ottawa	18	18	4	22	58
Pitre, Didier	Montreal	17	14	5	19	12
Skinner, Alf	Toronto	17	12	4	16	26
Cameron, Harry	Tor., Ott.	14	11	3	14	35
Darragh, Jack	Ottawa	14	11	3	14	33
Randall, Ken	Toronto	15	8	6	14	27
Cleghorn, Sprague	Ottawa	18	7	6	13	27

1919-20

Team	GP	W	L	T	GF	GA	PTS
*Ottawa	24	19	5	0	121	64	38
Montreal	24	13	11	0	129	113	26
Toronto	24	12	12	0	119	106	24
Quebec	24	4	20	0	91	177	8

Leading Scorers

Player	Club	GP	G	A	PTS	PIM
Malone, Joe	Quebec	24	39	10	49	12
Lalonde, Newsy	Montreal	23	37	9	46	34
Nighbor, Frank	Ottawa	23	26	15	41	18
Denneny, Corbett	Toronto	24	24	12	36	20
Darragh, Jack	Ottawa	23	22	14	36	22
Noble, Reg	Toronto	24	24	9	33	52
Arbour, Amos	Montreal	22	21	5	26	13
Wilson, Cully	Toronto	23	20	6	26	86
Pitre, Didier	Montreal	22	14	12	26	6
Broadbent, Punch	Ottawa	21	19	6	25	40

1920-21

Team	GP	W	L	T	GF	GA	PTS
Toronto	24	15	9	0	105	100	30
*Ottawa	24	14	10	0	97	75	28
Montreal	24	13	11	0	112	99	26
Hamilton	24	6	18	0	92	132	12

Leading Scorers

Player	Club	GP	G	A	PTS	PIM
Lalonde, Newsy	Montreal	24	33	10	43	36
Dye, Babe	Ham., Tor.	24	35	5	40	32
Denneny, Cy	Ottawa	24	34	5	39	10
Malone, Joe	Hamilton	20	28	9	37	6
Nighbor, Frank	Ottawa	24	19	10	29	10
Noble, Reg	Toronto	24	19	8	27	54
Cameron, Harry	Toronto	24	18	9	27	35
Prodgers, Goldie	Hamilton	24	18	9	27	8
Denneny, Corbett	Toronto	20	19	7	26	29
Darragh, Jack	Ottawa	24	11	15	26	20

1921-22

Team	GP	W	L	T	GF	GA	PTS
Ottawa	24	14	8	2	106	84	30
*Toronto	24	13	10	1	98	97	27
Montreal	24	12	11	1	88	94	25
Hamilton	24	7	17	0	88	105	14

Leading Scorers

Player	Club	GP	G	A	PTS	PIM
Broadbent, Punch	Ottawa	24	32	14	46	28
Denneny, Cy	Ottawa	22	27	12	39	20
Dye, Babe	Toronto	24	31	7	38	39
Cameron, Harry	Toronto	24	18	17	35	22
Malone, Joe	Hamilton	24	24	7	31	4
Denneny, Corbett	Toronto	24	19	9	28	28
Noble, Reg	Toronto	24	17	11	28	19
Cleghorn, Sprague	Montreal	24	17	9	26	80
Cleghorn, Odie	Montreal	23	21	3	24	26
Reise, Leo	Hamilton	24	9	14	23	11

1922-23

Team	GP	W	L	T	GF	GA	PTS
*Ottawa	24	14	9	1	77	54	29
Montreal	24	13	9	2	73	61	28
Toronto	24	13	10	1	82	88	27
Hamilton	24	6	18	0	81	110	12

Leading Scorers

Player	Club	GP	G	A	PTS	PIM
Dye, Babe	Toronto	22	26	11	37	19
Denneny, Cy	Ottawa	24	21	10	31	20
Adams, Jack	Toronto	23	19	9	28	42
Boucher, Billy	Montreal	24	23	4	27	52
Cleghorn, Odie	Montreal	24	19	7	26	14
Roach, Mickey	Hamilton	23	17	8	25	8
Boucher, George	Ottawa	23	15	9	24	44
Joliat, Aurel	Montreal	24	13	9	22	31
Noble, Reg	Toronto	24	12	10	22	41
Wilson, Cully	Hamilton	23	16	3	19	46

1923-24

Team	GP	W	L	T	GF	GA	PTS
Ottawa	24	16	8	0	74	54	32
*Montreal	24	13	11	0	59	48	26
Toronto	24	10	14	0	59	85	20
Hamilton	24	9	15	0	63	68	18

Leading Scorers

Player	Club	GP	G	A	PTS	PIM
Denneny, Cy	Ottawa	22	22	2	24	10
Boucher, George	Ottawa	21	13	10	23	38
Boucher, Billy	Montreal	23	16	6	22	48
Burch, Billy	Hamilton	24	16	6	22	6
Joliat, Aurel	Montreal	24	15	5	20	27
Dye, Babe	Toronto	19	16	3	19	23
Adams, Jack	Toronto	22	14	4	18	51
Noble, Reg	Toronto	23	12	5	17	79
Morenz, Howie	Montreal	24	13	3	16	20
Clancy, King	Ottawa	24	8	8	16	26

1924-25

Team	GP	W	L	T	GF	GA	PTS
Hamilton	30	19	10	1	90	60	39
Toronto	30	19	11	0	90	84	38
Montreal	30	17	11	2	93	56	36
Ottawa	30	17	12	1	83	66	35
Mtl. Maroons	30	9	19	2	45	65	20
Boston	30	6	24	0	49	119	12

Leading Scorers

Player	Club	GP	G	A	PTS	PIM
Dye, Babe	Toronto	29	38	8	46	41
Denneny, Cy	Ottawa	29	27	15	42	16
Joliat, Aurel	Montreal	24	30	11	41	85
Morenz, Howie	Montreal	30	28	11	39	46
Green, Red	Hamilton	30	19	15	34	81
Adams, Jack	Toronto	27	21	10	31	67
Boucher, Billy	Montreal	30	17	13	30	92
Burch, Billy	Hamilton	27	20	7	27	10
Herbert, Jimmy	Boston	30	17	7	24	55
Smith, Hooley	Ottawa	30	10	13	23	81

1925-26

Team	GP	W	L	T	GF	GA	PTS
Ottawa	36	24	8	4	77	42	52
*Mtl. Maroons	36	20	11	5	91	73	45
Pittsburgh	36	19	16	1	82	70	39
Boston	36	17	15	4	92	85	38
NY Americans	36	12	20	4	68	89	28
Toronto	36	12	21	3	92	114	27
Montreal	36	11	24	1	79	108	23

Leading Scorers

Player	Club	GP	G	A	PTS	PIM
Stewart, Nels	Mtl. Maroons	36	34	8	42	119
Denneny, Cy	Ottawa	36	24	12	36	18
Cooper, Carson	Boston	36	28	3	31	10
Herbert, Jimmy	Boston	36	26	5	31	47
Morenz, Howie	Montreal	31	23	3	26	39
Adams, Jack	Toronto	36	21	5	26	52
Joliat, Aurel	Montreal	35	17	9	26	52
Burch, Billy	NY Americans	36	22	3	25	33
Smith, Hooley	Ottawa	28	16	9	25	53
Nighbor, Frank	Ottawa	35	12	13	25	40

1926-27

CANADIAN DIVISION

Team	GP	W	L	T	GF	GA	PTS
*Ottawa	44	30	10	4	86	69	64
Montreal	44	28	14	2	99	67	58
Mtl. Maroons	44	20	20	4	71	68	44
NY Americans	44	17	25	2	82	91	36
Toronto	44	15	24	5	79	94	35

AMERICAN DIVISION

Team	GP	W	L	T	GF	GA	PTS
New York	44	25	13	6	95	72	56
Boston	44	21	20	3	97	89	45
Chicago	44	19	22	3	115	116	41
Pittsburgh	44	15	26	3	79	108	33
Detroit	44	12	28	4	76	105	28

Leading Scorers

Player	Club	GP	G	A	PTS	PIM
Cook, Bill	New York	44	33	4	37	58
Irvin, Dick	Chicago	43	18	18	36	34
Morenz, Howie	Montreal	44	25	7	32	49
Fredrickson, Frank	Det., Bos.	41	18	13	31	46
Dye, Babe	Chicago	41	25	5	30	14
Bailey, Ace	Toronto	42	15	13	28	82
Boucher, Frank	New York	44	13	15	28	17
Burch, Billy	NY Americans	43	19	8	27	40
Oliver, Harry	Boston	42	18	6	24	17
Keats, Gordon	Bos., Det.	42	16	8	24	52

1927-28

CANADIAN DIVISION

Team	GP	W	L	T	GF	GA	PTS
Montreal	44	26	11	7	116	48	59
Mtl. Maroons	44	24	14	6	96	77	54
Ottawa	44	20	14	10	78	57	50
Toronto	44	18	18	8	89	88	44
NY Americans	44	11	27	6	63	128	28

AMERICAN DIVISION

Team	GP	W	L	T	GF	GA	PTS
Boston	44	20	13	11	77	70	51
*New York	44	19	16	9	94	79	47
Pittsburgh	44	19	17	8	67	76	46
Detroit	44	19	19	6	88	79	44
Chicago	44	7	34	3	68	134	17

Leading Scorers

Player	Club	GP	G	A	PTS	PIM
Morenz, Howie	Montreal	43	33	18	51	66
Joliat, Aurel	Montreal	44	28	11	39	105
Boucher, Frank	New York	44	23	12	35	15
Hay, George	Detroit	42	22	13	35	20
Stewart, Nels	Mtl. Maroons	41	27	7	34	104
Gagne, Art	Montreal	44	20	10	30	75
Cook, Bun	New York	44	14	14	28	45
Carson, Bill	Toronto	32	20	6	26	36
Finnigan, Frank	Ottawa	38	20	5	25	34
Cook, Bill	New York	43	18	6	24	42
Keats, Gordon	Det., Chi.	38	14	10	24	60

1928-29

CANADIAN DIVISION

Team	GP	W	L	T	GF	GA	PTS
Montreal	44	22	7	15	71	43	59
NY Americans	44	19	13	12	53	53	50
Toronto	44	21	18	5	85	69	47
Ottawa	44	14	17	13	54	67	41
Mtl. Maroons	44	15	20	9	67	65	39

AMERICAN DIVISION

Team	GP	W	L	T	GF	GA	PTS
*Boston	44	26	13	5	89	52	57
New York	44	21	13	10	72	65	52
Detroit	44	19	16	9	72	63	47
Pittsburgh	44	9	27	8	46	80	26
Chicago	44	7	29	8	33	85	22

Leading Scorers

Player	Club	GP	G	A	PTS	PIM
Bailey, Ace	Toronto	44	22	10	32	78
Stewart, Nels	Mtl. Maroons	44	21	8	29	74
Cooper, Carson	Detroit	43	18	9	27	14
Morenz, Howie	Montreal	42	17	10	27	47
Blair, Andy	Toronto	44	12	15	27	41
Boucher, Frank	New York	44	10	16	26	8
Oliver, Harry	Boston	43	17	6	23	24
Cook, Bill	New York	43	15	8	23	41
Ward, Jimmy	Mtl. Maroons	43	14	8	22	46

Seven players tied with 19 points

1929-30

CANADIAN DIVISION

Team	GP	W	L	T	GF	GA	PTS
Mtl. Maroons	44	23	16	5	141	114	51
*Montreal	44	21	14	9	142	114	51
Ottawa	44	21	15	8	138	118	50
Toronto	44	17	21	6	116	124	40
NY Americans	44	14	25	5	113	161	33

AMERICAN DIVISION

Team	GP	W	L	T	GF	GA	PTS
Boston	44	38	5	1	179	98	77
Chicago	44	21	18	5	117	111	47
New York	44	17	17	10	136	143	44
Detroit	44	14	24	6	117	133	34
Pittsburgh	44	5	36	3	102	185	13

Leading Scorers

Player	Club	GP	G	A	PTS	PIM
Weiland, Cooney	Boston	44	43	30	73	27
Boucher, Frank	New York	42	26	36	62	16
Clapper, Dit	Boston	44	41	20	61	48
Cook, Bill	New York	44	29	30	59	56
Kilrea, Hec	Ottawa	44	36	22	58	72
Stewart, Nels	Mtl. Maroons	44	39	16	55	81
Morenz, Howie	Montreal	44	40	10	50	72
Himes, Normie	NY Americans	44	28	22	50	15
Lamb, Joe	Ottawa	44	29	20	49	119
Gainor, Norm	Boston	42	18	31	49	39

1930-31

CANADIAN DIVISION

Team	GP	W	L	T	GF	GA	PTS
*Montreal	44	26	10	8	129	89	60
Toronto	44	22	13	9	118	99	53
Mtl. Maroons	44	20	18	6	105	106	46
NY Americans	44	18	16	10	76	74	46
Ottawa	44	10	30	4	91	142	24

AMERICAN DIVISION

Team	GP	W	L	T	GF	GA	PTS
Boston	44	28	10	6	143	90	62
Chicago	44	24	17	3	108	78	51
New York	44	19	16	9	106	87	47
Detroit	44	16	21	7	102	105	39
Philadelphia	44	4	36	4	76	184	12

Leading Scorers

Player	Club	GP	G	A	PTS	PIM
Morenz, Howie	Montreal	39	28	23	51	49
Goodfellow, Ebbie	Detroit	44	25	23	48	32
Conacher, Charlie	Toronto	37	31	12	43	78
Cook, Bill	New York	43	30	12	42	39
Bailey, Ace	Toronto	40	23	19	42	46
Primeau, Joe	Toronto	38	9	32	41	18
Stewart, Nels	Mtl. Maroons	42	25	14	39	75
Boucher, Frank	New York	44	12	27	39	20
Weiland, Cooney	Boston	44	25	13	38	14
Cook, Bun	New York	44	18	17	35	72
Joliat, Aurel	Montreal	43	13	22	35	73

1931-32

CANADIAN DIVISION

Team	GP	W	L	T	GF	GA	PTS
Montreal	48	25	16	7	128	111	57
*Toronto	48	23	18	7	155	127	53
Mtl. Maroons	48	19	22	7	142	139	45
NY Americans	48	16	24	8	95	142	40

AMERICAN DIVISION

Team	GP	W	L	T	GF	GA	PTS
New York	48	23	17	8	134	112	54
Chicago	48	18	19	11	86	101	47
Detroit	48	18	20	10	95	108	46
Boston	48	15	21	12	122	117	42

Leading Scorers

Player	Club	GP	G	A	PTS	PIM
Jackson, Harvey	Toronto	48	28	25	53	63
Primeau, Joe	Toronto	46	13	37	50	25
Morenz, Howie	Montreal	48	24	25	49	46
Conacher, Charlie	Toronto	44	34	14	48	66
Cook, Bill	New York	48	34	14	48	33
Trottier, Dave	Mtl. Maroons	48	26	18	44	94
Smith, Reg	Mtl. Maroons	43	11	33	44	49
Siebert, Babe	Mtl. Maroons	48	21	18	39	64
Clapper, Dit	Boston	48	17	22	39	21
Joliat, Aurel	Montreal	48	15	24	39	46

1932-33

CANADIAN DIVISION

Team	GP	W	L	T	GF	GA	PTS
Toronto	48	24	18	6	119	111	54
Mtl. Maroons	48	22	20	6	135	119	50
Montreal	48	18	25	5	92	115	41
NY Americans	48	15	22	11	91	118	41
Ottawa	48	11	27	10	88	131	32

AMERICAN DIVISION

Team	GP	W	L	T	GF	GA	PTS
Boston	48	25	15	8	124	88	58
Detroit	48	25	15	8	111	93	58
*New York	48	23	17	8	135	107	54
Chicago	48	16	20	12	88	101	44

Leading Scorers

Player	Club	GP	G	A	PTS	PIM
Cook, Bill	New York	48	28	22	50	51
Jackson, Harvey	Toronto	48	27	17	44	43
Northcott, Baldy	Mtl. Maroons	48	22	21	43	30
Smith, Hooley	Mtl. Maroons	48	20	21	41	66
Haynes, Paul	Mtl. Maroons	48	16	25	41	18
Joliat, Aurel	Montreal	48	18	21	39	53
Barry, Marty	Boston	48	24	13	37	40
Cook, Bun	New York	48	22	15	37	35
Stewart, Nels	Boston	47	18	18	36	62
Morenz, Howie	Montreal	46	14	21	35	32
Gagnon, Johnny	Montreal	48	12	23	35	64
Shore, Eddie	Boston	48	8	27	35	102
Boucher, Frank	New York	47	7	28	35	4

1933-34

CANADIAN DIVISION

Team	GP	W	L	T	GF	GA	PTS
Toronto	48	26	13	9	174	119	61
Montreal	48	22	20	6	99	101	50
Mtl. Maroons	48	19	18	11	117	122	49
NY Americans	48	15	23	10	104	132	40
Ottawa	48	13	29	6	115	143	32

AMERICAN DIVISION

Team	GP	W	L	T	GF	GA	PTS
Detroit	48	24	14	10	113	98	58
*Chicago	48	20	17	11	88	83	51
New York	48	21	19	8	120	113	50
Boston	48	18	25	5	111	130	41

Leading Scorers

Player	Club	GP	G	A	PTS	PIM
Conacher, Charlie	Toronto	42	32	20	52	38
Primeau, Joe	Toronto	45	14	32	46	8
Boucher, Frank	New York	48	14	30	44	4
Barry, Marty	Boston	48	27	12	39	12
Dillon, Cecil	New York	48	13	26	39	10
Stewart, Nels	Boston	48	21	17	38	68
Jackson, Harvey	Toronto	38	20	18	38	38
Joliat, Aurel	Montreal	48	22	15	37	27
Smith, Hooley	Mtl. Maroons	47	18	19	37	58
Thompson, Paul	Chicago	48	20	16	36	17

1934-35

CANADIAN DIVISION

Team	GP	W	L	T	GF	GA	PTS
Toronto	48	30	14	4	157	111	64
*Mtl. Maroons	48	24	19	5	123	92	53
Montreal	48	19	23	6	110	145	44
NY Americans	48	12	27	9	100	142	33
St. Louis	48	11	31	6	86	144	28

AMERICAN DIVISION

Team	GP	W	L	T	GF	GA	PTS
Boston	48	26	16	6	129	112	58
Chicago	48	26	17	5	118	88	57
New York	48	22	20	6	137	139	50
Detroit	48	19	22	7	127	114	45

Leading Scorers

Player	Club	GP	G	A	PTS	PIM
Conacher, Charlie	Toronto	47	36	21	57	24
Howe, Syd	St.L., Det.	50	22	25	47	34
Aurie, Larry	Detroit	48	17	29	46	24
Boucher, Frank	New York	48	13	32	45	2
Jackson, Harvey	Toronto	42	22	22	44	27
Lewis, Herb	Detroit	47	16	27	43	26
Chapman, Art	NY Americans	47	9	34	43	4
Barry, Marty	Boston	48	20	20	40	33
Schriner, Sweeney	NY Americans	48	18	22	40	6
Stewart, Nels	Boston	47	21	18	39	45
Thompson, Paul	Chicago	48	16	23	39	20

1935-36

CANADIAN DIVISION

Team	GP	W	L	T	GF	GA	PTS
Mtl. Maroons	48	22	16	10	114	106	54
Toronto	48	23	19	6	126	106	52
NY Americans	48	16	25	7	109	122	39
Montreal	48	11	26	11	82	123	33

AMERICAN DIVISION

Team	GP	W	L	T	GF	GA	PTS
*Detroit	48	24	16	8	124	103	56
Boston	48	22	20	6	92	83	50
Chicago	48	21	19	8	93	92	50
New York	48	19	17	12	91	96	50

Leading Scorers

Player	Club	GP	G	A	PTS	PIM
Schriner, Sweeney	NY Americans	48	19	26	45	8
Barry, Marty	Detroit	48	21	19	40	16
Thompson, Paul	Chicago	45	17	23	40	19
Thoms, Bill	Toronto	48	23	15	38	29
Conacher, Charlie	Toronto	44	23	15	38	74
Smith, Hooley	Mtl. Maroons	47	19	19	38	75
Romnes, Doc	Chicago	48	13	25	38	6
Chapman, Art	NY Americans	47	10	28	38	14
Lewis, Herb	Detroit	45	14	23	37	25
Northcott, Baldy	Mtl. Maroons	48	15	21	36	41

1936-37

CANADIAN DIVISION

Team	GP	W	L	T	GF	GA	PTS
Montreal	48	24	18	6	115	111	54
Mtl. Maroons	48	22	17	9	126	110	53
Toronto	48	22	21	5	119	115	49
NY Americans	48	15	29	4	122	161	34

AMERICAN DIVISION

Team	GP	W	L	T	GF	GA	PTS
*Detroit	48	25	14	9	128	102	59
Boston	48	23	18	7	120	110	53
New York	48	19	20	9	117	106	47
Chicago	48	14	27	7	99	131	35

Leading Scorers

Player	Club	GP	G	A	PTS	PIM
Schriner, Sweeney	NY Americans	48	21	25	46	17
Apps, Syl	Toronto	48	16	29	45	10
Barry, Marty	Detroit	48	17	27	44	6
Aurie, Larry	Detroit	45	23	20	43	20
Jackson, Harvey	Toronto	46	21	19	40	12
Gagnon, Johnny	Montreal	48	20	16	36	38
Gracie, Bob	Mtl. Maroons	47	11	25	36	18
Stewart, Nels	Bos., NYA	43	23	12	35	37
Thompson, Paul	Chicago	47	17	18	35	28
Cowley, Bill	Boston	46	13	22	35	4

1937-38

CANADIAN DIVISION

Team	GP	W	L	T	GF	GA	PTS
Toronto	48	24	15	9	151	127	57
NY Americans	48	19	18	11	110	111	49
Montreal	48	18	17	13	123	128	49
Mtl. Maroons	48	12	30	6	101	149	30
AMERICAN DIVISION							
Boston	48	30	11	7	142	89	67
New York	48	27	15	6	149	96	60
*Chicago	48	14	25	9	97	139	37
Detroit	48	12	25	11	99	133	35

Leading Scorers

Player	Club	GP	G	A	PTS	PIM
Drillon, Gord	Toronto	48	26	26	52	4
Apps, Syl	Toronto	47	21	29	50	9
Thompson, Paul	Chicago	48	22	22	44	14
Mantha, Georges	Montreal	47	23	19	42	12
Dillon, Cecil	New York	48	21	18	39	6
Cowley, Bill	Boston	48	17	22	39	8
Schriner, Sweeney	NY Americans	49	21	17	38	22
Thoms, Bill	Toronto	48	14	24	38	14
Smith, Clint	New York	48	14	23	37	0
Stewart, Nels	NY Americans	48	19	17	36	29
Colville, Neil	New York	45	17	19	36	11

1938-39

Team	GP	W	L	T	GF	GA	PTS
*Boston	48	36	10	2	156	76	74
New York	48	26	16	6	149	105	58
Toronto	48	19	20	9	114	107	47
NY Americans	48	17	21	10	119	157	44
Detroit	48	18	24	6	107	128	42
Montreal	48	15	24	9	115	146	39
Chicago	48	12	28	8	91	132	32

Leading Scorers

Player	Club	GP	G	A	PTS	PIM
Blake, Toe	Montreal	48	24	23	47	10
Schriner, Sweeney	NY Americans	48	13	31	44	20
Cowley, Bill	Boston	34	8	34	42	2
Smith, Clint	New York	48	21	20	41	2
Barry, Marty	Detroit	48	13	28	41	4
Apps, Syl	Toronto	44	15	25	40	4
Anderson, Tom	NY Americans	48	13	27	40	14
Gottselig, Johnny	Chicago	48	16	23	39	15
Haynes, Paul	Montreal	47	5	33	38	27
Conacher, Roy	Boston	47	26	11	37	12
Carr, Lorne	NY Americans	46	19	18	37	16
Colville, Neil	New York	48	18	19	37	12
Watson, Phil	New York	48	15	22	37	42

1939-40

Team	GP	W	L	T	GF	GA	PTS
Boston	48	31	12	5	170	98	67
*New York	48	27	11	10	136	77	64
Toronto	48	25	17	6	134	110	56
Chicago	48	23	19	6	112	120	52
Detroit	48	16	26	6	90	126	38
NY Americans	48	15	29	4	106	140	34
Montreal	48	10	33	5	90	168	25

Leading Scorers

Player	Club	GP	G	A	PTS	PIM
Schmidt, Milt	Boston	48	22	30	52	37
Dumart, Woody	Boston	48	22	21	43	16
Bauer, Bobby	Boston	48	17	26	43	2
Drillon, Gord	Toronto	43	21	19	40	13
Cowley, Bill	Boston	48	13	27	40	24
Hextall, Bryan	New York	48	24	15	39	52
Colville, Neil	New York	48	19	19	38	22
Howe, Syd	Detroit	46	14	23	37	17
Blake, Toe	Montreal	48	17	19	36	48
Armstrong, M.	NY Americans	48	16	20	36	12

1940-41

Team	GP	W	L	T	GF	GA	PTS
*Boston	48	27	8	13	168	102	67
Toronto	48	28	14	6	145	99	62
Detroit	48	21	16	11	112	102	53
New York	48	21	19	8	143	125	50
Chicago	48	16	25	7	112	139	39
Montreal	48	16	26	6	121	147	38
NY Americans	48	8	29	11	99	186	27

Leading Scorers

Player	Club	GP	G	A	PTS	PIM
Cowley, Bill	Boston	46	17	45	62	16
Hextall, Bryan	New York	48	26	18	44	16
Drillon, Gord	Toronto	42	23	21	44	2
Apps, Syl	Toronto	41	20	24	44	6
Patrick, Lynn	New York	48	20	24	44	12
Howe, Syd	Detroit	48	20	24	44	8
Colville, Neil	New York	48	14	28	42	28
Wiseman, Eddie	Boston	48	16	24	40	10
Bauer, Bobby	Boston	48	17	22	39	2
Schriner, Sweeney	Toronto	48	24	14	38	6
Conacher, Roy	Boston	40	24	14	38	7
Schmidt, Milt	Boston	44	13	25	38	23

1941-42

Team	GP	W	L	T	GF	GA	PTS
New York	48	29	17	2	177	143	60
*Toronto	48	27	18	3	158	136	57
Boston	48	25	17	6	160	118	56
Chicago	48	22	23	3	145	155	47
Detroit	48	19	25	4	140	147	42
Montreal	48	18	27	3	134	173	39
Brooklyn	48	16	29	3	133	175	35

Leading Scorers

Player	Club	GP	G	A	PTS	PIM
Hextall, Bryan	New York	48	24	32	56	30
Patrick, Lynn	New York	47	32	22	54	18
Grosso, Don	Detroit	48	23	30	53	13
Watson, Phil	New York	48	15	37	52	48
Abel, Sid	Detroit	48	18	31	49	45
Blake, Toe	Montreal	47	17	28	45	19
Thoms, Bill	Chicago	47	15	30	45	8
Drillon, Gord	Toronto	48	23	18	41	6
Apps, Syl	Toronto	38	18	23	41	0
Anderson, Tom	Brooklyn	48	12	29	41	54

1942-43

Team	GP	W	L	T	GF	GA	PTS
*Detroit	50	25	14	11	169	124	61
Boston	50	24	17	9	195	176	57
Toronto	50	22	19	9	198	159	53
Montreal	50	19	19	12	181	191	50
Chicago	50	17	18	15	179	180	49
New York	50	11	31	8	161	253	30

Leading Scorers

Player	Club	GP	G	A	PTS	PIM
Bentley, Doug	Chicago	50	33	40	73	18
Cowley, Bill	Boston	48	27	45	72	10
Bentley, Max	Chicago	47	26	44	70	2
Patrick, Lynn	New York	50	22	39	61	28
Carr, Lorne	Toronto	50	27	33	60	15
Taylor, Billy	Toronto	50	18	42	60	2
Hextall, Bryan	New York	50	27	32	59	28
Blake, Toe	Montreal	48	23	36	59	28
Lach, Elmer	Montreal	45	18	40	58	14
O'Connor, Buddy	Montreal	50	15	43	58	2

1943-44

Team	GP	W	L	T	GF	GA	PTS
*Montreal	50	38	5	7	234	109	83
Detroit	50	26	18	6	214	177	58
Toronto	50	23	23	4	214	174	50
Chicago	50	22	23	5	178	187	49
Boston	50	19	26	5	223	268	43
New York	50	6	39	5	162	310	17

Leading Scorers

Player	Club	GP	G	A	PTS	PIM
Cain, Herb	Boston	48	36	46	82	4
Bentley, Doug	Chicago	50	38	39	77	22
Carr, Lorne	Toronto	50	36	38	74	9
Liscombe, Carl	Detroit	50	36	37	73	17
Lach, Elmer	Montreal	48	24	48	72	23
Smith, Clint	Chicago	50	23	49	72	4
Cowley, Bill	Boston	36	30	41	71	12
Mosienko, Bill	Chicago	50	32	38	70	10
Jackson, Art	Boston	49	28	41	69	8
Bodnar, Gus	Toronto	50	22	40	62	18

1944-45

Team	GP	W	L	T	GF	GA	PTS
Montreal	50	38	8	4	228	121	80
Detroit	50	31	14	5	218	161	67
*Toronto	50	24	22	4	183	161	52
Boston	50	16	30	4	179	219	36
Chicago	50	13	30	7	141	194	33
New York	50	11	29	10	154	247	32

Leading Scorers

Player	Club	GP	G	A	PTS	PIM
Lach, Elmer	Montreal	50	26	54	80	37
Richard, Maurice	Montreal	50	50	23	73	36
Blake, Toe	Montreal	49	29	38	67	15
Cowley, Bill	Boston	49	25	40	65	2
Kennedy, Ted	Toronto	49	29	25	54	14
Mosienko, Bill	Chicago	50	28	26	54	0
Carveth, Joe	Detroit	50	26	28	54	6
DeMarco, Ab	New York	50	24	30	54	10
Smith, Clint	Chicago	50	23	31	54	0
Howe, Syd	Detroit	46	17	36	53	6

1945-46

Team	GP	W	L	T	GF	GA	PTS
*Montreal	50	28	17	5	172	134	61
Boston	50	24	18	8	167	156	56
Chicago	50	23	20	7	200	178	53
Detroit	50	20	20	10	146	159	50
Toronto	50	19	24	7	174	185	45
New York	50	13	28	9	144	191	35

Leading Scorers

Player	Club	GP	G	A	PTS	PIM
Bentley, Max	Chicago	47	31	30	61	6
Stewart, Gaye	Toronto	50	37	15	52	8
Blake, Toe	Montreal	50	29	21	50	2
Smith, Clint	Chicago	50	26	24	50	2
Richard, Maurice	Montreal	50	27	21	48	50
Mosienko, Bill	Chicago	40	18	30	48	12
DeMarco, Ab	New York	50	20	27	47	20
Lach, Elmer	Montreal	50	13	34	47	34
Kaleta, Alex	Chicago	49	19	27	46	17
Taylor, Billy	Toronto	48	23	18	41	14
Horeck, Pete	Chicago	50	20	21	41	34

1946-47

Team	GP	W	L	T	GF	GA	PTS
Montreal	60	34	16	10	189	138	78
*Toronto	60	31	19	10	209	172	72
Boston	60	26	23	11	190	175	63
Detroit	60	22	27	11	190	193	55
New York	60	22	32	6	167	186	50
Chicago	60	19	37	4	193	274	42

Leading Scorers

Player	Club	GP	G	A	PTS	PIM
Bentley, Max	Chicago	60	29	43	72	12
Richard, Maurice	Montreal	60	45	26	71	69
Taylor, Billy	Detroit	60	17	46	63	35
Schmidt, Milt	Boston	59	27	35	62	40
Kennedy, Ted	Toronto	60	28	32	60	27
Bentley, Doug	Chicago	52	21	34	55	18
Bauer, Bobby	Boston	58	30	24	54	4
Conacher, Roy	Detroit	60	30	24	54	6
Mosienko, Bill	Chicago	59	25	27	52	2
Dumart, Woody	Boston	60	24	28	52	12

1947-48

Team	GP	W	L	T	GF	GA	PTS
*Toronto	60	32	15	13	182	143	77
Detroit	60	30	18	12	187	148	72
Boston	60	23	24	13	167	168	59
New York	60	21	26	13	176	201	55
Montreal	60	20	29	11	147	169	51
Chicago	60	20	34	6	195	225	46

Leading Scorers

Player	Club	GP	G	A	PTS	PIM
Lach, Elmer	Montreal	60	30	31	61	72
O'Connor, Buddy	New York	60	24	36	60	8
Bentley, Doug	Chicago	60	20	37	57	16
Stewart, Gaye	Tor., Chi.	61	27	29	56	83
Bentley, Max	Chi., Tor.	59	26	28	54	14
Poile, Bud	Tor., Chi.	58	25	29	54	17
Richard, Maurice	Montreal	53	28	25	53	89
Apps, Syl	Toronto	55	26	27	53	12
Lindsay, Ted	Detroit	60	33	19	52	95
Conacher, Roy	Chicago	52	22	27	49	4

1948-49

Team	GP	W	L	T	GF	GA	PTS
Detroit	60	34	19	7	195	145	75
Boston	60	29	23	8	178	163	66
Montreal	60	28	23	9	152	126	65
*Toronto	60	22	25	13	147	161	57
Chicago	60	21	31	8	173	211	50
New York	60	18	31	11	133	172	47

Leading Scorers

Player	Club	GP	G	A	PTS	PIM
Conacher, Roy	Chicago	60	26	42	68	8
Bentley, Doug	Chicago	58	23	43	66	38
Abel, Sid	Detroit	60	28	26	54	49
Lindsay, Ted	Detroit	50	26	28	54	97
Conacher, Jim	Det., Chi.	59	26	23	49	43
Ronty, Paul	Boston	60	20	29	49	11
Watson, Harry	Toronto	60	26	19	45	0
Reay, Billy	Montreal	60	22	23	45	33
Bodnar, Gus	Chicago	59	19	26	45	14
Peirson, Johnny	Boston	59	22	21	43	45

1949-50

Team	GP	W	L	T	GF	GA	PTS
*Detroit	70	37	19	14	229	164	88
Montreal	70	29	22	19	172	150	77
Toronto	70	31	27	12	176	173	74
New York	70	28	31	11	170	189	67
Boston	70	22	32	16	198	228	60
Chicago	70	22	38	10	203	244	54

Leading Scorers

Player	Club	GP	G	A	PTS	PIM
Lindsay, Ted	Detroit	69	23	55	78	141
Abel, Sid	Detroit	69	34	35	69	46
Howe, Gordie	Detroit	70	35	33	68	69
Richard, Maurice	Montreal	70	43	22	65	114
Ronty, Paul	Boston	70	23	36	59	8
Conacher, Roy	Chicago	70	25	31	56	16
Bentley, Doug	Chicago	64	20	33	53	28
Peirson, Johnny	Boston	57	27	25	52	49
Prystai, Metro	Chicago	65	29	22	51	31
Guidolin, Bep	Chicago	70	17	34	51	42

1950-51

Team	GP	W	L	T	GF	GA	PTS
Detroit	70	44	13	13	236	139	101
*Toronto	70	41	16	13	212	138	95
Montreal	70	25	30	15	173	184	65
Boston	70	22	30	18	178	197	62
New York	70	20	29	21	169	201	61
Chicago	70	13	47	10	171	280	36

Leading Scorers

Player	Club	GP	G	A	PTS	PIM
Howe, Gordie	Detroit	70	43	43	86	74
Richard, Maurice	Montreal	65	42	24	66	97
Bentley, Max	Toronto	67	21	41	62	34
Abel, Sid	Detroit	69	23	38	61	30
Schmidt, Milt	Boston	62	22	39	61	33
Kennedy, Ted	Toronto	63	18	43	61	32
Lindsay, Ted	Detroit	67	24	35	59	110
Sloan, Tod	Toronto	70	31	25	56	105
Kelly, Red	Detroit	70	17	37	54	24
Smith, Sid	Toronto	70	30	21	51	10
Gardner, Cal	Toronto	66	23	28	51	42

1951-52

Team	GP	W	L	T	GF	GA	PTS
*Detroit	70	44	14	12	215	133	100
Montreal	70	34	26	10	195	164	78
Toronto	70	29	25	16	168	157	74
Boston	70	25	29	16	162	176	66
New York	70	23	34	13	192	219	59
Chicago	70	17	44	9	158	241	43

Leading Scorers

Player	Club	GP	G	A	PTS	PIM
Howe, Gordie	Detroit	70	47	39	86	78
Lindsay, Ted	Detroit	70	30	39	69	123
Lach, Elmer	Montreal	70	15	50	65	36
Raleigh, Don	New York	70	19	42	61	14
Smith, Sid	Toronto	70	27	30	57	6
Geoffrion, Bernie	Montreal	67	30	24	54	66
Mosienko, Bill	Chicago	70	31	22	53	10
Abel, Sid	Detroit	62	17	36	53	32
Kennedy, Ted	Toronto	70	19	33	52	33
Schmidt, Milt	Boston	69	21	29	50	57
Peirson, Johnny	Boston	68	20	30	50	30

1952-53

Team	GP	W	L	T	GF	GA	PTS
Detroit	70	36	16	18	222	133	90
*Montreal	70	28	23	19	155	148	75
Boston	70	28	29	13	152	172	69
Chicago	70	27	28	15	169	175	69
Toronto	70	27	30	13	156	167	67
New York	70	17	37	16	152	211	50

Leading Scorers

Player	Club	GP	G	A	PTS	PIM
Howe, Gordie	Detroit	70	49	46	95	57
Lindsay, Ted	Detroit	70	32	39	71	111
Richard, Maurice	Montreal	70	28	33	61	112
Hergesheimer, W.	New York	70	30	29	59	10
Delvecchio, Alex	Detroit	70	16	43	59	28
Ronty, Paul	New York	70	16	38	54	20
Prystai, Metro	Detroit	70	16	34	50	12
Kelly, Red	Detroit	70	19	27	46	8
Olmstead, Bert	Montreal	69	17	28	45	83
Mackell, Fleming	Boston	65	27	17	44	63
McFadden, Jim	Chicago	70	23	21	44	29

1953-54

Team	GP	W	L	T	GF	GA	PTS
*Detroit	70	37	19	14	191	132	88
Montreal	70	35	24	11	195	141	81
Toronto	70	32	24	14	152	131	78
Boston	70	32	28	10	177	181	74
New York	70	29	31	10	161	182	68
Chicago	70	12	51	7	133	242	31

Leading Scorers

Player	Club	GP	G	A	PTS	PIM
Howe, Gordie	Detroit	70	33	48	81	109
Richard, Maurice	Montreal	70	37	30	67	112
Lindsay, Ted	Detroit	70	26	36	62	110
Geoffrion, Bernie	Montreal	54	29	25	54	87
Olmstead, Bert	Montreal	70	15	37	52	85
Kelly, Red	Detroit	62	16	33	49	18
Reibel, Earl	Detroit	69	15	33	48	18
Sandford, Ed	Boston	70	16	31	47	42
Mackell, Fleming	Boston	67	15	32	47	60
Mosdell, Ken	Montreal	67	22	24	46	64
Ronty, Paul	New York	70	13	33	46	18

1954-55

Team	GP	W	L	T	GF	GA	PTS
*Detroit	70	42	17	11	204	134	95
Montreal	70	41	18	11	228	157	93
Toronto	70	24	24	22	147	135	70
Boston	70	23	26	21	169	188	67
New York	70	17	35	18	150	210	52
Chicago	70	13	40	17	161	235	43

Leading Scorers

Player	Club	GP	G	A	PTS	PIM
Geoffrion, Bernie	Montreal	70	38	37	75	57
Richard, Maurice	Montreal	67	38	36	74	125
Beliveau, Jean	Montreal	70	37	36	73	58
Reibel, Earl	Detroit	70	25	41	66	15
Howe, Gordie	Detroit	64	29	33	62	68
Sullivan, Red	Chicago	69	19	42	61	51
Olmstead, Bert	Montreal	70	10	48	58	103
Smith, Sid	Toronto	70	33	21	54	14
Mosdell, Ken	Montreal	70	22	32	54	82
Lewicki, Danny	New York	70	29	24	53	8

1955-56

Team	GP	W	L	T	GF	GA	PTS
*Montreal	70	45	15	10	222	131	100
Detroit	70	30	24	16	183	148	76
New York	70	32	28	10	204	203	74
Toronto	70	24	33	13	153	181	61
Boston	70	23	34	13	147	185	59
Chicago	70	19	39	12	155	216	50

Leading Scorers

Player	Club	GP	G	A	PTS	PIM
Beliveau, Jean	Montreal	70	47	41	88	143
Howe, Gordie	Detroit	70	38	41	79	100
Richard, Maurice	Montreal	70	38	33	71	89
Olmstead, Bert	Montreal	70	14	56	70	94
Sloan, Tod	Toronto	70	37	29	66	100
Bathgate, Andy	New York	70	19	47	66	59
Geoffrion, Bernie	Montreal	59	29	33	62	66
Reibel, Earl	Detroit	68	17	39	56	10
Delvecchio, Alex	Detroit	70	25	26	51	24
Creighton, Dave	New York	70	20	31	51	43
Gadsby, Bill	New York	70	9	42	51	84

1956-57

Team	GP	W	L	T	GF	GA	PTS
Detroit	70	38	20	12	198	157	88
*Montreal	70	35	23	12	210	155	82
Boston	70	34	24	12	195	174	80
New York	70	26	30	14	184	227	66
Toronto	70	21	34	15	174	192	57
Chicago	70	16	39	15	169	225	47

Leading Scorers

Player	Club	GP	G	A	PTS	PIM
Howe, Gordie	Detroit	70	44	45	89	72
Lindsay, Ted	Detroit	70	30	55	85	103
Beliveau, Jean	Montreal	69	33	51	84	105
Bathgate, Andy	New York	70	27	50	77	60
Litzenberger, Ed	Chicago	70	32	32	64	48
Richard, Maurice	Montreal	63	33	29	62	74
McKenney, Don	Boston	69	21	39	60	31
Moore, Dickie	Montreal	70	29	29	58	56
Richard, Henri	Montreal	63	18	36	54	71
Ullman, Norm	Detroit	64	16	36	52	47

1957-58

Team	GP	W	L	T	GF	GA	PTS
*Montreal	70	43	17	10	250	158	96
New York	70	32	25	13	195	188	77
Detroit	70	29	29	12	176	207	70
Boston	70	27	28	15	199	194	69
Chicago	70	24	39	7	163	202	55
Toronto	70	21	38	11	192	226	53

Leading Scorers

Player	Club	GP	G	A	PTS	PIM
Moore, Dickie	Montreal	70	36	48	84	65
Richard, Henri	Montreal	67	28	52	80	56
Bathgate, Andy	New York	65	30	48	78	42
Howe, Gordie	Detroit	64	33	44	77	40
Horvath, Bronco	Boston	67	30	36	66	71
Litzenberger, Ed	Chicago	70	32	30	62	63
Mackell, Fleming	Boston	70	20	40	60	72
Beliveau, Jean	Montreal	55	27	32	59	93
Delvecchio, Alex	Detroit	70	21	38	59	22
McKenney, Don	Boston	70	28	30	58	22

1958-59

Team	GP	W	L	T	GF	GA	PTS
*Montreal	70	39	18	13	258	158	91
Boston	70	32	29	9	205	215	73
Chicago	70	28	29	13	197	208	69
Toronto	70	27	32	11	189	201	65
New York	70	26	32	12	201	217	64
Detroit	70	25	37	8	167	218	58

Leading Scorers

Player	Club	GP	G	A	PTS	PIM
Moore, Dickie	Montreal	70	41	55	96	61
Beliveau, Jean	Montreal	64	45	46	91	67
Bathgate, Andy	New York	70	40	48	88	48
Howe, Gordie	Detroit	70	32	46	78	57
Litzenberger, Ed	Chicago	70	33	44	77	37
Geoffrion, Bernie	Montreal	59	22	44	66	30
Sullivan, Red	New York	70	21	42	63	56
Hebenton, Andy	New York	70	33	29	62	8
McKenney, Don	Boston	70	32	30	62	20
Sloan, Tod	Chicago	59	27	35	62	79

1959-60

Team	GP	W	L	T	GF	GA	PTS
*Montreal	70	40	18	12	255	178	92
Toronto	70	35	26	9	199	195	79
Chicago	70	28	29	13	191	180	69
Detroit	70	26	29	15	186	197	67
Boston	70	28	34	8	220	241	64
New York	70	17	38	15	187	247	49

Leading Scorers

Player	Club	GP	G	A	PTS	PIM
Hull, Bobby	Chicago	70	39	42	81	68
Horvath, Bronco	Boston	68	39	41	80	60
Beliveau, Jean	Montreal	60	34	40	74	57
Bathgate, Andy	New York	70	26	48	74	28
Richard, Henri	Montreal	70	30	43	73	66
Howe, Gordie	Detroit	70	28	45	73	46
Geoffrion, Bernie	Montreal	59	30	41	71	36
McKenney, Don	Boston	70	20	49	69	28
Stasiuk, Vic	Boston	69	29	39	68	121
Prentice, Dean	New York	70	32	34	66	43

1960-61

Team	GP	W	L	T	GF	GA	PTS
Montreal	70	41	19	10	254	188	92
Toronto	70	39	19	12	234	176	90
*Chicago	70	29	24	17	198	180	75
Detroit	70	25	29	16	195	215	66
New York	70	22	38	10	204	248	54
Boston	70	15	42	13	176	254	43

Leading Scorers

Player	Club	GP	G	A	PTS	PIM
Geoffrion, Bernie	Montreal	64	50	45	95	29
Beliveau, Jean	Montreal	69	32	58	90	57
Mahovlich, Frank	Toronto	70	48	36	84	131
Bathgate, Andy	New York	70	29	48	77	22
Howe, Gordie	Detroit	64	23	49	72	30
Ullman, Norm	Detroit	70	28	42	70	34
Kelly, Red	Toronto	64	20	50	70	12
Moore, Dickie	Montreal	57	35	34	69	62
Richard, Henri	Montreal	70	24	44	68	91
Delvecchio, Alex	Detroit	70	27	35	62	26

1961-62

Team	GP	W	L	T	GF	GA	PTS
Montreal	70	42	14	14	259	166	98
*Toronto	70	37	22	11	232	180	85
Chicago	70	31	26	13	217	186	75
New York	70	26	32	12	195	207	64
Detroit	70	23	33	14	184	219	60
Boston	70	15	47	8	177	306	38

Leading Scorers

Player	Club	GP	G	A	PTS	PIM
Hull, Bobby	Chicago	70	50	34	84	35
Bathgate, Andy	New York	70	28	56	84	44
Howe, Gordie	Detroit	70	33	44	77	54
Mikita, Stan	Chicago	70	25	52	77	97
Mahovlich, Frank	Toronto	70	33	38	71	87
Delvecchio, Alex	Detroit	70	26	43	69	18
Backstrom, Ralph	Montreal	66	27	38	65	29
Ullman, Norm	Detroit	70	26	38	64	54
Hay, Bill	Chicago	60	11	52	63	34
Provost, Claude	Montreal	70	33	29	62	22

1962-63

Team	GP	W	L	T	GF	GA	PTS
*Toronto	70	35	23	12	221	180	82
Chicago	70	32	21	17	194	178	81
Montreal	70	28	19	23	225	183	79
Detroit	70	32	25	13	200	194	77
New York	70	22	36	12	211	233	56
Boston	70	14	39	17	198	281	45

Leading Scorers

Player	Club	GP	G	A	PTS	PIM
Howe, Gordie	Detroit	70	38	48	86	100
Bathgate, Andy	New York	70	35	46	81	54
Mikita, Stan	Chicago	65	31	45	76	69
Mahovlich, Frank	Toronto	67	36	37	73	56
Richard, Henri	Montreal	67	23	50	73	57
Beliveau, Jean	Montreal	69	18	49	67	68
Bucyk, John	Boston	69	27	39	66	36
Delvecchio, Alex	Detroit	70	20	44	64	8
Hull, Bobby	Chicago	65	31	31	62	27
Oliver, Murray	Boston	65	22	40	62	38

1963-64

Team	GP	W	L	T	GF	GA	PTS
Montreal	70	36	21	13	209	167	85
Chicago	70	36	22	12	218	169	84
*Toronto	70	33	25	12	192	172	78
Detroit	70	30	29	11	191	204	71
New York	70	22	38	10	186	242	54
Boston	70	18	40	12	170	212	48

Leading Scorers

Player	Club	GP	G	A	PTS	PIM
Mikita, Stan	Chicago	70	39	50	89	146
Hull, Bobby	Chicago	70	43	44	87	50
Beliveau, Jean	Montreal	68	28	50	78	42
Bathgate, Andy	NYR, Tor.	71	19	58	77	34
Howe, Gordie	Detroit	69	26	47	73	70
Wharram, Ken	Chicago	70	39	32	71	18
Oliver, Murray	Boston	70	24	44	68	41
Goyette, Phil	New York	67	24	41	65	15
Gilbert, Rod	New York	70	24	40	64	62
Keon, Dave	Toronto	70	23	37	60	6

1964-65

Team	GP	W	L	T	GF	GA	PTS
Detroit	70	40	23	7	224	175	87
*Montreal	70	36	23	11	211	185	83
Chicago	70	34	28	8	224	176	76
Toronto	70	30	26	14	204	173	74
New York	70	20	38	12	179	246	52
Boston	70	21	43	6	166	253	48

Leading Scorers

Player	Club	GP	G	A	PTS	PIM
Mikita, Stan	Chicago	70	28	59	87	154
Ullman, Norm	Detroit	70	42	41	83	70
Howe, Gordie	Detroit	70	29	47	76	104
Hull, Bobby	Chicago	61	39	32	71	32
Delvecchio, Alex	Detroit	68	25	42	67	16
Provost, Claude	Montreal	70	27	37	64	28
Gilbert, Rod	New York	70	25	36	61	52
Pilote, Pierre	Chicago	68	14	45	59	162
Bucyk, John	Boston	68	26	29	55	24
Backstrom, Ralph	Montreal	70	25	30	55	41
Esposito, Phil	Chicago	70	23	32	55	44

1965-66

Team	GP	W	L	T	GF	GA	PTS
*Montreal	70	41	21	8	239	173	90
Chicago	70	37	25	8	240	187	82
Toronto	70	34	25	11	208	187	79
Detroit	70	31	27	12	221	194	74
Boston	70	21	43	6	174	275	48
New York	70	18	41	11	195	261	47

Leading Scorers

Player	Club	GP	G	A	PTS	PIM
Hull, Bobby	Chicago	65	54	43	97	70
Mikita, Stan	Chicago	68	30	48	78	58
Rousseau, Bobby	Montreal	70	30	48	78	20
Beliveau, Jean	Montreal	67	29	48	77	50
Howe, Gordie	Detroit	70	29	46	75	83
Ullman, Norm	Detroit	70	31	41	72	35
Delvecchio, Alex	Detroit	70	31	38	69	16
Nevin, Bob	New York	69	29	33	62	10
Richard, Henri	Montreal	62	22	39	61	47
Oliver, Murray	Boston	70	18	42	60	30

1966-67

Team	GP	W	L	T	GF	GA	PTS
Chicago	70	41	17	12	264	170	94
Montreal	70	32	25	13	202	188	77
*Toronto	70	32	27	11	204	211	75
New York	70	30	28	12	188	189	72
Detroit	70	27	39	4	212	241	58
Boston	70	17	43	10	182	253	44

Leading Scorers

Player	Club	GP	G	A	PTS	PIM
Mikita, Stan	Chicago	70	35	62	97	12
Hull, Bobby	Chicago	66	52	28	80	52
Ullman, Norm	Detroit	68	26	44	70	26
Wharram, Ken	Chicago	70	31	34	65	21
Howe, Gordie	Detroit	69	25	40	65	53
Rousseau, Bobby	Montreal	68	19	44	63	58
Esposito, Phil	Chicago	69	21	40	61	40
Goyette, Phil	New York	70	12	49	61	6
Mohns, Doug	Chicago	61	25	35	60	58
Richard, Henri	Montreal	65	21	34	55	28
Delvecchio, Alex	Detroit	70	17	38	55	10

1967-68

EAST DIVISION

Team	GP	W	L	T	GF	GA	PTS
*Montreal	74	42	22	10	236	167	94
New York	74	39	23	12	226	183	90
Boston	74	37	27	10	259	216	84
Chicago	74	32	26	16	212	222	80
Toronto	74	33	31	10	209	176	76
Detroit	74	27	35	12	245	257	66

WEST DIVISION

Team	GP	W	L	T	GF	GA	PTS
Philadelphia	74	31	32	11	173	179	73
Los Angeles	74	31	33	10	200	224	72
St. Louis	74	27	31	16	177	191	70
Minnesota	74	27	32	15	191	226	69
Pittsburgh	74	27	34	13	195	216	67
Oakland	74	15	42	17	153	219	47

Leading Scorers

Player	Club	GP	G	A	PTS	PIM
Mikita, Stan	Chicago	72	40	47	87	14
Esposito, Phil	Boston	74	35	49	84	21
Howe, Gordie	Detroit	74	39	43	82	53
Ratelle, Jean	New York	74	32	46	78	18
Gilbert, Rod	New York	73	29	48	77	12
Hull, Bobby	Chicago	71	44	31	75	39
Ullman, Norm	Det., Tor.	71	35	37	72	28
Delvecchio, Alex	Detroit	74	22	48	70	14
Bucyk, John	Boston	72	30	39	69	8
Wharram, Ken	Chicago	74	27	42	69	18

1968-69

EAST DIVISION

Team	GP	W	L	T	GF	GA	PTS
*Montreal	76	46	19	11	271	202	103
Boston	76	42	18	16	303	221	100
New York	76	41	26	9	231	196	91
Toronto	76	35	26	15	234	217	85
Detroit	76	33	31	12	239	221	78
Chicago	76	34	33	9	280	246	77

WEST DIVISION

Team	GP	W	L	T	GF	GA	PTS
St. Louis	76	37	25	14	204	157	88
Oakland	76	29	36	11	219	251	69
Philadelphia	76	20	35	21	174	225	61
Los Angeles	76	24	42	10	185	260	58
Pittsburgh	76	20	45	11	189	252	51
Minnesota	76	18	43	15	189	270	51

Leading Scorers

Player	Club	GP	G	A	PTS	PIM
Esposito, Phil	Boston	74	49	77	126	79
Hull, Bobby	Chicago	74	58	49	107	48
Howe, Gordie	Detroit	76	44	59	103	58
Mikita, Stan	Chicago	74	30	67	97	52
Hodge, Ken	Boston	75	45	45	90	75
Cournoyer, Yvan	Montreal	76	43	44	87	31
Delvecchio, Alex	Detroit	72	25	58	83	8
Berenson, Red	St. Louis	76	35	47	82	43
Beliveau, Jean	Montreal	69	33	49	82	55
Mahovlich, Frank	Detroit	76	49	29	78	38
Ratelle, Jean	New York	75	32	46	78	26

1969-70

EAST DIVISION

Team	GP	W	L	T	GF	GA	PTS
Chicago	76	45	22	9	250	170	99
*Boston	76	40	17	19	277	216	99
Detroit	76	40	21	15	246	199	95
New York	76	38	22	16	246	189	92
Montreal	76	38	22	16	244	201	92
Toronto	76	29	34	13	222	242	71

WEST DIVISION

Team	GP	W	L	T	GF	GA	PTS
St. Louis	76	37	27	12	224	179	86
Pittsburgh	76	26	38	12	182	238	64
Minnesota	76	19	35	22	224	257	60
Oakland	76	22	40	14	169	243	58
Philadelphia	76	17	35	24	197	225	58
Los Angeles	76	14	52	10	168	290	38

Leading Scorers

Player	Club	GP	G	A	PTS	PIM
Orr, Bobby	Boston	76	33	87	120	125
Esposito, Phil	Boston	76	43	56	99	50
Mikita, Stan	Chicago	76	39	47	86	50
Goyette, Phil	St. Louis	72	29	49	78	16
Tkaczuk, Walt	New York	76	27	50	77	38
Ratelle, Jean	New York	75	32	42	74	28
Berenson, Red	St. Louis	67	33	39	72	38
Parise, Jean-Paul	Minnesota	74	24	48	72	72
Howe, Gordie	Detroit	76	31	40	71	58
Mahovlich, Frank	Detroit	74	38	32	70	59
Balon, Dave	New York	76	33	37	70	100
McKenzie, John	Boston	72	29	41	70	114

1970-71

EAST DIVISION

Team	GP	W	L	T	GF	GA	PTS
Boston	78	57	14	7	399	207	121
New York	78	49	18	11	259	177	109
*Montreal	78	42	23	13	291	216	97
Toronto	78	37	33	8	248	211	82
Buffalo	78	24	39	15	217	291	63
Vancouver	78	24	46	8	229	296	56
Detroit	78	22	45	11	209	308	55

WEST DIVISION

Team	GP	W	L	T	GF	GA	PTS
Chicago	78	49	20	9	277	184	107
St. Louis	78	34	25	19	223	208	87
Philadelphia	78	28	33	17	207	225	73
Minnesota	78	28	34	16	191	223	72
Los Angeles	78	25	40	13	239	303	63
Pittsburgh	78	21	37	20	221	240	62
California	78	20	53	5	199	320	45

Leading Scorers

Player	Club	GP	G	A	PTS	PIM
Esposito, Phil	Boston	78	76	76	152	71
Orr, Bobby	Boston	78	37	102	139	91
Bucyk, John	Boston	78	51	65	116	8
Hodge, Ken	Boston	78	43	62	105	113
Hull, Bobby	Chicago	78	44	52	96	32
Ullman, Norm	Toronto	73	34	51	85	24
Cashman, Wayne	Boston	77	21	58	79	100
McKenzie, John	Boston	65	31	46	77	120
Keon, Dave	Toronto	76	38	38	76	4
Beliveau, Jean	Montreal	70	25	51	76	40
Stanfield, Fred	Boston	75	24	52	76	12

1971-72

EAST DIVISION

Team	GP	W	L	T	GF	GA	PTS
*Boston	78	54	13	11	330	204	119
New York	78	48	17	13	317	192	109
Montreal	78	46	16	16	307	205	108
Toronto	78	33	31	14	209	208	80
Detroit	78	33	35	10	261	262	76
Buffalo	78	16	43	19	203	289	51
Vancouver	78	20	50	8	203	297	48

WEST DIVISION

Team	GP	W	L	T	GF	GA	PTS
Chicago	78	46	17	15	256	166	107
Minnesota	78	37	29	12	212	191	86
St. Louis	78	28	39	11	208	247	67
Pittsburgh	78	26	38	14	220	258	66
Philadelphia	78	26	38	14	200	236	66
California	78	21	39	18	216	288	60
Los Angeles	78	20	49	9	206	305	49

Leading Scorers

Player	Club	GP	G	A	PTS	PIM
Esposito, Phil	Boston	76	66	67	133	76
Orr, Bobby	Boston	76	37	80	117	106
Ratelle, Jean	New York	63	46	63	109	4
Hadfield, Vic	New York	78	50	56	106	142
Gilbert, Rod	New York	73	43	54	97	64
Mahovlich, Frank	Montreal	76	43	53	96	36
Hull, Bobby	Chicago	78	50	43	93	24
Cournoyer, Yvan	Montreal	73	47	36	83	15
Bucyk, John	Boston	78	32	51	83	4
Clarke, Bobby	Philadelphia	78	35	46	81	87
Lemaire, Jacques	Montreal	77	32	49	81	26

1972-73

EAST DIVISION

Team	GP	W	L	T	GF	GA	PTS
*Montreal	78	52	10	16	329	184	120
Boston	78	51	22	5	330	235	107
NY Rangers	78	47	23	8	297	208	102
Buffalo	78	37	27	14	257	219	88
Detroit	78	37	29	12	265	243	86
Toronto	78	27	41	10	247	279	64
Vancouver	78	22	47	9	233	339	53
NY Islanders	78	12	60	6	170	347	30

WEST DIVISION

Team	GP	W	L	T	GF	GA	PTS
Chicago	78	42	27	9	284	225	93
Philadelphia	78	37	30	11	296	256	85
Minnesota	78	37	30	11	254	230	85
St. Louis	78	32	34	12	233	251	76
Pittsburgh	78	32	37	9	257	265	73
Los Angeles	78	31	36	11	232	245	73
Atlanta	78	25	38	15	191	239	65
California	78	16	46	16	213	323	48

Leading Scorers

Player	Club	GP	G	A	PTS	PIM
Esposito, Phil	Boston	78	55	75	130	87
Clarke, Bobby	Philadelphia	78	37	67	104	80
Orr, Bobby	Boston	63	29	72	101	99
MacLeish, Rick	Philadelphia	78	50	50	100	69
Lemaire, Jacques	Montreal	77	44	51	95	16
Ratelle, Jean	NY Rangers	78	41	53	94	12
Redmond, Mickey	Detroit	76	52	41	93	24
Bucyk, John	Boston	78	40	53	93	12
Mahovlich, Frank	Montreal	78	38	55	93	51
Pappin, Jim	Chicago	76	41	51	92	82

1973-74

EAST DIVISION

Team	GP	W	L	T	GF	GA	PTS
Boston	78	52	17	9	349	221	113
Montreal	78	45	24	9	293	240	99
NY Rangers	78	40	24	14	300	251	94
Toronto	78	35	27	16	274	230	86
Buffalo	78	32	34	12	242	250	76
Detroit	78	29	39	10	255	319	68
Vancouver	78	24	43	11	224	296	59
NY Islanders	78	19	41	18	182	247	56

WEST DIVISION

Team	GP	W	L	T	GF	GA	PTS
*Philadelphia	78	50	16	12	273	164	112
Chicago	78	41	14	23	272	164	105
Los Angeles	78	33	33	12	233	231	78
Atlanta	78	30	34	14	214	238	74
Pittsburgh	78	28	41	9	242	273	65
St. Louis	78	26	40	12	206	248	64
Minnesota	78	23	38	17	235	275	63
California	78	13	55	10	195	342	36

Leading Scorers

Player	Club	GP	G	A	PTS	PIM
Esposito, Phil	Boston	78	68	77	145	58
Orr, Bobby	Boston	74	32	90	122	82
Hodge, Ken	Boston	76	50	55	105	43
Cashman, Wayne	Boston	78	30	59	89	111
Clarke, Bobby	Philadelphia	77	35	52	87	113
Martin, Rick	Buffalo	78	52	34	86	38
Apps, Syl	Pittsburgh	75	24	61	85	37
Sittler, Darryl	Toronto	78	38	46	84	55
MacDonald, Lowell	Pittsburgh	78	43	39	82	14
Park, Brad	NY Rangers	78	25	57	82	148
Hextall, Dennis	Minnesota	78	20	62	82	138

1974-75

PRINCE OF WALES CONFERENCE

Norris Division

Team	GP	W	L	T	GF	GA	PTS
Montreal	80	47	14	19	374	225	113
Los Angeles	80	42	17	21	269	185	105
Pittsburgh	80	37	28	15	326	289	89
Detroit	80	23	45	12	259	335	58
Washington	80	8	67	5	181	446	21

Adams Division

Team	GP	W	L	T	GF	GA	PTS
Buffalo	80	49	16	15	354	240	113
Boston	80	40	26	14	345	245	94
Toronto	80	31	33	16	280	309	78
California	80	19	48	13	212	316	51

CLARENCE CAMPBELL CONFERENCE

Patrick Division

Team	GP	W	L	T	GF	GA	PTS
*Philadelphia	80	51	18	11	293	181	113
NY Rangers	80	37	29	14	319	276	88
NY Islanders	80	33	25	22	264	221	88
Atlanta	80	34	31	15	243	233	83

Smythe Division

Team	GP	W	L	T	GF	GA	PTS
Vancouver	80	38	32	10	271	254	86
St. Louis	80	35	31	14	269	267	84
Chicago	80	37	35	8	268	241	82
Minnesota	80	23	50	7	221	341	53
Kansas City	80	15	54	11	184	328	41

Leading Scorers

Player	Club	GP	G	A	PTS	PIM
Orr, Bobby	Boston	80	46	89	135	101
Esposito, Phil	Boston	79	61	66	127	62
Dionne, Marcel	Detroit	80	47	74	121	14
Lafleur, Guy	Montreal	70	53	66	119	37
Mahovlich, Pete	Montreal	80	35	82	117	64
Clarke, Bobby	Philadelphia	80	27	89	116	125
Robert, Rene	Buffalo	74	40	60	100	75
Gilbert, Rod	NY Rangers	76	36	61	97	22
Perreault, Gilbert	Buffalo	68	39	57	96	36
Martin, Rick	Buffalo	68	52	43	95	72

1975-76

PRINCE OF WALES CONFERENCE

Norris Division

Team	GP	W	L	T	GF	GA	PTS
*Montreal	80	58	11	11	337	174	127
Los Angeles	80	38	33	9	263	265	85
Pittsburgh	80	35	33	12	339	303	82
Detroit	80	26	44	10	226	300	62
Washington	80	11	59	10	224	394	32

Adams Division

Team	GP	W	L	T	GF	GA	PTS
Boston	80	48	15	17	313	237	113
Buffalo	80	46	21	13	339	240	105
Toronto	80	34	31	15	294	276	83
California	80	27	42	11	250	278	65

CLARENCE CAMPBELL CONFERENCE

Patrick Division

Team	GP	W	L	T	GF	GA	PTS
Philadelphia	80	51	13	16	348	209	118
NY Islanders	80	42	21	17	297	190	101
Atlanta	80	35	33	12	262	237	82
NY Rangers	80	29	42	9	262	333	67

Smythe Division

Team	GP	W	L	T	GF	GA	PTS
Chicago	80	32	30	18	254	261	82
Vancouver	80	33	32	15	271	272	81
St. Louis	80	29	37	14	249	290	72
Minnesota	80	20	53	7	195	303	47
Kansas City	80	12	56	12	190	351	36

Leading Scorers

Player	Club	GP	G	A	PTS	PIM
Lafleur, Guy	Montreal	80	56	69	125	36
Clarke, Bobby	Philadelphia	76	30	89	119	13
Perreault, Gilbert	Buffalo	80	44	69	113	36
Barber, Bill	Philadelphia	80	50	62	112	104
Larouche, Pierre	Pittsburgh	76	53	58	111	33
Ratelle, Jean	Bos., NYR	80	36	69	105	18
Mahovlich, Pete	Montreal	80	34	71	105	76
Pronovost, Jean	Pittsburgh	80	52	52	104	24
Sittler, Darryl	Toronto	79	41	59	100	90
Apps, Syl	Pittsburgh	80	32	67	99	24

1976-77

PRINCE OF WALES CONFERENCE

Norris Division

Team	GP	W	L	T	GF	GA	PTS
*Montreal	80	60	8	12	387	171	132
Los Angeles	80	34	31	15	271	241	83
Pittsburgh	80	34	33	13	240	252	81
Washington	80	24	42	14	221	307	62
Detroit	80	16	55	9	183	309	41

Adams Division

Team	GP	W	L	T	GF	GA	PTS
Boston	80	49	23	8	312	240	106
Buffalo	80	48	24	8	301	220	104
Toronto	80	33	32	15	301	285	81
Cleveland	80	25	42	13	240	292	63

CLARENCE CAMPBELL CONFERENCE

Patrick Division

Team	GP	W	L	T	GF	GA	PTS
Philadelphia	80	48	16	16	323	213	112
NY Islanders	80	47	21	12	288	193	106
Atlanta	80	34	34	12	264	265	80
NY Rangers	80	29	37	14	272	310	72

Smythe Division

Team	GP	W	L	T	GF	GA	PTS
St. Louis	80	32	39	9	239	276	73
Minnesota	80	23	39	18	240	310	64
Chicago	80	26	43	11	240	298	63
Vancouver	80	25	42	13	235	294	63
Colorado	80	20	46	14	226	307	54

Leading Scorers

Player	Club	GP	G	A	PTS	PIM
Lafleur, Guy	Montreal	80	56	80	136	20
Dionne, Marcel	Los Angeles	80	53	69	122	12
Shutt, Steve	Montreal	80	60	45	105	28
MacLeish, Rick	Philadelphia	79	49	48	97	42
Perreault, Gilbert	Buffalo	80	39	56	95	30
Young, Tim	Minnesota	80	29	66	95	58
Ratelle, Jean	Boston	78	33	61	94	22
McDonald, Lanny	Toronto	80	46	44	90	77
Sittler, Darryl	Toronto	73	38	52	90	89
Clarke, Bobby	Philadelphia	80	27	63	90	71

1977-78

PRINCE OF WALES CONFERENCE

Team	GP	W	L	T	GF	GA	PTS
NORRIS DIVISION							
*Montreal	80	59	10	11	359	183	129
Detroit	80	32	34	14	252	266	78
Los Angeles	80	31	34	15	243	245	77
Pittsburgh	80	25	37	18	254	321	68
Washington	80	17	49	14	195	321	48
Adams Division							
Boston	80	51	18	11	333	218	113
Buffalo	80	44	19	17	288	215	105
Toronto	80	41	29	10	271	237	92
Cleveland	80	22	45	13	230	325	57
CLARENCE CAMPBELL CONFERENCE							
Patrick Division							
NY Islanders	80	48	17	15	334	210	111
Philadelphia	80	45	20	15	296	200	105
Atlanta	80	34	27	19	274	252	87
NY Rangers	80	30	37	13	279	280	73
Smythe Division							
Chicago	80	32	29	19	230	220	83
Colorado	80	19	40	21	257	305	59
Vancouver	80	20	43	17	239	320	57
St. Louis	80	20	47	13	195	304	53
Minnesota	80	18	53	9	218	325	45

Leading Scorers

Player	Club	GP	G	A	PTS	PIM
Lafleur, Guy	Montreal	79	60	72	132	26
Trottier, Bryan	NY Islanders	77	46	77	123	46
Sittler, Darryl	Toronto	80	45	72	117	100
Lemaire, Jacques	Montreal	76	36	61	97	14
Potvin, Denis	NY Islanders	80	30	64	94	81
Bossy, Mike	NY Islanders	73	53	38	91	6
O'Reilly, Terry	Boston	77	29	61	90	211
Perreault, Gilbert	Buffalo	79	41	48	89	20
Clarke, Bobby	Philadelphia	71	21	68	89	83
McDonald, Lanny	Toronto	74	47	40	87	54
Paiement, Wilf	Colorado	80	31	56	87	114

1978-79

PRINCE OF WALES CONFERENCE

Team	GP	W	L	T	GF	GA	PTS
Norris Division							
*Montreal	80	52	17	11	337	204	115
Pittsburgh	80	36	31	13	281	279	85
Los Angeles	80	34	34	12	292	286	80
Washington	80	24	41	15	273	338	63
Detroit	80	23	41	16	252	295	62
Adams Division							
Boston	80	43	23	14	316	270	100
Buffalo	80	36	28	16	280	263	88
Toronto	80	34	33	13	267	252	81
Minnesota	80	28	40	12	257	289	68
CLARENCE CAMPBELL CONFERENCE							
Patrick Division							
NY Islanders	80	51	15	14	358	214	116
Philadelphia	80	40	25	15	281	248	95
NY Rangers	80	40	29	11	316	292	91
Atlanta	80	41	31	8	327	280	90
Smythe Division							
Chicago	80	29	36	15	244	277	73
Vancouver	80	25	42	13	217	291	63
St. Louis	80	18	50	12	249	348	48
Colorado	80	15	53	12	210	331	42

Leading Scorers

Player	Club	GP	G	A	PTS	PIM
Trottier, Bryan	NY Islanders	76	47	87	134	50
Dionne, Marcel	Los Angeles	80	59	71	130	30
Lafleur, Guy	Montreal	80	52	77	129	28
Bossy, Mike	NY Islanders	80	69	57	126	25
MacMillan, Bob	Atlanta	79	37	71	108	14
Chouinard, Guy	Atlanta	80	50	57	107	14
Potvin, Denis	NY Islanders	73	31	70	101	58
Federko, Bernie	St. Louis	74	31	64	95	14
Taylor, Dave	Los Angeles	78	43	48	91	124
Gillies, Clark	NY Islanders	75	35	56	91	68

1979-80

PRINCE OF WALES CONFERENCE

Team	GP	W	L	T	GF	GA	PTS
Norris Division							
Montreal	80	47	20	13	328	240	107
Los Angeles	80	30	36	14	290	313	74
Pittsburgh	80	30	37	13	251	303	73
Hartford	80	27	34	19	303	312	73
Detroit	80	26	43	11	268	306	63
Adams Division							
Buffalo	80	47	17	16	318	201	110
Boston	80	46	21	13	310	234	105
Minnesota	80	36	28	16	311	253	88
Toronto	80	35	40	5	304	327	75
Quebec	80	25	44	11	248	313	61
CLARENCE CAMPBELL CONFERENCE							
Patrick Division							
Philadelphia	80	48	12	20	327	254	116
*NY Islanders	80	39	28	13	281	247	91
NY Rangers	80	38	32	10	308	284	86
Atlanta	80	35	32	13	282	269	83
Washington	80	27	40	13	261	293	67
Smythe Division							
Chicago	80	34	27	19	241	250	87
St. Louis	80	34	34	12	266	278	80
Vancouver	80	27	37	16	256	281	70
Edmonton	80	28	39	13	301	322	69
Winnipeg	80	20	49	11	214	314	51
Colorado	80	19	48	13	234	308	51

Leading Scorers

Player	Club	GP	G	A	PTS	PIM
Dionne, Marcel	Los Angeles	80	53	84	137	32
Gretzky, Wayne	Edmonton	79	51	86	137	21
Lafleur, Guy	Montreal	74	50	75	125	12
Perreault, Gilbert	Buffalo	80	40	66	106	57
Rogers, Mike	Hartford	80	44	61	105	10
Trottier, Bryan	NY Islanders	78	42	62	104	68
Simmer, Charlie	Los Angeles	64	56	45	101	65
Stoughton, Blaine	Hartford	80	56	44	100	16
Sittler, Darryl	Toronto	73	40	57	97	62
MacDonald, Blair	Edmonton	80	46	48	94	6
Federko, Bernie	St. Louis	79	38	56	94	24

1980-81

PRINCE OF WALES CONFERENCE

Team	GP	W	L	T	GF	GA	PTS
Norris Division							
Montreal	80	45	22	13	332	232	103
Los Angeles	80	43	24	13	337	290	99
Pittsburgh	80	30	37	13	302	345	73
Hartford	80	21	41	18	292	372	60
Detroit	80	19	43	18	252	339	56
Adams Division							
Buffalo	80	39	20	21	327	250	99
Boston	80	37	30	13	316	272	87
Minnesota	80	35	28	17	291	263	87
Quebec	80	30	32	18	314	318	78
Toronto	80	28	37	15	322	367	71
CLARENCE CAMPBELL CONFERENCE							
Patrick Division							
*NY Islanders	80	48	18	14	355	260	110
Philadelphia	80	41	24	15	313	249	97
Calgary	80	39	27	14	329	298	92
NY Rangers	80	30	36	14	312	317	74
Washington	80	26	36	18	286	317	70
Smythe Division							
St. Louis	80	45	18	17	352	281	107
Chicago	80	31	33	16	304	315	78
Vancouver	80	28	32	20	289	301	76
Edmonton	80	29	35	16	328	327	74
Colorado	80	22	45	13	258	344	57
Winnipeg	80	9	57	14	246	400	32

Leading Scorers

Player	Club	GP	G	A	PTS	PIM
Gretzky, Wayne	Edmonton	80	55	109	164	28
Dionne, Marcel	Los Angeles	80	58	77	135	70
Nilsson, Kent	Calgary	80	49	82	131	26
Bossy, Mike	NY Islanders	79	68	51	119	32
Taylor, Dave	Los Angeles	72	47	65	112	130
Stastny, Peter	Quebec	77	39	70	109	37
Simmer, Charlie	Los Angeles	65	56	49	105	62
Rogers, Mike	Hartford	80	40	65	105	32
Federko, Bernie	St. Louis	78	31	73	104	47
Richard, Jacques	Quebec	78	52	51	103	39
Middleton, Rick	Boston	80	44	59	103	16
Trottier, Bryan	NY Islanders	73	31	72	103	74

1981-82

CLARENCE CAMPBELL CONFERENCE

Team	GP	W	L	T	GF	GA	PTS
Norris Division							
Minnesota	80	37	23	20	346	288	94
Winnipeg	80	33	33	14	319	332	80
St. Louis	80	32	40	8	315	349	72
Chicago	80	30	38	12	332	363	72
Toronto	80	20	44	16	298	380	56
Detroit	80	21	47	12	270	351	54
Smythe Division							
Edmonton	80	48	17	15	417	295	111
Vancouver	80	30	33	17	290	286	77
Calgary	80	29	34	17	334	345	75
Los Angeles	80	24	41	15	314	369	63
Colorado	80	18	49	13	241	362	49
PRINCE OF WALES CONFERENCE							
Adams Division							
Montreal	80	46	17	17	360	223	109
Boston	80	43	27	10	323	285	96
Buffalo	80	39	26	15	307	273	93
Quebec	80	33	31	16	356	345	82
Hartford	80	21	41	18	264	351	60
Patrick Division							
*NY Islanders	80	54	16	10	385	250	118
NY Rangers	80	39	27	14	316	306	92
Philadelphia	80	38	31	11	325	313	87
Pittsburgh	80	31	36	13	310	337	75
Washington	80	26	41	13	319	338	65

Leading Scorers

Player	Club	GP	G	A	PTS	PIM
Gretzky, Wayne	Edmonton	80	92	120	212	26
Bossy, Mike	NY Islanders	80	64	83	147	22
Stastny, Peter	Quebec	80	46	93	139	91
Maruk, Dennis	Washington	80	60	76	136	128
Trottier, Bryan	NY Islanders	80	50	79	129	88
Savard, Denis	Chicago	80	32	87	119	82
Dionne, Marcel	Los Angeles	78	50	67	117	50
Smith, Bobby	Minnesota	80	43	71	114	82
Ciccarelli, Dino	Minnesota	76	55	51	106	138
Taylor, Dave	Los Angeles	78	39	67	106	130

1982-83

CLARENCE CAMPBELL CONFERENCE

Team	GP	W	L	T	GF	GA	PTS
Norris Division							
Chicago	80	47	23	10	338	268	104
Minnesota	80	40	24	16	321	290	96
Toronto	80	28	40	12	293	330	68
St. Louis	80	25	40	15	285	316	65
Detroit	80	21	44	15	263	344	57
Smythe Division							
Edmonton	80	47	21	12	424	315	106
Calgary	80	32	34	14	321	317	78
Vancouver	80	30	35	15	303	309	75
Winnipeg	80	33	39	8	311	333	74
Los Angeles	80	27	41	12	308	365	66
PRINCE OF WALES CONFERENCE							
Adams Division							
Boston	80	50	20	10	327	228	110
Montreal	80	42	24	14	350	286	98
Buffalo	80	38	29	13	318	285	89
Quebec	80	34	34	12	343	336	80
Hartford	80	19	54	7	261	403	45
Patrick Division							
Philadelphia	80	49	23	8	326	240	106
*NY Islanders	80	42	26	12	302	226	96
Washington	80	39	25	16	306	283	94
NY Rangers	80	35	35	10	306	287	80
New Jersey	80	17	49	14	230	338	48
Pittsburgh	80	18	53	9	257	394	45

Leading Scorers

Player	Club	GP	G	A	PTS	PIM
Gretzky, Wayne	Edmonton	80	71	125	196	59
Stastny, Peter	Quebec	75	47	77	124	78
Savard, Denis	Chicago	78	35	86	121	99
Bossy, Mike	NY Islanders	79	60	58	118	20
Dionne, Marcel	Los Angeles	80	56	51	107	22
Pederson, Barry	Boston	77	46	61	107	47
Messier, Mark	Edmonton	77	48	58	106	72
Goulet, Michel	Quebec	80	57	48	105	51
Anderson, Glenn	Edmonton	72	48	56	104	70
Nilsson, Kent	Calgary	80	46	58	104	10
Kurri, Jari	Edmonton	80	45	59	104	22

1983-84

CLARENCE CAMPBELL CONFERENCE

Norris Division

Team	GP	W	L	T	GF	GA	PTS
Minnesota	80	39	31	10	345	344	88
St. Louis	80	32	41	7	293	316	71
Detroit	80	31	42	7	298	323	69
Chicago	80	30	42	8	277	311	68
Toronto	80	26	45	9	303	387	61
Smythe Division							
*Edmonton	80	57	18	5	446	314	119
Calgary	80	34	32	14	311	314	82
Vancouver	80	32	39	9	306	328	73
Winnipeg	80	31	38	11	340	374	73
Los Angeles	80	23	44	13	309	376	59
PRINCE OF WALES CONFERENCE							
Adams Division							
Boston	80	49	25	6	336	261	104
Buffalo	80	48	25	7	315	257	103
Quebec	80	42	28	10	360	278	94
Montreal	80	35	40	5	286	295	75
Hartford	80	28	42	10	288	320	66
Patrick Division							
NY Islanders	80	50	26	4	357	269	104
Washington	80	48	27	5	308	226	101
Philadelphia	80	44	26	10	350	290	98
NY Rangers	80	42	29	9	314	304	93
New Jersey	80	17	56	7	231	350	41
Pittsburgh	80	16	58	6	254	390	38

Leading Scorers

Player	Club	GP	G	A	PTS	PIM
Gretzky, Wayne	Edmonton	74	87	118	205	39
Coffey, Paul	Edmonton	80	40	86	126	104
Goulet, Michel	Quebec	75	56	65	121	76
Stastny, Peter	Quebec	80	46	73	119	73
Bossy, Mike	NY Islanders	67	51	67	118	8
Pederson, Barry	Boston	80	39	77	116	64
Kurri, Jari	Edmonton	64	52	61	113	14
Trottier, Bryan	NY Islanders	68	40	71	111	59
Federko, Bernie	St. Louis	79	41	66	107	43
Middleton, Rick	Boston	80	47	58	105	14

1984-85

CLARENCE CAMPBELL CONFERENCE

Norris Division

Team	GP	W	L	T	GF	GA	PTS
St. Louis	80	37	31	12	299	288	86
Chicago	80	38	35	7	309	299	83
Detroit	80	27	41	12	313	357	66
Minnesota	80	25	43	12	268	321	62
Toronto	80	20	52	8	253	358	48
Smythe Division							
*Edmonton	80	49	20	11	401	298	109
Winnipeg	80	43	27	10	358	332	96
Calgary	80	41	27	12	363	302	94
Los Angeles	80	34	32	14	339	326	82
Vancouver	80	25	46	9	284	401	59
PRINCE OF WALES CONFERENCE							
Adams Division							
Montreal	80	41	27	12	309	262	94
Quebec	80	41	30	9	323	275	91
Buffalo	80	38	28	14	290	237	90
Boston	80	36	34	10	303	287	82
Hartford	80	30	41	9	268	318	69
Patrick Division							
Philadelphia	80	53	20	7	348	241	113
Washington	80	46	25	9	322	240	101
NY Islanders	80	40	34	6	345	312	86
NY Rangers	80	26	44	10	295	345	62
New Jersey	80	22	48	10	264	346	54
Pittsburgh	80	24	51	5	276	385	53

Leading Scorers

Player	Club	GP	G	A	PTS	PIM
Gretzky, Wayne	Edmonton	80	73	135	208	52
Kurri, Jari	Edmonton	73	71	64	135	30
Hawerchuk, Dale	Winnipeg	80	53	77	130	74
Dionne, Marcel	Los Angeles	80	46	80	126	46
Coffey, Paul	Edmonton	80	37	84	121	97
Bossy, Mike	NY Islanders	76	58	59	117	38
Ogrodnick, John	Detroit	79	55	50	105	30
Savard, Denis	Chicago	79	38	67	105	56
Federko, Bernie	St. Louis	76	30	73	103	27
Gartner, Mike	Washington	80	50	52	102	71

1985-86

CLARENCE CAMPBELL CONFERENCE

Norris Division

Team	GP	W	L	T	GF	GA	PTS
Chicago	80	39	33	8	351	349	86
Minnesota	80	38	33	9	327	305	85
St. Louis	80	37	34	9	302	291	83
Toronto	80	25	48	7	311	386	57
Detroit	80	17	57	6	266	415	40
Smythe Division							
Edmonton	80	56	17	7	426	310	119
Calgary	80	40	31	9	354	315	89
Winnipeg	80	26	47	7	295	372	59
Vancouver	80	23	44	13	282	333	59
Los Angeles	80	23	49	8	284	389	54
PRINCE OF WALES CONFERENCE							
Adams Division							
Quebec	80	43	31	6	330	289	92
*Montreal	80	40	33	7	330	280	87
Boston	80	37	31	12	311	288	86
Hartford	80	40	36	4	332	302	84
Buffalo	80	37	37	6	296	291	80
Patrick Division							
Philadelphia	80	53	23	4	335	241	110
Washington	80	50	23	7	315	272	107
NY Islanders	80	39	29	12	327	284	90
NY Rangers	80	36	38	6	280	276	78
Pittsburgh	80	34	38	8	313	305	76
New Jersey	80	28	49	3	300	374	59

Leading Scorers

Player	Club	GP	G	A	PTS	PIM
Gretzky, Wayne	Edmonton	80	52	163	215	52
Lemieux, Mario	Pittsburgh	79	48	93	141	43
Coffey, Paul	Edmonton	79	48	90	138	120
Kurri, Jari	Edmonton	78	68	63	131	22
Bossy, Mike	NY Islanders	80	61	62	123	14
Stastny, Peter	Quebec	76	41	81	122	60
Savard, Denis	Chicago	80	47	69	116	111
Naslund, Mats	Montreal	80	43	67	110	16
Hawerchuk, Dale	Winnipeg	80	46	59	105	44
Broten, Neal	Minnesota	80	29	76	105	47

1986-87

CLARENCE CAMPBELL CONFERENCE

Norris Division

Team	GP	W	L	T	GF	GA	PTS
St. Louis	80	32	33	15	281	293	79
Detroit	80	34	36	10	260	274	78
Chicago	80	29	37	14	290	310	72
Toronto	80	32	42	6	286	319	70
Minnesota	80	30	40	10	296	314	70
Smythe Division							
*Edmonton	80	50	24	6	372	284	106
Calgary	80	46	31	3	318	289	95
Winnipeg	80	40	32	8	279	271	88
Los Angeles	80	31	41	8	318	341	70
Vancouver	80	29	43	8	282	314	66
PRINCE OF WALES CONFERENCE							
Adams Division							
Hartford	80	43	30	7	287	270	93
Montreal	80	41	29	10	277	241	92
Boston	80	39	34	7	301	276	85
Quebec	80	31	39	10	267	276	72
Buffalo	80	28	44	8	280	308	64
Patrick Division							
Philadelphia	80	46	26	8	310	245	100
Washington	80	38	32	10	285	278	86
NY Islanders	80	35	33	12	279	281	82
NY Rangers	80	34	38	8	307	323	76
Pittsburgh	80	30	38	12	297	290	72
New Jersey	80	29	45	6	293	368	64

Leading Scorers

Player	Club	GP	G	A	PTS	PIM
Gretzky, Wayne	Edmonton	79	62	121	183	28
Kurri, Jari	Edmonton	79	54	54	108	41
Lemieux, Mario	Pittsburgh	63	54	53	107	57
Messier, Mark	Edmonton	77	37	70	107	73
Gilmour, Doug	St. Louis	80	42	63	105	58
Ciccarelli, Dino	Minnesota	80	52	51	103	92
Hawerchuk, Dale	Winnipeg	80	47	53	100	54
Goulet, Michel	Quebec	75	49	47	96	61
Kerr, Tim	Philadelphia	75	58	37	95	57
Bourque, Ray	Boston	78	23	72	95	36

1987-88

CLARENCE CAMPBELL CONFERENCE

Norris Division

Team	GP	W	L	T	GF	GA	PTS
Detroit	80	41	28	11	322	269	93
St. Louis	80	34	38	8	278	294	76
Chicago	80	30	41	9	284	328	69
Toronto	80	21	49	10	273	345	52
Minnesota	80	19	48	13	242	349	51
Smythe Division							
Calgary	80	48	23	9	397	305	105
*Edmonton	80	44	25	11	363	288	99
Winnipeg	80	33	36	11	292	310	77
Los Angeles	80	30	42	8	318	359	68
Vancouver	80	25	46	9	272	320	59
PRINCE OF WALES CONFERENCE							
Adams Division							
Montreal	80	45	22	13	298	238	103
Boston	80	44	30	6	300	251	94
Buffalo	80	37	32	11	283	305	85
Hartford	80	35	38	7	249	267	77
Quebec	80	32	43	5	271	306	69
Patrick Division							
NY Islanders	80	39	31	10	308	267	88
Washington	80	38	33	9	281	249	85
Philadelphia	80	38	33	9	292	292	85
New Jersey	80	38	36	6	295	296	82
NY Rangers	80	36	34	10	300	283	82
Pittsburgh	80	36	35	9	319	316	81

Leading Scorers

Player	Club	GP	G	A	PTS	PIM
Lemieux, Mario	Pittsburgh	76	70	98	168	92
Gretzky, Wayne	Edmonton	64	40	109	149	24
Savard, Denis	Chicago	80	44	87	131	95
Hawerchuk, Dale	Winnipeg	80	44	77	121	59
Robitaille, Luc	Los Angeles	80	53	58	111	82
Stastny, Peter	Quebec	76	46	65	111	69
Messier, Mark	Edmonton	77	37	74	111	103
Carson, Jimmy	Los Angeles	80	55	52	107	45
Loob, Hakan	Calgary	80	50	56	106	47
Goulet, Michel	Quebec	80	48	58	106	56

1988-89

CLARENCE CAMPBELL CONFERENCE

Norris Division

Team	GP	W	L	T	GF	GA	PTS
Detroit	80	34	34	12	313	316	80
St. Louis	80	33	35	12	275	285	78
Minnesota	80	27	37	16	258	278	70
Chicago	80	27	41	12	297	335	66
Toronto	80	28	46	6	259	342	62
Smythe Division							
*Calgary	80	54	17	9	354	226	117
Los Angeles	80	42	31	7	376	335	91
Edmonton	80	38	34	8	325	306	84
Vancouver	80	33	39	8	251	253	74
Winnipeg	80	26	42	12	300	355	64
PRINCE OF WALES CONFERENCE							
Adams Division							
Montreal	80	53	18	9	315	218	115
Boston	80	37	29	14	289	256	88
Buffalo	80	38	35	7	291	299	83
Hartford	80	37	38	5	299	290	79
Quebec	80	27	46	7	269	342	61
Patrick Division							
Washington	80	41	29	10	305	259	92
Pittsburgh	80	40	33	7	347	349	87
NY Rangers	80	37	35	8	310	307	82
Philadelphia	80	36	36	8	307	285	80
New Jersey	80	27	41	12	281	325	66
NY Islanders	80	28	47	5	265	325	61

Leading Scorers

Player	Club	GP	G	A	PTS	PIM
Lemieux, Mario	Pittsburgh	76	85	114	199	100
Gretzky, Wayne	Los Angeles	78	54	114	168	26
Yzerman, Steve	Detroit	80	65	90	155	61
Nicholls, Bernie	Los Angeles	79	70	80	150	96
Brown, Rob	Pittsburgh	68	49	66	115	118
Coffey, Paul	Pittsburgh	75	30	83	113	193
Mullen, Joe	Calgary	79	51	59	110	16
Kurri, Jari	Edmonton	76	44	58	102	69
Carson, Jimmy	Edmonton	80	49	51	100	36
Robitaille, Luc	Los Angeles	78	46	52	98	65

1989-90

CLARENCE CAMPBELL CONFERENCE

Norris Division

Team	GP	W	L	T	GF	GA	PTS
Chicago	80	41	33	6	316	294	88
St. Louis	80	37	34	9	295	279	83
Toronto	80	38	38	4	337	358	80
Minnesota	80	36	40	4	284	291	76
Detroit	80	28	38	14	288	323	70
Smythe Division							
Calgary	80	42	23	15	348	265	99
*Edmonton	80	38	28	14	315	283	90
Winnipeg	80	37	32	11	298	290	85
Los Angeles	80	34	39	7	338	337	75
Vancouver	80	25	41	14	245	306	64

PRINCE OF WALES CONFERENCE

Adams Division

Team	GP	W	L	T	GF	GA	PTS
Boston	80	46	25	9	289	232	101
Buffalo	80	45	27	8	286	248	98
Montreal	80	41	28	11	288	234	93
Hartford	80	38	33	9	275	268	85
Quebec	80	12	61	7	240	407	31
Patrick Division							
NY Rangers	80	36	31	13	279	267	85
New Jersey	80	37	34	9	295	288	83
Washington	80	36	38	6	284	275	78
NY Islanders	80	31	38	11	281	288	73
Pittsburgh	80	32	40	8	318	359	72
Philadelphia	80	30	39	11	290	297	71

Leading Scorers

Player	Club	GP	G	A	PTS	PIM
Gretzky, Wayne	Los Angeles	73	40	102	142	42
Messier, Mark	Edmonton	79	45	84	129	79
Yzerman, Steve	Detroit	79	62	65	127	79
Lemieux, Mario	Pittsburgh	59	45	78	123	78
Hull, Brett	St. Louis	80	72	41	113	24
Nicholls, Bernie	L.A., NYR	79	39	73	112	86
Turgeon, Pierre	Buffalo	80	40	66	106	29
LaFontaine, Pat	NY Islanders	74	54	51	105	38
Coffey, Paul	Pittsburgh	80	29	74	103	95
Sakic, Joe	Quebec	80	39	63	102	27
Oates, Adam	St. Louis	80	23	79	102	30

1990-91

CLARENCE CAMPBELL CONFERENCE

Norris Division

Team	GP	W	L	T	GF	GA	PTS
Chicago	80	49	23	8	284	211	106
St. Louis	80	47	22	11	310	250	105
Detroit	80	34	38	8	273	298	76
Minnesota	80	27	39	14	256	266	68
Toronto	80	23	46	11	241	318	57
Smythe Division							
Los Angeles	80	46	24	10	340	254	102
Calgary	80	46	26	8	344	263	100
Edmonton	80	37	37	6	272	272	80
Vancouver	80	28	43	9	243	315	65
Winnipeg	80	26	43	11	260	288	63

PRINCE OF WALES CONFERENCE

Adams Division

Team	GP	W	L	T	GF	GA	PTS
Boston	80	44	24	12	299	264	100
Montreal	80	39	30	11	273	249	89
Buffalo	80	31	30	19	292	278	81
Hartford	80	31	38	11	238	276	73
Quebec	80	16	50	14	236	354	46
Patrick Division							
*Pittsburgh	80	41	33	6	342	305	88
NY Rangers	80	36	31	13	297	265	85
Washington	80	37	36	7	258	258	81
New Jersey	80	32	33	15	272	264	79
Philadelphia	80	33	37	10	252	267	76
NY Islanders	80	25	45	10	223	290	60

Leading Scorers

Player	Club	GP	G	A	PTS	PIM
Gretzky, Wayne	Los Angeles	78	41	122	163	16
Hull, Brett	St. Louis	78	86	45	131	22
Oates, Adam	St. Louis	61	25	90	115	29
Recchi, Mark	Pittsburgh	78	40	73	113	48
Cullen, John	Pit., Hfd.	78	39	71	110	101
Sakic, Joe	Quebec	80	48	61	109	24
Yzerman, Steve	Detroit	80	51	57	108	34
Fleury, Theo	Calgary	79	51	53	104	136
MacInnis, Al	Calgary	78	28	75	103	90
Larmer, Steve	Chicago	80	44	57	101	79

1991-92

CLARENCE CAMPBELL CONFERENCE

Norris Division

Team	GP	W	L	T	GF	GA	PTS
Detroit	80	43	25	12	320	256	98
Chicago	80	36	29	15	257	236	87
St. Louis	80	36	33	11	279	266	83
Minnesota	80	32	42	6	246	278	70
Toronto	80	30	43	7	234	294	67
Smythe Division							
Vancouver	80	42	26	12	285	250	96
Los Angeles	80	35	31	14	287	296	84
Edmonton	80	36	34	10	295	297	82
Winnipeg	80	33	32	15	251	244	81
Calgary	80	31	37	12	296	305	74
San Jose	80	17	58	5	219	359	39

PRINCE OF WALES CONFERENCE

Adams Division

Team	GP	W	L	T	GF	GA	PTS
Montreal	80	41	28	11	267	207	93
Boston	80	36	32	12	270	275	84
Buffalo	80	31	37	12	289	299	74
Hartford	80	26	41	13	247	283	65
Quebec	80	20	48	12	255	318	52
Patrick Division							
NY Rangers	80	50	25	5	321	246	105
Washington	80	45	27	8	330	275	98
*Pittsburgh	80	39	32	9	343	308	87
New Jersey	80	38	31	11	289	259	87
NY Islanders	80	34	35	11	291	299	79
Philadelphia	80	32	37	11	252	273	75

Leading Scorers

Player	Club	GP	G	A	PTS	PIM
Lemieux, Mario	Pittsburgh	64	44	87	131	94
Stevens, Kevin	Pittsburgh	80	54	69	123	254
Gretzky, Wayne	Los Angeles	74	31	90	121	34
Hull, Brett	St. Louis	73	70	39	109	48
Robitaille, Luc	Los Angeles	80	44	63	107	95
Messier, Mark	NY Rangers	79	35	72	107	76
Roenick, Jeremy	Chicago	80	53	50	103	23
Yzerman, Steve	Detroit	79	45	58	103	64
Leetch, Brian	NY Rangers	80	22	80	102	26
Oates, Adam	St. L., Bos.	80	20	79	99	22

1992-93

CLARENCE CAMPBELL CONFERENCE

Norris Division

Team	GP	W	L	T	GF	GA	PTS
Chicago	84	47	25	12	279	230	106
Detroit	84	47	28	9	369	280	103
Toronto	84	44	29	11	288	241	99
St. Louis	84	37	36	11	282	278	85
Minnesota	84	36	38	10	272	293	82
Tampa Bay	84	23	54	7	245	332	53
Smythe Division							
Vancouver	84	46	29	9	346	278	101
Calgary	84	43	30	11	322	282	97
Los Angeles	84	39	35	10	338	340	88
Winnipeg	84	40	37	7	322	320	87
Edmonton	84	26	50	8	242	337	60
San Jose	84	11	71	2	218	414	24

PRINCE OF WALES CONFERENCE

Adams Division

Team	GP	W	L	T	GF	GA	PTS
Boston	84	51	26	7	332	268	109
Quebec	84	47	27	10	351	300	104
*Montreal	84	48	30	6	326	280	102
Buffalo	84	38	36	10	335	297	86
Hartford	84	26	52	6	284	369	58
Ottawa	84	10	70	4	202	395	24
Patrick Division							
Pittsburgh	84	56	21	7	367	268	119
Washington	84	43	34	7	325	286	93
NY Islanders	84	40	37	7	335	297	87
New Jersey	84	40	37	7	308	299	87
Philadelphia	84	36	37	11	319	319	83
NY Rangers	84	34	39	11	304	308	79

Leading Scorers

Player	Club	GP	G	A	PTS	PIM
Lemieux, Mario	Pittsburgh	60	69	91	160	38
LaFontaine, Pat	Buffalo	84	53	95	148	63
Oates, Adam	Boston	84	45	97	142	32
Yzerman, Steve	Detroit	84	58	79	137	44
Selanne, Teemu	Winnipeg	84	76	56	132	45
Turgeon, Pierre	NY Islanders	83	58	74	132	26
Mogilny, Alex.	Buffalo	77	76	51	127	40
Gilmour, Doug	Toronto	83	32	95	127	100
Robitaille, Luc	Los Angeles	84	63	62	125	100
Recchi, Mark	Philadelphia	84	53	70	123	95

1993-94

EASTERN CONFERENCE

Northeast Division

Team	GP	W	L	T	GF	GA	PTS
Pittsburgh	84	44	27	13	299	285	101
Boston	84	42	29	13	289	252	97
Montreal	84	41	29	14	283	248	96
Buffalo	84	43	32	9	282	218	95
Quebec	84	34	42	8	277	292	76
Hartford	84	27	48	9	227	288	63
Ottawa	84	14	61	9	201	397	37
Atlantic Division							
*NY Rangers	84	52	24	8	299	231	112
New Jersey	84	47	25	12	306	220	106
Washington	84	39	35	10	277	263	88
NY Islanders	84	36	36	12	282	264	84
Florida	84	33	34	17	233	233	83
Philadelphia	84	35	39	10	294	314	80
Tampa Bay	84	30	43	11	224	251	71

WESTERN CONFERENCE

Central Division

Team	GP	W	L	T	GF	GA	PTS
Detroit	84	46	30	8	356	275	100
Toronto	84	43	29	12	280	243	98
Dallas	84	42	29	13	286	265	97
St. Louis	84	40	33	11	270	283	91
Chicago	84	39	36	9	254	240	87
Winnipeg	84	24	51	9	245	344	57
Pacific Division							
Calgary	84	42	29	13	302	256	97
Vancouver	84	41	40	3	279	276	85
San Jose	84	33	35	16	252	265	82
Anaheim	84	33	46	5	229	251	71
Los Angeles	84	27	45	12	294	322	66
Edmonton	84	25	45	14	261	305	64

Leading Scorers

Player	Club	GP	G	A	PTS	PIM
Gretzky, Wayne	Los Angeles	81	38	92	130	20
Fedorov, Sergei	Detroit	82	56	64	120	34
Oates, Adam	Boston	77	32	80	112	45
Gilmour, Doug	Toronto	83	27	84	111	105
Bure, Pavel	Vancouver	76	60	47	107	86
Roenick, Jeremy	Chicago	84	46	61	107	125
Recchi, Mark	Philadelphia	84	40	67	107	46
Shanahan, Brendan	St. Louis	81	52	50	102	211
Andreychuk, Dave	Toronto	83	53	46	99	98
Jagr, Jaromir	Pittsburgh	80	32	67	99	61

Top 10 All-Time Career Goals Scored

894	Wayne Gretzky
801	Gordie Howe
731	Marcel Dionne
717	Phil Esposito
708	Mike Gartner
627	Mark Messier
627	Steve Yzerman
613	Mario Lemieux
610	Bobby Hull
610	Brett Hull

Top 10 All-Time Single Season Goals Scored

92	Wayne Gretzky	1981-82	Edmonton
87	Wayne Gretzky	1983-84	Edmonton
86	Brett Hull	1990-91	St. Louis
85	Mario Lemieux	1988-89	Pittsburgh
76	Phil Esposito	1970-71	Boston
76	Teemu Selanne	1992-93	Winnipeg
76	Alex. Mogilny	1992-93	Buffalo
73	Wayne Gretzky	1984-85	Edmonton
72	Brett Hull	1989-90	St. Louis
71	Wayne Gretzky	1982-83	Edmonton
71	Jari Kurri	1984-85	Edmonton

1994-95

EASTERN CONFERENCE

Northeast Division

Team	GP	W	L	T	GF	GA	PTS
Quebec	48	30	13	5	185	134	65
Pittsburgh	48	29	16	3	181	158	61
Boston	48	27	18	3	150	127	57
Buffalo	48	22	19	7	130	119	51
Hartford	48	19	24	5	127	141	43
Montreal	48	18	23	7	125	148	43
Ottawa	48	9	34	5	117	174	23
Atlantic Division							
Philadelphia	48	28	16	4	150	132	60
*New Jersey	48	22	18	8	136	121	52
Washington	48	22	18	8	136	120	52
NY Rangers	48	22	23	3	139	134	47
Florida	48	20	22	6	115	127	46
Tampa Bay	48	17	28	3	120	144	37
NY Islanders	48	15	28	5	126	158	35
WESTERN CONFERENCE							
Central Division							
Detroit	48	33	11	4	180	117	70
St. Louis	48	28	15	5	178	135	61
Chicago	48	24	19	5	156	115	53
Toronto	48	21	19	8	135	146	50
Dallas	48	17	23	8	136	135	42
Winnipeg	48	16	25	7	157	177	39
Pacific Division							
Calgary	48	24	17	7	163	135	55
Vancouver	48	18	18	12	153	148	48
San Jose	48	19	25	4	129	161	42
Los Angeles	48	16	23	9	142	174	41
Edmonton	48	17	27	4	136	183	38
Anaheim	48	16	27	5	125	164	37

Leading Scorers

Player	Club	GP	G	A	PTS	PIM
Jagr, Jaromir	Pittsburgh	48	32	38	70	37
Lindros, Eric	Philadelphia	46	29	41	70	60
Zhamnov, Alexei	Winnipeg	48	30	35	65	20
Sakic, Joe	Quebec	47	19	43	62	30
Francis, Ron	Pittsburgh	44	11	48	59	18
Fleury, Theoren	Calgary	47	29	29	58	112
Coffey, Paul	Detroit	45	14	44	58	72
Renberg, Mikael	Philadelphia	47	26	31	57	20
LeClair, John	Mtl., Phi.	46	26	28	54	30
Messier, Mark	NY Rangers	46	14	39	53	40
Oates, Adam	Boston	48	12	41	53	8

1995-96

EASTERN CONFERENCE

Northeast Division

Team	GP	W	L	T	GF	GA	PTS
Pittsburgh	82	49	29	4	362	284	102
Boston	82	40	31	11	282	269	91
Montreal	82	40	32	10	265	248	90
Hartford	82	34	39	9	237	259	77
Buffalo	82	33	42	7	247	262	73
Ottawa	82	18	59	5	191	291	41
Atlantic Division							
Philadelphia	82	45	24	13	282	208	103
NY Rangers	82	41	27	14	272	237	96
Florida	82	41	31	10	254	234	92
Washington	82	39	32	11	234	204	89
Tampa Bay	82	38	32	12	238	248	88
New Jersey	82	37	33	12	215	202	86
NY Islanders	82	22	50	10	229	315	54
WESTERN CONFERENCE							
Central Division							
Detroit	82	62	13	7	325	181	131
Chicago	82	40	28	14	273	220	94
Toronto	82	34	36	12	247	252	80
St. Louis	82	32	34	16	219	248	80
Winnipeg	82	36	40	6	275	291	78
Dallas	82	26	42	14	227	280	66
Pacific Division							
*Colorado	82	47	25	10	326	240	104
Calgary	82	34	37	11	241	240	79
Vancouver	82	32	35	15	278	278	79
Anaheim	82	35	39	8	234	247	78
Edmonton	82	30	44	8	240	304	68
Los Angeles	82	24	40	18	256	302	66
San Jose	82	20	55	7	252	357	47

Leading Scorers

Player	Club	GP	G	A	PTS	PIM
Lemieux, Mario	Pittsburgh	70	69	92	161	54
Jagr, Jaromir	Pittsburgh	82	62	87	149	96
Sakic, Joe	Colorado	82	51	69	120	44
Francis, Ron	Pittsburgh	77	27	92	119	56
Forsberg, Peter	Colorado	82	30	86	116	47
Lindros, Eric	Philadelphia	73	47	68	115	163
Kariya, Paul	Anaheim	82	50	58	108	20
Selanne, Teemu	Wpg., Ana.	79	40	68	108	22
Mogilny, Alex.	Vancouver	79	55	52	107	16
Fedorov, Sergei	Detroit	78	39	68	107	48

1996-97

EASTERN CONFERENCE

Northeast Division

Team	GP	W	L	T	GF	GA	PTS
Buffalo	82	40	30	12	237	208	92
Pittsburgh	82	38	36	8	285	280	84
Ottawa	82	31	36	15	226	234	77
Montreal	82	31	36	15	249	276	77
Hartford	82	32	39	11	226	256	75
Boston	82	26	47	9	234	300	61
Atlantic Division							
New Jersey	82	45	23	14	231	182	104
Philadelphia	82	45	24	13	274	217	103
Florida	82	35	28	19	221	201	89
NY Rangers	82	38	34	10	258	231	86
Washington	82	33	40	9	214	231	75
Tampa Bay	82	32	40	10	217	247	74
NY Islanders	82	29	41	12	240	250	70
WESTERN CONFERENCE							
Central Division							
Dallas	82	48	26	8	252	198	104
*Detroit	82	38	26	18	253	197	94
Phoenix	82	38	37	7	240	243	83
St. Louis	82	36	35	11	236	239	83
Chicago	82	34	35	13	223	210	81
Toronto	82	30	44	8	230	273	68
Pacific Division							
Colorado	82	49	24	9	277	205	107
Anaheim	82	36	33	13	245	233	85
Edmonton	82	36	37	9	252	247	81
Vancouver	82	35	40	7	257	273	77
Calgary	82	32	41	9	214	239	73
Los Angeles	82	28	43	11	214	268	67
San Jose	82	27	47	8	211	278	62

Leading Scorers

Player	Club	GP	G	A	PTS	PIM
Lemieux, Mario	Pittsburgh	76	50	72	122	65
Selanne, Teemu	Anaheim	78	51	58	109	34
Kariya, Paul	Anaheim	69	44	55	99	6
LeClair, John	Philadelphia	82	50	47	97	58
Gretzky, Wayne	NY Rangers	82	25	72	97	28
Jagr, Jaromir	Pittsburgh	63	47	48	95	40
Sundin, Mats	Toronto	82	41	53	94	59
Palffy, Zigmund	NY Islanders	80	48	42	90	43
Francis, Ron	Pittsburgh	81	27	63	90	20
Shanahan, Brendan	Hfd., Det.	81	47	41	88	131

Top 10 All-Time Career Assists

1963	Wayne Gretzky
1131	Paul Coffey
1117	Ray Bourque
1087	Mark Messier
1087	Ron Francis
1049	Gordie Howe
1040	Marcel Dionne
935	Steve Yzerman
926	Stan Mikita
910	Larry Murphy

Top 10 All-Time Career Points Scored

2857	Wayne Gretzky
1850	Gordie Howe
1771	Marcel Dionne
1714	Mark Messier
1590	Phil Esposito
1562	Steve Yzerman
1559	Ron Francis
1527	Paul Coffey
1520	Ray Bourque
1494	Mario Lemieux

Top 10 Defensemen Career Points Scored

1527	Paul Coffey
1520	Ray Bourque
1195	Larry Murphy
1130	Phil Housley
1104	Al MacInnis
1052	Denis Potvin
958	Larry Robinson
915	Bobby Orr
896	Brad Park
832	Chris Chelios

Top 10 All-Time Single Season Assists

163	Wayne Gretzky	1985-86	Edmonton
135	Wayne Gretzky	1984-85	Edmonton
125	Wayne Gretzky	1982-83	Edmonton
122	Wayne Gretzky	1990-91	Los Angeles
121	Wayne Gretzky	1986-87	Edmonton
120	Wayne Gretzky	1981-82	Edmonton
118	Wayne Gretzky	1983-84	Edmonton
114	Wayne Gretzky	1988-89	Los Angeles
114	Mario Lemieux	1988-89	Pittsburgh
109	Wayne Gretzky	1980-81	Edmonton
109	Wayne Gretzky	1987-88	Edmonton

Top 10 All-Time Single Season Points Scored

215	Wayne Gretzky	1985-86	Edmonton
212	Wayne Gretzky	1981-82	Edmonton
208	Wayne Gretzky	1984-85	Edmonton
205	Wayne Gretzky	1983-84	Edmonton
199	Mario Lemieux	1988-89	Pittsburgh
196	Wayne Gretzky	1982-83	Edmonton
183	Wayne Gretzky	1986-87	Edmonton
168	Mario Lemieux	1987-88	Pittsburgh
168	Wayne Gretzky	1988-89	Los Angeles
164	Wayne Gretzky	1980-81	Edmonton

Top 10 Rookie Point Scorers

132	Teemu Selanne	1992-93	Winnipeg
109	Peter Stastny	1980-81	Quebec
103	Dale Hawerchuk	1981-82	Winnipeg
102	Joe Juneau	1992-93	Boston
100	Mario Lemieux	1984-85	Pittsburgh
98	Neal Broten	1981-82	Minnesota
95	Bryan Trottier	1975-76	NY Islanders
92	Barry Pederson	1981-82	Boston
92	Joe Nieuwendyk	1987-88	Calgary
91	Mike Bossy	1977-78	NY Islanders

1997-98

EASTERN CONFERENCE

Northeast Division

Team	GP	W	L	T	GF	GA	PTS
Pittsburgh	82	40	24	18	228	188	98
Boston	82	39	30	13	221	194	91
Buffalo	82	36	29	17	211	187	89
Montreal	82	37	32	13	235	208	87
Ottawa	82	34	33	15	193	200	83
Carolina	82	33	41	8	200	219	74
Atlantic Division							
New Jersey	82	48	23	11	225	166	107
Philadelphia	82	42	29	11	242	193	95
Washington	82	40	30	12	219	202	92
NY Islanders	82	30	41	11	212	225	71
NY Rangers	82	25	39	18	197	231	68
Florida	82	24	43	15	203	256	63
Tampa Bay	82	17	55	10	151	269	44
WESTERN CONFERENCE							
Central Division							
Dallas	82	49	22	11	242	167	109
*Detroit	82	44	23	15	250	196	103
St. Louis	82	45	29	8	256	204	98
Phoenix	82	35	35	12	224	227	82
Chicago	82	30	39	13	192	199	73
Toronto	82	30	43	9	194	237	69
Pacific Division							
Colorado	82	39	26	17	231	205	95
Los Angeles	82	38	33	11	227	225	87
Edmonton	82	35	37	10	215	224	80
San Jose	82	34	38	10	210	216	78
Calgary	82	26	41	15	217	252	67
Anaheim	82	26	43	13	205	261	65
Vancouver	82	25	43	14	224	273	64

Leading Scorers

Player	Club	GP	G	A	PTS	PIM
Jagr, Jaromir	Pittsburgh	77	35	67	102	64
Forsberg, Peter	Colorado	72	25	66	91	94
Bure, Pavel	Vancouver	82	51	39	90	48
Gretzky, Wayne	NY Rangers	82	23	67	90	28
LeClair, John	Philadelphia	82	51	36	87	32
Palffy, Zigmund	NY Islanders	82	45	42	87	34
Francis, Ron	Pittsburgh	81	25	62	87	20
Selanne, Teemu	Anaheim	73	52	34	86	30
Allison, Jason	Boston	81	33	50	83	60
Stumpel, Jozef	Los Angeles	77	21	58	79	53

1998-99

EASTERN CONFERENCE

Northeast Division

Team	GP	W	L	T	GF	GA	PTS
Ottawa	82	44	23	15	239	179	103
Toronto	82	45	30	7	268	231	97
Boston	82	39	30	13	214	181	91
Buffalo	82	37	28	17	207	175	91
Montreal	82	32	39	11	184	209	75
Atlantic Division							
New Jersey	82	47	24	11	248	196	105
Philadelphia	82	37	26	19	231	196	93
Pittsburgh	82	38	30	14	242	225	90
NY Rangers	82	33	38	11	217	227	77
NY Islanders	82	24	48	10	194	244	58
Southeast Division							
Carolina	82	34	30	18	210	202	86
Florida	82	30	34	18	210	228	78
Washington	82	31	45	6	200	218	68
Tampa Bay	82	19	54	9	179	292	47
WESTERN CONFERENCE							
Central Division							
Detroit	82	43	32	7	245	202	93
St. Louis	82	37	32	13	237	209	87
Chicago	82	29	41	12	202	248	70
Nashville	82	28	47	7	190	261	63
Pacific Division							
*Dallas	82	51	19	12	236	168	114
Phoenix	82	39	31	12	205	197	90
Anaheim	82	35	34	13	215	206	83
San Jose	82	31	33	18	196	191	80
Los Angeles	82	32	45	5	189	222	69
Northwest Division							
Colorado	82	44	28	10	239	205	98
Edmonton	82	33	37	12	230	226	78
Calgary	82	30	40	12	211	234	72
Vancouver	82	23	47	12	192	258	58

Leading Scorers

Player	Club	GP	G	A	PTS	PIM
Jagr, Jaromir	Pittsburgh	81	44	83	127	66
Selanne, Teemu	Anaheim	75	47	60	107	30
Kariya, Paul	Anaheim	82	39	62	101	40
Forsberg, Peter	Colorado	78	30	67	97	108
Sakic, Joe	Colorado	73	41	55	96	29
Yashin, Alexei	Ottawa	82	44	50	94	54
Lindros, Eric	Philadelphia	71	40	53	93	120
Fleury, Theoren	Cgy., Col.	75	40	53	93	86
LeClair, John	Philadelphia	76	43	47	90	30
Demitra, Pavol	St. Louis	82	37	52	89	16

1999-2000

EASTERN CONFERENCE

Northeast Division

Team	GP	W	L	T	RT	GF	GA	PTS
Toronto	82	45	30	7	3	246	222	100
Ottawa	82	41	30	11	2	244	210	95
Buffalo	82	35	36	11	4	213	204	85
Montreal	82	35	38	9	4	196	194	83
Boston	82	24	39	19	6	210	248	73
Atlantic Division								
Philadelphia	82	45	25	12	3	237	179	105
*New Jersey	82	45	29	8	5	251	203	103
Pittsburgh	82	37	37	8	6	241	236	88
NY Rangers	82	29	41	12	3	218	246	73
NY Islanders	82	24	49	9	1	194	275	58
Southeast Division								
Washington	82	44	26	12	2	227	194	102
Florida	82	43	33	6	6	244	209	98
Carolina	82	37	35	10	0	217	216	84
Tampa Bay	82	19	54	9	7	204	310	54
Atlanta	82	14	61	7	4	170	313	39
WESTERN CONFERENCE								
Northeast Division								
St. Louis	82	51	20	11	1	248	165	114
Detroit	82	48	24	10	2	278	210	108
Chicago	82	33	39	10	2	242	245	78
Nashville	82	28	47	7	7	199	240	70
Pacific Division								
Dallas	82	43	29	10	6	211	184	102
Los Angeles	82	39	31	12	4	245	228	94
Phoenix	82	39	35	8	4	232	228	90
San Jose	82	35	37	10	7	225	214	87
Anaheim	82	34	36	12	3	217	227	83
Northwest Division								
Colorado	82	42	29	11	1	233	201	96
Edmonton	82	32	34	16	8	226	212	88
Vancouver	82	30	37	15	8	227	237	83
Calgary	82	31	41	10	5	211	256	77

Leading Scorers

Player	Club	GP	G	A	PTS	PIM
Jagr, Jaromir	Pittsburgh	63	42	54	96	50
Bure, Pavel	Florida	74	58	36	94	16
Recchi, Mark	Philadelphia	82	28	63	91	50
Kariya, Paul	Anaheim	74	42	44	86	24
Selanne, Teemu	Anaheim	79	33	52	85	12
Nolan, Owen	San Jose	78	44	40	84	110
Amonte, Tony	Chicago	82	43	41	84	48
Modano, Mike	Dallas	77	38	43	81	48
Sakic, Joe	Colorado	60	28	53	81	28
Yzerman, Steve	Detroit	78	35	44	79	34

Top 10 All-Time Games Played Leaders

1767	Gordie Howe
1558	Larry Murphy
1549	Alex Delvecchio
1540	John Bucyk
1532	Ray Bourque
1487	Wayne Gretzky
1479	Mark Messier
1446	Tim Horton
1432	Mike Gartner
1411	Harry Howell

Top 10 All-Time Career Shutouts

103	Terry Sawchuk
94	George Hainsworth
84	Glenn Hall
82	Jacques Plante
81	Tiny Thompson
81	Alex Connell
76	Tony Esposito
73	Lorne Chabot
71	Harry Lumley
67	Roy Worters

Top 10 All-Time Career Goals-Against Average

1.91	Alex Connell
1.93	George Hainsworth
2.02	Chuck Gardiner
2.04	Lorne Chabot
2.08	Tiny Thompson
2.15	Dave Kerr
2.20	Martin Brodeur
2.24	Ken Dryden
2.26	Dominik Hasek
2.27	Roy Worters

Top 10 Team Winning Percentages

.875	Boston Bruins	1929-30
.830	Montreal Canadiens	1943-44
.825	Montreal Canadiens	1976-77
.806	Montreal Canadiens	1977-78
.800	Montreal Canadiens	1944-45
.799	Detroit Red Wings	1995-96
.794	Montreal Canadiens	1975-76
.776	Boston Bruins	1970-71
.771	Boston Bruins	1938-39
.769	Montreal Canadiens	1972-73

Top 10 All-Time Single Season Shutouts

22	Geo. Hainsworth	1928-29	Montreal
15	Hal Winkler	1927-28	Boston
15	Alex Connell	1925-26	Ottawa
15	Alex Connell	1927-28	Ottawa
15	Tony Esposito	1969-70	Chicago
14	Geo. Hainsworth	1926-27	Montreal
13	Alex Connell	1926-27	Ottawa
13	Clint Benedict	1926-27	Mtl. Maroons
13	Geo. Hainsworth	1927-28	Montreal
13	Roy Worters	1928-29	NY Americans
13	John Ross Roach	1928-29	NY Rangers
13	Harry Lumley	1953-54	Toronto
13	Dominik Hasek	1997-98	Buffalo

Top 10 All-Time Single Season Goals-Against Average

0.92	Geo. Hainsworth	1928-29	Montreal
1.05	Geo. Hainsworth	1927-28	Montreal
1.12	Alex Connell	1925-26	Ottawa
1.15	Tiny Thompson	1928-29	Boston
1.15	Roy Worters	1928-29	NY Americans
1.24	Alex Connell	1927-28	Ottawa
1.37	Dolly Dolson	1928-29	Detroit
1.41	John Ross Roach	1928-29	NY Rangers
1.42	Clint Benedict	1926-27	Mtl. Maroons
1.43	Alex Connell	1928-29	Ottawa

CHAPTER 20

Maurice "Rocket" Richard

Three Perspectives on Hockey's Most Electrifying Performer

Fire on the Ice

Burning intensity, a champion's spirit, the pride of a man who knows the glory and loneliness of supremacy

Herbert Warren Wind

This piece originally appeared in Sports Illustrated *December 6, 1954. Reprinted with the author's permission.*

For all that has been said and written about the heights of fanatic devotion achieved by the fans of the Brooklyn Dodgers, the Notre Dame football team and the Australian Davis Cup defenders, it is doubtful if there is any group of sports addicts anywhere that, year in and year out, supports its team with quite the super-charged emotion and lavish pride expended by the citizens of bilingual Montreal on their hockey team, *les Canadiens*—the Canadians. In June each year, four months before the next season begins, every seat in the Montreal Forum, save 800 or so that the management holds for sale on the day of the game, has been sold out for the entire 70-game schedule. On playoff nights it is not uncommon for crowds seeking standing room to run into several thousands and to swarm over Ste-Catherine Street and beyond onto Atwater Park.

Hockey is deep in the Montrealer's blood. After a fine day by a member of the home team or, for that matter, of the visiting team, the Forum reverberates from the rinkside to the rafters with sharp enthusiastic applause. But many volts above this in feeling and many decibels above in volume is the singular and sudden pandemonium that shatters the Forum, like thunder and lightning, whenever the incomparable star of *les Canadiens*, Maurice "The Rocket" Richard, fights his way through the enemy defense and blasts the puck past the goalie. There is no sound quite like it in the whole world of sport.

A powerfully built athlete of 33 who stands 5'10" and now weighs 180, having put on about a pound a year since breaking in with *les Canadiens* in 1942, Joseph Henri Maurice Richard, Gallicly handsome and eternally intense, is generally regarded by most aficionados, be they Montrealers or *étrangers*, as the greatest player in the history of hockey. Whether he is or not, of course, is one of those sports arguments that boil down in the final analysis to a matter of personal opinion. However, as Richard's supporters invariably point out, hockey is in essence a game of scoring, and here there can be no argument; the Rocket stands in a class by himself, the outstanding scorer of all time.

It is not simply the multiplicity of Richard's goals nor their timeliness but, rather, the chronically spectacular manner in which he scores them that has made the fiery right wing the acknowledged Babe Ruth of hockey. "There are goals and there are Richard goals," Dick Irvin, who has coached the Canadiens the length of Richard's career, remarked not long ago. "He doesn't get lucky now. [Of his record 384 goals] 370 have had a flair. He can get to a puck and do things to it quicker than any man I've ever seen—even if he has to lug two defensemen with him, and he frequently had to. And his shots! They go in with such velocity that the whole net bulges."

The Seibert goal

One of the popular indoor pastimes year-round in Montreal is talking over old Richard goals—which one you thought was the most neatly set up, which one stirred you the most, etc., much in the way Americans used to hot stove about Ruth's home runs and do today about Willie Mays's various catches. In Irvin's opinion—and Hector "Toe" Blake and Elmer Lach, Richard's teammates on the famous Punch Line also feel this way—the Rocket's most sensational goal was "the Seibert goal," in the 1945–46 season. Earl Seibert, a strapping 200-pound defenseman who was playing for Detroit that season, hurled himself at Richard as he swept on a solo into the Detroit zone. Richard occasionally will bend his head and neck very low when he is trying to outmaneuver a defenseman. He did on this play. The two collided with a thud, and as they straightened up, there was Richard, still on his feet, still controlling the puck, and sitting on top of his shoulders, the burly Seibert. Richard not only carried Seibert with him on the way to the net, a tour de force in itself, but with that tremendous extra effort of which he is capable, faked the goalie out of position and with his one free hand somehow managed to hoist the puck into the far corner of the cage.

There are two interesting epilogues to this story. The first concerns Seibert and serves well to illustrate the enormous respect in which Richard is held by opposing players. When Seibert clambered into the dressing room after the game, Jack Adams, the voluble Detroit coach, eyed him scornfully. "Why, you dumb Dutchman," he began, "you go let that Richard"—"Listen, Mr. Adams," Seibert cut in, interrupting Adams for the first time in his career, "any guy who can carry me 60 feet and then put the puck into the net—well more power to him!" And that ended that. The second rider to the story is that Richard is perhaps the only hockey player who, to increase his ability to operate with a burden, has frequently spent an extra half hour after the regular practice sessions careening full steam around the rink with his young son, Maurice Jr., "The Petit Rocket," perched on his shoulders.

There is no question that Richard's most heroic winning goal was "the Boston goal"—the one he scored against the Bruins (on April 8, 1952) to lift Montreal into the finals of the Stanley Cup playoffs. It came late in the third period of a 1–1 game in which the Canadiens were playing badly, Richard in particular. Earlier in the game Maurice received a deep gash over his left eye. He was taken to the clinic inside the Forum, and the cut was hastily patched up. Blood was still trickling down from the dressing over his cheek when he returned to the bench and took his next turn on the ice. "I can see that goal now," Frank Selke Jr., the son of the Canadiens' managing director, reminisced recently. "Hundreds of us can. Richard sets off a chain reaction whenever he gets the puck, even if it is just a routine pass. It's strange and wonderful, the way he communicates with the crowd. Now, this time he got the puck at our own blue line and you knew—everybody knew—that the game was over right then."

For 10 years now because of his courage, his skill, and that magical uncultivatable quality—true magnetism—Maurice Richard has reigned in Montreal and throughout the province of Quebec as a hero whose hold on the public has no parallel in sport today unless it be the country-wide adoration that the people of Spain have from time to time heaped on their rare master matadors. The fact that 75 percent of the citizens of Montreal and a similar percentage of the Forum regulars are warm-blooded, excitable French-Canadians—and what is more, a hero-hungry people who think of themselves not as the majority group in their province but as the minority group in Canada—goes quite a distance in explaining their idolatry of Richard. "If Maurice were an English-Canadian or a Scottish-Canadian or a kid from the West he would be lionized, but not as much as he is now," an English-Canadian Richard follower declared last month. "I go to all the games with a French-Canadian friend of mine, a fellow named Roger Oulette. I know exactly what Roger thinks. He accepts the English as good as anyone. But he would hate to see the French population lose their language and their heritage generally. He doesn't like the fact that the government's pension checks are printed only in English. He feels that they should be printed in both English and French since the constitution of the Dominion provides for a two-language country. For Roger, Maurice Richard personifies French Canada and all that is great about it. Maybe you have to have French blood, really, to worship Richard, but you know, you only have to be a lover of hockey to admire him."

No cheap connections

As befits the Babe Ruth of hockey, Richard is the highest-paid player in the history of the game. While *les Canadiens* front office prefers not to divulge his exact salary, it amounts to a very healthy chunk of his estimated annual income of $50,000, which is filled out by his commissions for endorsing such products as a hair tonic and the Maurice Richard-model windbreaker, his cut from the sale of *Le Rocket de Hockey* and other publications about him during the offseason as a wrestling referee. "Maurice could earn much more than he does but he has been careful not to connect himself with anything cheap," Camil DesRoches, the Canadiens publicity director, says. "His appearance is enough to insure the success of any affair in the province, from wrestling to a church outing."

A few years ago, Richard and his teammate Kenny Reardon dropped in for lunch at the Canadian Club, a restaurant in Montreal. "When the other diners spotted Rocket," Reardon relates, "They began to pass the hat for him. It was a spontaneous gesture of appreciation. They collected $50, just like that. People can't do enough for him." Richard, in consequence, is the perfect companion to travel with should you journey anywhere in the province of Quebec. No one will let him pay for a meal, for lodgings, for transportation, for anything.

And what about *le Rocket*? How does he react to this fantastic adulation? Perhaps the surest key is the way he conducts himself after he scores one of his roof-raising goals. Down on the ice, below the tumult of tribute, Richard, while the referee is waiting for the clamor to subside before dropping the puck for the next face-off, cruises solemnly in slow circles, somewhat embarrassed by the strength of the ovation, his normally expressive dark eyes fixed expressionless on the ice. It is a brief moment of uncoiling, one of the few he is able to allow himself during the six-month-long season.

"Maurice," Toe Blake once remarked, "lives to score goals." It is not that Richard puts himself above his team or the game. Quite the contrary, in fact. But here—and he has never been any other way—is a terribly intense man who, like so many of the champions who have endured as champions, is forever driving himself to come up to the almost impossible high standard of performance he sets, whose pride in himself will not let him relax until he has delivered decisively and who, additionally, regards the veneration that has come his way as nothing less than a public trust that he must never let down. When Richard or *les Canadiens* lose, or when he is in the throes of a prolonged scoring slump, the Rocket will brood silently, sometimes for days at a time, limiting his conversations with his wife to "pass the butter" or "more water." Success affects Richard no less deeply. After his monumental playoff goal against the Bruins he broke down in tears in the dressing room. His father came in and they talked together for a while, and then Maurice was all right. Even today, when victory and frustration are old stories for him, he remains so highly charged that he has a great deal of trouble sleeping the night before a game when the team is on the road. "Maurice can relax," Elmer Lach has said, "but not during the hockey season. After the last game, Maurice is a different fellow."

Richard's teammates remember the tail end of the 1952–53 season as the time of his most alarming mood. This was the year that Gordie Howe (playing a 70-game schedule) was on the verge of breaking Richard's record for goals in one season, the 50 he had scored in 1944–45 when the league was playing a 50-game schedule. With one game to go, Howe stood at 49. The remaining game was in Detroit against the Canadiens. "The night of that game, that was the only time I ever was afraid to put a hockey player on the ice," Coach Irvin said not long ago. "I remember watching Rocket's eyes as we were going across the city in the cab. 'I can't play him tonight,' I said to myself. 'He'll kill somebody.' I played him but I made sure he wasn't going to be on the ice any time Howe was. In spite of my precautions, one time they were for a few seconds, I think Rocket was coming out of the penalty box. He skated straight across the ice and charged right at Howe. Then he turned around and skated back to the penalty box. Rocket was proud of his record, but it was more than that. He would have felt humiliated if Howe had beaten or tied it playing against him or his team. Anyway, Howe didn't score. After the game Richard was in the dressing room breathing hard and little Gerry McNeil, our goalie, went over to him. 'Well, Rocket,' Gerry told him with a big smile, 'Howe will have to start all over again with number one.' "

Stopping the Rocket

Because of his own scoring proclivities, Richard has for a dozen years been subjected to far more physical punishment than any other player since the National Hockey

League was organized back in 1917. To beat Montreal, you must stop the Rocket, and to stop him opposing teams assign one man and sometimes two to do nothing but stay with Richard "right into the dressing room" if necessary. Some of the men assigned to Richard play him cleanly but, more often than not, opposing "defensive specialists" resort to holding him, grabbing his jersey, hooking him, and whenever they get any kind of shot at him, belting him with their Sunday bodycheck. One of the best ways to stop Richard, of course, is to get him off the ice. With this in mind, some of the rival teams have made it a practice to use a left wing against him with instructions to ignite deliberately the Rocket's red glare. Then, if Richard retaliates and the referee calls a double penalty, Montreal loses Richard and the other team a far less valuable man.

If the Rocket always ranks near the top in goals, he also does in penalty time, and not all of his penalties, by any manner of means, are the result of self-protection. He probably holds the league record for misconduct penalties, 10-minute "rests" which are awarded for telling the referees off in overly pungent language. And the Rocket is always up among the leaders in major penalties, five-minute cool-off sessions for fighting. He has lost some fights, but only when he has been ganged up on. In man-to-man combat, he acquits himself extremely well.

The ambition of most Canadian boys is to be hockey players when they grow up, good enough to make the National Hockey League with their favorite team—*les Canadiens*, if the boy is of French descent. Maurice Richard was never confused by any other ambition. He was born on August 4, 1921, in Bordeaux, a typical parish on the reaches of Montreal, the oldest child of Onesime and Alice Laramee Richard. After Maurice came Georgette, Rene, Rollande, Jacques, Margaret, Henri and Claude. Henri, now 18, plays for the Montreal Royals, the Canadiens' farm team in the Quebec Hockey League. Not too hefty, Henri has a great deal of his older brother's dash and scoring flair, and has been dubbed "The Pocket Rocket." Claude is just 17 and also has the makings, in Maurice's opinion, of a pretty fair hockey player.

With a family soon on his hands, Richard *pere* was forced to give up any ideas he had about making a career in baseball. An accomplished center fielder although he stood not much over five feet tall, he continued to play semi-pro baseball until he was 45, but he earned his living, as he still does, as a workman in the machine shops of the Canadian-Pacific Railroad. Maurice began to skate when he was about four. In those days Canadian winters were much more severe than they are today. From October through April snow covered the outlying parishes like Bordeaux, and deliveries of milk and bread were made by sleigh. When the snow in the streets had been packed down into a hard crust, the children would skate to school on top of it. After school was out at 4 o'clock, Richard remembers he would play hockey till 5:30 when it was time to go home for supper. "Many days I kept my skates on while I ate," he says. "Then I would go out and play some more hockey until 10 o'clock."

A strong rugged forward

After finishing the ninth grade of elementary school, Maurice spent two years in the *Ecole Technique* in downtown Montreal studying the machinist's trade. He played for the school team and for about four others simultaneously, a strong, rugged forward but not a player for whom you would have been instantly able to predict a glowing future. (One of the teams on which Richard played represented the *Garage Paquette* and had been organized by a pal of his, Georges Norchet. The only significant upshot of the liaison was that Maurice met Georges's sister, Lucille, whom he later married.)

Late in 1940, Richard was given an opportunity to join the Verdun Maple Leafs, the bottom club in *les Canadiens'* farm system. He played with the Senior Canadiens in the Quebec Senior Amateur League the following two seasons, but it was impossible to get much of a line on him for he was laid up with injuries the better part of both years, first with a fractured left ankle, then with a fractured left wrist. He was invited to the Canadiens' training camp in September the next year but only because the team had been floundering at the bottom of the league and was grasping for any straw. He was kept on the squad only because Dick Irvin had never in his life seen a youngster so imbued with the desire to make good. The unknown quantity started off well with *les Canadiens*. He piled up five goals and six assists in the first 15 games. In the next game he fractured his right ankle in a collision with Jack Crawford. He was out for almost the entire season again, returning only for the final game.

A recurrent mystery in sports is how a player who has never shown any signs of greatness will suddenly and inexplicably "arrive" as a full-fledged star. When Richard reported to the Canadiens' training camp in Verdun prior to the 1943–44 campaign, everyone recognized that he was an altogether different and better hockey player. On the strength of his showing in these practice sessions, Coach Irvin, looking for someone to take Joe Benoit's place, gave Richard a crack at right wing on the first line with Elmer Lach, the superb center, and the veteran Toe Blake, "The Old Lamp Lighter," at left wing. Due to the scoring punch the new line supplied, *les Canadiens*, who had finished a floundering fourth the year before, won the league championship and went on to capture the team's first Stanley Cup playoff victory in a full 13 years. Richard eclipsed all playoff records by scoring 12 goals in nine games, and in one game against Toronto, went completely berserk and scored all five of the Canadiens' goals.

The Punch Line, as Blake, Lach and Richard came to be called, played together through the 1946–47 season, a stretch in which they led the Canadiens to three more league championships and one other Stanley Cup victory. They were a marvelous line to watch. Fast skating, spirited, and quick to take advantage of all opportunities offered them, they mapped out no set plays, but each of them, knowing his linemates' style perfectly and sharing an instinctive understanding of how a play should be developed (and the necessary alternative moves depending on how the defense reacted), always seemed to know, without looking, where the others should be.

A lefthanded right wing

If there was anything unorthodox about the Punch Line it was that Richard, a lefthanded shot, played right wing. "Right wing was good for Rocket because it gave him a bit more leverage on his shot and a bit more of the net to shoot at," Dick Irvin has said in explaining this move. "Besides, his backhand shot was as powerful as his forehand." Another aspect of Richard's sudden maturity was, oddly enough, the fact that he had fractured his right ankle the year before joining the Punch Line. After he had fractured his left ankle two years earlier, he had been inclined to overuse his right leg. After his right ankle was fractured he could no longer do this, and he began to skate with a far better distribution of leg drive. A long strider with amazingly quick acceleration, he rocks from side to side when he skates, a style that would be awkward in anyone else and which, if anything, has added to his deceptiveness. As for Richard himself, he considers that the great break of his entire career was that he was able to come back after three fractures in three consecutive years.

"Don't depend on me"

The first time he saw Richard play, Conn Smythe, the head man of the Toronto Maple Leafs, offered *les Canadiens* the (for hockey) fabulous sum of $50,000 for him. In making this offer to the Hon. Donat Raymond, owner of *les Canadiens*, Smythe declared in a characteristic Smythian comment, that he was willing to go this high even though Richard was a "one-way man"—a player not remarkably conspicuous on defense. Raymond was not at all interested in selling his new star but suggested to Smythe that if they made Richard a two-way man, it would be only proper for him to double his figure. (Only a short time ago, Smythe was offering $135,000 for Richard.) Jack Adams, the Detroit boss, after seeing Richard set a new league scoring record for a single game of five goals and three assists on the evening of December 28, 1944, declared him to be "the greatest hockey player I've seen in 20 years." This eight-point spree astonished Richard more than anyone. Before the game he had stretched out limply on a rubbing table in the dressing room. "I'm all tired out," he had yawned wearily to teammates who had gathered around him.

"Dis afternoon I move my apartment about t'ree blocks and can't get a truck. My brudder and me, we move every-t'ing. Tonight, don't depend too much on me." After he had tallied his eight points, to be sure, Richard's vitality perked up noticeably (Richard, by the way, spoke no English at the time he joined *les Canadiens*. He resented the fact that opponents made his broken English a target for wisecracks and it is typical of the pride he takes in everything he does, the way he dresses, the way he handles his hobbies, that today he speaks just about perfect English).

Richard's eight-point night was the high point of his second complete season, 1944–45, in which he set the league record of 50 goals. Since then he has not lost his standing in the affection of Montreal fans as the team's premier hero. New stars have come up, stalwarts like Bill Durnan (the six-time winner of the Vezina trophy for goalies), Butch Bouchard (the four-time all-star defenseman), Boom Boom Geoffrion, (the colorful, carefree youngster with the big shot who is married to Howie Morenz's daughter), and Jean Beliveau—who made so much money as the star of Quebec's amateur team that it was a financial hardship for him to turn professional. There is room for them all in the Canadiens fan's heart, but *le Rocket*—he has always been something special and apart. He is their *oriflamme*. They urge him on with a hundred different cries, but in a tight spot the Forum seems to rise up with one shout in particular. "*Envoyez, Maurice*!" This is a Canadian slang form of the imperative of the verb *envoyer*, to send or to expedite. "*Envoyez, Maurice*!"—"Let's expedite this game, Maurice!" "*Envoyez, Maurice*!"—"Let's go, Maurice!" "*Envoyez, Maurice*!"

Tempestuous and incident-prone

Maurice has never let his fans down but there have been moments when he has worried them sick. Largely because of his tempestuous temperament, he is what you might describe as incident-prone. A few years back, for instance, during a Red Wings-Canadiens game in Montreal that referee Hugh McLean was officiating, the Rocket swooped in from his wing to follow up a rebound and in the resulting melee before the Detroit goal, was sent sprawling to the ice by the Detroit center who practically used a headlock. There was no whistle for a penalty. Boiling with indignation, Richard skated up to McLean and demanded to know what the referee was going to do about it. McLean did something about it. He handed Richard a misconduct penalty for abusive language. Burned up by what he considered a vast miscarriage of justice, the Rocket tossed all night in his berth as the Canadiens traveled by train to New York for a game with the Rangers. The next day, still smoldering, he was sitting in the lobby of the Picadilly Hotel when he spotted McLean. He rushed over and grabbed the official by his coat collar, but before he had time to continue his protest, Camil DesRoches and some teammates jumped on him and managed to pull him away. It was very fortunate they did. For his assault on McLean, Richard was fined $500 by President Clarence Campbell of the NHL, the highest fine ever levied by the league, but he had been restrained in the nick of time. A real assault and Richard would have been suspended.

Last year this almost happened. In a game in New York, Ron Murphy of the Rangers swung at Geoffrion with his stick. He missed. Geoffrion, retaliating, caught Murphy on the head. The blow fractured Murphy's skull and he was out for the season. Geoffrion was suspended for all the remaining games against the Rangers that season. As Richard saw it, Geoffrion had been punished all out of proportion for a fight he had not started. Richard was then "writing" via a ghost, a column for the *Samedi Dimanche*, a French-language weekly. "If Mr. Campbell wants to throw me out of the league for daring to criticize him," Richard stated in his column, "let him do it. Geoffrion is no longer the same since his affair with Murphy... he is demoralized and humiliated for having dared to defend himself against a sneaky and deliberate attack by a third-class player. We know that on numerous occasions, he [President Campbell] has rendered decisions against Canadiens players... Let Mr. Campbell not try to gain publicity for himself by taking to task a good boy like Boom Boom Geoffrion simply because he is a French-Canadian... If this brings me reprisals, I will step out of hockey, and I know that any other players on the Canadiens team will do the same."

Well, this was something—a direct challenge to the authority of the president of the league. Richard was clearly miles out of line. The affair could have been disastrous, not only for Richard but for organized hockey, had it not been handled with consummate intelligence by Frank Selke, the managing director of *les Canadiens* who has been part of hockey since 1906. At the heart of the crisis *les Canadiens* returned to Montreal after a road trip. Selke was at the station to meet them. He collected Richard, Geoffrion, Ken Mosdell and their wives and took them to dinner at the Windsor Hotel. He never once mentioned what was on his mind and everyone's. The dinner over, Richard and Selke found themselves seated alone together in the hotel lobby for a moment.

"I'm surprised, Mr. Selke," Richard said, "I thought you were going to be very angry with me."

"Maurice," Selke said quietly, "I've never known you to do a rotten thing in your life before. You're accusing President Campbell of things that aren't true. That isn't like Maurice Richard. I don't believe you wrote that column."

"No, I didn't, but I authorized it," Richard replied. "I take full responsibility."

"I want you to act like a big leaguer," Selke went on. "President Campbell's office is just across the street. I know he works nights. I want you to come over with me and see him."

Richard sat silently for a moment. Then the two got up and called on Campbell. During the weeks that followed Richard's apology, which ended the affair, many of the French papers accused him of selling out. He never batted an eye. "Maurice Richard never disappoints you," Mr. Selke said recently. "We have had a lot of dealing. When a mistake is pointed out to him and he sees it is a mistake, he has the character to recognize it and to make genuine rectification. He has great class as a person."

The Richards live in a modest, trim home in Cartierville, which adjoins Bordeaux. During the hockey season Maurice spends the bulk of his free hours at home playing with his kids—Huguette, 11, a pretty girl who is a natural figure skater; Maurice Jr., 9, whom the family calls "Rocket" as matter-of-factly as if it were a prosaic nickname like Bud; Normand, 4; and Andre, an infant of six months. Richard is not just a devoted father, he is crazy about his kids. During the summer, at least once a week, Richard and his wife bundle the family into the car and head for the country for a day together in the open air. It is his truest pleasure.

Fishing, softball, and golf

Richard puts in some time in the summer as a sales representative for the Petrofina Company, a Belgian concern which operates gas stations in Canada, but a large part of every day goes to keeping himself in shape. It is his custom to take off on several three-day fishing trips when each hockey season is over. This is pure relaxation, but after that he plays his sports with an eye to preparing himself gradually for the coming hockey campaign. In June and July he plays some softball but principally he golfs. A 10-handicap, he responds so well to competition that for the last two season he and Elmer Lach have won the tournament for major league hockey players that takes place before the big Canadian golf tournament, the Labatt Open. Halfway through July he switches to tennis and handball. "I think they are very good sports for sharpening the eye and strengthening the legs," he told a friend not long ago. "When it is time to go to training camp, I find it not too hard to get into condition."

Richard has mellowed discernibly in recent years. In a relaxed mood he can be wonderful company, intelligent in conversation and very responsive to old friends. His shyness with strangers has lessened somewhat and he meets people far more gracefully. He has even displayed the edges of a dry sense of humor. Not long ago the exchange for Richard's telephone number was changed to Riverside. "Just dial RI," he said with a straight face to a rural photographer who had forgotten the exchange, "RI… for Richard." An old friend who stood by couldn't believe his ears.

Toward the 400th

Most of these relaxed moments, it goes without saying, take place from April to September. Then another hockey season is on, and while Richard today may be a shade less volcanic than formerly as he moves steadily toward his 400th goal, he still burns with a fierce sense of purpose. During a team slump or a personal scoring drought, he is still a good man to avoid. Silent and seething, he builds up intensity to such a pitch that, eventually, it must explode. Sometimes the Rocket explodes in fights, in arguments with referees, in overly aggressive if fruitless hockey. Sooner or later, though, he will explode with a splurge of dramatic goals. On these evenings, it is an experience to be in Montreal, for it is then that the Forum roars like one huge happy lion, the most jubilant hullabaloo you can hear in the sports world. It is not an extravagant tribute. After all, of all the great athletes of our time, none has played his game with more skill, more color, more competitive fire and more heart than Maurice Richard.

THE RICHARD HOCKEY RIOT

Sidney Katz

This piece originally appeared in Maclean's *magazine, September 17, 1955. Reprinted with permission.*

ON MARCH 17, 1955, AT EXACTLY 9:11 P.M., a tear-gas bomb exploded in the Montreal Forum where 16,000 people had gathered to watch a hockey match between the Montreal Canadiens and the Detroit Red Wings. The acrid yellowish fumes that filled the stadium sent the crowd rushing to the exits, crying, shrieking, coughing and retching. But it did more. It touched off the most destructive and frenzied riot in the history of Canadian sport.

The explosion of the bomb was the last straw in a long series of provocative incidents that swept away the last remnant of the crowd's restraint and decency. Many of the hockey fans had come to the game in an ugly mood. The day before, Clarence Campbell, president of the National Hockey League, had banished Maurice "The Rocket" Richard, the star of the Canadiens and the idol of the Montreal fans, from hockey for the remainder of the season. The suspension couldn't have come at a worse time for the Canadiens. They were leading Detroit by the narrow margin of two points. Richard's award for individual high scoring was at stake, too—he was only two points ahead of his teammate Bernie "Boom Boom" Geoffrion. Furthermore, it had been a long tough hockey season, full of emotional outbursts. Throughout the first period of play the crowd had vented their anger at Campbell by shouting, "*Va-t'en*, Campbell," ("Scram, Campbell") and showering him with rotten fruit, eggs, pickled pig's feet and empty bottles.

At one time there were as many as 10,000 people—patrons, demonstrators and onlookers—packed around the outside of the Forum. Many of them rushed around in bands shrieking like animals. For a time it looked as if a lynching might even be attempted: groups of rioters were savagely chanting in unison, "Kill Campbell! Kill Campbell!" The windows of passing streetcars were smashed and, for no apparent reason, cab drivers were hauled from their vehicles and pummeled. The mob smashed hundreds of windows in the Forum by throwing bricks, chunks of ice and even full bottles of beer. They pulled down signs and tore doors off their hinges. They toppled corner newsstands and telephones booths, doused them in oil and left them burning.

When the mob grew weary of the Forum they moved eastward down Ste-Catherine Street, Montreal's main shopping district. For 15 blocks they left in their path a swath of destruction. It looked like the aftermath of a wartime blitz in London. Hardly a store in those 15 blocks was spared. Display windows were smashed and looters carried away practically everything portable—jewelry, clothes, clocks, radios and cameras. The cost of the riot was added up later: an estimated $30,000 worth of damage due to looting and vandalism; 12 policemen and 25 civilians injured; eight police cars and several streetcars, taxicabs and private automobiles damaged. "It was the worst night I've had in my 33 years as a policeman," said Thomas Leggett, Montreal's director of police.

But the greatest damage done was not physical. Montrealers awoke ashamed and stunned after their emotional binge. *The Montreal Star* observed, "Nothing remains but shame." The *Toronto Star* commented "It's savagery which attacks the fundamentals of civilized behavior." Canadian hockey was given a black name on the front pages of newspapers as far apart as Los Angeles and London, England. "Ice hockey is rough," observed the London *News Chronicle*, "but it is now a matter of grim record that Canadian players are spring lambs compared to those who support them." A Dutch newspaper headlined the riot story: STADIUM WRECKED, 27 DEAD, 100 WOUNDED.

The newspapers and radio were blamed for whipping up public opinion against Campbell before the riot. Frank Hanley, of the Montreal city council, said that Mayor Jean Drapeau must accept at least some of the responsibility. Had he not publicly criticized Campbell's decision to suspend Richard instead of appealing to the public to accept it? Drapeau, in turn, blamed the riot on Campbell who "provoked it" by his presence at the game. Frank D. Corbett, a citizen of Westmount, expressed an opinion about the riot which many people thought about but few discussed publicly. In a letter to the editor of a local paper, he said bluntly that the outbreak was symptomatic of racial ill-feeling. "French and English relationships have deteriorated badly over the past 10 years and they have never been worse," he wrote. "The basic unrest is nationalism, which is ever present in Quebec. Let's face it ... the French Canadians want the English expelled from the province."

All of these observations contained some germ of truth but no single one of them explains satisfactorily what happened in Montreal on St. Patrick's Night. In the case history of the Richard riot, the night of March 13, four nights before the Montreal outburst, is important. On that night, the Montreal Canadiens were playing against the Boston Bruins in the Boston Gardens. An incident occurred six minutes before the end of the game that set the stage for the debacle in Montreal. Boston was leading 4–2, playing one man short because of a penalty. In a desperate effort to score, the Canadiens had removed their goalie and sent six men up the ice. Richard was skating across the Boston blue line past Boston defenseman Hal Laycoe when the latter put his stick up high and caught Richard on the left side of his head. It made a nasty gash that later required five stitches. Frank Udvari, the referee, signaled a penalty to Laycoe for high-sticking but allowed the game to go on because the Canadiens had the puck.

Richard skated behind the Boston net and had returned to the blue line when the whistle blew. He rubbed his head, then suddenly skated over to Laycoe who was a short distance away. Lifting his stick high over his head with both hands Richard pounded Laycoe over the face and shoulders with all his strength. Laycoe dropped his gloves and stick and motioned to Richard to come and fight with his fists. An official, linesman Cliff Thompson, grabbed Richard and took his stick away from him. Richard broke away, picked up a loose stick on the ice and again slashed away at Laycoe, this time breaking the stick on him. Again Thompson got hold of Richard, but again Richard escaped and with another stick slashed at the man who had injured him. Thompson subdued Richard for the third time by forcing him down to the ice. With the help of a teammate, Richard regained his feet and sprang at Thompson, bruising his face and blackening his eye. Thompson finally got Richard under control and sent him to the first-aid room for medical attention.

Richard was penalized for the remainder of the game and fined $100. Laycoe, who suffered body bruises and face wounds, was penalized five minutes for high-sticking and was given a further 10-minute penalty for tossing a blood-stained towel at referee Udvari as he entered the penalty box.

Richard's emotional and physical resistance were at a low ebb on the night of the Boston game. It was near the end of a long exhausting schedule. The Canadiens had played Boston only the previous night in Montreal. Richard had been hurled against a net and had injured his back. The back was so painful he hadn't been able to sleep on the train trip to Boston in spite of the application of ice packs. On the morning of the game he confided to a reporter, "My back still hurts like the dickens. I feel beat." He never considered sitting out the Boston game. There was too much at stake. With three scheduled games left, the Canadiens' chances of finishing first in the league were bright. Furthermore, Richard was narrowly leading the league for individual high scoring. If he won, he would receive a cup, $1,000 from the league and another $1,000 from his club. He was still brooding over an incident that had threatened his winning the top-scoring award. In Toronto the previous Thursday, he had been in a perfect position to score when he was hooked by Hugh Bolton of the Maple Leafs. Bolton was penalized but it still meant that Richard was deprived of a goal he desperately wanted.

Accustomed to the "win-at-any-cost" brand of hockey, some fans resort to violence of their own. Once in Boston, a woman jabbed Butch Bouchard, captain of the Canadiens, in the hip with a pin as he was entering the rink. Only a few months before the Richard riot, a Canadiens supporter sprinkled pepper on the towels used by the Boston Bruins to mop their faces. Many observers feel that the Richard riot was merely another example of how lawlessness can spread from players to spectators. Team owners, coaches and trainers have promoted disrespect for law and authority in hockey by their attitude. They complain bitterly when referees apply the rules strictly. A few weeks before the

Richard riot, coach Jimmy Skinner was using abusive language from the Detroit bench during a game. Campbell left his seat and approached him. "You've got to stop talking like that," he warned him. Skinner turned his abuse on Campbell. "Beat it, you—," he is reported to have said. "You're only a spectator here."

In this new brand of hockey which permits rough play and often ignores the rules, the most harassed player in the NHL is Richard. Thirty-four years old, 5'10" in height, Richard weighs 180 pounds and is handsome in a sullen kind of a way. His dark-brown hair is slicked back, he has bushy eyebrows, a small mouth and his characteristic expression is deadpan. His intense, penetrating dark eyes seem to perceive everything in microscopic detail. Talking to him at close range, you sometimes feel uneasy. It's possible that Richard is the greatest hockey player who ever lived. The Canadiens were once offered $135,000 for him—the highest value ever placed on a hockey player. Frank Selke, Canadiens managing director, refused, saying, "I'd sooner sell half the Forum."

Opposing teams fully recognize Richard's talent and use rugged methods to stop him. One and sometimes two players are specifically detailed to nettle him. They regularly hang on to him, put hockey sticks between his legs, body-check him and board him harder than necessary. Once he skated 20 feet with two men on his shoulders to score a goal.

His opponents also employ psychological warfare to unnerve him. Inspector William Minogue, who, as police officer in charge of the Forum, is regularly at the rinkside during games, frequently hears opposing players calling Richard "French pea soup" or "dirty French bastard" as they skate past. If these taunts result in a fight, both Richard and his provoker are sent to the penalty bench. Opposing teams consider this a good bargain.

Because of these tactics, Richard frequently explodes. But he is a rarity among men as well as among hockey players. He is an artist. He is completely dedicated to playing good hockey and scoring goals. "It's the most important thing in my life," he told me. In hockey, Richard has found a kind of personal destiny. "He's on fire inside all the time he's on the ice," says Frank Selke. "I've never had a player who tries so intensely." Even after 13 years of professional hockey Richard still approaches each game as though he were about to undergo a major surgical operation. He is in a brooding, uncommunicative mood. "I feel nervous the whole day," he told me. "I feel sick in the stomach. When we are lined up for the national anthem I pray silently to God that I might play a good game." As soon as the game starts, however, he loses his queasiness and is unaware of the crowd. "I think of only one thing," says Richard, "scoring goals." He has never been known to miss a practice or to be late for one. He doesn't want to be anything less than the greatest hockey player. "No one will have to tell me when to stop playing hockey," he told me. "When I stop scoring, I'll quit. I wouldn't be able to take that."

He suffers mental agony after a game in which he thinks he's done poorly. He'll slink quietly into the dressing room and sit on the bench for half an hour before making an attempt to get out of his uniform. On some such occasions he's been known to burst into tears. "A poor game makes me feel bad," he explains. "I'll go home and not talk to anybody, not even my wife. I'll sit by myself and think, over and over again, about all the chances I missed to score. I try to forget about it but I can't. I won't get to bed till about three or four in the morning." On the road, he'll sit on the edge of his berth repeating to himself, "I was lousy." He never offers alibis or blames a defeat on others.

There are better skaters, better stickhandlers, better checkers and better playmakers than Richard, but no better hockey player. He seems to have the power to summon forth all his strength at the very instant it's needed. "His strength comes all at once like the explosion of a bomb," says Kenny Reardon, an ex-hockey player who is now assistant manager of the Canadiens. Most of the time this concentrated outburst is channeled into the scoring of goals. But sometimes it is used to strike back at his tormentors—as it was in Boston on Sunday, March 13, when he assaulted Hal Laycoe and linesman Cliff Thompson.

On the night of the Boston fracas, Clarence Campbell was traveling from Montreal to New York by train to attend a meeting of the NHL Board of Governors where plans for the Stanley Cup playoffs were to be made. In Grand Central station next morning he read about the rumpus in the *New York Times*. Hurrying to his hotel, he phoned referee Frank Udvari and linesmen Sam Babcock and Cliff Thompson to get a verbal report. Disturbed by what he heard, he announced a hearing would be held in Montreal to ascertain all the facts and to decide on what punishment should be given to the players involved. The time set was two days later—Wednesday, March 16 at 10:30 a.m.

In the intervening time, the Boston incident was widely commented on. Dick Irvin was angry at his players. "What kind of spirit have we got on the Canadiens?" he asked. "There were four or five players on the ice and they hardly gave Richard any help!" He suggested that the Richard hearing be televised. Most of the comments were in a more serious vein. Richard's supporters contended that because of lax refereeing their hero had been badgered beyond his endurance. On the other hand, the *Toronto Star* described Richard as "a chronic blow-top and an habitual offender." Campbell was advised by many out-of-town newspapers to ground the Rocket long enough to teach him a lesson. Marshall Dann, a Boston columnist, said angrily that "if Richard is permitted to play one more game of hockey this season, Campbell should be fired. Richard is the most pampered player in the league. For his repeated misbehavior, he has drawn only mild wrist slaps or inconsequential fines from Campbell."

In January 1954, in his regular column in the Montreal weekly *Le Samedi-dimanche*, Richard denounced Campbell as a "dictator" who was prejudiced against the Canadiens and who "gloated when an opposing team scored a goal against us." He was required to apologize and post a $1,000 bond for good behavior. In December 1954, in Toronto, he charged into Bob Bailey with his stick, broke two of his front teeth, then turned and struck linesman George Hayes. He was given two 10-minute misconduct penalties and fined a total of $250.

And now, three months later, came the incident in Boston. Both Richard and Campbell refrained from making public statements until after the hearing. Richard, because of his head wound, spent most of the time under observation at the Montreal Western Hospital which was then located across from the Forum. On the morning of the hearing, March 16, he got dressed but did not shave. He looked pale and worried and wore a patch on the left side of his head. He walked across to the Forum where he picked up coach Dick Irvin and assistant manager Kenny Reardon. The three men got into a cab. On the way over to NHL headquarters about a mile away, Richard broke his silence only once to observe ruefully, "I always seem to be getting into trouble."

The NHL suite on the sixth floor of the Sun Life Building was a beehive of activity. A large group of young people from the adjoining offices, mostly girls, lined the corridors to catch a glimpse of their hockey hero. Reporters, photographers and TV cameramen had overflowed the outer office, sitting on the desks and monopolizing the phones. Richard posed unsmilingly for the photographers and forced a weak grin for the TV cameramen. When he entered Campbell's office with Irvin and Reardon, the other participants in the hearing were already seated around Campbell's desk: referee-in-chief Carl Voss, referee Frank Udvari, linesmen Cliff Thompson and Sammy Babcock, Hal Laycoe and Lynn Patrick, manager and coach of the Boston Bruins. The hearing was private.

It lasted for three hours. The officials read their reports of the incident and submitted to questioning. Everyone present was then invited to give his version of what happened. On some points, there were sharp differences. Campbell took notes busily. In defense of Richard, Irvin said that he had been temporarily stunned by the blow on his head and was unaware of what he was doing. Richard remained silent until asked if he had anything to say. "I don't remember what happened," he replied. Later, Richard told me: "When I'm hit, I get mad and I don't know what I do. Before each game I think about my temper and how I should control it, but as soon as I get on the ice I forget all that."

At 1:30 p.m. they filed out. They refused to comment to the 40 newsmen who had now gathered in the outer office. Richard returned to the hospital. Left alone, Campbell ordered a ham sandwich on brown bread and a cup of coffee and began studying his notes, preparatory to writing out his decision. "I had a hard time making up my mind," he told me later. By three o'clock Campbell had written out the first page of his decision. As each page was completed it was carried across the office by referee-in-chief Voss to a private office to be typed by Phyllis King, Campbell's secretary. He had made thousands of unpopular decisions—but none nearly so unpopular as the one he made public to the assembled newspapermen in his presidential office at four o'clock that March afternoon.

The attacks on Laycoe and Thompson were deliberate and persistent, he found. "An incident occurred less than three months ago in which the pattern of conduct of Richard was almost identical. . . Consequently, the time for leniency or probation is past. Whether this type of conduct is the product of temperamental instability or willful defiance doesn't matter. It's a type of conduct that cannot be tolerated." The room was completely silent as Campbell then pronounced the punishment. "Richard is suspended from playing in the remaining league and playoff games."

At about 4:30 p.m., Irvin, Reardon, Elmer Lach, a former Richard teammate, and Elmer Ferguson, of the *Montreal Herald*, were sitting around the Canadiens office when they heard the news on a radio broadcast. About 10 minutes later Richard came in. He had just been discharged from hospital. According to Ferguson this is what followed:

Richard asked, "Is the ruling out yet?"

Irvin was silent for a few seconds, then said quietly, "Be prepared for a shock, Rocket. You're out for the season—including the Stanley Cup playoffs."

Richard didn't believe it. "You're kidding—now tell me the truth."

Irvin said, "Sorry. That's the way it is, Rocket. No kidding."

Richard shrugged his shoulders, said good night and walked off to his car. Nobody spoke. A few seconds later Lach said, "There goes the greatest of them all."

Richard later told me that the decision came as a great shock. "I didn't expect it to be so severe. I had always been in the playoffs before. I was so disappointed I didn't know whether I would stay in Montreal or not. My first impulse was to go to Florida. But I changed my mind. I wanted to watch my team play. I didn't want the fans to get the idea that I was no longer interested just because I was suspended."

No sports decision ever hit the Montreal public with such impact. It seemed to strike at the very heart and soul of the city. Upon first hearing of the suspension a French speaking employee in the Gazette composing room broke down and cried. A bus driver became so upset by the news that he ignored a flashing railway-level-crossing signal and almost killed his passengers. The French station CKAC invited listeners to phone in their opinions: 97 percent said that although some punishment for Richard was justified the suspension for the playoffs was too severe. The switchboard became so jammed the station had to appeal to listeners to stop calling. The sports departments of the newspapers were so besieged by the phone calls and visitors that some of the writers had to go home to get their work done.

There were portents of what was to happen on the night of March 17 in the phone calls received by Campbell. Many of them were taken by Campbell's secretary, Phyllis King, an attractive, willowy blonde in her early 30s. "They were nearly all abusive and they seemed to grow worse as the day wore on," says Miss King. One of the first callers said, "Tell Campbell I'm an undertaker and he'll be needing me in a few days." Still another announced, "I'm no crank but I'm going to blow your place up." Many of the callers were so angry they could hardly talk. There were dozens of crying women on the phone. A 40-year-old secretary from Toronto ran up a $20 long-distance phone bill pleading with Campbell to call off the suspension.

The strong racial feelings engendered by the decision should have sounded an ominous warning. These were reflected in hundreds of letters that Campbell received. One of them said, "If Richard's name was Richardson you would have given a different verdict." From Verdun: "You're just another Englishman jealous of the French, who are much better than you."

There's abundant evidence that Richard holds a special place in the heart of French Canada. Perhaps ancient nationalist feelings would not have been as important a factor in causing the riot had people in positions of authority urged acceptance of Campbell's decision in the interest of law and order. Such mollifying statements were not forthcoming in sufficient number to influence public opinion. On the contrary, many prominent people added fuel to the fire. Mayor Jean Drapeau issued a statement castigating Campbell. "It would not be necessary to give too many such decisions to kill hockey in Montreal," he said.

The Montreal press, both English and French, reinforced the fans' feeling that Campbell had victimized them. *Le Devoir* called the punishment "unjust and too severe." One French weekly published a crude cartoon of Campbell's head on a platter, dripping blood, with the caption: "This is how we would like to see him." The English press followed a similar line, although somewhat more temperate in tone. Dink Carroll said "it was a harsh judgment" in the *Gazette*, while Baz O'Meara in the *Star* found the decision "tough and unexpectedly severe."

On March 17 at 11:30 a.m. came the first sign that Montreal fans would not be content to limit their protests to angry words. A dozen young men showed up at the Forum where Canadiens were scheduled to play Detroit that night. They bore signs saying "*Vive Richard*" and "*A Bas Campbell.*" At 1:30 p.m. about 20 young men arrived, apparently college students. They carried signs, one with a picture of a pig with Campbell's name on it; another had a picture of a pear which is the French equivalent of knucklehead. The police felt they weren't doing any harm and allowed them to march up and down. At about 3:30 another group of men between the ages of 18 and 35 arrived.

An air of excitement and anticipation hung over the city. Newspapers and radio stations headlined every new development. The crucial question now was: Would Campbell dare show himself in public at the game that night? When Campbell announced that he would definitely attend, excitement reached a fever pitch. At four o'clock, station CKVL dispatched a mobile sound unit to the Shell gas station across the road from the Forum and set up a direct line to its transmitter. "We were almost certain that there was going to be trouble," says Marcel Beauregard, feature editor of CKVL. "It was in the air." It was at about this time, too, according to a Montreal newspaper report, that an attempt was made to buy up a number of tickets near Campbell for the express purpose of tormenting him.

Why did Campbell decide to go to the game? As he saw it, he would be hanged either way. If he failed to go, he would be branded as a coward. "I never seriously considered not going to the game," he later said. "I'm a season ticketholder and a regular attendant and I have a right to go. I felt that the police could protect me. I didn't consult them and they didn't advise me not to attend."

Mayor Drapeau offers a different version. Campbell, he says, phoned the police during the afternoon to announce his attendance and ask for protection. A highly placed officer suggested that he stay away. Richard, the other central figure, was undecided about going until the last minute. His wife finally made up his mind for him. "She told me that she was going so I decided to go along too," he says.

The activity outside the Forum mounted steadily as the hour of the game approached. Bands of demonstrators moved up and down with signs saying "Unfair to French Canadians." At about 6:30 a number of panel trucks circled around Atwater Park, across from the Forum, a few times and discharged a number of young men in black leather windbreakers bearing white insignia. Their windbreakers had special significance for the police. They were the garb of youthful motorcyclists who had been involved in disorders on previous occasions. Other groups kept arriving steadily. By 8:30, when the game started, there were probably about 600 demonstrators. The Forum loudspeaker announced that all seats were now sold. A picketer shouted back, "We don't want seats. We want Campbell!" The cry was taken up and repeated endlessly with savage intensity.

A few minutes after the Canadiens-Detroit game started, Richard slipped into the Forum unnoticed and took a seat near the goal judge's cage at the south end of the rink. He gazed intently at the ice, a look of distress on his face: the Canadiens were playing sloppy hockey. At the 11th minute of the first period Detroit scored a second goal and the Canadiens saw their hopes of a league championship go up in smoke. It was at this minute that Clarence Campbell entered the arena. He couldn't have chosen a worse time.

As soon as Campbell sat down the crowd recognized him and pandemonium broke loose. They shifted their attention from the game to Campbell and set up a deafening roar "Shoo Campbell, Shoo Campbell" ... "*Va-t'en, Va-t'en.*" "The people didn't care if we got licked 100–1 that night," says Dick Irvin. "They were only interested in Campbell. Evidently our players were too because they paid no attention to their hockey." In the remaining nine minutes of the first period, Detroit was able to score another two goals, making the score 4–1. The next 40 minutes were to be sheer torture for Campbell. Vegetables, eggs, tomatoes, [toe] rubbers, bottles and programs rained down on him. They were from the $1.50 seats and standing section far above. Campbell was wearing a dark-green fedora and a dark-gray suit. They were soon smudged by oranges, eggs and tomatoes. At one point Campbell's hat was knocked off by a heavy flying object and an orange hit him square in the back.

Campbell's ordeal was shared by his neighbors. Jimmy Orlando, an ex-hockey player who sat below Campbell, was struck by a potato. Campbell's friends who shared his row—Audrey King, Hilda Hawkes, Mr. and Mrs. Cooper Smeaton and Dr. and Mrs. Jack Gerrie, were struck and splattered. A city hall employee who customarily sits near Campbell became alarmed by the violence. "Go home ... Please go home," he pleaded with Campbell.

But Campbell stood his ground. He was tight lipped but occasionally managed to smile. He tried to carry on his usual practice of making notes on the refereeing in a black notebook, but had to abandon it as the hail of peanuts, pig's feet and programs continued. Each time he got to brush the debris from his clothes, the clamor grew louder. Whenever the Detroit team scored the crowd's temper rose and the shower of objects on Campbell thickened. From his rinkside seat, Richard occasionally turned to see what was happening. "This is a disgrace," he said to physiotherapist Bill Head who was sitting beside him.

The first period ended. Ordinarily, Campbell spends the intermissions in the referees' room. Tonight he decided to remain in his seat, believing that this would cause less excitement. His friends in the same row did likewise. A woman going by leaned over and whispered in Campbell's ear, "I'm ashamed. I want to apologize for the crowd." She was close to tears. About a minute later, one Andre Robinson, a young man of 26 who resembles Marlon Brando, confronted Campbell. Without uttering a word he squashed two large tomatoes against Campbell's chest and rubbed them in. As he fled down the stairs Campbell kept pointing at him, signaling the two policemen to arrest him. At that moment, Frank Teskey, of the *Toronto Star*, aimed his camera for a shot. A grapefruit came whizzing down and knocked the camera out of his hand. Now hordes of people came rushing down from the seats above, surrounding Campbell. The ill feeling against Campbell was growing more intense by the second and there was nobody to help him.

Where were the police? On hockey nights the Forum is responsible for maintaining order inside the arena; the

Montreal police department, outside. Because of the special circumstances on March 17 the police stationed two of their constables near Campbell's seat. Frank Selke, manager of the Canadiens, employed eight plainclothesmen for similar duty, but they had to be rushed to guard the entrances against the demonstrators outside. Ordinarily, the Forum employs 350 ushers, 12 policemen and 24 firemen; for the Detroit game they added an extra 15 police—regular constables who were off duty. Ordinarily, the police have 25 men outside the Forum; on this night they had double that number to start with. But at 9:11, when Campbell was being surrounded by a hostile mob, none of them were there to protect him. At that critical moment he was delivered by the explosion of a tear-gas bomb 25 feet away. As the thick fumes fanned upward and outward, the crowd immediately forgot Campbell and began fighting their way to the fresh air outside.

Who threw the bomb? This question has never been answered. There is no evidence that the thrower intended to befriend Campbell but that's what he may have done. Chief of Detectives George Allain later observed, "The bomb-thrower protected Campbell's life by releasing it at precisely the right moment." The bomb, a type not on sale to the public, landed on a wet rubber mat on the aisle adjacent to the ice surface. The people nearby, of course, didn't know what it was. Some thought that the ammonia pipes had sprung a leak; others that a fire had broken out in the basement. Within a few seconds they were coughing and choking as the fumes clogged their eyes, throats, stomachs and lungs. To protect themselves as they hurried out they wrapped coats around their faces. Women were screaming. Somebody yelled "Fire!" A middle-aged man got stuck in one of the turnstiles in the lobby and was shouting to be released but nobody could hear him above the din. A pregnant woman fought her way to the fresh air outside and had to be taken to hospital. At the height of the exodus, with tears streaming from everybody's eyes, the organist high in the loft began playing "My Heart Cries For You."

Panic was averted by the fast work of police and firemen. When Tom Leggett, director of police, saw the bomb go off he immediately assigned his men, who were outside the Forum, to keep all exits open and to keep the crowd moving out. Jim Hunter, the superintendent of the building, hurriedly switched on his 13 powerful fans to suck the fumes out of the building. Campbell made his way to the first-aid center 50 feet away under the stands. Richard had also made his way to the first-aid center but never came face to face with Campbell because he was in a different room. He was aghast at what had happened. "This is terrible, awful," he said. "People might have been killed."

In the next 10 minutes the outcome of the Montreal-Detroit hockey game was to be decided. Armand Pare, head of the Montreal fire department, was unwilling to have the game continue. He felt that the temper of the crowd was such that there was real danger of panic and fire. Campbell sent the following note to Jack Adams, the Detroit general manager, after conferring with Selke: "The game has been forfeited to Detroit. You are entitled to take your team on its way anytime now. Selke agrees as the fire department has ordered this building closed."

Back in the Detroit dressing room, manager Jack Adams was in an angry mood. News of the forfeiture seemed to intensify it. "What's happened tonight makes me sick and ashamed," he said. He then turned to a group of newspapermen. "I blame you fellows for what's happened. You've turned Richard into an idol, a man whose suspension can turn hockey fans into shrieking idiots. Now hear this: Richard is no hero! He let his team down, he let hockey down, he let the public down. Richard makes me ashamed to be connected with this game."

Until the bomb exploded the demonstration outside the Forum was neither destructive nor out of control. The explosion, however, signaled a change of mood. When thousands of excited, frightened fans poured outside and joined the demonstrators it seemed to unleash an ugly mob spirit which ended in a shameful episode of physical violence, vandalism and looting.

In a mob riot only a small core of people are required to initiate violence. They act as a catalyst on the crowd. Other people are carried away by the excitement and drawn into their activities. In the Richard riot, the core of violence was made up of bands of teenagers and young adults. There were probably about 500 or 600 of them. Like packs of wolves, they moved up and down in front of the Forum, shrieking wildly and inflaming the crowd. They took rubbers off the feet of spectators and threw them at the police. There was soon a high pile of rubbers in front of the Forum. They attacked a side door of the building and tore it off its hinges. They hurled chunks of ice and empty bottles, smashing windows. Dissatisfied with this ammunition, they marched off to where a new hospital was being built half a block away and returned with chunks of brick and concrete.

The police had cleared a wide space directly in front of the Forum, pushing the crowd back to the park across the road. As soon as the rioters discharged their ammunition they sought shelter in the crowd. "It was dangerous to rush into the crowd to get them," says Chief Leggett. "It was full of women and children—some of them in carriages, some in arms. It was slippery. Had we used too much force, many people might have been trampled."

It is doubtful whether most of the troublemakers were hockey fans. Inspector William Minogue arrested a husky man in a black-and-red mackinaw. He identified himself as a lumberjack from Chalk River. "You must love Richard," said Minogue. A blank expression came over his face: "Richard? Who's he?"

Across the street CKVL broadcasters were giving the Montreal public a dramatic blow-by-blow description of the riot: "The bomb has gone off!... There goes another window!... The police are rushing the crowd!..." This marathon broadcast and others attracted thousands more people to the Forum.

By 11 p.m. the crowd numbered at least 10,000. It was too big for the police and the Forum was now virtually in a state of siege. It was unsafe to wander in the vicinity of the windows. Don Smith, manager of the box office, ordered Violet Trahan and Peggy Nibbs, the Forum telephone operators, to close down the switchboard and leave. Before abandoning the office himself he began to shove everything portable into the vault. As he was emptying the cash register a small rock came hurtling through the window, narrowly missing him and landing in the $10 compartment of the drawer. Eddie Quinn, a wrestling promoter whose office is on the east side of the Forum, invited a friend in for a chat. "Nobody will bother us here," he said. "Everybody knows I'm a Richard fan." He was referring to the fact that he employs Richard to referee wrestling matches during the summer. A few seconds later a large rock demolished his office window.

Frank Selke was sitting out the riot in the directors' room

along with other club officials and newsmen. He ordered the steward to make up a large batch of sandwiches and coffee. "Looks like we're going to be here for a while," he said. Campbell remained in the first-aid center. The trampling and shouting of the crowd and the shattering of glass were ominously audible. Everyone was tense. Did the crowd know where Campbell was? Would they attempt a raid to capture him? Later Campbell said, "I was never seriously afraid of being lynched. As a referee I learned something about mobs. They're cowards."

By about 11:15 p.m. the back entrance of the Forum was fairly quiet. Gaston Bettez, the Canadiens' trainer, drove Richard's car up to the door and hastily loaded Richard and his wife into it. "When I got home I listened to the riot on the radio," says Richard. "I felt badly. Once I felt like going downtown and telling the people over a loudspeaker to stop their nonsense. But it wouldn't have done any good. They would have carried me around on their shoulders. It's nice to have people behind you but not the way they did on the night of the Detroit game." The phone rang all night in the Richard home saying that Campbell got what he deserved. It was answered by the housekeeper. Richard himself retired at 4 a.m. and slept in the next morning.

At 11:30 p.m. Jim Hunter, the Forum building superintendent, entered the first-aid center and announced, "I think it's safe to go home now, Mr. Campbell." Leggett concurred. There was some discussion as to whether it would be safe for Campbell to spend the night alone at his home. Billy Wray, an undertaker and friend, was insisting that Campbell be his guest for the evening. Someone else suggested that he check into a hotel under an assumed name. Campbell refused both suggestions. Led by Hunter and a husky policeman, Campbell and Miss King made their way to the back of the building where Hunter's dark blue 1951 Ford was waiting inside. The policeman sat in front with the driver; Campbell and Miss King sat in the back.

Campbell, who lives four miles from the Forum, was dropped off first. As soon as he got home he phoned his father in Edmonton to say that he was safe. Although his phone is unlisted it started to ring incessantly. Most of the callers were abusive and spoke in broken English. He lifted the phone off the hook and went to bed about one o'clock. "I had a fine night's sleep," he said. He got up at his usual hour of 7:30 a.m.

By midnight the frenzy of the rioters outside the Forum became almost demoniacal. They were unaware of Campbell's departure. They attacked a newsstand at the southwest corner of Ste-Catherine and Closse Streets, sprinkled it with oil from a small stove they found inside and set it afire. Within a few minutes it was a pile of smoldering ashes. It was a wanton and tragic act. The stand belonged to Auguste Belanger, a 56-year-old father of four children. After a considerable struggle he had only recently managed to set himself up in business. "Why did they have to do such a thing to me?" he sobbed.

The rioters now turned their attention to the firms that rented space on the ground floor of the Forum, facing Ste-Catherine Street. They heaved rocks through the plate-glass windows of the Royal Bank of Canada. The supervisor and three salesgirls of a United Cigar Store had to barricade themselves in the stock room to escape injury. Patrick Maloney, proprietor of a jewelry store, took refuge in the small windowless room where he repairs watches. His windows and stock were demolished by chunks of rock, metal and bottles. Many objects were stolen, including a $490 diamond ring. Maloney passed the time brewing coffee. Occasionally, he would step into the store and pick up a full bottle of beer or pop that had been hurled in and drink it. Debris came flying through the windows of the York Tavern. Benny Parent, the manager, ordered that the building be evacuated. The police continued the hard task of arresting the rioters. Whenever they had a full load of them, the patrol wagon would rush off to the police station with its siren wailing. A young doctor from the hospital across from the Forum stepped outside for a minute to see what was going on; before he knew what was happening he was on his way to the police station in a wagon. A little old lady with fire in her eyes approached Chief Leggett. "Let's start getting tough with them," she said, "I'm with you."

The little old lady was not the only person offering advice to the director of police. Dozens of people urged him to use more forceful methods against the demonstrators. Had he wished to do so the means were at hand. Each constable was armed with a stick and a revolver; a police car stood by with a supply of tear-gas bombs; the firemen had a high-pressure water hose ready. But Leggett withheld the order to use any of these strong-arm methods. "It might have led to panic and hysteria—and that's when people get killed," he said. As it was, not a single person was seriously injured.

By midnight some people had left, but even more had arrived, drawn by the radio broadcasts. Finally, Pierre DesMarais, chief of Montreal's executive committee, appealed to the radio stations to stop broadcasting news of the trouble. He reached Marcel Beauregard, who was at the scene of the riot. "It would help the police if you went off the air," said DesMarais. Beauregard checked with his boss, Jack Tietolman, the proprietor of CKVL, who agreed. CKVL finally went off the air after more than seven hours of on-the-spot broadcasting. The other stations did likewise.

By one o'clock the crowd had thinned out. About 40 policemen, linked arm to arm, formed a solid chain across Ste-Catherine Street. They started moving slowly eastward, taking the crowd along with them. They felt that at last the riot was on the wane. But they were wrong. Ahead of them, hidden from view by hundreds of people, groups of demonstrators began smashing store windows and stealing their contents. A heavy safety-zone lantern was hurled through the window of the International Music store; instruments were smashed and looted. The mob noticed a picture of Richard and the Canadiens in the window of Adolph Stegmeier's photographic studio. To get at it, they hurled a 20-pound block of ice they found on the road at the window. Before they could reach in and seize the photograph their way was barred by tenants who occupied apartments above the studio. Signs at Red Cross headquarters were torn down. Costly plate-glass windows at Ogilvy's department store were shattered. When Gilles Rouleau, owner of a florist shop, heard the crowd approaching, he locked his doors, doused his lights and waited. The rioters passed him by. He noticed that the vandals were teenagers but that they were being egged on by older people, many of whom appeared to be drunk.

In the 15 blocks along Ste-Catherine Street, east of the Forum, 50 stores were damaged and looted. The stolen goods included kimonos, men's pants, dresses, high-chair pads, shoes, bracelets, cameras and assorted jewelry. At first it was believed that $100,000 worth of goods (including windows) had been damaged and stolen. Revised estimates scaled the amount down to $30,000 or less.

The police now sent out special patrols to find the vandals and recover the loot. They arrested one man who was carrying an armful of alarm clocks. By searching restaurants along Ste-Catherine Street they were able to pick up three other young men in possession of stolen goods. Only a few items of the pillaged goods were ever recovered. "Most of the stolen objects were mass-produced small items not easy to identify," says Chief Detective George Allain, "and there were no clues to follow." A few days after the riot A. Jeffries, proprietor of a photo-supply store, received a parcel in the mail containing a camera worth $100 that had been stolen from him. An unsigned note said, "My conscience has been bothering me ever since I took it from your window."

By 3 a.m. the last rock had been hurled, the last window had been smashed and the last blood-curdling shriek of "Kill Campbell!" had been uttered. The fury of the mob had spent itself. By the end of the riot the police had picked up 70 people and delivered them to No. 10 police station. Twenty-five were juveniles (under 18) and were driven home to their parents. The remainder were transferred to the cells at police headquarters on Gosford Street. They talked hockey for an hour or so, then stretched out and went to sleep. At seven in the morning a guard came in and announced (wrongly) that Campbell had resigned. The arrested men roused themselves, cheered, jumped up and down and broke out in a song. Addressing the offenders in municipal court the next morning, Judge Emmett J. McManamy intended his words to go far beyond his courtroom. "Last night's riot," he said, "brings home to the people of Montreal a terrible lesson of the narrow margin between order and disorder. It must never happen again."

The mood of most Montrealers following the riot was a mixture of shame and regret. It was well summed up by the terse opening sentence in Dink Carroll's column in the *Gazette* on March 18; "I am ashamed of my city." Others, like Mayor Jean Drapeau, were less remorseful. Drapeau issued a statement which, on the surface, seemed to absolve the public of all responsibility for the outbreak. It came about, he said, because of "provocation caused by Campbell's presence."

Campbell showed up at his office the next morning at the usual hour of 8:30. He refused a police offer of bodyguards. Newsmen were asking him for a statement. He said that he had no intention of resigning, as had been frequently suggested. Richard was still asleep when reporters knocked on the door of his home at eight o'clock. It was answered by his six-year-old son who said, "I hope you didn't come to talk to him about hockey." When the reporters returned later, Richard was attired in a white T-shirt and a pair of slacks. His face was lined with fatigue. "This certainly isn't the time for me to say anything," he said. "It might start something again." By three o'clock he changed his mind. He showed up in Frank Selke's office and said that he wanted to make a public statement. Selke said he could see no objection. At seven o'clock, seated in front of a battery of microphones, he made the following short speech in French:

> *"Because I always try so hard to win and had my troubles in Boston, I was suspended. At playoff time it hurts not be in the game with the boys. However I want to do what is good for the people of Montreal and the team. So that no further harm will be done, I would like to ask everyone to get behind the team and to help the boys win from the Rangers and Detroit. I will take my punishment and come back next year to help the club and younger players to win the Cup."*

As he repeated the speech in English, Richard appeared restless and upset. He rubbed his eyes, tugged at his tie and scratched his left ear. His words seemed to have a settling effect on the city. The question of his suspension was laid aside, at least for the time being. Mayor Drapeau and other leaders followed Richard with strong pleas for law and order. There was to be no further violence for the remainder of the season, despite the fact that the Canadiens lost the championship.

Rocket Inspires Thunderous Applause: Luminaries at Funeral Rise in Final Tribute

Ingrid Peritz and Tu Thanh Ha

This piece originally appeared June 1, 2000, the day following Maurice Richard's funeral in Montreal. Reprinted with permission from The Globe and Mail.

IN A TENDER, STIRRING FUNERAL MASS, Maurice "Rocket" Richard proved that even in death he has the power to inspire a standing ovation.

Jean-Claude Cardinal Turcotte, Archbishop of Montreal, had just finished delivering a moving homily on the late hockey icon yesterday when applause spontaneously broke out in the formal confines of Montreal's Notre Dame Basilica. The cardinal joined in, clapping his hands before Mr. Richard's rose-bedecked casket. Then, an entire church—premiers and prime ministers past and present, hockey Hall of Famers and hundreds of ordinary fans—rose to their feet in a thunderous sendoff to one of Canada's greatest hockey legends. Outside, several thousand fans watching the mass on a giant screen joined in the applause, some of them weeping abundantly.

"An entire nation is here to say adieu, to say thank you, Maurice," Cardinal Turcotte said in his homily to an estimated 2,700 mourners in the church. "Maurice Richard led his battles, on the ice and off the ice. He did it honestly, with all the tenacity and passion we've come to recognize."

Cardinal Turcotte ended by recalling Mr. Richard's love of fishing, a passion for a star who needed to escape the pressures of his celebrity. He said Mr. Richard could count on the company of other fishermen in heaven—several of Jesus's apostles.

"I can clearly see Maurice going to meet them," Cardinal Turcotte said. "They'll have a lot to say. Happy fishing, Maurice!"

The funeral mass was carried live on 11 television channels in the province, part of the blanket media coverage the Rocket's death has received.

Before yesterday's mass, thousands of people gathered along the cortege route through downtown Montreal, and office workers crowded to windows to catch a glimpse of the passing motorcade. It was a measure of the Rocket's status that the funeral of this modest son of a railway machinist and a stay-at-home wife would unfold amid the kind of pomp normally reserved for heads of state.

The mass for Mr. Richard, who insisted he was "just a hockey player," drew a who's who in politics and hockey. In attendance were Prime Minister Jean Chretien, Quebec Premier Lucien Bouchard and former prime minister Brian Mulroney, along with numerous federal and provincial cabinet ministers. It also drew hockey legends, such as Gordie Howe, Guy Lafleur, Jean Beliveau and Ken Dryden, along with members of the current Canadiens team, enabling captain Saku Koivu and center Sergei Zholtok to explain that Mr. Richard's fame had even reached their native Finland and Latvia, respectively.

But the Rocket's farewell was reserved for more than the funeral's 800 invited VIPs. At the Richard family's behest, 1,000 seats inside the basilica were specifically set aside for ordinary fans. They included people like Alexandra More, a former factory worker who arrived at the church by subway in a T-shirt and purple windbreaker. Inside, the diminutive 77-year-old took her place on the second-floor balcony.

"Mr. Richard knew how to be victorious, yet he was simple," she said, recalling watching games with her husband. "He loved the public, and we adored him back. My husband died in February, and now I know the two men will be together for eternity."

Mr. Richard's casket was accompanied into the grandiose interior of the historic church by eight former teammates, including younger brother Henri and Mr. Beliveau, who marched solemnly alongside it as a 26-member choir sang Gabriel Fauré's Requiem.

The Richard family declined an offer from the Quebec government protocol office to drape the province's Fleur-de-lis flag over the casket. Instead, it was covered by a large bouquet of yellow roses.

Maurice Richard Jr., the Rocket's eldest son, told the mourners that the family was touched by the outpouring of love witnessed in recent days.

"Maurice leaves us amid serenity and joy. We should not be sad. I'm sure that if he had watched from above what's happened over the last two or three days, he would be very proud," the younger Mr. Richard said.

Gordie Howe recalled facing off against Mr. Richard and his formidable skills numerous times, and said that despite being bitter adversaries, he always respected his opponent. "I think all of Canada should be proud of that man. He set the records for the rest of us to chase."

Another hockey great at the funeral, Frank Mahovlich, had been telling how, as a Maple Leaf rookie, he was assigned to cover the Rocket in a game. Hockey's fiercest player looked to Mr. Mahovlich and told him to back off. "Yes, Mr. Richard," Mr. Mahovlich remembered replying.

Mr. Richard's death from abdominal cancer on Saturday touched a chord in Quebec, even among a generation too young to have witnessed him on the ice. On Tuesday, an estimated 115,000 people filed past his casket. An hour before yesterday's mass, the funeral cortege left the Molson Centre, where Mr. Richard's body had been lying in state. Escorted by police officers on motorcycles, the hearse was followed by 14 black limousines carrying the relatives of Mr. Richard, who was the eldest of eight siblings and the father of seven children. As the procession passed, fans lining the streets burst into spontaneous applause. At one point, when the hearse slowed down, a woman rushed to it and placed a rose bouquet on its hood.

But for most of those who paid tribute, Maurice Richard, who retired in 1960, is only an abstract concept. Two-thirds of Quebec's population is under age 44 and would have been too young to have seen him play. For many, Mr. Richard's legend appears to have been handed down like a legacy from father to son. His death has made many Quebecers wax nostalgic for an earlier era.

"It's because we've talked about him from one generation to another," Bloc Quebecois leader Gilles Duceppe said. "I'm sure that my children, without ever having seen him play, will tell their children about him."

Mr. Bouchard recalled how "our fathers—and our mothers" admired the Rocket. "When we see him go today, we recall our youth, our childhood. He was the man of our childhood, for people of my generation. It's a bit of our childhood that disappears."

Federal Intergovernmental Affairs Minister Stephane Dion said his 12-year-old daughter had wondered what made Mr. Richard so famous 40 years after his retirement. Because, Mr. Dion said, "he represents for people courage and determination, and that's eternal."

CHAPTER 21

I Did It My Way

Five Players Reveal a Multitude of Routes to the NHL

Chris Tredree

PAT FLATLEY

Canadian High School and U.S. College Hockey

BORN AND RAISED IN HOCKEY-MAD TORONTO, Pat Flatley's childhood was no different than any other Canadian kid who loved hockey. He started playing the game as a five-year-old; he grew up playing ball hockey in the streets with his friends; he spent countless hours at public skates in the local suburban arenas and he played in the developmental system of minor hockey. Where his playing career differs from the traditional Canadian youngster is, he opted to play hockey in the school system rather than battle his way through the junior ranks en route to a 14-year career in the NHL.

"As a 14-year-old, I tried out for two bantam teams—the Toronto Marlies and the Mississauga Reps—and I was cut from both of them," said Flatley. "I remember the second tryout. There was about 200 players skating around the rink at once and it made no sense to me. My reaction when I got cut was 'this is ridiculous—I'm just going to play high school hockey and work hard there.' I felt like I had something to prove. Tony Tanti, who went on to play 11 years in the NHL (287 goals), was also cut from that Mississauga team."

Flatley went on to play for Henry Carr High School in Toronto where he spent four years honing his skills with his sights set on an athletic scholarship to a college in the United States. In his senior year, Henry Carr joined the Ontario Junior B ranks. Flatley captained the team.

"I knew right away that what I was doing made the most sense. We would practice most mornings for an hour at 6:30 and then would walk back from Albion Arena to school with our hockey bags over our shoulders. The whole team was also on the school's cross-country running team, and in the summers we would meet three times a week at the school and do running exercises to build strength and speed. Our coach, Peter Miller, was very big on building up your cardiovascular system. He had enthusiasm that was contagious."

Like the U.S. collegiate system, the high school hockey season in Canada consisted of very few games and constant practicing.

"Some of the practices would be just skating to music with no pucks," explained Flatley. "I knew that I was a bad skater so this type of practice could only help. One of the main reasons I got cut as a bantam was because of my skating. The Central Scouting report in my draft year said skating was a weakness, and I know that my skating would not have begun to develop had I not been on the ice every day at Henry Carr."

At the conclusion of his fourth year at Henry Carr, Flatley received scholarship offers from several schools in the United States. "I had set my goals one step at a time," he said. "When I was playing in high school, my goal was to get a scholarship at a U.S. college. I was drafted by the Ontario Hockey League's Sudbury Wolves in the first round, but I told them I was going to go to college.

"(Current Ottawa Senators general manager) Marshall Johnston was at the University of Denver and he came to see me in my last year at Henry Carr. He saw me play once and offered me a scholarship. After that, Grant Stanbrook from the University of Wisconsin came to see me play. I also went on a recruiting trip to Michigan Tech and Boston University. I favored Denver because of Marshall. He made a really good impression on me, but Grant was pretty relentless and would keep calling me. He came to see me at my house and said 'you have to see this video.' It was an inspirational video on their national championship. I was just being courteous, but as I'm watching, the phone rings and it was Marshall saying that he had just taken a job with New Jersey. I told him that he was the only reason I was going to go to Denver. I asked him what he thought of Wisconsin and he recommended it highly. I hung up the phone and told Grant that I wanted to go to Wisconsin."

Flatley arrived in Madison, Wisconsin, in September, 1981, making his NCAA debut with the University of Wisconsin Badgers as a 17-year-old freshman. Under the leadership of famed hockey coach Bob Johnson, Flatley posted 19 points (10 goals, nine assists) in 17 games in his first season, despite being sidelined for a month with a knee injury. Flatley made his first appearance in the NCAA Frozen Four that year as the Badgers finished second to North Dakota.

"My first memories of Bob are from my first practice. He made us skate wearing 20-pound weight vests. After the practice, he came by with a grin and said his famous line, 'it's a great day for hockey.' I'll always respect how he was able to encompass the game and make it the core of his being. We should all look at hockey as a gift. Being able to play it at any level is a privilege."

On June 9, 1982, the three-time defending Stanley Cup champion New York Islanders selected Flatley 21st overall to close the first round of the NHL Entry Draft. Jim Devellano, then a scout for the Islanders, introduced Flatley to the press and commented: "As you can see, Pat is a big, strong boy. He's also a good hockey player. He's a Bobby Nystrom, John Tonelli-type of player. He likes to knock people off the puck."

Johnson, who had just been named coach of the Calgary Flames, said, "Pat is a winner. When the puck goes into the corner, he's going in to get it. He's not a Mike Bossy. He's not lightning coming off his wing, Pat is more like Nystrom. He could play in the league tomorrow."

"During my first year at the University of Wisconsin, I got the sense that some NHL scouts were watching me and that there might be a chance to get drafted," said Flatley. "I was kind of oblivious to the whole thing. I just thought it was great to be at Wisconsin and it was great to be a part of a real good team.

"After the draft, playing in the NHL became a mission," Flatley recalls. "My dad and I took the train to Montreal for the draft and the day after I got home, I quit my summer job driving a shuttle for an airport hotel. Now I was going to focus on playing hockey. I started working out a lot more and, for the first time, dedicated my life to trying to make the NHL."

The Islanders made it clear that the best course for Flatley's development was to return to Wisconsin. In 1982–83, Flatley's stock skyrocketed as he was instrumental in leading the Badgers to their fourth NCAA title. With 17 goals and 24 assists in 26 games, he earned selections to the Western Collegiate Hockey Association's first all-star team and to the NCAA West first all-American team. He also was named to the NCAA Championship's all-tournament team.

"Wisconsin had 8,600 people for every game, and the Championships had 18,000. College hockey is huge," said Flatley. "The building is full, there are live marching bands and cheerleaders; the enthusiasm is overwhelming. They introduce you at the beginning of every game, and then after the game the whole campus is electric. Everyone's congratulating you. The atmosphere around college hockey is incredible."

In the fall of 1982, Flatley was invited to tryout for the Canadian national junior team. After a successful showing, Flatley was one of three NCAA players to make the team, joined by James Patrick and Gord Sherven of the University of North Dakota. At the age of 19, Flatley was one of the most senior players on a team that included 17-year-olds Mario Lemieux, Steve Yzerman and Sylvain Turgeon. Canada won a bronze medal in the tournament.

"At that time, U.S. college players were looked upon as being soft," he said. "I went to the Canadian national junior team tryout camp with the attitude of 'I'll show these guys.'

"After the World Juniors, I wanted to play in the Olympics. When I got drafted I started to feel that I was good enough to play in the NHL, but I knew I wanted to play in the Olympics first. That was the beauty of the Olympics back then because you had to make a choice—do you turn pro or do you play in the Olympics? I managed to make the national team and toured the world for the 1983–84 season before playing in the Olympics."

Flatley participated in the 1984 Winter Olympic Games in Sarajevo where Canada reached the medal round but finished fourth behind the Soviet Union, Czechoslovakia and Sweden. Following the Olympic tournament, he made his first NHL appearance, scoring on his first shot on February 29, 1984, against the Winnipeg Jets.

Flatley enjoyed 14 seasons in the NHL, including 13 with the Islanders. He retired at the conclusion of the 1996–97 season as a member of the New York Rangers. Flatley is now the NHL's Director of Alumni Relations.

"I knew that if I could get an education and play hockey at the same time, that was the way to go," said Flatley. "It's not just the schooling that's important, it's the whole social development that you gain from being in the university atmosphere. I think it's a better existence. When you compare the advantages and disadvantages, it really becomes an easy decision."

PHIL HOUSLEY

U.S. High School Superstar

CALGARY FLAMES DEFENSEMAN Phil Housley recalls a childhood that included dreams of hockey heroes, outdoor rinks and weekend games on television that helped shape his passion for the game.

"Hockey was as big in Minnesota as it was in Canada," said the St. Paul native. "We grew up in the 1970s watching the North Stars and Sunday hockey with Peter Puck. We played a lot of pond hockey, too. Minnesota has a lot of outdoor rinks, so we took advantage of that. We'd go out after school and on the weekends and skate all day. That's all we did. Hockey just consumed us and I really loved the game. I loved literally being a rink rat. I was fortunate enough to have a neighbor who flooded his yard and had lights out there so we could play at night until my dad whistled for us to come home. That experience was important before I started playing competitively in the amateur ranks of squirt, pee wee and bantam."

As a free-wheeling, high scoring center, Housley followed his older brother Larry to South St. Paul High School, where he was selected to the varsity hockey team as a 14-year-old freshman.

"I was fortunate to make the team because there was another person who was supposed to make it as a freshman but he broke his ankle and I got the opportunity to play. I spent four years at South St. Paul under the tutelage of head coach Doug Woog. He really helped me as a player. He taught me the game as it should be played.

"I was a center growing up until I made the high school team and my coach moved me back on defense. He felt that I could skate well and that there weren't a lot of good rushing defensemen in the NHL at that time. He also said that he could play me a lot more on defense. I owe a lot to him for making that move."

As a boy, Housley's dream of the NHL was a distant one since the focus of most young hockey players growing up in Minnesota is on playing high school hockey and, even more so, on participating in the prestigious state tournament.

Former American Olympic coach Herb Brooks once stated: "I don't care if the Vikings go to the Super Bowl or the Twins play in the World Series, the state high school hockey tournament is the biggest sports event in Minnesota, every year." Phil Housley agrees.

"One of the big things in Minnesota is making the state high school tournament," he said. "Every game was on TV and there were always a lot of pro scouts and college scouts eyeing players who might get a scholarship. With 18,000 fans for every game, I got an idea of what kind of effect playing in front of a big crowd can have on you."

Held annually at the St. Paul Civic Center, the single-elimination tournament consistently attracts more than 100,000 fans and is always a quick sell out. Housley led his team to consecutive appearances in the state tournament in his sophomore and junior years. As a junior, he was the leading goal scorer in the St. Paul Suburban Conference and finished second in scoring with 42 points, trailing his brother by one point.

"There were a lot of good hockey teams in South St. Paul, and even though we never won a state title, we did make it to the state tournament two of the four years I was there. It was a special feeling to play with your buddies and share with your high school friends something that's not an individual sport. I knew I was getting looked at by NHL scouts and some NCAA schools, but I always tried to be a bit humble and be a team player."

Concluding an extremely successful high school career that included recognition as an all-state, all-conference and all-Metro athlete in three consecutive years, Housley measured up his post-secondary options. Should he commit to an athletic scholarship from college or should he take a head-on approach to an immediate career in professional hockey?

"Getting a scholarship was pretty much what I wanted to do as a player. My dad had encouraged me to get good grades so that I wouldn't have to do the work he did as a construction worker.

"I did go to see some schools, including the University of Minnesota, University of Denver, University of Wisconsin, University of North Dakota and Notre Dame. I took advantage of the visits and got a feel for what the schools were like, but I knew I wanted to go to U of M [the University of Minnesota] and be close to home. I wanted my parents to have the chance to see me play. In the back of my mind, though, ever since I was a kid, I had always wanted to play in the NHL."

Beginning in 1980, when the NHL moved to a draft age of 18, clubs began to select players from high schools in the United States. That year, the Buffalo Sabres' selection of Jay North (62nd overall), a center from Minnesota's Bloomington-Jefferson High School, marked the first time a high school player was selected in the Entry Draft. There were only seven high school prospects taken in the 1980 draft, but the number increased to 17 in 1981, including Bobby Carpenter of St. John's Prep in Massachusetts, who was selected third overall by the Washington Capitals. The number of high schoolers taken in the NHL draft would increase every year before peaking in 1987 when 69 prospects were drafted from U.S. high schools (27.4 percent of the draft). Recently though, NHL clubs have turned their focus away from high school hockey. The number of high school prospects drafted fell from 28 in 1994 to only two in 1995. The NHL Entry Draft has averaged only six high school selections ever since.

"There were always those powerhouse schools who were going to the state tournaments," stated Housley about the talent in the high school system. "Some schools were more populated and, with more people to pick from, ultimately had better teams. I think high school hockey went to a tiered system to make it fair for everybody. It's given the smaller schools a better chance, but I think it has taken away from some of the powerhouse schools and resulted in less exposure for the game.

"A lot of the younger players are choosing to go to junior hockey now. They're not waiting to play in high school. They think they can learn more and develop more in junior because there is more competition. High school hockey isn't as exciting as it used to be because the schools are losing a lot of their great players. It's still a big thing in Minnesota though."

Back in 1981–82, his final year at South St. Paul, Phil Housley enjoyed a very eventful and successful year. Already a highly touted prospect for the NHL Entry Draft, he was selected to play with the United States team at the World Junior Championships in Minneapolis.

"I probably wouldn't even have been asked to join the team if it wasn't for me playing in the Minnesota high school system. Getting that exposure and the experience of playing in a couple of high school tournaments was the big break. I think that Tony [fellow Minnesota high school prospect Tony Kellin of Grand Rapids] and I were the only two high school players selected to play on the World Junior team," said Housley. "To get the opportunity to play against a lot of great players from other countries gave us a feel for how fast the game was. After we had played a couple games in the tournament, I got the chance to go back and watch South St. Paul play. After the World Junior experience, the high school game seemed a little slower."

Housley's hockey future became clearer as the 1982 NHL Entry Draft approached. At the conclusion of his high school season, he joined the St. Paul Vulcans, a local junior hockey club, which led to an opportunity to don his nation's colors for the second time.

"They really pushed for me to play a couple of exhibition games with the U.S. national team over in Germany. Doing that would really determine whether I would make the team to play in the World Championships in Finland. I made the team and I got to play."

While performing for the U.S. senior national team as an 18-year-old, Housley was facing some of the greatest hockey players in the world, including Canada's Wayne Gretzky, Bobby Clarke and Darryl Sittler, and Russia's Viacheslav Fetisov and Sergei Makarov. Although the United States finished the tournament in last place, the experience spoke volumes about the future career of Phil Housley.

"My last year of high school was when I started realistically thinking about the NHL. Playing in the World Juniors and the World Championships was a big stepping stone and an important sign. I felt I had the speed to keep up and the smarts and the hockey knowledge to play the game. Not only making the [U.S. national] team, but also doing something significant while I was there helped me to know that I could play in the NHL."

On June 9, 1982, a group of 252 NHL hopefuls was selected in the Entry Draft at the Montreal Forum. Housley, rated 11th by the NHL's Central Scouting Service, was taken sixth overall by the Buffalo Sabres, who made him the first U.S.-born selection, and the first of 47 high school draftees, that year.

"I flew to Toronto with my dad and Charlie Hallman, a sportswriter from St. Paul who covered me throughout my high school years. We took the train up to Montreal, where they showed me around. Buffalo had three picks in the first round, sixth, ninth (Paul Cyr) and 16th (Dave Andreychuk), and they made me their first choice. I remember meeting head coach Scotty Bowman. He seemed very intimidating because I knew all about his storied career and how much success he'd had as a coach. It was very exciting for me to go to Buffalo.

"I wanted to play in the NHL and I thought it would be a great challenge for me to play the next year. I worked extra hard that summer before going into my first training camp. My agent had told me that I would probably have to play in the minor leagues for a little bit before making the Sabres, so I used that as motivation and came to camp in excellent shape. They liked me and it went on from there."

Accustomed to high school hockey and its 25-game season, the transition to the NHL for a 19-year-old Housley was a difficult one. It was eased by the assistance of some of Buffalo's veteran players.

"Three players really come to mind," he said. "One is Larry Playfair, my roommate and my partner when I first made the team and began playing a regular shift. His presence kept guys away from me on the ice. Lindy Ruff and Mike Ramsey were two others who took me under their wings. They let me live at their place at the start of the season until I found my own place and showed me what it's like to be a professional hockey player; the discipline and all the little things that are such a demanding part of playing in the NHL. Those three guys really helped pave the way for me."

Eighteen NHL seasons later, Housley's career totals of 1,130 points (313 goals, 817 assists) in 1,288 games have distinguished him as the highest-scoring American-born player in NHL history. Commenting on his path to the NHL, Housley simply states: "I've been very fortunate and lucky that I haven't had to look back and think about how I could have changed things or done things differently. I'm positive I've made the right decisions."

MATS SUNDIN

Blue-Chip European First Overall Selection

ON JUNE 17, 1989, the Quebec Nordiques made hockey history when they drafted Swedish-born forward Mats Sundin, making him the first European player to be selected first overall in the NHL Entry Draft. The selection of the top-rated European player resulted immediately in a growing interest by the NHL in the international talent pool and in a renewed interest in the NHL by European fans and players.

"In Sweden, we didn't know what the draft really was," said Sundin. "It was a very new situation. A lot of people didn't really know how the draft worked, what it was all about, or how significant it was, until after I was drafted.

"I had flown to Minneapolis with my dad and my agent. We knew there was a chance that I might be picked in the top five, but we mainly went over to have some fun. We played some golf and toured around a bit. Obviously, at that age, you're just very excited to get the chance to go over to North America. After I got picked, the circus was on. People would ask me how I would deal with the pressure of being drafted first, but I didn't actually know what they were talking about. I found out when I got to Quebec my first year and started playing."

The 1989 Entry Draft saw 38 European players selected to NHL teams (15.1 percent of the draft). The European contingent grew to 53 players (21.2 percent) in 1990 and has consistently accounted for at least 20 percent in every Entry Draft since. The number of European prospects reached an all-time high when 141 Europeans (48.1 percent) were drafted in 2000.

Sundin was no stranger to success in sports. An accomplished athlete, he grew up playing soccer, hockey and bandy, a Swedish winter sport similar to field hockey but played on skates. *(See page 603.)* Although he was always one of the better players on all his teams, it was at hockey that he excelled.

"I played soccer and bandy until I was 16," said Sundin, "but hockey was the sport that I liked the most and had the most fun with. It was also the one that I had the most success with as a kid, so it was natural that hockey became the only sport."

Born in Bromma and raised in Sollentuna, both suburbs of Stockholm, Sundin began his journey toward the NHL at the age of five, learning to skate on a nearby lake. He developed his skills in the local hockey league before moving to a more advanced level of play with Djurgarden, a Stockholm-area team, as a 13-year-old. He would remain with Djurgarden until his jump to the NHL in 1990.

"I was fortunate to have played in Stockholm, a 20-minute car ride from home, until I turned pro. I think it was very important for me to stay in the community where I grew up and to have my family and friends around me. I never had to deal with moving away from home at an early age.

"Djurgarden is where I learned most of my hockey and that's where I developed as a hockey player," Sundin said. "We started to tour around quite a bit when I was 14. It was very common for Swedish teams to make trips to Finland, Norway and Czechoslovakia. I made my first North American trip as a 15-year-old in 1986. Djurgarden went to play in a tournament in Winnipeg. It was a great experience and we ended up winning."

As he began to develop into one of Djurgarden's most prized prospects, Sundin began to receive some attention within Sweden's hockey circles.

"I remember the first time I saw Mats," said former NHLer Anders Hedberg. "He was playing for Djurgarden and I was working for AIK as the general manager. Somebody in the stands told me I should look at this 15-year-old kid. He was with a Stockholm all-star team, and he was clearly the best player. Very tall, long stride, great skating. On one play, he came in from the left side, crashing the net. He stuck out his leg [to ward off the defender] and scored a goal. I knew right then he was a player."

Following consecutive appearances in the European Junior Championships in 1988 and 1989, and tallying 18 points (10 goals and eight assists) in 25 games with the Nacka Division 2 team in the 1988–89 season, Sundin was selected first in the NHL draft. Despite his top selection, the 6'2", 189-pound prospect was returned immediately to Sweden for the 1989–90 season.

"Physically, I wasn't ready [for the NHL] at all," Sundin said. "It was definitely right for me to go back. I grew so much the year I was drafted, and the rest of my body needed to catch up. I just wasn't strong enough to do my job."

The 1989–90 season marked Sundin's first year of professional hockey. He began with Djurgarden's Division 1 team and moved in and out of the lineup with their elite team. At the end of the season, Sundin became a regular with the elite team for the playoffs and helped Djurgarden capture their second of three consecutive Swedish league championships.

"The Elite League is the top league in Sweden," said Sundin of the Swedish hockey system. "Below that, it goes from Division 1 all the way to Division 5. Then there are the junior teams.

"Today, the NHL is probably followed as much in Sweden as the Swedish Elite League, but when I was growing up, making the Elite League and the national team were the big goals. Everybody knew about the NHL and followed it, but not too many [Swedish] players made it there. The NHL was a dream, but a distant one."

Sundin was able to fulfill another childhood dream when he was selected to perform for Sweden at the 1990 World Championships in Bern. Although he only appeared in four games, and didn't register a point, the experience and time to develop paid immediate dividends the following season.

"I didn't start to think seriously about the national team or the NHL until the European Junior tournaments," said Sundin. "The dream to play in the NHL had always been there since I was a kid, but not until I was 16 or 17—or even until I was drafted—did I realize there was an opportunity for me to play in the NHL."

The Nordiques called upon Sundin to perform as a 19-year-old rookie in 1990–91. He had a strong year, recording 59 points (23 goals and 36 assists) in 80 games to finish third in scoring among NHL rookies, but his status skyrocketed after he helped Sweden capture a gold medal at the 1991 World Championships. Sundin tied Finnish superstar Jari Kurri as the tournament's leading scorer with 12 points in 10 games and was named to the second all-star team. Later in the year, Sundin was selected to play in the Canada Cup. He led the Swedish squad in scoring, and was selected to the tournament's all-star team, despite being one of the youngest players (just 20 years old) at the event.

During his 10-year NHL career, Mats Sundin has performed in five World Championships, the Canada Cup, the World Cup of Hockey (1996), the Olympic Winter Games (1998) and in five NHL All-Star games (1996 to 2000). As captain of the Toronto Maple Leafs, he leads one of the most storied franchises in NHL history.

RADEK BONK

European Teenage Minor Pro

LIKE MOST KIDS GROWING UP in the small industrial town of Koprivnice in the north eastern part of what was then Czechoslovakia, Radek Bonk spent his time going to school and playing sports. A natural athlete, Bonk excelled in all the sports that were popular in his home country—soccer, tennis and hockey.

"My dad first brought me to the rink when I was five years old," said the Ottawa Senators' 6'3", 210-pound center. "I just remember having so much fun playing the game as a kid. Hockey was always the sport of choice for me.

"Growing up, everyone played soccer and tennis. I remember, there was a big tennis tournament in my hometown. I entered it and won. I went to tennis practice the next day, but half way through I said 'I have to go. I've got a hockey practice.' When the coaches told me I'd have to choose between hockey and tennis, I put my tennis racquet down and went to hockey practice. I love tennis and still play it, but hockey has always been number one."

Bonk achieved success at an early age. He was a perennial most valuable player and scoring champion for his minor hockey teams and was starring for HC Opava in the Czechoslovakian junior system (47 goals and 42 assists in 35 games in 1990–91) by the age of 14. Although hockey consumed his life, the NHL remained a very distant dream.

"In the Czech Republic, the NHL wasn't the biggest thing then because we didn't know too much about it," explained Bonk. "You would dream about playing for a Czechoslovakian team. Everybody wanted to play in the Elite League. That was the main goal.

"I was very serious about hockey right from the beginning. I started to think about playing professionally when I was about 15. That was when a team from the Czech Elite League called and said they wanted me to play for them. That's when I started to think that I could play professionally one day."

It was late in the summer of 1991 when the 15-year-old Bonk received a phone call from the coach of ZPS Zlin [pronounced Zleen], a Czech elite team that had finished seventh the previous year. They were looking for some new talent and expressed an interest in acquiring Bonk. After a brief meeting with the club's coach and general manager, Bonk packed his bags and moved to Zlin.

"I spent two years in Zlin. I played with their junior team in 1991–92 before I jumped to the Elite League in 1992–93. It was a big jump. Similar to Canada, there's a big difference between junior hockey and men's hockey. I started to play in the Elite League when I was 16. It was hard, but it wasn't a real big problem for me."

It is not uncommon for future stars to appear in the Czech Elite League as underage talents. Czech stars Jaromir Jagr, Bobby Holik and Robert Reichel all played in the Elite League prior to successful NHL careers. What really set Bonk apart was his next career decision: to play professional hockey in North America prior to his eligibility for the NHL Entry Draft.

"The decision to go to North America was made with my parents," he said. "My agents, Mike Barnett and Jiri Crha, gave me the opportunity. They told me that there was a chance to play with an International Hockey League team. I thought it would be a good idea to come over and learn the language and learn the style of living because it's very different from the Czech Republic."

In the summer of 1993, the 17-year-old Bonk signed a professional contract with the Las Vegas Thunder of the IHL. He became the first underaged European player to sign a professional hockey contract in North America and the youngest full-time player in IHL history.

"I just wanted to play men's hockey. I didn't want to come to North America to go back to playing junior. If I didn't have the chance to play in the IHL, I would have stayed in the Czech Republic, but I think it was the better decision to join an IHL team. My team in Zlin was disappointed, but that's what I wanted to do."

Bonk's signing made an immediate impact on hockey, paving the way for other young European talents to develop their skills at a professional level in North America. Two promising NHLers have already followed in Bonk's footsteps: Russian forward Sergei Samsonov (the 1998 Calder Trophy winner), who played for the Detroit Vipers of the IHL; and Czech center Patrik Stefan (the first choice overall in the 1999 Entry Draft), who played for the IHL's Long Beach Ice Dogs.

"Playing in Vegas was a lot of fun," said Bonk. "I had already played men's hockey for one year so it wasn't a really big jump. We had a great team and I adjusted really well because the style of hockey was similar to what I played back home. I'm a big player with good size and I always played a physical game."

Bonk's immediate success in the IHL thrust him into the spotlight as a season-long media frenzy surrounded the teenager. "The lifestyle was certainly different because back home I didn't have much media attention. In Zlin, the older guys on the team got all the attention, but in Las Vegas it was the opposite. Everyone started to talk to me because I was so young. I didn't speak English very well and I always had an interpreter to help me.

"All the guys on the team helped me along," said Bonk,

crediting his teammates for his successful transition to life in North America. "They were all very good. They showed me the ropes and if I ever had a problem with anything, they were always there for me. That's why I'll always remember that year in Vegas. It was a great year, both on and off the ice."

Bonk recorded 87 points (42 goals and 45 assists) in 76 games with the Ice Dogs, capturing the IHL's rookie of the year honors and being named the most popular athlete in Las Vegas—out-polling tennis star Andre Agassi and baseball's Greg Maddux in a newspaper vote.

Though the NHL's Central Scouting Service had rated Bonk as the top hockey talent in North America (another first for a European player), the 1994 NHL Entry Draft saw him picked third overall by the Ottawa Senators behind defenseman Ed Jovanovski (Florida) and Oleg Tverdovsky (Anaheim).

"I was very nervous," Bonk said. "Everyone was talking about me going one, two or three, but I just wanted everything to be over. I wanted to know what number I was so that I wouldn't have to think about it. Once I was picked, I was relieved and enjoyed the day. I spent it with my parents and my agent. It didn't matter where I went. I knew I was rated number one, but I wasn't disappointed that I hadn't been picked first."

Bonk made his NHL debut as a 19-year-old, scoring his first NHL goal on his first shot on net (January 27, 1995, at Pittsburgh). Six seasons later, Bonk has emerged as one of the Senators' leaders, recording a career-high 60 points (23 goals and 37 assists) in 80 games in 1999–2000.

"Going into the NHL was a much bigger jump than going from the Czech league to the IHL. The NHL is the best hockey league in the world and all the players are so much better. It was very hard to adjust."

LUC ROBITAILLE

Late-Round Draft Choice

SIXTEEN YEARS, 553 GOALS AND 597 ASSISTS LATER, the 16th greatest goal scorer in National Hockey League history still remembers the day as clearly as he sees the back of the net. He was just 18 years old at the time.

"It was a Saturday in June, 1984 (June 9), and the NHL Draft was taking place at the Montreal Forum," Luc Robitaille recalled. "It was shortly after 9:00 p.m., about six hours after the draft had started with the selection of Mario Lemieux by the Pittsburgh Penguins. The television cameras from the CBC broadcast of the first round had been gone for several hours, as was most of the crowd. Los Angeles Kings general manager Rogie Vachon announced my name over the Forum's p.a. system as the Kings' ninth choice, 171st overall. I remember that by the time I got down to the table on the arena floor (as is the custom for drafted players), Vachon was gone. Only a couple of people were left at the team's table, including Alex Smart—the scout who actually recommended that the team draft me. Alex was the guy who believed in me. Instead of receiving the jersey that they usually give to draft choices, they gave me a team pin."

In the highly competitive hockey world, the odds that a ninth-round pick will ever play in the NHL are very slim. Of the 79 players selected after Robitaille in 1984, only 13 went on to play in the NHL. However, although there were 170 names called before his, an optimistic Robitaille embraced the opportunity that had been presented.

"I left the Forum that night thinking that I had a chance to play in the NHL," he said. "I didn't think about how late in the draft I was selected, but rather that of all the kids in the world who want to play in the NHL, my name was now on a team's list. Now I had a chance. It was up to me to make it. Being the 171st selection was not a negative at all. I knew I was going to give pro hockey my best shot and not have any regrets when it came to an end."

Such is the attitude that Luc Robitaille has carried throughout his career. Given his statistics and accolades in hockey, it is hard to imagine that the Montreal native was so often considered a dark-horse talent.

"In my early years of playing hockey in Anjou (aged eight to 12), I was not the kid that hockey people thought would be one of the top players on the team. My family moved around quite a bit when I was younger, so people didn't really know me as a player. They would classify me a certain way early in the season and I would set out to prove them wrong."

In 1981–82, a 15-year-old Robitaille hoped to grab the attention of the Quebec Major Junior Hockey League while attempting to make the Montreal Bourassa team in the Quebec midget AAA, the QMJHL's primary developmental league. He would learn quickly that nothing would come easily.

"In my first year of midget, I didn't make the AAA team that I tried out for. Two days after the tryouts began, I got cut. My reaction was like any other 15-year-old kid—I was devastated. But I set a goal for myself: move down a level and have a really good year so that I would have a good shot of making AAA the next season.

"But I couldn't even get an invitation to tryout for the AA team in my hometown of Montreal North. I ended up playing for the Montreal North Midget BB—the third tier of hockey for my age group. I was even more devastated, but about half way through the season, I was leading the league in scoring and I got called up to play for the midget AA team."

Robitaille continued to work towards his goal and, following a strong season, was taken by the Bourassa AAA team for the 1982–83 season. He was shifted from center to left wing by coach Claude Therien.

"He told me that he did not have a spot for me at center, but asked me if I could play left wing. I told him I'd play anywhere!"

Starting the season as the fourth-line left wing, it wasn't long before Luc saw his first promotion. "After a few injuries to some of the top players in the first month of the season, I was moved up to the first line. The team really started to play well and that helped my confidence quite a bit."

Robitaille concluded the season with an impressive 93 points (36 goals, 57 assists) in 48 games, resulting in a favorable 11th-place ranking for the QMJHL midget draft. He was actually selected fourth overall by the Hull Olympiques. For the first time in his playing career, Robitaille had been recognized as a top player with a promising future.

"After that midget draft, I certainly never thought 'okay here's a chance for me to take another step toward making the NHL.' My only thought was that, having been selected in the first round, I had a good shot at playing for Hull. I spent that summer making sure I would be ready physically."

At age 17, Luc Robitaille entered his first year of major junior hockey in what was also his first year of eligibility for the NHL Entry Draft. Although the transition was a difficult one, he managed to finish second in team scoring (32 goals and 53 assists in 70 games) despite Hull's disappointing tenth place finish in the 11-team league. Following his selection by the Kings, Robitaille attended his first NHL training camp only to be returned to the Olympiques, an occurrence that would repeat itself the following year despite the fact that his progression had been dramatic during in his second season at Hull. Head coach Pat Burns had placed him on a line with Joe Foglieta and Sam Lang, creating one of the most successful combinations in the history of Canadian junior hockey. The trio combined for 148 goals and 225 assists and the team improved to second place in its division. Robitaille, with 55 goals and 94 assists, finished third in league scoring with 149 points.

The 1985–86 season that followed proved to be one of the most successful in Robitaille's career. The Olympiques acquired the previous season's scoring champion, Guy Rouleau (a center who had played on the Montreal Bourassa team that cut Robitaille four years earlier) and he and Robitaille would finish the 1985–86 campaign tied for the Quebec league's scoring title with 191 points apiece. They also led the Olympiques to a berth in the 1986 Memorial Cup tournament in Portland, Oregon.

When Robitaille was later named the Canadian Hockey League's player of the year, Pat Burns commented that "Luc has always been an honest player. He has good hands and works the corners well. For a couple of years, his skating was questioned. But he's worked hard on his skating and his shot and it shows. It doesn't look like he's going very fast but when you get next to him, he's motoring."

"I took a lot of criticism for my skating at the start of my junior career," Robitaille said. "People would say that I was not a very fast skater. It's something that I have worked on all my life. I had roller blades when I was 14 and would spend much of the summer doing sprints and quick starts. I have taken power-skating most of my life to get quicker and improve as much as I could. I always did the extra skating for one reason—to get better."

In addition to his success with Hull during the 1985–86 campaign, Robitaille was also given the opportunity to represent Canada at the 1986 World Junior Championships in Hamilton, Ontario. He helped the team win a silver medal, once again under the leadership of coach Pat Burns.

"The World Junior Championships were one of the best experiences of my career. I was only invited to the summer tryout camp after Stephane Richer decided at the last minute that he was not going to play, and I knew that I was not a big part of their plans, but I finished as the leading scorer during the week of scrimmages and forced them to invite me back in December. It was the first time that I played for my country and it was probably the most important time in my development towards a career in the NHL. When I came back to Hull after the World Juniors, the game seemed so much slower to me. I think that I was a totally different player after that experience. I always had the confidence in my abilities, but afterwards, the game seemed like it was that much easier to play."

With the experience of two NHL training camps, an award-winning season, a Memorial Cup tournament and the World Junior Championships, Luc was prepared for Los Angeles in the fall of 1986.

"The first two years that I went to training camp with the Kings, I was cut on the third day even though I felt I had pretty good camps. By my third training camp, I figured out that they had a short list of guys they were looking at and that I was now one of those guys. At the first two camps, I had to wear number 56 and was given old equipment, but at the third camp I got assigned number 20 and saw brand new equipment in my stall."

After posting 84 points (45 goals and 39 assists in 79 games) and winning the Calder Trophy as rookie of the year in 1986–87, Robitaille has gone on to earn five selections to the NHL's First All-Star Team. He also has two selections to the Second Team. In 1992–93, he set NHL single-season records for left wingers with 63 goals and 125 points and helped the Kings reach the Stanley Cup finals for the only time in franchise history. Luc Robitaille, L.A.'s ninth-round selection in 1984, will always be known as one of the NHL's greatest dark-horse talents.

CHAPTER 22

Hockey Demographics

When and Where NHL Players are Born

David Keon Jr. and Gary Meagher

THROUGH THE END OF THE 1998–99 SEASON, a total of 6,164 players had either played a game in the National Hockey League or were on an NHL club's reserve list. Of these, more have been born in January—711 or 11.5 percent of the total—than any other month. January's percentage is almost twice as high as that of December's—6.3 percent.

Following is a breakdown of the birth months of NHL players:

Month	Total Players	Percentage
January	711	11.5
February	577	9.4
March	598	9.7
April	592	9.6
May	557	9.1
June	500	8.1
July	492	8.0
August	417	6.8
September	481	7.8
October	450	7.3
November	404	6.6
December	385	6.3

While this analysis certainly does not suggest that hockey's future NHL stars are more likely to be born in the first month of the calendar year than in any other month, it is interesting to note both the quantity and quality of NHLers that have been born in January. Some of the league's all-time great wingers—Bobby Hull (Jan. 3); Dickie Moore (Jan. 6); Frank Mahovlich (Jan. 10); and Mike Bossy (Jan. 22)—were all born in January. A who's who of centermen—Syl Apps and Mark Messier (Jan. 18); Elmer Lach (Jan. 22); Wayne Gretzky (Jan. 26); and Joe Primeau (Jan. 29)—were also January born, as were defenseman Tim Horton (Jan. 12) and goaltenders Jacques Plante (Jan. 17); Bill Durnan (Jan. 22) and Dominik Hasek (Jan. 29).

Of note, it would seem that one January date—the 22nd—has produced more superstars than any other in the calendar year. Hall of Famers Durnan, Lach, Bossy and Serge Savard, along with another Montreal Canadiens great, defenseman Jean Claude Tremblay, were all born on that date.

Now before *Total Hockey II* gets accused of encouraging would-be parents of future NHL stars to have their children early in the calendar year, it is important (and obvious) to note that each of the other months has produced its share of superstars. Jaromir Jagr, Phil Esposito, Joe Malone and Eric Lindros were all born in February; Milt Schmidt, Roger Crozier, Bobby Orr, Gordie Howe and Dave Keon were born in March; and so on throughout the year.

The NHL's Director of Central Scouting, Frank Bonello, says that there are definite advantages for a youngster with an earlier birth date while growing up in the minor hockey system. "It sure helps a kid who is eight, 10 or 12 years old when he might have the benefit of being as much as 11 months older than the kids he is playing against. Just the size and strength factors of a kid with that age advantage are going to make a difference."

A significant birthdate for hockey players is September 15, the cut-off date for a player in the NHL Draft. (Players born on or before September 15 are eligible for that year's June draft; while players born from September 16 through the end of the calendar year must wait until the next June to be eligible for the Draft.) While numerous players in league history have been born around the September 15 date, two players—the San Jose Sharks' Patrick Marleau and the Atlanta Thrashers' Patrik Stefan—have most recently been affected by the cut-off date.

Marleau, born September 15, 1979, in Swift Current, Saskatchewan, was eligible for the 1997 draft by just hours and was selected second overall by the Sharks. Stefan, on the other hand, was born just one year and one day later than Marleau—September 16, 1980—but had to wait a full two years after Marleau to be drafted. The wait proved worth it for the Czech Republic native as he was selected first overall by the Thrashers in the 1999 Entry Draft.

Former Montreal Canadiens great Henri Richard is the answer to two interesting trivia questions: Name the player who has played on more Stanley Cup championship teams than any other? And, name the NHL's all-time leading scorer who was born in a leap year? Eleven Stanley Cup championships put Richard in a class by himself, but his February 29 birthdate puts "The Pocket Rocket" in a class with five other NHL players: Kari Eloranta (1956), Dan Daoust (1960), Jim Dobson (1960), Lyndon Byers (1964) and Simon Gagne (1980).

By the way, the most popular birth date for an NHL player is March 23. A total of 31 NHL players have been born on that date, including Don Marshall, Ted Green, John Tonelli, Bengt Gustafsson, Daren Puppa and Gord Murphy.

BIRTHPLACES OF CANADIAN NHLERS

With a population of approximately 29 million people and in excess of 500,000 youngsters enrolled in minor hockey associations on a yearly basis from St. John's, Newfoundland, to Victoria, British Columbia, it should surprise no one that throughout National Hockey League history, 72 percent of all players (4,444 in total) who have either played an NHL game, or are currently on an NHL team's reserve list, have been born in Canada.

With a population of almost 11 million people—or nearly 40 percent of hockey-mad Canada's entire population—it should also surprise no one that the province of Ontario has accounted for 45 percent of the total number of

Canadian-born NHLers in league history. The populous province of Quebec (second to Ontario with more than seven million people) ranks second at 16.7 percent.

Following is a breakdown of the number of players that each province and territory has produced. The numbers and information reflect a player's birthplace and not necessarily where the player was raised and/or played his minor hockey.

Province	Total Players	%	* Population
Ontario	1,999	45.0	10,753,573
Quebec	740	16.7	7,138,795
Alberta	462	10.4	2,696,826
Saskatchewan	451	10.2	990,237
Manitoba	343	7.8	1,113,898
British Columbia	282	6.3	3,724,500
Nova Scotia	63	1.4	909,282
New Brunswick	48	1.1	738,133
Prince Edward Island	25	0.6	134,557
Newfoundland	23	0.5	551,792
Northwest Territories	5	n/a	64,402
Yukon	3	n/a	30,766

* - all numbers based on 1996 Canadian census

Of the 885 cities, towns and villages across the country that have sent players to the NHL, Canada's largest city, Toronto, leads the way with 373 NHL players, followed by Montreal (250), Winnipeg (175) and Edmonton (162). But it is towns like Chemainus, British Columbia, (population 393) that have as much to do with the fabric of hockey in Canada as any of the urban centers. The tiny town located on Vancouver Island on Canada's west coast has had one native son (Doug Bodger) play more than 1,000 games in the NHL, while another, Robin Bawa, played just 61 games.

One can even look beyond the 10 provinces, to places in Canada's far north like Hay River, Northwest Territories (pop. 3,206), the birthplace of 10-year NHL veteran forward Geoff Sanderson. Or, Yellowknife, NWT, the home of Vic Mercredi and Greg Vaydik, who combined to play a total of just seven NHL games.

The Prairies – A Hockey Hotbed

What the analysis does uncover is what most hockey observers have believed for decades but have been unable to quantify—that the three western Canadian provinces of Alberta, Manitoba and Saskatchewan, despite accounting for just 16.6 percent of Canada's entire population, have sent almost 30 percent of the total number of Canadian-born players to the NHL. The prairie provinces, with strong minor hockey programs and a climate that permits youngsters to skate on outdoor ponds and lakes for in excess of four months, are a veritable hockey hotbed, producing 1,256 of Canada's 4,444 players.

The strength of these minor hockey programs can be found in the fact that, in the 1999–2000 season, just under 25 percent of the 500,000 minor hockey players in Canada were competing in leagues in the three prairie provinces.

Saskatchewan, with a population of about one million people, has sent more players to the NHL (451) per capita than any other Canadian province, American state or European country. This total reflects the strength of the province's minor hockey programs. In 1999–2000, there were 32,224 amateur players competing on 2,106 teams throughout the province, including 25,957 players who were aged 16 or younger.

In all, 135 cities, towns and villages—including Floral, home of "Mr. Hockey" Gordie Howe—scattered across the province of Saskatchewan have sent players to the NHL. The province's major cities of Regina and Saskatoon, each with populations of less than 200,000, have sent 80 and 67 players, respectively, to the NHL. Smaller cities such as Moose Jaw (pop. 33,593) and Prince Albert (pop. 34,181), have also produced significant numbers for the NHL, per capita, with 21 and 19 players, respectively.

But to measure the true impact of Saskatchewan's ability to develop world-class hockey players, one must look beyond the urban centers to towns like Delisle (pop. 874) with five NHL players to its credit. They include the Bentley brothers—Doug and Max, both of whom are in the Hockey Hall of Fame; and lesser known players like Reggie Bentley, Dick Butler and Jack Miller, who all played just a handful of games in the NHL but enjoyed outstanding minor pro careers. Other small towns—like Cudworth (pop. 727)—can lay claim to being the birthplace of Gerry Ehman, Orland Kurtenbach and Paul Shmyr, each of whom enjoyed lengthy NHL careers at various times from the 1950s through the early 1980's; or Oxbow (pop. 1,132), hometown to Theoren Fleury, Lindsay Carson and Reg Kerr.

The story of hockey in Saskatchewan can be similarly told in each of Canada's Western provinces. Alberta ranks third behind Ontario and Quebec with 462 NHLers to its credit. The province's main population centers—Edmonton (162 players) and Calgary (93 players)—have accounted for more than 50 percent of the players, but, like Saskatchewan, it is the 84 smaller cites and towns scattered across the province that have been as important in developing world class hockey players.

One of those small towns, Viking, Alberta, can legitimately lay claim to being the hometown of the sports world's most prominent family. Six Sutter brothers—Brian, Darryl, Duane, Brent, Rich and Ron—were all born and raised in Viking and went on to play more than 5,000 NHL games combined between 1976 and 2000. With a population of only 1,200 people, Viking is the pre-eminent example of a small town where hockey became a central part of its existence when the indoor arena was constructed in 1949. For the Sutters, the Carena (so named because construction of the rink was financed through the raffling of cars), along with a pond on the family farm, provided them with the sheets of ice that they would spend hours on each day en route to careers in the NHL.

If Viking is the home of hockey's first family, then Brandon, Manitoba, should surely rate consideration as "The Home of the Goaltender." Of the 26 players from Brandon (a town of less than 40,000 people, located just off the Trans-Canada highway) that have played in the NHL, five goaltenders—Hall of Famer Turk Broda, Ron Hextall, Ken Wregget, Bill Ranford and Glen Hanlon—enjoyed distinguished NHL careers. The five combined for 2,936 NHL games played, 1,230 wins, 122 shutouts and eight Stanley Cup championships.

Ontario and Quebec

Kirkland Lake & Rouyn-Noranda: The Ultimate Rivalry

Though separated by a provincial boundary, the towns of Rouyn-Noranda, Quebec, and Kirkland Lake, Ontario, are just 25 miles apart and have combined to send no fewer than 48 players to the National Hockey League. With populations of just 26,000 (Rouyn-Noranda) and 10,000 (Kirkland Lake), these two cities have arguably produced as great a group of players in NHL history as any neighboring towns.

Consider what games must have looked like at the local arena in Rouyn-Noranda during the 1950s with the likes of Dave Keon and Jacques Laperriere, future Hall of Famers who would go on to win four and six Stanley Cup titles, respectively, honing their skills. In Kirkland Lake, local minor hockey stars of that era included Dick Duff and Ralph Backstrom, each of whom would go on to win six Stanley Cups championships, while the Hillman brothers (Larry and Wayne) were beginning a journey that would eventually lead them to combine for five Stanley Cup titles.

In the 1960s, it was the Redmond brothers (Mickey and Dick), along with Bob Murdoch and Mike Walton, who developed their hockey skills as youngsters in Kirkland Lake before embarking on careers in the NHL that would see the foursome combine for six Stanley Cup titles. At the same time, down the road in Rouyn-Noranda, Rejean Houle began a minor hockey career that would culminate with his selection first overall in the 1969 Entry Draft. Houle would go on to win five Stanley Cup championships with the Montreal Canadiens before becoming the club's general manager. Dale Tallon of Rouyn-Noranda was the second-overall pick in the 1970 draft, while Paulin Bordeleau was 19th overall in 1973.

Hockey was a way of life in Kirkland Lake in the 1940s and 1950s. "Most of the men worked in the mines and played senior hockey," said Duff. "Good athletes were brought in to play hockey and fastball and they worked in the mines and brought up families. The Legion, Kiwanis, Lions Club and a few others sponsored teams, which made for a very competitive league. There were a lot of good people who put in time coaching and organizing because parents didn't seem to have the time. Hockey gave the people a place to go and socialize and provided a topic of conversation during the long days underground in the mines."

It took a little longer for the game to develop in Rouyn-Noranda. The minor hockey system there was similar to others in the surrounding area in that it grew at the same time as the economy. While Kirkland Lake flourished in the 1940s, Rouyn-Noranda came into its own in the 1950s. According to Rouyn-Noranda product Dave Keon, the rise of hockey and the economy very much paralleled each other. "Kirkland Lake had a good minor hockey system, as did Timmins," said Keon. "But as the mines slowed down in the area, people had to move to find work and the minor hockey system lost players. The minor hockey system in Rouyn-Noranda was able to benefit from this.

"We had a five-or six-team league that was extremely competitive. If a team won the local league, it would move on to play Kirkland Lake, Timmins, Sudbury and Sault Ste. Marie. Eventually, if you kept winning, you would end up in Southern Ontario playing teams like the Toronto Marlies for the Ontario championship," Keon added.

Half a century later, this area continues to flourish at hockey's highest level with the likes of Kirkland Lake native Daren Puppa and Rouyn-Noranda's Pierre Turgeon—like Houle, a first-overall selection in the Entry Draft. The 48 NHL players produced by Kirkland Lake and Rouyn-Noranda have combined for 42 Stanley Cups championships, including two recent winners in Eric Desjardins (Montreal, 1993) and Stephane Matteau (New York Rangers, 1994). This past season, Rouyn-Noranda product Jacques Caron was an assistant coach for the Stanley Cup Champion New Jersey Devils.

Following is the lineup of NHL players who were born in Rouyn-Noranda and Kirkland Lake along with their career statistics:

Rouyn-Noranda, Quebec

Skaters	GP	G	A	PTS	
Bob Blackburn	135	8	12	20	
Christian Bordeleau	205	38	65	103	1 Stanley Cup
Jean-Paul Bordeleau	519	97	126	223	Drafted 13th in 1969
Paulin Bordeleau	183	33	56	89	Drafted 19th in 1973
Roland Cloutier	34	8	9	17	
Wayne Connelly	543	133	174	307	
Jacques Cossete	64	8	6	14	
Eric Desjardins (active)	827	102	332	434	1 Stanley Cup
Chris Hayes	1	0	0	0	1 Stanley Cup
Rejean Houle	635	161	247	408	5 Stanley Cups
Dave Keon	1,296	396	590	986	4 Stanley Cups; HHOF
Jacques Laperriere	691	40	242	282	6 Stanley Cups; HHOF
Steve Larouche	26	9	9	18	
Jean Lemieux	204	23	63	86	
Pit Martin	1,101	324	485	809	
Stephane Matteau (active)	661	120	145	265	1 Stanley Cup
Bill McDonagh	4	0	0	0	
Andre St. Laurent	644	129	187	316	
Bob Sullivan	62	18	19	37	
Dale Tallon	642	98	238	336	Drafted 2nd in 1970
Pierre Turgeon (active)	929	423	640	1,063	Drafted 1st in 1987
Sylvain Turgeon	669	269	226	495	Drafted 2nd in 1983
TOTAL	**10,075**	**2,437**	**3,871**	**6,308**	**19 Stanley Cups**

Goaltenders	GP	W	L	T	Avg	SO
Jacques Caron	72	24	29	11	3.29	2
Jacques Cloutier	255	82	102	24	3.64	3
Jean Louis Levasseur	1	0	1	0	7.00	0
Ted Ouimet	1	0	1	0	2.00	0
Andre Racicot	68	26	23	8	3.50	2
TOTAL	**397**	**132**	**156**	**43**		**7**

Kirkland Lake, Ontario

Skaters	GP	G	A	PTS	
Ralph Backstrom	1,032	278	361	639	6 Stanley Cups
Don Blackburn	185	23	44	67	
Buddy Boone	34	5	3	8	
Dick Duff	1,030	283	289	572	6 Stanley Cups
Murray Hall	164	35	48	83	
Chuck Hamilton	4	0	2	2	
Earl Heiskala	127	13	11	24	
Larry Hillman	790	36	196	232	4 Stanley Cups
Wayne Hillman	691	18	86	104	1 Stanley Cup
Willie Marshall	33	1	5	6	
Bob Murdoch	757	60	218	278	2 Stanley Cups
Claude Noel	7	0	0	0	
Barclay Plager	614	44	187	231	
Bill Plager	263	4	34	38	
Bob Plager	644	20	126	146	
Dick Redmond	771	133	312	445	Drafted 5th in 1969
Mickey Redmond	538	233	195	428	2 Stanley Cups
Mike Walton	588	201	247	448	2 Stanley Cups
Dave Watson	18	0	1	1	
Tom Webster	102	33	42	75	
TOTAL	**8,392**	**1,420**	**2,407**	**3,827**	**23 Stanley Cups**

Goaltender	GP	W	L	T	Avg	SO
Daren Puppa (active)	429	179	161	54	3.03	19

ATLANTIC CANADA

While the combined population of Canada's four Atlantic Provinces of New Brunswick, Nova Scotia, Prince Edward Island and Newfoundland represents just eight percent of the country's total population, the region has been a vital cog in the development of National Hockey League talent through the years.

The four provinces have combined to send 159 players to

the NHL, including 63 from Nova Scotia, 48 from New Brunswick, 25 from Prince Edward Island and 23 from Newfoundland.

In Nova Scotia, the capital city of Halifax has sent more players to the NHL than any other (15), but it is the small town of New Glasgow (pop. 9,905) that has risen to prominence in the past two years with two citizens who were members of Stanley Cup championship teams. In 1998–99, rookie forward Jon Sim played with the Stanley Cup-winning Dallas Stars. A year later, rookie defenseman Colin White played a prominent role in helping the New Jersey Devils to the 2000 Stanley Cup title. Sim and White were both born in 1977 and become the third and fourth citizens of New Glasgow to compete in the NHL. Lowell MacDonald played 13 seasons with Detroit, Los Angeles and Pittsburgh from 1961–62 through 1977–78, while goaltender Troy Gamble played four seasons with the Vancouver Canucks before retiring in 1992.

Nova Scotia's Cape Breton Island has also been one of the country's hockey hotbeds. With a combined population of less than 35,000, the Cape Breton towns of Glace Bay, Inverness, North Sydney, Sydney and Sydney Mines have produced no fewer than 19 NHL players, including stars such as defenseman Al MacInnis of the St. Louis Blues (Inverness, pop. 2,013), former Montreal Canadien Bobby Smith (North Sydney, pop. 7,260); Mike McPhee (Sydney, pop. 26,063); Doug Sulliman (Glace Bay, pop. 19,501); and Tony Currie (Sydney Mines, pop. 7,551).

With a population of just 134,557 people, Canada's smallest province of Prince Edward Island has developed 25 NHL players, including 16 from the capital city of Charlottetown and six from the province's other major urban center of Summerside (pop. 7,474). The province's most famous NHLers include Charlottetown natives Al MacAdam, who scored 240 goals and totaled 591 points in a 12-year NHL career; Bobby and Billy MacMillan, who combined for more than 300 goals in 1,200 NHL games in the 1970s and 1980s; and Bobby Stewart. Summerside natives include Errol Thompson, Gerard Gallant and John Chabot, who all enjoyed solid NHL careers during the 1970s, 1980s and 1990s.

Grand Falls, a town of 6,000 in the northern reaches of the province of New Brunswick, has sent four of the 48 New Brunswick natives to the NHL, including Dave Pichette (322 games), Tony White (164), Gerry Ouellette (34) and Don Howse (33). The province's three largest cities—St. John, Moncton and Fredericton—each with a population of less than 75,000, have sent seven, nine and six players to the NHL, respectively.

While the province of Newfoundland cannot lay claim to any Hall of Famers, 50-goal scorers or Hart Trophy winners, it has produced its fair share of NHL players. With a population of about a half-million people, 23 NHL players call Newfoundland home. Perhaps the province's most famous son is former NHL defenseman Keith Brown (Corner Brook, pop. 22,410), who played 16 seasons with the Chicago Blackhawks and Florida Panthers from 1979–80 through 1994–95.

BREAKDOWN OF CANADIAN BIRTHPLACES

ONTARIO

Agincourt 1
Alliston 1
Ajax 1
Alexandria 1
Arnprior 2
Atikokan 1
Aurora 3
Ayr 1
Bancroft 2
Barrie 20
Barriefield 1
Barrys Bay 1
Beamsville 2
Beaverton 2
Beeton 3
Belle River 1
Belleville 18
Berlin (see Kitchener)
Blackburn 1
Blenheim 1
Blind River 2
Bolton 1
Bothwell 1
Bourget 2
Bowmanville 2
Bracebridge 5
Bradford 1
Bramalea 2
Brampton 12
Brantford 30
Brockville 9
Brussels 1
Burk's Falls 1
Burlington 10
Byron 1
Cache Bay 2
Callander 1
Cambridge 4
Campbellford 2
Capreol 3
Cardinal 2
Carleton Place..........2
Carlisle 1
Cayuga 2
Cedar Springs 1
Charlesbourg 1
Chapleau 4
Chatham 11
Chesley 4
Chesterville..............1
Charletone 1
Clinton 1
Cobalt......................3
Cobourg 4
Cochenour 1
Cochrane 1
Collingwood 10
Coniston 3
Cooksville 1
Copper Cliff..............4
Cornwall 22
Creighton Mines 2
Delhi 1
Deloro 1
Deseronto 2
Downeyville 1
Dresden 2
Dryden 4
Dublin......................1
Dunnville 4
Durham 2
Duro 1
Eardley 1
Earlton 2
East York 2
Eganville..................3
Elgin 1
Elliot Lake 1
Elmira......................2
Elmwood 1
Espanola..................5
Essex 2
Etobicoke 3
Exeter......................1
Falconbridge 1
Farrow's Point..........1
Fergus 3
Forest......................1
Forks of Credit 1
Fort Erie 5
Fort Frances 8
Fort William 31
Galt 9
Ganonoque 1
Garafraxa County 1
Georgetown 2
Geraldton 3
Gloucester 2
Goderich 5
Gore Bay..................1
Gravenhurst 1
Grimsby 2
Guelph 18
Hagersville 1
Haileybury 4
Haliburton 2
Hamilton 49
Hawkesbury 6
Hearst 1
Heathcote 1
Hespeler....................2
Highland Creek 1
Hillbrough 1
Holland Landing 1
Hornepayne 1
Humber Summit 1
Humberstone 1
Huntsville 2
Iroquois Falls 3
Kanata 2
Kapuskasing 4
Kemptville 1
Kenora 12
Kerr Lake 1
Keswick 2
King City....................1
Kincardine 6
Kingston 51
Kirkland Lake 21
Kitchener (incl. Berlin) ...47
Lambeth......................1
La Salle 3
Leamington..................6
Levack 2
Lindsay......................11
Listowel 5
Little Current 1
London 37
Lucknow......................1
Lynden 2
Manitouwadge 1
Manotick 1
Markdale 2
Marmora......................1
Massey 1
Matheson 1
Mattawa......................1
Meaford 4
Midland 4
Millbank 1
Milton..........................4
Mimico 2
Minesing......................1
Mississauga 11
Mitchell 1
Moose Factory 1
Morrisburg 1
Mount Albert 2
Mt. Dennis 1
Nanticoke 1
Napanee......................1
Naughton 1
Nepean 3
New Hamburg..............2
New Liskeard 7
New Toronto 1
Newmarket..................9
Newton Robinson 1
Niagara Falls..............25
Nilestown 1
Nobleton......................1
North Bay 25
North Gower 1
North York 7
Norwood......................1
Oakville 7
Ohsweken 1
Orillia 2
Orangeville 1
Oshawa 26
Osgoode 1
Ottawa 153
Owen Sound 16
Paisley 1
Palmerston 1
Paris 3
Parry Sound 6
Pembroke....................16
Penetanguishene..........5

Perth 5
Petawawa 1
Peterborough 41
Petersburg 1
Petrolia..................10
Pickering 1
Plattsville 1
Pointe Anne 2
Ponska 1
Port Arthur 22
Port Colborne 6
Port Credit 2
Port Dalhousie...........1
Port Hope 3
Port Perry 1
Portsmouth 1
Prescott 3
Preston 3
Randolph 1
Ravenswood 1
Red Lake 1
Renfrew 7
Rexdale 1
Richmond Hill 7
Ridgeway 1
Rockland 3
Ruthven 1
Sarnia 30
Sault Ste. Marie 38
Scarborough 29
Schomberg 1
Schumacher 5
Seaforth 5
Seaforth (Edmondville)...1
Seneca Township 1
Shawinigan Falls.........1
Shelbourne 1
Shelburne 1
Shumacher 1
Silver Mountain 1
Simcoe 6
Sioux Lookout 1
Skead 1
Smiths Falls 4
Smooth Rock Falls 3
South Porcupine 9
South River 1
St. Catharines 28
St. George 1
St. Lambert.................1
St. Mary's 2
St. Paul's 1
St. Thomas 4
Stirling 1
Stittsville....................2
Stoney Creek 3
Stouffville 1
Stratford 18
Strathroy 3
Sturgeon Falls.............3
Sudbury 67
Sundridge 3
Sutton West 1
Swansea.....................1
Synenham 1
Tecumseh 1
Terrace Bay 2
Thamesford 1
Thessalon 1
Thornhill 1
Thorold 3
Thunder Bay 37
Tilsonburg 1
Timmins 22
Timmons 1
Tinturn 1
Toronto 373
Trenton 7
Trout Creek.................1
Turgeon Falls 1
Unionville 1
Vankleek Hill 1
Varney 1
Victoria Harbour 1
Victoria Mines 1
Walkerton 1
Wallaceburg 1
Walpole Island 1
Waterford 1
Waterloo......................6
Waubaushene 2
Wawa...........................2
Webbwood 1
Welland 8
Weston 7
Wheatley 1
White River...................1
Willowdale 2
Williamstown 1
Winchester 4
Windsor 43
Wingham 1
Woodbridge 1
Woodstock 2
York 2
Total: 1999

QUEBEC

Acton Vale 2
Allomette 1
Amqui.........................1
Angegardien 1
Anjou 4
Arvida.........................3
Asbestos.....................4
Aylmer 1
Bagotville 1
Baie Comeau 2
Beauport.....................6
Bellefeuille 1
Blainville.....................1
Boucherville 2
Bout De L'isle 1
Bristol.........................2
Brownsburg 1
Buckingham 4
Cap-de-la-Madeleine ...2
Cap-Rouge 2
Caughnawaga...............1
Chambly 1
Chambly Basin 2
Chandler.....................1
Charlemagne 1
Charlesbourg 2
Chicoutimi 9
Cowansville 2
Dolbeau 1
Donnacona 2
Delson 1
Drummondville 14
Duparquet 1
East Broughton 1
Ferme-Neuve 3
Gaspe..........................4
Gatineau.....................5
Granby 4
Grand Baie 1
Grand'Mere.................4
Greenfield Park 1
Havre St. Pierre 1
Hauterive 1
Herbertville-Station 1
Hull 8
Ile Bizard 1
Ile Perrot......................1
Joliette 3
Jonquiere 1
Kenogami 2
Knowlton 1
L'Abord A Plouffe.........1
L'Annonciation 1
Labelle 1
Lac St. Charles 2
Lac St. Jean 2
Lachine 14
Lachute 5
LaSalle 10
La Sarre 1
Latbiniere 1
Laurierville 1
Lauzon 1
Laval 15
Laverlochere 1
Les Saulles 1
Levis 1
Longueuil 5
Magog 1
Malartic 3
Maniwaki 2
Masham 1
Mason 1
Massawippi 1
Matane 3
Matau..........................1
Mayo 1
Mont-Laurier 3
Mont Louis 1
Montmagny 1
Montmorency 1
Montreal 250
Notre Dame de la Salette...1
Nouvelle 1
Ormstown 1
Outremont 1
Padoue 1
Palmarolle 1
Papineau 1
Peribonka 1
Pierrefonds..................3
Pierreville 1
Pointe-aux-Trembles ...2
Pointe Claire 3
Pointe Gatineau 1
Pont Rouge 1
Pontiac 1
Quebec City 43
Repentigny 3
Richmond 1
Rimouski 1
Ripon 1
Riviere-du-loup 1
Robertsville 1
Rouyn-Noranda 27
Rosemere 1
Sept-Iles 3
Shawinigan..................2
Shawinigan Falls 9
Shawville 5
Sherbrooke 18
Sillery 1
Sorel 11
South Durham..............1
St-Agnes 1
St. Alexis-des-Monts ...1
St. Anicet 1
St.Antoine-de Pontbriand 1
St. Apollinaire 1
St. Bonaventure 1
St. Charles 1
St. Charles Bellechase ...1
St. Clec 1
St. Emile 1
St. Ephrem 1
St. Esprit.....................1
St-Eustache 1
St. Etienne 1
St. Francis D'Assisi 1
St. Gabriel-de-Brandon 1
St. Georges de Beauce 1
St. Hilaire 1
St. Hyacinthe 5
St. Janvier 1
St. Jean 3
St. Jerome 4
St. Lambert..................2
St. Leonard..................1
St. Malo 1
St. Maurice 1
St. Odilon 1
St. Prime 1
St-Raymond 1
St. Remi de Rinqwick 11
Ste-Adele 1
Ste-Agathe 1
Ste. Anne-de-Bellevue 24
Ste-Anne-des Plaines ...1
Ste. Elizabeth 1
Ste. Foy 3
Ste. Genevieve 2
Ste-Justine 1
Ste-Martine 1
Ste-Rose 1
Taschereau 1
Temiscamingue 4
Terrebonne 2
Thetford Mines 5
Thurso 2
Trois-Rivieres 11
Val d'Or 4
Valleyfield 8
Vanier..........................1
Verdun 19
Victoriaville 5
Ville de Vanier 1
Ville Ste. Pierre 1
Windsor 1
Yamaska......................1
Total: 740

ALBERTA

Banff 2
Bankhead 2
Bashaw 2
Bassano 1
Beaumont 1
Beaverlodge 2
Bentley 4
Blackie 1
Blairmore 1
Bonnyville 3
Bow Island 1
Cadomin......................1
Calahoo 2
Calgary 93
Camrose......................6
Canmore......................4
Carstairs......................1
Castor 1
Cold Lake 4
Coronation 2
Drayton Valley 1
Drumheller 1
Duchess 1
Edmonton 162
Edson 1
Elk Point 1
Fairview 1
Fort McMurray 2
Fort Saskatchewan 5
Fort Vermillon 1
Glendon 1
Grand Cache 1
Grand Center 1
Grande Prairie.............3
Grossfield 1
Halkirk 1
Hanna..........................2
Hardisty 1
High River 4
High Prairie 2
Hines Creek 1
Hinton 2
Hobbema 1
Hythe 1
Innisfail 2
Jasper 3
Lacombe 3
Lamont 1
Leduc...........................1
Lethbridge 14
Lloydminster 2
Mannville 3
Medicine Hat.............14
Milo 1
Morinville 1
Myrnam 1
Nanton 2
Olds 1
Onaway 1
Peace River..................6
Pincher Creek 3
Ponoka 4
Provost 2
Red Deer 18
Redwater 1
Rocky Mountain House 3
Sandon 1
Sexsmith 1
Sherwood Park 4
Slave Lake 1
Spruce Grove 4
St. Albert.....................3
Stettler 3
Swalwell......................1
Swan Hills 1
Trochu 1
Two Hills.....................1
Vegreville 2
Vermilion 3
Viking..........................6
Wainwright 2
Warburg 1
Westlock......................2
Wetaskiwin..................4
Willingdon 1
Youngstown 1
Total: 462

SASKATCHEWAN

Admiral 1
Allan 1
Asquith 1
Assiniboia 2
Balcarres 1
Battleford 1
Bengough 1
Big River.....................3
Birch Hills 1
Blaine Lake..................1
Borden 1
Canora 3
Carlisle 1
Central Butte 1
Churchbridge 2
Climax 2
Craik 2
Craven 1
Creelman 1
Cudworth 3
Cupar 1

Davidson 1
Delisle 5
Dinsmore 1
Diwide 1
Dodsland 3
Drake 1
Dunblane 1
Dysart 3
Edington 1
Esterhazy 2
Estevan 5
Fairlight 1
Fielding 1
Fillmore 1
Fleming 1
Floral 1
Foam Lake 3
Fort Qu'Appelle 2
Frobisher 1
Gainsborough 2
Goodsoil 1
Gravelbourg 1
Grenfell 2
Gull Lake 1
Hafford 2
Herbert 1
Hodgeville 1
Hudson Bay 3
Humboldt 8
Indian Head 1
Jansen 1
Kamsack 3
Kelvington 2
Kerrobert 1
Kindersley 9
Kinistino 2
Lac La Rouge 1
Lac Pelletier 1
Landis 2
Lang 2
Langenburg 1
Lanigan 3
Lashburn 1
Lloydminster 9
Loon Lake 1
Lucky Lake 2
Lumsden 4
Major 1
Manor.......................1
Maple Creek 2
Melfort 5
Melville 7
MacNutt 1
Maryfield 1
Meadow Lake 3
Milestone 1
Montmartre...............1
Moose Jaw 21
Moosomin 4
Neudorf 1
Nipawin 1
Nokomis 2
Norquay 2
North Battleford 13
Odessa 2
Oxbow 4
Paddockwood 1
Paradise Hills 1
Pense 1
Pierceland 1
Ponteix 1
Porcupine Plain 1
Prelate 1
Prince Albert 19
Punnicht 1
Quill Lake 3
Rama 1
Redvers 1
Regina 80
Rosetown 2
Rosthern 2
Sandy Lake Reserve ...1
Saskatoon...............67
Scepter 1
Semans 1
Shaunavon 2
Silton 1
Speers 1
Spy Hill 1
Star City 1
Stoughton 1
Strasbourg 1
Sutherland 2
Swift Current............10
Togo 1
Tubrose 1
Unity 1
Val Marie 1
Vanguard 1
Vonda.......................1
Wakaw 3
Waldheim 1
Wapella 1
Warman 1
Watrous 1
Watson 1
Wetaskawin 1
Weyburn...................9
White City 1
Wilcox 2
Wilkie 1
Wynard 1
Yellow Grass 1
Yorkton 7
Total: 451

MANITOBA

Ashburn 1
Baldur 1
Basswood 1
Beausejour 1
Birtle 2
Brandon 26
Carman 1
Carroll 2
Cowan 1
Dauphin 7
Deloraine 3
Dugald 1
Elkhorn 1
Eriksdale 2
Flin Flon 17
Foxwarren 2
Gilbert Plains 1
Gimley 1
Glenboro...................1
Gretna 1
Grosse Isle 1
Hamiota 4
Hartney 3
Holland 1
Lac du Bonnet 1
Lettelier 1
Manitou 1
Mariapolis 1
McCreary 1
Melita.......................1
Minnedosa 3
Neepawa 1
Neepouna 1
Oak Lake 1
Oakville 1
Pilot Mound 2
Pine Falls 1
Poplar Point 2
Portage La Prairie 8
Riverton 1
Russell 2
Selkirk 9
Sherridon 1
Snowflake 1
Souris.......................5
St. Boniface 18
St. Charles 1
St. James 2
St. Lazare 1
St. Vital 1
Ste. Rose 1
Steinbach 2
Stoney Mountain 3
Swan River 1
The Pas 3
Thompson 3
Transcona 1
Treheme 1
Virden.......................1
Winkler 1
Winnipeg 175
Winnipegosis 1
Total: 343

BRITISH COLUMBIA

100 Mile House 2
Abbotsford 1
Burnaby 14
Burn's Lake 1
Campbell 1
Campbell River 2
Cassiar 1
Castlegar 6
Chemainus 2
Chetwynd 1
Chilliwack 1
Christina Lake............1
Comox 1
Coal Creek 1
Coquitlam 2
Cranbrook..............14
Creston 3
Dawson Creek 4
Delta 2
Duncan 4
Fernie.......................4
Ft. McNeill 1
Fort St. James 4
Fort St. John 3
Golden 1
Grand Forks 2
Hazelton 3
Hope 1
Houston 1
Kamloops 12
Kelowna 3
Kimberley 4
Kitimat 1
Lake Cowachin 1
Lac La Hache 1
Ladysmith 1
Merritt 4
Miskel 1
Murrayville 2
Nakusp 1
Nanaimo...................5
Nelson 4
New Westminster 10
North Vancouver 6
Osoyoos 1
Penticton 3
Pitt Meadows 1
Port Alberni..............5
Port Alice 1
Port Hardy 1
Port McNeil...............1
Port Moody 1
Powell River 6
Prince George 7
Princeton 2
Quesnel 3
Revelstoke 1
Richmond 3
Rossland..................3
Salmon Arm 2
Sechelt 1
Sicamous 1
Smithers...................3
Summerland 1
Surrey 8
Shuswap 1
Terrace 3
Trail 17
Vancouver..............42
Vernon 8
Victoria..................15
White Rock 2
Total: 282

NOVA SCOTIA

Amherst 2
Antigonish 5
Bedford 1
Berwick 1
Cole Harbour 1
Glace Bay 3
Guysborough 1
Kentville 1
Halifax 15
Inverness 2
Liverpool 1
Middleton 1
Lockport 1
New Glasgow 4
New Waterford 1
North Sydney 4
Oxford 1
Parrsboro 1
Stellarton 1
Sydney 10
Sydney Mines 1
Truro 3
Wolfville 1
Yarmouth 1
Total: 63

NEW BRUNSWICK

Bayfield 3
Big Cove 1
Campbellton 4
Cape Tormentine 1
Causapscal 1
Chatham....................2
Dalhousie 1
Dorchester 1
Edmundston 1
Fredericton 6
Grand Falls 1
Lakeville Corner 1
Moncton 9
Newcastle 1
Port Elgin 1
Sackville....................1
Shediac 1
St. John 7
St. Stephen................1
Sussex 2
Woodstock 2
Total: 48

NEWFOUNDLAND

Baie Verte 1
Bishop Falls 1
Carbonear 1
Come-by-Chance 1
Corner Brook 3
Deer Lake 1
Grand Falls 4
Labrador City 2
Mt. Pearl 1
St. John's 8
Total: 23

PRINCE EDWARD ISLAND

Charlottetown 16
Montague 1
O'Leary 1
Summerdale 1
Summerside 6
Total: 25

NORTHWEST TERRITORIES

Hay River 1
Inuvik.......................2
Yellowknife 2
Total: 5

YUKON

Whitehorse 3
Total: 3

NHL BIRTHPLACES, U.S.A., BY STATE

The United States, led by strong youth programs in Minnesota, Massachusetts and Michigan, has produced 12.5 percent of NHL players, or 773 total players.

State	Total Players	%
Minnesota	187	24.2
Massachusetts	176	22.8
Michigan	92	11.9
New York	80	10.3
Illinois	37	4.8
Connecticut	20	2.6
Ohio	20	2.6
California	19	2.5
Rhode Island	17	2.2
Pennsylvania	16	2.1
Wisconsin	16	2.1
New Jersey	12	1.6
New Hampshire	8	1.0
Washington	8	1.0
Colorado	6	0.8
North Dakota	6	0.8
Alaska	5	0.6
Indiana	5	0.6
Missouri	4	0.5
Virginia	4	0.5
Florida	3	0.4
Maine	3	0.4
Maryland	3	0.4
Oklahoma	3	0.4
Oregon	3	0.4
Texas	3	0.4
Vermont	3	0.4
District of Columbia	2	0.3
Georgia	2	0.3
Idaho	2	0.3
Alabama	1	0.1
Arizona	1	0.1
Delaware	1	0.1
Iowa	1	0.1
Montana	1	0.1
Nebraska	1	0.1
South Dakota	1	0.1
Utah	1	0.1

NHL BIRTHPLACES, REST OF THE WORLD

Non-North American countries—led by hockey super powers Russia (213 players); Sweden (212 players); Czech Republic (157 players), Finland (135 players) and Slovakia (58 players), have produced 15 percent of NHL players (948 in total).

Country	Total Players	%
Russia	213	22.5
Sweden	212	22.4
Czech Republic	157	16.6
Finland	135	14.3
Slovakia	58	6.1
England	21	2.2
Ukraine	20	2.1
Scotland	19	2.0
Germany	18	1.9
Kazakhstan	14	1.5
Belarus	8	0.8
Latvia	8	0.8
Switzerland	8	0.8
Ireland	6	0.6
Poland	6	0.6
Austria	5	0.5
France	5	0.5
Norway	4	0.4
Wales	3	0.3
Yugoslavia	3	0.3
Brazil	2	0.2
Denmark	2	0.2
Italy	2	0.2
South Korea	2	0.2
Ukraine	2	0.2
Venezuela	2	0.2
Belgium	1	0.1
Estonia	1	0.1
Haiti	1	0.1
Hungary	1	0.1
Jamaica	1	0.1
Lebanon	1	0.1
Netherlands	1	0.1
Nigeria	1	0.1
Paraguay	1	0.1
Taiwan	1	0.1
Tanzania	1	0.1
South Africa	1	0.1

CHAPTER 23

Original Six and Then Some

Bronco Horvath's Hockey Odyssey

Fred Addis

THE ORIGINAL SIX ERA OF THE NHL produced many of hockey's most famous players. The exploits of Rocket Richard, Gordie Howe and Bobby Hull, to name but a few, are known wherever the game is played. Less known are the achievements of Bronco Horvath, a journeyman center from Port Colborne, Ontario. Yet Horvath has the distinction of holding one impressive Original Six record. He set the mark for the era's longest scoring streak when he tallied points in 22 consecutive games in 1959–60. This scoring feat is all the more remarkable in light of the fact that Bronco, along with Vic Lynn, Larry Hillman, Dave Creighton and Forbes Kennedy, is one of only five NHL players to have been the property of every Original Six team.

Bronco Horvath got his first break in pro hockey in the spring of 1950. His older brother, Johnny, was completing his second pro season with the Grand Rapids Rockets of the Eastern Hockey League. The team was shorthanded and needed some help heading down the home stretch of their season. Coincidentally, Bronco's Galt Black Hawks were finished for the year in the OHA Junior A loop. Answering his brother's call, Bronco caught the next train to Grand Rapids. He upstaged his big brother and stole the local headlines by scoring a hat trick in each of his first two pro games. Bronco's climb up the ladder through hockey's outposts had begun.

Horvath signed with Eddie Shore's Springfield franchise of the American Hockey League for the 1950–51 season. The following year Shore decided to flip the franchise to Syracuse, and Horvath skated for the Warriors for the next two seasons. Meanwhile, to protect the market, Shore entered a Springfield team in the Eastern Hockey League and then in the Quebec Hockey League for the 1953–54 season. Syracuse struggled in the AHL that season and ticket sales slumped as the Warriors fell out of contention midway through the campaign. Springfield, however, was drawing well and Shore, seeing a chance to turn a better dollar, asked his top Syracuse scoring line—Bronco Horvath, Walt Atanas and Vern Kaiser—to accept a transfer to his QHL team. Horvath's unit had no trouble scoring in the Quebec league, but unfortunately when they were not on the ice, the opposition seemed to score at will. Springfield finished dead last on the season, but when Horvath bumped into his boss at the end of the campaign, Shore peeled off $1,000 and passed it to him in appreciation for his loyalty in accepting the Quebec league demotion.

That summer Shore moved Horvath to the Edmonton Flyers in the Western Hockey League and Bronco got a chance to shine with the Detroit Red Wings affiliate. He won the WHL scoring title with 110 points, including 50 goals and 60 assists. His linemate Johnny Bucyk won WHL rookie honors. That same season, the parent Red Wings were hobbled by injuries in their Stanley Cup final series against Montreal and the call went out for reinforcements. Horvath and Bucyk were flown from Edmonton to join the Wings at practice in Toledo, Ohio.

Just hours before game seven at Detroit, NHL President Clarence Campbell ruled that both players were ineligible to play. Since Edmonton, which had won the WHL title, was awaiting the champion of the Quebec league in order to play an exhibition series for the Duke of Edinburgh Trophy, Campbell ruled that the Flyers had not finished their season and disqualified Horvath and Bucyk. Left to watch from behind the bench, the Edmonton farmhands witnessed the Wings defeat Montreal to capture the Stanley Cup. (The Shawinigan Falls Cataracts eventually defeated the Edmonton Flyers five games to two in the best-of-nine Duke of Edinburgh series.)

Back in Detroit general manager Jack Adams reshuffled his roster during the offseason and Edmonton teammate Norm Ullman was rated ahead of Horvath on the Wings depth chart. Meanwhile, the Rangers had penciled in prospect Ross Lowe at center but he died in a midsummer swimming accident. To fill the gap, Bronco and Dave Creighton were traded to New York for Billy Dea and Aggie Kukulowicz in August 1955.

That fall saw Bronco at the Rangers training camp in Saskatoon, Saskatchewan. He played pivot between Andy Hebenton and Wally Hergesheimer. With tongue in cheek, "Hergie" pointed out to anyone who would listen that among them they represented 100 goals: Horvath's 50 at Edmonton and Hebenton's 46 at Victoria (both in the Western Hockey League) added to Hergesheimer's four with the Rangers in a season shortened to 14 games by a broken leg.

Bronco made the cut at the Rangers camp and played his first season in the NHL under coach Phil Watson in 1955–56. Unfortunately, a lack of scoring led to less ice time and less ice time led to less scoring. Horvath had a reputation for being what some called "chirpy" or "yappy," and when Coach Watson would chide him on the bench saying, "Bronco, why don't you score?" Horvath would snap back, "It's tough to score sitting here." Something had to give, and with the 1956–57 campaign barely under way, Watson fingered Horvath for the Rangers farm club in Providence. When Bronco threatened to retire before reporting, his contract was sold to Montreal.

Horvath was assigned to the Canadiens new AHL franchise at Rochester where he quickly rediscovered his scoring touch. An injury to the Habs' Jean Beliveau in January, 1957 brought Bronco to Montreal, where he saw limited duty in a game against Toronto but did get out once on a power-play with Rocket Richard and Boom Boom Geoffrion. The Habs downed the Maple Leafs, 2–1, on a late goal by Donnie Marshall, but it would be Horvath's only game with the Habs. Coincidentally, it was the only game he played against his hometown hockey hero, Teeder Kennedy. Kennedy had retired the previous season but was coaxed back to playing with Toronto midway through the 1956–57 season.

After his debut at Montreal, Horvath was returned to Rochester where he closed out the season by finishing fifth in the AHL scoring race with 81 points in just 56 games. He tied Providence center Paul Larivee for AHL first all-star team honors. Rochester enjoyed a strong playoff that spring, but bowed out to Cleveland in the Calder Cup final. However, in the summer of 1957, Bronco was sold to the Boston Bruins and reunited with former Edmonton teammates Johnny Bucyk and Vic Stasiuk.

At Boston, Horvath also rejoined his old friend, southpaw goalie Don Simmons. The two were school chums and had both played minor hockey at Port Colborne and junior at Galt. Bronco credited Simmons with teaching him the finer points of how to beat big-league goaltending and he enjoyed his best years with the Bruins. His patented quick-release wrist shot and "shoot from anywhere" mentality were keys to his success.

Horvath's skill as a scorer was matched by his guts and determination. In October, 1958, both he and teammate Doug Mohns had their jaws broken by errant Leafs elbows in a game at Toronto. (The Maple Leafs had been the last team to comply with a league mandate to switch from the hard plastic-shell elbow pads to the softer padded variety.) After weeks of having his jaw wired shut and eating blended food through a drinking straw, Horvath returned to the lineup after Christmas. He was fitted with a full-face shield of rigid plexiglass to protect his jaw. Sporting this hot and cumbersome headgear he scored a hat trick, including two shorthand goals, on February 8, 1959, as the Bruins bested the Rangers, 4–1, at Boston Garden.

When the 1958–59 season concluded, the Boston Bruins and the New York Rangers traveled to Europe for a goodwill tour to promote the NHL. Bronco and his Bruins mates flew to London, England, along with the Rangers, to begin a whirlwind tour of 23 games in 26 days in 10 different cities across six countries. Some Rangers balked at the tour and their spots were filled by four volunteer recruits from the Chicago Black Hawks: Bobby Hull, Eric Nesterenko, Eddie Litzenberger and Pierre Pilote. However, the tour was plagued by poor promotion, low attendance and ice conditions which ranged from fair to poor. A league experiment with a fluorescent orange puck did not survive the trip.

The following season would be Bronco's best. Not only did he collect 17 goals and 18 assists while scoring in 22 consecutive games (an achievement that was overlooked until statisticians made the discovery in the mid 1970s) but Horvath also waged a season-long seesaw battle for the league scoring championship with Bobby Hull.

On the last day of the 1959–60, season Chicago was at Boston with the scoring race between Horvath and Hull knotted at 80 points each. Near the end of the first period, a Bruins point shot felled Horvath in front of the Hawks net and he was rushed to hospital for X-rays while the game continued. Hull registered an assist in Bronco's absence and when he returned from the hospital for the third period, he was unable to break free from the Hawks' intense checking. The match ended in a 5–5 tie, with Hull capturing the scoring crown by a single point. After the game, Hull sought out Bronco in the Bruins dressing room and congratulated and consoled his battered and dejected opponent. Bronco was named to the NHL's Second All-Star Team at center and also was winner of the Elizabeth C. Dufresne Trophy, presented annually to the Bruin who has been the most outstanding during home games. But at the time, the honors rang hollow in the face of the emotionally devastating loss of the scoring race and the fact that the Bruins had missed the playoffs.

Boston tumbled from contention again during the 1960–61 season and former Ranger coach Phil Watson was hired to right the ship. With his old adversary at the helm, Bronco's days were numbered. He was left unprotected in the June, 1961, Waiver Draft and was claimed by the Stanley Cup champion Chicago Black Hawks, piloted by his former junior coach, Rudy Pilous. The Hawks would return to the Stanley Cup finals in 1962, but they were no match for the surging Leafs, who rode the hot goaltending of Johnny Bower and Horvath's old friend, substitute Don Simmons.

Despite the trip to the championship round, June again was unkind to Bronco as he once more was left unprotected. He was claimed by the Rangers and reported for his second tour of duty on Broadway. With only seven goals in 41 games through January 1963, Horvath completed his Original Six circuit when he was placed on waivers and claimed by the Toronto Maple Leafs. He failed to impress coach and general manager Punch Imlach during a short stay in Toronto and was dispatched to the farm. Horvath found himself back in Rochester and the AHL.

Over the next eight years Bronco Horvath consistently would light up AHL netminders. He played on three Calder Cup championship teams and finished in the AHL's top 10 in scoring three times, including runner-up to the title on two occasions. Lonely Leaf farmhands, looking for the comfort of a home-cooked meal while in Rochester, invariably showed up at Bronco's house, where his wife, Dolly, would serve up her renowned spaghetti and meatballs for all comers. However, when Bronco broke this thumb during the 1967–68 AHL campaign he was assigned to the Leafs' Central Hockey League affiliate at Tulsa for a reconditioning stint.

Just as a death had given Horvath his first chance at the big time back in 1955, tragedy once again would send him to the NHL. When Minnesota forward Bill Masterton died after hitting his head on the ice during an NHL game on January 13, 1968, Horvath was loaned to the devastated North Stars. He provided good playmaking and a steadying influence while primarily being used to quarterback the North Stars power-play during 14 games in Minnesota. When general manager Wren Blair attempted to secure Horvath's contract outright, Punch Imlach's demands proved astronomical. A very disappointed Horvath was returned to Rochester. Later it would come to light that Bronco's father had offered Imlach $30,000 cash to let his son finish his career in Minnesota. As it was, he finished out the 1967–68 campaign in the AHL and retired 14 games into the 1969–70 season at the age of 40.

Bronco Horvath's professional hockey career spanned 21 seasons. The crafty center with the lightning-quick release left his mark not only in the National Hockey League, but also in the American Hockey League, where he is a member of the AHL Hall of Fame. In his retirement, he lives at Cape Cod, Massachusetts, and is an avid golfer.

CHAPTER 24

Johnny Bower

The Winningest Goalie of Them All

Ernie Fitzsimmons

As the new millennium begins and excitement is focused on Patrick Roy becoming the winningest goalie in NHL history, it is easy to overlook the fact that Johnny Bower is actually the winningest pro goaltender of them all. Bower's life in hockey was like two careers in one.

Orphaned at an early age, Bower was brought up by the Kizkan family of Prince Albert, Saskatchewan. (He used the last name Kizkan until he reverted to his original family name at age 21 in Cleveland.) After serving two years with the Canadian Army, Bower finished up his junior career by leading the Prince Albert Black Hawks to the Saskatchewan Junior Hockey League title in 1944–45—although it seems unlikely in looking back that he was really young enough for junior hockey.

In 1945–46 Bower and Prince Albert teammate Bob Solinger came east to try out with the Cleveland Barons of the American Hockey League. After learning the ropes as a pro from veteran Harvey Teno, young Johnny battled with Teno, Roger Bessette and Al Rollins for four years before becoming the main man in Cleveland in 1949–50. Four times in the next eight years, Bower topped the 40-win mark in 70-game seasons. He was above 30 in each of the other four years. Bower led his league in wins, goals-against average and shutouts four times each.

Over the course of his minor league career Bower was on first-place teams seven times in 12 seasons and backstopped his team to four Calder Cup titles as American Hockey League champions. He was the AHL MVP for three consecutive seasons starting in 1955–56.

During the late 1940s and early 1950s Cleveland was trying to win an NHL expansion franchise, so the team stockpiled many fine prospects. The Barons finally agreed to part with their 30-year-old veteran goaltender, dubbed "The China Wall" by Cleveland reporters, and allowed him to go to the New York Rangers, along with Eldred Kobussen, for Emile Francis, Neil Strain and cash on July 20, 1953.

For three years the Rangers had struggled defensively, giving up over 200 goals each season, but they tightened up and surrendered only 182 with Bower on the scene in 1953–54. The Rangers had posted a 17–37–16 record the year before he arrived, but Bower led them to a team-record 29 wins with a goals-against average of 2.60 that was the best by any Ranger goalie since Dave Kerr in 1940–41. Bower never let anybody handle his equipment and picked out all of his own sticks. He worked as hard in practice as he did in games and earned the respect of his teammates. He was also selected the most popular Ranger by New York fans.

With all he had going for him, it came as a great shock to Ranger fans, the media and most of all to Bower himself when the Rangers decided to go back to a younger Gump Worsley the following season. The 1954–55 campaign saw the Rangers drop back to a 17–35–18 record. Over the course of that season and the next, the team averaged over half-a-goal against per game more than they had in 1953–54. Meanwhile, Bower proceeded to lead the Western Hockey League in goals against (2.71) and shutouts (seven) in 1954–55. He followed up with an AHL-best 45 wins in 61 games for Providence in 1955–56.

Punch Imlach got a firsthand view of Bower's talents while coaching the Springfield Indians of the AHL in 1956–57 and 1957–58. One of his first acts when he took over as general manager in Toronto was to obtain Bower's rights from Cleveland in 1958.

At the time Bower was 34 years old and content in Cleveland after posting a league-best 2.19 goals-against in 1957–58 and performing brilliantly in shutting out Pittsburgh three times in the Calder Cup finals. Eventually, though, he gave in to Imlach's pleas and signed with the Leafs. There were many doubters when Bower struggled to a 15–17–7 record in his first year in Toronto, and at one time he was even removed from the Leafs roster. However, Bower soon settled into the number-one role and proceeded to give the Leafs the solid goaltending they needed to win the Stanley Cup four times between 1962 and 1967. Along the way he picked up 250 regular-season NHL wins and 35 more in the playoffs to add to his 421 victories in the minor leagues.

It seems a safe bet that if Bower had graduated to the NHL in 1949–50 and stayed there through those next eight great seasons, he would have topped 400 NHL victories and easily could have been number one overall in NHL wins. As it is, on the accompanying chart you will find Bower atop the list of the goaltenders with the most pro wins all-time. On it you will also see the names of several goalies who either didn't play in the NHL, or who played very little. Before casting aspersions on these players one must remember that playing in the big leagues is often just as much a case of opportunity as it is of talent.

When Bower first entered the NHL in 1953–54 the league had only six teams that carried one goalie each. They usually had two or three other backstops they kept in the minors. Compare that situation to the 1999–2000 season, in which 28 teams carried at least two goaltenders. This results in over 60 elite jobs for netminders.

If you were to ignore any goaltenders trained outside North America (as was the case in Bower's time) and reduce the current NHL to six teams with only one goalie each the cast might look something like this: Ed Belfour, Martin Brodeur, Curtis Joseph, Olaf Kolzig, Chris Osgood and Patrick Roy. Goaltenders like Byron Dafoe, Sean Burke, Trevor Kidd, Jeff Hackett, Jose Theodore, Mike Vernon and the rest would likely be playing in the minors.

On the other hand, if there had been 28 teams back in 1954 you would have to look outside of the four pro leagues that existed at the time in order to find enough starters for each NHL club. In order to staff the minors you would have had to strip the senior amateur leagues and lure some players who never gave the pro game a try.

Besides Bower, the NHL starters in 1954 were Jim Henry (Boston), Al Rollins (Chicago), Terry Sawchuk (Detroit) Gerry McNeil (Montreal) and Harry Lumley (Toronto). Other goalies who probably would have been starters in a 28-team league are: Ralph Almas, Gordie Bell, Harvey Bennett, Bill Brennan, Lucien Dechene, Emile Francis, Ray Frederick, Dave Gatherum, Jack Gelineau, Glenn Hall, Gordon Henry, Phil Hughes, Jean Marois, Gilles Mayer, Al Millar, Don O'Hearn, Andre Payette, Marcel Pelletier, Bob Perreault, Jacques Plante, Chuck Rayner and Gump Worsley. From this list only Francis, Gelineau, Hall, Plante, Rayner and Worsley ever played regularly in the NHL.

But even being given the chance to perform at the top level was no guarantee of an equal opportunity. For example, Gump Worsley played 186 of 210 games for the Rangers over his last three seasons in New York, but after being dealt to Montreal for Jacques Plante in 1963 he would only play eight games for the Canadiens his first year and 19 the second. (Worsley is the NHL's leader in losses with 352—one more than Gilles Meloche). Plante had averages of 2.86, 2.33 and 2.52 in his last three seasons with the powerful Habs, but ballooned to 3.91 and 3.67 in his first two years with the Rangers before being shipped to the minors.

Among the lesser-known goalies on the list of all-time winners, Lucien Dechene is the only one who never got a chance to play in the NHL. Still, for most of his career, Dechene was easily one of the top dozen goalies in the pro ranks. Playing a 70-game schedule, he won 38 games or more five times and led the WHL in shutouts for three straight years, from 1950–51 to 1952–53. Though Dechene is the WHL career leader with 389 wins and his record compares favorably with Bower, Glenn Hall and Worsley, who all played in that league, he never even got a glance from an NHL team. If not for Punch Imlach, Johnny Bower's name might by equally obscure today.

After playing for 24 years and registering 104 professional shutouts, Johnny Bower entered the new millennium as the biggest winner of them all. It may be a tough chore for anyone still playing to top his 706 victories. Though Patrick Roy enters the 2000–2001 season just two wins shy of Terry Sawchuk's NHL record of 446 wins, it will still take him at least three years of 40 wins per season (regular season and playoffs combined) to catch Bower who, it must be remembered, played in an era when eight was the most playoff wins he could record in one year.

GOALTENDERS' ALL-TIME PRO WINS

Because some minor pro statistics are incomplete, wins are approximated where noted.

Goaltender		Regular Season W	L	T	Playoffs W	L	T
Johnny Bower	NHL	250	195	90	35	34	0
	AHL	359	174	57	31	24	0
	WHL	30	25	8	1	4	0
	Total	639	394	155	67	62	0
	Overall	**706**	**456**	**155**			
Jacques Plante	NHL	435	247	145	71	36	0
	WHA	15	14	1			
	AHL	51	45	8	2	3	0
	Others	108	87	20	7	13	0
	Total	609	393	174	80	52	0
	Overall	**689**	**446**	**174**			
Gump Worsley	NHL	335	352	150	40	26	0
	AHL	79	42	5	4	5	0
	WHL	78	50	22	17	7	0
	Others	58	43	10	9	5	0
	Total	550	487	187	70	43	0
	Overall	**620**	**530**	**187**			
Terry Sawchuk	NHL	446	332	171	54	48	0
	AHL	69	37	22	8	2	0
	USHL	30	18	5	1	2	0
	Total	545	387	198	63	52	0
	Overall	**608**	**439**	**198**			
Glenn Hall	NHL	407	326	163	49	65	0
	AHL	22	40	6			
	WHL	94	75	30	28	16	0
	Total	523	341	199	77	81	0
	Overall	**600**	**422**	**199**			
Bob Perreault	NHL	8	16	7			
	AHL	229	172	36	46	36	0
	Others	200	157	25	28	18	0
	Total	437	345	68	74	54	0
(Statistics unavailable from 1969-70 to 1973-74. Minimum 80 addditional wins.)							
	Overall	**595**					

Goaltender		Regular Season W	L	T	Playoffs W	L	T
Gerry Cheevers	NHL	230	102	74	53	34	0
	WHA	99	78	9	7	12	0
	AHL	104	66	10	10	4	0
	Others	60	52	23	20	8	0
	Total	493	298	116	90	58	0
	Overall	**583**	**356**	**116**			
Marcel Pelletier	NHL	1	6	0			
	AHL	21	15	5	1	2	0
	WHL	297	324	50	25	26	0
	Others	163	107	34	41	31	0
	Total	482	452	89	67	59	0
(Missing statistics from 1966-68. Minimum 30 additional wins.)							
	Overall	**579**					
Patrick Roy	NHL	444	264	103	121	73	0
	AHL	1	0	0	10	3	0
	Total	445	264	103	131	76	0
	Overall	**576**	**340**	**103**			
Marv Edwards	NHL	15	34	7			
	AHL	7	11	1	1	3	0
	WHL	67	46	11	5	10	0
	Others	318	248	24	46	25	0
	Total	407	339	43	52	38	0
(Missing statistics from parts of four years. Minimum 85 additional wins.)							
	Overall	**548**					
Marcel Paille	NHL	32	52	22			
	WHA	2	8	0			
	AHL	329	309	58	49	38	0
	Others	80	92	17	1	4	0
	Total	443	461	97	50	42	0
(Missing statistics from 1953-54 and 1969-70. Minimum 50 additional wins.)							
	Overall	**543**					

GOALTENDERS' ALL-TIME PRO WINS

continued

Goaltender		Regular Season W	L	T	Playoffs W	L	T
Al Millar	NHL	1	4	1			
	AHL	55	106	10	3	2	0
	WHL	188	142	20	15	17	0
	Others	222	245	58	52	44	0
	Total	466	497	89	70	63	0
(Missing stats for parts of several seasons. Minimum 40 additional wins.)							
	Overall	**536**					
Grant Fuhr	NHL	403	295	114	92	50	0
	AHL	11	7	3			
	Total	414	302	117	92	50	0
	Overall	**506**	**352**	**117**			
Tony Esposito	NHL	423	306	151	45	53	0
	Others	35	40	6	0	1	0
	Total	458	346	158	45	54	0
	Overall	**503**	**400**	**157**			
Mike Vernon	NHL	371	241	86	77	56	0
	AHL	13	21	6			
	Others	36	17	2	2	4	0
	Total	420	279	94	79	60	0
	Overall	**499**	**339**	**94**			
Lucien Dechene	NHL	0	0	0	0	0	0
	AHL	5	10	0	3	4	0
	WHL	389	336	73	38	40	0
	Others	54	46	8			
	Total	448	392	81	41	44	0
	Overall	**489**	**436**	**81**			
Andy Moog	NHL	372	209	88	68	57	0
	Others	37	26	4	6	6	0
	Total	409	235	92	74	63	0
	Overall	**483**	**298**	**92**			
Gerry McNeil	NHL	119	105	52	17	18	0
	AHL	92	121	25	1	4	0
	Others	201	107	27	41	40	0
	Total	412	333	104	59	62	0
(Missing 1943-44 totals with a minimum 7 additional wins.)							
	Overall	**478**					

Goaltender		Regular Season W	L	T	Playoffs W	L	T
Harry Lumley	NHL	330	329	142	29	47	0
	AHL	89	97	25	1	4	0
	Others	18	41	4			
	Total	437	467	171	30	51	0
	Overall	**467**	**518**	**171**			
Ed Johnston	NHL	234	257	80	7	10	0
	WHL	82	83	8	9	10	0
	Others	73	47	14	26	16	0
	Total	389	387	102	42	36	0
(Statistics not available for 1959-60. Approximately 35 wins)							
	Overall	**465**					
Ed Giacomin	NHL	289	208	97	29	35	0
	AHL	112	130	10	3	6	0
	Others	6	10	0			
	Total	407	348	107	32	41	0
(Statistics not available for 1959-60 EHL. Minimum 20 additional wins.)							
	Overall	**459**					
Charlie Hodge	NHL	151	124	61	7	8	0
	AHL	86	89	19			
	Others	135	122	29	23	11	0
	Total	372	335	109	30	19	0
(Statistics are unavailable for IHL 1953-54. Approximately 40 additional wins.)							
	Overall	**442**					
G. Villemure	NHL	100	64	29	5	5	0
	AHL	119	85	31	18	15	0
	WHL	94	91	13	7	12	0
	Others	43	76	2			
	Total	356	316	75	30	32	0
(Statistics not available for AHL 1969-70. Approximately 35 additional wins.)							
	Overall	**421**					
Rogie Vachon	NHL	355	291	127	23	23	0
	AHL	6	4	0			
	CHL	17	12	5			
	Total	378	307	132	23	23	0
	Overall	**401**	**330**	**132**			

Notes on Early Goaltenders' Win Totals:

EARLY GOALTENDERS' WIN TOTALS if projected to 82-game seasons would match and, in some cases, exceed the numbers posted by Bower, Sawchuk and others.

Clint Benedict, Frank Brimsek, George Hainsworth and Georges Vezina would have had more than 700 wins. Hugh Lehman would likely have topped 600, while Andy Aitkenhead and Alfie Moore would certainly have finished near the 500-win mark.

CHAPTER 25

Lost in the Numbers

Observations on NHL Trophy and Award Winners

Kerry Banks

When Wayne Gretzky retired in April 1999, everyone wanted to know who would take the torch as the NHL's marquee player. Gretzky indicated that his successor would be Jaromir Jagr. Not that Jagr needed "The Great One's" blessing. The Czech's runaway 20-point victory in the 1998–99 scoring race was his second straight Art Ross Trophy title, a run that he extended to three in 1999–2000. The torch had been safely passed.

How long Jagr will rule the roost remains to be seen. More certain is that the bar of excellence has been raised to a new level by the two scoring champions that preceded him. Aside from the lockout-shortened 1994–95 season when Jagr won it, the Art Ross Trophy did not leave Gretzky and Mario Lemieux's sight for nearly two decades. The last time a player other than Jagr, Gretzky or Lemieux led the NHL in points was 1980, when Marcel Dionne did it with the Los Angeles Kings. That's 20 years worth of hardware owned by three players. That's dominance.

That's also the modern game. Despite adding more teams and players to the mix, expansion has not made the scoring title an entirely democratic pursuit. The Art Ross Trophy has remained the property of a small and elite club since 1951, the year a broad-shouldered Prairie boy named Gordie Howe won it for the first time.

It wasn't always this way. During the NHL's first three decades (1918 to 1950), the scoring title got passed around. In that era, only three players were able to cop the crown in consecutive years: Charlie Conacher, Sweeney Schriner and Max Bentley. Each time their reign lasted just two seasons. But beginning with Howe in 1951, the pattern changed.

Howe laid waste to the competition, putting up huge numbers and nailing four scoring titles in a row, six all told. Three Montreal marksmen—Jean Beliveau, Bernie Geoffrion and Dickie Moore—wrestled the trophy away from Howe in the latter half of the 1950s before the banner passed to a pair of gunners from the Windy City. Armed with their lethal banana blades, Chicago's Bobby Hull and Stan Mikita split seven scoring titles in the 1960s. Command next switched to Boston, where Phil Esposito and Bobby Orr kept the Art Ross Trophy under house arrest for seven straight seasons, from 1969 to 1975. After that, Guy Lafleur, the Gallic wonder, skated away with the trophy for three consecutive years. And then came #99.

Winning the Art Ross Trophy is a remarkably accurate predictor of greatness. All told, there have been 32 NHL scoring champions. Aside from Jagr, how many do you suppose are in the Hockey Hall of Fame? The answer: all but one. The outcast is Herb Cain, who led the scoring derby in 1943–44, tallying 82 points for the Boston Bruins in a 50-game schedule. The left wing's performance smashed Ralph "Cooney" Weiland's NHL record of 73 points, set with the Bruins in 1929–30. Cain's 82 points were 17 more than the previous year's scoring champion, Bryan Hextall, had earned. Seventeen points was the largest one-season leap in NHL history, but even that didn't make Cain a household word.

Admittedly, 1943–44 was an explosive season. Three other players also eclipsed Weiland's mark, and all of the top 10 scorers notched more points than Hextall had in 1942–43. The onslaught was due to a change in the rules. In 1943–44, the NHL introduced the center red line to open up the game. Although forward passing had previously been allowed in all three zones, the puck still had to be carried over both blue lines. Using strong forechecking, a team could bottle its opponent in their own end of the ice and limit scoring chances. But with the rule change, teams could now make passes out of their own zone right up to the red line. As a result, offense took off.

If Cain's record was tainted, it still took awhile for someone else to scale the same heights. His mark stood until Howe scored 86 points in 1950–51. But the Motor City legend set his mark in a 70-game schedule. Cain's feat of amassing 82 points in 50 games was not duplicated until Esposito did it during his record-shattering 1968–69 campaign. Cain's exclusion from hockey's Valhalla seems even more mysterious when one considers that he registered 400 career points, more than 10 Art Ross Trophy winners who are in the Hall.

Call it the mark of Cain.

Cain, at least, made the Second All-Star Team that year. No NHL scoring leader has ever failed to earn a berth on the two year-end All-Star Teams. But this prompts another question. Has an NHL goal-scoring leader ever not been named an All-Star? Surprisingly, it has happened several times, most recently in 1996–97 when left wing Keith Tkachuk popped a league-high 52 goals and finished behind Paul Kariya and John LeClair on the all-star ballots. In 1994–95, the loop's top sniper, right wing Peter Bondra, was edged in the voting by Jaromir Jagr and Theo Fleury. In 1938–39, left wing Roy Conacher led in goals but finished behind left wings Toe Blake and Johnny Gottselig; and in 1930–31, goal-scoring king Charlie Conacher lost to right wings Bill Cook and Dit Clapper.

But then the NHL record book is full of improbable occurrences. Take the case of Tommy "Cowboy" Anderson, whose nickname alone is more than a little unusual for someone born in Edinburgh, Scotland. Anderson must have been a remarkable player for at least one year. Against all odds, he bagged the Hart Trophy while patrolling the blue line for the last-place Brooklyn Americans in 1941–42. Defensemen who win MVP awards are rare at the best of times, but no rearguard besides Anderson has ever done it with a team that allowed the most goals in the league.

Anderson tied for eighth in league scoring with 41 points in 48 games, so he was obviously an offensive threat. But his election can also be viewed as a snub of the New York Rangers, who finished atop the NHL for the first time in club history. In Bryan Hextall, Lynn Patrick and Phil Watson, the Broadway Blues had three of the circuit's top four scorers, and in Patrick, the top goal-getter. But none of the three, evidently, was of MVP caliber. Instead, the coveted trophy went to a defenseman from the Rangers' cellar-dwelling crosstown rivals.

Brooklyn folded before the following season, leaving the Rangers the sole tenant of Madison Square Garden. Alone in the Big Apple spotlight, the Rangers promptly plunged to the basement in 1942–43. Anderson joined the Canadian armed forces and never again laced them up in the big show. He finished his career in 1947 in Hollywood, with the Wolves of the Pacific Coast Hockey League. You could say Cowboy went out on top. He remains the only player to never play another NHL game after being named MVP.

How about something even more unlikely? Has the league MVP ever failed to make the first or second All-Star Team? Incredibly, it's happened twice—and in consecutive years, no less. In 1954, Chicago Black Hawks goalie Al Rollins got the nod as MVP despite tending net for a last-place club, recording the league's worst goals-against average and setting a new record for losses in a season, 47.

No player has ever won the Hart Trophy with a worse team. The 1953–54 Blackhawks were a horror show; they won just 12 of 70 games and finished 43 points shy of a playoff spot. Rollins faced a steady hail of rubber all season. His courage under fire impressed the voters, although it's hard to imagine how much worse Chicago could have been without him. They should have given Rollins the Purple Heart.

The stress of being the last man back for the lowly Hawks took its toll. Rollins battled anxiety problems the next two seasons, and eventually lost his job to another goalie with a nervous stomach named Glenn Hall. A has-been at 31, Rollins left the NHL to play for the Calgary Stampeders of the Western Hockey League.

What made Rollins worthy of being the 1954 MVP, however, didn't make him an all-star. Employing a different set of criteria, the voters tabbed Harry Lumley and Terry Sawchuk as the year's two best puck stoppers. Their numbers were hard to ignore. The Red Wing great posted a sparkling 1.93 goals-against average and 12 shutouts, while "Apple Cheeks" was even better at 1.86 and 13 shutouts for the Maple Leafs. In contrast, Rollins, with his meager 3.23 average and five goose eggs, looked to be in a different league—which the Hawks almost were. Like Brooklyn in 1941–42, Chicago's franchise was on the verge of folding. Maybe Rollins's MVP award was meant as an inducement for the Hawks to stay.

The same voter schizophrenia surfaced again in 1954–55, as Toronto Maple Leafs center Ted Kennedy won the Hart Trophy despite scoring a mere 10 goals and placing 11th in the scoring race. Following the precedent they had set with Rollins, all-star voters ignored Kennedy and selected Jean Beliveau and Ken Mosdell of the Canadiens as the top two centers in 1954–55.

Leadership, not scoring stats, was always Kennedy's strength, but his MVP selection is still puzzling, as the Leafs finished third, with eight fewer points than they had the year before. Maybe this MVP award was meant as inducement for Kennedy to stay. Toronto's popular captain had indicated that he was considering retiring. If so, the strategy didn't work. At 30, Kennedy quit the game. He stayed away 18 months before returning, at the urging of Leafs g.m. Hap Day, for one final fling. It was an unsuccessful comeback. Even with Teeder back in the lineup, the Leafs missed the playoffs in 1956–57.

Although Kennedy and Rollins are the only two MVPs to be bypassed in the all-star voting, all-star status has eluded some prominent players throughout their entire careers. Despite scoring 708 goals, the fifth-highest total in NHL annals, Mike Gartner never was elected to an All-Star Team. In fact, the speedy right wing did not win a single award during his stellar 19-year career, not even the Stanley Cup. Gartner's best shot at getting his name on Lord Stanley's chalice vanished when he was traded by the Rangers late in the 1993–94 season, just as the Blueshirts made their curse-ending run to glory.

Playing a good chunk of his career for the Washington Capitals, not a Stanley Cup contender during these years, didn't help Gartner's cause, but his biggest enemy was his consistency. Gartner reached the 30-goal mark a record 17 seasons, three more times than Howe and Gretzky, but only made the 50-goal plateau once. Sustained excellence will get you into the Hall, but it doesn't always fill the trophy case.

Hall-of-Fame goalie Gerry Cheevers was never an all-star either. Like Gartner, he also failed to earn a single individual award. Although best remembered for his ghostly white mask with the Halloween stitch marks, winning—not flashy numbers—was Cheevers's strong suit. He still owns the record for the longest undefeated streak by an NHL netminder: 32 games with the Bruins in 1971–72.

Until recently, the best player never elected to an NHL All-Star Team was Steve Yzerman. The Detroit captain finally made the grade in 2000, earning a selection to the First Team after 16 barren years. According to the voters, there had always been at least two other centers in the league better than Yzerman, even in 1988–89, when he racked up 155 points. That's the most points ever collected by a player who didn't make the All-Star Team. It also happens to be the most points recorded in a season by anyone not named Wayne Gretzky or Mario Lemieux.

Unfortunately for Yzerman, he was outscored in 1988–89 by both Lemieux and Gretzky, who rang up 199 and 168 points, respectively. Having a good chunk of his career overlap with the world's two greatest centers is a factor in Stevie Wonder's blanking. Even so, several other pivots, including Adam Oates, Mark Messier, Eric Lindros, Pat LaFontaine, Sergei Fedorov and Alexei Zhamnov, were able to loosen the legendary pair's stranglehold on the all-star center slots.

Exactly how superior Lemieux and Gretzky were to Yzerman in 1988–89 is open to debate. Although Gretzky took home the Hart Trophy as MVP that year, Yzerman snared the Lester B. Pearson Award, which goes to the league's outstanding player as picked by the NHL players.

The Pearson, a major award without major-award status, lacks the clout of the trophies voted on by the media, even though it carries the same cash value. However, if you subscribe to the theory that true success comes when you are recognized by your peers, then the list of past Pearson winners is worth a second look.

Although the players and the media voted in lock step

throughout the 1990s, this wasn't always the case. During the 1970s and 1980s, the two camps often split over who was the MVP and who was the league's best player. Gretzky, for example, won the Hart Trophy nine times, including an amazing eight in a row from 1980 to 1987. Yet, he only won the Pearson five times. The players gave their award to Marcel Dionne in 1980, to Mike Liut in 1981, to Lemieux in 1986 and 1988 and to Yzerman in 1989. Maybe they were just trying to share the wealth.

A similar situation applies to Bobby Orr, who nabbed the Hart Trophy in three straight seasons from 1970 to 1972. But in 1971 and 1972—the first two years the Pearson was awarded—the players preferred Phil Esposito and Jean Ratelle. The choice of Ratelle over Orr in 1972 is doubly surprising, as the Rangers center missed 15 games with an ankle injury. In the view of his peers, Orr was the NHL's outstanding player only once: in 1975, a year in which the media backed Bobby Clarke as the league's MVP.

Aside from the Pearson, Orr had little trouble winning trophies. The pride of Parry Sound, Ontario, is still the only NHLer to capture four major awards in one year. In 1969–70, he won the Hart Trophy as league MVP, the Art Ross Trophy as leading scorer, the Norris Trophy as best defenseman and the Conn Smythe Trophy as MVP of the playoffs. Number four was always synonymous with Orr, and in 1970, the digit assumed a cosmic significance in the season's final second.

Boston won the Stanley Cup that year when Orr netted the game-winning goal in overtime. The dramatic moment, captured by Ray Lussier's famous photograph, shows Orr, arms outstretched in celebration, flying through the air after being tripped by St. Louis defenseman Noel Picard. Orr, of course, wore No. 4. So did Picard. The goal was Boston's fourth of the game, and it came in the fourth period (first overtime) of a 4–3 score. Boston swept the Blues in the final in four straight games. The Bruins also won 40 games that season.

It was Orr's fourth NHL campaign. He played 14 games in the 1970 playoffs. The winning goal was set up by Derek Sanderson who wore number 16, which is four squared. It was Sanderson's fourth assist of the playoffs. The goal was the Bruins' 344th goal of the season. Even eerier, Orr's game winner stopped the Boston Garden clock at 00:40. It gave Boston its first championship since 1941, and its fourth Cup in history.

NHL trophies and award winners are selected by the following: Vezina Trophy by team general managers; Jack Adams Award by the members of the NHL Broadcasters' Association; Hart, Norris, Calder, Selke, Lady Byng, Conn Smythe and Masterton trophies as well as First and Second All-Star Teams by members of the Professional Hockey Writers' Association; Lester B. Pearson Award by member of the NHL Players' Association. The King Clancy and Lester Patrick Trophy winners are selected by committees comprised of executives and former players. Voting takes place at the conclusion of the regular season with the exception of the Conn Smythe Trophy awarded to the playoff MVP.

NATIONAL HOCKEY LEAGUE INDIVIDUAL TROPHY AND AWARD WINNERS

ART ROSS TROPHY

Scoring leader

2000	Jaromir Jagr, Pit.
1999	Jaromir Jagr, Pit.
1998	Jaromir Jagr, Pit.
1997	Mario Lemieux, Pit.
1996	Mario Lemieux, Pit.
1995	Jaromir Jagr, Pit.
1994	Wayne Gretzky, L.A.
1993	Mario Lemieux, Pit.
1992	Mario Lemieux, Pit.
1991	Wayne Gretzky, L.A.
1990	Wayne Gretzky, L.A.
1989	Mario Lemieux, Pit.
1988	Mario Lemieux, Pit.
1987	Wayne Gretzky, Edm.
1986	Wayne Gretzky, Edm.
1985	Wayne Gretzky, Edm.
1984	Wayne Gretzky, Edm.
1983	Wayne Gretzky, Edm.
1982	Wayne Gretzky, Edm.
1981	Wayne Gretzky, Edm.
1980	Marcel Dionne, L.A.
1979	Bryan Trottier, NYI
1978	Guy Lafleur, Mtl.
1977	Guy Lafleur, Mtl.
1976	Guy Lafleur, Mtl.
1975	Bobby Orr, Bos.
1974	Phil Esposito, Bos.
1973	Phil Esposito, Bos.
1972	Phil Esposito, Bos.
1971	Phil Esposito, Bos.
1970	Bobby Orr, Bos.
1969	Phil Esposito, Bos.
1968	Stan Mikita, Chi.
1967	Stan Mikita, Chi.
1966	Bobby Hull, Chi.
1965	Stan Mikita, Chi.
1964	Stan Mikita, Chi.
1963	Gordie Howe, Det.
1962	Bobby Hull, Chi.
1961	Bernie Geoffrion, Mtl.
1960	Bobby Hull, Chi.
1959	Dickie Moore, Mtl.
1958	Dickie Moore, Mtl.
1957	Gordie Howe, Det.
1956	Jean Beliveau, Mtl.
1955	Bernie Geoffrion, Mtl.
1954	Gordie Howe, Det.
1953	Gordie Howe, Det.
1952	Gordie Howe, Det.
1951	Gordie Howe, Det.
1950	Ted Lindsay, Det.
1949	Roy Conacher, Chi.
1948*	Elmer Lach, Mtl.
1947	Max Bentley, Chi.
1946	Max Bentley, Chi.
1945	Elmer Lach, Mtl.
1944	Herb Cain, Bos.
1943	Doug Bentley, Chi.
1942	Bryan Hextall, NYR
1941	Bill Cowley, Bos.
1940	Milt Schmidt, Bos.
1939	Toe Blake, Mtl.
1938	Gordie Drillon, Tor.
1937	Dave Schriner, NYA
1936	Dave Schriner, NYA
1935	Charlie Conacher, Tor.
1934	Charlie Conacher, Tor.
1933	Bill Cook, NYR
1932	Harvey Jackson, Tor.
1931	Howie Morenz, Mtl.
1930	Cooney Weiland, Bos.
1929	Ace Bailey, Tor.
1928	Howie Morenz, Mtl.
1927	Bill Cook, NYR
1926	Nels Stewart, Mtl.M.
1925	Babe Dye, Tor.
1924	Cy Denneny, Ott.
1923	Babe Dye, Tor.
1922	Punch Broadbent, Ott.
1921	Newsy Lalonde, Mtl.
1920	Joe Malone, Que.
1919	Newsy Lalonde, Mtl.
1918	Joe Malone, Mtl.

* *Trophy first awarded in 1948. Scoring leader listed from 1918 to 1947.*

HART TROPHY

Most valuable player

2000	Chris Pronger, St.L.
1999	Jaromir Jagr, Pit.
1998	Dominik Hasek, Buf.
1997	Dominik Hasek, Buf.
1996	Mario Lemieux, Pit.
1995	Eric Lindros, Phi.
1994	Sergei Fedorov, Det.
1993	Mario Lemieux, Pit.
1992	Mark Messier, NYR
1991	Brett Hull, St.L.
1990	Mark Messier, Edm.
1989	Wayne Gretzky, L.A.
1988	Mario Lemieux, Pit.
1987	Wayne Gretzky, Edm.
1986	Wayne Gretzky, Edm.
1985	Wayne Gretzky, Edm.
1984	Wayne Gretzky, Edm.
1983	Wayne Gretzky, Edm.
1982	Wayne Gretzky, Edm.
1981	Wayne Gretzky, Edm.
1980	Wayne Gretzky, Edm.
1979	Bryan Trottier, NYI
1978	Guy Lafleur, Mtl.
1977	Guy Lafleur, Mtl.
1976	Bobby Clarke, Phi.
1975	Bobby Clarke, Phi.
1974	Phil Esposito, Bos.
1973	Bobby Clarke, Phi.
1972	Bobby Orr, Bos.
1971	Bobby Orr, Bos.
1970	Bobby Orr, Bos.
1969	Phil Esposito, Bos.
1968	Stan Mikita, Chi.
1967	Stan Mikita, Chi.
1966	Bobby Hull, Chi.
1965	Bobby Hull, Chi.
1964	Jean Beliveau, Mtl.
1963	Gordie Howe, Det.
1962	Jacques Plante, Mtl.
1961	Bernie Geoffrion, Mtl.
1960	Gordie Howe, Det.
1959	Andy Bathgate, NYR
1958	Gordie Howe, Det.
1957	Gordie Howe, Det.
1956	Jean Beliveau, Mtl.
1955	Ted Kennedy, Tor.
1954	Al Rollins, Chi.
1953	Gordie Howe, Det.
1952	Gordie Howe, Det.
1951	Milt Schmidt, Bos.
1950	Chuck Rayner, NYR
1949	Sid Abel, Det.
1948	Buddy O'Connor, NYR
1947	Maurice Richard, Mtl.
1946	Max Bentley, Chi.
1945	Elmer Lach, Mtl.
1944	Babe Pratt, Tor.
1943	Bill Cowley, Bos.
1942	Tom Anderson, Bro.
1941	Bill Cowley, Bos.
1940	Ebbie Goodfellow, Det.
1939	Toe Blake, Mtl.
1938	Eddie Shore, Bos.
1937	Babe Siebert, Mtl.
1936	Eddie Shore, Bos.
1935	Eddie Shore, Bos.
1934	Aurel Joliat, Mtl.
1933	Eddie Shore, Bos.
1932	Howie Morenz, Mtl.
1931	Howie Morenz, Mtl.
1930	Nels Stewart, Mtl.M.
1929	Roy Worters, NYA
1928	Howie Morenz, Mtl.
1927	Herb Gardiner, Mtl.
1926	Nels Stewart, Mtl.M.
1925	Billy Burch, Ham.
1924	Frank Nighbor, Ott.

LADY BYNG TROPHY

Gentlemanly conduct

2000	Pavol Demitra, St.L.
1999	Wayne Gretzky, L.A.
1998	Ron Francis, Pit.
1997	Paul Kariya, Ana.
1996	Paul Kariya, Ana.
1995	Ron Francis, Pit.
1994	Wayne Gretzky, L.A.
1993	Pierre Turgeon, NYI
1992	Wayne Gretzky, L.A.
1991	Wayne Gretzky, L.A.
1990	Brett Hull, St.L.
1989	Joe Mullen, Cgy.
1988	Mats Naslund, Mtl.
1987	Joe Mullen, Cgy.
1986	Mike Bossy, NYI
1985	Jari Kurri, Edm.
1984	Mike Bossy, NYI
1983	Mike Bossy, NYI
1982	Rick Middleton, Bos.
1981	Rick Kehoe, Pit.
1980	Wayne Gretzky, Edm.
1979	Bob MacMillan, Atl.
1978	Butch Goring, L.A.
1977	Marcel Dionne, L.A.
1976	Jean Ratelle, NYR-Bos.
1975	Marcel Dionne, Det.
1974	John Bucyk, Bos.
1973	Gilbert Perreault, Buf.
1972	Jean Ratelle, NYR
1971	John Bucyk, Bos.
1970	Phil Goyette, St.L.
1969	Alex Delvecchio, Det.
1968	Stan Mikita, Chi.
1967	Stan Mikita, Chi.
1966	Alex Delvecchio, Det.
1965	Bobby Hull, Chi.
1964	Ken Wharram, Chi.
1963	Dave Keon, Tor.
1962	Dave Keon, Tor.
1961	Red Kelly, Tor.
1960	Don McKenney, Bos.
1959	Alex Delvecchio, Det.
1958	Camille Henry, NYR
1957	Andy Hebenton, NYR
1956	Earl Reibel, Det.
1955	Sid Smith, Tor.
1954	Red Kelly, Det.
1953	Red Kelly, Det.
1952	Sid Smith, Tor.
1951	Red Kelly, Det.
1950	Edgar Laprade, NYR
1949	Bill Quackenbush, Det.
1948	Buddy O'Connor, NYR
1947	Bobby Bauer, Bos.
1946	Toe Blake, Mtl.
1945	Bill Mosienko, Chi.
1944	Clint Smith, Chi.
1943	Max Bentley, Chi.
1942	Syl Apps, Tor.
1941	Bobby Bauer, Bos.
1940	Bobby Bauer, Bos.
1939	Clint Smith, NYR
1938	Gordie Drillon, Tor.
1937	Marty Barry, Det.
1936	Doc Romnes, Chi.
1935	Frank Boucher, NYR
1934	Frank Boucher, NYR
1933	Frank Boucher, NYR
1932	Joe Primeau, Tor.
1931	Frank Boucher, NYR
1930	Frank Boucher, NYR
1929	Frank Boucher, NYR
1928	Frank Boucher, NYR
1927	Billy Burch, NYA
1926	Frank Nighbor, Ott.
1925	Frank Nighbor, Ott.

VEZINA TROPHY

Best goaltender

2000	Olaf Kolzig, Wsh.
1999	Dominik Hasek, Buf.
1998	Dominik Hasek, Buf.
1997	Dominik Hasek, Buf.
1996	Jim Carey, Wsh.
1995	Dominik Hasek, Buf.
1994	Dominik Hasek, Buf.
1993	Ed Belfour, Chi.
1992	Patrick Roy, Mtl.
1991	Ed Belfour, Chi.
1990	Patrick Roy, Mtl.
1989	Patrick Roy, Mtl.
1988	Grant Fuhr, Edm.
1987	Ron Hextall, Phi.
1986	John Vanbiesbrouck, NYR
1985	Pelle Lindbergh, Phi.
1984	Tom Barrasso, Buf.
1983	Pete Peeters, Bos.
1982**	Billy Smith, NYI
1981	Richard Sevigny, Mtl.
	Denis Herron, Mtl.
	Michel Larocque, Mtl.
1980	Bob Sauve, Buf.
	Don Edwards, Buf.
1979	Ken Dryden, Mtl.
	Michel Larocque, Mtl.
1978	Ken Dryden, Mtl.
	Michel Larocque, Mtl.
1977	Ken Dryden, Mtl.
	Michel Larocque, Mtl.
1976	Ken Dryden, Mtl.
1975	Bernie Parent, Phi.
1974	Bernie Parent, Phi. (tie)
	Tony Esposito, Chi. (tie)
1973	Ken Dryden, Mtl.
1972	Tony Esposito, Chi.
	Gary Smith, Chi.
1971	Ed Giacomin, NYR
	Gilles Villemure, NYR
1970	Tony Esposito, Chi.
1969	Jacques Plante, St.L.
	Glenn Hall, St.L.
1968	Gump Worsley, Mtl.
	Rogie Vachon, Mtl.
1967	Glenn Hall, Chi.
	Denis Dejordy, Chi.
1966	Gump Worsley, Mtl.
	Charlie Hodge, Mtl.
1965	Terry Sawchuk, Tor.
	Johnny Bower, Tor.
1964	Charlie Hodge, Mtl.
1963	Glenn Hall, Chi.
1962	Jacques Plante, Mtl.
1961	Johnny Bower, Tor.
1960	Jacques Plante, Mtl.
1959	Jacques Plante, Mtl.
1958	Jacques Plante, Mtl.
1957	Jacques Plante, Mtl.
1956	Jacques Plante, Mtl.
1955	Terry Sawchuk, Det.
1954	Harry Lumley, Tor.
1953	Terry Sawchuk, Det.
1952	Terry Sawchuk, Det.
1951	Al Rollins, Tor.
1950	Bill Durnan, Mtl.
1949	Bill Durnan, Mtl.
1948	Turk Broda, Tor.
1947	Bill Durnan, Mtl.
1946	Bill Durnan, Mtl.
1945	Bill Durnan, Mtl.
1944	Bill Durnan, Mtl.
1943	Johnny Mowers, Det.
1942	Frank Brimsek, Bos.
1941	Turk Broda, Tor.
1940	Dave Kerr, NYR
1939	Frank Brimsek, Bos.
1938	Tiny Thompson, Bos.
1937	Normie Smith, Det.
1936	Tiny Thompson, Bos.
1935	Lorne Chabot, Chi.
1934	Charlie Gardiner, Chi.
1933	Tiny Thompson, Bos.
1932	Charlie Gardiner, Chi.

** *Pre-1982, awarded for lowest goal-against average. Since 1982, awarded to top goaltender.*

VEZINA TROPHY *continued*

1931 Roy Worters, NYA
1930 Tiny Thompson, Bos.
1929 George Hainsworth, Mtl.
1928 George Hainsworth, Mtl.
1927 George Hainsworth, Mtl.

CALDER MEMORIAL TROPHY

Best Rookie

2000 Scott Gomez, N.J.
1999 Chris Drury, Col.
1998 Sergei Samsonov, Bos.
1997 Bryan Berard, NYI
1996 Daniel Alfredsson, Ott.
1995 Peter Forsberg, Que.
1994 Martin Brodeur, N.J.
1993 Teemu Selanne, Wpg.
1992 Pavel Bure, Van.
1991 Ed Belfour, Chi.
1990 Sergei Makarov, Cgy.
1989 Brian Leetch, NYR
1988 Joe Nieuwendyk, Cgy.
1987 Luc Robitaille, L.A.
1986 Gary Suter, Cgy.
1985 Mario Lemieux, Pit.
1984 Tom Barrasso, Buf.
1983 Steve Larmer, Chi.
1982 Dale Hawerchuk, Wpg.
1981 Peter Stastny, Que.
1980 Ray Bourque, Bos.
1979 Bobby Smith, Min
1978 Mike Bossy, NYI
1977 Willi Plett, Atl.
1976 Bryan Trottier, NYI
1975 Eric Vail, Atl.
1974 Denis Potvin, NYI
1973 Steve Vickers, NYR
1972 Ken Dryden, Mtl.
1971 Gilbert Perreault, Buf.
1970 Tony Esposito, Chi.
1969 Danny Grant, Min.
1968 Derek Sanderson, Bos.
1967 Bobby Orr, Bos.
1966 Brit Selby, Tor.
1965 Roger Crozier, Det.
1964 Jacques Laperriere, Mtl.
1963 Kent Douglas, Tor.
1962 Bobby Rousseau, Mtl.
1961 Dave Keon, Tor.
1960 Bill Hay, Chi.
1959 Ralph Backstrom, Mtl.
1958 Frank Mahovlich, Tor.
1957 Larry Regan, Bos.
1956 Glenn Hall, Det.
1955 Ed Litzenberger, Chi.
1954 Camille Henry, NYR
1953 Lorne Worsley, NYR
1952 Bernie Geoffrion, Mtl.
1951 Terry Sawchuk, Det.
1950 Jack Gelineau, Bos.
1949 Pentti Lund, NYR
1948 Jim McFadden, Det.
1947 Howie Meeker, Tor.
1946 Edgar Laprade, NYR
1945 Frank McCool, Tor.
1944 Gus Bodnar, Tor.
1943 Gaye Stewart, Tor.
1942 Grant Warwick, NYR
1941 Johnny Quilty, Mtl.
1940 Kilby MacDonald, NYR
1939 Frank Brimsek, Bos.
1938 Cully Dahlstrom, Chi.
1937 Syl Apps, Tor.
1936 Mike Karakas, Chi.
1935 Dave Schriner, NYA
1934 Russ Blinco, Mtl.M.
1933 Carl Voss, Det.

JAMES NORRIS TROPHY

Best defenseman

2000 Chris Pronger, St.L.
1999 Al MacInnis, St.L.
1998 Rob Blake, L.A.
1997 Brian Leetch, NYR
1996 Chris Chelios, Chi.
1995 Paul Coffey, Det.
1994 Ray Bourque, Bos.
1993 Chris Chelios, Chi.
1992 Brian Leetch, NYR
1991 Ray Bourque, Bos.
1990 Ray Bourque, Bos.
1989 Chris Chelios, Mtl.
1988 Ray Bourque, Bos.
1987 Ray Bourque, Bos.
1986 Paul Coffey, Edm.
1985 Paul Coffey, Edm.
1984 Rod Langway, Wsh.
1983 Rod Langway, Wsh.
1982 Doug Wilson, Chi.
1981 Randy Carlyle, Pit.
1980 Larry Robinson, Mtl.
1979 Denis Potvin, NYI
1978 Denis Potvin, NYI
1977 Larry Robinson, Mtl.
1976 Denis Potvin, NYI
1975 Bobby Orr, Bos.
1974 Bobby Orr, Bos.
1973 Bobby Orr, Bos.
1972 Bobby Orr, Bos.
1971 Bobby Orr, Bos.
1970 Bobby Orr, Bos.
1969 Bobby Orr, Bos.
1968 Bobby Orr, Bos.
1967 Harry Howell, NYR
1966 Jacques Laperriere, Mtl.
1965 Pierre Pilote, Chi.
1964 Pierre Pilote, Chi.
1963 Pierre Pilote, Chi.
1962 Doug Harvey, NYR
1961 Doug Harvey, Mtl.
1960 Doug Harvey, Mtl.
1959 Tom Johnson, Mtl.
1958 Doug Harvey, Mtl.
1957 Doug Harvey, Mtl.
1956 Doug Harvey, Mtl.
1955 Doug Harvey, Mtl.
1954 Red Kelly, Det.

MAURICE "ROCKET" RICHARD TROPHY

Most goals

2000 Pavel Bure, Fla.
1999 Teemu Selanne, Ana.

CONN SMYTHE TROPHY

Playoff MVP

2000 Scott Stevens, N.J.
1999 Joe Nieuwendyk, Dal.
1998 Steve Yzerman, Det.
1997 Mike Vernon, Det.
1996 Joe Sakic, Col.
1995 Claude Lemieux, N.J.
1994 Brian Leetch, NYR
1993 Patrick Roy, Mtl.
1992 Mario Lemieux, Pit.
1991 Mario Lemieux, Pit.
1990 Bill Ranford, Edm.
1989 Al MacInnis, Cgy.
1988 Wayne Gretzky, Edm.
1987 Ron Hextall, Phi.
1986 Patrick Roy, Mtl.
1985 Wayne Gretzky, Edm.
1984 Mark Messier, Edm.
1983 Billy Smith, NYI
1982 Mike Bossy, NYI
1981 Butch Goring, NYI
1980 Bryan Trottier, NYI
1979 Bob Gainey, Mtl.
1978 Larry Robinson, Mtl.
1977 Guy Lafleur, Mtl.
1976 Reggie Leach, Phi.
1975 Bernie Parent, Phi.
1974 Bernie Parent, Phi.
1973 Yvan Cournoyer, Mtl.
1972 Bobby Orr, Bos.
1971 Ken Dryden, Mtl.
1970 Bobby Orr, Bos.
1969 Serge Savard, Mtl.
1968 Glenn Hall, St.L.
1967 Dave Keon, Tor.
1966 Roger Crozier, Det.
1965 Jean Beliveau, Mtl.

FRANK J. SELKE TROPHY

Best defensive forward

2000 Steve Yzerman, Det.
1999 Jere Lehtinen, Dal.
1998 Jere Lehtinen, Dal.
1997 Michael Peca, Buf.
1996 Sergei Fedorov, Det.
1995 Ron Francis, Pit.
1994 Sergei Fedorov, Det.
1993 Doug Gilmour, Tor.
1992 Guy Carbonneau, Mtl.
1991 Dirk Graham, Chi.
1990 Rick Meagher, St.L.
1989 Guy Carbonneau, Mtl.
1988 Guy Carbonneau, Mtl.
1987 Dave Poulin, Phi.
1986 Troy Murray, Chi.
1985 Craig Ramsay, Buf.
1984 Doug Jarvis, Wsh.
1983 Bobby Clarke, Phi.
1982 Steve Kasper, Bos.
1981 Bob Gainey, Mtl.
1980 Bob Gainey, Mtl.
1979 Bob Gainey, Mtl.
1978 Bob Gainey, Mtl.

BILL MASTERTON TROPHY

Perseverance and dedication to hockey

2000 Ken Daneyko, N.J.
1999 John Cullen, T.B.
1998 Jamie McLennan, St.L.
1997 Tony Granato, S.J.
1996 Gary Roberts, Cgy.
1995 Pat LaFontaine, Buf.
1994 Cam Neely, Bos.
1993 Mario Lemieux, Pit.
1992 Mark Fitzpatrick, NYI
1991 Dave Taylor, L.A.
1990 Gord Kluzak, Bos.
1989 Tim Kerr, Phi.
1988 Bob Bourne, L.A.
1987 Doug Jarvis, Hfd.
1986 Charlie Simmer, Bos.
1985 Anders Hedberg, NYR
1984 Brad Park, Det.
1983 Lanny McDonald, Cgy.
1982 Chico Resch, Col.
1981 Blake Dunlop, St.L.
1980 Al MacAdam, Min.
1979 Serge Savard, Mtl.
1978 Butch Goring, L.A.
1977 Ed Westfall, NYI
1976 Rod Gilbert, NYR
1975 Don Luce, Buf.
1974 Henri Richard, Mtl.
1973 Lowell MacDonald, Pit.
1972 Bobby Clarke, Phi.
1971 Jean Ratelle, NYR
1970 Pit Martin, Chi.
1969 Ted Hampson, Oak.
1968 Claude Provost, Mtl.

KING CLANCY MEMORIAL TROPHY

Leadership on and off the ice

2000 Curtis Joseph, Tor.
1999 Rob Ray, Buf.
1998 Kelly Chase, St.L.
1997 Trevor Linden, Van.
1996 Kris King, Wpg.
1995 Joe Nieuwendyk, Cgy.
1994 Adam Graves, NYR
1993 Dave Poulin, Bos.
1992 Ray Bourque, Bos.
1991 Dave Taylor, L.A.
1990 Kevin Lowe, Edm.
1989 Bryan Trottier, NYI
1988 Lanny McDonald, Cgy.

JACK ADAMS AWARD

Coach of the year

2000 Joel Quenneville, St.L.
1999 Jacques Martin, Ott.
1998 Pat Burns, Bos.
1997 Ted Nolan, Buf.
1996 Scotty Bowman, Det.
1995 Marc Crawford, Que.
1994 Jacques Lemaire, N.J.
1993 Pat Burns, Tor.
1992 Pat Quinn, Van.
1991 Brian Sutter, St.L.
1990 Bob Murdoch, Wpg.
1989 Pat Burns, Mtl.
1988 Jacques Demers, Det.
1987 Jacques Demers, Det.
1986 Glen Sather, Edm.
1985 Mike Keenan, Phi.
1984 Bryan Murray, Wsh.
1983 Orval Tessier, Chi.
1982 Tom Watt, Wpg.
1981 Red Berenson, St.L.
1980 Pat Quinn, Phi.
1979 Al Arbour, NYI
1978 Bobby Kromm, Det.
1977 Scotty Bowman, Mtl.
1976 Don Cherry, Bos.
1975 Bob Pulford, L.A.
1974 Fred Shero, Phi.

WILLIAM M. JENNINGS TROPHY

Goaltender(s) on team allowing fewest goals

2000 Roman Turek, Dal.
1999 Ed Belfour, Dal.
Roman Turek
1998 Martin Brodeur, N.J.
1997 Martin Brodeur, N.J.
Mike Dunham, N.J.
1996 Chris Osgood, Det.
Mike Vernon, Det.
1995 Ed Belfour, Chi.
1994 Dominik Hasek, Buf.
Grant Fuhr, Buf.
1993 Ed Belfour, Chi.
1992 Patrick Roy, Mtl.
1991 Ed Belfour, Chi.
1990 Andy Moog, Bos.
Rejean Lemelin
1989 Patrick Roy, Mtl.
Brian Hayward
1988 Patrick Roy, Mtl.
Brian Hayward
1987 Patrick Roy, Mtl.
Brian Hayward
1986 Bob Froese, Phi.
Darren Jensen
1985 Tom Barrasso, Buf.
Bob Sauve
1984 Al Jensen, Wsh.
Pat Riggin
1983 Rollie Melanson, NYI
Billy Smith
1982 Rick Wamsley, Mtl.
Denis Herron

LESTER B. PEARSON AWARD

Outstanding player selected by NHLPA

2000 Jaromir Jagr, Pit.
1999 Jaromir Jagr, Pit.
1998 Dominik Hasek, Buf.
1997 Dominik Hasek, Buf.
1996 Mario Lemieux, Pit.
1995 Eric Lindros, Phi.
1994 Sergei Fedorov, Det.
1993 Mario Lemieux, Pit.
1992 Mark Messier, NYR
1991 Brett Hull, St.L.
1990 Mark Messier, Edm.
1989 Steve Yzerman, Det.
1988 Mario Lemieux, Pit.
1987 Wayne Gretzky, Edm.
1986 Mario Lemieux, Pit.
1985 Wayne Gretzky, Edm.
1984 Wayne Gretzky, Edm.
1983 Wayne Gretzky, Edm.
1982 Wayne Gretzky, Edm.
1981 Mike Liut, St.L.
1980 Marcel Dionne, L.A.
1978 Guy Lafleur, Mtl.
1979 Marcel Dionne, L.A.
1978 Guy Lafleur, Mtl.
1977 Guy Lafleur, Mtl.
1976 Guy Lafleur, Mtl.
1975 Bobby Orr, Bos.
1974 Phil Esposito, Bos.
1973 Bobby Clarke, Phi.
1972 Jean Ratelle, NYR

LESTER PATRICK TROPHY

Contributions to American hockey

2000 Mario Lemieux
Craig Patrick
Lou Vairo
1999 Harry Sinden
1998 U.S. Women's Olympic Hockey Team
1998 Peter Karmanos
Neal Broten
John Mayasich
Max McNab
1997 Seymour H. Knox III
Bill Cleary
Pat LaFontaine
1996 George Gund
Ken Morrow
Milt Schmidt
1995 Joe Mullen
Brian Mullen
Bob Fleming
1994 Wayne Gretzky
Robert Ridder
1993 *Frank Boucher
*Mervyn (Red) Dutton
Bruce McNall
Gil Stein
1992 Al Arbour
Art Berglund
Lou Lamoriello
1991 Rod Gilbert
Mike Ilitch
1990 Len Ceglarski
1989 Dan Kelly
Lou Nanne
*Lynn Patrick
Bud Poile
1988 Keith Allen
Fred Cusick
Bob Johnson
1987 *Hobey Baker
Frank Mathers

PATRICK TROPHY *continued*

1986 John MacInnes
Jack Riley
1985 Jack Butterfield
Arthur M. Wirtz
1984 John A. Ziegler Jr.
*Arthur Howie Ross
1983 Bill Torrey
1982 Emile P. Francis
1981 Charles M. Schulz
1980 Bobby Clarke
Edward M. Snider
Frederick A. Shero
1980 U.S. Olympic Hockey Team
1979 Bobby Orr
1978 Phil Esposito
Tom Fitzgerald
William T. Tutt
William W. Wirtz
1977 John P. Bucyk
Murray A. Armstrong
John Mariucci
1976 Stanley Mikita
George A. Leader
Bruce A. Norris
1975 Donald M. Clark
William L. Chadwick
Thomas N. Ivan
1974 Alex Delvecchio
Murray Murdoch
*Weston W. Adams, Sr.
*Charles L. Crovat
1973 Walter L. Bush, Jr.
1972 Clarence S. Campbell
John A. "Snooks" Kelly
Ralph "Cooney" Weiland
*James D. Norris
1971 William M. Jennings
*John B. Sollenberger
*Terrance G. Sawchuk
1970 Edward W. Shore
*James C. V. Hendy
1969 Robert M. Hull
*Edward J. Jeremiah
1968 Thomas F. Lockhart
*Walter A. Brown
*Gen. John R. Kilpatrick
1967 Gordon Howe
*Charles F. Adams
*James Norris, Sr.
1966 J.J. "Jack" Adams

* awarded posthumously

ROGER CROZIER MBNA SAVING GRACE AWARD

Best save percentage

2000 Ed Belfour, Dal.

BUD ICE PLUS–MINUS AWARD

Best plus–minus statistics

2000 Chris Pronger, St.L.
1999 John LeClair, Phi.
1998 Chris Pronger, St.L.
1997 John LeClair, Phi.

Team Award

PRESIDENTS' TROPHY

First place in the regular season

2000 St. Louis Blues
1999 Dallas Stars
1998 Dallas Stars
1997 Colorado Avalanche
1996 Detroit Red Wings
1995 Detroit Red Wings
1994 New York Rangers
1993 Pittsburgh Penguins
1992 New York Rangers
1991 Chicago Blackhawks
1990 Boston Bruins
1989 Calgary Flames
1988 Calgary Flames
1987 Edmonton Oilers
1986 Edmonton Oilers

CHAPTER 26

The Craft of Playing Defense

Evaluating the Contributions of Defensive Defensemen

Mark Paddock

IF YOU STOPPED EVERY FAN who was leaving an NHL rink after a game and asked how the players had performed, you would probably hear about Dominik Hasek's eye-catching saves or Jaromir Jagr's cunning assists. But how often would you hear an assessment of a game by a defenseman, especially one who rarely scores? Indeed, how could the fan decide if the defensive player had performed well or not? Can raw statistics tell the story the way saves, save percentage, goals and assists so often do?

These days, there are more statistical categories than ever, and several of them can be used to measure defensive contributions. Hits, ice time and plus-minus are three major ones, the latter being a traditional favorite of hockey journalists. One broadcaster, however, feels the need to tread carefully around it.

"Plus-minus as a bare statistic is very misleading," states former coach Harry Neale, "and very unfair to the defenseman who plays against the opposition's best line. He's more apt to be on the ice for more goals against. Also, you're often on the ice but have nothing to do with a goal against, yet you're charged the same penalty in plus-minus ratings as the guy who gave away the puck to the opponent that scored." In effect, the player becomes guilty by association.

Neale's argument is valid, though of course the statistic does have some meaning. In 1998–99, Joe Reekie (+11) and Calle Johansson (+12) were easily the best Capitals in the plus-minus category. Both are highly respected defensive forces who have enjoyed lengthy, if quiet, careers. On the other hand, Chris Pronger finished with a mediocre +3 that season with the St. Louis Blues and many experts thought he should have been an all-star.

How about the other categories?

"Ice time certainly is the greatest indicator of how much the coach thinks of a player, whatever position he plays," Neale believes. One of the reasons Pronger received so much acclaim for his 1999–2000 campaign was that he was on the ice for half of every game. This enabled him to influence the action more than anyone else. Defensemen have a built-in advantage over most forwards in this regard; they can take longer shifts, and the top ones average 23 to 30 minutes per match. At the same time, a defenseman can play a lot—out of necessity, or because the coach has faith in him—while having a poor year. Ice time does not always equate with success.

As for hits, the category obviously favors tough blueliners over finesse players. Reekie's hits for the 2000 season (99) pale next to those of his teammate Brendan Witt (322), but that doesn't prove he was a lesser player. It does suggest, though, that Witt is an intimidating opponent who can wear out forwards with his bodychecks.

"Statistically, it's very difficult to measure a defensive defenseman's performance, and that's probably why they're lower-paid than they should be, given their value to the team," Neale says. "I think it has to be measured by someone who watches the games and knows how much a player skates against the best opponents. Does he play in the last minute of every period? Does he play more with a 2–1 lead than with a 5–1 lead? Does he play half the overtime?"

Reaching this level of ability is hardly easy, and today, it's arguably more difficult than at any time in history. When hockey began, it was a game that developed in "straight-ahead, straight-line playing patterns," as Ken Dryden wrote in *The Game*. Defenders were often awkward skaters—but they had time to react to the limited set of options that attackers possessed. The rise of the speed and transition games, exemplified and partly instituted by Bobby Orr, changed that.

"There are a number of players who had good careers in the 1950s and 1960s who would have a tough time playing now," states Neale. "The defensemen are a lot bigger than they used to be and they are much speedier. In the 1940s, '50s and '60s, it was a vertical game: the wingers stayed on the wings and the centermen were only allowed to roam a little bit. It was not the crossover hockey we see today. There's a bigger premium on mobility and agility than there used to be."

In a swift game with ever-changing patterns, it becomes crucial for a defender to learn to make calm but instant decisions. In Montreal's final regular-season game in 2000, a must-win for the Canadiens, the Habs found themselves down 2–0 in the third period to Ottawa. Suddenly, Shayne Corson fumbled the puck at his blueline. Ottawa's Daniel Alfredsson stole it and raced toward the goal. A defender charged at Alfredsson but over-committed. Alfredsson slid past him and, in the lane the defender had just vacated, fired a perfect wrist shot into the net. The defenseman had reversed direction as soon as Alfredsson went past him, but the play was over in a second and he had no time to recover. It was the kind of mistake that occurs countless times in a season, but it dramatically illustrated the challenges that a blueliner must face.

Consider the following: a defenseman's team has puck possession deep in the offensive zone. What's going through his mind?

"He's got to seal off the blue line, so that if the puck comes to him, he can keep it in the zone," says Neale. "He should also be thinking about what the defensive wing is doing: 'Is he paying any attention to me at all? If he isn't, maybe I can slide into the slot and get a chance to score.' The score, who he's playing against, the length of time he's been on the ice and the time left in the period all factor into the decision he makes. You can't play every puck-control situation the same way. Some do, and the coach says, 'Didn't you realize we were winning 2–1? Didn't you realize Pavel Bure was on the ice? Didn't you realize you'd been out there for a minute?' The defender ought to be thinking about the worst thing that could happen and be ready for it."

Be ready for the worst: that is the first unwritten law of defensive play. Like a gloomy psychic, the defender constantly has to predict that the sky will fall; but unlike the fortune teller, he has to decide in advance how to hold it up.

Once the opposition gains possession and starts a breakout, the decision process becomes more complex and difficult.

"He's got to read the rush," Neale emphasizes. "He should realize who's got the puck. Is it a guy who can fly or stickhandle or one with a great shot? That's part of being a seasoned player. Secondly, he's got to know where his partner is and if he has a forward helping him. How many players are on the rush? If it's a three-on-two, he can't play one-on-one. If there's one backchecker to help both defensemen, then he can play one-on-one. Reading the rush is something more defensemen have trouble with than you might think. The defenders on the attacking team get involved a lot more often now, and you have to look back through the puck carrier to see if there's anyone else coming. Then, the defenseman also has to be ready for crossovers and ready to switch assignments. If they cross in front of you and you start crossing over with your partner, there's going to be a collision for sure if you have a backchecking wing involved. You need to be able to communicate, to yell at your own players or point to the man you're taking. I see that all the time. If the defender is only playing against one man, he's got to remember the puck is the puck carrier's problem, not his. He can't back in too deep so the carrier can use him as a screen. He should have time to see who it is and to ask himself what the player's favorite move is."

Clearly, without good vision on the ice, the defenseman will be in trouble. It's a trait Neale can't emphasize enough. "You have to be able to look into the depths of the rush, and that's really hard to do. Young defensemen have a terrible time learning this. That's why they practice three-on-twos, but it's hard to reproduce game situations." Of course, there's more to defense than playing the rush, but it's a fine example of the complex situations that defensemen have to learn to control. Speed, puck and player movement, stickhandling; it's all on full display there.

To a casual fan, the word "vision" may suggest that the player has superior eyesight, but if you equate vision with awareness, you have a more accurate definition.

"Vision just means you can comprehend the situation in a second when you're looking at it," Neale summarizes. "It's a skill the great players have. But you can learn it, too. Apart from practicing, the other way for young guys to learn it is through videotape. One of the defensive coach's assignments may be to make up a tape of the last 30 rushes a player had to put up with, showing him what he did right or wrong."

It's the blueliners with the best vision who will be found in overtime and in the final minutes of a close match. Given that every NHL defender needs a fair share of size, speed and skill nowadays, vision is arguably the most important trait they can have. And there's no statistic for that, so for the moment, at least, the defensive defenseman remains an under-appreciated breed outside the dressing room.

CHAPTER 27

Referees and Linesmen

A Comprehensive Register of NHL Officials

Glenn Cole

THIS IS THE FIRST PUBLISHED REGISTER of NHL referees and linesmen. Detailed records of officiating assignments were not kept in the early days of the NHL so even for some Hall of Fame referees, an accurate count of games worked is unavailable.

Many players worked as on-ice officials after their playing careers ended. King Clancy also served as the NHL's referee-in-chief, giving him a rare double hat trick: player, coach, manager, hockey ambassador, referee and director of officiating.

Referees and linesmen work their way up to the NHL in the same way that players do, through junior, minor pro and training camps. New officials are phased in, splitting assignments between the NHL and the minors for several seasons. The change to two referees plus the growth of the NHL from 21 to 30 teams over the last ten seasons has created new big-league jobs for qualified referees and linesmen. Note as well that some officials have two entries in this register, one as a referee and one as a linesman.

The register that follows lists regular-season games only.

Key: E – emergency replacement, **L** – linesman, **R** – referee, **T** – trainee,
***** – active in the NHL in 1999–2000, ◦ – worked in playoffs only,
Inducted into Hockey Hall of Fame…
…**§** – as a referee or linesman…• – as a player…≠ – as a builder.

	Name	Position	Games
	Derek Adams	L	1
	Scott A. Adams	L	9
	Lou Albrecht	L	1
*	Derek Amell	L	145
	Jim Anderson	R	2
*	Blaine Angus	R	174
	Larry Antoniuk	R	1
§	Neil Armstrong	L	1744
	Malcolm Ashford	L	440
	George Ashley	L	243
§	John Ashley	R	605
	Ron Asselstine	L	1364
	Walter Atanas	L	57
*	Stephane Auger	R	1
	Sam Babcock	L	663
	Charles Banfield	R	106
	Dominick Baolto	L	…
	Alex Barilko	L	…
	Robert Barrette	L	1
	Bill Beagan	R	16
	Claude Bechard	L	1118
	Bill Bell	L	17
	Bob Bell	L	5
	Ray Berry	L	31
	Robert Berry	L	31
	Bob Best	R	4
	Ken Bodendistel	R	10
*	Wayne Bonney	L	1456
	Darryl Borden	L	7
	Kevin Boschart	L	2
	Ryan Bozak	L	1589
*	David Brisebois	L	45
*	Gordon Broseker	L	1791
	Doug Brousseau	L	3
	John Brown	L	169
	Gorde Buchanan	R	3
	Vern Buffey	R	487
	Jerry Burt	L	5
	Ed Butler	l	125
*	Lonnie Cameron	L	259
	Bob Carse	L	7
	Brent Casselman	L	183
	Art Casterton	R	…
	Roger Castle	L	3
§	Bill Chadwick	R	778
*	Pierre Champoux	L	770
	Luc Charron	L	3
	Jim Christison	L	1252
	John Clancy	R	…
	Pat Clarke	L	8
	Bill Clements	L	…
	Dave Clutsan	L	40
	Frank Cole	R	3
*	Kevin Collins	L	1758
	Steve Corlyon	L	8
	Daniel Cournoyer	R	1
*	Michael Cvik	L	851
§	John D'Amico	L	1604
	Joe Dame	L	196
*	Pat Dapuzzo	L	1142
	Doug Davies	L	395
*	Bernard DeGrace	L	157
*	Bernard DeGrace	R	88
*	Alex Dell	E	1
*	Greg Devorski	L	431
*	Paul Devorski	R	603
	Bill Doiron	L	7
	Loring Doolittle	L	71
	Steve Dowling	R	7
*	Scott Driscoll	L	493
	James Dunn	L	53
	James Edgeworth	L	…
	Ron Ego	L	368
	Lou Farelli	R	60
	Brian Farley	L	2
*	Mark Faucette	R	702
	Gord Fevreau	L	25
	Ron Finn	L	1980
	Paul Flaherty	L	235
	Don Foreman	L	2
	Wayne Forsey	L	623
	Ron Fournier	R	462
	Michael Foy	R	8
	Ron Foyt	L	463
	Bob Frampton	L	176
*	Kerry Fraser	R	1263
	Bill Friday	R	470
	Brent Frizzell	E	1
*	Francois Gagnon	L	97
	Rick Galipeau	L	1
	Herbert Gallagher	L	185
	John Gallagher	R	2
	Mike Galletti	L	4
	Luke Galvin	T	1
	Jeff Gardner	L	5
	Bruce Garside	L	58
*	Gerard Gauthier	L	2138
	Real Gauthier	L	2
	Doug Geiger	L	44
	Ray Getliffe	L	90
*	Darren Gibbs	L	96
	Rodger Gilbertson	L	40
	Tom Gillespie	L	2
	Jim Gilligan	L	3
	Ray Gillmore	L	1
	Lloyd Gilmour	R	512
	Alan Glaspell	L	161
°	Vin Godleski	E	…
	Charles Good	L	1
	John Gould	L	4
	Sam Gowan	L	4
	Georges Gravel	R	303
*	Terry Gregson	R	1147
*	Conrad Hache	R	37
	Bob Hall	R	367
	Scott Hansen	T	1
	Ron Harris	R	127
	Wally Harris	R	954
	Chuck Harrison	R	2
§	George Hayes	L	…
	Rob Hearn	T	1
*	Don Henderson	L	248
	George Henderson	L	2
	Bob Henry	R	1
§	Bobby Hewitson	R	…
*	Shane Heyer	L	785
*	Shane Heyer	R	29
	Bob Hodges	L	1701
	Ron Hoggarth	R	1171
	Bruce Hood	R	1035
	Jim Houston	L	13
	Jeff Huber	L	3
	Scott Hughes	L	2
§	Mickey Ion	R	…
*	Dave Jackson	R	466
	Harold Jackson	L	57
*	Marc Joannette	R	3
	Russ Johnson	T	2
	Ray Jollimore	L	5
	Michel Joly	L	3
	Melville Keeling	R	…

Name	Position	Games
Jim Kehm	E	1
Marc Khedouri	L	7
Bob Kilger	R	326
* Greg Kimmerly	R	89
Chris Kit	L	4
William Knott	L	45
* Swede Knox	L	2046
* Don Koharski	L	163
* Don Koharski	R	1130
* Brad Kovachik	L	231
* Tom Kowal	R	5
Luc Lachapelle	R	6
* Dennis LaRue	R	289
* Brad Lazarowich	L	953
Scott Leavitt	R	6
* Chris Lee	R	1
* Mike Leggo	R	81
Alf LeJeune	R	243
Bernard Lemaitre	L	63
Bryan Lewis	R	1031
Darren Loraas	R	4
Bob Luther	L	745
Dave Lynch	T	13
Dalton MacArthur	R	133
Tim MacConaghy	R	4
Kenneth MacLeod	R	...
Gregg Madill	R	415
* Kevin Maguire	R	27
Kevin Mallin	R	4
Mush March	L	224
* Dan Marouelli	R	991
Brian Marshall	L	7
* Rob Martell	R	34
Lou Maschio	L	32
Saul Maslow	E	1
Stan McCabe	L	53
John McCauley	R	459
Dave McClellan	L	2
George McCorry	R	6
* Dan McCourt	L	1341
* Bill McCreary	R	1016
John McCutcheon	R	10
* Andy McElman	L	435
* Mick McGeough	R	591
° Paul McInnis	E	...
Bob McLaren	L	212
Hugh McLean	R	89
Morley McNeil	E	2
Jack Mehlenbacher	R	152
* Brad Meier	R	9
Eddie Mepham	L	3
Stephen Metcalfe	L	3
Stephen Meuris	L	14
Steve Miller	L	7
* Randy Mitton	L	1832
Don Moffatt	L	8
Peter Moffatt	R	44
Tom Monahan	R	5
Denis Morel	R	1142
Stewart Morgan	L	2
* Jean Morin	L	561
Bob Morley	R	5
Bill Morrison	L	148
Scotty Morrison	R	16
Kevin Muench	T	2
Ernie Mundey	L	34
Sibby Mundey	L	65
* Brian Murphy	L	714
* Brian Murphy	R	29
Leo Murray	L	3
Bob Myers	R	1233
Don Myers	L	1
Ian Nathanson	L	2
Ralph Nattress	L	7
* Thor Nelson	L	174
Dave Newell	R	1172
Earl Nicholson	L	2
Mike Noeth	R	166
Willard Norris	L	1472
* Tim Nowak	L	444
* Dan O'Halloran	R	156
* Dan O'Rourke	L	54
Jerry Olinski	R	81
Harry Ornest	L	1
Wille Papp	R	5
* Mark Pare	L	1538
* Baron Parker	L	363
Dennis Parrish	E	1
Jerry Pateman	L	568
§ Matt Pavelich	L	1745
* Tim Peel	R	10
Jim Peters	L	1
Ken Pierce	R	1
Terry Pierce	L	117
* Kevin Pollock	R	1
Bob Porter	L	3
Eddie Powers	R	414
Stanley Pratt	L	11
Jim Primeau	L	259
* Stephane Provost	L	407
* Pierre Racicot	L	466
Robert Read	L	3
Mike Rebus	R	2
Pete Reilly	L	1
Brien Ricci	R	4
Bill Roberts	L	162
* Lance Roberts	R	483
§ Mike Rodden	R	...
Jim Romeril	L	2
David Ross	R	1
Rob Rowatt	E	1
Brent Rutherford	R	5
Joseph Rys	L	1
Ian Sandercock	R	14
* Troy Sartison	L	59
* Ray Scapinello	L	2224
* Dan Schachte	L	1253
Bill Scherr	L	82
* Lyle Seitz	L	169
* Lyle Seitz	R	10
* Tony Sericolo	L	91
Randy Shantz	L	92
* Jay Sharrers	L	642
Dave Shaw	L	2
Greg Shepherd	R	5
Pat Shetler	L	423
Dave Shewchyk	R	174
* Rob Shick	R	785
Dennis Sholes	L	7
Bruce Sims	L	54
Art Skov	R	611
Bob Sloan	R	151
Mickey Slowik	L	2
§ Cooper Smeaton	R	...
David Smith	L	2
Tom Smith	R	41
Brian Sopp	L	75
Myles Spencer	L	3
Joseph Springer	L	37
Curt Stevens	L	6
Gaye Stewart	R	36
* Paul Stewart	R	804
Leon Stickle	L	1967
Alex Stobo	L	3
§ Red Storey	R	480
Rodger Strong	E	1
° Jim Sullivan	E	...
Drew Taylor	R	5
Jim Tedesco	L	3
Yves Tessier	R	...
Cliff Thompson	L	12
* Richard Trottier	R	477
Chip Tyson	L	3
§ Frank Udvari	R	718
Norm Usselman	L	19
§ Andy Van Hellemond	R	1475
* Don Van Massenhoven	R	402
Mark Vines	L	822
Rob Waddell	L	79
Jeff Walker	E	1
* Stephen Walkom	R	403
* Dean Warren	R	6
Derrick Wasiak	L	1
* Brad Watson	R	111
Ken Wheler	R	9
* Mark Wheler	L	515
Peter Wicklum	L	4
Ron Wicks	R	1112
John Wilken	L	3
George Wilson	R	3
Chuck Wynters	L	3
Douglas Young	L	...
* Scott Zelkin	R	90

NO STATISTICS AVAILABLE FOR THE FOLLOWING OFFICIALS:

Edward Barry
Robert Barry
Harry Batstone
Bell
Bellamer
Louis Berlinquette
Jack Blake
Jim Boddy
Johnny Brennan
Stan Burgoyne
Eddie Burke
• Harry Cameron
Jack Cameron
≠ Clarence Campbell
• King Clancy
William Cleary
Odie Cleghorn
Bert Corbeau
Eusebe Daigneault
• Hap Day
• Cy Denneny
Charlie Dinsmore
Art Duncan
• Babe Dye
• Frank Foyston
• Jimmy Gardner
Charles Ghedi
Jerry Goodman
Ted Graham
James Haggarty
Dr. Hamel
Mel Harwood
Bert Hedges
• Red Horner
• Harry Hyland
George Irvine
• Aurel Joliat
Dr. Labreque
Jerry Laflamme
Mel Lamport
• Percy LeSueur
George Mallinson
• Sylvio Mantha
Lou Marsh
• Jack Marshall
Dalton McArthur
Bert McCaffrey
Duke McCurry
Don McFadyen
Charlie McKinley
Archie McTeer
Rabbit McVeigh
Tom Melville
John Mitchell
Ken Mullins
• Reg Noble
F. O'Brien
Bill O'Hara
Eddie (Doc) O'Leary
Edward Panczak
Jack Paterson
Ken Paul
Dave Power
• Harvey Pulford
Arthur Reichert
A. Rekdahl
William Riley
Alex Romeril
• Art Ross
Orville Roulston
• Ernie Russell
Bill Shaver
Jeff Smith
Jess Spring
Harvey Sproule
F. Stevenson
Bill Stewart
Thomas Topping
Steve Vair
≠ Carl Voss
• Jack Walker
Maurice Walsh
• Harry (Rat) Westwick
Archie Wilcox

CHAPTER 28

"Foreign" Influence in the NHL

Tracking the Euro Style to North America

Shirley Fischler

IN 1935, MIKE BUCKNA, a forward of Czech-descent with the Smoke-Eaters team from Trail, British Columbia, accompanied a young Czech friend to the "old country" to choose a spouse. While in Prague, Mike attended some hockey games. One day he approached the rink manager, who also managed the local team, and asked for a tryout. When the manager saw how well Mike skated, he obliged the 21-year-old Czech-Canadian by immediately inviting him to join the Czech team. That is how young Mike Buckna came to play hockey in Czechoslovakia in 1935.

Buckna found Czech-style hockey laughably simple; the sole object was to prevent goals. Whenever a team lost the puck, five men would drop back to defend. Defensemen never touched the puck or moved from in front of the net, and the forwards had never heard of forechecking.

"The problem was the coaching," Mike recalled. "They either had old hockey players who taught the same things over and over, or coaches who'd never played hockey at all—maybe soccer or tennis."

In his first season in Prague, Mike was invited to hold coaching clinics. The next season, he was invited back to oversee the entire Czechoslovakian national hockey program. Mike coached and played on the Czech national team until the Canadian government insisted he come home in 1939, just prior to World War II. Buckna spent the duration of the war in Trail, but returned to Prague the minute he was allowed back into the country in 1946. He found that nine of the juniors he had coached before the war were now able seniors. In 1947, Buckna coached the team to its first World Championship. In 1948, they won the silver medal at the Winter Olympics in St. Moritz, Switzerland, tying Canada, 0–0, and losing the gold on goal-differential. That was Buckna's last year in Czechoslovakia, but the team he built went on to win the world title again in 1949.

When Mike Buckna left Canada for Prague in 1935, NHL hockey was being played without the red center line. Forwards played a passing game nicknamed "puck on a string" as exemplified by brothers Bill and Bun Cook and Frank Boucher of the New York Rangers. It was this style of game that Buckna took abroad and taught to the Czech national team. It was this same passing game that the Czechs later took to Moscow and introduced to the Russians. The Europeans never really saw the rigid "alley" style of play which became prevalent in the NHL by the 1950s and 1960s.

With plenty of cold weather to encourage the development and spread of the ice game, the Russian infatuation with hockey grew quickly. The Russians began to concentrate on a conditioning and training program geared to produce winning teams. If the Soviet Union took up a sport, they did their best to become the dominant force in that area of competition. The Soviet state-supported system of athletic competition strained the traditional concepts of "amateurism" beyond any previous boundaries but, because they technically were not paid to play, these Soviet athletes qualified as amateurs, nonetheless.

When the Russians first arrived at the World Championships in Stockholm in 1954, they indisputably were the underdog in the tourney. The favorite was a Canadian Senior B team called the East York Lyndhursts, sponsored by a car dealership in suburban Toronto. To everyone's surprise, the Lyndhursts found themselves facing the Soviets for the title. Even though the Canadian team was by this time riddled with injuries, whether or not they would win didn't seem to be an issue—the only question was by how much.

To everyone's amazement, the USSR pummeled Canada 7–2 in the final. Canadians extracted sweet revenge one year later when the Penticton Vees went over for the World Championships and squashed all of Europe, including the Russians. But Canada's world dominance was at an end. The trouncing the Russians had administered in 1954 turned out to be the proverbial tip of the iceberg. Soviet hockey—born from a Czech system originally taught by a Canadian—would dominate the world scene for decades.

Ironically, the advanced form of Mike Buckna's hockey game would come full circle and eventually would return to North America, first by copying European styles and coaching techniques then through the huge influx of European players to the NHL. How much has the advanced form of Buckna's game truly influenced North American hockey and the NHL? Most experts will admit privately, if not publicly, that the NHL has been profoundly influenced by Russian and European hockey.

Said Czech-born George Gross, once the sports editor of *The Toronto Sun*: "Before 1972, the NHL style was all up and down the alley, chase the puck in from the blue line and slam guys in the corners. After 1972, the NHL began to adapt more to the one-four system, with one forechecker up; less dumping, more passing and more interference with the goaltender."

As a modified version of "European hockey" began to invade the National Hockey League, ex-goaltender and longtime hockey executive Emile Francis said: "When the center red line was introduced to the NHL [back in 1943–44], puck control was sacrificed for pure scoring. When the Russians played the NHL in 1972, the whole idea of puck control was re-introduced to the NHL. Plus, they learned improvisation—not because that's what the Russians taught them, but because it was what worked against them!"

More exposure to the European game brought better awareness of the dangers of the player who didn't have the puck and changed the way the NHL thought about controlling and passing it. Players would no longer just patrol their side of the rink, they would strive to find open ice. In this type of game, speed became all-important.

Amateur and professional coaches from Canada and the United States began a new type of invasion of the European continent as the Cold War melted down. Walls and borders disappeared and NHL scouts began prowling the very rinks that had nurtured and extrapolated upon Mike Buckna's system of play. When Herb Brooks was coaching the New York Rangers, he was often called "the champion of European-style hockey." He went abroad several times to observe style and performance on the Continent. Lou Vairo, coach of the 1984 U.S. Olympic team and former assistant coach of the New Jersey Devils, coached in Italy for several years. He was followed by a horde of coaches and North American players who began to infiltrate European teams. Soon, every NHL team would have scouts who specialized on Eastern Europe instead of Western Saskatchewan.

Teams mimic success, so after the rough, tough Philadelphia Flyers won the Stanley Cup in consecutive years in the mid-1970s—making them the first expansion team to win it—every NHL club began pumping up the size of its players and expanding its bully corps. By the late 1970s, there wasn't a club that didn't carry at least one muscle-for-hire performer on its roster.

Then the trend shifted. In 1980, Herb Brooks's U.S. Olympic team won the gold medal by employing a hybrid North American/European style and the stock of the European model of hockey shot up. A year after the Olympics, Herb Brooks took the coaching job with the Rangers and taught them the much-admired, "motion" style—passing, swirling, skating—played abroad. Soon, more and more NHL clubs began experimenting with the European techniques.

But the new techniques didn't win Stanley Cup titles. The hard-nosed, grinding style of play, combined with a talented offense, was what won championships. The Islanders proved it between 1980 and 1983. The Oilers confirmed it when they had to learn to play a better team game in order to win the Cup five times in the next seven years. Montreal's Stanley Cup win in 1986 was also accomplished in this style. All those Cup-winning teams specialized in snipers, a workmanlike defense and outstanding goaltending—though the Edmonton style combined North American strength with European speed. All of these Stanley Cup teams also had a couple of goon-types to send out on the ice when necessary.

Then, with the arrival of the 1990s, the fall of the Berlin Wall and the dissolution of the Soviet Union, came the foreign flood into the NHL. No longer were the few overseas tourneys the only places where foreign techniques were witnessed and explored. Now, a veritable deluge of European players began crossing the Atlantic to dipsy-doodle in the expanding National Hockey League. Simultaneously, more and more U.S.-born players began to appear in the pro ranks, as well.

From rare U.S.-born players like Tommy Williams in the 1960s, to pioneering Scandinavians like Borje Salming in the 1970s, to brave defectors such as Peter Stastny and Alex Mogilny in the 1980s and 1990s, the National Hockey League of the new millennium has evolved into a truly multinational entity. There were so many Czechs and Slovaks on the Pittsburgh Penguins in 1999–2000 that general manager Craig Patrick brought in Ivan Hlinka, who briefly played in the NHL and later coached the Czech national squad to Olympic gold in 1998, to work as an associate coach with the team—under none other than Herb Brooks! A quartet of Russians on the 2000 Cup-winning New Jersey Devils benefitted greatly from the presence of assistant coach Slava Fetisov—once a huge star with the Red Army team who became one of the first Russian players to come to the NHL without defecting.

Finns, Ukrainians, Slovaks and Poles now all grace the NHL, and the first U.S.-born player of Hispanic descent, Scott Gomez, entered the league in 1999–2000 and got his name engraved on the Stanley Cup in his rookie season. Alongside Gomez's was the name of "rookie" Brian Rafalski, a 26-year-old American who had played four seasons in Sweden and Finland before being signed by New Jersey.

The National Hockey League—at least as constituted at the beginning of the third millennium—would now have to categorize "foreign" influence on the game as that coming from Asia, Antarctica, Australia, the Moon or Mars. Today, Canadian kids are going to U.S. colleges and European leagues to prepare for NHL hockey while European youngsters swarm through the minor professional leagues of North America. European-born players who could once be found only in the late rounds of the annual Entry Draft are now swelling the early rounds. In fact, in the final ranking of the NHL Central Scouting Service for the 2000 Entry Draft, the top 30 prospects (minus goaltenders and players still playing in Europe leagues) included eight U.S.-born players, three Czechs, a Russian and a Slovakian. The annual top-30 ranking in *The Hockey News* had a whopping 17 Europeans (including goaltenders and those playing in European leagues) and four U.S.-born players.

As the National Hockey League goes increasingly global, it is certainly worth keeping in mind the fact that the game brought to North America by the Europeans was, at heart, a more advanced version of the one that Mike Buckna, of Trail, British Columbia, took to Prague, Czechoslovakia, with a bride-seeking buddy back in 1935!

CHAPTER 29

NHL Barnstorming Tours

Taking the Game to the Fans

Dave Clamen

IT MAY BE HARD TO IMAGINE these days, but NHL teams actually used to play exhibition games in different cities at the conclusion—and often even during—the regular season. Back in the days before television, these games were the only way for people in different parts of North America to actually see their NHL heroes in action.

The NHL was only a few months old when the first mid-season exhibition game occurred. On February 22, 1918, the players of the Quebec Bulldogs, split up among the other NHL teams, were reunited for a game in their old hometown. Paddy Moran, Joe Hall, Harry Mummery, Joe Malone, Jack McDonald and George Carey thrilled the Quebec fans with a 4–3 win over the Montreal Canadiens. The crowd was large and enthusiastic, which leads one to wonder why the Bulldogs—who had been charter members of the NHL—were not able to put a team on the ice for the league's first two seasons.

Over the years, NHL teams would stage much more elaborate barnstorming tours. In the spring of 1936, the Gyros of Vancouver persuaded the Toronto Maple Leafs and the Chicago Black Hawks to play a postseason series in Vancouver. The proceeds would go to charity and the prize for the teams would be the Totem Trophy.

The two teams boarded a train in Toronto on April 16 and headed west. Not wishing to miss an opportunity for a few bucks and some publicity along the way, they played two games each in Winnipeg and Calgary (splitting in both cities). Lynn Patrick, a local favorite in Vancouver, was added to the Black Hawks roster.

The Leafs' train from Calgary rolled into Vancouver at 9:00 in the morning on April 25. They were greeted by civic dignitaries, but the players were more concerned with the fact that they would have to get dressed for the game in the small train compartments. A parade to the arena followed, where the game was played at 2:00 that afternoon. This was not part of the Totem series, but was a special exhibition for children who were let in for 25 cents each. After the game (won by Toronto 6-3), the players were mobbed by their adoring young fans.

The three games of the Totem series followed, and Toronto outscored Chicago 13–9. The play seemed to lack something, however, as the players were more concerned with their golf games than their hockey. Still, large crowds were attracted, lots of money was raised for charity, and the players got to bask in some hero worship. All in all, a very successful barnstorming tour.

Four years later, the Black Hawks made another visit to the West Coast. On March 22, 1940, Chicago had been eliminated by the Maple Leafs in the NHL playoffs. One day later it was announced that they would be traveling west to meet the Pacific Coast Hockey League champion Vancouver Lions in a four-game series. (It was later expanded to five.) Ten Chicago players would make the trip: Goodman, Seibert, Portland, Carse, Dahlstrom, Bentley, Hergesheimer, Allen, Gottselig and Cunningham.

Upon their arrival, the Black Hawks virtually got off the train and into the arena on March 29. The long train ride had obviously put them off their game, and they lost 6–0 to the minor leaguers. But the arena was full and the crowd was enthusiastic. Almost 20 years after a local team had last competed for the Stanley Cup, the city of Vancouver was abuzz at seeing an NHL team in action against their local heroes. The game was described as the biggest hockey event in Vancouver since the 1927 Allan Cup finals.

The NHLers also lost the second game (4–3), but showed their stuff in winning the last three (4–2, 7–6 and 7–3) before the golf clubs they brought with them finally got some use. By taking three of five games, the Black Hawks had done better in April than they did in February when they lost 4–3 to the St. Louis Flyers of the American Hockey Association. For making the postseason trip to Vancouver, each of the Chicago players made the princely sum of $500.

Canadian hockey players had been making their way to Europe since the early years of the 20th century, and Canadian senior amateur teams had been crossing the ocean fairly regularly since the 1920s, but not until 1938 was Europe introduced to NHL hockey. The Montreal Canadiens and the Detroit Red Wings strutted their stuff in Britain and France after the 1937–38 season. The immortal pioneers were:

MONTREAL	DETROIT
G Wilf Cude	G Norm Smith
D Babe Siebert	D Doug Young
D Walter Boswell	D Ebbie Goodfellow
D Red Groupille	D Pete Bessone
F Paul Haynes	F Marty Barry
F Johnny Gagnon	F Eddie Wares
F Toe Blake	F Carl Liscombe
F Pete Lepine	F Larry Aurie
F George Mantha	F Alex Motter
F Red Lorrain	F Mud Bruneteau
F Paul Drouin	F Hec Kilrea
	F Syd Howe

The two teams left Montreal by train on April 5, heading for Halifax and their ship to Britain. Along the way, they warmed up with three games in the Maritimes, showing off their stuff for the locals. Then, it was on to Europe, leaving on April 9 and arriving 10 days later.

The first game the Canadiens and the Red Wings played was at London's Empress Hall. The Habs won 5–4 in front of a sold-out crowd of 8,000. The game was punctuated by

Red Wings manager Jack Adams explaining to the fans some of the differences between amateur and NHL rules. During their stay, local newspapers played up the large salaries the NHLers got in relation to Britain's pro soccer players. Wilf Cude, who'd been born in Wales, became a local favorite—as did Pete Bessone, who had played in the British and French leagues.

The second game in London ended in a tie before the scene shifted to Paris for three games (of which Montreal won two). The teams then returned to London, where they split the final four games of their European tour. Familiarity began to breed contempt, with fights breaking out as the games got rougher, but the crowds were still large and enthusiastic. Canadiens manager Cecil Hart summed up the overseas excursion by saying: "We've had a successful and enjoyable trip. The boys played wonderful hockey and I'm sure that they sold the professional game in a big way to British and French fans."

Games had also been planned for Germany, but tensions there (the Nazis were in the process of annexing Austria) halted any such plans. These tensions, of course, led to World War II, and NHL teams were ready to do their part. Not only did many players enlist for the armed services in both Canada and the United States, but entire teams engaged in barnstorming tours to raise money for the war effort and morale on the home front. The New York Rangers beat a Navy team in Winnipeg 9–2 in October, 1939. In February, 1943, the Ottawa RCAF Flyers of the Ottawa Senior League played to a 5–4 loss in Detroit for war charities.

In April, 1943, the Montreal Canadiens and other NHL stars agreed to participate in a series of games, without compensation, on behalf of war charities. The first part would be a three-game playoff in San Diego between the San Diego Skyhawks of the Pacific Coast league and Victoria Navy of the Vancouver Island senior loop. Both teams were reinforced by NHL players, including the Bentley brothers and Turk Broda. Victoria won the set two games to one.

The second part of the series was a set of games between the Canadiens and Victoria in Los Angeles. Despite the addition of NHL stars, Victoria lost the series three games to one—but money was raised for the United States War Charities. Closer to home in New Westminster, British Columbia, Victoria was able to split two more games with the Habs following the California series.

The end of the war in 1945 did not mean the end of NHL barnstorming. In February, 1949, the Canadiens beat the Owen Sound Mercurys and then played the first game in the Cincinnati Arena, beating the Dallas Texans of the United States Hockey League. In January, 1950, the Habs played in Quebec and Kenora, while the Rangers beat a Quebec City junior team and the Red Wings started an annual series against the University of Michigan. In April, 1951, the Rangers played a series of games in the Canadian Maritimes against the Ottawa Senators of the Quebec Senior Hockey League. On April 1, 1951, Rangers netminder Chuck Rayner scored a goal in a game against a Maritime all-star team.

During the 1951–52 season, the Montreal Canadiens played local senior amateur opponents in Fredericton, New Brunswick, and in Sarnia and Sudbury, Ontario. Detroit played the Quebec Aces of the QSHL in front of 12,000 fans. In the 1952–53 season, the ever-popular Canadiens played against senior teams in the Ontario towns of Pembroke and Smiths Falls.

Games outside the confines of the NHL schedule were made possible in the six-team era by shorter seasons that did not stretch to even 70 games until 1949–50. Also, the fact that teams traveled by train, and were therefore able to stop along the way to an NHL opponent, made it easy to fit in an exhibition or two during the season. These games had several objectives: they showcased NHL talent at a time when people in small towns had no other way of actually seeing them play, and they raised funds that would help with local arena upkeep, and also publicize the senior team. The players on those teams would get a shot of hero worship—and perhaps the all-important chance to impress an NHL coach.

The coming of television in the 1950s started to put an end to the NHL's practice of barnstorming. People across Canada could now see these players on the small screen—a fact that also put an end to many local senior teams. By the 1960s, NHL expansion and the use of air travel made midseason exhibitions impractical. Yet barnstorming continues—in a fashion.

Every April and May, many NHL players pack up their bags and head to Europe to represent their native countries in the World Championships. This event gets big play overseas and it accomplishes many of the same things that the old barnstorming tours did: publicize the NHL, help local expenses and give players a chance to impress scouts and coaches.

CHAPTER 30

Rangers vs. Bruins 1959 European Tour

Barnstorming Across the Continent

Stan Fischler

THE 1958–59 NATIONAL HOCKEY LEAGUE SEASON was capped by an event that almost overshadowed the Stanley Cup finals between the defending champion Montreal Canadiens and Toronto Maple Leafs. For the first time since before the Second World War, a pair of NHL clubs—the Boston Bruins and the New York Rangers—embarked on a barnstorming tour of Europe.

To understand the significance of the 1959 tour, one must harken back to earlier trans-Atlantic crossings. In the late 1920s, the Bruins had enjoyed a postseason junket to France. Their stay in Paris was so appealing that once the club returned to Boston, the hit tune "Paree—How I Adore You" became the official club theme song. It was played by Boston Garden organist Frank Kiley whenever the home team stepped on the ice.

A number of North American teams (mostly amateur outfits) also had toured Europe before the outbreak of World War II, which effectively ended any hockey contact between the two continents. But once hostilities ended, a stickhandling renaissance evolved overseas and the desire for intercontinental play resumed.

The first meaningful postwar junket was organized by Rangers business manager Thomas F. Lockhart, who doubled as president of the Amateur Hockey Association of the United States (AHAUS). In the autumn of 1946, Lockhart and Frank Gentle, an official of the British Ice Hockey Association, worked out plans for an AHAUS squad to embark on a 37-game tour that would stretch 79 days and include dates against teams from Great Britain, Sweden and Czechoslovakia, among other countries. The team would cover 13,000 miles on the tour and eventually would play before 258,000 spectators.

There was a method to the matchmaking. Ever prescient, Lockhart realized the long-range possibilities of a trans-Atlantic hockey league. "Hockey leaders in America, England and Canada have long discussed the possibility of a postwar league in which hockey teams from those nations would play regularly-scheduled home-and-home games by flying the Atlantic." Lockhart and Gentle were hopeful that the 1946–47 tour would be a catalyst for such a league.

The twelve-man team that AHAUS sent to Europe that fall included skaters from Brooklyn, Boston, Woonsocket and Cambridge, as well as *Boston Globe* hockey writer Herb Ralby, who doubled as manager and coach. The club sailed to England on the steamship *Queen Elizabeth* and opened with two wins and a tie in Great Britain before eventually moving on to France, Switzerland and Sweden. Although they were outclassed at times—a Swedish team beat them 14–4, before the Americans then responded with a 6–2 victory—Uncle Sam's touring squad had succeeded in bridging the trans-Atlantic hockey gap, if not in launching a trans-Atlantic league.

In the immediate postwar years, other North American hockey clubs toured Europe, but none was of major-league caliber. It wasn't until the late 1950s that the NHL would show its stuff on the continent. The idea for a two-team NHL tournament began in an unlikely place with an even more unlikely promoter.

Otmar Delnon was a shy Swiss who, according to one observer, "wouldn't have been able to explain the difference between a slap shot and a pogo stick if he were pressed." That was a somewhat unfair accusation. Actually, Delnon had considerable experience as an amateur player, although he had made his fortune promoting miniature golf. His hockey experience infused him with the idea that money could also be made by featuring two NHL teams in the best ice palaces of England and the continent. His conviction was backed up by $250,000, which was locked in a Geneva bank prior to the tour launch.

For playing what would amount to one-third of a regular-season's slate of games in Europe, the players who made the journey would receive at least $1,000 in cash, engraved watches and luggage. Delnon would handle all other expenses.

Since the Montreal Canadiens were in the midst of their five-year (1956 to 1960) Stanley Cup dynasty, Delnon wanted the Habs to be one of the barnstorming teams. He met with Canadiens managing director Frank Selke and made an offer. Selke was interested, but also concerned about the safety of flying all his champions across the ocean in one plane.

"He told me his organization would not permit more than four of their players to travel on any single airplane," Delnon revealed. "That meant five planes would be necessary to take care of the Montreal club alone. It wasn't possible."

At the time, both Boston and New York had two of the NHL's best clubs. What's more, each was managed by a fun-loving brother: Murray "Muzz" Patrick with the Rangers and Lynn Patrick with the Bruins. Delnon met with the Patricks, who quickly agreed to the barnstorming proposition. He then enlisted Bunny Ahearne, a London travel agent who also was a British hockey official. Ahearne would plan the itinerary and handle the protocol. Members of the two barnstorming teams would share equally $70,000 as their cut for performing.

Ahearne assured both Rangers and Bruins management that their teams would stop at first-class hotels and be exposed to entertainment after the games. This moved *Toronto Star* columnist Milt Dunnell to opine: "By the time the tourists play 22 games in one month [actually 23], tap the wine vats of all nations and scale the stairs in the Tower of London for a look at the ancient armory, [Rangers goalie] Gump Worsley will be bigger than a barrel and hollow-eyed [Rangers coach] Phil Watson will be insulting the referees in Portuguese." Dunnell was not far off the mark.

Timing for the tour was excellent. By 1958, European hockey had surpassed its prewar quality level and new rinks were being built in many of the major cities. A brand-new arena had just been completed in Geneva and plans were afoot to erect a new hockey stadium in Prague. "If the Europeans like the sample displayed by the Bruins and Rangers," said a Canadian reporter, "there's every indication of a ready market for professional teams every spring."

As it happened, the Bruins had finished second during the 1958–59 NHL campaign with 73 points. After having held second place themselves for most of the season, the Rangers went into an uncontrollable nosedive with only two weeks remaining, blew a seven-point lead over Toronto and missed the playoffs on the final night of the season. While the Rangers waited to leave for Europe, the Bruins had to face the Maple Leafs in the opening playoff round.

Aware of the impending tour, several of the Boston players expressed their enthusiasm for their first trip to Europe. When the Bruins were upset four games to three by Toronto, one Boston reporter suggested that "some of the Bruins forwards played as if lacking in financial incentive. The income to be derived from the tour has been advanced as the reason."

Incensed at the accusation, Bruins coach Milt Schmidt shot back: "The players were told about the tour long ago but they didn't seem to be lacking in incentive when they finished in second place. Some of them disappointed me in the playoffs but I don't attribute it to lack of interest in the playoff money."

When it was revealed that some Rangers had decided not to make the trip overseas, the promoters contacted the Chicago Black Hawks, who supplied young left wings Bobby Hull and Ed Litzenberger. Although Hull had scored 18 goals and collected 32 assists in 1958–59, Chicago management believed that the youngster would benefit from the postseason experience.

One of the Rangers players who did not make the trip to Europe had been dropped because of an on-going feud with the coach. Crack penalty-killer Aldo Guidolin had been butting heads with Watson since the 1955–56 season and the Blueshirts coach never forgave him. "I was supposed to make the trip," Guidolin revealed, "but Watson deliberately dropped me from the squad."

The Rangers and Bruins flew to London on April 27, 1959. They played two games there before embarking on the following schedule: May 2, at Geneva, Switzerland; May 3, at Geneva; May 4 and 5, at Paris, France; May 6, 7 and 8, at Antwerp, Belgium; May 9 and 10, at Zurich, Switzerland; May 12 and 13, at Dortmund, West Germany; May 14 and 15, at Essen, West Germany; May 16 and 17, at Krefeld, West Germany; May 19, 20 and 21, at Berlin, West Germany; May 22, 23 and 24, at Vienna, Austria.

Most of the players who made the trip had never been to Europe before. Bruins coach Milt Schmidt, however, had served in England with the Royal Canadian Air Force during World War II. Rangers general manager Muzz Patrick had been with the United States army Army in Italy. Lynn Patrick had been in Europe to attend a world amateur tournament in Norway a year before the Rangers-Bruins tour.

"It's a great thrill for me," said Bruins forward Vic Stasiuk, expressing the general attitude of his teammates. "If I were to make a trip like this on my own it would cost me a great deal. Instead, I'm going with all expenses paid and I'm getting something extra besides."

Unfortunately, promoter Delnon received few extras, and many losses. Pregame promotion of the opening match at Wembley Pool Arena in London was non-existent. There was no notification in the London press of the two exhibitions. As a result, only 1,500 turned out for the opener and 4,500 for the second contest.

The public relations problem was improved by the time the teams arrived in Geneva for game three. A tour-record crowd of 11,000 turned out for the Swiss premiere, with 8,000 for the follow-up game. They would be the two biggest crowds for the entire exhibition series. The worst turnouts were in Paris—700 fans for each of the two games—and Antwerp, where only 500 paid to see the NHL performers. Some blamed high prices for the low attendance, while others claimed that the unseasonable weather on the continent was a factor. The tour concluded with a tie in Vienna before just 1,000 fans. Total attendance for 23 games was 71,000.

Though too few had seen it, the tourney had provided exciting hockey with the Rangers coming out on top by winning 11 games, losing nine and tying three. New York outscored Boston, 104–101. Despite the fact that the scores were relatively high, goaltenders Lorne Worsley and Don Simmons each received raves. Worsley recorded the lone shutout of the trip.

High scorer on the tour was Leo Labine of the Bruins, who netted 18 goals. Eddie Shack and Bobby Hull each scored 14 times to lead the Rangers. Hull's performance captured the attention of scouts, coaches and management, and the soon-to-be superstar would later credit the barnstorming tour as the turning point in his professional career. "Playing with so many veterans gave me confidence," Hull asserted. "When I came to training camp the following fall, I felt that I could accomplish a lot in the NHL."

Those journalists who had seen Hull in action shared his optimism about the future. In retrospect, the decision to add Hull to the Rangers roster was one of the best moves ever made by the Black Hawks. By 1961, he led Chicago to its first Stanley Cup championship since 1938.

Other high scorers for the Rangers on the tour were Dean Prentice and Ed Litzenberger, who scored 12 goals each. Bill Sweeney had 11, Jim Bartlett scored nine and Red Sullivan had eight. For Boston, Johnny Bucyk and Don McKenney each had 11 goals, while Jean-Guy Gendron, Bronco Horvath and Vic Stasiuk scored eight apiece. Hull carried off single-game scoring honors when he tallied four times before 5,000 fans in New York's 7–6 win over Boston in the tenth game at Zurich.

"The tour was a sporting success," concluded Muzz Patrick. "The boys played good hockey and the Europeans, who have had little if any professional material, were impressed."

But if it was an artistic triumph, the tour was a financial failure. Delnon didn't come close to meeting his expenses. Still, he remained optimistic and vowed to bring two other NHL teams to Europe in 1960. Apparently, he later re-evaluated his bankbook. No NHL encore ever took place. Nor did the trans-Atlantic hockey league envisioned by Tom Lockhart more than a half century ago ever come to pass—although such a scheme is still discussed to this day.

CHAPTER 31

NHL Franchise Histories

Profiles of Current and Former NHL Clubs

Mighty Ducks of Anaheim

The trade that sent Wayne Gretzky to the Los Angeles Kings in 1988 did more than anyone could have imagined to spark hockey interest in the United States. Still, the prospect of more than one team at that time in Southern California seemed unimaginable.

But, that was prior to 1992, when a $103-million arena began taking shape in the city of Anaheim. Once a small town better known as the butt of Jack Benny jokes, Anaheim had grown into prominence as the home of Disneyland, as well as one of the major satellite communities of Greater Los Angeles. Anaheim badly wanted to be known as a metropolis in Orange County and the arena would help enhance that image. Once the building was in place, a team would be sought. With that in mind, the city fathers erected a major-league facility that rivaled that of any city on the continent.

For a time, it appeared Anaheim's rink would turn into a white elephant bigger than Dumbo, but Michael Eisner would change all that. Eisner conferred with Bruce McNall, then-owner of the Kings, and learned the NHL might look kindly on a second major-league hockey team in Southern California. Since the building was there and Eisner—whose passion for hockey was deeply rooted—envisioned several positive possibilities for integrating it into his film business, all the pieces began to fall into place.

One of the first pieces was Disney's film The Mighty Ducks, which preceded the arena and became an instant hit. Grossing more than $50 million in North America, the movie whetted Eisner's appetite for an NHL franchise. This coincided with the transfer of NHL power from the conservative regime of president John Ziegler to Gary Bettman, who was named the league's first commissioner late in 1992.

Under Bettman, the NHL was encouraging strong ownership and, at the Board of Governors meetings in December, 1992, both Disney (Anaheim) and Wayne Huizenga (South Florida) were awarded expansion franchises. The expansion fee was $50 million. In the case of Anaheim, $25 million went to the NHL and the rest to McNall because of territorial indemnification.

"There's great growth in hockey," Eisner enthused. "In the way hockey is shot (on television), we can be creative in creating stars. We do it in the movie business."

That very "movie business" intruded heavily into hockey thinking from the very beginning in Anaheim, as, to the dismay of traditionalists, Eisner's team became the Mighty Ducks of Anaheim.

Tony Tavares, who had much experience in the arena business and had worked briefly with McNall, became point man for the management team and he, in turn, hired Jack Ferreira as g.m. and Pierre Gauthier as Ferreira's assistant.

A onetime goaltender for Boston University, Ferreira had considerable scouting and front-office experience with the New England Whalers, Calgary Flames and New York Rangers. The Montreal-born Gauthier won his spurs as scouting director for the Quebec Nordiques. Together they attended the NHL Expansion Draft in Quebec City in June, 1993, and picked goaltender Guy Hebert with their first choice after Florida had selected John Vanbiesbrouck. The Ducks' braintrust made an even more important first selection in the Entry Draft that immediately followed when they landed Paul Kariya from the University of Maine. The first freshman to win the Hobey Baker Award as the best collegiate player in the USA, Kariya had played for the NCAA titlists and was projected as a superstar despite his smallish physique, though he would spend a year with the Canadian national team before signing with the Ducks for their second season. For head coach, Anaheim chose Ron Wilson, an assistant with the Vancouver Canucks, who earlier had been an offensive-minded defenseman at Providence College and later in the pros.

The Mighty Ducks played their first exhibition game at Anaheim on September 18, 1993, against the Pittsburgh Penguins. A crowd of 16,673 proved a good barometer of sellouts to come: more than 12,000 season tickets had been sold along with more than 40 luxury boxes. Ducks fans began filling Arrowhead Pond early in the season and remained loyal throughout.

On the ice, the Mighty Ducks were just what had been expected of an expansion team: mediocre but promising. In fact, as the season progressed, it became evident that Wilson had devised a workable system to produce a competitive team. As late as March 6, 1994, the Mighty Ducks still had a shot at a playoff berth. Not surprisingly, they faded in the stretch and officially were eliminated from the race with five games remaining on the slate. But, there was one consolation; they did finish ahead of Los Angeles. "That gave us a great feeling," Wilson admitted.

The Mighty Ducks concluded 1993–94 with 71 points (33–46–5), setting a first-year record with Florida for most wins in a season. They had 19 road wins, most ever by a first-year club in the NHL. Of greater importance, the club captured the attention of Southern California hockey fans, while the rival Kings were in a tailspin.

There was no diminishing of popularity in 1994–95, although the NHL lockout permitted only a 48-game season that didn't begin until January, 1995. In the shortened schedule the Mighty Ducks were a microcosm of the 1993–94 team. They were competitive, staying in the playoff hunt through the homestretch, but were eliminated from contention with only two games remaining, although a strong finish provided optimism for the future. So did Kariya who, as a rookie, led the team in scoring with 39

With contributions from Mike Board, Tim Campbell, Bob Duff, Stan Fischler, Bruce Garrioch, Jeff Gordon, Chrys Goyens, Jay Greenberg, Brian McFarlane, Ross McKeon and Eric Zweig

points (18 goals, 21 assists) in 47 games. Rookie defenseman Oleg Tverdovsky blossomed into an offensive threat, while Guy Hebert's goaltending proved solid. A testimony to fan loyalty was the 24 consecutive home sellouts at Arrowhead Pond.

Disney marketing—not to mention a sequel to the original Mighty Ducks movie—was copied by other teams. Despite the Ducks' low standing, they managed to attract large crowds wherever they played, partly because of the Disney connection and the attraction of the jerseys. But, by far the most significant landmark in the team's evolution was a trade completed on February 7, 1996. Ferreira dealt potential stars Tverdovsky and Chad Kilger to Winnipeg for Finnish whiz Teemu Selanne.

Teamed with Kariya, Selanne averaged more than a point a game in the stretch and was a prime reason why the Ducks nearly qualified for a Western Conference playoff spot. They finished tied for eighth in the conference with Winnipeg, but lost the tie-breaker because the Jets had more wins. Nevertheless, Anaheim's 35 wins and 78 points were club records for one season and the combination of Selanne and Kariya virtually guaranteed that the upswing would continue into 1996–97.

By now Wilson had established himself as a first-rate coach and the playoff berth obtained in the spring of 1997 underlined the point. Judiciously employing Selanne and Kariya—Steve Rucchin usually was third man on the first line—Wilson energized Anaheim to a 7–3–4 record for 18 points in March, 1997, when his team needed it most. They followed that with an undefeated April (3–0–2) before qualifying for the playoffs.

With an overall mark of 36–33–13, the Mighty Ducks celebrated their first winning season. Selanne's 109 points trailed only Mario Lemieux in the NHL scoring race, while Kariya's 99 points in just 69 games ranked him third. Appropriately, the Ducks collided with Phoenix—formerly the Winnipeg Jets—in the opening playoff round, which exceeded dramatic expectations. After taking a two-games-to-none lead, Anaheim lost the next three in a row before rebounding for a 3–2 overtime win in game six. Kariya, on a pass from Selanne, scored at 7:29 of sudden death to send the series to a seventh game. This time Hebert stopped all 31 shots he faced in earning his first playoff shutout.

Advancing to the second round, Anaheim faced the eventual Stanley Cup-winning Detroit Red Wings. Three out of the four games went into overtime but each time the Motor City sextet won and they swept the series. Still it had been a highly successful season in Anaheim—though it would have a bitter aftermath.

A dispute between Wilson and upper management resulted in the hiring of Pierre Page as Wilson's replacement. (The latter moved on to become head coach of the Washington Capitals.) In addition, a contract dispute between Kariya and the high command left the superstar home in Vancouver while Selanne was compelled to carry the scoring load.

The disruptions left the Mighty Ducks in disarray, although Selanne nobly performed extraordinary feats of skill to at least keep his club competitive. Eventually, Kariya returned with a new, enlarged pact but his comeback would be aborted because of a serious concussion following a post-scoring hit delivered by Gary Suter of the Chicago Blackhawks.

Offseason changes prior to the 1998–99 campaign saw Pierre Gauthier succeed Jack Ferreira as general manager after two-plus seasons in Ottawa. Former Blackhawks coach Craig Hartsburg took over behind the bench. Most importantly, Kariya was able to defy doomsayers who thought he might never play again. With 101 points in 1998–99, he again finished third in the league, while Teemu Selanne placed second with 109 points—including a league-leading 47 goals that won him the Maurice Richard Trophy. The Ducks returned to the playoffs, but were ousted in four straight by the Red Wings.

Anaheim had a difficult season in 1999–2000 and failed to make the playoffs. Both Paul Kariya and Teemu Selanne saw their offensive totals decline, though both continued to rank among the league's top scorers. Lack of production from the rest of the lineup, and an uneven season from the usually reliable Guy Hebert in goal, hurt the Mighty Ducks. A power-play that had ranked first in the NHL the season before tumbled to 27th in the league midway through the 1999–2000 campaign. Traditionally slow starters throughout the brief history of the franchise, Anaheim was not able to make a late run for the playoffs in 1999–2000.

Mighty Ducks of Anaheim Year-by-Year Record

Season	GP	W	L	T	GF	GA	Pts	Finish	Division	Playoff Results
1993–94	84	33	46	5	229	251	71	4th	Pacific	Out of Playoffs
1994–95	48	16	27	5	125	164	37	6th	Pacific	Out of Playoffs
1995–96	82	35	39	8	234	247	78	4th	Pacific	Out of Playoffs
1996–97	82	36	33	13	245	233	85	2nd	Pacific	Lost Conf. Semifinal
1997–98	82	26	43	13	205	261	65	6th	Pacific	Out of Playoffs
1998–99	82	35	34	13	215	206	83	3rd	Pacific	Lost Conf. Quarterfinal
1999-2000	82	34	36	12	217	227	*83	5th	Pacific	Out of Playoffs

** Includes 3 points for regulation ties (RT)*

ATLANTA THRASHERS

On June 25, 1997, the National Hockey League awarded expansion teams to Nashville, Columbus, Minnesota and Atlanta. The awarding of the Atlanta franchise saw NHL hockey return to Georgia, which had first entered the league in 1972–73. The lack of a major television contract and a crumbling real estate empire saw the Atlanta Flames sold to Calgary in 1980. Fan support was never seen as an issue in Atlanta, and TV and ownership shouldn't be a problem this time under Ted Turner and the Turner Broadcasting System, Inc.

Turner Sports president Dr. Harvey Schiller, former executive director of the United States Olympic Committee, became club president when the franchise was obtained. The nickname Thrashers for the Atlanta hockey club was announced on February16, 1998. It was taken from the state bird of Georgia—the Brown Thrasher. The team logo communicates the characteristics of fierce determination and speed.

Almost a year to the day after the franchise was awarded, Don Waddell was hired as the Thrashers' general manager on June 23, 1998. An assistant g.m. in Detroit during the 1997–98 season, Waddell had previously served as the vice president and general manager of the International Hockey League's Orlando Solar Bears from 1995 to 1997. Prior to the Solar Bears, he held the same role with the IHL's San Diego Gulls from 1990 to 1995. Waddell's playing career included three seasons in the Los Angeles Kings' farm system. He was a member of the United States national team in 1983. An injury kept him from appearing with the 1980 "Miracle on Ice" United States Olympic hockey team.

For the first head coach in Atlanta, Waddell turned to former NHL player Curt Fraser, who had coached for him previously with Orlando. In fact, the Solar Bears reached the Turner Cup finals under Fraser as a first-year expansion team in 1995–96.

Waddell had begun the process of building his team before hiring Fraser on July 14, 1999. Slightly less than one month earlier (June 18) the club had acquired its first player when goaltender Damian Rhodes was obtained from the Ottawa Senators for future considerations. Andrew Brunette was picked up from Nashville three days later. The bulk of the first-year roster was obtained in the Expansion Draft on June 25. Players picked up that day included Yannick Tremblay from Toronto, Johan Garpenlov from Florida, Kelly Buchberger from Edmonton and David Harlock from the New York Islanders. However, the player on which the Atlanta brass has pinned its hopes for the future was acquired in the Entry Draft on June 26, 1999.

Though the concussion he had suffered while playing for the IHL's Long Beach Ice Dogs scared off some teams, Waddell was determined to land Patrik Stefan for the Thrashers. A series of draft-day deals saw Atlanta move up from the second choice to the first, which they used to obtain the player who was seen as the most physically mature prospect available. The youngest member of the Thrashers would soon be joined by veterans like Nelson Emerson and Ray Ferraro, who were acquired as free agents in July and August respectively.

The NHL was a 28-team league (on its way to 30) when the Thrashers came on board for the 1999–2000 season. Playing out of the Southeast Division of the Eastern Conference with the Carolina Hurricanes, Florida Panthers, Tampa Bay Lightning and Washington Capitals, Atlanta played its first regular-season game on October 2, 1999. A capacity crowd of 18,545 filled the Philips Arena, the new facility the Thrashers share with the NBA's Atlanta Hawks to watch the New Jersey Devils beat the home side 4–1. Captain Kelly Buchberger scored the Thrashers' goal.

After a 7–1 loss to the Detroit Red Wings in their second game, Atlanta picked up its first point in a 5–5 tie with Buffalo on October 9. Stefan starred in that contest, collecting two goals against Sabres goalie—and fellow Czech native—Dominik Hasek. He also picked up an assist. Stefan set up a key goal in a road game five nights later when the Thrashers scored the first win in franchise history. He set up Buchberger for the clinching goal in a 2–0 win over the New York Islanders. The Thrashers picked up their first home-ice victory on October 26 against Atlanta's prior incarnation the Calgary Flames. Nelson Emerson and Andrew Brunette had the goals, but it was Damian Rhodes who was the hero that night in a 2–1 victory. Unfortunately for Atlanta, injuries would keep Rhodes out for much of the season. Norm Maracle assumed the number-one role.

Still, crowds flocked to Philips Arena—the Thrashers became the first NHL expansion team to average better than 17,000 per game—but it was a long season for Atlanta hockey fans. Particularly trying was a record-tying 17-game home winless streak (two ties, 15 losses) that lasted until April 2. In all, the team won just 14 games—and six of those were against either the Islanders or the Tampa Bay Lightning. Bright spots for the team included the play of Andrew Brunette, who led the club in goals (23) and assists (27) and Ray Ferraro, who matched his totals of the two previous seasons combined when he scored 19 goals, including a team-leading 10 on the power-play. Patrick Stefan suffered through a prolonged scoring drought and finished the season with just five goals and 20 assists, but still offers much hope for the future.

Atlanta Thrashers Year-by-Year Record

Season	GP	W	L	T	GF	GA	Pts	Finish	Division	Playoff Results
1999-2000	82	14	16	7	170	313	*39	5th	Southeast	Out of Playoffs

** Includes 4 points for regulation ties (RT)*

BOSTON BRUINS

WHEN THE NHL WAS FORMED IN 1917, the Boston Athletic Association was the defending American Amateur Hockey League champion. Boston was already a hockey hub, and it was appropriate that the Bruins would become the first American team in the National Hockey League.

Grocery store magnate Charles Adams had sponsored an amateur club in Boston, but became disenchanted after discovering that several rivals were spreading rather large gratuities among their players. Ripe for a professional franchise, Adams was lobbied by a group that included Tom Duggan, Frank Sullivan and Russ Layton who insisted that a firsthand view of an NHL game would persuade the millionaire to invest his money in professional hockey. Adams agreed to attend the 1924 Stanley Cup finals between the Calgary Tigers and a Montreal Canadiens club loaded with such legends as Georges Vezina, Howie Morenz, Aurel Joliat and Sprague Cleghorn. He was hooked.

Adams wasted little time organizing his new enterprise. During his Canadian excursion he had met early hockey legend Art Ross. Adams liked the man and promptly named him coach, general manager and scout of the new team. However, when the 1924–25 season ended, the Bruins' only claim to fame was that they were America's first NHL team. They barely held up the bottom of the six-team league with a feeble record of six wins and 24 losses.

Despite their misfortune, the Bruins made a singular impact on Bostonians, who began filling Boston Arena. Adams responded after two years by spending $50,000 on a massive infusion of talent. He landed Duke Keats, Perk Galbraith, Harry Oliver and Harry Meeking as well as the inimitable Eddie Shore from the folding Western Hockey League. With Shore as its centerpiece, the Bruins began muscling their way to a more prominent place in the NHL. Within three seasons of the Bruins' birth, Boston had a Stanley Cup contender. Although Art Ross's team lost to Ottawa in the 1927 finals, more than 29,000 applications were received by the Bruins for tickets.

Responding to the hockey mania, and with the backing of Madison Square Garden money, promoters built a new arena for the 1928–29 season. Originally named "Boston Madison Square Garden," the rink opened on November 20, 1928. By season's end, the Bruins had reached the finals again, this time against the Rangers. On March 29, 1929, the visiting Bostonians defeated New York 2–1 to bring the Stanley Cup to the Hub for the first time.

Having acquired Cecil "Tiny" Thompson from the Minneapolis Millers, Ross's Bruins boasted some of the best goaltending the league had ever seen. Thompson twice blanked the Canadiens in a three-game semifinal series, and then held New York to only one goal in two games in the finals. He finished with a 0.60 goals-against average through the five playoff games and would eventually win the Vezina Trophy four times before being dealt to the Detroit Red Wings.

Nevertheless, Shore was the draw at Boston Garden. The defenseman—equally renowned for his end-to-end rushes and bruising physical play—symbolized the macho hockey man of the early NHL days. After an injury left his ear hanging tenuously from the side of his head, Shore insisted on sewing it back on while an incredulous doctor held the mirror for him. Despite his heroics, Shore's career was marred by an ugly episode that nearly resulted in the death of Toronto Maple Leafs stickhandling expert Ace Bailey. The game, played at Boston Garden on the night of December 12, 1933, was a typically robust Toronto/Boston encounter, aggravated by the intense rivalry between Ross and Leafs boss Conn Smythe. The incident, which to this day remains one of the most discussed in league history, began when King Clancy and Red Horner of Toronto simultaneously checked Shore into the boards near the Maple Leafs net.

"I looked back," Clancy recalled, "saw Shore scrambling to his feet and then hit Bailey across the back of the legs. Eddie thought he was retaliating against me. I know he never meant it to be that bad." It was worse. Bailey nearly died in the hospital. After two delicate brain operations, Ace's recuperation was miraculous but he never played hockey again. Shore was suspended for 16 games, which Clancy called "fitting."

Shore's marquee personality tended to overshadow other Bruins who were outstanding in their own right. Aubrey "Dit" Clapper was a star forward who would conclude his 20-year Boston career as a defenseman of equal ability. Lionel Hitchman was every bit as good as Shore on the blue line but less belligerent. Frank Fredrickson, Harry Oliver, Norman "Dutch" Gainor and Ralph "Cooney" Weiland were among the other starry Bruins in their early years. Boston's "Dynamite Line" of Weiland, Clapper and Gainor was one of the better trios ever to don a Bruins uniform. They helped Boston finish first five times in the American Division in the nine seasons between 1929–30 and 1937–38.

Ever the insightful thinker, Art Ross was the first NHL coach to pull his goaltender in a Stanley Cup playoff game. Unheard of at the time, the tactic was employed on March 26, 1931. Ross pulled Tiny Thompson for a sixth attacker in the last minute but the Montreal Canadiens were able to hold their 1–0 lead. By 1934, Ross had decided he wanted to concentrate on managing and hired Frank Patrick as coach. The salary of $10,500 was considered high for the time. Patrick lasted two seasons behind the bench, doing well in the regular season but losing the first playoff round in successive years. Ross removed Patrick at the start of the 1936–37 season and returned to the bench himself. His sense of timing was excellent. The Bruins had signed a hard-nosed center from Kitchener, Ontario, named Milt Schmidt and soon would add the kid's two pals, Bobby Bauer and Woody Dumart, who would form the outstanding Kraut Line.

When the NHL's two divisions amalgamated in 1938–39, Boston became the scourge of big-league hockey. Frank Brimsek replaced Tiny Thompson in goal and blossomed into one of the best goalies of all time. Another hero of what would prove to be Boston's second Stanley Cup-winning season was "Sudden Death" Mel Hill, who specialized for a brief 12 days in beating the Rangers in overtime. Boston won the best-of-seven semifinal series with New York four games to three; Hill secured three of the wins with overtime goals. He didn't provide any heroics in the Cup finals against Toronto, but none were needed. The Bruins dispatched the Leafs in five games and the team was hailed by many critics as the greatest of all time.

Even after Shore left Boston to play for the New York Americans in 1940, the Bostonians continued to rule. In 1940–41, paced by the Krauts and Brimsek, the Bruins were coached by Cooney Weiland, who had moved behind the bench to replace Ross the year before. Weiland directed his club to a seven-game semifinal playoff win over Toronto and then whipped Detroit four straight. The Krauts were magnificent, but no one was better than a deft center named Bill Cowley, who had won the scoring championship and reached new levels of stickhandling agility.

Cowley would play consecutively through the 1946–47 season, but the club's core soon would be demolished by World War II enlistments. Brimsek enlisted in the U.S. Coast Guard, while Schmidt, Dumart and Bauer signed up as a unit in the Royal Canadian Air Force. The Bruins would never be the same. At war's end, the four veterans returned to Boston, each having lost an edge during their service stint. Brimsek eventually was traded to Chicago and Bauer hung up his skates after the 1946–47 season—he returned for a one-game cameo appearance in 1951–52—leaving Schmidt and Dumart to carry the load. The former was superb for several years while the latter played a workmanlike checking role, which climaxed in the 1953 playoffs when Woody shadowed Gordie Howe efficiently enough to gain Boston an upset of the defending Stanley Cup champion Red Wings.

After retiring, Schmidt became Bruins coach in 1954–55—with modest success. By the early 1960s, Uke Line stars Bronco Horvath, Vic Stasiuk and Johnny Bucyk ranked among the league's best, but the Bruins missed the playoffs eight years in a row through 1966–67. That season, Harry Sinden, an intense 34-year-old coach who never played a game in the NHL, was given control of the club. When Schmidt became general manager in 1967–68, he produced one of the most one-sided trades ever. From the Chicago Black Hawks, the Bruins obtained Phil Esposito, Fred Stanfield and Ken Hodge for Jack Norris, Pit Martin and Gilles Marotte. That year, the Bruins began their ascent, abetted by the maturing wunderkind Bobby Orr, who was in the process of revolutionizing the game.

A Boston farmhand since the age of 14, Orr had joined the Bruins as an 18-year-old in 1966–67. Listed as a defenseman, Orr employed extraordinary speed, puck control and shooting ability. Rather than stick to defensive play, he would lead attack after attack, combining like perfectly meshed gears with the finishing genius, Esposito. Together, Orr and Espo helped end the Bruins' Stanley Cup drought with a four-straight sweep of St. Louis in the 1970 finals. The feat was minimized by some because Boston's opponent, the Blues, was an expansion team loaded with retreads and assorted castaways. Yet the image that remains firmly set in the minds of Bostonians is that of an exuberant Orr flying through the air past St. Louis defenseman Noel Picard after the Beantown hero had fired the Cup-winning sudden-death goal past goalie Glenn Hall.

The triumph was partially marred by Sinden's unexpected resignation over a salary dispute. He was replaced by Tom Johnson, the Hall of Fame defenseman who had been Boston's assistant general manager. Although Johnson coached the Bruins to a first-place finish in the East

Division, there were concerns about the team's country-club attitude. Favored to repeat as Cup champs, Esposito, Orr & Co. encountered a Montreal team that started an inexperienced rookie goalie named Ken Dryden. As expected, Boston won the opener, but Dryden grew progressively stronger as the series unfolded, while the Bruins became more and more frustrated by the tall Cornell grad. The series ran a full seven games, ending with a remarkable Montreal victory.

Few teams ever have been more determined to atone for a humiliation than the 1971–72 Bruins, one of the most powerful teams ever assembled. They finished the season with the best record—Esposito was leading scorer and Orr the most valuable player—and then marched all the way to the finals where they collided with a mighty Rangers team thirsting for New York's first Cup in 32 years. At times the Rangers appeared on the verge of a breakthrough but, with the series three games to two in Boston's favor, the Bruins came to Madison Square Garden and let Orr do the skating and shooting. He ended a scoreless tie with a dazzling pirouette and then fired what would be the winning goal in what ultimately was a 3–0 decision for the Bruins.

The Bruins had the makings of a dynasty. Eddie Johnston and Gerry Cheevers provided splendid goaltending, while the Orr-centered defense was balanced and robust. Esposito, Ken Hodge, Derek Sanderson and Ed Westfall each provided diverse ingredients necessary to win a Stanley Cup championship.

But, few could have forecast the upheaval that was ahead. The simultaneous arrival of the World Hockey Association and NHL expansion would rob the Bruins of pivotal players. Cheevers, Sanderson and Ted Green immigrated to the new WHA, while Westfall was claimed by the expansion New York Islanders in 1972. The results were devastating for Boston. Johnson was fired in midseason and replaced by former Bruin Armand "Bep" Guidolin. The Canadiens swept past them in the regular-season race, although Esposito won the scoring championship and Orr won the Norris Trophy as the best defenseman. But, the playoffs were a disaster. Esposito was crippled by a knee injury, leaving the Bruins without a top sniper, and the Rangers knocked Boston out of the first round in five games.

The shock was almost as bad as it had been two years earlier and once again the Bruins vowed to regroup. True to their word, they finished an impressive first (52–17–9) in 1973–74 with the usual prizes. Esposito took both the Hart and Art Ross trophies, while Orr again earned the Norris Trophy and Johnny Bucyk won the Lady Byng Trophy. Most of the hockey world expected the Bruins to annex the Stanley Cup when they took on the expansion Philadelphia Flyers in the finals. But, once again a hot goaltender—this time Bernie Parent—did them in and Boston exited in six games. Despite Orr's heroics, the would-be dynasty was no more. Orr won the Norris Trophy yet again in 1975, but when the finals arrived it was Philadelphia versus Buffalo with Boston long gone.

Slowly yet relentlessly the Bruins lost their luster, and eventually lost Phil Esposito and Bobby Orr as well. Esposito was traded to the Rangers with Carol Vadnais for Brad Park, Jean Ratelle and Joe Zanussi on November 7, 1975. On June 24, 1976, Orr, the defenseman who symbolized Bruins hockey as much as Eddie Shore had in an earlier era, signed as a free agent with the Chicago Black Hawks.

Devastating as the losses may have been, the Bruins were revitalized in a curious way. New owners—Sports Systems Corp., led by brothers Jeremy, Max and Lawrence Jacobs of Eggerts, New York—assumed control of the club on August 28, 1975. A career minor-leaguer, Don Cherry, was hired as coach and infused an already rugged Boston squad with even more fire. They finished first in the Adams Division in 1976–77 and went all the way to the Stanley Cup finals before being dispatched by the Canadiens in four straight. Cherry again brought them to the last round of the playoffs against Montreal the following spring and even managed to win the first two games played at Boston Garden—tying the series at two apiece—before losing in six games.

By now Cherry's exuberance had made him the coaching toast of the league. Everyone seemed to love him except g.m. Harry Sinden. A simmering feud was kept from exploding because Cherry delivered another first-place finish in 1978–79 and a four-game playoff sweep of Pittsburgh in the quarterfinals. He peaked in the semifinals, bringing Boston back from a three-games-to-two deficit against Montreal. Game seven was a classic, with the Bruins leading until late in the third period when a too-many-men-on-the-ice penalty was called against them. Guy Lafleur scored for the Habs to tie it up, and Montreal won the game and the series in overtime.

Cherry was fired. A year later, the Bruins were eliminated from playoff contention by the Islanders, in 1981 by Minnesota and in 1982 by Quebec. They did have the 1982 Lady Byng Trophy winner in Rick Middleton, a top scorer in Barry Pederson and solid goaltending from Pete Peeters, but the Islanders proved too formidable in the playoffs. Over the years, Sinden's adroit managing kept the Bruins in contention and they gained a playoff berth every season for 29 years until 1996–97, when their record streak was ended. They were able to remain a top club because of Orr's successor as defense hero, Raymond Bourque.

Less flamboyant than Orr or Shore, Bourque nevertheless was exceptionally skilled as a skater, shooter and stickhandler and, unlike Orr, was miraculously durable. He helped Boston to the Stanley Cup finals in 1988—a four-games-to-none loss to Edmonton—and again in 1990 when they took one game from a strong Oilers squad. Even though Bourque was a perpetual Norris Trophy candidate, his supporting cast was never sufficient to win the silver mug.

The deteriorating state of Boston Garden was never more apparent then on the night of May 24, 1988, when an electrical failure plunged the building into darkness and forced postponement of the fourth game of the Stanley Cup finals. Construction would begin less than five years later on a modern replacement, FleetCenter. The new facility opened prior to the 1995-96 season and played host to the NHL All-Star Game in January, 1996.

Following a non-playoff year in 1996–97, Sinden fired coach Steve Kasper and replaced him with the veteran Pat Burns. The new coach was presented with two first-round draft picks—Joe Thornton and Sergei Samsonov—as well as good goaltending from former second-stringer Byron Dafoe.

While most critics believed that the Bostonians were too shallow to even reach a playoff berth in 1997–98, they surprised almost everyone by quickly moving over the .500 mark and remaining there throughout the season. Thornton initially was a disappointment, but Samsonov—the Calder Trophy winner—led all rookies in scoring with 22 goals and 47 points while Jason Allison emerged as top-10 talent with 83 points. Mostly, though, it was the improved defense credited to Pat Burns's coaching system that saw the Bruins climb to fifth in the Eastern Conference. A succession of bad breaks, as much as anything, saw Boston fall to the Washington Capitals in six games in the opening round of the 1998 playoffs.

The Bruins posted a 39–30–13 record in 1998–99 in their second season under Burns, with Allison, Samsonov and Dmitri Khristich enjoying strong seasons and Joe Thornton beginning to deliver on his promise as a first-overall draft choice. However, it was a defense led by Bourque and Dafoe that remained the team's strength. Dafoe led the league with 10 shutouts, and his 1.99 goals-against average made him just the fourth netminder in Bruins history to post an average below 2.00 and the first since Frank Brimsek 60 years before. In the playoffs, Boston eliminated the Carolina Hurricanes before being knocked out by the Buffalo Sabres. It was the second year in a row that the Bruins had been defeated by the team that would go on to represent the Eastern Conference in the Stanley Cup finals.

Despite his having led the Bruins with 29 goals in each of the previous two seasons, Harry Sinden refused to meet Dmitri Khristich's multi-million dollar arbitration award prior to the 1999–2000 season. Byron Dafoe also presented problems, holding out for a better contract. Khristich was eventually dealt to Toronto, while Dafoe was re-signed after the team's slow start. Unfortunately, the team never seemed to recover. A wrist injury to Jason Allison eventually sidelined him for much of the season, which only added to the Bruins' woes. Among the bright spots of a disappointing season was the play of Joe Thornton. The first-overall draft choice in 1997 wound up leading the team in scoring. Anson Carter, who scored 24 goals in 1998–99, continued to be an effective player.

The 1999–2000 season marked the end of an era in Boston. Hoping to finally add a Stanley Cup victory to his Hall of Fame resumé, Raymond Bourque asked for a trade to a contending team. Harry Sinden granted his star defenseman's request and dealt him to the Colorado Avalanche. After 20-plus seasons, Bourque left Boston as the Bruins' all-time leader in games played, assists and points.

Boston Bruins Year-by-Year Record

Season	GP	W	L	T	GF	GA	Pts	Finish	Division	Playoff Results
1924–25	30	6	24	0	49	119	12	6th		Out of Playoffs
1925–26	36	17	15	4	92	85	38	4th		Out of Playoffs
1926–27	44	21	20	3	97	89	45	2nd	American	Lost Final
1927–28	44	20	13	11	77	70	51	1st	American	Lost Semifinal
1928–29	44	26	13	5	89	52	57	1st	American	Won Stanley Cup
1929–30	44	38	5	1	179	98	77	1st	American	Lost Final
1930–31	44	28	10	6	143	90	62	1st	American	Lost Semifinal
1931–32	48	15	21	12	122	117	42	4th	American	Out of Playoffs
1932–33	48	25	15	8	124	88	58	1st	American	Lost Semifinal
1933–34	48	18	25	5	111	130	41	4th	American	Out of Playoffs
1934–35	48	26	16	6	129	112	58	1st	American	Lost Semifinal
1935–36	48	22	20	6	92	83	50	2nd	American	Lost Quarterfinal
1936–37	48	23	18	7	120	110	53	2nd	American	Lost Quarterfinal
1937–38	48	30	11	7	142	89	67	1st	American	Lost Semifinal
1938–39	48	36	10	2	156	76	74	1st		Won Stanley Cup
1939–40	48	31	12	5	170	98	67	1st		Lost Semifinal
1940–41	48	27	8	13	168	102	67	1st		Won Stanley Cup
1941–42	48	25	17	6	160	118	56	3rd		Lost Semifinal
1942–43	50	24	17	9	195	176	57	2nd		Lost Final
1943–44	50	19	26	5	223	268	43	5th		Out of Playoffs
1944–45	50	16	30	4	179	219	36	4th		Lost Semifinal
1945–46	50	24	18	8	167	156	56	2nd		Lost Final
1946–47	60	26	23	11	190	175	63	3rd		Lost Semifinal
1947–48	60	23	24	13	167	168	59	3rd		Lost Semifinal
1948–49	60	29	23	8	178	163	66	2nd		Lost Semifinal
1949–50	70	22	32	16	198	228	60	5th		Out of Playoffs
1950–51	70	22	30	18	178	197	62	4th		Lost Semifinal
1951–52	70	25	29	16	162	176	66	4th		Lost Semifinal
1952–53	70	28	29	13	152	172	69	3rd		Lost Final
1953–54	70	32	28	10	177	181	74	4th		Lost Semifinal
1954–55	70	23	26	21	169	188	67	4th		Lost Semifinal
1955–56	70	23	34	13	147	185	59	5th		Out of Playoffs
1956–57	70	34	24	12	195	174	80	3rd		Lost Final
1957–58	70	27	28	15	199	194	69	4th		Lost Final
1958–59	70	32	29	9	205	215	73	2nd		Lost Semifinal
1959–60	70	28	34	8	220	241	64	5th		Out of Playoffs
1960–61	70	15	42	13	176	254	43	6th		Out of Playoffs
1961–62	70	15	47	8	177	306	38	6th		Out of Playoffs
1962–63	70	14	39	17	198	281	45	6th		Out of Playoffs
1963–64	70	18	40	12	170	212	48	6th		Out of Playoffs
1964–65	70	21	43	6	166	253	48	6th		Out of Playoffs
1965–66	70	21	43	6	174	275	48	5th		Out of Playoffs
1966–67	70	17	43	10	182	253	44	6th		Out of Playoffs
1967–68	74	37	27	10	259	216	84	3rd	East	Lost Quarterfinal
1968–69	76	42	18	16	303	221	100	2nd	East	Lost Semifinal
1969–70	76	40	17	19	277	216	99	2nd	East	Won Stanley Cup
1970–71	78	57	14	7	399	207	121	1st	East	Lost Quarterfinal
1971–72	78	54	13	11	330	204	119	1st	East	Won Stanley Cup
1972–73	78	51	22	5	330	235	107	2nd	East	Lost Quarterfinal
1973–74	78	52	17	9	349	221	113	1st	East	Lost Final
1974–75	80	40	26	14	345	245	94	2nd	Adams	Lost Prelim. Round
1975–76	80	48	15	17	313	237	113	1st	Adams	Lost Semifinal
1976–77	80	49	23	8	312	240	106	1st	Adams	Lost Final
1977–78	80	51	18	11	333	218	113	1st	Adams	Lost Final
1978–79	80	43	23	14	316	270	100	1st	Adams	Lost Semifinal
1979–80	80	46	21	13	310	234	105	2nd	Adams	Lost Quarterfinal
1980–81	80	37	30	13	316	272	87	2nd	Adams	Lost Prelim. Round
1981–82	80	43	27	10	323	285	96	2nd	Adams	Lost Div. Final
1982–83	80	50	20	10	327	228	110	1st	Adams	Lost Conf. Final
1983–84	80	49	25	6	336	261	104	1st	Adams	Lost Div. Semifinal
1984–85	80	36	34	10	303	287	82	4th	Adams	Lost Div. Semifinal
1985–86	80	37	31	12	311	288	86	3rd	Adams	Lost Div. Semifinal
1986–87	80	39	34	7	301	276	85	3rd	Adams	Lost Div. Semifinal
1987–88	80	44	30	6	300	251	94	2nd	Adams	Lost Final
1988–89	80	37	29	14	289	256	88	2nd	Adams	Lost Div. Final
1989–90	80	46	25	9	289	232	101	1st	Adams	Lost Final
1990–91	80	44	24	12	299	264	100	1st	Adams	Lost Conf. Final
1991–92	80	36	32	12	270	275	84	2nd	Adams	Lost Conf. Final
1992–93	84	51	26	7	332	268	109	1st	Adams	Lost Div. Semifinal
1993–94	84	42	29	13	289	252	97	2nd	Northeast	Lost Conf. Semifinal
1994–95	48	27	18	3	150	127	57	3rd	Northeast	Lost Conf. Quarterfinal
1995–96	82	40	31	11	282	269	91	2nd	Northeast	Lost Conf. Quarterfinal
1996–97	82	26	47	9	234	300	61	6th	Northeast	Out of Playoffs
1997–98	82	39	30	13	221	194	91	2nd	Northeast	Lost Conf. Quarterfinal
1998–99	82	39	30	13	214	181	91	3rd	Northeast	Lost Conf. Semifinal
1999-2000	82	24	39	19	210	248	*73	5th	Northeast	Out of Playoffs

** Includes 6 points for regulation ties (RT)*

BUFFALO SABRES

THE STORY OF THE BUFFALO SABRES begins in the mid-1960s. Seymour Knox III and Northrup Knox spearheaded a drive for a Buffalo franchise when the NHL announced a doubling of the number of teams for the 1967–68 season. Despite a splendid written and oral presentation to the NHL Board of Governors at that time, the city was not included in the list of six new franchises.

Discouraged but unwilling to give up, the Knoxes joined the fraternity of NHL owners by buying shares in the Oakland Seals. When the NHL decided to add two clubs for the 1970–71 season—at triple the 1967 cost—the Knoxes were still interested on behalf of Buffalo. On December 2, 1969, for a fee of $6 million apiece, Buffalo and Vancouver were named the newest members of the NHL. On January 16, 1970, the yet-to-be-named Buffalo club announced the signing of George "Punch" Imlach as general manager and coach of the new franchise. Imlach had been fired by the Toronto Maple Leafs in 1969 after guiding the club to four Stanley Cup titles. "Running the Buffalo club will be the toughest job in pro hockey," Imlach said. "But, the tougher it is, the better I like it."

Imlach could not resist a dig at his former employers in

Toronto. He chose uniforms similar to those worn by his old Cup-winning Maple Leaf teams, but instead of blue and white he wanted blue and gold because, "We're classier than the Leafs."

A "Name the Team" contest in the spring of 1970 brought forth 13,000 suggestions. The club rejected candidates like Mugwumps and Flying Zeppelins before settling on Sabres, because the name reflected the steely determination to succeed at a lightning quick pace. Next came the annual June draft in Montreal and the dispersal of the best amateur talent. The two most coveted players were Gilbert Perreault from the Montreal Junior Canadiens and Dale Tallon of the Toronto Marlboros. A "spin of the wheel" gave Buffalo first choice, and Imlach selected Perreault. (Perreault's number 11 commemorated the result of that fateful spin of the wheel. Vancouver would get first pick if an even number came up; but when the pointer clicked to a stop on 11, Perreault was headed for Buffalo.)

During the Sabres' first season of 1970–71, the Boston Bruins set 37 team records and topped the NHL standings with 57 wins and 121 points. The Sabres turned in a respectable 24 wins and 63 points and finished ahead of Vancouver (56 points) and Detroit (55) for fifth place in the East Division. Perreault proved he needed no further seasoning in the minors, as he set a goal-scoring record for rookies with 38 and earned the Calder Trophy.

Left wing Rick Martin was the Sabres' top pick in the 1971 draft. In a normal year, Martin's 44 goals and 74 points would have made him a shoo-in as rookie of the year. But, Ken Dryden's great goaltending for Montreal, in the eyes of the voters, was even more impressive. The 1971 Amateur Draft also produced Craig Ramsay and Bill Hajt. That year, general manager and coach Punch Imlach suffered heart problems and was persuaded to hand over the coaching duties to his longtime friend, Joe Crozier.

Martin and Perreault played brilliantly together while a search went on to find a right wing to fit their style. It ended in 1972, when the Sabres sent Eddie Shack to Pittsburgh for unheralded Rene Robert and the French Connection Line was born. Defenseman Jim Schoenfeld was the team's number-one draft choice in 1972, and the 1972–73 season saw the Sabres reach the playoffs in just their third year. They qualified by defeating the St. Louis Blues 3–1 in the final game of the regular season, then went on to give Montreal a fright in the first round before bowing out in six games.

Floyd Smith replaced Joe Crozier as the Sabres' coach for the 1974–75 season and guided the club to 49 wins and 113 points, still the best numbers in the history of the franchise. Danny Gare joined the club that season and scored 31 goals. His first came 18 seconds after the opening whistle in his first NHL game, three seconds shy of the fastest goal by a rookie (Gus Bodnar in 1943). The following year, Gare would jump to 50 goals.

The Sabres remained hot in the 1975 playoffs, ousting the Chicago Black Hawks in five games, then eliminating a powerful Montreal club to earn a ticket to the Stanley Cup finals against the Philadelphia Flyers, the defending champions.

The final series matched the French Connection against the Flyers' potent combination of Bobby Clarke, Bill Barber and Reggie Leach. The Flyers captured the first two games, but the Sabres rebounded for a pair of wins on home ice. The Sabres, who had never won at the Philadelphia Spectrum, lost game five by a 5–1 score. Back in Buffalo for game six, Roger Crozier replaced Gerry Desjardins in the Sabres goal, but was outdueled by Bernie Parent in a 2–0 Flyers victory. "We were a good young team then," forward Craig Ramsay would say later. "We thought we'd be back every year, taking a run at the Stanley Cup."

But, it was not to be. A team that boasted five 30-plus goal scorers and a powerful defense remained one of the NHL's elite, but could never again generate enough playoff wins to reach the Stanley Cup finals. Despite its string of playoff disappointments, Buffalo remained near the top of the NHL regular-season standings from the mid 1970s onward. From 1974–75 through 1977–78 the team never failed to top the 100-point plateau. One of the highlights of the Sabres' first decade would come from the All-Star Game, held in Buffalo in 1978. Rick Martin and Gilbert Perreault led the Wales Conference to an exciting 3–2 victory. Martin scored the tying goal with 1:39 left in the third period, and Perreault scored the winner after 3:55 of overtime.

Punch Imlach was fired after the 1978 playoffs, and coach Marcel Pronovost also lost his job when the Sabres got off to a slow start in 1978–79. John Anderson was named interim manager until the Sabres were able to land renowned hockey man Scotty Bowman in 1979. Bowman just had coached the Montreal Canadiens to four consecutive Stanley Cup titles and wanted to add general manager's duties to his portfolio.

Bowman spent the next few seasons making widespread changes. He added players Mike Ramsey, Lindy Ruff, Hannu Virta, Phil Housley, Mike Foligno, Dave Andreychuk and goalies Tom Barrasso and Daren Puppa. Bowman's maneuvers and coaching acumen bore results. In 1979–80 the Sabres had 110 points, and from 1980–81 through 1984–85 they never had fewer than 89 points. The club missed the playoffs with 80 points in 1985–86 and sputtered in 1986–87, resulting in Bowman's dismissal. He was replaced as g.m. by Gerry Meehan. Ted Sator took over as coach.

In 1987, after 17 years, 512 goals and 1,326 points, Gilbert Perreault announced his retirement. Despite an offer from the club, he passed up a front office job, returned home to Quebec and would become a successful junior team owner and coach. At the NHL Entry Draft in 1987, Gerry Meehan snared Pierre Turgeon with the number-one pick, hoping that he'd landed a player of Perreault's stature. Turgeon rewarded Meehan with 88 and 106 points in his second and third seasons, but never quite replaced Perreault in the hearts of Sabres fans. In October, 1991, he would be traded to the Islanders, the key player in a deal that would bring Pat LaFontaine to Buffalo.

Meanwhile, with Ted Sator at the helm for the 1987–88 season, the team improved by 21 points. Sator would guide the team to two third-place finishes in the Adams Division and two first-round playoff eliminations. Former Sabre Rick Dudley became the club's coach in 1989, and Buffalo made another impressive leap forward, finishing third overall with 45 wins and 98 points in 1989–90. During the season, the club sought the help of a psychologist for talented Soviet defector Alexander Mogilny, who revealed he had a fear of flying. There was more playoff disappointment in Buffalo this year when the Sabres, who'd finished with more wins, more points and more goals than Montreal, fell to the Canadiens in six games in the first round.

Prior to the 1991–92 season, former Edmonton Oilers coach John Muckler was hired as director of hockey operations. Islanders star Pat LaFontaine, involved in a contract dispute with his team, was acquired by Buffalo in a multi-player deal, yet the Sabres were ousted in the first round of the playoffs for the fifth year in a row. Muckler took over as coach of the Sabres for 1992–93. Mogilny set a club record with 76 goals, while LaFontaine had 95 assists and 148 points. In the playoffs, the Sabres surprised the Boston Bruins with a four-game sweep and advanced past the first round for the first time since 1983. In round two, Mogilny suffered a broken leg and the Canadiens swept the series, then defeated the Islanders and the Los Angeles Kings to capture the Stanley Cup.

Dominik Hasek, who had been named the top player in Czechoslovakia in 1987, 1989 and 1990, had joined the Sabres prior to the 1992–93 season. After playing 28 games in that first campaign, he became Buffalo's number-one goal-tender in 1993–94. "The Dominator" responded by recording a 1.95 goal-against average, the lowest mark seen in the NHL since Bernie Parent's 1.89 in 1973–74. Hasek's .930 save percentage was the highest recorded since the NHL began to keep this statistic in the early 1980s. He was rewarded with the Vezina Trophy and a First All-Star Team selection.

Hasek's unorthodox and acrobatic goaltending made him a sensation in Buffalo and throughout the NHL. In the 1994 playoffs, he made 70 saves in game six of a first-round playoff matchup against New Jersey. The game was decided in the fourth overtime period, with Buffalo winning on Dave Hannan's goal. It was the longest game in Sabres' history and ranked as the sixth-longest ever played in the NHL to that time. However, the Devils went on to win the series in the seventh game by a 2–1 score.

Pat LaFontaine had ranked second in the NHL behind Mario Lemieux with his 148 points in 1992–93, but missed most of the next two seasons with a serious knee injury. He returned in time to help Buffalo reach the playoffs in 1994–95, but the Sabres suffered yet another first-round defeat—this time to Philadelphia. Hasek continued to frustrate the NHL's best scorers, winning the Vezina Trophy for the second straight year, while Pat LaFontaine was awarded the Bill Masterton Trophy for sportsmanship and dedication to hockey.

On July 8, 1995, the Sabres traded Alexander Mogilny to Vancouver in a deal that brought Michael Peca to Buffalo. Ted Nolan left the St. Louis Blues to join the Sabres in 1995–96, but the team missed the playoffs that year.

On May 22, 1996, Seymour Knox III passed away at age 70. Among his many legacies to the city of Buffalo was the new Marine Midland Arena, which would open that fall. The opening of the new facility (later to become the HSBC Center), plus new team colors, logo and uniforms, coincided with on-ice improvement in 1996–97. With Ted Nolan in his second season as coach, the Sabres leaped to the top of the Northeast Division standings and finished with 92 points. For spearheading the turnaround, Dominik Hasek would become the first goalie since Jacques Plante in 1962 to be awarded the Hart Trophy as the NHL's most valuable player. In the playoffs, however, Hasek sustained a knee injury in the opening round against Ottawa. The Sabres called on backup goalie Steve Shields and survived the Senators in seven games before Philadelphia eliminated them in the second round.

Despite a measure of on-ice success, antagonism had developed between Hasek and coach Nolan and between Nolan and g.m. John Muckler. Both Nolan and Muckler were replaced before the 1997–98 campaign. With Darcy Regier in the front office and ex-Sabre Lindy Ruff behind the bench, Buffalo started the new season poorly but when Hasek moved his game into high gear in December, the Sabres became one of the league's best teams in the second half of the schedule. Hasek also starred for his native Czech Republic in a gold medal performance at the Nagano Olympics.

Though only eight teams would score fewer goals than Buffalo in 1997–98, Hasek's brilliance was enough to get the Sabres into the playoffs with plenty of room to spare. His 13 shutouts were the most since Tony Esposito posted 15 in 1969–70, and he again earned both the Hart and Vezina trophies. In the postseason, Hasek's fine play, and the Sabres overall team speed, saw Buffalo upset the Philadelphia Flyers in the first round. The Sabres then swept the Montreal Canadiens before bowing out against the Washington Capitals in a six-game Eastern Conference final. A groin injury cut into Hasek's playing time in 1998–99, and he relinquished his hold on the Hart, though he again won the Vezina Trophy. He also helped the Sabres reach the Stanley Cup finals for just the second time in team history. Buffalo pushed the Dallas Stars to six games before losing the series in triple overtime.

During the offseason, Dominik Hasek announced that the 1999–2000 campaign would be his last in the NHL. Still bothered by his tender groin, both Hasek and the Sabres got off to a slow start. The Dominator was forced out of the lineup on October 29 and did not return until February 1. On February 14, he announced he would return to Buffalo for one more year.

Though Martin Biron had posted five shutouts in Hasek's absence, the Sabres struggled. Michael Peca was playing below the form of recent years and Miroslav Satan was below the pace that had seen him score 40 goals the year before. He would eventually net 33, and Peca did pick up the pace; however, it was the acquisition of Doug Gilmour at the trade deadline that seemed to breathe new life into the Sabres. Chris Gratton was also a late addition as the defending Stanley Cup finalists came on strong and nailed down the final Eastern Conference playoff berth on the last day of the season. Buffalo carried a full head of steam into the postseason and many felt they were poised to do some damage, but there would be no return to the finals this year. Philadelphia ended the Sabres' season early with a five-game victory in the first round of the playoffs.

Buffalo Sabres Year-by-Year Record

Season	GP	W	L	T	GF	GA	Pts	Finish	Division	Playoff Results
1970–71	78	24	39	15	217	291	63	5th	East	Out of Playoffs
1971–72	78	16	43	19	203	289	51	6th	East	Out of Playoffs
1972–73	78	37	27	14	257	219	88	4th	East	Lost Quarterfinal
1973–74	78	32	34	12	242	250	76	5th	East	Out of Playoffs
1974–75	80	49	16	15	354	240	113	1st	Adams	Lost Final
1975–76	80	46	21	13	339	240	105	2nd	Adams	Lost Quarterfinal
1976–77	80	48	24	8	301	220	104	2nd	Adams	Lost Quarterfinal
1977–78	80	44	19	17	288	215	105	2nd	Adams	Lost Quarterfinal
1978–79	80	36	28	16	280	263	88	2nd	Adams	Lost Prelim. Round
1979–80	80	47	17	16	318	201	110	1st	Adams	Lost Semifinal
1980–81	80	39	20	21	327	250	99	1st	Adams	Lost Quarterfinal
1981–82	80	39	26	15	307	273	93	3rd	Adams	Lost Div. Semifinal
1982–83	80	38	29	13	318	285	89	3rd	Adams	Lost Div. Final
1983–84	80	48	25	7	315	257	103	2nd	Adams	Lost Div. Semifinal
1984–85	80	38	28	14	290	237	90	3rd	Adams	Lost Div. Semifinal
1985–86	80	37	37	6	296	291	80	5th	Adams	Out of Playoffs
1986–87	80	28	44	8	280	308	64	5th	Adams	Out of Playoffs
1987–88	80	37	32	11	283	305	85	3rd	Adams	Lost Div. Semifinal

Season	GP	W	L	T	GF	GA	Pts	Finish	Division	Playoff Results
1988–89	80	38	35	7	291	299	83	3rd	Adams	Lost Div. Semifinal
1989–90	80	45	27	8	286	248	98	2nd	Adams	Lost Div. Semifinal
1990–91	80	31	30	19	292	278	81	3rd	Adams	Lost Div. Semifinal
1991–92	80	31	37	12	289	299	74	3rd	Adams	Lost Div. Semifinal
1992–93	84	38	36	10	335	297	86	4th	Adams	Lost Div. Final
1993–94	84	43	32	9	282	218	95	4th	Northeast	Lost Conf. Quarterfinal
1994–95	48	22	19	7	130	119	51	4th	Northeast	Lost Conf. Quarterfinal
1995–96	82	33	42	7	247	262	73	5th	Northeast	Out of Playoffs
1996–97	82	40	30	12	237	208	92	1st	Northeast	Lost Conf. Semifinal
1997–98	82	36	29	17	211	187	89	3rd	Northeast	Lost Conf. Final
1998–99	82	37	28	17	207	175	91	4th	Northeast	Lost Final
1999-2000	82	35	36	11	213	204	*85	3rd	Northeast	Lost Conf. Quarterfinal

** Includes 4 points for regulation ties (RT)*

CALGARY/ATLANTA FLAMES

WHEN THE ATLANTA FLAMES became the Calgary Flames in 1980, hockey immediately became the main sport and the hottest ticket in town. The flaming "A" was replaced by a flaming "C" and there was hardly a heartbeat missed. The NHL officially arrived on October 9, 1980, when the newborn Calgary Flames tied the Quebec Nordiques, 5–5.

Playing to raucous crowds in the 6,500-seat Stampede Corral rink that first year, it looked as though the city had inherited a pretty good team to cheer for. "Nobody could beat us in the Corral," recalls then-general manager Cliff Fletcher, the silver-haired wheeler-dealer who was with the organization for 20 years. "It was a very successful first season." With a 25–5–10 record in the Corral and a 39–27–14 record overall, the Flames finished third in the Patrick Division and seventh overall in the league. They then defeated Chicago and Philadelphia before losing to Minnesota in the Stanley Cup semifinals.

With a new 20,000-seat rink being built across the street from the Corral, the future looked bright. Kent Nilsson, the supremely talented Swede, had a franchise-record 82 assists and 131 points that first season in Calgary and just missed the 50-goal plateau, scoring 49. Pat Riggin had 21 wins in net. Jim Peplinski was a rookie, just beginning his famous glove-in-the-face rubs en route to becoming one of the captains on Calgary's championship team of the future. Willi Plett hacked his way to 239 penalty minutes, but also scored 38 goals. Guy Chouinard had 83 points.

The Flames franchise had begun playing in the league in Atlanta in 1972–73. It appeared that Omni Sports group, a consortium of businessmen from the area headed by Tom Cousins, was on solid ground, but that same year the wildcat World Hockey Association began operation and players were jumping from the NHL to the WHA for the big money being offered by the new league. That, in turn, threw a big wrench into the financing of the Atlanta franchise. Still, the team persevered for eight seasons, missing the playoffs only during its first and third years of operation. These early Flames were competitive, too. Teams that probably should have done better in the postseason instead lost every first-round playoff matchup they entered.

As time went on, the businessmen that Cousins had recruited faded from the picture, unwilling to put more money into the operation of a hockey franchise. When he sold the team to Nelson Skalbania, a Vancouver-based businessman, Cousins' stake in the team had increased from 20 percent to 89 percent. But, Cousins sold the team for $16 million U.S., a record amount for an NHL team at the time. "It turned his whole experience into a profitable one," says Fletcher.

Skalbania had, in fact, jumped into the bidding late, had gone high on his bid, and basically had undermined what three Calgary businessmen had been negotiating. Doc and B.J. Seaman were the two instigators in placing an NHL team in Calgary. Harley Hotchkiss, another local businessman with ties to the oil patch that makes Calgary go around, was brought into the picture very early.

Behind the scenes, the Calgary group headed by the Seamans was well along in brokering the deal to purchase the Atlanta franchise, when Canadian financier Skalbania entered the fray. In the end, Skalbania would play a major bartering role in the Calgary franchise, but one that drove the cost of the team much higher than what it probably was worth. Using a $6-million deal with Molson that gave them television rights for 10 years, Skalbania was able to make his deal. However, being based in Vancouver, he immediately found it difficult to negotiate with the parties that the Seamans had been dealing with and called upon Norm Green, a Calgary businessman with whom he had previously dealt. In May, 1980, Green brought the two parties together and a deal was struck: Calgary interests would own 50 percent of the team and Skalbania the other 50 percent.

The Calgary owners were the Seamans, Hotchkiss, Green, Ralph Scurfield, then owner of a Banff ski area called Sunshine Village, and Norm Kwong, a former running back with the Edmonton Eskimos who had a one-percent share. By August, 1981, the local ownership had bought out Skalbania in two separate transactions. When all was settled, the two Seamans, Hotchkiss, Scurfield and Green equally shared 90 percent of the team while Kwong increased his share to 10 percent. Skalbania had paid $16 million U.S., but by the time the dust had settled, the Calgary owners had spent between $20 and $30 million to complete the deal. With the raging success of the first season, however, there were few complaints.

The Flames moved from the Patrick Division to the Smythe Division for their second season in Calgary, one that began with much optimism but ended in disappointment. It was the year the man with hockey's best-known moustache, Lanny McDonald, joined the team in a trade with the Colorado Rockies. McDonald would finish his playing career in Calgary, scoring a club record 66 goals in 1982–83 and serving as co-captain of the Stanley Cup champion team in 1989.

McDonald retired that summer and has since had his jersey raised to the roof of the current rink, the Saddledome, the only Flames jersey to be retired. McDonald still works in the Flames offices vice president, corporate development and there was a time when many figured he could have run for mayor and been elected in a landslide. But, not even his presence could help the Flames in their second Alberta season as they finished with a 29–34–17 record and then bowed out in the first round of the playoffs to Vancouver, who went on to the Stanley Cup finals.

That would be a trend for Calgary, losing to teams that reached the Stanley Cup finals after beating the Flames in the first round of the playoffs. Usually it was Edmonton. But, Vancouver in 1994 and Los Angeles in 1993 also handed Calgary first-round playoff defeats and proceeded all the way to the Stanley Cup finals.

After that second-year disappointment, the Flames changed direction on the ice. "That's when we realized we really did have a long way to go to build a winner," says Fletcher. "We only had to look 180 miles north to

Edmonton to see an emerging dynasty." The 1982–83 season became a rebuilding year. The ultra-positive "Badger Bob" Johnson replaced Al MacNeil as coach. With Johnson's college background, the Flames began recruiting college free agents such as Neil Sheehy, Joel Otto and Colin Patterson, later drafting future captain and 50-goal scorer Joe Nieuwendyk out of Cornell.

Riding Nilsson's 104-point season and McDonald's 66 goals, the Flames reached the playoffs in 1982–83, defeated Vancouver in the first round and then lost to nemesis Edmonton in the division final. The Oilers would win the Stanley Cup the next two seasons, while Fletcher and his staff hustled, traded and pieced together a team that could score, skate and hit with the Oilers. For toughness and grit he added Doug Risebrough. In the skill department he added a young Dan Quinn, Al MacInnis and Hakan Loob. Calgary-born Mike Vernon was added to the goaltending mix and the beginnings of the championship team were born.

In the fall of 1983, the Flames moved into what was then called the Olympic Saddledome, a unique-looking building that fit into the western flavor of the city, as the roof is shaped like the saddle of a horse. That year the Flames took Edmonton to seven games in the Smythe Division finals, the closest the team had come to beating the Oilers, who won the Stanley Cup for the first time that season.

It was then, perhaps, that one of the greatest hockey rivalries of the modern era developed. Those games were wars. As Wayne Gretzky and Paul Coffey and Hakan Loob, Kent Nilsson and Lanny McDonald battled on the skill side of the game, the likes of Doug Risebrough, Neil Sheehy, Tim Hunter and Jim Peplinski fought against Ken Linesman, Dave Semenko and Don Jackson in the trenches. They were games that meant everything to both teams. "It was tremendous. Anytime you played the Oilers you could feel the electricity in the building, playoffs or regular season," says Fletcher.

In 1984-85, the team achieved a high in points with 94, but bowed out disappointingly in the first round to Winnipeg. The next season was the turning point. "That's when we caught the Oilers and went to the finals," says Fletcher, who dealt for scorer Joe Mullen, the first American-born player to score 500 goals. Gary Suter, a late-round draft pick, won the Calder Trophy, scoring 68 points from the blue line. Late in the season, Fletcher acquired the gritty John Tonelli. Mike Vernon won 12 playoff games.

The key for the organization was that they had found a way to beat the Oilers, winning game seven in Edmonton on a goal that rookie Oiler defenseman Steve Smith put in his own net. Coincidentally, Smith would return to Calgary as a coach in 1997 before making a comeback as a player with the Flames in 1998–99.

"It was the most exhilarating experience in my hockey career," says Fletcher of that win in Edmonton and the short, 30-minute fight home. "We got to the airport and there were 25,000 people there. It was quite a scene. We felt a sense of accomplishment. In the minds of the southern Albertans, it was probably better than winning the Stanley Cup."

Which Calgary didn't do in 1986 as Montreal, led by Larry Robinson and a young Chris Chelios and Patrick Roy, eliminated the Flames in a five-game final.

In 1986, one of the team's original owners, Ralph Scurfield, died in an avalanche. His wife, Sonia took over his share of the Flames. For 10 years, no other ownership changes took place. Since that time, a number have occurred.

In 1991, Green bought the Minnesota North Stars and the remaining Calgary owners bought up his shares. In 1994, the ownership again underwent a restructuring. By 1995, the owners, the city and the federal government had combined to spend $40 million in renovations to the Saddledome as a way of increasing revenue for the team. As well, the owners took control of the building on a long-term lease, no longer having to deal with the intermediary Calgary Stampede, which had operated the building since its inception in 1983. By 1998, there were nine owners in the Flames operation. Hotchkiss, the Seamans, local private merchant banker Murray Edwards and Tim Horton Donuts owner Ronald Joyce each own about 23 percent. The remainder is divided evenly among businessmen from Calgary: Allan Markin, Alvin Libin, Grant Bartlett and J.R. McCaig.

On the ice, the Edmonton Oilers would win the Stanley Cup in 1987 and 1988, although the Flames won the Presidents' Trophy in 1987–88 with a 48–23–9 regular season record, the same year Joe Nieuwendyk won the Calder Trophy. Edmonton, however, disposed of Calgary in four games in the Smythe Division finals. From 1986 to 1991, the Flames had one of the best records in the NHL, and twice captured the Presidents' Trophy. Their playoff puzzle came together with a Stanley Cup win in 1989.

Coach Bob Johnson had left Calgary in 1987 to join the Amateur Hockey Association of the United States in Colorado Springs. ("Badger Bob" would later return to the NHL and coach Pittsburgh to a Stanley Cup title before passing away after a battle with cancer.) Terry Crisp took over as coach while Fletcher continued to assemble a winning roster.

Doug Gilmour was brought on in a trade with St. Louis in 1988–89. Theo Fleury, who would become the team's franchise player, was a rookie fourth-liner.

Gilmour, Mullen, Loob, Nieuwendyk, Suter and MacInnis formed perhaps the best power play the Flames have ever assembled. It had all the ingredients, including the rocket from the blue line that was MacInnis's shot. Oddly, the year they won the Cup they did not have to go through Edmonton, instead squeaking by Vancouver, thumping Los Angeles, grinding it out against Chicago and, finally, defeating Montreal at the Forum in game six to claim the Cup. It was the first time the Canadiens had lost a Stanley Cup final series on home ice.

Lanny McDonald scored the final goal of his Hall of Fame career in game six at 4:24 of the second period, giving Calgary a 2–1 lead. Doug Gilmour scored the game winner at 11:02 on the power-play before adding an empty-netter for the 4–2 Calgary win. They had reached the pinnacle. And since then they have not come close. Crisp, the coach who took them to the Holy Grail of hockey, was fired a year later.

Crisp was replaced on the bench by Doug Risebrough in 1990–91, a season that would be the last for Fletcher in the Flames organization. Fittingly, the team lost to Edmonton in the first round of the playoffs. The team Fletcher had chased all those years had chased him, too.

Fletcher's leaving caused quite the stir in Calgary. After all, he was the only architect the team had known. "It had been 19 years. I just thought it was time for a change to get the juices going to 100 percent again," says Fletcher, who moved to Toronto as president and general manager.

Risebrough, who had been under Fletcher's wing in the front office, took on the dual role of g.m. and coach. Fletcher then picked the pocket of his pupil in January, 1992, acquiring Doug Gilmour, who had walked out on the Flames in a contract dispute, Jamie Macoun, Ric Nattress, Kent Manderville and Rick Wamsley for Gary Leeman, Alexander Godynyuk, Jeff Reese, Michel Petit and Craig Berube. It was the largest trade in NHL history at the time and one that turned out to highly favor Toronto. Two seasons later, not one of the players Calgary had acquired was with the team and only Craig Berube, who by then was playing with Washington, was taking a regular shift in the league. The Flames missed the playoffs that season, although Gary Roberts scored 53 goals and vowed to name his next child after setup man Sergei Makarov.

The Flames had broken new ground in bringing Russian players to the NHL when they signed Sergei Priakin to a contract in 1988–89. "What we were trying to do was set up things for down the road but eventually they eased the restrictions," recalls Fletcher. Makarov, a veteran Soviet star, won the Calder Trophy as NHL rookie of the year in 1989–90.

Having missed the playoffs for the first time since moving to Calgary, the Flames gave Dave King, the former Canadian national team coach, his first NHL coaching job in 1992–93. In his three seasons behind the bench, he directed the Flames to very credible regular-season records—all in the top 10 overall. But, the team failed miserably in the playoffs, losing in the first round three consecutive seasons. It was also during these seasons that salaries began to rise, the league went through the lockout and running a small-market team became a very different proposition.

One by one the Flames watched superstars depart: Mike Vernon to Detroit, Al MacInnis to St. Louis, Joe Nieuwendyk to Dallas, Gary Suter to Chicago, Gary Roberts, after two neck surgeries, to Carolina. Pierre Page replaced King behind the bench in 1995–96. After a terrible start to the season, Risebrough was fired as general manager and replaced by Al Coates. The Flames scraped into the playoffs but were swept by Chicago. Rebuilding was the order of the day.

The Flames missed the playoffs in Page's second year, finishing 21st overall in the league. Albertan and taskmaster Brian Sutter was named coach for 1997–98 as the rebuilding and the on-ice struggles continued. Calgary actually finished six points worse (with 67) under Sutter than they had under Page, and though they remained within hailing distance of eighth place in the Western Conference for much of the season, the Flames were never really playoff contenders.

The Flames would show only modest improvement under Sutter in his second season of 1998–99, though they surprised many by remaining in playoff contention after dealing Fleury to the Colorado Avalanche late in the season. Injuries forced the Flames to use six goaltenders during the year. Former nemesis Grant Fuhr was signed for the 1999–2000 season to shore up the goaltending, and to lend experience to promising youngsters like Fred Brathwaite and Jean-Sebastien Giguere. Unfortunately, injuries limited Fuhr to just 23 games. Once again in 1999–2000, the Flames remained on the edge of playoff contention but ultimately came up short. A fourth straight season out of the playoffs cost both Brian Sutter and g.m. Al Coates their jobs. Former Dallas Stars director of player personnel Craig Button took over as general manager.

On the ice Phil Housley provides a veteran example for defensemen like Derek Morris and Cale Hulse, while offensive leadership comes from Valeri Bure, who enjoyed a breakthrough season in 1999–2000, and Jarome Iginla. At the 2000 Entry Draft hosted by the Flames in the Saddledome, more positive moves were made highlighted by the return to Calgary of veteran goaltender Mike Vernon and the drafting of local junior star Brent Krahn. These players, and youngsters like Daniel Tkachuk and Rico Fata, offer hope for the future.

Calgary Flames Year-by-Year Record

Season	GP	W	L	T	GF	GA	Pts	Finish	Division	Playoff Results
1972–73*	78	25	38	15	191	239	65	7th	West	Out of Playoffs
1973–74*	78	30	34	14	214	238	74	4th	West	Lost Quarterfinal
1974–75*	80	34	31	15	243	233	83	4th	Patrick	Out of Playoffs
1975–76*	80	35	33	12	262	237	82	3rd	Patrick	Lost Prelim. Round
1976–77*	80	34	34	12	264	265	80	3rd	Patrick	Lost Prelim. Round
1977–78*	80	34	27	19	274	252	87	3rd	Patrick	Lost Prelim. Round
1978–79*	80	41	31	8	327	280	90	4th	Patrick	Lost Prelim. Round
1979–80*	80	35	32	13	282	269	83	4th	Patrick	Lost Prelim. Round
1980–81	80	39	27	14	329	298	92	3rd	Patrick	Lost Semifinal
1981–82	80	29	34	17	334	345	75	3rd	Smythe	Lost Div. Semifinal
1982–83	80	32	34	14	321	317	78	2nd	Smythe	Lost Div. Final
1983–84	80	34	32	14	311	314	82	2nd	Smythe	Lost Div. Final
1984–85	80	41	27	12	363	302	94	3rd	Smythe	Lost Div. Semifinal
1985–86	80	40	31	9	354	315	89	2nd	Smythe	Lost Final
1986–87	80	46	31	3	318	289	95	2nd	Smythe	Lost Div. Semifinal
1987–88	80	48	23	9	397	305	105	1st	Smythe	Lost Div. Final
1988–89	80	54	17	9	354	226	117	1st	Smythe	Won Stanley Cup
1989–90	80	42	23	15	348	265	99	1st	Smythe	Lost Div. Semifinal
1990–91	80	46	26	8	344	263	100	2nd	Smythe	Lost Div. Semifinal
1991–92	80	31	37	12	296	305	74	5th	Smythe	Out of Playoffs
1992–93	84	43	30	11	322	282	97	2nd	Smythe	Lost Div. Semifinal
1993–94	84	42	29	13	302	256	97	1st	Pacific	Lost Conf. Quarterfinal
1994–95	48	24	17	7	163	135	55	1st	Pacific	Lost Conf. Quarterfinal
1995–96	82	34	37	11	241	240	79	2nd	Pacific	Lost Conf. Quarterfinal
1996–97	82	32	41	9	214	239	73	5th	Pacific	Out of Playoffs
1997–98	82	26	41	15	217	252	67	5th	Pacific	Out of Playoffs
1998–99	82	30	40	12	211	234	72	3rd	Northwest	Out of Playoffs
1999-2000	82	31	41	10	211	256	§77	4th	Northwest	Out of Playoffs

* *Atlanta Flames*

§ *Includes 5 points for regulation ties (RT)*

CALIFORNIA/OAKLAND SEALS AND CLEVELAND BARONS

WITH ITS LONG TRADITION OF MINOR LEAGUE HOCKEY, the state of California was a natural target of growth for NHL expansion in 1967. The Los Angeles entry went to Jack Kent Cooke, while the leader in Northern California was a 28-year-old friend of New York Rangers president William Jennings. Barend (Barry) Van Gerbig was a jet-setting beachboy who owned pieces of Standard Oil and Union Carbide. He had played goal for the varsity team at Princeton, and graduated to marry the daughter of film icon Douglas Fairbanks, Jr. His godfather was Bing Crosby.

The seemingly well-heeled Van Gerbig and his partners purchased the San Francisco Seals of the Western Hockey League, a team that had played its home games out of the creaky Cow Palace in Daly City. In 1966-67, their final WHL season, Seals games were moved to a relatively palatial facility across the Bay in Oakland. Though San Francisco would have been an ideal site for an NHL expansion club, it lacked a suitable arena. By contrast, the Bay Area's second—and noticeably lesser—city, boasted a brand-new hockey facility. As such, the Oakland-Alameda County Coliseum was chosen by Van Gerbig as home for his Oakland Seals. The decision to leave San Francisco would prove a mistake.

Bert Olmstead was hired as general manager and coach

of the new Oakland team, and he selected what looked like a winning lineup in the 1967 Expansion Draft. Goalie Charlie Hodge had considerable NHL experience with the Canadiens, while Bob Baun and Kent Douglas had skated for Stanley Cup winners in Toronto. Gerry Ehman had been a proven goal scorer, and Bill Hicke once had been touted as the natural heir to Maurice Richard in Montreal. The Seals also drafted the young sons of former stars King Clancy, Babe Pratt and Bryan Hextall. However, Olmstead's crew was a dismal 11–37–16 when he was fired late in the 1967–68 season.

The Seals were the only club in the newly created West Division that was never in playoff contention. Even worse, attendance was terrible. Early in the season Van Gerbig had threatened to move the team if more fans didn't show up. By the time the NHL Board of Governors convened for its March meeting, there were changes afoot. Labatt Breweries of Canada offered a loan of $680,000 (the amount that the league specified the Seals had to come up with by May 15) in order to move the franchise to Vancouver. Other interested parties included Ralph Wilson, owner of the Buffalo Bills football team. A move to Vancouver was vetoed by an 8–4 vote, as the league was in no mood to depart from a large population area so vital to any television plans. (The CBS TV contract specifically stipulated the inclusion of the Bay Area.)

Aided by the loan from Labatt, the Seals were purchased in August by the owners of the Harlem Globetrotters—Potter Palmer and George Gillett of Chicago, and John O'Neil Jr. of Miami. The three also had financial interests in the Atlanta Braves, the Miami Dolphins and the Atlanta Chiefs soccer team. Palmer and O'Neil had been partners of Van Gerbig, who would now serve the team in an advisory capacity only. President Frank Selke Jr. became the general manager. Fred Glover was the new coach.

Glover was not the only new face in the Seals dressing room for the 1968–69 season. Only seven of the 20 players originally drafted by the club remained. It was hoped that newcomers like Bryan Watson, Carol Vadnais, Gary Jarrett and Doug Roberts would help Glover move the Seals upward. In goal, the new coach inherited Charlie Hodge and Gary Smith who, while promising, had shown an alarming tendency to stickhandle the puck across the blue line in his first season. Few NHL goalies have been bombarded the way Smith would be during the 1969–70 and 1970–71 seasons.

Prior to the 1970–71 campaign, flamboyant Oakland A's baseball owner Charles Finley bought the hockey club and changed its name to the California Golden Seals. Finley added colored skates, new jerseys and several other gimmicks, but the Seals finished with the worst record in the league. One disaster led to another until February 1974, when the team was purchased by the NHL. League president Clarence Campbell named Munson Campbell as club president. Campbell was a man with over 30 years experience in the inner workings of professional hockey. He had been named vice president of the California Seals under Finley in 1971, but left a year later to return to private business.

As president, Campbell attempted to find new ownership for the foundering Seals. He eventually came up with hotelier Mel Swig, a former owner of the San Francisco Seals and another suitor who had been interested in purchasing the club during its original troubles in 1968. The hope now was that a proposed new arena would be built in San Francisco for the Seals, but when it became apparent that the plans never would become reality, the club moved to Cleveland in 1976. Swig's ownership gave way to the Gund family in June, 1977, but the Gunds could not solve the arena problem that had bedeviled the Seals in San Francisco.

The new Cleveland Barons played their home games at the Coliseum in Richfield, Ohio. While it listed the largest seating capacity in the NHL at the time (18,544), the Coliseum was located in farm country far from downtown Cleveland and suffered sparse crowds. Of course, the Barons' record hardly encouraged sellouts. Under coach Jack Evans, Cleveland finished the 1977–78 season with a 22–45–13 record and last place in the Adams Division. So poor was the club's financial condition that prior to the 1978–79 season the Gunds merged with the Minnesota North Stars. In 1990, the Gunds would agree to sell the North Stars in exchange for the rights to an expansion team that would return hockey to Northern California—the San Jose Sharks.

California/Oakland/Cleveland Year-by-Year Record

Season	GP	W	L	T	GF	GA	Pts	Finish	Division	Playoff Results
1967–68	74	15	42	17	153	219	47	6th	West	Out of Playoffs
1968–69	76	29	36	11	219	251	69	2nd	West	Lost Quarterfinal
1969–70	76	22	40	14	169	243	58	4th	West	Lost Quarterfinal
1970–71	78	20	53	5	199	320	45	7th	West	Out of Playoffs
1971–72	78	21	39	18	216	288	60	6th	West	Out of Playoffs
1972–73	78	16	46	16	213	323	48	8th	West	Out of Playoffs
1973–74	78	13	55	10	195	342	36	8th	West	Out of Playoffs
1974–75	80	19	48	13	212	316	51	4th	Adams	Out of Playoffs
1975–76	80	27	42	11	250	278	65	4th	Adams	Out of Playoffs
1976–77	80	25	42	13	240	292	63	4th	Adams	Out of Playoffs
1977–78	80	22	45	13	230	325	57	4th	Adams	Out of Playoffs

CAROLINA HURRICANES AND HARTFORD WHALERS

THE CAROLINA HURRICANES started their existence as the New England Whalers and are the culmination of a saga that has moved from Boston to Springfield to Hartford to Greensboro and, finally, to Raleigh. The seeds of the franchise were planted in October, 1971, by a pair of young sportsmen, Howard Baldwin and John Coburn Jr., who originally had planned to build a small hockey arena near Cape Cod. Out of this blueprint emerged one of the most powerful teams in the World Hockey Association. Baldwin, a former business manager of the Jersey Devils of the old Eastern Hockey League, hired Jack Kelley, the Boston University coach, to manage and coach the Whalers.

Former Montreal Canadiens center Larry Pleau of Lynn, Massachusetts, was the first Whaler signed by Kelley, followed by NHL regulars Brad Selwood, Rick Ley and Jim Dorey, all former Toronto Maple Leafs. On July 27, 1972, the Whalers signed former Boston Bruins defenseman Ted Green as captain, and then signed other NHL aces such as Tom Webster, Al Smith and Tom Williams. On October 12, 1972, the Whalers played their first home game at Boston Garden before a crowd of 14,442, defeating the Philadelphia Blazers, 4–3. The Whalers went on to finish first and win the Avco World Cup.

Kelley gave assistant coach Ron Ryan the head coaching position in 1973–74, and once again the Whalers moved to the top of the East Division. However, the team was encountering financial problems because of competition from the NHL's Boston Bruins. Attendance was less than satisfactory at Boston Garden in the second season, so Baldwin began entertaining offers from other cities that coveted the franchise. He finally selected Hartford, which was building a new arena in the Connecticut city's civic center.

Instead of waiting until the end of the 1973–74 season, the Whalers moved their home games to the Eastern States Coliseum in Springfield, Massachusetts, because their new home in Hartford had yet to be completed. Playing their final games in Springfield late in the 1973–74 season had a negative effect on the Whalers, who were eliminated from the playoffs in a first-round upset by the Chicago Cougars.

The Whalers continued to excel during the 1974–75 campaign, which was launched in Springfield and continued in Hartford late in the season upon completion of the 10,400-seat Civic Center arena. Once again they finished first in their division, but not without problems. En route to a match in Toronto on March 30, coach Ryan collapsed and was rushed to a hospital. He was replaced behind the bench by Kelley. On the plus side, the Whalers became an instant hit in Hartford, frequently selling out the new building.

During their WHA existence, the Whalers boasted several luminaries, not the least of whom were Gordie Howe and Dave Keon. Baldwin would become president of the league and was the prime architect in hammering out the merger that saw the Whalers, Edmonton Oilers, Winnipeg Jets and Quebec Nordiques become NHL members. The venerable Gordie Howe returned to the NHL at the age of 51 in 1979–80 as a member of Hartford. He finished his 32nd and final NHL season with 15 goals, including his 800th career regular-season tally. That same year, the Whalers traded for another Hall of Famer, Bobby Hull, and the two played on the same line for nine games.

The 1980–81 season saw first-ever Whalers player Larry Pleau take over as coach, replacing the fired Don Blackburn. Also that summer, Pleau drafted an 18-year-old center fourth overall. Less than six months after being selected, Ron Francis was brought up to Hartford. He made an immediate impact, finishing the year third in team scoring with 68 points in 56 games and helping to turn the 21st-ranked power-play into the best in the league for a three-month stretch. Despite missing the playoffs for the second straight year, the Whalers seemed destined for greatness. But, the 1982–83 campaign saw Larry Pleau return as bench boss, replacing another fired coach, Larry Kish, and the Whalers did not qualify for postseason play, finishing with only 19 wins.

The 1983 offseason saw a total overhaul to the Hartford front office. Now coaching was Jack Evans, and hired as general manager was Emile "the Cat" Francis. In two years, this tandem would eventually lead the hapless Whalers to unseen heights in the NHL. After missing the playoffs yet again in the 1984–85 season, the Whalers traded for goalie (and Ron Francis's first cousin) Mike Liut. Liut helped the Whale to their first winning finish in seven years and put them in the playoffs for the first time since their initial NHL season. Hartford then upset the Quebec Nordiques before pushing the Montreal Canadiens to seven games in a thrilling Adams Division final. Emile Francis was named NHL executive of the year by both The Hockey News and The Sporting News.

The next season, 1986–87, saw the Whalers capture their first and only regular-season Adams Division championship. The celebration, however, was short-lived as the Nordiques upset the Whalers in the first playoff round. Hartford returned to the postseason the following year, but was again ousted in the first round, this time by rival Montreal. Following 1988–89, and another first-round loss to the Canadiens, Emile Francis was made team president and former goaltender Ed Johnston was named g.m. Pleau, who had returned to the bench for a third time the previous season, was fired and replaced by former Whaler Rick Ley. But, the next two seasons saw little excitement as the Whalers still could not win a playoff round.

En route to their worst finish in seven seasons, in March, 1991, Ron Francis, owner of most Hartford Whalers offensive records, was traded to Pittsburgh in a multiplayer deal. Francis would go on to win the Stanley Cup that year and the next, and the Whalers never seemed to recover. The next three years saw three separate coaches: Jimmy Roberts, Paul Holmgren and Pierre Maguire. Emile Francis retired after a 47-year hockey career. Brian Burke replaced Johnston as g.m., but soon resigned to become senior vice president and director of hockey operations for the NHL. He was replaced by Holmgren. On the day the 1994 NHL Entry Draft was held in Hartford, the team was sold to Compuware owner Peter Karmanos, Thomas Thewes and former NHL goaltender Jim Rutherford for $47.5 million. Rutherford became g.m. and president, and Holmgren was named head coach.

Two more non-playoff seasons followed, and the end was near for the Hartford Whalers. On March 26, 1997, near the end of yet another lackluster season, Peter Karmanos confirmed suspicions as he announced that the franchise would be playing elsewhere come the 1997–98 season. While some die-hard fans did their best to prevent the move, launching a "Save the Whale" campaign in an effort to sell more tickets, it was announced that the Whalers would relocate to Raleigh, North Carolina. A new arena would be built there for the Hurricanes, but meanwhile the team would be playing at Greensboro Coliseum, which overnight became one of the NHL's largest arenas. Kevin Dineen scored the last Whaler goal in history as Hartford defeated the Tampa Bay Lightning, 2–1, in an emotional game on April 13, 1997. The Whalers finished out of the playoffs, but Karmanos predicted that the move to Carolina would be good for another 10 to 15 points.

It wasn't to be. The Carolina Hurricanes' first season was, to put it mildly, a stormy one. Deep in the heart of college basketball and NASCAR country in Greensboro, the Hurricanes did not attract as much attention as they had wished. There were problems with the personnel as well. Geoff Sanderson, the leading scorer of the 1996–97 team, was unhappy. He was traded away. Goalie Sean Burke, who had won four consecutive awards as the team MVP, did not play up to his usual standards. Plagued by this, as well as some off-ice problems, the successful goaltender also was traded. And finally, the team owners tried to lure all-star Sergei Fedorov away from the Detroit Red Wings with a $38 million offer sheet designed to sink the Wings' chances of matching. But, match they did, leaving Carolina without the superstar center.

But, there were some silver linings among the gray storm clouds that hung over the transferred franchise. Captain and team leader Keith Primeau was an important part of Canada's entry at the 1998 Nagano Olympics and led the Hurricanes in scoring. Power forward Gary Roberts, who had played only 43 games since the end of the 1993–94 season because of injuries, joined the team after one year of retirement and went on to be the third-leading scorer with 20 goals and 29 assists in only 61 games. And forward Sami Kapanen had a breakthrough year, amassing 63 points for a share of first place in team scoring, and turning a few heads in the league in the process.

Still commuting to Greensboro for games, Primeau and Kapanen led the 'Canes again in 1998–99. With the addition of goaltender Arturs Irbe and the free-agent acquisition of former Whalers great Ron Francis, Carolina won the newly created Southeast Division and made the playoffs for the first time in six years. In 1999–2000, the Hurricanes opened the season with nine straight road games before finally opening their brand-new arena in Raleigh on October 29, 1999. A sellout crowd of 18,730 saw the party spoiled by the New Jersey Devils, who scored a 4–2 victory. The Hurricanes averaged 12,400 fans per game at the Raleigh Entertainment and Sports Arena for an increase of over 4,000 per game from the season before in Greensboro. Despite the move to their new home, the dominant story for the first half of the Hurricanes' season was the holdout of Keith Primeau, who was eventually traded to the Philadelphia Flyers for Rod Brind'amour.

With a final record of 37–35–10–0, Carolina posted back-to-back .500-plus seasons for the first time since 1985–86 and 1986–87. Unfortunately, the Hurricanes were eliminated from playoff contention on the final day of the regular season as they finished one point behind the eighth-place Buffalo Sabres. Highlights of the season included Arturs Irbe setting franchise records for games (75) and wins (34) by a goaltender and Paul Maurice becoming the franchise's winningest coach. Ron Francis and Paul Coffey became the first teammates to top the 1,500-point plateau in the same season. They were just the sixth and eighth players, respectively, in NHL history to score 1,500 points. Francis led the team in scoring with 73 points, with Gary Roberts, Jeff O'Neill and Sami Kapanen each also scoring at least 23 goals. The Hurricanes solidified their blue line by dealing for star defenseman Sandis Ozolinsh at the 2000 Entry Draft

Carolina Hurricanes Year-by-Year Record

Season	GP	W	L	T	GF	GA	Pts	Finish	Division	Playoff Results
1979–80*	80	27	34	19	303	312	73	4th	Norris	Lost Prelim. Round
1980–81*	80	21	41	18	292	372	60	4th	Norris	Out of Playoffs
1981–82*	80	21	41	18	264	351	60	5th	Adams	Out of Playoffs
1982–83*	80	19	54	7	261	403	45	5th	Adams	Out of Playoffs
1983–84*	80	28	42	10	288	320	66	5th	Adams	Out of Playoffs
1984–85*	80	30	41	9	268	318	69	5th	Adams	Out of Playoffs
1985–86*	80	40	36	4	332	302	84	4th	Adams	Lost Div. Final
1986–87*	80	43	30	7	287	270	93	1st	Adams	Lost Div. Semifinal
1987–88*	80	35	38	7	249	267	77	4th	Adams	Lost Div. Semifinal
1988–89*	80	37	38	5	299	290	79	4th	Adams	Lost Div. Semifinal
1989–90*	80	38	33	9	275	268	85	4th	Adams	Lost Div. Semifinal
1990–91*	80	31	38	11	238	276	73	4th	Adams	Lost Div. Semifinal
1991–92*	80	26	41	13	247	283	65	4th	Adams	Lost Div. Semifinal
1992–93*	84	26	52	6	284	369	58	5th	Adams	Out of Playoffs
1993–94*	84	27	48	9	227	288	63	6th	Northeast	Out of Playoffs
1994–95*	48	19	24	5	127	141	43	5th	Northeast	Out of Playoffs
1995–96*	82	34	39	9	237	259	77	4th	Northeast	Out of Playoffs
1996–97*	82	32	39	11	226	256	75	5th	Northeast	Out of Playoffs
1997–98	82	33	41	8	200	219	74	6th	Northeast	Out of Playoffs
1998–99	82	34	30	18	210	202	86	1st	Southeast	Lost Conf. Quarterfinal
1999-2000	82	37	35	10	217	216	84	3rd	Southeast	Out of Playoffs

** Hartford Whalers*

CHICAGO BLACKHAWKS

THE SAGA OF THE CHICAGO BLACKHAWKS began during the mid-1920s with a telephone call to Major Frederic McLaughlin, a millionaire coffee baron and prominent American polo player. The Patrick brothers, Frank and Lester, who were disbanding the Western Hockey League, were on the other end of the wire. The WHL no longer could compete with the higher-salaried NHL and the Patricks were holding a fire sale. They convinced McLaughlin that there was money to be made out of hockey and that Chicago could have a ready-made team by purchasing the Portland (Oregon) Rosebuds for $200,000. Fortified with about one hundred of his aristocratic Windy City friends, including H.R. Hardwick, the Major formed a consortium, bought the franchise, moved the Rosebuds to Illinois and changed their name.

As a commander of the 333rd Machine Gun Battalion of the U.S. Army's World War I Expeditionary Force, the Major belonged to the 85th Blackhawk Division and felt a many-faceted affection for the name. He also was aware that a Chief Blackhawk headed an Indian tribe that roamed the plains of the Midwest. After McLaughlin named the team, his wife Irene Castle—a world-renowned ballroom dancer who had teamed with her former husband Vernon before he had died—designed the unique black-and-white striped uniforms with the head of Chief Blackhawk on the logo.

McLaughlin and friends found a home for the Black Hawks at the 6,000-seat Chicago Coliseum. More often than not the arena was home to cattle shows, but with the aid of an ice plant, the Black Hawks were ready for play in the 1926–27 season. (Until 1985–86, the name "Black Hawks" usually was written as two words.)

Thanks to the Patricks, McLaughlin not only acquired a coach in Pete Muldoon but a package of players that included coach-in-waiting Dick Irvin, Rabbit McVeigh, Mickey MacKay, George Hay, Percy Traub and Bob Trapp. For added scoring power, Babe Dye was obtained from the Toronto St. Pats. Dye was a poor skater, but was reputed to have the hardest shot in hockey and had been a top goal scorer throughout the 1920s. With 25 goals in 1926–27, Dye tied for second in the NHL and helped the Black Hawks finish third in the new American Division, whereupon McLaughlin—displaying an impatience that would be his hallmark—promptly fired coach Muldoon.

Whether the story is apocryphal remains debatable to this day, but legend has it that when Muldoon was fired he warned the Major that he would be sorry. "The Hawks will never finish first!" Muldoon hollered. "I'll put a curse on this team that will hoodoo it."

True hoodoo or not, the Chicagoans did seem cursed. During the 1927–28 training camp, Dye broke his leg in a scrimmage prank and the injury virtually ended his playing career. Without Dye to bolster their attack, the Hawks finished fifth in the American Division and wound up out of the playoffs. If they had anything worth cheering about, it was a young goaltender imported from the Winnipeg Maroons. His name was Charlie Gardiner, and he was slowly developing into one of the finds of the decade.

The 1928–29 season was another poor one for the Black Hawks, who scored just 33 goals in 44 games and were shut out in eight straight late in the season. With the Chicago Stadium slated to open the following season, Major

McLaughlin managed to let his lease with the Coliseum lapse, and the Black Hawks were forced to close out the year by playing home games on the road in Buffalo, Fort Erie, Detroit and Windsor. Things finally began to look up in 1929–30 when the Black Hawks moved their home base to the mammoth new structure on West Madison Street. The Chicago Stadium would hold more than 18,000 people, making it the largest rink in the NHL. By that season, Gardiner had improved so much that he finished second to Tiny Thompson of the Boston Bruins in the race for the Vezina Trophy. In 1932, he finally would win the coveted prize. The 1929–30 season saw the Black Hawks finish second to Boston, albeit a distant second, but they were eliminated by the Canadiens in the Stanley Cup semifinals. A year later they were runners-up to the Bruins again. However, this time they eliminated Toronto in the first round, New York in the second round, and advanced to the Cup finals before losing to the Canadiens. After coaching the team in 1930–31, Dick Irvin was released and later accepted a similar job with the Maple Leafs. It was too much to expect Major McLaughlin to follow Irvin with an equally competent coach. Instead, the Major chose a chap named Godfrey Matheson, who had absolutely no big-league hockey coaching experience.

Despite the Major's machinations, the Black Hawks had sold Chicagoans on big-league hockey and the NHL was so popular that grain millionaire James Norris, a Canadian with ties to the Montreal Athletic Association, applied for a second Windy City franchise to share Chicago with the Black Hawks. The Major wanted no part of that and stopped the Norris bid. But, Norris went to war and organized a competitive team, the Chicago Shamrocks, and entered them in the American Hockey Association in 1930–31. Norris further embarrassed McLaughlin by hiring Tom Shaughnessy—recently fired by the Major—as Shamrocks coach.

Playing at the Chicago Stadium (which was owned by Norris), the Shamrocks drew healthy crowds and won the AHA title in 1931–32. At season's end, Norris even issued a challenge for the Stanley Cup but was rejected by the NHL. Prior to the 1932–33 season, Norris bought into the Detroit Red Wings and folded the Shamrocks. McLaughlin and his Black Hawks now had the run of the Stadium, and they continued their futile pursuit of the Stanley Cup.

Charlie Gardiner's superlative goaltending kept the Hawks competitive. In 1933–34, Chicago finished second to Detroit in the American Division while Gardiner allowed only 83 goals in 48 games and posted 10 shutouts. In 14 other games, he permitted just one goal. But, astute Gardiner-watchers perceived that there was something unusual about the goalie's deportment. The goaltender had lost his jovial manner and appeared melancholy. There were many explanations, but it soon became apparent that Gardiner had been gravely ill all season. Two months after his heroic goaltending had led Chicago to its first Stanley Cup title, Gardiner collapsed and died of a brain hemorrhage in his hometown of Winnipeg. He was 29 years old.

Without Gardiner, the Black Hawks were no longer a Stanley Cup contender. But, McLaughlin had an arresting idea for bringing glory back to his hockey club. An ardent nationalist, he resented Canada's grip on hockey and believed that a team of all American-born players could well represent Chicago in the NHL.

He started with Mike Karakas (Aurora, Minnesota), Alex Levinsky (Syracuse, New York), Doc Romnes (White Bear, Minnesota) and Lou Trudel (Salem, Massachusetts). Although Canadian-born managers throughout the league mocked him, the Major urged his high command to add Americans whenever possible. By the 1937–38 season even the coach, Bill Stewart, was American.

The Americanized Black Hawks managed to plod along through the schedule at a slightly quicker pace than the Red Wings. The result was that Chicago finished third in the American Division, just two points ahead of its Detroit pursuers, but a good 30 points behind division-leading Boston. Their chances for winning the Stanley Cup were considered no better than 100–1. To begin with, the Hawks were the only one of the six qualifying teams to have less than a .500 record (14–25–9), and their first-round opponents were the Montreal Canadiens. Further complicating matters for Chicago was the fact that two of the three games would be played in the Montreal Forum.

Predictably, the Canadiens won the first match, 6–4. But, when the series shifted to Chicago, goalie Karakas shut out the Montrealers, 4–0. Suddenly the Black Hawks were coming on strong. The final game was tied 2–2 after regulation time. It was decided in Chicago's favor when Lou Trudel's shot bounced off Paul Thompson and into Montreal's cage, although some observers insist that the puck was shot home by Mush March.

Now the Black Hawks were to face an equally aroused New York American sextet that had just routed the archrival Rangers in three games. Once again, the Hawks would have the benefit of only one home game in the best-of-three series, but once again the Chicago team prevailed and advanced into the Stanley Cup finals against the Toronto Maple Leafs.

By now the betting odds had dropped considerably in Chicago's favor. But, they soared again when it was learned that Karakas had suffered a broken big toe in the final game with the Americans. Karakas didn't realize the extent of the damage until he attempted to lace on his skates for the game with Toronto. He just couldn't make it, and the Hawks suddenly became desperate for a goaltender. With the Leafs blocking Chicago's efforts to borrow Rangers goalie Dave Kerr, the Black Hawks turned to Alfie Moore, a minor-league goalie who purportedly was quaffing liquid refreshment in a Toronto pub when he was drafted to climb into the barrel for the Chicagoans. Moore answered the call and went into the Chicago nets on April 5, 1938, defeating Toronto 4–1 in the opening game of the series at Maple Leaf Gardens. Moore was deemed ineligible for game two, but with Karakas back by the third game, Chicago went on to defeat Toronto in what was one of the singular upsets in Cup history.

Stewart was the coaching hero of Chicago until the following season when McLaughlin fired him after 21 games. From that point on, for more than two decades, the Windy City's hockey fortunes dipped. There would not be another championship at Chicago Stadium for almost a quarter of a century. There were, however, some fun years, particularly at the outset of World War II, when a pair of fleet youngsters named Max and Doug Bentley teamed with Bill Mosienko to form the Pony Line, one of the best offensive trios the league has known.

In both 1945–46 and 1946–47, Max Bentley led the league in scoring, but Chicago was going nowhere and, early in the 1947–48 season, the Black Hawks sent Bentley to the Toronto Maple Leafs. The Leafs dispatched Gaye Stewart, Gus Bodnar, and Bud Poile—an entire forward line—as well as defensemen Bob Goldham and Ernie Dickens, to Chicago in return for Bentley and an unobtrusive forward named Cy Thomas. The deal correctly was called one of the most extraordinary ever made. Conn Smythe, the Toronto boss, immediately claimed the trade would become the basis for a hockey dynasty—and he was right. With centers such as Syl Apps, Ted Kennedy and Bentley, he had the best offense in the league. The Leafs finished first that season and romped to the Cup.

In contrast, the Hawks, even augmented with the ex-Leafs, continued to struggle. They always seemed to come up with adequate scorers, but defense never seemed to be part of their vocabulary. The team acquired new ownership on September 11, 1952, when James Norris Sr., James D. Norris Jr. and Arthur Wirtz obtained control of the team. The Norrises already owned the Detroit Red Wings and had an interest in Madison Square Garden. By 1954, brothers Arthur and Michael Wirtz held controlling interest. Bill Wirtz also joined his father and uncle in reinvigorating the Black Hawks organization.

The Red Wings and Black Hawks became frequent trading partners, and in 1952–53 a collection of ex-Detroiters including Jim McFadden, Jimmy Peters, George Gee, Gerry Couture and Lidio "Lee" Fogolin lifted Chicago to a fourth-place finish. With ex-Red Wing Sid Abel coaching while also doing considerable work at center, the Black Hawks marched into the Stanley Cup playoffs for the first time since the Bentley trade. The Black Hawks' most important asset was the goaltending of angular Al Rollins, perhaps the most underrated goalie the NHL has known. A former Maple Leaf, Rollins would win the Hart Trophy in 1953–54 despite Chicago's last-place finish that season. That season marked the first of five consecutive non-playoff years.

The decline of the Hawks nearly caused owner Jim Norris to forsake the game for more lucrative ventures. But, Norris finally was persuaded to invest a few million dollars in the rejuvenation of the franchise. He imported Tommy Ivan from the Detroit system and ordered him to develop a farm system from which Chicago could obtain a constant flow of young players. In the meantime, a few members of the league sympathized enough with the Chicago plight to promise help in some form or other. The talent-rich Canadiens finally cooperated by dealing the Hawks Ed Litzenberger, a muscular young forward of great promise.

By the 1955–56 season, the first trickles of new talent began flowing into Chicago Stadium. Such youngsters as Ken Wharram and Pierre Pilote pulled on Black Hawk jerseys and hardly seemed out of place against their more accomplished opponents. Soon the St. Catharines farm club began funneling such young talents as Bobby Hull and Hank Ciesla, and veterans were traded for hopefully better prospects. Chicago finished fifth in 1957–58, but the signs were clear that better days were ahead. The next season, they leaped into third place and gave Montreal a six-game run in the playoffs.

With Rudy Pilous at the helm, guiding the likes of Litzenberger, Hull, Pilote and Stan Mikita, Chicago remained a solid third-place team without making any playoff progress until 1961, when they again ran head-long into the Canadiens. Led by Glenn Hall's exceptional goaltending, Chicago captured the series, 4–2, and then defeated Detroit in six games. It had taken 23 long and often miserable years for the Hawks to win the Stanley Cup.

With the Stanley Cup finally returned to Chicago, the Hawks appeared ready for an assault on "The Muldoon Jinx." Certainly, with such stars as Hull, Hall, Mikita, and Pilote, they were the equal of any club in the league. But, when the chips were down, they didn't produce. They looked like sure champs in 1962–63, but they bowed out in the stretch, and as a result coach Pilous was fired. His successor, Billy Reay, who had once been fired by the Leafs, was imported from Buffalo in the American Hockey League. But, the next season the Black Hawks missed again and landed in second place, just a solitary point behind the champion Canadiens. In fact, the Black Hawks would not finish first in the NHL standings until the 1966–67 season. But, there were some highlights along the way, most notably in the 1965–66 season when Bobby Hull became the first player to break the 50-goal barrier when he collected his 51st against Cesare Maniago on March 12, 1966. He finished with 54 goals and broke the league points record with 97.

Following the NHL's expansion from six to 12 teams in 1967, one of the most damaging events in franchise history occurred when Black Hawks general manager Tommy Ivan dealt Phil Esposito, Ken Hodge and Fred Stanfield to Boston for Gilles Marotte, Pit Martin and a minor-league goalie named Jack Norris. The three ex-Hawks, all young forwards, were responsible for a Boston surge. The rangy Esposito set an NHL record for points in a single season with 126 for the Bruins in 1968–69, while the Black Hawks fell into last place in the East Division. But, the Black Hawks weren't dead for long. With Phil's brother Tony Esposito starring in goal, Chicago finished first in the East in 1969–70, and then were transferred to the West Division after further expansion in 1970–71 and finished on top once more. In the playoffs, they went all the way to the seventh game of the Stanley Cup finals before being defeated by the Montreal Canadiens.

Another telling blow occurred in 1972 when a contract dispute with the Wirtz family resulted in Windy City hero Bobby Hull bolting to the newly organized World Hockey Association. Despite NHL assertions that the WHA would quickly fold—causing Hull to return to the Black Hawks—it remained in business through the 1970s and Chicago lost its most colorful drawing card. But, once again the Black Hawks survived and, in some cases, thrived. Thanks to productive performers such as Stan Mikita, Jim Pappin and Ivan Boldirev, the Black Hawks remained competitive throughout the WHA years.

Stars like Denis Savard and Doug Wilson kept the club strong throughout the 1980s, but it wasn't until the 1991–92 season under coach Mike Keenan that the Blackhawks reached the Stanley Cup finals again. Despite the heroics of Ed Belfour, Jeremy Roenick, Steve Larmer and Chicago native Chris Chelios, they were eliminated by Pittsburgh in four straight games and have yet to reach similar heights again.

After 65 years in the historic Chicago Stadium, the Hawks moved across Madison Street for the 1994–95 season and into their new home, the United Center. However, by 1997–98, only Chelios remained of the Blackhawks' all-star nucleus from the early 1990s. Bob Pulford had departed as general manager after 20 years at the helm, turning over the position to Bob Murray. After a disastrous start to the season, the Blackhawks appeared to have their new house in order, but a weak finish saw the club miss post-season play for the first time since 1968–69. Third-year coach Craig Hartsburg lost his job, and the rebuilding process began anew with the hiring of former Blackhawk captain Dirk Graham to coach the team. However, Graham did not even last the entire 1998–99 season. The Blackhawks improved under new coach Lorne Molleken, who led them to a 13–6–4 record, but the team was never really in playoff contention. Tony Amonte had a fine season, leading the club in scoring for the third straight year, but expensive free-agent acquisition Doug Gilmour was less effective than hoped in a season cut short by injuries. Late in the year, Chelios was sent to the Detroit Red Wings for a package of prospects.

The club's hot finish under Molleken in 1998–99 did not carry over to the start of the 1999–2000 season. In December, Bob Pulford was brought out of semi-retirement in the upper levels of the front office to replace both Murray and Molleken, though Molleken stayed on as an associate coach. Mike Smith was added to the management team following a power struggle that had seen him lose his job in Toronto after the 1998–99 season. The changes led to only minimal improvements on the ice and the Blackhawks were never in playoff contention. Hampered by goaltending problems early in the season and the holdout of defenseman Boris Mironov, Chicago had slumped to last in the Western Conference at the midway point in the season, though once again they finished the year strongly. Amonte enjoyed another excellent year, ranking third in the NHL with 43 goals and seventh in scoring with 84 points.

Having missed the playoffs three seasons in a row, Mike Smith got an early start on the rebuilding process when he dealt Gilmour to the Buffalo Sabres at the 2000 trade deadline. Shortly after the season ended, he fired Lorne Molleken and made Alpo Suhonen, who had worked under him in both Winnipeg and Toronto, the first man born and raised in Europe to become a head coach in the NHL. Chicago fans hope that Smith will be as successful in salvaging the Blackhawks as he was in helping turn around the Maple Leafs.

Chicago Blackhawks Year-by-Year Record Record

Season	GP	W	L	T	GF	GA	Pts	Finish	Division	Playoff Results
1926–27	44	19	22	3	115	116	41	3rd	American	Lost Quarterfinal
1927–28	44	7	34	3	68	134	17	5th	American	Out of Playoffs
1928–29	44	7	29	8	33	85	22	5th	American	Out of Playoffs
1929–30	44	21	18	5	117	111	47	2nd	American	Lost Quarterfinal
1930–31	44	24	17	3	108	78	51	2nd	American	Lost Final
1931–32	48	18	19	11	86	101	47	2nd	American	Lost Quarterfinal
1932–33	48	16	20	12	88	101	44	4th	American	Out of Playoffs
1933–34	48	20	17	11	88	83	51	2nd	American	Won Stanley Cup
1934–35	48	26	17	5	118	88	57	2nd	American	Lost Quarterfinal
1935–36	48	21	19	8	93	92	50	3rd	American	Lost Quarterfinal
1936–37	48	14	27	7	99	131	35	4th	American	Out of Playoffs
1937–38	48	14	25	9	97	139	37	3rd	American	Won Stanley Cup
1938–39	48	12	28	8	91	132	32	7th		Out of Playoffs
1939–40	48	23	19	6	112	120	52	4th		Lost Quarterfinal
1940–41	48	16	25	7	112	139	39	5th		Lost Semifinal
1941–42	48	22	23	3	145	155	47	4th		Lost Quarterfinal
1942–43	50	17	18	15	179	180	49	5th		Out of Playoffs
1943–44	50	22	23	5	178	187	49	4th		Lost Final
1944–45	50	13	30	7	141	194	33	5th		Out of Playoffs
1945–46	50	23	20	7	200	178	53	3rd		Lost Semifinal
1946–47	60	19	37	4	193	274	42	6th		Out of Playoffs
1947–48	60	20	34	6	195	225	46	6th		Out of Playoffs
1948–49	60	21	31	8	173	211	50	5th		Out of Playoffs
1949–50	70	22	38	10	203	244	54	6th		Out of Playoffs
1950–51	70	13	47	10	171	280	36	6th		Out of Playoffs
1951–52	70	17	44	9	158	241	43	6th		Out of Playoffs
1952–53	70	27	28	15	169	175	69	4th		Lost Semifinal
1953–54	70	12	51	7	133	242	31	6th		Out of Playoffs
1954–55	70	13	40	17	161	235	43	6th		Out of Playoffs
1955–56	70	19	39	12	155	216	50	6th		Out of Playoffs
1956–57	70	16	39	15	169	225	47	6th		Out of Playoffs
1957–58	70	24	39	7	163	202	55	5th		Out of Playoffs
1958–59	70	28	29	13	197	208	69	3rd		Lost Semifinal
1959–60	70	28	29	13	191	180	69	3rd		Lost Semifinal
1960–61	70	29	24	17	198	180	75	3rd		Won Stanley Cup
1961–62	70	31	26	13	217	186	75	3rd		Lost Final
1962–63	70	32	21	17	194	178	81	2nd		Lost Semifinal
1963–64	70	36	22	12	218	169	84	2nd		Lost Semifinal
1964–65	70	34	28	8	224	176	76	3rd		Lost Final
1965–66	70	37	25	8	240	187	82	2nd		Lost Semifinal
1966–67	70	41	17	12	264	170	94	1st		Lost Semifinal
1967–68	74	32	26	16	212	222	80	4th	East	Lost Semifinal
1968–69	76	34	33	9	280	246	77	6th	East	Out of Playoffs
1969–70	76	45	22	9	250	170	99	1st	East	Lost Semifinal
1970–71	78	49	20	9	277	184	107	1st	West	Lost Final
1971–72	78	46	17	15	256	166	107	1st	West	Lost Semifinal
1972–73	78	42	27	9	284	225	93	1st	West	Lost Final
1973–74	78	41	14	23	272	164	105	2nd	West	Lost Semifinal
1974–75	80	37	35	8	268	241	82	3rd	Smythe	Lost Quarterfinal
1975–76	80	32	30	18	254	261	82	1st	Smythe	Lost Quarterfinal
1976–77	80	26	43	11	240	298	63	3rd	Smythe	Lost Prelim. Round
1977–78	80	32	29	19	230	220	83	1st	Smythe	Lost Quarterfinal
1978–79	80	29	36	15	244	277	73	1st	Smythe	Lost Quarterfinal
1979–80	80	34	27	19	241	250	87	1st	Smythe	Lost Quarterfinal
1980–81	80	31	33	16	304	315	78	2nd	Smythe	Lost Prelim. Round
1981–82	80	30	38	12	332	363	72	4th	Norris	Lost Conf. Final
1982–83	80	47	23	10	338	268	104	1st	Norris	Lost Conf. Final
1983–84	80	30	42	8	277	311	68	4th	Norris	Lost Div. Semifinal
1984–85	80	38	35	7	309	299	83	2nd	Norris	Lost Conf. Final
1985–86	80	39	33	8	351	349	86	1st	Norris	Lost Div. Semifinal
1986–87	80	29	37	14	290	310	72	3rd	Norris	Lost Div. Semifinal
1987–88	80	30	41	9	284	328	69	3rd	Norris	Lost Div. Semifinal
1988–89	80	27	41	12	297	335	66	4th	Norris	Lost Conf. Final
1989–90	80	41	33	6	316	294	88	1st	Norris	Lost Conf. Final
1990–91	80	49	23	8	284	211	106	1st	Norris	Lost Div. Semifinal
1991–92	80	36	29	15	257	236	87	2nd	Norris	Lost Final
1992–93	84	47	25	12	279	230	106	1st	Norris	Lost Div. Semifinal
1993–94	84	39	36	9	254	240	87	5th	Central	Lost Conf. Quarterfinal
1994–95	48	24	19	5	156	115	53	3rd	Central	Lost Conf. Final
1995–96	82	40	28	14	273	220	94	2nd	Central	Lost Conf. Semifinal
1996–97	82	34	35	13	223	210	81	5th	Central	Lost Conf. Quarterfinal
1997–98	82	30	39	13	192	199	73	5th	Central	Out of Playoffs
1998–99	82	29	41	12	202	248	70	3rd	Central	Out of Playoffs
1999-2000	82	33	39	10	242	245	*78	3rd	Central	Out of Playoffs

** Includes 2 points for regulation ties (RT)*

COLORADO AVALANCHE AND QUEBEC NORDIQUES

THE QUEBEC NORDIQUES strived for equal billing with the Montreal Canadiens in the province of Quebec for 23 years, seven of them spent in the World Hockey Association and 16 in the NHL. No matter how arduous the task, the Nordiques would enjoy their share of success in "The Battle of Quebec." Ironically, when the franchise relocated to Colorado, the influence of the Montreal Canadiens would be felt in a much more positive way.

In 1971, Guy Lafleur was the latest in a long line of homegrown superstars who had excelled in junior hockey in Quebec City and then graduated to the Canadiens. This grated on the provincial capital. Lafleur was in the second month of his rookie season with Montreal when news came on November 1, 1971, of a new professional league. The World Hockey Association would begin play the following October with 12 franchises. In February, a group of six Quebec businessmen purchased the rights of the San Francisco franchise and moved it to Quebec, where they would play as the Nordiques, a term that roughly translates to "North-men."

The Montreal influence was all pervasive, even as the infant franchise took its first steps. Veteran Montreal defenseman Jean-Claude Tremblay was the first player signed by the new team, on July 20, 1972, and Maurice Richard joined him as the team's first coach. The new team even managed a $1 million offer for Jean Beliveau to come out of retirement, but the former Quebec City star and Canadiens legend opted to remain in the Montreal head office. The Nordiques played their first WHA game on October 11, 1972, a 3–0 loss to Gerry Cheevers and the Cleveland Crusaders. Three days later, Richard admitted that he wasn't suited to coaching and resigned. Shortly thereafter, Hall of Fame netminder Jacques Plante joined the team as general manager.

Other former Canadiens, including the young duo of Marc Tardif and Rejean Houle (the team's top two draft picks in 1969), joined a mix of veteran NHL and minor pro stars that made Quebec a competitive team in its first seasons. Le Colisee was one of the best-attended WHA arenas. While other franchises in Canada and the United States foundered, the Nordiques built a loyal following in the province. Young stars in the Quebec Junior League now had an alternative to the Canadiens and the NHL when draft time came. The Nordiques scored a coup in 1974 when they signed 18-year-old Quebec Remparts star Real Cloutier.

The Nordiques challenged for the Avco Cup in their third season of 1974–75, but were swept in the finals by the Houston Aeros, who boasted the unique trio of Gordie Howe and his two sons, Mark and Marty. Two years later a local brewery invested $2 million in the team, and rookie coach Marc Boileau led the Nordiques to their first championship when the team edged out the Winnipeg Jets and Bobby Hull in seven games. That victory was savored in Quebec City, but paled against the exploits of the Canadiens. With Guy Lafleur in a six-year run of 50-goal seasons, the Canadiens captured the second of four straight Stanley Cup titles and were recognized as the power in hockey.

Although some fans cried out for a championship series between the Stanley Cup and Avco Cup winners, few executives in pro hockey paid much mind. Though they didn't know it, the fans were a lot closer to a reunification championship than they dared hope, as talks of a merger between the leagues, which had begun in 1974, were now being taken seriously. With the WHA providing a windfall in players' salaries, and the new league siphoning off junior-aged talents such as Wayne Gretzky, Mark Messier and Rod Langway, as well as opening the doors wide to such skilled Europeans as Ulf and Kent Nilsson and Anders Hedberg of Sweden, the NHL sought to institute damage control. During the 1978–79 season it was announced that four WHA teams would enter the NHL the following September. Although six WHA teams remained, only Quebec, Winnipeg, New England and Edmonton would join the league. The Cincinnati Stingers and the Birmingham Bulls would be dissolved. Significant talent was involved, and dispersed throughout the newly expanded NHL via the Entry Draft.

Coach Jacques Demers had several veterans available to him in Quebec's first NHL season, among them Marc Tardif, Real Cloutier, Robbie Ftorek, Dale Hoganson, Gerry Hart and Serge Bernier, and the team was astute in its inaugural pass at the drafting table, picking up Michel Goulet as well as junior stalwarts Dale Hunter and Lee Norwood. A more significant draft was that of Czech star Anton Stastny, although it seemed the big wing might never make it across the Atlantic because the powerhouses of Eastern Europe jealously protected their talent. Still, at season's end, none of the former WHA teams had a winning record. Only Edmonton and Hartford made the playoffs, but both were swept in their best-of-five division semifinals, although the Whalers may have cost the Canadiens a second shot at five straight championships when wing Pat Boutette downed Lafleur with a season-ending knee injury.

The Nordiques showed great improvement during the 1980–81 season and gave indications of future greatness. Quebec's success was the result of several factors: the hiring of a feisty coach from Quebec's junior league, Michel Bergeron; some judicious draft choices; and a special scouting expedition to Europe by team president Marcel Aubut and chief scout Gilles Leger. With the suspense and secrecy of a spy thriller, the Nordiques braintrust spirited away 1979 draft choice Anton Stastny—and netted a bigger prize, older brother Peter—from Czechoslovakia in the summer of 1980.

With the emergence of Jacques Richard (52 goals) and Goulet (32 goals), the arrival of Hunter (19 goals), young defensemen Mario Marois and Normand Rochefort and newly acquired goalie Daniel Bouchard, the Nordiques surged immediately. But the biggest influence by far was the Stastny brothers. Both scored 39 goals, and Peter added 70 assists to finish his Calder Trophy-winning season with 109 points. The Nordiques were now seen as a rising force, while Montreal apparently was floundering, both on the ice and in the front office.

"The Battle of Quebec" emerged as a premier NHL matchup in 1981–82 for several reasons. First and foremost, the Canadiens and Nordiques found themselves in the same division, the Adams, which meant a full slate of games at the Forum and Le Colisee each winter. Each game was no-holds-barred, and the same could be said for their first post-season meeting in April, 1982. The Canadiens had rebounded to claim first in the Adams with 118 points, 43 better than the fourth-place Nordiques, but all observers agreed that regular-season statistics would have little bearing on the playoffs.

The Canadiens handily defeated Quebec, 5–1, in the series opener, but the Nords rebounded 3–2 in the second game at the Forum and returned to Quebec with home-ice advantage to bounce the Canadiens, 2–1. With Montreal on the ropes, it was Quebec's turn to falter and Montreal silenced a boisterous Colisee crowd with a 6–2 walkover. Game five was the stuff of legend, with the Nordiques taking a 2–0 lead into the third period, even though they had been outplayed significantly by the home team. Mario Tremblay, a fiery wing who became famous for his confrontations with Nordiques coach Bergeron, pulled the Habs within one at 10:49, and then Robert Picard drew Montreal even 80 seconds later.

The teams were tied 2–2 after regulation play, although the Canadiens had swarmed the Quebec net. Early in overtime, Montreal attacked the Quebec zone but it was the Nordiques who would emerge victorious on a goal by Dale Hunter. From that point on, the two teams would meet as equals.

The Canadiens and Nordiques would face off in 113 regular-season games between 1979 and 1995. The Canadiens won 62, lost 39 and played 12 ties. The teams would meet five times in the playoffs. The Canadiens eliminated Quebec on three occasions (twice going on to win the Stanley Cup), while the Nordiques got the best of the Canadiens on the two other occasions but never went on to win the NHL's top prize. Nords–Habs playoffs were fraught with drama, including Peter Stastny's overtime goal in game seven of the 1985 division finals and Montreal's seven-game victory in 1987. The series that may have hurt the Quebec franchise the most came in 1993, the year

Montreal would go on to win its 24th Stanley Cup title.

After missing the playoffs for five straight seasons, which enabled the Nordiques to stockpile an impressive inventory of draft choices, Quebec fought the Bruins and Canadiens tooth-and-nail in the Adams Division, finishing second with 104 points—five behind Boston and two ahead of Montreal. Those five years had been torture for the Nordiques' faithful, and they sought vindication when the Adams Division semifinals began. The only relief of sorts during the five-year power outage had been the return of Guy Lafleur to Quebec. "The Flower" had retired from Montreal during the 1984–85 season, despondent over his apparently waning talent. After sitting out three seasons, during which he was inducted into the Hockey Hall of Fame, Lafleur came back for a single season with the Rangers and coach Michel Bergeron, and then the two were reunited in Quebec the following season. Lafleur would play two seasons for Quebec before putting a proper close to his playing career.

Lining up for the Nordiques against Montreal in 1993 were the harvests of so many rich draft years: Joe Sakic (1987, #15), Valeri Kamensky (1987, #129), Mats Sundin (1989, #1), Adam Foote (1989, #22) and Owen Nolan (1990, #1). Not in the lineup, however, was the biggest draft prize, Eric Lindros. Lindros had told the hockey world that he would not play in Quebec, but the Nordiques made him the top choice in 1991, anyway. Both sides became involved in a year-long soap opera that finally came to a head at the 1992 Entry Draft when Aubut entertained offers from all comers. He eventually decided on a five-player package plus cash, offered by the New York Rangers.

At this point, Philadelphia vice president Jay Snider complained his team's offer had been verbally accepted by the Nordiques, and he took his contention to the league. Independent arbitrator Larry Bertuzzi, a Toronto-based lawyer, was appointed and he eventually ruled in favor of Philadelphia. While that decision may have been embarrassing to the Nordiques president, the decision definitely would help the team. Coming to Quebec were forwards Peter Forsberg, Chris Simon and Mike Ricci, defensemen Kerry Huffman and Steve Duchesne, goalie Ron Hextall, draft choices in 1993 (Jocelyn Thibault) and 1994 (traded) and $15 million cash.

All but Huffman and Thibault were in the Quebec lineup against Montreal in 1993, as were other solid players such as Czech Martin Rucinsky and Russian Andrei Kovalenko. The Nordiques immediately jumped to a 2–0 series lead, but Montreal got back into the series with a 2–1 overtime win, then evened things with a 3–2 victory at the Forum. The game that took Quebec out of the series was played at Le Colisee, a 5–4 win by Montreal on Kirk Muller's overtime goal through Ron Hextall's legs. Two nights later, the aroused Habs thumped the dispirited Nords, 6–2, at the Forum and their season was over. It was the last playoff meeting between the teams.

While the Nordiques players were struggling on the ice in the 1993–94 season, dropping to fifth place in the Adams and out of the playoffs, a similar uphill battle was being waged off the ice by their president. Marcel Aubut, who represented a consortium of owners of the team, had taken his case to his community, his city government and the provincial government.

The Nordiques were victims of the 1990s disease in sports, an outdated facility and too few revenue streams, and the only cure would be a state-of-the-art new building, with control of concessions and parking, and tax breaks. The war of words was waged for two years, and the spirits and hopes of Quebec fans were raised in 1994–95 when the team, under new coach Marc Crawford, soared to the top of the Adams Division in a lockout-shortened season. Mats Sundin had been moved to Toronto for veteran wing Wendel Clark and defenseman Sylvain Lefebvre, and the young goaltending tandem of Jocelyn Thibault and Stephane Fiset showed poise beyond its years.

And then the bad news came all at once. The Nordiques were swept aside in six games by the Rangers, and three levels of government said no. Quebec's last game was a 4–2 loss at Madison Square Garden on May 16.

Nine days later, the Nordiques ownership group signed an agreement in principle with COMSAT Entertainment Group to sell the team. Ironically, it was on Canada Day, July 1, 1995, that the Nordiques announced that they were moving to Colorado. The Battle of Quebec was stilled forever. Despite the move, the long-reaching shadow of the Forum and the Montreal Canadiens would touch the hockey team once again, albeit in a positive manner.

The team's new home, Denver, had a tenuous connection with professional hockey, playing host to a succession of minor league teams and a WHA franchise called the Spurs over the years before the Kansas City Scouts moved to the Mile High City in 1976 and became the Colorado Rockies. A succession of coaches, including the colorful Don Cherry, led the team, and talented young stars like Rob Ramage, Barry Beck, Wilf Paiement and Lanny McDonald plied their trade with the Rockies until the franchise was moved to New Jersey after the 1981–82 season. Denver attempted half-hearted efforts at pro hockey after that until the Grizzlies entered the International Hockey League in 1993. A strong entry in the "I," the Grizzlies captured the Calder Cup championship in their inaugural season and averaged 12,000 fans per game at McNichols Arena. When the Avalanche came to town two years later, the Grizzlies moved to Salt Lake City.

It is rare that a team in a new city is competitive, and unlike the case of the Scouts/Rockies, this time Denver was getting a serious Stanley Cup contender. The team became a threat during the season, thanks to the influence of the Montreal Canadiens. The first move was made October 3, 1995, when former Montreal wing Claude Lemieux was acquired from New Jersey in a three-way deal. Lemieux had debuted with the Canadiens late in the 1985–86 season and scored 10 goals during the playoffs. Four months before joining Colorado, he had led New Jersey to its first Stanley Cup title and won the Conn Smythe Trophy as playoff MVP. Three weeks later, the Avalanche traded power forward Owen Nolan to San Jose to acquire the defensive quarterback they needed in Sandis Ozolinsh, but the team's biggest move still was two months away and came in the form of an early Christmas present from Montreal. On December 6, 1995, four days after a feud with coach Mario Tremblay became public knowledge, Patrick Roy was dealt to the Avalanche along with Canadiens captain Mike Keane in a blockbuster deal engineered by g.m. Pierre Lacroix. Goalie Jocelyn Thibault and forwards Andrei Kovalenko and Martin Rucinsky were sent to Montreal. Avalanche defenseman Uwe Krupp was driving around Denver when he heard the news and said to himself, "We've got a great chance to win the whole thing now."

On June 10, 1996, less than a year after acquiring an NHL franchise, Colorado won the Stanley Cup on a goal by Krupp in the third overtime period after a masterful postseason by Roy. While the Colorado sweep over the Florida Panthers in the finals was the stuff of champions, the real victory came in the conference finals when the Avalanche bested favored Detroit, a team that had won an NHL-record 62 games during the regular season, in a masterful six-game set.

The Avalanche have remained at the top of their conference with Detroit and the Dallas Stars since 1996, although the team has not returned to the Stanley Cup finals. Led by the likes of Sakic, Forsberg, Roy, Ozolinsh, Kamensky, Lemieux and Adam Deadmarsh, Colorado followed up its Stanley Cup championship with a Presidents' Trophy win in 1996–97, but dropped the Western Conference championship to the rival Red Wings, who finally went on to win the Stanley Cup. A year later, the Avalanche suffered a shocking first-round playoff loss to the Edmonton Oilers.

NHL realignment saw Colorado shifted into the newly created Northwest Division in 1998–99, and the club won its fifth straight division title. The emergence of rookies Milan Hejduk and Chris Drury (the Calder Trophy winner) as stars, and the late-season acquisition of Theo Fleury in a deal with Calgary made the Avalanche a Stanley Cup favorite heading into the playoffs. The Avalanche downed San Jose in six games before dropping the first two games of their second-round series with Detroit. The Avalanche rallied for four straight victories to eliminate the Red Wings, then took a three-games-to-two lead over Dallas in the Western Conference final before falling to the eventual Stanley Cup winners in seven games.

The offseason prior to the 1999–2000 season was an eventful one, as the Avalanche lost Fleury and Kamensky to the New York Rangers via free agency, but gained a new owner in Donald L. Strum of Liberty Media, who purchased the Avalanche, the Denver Nuggets basketball team and the Pepsi Center. (The entire package would later be purchased by Wal-Mart heir Stanley Kroenke, who is also part-owner of the St. Louis Rams football team. NHL approval of this purchase was given on June 20, 2000.) The Avalanche made their debut in the new 18,129-seat Pepsi Center on October 15, 1999, but with Peter Forsberg out because of offseason shoulder surgery and Joe Sakic also sidelined by injuries, Colorado started the new season slowly. Hedjuk and Drury continued to shine, as did rookie Alex Tanguay, but by early March, the Avalanche trailed the Edmonton Oilers in the Northwest Division standings.

On March 6, 2000, Colorado acquired Ray Bourque from the Bruins. After 20-plus seasons in Boston, Bourque had asked for a trade to a contender—though Colorado hardly looked like potential Stanley Cup champions when he arrived. However, the future Hockey Hall of Famer collected eight goals and six assists in his first 13 games with the Avalanche, sparking the team to a 10–2–1 record and its sixth straight division crown. Colorado carried an eight-game winning streak into the playoffs and wiped out the Phoenix Coyotes in five games. Facing Detroit in the second round for the second straight year, the Avalanche disposed of their rivals with relative ease in another five-game series. Bourque was hurt during the fourth game, and did not return until game three of the Conference final against Dallas. Bourque was key in a game-six victory that kept Colorado alive, but for the second year in a row the Avalanche fell to the Stars in seven games. Shortly after their season ended, Bourque, who could have become a free agent, signed a one-year deal to stay in Colorado.

Colorado Avalanche Year-by-Year Record

Season	GP	W	L	T	GF	GA	Pts	Finish	Division	Playoff Results
1979–80*	80	25	44	11	248	313	61	5th	Adams	Out of Playoffs
1980–81*	80	30	32	18	314	318	78	4th	Adams	Lost Prelim. Round
1981–82*	80	33	31	16	356	345	82	4th	Adams	Lost Conf. Final
1982–83*	80	34	34	12	343	336	80	4th	Adams	Lost Div. Semifinal
1983–84*	80	42	28	10	360	278	94	3th	Adams	Lost Div. Final
1984–85*	80	41	30	9	323	275	91	2nd	Adams	Lost Conf. Final
1985–86*	80	43	31	6	330	289	92	1st	Adams	Lost Div. Semifinal
1986–87*	80	31	39	10	267	276	72	4th	Adams	Lost Div. Final
1987–88*	80	32	43	5	271	306	69	5th	Adams	Out of Playoffs
1988–89*	80	27	46	7	269	342	61	5th	Adams	Out of Playoffs
1989–90*	80	12	61	7	240	407	31	5th	Adams	Out of Playoffs
1990–91*	80	16	50	14	236	354	46	5th	Adams	Out of Playoffs
1991–92*	80	20	48	12	255	318	52	5th	Adams	Out of Playoffs
1992–93*	84	47	27	10	351	300	104	2nd	Adams	Lost Div. Semifinal
1993–94*	84	34	42	8	277	292	76	5th	Northeast	Out of Playoffs
1994–95*	48	30	13	5	185	134	65	1st	Northeast	Lost Conf. Quarterfinal
1995–96	82	47	25	10	326	240	104	1st	Pacific	Won Stanley Cup
1996–97	82	49	24	9	277	205	107	1st	Pacific	Lost Conf. Final
1997–98	82	39	26	17	231	205	95	1st	Pacific	Lost Conf. Quarterfinal
1998–99	82	44	28	10	239	205	98	1st	Northwest	Lost Conf. Final
1999-2000	82	42	29	11	233	201	§96	1st	Northwest	Lost Conf. Final

** Quebec Nordiques*

§ Includes 1 point for a regulation tie (RT)

COLUMBUS BLUE JACKETS

THE ADDITION OF TEAMS in Columbus and Minnesota to the National Hockey League for the 2000–2001 season sees the league become a 30-club circuit and completes a wave of expansion that began on June 25, 1997, when those two cities were formally admitted into the NHL along with Nashville and Atlanta. Columbus will play in the Central Division of the Western Conference with the Chicago Blackhawks, Detroit Red Wings, Nashville Predators and St. Louis Blues.

Principal owner of the NHL's Columbus franchise is John H. McConnell, who announced the selection of the team name Blue Jackets on November 11, 1997. "We wanted a name that reflected the spirit and pride that exists in Columbus," McConnell said. "The Blue Jacket [an insect] is aggressive, industrious, multi-tasked, resourceful and fast—many of the qualities exemplified by our community." The name was selected after a name-the-team contest which drew over 14,000 entries and thousands of different suggestions.

The Blue Jackets were quick to start the process of putting some sting in their on-ice activities, hiring former Florida Panthers head coach Doug MacLean in February, 1998 as the franchise's first general manager. MacLean assembled a staff of scouts and consultants that includes former Los Angeles Kings general manager Sam McMaster and former NHL goaltender Rick Wamsley. Guiding the team on the ice will be Dave King, former coach of the Canadian national team whose previous NHL experience includes a head coaching job with the Calgary Flames and an assistant's role with the Montreal Canadiens.

The Blue Jackets will play out of Nationwide Arena, a $150-million facility privately financed by Nationwide Insurance Enterprises and the Dispatch Printing Company. Excavation for the arena began in June, 1998, with a formal groundbreaking ceremony on July 23. The mixed-use glass, brick and steel structure seats 18,500 for hockey and also houses an adjoining practice rink, an office building, retail space and restaurants.

COLUMBUS EXPANSION DRAFT SELECTIONS

PLAYER	POSITION	PREVIOUS CLUB
Rick Tabaracci	G	Colorado
Frederic Chabot	G	Montreal
Dwayne Roloson	G	Buffalo
Mattias Timander	D	Boston
Bert Robertsson	D	Edmonton
Tommi Rajamaki	D	Toronto
Jamie Pushor	D	Dallas
Lyle Odelein	D	Phoenix
Radim Bicanek	D	Chicago
Mathieu Schneider	D	NY Rangers
J. Andersson-Junkka	D	Pittsburgh
Geoff Sanderson	LW	Buffalo
Turner Stevenson	RW	Montreal
Robert Kron	LW	Carolina
Steve Heinze	RW	Boston
Tyler Wright	C	Pittsburgh
Kevyn Adams	C	Toronto
Dmitri Subbotin	LW	NY Rangers
Dallas Drake	RW	Phoenix
Bruce Gardiner	C	Tampa Bay
Barrie Moore	LW	Washington
Martin Streit	LW	Philadelphia
Kevin Dineen	RW	Ottawa
Jeff Williams	C	New Jersey
Sergei Luchinkin	LW	Dallas
Ted Drury	C	NY Islanders

DALLAS STARS AND MINNESOTA NORTH STARS

WITH THE EXCEPTION of the Canadian provinces, no similar region produces as many hockey players, nor is the game played as much per square mile, as in Minnesota. So when the NHL decided to expand to 12 teams in 1967, it was not surprising that the state was included.

In order to enter the NHL, Minnesota had to produce a suitable arena. This requirement was fulfilled when the splendid Metropolitan Sports Center was completed in Bloomington just prior to the start of the 1967–68 season. And with such eminent sportsmen as Gordon Ritz, Walter Bush, W. John Driscoll, Robert McNulty, Robert Ridder and Harry McNeely, Jr. on the North Stars' board, success was virtually guaranteed. Wren Blair, a veteran hockey organizer, was named coach and general manager and the building of the North Stars was under way. The first game of the season was held at Bloomington on October 21, 1967. The North Stars beat the Oakland Seals 3–1.

The young franchise was was dealt a stunning blow early in its existence with the death of 29-year-old Bill Masterton on January 15, 1968, two days after he sustained a brain injury in a game against Oakland. "Because he had the habit of giving everything he had for every second he was on the ice, Bill was the type of player who didn't have to score a lot of goals to help a club," said Wren Blair. Soon after the 1967–68 season, the NHL inaugurated a memorial award, the Bill Masterton Trophy, for perseverance, sportsmanship and dedication to hockey.

The North Stars finished fourth in the West Division and reached the NHL playoffs in their rookie season. They eliminated the Los Angeles Kings in a rugged seven-game first-round series, fighting back from 2–0 and 3–2 deficits. In the semifinals, Minnesota went up against the St. Louis Blues and carried the foe to seven games before losing 2–1 in double overtime.

The North Stars fell to the worst record in the NHL in their second season, but a complete house-cleaning by Blair turned things around in 1969–70. In 1970–71, he turned over coaching duties to Jack Gordon, and also infused the playing roster with significant names: defenseman Ted Harris, a hardrock ex-Canadien who became the team captain, veterans Doug Mohns and Lorne "Gump" Worsley, plus youngsters Jude Drouin and Barry Gibbs. Despite a fourth-place finish, the North Stars played mightily in the Stanley Cup competition, defeating the heavily favored St. Louis Blues in the first round.

Every young franchise requires a significant series to make it respectable. For the North Stars, it came in April, 1971 in a series with the fabled Montreal Canadiens. Conspicuous underdogs, the North Stars lost the series in six games, but not before giving the Montrealers considerable consternation. "None of us realized that the North Stars were that good," said Peter Mahovlich of the Canadiens. The Minnesotans obtained another measure of glory in the 1971–72 season, challenging Chicago for first place in the West before settling for a strong second-place position. Their eventual defeat by the Blues in the seventh game of the opening Cup round has gone down as a Stanley Cup classic.

Computations revealed that the North Stars' average attendance was 11,800 fans in their first NHL season, in a rink with a seating capacity of 15,095. By the third season the average had jumped to 14,351, and in the 1971–72 season it was next to impossible to find an empty seat in the building at any time. One reason for the club's popularity was its cast of characters.

It is doubtful that any NHL team ever boasted two such competent yet contrasting goaltenders as the Mutt and Jeff combination of Gump Worsley and Cesare Maniago. Worsley was short and round and tended his goal without the benefit of a protective face mask; tall and lean, Maniago wore a white mask with huge openings around the eyes that was suggestive of a World War I gas mask. Another marquee player was big, blond right wing Bill Goldsworthy, who played with flair and a shuffle that endeared him to rooters at the Met Center.

Led by Dennis Hextall, who tallied 30 goals and 52 assists, and all-stars Barry Gibbs and J.P. Parise, the North Stars enjoyed another solid season in 1972–73, but were defeated in the opening round of the playoffs by Philadelphia. The next five seasons were disappointing, as the North Stars were transformed into also-rans. The 1976–77 season did offer some hope, as Tim Young led the team in scoring with 95 points and Roland Eriksson (Minnesota's first Swedish import) added some scoring punch. Minnesota managed to finish second in the Smythe despite a mediocre 23–39–18 record, but whatever high hopes fans could have for a gallant playoff run reminiscent of the early 1970s was extinguished in the first round when the Buffalo Sabres swept a best-of-three series. The Stars' fell back to the bottom of the NHL pack in 1977–78. They managed just 18 wins and nine ties—and a whopping 53 losses.

Popular player Lou Nanne took over as coach and general manager late in the 1977–78 season. As g.m., he would soon help turn the franchise around, but things looked bleak for the financially struggling North Stars until an unprecedented merger with another cash-strapped franchise breathed some life into their roster.

The Minnesota franchise had been owned by a group of

investors led by team president Gordon Ritz since the club's inception. With the team fighting for its fiscal life, Ritz and company looked to cut their losses and sell to new investors, who, it so happened, were already owners of another struggling NHL franchise. Brothers George and Gordon Gund had also been suffering heavy monetary losses since they purchased the former Oakland Seals and moved them to Cleveland in 1976.

The Gunds knew it would be economic suicide to manage two losing hockey clubs at once. The solution? The two franchises merged and the Gunds assumed ownership of the Minnesota club while Cleveland folded. More significantly, all the players who had a contract with Cleveland were transferred to Minnesota, and the 1978–79 North Stars hit the ice with eight former Cleveland Barons. Right wing Al MacAdam and goaltender Gilles Meloche proved to be the best of a bunch.

But the most promising newcomer of 1978-79 was first-round draft choice Bobby Smith, a talented young center who burst on the scene in Minnesota with 30 goals and 44 assists that season. Smith's production earned him the team lead in scoring and the Calder Trophy as the NHL's rookie of the year.

These new players left the North Stars much improved. In 1980, they ended Montreal's bid for a fifth straight Stanley Cup title with a thrilling four-games-to-three victory in the quarterfinals. In 1981, they were demonstrating their proficiency by advancing to the Stanley Cup finals against the defending champion New York Islanders. Badly outgunned, the Minnesotans played gamely and averted a sweep with a 4–2 win in game four at home. The Islanders would clinch their second consecutive Cup title in with a 5–1 win in game five. The North Stars followed up their Stanley Cup appearance with a 94-point season to lead the Norris Division in 1981–82, but dropped an opening-round playoff series to Chicago. The Black Hawks would eliminate Minnesota again one year later, this time in the second round.

Bobby Smith was traded to Montreal 10 games into the 1983–84 season, but still the Stars regained the Norris Division title. Helping to fill the void created by Smith's absence was Brian Bellows, who contributed 44 goals. In the first round of the playoffs, the Stars faced and defeated their nemesis from Chicago in a tough five-game series. The second-round series against the St. Louis Blues also went the distance, with Minnesota prevailing at 6:00 of overtime in game seven on a goal by Steve Payne. But the powerhouse Edmonton Oilers steamrollered the Stars with a fast four-game sweep in the Campbell Conference finals.

The North Stars' loss seemed to affect them the following season. They finished 18 games under .500, but did earn a playoff berth, albeit against first-place St. Louis. Most were anticipating a quick series. And indeed it was—but it was Minnesota that blindsided the Blues with a sweep in the best-of-five first round. Keith Acton, who had been acquired from Montreal in the Bobby Smith trade, scored two game-winners in the series. The Stars were brought back down to earth in round two by—who else?—the Chicago Black Hawks.

The 1985–86 season was something of a bounce-back year. Broten bumped his numbers over 100 points for the first time in his career, Dino Ciccarelli, who had scored 55 goals in 1981–82 but just 15 in 51 games in 1984–85, was back with 44 goals. Bellows popped in 31 more. The Stars finished in second in their division, but this year St. Louis would turn the tables and eliminate them in the opening round of the playoffs. It would be the last postseason action the Stars would see for some time.

Thanks to a pair of key trades, the North Stars found themselves back in the pack for the playoffs of 1989. Dave Gagner, who had been acquired from the New York Rangers in 1987, came out of nowhere to lead the Stars in scoring in 1988–89 with 78 points. Mike Gartner, on the other hand, was already an established star in Washington when Minnesota traded fan-favorite Dino Ciccarelli for him in March, 1989. Also coming into prominence with the North Stars that year was goaltender Jon Casey. Led by this new corps—and, of course, Broten and Bellows—the Stars locked up third place in the Norris Division. Once again, however, they were knocked out of the playoffs by St. Louis. Making matters worse, the Gartner gamble didn't pay off; he went scoreless in the series and the Stars traded him to the Rangers for Ulf Dahlen next season.

In 1989–90, Minnesota fans got their first true glimpse of the man who would ultimately become their team's biggest star. Speedy center Mike Modano had 29 goals and 46 assists in his rookie campaign, earning him kudos as the rookie of the year as chosen by The Hockey News.

Meanwhile, Bellows banged home an impressive 55 goals that season and Broten's playmaking was as good as ever. But once again an old nemesis was there to ground the Stars: Chicago ousted them in the first round of a hard-fought seven-game series.

But the 1989–90 season was tumultuous in other ways for the Stars. Owners George and Gordon Gund threatened to move the team elsewhere (San Jose) if they didn't find a buyer who would pay $50 million. At the 11th hour Howard Baldwin and Norm Green pulled together the resources and purchased the team. The Gunds were granted an NHL expansion franchise for San Jose and reached an agreement that would see them retain a portion of the players on the Minnesota reserve list. The new San Jose team—later called the Sharks—would select players from the Minnesota system at a dispersal draft after the 1990-91 season.

The old regime, headed by general manager Jack Ferreira and coach Pierre Page, was replaced by a new one featuring former Flyers captain Bob Clarke as g.m. and ex-Montreal hero Bob Gainey as coach, but the 1990–91 season began ominously for the North Stars. They managed only one win in their first nine contests and continued to play poorly until January. A late-season slump nearly cost them a playoff spot, but the North Stars managed to hold on. What followed can only be described as a miracle run.

The North Stars—a fourth-place team that had finished 12 games under .500—defeated their traditional playoff foes in the next three rounds. First it was a 4–2 series win over Norris Division champs Chicago, then a 4–2 win over St. Louis in round two. Goalie Jon Casey outplayed rookie of the year counterpart Ed Belfour in round one, and shut down the deadly duo of 86-goal scorer Brett Hull and super-playmaker Adam Oates in round two. Minnesota hadn't won in Edmonton in more than 11 years, but needed only five games to defeat the Oilers for the Campbell Conference championship.

The Stanley Cup finals pitted two surprise American teams: Minnesota, who had finished 16th overall in the 21-team NHL, and Mario Lemieux's Pittsburgh Penguins, playoff participants only once in the previous eight years. The teams split the first two games before Minnesota took the third 3–1. Lemieux had sat out the match with recurring back spasms, but when he returned to the lineup in time for game four the Penguins' offense kicked into high gear. Behind Super Mario, the Pens took control of the series with a pair of victories before Lemieux's four-point outburst triggered an 8–0 victory over the shell-shocked Stars in game six. The 1991 trip to the finals would prove to be Minnesota's final flirtation with a Stanley Cup title.

The dispersal draft to stock the new San Jose franchise was held on May 30, 1991. As per prior agreement the Sharks claimed four players from the Stars' NHL roster and 10 from their farm system. As compensation, the North Stars were allowed to select players from other NHL clubs in the 1991 Expansion Draft.

By this time, owner Norman Green's stewardship of the club had become ensnared with financial and legal problems, and the North Stars followed up their gallant playoff run by finishing in fourth place in the Norris Division in 1991–92 and losing to Detroit in seven games in the first playoff round. As if to add to the troubles, the Met Center itself, once a jewel among ice rinks, suddenly became an also-ran among arenas when the Target Center opened in downtown Minneapolis. Arrangements to move the North Stars from Bloomington's suburbs to the inner city failed.

After 1991–92, Bob Clarke moved on to run the expansion Florida Panthers, leaving Bob Gainey to add general manager's duties to his coaching role. Despite Gainey's competence and Hall of Fame status, the Stars finished out of the playoffs in 1992–93.

Minnesota lost its NHL franchise in 1993. The North Stars were transferred to Dallas and became the first Texas-based team in the league. The word "North" was erased from the name. Thus truncated, the Dallas Stars' home games would be played at the 16,924-seat Reunion Arena, home of the NBA Mavericks. Before the season began the Stars made one more drastic change, sending goalie Jon Casey to Boston for Andy Moog to complete an earlier deal.

The Stars enjoyed a stellar first season in Texas, but showed signs of weakness one season later during the lockout-shortened 1994–95 campaign. Norman Green sold the club to media mogul Tom Hicks in December, 1995, but despite the infusion of cash and new blood, the Stars gave a harsh welcome to their new bosses when they finished with a 26–42–14 mark and didn't qualify for the 1995–96 postseason. On January 8, 1996, Gainey formally stepped down as coach to concentrate on his g.m. duties and brought Ken Hitchcock in to replace him. A highly successful junior coach, Hitchcock was guiding the Stars' International Hockey League affiliate in Kalamazoo when he got the call.

The addition of Hitchcock and dependable veterans like Guy Carbonneau and Joe Nieuwendyk couldn't help the Stars in what was ultimately a lost season—but they did lay the groundwork for a dramatic franchise turnaround. Dallas won the Central Division crown with a 38-point jump in 1996–97, but the Stars were upset in the first round of the playoffs by a red-hot Curtis Joseph in net for the Edmonton Oilers.

Taking much of the blame for the crushing upset was Moog, who was not re-signed by the Stars. For a new goaltender, Gainey looked to Ed Belfour, who had been traded by Chicago to San Jose and had no intentions of re-signing with the struggling Sharks. Gainey also signed free-agent defenseman Shawn Chambers, late of the 1995 New Jersey Cup-winning team. Later in the season, Dallas obtained forwards Mike Keane and Brian Skrudland from the Rangers. Both had prior experience as team captains, and both had played on Stanley Cup champions.

In a neck-and-neck race with the Devils and Red Wings for the best overall points record in 1997-98, the Stars won the Presidents' Trophy with 109 points (49–22–11) before taking a more determined run at the Stanley Cup. The road to the top wasn't easy, though. The Stars battled injuries during the entire season and at one time or another were missing such potent offensive forces as Nieuwendyk, Selke Trophy winner Jere Lehtinen and superstar Mike Modano. Leading the way in spite of those potentially disastrous absences were defensemen Sergei Zubov and Derian Hatcher.

With Belfour playing some of the best hockey of his life, Dallas eliminated San Jose in six games in the first round before exacting revenge on the Oilers in a five-game second-round test. But more injuries, particularly to Nieuwendyk (who was hurt in the first game against San Jose) caught up with the Stars in the Western Conference final. The Red Wings defeated Dallas in six games and went on to capture their second straight Stanley Cup championship. However the Stars would not be denied in 1998–99.

With Modano's 34 goals and 81 points leading the way, Dallas established club records with 51 wins and 114 points and captured the Presidents' Trophy for the second straight year. A four-game sweep of the Oilers was followed up with a tough six-game victory over the St. Louis Blues that featured four overtime games, including Dallas's 2–1 win in the clincher. Belfour, who had combined with Roman Turek to win the Jennings Trophy, then outdueled Patrick Roy as the Stars defeated Colorado in seven games to win the Western Conference championship. Belfour got the better of Dominik Hasek in the Stanley Cup finals, as Dallas captured the franchise's first NHL title in six games. Free-agent acquisition Brett Hull scored the Cup-winning goal for Dallas in triple overtime. Nieuwendyk led all playoff performers with 11 goals and won the Conn Smythe Trophy.

Having assembled a Stanley Cup winner, Bob Gainey was not about to rest on his laurels. To make room for promising youngsters like Blake Sloan, Brenden Morrow and Jonathan Sim, veterans like Pat Verbeek and Benoit Hogue were not re-signed. To avoid losing him in the expansion draft, Roman Turek was traded to St. Louis. However, the Stars struggled to start the 1999–2000 season—a situation that was compounded by the club's many injuries. The slow start had both Brett Hull and Mike Modano questioning Ken Hitchcock's defensive system. Though Modano ended the year with 38 goals (his most since scoring 50 in 1993–94) and Hull matched his father with 610 career scores, it was defense that continued to win in Dallas as the Stars soon got back on the winning track and topped 100 points for the fifth straight year in cruising to their fifth consecutive division title. Remarkably, Ed Belfour's 2.10 goals-against average was the highest of this three seasons with the Stars, but his .919 save percentage was the NHL's best by a thread over Jose Theodore of Montreal.

In the playoffs, the defending Stanley Cup champions once again knocked off the Edmonton Oilers in the first round (this time in five games), then beat the San Jose Sharks in five to set up a Western Conference final rematch with Colorado. Once again the series went seven tough games before Dallas emerged victorious. Ed Belfour had been brilliant throughout the playoffs so far, but he surrendered six goals in a stunning 7–3 loss to the New Jersey

Devils in game one of the Stanley Cup finals. Belfour blamed the flu and cold medications for his poor performance, and certainly looked more like himself in a second game victory. The Stars returned home with the series tied 1–1, but were beaten in two straight games and were on the verge of elimination when the series shifted back to the Meadowlands for game five. Beflour dug out the skates he had not worn since game six against Buffalo the year before and, in a contest that was remarkably similar, he blanked the Devils through more than 100 minutes of playing time before Mike Modano scored at 6:21 of triple overtime to give the Stars a 1–0 victory. But the Stars run as Stanley Cup champions ended at home two nights later when Jason Arnott scored for the Devils in double overtime.

Though the loss to New Jersey proved just how difficult it is to stay on top in the modern NHL, Dallas should rank among the league's elite for years to come. In the fall of 2001 the Stars are scheduled to move into the new American Airlines Center.

Dallas Stars Year-by-Year Record

Season	GP	W	L	T	GF	GA	Pts	Finish	Division	Playoff Results
1967–68*	74	27	32	15	191	226	69	4th	West	Lost Semifinal
1968–69*	76	18	43	15	189	270	51	6th	West	Out of Playoffs
1969–70*	76	19	35	22	224	257	60	3rd	West	Lost Quarterfinal
1970–71*	78	28	34	16	191	223	72	4th	West	Lost Semifinal
1971–72*	78	37	29	12	212	191	86	2nd	West	Lost Quarterfinal
1972–73*	78	37	30	11	254	230	85	3rd	West	Lost Quarterfinal
1973–74*	78	23	38	17	235	275	63	7th	West	Out of Playoffs
1974–75*	80	23	50	7	221	341	53	4th	Smythe	Out of Playoffs
1975–76*	80	20	53	7	195	303	47	4th	Smythe	Out of Playoffs
1976–77*	80	23	39	18	240	310	64	2nd	Smythe	Lost Prelim. Round
1977–78*	80	18	53	9	218	325	45	5th	Smythe	Out of Playoffs
1978–79*	80	28	40	12	257	289	68	4th	Adams	Out Of Playoffs
1979–80*	80	36	28	16	311	253	88	3rd	Adams	Lost Semifinal
1980–81*	80	35	28	17	291	263	87	3rd	Adams	Lost Final
1981–82*	80	37	23	20	346	288	94	1st	Norris	Lost Div. Semifinal
1982–83*	80	40	24	16	321	290	96	2nd	Norris	Lost Div. Final
1983–84*	80	39	31	10	345	344	88	1st	Norris	Lost Conf. Final
1984–85*	80	25	43	12	268	321	62	4th	Norris	Lost Div. Final
1985–86*	80	38	33	9	327	305	85	2nd	Norris	Lost Div. Semifinal
1986–87*	80	30	40	10	296	314	70	5th	Norris	Out of Playoffs
1987–88*	80	19	48	13	242	349	51	5th	Norris	Out of Playoffs
1988–89*	80	27	37	16	258	278	70	3rd	Norris	Lost Div. Semifinal
1989–90*	80	36	40	4	284	291	76	4th	Norris	Lost Div. Semifinal
1990–91*	80	27	39	14	256	266	68	4th	Norris	Lost Final
1991–92*	80	32	42	6	246	278	70	4th	Norris	Lost Div. Semifinal
1992–93*	84	36	38	10	272	293	82	5th	Norris	Out of Playoffs
1993–94	84	42	29	13	286	265	97	3rd	Central	Lost Conf. Semifinal
1994–95	48	17	23	8	136	135	42	5th	Central	Lost Conf. Quarterfinal
1995–96	82	26	42	14	227	280	66	6th	Central	Out of Playoffs
1996–97	82	48	26	8	252	198	104	1st	Central	Lost Conf. Quarterfinal
1997–98	82	49	22	11	242	167	109	1st	Central	Lost Conf. Final
1998–99	82	51	19	12	236	168	114	1st	Pacific	Won Stanley Cup
1999-2000	82	43	29	10	211	184	§102	1st	Pacific	Lost Final

** Minnesota North Stars*

§ Includes 6 points for regulation ties (RT)

DETROIT RED WINGS

THE MOTOR CITY'S PASSION for the game is etched at center ice of Joe Louis Arena. Detroit is Hockeytown. Has been for more than three-quarters of a century.

As the most successful American-based franchise in National Hockey League history, only the Montreal Canadiens and Toronto Maple Leafs have won more Stanley Cup titles than the nine captured by the Red Wings. The Detroit franchise has been part of the NHL since 1926. American expansion by the NHL brought the Boston Bruins into the fold in 1924, with the Pittsburgh Pirates and the New York Americans joining the following year.

The success of these moves led to more U.S. cities clamoring for NHL hockey, and the league had no fewer than 11 bids for NHL franchises from American-based groups at its 1926 spring meetings, including five from Detroit. As early as March, 1926, one of the groups made a bold attempt to acquire the rights to Edmonton's franchise in the Western Hockey League and move it to Detroit. "Detroit will have professional hockey, of that there is no doubt," said James Connors, a representative of the Detroit Hockey Club.

On May 15, a group that included former pro netminder Percy LeSueur was awarded the franchise. Charles King was named club president. Players were secured when the roster of the WHL's Victoria Cougars was purchased for $100,000. Art Duncan, who led the Pacific Coast Hockey Association in scoring with Vancouver in 1923–24, was signed and named player-manager.

On paper, it appeared Detroit had bought itself instant status as a contender. Victoria had won the Stanley Cup in 1925 and was the losing finalist in 1926. Among the players acquired were goaltender Harry "Hap" Holmes, who had backstopped four teams to Stanley Cup victories, and Frank Fredrickson, Jack Walker and Frank Foyston, superstars of the western circuits.

But, the Stanley Cup is won on the ice and the Detroit club, which kept the Cougars nickname, soon found the nucleus of its roster was past its prime and no longer had what it took to contend. Detroit played its home games in Windsor, Ontario, making it the first professional franchise to have a foreign country as home base. A disappointing first campaign concluded with a 12–28–4 record and a last-place finish in the NHL's five-team American Division. Financially, the team was more than $80,000 in the hole after just one season.

There would be plenty of changes before the puck would drop again. The most significant came May 16, 1927, when the Cougars announced that Jack Adams had been signed as manager. A star player who had just helped Ottawa win the Stanley Cup, Adams was chosen after the owners failed to lure Lester Patrick, who had coached the Cougars in the WHL, away from the New York Rangers.

The Olympia, Detroit's new rink, finally debuted on November 22, 1927. Johnny Sheppard scored for the Cougars, who lost, 2–1, to the Stanley Cup champion Senators.

Tight-fisted, indecisive ownership would be the trademark of Detroit's early years. Detroit made the playoffs just twice in its first seven seasons, losing in the first round on both occasions. The club tried changing players, changing sweaters and changing names, going from the Cougars to the Falcons in 1930, but where the Cougars hadn't roared, the Falcons couldn't soar.

Distraught during one of his team's many slumps, Adams concluded that it was because the Cougars had loaned backup goalie Porky Levine to Seattle of the Pacific Coast League, thus leaving his club with only one goalie to shoot at during practice. Team officials would not allow him to sign another netminder, so Adams had a wooden effigy of Porky constructed and outfitted in goalie equipment, including skates. The Detroit players pushed their pine Porky into place in front of the net during practice and sometimes took it out for pregame warmups.

Carving goaltenders out of plywood was a fact of life for Adams until the summer of 1932, when grain millionaire James Norris purchased the Detroit franchise. Norris had been a member of the Montreal Amateur Athletic

Association, a sporting club with cycling roots. The MAAA's teams were known by their club emblem and these Winged Wheelers were the first winners of the Stanley Cup in 1893. Norris decided a version of their logo was perfect for a team playing in the Motor City and on October 5, 1932, the club was renamed the Red Wings.

The winged wheel also was suitable, because this was a franchise that was about to turn things around and take off. Adams had used his eye for talent to methodically assemble the basis of a decent club. He added defenseman Doug Young and forwards Herbie Lewis, John Sorrell and Larry Aurie from the minor leagues, and acquired the rights to amateur Ebbie Goodfellow from the New York Americans.

Detroit reached the Stanley Cup semifinals the first season with Norris as owner and in 1933–34, bolstered by the midseason acquisition of goalie Wilf Cude on loan from the Montreal Canadiens, Detroit reached the Stanley Cup finals for the first time. Although the Red Wings lost the final to the Chicago Black Hawks, excitement finally was gripping the hockey fans of Detroit. But, just when everything seemed rosy, a large hole was cut in the lineup when Cude was recalled by the Habs.

Minus its goalie, Detroit fell out of the playoff picture again in 1934–35, but Adams still was looking ahead. He dispatched $50,000 and defenseman Teddy Graham to the St. Louis Eagles for forward Syd Howe and defenseman Ralph (Scotty) Bowman. Adams also acquired Normie Smith from the Eagles to fill the void in net. He converted Goodfellow, who had been the club's scoring leader, from forward to defense.

The final piece of the puzzle fell into place when Adams met with Boston coach Frank Patrick during the 1935 Cup finals in Montreal. "If I had Cooney Weiland, my club would be here," Patrick said of the Detroit wing. "If I had Marty Barry," responded Adams, referring to Boston's number-one center, "we'd win the Cup." On June 30, 1935, the deal was consummated—Barry and Art Giroux to Detroit for Weiland and Walt Buswell.

Adams proved a prophet. With Barry playing between Lewis and Aurie on the club's top forward unit, the Wings soared to the top of the NHL standings in 1935–36. Under the playoff format of the day, the first-place finishers from the league's two divisions would meet in the first round of the playoffs, with the winner advancing to the final. That meant Detroit would open at Montreal against the defending champion Maroons on March 24.

The game was scoreless after 60 minutes and through five overtime periods neither goaltender—Smith or Montreal's Lorne Chabot—had faltered. At 4:47 of the sixth overtime period, the game became the longest in NHL history, surpassing the 164:46 mark set by Boston and Toronto in 1933.

Late in the sixth overtime, wing Mud Bruneteau, recalled from the minors just two weeks earlier, came over the boards with Howe and Hec Kilrea. After Smith thwarted a Montreal rush, Kilrea broke down ice, Bruneteau at his side. He fed Bruneteau, who deked the sliding Chabot and ended hockey's longest game after 176 minutes and 30 seconds.

Smith stopped 89 shots in the game, which ended at 2:25 a.m. on March 25. He also shut out the Maroons in game two and his shutout sequence of 248:32 remains a playoff record. After sweeping the Maroons, the Red Wings bounced the Toronto Maple Leafs in the finals to win their first Stanley Cup title.

Detroit became the first American-based franchise to win consecutive Stanley Cup championships when the Wings downed the New York Rangers in 1937, even though minor-league goalie Earl Robertson, filling in for an injured Smith, played the final series. Buoyed by Robertson's performance, Adams sold minor-league goalie Turk Broda to Toronto shortly after the playoffs. It was a move he would live to regret.

The 1937–38 season would play a large role in mapping out Adams's future plans. Sticking with the same nucleus, he watched as his two-time Cup champs slipped out of the playoffs. Afterwards, Adams developed a theory that championship-caliber squads had a shelf life of approximately five years—a theory he would continue to put into practice.

The war years saw Detroit play in three straight finals. The Wings lost in 1941, won in 1943 and gained infamy in 1942. Taking a 3–0 lead in the best-of-seven series, Detroit lost game four and its coach when Adams was suspended by the NHL after assaulting referee Mel Harwood. Amazingly, Toronto—behind the goaltending of Broda—won four straight, the only time a team has rallied from a 3–0 deficit to win a best-of-seven Stanley Cup finals.

Goaltender John Mowers, defenseman Black Jack Stewart and center Syd Howe were Detroit stars of this era. In a club-record 15–0 win over the Rangers on January 23, 1944, Howe posted a hat trick to surpass Lewis (148) as Detroit's career goal-scoring leader. Eleven days later, also against the Rangers, Howe set another club mark, scoring six times in a 12–2 win. "I wonder what the boys in the shop will say now," pondered the soft-spoken Howe, who, like many U.S.-based NHLers during World War II, worked a day job at a war plant.

By now, the face of the NHL had changed—shrinking from 10 teams to six. Sponsorship of amateur teams by NHL clubs was now being employed to develop future talent. The league allotted each club the rights to all players playing within a 50-mile radius of that NHL city. That was good news for Toronto and Montreal and even Detroit, which could grab players from Southwestern Ontario. It didn't do much good at all for Boston, New York or Chicago, which might explain why the Maple Leafs, Canadiens and Red Wings were the only teams to win the Stanley Cup from 1942 to 1960.

Detroit reached the finals in 1945 and nearly turned the tables on Toronto. The Leafs won the first three games, Detroit the next three, but Toronto rallied to take the deciding contest. Even though his club had played in four Stanley Cup finals in five seasons, Adams stuck to his five-year plan. Harry Lumley replaced Mowers in goal. A rugged wing named Ted Lindsay and a slick center named Sid Abel also moved into the lineup.

If the NHL's modern era is designated by the advent of the red line in 1943, the golden era of the Detroit franchise is earmarked by the arrival of Gordie Howe in 1946. Labeled "the best prospect I've seen in 20 years" by Adams, Howe had a goal in his first NHL game against Toronto and two games later displayed his legendary mean streak for the first time, running Chicago goalie Paul Bibeault when he wandered from his net to play the puck.

Detroit finished first in 1948–49, starting a streak of seven first-place finishes—an NHL record. The Wings reached the finals in both 1948 and 1949, but both times were vanquished by their nemesis Broda and the Maple Leafs.

By this time, Howe was considered the NHL's most

complete player and Detroit's Production Line of Lindsay, Abel and Howe finished 1–2–3 in NHL scoring in 1949–50. This time, Detroit got the better of Broda and the Leafs in the playoffs, even though they had to do so without Howe. Howe suffered a severe head injury—but not a fractured skull, as is often reported—in Detroit's first playoff game in Toronto when he tried to hit Toronto's Teeder Kennedy, but miscalculated and put himself head-first into the boards.

"I enjoyed my last three Stanley Cups," reflected Howe, a six-time Hart Trophy winner, who captured the first of four consecutive NHL scoring crowns in 1950–51. "I don't remember much about the first one." His other three scoring titles would come in the next four seasons. Terry Sawchuk replaced Lumley in goal, and Red Kelly, veteran Bob Goldham and Marcel Pronovost, pilfered out of Quebec from right under the Canadiens' noses, anchored the defense. Classy forward Alex Delvecchio, who would play 24 seasons in Detroit, was added to the mix.

Detroit beat the New York Rangers in the 1950 final, and had Stanley Cup wins over Montreal in 1952, 1954 and 1955. In 1952, the Red Wings became the first team to sweep through the playoffs, going 8–0. Sawchuk, considered by many to be the greatest goaltender in the game, posted four shutouts.

Wins in 1950 and 1954 had come in more dramatic fashion—game-seven overtime goals. Pete Babando (1950) and Tony Leswick (1954) were the scorers. Detroit also vanquished the Canadiens in a seven-game final in 1955, prompting The Hockey News to predict that Detroit was plotting "to imprison the Stanley Cup for all time." Ever the wheeler-dealer, Adams went to work on another rebuilding project shortly after the 1955 Cup win. He made a nine-player deal with Chicago and an eight-player trade with Boston, which sent Sawchuk to the Bruins.

This time, the moves backfired. "He definitely took the heart and character out of that team with those trades and he didn't get much in return," said Hall of Fame defenseman Pronovost. Adams took issue with Lindsay's attempts to organize a player's union in 1957 and shipped him and goalie Glenn Hall to Chicago. He dealt talented young forward John Bucyk to Boston to get Sawchuk back. By 1958–59, the once-mighty Wings were a last-place club. Adams was gone in 1962, retiring to take over as president of the Central Hockey League.

The Red Wings reached the finals again in 1961, 1963, 1964 and 1966, but each time came out a loser, blowing the 1966 series after winning the first two games in Montreal. From 1967 to 1986, Detroit would reach the playoffs just four times. "They just got rid of so much great talent," said Howe, who retired in 1971 as the NHL's all-time scoring leader, having worn the winged wheel for a quarter-century. He was selected to 21 NHL All-Star teams in 26 seasons. "They made bad trades, the people didn't come up through the system and they made more bad trades trying to fill the holes."

Another Detroit revival was launched in 1982, when Mike and Marian Ilitch purchased the club from the Norris family, installing Jim Devellano as general manager. Devellano picked center Steve Yzerman in the first round of the 1983 NHL draft. Yzerman remains the pillar of the franchise today.

Under coach Jacques Demers, workmanlike Detroit clubs reached the Stanley Cup semifinals in 1987 and 1988, reviving fan interest. But, the best was yet to come. In the 1989 draft, the Wings raided Europe for defensemen Nicklas Lidstrom and Vladimir Konstantinov and forward Sergei Fedorov. All were playing key roles in Detroit by the early 1990s.

Scotty Bowman, the NHL's winningest coach, was hired in 1993. A year later, the club acquired veteran goalie Mike Vernon from Calgary and reached the Stanley Cup finals for the first time since the 1966 fiasco.

Although swept by New Jersey, the Wings rebounded to set an NHL record with 62 wins (62–13–7) in 1995–96. Bowman picked up legends Igor Larionov and Slava Fetisov to play with Fedorov, Konstantinov and Slava Kozlov as part of an all-Russian unit. Rugged wing Brendan Shanahan and skilled defender Larry Murphy came aboard in 1997, and in a sweep of Philadelphia, returned the Stanley Cup to the Motor City for the first time in 42 years.

The euphoria was short-lived. Konstantinov and team masseur Sergei Mnatsakanov suffered life-threatening head injuries in an automobile accident just a week after the final game. Vernon, who won the Conn Smythe Trophy as the most valuable player in the playoffs, was dealt to San Jose, following in the tradition of Jack Adams who had dealt away Harry Lumley (1950) and Sawchuk (1955) shortly after they'd won Cup titles.

In 1997–98, the Red Wings finished behind the Dallas Stars and the New Jersey Devils with the third-best record overall. In the playoffs, Chris Osgood provided steady goaltending and rebounded heroically from the occasional weak goal. The Red Wings won 16 games to match Konstantinov's jersey number 16, concluding the postseason on June 16 with a sweep of the Washington Capitals for their second straight Stanley Cup title. After he accepted the NHL's top prize (and his first major individual honor, the Conn Smythe Trophy as playoff MVP), captain Steve Yzerman placed the Stanley Cup in the lap of Konstantinov, who had been brought onto the ice in his wheelchair.

The Red Wings entered the 1998–99 season as favorites to win the Stanley Cup once again. Detroit got off to a quick start under the guidance of associate coaches Dave Lewis and Barry Smith while Scotty Bowman recovered from off-season surgery, but the Red Wings were a very ordinary team for most of the season. Not until deals at the trade deadline added Wendel Clark and Bill Ranford from Tampa Bay, Chris Chelios from Chicago and Ulf Samuelsson from the Rangers did Detroit finally look capable of winning a third straight Stanley Cup title. The Red Wings ended the regular season with 93 points and the top spot in the Central Division. They opened the playoffs with a convincing four-game sweep of Anaheim, and though Chris Osgood hurt his knee in the clinching victory over the Mighty Ducks, Ranford stepped in to score two straight victories over the Avalanche in Colorado.

Heading back to Detroit, the Red Wings seemed poised for a sweep of their fierce Western Conference rivals. Suddenly Ranford seemed to lose the magic and the Avalanche evened the series. Even the return of Osgood for game five couldn't stop the sudden and surprising slide, and Colorado wrapped up the series in six.

Anxious to atone in 1999–2000, the Red Wings came out strongly and had the NHL's best record through the first half of the season. Year's end would find them with 48 wins for their best total since their record-breaking 62-win campaign, though their 108 points were only good for second overall, and second place in the Central Division, behind the St.

Louis Blues. Detroit did lead the NHL with 279 goals—the league's highest total in four years. The Red Wings were led by captain Steve Yzerman, who topped the team with 79 points and cracked the top 10 in the NHL for the first time since 1992–93. (Yzerman would also be named a First Team All-Star, the first all-star honor of his career.) Brendan Shanahan led Detroit with 41 goals. Pat Verbeek, picked up after he was released by the Dallas Stars, added 22 tallies to the Red Wings total, including the 500th of his career. Chris Chelios proved a good fit among a veteran defense corp led by Nicklas Lidstrom. The former Blackhawk recorded a +48 to trail only Chris Pronger of St. Louis among the league leaders. But, the true measure of success in Detroit these days comes in the playoffs, and after sweeping the Los Angeles Kings in the opening round, the Red Wings were ousted by the Avalanche in the second round for the second straight year—this time in only five games.

As the NHL's most successful team in the 1990s, the Red Wings may now need to rethink their direction, but Detroit should continue to contend in the new millennium. Solid ownership and management and a raucous fan base will ensure that this is the case. "Winning has always been a priority around here," Yzerman has said.

Hockeytown wouldn't have it any other way.

Detroit Red Wings Year-by-Year Record

Season	GP	W	L	T	GF	GA	Pts	Finish	Division	Playoff Results
1926–27***	44	12	28	4	76	105	28	5th	American	Out of Playoffs
1927–28	44	19	19	6	88	79	44	4th	American	Out of Playoffs
1928–29	44	19	16	9	72	63	47	3rd	American	Lost Quarterfinal
1929–30	44	14	24	6	117	133	34	4th	American	Out of Playoffs
1930–31**	44	16	21	7	102	105	39	4th	American	Out of Playoffs
1931–32	48	18	20	10	95	108	46	3rd	American	Lost Quarterfinal
1932–33*	48	25	15	8	111	93	58	2nd	American	Lost Semifinal
1933–34	48	24	14	10	113	98	58	1st	American	Lost Final
1934–35	48	19	22	7	127	114	45	4th	American	Out of Playoffs
1935–36	48	24	16	8	124	103	56	1st	American	Won Stanley Cup
1936–37	48	25	14	9	128	102	59	1st	American	Won Stanley Cup
1937–38	48	12	25	11	99	133	35	4th	American	Out of Playoffs
1938–39	48	18	24	6	107	128	42	5th		Lost Semifinal
1939–40	48	16	26	6	90	126	38	5th		Lost Semifinal
1940–41	48	21	16	11	112	102	53	3rd		Lost Final
1941–42	48	19	25	4	140	147	42	5th		Lost Final
1942–43	50	25	14	11	169	124	61	1st		Won Stanley Cup
1943–44	50	26	18	6	214	177	58	2nd		Lost Semifinal
1944–45	50	31	14	5	218	161	67	2nd		Lost Final
1945–46	50	20	20	10	146	159	50	4th		Lost Semifinal
1946–47	60	22	27	11	190	193	55	4th		Lost Semifinal
1947–48	60	30	18	12	187	148	72	2nd		Lost Final
1948–49	60	34	19	7	195	145	75	1st		Lost Final
1949–50	70	37	19	14	229	164	88	1st		Won Stanley Cup
1950–51	70	44	13	13	236	139	101	1st		Lost Semifinal
1951–52	70	44	14	12	215	133	100	1st		Won Stanley Cup
1952–53	70	36	16	18	222	133	90	1st		Lost Semifinal
1953–54	70	37	19	14	191	132	88	1st		Won Stanley Cup
1954–55	70	42	17	11	204	134	95	1st		Won Stanley Cup
1955–56	70	30	24	16	183	148	76	2nd		Lost Final
1956–57	70	38	20	12	198	157	88	1st		Lost Semifinal
1957–58	70	29	29	12	176	207	70	3rd		Lost Semifinal
1958–59	70	25	37	8	167	218	58	6th		Out of Playoffs
1959–60	70	26	29	15	186	197	67	4th		Lost Semifinal
1960–61	70	25	29	16	195	215	66	4th		Lost Final
1961–62	70	23	33	14	184	219	60	5th		Out of Playoffs
1962–63	70	32	25	13	200	194	77	4th		Lost Final
1963–64	70	30	29	11	191	204	71	4th		Lost Final
1964–65	70	40	23	7	224	175	87	1st		Lost Semifinal
1965–66	70	31	27	12	221	194	74	4th		Lost Final
1966–67	70	27	39	4	212	241	58	5th		Out of Playoffs
1967–68	74	27	35	12	245	257	66	6th	East	Out of Playoffs
1968–69	76	33	31	12	239	221	78	5th	East	Out of Playoffs
1969–70	76	40	21	15	246	199	95	3rd	East	Lost Quarterfinal
1970–71	78	22	45	11	209	308	55	7th	East	Out of Playoffs
1971–72	78	33	35	10	261	262	76	5th	East	Out of Playoffs
1972–73	78	37	29	12	265	243	86	5th	East	Out of Playoffs
1973–74	78	29	39	10	255	319	68	6th	East	Out of Playoffs
1974–75	80	23	45	12	259	335	58	4th	Norris	Out of Playoffs
1975–76	80	26	44	10	226	300	62	4th	Norris	Out of Playoffs
1976–77	80	16	55	9	183	309	41	5th	Norris	Out of Playoffs
1977–78	80	32	34	14	252	266	78	2nd	Norris	Lost Quarterfinal
1978–79	80	23	41	16	252	295	62	5th	Norris	Out of Playoffs
1979–80	80	26	43	11	268	306	63	5th	Norris	Out of Playoffs
1980–81	80	19	43	18	252	339	56	5th	Norris	Out of Playoffs
1981–82	80	21	47	12	270	351	54	6th	Norris	Out of Playoffs
1982–83	80	21	44	15	263	344	57	5th	Norris	Out of Playoffs
1983–84	80	31	42	7	298	323	69	3rd	Norris	Lost Div. Semifinal
1984–85	80	27	41	12	313	357	66	3rd	Norris	Lost Div. Semifinal
1985–86	80	17	57	6	266	415	40	5th	Norris	Out of Playoffs
1986–87	80	34	36	10	260	274	78	2nd	Norris	Lost Conf. Final
1987–88	80	41	28	11	322	269	93	1st	Norris	Lost Conf. Final
1988–89	80	34	34	12	313	316	80	1st	Norris	Lost Div. Semifinal
1989–90	80	28	38	14	288	323	70	5th	Norris	Out of Playoffs
1990–91	80	34	38	8	273	298	76	3rd	Norris	Lost Div. Semifinal
1991–92	80	43	25	12	320	256	98	1st	Norris	Lost Div. Final
1992–93	84	47	28	9	369	280	103	2nd	Norris	Lost Div. Semifinal
1993–94	84	46	30	8	356	275	100	1st	Central	Lost Conf. Quarterfinal
1994–95	48	33	11	4	180	117	70	1st	Central	Lost Final
1995–96	82	62	13	7	325	181	131	1st	Central	Lost Conf. Final
1996–97	82	38	26	18	253	197	94	2nd	Central	Won Stanley Cup
1997–98	82	44	23	15	250	196	103	2nd	Central	Won Stanley Cup
1998–99	82	43	32	7	245	202	93	1st	Central	Lost Conf. Semifinal
1999-2000	82	48	24	10	278	210	§108	2nd	Central	Lost Conf. Semifinal

** Team name changed to Red Wings. ** Team name changed to Falcons. *** Team named Cougars.*

§ Includes 2 points for regulation ties (RT)

EDMONTON OILERS

THE EDMONTON OILERS were facing an uncertain future in the spring of 1998. The team was up for sale. Local sportsmen were scrambling around, talking to bank managers, financial wizards and potential investors, attempting to raise millions of dollars in time to meet a Friday, March 13 deadline. Their goal was to save the team and keep it in Edmonton. On deadline day, a local ownership group of 17 investors did rescue the franchise by announcing its decision to purchase. The sale was approved by the NHL on April 27. By the 1999–2000 season, the team was headed up by a 37-person ownership group.

The Oilers will face a new challenge in 2000–2001 when they open the season without Glen Sather, architect of the club's Stanley Cup dynasty. Sather had joined the team in 1976 and served in the dual role of coach and general manager when the club entered the NHL in 1979. He soon added the role of president to his resumé and became one of the league's most respected administrators. Sather stepped down from the Oilers' front office on May 19, 2000, and joined the New York Rangers. In his place, the club named former defenseman and coach Kevin Lowe to the general manager's job while Craig MacTavish, who had served as an assistant in 1999-2000, became the head coach.

The history of the Oilers franchise dates back to 1972 and the inaugural season of the World Hockey Association. Despite predictions by NHL moguls that "a rival league will never get off the ground or on the ice," the WHA opened for business as a 12-team circuit with Eastern and Western divisions. The Alberta Oilers, with Bill Hunter as spokesman, Ray Kinasewich as coach and Jim Harrison as the new league's early scoring leader, were named for the province because initially the franchise was to split its games between Calgary and Edmonton. This idea was abandoned before the WHA opened for business. In 1973–74, the team name was changed to Edmonton Oilers. Later, Edmonton and Calgary would become fierce rivals in the NHL.

Prior to the 1977–78 season, six WHA cities—Edmonton, Quebec, Hartford, Winnipeg, Houston and Cincinnati—were told they would be welcomed into the NHL fold—for $2.9 million apiece. But, at a subsequent meeting, Toronto Maple Leafs owner Harold Ballard persuaded some of the NHL governors to kill any merger plans. The war between the two leagues continued. The Oilers could not decide whether to continue operating or to fold. Two weeks before the season opener, two schedules were in place: one including the Oilers and one without. New owner Peter Pocklington was said to be trying to buy the NHL's Colorado Rockies. Meanwhile, the Oilers decided to continue playing and finished in fifth place in the revamped eight-team league. The Oilers were eliminated in the playoffs by New England, whose most famous player, Gordie Howe, became a grandfather during the series.

Early in the 1978–79 season, the Edmonton Oilers announced the acquisition of teenage sensation Wayne Gretzky from the Indianapolis Racers. The announced price for Gretzky, Eddie Mio and Peter Driscoll was $850,000. In Edmonton, Gretzky signed a 21-year personal services contract with Peter Pocklington, the longest player agreement in hockey history, and one said to be worth between $4 and $5 million. The pact was signed at center ice before 12,000 fans on January 26, 1979—Gretzky's 18th birthday.

The NHL, by a vote of 14–3, agreed to accept four WHA clubs for the 1979–80 season. Edmonton was one of them. Cost of entry was $6 million. During the final WHA season of 1978–79, the Oilers led all clubs with 48 wins and 98 points. Gretzky was third in league scoring with 46 goals and 110 points. Edmonton was upset by the Winnipeg Jets in the final series for the Avco Cup, and fans wondered if Wayne Gretzky would find life more difficult in the NHL.

Upon entry into the NHL, the Oilers used one of their two Expansion Draft priority selections to retain Gretzky. In the annual NHL Entry Draft, the Oilers selected teenager Mark Messier who had jumped from Tier II junior hockey to the Cincinnati Stingers of the WHA the previous season. Edmonton was placed in the Smythe Division of the NHL in 1979–80, along with its fellow WHA refugees from Winnipeg. Gretzky set a scoring record for first-year players with 137 points, but was declared ineligible for the Calder Trophy because of his WHA service. Gretzky's 137 points tied the Kings' Marcel Dionne atop the NHL scoring list, but Dionne won the Art Ross Trophy by virtue of having scored 53 goals to Gretzky's 51. The Oilers finished the season in fourth place in their division, but were swept aside by Philadelphia in the first round of the playoffs.

Bryan Watson was behind the Oiler bench for the 1980–81 season, but was fired after just 18 games and replaced by team president and general manager Glen Sather, who had coached the club in its first year. Gretzky finished the 1980–81 season with a league-record 164 points, then led the Oilers to a major playoff upset as the 14th-place club stunned the third-place Montreal Canadiens in three straight games. "I guess we've come of age," chuckled rookie defenseman Paul Coffey. The Oilers then carried the New York Islanders to six games before bowing out in the quarterfinals. Gretzky won both the Art Ross and Hart trophies.

During the 1981–82 season, Wayne Gretzky signed a new contract calling for $20 million over the next 15 years and making him the NHL's highest-paid player. Gretzky scored 50 goals through the first 39 games of the season and broke Phil Esposito's record of 76 goals in his 64th game. His year-end accomplishments included a record 92 goals, 120 assists and 212 points. The Oilers cruised to top spot in the Smythe Division but were then shocked when the lowly Los Angeles Kings eliminated them in the first round of the playoffs.

Gretzky captured most of the headlines again in 1982–83, winning the scoring crown for the third straight season. The Oilers finished third overall with 106 points, but they amassed a record number of goals—424—and Gretzky, Messier and Glenn Anderson all topped 100 points. The Oilers reached the Stanley Cup finals, only to be ousted in four games by the Islanders.

They would not be denied in 1983–84.

Gretzky had yet another remarkable season with 87 goals, 118 assists and 205 points as the Oilers smashed their own record for goals in a season with 446. In the spring of 1984, the Oilers overpowered the Islanders to win the Stanley Cup in five games. Peter Pocklington said: "No question. I can see we're going to keep the Cup in Edmonton." On May 30, 1985, at Northlands Coliseum, the Oilers bounced the Philadelphia Flyers, 8–3, in game five of the final series and captured their second Stanley Cup title. Gretzky compiled a record 30 assists and 47 playoff points in just 18 games.

The 1985–86 season saw Gretzky collect an amazing 215 points, breaking his own record. His 163 assists represented more points than any other player had ever scored in a season. Paul Coffey, with 48 goals, broke Bobby Orr's record for most goals by a defenseman. Jari Kurri became the first European player to win the goal-scoring title with 68. The Oilers finished on top of the standings with 119 points, but lost to Calgary in the playoffs when rookie defenseman Steve Smith's clearing attempt resulted in an accidental goal against the Oilers in game seven. Intent on redeeming themselves, the Oilers finished on top of the overall standings with 106 points in 1986–87, and advanced to the Stanley Cup finals against the Philadelphia Flyers. The Oilers won the series in seven games and celebrated their third Stanley Cup victory.

Prior to the 1987–88 season, Paul Coffey announced: "It will be impossible for me to wear the Oiler jersey ever again." He was irate over remarks made by Peter Pocklington that allegedly questioned the two-time Norris Trophy winner's courage. Coffey was traded to Pittsburgh in return for Craig Simpson and defenseman Chris Joseph.

That season, Gretzky scored a goal to tie Mike Bossy for fifth place in career goals (573) but on the play he injured a knee and missed 13 games. Later, Gretzky passed Gordie Howe to become the National Hockey League's all-time assists leader. The Oilers slipped to second place behind Calgary in the Smythe Division, but managed to eliminate the Flames in four games in the division final. The Oilers moved on to oust the Detroit Red Wings in the conference final. In the Cup finals, they easily defeated Boston in four games to win their fourth Cup title in five years. Gretzky won the Conn Smythe Trophy after compiling 43 playoff points, but Mario Lemieux captured the Hart Trophy, ending Gretzky's eight-year reign as hockey's top player.

Hockey's most publicized wedding took place in Edmonton on July 16, 1988, when Gretzky married Hollywood actress Janet Jones. On August 9, 1988, news of the greatest trade in history rocked the hockey world as Gretzky was dealt to the Los Angeles Kings. The Oilers received $15 million as part of the multiplayer deal. Without Gretzky, Edmonton slid to third place in the Smythe Division behind Los Angeles and first-place Calgary. In the first round of the playoffs, the Oilers blew a 3–1 lead in games and lost to Gretzky and the Kings.

The 1989–90 season got under way with John Muckler

behind the Oiler bench. On October 15, 1989, Gretzky returned to Edmonton as a visiting player with the Kings and scored the tying goal against Bill Ranford late in the game. The goal marked his 1,851st regular-season point and broke Gordie Howe's record of 1,850. He then scored the game-winning goal in overtime. That same week, Jimmy Carson (a 100-point scorer for the Oilers in 1988–89 after coming over in the Gretzky trade) announced his retirement from hockey because he "can't get mentally up for the games." Glen Sather suspended him, then traded him to Detroit in a deal that brought Joe Murphy, Adam Graves and Petr Klima to Edmonton. All three would be key contributors when the Oilers beat Boston to win the Stanley Cup in 1990. Goalie Bill Ranford captured the Conn Smythe Trophy. At the victory celebration, Mark Messier said: "This one's for you, Gretz." Messier was named winner of the Hart Trophy for 1989–90.

Prior to the 1990–91 season, Jari Kurri returned to Europe to play hockey. Goalie Grant Fuhr received a one-year suspension after admitting to past substance abuse. Later, Fuhr's suspension was reduced to 60 games. The Oilers won just two of their first 15 games and almost slid into the basement. Come the playoffs, the Oilers, with Fuhr back in goal, ousted Calgary in seven games and the Kings in six. Mark Messier was severely hobbled by injuries in the Conference finals and the Oilers lost to the Minnesota North Stars in six games.

In 1991–92, Ted Green replaced John Muckler as coach, but after Fuhr and Anderson were traded to Toronto, the Oilers were only a pale imitation of their former selves. In 1992–93, they missed the playoffs for the first time. Owner Peter Pocklington announced he'd move the Oilers to Hamilton if he didn't get a better lease arrangement. He later filed a letter with the league requesting permission to move the Oilers.

In 1993–94, the Oilers slipped to the bottom of the renamed Pacific Division with a 25–45–14 record. Rookie coach George Burnett took over in 1994–95, but was fired after 35 games and replaced by Ron Low. Still, the Oilers finished just one point ahead of the expansion Mighty Ducks of Anaheim during the lockout-shortened 48-game season. In 1995–96, the Oilers missed the playoffs for the fourth year in a row.

In September, 1996, NHL commissioner Gary Bettman announced that Oilers season ticket sales must rise from 6,800 to 13,000 for the team to qualify for the NHL's Canadian Assistance Plan. Oiler fans bought the tickets. They were rewarded when the Oilers crept close to .500 hockey with a 36–37–9 record and a third-place finish in the Pacific Division. In the playoffs, Curtis Joseph starred as the Oilers ousted the Dallas Stars (second overall) in seven games. But, the Oilers couldn't match the speed and scoring of the Avalanche in round two and fell in five games. Coach Low was rewarded with a contract extension.

Led by Doug Weight, the Oilers qualified for the 1998 playoffs and proceeded to engineer another upset, defeating the Colorado Avalanche in seven games after trailing three games to one. Goaltending by Joseph and strong team defense held the Avalanche to just one goal over the final three games of the series. Facing the Stars in the second round, Edmonton could not continue the Cinderella story and was dropped by Dallas in five games.

Curtis Joseph had been the star of two great Oilers playoff runs, but after the 1997–98 season, he signed with the Toronto Maple Leafs as a free agent. Mikhail Shtalenkov and Bob Essensa shared goaltending duties, but it was not until Tommy Salo was acquired from the Islanders on March 20, 1999, that Edmonton was able to outdistance Calgary for the final playoff spot in the West. There would be no playoff miracles, as the Stars swept the Oilers in the opening round.

Under new coach (and former Oilers star) Kevin Lowe, Edmonton opened the 1999–2000 season without sniper Bill Guerin, who was holding out for a new contract. Guerin slumped after returning to the lineup, but the scoring slack was picked up by Alexander Selivanov, who emerged as one of the NHL's most productive goal-getters in the early going. Selivanov's production would decline, be he would still wind up with 27 goals, second on the club behind Ryan Smyth's 28. Guerin rebounded to net 24, but the top offensive player in Edmonton was Doug Weight. He recovered from an injury plagued 1998–99 campaign to lead the club in scoring for the sixth time in seven years with 72 points. Jason Smith anchored the Oilers blueline, but the club's key performer was netminder Tommy Salo. His solid play was the main reason Edmonton battled Colorado for top spot in the Northeast Division for much of the season. A strong finish by the Avalanche relegated the Oilers to a battle with the Phoenix Coyotes and San Jose Sharks for the sixth, seventh and eighth seeds in the Western Conference playoffs. Edmonton wound up seventh and had to face Dallas once again in the first round of the playoffs. Though they battled hard, the Oilers were defeated in five games.

Shortly after the Oilers were eliminated from the playoffs, stories began to spread that Wayne Gretzky was going to become a minority owner of the Phoenix Coyotes (which he did) and that Glen Sather might join him in the desert (which he did not). There were also reports that Sather might wind up in Calgary, though the most persistent—and ultimately true—talk was that Sather would wind up in New York with the Rangers. Though there were also reports that Kevin Lowe would follow Sather to New York, he remained in Edmonton and succeeded Slats as general manager. Assistant coach Craig MacTavish was bumped up to head man behind the bench.

Edmonton Oilers Year-by-Year Record

Season	GP	W	L	T	GF	GA	Pts	Finish	Division	Playoff Results
1979–80	80	28	39	13	301	322	69	4th	Smythe	Lost Prelim. Round
1980–81	80	29	35	16	328	327	74	4th	Smythe	Lost Quarterfinal
1981–82	80	48	17	15	417	295	111	1st	Smythe	Lost Div. Semifinal
1982–83	80	47	21	12	424	315	106	1st	Smythe	Lost Final
1983–84	80	57	18	5	446	314	119	1st	Smythe	Won Stanley Cup
1984–85	80	49	20	11	401	298	109	1st	Smythe	Won Stanley Cup
1985–86	80	56	17	7	426	310	119	1st	Smythe	Lost Div. Final
1986–87	80	50	24	6	372	284	106	1st	Smythe	Won Stanley Cup
1987–88	80	44	25	11	363	288	99	2nd	Smythe	Won Stanley Cup
1988–89	80	38	34	8	325	306	84	3rd	Smythe	Lost Div. Semifinal
1989–90	80	38	28	14	315	283	90	2nd	Smythe	Won Stanley Cup
1990–91	80	37	37	6	272	272	80	3rd	Smythe	Lost Conf. Final
1991–92	80	36	34	10	295	297	82	3rd	Smythe	Lost Conf. Final
1992–93	84	26	50	8	242	337	60	5th	Smythe	Out of Playoffs
1993–94	84	25	45	14	261	305	64	6th	Pacific	Out of Playoffs
1994–95	48	17	27	4	136	183	38	5th	Pacific	Out of Playoffs
1995–96	82	30	44	8	240	304	68	5th	Pacific	Out of Playoffs
1996–97	82	36	37	9	252	247	81	3rd	Pacific	Lost Conf. Semifinal
1997–98	82	35	37	10	215	224	80	3rd	Pacific	Lost Conf. Semifinal
1998–99	82	33	37	12	230	226	78	2nd	Northwest	Lost Conf. Quarterfinal
1999-2000	82	32	34	16	226	212	*88	2nd	Northwest	Lost Conf. Quarterfinal

* *Includes 8 points for regulation ties (RT)*

FLORIDA PANTHERS

IN 1972, THE WORLD HOCKEY ASSOCIATION granted a franchise to Miami for its inaugural season. But, the Screaming Eagles never got off the ground. Twenty years later, in November, 1992, H. Wayne Huizenga launched his NHL project.

Huizenga, who spent his early years in Chicago, was part-owner of the National Football League Miami Dolphins and also had purchased the expansion Florida Marlins baseball team. As chairman of Blockbuster Entertainment, he already had established himself as a major player in merchandising, but he had no interest in hockey until a chance meeting with then-NHL board chairman and Los Angeles Kings head Bruce McNall. McNall and interim NHL president Gil Stein informed Huizenga that Disney soon would be admitted to the league as owners of an Anaheim franchise and another nationally known company like Blockbuster would be welcome at the same time. Although Huizenga may have had doubts about including a major-league hockey team in his portfolio, he took the gamble and on December 10, 1992, NHL owners approved both the Miami and Anaheim applications. The new franchises would begin operations for the 1993–94 season, which meant there was precious little time to organize an office staff and no time to build a new rink for the team-to-be. The club would play out of the Miami Arena, home to the NBA Heat, until a state-of-the-art facility could be constructed.

As for the club's high command, the key selection would be the team's general manager and the race narrowed to Washington Capitals g.m. David Poile and Philadelphia Flyers senior vice president Bob Clarke, whose position was largely ceremonial. Clarke was hired on March 1, 1993. Needing a president to oversee the operation, Huizenga opted for Bill Torrey, architect of the New York Islanders' Stanley Cup dynasty of the early 1980s. As a nickname, Huizenga settled on "Panthers," in part because the Florida panther had been designated the official state animal—even though there were fewer than 100 left in the wild.

For the team's first coach, Clarke selected Roger Neilson, who had directed the New York Rangers to their most productive record in a half-century in 1991–92. When it came to stocking the team, the Panthers were fortunate. The NHL created more favorable rules—better than those accorded Ottawa and Tampa Bay—for Miami and Anaheim, and the Panthers hit the ground running. With Torrey and Clarke masterminding the selections, Neilson got the tough defensive team he wanted. Brian Skrudland, who would become team captain, was renowned for his work ethic, as were players such as Bill Lindsay, Tom Fitzgerald, Mike Hough and Dave Lowry. Others such as Gord Murphy and Scott Mellanby also were proven big leaguers.

Goaltending can make or break a club, and in that department Neilson got a big break. Onetime Rangers hero John Vanbiesbrouck was made available and was promptly snapped up by the Panthers. To serve as backup, the Panthers picked former Islander Mark Fitzpatrick. Torrey made further use of his Long Island past when he landed Billy Smith as a goaltending coach.

Surrounding the veterans with first-rate young players was the next objective, which meant adroit scouting among the Canadian junior ranks. Clarke's prize selection was Rob Niedermayer, a big, highly touted forward (and kid brother of New Jersey Devils ace defenseman Scott Niedermayer) who was believed to be ready to make the difficult jump to the NHL directly from amateur hockey.

The brand-new Panthers opened training camp on September 10, 1993, and kicked off their first season on October 6 against the Blackhawks at Chicago Stadium. Despite suggestions that the new club could not help but be overwhelmed by one of the Original Six, the final score was 4–4. A loss to St. Louis in game two was followed by a match at Tampa Bay's ThunderDome, viewed by an NHL record 27,227. Vanbiesbrouck registered a 2–0 shutout and Florida had posted its first NHL victory. More important than wins and losses, South Florida sports fans had instantly taken to the team. They jammed Miami Arena all season long.

Past the halfway mark and into the home stretch, the Panthers continued to be competitive. At one point they were five games over .500, but then the dreaded slump occurred and the Panthers plummeted. They were knocked out of playoff contention during the final week of the season. Still, the first-year results were impressive. The Panthers won 33 games and finished with 83 points. Their .494 won-lost percentage was the best for a first-year team in modern pro sports history. However, the front office suffered a blow when Clarke returned to Philadelphia to run the Flyers organization. His replacement would be Bryan Murray, who had established a good reputation in both coaching (for Washington) and managing (for Detroit).

With first pick in the 1994 Entry Draft, the Panthers selected Ed Jovanovski, a rugged defenseman from the Windsor Spitfires. Murray also obtained productive veterans such as Ray Sheppard, but in a lockout-shortened 1994–95 season, the Panthers didn't begin play until January 21, 1995, when they opened against the Islanders at Nassau Coliseum. The 2–1 loss would set a tone for the rest of the season. Neilson brought his club to the brink in the final days of the schedule but had to settle for another non-playoff year. Granted, the Panthers missed by only one point, but that fact rankled management and the scapegoat was Neilson. Doug MacLean was appointed coach on July 24, 1995. Management claimed Neilson's defense-first orientation had slowed the club's progress.

Under Neilson, the Panthers were lacking something to set them apart from the NHL's other new franchises. This would change in the second game of the 1995–96 season at Miami Arena. A few minutes before game time, a rat darted into the Panthers locker room, heading straight for Scott Mellanby. The Florida forward grabbed his stick and used the rat as a puck, slapping it so hard it catapulted across the room and off the wall—dead. An hour later, he starred in the Panthers' 4–3 win over Calgary, scoring two goals. Following the victory, several reporters approached Mellanby, who was being kidded by Vanbiesbrouck. The three-goal hat trick was replaced at Miami Arena by the two-goal "rat trick."

Newspapers reported the rodent assault a day later, and a number of fans picked up on it. When Mellanby registered another hot night, his goals were greeted with a shower of plastic and rubber rats. "Pretty soon they were throwing rats no matter who scored," Mellanby recalled, "and all of a sudden, we had an identity." And because the club was enjoying its best season yet, the population of ersatz rats increased as the wins multiplied and enthusiasm grew.

Under MacLean's direction, the Panthers had become a better team than they had been in their previous two seasons. After 50 games, the club boasted a 31–14–5 mark and ranked among the NHL elite. Although a slump followed, the Panthers managed to stumble to the finish line with enough points to earn a playoff berth.

They were not expected to advance beyond the opening playoff round, since their first-round foe was the Boston Bruins, then the league's hottest team. But, a three-goal outburst in the first period of the Panthers' initial playoff game set a tone for the series. They stunned Boston with a four-games-to-one upset and next faced a daunting challenge in the Philadelphia Flyers. The series would not prove as easy as the opener with Boston, but Florida prevailed again, this time in six games. Among the highlights was the neutralizing of Philadelphia behemoth Eric Lindros by rookie sensation Ed Jovanovski.

Having disposed of the Broad Street Bullies, the Panthers then stunned Mario Lemieux and the Pittsburgh Penguins in seven games.The main man for the Panthers, as he had been throughout the playoffs, was Vanbiesbrouck. He thwarted the best Lemieux had to offer in a throbbing seventh match that was tied 1–1 early in the third period. Instead of faltering, the Panthers went on to score an improbable 3–1 victory. In only its third year, the expansion club was headed for the Stanley Cup finals.

Facing the Panthers for the Cup were the transplanted Quebec Nordiques, now playing out of Denver as the Colorado Avalanche. The series lasted only four games, but the fact that Florida went down in a sweep was deceptive. In game four, which went into three sudden-death overtime periods, the Panthers hurled 63 shots at Avalanche goalie Patrick Roy. Deadlocked at 0–0, the game lasted beyond 1 a.m. on a damp Miami morning before Uwe Krupp, the hulking Colorado defenseman, blasted a slapshot past Vanbiesbrouck at 4:31 of the sixth period of play.

Disheartened though they were, South Floridians had become dedicated to their club. Approval had been given for construction of a new arena in the city of Sunrise, which would be home to the Panthers by the start of the 1998–99 season. In the meantime, the team continued filling Miami Arena through 1996–97 with a zestful brand of hockey that was good enough for a second straight playoff berth. Optimism prevailed as the Panthers entered the playoffs against Wayne Gretzky, Mark Messier and the rest of the New York Rangers.

For a brief moment, it appeared that the 1996 playoff success would be repeated. Vanbiesbrouck thwarted New York 3–0 in the opener at Miami Arena, but the Rangers rebounded for four wins in a row.

Overall, two playoffs in two years was a major positive for the young franchise, which appeared on the rise—until its high command changed in the offseason. When Lindy Ruff resigned as assistant coach to become head coach of the Buffalo Sabres in 1997–98, the Panthers lost a valuable resource behind the bench. Once the season began, the evidence suggested problems. Jovanovski's declining play continued to be a problem, Vanbiesbrouck could not hold the club together on his own, and a perilous slump produced a major shakeup in the front office.

Murray fired MacLean and assumed the coach's role while remaining the manager. (After the season he would hire his brother, Terry, who had previously been an NHL head coach in Washington and Philadelphia.) By late March, 1998, the Panthers had lost 13 consecutive games. "The underdog team that charmed South Florida and reached the Stanley Cup Finals only two years ago is no more," commented Miami Herald columnist Greg Cote.

Florida was eliminated from playoff contention long before the season's end, leaving a bitter taste with fans. But, if there was a sweet use of the adversity, it was the prospect that starting in October, 1998, the still-young franchise would play its home games at a spanking new rink in suburban Sunrise—the National Car Rental Center. The Panthers did lose John Vanbiesbrouck to free agency, but the 1998–99 season saw the team pick up its first offensive superstar. On January 17, 1999, Florida sent a package of players including Ed Jovanovski to Vancouver in a deal that brought them Pavel Bure in return. "The Russian Rocket" scored 13 goals in just 11 games for Florida before a knee injury cut short his season. The loss of Bure effectively ended any chances of catching the Carolina Hurricanes in the newly created Southeast Division, and once again the Panthers missed the playoffs.

Though Bure battled injuries early in the 1999–2000 campaign, he certainly delivered everything the Panthers could have hoped for. His 58 goals were 14 more than anyone else in the NHL and represented the league's best total since Mario Lemieux scored 69 in 1995–96. Bure won the Maurice Richard Trophy as the league's top goal scorer and his 94 points saw him finish just two behind Jaromir Jagr in the battle for the Art Ross Trophy. Goaltender Trevor Kidd was another reason why the Panthers got off to a fast start. His shoulder injury in December could have been a severe blow, but the acquisition of Mike Vernon from the San Jose Sharks kept the Panthers in contention not only for the Southeast Division title but also for the best-overall record in the Eastern Conference. The Panthers eventually recorded the fifth-best record with a franchise high 43 wins and 98 points. There would be no miracle run to the Stanley Cup finals this time, though. Scott Stevens did an effective job of shutting down Bure, and the New Jersey Devils scored three straight one-goal victories en route to a series sweep in the first round of the playoffs that sent them on their way to an eventual Stanley Cup championship.

Florida Panthers Year-by-Year Record

Season	GP	W	L	T	GF	GA	Pts	Finish		Playoff Results
1993–94	84	33	34	17	233	233	83	5th	Atlantic	Out of Playoffs
1994–95	48	20	22	6	115	127	46	5th	Atlantic	Out of Playoffs
1995–96	82	41	31	10	254	234	92	3rd	Atlantic	Lost Final
1996–97	82	35	28	19	221	201	89	3rd	Atlantic	Lost Conf. Quarterfinal
1997–98	82	24	43	15	203	256	63	6th	Atlantic	Out of Playoffs
1998–99	82	30	34	18	210	228	78	2nd	Southeast	Out of Playoffs
1999-2000	82	43	33	6	244	209	*98	2nd	Southeast	Lost Conf. Quarterfinal

* *Includes 6 points for regulation ties (RT)*

HAMILTON TIGERS

HAMILTON'S FIRST ATTEMPT to attract an NHL franchise came during the league's inaugural season of 1917–18. Arena owners in the city offered to take in the Montreal Wanderers after fire destroyed the Montreal Arena on January 2, 1918, but Wanderers' owner Sam Lichtenhein chose to withdraw his franchise instead. Hamilton would have to wait three more years before attracting another unwanted franchise. Amid rumors that a rival league with teams in Toronto, Hamilton and Cleveland was being organized by E.J. Livingstone (the former Toronto owner who had been frozen out when the NHL was created), the owners of the Abso-Pure Ice Company paid

$5,000 for the NHL franchise in Quebec City. Abso-Pure recently had built a 3,800-seat artificial ice rink in Hamilton, and was looking for a hockey team to fill it.

The Quebec club that became the Hamilton Tigers had recorded just four wins against 20 losses during the 1919–20 season. Former Quebec players Eddie Carpenter, George Carey, Tom McCarthy and goalie Howie Lockhart were retained, but the NHL recognized that more than a new name was needed to attract fans in the new city. The Montreal Canadiens provided Billy Coutu, while the Toronto St. Pats supplied Joe Matte, Goldie Prodgers and Babe Dye (though they quickly recalled Dye and sent Mickey Roach to Hamilton instead). Four games into the 1920–21 season, Quebec star Joe Malone signed with the Tigers. He went on to rank among the league leaders with 28 goals, but Hamilton finished last in both halves of the NHL season, going 3–7–0 and 3–11–0. The Tigers showed little improvement with a record of 7–17–0 when the split schedule was abandoned in 1921–22.

Percy Thompson originally had been hired by the Abso-Pure Ice Company to coach and manage its hockey team, but he gave up his coaching duties after the 1921–22 season. Concentrating on building the Hamilton team, Thompson made several astute moves heading into the 1922–23 season—although improvement would still take time. Thompson signed former Toronto St. Pats goalie Jake Forbes to replace "Holes" Lockhart, and inked amateur star Billy Burch to his first pro contract. His most controversial move was trading Joe Malone to the Montreal Canadiens for Bert Corbeau and Edmond Bouchard. This deal worked out to the Tigers' advantage, as Malone scored just one goal in 20 games in Montreal while Bouchard led the NHL with 12 assists. Unfortunately, Hamilton posted a 6–18–0 record under coach Art Ross for yet another last-place finish. In 1923–24, the Tigers finished last again under Percy LeSueur. However, two newcomers to the Hamilton lineup that year would help make the difference in 1924–25.

Brothers Red and Shorty Green had been amateur stars in their hometown of Sudbury, Ontario. Thompson convinced them to turn pro with two-year deals reportedly worth $6,000—about twice the going rate—and placed them on a line with Billy Burch. The NHL had been courting Shorty Green since 1920, and Hamilton's acquisition of the brothers was seen as a major coup. When Thompson signed ex-Sudbury stars Alex McKinnon and Charlie Langlois for the Tigers' defense in 1924–25, Hamilton was poised for a breakthrough.

In an era when a team's starting players still played almost the entire game, having the four long-time Sudbury teammates in Hamilton made all the difference to the Tigers' teamwork. Under new coach Jimmy Gardiner, the Tigers raced out to a 10–4–1 record by the season's midpoint, then held off the hard-charging Toronto St. Pats to finish in first place by one point with a record of 19–10–1. Billy Burch earned the Hart Trophy as the most valuable player as Hamilton went from worst to first. But, on March 9, 1925, the 10 Tigers players promptly informed Percy Thompson that they would not take part in the upcoming playoffs unless each man received an additional $200. The dispute became public two days later when the St. Pats and the Montreal Canadiens began the semifinal series that was supposed to determine the Tigers' playoff opponent.

The Hamilton players had legitimate reasons to feel they were entitled to additional money. The NHL had undergone significant changes prior to the 1924–25 campaign. Expanding for the first time, the league had added a second franchise in Montreal and made its first foray into the United States with the admission of the Boston Bruins. With six teams instead of four, NHL owners had decided to increase the length of the season from 24 to 30 games and to increase the playoffs from one round to two. All the profits from the expanded playoffs would be divided evenly among the six NHL owners, with no money guaranteed to go to the players. The Hamilton owners had already turned a record profit due to the Tigers' first winning season, while the players had worked harder than ever under contracts originally signed for a 24-game schedule. Other teams had given raises to their players, or had provided generous Christmas bonuses. Hamilton had not. And now the Tigers would have to play at least two unpaid playoff games.

NHL president Frank Calder was not sympathetic. He stated that their contracts required players to make their services available from December 1 to March 31, regardless of the length of the season. (It is interesting to note, however, that the 1924–25 NHL season had actually begun on November 29.) Calder announced that the players would be fined or suspended if they refused to play, but the players stated they would quit the sport rather than be taken advantage of. Shorty Green met with Calder on March 13, 1925, during the final game of the Toronto–Montreal playoff series, but no compromise could be reached. The players were suspended and fined $200, and Hamilton was disqualified from the NHL finals. A plan to have the fourth-place Ottawa Senators meet the victorious Canadiens proved unpopular, so Montreal was simply declared league champions and sent to meet the winners of the Western Canada Hockey League. The Canadiens proved no match for the Victoria Cougars, who became the last non-NHL team to win the Stanley Cup.

On April 17, 1925, the NHL announced it would place a team in New York for the 1925–26 season. "Big Bill" Dwyer, New York's most-celebrated Prohibition bootlegger, would own the team. Tommy Gorman would operate it out of the newly completed 18,000-seat Madison Square Garden. In order to assure a solid showing in the most important American market, Dwyer bought the Hamilton franchise from Percy Thompson and Abso-Pure for $75,000. The Hamilton owners were only too happy to sell, having become convinced the league had outgrown their 3,800-seat arena and knowing that their players had stated publicly that they would never play for them again.

Now known as the New York Americans, the former Hamilton players all received raises, with Shorty Green's salary reportedly bumped from $3,000 to $5,000. Billy Burch signed a three-year deal said to be worth between $18,000 and $25,000. Born in Yonkers, New York, and being the league's reigning MVP, Burch was promoted as "The Babe Ruth of Hockey." However, before the former Hamilton players could suit up in New York there was the matter of their fines and suspensions. Frank Calder required every player to offer an apology, and to request readmission to the league in writing. After a series of letters in which most players began by maintaining that they had been right to strike, Calder finally received the apologies he wanted. As for the fines, it remains unclear whether they were paid by the players, by Tommy Gorman, or at all.

The NHL has yet to return to Canada's Steel City, but Hamilton's loss ultimately proved to be hockey's gain.

Though the New York Americans would prove unsuccessful, they did help to sell the sport in the United States at a time when the NHL was struggling to establish itself south of the border.

Hamilton Tigers Year-by-Year Record

Season	GP	W	L	T	GF	GA	Pts	Finish	Playoff Results
1920–21	24	6	18	0	92	132	12	4th	Out of Playoffs
1921–22	24	7	17	0	88	105	14	4th	Out of Playoffs
1922–23	24	6	18	0	81	110	12	4th	Out of Playoffs
1923–24	24	9	15	0	63	68	18	4th	Out of Playoffs
1924–25	30	19	10	1	90	60	39	1st	Suspended

LOS ANGELES KINGS

AT ONE TIME, the thriving Pacific Coast Hockey League (later the Western Hockey League) embraced teams in Los Angeles. During the immediate postwar years, the PCHL's Hollywood Wolves were linked with the NHL's Toronto Maple Leafs. The Wolves' most significant contribution as a farm team was defenseman Bill Barilko, who would in time score the 1951 Stanley Cup-winning goal for Toronto against the Montreal Canadiens. Despite the rapid growth of Southern California in the 1940s and 1950s, the NHL ignored the area for several reasons, not the least of which was the absence of a major-league arena in which to hold games.

By the early 1960s, Canadian-born entrepreneur Jack Kent Cooke recognized the potential for major-league hockey in the Los Angeles area. He paid $2 million for an expansion franchise for the 1967–68 season when the NHL doubled in size from six to 12 teams. Asked where he proposed to play home games, Cooke replied, "I'm going to build the most beautiful arena in the world, and it will be ready sometime in the opening season." True to his word, Cooke supervised construction of his "Fabulous Forum" in suburban Inglewood, and the $20 million project opened to rave reviews.

For his first coach, Cooke hired Leonard "Red" Kelly, the former Detroit Red Wings and Toronto Maple Leafs star. He also purchased the Springfield Indians of the American Hockey League in order to develop minor-leaguers for his organization. In addition to Kelly, Cooke surrounded himself with top personnel, including Larry Regan, a former Leafs center, as general manager. Los Angeles finished its first season in the expansion West Division only one point out of first place, and Cooke was voted executive of the year by The Hockey News.

The Kings were fourth in the West during their sophomore year, but managed to make it to the semifinals. By this time the best-laid plans of Cooke had become damaged by fate and mismanagement. The Kings then missed the playoffs for four years straight, as Cooke proved more a problem than a blessing. Because of his brash style, he angered key members of the NHL Board of Governors, none of whom would do him any favors in the draft or anywhere else. In 1969, Kelly quit the club to coach in Pittsburgh, and in 1971–72 Regan was replaced by Fred Glover, who had been fired recently by the California Seals.

The result was the Kings' worst finish ever, a mere 49 points, 11 fewer than the sickly Seals. There were major changes the next year. Veteran center Bob Pulford retired to go behind the bench, while the defense was boosted by ex-Canadien Terry Harper and former Black Hawk Gilles Marotte. Los Angeles returned to playoff competition in 1973–74, but lacked a marquee superstar to tantalize the demanding California fans. A dispute a couple of thousand miles away turned out to be the solution to the Kings' quest for a big-name player.

Marcel Dionne had been the captain and foremost scorer on the Detroit Red Wings. In 1974–75 he had his finest season as a Red Wing, amassing 47 goals and 74 assists. His 121 points placed him behind only Phil Esposito and Bobby Orr in the NHL scoring race.

Despite his productive campaign, Dionne still felt underappreciated in Detroit; so, once the season ended, Marcel's agent Alan Eagleson informed the Red Wings that Dionne would be taking his services elsewhere.

Six teams were in the early running—the Kings, the Canadiens, the Blues, the Sabres, the Maple Leafs and the Edmonton Oilers (of the World Hockey Association). Dionne's demands were high, as were those of the Red Wings, who were entitled to compensation from the team that signed him. Ultimately, the Kings, whose owner Jack Kent Cooke had just acquired Kareem Abdul-Jabbar for his basketball Lakers, offered the most money.

The Kings won the bidding war, and surrendered veteran defenseman Terry Harper and rugged forward Dan Maloney to Detroit. Cooke signed Marcel to a five-year, $1.5 million pact. Although Dionne and Cooke were pleased, Kings coach Bob Pulford wondered how well the newcomer would fit in with the team's disciplined defensive style. The Kings previously had enjoyed an extremely successful season. Los Angeles had the fourth-best won-lost record in the league, and only the Stanley Cup champion Philadelphia Flyers allowed fewer goals.

Pulford explained the situation: "I told Marcel that he couldn't float around center ice here the way he had in Detroit. He should retreat into the defensive end and work with the defensemen to get the puck out. That type of discipline was new to him, and I knew it would take time for him to learn our system."

"The Little Beaver" was up to the new challenge. After a brief period of adjustment with his new team, Dionne scored 40 goals and 54 assists for 94 points. However, the Kings no longer were the stingy defensive team they had been the year before. They gave up more goals, and instead of battling Montreal for first place in the NHL's Norris Division, the club found itself far back of the leader.

It was a tough adjustment for Dionne to adapt to the Kings' style, but he made the necessary changes and was ready for the 1976–77 season, playing both at center and right wing. Dionne became a new man, scoring goals and setting up teammates unselfishly, while diligently attending to the less-glamorous job on defense. He was the only player to stay close to the Canadiens' Guy Lafleur in the scoring race. Marcel finished the 1976–77 season with 53 goals and 69 assists, and, for a pleasant change, earned rave reviews for his positive attitude.

"He was the complete opposite of everything the Detroit people said he was," said former Kings general manager Jake Milford. "In our games in Los Angeles he never wanted to be picked a star of the game and I don't even think he ever worried about the scoring race. He had become that much of a team player."

Unfortunately, Dionne's improvement failed to help the Kings cope with the powerful Canadiens in the 1976–77 Norris Division race. In the playoffs, the Kings again failed to get past the quarterfinal round, although they hung tough against the feisty Boston Bruins after losing the first three games, finally bowing out in six.

Dionne won the Lady Byng Trophy and was named to the First All-Star Team in 1976–77. He was a Second Team All-Star in 1978–79 and went on to his best season in 1979–80, leading the NHL in scoring with 53 goals and 84 assists for a career-high 137 points. He also was named a First Team All-Star and won the Lester Pearson Award as the NHL player of the year as selected by his fellow players.

A prime reason for Dionne's point surplus was the quality of his linemates. Until the 1979–80 season, left wing Charlie Simmer bounced between the minors and the NHL, making no significant impact. But in 1979–80, Simmer became Dionne's regular linemate and tallied a league-leading 56 goals in only 64 games.

Filling out the Triple Crown Line was big right wing Dave Taylor who had been drafted by the Kings in June, 1975. Taylor was chosen in the 15th round, 210th overall. Taylor's grit and artistry produced 37 goals and 53 assists over 61 games in 1979–80 and set the stage for his great leap forward. In 72 games a season later, he produced 47 goals and 65 assists for 112 points.

Taylor, who would become general manager of the Kings after the 1996–97 season, emerged as one of the NHL's most appealing athletes. When he was in his early years in California, Dave battled and eventually licked a stuttering problem. Beloved by his teammates, he was recognized by the NHL in 1991, when he became the only player to win the King Clancy Trophy for outstanding community service and the Masterton Trophy for dedication to hockey in the same season. He also reached the 1,000-point milestone in 1990-91.

In addition to the members of the Triple Crown Line, another King with extraordinary appeal was goalie Rogatien Vachon. Vachon came to Los Angeles in 1971–72 after winning Stanley Cup championships with Montreal in 1968, 1969 and 1971. Almost minuscule between the pipes, Vachon emerged as a heroic figure to the audience at Inglewood and would become one of California's most popular athletes. "When you're my size," said Vachon, "you've got to be a stand-up kind of person. I take my bruises but I won't back down. Never."

Unquestionably, Vachon ranks as the most competent goaltender in Kings history. He was especially effective in the 1976 playoffs. The Kings eliminated Atlanta two games to none and then faced a powerful Boston Bruins team. Despite a 4–0 drubbing in the opening match at Boston Garden, Los Angeles rebounded with a 3–2 overtime win on the road and extended the favorites to a seventh game before succumbing.

Vachon remained with Los Angeles through the 1977–78 season, during which time the Kings earned regular berths in the playoffs but never developed significant headway. He was traded to Detroit for the 1978–79 campaign without ever being adequately replaced.

Dionne notwithstanding, the Kings remained a club mired in mediocrity during the early 1980s. They missed the playoffs in 1982–83 and 1983–84 as well as 1985–86. But, better days and nights were on the horizon when Bruce McNall became co-owner of the Kings during the 1986–87 season and was named club president in September, 1987. With gifted youngsters such as Luc Robitaille and Steve Duchesne, the Kings were positioned for a leap forward if they could obtain a major scorer and leader. That would happen on August 9, 1988, when Wayne Gretzky was acquired by Los Angeles along with Marty McSorley and Mike Krushelnyski for Jimmy Carson, Martin Gelinas, three first-round draft picks over the next five years and $15 million.

The Gretzky era in Los Angeles produced unprecedented attention for the NHL, as well as a few successful years for the Kings. "The Great One" still possessed enormous scoring skills and in 1992–93 actually orchestrated a march to the Stanley Cup finals, a first in Los Angeles hockey history. After defeating Montreal in game one, the Kings led the Canadiens late in game two when McSorley was penalized for carrying an illegal stick. The Habs capitalized on the power-play, sending the game into overtime. Montreal scored the winner and went on to capture the Cup. That launched the downfall of Gretzky in California and the Kings as a contender. They missed the playoffs in the next four seasons, during which time Gretzky moved on to St. Louis and, eventually, New York.

Although it wasn't readily apparent at the time, another turning point in the Kings history took place on July 25, 1989. On that date, the team signed Hall of Fame defenseman Larry Robinson as a free agent. He anchored the Kings defense in 1989–90 and spent three seasons on the blue line for Los Angeles. He was the second-highest scoring defenseman on the Kings in 1989–90 with 39 points (seven goals and 32 assists) and helped the team to a first-place finish in the Smythe Division in 1990–91.

During his three years with the Kings, Robinson made an indelible imprint not only because of his playing ability but also because of his character. After his retirement, he was named assistant coach of the New Jersey Devils beginning in 1993–94. Working with coach Jacques Lemaire, Robinson helped turn the Devils into a contender and, in 1995, into a Stanley Cup champion. It was evident that he was head coaching material and on July 26, 1995, the Kings gave him the opportunity to prove himself.

Assuming command of a foundering ship, Robinson patiently put it on an even keel and by 1997–98 had turned the Kings into a playoff contender once more. Under his guidance, Los Angeles finished with a plus-.500 record for the first time since 1992–93 and earned a playoff berth.

Nothing underlined the value of Robinson's coaching ability more than the improvement he brought about in defenseman Rob Blake, who had been named team captain prior to the 1996–97 campaign. If Robinson was symbolic of one aspect of the franchise's rebound, Blake was part of another. A fourth-round pick in the 1988 Entry Draft, Blake joined the Kings at the end of the 1989–90 season and had one goal and three assists for four points in eight playoff games. In his first full season as a King, Blake was named to the NHL's All-Rookie Team, as he led all rookie defensemen in scoring with 12 goals and 34 assists for 46 points. He has paced Kings defensemen in scoring in every season in which he has been healthy enough to play most of the year. Blake would play only 30 games over the 1994–95 and 1995–96 seasons due to a host of injuries, from a nagging groin to a torn ligament in his left knee. His spirited comeback was slow but in the end it was well worth the wait.

The addition of Robinson, Blake's childhood idol, as head coach pushed him to the next level, as he was named winner of the Norris Trophy after the 1997–98 season. Rob Blake had finally arrived. Blake and Robinson were not the only elements of the Kings renaissance that season. New g.m. Dave Taylor worked closely with Robinson, bringing in younger talent. Three 1997 deals had a major impact on the franchise, starting with a March 18, 1997, trade that brought Glen Murray to Los Angeles for Ed Olczyk. Taylor and Robinson looked to rebuild around character and youth. Subsequent trades were made for Jozef Stumpel, Sandy Moger and Luc Robitaille (on his second tour of duty with the Kings). Each played a role in the Kings' resurgence in 1997–98. An even earlier trade paid benefits as Mattias Norstrom became a dependable everyday defenseman.

Off the ice, another epoch of redevelopment had begun in October, 1995, when Philip Anschutz and Edward Roski Jr. assumed ownership of the team. Apart from putting a winning product on the ice, the new ownership began thinking long-range—well into the 21st century. The cornerstone of their planning would be a new, state-of-the-art arena, located not in the suburbs but rather in downtown Los Angeles. Plans for the new arena were unveiled late in the 1997–98 season, thus ushering in a truly new era of major-league hockey.

Robitaille returned to the upper echelons of NHL scorers in 1998–99, collecting 39 goals, but Rob Blake was again bothered by injuries and the Kings slumped to 69 points. Robinson was fired the day after the season ended and the team turned to Andy Murray, a former Canadian national team coach who had spent seven seasons as an NHL assistant. Murray had coached Shattuck-St. Mary's prep school to the Midget Triple A USA Hockey national championship in 1998–99, and he brought a high school-like enthusiasm to the Kings in 1999–2000. The team was further aided by the addition of Zigmund Palffy in an off-season deal and the opening of the brand new Staples Center. Los Angeles began the season with 12 wins and four ties in the first 20 games to race out to top spot in the Pacific Division. Year's end found them with 39 wins and 94 points—the most since they topped 100 back in 1990–91. Robitaille led the club with 36 goals and combined with Palffy and Jozef Stumpel to give the Kings a potent first line that helped the team rank fifth in the league with 245 goals. Meanwhile, a healthy Rob Blake once again proved to be among the NHL's best defensemen. However, having reached the playoffs for just the second time in seven seasons, the Kings were swept aside in the first round by Detroit, just as they had been in 1998.

Los Angeles Kings Year-by-Year Record

Season	GP	W	L	T	GF	GA	Pts	Finish	Division	Playoff Results
1967–68	74	31	33	10	200	224	72	2nd	West	Lost Quarterfinal
1968–69	76	24	42	10	185	260	58	4th	West	Lost Semifinal
1969–70	76	14	52	10	168	290	38	6th	West	Out of Playoffs
1970–71	78	25	40	13	239	303	63	5th	West	Out of Playoffs
1971–72	78	20	49	9	206	305	49	7th	West	Out of Playoffs
1972–73	78	31	36	11	232	245	73	6th	West	Out of Playoffs
1973–74	78	33	33	12	233	231	78	3rd	West	Lost Quarterfinal
1974–75	80	42	17	21	269	185	105	2nd	Norris	Lost Prelim. Round
1975–76	80	38	33	9	263	265	85	2nd	Norris	Lost Quarterfinal
1976–77	80	34	31	15	271	241	83	2nd	Norris	Lost Quarterfinal
1977–78	80	31	34	15	243	245	77	3rd	Norris	Lost Prelim. Round
1978–79	80	34	34	12	292	286	80	3rd	Norris	Lost Prelim. Round
1979–80	80	30	36	14	290	313	74	2nd	Norris	Lost Prelim. Round
1980–81	80	43	24	13	337	290	99	2nd	Norris	Lost Prelim. Round
1981–82	80	24	41	15	314	369	63	4th	Smythe	Lost Div. Final
1982–83	80	27	41	12	308	365	66	5th	Smythe	Out of Playoffs
1983–84	80	23	44	13	309	376	59	5th	Smythe	Out of Playoffs
1984–85	80	34	32	14	339	326	82	4th	Smythe	Lost Div. Semifinal
1985–86	80	23	49	8	284	389	54	5th	Smythe	Out of Playoffs
1986–87	80	31	41	8	318	341	70	4th	Smythe	Lost Div. Semifinal
1987–88	80	30	42	8	318	359	68	4th	Smythe	Lost Div. Semifinal
1988–89	80	42	31	7	376	335	91	2nd	Smythe	Lost Div. Final
1989–90	80	34	39	7	338	337	75	4th	Smythe	Lost Div. Final
1990–91	80	46	24	10	340	254	102	1st	Smythe	Lost Div. Final
1991–92	80	35	31	14	287	296	84	2nd	Smythe	Lost Div. Semifinal
1992–93	84	39	35	10	338	340	88	3rd	Smythe	Lost Final
1993–94	84	27	45	12	294	322	66	5th	Pacific	Out of Playoffs
1994–95	48	16	23	9	142	174	41	4th	Pacific	Out of Playoffs
1995–96	82	24	40	18	256	302	66	6th	Pacific	Out of Playoffs
1996–97	82	28	43	11	214	268	67	6th	Pacific	Out of Playoffs
1997–98	82	38	33	11	227	225	87	2nd	Pacific	Lost Conf. Quarterfinal
1998–99	82	32	45	5	189	222	69	5th	Pacific	Out of Playoffs
1999-2000	82	39	31	12	245	228	*94	2nd	Pacific	Lost Conf. Quarterfinal

** Includes 4 points for regulation ties (RT)*

MINNESOTA WILD

THE NATIONAL HOCKEY LEAGUE announced its return to the Minneapolis–St. Paul area on June 25, 1997, when the league also welcomed Nashville, Atlanta and Columbus as new expansion cities. The hotbed of American high school and college hockey is once again part of the NHL scene, beginning with the 2000–2001 season. Minnesota joins the Calgary Flames, Colorado Avalanche, Edmonton Oilers and Vancouver Canucks in the Northwest Division of the Western Conference in the 30-team NHL.

The team name Wild for the Minnesota franchise was announced on January 22, 1998, following a name-the-team contest that ran for six months. The Minnesota Wild word logo was introduced in January, 1997, and adorns the shoulders of the club's jersey. The home sweater, which was unveiled on November 18, 1999, quickly became a bestseller. The crest incorporates a wild animal, the North Star, evergreen trees, a red sky, the sun and/or moon and a stream. "The Wild home sweater reflects the power, energy and speed prevalent in both the Minnesota wilderness and the sport of hockey," stated club CEO Jac K. Sperling.

The home of the Minnesota Wild is the Excel Energy Center. Plans for the 18,600-seat arena were unveiled on June 17, 1998, with the groundbreaking ceremony held six days later. Overseeing construction of the on-ice product is Doug Risebrough. The former Montreal Canadiens star and front office employee in Calgary and Edmonton was hired as the club's executive vice president and general manager on September 2, 1999. Risebrough was made responsible for the entire Minnesota Wild hockey operation, overseeing a scouting department headed up by Tom Thompson and his former Montreal teammate, Guy Lapointe. Another former Canadiens teammate, Jacques Lemaire, was hired as the club's first head coach on June 19, 2000. Lemaire's past successes behind the bench in Montreal and, particularly, New Jersey, should ensure that the Wild will be well-schooled in the fundamentals when they take to the ice for their inaugural season.

MINNESOTA EXPANSION DRAFT SELECTIONS

PLAYER	POSITION	PREVIOUS CLUB
Jamie McLennan	G	St. Louis
Mike Vernon	G	Florida
Chris Terreri	G	New Jersey
Zac Bierk	G	Tampa Bay
Sean O'Donnell	D	Los Angeles
Curtis Leschyshyn	D	Carolina
Ladislav Benysek	D	Anaheim
Chris Armstrong	D	San Jose
Filip Kuba	D	Calgary
Oleg Orekhovsky	D	Washington
Ian Herbers	D	NY Islanders
Artem Anisimov	D	Philadelphia

MINNESOTA EXPANSION DRAFT SELECTIONS *continued*

Player	Position	Previous Club
Stacy Roest	C	Detroit
Darryl Laplante	C	Detroit
Scott Pellerin	LW	St. Louis
Jim Dowd	C	Edmonton
Sergei Krivokrasov	RW	Calgary
Jeff Nielsen	RW	Anaheim
Jeff Odgers	RW	Colorado
Steve McKenna	LW	Los Angeles
Michal Bros	C	San Jose
Joe Juneau	C	Ottawa
Darby Hendrickson	C	Vancouver
Jeff Daw	C	Chicago
Steffan Nilsson	C	Vancouver
Cam Stewart	LW	Florida

Montreal Canadiens

The Montreal Canadiens Hockey Club was born on December 4, 1909—designed to add a French face to hockey in Montreal, until then predominantly the preserve of the mercantile English with clubs like the Shamrocks, Wanderers and Victorias. Ironically, the first owner, J. Ambrose O'Brien, was neither a Montrealer nor a French Canadian. The scion of a wealthy mine-owning family, he sought to establish a French-Canadian club in the National Hockey Association, where he already had an interest in a team in his hometown of Renfrew, Ontario. It was agreed that when French-speaking owners from Montreal could be found, ownership would be transferred as soon as possible. Jack Laviolette was hired to form and manage the team, and the first lineup included the stars such as Newsy Lalonde, Didier Pitre, Art Bernier and Skinner Poulin.

Early in its history, the club acquired the nickname "les Habitants" or "the Habs," a French term first used to describe rugged farmer-settlers in New France, the 17th-century predecessor of what is now Quebec. The French usage of the word "Canadien" at the time the team was formed had a similar meaning, and referred to the hard-working local people of Montreal.

The Canadiens played their first National Hockey Association game on natural ice at the Jubilee Arena on January 5, 1910, defeating the Cobalt Silver Kings 7–6. They were the real bleu-blanc-rouge (blue, white and red, the colors of the French flag). They wore blue sweaters featuring a simple "C" of white; short, white pants, and long, red wool socks. O'Brien's right to call his team les Canadiens was challenged by Georges Kendall, owner of a sporting association known as le Club Athlétique Canadien. The resulting out-of-court settlement saw ownership of the hockey team transferred to Kendall's athletic club. (Kendall used the name "George Kennedy" in his dealings with the predominately English-speaking commercial society that controlled business affairs in Montreal at this time.) Within three years, the team petitioned the league and was given the right to hire English-speaking players—homegrown French players being in short supply.

The Canadiens, now sporting the red, white and blue uniforms they wear to this day, but with a "CA" crest (Club Athlétique), won the franchise's first Stanley Cup title on March 30, 1916, defeating the Portland Rosebuds of the Pacific Coast Hockey Association in a five-game series. Upon joining the fledgling National Hockey League as a founding member in November, 1917, the team officially changed its name to le club de hockey Canadien and added the now-famous letters "CH" to its familiar uniform.

Two years later, the Canadiens were poised for a second Stanley Cup victory when tragedy struck. After winning the National Hockey League title in a five-game series with Ottawa, Montreal journeyed west to challenge the Seattle Metropolitans of the PCHA. After five games, the spirited series was deadlocked at two wins and a tie for each team, when fate intervened in the form of the Spanish Influenza pandemic that would kill an estimated 25 million from 1918 to 1920. The final game of the 1919 series was scheduled for April 1, but with Newsy Lalonde, Billy Coutu, Louis Berlinquette, Jack McDonald, Joe Hall and manager Kendall/Kennedy all down with the flu, the Canadiens were unable to ice a team. The game was canceled and, for the only time in Stanley Cup history, no champion was declared. Four days later, "Bad" Joe Hall died in a Seattle hospital. Within a year, Kendall/Kennedy was dead of complications related to influenza.

While O'Brien put the first team on the ice, and Kendall/Kennedy nursed it through its first decade, the Canadiens did not acquire much of their mythic aura until a Franco-American from Bourbonnais, Illinois, came along to take control of the franchise. He was Leo Dandurand, a dandy who made and lost several fortunes in the sports world, especially in horse racing, where he was an owner of famous thoroughbreds, as well as head of the Montreal Jockey Club for years.

Dandurand plus partners Joseph Cattarinich and Louis Letourneau purchased the Canadiens from the widow of Kendall/Kennedy in 1921. Cecil Hart, who would serve as a club director and later the coach, represented Dandurand *et al.* at the sale. Tommy Duggan, who ran the Mount Royal Arena, where the Canadiens were now playing, also wanted the team, as did a group based in Ottawa. According to stories, Duggan arrived at the negotiating session with ten $1,000 bills. Hart made a phone call to Dandurand and convinced him to go to $11,000. When the Ottawa group could not go above $8,500, the team was sold to the trio that would become known as the Three Musketeers of Sport. (When Dandurand and Cattarinich sold the club in 1935—they had previously bought out Letourneau—the price was $165,000.)

With the fledgling NHL attempting to break out of its eastern Canadian niche and into the northeastern United States, Dandurand was the right man in the right spot. He was a promoter extraordinaire who traveled in the same circles as New York's legendary Tex Rickard and Chicago's Major Frederic McLaughlin. If hockey was to make a go in markets such as New York, Boston and Chicago, the visiting teams would have to capture the imagination of the American fans who were new to the game. Dandurand's Flying Frenchmen—a term first used to describe some of the earliest Canadiens teams—were up to the task.

The Montreal Canadiens of this era boasted Aurel Joliat and Johnny "Black Cat" Gagnon, as well as Georges Vezina, Billy Boucher, the Mantha brothers Sylvio and Georges, and the hardrock Cleghorn brothers, Odie and Sprague, but the man who would become professional hockey's superstar in the Roaring Twenties was Howie Morenz.

William Howard Morenz, a German-Canadian born in Mitchell, Ontario, was spirited away by Cecil Hart and Leo Dandurand from under the noses of the Toronto St. Pats after representing a team from Stratford, Ontario, in a railway league final in Montreal. Morenz was signed for the 1923–24 season for $850, but as training camp approached, he tried to get out of the deal. Morenz was afraid that he wasn't good enough for the NHL and that he would lose his amateur standing because there was no minor professional league at the time. Dandurand stuck to his guns and a tearful Morenz was forced to join the Canadiens. The following March, he led all playoff scorers as the Canadiens won the Stanley Cup.

Morenz, Joliat, Gagnon and the rest sold hockey on both sides of the border in the 1920s, helping new franchises take root in Boston, New York, Detroit and Chicago. As well, Dandurand's skill as a promoter and Morenz's on-ice heroics helped in the creation of another franchise in Montreal, the Maroons, who would represent English Montreal against the darlings of French Montreal, les Canadiens.

A modern ice palace with the latest in artificial-ice technology would accompany the Maroons' arrival in the NHL. Called the Forum, it was constructed in 159 days in 1924 and was ready for action in late November when the new National Hockey League season got under way. Ironically, it would be inaugurated by the Canadiens, whose own Mount Royal Arena and its newly installed artificial-ice plant was plagued by electrical problems. On November 29, 1924, the Canadiens took part in the first game ever played at the Forum, thumping the Toronto St. Pats, 7–1. It took Billy Boucher only 56 seconds to score the first goal at what would become hockey's most venerated shrine.

For its first two seasons, the Forum was home to the Maroons exclusively. The Canadiens joined them starting with the 1926–27 season and would play there for another 70 years. The Maroons-Canadiens rivalry would galvanize Montreal hockey fans for more than a decade. The Maroons would win the Stanley Cup in 1926 and 1935, but by the late 1930s, Montreal no longer could support two teams during The Great Depression and the Maroons were sold.

In the meantime, the Maroons era made Montreal the hockey hotbed of the league. Morenz and the Flying Frenchmen returned to prominence when they won consecutive Stanley Cup championships in 1930 and 1931. With the win in 1924, and the two titles by the Maroons, Montreal was the summer home to the Cup for five of 11 seasons. That kind of success could not prepare Montreal fans for what would become known as the grand noirceur or "great darkness" of the period between the Maroons' Cup in 1935 and the next success by a Montreal team in 1944. And nothing could prepare the hockey world for the unspeakable tragedy that would befall Howie Morenz in 1937.

As age gained on "the Stratford Streak," the rocketing speed and rink-long dashes that had thrilled fans in all NHL cities was being displayed less and less often. In 1934, he was traded to Chicago. After a year-and-a-half with the Black Hawks and half a season with the Rangers, Morenz rejoined the Canadiens late in the summer of 1936.

On January 28, 1937, in a rush that evoked Morenz at the peak of his powers, he burst into the Chicago zone at full speed. Chicago defenseman Earl Seibert caught the Canadiens center with a hip check and Morenz lost his balance. He fell toward the boards and, somehow, his skate jammed in a crack in the boards. When Seibert collided with him again, the sound of the leg breaking could be heard throughout the Forum.

Hospitalized, Howie Morenz kept up a brave appearance, but told teammate Aurel Joliat he never would skate again. Still in hospital nearly two months later, weak and depressed, Morenz died suddenly on March 8, 1937, of a coronary embolism. Three days later, more than 10,000 people sat in silence in a jam-packed Forum during Morenz's funeral service. The city of Montreal was in mourning for Morenz for months. On the ice, the mourning period was extended some seven more years, until the arrival of the next Montreal superhero.

Montreal's previous superstar had come out of the machine shops of the Canadian Pacific Railway. The next one was the son of a machinist in the Montreal shops of the same CPR. Born Joseph Henri Maurice Richard, he would come to be known as "The Rocket" and would carry professional hockey and the NHL through the World War II era and into the modern age. After suffering a season-ending ankle injury in his first campaign, Richard settled into the NHL during the 1943–44 season. Significantly, that ankle injury would keep him out of military service.

A bone of contention in English Canada during the 1940s was French Quebec's reluctance to embrace the war, which involved the entire British Commonwealth. Anti-conscription riots broke out in Montreal and other Quebec centers, and local draft boards were seen from outside the province as notoriously lax. And although the Canadiens had their share of players in the country's uniform, the team was to all intents and purposes left intact. Veterans Hector "Toe" Blake and Elmer Lach teamed up with a "Rocket" right wing in 1943–44, and the Canadiens took off, posting an astonishing 38–5–7 record in a 50-game schedule. In nine playoff games, Richard scored 12 goals and the Canadiens had their first Stanley Cup victory since 1931.

A year later, with the war winding down in Europe, Richard's scoring exploits began taking over the front pages, as the fiery competitor maintained a goal-a-game clip into January and then February. War-depleted lineups or not, opposing teams tried everything to stop Montreal's scoring machine, and the superstar spent a significant amount of playing time in the penalty box for defending himself against all comers. Late in February, his two goals against Detroit gave Montreal a 5–2 win and Richard 43 in 38 games, tying Cooney Weiland for the second-highest season total in league history. A week later, a score against Toronto tied the legendary Joe Malone at 44, and he passed Malone in a Forum encounter against the Leafs several days later. With eight games remaining in the season, could Richard possibly tally five more for a magical 50?

By game 49, Richard had 49 goals and an emotional crowd was crammed into every nook and cranny of the Forum on the last Saturday of the season. Late in the game, a Chicago defenseman tripped Richard and the Rocket was awarded a penalty shot… and missed. It was not to be—at home, anyway. The following night, Richard scored his 50th goal of the season in Boston.

The arrival of Richard heralded a new era for the Canadiens, and though the team would win another Stanley Cup in 1946, Montreal's leap into the upper echelons of the league was the result of another new recruit. On August 1, 1946, the victim of a Toronto purge by Conn Smythe began work at the Forum as the Canadiens' manager. The diminutive new leader was Frank Selke, and he would build the farm system that would allow the team to rival the Leafs and Red Wings during the late 1940s and then surpass all comers in the golden 1950s. Not only did Selke's wide-reaching farm system ensure the Canadiens a rich bounty each season, it soon began to pay for itself with the sales of prospects to other NHL teams.

Richard had joined a team that included veterans Blake and Lach, as well as Ken Reardon and Butch Bouchard. It soon added goalie Bill Durnan and defenseman Doug Harvey, arguably the greatest rearguard of his era. However, the Montreal team that would emerge in the mid-1950s was based on Selke's star harvests, and future Hall of Famers, Bernard "Boom Boom" Geoffrion, Jean Beliveau, Richard's younger brother Henri, Dickie Moore, Bert Olmstead, Jean-Guy Talbot, Phil Goyette, Don Marshall, Ralph Backstrom and the greatest character of them all, goaltender Jacques Plante.

Elements of the old and the new came together to win the Stanley Cup in 1953, but it would not be until the spring of 1956 that the team would take off in postseason play, setting a raft of records in the process. Local fans argue that the Canadiens might have won eight Cup titles in a row if not for a bit of bad luck and a decision by NHL president Clarence Campbell that ignited Montreal in 1955. In 1954, the Canadiens and Red Wings played to overtime in the seventh game of the finals, with Detroit's Tony Leswick sealing the issue. In 1955, although the team would go down in a seventh game at Detroit, the Cup actually had been lost weeks before, in Boston and Montreal. Late that season, with the Canadiens and Wings battling neck-and-neck for first place, Rocket Richard attacked Hal Laycoe after the Bruins defenseman cut him with a swinging stick. During the ensuing brawl, Richard twice punched linesman Cliff Thompson. He was ejected immediately with a match penalty and was ordered to a meeting at league headquarters in Montreal two days later.

A year earlier, Richard had emerged unscathed from a similar incident with an official in Toronto, and Conn Smythe of the Leafs and Detroit's Jack Adams took great pains to remind Campbell of the results of his previous clemency. This time, the president suspended Richard for the rest of the regular season (three games) and all of the playoffs. Montreal went into shock, and then, rage, with the French media and French-speaking mayor Jean Drapeau accusing Campbell of anti-French bias. The English media adopted a law-and-order stance.

A restive crowd thronged the Forum on March 17 for a first-place showdown with the visiting Wings, with another 10,000 or so fans milling about outside the building. Late in the first period, with Detroit leading the dispirited Canadiens 4–1, Campbell sat down at his seat and was attacked in short order by a fan. Then a tear-gas canister was set off, driving fans out of the building as the first period came to an end. Inside the Forum, a fire marshal declared that the game was over. (It would be forfeited to the Red Wings.) Outside the Forum, Montreal erupted into a riot that trashed the downtown core and had the city seething for more than 24 hours. It took a special radio appeal by the Rocket to call an end to what would become known as "The Richard Riot." Detroit went on to capture first place and home-ice advantage in the playoffs, and Boom Boom Geoffrion won the scoring title, only to be vilified by his own fans for surpassing their beloved Rocket.

Montreal would not win the Cup that year, but it would be the last loss during Maurice Richard's career. On April 12, 1960, Richard scored on a backhand against Toronto's Johnny Bower as Montreal went on to a fifth straight Stanley Cup title. It was his 82nd playoff goal, 34th in the finals and the last of his career. Eventually all of his scoring records, 544 regular-season goals, 988 points, would be surpassed. But, no player would match the Rocket's impact during his era.

It was a testament to Frank Selke's skill as a hockey manager and administrator that his team took the powerful Red Wings to seven games in 1954 and 1955 minus several important players. Selke had built a juggernaut by then, and team leadership was moving from Maurice Richard and Butch Bouchard to Doug Harvey, Jean Beliveau, Henri Richard and Dickie Moore. The most distinctive of all was the 6'3" Beliveau, an elegant center with soft hands who had the strength to fight off opposing defensemen while scoring spectacular goals. The Canadiens had the luxury of two all-star lines. The Richard brothers and Moore terrorized opposition defenses, only to be replaced by the trio of Beliveau, Geoffrion and Olmstead. With Hall of Famers like Harvey, Tom Johnson and Jean-Guy Talbot on the blue line and five-time Vezina Trophy winner Plante in nets, the Canadiens were challenged rarely as they won the Stanley Cup five times in a row. These championships were won under Toe Blake, who replaced Dick Irvin as coach after the 1954–55 season because it was believed that Blake would have a calming influence on his former linemate, the Rocket.

With Geoffrion winning the scoring title in 1954–55 and Beliveau winning it the following year, the Montreal offense proved so powerful during the team's Stanley Cup run that the league was forced to change the rule governing minor penalties. Previous to the change, minors were served in their entirety even if a goal was scored on the shorthanded team. The Canadiens offense was so potent that the team sometimes scored two or three goals per opposition minor, putting games out of reach in the first period. The amended rule allowed the penalized player to return to the ice if a goal was scored against his team. Rule change notwithstanding, Dickie Moore managed to win the scoring title in 1957–58 and 1958–59. At the other end of the ice, the Canadiens allowed the fewest goals for five years running.

The Canadiens finally relinquished the Stanley Cup to Chicago in 1961, but after Punch Imlach's Leafs captured three straight championships, the Habs were back in contention in 1965. Although many veterans of the five-straight team remained, direction of the team had moved from Frank Selke to Sam Pollock, and the astute managing director would guide the team into the modern era.

Montreal won the Cup in 1965 and 1966 with a team built primarily through its farm system, and then came back with victories in 1968, 1969, 1971 and 1973 with teams built by trades and draft choices acquired by Pollock. By the time the league had welcomed six new teams with the Expansion Draft in 1967, Pollock had dismantled Selke's vast farm system and shipped more that 70 players throughout the league, stockpiling draft selections as he went. Teams like St. Louis, Minnesota and Oakland immediately were competitive thanks to former Canadiens farmhands, but Montreal's future throughout the coming decade was assured. Stars like Guy Lafleur, Larry Robinson and Steve Shutt were all accumulated in this fashion. Occasionally, "Trader Sam" got lucky as well, such as when he acquired goalie Ken Dryden from the Boston farm system.

The acquisition of Guy Lafleur provides a classic example of Pollock's foresight. The Canadiens owned Oakland's first pick for the 1971 draft, and with the Seals in last place in the Western Division, it appeared that the selection would be first overall. Late in the season, however, the Los Angeles Kings began to falter and threatened to sink below the Seals in the standings. Pollock immediately dispatched veteran center Ralph Backstrom to Los Angeles and his leadership got the Kings over the hump. On June 9, 1971, Jean Beliveau announced his retirement, but a day later, the Canadiens obtained his replacement in Lafleur by using the Oakland draft choice. For good measure, the team also picked up future Hall of Fame defenseman Larry Robinson in the same draft.

In the mid-1960s, the Canadiens had been a veteran team that included Beliveau, Henri Richard, Talbot, Ralph Backstrom and Claude Provost, bolstered by a large and strong defense corps that included newcomers Jacques Laperriere, Terry Harper and Ted Harris. They were strengthened up front by the addition of tough wings Claude Larose and John Ferguson and the sheer explosiveness of Yvan Cournoyer.

Pollock tinkered with his team yearly. The club that won in 1965 and 1966 saw players like Jean-Guy Talbot, Leon Rochefort, Charlie Hodge and Dave Balon moved to make room for newcomers Rogatien Vachon, Serge Savard, Guy Lapointe, Jacques Lemaire, Pete Mahovlich and Mickey Redmond. The reconstructed Canadiens then turned around and burned the rising Bruins and Black Hawks in the 1968 and 1969 playoffs. By 1971, Gump Worsley had departed from the goal, as had scorers Redmond and Danny Grant. These moves made room for Ken Dryden and Frank Mahovlich, who would both star in the team's 1971 Stanley Cup triumph. Dryden, who had played just six games late in the regular season, almost singlehandedly eliminated the first-place Bruins to open the playoffs and went on to win the Conn Smythe Trophy before he had even qualified as an NHL rookie.

In the period between the 1964–65 and 1972–73 seasons, Pollock managed to remake his entire team and still win the Stanley Cup six times. Only five players, Henri Richard, Yvan Cournoyer, Jacques Laperriere, Jim Roberts and Claude Larose, played for both the 1965 and 1973 Cup winners, and the latter two had been traded away and reacquired in the interim. Yet some Canadiens players accumulated individual postseason statistics that are staggering in today's context: Henri Richard won 11 championships, while Beliveau and Cournoyer each won 10. Provost was a part of nine Cup teams; Lemaire, eight; Talbot, seven, and a raft of others won six or five championships.

Ice generalship was not a factor. When the popular and demanding Toe Blake asked to be replaced behind the Canadiens bench in 1968 after eight titles in 13 years, Pollock's team was strong enough to win the 1969 championship with rookie coach Claude Ruel calling the shots. Two years later, another rookie coach, Al MacNeil, replaced Ruel midway through the season and led the team to a championship, only to be replaced by Scotty Bowman the following September. Bowman would win five titles with Montreal in the 1970s before shuffling off to Buffalo.

The onset of the World Hockey Association in 1972 saw the Canadiens lose some players (Rejean Houle, Marc Tardif, J.C. Tremblay and Frank Mahovlich) to the new league, but the team was in better shape than most NHL entries. Lafleur struggled in his first three seasons, alternating between right wing and center on different lines, but finally emerged a top-rank superstar in 1974–75. A cross between the elegance of Beliveau and the fire of the Rocket, he electrified NHL audiences with his rink-long dashes, blond hair streaming behind him. Pollock put together a stellar supporting cast that included Cournoyer, Shutt, Lemaire, Peter Mahovlich, Doug Risebrough, Yvon Lambert, Mario Tremblay and the incomparable Bob Gainey on the forward lines, and "The Big Three" of Larry Robinson, Guy Lapointe and Serge Savard anchoring an airtight defense backstopped by Dryden.

That Montreal team ended the "three-peat" aspirations of the Philadelphia Flyers in May, 1976, outdueling the Broad Street Bullies in the corners, with bangers like Pierre Bouchard, Lambert and Rick Chartraw, and outfinessing them with the likes of Lafleur, Shutt and Mahovlich. Four straight championships resulted, as the Habs fended off strong teams in Boston, Buffalo and New York (Islanders) until injury and age caught up with them in 1980. The last Canadiens dynasty came to an end on April 27, 1980, in a 3–2 Forum loss to the youthful Minnesota North Stars. Gone a year earlier to retirement were young Jacques Lemaire, 33, and Ken Dryden, 31. Gone also was Scotty Bowman, miffed because Sam Pollock would not name him as his own replacement. Pollock selected Irving Grundman, his assistant in the previous decade, who was not a hockey man. Although Grundman managed a Cup winner in his "rookie" season of 1978–79, his leadership was under perpetual challenge by the strident Montreal media.

Grundman made a major mistake when he attempted to replace Bowman with the colorful Bernie Geoffrion, who had coached the Rangers and later the expansion Atlanta Flames, stepping down both times for health reasons. Boomer lasted just 30 games in Montreal and was replaced, as Toe Blake had been, by Claude Ruel. The team still was competitive, but the early 1980s belonged to the Islanders and the Edmonton Oilers. A nucleus of talent that included Robinson, Savard and Gainey, and quality additions like Ryan Walter, Bobby Smith, Rick Green, Chris Chelios and Mats Naslund kept the team near the top of the league standings. Montreal could not afford to dwell on the successes of the Oilers and Islanders, however, because the challenge to their hegemony came from their own backyard. In 1979, the NHL expanded to include four teams from the WHA, and suddenly the province of Quebec was no longer the exclusive preserve of the Canadiens, with the Nordiques challenging them from the provincial capital.

When Quebec managed to eliminate Montreal in their first playoff confrontation, a best-of-five series in 1982, the second floor at the Forum went into shock. With Quebec now claiming to be the province's "French" team, the Canadiens responded with the hiring of Ronald Corey as team president, and his decision was to replace Grundman with former star Serge Savard.

In the spring of 1984, the Canadiens gained a measure of revenge by ousting the Nordiques in the bitterly fought six-game Adams Division finals, which included a huge Good Friday brawl in the final contest. Montreal went on to lose to the Islanders in six games in the conference finals, but the Canadiens had given notice that they were back in the chase. In June, 1984, Savard and the Canadiens had a dream draft, selecting Czech defector Petr Svoboda and Shayne Corson in the first round, adding Stephane Richer in the second and goaltender Patrick Roy in the third. They once again lost to the Nordiques in the playoffs, but were poised to challenge the league in 1985–86, when Svoboda, Richer and Roy, joined the team as regulars.

When Montreal had fallen to Quebec in 1985, the scapegoat was goaltender Steve Penney, a journeyman who had enjoyed two decent seasons in Montreal but was unable to provide the championship backstopping the team needed. That changed in 1986 with Patrick Roy.

Roy was a cross between Jacques Plante and Ken Dryden, impressive credentials indeed in Montreal. And like Plante and Dryden before him, he took the team to a Stanley Cup triumph in his rookie season. Roy was unbeatable in the playoffs, helping the Canadiens to sweep the Bruins 3–0 in their best-of-five division semifinals, and then out-battling Hartford's Mike Liut in a division final that went to overtime in game seven before rookie Claude Lemieux ended it. The Canadiens disposed of the Rangers in five games, including a spectacular overtime win in game three (again on a goal by Lemieux) that saw Roy hold off the aroused Rangers single-handedly, including 13 stops (44 overall) in extra time. The final was a formality. Montreal defeated Calgary in five close games, and Roy posed happily in the team's dressing room at the Saddledome with his arms around the Conn Smythe Trophy and the Stanley Cup.

Roy remained one of the league's best goaltenders over the years, but was truly at his best seven years later when he led a much-changed team—only he and Guy Carbonneau remained from the 1986 champions—to the franchise's 24th Stanley Cup and 23rd in the team's NHL history. The 1986 and 1993 victories gave Montreal a unique and enviable record in professional sports in North America, making them the only long-established team to win a league championship in each decade in which it has played. However, just two seasons later, Montreal would miss the playoffs for the first time since 1970 and just the second time since 1948.

In March, 1996, the fabulous Forum closed its doors with a touching ceremony after a 4–1 win over the Dallas Stars. The team moved across town to the spanking-new Molson Centre, but the team that made the move had few connections with the Stanley Cup, including the championship won less than three years before. In the fashion of professional sport in the 1990s and the new world of free agency and liberal player movement, only four Canadiens remained from the team that had won Cup #24.

Gone to Philadelphia were John LeClair and the memories of his two overtime goals in "The Fabulous Forum" in Inglewood that eviscerated Wayne Gretzky and the Kings. Joining "Marmaduke" in the Philly shuffle was Eric Desjardins, whose three goals, including one in overtime, in the pivotal second game of the Kings series, set Montreal on the road to the championship.

Gone were longtime NHL stars Kirk Muller, Brian Bellows, Denis Savard, Guy Carbonneau and Mathieu Schneider. Gone, too, were players who had huge roles in the 1993 conquest: Lyle Odelein, Jean-Jacques Daigneault, Gilbert Dionne, Paul DiPietro, Mike Keane, Andre Racicot and Kevin Haller. Farthest gone was King Patrick, in a spectacular and very public tantrum against rookie coach Mario Tremblay seen nationwide on *Hockey Night in Canada* during an 11–1 Forum shellacking at the hands of Detroit. Roy's snubbing of his coach and embarrassing of team president Ronald Corey forced the reluctant Canadiens to trade him to Colorado, where he won the Stanley Cup six months later.

Montreal's 1993 champions were an all-North American aggregation, not a whiff of Europe to them. That would change quickly. Not only would Andrei Kovalenko, Martin Rucinsky and Vladimir Malakhov arrive by trades, the Canadiens would find European-trained talent on both sides of the Atlantic, adding Valeri Bure, brother of Vancouver's Pavel, who played his junior hockey in Spokane, and a feisty Finnish centre, Saku Koivu, from Turku's TPS team.

However, the late 1990s would prove to be turbulent times in Montreal. Such popular players as Pierre Turgeon, Vincent Damphousse and Mike Recchi were all shipped out as the team's fortunes took a turn for the worse. The club fell out of the playoff picture in 1998–99. Ronald Corey resigned. He was replaced as president by Pierre Boivin, who joined the team from the sporting goods industry. With top players like Shayne Corson, Brian Savage, Saku Koivu and Trevor Linden all missing significant time due to injuries, the Canadiens appeared to tumble hopelessly out of contention in the first half of the 1999–2000 season. Among the most serious of Montreal's many injuries was that of Trent McCleary, who was struck in the throat by a puck, damaging his windpipe.

Though the injuries continued to pile up, the Canadiens were able to turn around their season in the second half. Led by the spectacular goaltending of Jose Theodore and Jeff Hackett, Montreal climbed to as high as seventh overall in the Eastern Conference standings. However, when returning players such as Koivu and Linden were again knocked out of the lineup, the rally lost steam and the Canadiens were eliminated from playoff contention on the final Saturday night of the regular season. It marked the first time that Montreal had failed to reach the playoffs in consecutive years since the early 1920s. With eight seasons between Stanley Cup victories, Montreal is also in the midst of its longest championship drought since before World War II. Canadiens fans can only hope that the club will respond as it always has in the past.

Montreal Canadiens Year-by-Year Record

Season	GP	W	L	T	GF	GA	Pts	Finish	Division	Playoff Results
1917–18	22	13	9	0	115	84	26	1st and 3rd*		Lost NHL Final
1918–19	18	10	8	0	88	78	20	1st and 2nd*		NHL Champion **
1919–20	24	13	11	0	129	113	26	2nd and 3rd*		Out of Playoffs
1920–21	24	13	11	0	112	99	26	3rd and 2nd*		Out of Playoffs
1921–22	24	12	11	1	88	94	25	3rd		Out of Playoffs
1922–23	24	13	9	2	73	61	28	2nd		Lost NHL Final
1923–24	24	13	11	0	59	48	26	2nd		Won Stanley Cup
1924–25	30	17	11	2	93	56	36	3rd		Lost Final
1925–26	36	11	24	1	79	108	23	7th		Out of Playoffs
1926–27	44	28	14	2	99	67	58	2nd	Canadian	Lost Semifinal
1927–28	44	26	11	7	116	48	59	1st	Canadian	Lost Semifinal
1928–29	44	22	7	15	71	43	59	1st	Canadian	Lost Semifinal
1929–30	44	21	14	9	142	114	51	2nd	Canadian	Won Stanley Cup
1930–31	44	26	10	8	129	89	60	1st	Canadian	Won Stanley Cup
1931–32	48	25	16	7	128	111	57	1st	Canadian	Lost Semifinal
1932–33	48	18	25	5	92	115	41	3rd	Canadian	Lost Quarterfinal
1933–34	48	22	20	6	99	101	50	2nd	Canadian	Lost Quarterfinal
1934–35	48	19	23	6	110	145	44	3rd	Canadian	Lost Quarterfinal
1935–36	48	11	26	11	82	123	33	4th	Canadian	Out of Playoffs
1936–37	48	24	18	6	115	111	54	1st	Canadian	Lost Semifinal
1937–38	48	18	17	13	123	128	49	3rd	Canadian	Lost Quarterfinal
1938–39	48	15	24	9	115	146	39	6th		Lost Quarterfinal
1939–40	48	10	33	5	90	167	25	7th		Out of Playoffs
1940–41	48	16	26	6	121	147	38	6th		Lost Quarterfinal
1941–42	48	18	27	3	134	173	39	6th		Lost Quarterfinal
1942–43	50	19	19	12	181	191	50	4th		Lost Semifinal
1943–44	50	38	5	7	234	109	83	1st		Won Stanley Cup
1944–45	50	38	8	4	228	121	80	1st		Lost Semifinal
1945–46	50	28	17	5	172	134	61	1st		Won Stanley Cup
1946–47	60	34	16	10	189	138	78	1st		Lost Final
1947–48	60	20	29	11	147	169	51	5th		Out of Playoffs
1948–49	60	28	23	9	152	126	65	3rd		Lost Semifinal
1949–50	70	29	22	19	172	150	77	2nd		Lost Semifinal
1950–51	70	25	30	15	173	184	65	3rd		Lost Final
1951–52	70	34	26	10	195	164	78	2nd		Lost Final
1952–53	70	28	23	19	155	148	75	2nd		Won Stanley Cup

Season	GP	W	L	T	GF	GA	Pts	Finish	Division	Playoff Results
1953–54	70	35	24	11	195	141	81	2nd		Lost Final
1954–55	70	41	18	11	228	157	93	2nd		Lost Final
1955–56	70	45	15	10	222	131	100	1st		Won Stanley Cup
1956–57	70	35	23	12	210	155	82	2nd		Won Stanley Cup
1957–58	70	43	17	10	250	158	96	1st		Won Stanley Cup
1958–59	70	39	18	13	258	158	91	1st		Won Stanley Cup
1959–60	70	40	18	12	255	178	92	1st		Won Stanley Cup
1960–61	70	41	19	10	254	188	92	1st		Lost Semifinal
1961–62	70	42	14	14	259	166	98	1st		Lost Semifinal
1962–63	70	28	19	23	225	183	79	3rd		Lost Semifinal
1963–64	70	36	21	13	209	167	85	1st		Lost Semifinal
1964–65	70	36	23	11	211	185	83	2nd		Won Stanley Cup
1965–66	70	41	21	8	239	173	90	1st		Won Stanley Cup
1966–67	70	32	25	13	202	188	77	2nd		Lost Final
1967–68	74	42	22	10	236	167	94	1st	East	Won Stanley Cup
1968–69	76	46	19	11	271	202	103	1st	East	Won Stanley Cup
1969–70	76	38	22	16	244	201	92	5th	East	Out of Playoffs
1970–71	78	42	23	13	291	216	97	3rd	East	Won Stanley Cup
1971–72	78	46	16	16	307	205	108	3rd	East	Lost Quarterfinal
1972–73	78	52	10	16	329	184	120	1st	East	Won Stanley Cup
1973–74	78	45	24	9	293	240	99	2nd	East	Lost Quarterfinal
1974–75	80	47	14	19	374	225	113	1st	Norris	Lost Semifinal
1975–76	80	58	11	11	337	174	127	1st	Norris	Won Stanley Cup
1976–77	80	60	8	12	387	171	132	1st	Norris	Won Stanley Cup
1977–78	80	59	10	11	359	183	129	1st	Norris	Won Stanley Cup
1978–79	80	52	17	11	337	204	115	1st	Norris	Won Stanley Cup
1979–80	80	47	20	13	328	240	107	1st	Norris	Lost Quarterfinal
1980–81	80	45	22	13	332	232	103	1st	Norris	Lost Prelim. Round
1981–82	80	46	17	17	360	223	109	1st	Adams	Lost Div. Semifinal
1982–83	80	42	24	14	350	286	98	2nd	Adams	Lost Div. Semifinal
1983–84	80	35	40	5	286	295	75	4th	Adams	Lost Conf. Final
1984–85	80	41	27	12	309	262	94	1st	Adams	Lost Div. Final
1985–86	80	40	33	7	330	280	87	2nd	Adams	Won Stanley Cup
1986–87	80	41	29	10	277	241	92	2nd	Adams	Lost Conf. Final
1987–88	80	45	22	13	298	238	103	1st	Adams	Lost Div. Final
1988–89	80	53	18	9	315	218	115	1st	Adams	Lost Final
1989–90	80	41	28	11	288	234	93	3rd	Adams	Lost Div. Final
1990–91	80	39	30	11	273	249	89	2nd	Adams	Lost Div. Final
1991–92	80	41	28	11	267	207	93	1st	Adams	Lost Div. Final
1992–93	84	48	30	6	326	280	102	3rd	Adams	Won Stanley Cup
1993–94	84	41	29	14	283	248	96	3rd	Northeast	Lost Conf. Quarterfinal
1994–95	48	18	23	7	125	148	43	6th	Northeast	Out of Playoffs
1995–96	82	40	32	10	265	248	90	3rd	Northeast	Lost Conf. Quarterfinal
1996–97	82	31	36	15	249	276	77	4th	Northeast	Lost Conf. Quarterfinal
1997–98	82	37	32	13	235	208	87	4th	Northeast	Lost Conf. Semifinal
1998–99	82	32	39	11	184	209	75	5th	Northeast	Out of Playoffs
1999-2000	82	35	38	9	196	194	§83	4th	Northeast	Out of Playoffs

* *Season played in two halves with no combined standing at end.*
From 1917–18 through 1925–26 NHL champions played against western champions for Stanley Cup.
** *Stanley Cup series with Seattle of the PCHA suspended due to influenza epidemic.*
§ *Includes 4 points for regulation ties (RT)*

MONTREAL MAROONS

DURING 14 SEASONS IN THE NHL, the Montreal Maroons boasted some of the top stars of the era, including Nels Stewart, the NHL's first 300-goal scorer. They won the Stanley Cup twice. But, the Maroons' greatest legacy to their city and the NHL was the Montreal Forum.

Montreal had been left without a top-rate hockey facility, and without a team to represent its anglophone population, when fire destroyed the Montreal Arena on January 2, 1918. The Mount Royal Arena was built to house the Montreal Canadiens in 1920, but its natural ice surface was unreliable in mild weather. By March, 1922, English Montreal was mobilizing to build a new hockey showcase and to return to the NHL. Ironically, French Canadian Donat Raymond would make it happen. He and William Northey appealed to Canadian Pacific Railway Chairman Edward W. Beatty, whose influence and financial support led to the creation of the Canadian Arena Company in January, 1924. Construction began in late spring, and by fall the Montreal Forum stood at the corner of St. Catherine and Atwater.

To provide a team for the new arena, Raymond and Northey turned to James Strachan who had created the Montreal Wanderers in 1903. On October 12, 1924, it was reported that Strachan and Raymond would be granted an NHL franchise for $15,000. The NHL formally admitted the new Montreal team, along with its first American entry, the Boston Bruins, on November 1, 1924. Yet another French Canadian had been instrumental behind the scenes. Leo Dandurand facilitated the admittance of the English Montreal team as part of a gentlemen's agreement that would allow him to move his Canadiens into the Forum when the lease expired at the Mount Royal Arena in 1926. In fact, the Canadiens played the first game at the Forum on November 29, 1924, because the natural ice surface at the Arena was not ready for the 1924–25 season opener.

The new Montreal team was formally known as the Montreal Professional Hockey Club during its first season. The owners had hoped to use the Wanderers name, but the rights apparently belonged to former Wanderers player and manager Dickie Boon. The Montreal roster comprised mostly veteran castoffs, though Clint Benedict, Punch Broadbent and Reg Noble would prove they had some life left. Rookies included Dunc Munro, a prized acquisition from the Toronto Granites, who had won an Olympic gold medal in February 1924. Still, the team was only spared from last place by the woeful record of its expansion cousins in Boston. However, with sellout crowds flocking to the Forum, success would come as quickly.

By January of the club's first season, newspapers had taken to calling Montreal's new hockey team the Maroons. In 1925–26, the team officially became known by the color of its uniforms. Two players acquired to wear those uniforms—Nels Stewart and Babe Siebert—led the Montreal Maroons from second last to second place in the club's second season. Stewart was a slow, plodding skater, but he had size and strength and would become known as "Old Poison" for the deadly accuracy of his shot. It found the net a league-leading 34 times in 1925–26, not only earning Stewart a scoring title but also the Hart Trophy as the NHL's most valuable player.

The Maroons defeated the Pittsburgh Pirates in their playoff debut, but the first-place Ottawa Senators were favored to defeat them in the NHL championship series. However ex-Senator Punch Broadbent scored for Montreal in a 1–1 tie in the first game, while former Ottawa star Clint Benedict recorded a shutout in game two. Babe Siebert's goal gave the Maroons a 2–1 total-goals series victory that entitled them to play the Western Hockey League's Victoria Cougars for the Stanley Cup. Nels Stewart fired six goals in four games against Victoria, including both goals in the 2–0 victory that gave the Maroons the series three games to one.

The NHL expanded to 10 teams in 1926–27, and split into Canadian and American divisions. The defending Stanley Cup champion Maroons slumped to third place in the Canadian Division and were knocked out of the playoffs by their fellow Forum tenants. Crowds of more than 11,000 fans jammed the arena—whose capacity was said to be only 10,000—for each of the two-game quarterfinal series. Howie Morenz won it for the Canadiens with an overtime goal in game two. The Maroons got their revenge the following year with a semifinal victory over the Canadiens that put them into the Stanley Cup finals against the New York Rangers. Though every game of the 1928 final was played at the Forum because the circus was performing at Madison Square Garden, the Rangers beat the Maroons three games to two. This was the series in which Rangers coach Lester Patrick made an emergency appearance in goal.

The Maroons fell to last place in the Canadian Division in 1928–29, but rebounded to remain a power in the league well into the 1930s. Nels Stewart again was the most valuable player in 1929–30, and the S-Line of Stewart, Babe Siebert and Hooley Smith remained among the league's most dangerous units until Stewart and Siebert were traded in 1932. By then, Baldy Northcott, Dave Trottier and Jimmy Ward had emerged as new stars, and with Russ Blinco named rookie of the year in 1933–34, the Maroons were able to compensate for the loss of the two future Hall of Famers.

Tommy Gorman joined the club in 1934–35 after winning the Stanley Cup in Chicago. The new coach and general manager acquired Alex Connell, who gave the Maroons their first star goaltender since Clint Benedict's departure in 1930. (Ironically, it was Connell's arrival in Ottawa in 1924 that had convinced the Senators to sell Benedict to Montreal.) Connell led the league with nine shutouts, then sparkled in the playoffs as the Maroons won the Stanley Cup again. With the line of Hooley Smith, Baldy Northcott and Jimmy Ward leading the way, the Maroons followed up their Stanley Cup victory with a Canadian Division title in 1935–36. But, attendance had been in decline in Montreal and around the league since the onset of the Depression, and now the Maroons began to feel the economic pinch.

Hooley Smith was an all-star in 1935–36, but salary concerns saw him peddled to the Boston Bruins. Without him, the Maroons opened the 1936–37 season poorly and attendance suffered all the more. The retirement of Lionel Conacher and Alex Connell further weakened the team in 1937–38, but Gorman hoped that hiring King Clancy as coach would fill the Maroons with a fighting spirit. It didn't. Clancy resigned on December 31, 1937, with the team in last place. At the time it was said that Clancy hadn't enforced enough discipline; others put the blame for the team's poor play on the low wages Gorman was paying. The Maroons continued to slump with Gorman behind the bench, and attendance worsened amid talk the city might be better served by just one professional hockey team. A 6–3 loss to the Canadiens on March 17, 1938, saw the Maroons finish the season with the league's worst record and miss the playoffs for the first time in nine years. It was the last game they ever played.

With the threat of war in Europe making the economic future even more uncertain, the team requested permission to suspend operations for one year, which the NHL granted on August 25, 1938. On May 13, 1939, the Montreal Maroons advised the NHL that they would no longer operate a franchise. Within a year, the Canadian Arena Company acquired the complete stock and assets of the Montreal Canadiens. The city's French team was also drawing poorly, but Donat Raymond would assure that at least one Montreal club survived. While the man who had built the Forum and created the Maroons continued to absorb financial losses, Tommy Gorman and coach Dick Irvin rebuilt the Canadiens into the team that would become the most successful franchise in hockey history.

Montreal Maroons Year-by-Year Record

Season	GP	W	L	T	GF	GA	Pts	Finish	Division	Playoff Results
1924–25	30	9	19	2	45	65	20	5th		Out of Playoffs
1925–26	36	20	11	5	91	73	45	2nd		Won Stanley Cup
1926–27	44	20	20	4	71	68	44	3rd	Canadian	Lost Quarterfinal
1927–28	44	24	14	6	96	77	54	2nd	Canadian	Lost Final
1928–29	44	15	20	9	67	65	39	5th	Canadian	Out of Playoffs
1929–30	44	23	16	5	141	114	51	1st	Canadian	Lost Semifinal
1930–31	44	20	18	6	105	106	46	3rd	Canadian	Lost Quarterfinal
1931–32	48	19	22	7	142	139	45	3rd	Canadian	Lost Semifinal
1932–33	48	22	20	6	135	119	50	2nd	Canadian	Lost Quarterfinal
1933–34	48	19	18	11	117	122	49	3rd	Canadian	Lost Semifinal
1934–35	48	24	19	5	123	92	53	2nd	Canadian	Won Stanley Cup
1935–36	48	22	16	10	114	106	54	1st	Canadian	Lost Semifinal
1936–37	48	22	17	9	126	110	53	2nd	Canadian	Lost Semifinal
1937–38	48	12	30	6	101	149	30	4th	Canadian	Out of Playoffs

MONTREAL WANDERERS

THOUGH THEY HAVE BEEN GONE FOR MORE THAN 80 YEARS, the Montreal Wanderers remain one of the legendary teams in hockey history. Sixteen future Hockey Hall of Famers played for the Wanderers during the club's 15-year existence. The team won Stanley Cup championships in 1906, 1907, 1908 and 1910. But, even more than success, controversy defined the Montreal Wanderers.

The Wanderers were charter members of the Federal Amateur Hockey League, which was formed on December 5, 1903, to accommodate Wanderers founder James Strachan (a member of a prominent Montreal bakery family who would later help form the Montreal Maroons). Strachan's team was not welcome in the Canadian Amateur Hockey League because he had raided the roster of the Montreal Amateur Athletic Association hockey club. Jack Marshall, Jimmy Gardner, Cecil Blachford, Dickie Boon, Billy Bellingham and Billy Nicholson all had been with the rival Montreal organization the previous season. All except Blachford also had been members of the AAA's Stanley Cup-winning team of 1902. That team had been dubbed "The Little Men of Iron" for the tenacious way they hung on to defeat the Winnipeg Victorias. In later years the nickname was applied frequently to the Wanderers.

The Wanderers' powerful aggregation of former champions had little trouble with the competition in the FAHL, romping to the championship with a perfect 6–0 record. A two-game, total-goals Stanley Cup challenge match then was arranged between the Wanderers and the Ottawa Silver Seven. Ottawa, too, had seen its share of controversy that year, as the club had resigned from the CAHL in midseason. The Stanley Cup series between the season's two most troublesome teams provided even more problems after an extremely physical game on March 2, 1904 ended in a 5–5 tie after 60 minutes. Unhappy with the refereeing, the Wanderers refused to play overtime. The Stanley Cup trustees ordered a new two-game set with both games to be played in Ottawa. The Wanderers refused to take part unless the tied game was replayed in Montreal, and the series had to be abandoned.

The Silver Seven joined the Wanderers in the Federal League in 1904–05, although there were rumors that both teams would abandon the FAHL if the CAHL would accept them. The rumors heated up again prior to the 1905–06 season, but the Wanderers would be in on a much more surprising development when a new league was formed on December 11, 1906. The Eastern Canada Amateur Hockey Association consisted of the Wanderers and Ottawa from the FAHL, and the Montreal Victorias, Quebec Bulldogs, Montreal AAA and Montreal Shamrocks of the CAHL.

Bolstered by the addition of future Hall of Famers Lester Patrick, Moose Johnson and Ernie Russell, the Wanderers proved the equal of the defending Stanley Cup champions from Ottawa and the two teams finished the first ECAHA season with identical 9–1 records. To break the tie, a two-game, total-goals playoff was scheduled. The winner would not only claim the league title but also the Stanley Cup. The first game was played in Montreal on March 14, 1906, and resulted in a 9–1 victory for the Wanderers. Game two was played in Ottawa three nights later. Amazingly, Ottawa stormed back to even the series score at 10–10 before Lester Patrick ended the Silver Seven's Stanley Cup reign with a pair of late goals.

Not content to rest on their championship laurels, James Strachan and the Wanderers began to stir up new trouble at the annual meeting of the Eastern Canada Amateur Hockey Association on November 11, 1906. Strachan led the move to allow professional players into the ECAHA along with amateurs, then threatened to withdraw from the league unless the Wanderers were permitted to meet a team from New Glasgow, Nova Scotia, in a preseason Stanley Cup challenge match in December. Permission was granted, and the Wanderers scored easy 10–3 and 7–2 victories. Strachan's team then took time out from the ECAHA season in mid-January to entertain another Stanley Cup challenge. This time, however, the Wanderers were defeated by the Kenora Thistles, 4–2 and 8–6.

Spurred on by the desire to win back the trophy, the Wanderers blazed through the remainder of the regular season. With Ernie Russell scoring 42 goals in nine league games, the Wanderers romped to a 10–0 record and headed west to Winnipeg for a Stanley Cup rematch with Kenora. The Wanderers scored a 7–2 victory in the first game on March 23, 1907, and though the Thistles won the second game, 6–5, the Wanderers took the total-goals series, 12–8, and were Stanley Cup champions once again. Another ECAHA title in 1907–08, and successful defenses against teams from Ottawa, Toronto, Winnipeg and Edmonton kept the Stanley Cup in Montreal through one more year. Lester Patrick had gone west to British Columbia to work in the family lumber business and Hod Stuart had drowned during the summer of 1907, but the addition of Art Ross and Hod's brother, Bruce Stuart, helped the Wanderers offset their losses.

The 1908–09 season saw the Eastern Canada Amateur Hockey Association become the Eastern Canada Hockey Association after the withdrawal of the strictly amateur Montreal Victorias and Montreal AAA. Ottawa (now known as the Senators) beat the Wanderers in the final game of the season to win the ECHA title and the Stanley Cup, but the Wanderers would return to the top in 1910—though not without more controversy.

By this time the Wanderers had been sold to P.J. Doran, who owned the Jubilee Arena in Montreal. Although his arena had about half the capacity of the team's previous home, Doran proposed to move the Wanderers into his rink for the 1909–10 season. Facing a dwindling share of the gate receipts, Doran's fellow owners voted the ECHA out of existence on November 25, 1909, and created the new Canadian Hockey Association. This league would not include the Wanderers, nor the team from Renfrew, Ontario, that the Wanderers supported for inclusion in the ECHA.

Having both been snubbed, the Wanderers and Renfrew joined to form a rival hockey league—the National Hockey Association. Backed by Renfrew millionaire M.J. O'Brien and run by his son Ambrose, the NHA proved more viable than the CHA and by mid-January, 1910, the Montreal Shamrocks and Ottawa Senators abandoned the CHA for the new league. The Wanderers posted an 11–1 record during the 1909–10 season to win both the NHA title and the Stanley Cup.

Ownership of the Wanderers again changed hands for the 1910–11 season, and the team moved back to the larger Montreal Arena. However, the glory days of the franchise were over. The period of Sam Lichtenhein's ownership was marked by financial struggles. The war over players with the rival Pacific Coast Hockey Association drove up salaries, while the war in Europe depleted rosters and lessened hockey's box-office appeal. The Wanderers were included when the teams of the NHA reorganized to form the NHL in November, 1917, but Lichtenhein's team was clearly in trouble. As late as December 12, 1917, it appeared the Wanderers might not be able to produce a team because of injuries and military commitments. However, when the NHL season opened seven days later, the Wanderers' cast of aging veterans and unproven youngsters defeated Toronto 10–9—though only 700 fans saw the game. Two nights later, the rival Canadiens crushed the Wanderers, 11–2, and Lichtenhein threatened to withdraw from the NHL unless he could get more players. Two more lopsided losses followed.

On January 2, 1918, fire destroyed the Montreal Arena. The blaze was attributed to an unknown cause in the Wanderers dressing room. The Montreal Canadiens announced they would play out the season in the Wanderers' old home, the Jubilee Arena. Hamilton, Ontario, offered to take in the Wanderers, but when the other NHL teams refused to provide additional players, Lichtenhein withdrew his club on January 4, 1918. A colorful and controversial era in hockey history was over.

Montreal Wanderers Year-by-Year Record

Season	GP	W	L	T	GF	GA	Pts	Finish	Playoff Results
1917–18	*6	1	*5	0	17	35	2	Withdrew	–

** includes two defaulted games*

NASHVILLE PREDATORS

NASHVILLE WAS THE FIRST TEAM TO BEGIN PLAY after being welcomed into the National Hockey League with Atlanta, Minnesota and Columbus as expansion clubs on June 25, 1997. The Predators were placed in the Central Division of the Western Conference along with the Chicago Blackhawks, Detroit Red Wings and St. Louis Blues for the 1997–98 season. (The Columbus Blue Jackets were added to the division for the 2000–2001 campaign.) Their home rink is the Gaylord Entertainment Center, which was known as the Nashville Arena when it opened for the club's inaugural year.

The first major order of business for team president Jack Diller was to hire David Poile as executive vice president of hockey operations and general manager on July 9, 1997. Poile had served as general manager of the Washington Capitals since 1982, and had helped build the team into a perennial contender. He had begun his career in hockey administration with the expansion Atlanta Flames in 1972, and worked himself up to the position of assistant general manager in both Atlanta and Calgary. His father, Bud Poile, had played seven years in the NHL and was the general manager of expansion teams in both Philadelphia and Vancouver. A little less than a month after his own hiring in

Nashville, Poile signed Barry Trotz as the team's first head coach. Trotz had spent four seasons as the head coach of the Portland Pirates, Washington's farm club in the American Hockey League.

The Predators name was announced for Nashville's first major-league sports franchise on November 13, 1997, by club chairman and majority owner Craig Leipold and Diller. "Given the intense nature of hockey, combined with the game's speed and skill, Predators is a natural fit," said Leipold, "and it is the name Nashville fans chose for their team." Added Diller: "The image of a predator is one who succeeds and wins, something we hope our team will do often when we begin play." For a logo, the team chose a dramatic profile of a saber-toothed cat, which was native in prehistoric times to the region that is now Nashville.

On June 1, 1998, the Predators acquired their first player when they obtained Marian Cisar from the Los Angeles Kings for future considerations. (Cisar was later assigned to Nashville's AHL farm club in Milwaukee.) Free agents Jayson More, Rob Valicevic and Mark Mowers, who were signed later in June, all saw action for Nashville during the inaugural 1998–99 season, but roster-building began in earnest on June 26, 1998, at the Expansion Draft in Buffalo. Greg Johnson and Andrew Brunette, as well as goaltenders Mike Dunham and Tomas Vokoun, were key members of the inaugural club. Such players as Sergei Krivokrasov, Jan Vopat and Sebastien Bordeleau were picked up in trades later in the day.

One day after the Expansion Draft, a trade with the San Jose Sharks landed Nashville the second pick in the NHL Entry Draft. The Predators chose highly regarded junior prospect David Legwand. A rookie in the Ontario Hockey League in 1997–98, Legwand had 54 goals and 51 assists in just 59 games for the Plymouth Whalers and became the first rookie (and second American-born player) to be named the OHL's most valuable player. Tom Fitzgerald, who had been the first forward selected by the Florida Panthers in the 1993 Expansion Draft, joined the Predators as a free agent on July 6, 1998, and became the club's first captain.

The Nashville Predators played their first game on October 10, 1998, entering the arena on a red carpet in front of a sellout crowd of 17,298. Even a 1–0 loss to the Florida Panthers couldn't dampen the enthusiasm generated that evening. Three nights later, the Predators had their first victory when they defeated the Carolina Hurricanes 3–2 on home ice. Andrew Brunette scored the club's first goal, while Mike Dunham earned the first victory. By month's end, the team had a respectable record of 3–5–1, including a 3–2 victory over the Colorado Avalanche on October 31. Even more important than a victory over one of the NHL's top clubs was the trade that day that brought Cliff Ronning to Nashville from the Phoenix Coyotes. Ronning's 35 assists and 53 points in 72 games as a Predator led all Nashville players during the club's first season. Krivokrasov's 25 goals were also tops on the team.

Among the highlights of the Predators' first season was the one and only visit by Wayne Gretzky to Nashville. Gretzky had four assists as the New York Rangers raced out to a 6–0 lead midway through the second period and, despite the lopsided score, the performance of "The Great One" had the crowd buzzing. Live country music being played in the aisles added to the festive atmosphere, which reached frenzied proportions when the Predators scored four straight goals. A fifth assist by Gretzky capped an eventual 7–4 Rangers win.

Though Nashville ended its inaugural season with four straight losses to drop its record to 28–47–7, the club attracted sellout crowds for six straight games to close out the schedule. The Predators drew 664,000 fans during their first season for an average attendance of 16,202 (94% of capacity). The season finalé, on April 18, 1999, featured the NHL debut of David Legwand, who had signed with the team two days earlier after playing out the season in Plymouth. Legwand had two shots on goal in a game won 4–1 by the Devils. The success of the Predators' inaugural campaign was reflected in the contract extensions offered to Barry Trotz and his assistant coaches, Paul Gardner and Brent Peterson, a month after the season ended.

Few personnel changes were made prior to the 1999–2000 season, as the Predators kept the core of the first-year team together. David Legwand, still only 19 years old, earned a spot on the Nashville roster to start the 1999–2000 season. He had a landmark game in Toronto on October 11, 1999, when he collected the first goal and the first assist of his NHL career. Legwand's goal against the Maple Leafs goaltender Glenn Healy came with 1:03 remaining in the third period. It broke a 2–2 tie and sparked the Predators to a 4–2 victory. The win was the first of the season for the second-year club. Legwand wound up playing 71 games for the Predators and ranked among the rookie scoring leaders with 28 points. Once again Cliff Ronning was the team's top scorer, but the club will need Legwand and other youngsters in the system like Denis Arkhipov and Martin Bartek to begin to make offensive contributions in coming seasons. Among the most pleasant surprises of 1999–2000 was the play of rookie defenseman Karlis Skrastins.

Like their inaugural season, the Predators were able to play consistent hockey through the first half of the schedule—and even dreamed of the postseason—until the club hit a February swoon. They wound up the 1999–2000 campaign with an identical won-loss-tied record of 28–47–7, but did gain seven extra points in the standings due to the new rule providing a point for losses in overtime.

Nashville Predators Year-by-Year Record

Season	GP	W	L	T	GF	GA	Pts	Finish	Division	Playoff Results
1998–99	82	28	47	7	190	261	63	4th	Central	Out of Playoffs
1999-2000	82	28	47	7	199	240	70	4th	Central	Out of Playoffs

** Includes 7 points for regulation ties (RT)*

New Jersey Devils, Colorado Rockies and Kansas City Scouts

During the 1990s, the New Jersey Devils were able to erase their image as the league's laughing stock and establish themselves as a Stanley Cup champion and consistent challenger for the Presidents' Trophy as the NHL's regular-season champion.

The Devils began their existence not in New Jersey, but in Missouri as the Kansas City Scouts. They entered the league with the Washington Capitals in 1974–75. Playing out of the brand-new Kemper Arena, the Scouts had little to offer in their rookie season. Facing competition from the two-year-old World Hockey Association, the Scouts scrambled for talent and had little apart from the solid goaltending of Denis Herron, the power shooting of Simon Nolet and the hope that high-priced rookie Wilf Paiement would make his three-year, $500,000 contract look worthwhile.

Former Detroit Red Wings hero Sid Abel was named general manager, and he did the best with what he had but, admittedly, it was not much. "Neither the Capitals nor ourselves were exactly overloaded with stars," said Abel. By comparison with the Capitals, the Scouts did relatively well. Kansas City finished with 41 points, 20 more than Washington, but that was the extent of the jubilation. A year later Kansas City slipped to 36 points while attendance slipped to the point of no return. With the NHL's approval, the franchise was moved to Denver, where it was rechristened the Colorado Rockies and continued to lose hockey games.

Under coach Johnny Wilson, the Rockies finished last in the Smythe Division and offered little to attract the Rocky Mountain fans other than Paiement, who began fulfilling his early notices. There was little difference between the franchise in Kansas City and Denver other than the fact that Rockies lasted six years rather than two and for a brief, colorful period had Don Cherry as their coach.

By the 1980–81 season it had become obvious that Denver was not buying into the Rockies. New Jersey trucking executive Arthur Imperatore, who had purchased the team, threatened to move the franchise to a new arena in his home state's Meadowlands within view of the Manhattan skyline. But the Rangers, Islanders and Flyers—each of whom had veto power—nixed the idea, whereupon Imperatore sold the club to Buffalo cable television magnate Peter Gilbert and former Colorado lieutenant governor Mark Hogan.

After another dreadful season in 1981–82, Gilbert wanted out and found a buyer in Dr. John J. McMullen. Renowned in sporting circles, Dr. McMullen first ventured into baseball as a limited partner of the New York Yankees and later would own the Houston Astros.

A New Jersey native, McMullen became convinced that his native state could support an NHL team at The Meadowlands. On May 27, 1982, it became official. McMullen, along with John C. Whitehead, now the chairman of AEA Investors, Inc., and former New Jersey governor Brendan T. Byrne, purchased the Rockies and received NHL approval to shift the franchise to The Meadowlands. It was not, however, a simple transaction. McMullen had to indemnify the Flyers, Rangers and Islanders handsomely for "invading" their territory. McMullen named longtime hockey executive Max McNab vice president in charge of hockey operations and Billy MacMillan as general manager and coach.

The New Jersey Devils played their first home game on September 21, 1982, in a preseason contest with the New York Rangers. Dr. McMullen accelerated the future rivalry by twitting the denizens of Madison Square Garden in a pregame comment that was well-covered by the media. "I believe we're going to be a lot more aggressive than the Rangers," said McMullen. "They're complacent because they're sold out." Seizing on the observation, the *New York Post* headlined the story "Rangers Angry Over McMullen Remark."

Perhaps they were, but McMullen couldn't have cared less. He wanted his team to put on a good showing against the 56-year-old franchise from across the Hudson River. The Devils did not win, but the 9,193 fans were well entertained. Billy MacMillan was disappointed with the result. "We still have a long way to go," he opined.

It is doubtful that McMullen realized precisely how long it would take for his Devils to become a playoff contender. They finished their first season with a record of 17–49–14, placing them fifth in the six-team Patrick Division. "We're making some progress," said Aaron Broten. "Last year we didn't know if the team would be in Denver or wherever. Now we know we're going to be in New Jersey next year."

But 1983–84 was no kinder to New Jersey's franchise. If one episode could encapsulate the club's futility, it would be a game at Northlands Coliseum in Edmonton on November 19, 1983. Ron Low started in goal for New Jersey. He was well-known to Edmonton fans and players, having played for the Oilers over four seasons before being traded to the Devils.

Much as they liked Low, the Oilers were merciless in their treatment of him that evening. They pumped eight goals past him through two periods of play and were so overwhelming that MacMillan felt obligated to pull his starter and replace Ron with Glenn "Chico" Resch for the third period. The final tally was 13–4, representing the largest score ever run up against the franchise. And the swarming was not over.

Reporters descended on the Oilers dressing room for comments, especially from Wayne Gretzky who had recorded three goals and five assists.

Prodded with leading questions from the newsmen, Gretzky was lured into a denunciation that he might have avoided. But he answered spontaneously when queried about the bombardment of his buddy Low. "It got to a point where it wasn't even funny," said Gretzky. "They're ruining the whole league. They had better stop running a Mickey Mouse operation and put somebody on ice."

The 13–4 game took place on Saturday night in Edmonton, after most of the New Jersey-New York newspapers had their last editions put to bed. Little other than the scoring results appeared in most Sunday papers, but by Monday the headlines were blaring all over the country. "Gretzky Takes a Slap at Devils Organization" barked the headline in *USA Today. The New York Post* was more direct: "Gretzky: Devils are a Mickey Mouse Team."

To his surprise, Gretzky began feeling the heat. He was surprised by the groundswell of public opinion against his tirade. "You'd have thought I'd criticized Miss Newark or something," said Gretzky. "The fans went crazy against me."

The fallout from the Gretzky fiasco led to MacMillan being dismissed. Max McNab was named general manager and Tom McVie, who had been coaching the Maine Mariners, was promoted to head coach. The results were insignificant. Not only did the Devils finish fifth again, now they had the stigma of Gretzky's insult tarnishing their image. If there was hope, it was provided by draft choices such as Kirk Muller and John MacLean, who infused energy into the machine if not sufficient wins. Soon rugged, young defenseman Ken Daneyko would established himself as a fan favorite.

Management appointed Doug Carpenter as head coach in 1985–86, and while the redhead provided a sense of discipline and purpose in the young club, the coveted playoff berth was still beyond reach. The club's turning point began on April 24, 1987, when president Bob Butera resigned and McMullen named Lou Lamoriello as his successor. For two decades Lamoriello had been the guiding force behind Providence College's hockey success. When Max McNab was moved up to a vice presidency, Lamoriello became general manager as well. On January 26, 1988, he introduced Jim Schoenfeld as the Devils' new bench boss.

Schoenfeld was one of two key additions who would transform the Devils from perennial losers to a playoff team. The other was goaltender Sean Burke, who had been drafted by New Jersey in 1985 and had come to the team following the 1988 Winter Olympic Games at Calgary. In his first game as a Devil at Boston Garden, Burke defeated the Bruins 7–6 in overtime. Although nobody knew it for sure at the time, this was the start of something big. Slowly, relentlessly, the Devils began a long climb toward a playoff berth that culminated with a decisive game at Chicago Stadium on April 3, 1988. Trailing the Rangers throughout the homestretch, the Devils could oust their rivals by defeating the Blackhawks. The game went into overtime before John MacLean beat goalie Darren Pang at 2:21 to give New Jersey its victory and first taste of postseason play.

The Devils then upset the first-place Islanders in the opening round and followed that with a seven-game series win—again MacLean scored the decisive goal—over favored Washington. Facing Boston in the third round, the Devils unexpectedly became involved in a brouhaha at the end of game three at Byrne Arena. Coach Jim Schoenfeld engaged in a verbal bout with referee Don Koharski that continued in a hallway leading from the ice to the dressing rooms. When NHL vice president Brian O'Neill—NHL president John Ziegler was reportedly out-of-town—suspended Schoenfeld, the Devils charged that no hearing had been held and the right of appeal should be honored.

Taking their case to court, the Devils won a temporary restraining order that lifted Schoenfeld's suspension. The decision was rendered minutes before game time on Mother's Day, May 8, the night on which game four was to be played. Upon hearing of the judge's decision, the referee and linesmen refused to take the ice. The NHL responded by hiring three off-ice officials—Paul McInnis, Vin Godleski and Jim Sullivan—to officiate the game. Skates were found for all three. Only one had a striped shirt. The other two donned yellow practice jerseys and took the ice one hour and six minutes after the scheduled start of the game. (Two more striped shirts were found for the start of period two.) The Devils won 3–1 and the replacement officials won praise for their efforts.

New Jersey took Boston to seven games before succumbing 6–2 in the finalé at Boston Garden. "Our club has proven that we no longer will be two easy points for every opponent," said Lamoriello. But instead of providing an impetus for bigger things, the big run to the playoffs proved illusory. In 1988–89, the Devils missed the postseason again, but they rebounded the following season with a second-place finish after John Cunniff had replaced Schoenfeld as coach. A first-round exit dimmed the luster, and Cunniff exited in the middle of the 1990–91 season in favor of Tom McVie. The Devils continued to play competitively, reaching the playoffs but never advancing past the first round, even after Herb Brooks succeeded McVie for the 1992–93 campaign.

A new era dawned on June 28, 1993, when Jacques Lemaire, a member of eight Stanley Cup-winning Montreal Canadiens teams, was named New Jersey's seventh head coach, with former teammate Larry Robinson coming aboard as assistant. Lemaire introduced a defensive system that would become known as the neutral zone trap, and the results were remarkable. The Devils recorded their best-ever record, 47–25–12, good for second place in the division. They then defeated Boston and Buffalo in the first two playoff rounds before extending the Rangers to double-overtime of the seventh game of a thrilling Eastern Conference championship.

A year later, in a lockout-shortened season, the Devils finished second again and entered the playoffs as distinct underdogs to the Boston Bruins. Paced by Claude Lemieux and Stephane Richer, New Jersey opened with a 5–0 win on the road and proceeded to demolish the Bruins in five games. Facing Pittsburgh, the Devils fell behind by a game, then closed out the series with four wins in a row.

Next on the agenda was Philadelphia, with the Devils again opening on the road. It hardly mattered. They beat the Flyers in two straight at the Spectrum and won the series in six. Lemieux, Richer and goalie Martin Brodeur continued to excel as New Jersey reached the finals against the Red Wings at Joe Louis Arena. Employing their trap to perfection, the Devils shut down the high-flying Wings in a surprising four-game sweep, wrapping up the series with consecutive 5–2 victories before capacity crowds of 19,040 at the Meadowlands. NHL commissioner Gary Bettman presented the Cup to captain Scott Stevens and then congratulated John McMullen. The new NHL champs boasted 12 American-born players in their lineup, a record for a Stanley Cup winner.

But the days of celebration were clouded in uncertainty. In a dispute with the New Jersey Sports and Exposition Authority—the landlord of Byrne Arena—McMullen threatened to move his club to Nashville where a brand-new rink was being completed and financial enticements were difficult to refuse. After a summer of intense negotiations with the involvement of Bettman, a compromise was hammered out which included a new lease at what would become known as Continental Airlines Arena.

In their defense of the Stanley Cup, the Devils proved a disappointment. Although their record in 1995–96 was 37–33–12, good for 86 points, New Jersey was eliminated from playoff contention on the final weekend of the season, losing to Ottawa at home and thus enabling the Tampa Bay Lightning to earn their first playoff berth. However, Lemaire was able to galvanize his team the following year, lifting New Jersey to first place both in the division and the conference. Martin Brodeur had established himself as one of the league's foremost goaltenders while Scott Stevens was a rock on the blue line. Lacking a gunner, the Devils nevertheless spread the goals among four well-balanced lines led by the likes of Bobby Holik, Dave Andreychuk and Randy McKay.

The Devils seemed on course for another long playoff run in the spring of 1997 until Andreychuk—the club's best two-way forward—badly broke his ankle in the final game of the season at Philadelphia. Although New Jersey defeated Montreal in a five-game opening playoff round, they went down to the Rangers in round two—losing four in a row after a game-one victory.

Lamoriello made some lineup alterations for 1997–98, dipping into his Albany River Rats farm club for reinforcements. Youngsters such as Brad Bombardir, Patrik Elias and Sheldon Souray were added to the lineup and paid off handsomely. New Jersey finished with a club record 107 points (48–23–11), falling just short of winning the Presidents' Trophy. First in their division and first in their conference, the Devils were rated among the Stanley Cup favorites. However, New Jersey was stunned by an Ottawa Senators team that eliminated them in six games. Jacques Lemaire stepped down as coach after the season and was replaced by Robbie Ftorek.

Despite the disappointing finish, New Jersey had established itself as a formidable organization. Attendance reached an all-time high during the 1997–98 season with an average of more than 17,000 per game, and the Albany farm club continued to excel in the American Hockey League. Ftorek would relax the Devils' tight defensive system in 1998–99, and for the first time in three years the team did not allow the fewest goals against, although Martin Brodeur did lead the league with 39 victories. The Devils set an NHL road record with 28 wins away from home (28–10–3) and led the Eastern Conference with 105 points. However, the season ended almost identically to the year before, as once again the Devils were eliminated in the first round of the playoffs, this time by Pittsburgh.

Patrick Elias and Hispanic-Alaskan rookie Scott Gomez feuled the Devils offense in 1999–2000, but once again the team's top performer was Martin Brodeur who led the NHL with 43 victories. Scott Stevens continued to lead a defense that was among the league's stingiest. Rookies John Madden and Brian Rafalski proved to be key additions. Rafalski had played four years in Europe after being undrafted out of the University of Wisconsin. Another rookie, Colin White, would prove his value in the playoffs as a blueliner in the Stevens image.

The Devils topped the Eastern Conference standings for much of the year, but a late slump cost Robbie Ftorek his job with just eight games left in the season. The Devils limped to a 4–4 finish under new coach Larry Robinson and allowed Philadelphia to slip past them for first place in both the Atlantic Division and the East. Though New Jersey's 103 points was the second-best total in the conference they were seeded fourth in the playoffs behind the division-winning Capitals and Toronto Maple Leafs.

The Devils seemed to shake off their late-season slide when they swept the Florida Panthers in the opening round of the playoffs. New Jersey's stifling defense shut down Pavel Bure, and was even more effective against Toronto's top line of Mats Sundin, Steve Thomas and Jonas Hogland in round two. That victory required six games, but the Maple Leafs were limited to just six shots in the series finalé, an all-time playoff low. New Jersey's hot playoff run seemed about to end when they fell behind the Flyers three games to one in the Eastern Conference final, but the Devils rallied for three straight wins and advanced to meet the defending champion Dallas Stars for the Stanley Cup. After stunning the Stars with a 7–3 victory in game one, it was the Devils who jumped out to a 3–1 series lead this time. With a chance to wrap up the series on home ice in game five, the Devils were instead shut out through more than five periods of hockey before Mike Modano finally gave Dallas a 1–0 victory in triple overtime. Two nights later in Dallas, the two teams battled into double overtime before Jason Arnott beat Ed Belfour to make the Devils Stanley Cup champions for the first time since 1995. Scott Stevens, whose crushing bodychecks had neutralized opposition scorers throughout the playoffs, earned the Conn Smythe Trophy as playoff MVP.

The Stanley Cup victory marked a fitting send off for John McMullen, whose effective ownership had allowed Lou Lamoriello to build the Devils into a powerhouse.

New Jersey Devils Year-by-Year Record

Season	GP	W	L	T	GF	GA	Pts	Finish	Division	Playoff Results
1974–75*	80	15	54	11	184	328	41	5th	Smythe	Out of Playoffs
1975–76*	80	12	56	12	190	351	36	5th	Smythe	Out of Playoffs
1976–77**	80	20	46	14	226	307	54	5th	Smythe	Out of Playoffs
1977–78**	80	19	40	21	257	305	59	2nd	Smythe	Lost Prelim. Round
1978–79**	80	15	53	12	210	331	42	4th	Smythe	Out of Playoffs
1979–80**	80	19	48	13	234	308	51	6th	Smythe	Out of Playoffs
1980–81**	80	22	45	13	258	344	57	5th	Smythe	Out of Playoffs
1981–82**	80	18	49	13	241	362	49	5th	Smythe	Out of Playoffs
1982–83	80	17	49	14	230	338	48	5th	Patrick	Out of Playoffs
1983–84	80	17	56	7	231	350	41	5th	Patrick	Out of Playoffs
1984–85	80	22	48	10	264	346	54	5th	Patrick	Out of Playoffs
1985–86	80	28	49	3	300	374	59	6th	Patrick	Out of Playoffs
1986–87	80	29	45	6	293	368	64	6th	Patrick	Out of Playoffs
1987–88	80	38	36	6	295	296	82	4th	Patrick	Lost Conf. Final
1988–89	80	27	41	12	281	325	66	5th	Patrick	Out of Playoffs
1989–90	80	37	34	9	295	288	83	2nd	Patrick	Lost Div. Semifinal
1990–91	80	32	33	15	272	264	79	4th	Patrick	Lost Div. Semifinal
1991–92	80	38	31	11	289	259	87	4th	Patrick	Lost Div. Semifinal
1992–93	84	40	37	7	308	299	87	4th	Patrick	Lost Div. Semifinal
1993–94	84	47	25	12	306	220	106	2nd	Atlantic	Lost Conf. Final
1994–95	48	22	18	8	136	121	52	2nd	Atlantic	Won Stanley Cup
1995–96	82	37	33	12	215	202	86	6th	Atlantic	Out of Playoffs
1996–97	82	45	23	14	231	182	104	1st	Atlantic	Lost Conf. Semifinal
1997–98	82	48	23	11	225	166	107	1st	Atlantic	Lost Conf. Quarterfinal
1998–99	82	47	24	11	248	196	105	1st	Atlantic	Lost Conf. Quarterfinal
1999-2000	82	45	29	8	251	203	§103	2nd	Atlantic	Won Stanley Cup

** Kansas City Scouts. ** Colorado Rockies.*

§ Includes 5 points for regulation ties (RT)

NEW YORK AMERICANS

Though they were the first NHL team in Manhattan, the New York Americans played second-fiddle to the New York Rangers during most of their run on Broadway. Yet in their own bizarre way, the star-spangled skaters generated excitement both on the ice and off. They entered the NHL for the 1925–26 season, one year before the Rangers were granted a franchise, and became a barometer for future NHL expansion.

At a time when journalist Damon Runyon was glorifying the guys and dolls of Broadway, the New York Americans boasted a list of characters that could have filled Runyon's columns. By far the best was William V. Dwyer, founder of the Amerks (as the newspapers called them), who also happened to be one of America's most notorious bootleggers during the Prohibition years of the Roaring Twenties.

Not especially versed in hockey, Dwyer happened upon the Americans in a curious way. Having already expanded to Boston, the NHL targeted Manhattan as its next site but lacked a buyer. William MacBeth, a Canadian who wrote for the New York Herald-Tribune, knew about the NHL's interest and believed that hockey would become a cash cow in America's largest city. Friendly with Dwyer, MacBeth persuaded the liquor boss to buy the waiting New York franchise, knowing that George "Tex" Rickard, impresario of the new Madison Square Garden, had been persuaded to include ice-making facilities in his arena. Since Rickard was lukewarm to hockey, Dwyer made his move.

Understanding the importance of a strong Broadway opening, Dwyer purchased the Hamilton Tigers and moved them to New York. The Tigers had finished in first place during the 1924–25 season, but the franchise was ripe for relocation because the Hamilton players had pulled a protest walkout during the playoffs. For $75,000 Dwyer was able to obtain a team that was primed to be instantly competitive, with top talents like Billy Burch and brothers Red and Shorty Green—plus a speedy addition from Western Canada who would immediately catch the fans' fancy, "Bullet" Joe Simpson.

The Americans played their first NHL game at the Garden on December 15, 1925, against the Montreal Canadiens. Although they lost, 3–1, the Amerks impressed everyone, including the legion of New York City bluebloods who graced the arena. With MacBeth handling their publicity and Tommy Gorman managing them, the Americans became an instant hit. Unfortunately, the press agent overplayed his hand in touting Simpson as "The Blue Streak from Saskatoon" and Burch as "The Babe Ruth of Hockey." Unschooled in the fundamentals, New York fans seized upon the nicknames. They immediately made these two players their favorites, and demanded goals from them.

"Every time one of them passed to another player," wrote Frank Graham Sr., who covered sports for the New York Sun, "the spectators howled in rage and disappointment. Seeking to please the customers, Billy and Joe did as little passing as possible. This resulted in spectacular but futile one-man raids on enemy nets and a rapid disintegration of the team play necessary to ensure victories."

Still, the Americans proved so popular that Madison Square Garden ownership decided to obtain a big-league team of its own despite the fact that Dwyer had an unwritten "guarantee" from the Garden that his club would have sole rights to the New York area. Unfortunately, the bootlegger was in no position to take issue with Garden president Colonel John Hammond. Dwyer had been nailed by the feds over an elaborate rum-running scheme. (He would be dispatched to Atlanta Penitentiary for two years in June, 1927.) Meanwhile, what infuriated Dwyer most about the Garden's New York Rangers was the rent-free status emjoyed by the new franchise compared with his Amerks, whose own rent bill grew steeper by the season. These indignities sparked a rivalry that quickly flamed into one of the best in a city that featured the Brooklyn Dodgers versus the New York Giants and, if a World Series meeting took place, either of these clubs against the New York Yankees.

Despite Roy Worters' peerless goaltending, the Americans rarely were as good as the Rangers. When the Broadway Blueshirts won their first Stanley Cup in their second season (1927–28), they instantly became the darlings of New York hockey while the Amerks took on the image of also-rans. By 1933, the Americans were still Cupless while the Rangers had won their second championship. Although Dwyer remained a member of the NHL Board of Governors until 1937, his fiscal infusions into his hockey club had ended. Big Bill went broke after the government won a $3.7 million action against him, causing the league to take over the team in 1936–37. That, plus the end of Prohibition, finished Dwyer but not the Amerks.

Mervyn "Red" Dutton, who had become playing coach, was the scion of a wealthy western Canadian contracting family. With the Great Depression playing havoc with finances, Dutton occasionally had shelled out money to Dwyer. Now the team was his to run. Despite the Depression and other hardships, Dutton managed to keep the Americans afloat. Deft trades for veteran castoffs and the addition of unproven rookies enabled him to ice a competitive team that nearly challenged for the Stanley Cup in 1937–38. That year the Americans finished second in the Canadian Division and faced the Rangers in a best-of-three series to open the playoffs. The clubs split the first two games before the largest crowd of the season (16,340) jammed the arena for the deciding contest. The Rangers jumped into a 2–0 lead, but Lorne Carr and Nels Stewart tied the game for the Amerks and sent it into overtime. Neither team could break the tie for three sudden-death periods until Carr finally scored the winner for Dutton and Company.

"That," Dutton stated, "was the greatest thrill I ever got in hockey. The Rangers had a high-priced team then, and beating them was like winning the Stanley Cup to us."

Unfortunately, the Americans were knocked out of the playoffs by Chicago in the next round and were never to achieve such lofty heights again. They did reach the playoffs in each of the next two seasons, but they finished dead last in 1940–41. By then World War II had broken out, and many Canadian-born players quit hockey to join the armed forces. Dutton lost 14 of 16 players to the Canadian army and other branches of the services.

When the 1941–42 season started, Dutton changed the club's name to the Brooklyn Americans. "We had fans mostly from Brooklyn," he said, "while the Rangers had the hotsy-totsy ones from New York." However, all Americans' home games were still played at the Garden and this token gesture did little to stimulate a Brooklyn–New York rivalry. The Amerks finished last again, but had come up with young players like goalie Chuck Rayner and defenseman Pat Egan, who showed considerable promise. However, the war effort soon took Rayner and several other Americans, and at the start of the 1942–43 season, Dutton was forced to fold the club just when he was starting to pull out from under the debris of the Dwyer days. "It looked as though we were going to come out of it all right. A couple more years and we would have run the Rangers right out of the rink." Instead, the Americans vanished and a glorious hockey era came to a sad close.

New York Americans Year-by-Year Record

Season	GP	W	L	T	GF	GA	Pts	Finish	Division	Playoff Results
1925–26	36	12	20	4	68	89	28	4th	Canadian	Out of Playoffs
1926–27	44	17	25	2	82	91	36	4th	Canadian	Out of Playoffs
1927–28	44	11	27	6	63	128	28	5th	Canadian	Out of Playoffs
1928–29	44	19	13	12	53	53	50	2nd	Canadian	Lost Quarterfinal
1929–30	44	14	25	5	113	161	33	5th	Canadian	Out of Playoffs
1930–31	44	18	16	10	76	74	46	4th	Canadian	Out of Playoffs
1931–32	48	16	24	8	95	142	40	4th	Canadian	Out of Playoffs
1932–33	48	15	22	11	91	118	41	4th	Canadian	Out of Playoffs
1933–34	48	15	23	10	104	132	40	4th	Canadian	Out of Playoffs
1934–35	48	12	27	9	100	142	33	4th	Canadian	Out of Playoffs
1935–36	48	16	25	7	109	122	39	3rd	Canadian	Lost Semifinal
1936–37	48	15	29	4	122	161	34	4th	Canadian	Out of Playoffs
1937–38	48	19	18	11	110	111	49	2nd	Canadian	Lost Semifinal
1938–39	48	17	21	10	119	157	44	4th		Lost Quarterfinal
1939–40	48	15	29	4	106	140	34	6th		Lost Quarterfinal
1940–41	48	8	29	11	99	186	27	7th		Out of Playoffs
1941–42	48	16	29	3	133	175	35	7th		Out of Playoffs

NEW YORK ISLANDERS

THE HISTORY OF HOCKEY in Nassau and Suffolk counties, which comprise Long Island, dates back to amateur leagues of the 1930s and various minor pro clubs that emerged in the years after World War II. When Nassau Veterans' Memorial Coliseum was designed in 1970, the NHL decided to place an expansion franchise on Long Island as well as another in Atlanta. Businessman Roy Boe, who already owned the New York Nets of the infant American Basketball Association, badly wanted to add big-league hockey to his portfolio.

The NHL was asking $6 million per franchise, so Boe persuaded 19 other investors besides him to purchase the franchise and pay off a $4 million territorial fee to the Rangers, who were a mere 25 miles away. He also hired William Arthur (Bill) Torrey, who had previously been chief executive of the Oakland Seals, as his general manager. Torrey's task was daunting because the World Hockey Association was also set to debut in October, 1972.

Torrey's opening season nucleus included coach Phil Goyette, a former Montreal Canadiens and Rangers ace; top draft pick Billy Harris, a fleet right wing with a powerful shot; versatile checking forward Ed Westfall, who had played for two Stanley Cup-winning Bruins teams; and rugged defenseman Gerry Hart.

Other members of the first-year club included Gerry Desjardins, the former Chicago goalie who had a permanently bent arm following an injury, and flame-haired Terry Crisp, who had been an effective utility player with the St. Louis Blues. One of Torrey's most colorful additions would be a 24-year-old out of the U.S. hockey system—goaltender Glenn "Chico" Resch, though Resch would not reach the NHL for a few seasons yet.

The Islanders' first season opened on October 7, 1972, when a crowd of 12,221 turned out to see the Islanders lose 3–2 to the Flames. Westfall scored the first goal in Islanders' history and would prove to be a formidable captain during the team's formative years. On October 12, 1972, the Isles won their first NHL game, beating the Kings 3–2 at Inglewood, but after 25 games, the Islanders had only three wins, two ties and 20 losses. Although the club admittedly was weak, it had hoped to be more competitive. After considerable review, Torrey decided in midseason to replace Goyette with Earl Ingarfield.

Ingarfield replaced Goyette as coach on January 29, 1973, but the results were hardly encouraging. No fewer than 32 players would wear the blue and orange that first season, and none of them would collect more than 50 points. As expected, Billy Harris, the Long Island hunk, led the team with 28 goals; no one else had more than 19. At one point, the team lost 12 straight games, never won more than three in a row, and in one particularly futile stretch compiled a 1–20–1 record on the road.

The team's overall won-lost record showed that the Islanders had captured only 12 games, a record low, and lost 60, a record high. They finished 72 points behind the Rangers, who nevertheless had helped the Islanders forge the kind of white-hot rivalry Boe had envisioned—even though the Rangers won all six regular-season meetings by outscoring the upstarts from Long Island, 25–5. Among the rookies, the most encouraging were pugnacious Garry Howatt and hard-working Bob Nystrom, who were elevated to the big club in March, 1973.

The Islanders' last-place finish guaranteed them the first pick in the Amateur Draft, which was one of the best in history. Torrey resisted several offers from Canadiens general manager Sam Pollock, and made Denis Potvin of the Ottawa 67's his top choice. When Ingarfield asked to be relieved of the coaching job, Torrey offered the position to bespectacled Al Arbour.

The addition of Arbour to his general staff was one of Torrey's most meaningful moves. Arbour quickly brought discipline and toughness to the sophomore—and sometimes sophomoric—Islanders. Under Goyette, the team regularly had broken training rules, but Arbour changed all that. An 11 p.m. curfew on the eve of games was instituted and rigorously enforced, and Arbour began fining players who were late, whether it was for the bus, the plane or practice. The strict new regime began on the first day of training camp, when Arbour insisted that each and every player jog from the motel to the practice rink.

Even with Arbour, Potvin and Westfall, the Islanders struggled in 1973–74, finishing last (19–41–18) in the Eastern Division with the second-worst record in the entire league. They did gain respect in goal. Billy Smith had emerged as a combative netminder with a knack of making the hardest saves at the most critical moments. Smith and Resch would become a tandem through the club's first Stanley Cup season.

It wasn't until the autumn of 1974 that the Isles began turning the competitive corner. Torrey had selected Clark Gillies, a big left wing, as his first draft pick and later added Gillies's pal, Bob Bourne, a swift left wing. At midseason, Torrey completed a landmark trade with Minnesota, obtaining left wing J.P. Parise and center Jude Drouin. Working with Westfall, Parise and Drouin provided New York with a dependable scoring and checking line. In a neck-and-neck battle with Atlanta for a final playoff berth, the Islanders prevailed in the homestretch, finishing with 33 wins compared to 19 the previous season.

The 1975 playoff experience figured to be remarkably short. Facing the Islanders in the first round was a powerful Rangers squad sprinkled with future Hall of Famers such as Rod Gilbert, Brad Park and Ed Giacomin. The best-of-three series was expected to be completed with a two-straight Rangers rout because of experience and talent.

Instead, the Islanders won with a stirring sudden-death victory on Parise's goal—on a pass from Drouin—with only 11 seconds elapsed in overtime. They advanced to the second round against a Pittsburgh Penguins franchise that also was rated a prohibitive favorite. For three games, the Isles appeared lost, but, facing elimination, they won three in a row. Not only did they tie the series but a folk hero was born after goalie Chico Resch smothered a shot by Ron Schock that had rebounded to him after it had hit the goal post. Resch pulled himself to his feet and kissed the red piping, an act that forever endeared him to the fans.

In another melodramatic moment, Westfall ended the series by breaking a 0–0 tie late in the third period of the seventh game with a backhand past goalie Gary Inness. Thus the Isles found their place in history alongside the 1942 Toronto Maple Leafs, as the only NHL clubs to have surmounted a three-game deficit in the playoffs to win four straight.

Defying all odds, the Islanders took on the defending champion Philadelphia Flyers, lost three straight and then rebounded for another remarkable comeback. With the series tied at three and the deciding game in Philadelphia, the Flyers produced the ultimate good luck charm.

Kate Smith had sung "God Bless America" before many Flyers games—either in person or on tape—and Philadelphia had a record of 40–3–1 on those occasions. Islanders captain Ed Westfall attempted to change the luck by presenting Kate with a bouquet of yellow roses. It didn't work; Philadelphia triumphed, 4–1. But, the Isles' miracle run had a long-term benefit for the team. Beating the Rangers gave them bragging rights in the New York Metropolitan area, and the two separate comeback performances captured the imagination of NHL fans, while boosting the young club's confidence. Meanwhile, Torrey continued building the foundation of what eventually would be a dynasty.

To his promising attacking corps he added rugged center

Bryan Trottier for the 1975–76 season and a year later Mike Bossy was picked first (15th overall) in the 1977 draft. Gillies, Trottier and Bossy would in time become Trio Grande, the best line ever to skate in Nassau. Gifted though they were, the Islanders were missing a key element in team chemistry and balance. This was evident when underdog Toronto eliminated them in a vicious, seven-game 1978 playoff that was followed a year later by a humiliating six-game series loss to the Rangers after the Isles had become the first expansion team to lead the NHL with a 51–15–14 mark.

Torrey made key changes. He added World Hockey Association defenseman Dave Langevin and gold medal Olympian Ken Morrow after the U.S. won at Lake Placid in 1980. But, his most important move was obtaining center Butch Goring from Los Angeles.

"With Butchie at center," said Denis Potvin, "there was a sense of hope we didn't have before." Sure enough, the revitalized Islanders reached the Stanley Cup finals against the Flyers. Leading three games to two, the Isles hosted the sixth game on a warm spring afternoon. The game was tied 4–4 when the biggest goal in franchise history was scored. Bob Nystrom took a pass from John Tonelli and beat Pete Peeters at 7:11 of overtime.

Nystrom's goal was the start of something big. The Islanders won additional Stanley Cup titles in 1981, 1982 and 1983. The victims, successively, were Minnesota, Vancouver and Edmonton, the latter two exiting in four straight games while the North Stars lasted five.

To maintain the dynasty, Torrey continually juggled his roster. Additions such as defensemen Gord Lane and Mike McEwen played pivotal roles in the Cup years, as did forwards Wayne Merrick and Anders Kallur. But, the steady work of tempestuous goalie Billy Smith provided the last line of defense so necessary to a champion. For grit there was the Sutter brothers, Duane and Brent, as well as underrated defensemen Stefan Persson and fellow Swede Tomas Jonsson.

In their "Drive for Five," the Islanders came close. They etched their names in the history book by completing a total of 19 consecutive playoff series victories when they won the first three rounds of the 1984 playoffs. But, by the time they reached the finals against a young, healthy Edmonton team, Al Arbour's skaters were wounded beyond repair. They split the first two games on Long Island before flying to Edmonton and three straight games at Northlands Coliseum. By the end of the fifth game, the league had a new champion and Torrey returned to the drawing board to reshape his squad.

Two key additions—forwards Pat LaFontaine and Patrick Flatley—fortified the attack, while Kelly Hrudey was designated the number-two goalie behind Bill Smith. But, the shocker was Arbour's decision to retire after 13 seasons behind the Islanders bench. He was replaced by Terry Simpson, who was pacing the matting on April 18–19, 1987, when the Islanders participated in their longest game. Played at Capital Centre in Landover, Maryland, the seventh game of the Washington–Islanders series lasted until 8:47 of the fourth overtime period when LaFontaine beat goalie Bob Mason just seconds before 2 a.m.

The Islanders remained competitive through the late 1980s under the ownership of John Pickett. In 1987–88, they won the Patrick Division title and faced New Jersey in the opening playoff round. The Devils had gained a playoff berth on the final night of the season and seemed to be easy pickings, but New Jersey physically manhandled the Islanders and wiped them out in six games. Not only were the Isles eliminated but they lost their best defenseman, Denis Potvin, to retirement, and a severe depression settled over the club in 1988–89 when they finished with a record of 28–47–5, their worst season since the second year of the franchise. Bill Smith retired, leaving youthful Mark Fitzpatrick and Jeff Hackett to battle for the goaltending job.

Torrey persuaded Arbour to come out of retirement, but there was little improvement until late in the 1989–90 season when the Isles were able to clinch a playoff berth on the final night of the season by beating Philadelphia while Buffalo toppled Pittsburgh.

It was the next-to-last high point of what would become a terribly disappointing decade. Only in 1992–93 was there a renaissance, as a gutsy team including Ray Ferraro, Steve Thomas, Benoit Hogue and Tom Fitzgerald kept them competitive, while Pierre Turgeon—obtained from Buffalo in a deal for Pat LaFontaine—led the scoring and ebullient Glenn Healy surfaced as the new netminding favorite.

The Islanders beat Washington in six games to open the playoffs, but the bad news was a blindside cheap shot delivered by Dale Hunter of the Capitals against Turgeon that left the star with a shoulder separation and concussion. Undaunted, the Isles next took favored Pittsburgh to a seventh game and won it at the Igloo when Czech-born David Volek steered a Ferraro pass behind Tom Barrasso at 5:16 of overtime to complete the upset. The dream ended in the next round as the eventual Stanley Cup-winning Montreal Canadiens ousted the Islanders in five games.

A number of personnel moves changed the team's chemistry, although it did manage another playoff berth in 1994. With Healy moved to the Rangers, Ron Hextall became the resident goaltender. On some nights he was peerless and others powerless. But, in a tense stretch drive, he enabled his new club to gain a playoff berth with a 2–0 win over the Lightning at Tampa Bay during the last week of the regular season.

Facing the Rangers in the first round, the Islanders—especially Hextall—disintegrated, losing four straight and setting the stage for a dismal playoff drought through the remainder of the 1990s. Adding insult to injury was Pickett's decision to sell the team to so-called tycoon John Spano. Before the sale could be consummated, Spano was indicted on several fraud counts and eventually sentenced to prison.

Pickett regained control of the team and in 1997 sold the Islanders to New York Sports Ventures, a group headed by Steven Gluckstern, Howard Milstein, Edward Milstein and David Seldin. The new owners took command during the 1997–98 season, another disappointing year during which general manager Mike Milbury fired coach Rick Bowness and finished the year behind the bench himself. Trades dominated the Islanders agenda in 1998–99 and 1999–2000, with players such as 1997 Calder Trophy winner Bryan Berard, scoring star Zigmund Palffy and captain Trevor Linden all shipped out. Hope for the future exists in former Stanley Cup star Butch Goring, who was hired to coach the team on April 30, 1999, and in the first-overall 2000 Entry Draft selection of Boston University goaltending Rick DiPietro. The team's goaltending position was further solidified with acquisition of veteran John Vanbiesbrouck.

Most important of all, the Islanders' ownership has been resolved with the $175 million sale of the team to software billionaire Charles Wang of Long Island-based Computer

Associates in April 2000. The NHL Board of Governors approved the sale to Wang and Sanjay Kumar on June 20, 2000. Says NHL commissioner Gary Bettman: "We are optimistic we will see some positive steps that will begin to put the franchise back on the firm footing it had for so many years."

New York Islanders Year-by-Year Record

Season	GP	W	L	T	GF	GA	Pts	Finish	Division	Playoff Results
1972–73	78	12	60	6	170	347	30	8th	East	Out of Playoffs
1973–74	78	19	41	18	182	247	56	8th	East	Out of Playoffs
1974–75	80	33	25	22	264	221	88	3rd	Patrick	Lost Semifinal
1975–76	80	42	21	17	297	190	101	2nd	Patrick	Lost Semifinal
1976–77	80	47	21	12	288	193	106	2nd	Patrick	Lost Semifinal
1977–78	80	48	17	15	334	210	111	1st	Patrick	Lost Quarterfinal
1978–79	80	51	15	14	358	214	116	1st	Patrick	Lost Semifinal
1979–80	80	39	28	13	281	247	91	2nd	Patrick	Won Stanley Cup
1980–81	80	48	18	14	355	260	110	1st	Patrick	Won Stanley Cup
1981–82	80	54	16	10	385	250	118	1st	Patrick	Won Stanley Cup
1982–83	80	42	26	12	302	226	96	2nd	Patrick	Won Stanley Cup
1983–84	80	50	26	4	357	269	104	1st	Patrick	Lost Final
1984–85	80	40	34	6	345	312	86	3rd	Patrick	Lost Div. Final
1985–86	80	39	29	12	327	284	90	3rd	Patrick	Lost Div. Semifinal
1986–87	80	35	33	12	279	281	82	3rd	Patrick	Lost Div. Final
1987–88	80	39	31	10	308	267	88	1st	Patrick	Lost Div. Semifinal
1988–89	80	28	47	5	265	325	61	6th	Patrick	Out of Playoffs
1989–90	80	31	38	11	281	288	73	4th	Patrick	Lost Div. Semifinal
1990–91	80	25	45	10	223	290	60	6th	Patrick	Out of Playoffs
1991–92	80	34	35	11	291	299	79	5th	Patrick	Out of Playoffs
1992–93	84	40	37	7	335	297	87	3rd	Patrick	Lost Conf. Final
1993–94	84	36	36	12	282	264	84	4th	Atlantic	Lost Conf. Quarterfinal
1994–95	48	15	28	5	126	158	35	7th	Atlantic	Out of Playoffs
1995–96	82	22	50	10	229	315	54	7th	Atlantic	Out of Playoffs
1996–97	82	29	41	12	240	250	70	7th	Atlantic	Out of Playoffs
1997–98	82	30	41	11	212	225	71	4th	Atlantic	Out of Playoffs
1998–99	82	24	48	10	194	244	58	5th	Atlantic	Out of Playoffs
1999-2000	82	24	49	9	194	275	*58	5th	Atlantic	Out of Playoffs

* *Includes 1 point for a regulation tie (RT)*

NEW YORK RANGERS

THE RANGERS WERE BORN out of a New York City hockey boom that was rooted in a popular series of exhibition games played at the old St. Nicholas Arena on Manhattan's Upper West Side shortly after the turn of the century. But, it wasn't until the ice game's popularity was confirmed on a big-league level in 1925–26 by the New York Americans that the Broadway Blueshirts finally were awarded an NHL franchise.

None of this would have been possible had a Kansas City-born, Texas-bred entrepreneur named George Lewis Rickard not made a fortune promoting fights in New York. By 1924, when the New York Life Insurance Company decided to raze old Madison Square Garden and build a 40-story office building, Rickard had become Manhattan's most renowned sportsman. He rounded up a syndicate of businessmen—his self-proclaimed "600 millionaires"—and organized the Madison Square Garden Corporation. By December 15, 1925, the new Garden was up and flourishing, with its lone NHL tenant, the New York Americans, playing the Montreal Canadiens.

Once Rickard realized that hockey was a hit on Broadway, he concluded that the Garden should organize its own team—the Americans were merely renting the arena—and, along with MSG president Colonel John S. Hammond, laid the groundwork for a second New York franchise. Rickard and Hammond designated Conn Smythe, a bright, young Torontonian who already had a reputation for successfully managing hockey teams, to organize the Rangers. Since the strong-willed Hammond paid close attention to the hockey club, the Colonel and Smythe developed a strong but stormy relationship.

Smythe adroitly signed a nucleus of superb players, including the amateur defense pair of Ivan "Ching" Johnson and Clarence "Taffy" Abel, names soon to become bywords among New York sports fans. By far Smythe's best moves were the acquisitions of center Frank Boucher, left wing Fred "Bun" Cook and right wing Bill Cook. The brothers Cook and Boucher—all Hall of Famers—would comprise one of the finest forward lines ever to grace the NHL.

Smythe also chose wisely in goal with Lorne Chabot and when the Rangers gathered for their first training camp at Toronto's little Ravina rink in the fall of 1926, their roster appeared competitive if not downright formidable. Unfortunately for Smythe, Hammond disagreed. He wanted more recognizable names for the New York club. Hammond wanted Smythe to sign Babe Dye, a leading scorer throughout the 1920s, but Smythe didn't feel Dye would fit in with the team-first approach he wanted his players to take. His refusal to sign Dye led to him being fired before training camp was finished.

The Colonel had been well prepared for this moment, having already summoned former Pacific Coast Hockey Association co-organizer and former player Lester Patrick to Toronto. The moment Smythe departed, Patrick became coach of the Rangers for the then astronomical fee of $18,000 a year. It marked the beginning of a long and lovely relationship.

Patrick not only oozed the kind of class that Rickard revered, he also knew as much about hockey as Smythe and proved it by taking over the Rangers without missing a beat. Beginning with an opening night 1–0 victory over the powerful Montreal Maroons on November 17, 1926, the Rangers obliged Patrick by recording a first-place finish in the newly created American Division. They also proved Smythe had been correct in his assessment of the team.

Paced by the Cook-Boucher line, as well as stout defense and solid goaltending, the Rangers became immediate contenders, while coach Patrick emerged as a major personality in the Big Apple along with Babe Ruth and Lou Gehrig. "Lester didn't adjust to New York," said Americans manager Tommy Gorman, "New York adjusted to him." In only their second NHL season, the Rangers reached the Stanley Cup finals against the Maroons. They had achieved a rare balance from goal through defense to the forward lines but they had one obstacle that was unconquerable: they couldn't defeat Ringling Brothers and Barnum and Bailey.

The appearance of the elephants at playoff time would haunt the Blueshirts for nearly four decades, but playing all games on the Maroons' home ice in 1928 was hardly daunting for the Rangers. More challenging was the search for a goaltender after Chabot was injured during the second game. In an era when NHL clubs carried only one goalie, it was commonplace for teams to "borrow" a neutral netminder. Patrick asked permission to use either Alex Connell of the Ottawa Senators or a minor-leaguer, Hughie McCormick, both of whom were in the stands. When Maroons manager Eddie Gerard refused, Patrick went to his dressing room, huddled with Bun Cook and Boucher, then decided to play goal himself.

Already down one game to none, the Rangers desperately needed this win and Patrick heroically stopped all but one shot as the teams completed regulation time tied 1–1. According to Montreal Star columnist Baz O'Meara, Patrick performed "prodigious feats of netminding." The climax to the remarkable evening came when Boucher scored the game winner in overtime.

For the remainder of the series, Patrick was replaced in goal by an obscure netminder named Joe Miller, on loan from the Americans. Tied at two games apiece, the Rangers and Maroons met in game five to decide the championship. As coach Patrick had earlier, Miller held Montreal to one goal while Boucher managed both scores for New York. The final score was 2–1. In their second NHL season, the Rangers had won their first Stanley Cup. Upon returning to Manhattan, the Blueshirts were suitably hailed as conquering heroes. They were greeted on the steps of City Hall by a beaming Mayor Jimmy Walker, who was a regular at Madison Square Garden games, and a crowd of proud New Yorkers. The Rangers had arrived.

Under Patrick's orchestration, the Rangers' standard of excellence was maintained through the early 1930s, although they didn't win another Stanley Cup title until 1933. The core of the original Cup-winners was intact except for Chabot and Abel, who had been traded, when they faced Toronto in the 1933 finals. Ironically, Smythe, who was running the Maple Leafs, watched in frustration as the very players he had signed for New York dominated his Toronto skaters. Bill Cook led the Rangers to a 1–0 victory in the fourth and final game, although he was now 35 years old and supposedly past his prime.

Two Stanley Cup titles in only seven seasons were a laudable achievement for Patrick and his Rangers, who were feted in a glittering victory party at the Astor Hotel in the center of Times Square. The celebration was significant in another way because it served as an introductory platform for the Rangers' new president, General John Reed Kilpatrick. A World War I hero, Kilpatrick was the ideal boss for Patrick and the two set out to rejuvenate what was an aging hockey team. The feat was accomplished by means of an elaborate farm system that would eventually comprise the Three Rs—New Haven Ramblers, New York Rovers and Lake Placid Roamers.

However, the original revivifying sources came from Patrick's American League farm club in Philadelphia, not to mention Lester's own family. His sons, Lynn—the eldest and most productive as a scorer—and Murray had been outstanding athletes in hockey, track, bicycling, baseball, rugby, football and basketball. Murray, later known as Muzz, was so adept in the ring that he became an amateur boxing champion. As the Cooks and Boucher were phased out of the lineup, the likes of Bryan Hextall, Phil Watson, Dutch Hiller, the Colville Brothers (Neil and Mac), Alex Shibicky and goalie Davey Kerr moved in, along with Lynn up front and Muzz on defense. By the time World War II had exploded in the fall of 1939, Patrick's Rangers were as powerful as his club of a dozen years earlier. Only this time, Boucher was behind the bench coaching instead of occupying his familiar spot on the ice at center.

The 1939–40 Rangers were an extraordinary group of players. At one point they had recorded 24 victories or ties in 25 games. They developed the strategy of offensive penalty-killing and popularized pulling the goalie for a sixth attacker in the final minute of play. With exquisite irony, they advanced to the Stanley Cup finals against Smythe's Maple Leafs once more and defeated them in six games. Forced out of their Madison Square Garden home by the circus, the Rangers played the last two games at Maple Leaf Gardens, winning both in overtime. Lester accepted the Stanley Cup from NHL president Frank Calder and then posed for an historic picture: a father and two sons on a Cup-winner at the same time.

Since their inception, the Rangers now had won the Stanley Cup three times and, with a young roster, it appeared that more championships were in the offing. But, World War II would change that. Within months, the Blueshirts roster was decimated by armed forces enlistments and by 1942, both Muzz and Lynn were in uniform. It was the beginning of a long and dismal run for the Rangers, with relief not coming until well after the war's end. By that time Lester had retired and Boucher took over both managing and coaching. New York's only bright season was 1949–50 when some adroit trades elevated the Rangers to playoff contention. They reached the finals—naturally playing all home games on the road—against Detroit and forced the Red Wings to double overtime in the seventh game before losing on a Pete Babando goal.

The Frank Boucher era ended with his dismissal at the end of the 1954–55 season, just after he had successfully reorganized the farm system, centered on the Guelph Biltmore Madhatters of the Ontario Hockey Association. Future Hall of Famers such as Harry Howell and Andy Bathgate graduated to the Blueshirts, along with goalie Lorne "Gump" Worsley, who had been developed on the Rangers' Eastern League farm club, the Rovers.

With Muzz Patrick managing and Phil Watson coaching, the club enjoyed a few bright moments in the late 1950s before fading again under Watson's tyrannical rule. By 1964, Patrick was gone, replaced by onetime—though only briefly—Ranger goalie Emile "the Cat" Francis. A native of North Battleford, Saskatchewan, Francis restored the franchise to a modicum of dignity and championship potential.

Francis's goaltending discovery Ed Giacomin anchored an impressive lineup that included the G-A-G (Goal-A-Game) Line centered by Jean Ratelle and flanked by Rod Gilbert on the right and Vic Hadfield. Although not as popular as Patrick, Francis became a Big Apple favorite who enjoyed innovation as much as his predecessor. "The Cat" even lured onetime NHL scoring champion Bernie "Boom Boom" Geoffrion out of retirement in a move that paid immediate dividends: a second playoff berth in two years in 1967–68. Try as he might, Francis could not craft a Cup-winner, although the 1971–72 team reached the finals before losing to Bobby Orr and the Boston Bruins in six games. Unable to replenish his aging lineup with young stars, Francis lost favor with management and soon was replaced by former Ranger-basher John Ferguson.

This was a trying time for Rangers fans. An expansion franchise in adjoining Nassau County had become a winner faster than anyone had expected. In the 1974–75 season—only the third in franchise history—the New York Islanders not only reached the playoffs but unceremoniously ousted the vaunted Rangers in the opening round. Revenge, of sorts, was obtained four seasons later when the Blueshirts, now guided by former Philadelphia Flyers coach Fred Shero, upset the Islanders in a six-game series and reached the Stanley Cup finals against the defending champion Montreal Canadiens. A New York victory in the opener at the Forum was followed by a two-goal Rangers lead in game two, but the Habs soon counterattacked and won four straight games and another Cup title.

One by one, New York coaches and managers came and went, but that coveted fourth Stanley Cup appeared more distant than ever. Craig Patrick—Lynn's son and grandson of Lester—provided hope in the early 1980s, along with

Lake Placid Olympic hero Herb Brooks. With the latter behind the bench, the Blueshirts introduced a revolutionary game plan that blended European and North American hockey styles. During the 1983–84 playoffs, Brooks's Rangers extended the four-time Cup-champion Islanders to a full five games before losing in sudden-death overtime. Again, the team crested and then plummeted while management desperately searched for a Cup-winning formula. Meanwhile, expansion teams were passing them by as Philadelphia had won two championships, Edmonton crafted a late 1980s Stanley Cup dynasty and Calgary won a title before the decade was over. The likes of Phil Esposito in the front office and Michel Bergeron behind the bench did little to bring the club closer to a championship.

The gloom over Broadway was lifted at the start of the 1990s when Craig Patrick draftee Brian Leetch established himself as a premier defenseman on the Rangers blue line. "He's reminiscent of the great Doug Harvey," said Esposito. Leetch won the Norris Trophy in 1992, not coincidentally in the same season that Mark Messier was lured away from Edmonton in a colossal deal that saw Rangers' young general manager Neil Smith dispatch minor-league prospects Louie DeBrusk and Steven Rice to the Oilers along with popular center Bernie Nicholls and an unnamed but substantial amount of cash.

For the first time in 50 years, the Rangers had the best NHL record in 1991–92 (50–25–5), thanks in large part to Messier's leadership, his 107 points and an all-round performance that earned him the Hart Trophy. Still, it wasn't enough. Pittsburgh won the Stanley Cup for the second straight year. Messier's presence notwithstanding, the Rangers fell to the bottom of the division in 1992–93 and missed the playoffs as injuries and personnel strife disrupted the organization. Messier was openly critical of coach Roger Neilson, who was fired and replaced by Mike Keenan.

The turnabout was dramatic. Under Keenan's rule, the Rangers rebounded to the top, finishing with the league's best regular-season record (52–24–8) before embarking on a relentless march through the playoffs. They stumbled in a third-round encounter with the New Jersey Devils, falling behind three games to two. But, Messier scored a hat trick in game six and third-liner Stephane Matteau put them in the finals with an overtime goal in the seventh match.

New York required seven games before disposing of Vancouver in the 1994 finals. Leetch, who tallied 34 points and won the Conn Smythe Trophy, detonated the seventh-game win with a goal in the first period. Goalie Mike Richter withstood a late-game Canucks assault to preserve the victory and give the Big Apple its first Stanley Cup since 1940. A sign carried by one fan in the stands read "Now I can die in peace." There was, however, no peace in the Rangers front office.

Keenan and Smith had been feuding all season and, instead of bringing the high command together, the Cup triumph pulled them farther apart. By mid-summer, 1994, Keenan had left New York to become general manager and coach of the St. Louis Blues. Smith replaced him with assistant coach Colin Campbell.

In a lockout-shortened 1994–95 season, the Rangers betrayed their age by playoff time. Messier proved no match for the younger, stronger Eric Lindros, and his teammates saw their one-year reign collapse. Smith moved quickly, obtaining Wayne Gretzky—"The Great One" had moved from Edmonton, to Los Angeles, to St. Louis—and suddenly Broadway was abuzz with hockey frenzy. The former Oilers cronies, Gretzky and Messier, infused the Rangers with new life. Along with Adam Graves, Alexei Kovalev, Ulf Samuelsson, Richter and Leetch, the Rangers had elite written all over them, although their regular-season record was less than awesome. But, once the playoffs began, the old pros delivered. Gretzky personally took over the opening-round series against Florida and delivered a five-game victory. Second-round opponent New Jersey looked impressive, shutting out the Rangers in game one, but Richter turned impregnable and again the New Yorkers annexed a series in five.

An opening-game win in round three against Philadelphia suggested that the finals—and even the Cup—were reachable. But, injuries and age combined to enervate the Blueshirts. Lindros and company rolled over them in the next four games, ending hopes for a Gretzky-Messier return to the finals. As captain, Messier had been an unqualified leader on Broadway, but the general staff had more and more come to the conclusion that he was overstepping his power base. A dismal performance in the Philadelphia series led general manager Smith to conclude that Messier's value would diminish in the seasons ahead. The Rangers did make the captain an offer to return, but it was not deemed suitable by Messier. Instead, he chose a more lucrative Canucks contract and signed with Vancouver.

The decision caused shockwaves up and down Seventh Avenue. Garden officials were assailed for failing to retain the captain, but Smith and others countered that a reasonable offer was made and rejected by the Messier camp. Instead, the Rangers obtained Pat LaFontaine from Buffalo, sending a second-round draft pick to the Sabres. Smith also obtained free agent veterans Brian Skrudland and Mike Keane. Prior to the opening game, fellow general managers told Smith that he had a potential Stanley Cup-winner if LaFontaine had fully recovered from the concussions that had sidelined him in Buffalo. Unfortunately, another head injury to LaFontaine late in the 1997–98 campaign not only ended his season early, it ended his career. John Muckler replaced Colin Campbell as coach in February, but despite strong play by Wayne Gretzky over the last two months of the season, the Rangers missed the playoffs. Skrudland and Keane were shipped out to Dallas before the year was through.

The 1998–99 season proved to be another disappointing one in New York, with the club missing the playoffs for the second year in a row. As Gretzky struggled through injuries, rumors began to spread that he would retire. "The Great One" confirmed this during the season's final week. He formally announced his retirement on April 16, 1999, and played his final game two days later. The Rangers lost, 2–1, to Pittsburgh in overtime.

Looking to retool for 1999–2000, the Rangers signed free agents Theo Fleury, Valeri Kamensky, Sylvain Lefebvre and Kirk McLean, which bloated the payroll to an NHL-high $61 million. Not one made the contribution that was expected of him. Though injuries to Brian Leetch and Mike Richter also contributed, the Rangers' disappointing play again in 1999–2000 cost John Muckler and g.m. Neil Smith their jobs with four games left in the regular season. On June 1, 2000, the Rangers announced that former Edmonton Oilers president and g.m. Glen Sather had been hired to serve the same dual role in New York. In July, 2000, Ron Low was hired as coach and Mark Messier returned as captain after a three-year absence.

Peter Nedved had led the club in points in 1999–2000, but the team's best player was rookie Michael York who led the club with 26 goals. Another youngster who may help in future is Pavel Brendl. The fourth selection overall at the 1999 NHL Entry Draft, he led the Western Hockey League in points in 1998–99 and in goals in 1999–2000.

New York Rangers Year-by-Year Record

Season	GP	W	L	T	GF	GA	Pts	Finish	Division	Playoff Results
1926–27	44	25	13	6	95	72	56	1st	American	Lost Quarterfinal
1927–28	44	19	16	9	94	79	47	2nd	American	Won Stanley Cup
1928–29	44	21	13	10	72	65	52	2nd	American	Lost Final
1929–30	44	17	17	10	136	143	44	3rd	American	Lost Semifinal
1930–31	44	19	16	9	106	87	47	3rd	American	Lost Semifinal
1931–32	48	23	17	8	134	112	54	1st	American	Lost Final
1932–33	48	23	17	8	135	107	54	3rd	American	Won Stanley Cup
1933–34	48	21	19	8	120	113	50	3rd	American	Lost Quarterfinal
1934–35	48	22	20	6	137	139	50	3rd	American	Lost Semifinal
1935–36	48	19	17	12	91	96	50	4th	American	Out of Playoffs
1936–37	48	19	20	9	117	106	47	3rd	American	Lost Final
1937–38	48	27	15	6	149	96	60	2nd	American	Lost Quarterfinal
1938–39	48	26	16	6	149	105	58	2nd		Lost Semifinal
1939–40	48	27	11	10	136	77	64	2nd		Won Stanley Cup
1940–41	48	21	19	8	143	125	50	4th		Lost Quarterfinal
1941–42	48	29	17	2	177	143	60	1st		Lost Semifinal
1942–43	50	11	31	8	161	253	30	6th		Out of Playoffs
1943–44	50	6	39	5	162	310	17	6th		Out of Playoffs
1944–45	50	11	29	10	154	247	32	6th		Out of Playoffs
1945–46	50	13	28	9	144	191	35	6th		Out of Playoffs
1946–47	60	22	32	6	167	186	50	5th		Out of Playoffs
1947–48	60	21	26	13	176	201	55	4th		Lost Semifinal
1948–49	60	18	31	11	133	172	47	6th		Out of Playoffs
1949–50	70	28	31	11	170	189	67	4th		Lost Final
1950–51	70	20	29	21	169	201	61	5th		Out of Playoffs
1951–52	70	23	34	13	192	219	59	5th		Out of Playoffs
1952–53	70	17	37	16	152	211	50	6th		Out of Playoffs
1953–54	70	29	31	10	161	182	68	5th		Out of Playoffs
1954–55	70	17	35	18	150	210	52	5th		Out of Playoffs
1955–56	70	32	28	10	204	203	74	3rd		Lost Semifinal
1956–57	70	26	30	14	184	227	66	4th		Lost Semifinal
1957–58	70	32	25	13	195	188	77	2nd		Lost Semifinal
1958–59	70	26	32	12	201	217	64	5th		Out of Playoffs
1959–60	70	17	38	15	187	247	49	6th		Out of Playoffs
1960–61	70	22	38	10	204	248	54	5th		Out of Playoffs
1961–62	70	26	32	12	195	207	64	4th		Lost Semifinal
1962–63	70	22	36	12	211	233	56	5th		Out of Playoffs
1963–64	70	22	38	10	186	242	54	5th		Out of Playoffs
1964–65	70	20	38	12	179	246	52	5th		Out of Playoffs
1965–66	70	18	41	11	195	261	47	6th		Out of Playoffs
1966–67	70	30	28	12	188	189	72	4th		Lost Semifinal
1967–68	74	39	23	12	226	183	90	2nd	East	Lost Quarterfinal
1968–69	76	41	26	9	231	196	91	3rd	East	Lost Quarterfinal
1969–70	76	38	22	16	246	189	92	4th	East	Lost Quarterfinal
1970–71	78	49	18	11	259	177	109	2nd	East	Lost Semifinal
1971–72	78	48	17	13	317	192	109	2nd	East	Lost Final
1972–73	78	47	23	8	297	208	102	3rd	East	Lost Semifinal
1973–74	78	40	24	14	300	251	94	3rd	East	Lost Semifinal
1974–75	80	37	29	14	319	276	88	2nd	Patrick	Lost Prelim. Round
1975–76	80	29	42	9	262	333	67	4th	Patrick	Out of Playoffs
1976–77	80	29	37	14	272	310	72	4th	Patrick	Out of Playoffs
1977–78	80	30	37	13	279	280	73	4th	Patrick	Lost Prelim. Round
1978–79	80	40	29	11	316	292	91	3rd	Patrick	Lost Final
1979–80	80	38	32	10	308	284	86	3rd	Patrick	Lost Quarterfinal
1980–81	80	30	36	14	312	317	74	4th	Patrick	Lost Semifinal
1981–82	80	39	27	14	316	306	92	2nd	Patrick	Lost Div. Final
1982–83	80	35	35	10	306	287	80	4th	Patrick	Lost Div. Final
1983–84	80	42	29	9	314	304	93	4th	Patrick	Lost Div. Semifinal
1984–85	80	26	44	10	295	345	62	4th	Patrick	Lost Div. Semifinal
1985–86	80	36	38	6	280	276	78	4th	Patrick	Lost Conf. Final
1986–87	80	34	38	8	307	323	76	4th	Patrick	Lost Div. Semifinal
1987–88	80	36	34	10	300	283	82	5th	Patrick	Out of Playoffs
1988–89	80	37	35	8	310	307	82	3rd	Patrick	Lost Div. Semifinal
1989–90	80	36	31	13	279	267	85	1st	Patrick	Lost Div. Final
1990–91	80	36	31	13	297	265	85	2nd	Patrick	Lost Div. Semifinal
1991–92	80	50	25	5	321	246	105	1st	Patrick	Lost Div. Final
1992–93	84	34	39	11	304	308	79	6th	Patrick	Out of Playoffs
1993–94	84	52	24	8	299	231	112	1st	Atlantic	Won Stanley Cup
1994–95	48	22	23	3	139	134	47	4th	Atlantic	Lost Conf. Semifinal
1995–96	82	41	27	14	272	237	96	2nd	Atlantic	Lost Conf. Semifinal
1996–97	82	38	34	10	258	231	86	4th	Atlantic	Lost Conf. Final
1997–98	82	25	39	18	197	231	68	5th	Atlantic	Out of Playoffs
1998–99	82	33	38	11	217	227	77	4th	Atlantic	Out of Playoffs
1999-2000	82	29	41	12	218	246	*73	4th	Atlantic	Out of Playoffs

** Includes 3 points for regulation ties (RT)*

OTTAWA SENATORS 1917–18 TO 1933–34

TEAMS FROM CANADA'S CAPITAL have brought honor and distinction to the city almost from the beginning of hockey history. At the second Montreal Winter Carnival in 1884, an Ottawa team competed against four Montreal squads and beat McGill University in the finals. After Lord Stanley arrived in Ottawa in 1888 to begin his term as Canada's Governor-General, the excitement of the hockey scene he found there inspired him to donate the Stanley Cup. Though it would take 10 years for an Ottawa team to win it after the Stanley Cup was first presented in 1893, Ottawa's team enjoyed nine championship seasons through 1927—a mark unprecedented at the time.

The famed Ottawa Silver Seven won the Stanley Cup in 1903, and retained it until being dethroned by the Montreal Wanderers in 1906. The Silver Seven boasted six future members of the Hockey Hall of Fame, including the legendary Frank McGee. The Silver Seven became known as the Ottawa Senators after their Stanley Cup reign ended, and, by 1909, the great Cyclone Taylor had led the team to another championship. Stars like Percy LeSueur, Marty Walsh and Dubbie Kerr brought the Stanley Cup back to Ottawa again in 1911.

The Senators were charter members of the National Hockey League when it was formed in 1917, and Ottawa quickly established itself as the NHL's best team. Boasting such stars as Clint Benedict, Eddie Gerard, Frank Nighbor and Cy Denneny, the Senators won both halves of the 1919–20 season's split schedule to eliminate the need for a playoff to determine the NHL champion. The Senators then hosted the Pacific Coast Hockey League's Seattle Metropolitans for the Stanley Cup, and defeated them in five games—though mild weather in Ottawa saw the final two games moved to the artificial ice surface of Toronto's Mutual Street Arena.

In 1921, Ottawa won the first half of the NHL's split-season schedule, but slumped to third place in the second half before catching fire in the playoffs and winning the right to meet the Vancouver Millionaires in Vancouver for the Stanley Cup. An estimated 51,000 fans saw the five games played in the West Coast city. Thousands had to be turned away from the final game on April 4, which Ottawa won, 2–1, on a pair of goals by Jack Darragh. Cyclone Taylor, the star of Ottawa's 1909 Stanley Cup victory, suited up for the Millionaires that night in one of the final games of his brilliant career.

The 1921–22 season saw the Senators top the standings in the year in which the NHL did away with its split-season format. However, Ottawa was defeated by the second-place Toronto St. Pats under the new NHL playoff format. A year later, the Senators edged out the Montreal Canadiens by a single point to finish first again, then scored a 3–2 victory in a two-game, total-goals playoff. The victory entitled the banged-up Ottawa team to face Vancouver once again in the 1923 Stanley Cup playoffs. The Senators took the series three games to one, and were described by Vancouver's Frank Patrick as "the greatest team I have ever seen." However, there still was the matter of the Western Canada Hockey League's Edmonton Eskimos, whom the Senators beat in two straight games to claim the Stanley Cup championship.

It was in game two of the Edmonton series that Ottawa star Frank "King" Clancy is said to have played every position on the ice, including goal. In that era, goaltenders served their own penalties and when Senator netminder Clint Benedict was banished to the box for two minutes, he casually handed his goal stick to Clancy, who guarded the net until Benedict returned.

Artificial ice finally came to Ottawa on November 30, 1923, when the Auditorium opened for hockey business. Playing at their new arena, the Senators topped the NHL standings again for three of the next four seasons. By 1926–27, the rival professional leagues of the west had collapsed and the Stanley Cup had become exclusively an NHL trophy. The final Stanley Cup championship won by an Ottawa team came from a tight 1927 playoff series that saw the Senators beat the Boston Bruins two games to nothing, although two other games ended in ties. After the fourth and final game, Boston's Billy Coutu assaulted one of the game officials in the corridor and received a lifetime suspension from the NHL.

Despite the Senators' success on the ice, NHL expansion into the United States had left Ottawa as the smallest market in the NHL by far. Owner Frank Ahearn had been absorbing financial losses for years, but the first official notice of the difficulties the team was facing came at the NHL meetings in September, 1927, when Ottawa management requested that the team receive a larger percentage of the box office receipts from road games. (As perennial champions, the Senators were always a large draw on the road.) Next, the Senators sold Hooley Smith to the Montreal Maroons. Ed Gorman was sold to Toronto, and Jack Adams was permitted to retire. The defending Stanley Cup champions slipped to third in the standings of the NHL's Canadian Division, and were eliminated by the Montreal Maroons in the first round of the playoffs.

The Senators continued to ship out expensive talent in 1928–29 when they sent Cy Denneny to the Bruins and Punch Broadbent to the New York Americans. Ottawa fell to fourth in the standings and missed the playoffs. Prior to the 1929–30 season, the Senators again requested an increased share of the road receipts. In January, they shipped an aging Frank Nighbor to the Toronto Maple Leafs. With King Clancy and Alex Connell as the only stars left in Ottawa, the Senators managed to slip into the playoffs that year, but were handled easily by the New York Rangers in the opening round.

Prior to the 1930–31 season, one of hockey's biggest deals took place when Conn Smythe purchased Clancy from the Senators. The $35,000 Ottawa received wasn't enough to solve the Senators' financial woes, and reports began circulating that the team might be sold. Before the start of the 1931–32 season, the Senators requested a year's leave of absence from the NHL. Ottawa players were distributed around the league. The Senators returned under new management in 1932–33, but finished with the worst record in the league the next two years. Arrangements were made to transfer the once-proud franchise to St. Louis.

The original Ottawa Senators played their final home game on March 15, 1934. The New York Americans defeated the Senators 3–2. When Americans goalie Roy Worters received a deep gash over the eye in this match, Ottawa loaned the visitors Alex Connell, who had been relegated to a backup role earlier in the season. Connell played brilliantly for the visitors and was the number-one star of the contest. Over 6,500 fans applauded Connell, then left the Auditorium with solemn faces, knowing it was the end of a memorable era in Canadian hockey.

Ottawa Senators Year-by-Year Record, 1917–1934

Season	GP	W	L	T	GF	GA	Pts	Finish	Division	Playoff Results
1917–18	22	9	13	0	102	114	18	3rd		Out of Playoffs
1918–19	18	12	6	0	71	53	24	1st		Lost NHL Final
1919–20	24	19	5	0	121	64	38	1st		Won Stanley Cup
1920–21	24	14	10	0	97	75	28	2nd		Won Stanley Cup
1921–22	24	14	8	2	106	84	30	1st		Lost NHL Final
1922–23	24	14	9	1	77	54	29	1st		Won Stanley Cup
1923–24	24	16	8	0	74	54	32	1st		Lost NHL Final
1924–25	30	17	12	1	83	66	35	4th		Out of Playoffs
1925–26	36	24	8	4	77	42	52	1st		Lost NHL Final
1926–27	44	30	10	4	86	69	64	1st	Canadian	Won Stanley Cup
1927–28	44	20	14	10	78	57	50	3rd	Canadian	Lost Quarterfinal
1928–29	44	14	17	13	54	67	41	4th	Canadian	Out of Playoffs
1929–30	44	21	15	8	138	118	50	3rd	Canadian	Lost Quarterfinal
1930–31	44	10	30	4	91	142	24	5th	Canadian	Out of Playoffs
1931–32	Suspended operations for one season									
1932–33	48	11	27	10	88	131	32	5th	Canadian	Out of Playoffs
1933–34	48	13	29	6	115	143	32	5th	Canadian	Out of Playoffs

OTTAWA SENATORS 1992–93 TO DATE

THOUGH THE HISTORY OF HOCKEY in Ottawa is long and rich, the original attempt by Terrace Investments to bring the NHL back to Canada's capital city was not taken seriously.

"It's not that the area isn't big enough to support a professional hockey team," said former Ottawa mayor Jim Durrell, who later joined the Senators as team president. "It's just that we're not going to get it."

For a year, Bruce Firestone, Randy Sexton and Cyril Leeder lobbied NHL owners, governors and general managers in an attempt to get them to believe in the city. They fought political types constantly, trying to get land re-zoned in order to build the Ottawa Palladium (later the Corel Centre). The battle proved difficult. It was obvious the city wanted hockey, but nobody wanted to say for sure that these were the men who could make it happen. Firestone was ripped in the media. People wondered if he actually had the backing to get the job done.

Armed with an impressive hardcover book outlining their bid, the Senators made their way to the NHL Board of Governors meeting at The Breakers in West Palm Beach, Florida. The Ottawa group received little indication that its bid had been well-received, but on December 6, 1990, with the announcement imminent, Firestone was summoned to a room where the governors were gathered prior to a press conference. He was handed a piece of paper that contained just two words—"Tampa" and "Ottawa." With that simple gesture, Firestone burst into tears. Ottawa had scored.

There was joy at the announcement and season tickets were snapped up by fans immediately after they went on sale. Still, raising the $50 million (U.S.) franchise fee and getting the funding for the $150 million Palladium—which had been downsized from 22,500 to 18,500 seats—would prove difficult. That's when Rod Bryden entered the picture. A local businessman and friend of Firestone's, Bryden was brought on board to find investors in the team.

Once the expansion fee was paid and the franchise's future secured, the team began to build its hockey department. Sexton was the man in charge. Mel Bridgman, a 14-year NHL player with an impressive education from the Wharton School of Business, was assigned the tough job of building the team with the help of former Montreal Canadiens great John Ferguson. Only days before the

Expansion Draft, highly touted coach Rick Bowness was fired by the Boston Bruins and immediately hired as the Senators' first coach.

The first mistake by Bridgman, and one of the most embarrassing for the franchise, came at the Expansion Draft in a downtown hotel in Montreal. The final list was misplaced by Ferguson, and the Senators attempted to draft two players who were ineligible. Twice they were told to make a new selection. It left the organization looking bad from the start. "Ottawa apologizes," said Bridgman.

Only days later, at the Entry Draft in Montreal, fans could have cut the silence with a knife after the club made relative unknown Alexei Yashin from the Moscow Dynamo its number-one pick and the second overall selection. The top-rated player in the draft, Roman Hamrlik, went to Tampa Bay. A trainload of people from Ottawa clapped politely. Ferguson talked about Yashin's star potential. Nobody knew it would become a reality.

The new Ottawa Senators played their first NHL game on October 8, 1992, against the Montreal Canadiens. Fans packed the cozy 10,500-seat Civic Centre—the club's temporary home—and with a national television audience watching on Hockey Night in Canada, the Senators beat the Habs, 5–3. It was a special night, though it would be the last bit of joy for the season. The team finished with a 10–70–4 record for 24 points, which made them one of the worst expansion teams of all time. Yashin had decided to stay in Russia an extra year. Laurie Boschman, the man assigned the captaincy, showed he could not do it anymore. Instead, the player who carried the torch was defenseman Brad Marsh.

Asked to breakfast by Bryden—who had been installed as chief operating officer—the morning after getting a vote of confidence on local television, Bridgman was fired unceremoniously. What was the meeting like? "Well, I didn't eat my breakfast," said Bridgman. Sexton was installed as g.m.—the job he always had coveted—and a new era in Ottawa NHL hockey began.

Ottawa's last-place finish had sealed up the number-one pick at the 1993 NHL Entry Draft, and the Senators made no secret of the fact they would use the selection for highly touted Victoriaville Tigres superstar Alexandre Daigle. Daigle was young, French and had superstar quality. Believing he would be just the tonic the franchise needed, management handed him an unprecedented five-year, $12.5 million contract.

The next season started with promise and hope. Yashin reported to camp and looked brilliant. Daigle had his flashy speed. It couldn't get worse than the season before. The team looked like it was going places. Even financing for the Palladium was falling into place and there was a belief in the region the rink was going to get built. The Senators actually were surrounded by excitement.

Yashin finished with 77 points—including 35 goals—and was voted to play in the NHL All-Star Game, while Daigle had 20 goals and 31 assists. Unfortunately, the record didn't get much better on the ice. The team finished with 37 points. Questions started about Sexton's leadership because Yashin and agent Mark Gandler claimed the organization had made a verbal promise to renegotiate Yashin's contract.

A war of words stretched through the summer. Yashin didn't report to training camp and 1995 number-one selection Bryan Berard walked out because Sexton didn't make him a contract offer. While the NHL lockout stole the headlines, Yashin worked out with the Ottawa 67's junior team. A deal was struck to bring Yashin back into the fold just hours before the team left to play its first game of the shortened 48-game schedule in January when the lockout was settled. Again, all seemed well in the world.

But, another disappointing season passed under Sexton and Bowness. Then, another battle with Yashin broke out and confidence in management reached an all-time low. Ferguson walked out on the team because he didn't agree with the club's position to trade Yashin. "Just get the guy signed and get him into camp," said Ferguson. "You don't trade talent like that."

On opening night of the 1995–96 season, Yashin was on the front page of the local newspaper with his sticks packed up and headed for Russia. He practiced for a week with Moscow Dynamo and suited up for a couple of games before the International Ice Hockey Federation suspended him. An attempt to have his contract declared null and void by an NHL arbitrator was turned down. Twenty games into the year, Bowness was fired and Dave Allison—a career minor-leaguer with no NHL coaching experience—was Sexton's hand-picked successor. The move didn't work. Only weeks later, Sexton was shown the door by Bryden, with Anaheim Mighty Ducks assistant g.m. Pierre Gauthier hired to take over the hockey operation. He moved swiftly by bringing Yashin back into the fold—signing him to a five-year, $13 million U.S. contract. Excitement was building, the team was ready to move into the Palladium in January, 1996, and there was a sense of direction to the franchise. But, Gauthier wasn't finished.

Allison, who had only two victories since taking over from Bowness, was fired on January 24 and replaced by Colorado Avalanche assistant Jacques Martin. The move came only hours after Gauthier pulled off an important three-way trade with the Toronto Maple Leafs and New York Islanders that brought the club young defenseman Wade Redden and goaltender Damian Rhodes. It was a move that signalled there was a new era in Ottawa. The move to get Rhodes injected life into the team. Swede Daniel Alfredsson was selected the NHL's rookie of the year, and by the time the season ended, fans had confidence. Former L.A. Kings president Roy Mlakar, who carried a strong background in marketing, was installed to take over in Ottawa.

The summer of 1996 was a flurry of activity. By the time training camp ended, Gauthier and Martin had made 10 changes to the roster. The only consistency in the lineup was Yashin, Alfredsson, Daigle, Redden and Rhodes, along with 1994 number-one selection Radek Bonk and veteran captain Randy Cunneyworth. Virtually every other part had changed, but the Senators were expected to compete for a playoff spot.

Goaltender Ron Tugnutt, signed in the offseason to back up Rhodes, emerged as the hero down the stretch when the latter went down with a season-ending ankle injury in late February. The Senators needed help getting into the playoffs, but did themselves a favor by going 9–3–1 down the stretch to seal up seventh place in the Eastern Conference on the final night of the season. Defenseman Steve Duchesne fired the shot heard around Ottawa with a late goal that broke a 0–0 tie with Buffalo and vaulted the Senators into the playoffs.

Backed by Tugnutt, the "Cinderella" Senators faced the Sabres in the first round. With Dominik Hasek injured, it appeared Ottawa was going to knock off Buffalo after taking a 3–2 lead in the series, but a 3–0 loss at home in the sixth game set the stage for a dramatic game seven at the Marine Midland Arena. The Senators lost, 3–2, in overtime. After the initial disappointment passed, the Senators viewed their run to the playoffs as a good sign for the future. Changes were kept to a minimum in the summer. Tugnutt was signed to a new three-year deal. Defenseman Chris Phillips, the club's top draft pick in 1996 from the Western Hockey League's Prince Albert Raiders, was added to the roster at the start of the 1997–98 season. Alfredsson joined the club six games into the season after signing a new five-year, $10 million U.S. deal. The average attendance in the building leaped by more than 2,000 additional tickets sold per game.

Not everything stayed the same. Daigle left. Gauthier shipped him to the Philadelphia Flyers for Pat Falloon and prospect Vaclav Prospal. Carrying the weight of the rookie contract he had signed, Daigle never had success in Ottawa.

After finishing the regular schedule with a franchise-record 83 points, the Senators faced the powerful New Jersey Devils in the opening round of the 1998 playoffs. Although some insiders thought the speedy Senators were capable of beating the older, slower Devils, Ottawa's domination during a six-game playoff victory was considered a major upset. Though a five-game loss to the Washington Capitals followed, 1997–98 had been a very successful season.

Shortly after the 1998 NHL Entry Draft, Pierre Gauthier announced his resignation. Soon he would resurface in Anaheim. Rick Dudley, who previously was g.m. of the successful Detroit Vipers franchise in the International Hockey League, was hired as the Senators' fourth general manager.

Ottawa had come of age when they knocked off the Devils in the playoffs, but their improvement in 1998-99 went beyond most predictions. Alexei Yashin showed that he belonged among the league's elite, collecting 44 goals and 50 assists. With players like Marian Hossa and Magnus Arvedson emerging among the team's corp of young stars, the Senators had excellent team speed and solid defense backed up by the stellar goaltending of Ron Tugnutt (whose league-leading goals-against average of 1.79 was the lowest in the NHL since Tony Esposito's 1.77 in 1971-72). Ottawa was also the least-penalized team in the NHL.

The Senators not only led the Northeast Division with 103 points, they topped the entire Eastern Conference for much of the year. Only a late-season slump allowed the New Jersey Devils to claim top spot with 105 points. However, the season ended in disappointment when the Buffalo Sabres swept the Senators to open the playoffs.

Though the 1999–2000 season would be another productive one on the ice, there were plenty of distractions off of it. Dudley bolted the team for a similar job in Tampa Bay, and Marshall Johnston became the club's fifth general manager in its eight-year history. Once again Yashin refused to report unless the club agreed to renegotiate his contract, and this time his holdout/suspension played out as a season-long soap opera. Many expected Ottawa to deal him at the trade deadline, but the Senators held firm to their position that he would not be moved.

Most problematic of all for Ottawa was the possibility that owner Rod Bryden would be forced to sell and/or relocate the franchise unless the Canadian government agreed to provide financial assistance and/or tax concessions. The Canadian government did announce a subsidy plan on January 18, 2000, but revoked the plan just two days later. A show of support by Ottawa fans when Bryden announced the team needed to sell more tickets convinced him not to put the club on the market.

With the absence of Alexei Yashin, Daniel Alfredsson was named team captain. Radek Bonk and Marian Hossa helped pick up the offensive slack, as Bonk led the team with 60 points and Hossa topped all scorers with 29 goals. Wade Redden continued to develop into one of the NHL's best young defensemen. The decision to deal Damian Rhodes to the expansion Atlanta Thrashers before the season left Tugnutt to assume the role of the number-one goaltender, but he was dealt to the Pittsburgh Penguins for Tom Barrasso at the trade deadline.

While not quite able to live up to the previous year's performance, Ottawa was able to keep the pressure on Toronto in the race for first place in the Northeast Division. Though the Maple Leafs wound up on top, the Senators had their chance for revenge in the first round of the playoffs, as the teams hooked up in "The Battle of Ontario." After losing the first two games in Toronto, Ottawa fought back to make a series of it before eventually surrendering in six. The Senators could only manage 10 goals against Curtis Joseph, with their top line of Bonk, Hossa and Arvedson being held without a point.

Ottawa Senators Year-by-Year Record, 1992–2000

Season	GP	W	L	T	GF	GA	Pts	Finish	Division	Playoff Results
1992–93	84	10	70	4	202	395	24	6th	Adams	Out of Playoffs
1993–94	84	14	61	9	201	397	37	7th	Northeast	Out of Playoffs
1994–95	48	9	34	5	117	174	23	7th	Northeast	Out of Playoffs
1995–96	82	18	59	5	191	291	41	6th	Northeast	Out of Playoffs
1996–97	82	31	36	15	226	234	77	3rd	Northeast	Lost Conf. Quarterfinal
1997–98	82	34	33	15	193	200	83	5th	Northeast	Lost Conf. Semifinal
1998–99	82	44	23	15	239	179	103	1st	Northeast	Lost Conf. Quarterfinal
1999-2000	82	41	30	11	244	210	*95	2nd	Northeast	Lost Conf. Quarterfinal

* *Includes 2 points for regulation ties (RT)*

PHILADELPHIA FLYERS

ED SNIDER WAS A FOOTBALL EXECUTIVE talking business with team banker Bill Putnam in 1965 when he got the tip that led to the birth of one of the NHL's most enduringly successful franchises. Putnam mentioned he would soon be leaving to prepare Jack Kent Cooke's bid for an NHL franchise for Los Angeles and referred Snider to Bill Jennings, the president of the New York Rangers and chairman of the expansion committee.

Jennings was both intrigued by the nation's fourth-largest market and skeptical of its historically poor support of a variety of minor-league teams. The last, the Ramblers of the Eastern Hockey League, had abandoned the ramshackle Philadelphia Arena in 1964 for another shabby arena in the New Jersey suburbs.

Meanwhile, Snider, who was the Philadelphia Eagles' point man for a proposed baseball/football stadium in South Philadelphia, was asked by Ike Richman, part-owner of the NBA's Philadelphia 76ers, whether Jerry Wolman, the wildly successful developer who owned the Eagles, had any interest in building an arena. Snider went to Wolman, who agreed that a building with twin hockey/basketball tenants could be viable.

When Putnam subsequently decided to leave Cooke, he joined the Snider-Wolman partnership and began the bid for an NHL franchise. It was granted, to the surprise of many who expected it to go to Baltimore, on February 9, 1966. Ground was broken for the arena (the Spectrum) in May at the corner of Broad Street and Pattison Avenue. Team colors of orange, black and white were selected by Putnam, both because of their boldness and because of his old loyalties to the University of Texas, where he had played football. Snider's sister, Phyllis, came up with the name Flyers, as did enough voters in a name-the-team contest that the franchise could justify its selection over suggestions like Quakers and Liberty Bells.

Before payment of the $2-million franchise fee was due in June, 1967, Snider acquired Wolman's 22 percent stake in the team in exchange for his own 40 percent share in the Spectrum. Snider also bought out Jerry Schiff, giving him 60 percent of the Flyers. Wolman reiterated his pledge to put up half of the $2 million franchise fee, but with less than two weeks to go before the money was due at the expansion draft, he admitted he didn't have it. Snider and Putnam had to scramble. The last $500,000 was not procured until 48 hours before the deadline. A 15 percent share in the team later was sold to Joe Scott, a well-known local beer baron who would work tirelessly to sell tickets and open doors to a business community that was slow to respond to a perceived foreign sport.

On June 6, 1967, general manager Bud Poile, a longtime minor-league executive in the Detroit organization hired by Putnam on the advice of Jack Adams, and coach Keith Allen supervised the Flyers in a drafting approach that differed from the other five new teams. Starting with their two goaltender selections, Bernie Parent and Doug Favell, the Flyers focused on young players, only four of whom—Joe Watson, Ed Van Impe, Lou Angotti and Brit Selby—had spent more than token time in the NHL.

The Flyers debuted with a 5–1 loss at Oakland on October 11, 1967. The team's first victory was a 2–1 win in St. Louis on October 18. The following night, with signs of unfinished construction all around the Spectrum, they drew 7,812 for their initial home game, a 1–0 victory over Pittsburgh. Winger Bill Sutherland, who had to sneak into the building after an overzealous usher refused to believe he was a player, scored the winning goal in the third period.

With a base of only 2,100 season tickets and no radio contract, the team endured crowds as embarrassingly low as 4,203 in the early weeks. But, momentum began to build. In February, the team had just drawn consecutive sellouts of home games against Toronto and Chicago when high winds tore portions of tarpaper off the Spectrum roof during a performance of the Ice Capades. The building was quickly repaired, but 12 days later more wind did greater damage to a building that, it was learned, had never received a final safety inspection before opening.

The Flyers were orphaned, moving the first two of seven remaining home games to Madison Square Garden and Maple Leaf Gardens before settling in Quebec City, where they owned their farm club. Nevertheless, the team persevered to be crowned champions of the expansion West Division and returned home to the re-opened Spectrum for the playoffs. They lost a tough seven-game series to St. Louis, but left to a standing ovation that was symbolic of how they had captured the city's heart. A year later, after the Flyers were physically abused by the Blues in four straight, the team prioritized size in the draft. But first, they struck gold with the selection of center Bobby Clarke. Though a dominating junior player, Clarke had been passed over by ten teams, including the Flyers, in the 1969 draft because he had been diagnosed as a diabetic.

By this time, Poile was losing favor with Snider, who had become increasingly impressed with Allen. Bumped up to assistant general manager at the end of the second season, Allen was elevated to g.m. when Poile was fired midway through the third. With the departure of the g.m. he had selected, Putnam sold his shares and left.

When a late-season slump cost the Flyers a playoff spot in 1970–71, the decision was made to move one of the team's young goalies for some scoring. Allen traded Parent to Toronto in a three-way deal with the Leafs and Bruins for Rick MacLeish. Philadelphia made the playoffs in their fourth year, but were uncompetitive in a first-round sweep by Chicago. In 1971–72, an eight-player trade with Los Angeles brought a player of lasting impact, left wing Ross Lonsberry, but the team missed the playoffs after losing the last game of the season. The loss seemed a devastating setback to the modest progress the team had made in the second half under first-year coach Fred Shero, but Allen and Snider stayed the course.

The next season, the heretofore disappointing MacLeish blossomed dramatically into a 50-goal scorer while Bill Barber added offensive punch and poise well beyond his years. Also, the organization's bulk-up plan, four years in the works, came to fruition with the promotion of enforcer Dave Schultz. A trade with St. Louis for defenseman Andre Dupont added a bouncer to a defense anchored by Watson and Van Impe and bolstered by the development of Barry Ashbee. Rambunctious wing Bob Kelly now had some muscle on his side, and Shero showed no hesitation to use. The scrawny little Flyers had become "The Broad Street Bullies" and, with Clarke breaking 100 points and winning the Hart Trophy, they completed their first winning season in 1972–73. Philadelphia had emerged not only as the NHL's most notorious team, but also as one of its best.

Allen reacquired Parent, who had matured under the tutelage of Jacques Plante in Toronto, and with the balance of excellent goaltending, the discipline of Shero's dump-and-chase system, large doses of terror tactics, and a charmed home record whenever Kate Smith sang "God Bless America," the 1973–74 Flyers rolled to a division title and then past the Atlanta Flames into the semifinals.

In seven ferocious games with the New York Rangers, during which Ashbee lost his playing career to a puck in the eye, Philadelphia held off the Rangers 4–3 in a desperate seventh game at the Spectrum and became the first expansion team to beat an old guard club. After losing game one of the finals to the heavily favored Bruins at Boston Garden, the Flyers won game two when Clarke put in his own rebound 12:01 into overtime. Having obtained their first victory in Boston in six-plus seasons, the Flyers then scored a 4–1 victory over the suddenly passive Bruins in game three. The series went to six, but with Kate Smith making her second live appearance at the Spectrum, the Flyers played the game of their lives. They won the Cup in a 1–0 classic on a first-period tip-in by MacLeish, relentless bumping and checking of Orr, and a flawless performance by Parent. The Flyers made it two in a row in 1975, beating the Sabres in six. Once again, Bernie Parent blanked the opposition in the decisive game as Philadelphia scored a

2–0 victory. Parent won the Conn Smythe Trophy for the second time.

Five months later, the best goaltender in the game had to leave training camp for neck disc surgery. Still, the well-oiled Flyers rolled to their best-yet regular-season record. They also scored a victory in one of the most storied international sports events in history, beating the Central Red Army, 4–1, after the visiting Soviet League champions had gone undefeated through the first three games of an unprecedented four-game tour of NHL teams.

Parent was back by playoff time, but struggled during the team's unexpectedly difficult seven-game first-round triumph over Toronto. He was benched, and backup Wayne Stephenson led the Flyers past Boston in five games and into one of the most anticipated finals in years against a swift and powerful Montreal team that had outlasted Philadelphia for the league's best record. Without Parent or MacLeish, who had suffered a season-ending knee injury in February, and with Clarke hobbled by a bad knee, Montreal won four straight games by a total margin of five goals to end the Flyers' reign, despite a record 19-goal playoff by Reggie Leach.

Another Patrick Division title followed in 1976–77, but the Flyers were emotionally worn by the death of Barry Ashbee (now an assistant coach) from leukemia in the spring of 1977, and were swept by the Bruins in the semifinals. When Boston eliminated Philadelphia one step short of the finals again in 1978, Allen made the decision to rebuild.

Shero, who wanted more control over personnel decisions, left to become the coach and general manager of the Rangers, who routed the rebuilding Flyers and rookie head coach Pat Quinn in the 1979 quarterfinals. But, two high draft picks, center Ken Linseman and defenseman Behn Wilson, plus the emergence of bedrock right wing Paul Holmgren as a scorer and leader, brought the Flyers back strong the following season.

After dropping the second contest of the year, the Flyers did not lose again for 84 days, running their mind-boggling streak to 35 games (25–0–10). During a tough playoff run, the battered Flyers ultimately proved deeper in enthusiasm than they were on defense, and the Islanders defeated them for the Stanley Cup on Bob Nystrom's overtime goal in game six.

More major changes followed a 1981 upset by Calgary in the quarterfinals, and a 1982 first-round loss to the Rangers. The acquisition of defenseman Mark Howe from Hartford in a trade for Linseman stabilized a defense that was hanging in tatters. Under coach Bob McCammon, who had succeeded the fired Quinn late in the 1981–82 season, the Flyers bounced back strongly with a 106-point season and a Patrick Division championship. After the speedier Rangers took them apart in three straight first-round games, Allen was pushed upstairs and McCammon was given the dual role of coach and general manager. He then was let go by new team president Jay Snider, the owner's son, after a third consecutive first-round loss in 1984.

Clarke retired to become general manager, and Barber's career ended with a knee injury. Nevertheless, in what was expected to be a rebuilding season, the youngest team in the NHL was directed by rookie coach Mike Keenan to the NHL's best record. Keyed by the emergence of a new 50-goal scorer, Tim Kerr, anchored by the flawless defense of Howe and brilliant goaltending by Swedish import Pelle Lindbergh, plus injected with three energetic rookies—Rick Tocchet, Peter Zezel and Derrick Smith—the Flyers ended their playoff misery by advancing all the way to the Stanley Cup finals. Their loss there to the defending champion Oilers became inconsequential five months later when Lindbergh, the Vezina Trophy winner, was killed in an automobile accident.

Despite the loss of Lindbergh, the Flyers came within three points of the previous season's 113 before a first-round playoff loss to the Rangers brought the season to a crashing halt. The following year, Keenan turned over the goaltending duties from Bob Froese to rookie Ron Hextall, whose unprecedented puck-handling skills and fiery demeanor carried an injury-racked team to another 100-point season. A brilliant playoff performance by Hextall saw the Flyers return to the finals for a second crack at Edmonton and the Cup in three years. This time Philadelphia rallied from a three-games-to-one deficit before falling to the Oilers in seven.

The Flyers began the 1987–88 season looking burned out from their record 26-game playoff ordeal, and struggled in the continuing absence of Kerr, who needed multiple operations on a shoulder that had forced him out of the final two series. They started to come on in late November and made history on December 8 against Boston when Hextall became the first NHL goalie to shoot and score a goal. But, they struggled down the stretch and blew a 3–1 series lead in the first round to Washington, failing to hold a 3–0 edge in a 5–4 overtime loss in game seven at the Capital Centre.

Clarke perceived mental fatigue from four years under the hard-driving Keenan and fired the coach, promoting assistant Holmgren. The Flyers suffered through their first losing season in 17 years, but got hot in the playoffs and advanced to the semifinals. However, this turned out to be the last hurrah for the era. In 1989–90, the team missed the playoffs for the first time in 18 seasons. Clarke, who had lost the confidence of Jay Snider over a perceived reluctance to rebuild, was fired and new g.m. Russ Farwell struggled to right the team's direction after years of poor drafting. After two more years of missing the playoffs, the Sniders and Farwell decided it was time to do something bold. They pursued a trade with the Quebec Nordiques for Eric Lindros, heralded as the prospect of the decade.

The Flyers agreed to give up six players—including the injury-racked Hextall and their last two number-one draft picks, center Mike Ricci and Peter Forsberg. They spiced the package with two future first-round picks, plus $15 million. When Nordiques president Marcel Aubut claimed he had never finalized the deal and announced he had reached an agreement for Lindros with the New York Rangers, Jay Snider protested to the league and arbitrator Larry Bertuzzi decided in favor of the Flyers, consummating one of the biggest deals in sports.

Despite missing 40 games with various injuries in his first two seasons, Lindros performed well. Still, the lineup gaps left by the massive trade doomed the Flyers to fourth and fifth consecutive seasons without a playoff spot.

Jay Snider resigned to go into private business, and Ed Snider, returned to an active role in running the team as he negotiated to build a new arena, brought back Clarke as general manager. His trade of Mark Recchi to Montreal brought defenseman Eric Desjardins and left wing John LeClair and reestablished the Flyers as an elite team.

With a reacquired Hextall, the Flyers, under coach Terry

Murray, reached the conference finals before losing to the eventual champion New Jersey Devils in six games, but Lindros joined Clarke to become just the second Flyer to win the Hart Trophy. In 1996–97, the Flyers' first in the new 19,519-seat First Union Center, they returned to the Stanley Cup finals, but were overwhelmed in four straight by Detroit, leading to the firing of Murray.

Lindros missed 18 games just before the 1998 playoffs with a concussion and was ineffective as the Flyers, under veteran coach Roger Neilson, lost in the first round to Buffalo. In 1998–99, Lindros was having his most complete season when he suffered a collapsed lung that left the Flyers without him for the playoffs, where they lost in six games to Toronto.

After backing up John Vanbiesbrouck for a year, Ron Hextall retired prior to the 1999–2000 campaign, but the Flyers entered the new season with few changes to the line-up. The club started poorly, but was in top form by December when it was learned coach Roger Neilson had bone-marrow cancer. Though he continued to coach while undergoing treatment, he was forced to step aside on February 20, 2000, and was replaced by assistant coach Craig Ramsay. (Ramsay would be formally named the club's new head coach after the playoffs.) On the ice, meanwhile, Mark Recchi (who had been reacquired late in the 1998–99 season) reestablished himself as a top-notch NHL star, leading the league with 63 assists and finishing third in scoring behind Jaromir Jagr and Pavel Bure. John LeClair scored 40 goals. Simon Gagne, the club's first draft choice in 1998, proved to have a scoring touch with 20 goals, while fellow rookie Brian Boucher, the club's top pick in 1997, emerged as the number-one goaltender. In 35 games played, Boucher posted a 1.91 goals-against average to lead the league and become the first rookie netminder with an average below 2.00 since 1950–51.

All was not well with Eric Lindros, however.

Having already missed some time due to back spasms, Lindros was sidelined by a concussion late in the season. (He would suffer yet another head injury when he returned to action against New Jersey in the playoffs.) While he was out, Eric Desjardins replaced Lindros as captain.

The club plyayed well down the stretch, riding a hot finish to overhaul the Devils for first place overall in the Eastern Conference.

Though some thought the eighth-seeded Buffalo Sabres had a chance to do some damage in the playoffs, the Flyers handled them easily for an opening-round victory in five games. Roger Neilson received medical clearance to rejoin the team for the conference semifinals and returned to assist Craig Ramsay and the coaching staff for the series with Pittsburgh. The Flyers dropped the first two games of the second-round set on home ice and the Penguins seemed poised for an upset before the Flyers won two in a row on the road, including a 2–1 victory in game four that required five overtime periods. After winning the third-longest game in NHL history, Philadelphia posted two more wins to take the series in six and advance to play New Jersey in the Conference final. Though the Flyers raced to a 3–1 series lead, the Devils got their revenge when they stormed back to take the series in seven games.

Philadelphia Flyers Year-by-Year Record

Season	GP	W	L	T	GF	GA	Pts	Finish	Division	Playoff Results
1967–68	74	31	32	11	173	179	73	1st	West	Lost Quarterfinal
1968–69	76	20	35	21	174	225	61	3rd	West	Lost Quarterfinal
1969–70	76	17	35	24	197	225	58	5th	West	Out of Playoffs
1970–71	78	28	33	17	207	225	73	3rd	West	Lost Quarterfinal
1971–72	78	26	38	14	200	236	66	5th	West	Out of Playoffs
1972–73	78	37	30	11	296	256	85	2nd	West	Lost Semifinal
1973–74	78	50	16	12	273	164	112	1st	West	Won Stanley Cup
1974–75	80	51	18	11	293	181	113	1st	Patrick	Won Stanley Cup
1975–76	80	51	13	16	348	209	118	1st	Patrick	Lost Final
1976–77	80	48	16	16	323	213	112	1st	Patrick	Lost Semifinal
1977–78	80	45	20	15	296	200	105	2nd	Patrick	Lost Semifinal
1978–79	80	40	25	15	281	248	95	2nd	Patrick	Lost Quarterfinal
1979–80	80	48	12	20	327	254	116	1st	Patrick	Lost Final
1980–81	80	41	24	15	313	249	97	2nd	Patrick	Lost Quarterfinal
1981–82	80	38	31	11	325	313	87	3rd.	Patrick	Lost Div. Semifinal
1982–83	80	49	23	8	326	240	106	1st	Patrick	Lost Div. Semifinal
1983–84	80	44	26	10	350	290	98	3rd	Patrick	Lost Div. Semifinal
1984–85	80	53	20	7	348	241	113	1st	Patrick	Lost Final
1985–86	80	53	23	4	335	241	110	1st	Patrick	Lost Div. Semifinal
1986–87	80	46	26	8	310	245	100	1st	Patrick	Lost Final
1987–88	80	38	33	9	292	292	85	3rd	Patrick	Lost Div. Semifinal
1988–89	80	36	36	8	307	285	80	4th	Patrick	Lost Conf. Final
1989–90	80	30	39	11	290	297	71	6th	Patrick	Out of Playoffs
1990–91	80	33	37	10	252	267	76	5th	Patrick	Out of Playoffs
1991–92	80	32	37	11	252	273	75	6th	Patrick	Out of Playoffs
1992–93	84	36	37	11	319	319	83	5th	Patrick	Out of Playoffs
1993–94	84	35	39	10	294	314	80	6th	Atlantic	Out of Playoffs
1994–95	48	28	16	4	150	132	60	1st	Atlantic	Lost Conf. Final
1995–96	82	45	24	13	282	208	103	1st	Atlantic	Lost Conf. Semifinal
1996–97	82	45	24	13	274	217	103	2nd	Atlantic	Lost Final
1997–98	82	42	29	11	242	193	95	2nd	Atlantic	Lost Conf. Quarterfinal
1998–99	82	37	26	19	231	196	93	2nd	Atlantic	Lost Conf. Quarterfinal
1999-2000	82	45	25	12	237	179	*105	1st	Atlantic	Lost Conf. Final

* *Includes 3 points for regulation ties (RT)*

PHILADELPHIA QUAKERS

IT WAS 1930 when the NHL first arrived in the City of Brotherly Love. The Pittsburgh Pirates moved across state to become the Philadelphia Quakers, taking their name from the religious community of the Pennsylvania countryside.

Pittsburgh had become the third American city in the NHL (after Boston and New York) when the Pirates were granted a franchise in 1925. Though the city had a long hockey tradition, the Pirates were not a financial success. One year after the stock market crash of October, 1929 weakened the city's steel industry, Benny Leonard, the ex-boxer and fight promoter who had joined the hockey club's ownership group in 1928, decided to relocate. The transfer of Pittsburgh's home games to Philadelphia was accepted by the NHL's Board of Governors on October 18, 1930.

Twelve players who had worn the yellow and black of the Pittsburgh Pirates in 1929–30 suited up in the orange and black of the Philadelphia Quakers in 1930–31. Harry Darragh, Hib Milks, Tex White and Herb Drury had been with the franchise since its NHL debut in 1925–26, though only Milks would suffer through the entire season in Philadelphia. Future Hockey Hall of Fame referee Cooper Smeaton had resigned as the NHL's referee-in-chief to coach the Quakers. The roster was bolstered by future star Syd Howe and new goalie Wilf Cude, but Smeaton would be refereeing again by 1931–32.

The first NHL game in Philadelphia took place on November 11, 1930, with the New York Rangers defeating the Quakers, 3–0. It would take until their third game before the Quakers scored their first goal. Their first victory came in game six against the Toronto Maple Leafs on November 25, but the Quakers' next win would not come until January 10, 1931, when they beat the Montreal Maroons to "improve" to 2–19–1. The Quakers finished the season with a record of 4–36–4. Philadelphia's 76 goals in 1930–31 tied the New York Americans for fewest in the league, while the Quakers' 184 goals against was 42 more than the next worst team (the Ottawa Senators) and almost double the average of 97 goals allowed by the NHL's other nine clubs. Philadelphia's winning percentage of .136 would remain the worst in NHL history until the Washington Capitals went 8–67–5 for a .131 mark in 1974–75.

At the NHL Board of Governors meeting on September 26, 1931, it was announced that both the Ottawa Senators and the Pittsburgh-Philadelphia franchise would suspend operations for 1931–32. The Pennsylvania club continued to receive permission to suspend operations until May 7, 1936, when the franchise was formally canceled. The NHL did not return to Pittsburgh or Philadelphia until 1967.

Philadelphia Quakers Year-by-Year Record

Season	GP	W	L	T	GF	GA	Pts	Finish	Divsion	Playoff Results
1930–31	44	4	36	4	76	184	12	5th	American	Out of Playoffs

PHOENIX COYOTES AND WINNIPEG JETS

THREE-TIME CHAMPIONS in the seven-year history of the World Hockey Association, the Winnipeg Jets enjoyed good times and bad in the NHL. At their best during the heyday of the Edmonton Oilers, Winnipeg iced strong teams that never could get out of their division in the playoffs. Left in a competitive desert as the smallest of small-market teams, the Jets left Winnipeg for Phoenix in 1996 and rose from the ashes as the Coyotes.

The original Winnipeg Jets franchise began in the Western Canada Junior Hockey League in 1967. Spearheaded by entrepreneur Ben Hatskin, the team was named simply because Hatskin was a friend and admirer of Sonny Werblin, owner of the National Football League's New York Jets. The new hockey team met with only limited success, but Hatskin was hooked on both the game and ownership. When Gary Davidson and Dennis Murphy created a pro league to rival the NHL, Hatskin joined the 12-team World Hockey Association in 1971. The WHA's first games were played in 1972-73.

The rival league wasn't regarded with much interest or credibility by hockey's establishment, until a couple of high-profile signings changed everything. Talented goalie Bernie Parent led the defections to the WHA, and Hatskin was not far behind with his coup de grace. His target was Bobby Hull.

"The Golden Jet" found most of Hatskin's early overtures merely a nuisance, and jokingly told the Winnipeg organization that he needed a million dollars to jump leagues. Hull soon found out that Hatskin and his new partners weren't kidding around.

Some intense negotiations and deal-brokering with other WHA franchises to contribute half of a $2.75 million contract led to Hull's decision to switch leagues. He inked the deal June 27, 1972, and jetted off to Winnipeg for a symbolic signing at the city's epicenter, the corner of Portage Avenue and Main Street. Hull's signing touched off a flurry of NHL defections that numbered 60 by the time the first WHA schedule had begun.

The defections were followed as quickly by lawsuits from NHL clubs, who held that the reserve clause bound players to teams, even if their contracts had expired. Legal actions continued into August 1972 (costing Hull a spot on Team Canada's 1972 roster), but the Jets did not sit still. Not only did they name Hull as the team's first coach, but they hired Nick Mickoski as his assistant and named Ab McDonald their first captain. Hull did not suit up for the franchise's first pro game, a 6–4 win over the New York Raiders at Madison Square Garden on October 12, 1972. In fact, he missed 15 games before an American judge tossed out the NHL suits as "harassment."

Despite the forced hiatus, "The Golden Jet" fired 51 goals and 103 points that inaugural season. Playing on the Luxury Line with Christian Bordeleau and Normie Beaudin, Hull and the Jets went all the way to the Avco Cup finals before losing to New England. After a mediocre second year, Hatskin dispatched confidant and scout Billy Robinson to Sweden to bolster the club's lineup—a philosophy much ahead of its time. The mission brought Ulf Nilsson, Anders Hedberg, defenseman Lars-Erik Sjoberg and others to Winnipeg, and became the catalyst for a new and high-tempo brand of offensive hockey that made the Jets immensely successful in the remaining WHA years. Playing with Nilsson and Hedberg, Hull scored a record 77 goals in 1974–75.

While the Jets were dominating the WHA in the late 1970s, the league eventually ran up against some insurmountable problems, most of them financial. However, as one of the league's strongest entities, the Jets eventually became one of four clubs that were accepted into the NHL's expansion of 1979. About a year earlier, a local lawyer named Barry Shenkarow and Winnipeg businessman Michael Gobuty had become part of the ownership team. The deal cut to admit the Jets, Edmonton, Hartford and Quebec into the NHL came with some harsh conditions attached. Jets general manager John Ferguson was allowed to retain only two skaters and two goaltenders before the Expansion Draft, and the successful hockey team Winnipeggers had come to love was more or less disbanded.

Under coach Tom McVie and his assistant Billy Sutherland, the Jets opened their first NHL season in Pittsburgh, October 10, 1979, with a 4–2 loss. Their first NHL goal came from Morris Lukowich, who went on to lead the club in scoring that first rag-tag season. It produced 20 wins, as the Jets managed to tie Colorado for last place with 51 points. The team found the going even rougher in year two. The Jets went 30 games without a victory in one stretch, went through three coaches (McVie, Sutherland and future g.m. Mike Smith) and ended up a distant last in the NHL with only nine wins (9–57–14) and 32 points. The Jets' rebound in the 1981–82 season was one of the most dramatic on record. The club posted a .500 mark that year, 33–33–14, finishing second in the Norris Division to Minnesota.

There were reasons for this turnaround. Having the worst record the year before had allowed the Jets to select Dale Hawerchuk first overall in the 1981 Entry Draft. Hawerchuk's scoring exploits from junior translated instantly into the pro game, amounting to 45 goals and 103 points. Thomas Steen also made his debut in Winnipeg. The Jets had hired career college coach Tom Watt from the University of Toronto, and the additions were enough to bring them immediate respectability. Hawerchuk won the

Calder Trophy, and Watt was rewarded with the Jack Adams Award as NHL coach of the year.

An ominous tendency for early playoff exits began in that spring of 1982, when the Jets lost four straight to St. Louis in the first round. In the following two years, it happened against the powerful Oilers. A minor breakthrough occurred in the spring of 1985, when a very balanced Jets team dropped the Calgary Flames in the first round, but lost Hawerchuk to a broken rib. An Edmonton sweep in the second round took away from many of the positives in a season where six different Jets had at least 30 goals. An experienced defense led by Randy Carlyle and Dave Ellett also had been promising. Under coach Barry Long, the Jets had hit a high-water mark of 43 wins and 96 points.

The Jets fell back to 59 points the very next season, and the yo-yo trend of good season followed by bad was well under way. Long was replaced by Dan Maloney who, as per the script, brought the team back up to 88 points in 1986–87.

That was another exciting spring in Winnipeg. The Jets won a stirring first-round playoff matchup against the Calgary Flames in six games—the last time the team made it past the first round—but it was the same old story against the Oilers. The second-round series lasted the minimum four games, taking the Jets' postseason record against Edmonton to 0–14. From 88 points, the Jets slipped back again the following season to 77 and the 1988 playoffs brought a familiar opponent, the Oilers. A five-game triumph for Edmonton left the overall tally at 1–18. That, as much as anything, cost the always-boisterous Ferguson his job in October, 1988.

Longtime scout and assistant g.m. Mike Smith was brought in as general manager, first on an interim basis and then as a permanent appointment. But, by the time he started rearranging the team's role players and depth, the season was lost. Maloney was a casualty, and the Jets finished under Rick Bowness. Bob Murdoch took over as the new coach in 1989–90, and the team perked up once again. It rebounded to 85 points with a very workmanlike approach. In the playoffs, Winnipeg jumped out to a 3–1 series lead over Edmonton, including Dave Ellett's double-overtime marker that for many Jets fans remains one of the club's greatest NHL moments. But, Jari Kurri, Mark Messier and company still proved too much for Winnipeg in seven games and the Oilers marched on to the Stanley Cup.

Over the years, Smith's management style became the subject of much scrutiny. The introspective and highly educated g.m. made frequent trades (71 during his five-year tenure) and stocked the Winnipeg reserve list with European players, mainly Russians. Smith also became known as a frugal manager and formidable negotiator, a trait that may have been good for the team's bottom line but alienated several important players.

Hawerchuk eventually became disgruntled and his trade request was granted by Smith after the seven-game loss to the Oilers in 1990. The haul was Buffalo's highly talented defenseman Phil Housley, who himself became a contractual headache and was traded to St. Louis in September, 1993. The same fate befell goalie Bob Essensa, who was a Vezina Trophy finalist in 1991–92, and later won the first $1 million arbitration award in NHL history. Essensa, however, was traded in March, 1994.

After the Hawerchuk trade, the Jets had sagged to 63 points under Murdoch in 1990-91 and the coach was replaced by Oak River, Manitoba, native John Paddock. Paddock had spent most of his playing time in the minors and had assembled an impressive resume behind the bench of several successful American Hockey League clubs. He took over in the fall of 1991 and moved the team to two straight playoff berths, with improved point totals each year—a first for the franchise. But, the Vancouver Canucks defeated the Jets in the playoffs in both 1992 and 1993.

Paddock had benefited from the introduction of Teemu Selanne to the NHL in the fall of 1992. With speed, skill and charisma, "The Finnish Flash" vaulted to instant stardom in Winnipeg and around the NHL. Selanne smashed records for goals by freshmen with 76 (tying Alexander Mogilny for the overall league lead) and points with 132. He was the unanimous selection (all 50 first-place votes) as the Calder Trophy winner over the likes of Eric Lindros and Felix Potvin.

Mike Smith was responsible for drafting or bringing much of the new wave of talent to the franchise—including Selanne, Teppo Numminen, Alexei Zhamnov, Keith Tkachuk and goalie Nikolai Khabibulin. But Shenkarow, the team's president, could go no further with Smith and dismissed him in January, 1994. Paddock the coach became Paddock the coach/general manager.

The lockout-shortened season of 1994–95 proved to be the beginning of the end for the franchise in Winnipeg. Burdened with the city's decaying arena (built in the 1950s and renovated several times) and escalating NHL salaries, Shenkarow and his private ownership group (holding 64 percent) were caught in a financial squeeze. Provincial and city governments held a 36 percent stake and had a grip on the team's purse strings after agreeing to fund any operating losses in 1991.

The covering of losses was the panacea to Shenkarow to be patient. It also turned out to be a short-sighted guarantee in the wake of rising salaries, and eventually became a political lightning rod that damaged whatever hope there might have been to save the franchise in Winnipeg.

Two distinct groups emerged to try to rescue the situation in 1994 and 1995. Manitoba Entertainment Complex (MEC) was the first group to try to arrange the purchase of the team and construction of a new, revenue-enhancing arena. Shenkarow, in his 1991 agreement with governments, had agreed to sell the franchise to approved buyers for $32 million Canadian by 1996. MEC, however, after first blaming NHL commissioner Gary Bettman, couldn't finalize an agreement with Shenkarow on the sale of the team or with different government bodies on the arena financing, and flew the white flag in early May.

After missing the playoffs, an emotional in-arena funeral to retire the team logo and Thomas Steen's number 25 was held only days before a second group called Spirit of Manitoba surfaced. However, Shenkarow's August deadline to consummate a deal with the group could not be met.

Mostly, the deal was just too complicated, but Bettman's summation of the mess was painfully accurate—that it was a simple case that nobody in the Manitoba capital wanted to step up and own the team. Winnipeg fans and taxpayers had run the emotional gamut from death to life, back to the inevitable and impending departure. Winnipeg was left with a lame-duck team for the 1995–96 season because all the political and financial wrangling went past the league deadline for transferring locations.

And so they played their final season, to poor crowds that eventually averaged 11,316 (74 percent of capacity). The club's 36–40–6 record was overshadowed by Tkachuk's huge new five-year contract, the terms of which were dictated by an offer sheet tendered by the Chicago Blackhawks, and by the unpopular trade of Teemu Selanne to Anaheim.

On the ice, the club struggled to the bitter end to squeeze into the playoffs. Tkachuk's 50th goal in the second-to-last game of the season sparked a final burst of enthusiasm for the team, though the Jets had drawn the powerful, first-seeded Detroit Red Wings in the first round of the Western Conference playoffs. Winnipeg, with its white-clad, frenzied fans, got in its licks to take the Wings to six games, but Norm Maciver's goal in the 3–1, game six loss on April 28, 1996, closed the book on Winnipeg in the NHL.

Exactly 1,400 regular and postseason NHL games had been played by the Jets, who were turned into the Phoenix Coyotes after a $68-million (U.S.) purchase by Richard Burke and Steven Gluckstern. Coach Terry Simpson lost his job in the transition as ties to Winnipeg were cut by the new owners. Paddock, who had stepped aside as coach in the spring of 1995, also was a casualty just two months into the team's new season in Phoenix. Vice president Bobby Smith, hired by Burke, took over the job of running the team.

With rookie Don Hay running the show, the Coyotes played inconsistently again, but eventually finished at 38–37–7, in spite of a losing record in their new home rink, America West Arena. Tkachuk scored 52 goals to become the first American-born player to lead the league. The team survived a lengthy holdout by Jeremy Roenick, who was acquired for Zhamnov during the offseason, and matched up against the Mighty Ducks of Anaheim in the first playoff round.

From Winnipeg, Phoenix imported the "white-out" tradition of fans all wearing white to home games in the postseason, but all it brought them was the same old grief. The Coyotes were knocked out by the Ducks in a seventh game. The defeat surprisingly prompted Smith to dismiss Hay, and Jim Schoenfeld was brought in to coach year number two in Phoenix. Rick Tocchet was signed as a free agent to add on-ice leadership. Again the club qualified for the playoffs, only to be knocked out in the first round, this time by the eventual Stanley Cup champions from Detroit.

The Coyotes kept pace with the eventual Stanley Cup champions in Dallas in the very early going in 1998–99, but a midseason slump knocked them far out of contention for top spot. Still, the Coyotes enjoyed a 90-point campaign and the club's best season since its move to Phoenix. In the playoffs, the Coyotes jumped out to a 3–1 series lead—only to fall to the St. Louis Blues in seven games. The unsettling playoff departure cost Jim Schoenfeld his job, as the Coyotes turned to Bob Francis, a successful minor-league coach and son of Emile Francis.

Since the move to Phoenix, Nikolai Khabibulin had established himself as a front line goaltender in the NHL, yet the Coyotes refused to meet his contract demands and the netminder held out before eventually playing out the season with the Long Beach Ice Dogs of the International Hockey League. Still, with former Jet Bob Essensa and Sean Burke providing solid goaltending, and Jeremy Roenick rediscovering the form from his Chicago days, the Coyotes raced out of the starting blocks. Despite a seven-game losing streak in March that represented the club's worst slide since leaving Winnipeg, Phoenix still was able to match the 39 wins and 90 points of the previous season. Injuries limited Keith Tkachuk to just 22 goals in 50 games.

Though Phoenix had pulled out of its late-season funk by playoff time, the Colorado Avalanche handed the team its ninth consecutive first-round defeat. During the series it was announced that an agreement of terms had been reached in the sale of the club by Richard Burke to The Ellman Companies, a real estate development group planning a new arena for the hockey team in neighboring Scottsdale. Construction is due to be completed by the 2002–2003 season. Buying in as a minority owner in Steve Ellman's investment is Wayne Gretzky, who is expected to take an active role in the team's hockey operations.

Phoenix Coyotes Year-by-Year Record

Season	GP	W	L	T	GF	GA	Pts	Finish	Division	Playoff Results
1979–80*	80	20	49	11	214	314	51	5th	Smythe	Out of Playoffs
1980–81*	80	9	57	14	246	400	32	6th	Smythe	Out of Playoffs
1981–82*	80	33	33	14	319	332	80	2nd	Norris	Lost Div. Semifinal
1982–83*	80	33	39	8	311	333	74	4th	Smythe	Lost Div. Semifinal
1983–84*	80	31	38	11	340	374	73	4th	Smythe	Lost Div. Semifinal
1984–85*	80	43	27	10	358	332	96	2nd	Smythe	Lost Div. Final
1985–86*	80	26	47	7	295	372	59	3rd	Smythe	Lost Div. Semifinal
1986–87*	80	40	32	8	279	271	88	3rd	Smythe	Lost Div. Final
1987–88*	80	33	36	11	292	310	77	3rd	Smythe	Lost Div. Semifinal
1988–89*	80	26	42	12	300	355	64	5th	Smythe	Out of Playoffs
1989–90*	80	37	32	11	298	290	85	3rd	Smythe	Lost Div. Semifinal
1990–91*	80	26	43	11	260	288	63	5th	Smythe	Out of Playoffs
1991–92*	80	33	32	15	251	244	81	4th	Smythe	Lost Div. Semifinal
1992–93*	84	40	37	7	322	320	87	4th	Smythe	Lost Div. Semifinal
1993–94*	84	24	51	9	245	344	57	6th	Central	Out of Playoffs
1994–95*	48	16	25	7	157	177	39	6th	Central	Out of Playoffs
1995–96*	82	36	40	6	275	291	78	5th	Central	Lost Conf. Quarterfinal
1996–97	82	38	37	7	240	243	83	3rd	Central	Lost Conf. Quarterfinal
1997–98	82	35	35	12	224	227	82	4th	Central	Lost Conf. Quarterfinal
1998–99	82	39	31	12	205	197	90	2nd	Pacific	Lost Conf. Quarterfinal
1999-2000	82	39	35	8	232	228	§90	3rd	Pacific	Lost Conf. Quarterfinal

** Winnipeg Jets*

§ Includes 4 points for regulation ties (RT)

PITTSBURGH PENGUINS

PITTSBURGH ENTERED THE NHL during the great expansion of 1967–68. The winning name in the contest to give the team an identifying symbol was Penguins. However, the team symbol, a penguin skating along, stick in hand, flowing scarf from neck, was nowhere to be seen on the uniform. Only the word "Pittsburgh" adorned the front of each jersey. (In 1969, the Penguins symbol, sans scarf, was added in a new uniform design.) One particularly plausible answer as to why "Penguins" was chosen is that the Civic Arena, completed in 1961 at the cost of $22 million, is called "The Igloo" because of its domed roof.

The NHL's first franchise in Pittsburgh joined the league in 1925. The Pirates, who took their name from the National League baseball team, moved to Philadelphia after the 1929–30 season, when The Great Depression damaged the city's steel industry. From the mid-1930s, when John H. Harris bought a franchise in the AHL, the Hornets had been symbolic of Pittsburgh hockey and a training ground, first for Detroit but later, and more famously, for Toronto Maple Leafs farmhands. When the old Duquesne Gardens on Craig Street was torn down in the 1950s, there was an absence of hockey in Pittsburgh for five years until the Civic Arena opened and the Hornets returned for the 1961–62 season. The year before the NHL came to town, Pittsburgh won both the AHL title and the Calder Cup. Although they would now see Howe, Hull and Beliveau, the ice fans in the Steel City no longer had a team they identified with and they had to be won over.

In the Expansion Draft of 1967, general manager Jack Riley and coach Red Sullivan sought players with experience and wound up with the oldest club—average age 32. Explained Riley, a popular hockey man who had run the Rochester team of the AHL, and then became president of that league before joining the Penguins: "[Pittsburgh] won the Calder Cup last year. Our fans don't want a building program, they're used to winners. We felt we had to put quality on the ice immediately.... The older players have been winning in hockey in recent years, so that's the way we went."

Three of the important draftees were Earl Ingarfield, Ken Schinkel and Andy Bathgate. All were over 30 and each had something else in common. They had played for the New York Rangers, where the Penguins' coach, Sullivan, had played and coached. In fact, the Pittsburgh roster began to resemble an old Rangers list with defenseman Al MacNeil and forwards Val Fonteyne and Mel Pearson.

Before the 1966–67 season, Pittsburgh had purchased three defensemen—Ted Lanyon, Dick Mattiussi and Bill Speer—and goaltender Les Binkley from the Cleveland Barons. At the time, the Pens had no farm team of their own ,so the four were spread around the minors and convened with the rest of the squad at Brantford, Ontario, for the first training camp. A hot battle for the two goaltending jobs developed among Binkley, rookie Joe Daley, veteran Hank Bassen and amateur Marv Edwards. Bassen, who as a Hornet had led his team to the Calder Cup the previous year, was garnered in a trade with Detroit just before the season opened. He figured to do a job and be colorfully popular at the same time. What he hadn't anticipated was just how good Binkley was.

Binkley posted six shutouts in 1967–68, tying him for second place in that department with Lorne Worsley and Cesare Maniago behind Ed Giacomin's eight. In 54 games he compiled a solid 2.87 goals-against average. However, in the futile pursuit of a playoff berth, Binkley broke his finger in a 6–6 tie in Oakland. The Penguins blew a big lead and lost a vital point along with their ace goalie. To their credit, they kept battling to the end of the campaign. Binkley, having recovered, returned in time to lead them to victory in three of their last four winning games. When it was all over, they had as many wins as the North Stars but two fewer points.

Despite missing the playoffs, there were signs of encouragement in the Penguin nest. Pittsburgh fandom, resentful and skeptical at first, had been won over, and late in the season the club's majority interest was sold to a group of Michigan investors, headed by Donald H. Parsons, board chairman of the Bank of the Commonwealth of Detroit, who announced that the Penguins would remain in Pittsburgh. Early in the 1967–68 season, a bid to purchase the team by owners of the baseball Braves had led to rumors that the Penguins might move to Atlanta.

The Pens kept plugging away and gained their first playoff berth in April, 1970, under the coaching of Red Kelly (who would add general managers duties the following year). Pittsburgh moved into the semifinals before being eliminated by St. Louis. Delighted with the play of rookie forward Michel Briere, the Penguins looked forward to next year, but tragedy struck shortly after the 1969–70 season. Briere was seriously injured in an automobile accident in Northern Quebec and never recovered. After a long convalescence, the young player died during the 1971 playoffs. Without Briere, the Penguins had been unable to gain a playoff berth in 1971.

That year did see the team sold again, this time to a Pittsburgh-based group led by Thayer R. "Tad" Potter, who installed himself as general partner and CEO. Other changes included Kelly stepping down as general manager and Jack Riley replacing him, and the acquisition of the flamboyant Eddie Shack in exchange for future Buffalo Sabres star Rene Robert. All these moves didn't help the on-ice product, though, as Pittsburgh was swept in the first round of the playoffs by Chicago. The Penguins continued their hot and cold ways for the next three seasons. Despite setting a still-enduring NHL record for the fastest five goals scored by one team (two minutes, seven seconds) and Greg Polis winning the 1972–73 All-Star Game MVP award, they missed the playoffs that season and the next.

But, there was a turnaround in the 1974–75 campaign. Behind Jean Pronovost, Syl Apps (that year's All-Star MVP) and rookie Pierre Larouche, Pittsburgh climbed to a 37–28–15 record, third-best in the new Norris Division. After sweeping the Blues in the preliminary round, the Penguins went into the quarterfinals against the New York Islanders and quickly established a three-games-to-none lead going into game four.

It was then that Pittsburgh suffered one of the most ignominious setbacks in playoff history. They lost four games in a row, including a 1–0 defeat in game seven that left Penguins fans in a state of shock. The following seasons didn't help ease the pain, as the Penguins suffered consecutive preliminary-round losses to Toronto in the 1976 and 1977 playoffs and were a no-show in 1978. Although the 1978–79 Penguins finished second in their division, they too didn't fare well, surrendering to the Boston Bruins in straight games in the quarterfinals.

The Penguins unveiled a new uniform in 1979, doffing the old blue-and-white and adopting the black-and-gold color scheme of the baseball Pirates and football Steelers. This didn't sit well with Boston, which had been wearing almost identical hues. The Bruins protested, but to no avail as the Penguins cited a precedent set by the Pittsburgh Hockey Club of the 1920s, similar wearers of black and gold uniforms. First-round playoff losses in 1980, 1981 and 1982 followed in what would prove to be the franchise's only playoff appearances until 1989.

Because of a last-place finish in 1983–84, the Penguins were able to select Mario Lemieux first in the 1984 Entry draft. Considered the finest young player to arrive in the NHL since Wayne Gretzky, Lemieux arrived at training camp in 1984 and immediately dazzled onlookers with his comprehensive talent. Lemieux won the Calder Trophy as rookie of the year in 1984–85, and followed that with nomination to the Second All-Star Team in 1986 and 1987. A season later, he won the Hart Trophy as most valuable player as well as the Art Ross Trophy as leading scorer. Despite these accomplishments, the Penguins missed the playoffs every season through 1987–88. During this time, former goaltenders Ed Johnston and Tony Esposito called the shots as g.m. Bob Berry and Pierre Creamer worked behind the bench.

Finally, in 1988–89, Gene Ubriaco coached Pittsburgh to second in the Patrick Division and a berth in the playoffs. Despite this measure of success. Ubriaco and Lemieux never saw eye-to-eye.

When Craig Patrick was named general manager on December 5, 1989, a new era in Pittsburgh hockey leadership was launched. One of Patrick's most crucial moves was made at the 1990 Entry Draft, where Pittsburgh held the fifth selection overall. While Owen Nolan, Petr Nedved, Keith Primeau and Mike Ricci were picked in that order, the Penguins g.m. opted for a tall, gangly Czech named Jaromir Jagr, who would emerge as the second coming of Lemieux.

On June 12, 1990, Patrick hired collegiate legend "Badger" Bob Johnson as head coach. With Johnson at the helm, the Penguins would win their first division title in 1990–91. Patrick's most significant move was a multiplayer trade he completed on March 4, 1991. To the Hartford Whalers went John Cullen, Zarley Zalapski and Jeff Parker; coming to the Igloo were Ulf Samuelsson, Grant Jennings and the symbol of Hartford hockey, Ron Francis. All three players became key components as the Penguins proceeded to defeat Minnesota in six games to win the Stanley Cup. Lemieux won the Conn Smythe Trophy as the playoffs' most valuable player and had surpassed Gretzky as the NHL's dominant performer.

A significant ownership change took place in 1991 when the DeBartolo family sold the franchise to a partnership that included Howard Baldwin, Morris Belzberg and Thomas Ruta. Baldwin, who had been president of the World Hockey Association and head of the Hartford Whalers, became the hands-on leader of the hockey club as it was entering its golden era. However, tragedy marred the 1991–92 season for the Penguins. On August 29, 1991, Bob Johnson was diagnosed with brain tumors and was replaced behind the bench on October 1 by Scott Bowman, who had been the club's director of player development and Johnson's consigliere during the first Cup triumph. Johnson died at the age of 60 on November 26, 1991 in Colorado Springs.

Despite the loss, Lemieux's dominance continued through 1991–92. He swept the Hart and Art Ross trophies with a combination of stickhandling and shooting artistry. He also was the NHL's plus-minus leader. Not surprisingly, Pittsburgh gained its second consecutive Stanley Cup championship with a four-game sweep of Chicago. The Penguins closed the playoffs with 11 straight victories, tying an NHL record set by the Blackhawks earlier in the postseason.

With Bowman retained to guide the team once again, Pittsburgh expected a third straight Stanley Cup title in 1993. The Penguins underlined the point by finishing first in the Patrick Division and winning the Presidents' Trophy for most points in the league. But, tragedy struck again. Mario Lemieux, who had previously battled debilitating back injuries, was diagnosed with Hodgkin's disease, a form of cancer. Radiation treatments lasted from February 1 to March 2. Amazingly, Lemieux returned to the lineup immediately and won another scoring title.

The Penguins began the playoffs with a five-game opening-round victory over the New Jersey Devils. However, the dynasty was derailed when the New York Islanders scored one of the league's most extraordinary upsets. Game seven proved to be a classic on every level. Rallying to tie the game 3–3 in the final minutes of the third period, the Penguins appeared ready to win the game in overtime until David Volek stunned the capacity crowd by beating Tom Barrasso after 5:16 of extra time.

Although the Penguins finished first again in 1993–94, they were without Lemieux for all but 22 games because of illness. They were eliminated by Washington in the first round and began retooling for the future. This was made even more imperative after Lemieux announced in August, 1994, that he would take a one-year leave of absence from the game. Jagr inherited the leadership role and won the Art Ross Trophy in the lockout-shortened 1994–95 season.

Lemieux startled the hockey world with his return from medical leave in October, 1995. He scored his 500th career goal on October 28, 1995, and finished the season with an Art Ross Trophy-winning 69 goals and 92 assists for 161 points in just 70 games. Jagr was runner-up with 149 points.

Uncertainty characterized the Penguins' play during 1996–97, culminating with the firing of coach Ed Johnston on March 3, 1997. He was replaced on an interim basis by g.m. Patrick. Lemieux retired at the conclusion of the 1996–97 season after Pittsburgh was eliminated in a five-game opening-round series with Philadelphia.

In May, 1997, Roger Marino joined Howard Baldwin as co-owner and co-managing director of the franchise. During the offseason, Craig Patrick named the defense-oriented Kevin Constantine as head coach. Although Constantine occasionally clashed with Jagr over his disciplinary tactics and heavy defensive orientation, the Penguins surprised the critics with a strong performance, finishing first in the Northeast Division with 98 points. Jagr won the Art Ross Trophy while Tom Barrasso turned in a strong comeback effort in goal. The year would end in disappointment, however, as the Montreal Canadiens eliminated the Penguins in six games in the opening round of the 1998 playoffs.

On October 13, 1998, Marino and Baldwin declared bankruptcy, claiming $100 million in debt. Facing the loss of millions of dollars in deferred monies owed to him, Lemieux organized a group of investors. In March, 1999, they filed a plan of reorganization that was acknowledged by the U.S. Bankruptcy court on June 24, leading to several more months of negotiations with partners and creditors.

The Penguins played most of the 1998–99 season in uncertainty. In the competitive Eastern Conference, Pittsburgh's 90 points were good only for the eighth and final playoff position, but the fact the Penguins could compete at all was due mainly to Jaromir Jagr. His 44 goals and 83 assists gave him a league-leading 127 points. Not only did Jagr win the Art Ross Trophy for the second straight season, he also was rewarded with the Hart Trophy as MVP. In the playoffs, he returned from a serious groin injury to engineer a seven-game upset of the conference-leading New Jersey Devils. However, when the Penguins lost their second-round series to Toronto on May 17, 1999, there was the chance that they might have played their last game in Pittsburgh.

On September 3, 1999, Judge Bernard Markovitz approved Lemieux's purchase of the Penguins. Two days earlier, the NHL Board of Governors had voted in favor of Lemieux's bid. A month later, the Penguins opened the 1999–2000 season. Despite Jagr's continued brilliance, the team struggled and in December Craig Patrick replaced Kevin Constantine with Herb Brooks. The former coach of the 1980 "Miracle on Ice" U.S. Olympic team had been a Penguins scout since 1995. Ivan Hlinka, former Czechoslovakian national team star and coach of the 1998 Czech Republic Olympic gold medal team, was brought in as an associate coach. (He would be named the club's head coach after the season.) However, injuries to Jagr almost saw the team fall out of playoff contention.

Though he was only able to play 63 games, Jagr still led the NHL in scoring for the third straight season (96 points) and returned to the lineup in time to help Pittsburgh nail down a playoff spot in the Eastern Conference. Once in the playoffs, Jagr turned in a dominating effort as the seventh-seeded Penguins knocked off the Southeast Division champion Washington Capitals in the first round. Ron Tugnutt, acquired in a deal with Ottawa for Tom Barrasso at the trade deadline, also sparkled. Pittsburgh jumped out to a 2–0 lead in games in a second-round matchup with Philadelphia, but with injuries again hampering Jagr, the Flyers rebounded for four straight wins. The back-breaker for the Penguins was a 2–1 loss in game four that required five overtime periods, the third-longest game in NHL history.

Pittsburgh Penguins Year-by-Year Record

Season	GP	W	L	T	GF	GA	Pts	Finish	Division	Playoff Results
1967–68	74	27	34	13	195	216	67	5th	West	Out of Playoffs
1968–69	76	20	45	11	189	252	51	5th	West	Out of Playoffs
1969–70	76	26	38	12	182	238	64	2nd	West	Lost Semifinal
1970–71	78	21	37	20	221	240	62	6th	West	Out of Playoffs
1971–72	78	26	38	14	220	258	66	4th	West	Lost Quarterfinal
1972–73	78	32	37	9	257	265	73	5th	West	Out of Playoffs
1973–74	78	28	41	9	242	273	65	5th	West	Out of Playoffs
1974–75	80	37	28	15	326	289	89	3rd	Norris	Lost Quarterfinal
1975–76	80	35	33	12	339	303	82	3rd	Norris	Lost Prelim. Round
1976–77	80	34	33	13	240	252	81	3rd	Norris	Lost Prelim. Round
1977–78	80	25	37	18	254	321	68	4th	Norris	Out of Playoffs
1978–79	80	36	31	13	281	279	85	2nd	Norris	Lost Quarterfinal
1979–80	80	30	37	13	251	303	73	3rd	Norris	Lost Prelim. Round
1980–81	80	30	37	13	302	345	73	3rd	Norris	Lost Prelim. Round
1981–82	80	31	36	13	310	337	75	4th	Patrick	Lost Div. Semifinal
1982–83	80	18	53	9	257	394	45	6th	Patrick	Out of Playoffs
1983–84	80	16	58	6	254	390	38	6th	Patrick	Out of Playoffs
1984–85	80	24	51	5	276	385	53	6th	Patrick	Out of Playoffs
1985–86	80	34	38	8	313	305	76	5th	Patrick	Out of Playoffs
1986–87	80	30	38	12	297	290	72	5th	Patrick	Out of Playoffs
1987–88	80	36	35	9	319	316	81	6th	Patrick	Out of Playoffs
1988–89	80	40	33	7	347	349	87	2nd	Patrick	Lost Div. Final
1989–90	80	32	40	8	318	359	72	5th	Patrick	Out of Playoffs
1990–91	80	41	33	6	342	305	88	1st	Patrick	Won Stanley Cup
1991–92	80	39	32	9	343	308	87	3rd	Patrick	Won Stanley Cup
1992–93	84	56	21	7	367	268	119	1st	Patrick	Lost Div. Final
1993–94	84	44	27	13	299	285	101	1st	Northeast	Lost Conf. Quarterfinal
1994–95	48	29	16	3	181	158	61	2nd	Northeast	Lost Conf. Semifinal
1995–96	82	49	29	4	362	284	102	1st	Northeast	Lost Conf. Final
1996–97	82	38	36	8	285	280	84	2nd	Northeast	Lost Conf. Quarterfinal
1997–98	82	40	24	18	228	188	98	1st	Northeast	Lost Conf. Quarterfinal
1998–98	82	38	30	14	242	225	90	3rd	Atlantic	Lost Conf. Semifinal
1999-2000	82	37	37	8	241	236	*88	3rd	Atlantic	Lost Conf. Semifinal

§ *Includes 6 points for regulation ties (RT)*

PITTSBURGH PIRATES

THE NHL'S THIRD FRANCHISE in the United States was granted on November 7, 1925, when Pittsburgh formally joined the Boston Bruins and New York Americans in the seven-team circuit. Though there were published reports saying Americans owner William Dwyer would have a hand in Pittsburgh ownership, the team belonged to Henry Townsend, who, with an investment from attorney James F. Callahan, had purchased the Pittsburgh Yellow Jackets—United States Amateur Hockey Association champions in 1924 and 1925.

Lionel Conacher, Canada's greatest all-around athlete, had been the leader of the Yellow Jackets since his formal arrival in Pittsburgh in the fall of 1923. (He had actually come to play football, which he did briefly at Duquesne University in 1924.) Conacher helped recruit friends like goalie Roy Worters, Harry Darragh, and Harold "Baldy" Cotton from top amateur clubs in Toronto and Ottawa to join him in Pittsburgh. They all accepted the offer to turn pro when the NHL arrived in town, as did Yellow Jackets teammates Hib Milks, Duke McCurry, Tex White and Herb Drury. As professionals, they would be known as the Pittsburgh Pirates—the same as the city's baseball team.

Odie Cleghorn left Montreal to operate the Pirates (and would occasionally see ice time as well—including a game in goal when Worters had pneumonia). Because his team did not have the star talent others did, Cleghorn employed three set forward lines at a time when most teams simply used their best players for as long as possible. He also became the first NHL coach to change his players on the fly. Little had been expected from Cleghorn's roster of amateurs, but his innovative coaching tactics—and Worters' great goaltending—saw the Pirates finish in third place with a record of 19–16–1 and beat out the Bruins by one point for the final playoff spot. The Montreal Maroons then defeated the Pirates 6–4 in a two-game, total-goals series, and went on to win the Stanley Cup.

The 1926–27 season saw the NHL add the New York Rangers, Chicago Black Hawks, and Detroit Cougars (later the Falcons, then the Red Wings), who joined Pittsburgh and Boston in the newly created American Division. The league also was bolstered by an influx of talent after the Western Hockey League ceased operations. Most of the western players stocked the rosters of the NHL's newest teams, though future stars like Eddie Shore (Bruins) and George Hainsworth (Montreal Canadiens) found their way onto existing clubs. The Pirates' only acquisition was Ty Arbour from the Vancouver Maroons.

Pittsburgh headed into its second season with virtually the same roster as the year before, but Lionel Conacher was soon traded to the New York Americans. "The Big Train" was sorely missed, as the Pirates' defensive record ballooned to second-worst in the NHL. Pittsburgh finished the year fourth in the American Division and missed the playoffs. A few minor roster adjustments and Roy Worters' return to form saw the Pirates reach the playoffs again in 1927–28. As in 1926, Pittsburgh was beaten in the first round by the team that would go on to win the Stanley Cup—this time the New York Rangers.

Even with their success on the ice, the Pirates were not receiving much fan support in Pittsburgh. Despite new ownership by ex-boxer and fight-promoter Benny Leonard (Townsend had died in January, 1927, though the team remained in his family through the 1927–28 season), the Pirates, like the Ottawa Senators, began peddling talent to help their finances—most notably Roy Worters, who joined the New York Americans. The Pirates plummeted to 9–27–8 in 1928–29 and were only spared last place in the NHL by the dreadful Chicago Black Hawks.

Odie Cleghorn resigned after the 1928–29 campaign and became an NHL referee. Frank Fredrickson took over as playing coach in Pittsburgh (though a serious knee injury would limit his playing to just nine games), but he could do nothing to change the team's fortunes. The Pirates suffered through a 5–36–3 season, and the combination of a last-place team plus the stock market crash, which had seriously depressed the steel industry, doomed professional hockey in Pittsburgh. The Pirates were transferred to Philadelphia in 1930, but the results were even worse. After a 4–36–4 season, the Pittsburgh–Philadelphia franchise was given permission to suspend operations at the NHL Board of Governors meeting on September 26, 1931. Not until the NHL meetings on May 7, 1936, was the franchise formally canceled. It would be more than 30 years before the NHL returned to the state of Pennsylvania.

Pittsburgh Pirates Year-by-Year Record

Season	GP	W	L	T	GF	GA	Pts	Finish	Division	Playoff Results
1925–26	36	19	16	1	82	70	39	3rd		Lost NHL Semifinal
1926–27	44	15	26	3	79	108	33	4th	American	Out of Playoffs
1927–28	44	19	17	8	67	76	46	3rd	American	Lost Quarterfinal
1928–29	44	9	27	8	46	80	26	4th	American	Out of Playoffs
1929–30	44	5	36	3	102	185	13	5th	American	Out of Playoffs

QUEBEC BULLDOGS

THE HISTORY OF HOCKEY IN QUEBEC CITY dates back to at least the first Montreal Winter Carnival in 1883. The roots of the Quebec Bulldogs can be traced to 1886 and the formation of the Amateur Hockey Association of Canada (the first national hockey league). Quebec continued to be represented in a variety of top Canadian leagues until 1909–10, when the Bulldogs were left out during the formation of the National Hockey Association. A realignment of the NHA in 1910–11 brought Quebec back into the fold. By 1912, the Bulldogs were Stanley Cup champions. Quebec retained the Stanley Cup in 1913, but the Bulldogs' championship reign came to an end in 1914.

Quebec's roster from the Stanley Cup years boasted future Hall of Famers Joe Malone, Paddy Moran, Joe Hall, Tommy Smith and Russell Crawford. All were of English, Irish, or Scottish descent, as was the entire team. In fact, though it represented the capital city of the province of Quebec, there are no more than a handful of French Canadians who ever played for the team. Even the Bulldogs nickname (which dates to at least 1909) was chosen to evoke the ideals of courage and determination represented by 19th century Britain.

Joe Malone was the greatest star in the history of the Quebec franchise. He joined the club as a 19-year-old in 1908–09, and his goal-scoring feats became legendary during seven seasons in the NHA. His greatest year came in the first season of the NHL, when he scored 44 goals in 20 games for the Montreal Canadiens. The Bulldogs had been charter members when the NHL was formed in November, 1917, but the financially troubled franchise did not operate a team that year and its players were dispersed throughout the NHL. They did reassemble for an exhibition game against the Canadiens in February.

Quebec finally did ice a team during the NHL's third season, 1919–20, and although many of the Bulldogs' star players returned, only Malone proved still capable. He led the NHL with 39 goals (including a record seven in one game on January 31, 1920) and 49 points, but Quebec was a dismal 4–20–0. Prior to the 1920–21 season, the Bulldogs became the Hamilton Tigers. After five seasons in the Ontario city, the team moved again and became the New York Americans. Quebec City did not return to the NHL until 1979 when the Nordiques were absorbed from the World Hockey Association. That team, too, wound up in the United States when it became the Colorado Avalanche in 1995.

Quebec Bulldogs Year-by-Year Record

Season	GP	W	L	T	GF	GA	Pts	Finish	Playoff Results
1919–20	24	4	20	0	91	177	8	4th	Out of Playoffs

ST. LOUIS BLUES

SINCE ENTERING THE NHL, the St. Louis Blues have employed some of the greatest players in history. Such old-time hockey heroes as Dickie Moore, Doug Harvey, Glenn Hall and Jacques Plante helped give the team its start. Later, stars such as Wayne Gretzky, Dale Hawerchuk and Peter Stastny also would spend time in St. Louis. Legendary architects Lynn Patrick and Emile Francis once ran the Blues, and championship team builders Cliff Fletcher and Jimmy Devellano had stints on the St. Louis hockey staff. Coaches include Stanley Cup champions Scotty Bowman, Al Arbour and Jacques Demers.

The Blues enjoyed some team success, too, reaching the Cup finals in the first three seasons out of the expansion bracket. From 1979 through 1999–2000, the club reached the playoffs 21 times in a row…yet the team still seeks its first Stanley Cup title after 33 seasons. The franchise has also been scarred by tragedies. Young defenseman Bobby Gassoff was killed in a motorcycle crash after attending a team function. Broadcaster Dan Kelly lost his battle with cancer while still in his prime. Barclay Plager succumbed to brain tumors while serving as an assistant coach.

Hockey began auspiciously in St. Louis in 1967–68. The Blues were the best of the NHL's six expansion teams, playing a disciplined defensive game that allowed them to outperform the other fledgling franchises. Midway through their inaugural campaign, Scotty Bowman convinced future Hall of Fame forward Dickie Moore to make a comeback. Moore, who hadn't laced up the blades since retiring at the end of the 1964–65 season, quickly established himself as the team leader.

With Moore and, later, Doug Harvey providing the emotional lift, the Blues survived two gruelling seven-game marathons against Los Angeles and Minnesota before reaching the Stanley Cup finals. Waiting there to welcome them were the well-rested Montreal Canadiens, still steaming from their loss to the underdog Toronto Maple Leafs 12 months earlier. The Blues fought hard, losing in four one-goal games, but it was clear the gap in talent was too wide for the Blues to overcome.

Still, the franchise flourished for the game's ultimate players' owner, Sidney J. Salomon Jr. His family had bought the team for $2 million and the St. Louis Arena from Chicago Black Hawks owners Arthur and Bill Wirtz for $4 million. The Original Six teams were run by strict and penurious men, but Salomon provided cars for his players and treated them to Florida vacations. The Blues acquired a bunch of all-stars in the twilight of their careers and they loved St. Louis. "It was unique compared to what was going on in the league," Glenn Hall said. "You were just like cattle, bought and sold and auctioned off. The only way we could return the favor to the Salomons was to go out and give a good effort every night."

Hall and Plante were stellar in goal and the Plager brothers, Barclay and Bob, led a gritty defense that also featured Al Arbour and Harvey. Red Berenson, Ab McDonald and Gary Sabourin led the offense. Berenson's six-goal game in Philadelphia during the 1968–69 season remains one of the great milestones for the franchise.

Bowman added the general manager's portfolio to his resume in 1968 and he continued to mold his oldtimers into a lovable team that filled the old St. Louis Arena. Alas, the good times would not last. The Blues continued to be the best of the bunch in the West Division, reaching the Stanley Cup finals again in both 1969 and 1970. Once there, however, they were unable to win a game against their Original Six opponents, dropping four-game decisions to Montreal and Boston. Then, in 1971, Sidney Salomon III took a larger role in running his father's franchise and the result was constant upheaval from 1971, when Bowman left, until 1977.

The coaches came and went, with Arbour, Sid Abel, Bill McCreary, Jean-Guy Talbot, Lou Angotti, Garry Young, Leo Boivin and Emile Francis spending time behind the bench. General managers also came and went, with Abel, Charles Catto, Gerry Ehman and Dennis Ball holding the job from 1972 to 1976. Only Garry Unger's flashy scoring kept fans interested until the Salomons' final day. The challenge of the World Hockey Association, escalating costs and declining revenues pushed the franchise to the brink of financial ruin. Out of the gloom came Emile "The Cat" Francis, who took over as general manager, caretaker, security guard and saviour. If "The Cat" was going to save the Blues, he would need all of his nine lives to do it.

After a financially devastating 1976–77 season that saw the Blues pare down their staff to three employees, Francis was able to convince Ralston Purina chairman R. Hal Dean to invest in the team. On July 27, 1977, Francis announced the St. Louis Blues had been reborn. On paper, at least. In 1978–79, the Blues slipped off the bottom rung of the NHL ladder, winning just 18 games under coach Barclay Plager. Yet, once again, Francis was able to rebuild the crumbling foundation. Ralston Purina repainted the old bandbox known as the Arena and rechristened it the Checkerdome. In the 1976 Amateur Draft, Francis had selected Bernie Federko, Brian Sutter and Mike Liut, who would go on to become the cornerstones of the team in the 1980s. Such runners-and-gunners as Wayne Babych (picked third overall in 1978) and Perry Turnbull (taken second in 1979) were added to the nucleus and by 1980–81, the Blues had a 107-point juggernaut for Red Berenson, who had taken over as coach during the previous season.

"It was a very exciting time for me," Francis says. "There we were, on the brink of extinction, then to come all the way back the way we did and get the support we needed ... that was like a dream come true." Almost as quickly, it all came tumbling down. The Blues finished eight games under .500 in 1981–82 and slid to 65 points the following season, the fourth-lowest total in club history. Berenson got canned, Dean retired and Ralston Purina soon lost interest in hockey. Citing losses of $1.8 million per year, the company put the team up for sale. When the league blocked the sale of the Blues to Saskatoon interests in 1983, the company padlocked the Checkerdome and left the franchise on the NHL's doorstep. The Blues, with their ownership unresolved, did not participate in the 1983 NHL Entry Draft.

Enter entrepreneur Harry Ornest, who bought the franchise off the scrap heap. He, new general manager Ron Caron and coach Jacques Demers quickly made the Blues profitable and competitive. Federko, Sutter and Doug Gilmour, a gritty two-way center whose desire and determination more than made up for his lack of size, led the charge back up the NHL ladder. Caron traded furiously, shuffling stars (like Liut and Mullen) and draft picks for lots of affordable, competent veterans whose work ethic helped transform the team into the type of blue-collar hockey club that the city had rallied behind so vigorously in the early years.

This regime peaked in the 1986 playoffs with the "Monday Night Miracle" game. After being stretched to the limit to eliminate Minnesota and Toronto, the Blues had their backs against the wall once again in their semifinal series against the Calgary Flames. Needing a home-ice victory to force a seventh game, the Blues trailed 5–2 with less than 12 minutes remaining in the game and their season. The unlikely hero on this madcap Monday night was Greg Paslawski, a hard-plugging foot soldier. "Paws" notched a pair of late third-period goals to even the affair after Brian Sutter had lit the comeback torch at 8:08.

Twenty minutes later, Doug Wickenheiser—who had received his fair share of hard knocks when the Montreal Canadiens selected him ahead of hometown hero Denis Savard in the 1980 Entry Draft—slipped a rebound past Mike Vernon to give the Blues a comeback win for the ages. Paslawski notched 10 playoff goals in the greatest spring of his career, more than he would score in the rest of his postseason career combined. The 6–5 victory forced a decisive seventh game of the Western Conference finals, but the Flames extinguished the Blues' Stanley Cup aspirations with a 2–1 win back in the Saddledome. Doug Gilmour and Bernie Federko tied for the playoff lead in points, becoming the first players to lead the postseason scoring parade without making it to the finals.

Demers left for Detroit after that season and Ornest, like the other owners before him, also decided to move on. He sold the team to a local ownership group led by Michael Shanahan during the 1986–87 season. However, with Ron Caron still aboard, the club remained in capable hands. Within two years, Caron had landed Brett Hull, Adam Oates and Curtis Joseph. Later, through astute trades and eye-opening free agent acquisitions, Caron brought such high-profile names as Scott Stevens, Brendan Shanahan, Phil Housley and Al MacInnis into the St. Louis fold. Still, the manager's coup remained the steal of Brett Hull from the Calgary Flames.

Deemed uncoachable, lazy and uninterested in improving his game, Hull was an enigma to many of the scouts and coaches who took him under their wing. In St. Louis, however, the offensive system was molded around Hull, his deadly accurate shot and his uncanny ability to find open ice, and once there, deliver the goods. With Adam Oates supplying picture-perfect passes, Hull became the NHL's top sniper. Hull reached the 70-goal plateau in three consecutive seasons, including his Hart Trophy-winning campaign of 1990–91, when he slipped 86 pucks past enemy goaltenders—the most by any player in NHL history not named Gretzky. Hull's exploits helped to broaden local interest in the team. The Blues filled the arena, made the playoffs every year and began multiplying both their revenue and payroll in a giddy bid for greatness.

In 1990–91, the Blues had a breakout 105-point season behind Hull but the club couldn't get past the second round of the playoffs. Though this front office never got to the final four with coaches Jacques Martin, Brian Sutter, Bob Plager and Bob Berry, it did turn the Blues into a mainstream sports success. The team's success inspired the top St. Louis corporations to come together, buy the team from Shanahan and build the new Kiel Center, which opened in downtown St. Louis in 1994.

Shanahan's last stab at glory was to hire Mike Keenan as general manager and coach. Keenan brought a lot of baggage with him, but he also carried a reputation as a winner. He tested the patience of the Blues fans early, unloading Petr

Nedved, Craig Janney and Brendan Shanahan within a year of stepping into the front office. Many of the dedicated St. Louis fans never forgave Keenan for casting off Shanahan. The quick-witted power forward was a local favorite and one of the most outgoing of all the pro athletes in the city, who generously gave his time and effort to charities and special events. There was another tempest brewing, as well.

Relations between Keenan and Brett Hull were acrimonious at best, and when Iron Mike stripped Hull of his captaincy, the battle of wills was on. In an effort to stem the tide of unrest, Keenan made a bold move, acquiring potential free agent Wayne Gretzky for the final playoff push in the 1995–96 season. Any hopes for a lengthy playoff run were dashed early when Grant Fuhr suffered a season-ending knee injury in the first game of the postseason against the Toronto Maple Leafs. Although backup Jon Casey performed admirably, the Blues lacked the consistent offensive attack required to reach the highest level. Gretzky came close to resurrecting the club's Stanley Cup hopes with 16 points in 13 games, but in the end, the Blues' lack of firepower caught up to them. The Blues did manage to stretch Detroit to double overtime in the seventh game in the Western Conference semifinal, but a Steve Yzerman goal gave the Wings a 1–0 victory and ended Keenan's quest for the Cup.

After the season, Gretzky joined the New York Rangers via free agency. The war of words between Keenan and Hull escalated and the product on the ice suffered. Finally, on December 19, 1996, the Keenan era ended, with both him and Jack Quinn being ushered out of town. Ron Caron came out of quasi-retirement to serve as interim general manager, helping new team president Mark Sauer hire coach Joel Quenneville and general manager Larry Pleau. Together, they tried to get the franchise back to the basics of drafting talent, grooming players and building up for another run at the Stanley Cup.

The Blues made another remarkable recovery in 1997–98. Even Brett Hull bought into Quenneville's defense-first philosophy, proving himself a better-than-adequate penalty killer and checker. Still, the Blues had enough all-around firepower to lead the NHL with 256 goals and finished with 98 points for the league's fourth-best record. The Blues overwhelmed the Los Angeles Kings with a four-game sweep to open the playoffs and were given an excellent chance of knocking off defending champion Detroit in round two. It was not to be, however, as the Red Wings eliminated St. Louis for the third year in a row en route to their second straight Stanley Cup title.

The Brett Hull era came to a close in St. Louis, after a decade of highlight reel goals and mile-wide smiles, when Hull signed as a free agent with Dallas. The Blues did re-sign veteran rearguard Al MacInnis, ensuring that the league's most powerful shooter will finish his career in St. Louis. MacInnis won the Norris Trophy as the NHL's best defenseman for the first time in his career in 1998–99. The emergence of Chris Pronger as a potential superstar continued. Pavol Demitra developed into a top-flight scorer with 37 goals and helped St. Louis overcome the loss of Hull. In the playoffs, the Blues rebounded from a 3–1 deficit in games to eliminate Phoenix, then engaged in a thrilling six-game series with Dallas that featured four overtime matches before the Blues were beaten by the eventual Stanley Cup champions for the third straight season.

In September, 1999, the consortium of 19 St. Louis companies which owned the Blues and the Kiel Center announced that the team and the rink had been sold to Bill and Nancy Laurie. (Nancy is the daughter of Wal-Mart co-founder James "Bud" Walton.) New on the ice that season was Roman Turek, who had been acquired from Dallas within days of the Stars' 1999 Stanley Cup title. He proved to be a dominant netminder in 1999–2000. Turek led the league with seven shutouts, while his 1.95 goals-against average was just edged out by Brian Boucher of the Philadelphia Flyers. He also posted a club-record 42 victories in leading St. Louis to a franchise high 51 wins and 114 points and the first Presidents' Trophy title in club history. With a defense led by Pronger and MacInnis, the Blues also won the Jennings Trophy by allowing the fewest goals in the NHL. In fact, with just 165 goals against, the Blues allowed the fewest goals in any full season since 1973–74 when both Philadelphia and Chicago surrendered 164 goals in 78 games. Offensively, the club was once again led by Pavol Demitra, who collected 28 goals and 75 points (though an injury late in the season would keep him out of the playoffs). Pierre Turgeon had 26 goals and 40 assists in just 52 games. Even with the club's defensive brilliance, only the Red Wings and the New Jersey Devils scored more goals than St. Louis, which netted 248.

Hopes were high for the club's first Stanley Cup championship entering the playoffs. But after taking game one from the San Jose Sharks, St. Louis suddenly lost three in a row and was down three games to one. Things looked good for yet another comeback, especially after the Blues trounced the Sharks 6–2 in San Jose in game six, but a 3–1 loss in game seven made St. Louis the first first-place club to be bounced in the opening round of the playoffs since the 1991 Chicago Blackhawks. At least there was some consolation at the 2000 NHL Awards, where Chris Pronger won the Hart Trophy as the league's most valuable player, Pavol Demitra earned the Lady Byng Trophy for gentlemanly play and Joel Quenneville won the Jack Adams Award as coach of the year.

St. Louis Blues Year-by-Year Record

Season	GP	W	L	T	GF	GA	Pts	Finish	Division	Playoff Results
1967–68	74	27	31	16	177	191	70	3rd	West	Lost Final
1968–69	76	37	25	14	204	157	88	1st	West	Lost Final
1969–70	76	37	27	12	224	179	86	1st	West	Lost Final
1970–71	78	34	25	19	223	208	87	2nd	West	Lost Quarterfinal
1971–72	78	28	39	11	208	247	67	3rd	West	Lost Semifinal
1972–73	78	32	34	12	233	251	76	4th	West	Lost Quarterfinal
1973–74	78	26	40	12	206	248	64	6th	West	Out of Playoffs
1974–75	80	35	31	14	269	267	84	2nd	Smythe	Lost Prelim. Round
1975–76	80	29	37	14	249	290	72	3rd	Smythe	Lost Prelim. Round
1976–77	80	32	39	9	239	276	73	1st	Smythe	Lost Quarterfinal
1977–78	80	20	47	13	195	304	53	4th	Smythe	Out of Playoffs
1978–79	80	18	50	12	249	348	48	3rd	Smythe	Out of Playoffs
1979–80	80	34	34	12	266	278	80	2nd	Smythe	Lost Prelim. Round
1980–81	80	45	18	17	352	281	107	1st	Smythe	Lost Quarterfinal
1981–82	80	32	40	8	315	349	72	3rd	Norris	Lost Div. Final
1982–83	80	25	40	15	285	316	65	4th	Norris	Lost Div. Semifinal
1983–84	80	32	41	7	293	316	71	2nd	Norris	Lost Div. Final
1984–85	80	37	31	12	299	288	86	1st	Norris	Lost Div. Semifinal
1985–86	80	37	34	9	302	291	83	3rd	Norris	Lost Conf. Final
1986–87	80	32	33	15	281	293	79	1st	Norris	Lost Div. Semifinal
1987–88	80	34	38	8	278	294	76	2nd	Norris	Lost Div. Final
1988–89	80	33	35	12	275	285	78	2nd	Norris	Lost Div. Final
1989–90	80	37	34	9	295	279	83	2nd	Norris	Lost Div. Final
1990–91	80	47	22	11	310	250	105	2nd	Norris	Lost Div. Final
1991–92	80	36	33	11	279	266	83	3rd	Norris	Lost Div. Semifinal
1992–93	84	37	36	11	282	278	85	4th	Norris	Lost Div. Final
1993–94	84	40	33	11	270	283	91	4th	Central	Lost Conf. Quarterfinal
1994–95	48	28	15	5	178	135	61	2nd	Central	Lost Conf. Quarterfinal
1995–96	82	32	34	16	219	248	80	4th	Central	Lost Conf. Semifinal
1996–97	82	36	35	11	236	239	83	4th	Central	Lost Conf. Quarterfinal
1997–98	82	45	29	8	256	204	98	3rd	Central	Lost Conf. Semifinal
1998–99	82	37	32	13	237	209	87	2nd	Central	Lost Conf. Semifinal
1999-2000	82	51	20	11	248	165	*114	1st	Central	Lost Conf. Quarterfinal

** Includes 1 point for a regulation tie (RT)*

St. Louis Eagles

Despite four Stanley Cup titles during the 1920s, the Ottawa Senators fell victim to the Great Depression. Senators owner Tommy Ahearne absorbed losses for years, but at the NHL Board of Governors meeting on September 22, 1934, the directors of the Ottawa club sought permission to move their team to St. Louis. Permission was granted, even though a franchise application from the city had been rejected at an NHL meeting two years earlier because of excessive travel expenses. Redmond Quinn would continue to guide operations from Ottawa, while Clare Brunton ran the team in Missouri. The Ottawa Senators were now the St. Louis Eagles, but the city was already home to an American Hockey Association team called the Flyers. Owners of this club contended that there was an agreement between the AHA and the NHL that prevented the latter from placing a team west of the Mississippi. However, a threatened $200,000 damage suit was never filed.

The Eagles began the 1934–35 season with much the same roster the Senators had employed in 1933–34, but an NHL team that had gone 13–29–6 the previous season did not excite fans in St. Louis any more than it had in Ottawa. Attendance began at 12,600 on opening night (November 8, 1934) but crowds quickly decreased. By early December, financial concerns saw the Eagles begin to trade away players, and when the team tumbled to 2–11–0 on December 9, coach Eddie Gerard was fired in favor of George Boucher. By February, Brunton and Quinn were denying rumors that home games would be switched back to Ottawa. However, star player Syd Howe was promptly sold to the Detroit Red Wings. Frank Finnigan was bought by the Toronto Maple Leafs. Season's end found the Eagles last overall in the NHL.

The annual NHL meeting on May 11, 1935, left the status of the Ottawa-St. Louis franchise unsettled, but at a league meeting on September 28, Redmond Quinn asked if the team could suspend operations for a year as it had done in Ottawa in 1931–32. On October 15 the NHL governors decided to terminate the team instead, buying out the franchise and distributing the players through the league via draft. The prize pick wound up going to the Boston Bruins, who selected sixth. Bill Cowley had attracted little attention as a rookie in St. Louis, but would go on to become one of the league's top stars. The NHL finally returned to St. Louis in 1967. It was not back in Ottawa until 1992.

St. Louis Eagles Year-by-Year Record

Season	GP	W	L	T	GF	GA	Pts	Finish	Division	Playoff Results
1934–35	48	11	31	6	86	144	28	5th	Canadian	Out of Playoffs

San Jose Sharks

Pro hockey was no stranger to the San Francisco Bay Area, but success and longevity never had gone hand-in-hand. A series of minor-league teams had called the area home over a period from 1928 to 1967, when the Oakland Seals entered the NHL, one of six new franchises as the NHL doubled from its Original Six to 12 teams. Struggling at the gate and in the standings, the Seals went through numerous owners before ending a nine-year run in the Bay Area by moving to Cleveland in 1976, where they would be owned by George and Gordon Gund. The franchise merged with the Minnesota North Stars after two more unsuccessful seasons.

On May 9, 1990, the National Hockey League granted approval for the Gund brothers to sell the North Stars in return for the rights to an expansion franchise in the San Francisco Bay Area. The new club would begin to play in the 1991–92 season. Despite past failures, the league was attracted to the region because it had grown to boast eight million residents and represented the fourth-largest media market in the United States.

On September 6, 1990, it was announced that the newest Bay Area franchise would be known as the Sharks. A week later, the team's majority owner George Gund and San Jose mayor Tom McEnery announced that the South Bay city would be the permanent home for the NHL franchise. The Sharks would play two years at the Cow Palace in Daly City, located just outside the San Francisco city limits, before moving to a new arena in downtown San Jose for the 1993–94 campaign. The team colors of Pacific teal, gray, black and white were unveiled on February 12, 1991. Two months later, the Sharks chose George Kingston to be the team's initial head coach. The 52-year-old had little previous NHL experience among his 30 years in hockey.

Nine days after paying the league the balance of a $50-million entrance fee, the Sharks obtained their first 34 players in dispersal and expansion drafts held on May 30, 1991. San Jose inherited 24 players from Minnesota's reserve list, mostly young players from the North Stars affiliate, Kalamazoo of the International Hockey League, or those playing in the college or junior ranks. Among those players were Arturs Irbe, Brian Hayward, Neil Wilkinson, Rob Zettler and Link Gaetz. The Sharks also selected 10 players from other NHL teams' unprotected lists in the Expansion Draft. Goalie Jeff Hackett was among those chosen.

On June 22, 1991, the Sharks participated in their first NHL Entry Draft and selected right wing Pat Falloon from the Western Hockey League's Spokane Chiefs with the second-overall pick. The Sharks also picked Ray Whitney and Sandis Ozolinsh. Just as the team was preparing to begin its first training camp, general manager Jack Ferreira engineered a trade with Chicago to bring popular defenseman Doug Wilson to the Sharks. The 14-year Blackhawk became San Jose's first captain.

The Sharks first game, on October 4, 1991, ended in a 4–3 loss at Vancouver. The visitors rallied for three goals in the final period to tie the score before Trevor Linden provided the game winner with just 19 seconds remaining in regulation. Journeyman forward Craig Coxe scored the first goal in club history. In the second game at the Cow Palace on October 8, the Sharks posted their first win against the Calgary Flames.

San Jose faced a lot of adversity in its first season. The Sharks experienced an early-season 13-game losing streak, three four-game skids and two stretches of seven consecutive losses—including one to close out the year. In addition, they surrendered a league-high 359 goals. They led the league with 17 one-goal losses and dropped 13 of 14 two-goal decisions. San Jose finished last in the six-team Smythe Division with a 17–58–5 record in a season that included a 10-day work stoppage.

It didn't take long once the season ended for changes to occur. Jack Ferreira, a highly respected manager around the league, was fired on June 26, 1992. Chuck Grillo, director of player personnel, convinced initial team president Art Savage a change was needed. Besides remaining in his capacity, Grillo was elevated to vice president and given one-third of the general manager's responsibilities to share with Kingston and former assistant g.m. Dean Lombardi.

The Sharks' second season would be their last one in the intimate and sometimes odorous confines of the Cow Palace. An opening-night 4–3 win against visiting Winnipeg in overtime provided a false illusion of how 1992–93 would unfold. The Sharks proceeded to lose their next nine games and were mired in last place, hopelessly out of playoff contention, at 6–31–2 by January 3. The next night they would embark on an NHL record-tying 17-game losing streak. Along the way, the Sharks suffered a franchise-worst loss with a 13–1 shellacking in Calgary. The ineptitude finally ended with a 3–2 victory over Winnipeg on February 14, 1993. However, the Sharks would win just four more times in their last 26 outings. Losing 16 of its final 17 games, San Jose ended a miserable second season with an 11–71–2 record to set a league record for most losses in a single campaign. Four days into the offseason, Kingston was fired.

Latvian goaltender Arturs Irbe, who would develop into a fan favorite, won only seven of 33 decisions in his first full season in the NHL. He did provide one of the season's few highlights by stopping 39 Los Angeles shots during a 6–0 victory on November 17, 1992, the first Sharks shutout. Rookie right wing Rob Gaudreau made a splash by recording the team's first hat trick in just his second NHL game. It came during a 7–5 loss to visiting Hartford on December 3, 1992.

The Sharks opened their third season in the San Jose Arena, a state-of-the-art building that featured 64 luxury boxes and seating for 17,190 at a cost of $162.5 million. Replacing Kingston behind the bench was Kevin Constantine. The 35-year-old entered the season as the league's youngest coach. One year removed from winning the Turner Cup with San Jose's minor-league affiliate, Kansas City of the International Hockey League, Constantine was familiar with San Jose's personnel and direction since he'd been part of the franchise from its inception.

The Sharks would make their initial season in San Jose a memorable one. Despite getting off to an 0–8–1 start, the players rallied behind Constantine's defense-first approach to make the playoffs for the first time, as they established an NHL record for the greatest single-season turnaround—finishing 58 points better than 1992–93's total of 24. The reunion of Russian hockey greats Sergei Makarov and Igor Larionov to form two-thirds of a potent first line, the maturation of young defenseman Sandis Ozolinsh and the workmanlike goaltending of Arturs Irbe sparked the team to a 33–35–16 record and an eighth-place finish in the Western Conference standings. But, the Sharks were not finished there. In the first round of the playoffs they drew top-seed Detroit, a team they had beaten only once in 11 previous meetings. Amazingly, the Sharks took the series in seven games. Against Toronto in the second round, San Jose jumped out to a 3–2 lead in the series before the Cinderella season ended with a seventh-game defeat.

The lovefest in the Bay Area that was now Sharks hockey had to wait until late January, 1995, to resume because of a labor lockout. San Jose picked up where it left off, shooting 5–1–1 out of the gate to raise already high expectations. Qualifying for a second straight postseason would become a challenge, however, as the team slumped by losing 10 of its next 16 before having a home game on March 10 against Detroit postponed because of heavy rain and flooding around San Jose Arena. Knowing a loss in the season finalé would preclude an invitation to the playoffs, the Sharks tied Vancouver, 3–3, to sneak into seventh place with an otherwise disappointing 19–25–4 record.

Like its first-round opponent a season ago, the Sharks drew a foe that was ripe for an upset. Calgary had lost six straight first-round matchups since its Stanley Cup triumph in 1989, and the streak reached seven when San Jose scored a seven-game victory. Revenge-seeking Detroit was waiting in round two and they destroyed the Sharks in four straight games, outscoring them, 24–6. The postseason disappointment was softened by the outstanding showing of rookie Jeff Friesen, who stepped right into the lineup after being selected 11th overall the previous June. He was the first Shark to be named to an NHL All-Rookie Team.

All the success and giddiness that surrounded the seemingly up-and-coming franchise would come crashing down, however. One by one, the heroes fell. His confidence already shaken by the loss of his status as the team's number-one goalie, Irbe experienced an offseason mishap when he was attacked by his dog. He required delicate surgery to repair injuries to his hands and left wrist. He and Wade Flaherty would get off to awful starts in 1995–96. An out-of-shape Makarov never made it out of training camp. A frustrated Larionov had a run-in with Constantine and was traded on October 24. Ozolinsh was dealt two days later to Colorado in return for a much-needed scorer, Owen Nolan. Constantine didn't last much longer. Despite having signed a new three-year deal the first week of the season, he was fired on December 2 after the team managed to win only three of its first 25 games (3–18–4). Interim coach Jim Wiley could do little with a group that quit and malingered throughout the sorry campaign. The team's first draft choice, Pat Falloon, was traded. San Jose gave up on Irbe when it acquired Chris Terreri. Grillo was fired and Dean Lombardi was named general manager. The Sharks finished ahead of only Ottawa in the overall standings at 20–55–7. Surprisingly, they sold out all 41 home games.

Rebuilding would prove tedious, as Lombardi started over from scratch. He had to weed the organization of veterans who had gotten used to losing, evaluate youth to determine who had viable NHL potential, and acquire players who would compete on a nightly basis. Lombardi turned the roster over before the 1996–97 season, securing no fewer than eight seasoned veterans with a winning track record, including Todd Gill, Al Iafrate, Kelly Hrudey, Marty McSorley, Tony Granato and Bernie Nicholls. Once the new campaign began, Lombardi continued adding players. In his boldest move, he gambled on acquiring veteran goalie Ed Belfour from Chicago. Belfour would be an unrestricted free agent at season's end.

The one move by Lombardi that did not pan out was the hiring of ex-Anaheim assistant Al Sims as the team's fourth head coach. Sims's Sharks finished 25th overall again, posting a 27–47–8 record. They produced a league-low 211 goals and fell 19 points short of a playoff spot.

Sims was fired on May 9. Exactly one month later, former Blackhawks coach Darryl Sutter was lured out of retirement and hired to lead San Jose into the 1997–98 season. Though Belfour bolted for Dallas, Lombardi acquired 1997 Conn

Smythe Trophy winner Mike Vernon from Detroit. The two-time champion would handle the job of number-one goaltender as the Sharks also welcomed newcomers Murray Craven, Stephane Matteau, Shawn Burr, Bill Houlder and rookies Patrick Marleau and Marco Sturm.

The 1997–98 season proved to be a success. The Sharks won a franchise-high 34 games and returned to the playoffs after a two-year absence. Unfortunately, San Jose hooked up with the regular season's strongest team when they faced the Dallas Stars to open the postseason. Although they won twice on home ice, the Sharks were eliminated in six games. A six-game loss to the Colorado Avalanche knocked San Jose out of the playoffs in 1998–99.

The Sharks picked up Vincent Damphousse from the Montreal Canadiens late in the 1998–99 season, and the 31-year-old veteran helped bring big changes to a team that never had finished above .500. Damphousse, Nolan, Granato and Mike Ricci gave the Sharks a solid veteran presence, while Friesen and emerging stars like Marleau, Sturm, Alex Korolyuk and Niklas Sundstrom provided a youthful talent core. The need for a greater physical presence was addressed during the 1999–2000 campaign when Mike Vernon was dealt to the Florida Panthers in a three-way deal that brought in Todd Harvey from the New York Rangers. The trade installed Steve Shields as the number-one goaltender in San Jose.

The Sharks started the 1999–2000 season strongly and were battling for top spot in the tough Pacific Division through the first two months until the club began to slide in December. Though Owen Nolan continued to score (his 44 goals were topped only by Pavel Bure's 58), San Jose did not nail down the final playoff berth in the Western Conference until the final week of the season. Finishing eighth meant a playoff matchup with the NHL's best team—the St. Louis Blues—but after dropping the first game, the Sharks won the next three and suddenly seemed to have the series well in hand.

Game five saw St. Louis storm out to an early 3–0 lead, but the Sharks rallied to tie the game before suffering a 5–3 defeat. Heading back home with another chance to wrap up the series, the Sharks were blown out 6–2 and suddenly St. Louis seemed to be in command. But, just like against Detroit back in 1994, San Jose shook off a game-six shellacking and wrapped up the series in seven. The return to form of Steve Shields and an Owen Nolan goal from near center ice with 10 seconds left in the first period were the keys to a 3–1 victory. The Sharks battled hard in round two against the defending Stanley Cup champions from Dallas, but went down to defeat in five games.

San Jose Sharks Year-by-Year Record

Season	GP	W	L	T	GF	GA	Pts	Finish	Division	Playoff Results
1991–92	80	17	58	5	219	359	39	6th	Smythe	Out of Playoffs
1992–93	84	11	71	2	218	414	24	6th	Smythe	Out of Playoffs
1993–94	84	33	35	16	252	265	82	3rd	Pacific	Lost Conf. Semifinal
1994–95	48	19	25	4	129	161	42	3rd	Pacific	Lost Conf. Semifinal
1995–96	82	20	55	7	252	357	47	7th	Pacific	Out of Playoffs
1996–97	82	27	47	8	211	278	62	7th	Pacific	Out of Playoffs
1997–98	82	34	38	10	210	216	78	4th	Pacific	Lost Conf. Quarterfinal
1998–99	82	31	33	18	196	191	80	4th	Pacific	Lost Conf. Quarterfinal
1999-2000	82	35	37	10	225	214	*87	4th	Pacific	Lost Conf. Semifinal

** Includes 7 points added for regulation-time tie games lost in overtime*

TAMPA BAY LIGHTNING

PRIOR TO THE LATE 1980S, there had been considerable skepticism about the possibility of major-league hockey in steamy Florida. An attempt by the World Hockey Association to establish a foothold in Miami during the early 1970s ended in failure before a game was ever played. But, in December, 1989, the NHL announced a grand plan to expand, and in March of the next year, Hall of Famer Phil Esposito came to the conclusion that the Tampa-St. Petersburg area was prime for NHL expansion.

Teaming with Florida attorney Henry Lee Paul, son of longtime baseball executive Gabe Paul, and Mel Lowell, a former Madison Square Garden official, Esposito laid the groundwork for acceptance. His first move was to promote an exhibition game at the massive Florida Suncoast Dome between the Los Angeles Kings and Pittsburgh Penguins on September 19, 1990. The game drew a crowd of 25,581—the largest in NHL history—and Tampa Coliseum, Inc. agreed to finance construction of a multi-purpose arena next to Tampa Stadium.

Still cautious, the NHL dispatched an expeditionary force to Tampa on November 1, 1990, to gauge interest. Less than five weeks later, Tampa Bay and Ottawa were awarded conditional franchises to play in 1992–93.

It had been expected that the Pritzger family, owner of the Hyatt Corporation among other holdings, would put up the $50 million expansion fee. Pritzger decided to stay out of the hockey business. Esposito then jetted to the Orient in search of funding.

He started with a $2 million infusion and eventually boosted it with support from such Japanese firms as Kokusai Green, Nippon Green and Tokyo Tower. Esposito liked to humorously recall that some of the negotiations took place between drinks. "The more we drank," said Esposito, "the more it [the deal] made sense."

Fiscal clouds appeared in June, 1991, when the team missed a $22.5-million franchise installment payment. That moved Kokusai Green into action, and it felt obliged to take a majority stake in the franchise.

In September, 1991, the Lightning received league approval for a restructured partnership with Lightning Partners—owned by Kokusai Green—assuming the role of general partner. Esposito's group now had been formally replaced by the Japanese majority owners.

In December, 1991, the NHL granted permanent membership status to both the Lightning and Ottawa Senators. On the operating front, Phil Esposito emerged as the general manager, with brother Tony heading the scouting division. Terry Crisp would be the team's first coach. As for a playing venue, the club opted for the Florida State Fairgrounds Expo Hall as a temporary home until a permanent arena was built in Tampa.

During the club's first training camp, Esposito stunned the hockey world by signing female goaltender Manon Rheaume to a tryout form. The attractive French Canadian made history on September 23, 1992, by becoming the first woman to play one of the four major professional sports when she started against St. Louis in a preseason game. Rheaume made seven saves during 20 minutes of action and later was awarded a contract with Atlanta, Tampa Bay's International Hockey League affiliate.

On opening night, a sellout crowd of 10,425 jammed Expo Hall cheering the Lightning to a 7–3 victory over

Chicago. Chris Kontos, a reject of several NHL teams, scored four goals for Tampa Bay. As expected, the Lightning played like an expansion team, although there were conspicuous highlights. One of the earliest took place on November 7, 1992, when defenseman Doug Crossman collected six points in a 6–5 win over the New York Islanders.

Of all the discards picked up by Esposito, the most impressive was Brian Bradley, who finished the season with a team-leading 42 goals and 44 assists. In the end, Tampa Bay finished sixth in the Norris Division (23–54–7) and missed the playoffs.

For their second season, the Lightning moved out of the drafty, barn-like Expo Hall to St. Petersburg's Florida Suncoast Dome, which was designed as a baseball stadium but was reconfigured to handle hockey. It would have 28,000 seats for NHL games and would later be renamed the Thunderdome.

Underlying all the excitement were negative fiscal currents. Starting in 1992, the club was so cash-strapped that Lightning officials were constantly concerned about failure to make payroll and the potential collapse of the team. Nevertheless, Phil Esposito continued to fortify his lineup. With his first selection (third overall) in the 1993 Entry Draft, Esposito selected Chris Gratton, a big forward. He also acquired five-time 30-goal scorer Petr Klima from Edmonton for future considerations.

Klima led the Lightning in scoring with 28 goals in 1993–94, while Daren Puppa, who was obtained from the Florida Panthers in phase two of the 1993 Expansion Draft, proved to be the formidable goaltender the club required to remain competitive.

Any doubts that the Tampa Bay area was hockey country were dispelled on October 9, 1993, when the club set an NHL single-game attendance mark with 27,227 fans witnessing the Lightning home-opener against Florida. The team's record of 30–43–11was a further boost, despite a second straight year without making the playoffs. The team drew 805,901 over 41 games, for an average of 19,656, but many of the seats were low-priced or giveaways and the financial woes continued.

During the autumn of 1994, the Internal Revenue Service and the State of Florida were prepared to file liens on the Lightning for $750,000 in past-due taxes. Other debts also were piling up, and to handle them, Kokusai Green borrowed against many of the team's revenue streams. Further financial troubles in 1995 saw Mel Lowell leave his job as executive vice president when his contract was not renewed.

These events coincided with yet another non-playoff season during the lockout-shortened 1994–95 campaign. The turnabout for the Lightning's fortunes took place in October, 1995 when Paul Ysebaert was named the first captain in team history and young defenseman Roman Hamrlik surfaced as one of the best offensive point men in the NHL. Between Puppa's goaltending, Hamrlik's versatility on defense and attack and Terry Crisp's spirited coaching, the Lightning earned their first playoff berth when they edged out the defending champion New Jersey Devils for the final postseason spot.

A powerful Philadelphia club faced the Lightning and won 7–3 at the Spectrum in the opener, but an overtime goal by Brian Bellows provided the underdogs with a 2–1 win in game two. Then came the stunner: returning to the confines of their home rink, the Lightning defeated Philadelphia, 5–4, on Alexander Selivanov's goal in overtime.

It proved to be the Lightning's last gasp, as the Flyers next ran off three straight victories to capture the series. However, fan support was stronger than ever and on April 23, 1996, the Lightning set an all-time NHL attendance record of 28,183 for game four of the playoff series. Even more encouraging was news that the club's new home, the Tampa-based Ice Palace, was ready for occupancy at the start of the 1996–97 season.

Opening night at the new building was October 20, 1996, when the home team defeated the New York Rangers 5–3 in front of 20,543 fans. It was an auspicious debut for a season of disappointment. A troublesome back kayoed Puppa, causing coach Crisp to alternate Corey Schwab and Rick Tabaracci in goal. Strong offensive efforts by Dino Ciccarelli and John Cullen enabled the Lightning to stay in the playoff hunt, but it was not to be.

By this time the Japanese-based ownership had begun a determined effort to sell the team. The organization's debt had passed $50 million and would reach $100 million by 1998. The Las Vegas-based Maloof family spent eight months trying to hammer out a deal but never was able to personally contact the mysterious Japanese owner Takashi Okubo. Instead of buying the Lightning, the Maloofs purchased the NBA Sacramento Kings.

Okubo, who had poured $90 million into the team but had never attended a game, became more and more the subject of scrutiny as the 1997–98 season unfolded. It would be a traumatic year for the Lightning.

Among the many misfortunes to face the team was the fact that John Cullen, who had been diagnosed with cancer, learned in September, 1997 that radiation and chemotherapy treatments had not been successful. He would have to undergo a bone-marrow transplant, and doctors now reported that his chances of recovery—once reported to be better than 90 percent—were no better than 75 percent.

On a purely hockey front, the most egregious loss for Tampa was that of Chris Gratton, the 6'4", 218-pound center who received a five-year, $16.5-million, free-agent offer sheet from the Philadelphia Flyers in the summer of 1997.

Unable to match the bid, Phil Esposito later explained to an arbitrator that he couldn't decipher Philadelphia's proposal because some of the numbers on the fax were smudged. The Lightning escaped a total disaster when Philadelphia agreed to trade Mikael Renberg and Karl Dykhuis to Tampa Bay for the four first-round draft picks that the Flyers would have lost to the Lightning in the original offer sheet plan. But, by December, 1997, Renberg had broken his wrist and was lost for a month. (Gratton would prove to be a bust in Philly, and was traded back to Tampa for Renberg during the 1998–99 season. He was later dealt to the Buffalo Sabres in 1999–2000.)

Meanwhile, Phil Esposito had fired Terry Crisp, placed Rick Paterson in the head coaching slot, and then replaced him with Jacques Demers. No matter who was behind the bench, the Lightning required Puppa's top goaltending to survive, but in a game against Boston in December, 1997, the goalie left complaining of back spasms. He was unable to play for the rest of the season. The club concluded the 1997–98 season with the worst record of its six-year existence. With only 17 wins in 82 games, the Lightning lost 55 matches, one more than in their maiden season.

At season's end, NHL commissioner Gary Bettman revealed that the league was diligently working to consummate a sale of the team that would eliminate "99.9 percent" of the team's problems. "There are difficulties in having distant ownership," said Bettman, "particularly if that ownership is not familiar with the sports business. At this point I'll define 'local interest' as North America. I'll take somebody within a six-hour flight!"

Insurance magnate Art Williams purchased the club on June 25, 1998, just a few weeks after John Cullen learned that his cancer was in remission. He returned to play briefly in 1998–99 before retiring to become an assistant coach.

The club's on-ice future received a considerable boost in 1998–99, with first overall 1998 draft choice Vincent Lecavalier. Still, the team posted the NHL's worst record amid a season of upheaval. Just two games in, Art Williams fired Phil Esposito and gave his general manager's job to coach Jacques Demers. Later in the year, Williams sold the team to Bill Davidson, owner of the Detroit Pistons of the National Basketball Association and the Detroit Vipers of the International Hockey League. After the season, Davidson hired former Vipers coach and g.m. Rick Dudley away from the Ottawa Senators to head up hockey operations in Tampa. (The move cost the Lightning Rob Zamuner as compensation.) Dudley hired Steve Ludzik, who had coached for him in Detroit, as the Lightning's bench boss

Despite the changes, the Lightning became just the second club in NHL history to lose at least 50 games three seasons in a row. But, like the Pittsburgh Penguins, whose three years of futility helped them land Mario Lemieux, there is reason for optimism in Tampa. Lecavalier became the youngest captain in NHL history in 1999–2000 and he improved in every facet of his game. Acquisitions like former Toronto Maple Leafs Mike Johnson and Fredrik Modin help bolster the offense, while young defensemen Pavel Kubina, Paul Mara and Ben Clymer offer more hope for the future. Unfortunately, plans to ease Dan Cloutier into the number-one goaltending job had to be accelerated when Daren Puppa was injured for the fourth straight season. In fact, injuries forced Tampa Bay to use six different goalies in 1999–2000 and the club struggled to the NHL's second-worst defensive record, behind only the expansion Atlanta Thrashers.

Tampa Bay Lightning Year-by-Year Record

Season	GP	W	L	T	GF	GA	Pts	Finish	Division	Playoff Results
1992–93	84	23	54	7	245	332	53	6th	Norris	Out of Playoffs
1993–94	84	30	43	11	224	251	71	7th	Atlantic	Out of Playoffs
1994–95	48	17	28	3	120	144	37	6th	Atlantic	Out of Playoffs
1995–96	82	38	32	12	138	248	88	6th	Atlantic	Lost Conf. Quarterfinal
1996–97	82	32	40	10	217	247	74	6th	Atlantic	Out of Playoffs
1997–98	82	17	55	10	151	269	44	7th	Atlantic	Out of Playoffs
1998–99	82	19	54	9	179	292	47	4th	Southeast	Out of Playoffs
1999-2000	82	19	54	9	204	310	*54	4th	Southeast	Out of Playoffs

** Includes 7 points added for regulation-time tie games lost in overtime*

TORONTO MAPLE LEAFS

THE NHL, FORMED IN A SERIES of meetings between November 22 and November 26, 1917, originally comprised teams from Quebec, Ottawa and two clubs from Montreal—the Canadiens and the Wanderers. Toronto was included in the mix with the stipulation that former owner Eddie Livingstone not be involved in any way. Livingstone was not a popular chap among his hockey brethren. The Toronto team was admitted to the NHL under the ownership of the city's Mutual Street Arena, hence the name the Toronto Arenas. (This name has been traditionally attached to Toronto's NHL team of 1917–18, but it appears that the name was not actually used until the following season.)

Toronto played its first NHL game on December 19, 1917, and lost, 10–9, to the Montreal Wanderers. Despite the fact those original Toronto players quarreled with management and were hit by fines for breaking training, the team won the second half of the NHL's split schedule, defeated the Montreal Canadiens in a playoff series and captured the Stanley Cup by winning a best-of-five series with the Vancouver Millionaires of the Pacific Coast Hockey Association. And they did it on a surface of artificial ice—the only such surface in the NHL.

While the victory in 1918 was Toronto's first Cup win under the NHL banner, a 1914 team playing in the National Hockey Association is credited with first bringing Lord Stanley's basin to the city. The 1914 Toronto Blueshirts featured goaltender Harry Holmes and defenseman Harry Cameron, who also played on the 1918 championship team. Why not? They were well paid for their efforts. By 1918, Holmes was earning $700 per season, Cameron $900. The total payroll for the 10 players on the Toronto roster was $6,150.

Despite winning the Stanley Cup in the NHL's first season, the Toronto Arenas struggled in 1918–19 and, in fact, withdrew from the league on February 20, 1919. The team was back for the 1919–20 season after having been reorganized as the Toronto St. Patricks. In 1922, the St. Pats squad surprised the hockey world by defeating the Ottawa Senators in the NHL playoffs and then toppling Vancouver in five games in the finals for the Stanley Cup. Toronto's Babe Dye led all playoff scorers with 11 goals in seven games. Dye had been the NHL's top goal scorer in 1920–21 (35 goals) and would top the league again with 26 in 1922–23. His 38 goals in 1924–25 were a career high and his 44 points that season also led the NHL.

By 1926–27 the NHL had expanded to 10 teams. Young Conn Smythe was hired to assemble the original New York Rangers, but was fired before the first game was played. Lester Patrick, older and more experienced, was signed to replace him. New York's loss soon became Toronto's gain.

Following his dismissal in New York, Smythe managed to raise $160,000 and purchased the last-place St. Pats in February, 1927. He promptly renamed the team the Toronto Maple Leafs, and switched the uniform colors from green and white to blue and white.

Meanwhile, in March, 1923, a 20-year-old newspaper reporter named Foster Hewitt had begun broadcasting hockey games from Mutual Street Arena on the *Toronto Star*'s new radio station, CFCA. Soon, Hewitt's broadcasts of Maple Leaf games were attracting more and more fans to the Arena and Smythe began formulating plans for a new ice palace—Maple Leaf Gardens.

When financing the project became a major undertaking, Smythe and his energetic assistant Frank Selke turned to the trade unions and bartered Gardens stock in return for labor. In what has been called "a miracle of engineering," the new ice palace was erected in six months and at a bargain price of $1.5 million. It opened for business on November 12, 1931. With Hap Day and King Clancy on defense and the Kid Line of Charlie Conacher, Joe Primeau and Busher Jackson up front, the Leafs became a powerful force in the NHL. Through the decades that followed, the Gardens was always full to overflowing.

In 1931–32, their first year on Gardens ice, the Leafs swept to the Stanley Cup, ousting the Rangers in the finals in three straight games. Early in the season, Smythe had replaced coach Art Duncan with Dick Irvin, who had been fired by Chicago the previous season. Irvin brought the Leafs from last place to first place within a month. The Leafs would reach the Stanley Cup finals six times in eight years following their victory in 1932.

In 1940, Dick Irvin resigned as Leafs coach and accepted a similar position with the Montreal Canadiens. Hap Day was Irvin's successor and figured prominently in one of hockey's most dramatic comebacks. In 1942, after Detroit took a 3–0 lead in games over Toronto in the Stanley Cup finals, Day made some player changes and the Leafs roared back with three straight wins to tie the series. They won the Cup with a 3–1 victory in a thrilling seventh game. It's the only time a club has come back from such a deficit in the Stanley Cup finals.

Goaltender Frank McCool was a Toronto hero in the Stanley Cup finals of 1945 when he set a record with three shutouts. The Leafs won the series in seven games. One of the stars of that team was defenseman Babe Pratt, who had won the Hart Trophy in 1944. Pratt would be expelled from hockey in 1945–46 for wagering on games and, although he was reinstated on February 14, 1946, his days in Toronto were numbered. Pratt was traded to the Boston Bruins after the season and finished his playing days in the minors.

The Leafs regained the Stanley Cup in the spring of 1947, with Ted Kennedy scoring the winning goal in a 2–1 victory over Montreal in game six of the finals. Early the following season, Conn Smythe traded several players to Chicago in order to land Max Bentley, who helped the Leafs retain the Cup in 1948 and 1949. The 1950–51 season is remembered for Bill Barilko's Stanley Cup-winning goal, capping a series in which all five games required overtime. Barilko perished in a plane crash a few weeks later.

On February 1, 1955, Conn Smythe stepped down as general manager of the Leafs and handed the position to Hap Day. Leaf fans, however, had little to cheer about during this era. The club finished in last place for the first time in history in 1956–57, but things were about to get better.

In August, 1958, Toronto signed 33-year-old minor-league goaltender Johnny Bower and rookie defenseman Carl Brewer. Defenseman Allan Stanley was acquired from Boston and assistant general manager Punch Imlach took over as general manager in November. One of his first moves was to fire Billy Reay and add the coaching job to his own portfolio. He installed rookie Dave Keon at center and grabbed roustabout wing Eddie Shack from the Rangers in a deal. Imlach's "Cinderella Leafs" climbed from last place into the playoffs that season but lost in the finals to a powerful Montreal club. In February, 1960, Imlach snared Red Kelly from Detroit and switched him from defense to center. Once again the Leafs reached the finals and once again they lost to Montreal, who captured their fifth straight Stanley Cup championship.

In November, 1961, Conn Smythe officially stepped aside and sold his 50,000 shares in the Maple Leafs franchise (60 percent of the voting rights) to his son Stafford, Harold Ballard and *Toronto Telegram* owner John Bassett for $2 million dollars. Under this new ownership group, the Leafs won the Stanley Cup in 1962 and 1963. The following season, Punch Imlach dealt forwards Dick Duff, Bob Nevin and Bill Collins, plus defensemen Arnie Brown and Rod Seiling, to the Rangers in return for Andy Bathgate and Don McKenney. Bathgate and McKenney proved a big help as the Leafs won their third consecutive Cup title in 1964. In the final series against Detroit, hardrock defenseman Bobby Baun scored the winning goal in game six in overtime while playing on a cracked anklebone. Toronto captured the Cup once more in the 1960s. With NHL expansion looming, Imlach's veterans—the oldest club ever to reach the finals—ousted Montreal in six games in 1967 behind the superb goaltending of Terry Sawchuk and Johnny Bower.

When his team slumped in 1967–68, Imlach sent Frank Mahovlich (a player he couldn't get along with), Pete Stemkowski and Garry Unger, along with the rights to retired Carl Brewer (another Leaf who drove Imlach to distraction), to Detroit for Norm Ullman, Paul Henderson and Floyd Smith. But the Leafs were no longer championship material. After they were eliminated by Boston in the 1969 playoffs, Imlach was fired by Stafford Smythe. Jim Gregory took over as general manager and John McLellan was assigned the coaching job.

In the summer of 1969, Harold Ballard and Stafford Smythe faced charges of tax evasion. John Bassett, unwilling to be associated with partners who faced jail terms, sold his shares to Ballard and Smythe for close to $6 million. Smythe died before he could be sentenced. Ballard then bought Smythe's shares, with help from his friend Don Giffin, who arranged for a loan of $7.4 million. Ballard, now in full control of the franchise and the Gardens, had his jail sentenced postponed until after the Canada–Soviet series of 1972. Then he was whisked off to jail to serve three concurrent three-year terms. He served only a year, and returned to put his personal ruinous stamp on hockey at Maple Leaf Gardens for most of the next two decades.

Upon his return to Toronto, Ballard scoffed at reports the newly formed World Hockey Association would give him any trouble. As a result, his organization lost no fewer than 14 players to the rival loop, including such young stars as Brad Selwood, Rick Ley, Jim Harrison and the brilliant young goaltender Bernie Parent.

Though they were no longer the powerhouse club of the 1960s, Ballard's Leafs played decent hockey throughout most of the 1970s. One of the game's great moments took place on February 7, 1976, when Leaf captain Darryl Sittler scored a record 10 points (six goals and four assists) in a game against Boston. Sittler capped an outstanding year by scoring five goals in a playoff game against Philadelphia, and later scored in overtime for Team Canada against Czechoslovakia in the final of the inaugural Canada Cup tournament in September, 1976. In 1977–78, the Leafs, with new coach Roger Neilson replacing Red Kelly behind the bench, stunned the New York Islanders in the playoff quarterfinals, winning in overtime in game seven on a Lanny McDonald goal.

Late in the 1978–79 season, Ballard fired Neilson after a March 1 loss to Montreal, then found he had nobody to replace him. He rehired Neilson prior to the next game, then fired him a second time a few weeks later. He also fired Jim Gregory and dumped chief scout Bob Davidson. The Leafs were about to head into a steep decline. Ballard talked of hiring Scotty Bowman to run his team. Then it was Don Cherry. Instead, he wound up bringing back Punch Imlach and promising him full control. It proved a huge mistake.

Imlach's dictatorial ways had paid big dividends for the Maple Leafs of the 1960s, but his tactics didn't work with the Leafs of the 1980s. When players raised his ire he got rid of them. He feuded with Darryl Sittler and fumed because Sittler had a no-trade clause in his contract. Maliciously, he traded Sittler's best friend Lanny McDonald to Colorado. He sent Pat Boutette to Hartford, Dave Hutchison to Chicago and Tiger Williams to Vancouver. Imlach brought back retired players in Larry Carriere and Carl Brewer, and installed old pals as coaches, first Floyd Smith and then Joe Crozier. When Imlach suffered two heart attacks and required bypass surgery during the 1980–81 season, Ballard didn't fire him. He simply said his manager wouldn't be back because of ill health. When Imlach did return, his parking spot was gone.

When Imlach was pushed aside, Ballard took over. He appointed Gerry McNamara as general manager. It was another unpopular move, but McNamara remained on the job through the 1987–88 season. Thirty-year-old Gord Stellick (who had begun working for the Leafs while still in high school) and loyal Floyd Smith followed McNamara in the general manager's chair, while Leaf coaches in the 1980s included Joe Crozier, Mike Nykoluk, Dan Maloney, John Brophy, Doug Carpenter and George Armstrong.

Team founder Conn Smythe passed away at age 85 on November 18, 1980.

Darryl Sittler had resigned as Leaf captain under Imlach, but later was persuaded by Ballard to resume that role. Sittler was grossly underpaid compared to other stars in the league, and when he requested a raise, Ballard told him to think about joining another team. During the 1981–82 season, Sittler agreed to join the Philadelphia Flyers. He had set club records for goals (389), assists (527) and points (916) during his career in Toronto.

Though the club missed the playoffs four times in eight years during the mid-1980s, Leaf fans at least could witness some impressive individual efforts. Rick Vaive became the first Leaf player to score 50 or more goals in a season with 54 in 1981–82, and topped 50 again each of the next two years. Later in the decade, Gary Leeman totaled 51 goals.

In November, 1986, King Clancy died after a gall bladder operation. The death of his great friend left Harold Ballard devastated despite the consoling words of Yolanda, the lady in his life. In the later years of his own life, the saga of Harold and Yolanda would play out like a soap opera in the Toronto media. In April, 1990, Ballard passed away at age 86, leaving a once-great hockey franchise in tatters.

Donald Giffin, Steve Stavro and Donald Crump stepped in as executors of the Ballard estate to sort out the mess both on and off the ice, which included a debt of $60 million. On June 4, 1991, Giffin hired Cliff Fletcher as president, chief operating officer and general manager of the Leafs.

Fletcher was signed to a five-year, $4 million contract. He immediately reshaped the front office, named popular Wendel Clark as captain, and masterminded a number of shrewd deals to improve the questionable product on the ice. On January 2, 1992, he hit the jackpot by sweet-talking his Calgary counterpart, Doug Risebrough, into giving up Doug Gilmour, Jamie Macoun, Ric Nattress, Kent Manderville and Rick Wamsley in return for Gary Leeman, Michel Petit, Alexander Godynyuk, Craig Berube and Jeff Reese. Gilmour, always a prolific scorer, was the plum in the pudding. He swiftly became a superstar in Toronto.

Fletcher's next major move was to sign Pat Burns as coach, replacing Tom Watt. Burns had resigned from the Montreal Canadiens in May, 1992. Within hours, he was a Maple Leaf. Together, Fletcher and Burns resurrected the franchise. The Leafs recorded a club-record 99 points in 1992–93. Thrilling seven-game playoff victories over Detroit and St. Louis saw Toronto reach the Campbell Conference final, where the most exciting hockey season in Toronto in recent memory ended with a seventh-game loss to Wayne Gretzky and the Los Angeles Kings.

In the playoffs of 1994, the Leafs eliminated Chicago in six and San Jose in seven. But, a five-game playoff loss to Vancouver ended their season. Undaunted, Fletcher kept making moves. At the annual draft sessions in Hartford, Fletcher traded Wendel Clark, Sylvain Lefebvre and Landon Wilson to Quebec for Mats Sundin, Garth Butcher and Todd Warriner. This time, the dealing took its toll and the team began to tumble. Burns was fired late in 1995–96 after a devastating midseason slump.

Ordered by owner Steve Stavro to trim the payroll, on June 22, 1996, Fletcher traded Mike Gartner to Phoenix (Gartner claimed he had a verbal no-trade agreement with the g.m.) and Dave Gagner to Calgary. During the 1996–97 season, Doug Gilmour was traded to New Jersey, along with Dave Ellett, for Steve Sullivan, Jason Smith and Alyn McCauley, a junior star. At the trade deadline, Fletcher sent Larry Murphy to Detroit and Kirk Muller to the Panthers.

Despite the many moves in an attempt to salvage the season, Toronto finished in last place in the Central Division and missed the playoffs. The next move would involve Fletcher himself. He was dismissed on May 24, 1997.

In a surprise move six days after Fletcher's departure, Hall of Fame goaltender Ken Dryden accepted the job as president of the Toronto Maple Leafs. Though he had no managerial experience, Dryden promised everything from a better team on the ice to better hot dogs at the concession stands. "I'm here because it feels right to be here," Dryden said.

On August 20, 1997, Dryden named himself to the position of general manager and named Anders Hedberg, Mike Smith and Bill Watters to his management team. Mike Murphy was retained as coach, but was presented with perhaps an even less-talented roster than the team that had missed the playoffs in Fletcher's final season. With only Mats Sundin proving capable offensively, the Leafs struggled to score goals throughout the 1997–98 season and missed the playoffs for the second year in a row. Dryden fired Murphy on June 23, 1998, and replaced him with Pat Quinn three days later.

An era in NHL history ended during the 1998–99 season when the Toronto Maple Leafs bid farewell to their home of 68 years and moved into Air Canada Centre (which would also house the NBA's Toronto Raptors, who had been purchased by Maple Leaf Sports and Entertainment). The last remaining Original Six arena played host to its final game on February 13, 1999. Unfortunately for Toronto fans, Maple Leaf Gardens closed much as it opened, with the Chicago Blackhawks scoring a 6–2 victory (Chicago had beaten the Maple Leafs, 2–1, back in 1931).

The loss to the Blackhawks was one of very few disappointments in Toronto, as the Maple Leafs made a surprising return to the upper echelon of the NHL. The good things began in the offseason, when Dryden negotiated Toronto back into the Eastern Conference and into the Northeast Division with Ottawa, Buffalo, Boston and Montreal.

Most important to the Leafs' on-ice success in 1998–99 was the decision to sign Curtis Joseph. "Cujo" provided clutch goaltending that allowed Quinn to employ an offensive approach and saw the Leafs lead the league with 268 goals while winning a team-record 45 games. Joseph himself established a franchise high with 35 victories. The acquisition of Joseph made Felix Potvin expendable, though associate general manager Mike Smith held on to him until he could get the deal he wanted. Smith was finally able to land talented young defenseman Bryan Berard when he shipped Potvin to the New York Islanders in January. (Sadly, Berard would find his career in jeopardy when he suffered a serious eye injury against the Ottawa Senators on March 11, 2000.)

The Maple Leafs finished the 1998–99 season with 97 points, good for second in their division behind the surprising Senators. They then defeated Philadelphia and Pittsburgh in the playoffs before bowing out to the Buffalo Sabres in the Eastern Conference final.

During the offseason, Smith left the team. He would resurface in Chicago. Anders Hedberg also departed, and would work in Edmonton before returning to Europe to manage Sweden's national team program. Pat Quinn was promoted to general manager, making him the first man since Punch Imlach to hold the dual role of coach and g.m. in Toronto.

The club's failure to make significant additions to the on-ice talent worried fans heading into the 1999–2000 season, but newcomer Jonas Hoglund proved a key addition to the club's top line alongside Mats Sundin and Steve Thomas. Nik Antropov, drafted 10th overall out of Kazakhstan in 1997, showed promise as a rookie after being called up early in the season. Other additions as the year wore on included Dmitri Khristich from Boston and the return of Wendel Clark. Deals for Darcy Tucker and Gerald Diduck added to the team's toughness, but the biggest key to Toronto's success continued to be Curtis Joseph. He broke his own team record with 36 victories as Toronto posted the first 100-point season in franchise history. By coming in first in the Northeast Division, Toronto finished atop the standings for the first time since finishing first overall in the six-team NHL back in 1962–63.

Hopes for the franchise's first Stanley Cup title since 1967 were dashed in the second round of the playoffs. After beating the Senators in six games in the opening round, the Leafs were then defeated in six games by the New Jersey Devils.

Toronto Maple Leafs Year-by-Year Record

Season	GP	W	L	T	GF	GA	Pts	Finish	Division	Playoff Results
1917–18	22	13	9	0	108	109	26	2nd and 1st***		Won Stanley Cup
1918–19	18	5	13	0	64	92	10	3rd and 3rd***		Out of Playoffs
1919–20**	24	12	12	0	119	106	24	3rd and 2nd***		Out of Playoffs
1920–21	24	15	9	0	105	100	30	2nd and 1st***		Lost NHL Final
1921–22	24	13	10	1	98	97	27	2nd		Won Stanley Cup
1922–23	24	13	10	1	82	88	27	3rd		Out of Playoffs
1923–24	24	10	14	0	59	85	20	3rd		Out of Playoffs
1924–25	30	19	11	0	90	84	38	2nd		Lost NHL Semifinal
1925–26	36	12	21	3	92	114	27	6th		Out of Playoffs
1926–27*	44	15	24	5	79	94	35	5th	Canadian	Out of Playoffs
1927–28	44	18	18	8	89	88	44	4th	Canadian	Out of Playoffs
1928–29	44	21	18	5	85	69	47	3rd	Canadian	Lost Semifinal
1929–30	44	17	21	6	116	124	40	4th	Canadian	Out of Playoffs
1930–31	44	22	13	9	118	99	53	2nd	Canadian	Lost Quarterfinal
1931–32	48	23	18	7	155	127	53	2nd	Canadian	Won Stanley Cup
1932–33	48	24	18	6	119	111	54	1st	Canadian	Lost Final
1933–34	48	26	13	9	174	119	61	1st	Canadian	Lost Semifinal
1934–35	48	30	14	4	157	111	64	1st	Canadian	Lost Final
1935–36	48	23	19	6	126	106	52	2nd	Canadian	Lost Final
1936–37	48	22	21	5	119	115	49	3rd	Canadian	Lost Quarterfinal
1937–38	48	24	15	9	151	127	57	1st	Canadian	Lost Final
1938–39	48	19	20	9	114	107	47	3rd		Lost Final
1939–40	48	25	17	6	134	110	56	3rd		Lost Final
1940–41	48	28	14	6	145	99	62	2nd		Lost Semifinal
1941–42	48	27	18	3	158	136	57	2nd		Won Stanley Cup
1942–43	50	22	19	9	198	159	53	3rd		Lost Semifinal
1943–44	50	23	23	4	214	174	50	3rd		Lost Semifinal
1944–45	50	24	22	4	183	161	52	3rd		Won Stanley Cup
1945–46	50	19	24	7	174	185	45	5th		Out of Playoffs
1946–47	60	31	19	10	209	172	72	2nd		Won Stanley Cup
1947–48	60	32	15	13	182	143	77	1st		Won Stanley Cup
1948–49	60	22	25	13	147	161	57	4th		Won Stanley Cup
1949–50	70	31	27	12	176	173	74	3rd		Lost Semifinal
1950–51	70	41	16	13	212	138	95	2nd		Won Stanley Cup
1951–52	70	29	25	16	168	157	74	3rd		Lost Semifinal
1952–53	70	27	30	13	156	167	67	5th		Out of Playoffs
1953–54	70	32	24	14	152	131	78	3rd		Lost Semifinal
1954–55	70	24	24	22	147	135	70	3rd		Lost Semifinal
1955–56	70	24	33	13	153	181	61	4th		Lost Semifinal
1956–57	70	21	34	15	174	192	57	5th		Out of Playoffs
1957–58	70	21	38	11	192	226	53	6th		Out of Playoffs
1958–59	70	27	32	11	189	201	65	4th		Lost Final
1959–60	70	35	26	9	199	195	79	2nd		Lost Final
1960–61	70	39	19	12	234	176	90	2nd		Lost Semifinal
1961–62	70	37	22	11	232	180	85	2nd		Won Stanley Cup
1962–63	70	35	23	12	221	180	82	1st		Won Stanley Cup
1963–64	70	33	25	12	192	172	78	3rd		Won Stanley Cup
1964–65	70	30	26	14	204	173	74	4th		Lost Semifinal
1965–66	70	34	25	11	208	187	79	3rd		Lost Semifinal
1966–67	70	32	27	11	204	211	75	3rd		Won Stanley Cup
1967–68	74	33	31	10	209	176	76	5th	East	Out of Playoffs
1968–69	76	35	26	15	234	217	85	4th	East	Lost Quarterfinal
1969–70	76	29	34	13	222	242	71	6th	East	Out of Playoffs
1970–71	78	37	33	8	248	211	82	4th	East	Lost Quarterfinal
1971–72	78	33	31	14	209	208	80	4th	East	Lost Quarterfinal
1972–73	78	27	41	10	247	279	64	6th	East	Out of Playoffs
1973–74	78	35	27	16	274	230	86	4th	East	Lost Quarterfinal
1974–75	80	31	33	16	280	309	78	3rd	Adams	Lost Quarterfinal
1975–76	80	34	31	15	294	276	83	3rd	Adams	Lost Quarterfinal
1976–77	80	33	32	15	301	285	81	3rd	Adams	Lost Quarterfinal
1977–78	80	41	29	10	271	237	92	3rd	Adams	Lost Semifinal
1978–79	80	34	33	13	267	252	81	3rd	Adams	Lost Quarterfinal
1979–80	80	35	40	5	304	327	75	4th	Adams	Lost Prelim. Round
1980–81	80	28	37	15	322	367	71	5th	Adams	Lost Prelim. Round
1981–82	80	20	44	16	298	380	56	5th	Norris	Out of Playoffs
1982–83	80	28	40	12	293	330	68	3rd	Norris	Lost Div. Semifinal
1983–84	80	26	45	9	303	387	61	5th	Norris	Out of Playoffs
1984–85	80	20	52	8	253	358	48	5th	Norris	Out of Playoffs
1985–86	80	25	48	7	311	386	57	4th	Norris	Lost Div. Final
1986–87	80	32	42	6	286	319	70	4th	Norris	Lost Div. Final
1987–88	80	21	49	10	273	345	52	4th	Norris	Lost Div. Semifinal
1988–89	80	28	46	6	259	342	62	5th	Norris	Out of Playoffs
1989–90	80	38	38	4	337	358	80	3rd	Norris	Lost Div. Semifinal
1990–91	80	23	46	11	241	318	57	5th	Norris	Out of Playoffs
1991–92	80	30	43	7	234	294	67	5th	Norris	Out of Playoffs
1992–93	84	44	29	11	288	241	99	3rd	Norris	Lost Conf. Final
1993–94	84	43	29	12	280	243	98	2nd	Central	Lost Conf. Final
1994–95	48	21	19	8	135	146	50	4th	Central	Lost Conf. Quarterfinal
1995–96	82	34	36	12	247	252	80	3rd	Central	Lost Conf. Quarterfinal
1996–97	82	30	44	8	230	273	68	6th	Central	Out of Playoffs
1997–98	82	30	43	9	194	237	69	6th	Central	Out of Playoffs
1998–99	82	45	30	7	268	231	97	2nd	Northeast	Lost Conf. Final
1999-2000	82	45	30	7	246	222	§100	1st	Northeast	Lost Conf. Semifinal

* *Name changed from St. Patricks to Maple Leafs.*
** *Name changed from Arenas to St. Patricks.*
*** *Season played in two halves with no combined standing at end.*
§ *Includes 3 points added for regulation-time tie games lost in overtime*

VANCOUVER CANUCKS

WHEN THE VANCOUVER CANUCKS played their first NHL game, a 3–1 loss to the Los Angeles Kings, on October 9, 1970, it marked the first major professional hockey game in the British Columbia city since the 1920s.

The Vancouver Millionaires had played some glorious hockey in the old Pacific Coast Hockey Association, a creation of brothers Frank and Lester Patrick. Featuring future Hockey Hall of Famers Cyclone Taylor, Frank Nighbor and Hugh Lehman, the Millionaires had won Vancouver's one and only Stanley Cup in 1915. The team was known as the Vancouver Maroons by the time pro hockey collapsed in the west in 1926. In the years that followed, Vancouver would be home to several minor pro teams and leagues.

In 1965, when the NHL announced plans to expand into

six additional hockey markets, Vancouver representatives were front-and-center seeking a franchise to represent western Canada. Fred Hume, former mayor of the city and owner of the minor-league Vancouver Canucks, announced that he would apply for a franchise.

Initially, Cyrus McLean, chairman of the board of B.C. Telephone, and the legendary broadcaster Foster Hewitt were named as the prospective owners of the Vancouver entry in the NHL. McLean had purchased the minor-league Canucks from Fred Hume, who was then in failing health. But, the McLean/Hewitt presentation to the league governors at a 1966 meeting in New York was sloppily prepared. Another reason the bid for a team failed may have stemmed from Toronto Maple Leafs owner Stafford Smythe's distaste for Vancouver after the city failed to approve a Smythe plan to build an arena on city-owned land a few months earlier. Yet another reason for denial may be attributed to Chicago Black Hawks' influential owner James D. Norris. It was said Norris would have preferred to see some of his personal friends involved in the Vancouver bid—men like Frank McMahon, Max Bell and Red Dutton, all powerful figures in sports and business in western Canada.

Meanwhile, Captain Harry Terry, president of the Pacific National Exhibition, had decided that a new rink should adorn the Vancouver Exhibition grounds. Terry knew that the federal government would come through with low-interest loans and grants for such an edifice because of new legislation promising funding of winter and summer fairs, etc. It was agreed that the federal and provincial governments would put up $2 million each; the city would be liable for another $1 million. Through private funding, the city would also commit another $1 million to the arena project.

Pacific Coliseum was dedicated on January 8, 1968. A month later, the first hockey game was played between the Montreal Oldtimers and the Western All-Stars. It attracted 16,511 fans—the largest crowd to see a game in Canada at that time. Obviously, Vancouver had a thirst for hockey. Now it hungered for an NHL team.

By the time of the follow-up NHL expansion in 1970–71, the Vancouver ownership picture had changed. Foster Hewitt was no longer involved and Cyrus McLean was thrust into a secondary role among the new majority owners, the Medicor Group of Minneapolis. The new ownership group had bought the minor-league Western Hockey League Vancouver Canucks and successfully negotiated with the NHL for an expansion franchise. At a cost of $6 million apiece, both the new Vancouver Canucks and the Buffalo Sabres were admitted into the league. In an effort to maintain the NHL's competitive balance, both Buffalo and Vancouver were placed in the East Division, despite the geographical contradiction.

The first general manager of the Canucks was Norman "Bud" Poile, former g.m. of the Philadelphia Flyers, who had entered the league in 1967. There was grumbling in some quarters when Poile was selected over Joe Crozier, who had run the minor-league Canucks with much success. Poile in turn selected Hal Laycoe, formerly of the Los Angeles Kings, to coach the Canucks in their inaugural season.

Despite a restrictive Expansion Draft procedure, the Canucks were relatively pleased with their new talent. Their first choice was Gary Doak, a former Boston Bruin who was thought of as a young defenseman with promise. Also chosen was Orland Kurtenbach, a tough forward and future team leader. Wayne Maki, who scored only seven goals in 66 games with Chicago and St. Louis, contributed a career-high 25 goals (and 63 points) in that first season—a pleasant surprise.

After the June, 1970, Expansion Draft, the immediate future of the Canucks—and the Sabres—depended largely on the Amateur Draft of junior players. A "spin of the wheel" at the June 9 draft meetings in Montreal determined that the Canucks would pick second. After Buffalo grabbed Gilbert Perreault, Poile selected defenseman Dale Tallon as the Canucks' first choice.

The Canucks finished their first season out of the playoffs, but achieved 56 points in a 78-game schedule. They finished seven points below their expansion cousins in Buffalo, but did manage to finish one point ahead of Detroit, an Original Six team, in the East Division standings.

The Canucks struggled through the next three seasons, finishing with 48, 53 and 59 points. Then, with a happy-go-lucky goaltender named Gary Smith in the net, obtained from Chicago with Jerry Korab in return for Tallon, they soared to first place in the Smythe Division with 86 points in their fifth season of 1974–75. In the playoffs, the Canucks lost in overtime to a powerful Montreal club in the fifth game of the quarterfinals.

Meanwhile, when the Medicor people stepped away from hockey and the club was put up for sale, the Griffiths family moved forward to rescue the organization. Frank Griffiths' wife Emily is often credited with making the final decision to purchase the club in 1974. Griffiths had been highly successful in the broadcast business and he genuinely wanted to put something back into the community.

The new ownership provided a degree of stability and things began to look up on the ice. By 1982 the Canucks found themselves sailing into the Stanley Cup finals. Coach Harry Neale, suspended for 10 games after challenging some fans in Quebec, wasn't around for the fun. His assistant, Roger Neilson, took the spotlight behind the bench, and captured headlines after he waved a white towel at referee Bob Myers in mock surrender during a playoff game in Chicago. Tiger Williams and the other Canucks followed suit, hoisting towels on their hockey sticks. The club was fined $10,000 for ridiculing the game officials. When the team returned home for the next game, almost every Vancouver fan waved a white towel enthusiastically.

The Canucks disposed of the Black Hawks and advanced to the finals against the Islanders, only to lose in four straight games. One day after their defeat, 100,000 Vancouverites honored their underdog heroes with a civic parade. Thomas Gradin, Stan Smyl and Ivan Boldirev were the team's top scorers, but the star of the surprising playoff run had been goaltender Richard Brodeur. Unfortunately, the success of 1982 did not carry over into subsequent seasons, as the team struggled annually to reach the playoffs and failed to advance beyond the first round when it did.

A turning point in team history occured on January 9, 1987, when the Canucks announced that Pat Quinn had accepted the position of general manager and president in Vancouver. Quinn was under contract as coach of the Los Angeles Kings at the time, and league president John Ziegler issued a fine of $310,000 (later reduced to $10,000 by the B.C. Supreme Court) for tampering. Quinn was not permitted to assume his dual roles until May 1, and soon after, hired Bob McCammon as his coach and Brian Burke as director of hockey operations. After collecting just 59 points during the 80-game 1987–88 season, the Canucks used the second selection overall in the 1988 Entry Draft to obtain Trevor Linden.

Linden entered the NHL as the league's youngest player in 1988–89 after having helped the Medicine Hat Tigers win consecutive Memorial Cup championships. He set a Canucks rookie record with 30 goals and was named Vancouver's most valuable player while finishing as the runner-up to New York Rangers defenseman Brian Leetch in voting for the Calder Trophy as rookie of the year. In the playoffs, Vancouver was beaten in the first round, but they were the only team to take the eventual Stanley Cup champion Calgary Flames to the seven-game limit, losing 4–3 in overtime in the final game.

On July 1, 1989, the Canucks signed former Soviet star Igor Larionov. The move came just a few days after Vancouver had selected Pavel Bure in the fourth round of the 1989 Entry Draft. Bure's draft eligibility was questioned, but was resolved in the Canucks' favor several months later. He joined the Canucks for the 1991–92 season, scoring 34 goals to break Linden's club rookie record. "The Russian Rocket" also became the first Canucks player to win a major postseason award when he was named the winner of the Calder Trophy. Pat Quinn, who had added coaching duties to his portfolio in January, 1991, joined Bure on the winners' podium as he captured the Jack Adams Award as coach of the year. With a record of 42–26–12, Quinn had guided the Canucks to first place in the Smythe Division for the first time since 1974–75.

It was another first-place finish in 1992–93, as two club records set the preceding season were shattered when the Canucks registered 47 wins and 101 points. Bure became the first Canuck to top 50 goals and 100 points, finishing the season with 60 and 110. On April 2, 1993, team owner Frank Griffiths was inducted into the Hockey Hall of Fame. A year later he passed away after a lengthy illness.

On April 13, 1994, Bure reached 60 goals for the second straight season. Later in the month, Bure scored at 2:20 of the second overtime to give Vancouver a 4–3 win over Calgary. It was the club's third straight overtime win in a come-from-behind, seven-game playoff victory. After eliminating the Dallas Stars, goalie Kirk McLean blanked the Leafs in consecutive playoff games en route to a five-game victory in the Campbell Conference finals. The Canucks advanced to the Stanley Cup finals for the second time in their history.

Greg Adams's goal at 19:26 of overtime gave the Canucks a 3–2 win over the Rangers in game one of the finals before New York reeled off three straight wins. Heading back to Madison Square Garden for game five, the Canucks stayed alive with a 6–3 victory, then forced a seventh game with a 4–1 win at home. Back in New York, the Rangers sweated out a 3–2 victory for their first Stanley Cup triumph in 54 years. Bure's 16 goals led all playoff performers.

In March, 1995, Seattle businessman John E. McCaw purchased a majority interest in the Canucks and also gained control of the new $163-million General Motors Place arena and the NBA's Vancouver Grizzlies.

The Canucks reunited former junior hockey teammates Alexander Mogilny and Pavel Bure when they acquired Mogilny from Buffalo for the 1995–96 season. He would go on to collect 55 goals and 107 points. On October 9, 1995, the Canucks played their first regular-season game at General Motors Place and lost 5–3 to Detroit. Mike Ridley scored the first regular-season goal in the new ice palace.

After the season, Quinn hired former Canadian national team coach Tom Renney to coach the Canucks. The team had difficulty adjusting to Renney's checking system, and the Canucks finished out of the playoffs. In June, 1997, the club introduced new team colors and a logo of a killer whale breaking through ice shaped in the letter C. Mark Messier was signed as an expensive free agent (three years at more than $20 million) and Linden chose to relinquish the captaincy to the newly acquired team leader. The 1997–98 season, however, proved to be a disaster. Quinn was fired after a poor start and Renney was released a short time later. Mike Keenan was brought in to coach and, by the end of January, was given the authority to make personnel changes. Keenan had feuded with Linden since his arrival and traded the popular player to the New York Islanders in February. Though Keenan's shakeups improved the team marginally, Vancouver still missed the playoffs for the second year in a row. In June, 1998, Brian Burke returned to the Canucks as the club's general manager.

Though Burke and Keenan stated for the record that they would have no problem working together, the club's poor record during the 1998–99 season saw former Colorado Avalanche boss Marc Crawford brought in to coach the Canucks in January. Just a few weeks earlier, Burke had dealt Pavel Bure to the Florida Panthers in a package deal that brought Ed Jovanovski to Vancouver. Bure had refused to suit up for the Canucks after demanding a trade in the offseason. The emergence of Adrian Aucoin was one bright spot during the season, as he led all NHL defensemen with 23 goals. Injuries would limit his effectiveness in 1999–2000.

After a decent start to the new season, the Canucks endured a dismal December that saw them win just twice in 11 games. Though the slump continued through January, the Canucks began to pick up the pace after the All-Star break. Newly acquired Felix Potvin started to flash the form he had displayed earlier in his career. Mark Messier returned from injuries and though there were rumors that he would be dealt at the trade deadline, the team was suddenly in playoff contention and Messier's leadership was key. Alexander Mogilny, however, was dealt to the New Jersey Devils for Brendan Morrison and Denis Pederson. Ultimately, the Canucks came up short of a playoff spot.

Despite the poor results of recent years, Canucks fans need look no further than the 1999 Entry Draft for hopes for the future. Though it cost him Bryan McCabe and the club's first-round choice in the 2000 draft, Burke was able to gain the second overall draft position in addition to Vancouver's third choice, which allowed him to select talented Swedish twins Daniel and Henrik Sedin, both of whom could begin their NHL careers in 2000–2001.

Vancouver Canucks Year-by-Year Record

Season	GP	W	L	T	GF	GA	Pts	Finish	Division	Playoff Results
1970–71	78	24	46	8	229	296	56	6th	East	Out of Playoffs
1971–72	78	20	50	8	203	297	48	7th	East	Out of Playoffs
1972–73	78	22	47	9	233	339	53	7th	East	Out of Playoffs
1973–74	78	24	43	11	224	296	59	7th	East	Out of Playoffs
1974–75	80	38	32	10	271	254	86	1st	Smythe	Lost Quarterfinal
1975–76	80	33	32	15	271	272	81	2nd	Smythe	Lost Prelim. Round
1976–77	80	25	42	13	235	294	63	4th	Smythe	Out of Playoffs
1977–78	80	20	43	17	239	320	57	3rd	Smythe	Out of Playoffs
1978–79	80	25	42	13	217	291	63	2nd	Smythe	Lost Prelim. Round
1979–80	80	27	37	16	256	281	70	3rd	Smythe	Lost Prelim. Round
1980–81	80	28	32	20	289	301	76	3rd	Smythe	Lost Prelim. Round
1981–82	80	30	33	17	290	286	77	2nd	Smythe	Lost Final
1982–83	80	30	35	15	303	309	75	3rd	Smythe	Lost Div. Semifinal
1983–84	80	32	39	9	306	328	73	3rd	Smythe	Lost Div. Semifinal

Season	GP	W	L	T	GF	GA	Pts	Finish	Division	Playoff Results
1984–85	80	25	46	9	284	401	59	5th	Smythe	Out of Playoffs
1985–86	80	23	44	13	282	333	59	4th	Smythe	Lost Div. Semifinal
1986–87	80	29	43	8	282	314	66	5th	Smythe	Out of Playoffs
1987–88	80	25	46	9	272	320	59	5th	Smythe	Out of Playoffs
1988–89	80	33	39	8	251	253	74	4th	Smythe	Lost Div. Semifinal
1989–90	80	25	41	14	245	306	64	5th	Smythe	Out of Playoffs
1990–91	80	28	43	9	243	315	65	4th	Smythe	Lost Div. Semifinal
1991–92	80	42	26	12	285	250	96	1st	Smythe	Lost Div. Final
1992–93	84	46	29	9	346	278	101	1st	Smythe	Lost Div. Final
1993–94	84	41	40	3	279	276	85	2nd	Pacific	Lost Final
1994–95	48	18	18	12	153	148	48	2nd	Pacific	Lost Conf. Semifinal
1995–96	82	32	35	15	278	278	79	3rd	Pacific	Lost Conf. Quarterfinal
1996–97	82	35	40	7	257	273	77	4th	Pacific	Out of Playoffs
1997–98	82	25	43	14	224	273	64	7th	Pacific	Out of Playoffs
1998–99	82	23	47	12	192	258	58	4th	Northwest	Out of Playoffs
1999-2000	82	30	37	15	227	237	*83	3rd	Northwest	Out of Playoffs

** Includes 8 points added for regulation-time tie games lost in overtime*

WASHINGTON CAPITALS

WHEN ABE POLLIN announced in 1972 that he planned to bring an NHL team to America's national capital, the Washington sportsman—who had headed his own construction firm—was advised by a Las Vegas bookmaker that the odds were 600–1 against him. Undaunted, Pollin personally delivered his application to the NHL office in Montreal on the day of the deadline to submit it. He made his presentation at the Board of Governors meetings in May, 1972. Aware that he was an underdog among 10 competitors for two expansion franchise openings, Pollin spent five days in a Montreal hotel, lobbying hockey's power brokers on Washington's behalf. His presentation was impressive enough to get him the franchise, on the condition that a suitable arena would be available by 1974–75.

Pollin, who already owned the NBA Baltimore Bullets, envisioned a new arena that would house both his major-league teams somewhere in the Capital District. But bickering and bureaucratic delays over who—or which city—would build the arena frustrated his plans. Finally he decided to construct the rink with his own funds, on a site he personally would choose. Pollin bypassed both Washington and Baltimore for a tract of former farmland in Landover, Maryland, where he planned to build an $18-million arena to be known as the Capital Centre.

The minimum target date for completion was thought to be two years. Instead, the arena was completed in 15 months. It seated 17,962 for hockey and boasted that every spectator was guaranteed a seat no further than 200 feet from center ice. Furthermore, at a time when other NHL arenas were not even considering premium seating, Pollin arranged for 40 luxury sky suites to be clustered along the upper levels.

For their first season, the Washington Capitals had former American Hockey League star Jimmy Anderson behind the bench and Hall of Famer Milt Schmidt as general manager. However, the Capitals were competing against the three-year-old World Hockey Association and the NHL expansion Kansas City Scouts for players. The result was a patchwork conspicuously lacking in talent on both the attack and defense. Washington's leading scorer, Tommy Williams (22 goals, 36 assists), was a Boston Bruins discard, and the supporting cast, with the notable exception of heroic goalie Ron Low, had even fewer credentials. The team's major hope was an African-Canadian named Mike Marson who had been the top scorer with the Sudbury Wolves in the Ontario Hockey Association. Marson was only the second black to reach the NHL, the first having been Willie O'Ree, who had played briefly for the Boston Bruins beginning in 1957–58. Marson finished as the Caps' third-leading scorer with 16 goals and 28 points.

Precisely how Washingtonians would respond to hockey was underscored on opening night, October 9, 1974, when a crowd of 17,500 turned out to see the New York Rangers defeat the Caps 6–3. Sellouts were not the norm, but there were enough substantial gates to persuade Pollin he had made a good move despite the fact that the team went just 8–67–5 and set records for fewest wins (minimum 70 games), most losses (since broken), most consecutive losses (17—later tied by San Jose) and most goals-against (446).

It would have been difficult for Pollin's puckchasers to do worse in their second season, but the improvement proved to be minuscule. The Capitals launched the season with Schmidt managing and coaching. After 36 games, his record was three wins, five ties and 28 losses, and Pollin made a wholesale change. Central Hockey League president Max McNab was imported as general manager, and McNab in turn hired Tom McVie to handle the team. The Caps finished the year 11–59–10. McVie, who won eight, tied five and lost 31, was retained to coach the following year.

McNab's regime was marked by a significant improvement. In 1976–77, the team's record leaped to a more reasonable 24–42–14 thanks to key acquisitions such as Guy Charron, Bryan Watson and Gerry Meehan. Unfortunately for McVie, the upward trend didn't continue. In 1977–78, the Caps' record dropped to 17–49–14.

"It was the low point in my career," McVie allowed. "It was my first NHL job and I gave my soul. I put the team ahead of my family and health. I took a day off once with my wife, and when I came back, Danny Belisle was in my coach's chair. They said, 'You're gone!' That taught me a lesson. Ever since then, I take my chair with me and never go on vacations."

With Belisle coaching in their fifth year of existence (1978–79), the Capitals registered their best record yet with 63 points (24–41–15)—but still missed the playoffs. Fleet little Dennis Maruk became an overnight sensation as he led the team in scoring with 90 points.

Belisle's tenure was short-lived, however. The victim of a poor start (4–10–2) in 1979–80, he was yanked after 16 games in favor of a youthful Gary Green. The 26-year-old Green was the youngest coach in NHL history.

Green produced the best-yet Capitals coaching record (23–30–11), but it was a case of too little, too late and a playoff berth eluded the franchise for the sixth consecutive year in spite of starry efforts by Maruk, Mike Gartner and Ryan Walter that offered hope for the future.

Green could not shake the Capitals' playoffs jinx in 1980–81, either. The club finished with a 26–36–18 record, but Green simply couldn't find the necessary mix. He lasted 13 games into the 1981–82 season, winning but a single game and losing a dozen before he got the hook. Assistant g.m. Roger Crozier handled one game (a tie) until Bryan Murray could be named the head coach.

Still, the ongoing playoff drought finally compelled Pollin to make another change in his general staff. On August 30, 1982, McNab was dropped as general manager in favor of 33-year-old David Poile, who became the youngest g.m. in NHL history. David's father, Norman "Bud" Poile, had been an NHL star and later a top hockey executive, and David had done his front office basic training with Atlanta and Calgary before moving to Landover.

On September 10, 1982, shortly after training camp started, Poile sent defenseman Rick Green and forward Ryan Walter to Montreal for defensemen Rod Langway and Brian Engblom as well as forwards Doug Jarvis and Craig Laughlin. Few deals for any team at any time have ever produced a more dramatic impact. The former Canadiens infused the Capitals with a winning spirit that was translated into the club's first season above .500.

Washington finished third in the Patrick Division with a record of 39–25–16 before losing their first playoff series to the Stanley Cup champion New York Islanders. Langway won the Norris Trophy as the NHL's best defenseman and Scott Stevens made an instant impact as a rookie defenseman. With Langway leading the way on the ice and in the dressing room, Washington improved to second place (48–27–5) in 1983–84. The captain again won the Norris Trophy, Doug Jarvis the Selke Trophy as the NHL's best defensive forward, the goaltending tandem of Al Jensen and Pat Riggin the Jennings Trophy for having the fewest goals against, and to top off Washington's biggest year yet for awards, Murray took the Jack Adams Award as coach of the year. Still, the defending champion Islanders once more eliminated them from the Stanley Cup run, four games to one.

Murray's effervescent coaching continued to keep the Capitals near the top of the Patrick Division. In 1984–85, they finished third overall with 101 points and featured two 50-goal scorers in Bobby Carpenter (53) and Mike Gartner (50). "It was a positive development," says Poile. "But, the problem was that too much of our scoring was concentrated in those two people."

After winning 50 regular-season games for the first time in franchise history in 1985–86, Murray appeared to have a Cup-worthy team. Carpenter, Gartner, Dave Christian and Bengt Gustafsson paced the attack while Al Jensen provided grade-A goaltending. Heavy favorites to defeat the Rangers in the playoffs, the Capitals were upset four games to two and by now had taken on the distinct image of playoff chokers, a state of affairs that moved Poile to action.

Once again he executed an arresting deal. On New Year's Day, 1987, he delivered Carpenter and a second-round draft choice to the Rangers for Kelly Miller, Mike Ridley and Bob Crawford. Carpenter was a bust on Broadway, while Ridley and Miller excelled in a dual capacity as scoring threats and penalty killers. Remarkably, defenseman Larry Murphy led Washington in points (81); Gartner's 41 goals were tops in that department.

Still nothing changed with regard to the playoffs. After a 38–32–10 season, the Caps encountered their traditional nemesis, the Islanders, in the divisional semifinals. The series wound down to an excruciatingly close seventh game at Capital Centre. When the fans finally departed, it was six hours after the opening face-off and they had witnessed the most memorable game of the 1980s—a quadruple-overtime thriller in which the Isles ultimately prevailed, 3–2. It was at 1:56 a.m. on Easter Sunday when Pat LaFontaine launched a turnaround slapshot that put the Caps out of their misery. Washington had suffered another premature season's end.

The pattern of playoff futility continued through the Bryan Murray regime in spite of heartening regular-season efforts. Finally, the 1989–90 campaign brought a breakthrough. After going 18–24–4 in the first half of the season, Poile replaced head coach Bryan Murray with his brother, Terry. This time there was an improvement: Washington reached the third round of the playoffs before losing to Boston in four straight games.

Meanwhile, the face of the Capitals was changing. In 1990–91, rookie Peter Bondra showed flashes of brilliance behind usual point producers Mike Ridley and Michal Pivonka. The blue line was solidified with Kevin Hatcher and smooth-skating Calle Johansson. In 1994, the Caps acquired playmaker Joe Juneau from Boston for defenseman Al Iafrate. Rounding out the new look was goalie Jim Carey, who posted a stunning 18–6–3 record in his rookie year, then went 35–24–9 with nine shutouts the year after and captured the 1996 Vezina Trophy. The final step in the process of change saw the Capital Centre renamed the U.S. Air Arena.

Despite the many alterations, the Caps' legendary lack of luck in the playoffs continued. Every year that Washington failed to reach the Stanley Cup finals brought Poile under more fire from the hometown media. Still, he retained Pollin's confidence until the end of the 1996–97 season. This time, for the first time in 15 years, the Caps didn't even get to the playoffs.

Poile executed a late-season deal that at first seemed to save his job when he sent the suddenly struggling Carey and young forwards Anson Carter and Jason Allison to Boston for top playmaker Adam Oates, former Philadelphia captain Rick Tocchet and one-time Conn Smythe Trophy-winning goalie Bill Ranford. But, it wasn't enough. Pollin replaced Poile with former left wing George McPhee on June 9, 1997. (As many suspected, Poile wasn't out of work long. By the end of the summer, he had been hired as g.m. of the expansion Nashville Predators.) Also released was head coach Jim Schoenfeld, who had replaced Terry Murray in 1993–94.

The first major coup of the McPhee era was hiring Ron Wilson as head coach. Wilson had coached the Anaheim Mighty Ducks to their first playoff berth in 1996, then guided Team USA to a victory at the World Cup of Hockey. A dispute with Anaheim high command paved the way for Wilson's arrival on Capital Hill, where he discovered a major change in the Capitals' ambience. After playing in Landover for 24 years, the team moved into a spanking-new arena in downtown Washington. Commercially named MCI Center, the rink signaled a gamble that Pollin could lure the suburban fans from Maryland and Virginia into the inner city that had been off-limits to many of them in the past, but the change of venue was temporarily disappointing in terms of attendance. Crowds were smaller than anticipated until the Capitals turned on the heat in the homestretch of 1997–98 and reached the playoffs.

Under Wilson, the Caps suffered through a season pockmarked by injuries but still finished third in the Atlantic Division with a 40–30–12 record and eliminated Boston in the first round of the playoffs. At least part of the success came from Wilson's unorthodox coaching: using popsicle sticks to illustrate plays and having water pistol fights to stimulate his skaters in practice.

Wilson guided Washington into the second playoff round against Ottawa and the battle between the two national capitals went to the American city in five games. Goaltender Olaf Kolzig had enjoyed an excellent season in 1997–98. His 33 wins, five shutouts and 2.20 goals-against average had all ranked among the best in the game, but in the postseason, "Olie the Goalie" truly came into his own. He outplayed Dominik Hasek as Washington beat Buffalo to win the Eastern Conference championship and advance to the Stanley Cup finals for the first time. But, the ultimate mission would not be accomplished. Though Wilson scoffed at speculation that the Detroit Red Wings would complete the Stanley Cup's fourth consecutive sweep, the defending champions did just that and retained their title with four straight wins.

The 1998–99 season proved to be a tremendous disappointment as the Capitals tumbled out of the playoffs with just 68 points, finishing ahead of only the Tampa Bay Lightning in the newly created Southeast Division. Injuries limited the effectiveness of Peter Bondra and Adam Oates, though defenseman Sergei Gonchar helped pick up the slack with 21 goals in just 53 games. Longtime fan favorite Dale Hunter was traded late in the season, but returned to Washington in a front-office capacity for 1999–2000.

The Capitals changed hands on May 12, 1999, when Pollin sold the franchise to a small investment group headed by America Online president Ted Leonsis. The struggle continued on the ice through the first half of the 1999–2000 season. At the Christmas break, Washington stood 11th in the Eastern Conference. And then the team started to win. Though Peter Bondra struggled for goals (he would only score 21), Chris Simon picked up much of the slack by almost doubling his previous best with 29. Sergei Gonchar scored 18 times. Adam Oates led the club with 71 points and reached milestones with his 300th career goal and 900th assist. Sparking the turnaround that would see Washington win the Southeast Division with 102 points was the play of Olaf Kolzig. "Olie the Goalie" recaptured his form of 1997–98 and then some. He won the Vezina Trophy after setting club records for games (73), minutes (4,371) and, of greatest importance, wins with 41. His 2.24 goals-against average and .917 save percentage also ranked high among the league leaders. However, the Capitals ran into Pittsburgh and a red-hot Jaromir Jagr in the first round of the playoffs.

Apparently fully recovered from injuries that had sidelined him for much of the last half of the regular season, Jagr recorded four assists to lead the Pittsburgh Penguins to a 7–0 victory in the playoff opener. The Capitals never seemed to recover. Pittsburgh raced out to a 3–0 series lead and eliminated Washington in five games.

Washington Capitals Year-by-Year Record

Season	GP	W	L	T	GF	GA	Pts	Finish	Division	Playoff Results
1974–75	80	8	67	5	181	446	21	5th	Norris	Out of Playoffs
1975–76	80	11	59	10	224	394	32	5th	Norris	Out of Playoffs
1976–77	80	24	42	14	221	307	62	4th	Norris	Out of Playoffs
1977–78	80	17	49	14	195	321	48	5th	Norris	Out of Playoffs
1978–79	80	24	41	15	273	338	63	4th	Norris	Out of Playoffs
1979–80	80	27	40	13	261	293	67	5th	Patrick	Out of Playoffs
1980–81	80	26	36	18	286	317	70	5th	Patrick	Out of Playoffs
1981–82	80	26	41	13	319	338	65	5th	Patrick	Out of Playoffs
1982–83	80	39	25	16	306	283	94	3rd	Patrick	Lost Div. Semifinal
1983–84	80	48	27	5	308	226	101	2nd	Patrick	Lost Div. Final
1984–85	80	46	25	9	322	240	101	2nd	Patrick	Lost Div. Semifinal
1985–86	80	50	23	7	315	272	107	2nd	Patrick	Lost Div. Final
1986–87	80	38	32	10	285	278	86	2nd	Patrick	Lost Div. Semifinal
1987–88	80	38	33	9	281	249	85	2nd	Patrick	Lost Div. Final
1988–89	80	41	29	10	305	259	92	1st	Patrick	Lost Div. Semifinal
1989–90	80	36	38	6	284	275	78	3rd	Patrick	Lost Conf. Final
1990–91	80	37	36	7	258	258	81	3rd	Patrick	Lost Div. Final
1991–92	80	45	27	8	330	275	98	2nd	Patrick	Lost Div. Semifinal
1992–93	84	43	34	7	325	286	93	2nd	Patrick	Lost Div. Semifinal
1993–94	84	39	35	10	277	263	88	3rd	Atlantic	Lost Conf. Semifinal
1994–95	48	22	18	8	136	120	52	3rd	Atlantic	Lost Conf. Quarterfinal
1995–96	82	39	32	11	234	204	89	4th	Atlantic	Lost Conf. Quarterfinal
1996–97	82	33	40	9	214	231	75	5th	Atlantic	Out of Playoffs
1997–98	82	40	30	12	219	202	92	3rd	Atlantic	Lost Final
1998–98	82	31	45	6	200	218	68	3rd	Southeast	Out of Playoffs
1999-2000	82	44	26	12	227	194	*102	1st	Southeast	Lost Conf. Quarterfinal

** Includes 2 points added for regulation-time tie games lost in overtime*

CHAPTER 32

Year-by-Year

NHL Regular-season and Playoff Summaries

Eric Zweig

IN A SERIES OF MEETINGS held between November 22 and November 26, 1917, team owners from the National Hockey Association met to form a new league, the National Hockey League. Former NHA secretary Frank Calder was chosen as the new circuit's first president. Notably absent from the meetings was Toronto owner Eddie Livingstone, who was not popular among his fellow owners; instead, the NHL's Toronto franchise was given to the directors of the Arena Gardens.

In addition to Toronto, the NHL's charter members were the Montreal Canadiens, Montreal Wanderers, Ottawa Senators and Quebec Bulldogs. The Bulldogs, however, elected not to operate their team until the 1919–20 season and the Wanderers withdrew from the league after just six games when their home arena burned down.

1917–18

The star of the NHL's first season was Joe Malone of the Canadiens, who had 44 goals in just 20 games.

Clubs played a split schedule. The Canadiens won the first half, but were defeated in a playoff for the NHL championship by the leaders of the second half, the Torontos—or the Arenas as they are more commonly known.

In the rival Pacific Coast Hockey Association, Gordie Roberts and Bernie Morris led the Seattle Metropolitans to a first–place finish, but league scoring champion Cyclone Taylor and the Vancouver Millionaires knocked them out in the playoffs, earning the right to travel east to play Toronto for the Stanley Cup.

The Stanley Cup series went the full five-game limit, with Toronto emerging victorious. Incidentally, the PCHA still played seven-man hockey (using a rover) and also allowed limited forward passing, which was not added in the NHL until the following season. To accommodate for the differences, the teams alternated between eastern and western rules during the series. Each team won the games played under its rules.

1918–19

The NHL fielded only three teams in the 1918–19 season and a 20-game split schedule was drawn up, with the winners of the two halves to meet for the league title. The Montreal Canadiens, led by Newsy Lalonde (who would claim the league scoring title with 23 goals and 10 assists), were the class of the NHL's first half, posting a 7–3 record. In the second half, the Ottawa Senators had won seven of eight games when the season was cut short because the Toronto Arenas ran into financial difficulties and had to withdraw from the league.

Left with only two teams, the NHL decided to stage a best-of-seven series between Ottawa and Montreal to determine a league champion. The Canadiens proved to be surprisingly easy winners of this showdown, taking the first three games and winning the series in five.

The NHL championship entitled Montreal to play the Seattle Metropolitans of the Pacific Coast Hockey Association for the Stanley Cup. Reversing the results of the previous season, Seattle had finished second in the PCHA before knocking off the first-place Vancouver Millionaires in the playoffs. The Victoria Aristocrats once again missed the playoffs.

The Stanley Cup finals were played in Seattle, with the Mets taking the opener 7–0 under western rules that included the use of the rover. As was the custom, alternate games were played under eastern and western rules. The series proved hard-fought and evenly matched, as each team had recorded two wins and a tie through five games. The deciding game was scheduled for April 1, but the onset of a worldwide Spanish influenza epidemic intervened. Several Canadiens players were too sick to continue and the series was abandoned. Canadiens star "Bad Joe" Hall lost his life to the illness four days later. It was the only year that no Stanley Cup champion would be declared.

1919–20

The 1919–20 season saw the NHL regrouping after a rocky 1918–19 campaign. On the eve of the regular season, the Toronto club found new owners, was renamed the St. Patricks and rejoined the NHL. Meanwhile the Quebec Bulldogs, one of the NHL's founding members, finally exercised its franchise and iced a team. A number of players who'd taken jobs elsewhere returned to Quebec City, most notably Joe Malone. Though Quebec would post a dismal 4–20 record, Malone was the league's top scorer with 39 goals and 10 assists for 49 points. On January 31, 1920, Malone also set an NHL record that still stands when he scored seven goals in a single game in the Bulldogs' 10–6 victory over Toronto.

The NHL again played a split season, but this year the Ottawa Senators negated the need for a playoff by winning both halves. Led by stars Frank Nighbor, Cy Denneny, Jack Darragh, Punch Broadbent and goalie Clint Benedict, the Senators were 9–3 in the first half and 10–2 in the second.

The competition was much tighter in the Pacific Coast Hockey Association, where just two wins separated the three teams. The Seattle Metropolitans clinched first place on the second-last night of the season and finished 12–10. The Vancouver Millionaires went 11–11, while the Victoria Aristocrats again missed the playoffs with a 10–12 record.

Vancouver beat the Mets 3–1 in game one in Seattle, but lost 6–0 at home as the Metropolitans advanced to the Stanley Cup finals with a 7–3 victory in the two-game, total-goals series.

The Stanley Cup finals were slated for Ottawa, but warm weather forced the final two games to be moved to the artificial ice of Toronto's Arena Gardens. Despite the disruption, the Senators prevailed with a 6–1 victory in the fifth and deciding game of the best-of-five affair.

1920–21

The first franchise shift in NHL history took place as the Quebec Bulldogs moved to Hamilton and became the Tigers. The change of venue did little to improve the team's fortunes: Though other NHL teams contributed players to bolster Hamilton's roster, the Tigers finished last in both halves of the split season, going 3–7 and 3–11.

The defending Stanley Cup champion Ottawa Senators were the best team in the NHL's first half, posting an 8–2 record, but they slumped to third place in the second half. Former Senator Sprague Cleghorn helped Toronto post a 10–4 record to win the second half, edging out the 9–5 Canadiens. Toronto's Babe Dye led the league with 35 goals, one better than Ottawa's Cy Denneny. Montreal's Newsy Lalonde had 32 goals, but his 11 assists gave him 43 points to lead the league. Despite poor support, Hamilton's Joe Malone was fourth in both goals and points, with 28 goals and nine assists. It was defense, though, that made the difference in the playoffs, as Ottawa twice blanked Toronto, 5–0 and 2–0, for an easy win in the total-goals series. Clint Benedict was brilliant in net, while Eddie Gerard and George Boucher were solid on defense.

Ottawa traveled west to face the Vancouver Millionaires of the Pacific Coast Hockey Association for the Stanley Cup. For the second straight year, the PCHA had gone down to the wire. The Millionaires were 13–11–0 to Seattle's 12–11–1. The Victoria Aristocrats were in their usual third-place spot at 10–13–1, but the debut this season of Frank Fredrickson offered hope for future improvement. Vancouver crushed the Metropolitans 7–0 and 6–2 in the playoffs.

The first game of the Stanley Cup series drew a record crowd of 10,000 fans, as Vancouver beat Ottawa 3–1. The Senators, though, were able to retain the trophy with a victory in five games that were witnessed by an estimated 51,000 fans.

1921–22

Professional hockey prospered as the 1920s roared. In November 1921 the Montreal Canadiens were sold to Leo Dandurand, Joseph Cattarinich and Louis Letourneau for a reported $11,000. Bigger news came out of the Prairies with the rise of a third professional league to rival the NHL and Pacific Coast Hockey Association. The Western Canada Hockey League boasted teams in Calgary, Edmonton, Regina and Saskatoon.

The NHL abandoned the split-season format for 1921–22, adopting the PCHA's playoff scheme that saw the first- and second-place teams meet for the league championship. The defending Stanley Cup champion Ottawa Senators, who added King Clancy and Frank Boucher to a star-studded lineup, were again the NHL's best with a 14–8–2 record. Ottawa's Punch Broadbent led the NHL in scoring with 32 goals and 14 assists and established an NHL record that still stands today, scoring in 16 consecutive games. Still, the second-place Toronto St. Pats pulled off an upset in the two-game, total-goals playoff.

In the west, the PCHA had another tight finish, with Seattle going 12–11–1, Vancouver finishing 12–12–0 and Victoria 11–12–1. The Millionaires then defeated the first-place Metropolitans with a pair of 1–0 shutouts by Hugh Lehman. Edmonton was the first-place club in the WCHL's inaugural season, but the Regina Capitals, having first knocked off the Calgary Tigers in a playoff to determine second place, defeated the Eskimos to claim the first league championship.

Regina and Vancouver met in a two-game, total-goals series to determine the western challenger for the Stanley Cup. After a 2–1 win, Regina was shut out 4–0 and it was the Millionaires who earned the right to go to Toronto to play for the Stanley Cup. The final went a full five games before the St. Patricks emerged victorious. Babe Dye of Toronto was the series star with nine goals.

1922–23

A controversial deal marked the preseason in 1922–23. Veteran star Newsy Lalonde of the Montreal Canadiens was sold to the Western Canada league's Saskatoon Crescents without being offered on waivers to other NHL clubs. The dispute was resolved when NHL president Frank Calder ruled Lalonde would be considered traded for a top Saskatoon prospect named Aurel Joliat. Joliat became an instant star in Montreal and helped the Canadiens edge out the Toronto St. Pats for second place and a playoff spot behind the Ottawa Senators.

Ottawa won the playoff opener 2–0 despite the dirty play of Montreal defensemen Sprague Cleghorn and Bill Couture. The pair were suspended from game two by Canadiens owner Leo Dandurand. Still, Montreal hung on in the second game, taking a 2–0 lead, but Cy Denneny scored for Ottawa and gave the Senators a 3–2 victory in the total-goals series.

Out west, the Pacific Coast Hockey Association finally made the switch to six-man hockey, abandoning the rover position. The move allowed the PCHA and the WCHL to play an interlocking schedule, though the two leagues would maintain separate standings and playoffs. Vancouver finished first in the PCHA, but the real story was in Victoria where Frank Fredrickson's scoring exploits led the Aristocrats to the playoffs for the first time in 10 years. Still, it was Vancouver, now known as the Maroons, who won the league title in the playoffs. Newsy Lalonde won the WCHL scoring title, though his Saskatoon club finished last. Edmonton's 19–10–1 record had the Eskimos comfortably in first place, though they needed overtime to beat Regina 4–3 in the two-game, total-goals playoff.

The NHL champion Senators first defeated Vancouver three games to one in a best-of-five affair, then swept the WCHL champion Eskimos 2–0 in a best-of-three series to claim their third Stanley Cup title in four years.

1923–24

The defending Stanley Cup champion Ottawa Senators were under new ownership for the 1923–24 season, and moved into the new 11,000-seat Ottawa Auditorium.

Longtime star and captain Eddie Gerard was forced to retire because of illness, but the Senators were still the class of the NHL, cruising to a first-place finish with a 16–8–0 record. Ottawa's Frank Nighbor was the first winner of the Hart Trophy—donated by Dr. David Hart, father of Montreal Canadiens coach and manager Cecil Hart, to recognize the league's most valuable player.

The Canadiens introduced a talented newcomer named Howie Morenz this season, and finished comfortably ahead of Toronto and Hamilton (who finished last for the fourth straight year) to make the playoffs. Montreal then surprised Ottawa with victories of 1–0 and 4–2 to claim the NHL championship.

On the other side of the continent, the Pacific Coast Hockey Association and Western Canada Hockey League once again played an interlocking schedule, with Seattle proving to be the PCHA's best. As in the NHL, there was a playoff upset as second-place Vancouver eliminated Seattle. In the WCHL, future NHL star Bill Cook led the loop in scoring, but his Saskatoon team finished out of the playoffs behind Calgary and Regina. Calgary was the only first-place team to survive the postseason.

Canadiens owner Leo Dandurand wanted the two western champions to face each other in a playoff to send only one team east, but Frank Patrick of the PCHA insisted the NHL champs play both Vancouver and Calgary. Montreal gave in and swept both teams in two straight games. Howie Morenz scored seven goals in the Canadiens' six playoff games as Montreal won its first Stanley Cup championship since the club was part of the old NHA in 1916.

1924–25

There were changes throughout professional hockey in 1924–25. The NHL expanded to six teams, adding its first American club, the Boston Bruins, and a second Montreal team (later known as the Maroons) that would play its home games at the new Montreal Forum. In the west, the Seattle Metropolitans folded, marking the end of the Pacific Coast Hockey Association. Vancouver and Victoria joined Calgary, Edmonton, Regina and Saskatoon in a revamped Western Canada Hockey League.

With expansion, the NHL extended its season from 24 to 30 games and changed the playoff structure. The first-place team would now receive a bye into the finals and meet the winner of a series between the second- and third-place teams. The Hamilton Tigers, who'd placed last in each of the previous four seasons, went 19–10–1 this year to finish one point ahead of the Toronto St. Pats for first place. But the Tigers players were upset that the season had been lengthened by 25 percent without a comparable increase in their salaries and they refused to take part in the playoffs unless they received an extra $200 each. President Frank Calder suspended the players and announced that the winner of a playoff between the Canadiens and St. Patricks would receive the new Prince of Wales Trophy as the NHL's regular-season champion. Montreal won and earned the right to play for the Stanley Cup.

In the west, Victoria had added Seattle stars Jack Walker, Frank Foyston and Hap Holmes to a roster that already boasted future Hall of Famer Frank Fredrickson, and though they only finished third, the Cougars (as they were now known) beat Saskatoon and Calgary in the playoffs to earn a chance at hockey's top prize. Victoria then beat Montreal to become the last non-NHL team to win the Stanley Cup.

1925–26

On September 22, 1925, the NHL held its first meeting in the United States, when a special session was convened in New York to discuss the admission of a new expansion team for that city. The Hamilton Tigers were being dropped and the New York Americans would take Hamilton's place and employ its players. Another new team, the Pittsburgh Pirates, also joined the league for 1925–26, bringing membership to seven teams. The Pirates were stocked with players from the American amateur champion Pittsburgh Yellow Jackets and included such stars as Lionel Conacher and Roy Worters.

Coached by Odie Cleghorn, Pittsburgh finished in third place and made the playoffs in its first season. The Pirates were just ahead of the much-improved Boston Bruins, but the Montreal Maroons showed even greater improvement. Young stars like Babe Siebert and Nels Stewart (who won the NHL scoring title and the Hart Trophy) helped lift the Maroons into second place, beat Pittsburgh in the playoffs, then knock off the first-place Ottawa Senators for the NHL championship.

In the Western Canada Hockey League, poor fan support in Regina saw the franchise transferred to Portland, Oregon. Consequently, the word "Canada" was dropped from the league's name. The defending Stanley Cup champion Victoria Cougars limped through the first half of the season, but came alive late to finish third. Victoria then knocked off Saskatoon and Edmonton to claim the Western Hockey League championship.

Victoria came east to Montreal in what proved to be the last Stanley Cup finals involving a team from a league other than the NHL. The Maroons won the best-of-five series in four games, claiming the first of what would be many Stanley Cup championships won on Forum ice.

1926–27

With American expansion proving successful, the NHL prepared to add three more U.S. teams for the 1926–27 season. Much of that growth was at the expense of the Western Hockey League which, lacking the larger, richer markets of the east, closed its doors. The NHL's new Chicago franchise, the Black Hawks, bought the entire roster of the WHL's Portland Rosebuds. Similarly, the Victoria Cougars were sold to eastern interests and joined the NHL as the Detroit Cougars.

The Bruins acquired defenseman Eddie Shore from the Edmonton Eskimos, while the newly formed New York Rangers used such WHL stars as Frank Boucher and brothers Bill and Bun Cook to hit the ground running in the NHL. Conn Smythe was originally hired to build, coach and manage the Rangers, but a clash with management saw him ousted in favor of WHL impresario Lester Patrick. Smythe bought the Toronto St. Patricks later in the 1926–27 season and renamed them the Maple Leafs.

With league membership now at 10 teams, the NHL was split into Canadian and American Divisions. Boston, Pittsburgh, Chicago, Detroit and the Rangers comprised the American Division, while Ottawa, Toronto, the Montreal Maroons and Canadiens and, oddly enough, the New York

Americans made up the Canadian Division. The top three teams from each division would make the playoffs, with the first-place teams earning a bye into their division finals.

The Rangers were first in the American Division, but Boston beat Chicago before upsetting New York to become the first U.S.-based NHL team to reach the Stanley Cup finals. Ottawa won the Canadian Division, then beat the Bruins to claim their fourth Cup title of the decade.

1927–28

The NHL was now hockey's undisputed major professional league and business was booming. As a sign of the league's growing confidence, it did away with salary cap restrictions and increased the transfer fee for players on waivers from $2,500 to $5,000. There was, however, one cause for concern. The powerhouse Ottawa Senators, playing in what was now the league's smallest market, were losing money despite their Stanley Cup success, and were forced to sell Hooley Smith to the Montreal Maroons.

Stars from the NHL's early days were now retired or reaching the ends of their careers and a new generation of superstars was taking their place. The New York Rangers had Frank Boucher and Bill and Bun Cook. Boston boasted Eddie Shore, Dit Clapper and Cooney Weiland. The Maroons would soon team Hooley Smith with Nels Stewart and Babe Siebert to form the powerful S Line, but the Montreal Canadiens had the greatest star of all in Howie Morenz.

Morenz led the NHL in scoring in 1927–28 with 33 goals and 18 assists in the 44-game regular season and won the Hart Trophy as the Canadiens finished first in the Canadian Division. The Habs were upset, however, by the rival Maroons in the playoffs.

In the American Division, Boston finished first, but the second-place Rangers beat the Pittsburgh Pirates and eliminated the Bruins to advance to the Stanley Cup finals. Because a circus was booked into Madison Square Garden, all five games of the series were played at the Montreal Forum. The second game provided a legendary moment when 44-year-old Ranger coach Lester Patrick took over in goal after an injury to Lorne Chabot. Patrick's Rangers won the game 2–1 in overtime and went on to become only the second American team (after the 1917 Seattle Metropolitans) to win the Stanley Cup with a victory in the full five games.

1928–29

In 1919–20, the league's four clubs had averaged nearly five goals each per game, but during the ensuing decade an emphasis on defense meant only the top-scoring teams approached three per game. But 1928–29 was the year the NHL reached its offensive low point—the 10 teams scored fewer than 1.5 goals per game, with last-place Chicago netting just 33 in 44 games. Ace Bailey of the Toronto Maple Leafs led the league with just 22 goals and 10 assists, and Nels Stewart of the Maroons, with 21, was the only other man in the league to score more than 20.

Meanwhile, all but two of the league's first-string goalies recorded at least 10 shutouts. The Montreal Canadiens' George Hainsworth led the way, setting a record that still stands with 22 shutouts, and posting a remarkable 0.92 goals-against average on his way to his third consecutive Vezina Trophy win.

The playoff format was altered this year. The top three teams from both the Canadian and American divisions still made the playoffs, but each second- and third-place finisher would meet its counterpart from the other division in a two-game, total-goals series. The winners would compete in a best-of three-series for a berth in the Stanley Cup finals. Meanwhile, the two first-place teams played a best-of-five series for the other spot in the finals.

The Canadiens and Bruins finished atop their respective divisions and engaged in a close-checking semifinal. Boston recorded 1–0 victories in each of the first two games, as Tiny Thompson turned away every shot he faced and Cooney Weiland scored both Bruin goals. They completed the sweep with a 3–2 victory in game three. The Rangers knocked off the Americans and then the Toronto Maple Leafs to provide Boston's opposition in the first all-American Stanley Cup finals. The best-of-three set went to the Bruins in two straight as Boston celebrated its first Stanley Cup victory.

1929–30

After the previous season's offensive drought, the NHL made significant rule changes to increase scoring in 1929–30. The most important new rule allowed forward passing in the offensive zone—previously it had only been allowed in a team's neutral and defensive zones. But the changes quickly proved too effective, as forwards began to station themselves in front of the opposition goal and wait for passes. So, on December 21, 1929, the NHL legislated that no attacking player would be allowed to precede the puck across the blue line. The modern offside rule was born.

Bruins coach Art Ross had schooled his players well in the new rules and Boston was by far the best team in the NHL, posting a 38–5–1 record for an .875 winning percentage that still remains a league record. Cooney Weiland's league-leading 43 goals nearly doubled Ace Bailey's high of 22 the year before, and his 73 points were by far a new league record. Linemate Dit Clapper had 41 goals, while Dutch Gainor, the third member of the Dynamite Line, recorded 31 assists, second-best in the league. Boston's Tiny Thompson won the Vezina Trophy, though his 2.19 goals-against average was nearly double what it had been the year before. Veteran goaltender Clint Benedict chose to retire from the NHL late in the season after a crude leather facemask failed to adequately protect his broken nose.

The Bruins cruised into the Stanley Cup finals after sweeping the Montreal Maroons to open the playoffs. The Canadiens provided the opposition after beating the Black Hawks and Rangers. Boston was heavily favored, but Montreal swept the best-of-three series, handing the Bruins consecutive losses for the first time all season. Partly as a result of the surprising sweep, the Stanley Cup finals would be increased to a best-of-five affair in the future.

1930–31

The Great Depression began to take its toll on the NHL by the 1930–31 season. Even in the best of times, the Ottawa Senators had been finding the economic going rough. Now, the situation was even worse. Several Senators were sold off prior to the start of the season, most notably King Clancy, who was purchased by the Toronto Maple

Leafs for $35,000 and two players. Toronto immediately improved to second place in the Canadian Division, while Ottawa slumped to last place with a 10–30–4 mark.

The Pittsburgh Pirates had also been been in trouble for several years, and, after a 5–36–3 season in 1929–30, the franchise was moved to Philadelphia. Renamed the Quakers, the relocated team proved even worse that year as they limped through a 4–36–4 campaign.

At the other end of the spectrum, the Boston Bruins were the NHL's best for the second year in a row, finishing atop the American Division with a 28–10–6 record. League-leading scorer Howie Morenz powered the Montreal Canadiens to top spot in the Canadian Division and earned the Hart Trophy as MVP for the second time.

In a rematch of the previous season's Stanley Cup finals, the Canadiens beat Boston in five games to open the playoffs. The Chicago Black Hawks made their first appearance in the finals after knocking off the Toronto Maple Leafs and the New York Rangers.

The series opened before huge crowds at the Chicago Stadium, where the teams split two games before concluding the series at the Montreal Forum. The Black Hawks won game three before the Canadiens rallied to defend their Cup title by winning the fourth and fifth games.

1931–32

The NHL's fortunes between the two world wars matched those of the countries it played in. The league had grown from four to 10 teams in the space of just four seasons in the Roaring Twenties, but this season would see it suffering from the impact of the Great Depression. One of the casualties was the Philadelphia Quakers, who closed shop after only one year following five seasons in Pittsburgh as the Pirates. More shocking was the decision of the Ottawa Senators to withdraw from play. Ottawa was a founding member of the NHL, had won its first Stanley Cup in 1903 (long before the NHL even existed) and had won the Cup four times in the 1920s.

Meanwhile, Conn Smythe's Toronto Maple Leafs seemed to be the picture of optimism. Against long odds, Conn Smythe had built his hockey palace, Maple Leaf Gardens, which opened on November 12, 1931, with a disappointing 2–1 loss to Chicago. The Leafs rebounded to win a club-record 23 games (23–18–7) in the newly expanded 48-game season and their Kid Line of Joe Primeau, Busher Jackson and Charlie Conacher emerged as full-fledged superstars. Jackson led the league with 53 points on 28 goals and 25 assists and Primeau's 37 assists topped the loop, while Conacher's 34 goals tied him with Bill Cook for top spot in the NHL.

Toronto finished second behind the Montreal Canadiens in the Canadian Division, but advanced to the Stanley Cup finals with playoff victories over the Chicago Black Hawks and Montreal Maroons. Meanwhile, the Canadiens were eliminated by the American Division-winning New York Rangers. The Rangers had a week off before meeting Toronto in the Stanley Cup finals, but the rest was of no benefit. Toronto took the opener 6–4 in New York, won game two 6–2 in Boston after the circus forced the series out of Madison Square Garden, then completed the sweep with a 6–4 victory at home. It was Toronto's first Stanley Cup victory since the St. Patricks won it 10 years before.

1932–33

After a one-year absence, the Ottawa Senators returned to the NHL for the 1932–33 season, but finished last in the league with an 11–27–10 mark. In Toronto, the defending Stanley Cup champions climbed to top spot in the Canadian Division, and starting this year, Foster Hewitt's broadcasts from Maple Leaf Gardens could be heard nationally over a network of 20 radio stations. The Montreal Maroons placed second to Toronto, while their rink-mates, the Canadiens, edged the New York Americans for the final playoff spot.

In the American Division, the Rangers, Boston and Detroit (now under new ownership and renamed the Red Wings) battled for top spot, with only Chicago out of the running. The Black Hawks fired two coaches before settling on Tommy Gorman. A dispute over rent at the Chicago Stadium saw the team spend the first month of the season at the old Chicago Coliseum. Eddie Shore won the Hart Trophy for the first of four times in his career as the Bruins finished on top of the division. Detroit finished second despite an identical 25–15–8 record. The Rangers finished third but came on strong in the postseason, knocking off the Canadiens and Red Wings to advance to the Stanley Cup finals.

In the battle of first-place finishers, Toronto beat Boston in five games. The series finalé on April 3 was the longest game to date in NHL history, as Ken Doraty scored at 4:46 of the sixth overtime period to give the Maple Leafs a 1–0 victory. The game ended at 1:50 a.m. on the 4th, but the Leafs were in New York later that night to open the Stanley Cup finals. The Rangers breezed to a 5–1 victory and won the series in four games, avenging their sweep at the hands of the Leafs the previous spring.

1933–34

As the Great Depression worsened, so did its effect on the NHL. Although the Detroit Red Wings were now safely under the ownership of multimillionaire James Norris and his son James D. Norris of Olympia Incorporated, the Ottawa Senators were on shaky financial ground after 1932–33, and so were the New York Americans. NHL president Frank Calder quickly put down rumors that the teams might merge. Meanwhile in Montreal, it was beginning to look as if there was room for only one team, as the Montreal Maroons were having trouble drawing fans to the Forum, the rink they shared with the Canadiens.

Despite league-wide economic hardship, Boston's Eddie Shore refused to accept a pay cut after winning the Hart Trophy and sat out the first three games of the season before agreeing to a $7,500 contract. Shore would be in the hockey headlines again a month later after one of the darkest incidents in NHL history.

On December 12, 1933, the Toronto Maple Leafs were in Boston to play the Bruins. The game got chippy and Shore was tripped by King Clancy after a rink-long rush. Shore retaliated angrily by checking the first Leaf he could see, Ace Bailey, from behind. Bailey's skull was fractured as he fell over backward and his head hit the ice. It was 10 days before doctors were even sure the wounded Maple Leaf would live. As it was, Bailey's hockey career was over. Shore was suspended for 16 games—one-third of the 48-game schedule. On February 14, 1934, an NHL All-Star Game was played to benefit Bailey and his family.

The Chicago Black Hawks, led by the exploits of goaltender Charlie Gardiner, won their first Stanley Cup championship. Gardiner played in the Bailey benefit game and also earned the Vezina Trophy that year for the second time. Shortly after Chicago's Stanley Cup victory, Gardiner died of a brain tumor. He was 29 years old.

1934–35

The Ottawa Senators finally succumbed to financial woes prior to the 1934–35 season, as the once proud franchise abandoned the Canadian capital to become the St. Louis Eagles. The change of venue did not improve the club's fortunes, however, and, after finishing last with an 11–31–6 record, the club folded for good. Meanwhile, driven by hard economic times, the NHL lowered its salary cap to $62,500 per team and a maximum of $7,000 per player. The move didn't help the New York Americans players, who complained that they weren't being paid.

Because of the salary cap, the Montreal Canadiens were forced to trade aging superstar Howie Morenz to the Chicago Black Hawks. Goalie Lorne Chabot was included in the deal to replace the late Charlie Gardiner. Chabot would enjoy a career year and win the Vezina Trophy. The Canadiens received Lionel Conacher and two other players, then they dealt Conacher to the Montreal Maroons, where he was reunited with coach Tommy Gorman, who, despite winning the Stanley Cup in 1934, had been fired by the Black Hawks.

On the ice, Charlie Conacher led the league in scoring and his Toronto Maple Leafs easily outdistanced the Maroons for top spot in the Canadian Division. The Boston Bruins, who had fallen to last place the previous year, regained their usual perch atop the American Division standings and Eddie Shore took home the Hart Trophy for a second time. The Lady Byng Trophy, for sportsmanship, was won by Frank Boucher of the New York Rangers. It was the seventh time in eight years Boucher had won the award and, in recognition of that fact, he was given permanent possession of the original trophy.

In the playoffs, Toronto knocked off Boston to advance to the Stanley Cup finals, while the Maroons defeated the Black Hawks and Rangers before upsetting the Leafs for the league championship.

1935–36

Despite their Stanley Cup win, the Montreal Maroons continued to struggle at the box office. So did the Canadiens, who were sold by Leo Dandurand and Joseph Cattarinich to the Canadian Arena Company prior to the 1935–36 season.

A dispersal draft was held to distribute the players belonging to the defunct St. Louis Eagles, and the Boston Bruins got a diamond in the rough in Bill Cowley who would blossom into a superstar. Boston also traded Marty Barry to the Detroit Red Wings, where he teamed with Larry Aurie and Herbie Lewis to form one of the league's top lines.

The Wings emerged as the best in the league this season, winning the American Division with a 24–16–8 record. The Maroons won the Canadian Division with the nearly identical mark of 22–16–10. The teams were so evenly matched in the first game of their playoff series that it took until 16:30 of the sixth overtime period for Mud Bruneteau to beat Lorne Chabot for the game's only goal.

Not only had Detroit's Normie Smith recorded a shutout in the longest game in NHL history, he went on to blank the Maroons for 60 minutes more in game two—another 1–0 victory—then allowed only one goal in a 2–1 win that swept the series. Smith's goals-against average for the series was a minuscule 0.20.

The New York Americans made the playoffs for the first time since 1929 and beat the Chicago Black Hawks in their first series before falling to the Toronto Maple Leafs. It was the Leafs' fourth trip to the finals in five years, but they would come away empty-handed for the third year in a row as the Red Wings earned their first NHL championship.

1936–37

The Toronto Maple Leafs unveiled several new players for the 1936–37 season. Center Syl Apps would earn honors as rookie of the year, as his playmaking skills blended perfectly with first-year sniper Gordie Drillon. Goalie Turk Broda also made his debut this season. In Montreal, it was an old name that made headlines, as Howie Morenz returned to the Canadiens after stints with the Black Hawks and Rangers. Morenz took his place at center between his old linemates Aurel Joliat and Johnny Gagnon. The three were now past their prime, but the Canadiens were showing much improvement over the previous year's last-place finish, thanks largely to youngster Toe Blake, who shouldered most of the offensive load.

Meanwhile, reaching the playoffs the previous season had done little to help the New York Americans' bottom line; the NHL was forced to take over operation of the club before the start of the season.

On January 28, 1937, Morenz caught the tip of his skate in the boards at the Montreal Forum, badly breaking his leg above the ankle. On March 8, the hockey world was stunned to learn that Morenz had died in hospital. A pulmonary embolism was given as the cause of death. Thousands of fans filed past Morenz's body, which lay in state at the Forum, and thousands more lined the route of the funeral procession that took him to the cemetery.

Despite the loss of their great superstar, the Canadiens won the Canadian Division, but were knocked out of the playoffs by the Red Wings. Detroit then became the first American franchise to win consecutive Stanley Cup titles when they defeated the New York Rangers.

1937–38

The NHL had lost its first great superstar the year before and so the 1937–38 season began with a memorial All-Star Game in honor of Howie Morenz. A team made up of Montreal Canadiens and Maroons took on the best from the NHL's other six teams. The event raised over $11,000 for the Morenz family.

Nels Stewart, who'd overtaken Morenz as the NHL's all-time career goal-scoring leader the year before, notched his 300th goal in 1937–38, while Boston's Eddie Shore returned from a serious back injury the previous year to win the Hart Trophy for the fourth and final time.

Shore's Bruins were the best in the NHL in the regular season, winning the American Division over a strong New York Ranger squad. The Chicago Black Hawks snuck into the playoffs with a weak 14–25–9 third-place finish. The

Toronto Maple Leafs won the Canadian Division behind the stellar play of scoring leader Gordie Drillon and runner-up Syl Apps. Boston's stronger defense had them favored to beat Toronto in the playoffs, but Turk Broda's stellar goaltending sparked an upset as the Leafs advanced to the Stanley Cup finals for the fifth time in seven years.

Despite a poor regular season (and spared a last-place finish only by Detroit's shocking collapse from first to worst), the Black Hawks came alive in the playoffs. Chicago upset the Canadiens and Americans, though their win over New York cost them the services of netminder Mike Karakas, who suffered a broken toe. Ex-NHLer Alfie Moore took over in goal and stunned the Leafs with a 3–1 victory in game one. Moore was then declared ineligible and Chicago lost game two 5–1 with farmhand Paul Goodman between the pipes. Karakas subsequently returned, wearing a specially fitted skate, and the Black Hawks won the next two games to take the Stanley Cup. Two facts distinguished the Chicago win: they were the first club with a losing record to win the Cup, and they did it with a roster made up of an equal number of Canadian and American players.

1938–39

The Montreal Maroons' last-place finish in 1937–38 proved the final nail in their coffin. They suspended operations prior to the 1938–39 season, leaving the NHL with just seven teams. As a result, the league reverted to a single division for the first time since 1926–27. Six of the seven teams would qualify for the postseason: the first- and second-place clubs would play a seven-game semifinal, while the third- and fourth-place teams would meet in a best-of-three quarterfinal, as did the fifth- and sixth-place finishers. The quarterfinal winners would then compete in a three-game semifinal series. The Stanley Cup finals would be a best-of-seven series.

The Detroit Red Wings replaced goaltender Normie Smith at the start of the season. Manager Jack Adams purchased Tiny Thompson from the Boston Bruins. Thompson had won the Vezina Trophy for the fourth time the year before—then a league record—but Bruins manager Art Ross knew he had a worthy replacement in Frank Brimsek. "Mr. Zero," as he became known, led the league with 10 shutouts, won the Vezina Trophy with a 1.56 goals-against average, and was named to the First All-Star Team as the Bruins cruised to a first-place finish.

Though the 36–10–2 Bruins had 10 more victories and 16 more points than the second-place Rangers, it took Boston the full seven games to eliminate New York in the semifinals. Mel Hill earned the nickname "Sudden Death" by scoring three overtime goals in the series. The third-place Leafs beat the Americans and Red Wings to reach the finals, then lost to the Bruins in five games as the Stanley Cup returned to Boston for the first time in 10 years.

1939–40

War broke out in Europe before the NHL started the 1939–40 season, but the league was determined to continue operations with as little disruption as possible. Economic conditions were beginning to improve with the end of the Great Depression, but the New York Americans were still strapped for cash. As a result, they peddled their best player, Sweeney Schriner, to the Toronto Maple Leafs for cash and four players, including the aging Busher Jackson. Jackson would team with ex-Kid Line mate Charlie Conacher on an Americans roster that had become something of a haven for fading stars. Former Bruin great Eddie Shore would play out his career alongside the two ex-Leafs, but the Americans would tumble to sixth place, ahead of only the Montreal Canadiens, who were in the cellar for the first time since 1925–26.

The loss of Shore did not hinder the Bruins in 1939–40, as Kraut Line stars Milt Schmidt, Woody Dumart and Bobby Bauer finished 1–2–3 in the league scoring race. Teammate Bill Cowley came in fifth. The defending Stanley Cup champions posted the best record in the NHL for the third consecutive season, but were upset by the second-place New York Rangers in six games in their semifinal. New York's opposition in the finals was third-place Toronto, who had advanced with wins over the Chicago Black Hawks and Detroit Red Wings.

The Stanley Cup series opened in New York, with the Rangers winning the first two games. As happened so many times to the Rangers over the years, the circus at Madison Square Garden forced the rest of the series to be played in Toronto. The Leafs won games three and four, but a pair of overtime victories gave the Rangers their third Stanley Cup title in 13 seasons. It would be 54 years before the Rangers won the Stanley Cup again.

1940–41

Determined to rebuild after their last-place finish in 1939-40, the Canadiens hired a new coach—Dick Irvin, who had enjoyed great success with the Toronto Maple Leafs in the 1930s. Though he would help the Canadiens qualify for the playoffs this season, the return to glory in Montreal was still several seasons in the offing.

At the other end of the spectrum, the Boston Bruins—despite failing to repeat as Stanley Cup champions in 1940—kept their team intact for 1940–41. General manager Art Ross's patience was rewarded with a fourth consecutive first-place finish and the team's second Stanley Cup title in three years. Bill Cowley led the NHL in scoring with 62 points, 18 more than the five players who finished tied for second. Bruins teammates Eddie Wiseman, Bobby Bauer, Roy Conacher and Milt Schmidt all joined Cowley in the top 10, while Frank Brimsek led the league with six shutouts. The Bruins set an NHL record with a 23-game undefeated streak, and they set another record on March 4, 1941, when they fired 83 shots against the Black Hawks. Chicago goalie Sam LoPresti made 80 saves in a 3–2 loss.

In the playoffs, Boston defeated the second-place Maple Leafs in a thrilling seven-game semifinal. Third-place Detroit supplied the opposition for the Stanley Cup after the Red Wings eliminated the New York Rangers and Chicago. Boston then beat Detroit in the first four-game sweep in Stanley Cup history. The victory would prove to be Boston's last until 1970.

1941–42

After the 1940–41 season, the NHL turned over ownership of the New York Americans to club manager Red Dutton. He tried to spark a local rivalry by changing the team's name to the Brooklyn Americans. Dutton even moved to the borough, and encouraged his players to do the same. Although the club practiced in Brooklyn, games would continue to be played at Madison Square Garden. Still, the cash-strapped team was forced to sell off its few remaining stars, and the 1941–42 season would prove to be the Amerks' swan song.

The rival New York Rangers enjoyed much more success than their crosstown cousins. The team had slumped after their 1940 Stanley Cup victory, but rebounded to first place in 1941–42. Bryan Hextall led the way, winning the NHL scoring title. His 54 points were two more than runner-up and linemate Lynn Patrick, and four more than his other linemate, Phil Watson, who finished fourth in the scoring race. The Rangers held off the Toronto Maple Leafs in a tight race for top spot. The Boston Bruins finished a close third despite losing their entire Kraut Line to military service midway through the season.

In the playoffs, the Maple Leafs upset the Rangers in the semifinals, but dropped the first three games of the finals to the Detroit Red Wings. Then coach Hap Day shook up his roster, benching Gordie Drillon and Bucko McDonald in favor of Don Metz and Hank Goldup, and the team roared back to win the next four games and the Stanley Cup. Though this was their seventh trip to the finals since 1932, it was the Maple Leafs' first Stanley Cup title since then.

1942–43

With the departure of the Brooklyn Americans, the National Hockey League, after growing to as many as 10 teams, was reduced in 1942–43 to what would become known as the Original Six. There were concerns that even the six surviving teams would be sidelined if the increased Canadian and American participation in World War II forced the cancelation of hockey, but such fears were put to rest by NHL President Frank Calder. On September 28, 1942, he announced that government officials in both the United States and Canada had decided the game should continue "in the interest of public morale."

Still, with at least 80 players serving in the armed forces, the NHL's clubs faced severe manpower shortages. The Boston Bruins had lost their entire Kraut Line of Milt Schmidt, Woody Dumart and Bobby Bauer, while seven Toronto Maple Leaf players were in the army. The New York Rangers were hit particularly hard, losing brothers Neil and Mac Colville, Alex Shibicky, Jim Henry and Art Coulter to wartime service.

On November 21, three weeks after the start of the 1942–43 season, the league announced regular-season overtime was being discontinued because of wartime travel restrictions. It was the last major decision president Frank Calder would ever make, as he died of heart failure on February 4, 1943. Former New York Americans player and manager Mervyn "Red" Dutton succeeded him as the NHL's second president.

Offense increased during the 1942–43 season, and the Chicago Black Hawks' Doug Bentley led the NHL with 73 points (tying Cooney Weiland's single-season record set back in 1929–30). Though the Detroit Red Wings failed to produce a top-10 scorer, they finished first in the regular-season standings and captured the Stanley Cup, avenging the previous year's defeat when they had lost to Toronto after leading the series three games to none.

1943–44

The National Hockey League Board of Governors made a decision at the league meetings in September 1943 that has since been interpreted as the beginning of hockey's modern era: they voted to add a red line at center ice. Players could now pass the puck from their own zone into the neutral zone, as far as the red line. The idea was to reduce the number of offside calls, thus opening up the defensively oriented style of play that dominated. It was hoped that a game that offered more offense would keep customers clicking through the turnstiles while NHL owners suffered through both player and cash shortages during World War II.

Military obligations continued to take talent from NHL rosters during the 1943–44 campaign. The Stanley Cup champion Detroit Red Wings lost nine starters to military service, while the New York Rangers, already badly depleted, lost five more players, including top scorer Lynn Patrick. The Rangers suffered through a horrendous 6–39–5 season in 1943–44, allowing a then-record 310 goals in just 50 games. Goaltender Ken "Tubby" McAuley's 6.20 goals-against average is still the highest single-season mark in league history among goalies appearing in at least 30 games.

The Rangers' woefully inept defense played a part in a league-wide offensive explosion. Four teams scored 200 or more goals, and three players, led by Herb Cain's 82 points for the Boston Bruins, eclipsed the old single-season scoring record of 73 points. On February 3, 1944, Detroit's Syd Howe scored six goals in a single game. The Montreal Canadiens led the league with a record 234 goals and also posted the NHL's best defensive record as they cruised home as regular-season champions, 25 points ahead of their closest competitor, the Detroit Red Wings.

The Habs' Rocket Richard scored 12 goals in nine postseason games—including five in one game against the Toronto Maple Leafs—to lead the Canadiens to their first Stanley Cup title in 14 years.

1944–45

With the war in Europe winding down, players who had performed military service slowly began trickling back to NHL rosters in 1944–45, though most teams were still thinly stocked. Picking up the slack were several talented newcomers who made their NHL debuts this season, including Ted Lindsay and Harry Lumley with the Detroit Red Wings, Toronto's Frank McCool, and Bill Moe with the New York Rangers. The undisputed star of the 1944–45 season, though, was Rocket Richard.

Scoring at a season-long pace of a goal per game, the Canadiens right wing enjoyed a record-setting night on December 28, 1944, scoring five goals and adding three assists in a 9–1 Montreal victory over the Detroit Red Wings. Later in the season, Richard surpassed Joe Malone's single-season scoring record of 44 goals (set during the NHL's 22-game inaugural season of 1917–18) when he scored his 45th on February 25, 1945. By season's end, Richard had scored 50 goals in 50 games.

The Rocket was not the only record-setting player during the 1944–45 campaign. His linemate Elmer Lach set a new standard with 54 assists en route to winning the league scoring title with 80 points. Syd Howe's 515th career point during that season put him ahead of Nels Stewart as the NHL's all-time leader, while his Detroit Red Wings teammate Flash Hollett became the first defenseman to score 20 goals in a season.

Montreal's Bill Durnan won the Vezina Trophy for the second consecutive time, as the Canadiens once again finished first. In the playoffs, however, the Canadiens were the targets of a semifinal upset by the Toronto Maple Leafs. Leaf goalie Frank McCool, 1945's rookie of the year, opened the finals with three consecutive shutouts as the Leafs held on to beat Detroit in seven games and win the Stanley Cup.

1945–46

With World War II over, more than 40 players returned from military service to their respective NHL rosters for the start of training camp in 1945. The Boston Bruins welcomed back Milt Schmidt, Woody Dumart, Bobby Bauer and goaltender Frank Brimsek. Art Ross, deciding to concentrate on his role as general manager, turned over the coaching honors to Dit Clapper, who would also continue to play for Boston. The revitalized Bruins battled the Montreal Canadiens for much of the 1945–46 season before settling for second place.

The New York Rangers welcomed back stars Lynn and Muzz Patrick, Neil Colville and goalie Chuck Rayner. Their lineup also boasted rookie of the year Edgar Laprade, but hard times continued as the club finished last in every major statistical category for the third year in a row and wound up in last place again. The going was also tough in Toronto, where the Maple Leafs opened the season without goaltender Frank McCool. Even Turk Broda's return from the military in January 1946 could not salvage a season that saw Toronto become just the second NHL team to miss the playoffs the year after winning the Stanley Cup.

The Montreal Canadiens endured a scoring slump by the Punch Line of Rocket Richard, Elmer Lach and Toe Blake, as well as an injury to goalie Bill Durnan, yet they once again finished first in the regular season. Their top trio regained its scoring touch in the playoffs, finishing 1–2–3 in postseason scoring as the Canadiens won the Stanley Cup for the second time in three seasons, beating Boston in the final.

1946–47

Postwar reconstruction of the NHL began in earnest prior to the 1946–47 season. Clarence Campbell was named the NHL's third president, succeeding Red Dutton, rosters were replenished with returning veterans, and the regular season was extended from 50 to 60 games.

In Toronto, Frank Selke, who had guided the Maple Leafs during Conn Smythe's military service, lost a power struggle with the team's board of directors and left to run the Montreal Canadiens. Fully in charge of his team again, Smythe cleared out a number of aging stars to make room for youngsters like Bill Barilko, Sid Smith, Calder Trophy-winner Howie Meeker and Garth Boesch, and hockey's newest dynasty was formed.

Max Bentley, playing on the Chicago Black Hawks' Pony Line with brother Doug and Bill Mosienko, led the NHL with 72 points, and Punch Line star Rocket Richard regained his scoring touch to pot 45 goals. Milt Schmidt and Woody Dumart of Boston's Kraut Line also returned to the NHL's top 10 scorers in 1946–47. On March 16, 1947, Billy Taylor of the Detroit Red Wings collected a record seven assists in a single game, while the Leafs' Howie Meeker set a rookie record on January 8 with five goals in one contest.

The Leafs finished the regular season in second place behind Montreal and knocked off the Red Wings in five games in the semifinals. Toronto dropped the opening game of the finals 6–0 to the Canadiens before winning the Stanley Cup in six games.

1947–48

The 1947–48 NHL season began with the All-Star Game, an idea which had been proposed the previous season. A collection of NHL greats defeated the defending Stanley Cup champion Toronto Maple Leafs 4–3. Unfortunately, this spirited game was marred by an injury to Chicago Black Hawks star Bill Mosienko, who suffered a fractured ankle. A similar injury later in the season ended the career of Toe Blake, thus breaking up the Montreal Canadiens' much-feared Punch Line. It was also the end of an era in Boston, where Bobby Bauer's retirement broke up the Kraut Line. Meanwhile Detroit saw the rise of a new offensive force when Red Wings coach Tommy Ivan teamed second-year forward Gordie Howe on a line with Ted Lindsay and Sid Abel, creating the Production Line.

In Toronto, Conn Smythe was not satisfied with the defending Stanley Cup champions' depth. He wanted a third center to complement Syl Apps and Teeder Kennedy, a need made all the more pressing by Apps's talk of retirement. The Leafs opened the season undefeated in six games, but after a loss to the Rangers on November 2, Smythe orchestrated the biggest trade in NHL history, sending Bud Poile, Bob Goldham, Ernie Dickens, Gaye Stewart and Gus Bodnar to the Chicago Black Hawks for perennial All-Star and slick stickhandler Max Bentley, along with rookie Cy Thomas.

With Bentley bolstering their attack, the Leafs soared to a 32–15–13 record and a first-place finish. In the playoffs, Toronto downed the Bruins in five games before sweeping the Detroit Red Wings for their second consecutive Stanley Cup championship.

On a dark note, two of the league's finest playmakers, Billy Taylor of the Rangers and Boston's Don Gallinger, were handed lifetime suspensions for gambling.

1948–49

The 1948–49 season opened on a sour note for the New York Rangers. The team was enjoying a productive training camp when Bill Moe, Edgar Laprade, Buddy O'Connor, Frank Eddolls and Tony Leswick were all injured in a car accident. Three of the five sustained only minor injuries, but O'Connor and Eddolls would be lost for at least two months. The Rangers opened the season 6–11–6, costing Frank Boucher his coaching job. Lynn Patrick took over behind the bench, but the Rangers still wound up missing the playoffs by 10 points.

Joining New York on the sidelines come postseason were the Chicago Black Hawks, who finished fifth in the six-team league despite the fact that teammates Roy Conacher and Doug Bentley were a comfortable 1–2 atop the NHL scoring leaders. For much of the season, it appeared the two-time Cup-champion Maple Leafs would miss the playoffs. Hurt by the retirements of Nick Metz and Syl Apps, and besieged by injuries all season, only a late-season collapse by the Rangers and Hawks got the Leafs into the playoffs. The brilliant goaltending of Bill Durnan, who had 10 shutouts on the season—including a modern-day record four in a row at one stretch—carried the Montreal Canadiens to a third-place finish. The Detroit Red Wings easily topped the Boston Bruins to wind up first in the regular-season standings.

In the playoffs, the Leafs came to life. Healthy for the first time all season, Toronto downed Boston in five games, then swept Detroit for the second straight year to win their third consecutive Stanley Cup title. They were the first fourth-place regular-season finisher to win the trophy.

1949–50

The Detroit Red Wings won eight of their first 10 games to start the 1949–50 season and they never looked back. Despite a surprising trade that saw them swap star defenseman Bill Quackenbush to the Boston Bruins for four players, and an injury to goalie Harry Lumley, the Red Wings were the best in hockey. The Quackenbush trade allowed Red Kelly to take a more prominent role on the club's defense, while the Lumley injury let Detroit preview goaltender Terry Sawchuk. Offensively, the Production Line of Ted Lindsay, Sid Abel and Gordie Howe finished 1–2–3 in league scoring.

In Montreal, goalie Bill Durnan won the Vezina Trophy for the sixth time in seven seasons, and Rocket Richard returned to form with 43 goals, but the Canadiens finished a distant second to Detroit in the standings. The Toronto Maple Leafs were third, while the disappointing Bruins dropped to fifth and missed the playoffs. Despite a lineup that featured five 20-goal scorers, the Chicago Black Hawks finished last and had problems drawing fans.

The surprise of the 1949–50 season was the Broadway revival of the New York Rangers. A well-balanced attack and the stellar goaltending of Chuck Rayner, who earned the Hart Trophy as most valuable player, led the Rangers to a fourth-place finish and just their second postseason appearance since 1943.

In the playoffs, the Red Wings knocked off Toronto despite a severe head injury to Gordie Howe. The Rangers defeated Montreal in the semifinals, but were forced to play the entire final series against Detroit on the road because the circus was booked into Madison Square Garden. Still, the Rangers pushed the Red Wings to seven games before Pete Babando (acquired in the Quackenbush trade) scored in the second overtime to give Detroit the Stanley Cup.

1950–51

The Detroit Red Wings were defending Stanley Cup champions and clear favorites to repeat, but there were changes in the Motor City for 1950–51. In the biggest trade in NHL history, Detroit sent Harry Lumley, Jack Stewart, Al Dewsbury, Don Morrison and Pete Babando to the Chicago Black Hawks for Jim Henry, Bob Goldham, Gaye Stewart and Metro Prystai. Lumley had been the NHL's winningest goalie the previous two seasons, but was deemed expendable with the emergence of Terry Sawchuk.

During the offseason, the NHL decided to maintain the 70-game schedule introduced the year before, and Detroit took advantage of the extra 10 games to rewrite the record book, winning 44 games and posting 101 points—the first 100-point season in NHL history. Sawchuk was in net for each of the victories, setting an individual record, and he won the Calder Trophy as rookie of the year. Gordie Howe bounced back from a head injury suffered in last year's playoffs to win the Art Ross Trophy with an all-time NHL high of 86 points. Despite their great success, however, the Red Wings were eliminated in six games in the semifinals by the third-place Montreal Canadiens.

Under new coach Joe Primeau, the Toronto Maple Leafs had battled Detroit all season long and established a club record with 95 points. The Maple Leafs knocked off the fourth-place Boston Bruins in five games, then beat Montreal in five for their fifth Stanley Cup victory in seven years. Each of the five games in the finals went to overtime, with Bill Barilko scoring the series-winner. Three months later, Barilko disappeared on a fishing trip to northern Ontario. The wreckage of the plane that contained his body would not be discovered until 1962. By strange coincidence, the Leafs would not win the Cup again until that same year.

1951–52

For the second year in a row, the Detroit Red Wings made changes to a talented roster and came out ahead. Six players were sold to the Chicago Black Hawks, with Jack Adams convinced that rookie Alex Delvecchio and newcomer Tony Leswick would help pick up the slack. Adams was right, as the Red Wings cruised to their second straight 44-win season and easily finished atop the NHL standings with 100 points. Gordie Howe earned both the Hart and Art Ross trophies, while Terry Sawchuk won the Vezina Trophy with a 1.90 goals-against average and 12 shutouts.

The Montreal Canadiens finished in second place in 1951–52. The team was without Rocket Richard due to injuries for much of the season, but Bernie "Boom Boom" Geoffrion bolstered the offense with 30 goals and was named rookie of the year. Dickie Moore joined the team in December and recorded 33 points in 33 games. The Toronto Maple Leafs, struggling to score goals throughout the season, finished four points behind Montreal for third place. The Boston Bruins claimed the last playoff spot, while the New York Rangers and Chicago Black Hawks finished fifth and sixth respectively. On the last night of the regular season, Chicago's Bill Mosienko put his name in the record book by scoring three goals in 21 seconds during a 7–6 win over the Rangers.

The Red Wings proved to be even better in the playoffs than during the regular season, sweeping Toronto in the semifinals and then sweeping Montreal in the finals to capture the Stanley Cup in just eight games, the minimum number required. Terry Sawchuk did not allow a single goal on home ice during both rounds of the playoffs, posting a 0.62 goals-against average and recording four shutouts in postseason play.

1952–53

Big changes in Chicago this season saw the Black Hawks make the playoffs for the first time since 1946. On September 11, 1952, the three owners of the Chicago Stadium—James Norris, Sr., James D. Norris, and Arthur Wirtz—acquired control of the hockey team. They lured Sid Abel away from the Detroit Red Wings to become a playing coach, and they dealt goalie Harry Lumley to the Toronto Maple Leafs for Al Rollins, Ray Hannigan, Gus Mortson and Cal Gardner.

Despite the loss of Abel, the Red Wings remained the NHL's best team. Alex Delvecchio joined Gordie Howe and Ted Lindsay on the team's top line, which remained as productive as ever. Gordie Howe netted 49 goals during the 1952–53 season and won the Art Ross Trophy with a league-record 95 points. Detroit finished the regular season in first place for the fifth straight season, while the Montreal Canadiens again finished second. Rocket Richard scored his 325th career goal during the season, surpassing Nels Stewart as the NHL's all-time leader.

There was concern in Toronto that the Maple Leafs were getting old as the team struggled to score goals for the second year in a row. The fears proved well-founded as the Leafs missed the playoffs, finishing two points back of Chicago and the Boston Bruins, who were tied with 69 points. The Rangers dropped to the basement, but the debuts of Gump Worsley, Andy Bathgate, Dean Prentice and Harry Howell provided reason for optimism at Madison Square Garden.

Chicago's return to the postseason lasted seven games before Montreal, with Jacques Plante starring in goal, eliminated them. The Bruins then stunned the Red Wings in a six-game semifinal, but fell to the Canadiens in five in the Stanley Cup finals.

1953–54

A familiar cast of characters led the Detroit Red Wings to their sixth first-place finish in a row. Gordie Howe won the Art Ross Trophy for the fourth consecutive year as the NHL's leading scorer. Terry Sawchuk registered 12 shutouts and a 1.92 goals-against average and Red Kelly became the first winner of the James Norris Memorial Trophy as the NHL's best defenseman.

After a prolonged courtship, the Montreal Canadiens finally signed Jean Beliveau this season, but injuries would limit him to just 44 games. Injuries also sidelined Dickie Moore, while a pair of suspensions forced the Habs to do without Boom Boom Geoffrion for 16 games. Rocket Richard led the league with 37 goals, and his 67 points were second only to Gordie Howe as Montreal still managed to finish the regular season in second place.

King Clancy took over the coaching reins in Toronto and, emphasizing defense, led the Maple Leafs back into the playoffs with a third-place finish. Goalie Harry Lumley had 13 shutouts and a 1.86 goals-against average to win the Vezina Trophy. The Boston Bruins grabbed fourth place, while the New York Rangers and Chicago Black Hawks missed the playoffs. The Black Hawks were a woeful 12–51–7 and yet goalie Al Rollins still managed to compile a decent 3.23 goals-against average and was rewarded with the Hart Trophy as the player most valuable to his team.

In the playoffs, the Red Wings, still stinging from last year's postseason disappointment, were not be denied. They downed Toronto in five games, while Montreal swept Boston. The finals came down to a seventh game, with Detroit's Tony Leswick scoring the Stanley Cup winner on a bad bounce in overtime for a 2–1 victory.

1954–55

Conn Smythe stepped aside as general manager of the Toronto Maple Leafs prior to the 1954–55 season, turning over the job to Hap Day. Boston's general manager Art Ross also retired after running the Bruins since their inception in 1924. In Chicago, Sid Abel resigned as Black Hawks' coach amid fears the franchise might fold and Tommy Ivan gave up coaching the Detroit Red Wings to become Chicago's general manager. Elmer Lach retired in Montreal and Jacques Plante took over from Gerry McNeil in the Canadiens' goal, but there would be a much bigger story involving the Habs this season.

Though he was the NHL's greatest goal scorer, Rocket Richard had never won the Art Ross Trophy. He appeared destined to capture his first scoring title in 1954–55, until his legendary temper got the better of him. On March 13, 1955, Richard punched linesman Cliff Thompson after a stick-swinging incident with Boston's Hal Laycoe. NHL president Clarence Campbell suspended Richard for the season's final three games and all of the playoffs. When Campbell showed up at the Montreal Forum on the night of March 17, a riot broke out. Only a radio plea by Richard the following day was able to restore peace to the city.

At the time of his suspension, the Rocket led Boom Boom Geoffrion by two points in the NHL scoring race and the Canadiens were two points up on Detroit for top spot in the standings. With Richard out, Geoffrion passed him for the scoring title and Detroit claimed first place for the seventh consecutive season. In the playoffs, the Red Wings swept Toronto, while Montreal beat Boston in five. In the finals, the Red Wings again got the better of the Canadiens, winning the Stanley Cup in seven games.

1955–56

After two straight losses to the Detroit Red Wings in the Stanley Cup finals, the Montreal Canadiens made several key changes for the 1955–56 season, in the process assembling the greatest dynasty in NHL history. With Doug Harvey now the key to the Canadiens' defense, veteran Butch Bouchard was phased out, opening a spot for newcomer Bob Turner. Henri Richard, the Rocket's brother, and Claude Provost were also added to the lineup. The key change, however, was the decision to replace coach Dick Irvin with Toe Blake. Irvin returned to Chicago, where he'd begun his NHL playing and coaching careers, to try and resurrect the Black Hawks.

There were more changes in Detroit in 1955–56, but unlike past moves, this season's trade hurt the team. With Glenn Hall emerging as a top-notch goaltender, Jack Adams dealt Terry Sawchuk and three other players to the Boston Bruins, but of the five players Detroit received in return only Warren Godfrey lasted the entire season.

With Jean Beliveau's 47 goals and 88 points leading the league, and Jacques Plante winning the Vezina Trophy in goal, the Canadiens cruised to an NHL-record 45 victories and the first 100-point season in franchise history. Detroit was a distant second with 76 points, while the New York Rangers established franchise highs with 32 wins and 74 points. The Toronto Maple Leafs slipped into the final playoff spot, with two more points than Boston's 59.

In the playoffs, Montreal disposed of New York in five games while Detroit dispatched Toronto just as easily. This year, the Red Wings proved no match for the Canadiens as Montreal won the Stanley Cup in five games. No other team would win it for the rest of the decade.

1956–57

After losing both their regular-season and Stanley Cup crowns to the Montreal Canadiens, it was expected that the Detroit Red Wings would make big changes for the 1956–57 season, but Jack Adams made only minor adjustments. His team responded with a first-place finish. Injuries to Montreal stars Boom Boom Geoffrion, Rocket Richard, Henri Richard and Jacques Plante helped Detroit's cause, but so too did the play of Gordie Howe. Howe edged teammate Ted Lindsay by four points to win the Art Ross Trophy for the fifth time and also took home the Hart as most valuable player.

The Boston Bruins proved a pleasant surprise this season, though injuries and illness forced them to replace goalie Terry Sawchuk with rookie Don Simmons for much of the year. A solid offense, led by Real Chevrefils's 31 goals, saw Boston finish just two points behind Montreal for third place in the standings. The New York Rangers grabbed the final playoff spot, while the Toronto Maple Leafs fell to fifth place under rookie coach Howie Meeker. Tommy Ivan replaced an ailing Dick Irvin as coach in Chicago, but the Black Hawks finished in the league basement for the fourth year in a row.

In the semifinals, Boston threw a tight-checking blanket over Detroit's top line of Lindsay, Howe and Alex Delvecchio enabling them to upset the first-place Red Wings in five games. Montreal needed just five games to knock off New York, with Rocket Richard scoring the series winner in overtime. Two nights later, Richard opened the Stanley Cup finals with a four-goal effort in a 5–1 Canadiens win. Montreal cruised to its second consecutive Stanley Cup title in five games.

1957–58

In February 1957, a group of NHL players tried to form a union. The attempt was not welcomed by NHL owners, who crushed the fledgling association during the 1957–58 season. Ted Lindsay had been the leader of the players' fight for rights, and Jack Adams punished his great star with a trade to the lowly Chicago Black Hawks. Lindsay and goalie Glenn Hall were both dealt to Chicago, who also introduced a rookie named Bobby Hull this season and finally began to show signs of improvement after years of horrible hockey—though they would miss the playoffs again this season.

The Boston Bruins also proved beneficiaries of Jack Adams's wheeling and dealing, acquiring John Bucyk in a deal that returned Terry Sawchuk to Detroit. Another key Bruins addition was Bronco Horvath, who came over from the Montreal Canadiens. The star-studded Canadiens, who kept their team basically intact, set an NHL record with 250 goals and cruised to first place in the standings. Dickie Moore led the league in goals and points, while Henri Richard topped the loop in assists. Jacques Plante won the Vezina Trophy, while Rocket Richard became the first player in league history to score 500 goals. The New York Rangers finished a surprising second to Montreal. The Toronto Maple Leafs, who fired general manager Howie Meeker before the club had even played a game, slipped to last place for the first time since 1919 when the team had been known as the Arenas.

Montreal swept Detroit in the semifinals while Boston upset New York to set up a rematch of the previous year's final. This time, the Bruins proved a stubborn foe, but the powerful Canadiens prevailed in six games to capture their third consecutive Stanley Cup championship.

1958–59

The Montreal Canadiens were the class of the NHL again in 1958–59, finishing well atop the regular-season standings and becoming the first team in league history to win four consecutive Stanley Cup titles. Jacques Plante won the Vezina Trophy for the fourth straight season, while Tom Johnson won the Norris Trophy as top defenseman, ending teammate Doug Harvey's four-year reign. Dickie Moore earned the Art Ross Trophy for the second consecutive season, setting a new NHL scoring record with 96 points.

The Boston Bruins climbed to second place, while the Chicago Black Hawks, backed by the solid goaltending of Glenn Hall, reached the playoffs for just the second time in 13 years. The Hawks featured an excellent defense, and a young Bobby Hull complemented a veteran forward unit that included Ted Lindsay and Tod Sloan. The Canadiens' fierce rival for much of the decade, the Detroit Red Wings, fell to last place.

The New York Rangers appeared to have the fourth and final playoff spot sewn up before one of the great collapses in hockey history. Punch Imlach, who'd been named general manager of the Toronto Maple Leafs early in the 1958–59 season, had promptly named himself head coach. But the Leafs, who had missed the playoffs two years in a row, were slow to respond. In fact, with just five games left in the season, Toronto was still seven points behind the Rangers. But the Leafs won those last five games, while New York dropped six of seven, and the Leafs clinched a playoff spot on the last night of the season.

Toronto's roll continued into the playoffs, as they defeated Boston in the semifinals in seven games. The Canadiens, however, needed just five games to cool off the Leafs and claim an NHL record-setting fourth consecutive Stanley Cup championship.

1959–60

Bobby Hull emerged as an NHL superstar in 1959–60. Teamed on a line with Bill Hay and Murray Balfour, the Chicago Black Hawks' "Golden Jet" was involved in a season-long battle for the NHL scoring title with Bronco Horvath of the Boston Bruins. Hull emerged victorious, ending the year with 39 goals and 42 assists to Horvath's 39 and 41. A promising newcomer was added to the Chicago roster, as Stan Mikita centered a line with Ted Lindsay and Kenny Wharram. Glenn Hall, as always, was solid in goal as the Black Hawks emerged from an early-season slump to finish in third place and reach the playoffs in consecutive seasons for the first time since the early 1940s.

The Toronto Maple Leafs, who had rallied into the playoffs the previous season under Punch Imlach, enjoyed a solid second-place finish in 1959–60, as once again the Montreal Canadiens came out on top. The Detroit Red Wings rebounded from last season's trip to the cellar, climbing into fourth place. The Boston Bruins and New York Rangers missed the playoffs.

In their semifinal series, the Canadiens assigned Claude Provost to shadow Bobby Hull and he limited the NHL's scoring leader to just one goal in a four-game sweep as Montreal reached the Stanley Cup finals for the tenth year in a row. The other semifinal featured Toronto and Detroit, with the Leafs winning in six. The Canadiens were heavy favorites in the finals and had little trouble with the Leafs, winning in four to duplicate Detroit's 1952 feat of sweeping the playoffs, and setting a new standard with five consecutive Stanley Cup wins. Rocket Richard scored what would prove to be the final goal of his legendary career in the third game of the Leafs series.

1960–61

Throughout the summer, Montreal newspapers were filled with rumors about Rocket Richard's imminent retirement. Although Richard was with the Canadiens when they opened training camp, he announced on September 15, 1960—only hours after scoring four goals in an intrasquad scrimmage—that his brilliant career was over. He had scored a record 544 goals in the regular season and added 82 more in the playoffs. Even more importantly, he had been the heart and soul of hockey in Montreal.

As Richard made his exit, two players took aim at one of his most legendary accomplishments. Though the NHL season had lengthened from 50 games to 70, no one had so far managed to duplicate Richard's 50-goal season of 1944–45. This year, Frank Mahovlich of the Toronto Maple Leafs was scoring at a record rate, but he slumped down the stretch just as Montreal's Boom Boom Geoffrion got red hot. Season's end found Mahovlich with 48 goals, but Geoffrion reached the magic 50 and added 45 assists to win the Art Ross Trophy. Punch Imlach had much improved his Toronto club, putting ex-defenseman Red Kelly at center on a line with Mahovlich and rookie Bob Nevin. Another first-year Leaf, center Dave Keon, was also impressive, scoring 20 goals and winning the Calder Trophy.

The four playoff qualifiers finished in the same order as last year: Montreal, Toronto, Chicago, Detroit. The Chicago Black Hawks surprised Montreal in the semifinals, winning in six games and dashing the Canadiens' hopes of a sixth consecutive Cup win. The fourth-place Red Wings upset Toronto, setting up the first all-U.S. final since 1950, but they could not contain the Black Hawks, who won in six games to capture their first Stanley Cup title since 1938.

1961–62

Though their five-year reign as Stanley Cup champions had ended the previous spring, the Montreal Canadiens resisted the urge to overhaul their aging roster for 1961–62. One major change, though, saw the Canadiens allow superstar defenseman Doug Harvey to move to the New York Rangers, where he became a playing coach. The Canadiens received tough guy Lou Fontinato in return. The Rangers responded by climbing to fourth place and back into the postseason, though the play of Andy Bathgate was probably more responsible than Harvey's coaching.

All season long, Bathgate and Bobby Hull of the defending Stanley Cup champion Chicago Black Hawks battled for the scoring title. The duel between the slick playmaker and powerful goal scorer went right down to the final game, when Hull became just the third player in history to score 50 goals by beating the Rangers' Gump Worsley. Bathgate collected his 56th assist against the Black Hawks that night, and the two players ended tied with 88 points. Hull was awarded the Art Ross Trophy because he had more goals.

For the third year in a row, the top two teams in the regular season were the Canadiens and the Toronto Maple Leafs. The Detroit Red Wings missed the playoffs, while the Boston Bruins were a dismal 15–47–8 and finished last for the second year running. The Canadiens took the first two games from Chicago in their semifinal series, but then lost four in a row as the Black Hawks returned to the finals. The Leafs beat New York in six games. An injury to Johnny Bower forced the Leafs to switch to Don Simmons in goal after four games with Chicago, and he led Toronto to victory in six. It was Toronto's first Stanley Cup triumph since their overtime thriller in 1951.

1962–63

Having won the Cup the previous spring, Punch Imlach and the Toronto Maple Leafs entered the 1962–63 season with the team virtually intact, though top scorer Frank Mahovlich was nearly sold to the Chicago Black Hawks for $1 million. Only five points separated the first- and fourth-place teams in the tightest season-long competition in league history, with the Leafs finishing on top for the first time since 1947–48. The Black Hawks' 81 points were just one behind Toronto, though a remarkable streak ended in Chicago when a sore back forced Glenn Hall out of goal after playing 502 consecutive complete games. Injuries also hampered the Montreal Canadiens, who slipped to third for their worst performance since 1950–51. The Detroit Red Wings finished fourth in a rebuilding year that saw Jack Adams step down after 35 years as general manager.

Sid Abel added the general manager's portfolio to his Detroit coaching duties, and it was his former Production Line-mate Gordie Howe who led the resurgence. Mr. Hockey earned the Art Ross Trophy as the NHL's leading scorer with 86 points, while also garnering the Hart Trophy as MVP. It was the sixth and final time he'd receive either honor. Andy Bathgate was runner-up for the Art Ross for the second year in a row, though his New York Rangers slipped to fifth place. The Boston Bruins occupied the basement for the third straight year.

Toronto and Montreal met in the semifinals, with Johnny Bower collecting two shutouts and allowing the Canadiens just six goals in a five-game Leafs victory. The Black Hawks took the first two games from Detroit in their series before the Red Wings rallied to win in six. The finals featured tight defensive play, in which the Leafs prevailed in five evenly matched games to win their second consecutive Stanley Cup title.

1963–64

After three early playoff exits, the Montreal Canadiens swung a major trade with the New York Rangers prior to the 1963–64 season. The Habs sent Jacques Plante, Phil Goyette and Don Marshall to New York for Dave Balon, Len Ronson, Leon Rochefort and Gump Worsley, though it would be Charlie Hodge rather than Worsley who would see most of the action in the Canadiens' goal. Tom Johnson went to the Boston Bruins, and Dickie Moore retired and was replaced by John Ferguson. Montreal responded to the changes with a first-place finish, one point ahead of the Chicago Black Hawks.

Billy Reay was the new coach in Chicago, where teammates Bobby Hull and Stan Mikita dueled for the scoring title. Hull led the league with 43 goals, but Mikita's 89 points on 39 goals and 50 assists were two better than the Golden Jet. Two major career records were broken by Detroit Red Wings players during the 1963–64 season—Gordie Howe surpassed Rocket Richard's mark of 544 goals, while Terry Sawchuk passed George Hainsworth with his 95th career shutout. The Red Wings slumped in the early going under the pressure of Howe's record chase, but rallied to a fourth-place finish.

The defending Stanley Cup champion Toronto Maple Leafs also found the going rough until a huge late-season trade saw them acquire Andy Bathgate and Don McKenney from the New York Rangers for five players. The Leafs ended the season in third place while New York missed the playoffs for the second year in a row. The Boston Bruins finished last for the fourth straight season.

For the first time since the best-of-seven format was introduced in 1939, all three playoff series went the distance, with the Maple Leafs knocking off Montreal and Detroit for their third consecutive Stanley Cup triumph.

1964–65

After 18 seasons, during which he had built the greatest dynasty in hockey history, Frank Selke retired as managing director of the Montreal Canadiens prior to the 1964–65 season. He was succeeded by Sam Pollock. Several youngsters were also added to the roster to replace aging and departing veterans, but it was the play of long-time greats Jean Beliveau and Henri Richard that had the Canadiens off to a flying start. Injuries, though, saw Montreal slump to a second-place finish in the regular season.

The top team in the NHL this season was the Detroit Red Wings, who had not finished first since 1956–57. The team was sparked by the comeback of Ted Lindsay after a four-year retirement, but it was the play of young goalie Roger Crozier, as well as the offensive power of Gordie Howe, Alex Delvecchio and Norm Ullman that fueled the Red Wings' resurgence. Ullman led the NHL with 42 goals, and his 83 points trailed only Stan Mikita's 87. Mikita and the Chicago Black Hawks fought Montreal and Detroit in a three-way battle for first place, but had to settle for third. A string of injuries saw the three-time defending Stanley Cup champion Toronto Maple Leafs fall into fourth place, while, for the fifth time in six years, the New York Rangers and Boston Bruins both failed to make the playoffs.

The Leafs' reign as Stanley Cup champions came to an early end when the Canadiens beat them in a six-game semifinal. Chicago knocked off Detroit in seven games, reversing the results of a season ago. The Canadiens then knocked off Chicago in a tough seven-game series to win the Stanley Cup. Jean Beliveau was named the inaugural winner of the Conn Smythe Trophy as playoff MVP.

1965–66

Bobby Hull became hockey's all-time single-season scoring leader in 1965–66, collecting 54 goals and 97 points, both league records. Goal number 51 came on March 12, 1966, before a packed house at Chicago Stadium. Hull won the Art Ross Trophy for the third time, as well as earning his second consecutive Hart Trophy selection as league MVP. The Golden Jet's brilliant play had the Chicago Black Hawks in a season-long battle for top spot with the Montreal Canadiens, though they would have to settle for second place this year.

The Detroit Red Wings, who had finished first the previous season but been eliminated in the first playoff round, made some lineup adjustments, including an eight-player swap with the Toronto Maple Leafs in which the principals were rugged defenseman Marcel Pronovost—headed for Toronto—and center Andy Bathgate—going to the Wings. Detroit was further buoyed by Gordie Howe's 600th goal, but a career-ending injury to defenseman Doug Barkley saw them slump to fourth place. The aging Maple Leafs came in third. The Boston Bruins finally climbed out of last place, finishing one point ahead of the New York Rangers. Promising youngsters like Ted Green, Don Awrey and Gerry Cheevers gave reason for optimism in Boston once the league expanded for the 1967–68 season—a decision that the league announced on February 9, 1966.

For the third year in a row, Detroit met the Black Hawks in the semifinals. Chicago was heavily favored, but the Red Wings won in six games. Montreal knocked off Toronto in four, and claimed their second straight Stanley Cup title with a six-game victory over Detroit. Red Wings goalie Roger Crozier won the Conn Smythe Trophy as playoff MVP for his outstanding play in a losing effort.

1966–67

The NHL's final season as a six-team loop saw the Chicago Black Hawks finish in first place for the first time in franchise history, which dated back to 1926. Bobby Hull's 52 goals led the league as Chicago established a new team goal-scoring record with 264, but Stan Mikita was the big story as he won the Art Ross Trophy with 97 points and the Hart Trophy as MVP. The reformed tough guy also won the Lady Byng Trophy, becoming in the process the first NHL player to capture three major awards in one season.

The two-time defending Stanley Cup champion Montreal Canadiens finished second to Chicago in the regular season, though their 77 points left them 17 out of top spot. A veteran band of Toronto Maple Leafs, augmented by youngsters like Jim Pappin and Pete Stemkowski, finished third, while the New York Rangers returned to the postseason after missing the playoffs in seven of eight previous seasons. The Detroit Red Wings fell into fifth place, while the Boston Bruins slipped back into the basement. The debut of Bobby Orr and the appointment of Harry Sinden as coach suggested their days as also-rans were coming to an end.

New York's return to the playoffs was short-lived, as Montreal swept them out of the semifinals. Toronto and goalie Terry Sawchuk stunned Chicago in six games to set up an all-Canadian final in Canada's centennial year. The Canadiens were expected to add a Stanley Cup win to Montreal's Expo 67 festivities (a place had been reserved for the trophy in the Quebec pavilion at the world's fair) but instead, an aging gang of Toronto players, including Sawchuk, George Armstrong, Johnny Bower, Allan Stanley and Red Kelly, closed out hockey's six-team era with what would prove to be coach Punch Imlach's fourth and last Stanley Cup victory.

1967–68

The NHL doubled its membership for 1967–68, adding the Philadelphia Flyers, Los Angeles Kings, St. Louis Blues, Minnesota North Stars, Pittsburgh Penguins and Oakland Seals. The expanded 12-team league was split into two divisions, with the Original Six teams in the East Division and the new clubs in the West. The regular season was expanded to 74 games, with each team playing 50 against divisional rivals and 24 against the other division. The top four teams in each division would make the playoffs, with the quarterfinals and semifinals determining the champion of each division, who would then play for the Stanley Cup. This playoff format guaranteed an established team would meet an expansion team in the final round.

An elaborate expansion draft, plus much preseason wheeling and dealing, meant the NHL's newest clubs all had some veteran talent, though two of the more interesting trades involved only the old-line teams. The Boston Bruins acquired Phil Esposito, Ken Hodge and Fred Stanfield from Chicago for Gilles Marotte, Pit Martin and Jack Norris, while the Maple Leafs sent Frank Mahovlich, Pete Stemkowski, Garry Unger and the rights to Carl Brewer to the Red Wings for Norm Ullman, Paul Henderson and Floyd Smith. Both Toronto and Detroit failed to make the playoffs, but Boston's big deal helped the Bruins return to the postseason for the first time since 1959. Bobby Orr helped too, winning the Norris Trophy as best defenseman in only his second season.

Except for Oakland, the expansion teams were evenly matched, with just six points separating the top five teams. Philadelphia took first place, but St. Louis proved the best in the playoffs. The Blues were no match for the East champion Canadiens, though, as Montreal swept St. Louis to win the Stanley Cup.

1968–69

The 1968–69 season saw the Boston Bruins' emergence as an NHL powerhouse. Bobby Orr was by far the league's best defenseman and Phil Esposito proved to be its best offensive star. Esposito became the first player to top 100 points when he finished the season with 49 goals and 77 assists. New York's Goal-A-Game Line of Jean Ratelle, Vic Hadfield and Rod Gilbert was also leading the Rangers back to respectability.

In Chicago, the Black Hawks signed Bobby Hull to a three-year deal worth $100,000 per season and he responded with a record 58 goals. Hull and Detroit's ageless Gordie Howe also topped 100 points this season, though their teams failed to make the playoffs in the East. Montreal was the top club in the regular season with 103 points (three more than Boston) and once again advanced to the Stanley Cup finals with a pair of playoff series victories.

For the second year in a row, St. Louis proved to be the best in the West, topping all the new teams with 88 points. The Blues had enticed Jacques Plante out of retirement to join Glenn Hall in a stellar goaltending tandem. The veterans combined for 13 shutouts and shared the Vezina Trophy by backstopping the league's stingiest defense. The Blues also had some offensive talent, as Red Berenson tied an NHL record with six goals in a single game. He finished the year with 35 goals and 47 assists and was the only West Division player to crack the top 10 in league scoring.

For the second year in a row, future Canadiens coach Scotty Bowman led the St. Louis Blues against Montreal in the Stanley Cup finals and, for the second year in a row, the Canadiens swept the series in four close games.

1969–70

There was a fierce battle for playoff spots in the East Division in 1969–70, with the two-time defending Stanley Cup champion Montreal Canadiens missing the postseason despite a 92-point season that topped any team in the West. The Toronto Maple Leafs were last in the East with 71 points, making it the first time in NHL history that no Canadian teams qualified for the playoffs.

Bobby Hull joined Gordie Howe and Rocket Richard in the 500-goal club, but the highlight of the season for the first-place Black Hawks was the remarkable goaltending of Tony Esposito. The rookie netminder posted a modern-era record 15 shutouts and won both the Vezina and Calder trophies. Bobby Orr enjoyed a sizzling record-breaking season in Boston, becoming the first defenseman to lead the NHL in scoring. In addition to winning the Art Ross Trophy as scoring leader, Orr also won the Norris Trophy as the league's best blueliner for the third year in a row.

Once again, the St. Louis Blues were the top team in the West Division, finishing well ahead of the Pittsburgh Penguins. The Blues advanced to their third consecutive Stanley Cup finals by eliminating the Minnesota North Stars, then Pittsburgh in the playoffs. This year, Boston would be their opponent in the finals. The Bruins needed six games to defeat the New York Rangers, then surprised Chicago with a four-game sweep.

Long-suffering Bruins star John Bucyk celebrated his first appearance in the Stanley Cup finals since 1958 with a hat trick in game one. Following two more Bruins victories, Bobby Orr completed the series sweep with an overtime goal in game four and became the subject of one of hockey's most famous photographs when he went flying through the air after being upended by the Blues' Noel Picard. The Stanley Cup was back in Boston for the first time since 1941.

1970–71

Two cities that narrowly missed joining the NHL in 1967 were added to the league in 1970–71. Despite the geographic contradiction, the Buffalo Sabres and Vancouver Canucks were both placed in the East Division. To improve the competitive balance between the two divisions, the Chicago Black Hawks moved into the West, and the season, extended to 78 games, featured a balanced schedule. The playoff format was also altered so that teams would cross divisional lines after the opening round.

The Boston Bruins, as their Stanley Cup predecessors

had done in 1929, followed up their championship with a record-breaking season. The 1970–71 edition of the Bruins set NHL all-time single-season records with 57 victories, 121 points and 399 goals. Phil Esposito set new records with 76 goals and 152 points, while Bobby Orr established a new mark with 102 assists. Esposito, Orr, John Bucyk and Ken Hodge finished 1–2–3–4 in the NHL scoring race as all four topped 100 points, while Espo and Bucyk became the first teammates to top 50 goals in a single season. Unfortunately, these Bruins were also like that 1929–30 team in that they couldn't get past the Montreal Canadiens.

Though he had played just six games late in the regular season, Montreal made Ken Dryden their number-one goalie for their quarterfinal series against Boston. Dryden completely stymied the powerful Bruins as Montreal pulled off a stunning seven-game upset. The Canadiens then defeated the Minnesota North Stars to advance to the finals. Chicago provided the opposition, but the Stanley Cup returned to Montreal in a tight seven-game series. Henri Richard scored the Cup-winning goal after feuding with coach Al MacNeil earlier in the series. Dryden earned the Conn Smythe Trophy as playoff MVP.

The NHL lost two of its greats when Jean Beliveau and Gordie Howe announced their retirements—although Howe, it would turn out, was not done just yet.

1971–72

The Montreal Canadiens made two moves before the 1971–72 season that ensured the success of the franchise for years to come. Scotty Bowman was hired as coach and, after a series of trades to ensure they landed the number-one pick, Guy Lafleur was selected in the draft. "The Flower" slowly blossomed into the league's top star, while Rick Martin, selected fifth overall by Buffalo, provided the Sabres with more immediate benefits. Martin set a rookie record with 44 goals, but the Calder Trophy went to Ken Dryden, who had not played enough regular-season games in 1970–71 to lose his rookie status.

For the second straight year, the Boston Bruins and New York Rangers proved to be the top teams in the regular season. Boston's Phil Esposito and Bobby Orr finished 1–2 in the NHL scoring race, while New York's Goal-A-Game Line of Jean Ratelle, Vic Hadfield and Rod Gilbert finished 3–4–5. Bobby Clarke of the Philadelphia Flyers was establishing himself as a star and was the only player from an expansion team to crack the top 10.

With the previous year's playoff upset still in mind, the Bruins downed the Toronto Maple Leafs in five games, then swept the St. Louis Blues in four to advance to the Stanley Cup finals. The Rangers, who had edged Montreal by just one point in the regular-season standings, knocked off the Canadiens in six, then swept the West Division-leading Chicago Black Hawks to reach the finals for the first time since 1950.

The Boston–New York Stanley Cup matchup was the first since 1960 to feature the NHL's top two regular-season teams, and the first-place Bruins emerged victorious in six games. Bobby Orr became the first two-time winner of the Conn Smythe Trophy, earning playoff MVP honors as he had in 1970.

1972–73

The hockey universe changed forever in 1972. The NHL had a major professional rival for the first time since the 1926 demise of the old Western Hockey League with the establishment of the World Hockey Association. The new 12-team league featured the Alberta Oilers, Winnipeg Jets, Chicago Cougars, Houston Aeros, Los Angeles Sharks and Minnesota Fighting Saints in the Western Division, while the Eastern Division was comprised of the Cleveland Crusaders, New England Whalers, Quebec Nordiques, Ottawa Nationals, Philadelphia Blazers and New York Raiders.

The WHA raided NHL rosters of talent, securing such players as Bernie Parent, Gerry Cheevers and J.C. Tremblay, though the real coup was Winnipeg's signing of Bobby Hull to a 10-year deal worth $2.75 million. The league was also a place for NHL journeymen such as Andre Lacroix and Danny Lawson to shine. Lawson scored a league-leading 61 goals, while Lacroix topped the loop with 124 points. The Whalers beat Hull's Jets in the Avco Cup finals to claim the first WHA championship.

Before either league opened its 1972–73 schedule, hockey fans around the world focused their attention on an eight-game series pitting an all-NHL Team Canada against the Soviet Union's national team. The Soviets were perennial amateur champions, but Canadian fans were confident their top professionals would put the Russians in their place. The Canadians quickly found that the Soviets were a superb team and struggled valiantly to raise their play to meet the challenge. Only Paul Henderson's goal with 34 seconds to play in game eight secured a narrow victory for Team Canada. The Soviets' superior training techniques and strong skating and passing skills would influence the future of hockey in North America.

The NHL responded to the WHA's challenge by adding the New York Islanders and Atlanta Flames this year, but the season's best performances came from traditional favorites. The Boston Bruins' Phil Esposito won his third consecutive scoring title, while the Montreal Canadiens finished first overall in the regular season and later beat the Chicago Black Hawks in six games in the finals to win the Stanley Cup. A one-game challenge issued by the WHA champion Whalers went unheeded by the NHL.

1973–74

During the 1972–73 season, Bobby Clarke had finished second to Phil Esposito in NHL scoring with 104 points, making him the first player from an expansion team to top the 100-point plateau. His Philadelphia Flyers had finished 37–30–11 for their first winning season, and the Flyers' captain was the first member of a non-Original Six team to win the Hart Trophy as most valuable player. During the 1973–74 campaign, the Flyers would emerge as the new NHL powerhouse.

Known as "The Broad Street Bullies" for their intimidating play, the Flyers featured offensive talent in Clarke, Bill Barber and Rick MacLeish, a strong defense boasting Tom Bladon and Andre "Moose" Dupont, and prototypical tough guys like Dave Schultz and Don Saleski, all extremely well coached by Fred Shero. Bernie Parent, back with the Flyers after a season with the WHA's Philadelphia Blazers, provided excellent goaltending, sharing the Vezina Trophy with Tony Esposito of the Chicago Black Hawks. The Flyers recorded a 50–16–12 mark to lead the West Division with 112 points, just one point behind the Boston Bruins for top spot overall. Boston's Phil Esposito, Bobby Orr, Ken Hodge and Wayne Cashman finished 1–2–3–4 on the NHL scoring list.

In the postseason, the Bruins and Philadelphia continued to be the league's best teams as they marched through the playoffs toward a showdown for the Stanley Cup. Boston won game one of the final 3–2 on a late goal by Bobby Orr, but the Flyers became the first expansion team to win a Stanley Cup final-series game with a 3–2 victory of their own in game two. By game six, with Kate Smith belting out *God Bless America*, Philadelphia was the NHL's first expansion champion after a 1–0 triumph. Rick MacLeish had the game's only goal, while Bernie Parent's shutout sealed his selection as Conn Smythe Trophy winner.

The World Hockey Association was back with a 12-team lineup for the 1973–74 season, although franchise shifts had landed teams in Toronto (the Toros, formerly the Ottawa Nationals) and Vancouver (the former Philadelphia Blazers). The rival league dropped another bombshell when Gordie Howe ended a two-year retirement to join sons Mark and Marty with the Houston Aeros. The 45-year-old wonder scored 31 goals and added 69 assists and helped Houston win the Avco Cup. Former NHLer Mike Walton led WHA scorers with 57 goals and 117 points.

1974–75

It was another expansion year for the NHL, which added the Kansas City Scouts and Washington Capitals and the 18-team league was reorganized into four divisions named after some of the game's builders. The Norris and Adams divisions made up the Prince of Wales Conference, while the Clarence Campbell Conference housed the Patrick and Smythe divisions. The Philadelphia Flyers, Buffalo Sabres and Montreal Canadiens led the Patrick, Adams and Norris divisions respectively, each finishing with 113 points, while the Vancouver Canucks were the surprise winners of the Smythe Division with 86 points in the newly expanded 80-game season. Under a new playoff format, the top three teams in each division qualified, with the four first-place teams receiving a bye into the quarterfinals while the others battled through a preliminary round.

The 1975 Stanley Cup finals marked the first battle between two expansion teams. The Flyers, buoyed by Bobby Clarke's second Hart Trophy performance in as many years and Bernie Parent's Vezina win, led the league with 51 wins and eliminated the Toronto Maple Leafs and New York Islanders to reach the finals for the second year in a row. The Islanders had battled back from a 3–0 deficit to beat Pittsburgh in the quarterfinals, and nearly duplicated the feat against Philadelphia. Meanwhile, the Sabres knocked off the Black Hawks and the Canadiens to play for the Stanley Cup in only their fifth season. The Flyers successfully defended their Cup title in a six-game final series remembered for the fog that rose from the ice at Buffalo's Memorial Auditorium and frequently interrupted play.

The regular season also saw the emergence of new individual talents. Veterans Bobby Orr and Phil Esposito finished 1–2 atop the NHL scoring list, but right behind them were Marcel Dionne and Guy Lafleur, who were finally showing the promise that had made them the top two selections in the 1971 Amateur Draft.

The WHA also expanded this year, adding the Phoenix Roadrunners and Indianapolis Racers, although several of the 12 "established" franchises moved before (and even during) the season. The innovative league created a Canadian Division of Vancouver, Edmonton, Winnipeg, Toronto and Quebec. Bobby Hull set a pro hockey record with 77 goals for Winnipeg, while Andre Lacroix of San Diego had a record 106 assists, but Gordie Howe's Houston Aeros emerged on top, winning their second Avco Cup title.

1975–76

The Montreal Canadiens returned to the NHL's summit in 1975–76, collecting a league-record 58 wins and 127 points. Guy Lafleur won the first of three consecutive scoring titles, leading the league with 56 goals and 125 points, while Ken Dryden earned the Vezina Trophy with a 2.03 goals-against average. The Norris Trophy this year went to Denis Potvin of the New York Islanders, ending Bobby Orr's streak of eight consecutive Norris Trophy wins. Orr was forced to undergo two knee operations and played just 10 games during the 1975–76 season.

Orr's was not the only significant absence from the Boston Bruins' lineup. In November, Harry Sinden stunned the hockey world by dealing Phil Esposito and Carol Vadnais to the New York Rangers for Jean Ratelle, Brad Park and Joe Zanussi. The blockbuster helped revitalize an aging roster, allowing Boston to claim top spot in the Adams Division and to remain one of the NHL's top clubs for years to come. In another surprising move, Marcel Dionne left the Detroit Red Wings as a free agent. He was signed by the Los Angeles Kings, who sent Dan Maloney, Terry Harper and a draft choice to Detroit as compensation.

The two-time defending Stanley Cup champion Philadelphia Flyers enjoyed another outstanding season, leading the Patrick Division with 118 points. Philadelphia beat the Toronto Maple Leafs in a quarterfinal series that saw both Reggie Leach and Toronto's Darryl Sittler tie the playoff record of five goals in a game, then the Flyers defeated Boston to reach the finals. Montreal advanced with wins over the Chicago Black Hawks and the Islanders, capping their season with a Stanley Cup sweep.

The WHA once again opened the season with 14 teams playing in the Canadian, Eastern and Western divisions, though the Cincinnati Stingers and Denver Spurs replaced teams in Chicago and Baltimore, and the Vancouver Blazers became the Calgary Cowboys.

The Spurs and the Minnesota Fighting Saints both folded before the season's end. Quebec enjoyed the year's best individual performances, as Marc Tardif led the league with 71 goals and 148 points and tied teammate J.C. Tremblay with 77 assists, while goalie Richard Brodeur had 44 wins. But the Winnipeg Jets, led by Bobby Hull, Ulf Nilsson and Anders Hedberg, won the Avco Cup, denying Houston a third straight title with a four-game sweep in the finals.

1976–77

Two of the NHL's weakest clubs found new homes for the 1976–77 season—the first franchise shifts since the Ottawa Senators moved to St. Louis in 1934–35. The Kansas City Scouts headed for Denver, where they would now be known as the Colorado Rockies, while the California Golden Seals left Oakland for the Rust Belt, setting up shop as the Cleveland Barons. Wilf Paiement scored 41 goals for the Rockies, who improved by 18 points over their last year in Kansas City, but both Colorado and Cleveland finished last in their respective divisions. Only the woeful 41-point effort by the Detroit Red Wings kept the two transplanted clubs out of the NHL cellar.

At the other end of the standings, the Montreal Canadiens surpassed their brilliant record of the previous season with a mark of 60–8–12 for 132 points. The Canadiens lost just once on home ice, going 33–1–6 at the Forum. Guy Lafleur won his second straight scoring title with 136 points and also won the Hart Trophy as MVP. Steve Shutt led the NHL with 60 goals, Larry Robinson won the Norris Trophy as best defenseman, and Ken Dryden and Michel "Bunny" Larocque shared the Vezina Trophy. The Philadelphia Flyers also had another great year, leading the Patrick Division with 112 points. The New York Islanders were second with 106, a point total that was good enough for Boston to win the Adams Division title. The Bruins and New York Rangers made another trade—though not as sensational as the previous year's Esposito deal—acquiring Rick Middleton for Ken Hodge. Still, the deal would pay dividends for Boston.

St. Louis, with just 73 points in 80 games, finished first in the Smythe Division but was swept out of the playoffs by the Canadiens, who then beat the Islanders to return to the Stanley Cup finals. Boston provided the opposition after eliminating the Los Angeles Kings and Philadelphia. The Canadiens won the first three games, with Boston playing their best hockey of the series in game four before Jacques Lemaire scored in overtime to complete the sweep.

The WHA opened the 1976–77 season with 12 teams, the same number as at the end of 1975–76, but there were two more franchise shifts. The Toronto Toros moved to Alabama, becoming the Birmingham Bulls, while the Cleveland Crusaders moved to Minnesota as the second incarnation of the Fighting Saints. The new Saints proved no more viable than the old, folding before season's end.

Anders Hedberg of Winnipeg led the league with 70 goals, while teammate Ulf Nilsson was tops with 85 assists. The scoring title went to Quebec's Real Cloutier with 66 goals and 75 assists for 141 points. The Nordiques beat the Jets for the Avco Cup in a seven-game championship series.

1977–78

The offseason was eventful for the World Hockey Association, as six teams applied for entry into the NHL. The vote among NHL owners was close, but not close enough, and with Phoenix, Calgary and San Diego ceasing operations, the WHA entered its sixth season with just eight teams. The Houston Aeros, a perennial power, were weakened by the departure of Marty, Mark and Gordie Howe to the New England Whalers, and would also fold in the spring of 1978. Bolstered by the arrival of Gordie and sons, the Whalers beat the Winnipeg Jets for the Avco Cup. Meanwhile, Marc Tardif of the Quebec Nordiques was the league's top scorer with 65 goals and 89 assists.

In the NHL, the Montreal Canadiens dominated play for the third consecutive season. The Canadiens were 59–10–11 on the year and their 129 points led the Norris Division by 51 points over a much-improved Detroit Red Wings team. Guy Lafleur won the Art Ross Trophy for the third year in succession and won the Hart Trophy for the second straight year. Ken Dryden and Bunny Larocque again shared the Vezina Trophy. Bob Gainey won the newly created Selke Trophy as the NHL's best defensive forward. It was an honor he would win again in each of the next three seasons.

The New York Islanders won their first Patrick Division title this year with 111 points. Bryan Trottier's 123 points were second behind Lafleur's 132 in the NHL scoring race, while teammate Mike Bossy set a rookie record with 53 goals. Denis Potvin finished fifth in scoring with 30 goals and 64 assists and earned his second Norris Trophy win as the league's best defenseman. But despite their great regular season, the Islanders' year ended in disappointment when Lanny McDonald's seventh-game overtime goal gave the Toronto Maple Leafs a quarterfinal series upset. Toronto had enjoyed a 92-point year under rookie coach Roger Neilson, but couldn't get past Montreal in the semifinals as the Canadiens swept Toronto en route to the finals.

For the second year in a row, Don Cherry's Bruins faced Montreal in the final. Boston had won the Adams Division with 113 points and had needed just nine games to eliminate the Chicago Black Hawks and Philadelphia Flyers. Boston provided much tougher competition this year, but the Canadiens still made it three straight Stanley Cup titles with a six-game victory. Larry Robinson and Guy Lafleur tied for the postseason scoring lead, with the big defenseman taking home the Conn Smythe Trophy as playoff MVP.

1978–79

After another summer of fruitless merger talks with the NHL, the World Hockey Association prepared for its seventh season with seven teams lumped into a single division. Early in the year, the Indianapolis Racers went out of business. The team made one significant deal before folding, selling the contract of 17-year-old Wayne Gretzky to the Edmonton Oilers. Gretzky scored 46 goals and added 64 assists as a rookie and led Edmonton to a first-place finish. His 110 points ranked third in WHA scoring. The Quebec Nordiques' Real Cloutier led the league again with 75 goals and 54 assists.

In the playoffs, the Winnipeg Jets beat the Oilers for the last-ever Avco Cup championship. On March 29, 1979, the NHL had announced it would take in four WHA teams the following season: Edmonton, Winnipeg, Quebec, and the New England Whalers. The two remaining clubs, the Cincinnati Stingers and Birmingham Bulls, were paid to go out of business.

The WHA's instability had many of its top players rushing to sign with NHL clubs prior to the 1978–79 season. The New York Rangers doled out big bucks for Swedish stars Ulf Nilsson and Anders Hedberg, who got two-year contracts worth $1 million. The Rangers also hired former Philadelphia Flyers coach Fred Shero to fill the dual role of coach and general manager. New York's 91 points this season were 18 better than the previous year, but good for only third place in the Patrick Division. First place in the Patrick belonged to New York Islanders, whose 116 points edged out the Montreal Canadiens at 115 for top spot in the overall standings. Bryan Trottier earned both the Art Ross and Hart trophies, but once again a great Islanders season would end in playoff disappointment. Phil Esposito had led the Rangers to victories over the Los Angeles Kings and Philadelphia, but it was goalie John Davidson who made the difference when the team knocked off the Islanders in a six-game semifinal.

The Rangers' opponent for the Stanley Cup was Montreal, who had reached the final for the fourth consecutive year after a thrilling seven-game semifinal with the Bruins. The deciding game had turned on a late Boston bench minor for having too many men on the ice. On the ensuing power-play, Montreal tied the score and went on to win in overtime. The Rangers took full advantage of the Canadiens' fatigue in a 4–1 series-opening victory, but Montreal stormed back to take the next four games for their fourth consecutive Stanley Cup championship. Bob Gainey earned the Conn Smythe Trophy as playoff MVP.

1979–80

A year after the struggling Cleveland Barons merged with the Minnesota North Stars, reducing the NHL to 17 teams, the league was growing again as it absorbed the four survivors of the World Hockey Association: the Edmonton Oilers, Winnipeg Jets, Quebec Nordiques and Hartford (formerly New England) Whalers.

The National Hockey League benefited from an influx of talent created by the WHA's demise. Most notable was the return of legends Bobby Hull, Dave Keon and 51-year-old Gordie Howe, who would score 15 goals for Hartford. At the other end of their careers were young players like Mike Gartner, Rick Vaive, Michel Goulet and Mark Messier, who'd played in the WHA as underage pros. But it was the youngest of the WHA's refugees who would prove to be the greatest NHLer of all.

Beginning his pro career at the age of 17, Wayne Gretzky had finished third in WHA scoring in 1978–79. He had been a point-scoring machine all his young life, but few expected his WHA performance to translate into NHL success. Getting better as the year progressed, Gretzky proved the doubters wrong, enjoying a late-season surge that saw him tie Marcel Dionne for the league lead with 137 points. The Art Ross Trophy, however, went to the Los Angeles Kings superstar because his 53 goals were two more than Gretzky's 51. "The Great One", as Gretzky would become known, was also denied the Calder Trophy because the season he spent in the WHA meant he wasn't considered an NHL rookie, but his brilliance was recognized with both the Hart and Lady Byng trophies. Gretzky's great play also managed to sneak Edmonton into the 16th and final playoff spot, though the Oilers were knocked off in three straight games by Philadelphia. The Flyers set a professional sports record during the season with a 35-game unbeaten streak en route to a first-place finish in the overall standings.

The four-time defending Stanley Cup champion Montreal Canadiens underwent a major overhaul before the 1979–80 season. Goalie Ken Dryden announced his retirement and Scotty Bowman resigned as coach to run the Buffalo Sabres. Bowman was replaced by Canadiens legend Boom Boom Geoffrion, who in turn gave way to Claude Ruel during the season. Montreal managed to finish atop the Norris Division with 107 points, but a quarterfinal defeat at the hands of the Minnesota North Stars ended the team's quest for a record-tying fifth straight Stanley Cup championship. The Cup wound up instead with the New York Islanders when Bob Nystrom's overtime goal upset favored Philadelphia in a six-game final.

1980–81

The defending Stanley Cup champion New York Islanders proved to be the best again during the 1980–81 season. The Islanders' 110 points topped both the Patrick Division and the overall NHL standings, just three points ahead of the Smythe Division's surprising St. Louis Blues. The Canadiens were the NHL's third-best team with 103 points, but Montreal was stunned in the first round of the playoffs when the Edmonton Oilers eliminated them in three straight games. The victory was a clear sign that the balance of power in the NHL had shifted from the older, established teams. Edmonton's playoff success continued as they lasted six games in the second round before bowing out against the Islanders.

The Oilers featured a host of talented young players—Glenn Anderson, Jari Kurri, Paul Coffey, Kevin Lowe and Mark Messier—but the undisputed leader was Wayne Gretzky, who began to rewrite the NHL record book this year. He broke Bobby's Orr's single-season assist record by seven with 109, and his 55 goals gave him 164 points, easily breaking Phil Esposito's record of 152. It was the first of seven consecutive Art Ross Trophy wins for Gretzky, and the second of eight straight Hart Trophy selections. The Oilers had a provincial rival this season, as the Atlanta Flames moved north to Calgary.

Two of Edmonton's fellow WHA refugees did not fare as well in 1980–81. The Hartford Whalers, now without the retired Gordie Howe, fell out of the playoffs, while the Jets suffered through one of the worst season's in hockey history. Winnipeg's 9–57–14 mark was the worst in the NHL since the Washington Capitals went 8–67–5 in 1974–75. The Jets suffered through 30 games without a victory at one point, establishing a new NHL record for futility.

Meanwhile, the Quebec Nordiques unveiled brothers Anton and Peter Stastny this season, with 25-year-old Peter setting a rookie scoring record with 109 points. A third Stastny brother, Marian, would join Quebec in 1981–82. Another new name appeared among the NHL scoring leaders this season, as Calgary's Kent Nilsson placed third with 131 points. The NHL goal-scoring crown went to Mike Bossy of the Islanders, who netted 68 goals and equaled Rocket Richard's legendary feat of 50 goals in 50 games.

After eliminating the Oilers in the quarterfinals, Bossy and the Islanders swept the Rangers to return to the Stanley Cup finals. Their opponents were the upstart Minnesota North Stars, but the Islanders proved too powerful, needing only five games to win their second consecutive Cup title. Bossy, Bryan Trottier and Denis Potvin were the offensive stars, but the determined hustle of Butch Goring was rewarded with the Conn Smythe Trophy.

1981–82

In just their third season in the NHL, the Edmonton Oilers arrived as a powerhouse in 1981–82, winning the

Smythe Division with 111 points and finishing second overall to the two-time defending Stanley Cup champion New York Islanders. Wayne Gretzky was the story of the regular season, collecting goals and assists in bunches from the very beginning of the schedule. A year after Mike Bossy had duplicated Rocket Richard's mark of 50 goals in 50 games, Gretzky obliterated this record. His five-goal performance on December 30, 1981, gave him 50 in just 39 games. On February 24, 1982, Gretzky broke Phil Esposito's single-season record with his 77th goal and pushed his total to 92 by season's end. The Great One also broke his own record with 120 assists, giving him an astounding total of 212 points. The Oilers set a new NHL record with 417 goals this year, though none of their other improving young stars managed to join Gretzky in the league's top 10. Edmonton unveiled goalie Grant Fuhr this season and his netminding would soon prove the perfect complement to the team's high-powered offense.

The NHL realigned geographically this year and changed its playoff format to emphasize divisional play. Teams played for division, then conference titles, to determine the two Stanley Cup finalists. The Oilers finished 48 points ahead of fourth-place Los Angeles, but were eliminated by the Kings in the first round of the Smythe Division playoffs. The third game of the best-of-five series saw the Kings rebound from a 5–0 deficit to win in overtime in a game that became known as "The Miracle on Manchester" after the site of the Los Angeles Forum.

There were plenty of other playoff upsets in the Campbell Conference this year, with the Vancouver Canucks (third in the Smythe) and Chicago Black Hawks (fourth in the Norris) advancing to the conference final. In the Prince of Wales Conference, the fourth-place Nordiques eliminated the first-place Montreal Canadiens in "The Battle of Quebec," then beat the Boston Bruins for the Adams Division title. Only in the Patrick Division did things go according to expectations, as the Islanders emerged victorious. The New York club then swept Quebec to return to the Stanley Cup finals against Vancouver.

Game one found the Canucks leading 5–4 with only seven minutes to play before Mike Bossy tied it up and then won it in overtime. Richard Brodeur provided Vancouver with excellent goaltending, which kept the games close, but the Islanders claimed their third straight Stanley Cup title with a series sweep. The Conn Smythe Trophy for playoff MVP went to Bossy, whose 17 postseason goals led all scorers.

1982–83

The Boston Bruins returned to the top of the NHL standings for the first time since 1973–74 with 110 points. Barry Pederson's 46 goals and 61 assists placed him among the NHL's top 10 in scoring and Rick Middleton's 49 goals led the team, but defense was the key to the Bruins' success. Ray Bourque was named to the Second All-Star Team—the fourth all-star selection of his four-year career—while Pete Peeters earned the Vezina Trophy with 40 wins and a 2.36 goals-against average. His eight shutouts this season would prove to be the best single-season total of the 1980s. A sad note in Boston this season was the brain hemorrhage suffered by second-year wing Normand Leveille. He survived the illness, but his hockey career was over.

The three-time defending Stanley Cup champion New York Islanders started the season slowly, but came on strong. Still, they wound up in second place in the Patrick Division behind the Philadelphia Flyers. (The Patrick Division included a new team this year, as the Colorado Rockies had become the New Jersey Devils.) In the playoffs, Philadelphia lost to the New York Rangers in the first round, while the Islanders beat the Washington Capitals and then the Rangers to set up a Wales Conference showdown with Boston. The Bruins had defeated the Quebec Nordiques and Buffalo Sabres, but after a six-game conference final, the Islanders were headed back to the Stanley Cup finals for the fourth year in a row.

In the Campbell Conference, the Chicago Black Hawks enjoyed an excellent season. Denis Savard finished third in the league with 121 points, Al Secord scored 54 goals, and rookie of the year Steve Larmer notched 43. Chicago topped the Norris Division with 104 points and beat the St. Louis Blues and Minnesota North Stars in the playoffs before falling to the Edmonton Oilers in the conference final.

After the playoff disappointment of the previous season, the Oilers had rebounded. Although Wayne Gretzky "slumped" to 71 goals, his 125 assists were a new league high and his 196 points were 72 more than runner-up Peter Stastny—the widest gap ever between first and second place in the scoring derby. Gretzky's teammates Mark Messier, Glenn Anderson and Jari Kurri each collected at least 40 goals and 100 points and joined him among the top 10 scorers this season as the Oilers broke their own league record with 424 goals.

The Stanley Cup finals between the Oilers and Islanders was much anticipated, but the high-flying newcomers did not yet have the experience necessary to better the defending champions. The Islanders kept Gretzky off the scoresheet and held the Oilers to just six goals as they won their fourth consecutive Stanley Cup title in a four-game sweep.

1983–84

Overtime returned to the NHL regular season for the first time since 1942, when wartime travel restrictions had curtailed the practice. In the event of a tie after 60 minutes, teams would play a five-minute sudden-death session. If no one scored, the game would remain a tie.

Following their Stanley Cup loss to the New York Islanders the previous year, the Edmonton Oilers posted a 119-point season in 1983–84 and, for the third year in a row, set an all-time record with 446 goals. Not surprisingly, it was Wayne Gretzky who led the way as he tallied 87 goals and 118 assists for 205 points. Paul Coffey emerged as the best offensive defenseman since Bobby Orr, collecting 40 goals and 86 assists to finish second to Gretzky in the league scoring race. Jari Kurri had 52 goals and 61 assists to finish seventh in scoring, while Glenn Anderson had 54 goals as the Oilers become the first team to boast three 50-goal scorers in one season.

The New York Islanders showed every indication in the regular season that they were a legitimate threat to equal the Montreal Canadiens' record of five consecutive Stanley Cup championships. The Islanders posted 104 points to lead the Patrick Division after a tight race with the much-improved Washington Capitals, who set a franchise high with 101 points. The Boston Bruins, also with 104 points, won the Adams Division by a single point over the Buffalo Sabres. Buffalo was sparked by 18-year-old goalie Tom Barrasso, who won both the Calder and Vezina trophies.

The Montreal Canadiens tumbled to fourth place in the division with their first sub-.500 season since 1948–49.

In a move reminiscent of their 1971 decision to go with Ken Dryden, the Habs elected to open the playoffs with rookie Steve Penney in goal, even though he had played only four games during the season. Penney responded by leading Montreal to upsets of Boston and the Quebec Nordiques. His hot hand even carried the Canadiens to two wins to open the Prince of Wales Conference championship before the Islanders recovered to win four in a row and advance to play for the Stanley Cup once again.

Playoff victories over the Winnipeg Jets, Calgary Flames and Minnesota North Stars meant Edmonton would face the Islanders in the finals for the second year in a row. The teams split the first two games before the Oilers' offense clicked into high gear. Edmonton won three in a row, outscoring the Isles 19–6, to take the series in five and deny the Islanders a fifth straight Stanley Cup title. Wayne Gretzky led all playoff performers with 35 points, but the Conn Smythe Trophy for playoff MVP went to rugged teammate Mark Messier.

1984–85

Chosen first overall in the 1984 Entry Draft, Pittsburgh center Mario Lemieux recorded 43 goals and 57 assists en route to winning the Calder Trophy as rookie of the year. Within a few seasons, Lemieux would be credited with saving the Penguins franchise and would rival Wayne Gretzky as the greatest player in the game. This year, however, the Penguins recorded just 53 points and finished ahead of only the Toronto Maple Leafs in the NHL's overall standings.

Meanwhile, Gretzky and his Edmonton Oilers continued to dominate the league. Gretzky set yet another single-season record with 135 assists, and he added 73 goals for a total of 208 points. Linemate Jari Kurri's 71 goals and 135 points trailed only Gretzky in the league scoring race. Edmonton's Smythe Division rivals, the Winnipeg Jets and Calgary Flames, were also among the league's best this season and the league's top five scorers were all from the Smythe Division: Gretzky, Kurri, Winnipeg's Dale Hawerchuk, Marcel Dionne of Los Angeles and Oiler defenseman Paul Coffey.

The top team overall, however, was the Philadelphia Flyers. Former captain Bobby Clarke was now the general manager and new coach Mike Keenan got 53 wins and 113 points out of his troops. Tim Kerr led the team with 54 goals, but it was a stingy defense, led by Mark Howe and the Vezina Trophy-winning goaltending of Pelle Lindbergh, that was key to Philadelphia's success. The Flyers outdistanced the Washington Capitals for top spot in the Patrick Division, while the New York Islanders slipped to third place. The Islanders upset Washington in the playoffs, but suffered their earliest postseason ouster since 1979 when they lost to Philadelphia in the second round. The Montreal Canadiens survived the midseason retirement of Guy Lafleur to lead the Adams Division, but lost to Quebec in the playoffs. The Nordiques then fell to the Flyers in the Wales Conference final.

Bernie Federko's 103 points led the St. Louis Blues to first place in the Norris Division, but it was the Chicago Black Hawks who survived the playoffs before falling to Edmonton in a six-game Campbell Conference final that saw the powerful Oilers score a record 44 goals. Philadelphia beat Edmonton 4–1 in game one of the finals, before the Oilers won three tight games to take a commanding lead in the series. The Oilers wrapped it up with an offensive explosion that resulted in an 8–3 victory in game five and their second straight Stanley Cup title. Jari Kurri tied former Flyer Reggie Leach's record with 19 goals in the postseason, while Wayne Gretzky had 17 goals and 30 assists for a playoff-record 47 points, earning him the Conn Smythe Trophy.

1985–86

Just as the explosive Montreal Canadiens power-play of the late 1950s had caused the NHL to change its rules (allowing a penalized player to return to the ice before the two minutes expired if a goal was scored), the Edmonton Oilers' abundance of firepower caused the league to allow player substitutions on coincidental minor penalties, virtually eliminating the four-on-four situations that favored teams with superior skill.

The rule change did little to put the brakes on the Oilers, as the two-time defending Stanley Cup champions wrapped up their fifth consecutive Smythe Division title. The Oilers also returned to the top spot in the overall standings with 119 points and became the inaugural winners of the Presidents' Trophy for finishing in first place. Wayne Gretzky broke his own single-season record with 215 points, mainly by shattering his assist record with an astounding total of 163. Gretzky's assist total alone would have been enough to win the scoring title, as Mario Lemieux of the Pittsburgh Penguins finished second with 141 points. Paul Coffey also enjoyed a record-breaking year, surpassing Bobby Orr's standard of 46 goals by a defenseman with 48. Coffey added 90 assists to finish third in the scoring race. Jari Kurri's 68 goals and 63 assists saw him finish fourth.

As in Wayne Gretzky's 212-point campaign of 1981–82, regular-season records didn't translate into playoff prosperity as the rival Calgary Flames eliminated the Oilers in a seven-game Smythe Division final. The series-winning goal came when Edmonton defenseman Steve Smith bounced a clearing pass off goalie Grant Fuhr into his own net. Calgary then defeated the Norris Division champion St. Louis Blues in seven games to reach the Stanley Cup finals.

Upsets also abounded in the Prince of Wales Conference, where the Montreal Canadiens prevailed, setting up the first all-Canadian final since 1967. Mats Naslund's 110 points made him the first Hab to crack the top 10 in scoring since Guy Lafleur in 1980. Rookie Brian Skrudland scored the fastest overtime goal in history after just nine seconds for a 3–2 win over Calgary in game two of the Stanley Cup finals, and newcomer Claude Lemieux had 10 goals in the playoffs. But the most important rookie of all was Patrick Roy. He posted a 1.92 goals-against average in the playoffs and backstopped Montreal to a five-game Stanley Cup victory. Roy was the first rookie since Harry Lumley in 1945 to register a shutout in the finals when he blanked the Flames for a 1–0 victory in game four and was a deserving recipient of the Conn Smythe Trophy as playoff MVP.

1986–87

Numerous coaching changes took place before and during the 1986–87 season. The New York Islanders named Terry Simpson their new head coach and promoted four-time Stanley Cup winner Al Arbour to vice president. The New York Rangers named Phil Esposito their new general manager, and he made 19 trades during the course of the year. He also fired coach Ted Sator after just 19 games and took over the chores himself when an inner-ear infection sidelined Sator's replacement, Tom Webster. Sator was hired by the Buffalo Sabres, replacing Craig Ramsay, who had replaced Scotty Bowman. In Boston, the Bruins fired Butch Goring and hired Terry O'Reilly.

Four of the five Norris Division teams made coaching changes. Jacques Demers left St. Louis for the Detroit Red Wings and the Blues replaced him with Jacques Martin. In Minnesota, the North Stars sacked Glen Sonmor in favor of Lorne Henning and the Toronto Maple Leafs turned to John Brophy after firing Dan Maloney. Bob Pulford stayed on as Chicago's coach, but the team did change the spelling of its nickname from Black Hawks to Blackhawks after discovering that the moniker had been spelled as one word in the club's original NHL charter.

In an attempt to limit upsets, the first round of the playoffs was extended to a best-of-seven series. The New York Islanders and Washington Capitals took the new format to its limit—and then some. Pat LaFontaine's goal in the fourth overtime period of game seven provided the Islanders with the victory.

Fueled by their playoff defeat in 1986, the Edmonton Oilers again led the regular season, though their 106 points were the fewest by a first-place team since 1969–70. Wayne Gretzky won the Art Ross Trophy for the seventh consecutive season with 62 goals and 121 assists. He was awarded the Hart Trophy as MVP for an eighth consecutive season as well. After playoff victories over the Los Angeles Kings, Winnipeg Jets and Detroit Red Wings, Edmonton faced Philadelphia, the NHL's only other 100-point team, for the Stanley Cup.

The Oilers jumped out to a three-games-to-one lead in the finals, but the Flyers rallied to tie the series. It was Edmonton's turn to come back in game seven as they turned an early 1–0 deficit into a 3–1 victory and their third Cup championship. Wayne Gretzky hoisted the Stanley Cup and then passed it to Steve Smith, whose errant clearing pass the year before had knocked Edmonton out of the playoffs. Flyers goalie Ron Hextall played well enough in defeat to win the Conn Smythe Trophy as, for the second year in a row, a rookie goalie was named playoff MVP. Hextall also won the Vezina Trophy as the NHL's top goaltender.

1987–88

During the late summer of 1987, the fourth Canada Cup tournament took place and it marked the rise of Mario Lemieux as a true superstar. Playing on a line with Wayne Gretzky, Lemieux's work ethic and mental approach finally caught up with his immense physical skills. He was the tournament's top goal scorer and netted the dramatic series-winning goal against the Soviets on a feed from Gretzky late in the final game. By the end of the regular season, Lemieux had unseated Gretzky as NHL scoring champion and ended his eight-year hold on the Hart Trophy.

Lemieux's brilliant play and the acquisition of Paul Coffey from the Edmonton Oilers saw Pittsburgh post its best record in 10 years, but the Penguins' 81 points were still not enough to make the playoffs in the tight Patrick Division where only seven points separated the six teams. The New York Islanders finished first, followed by the Washington Capitals and Philadelphia Flyers. In a game against Boston on December 8, 1987, Flyers goalie Ron Hextall became the first NHL netminder to shoot the puck the length of the ice for a goal into an empty net.

Fourth place in the Patrick Division went to the New Jersey Devils, who made the playoffs for the first time in 10 years and just the second time in franchise history. Led by the goaltending of Canadian national team star Sean Burke, the surprising Devils reached the Wales Conference final before they fell to the Bruins. Boston had finished second behind the Montreal Canadiens—who boasted the league's best defensive record as well as 50-goal scorer Stephane Richer—in the Adams Division, but the Bruins prevailed in the division final, beating Montreal for the first time in 18 playoff series dating back to 1945.

The Presidents' Trophy for first place overall went to Calgary with 105 points, but their Alberta rivals, the defending Stanley Cup champion Edmonton Oilers, made easy work of the Flames in the Smythe Division final, sweeping the series in four games.

The Oilers went on to beat the Detroit Red Wings, the Norris Division champions, to play Boston for the Stanley Cup. Edmonton swept the Bruins to win their fourth Stanley Cup championship in five years, although the series actually went five games—late in the second period of game four, with the score tied 3–3, a power failure at Boston Garden forced the game's suspension. Wayne Gretzky won the Conn Smythe Trophy after setting a new record with 13 points in the finals. The Oilers celebrated their Stanley Cup triumph with an impromptu group photo at center ice. Little did anyone know that the picture documented the end of an era.

1988–89

The hockey world was shocked on August 9, 1988, when the Edmonton Oilers and Los Angeles Kings announced a trade virtually without parallel in sports history. Wayne Gretzky, Mike Krushelnyski and Marty McSorley were L.A.-bound, while the Oilers would receive Jimmy Carson, Martin Gelinas, the Kings' first-round draft choices in 1989, 1991 and 1993, plus a reported $15 million in cash. Fans in Edmonton, and across Canada, bemoaned the loss of the Great One, while the citizens of southern California would be turned on to hockey as never before.

Showing a flair for the dramatic worthy of his Hollywood surroundings, Gretzky scored a goal on his very first shot of the 1988–89 season. He led the Kings to a 91-point season, good for second place in the Smythe Division and the team's best showing since 1981. His 114 assists tied Mario Lemieux for top spot in the NHL, and though Lemieux's 85 goals to Gretzky's 54 meant Mario retained the Art Ross Trophy, Gretzky was awarded the Hart Trophy as MVP for the ninth time. Gretzky also brought out the greatest in his Los Angeles teammates—Bernie Nicholls, with 70 goals and 80 assists, and Luc Robitaille, with 46 goals and 52 assists, were also among the top 10 in scoring.

L.A. faced Edmonton in the first round of the playoffs and defeated Gretzky's former teammates in seven games. The Kings were swept aside in the Smythe Division final, however, by the Calgary Flames, the NHL's best team during the regular season with 117 points. Joe Mullen set career highs with 51 goals and 110 points, while Joe

Nieuwendyk followed up his 51-goal rookie performance with another 51 goals this season. In the Norris Division, Flames castoff Brett Hull emerged as a star, scoring 41 goals for the St. Louis Blues, while in Detroit, Steve Yzerman led the Red Wings with 65 goals and 90 assists. Still, it was the Chicago Blackhawks who emerged from the Norris Division before falling to the Flames in five games.

Led by Mario Lemieux, Pittsburgh was back in the playoffs after six years. The Penguins took on the New York Rangers—who boasted rookie stars Brian Leetch and Tony Granato, and who had convinced Guy Lafleur to come out of retirement—and eliminated the Blueshirts in the first round. The Philadelphia Flyers knocked Pittsburgh out, then went on to lose to the Montreal Canadiens—led by rookie coach Pat Burns to the league's second-best record with 115 points—in the Prince of Wales Conference final.

Calgary opened the Cup finals at home with a 3–2 victory and, after splitting the next four games, took a one-game series lead back to Montreal for game six. The Canadiens had never allowed an opponent to beat them for the Stanley Cup on Forum ice, but the Flames defied history with a 4–2 victory. Lanny McDonald, who had recorded his 500th goal and 1,000th point during the season—scored a key goal in the final game and retired a Stanley Cup champion.

1989–90

The NHL enjoyed unprecedented box-office success in 1989–90, as attendance was up for the 11th year in a row. But the story this season was growing parity and tight divisional races. Under rookie coach Mike Milbury, the Boston Bruins won the Presidents' Trophy with 101 points, marking the first season since 1970–71 that only one team broke the 100-point barrier. Cam Neely led the offense with 55 goals, while Ray Bourque earned his third Norris Trophy win in four years as the NHL's best defenseman. Goalies Reggie Lemelin and Andy Moog allowed the fewest goals in the league and shared the Jennings Trophy. The Bruins survived a seven-game scare from the Hartford Whalers in the first round of playoffs before beating the Montreal Canadiens and Washington Capitals to reach the Stanley Cup finals for the second time in three years. At the other end of the standings, the return of Guy Lafleur to the city where he'd starred as a Junior couldn't save the Quebec Nordiques, whose 61 losses and 31 points were the worst the league had seen since 1975.

An injury to Mario Lemieux kept him out of 21 games this season and saw the Pittsburgh Penguins miss the playoffs. His absence made it possible for Wayne Gretzky to reclaim the Art Ross Trophy. Although his 142 points represented his lowest total since his first NHL season, the Great One continued his assault on the record book. On October 15, 1989, Gretzky became the NHL's all-time scoring leader when he surpassed Gordie Howe's career total of 1,850 points—fittingly enough, in a game at Edmonton's Northlands Coliseum. His former Oilers teammate Mark Messier established a career high with 129 points on 45 goals and 84 assists, earning him the Hart Trophy as most valuable player. Brett Hull of the St. Louis Blues led the NHL, and set a new record for right wingers, with 72 goals.

Fourth-place Los Angeles upset the defending Stanley Cup champion Calgary Flames in the Smythe Division semifinals before falling to Messier and the Oilers in four straight. Edmonton advanced to play for the Stanley Cup after a six-game Campbell Conference final victory over the Chicago Blackhawks, who had won the Norris Division in their second year under former Philadelphia Flyers coach Mike Keenan.

Game one of the Stanley Cup finals needed 55 minutes of overtime before Petr Klima gave Edmonton a 3–2 victory. A 7–2 win followed in game two, and the Oilers rolled to victory in five games. Messier, Glenn Anderson, Jari Kurri and Kevin Lowe all earned their fifth Stanley Cup rings, and the play of youngsters Adam Graves, Joe Murphy and Martin Gelinas had also figured prominently. The Conn Smythe Trophy for playoff MVP went to goalie Bill Ranford, who was in net for all 16 of Edmonton's postseason victories.

1990–91

The 1990–91 season featured a great race for the Presidents' Trophy, with five teams, representing three of the league's four divisions, in the hunt for first place overall. The Boston Bruins again proved the best in the Adams Division with 100 points. Ray Bourque won the Norris Trophy for the fourth time and Cam Neely scored 51 goals. The Calgary Flames also had 100 points this season, but top spot in the Smythe Division went to the Los Angeles Kings, first-place finishers for the first time in franchise history with 102 points. The Kings were led by Wayne Gretzky, who earned his ninth scoring title with 41 goals and 122 assists. Gretzky also took home the Lady Byng Trophy.

But the battle for first place overall came down to Norris Division rivals St. Louis and Chicago. The Blues had Hart Trophy winner Brett Hull's 86 goals on their side, but the Blackhawks edged them out with 106 points to the Blues' 105. Defense was the key in Chicago, where goalie Ed Belfour won the Vezina Trophy as well as the Calder as rookie of the year. In the playoffs, both Norris Division titans were eliminated by the surprising Minnesota North Stars, who racked up a third playoff upset when they knocked off the Edmonton Oilers in the Campbell Conference finals. The defending Stanley Cup champions, who'd slipped to a third-place .500 record, had upset Calgary and Los Angeles before falling to Minnesota.

In the Patrick Division, the Pittsburgh Penguins opened the season without Mario Lemieux (who missed 54 games because of back surgery), but developed a balanced attack led by Mark Recchi, Kevin Stevens and Paul Coffey. Lemieux's late-season return, and a trade that brought Ron Francis and Ulf Samuelsson from Hartford, propelled the Penguins to their first-ever division title with 88 points. Pittsburgh defeated the New Jersey Devils and Washington Capitals to reach the Wales Conference final for the first time. After dropping the first two games to Boston, the Penguins won four in a row and advanced to play Minnesota for the Stanley Cup.

The matchup of Pittsburgh and Minnesota marked the first time since 1934, when the Detroit Red Wings faced Chicago, that neither finalist had ever won the Stanley Cup. The North Stars won games one and three of the series, but Pittsburgh held a 3–2 lead after five games. The Penguins' offensive power finally proved too great in game six, and Pittsburgh claimed its first Stanley Cup title with an 8–0 victory. Mario Lemieux led all postseason performers with 44 points to win the Conn Smythe Trophy as playoff MVP.

1991–92

The 1991–92 season was the league's 75th, and the Original Six franchises—Boston, Chicago, Detroit, Montreal, New York Rangers and Toronto—commemorated the occasion by wearing vintage uniforms for selected games. The Rangers were the season's top team with 105 points on a club-record 50 victories, leading the league for the first time since 1941–42. Mark Messier, traded to New York by the Edmonton Oilers just before the start of the season, won the Hart Trophy, becoming only the second player after former teammate Wayne Gretzky to be named the league's most valuable player with two different teams.

Gretzky and Mario Lemieux both lost time to injuries this season, but Lemieux regained the NHL scoring title with 44 goals and 87 assists. Pittsburgh Penguins teammate Kevin Stevens was second in scoring with 123 points, while Gretzky was third with 31 goals and 90 assists. For the third season in a row, Brett Hull of the St. Louis Blues led the league in goals, this time with 70.

A 10-day players' strike late in year jeopardized the conclusion of the season and pushed back the start of the playoffs to April 18, the latest date in history. The delayed first round proved to be one of the most exciting in history, as six of the eight series went to the full seven games. Boston, Detroit, the Pittsburgh Penguins and Vancouver Canucks all rebounded from 3–1 deficits to win their series. For the first time since 1980, all four division leaders (Montreal, the Rangers, Detroit and Vancouver) advanced to the second round, though each team lost in their respective division finals. Chicago got past Edmonton to advance to the Stanley Cup finals from the Campbell Conference, while Pittsburgh beat Boston for the Wales Conference championship.

The Penguins' season had been eventful: new owners had taken over and popular coach Bob Johnson had died in November 1991. The team was not to be denied under interim coach Scotty Bowman, even though the Blackhawks had set a playoff record with 11 consecutive wins en route to the Stanley Cup finals, and took an early 3–0 lead in game one before Pittsburgh rallied for a last-minute 5–4 win. The Penguins went on to sweep the series, with their four straight victories giving them 11 consecutive playoff wins. The Conn Smythe Trophy for playoff MVP went to Mario Lemieux, who joined Bernie Parent of the Philadelphia Flyers as the only players to win the award two years in a row.

The league awarded its first new franchise since 1979, adding the San Jose Sharks, as NHL hockey returned to the San Francisco Bay area for the first time since 1976. The Sharks' teal and black jersey with its shark-biting-stick logo quickly became a top seller, ushering in a new era of marketing and merchandising consciousness around the NHL.

1992–93

Major changes took place during the summer of 1992. League president John Ziegler resigned and was replaced for a short time by Gil Stein. A new position of commissioner was created in December 1992 with the election of Gary Bettman. Meanwhile, NHL membership reached 24 teams with the addition of the Tampa Bay Lightning and Ottawa Senators. The Senators' home opener marked the first NHL game played in the Canadian capital since 1934, but there were even more amazing resurrections during the Stanley Cup's 100th-anniversary season.

The Toronto Maple Leafs repaid their long-suffering fans with a return to the upper echelon under former Montreal Canadiens coach Pat Burns. Longtime Atlanta-Calgary Flames executive Cliff Fletcher had taken over as president and general manager the year before and acquired Doug Gilmour and Grant Fuhr in a pair of blockbuster trades. With Felix Potvin now ready to emerge as the number-one goalie, Fletcher traded Fuhr to the Buffalo Sabres during the 1992–93 season for sniper Dave Andreychuk. With Andreychuk converting his passes, Gilmour enjoyed career highs with 95 assists and 127 points, and with the Leafs adhering to Burns's defensive philosophy, Toronto set club records with 44 wins and 99 points during the expanded 84-game season. In the playoffs, the Leafs knocked off the Detroit Red Wings in a thrilling seven-game Norris Division semifinal, then beat the St. Louis Blues to win the division final.

Wayne Gretzky also enjoyed a brilliant comeback. The Great One missed the first 39 games of the season due to a career-threatening back injury, but he returned to action on January 6, 1993, and collected 65 points in 45 games. Gretzky was in top form by the playoffs, leading the Los Angeles Kings to victories over the Calgary Flames and Vancouver Canucks before eliminating the Leafs in seven games to reach the Stanley Cup finals for the first time in franchise history.

One day before Gretzky's return to the Kings, the Pittsburgh Penguins announced that Mario Lemieux had Hodgkin's disease, a form of cancer. Lemieux missed 24 games while receiving treatment, then returned to claim the NHL scoring title and spark Pittsburgh to a record 17-game winning streak that led the Penguins to first place overall. Lemieux was bothered by back spasms in the playoffs and the New York Islanders stunned the Penguins in the Patrick Division final before falling to the Montreal Canadiens in the Wales Conference championship.

The 100th anniversary of the Stanley Cup matched the game's greatest franchise against arguably its greatest player and it was the Montreal Canadiens who came out ahead of Wayne Gretzky and the Los Angeles Kings in five games. Montreal won its 24th Stanley Cup title on Patrick Roy's brilliant playoff goaltending and an amazing streak of victories in 10 consecutive overtime games, including three against Los Angeles.

1993–94

The 1993–94 season was the NHL's third consecutive expansion year as the Miami-based Florida Panthers and the Mighty Ducks of Anaheim joined the fold. The league moved into another southern city as the Minnesota North Stars relocated to Texas, becoming the Dallas Stars. The division and conference names were also changed to geographic designations: the Adams, Patrick, Norris and Smythe divisions became the Northeast, Atlantic, Central and Pacific. The Prince of Wales and Clarence Campbell conferences were now known respectively as the Eastern and Western.

Previous expansions had all produced an explosion of offense, but defense came to the forefront in the new 26-team NHL. In 1992–93 only two goaltenders had posted goals-against averages below 3.00; in 1993–94, 19 goalies broke that barrier, led by Vezina Trophy winner Dominik Hasek of the Buffalo Sabres, whose 1.95 average made him the first netminder below 2.00 since Bernie Parent of the Philadelphia Flyers in 1973–74.

Pittsburgh Penguins superstar Mario Lemieux did not figure in the scoring race this season, as injuries and illness limited him to just 22 games. Pat LaFontaine of the Buffalo Sabres, runner-up to Lemieux in 1992–93, missed 68 games with a knee injury. Teemu Selanne of the Winnipeg Jets, who scored 76 goals as a rookie the year before, played just 51 games, while budding superstar Eric Lindros of the Philadelphia Flyers missed 19 games with injuries.

Despite the drop in offense, Wayne Gretzky still managed to become the greatest goal scorer in NHL history. On March 23, 1994, the Los Angeles Kings superstar was set up by teammates Marty McSorley and Luc Robitaille and beat Kirk McLean of the Vancouver Canucks for his 802nd career goal, breaking Gordie Howe's record of 801. Gretzky finished the year with 38 goals and 92 assists, earning his 10th scoring title. The Hart Trophy went to Sergei Fedorov of the Detroit Red Wings, who was runner-up to Gretzky for the Art Ross and also earned the Selke Trophy as the NHL's best defensive forward.

The New York Rangers proved to be the best in the NHL this year, setting franchise records with 52 wins and 112 points under coach Mike Keenan. They beat the New York Islanders and Washington Capitals before defeating the New Jersey Devils in a thrilling seven-game Eastern Conference final. The Vancouver Canucks provided the opposition for the Stanley Cup. Vancouver won game one, but the Rangers took the next three in a row. The Canucks rallied for two wins to force a seventh game, but the Rangers finally snapped their 54-year Stanley Cup jinx with a 3–2 victory.

1994–95

A 103-day lockout resulted in the NHL's shortest regular season in 53 years. The 1994–95 season did not begin until January 20, 1995, but the abbreviated 48-game schedule was packed with plenty of excitement.

The Pittsburgh Penguins were without Mario Lemieux for the entire year, as he took the season off to recuperate from the lingering effects of back injuries and his battle with cancer, but the team remained in fine form, opening the season with a 12–0–1 mark. The Quebec Nordiques, not to be outdone, streaked out of the gate at 12–1–0 and the two teams battled for top spot in the Northeast Division until the final night of the season. Quebec, who had swapped Mats Sundin to Toronto in a deal for Wendel Clark and Sylvain Lefebvre, emerged victorious with 65 points to Pittsburgh's 61.

The Penguins' Jaromir Jagr broke through as a superstar, leading the NHL with 70 points on 32 goals and 38 assists. Eric Lindros earned the Hart Trophy for leading the Philadelphia Flyers to top spot in the Atlantic Division. Lindros equaled Jagr's 70 points, but missed out on the Art Ross Trophy because he had only scored 29 goals.

The defending Stanley Cup champion New York Rangers battled all season just to earn a berth in the playoffs. They snuck in as the eighth and final qualifier in the Eastern Conference. Montreal wasn't so lucky. Despite acquiring Mark Recchi for John LeClair in a blockbuster deal with Philadelphia, and swapping captain Kirk Muller to the New York Islanders for Pierre Turgeon, the Canadiens missed the playoffs for the first time in 25 years. The Rangers managed to upset the Quebec Nordiques in the first round before losing to Philadelphia. Pittsburgh reached the second round before falling to the New Jersey Devils, who then beat the Flyers to advance to the Stanley Cup finals for the first time in franchise history.

In the Western Conference, the Detroit Red Wings cruised to top spot in the Central Division with a record of 33–11–4 and finished first overall in the NHL standings for the first time since 1964–65. The Red Wings then beat the Dallas Stars before avenging the previous year's first-round loss to the San Jose Sharks with a four-game sweep. After a five-game victory over the Chicago Blackhawks for the Western Conference title, Detroit was back in the Stanley Cup finals for the first time in 29 years.

Under coach Jacques Lemaire, the Devils had successfully employed a defensive scheme known as the "neutral-zone trap" throughout the Eastern Conference playoffs, but their detractors doubted they could shut down the powerful Red Wings. The Devils proved the pundits wrong, completely closing down Detroit's attack in a surprising four-game sweep of the Stanley Cup finals.

1995–96

After their first-place finish the year before, most expected the Detroit Red Wings to come out flying in 1995–96 and they didn't disappoint. Coach Scotty Bowman's squad exceeded even his great Montreal Canadiens teams of the late 1970s with an NHL-record 62 victories, though Detroit's 62–13–7 mark produced one fewer points than the record 132 collected by Bowman's 60–8–12 Canadiens of 1976–77. Meanwhile, 1994–95's top Eastern Conference team, the Quebec Nordiques, moved to Denver, becoming the Colorado Avalanche and playing in the Pacific Division. The Avalanche would beat the Wings in a six-game Western Conference final.

After sitting out the 1994–95 season, Mario Lemieux came back to score 69 goals in 70 games and win his fifth scoring title with 161 points. Lemieux won the Hart Trophy as most valuable player for the third time. Things did not go as well for Wayne Gretzky this season. The Great One and his Los Angeles Kings were both slumping when he was dealt to the St. Louis Blues in February. Another significant trade this season saw Patrick Roy swapped to Colorado after a dispute with Canadiens coach Mario Tremblay.

Several young players took their place among the NHL's elite. Jaromir Jagr followed up his Art Ross performance of the previous season with 149 points, while Joe Sakic of the Avalanche finished third in league scoring with 120 points. Teammate Peter Forsberg (rookie of the year in 1994–95) collected 116 points, while Eric Lindros of the Philadelphia Flyers had 115. Paul Kariya fulfilled the promise expected of him with 50 goals and 58 assists for the Mighty Ducks of Anaheim and was teamed with a linemate who complemented his talents when Teemu Selanne was acquired from the Winnipeg Jets.

In the Eastern Conference, the Florida Panthers made the playoffs in just their third season and rode the hot goaltending of John Vanbiesbrouck past the Boston Bruins, Philadelphia Flyers and Pittsburgh Penguins to the Stanley Cup finals, which opened in Denver with the Avalanche scoring 3–1 and 8–1 victories. The Panthers played better when the series moved to Miami, but Colorado completed the sweep with 3–2 and 1–0 wins. Uwe Krupp scored the

Stanley Cup-winning goal at 4:31 of the third overtime period. Joe Sakic won the Conn Smythe Trophy, while Claude Lemieux (previously a winner in Montreal and New Jersey) became only the fourth player in history to celebrate Stanley Cup titles with three different teams.

1996–97

There were many changes throughout the 1996–97 season, beginning with the United States dethroning Canada as the top hockey nation at the inaugural World Cup of Hockey. Major trades this season involved Jeremy Roenick, Brendan Shanahan, Paul Coffey, Adam Oates, Bill Ranford, Ed Belfour and Doug Gilmour. Wayne Gretzky took his act to Broadway, signing as a free agent with the New York Rangers, and Mario Lemieux staged a farewell tour, retiring at season's end at the age of 31. Lemieux went out in style, winning the Art Ross Trophy for a sixth time with 122 points. Wayne Gretzky tied Lemieux for the league lead with 72 assists and added 25 goals to lead the Rangers in scoring with 97 points. Lemieux and Teemu Selanne were the only players to top 100 points in a season dominated by defense. The southward migration of NHL franchises also continued this year as the Winnipeg Jets moved to Phoenix, setting up shop as the Coyotes.

Goaltenders all around the league posted outstanding numbers, but Martin Brodeur of the New Jersey Devils was the most impressive. His 1.88 goals-against average was the lowest in the NHL since Tony Esposito's 1.77 in 1971–72 and his 10 shutouts made him the first to reach double digits since Ken Dryden in 1976–77. Brodeur and backup Mike Dunham shared the Jennings Trophy, but the Vezina Trophy went to Dominik Hasek. The Buffalo star also became the first goaltender since Jacques Plante in 1962 to win the Hart Trophy after leading the Sabres to a surprising first-place finish in the Northeast Division.

The Sabres needed overtime in the seventh game to subdue an improved Ottawa Senators team in the first round of the playoffs. The Philadelphia Flyers—en route to the Stanley Cup finals—then eliminated the Sabres and New York to advance.

In the Western Conference, the defending Stanley Cup champion Colorado Avalanche topped the NHL standings with 107 points. The Detroit Red Wings followed up their record-breaking season with an "ordinary" 94-point campaign and they had trouble getting past the St. Louis Blues to open the playoffs. A four-game sweep of the Mighty Ducks of Anaheim followed before the Red Wings avenged the previous spring's loss to the Avalanche with a six-game victory for the Western Conference championship. The Stanley Cup then returned to Detroit for the first time since 1955 as the Red Wings defeated the Philadelphia Flyers in four consecutive games. Goalie Mike Vernon won the Conn Smythe Trophy as playoff MVP.

1997–98

The 1997-98 season saw the Red Wings win their second consecutive Stanley Cup title with a four-game sweep of the Washington Capitals. The Red Wings had been the third-best team during the regular season, posting 103 points to trail both the Dallas Stars and New Jersey Devils. Detroit's success had been a true team effort; their team total of 250 goals was the second-highest in the NHL (behind the St. Louis Blues' 256) despite the fact that no Detroit player ranked among the NHL's top 20 scorers.

Jaromir Jagr was the league's leading scorer with 102 points. His total was the lowest to top the NHL in a full season since Stan Mikita's 87 points in 1967–68 and marked the first time since Bobby Orr in 1969–70 that only one NHL player had more than 100 points. Jagr's strong play helped the Pittsburgh Penguins to a surprising first-place finish in the Northeast Division in the first season following the retirement of Mario Lemieux. Jagr also helped the Czech Republic win a gold medal in hockey at the Winter Olympics in Nagano, Japan.

The participation of NHL players at the Winter Olympics resulted in the most evenly matched hockey competition in Winter Games history. North American fans were disappointed by the early elimination of the United States and by Canada's fourth-place finish. The Russians, led by Pavel Bure, appeared headed for the gold until they ran into Dominik Hasek in the championship game. Hasek blanked Russia 1–0 to clinch the Czech Republic's first Olympic gold medal.

Hasek enjoyed another brilliant season in 1997–98. He shook off a slow start to lead the NHL with 13 shutouts, and his 33 wins and 2.09 goals-against average also ranked among the leaders. With his second consecutive Hart Trophy win, he became the first goalie to earn multiple MVP awards. Hasek's play led Buffalo to the Eastern Conference finals, where the Sabres lost to Washington in six games. Upsets had marked the Eastern playoffs, particularly in the first round where the Sabres knocked off the Philadelphia Flyers, the Montreal Canadiens surprised Pittsburgh, and the Ottawa Senators stunned the Devils.

The playoffs went more according to form in the Western Conference, as Detroit defeated Phoenix and St. Louis to meet a Dallas team that had knocked off the San Jose Sharks and Edmonton Oilers. The Western Conference final matchup of the defending Cup champion (Detroit) against the league's best club in the regular season (Dallas) was compelling, but the Red Wings, led by captain Steve Yzerman, eliminated the Stars in six games.

1998–99

There were many compelling plot lines during the 1998-99 regular season: the realignment of the league into six divisions; the rebirth of the Toronto Maple Leafs; the rise to prominence of the Ottawa Senators; and the season-long excellence of the Dallas Stars. But, come the final week of the regular season, one story overshadowed them all.

On April 16, 1999, Wayne Gretzky announced his retirement from the NHL. He played his final game two days later. Gretzky retired with 894 goals and 1,963 assists for a total of 2,857 points. Those totals represent just three of the 61 NHL records that Wayne Gretzky holds or shares. His final goal on March 29, 1999, gave Gretzky 1,072 in his career (NHL and WHA, regular season and playoffs combined)—one more than Gordie Howe scored during his career.

Wayne Gretzky's New York Rangers lost the final game of the Great One's career, dropping a 2–1 decision to the Pittsburgh Penguins. Jaromir Jagr scored the winning goal in overtime, and Gretzky spoke of the torch being passed. Jagr had a brilliant season, winning the Art Ross Trophy for the second straight season with 127 points (44 goals, 83 assists). He also knocked off Dominik Hasek for the Hart

Trophy as MVP. Trailing Jagr in the scoring race were Mighty Ducks teammates Teemu Selanne (107 points) and Paul Kariya (101). Selanne's total included a league-leading 47 goals, which made him the first recipient of the new Maurice "Rocket" Richard Trophy. Kariya's season represented a significant comeback from serious injuries that had kept him out of almost the entire 1997–98 season.

The NHL's realignment for the 1998-99 season brought Toronto back into the Eastern Conference, where the surprising Maple Leafs battled the Ottawa Senators for top spot in the Northeast Division. Ottawa won out, topped only in the Conference by the Atlantic Division-leading New Jersey Devils. The new Southeast Division was won by the Carolina Hurricanes. Out west, the Detroit Red Wings won the Central Division, while the Colorado Avalanche topped the Northwest. The best team in the league was the Dallas Stars, who took the Pacific Division with a team-record 51 wins and 114 points. This marked the second straight year Dallas won the Presidents' Trophy.

It had been five years since the NHL's best regular-season team was also the league's playoff champion, but this year the Stars would not be denied. Dallas swept the Edmonton Oilers to open the playoffs, then defeated the St. Louis Blues before taking on Colorado. The Avalanche had knocked off the two-time defending Stanley Cup champions from Detroit in the second round, but then fell to Dallas in seven games. The Eastern Conference playoffs saw the Buffalo Sabres upset Ottawa, then beat Boston before toppling Toronto in five games. Dallas and Buffalo provided the most competitive Stanley Cup finals in years before the Stars took the series in six. Brett Hull scored the Stanley Cup-winning goal with 5:09 left in the third overtime session, ending the second-longest game in the history of the Stanley Cup finals.

1999–2000

In the first NHL season of the post-Gretzky era, Jaromir Jagr became the first player to lead the league in scoring for three consecutive seasons since "The Great One" won the Art Ross Trophy eight times in a row, starting in 1980–81. Though injuries limited Jagr to just 63 games, his 96 points were still two more than Pavel Bure, who led the league with 58 goals. The Russian Rocket won the Maurice "Rocket" Richard Trophy by a margin of 14 goals over Owen Nolan. Maurice Richard, the NHL's first 50-goal scorer, passed away on May 27, 2000.

Among the netminding fraternity, several new names emerged to join more familiar ones atop the 1999–2000 goaltenders statistics. Brian Boucher (1.91), Roman Turek (1.95) and Jose Theodore (2.10) finished 1–2–3 in goals-against average. Turek also topped the league with seven shutouts. Martin Brodeur led the league in wins (43) for the second straight season, while Ed Belfour edged out Theodore for the NHL's best save percentage at .919. Patrick Roy won 32 games to give him 444 victories in his career, three short of Terry Sawchuk's all-time record.

Philadelphia, New Jersey, Toronto and Washington were the top teams in the Eastern Conference. The Flyers edged out the Devils for top spot in the regular season but New Jersey rallied from a three-games-to-one deficit to eliminate Philadelphia in the Conference final. Earlier in the playoffs, the Flyers had defeated Pittsburgh 2–1 in a marathon game that needed 92 minutes of overtime.

Out west, St. Louis won the Presidents' Trophy for the first time, but was eliminated by San Jose in the first round. Dallas won the Pacific Division, while Colorado added Ray Bourque from Boston at the trade deadline and went on to finish first in the Northwest. The teams met in the Western Conference final with Dallas again winning in seven games. The Stanley Cup finals between the Devils and Stars opened with a 7–3 New Jersey win in game one and ended with New Jersey taking the series in six games. Jason Arnott scored the Cup-winning goal for the Devils in double overtime.

CHAPTER 33

The NHL Entry Draft

7,221 Dreams of Hockey Glory

THE NHL'S ENTRY DRAFT and its predecessor, the Amateur Draft, have been the gateway to the National Hockey League for players from all over the world. There have been 7,221 selections made since the first NHL draft in 1963 including a record total of 293 picks at the 2000 Entry Draft.

The Amateur Draft was created by the NHL in 1963 as a means of phasing out the sponsorship of amateur teams by the league's member clubs. However, since most of hockey's top junior players had already been assigned to NHL clubs through sponsored junior teams, few top prospects were eligible in the early years. As a result, even though each of the NHL's "Original Six" clubs was allowed to select four players, not all of the choices would be exercised every year. In 1965, for example, only 11 players where drafted—even though teams from the American Hockey League, the Western Hockey League and the Central Pro league were allowed to select junior prospects as part of the draft. Even after the NHL added six new teams in 1967, no more than 24 players were selected in one season through 1968. The draft in 1968 marked the first time that teams selected in the reverse order of the final standings. Previously, the draft order had rotated on an annual basis.

On June 12, 1969, the National Hockey League staged its first universal Amateur Draft. All junior prospects were eligible to be drafted because the old sponsorship system had been phased out. Every team had an equal opportunity to acquire the best junior talent—with one exception: Since the first draft in 1963, the Montreal Canadiens had held the option of selecting two French-Canadian players before any other NHL team made its first choice. Using this rule, and some clever trading, the Canadiens had acquired the first three picks in the 1968 draft. In 1969, they used the first two picks to land Rejean Houle and Marc Tardif. This territorial exemption was discontinued beginning in 1970.

Eighty-four players were selected in the 1969 Amateur Draft—almost four times more than had ever been picked before. The number of selections reached 115 the following year and, as the NHL continued to expand through the 1970s, topped 200 for the first time in 1978. When, in 1979, the NHL expanded to include four teams that had previously played in the World Hockey Association, the Amateur Draft was renamed the Entry Draft to reflect the fact that young players who previously had played professionally in the now-defunct WHA now were eligible to be drafted by NHL clubs.

Though Garry Monahan was just 16 years and seven months old when he became the first player drafted in 1963, the eligibility age had risen to 20 by 1967. Competiton from WHA teams in the mid-1970s resulted in the age limit dropping to 18 in certain cases. Between 1980 and 1995, all 18-, 19- and 20-year-old North American players were eligible for the Entry Draft. From 1987 to 1991, the selection of 18- and 19-year-old players was generally restricted to the first three rounds. Since the 1995 Entry Draft, all 18-year-old players are required to declare themselves eligible by signing what is called an "opt-in" form.

Players from outside North America are also draft eligible from the age of 18. Non-North American players over the age of 20 must be drafted as well.

In order to be eligible for the draft, a player must be 18 years old by September 15 of his draft year.

Players have been eligible to re-enter the draft since 1978. League rules state that any North American player age 20 or under who does not receive a bona fide offer from his NHL club within one year, or, has not signed a contract within two years of being selected is eligible to re-enter the draft. If a player is drafted twice, he is not eligible for further re-entry. Since 1995, the NHL has awarded compensatory picks to clubs in two circumstances: i) if a club is unable to sign a first-round draft choice and ii) if a club loses a player to Group III (unrestricted) free agency.

Though Canadian major junior hockey always has supplied the largest number of players selected, the international flavor of the Entry Draft dates back to its Amateur days. The first player to be selected from an American university was Al Karlander (17th overall in 1967), a Canadian who attended Michigan Tech. The first American-born player drafted into the NHL was another Michigan Tech player, Herb Boxer (17th overall in 1968). Brian Lawton became the first American to be chosen number-one in the draft when the Minnesota North Stars selected him in 1983.

In 1969, the St. Louis Blues made Finnish-born Tommi Salmelainen (66th overall) the first European player to be selected in the draft. By the late 1970s, and throughout the 1980s, many NHL teams used late-round selections to take a chance on Russians and Czechs who would have had to defect in order to enter the NHL. Sergei Priakin, the first Russian to play with permission in the NHL, was the last player drafted in 1988 when the Calgary Flames claimed him with the 252nd choice. One year later, Sweden's Mats Sundin became the first European player selected atop the draft when the Quebec Nordiques chose him first overall.

NOTE: Where available, brief comments have been added for players drafted in the first or second rounds who have not appeared in an NHL regular-season game.

1963

			DRAFTED	NHL PLAYERS: POS	GP	G	A	PTS	PIM
PICK	TEAM	NAME	FROM	NHL GOALTENDERS: POS	GP	W	GA	SO	AVG
1	MTL	Garry Monahan	St. Michael's Juveniles	LW	748	116	169	285	484
2	DET	Pete Mahovlich	St. Michael's Juveniles	C	884	288	485	773	916
3	BOS	Orest Romashyma	New Hamburg Jr. C		Did not play professionally				
4	NYR	Al Osborne	Weston Jr. B	RW	Played 8 years in OHA-Sr.				
5	CHI	Art Hampson	Trenton Midgets		Did not play professionally				
6	TOR	Walt McKechnie	London Jr. B	C	955	214	392	606	469
7	MTL	Rodney Presswood	Georgetown Midgets		Did not play professionally				
8	DET	Bill Cosburn	Bick's Pickles		Did not play professionally				
9	BOS	Terrance Lane	Georgetown Midgets		Did not play professionally				
10	NYR	Terry Jones	Weston Midgets		Two 70PT years in EHL				
11	CHI	Wayne Davidson	Georgetown Midgets		Did not play professionally				
12	TOR	Neil Clairmont	Parry Sound Midgets	LW	10 seasons in EHL, IHL, NAHL				
13	MTL	Roy Pugh	Aurora Jr. C	C					
14	BOS	Roger Bamburak	Isaac Brock	RW					
15	NYR	Mike Cummings	Georgetown Midgets						
16	CHI	Bill Carson	Brampton Midgets	D					
17	TOR	Jim McKenny	Neil McNeil Jr. A	D	604	82	247	329	294
18	MTL	Glen Shirton	Port Colborne Midgets	D					
19	BOS	Jim Blair	Georgetown Midgets						
20	NYR	Campbell Alleson	Portage la Prairie Jr.						
21	TOR	Gerry Meehan	Neil McNeil Jr. A	C	670	180	243	423	111

1964

PICK	TEAM	NAME	DRAFTED FROM	POS	GP	G / W	A / GA	PTS / SO	PIM / AVG
				NHL PLAYERS: POS	GP	G	A	PTS	PIM
				NHL GOALTENDERS: POS	GP	W	GA	SO	AVG
1	DET	Claude Gauthier	Rosemount Midgets		Did not play professionally				
2	BOS	Alec Campbell	Strathroy Midgets	RW	71 career IHL games				
3	NYR	Robert Graham	Toronto Marlboro Midgets	D	68 career EHL games				
4	CHI	Richard Bayes	Dixie Midgets	C	17 career NAHL goals				
5	TOR	Tom Martin	Toronto Marlboro Midgets	RW	3	1	0	1	0
6	MTL	Claude Chagnon	Rosemount Midgets		3 junior seasons – Montreal				
7	DET	Brian Watts	Toronto Marlboro Midgets	LW	4	0	0	0	0
8	BOS	Jim Booth	Sault Ste. Marie	LW	3 pro seasons in CHL and IHL				
9	NYR	Tim Ecclestone	Etobicoke Jr. B	LW	692	126	233	359	344
10	CHI	Jan Popiel	Georgetown Midgets	LW	160PTS in 296 WHA games				
11	TOR	Dave Cotey	Aurora Jr. C		Did not play professionally				
12	MTL	Guy Allen	Stamford Jr. B	D	4 years CHL/IHL/EHL				
13	DET	Ralph Buchanan	Montreal East Intermediates	D					
14	BOS	Ken Dryden	Etobicoke Jr. B	G	397	258	870	46	2.24
15	NYR	Gordon Lowe	Toronto Marlboro Midgets	D					
16	CHI	Carl Hadfield	Dixie Jr. B	RW					
17	TOR	Mike Pelyk	Toronto Marlboro Midgets	D	441	26	88	114	566
18	MTL	Paul Reid	Kingston Midgets						
19	DET	Rene Leclerc	Hamilton Jr. B	RW	87	10	11	21	105
20	BOS	Blair Allister	Ingersoll Jr. B						
21	NYR	Syl Apps Jr.	Kingston Midgets	C	727	183	423	606	311
22	CHI	Moe L'Abbe	Rosemount Midgets	RW	5	0	1	1	0
23	TOR	Jim Dorey	Stamford Jr. B	D	232	25	74	99	553
24	MTL	Michel Jacques	Megantic Jr. B	LW					

1965

PICK	TEAM	NAME	DRAFTED FROM	POS	GP	G / W	A / GA	PTS / SO	PIM / AVG
				NHL PLAYERS: POS	GP	G	A	PTS	PIM
				NHL GOALTENDERS: POS	GP	W	GA	SO	AVG
1	NYR	Andre Veilleux	Montreal Jr. B	RW	Played in QJHL-B				
2	CHI	Andrew Culligan	St. Michael's Jr. B		1 career IHL game				
3	DET	George Forgie	Flin Flon	D	2 years IHL, 405 PIM				
4	BOS	Joe Bailey	St. Thomas Jr. B		5 games – Niagara Falls				
5	MTL	Pierre Bouchard	St. Vincent de Paul Jr. B	D	595	24	82	106	433
6	NYR	George Surmay	Kelvin Juveniles	G	3 years EHL/CHL/WHL				
7	CHI	Brian McKenney	Smiths Falls Jr.		Did not play professionally				
8	DET	Bob Birdsell	Settler	RW	4 years WHL/CHL/AHL				
9	BOS	Bill Ramsay	Winnipeg		Did not play professionally				
10	NYR	Michel Parizeau	Montreal Jr. B	C	58	3	14	17	18
11	PIT(AHL)	Gary Beattie	Gananoque Jr. C		Did not play professionally				

1966

PICK	TEAM	NAME	DRAFTED FROM	POS	GP	G / W	A / GA	PTS / SO	PIM / AVG
				NHL PLAYERS: POS	GP	G	A	PTS	PIM
				NHL GOALTENDERS: POS	GP	W	GA	SO	AVG
1	BOS	Barry Gibbs	Estevan	D	797	58	224	282	945
2	NYR	Brad Park	Toronto	D	1113	213	683	896	1429
3	CHI	Terry Caffery	Toronto	C	14	0	0	0	0
4	TOR	John Wright	West Clair Jr. B	C	127	16	36	52	67
5	MTL	Phil Myre	Shawinigan	G	439	149	1482	14	3.53
6	DET	Steve Atkinson	Niagara Falls	RW	302	60	51	111	104
7	BOS	Rick Smith	Hamilton	D	687	52	167	219	560
8	NYR	Joey Johnston	Peterborough	LW	331	85	106	191	320
9	CHI	Ron Dussiaume	Oshawa	LW	5 years in the CHL and AHL				
10	TOR	Cam Crosby	Toronto		4 seasons – Toronto/Kitchener				
11	MTL	Maurice St. Jacques	London	C	52G and 95PTS in 1969-70				
12	DET	Jim Whittaker	Oshawa	D	3 years EHL/IHL				
13	BOS	Garnet Bailey	Edmonton	LW	568	107	171	278	633
14	NYR	Don Luce	Kitchener	C	894	225	329	554	364
15	CHI	Larry Gibbons	Markham Jr. B	D					
16	TOR	Rick Ley	Niagara Falls	D	310	12	72	84	528
17	MTL	Jude Drouin	Verdun	C	666	151	305	456	346
18	DET	Lee Carpenter	Hamilton Jr. B	D					
19	BOS	Tom Webster	Niagara Falls	RW	102	33	42	75	61
20	NYR	Jack Egers	Kitchener Jr. B	RW	284	64	69	133	154
21	CHI	Brian Morenz	Oshawa	LW					
22	TOR	Dale MacLeish	Peterborough	C					
23	MTL	Bob Pate	Montreal	D					
24	DET	Grant Cole	St. Michael's Jr. B	G					

1967

PICK	TEAM	NAME	DRAFTED FROM	POS	GP	G / W	A / GA	PTS / SO	PIM / AVG
				NHL PLAYERS: POS	GP	G	A	PTS	PIM
				NHL GOALTENDERS: POS	GP	W	GA	SO	AVG
1	L.A.	Rick Pagnutti	Garson	D	10 pro years in 5 leagues				
2	PIT	Steve Rexe	Belleville Sr.	G	3 years EHL/AHL				
3	OAK	Ken Hicks	Brandon		5 years EHL/USHL				
4	MIN	Wayne Cheesman	Whitby Jr. B	D	2 years in OHL-Sr.				
5	PHI	Serge Bernier	Sorel	RW	302	78	119	197	234
6	NYR	Robert Dickson	Chatham Jr. B	LW	25 points in EHL/IHL				
7	CHI	Bob Tombari	Sault Ste. Marie	LW	716PTS – Muskegon 1967-78				
8	MTL	Elgin McCann	Weyburn Jr. A	RW	9 pro seasons in 5 leagues				
9	DET	Ron Barkwell	Flin Flon		1 year EHL/IHL				
10	BOS	Meehan Bonnar	St. Thomas Jr. B	RW	6 years, 4 leagues				
11	PIT	Bob Smith	Sault Ste. Marie	C	5 years IHL and CHL				
12	OAK	Garry Wood	Fort Frances	D	9 pro seasons in 4 leagues				
13	MIN	Larry Mick	Pembroke Jr. A		29PTS in 75 EHL games				
14	PHI	Al Sarault	Pembroke Jr. A	D	28PTS in 81 EHL games				
15	NYR	Brian Tosh	Smiths Falls Jr.	D	13PTS in 68 IHL games				
16	TOR	Bob Kelly	Port Arthur Jr.	LW	425	87	109	196	687
17	DET	Al Karlander	Michigan Tech	C	212	36	56	92	70
18	OAK	Kevin Smith	Halifax Jr.	D	Did not play professionally				

1968

PICK	TEAM	NAME	DRAFTED FROM	POS	GP	G / W	A / GA	PTS / SO	PIM / AVG
				NHL PLAYERS: POS	GP	G	A	PTS	PIM
				NHL GOALTENDERS: POS	GP	W	GA	SO	AVG
1	MTL	Michel Plasse	Drummondville	G	299	92	1058	2	3.79
2	MTL	Roger Belisle	Montreal North Beavers		11 career IHL games				
3	MTL	Jim Pritchard	Winnipeg	D	2 WHA games – Chicago				
4	PIT	Garry Swain	Niagara Falls	C	9	1	1	2	0
5	MIN	Jim Benzelock	Winnipeg	RW	45 points in 166 WHA games				
6	ST.L.	Gary Edwards	Toronto	G	286	88	973	11	3.65
7	L.A.	Jim McInally	Hamilton	D	3 years AHL/EHL/IHL				
8	PHI	Lew Morrison	Flin Flon	RW	564	39	52	91	107
9	CHI	John Marks	North Dakota	LW	657	112	163	275	330
10	TOR	Brad Selwood	Niagara Falls	D	163	7	40	47	153
11	DET	Steve Andrascik	Flin Flon	RW	1 NHL playoff game – Rangers				
12	BOS	Danny Schock	Estevan	LW	20	1	2	3	0
13	OAK	Doug Smith	Winnipeg	C	4 pro seasons in 4 leagues				
14	PIT	Ron Snell	Regina	RW	7	3	2	5	6
15	MIN	Marc Rioux	Verdun	C	Did not play professionally				
16	ST.L.	Curt Bennett	Brown	LW	580	152	182	334	347
17	DET	Herb Boxer	Michigan Tech	RW	5 years, 4 leagues				
18	BOS	Fraser Rice	Halifax Jr.	C	2 years EHL/CHL				
19	NYR	Bruce Buchanan	Weyburn Jr. A	D	Did not play professionally				
20	OAK	Jim Trewin	Flin Flon	D					
21	PIT	Dave Simpson	Port Arthur Jr.	D					
22	MIN	Glen Lindsay	Saskatoon	G					
23	MTL	Don Grierson	North Bay Jr. A	RW					
24	BOS	Brian St. John	U. of Toronto	C					

1969

PICK	TEAM	NAME	DRAFTED FROM	POS	GP	G / W	A / GA	PTS / SO	PIM / AVG
				NHL PLAYERS: POS	GP	G	A	PTS	PIM
				NHL GOALTENDERS: POS	GP	W	GA	SO	AVG
FIRST ROUND									
1	MTL	Rejean Houle	Montreal	L/RW	635	161	247	408	395
2	MTL	Marc Tardif	Montreal	LW	517	194	207	401	443
3	BOS	Don Tannahill	Niagara Falls	LW	111	30	33	63	25
4	BOS	Frank Spring	Edmonton	RW	61	14	20	34	12
5	MIN	Dick Redmond	St. Catharines	D	771	133	312	445	504
6	PHI	Bob Currier	Cornwall	C	5 pro seasons in 3 leagues				
7	OAK	Tony Featherstone	Peterborough	RW	130	17	21	38	65
8	NYR	Andre Dupont	Montreal	D	800	59	185	244	1986
9	TOR	Ernie Moser	Estevan	RW	91PTS – Flint (IHL) in 72-73				
10	DET	Jim Rutherford	Hamilton	G	457	151	1576	14	3.65
11	BOS	Ivan Boldirev	Oshawa	C	1052	361	505	866	507
12	NYR	Pierre Jarry	Ottawa	LW	344	88	117	205	142
13	CHI	J.P. Bordeleau	Montreal	RW	519	97	126	223	143
SECOND ROUND									
14	MIN	Dennis O'Brien	St. Catharines	D	592	31	91	122	1017
15	PIT	Rick Kessell	Oshawa	C	135	4	24	28	6
16	L.A.	Dale Hoganson	Estevan	D	343	13	77	90	186
17	PHI	Bobby Clarke	Flin Flon	C	1144	358	852	1210	1453
18	OAK	Ron Stackhouse	Peterborough	D	889	87	372	459	824
19	ST.L.	Mike Lowe	Loyola College	C	Loyola grad – 24PTS in CHL				
20	TOR	Doug Brindley	Niagara Falls	LW/C	3	0	0	0	0
21	DET	Ron Garwasiuk	Regina	LW	19PTS in 51 WHA games				
22	BOS	Art Quoquochi	Montreal	RW	3 pro seasons in 4 leagues				
23	NYR	Bert Wilson	London	LW	478	37	44	81	646
24	CHI	Larry Romanchych	Flin Flon	RW	298	68	97	165	102
OTHER ROUNDS									
25	MIN	Gilles Gilbert	London	G	416	192	1290	18	3.27
26	PIT	Michel Briere	Shawinigan	C	76	12	32	44	20
27	L.A.	Gregg Boddy	Edmonton	D	273	23	44	67	263
28	PHI	Willie Brossart	Estevan	LW	129	1	14	15	88
29	OAK	Don O'Donoghue	St. Catharines	RW	125	18	17	35	35
30	ST.L.	Bernard Gagnon	Michigan	C					
31	TOR	Larry McIntyre	Moose Jaw	D	41	0	3	3	26
32	MTL	Bobby Sheehan	St. Catharines	C	310	48	63	111	40
33	DET	Wayne Hawrysh	Flin Flon	RW					
34	BOS	Nels Jacobson	Winnipeg	LW					

PICK	TEAM	NAME	DRAFTED FROM	NHL PLAYERS: POS / NHL GOALTENDERS: POS	GP / GP	G / W	A / GA	PTS / SO	PIM / AVG
35	NYR	Kevin Morrison	St-Jerome	D	41	4	11	15	23
36	CHI	Milt Black	Winnipeg	RW					
37	MIN	Fred O'Donnell	Oshawa	RW	115	15	11	26	98
38	PIT	Yvon Labre	Toronto	D	371	14	87	101	788
39	L.A.	Bruce Landon	Peterborough	G					
40	PHI	Michel Belhumeur	Drummondville	G	65	9	254	0	4.61
41	OAK	Pierre Farmer	Shawinigan	D					
42	ST.L.	Vic Teal	St. Catharines	RW	1	0	0	0	0
43	TOR	Frank Hughes	Edmonton	LW	5	0	0	0	0
44	MTL	Murray Anderson	Flin Flon	D	40	0	1	1	68
45	DET	Wayne Chernecki	Winnipeg	C					
46	BOS	Ron Fairbrother	Saskatoon	LW					
47	NYR	Bruce Hellemond	Moose Jaw	LW					
48	CHI	Daryl Maggs	Calgary	D	135	14	19	33	54
49	MIN	Pierre Jutras	Shawinigan	LW					
50	PIT	Ed Patenaude	Calgary	RW					
51	L.A.	Butch Goring	Dauphin Jr. A	C	1107	375	513	888	102
52	PHI	Dave Schultz	Sorel	LW	535	79	121	200	2294
53	OAK	Warren Harrison	Sorel	C					
54	ST.L.	Brian Glenwright	Kitchener	LW					
55	TOR	Brian Spencer	Swift Current	LW	553	80	143	223	634
56	MTL	Garry Doyle	Ottawa	G					
57	DET	Wally Olds	Minnesota-Duluth	D					
58	BOS	Jeremy Wright	Calgary	C					
59	NYR	Gordon Smith	Cornwall	D					
60	CHI	Mike Baumgartner	North Dakota	D	17	0	0	0	0
61	MIN	Bob Walton	Niagara Falls	C					
62	PIT	Paul Hoganson	Toronto	G	2	0	7	0	7.37
63	MTL	Guy Delparte	London	LW	48	1	8	9	18
64	PHI	Don Saleski	Regina	RW	543	128	125	253	629
65	OAK	Neil Nicholson	London	D	39	3	1	4	23
66	ST.L.	Tommi Salmelainen	HIFK Helsinki, FIN	LW					
67	TOR	Bob Neufeld	Dauphin Jr. A	LW					
68	MTL	Lynn Powis	U. of Denver	C	130	19	33	52	25
69	BOS	Jim Jones	Peterborough	D	2	0	0	0	0
70	ST.L.	Dale Yutsyk	Colorado College	LW					
71	CHI	Dave Hudson	North Dakota	C	409	59	124	183	89
72	MIN	Rick Thompson	Niagara Falls	D					
73	ST.L.	Bob Collyard	Colorado College	C	10	1	3	4	4
74	MTL	Ian Wilkie	Edmonton	G					
75	MTL	Dale Power	Peterborough	C					
76	OAK	Pete Vipond	Oshawa	LW	3	0	0	0	0
77	ST.L.	Dave Pulkkinen	Oshawa	LW/D	2	0	0	0	0
78	MIN	Cal Russell	Hamilton	RW					
79	MTL	Frank Hamill	Toronto	RW					
80	ST.L.	Pat Lange	Sudbury						
81	PHI	Claude Chartre	Drummondville	C					
82	ST.L.	John Converse	Estevan						
83	MTL	Gilles Drolet	Quebec						
84	MTL	Darrel Knibbs	Lethbridge	C					

1970

PICK	TEAM	NAME	DRAFTED FROM	NHL PLAYERS: POS / NHL GOALTENDERS: POS	GP / GP	G / W	A / GA	PTS / SO	PIM / AVG
FIRST ROUND									
1	BUF	Gilbert Perreault	Montreal	C	1191	512	814	1326	500
2	VAN	Dale Tallon	Toronto	D	642	98	238	336	568
3	BOS	Reggie Leach	Flin Flon	RW	934	381	285	666	387
4	BOS	Rick MacLeish	Peterborough	C	846	349	410	759	434
5	MTL	Ray Martynuik	Flin Flon	G	8 pro seasons in 5 leagues				
6	MTL	Chuck Lefley	Canadian National	LW	407	128	164	292	137
7	PIT	Greg Polis	Estevan	LW	615	174	169	343	391
8	TOR	Darryl Sittler	London	C	1096	484	637	1121	948
9	BOS	Ron Plumb	Peterborough	D	26	3	4	7	14
10	CAL	Chris Oddleifson	Winnipeg	C	524	95	191	286	464
11	NYR	Norm Gratton	Montreal	LW	201	39	44	83	64
12	DET	Serge Lajeunesse	Montreal	D/RW	103	1	4	5	103
13	BOS	Bob Stewart	Oshawa	D	575	27	101	128	809
14	CHI	Dan Maloney	London	LW	737	192	259	451	1489
SECOND ROUND									
15	BUF	Butch Deadmarsh	Brandon	LW	137	12	5	17	155
16	VAN	Jim Hargreaves	Winnipeg	D	66	1	7	8	105
17	MIN	Buster Harvey	Hamilton	RW	407	90	118	208	131
18	PHI	Bill Clement	Ottawa	C	719	148	208	356	383
19	CAL	Pete Laframboise	Ottawa	LW/C	227	33	55	88	70
20	MIN	Fred Barrett	Toronto	D	745	25	123	148	671
21	PIT	John Stewart	Flin Flon	LW	258	58	60	118	158
22	TOR	Errol Thompson	Charlottetown Sr.	LW	599	208	185	393	184
23	ST.L.	Murray Keogan	Minnesota-Duluth	C	84PTS in 124 WHA games				
24	L.A.	Al McDonough	St. Catharines	RW	237	73	88	161	73
25	NYR	Mike Murphy	Toronto	RW	831	238	318	556	514
26	DET	Bobby Guindon	Montreal	LW	6	0	1	1	0
27	BOS	Dan Bouchard	London	G	655	286	2061	27	3.26
28	CHI	Michel Archambault	Drummondville	LW	3	0	0	0	0
OTHER ROUNDS									
29	BUF	Steve Cuddie	Toronto	D					
30	VAN	Ed Dyck	Calgary	G	49	8	178	1	4.35
31	MTL	Steve Carlyle	Red Deer Jr. A	D					
32	PHI	Bob Kelly	Oshawa	LW	837	154	208	362	1454
33	CAL	Randy Rota	Calgary	C/LW	212	38	39	77	60
34	MIN	Dennis Patterson	Peterborough	D	138	6	22	28	67
35	PIT	Larry Bignell	Edmonton	D	20	0	3	3	2
36	TOR	Gerry O'Flaherty	Kitchener	LW	438	99	95	194	168
37	ST.L.	Ron Climie	Hamilton	LW					
38	L.A.	Terry Holbrook	London	RW	43	3	6	9	4
39	NYR	Wendell Bennett	Weyburn Jr. A	D					
40	DET	Yvon Lambert	Drummondville	LW	683	206	273	479	340
41	BOS	Ray Brownlee	U. of Brandon	C					
42	CHI	Len Frig	Calgary	D	311	13	51	64	479
43	BUF	Randy Wyrozub	Edmonton	C	100	8	10	18	10
44	VAN	Brent Taylor	Estevan	RW					
45	MTL	Cal Hammond	Flin Flon	G					
46	PHI	Jacques Lapierre	Shawinigan	D					
47	CAL	Ted McAneeley	Edmonton	D	158	8	35	43	141
48	MIN	Dave Cressman	Kitchener	LW	85	6	8	14	37
49	PIT	Connie Forey	Ottawa	LW	4	0	0	0	2
50	TOR	Bob Gryp	Boston U.	LW	74	11	13	24	33
51	ST.L.	Gord Brooks	London	RW	70	7	18	25	37
52	MTL	John French	Toronto	LW					
53	NYR	Andre St. Pierre	Drummondville	D					
54	DET	Tom Johnston	Toronto	RW					
55	BOS	Gordon Davies	Toronto	LW					
56	CHI	Walt Ledingham	Minnesota-Duluth	LW	15	0	2	2	4
57	BUF	Mike Morton	Shawinigan	RW					
58	VAN	Bill McFadden	Swift Current	F					
59	L.A.	Billy Smith	Cornwall	G	680	305	2031	22	3.17
60	PHI	Doug Kerslake	Edmonton	RW					
61	OAK	Ray Gibbs	Charlottetown Sr.	G					
62	MIN	Henri Lehvonen	Kitchener	D	4	0	0	0	0
63	PIT	Steve Cardwell	Oshawa	LW	53	9	11	20	35
64	TOR	Luc Simard	Trois-Rivieres	RW					
65	ST.L.	Mike Stevens	Minnesota-Duluth	D					
66	MTL	Rick Wilson	North Dakota	D	239	6	26	32	165
67	NYR	Gary Coalter	Hamilton	RW	34	2	4	6	2
68	DET	Tom Mellor	Boston College	D	26	2	4	6	25
69	BOS	Robert Roselle	Sorel	LW					
70	CHI	Gilles Meloche	Verdun	G	788	270	2756	20	3.64
71	BUF	Mike Keeler	Niagara Falls	D					
72	VAN	Dave Gilmour	London	LW					
73	L.A.	Gerry Bradbury	London	C					
74	PHI	Dennis Giannini	London	LW					
75	OAK	Doug Moyes	Sorel	RW					
76	MIN	Murray McNeill	Calgary	LW					
77	PIT	Bob Fitchner	Brandon	C	78	12	20	32	59
78	TOR	Calvin Booth	Weyburn Jr. A	LW					
79	ST.L.	Claude Moreau	Montreal	D					
80	MTL	Robert Brown	Boston U.	D					
81	NYR	Duane Wylie	St. Catharines	C	14	3	3	6	2
82	DET	Bernie MacNeil	Espanola Jr.	LW	4	0	0	0	0
83	BOS	Murray Wing	North Dakota	D	1	0	1	1	0
84	BUF	Tim Regan	Boston U.	G					
85	ST.L.	Jack Taggart	U. of Denver	D					
86	L.A.	Brian Carlin	Calgary	LW	5	1	0	1	0
87	PHI	Hank Nowak	Oshawa	LW	180	26	29	55	161
88	OAK	Terry Murray	Ottawa	D	302	4	76	80	199
89	MIN	Gary Geldart	London	D	4	0	0	0	5
90	PIT	Jim Pearson	St. Catharines	RW					
91	TOR	Paul Larose	Quebec	RW					
92	ST.L.	Terry Marshall	Brandon	D					
93	MTL	Bob Fowler	Estevan	RW					
94	NYR	Wayne Bell	Estevan	G					
95	DET	Ed Hays	U. of Denver	C					
96	BOS	Glen Siddall	Kitchener	LW					
97	BUF	Doug Rombough	St. Catharines	C	150	24	27	51	80
98	L.A.	Brian Chinnick	Peterborough	C					
99	PHI	Garry Cunningham	St. Catharines	D					
100	OAK	Al Henry	North Dakota	D					
101	MIN	Mickey Donaldson	Peterborough	LW					
102	PIT	Cam Newton	Kitchener	G	16	4	51	0	3.76
103	TOR	Ron Low	Dauphin Jr. A	G	382	102	1463	4	4.28
104	ST.L.	Dave Tataryn	Niagara Falls	G	2	1	10	0	7.50
105	MTL	Rick Jordan	Boston U.	D					
106	NYR	Pierre Brind'Amour	Montreal	LW					
107	BUF	Luc Nadeau	Drummondville	C					
108	ST.L.	Bob Winograd	Colorado College	D					
109	PHI	Jean Daigle	Sorel	LW					
110	PIT	Ron Lemieux	Dauphin Jr. A	RW					
111	ST.L.	Mike Lampman	U. of Denver	LW	96	17	20	37	34
112	ST.L.	Jeff Rotsch	Wisconsin	D					
113	ST.L.	Al Calver	Kitchener	D					
114	ST.L.	Gerry MacDonald	St. Francis Xavier	D					
115	ST.L.	Gerald Haines	Kenora						

1971

PICK	TEAM	NAME	DRAFTED FROM	NHL PLAYERS: POS / NHL GOALTENDERS: POS	GP / GP	G / W	A / GA	PTS / SO	PIM / AVG
FIRST ROUND									
1	MTL	Guy Lafleur	Quebec	RW	1126	560	793	1353	399
2	DET	Marcel Dionne	St. Catharines	C	1348	731	1040	1771	600
3	VAN	Jocelyn Guevremont	Montreal	D	571	84	223	307	319
4	ST.L.	Gene Carr	Flin Flon	C	465	79	136	215	365
5	BUF	Rick Martin	Montreal	LW	685	384	317	701	477
6	BOS	Ron Jones	Edmonton	D	54	1	4	5	31
7	MTL	Chuck Arnason	Flin Flon	RW	401	109	90	199	122
8	PHI	Larry Wright	Regina	C	106	4	8	12	19
9	PHI	Pierre Plante	Drummondville	RW	599	125	172	297	599
10	NYR	Steve Vickers	Toronto	LW	698	246	340	586	330
11	MTL	Murray Wilson	Ottawa	LW	386	94	95	189	162
12	CHI	Dan Spring	Edmonton	C	90 points in 201 WHA games				
13	NYR	Steve Durbano	Toronto	D	220	13	60	73	1127
14	BOS	Terry O'Reilly	Oshawa	RW	891	204	402	606	2095
SECOND ROUND									
15	CAL	Ken Baird	Flin Flon	D	10	0	2	2	15
16	DET	Henry Boucha	U.S. Nationals	C	247	53	49	102	157
17	VAN	Bobby Lalonde	Montreal	C	641	124	210	334	298
18	PIT	Brian McKenzie	St. Catharines	LW	6	1	1	2	4
19	BUF	Craig Ramsay	Peterborough	LW	1070	252	420	672	201
20	MTL	Larry Robinson	Kitchener	D	1384	208	750	958	793
21	MIN	Rod Norrish	Regina	LW	21	3	3	6	2
22	TOR	Rick Kehoe	Hamilton	RW	906	371	396	767	120
23	TOR	Dave Fortier	St. Catharines	D	205	8	21	29	335
24	MTL	Michel Deguise	Sorel	G	Won 18 games in 2 WHA yrs.				
25	MTL	Terry French	Ottawa	C	Injury-plagued 62-game career				
26	CHI	Dave Kryskow	Edmonton	LW	231	33	56	89	174
27	NYR	Tom Williams	Hamilton	LW	397	115	138	253	73
28	BOS	Curt Ridley	Portage la Prairie Jr.	G	104	27	355	1	3.87
OTHER ROUNDS									
29	CAL	Rich LeDuc	Trois-Rivieres	C	130	28	38	66	69
30	DET	Ralph Hopiavuouri	Toronto	D					
31	MTL	Jim Cahoon	North Dakota	C					
32	PIT	Joe Noris	Toronto	C/D	55	2	5	7	22
33	BUF	Bill Hajt	Saskatoon	D	854	42	202	244	433
34	L.A.	Vic Venasky	U. of Denver	C	430	61	101	162	66
35	MIN	Ron Wilson	Flin Flon	D					
36	PHI	Glen Irwin	Estevan	D					
37	TOR	Gavin Kirk	Toronto	C					
38	ST.L.	John Garrett	Peterborough	G	207	68	837	1	4.27
39	VAN	Richard Lemieux	Montreal	C	274	39	82	121	132
40	CHI	Bob Peppler	St. Catharines	LW					
41	NYR	Terry West	London	C					
42	BOS	Dave Bonter	Estevan	C					
43	CAL	Hartland Monahan	Montreal	RW	334	61	80	141	163
44	DET	George Hulme	St. Catharines	G					
45	MTL	Ed Sidebottom	Estevan	D					
46	PIT	Gerald Methe	Oshawa	D					
47	BUF	Bob Richer	Trois-Rivieres	C	3	0	0	0	0
48	L.A.	Neil Komadoski	Winnipeg	D	502	16	76	92	632
49	MIN	Mike Legge	Winnipeg	LW					
50	PHI	Ted Scharf	Kitchener	RW					
51	TOR	Rick Cunningham	Peterborough	D					
52	ST.L.	Derek Harker	Edmonton	D					
53	MTL	Greg Hubick	Minnesota-Duluth	D	77	6	9	15	10
54	CHI	Clyde Simon	St. Catharines	RW					
55	NYR	Jerry Butler	Hamilton	RW	641	99	120	219	515
56	BOS	Dave Hynes	Harvard	LW	22	4	0	4	2
57	CAL	Ray Belanger	Shawinigan	G					
58	DET	Earl Anderson	North Dakota	RW	109	19	19	38	22
59	VAN	Mike McNiven	Halifax Jr.	D					
60	PIT	Dave Murphy	North Dakota	G					
61	BUF	Steve Warr	Clarkson	D					
62	L.A.	Gary Crosby	Michigan Tech	C					
63	MIN	Brian McBratney	St. Catharines	D					
64	PHI	Don McCulloch	Niagara Falls	D					
65	TOR	Bob Sykes	Sudbury	LW	2	0	0	0	0
66	ST.L.	Wayne Gibbs	Calgary	D					
67	MTL	Mike Busniuk	U. of Denver	D	143	3	23	26	297
68	CHI	Dean Blais	U. of Minnesota	LW					
69	NYR	Fraser Robertson	Lethbridge	D					
70	BOS	Bert Scott	Edmonton	C					
71	CAL	Gerry Egers	Sudbury	D					
72	DET	Charlie Shaw	Toronto	D					
73	VAN	Tim Steeves	Prince Edward Islanders Jr.	D					
74	PIT	Ian Williams	U. of Notre Dame	RW					
75	BUF	Pierre Duguay	Quebec	C					
76	L.A.	Camille Lapierre	Montreal	C					
77	MIN	Al Globensky	Montreal	D					
78	PHI	Yvon Bilodeau	Estevan	D					
79	TOR	Mike Ruest	Cornwall	D					
80	ST.L.	Bernie Doan	Calgary	D					
81	MTL	Ross Butler	Winnipeg	LW					
82	CHI	Jim Johnston	Wisconsin	C					
83	NYR	Wayne Wood	Montreal	G					
84	BOS	Bob McMahon	St. Catharines	G					
85	CAL	Al Simmons	Winnipeg	D	11	0	1	1	21
86	DET	Jim Nahrgang	Michigan Tech	D	57	5	12	17	34
87	VAN	Bill Green	U. of Notre Dame	D					
88	PIT	Doug Elliott	Harvard	D					
89	L.A.	Peter Harasym	Clarkson	LW					
90	L.A.	Norm Dube	Sherbrooke	LW	57	8	10	18	54
91	MIN	Bruce Abbey	Peterborough	D					
92	PHI	Bob Gerrard	Regina	RW					
93	TOR	Dale Smedsmo	Bemidji State College	LW	4	0	0	0	0
94	ST.L.	Dave Smith	Regina	D					
95	MTL	Peter Sullivan	Oshawa	C	126	28	54	82	40
96	NYR	Douglas Keeler	Ottawa	C					
97	NYR	Jean Denis Royal	St-Jerome	D					
98	TOR	Steve Johnson	Verdun	D					
99	CAL	Angus Beck	Charlottetown Jr.	C					
100	DET	Bob Boyd	Michigan State	D					
101	VAN	Norm Cherry	Wisconsin	RW					
102	VAN	Bob Murphy	Cornwall	LW					
103	L.A.	Lorne Stamler	Michigan Tech	LW	116	14	11	25	16
104	CAL	Red Lyons	Halifax Jr.	LW					
105	MIN	Russ Frieson	Hamilton	C					
106	PHI	Jerome Mrazek	Minnesota-Duluth	G	1	0	1	0	10.00
107	TOR	Bob Burns	Cdn. Armed Forces	D					
108	ST.L.	Jim Collins	Flin Flon	LW					
109	NYR	Gene Sobchuk	Regina	LW/C	1	0	0	0	0
110	NYR	Jim Ivison	Brandon	D					
111	NYR	Andre Peloffy	Rosemount Jr. A	C	9	0	0	0	0
112	NYR	Elston Evoy	Sault Ste. Marie	C					
113	MIN	Mike Antonovich	Minnesota-Duluth	C	87	10	15	25	37
114	NYR	Gerald Lecompte	Sherbrooke	D					
115	NYR	Wayne Forsey	Swift Current	LW					
116	NYR	Bill Forrest	Hamilton	D					
117	MIN	Richard Coutu	Rosemount Jr. A	G					

1972

PICK	TEAM	NAME	DRAFTED FROM	NHL PLAYERS: POS / NHL GOALTENDERS: POS	GP / GP	G / W	A / GA	PTS / SO	PIM / AVG
FIRST ROUND									
1	NYI	Billy Harris	Toronto	RW	897	231	327	558	394
2	ATL	Jacques Richard	Quebec	LW	556	160	187	347	307
3	VAN	Don Lever	Niagara Falls	LW	1020	313	367	680	593
4	MTL	Steve Shutt	Toronto	LW	930	424	393	817	410
5	BUF	Jim Schoenfeld	Niagara Falls	D	719	51	204	255	1132
6	MTL	Michel Larocque	Ottawa	G	312	160	978	17	3.33
7	PHI	Bill Barber	Kitchener	LW	903	420	463	883	623
8	MTL	Dave Gardner	Toronto	C	350	75	115	190	41
9	ST.L.	Wayne Merrick	Ottawa	C	774	191	265	456	303
10	NYR	Albert Blanchard	Kitchener	LW	4 pro seasons in AHL and IHL				
11	TOR	George Ferguson	Toronto	C	797	160	238	398	431
12	MIN	Jerry Byers	Kitchener	LW	43	3	4	7	15
13	CHI	Phil Russell	Edmonton	D	1016	99	325	424	2038
14	MTL	John Van Boxmeer	Guelph	D	588	84	274	358	465
15	NYR	Bob MacMillan	St. Catharines	RW	753	228	349	577	260
16	BOS	Mike Bloom	St. Catharines	LW	201	30	47	77	215
SECOND ROUND									
17	NYI	Lorne Henning	New Westminster	C	544	73	111	184	102
18	ATL	Dwight Bialowas	Regina	D	164	11	46	57	46
19	VAN	Bryan McSheffrey	Ottawa	RW	90	13	7	20	44
20	L.A.	Don Kozak	Edmonton	RW	437	96	86	182	480
21	NYR	Larry Sacharuk	Saskatoon	D	151	29	33	62	42
22	CAL	Tom Cassidy	Kitchener	C	26	3	4	7	15
23	PHI	Tom Bladon	Edmonton	D	610	73	197	270	392
24	PIT	Jack Lynch	Oshawa	D	382	24	106	130	336
25	BUF	Larry Carriere	Loyola College	D	367	16	74	90	462
26	DET	Pierre Guite	St. Catharines	LW	197 points in 377 WHA games				
27	TOR	Randy Osburn	London	LW	27	0	2	2	0
28	CAL	Stan Weir	Medicine Hat	C	642	139	207	346	183
29	CHI	Brian Ogilvie	Edmonton	C	90	15	21	36	29
30	PIT	Bernie Lukowich	New Westminster	RW	79	13	15	28	34
31	NYR	Rene Villemure	Shawinigan	LW	93PTS w/ Beauce in 75-76				
32	BOS	Wayne Elder	London	D	2 pro seasons in AHL & CHL				
OTHER ROUNDS									
33	NYI	Bob Nystrom	Calgary	RW	900	235	278	513	1248
34	ATL	Jean Lemieux	Sherbrooke	D	204	23	63	86	39
35	VAN	Paul Raymer	Peterborough	LW					
36	L.A.	Dave Hutchison	London	D	584	19	97	116	1550
37	BUF	Jim McMasters	Calgary	D					
38	CAL	Paul Shakes	St. Catharines	D	21	0	4	4	12
39	PHI	Jimmy Watson	Calgary	D	613	38	148	186	492
40	PIT	Denis Herron	Trois-Rivieres	G	462	146	1579	10	3.70

PICK	TEAM	NAME	DRAFTED FROM	NHL PLAYERS: POS / NHL GOALTENDERS: POS	GP / GP	G / W	A / GA	PTS / SO	PIM / AVG
41	ST.L.	Jean Hamel	Drummondville	D	699	26	95	121	766
42	DET	Bob Krieger	U. of Denver	C					
43	TOR	Denis Deslauriers	Shawinigan	D					
44	MIN	Terry Ryan	Hamilton	C					
45	CHI	Mike Veisor	Peterborough	G	139	41	532	5	4.09
46	MTL	Ed Gilbert	Hamilton	C	166	21	31	52	22
47	NYR	Gerry Teeple	Cornwall	C					
48	BOS	Michel Boudreau	Laval	C					
49	NYI	Ron Smith	Cornwall	D	11	1	1	2	14
50	ATL	Don Martineau	New Westminster	RW	90	6	10	16	63
51	VAN	Ron Homenuke	Calgary	RW	1	0	0	0	0
52	L.A.	John Dobie	Regina	D					
53	BUF	Richard Campeau	Sorel	D					
54	CAL	Claude St. Sauveur	Sherbrooke	C	79	24	24	48	23
55	PHI	Al MacAdam	University of PEI	RW	864	240	351	591	509
56	PIT	Ron Lalonde	Peterborough	C	397	45	78	123	106
57	ST.L.	Murray Myers	Saskatoon	D					
58	DET	Danny Gruen	Thunder Bay Jr. A	LW	49	9	13	22	19
59	TOR	Brian Bowles	Cornwall	D					
60	MIN	Tom Thomson	Toronto	D					
61	CHI	Tom Peluso	U. of Denver	LW					
62	MTL	Dave Ellenbaas	Cornell	G					
63	NYR	Doug Horbul	Calgary	LW	4	1	0	1	2
64	BOS	Les Jackson	New Westminster	LW					
65	NYI	Richard Grenier	Verdun	C	10	1	1	2	2
66	MTL	Bill Nyrop	U. of Notre Dame	D	207	12	51	63	101
67	VAN	Larry Bolonchuk	Winnipeg	D	74	3	9	12	97
68	L.A.	Bernie Germaine	Regina	G					
69	BUF	Gilles Gratton	Oshawa	G	47	13	154	0	4.02
70	CAL	Tim Jacobs	St. Catharines	D	46	0	10	10	35
71	PHI	Daryl Fedorak	Victoria	G					
72	PIT	Brian Walker	Calgary	C					
73	ST.L.	Dave Johnson	Cornwall	LW					
74	DET	Dennis Johnson	North Dakota	LW					
75	TOR	Michel Plante	Drummondville	LW					
76	MIN	Chris Ahrens	Kitchener	D	52	0	3	3	84
77	CHI	Rejean Giroux	Quebec	RW					
78	ATL	Jean-Paul Martin	Shawinigan	C					
79	NYR	Martin Gateman	Hamilton	D					
80	BOS	Brian Coates	Brandon	LW					
81	NYI	Derek Black	Calgary	LW					
82	ATL	Frank Blum	Sarnia Jr. B	G					
83	VAN	Dave McLelland	Brandon	G	2	1	10	0	5.00
84	L.A.	Mike Usitalo	Michigan Tech	LW					
85	BUF	Peter McNab	U. of Denver	C	954	363	450	813	179
86	CAL	Jacques Lefebvre	Shawinigan	G					
87	PHI	Dave Hastings	Charlottetown Jr.	G					
88	PIT	Jeff Ablett	Medicine Hat	LW					
89	ST.L.	Tom Simpson	Oshawa	RW					
90	DET	Bill Miller	Medicine Hat	D					
91	TOR	Dave Shardlow	Flin Flon	LW					
92	MIN	Steve West	Oshawa	C					
93	CHI	Rob Palmer	U. of Denver	C	16	0	3	3	2
94	MTL	D'Arcy Ryan	Yale	LW					
95	NYR	Ken Ireland	New Westminster	C					
96	BOS	Peter Gaw	Ottawa	RW					
97	NYI	Richard Brodeur	Cornwall	G	385	131	1410	6	3.85
98	ATL	Scott Smith	Regina	LW					
99	VAN	Dan Gloor	Peterborough	C	2	0	0	0	0
100	L.A.	Glen Toner	Regina	LW					
101	NYI	Don McLaughlin	Brandon	LW					
102	CAL	Mike Amodeo	Oshawa	D	19	0	0	0	2
103	PHI	Serge Beaudoin	Trois-Rivieres	D	3	0	0	0	0
104	PIT	D'Arcy Keating	U. of Notre Dame	RW					
105	ST.L.	Brian Coughlin	Verdun	D					
106	DET	Glenn Seperich	Kitchener	G					
107	TOR	Monte Miron	Clarkson	D					
108	MIN	Chris Meloff	Kitchener	D					
109	CHI	Terry Smith	Edmonton	C					
110	MTL	Yves Archambault	Sorel	G					
111	NYR	Jeff Hunt	Winnipeg	LW					
112	BOS	Gordie Clark	New Hampshire	RW	8	0	1	1	0
113	NYI	Derek Kuntz	Medicine Hat	LW					
114	ATL	Dave Murphy	Hamilton	C					
115	VAN	Dennis McCord	London	D	3	0	0	0	6
116	MIN	Scott MacPhail	Montreal	RW					
117	NYI	Rene Lavasseur	Shawinigan	D					
118	CAL	Brent Meeke	Niagara Falls	D	75	9	22	31	8
119	PHI	Pat Russell	Vancouver	RW					
120	PIT	Yves Bergeron	Shawinigan	RW	3	0	0	0	0
121	ST.L.	Gary Winchester	Wisconsin	C					
122	DET	Mike Ford	Brandon	D					
123	TOR	Peter Williams	University of PEI	D					
124	MIN	Bob Lundeen	Wisconsin	D					
125	CHI	Billy Reay Jr.	Wisconsin	RW					
126	MTL	Graham Parsons	Red Deer Jr. A	G					
127	NYR	Yvon Blais	Cornwall	LW					
128	BOS	Roy Carmichael	New Westminster	D					
129	NYI	Yvan Rolando	Drummondville	RW					
130	ATL	Pierre Roy	Quebec	D					
131	VAN	Steve Stone	Niagara Falls	RW	2	0	0	0	0
132	ATL	Jean Lamarre	Quebec	RW					
133	NYI	Bill Ennos	Vancouver	RW					
134	CAL	Denis Meloche	Drummondville	C					
135	PHI	Ray Boutin	Sorel	G					
136	PIT	Jay Babcock	London	D					
137	NYR	Pierre Archambault	St-Jerome	D					
138	DET	George Kuzmicz	Cornell	D					
139	TOR	Pat Boutette	Minnesota-Duluth	C/RW	756	171	282	453	1354
140	MIN	Glen Mikkelson	Brandon	RW					
141	CHI	Gary Donaldson	Victoria	RW	1	0	0	0	0
142	MTL	Edward Bumbacco	U. of Notre Dame	LW					
143	TOR	Gary Schofield	Clarkson	D					
144	NYI	Garry Howatt	Flin Flon	LW	720	112	156	268	1836
145	MIN	Steve Lyon	Peterborough	D/RW	3	0	0	0	2
146	NYI	Rene Lambert	St-Jerome	RW					
147	MIN	Juri Kudrosov	Kitchener	C					
148	MIN	Marcel Comeau	Edmonton	C					
149	PIT	Don Atchison	Saskatoon	G					
150	DET	Dave Arundel	Wisconsin	D					
151	MTL	Fred Riggall	Dartmouth	RW					
152	MTL	Ron Leblanc	U. of Moncton	RW					

1973

FIRST ROUND

PICK	TEAM	NAME	DRAFTED FROM	NHL PLAYERS: POS / NHL GOALTENDERS: POS	GP / GP	G / W	A / GA	PTS / SO	PIM / AVG
1	NYI	Denis Potvin	Ottawa	D	1060	310	742	1052	1356
2	ATL	Tom Lysiak	Medicine Hat	C	919	292	551	843	567
3	VAN	Dennis Ververgaert	London	RW	583	176	216	392	247
4	TOR	Lanny McDonald	Medicine Hat	RW	1111	500	506	1006	899
5	ST.L.	John Davidson	Calgary	G	301	123	1004	7	3.52
6	BOS	Andre Savard	Quebec	C	790	211	271	482	411
7	PIT	Blaine Stoughton	Flin Flon	RW	526	258	191	449	204
8	MTL	Bob Gainey	Peterborough	LW	1160	239	262	501	585
9	VAN	Bob Dailey	Toronto	D	561	94	231	325	814
10	TOR	Bob Neely	Peterborough	LW	283	39	59	98	266
11	DET	Terry Richardson	New Westminster	G	20	3	85	0	5.63
12	BUF	Morris Titanic	Sudbury	LW	19	0	0	0	0
13	CHI	Darcy Rota	Edmonton	LW	794	256	239	495	973
14	NYR	Rick Middleton	Oshawa	RW	1005	448	540	988	157
15	TOR	Ian Turnbull	Ottawa	D	628	123	317	440	736
16	ATL	Vic Mercredi	New Westminster	C	2	0	0	0	0

SECOND ROUND

PICK	TEAM	NAME	DRAFTED FROM	POS	GP	G	A	PTS	PIM
17	MTL	Glenn Goldup	Toronto	RW	291	52	67	119	303
18	MIN	Blake Dunlop	Ottawa	C	550	130	274	404	172
19	VAN	Paulin Bordeleau	Toronto	RW	183	33	56	89	47
20	PHI	Larry Goodenough	London	D	242	22	77	99	179
21	ATL	Eric Vail	Sudbury	LW	591	216	260	476	281
22	MTL	Peter Marrin	Toronto	C	193PTS 277 WHA games				
23	PIT	Wayne Bianchin	Flin Flon	LW	276	68	41	109	137
24	ST.L.	George Pesut	Saskatoon	D	92	3	22	25	130
25	MIN	John Rogers	Edmonton	RW	14	2	4	6	0
26	PHI	Brent Leavins	Swift Current	LW	Broke both legs in auto crash				
27	PIT	Colin Campbell	Peterborough	D	636	25	103	128	1292
28	BUF	Jean Landry	Quebec	D	4 pro seasons in 3 leagues				
29	CHI	Reg Thomas	London	LW	39	9	7	16	6
30	NYR	Pat Hickey	Hamilton	LW	646	192	212	404	351
31	BOS	Jimmy Jones	Peterborough	RW	148	13	18	31	68
32	MTL	Ron Andruff	Flin Flon	C	153	19	36	55	54

OTHER ROUNDS

PICK	TEAM	NAME	DRAFTED FROM	POS	GP	G	A	PTS	PIM
33	NYI	Dave Lewis	Saskatoon	D	1008	36	187	223	953
34	CAL	Jeff Jacques	St. Catharines	RW					
35	VAN	Paul Sheard	Ottawa	RW					
36	BOS	Doug Gibson	Peterborough	C	63	9	19	28	0
37	MTL	Ed Humphreys	Saskatoon	G					
38	L.A.	Russ Walker	Saskatoon	RW	17	1	0	1	41
39	DET	Nelson Pyatt	Oshawa	C	296	71	63	134	69
40	PHI	Bob Stumpf	New Westminster	RW/D	10	1	1	2	20
41	MIN	Rick Chinnick	Peterborough	RW	4	0	2	2	0
42	PHI	Mike Clarke	Calgary	C					
43	DET	Robbie Neale	Brandon	LW					
44	BUF	Andre Deschamps	Quebec	LW					
45	CHI	Randy Holt	Sudbury	D	395	4	37	41	1438
46	NYR	John Campbell	Sault Ste. Marie	C					
47	BOS	Al Sims	Cornwall	D	475	49	116	165	286
48	ST.L.	Bob Gassoff	Medicine Hat	D	245	11	47	58	866
49	NYI	Andre St. Laurent	Montreal	C	644	129	187	316	749
50	CAL	Ron Serafini	St. Catharines	D	2	0	0	0	2
51	VAN	Keith Mackie	Edmonton	D					
52	TOR	Francois Rochon	Sherbrooke	LW					

PICK	TEAM	NAME	DRAFTED FROM	NHL PLAYERS: POS / NHL GOALTENDERS: POS	GP / GP	G / W	A / GA	PTS / SO	PIM / AVG
53	ATL	Dean Talafous	Wisconsin	RW	497	104	154	258	163
54	L.A.	Jim McCrimmon	Medicine Hat	D	2	0	0	0	0
55	PIT	Dennis Owchar	Toronto	D	288	30	85	115	200
56	MTL	Al Hangsleben	North Dakota	D	185	21	48	69	396
57	MIN	Tom Colley	Sudbury	C	1	0	0	0	2
58	PHI	Dale Cook	Victoria	LW					
59	DET	Mike Korney	Winnipeg	RW	77	9	10	19	59
60	BUF	Yvon Dupuis	Quebec	RW					
61	CHI	Dave Elliott	Winnipeg	LW					
62	NYR	Brian Molvik	Calgary	D					
63	BOS	Steve Langdon	London	LW	7	0	1	1	2
64	MTL	Richard Latulippe	Quebec	C					
65	NYI	Ron Kennedy	New Westminster	RW					
66	CAL	Jim Moxey	Hamilton	RW	127	22	27	49	59
67	VAN	Paul O'Neil	Boston U.	C/RW	6	0	0	0	0
68	TOR	Gord Titcomb	St. Catharines	LW					
69	ATL	John Flesch	Lake Superior State	LW	124	18	23	41	117
70	L.A.	Dennis Abgrall	Saskatoon	RW	13	0	2	2	4
71	PIT	Guido Tenesi	Oshawa	D					
72	ST.L.	Bill Laing	Saskatoon	LW					
73	MIN	Lowell Ostlund	Saskatoon	D					
74	PHI	Michel Latreille	Montreal	D					
75	DET	Blair Stewart	Winnipeg	C	229	34	44	78	326
76	BUF	Bob Smulders	Peterborough	RW					
77	CHI	Dan Hinton	Sault Ste. Marie	LW	14	0	0	0	16
78	NYR	Pierre Laganiere	Sherbrooke	RW					
79	BOS	Peter Crosbie	London	G					
80	MTL	Gerry Gibbons	St. Mary's U.	D					
81	NYI	Keith Smith	Brown	D					
82	CAL	William Trognitz	Thunder Bay Jr. A	LW					
83	VAN	Jim Cowell	Ottawa	C					
84	TOR	Doug Marit	Regina	D					
85	ATL	Ken Houston	Chatham Jr. B	RW	570	161	167	328	624
86	L.A.	Blair MacDonald	Cornwall	RW	219	91	100	191	65
87	PIT	Don Seiling	Oshawa	LW					
88	ST.L.	Randy Smith	Edmonton	C	3	0	0	0	0
89	MIN	David Lee	Ottawa	LW					
90	PHI	Doug Ferguson	Hamilton	D					
91	DET	Glenn Cickello	Hamilton	D					
92	BUF	Neil Korzack	Peterborough	LW					
93	CHI	Gary Doerksen	Winnipeg	C					
94	NYR	Dwayne Pentland	Brandon	D					
95	BOS	Jean-Pierre Bourgouyne	Shawinigan	D					
96	MTL	Dennis Patry	Drummondville	RW					
97	NYI	Don Cutts	RPI	G	6	1	16	0	3.57
98	CAL	Paul Tantardini	Downsview Jr.	LW					
99	VAN	Clay Hebenton	Portland	G					
100	TOR	Dan Follett	Downsview Jr.	G					
101	ATL	Tom Machowski	Wisconsin	D					
102	L.A.	Roly Kimble	Hamilton	G					
103	PIT	Terry Ewasiuk	Victoria	LW					
104	ST.L.	John Wensink	Cornwall	LW	403	70	68	138	840
105	MIN	Lou Nistico	London	C	3	0	0	0	0
106	PHI	Tom Young	Sudbury	D					
107	DET	Brian Middleton	U. of Alberta	D					
108	BUF	Bob Young	U. of Denver	D					
109	CHI	Wayne Dye	New Westminster	LW					
110	NYI	Dennis Anderson	New Westminster	D					
111	BOS	Walter Johnson	Oshawa	RW					
112	MTL	Michel Belisle	Montreal	C					
113	NYI	Mike Kennedy	Kitchener	RW					
114	CAL	Bruce Greig	Vancouver	LW	9	0	1	1	46
115	VAN	John Senkpiel	Vancouver	LW					
116	TOR	Les Burgess	Kitchener	LW					
117	ATL	Bob Law	North Dakota	RW					
118	DET	Dennis Polonich	Flin Flon	C/RW	390	59	82	141	1242
119	PIT	Fred Comrie	Edmonton	C					
120	ST.L.	John Tetreault	Drummondville	LW					
121	MIN	George Beveridge	Kitchener	D					
122	PHI	Norm Barnes	Michigan State	D	156	6	38	44	178
123	DET	George Lyle	Michigan Tech	LW	99	24	38	62	51
124	BUF	Tim O'Connell	Vermont	RW					
125	CHI	Jim Koleff	Hamilton	C					
126	NYI	Denis Desgagnes	Sorel	C					
127	BOS	Virgil Gates	Swift Current	D					
128	MTL	Mario Desjardins	Sherbrooke	LW					
129	NYI	Bob Lorimer	Michigan Tech	D	529	22	90	112	431
130	CAL	Larry Patey	Braintree H.S.	C	717	153	163	316	631
131	VAN	Peter Folco	Quebec	D	2	0	0	0	0
132	TOR	Dave Pay	Wisconsin	LW					
133	ATL	Bob Bilodeau	New Westminster	D					
134	PIT	Gord Lane	New Westminster	D	539	19	94	113	1228
135	DET	Dennis O'Brien	Laurentian	D					
136	MIN	Jim Johnston	Peterborough	C					
137	PHI	Dan O'Donohue	Sault Ste. Marie	D					
138	DET	Tom Newman	Kitchener	D					
139	DET	Ray Bibeau	Montreal	D					
140	CHI	Jack Johnson	Wisconsin	LW					
141	CHI	Steve Alley	Wisconsin	LW	15	3	3	6	11
142	BOS	Jim Pettie	St. Catharines	G	21	9	71	1	3.68
143	MTL	Bob Wright	Pembroke Jr. A						
144	TOR	Lee Palmer	Clarkson	D					
145	CAL	Doug Mahood	Sault Ste. Marie	RW					
146	VAN	Terry McDougall	Swift Current	C					
147	TOR	Bob Peace	Cornell	F					
148	ATL	Glen Surbey	Loyola College	D					
149	ATL	Guy Ross	Sherbrooke	D					
150	PIT	Randy Aimoe	Medicine Hat	D					
151	DET	Kevin Neville	Toronto	G					
152	MIN	Sam Clegg	Medicine Hat	G					
153	PHI	Brian Dick	Winnipeg	RW					
154	DET	Ken Gibb	North Dakota	D					
155	DET	Mitch Brandt	U. of Denver						
156	CHI	Rick Clubbe	North Dakota	RW					
157	BOS	Yvan Bouillon	Cornwall	C					
158	MTL	Alain Labrecque	Trois-Rivieres	C					
159	TOR	Norm McLeod	Ottawa M&W Rangers	LW					
160	CAL	Angelo Moretto	Michigan	C	5	1	2	3	2
161	MIN	Russ Wiechnik	Calgary	C					
162	ATL	Greg Fox	Michigan	D	494	14	92	106	637
163	MIN	Max Hansen	Sudbury	LW					
164	PIT	Don McLeod	Saskatoon	G	18	3	74	0	5.05
165	CHI	Gene Strate	Edmonton	D					
166	MTL	Gord Halliday	U. of Pennsylvania						
167	MTL	Cap Raeder	New Hampshire	G					
168	MTL	Louis Chiasson	Trois-Rivieres	C					

1974

PICK	TEAM	NAME	DRAFTED FROM	NHL PLAYERS: POS / NHL GOALTENDERS: POS	GP / GP	G / W	A / GA	PTS / SO	PIM / AVG
FIRST ROUND									
1	WSH	Greg Joly	Regina	D	365	21	76	97	250
2	K.C.	Wilf Paiement	St. Catharines	RW	946	356	458	814	1757
3	CAL	Rick Hampton	St. Catharines	LW/D	337	59	113	172	147
4	NYI	Clark Gillies	Regina	LW	958	319	378	697	1023
5	MTL	Cam Connor	Flin Flon	RW	89	9	22	31	256
6	MIN	Doug Hicks	Flin Flon	D	561	37	131	168	442
7	MTL	Doug Risebrough	Kitchener	C	740	185	286	471	1542
8	PIT	Pierre Larouche	Sorel	C	812	395	427	822	237
9	DET	Bill Lochead	Oshawa	LW	330	69	62	131	180
10	MTL	Rick Chartraw	Kitchener	D/RW	420	28	64	92	399
11	BUF	Lee Fogolin Jr.	Oshawa	D	924	44	195	239	1318
12	MTL	Mario Tremblay	Montreal	RW	852	258	326	584	1043
13	TOR	Jack Valiquette	Sault Ste. Marie	C	350	84	134	218	79
14	NYR	Dave Maloney	Kitchener	D	657	71	246	317	1154
15	MTL	Gord McTavish	Sudbury	C	11	1	3	4	2
16	CHI	Grant Mulvey	Calgary	RW	586	149	135	284	816
17	CAL	Ron Chipperfield	Brandon	C	83	22	24	46	34
18	BOS	Don Larway	Swift Current	RW	186 points in 324 WHA games				
SECOND ROUND									
19	WSH	Mike Marson	Sudbury	LW	196	24	24	48	233
20	K.C.	Glen Burdon	Regina	C	11	0	2	2	0
21	CAL	Bruce Affleck	U. of Denver	D	280	14	66	80	86
22	NYI	Bryan Trottier	Swift Current	C	1279	524	901	1425	912
23	VAN	Ron Sedlbauer	Kitchener	LW	430	143	86	229	210
24	MIN	Rich Nantais	Quebec	LW	63	5	4	9	79
25	BOS	Mark Howe	Toronto	D	929	197	545	742	455
26	ST.L.	Bob Hess	New Westminster	D	329	27	95	122	178
27	PIT	Jacques Cossette	Sorel	RW	64	8	6	14	29
28	ATL	Guy Chouinard	Quebec	C	578	205	370	575	120
29	BUF	Danny Gare	Calgary	RW	827	354	331	685	1285
30	MTL	Gary MacGregor	Cornwall	C	160 points in 251 WHA games				
31	TOR	Tiger Williams	Swift Current	LW	962	241	272	513	3966
32	NYR	Ron Greschner	New Westminster	D	982	179	431	610	1226
33	MTL	Gilles Lupien	Montreal	D	226	5	25	30	416
34	CHI	Alain Daigle	Trois-Rivieres	RW	389	56	50	106	122
35	PHI	Don McLean	Sudbury	D	9	0	0	0	6
36	BOS	Peter Sturgeon	Kitchener	LW	6	0	1	1	2
OTHER ROUNDS									
37	WSH	John Paddock	Brandon	RW	87	8	14	22	86
38	K.C.	Bob Bourne	Saskatoon	C	964	258	324	582	605
39	CAL	Charlie Simmer	Sault Ste. Marie	LW	712	342	369	711	544
40	NYI	Brad Anderson	Victoria	C					
41	VAN	John Hughes	Toronto	D	70	2	14	16	211
42	MIN	Pete LoPresti	U. of Denver	G	175	43	668	5	4.07
43	ST.L.	Gord Buynak	Kingston	D	4	0	0	0	2
44	DET	Dan Mandryk	Calgary	C					
45	DET	Bill Evo	Peterborough	RW					
46	ATL	Dick Spannbauer	Minnesota-Duluth	D					
47	BUF	Michel Deziel	Sorel	LW					
48	L.A.	Gary Sargent	Fargo-Moorhead	D	402	61	161	222	273

PICK	TEAM	NAME	DRAFTED FROM	NHL PLAYERS: POS / NHL GOALTENDERS: POS	GP / GP	G / W	A / GA	PTS / SO	PIM / AVG
49	TOR	Per Arne Alexandersson	Leksand, SWE	C					
50	NYR	Jerry Holland	Calgary	LW	37	8	4	12	6
51	MTL	Marty Howe	Toronto	D	197	2	29	31	99
52	CHI	Bob Murray	Cornwall	D	1008	132	382	514	873
53	PHI	Bob Sirois	Montreal	RW	286	92	120	212	42
54	BOS	Tom Edur	Toronto	D	158	17	70	87	67
55	WSH	Paul Nicholson	London	LW	62	4	8	12	18
56	K.C.	Roger Lemelin	London	D	36	1	2	3	27
57	CAL	Tom Price	Ottawa	D	29	0	2	2	12
58	ATL	Pat Ribble	Oshawa	D	349	19	60	79	365
59	VAN	Harold Snepsts	Edmonton	D	1033	38	195	233	2009
60	MIN	Kim MacDougall	Regina	D	1	0	0	0	0
61	MTL	Barry Legge	Winnipeg	D	107	1	11	12	144
62	PIT	Mario Faubert	St. Louis U.	D	231	21	90	111	292
63	DET	Michel Bergeron	Sorel	RW	229	80	58	138	165
64	ATL	Cam Botting	Niagara Falls	RW	2	0	1	1	0
65	BUF	Paul McIntosh	Peterborough	D	48	0	2	2	66
66	L.A.	Brad Winton	Toronto	C					
67	TOR	Peter Driscoll	Kingston	LW	60	3	8	11	97
68	NYR	Boyd Anderson	Medicine Hat	LW					
69	MTL	Mike McKegney	Kitchener	RW					
70	CHI	Terry Ruskowski	Swift Current	C	630	113	313	426	1354
71	PHI	Randy Andreachuk	Kamloops	C					
72	BOS	Bill Reed	Sault Ste. Marie	D					
73	WSH	Jack Patterson	Kamloops	C					
74	K.C.	Mark Lomenda	Victoria	RW					
75	CAL	Jim Warden	Michigan Tech	G					
76	NYI	Carlo Torresan	Sorel	D					
77	VAN	Mike Rogers	Calgary	C	484	202	317	519	184
78	MIN	Ron Ashton	Saskatoon	D					
79	ST.L.	Mike Zuke	Michigan Tech	C	455	86	196	282	220
80	PIT	Bruce Aberhart	London	G					
81	DET	John Taft	Wisconsin	D	15	0	2	2	4
82	ATL	Jerry Badiuk	Kitchener	D					
83	BUF	Garry Lariviere	St. Catharines	D	219	6	57	63	167
84	L.A.	John Paul Evans	Kitchener	C	103	14	25	39	34
85	TOR	Mike Palmateer	Toronto	G	356	149	1183	17	3.53
86	NYR	Dennis Olmstead	Wisconsin	C					
87	ST.L.	Donald Wheldon	London	D	2	0	0	0	0
88	CHI	Dave Logan	Laval	D	218	5	29	34	470
89	PHI	Dennis Sobchuk	Regina	C	35	5	6	11	2
90	BOS	Jim Bateman	Quebec	LW					
91	WSH	Brian Kinsella	Oshawa	C	10	0	1	1	0
92	K.C.	John Shewchuk	St. Paul Jr. A	C					
93	CAL	Tom Sundberg	St. Paul Jr. A	C/LW					
94	NYI	Sid Prysunka	New Westminster	W					
95	VAN	Andy Spruce	London	LW	172	31	42	73	111
96	MIN	John Sheridan	Minnesota-Duluth	C					
97	ST.L.	Mike Thompson	Victoria	D					
98	PIT	William Schneider	Minnesota-Duluth	LW					
99	DET	Don Dufek	Michigan	LW					
100	ATL	Bill Moen	U. of Minnesota	G					
101	BUF	Dave Given	Brown	D					
102	L.A.	Marty Mathews	Flin Flon	LW					
103	TOR	Bill Hassard	Wexford Jr.	C					
104	NYR	Eddie Johnstone	Medicine Hat	RW	426	122	136	258	375
105	MTL	John Stewart	Bowling Green	C	2	0	0	0	0
106	CHI	Bob Volpe	Sudbury	G					
107	PHI	Willie Friesen	Swift Current	LW					
108	BOS	Bill Best	Sudbury	LW					
109	WSH	Garth Malarchuk	Calgary	G					
110	K.C.	Mike J. Boland	Sault Ste. Marie	D	23	1	2	3	29
111	CAL	Tom Anderson	St. Paul Jr. A	D					
112	NYI	Dave Langevin	Minnesota-Duluth	D	513	12	107	119	530
113	VAN	Jim Clarke	Toronto	D					
114	MIN	Dave Heitz	Fargo-Moorhead	G					
115	ST.L.	Terry Casey	St. Catharines	RW					
116	PIT	Robbie Laird	Regina	LW	1	0	0	0	0
117	DET	Jack Carlson	Marquette Sr.	LW	236	30	15	45	417
118	ATL	Peter Brown	Boston U.	D					
119	BUF	Bernard Noreau	Laval	RW					
120	L.A.	Harvey Stewart	Flin Flon	G					
121	TOR	Kevin Devine	Toronto	LW	2	0	1	1	8
122	NYR	John Memryk	Winnipeg	G					
123	MTL	Joe Micheletti	Minnesota-Duluth	D	158	11	60	71	114
124	CHI	Eddie Mio	Colorado College	G	192	64	705	4	4.06
125	PHI	Reggie Lemelin	Sherbrooke	G	507	236	1613	12	3.46
126	BOS	Ray Maluta	Flin Flon	D	25	2	3	5	6
127	WSH	John Nazar	Cornwall	LW					
128	CAL	Jim McCabe	Welland Jr. B	C					
129	NYI	David Inkpen	Edmonton	D					
130	VAN	Robbie Watt	Flin Flon	LW					
131	MIN	Roland Eriksson	Tunabro, SWE	C	193	48	95	143	26
132	ST.L.	Rod Tordoff	Swift Current	D					
133	PIT	Larry Finck	St. Catharines	D					
134	DET	Greg Steele	Calgary	D					
135	ATL	Tom Lindskog	Michigan	D					
136	BUF	Charles Constantin	Quebec	C					
137	L.A.	John Held	London	D					
138	TOR	Kevin Kemp	Ottawa	D	3	0	0	0	4
139	NYR	Greg Holst	Kingston	C	11	0	0	0	0
140	MTL	Jamie Hislop	New Hampshire	RW	345	75	103	178	86
141	CHI	Mike St. Cyr	Kitchener	D					
142	PHI	Steve Short	Minnesota Jr. Stars	LW	6	0	0	0	2
143	BOS	Darryl Drader	North Dakota	D					
144	WSH	Kelvin Erickson	Calgary	G					
145	K.C.	Brian Kurliak	North Bay	LW					
146	NYI	Jim Foubister	Victoria	G					
147	VAN	Marc Gaudreault	Lake Superior State	D					
148	MIN	Dave Staffen	Ottawa	C					
149	ST.L.	Paul-Andre Touzin	Shawinigan	G					
150	PIT	James Chicoyne	Brandon	D					
151	DET	Glenn McLeod	Sudbury	D					
152	ATL	Larry Hopkins	Oshawa	LW	60	13	16	29	26
153	BUF	Rick Jodzio	Hamilton	LW	70	2	8	10	71
154	L.A.	Mario Lessard	Sherbrooke	G	240	92	843	9	3.74
155	TOR	Dave Syvret	St. Catharines	D					
156	NYR	Claude Arvisais	Shawinigan	C					
157	MTL	Gord Stewart	Kamloops	C					
158	CHI	Stephen Colp	Michigan State	C					
159	PHI	Peter McKenzie	St. Francis Xavier	D					
160	BOS	Peter Roberts	St. Cloud Jr.	C					
161	WSH	Tony White	Kitchener	LW	164	37	28	65	104
162	K.C.	Denis Carufel	Sorel	D					
163	NYI	Bob Ferguson	Cornwall	C					
164	MIN	Brian Anderson	New Westminster	D					
165	ST.L.	Jack Ahern	Brown	D					
166	PIT	Rick Uhrich	Regina	RW					
167	ATL	Louis Loranger	Shawinigan	C					
168	BUF	Derek Smith	Ottawa	C/LW	335	78	116	194	60
169	L.A.	Derrick Emerson	Montreal	RW					
170	TOR	Andy Stoesz	Selkirk Jr.	G					
171	NYR	Ken Dodd	New Westminster	LW					
172	MTL	Charlie Luksa	Kitchener	D	8	0	1	1	4
173	CHI	Rick Fraser	Oshawa	D					
174	PHI	Marcel Labrosse	Shawinigan	C					
175	BOS	Peter Waselovich	North Dakota	G					
176	WSH	Ron Pronchuk	Brandon	D					
177	K.C.	Soren Johansson	Djurgarden Stockholm, SWE	C					
178	NYI	Murray Fleck	Estevan	D					
179	MIN	Duane Bray	Flin Flon	D					
180	ST.L.	Mitch Babin	North Bay	C	8	0	0	0	0
181	PIT	Serge Gamelin	Sorel	RW					
182	ATL	Randy Montgomery	Welland Jr. B	LW					
183	BUF		invalid claim						
184	L.A.	Jacques Locas	Quebec	C					
185	TOR	Martin Feschuk	Saskatoon	D					
186	NYR	Ralph Krentz	Brandon	LW					
187	MTL	Cliff Cox	New Hampshire	C					
188	CHI	Jean Bernier	Shawinigan	D					
189	PHI	Scott Jessee	Michigan Tech	RW					
190	WSH	Dave McKee	Oshawa	RW					
191	K.C.	Mats Ulander	Boden, SWE	D					
192	NYI	David Rooke	Cornwall	D					
193	MIN	Don Hay	New Westminster	RW					
194	ST.L.	Doug Allan	New Westminster	G					
195	PIT	Richard Perron	Quebec	D					
196	BUF	Bob Geoffrion	Cornwall	LW					
197	L.A.	Lindsay Thomson	U. of Denver	C					
198	NYR	Larry Jacques	Ottawa	RW					
199	MTL	Dave Lumley	New Hampshire	RW	437	98	160	258	680
200	CHI	Dwane Byers	Sherbrooke	RW					
201	PHI	Richard Guay	Chicoutimi	G					
202	WSH	Scott Mabley	Sault Ste. Marie	D					
203	K.C.	Edward Pizunski	Peterborough	D					
204	NYI	Neil Smith	Brockville Jr. A	D					
205	MIN	Brian Holderness	Saskatoon	G					
206	PIT	Richard Hindmarch	U. of Calgary	RW					
207	L.A.	Craig Brickley	U. of Pennsylvania	C					
208	NYR	Tom Gastle	Peterborough	LW					
209	MTL	Mike Hobin	Hamilton	C					
210	CHI	Glen Ing	Victoria	RW					
211	PHI	Brad Morrow	Minnesota-Duluth	D					
212	WSH	Bernard Plante	Trois-Rivieres	LW					
213	K.C.	Willie Wing	Hamilton	RW					
214	NYI	Stefan Persson	Brynas Gavle, SWE	D	622	52	317	369	574
215	MIN	Frank Taylor	Brandon	D					
216	PIT	Bill Davis	Colgate	D					
217	L.A.	Brad Kuglin	U. of Pennsylvania	LW					
218	NYR	Eric Brubacher	Kingston	C					
219	PHI	Craig Arvidson	Minnesota-Duluth	LW					
220	WSH	Jacques Chiasson	Drummondville	RW					
221	NYI	Dave Otness	Wisconsin	C					
222	MIN	Jeff Hymanson	St. Cloud Jr.	D					

PICK	TEAM	NAME	DRAFTED FROM	NHL PLAYERS: POS	GP	G	A	PTS	PIM
				NHL GOALTENDERS: POS	GP	W	GA	SO	AVG
223	PIT	James Mathers	Northeastern	D					
224	NYR	Russell Hall	Winnipeg	RW					
225	WSH	Bill Bell	Regina	LW					
226	NYI	Jim Murray	Michigan State	D					
227	NYR	Bill Kriski	Winnipeg	G					
228	WSH	Robert Blanchet	Kitchener	G					
229	NYI	Mike Dibble	Wisconsin	G					
230	NYR	Kevin Treacy	Cornwall	RW					
231	WSH	Johnny Bower	Downsview Jr.	G					
232	NYI	Brian Bye	Kitchener	LW					
233	NYR	Ken Gassoff	Medicine Hat	C					
234	WSH	Yves Plouffe	Sorel	D					
235	NYI	Martti Jarkko	Tappara Tampere, FIN	D					
236	NYR	Cliff Bast	Medicine Hat	D					
237	WSH	Terry Bozack	Pembroke Jr. A	D					
238	NYI	Ron Phillips	St. Catharines	D					
239	NYR	Jim Mayer	Michigan Tech	RW	4	0	0	0	0
240	WSH	Gord Cole	Brandon	LW					
241	NYR	Warren Miller	Minnesota-Duluth	RW	262	40	50	90	137
242	WSH	Mike Cosentino	Hamilton	C					
243	NYR	Kevin Walker	Cornell	D					
244	WSH	John Duncan	Cornwall	D					
245	NYR	Jim Warner	Minnesota Jr.	RW	32	0	3	3	10
246	WSH	Barry Kerfoot	Smiths Falls Jr.	RW					
247	WSH	Ron Poole	Kamloops	C					

1975

PICK	TEAM	NAME	DRAFTED FROM	NHL PLAYERS: POS	GP	G	A	PTS	PIM
				NHL GOALTENDERS: POS	GP	W	GA	SO	AVG
FIRST ROUND									
1	PHI	Mel Bridgman	Victoria	C	977	252	449	701	1625
2	K.C.	Barry Dean	Medicine Hat	LW	165	25	56	81	146
3	CAL	Ralph Klassen	Saskatoon	C	497	52	93	145	120
4	MIN	Bryan Maxwell	Medicine Hat	D	331	18	77	95	745
5	DET	Rick Lapointe	Victoria	D	664	44	176	220	831
6	TOR	Don Ashby	Calgary	C	188	40	56	96	40
7	CHI	Greg Vaydik	Medicine Hat	C	5	0	0	0	0
8	ATL	Richard Mulhern	Sherbrooke	D	303	27	93	120	217
9	MTL	Robin Sadler	Edmonton	D	Played in Europe 1976-1989				
10	VAN	Rick Blight	Brandon	RW	326	96	125	221	170
11	NYI	Pat Price	Saskatoon	D	726	43	218	261	1456
12	NYR	Wayne Dillon	Toronto	C	229	43	66	109	60
13	PIT	Gord Laxton	New Westminster	G	17	4	74	0	5.55
14	BOS	Doug Halward	Peterborough	D	653	69	224	293	774
15	MTL	Pierre Mondou	Montreal	C	548	194	262	456	179
16	L.A.	Tim Young	Ottawa	C	628	195	341	536	438
17	BUF	Bob Sauve	Laval	G	420	182	1377	8	3.48
18	WSH	Alex Forsyth	Kingston	C	1	0	0	0	0
SECOND ROUND									
19	WSH	Peter Scamurra	Peterborough	D	132	8	25	33	59
20	K.C.	Don Cairns	Victoria	LW	9	0	1	1	2
21	CAL	Dennis Maruk	London	C	888	356	522	878	761
22	MTL	Brian Engblom	Wisconsin	D	659	29	177	206	599
23	DET	Jerry Rollins	Winnipeg	D	27 points in 130 WHA games				
24	TOR	Doug Jarvis	Peterborough	C	964	139	264	403	263
25	CHI	Daniel Arndt	Saskatoon	LW	39 points in 120 WHA games				
26	ATL	Rick Bowness	Montreal	RW	173	18	37	55	191
27	ST.L.	Ed Staniowski	Regina	G	219	67	818	2	4.06
28	VAN	Brad Gassoff	Kamloops	LW	122	19	17	36	163
29	NYI	Dave Salvian	St. Catharines	RW	1 playoff game with NY Islanders				
30	NYR	Doug Soetaert	Edmonton	G	284	110	1030	6	3.97
31	PIT	Russ Anderson	Minnesota-Duluth	D	519	22	99	121	1086
32	BOS	Barry Smith	New Westminster	C	114	7	7	14	10
33	L.A.	Terry Bucyk	Lethbridge	RW	3 pro seasons in 3 leagues				
34	MTL	Kelly Greenbank	Winnipeg	RW	Played in Europe until 1990				
35	BUF	Ken Breitenbach	St. Catharines	D	68	1	13	14	49
36	ST.L.	Jamie Masters	Ottawa	D	33	1	13	14	2
OTHER ROUNDS									
37	DET	Al Cameron	New Westminster	D	282	11	44	55	356
38	K.C.	Neil Lyseng	Kamloops	RW					
39	CAL	John Tweedle	Lake Superior State	RW					
40	MIN	Paul Harrison	Oshawa	G	109	28	408	2	4.22
41	MIN	Alex Pirus	U. of Notre Dame	RW	159	30	28	58	94
42	TOR	Bruce Boudreau	Toronto	C	141	28	42	70	46
43	CHI	Mike O'Connell	Kingston	D	860	105	334	439	605
44	BUF	Terry Martin	London	LW	479	104	101	205	202
45	DET	Blair Davidson	Flin Flon	D					
46	VAN	Normand Lapointe	Trois-Rivieres	G					
47	NYI	Joe Fortunato	Kitchener	LW					
48	NYR	Greg Hickey	Hamilton	LW	1	0	0	0	0
49	PIT	Paul Baxter	Winnipeg	D	472	48	121	169	1564
50	DET	Clarke Hamilton	U. of Notre Dame	LW					
51	MTL	Paul Woods	Sault Ste. Marie	LW	501	72	124	196	276
52	MTL	Pat Hughes	Michigan	RW	573	130	128	258	646
53	BUF	Gary McAdam	St. Catharines	LW	534	96	132	228	243
54	PHI	Bob Ritchie	Sorel	LW	29	8	4	12	10
55	WSH	Blair MacKasey	Montreal	D	1	0	0	0	2
56	K.C.	Ron Delorme	Lethbridge	C	524	83	83	166	667
57	CAL	Greg Smith	Colorado College	D	829	56	232	288	1110
58	MIN	Steve Jensen	Michigan Tech	LW	438	113	107	220	318
59	DET	Mike Wirachowsky	Regina	D					
60	BOS	Rick Adduono	St. Catharines	C	4	0	0	0	2
61	CHI	Pierre Giroux	Hull	C	6	1	0	1	17
62	ATL	Dale Ross	Ottawa	LW					
63	ST.L.	Rick Bourbonnais	Ottawa	RW	71	9	15	24	29
64	VAN	Glen Richardson	Hamilton	LW	24	3	6	9	19
65	NYI	Andre Lepage	Montreal	G					
66	NYR	Bill Cheropita	St. Catharines	G					
67	PIT	Stuart Younger	Michigan State	LW					
68	BOS	Denis Daigle	Montreal	LW					
69	L.A.	Andre Leduc	Sherbrooke	D					
70	MTL	Dave Gorman	St. Catharines	RW	3	0	0	0	0
71	BUF	Greg Neeld	Calgary	D					
72	PHI	Rick St. Croix	Oshawa	G	130	49	451	2	3.71
73	WSH	Craig Crawford	Toronto	LW					
74	K.C.	Terry McDonald	Kamloops	D	8	0	1	1	6
75	CAL	Doug Young	Michigan Tech	D					
76	MIN	David Norris	Hamilton	LW					
77	DET	Mike Wong	Montreal	C	22	1	1	2	12
78	TOR	Ted Long	Hamilton	D					
79	CHI	Bob Hoffmeyer	Saskatoon	D	198	14	52	66	325
80	ATL	Willi Plett	St. Catharines	RW	834	222	215	437	2572
81	ST.L.	Jim Gustafson	Victoria	C					
82	VAN	Doug Murray	Brandon	LW					
83	NYI	Denis McLean	Calgary	LW					
84	NYR	Larry Huras	Kitchener	D	2	0	0	0	0
85	PIT	Kim Clackson	Victoria	D	106	0	8	8	370
86	BOS	Stan Jonathan	Peterborough	LW	411	91	110	201	751
87	L.A.	Dave Miglia	Trois-Rivieres	D					
88	MTL	Jim Turkiewicz	Peterborough	D					
89	BUF	Don Edwards	Kitchener	G	459	208	1449	16	3.32
90	PHI	Gary Morrison	Michigan	RW	43	1	15	16	70
91	WSH	Roger Swanson	Flin Flon	G					
92	K.C.	Eric Sanderson	Victoria	LW					
93	CAL	Larry Hendrick	Calgary	G					
94	MIN	Greg Clause	Hamilton	RW					
95	DET	Mike Harazny	Regina	D					
96	TOR	Kevin Campbell	St. Lawrence U.	D					
97	CHI	Tom Ulseth	Wisconsin	RW					
98	ATL	Paul Heaver	Oshawa	D					
99	ST.L.	Jack Brownschidle	U. of Notre Dame	D	494	39	162	201	151
100	VAN	Bob Watson	Flin Flon	RW					
101	NYI	Mike Sleep	New Westminster	RW					
102	NYR	Randy Koch	Vermont	LW					
103	PIT	Peter Morris	Victoria	LW					
104	BOS	Matti Hagman	HIFK Helsinki, FIN	C	237	56	89	145	36
105	L.A.	Bob Russell	Sudbury	C					
106	MTL	Michel Lachance	Montreal	D	21	0	4	4	22
107	BUF	Jim Minor	Regina	LW					
108	PHI	Paul Holmgren	U. of Minnesota	RW	527	144	179	323	1684
109	WSH	Clark Jantzie	U. of Alberta	LW					
110	K.C.	Bill Oleschuk	Saskatoon	G	55	7	188	1	3.98
111	CAL	Rick Shinske	New Westminster	C	63	5	16	21	10
112	MIN	Francois Robert	Sherbrooke	D					
113	DET	Jean-Luc Phaneuf	Montreal	C					
114	TOR	Mario Rouillard	Trois-Rivieres	RW					
115	CHI	Ted Bulley	Hull	LW	414	101	113	214	704
116	ATL	Dale McMullin	Brandon	LW					
117	ST.L.	Doug Lindskog	Michigan	LW					
118	VAN	Brian Shmyr	New Westminster	C					
119	NYI	Richie Hansen	Sudbury	C	20	2	8	10	4
120	NYR	Claude Larose	Sherbrooke	LW	25	4	7	11	2
121	PIT	Mike Will	Edmonton	C					
122	BOS	Gary Carr	Toronto	G					
123	L.A.	Dave Faulkner	Regina	C					
124	MTL	Tim Burke	New Hampshire	D					
125	BUF	Grant Rowe	Ottawa	D					
126	PHI	Dana Decker	Michigan Tech	LW					
127	WSH	Mike Fryia	Peterborough	LW					
128	K.C.	Joe Baker	Minnesota-Duluth	D					
129	CAL	Doug Schoenfeld	Cambridge Sr.	D					
130	MIN	Dean Magee	Colorado College	LW	7	0	0	0	4
131	DET	Steve Carlson	Johnstown NAHL	C	52	9	12	21	23
132	TOR	Ron Wilson	Providence	D	177	26	67	93	68
133	CHI	Paul Jensen	Michigan Tech	D					
134	ATL	Rick Piche	Brandon	D					
135	ST.L.	Dick Lamby	Salem State	D	22	0	5	5	22
136	VAN	Allan Fleck	New Westminster	LW					
137	NYI	Bob Sunderland	Boston U.	D					
138	NYR	Bill Hamilton	St. Catharines	RW					
139	PIT	Tapio Levo	Assat Pori, FIN	D	107	16	53	69	36

PICK	TEAM	NAME	DRAFTED FROM	NHL PLAYERS: POS / NHL GOALTENDERS: POS	GP / GP	G / W	A / GA	PTS / SO	PIM / AVG
140	BOS	Bo Berglund	Djurgarden Stockholm, SWE	LW					
141	L.A.	Bill Reber	Vermont	RW					
142	MTL	Craig Norwich	Wisconsin	D	104	17	58	75	60
143	BUF	Alex Tidey	Lethbridge	RW	9	0	0	0	8
144	WSH	Jim Ofrim	U. of Alberta	C					
145	K.C.	Scott Williams	Flin Flon	LW					
146	CAL	Jim Weaver	Kingston	G					
147	MIN	Terry Angel	Oshawa	RW					
148	DET	Gary Vaughn	Medicine Hat	RW					
149	TOR	Paul Evans	Peterborough	C/LW	11	1	1	2	21
150	ATL	Nick Sanza	Sherbrooke	G					
151	ST.L.	Dave McNab	Wisconsin	G					
152	VAN	Bob McNeice	New Westminster	D					
153	NYI	Don Blair	Ottawa	RW					
154	NYR	Bud Stefanski	Oshawa	C	1	0	0	0	0
155	PIT	Bryan Shutt	Bowling Green	LW					
156	BOS	Joe Rando	New Hampshire	D					
157	L.A.	Sean Sullivan	Hamilton	D					
158	MTL	Paul Clarke	U. of Notre Dame	D					
159	BUF	Andy Whitby	Oshawa	RW					
160	PHI	Viktor Khatulev	Dynamo Riga, USSR	C					
161	WSH	Malcolm Zinger	Kamloops	RW					
162	ST.L.	Greg Agar	Merritt Jr. A	RW					
163	MIN	Michel Blais	Kingston	D					
164	DET	Jean Thibodeau	Shawinigan	C					
165	TOR	Jean Latendresse	Shawinigan	D					
166	TOR	Paul Crowley	Sudbury	RW					
167	ATL	Brian O'Connell	St. Louis U.	G					
168	NYI	Joey Girardin	Winnipeg	D					
169	NYR	Daniel Beaulieu	Quebec	LW					
170	PIT	Frank Salive	Peterborough	G					
171	BOS	Kevin Nugent	U. of Notre Dame	G					
172	L.A.	Brian Petrovek	Harvard	G					
173	MTL	Bob Ferriter	Boston College	C					
174	BUF	Len Moher	U. of Notre Dame	G					
175	PHI	Duffy Smith	Bowling Green	D					
176	DET	David Hanson	Colorado College	D					
177	MIN	Earl Sargent	Fargo-Moorhead	RW					
178	DET	Robin Larson	Minnesota-Duluth	D					
179	TOR	Dan D'Alvise	Royal York Jr.	C					
180	TOR	Jack Laine	Bowling Green	RW					
181	ATL	Joe Augustine	Austin Prep	D					
182	VAN	Sid Veysey	Sherbrooke	C	1	0	0	0	0
183	NYI	Geoff Green	Sudbury	RW					
184	NYR	John McMorrow	Providence	C					
185	PIT	John Glynne	Vermont	D					
186	L.A.	Tom Goddard	North Dakota	RW					
187	MTL	David Bell	Harvard	C					
188	TOR	Ken Holland	Medicine Hat	G	4	0	17	0	4.95
189	TOR	Bob Barnes	Hamilton	D					
190	MIN	Gilles Cloutier	Shawinigan	G					
191	TOR	Gary Burns	New Hampshire	LW/C	11	2	2	4	18
192	ATL	Torbjorn Nilsson	Skelleftea, SWE	RW					
193	TOR	Jim Montgomery	Hull	C					
194	NYI	Kari Makkonen	Assat Pori, FIN	RW	9	2	2	4	0
195	NYR	Tom McNamara	Vermont	G					
196	PIT	Lex Hudson	U. of Denver	D	2	0	0	0	0
197	L.A.	Mario Viens	Cornwall	G					
198	MTL	Carl Jackson	U. of Pennsylvania	C					
199	TOR	Rick Martin	London	RW					
200	NYR	Steve Roberts	Providence	D					
201	NYR	Paul Dionne	Princeton	D					
202	PIT	Dan Tsubouchi	St. Louis U.	RW					
203	L.A.	Chuck Carpenter	Yale	C					
204	MTL	Michel Brisebois	Sherbrooke	C					
205	NYR	Cecil Luckern	New Hampshire	LW					
206	PIT	Bronislav Stankovsky	Fargo-Moorhead	LW					
207	L.A.	Bob Fish	Fargo-Moorhead	LW					
208	MTL	Roger Bourque	U. of Notre Dame	D					
209	NYR	John Corriveau	New Hampshire	RW					
210	L.A.	Dave Taylor	Clarkson	RW	1111	431	638	1069	1589
211	MTL	Jim Lundquist	Brown	D					
212	NYR	Tom Funke	Fargo-Moorhead	LW					
213	L.A.	Robert Shaw	Clarkson	D					
214	MTL	Don Madson	Fargo-Moorhead	C					
215	MTL	Bob Bain	New Hampshire	D					
216	ATL	Gary Gill	Sault Ste. Marie	LW					
217	PIT	Kelly Secord	New Westminster	RW					

1976

FIRST ROUND

PICK	TEAM	NAME	DRAFTED FROM	NHL PLAYERS: POS / NHL GOALTENDERS: POS	GP / GP	G / W	A / GA	PTS / SO	PIM / AVG
1	WSH	Rick Green	London	D	845	43	220	263	588
2	PIT	Blair Chapman	Saskatoon	RW	402	106	125	231	158
3	MIN	Glen Sharpley	Hull	C	389	117	161	278	199
4	DET	Fred Williams	Saskatoon	C	44	2	5	7	10
5	CAL	Bjorn Johansson	Orebro, SWE	D	15	1	1	2	10
6	NYR	Don Murdoch	Medicine Hat	RW	320	121	117	238	155
7	ST.L.	Bernie Federko	Saskatoon	C	1000	369	761	1130	487
8	ATL	Dave Shand	Peterborough	D	421	19	84	103	544
9	CHI	Real Cloutier	Quebec	RW	317	146	198	344	119
10	ATL	Harold Phillipoff	New Westminster	LW	141	26	57	83	267
11	K.C.	Paul Gardner	Oshawa	C	447	201	201	402	207
12	MTL	Peter Lee	Ottawa	RW	431	114	131	245	257
13	MTL	Rod Schutt	Sudbury	LW	286	77	92	169	177
14	NYI	Alex McKendry	Sudbury	L/RW	46	3	6	9	21
15	WSH	Greg Carroll	Medicine Hat	C	131	20	34	54	44
16	BOS	Clayton Pachal	New Westminster	C/LW	35	2	3	5	95
17	PHI	Mark Suzor	Kingston	D	64	4	16	20	60
18	MTL	Bruce Baker	Ottawa	RW	5 seasons – Nova Scotia (AHL)				

SECOND ROUND

PICK	TEAM	NAME	DRAFTED FROM	NHL PLAYERS: POS / NHL GOALTENDERS: POS	GP / GP	G / W	A / GA	PTS / SO	PIM / AVG
19	PIT	Greg Malone	Oshawa	C	704	191	310	501	661
20	ST.L.	Brian Sutter	Lethbridge	LW	779	303	333	636	1786
21	L.A.	Steve Clippingdale	New Westminster	LW	19	1	2	3	9
22	DET	Reed Larson	Minnesota-Duluth	D	904	222	463	685	1391
23	CAL	Vern Stenlund	London	C	4	0	0	0	0
24	NYR	Dave Farrish	Sudbury	D	430	17	110	127	440
25	ST.L.	John Smrke	Toronto	LW	103	11	17	28	33
26	VAN	Bob Manno	St. Catharines	D	371	41	131	172	274
27	CHI	Jeff McDill	Victoria	RW	1	0	0	0	0
28	ATL	Bobby Simpson	Sherbrooke	LW	175	35	29	64	98
29	PIT	Peter Marsh	Sherbrooke	RW	278	48	71	119	224
30	TOR	Randy Carlyle	Sudbury	D	1055	148	499	647	1400
31	MIN	Jim Roberts	Ottawa	LW	106	17	23	40	33
32	NYI	Mike Kaszycki	Sault Ste. Marie	C	226	42	80	122	108
33	BUF	Joe Kowal	Hamilton	LW	22	0	5	5	13
34	BOS	Lorry Gloeckner	Victoria	D	13	0	2	2	6
35	PHI	Drew Callander	Regina	C/RW	39	6	2	8	7
36	MTL	Barry Melrose	Kamloops	D	300	10	23	33	728

OTHER ROUNDS

PICK	TEAM	NAME	DRAFTED FROM	NHL PLAYERS: POS / NHL GOALTENDERS: POS	GP / GP	G / W	A / GA	PTS / SO	PIM / AVG
37	WSH	Tom Rowe	London	RW	357	85	100	185	615
38	K.C.	Mike Kitchen	Toronto	D	474	12	62	74	370
39	MIN	Don Jackson	U. of Notre Dame	D	311	16	52	68	640
40	DET	Fred Berry	New Westminster	C	3	0	0	0	0
41	CAL	Mike Fidler	Boston U.	LW	271	84	97	181	124
42	NYR	Mike McEwen	Toronto	D	716	108	296	404	460
43	ST.L.	Jim Kirkpatrick	Toronto	D					
44	VAN	Rob Flockhart	Kamloops	LW	55	2	5	7	14
45	CHI	Thomas Gradin	MoDo Ornskoldsvik, SWE	C	677	209	384	593	298
46	ATL	Rick Hodgson	Calgary	D	6	0	0	0	6
47	PIT	Morris Lukowich	Medicine Hat	LW	582	199	219	418	584
48	TOR	Alain Belanger	Sherbrooke	RW	9	0	1	1	6
49	L.A.	Don Moores	Kamloops	C					
50	NYI	Garth MacGuigan	Montreal	C	5	0	1	1	2
51	MIN	Ron Zanussi	London	RW	299	52	83	135	373
52	TOR	Gary McFayden	Hull	RW					
53	PHI	Craig Hamner	St. Paul Jr. A	D					
54	MTL	Bill Baker	Minnesota-Duluth	D	143	7	25	32	175
55	WSH	Al Glendinning	Calgary	D					
56	ST.L.	Mike Liut	Bowling Green	G	663	293	2219	25	3.49
57	MIN	Mike Fedorko	Hamilton	D					
58	DET	Kevin Schamehorn	New Westminster	RW	10	0	0	0	17
59	CAL	Warren Young	Michigan Tech	C	236	72	77	149	472
60	NYR	Claude Periard	Trois-Rivieres	LW					
61	ST.L.	Paul Skidmore	Boston College	G	2	1	6	0	3.00
62	VAN	Elmer Ray	Calgary	LW					
63	CHI	Dave Debol	Michigan	C	92	26	26	52	4
64	ATL	Kent Nilsson	Djurgarden Stockholm, SWE	C	553	264	422	686	116
65	PIT	Greg Redquest	Oshawa	G	1	0	3	0	13.85
66	TOR	Tim Williams	Victoria	D					
67	L.A.	Bob Mears	Kingston	G					
68	NYI	Ken Morrow	Bowling Green	D	550	17	88	105	309
69	BUF	Henry Maze	Edmonton	LW					
70	BOS	Bob Miller	Ottawa	C	404	75	119	194	220
71	PHI	Dave Hynek	Kingston	LW					
72	MTL	Ed Clarey	Cornwall	RW					
73	WSH	Doug Patey	Sault Ste. Marie	RW	45	4	2	6	8
74	K.C.	Rick McIntyre	Oshawa	LW					
75	MIN	Phil Verchota	Minnesota-Duluth	C					
76	DET	Dwight Schofield	London	D	211	8	22	30	631
77	CAL	Darcy Regier	Lethbridge	D	26	0	2	2	35
78	NYR	Doug Gaines	St. Catharines	C					
79	CAL	Cal Sandbeck	U. of Denver	D					
80	VAN	Rick Durston	Victoria	LW					
81	CHI	Terry McDonald	Edmonton	C					

PICK	TEAM	NAME	DRAFTED FROM	NHL PLAYERS: POS / NHL GOALTENDERS: POS	GP / GP	G / W	A / GA	PTS / SO	PIM / AVG
82	ATL	Mark Earp	Kamloops	G					
83	PIT	Brendan Lowe	Sherbrooke	D					
84	TOR	Greg Hotham	Kingston	D	230	15	74	89	139
85	L.A.	Robert Palmer	Michigan	D	320	9	101	110	115
86	NYI	Mike Hordy	Sault Ste. Marie	D	11	0	0	0	7
87	BUF	Ron Roscoe	Hamilton	D					
88	BOS	Peter Vandemark	Oshawa	LW					
89	PHI	Robin Lang	Cornell	D					
90	MTL	Maurice Barrette	Quebec	G					
91	WSH	Jim Bedard	Sudbury	G	73	17	278	1	3.94
92	K.C.	Larry Skinner	Ottawa	C	47	10	12	22	8
93	MIN	Dave Delich	Colorado College	C					
94	DET	Tony Horvath	Sault Ste. Marie	D					
95	CAL	Jouni Rinne	Lukko Rauma, FIN	RW					
96	NYR	Barry Scully	Kingston	RW					
97	ST.L.	Nels Goddard	Michigan Tech	D					
98	VAN	Rob Tudor	Regina	RW/C	28	4	4	8	19
99	CHI	John Peterson	U. of Notre Dame	G					
100	WSH	Don Wilson	St. Catharines	D					
101	PIT	Vic Sirko	Oshawa	D					
102	TOR	Dan Djakalovic	Kitchener	C					
103	L.A.	Larry McRae	Windsor	G					
104	NYI	Yvon Vautour	Laval	RW	204	26	33	59	401
105	BUF	Don Lemieux	Trois-Rivieres	D					
106	BOS	Ted Olson	Calgary	LW					
107	PHI	Paul Klasinski	St. Paul Jr. A	LW					
108	MTL	Pierre Brassard	Cornwall	LW					
109	WSH	Dale Rideout	Flin Flon	G					
110	MIN	Jeff Barr	Michigan State	D					
111	DET	Fern LeBlanc	Sherbrooke	C	34	5	6	11	0
112	NYR	Remi Levesque	Quebec	C					
113	ST.L.	Mike Eaves	Wisconsin	C	324	83	143	226	80
114	VAN	Brad Rhiness	Kingston	C					
115	CHI	John Rothstein	Minnesota-Duluth	RW					
116	TOR	Chuck Skjodt	Windsor	C					
117	PHI	Ray Kurpis	Austin Prep	RW					
118	MTL	Rick Gosselin	Flin Flon	C					
119	WSH	Allan Dumba	Regina	RW					
120	DET	Claude Legris	Sorel	G	4	0	4	0	2.64
121	ST.L.	Jacques Soguel	Davos, SUI	C					
122	VAN	Stu Ostlund	Michigan Tech	C					
123	MTL	John Gregory	Wisconsin	D					
124	ST.L.	David Dornself	Providence	D					
125	MTL	Bruce Horsch	Michigan Tech	G					
126	ST.L.	Brad Wilson	Providence	C					
127	MTL	John Tavella	Sault Ste. Marie	LW					
128	ST.L.	Don Hoene	Michigan	RW					
129	MTL	Mark Davidson	Flin Flon	RW					
130	ST.L.	Goran Lindblom	Skelleftea, SWE	D					
131	MTL	Bill Wells	Cornwall	LW					
132	ST.L.	Jim Bales	U. of Denver	G					
133	MTL	Ron Wilson	St. Catharines	C	832	110	216	326	415
134	ST.L.	Anders Hakansson	AIK Solna, SWE	LW	330	52	46	98	141
135	ST.L.	Juhani Wallenius	Lukko Rauma, FIN	C					

1977

PICK	TEAM	NAME	DRAFTED FROM	NHL PLAYERS: POS / NHL GOALTENDERS: POS	GP / GP	G / W	A / GA	PTS / SO	PIM / AVG
FIRST ROUND									
1	DET	Dale McCourt	St. Catharines	C	532	194	284	478	124
2	COL	Barry Beck	New Westminster	D	615	104	251	355	1016
3	WSH	Robert Picard	Montreal	D	899	104	319	423	1025
4	VAN	Jere Gillis	Sherbrooke	LW	386	78	95	173	230
5	CLE	Mike Crombeen	Kingston	RW	475	55	68	123	218
6	CHI	Doug Wilson	Ottawa	D	1024	237	590	827	830
7	MIN	Brad Maxwell	New Westminster	D	612	98	270	368	1292
8	NYR	Lucien DeBlois	Sorel	C	993	249	276	525	814
9	ST.L.	Scott Campbell	London	D	80	4	21	25	243
10	MTL	Mark Napier	Toronto	RW	767	235	306	541	157
11	TOR	John Anderson	Toronto	RW	814	282	349	631	263
12	TOR	Trevor Johansen	Toronto	D	286	11	46	57	282
13	NYR	Ron Duguay	Sudbury	C/RW	864	274	346	620	582
14	BUF	Ric Seiling	St. Catharines	RW/C	738	179	208	387	573
15	NYI	Mike Bossy	Laval	RW	752	573	553	1126	210
16	BOS	Dwight Foster	Kitchener	RW	541	111	163	274	420
17	PHI	Kevin McCarthy	Winnipeg	D	537	67	191	258	527
18	MTL	Norm Dupont	Montreal	LW	256	55	85	140	52
SECOND ROUND									
19	CHI	Jean Savard	Quebec	C	43	7	12	19	29
20	ATL	Miles Zaharko	New Westminster	D	129	5	32	37	84
21	WSH	Mark Lofthouse	New Westminster	RW/C	181	42	38	80	73
22	VAN	Jeff Bandura	Portland	D	2	0	1	1	0
23	CLE	Dan Chicoine	Sherbrooke	RW	31	1	2	3	12
24	TOR	Bob Gladney	Oshawa	D	14	1	5	6	4
25	MIN	Dave Semenko	Brandon	LW	575	65	88	153	1175
26	NYR	Mike Keating	St. Catharines	LW	1	0	0	0	0
27	ST.L.	Neil Labatte	Toronto	C/D	26	0	2	2	19
28	ATL	Don Laurence	Kitchener	C	79	15	22	37	14
29	TOR	Rocky Saganiuk	Lethbridge	RW/C	259	57	65	122	201
30	PIT	Jim Hamilton	London	RW	95	14	18	32	28
31	ATL	Brian Hill	Medicine Hat	RW	19	1	1	2	4
32	BUF	Ron Areshenkoff	Medicine Hat	C	4	0	0	0	0
33	NYI	John Tonelli	Toronto	LW	1028	325	511	836	911
34	BOS	Dave Parro	Saskatoon	G	77	21	274	2	4.09
35	PHI	Tom Gorence	U. of Minnesota	RW	303	58	53	111	89
36	MTL	Rod Langway	New Hampshire	D	994	51	278	329	849

OTHER ROUNDS

PICK	TEAM	NAME	DRAFTED FROM	NHL PLAYERS: POS / NHL GOALTENDERS: POS	GP / GP	G / W	A / GA	PTS / SO	PIM / AVG
37	DET	Rick Vasko	Peterborough	D	31	3	7	10	29
38	COL	Doug Berry	U. of Denver	C	121	10	33	43	25
39	WSH	Eddy Godin	Quebec	RW	27	3	6	9	12
40	VAN	Glen Hanlon	Brandon	G	477	167	1561	13	3.60
41	CLE	Reg Kerr	Kamloops	LW	263	66	94	160	169
42	CLE	Guy Lash	Winnipeg	RW					
43	MTL	Alain Cote	Chicoutimi	LW	696	103	190	293	383
44	NYR	Steve Baker	Union College	G	57	20	190	3	3.70
45	ST.L.	Tom Roulston	Winnipeg	C/RW	195	47	49	96	74
46	MTL	Pierre Lagace	Quebec	LW					
47	COL	Randy Pierce	Sudbury	RW	277	62	76	138	223
48	PIT	Kim Davis	Flin Flon	C	36	5	7	12	51
49	MTL	Moe Robinson	Kingston	D	1	0	0	0	0
50	NYI	Hector Marini	Sudbury	RW	154	27	46	73	246
51	NYI	Bruce Andres	New Westminster	LW					
52	BOS	Mike Forbes	St. Catharines	D	50	1	11	12	41
53	PHI	Dave Hoyda	Portland	LW	132	6	17	23	299
54	MTL	Gordie Roberts	Victoria	D	1097	61	359	420	1582
55	DET	John Hilworth	Medicine Hat	D	57	1	1	2	89
56	VAN	Dave Morrow	Calgary	C/D					
57	WSH	Nelson Burton	Quebec	LW	8	1	0	1	21
58	VAN	Murray Bannerman	Victoria	G	289	116	1051	8	3.83
59	CLE	John Baby	Sudbury	D	26	2	8	10	26
60	CHI	Randy Ireland	Portland	G	Re-entered Draft in 1978				
61	MIN	Kevin McCloskey	Calgary	D					
62	NYR	Mario Marois	Quebec	D	955	76	357	433	1746
63	ST.L.	Tony Currie	Portland	RW	290	92	119	211	83
64	MTL	Robbie Holland	Montreal	G	44	11	171	1	4.08
65	TOR	Dan Eastman	London	C	Re-entered Draft in 1978				
66	PIT	Mark Johnson	Wisconsin	C	669	203	305	508	260
67	PHI	Yves Guillemette	Shawinigan	G					
68	BUF	Bill Stewart	Niagara Falls	D	261	7	64	71	424
69	NYI	Steve Stoyanovich	RPI	C	23	3	5	8	11
70	BOS	Brian McGregor	Saskatoon	RW					
71	PHI	Rene Hamelin	Shawinigan	LW					
72	ATL	Jim Craig	Boston U.	G	30	11	100	0	3.78
73	DET	Jim Korn	Providence	D	597	66	122	188	1801
74	COL	Mike Dwyer	Niagara Falls	LW	31	2	6	8	25
75	WSH	Denis Turcotte	Quebec	C					
76	VAN	Steve Hazlett	St. Catharines	LW	1	0	0	0	0
77	CLE	Owen Lloyd	Medicine Hat	D					
78	CHI	Gary Platt	Sorel	D					
79	MIN	Robert Parent	Kingston	D					
80	NYR	Benoit Gosselin	Trois-Rivieres	LW	7	0	0	0	33
81	ST.L.	Bruce Hamilton	Saskatoon	LW					
82	ATL	Kurt Christoferson	Colorado College	D					
83	TOR	John Wilson	Windsor	LW					
84	L.A.	Julian Baretta	Wisconsin	G					
85	L.A.	Warren Holmes	Ottawa	C	45	8	18	26	7
86	BUF	Richard Sirois	Laval	G	Re-entered Draft in 1978				
87	NYI	Markus Mattsson	Ilves Tampere, FIN	G	92	21	343	6	4.11
88	BOS	Douglas Butler	St. Louis U.	D					
89	PHI	Dan Clark	Kamloops	D	Re-entered Draft in 1978				
90	MTL	Gaetan Rochette	Shawinigan	LW					
91	DET	Jim Baxter	Union College	G					
92	COL	Dan Lempe	Minnesota-Duluth	C					
93	WSH	Perry Schnarr	U. of Denver	RW					
94	VAN	Brian Drumm	Peterborough	LW					
95	CLE	Jeff Allan	Hull	D	4	0	0	0	2
96	CHI	Jack O'Callahan	Boston U.	D	389	27	104	131	541
97	MIN	Jamie Gallimore	Kamloops	RW	2	0	0	0	0
98	NYR	John Bethel	Boston U.	LW	17	0	2	2	4
99	ST.L.	Gary McMonagle	Peterborough	C					
100	ATL	Bernard Harbec	Laval	C					
101	TOR	Roy Sommer	Calgary	LW/C	3	1	0	1	7
102	PIT	Greg Millen	Peterborough	G	604	215	2281	17	3.87
103	L.A.	Randy Rudnyk	New Westminster	RW					
104	BUF	Wayne Ramsey	Brandon	D	2	0	0	0	0
105	NYI	Steve Letzgus	Michigan Tech	D					
106	BOS	Keith Johnson	Saskatoon	D					
107	PHI	Alain Chaput	Sorel	C					
108	MTL	Bill Himmelright	North Dakota	D					
109	DET	Randy Wilson	Providence	LW					

PICK	TEAM	NAME	DRAFTED FROM	POS	GP	G / W	A / GA	PTS / SO	PIM / AVG
				NHL PLAYERS: POS	GP	G	A	PTS	PIM
				NHL GOALTENDERS: POS	GP	W	GA	SO	AVG
110	COL	Rick Doyle	London	LW					
111	WSH	Rollie Boutin	Lethbridge	G	22	7	75	0	3.96
112	VAN	Ray Creasey	New Westminster	C					
113	CLE	Mark Toffolo	Chicoutimi	D	Re-entered Draft in 1978				
114	CHI	Floyd Lahache	Sherbrooke	RW					
115	MIN	Jean-Pierre Sanvido	Trois-Rivieres	G					
116	NYR	Bob Sullivan	Chicoutimi	LW	62	18	19	37	18
117	ST.L.	Matti Forss	Lukko Rauma, FIN	C					
118	ATL	Bobby Gould	New Hampshire	RW	697	145	159	304	572
119	TOR	Lynn Jorgensen	Toronto	LW					
120	L.A.	Robert Suter	Wisconsin	D					
121	NYI	Harald Luckner	Farjestad Karlstad, SWE	C	Re-entered Draft in 1978				
122	BOS	Ralph Cox	New Hampshire	RW					
123	PHI	Richard Dalpe	Trois-Rivieres	C					
124	MTL	Richard Sevigny	Sherbrooke	G	176	80	507	5	3.21
125	DET	Raymond Roy	Sherbrooke	C					
126	COL	Joe Contini	St. Catharines	C	68	17	21	38	34
127	WSH	Brent Tremblay	Trois-Rivieres	D	10	1	0	1	6
128	CLE	Grant Eakin	Lethbridge	LW					
129	CHI	Jeff Geiger	Ottawa	D					
130	MIN	Greg Tebbutt	Victoria	D	26	0	3	3	35
131	NYR	Lance Nethery	Cornell	C	41	11	14	25	14
132	ST.L.	Raimo Hirvonen	HIFK Helsinki, FIN	C					
133	ATL	Jim Bennett	Brown	LW					
134	TOR	Kevin Howe	Sault Ste. Marie	C/D					
135	PHI	Pete Peeters	Medicine Hat	G	489	246	1424	21	3.08
136	PHI	Clint Eccles	Kamloops	LW					
137	MTL	Keith Hendrickson	U. of Minnesota	D					
138	BOS	Mario Claude	Sherbrooke	D					
139	PHI	Mike Greeder	St. Paul Jr. A	D					
140	MTL	Mike Reilly	Colorado College	RW					
141	DET	Kip Churchill	Union College	C					
142	COL	Jack Hughes	Harvard	D	46	2	5	7	104
143	WSH	Don Michiletti	U. of Minnesota	LW					
144	CHI	Stephen Ough	Laval	D					
145	MIN	Keith Hanson	Austin Prep	D	25	0	2	2	77
146	NYR	Alex Jeans	U. of Toronto	RW					
147	ST.L.	Bjorn Olsson	Farjestad Karlstad, SWE	D					
148	ATL	Tim Harrer	U. of Minnesota	RW	3	0	0	0	2
149	TOR	Ray Robertson	St. Lawrence U.	D					
150	PHI	Tom Bauer	Providence	LW					
151	PHI	Mike Bauman	Hull	LW					
152	MTL	Barry Borrett	Cornwall	G					
153	PHI	Bruce Crowder	New Hampshire	RW	243	47	51	98	156
154	MTL	Sid Tanchak	Clarkson	C					
155	DET	Lance Gatoni	U. of Toronto	D					
156	WSH	Archie Henderson	Victoria	RW	23	3	1	4	92
157	NYR	Peter Raps	Western Michigan	LW					
158	PHI	Rob Nicholson	St. Paul Jr. A	D					
159	PHI	Dave Isherwood	Winnipeg	C					
160	MTL	Mark Holden	Brown	G	8	2	25	0	4.03
161	PHI	Steve Jones	Ohio State	G					
162	MTL	Craig Laughlin	Clarkson	RW	549	136	205	341	364
163	DET	Rob Plumb	Kingston	LW	14	3	2	5	2
164	NYR	Mike Brown	Western Michigan	RW					
165	PHI	Jim Trainor	Harvard	D					
166	PHI	Daniel Duench	Kitchener	D					
167	MTL	Daniel Poulin	Chicoutimi	D	3	1	1	2	2
168	PHI	Rod McNair	Ohio State	D					
169	MTL	Tom McDonnell	Ottawa	C					
170	DET	Alain Belanger	Trois-Rivieres	RW					
171	NYR	Mark Miller	Michigan	LW					
172	PHI	Mike Laycock	Brown	G					
173	MTL	Gary Farelli	Toronto	C/RW					
174	MTL	Carey Walker	New Westminster	G					
175	DET	Dean Willers	Union College	C					
176	MTL	Mark Wells	Bowling Green	C					
177	MTL	Stan Palmer	U. of Minnesota	D					
178	DET	Roland Cloutier	Trois-Rivieres	C	34	8	9	17	2
179	MTL	Jean Belisle	Chicoutimi	G					
180	MTL	Bob Daly	Ottawa	G					
181	DET	Edward Hill	Vermont	RW					
182	MTL	Bob Boileau	Boston U.	RW					
183	MTL	John Costello	Lowell Tech College	C					
184	DET	Val James	Quebec	LW	11	0	0	0	30
185	DET	Grant Morin	Calgary	RW					

1978

FIRST ROUND

PICK	TEAM	NAME	DRAFTED FROM	POS	GP	G / W	A / GA	PTS / SO	PIM / AVG
1	MIN	Bobby Smith	Ottawa	C	1077	357	679	1036	917
2	WSH	Ryan Walter	Seattle	C/LW	1003	264	382	646	946
3	ST.L.	Wayne Babych	Portland	RW	519	192	246	438	498
4	VAN	Bill Derlago	Brandon	C	555	189	227	416	247
5	COL	Mike Gillis	Kingston	LW	246	33	43	76	186
6	PHI	Behn Wilson	Kingston	D	601	98	260	358	1480
7	PHI	Ken Linseman	Kingston	C	860	256	551	807	1727
8	MTL	Danny Geoffrion	Cornwall	RW	111	20	32	52	99
9	DET	Willie Huber	Hamilton	D	655	104	217	321	950
10	CHI	Tim Higgins	Ottawa	RW	706	154	198	352	719
11	ATL	Brad Marsh	London	D	1086	23	175	198	1241
12	DET	Brent Peterson	Portland	C	620	72	141	213	484
13	BUF	Larry Playfair	Portland	D	688	26	94	120	1812
14	PHI	Danny Lucas	Sault Ste. Marie	RW	6	1	0	1	0
15	NYI	Steve Tambellini	Lethbridge	C	553	160	150	310	105
16	BOS	Al Secord	Hamilton	LW	766	273	222	495	2093
17	MTL	Dave Hunter	Sudbury	LW	746	133	190	323	918
18	WSH	Tim Coulis	Hamilton	LW	47	4	5	9	138

SECOND ROUND

PICK	TEAM	NAME	DRAFTED FROM	POS	GP	G / W	A / GA	PTS / SO	PIM / AVG
19	MIN	Steve Payne	Ottawa	LW	613	228	238	466	435
20	WSH	Paul Mulvey	Portland	LW	225	30	51	81	613
21	TOR	Joel Quenneville	Windsor	D	803	54	136	190	705
22	VAN	Curt Fraser	Victoria	LW	704	193	240	433	1306
23	WSH	Paul MacKinnon	Peterborough	D	147	5	23	28	91
24	MIN	Steve Christoff	Minnesota-Duluth	C	248	77	64	141	108
25	PIT	Mike Meeker	Peterborough	RW	4	0	0	0	5
26	NYR	Don Maloney	Kitchener	LW	765	214	350	564	815
27	COL	Merlin Malinowski	Medicine Hat	C	282	54	111	165	121
28	DET	Glenn Hicks	Flin Flon	LW	108	6	12	18	127
29	CHI	Doug Lecuyer	Portland	LW	126	11	31	42	178
30	MTL	Dale Yakiwchuk	Portland	C	3 100 pt. seasons in EHL, IHL				
31	DET	Al Jensen	Hamilton	G	179	95	557	8	3.35
32	BUF	Tony McKegney	Kingston	LW	912	320	319	639	517
33	PHI	Mike Simurda	Kingston	RW	2 pro seasons in AHL & IHL				
34	NYI	Randy Johnston	Peterborough	D	4	0	0	0	4
35	BOS	Graeme Nicolson	Cornwall	D	52	2	7	9	60
36	MTL	Ron Carter	Sherbrooke	RW	2	0	0	0	0

OTHER ROUNDS

PICK	TEAM	NAME	DRAFTED FROM	POS	GP	G / W	A / GA	PTS / SO	PIM / AVG
37	PHI	Gord Salt	Michigan Tech	RW					
38	WSH	Glen Currie	Laval	C	326	39	79	118	100
39	ST.L.	Steve Harrison	Toronto	D					
40	VAN	Stan Smyl	New Westminster	RW	896	262	411	673	1556
41	COL	Paul Messier	U. of Denver	C	9	0	0	0	4
42	MTL	Richard David	Trois-Rivieres	LW	31	4	4	8	10
43	NYR	Ray Markham	Flin Flon	C	14	1	1	2	21
44	NYR	Dean Turner	Michigan	D	35	1	0	1	59
45	WSH	Jay Johnston	Hamilton	D	8	0	0	0	13
46	CHI	Rick Paterson	Cornwall	C	430	50	43	93	136
47	ATL	Tim Bernhardt	Cornwall	G	67	17	267	0	4.27
48	TOR	Mark Kirton	Peterborough	C	266	57	56	113	121
49	BUF	Rob McClanahan	Minnesota-Duluth	C	224	38	63	101	126
50	PHI	Glen Cochrane	Victoria	D	411	17	72	89	1556
51	NYI	Dwayne Lowdermilk	Seattle	D	2	0	1	1	2
52	BOS	Brad Knelson	Lethbridge	D					
53	DET	Doug Derkson	New Westminster	C					
54	MIN	Curt Giles	Minnesota-Duluth	D	895	43	199	242	733
55	WSH	Bengt-Ake Gustafsson	Farjestad Karlstad, SWE	RW	629	196	359	555	196
56	VAN	Harald Luckner	Farjestad Karlstad, SWE	C					
57	VAN	Brad Smith	Sudbury	RW	222	28	34	62	591
58	COL	Dave Watson	Sault Ste. Marie	LW	18	0	1	1	10
59	NYR	Dave Silk	Boston U.	RW	249	54	59	113	271
60	NYR	Andre Dore	Quebec	D	257	14	81	95	261
61	PIT	Shane Pearsall	Ottawa	LW					
62	DET	Bjorn Skaare	Ottawa	C	1	0	0	0	0
63	CHI	Brian Young	New Westminster	D	8	0	2	2	6
64	ATL	Jim MacRae	London	LW					
65	TOR	Bob Parent	Kitchener	G	3	0	15	0	5.63
66	BUF	Mike Gazdic	Sudbury	D					
67	PHI	Russ Wilderman	Seattle	C					
68	BOS	George Buat	Seattle	RW					
69	MTL	Kevin Reeves	Montreal	C					
70	MIN	Roy Kerling	Cornell	LW					
71	WSH	Lou Franceschetti	Niagara Falls	RW	459	59	81	140	747
72	ST.L.	Kevin Willison	Billings	D					
73	COL	Tim Thomlison	Billings	G					
74	COL	Rod Guimont	Lethbridge	RW					
75	PIT	Rob Garner	Toronto	C	1	0	0	0	0
76	NYR	Mike McDougal	Port Huron IHL	RW	61	8	10	18	43
77	L.A.	Paul Mancini	Sault Ste. Marie	LW					
78	DET	Ted Nolan	Sault Ste. Marie	C	78	6	16	22	105
79	CHI	Mark Murphy	Toronto	LW					
80	ATL	Gord Wappel	Regina	D	20	1	1	2	10
81	TOR	Jordy Douglas	Flin Flon	LW	268	76	62	138	160
82	BUF	Randy Ireland	Portland	G	2	0	3	0	6.00
83	PHI	Brad Tamblyn	U. of Toronto	D					
84	NYI	Greg Hay	Michigan Tech	LW					
85	BOS	Darryl MacLeod	Boston U.	LW					
86	MTL	Mike Boyd	Sault Ste. Marie	D					
87	MIN	Bob Bergloff	Minnesota-Duluth	D	2	0	0	0	5
88	WSH	Vince Magnan	U. of Denver	LW					
89	ST.L.	Jim Nill	Medicine Hat	RW	524	58	87	145	854
90	VAN	Gerry Minor	Regina	C	140	11	21	32	173

PICK	TEAM	NAME	DRAFTED FROM	NHL PLAYERS: POS NHL GOALTENDERS: POS	GP GP	G W	A GA	PTS SO	PIM AVG
91	COL	John Hynes	Harvard	G					
92	TOR	Mel Hewitt	Calgary	D/LW					
93	NYR	Tom Laidlaw	Northern Michigan	D	705	25	139	164	717
94	L.A.	Doug Keans	Ottawa	G	210	96	666	4	3.51
95	DET	Sylvain Locas	Sherbrooke	C					
96	CHI	Dave Feamster	Colorado College	D	169	13	24	37	154
97	ATL	Greg Meredith	U. of Notre Dame	RW	38	6	4	10	8
98	TOR	Normand Lefebvre	Trois-Rivieres	RW					
99	BUF	Cam MacGregor	Cornwall	LW					
100	PHI	Mark Taylor	North Dakota	C	209	42	68	110	73
101	NYI	Kelly Davis	Flin Flon	LW/D					
102	BOS	Jeff Brubaker	Peterborough	LW	178	16	9	25	512
103	MTL	Keith Acton	Peterborough	C	1023	226	358	584	1172
104	MIN	Kim Spencer	Victoria	D					
105	WSH	Mats Hallin	Sodertalje, SWE	LW	152	17	14	31	193
106	ST.L.	Steve Stockman	Cornwall	C					
107	VAN	Dave Ross	Portland	W					
108	COL	Andy Clark	Lake Superior State	D					
109	ST.L.	Paul MacLean	Hull	RW	719	324	349	673	968
110	NYR	Dan Clark	Milwaukee IHL	D	4	0	1	1	6
111	L.A.	Don Waddell	Northern Michigan	D	1	0	0	0	0
112	DET	Wes George	Saskatoon	LW					
113	CHI	Dave Mancuso	Windsor	D					
114	ATL	Dave Hindmarch	U. of Alberta	RW	99	21	17	38	25
115	TOR	John Scammel	Lethbridge	D					
116	BUF	Dan Eastman	Saginaw IHL	C					
117	PHI	Mike Ewanouski	Boston College	RW					
118	NYI	Richard Pepin	Laval	RW					
119	BOS	Murray Skinner	Lake Superior State	G					
120	MTL	Jim Lawson	Brown	RW					
121	MIN	Mike Cotter	Bowling Green	D					
122	WSH	Rick Sirois	Milwaukee IHL	G					
122	WSH	Richard Sirois	Milwaukee IHL	G					
123	ST.L.	Denis Houle	Hamilton	RW					
124	VAN	Steve O'Neill	Providence	LW					
125	COL	John Olver	Michigan	RW/C					
126	PHI	Jerry Price	Portland	G					
127	NYR	Greg Kostenko	Ohio State	D					
128	L.A.	Rob Mierkalns	Hamilton	C					
129	DET	John Barrett	Windsor	D	488	20	77	97	604
130	CHI	Sandy Ross	Colgate	D					
131	ATL	Dave Morrison	Calgary	RW					
132	TOR	Kevin Reinhart	Kitchener	D					
133	BUF	Eric Strobel	Minnesota-Duluth	C					
134	PHI	Darre Switzer	Medicine Hat	D					
135	NYI	Dave Cameron	University of PEI	C	168	25	28	53	238
136	BOS	Richard Hehir	Boston College	C					
137	MTL	Larry Landon	RPI	RW	9	0	0	0	2
138	MIN	Brent Gogol	Billings	D					
139	WSH	Denis Pomerleau	Trois-Rivieres	RW					
140	ST.L.	Tony Meagher	Boston U.	RW					
141	VAN	Charlie Antetomaso	Boston College	D					
142	COL	Kevin Krook	Regina	D	3	0	0	0	2
143	ST.L.	Rick Simpson	Medicine Hat	C/RW					
144	NYR	Brian McDavid	Kitchener	D					
145	L.A.	Ric Scully	Brown	LW					
146	DET	Jim Malazdrewicz	St. Boniface Jr. A	LW					
147	CHI	Mark Locken	Niagara Falls	G					
148	ATL	Doug Todd	Michigan	RW					
149	TOR	Mike Waghorne	New Hampshire	D					
150	BUF	Eugene O'Sullivan	Calgary	C					
151	PHI	Greg Francis	St. Lawrence U.	D					
152	NYI	Paul Joswiak	Minnesota-Duluth	G					
153	BOS	Craig MacTavish	University of Lowell	C	1093	213	267	480	891
154	MTL	Kevin Constantine	RPI	G					
155	MIN	Mark Seide	Bloomington Jr.	LW/D					
156	WSH	Barry Heard	London	G					
157	ST.L.	Jim Lockhurst	Kingston	G					
158	VAN	Richard Martens	New Westminster	G					
159	COL	Jeff Jensen	Lake Superior State	LW					
160	ST.L.	Bob Froese	Niagara Falls	G	242	128	694	13	3.10
161	NYR	Mark Rodrigues	Yale	G					
162	L.A.	Brad Thiessen	Toronto	C					
163	DET	Geoff Shaw	Hamilton	RW					
164	CHI	Glenn Van	Colorado College	D					
165	ATL	Mark Green	Sherbrooke	C					
166	TOR	Laurie Cuvelier	St. Francis Xavier	D					
167	PHI	Rick Berard	St. Mary's U.	LW/D					
168	PHI	Don Lucia	U. of Notre Dame	D					
169	NYI	Scott Cameron	U. of Notre Dame	D					
170	ST.L.	Dan Lerg	Michigan	C					
171	MTL	John Swan	McGill University	C					
172	WSH	Mark Toffolo	Port Huron IHL	D					
173	ST.L.	Risto Siltanen	Ilves Tampere, FIN	D	562	90	265	355	266
174	COL	Bo Ericson	AIK Solna, SWE	D					
175	ST.L.	Dan Hermansson	Karlskoga, SWE	LW					
176	NYR	Steve Weeks	Northern Michigan	G	290	111	989	5	3.74
177	L.A.	Jim Armstrong	Clarkson	LW/C					
178	DET	Carl Van Harrewyn	New Westminster	D/RW					
179	CHI	Darryl Sutter	Lethbridge	LW	406	161	118	279	288
180	ATL	Robert Sullivan	New Haven/Toledo IHL	C/LW					
181	ST.L.	Jean-Francois Boutin	Verdun	LW					
182	PHI	Mark Berge	North Dakota	D					
183	PHI	Ken Moore	Clarkson	G					
184	NYI	Christer Lowdahl	Oreboro, SWE	C/LW					
185	ST.L.	John Sullivan	Providence	RW					
186	MTL	Daniel Metivier	Hull	RW					
187	WSH	Paul Hogan	Regina	LW					
188	ST.L.	Serge Menard	Montreal	RW					
189	WSH	Steve Barger	Boston College	RW					
190	COL	Jari Viitala	Ilves Tampere, FIN	C/LW					
191	ST.L.	Don Boyd	RPI	D/C					
192	NYR	Pierre Daigneault	St. Laurent College	LW					
193	L.A.	Claude Larochelle	Hull	C					
194	DET	Ladislav Svozil	TJ Vitkovice, TCH	LW					
195	PHI	Jim Olson	St. Paul Jr. A	C					
196	ATL	Bernhard Englbrecht	Landshut, FRG	G					
197	ST.L.	Paul Stasiuk	Providence	LW					
198	PHI	Anton Stastny	Slovan Bratislava, TCH	LW	Re-entered Draft in 1979				
199	NYI	Gunnar Persson	Brynas Gavle, SWE	D					
200	ST.L.	Gerd Truntschka	Landshut, FRG	C/LW					
201	MTL	Viacheslav Fetisov	CSKA Moscow, USSR	D	Re-entered Draft in 1983				
202	WSH	Rod Pacholsuk	Michigan	D					
203	ST.L.	Viktor Shkurdyuk	SKA Leningrad, USSR	RW					
204	COL	Ulf Zetterstrom	Kiruna, SWE	LW					
205	ST.L.	Carl Bloomberg	St. Louis U.	G					
206	NYR	Chris McLaughlin	Dartmouth	D					
207	ST.L.	Terry Kitching	St. Louis U.	LW					
208	DET	Tom Bailey	Kingston	RW					
209	ST.L.	Brian O'Connor	Boston U.	D					
210	ST.L.	Brian Crombeen	Kingston	D					
211	ST.L.	Mike Pidgeon	Oshawa	C					
212	MTL	Jeff Mars	Michigan	RW					
213	WSH	Wes Jarvis	Windsor	C	237	31	55	86	98
214	ST.L.	John Cochrane	Harvard	RW					
215	WSH	Ray Irwin	Oshawa	D					
216	ST.L.	Joe Casey	Boston College	D					
217	NYR	Todd Johnson	Boston U.	C					
218	ST.L.	Jim Farrell	Princeton	C					
219	DET	Larry Lozinski	Flin Flon	G	30	6	105	0	4.32
220	ST.L.	Frank Johnson	Providence	D					
221	ST.L.	Blair Wheeler	Yale	D					
222	MTL	Greg Tiganelli	Northern Michigan	LW					
223	NYR	Dan McCarthy	Sudbury	C	5	4	0	4	4
224	DET	Randy Betty	New Westminster	LW					
225	MTL	George Goulakos	St. Lawrence U.	LW					
226	DET	Brian Crawley	St. Lawrence U.	D					
227	MTL	Ken Moodie	Colgate	RW					
228	DET	Doug Feasby	Toronto	C					
229	MTL	Serge Leblanc	Vermont	D					
230	MTL	Bob Magnuson	Merrimack	C					
231	MTL	Chris Nilan	Northeastern	RW	688	110	115	225	3043
232	MTL	Rick Wilson	St. Lawrence U.	G					
233	MTL	Louis Sleigher	Chicoutimi	RW	194	46	53	99	146
234	MTL	Doug Robb	Billings	RW					

1979

FIRST ROUND

PICK	TEAM	NAME	DRAFTED FROM	NHL PLAYERS: POS NHL GOALTENDERS: POS	GP GP	G W	A GA	PTS SO	PIM AVG
1	COL	Rob Ramage	London	D	1044	139	425	564	2226
2	ST.L.	Perry Turnbull	Portland	C	608	188	163	351	1245
3	DET	Mike Foligno	Sudbury	RW	1018	355	372	727	2049
4	WSH	Mike Gartner	Niagara Falls	RW	1432	708	627	1335	1159
5	VAN	Rick Vaive	Sherbrooke	RW	876	441	347	788	1445
6	MIN	Craig Hartsburg	Sault Ste. Marie	D	570	98	315	413	818
7	CHI	Keith Brown	Portland	D	876	68	274	342	916
8	BOS	Ray Bourque	Verdun	D	1532	403	1117	1520	1093
9	TOR	Laurie Boschman	Brandon	C	1009	229	348	577	2265
10	MIN	Tom McCarthy	Oshawa	LW	460	178	221	399	330
11	BUF	Mike Ramsey	Minnesota-Duluth	D	1070	79	266	345	1012
12	ATL	Paul Reinhart	Kitchener	D	648	133	426	559	277
13	NYR	Doug Sulliman	Kitchener	RW	631	160	168	328	175
14	PHI	Brian Propp	Brandon	LW	1016	425	579	1004	830
15	BOS	Brad McCrimmon	Brandon	D	1222	81	322	403	1416
16	L.A.	Jay Wells	Kingston	D	1098	47	216	263	2359
17	NYI	Duane Sutter	Lethbridge	RW	731	139	203	342	1333
18	HFD	Ray Allison	Brandon	RW	238	64	93	157	223
19	WPG	Jimmy Mann	Sherbrooke	RW	293	10	20	30	895
20	QUE	Michel Goulet	Quebec	LW	1089	548	604	1152	825
21	EDM	Kevin Lowe	Quebec	D	1254	84	347	431	1498

PICK	TEAM	NAME	DRAFTED FROM	NHL PLAYERS: POS / NHL GOALTENDERS: POS	GP / GP	G / W	A / GA	PTS / SO	PIM / AVG
SECOND ROUND									
22	PHI	Blake Wesley	Portland	D	298	18	46	64	486
23	ATL	Mike Perovich	Brandon	D	4 pro seasons in CHL & AHL				
24	WSH	Errol Rausse	Seattle	LW	31	7	3	10	0
25	NYI	Tomas Jonsson	MoDo Ornskoldsvik, SWE	D	552	85	259	344	482
26	VAN	Brent Ashton	Saskatoon	LW	998	284	345	629	635
27	MTL	Gaston Gingras	Hamilton	D	476	61	174	235	161
28	CHI	Tim Trimper	Peterborough	LW	190	30	36	66	153
29	L.A.	Dean Hopkins	London	RW	223	23	51	74	306
30	L.A.	Mark Hardy	Montreal	D	915	62	306	368	1293
31	PIT	Paul Marshall	Brantford	LW	95	15	18	33	17
32	BUF	Lindy Ruff	Lethbridge	D/LW	691	105	195	300	1264
33	ATL	Pat Riggin	London	G	350	153	1135	11	3.43
34	NYR	Ed Hospodar	Ottawa	D	450	17	51	68	1314
35	PHI	Pelle Lindbergh	AIK Solna, SWE	G	157	87	503	7	3.30
36	BOS	Doug Morrison	Lethbridge	RW	23	7	3	10	15
37	MTL	Mats Naslund	Brynas Gavle, SWE	LW	651	251	383	634	111
38	NYI	Billy Carroll	London	C	322	30	54	84	113
39	HFD	Stu Smith	Peterborough	D	77	2	10	12	95
40	WPG	Dave Christian	North Dakota	RW	1009	340	433	773	284
41	QUE	Dale Hunter	Sudbury	C	1407	323	697	1020	3565
42	MIN	Neal Broten	Minnesota-Duluth	C	1099	289	634	923	569
OTHER ROUNDS									
43	MTL	Craig Levie	Edmonton	D	183	22	53	75	177
44	MTL	Guy Carbonneau	Chicoutimi	C	1318	260	403	663	820
45	DET	Jody Gage	Kitchener	RW	68	14	15	29	26
46	DET	Boris Fistric	New Westminster	D					
47	VAN	Ken Ellacott	Peterborough	G	12	2	41	0	4.43
48	EDM	Mark Messier	St. Albert Jr. A	LW/C	1479	627	1087	1714	1717
49	CHI	Bill Gardner	Peterborough	C	380	73	115	188	68
50	L.A.	John Paul Kelly	New Westminster	LW	400	54	70	124	366
51	TOR	Norm Aubin	Verdun	C	69	18	13	31	30
52	PIT	Bennett Wolf	Kitchener	D	30	0	1	1	133
53	BUF	Mark Robinson	Victoria	D					
54	ATL	Tim Hunter	Seattle	RW	815	62	76	138	3146
55	BUF	Jacques Cloutier	Trois-Rivieres	G	255	82	778	3	3.64
56	PHI	Lindsay Carson	Billings	C	373	66	80	146	524
57	BOS	Keith Crowder	Peterborough	RW	662	223	271	494	1354
58	MTL	Rick Wamsley	Brantford	G	407	204	1287	12	3.34
59	NYI	Rollie Melanson	Windsor	G	291	129	995	6	3.63
60	HFD	Don Nachbaur	Billings	C	223	23	46	69	465
61	WPG	Bill Whelton	North Dakota	D	2	0	0	0	0
62	QUE	Lee Norwood	Oshawa	D	503	58	153	211	1099
63	MIN	Kevin Maxwell	North Dakota	C	66	6	15	21	61
64	COL	Steve Peters	Oshawa	C	2	0	1	1	0
65	ST.L.	Bob Crawford	Cornwall	RW	246	71	71	142	72
66	DET	John Ogrodnick	New Westminster	LW	928	402	425	827	260
67	WSH	Harvie Pocza	Billings	LW	3	0	0	0	2
68	VAN	Art Rutland	Sault Ste. Marie	C					
69	EDM	Glenn Anderson	U. of Denver	RW	1129	498	601	1099	1120
70	CHI	Lou Begin	Sherbrooke	LW					
71	L.A.	John Gibson	Niagara Falls	D	48	0	2	2	120
72	TOR	Vincent Tremblay	Quebec	G	58	12	223	1	4.80
73	PIT	Brian Cross	Brantford	D					
74	BUF	Gilles Hamel	Laval	LW	519	127	147	274	276
75	ATL	Jim Peplinski	Toronto	RW	711	161	263	424	1467
76	NYR	Pat Conacher	Saskatoon	LW	521	63	76	139	235
77	PHI	Don Gillen	Brandon	RW	35	2	4	6	22
78	BOS	Larry Melnyk	New Westminster	D	432	11	63	74	686
79	MTL	Dave Orleski	New Westminster	LW	2	0	0	0	0
80	NYI	Tim Lockridge	Brandon	D					
81	HFD	Ray Neufeld	Edmonton	RW	595	157	200	357	816
82	WPG	Pat Daley	Montreal	LW	12	1	0	1	13
83	QUE	Anton Stastny	Slovan Bratislava, TCH	LW	650	252	384	636	150
84	EDM	Maxwell Kostovich	Portland	LW					
85	COL	Gary Dillon	Toronto	C	13	1	1	2	29
86	ST.L.	Mark Reeds	Peterborough	RW	365	45	114	159	135
87	DET	Joe Paterson	London	LW	291	19	37	56	829
88	WSH	Tim Tookey	Portland	C	106	22	36	58	71
89	VAN	Dirk Graham	Regina	L/RW	772	219	270	489	917
90	MIN	Jim Dobson	Portland	RW	12	0	0	0	6
91	CHI	Lowell Loveday	Kingston	D					
92	L.A.	Jim Brown	U. of Notre Dame	D	3	0	1	1	5
93	TOR	Frank Nigro	London	C	68	8	18	26	39
94	PIT	Nick Ricci	Niagara Falls	G	19	7	79	0	4.36
95	BUF	Alan Haworth	Sherbrooke	C	524	189	211	400	425
96	ATL	Brad Kempthorne	Brandon	C/RW					
97	NYR	Dan Makuch	Clarkson	RW					
98	PHI	Thomas Eriksson	Djurgarden Stockholm, SWE	D	208	22	76	98	107
99	BOS	Marco Baron	Montreal	G	86	34	292	1	3.63
100	MTL	Yvan Joly	Ottawa	RW	2	0	0	0	0
101	NYI	Glenn Duncan	Toronto	LW					
102	HFD	Mark Renaud	Niagara Falls	D	152	6	50	56	86
103	WPG	Thomas Steen	Leksand, SWE	C	950	264	553	817	753
104	QUE	Pierre Lacroix	Trois-Rivieres	D	274	24	108	132	197
105	EDM	Mike Toal	Portland	C	3	0	0	0	0
106	COL	Bob Attwell	Peterborough	RW	22	1	5	6	0
107	ST.L.	Gilles Leduc	Verdun	LW					
108	DET	Carmine Cirella	Peterborough	LW					
109	WSH	Greg Theberge	Peterborough	D	153	15	63	78	73
110	VAN	Shane Swan	Sudbury	D					
111	MIN	Brian Gualazzi	Sault Ste. Marie	D					
112	CHI	Doug Crossman	Ottawa	D	914	105	359	464	534
113	L.A.	Jay MacFarlane	Wisconsin	D					
114	TOR	Bill McCreary Jr.	Colgate	RW	12	1	0	1	4
115	PIT	Marc Chorney	North Dakota	D	210	8	27	35	209
116	BUF	Rick Knickle	Brandon	G	14	7	44	0	3.74
117	ATL	Glenn Johnson	U. of Denver	C					
118	NYR	Stan Adams	Niagara Falls	C					
119	PHI	Gord Williams	Lethbridge	RW	2	0	0	0	2
120	BOS	Mike Krushelnyski	Montreal	LW/C	897	241	328	569	699
121	MTL	Greg Moffett	New Hampshire	LW					
122	NYI	John Gibb	Bowling Green	D					
123	HFD	Dave McDonald	Brandon	LW					
124	WPG	Tim Watters	Michigan Tech	D	741	26	151	177	1289
125	QUE	Scott McGeown	Toronto	D					
126	EDM	Blair Barnes	Windsor	RW	1	0	0	0	0

1980

PICK	TEAM	NAME	DRAFTED FROM	NHL PLAYERS: POS / NHL GOALTENDERS: POS	GP / GP	G / W	A / GA	PTS / SO	PIM / AVG
FIRST ROUND									
1	MTL	Doug Wickenheiser	Regina	C	556	111	165	276	286
2	WPG	Dave Babych	Portland	D	1195	142	581	723	970
3	CHI	Denis Savard	Montreal	C	1196	473	865	1338	1336
4	L.A.	Larry Murphy	Peterborough	D	1558	285	910	1195	1072
5	WSH	Darren Veitch	Regina	D	511	48	209	257	296
6	EDM	Paul Coffey	Kitchener	D	1391	396	1131	1527	1772
7	VAN	Rick Lanz	Oshawa	D	569	65	221	286	448
8	HFD	Fred Arthur	Cornwall	D	80	1	8	9	49
9	PIT	Mike Bullard	Brantford	C	727	329	345	674	703
10	L.A.	Jim Fox	Ottawa	RW	578	186	293	479	143
11	DET	Mike Blaisdell	Regina	RW	343	70	84	154	166
12	ST.L.	Rik Wilson	Kingston	D	251	25	65	90	220
13	CGY	Denis Cyr	Montreal	RW	193	41	43	84	36
14	NYR	Jim Malone	Toronto	C	3 pro seasons – AHL, CHL, IHL				
15	CHI	Jerome Dupont	Toronto	D	214	7	29	36	468
16	MIN	Brad Palmer	Victoria	LW	168	32	38	70	58
17	NYI	Brent Sutter	Red Deer Jr. A	C	1111	363	466	829	1054
18	BOS	Barry Pederson	Victoria	C	701	238	416	654	472
19	COL	Paul Gagne	Windsor	LW	390	110	101	211	127
20	BUF	Steve Patrick	Brandon	RW	250	40	68	108	242
21	PHI	Mike Stothers	Kingston	D	30	0	2	2	65
SECOND ROUND									
22	COL	Joe Ward	Seattle	C	4	0	0	0	2
23	WPG	Moe Mantha	Toronto	D	656	81	289	370	501
24	QUE	Normand Rochefort	Quebec	D	598	39	119	158	570
25	TOR	Craig Muni	Kingston	D	819	28	119	147	775
26	TOR	Bob McGill	Victoria	D	705	17	55	72	1766
27	MTL	Ric Nattress	Brantford	D	536	29	135	164	377
28	CHI	Steve Ludzik	Niagara Falls	C	424	46	93	139	333
29	HFD	Michel Galarneau	Hull	C	78	7	10	17	34
30	CHI	Ken Solheim	Medicine Hat	LW	135	19	20	39	34
31	CGY	Tony Curtale	Brantford	D	2	0	0	0	0
32	CGY	Kevin LaVallee	Brantford	LW	366	110	125	235	85
33	L.A.	Greg Terrion	Brantford	LW	561	93	150	243	339
34	L.A.	Dave Morrison	Peterborough	RW	39	3	3	6	4
35	NYR	Mike Allison	Sudbury	LW	499	102	166	268	630
36	CHI	Len Dawes	Victoria	D	43 career AHL games				
37	MIN	Don Beaupre	Sudbury	G	668	268	2154	17	3.45
38	NYI	Kelly Hrudey	Medicine Hat	G	677	271	2174	17	3.43
39	CGY	Steve Konroyd	Oshawa	D	895	41	195	236	863
40	MTL	John Chabot	Hull	C	508	84	228	312	85
41	BUF	Mike Moller	Lethbridge	RW	134	15	28	43	41
42	PHI	Jay Fraser	Ottawa	LW	Played with 5 minor pro teams				
OTHER ROUNDS									
43	TOR	Fred Boimistruck	Cornwall	D	83	4	14	18	45
44	WPG	Murray Eaves	Michigan	C	57	4	13	17	9
45	MTL	John Newberry	Nanaimo	C	22	0	4	4	6
46	DET	Mark Osborne	Niagara Falls	LW	919	212	319	531	1152
47	WSH	Don Miele	Providence	RW					
48	EDM	Shawn Babcock	Windsor	RW					
49	VAN	Andy Schliebener	Peterborough	D	84	2	11	13	74
50	HFD	Mickey Volcan	North Dakota	D	162	8	33	41	146
51	PIT	Randy Boyd	Ottawa	D	257	20	67	87	328
52	L.A.	Steve Bozek	Northern Michigan	LW	641	164	167	331	309
53	MIN	Randy Velischek	Providence	D	509	21	76	97	401
54	ST.L.	Jim Pavese	Kitchener	D	328	13	44	57	689

PICK	TEAM	NAME	DRAFTED FROM	NHL PLAYERS: POS / NHL GOALTENDERS: POS	GP / GP	G / W	A / GA	PTS / SO	PIM / AVG
55	WSH	Torrie Robertson	Victoria	LW	442	49	99	148	1751
56	BUF	Sean McKenna	Sherbrooke	RW	414	82	80	162	181
57	CHI	Troy Murray	St. Albert Jr. A	C	915	230	354	584	875
58	CHI	Marcel Frere	Billings	LW					
59	NYI	Dave Simpson	London	C					
60	BOS	Tom Fergus	Peterborough	C	726	235	346	581	499
61	MTL	Craig Ludwig	North Dakota	D	1256	38	184	222	1437
62	BUF	Jay North	Bloomington-Jefferson H.S.	C					
63	PHI	Paul Mercier	Sudbury	D					
64	COL	Rick LaFerriere	Peterborough	G	1	0	1	0	3.00
65	WPG	Guy Fournier	Shawinigan	C					
66	QUE	Jay Miller	New Hampshire	LW	446	40	44	84	1723
67	CHI	Carey Wilson	Dartmouth	C	552	169	258	427	314
68	NYI	Monty Trottier	Billings	C					
69	EDM	Jari Kurri	Jokerit Helsinki, FIN	RW	1251	601	797	1398	545
70	VAN	Marc Crawford	Cornwall	LW	176	19	31	50	229
71	HFD	Kevin McClelland	Niagara Falls	RW	588	68	112	180	1672
72	PIT	Tony Feltrin	Victoria	D	48	3	3	6	65
73	L.A.	Bernie Nicholls	Kingston	C	1127	475	734	1209	1292
74	TOR	Stew Gavin	Toronto	LW	768	130	155	285	584
75	ST.L.	Bob Brooke	Yale	C	447	69	97	166	520
76	CGY	Marc Roy	Trois-Rivieres	RW					
77	NYR	Kurt Kleinendorst	Providence	C					
78	CHI	Brian Shaw	Portland	RW					
79	MIN	Mark Huglen	Roseau H.S.	D					
80	NYI	Greg Gilbert	Toronto	LW	837	150	228	378	576
81	BOS	Steve Kasper	Verdun	C	821	177	291	468	554
82	MTL	Jeff Teal	U. of Minnesota	RW	6	0	1	1	0
83	BUF	Jim Wiemer	Peterborough	D	325	29	72	101	378
84	PHI	Taras Zytynsky	Montreal	D					
85	COL	Ed Cooper	Portland	LW	49	8	7	15	46
86	WPG	Glen Ostir	Portland	D					
87	QUE	Basil McRae	London	LW	576	53	83	136	2457
88	DET	Mike Corrigan	Cornwall	RW					
89	WSH	Timo Blomqvist	Jokerit Helsinki, FIN	D	243	4	53	57	293
90	EDM	Walt Poddubny	Kingston	LW	468	184	238	422	454
91	VAN	Darrell May	Portland	G	6	1	31	0	5.11
92	HFD	Darren Jensen	North Dakota	G	30	15	95	2	3.81
93	PIT	Doug Shedden	Sault Ste. Marie	C	416	139	186	325	176
94	L.A.	Alan Graves	Seattle	LW					
95	TOR	Hugh Larkin	Sault Ste. Marie	RW					
96	ST.L.	Alain Lemieux	Chicoutimi	C	119	28	44	72	38
97	CGY	Randy Turnbull	Portland	D	1	0	0	0	2
98	NYR	Scot Kleinendorst	Providence	D	281	12	46	58	452
99	CHI	Kevin Ginnell	Medicine Hat	C					
100	MIN	David Jensen	Minnesota-Duluth	D	18	0	2	2	11
101	NYI	Ken Leiter	Michigan State	D	143	14	36	50	62
102	BOS	Randy Hillier	Sudbury	D	543	16	110	126	906
103	MTL	Remi Gagne	Chicoutimi	RW					
104	BUF	Dirk Rueter	Sault Ste. Marie	D					
105	PHI	Dan Held	Seattle	C					
106	COL	Aaron Broten	Minnesota-Duluth	LW/C	748	186	329	515	441
107	WPG	Ron Loustel	Saskatoon	G	1	0	10	0	10.00
108	QUE	Mark Kumpel	University of Lowell	RW	288	38	46	84	113
109	DET	Wayne Crawford	Toronto	C					
110	WSH	Todd Bidner	Toronto	LW	12	2	1	3	7
111	EDM	Mike Winther	Brandon	C					
112	VAN	Ken Berry	Canadian Olympic	LW	55	8	10	18	30
113	HFD	Mario Cerri	Ottawa	C					
114	PIT	Pat Graham	Niagara Falls	LW	103	11	17	28	136
115	L.A.	Darren Eliot	Cornell	G	89	25	377	1	4.59
116	TOR	Ron Dennis	Princeton	G					
117	ST.L.	Perry Anderson	Brantford	LW	400	50	59	109	1051
118	CGY	John Multan	Portland	RW					
119	NYR	Reijo Ruotsalainen	Karpat Oulu, FIN	D	446	107	237	344	180
120	CHI	Steve Larmer	Niagara Falls	RW	1006	441	571	1012	532
121	MIN	Dan Zavarise	Cornwall	D					
122	NYI	Dan Revell	Oshawa	RW					
123	BOS	Steve Lyons	Matignon H.S.	LW					
124	MTL	Mike McPhee	RPI	LW	744	200	199	399	661
125	BUF	Daniel Naud	Verdun	D					
126	PHI	Brian Tutt	Calgary	D	7	1	0	1	2
127	COL	Dan Fascinato	Ottawa	D					
128	WPG	Brian Mullen	U.S. Jr. Nationals	RW	832	260	362	622	414
129	QUE	Gaston Therrien	Quebec	D	22	0	8	8	12
130	DET	Mike Braun	Niagara Falls	D					
131	WSH	Frank Perkins	Sudbury	RW					
132	EDM	Andy Moog	Billings	G	713	372	2097	28	3.13
133	VAN	Doug Lidster	Colorado College	D	897	75	268	343	679
134	HFD	Mike Martin	Sudbury	D					
135	WPG	Mike Lauen	Michigan Tech	RW	4	0	1	1	0
136	L.A.	Mike O'Connor	Michigan Tech	D					
137	TOR	Russ Adam	Kitchener	C	8	1	2	3	11
138	ST.L.	Roger Hagglund	Bjorkloven Umea, SWE	D	3	0	0	0	0
139	CGY	Dave Newsom	Brantford	LW					
140	NYR	Bob Scurfield	Western Michigan	C					
141	CHI	Sean Simpson	Ottawa	C					
142	MIN	Bill Stewart	U. of Denver	RW					
143	NYI	Mark Hamway	Michigan State	RW	53	5	13	18	9
144	BOS	Tony McMurchy	New Westminster	C					
145	MTL	Bill Norton	Clarkson	LW					
146	BUF	Jari Paavola	TPS Turku, FIN	G					
147	PHI	Ross Fitzpatrick	Western Michigan	C	20	5	2	7	0
148	COL	Andre Hidi	Peterborough	LW	7	2	1	3	9
149	WPG	Sandy Beadle	Northeastern	LW	6	1	0	1	2
150	QUE	Michel Bolduc	Chicoutimi	D	10	0	0	0	6
151	DET	John Beukeboom	Peterborough	D					
152	WSH	Bruce Raboin	Providence	D					
153	EDM	Rob Polman Tuin	Michigan Tech	G					
154	VAN	John O'Connor	Vermont	D					
155	HFD	Brent Denat	Michigan Tech	LW					
156	PIT	Bob Geale	Portland	C	1	0	0	0	2
157	L.A.	Bill O'Dwyer	Boston College	C	120	9	13	22	108
158	TOR	Fred Perlini	Toronto	C	8	2	3	5	0
159	ST.L.	Pat Rabbit	Billings	LW					
160	CGY	Claude Drouin	Quebec	C					
161	NYR	Bart Wilson	Toronto	D					
162	CHI	Jim Ralph	Ottawa	G					
163	MIN	Jeff Walters	Peterborough	RW					
164	NYI	Morrison Gare	Penticton Jr. A	RW					
165	BOS	Mike Moffat	Kingston	G	19	7	70	0	4.29
166	MTL	Steve Penney	Shawinigan	G	91	35	313	1	3.62
167	BUF	Randy Cunneyworth	Ottawa	LW	866	189	225	414	1280
168	PHI	Mark Botell	Brantford	D	32	4	10	14	31
169	COL	Shawn MacKenzie	Windsor	G	4	0	15	0	6.92
170	WPG	Edward Christian	Warroad H.S.	LW					
171	QUE	Christian Tanguay	Trois-Rivieres	RW	2	0	0	0	0
172	DET	Dave Miles	Brantford	RW					
173	WSH	Peter Andersson	Timra, SWE	D	172	10	41	51	81
174	EDM	Lars-Gunnar Petterson	Lulea, SWE	D					
175	VAN	Patrik Sundstrom	Bjorkloven Umea, SWE	C	679	219	369	588	349
176	HFD	Paul Fricker	Michigan	G					
177	PIT	Brian Lundberg	Michigan	D	1	0	0	0	2
178	L.A.	Daryl Evans	Niagara Falls	LW	113	22	30	52	25
179	TOR	Darwin McCutcheon	Toronto	D	1	0	0	0	2
180	ST.L.	Peter Lindgren	Hammarby Stockholm, SWE	D					
181	CGY	Hakan Loob	Farjestad Karlstad, SWE	RW	450	193	236	429	189
182	NYR	Chris Wray	Boston College	RW					
183	CHI	Don Dietrich	Brandon	D	28	0	7	7	10
184	MIN	Bob Lakso	Aurora H.S.	LW					
185	NYI	Peter Steblyk	Medicine Hat	D					
186	BOS	Michael Thelven	Djurgarden Stockholm, SWE	D	207	20	80	100	217
187	MTL	John Schmidt	U. of Notre Dame	D					
188	BUF	Dave Beckon	Peterborough	C					
189	PHI	Peter Dineen	Kingston	D	13	0	2	2	13
190	COL	Bob Jansch	Victoria	RW					
191	WPG	Dave Chartier	Brandon	C	Re-entered Draft in 1982				
192	QUE	William Robinson	Acton-Boxboro H.S.	D					
193	DET	Brian Rorabeck	Niagara Falls	D					
194	WSH	Tony Camazzola	Brandon	D	3	0	0	0	4
195	PHI	Bob O'Brien	Dixie Jr. B	RW					
196	VAN	Grant Martin	Kitchener	LW	44	0	4	4	55
197	HFD	Lorne Bokshowan	Saskatoon	C					
198	PIT	Steve McKenzie	St. Albert Jr. A	D					
199	L.A.	Kim Collins	Bowling Green	LW					
200	TOR	Paul Higgins	Henry Carr H.S.	RW	25	0	0	0	152
201	ST.L.	John Smyth	Calgary	D					
202	CGY	Steven Fletcher	Hull	LW/D	3	0	0	0	5
203	NYR	Anders Backstrom	Brynas Gavle, SWE	D					
204	CHI	Dan Frawley	Sudbury	RW	273	37	40	77	674
205	MIN	Dave Richter	Michigan	D	365	9	40	49	1030
206	NYI	Glenn Johannesen	Red Deer Jr. A	LW	2	0	0	0	0
207	BOS	Jens Ohling	Djurgarden Stockholm, SWE	LW					
208	MTL	Scott Robinson	U. of Denver	G					
209	BUF	John Bader	Irondale H.S.	LW					
210	PHI	Andy Brickley	Bowling Green	LW/C	385	82	140	222	81

1981

PICK	TEAM	NAME	DRAFTED FROM	NHL PLAYERS: POS / NHL GOALTENDERS: POS	GP / GP	G / W	A / GA	PTS / SO	PIM / AVG
FIRST ROUND									
1	WPG	Dale Hawerchuk	Cornwall	C	1188	518	891	1409	730
2	L.A.	Doug Smith	Ottawa	C	535	115	138	253	624
3	WSH	Bob Carpenter	St. John's Prep	C	1178	320	408	728	919
4	HFD	Ron Francis	Sault Ste. Marie	C	1407	472	1087	1559	885
5	COL	Joe Cirella	Oshawa	D	828	64	211	275	1446
6	TOR	Jim Benning	Portland	D	605	52	191	243	461
7	MTL	Mark Hunter	Brantford	RW	628	213	171	384	1426
8	EDM	Grant Fuhr	Victoria	G	868	403	2756	25	3.38
9	NYR	James Patrick	Prince Albert	D	1046	132	454	586	693
10	VAN	Garth Butcher	Regina	D	897	48	158	206	2302
11	QUE	Randy Moller	Lethbridge	D	815	45	180	225	1692

PICK	TEAM	NAME	DRAFTED FROM	NHL PLAYERS: POS / NHL GOALTENDERS: POS	GP / GP	G / W	A / GA	PTS / SO	PIM / AVG
12	CHI	Tony Tanti	Oshawa	RW	697	287	273	560	661
13	MIN	Ron Meighan	Niagara Falls	D	48	3	7	10	18
14	BOS	Normand Leveille	Chicoutimi	LW	75	17	25	42	49
15	CGY	Al MacInnis	Kitchener	D	1203	301	803	1104	1330
16	PHI	Steve Smith	Sault Ste. Marie	D	18	0	1	1	15
17	BUF	Jiri Dudacek	Poldi SNOP Kladno, TCH	RW	Played in Europe until 1992				
18	MTL	Gilbert Delorme	Chicoutimi	D	541	31	92	123	520
19	MTL	Jan Ingman	Farjestad Karlstad, SWE	LW	Played w/ Farjestads 1981-90				
20	ST.L.	Marty Ruff	Lethbridge	D	2 pro seasons in IHL				
21	NYI	Paul Boutilier	Sherbrooke	D	288	27	83	110	358
SECOND ROUND									
22	WPG	Scott Arniel	Cornwall	LW	730	149	189	338	599
23	DET	Claude Loiselle	Windsor	C	616	92	117	209	1149
24	TOR	Gary Yaremchuk	Portland	C	34	1	4	5	28
25	CHI	Kevin Griffin	Portland	LW	Played pro in Britain until 1990				
26	COL	Rich Chernomaz	Victoria	RW	51	9	7	16	18
27	MIN	Dave Donnelly	St. Albert Jr. A	C	137	15	24	39	150
28	PIT	Steve Gatzos	Sault Ste. Marie	RW	89	15	20	35	83
29	EDM	Todd Strueby	Regina	LW	5	0	1	1	2
30	NYR	Jan Erixon	Skelleftea, SWE	LW	556	57	159	216	167
31	MIN	Mike Sands	Sudbury	G	6	0	26	0	5.17
32	MTL	Lars Eriksson	Brynas Gavle, SWE	G	Never played outside Europe				
33	MIN	Tom Hirsch	Patrick Henry H.S.	D	31	1	7	8	30
34	MIN	Dave Preuss	St. Thomas Academy	RW	No pro play after Minnesota				
35	BOS	Luc Dufour	Chicoutimi	LW	167	23	21	44	199
36	ST.L.	Hakan Nordin	Farjestad Karlstad, SWE	D	Played w/ Farjestads all career				
37	PHI	Rich Costello	Natick H.S.	C	12	2	2	4	2
38	BUF	Hannu Virta	TPS Turku, FIN	D	245	25	101	126	66
39	L.A.	Dean Kennedy	Brandon	D	717	26	108	134	1118
40	MTL	Chris Chelios	Moose Jaw	D	1157	168	664	832	2385
41	MIN	Jali Wahlsten	TPS Turku, FIN	C	Played in Europe until 1994				
42	NYI	Gord Dineen	Sault Ste. Marie	D	528	16	90	106	695
OTHER ROUNDS									
43	WPG	Jyrki Seppa	Ilves Tampere, FIN	D	13	0	2	2	6
44	DET	Corrado Micalef	Sherbrooke	G	113	26	409	2	4.24
45	WSH	Eric Calder	Cornwall	D	2	0	0	0	0
46	MTL	Dieter Hegen	ESV Kaufbeuern, FRG	LW					
47	PHI	Barry Tabobondung	Oshawa	LW					
48	COL	Uli Hiemer	Fussen, FRG	D	143	19	54	73	176
49	PIT	Tom Thornbury	Niagara Falls	D	14	1	8	9	16
50	NYR	Peter Sundstrom	Bjorkloven Umea, SWE	LW	338	61	83	144	120
51	NYR	Mark Morrison	Victoria	C	10	1	1	2	0
52	VAN	Jean-Marc Lanthier	Sorel	RW	105	16	16	32	29
53	QUE	Jean-Marc Gaulin	Sorel	RW	26	4	3	7	8
54	CHI	Darrel Anholt	Calgary	D	1	0	0	0	0
55	TOR	Ernie Godden	Windsor	C	5	1	1	2	6
56	CGY	Mike Vernon	Calgary	G	722	371	2047	23	2.97
57	NYI	Ron Handy	Sault Ste. Marie	LW	14	0	3	3	0
58	PHI	Ken Strong	Peterborough	LW	15	2	2	4	6
59	BUF	Jim Aldred	Kingston	LW					
60	BUF	Colin Chisholm	Calgary	D	1	0	0	0	0
61	HFD	Paul MacDermid	Windsor	RW	690	116	142	258	1303
62	ST.L.	Gord Donnelly	Sherbrooke	D	554	28	41	69	2069
63	NYI	Neal Coulter	Toronto	RW	26	5	5	10	11
64	WPG	Kirk McCaskill	Vermont	C					
65	PHI	Dave Michayluk	Regina	LW	14	2	6	8	8
66	COL	Gus Greco	Windsor	C					
67	HFD	Mike Hoffman	Brantford	LW	9	1	3	4	2
68	WSH	Tony Kellin	Grand Rapids H.S.	D					
69	MIN	Terry Tait	Sault Ste. Marie	C					
70	PIT	Norm Schmidt	Oshawa	D	125	23	33	56	73
71	EDM	Paul Houck	Kelowna	RW	16	1	2	3	2
72	NYR	John Vanbiesbrouck	Sault Ste. Marie	G	829	358	2367	38	2.99
73	VAN	Wendell Young	Kitchener	G	187	59	618	2	3.94
74	QUE	Clint Malarchuk	Portland	G	338	141	1100	12	3.47
75	CHI	Perry Pelensky	Portland	RW	4	0	0	0	5
76	MIN	Jim Malwitz	Grand Rapids H.S.	C					
77	BOS	Scott McLellan	Niagara Falls	RW	2	0	0	0	0
78	CGY	Peter Madach	HV 71 Jonkoping, SWE	C					
79	PHI	Ken Latta	Sault Ste. Marie	RW					
80	BUF	Jeff Eatough	Cornwall	RW	1	0	0	0	0
81	L.A.	Marty Dallman	RPI	C	6	0	1	1	0
82	MTL	Kjell Dahlin	Timra, SWE	RW	166	57	59	116	10
83	BUF	Anders Wikberg	Timra, SWE	LW					
84	NYI	Todd Lumbard	Brandon	G					
85	WPG	Marc Behrend	Wisconsin	G	39	12	160	1	4.82
86	DET	Larry Trader	London	D	91	5	13	18	74
87	COL	Doug Speck	Peterborough	D					
88	MTL	Steve Rooney	Canton H.S.	LW	154	15	13	28	496
89	WSH	Mike Siltala	Kingston	RW	7	1	0	1	2
90	TOR	Normand Lefrancois	Trois-Rivieres	LW					
91	WSH	Peter Sidorkiewicz	Oshawa	G	246	79	832	8	3.60
92	EDM	Phil Drouillard	Niagara Falls	LW					
93	HFD	Bill Maguire	Niagara Falls	D					
94	NYI	Jacques Sylvestre	Sorel	C					
95	QUE	Edward Lee	Princeton	RW	2	0	0	0	5
96	CHI	Doug Chessell	London	G					
97	MIN	Kelly Hubbard	Portland	D					
98	BOS	Joe Mantione	Cornwall	G					
99	CGY	Mario Simioni	Toronto	RW					
100	PHI	Justin Hanley	Kingston	C					
101	BUF	Mauri Eivola	TPS Turku, FIN	C					
102	TOR	Barry Bringley	Calgary	C					
103	HFD	Dan Bourbonnais	Calgary	LW	59	3	25	28	11
104	ST.L.	Mike Hickey	Sudbury	C					
105	VAN	Moe Lemay	Ottawa	LW	317	72	94	166	442
106	WPG	Bob O'Connor	Boston College	G					
107	DET	Gerard Gallant	Sherbrooke	LW	615	211	269	480	1674
108	COL	Bruce Driver	Wisconsin	D	922	96	390	486	670
109	PIT	Paul Edwards	Oshawa	D					
110	WSH	Jim McGeough	Billings	C	57	7	10	17	32
111	EDM	Steve Smith	London	D	791	72	301	373	2122
112	PIT	Rod Buskas	Medicine Hat	D	556	19	63	82	1294
113	EDM	Marc Habscheid	Saskatoon	RW/C	345	72	91	163	171
114	NYR	Eric Magnuson	RPI	C					
115	VAN	Stu Kulak	Victoria	RW	90	8	4	12	130
116	QUE	Mike Eagles	Kitchener	C/LW	853	74	122	196	928
117	CHI	Bill Schafhauser	Northern Michigan	D					
118	MIN	Paul Guay	Mount St. Charles H.S.	RW	117	11	23	34	92
119	BOS	Bruce Milton	Boston U.	D					
120	CGY	Todd Hooey	Windsor	RW					
121	PHI	Andre Villeneuve	Chicoutimi	D					
122	BUF	Ali Butorac	Ottawa	D/LW					
123	L.A.	Brad Thompson	London	D					
124	MTL	Tom Anastos	Paddock Pool H.S.	RW					
125	ST.L.	Peter Aslin	AIK Solna, SWE	G					
126	NYI	Chuck Brimmer	Kingston	C					
127	WPG	Peter Nilsson	Hammarby Stockholm, SWE	C					
128	DET	Greg Stefan	Oshawa	G	299	115	1068	5	3.92
129	COL	Jeff Larmer	Kitchener	LW	158	37	51	88	57
130	HFD	John Mokosak	Victoria	D	41	0	2	2	96
131	WSH	Risto Jalo	Ilves Tampere, FIN	C	3	0	3	3	0
132	TOR	Andrew Wright	Peterborough	D					
133	PIT	Geoff Wilson	Winnipeg	RW					
134	L.A.	Craig Hurley	Saskatoon	D					
135	NYR	Mike Guentzel	Greenway/Coleraine H.S.	D					
136	VAN	Bruce Holloway	Regina	D	2	0	0	0	0
137	PHI	Vladimir Svitek	VSZ Kosice, TCH	RW					
138	CHI	Marc Centrone	Lethbridge	C/RW					
139	MIN	Jim Archibald	Moose Jaw	RW	16	1	2	3	45
140	BOS	Mats Thelin	AIK Solna, SWE	D	163	8	19	27	107
141	CGY	Rick Heppner	Mount View H.S.	D					
142	PHI	Gil Hudon	Prince Albert	G					
143	BUF	Heikki Leime	TPS Turku, FIN	D					
144	L.A.	Peter Sawkins	St. Paul Academy	D					
145	MTL	Tom Kurvers	Minnesota-Duluth	D	659	93	328	421	350
146	ST.L.	Erik Holmberg	Sodertalje, SWE	C					
147	NYI	Teppo Virta	TPS Turku, FIN	RW					
148	WPG	Dan McFall	Buffalo Jr. Sabres	D	9	0	1	1	0
149	DET	Rick Zombo	Austin Prep	D	652	24	130	154	728
150	COL	Tony Arima	Jokerit Helsinki, FIN	LW					
151	HFD	Denis Doré	Chicoutimi	RW					
152	WSH	Gaetan Duchesne	Quebec	LW	1028	179	254	433	617
153	TOR	Richard Turmel	Shawinigan	D					
154	PIT	Mitch Lamoureux	Oshawa	C	73	11	9	20	59
155	EDM	Mike Sturgeon	Kelowna	D					
156	NYR	Ari Lahtenmaki	HIFK Helsinki, FIN	RW					
157	VAN	Petri Skriko	SaiPa Lappeenranta, FIN	LW	541	183	222	405	246
158	QUE	Andre Cote	Quebec	RW					
159	CHI	Johan Mellstrom	Falun, SWE	LW					
160	MIN	Kari Kanervo	TPS Turku, FIN	C					
161	BOS	Armel Parisee	Chicoutimi	D					
162	CGY	Dale DeGray	Oshawa	D	153	18	47	65	195
163	PHI	Steve Taylor	Providence	LW					
164	BUF	Gates Orlando	Providence	C	98	18	26	44	51
165	L.A.	Dan Brennan	North Dakota	LW	8	0	1	1	9
166	MTL	Paul Gess	Jefferson H.S.	RW					
167	ST.L.	Alain Vigneault	Trois-Rivieres	D	42	2	5	7	82
168	NYI	Bill Dowd	Ottawa	D					
169	WPG	Greg Dick	St. Mary's H.S.	G					
170	DET	Don Leblanc	Moncton Jr.	LW					
171	COL	Tim Army	Providence	C					
172	HFD	Jeff Poeschl	Northern Michigan	G					
173	WSH	George White	New Hampshire	LW					
174	TOR	Greg Barber	Victoria	D					
175	PIT	Dean Defazio	Brantford	LW	22	0	2	2	28
176	EDM	Miloslav Horava	Poldi SNOP Kladno, TCH	D	80	5	17	22	38
177	NYR	Paul Reifenberger	Anoka H.S.	C					
178	VAN	Frank Caprice	London	G	102	31	391	1	4.20
179	QUE	Marc Brisebois	Sorel	RW					
180	CHI	John Benns	Billings	LW					
181	MIN	Scott Bjugstad	Minnesota-Duluth	RW	317	76	68	144	144
182	BOS	Don Sylvestri	Clarkson	G	3	0	6	0	3.53

PICK	TEAM	NAME	DRAFTED FROM	NHL PLAYERS: POS / NHL GOALTENDERS: POS	GP / GP	G / W	A / GA	PTS / SO	PIM / AVG
183	CGY	George Boudreau	Matignon H.S.	D					
184	PHI	Len Hachborn	Brantford	C	102	20	39	59	29
185	BUF	Venci Sebek	Niagara Falls	D					
186	L.A.	Allan Tuer	Regina	D	57	1	1	2	208
187	MTL	Scott Ferguson	Edina West H.S.	D					
188	ST.L.	Dan Wood	Kingston	RW					
189	NYI	Scott MacLellan	Burlington Jr. B	RW					
190	WPG	Vladimir Kadlec	TJ Vitkovice, TCH	D					
191	DET	Robert Nordmark	Lulea, SWE	D					
192	COL	John Johannson	Wisconsin	C	5	0	0	0	0
193	HFD	Larry Power	Kitchener	C					
194	WSH	Chris Valentine	Sorel	C	105	43	52	95	127
195	TOR	Marc Magnan	Lethbridge	LW	4	0	1	1	5
196	PIT	Dave Hannan	Brantford	C	841	114	191	305	942
197	EDM	Gord Sherven	Weyburn Jr. A	C	97	13	22	35	33
198	NYR	Mario Proulx	Providence	G					
199	VAN	Rejean Vignola	Shawinigan	C	Re-entered Draft in 1984				
200	QUE	Kari Takko	Assat Pori, FIN	G					
201	CHI	Sylvain Roy	Hull	D					
202	MIN	Steve Kudebeh	Breck H.S.	G					
203	BOS	Richard Bourque	Sherbrooke	LW					
204	CGY	Bruce Eakin	Saskatoon	C	13	2	2	4	4
205	PHI	Steve Tsujiura	Medicine Hat	C					
206	BUF	Warren Harper	Prince Albert	RW					
207	L.A.	Jeff Baikie	Cornell	LW					
208	MTL	Danny Burrows	Belleville	G					
209	ST.L.	Richard Zemlak	Spokane	RW	132	2	12	14	587
210	NYI	Dave Randerson	Stratford Jr. B	RW					
211	WPG	Dave Kirwin	Irondale H.S.	D					

1982

PICK	TEAM	NAME	DRAFTED FROM	NHL PLAYERS: POS / NHL GOALTENDERS: POS	GP / GP	G / W	A / GA	PTS / SO	PIM / AVG
FIRST ROUND									
1	BOS	Gord Kluzak	Nanaimo	D	299	25	98	123	543
2	MIN	Brian Bellows	Kitchener	LW	1188	485	537	1022	718
3	TOR	Gary Nylund	Portland	D	608	32	139	171	1235
4	PHI	Ron Sutter	Lethbridge	C	1072	204	326	530	1340
5	WSH	Scott Stevens	Kitchener	D	1353	179	649	828	2607
6	BUF	Phil Housley	South St. Paul H.S.	D	1288	313	817	1130	738
7	CHI	Ken Yaremchuk	Portland	C	235	36	56	92	106
8	N.J.	Rocky Trottier	Nanaimo	RW	38	6	4	10	2
9	BUF	Paul Cyr	Victoria	LW	470	101	140	241	623
10	PIT	Rich Sutter	Lethbridge	RW	874	149	166	315	1411
11	VAN	Michel Petit	Sherbrooke	D	827	90	238	328	1839
12	WPG	Jim Kyte	Cornwall	D	598	17	49	66	1342
13	QUE	David Shaw	Kitchener	D	769	41	153	194	906
14	HFD	Paul Lawless	Windsor	LW	239	49	77	126	54
15	NYR	Chris Kontos	Toronto	LW/C	230	54	69	123	103
16	BUF	Dave Andreychuk	Oshawa	LW	1287	552	624	1176	892
17	DET	Murray Craven	Medicine Hat	LW	1071	266	493	759	524
18	N.J.	Ken Daneyko	Seattle	D	1070	34	125	159	2339
19	MTL	Alain Heroux	Chicoutimi	LW	20PTS in 53 AHL games				
20	EDM	Jim Playfair	Portland	D	21	2	4	6	51
21	NYI	Pat Flatley	Wisconsin	RW	780	170	340	510	686
SECOND ROUND									
22	BOS	Brian Curran	Portland	D	381	7	33	40	1461
23	DET	Yves Courteau	Laval	RW	22	2	5	7	4
24	TOR	Gary Leeman	Regina	RW	667	199	267	466	531
25	TOR	Peter Ihnacak	Sparta Praha, TCH	C	417	102	165	267	175
26	BUF	Mike Anderson	North St. Paul H.S.	C	Played 25 AHL games– 85-86				
27	L.A.	Michael Heidt	Calgary	D	6	0	1	1	7
28	CHI	Rene Badeau	Quebec	D	2 pro seasons in IHL & AHL				
29	CGY	Dave Reierson	Prince Albert	D	2	0	0	0	2
30	BUF	Jens Johansson	Pitea, SWE	D	Never played outside Europe				
31	MTL	Jocelyn Gauvreau	Granby	D	2	0	0	0	0
32	MTL	Kent Carlson	St. Lawrence U.	D	113	7	11	18	148
33	MTL	David Maley	Edina H.S.	LW	466	43	81	124	1043
34	QUE	Paul Gillis	Niagara Falls	C	624	88	154	242	1498
35	HFD	Mark Paterson	Ottawa	D	29	3	3	6	33
36	NYR	Tomas Sandstrom	Farjestad Karlstad, SWE	RW	983	394	462	856	1193
37	CGY	Rich Kromm	Portland	LW	372	70	103	173	138
38	PIT	Tim Hrynewich	Sudbury	LW	55	6	8	14	82
39	BOS	Lyndon Byers	Regina	RW	279	28	43	71	1081
40	MTL	Scott Sandelin	Hibbing H.S.	D	25	0	4	4	2
41	EDM	Steve Graves	Sault Ste. Marie	LW	35	5	4	9	10
42	NYI	Vern Smith	Lethbridge	D	1	0	0	0	0
OTHER ROUNDS									
43	N.J.	Pat Verbeek	Sudbury	R/LW	1293	500	513	1013	2760
44	DET	Carmine Vani	Kingston	LW					
45	TOR	Ken Wregget	Lethbridge	G	575	225	1917	9	3.63
46	PHI	Miroslav Dvorak	Motor Ceske Budejovice, TCH	D	193	11	74	85	51
47	PHI	Bill Campbell	Montreal	D					
48	L.A.	Steve Seguin	Kingston	L/RW	5	0	0	0	9
49	CHI	Tom McMurchy	Brandon	RW	55	8	4	12	65
50	ST.L.	Mike Posavad	Peterborough	D	8	0	0	0	0
51	CGY	Jim Laing	Clarkson	D					
52	PIT	Troy Loney	Lethbridge	LW	624	87	110	197	1091
53	VAN	Yves Lapointe	Shawinigan	LW					
54	N.J.	Dave Kasper	Sherbrooke	C					
55	QUE	Mario Gosselin	Shawinigan	G	241	91	801	6	3.74
56	HFD	Kevin Dineen	U. of Denver	RW	1059	342	390	732	2029
57	NYR	Corey Millen	Cloquet H.S.	C	335	90	119	209	236
58	WSH	Milan Novy	Poldi SNOP Kladno, TCH	C	73	18	30	48	16
59	MIN	Wally Chapman	Edina H.S.	C					
60	BOS	Dave Reid	Peterborough	LW	888	164	195	359	232
61	MTL	Scott Harlow	S.S. Braves H.S.	LW	1	0	1	1	0
62	EDM	Brent Loney	Cornwall	LW					
63	NYI	Garry Lacey	Toronto	LW					
64	L.A.	Dave Gans	Oshawa	C	6	0	0	0	2
65	CGY	Dave Meszaros	Toronto	G					
66	DET	Craig Coxe	St. Albert Jr. A	LW	235	14	31	45	713
67	HFD	Ulf Samuelsson	Leksand, SWE	D	1080	57	275	332	2453
68	BUF	Timo Jutila	Tappara Tampere, FIN	D	10	1	5	6	13
69	MTL	John Devoe	Edina H.S.	RW					
70	CHI	Bill Watson	Prince Albert	RW	115	23	36	59	12
71	VAN	Shawn Kilroy	Peterborough	G					
72	CGY	Mark Lamb	Nanaimo	C	403	46	100	146	291
73	TOR	Vladimir Ruzicka	CHZ Litvinov, TCH	C	233	82	85	167	129
74	WPG	Tom Martin	Kelowna Jr. A	LW	92	12	11	23	249
75	WPG	Dave Ellett	Ottawa Jr. A	D	1129	153	415	568	985
76	QUE	Jiri Lala	Dukla Jihlava, TCH	RW					
77	PHI	Mikael Hjalm	MoDo Ornskoldsvik, SWE	R/LW					
78	NYR	Chris Jensen	Kelowna Jr. A	RW	74	9	12	21	27
79	BUF	Jeff Hamilton	Providence	R/LW					
80	MIN	Bob Rouse	Nanaimo	D	1061	37	181	218	1559
81	MIN	Dusan Pasek	Slovan Bratislava, TCH	C	48	4	10	14	30
82	L.A.	Dave Ross	Seattle	G					
83	EDM	Jaroslav Pouzar	Motor Ceske Budejovice, TCH	LW	186	34	48	82	135
84	NYI	Alan Kerr	Seattle	RW	391	72	94	166	826
85	N.J.	Scott Brydges	Mariner H.S.	D					
86	DET	Brad Shaw	Ottawa	D	377	22	137	159	208
87	TOR	Eduard Uvira	CHZ Litvinov, TCH	D					
88	HFD	Ray Ferraro	Penticton Jr. A	C	1101	365	420	785	1123
89	WSH	Dean Evason	Kamloops	C	803	139	233	372	1002
90	L.A.	Darcy Roy	Ottawa	LW					
91	CHI	Brad Beck	Penticton Jr. A	D					
92	ST.L.	Scott Machej	Calgary	C/LW					
93	CGY	Lou Kiriakou	Toronto	D					
94	PIT	Grant Sasser	Portland	C	3	0	0	0	0
95	L.A.	Ulf Isaksson	AIK Solna, SWE	LW	50	7	15	22	10
96	WPG	Tim Mishler	East Grand Forks H.S.	C					
97	QUE	Phil Stanger	Seattle	LW					
98	PHI	Todd Bergen	Prince Albert	C	14	11	5	16	4
99	TOR	Sylvain Charland	Shawinigan	LW					
100	BUF	Robert Logan	West Island Jr.	RW	42	10	5	15	0
101	MIN	Marty Wiitala	Superior H.S.	C					
102	BOS	Bob Nicholson	London	D					
103	MTL	Kevin Houle	Acton-Boxboro H.S.	LW					
104	EDM	Dwayne Boettger	Toronto	D					
105	NYI	Rene Breton	Granby	C					
106	N.J.	Mike Moher	Kitchener	RW	9	0	1	1	28
107	DET	Claude Vilgrain	Laval	RW	89	21	32	53	78
108	TOR	Ron Dreger	Saskatoon	LW					
109	HFD	Randy Gilhen	Winnipeg	C	457	55	60	115	314
110	WSH	Ed Kastelic	London	R/LW	220	11	10	21	719
111	BUF	Jeff Parker	Mariner H.S.	RW	141	16	19	35	163
112	CHI	Mark Hatcher	Niagara Falls	D					
113	ST.L.	Perry Ganchar	Saskatoon	RW	42	3	7	10	36
114	CGY	Jeff Vaive	Ottawa	C					
115	TOR	Craig Kales	Niagara Falls	RW					
116	VAN	Taylor Hall	Regina	LW	41	7	9	16	29
117	MTL	Ernie Vargas	Coon Rapids H.S.	C					
118	CGY	Mats Kihlstrom	Sodertalje, SWE	D					
119	PHI	Ron Hextall	Brandon	G	608	296	1723	23	2.97
120	NYR	Tony Granato	Northwood Prep	RW	713	244	239	483	1360
121	BUF	Jacob Gustavsson	Almtuna, SWE	G					
122	MIN	Todd Carlile	North St. Paul H.S.	D					
123	BOS	Bob Sweeney	Acton-Boxboro H.S.	C/RW	639	125	163	288	799
124	MTL	Michael Dark	Sarnia Jr. B	D	43	5	6	11	14
125	EDM	Raimo Summanen	Reipas Lahti, FIN	LW	151	36	40	76	35
126	NYI	Roger Kortko	Saskatoon	C	79	7	17	24	28
127	N.J.	Paul Fulcher	London	LW					
128	DET	Greg Hudas	Redford Jr.	D					
129	TOR	Dom Campedelli	Cohasset H.S.	D	2	0	0	0	0
130	HFD	Jim Johannson	Rochester Mayo H.S.	C					
131	QUE	Daniel Poudrier	Shawinigan	D	25	1	5	6	10
132	L.A.	Viktor Nechayev	SKA Leningrad, USSR	C	3	1	0	1	0
133	CHI	Jay Ness	Roseau H.S.	C					
134	ST.L.	Doug Gilmour	Cornwall	C	1271	422	883	1305	1147
135	CGY	Brad Ramsden	Peterborough	RW					

PICK	TEAM	NAME	DRAFTED FROM	NHL PLAYERS: POS	GP	G	A	PTS	PIM
				NHL GOALTENDERS: POS	GP	W	GA	SO	AVG
136	PIT	Brent Couture	Lethbridge	D					
137	VAN	Parie Proft	Calgary	D					
138	WPG	Derek Ray	Seattle Jr. B	LW					
139	TOR	Jeff Triano	Toronto	D					
140	PHI	David Brown	Saskatoon	RW	729	45	52	97	1789
141	NYR	Sergei Kapustin	Spartak Moscow, USSR	LW					
142	BUF	Allen Bishop	Niagara Falls	D					
143	MIN	Viktor Zhluktov	CSKA Moscow, USSR	LW					
144	BOS	John Meulenbroeks	Brantford	D					
145	MTL	Hannu Jarvenpaa	Karpat Oulu, FIN	RW	Re-entered Draft in 1985				
146	EDM	Brian Small	Ottawa	RW					
147	NYI	John Tiano	Winthrop H.S.	C					
148	N.J.	John Hutchings	Oshawa	D					
149	DET	Pat Lahey	Windsor	C					
150	MTL	Steve Smith	St. Lawrence U.	D					
151	HFD	Mickey Kramptoich	Hibbing H.S.	C					
152	WSH	Wally Schreiber	Regina	RW	41	8	10	18	12
153	L.A.	Peter Helander	Skelleftea, SWE	D	7	0	1	1	0
154	CHI	Jeff Smith	London	LW					
155	ST.L.	Chris Delaney	Boston College	LW					
156	CGY	Roy Myllari	Cornwall	D					
157	PIT	Peter Derksen	Portland	LW					
158	VAN	Newell Brown	Michigan State	C					
159	WPG	Guy Gosselin	John Marshall H.S.	D	5	0	0	0	6
160	NYR	Brian Glynn	Buffalo Jr.	C					
161	PHI	Alain Lavigne	Shawinigan	RW					
162	NYR	Jan Karlsson	Kiruna, SWE	D					
163	BUF	Claude Verret	Trois-Rivieres	C	14	2	5	7	2
164	MIN	Paul Miller	Crookston H.S.	C					
165	BOS	Tony Fiore	Montreal	C					
166	MTL	Tom Kolioupoulos	Fraser H.S.	RW					
167	EDM	Dean Clark	St. Albert Jr. A	D	1	0	0	0	0
168	NYI	Todd Okerlund	Burnsville H.S.	RW	4	0	0	0	2
169	N.J.	Alan Hepple	Ottawa	D	3	0	0	0	7
170	DET	Gary Cullen	Cornell	C					
171	TOR	Miroslav Ihnacak	VSZ Kosice, TCH	LW	56	8	9	17	39
172	HFD	Kevin Skilliter	Cornwall	D					
173	WSH	Jamie Reeve	Saskatoon Jr. A	G					
174	L.A.	Dave Chartier	Saskatoon	C	1	0	0	0	0
175	CHI	Phil Patterson	Ottawa	RW					
176	ST.L.	Matt Christensen	Aurora H.S.	C					
177	CGY	Ted Pearson	Wisconsin	LW					
178	PIT	Greg Gravel	Windsor	C					
179	VAN	Don McLaren	Ottawa	RW					
180	WPG	Tom Ward	Richfield H.S.	D					
181	QUE	Mike Hough	Kitchener	LW	707	100	156	256	675
182	PHI	Magnus Roupe	Farjestad Karlstad, SWE	LW	40	3	5	8	42
183	NYR	Kelly Miller	Michigan State	LW	1057	181	282	463	512
184	BUF	Rob Norman	Cornwall	RW					
185	MIN	Pat Micheletti	Hibbing H.S.	C	12	2	0	2	8
186	BOS	Doug Kostynski	Kamloops	C	15	3	1	4	4
187	MTL	Brian Williams	Sioux City Jr. A	C					
188	EDM	Ian Wood	Penticton Jr. A	G					
189	NYI	Gord Paddock	Saskatoon Jr. A	D					
190	N.J.	Brent Shaw	Seattle	RW					
191	DET	Brent Meckling	Calgary Jr. A	D					
192	TOR	Leigh Verstraete	Calgary	RW	8	0	1	1	14
193	NYR	Simo Saarinen	HIFK Helsinki, FIN	D	8	0	0	0	0
194	WSH	Juha Nurmi	Tappara Tampere, FIN	C					
195	L.A.	John Franzosa	Brown	G					
196	CHI	James Camazzola	Penticton Jr. A	LW	3	0	0	0	0
197	ST.L.	John Shumski	RPI	C/RW					
198	CGY	Jim Uens	Oshawa	C/RW					
199	PIT	Stu Wenaas	Winnipeg	D					
200	VAN	Alain Raymond	Niagara Falls	LW					
201	WPG	Mike Savage	Sudbury	LW					
202	QUE	Vincent Lukac	Dukla Jihlava, TCH	RW					
203	PHI	Tom Allen	Michigan Tech	G					
204	NYR	Bob Lowes	Prince Albert	C					
205	BUF	Mike Craig	Nanaimo	G					
206	MIN	Arnold Kadlec	CHZ Litvinov, TCH	D					
207	BOS	Tony Gilliard	Niagara Falls	LW					
208	MTL	Bob Emery	Matignon H.S.	D					
209	EDM	Grant Dion	Cowichan Valley Jr.	D					
210	NYI	Eric Faust	Henry Carr Jr. B	D					
211	N.J.	Scott Fusco	Harvard	LW					
212	DET	Mike Stern	Oshawa	LW					
213	TOR	Tim Loven	Red River H.S.	D					
214	HFD	Martin Linse	Djurgarden Stockholm, SWE	C					
215	WSH	Wayne Prestage	Seattle	C					
216	L.A.	Ray Shero	St. Lawrence U.	LW					
217	CHI	Mike James	Ottawa	D					
218	ST.L.	Brian Ahern	West St. Paul H.S.	LW					
219	CGY	Rick Erdall	Minnesota-Duluth	C					
220	PIT	Chris McCauley	London	RW					
221	VAN	Steve Driscoll	Cornwall	LW					
222	WPG	Bob Shaw	Penticton Jr. A	RW					
223	QUE	Andre Martin	Montreal	D					
224	PHI	Rick Gal	Lethbridge	LW					
225	NYR	Andy Otto	Northwood Prep	D					
226	BUF	Jim Plankers	Cloquet H.S.	D					
227	MIN	Scott Knutson	Warroad H.S.	C					
228	BOS	Tommy Lehman	Stocksund, SWE	C	36	5	5	10	16
229	MTL	Darren Acheson	Fort Saskatchewan	C					
230	EDM	Chris Smith	Regina	G					
231	NYI	Pat Goff	Alexander Ramsey H.S.	D					
232	N.J.	Dan Dorion	Austin Prep	C	4	1	1	2	2
233	DET	Shaun Reagan	Brantford	RW					
234	TOR	Jim Appleby	Winnipeg	G					
235	HFD	Randy Cameron	Winnipeg	D					
236	WSH	Jim Holden	Peterborough	G					
237	L.A.	Mats Ulander	AIK Solna, SWE	RW					
238	CHI	Bob Andrea	Dartmouth Jr.	D					
239	ST.L.	Peter Smith	U. of Maine	G					
240	CGY	Dale Thompson	Calgary Jr. A	RW					
241	PIT	Stan Bautch	Hibbing H.S.	G					
242	VAN	Shawn Green	Victoria	RW					
243	WPG	Jan Urban Ericson	AIK Solna, SWE	LW					
244	QUE	Jozef Lukac	VSZ Kosice, TCH	C					
245	PHI	Mark Vichorek	Sioux City Jr. A	D					
246	NYR	Dwayne Robinson	New Hampshire	D					
247	WSH	Marco Kallas	St. Louis Jr. B	C					
248	QUE	Jan Jasko	Slovan Bratislava, TCH	LW					
249	BOS	Bruno Campese	Northern Michigan	G					
250	MTL	Bill Brauer	Edina H.S.	D					
251	EDM	Jeff Crawford	Regina	LW					
252	NYI	Jim Koudys	Sudbury	D					

1983

PICK	TEAM	NAME	DRAFTED FROM	NHL PLAYERS: POS	GP	G	A	PTS	PIM
				NHL GOALTENDERS: POS	GP	W	GA	SO	AVG
FIRST ROUND									
1	MIN	Brian Lawton	Mount St. Charles H.S.	LW	483	112	154	266	401
2	HFD	Sylvain Turgeon	Hull	LW	669	269	226	495	691
3	NYI	Pat LaFontaine	Verdun	C	865	468	545	1013	552
4	DET	Steve Yzerman	Peterborough	C	1256	627	935	1562	816
5	BUF	Tom Barrasso	Acton-Boxboro H.S.	G	733	353	2276	35	3.27
6	N.J.	John MacLean	Oshawa	RW	1144	406	424	830	1294
7	TOR	Russ Courtnall	Victoria	RW	1029	297	447	744	557
8	WPG	Andrew McBain	North Bay	RW	608	129	172	301	633
9	VAN	Cam Neely	Portland	RW	726	395	299	694	1241
10	BUF	Normand Lacombe	New Hampshire	RW	319	53	62	115	196
11	BUF	Adam Creighton	Ottawa	C	708	187	216	403	1077
12	NYR	Dave Gagner	Brantford	C	946	318	401	719	1018
13	CGY	Dan Quinn	Belleville	C	805	266	419	685	533
14	WPG	Bobby Dollas	Laval	D	625	41	95	136	449
15	PIT	Bob Errey	Peterborough	LW	895	170	212	382	1005
16	NYI	Gerald Diduck	Lethbridge	D	918	56	156	212	1594
17	MTL	Alfie Turcotte	Portland	C	112	17	29	46	49
18	CHI	Bruce Cassidy	Ottawa	D	36	4	13	17	10
19	EDM	Jeff Beukeboom	Sault Ste. Marie	D	804	30	129	159	1890
20	HFD	David Jensen	Lawrence Academy	C	69	9	13	22	22
21	BOS	Nevin Markwart	Regina	LW	309	41	68	109	794
SECOND ROUND									
22	PIT	Todd Charlesworth	Oshawa	D	93	3	9	12	47
23	HFD	Ville Siren	Ilves Tampere, FIN	D	290	14	68	82	276
24	N.J.	Shawn Evans	Peterborough	D	9	1	0	1	2
25	DET	Lane Lambert	Saskatoon	RW	283	58	66	124	521
26	MTL	Claude Lemieux	Trois-Rivieres	RW	1001	345	353	698	1584
27	MTL	Sergio Momesso	Shawinigan	LW	710	152	193	345	1557
28	TOR	Jeff Jackson	Brantford	LW	263	38	48	86	313
29	WPG	Brad Berry	St. Albert Jr. A	D	241	4	28	32	323
30	VAN	David Bruce	Kitchener	LW	234	48	39	87	338
31	BUF	John Tucker	Kitchener	C	656	177	259	436	285
32	QUE	Yves Heroux	Chicoutimi	RW	1	0	0	0	0
33	NYR	Randy Heath	Portland	LW	13	2	4	6	15
34	BUF	Richard Hajdu	Kamloops	LW	5	0	0	0	4
35	MTL	Todd Francis	Brantford	RW	Played until 1995 in 3 leagues				
36	MIN	Malcolm Parks	St. Albert Jr. A	C	Played 4 years at N-Dakota				
37	NYI	Garnet McKechney	Kitchener	RW	5 pro seasons in 3 leagues				
38	MIN	Frantisek Musil	Tesla Pardubice, TCH	D	784	34	104	138	1237
39	CHI	Wayne Presley	Kitchener	RW	684	155	147	302	953
40	EDM	Mike Golden	Reading H.S.	C	U-Maine grad played until '91				
41	PHI	Peter Zezel	Toronto	C	873	219	389	608	435
42	BOS	Greg Johnston	Toronto	RW	187	26	29	55	124
OTHER ROUNDS									
43	WPG	Peter Taglianetti	Providence	D	451	18	74	92	1106
44	PHI	Derrick Smith	Peterborough	LW	537	82	92	174	373
45	MTL	Daniel Letendre	Quebec	RW					
46	DET	Bob Probert	Brantford	LW	795	155	206	361	3021
47	L.A.	Bruce Shoebottom	Peterborough	D	35	1	4	5	53

PICK	TEAM	NAME	DRAFTED FROM	NHL PLAYERS: POS / NHL GOALTENDERS: POS	GP / GP	G / W	A / GA	PTS / SO	PIM / AVG
48	ST.L.		no selection						
49	TOR	Allan Bester	Brantford	G	219	73	786	7	4.01
50	NYR	Vesa Salo	Lukko Rauma, FIN	D					
51	VAN	Scott Tottle	Peterborough	RW					
52	CGY	Brian Bradley	London	C	651	182	321	503	528
53	QUE	Bruce Bell	Windsor	D	209	12	64	76	113
54	NYR	Gord Walker	Portland	RW	31	3	4	7	23
55	QUE	Iiro Jarvi	HIFK Helsinki, FIN	RW	116	18	43	61	58
56	CGY	Perry Berezan	St. Albert Jr. A	C	378	61	75	136	279
57	MIN	Mitch Messier	Notre Dame Juvenile	C	20	0	2	2	11
58	NYI	Mike Neill	Sault Ste. Marie	D					
59	PIT	Mike Rowe	Toronto	D	11	0	0	0	11
60	CHI	Marc Bergevin	Chicoutimi	D	992	32	123	155	997
61	EDM	Mike Flanagan	Acton-Boxboro H.S.	D					
62	HFD	Leif Karlsson	Mora, SWE	D					
63	BOS	Greg Puhalski	Kitchener	LW					
64	PIT	Frank Pietrangelo	Minnesota-Duluth	G	141	46	490	1	4.12
65	HFD	Dave MacLean	Belleville	RW					
66	NYI	Mikko Makela	Ilves Tampere, FIN	LW	423	118	147	265	139
67	CGY	John Bekkers	Regina	C					
68	L.A.	Guy Benoit	Shawinigan	C					
69	ST.L.		no selection						
70	DET	David Korol	Winnipeg	D					
71	WPG	Bob Essensa	Henry Carr Jr. B	G	398	155	1161	17	3.19
72	VAN	Tim Lorentz	Portland	LW					
73	CGY	Kevan Guy	Medicine Hat	D	156	5	20	25	138
74	HFD	Ron Chyzowski	St. Albert Jr. A	C					
75	NYR	Peter Andersson	Orebro, SWE	D	47	6	13	19	20
76	BUF	Daren Puppa	Kirkland Lake	G	429	179	1204	19	3.03
77	WSH	Tim Bergland	Lincoln H.S.	RW	182	17	26	43	75
78	MIN	Brian Durand	Cloquet H.S.	C					
79	CGY	Bill Claviter	Virginia H.S.	LW					
80	MTL	John Kordic	Portland	RW	244	17	18	35	997
81	CHI	Tarek Howard	Olds Jr. A	D					
82	EDM	Esa Tikkanen	HIFK Helsinki, FIN	LW	877	244	386	630	1077
83	PHI	Alan Bourbeau	Acton-Boxboro H.S.	C					
84	BOS	Alain Larochelle	Saskatoon	G					
85	TOR	Dan Hodgson	Prince Albert	C	114	29	45	74	64
86	NYI	Bob Caulfield	Detroit Lakes H.S.	RW					
87	N.J.	Chris Terreri	Providence	G	388	147	1104	9	3.08
88	DET	Petr Klima	Dukla Jihlava, TCH	R/LW	786	313	260	573	671
89	L.A.	Bob LaForest	North Bay	RW	5	1	0	1	2
90	ST.L.		no selection						
91	DET	Joe Kocur	Saskatoon	RW	820	80	82	162	2519
92	WPG	Harry Armstrong	Dubuque Jr. A	D					
93	VAN	Doug Quinn	Nanaimo	D					
94	CGY	Igor Liba	Dukla Jihlava, TCH	LW	37	7	18	25	36
95	QUE	Luc Guenette	Quebec	G					
96	NYR	Jim Andonoff	Belleville	RW					
97	BUF	Jayson Meyer	Regina	D					
98	WSH	Martin Bouliane	Granby	C					
99	MIN	Rich Geist	St. Paul Academy	C					
100	NYI	Ron Viglasi	Victoria	D					
101	MTL	Dan Wurst	Edina H.S.	D					
102	CHI	Kevin Robinson	Toronto	D					
103	L.A.	Garry Galley	Bowling Green	D	1093	119	461	580	1159
104	PHI	Jerome Carrier	Verdun	D					
105	BOS	Allen Pedersen	Medicine Hat	D	428	5	36	41	487
106	PIT	Patrick Emond	Hull	C					
107	HFD	Brian Johnson	Silver Bay H.S.	RW	3	0	0	0	5
108	N.J.	Gordon Mark	Kamloops	D	85	3	10	13	187
109	DET	Chris Pusey	Abbotsford Jr.	G	1	0	3	0	4.50
110	L.A.	Dave Lundmark	Virginia H.S.	D					
111	ST.L.		no selection						
112	L.A.	Kevin Stevens	Silver Lake H.S.	LW	787	318	371	689	1372
113	WPG	Joel Baillargeon	Hull	LW	20	0	2	2	31
114	VAN	Dave Lowry	London	LW	891	133	149	282	1060
115	CGY	Grant Blair	Harvard	G					
116	QUE	Brad Walcott	Kingston	D					
117	NYR	Bob Alexander	Rosemount H.S.	D					
118	BUF	Jim Hofford	Windsor	D	18	0	0	0	47
119	CHI	Jari Torkki	Lukko Rauma, FIN	LW	4	1	0	1	0
120	MIN	Tom McComb	Mount St. Charles H.S.	D					
121	NYI	Darin Illikainen	Hermantown H.S.						
122	MTL	Arto Javanainen	Assat Pori, FIN	RW	Re-entered Draft in 1984				
123	CHI	Mark LaVarre	Stratford Jr. B	RW	78	9	16	25	58
124	EDM	Don Barber	Kelowna	R/LW	115	25	32	57	64
125	PHI	Rick Tocchet	Sault Ste. Marie	RW	1070	426	488	914	2863
126	BOS	Terry Taillefer	St. Albert Jr. A	G					
127	PIT	Paul Ames	Billerica H.S.	D					
128	HFD	Joe Reekie	North Bay	D	Re-entered Draft in 1985				
129	N.J.	Greg Evtushevski	Kamloops	RW					
130	DET	Bob Pierson	London	LW					
131	L.A.	Tim Burgess	Oshawa	D					
132	ST.L.		no selection						
133	TOR	Cam Plante	Brandon	D	2	0	0	0	0
134	WPG	Iain Duncan	North York Jr. B	LW	127	34	55	89	149
135	VAN	Terry Maki	Brantford	LW					
136	CGY	Jeff Hogg	Oshawa	G					
137	QUE	Craig Mack	East Grand Forks H.S.	D					
138	NYR	Steve Orth	St. Cloud Tech H.S.	C					
139	BUF	Christian Ruuttu	Assat Pori, FIN	C	621	134	298	432	714
140	WSH	Dwaine Hutton	Kelowna	C					
141	MIN	Sean Toomey	Cretin H.S.	LW	1	0	0	0	0
142	NYI	Jim Sprenger	Cloquet H.S.	D					
143	MTL	Vladislav Tretiak	CSKA Moscow, USSR	G					
144	CHI	Scott Birnie	Cornwall	RW					
145	EDM	Dale Derkatch	Regina	C					
146	PHI	Bobby Mormina	Longueuil	D					
147	BOS	Ian Armstrong	Peterborough	D					
148	HFD	Chris Duperron	Chicoutimi	D					
149	HFD	James Falle	Clarkson	G					
150	N.J.	Viacheslav Fetisov	CSKA Moscow, USSR	D	546	36	192	228	656
151	DET	Craig Butz	Kelowna	D					
152	L.A.	Ken Hammond	RPI	D	193	18	29	47	290
153	ST.L.		no selection						
154	TOR	Paul Bifano	Burnaby Jr.	LW					
155	WPG	Ron Pessetti	Western Michigan	D					
156	VAN	John Labatt	Minnetonka H.S.	C					
157	CGY	Chris MacDonald	Western Michigan	D					
158	QUE	Tommy Albelin	Djurgarden Stockholm, SWE	D	715	40	174	214	379
159	NYR	Peter Marcov	Welland Jr. B	LW					
160	BUF	Don McSween	Regina Jr. A	D	47	3	10	13	55
161	WSH	Marty Abrams	Pembroke Jr. A	G					
162	MIN	Don Biggs	Oshawa	C	12	2	0	2	8
163	NYI	Dale Henry	Saskatoon	LW	132	13	26	39	263
164	MTL	Rob Bryden	Henry Carr Jr. B	LW					
165	CHI	Kent Paynter	Kitchener	D	37	1	3	4	69
167	PHI	Per-Erik Eklund	AIK Solna, SWE	C	594	120	335	455	109
168	BOS	Francois Olivier	St-Jean	LW					
169	PIT	Marty Ketola	St. Cloquet H.S.	RW					
170	HFD	Bill Fordy	Guelph	LW					
171	N.J.	Jay Octeau	Mount St. Charles H.S.	D					
172	DET	Dave Sikorski	Cornwall	D					
173	L.A.	Bruce Fishback	Mariner H.S.	C					
174	ST.L.		no selection						
175	TOR	Cliff Albrecht	Princeton	D					
176	WPG	Todd Flichel	Gloucester	D	6	0	1	1	4
177	VAN	Allan Measures	Calgary	D					
178	CGY	Rob Kivell	Victoria	D					
179	QUE	Wayne Groulx	Sault Ste. Marie	C	1	0	0	0	0
180	NYR	Paul Jerrard	Notre Dame Jr. A	D	5	0	0	0	4
181	BUF	Tim Hoover	Sault Ste. Marie	D					
182	WSH	David Cowan	Washburn H.S.	LW					
183	MIN	Paul Pulis	Hibbing H.S.	RW					
184	NYI	Kevin Vescio	North Bay	D					
185	MTL	Grant MacKay	U. of Calgary	D					
186	CHI	Brian Noonan	Archbishop Williams H.S.	RW	629	116	159	275	518
187	EDM	Dave Roach	New Westminster	G					
188	PHI	Rob Nichols	Kitchener	LW					
189	BOS	Harri Laurila	Reipas Lahti, FIN	D					
190	PIT	Alec Haidy	Sault Ste. Marie	RW					
191	TOR	Greg Rolston	Michael Power H.S.	RW					
192	N.J.	Alexander Chernykh	Khimik Voskresensk, USSR	C					
193	DET	Stu Grimson	Regina	LW	Re-entered Draft in 1985				
194	L.A.	Thomas Ahlen	Skelleftea, SWE	D					
195	ST.L.		no selection						
196	TOR	Brian Ross	Kitchener	D					
197	WPG	Cory Wright	Dubuque Jr. A	RW					
198	VAN	Roger Grillo	U. of Maine	D					
199	CGY	Tom Pratt	Kimball Union Academy	D					
200	QUE	Scott Shaunessy	St. John's Prep	D/LW	7	0	0	0	23
201	HFD	Reine Karlsson	Sodertalje, SWE	LW					
202	BUF	Mark Ferner	Kamloops	D	91	3	10	13	51
203	WSH	Yves Beaudoin	Shawinigan	D	11	0	0	0	5
204	MIN	Milos Riha	TJ Gottwaldov, TCH	LW					
205	NYI	Dave Shellington	Cornwall	LW					
206	MTL	Thomas Rundqvist	Farjestad Karlstad, SWE	C	2	0	1	1	0
207	CHI	Dominik Hasek	Tesla Pardubice, TCH	G	449	210	977	45	2.26
208	EDM	Warren Yadlowski	Calgary	C					
209	PHI	William McCormick	Westminster Heights H.S.	C					
210	BOS	Paul Fitzsimmons	Northeastern	D					
211	PIT	Garth Hildebrand	Calgary	LW					
212	HFD	Allan Acton	Saskatoon	LW					
213	N.J.	Allan Stewart	Prince Albert	LW	64	6	4	10	243
214	DET	Jeff Frank	Regina	RW					
215	L.A.	Miroslav Blaha	Motor Ceske Budejovice, TCH	RW					
216	ST.L.		no selection						
217	TOR	Mike Tomlak	Cornwall	C/LW	141	15	22	37	103
218	WPG	Eric Cormier	St. Georges	LW					
219	VAN	Steve Kayser	Vermont	D					
220	CGY	Jaroslav Benak	Dukla Jihlava, TCH	LW					
221	MIN	Oldrich Valek	Dukla Jihlava, TCH	RW					
222	NYR	Bryan Walker	Portland	D					

PICK	TEAM	NAME	DRAFTED FROM	NHL PLAYERS: POS / NHL GOALTENDERS: POS	GP / GP	G / W	A / GA	PTS / SO	PIM / AVG
223	BUF	Uwe Krupp	Koln, FRG	D	717	69	211	280	642
224	WSH	Alain Raymond	Trois-Rivieres	G	1	0	2	0	3.00
225	WSH	Anders Huss	Brynas Gavle, SWE	C					
226	NYI	John Bjorkman	Warroad H.S.	C					
227	MTL	Jeff Perpich	Hibbing H.S.	D					
228	CHI	Steve Pepin	St-Jean	C					
229	EDM	John Miner	Regina	D	14	2	3	5	16
230	PHI	Brian Jopling	Williston Academy	G					
231	BOS	Norm Foster	Penticton Jr. A	G	13	7	34	0	3.27
232	PIT	Dave Goertz	Regina	D	2	0	0	0	2
233	HFD	Darcy Kaminski	Lethbridge	D					
234	N.J.	Alexei Kasatonov	CSKA Moscow, USSR	D	383	38	122	160	326
235	DET	Charles Chiatto	Cranbrook H.S.	C					
236	L.A.	Chad Johnson	Roseau H.S.	C					
237	ST.L.		no selection						
238	TOR	Ron Choules	Trois-Rivieres	LW					
239	WPG	Jamie Husgen	Des Moines Jr. A	D					
240	VAN	Jay Mazur	Breck H.S.	C/RW	47	11	7	18	20
241	CGY	Sergei Makarov	CSKA Moscow, USSR	RW	424	134	250	384	317
242	QUE	Bo Berglund	Djurgarden Stockholm, SWE	RW	130	28	39	67	40
243	NYR	Ulf Nilsson	Skelleftea, SWE	C	170	57	112	169	85
244	BUF	Marc Hamelin	Shawinigan	G					
245	BUF	Kermit Salfi	Northwood Prep	LW					
246	MIN	Paul Roff	Edina H.S.	RW					
247	NYI	Peter McGeough	Henricken H.S.	RW					
248	MTL	Jean-Guy Bergeron	Shawinigan	D					
249	QUE	Jindrich Kokrment	CHZ Litvinov, TCH	C					
250	EDM	Steve Woodburn	Verdun	D					
251	PHI	Harold Duvall	Belmont Hill H.S.	LW					
252	BOS	Greg Murphy	Trinity-Pawling H.S.	D					

1984

PICK	TEAM	NAME	DRAFTED FROM	NHL PLAYERS: POS / NHL GOALTENDERS: POS	GP / GP	G / W	A / GA	PTS / SO	PIM / AVG
FIRST ROUND									
1	PIT	Mario Lemieux	Laval	C	745	613	881	1494	737
2	N.J.	Kirk Muller	Guelph	LW	1161	345	568	913	1151
3	CHI	Ed Olczyk	Team USA	C	1031	342	452	794	874
4	TOR	Al Iafrate	Belleville	D	799	152	311	463	1301
5	MTL	Petr Svoboda	CHZ Litvinov, TCH	D	1009	57	338	395	1564
6	L.A.	Craig Redmond	U. of Denver	D	191	16	68	84	134
7	DET	Shawn Burr	Kitchener	LW/C	878	181	259	440	1069
8	MTL	Shayne Corson	Brantford	LW	942	241	368	609	1970
9	PIT	Doug Bodger	Kamloops	D	1071	106	422	528	1007
10	VAN	J.J. Daigneault	Longueuil	D	898	53	197	250	685
11	HFD	Sylvain Cote	Quebec	D	1032	112	291	403	497
12	CGY	Gary Roberts	Ottawa	LW	792	314	335	649	2079
13	MIN	David Quinn	Kent Prep	D	Blood disease ended career				
14	NYR	Terry Carkner	Peterborough	D	858	42	188	230	1588
15	QUE	Trevor Stienburg	Guelph	RW	71	8	4	12	161
16	PIT	Roger Belanger	Kingston	C	44	3	5	8	32
17	WSH	Kevin Hatcher	North Bay	D	1100	223	436	659	1354
18	BUF	Mikael Andersson	Vastra Frolunda, SWE	LW	761	95	169	264	134
19	BOS	Dave Pasin	Prince Albert	RW	76	18	19	37	50
20	NYI	Duncan MacPherson	Saskatoon	D	Played 3 pro seasons in AHL				
21	EDM	Selmar Odelein	Regina	D	18	0	2	2	35
SECOND ROUND									
22	PHI	Greg Smyth	London	D	229	4	16	20	783
23	N.J.	Craig Billington	Belleville	G	298	102	954	9	3.69
24	L.A.	Brian Wilks	Kitchener	C	48	4	8	12	27
25	TOR	Todd Gill	Windsor	D	898	79	259	338	1136
26	ST.L.	Brian Benning	Portland	D	568	63	233	296	963
27	PHI	Scott Mellanby	Henry Carr Jr. B	RW	1016	274	346	620	1945
28	DET	Doug Houda	Calgary	D	560	19	63	82	1102
29	MTL	Stephane Richer	Granby	RW	986	407	384	791	600
30	WPG	Peter Douris	New Hampshire	RW	321	54	67	121	80
31	VAN	Jeff Rohlicek	Portland	C	9	0	0	0	8
32	ST.L.	Tony Hrkac	Orillia Jr. A	C	518	92	171	263	118
33	CGY	Ken Sabourin	Sault Ste. Marie	D	74	2	8	10	201
34	WSH	Stephen Leach	Matignon H.S.	RW	702	130	153	283	978
35	NYR	Raimo Helminen	Ilves Tampere, FIN	C	117	13	46	59	16
36	QUE	Jeff Brown	Sudbury	D	747	154	430	584	498
37	PHI	Jeff Chychrun	Kingston	D	262	3	22	25	744
38	CGY	Paul Ranheim	Edina H.S.	LW	786	143	180	323	222
39	BUF	Doug Trapp	Regina	LW	2	0	0	0	0
40	BOS	Ray Podloski	Portland	C	8	0	1	1	17
41	NYI	Bruce Melanson	Oshawa	RW	Died of heart failure in 1985				
42	EDM	Daryl Reaugh	Kamloops	G	27	8	72	1	3.47
OTHER ROUNDS									
43	PHI	David McLay	Kelowna	LW					
44	N.J.	Neil Davey	Michigan State	D					
45	CHI	Trent Yawney	Saskatoon	D	593	27	102	129	783
46	MIN	Ken Hodge	St. John's Prep	C/RW	142	39	48	87	32
47	PHI	John Stevens	Oshawa	D	53	0	10	10	48
48	L.A.	John English	Sault Ste. Marie	D	3	1	3	4	4
49	DET	Milan Chalupa	Dukla Jihlava, TCH	D	14	0	5	5	6
50	ST.L.	Toby Ducolon	Bellows Academy	RW					
51	MTL	Patrick Roy	Granby	G	841	444	2155	48	2.63
52	VAN	David Saunders	St. Lawrence U.	LW	56	7	13	20	10
53	ST.L.	Robert Dirk	Regina	D	402	13	29	42	786
54	MTL	Graeme Bonar	Sault Ste. Marie	RW					
55	VAN	Landis Chaulk	Calgary	LW					
56	ST.L.	Alan Perry	Mount St. Charles H.S.	G					
57	QUE	Steven Finn	Laval	D	725	34	78	112	1724
58	VAN	Mike Stevens	Kitchener	LW	23	1	4	5	29
59	WSH	Michal Pivonka	Poldi SNOP Kladno, TCH	C	825	181	418	599	478
60	BUF	Ray Sheppard	Cornwall	RW	817	357	300	657	212
61	BOS	Jeff Cornelius	Toronto	D					
62	NYI	Jeff Norton	Cushing Academy	D	725	50	316	366	577
63	EDM	Todd Norman	Hill-Murray H.S.	C					
64	PIT	Mark Teevens	Peterborough	RW					
65	MTL	Lee Brodeur	Grafton H.S.	RW					
66	CHI	Tommy Eriksson	MoDo Ornskoldsvik, SWE	C					
67	TOR	Jeff Reese	London	G	174	53	529	5	3.66
68	WPG	Chris Mills	Bramalea Jr. B	D					
69	L.A.	Thomas Glavine	Billerica H.S.	C					
70	NYI	Doug Wieck	Rochester Mayo H.S.	LW					
71	ST.L.	Graham Herring	Longueuil	D					
72	WPG	Sean Clement	Brockville Jr. A	D					
73	VAN	Brian Bertuzzi	Kamloops	C					
74	N.J.	Paul Ysebaert	Petrolia Jr. B	C	532	149	187	336	217
75	CGY	Petr Rosol	Dukla Jihlava, TCH	LW					
76	MIN	Miroslav Maly	Bayreuth, FRG	D					
77	NYR	Paul Broten	Roseau H.S.	RW	322	46	55	101	264
78	QUE	Terry Perkins	Portland	RW					
79	PHI	Dave Hanson	U. of Denver	C					
80	WSH	Kris King	Peterborough	LW	836	65	85	150	2022
81	BUF	Bob Halkidis	London	D	256	8	32	40	825
82	BOS	Bob Joyce	Notre Dame Jr. A	LW	158	34	49	83	90
83	NYI	Ari Haanpaa	Ilves Tampere, FIN	LW	60	6	11	17	37
84	EDM	Rich Novak	Richmond Jr.	RW					
85	PIT	Arto Javanainen	Assat Pori, FIN	RW	14	4	1	5	2
86	N.J.	Jon Morris	Chelmsford H.S.	C	103	16	33	49	47
87	L.A.	David Grannis	South St. Paul H.S.	RW					
88	TOR	Jack Capuano	Kent Prep	D	6	0	0	0	0
89	MIN	Jiri Poner	Landshut, FRG	RW					
90	CHI	Timo Lehkonen	Jokerit Helsinki, FIN	D					
91	DET	Mats Lundstrom	Skelleftea, SWE	LW					
92	ST.L.	Scott Paluch	Chicago Jr.	D					
93	WPG	Scott Schneider	Colorado College	C					
94	VAN	Brett MacDonald	North Bay	D	1	0	0	0	0
95	MTL	Gerald Johannson	Swift Current	D					
96	CGY	Joel Paunio	HIFK Helsinki, FIN	LW					
97	MIN	Kari Takko	Assat Pori, FIN	G	142	37	475	1	3.90
98	NYR	Clark Donatelli	Stratford Jr. B	LW	35	3	4	7	39
99	WPG	Brent Severyn	Seattle	LW	328	10	30	40	825
100	PHI	Brian Dobbin	London	RW	63	7	8	15	61
101	CHI	Darin Sceviour	Lethbridge	RW	1	0	0	0	0
102	BUF	Joel Rampton	Sault Ste. Marie	LW					
103	BOS	Mike Bishop	London	G					
104	NYI	Mike Murray	London	C	1	0	0	0	0
105	EDM	Richard Lambert	Henry Carr Jr. B	LW					
106	EDM	Emanuel Viveiros	Prince Albert	D	29	1	11	12	6
107	N.J.	Kirk McLean	Oshawa	G	589	237	1833	22	3.25
108	L.A.	Greg Strome	North Dakota	G					
109	TOR	Fabian Joseph	Victoria	C					
110	HFD	Mike Millar	Brantford	RW	78	18	18	36	12
111	CHI	Chris Clifford	Kingston	G	2	0	0	0	0.00
112	DET	Randy Hansch	Victoria	G					
113	ST.L.	Steve Tuttle	Richmond Jr.	RW	144	28	28	56	12
114	WPG	Gary Lorden	Bishop Hendricken H.S.	D					
115	VAN	Jeff Korchinski	Clarkson	D					
116	MTL	Jim Nesich	Verdun	RW/C					
117	CGY	Brett Hull	Penticton Jr. A	RW	940	610	494	1104	371
118	MIN	Gary McColgan	Oshawa	LW					
119	NYR	Kjell Samuelsson	Leksand, SWE	D	813	48	138	186	1225
120	QUE	Darren Cota	Kelowna	RW					
121	PHI	John Dzikowski	Brandon	LW					
122	WSH	Vito Cramarossa	Toronto	RW					
123	BUF	James Gasseau	Drummondville	D					
124	BOS	Randy Oswald	Michigan Tech	D					
125	NYI	Jim Wilharm	Minnetonka H.S.	D					
126	EDM	Ivan Dornic	Dukla Trencin, TCH	LW					
127	PIT	Tom Ryan	Newton North H.S.	D					
128	N.J.	Ian Ferguson	Oshawa	D					
129	L.A.	Timothy Hanley	Deerfield Academy	C					
130	TOR	Joseph McInnis	Watertown H.S.	C					
131	HFD	Mike Vellucci	Belleville	D	2	0	0	0	11
132	CHI	Mike Stapleton	Cornwall	C	645	69	105	174	332
133	DET	Stefan Larsson	Vastra Frolunda, SWE	D					
134	ST.L.	Cliff Ronning	New Westminster	C	856	242	439	681	367

PICK	TEAM	NAME	DRAFTED FROM	NHL PLAYERS: POS / NHL GOALTENDERS: POS	GP / GP	G / W	A / GA	PTS / SO	PIM / AVG
135	WPG	Luciano Borsato	Bramalea Jr. B	C	203	35	55	90	113
136	VAN	Blaine Chrest	Portland	C					
137	MTL	Scott MacTavish	Fredericton H.S.	D					
138	CGY	Kevan Melrose	Red Deer Jr. A	D					
139	MIN	Vladimir Kyhos	CHZ Litvinov, TCH	LW					
140	NYR	Thomas Hussey	St. Andrew's H.S.	LW					
141	QUE	Henrik Cedegren	Brynas Gavle, SWE	RW					
142	PHI	Tom Allen	Kitchener	D					
143	WSH	Timo Iljima	Karpat Oulu, FIN	C					
144	BUF	Darcy Wakaluk	Kelowna	G	191	67	524	9	3.22
145	BOS	Mark Thietke	Saskatoon	C					
146	NYI	Kelly Murphy	Notre Dame Jr. A	D					
147	EDM	Heikki Riihijarvi	Kiekko-Espoo, FIN	D					
148	ST.L.	Don Porter	Michigan Tech	LW					
149	N.J.	Vladimir Kames	Dukla Jihlava, TCH	C					
150	L.A.	Shannon Deegan	Vermont	C					
151	TOR	Derek Laxdal	Brandon	RW	67	12	7	19	88
152	DET	Lars Karlsson	Farjestad Karlstad, SWE	LW					
153	CHI	Glen Greenough	Sudbury	RW					
154	DET	Urban Nordin	MoDo Ornskoldsvik, SWE	C					
155	ST.L.	Jim Vesey	Columbus H.S.	C/RW	15	1	2	3	7
156	WPG	Brad Jones	Michigan	LW	148	25	31	56	122
157	VAN	Jim Agnew	Brandon	D	81	0	1	1	257
158	MTL	Brad McCaughey	Ann Arbor H.S.	RW					
159	CGY	Jiri Hrdina	Sparta Praha, TCH	C	250	45	85	130	92
160	MIN	Darin MacInnis	Kent Prep	G					
161	NYR	Brian Nelson	Willmar H.S.	C					
162	QUE	Jyrki Maki	Simley H.S.	D					
163	PHI	Luke Vitale	Henry Carr Jr. B	C					
164	WSH	Frank Joo	Regina	D					
165	BUF	Orvar Stambert	Djurgarden Stockholm, SWE	D					
166	BOS	Don Sweeney	St Paul's Prep	D	832	44	180	224	578
167	NYI	Franco Desantis	Verdun	D					
168	EDM	Todd Ewen	New Westminster	RW	518	36	40	76	1911
169	PIT	John Del Col	Toronto	LW					
170	N.J.	Mike Roth	Hill-Murray H.S.	D					
171	L.A.	Luc Robitaille	Hull	LW	1042	553	597	1150	915
172	TOR	Dan Turner	Medicine Hat	LW					
173	HFD	John Devereaux	Scituate H.S.	C					
174	CHI	Ralph Difiore	Shawinigan	D					
175	DET	Bill Shibicky	Michigan State	C					
176	ST.L.	Daniel Jomphe	Granby	LW					
177	WPG	Gord Whitaker	Colorado College	RW					
178	VAN	Rex Grant	Kamloops	G					
179	MTL	Eric Demers	Shawinigan	LW					
180	CGY	Gary Suter	Wisconsin	D	995	187	591	778	1208
181	MIN	Duane Wahlin	Johnson H.S.	RW					
182	NYR	Ville Kentala	HIFK Helsinki, FIN	LW					
183	QUE	Guy Ouellette	Quebec	C					
184	PHI	Billy Powers	Matignon H.S.	C					
185	WSH	Jim Thomson	Toronto	RW	115	4	3	7	416
186	BOS	Kevin Heffernan	Weymouth H.S.	C					
187	NYI	Tom Warden	North Bay	D					
188	NYR	Heinz Ehlers	Leksand, SWE	C					
189	PIT	Steve Hurt	Hill-Murray H.S.	RW					
190	N.J.	Mike Peluso	Greenway H.S.	LW	458	38	52	90	1951
191	L.A.	Jeff Crossman	Western Michigan	C					
192	TOR	David Buckley	Trinity-Pawling H.S.	D					
193	HFD	Brent Regan	St. Albert Jr. A	RW					
194	CHI	Joakim Persson	S/G Hockey 83 Gavle, SWE	RW					
195	DET	Jay Rose	New Prep H.S.	D					
196	ST.L.	Tom Tilley	Orillia Jr. A	D	174	4	38	42	89
197	WPG	Rick Forest	Melville Jr. A	LW					
198	VAN	Ed Lowney	Boston U.	RW					
199	MTL	Ron Annear	San Diego U.	D					
200	CGY	Petr Rucka	Sparta Praha, TCH	C					
201	MIN	Michael Orn	Stillwater H.S.	C					
202	NYR	Kevin Miller	Redford Jr.	C	616	150	183	333	429
203	QUE	Ken Quinney	Calgary	RW	59	7	13	20	23
204	PHI	Daryn Fersovich	St. Albert Jr. A	C					
205	WSH	Paul Cavallini	Henry Carr Jr. B	D	564	56	177	233	750
206	BUF	Brian McKinnon	Ottawa	C					
207	BOS	J. D. Urbanic	Windsor	LW					
208	NYI	David Volek	Slavia Praha, TCH	L/RW	396	95	154	249	201
209	EDM	Joel Curtis	Oshawa	LW					
210	PIT	Jim Steen	Moorehead H.S.	C					
211	N.J.	Jarkko Piiparinen	Kiekkoreipas, FIN.	C					
212	L.A.	Paul Kenny	Cornwall	G					
213	TOR	Mikael Wurst	Ohio State	LW					
214	HFD	Jim Culhane	Western Michigan	D	6	0	1	1	4
215	CHI	Bill Brown	Simley H.S.	C					
216	DET	Tim Kaiser	Guelph	RW/D					
217	ST.L.	Mark Cupolo	Guelph	LW					
218	WPG	Mike Warus	Lake Superior State	RW					
219	VAN	Doug Clarke	Colorado College	D					
220	MTL	Dave Tanner	Notre Dame Jr. A	D					
221	CGY	Stefan Jonsson	Sodertalje, SWE	D					
222	MIN	Tom Terwilliger	Edina H.S.	D					
223	NYR	Tom Lorentz	Brady H.S.	C					
224	CHI	David Mackey	Victoria	LW	126	8	12	20	305
225	WSH	Mikhail Tatarinov	Sokol Kiev, USSR	D	161	21	48	69	184
226	BUF	Grant Delcourt	Kelowna	RW					
227	BOS	Bill Kopecky	Austin Prep	C					
228	NYI	Russ Becker	Virginia H.S.	D					
229	EDM	Simon Wheeldon	Victoria	C	15	0	2	2	10
230	PIT	Mark Ziliotto	Streetsville Jr. B	LW					
231	N.J.	Chris Kiene	Springfield Jr. B	D					
232	L.A.	Brian Martin	Belleville	C					
233	TOR	Peter Slanina	VSZ Kosice, TCH	D					
234	HFD	Peter Abric	North Bay	G					
235	CHI	Dan Williams	Chicago Jr.	D					
236	DET	Tom Nickolau	Guelph	C					
237	ST.L.	Mark Lanigan	U. of Waterloo	D					
238	WPG	Jim Edmonds	Cornell	G					
239	VAN	Ed Kister	London	D					
240	MTL	Troy Crosby	Verdun	G					
241	CGY	Rudolf Suchanek	Motor Ceske Budejovice, TCH	D					
242	MIN	Mike Nightengale	Simley H.S.	D					
243	NYR	Scott Brower	Lloydminster Jr.	G					
244	QUE	Peter Loob	Sodertalje, SWE	D	8	1	2	3	0
245	PHI	Juraj Bakos	VSZ Kosice, TCH	D					
246	WSH	Per Schedrin	Brynas Gavle, SWE	D					
247	BUF	Sean Baker	Seattle	LW					
248	BOS	Jim Newhouse	Matignon H.S.	LW					
249	NYI	Allister Brown	New Hampshire	D					
250	EDM	Darren Gani	Belleville	D					

1985

PICK	TEAM	NAME	DRAFTED FROM	NHL PLAYERS: POS / NHL GOALTENDERS: POS	GP / GP	G / W	A / GA	PTS / SO	PIM / AVG
FIRST ROUND									
1	TOR	Wendel Clark	Saskatoon	LW/D	793	330	234	564	1690
2	PIT	Craig Simpson	Michigan State	LW	634	247	250	497	659
3	N.J.	Craig Wolanin	Kitchener	D	695	40	133	173	894
4	VAN	Jim Sandlak	Calgary	RW	549	110	119	229	821
5	HFD	Dana Murzyn	London	D	838	52	152	204	1571
6	NYI	Brad Dalgarno	Hamilton	RW	321	49	71	120	332
7	NYR	Ulf Dahlen	Ostersund, SWE	RW	761	246	272	518	202
8	DET	Brent Fedyk	Regina	LW	470	97	112	209	308
9	L.A.	Craig Duncanson	Sudbury	LW	38	5	4	9	61
10	L.A.	Dan Gratton	Oshawa	C	7	1	0	1	5
11	CHI	Dave Manson	Prince Albert	D	982	98	279	377	2666
12	MTL	Jose Charbonneau	Drummondville	RW	71	9	13	22	67
13	NYI	Derek King	Sault Ste. Marie	LW	830	261	351	612	417
14	BUF	Calle Johansson	Vastra Frolunda, SWE	D	932	107	369	476	463
15	QUE	David Latta	Kitchener	LW	36	4	8	12	4
16	MTL	Tom Chorske	Minneapolis SW H.S.	LW	596	115	122	237	225
17	CGY	Chris Biotti	Belmont Hill H.S.	D	Played 3 pro seasons in IHL				
18	WPG	Ryan Stewart	Kamloops	C	3	1	0	1	0
19	WSH	Yvon Corriveau	Toronto	LW	280	48	40	88	310
20	EDM	Scott Metcalfe	Kingston	LW	19	1	2	3	18
21	PHI	Glen Seabrooke	Peterborough	C	19	1	6	7	4
SECOND ROUND									
22	TOR	Ken Spangler	Calgary	D	Lengthy career w/ Flint Gens				
23	PIT	Lee Giffin	Oshawa	RW	27	1	3	4	9
24	N.J.	Sean Burke	Toronto	G	571	218	1704	22	3.16
25	VAN	Troy Gamble	Medicine Hat	G	72	22	229	1	3.61
26	HFD	Kay Whitmore	Peterborough	G	149	59	487	4	3.51
27	CGY	Joe Nieuwendyk	Cornell	C	883	440	417	857	493
28	NYR	Mike Richter	Northwood Prep	G	553	252	1505	22	2.85
29	DET	Jeff Sharples	Kelowna	D	105	14	35	49	70
30	L.A.	Par Edlund	Bjorkloven Umea, SWE	RW	Continues to play in Sweden				
31	BOS	Alain Cote	Quebec	D	119	2	18	20	124
32	N.J.	Eric Weinrich	North Yarmouth Academy	D	759	52	225	277	617
33	MTL	Todd Richards	Armstrong H.S.	D	8	0	4	4	4
34	NYI	Brad Lauer	Regina	LW	323	44	67	111	218
35	BUF	Benoit Hogue	St-Jean	C	771	212	306	518	814
36	QUE	Jason Lafreniere	Hamilton	C	146	34	53	87	22
37	ST.L.	Herb Raglan	Kingston	RW	343	33	56	89	775
38	CGY	Jeff Wenaas	Medicine Hat	C	Canada Nat-Team and IHL				
39	WPG	Roger Ohman	Leksand, SWE	D	Continues to play in Germany				
40	WSH	John Druce	Peterborough	RW	531	113	126	239	347
41	EDM	Todd Carnelley	Kamloops	D	Canada Nat-Team and IHL				
42	PHI	Bruce Rendall	Chatham Jr. B	LW	Mich-State grad played to '99				
OTHER ROUNDS									
43	TOR	Dave Thomlinson	Brandon	LW	42	1	3	4	50
44	ST.L.	Nelson Emerson	Stratford Jr. A	RW	652	179	280	459	496
45	N.J.	Myles O'Connor	Notre Dame Jr. A	D	43	3	4	7	69
46	VAN	Shane Doyle	Belleville	D					
47	MTL	Rocky Dundas	Spokane	RW	5	0	0	0	14
48	PHI	Darryl Gilmour	Moose Jaw	G					

PICK	TEAM	NAME	DRAFTED FROM	NHL PLAYERS: POS / NHL GOALTENDERS: POS	GP / GP	G / W	A / GA	PTS / SO	PIM / AVG
49	NYR	Sam Lindstahl	Sodertalje, SWE	G					
50	DET	Steve Chiasson	Guelph	D	751	93	305	398	1107
51	MIN	Stephane Roy	Granby	C	12	1	0	1	0
52	BOS	Bill Ranford	New Westminster	G	647	240	2042	15	3.41
53	CHI	Andy Helmuth	Ottawa	G					
54	ST.L.	Ned Desmond	Hotchkiss H.S.	D					
55	NYI	Jeff Finley	Portland	D	441	10	52	62	309
56	BUF	Keith Gretzky	Windsor	C					
57	QUE	Max Middendorf	Sudbury	RW	13	2	4	6	6
58	PIT	Bruce Racine	Northeastern	G	11	0	12	0	3.13
59	CGY	Lane Macdonald	Harvard	LW					
60	WPG	Daniel Berthiaume	Chicoutimi	G	215	81	714	5	3.67
61	WSH	Rob Murray	Peterborough	C	107	4	15	19	111
62	EDM	Michael Ware	Hamilton	RW	5	0	1	1	15
63	PHI	Shane Whelan	Oshawa	C					
64	TOR	Greg Vey	Peterborough	C					
65	QUE	Peter Massey	New Hampton H.S.	LW					
66	N.J.	Gregg Polak	Lincoln H.S.	LW					
67	VAN	Randy Siska	Medicine Hat	C					
68	HFD	Gary Callaghan	Belleville	C					
69	MIN	Mike Berger	Lethbridge	D	30	3	1	4	67
70	NYR	Pat Janostin	Notre Dame Jr. A	D					
71	DET	Mark Gowans	Windsor	G					
72	L.A.	Perry Florio	Kent Prep	D					
73	BOS	Jaime Kelly	Scituate H.S.	RW					
74	CHI	Dan Vincelette	Drummondville	LW	193	20	22	42	351
75	MTL	Martin Desjardins	Trois-Rivieres	C	8	0	2	2	2
76	NYI	Kevin Herom	Moose Jaw	LW					
77	BUF	Dave Moylan	Sudbury	D					
78	QUE	David Espe	White Bear Lake H.S.	D					
79	MTL	Brent Gilchrist	Kelowna	LW	646	130	154	284	331
80	CGY	Roger Johansson	Troja-Ljungby, SWE	D	161	9	34	43	163
81	WPG	Fredrik Olausson	Farjestad Karlstad, SWE	D	931	143	415	558	406
82	WSH	Bill Houlder	North Bay	D	601	53	167	220	286
83	WSH	Larry Shaw	Peterborough	D					
84	PHI	Paul Marshall	Northwood Prep	D					
85	TOR	Jeff Serowik	Lawrence Academy	D	28	0	6	6	16
86	PIT	Steve Gotaas	Prince Albert	C	49	6	9	15	53
87	CHI	Rick Herbert	Portland	D					
88	VAN	Robert Kron	Zetor Brno, TCH	LW	653	132	172	304	105
89	NYI	Tommy Hedlund	AIK Solna, SWE	D					
90	MIN	Dwight Mullins	Lethbridge	C					
91	NYR	Brad Stephan	Hastings H.S.	LW					
92	DET	Chris Luongo	St. Clair Shores H.S.	D	218	8	23	31	176
93	L.A.	Petr Prajsler	Tesla Pardubice, TCH	D	46	3	10	13	51
94	BOS	Steve Moore	London Jr. B	D					
95	CHI	Brad Belland	Sudbury	C					
96	MTL	Tom Sagissor	Hastings H.S.	C					
97	NYI	Jeff Sveen	Boston U.	C					
98	BUF	Ken Priestlay	Victoria	C	168	27	34	61	63
99	QUE	Bruce Major	Richmond Jr.	C	4	0	0	0	0
100	ST.L.	Dan Brooks	St. Thomas Academy	D					
101	CGY	Esa Keskinen	TPS Turku, FIN	C					
102	WPG	John Borrell	Burnsville H.S.	RW					
103	WSH	Claude Dumas	Granby	C					
104	EDM	Tomas Kapusta	TJ Gottwaldov, TCH	C					
105	PHI	Daril Holmes	Kingston	RW					
106	TOR	Jiri Latal	Sparta Praha, TCH	D	92	12	36	48	24
107	PIT	Kevin Clemens	Regina	LW					
108	N.J.	Bill McMillan	Peterborough	RW					
109	VAN	Martin Hrstka	Ingstav Brno, TCH	LW					
110	HFD	Shane Churla	Medicine Hat	RW	488	26	45	71	2301
111	MIN	Michael Mullowney	Deerfield Academy	D					
112	NYR	Brian McReynolds	Orillia Jr. A	C	30	1	5	6	8
113	DET	Randy McKay	Michigan Tech	RW	711	126	157	283	1537
114	PIT	Stuart Marston	Longueuil	D					
115	BOS	Gord Hynes	Medicine Hat	D	52	3	9	12	22
116	CHI	Jonas Heed	Sodertalje, SWE	D					
117	MTL	Donald Dufresne	Trois-Rivieres	D	268	6	36	42	258
118	NYI	Rod Dallman	Prince Albert	LW	6	1	0	1	26
119	BUF	Joe Reekie	Cornwall	D	773	21	124	145	1180
120	QUE	Andy Akervik	Claire H.S.	C					
121	ST.L.	Rich Burchill	Catholic Memorial H.S.	G					
122	CGY	Tim Sweeney	Weymouth North H.S.	LW	291	55	83	138	123
123	WPG	Danton Cole	Aurora Jr. A	C/RW	318	58	60	118	125
124	WSH	Doug Stromback	Kitchener	RW					
125	EDM	Brian Tessier	North Bay	G					
126	PHI	Ken Alexander	Kitchener	D					
127	TOR	Tim Bean	North Bay	LW					
128	PIT	Steve Titus	Cornwall	G					
129	N.J.	Kevin Schrader	Burnsville H.S.	D					
130	VAN	Brian McFarlane	Seattle	RW					
131	HFD	Chris Brant	Sault Ste. Marie	LW					
132	MIN	Michael Kelfer	St. John's Prep	C					
133	NYR	Neil Pilon	Kamloops	D					
134	DET	Thomas Bjur	AIK Solna, SWE	RW					
135	L.A.	Tim Flannigan	Michigan Tech	RW					
136	BOS	Per Martinelle	AIK Solna, SWE	RW					
137	CHI	Victor Posa	Wisconsin	LW/D	2	0	0	0	2
138	ST.L.	Pat Jablonski	Detroit Compuware Jr. A	G	128	28	413	1	3.74
139	NYI	Kurt Lackten	Moose Jaw	RW					
140	BUF	Petri Matikainen	SaPKo Savolinna, FIN	D					
141	QUE	Mike Oliverio	Sault Ste. Marie	C					
142	MTL	Ed Cristofoli	Penticton Jr. A	RW	9	0	1	1	4
143	CGY	Stu Grimson	Regina	LW	627	13	19	32	1802
144	WPG	Brent Mowery	Summerland Jr.	LW					
145	WSH	Jamie Nadjiwan	Sudbury	LW					
146	EDM	Shawn Tyers	Kitchener	RW					
147	PHI	Tony Horacek	Kelowna	LW	154	10	19	29	316
148	TOR	Andy Donahue	Belmont Hill H.S.	C					
149	PIT	Paul Stanton	Catholic Memorial H.S.	D	295	14	49	63	262
150	N.J.	Ed Krayer	St. Paul's H.S.	C					
151	VAN	Hakan Ahlund	Orebro, SWE	RW					
152	HFD	Brian Puhalsky	Notre Dame Jr. A	LW					
153	MIN	Ross Johnson	Mayo H.S.	C					
154	NYR	Larry Bernard	Seattle	LW					
155	DET	Mike Luckraft	Burnsville H.S.	D					
156	L.A.	John Hyduke	Hibbing H.S.	D					
157	BOS	Randy Burridge	Peterborough	LW	706	199	251	450	458
158	CHI	John Reid	Belleville	G					
159	ST.L.	Scott Brickey	Port Huron Jr.	RW					
160	NYI	Hank Lammens	St. Lawrence U.	D	27	1	2	3	22
161	BUF	Trent Kaese	Lethbridge	RW	1	0	0	0	0
162	QUE	Mario Brunetta	Quebec	G	40	12	128	0	3.90
163	MTL	Mike Claringbull	Medicine Hat	D					
164	CGY	Nate Smith	Lawrence Academy	D					
165	WPG	Tom Draper	Vermont	G	53	19	173	1	3.70
166	WSH	Mark Haarmann	Oshawa	D					
167	EDM	Tony Fairfield	St. Albert Jr. A	RW					
168	PHI	Mike Cusack	Dubuque Jr. A	RW					
169	TOR	Todd Whittemore	Kent Prep	C					
170	PIT	Jim Paek	Oshawa	D	217	5	29	34	155
171	N.J.	Jamie Huscroft	Seattle	D	352	5	33	38	1065
172	VAN	Curtis Hunt	Prince Albert	D					
173	HFD	Greg Dornbach	Miami of Ohio	C					
174	MIN	Tim Helmer	Ottawa	C					
175	NYR	Stephane Brochu	Quebec	D	1	0	0	0	0
176	DET	Rob Schenna	St. John's Prep	D					
177	L.A.	Steve Horner	Henry Carr Jr. B	RW					
178	BOS	Gord Cruickshank	Providence	C					
179	CHI	Richard Laplante	Vermont	C					
180	ST.L.	Jeff Urban	Minnetonka H.S.	LW					
181	NYI	Rich Wiest	Lethbridge	C					
182	BUF	Jiri Sejba	Dukla Jihlava, TCH	LW	11	0	2	2	8
183	QUE	Brit Peer	Sault Ste. Marie	RW					
184	MTL	Roger Beedon	Sarnia Jr. B	G					
185	CGY	Darryl Olsen	St. Albert Jr. A	D	1	0	0	0	0
186	WPG	Nevin Kardum	Henry Carr Jr. B	C					
187	WSH	Steve Hollett	Sault Ste. Marie	C					
188	EDM	Kelly Buchberger	Moose Jaw	RW	876	89	171	260	1899
189	PHI	Gord Murphy	Oshawa	D	820	82	225	307	643
190	TOR	Bobby Reynolds	St. Clair Shores H.S.	LW	7	1	1	2	0
191	PIT	Steve Shaunessy	Reading H.S.	D					
192	N.J.	Terry Shold	International Falls H.S.	LW					
193	VAN	Carl Valimont	University of Lowell	D					
194	HFD	Paul Tory	Illinois-Chicago	C					
195	MIN	Gordon Ernst	Cranston East H.S.	C					
196	NYR	Steve Nemeth	Lethbridge	C	12	2	0	2	2
197	DET	Erik Hamalainen	Lukko Rauma, FIN	D					
198	MTL	Maurice Mansi	RPI	C					
199	BOS	Dave Buda	Streetsville Jr. B	LW					
200	CHI	Brad Hamilton	Aurora Jr. A	D					
201	ST.L.	Vince Guidotti	Noble and Greenough H.S.	D					
202	NYI	Real Arsenault	Prince Andrew H.S.	LW					
203	BUF	Boyd Sutton	Stratford Jr. B	C					
204	QUE	Tom Sasso	Babson College	C					
205	MTL	Chad Arthur	Stratford Jr. B	LW					
206	CGY	Peter Romberg	Iserlohn, FRG	D					
207	WPG	Dave Quigley	U. of Moncton	G					
208	WSH	Dallas Eakins	Peterborough	D	100	0	8	8	193
209	EDM	Mario Barbe	Chicoutimi	D					
210	BOS	Bob Beers	Buffalo Jr.	D	258	28	79	107	225
211	TOR	Tim Armstrong	Toronto	C	11	1	0	1	6
212	PIT	Doug Greschuk	St. Albert Jr. A	D					
213	N.J.	Jamie McKinley	Guelph	C					
214	VAN	Igor Larionov	CSKA Moscow, USSR	C	663	138	369	507	318
215	HFD	Jerry Pawlowski	Harvard	C					
216	MIN	Ladislav Lubina	Tesla Pardubice, TCH	RW					
217	NYR	Robert Burakovsky	Leksand, SWE	RW	23	2	3	5	6
218	DET	Bo Svanberg	Farjestad Karlstad, SWE	C					
219	L.A.	Trent Ciprick	Brandon	RW					
220	BOS	John Byce	Madison Memorial H.S.	C	21	2	3	5	6
221	CHI	Ian Pound	Kitchener	D					
222	ST.L.	Ron Saatzer	Hopkins H.S.	C					

PICK	TEAM	NAME	DRAFTED FROM	NHL PLAYERS: POS / NHL GOALTENDERS: POS	GP / GP	G / W	A / GA	PTS / SO	PIM / AVG
223	NYI	Mike Volpe	St. Mary's U.	G					
224	BUF	Guy Larose	Guelph	C	70	10	9	19	63
225	QUE	Gary Murphy	Arlington Catholic H.S.	D					
226	MTL	Mike Bishop	Sarnia Jr. B	D					
227	CGY	Alexander Kozhevnikov	Spartak Moscow, USSR	LW					
228	WPG	Chris Norton	Cornell	D					
229	WSH	Steve Hrynewich	Ottawa	LW					
230	EDM	Peter Headon	Notre Dame Jr. A	C					
231	PHI	Rod Williams	Kelowna	RW					
232	TOR	Mitch Murphy	St. Paul's H.S.	G					
233	PIT	Gregory Choules	Chicoutimi	LW					
234	N.J.	David Williams	Choate	D	173	11	53	64	157
235	VAN	Darren Taylor	Calgary	LW					
236	HFD	Bruce Hill	U. of Denver	LW					
237	MIN	Tommy Sjodin	Timra, SWE	D	106	8	40	48	52
238	NYR	Rudy Poeschek	Kamloops	RW/D	364	6	25	31	817
239	DET	Mikael Lindman	AIK Solna, SWE	D					
240	L.A.	Marian Horwath	Slovan Bratislava, TCH	LW					
241	BOS	Marc West	Burlington Jr. B	C					
242	CHI	Rick Braccia	Avon Old Farms H.S.	LW					
243	ST.L.	Dave Jecha	Minnetonka H.S.	D					
244	NYI	Tony Grenier	Prince Albert	C					
245	BUF	Ken Baumgartner	Prince Albert	LW	696	13	41	54	2244
246	QUE	Jean Bois	Trois-Rivieres	LW					
247	MTL	John Ferguson Jr.	Winnipeg South Blues Jr.	LW					
248	CGY	Bill Gregoire	Victoria	D					
249	WPG	Anssi Melametsa	HIFK Helsinki, FIN	LW	27	0	3	3	2
250	WSH	Frank Di Muzio	Belleville	C					
251	EDM	John Haley	Hull H.S.	G					
252	PHI	Paul Maurice	Windsor	D					

1986

FIRST ROUND

PICK	TEAM	NAME	DRAFTED FROM	NHL PLAYERS: POS / NHL GOALTENDERS: POS	GP / GP	G / W	A / GA	PTS / SO	PIM / AVG
1	DET	Joe Murphy	Michigan State	RW	765	232	290	522	790
2	L.A.	Jimmy Carson	Verdun	C	626	275	286	561	254
3	N.J.	Neil Brady	Medicine Hat	C	89	9	22	31	95
4	PIT	Zarley Zalapski	Canadian National	D	637	99	285	384	684
5	BUF	Shawn Anderson	Canadian National	D	255	11	51	62	117
6	TOR	Vincent Damphousse	Laval	C	1087	368	631	999	936
7	VAN	Dan Woodley	Portland	RW	5	2	0	2	17
8	WPG	Pat Elynuik	Prince Albert	RW	506	154	188	342	459
9	NYR	Brian Leetch	Avon Old Farms H.S.	D	857	184	597	781	419
10	ST.L.	Jocelyn Lemieux	Laval	RW	598	80	84	164	740
11	HFD	Scott Young	Boston U.	RW	822	234	302	536	296
12	MIN	Warren Babe	Lethbridge	LW	21	2	5	7	23
13	BOS	Craig Janney	Boston College	C	760	188	563	751	170
14	CHI	Everett Sanipass	Verdun	LW	164	25	34	59	358
15	MTL	Mark Pederson	Medicine Hat	LW	169	35	50	85	77
16	CGY	George Pelawa	Bemidji H.S.	RW	Died in car accident				
17	NYI	Tom Fitzgerald	Austin Prep	RW/C	731	107	140	247	517
18	QUE	Ken McRae	Sudbury	C	137	14	21	35	364
19	WSH	Jeff Greenlaw	Canadian National	LW	57	3	6	9	108
20	PHI	Kerry Huffman	Guelph	D	401	37	108	145	361
21	EDM	Kim Issel	Prince Albert	RW	4	0	0	0	0

SECOND ROUND

PICK	TEAM	NAME	DRAFTED FROM	POS	GP	G	A	PTS	PIM
22	DET	Adam Graves	Windsor	C	907	293	248	541	1064
23	PHI	Jukka Seppo	Sport Vaasa, FIN	LW	Continues to play in Germany				
24	N.J.	Todd Copeland	Belmont Hill H.S.	D	Grinder played 7 pro seasons				
25	PIT	Dave Capuano	Mount St. Charles H.S.	LW	104	17	38	55	56
26	BUF	Greg Brown	St. Mark's H.S.	D	94	4	14	18	86
27	MTL	Benoit Brunet	Hull	LW	443	89	136	225	205
28	PHI	Kent Hawley	Ottawa	C	Offensive wizard in ColHL/UHL				
29	WPG	Teppo Numminen	Tappara Tampere, FIN	D	872	84	341	425	319
30	MIN	Neil Wilkinson	Selkirk Jr.	D	460	16	67	83	813
31	ST.L.	Mike Posma	Buffalo Jr.	D	Continues to play in Switz-2				
32	HFD	Marc Laforge	Kingston	LW	14	0	0	0	64
33	MIN	Dean Kolstad	Prince Albert	D	40	1	7	8	69
34	BOS	Pekka Tirkkonen	SaPKo Savolinna, FIN	C	Continues to play in Finland				
35	CHI	Mark Kurzawski	Windsor	D	Played 85 games in IHL				
36	TOR	Darryl Shannon	Windsor	D	537	28	110	138	517
37	CGY	Brian Glynn	Saskatoon	D	431	25	79	104	410
38	NYI	Dennis Vaske	Armstrong H.S.	D	235	5	41	46	253
39	QUE	Jean-Marc Routhier	Hull	RW	8	0	0	0	9
40	WSH	Steve Seftel	Kingston	LW	4	0	0	0	2
41	QUE	Stephane Guerard	Shawinigan	D	34	0	0	0	40
42	EDM	Jamie Nichols	Portland	LW	Played 11years in France/USA				

OTHER ROUNDS

PICK	TEAM	NAME	DRAFTED FROM	NHL PLAYERS: POS / NHL GOALTENDERS: POS	GP / GP	G / W	A / GA	PTS / SO	PIM / AVG
43	DET	Derek Mayer	U. of Denver	D	17	2	2	4	8
44	L.A.	Denis Larocque	Guelph	D	8	0	1	1	18
45	N.J.	Janne Ojanen	Tappara Tampere, FIN	C	98	21	23	44	28
46	PIT	Brad Aitken	Sault Ste. Marie	LW	14	1	3	4	25
47	BUF	Bob Corkum	U. of Maine	C	570	87	91	178	239
48	TOR	Sean Boland	Toronto	D					
49	VAN	Don Gibson	Winkler Jr. A	D	14	0	3	3	20
50	WPG	Esa Palosaari	Karpat Oulu, FIN	RW					
51	NYR	Bret Walter	U. of Alberta	C					
52	ST.L.	Tony Hejna	Nichols H.S.	LW					
53	NYR	Shawn Clouston	U. of Alberta	RW					
54	MIN	Rick Bennett	Wilbraham Monson H.S.	LW	15	1	1	2	13
55	MIN	Rob Zettler	Sault Ste. Marie	D	491	4	57	61	809
56	BUF	Kevin Kerr	Windsor	RW					
57	MTL	Jyrki Lumme	Ilves Tampere, FIN	D	788	100	313	413	508
58	MIN	Brad Turner	Calgary	D	3	0	0	0	0
59	NYI	Bill Berg	Toronto	LW	546	55	67	122	488
60	WSH	Shawn Simpson	Sault Ste. Marie	G					
61	WSH	Jim Hrivnak	Merrimack	G	85	34	262	0	3.73
62	N.J.	Marc Laniel	Oshawa	D					
63	EDM	Ron Shudra	Kamloops	D	10	0	5	5	6
64	DET	Tim Cheveldae	Saskatoon	G	340	149	1116	10	3.49
65	L.A.	Sylvain Couturier	Laval	C	33	4	5	9	4
66	N.J.	Anders Carlsson	Sodertalje, SWE	C	104	7	26	33	34
67	PIT	Rob Brown	Kamloops	RW	543	191	248	438	599
68	BUF	David Baseggio	Yale	D					
69	TOR	Kent Hulst	Windsor	C					
70	VAN	Ron Stern	Longueuil	RW	638	75	86	161	2077
71	WPG	Hannu Jarvenpaa	Karpat Oulu, FIN	RW	114	11	26	37	83
72	NYR	Mark Janssens	Regina	C	683	40	73	113	1389
73	ST.L.	Glen Featherstone	Windsor	D	384	19	61	80	939
74	HFD	Brian Chapman	Belleville	D	3	0	0	0	29
75	MIN	Kirk Tomlinson	Hamilton	C	1	0	0	0	0
76	BOS	Dean Hall	St. James Jr. A	C					
77	CHI	Frantisek Kucera	Sparta Praha, TCH	D	354	21	75	96	227
78	MTL	Brent Bobyck	Notre Dame Midgets	LW					
79	CGY	Tom Quinlan	Hill-Murray H.S.	RW					
80	NYI	Shawn Byram	Regina	LW	5	0	0	0	14
81	QUE	Ron Tugnutt	Peterborough	G	398	134	1159	15	3.22
82	WSH	Erin Ginnell	Calgary	C					
83	PHI	Mark Bar	Peterborough	D					
84	EDM	Dan Currie	Sault Ste. Marie	LW	22	2	1	3	4
85	DET	Johan Garpenlov	Nacka, SWE	LW	609	114	197	311	276
86	L.A.	Dave Guden	Roxbury Latin	LW					
87	ST.L.	Michael Wolak	Kitchener	C					
88	PIT	Sandy Smith	Brainerd H.S.	C					
89	BUF	Larry Rooney	Thayer Academy	F					
90	TOR	Scott Taylor	Kitchener	D					
91	VAN	Eric Murano	Calgary	C					
92	WPG	Craig Endean	Seattle	LW	2	0	1	1	0
93	NYR	Jeff Bloemberg	North Bay	D	43	3	6	9	25
94	MTL	Eric Aubertin	Granby	LW					
95	HFD	Bill Horn	Western Michigan	G					
96	MIN	Jari Gronstrand	Tappara Tampere, FIN	D	185	8	26	34	135
97	BOS	Matt Pesklewis	St. Albert Jr. A	LW					
98	CHI	Lonnie Loach	Guelph	LW	56	10	13	23	29
99	MTL	Mario Milani	Verdun	RW					
100	CGY	Scott Bloom	Burnsville H.S.	LW					
101	NYI	Dean Sexsmith	Brandon	C					
102	QUE	Gerald Bzdel	Regina	D					
103	WSH	John Purves	Hamilton	RW	7	1	0	1	0
104	NYI	Todd McLellan	Saskatoon	C	5	1	1	2	0
105	EDM	David Haas	London	LW	7	2	1	3	7
106	DET	Jay Stark	Portland	D					
107	L.A.	Robb Stauber	Duluth Denfield H.S.	G	62	21	209	1	3.81
108	N.J.	Troy Crowder	Hamilton	RW	150	9	7	16	433
109	PIT	Jeff Daniels	Oshawa	LW	234	12	20	32	48
110	BUF	Miguel Baldris	Shawinigan	D					
111	TOR	Stephane Giguere	St-Jean	LW					
112	VAN	Steve Herniman	Cornwall	D					
113	WPG	Robertson Bateman	St. Laurent College	RW					
114	NYR	Darren Turcotte	North Bay	C	635	195	216	411	301
115	ST.L.	Mike O' Toole	Markham Jr. B	W					
116	HFD	Joe Quinn	Calgary	RW					
117	QUE	Scott White	Michigan Tech	D					
118	BOS	Garth Premak	New Westminster	D					
119	CHI	Mario Doyon	Drummondville	D	28	3	4	7	16
120	MTL	Steve Bisson	Sault Ste. Marie	D					
121	CGY	John Parker	White Bear Lake H.S.	C					
122	NYI	Tony Schmalzbauer	Hill-Murray H.S.	D					
123	QUE	Morgan Samuelsson	Boden, SWE	F					
124	WSH	Stefan Nilsson	Lulea, SWE	C	Re-entered Draft in 1988				
125	PHI	Steve Scheifele	Stratford Jr. B	RW					
126	EDM	Jim Ennis	Boston U.	D	5	1	0	1	10
127	DET	Per Djoos	Mora, SWE	D	82	2	31	33	58
128	L.A.	Sean Krakiwsky	Calgary	RW					
129	N.J.	Kevin Todd	Prince Albert	C	383	70	133	203	225
130	PIT	Doug Hobson	Prince Albert	D					
131	BUF	Mike Hartman	North Bay	LW	397	43	35	78	1388
132	TOR	Danny Hie	Ottawa	C					
133	VAN	Jon Helgeson	Roseau H.S.	C					
134	QUE	Mark Vermette	Lake Superior State	RW	67	5	13	18	33
135	NYR	Robb Graham	Guelph	RW					
136	ST.L.	Andy May	Bramalea Jr. B						
137	HFD	Steve Torrel	Hibbing H.S.	C					

PICK	TEAM	NAME	DRAFTED FROM	NHL PLAYERS: POS / NHL GOALTENDERS: POS	GP / GP	G / W	A / GA	PTS / SO	PIM / AVG
138	NYI	Will Anderson	Victoria						
139	BOS	Paul Beraldo	Sault Ste. Marie	RW	10	0	0	0	4
140	CHI	Mike Hudson	Sudbury	C/LW	416	49	87	136	414
141	MTL	Lyle Odelein	Moose Jaw	D	721	34	155	189	1885
142	CGY	Rick Lessard	Ottawa	D	15	0	4	4	18
143	NYI	Rich Pilon	Prince Albert AAA	D	554	6	58	64	1561
144	QUE	Jean F. Nault	Granby	C					
145	WSH	Peter Choma	Belleville	RW					
146	PHI	Sami Wahlsten	TPS Turku, FIN	W					
147	EDM	Ivan Matulik	Slovan Bratislava, TCH	LW					
148	DET	Dean Morton	Oshawa	D	1	1	0	1	2
149	L.A.	Rene Chapdelaine	Lake Superior State	D	32	0	2	2	32
150	N.J.	Ryan Pardoski	Calgary	LW					
151	PIT	Steve Rohlik	Hill-Murray H.S.						
152	BUF	Francois Guay	Laval	C	1	0	0	0	0
153	TOR	Stephen Brennan	New Prep H.S.	W					
154	VAN	Jeff Noble	Kitchener	C					
155	WPG	Frank Furlan	Sherwood Park Jr. A	G					
156	NYR	Barry Chyzowski	St. Albert Jr. A	C					
157	ST.L.	Randy Skarda	St. Thomas Academy	D	26	0	5	5	11
158	HFD	Ron Hoover	Western Michigan	C	18	4	0	4	31
159	MIN	Scott Mathias	U. of Denver	C					
160	BOS	Brian Ferreira	Falmouth H.S.	RW					
161	CHI	Marty Nanne	Minnesota-Duluth	RW					
162	MTL	Rick Hayward	Hull	D	4	0	0	0	5
163	CGY	Mark Olsen	Colorado College	D					
164	NYI	Peter Harris	Haverhill H.S.	G					
165	QUE	Keith Miller	Guelph	LW					
166	WSH	Lee Davidson	Penticton Jr. A	C					
167	PHI	Murray Baron	Vernon Jr. A	D	687	28	71	99	1055
168	EDM	Nicolas Beaulieu	Drummondville	LW					
169	DET	Marc Potvin	Stratford Jr. B	RW	121	3	5	8	456
170	L.A.	Trevor Pochipinski	Penticton Jr. A	D					
171	N.J.	Scott McCormack	St Paul's Prep						
172	PIT	Dave McLlwain	North Bay	C/RW	501	100	107	207	292
173	BUF	Shawn Whitham	Providence	D					
174	TOR	Brian Bellefeuille	Canterbury H.S.	LW					
175	VAN	Matt Merton	Stratford Jr. B	G					
176	WPG	Mark Green	New Hampton H.S.	C					
177	NYR	Pat Scanlon	Cretin H.S.						
178	ST.L.	Martyn Ball	St. Michael's Jr. B	LW					
179	HFD	Robert Glasgow	Sherwood Park Jr. A	RW					
180	MIN	Lance Pitlick	Cooper H.S.	D	290	14	30	44	244
181	BOS	Jeff Flaherty	Weymouth H.S.	RW					
182	CHI	Geoff Benic	Windsor	LW					
183	MTL	Antonin Routa	Poldi SNOP Kladno, TCH	D					
184	CGY	Scott Sharples	Penticton Jr. A	G	1	0	4	0	3.69
185	NYI	Jeff Jablonski	London Jr. B	LW					
186	QUE	Pierre Millier	Chicoutimi	D					
187	WSH	Tero Toivola	Tappara Tampere, FIN	W					
188	PHI	Blaine Rude	Fergus Falls	RW					
189	EDM	Mike Greenlay	Calgary Midget AAA	G	2	0	4	0	12.00
190	DET	Scott King	Vernon Jr. A	G	2	0	3	0	2.95
191	L.A.	Paul Kelly	Guelph	D					
192	N.J.	Frederic Chabot	St. Foy Midget AAA	G	32	4	62	0	2.95
193	PIT	Kelly Cain	London	C					
194	BUF	Kenton Rein	Prince Albert	G					
195	TOR	Sean Davidson	Toronto	RW					
196	VAN	Marc Lyons	Kingston	D					
197	WPG	John Blue	Minnesota-Duluth	G	46	16	126	1	3.00
198	NYR	Joe Ranger	London	D					
199	ST.L.	Rod Thacker	Hamilton	D					
200	HFD	Sean Evoy	Cornwall	G					
201	MIN	Dan Keczmer	Detroit Little Caesar's	D	235	8	38	46	212
202	BOS	Greg Hawgood	Kamloops	D	456	58	159	217	418
203	CHI	Glen Lowes	Toronto						
204	MTL	Eric Bohemier	Hull	G					
205	CGY	Doug Pickell	Kamloops	LW					
206	NYI	Kerry Clark	Saskatoon	RW					
207	QUE	Chris Lappin	Canterbury H.S.	D					
208	WSH	Bobby Babcock	Sault Ste. Marie	D	2	0	0	0	2
209	PHI	Shaun Sabol	St. Paul Jr. A	D	2	0	0	0	0
210	EDM	Matt Lanza	Winthrop H.S.	D					
211	DET	Tom Bissett	Michigan Tech	C	5	0	0	0	0
212	L.A.	Russ Mann	St. Lawrence U.	D					
213	N.J.	John Andersen	Oshawa	LW					
214	PIT	Stan Drulia	Belleville	RW	92	13	23	36	34
215	BUF	Tony Arndt	Portland	D					
216	TOR	Mark Holick	Saskatoon	RW					
217	VAN	Todd Hawkins	Belleville	L/RW	10	0	0	0	15
218	WPG	Matt Cote	Lake Superior State						
219	NYR	Russell Parent	South Winnipeg Jr.	D					
220	ST.L.	Terry MacLean	Longueuil	C					
221	HFD	Cal Brown	Penticton Jr. A	D					
222	MIN	Garth Joy	Hamilton	D					
223	BOS	Steffan Malmqvist	Leksand, SWE	F					
224	CHI	Chris Thayer	Kent Prep	C					
225	MTL	Charlie Moore	Belleville	LW					
226	CGY	Anders Lindstrom	Timra, SWE	C					
227	NYI	Dan Beaudette	St. Thomas Academy						
228	QUE	Martin Latreille	Laval	D					
229	WSH	John Schratz	Amherst Jr. B	D					
230	PHI	Brett Lawrence	Rochester Jr. B	RW					
231	EDM	Mojmir Bozik	VSZ Kosice, TCH	D					
232	DET	Peter Ekroth	Sodertalje, SWE	D					
233	L.A.	Brian Hayton	Guelph	LW					
234	ST.L.	Bill Butler	Northwood Prep	LW					
235	PIT	Rob Wilson	Sudbury	D					
236	N.J.	Doug Kirton	Orillia Jr. A	W					
237	TOR	Brian Hoard	Hamilton	D					
238	VAN	Vladimir Krutov	CSKA Moscow, USSR	LW	61	11	23	34	20
239	WPG	Arto Blomsten	Djurgarden Stockholm, SWE	D	25	0	4	4	8
240	NYR	Soren True	Skovbakken, DEN	W					
241	ST.L.	David O'Brien	Northeastern	RW					
242	HFD	Brian Verbeek	Kingston	C					
243	MIN	Kurt Stahura	Williston Academy	LW					
244	BOS	Joel Gardner	Sarnia Jr. B	C					
245	CHI	Sean Williams	Oshawa	C	2	0	0	0	4
246	MTL	Karel Svoboda	Skoda Plzen, TCH	W					
247	CGY	Antonin Stavjana	TJ Gottwaldov, TCH	D					
248	NYI	Paul Thompson	Northern Manitoba AAA	D					
249	QUE	Sean Boudreault	Mount St. Charles H.S.	F					
250	WSH	Scott McCrory	Oshawa	C					
251	PHI	Daniel Stephano	Northwood Prep	G					
252	EDM	Tony Hand	Murrayfield Racers, GBR	C					

1987

PICK	TEAM	NAME	DRAFTED FROM	NHL PLAYERS: POS / NHL GOALTENDERS: POS	GP / GP	G / W	A / GA	PTS / SO	PIM / AVG
FIRST ROUND									
1	BUF	Pierre Turgeon	Granby	C	929	423	640	1063	319
2	N.J.	Brendan Shanahan	London	LW	947	435	444	879	1854
3	BOS	Glen Wesley	Portland	D	955	113	337	450	717
4	L.A.	Wayne McBean	Medicine Hat	D	211	10	39	49	168
5	PIT	Chris Joseph	Seattle	D	467	38	108	146	531
6	MIN	Dave Archibald	Portland	C/LW	323	57	67	124	139
7	TOR	Luke Richardson	Peterborough	D	947	28	115	143	1571
8	CHI	Jimmy Waite	Chicoutimi	G	106	28	293	4	3.35
9	QUE	Bryan Fogarty	Kingston	D	156	22	52	74	119
10	NYR	Jay More	New Westminster	D	406	18	54	72	702
11	DET	Yves Racine	Longueuil	D	508	37	194	231	439
12	ST.L.	Keith Osborne	North Bay	RW	16	1	3	4	16
13	NYI	Dean Chynoweth	Medicine Hat	D	241	4	18	22	667
14	BOS	Stephane Quintal	Granby	D	750	48	142	190	1021
15	QUE	Joe Sakic	Swift Current	C	852	403	657	1060	368
16	WPG	Bryan Marchment	Belleville	D	586	27	94	121	1603
17	MTL	Andrew Cassels	Ottawa	C	728	151	369	520	308
18	HFD	Jody Hull	Peterborough	RW	665	112	119	231	126
19	CGY	Bryan Deasley	Michigan	LW	Mich-grad played 4 years in IHL				
20	PHI	Darren Rumble	Kitchener	D	157	10	22	32	181
21	EDM	Peter Soberlak	Swift Current	LW	Played 3 pro seasons in AHL				
SECOND ROUND									
22	BUF	Brad Miller	Regina	D	82	1	5	6	321
23	N.J.	Ricard Persson	Ostersund, SWE	D	162	7	29	36	185
24	VAN	Rob Murphy	Laval	C	125	9	12	21	152
25	CGY	Stephane Matteau	Hull	LW	661	120	145	265	668
26	PIT	Rick Tabaracci	Cornwall	G	286	93	760	15	2.99
27	L.A.	Mark Fitzpatrick	Medicine Hat	G	329	113	953	8	3.12
28	TOR	Daniel Marois	Chicoutimi	RW	350	117	93	210	419
29	CHI	Ryan McGill	Swift Current	D	151	4	15	19	391
30	PHI	Jeff Harding	St. Michael's Jr. B	RW	15	0	0	0	47
31	NYR	Daniel Lacroix	Granby	LW	188	11	7	18	379
32	DET	Gord Kruppke	Prince Albert	D	23	0	0	0	32
33	MTL	John LeClair	Bellows Academy	LW	665	309	306	615	331
34	NYI	Jeff Hackett	Oshawa	G	403	132	1106	22	2.92
35	MIN	Scott McCrady	Medicine Hat	D	Injuries ended career in 1992				
36	WSH	Jeff Ballantyne	Ottawa	D	Did not play professionally				
37	WPG	Patrik Ericksson	Brynas Gavle, SWE	C	Continues to play in Sweden				
38	MTL	Eric Desjardins	Granby	D	827	102	332	434	564
39	HFD	Adam Burt	North Bay	D	710	37	113	150	934
40	CGY	Kevin Grant	Kitchener	D	Continues to play in Germany				
41	DET	Bob Wilkie	Swift Current	D	18	2	5	7	10
42	EDM	Brad Werenka	Northern Michigan	D	287	18	57	75	283
OTHER ROUNDS									
43	L.A.	Ross Wilson	Peterborough	RW					
44	MTL	Mathieu Schneider	Cornwall	D	708	115	260	375	710
45	VAN	Steve Veilleux	Trois-Rivieres	D					
46	NYR	Simon Gagne	Laval	RW					
47	PIT	Jamie Leach	Hamilton	RW	81	11	9	20	12
48	MIN	Kevin Kaminski	Saskatoon	C	139	3	10	13	528
49	TOR	John McIntyre	Guelph	C	351	24	54	78	516

PICK	TEAM	NAME	DRAFTED FROM	NHL PLAYERS: POS / NHL GOALTENDERS: POS	GP / GP	G / W	A / GA	PTS / SO	PIM / AVG
50	CHI	Cam Russell	Hull	D	396	9	21	30	872
51	QUE	Jim Sprott	London	D					
52	DET	Dennis Holland	Portland	C					
53	BUF	Andrew MacVicar	Peterborough	LW					
54	ST.L.	Kevin Miehm	Ottawa	C	22	1	4	5	8
55	NYI	Dean Ewen	Spokane	LW					
56	BOS	Todd Lalonde	Sudbury	LW					
57	WSH	Steve Maltais	Cornwall	LW	94	9	15	24	41
58	MTL	Francois Gravel	Shawinigan	G					
59	ST.L.	Robert Nordmark	Lulea, SWE	D	236	13	70	83	254
60	CHI	Mike Dagenais	Peterborough	D					
61	CGY	Scott Mahoney	Oshawa	LW					
62	PHI	Martin Hostak	Sparta Praha, TCH	C	55	3	11	14	24
63	EDM	Geoff Smith	St. Albert Jr. A	D	462	18	73	91	282
64	EDM	Peter Eriksson	HV 71 Jonkoping, SWE	LW	20	3	3	6	24
65	N.J.	Brian Sullivan	Springfield Jr. B	RW	2	0	1	1	0
66	VAN	Doug Torrel	Hibbing H.S.	C					
67	BOS	Darwin McPherson	New Westminster	D					
68	PIT	Risto Kurkinen	JyP HT Jyvaskyla, FIN	LW					
69	NYR	Mike Sullivan	Boston U.	C	595	48	76	124	171
70	CGY	Tim Harris	Pickering Jr. B	RW					
71	TOR	Joe Sacco	Medford H.S.	RW	570	86	100	186	302
72	QUE	Kip Miller	Michigan State	C	241	43	80	123	67
73	MIN	John Weisbrod	Choate	C					
74	DET	Mark Reimer	Saskatoon	G					
75	ST.L.	Darren Smith	North Bay	LW					
76	NYI	George Maneluk	Brandon	G	4	1	15	0	6.43
77	BOS	Matt DelGuidice	St. Anselm College	G	11	2	28	0	3.87
78	WSH	Tyler Larter	Sault Ste. Marie	C	1	0	0	0	0
79	WPG	Don McLennan	U. of Denver	D					
80	MTL	Kris Miller	Greenway H.S.	D					
81	HFD	Terry Yake	Brandon	C	391	77	117	194	212
82	ST.L.	Andy Rymsha	Western Michigan	D	6	0	0	0	23
83	PHI	Tomaz Eriksson	Djurgarden Stockholm, SWE	LW					
84	BUF	John Bradley	New Hampton H.S.	G					
85	BUF	David Pergola	Belmont Hill H.S.	RW					
86	N.J.	Kevin Dean	Culver Military Academy	D	262	7	37	44	108
87	VAN	Sean Fabian	Hill-Murray H.S.	D					
88	MIN	Teppo Kivela	Jokerit Helsinki, FIN	C					
89	PIT	Jeff Waver	Hamilton	D					
90	L.A.	Mike Vukonich	Duluth Denfield H.S.	C					
91	TOR	Mike Eastwood	Pembroke Jr. A	C	483	67	94	161	213
92	CHI	Ulf Sandstrom	MoDo Ornskoldsvik, SWE	RW					
93	QUE	Rob Mendel	Wisconsin	D					
94	NYR	Eric O'Borsky	Yale	C					
95	DET	Radomir Brazda	Tesla Pardubice, TCH	D					
96	WPG	Ken Gernander	Greenway H.S.	C	10	2	3	5	4
97	NYI	Petr Vlk	Dukla Jihlava, TCH	LW					
98	BOS	Ted Donato	Catholic Memorial H.S.	LW	614	134	174	308	342
99	WSH	Pat Beauchesne	Moose Jaw	D					
100	WPG	Darrin Amundson	Duluth East H.S.	C					
101	MTL	Steve McCool	Hill H.S.	D					
102	HFD	Marc Rousseau	U. of Denver	D					
103	CGY	Tim Corkery	Ferris State	D					
104	PHI	Bill Gall	New Hampton H.S.	RW					
105	EDM	Shaun Van Allen	Saskatoon	C	511	55	126	181	293
106	BUF	Chris Marshall	Boston College H.S.	LW					
107	N.J.	Ben Hankinson	Edina H.S.	RW	43	3	3	6	45
108	VAN	Garry Valk	Sherwood Park Jr. A	LW	624	87	127	214	667
109	MIN	D'arcy Norton	Kamloops	LW					
110	PIT	Shawn McEachern	Matignon H.S.	LW	593	180	192	372	266
111	L.A.	Greg Batters	Victoria	RW					
112	TOR	Damian Rhodes	Richfield H.S.	G	256	90	657	12	2.72
113	CHI	Mike McCormick	Richmond Jr.	D					
114	QUE	Garth Snow	Mount St. Charles H.S.	G	206	77	515	9	2.79
115	NYR	Ludek Cajka	Dukla Jihlava, TCH	D					
116	DET	Sean Clifford	Ohio State	D					
117	ST.L.	Rob Robinson	Miami of Ohio	D	22	0	1	1	8
118	NYI	Rob DiMaio	Medicine Hat	C	560	71	110	181	603
119	BOS	Matt Glennon	Archbishop Williams H.S.	LW	3	0	0	0	2
120	WSH	Rich Defreitas	St. Mark's H.S.	D					
121	WPG	Joe Harwell	Hill-Murray H.S.	D					
122	MTL	Les Kuntar	Nichols H.S.	G	6	2	16	0	3.18
123	HFD	Jeff St. Cyr	Michigan Tech	D					
124	CGY	Joe Aloi	Hull	D					
125	PHI	Tony Link	Dimond H.S.	D					
126	EDM	Radek Toupal	Motor Ceske Budejovice, TCH	RW					
127	BUF	Paul Flanagan	New Hampton H.S.	D					
128	N.J.	Tom Neziol	Miami of Ohio	LW					
129	VAN	Todd Fanning	Ohio State	G					
130	MIN	Timo Kulonen	KalPa Kuopio, FIN	D					
131	PIT	Jim Bodden	Chatham Jr. B	C					
132	L.A.	Kyosti Karjalainen	Brynas Gavle, SWE	RW	28	1	8	9	12
133	TOR	Trevor Jobe	Moose Jaw	LW					
134	CHI	Stephen Tepper	Westboro H.S.	RW	1	0	0	0	0
135	QUE	Tim Hanus	Minnetonka H.S.	LW					
136	NYR	Clint Thomas	Bartlet H.S.	D					
137	DET	Mike Gober	Laval	LW					
138	ST.L.	Todd Crabtree	Governor Dummer H.S.	D					
139	NYI	Knut Walbye	Furuset Oslo, NOR	C					
140	BOS	Rob Cheevers	Boston College	C					
141	WSH	Devon Oleniuk	Kamloops	D					
142	WPG	Todd Hartje	Harvard	C					
143	MTL	Rob Kelley	Matignon H.S.	LW					
144	HFD	Greg Wolf	Buffalo Regal Midgets	D					
145	CGY	Peter Ciavaglia	Nichols H.S.	C	5	0	0	0	0
146	PHI	Mark Strapon	Hayward H.S.	D					
147	EDM	Tomas Srsen	Zetor Brno, TCH	RW	2	0	0	0	0
148	BUF	Sean Dooley	Groton	D					
149	N.J.	Jim Dowd	Brick H.S.	C	214	22	55	77	80
150	VAN	Viktor Tyumenev	Spartak Moscow, USSR	C					
151	MIN	Don Schmidt	Kamloops	D					
152	PIT	Jiri Kucera	Dukla Jihlava, TCH	C					
153	BUF	Tim Roberts	Deerfield Academy	C					
155	CHI	John Reilly	Phillips Andover H.S.	LW					
156	QUE	Jake Enebak	Northfield H.S.	LW					
157	NYR	Charles Wiegand	Essex Junction H.S.	C					
158	DET	Kevin Scott	Vernon Jr. A	C					
159	ST.L.	Guy Hebert	Hamilton College	G	437	174	1150	26	2.77
160	NYI	Jeff Saterdalen	Jefferson H.S.	RW					
161	BOS	Chris Winnes	Northwood Prep	RW	33	1	6	7	6
162	WSH	Thomas Sjogren	Vastra Frolunda, SWE	RW					
163	WPG	Markku Kyllonen	Karpat Oulu, FIN	LW	9	0	2	2	2
164	MTL	Will Geist	St. Paul Academy	D					
165	HFD	John Moore	Yale	C					
166	CGY	Theoren Fleury	Moose Jaw	RW	886	389	529	918	1425
167	PHI	Darryl Ingham	U. of Manitoba	RW					
168	EDM	Age Ellingsen	Storhamar, NOR	D					
169	BUF	Grant Tkachuk	Saskatoon	LW					
170	N.J.	John Blessman	Toronto	D					
171	VAN	Greg Daly	New Hampton H.S.	D					
172	MIN	Jarmo Myllys	Lukko Rauma, FIN	G	39	4	161	0	5.23
173	PIT	Jack MacDougall	New Prep H.S.	RW					
174	L.A.	Jeff Gawlicki	Northern Michigan	LW					
175	TOR	Brian Blad	Belleville	D					
176	CHI	Lance Werness	Burnsville H.S.	RW					
177	QUE	Jaroslav Sevcik	Zetor Brno, TCH	LW	13	0	2	2	2
178	NYR	Eric Burrill	Tartan H.S.	RW					
179	DET	Mikko Haapakoski	Karpat Oulu, FIN	D					
180	ST.L.	Robert Dumas	Seattle	D					
181	NYI	Shawn Howard	Penticton Jr. A	D					
182	BOS	Paul Ohman	St. John's Prep	D					
183	QUE	Ladislav Tresl	Zetor Brno, TCH	C					
184	WPG	Jim Fernholz	White Bear Lake H.S.	RW					
185	MTL	Eric Tremblay	Drummondville	D					
186	HFD	Joe Day	St. Lawrence U.	C	72	1	10	11	87
187	CGY	Mark Osiecki	Madison Jr. A	D	93	3	11	14	43
188	PHI	Bruce McDonald	Loomis-Chaffee H.S.	RW					
189	EDM	Gavin Armstrong	RPI	G					
190	BUF	Ian Herbers	Swift Current	D	65	0	5	5	79
191	N.J.	Peter Fry	Victoria	G					
192	VAN	John Fletcher	Clarkson	G					
193	MIN	Larry Olimb	Warroad H.S.	D					
194	PIT	Daryn McBride	U. of Denver	C					
195	L.A.	John Preston	Boston U.	C					
196	TOR	Ron Bernacci	Hamilton College	C					
197	CHI	Dale Marquette	Brandon	LW					
198	QUE	Darren Nauss	North Battleford Jr.	RW					
199	NYR	David Porter	Northern Michigan	LW					
200	DET	Darin Bannister	Illinois-Chicago	D					
201	ST.L.	David Marvin	Warroad H.S.	D					
202	NYI	John Herlihy	Babson College	RW					
203	BOS	Casey Jones	Cornell	C					
204	WSH	Chris Clarke	Pembroke Jr. A	D					
205	NYR	Brett Barnett	Wexford Jr. B	RW					
206	MTL	Barry McKinlay	Illinois-Chicago	D					
207	ST.L.	Andy Cesarski	Culver Military Academy	D					
208	CGY	William Sedergren	Springfield Jr. B	D					
209	PHI	Steve Morrow	Westminster H.S.	D					
210	EDM	Mike Tinkham	Newburyport H.S.	RW					
211	BUF	David Littman	Boston College	G	3	0	14	0	5.96
212	N.J.	Alain Charland	Drummondville	C					
213	VAN	Roger Hansson	Rogle Angelholm, SWE	LW					
214	MIN	Mark Felicio	Northwood Prep	G					
215	PIT	Mark Carlson	Philadelphia Jr.	LW					
216	L.A.	Rostislav Vlach	TJ Gottwaldov, TCH	RW					
217	TOR	Ken Alexander	Hamilton	LW					
218	CHI	Bill Lacouture	Natick H.S.	RW					
219	QUE	Mike Williams	Ferris State	G					
220	NYR	Lance Marciano	Choate	D					
221	DET	Craig Quinlan	Hill-Murray H.S.	D					
222	ST.L.	Dan Rolfe	Brockville Jr. A	D					
223	NYI	Michael Erickson	St. John's Hill H.S.	D					
224	BOS	Eric Lemarque	Northern Michigan	RW					

PICK	TEAM	NAME	DRAFTED FROM	NHL PLAYERS: POS / NHL GOALTENDERS: POS	GP / GP	G / W	A / GA	PTS / SO	PIM / AVG
225	WSH	Milos Vanik	Freiburg, FRG	C					
226	WPG	Roger Rougelot	Madison Jr. A	G					
227	MTL	Ed Ronan	Andover Academy	RW	182	13	23	36	101
228	HFD	Kevin Sullivan	Princeton	RW					
229	CGY	Peter Hasselblad	Orebro, SWE	D					
230	PHI	Darius Rusnak	Slovan Bratislava, TCH	C					
231	EDM	Jeff Pauletti	Minnesota-Duluth	D					
232	BUF	Allan MacIsaac	Guelph	LW					
233	VAN	Neil Eisenhut	Langley Eagles (BCJHL)	C	16	1	3	4	21
234	VAN	Matt Evo	Country Day H.S.	LW					
235	MIN	Dave Shields	U. of Denver	C					
236	PIT	Ake Lilljebjorn	Brynas Gavle, SWE	G					
237	L.A.	Mikael Lindholm	Brynas Gavle, SWE	C	18	2	2	4	2
238	TOR	Alex Weinrich	North Yarmouth Academy	C					
239	CHI	Mike Lappin	Northwood Prep	C					
240	WSH	Dan Brettschneider	Burnsville H.S.	RW					
241	EDM	Jesper Duus	Rodovre, DEN	D					
242	DET	Tomas Jansson	IK Talje, SWE	D					
243	ST.L.	Ray Savard	Regina	C					
244	NYI	Will Averill	Belmont Hill H.S.	D					
245	BOS	Sean Gorman	Matignon H.S.	D					
246	WSH	Ryan Kummo	RPI	D					
247	WPG	Hans Goran Elo	Djurgarden Stockholm, SWE	G					
248	MTL	Bryan Herring	Dubuque Jr. A	C					
249	HFD	Steve Laurin	Dartmouth	G					
250	CGY	Magnus Svensson	Leksand, SWE	D	46	4	14	18	31
251	PHI	Dale Roehl	Minnetonka H.S.	G					
252	EDM	Igor Vyazmikin	CSKA Moscow, USSR	R/LW	4	1	0	1	0

1988

PICK	TEAM	NAME	DRAFTED FROM	NHL PLAYERS: POS / NHL GOALTENDERS: POS	GP / GP	G / W	A / GA	PTS / SO	PIM / AVG
FIRST ROUND									
1	MIN	Mike Modano	Prince Albert	C	787	349	467	816	548
2	VAN	Trevor Linden	Medicine Hat	C/RW	859	288	375	663	644
3	QUE	Curtis Leschyshyn	Saskatoon	D	779	42	139	181	572
4	PIT	Darrin Shannon	Windsor	LW	506	87	163	250	344
5	QUE	Daniel Dore	Drummondville	RW	17	2	3	5	59
6	TOR	Scott Pearson	Kingston	LW	292	56	42	98	615
7	L.A.	Martin Gelinas	Hull	LW	744	195	192	387	474
8	CHI	Jeremy Roenick	Thayer Academy	C	828	378	493	871	1020
9	ST.L.	Rod Brind'Amour	Notre Dame Jr. A	C	823	282	443	725	724
10	WPG	Teemu Selanne	Jokerit Helsinki, FIN	RW	564	346	383	729	197
11	HFD	Chris Govedaris	Toronto	LW	45	4	6	10	24
12	N.J.	Corey Foster	Peterborough	D	45	5	6	11	24
13	BUF	Joel Savage	Victoria	RW	3	0	1	1	0
14	PHI	Claude Boivin	Drummondville	LW	132	12	19	31	364
15	WSH	Reggie Savage	Victoriaville	C	34	5	7	12	28
16	NYI	Kevin Cheveldayoff	Brandon	D	Played 4 pro years in AHL/IHL				
17	DET	Kory Kocur	Saskatoon	RW	Played 4 pro seasons in AHL				
18	BOS	Robert Cimetta	Toronto	L/RW	103	16	16	32	66
19	EDM	Francois Leroux	St-Jean	D	249	3	20	23	577
20	MTL	Eric Charron	Trois-Rivieres	D	130	2	7	9	127
21	CGY	Jason Muzzatti	Michigan State	G	62	13	167	1	3.32
SECOND ROUND									
22	NYR	Troy Mallette	Sault Ste. Marie	LW	456	51	68	119	1226
23	N.J.	Jeff Christian	London	LW	18	2	2	4	17
24	QUE	Stephane Fiset	Victoriaville	G	381	161	1088	16	3.06
25	PIT	Mark Major	North Bay	LW	2	0	0	0	5
26	NYR	Murray Duval	Spokane	RW	Played in ECHL, IHL and AHL				
27	TOR	Tie Domi	Peterborough	RW	628	55	86	141	2656
28	L.A.	Paul Holden	London	D	Continues to play in Europe				
29	NYI	Wayne Doucet	Hamilton	LW	5 seasons in AHL/IHL/ColHL				
30	ST.L.	Adrien Plavsic	New Hampshire	D	214	16	56	72	161
31	WPG	Russell Romaniuk	St. Boniface Jr. A	LW	102	13	14	27	63
32	HFD	Barry Richter	Culver Military Academy	D	149	11	34	45	74
33	VAN	Leif Rohlin	Vasteras, SWE	D	96	8	24	32	40
34	MTL	Martin St. Amour	Verdun	LW	1	0	0	0	2
35	PHI	Pat Murray	Michigan State	LW	25	3	1	4	15
36	WSH	Tim Taylor	London	C	343	48	51	99	291
37	NYI	Sean Lebrun	New Westminster	LW	4 seasons in AHL and ECHL				
38	DET	Serge Anglehart	Drummondville	D	Injuries ended career in 1994				
39	EDM	Petro Koivunen	Kiekko-Espoo, FIN	C	Continues to play in Finland				
40	MIN	Link Gaetz	Spokane	D	65	6	8	14	412
41	WSH	Wade Bartley	Dauphin Jr. A	D	Played in six leagues until '98				
42	CGY	Todd Harkins	Miami of Ohio	C	48	3	3	6	78
OTHER ROUNDS									
43	MIN	Shaun Kane	Springfield Jr. B	D					
44	VAN	Dane Jackson	Vernon Jr. A	RW	45	12	6	18	58
45	QUE	Petri Aaltonen	HIFK Helsinki, FIN	C					
46	MTL	Neil Carnes	Verdun	C					
47	DET	Guy Dupuis	Hull	D					
48	TOR	Peter Ing	Windsor	G	74	20	266	1	4.05
49	L.A.	John Van Kessel	North Bay	RW					
50	CHI	Trevor Dam	London	RW					
51	ST.L.	Rob Fournier	North Bay	G					
52	WPG	Stephane Beauregard	St-Jean	G	90	19	268	2	3.65
53	EDM	Trevor Sim	Seattle	RW	3	0	1	1	2
54	N.J.	Zdeno Ciger	ZTS Martin, TCH	LW	296	82	121	203	75
55	BUF	Darcy Loewen	Spokane	LW	135	4	8	12	211
56	PHI	Craig Fisher	Oshawa Jr. B	C	12	0	0	0	2
57	WSH	Duane Derksen	Winkler Jr. A	G					
58	NYI	Danny Lorenz	Seattle	G	8	1	25	0	4.20
59	DET	Petr Hrbek	Sparta Praha, TCH	RW					
60	BOS	Steve Heinze	Lawrence Academy	RW	515	131	108	239	275
61	EDM	Collin Bauer	Saskatoon	D					
62	PIT	Daniel Gauthier	Victoriaville	LW	5	0	0	0	0
63	PHI	Dominic Roussel	Trois-Rivieres	G	184	74	503	7	3.12
64	MIN	Jeffrey Stolp	Greenway H.S.	G					
65	N.J.	Matt Ruchty	Bowling Green	LW					
66	QUE	Darin Kimble	Prince Albert	RW	311	23	20	43	1082
67	PIT	Mark Recchi	Kamloops	RW	863	361	572	933	619
68	NYR	Tony Amonte	Thayer Academy	RW	697	290	304	594	482
69	TOR	Ted Crowley	Lawrence Academy	D	34	2	4	6	12
70	L.A.	Rob Blake	Bowling Green	D	608	121	259	380	982
71	CHI	Stefan Elvenas	Rogle Angelholm, SWE	RW					
72	ST.L.	Jaan Luik	Miami of Ohio	D					
73	WPG	Brian Hunt	Oshawa	C					
74	HFD	Dean Dyer	Lake Superior State	C					
75	N.J.	Scott Luik	Miami of Ohio	RW					
76	BUF	Keith Carney	Mount St. Charles H.S.	D	506	25	96	121	519
77	PHI	Scott Lagrand	Hotchkiss H.S.	G					
78	WSH	Bob Krauss	Lethbridge	D					
79	NYI	Andre Brassard	Trois-Rivieres	D					
80	DET	Sheldon Kennedy	Swift Current	RW	310	49	58	107	233
81	BOS	Joe Juneau	RPI	C	547	127	339	466	194
82	EDM	Cam Brauer	RPI	D					
83	MTL	Patrik Kjellberg	Falun, SWE	LW	160	34	43	77	40
84	CGY	Gary Socha	Tabor Academy	C					
85	CGY	Tomas Forslund	Leksand, SWE	RW	44	5	11	16	12
86	TOR	Len Esau	Humboldt Jr. A	D	27	0	10	10	24
87	QUE	Stephane Venne	Vermont	D					
88	PIT	Greg Andrusak	Minnesota-Duluth	D	28	0	6	6	16
89	BUF	Alexander Mogilny	CSKA Moscow, USSR	RW	705	353	405	758	351
90	CGY	Scott Matusovich	Canterbury H.S.	D					
91	L.A.	Jeff Robison	Mount St. Charles H.S.	D					
92	CHI	Joe Cleary	Stratford Jr. B	D					
93	MTL	Peter Popovic	Vasteras, SWE	D	425	9	57	66	243
94	WPG	Tony Joseph	Oshawa	RW	2	1	0	1	0
95	HFD	Scott Morrow	Northwood Prep	LW	4	0	0	0	0
96	N.J.	Chris Nelson	Rochester Jr. A	D					
97	BUF	Rob Ray	Cornwall	RW	714	34	41	75	2687
98	PHI	Edward O'Brien	Cushing Academy	LW					
99	NYR	Martin Bergeron	Drummondville	C					
100	NYI	Paul Rutherford	Ohio State	C					
101	WPG	Benoit Lebeau	Merrimack	LW					
102	BOS	Daniel Murphy	Gunnery H.S.	D					
103	EDM	Don Martin	London	LW					
104	MTL	Jean-Claude Bergeron	Verdun	G	72	21	232	1	3.69
105	ST.L.	Dave Lacouture	Natick H.S.	RW					
106	BUF	David Di Vita	Lake Superior State	G					
107	VAN	Corrie D'Alessio	Cornell	G	1	0	0	0	0.00
108	QUE	Ed Ward	Michigan	RW	274	23	25	48	348
109	L.A.	Micah Aivazoff	Victoria	C	92	4	6	10	46
110	NYR	Dennis Vial	Hamilton	LW	242	4	15	19	794
111	NYI	Pavel Gross	Sparta Praha, TCH	RW					
112	L.A.	Robert Larsson	Skelleftea, SWE	D					
113	CHI	Justin Lafayette	Ferris State	LW					
114	ST.L.	Dan Fowler	U. of Maine	D					
115	WPG	Ronald Jones	Windsor	RW					
116	HFD	Corey Beaulieu	Seattle	D					
117	N.J.	Chad Johnson	Rochester Jr. A	C					
118	BUF	Mike McLaughlin	Choate	LW					
119	PHI	Gordie Frantti	Calumet H.S.	C					
120	WSH	Dmitri Khristich	Sokol Kiev, USSR	LW/C	680	237	300	537	394
121	NYI	Jason Rathbone	Brookline H.S.	RW					
122	VAN	Phil Von Stefenelli	Boston U.	D	33	0	5	5	23
123	BOS	Derek Geary	Gloucester	RW					
124	EDM	Len Barrie	Victoria	C	124	14	27	41	155
125	MTL	Patrik Carnback	Vastra Frolunda, SWE	C	154	24	38	62	122
126	CGY	Jonas Bergqvist	Leksand, SWE	RW	22	2	5	7	10
127	WPG	Markus Akerblom	Bjorkloven Umea, SWE	C					
128	VAN	Dixon Ward	Red Deer Jr. A	RW	466	90	116	206	364
129	QUE	Valeri Kamensky	CSKA Moscow, USSR	LW	518	179	267	446	327
130	PIT	Troy Mick	Portland	LW					
131	NYR	Mike Rosati	Hamilton	G	1	1	0	0	0.00
132	TOR	Matt Mallgrave	St Paul's Prep	C					
133	L.A.	Jeff Kruesel	John Marshall H.S.	G					
134	CHI	Craig Woodcroft	Colgate	LW					
135	ST.L.	Matt Hayes	New Hampton H.S.	D					
136	WPG	Jukka Marttila	Tappara Tampere, FIN	D					

PICK	TEAM	NAME	DRAFTED FROM	NHL PLAYERS: POS / NHL GOALTENDERS: POS	GP / GP	G / W	A / GA	PTS / SO	PIM / AVG
137	HFD	Kerry Russell	Michigan State	RW					
138	N.J.	Chad Erickson	Warroad H.S.	G	2	1	9	0	4.50
139	BUF	Mike Griffith	Ottawa	RW					
140	PHI	Jamie Cooke	Bramalea Jr. B	RW					
141	WSH	Keith Jones	Niagara Falls Jr. B	RW	483	117	141	258	761
142	NYI	Yves Gaucher	Chicoutimi	LW					
143	DET	Kelly Hurd	Michigan Tech	RW					
144	WSH	Brad Schlegel	London	D	48	1	8	9	10
145	EDM	Mike Glover	Sault Ste. Marie	RW					
146	MTL	Tim Chase	Tabor Academy	C					
147	CGY	Stefan Nilsson	HV 71 Jonkoping, SWE	C					
148	MIN	Ken MacArthur	U. of Denver	D					
149	VAN	Greg Geldart	St. Albert Jr. A	C					
150	QUE	Sakari Lindfors	HIFK Helsinki, FIN	G					
151	PIT	Jeff Blaeser	St. John's Prep	LW					
152	NYR	Eric Couvrette	St-Jean	LW					
153	TOR	Peter Elvenas	Rogle Angelholm, SWE	C					
154	L.A.	Timo Peltomaa	Ilves Tampere, FIN	RW					
155	CHI	Jon Pojar	Roseville H.S.	LW					
156	ST.L.	John McCoy	Edina H.S.	LW					
157	WPG	Mark Smith	Trinity-Pawling H.S.	C					
158	HFD	Jim Burke	U. of Maine	D					
159	N.J.	Bryan Lafort	Waltham H.S.	G					
160	BUF	Daniel Ruoho	Madison Memorial H.S.	D					
161	PHI	Johan Salle	Malmo, SWE	D					
162	WSH	Todd Hilditch	Penticton Jr. A	D					
163	NYI	Marty McInnis	Milton Academy	LW	565	130	201	331	219
164	DET	Brian McCormack	St Paul's Prep	D					
165	BOS	Mark Krys	Boston U.	D					
166	EDM	Shjon Podein	Minnesota-Duluth	LW	485	73	73	146	302
167	MTL	Sean Hill	Duluth East H.S.	D	400	31	101	132	421
168	CGY	Troy Kennedy	Brandon	RW					
169	MIN	Travis Richards	Armstrong H.S.	D	3	0	0	0	2
170	VAN	Roger Akerstrom	Lulea, SWE	D					
171	QUE	Dan Wiebe	U. of Alberta	LW					
172	PIT	Rob Gaudreau	Bishop Hendricken H.S.	RW	231	51	54	105	69
173	NYI	Shorty Forrest	St. Cloud State	D					
174	TOR	Mike Delay	Canterbury H.S.	D					
175	L.A.	Jim Larkin	Mount St. Charles H.S.	LW					
176	CHI	Mathew Hentges	Edina H.S.	D					
177	ST.L.	Tony Twist	Saskatoon	LW	445	10	18	28	1121
178	WPG	Mike Helber	Ann Arbor H.S.	C					
179	HFD	Mark Hirth	Michigan State	C					
180	N.J.	Sergei Svetlov	Dynamo Moscow, USSR	RW					
181	BUF	Wade Flaherty	Victoria	G	93	19	268	4	3.57
182	PHI	Brian Arthur	Etobicoke Jr. B	D					
183	WSH	Petr Pavlas	Dukla Trencin, TCH	D					
184	NYI	Jeff Blumer	U. of St. Thomas	RW					
185	DET	Jody Praznik	Colorado College	D					
186	BOS	Jon Rohloff	Grand Rapids H.S.	D	150	7	25	32	129
187	EDM	Tim Cole	Woburn H.S.	G					
188	MTL	Harijs Vitolinsh	Dynamo Riga, USSR	C	Re-entered Draft in 1993				
189	CGY	Brett Peterson	St. Paul Jr. A	D					
190	MIN	Ari Matilainen	Assat Pori, FIN	RW					
191	VAN	Paul Constantin	Burlington Jr. B	C					
192	WSH	Mark Sorensen	Michigan	D					
193	PIT	David Pancoe	Hamilton	LW					
194	NYR	Paul Cain	Cornwall	C					
195	TOR	David Sacco	Medford H.S.	RW	35	5	13	18	22
196	L.A.	Brad Hyatt	Windsor	D					
197	CHI	Daniel Maurice	Chicoutimi	C					
198	ST.L.	Bret Hedican	North St. Paul H.S.	D	518	27	130	157	460
199	WPG	Pavel Kostichkin	CSKA Moscow, USSR	C					
200	HFD	Wayde Bucsis	Prince Albert	RW					
201	N.J.	Bob Woods	Brandon	D					
202	NYR	Eric Fenton	North Yarmouth Academy	C					
203	PHI	Jeff Dandretta	Cushing Academy	RW					
204	WSH	Claudio Scremin	U. of Maine	D	17	0	1	1	29
205	NYI	Jeff Kampersal	St. John's Prep	D					
206	DET	Glen Goodall	Seattle	C					
207	N.J.	Alexander Semak	Dynamo Moscow, USSR	C	289	83	91	174	187
208	EDM	Vladimir Zubkov	CSKA Moscow, USSR	D					
209	MTL	Yuri Krivokhizha	Dynamo Minsk, USSR	D					
210	CGY	Guy Darveau	Victoriaville	D					
211	MIN	Grant Bischoff	Minnesota-Duluth	LW					
212	VAN	Chris Wolanin	Illinois-Chicago	D					
213	QUE	Alexei Gusarov	CSKA Moscow, USSR	D	556	38	120	158	295
214	PIT	Cory Laylin	St. Cloud Appollo H.S.	LW					
215	NYR	Peter Fiorentino	Sault Ste. Marie	D	1	0	0	0	0
216	TOR	Mike Gregorio	Cushing Academy	G					
217	L.A.	Doug Laprade	Lake Superior State	RW					
218	CHI	Dirk Tenzer	St. Paul's H.S.	D					
219	ST.L.	Heath DeBoer	Spring Lake Park H.S.	D					
220	WPG	Kevin Heise	Lethbridge	LW					
221	HFD	Rob White	St. Lawrence U.	D					
222	N.J.	Charles Hughes	Catholic Memorial H.S.	G					
223	BUF	Thomas Nieman	Choate	RW					
224	PHI	Scott Billey	Madison Jr. A	RW					
225	WSH	Chris Venkus	Western Michigan	RW					
226	NYI	Phillip Neururer	Osseo H.S.	D					
227	DET	Darren Colbourne	Cornwall	RW					
228	BOS	Eric Reisman	Ohio State	D					
229	EDM	Darin MacDonald	Boston U.	LW					
230	MTL	Kevin Dahl	Bowling Green	D	184	7	22	29	151
231	CGY	Dave Tretowicz	Clarkson	D					
232	MIN	Trent Andison	Cornwall	LW					
233	VAN	Steffan Nilsson	Troja-Ljungby, SWE	LW					
234	QUE	Claude Lapointe	Laval	C	597	96	132	228	537
235	PIT	Darren Stolk	Lethbridge	D					
236	NYR	Keith Slifstein	Choate	RW					
237	TOR	Peter DeBoer	Windsor	RW					
238	L.A.	Joe Flanagan	Canterbury H.S.	C					
239	CHI	Andreas Lupzig	Landshut, FRG	C					
240	ST.L.	Michael Francis	Harvard	G					
241	WPG	Kyle Galloway	U. of Manitoba	D					
242	HFD	Dan Slatalla	Deerfield Academy	LW					
243	BUF	Michael Pohl	Rosenheim, FRG	C					
244	N.J.	Robert Wallwork	Miami of Ohio	C					
245	PHI	Drahomir Kadlec	Dukla Jihlava, TCH	D					
246	WSH	Ron Pascucci	Belmont Hill H.S.	D					
247	NYI	Joe Caprinni	Babson College	G					
248	DET	Donald Stone	Michigan	C					
249	BOS	Doug Jones	Kitchener	D					
250	EDM	Tim Tisdale	Swift Current	C					
251	MTL	Dave Kunda	U. of Guelph	D					
252	CGY	Sergei Priakin	Krylja Sovetov Mosc., USSR	RW	46	3	8	11	2

1989

PICK	TEAM	NAME	DRAFTED FROM	NHL PLAYERS: POS / NHL GOALTENDERS: POS	GP / GP	G / W	A / GA	PTS / SO	PIM / AVG
FIRST ROUND									
1	QUE	Mats Sundin	Nacka, SWE	C/RW	766	328	460	788	589
2	NYI	Dave Chyzowski	Kamloops	LW	126	15	16	31	144
3	TOR	Scott Thornton	Belleville	C	494	55	62	117	896
4	WPG	Stu Barnes	Tri-City	C	596	161	193	354	230
5	N.J.	Bill Guerin	Springfield Jr. B	RW	570	175	178	353	805
6	CHI	Adam Bennett	Sudbury	D	69	3	8	11	69
7	MIN	Doug Zmolek	John Marshall H.S.	D	467	11	53	64	905
8	VAN	Jason Herter	North Dakota	D	1	0	1	1	0
9	ST.L.	Jason Marshall	Vernon Jr. A	D	299	6	26	32	605
10	HFD	Bobby Holik	Dukla Jihlava, TCH	LW	717	200	247	447	760
11	DET	Mike Sillinger	Regina	C	530	99	148	247	285
12	TOR	Rob Pearson	Belleville	RW	269	56	54	110	645
13	MTL	Lindsay Vallis	Seattle	D	1	0	0	0	0
14	BUF	Kevin Haller	Regina	D	611	40	92	132	849
15	EDM	Jason Soules	Niagara Falls	D	Played 51 games in the AHL				
16	PIT	Jamie Heward	Regina	D	142	13	27	40	76
17	BOS	Shayne Stevenson	Kitchener	RW	27	0	2	2	35
18	N.J.	Jason Miller	Medicine Hat	LW	6	0	0	0	0
19	WSH	Olaf Kolzig	Tri-City	G	272	114	637	16	2.49
20	NYR	Steven Rice	Kitchener	RW	329	64	61	125	275
21	TOR	Steve Bancroft	Belleville	D	1	0	0	0	0
SECOND ROUND									
22	QUE	Adam Foote	Sault Ste. Marie	D	558	28	103	131	868
23	NYI	Travis Green	Spokane	C	567	135	194	329	400
24	CGY	Kent Manderville	Notre Dame Jr. A	LW	444	27	47	74	243
25	WPG	Dan Ratushny	Cornell	D	1	0	1	1	2
26	N.J.	Jarrod Skalde	Oshawa	C	95	12	19	31	40
27	CHI	Michael Speer	Guelph	D	Returned to school w/ U of T				
28	MIN	Mike Craig	Oshawa	RW	421	71	97	168	548
29	VAN	Robert Woodward	Deerfield Academy	LW	Retired in 93. Back in IHL in 98				
30	MTL	Patrice Brisebois	Laval	D	499	52	161	213	394
31	ST.L.	Rick Corriveau	London	D	Re-entered Draft in 1991				
32	DET	Bob Boughner	Sault Ste. Marie	D	329	8	25	33	797
33	PHI	Greg Johnson	Thunder Bay Jr. A	C	433	79	146	225	196
34	PHI	Patrik Juhlin	Vasteras, SWE	LW	56	7	6	13	23
35	WSH	Byron Dafoe	Portland	G	271	105	693	20	2.73
36	EDM	Richard Borgo	Kitchener	G	Five seasons in AHL, ECHL				
37	PIT	Paul Laus	Niagara Falls	RW	460	9	53	62	1479
38	BOS	Mike Parson	Guelph	G	Journeyman - 11 pro teams				
39	L.A.	Brent Thompson	Medicine Hat	D	121	1	10	11	352
40	NYR	Jason Prosofsky	Medicine Hat	RW	Played 59 games in 4 seasons				
41	MTL	Steve Larouche	Trois-Rivieres	C	26	9	9	18	10
42	CGY	Ted Drury	Fairfield Prep	C	413	41	52	93	367
OTHER ROUNDS									
43	QUE	Stephane Morin	Chicoutimi	C	90	16	39	55	52
44	NYI	Jason Zent	Nichols H.S.	LW	27	3	3	6	13
45	NYR	Rob Zamuner	Guelph	LW	541	94	130	224	357
46	WPG	Jason Cirone	Cornwall	C	3	0	0	0	2
47	N.J.	Scott Pellerin	U. of Maine	LW	346	56	79	135	230
48	CHI	Bob Kellogg	Springfield Jr. B	D					
49	NYR	Louie DeBrusk	London	LW	358	24	17	41	1075

PICK	TEAM	NAME	DRAFTED FROM	NHL PLAYERS: POS / NHL GOALTENDERS: POS	GP / GP	G / W	A / GA	PTS / SO	PIM / AVG
50	CGY	Veli-Pekka Kautonen	HIFK Helsinki, FIN	D					
51	MTL	Pierre Sevigny	Trois-Rivieres	LW	78	4	5	9	64
52	HFD	Blair Atcheynum	Moose Jaw	RW	177	26	31	57	34
53	DET	Nicklas Lidstrom	Vasteras, SWE	D	693	121	375	496	182
54	QUE	John Tanner	Peterborough	G	21	2	65	1	3.60
55	ST.L.	Denny Felsner	Michigan	LW	18	1	4	5	6
56	BUF	Scott Thomas	Nichols H.S.	RW	39	3	3	6	23
57	BOS	Wes Walz	Lethbridge	C	169	27	51	78	71
58	PIT	John Brill	Grand Rapids H.S.						
59	WSH	Jim Mathieson	Regina	D	2	0	0	0	4
60	MIN	Murray Garbutt	Medicine Hat	C					
61	WSH	Jason Woolley	Michigan State	D	408	44	155	199	243
62	WPG	Kris Draper	Canadian National	C	418	47	59	106	319
63	CGY	Corey Lyons	Lethbridge	RW					
64	WPG	Mark Brownschidle	Boston U.	D					
65	NYI	Brent Grieve	Oshawa	LW	97	20	16	36	87
66	TOR	Matt Martin	Avon Old Farms H.S.	D	76	0	5	5	71
67	NYR	Jim Cummins	Michigan State	RW	365	18	28	46	1193
68	QUE	Niklas Andersson	Vastra Frolunda, SWE	LW	153	29	52	81	81
69	WPG	Allain Roy	Harvard	G					
70	CGY	Robert Reichel	CHZ Litvinov, TCH	C	602	209	298	507	306
71	VAN	Brett Hauer	Richfield H.S.	D	34	4	4	8	32
72	PHI	Reid Simpson	Prince Albert	LW	184	10	15	25	537
73	HFD	Jim McKenzie	Victoria	LW	623	38	34	72	1321
74	DET	Sergei Fedorov	CSKA Moscow, USSR	C	672	301	433	734	459
75	MIN	Jean-Francois Quintin	Shawinigan	LW	22	5	5	10	4
76	MTL	Eric Dubois	Laval	D					
77	BUF	Doug MacDonald	Wisconsin	LW	11	1	0	1	2
78	EDM	Josef Beranek	CHZ Litvinov, TCH	LW/C	461	109	130	239	355
79	PIT	Todd Nelson	Prince Albert	D	3	1	0	1	2
80	BOS	Jackson Penney	Victoria	C					
81	L.A.	Jim Maher	Illinois-Chicago	D					
82	WSH	Trent Klatt	Osseo H.S.	RW	507	89	134	223	212
83	MTL	Andre Racicot	Granby	G	68	26	196	2	3.50
84	CGY	Ryan O'Leary	Hermantown H.S.	C					
85	QUE	Kevin Kaiser	Minnesota-Duluth	LW					
86	NYI	Jace Reed	Grand Rapids H.S.	D					
87	MIN	Pat MacLeod	Kamloops	D	53	5	13	18	14
88	NYR	Aaron Miller	Niagara Jr. A	D	255	13	37	50	150
89	N.J.	Mike Heinke	Avon Old Farms H.S.	G					
90	NYI	Steve Young	Moose Jaw	RW					
91	MIN	Bryan Schoen	Minnetonka H.S.	G					
92	EDM	Peter White	Michigan State	C	86	11	17	28	8
93	ST.L.	Daniel Laperriere	St. Lawrence U.	D	48	2	5	7	27
94	HFD	James Black	Portland	LW	310	57	52	109	80
95	DET	Shawn McCosh	Niagara Falls	C	9	1	0	1	6
96	TOR	Keith Carney	Mount St. Charles H.S.	D					
97	MIN	Rhys Hollyman	Miami of Ohio	D					
98	BUF	Ken Sutton	Saskatoon	D	314	22	71	93	293
99	NYI	Kevin O'Sullivan	Catholic Memorial H.S.	D					
100	PIT	Tom Nevers	Edina H.S.	C					
101	BOS	Mark Montanari	Kitchener	C					
102	L.A.	Eric Ricard	Granby	D					
103	L.A.	Thomas Newman	Blaine H.S.	G					
104	MTL	Marc Deschamps	Cornell	D					
105	CGY	Toby Kearney	Belmont Hill H.S.	LW					
106	QUE	Dan Lambert	Swift Current	D	29	6	9	15	22
107	BUF	Bill Pye	Northern Michigan	G					
108	TOR	David Burke	Cornell	D					
109	WPG	Dan Bylsma	Bowling Green	RW	220	9	21	30	122
110	N.J.	David Emma	Boston College	C	28	5	6	11	2
111	CHI	Tommi Pullola	Sport Vaasa, FIN	C					
112	MIN	Scott Cashman	Kanata Jr.	G					
113	VAN	Pavel Bure	CSKA Moscow, USSR	RW	513	325	263	588	348
114	ST.L.	David Roberts	Avon Old Farms H.S.	LW	125	20	33	53	85
115	HFD	Jerome Bechard	Moose Jaw	LW					
116	DET	Dallas Drake	Northern Michigan	RW	501	110	191	301	458
117	PHI	Niklas Eriksson	Leksand, SWE	C					
118	NYR	Joby Messier	Michigan State	D	25	0	4	4	24
119	BUF	Mike Barkley	U. of Maine	RW					
120	EDM	Anatoli Semenov	Dynamo Moscow, USSR	C/LW	362	68	126	194	122
121	PIT	Mike Markovich	U. of Denver	D					
122	BOS	Stephen Foster	Catholic Memorial H.S.	D					
123	L.A.	Daniel Rydmark	Farjestad Karlstad, SWE	C					
124	ST.L.	Derek Frenette	Ferris State	LW					
125	TOR	Michael Doers	Northwood Prep	RW					
126	PIT	Mike Needham	Kamloops	RW	86	9	5	14	16
127	QUE	Sergei Mylnikov	Traktor Chelyabinsk, USSR	G	10	1	47	0	4.96
128	NYI	Jon Larson	Roseau H.S.	D					
129	TOR	Keith Merkler	Portledge H.S.	LW					
130	WPG	Pekka Peltola	HPK Hameenlinna, FIN	RW					
131	WPG	Doug Evans	Peterborough	D					
132	CHI	Tracy Egeland	Prince Albert	LW					
133	NYI	Brett Harkins	Detroit Compuware Jr. A	LW	53	4	18	22	14
134	VAN	James Revenberg	Windsor	RW					
135	ST.L.	Jeff Batters	Alaska-Anchorage	D	16	0	0	0	28
136	HFD	Scott Daniels	Regina	LW	149	8	12	20	667
137	DET	Scott Zygulski	Culver Military Academy	D					
138	PHI	John Callahan Jr.	Belmont Hill H.S.	C					
139	NYR	Greg Leahy	Portland	C					
140	EDM	Davis Payne	Michigan Tech	LW	22	0	1	1	14
141	EDM	Sergei Yashin	Dynamo Moscow, USSR	LW					
142	PIT	Patrick Schafhauser	Hill-Murray H.S.	D					
143	BOS	Otto Hascak	Dukla Trencin, TCH	RW					
144	L.A.	Ted Kramer	Michigan	RW					
145	WSH	Dave Lorentz	Peterborough	LW					
146	MTL	Craig Ferguson	Yale	C	27	1	1	2	6
147	CGY	Alex Nikolic	Cornell	LW					
148	QUE	Paul Krake	Alaska-Anchorage	G					
149	NYI	Phil Huber	Kamloops	LW					
150	TOR	Derek Langille	North Bay	D					
151	WPG	Jim Solly	Bowling Green	C					
152	N.J.	Sergei Starikov	CSKA Moscow, USSR	D	16	0	1	1	8
153	CHI	Milan Tichy	Skoda Plzen, TCH	D	23	0	5	5	40
154	MIN	Jonathon Pratt	Pingree Prep	C					
155	VAN	Rob Sangster	Kitchener	LW					
156	ST.L.	Kevin Plager	Parkway North H.S.	RW					
157	HFD	Raymond Saumier	Trois-Rivieres	RW					
158	DET	Andy Suhy	Western Michigan	D					
159	PHI	Sverre Sears	Belmont Hill H.S.	D					
160	NYR	Greg Spenrath	Tri-City	LW					
161	BUF	Derek Plante	Cloquet H.S.	C	438	95	150	245	134
162	EDM	Darcy Martini	Michigan Tech	D	2	0	0	0	0
163	PIT	Dave Shute	Victoria	D					
164	BOS	Rick Allain	Kitchener	D					
165	L.A.	Sean Whyte	Guelph	RW	21	0	2	2	12
166	WSH	Dean Holoien	Saskatoon	D					
167	MTL	Patrick Lebeau	St-Jean	LW	15	3	2	5	6
168	CGY	Kevin Wortman	American International College	D	5	0	0	0	2
169	QUE	Viacheslav Bykov	CSKA Moscow, USSR	C					
170	NYI	Matthew Robbins	New Hampton H.S.	C					
171	TOR	Jeffrey St. Laurent	Berwick H.S.	RW					
172	WPG	Stephane Gauvin	Cornell	LW					
173	N.J.	Andre Faust	Princeton	C	47	10	7	17	14
174	CHI	Jason Greyerbiehl	Colgate	LW					
175	MIN	Kenneth Blum	St. Joseph H.S.	C					
176	VAN	Sandy Moger	Lake Superior State	C	236	41	38	79	212
177	ST.L.	John Roderick	Rindge and Latin Academy	D					
178	HFD	Michel Picard	Trois-Rivieres	LW	159	27	38	65	103
179	DET	Bob Jones	Sault Ste. Marie	LW	2	0	0	0	0
180	PHI	Glen Wisser	Philadelphia Jr.	RW					
181	NYR	Mark Bavis	Cushing Academy	C					
182	L.A.	Jim Giacin	Culver Military Academy	LW					
183	BUF	Donald Audette	Laval	RW	521	201	167	368	431
184	PIT	Andrew Wolf	Victoria	D					
185	BOS	James Lavish	Deerfield Academy	RW					
186	L.A.	Martin Maskarinec	Sparta Praha, TCH	D					
187	WSH	Victor Gervais	Seattle	C					
188	MTL	Roy Mitchell	Portland	D	3	0	0	0	0
189	CGY	Sergei Gomolyako	Traktor Chelyabinsk, USSR	C					
190	QUE	Andrei Khomutov	CSKA Moscow, USSR	RW					
191	NYI	Vladimir Malakhov	CSKA Moscow, USSR	D	466	70	201	271	477
192	TOR	Justin Tomberlin	Greenway H.S.	C					
193	WPG	Joe Larson	Minnetonka H.S.	C					
194	BUF	Mark Astley	Lake Superior State	D	75	4	19	23	92
195	CHI	Matt Saunders	Northeastern	LW					
196	MIN	Arturs Irbe	Dynamo Riga, USSR	G	396	149	1084	24	2.92
197	VAN	Gus Morschauser	Kitchener	G					
198	ST.L.	John Valo	Detroit Compuware Jr. A	D					
199	HFD	Trevor Buchanan	Kamloops	LW					
200	DET	Greg Bignell	Belleville	D					
201	PHI	Al Kummu	Humboldt Jr. A	D					
202	NYR	Roman Oksiuta	Khimik Voskresensk, USSR	RW	153	46	41	87	100
203	BUF	John Nelson	Toronto	C					
204	DET	Rick Judson	Illinois-Chicago	LW					
205	PIT	Greg Hagen	Hill-Murray H.S.	RW					
206	BOS	Geoff Simpson	Estevan Jr. A	D					
207	L.A.	Jim Hiller	Melville Jr. A	RW	63	8	12	20	116
208	WSH	Jiri Vykoukal	DS Olomouc, TCH	D					
209	MTL	Ed Henrich	Nichols H.S.	D					
210	CGY	Dan Sawyer	Ramapo Jr.	D					
211	QUE	Byron Witkowski	Nipiwan Jr. A	LW					
212	NYI	Kelly Ens	Lethbridge	C					
213	TOR	Mike Jackson	Toronto	RW					
214	WPG	Bradley Podiak	Wayzata H.S.	LW					
215	N.J.	Jason Simon	Windsor	LW	5	0	0	0	34
216	CHI	Mike Kozak	Clarkson	RW					
217	MIN	Tom Pederson	Minnesota-Duluth	D	240	20	49	69	142
218	VAN	Hayden O'Rear	Lathrop H.S.	D					
219	ST.L.	Brian Lukowski	Niagara Jr. A	G					
220	HFD	John Battice	London	D					
221	DET	Vladimir Konstantinov	CSKA Moscow, USSR	D	446	47	128	175	838
222	PHI	Matt Brait	St. Michael's Jr. B	D					
223	NYR	Steve Locke	Niagara Falls	LW					

PICK	TEAM	NAME	DRAFTED FROM	NHL PLAYERS: POS / NHL GOALTENDERS: POS	GP / GP	G / W	A / GA	PTS / SO	PIM / AVG
224	BUF	Todd Henderson	Thunder Bay Jr. A	G					
225	EDM	Roman Bozek	Motor Ceske Budejovice, TCH	RW					
226	PIT	Scott Farrell	Spokane	D					
227	BOS	David Franzosa	Boston College	LW					
228	L.A.	Steve Jaques	Tri-City	D					
229	WSH	Sidorov Sidorov	Sokol Kiev, USSR						
230	MTL	Justin Duberman	North Dakota	RW	4	0	0	0	0
231	CGY	Alexander Yudin	Dynamo Moscow, USSR	D					
232	QUE	Noel Rahn	Edina H.S.	C					
233	NYI	Iain Fraser	Oshawa	C	94	23	23	46	31
234	TOR	Steve Chartrand	Drummondville	LW					
235	WPG	Evgeny Davydov	CSKA Moscow, USSR	LW	155	40	39	79	120
236	N.J.	Peter Larsson	Sodertalje, SWE	C					
237	CHI	Michael Doneghey	Catholic Memorial H.S.	G					
238	MIN	Helmut Balderis	Dynamo Riga, USSR	RW	26	3	6	9	2
239	VAN	Darcy Cahill	Cornwall	C					
240	WPG	Sergei Kharin	Krylja Sovetov Mosc., USSR	RW	7	2	3	5	2
241	HFD	Peter Kasowski	Swift Current	C					
242	DET	Joseph Frederick	Madison Jr. A	RW					
243	PHI	James Pollio	Vermont Academy	LW					
244	NYR	Ken MacDermid	Hull	LW					
245	BUF	Michael Bavis	Cushing Academy	RW					
246	DET	Jason Glickman	Hull	G					
247	PIT	Jason Smart	Saskatoon	C					
248	VAN	Jan Bergman	Sodertalje, SWE	D					
249	L.A.	Kevin Sneddon	Harvard	D					
250	WSH	Ken House	Miami of Ohio	C					
251	MTL	Steve Cadieux	Shawinigan	C					
252	CGY	Kenneth Kennholt	Djurgarden Stockholm, SWE	D					

1990

PICK	TEAM	NAME	DRAFTED FROM	NHL PLAYERS: POS / NHL GOALTENDERS: POS	GP / GP	G / W	A / GA	PTS / SO	PIM / AVG
FIRST ROUND									
1	QUE	Owen Nolan	Cornwall	RW	643	254	264	518	1215
2	VAN	Petr Nedved	Seattle	C	573	202	250	452	410
3	DET	Keith Primeau	Niagara Falls	C	620	186	237	423	1158
4	PHI	Mike Ricci	Peterborough	C	708	174	257	431	704
5	PIT	Jaromir Jagr	Poldi Kladno, TCH	RW	725	387	571	958	551
6	NYI	Scott Scissons	Saskatoon	C	2	0	0	0	0
7	L.A.	Darryl Sydor	Kamloops	D	623	63	226	289	474
8	MIN	Derian Hatcher	North Bay	D	585	57	159	216	1110
9	WSH	John Slaney	Cornwall	D	263	22	67	89	99
10	TOR	Drake Berehowsky	Kingston	D	349	21	67	88	573
11	CGY	Trevor Kidd	Brandon	G	278	114	687	16	2.68
12	MTL	Turner Stevenson	Seattle	RW	385	45	66	111	611
13	NYR	Michael Stewart	Michigan State	D	Continues to play in IHL				
14	BUF	Brad May	Niagara Falls	LW	577	91	110	201	1556
15	HFD	Mark Greig	Lethbridge	RW	113	12	25	37	84
16	CHI	Karl Dykhuis	Hull	D	423	28	71	99	383
17	EDM	Scott Allison	Prince Albert	C	Continues to play in Germany				
18	VAN	Shawn Antoski	North Bay	LW	183	3	5	8	599
19	WPG	Keith Tkachuk	Malden Catholic H.S.	LW	576	294	258	552	1400
20	N.J.	Martin Brodeur	St-Hyacinthe	G	447	244	950	42	2.20
21	BOS	Bryan Smolinski	Michigan State	C/RW	523	151	194	345	338
SECOND ROUND									
22	QUE	Ryan Hughes	Cornell	C	3	0	0	0	0
23	VAN	Jiri Slegr	CHZ Litvinov, TCH	D	417	34	130	164	592
24	N.J.	David Harlock	Michigan	D	128	2	12	14	108
25	PHI	Chris Simon	Ottawa	LW	314	72	82	154	952
26	CGY	Nicolas Perreault	Hawkesbury Jr. A	D	Still plays in QSPHL				
27	NYI	Chris Taylor	London	C	70	4	10	14	18
28	L.A.	Brandy Semchuk	Canadian Olympic	RW	1	0	0	0	2
29	N.J.	Chris Gotziaman	Roseau H.S.	RW	Injuries hampered career				
30	WSH	Rod Pasma	Cornwall	D	Evaluates minor pro officials				
31	TOR	Felix Potvin	Chicoutimi	G	436	179	1216	13	2.88
32	CGY	Vesa Viitakoski	SaiPa Lappeenranta, FIN	LW	23	2	4	6	8
33	ST.L.	Craig Johnson	Hill-Murray H.S.	LW	325	53	64	117	170
34	NYR	Doug Weight	Lake Superior State	C	624	155	402	557	514
35	WPG	Mike Muller	Wayzata H.S.	D	Continues to play in Europe				
36	HFD	Geoff Sanderson	Swift Current	LW	656	225	212	437	263
37	CHI	Ivan Droppa	Liptovsky Mikulas, TCH	D	19	0	1	1	14
38	EDM	Alexandre Legault	Boston U.	RW	Boston U. grad played 1 year				
39	MTL	Ryan Kuwabara	Ottawa	RW	Continues to play in Japan				
40	PHI	Mikael Renberg	Pitea, SWE	RW	464	150	202	352	250
41	CGY	Etienne Belzile	Cornell	D	Did not play beyond College				
42	PHI	Terran Sandwith	Tri-City	D	8	0	0	0	6
OTHER ROUNDS									
43	QUE	Brad Zavisha	Seattle	LW	2	0	0	0	0
44	PHI	Kimbi Daniels	Swift Current	C	27	1	2	3	4
45	DET	Vyacheslav Kozlov	Khimik Voskresensk, USSR	C	535	182	195	377	346
46	PHI	Bill Armstrong	Oshawa	D					
47	PHI	Chris Therien	Northwood Prep	D	433	21	89	110	385
48	NYI	Dan Plante	Edina H.S.	RW	159	9	14	23	135
49	L.A.	Bill Berg	Belleville	LW					
50	MIN	Laurie Billeck	Prince Albert	D					
51	WSH	Chris Longo	Peterborough	RW					
52	PHI	Al Kinisky	Seattle	LW					
53	N.J.	Mike Dunham	Canterbury H.S.	G	137	48	345	4	2.82
54	ST.L.	Patrice Tardif	Lennoxville Jr.	C	65	7	11	18	78
55	NYR	John Vary	North Bay	D					
56	N.J.	Brad Bombardir	Powell River Jr. A	D	131	5	13	18	30
57	HFD	Mike Lenarduzzi	Sault Ste. Marie	G	4	1	10	0	3.17
58	MTL	Charles Poulin	St-Hyacinthe	C					
59	EDM	Joe Crowley	Lawrence Academy	LW					
60	MTL	Robert Guillet	Longueuil	RW					
61	PIT	Joe Dziedzic	Edison H.S.	LW	130	14	14	28	131
62	CGY	Glen Mears	Rochester Jr. A	D					
63	BOS	Cam Stewart	Elmira Jr. B	LW	148	12	14	26	102
64	N.J.	Mike Bodnarchuk	Kingston	RW					
65	VAN	Darin Bader	Saskatoon	LW					
66	DET	Stewart Malgunas	Seattle	D	129	1	5	6	144
67	EDM	Joel Blain	Hull	LW					
68	PIT	Chris Tamer	Michigan	D	374	11	34	45	771
69	NYR	Jeff Nielsen	Grand Rapids H.S.	RW	193	17	19	36	66
70	MIN	Cal McGowan	Kamloops	C					
71	MIN	Frank Kovacs	Regina	LW					
72	WSH	Randy Pearce	Kitchener	LW					
73	TOR	Darby Hendrickson	Richfield H.S.	C	316	35	30	65	264
74	WPG	Roman Meluzin	Zetor Brno, TCH	RW					
75	WPG	Scott Levins	Tri-City	C/RW	124	13	20	33	316
76	NYR	Rick Willis	Pingree Prep	LW					
77	WPG	Alexei Zhamnov	Dynamo Moscow, USSR	C	526	187	312	499	433
78	HFD	Chris Bright	Moose Jaw	C					
79	CHI	Chris Tucker	Jefferson H.S.	C					
80	TOR	Greg Walters	Ottawa	C					
81	MTL	Gilbert Dionne	Kitchener	LW	223	61	79	140	108
82	BUF	Brian McCarthy	Pingree Prep	C					
83	CGY	Paul Kruse	Kamloops	LW	422	38	33	71	1069
84	BOS	Jerome Buckley	Northwood Prep	RW					
85	NYR	Sergei Zubov	CSKA Moscow, USSR	D	538	83	332	415	161
86	VAN	Gino Odjick	Laval	LW	539	58	66	124	2391
87	DET	Tony Burns	Duluth Denfield H.S.	D					
88	PHI	Dan Kordic	Medicine Hat	LW	197	4	8	12	584
89	PIT	Brian Farrell	Avon Old Farms H.S.	C					
90	NYI	Chris Marinucci	Grand Rapids H.S.	C	13	1	4	5	2
91	L.A.	David Goverde	Sudbury	G	5	1	29	0	6.26
92	MIN	Enrico Ciccone	Trois-Rivieres	D	371	10	18	28	1455
93	WSH	Brian Sakic	Tri-City	C					
94	WSH	Mark Ouimet	Michigan	C					
95	N.J.	Dean Malkoc	Kamloops	D	116	1	3	4	299
96	ST.L.	Jason Ruff	Lethbridge	LW	14	3	3	6	10
97	BUF	Richard Smehlik	TJ Vitkovice, TCH	D	473	41	117	158	373
98	WPG	Craig Martin	Hull	RW	21	0	1	1	24
99	NYR	Lubos Rob	Motor Ceske Budejovice, TCH	C					
100	BUF	Todd Bojcun	Peterborough	G					
101	EDM	Greg Louder	Cushing Academy	G					
102	MTL	Paul Di Pietro	Sudbury	C	192	31	49	80	96
103	BUF	Brad Pascall	North Dakota	D					
104	N.J.	Petr Kuchyna	Dukla Jihlava, TCH	D					
105	BOS	Mike Bales	Ohio State	G	23	2	77	0	4.13
106	QUE	Jeff Parrott	Minnesota-Duluth	D					
107	PIT	Ian Moran	Belmont Hill H.S.	RW	259	14	25	39	153
108	DET	Claude Barthe	Victoriaville	D					
109	PHI	Viacheslav Butsayev	CSKA Moscow, USSR	C	132	17	26	43	133
110	PIT	Denis Casey	Colorado College	G					
111	NYI	Joni Lehto	Ottawa	D					
112	L.A.	Erik Andersson	Danderyd, SWE	C	Re-entered Draft in 1997				
113	MIN	Roman Turek	VTJ Pisek, TCH	G	122	72	235	9	2.03
114	WSH	Andrei Kovalev	Dynamo Moscow, USSR	RW					
115	TOR	Alexander Godynyuk	Sokol Kiev, USSR	D	223	10	39	49	224
116	N.J.	Lubomir Kolnik	Dukla Trencin, TCH	RW					
117	ST.L.	Kurtis Miller	Rochester Jr. A	LW					
118	NYR	Jason Weinrich	Springfield Jr. B	D					
119	WPG	Daniel Jardemyr	Uppsala, SWE	D					
120	HFD	Cory Keenan	Kitchener	D					
121	CHI	Brett Stickney	St. Paul's H.S.	C					
122	EDM	Keijo Sailynoja	Jokerit Helsinki, FIN	LW					
123	MTL	Craig Conroy	Northwood Prep	C	303	47	80	127	165
124	CHI	Derek Edgerly	Stoneham H.S.	C					
125	CGY	Chris Tschupp	Trinity-Pawling H.S.	C					
126	BOS	Mark Woolf	Spokane	RW					
127	QUE	Dwayne Norris	Michigan State	RW	20	2	4	6	8
128	VAN	Daryl Filipek	Ferris State	D					
129	DET	Jason York	Kitchener	D	419	24	116	140	341
130	PIT	Mika Valila	Tappara Tampere, FIN	C					
131	PIT	Ken Plaquin	Michigan Tech	D					
132	NYI	Michael Guilbert	Governor Dummer H.S.	D					
133	L.A.	Robert Lang	CHZ Litvinov, TCH	C	351	72	117	189	80
134	MIN	Jeff Levy	Rochester Jr. A	G					
135	WSH	Roman Kontsek	Dukla Trencin, TCH	RW					
136	TOR	Eric Lacroix	Governor Dummer H.S.	LW	417	65	66	131	318

PICK	TEAM	NAME	DRAFTED FROM	NHL PLAYERS: POS / NHL GOALTENDERS: POS	GP / GP	G / W	A / GA	PTS / SO	PIM / AVG
137	N.J.	Chris McAlpine	Roseville H.S.	D	178	6	13	19	153
138	ST.L.	Wayne Conlan	Trinity-Pawling H.S.	C					
139	NYR	Brian Lonsinger	Choate	D					
140	WPG	John Lilley	Cushing Academy	RW	23	3	8	11	13
141	HFD	Jergus Baca	VSZ Kosice, TCH	D	10	0	2	2	14
142	BUF	Viktor Gordiouk	Krylja Sovetov Mosc., USSR	LW	26	3	8	11	0
143	EDM	Mike Power	Western Michigan	G					
144	MTL	Stephen Rohr	Culver Military Academy	RW					
145	PIT	Pat Neaton	Michigan	D	9	1	1	2	12
146	CGY	Dimitri Frolov	Dynamo Moscow, USSR	D					
147	BOS	Jim Mackey	Hotchkiss H.S.	D					
148	QUE	Andrei Kovalenko	CSKA Moscow, USSR	RW	544	157	185	342	362
149	VAN	Paul O'Hagan	Oshawa	D					
150	DET	Wes McCauley	Michigan State	D					
151	PHI	Patrik Englund	AIK Solna, SWE	LW					
152	PIT	Petteri Koskimaki	Boston U.	C					
153	NYI	Sylvain Fleury	Longueuil	LW					
154	L.A.	Dean Hulett	Lake Superior State	RW					
155	MIN	Doug Barrault	Lethbridge	RW	4	0	0	0	2
156	WSH	Peter Bondra	HC Kosice, TCH	RW	672	337	246	583	465
157	TOR	Dan Stiver	Michigan	RW					
158	QUE	Alexander Karpovtsev	Dynamo Moscow, USSR	D	405	27	114	141	317
159	WSH	Steve Martell	London	RW					
160	NYR	Todd Hedlund	Roseau H.S.	RW					
161	WPG	Henrik Andersson	Vasteras, SWE	D					
162	HFD	Martin D'Orsonnens	Clarkson	D					
163	CHI	Hugo Belanger	Clarkson	LW					
164	EDM	Roman Mejzlik	Dukla Jihlava, TCH	LW/C					
165	MTL	Brent Fleetwood	Portland	LW					
166	BUF	Milan Nedoma	Zetor Brno, TCH	D					
167	CGY	Shawn Murray	Hill-Murray H.S.	G					
168	BOS	John Gruden	Waterloo Jr. A	D	81	0	8	8	40
169	QUE	Pat Mazzoli	Humboldt Jr. A	G					
170	VAN	Mark Cipriano	Victoria	RW					
171	DET	Anthony Gruba	Hill-Murray H.S.	RW					
172	PHI	Toni Porkka	Lukko Rauma, FIN	D					
173	PIT	Ladislav Karabin	Slovan Bratislava, TCH	LW	9	0	0	0	2
174	NYI	John Joyce	Avon Old Farms H.S.	C					
175	L.A.	Denis Leblanc	St-Hyacinthe	C					
176	MIN	Joe Biondi	Minnesota-Duluth	C					
177	WSH	Ken Klee	Bowling Green	D	378	32	40	72	421
178	TOR	Robert Horyna	Dukla Jihlava, TCH	G					
179	N.J.	Jaroslav Modry	Motor Ceske Budejovice, TCH	D	186	14	40	54	105
180	ST.L.	Parris Duffus	Melfort Jr. A	G	1	0	1	0	2.07
181	NYR	Andrew Silverman	Beverly H.S.	D					
182	WPG	Rauli Raitanen	Assat Pori, FIN	C					
183	HFD	Corey Osmak	Nipiwan Jr. A	C					
184	CHI	Owen Lessard	Owen Sound	LW					
185	EDM	Richard Zemlicka	Sparta Praha, TCH	R/LW					
186	MTL	Derek Maguire	Delbarton H.S.	D					
187	BUF	Jason Winch	Niagara Falls	LW					
188	CGY	Mike Murray	Cushing Academy	RW					
189	BOS	Darren Wetherill	Minot Jr. A	D					
190	QUE	Scott Davis	U. of Manitoba	D					
191	VAN	Troy Neumier	Prince Albert	D					
192	DET	Travis Tucker	Avon Old Farms H.S.	D					
193	PHI	Greg Hanson	Bloomington-Kennedy H.S.	D					
194	PIT	Timothy Fingerhut	Canterbury H.S.	LW					
195	NYI	Richard Enga	Culver Military Academy	C					
196	L.A.	Patrik Ross	HV 71 Jonkoping, SWE	RW					
197	MIN	Troy Binnie	Ottawa	RW					
198	WSH	Michael Boback	Providence	C					
199	TOR	Rob Chebator	Arlington Catholic H.S.	D					
200	N.J.	Corey Schwab	Seattle	G	103	23	268	3	3.20
201	ST.L.	Steve Widmeyer	U. of Maine	RW					
202	NYR	Jon Hillebrandt	Monona Grove H.S.	G					
203	WPG	Mika Alatalo	KooKoo Kouvola, FIN	LW	82	10	17	27	36
204	HFD	Espen Knutsen	Valerengen, NOR	C	19	3	0	3	6
205	CHI	Erik Peterson	Brockton H.S.	C					
206	EDM	Petr Korinek	Skoda Plzen, TCH	C					
207	MTL	Mark Kettelhut	Duluth East H.S.	D					
208	BUF	Sylvain Naud	Laval	RW					
209	CGY	Rob Sumner	Victoria	D					
210	BOS	Dean Capuano	Mount St. Charles H.S.	D					
211	QUE	Mika Stromberg	Jokerit Helsinki, FIN	D					
212	VAN	Tyler Ertel	North Bay	C					
213	DET	Brett Larson	Duluth Denfield H.S.	D					
214	PHI	Tommy Soderstrom	Djurgarden Stockholm, SWE	G	156	45	496	10	3.63
215	PIT	Michael Thompson	Michigan State	RW					
216	NYI	Martin Lacroix	St. Lawrence U.	RW					
217	L.A.	K.J.(Kevin) White	Windsor	C					
218	MIN	Ole-Eskild Dahlstrom	Furuset Oslo, NOR	C					
219	WSH	Alan Brown	Colgate	D					
220	TOR	Scott Malone	Northfield H.S.	D					
221	N.J.	Valeri Zelepukin	Khimik Voskresensk, USSR	LW	559	114	173	287	509
222	ST.L.	Joe Hawley	Peterborough	RW					
223	NYR	Brett Lievers	Wayzata H.S.	C					
224	WPG	Sergei Selyanin	Khimik Voskresensk, USSR	D					
225	HFD	Tommie Eriksen	Prince Albert	D					
226	CHI	Steve Dubinsky	Clarkson	C	258	13	33	46	113
227	EDM		invalid claim						
228	MTL	John Uniac	Kitchener	D					
229	BUF	Kenneth Martin	Belmont Hill H.S.	LW					
230	CGY		invalid claim						
231	BOS	Andy Bezeau	Niagara Falls	LW					
232	QUE	Wade Klippenstein	Alaska-Fairbanks	LW					
233	VAN	Karri Kivi	Ilves Tampere, FIN	D					
234	DET	John Hendry	Lake Superior State	LW					
235	PHI	William Lund	Roseau H.S.	C					
236	PIT	Brian Bruininks	Colorado College	D					
237	NYI	Andy Shier	Detroit Compuware Jr. A	C					
238	L.A.	Troy Mohns	Colgate	D					
239	MIN	John McKersie	West H.S.	G					
240	WSH	Todd Hlushko	London	C	79	8	13	21	84
241	TOR	Nick Vachon	Governor Dummer H.S.	C	1	0	0	0	0
242	N.J.	Todd Reirden	Tabor Academy	D	73	6	24	30	52
243	ST.L.	Joe Fleming	Xaverian H.S.	D					
244	NYR	Sergei Nemchinov	Krylja Sovetov Mosc., USSR	C	628	139	166	305	225
245	WPG	Keith Morris	Alaska-Anchorage	C					
246	HFD	Denis Chalifoux	Laval	C					
247	CHI	Dino Grossi	Northeastern	RW					
248	EDM	Sami Nuutinen	Kiekko-Espoo, FIN	D					
249	MTL	Sergei Martynyuk	Torpedo Yaroslavl, USSR	LW					
250	BUF	Brad Rubachuk	Lethbridge	C					
251	CGY	Leo Gudas	Sparta Praha, TCH	D					
252	BOS	Ted Miskolczi	Belleville	D					

1991

PICK	TEAM	NAME	DRAFTED FROM	NHL PLAYERS: POS / NHL GOALTENDERS: POS	GP / GP	G / W	A / GA	PTS / SO	PIM / AVG
FIRST ROUND									
1	QUE	Eric Lindros	Oshawa	C	486	290	369	659	946
2	S.J.	Pat Falloon	Spokane	RW	575	143	179	322	141
3	N.J.	Scott Niedermayer	Kamloops	D	597	70	245	315	320
4	NYI	Scott Lachance	Boston U.	D	524	27	86	113	381
5	WPG	Aaron Ward	Michigan	D	203	12	22	34	181
6	PHI	Peter Forsberg	MoDo Ornskoldsvik, SWE	C	393	142	349	491	390
7	VAN	Alek Stojanov	Hamilton	RW	107	2	5	7	222
8	MIN	Richard Matvichuk	Saskatoon	D	430	23	76	99	376
9	HFD	Patrick Poulin	St-Hyacinthe	C	554	92	118	210	280
10	DET	Martin Lapointe	Laval	RW	470	81	92	173	761
11	N.J.	Brian Rolston	Detroit Compuware Jr. A	C	414	94	111	205	93
12	EDM	Tyler Wright	Swift Current	C	279	20	17	37	387
13	BUF	Philippe Boucher	Granby	D	275	30	66	96	184
14	WSH	Pat Peake	Detroit	C	134	28	41	69	105
15	NYR	Alexei Kovalev	Dynamo Moscow, USSR	RW	547	165	222	387	590
16	PIT	Markus Naslund	MoDo Ornskoldsvik, SWE	RW	477	126	150	276	295
17	MTL	Brent Bilodeau	Seattle	D	Contiues to play minor pro				
18	BOS	Glen Murray	Sudbury	RW	514	133	128	261	341
19	CGY	Niklas Sundblad	AIK Solna, SWE	RW	2	0	0	0	0
20	EDM	Martin Rucinsky	CHZ Litvinov, TCH	LW	542	151	206	357	459
21	WSH	Trevor Halverson	North Bay	LW	17	0	4	4	28
22	CHI	Dean McAmmond	Prince Albert	C	396	76	124	200	223
SECOND ROUND									
23	S.J.	Ray Whitney	Spokane	LW	439	136	185	321	133
24	QUE	Rene Corbet	Drummondville	LW	319	50	65	115	363
25	WSH	Eric Lavigne	Hull	D	1	0	0	0	0
26	NYI	Ziggy Palffy	AC Nitra, TCH	RW	395	195	202	397	205
27	ST.L.	Steve Staios	Niagara Falls	D/RW	236	8	23	31	349
28	MTL	Jim Campbell	Northwood Prep	RW	217	51	63	114	209
29	VAN	Jassen Cullimore	Peterborough	D	265	11	24	35	277
30	S.J.	Sandis Ozolinsh	Dynamo Riga, USSR	D	506	115	254	369	369
31	HFD	Martin Hamrlik	TJ Zlin, TCH	D	Continues to play Czech-Rep				
32	DET	Jamie Pushor	Lethbridge	D	276	7	25	32	392
33	N.J.	Donevan Hextall	Prince Albert	LW	Played 116 games in pros				
34	EDM	Andrew Verner	Peterborough	G	Continues to play in Sweden				
35	BUF	Jason Dawe	Peterborough	RW	365	86	90	176	162
36	WSH	Jeff Nelson	Prince Albert	C	52	3	8	11	20
37	NYR	Darcy Werenka	Lethbridge	D	Played in Europe, AHL, IHL				
38	PIT	Rusty Fitzgerald	Duluth East H.S.	C	25	2	2	4	12
39	CHI	Mike Pomichter	Springfield Jr. B	C	Contiues to play minor pro				
40	BOS	Jozef Stumpel	AC Nitra, TCH	C	472	105	242	347	127
41	CGY	Francois Groleau	Shawinigan	D	8	0	1	1	6
42	L.A.	Guy Leveque	Cornwall	C	17	2	2	4	21
43	MTL	Craig Darby	Albany Academy	C	111	9	18	27	16
OTHER ROUNDS									
44	CHI	Jamie Matthews	Sudbury	C	Re-entered Draft in 1993				
45	S.J.	Dody Wood	Seattle	C	106	8	10	18	471
46	QUE	Rich Brennan	Tabor Academy	D	37	2	5	7	25
47	TOR	Yanic Perreault	Trois-Rivieres	C	371	104	118	222	152

PICK	TEAM	NAME	DRAFTED FROM	NHL PLAYERS: POS	GP	G	A	PTS	PIM
				NHL GOALTENDERS: POS	GP	W	GA	SO	AVG
48	NYI	Jamie McLennan	Lethbridge	G	138	55	330	7	2.63
49	WPG	Dmitri Filimonov	Dynamo Moscow, USSR	D	30	1	4	5	18
50	PHI	Yanick Dupre	Drummondville	LW	35	2	0	2	16
51	VAN	Sean Pronger	Bowling Green	C	153	13	28	41	79
52	CGY	Sandy McCarthy	Laval	RW	441	41	43	84	1081
53	HFD	Todd Hall	Hamden H.S.	LW					
54	DET	Chris Osgood	Medicine Hat	G	337	196	773	29	2.36
55	N.J.	Fredrik Lindquist	Djurgarden Stockholm, SWE	C	8	0	0	0	2
56	EDM	George Breen	Cushing Academy	RW					
57	BUF	Jason Young	Sudbury	LW					
58	WSH	Steve Konowalchuk	Portland	C	500	105	145	250	438
59	HFD	Michael Nylander	Huddinge, SWE	C	386	82	166	248	150
60	PIT	Shane Peacock	Lethbridge	D					
61	MTL	Yves Sarault	St-Jean	LW	85	5	6	11	25
62	BOS	Marcel Cousineau	Beauport	G	26	4	51	1	2.92
63	CGY	Brian Caruso	Minnesota-Duluth	LW					
64	ST.L.	Kyle Reeves	Tri-City	RW					
65	ST.L.	Nathan LaFayette	Cornwall	C	187	17	20	37	103
66	CHI	Bobby House	Brandon	RW					
67	S.J.	Kerry Toporowski	Spokane	D					
68	QUE	Dave Karpa	Ferris State	D	383	13	62	75	1070
69	TOR	Terry Chitaroni	Sudbury	C					
70	NYI	Milan Hnilicka	Poldi Kladno, TCH	G	2	0	5	0	3.49
71	CHI	Igor Kravchuk	CSKA Moscow, USSR	D	562	59	174	233	210
72	BUF	Peter Ambroziak	Ottawa	LW	12	0	1	1	0
73	MTL	Vladimir Vujtek	Tri-City	LW	105	7	29	36	38
74	MIN	Mike Torchia	Kitchener	G	6	3	18	0	3.30
75	HFD	Jim Storm	Michigan Tech	LW	84	7	15	22	44
76	DET	Mike Knuble	Kalamazoo Jr. A	RW	217	35	34	69	68
77	N.J.	Bradley Willner	Richfield H.S.	D					
78	EDM	Mario Nobili	Longueuil	LW					
79	L.A.	Keith Redmond	Bowling Green	LW	12	1	0	1	20
80	WSH	Justin Morrison	Kingston	C					
81	L.A.	Alexei Zhitnik	Sokol Kiev, USSR	D	584	65	211	276	688
82	PIT	Joe Tamminen	Virginia H.S.	C					
83	MTL	Sylvain Lapointe	Clarkson	D					
84	BOS	Brad Tiley	Sault Ste. Marie	D	9	0	0	0	0
85	CGY	Steven Magnusson	Anoka H.S.	C					
86	PHI	Aris Brimanis	Bowling Green	D	39	2	4	6	18
87	ST.L.	Grayden Reid	Owen Sound	C					
88	CHI	Zac Boyer	Kamloops	RW	3	0	0	0	0
89	S.J.	Dan Ryder	Sudbury	G					
90	QUE	Patrick Labrecque	St-Jean	G	2	0	7	0	4.29
91	WPG	Juha Ylonen	Kiekko-Espoo, FIN	C	192	13	51	64	42
92	NYI	Steve Junker	Spokane	LW	5	0	0	0	0
93	EDM	Ryan Haggerty	Westminster H.S.	C					
94	PHI	Yanick Degrace	Trois-Rivieres	G					
95	VAN	Dan Kesa	Prince Albert	RW	139	8	22	30	66
96	NYR	Corey Machanic	Vermont	D					
97	MIN	Mike Kennedy	U. of British Columbia	C	145	16	36	52	112
98	DET	Dimitri Motkov	CSKA Moscow, USSR	D					
99	WPG	Yan Kaminsky	Dynamo Moscow, USSR	RW	26	3	2	5	4
100	MTL	Brad Layzell	RPI	D					
101	BUF	Steve Shields	Michigan	G	135	49	322	8	2.54
102	TOR	Alexei Kudashov	Krylja Sovetov Mosc., USSR	C	25	1	0	1	4
103	QUE	Bill Lindsay	Tri-City	LW	590	77	116	193	608
104	PIT	Robert Melanson	Hull	D					
105	MTL	Tony Prpic	Culver Military Academy	RW					
106	BOS	Mariusz Czerkawski	GKS Tychy, POL	RW	422	125	124	249	136
107	CGY	Jerome Butler	Roseau H.S.	G					
108	L.A.	Pauli Jaks	Ambri-Piotta, SUI	G	1	0	2	0	3.00
109	ST.L.	Jeff Callinan	Minnetonka H.S.	G					
110	CHI	Maco Balkovec	Merritt Jr. A	D					
111	S.J.	Frank Nilsson	Vasteras, SWE	C					
112	CHI	Kevin St. Jacques	Lethbridge	LW					
113	TOR	Jeff Perry	Owen Sound	LW					
114	NYI	Robert Valicevic	Detroit Red Wings Jr. A	RW	99	18	13	31	23
115	WPG	Jeff Sebastian	Seattle	D					
116	PHI	Clayton Norris	Medicine Hat	RW					
117	VAN	John Namestnikov	Torpedo Niz. Novogord, USSR	D	43	0	9	9	24
118	MIN	Mark Lawrence	Detroit	RW	106	15	22	37	83
119	HFD	Mike Harding	Northern Michigan	RW					
120	TOR	Alexander Kuzminsky	Sokol Kiev, USSR	C					
121	N.J.	Curt Regnier	Prince Albert	RW					
122	PHI	Dimitri Yushkevich	Torpedo Yaroslavl, USSR	D	567	29	139	168	535
123	BUF	Sean O'Donnell	Sudbury	D	381	12	59	71	799
124	BUF	Brian Holzinger	Detroit Compuware Jr. A	C	366	73	100	173	223
125	NYR	Fredrik Jax	Leksand, SWE	RW					
126	PIT	Brian Clifford	Nichols H.S.	C					
127	MTL	Oleg Petrov	CSKA Moscow, USSR	RW	156	22	50	72	47
128	NYR	Barry Young	Sudbury	D					
129	CGY	Bobby Marshall	Miami of Ohio	D					
130	L.A.	Brett Seguin	Ottawa	C					
131	ST.L.	Bruce Gardiner	Colgate	C	232	25	38	63	183
132	CHI	Jacques Auger	Wisconsin	D					
133	S.J.	Jaroslav Otevrel	TJ Zlin, TCH	LW	16	3	4	7	2
134	QUE	Mikael Johansson	Djurgarden Stockholm, SWE	C					

PICK	TEAM	NAME	DRAFTED FROM	NHL PLAYERS: POS	GP	G	A	PTS	PIM
				NHL GOALTENDERS: POS	GP	W	GA	SO	AVG
135	TOR	Martin Prochazka	Poldi Kladno, TCH	RW	32	2	5	7	8
136	NYI	Andreas Johansson	Falun, SWE	C	204	35	46	81	96
137	MIN	Geoff Finch	Brown	G					
138	PHI	Andrei Lomakin	Dynamo Moscow, USSR	RW	215	42	62	104	92
139	VAN	Brent Thurston	Spokane	LW					
140	CGY	Matt Hoffman	Oshawa	LW					
141	HFD	Brian Mueller	South Kent H.S.	D					
142	DET	Igor Malykhin	CSKA Moscow, USSR	D					
143	N.J.	David Craievich	Oshawa	D					
144	EDM	David Oliver	Michigan	RW	181	42	41	83	68
145	BUF	Chris Snell	Ottawa	D	34	2	7	9	24
146	WSH	Dave Morissette	Shawinigan	LW	11	0	0	0	57
147	NYR	John Rushin	Kennedy H.S.	C					
148	PIT	Ed Patterson	Kamloops	RW	68	3	3	6	56
149	MTL	Brady Kramer	Haverford H.S.	C					
150	BOS	Gary Golczewski	Trinity-Pawling H.S.	LW					
151	CGY	Kelly Harper	Michigan State	C					
152	L.A.	Kelly Fairchild	Grand Rapids H.S.	C	24	0	3	3	4
153	ST.L.	Terry Hollinger	Lethbridge	D	7	0	0	0	2
154	CHI	Scott Kirton	Powell River Jr. A	RW					
155	S.J.	Dean Grillo	Warroad H.S.	RW					
156	QUE	Janne Laukkanen	Reipas Lahti, FIN	D	291	11	69	80	265
157	QUE	Aaron Asp	Ferris State	C					
158	NYI	Todd Sparks	Hull	LW					
159	WPG	Jeff Ricciardi	Ottawa	D					
160	TOR	Dmitri Mironov	Krylja Sovetov Mosc., USSR	D	520	51	201	252	562
161	VAN	Eric Johnson	Armstrong H.S.	RW					
162	BUF	Jiri Kuntos	Dukla Jihlava, TCH	D					
163	HFD	Steve Yule	Kamloops	D					
164	TOR	Robb McIntyre	Dubuque Jr. A	LW					
165	N.J.	Paul Wolanski	Niagara Falls	D					
166	EDM	Gary Kitching	Thunder Bay Jr. A	C					
167	TOR	Tomas Kucharcik	Dukla Jihlava, TCH	C					
168	WSH	Rick Corriveau	London	D					
169	NYR	Corey Hirsch	Kamloops	G	105	33	297	4	3.15
170	PIT	Peter McLaughlin	Belmont Hill H.S.	D					
171	MTL	Brian Savage	Miami of Ohio	RW	352	120	91	211	169
172	BOS	Jay Moser	Park H.S.	D					
173	CGY	David St. Pierre	Longueuil	C					
174	MIN	Michael Burkett	Michigan State	LW					
175	ST.L.	Chris Kenady	St. Paul Jr. A	RW	7	0	2	2	0
176	CHI	Roch Belley	Niagara Falls	G					
177	S.J.	Corwin Saurdiff	Waterloo Jr. A	G					
178	QUE	Adam Bartell	Niagara Jr. A	D					
179	TOR	Guy Lehoux	Drummondville	D					
180	NYI	John Johnson	Niagara Falls	C					
181	WPG	Sean Gauthier	Kingston	G	1	0	0	0	0.00
182	PHI	James Bode	Armstrong H.S.	RW					
183	VAN	David Neilson	Prince Albert	LW					
184	MIN	Derek Herlofsky	St. Paul Jr. A	G					
185	HFD	Chris Belanger	Western Michigan	D					
186	DET	Jim Bermingham	Laval	C					
187	N.J.	Daniel Reimann	Anoka H.S.	D					
188	QUE	Brent Brekke	Western Michigan	D					
189	BUF	Tony Iob	Sault Ste. Marie	LW					
190	WSH	Trevor Duhaime	St-Jean	RW					
191	NYR	Vyachesl Uvayev	Spartak Moscow, USSR	D					
192	PIT	Jeff Lembke	Omaha Jr. A	G					
193	MTL	Scott Fraser	Dartmouth	C	72	16	15	31	24
194	BOS	Daniel Hodge	Merrimack	D					
195	CGY	David Struch	Saskatoon	C	4	0	0	0	4
196	L.A.	Craig Brown	Western Michigan	G					
197	ST.L.	Jed Fiebelkorn	Osseo H.S.	RW					
198	CHI	Scott MacDonald	Choate	D					
199	S.J.	Dale Craigwell	Oshawa	C	98	11	18	29	28
200	QUE	Paul Koch	Omaha Jr. A	D					
201	TOR	Gary Miller	North Bay	D					
202	NYI	Robert Canavan	Hingham H.S.	LW					
203	WPG	Igor Ulanov	Khimik Voskresensk, USSR	D	484	15	85	100	901
204	PHI	Josh Bartell	Rome Free Academy	D					
205	VAN	Brad Barton	Kitchener	D					
206	MIN	Tom Nemeth	Cornwall	LW					
207	HFD	Jason Currie	Clarkson	G					
208	DET	Jason Firth	Kitchener	C					
209	WSH	Rob Leask	Hamilton	D					
210	EDM	Vegar Barlie	Valerengen, NOR	RW					
211	BUF	Spencer Meany	St. Lawrence U.	RW					
212	WSH	Carl Leblanc	Granby	D					
213	NYR	Jamie Ram	Michigan Tech	G	1	0	0	0	0.00
214	PIT	Chris Tok	Greenway H.S.	D					
215	MTL	Greg MacEachern	Laval	D					
216	BOS	Steve Norton	Michigan State	D					
217	CGY	Sergei Zolotov	Krylja Sovetov Mosc., USSR	LW					
218	L.A.	Mattias Olsson	Farjestad Karlstad, SWE	D					
219	ST.L.	Chris MacKenzie	Colgate	LW					
220	CHI	Alexander Andrievski	Dynamo Moscow, USSR	RW	1	0	0	0	0
221	S.J.	Aaron Kriss	Cranbrook H.S.	D					

PICK	TEAM	NAME	DRAFTED FROM	NHL PLAYERS: POS / NHL GOALTENDERS: POS	GP / GP	G / W	A / GA	PTS / SO	PIM / AVG
222	QUE	Doug Friedman	Boston U.	LW	18	0	1	1	34
223	TOR	Johnathon Kelley	Arlington Catholic H.S.	C					
224	NYI	Marcus Thuresson	Leksand, SWE	C					
225	WPG	Jason Jennings	Western Michigan	RW					
226	PHI	Neil Little	RPI	G					
227	VAN	Jason Fitzsimmons	Moose Jaw	G					
228	MIN	Shayne Green	Kamloops	RW					
229	HFD	Mike Santonelli	Matignon H.S.	C					
230	DET	Bart Turner	Michigan State	LW					
231	N.J.	Kevin Riehl	Medicine Hat	C					
232	EDM	Yevgeny Belosheiken	CSKA Moscow, USSR	G					
233	BUF	Mikhail Volkov	Krylja Sovetov Mosc., USSR	RW					
234	WSH	Rob Puchniak	Lethbridge	D					
235	NYR	Vitali Chinakhov	Torpedo Yaroslavl, USSR	C					
236	PIT	Paul Dyck	Moose Jaw	D					
237	MTL	Paul Lepler	Rochester Jr. A	D					
238	BOS	Stephen Lombardi	Deerfield Academy	C					
239	CGY	Marko Jantunen	Reipas Lahti, FIN	C	3	0	0	0	0
240	L.A.	Andre Bouliane	Longueuil	G					
241	ST.L.	Kevin Rappana	Duluth East H.S.	D					
242	CHI	Mike Larkin	Rice Memorial H.S.	D					
243	S.J.	Mikhail Kravets	SKA Leningrad, USSR	RW	2	0	0	0	0
244	QUE	Eric Meloche	Drummondville	RW					
245	TOR	Chris O'Rourke	Alaska-Fairbanks	D					
246	NYI	Marty Schriner	North Dakota	C					
247	WPG	Sergei Sorokin	Dynamo Moscow, USSR	D					
248	PHI	John Porco	Belleville	C					
249	VAN	Xavier Majic	RPI	C					
250	MIN	Jukka Suomalainen	GrIFK Kauniainen, FIN	D					
251	HFD	Rob Peters	Ohio State	D					
252	DET	Andrew Miller	Wexford Jr. B	RW					
253	N.J.	Jason Hehr	Kelowna Jr. A	D					
254	EDM	Juha Riihijarvi	Karpat Oulu, FIN	RW					
255	BUF	Michael Smith	Lake Superior State	D					
256	WSH	Bill Kovacs	Sudbury	LW					
257	NYR	Brian Wiseman	Michigan	C	3	0	0	0	0
258	PIT	Pasi Huura	Ilves Tampere, FIN	D					
259	MTL	Dale Hooper	Springfield Jr. B	D					
260	BOS	Torsten Kienass	Dynamo Berlin, FRG	D					
261	CGY	Andrei Trefilov	Dynamo Moscow, USSR	G	54	12	153	2	3.45
262	L.A.	Michael Gaul	St. Lawrence U.	D	1	0	0	0	0
263	ST.L.	Mike Veisor	Springfield Jr. B	G					
264	CHI	Scott Dean	Lake Forest H.S.	D					

1992

PICK	TEAM	NAME	DRAFTED FROM	NHL PLAYERS: POS / NHL GOALTENDERS: POS	GP / GP	G / W	A / GA	PTS / SO	PIM / AVG
FIRST ROUND									
1	T.B.	Roman Hamrlik	ZPS Zlin, TCH	D	573	74	214	288	660
2	OTT	Alexei Yashin	Dynamo Moscow, CIS	C	422	178	225	403	192
3	S.J.	Mike Rathje	Medicine Hat	D	376	13	66	79	249
4	QUE	Todd Warriner	Windsor	LW	308	47	61	108	151
5	NYI	Darius Kasparaitis	Dynamo Moscow, CIS	D	491	16	80	96	866
6	CGY	Cory Stillman	Windsor	C	327	88	102	190	147
7	PHI	Ryan Sittler	Nichols H.S.	LW	Played 5 injury-plagued years				
8	TOR	Brandon Convery	Sudbury	C	72	9	19	28	36
9	HFD	Robert Petrovicky	Dukla Trencin, TCH	C	197	27	38	65	114
10	S.J.	Andrei Nazarov	Dynamo Moscow, CIS	LW	321	41	60	101	699
11	BUF	David Cooper	Medicine Hat	D	28	3	7	10	24
12	CHI	Sergei Krivokrasov	CSKA Moscow, CIS	RW	370	77	91	168	232
13	EDM	Joe Hulbig	St. Sebastian's H.S.	LW	48	4	4	8	12
14	WSH	Sergei Gonchar	Traktor Chelyabinsk, CIS	D	364	74	110	184	293
15	PHI	Jason Bowen	Tri-City	D	77	2	6	8	109
16	BOS	Dmitri Kvartalnov	San Diego IHL	LW	112	42	49	91	26
17	WPG	Sergei Bautin	Dynamo Moscow, CIS	D	132	5	25	30	176
18	N.J.	Jason Smith	Regina	D	418	12	49	61	394
19	PIT	Martin Straka	HC Skoda Plzen, TCH	C	521	132	222	354	202
20	MTL	David Wilkie	Kamloops	D	166	10	26	36	163
21	VAN	Libor Polasek	TJ Vitkovice, TCH	C	Continues to play Czech-Rep				
22	DET	Curtis Bowen	Ottawa	LW	Continues to play in Britain				
23	TOR	Grant Marshall	Ottawa	RW	327	39	58	97	428
24	NYR	Peter Ferraro	Waterloo Jr. A	C	88	9	14	23	58
SECOND ROUND									
25	OTT	Chad Penney	North Bay	LW	3	0	0	0	2
26	T.B.	Drew Bannister	Sault Ste. Marie	D	160	5	25	30	161
27	WPG	Boris Mironov	CSKA Moscow, CIS	D	455	58	177	235	639
28	QUE	Paul Brousseau	Hull	RW	25	1	3	4	29
29	QUE	Tuomas Gronman	Tacoma	D	38	1	3	4	38
30	CGY	Chris O'Sullivan	Catholic Memorial H.S.	D	60	2	16	18	16
31	PHI	Denis Metlyuk	Lada Togliatti, CIS	C	Contiues to play minor pro				
32	WSH	Jim Carey	Catholic Memorial H.S.	G	172	79	416	16	2.58
33	MTL	Valeri Bure	Spokane	RW	393	112	135	247	147
34	MIN	Jarkko Varvio	HPK Hameenlinna, FIN	RW	13	3	4	7	4
35	BUF	Jozef Cierny	ZTK Zvolen, TCH	LW	1	0	0	0	0
36	CHI	Jeff Shantz	Regina	C	455	61	115	176	225
37	EDM	Martin Reichel	Freiburg, GER	RW	Continues to play in Germany				
38	ST.L.	Igor Korolev	Dynamo Moscow, CIS	C/LW	530	93	173	266	230
39	L.A.	Justin Hocking	Spokane	D	1	0	0	0	0
40	VAN	Michael Peca	Ottawa	C	400	102	127	229	384
41	CHI	Sergei Klimovich	Dynamo Moscow, CIS	C	1	0	0	0	2
42	N.J.	Sergei Brylin	CSKA Moscow, CIS	C	234	28	39	67	102
43	PIT	Marc Hussey	Moose Jaw	D	Continues to play in Britain				
44	MTL	Keli Corpse	Kingston	C	Contiunes to play minor pro				
45	VAN	Mike Fountain	Oshawa	G	10	2	25	1	3.54
46	DET	Darren McCarty	Bellevile	RW	393	83	123	206	866
47	HFD	Andrei Nikolishin	Dynamo Moscow, CIS	LW	358	56	117	173	146
48	NYR	Mattias Norstrom	AIK Solna, SWE	D	367	7	58	65	324
OTHER ROUNDS									
49	T.B.	Brent Gretzky	Belleville	C	13	1	3	4	2
50	OTT	Patrick Traverse	Shawinigan	D	117	7	26	33	45
51	S.J.	Alexander Cherbayev	Khimik Voskresensk, CIS	LW					
52	QUE	Manny Fernandez	Laval	G	33	12	74	1	2.48
53	WSH	Stefan Ustorf	ESV Kaufbeuren, GER	C	54	7	10	17	16
54	CGY	Mathias Johansson	Farjestad Karlstad, SWE	C					
55	BOS	Sergei Zholtok	Rigas Stars, CIS	C	298	57	58	115	71
56	NYI	Jarrett Deuling	Kamloops	LW	15	0	1	1	11
57	HFD	Jan Vopat	HC Chemopetrol Litvinov, TCH	D	126	11	20	31	70
58	MIN	Jeff Bes	Guelph	C					
59	BUF	Ondrej Steiner	HC Skoda Plzen, TCH	C					
60	WPG	Jeremy Stevenson	Cornwall	LW	Re-entered Draft in 1994				
61	EDM	Simon Roy	Shawinigan	D					
62	ST.L.	Vitali Karamnov	Dynamo Moscow, CIS	LW	92	12	20	32	65
63	L.A.	Sandy Allan	North Bay	G					
64	ST.L.	Vitali Prokhorov	Spartak Moscow, CIS	LW	83	19	11	30	35
65	EDM	Kirk Maltby	Owen Sound	RW	395	53	45	98	412
66	N.J.	Cale Hulse	Portland	D	273	10	43	53	444
67	PIT	Travis Thiessen	Moose Jaw	D					
68	MTL	Craig Rivet	Kingston	D	247	6	33	39	348
69	VAN	Jeff Connolly	St. Sebastian's H.S.	C					
70	DET	Sylvain Cloutier	Guelph	C	7	0	0	0	0
71	WSH	Martin Gendron	St-Hyacinthe	RW	30	4	2	6	10
72	NYR	Eric Cairns	Detroit	D	155	2	14	16	458
73	OTT	Radek Hamr	Sparta Praha, TCH	D	11	0	0	0	0
74	T.B.	Aaron Gavey	Sault Ste. Marie	C	204	25	24	49	180
75	S.J.	Jan Caloun	HC Chemopetrol Litvinov, TCH	RW	13	8	3	11	0
76	QUE	Ian McIntyre	Beauport	D					
77	TOR	Nikolai Borschevsky	Spartak Moscow, CIS	RW	162	49	73	122	44
78	CGY	Robert Svehla	Dukla Trencin, TCH	D	409	48	185	233	440
79	HFD	Kevin Smyth	Moose Jaw	LW	58	6	8	14	31
80	BUF	Dean Melanson	St-Hyacinthe	D	5	0	0	0	4
81	HFD	Jason McBain	Portland	D	9	0	0	0	0
82	MTL	Louis Bernard	Drummondville	D					
83	BUF	Matthew Barnaby	Beauport	RW	399	61	93	154	1479
84	WPG	Mark Visheau	London	D	29	1	3	4	107
85	NYR	Chris Ferraro	Waterloo Jr. A	C/RW	73	7	8	15	57
86	ST.L.	Lee Leslie	Prince Albert	LW					
87	L.A.	Kevin Brown	Belleville	RW	64	7	9	16	28
88	MIN	Jere Lehtinen	Kiekko-Espoo, FIN	RW	283	68	105	173	56
89	CHI	Andy MacIntyre	Saskatoon	LW					
90	N.J.	Vitali Tomilin	Krylja Sovetov Mosc., CIS	C					
91	PIT	Todd Klassen	Tri-City	D					
92	MTL	Marc Lamothe	Kingston	G	2	1	10	0	5.17
93	VAN	Brent Tully	Peterborough	D					
94	N.J.	Scott McCabe	GPD Midgets	D					
95	TOR	Mark Raiter	Saskatoon	D					
96	EDM	Ralph Intranuovo	Sault Ste. Marie	C	22	2	4	6	4
97	T.B.	Brantt Myhres	Lethbridge	RW	128	6	2	8	599
98	OTT	Daniel Guerard	Victoriaville	RW	2	0	0	0	0
99	S.J.	Marcus Ragnarsson	Djurgarden Stockholm, SWE	D	356	19	91	110	274
100	QUE	Charlie Wasley	St. Paul Jr. A	D					
101	TOR	Janne Gronvall	Lukko Rauma, FIN	D					
102	CGY	Sami Helenius	Jokerit Helsinki, FIN	D	44	1	1	2	69
103	PHI	Vladislav Buljin	Dizelist Penza, CIS	D					
104	NYI	Thomas Klimt	HC Skoda Plzen, TCH	C					
105	NYI	Ryan Duthie	Spokane	C					
106	TOR	Chris Deruiter	Kingston Jr. A	RW					
107	BUF	Markus Ketterer	Jokerit Helsinki, FIN	G					
108	BUF	Yuri Khmylev	Krylja Sovetov Mosc., CIS	LW	263	64	88	152	133
109	EDM	Joaquin Gage	Portland	G	18	2	52	0	3.82
110	VAN	Brian Loney	Ohio State	RW	12	2	3	5	6
111	L.A.	Jeff Shevalier	North Bay	LW	32	5	9	14	8
112	BOS	Scott Bailey	Spokane	G	19	6	55	0	3.42
113	CHI	Tim Hogan	Michigan	D					
114	N.J.	Ryan Black	Peterborough	LW					
115	PIT	Philippe DeRouville	Verdun	G	3	1	9	0	3.16
116	MTL	Don Chase	Springfield Jr. B	C					
117	VAN	Adrian Aucoin	Boston U.	D	294	46	58	104	225
118	DET	Mike Sullivan	Reading H.S.	C					
119	WSH	John Varga	Tacoma	LW					
120	NYR	Dmitri Starostenko	CSKA Moscow, CIS	LW					

PICK	TEAM	NAME	DRAFTED FROM	NHL PLAYERS: POS NHL GOALTENDERS: POS	GP GP	G W	A GA	PTS SO	PIM AVG
121	OTT	Al Sinclair	Michigan	D					
122	T.B.	Martin Tanguay	Verdun	C					
123	S.J.	Michal Sykora	Tacoma	D	218	10	43	53	159
124	QUE	Paxton Schulte	Spokane	LW	2	0	0	0	4
125	TOR	Mikael Hakansson	Nacka, SWE	C					
126	CGY	Ravil Yakubov	Dynamo Moscow, CIS	C					
127	PHI	Roman Zolotov	Dynamo Moscow, CIS	D					
128	NYI	Derek Armstrong	Sudbury	C	83	9	10	19	56
129	CGY	Joel Bouchard	Verdun	D	244	14	27	41	195
130	MIN	Michael Johnson	Ottawa	D					
131	BUF	Paul Rushforth	North Bay	C					
132	WPG	Alexander Alexeyev	Sokol Kiev, CIS	D					
133	BOS	Jiri Dopita	DS Olomouc, TCH	C	Re-entered Draft in 1998				
134	ST.L.	Bob Lachance	Springfield Jr. B	RW					
135	L.A.	Rem Murray	Michigan State	C/LW	265	50	52	102	83
136	BOS	Grigori Panteleev	Rigas Stars, CIS	LW	54	8	6	14	12
137	CHI	Gerry Skrypec	Ottawa	D					
138	N.J.	Daniel Trebil	Bloomington-Jefferson H.S.	D	59	4	4	8	25
139	PIT	Artem Kopot	Traktor Chelyabinsk, CIS	D					
140	MTL	Martin Sychra	Zetor Brno, TCH	C					
141	VAN	Jason Clark	St. Thomas Jr. B	C					
142	DET	Jason MacDonald	Owen Sound	RW					
143	HFD	Jarrett Reid	Sault Ste. Marie	C					
144	NYR	David Dal Grande	Ottawa Jr. A	D					
145	T.B.	Derek Wilkinson	Detroit	G	22	3	57	0	3.67
146	OTT	Jaroslav Miklenda	DS Olomouc, TCH	G					
147	S.J.	Eric Bellerose	Trois-Rivieres	LW					
148	QUE	Martin Lepage	Hull	D					
149	TOR	Patrik Augusta	Dukla Jihlava, TCH	RW	4	0	0	0	0
150	CGY	Pavel Rajnoha	ZPS Zlin, TCH	D					
151	PHI	Kirk Daubenspeck	Culver Military Academy	G					
152	NYI	Vladimir Grachev	Dynamo-2 Moscow, CIS	LW					
153	HFD	Ken Belanger	Ottawa	LW	156	7	10	17	465
154	MIN	Kyle Peterson	Thunder Bay Jr. A	C					
155	WPG	Artur Oktyabrev	CSKA Moscow, CIS	D					
156	WPG	Andrei Raisky	Ust-Kamenogorsk, RUS, CIS	C					
157	EDM	Steve Gibson	Windsor	LW					
158	ST.L.	Ian Laperriere	Drummondville	C	399	45	78	123	796
159	NYI	Steve O'Rourke	Tri-City	RW					
160	ST.L.	Lance Burns	Lethbridge	C					
161	CHI	Mike Prokopec	Cornwall	RW	15	0	0	0	11
162	N.J.	Geordie Kinnear	Peterborough	D	4	0	0	0	13
163	PIT	Jan Alinc	HC Chemopetrol Litvinov, TCH	C					
164	MTL	Christian Proulx	St-Jean	D	7	1	2	3	20
165	VAN	Scott Hollis	Oshawa	RW					
166	DET	Greg Scott	Niagara Falls	G					
167	WSH	Mark Matier	Sault Ste. Marie	D					
168	NYR	Matt Oates	Miami of Ohio	LW					
169	OTT	Jay Kenney	Canterbury H.S.	D					
170	T.B.	Dennis Maxwell	Niagara Falls	C					
171	S.J.	Ryan Smith	Brandon	D					
172	QUE	Mike Jickling	Spokane	C					
173	TOR	Ryan Vandenbussche	Cornwall	RW	89	2	2	4	233
174	CGY	Ryan Mulhern	Canterbury H.S.	C	3	0	0	0	0
175	PHI	Claude Jutras Jr.	Hull	RW					
176	NYI	Jason Widmer	Lethbridge	D	7	0	1	1	7
177	HFD	Konstantin Korotkov	Spartak Moscow, CIS	C					
178	MIN	Juha Lind	Jokerit Helsinki, FIN	C	86	6	9	15	16
179	BUF	Dean Tiltgen	Tri-City	C					
180	ST.L.	Igor Boldin	Spartak Moscow, CIS	C					
181	EDM	Kyuin Shim	Sherwood Park Jr. A	RW					
182	ST.L.	Nick Naumenko	Dubuque Jr. A	D					
183	DET	Justin Krall	Omaha Jr. A	D					
184	BOS	Kurt Seher	Seattle	D					
185	CHI	Layne Roland	Portland	RW					
186	N.J.	Stephane Yelle	Oshawa	C	382	45	67	112	184
187	PIT	Fran Bussey	Duluth East H.S.	C					
188	MTL	Michael Burman	North Bay	D					
189	DET	C. J. Denomme	Kitchener	G					
190	EDM	Colin Schmidt	Regina Midgets	C					
191	WSH	Mike Mathers	Kamloops	LW					
192	NYR	Mickey Elick	Wisconsin	D					
193	T.B.	Andrew Kemper	Seattle	D					
194	OTT	Claude Jr. Savoie	Victoriaville	RW					
195	S.J.	Chris Burns	Thunder Bay Jr. A	G					
196	QUE	Steve Passmore	Victoria	G	30	8	80	1	2.74
197	TOR	Wayne Clarke	RPI	RW					
198	CGY	Brandon Carper	Bowling Green	D					
199	PHI	Jonas Hakansson	Malmo, SWE	LW					
200	NYI	Daniel Paradis	Chicoutimi	C					
201	HFD	Greg Zwakman	Edina H.S.	D					
202	MIN	Lars Edstrom	Lulea, SWE	LW					
203	BUF	Todd Simon	Niagara Falls	C	15	0	1	1	0
204	WPG	Nikolai Khabibulin	CSKA Moscow, CIS	G	284	126	735	21	2.75
205	EDM	Marko Tuomainen	Clarkson	RW	67	9	8	17	80
206	ST.L.	Todd Harris	Tri-City	D					
207	L.A.	Magnus Wernblom	MoDo Ornskoldsvik, SWE	RW					
208	BOS	Mattias Timander	MoDo Ornskoldsvik, SWE	D	146	2	23	25	52
209	CHI	David Hymovitz	Thayer Academy	LW					
210	N.J.	Jeff Toms	Sault Ste. Marie	LW	122	8	21	29	31
211	PIT	Brian Bonin	White Bear Lake H.S.	C	5	0	0	0	0
212	MTL	Earl Cronan	St. Mark's H.S.	LW					
213	VAN	Sonny Mignacca	Medicine Hat	G					
214	DET	Jeff Walker	Peterborough	D					
215	WSH	Brian Stagg	Kingston	RW					
216	NYR	Daniel Brierley	Choate	D					
217	OTT	Jake Grimes	Belleville	C					
218	T.B.	Marc Tardif	Shawinigan	LW					
219	S.J.	Alexander Kholomeyev	Izoherts St. Petersburg, CIS	LW					
220	QUE	Anson Carter	Wexford Jr. A	C	230	73	75	148	76
221	TOR	Sergei Simonov	Kristall Saratov, CIS	D					
222	CGY	Jonas Hoglund	Farjestad Karlstad, SWE	RW	302	68	66	134	60
223	PHI	Chris Herperger	Swift Current	LW	9	0	0	0	5
224	NYI	David Wainwright	Thayer Academy	D					
225	HFD	Steven Halko	Thornhill Jr. A	D	96	0	13	13	59
226	MIN	Jeff Romfo	Blaine H.S.	C					
227	BUF	Rick Kowalsky	Sault Ste. Marie	RW					
228	WPG	Yevgeny Garanin	Khimik Voskresensk, CIS	C					
229	WPG	Teemu Numminen	Stoneham H.S.	C					
230	ST.L.	Yuri Gunko	Sokol Kiev, CIS	D					
231	L.A.	Ryan Pisiak	Prince Albert	RW					
232	BOS	Chris Crombie	London	LW					
233	CHI	Richard Raymond	Cornwall	D					
234	N.J.	Heath Weenk	Regina	D					
235	PIT	Brian Callahan	Belmont Hill H.S.	C					
236	MTL	Trent Cavicchi	Dartmouth Midgets	G					
237	VAN	Mark Wotton	Saskatoon	D	42	3	6	9	25
238	DET	Dan McGillis	Hawkesbury Jr. A	D	299	29	87	116	277
239	WSH	Gregory Callahan	Belmont Hill H.S.	D					
240	NYR	Vladimir Vorobjev	Metallurg Cherepovets, CIS	LW	33	9	7	16	14
241	T.B.	Tom MacDonald	Sault Ste. Marie	C					
242	OTT	Tomas Jelinek	HPK Hameenlinna, FIN	RW	49	7	6	13	52
243	S.J.	Victor Ignatjev	Rigas Stars, CIS	D	11	0	1	1	6
244	QUE	Aaron Ellis	Culver Military Academy	G					
245	TOR	Nathan Dempsey	Regina	D	20	1	3	4	4
246	CGY	Andrei Potaichuk	Krylja Sovetov Mosc., CIS	RW					
247	PHI	Patrice Paquin	Beauport	LW					
248	NYI	Andrei Vasilyev	CSKA Moscow, CIS	LW	16	2	5	7	6
249	HFD	Joacim Esbjors	Vastra Frolunda, SWE	D					
250	MIN	Jeffrey Moen	Roseville H.S.	G					
251	BUF	Chris Clancy	Cornwall	LW					
252	WPG	Andrei Karpovstev	Dynamo Moscow, CIS	RW					
253	EDM	Bryan Rasmussen	St. Louis Park H.S.	LW					
254	WPG	Ivan Vologzhaninov	Sokol Kiev, CIS	RW					
255	L.A.	Jukka Tiilikainen	Kiekko-Espoo, FIN	LW					
256	BOS	Denis Chervyakov	Rigas Stars, CIS	D	2	0	0	0	2
257	BOS	Yevgeny Pavlov	SKA St. Petersburg, CIS	LW					
258	N.J.	Vladislav Yakovenko	Argus Moscow, CIS	LW					
259	ST.L.	Wade Salzman	Duluth East H.S.	G					
260	MTL	Hiroyuki Miura	Kushiro High School, JPN	D					
261	VAN	Aaron Boh	Spokane	D					
262	DET	Ryan Bach	Notre Dame Jr. A.	G	3	0	8	0	4.44
263	WSH	Billy Jo MacPherson	Oshawa	LW					
264	OTT	Petter Ronnqvist	Nacka, SWE	G					

1993

PICK	TEAM	NAME	DRAFTED FROM	NHL PLAYERS: POS NHL GOALTENDERS: POS	GP GP	G W	A GA	PTS SO	PIM AVG
FIRST ROUND									
1	OTT	Alexandre Daigle	Victoriaville	C	459	100	141	241	152
2	HFD	Chris Pronger	Peterborough	D	508	64	184	248	805
3	T.B.	Chris Gratton	Kingston	C	526	112	202	314	956
4	ANA	Paul Kariya	U. of Maine	LW	376	210	254	464	117
5	FLA	Rob Niedermayer	Medicine Hat	C	451	89	145	234	385
6	S.J.	Viktor Kozlov	Dynamo Moscow, CIS	C	365	74	139	213	104
7	EDM	Jason Arnott	Oshawa	C	471	154	210	364	640
8	NYR	Niklas Sundstrom	MoDo Ornskoldsvik, SWE	LW	394	77	123	200	100
9	DAL	Todd Harvey	Detroit	C	347	60	85	145	661
10	QUE	Jocelyn Thibault	Sherbrooke	G	327	136	846	15	2.77
11	WSH	Brendan Witt	Seattle	D	287	9	24	33	486
12	TOR	Kenny Jonsson	Rogle Angelholm, SWE	D	395	32	119	151	196
13	N.J.	Denis Pederson	Prince Albert	C	283	47	51	98	243
14	QUE	Adam Deadmarsh	Portland	C	414	125	137	262	664
15	WPG	Mats Lindgren	Skelleftea, SWE	C	254	43	49	92	102
16	EDM	Nick Stajduhar	London	D	2	0	0	0	4
17	WSH	Jason Allison	London	C	305	76	152	228	190
18	CGY	Jesper Mattsson	Malmo, SWE	C	Continues to play in Sweden				
19	TOR	Landon Wilson	Dubuque Jr. A	RW	146	14	23	37	120
20	VAN	Mike Wilson	Sudbury	D	295	15	39	54	222
21	MTL	Saku Koivu	TPS Turku, FIN	C	290	68	155	223	178
22	DET	Anders Eriksson	MoDo Ornskoldsvik, SWE	D	235	12	63	75	98
23	NYI	Todd Bertuzzi	Guelph	C	326	74	87	161	442

PICK	TEAM	NAME	DRAFTED FROM	NHL PLAYERS: POS / NHL GOALTENDERS: POS	GP / GP	G / W	A / GA	PTS / SO	PIM / AVG
24	CHI	Eric Lecompte	Hull	LW	Continues to play in Germany				
25	BOS	Kevyn Adams	Miami of Ohio	C	58	5	8	13	46
26	PIT	Stefan Bergkvist	Leksand, SWE	D	7	0	0	0	9

SECOND ROUND

PICK	TEAM	NAME	DRAFTED FROM	POS	GP	G/W	A/GA	PTS/SO	PIM/AVG
27	OTT	Radim Bicanek	Dukla Jihlava, TCH	D	53	0	4	4	22
28	S.J.	Shean Donovan	Ottawa	RW	347	42	43	85	220
29	T.B.	Tyler Moss	Kingston	G	17	5	43	0	2.81
30	ANA	Nikolai Tsulygin	Salavat Yulayev Ufa, CIS	D	22	0	1	1	8
31	WPG	Scott Langkow	Portland	G	20	3	68	0	4.33
32	N.J.	Jay Pandolfo	Boston U.	LW	210	28	32	60	24
33	EDM	David Vyborny	Sparta Praha, TCH	RW	61 points in lone pro season				
34	NYR	Lee Sorochan	Lethbridge	D	3	0	0	0	0
35	DAL	Jamie Langenbrunner	Cloquet H.S.	C	311	68	111	179	250
36	PHI	Janne Niinimaa	Karpat Oulu, FIN	D	316	20	128	148	297
37	ST.L.	Maxim Bets	Spokane	LW	3	0	0	0	0
38	BUF	Denis Tsygurov	Lada Togliatti, CIS	D	51	1	5	6	45
39	N.J.	Brendan Morrison	Penticton Jr. A	C	143	25	65	90	36
40	NYI	Bryan McCabe	Spokane	D	394	32	89	121	789
41	FLA	Kevin Weekes	Owen Sound	G	78	16	228	2	3.39
42	L.A.	Shayne Toporowski	Prince Albert	RW	3	0	0	0	7
43	WPG	Alexei Budayev	Kristall Elektrostal, CIS	C	10 points – HK Omsk in 99-00				
44	CGY	Jamie Allison	Detroit	D	162	6	13	19	303
45	S.J.	Vlastimil Kroupa	HC Chemopetrol Litvinov, TCH	D	105	4	19	23	66
46	VAN	Rick Girard	Swift Current	C	Continues to play in Germany				
47	MTL	Rory Fitzpatrick	Sudbury	D	51	0	3	3	28
48	DET	Jon Coleman	Andover Academy	D	Continues to play minor pro				
49	QUE	Ashley Buckberger	Swift Current	RW	Continues to play minor pro				
50	CHI	Eric Manlow	Kitchener	C	Continues to play minor pro				
51	BOS	Matt Alvey	Springfield Jr. B	RW	Continues to play minor pro				
52	PIT	Domenic Pittis	Lethbridge	C	11	1	0	1	8

OTHER ROUNDS

PICK	TEAM	NAME	DRAFTED FROM	POS	GP	G/W	A/GA	PTS/SO	PIM/AVG
53	OTT	Patrick Charbonneau	Victoriaville	G					
54	CHI	Bogdan Savenko	Niagara Falls	RW					
55	T.B.	Allan Egeland	Tacoma	C	17	0	0	0	16
56	ANA	Valeri Karpov	Traktor Chelyabinsk, CIS	RW	76	14	15	29	32
57	FLA	Chris Armstrong	Moose Jaw	D					
58	S.J.	Ville Peltonen	HIFK Helsinki, FIN	LW	152	15	41	56	38
59	EDM	Kevin Paden	Detroit	C/LW					
60	EDM	Alexander Kerch	Pardaugava Riga, CIS	LW	5	0	0	0	2
61	NYR	Maxim Galanov	Lada Togliatti, CIS	D	97	8	7	15	36
62	PIT	Dave Roche	Peterborough	C	170	15	15	30	334
63	ST.L.	Jamie Rivers	Sudbury	D	228	7	30	37	175
64	BUF	Ethan Philpott	Andover Academy	RW					
65	N.J.	Krzysztof Oliwa	Welland Jr. B	LW	207	13	20	33	724
66	NYI	Vladimir Chebaturkin	Kristall Elektrostal, CIS	D	27	1	3	4	20
67	FLA	Mikael Tjallden	MoDo Ornskoldsvik, SWE	D					
68	L.A.	Jeff Mitchell	Detroit	C/RW	7	0	0	0	7
69	WSH	Patrick Boileau	Laval	D	5	0	1	1	2
70	CGY	Dan Tompkins	Omaha Jr. A	LW					
71	PHI	Vaclav Prospal	Motor Ceske Budejovice, TCH	C	232	43	88	131	123
72	HFD	Marek Malik	TJ Vitkovice, TCH	D	164	7	25	32	153
73	MTL	Sebastien Bordeleau	Hull	C	217	34	54	88	94
74	DET	Kevin Hilton	Michigan	C					
75	QUE	Bill Pierce	Lawrence Academy	C					
76	CHI	Ryan Huska	Kamloops	LW	1	0	0	0	0
77	PHI	Milos Holan	TJ Vitkovice, TCH	D	49	5	11	16	42
78	FLA	Steve Washburn	Ottawa	C	90	14	15	29	42
79	WPG	Ruslan Batyrshin	Dynamo Moscow, CIS	D	2	0	0	0	6
80	S.J.	Alexander Osadchy	CSKA Moscow, CIS	D					
81	T.B.	Marian Kacir	Owen Sound	RW					
82	ANA	Joel Gagnon	Oshawa	G					
83	FLA	Bill McCauley	Detroit	C	Re-entered Draft in 1995				
84	HFD	Trevor Roenick	Boston Jr.	RW					
85	MTL	Adam Wiesel	Springfield Jr. B	D					
86	NYR	Sergei Olimpiyev	Dynamo Minsk, CIS	LW					
87	DAL	Chad Lang	Peterborough	G					
88	BOS	Charles Paquette	Sherbrooke	D					
89	ST.L.	Jamal Mayers	Western Michigan	C	119	11	16	27	132
90	CHI	Eric Daze	Beauport	LW	366	129	87	216	108
91	OTT	Cosmo Dupaul	Victoriaville	C					
92	NYI	Warren Luhning	Calgary Jr. A	RW	29	0	1	1	21
93	WPG	Ravil Gusmanov	Traktor Chelyabinsk, CIS	LW	4	0	0	0	0
94	L.A.	Bob Wren	Detroit	C	3	0	0	0	0
95	CGY	Jason Smith	Princeton	D					
96	CGY	Marty Murray	Brandon	C	19	3	3	6	6
97	DET	John Jakopin	St. Michael's Jr. B	D	22	0	0	0	30
98	VAN	Dieter Kochan	Kelowna Jr. A	G	5	1	17	0	4.29
99	MTL	Jean-Francois Houle	Northwood Prep	LW					
100	DET	Benoit Larose	Laval	D					
101	QUE	Ryan Tocher	Niagara Falls	D					
102	CHI	Patrik Pysz	Augsburg, GER	C					
103	BOS	Shawn Bates	Medford H.S.	C	90	12	11	23	18
104	PIT	Jonas Andersson-Junkka	Kiruna, SWE	D					
105	L.A.	Frederick Beaubien	St-Hyacinthe	G					
106	S.J.	Andrei Buschan	Sokol Kiev, CIS	D					
107	T.B.	Ryan Brown	Swift Current	D					
108	ANA	Mikhail Shtalenkov	Milwaukee IHL	G	190	62	480	8	2.89
109	FLA	Todd MacDonald	Tacoma	G					
110	N.J.	John Guirestante	London	RW					
111	EDM	Miroslav Satan	Dukla Trencin, TCH	LW	379	138	114	252	158
112	NYR	Gary Roach	Sault Ste. Marie	D					
113	MTL	Jeff Lank	Prince Albert	D	Re-entered Draft in 1995				
114	PHI	Vladimir Krechin	Traktor Chelyabinsk, CIS	LW					
115	HFD	Nolan Pratt	Portland	D	157	4	19	23	235
116	BUF	Richard Safarik	AC Nitra, TCH	RW					
117	L.A.	Jason Saal	Detroit	G					
118	NYI	Tommy Salo	Vasteras, SWE	G	270	97	677	16	2.63
119	WPG	Larry Courville	Newmarket	LW	Re-entered Draft in 1995				
120	L.A.	Tomas Vlasak	Slavia Praha, TCH	C					
121	CGY	Darryl Lafrance	Oshawa	C					
122	CGY	John Emmons	Yale	C	10	0	0	0	6
123	TOR	Zdenek Nedved	Sudbury	RW	31	4	6	10	14
124	VAN	Scott Walker	Owen Sound	C	337	32	80	112	659
125	MTL	Dion Darling	Spokane	D					
126	DET	Norm Maracle	Saskatoon	G	52	12	131	1	3.00
127	QUE	Anders Myrvold	Farjestad Karlstad, SWE	D	13	0	3	3	10
128	CHI	Jonni Vauhkonen	Reipas Lahti, FIN	RW					
129	BOS	Andrei Sapozhnikov	Traktor Chelyabinsk, CIS	D					
130	PIT	Chris Kelleher	St. Sebastian's H.S.	D					
131	OTT	Rick Bodkin	Sudbury	C					
132	S.J.	Petri Varis	Assat Pori, FIN	LW	1	0	0	0	0
133	T.B.	Kiley Hill	Sault Ste. Marie	LW					
134	ANA	Antti Aalto	TPS Turku, FIN	C	139	10	16	26	50
135	FLA	Alain Nasreddine	Drummondville	D	15	0	0	0	52
136	DAL	Rick Mrozik	Cloquet H.S.	D					
137	QUE	Nicholas Checco	Bloomington-Jefferson H.S.	C					
138	NYR	Dave Trofimenkoff	Lethbridge	G					
139	DAL	Per Svartvadet	MoDo Ornskoldsvik, SWE	C	38	3	4	7	6
140	PHI	Mike Crowley	Bloomington-Jefferson H.S.	D	28	4	5	9	24
141	ST.L.	Todd Kelman	Vernon Jr. A	D					
142	BUF	Kevin Pozzo	Moose Jaw	D					
143	N.J.	Steve Brule	St-Jean	RW					
144	NYI	Peter LeBoutillier	Red Deer	RW	Re-entered Draft in 1995				
145	WPG	Michal Grosek	ZPS Zlin, TCH	LW	350	67	104	171	332
146	L.A.	Jere Karalahti	HIFK Helsinki, FIN	D	48	6	10	16	18
147	WSH	Frank Banham	Saskatoon	RW	27	9	2	11	14
148	CGY	Andreas Karlsson	Leksand, SWE	C	51	5	9	14	14
149	TOR	Paul Vincent	Cushing Academy	C					
150	VAN	Troy Creurer	Notre Dame Jr. A	D					
151	MTL	Darcy Tucker	Kamloops	C	309	56	78	134	595
152	DET	Tim Spitzig	Kitchener	RW					
153	QUE	Christian Matte	Granby	RW	22	2	3	5	10
154	S.J.	Fredrik Oduya	Ottawa	LW					
155	BOS	Milt Mastad	Seattle	D					
156	PIT	Patrick Lalime	Shawinigan	G	77	40	180	6	2.64
157	OTT	Sergei Poleschuk	Kryljа Sovetov, CIS	D					
158	S.J.	Anatoli Filatov	Ust-Kamenogorsk, RUS, CIS	RW					
159	T.B.	Matthieu Raby	Victoriaville	D					
160	ANA	Matt Peterson	Osseo H.S.	D					
161	FLA	Trevor Doyle	Kingston	D					
162	NYR	Sergei Kondrashkin	Metallurg Cherepovets, CIS	RW					
163	EDM	Alexander Zhurik	Dynamo Minsk, CIS	D					
164	NYR	Todd Marchant	Clarkson	C	449	91	119	210	350
165	DAL	Jeremy Stasiuk	Spokane	RW					
166	PHI	Aaron Israel	Harvard	G					
167	ST.L.	Mike Buzak	Michigan State	G					
168	BUF	Sergei Petrenko	Dynamo Moscow, CIS	LW	14	0	4	4	0
169	N.J.	Nikolai Zavarukhin	Salavat Yulayev Ufa, CIS	C					
170	NYI	Darren Van Impe	Red Deer	D	299	18	71	89	287
171	WPG	Martin Woods	Victoriaville	D					
172	L.A.	Justin Martin	Essex Junction H.S.	RW					
173	WSH	Daniel Hendrickson	St. Paul Jr. A	RW					
174	WSH	Andrew Brunette	Owen Sound	LW	220	52	69	121	80
175	TOR	Jeff Andrews	North Bay	LW					
176	VAN	Yevgeni Babariko	Torpedo Nizhny Novogord, CIS	C					
177	MTL	David Ruhly	Culver Military Academy	LW					
178	DET	Yuri Yeresko	CSKA Moscow, CIS	D					
179	QUE	David Ling	Kingston	RW	3	0	0	0	0
180	CHI	Tom White	Westminster H.S.	C					
181	BOS	Ryan Golden	Reading H.S.	C					
182	PIT	Sean Selmser	Red Deer	LW					
183	OTT	Jason Disher	Kingston	D					
184	S.J.	Todd Holt	Swift Current	RW					
185	T.B.	Ryan Nauss	Peterborough	LW					
186	ANA	Tom Askey	Ohio State	G	7	0	12	0	2.64
187	FLA	Briane Thompson	Sault Ste. Marie	D					
188	HFD	Manny Legace	Niagara Falls	G	21	6	50	0	2.63
189	EDM	Martin Bakula	Alaska-Anchorage	D					
190	NYR	Ed Campbell	Omaha Jr. A	D					
191	DAL	Rob Lurtsema	Burnsville H.S.	LW					
192	PHI	Paul Healey	Prince Albert	RW	6	0	0	0	12
193	ST.L.	Eric Boguniecki	Westminster H.S.	C	4	0	0	0	2
194	BUF	Mike Barrie	Victoria	C					

PICK	TEAM	NAME	DRAFTED FROM	POS	GP	G / W	A / GA	PTS / SO	PIM / AVG
195	N.J.	Thomas Cullen	Wexford Jr. A	D					
196	NYI	Rod Hinks	Sudbury	C					
197	WPG	Adrian Murray	Newmarket	D					
198	L.A.	John-Tra Dillabough	Wexford Jr. A	C					
199	WSH	Joel Poirier	Sudbury	LW					
200	CGY	Derek Sylvester	Niagara Falls	RW					
201	TOR	David Brumby	Tri-City	G					
202	VAN	Sean Tallaire	Lake Superior State	RW					
203	MTL	Alan Letang	Newmarket	D	8	0	0	0	2
204	DET	Vitezslav Skuta	TJ Vitkovice, TCH	D					
205	QUE	Petr Franek	HC Chemopetrol Litvinov, TCH	G					
206	CHI	Sergei Petrov	Cloquet H.S.	LW					
207	BOS	Hal Gill	Nashoba H.S.	D	229	8	20	28	161
208	PIT	Larry McMorran	Seattle	C					
209	OTT	Toby Kvalevog	Bemidji State College	G					
210	S.J.	Jonas Forsberg	Djurgarden Stockholm, SWE	G					
211	T.B.	Alexandre Laporte	Victoriaville	D					
212	ANA	Vitali Kozel	Khimik Novopolotsk, CIS	C					
213	FLA	Chad Cabana	Tri-City	LW					
214	HFD	Dmitri Gorenko	CSKA Moscow, CIS	LW					
215	EDM	Brad Norton	Cushing Academy	D					
216	NYR	Ken Shepard	Oshawa	G					
217	WPG	Vladimir Potapov	Kristall Elektrostal, CIS	RW					
218	PHI	Tripp Tracy	Harvard	G					
219	ST.L.	Michael Grier	St. Sebastian's H.S.	RW	292	53	69	122	240
220	BUF	Barrie Moore	Sudbury	LW	39	2	6	8	18
221	N.J.	Judd Lambert	Chilliwack Jr. A	G					
222	NYI	Daniel Johansson	Rogle Angelholm, SWE	D					
223	WPG	Ilja Stashenkov	Krylja Sovetov Mosc., CIS	D					
224	L.A.	Martin Strbak	ZPA Presov, TCH	D					
225	WSH	Jason Gladney	Kitchener	D					
226	PHI	E.J. Bradley	Tabor Academy	C					
227	OTT	Pavol Demitra	Dukla Trencin, TCH	LW	281	102	143	245	58
228	WPG	Harijs Vitolinsh	Chur, SUI	C	8	0	0	0	4
229	MTL	Alexandre Duchesne	Drummondville	LW					
230	DET	Ryan Shanahan	Sudbury	RW					
231	QUE	Vincent Auger	Hawkesbury Jr. A	C					
232	CHI	Mike Rusk	Guelph	D					
233	BOS	Joel Prpic	Waterloo Jr. B	C	15	0	3	3	2
234	PIT	Timothy Harberts	Wayzata H.S.	C					
235	OTT	Rick Schuwerk	Canterbury H.S.	D					
236	S.J.	Jeff Salajko	Ottawa	G					
237	T.B.	Brett Duncan	Seattle	D					
238	ANA	Anatoli Fedotov	Moncton AHL	D	4	0	2	2	0
239	FLA	John Demarco	Archbishop Williams H.S.	D					
240	HFD	Wes Swinson	Kitchener	D					
241	EDM	Oleg Maltsev	Traktor Chelyabinsk, CIS	LW					
242	NYR	Andrei Kudinov	Traktor Chelyabinsk, CIS	RW					
243	DAL	Jordan Willis	London	G	1	0	1	0	3.16
244	PHI	Jeff Staples	Brandon	D					
245	ST.L.	Libor Prochazka	Poldi Kladno, TCH	D					
246	BUF	Chris Davis	Calgary Jr. A	G					
247	N.J.	Jimmy Provencher	St-Jean	RW					
248	NYI	Stephane Larocque	Sherbrooke	RW					
249	DAL	Bill Lang	North Bay	C					
250	L.A.	Kimmo Timonen	KalPa Kuopio, FIN	D	101	12	33	45	56
251	WSH	Mark Seliger	Rosenheim, FRG	G					
252	CGY	German Titov	TPS Turku, FIN	C	487	135	195	330	214
253	TOR	Kyle Ferguson	Michigan Tech	RW					
254	VAN	Bert Robertsson	Sodertalje, SWE	D	121	4	10	14	71
255	MTL	Brian Larochelle	Phillips-Exeter H.S.	G					
256	DET	James Kosecki	Berkshire H.S.	G					
257	QUE	Mark Pivetz	Saskatoon Jr. A	D					
258	CHI	Mike McGhan	Prince Albert	LW					
259	BOS	Joakim Persson	Hammarby Stockholm, SWE	G					
260	PIT	Leonid Toropchenko	Springfield AHL	C					
261	NYR	Pavel Komarov	Torpedo Nizhny Novogord, CIS	D					
262	S.J.	Jamie Matthews	Sudbury	C					
263	T.B.	Mark Szoke	Lethbridge	LW					
264	ANA	David Penney	Worcester Academy	LW					
265	FLA	Eric Montreuil	Chicoutimi	C					
266	HFD	Igor Chibirev	Fort Wayne IHL	C	45	7	12	19	2
267	EDM	Ilja Byakin	Landshut, GER	D	57	8	25	33	44
268	NYR	Maxim Smelnitsky	Traktor Chelyabinsk, CIS	RW					
269	DAL	Cory Peterson	Bloomington-Jefferson H.S.	D					
270	PHI	Ken Hemenway	Alaska All-Stars	D					
271	ST.L.	Alexander Vasilevski	Victoria	RW	4	0	0	0	2
272	BUF	Scott Nichol	Portland	C	5	0	0	0	14
273	N.J.	Mike Legg	London Jr. B	RW					
274	NYI	Carl Charland	Hull	LW					
275	ST.L.	Christer Olsson	Brynas Gavle, SWE	D	56	4	12	16	24
276	L.A.	Patrick Howald	Lugano, SUI	LW					
277	WSH	Dany Bousquet	Penticton Jr. A	C					
278	CGY	Burke Murphy	St. Lawrence U.	LW					
279	TOR	Mikhail Lapin	Western Michigan	D					
280	VAN	Sergei Tkachenko	Hamilton AHL	G					
281	MTL	Russell Guzior	Culver Military Academy	C					
282	DET	Gordon Hunt	Detroit Compuware Jr. A	C					
283	QUE	John Hillman	St. Paul Jr. A	C					
284	CHI	Tom Noble	Catholic Memorial H.S.	G					
285	WPG	Russell Hewson	Swift Current	LW					
286	PIT	Hans Jonsson	MoDo Ornskoldsvik, SWE	D	68	3	11	14	12

1994

PICK	TEAM	NAME	DRAFTED FROM	POS	GP	G / W	A / GA	PTS / SO	PIM / AVG
FIRST ROUND									
1	FLA	Ed Jovanovski	Windsor	D	359	36	84	120	647
2	ANA	Oleg Tverdovsky	Krylja Sovetov Mosc., CIS	D	410	49	143	192	159
3	OTT	Radek Bonk	Las Vegas IHL	C	397	70	102	172	195
4	EDM	Jason Bonsignore	Niagara Falls	C	79	3	13	16	34
5	HFD	Jeff O'Neill	Guelph	C	366	82	108	190	285
6	EDM	Ryan Smyth	Moose Jaw	LW	351	102	88	190	268
7	L.A.	Jamie Storr	Owen Sound	G	102	45	228	7	2.51
8	T.B.	Jason Wiemer	Portland	C	386	50	52	102	716
9	NYI	Brett Lindros	Kingston	RW	51	2	5	7	147
10	WSH	Nolan Baumgartner	Kamloops	D	18	0	2	2	2
11	S.J.	Jeff Friesen	Regina	C	448	137	177	314	260
12	QUE	Wade Belak	Saskatoon	D	84	1	4	5	254
13	VAN	Mattias Ohlund	Pitea, SWE	D	193	20	65	85	183
14	CHI	Ethan Moreau	Niagara Falls	LW	297	51	47	98	354
15	WSH	Alexander Kharlamov	CSKA Moscow, CIS	C	41PTS – Tacoma in 99-00				
16	TOR	Eric Fichaud	Chictoutimi	G	93	22	247	2	3.13
17	BUF	Wayne Primeau	Owen Sound	C	242	21	28	49	252
18	MTL	Brad Brown	North Bay	D	131	1	16	17	361
19	CGY	Chris Dingman	Brandon	LW	141	11	6	17	305
20	DAL	Jason Botterill	Michigan	LW	48	1	4	5	59
21	BOS	Evgeni Ryabchikov	Molot Perm, CIS	G	Played 4 seasons w/ 7 teams				
22	QUE	Jeff Kealty	Catholic Memorial H.S.	D	Head injury may end career				
23	DET	Yan Golubovsky	Dynamo-2 Moscow, CIS	D	50	1	5	6	30
24	PIT	Chris Wells	Seattle	C	195	9	20	29	193
25	N.J.	Vadim Sharifijanov	Salavat Yulayev Ufa, CIS	RW	92	16	21	37	50
26	NYR	Dan Cloutier	Sault Ste. Marie	G	86	19	217	0	3.14
SECOND ROUND									
27	FLA	Rhett Warrener	Saskatoon	D	291	5	26	31	406
28	ANA	Johan Davidsson	HV 71 Jonkoping, SWE	C	83	6	9	15	16
29	OTT	Stanislav Neckar	HC Ceske Budejovice, CZE	D	293	8	25	33	178
30	WPG	Deron Quint	Seattle	D	224	21	46	67	86
31	FLA	Jason Podollan	Spokane	RW	40	1	5	6	17
32	EDM	Mike Watt	Stratford Jr. B	LW	134	14	25	39	33
33	L.A.	Matt Johnson	Peterborough	LW	246	8	13	21	825
34	T.B.	Colin Cloutier	Brandon	C	84 pro games in AHL/ECHL				
35	QUE	Josef Marha	Dukla Jihlava, CZE	C	144	21	29	50	26
36	FLA	Ryan Johnson	Thunder Bay Jr. A	C	91	5	16	21	16
37	S.J.	Angel Nikolov	Chemopetrol Litvinov, CZE	D	21PTS – CHZ Litvinov 99-00				
38	NYI	Jason Holland	Kamloops	D	24	1	1	2	12
39	VAN	Robb Gordon	Powell River Jr. A	C	4	0	0	0	2
40	CHI	Jean-Yves Leroux	Beauport	LW	161	12	18	30	124
41	WSH	Scott Cherrey	North Bay	LW	Played at UNB and minor pro				
42	VAN	Dave Scatchard	Portland	C	223	38	42	80	422
43	BUF	Curtis Brown	Moose Jaw	C	248	55	76	131	152
44	MTL	Jose Theodore	St-Jean	G	65	21	162	6	2.86
45	CGY	Dmitri Ryabykin	Dynamo-2 Moscow, CIS	D	15 points – HK Omsk 99-00				
46	DAL	Lee Jinman	North Bay	C	Continues to play minor pro				
47	BOS	Daniel Goneau	Laval	LW	Re-entered Draft in 1996				
48	TOR	Sean Haggerty	Detroit	LW	11	1	1	2	4
49	DET	Mathieu Dandenault	Sherbrooke	RW/D	323	23	50	73	156
50	PIT	Richard Park	Belleville	C	91	5	10	15	56
51	N.J.	Patrik Elias	HC Kladno, CZE	LW	238	72	92	164	122
52	NYR	Rudolf Vercik	Slovan Bratislava, SVK	LW	23PTS – HC Bratislava 99-00				
OTHER ROUNDS									
53	EDM	Corey Neilson	North Bay	D					
54	MTL	Chris Murray	Kamloops	RW	242	16	18	34	550
55	T.B.	Vadim Epanchintsev	Spartak Moscow, CIS	C					
56	WPG	Dorian Anneck	Victoria	C					
57	PIT	Sven Butenschon	Brandon	D	28	0	0	0	12
58	WPG	Tavis Hansen	Tacoma	C	27	2	1	3	12
59	L.A.	Vitali Yachmenev	North Bay	RW	272	52	83	135	52
60	EDM	Brad Symes	Portland	D					
61	QUE	Sebastien Bety	Drummondville	D					
62	PHI	Artem Anisimov	Itil Kazan, CIS	D					
63	NYI	Jason Strudwick	Kamloops	D	157	1	8	9	250
64	TOR	Fredrik Modin	Yepandhin Dev Timra, SWE	LW	297	60	64	124	109
65	VAN	Chad Allan	Saskatoon	D					
66	S.J.	Alexei Yegorov	SKA St. Petersburg, CIS	RW	11	3	3	6	2
67	ANA	Craig Reichert	Red Deer	RW	3	0	0	0	0
68	ST.L.	Stephane Roy	Val d'Or	C					
69	BUF	Rumun Ndur	Guelph	D	69	2	3	5	137
70	MTL	Marko Kiprusoff	TPS Turku, FIN	D	24	0	4	4	8
71	N.J.	Sheldon Souray	Tri-City	D	201	7	22	29	309
72	QUE	Chris Drury	Fairfield Prep	C	161	40	71	111	104

Column headings: NHL PLAYERS: POS, GP, G, A, PTS, PIM; NHL GOALTENDERS: POS, GP, W, GA, SO, AVG.

PICK	TEAM	NAME	DRAFTED FROM	NHL PLAYERS: POS / NHL GOALTENDERS: POS	GP / GP	G / W	A / GA	PTS / SO	PIM / AVG
73	PIT	Greg Crozier	Lawrence Academy	LW					
74	MTL	Martin Belanger	Granby	D					
75	DET	Sean Gillam	Spokane	D					
76	PIT	Alexei Krivchenkov	CSKA Moscow, CIS	D					
77	CGY	Chris Clark	Springfield Jr. B	RW	22	0	1	1	14
78	NYR	Adam Smith	Tacoma	D					
79	EDM	Adam Copeland	Burlington Jr. B	RW					
80	ANA	Byron Briske	Red Deer	D					
81	OTT	Bryan Masotta	Hotchkiss H.S.	G					
82	WPG	Steve Cheredaryk	Medicine Hat	D					
83	HFD	Hnat Domenichelli	Kamloops	C	136	28	33	61	42
84	FLA	David Nemirovsky	Ottawa	RW	91	16	22	38	42
85	CHI	Steve McLaren	North Bay	LW					
86	T.B.	Dmitri Klevakin	Spartak Moscow, CIS	RW					
87	QUE	Milan Hejduk	HC Pardubice, CZE	RW	164	50	70	120	42
88	PHI	Adam Magarrell	Brandon	D					
89	S.J.	Vaclav Varada	HC Vitkovice, CZE	RW	181	22	57	79	140
90	NYI	Brad Lukowich	Kamloops	D	78	4	4	8	71
91	CGY	Ryan Duthie	Spokane	C					
92	VAN	Mike Dubinsky	Brandon	RW					
93	WSH	Matt Herr	Hotchkiss H.S.	C	30	2	2	4	8
94	ST.L.	Tyler Harlton	Vernon Jr. A	D					
95	EDM	Jussi Tarvainen	KalPa Kuopio, FIN	RW					
96	MTL	Arto Kuki	Kiekko-Espoo, FIN	C					
97	CGY	Johan Finnstrom	Rogle Angelholm, SWE	D					
98	DAL	Jamie Wright	Guelph	LW	55	5	6	11	18
99	BOS	Eric Nickulas	Cushing Academy	C	22	5	6	11	12
100	NYR	Alexander Korobolin	Traktor Chelyabinsk, CIS	D					
101	PHI	Sebastien Vallee	Victoriaville	LW					
102	PIT	Tom O'Connor	Springfield Jr. B	D					
103	N.J.	Zdenek Skorepa	Chemopetrol Litvinov, CZE	RW					
104	NYR	Sylvain Blouin	Laval	LW	12	0	0	0	42
105	FLA	Dave Geris	Windsor	D					
106	ANA	Pavel Trnka	HC Skoda Plzen, CZE	D	168	5	23	28	134
107	CGY	Nils Ekman	Hammarby Stockholm, SWE	LW	28	2	2	4	36
108	WPG	Craig Mills	Belleville	RW	31	0	5	5	36
109	HFD	Ryan Risidore	Guelph	D					
110	EDM	Jon Gaskins	Dubuque Jr. B	D					
111	L.A.	Chris Schmidt	Seattle	C					
112	NYI	Mark McArthur	Guelph	G					
113	QUE	Tony Tuzzolino	Michigan State	RW	1	0	0	0	2
114	DET	Frederic Deschenes	Granby	G					
115	S.J.	Brian Swanson	Omaha Jr. A	C					
116	NYI	Albert O'Connell	St. Sebastian's H.S.	LW					
117	VAN	Yanick Dube	Laval	C					
118	CHI	Marc Dupuis	Belleville	D					
119	WSH	Yanick Jean	Chicoutimi	D					
120	ST.L.	Edvin Frylen	Vasteras, SWE	D					
121	BUF	Sergei Klimentiev	Medicine Hat	D					
122	MTL	Jimmy Drolet	St-Hyacinthe	D					
123	CGY	Frank Appel	Dusseldorf, GER	D					
124	DAL	Marty Turco	Cambridge Jr. B	G					
125	BOS	Darren Wright	Prince Albert	D					
126	TOR	Mark Deyell	Saskatoon	C					
127	DET	Doug Battaglia	Brockville Jr. A	LW					
128	PIT	Clint Johnson	Duluth East H.S.	LW					
129	N.J.	Christian Gosselin	St-Hyacinthe	D					
130	NYR	Martin Ethier	Beauport	D					
131	OTT	Mike Gaffney	St. John's Prep	D					
132	ANA	Bates Battaglia	Caledon Jr. A	LW	170	25	33	58	146
133	OTT	Daniel Alfredsson	Vastra Frolunda, SWE	RW	328	99	170	269	118
134	N.J.	Ryan Smart	Meadville H.S.	C					
135	NYR	Yuri Litvinov	Krylja Sovetov Mosc., CIS	C					
136	EDM	Terry Marchant	Niagara Jr. A	LW					
137	T.B.	Daniel Juden	Governor Dummer H.S.	RW					
138	T.B.	Bryce Salvador	Lethbridge	D					
139	QUE	Nicholas Windsor	Cornwall	D					
140	PHI	Alex Selivanov	Spartak Moscow, CIS	RW	400	113	103	216	341
141	S.J.	Alexander Korolyuk	Krylja Sovetov Mosc., CIS	RW	131	28	42	70	67
142	NYI	Jason Stewart	Simley H.S.	RW					
143	WPG	Steve Vezina	Beauport	G					
144	CHI	Jim Enson	North Bay	C					
145	WSH	Dmitri Mekeshkin	Avangard Omsk, CIS	D					
146	WPG	Chris Kibermanis	Red Deer	D					
147	BUF	Cal Benazic	Medicine Hat	D					
148	MTL	Joel Irving	Regina Midgets	C					
149	CGY	Patrick Haltia	Grums, SWE	G					
150	DAL	Evgeny Petrochinin	Spartak Moscow, CIS	D					
151	BOS	Andre Roy	Chicoutimi	LW	86	4	5	9	157
152	TOR	Karri White	Newmarket	D					
153	DET	Pavel Agarkov	Krylja Sovetov Mosc., CIS	RW					
154	PIT	Valentin Morozov	CSKA Moscow, CIS	C					
155	N.J.	Luciano Caravaggio	Michigan Tech	G					
156	NYR	David Brosseau	Shawinigan	C					
157	FLA	Matt O'Dette	Kitchener	D					
158	ANA	Rocky Welsing	Wisconsin Jr. A	D					
159	OTT	Doug Sproule	Hotchkiss H.S.	LW					
160	EDM	Chris Sheptak	Olds Jr. A	LW					
161	PIT	Serge Aubin	Granby	C	16	2	1	3	6
162	EDM	Dmitri Shulga	Tivali Minsk, CIS	RW					
163	L.A.	Luc Gagne	Sudbury	RW					
164	T.B.	Chris Maillet	Red Deer	D					
165	QUE	Calvin Elfring	Powell River Jr. A	D					
166	PHI	Colin Forbes	Sherwood Park Jr. A	LW	199	27	20	47	150
167	S.J.	Sergei Gorbachev	Dynamo Moscow, CIS	RW					
168	BUF	Steve Plouffe	Granby	G					
169	VAN	Yuri Kuznetsov	Avangard Omsk, CIS	C					
170	CHI	Tyler Prosofsky	Tacoma	C	Re-entered Draft in 1996				
171	WSH	Daniel Reja	London	C					
172	ST.L.	Roman Vopat	Chemopetrol Litvinov, CZE	C	133	6	14	20	253
173	BUF	Shane Hnidy	Prince Albert	D					
174	MTL	Jessie Rezansoff	Regina	RW					
175	CGY	Ladislav Kohn	Swift Current	RW	102	7	20	27	33
176	BUF	Steve Webb	Peterborough	RW	171	2	7	9	314
177	BOS	Jeremy Schaefer	Medicine Hat	LW					
178	TOR	Tommi Rajamaki	Assat Pori, FIN	D					
179	EDM	Chris Wickenheiser	Red Deer	G					
180	PIT	Drew Palmer	Seattle	D					
181	N.J.	Jeff Williams	Guelph	C					
182	NYR	Alexei Lazarenko	CSKA-2 Moscow, CIS	LW					
183	FLA	Jason Boudrias	Laval	C					
184	ANA	Brad Englehart	Kimball Union Academy	C					
185	EDM	Rob Guinn	Newmarket	D					
186	WPG	Ramil Saifullin	Avangard Omsk, CIS	C					
187	HFD	Tom Buckley	St. Joseph H.S.	C					
188	EDM	Jason Reid	St. Andrew's H.S.	D					
189	L.A.	Andrew Dale	Sudbury	RW					
190	T.B.	Alexei Baranov	Dynamo-2 Moscow, CIS	C					
191	QUE	Jay Bertsch	Spokane	RW	Re-entered Draft in 1996				
192	PHI	Derek Diener	Lethbridge	D					
193	S.J.	Eric Landry	Guelph	RW					
194	NYI	Mike Loach	Windsor	C					
195	VAN	Rob Trumbley	Moose Jaw	C					
196	CHI	Mike Josephson	Kamloops	LW					
197	WSH	Chris Patrick	Kent Prep	LW					
198	ST.L.	Steve Noble	Stratford Jr. B	C					
199	BUF	Bob Westerby	Kamloops	LW					
200	MTL	Peter Strom	Vastra Frolunda, SWE	LW					
201	CGY	Keith McCambridge	Swift Current	D					
202	PHI	Ray Giroux	Powasson Jr.	D	14	0	9	9	10
203	NYI	Peter Hogardh	Vastra Frolunda, SWE	C					
204	TOR	Rob Butler	Niagara Jr. A	LW					
205	DET	Jason Elliot	Kimberley Jr. A	G					
206	PIT	Boris Zelenko	CSKA Moscow, CIS	LW					
207	N.J.	Eric Bertrand	Granby	LW	12	0	0	0	4
208	NYR	Craig Anderson	Park Center H.S.	D					
209	NYR	Vitali Yeremeyev	Ust-Kamenogorsk, RUS, CIS	G					
210	OTT	Frederic Cassivi	St-Hyacinthe	G					
211	OTT	Danny Dupont	Laval	D					
212	WPG	Henrik Smangs	Leksand, SWE	G					
213	HFD	Ashlin Halfnight	Harvard	D					
214	EDM	Jeremy Jablonski	Victoria	G					
215	L.A.	Jan Nemecek	HC Ceske Budejovice, CZE	D	7	1	0	1	4
216	T.B.	Yuri Smirnov	Spartak Moscow, CIS	C					
217	QUE	Tim Thomas	Vermont	G					
218	PHI	Johan Hedberg	Leksand, SWE	G					
219	S.J.	Evgeni Nabokov	Ust-Kamenogorsk, RUS, CIS	G	11	2	15	1	2.17
220	NYI	Gord Walsh	Kingston	LW					
221	VAN	Bill Muckalt	Kelowna Jr. A	RW	118	24	31	55	119
222	CHI	Lubomir Jandera	Chemopetrol Litvinov, CZE	D					
223	WSH	John Tuohy	Kent Prep	D					
224	ST.L.	Marc Stephan	Tri-City	C					
225	BUF	Craig Millar	Swift Current	D	93	7	13	20	57
226	MTL	Tomas Vokoun	HC Kladno, CZE	G	71	21	187	2	2.91
227	CGY	Jorgen Jonsson	Rogle Angelholm, SWE	LW	81	12	19	31	16
228	DAL	Marty Flichel	Tacoma	RW					
229	BOS	John Grahame	Sioux City Jr. A	G	24	7	55	2	2.46
230	HFD	Matt Ball	Detroit	RW					
231	DET	Jeff Mikesch	Michigan Tech	C					
232	PIT	Jason Godbout	Hill-Murray H.S.	D					
233	N.J.	Steve Sullivan	Sault Ste. Marie	C	276	70	110	180	169
234	NYR	Eric Boulton	Oshawa	LW					
235	FLA	Tero Lehtera	Kiekko-Espoo, FIN	LW					
236	ANA	Tommi Miettinen	KalPa Kuopio, FIN	C					
237	OTT	Stephen MacKinnon	Cushing Academy	LW					
238	WPG	Mike Mader	Loomis-Chaffee H.S.	RW					
239	HFD	Brian Regan	Westminster H.S.	G					
240	S.J.	Tomas Pisa	HC Pardubice, CZE	RW					
241	L.A.	Sergei Shalomai	Spartak Moscow, CIS	LW					
242	T.B.	Shawn Gervais	Seattle	C					
243	QUE	Chris Pittman	Kitchener	LW					
244	PHI	Andre Payette	Sault Ste. Marie	C					
245	S.J.	Aniket Dhadphale	Marquette Elec. AAA	LW					
246	NYI	Kirk Dewaele	Lethbridge	D					

PICK	TEAM	NAME	DRAFTED FROM	NHL PLAYERS: POS / NHL GOALTENDERS: POS	GP / GP	G / W	A / GA	PTS / SO	PIM / AVG
247	VAN	Tyson Nash	Kamloops	LW	68	4	9	13	155
248	CHI	Lars Weibel	Lugano, SUI	G					
249	WSH	Richard Zednik	IS Banska Bystrica, SVK	LW	195	47	34	81	136
250	ST.L.	Kevin Harper	Wexford Jr. A	D					
251	BUF	Mark Polak	Medicine Hat	C					
252	MTL	Chris Aldous	Northwood Prep	D					
253	CGY	Mike Peluso	Omaha Jr. A	RW					
254	DAL	Jimmy Roy	Thunder Bay Jr. A	C					
255	BOS	Neil Savary	Hull	G					
256	TOR	Sergei Berezin	Khimik Voskresensk, CIS	LW	278	104	66	170	26
257	DET	Tomas Holmstrom	Boden, SWE	LW	258	37	63	100	189
258	PIT	Mikhail Kazakevich	Torpedo Yaroslavl, CIS	LW					
259	N.J.	Scott Swanjord	Waterloo Jr. A	G					
260	NYR	Radoslav Kropac	Slovan Bratislava, SVK	RW					
261	FLA	Per Gustafsson	HV 71 Jonkoping, SWE	D	89	8	27	35	38
262	ANA	Jeremy Stevenson	Sault Ste. Marie	LW	56	3	6	9	134
263	CHI	Rob Mara	Belmont Hill H.S.	RW					
264	WPG	Jason Issel	Prince Albert	LW					
265	HFD	Steve Nimigon	Niagara Falls	LW					
266	EDM	Ladislav Benysek	HC Olomouc Jr., CZE	D	2	0	0	0	0
267	NYR	Jamie Butt	Tacoma	LW					
268	T.B.	Brian White	Arlington Catholic H.S.	D	2	0	0	0	0
269	N.J.	Mike Hanson	Minot H.S.	C					
270	PHI	Jan Lipiansky	Slovan Bratislava, SVK	LW					
271	S.J.	David Beauregard	St-Hyacinthe	LW					
272	NYI	Dick Tarnstrom	AIK Solna, SWE	D					
273	VAN	Robert Longpre	Medicine Hat	C					
274	OTT	Antti Tormanen	Jokerit Helsinki, FIN	RW	50	7	8	15	28
275	WSH	Sergei Tertyshny	Traktor Chelyabinsk, CIS	D					
276	ST.L.	Scott Fankhouser	Loomis-Chaffe H.S.	G	16	2	49	0	3.20
277	BUF	Shayne Wright	Owen Sound	D					
278	MTL	Ross Parsons	Regina	D					
279	CGY	Pavel Torgaev	TPS Turku, FIN	LW	55	6	14	20	20
280	DAL	Chris Szysky	Swift Current	RW					
281	BOS	Andrei Yakhanov	Salavat Yulayev Ufa, CIS	D					
282	TOR	Doug Nolan	Catholic Memorial H.S.	LW					
283	DET	Toivo Suursoo	Krylja Sovetov Mosc., CIS	LW					
284	PIT	Brian Leitza	Sioux City Jr. A	G					
285	QUE	Steven Low	Sherbrooke	D					
286	NYR	Kim Johnsson	Malmo, SWE	D	76	6	15	21	46

1995

FIRST ROUND

PICK	TEAM	NAME	DRAFTED FROM	NHL PLAYERS: POS / NHL GOALTENDERS: POS	GP / GP	G / W	A / GA	PTS / SO	PIM / AVG
1	OTT	Bryan Berard	Detroit	D	290	34	124	158	235
2	NYI	Wade Redden	Brandon	D	315	32	85	117	171
3	L.A.	Aki Berg	Kiekko-67 Turku, FIN	D	234	5	34	39	159
4	ANA	Chad Kilger	Kingston	C	247	32	36	68	109
5	T.B.	Daymond Langkow	Tri-City	C	311	55	79	134	192
6	EDM	Steve Kelly	Prince Albert	C	86	4	6	10	56
7	WPG	Shane Doan	Kamloops	RW	330	48	65	113	305
8	MTL	Terry Ryan	Tri-City	LW	8	0	0	0	36
9	BOS	Kyle McLaren	Tacoma	D	321	29	70	99	298
10	FLA	Radek Dvorak	HC Ceske Budejovice, TCH	RW	382	80	115	195	128
11	DAL	Jarome Iginla	Kamloops	RW	311	91	105	196	150
12	S.J.	Teemu Riihijarvi	Kiekko-Espoo, FIN	LW	Continues to play in Finland				
13	HFD	Jean-Sebastien Giguere	Halifax	G	30	8	85	0	3.22
14	BUF	Jay McKee	Niagara Falls	D	250	7	41	48	204
15	TOR	Jeff Ware	Oshawa	D	21	0	1	1	12
16	BUF	Martin Biron	Beauport	G	50	20	110	5	2.51
17	WSH	Brad Church	Prince Albert	LW	2	0	0	0	0
18	N.J.	Petr Sykora	Detroit	C	299	89	132	221	106
19	CHI	Dmitri Nabokov	Krylja Sovetov Mosc., CIS	C	55	11	13	24	28
20	CGY	Denis Gauthier	Drummondville	D	104	4	5	9	134
21	BOS	Sean Brown	Belleville	D	146	4	16	20	427
22	PHI	Brian Boucher	Tri-City	G	35	20	65	4	1.91
23	WSH	Miika Elomo	Kiekko-67 Turku, FIN	LW	2	0	1	1	2
24	PIT	Aleksey Morozov	Krylja Sovetov Mosc., CIS	RW	211	34	42	76	36
25	COL	Marc Denis	Chicoutimi	G	28	10	63	3	2.55
26	DET	Maxim Kuznetsov	Dynamo Moscow, CIS	D	44 games – Cincinnati 99-00				

SECOND ROUND

PICK	TEAM	NAME	DRAFTED FROM	NHL PLAYERS: POS / NHL GOALTENDERS: POS	GP / GP	G / W	A / GA	PTS / SO	PIM / AVG
27	OTT	Marc Moro	Kingston	D	9	0	0	0	40
28	NYI	Jan Hlavac	Sparta Praha, CZE	LW	67	19	23	42	16
29	ANA	Brian Wesenberg	Guelph	RW	1	0	0	0	5
30	T.B.	Mike McBain	Red Deer	D	64	0	7	7	22
31	EDM	Georges Laraque	St-Jean	RW	126	11	10	21	239
32	WPG	Marc Chouinard	Beauport	C	17G, 33PTS – Cincinnati 99-00				
33	L.A.	Donald MacLean	Beauport	C	22	5	2	7	4
34	WPG	Jason Doig	Laval	D	35	1	4	5	72
35	HFD	Sergei Fedotov	Dynamo Moscow, CIS	D	Continues to play minor pro				
36	FLA	Aaron MacDonald	Swift Current	G	4.51GAA – Ft. Wayne in 99-00				
37	DAL	Patrick Cote	Beauport	LW	99	1	2	3	359
38	S.J.	Peter Roed	White Bear Lake H.S.	C	13G, 32PTS – Kentucky 99-00				
39	NYR	Christian Dube	Sherbrooke	C	33	1	1	2	4
40	VAN	Chris McAllister	Saskatoon	D	120	2	8	10	276
41	NYI	D.J. Smith	Windsor	D	11	0	1	1	12
42	BUF	Mark Dutiaume	Brandon	LW	20G, 66PTS – BC Icemen				
43	WSH	Dwayne Hay	Guelph	LW	30	1	1	2	6
44	N.J.	Nathan Perrott	Oshawa	RW	12G, 21PTS – Cleveland 99-00				
45	CHI	Christian Laflamme	Beauport	D	214	2	31	33	171
46	CGY	Pavel Smirnov	Molot Perm, CIS	C/RW	Injured most of 99-00				
47	BOS	Paxton Schafer	Medicine Hat	G	3	0	6	0	4.68
48	PHI	Shane Kenny	Owen Sound	D	61 games w/ 3 teams 99-00				
49	ST.L.	Jochen Hecht	Mannheim, GER	C	66	13	21	34	28
50	L.A.	Pavel Rosa	Chemopetrol Litvinov, CZE	RW	32	4	12	16	6
51	COL	Nic Beaudoin	Detroit	LW	73PTS – Mohawk Valley 99-00				
52	DET	Philippe Audet	Granby	LW	4	0	0	0	0

OTHER ROUNDS

PICK	TEAM	NAME	DRAFTED FROM	NHL PLAYERS: POS / NHL GOALTENDERS: POS	GP / GP	G / W	A / GA	PTS / SO	PIM / AVG
53	OTT	Brad Larsen	Swift Current	LW	Re-entered Draft in 1997				
54	TOR	Ryan Pepperall	Kitchener	RW					
55	ANA	Mike Leclerc	Brandon	LW	88	9	12	21	80
56	T.B.	Shane Willis	Prince Albert	RW	Re-entered Draft in 1997				
57	EDM	Lukas Zib	HC Ceske Budejovice, CZE	D					
58	DET	Darryl Laplante	Moose Jaw	C	35	0	6	6	10
59	L.A.	Vladimir Tsyplakov	Fort Wayne IHL	LW	295	62	94	156	80
60	MTL	Miloslav Guren	ZPS Zlin, CZE	D	36	1	3	4	16
61	VAN	Larry Courville	Oshawa	LW	33	1	2	3	16
62	FLA	Mike O'Grady	Lethbridge	D					
63	DAL	Petr Buzek	Dukla Jihlava, CZE	D	67	5	14	19	45
64	S.J.	Marko Makinen	TPS Turku, FIN	RW					
65	NYR	Mike Martin	Windsor	D					
66	VAN	Peter Schaefer	Brandon	LW	96	20	19	39	28
67	WPG	Brad Isbister	Portland	RW	162	35	32	67	248
68	BUF	Mathieu Sunderland	Drummondville	RW					
69	DAL	Sergey Gusev	CSK VVS Samara, CIS	D	73	3	10	13	24
70	N.J.	Sergei Vyshedkevich	Dynamo Moscow, CIS	D	7	1	3	4	2
71	CHI	Kevin McKay	Moose Jaw	D					
72	CGY	Rocky Thompson	Medicine Hat	RW	15	0	0	0	86
73	BOS	Bill McCauley	Detroit	C					
74	MTL	Martin Hohenberger	Prince George	LW					
75	ST.L.	Scott Roche	North Bay	G					
76	PIT	Jean-Sebastien Aubin	Sherbrooke	G	68	27	148	4	2.50
77	COL	John Tripp	Oshawa	RW	Re-entered Draft in 1997				
78	N.J.	David Gosselin	Sherbrooke	RW	10	2	1	3	6
79	N.J.	Alyn McCauley	Ottawa	C	144	20	30	50	18
80	FLA	Dave Duerden	Peterborough	LW	2	0	0	0	0
81	COL	Tomi Kallio	Kiekko-67 Turku, FIN	LW					
82	CHI	Chris Van Dyk	Windsor	D					
83	EDM	Mike Minard	Chilliwack Jr. A	G	1	1	3	0	3.00
84	WPG	Justin Kurtz	Brandon	D					
85	HFD	Ian MacNeil	Oshawa	C					
86	MTL	Jonathan Delisle	Hull	RW	1	0	0	0	0
87	HFD	Sami Kapanen	HIFK Helsinki, FIN	LW	318	92	112	204	46
88	FLA	Daniel Tjarnqvist	Rogle Angelholm, SWE	D					
89	OTT	Kevin Bolibruck	Peterborough	D					
90	S.J.	Vesa Toskala	Ilves Tampere, FIN	G					
91	NYR	Marc Savard	Oshawa	C	176	32	72	104	98
92	VAN	Lloyd Shaw	Seattle	D					
93	WSH	Sebastien Charpentier	Laval	G					
94	BUF	Matt Davidson	Portland	RW					
95	WSH	Joel Theriault	Beauport	D					
96	N.J.	Henrik Rehnberg	Farjestad Karlstad, SWE	D					
97	CHI	Pavel Kriz	Tri-City	D					
98	CGY	Jan Labraaten	Farjestad Karlstad, SWE	LW					
99	BOS	Cameron Mann	Peterborough	RW	74	13	7	20	34
100	PHI	Radovan Somik	ZTS Martin, SVK	LW					
101	ST.L.	Michal Handzus	IS Banska Bystrica, SVK	C	147	29	40	69	74
102	PIT	Oleg Belov	CSKA Moscow, CIS	C					
103	OTT	Kevin Boyd	London	LW					
104	DET	Anatoli Ustyugov	Torpedo Yaroslavl, CIS	LW					
105	WSH	Benoit Gratton	Laval	LW	32	4	6	10	32
106	NYI	Vladimir Orszagh	IS Banska Bystrica, SVK	RW	34	3	2	5	12
107	ANA	Igor Nikulin	Severstal Cherepovets, CIS	RW					
108	T.B.	Konstantin Golokhvastov	Dynamo Moscow, CIS	RW					
109	EDM	Jan Snopek	Oshawa	D					
110	NYR	Alexei Vasiliev	Torpedo-2 Yaroslavl, CIS	D	1	0	0	0	2
111	BUF	Marian Menhart	Chemopetrol Litvinov, CZE	D					
112	MTL	Niklas Anger	Djurgarden Stockholm, SWE	RW					
113	HFD	Hugh Hamilton	Spokane	D					
114	FLA	Francois Cloutier	Hull	LW					
115	DAL	Wade Strand	Regina	D					
116	S.J.	Miikka Kiprusoff	TPS Turku, FIN	G					
117	NYR	Dale Purinton	Tacoma	D	1	0	0	0	7
118	L.A.	Jason Morgan	Kingston	C	14	1	0	1	4
119	BUF	Kevin Popp	Seattle	D					
120	VAN	Todd Norman	Guelph	LW					
121	WPG	Brian Elder	Brandon	G					
122	N.J.	Chris Mason	Prince George	G	3	0	6	0	5.22

PICK	TEAM	NAME	DRAFTED FROM	NHL PLAYERS: POS / NHL GOALTENDERS: POS	GP / GP	G / W	A / GA	PTS / SO	PIM / AVG
123	BUF	Daniel Bienvenue	Val d'Or	LW					
124	WSH	Joel Cort	Guelph	D					
125	DET	Chad Wilchynski	Regina	D					
126	DET	David Arsenault	Drummondville	G					
127	ST.L.	Jeff Ambrosio	Belleville	LW					
128	PIT	Jan Hrdina	Seattle	C	152	26	62	88	83
129	COL	Brent Johnson	Owen Sound	G	6	3	10	0	2.10
130	S.J.	Michal Bros	HC Olomouc, CZE	C					
131	OTT	David Hruska	Banik Sokolov, CZE	RW					
132	PHI	Dimitri Tertyshny	Traktor Chelyabinsk, CIS	D	62	2	8	10	30
133	ANA	Peter LeBoutillier	Red Deer	RW	35	2	1	3	176
134	T.B.	Eduard Pershin	Dynamo Moscow, CIS	RW					
135	PHI	Jamie Sokolsky	Belleville	D					
136	WPG	Sylvain Daigle	Shawinigan	G					
137	L.A.	Igor Melyakov	Torpedo Yaroslavl, CIS	LW					
138	MTL	Boyd Olson	Tri-City	C					
139	TOR	Doug Bonner	Seattle	G					
140	S.J.	Timo Hakanen	Assat Pori, FIN	C					
141	DAL	Dominic Marleau	Victoriaville	D					
142	S.J.	Jaroslav Kudrna	Penticton Jr. A	LW					
143	NYR	Peter Slamiar	ZTK Zvolen, SVK	LW					
144	VAN	Brent Sopel	Swift Current	D	23	3	4	7	16
145	TOR	Yannick Tremblay	Beauport	D	153	14	32	46	44
146	CHI	Marc Magliarditi	Des Moines Jr. A	G					
147	WSH	Frederick Jobin	Laval	D					
148	N.J.	Adam Young	Windsor	D					
149	CHI	Marty Wilford	Oshawa	D					
150	CGY	Clarke Wilm	Saskatoon	C	156	20	20	40	120
151	BOS	Yevgeny Shaldybin	Torpedo Yaroslavl, CIS	D	3	1	0	1	0
152	PHI	Martin Spanhel	ZPS Zlin, CZE	RW					
153	ST.L.	Denis Hamel	Chicoutimi	LW	3	1	0	1	0
154	PIT	Alexei Kolkunov	Krylja Sovetov Mosc., CIS	C					
155	COL	John Cirjak	Spokane	RW					
156	DET	Tyler Perry	Seattle	C					
157	L.A.	Benoit Larose	Sherbrooke	D					
158	NYI	Andrew Taylor	Detroit	LW					
159	ANA	Mike LaPlante	Calgary	D					
160	T.B.	Cory Murphy	Sault Ste. Marie	D					
161	EDM	Martin Cerven	Dukla Trencin, SVK	C					
162	WPG	Paul Traynor	Kitchener	D					
163	L.A.	Juha Vuorivirta	Tappara Tampere, FIN	C					
164	MTL	Stephane Robidas	Shawinigan	D	1	0	0	0	0
165	HFD	Byron Ritchie	Lethbridge	C	29	0	2	2	17
166	FLA	Peter Worrell	Hull	LW	129	7	11	18	580
167	S.J.	Brad Mehalko	Lethbridge	RW					
168	S.J.	Robert Dindrich	HC Interconex Plzen, CZE	D					
169	NYR	Jeff Heil	Wisconsin-River Falls	G					
170	VAN	Stewart Bodtker	Colorado College	C					
171	TOR	Marek Melenovsky	Dukla Jihlava, CZE	C					
172	BUF	Brian Scott	Kitchener	LW					
173	DAL	Jeff Dewar	Moose Jaw	RW					
174	N.J.	Richard Rochefort	Sudbury	C					
175	CHI	Steve Tardif	Drummondville	C					
176	CGY	Ryan Gillis	North Bay	D					
177	BOS	P.J. Axelsson	Vastra Frolunda, SWE	LW	240	25	45	70	80
178	PHI	Martin Streit	HC Olomouc, CZE	LW					
179	ST.L.	Jean-Luc Grand-Pierre	Val d'Or	D	27	0	1	1	32
180	PIT	Derrick Pyke	Halifax	RW					
181	COL	Dan Smith	U. of British Columbia	D	15	0	0	0	9
182	DET	Per Eklund	Djurgarden Stockholm, SWE	LW					
183	OTT	Kaj Linna	Boston U.	D					
184	OTT	Ray Schultz	Tri-City	D	26	0	2	2	82
185	ANA	Igor Karpenko	Sokol Kiev, CIS	G					
186	T.B.	Joe Cardarelli	Spokane	LW					
187	EDM	Stephen Douglas	Niagara Falls	D					
188	WPG	Jaroslav Obsut	North Battleford	D					
189	WPG	Fredrik Loven	Djurgarden Stockholm, SWE	C					
190	MTL	Greg Hart	Kamloops	RW					
191	HFD	Milan Kostolny	Detroit	RW					
192	FLA	Filip Kuba	HC Vitkovice, CZE	D	18	1	6	7	2
193	DAL	Anatoli Koveshnikov	Sokol Kiev, CIS	RW					
194	S.J.	Ryan Kraft	Minnesota-Duluth	C					
195	NYR	Ilja Gorokhov	Torpedo Yaroslavl, CIS	D					
196	VAN	Tyler Willis	Swift Current	RW					
197	TOR	Mark Murphy	Stratford Jr. B	LW					
198	BUF	Mike Zanutto	Oshawa	C					
199	WSH	Vasili Turkovsky	CSKA Moscow, CIS	D					
200	N.J.	Frederic Henry	Granby	G					
201	CHI	Casey Hankinson	Minnesota-Duluth	LW					
202	DAL	Sergei Luchinkin	Dynamo Moscow, CIS	LW					
203	BOS	Sergei Zhukov	Torpedo Yaroslavl, CIS	D					
204	PHI	Ruslan Shafikov	Salavat Yulayev Ufa, CIS	C					
205	ST.L.	Derek Bekar	Powell River Jr. A	LW	1	0	0	0	0
206	PIT	Sergei Voronov	Dynamo Moscow, CIS	D					
207	COL	Tomi Hirvonen	Ilves Tampere, FIN	C					
208	DET	Andrei Samokhvalov	Ust-Kamenogorsk, RUS, CIS	RW					
209	ST.L.	Libor Zabransky	HC Ceske Budejovice, TCH	D	40	1	6	7	50
210	NYI	David MacDonald	Sudbury	G					
211	NYI	Mike Broda	Moose Jaw	LW					
212	T.B.	Zac Bierk	Peterborough	G	26	5	63	0	3.78
213	EDM	Jiri Antonin	HC Pardubice, CZE	D					
214	WPG	Rob Deciantis	Kitchener	C					
215	L.A.	Brian Stewart	Sault Ste. Marie						
216	MTL	Eric Houde	Halifax	C	30	2	3	5	4
217	HFD	Mike Rucinski	Detroit	D	24	0	2	2	10
218	FLA	David Lemanowicz	Spokane	G					
219	DAL	Stephen Lowe	Sault Ste. Marie	C					
220	S.J.	Mikko Markkanen	TPS Turku, FIN	RW					
221	NYR	Bob Maudie	Kamloops	C					
222	VAN	Jason Cugnet	Kelowna Jr. A	G					
223	TOR	Danny Markov	Spartak Moscow, CIS	D	141	6	23	29	103
224	BUF	Rob Skrlac	Kamloops	LW					
225	WSH	Scott Swanson	Omaha Jr. A	D					
226	N.J.	Colin O'Hara	Winnipeg Jr. A	D					
227	CHI	Mike Pittman	Guelph	C					
228	COL	Chris George	Sarnia	RW					
229	BOS	Jonathon Murphy	Peterborough	D					
230	PHI	Jeff Lank	Prince Albert	D	2	0	0	0	2
231	OTT	Erik Kaminski	Cleveland Jr.	RW					
232	PIT	Frank Ivankovic	Oshawa	G					
233	CGY	Steve Shirreffs	Hotchkiss H.S.	D					
234	DET	David Engblom	Vallentuna, SWE	C					

1996

PICK	TEAM	NAME	DRAFTED FROM	NHL PLAYERS: POS / NHL GOALTENDERS: POS	GP / GP	G / W	A / GA	PTS / SO	PIM / AVG
FIRST ROUND									
1	OTT	Chris Phillips	Prince Albert	D	171	13	28	41	109
2	S.J.	Andrei Zyuzin	Salavat Yulayev Ufa, CIS	D	115	11	17	28	137
3	NYI	Jean-Pierre Dumont	Val d'Or	RW	72	19	14	33	28
4	WSH	Alexandre Volchkov	Barrie	C	3	0	0	0	0
5	DAL	Richard Jackman	Sault Ste. Marie	D	22	1	2	3	6
6	EDM	Boyd Devereaux	Kitchener	C	175	15	31	46	49
7	BUF	Erik Rasmussen	Minnesota-Duluth	C	130	13	16	29	94
8	BOS	Johnathan Aitken	Medicine Hat	D	3	0	0	0	0
9	ANA	Ruslan Salei	Las Vegas IHL	D	241	12	30	42	266
10	N.J.	Lance Ward	Red Deer	D	Re-entered Draft in 1998				
11	PHX	Dan Focht	Tri-City	D	Played Finland, AHL in 99-00				
12	VAN	Josh Holden	Regina	C	36	3	9	12	12
13	CGY	Derek Morris	Regina	D	231	25	76	101	241
14	ST.L.	Marty Reasoner	Boston College	C	54	13	21	34	28
15	PHI	Dainius Zubrus	Pembroke Jr. A	RW	290	36	76	112	147
16	T.B.	Mario Larocque	Hull	D	5	0	0	0	16
17	WSH	Jaroslav Svejkovsky	Tri-City	RW	113	23	19	42	56
18	MTL	Matt Higgins	Moose Jaw	C	51	1	2	3	4
19	EDM	Matthieu Descoteaux	Shawinigan	D	18pts w/ Hamilton/Quebec				
20	FLA	Marcus Nilson	Djurgarden Stockholm, SWE	RW	17	1	3	4	7
21	S.J.	Marco Sturm	Landshut, GER	C	226	38	57	95	114
22	NYR	Jeff Brown	Sarnia	D	25pts – Charlotte 99-00				
23	PIT	Craig Hillier	Ottawa	G	28 games w/ 4 teams in 99-00				
24	PHX	Daniel Briere	Drummondville	C	82	10	15	25	32
25	COL	Peter Ratchuk	Shattuck St. Mary's H.S.	D	24	1	1	2	10
26	DET	Jesse Wallin	Red Deer	D	1	0	0	0	0
SECOND ROUND									
27	BUF	Cory Sarich	Saskatoon	D	63	0	6	6	77
28	PIT	Pavel Skrbek	Poldi Kladno, CZE	D	4	0	0	0	2
29	NYI	Dan Lacouture	Springfield Jr.	LW	8	0	0	0	10
30	L.A.	Josh Green	Medicine Hat	LW	76	13	17	30	49
31	CHI	Remi Royer	St-Hyacinthe	D	18	0	0	0	67
32	EDM	Chris Hajt	Guelph	D	Continues to improve in AHL				
33	BUF	Darren Van Oene	Brandon	LW	20g, 38pts – Rochester 99-00				
34	HFD	Trevor Wasyluk	Medicine Hat	LW	26pts w/ 2 teams in IHL 99-00				
35	ANA	Matt Cullen	St. Cloud State	C	216	30	61	91	94
36	TOR	Marek Posmyk	Dukla Jihlava, CZE	D	18	1	2	3	20
37	L.A.	Marian Cisar	Slovan Bratislava, SVK	RW	3	0	0	0	4
38	N.J.	Wes Mason	Sarnia	LW	77pts w/ 3 teams in 3 leagues				
39	CGY	Travis Brigley	Lethbridge	LW	19	0	2	2	6
40	CGY	Steve Begin	Val d'Or	C	18	1	1	2	41
41	N.J.	Josh DeWolf	Twin Cities Jr.	D	15pts w/ 2 AHL teams 99-00				
42	CHI	Jeff Paul	Niagara Falls	D	69 games – Cleveland 99-00				
43	WSH	Jan Bulis	Barrie	C	142	21	49	70	54
44	MTL	Mathieu Garon	Victoriaville	G	3.10gaa w/ Quebec 99-00				
45	BOS	Henry Kuster	Medicine Hat	RW	35pts – 3 teams in 2 leagues				
46	CHI	Geoff Peters	Niagara Falls	C	10 g, 68 games – Cleveland				
47	N.J.	Pierre Dagenais	Moncton	LW	Re-entered Draft in 1998				
48	NYR	Daniel Goneau	Granby	LW	53	12	3	15	14
49	N.J.	Colin White	Hull	D	21	2	1	3	40
50	TOR	Francis Larivee	Laval	G	4.73gaa – Greensboro 99-00				
51	COL	Yuri Babenko	Krylja Sovetov Mosc., CIS	C	20g, 45pts w/ Hershey 99-00				
52	DET	Aren Miller	Spokane	G	3.33gaa – Cincinnati 99-00				

OTHER ROUNDS

PICK	TEAM	NAME	DRAFTED FROM	NHL PLAYERS: POS	GP	G	A	PTS	PIM
				NHL GOALTENDERS: POS	GP	W	GA	SO	AVG
53	BOS	Eric Naud	St-Hyacinthe	LW					
54	BUF	Francois Methot	St-Hyacinthe	C					
55	S.J.	Terry Friesen	Swift Current	G					
56	NYI	Zdeno Chara	Dukla Trencin, SVK	D	149	4	16	20	190
57	L.A.	Greg Phillips	Saskatoon	RW					
58	WSH	Sergei Zimakov	Krylja Sovetov Mosc., CIS	D					
59	EDM	Tom Poti	Cushing Academy	D	149	14	42	56	107
60	FLA	Chris Allen	Kingston	D	2	0	0	0	2
61	HFD	Andrei Petrunin	CSKA Moscow, CIS	RW					
62	PHX	Per-Anton Lundstrom	MoDo Ornskoldsvik, SWE	D					
63	N.J.	Scott Parker	Kelowna	RW	Re-entered Draft in 1998				
64	PHI	Chester Gallant	Niagara Falls	RW					
65	FLA	Oleg Kvasha	CSKA Moscow, CIS	LW	146	17	33	50	79
66	TOR	Mike Lankshear	Guelph	D					
67	ST.L.	Gordie Dwyer	Beauport	LW	Re-entered Draft in 1998				
68	TOR	Konstantin Kalmikov	Detroit	LW					
69	T.B.	Curtis Tipler	Regina	RW					
70	DAL	Jonathan Sim	Sarnia	C	32	6	3	9	22
71	MTL	Arron Asham	Red Deer	RW	40	4	2	6	24
72	PIT	Boyd Kane	Regina	LW	Re-entered Draft in 1998				
73	CGY	Dmitri Vlasenkov	Torpedo Yaroslavl, CIS	LW					
74	WSH	Dave Weninger	Michigan Tech	G					
75	VAN	Zenith Komarniski	Tri-City	D	18	1	1	2	8
76	NYR	Dmitri Subbotin	CSKA Moscow, CIS	LW					
77	PIT	Boris Protsenko	Calgary	RW					
78	WSH	Shawn McNeil	Kamloops	C					
79	COL	Mark Parrish	St. Cloud State	LW	154	50	31	81	64
80	BOS	Jason Doyle	Owen Sound	RW	Re-entered Draft in 1998				
81	OTT	Antti-Jussi Niemi	Jokerit Helsinki, FIN	D					
82	FLA	Joey Tetarenko	Portland	D					
83	NYI	Tyrone Garner	Oshawa	G	3	0	12	0	5.18
84	L.A.	Mikael Simons	Mora, SWE	C					
85	WSH	Justin Davis	Kingston	RW					
86	TOR	Jason Sessa	Lake Superior State	RW					
87	BUF	Kurt Walsh	Owen Sound	RW					
88	HFD	Craig MacDonald	Harvard	C	11	0	0	0	0
89	CGY	Toni Lydman	Reipas Lahti, FIN	D					
90	DAL	Mike Hurley	Tri-City	RW					
91	N.J.	Josef Boumedienne	Huddinge, SWE	D					
92	MTL	Kim Staal	Malmo, SWE	C					
93	VAN	Jonas Soling	Huddinge, SWE	RW					
94	CGY	Christian Lefebvre	Granby	D	Re-entered Draft in 1998				
95	ST.L.	Jonathan Zukiwsky	Red Deer	C					
96	L.A.	Eric Belanger	Beauport	C					
97	ST.L.	Andrei Petrakov	Avtomo. Yekaterinburg, CIS	RW					
98	COL	Ben Storey	Harvard	D					
99	MTL	Etienne Drapeau	Beauport	C					
100	BOS	Trent Whitfield	Spokane	C					
101	N.J.	Josh MacNevin	Vernon Jr. A	D					
102	S.J.	Matt Bradley	Kingston	RW					
103	TOR	Vladimir Antipov	Torpedo Yaroslavl, CIS	RW					
104	HFD	Steve Wasylko	Detroit	C					
105	PIT	Michal Rozsival	Dukla Jihlava, CZE	D	75	4	17	21	48
106	BUF	Mike Martone	Peterborough	D					
107	COL	Randy Petruk	Kamloops	G					
108	DET	Johan Forsander	HV 71 Jonkoping, SWE	LW					
109	NYI	Andy Berenzweig	Michigan	D	2	0	0	0	0
110	TOR	Peter Cava	Sault Ste. Marie	C					
111	TOR	Brandon Sugden	London	D					
112	DAL	Ryan Christie	Owen Sound	LW	5	0	0	0	0
113	DAL	Yevgeny Tsybuk	Torpedo Yaroslavl, CIS	D					
114	EDM	Brian Urick	U. of Notre Dame	RW					
115	BUF	Alexei Tezikov	Lada Togliatti, CIS	D	28	1	1	2	2
116	HFD	Mark McMahon	Kitchener	D					
117	ANA	Brendan Buckley	Boston College	D					
118	N.J.	Glenn Crawford	Windsor	C					
119	PHX	Richard Lintner	Dukla Trencin, SVK	D	33	1	5	6	22
120	L.A.	Jesse Black	Niagara Falls	D					
121	VAN	Tyler Prosofsky	Kelowna	C					
122	CGY	Josef Straka	Chemopetrol Litvinov, CZE	C					
123	L.A.	Peter Hogan	Oshawa	D					
124	PHI	Per-Ragnar Bergqvist	Leksand, SWE	G					
125	T.B.	Jason Robinson	Niagara Falls	D					
126	WSH	Matthew Lahey	Peterborough	LW					
127	MTL	Daniel Archambault	Val d'Or	D					
128	NYI	Peter Sachl	HC Ceske Budejovice, CZE	C					
129	FLA	Andrew Long	Guelph	C					
130	CHI	Andy Johnson	Peterborough	D					
131	NYR	Colin Pepperall	Niagara Falls	LW					
132	BOS	Elias Abrahamsson	Halifax	D					
133	PHI	Jesse Boulerice	Detroit	RW					
134	COL	Luke Curtin	Kelowna	LW					
135	DET	Michal Podolka	Sault Ste. Marie	G					
136	OTT	Andreas Dackell	Brynas Gavle, SWE	RW	320	52	97	149	80
137	S.J.	Michel Larocque	Boston U.	G					
138	NYI	Todd Miller	Sarnia	C					
139	PHX	Robert Esche	Detroit	G	11	2	30	0	3.35
140	TOR	Dmitri Yakushin	Pembroke Jr. A	D	2	0	0	0	2
141	EDM	Bryan Randall	Medicine Hat	C					
142	BUF	Ryan Davis	Owen Sound	RW					
143	HFD	Aaron Baker	Tri-City	G					
144	DET	Magnus Nilsson	Vita Hasten, SWE	RW					
145	N.J.	Sean Ritchlin	Michigan	RW					
146	COL	Brian Willsie	Guelph	RW	1	0	0	0	0
147	VAN	Nolan McDonald	Vermont	G					
148	TOR	Chris Bogas	Michigan State	D					
149	ANA	Blaine Russell	Prince Albert	G					
150	PIT	Peter Bergman	Kamloops	C					
151	TOR	Lucio DeMartinis	Shawinigan	LW					
152	T.B.	Nikolai Ignatov	CSKA Moscow, CIS	D					
153	WSH	Andrew Van Bruggen	Northern Michigan	RW					
154	MTL	Brett Clark	U. of Maine	D	116	3	3	6	40
155	BOS	Chris Lane	Spokane	D					
156	FLA	Gaetan Poirier	Merrimack	LW					
157	T.B.	Xavier Delisle	Granby	C	2	0	0	0	0
158	NYR	Ola Sandberg	Djurgarden Stockholm, SWE	D					
159	ST.L.	Stephen Wagner	Olds Jr. A	G					
160	COL	Kai Fischer	Dusseldorf, GER	G					
161	BUF	Darren Mortier	Sarnia	C					
162	DET	Alexandre Jacques	Shawinigan	C					
163	OTT	Francois Hardy	Val d'Or	D					
164	S.J.	Jake Deadmarsh	Kamloops	D					
165	NYI	J.R. Prestifilippo	Hotchkiss H.S.	G					
166	DAL	Eoin McInerney	London	G					
167	COL	Dan Hinote	Army	RW	27	1	3	4	10
168	EDM	David Bernier	St-Hyacinthe	C					
169	ST.L.	Daniel Corso	Victoriaville	C					
170	EDM	Brandon Lafrance	Ohio State	RW					
171	HFD	Greg Kuznik	Seattle	D					
172	ANA	Timo Ahmaoja	JyP HT Jyvaskyla, FIN	D					
173	N.J.	Daryl Andrews	Melfort Jr. A	D					
174	PHX	Trevor Letowski	Sarnia	C	96	21	22	43	22
175	VAN	Clint Cabana	Medicine Hat	D					
176	COL	Samual Pahlsson	MoDo Ornskoldsvik, SWE	C					
177	ST.L.	Reed Low	Moose Jaw	RW					
178	TOR	Reggie Berg	Minnesota-Duluth	C					
179	T.B.	Pavel Kubina	HC Vitkovice, CZE	D	147	18	32	50	195
180	WSH	Michael Anderson	Minnesota-Duluth	RW					
181	MTL	Timo Vertala	JyP HT Jyvaskyla, FIN	LW					
182	BOS	Thomas Brown	Sarnia	D					
183	FLA	Alexandre Couture	Victoriaville	D					
184	CHI	Mike Vellinga	Guelph	D					
185	NYR	Jeff Dessner	Taft H.S.	D					
186	PIT	Eric Meloche	Cornwall	RW					
187	PHI	Roman Malov	Avangard Omsk, CIS	LW					
188	COL	Roman Pylner	Chemopetrol Litvinov, CZE	C					
189	DET	Colin Beardsmore	North Bay	C					
190	L.A.	Stephen Valiquette	Sudbury	G	6	2	6	0	1.87
191	S.J.	Cory Cyrenne	Brandon	C					
192	NYI	Evgeny Korolev	Peterborough	D	Re-entered Draft in 1998				
193	L.A.	Kai Nurminen	HV 71 Jonkoping, SWE	LW	67	16	11	27	22
194	DAL	Joel Kwiatkowski	Prince George	D					
195	EDM	Fernando Pisani	St. Albert Jr. A	C/LW					
196	ST.L.	Andrei Podkonicky	ZTK Zvolen, SVK	C					
197	HFD	Kevin Marsh	Calgary	LW					
198	ANA	Kevin Kellett	Prince Albert	D					
199	N.J.	Willie Mitchell	Melfort Jr. A	D	2	0	0	0	0
200	PHX	Nicholas Lent	Omaha Jr. A	RW					
201	VAN	Jeff Scissons	Vernon Jr. A	C					
202	CGY	Ryan Wade	Kelowna	RW					
203	ST.L.	Tony Hutchins	Lawrence Academy	C					
204	TOR	Tomas Kaberle	Poldi Kladno, CZE	D	139	11	51	62	36
205	N.J.	Jay Bertsch	Spokane	RW					
206	WSH	Oleg Orekhovsky	Dynamo Moscow, CIS	D					
207	MTL	Mattia Baldi	Ambri-Piotta, SUI	F					
208	BOS	Bob Prier	St. Lawrence U.	RW					
209	FLA	Denis Khloptonov	CSKA Moscow, CIS	G					
210	CHI	Chris Twerdun	Moose Jaw	D					
211	NYR	Ryan McKie	London	D					
212	OTT	Erich Goldmann	Mannheim, GER	D	1	0	0	0	0
213	PHI	Jeff Milleker	Moose Jaw	C					
214	COL	Matthew Scorsune	Hotchkiss H.S.	D					
215	DET	Craig Stahl	Tri-City	RW					
216	OTT	Ivan Ciernik	HC Nitra, SVK	LW	2	0	0	0	0
217	S.J.	David Thibeault	Drummondville	LW					
218	NYI	Mike Muzechka	Calgary	D					
219	L.A.	Sebastien Simard	Drummondville	LW					

PICK	TEAM	NAME	DRAFTED FROM	NHL PLAYERS: POS / NHL GOALTENDERS: POS	GP / GP	G / W	A / GA	PTS / SO	PIM / AVG
220	DAL	Nick Bootland	Guelph	LW					
221	EDM	John Hultberg	Kingston	G					
222	BUF	Scott Buhler	Medicine Hat	G					
223	HFD	Craig Adams	Harvard	RW					
224	ANA	Tobias Johansson	Malmo, SWE	LW					
225	N.J.	Pasi Petrilainen	Tappara Tampere, FIN	D					
226	PHX	Marc-Etienne Hubert	Laval	C					
227	VAN	Lubomir Vaic	HC Kosice, SVK	C	9	1	1	2	2
228	CGY	Ronald Petrovicky	Prince George	RW					
229	ST.L.	Konstantin Shafranov	Fort Wayne IHL	RW	5	2	1	3	0
230	TOR	Jared Hope	Spokane	C					
231	HFD	Askhat Rakhmatullin	Salavat Yulayev Ufa, CIS	LW					
232	WSH	Chad Cavanagh	London	C					
233	MTL	Michel Tremblay	Shawinigan	LW					
234	BOS	Anders Soderberg	MoDo Ornskoldsvik, SWE	RW					
235	FLA	Russell Smith	Hull	D					
236	CHI	Andrei Kozyrev	Severstal Cherepovets, CIS	D					
237	NYR	Ronnie Sundin	Vastra Frolunda, SWE	D	1	0	0	0	0
238	PIT	Timo Seikkula	Junkkarit Kalajoki, FIN	C					
239	OTT	Sami Salo	TPS Turku, FIN	D	98	13	20	33	26
240	COL	Justin Clark	Michigan	RW					
241	DET	Eugeny Afanasiev	Detroit Little Caesar's	LW					

1997

FIRST ROUND

PICK	TEAM	NAME	DRAFTED FROM	POS	GP / GP	G / W	A / GA	PTS / SO	PIM / AVG
1	BOS	Joe Thornton	Sault Ste. Marie	C	217	42	66	108	170
2	S.J.	Patrick Marleau	Seattle	C	236	51	66	117	74
3	L.A.	Olli Jokinen	HIFK Helsinki, FIN	C	156	20	22	42	130
4	NYI	Roberto Luongo	Val d'Or	G	24	7	70	1	3.25
5	NYI	Eric Brewer	Prince George	D	89	5	8	13	52
6	CGY	Daniel Tkaczuk	Barrie	C	25G, 66PTS in AHL 99-20				
7	T.B.	Paul Mara	Sudbury	D	55	8	12	20	73
8	BOS	Sergei Samsonov	Detroit	LW	237	66	77	143	30
9	WSH	Nick Boynton	Ottawa	D	Re-entered Draft in 1999				
10	VAN	Brad Ference	Spokane	D	13	0	2	2	46
11	MTL	Jason Ward	Erie	RW	32	2	1	3	10
12	OTT	Marian Hossa	Dukla Trencin, SVK	LW	145	44	43	87	69
13	CHI	Daniel Cleary	Belleville	LW	58	7	7	14	32
14	EDM	Michel Riesen	Biel-Bienne, SUI	RW	29G, 60PTS in AHL 99-00				
15	L.A.	Matt Zultek	Ottawa	C	Re-entered Draft in 1999				
16	CHI	Ty Jones	Spokane	RW	8	0	0	0	12
17	PIT	Robert Dome	Las Vegas IHL	RW	52	7	7	14	12
18	ANA	Mikael Holmqvist	Djurgarden Stockholm, SWE	C	Played – TPS Turku in 99-00				
19	NYR	Stefan Cherneski	Brandon	RW	Leg injury in 98 slow to heal				
20	FLA	Mike Brown	Red Deer	LW	13G, 31PTS in AHL 99-00				
21	BUF	Mika Noronen	Tappara Tampere, FIN	G	54 games – Rochester 99-00				
22	CAR	Nikos Tselios	Belleville	D	22PTS – Cincinnati 99-00				
23	S.J.	Scott Hannan	Kelowna	D	35	1	4	5	16
24	N.J.	J-F Damphousse	Moncton	G	13 wins in ECHL, AHL 99-00				
25	DAL	Brenden Morrow	Portland	LW	64	14	19	33	81
26	COL	Kevin Grimes	Kingston	D	45 games in ECHL, IHL 99-00				

SECOND ROUND

PICK	TEAM	NAME	DRAFTED FROM	POS	GP / GP	G / W	A / GA	PTS / SO	PIM / AVG
27	BOS	Ben Clymer	Minnesota-Duluth	D	60	2	6	8	87
28	CAR	Brad DeFauw	North Dakota	LW	22PTS – N-Dakota 99-00				
29	L.A.	Scott Barney	Peterborough	C	DNP in 99-00 – back injury				
30	PHI	Jean-Marc Pelletier	Cornell	G	1	0	5	0	5.00
31	NYI	Jeff Zehr	Windsor	LW	4	0	0	0	2
32	CGY	Evan Lindsay	Prince Albert	G	Re-entered Draft in 1999				
33	T.B.	Kyle Kos	Red Deer	D	56 games – Detoit/Utah in IHL				
34	VAN	Ryan Bonni	Saskatoon	D	3	0	0	0	0
35	WSH	Jean-Francois Fortin	Sherbrooke	D	10PTS in ECHL & AHL 99-00				
36	VAN	Harold Druken	Detroit	C	33	7	9	16	10
37	MTL	Gregor Baumgartner	Laval	LW	Re-entered Draft in 1999				
38	N.J.	Stanislav Gron	Slovan Bratislava, SVK	C	29PTS w/ Albany 99-00				
39	CHI	Jeremy Reich	Seattle	C	91PTS/ w/ Swift Current 99-00				
40	ST.L.	Tyler Rennette	North Bay	C	25PTS – Worcester 99-00				
41	EDM	Patrick Dovigi	Erie	G	4.05GAA w/ St. Mike's Jr. A				
42	CGY	John Tripp	Oshawa	RW	39PTS in ECHL & AHL 99-00				
43	PHX	Juha Gustafsson	Kiekko-Espoo, FIN	D	Played – Espoo Blues 99-00				
44	PIT	Brian Gaffaney	North Iowa Jr. A	D	Played St. Cloud State 99-00				
45	ANA	Maxim Balmochnykh	Lada Togliatti, RUS	LW	6	0	1	1	2
46	NYR	Wes Jarvis	Kitchener	D	43 games–Canada Nat-Team				
47	FLA	Kristian Huselius	Farjestad Karlstad, SWE	RW	21G, 44PTS – Frolunda 99-00				
48	BUF	Henrik Tallinder	AIK Solna, SWE	D	2 years in Sweden				
49	DET	Yuri Butsayev	Lada Togliatti, RUS	C	57	5	3	8	12
50	PHI	Pat Kavanagh	Peterborough	RW	12G, 20PTS - Syracuse 99-00				
51	CGY	Dmitri Kokorev	Dynamo-2 Moscow, RUS	D	Played 99-00 D'amo Moscow				
52	DAL	Roman Lyashenko	Torpedo Yaroslavl, RUS	C	58	6	6	12	10
53	COL	Graham Belak	Edmonton	D	Played Kootenay Jr. 99-00				

OTHER ROUNDS

PICK	TEAM	NAME	DRAFTED FROM	POS	GP / GP	G / W	A / GA	PTS / SO	PIM / AVG
54	BOS	Mattias Karlin	MoDo Ornskoldsvik, SWE	C/RW					
55	COL	Rick Berry	Seattle	D					
56	FLA	Vratislav Cech	Kitchener	D					
57	TOR	Jeff Farkas	Boston College	C					
58	OTT	Jani Hurme	TPS Turku, FIN	G	1	1	2	0	2.00
59	NYI	Jarrett Smith	Prince George	C					
60	CGY	Derek Schutz	Spokane	C					
61	T.B.	Matt Elich	Windsor	RW	8	1	1	2	0
62	PHI	Kris Mallette	Kelowna	D					
63	BOS	Lee Goren	North Dakota	RW					
64	VAN	Kyle Freadrich	Regina	LW	10	0	0	0	39
65	MTL	Ilkka Mikkola	Karpat Oulu, FIN	D					
66	OTT	Josh Langfeld	Lincoln Jr.	RW					
67	CHI	Mike Souza	New Hampshire	LW					
68	EDM	Sergei Yerkovich	Las Vegas IHL	D					
69	BUF	Maxim Afinogenov	Dynamo Moscow, RUS	RW	65	16	18	34	41
70	CGY	Erik Andersson	U. of Denver	C	12	2	1	3	8
71	PIT	Josef Melichar	HC Ceske Budejovice, CZE	D					
72	ANA	Jay Legault	London	LW					
73	NYR	Burke Henry	Brandon	D					
74	FLA	Nick Smith	Barrie	C					
75	BUF	Jeff Martin	Windsor	C					
76	DET	Petr Sykora	HC Pojis. IB Pardubice, CZE	C	2	0	0	0	0
77	DAL	Steve Gainey	Kamloops	LW					
78	COL	Ville Nieminen	Tappara Tampere, FIN	LW	1	0	0	0	0
79	NYI	Robert Schnabel	Slavia Praha, CZE	D	Re-entered Draft in 1998				
80	CAR	Francis Lessard	Val d'Or	D					
81	BOS	Karol Bartanus	Drummondville	RW					
82	S.J.	Adam Colagiacomo	Oshawa	RW					
83	L.A.	Joseph Corvo	Western Michigan	D					
84	TOR	Adam Mair	Owen Sound	C	8	1	0	1	6
85	NYI	Petr Mika	Slavia Praha, CZE	LW	3	0	0	0	0
86	ST.L.	Didier Tremblay	Halifax	D					
87	COL	Brad Larsen	Swift Current	LW	1	0	0	0	0
88	CAR	Shane Willis	Lethbridge	RW	9	0	0	0	0
89	WSH	Curtis Cruickshank	Kingston	G					
90	VAN	Chris Stanley	Belleville	C					
91	MTL	Daniel Tetrault	Brandon	D					
92	CGY	Chris St. Croix	Kamloops	D					
93	NYR	Tomi Kallarsson	HPK Hameenlinna, FIN	D					
94	EDM	Jonas Elofsson	Farjestad Karlstad, SWE	D					
95	FLA	Ivan Novoseltsev	Krylja Sovetov Mosc., RUS	LW	14	2	1	3	8
96	PHX	Scott McCallum	Tri-City	D					
97	PIT	Alexandre Mathieu	Halifax	LW					
98	ST.L.	Jan Horacek	Slavia Praha, CZE	D					
99	L.A.	Sean Blanchard	Ottawa	D					
100	CGY	Ryan Ready	Belleville	LW					
101	BUF	Luc Theoret	Lethbridge	D					
102	DET	Quintin Laing	Kelowna	LW					
103	PHI	Mikhail Chernov	Torpedo-2 Yaroslavl, RUS	D					
104	N.J.	Lucas Nehrling	Sarnia	D					
105	DAL	Marc Kristofferson	Mora, SWE	RW					
106	ST.L.	Jame Pollock	Seattle	D					
107	S.J.	Adam Nittel	Erie	RW					
108	T.B.	Mark Thompson	Regina	D					
109	T.B.	Jan Sulc	Chemopetrol Litvinov, CZE	C					
110	CHI	Benjamin Simon	U. of Notre Dame	C					
111	TOR	Frantisek Mrazek	HC Ceske Budejovice, CZE	LW					
112	T.B.	Karel Betik	Kelowna	D	3	0	2	2	2
113	CGY	Martin Moise	Beauport	LW					
114	VAN	David Darguzas	Edmonton	C					
115	NYI	Adam Edinger	Bowling Green	C					
116	WSH	Kevin Caulfield	Boston College	RW					
117	VAN	Matt Cockell	Saskatoon	G					
118	MTL	Konstantin Sidulov	Traktor Chelyabinsk, RUS	D					
119	OTT	Magnus Arvedsson	Farjestad Karlstad, SWE	C	188	47	54	101	122
120	CHI	Peter Gardiner	RPI	RW					
121	EDM	Jason Chimera	Medicine Hat	C					
122	MTL	Gennady Razin	Kamloops	D					
123	PHX	Curtis Suter	Spokane	LW					
124	PIT	Harlan Pratt	Prince Albert	D					
125	ANA	Luc Vaillancourt	Beauport	G					
126	NYR	Jason McLean	Moose Jaw	G					
127	FLA	Pat Parthenais	Detroit	D					
128	BUF	Torrey DiRoberto	Seattle	C					
129	DET	John Wikstrom	Lulea, SWE	D					
130	CHI	Kyle Calder	Regina	C	8	1	1	2	2
131	N.J.	Jiri Bicek	HC Kosice, SVK	LW					
132	DAL	Teemu Elomo	TPS Turku, FIN	LW					
133	COL	Aaron Miskovich	Green Bay	C					
134	NYR	Johan Lindbom	HV 71 Jonkoping, SWE	LW	38	1	3	4	28
135	BOS	Denis Timofeyev	CSKA-2 Moscow, RUS	D					
136	NYR	Mike York	Michigan State	C	82	26	24	50	18
137	L.A.	Richard Seeley	Prince Albert	D					
138	TOR	Eric Gooldy	Detroit	LW					
139	NYI	Bobby Leavins	Brandon	LW					

PICK	TEAM	NAME	DRAFTED FROM	NHL PLAYERS: POS	GP	G	A	PTS	PIM
				NHL GOALTENDERS: POS	GP	W	GA	SO	AVG
140	CGY	Ilja Demidov	Dynamo-2 Moscow, RUS	D					
141	EDM	Peter Sarno	Windsor	C					
142	CAR	Kyle Dafoe	Owen Sound	D					
143	WSH	Henrik Petre	Djurgarden Stockholm, SWE	D					
144	VAN	Matt Cooke	Windsor	LW	81	5	9	14	66
145	MTL	Jonathan Desroches	Granby	D					
146	OTT	Jeff Sullivan	Halifax	D					
147	CHI	Heath Gordon	Green Bay	RW					
148	VAN	Larry Shapley	Welland Jr. B	D					
149	ST.L.	Nicholas Bilotto	Beauport	D					
150	L.A.	Jeff Katcher	Brandon	D					
151	PHX	Robert Francz	Peterborough	LW					
152	PIT	Petr Havelka	Sparta Praha, CZE	LW					
153	T.B.	Andrei Skopintsev	TPS Turku, FIN	D	23	1	1	2	16
154	NYR	Shawn Degagne	Kitchener	G					
155	FLA	Keith Delaney	Barrie	C					
156	BUF	Brian Campbell	Ottawa	D	12	1	4	5	4
157	DET	B.J. Young	Red Deer	RW	1	0	0	0	0
158	PHI	Jordon Flodell	Moose Jaw	D					
159	N.J.	Sascha Goc	Schwenningen, GER	D					
160	DAL	Alexei Timkin	Torpedo-2 Yaroslavl, RUS	RW					
161	COL	David Aebischer	Fribourg-Gotteron, SUI	G					
162	BOS	Joel Trottier	Ottawa	RW					
163	S.J.	Joe Dusabek	U. of Notre Dame	RW					
164	PHI	Todd Fedoruk	Kelowna	LW					
165	TOR	Hugo Marchand	Victoriaville	D					
166	NYI	Kris Knoblauch	Edmonton	LW					
167	CGY	Jeremy Rondeau	Swift Current	LW					
168	T.B.	Justin Jack	Kelowna	RW					
169	CAR	Andrew Merrick	Michigan	C					
170	T.B.	Eero Somervuori	Jokerit Helsinki, FIN	RW					
171	VAN	Rod Leroux	Seattle	D					
172	MTL	Ben Guite	U. of Maine	RW					
173	OTT	Robin Bacul	Slavia Praha Jr., CZE	RW					
174	CHI	Jerad Smith	Portland	D					
175	NYR	Johan Holmqvist	Brynas Gavle, SWE	G					
176	EDM	Kevin Bolibruck	Peterborough	D					
177	ST.L.	Ladislav Nagy	Dragon Presov	C	11	2	4	6	2
178	ANA	Tony Mohagen	Seattle	LW					
179	PIT	Mark Moore	Harvard	D					
180	BOS	Jim Baxter	Oshawa	D	Re-entered Draft in 1999				
181	ANA	Mat Snesrud	North Iowa Jr. A	D					
182	NYR	Mike Mottau	Boston College	D					
183	FLA	Tyler Palmer	Lake Superior State	D					
184	BUF	Jeremy Adduono	Sudbury	RW					
185	T.B.	Samuel St. Pierre	Victoriaville	RW					
186	DET	Mike Laceby	Kingston	C					
187	EDM	Chad Hinz	Moose Jaw	RW					
188	N.J.	Mathieu Benoit	Chicoutimi	RW					
189	DAL	Jeff McKercher	Barrie	D					
190	TOR	Shawn Thornton	Peterborough	RW					
191	BOS	Antti Laaksonen	U. of Denver	LW	38	7	5	12	4
192	S.J.	Cam Severson	Prince Albert	LW					
193	L.A.	Jay Kopischke	North Iowa Jr. A	LW					
194	TOR	Russ Bartlett	Phillips-Exeter H.S.	C					
195	CAR	Niklas Nordgren	MoDo Ornskoldsvik, SWE	LW					
196	NYI	Jeremy Symington	Petrolia Jr. B	G					
197	MTL	Petr Kubos	Petra Vsetin, CZE	D					
198	T.B.	Shawn Skolney	Seattle	D					
199	CAR	Randy Fitzgerald	Detroit	LW					
200	WSH	Pierre-Luc Therrien	Drummondville	G					
201	VAN	Denis Martynyuk	CSKA-2 Moscow, RUS	LW					
202	MTL	Andrei Sidyakin	Salavat Yulayev Ufa, CIS	RW					
203	OTT	Nick Gillis	Cushing Academy	RW					
204	CHI	Sergei Shikhanov	Lada Togliatti, RUS	RW					
205	EDM	Chris Kerr	Sudbury	D					
206	ST.L.	Bobby Haglund	Des Moines Jr. A	LW					
207	PHX	Alexander Andreyev	Weyburn Jr. A	D					
208	PIT	Andrew Ference	Portland	D	30	2	4	6	20
209	ANA	Rene Stussi	Thurgau, SUI	C					
210	NYR	Andrew Proskurnicki	Sarnia	LW					
211	FLA	Doug Schueller	Twin Cities Jr.	D					
212	BUF	Kamil Piros	Chemopetrol Litvinov, CZE	C					
213	DET	Steve Willejto	Prince Albert	C					
214	PHI	Marko Kauppinen	JYP HT Jyvaskyla Jr., FIN	D					
215	N.J.	Scott Clemmensen	Des Moines Jr. A	G					
216	DAL	Alexei Komarov	Dynamo-2 Moscow, RUS	D					
217	COL	Doug Schmidt	Waterloo Jr. A	D					
218	BOS	Eric Van Acker	Chicoutimi	D					
219	S.J.	Mark Smith	Lethbridge	C					
220	L.A.	Konrad Brand	Medicine Hat	D					
221	TOR	Jonathan Hedstrom	Skelleftea, SWE	RW					
222	NYI	Ryan Clark	Lincoln Jr. A	D					
223	CGY	Dustin Paul	Moose Jaw	RW					
224	T.B.	Paul Comrie	U. of Denver	C	15	1	2	3	4
225	CAR	Kent McDonell	Guelph	RW	Re-entered Draft in 1999				
226	WSH	Matt Oikawa	St. Lawrence U.	RW					
227	VAN	Peter Brady	Powell River Jr. A	G					
228	MTL	Jarl Espen Ygranes	Furuset Oslo, NOR	D					
229	OTT	Karel Rachunek	ZPS Zlin Jr., CZE	D	6	0	0	0	2
230	CHI	Chris Feil	Ohio State	D					
231	EDM	Alexander Fomitchev	St. Albert Jr. A	G					
232	ST.L.	Dmitri Plekhanov	Neftekhimik Nizhnekamsk, RUS	D					
233	PHX	Wyatt Smith	Minnesota-Duluth	C	2	0	0	0	0
234	PIT	Eric Lind	Avon Old Farms H.S.	D					
235	ANA	Tommi Degerman	Boston U.	LW					
236	NYR	Richard Miller	Providence	D					
237	FLA	Benoit Cote	Shawinigan	C					
238	BUF	Dylan Kemp	Lethbridge	D					
239	DET	Greg Willers	Kingston	D					
240	PHI	Par Styf	MoDo Ornskoldsvik, SWE	D					
241	N.J.	Jan Srdinko	Petra Vsetin, CZE	D					
242	DAL	Brett McLean	Kelowna	C					
243	COL	Kyle Kidney	Salisbury H.S.	LW					
244	ST.L.	Marek Ivan	Lethbridge	C					
245	COL	Stephen Lafleur	Belleville	D					
246	BOS	Jay Henderson	Edmonton	LW	20	1	3	4	11

1998

FIRST ROUND

PICK	TEAM	NAME	DRAFTED FROM	POS	GP	G	A	PTS	PIM
1	T.B.	Vincent Lecavalier	Rimouski	C	162	38	57	95	66
2	NSH	David Legwand	Plymouth	C	72	13	15	28	30
3	S.J.	Brad Stuart	Regina	D	82	10	26	36	32
4	VAN	Bryan Allen	Oshawa	D	Shoulder injury, out 6 months				
5	ANA	Vitaly Vishnevski	Torpedo-2 Yaroslavl, RUS	D	31	1	1	2	26
6	CGY	Rico Fata	London	C	22	0	1	1	4
7	NYR	Manny Malhotra	Guelph	C	100	8	8	16	17
8	CHI	Mark Bell	Ottawa	C	72PTS – Ottawa 67's 99-00				
9	NYI	Michael Rupp	Erie	LW	Re-entered Draft in 2000				
10	TOR	Nikolai Antropov	Ust-Kamenogorsk, RUS	C	66	12	18	30	41
11	CAR	Jeff Heerema	Sarnia	RW	77PTS – Sarnia Sting 99-00				
12	COL	Alex Tanguay	Halifax	C	76	17	34	51	22
13	EDM	Michael Henrich	Barrie	RW	86PTS – Barrie Colts 99-00				
14	PHX	Patrick Desrochers	Sarnia	G	21 wins – Springfield 99-00				
15	OTT	Mathieu Chouinard	Shawinigan	G	Re-entered Draft in 2000				
16	MTL	Eric Chouinard	Quebec	C	104PTS – Quebec Jr. 99-00				
17	COL	Martin Skoula	Barrie	D	80	3	13	16	20
18	BUF	Dmitri Kalinin	Traktor Chelyabinsk, RUS	D	4	0	0	0	4
19	COL	Robyn Regehr	Kamloops	D	57	5	7	12	46
20	COL	Scott Parker	Kelowna	RW	27	0	0	0	71
21	L.A.	Mathieu Biron	Shawinigan	D	60	4	4	8	38
22	PHI	Simon Gagne	Quebec	C	80	20	28	48	22
23	PIT	Milan Kraft	Keramika Plzen Jr.	C	69PTS- Prince Albert 99-00				
24	ST.L.	Christian Backman	Vastra Frolunda Jr., SWE	D	Played – V-Frolunda 99-00				
25	DET	Jiri Fischer	Hull	D	52	0	8	8	45
26	N.J.	Mike Van Ryn	U. of Michigan	D	Played – Sarnia Sting 99-00				
27	N.J.	Scott Gomez	Tri-City	C	82	19	51	70	78

SECOND ROUND

PICK	TEAM	NAME	DRAFTED FROM	POS	GP	G	A	PTS	PIM
28	COL	Ramzi Abid	Chicoutimi	LW	Re-entered Draft in 2000				
29	S.J.	Jonathan Cheechoo	Belleville	RW	91PTS – Belleville 99-00				
30	FLA	Kyle Rossiter	Spokane	D	22PTS – Spokane 99-00				
31	VAN	Artem Chubarov	Dynamo Moscow, RUS	C	49	1	8	9	10
32	ANA	Stephen Peat	Red Deer	D	Played w/ Tri-City & Calgary				
33	CGY	Blair Betts	Prince George	C	24G, 59PTS – Prince George				
34	BUF	Andrew Peters	Oshawa	LW	19PTS w/ Kitchener 99-00				
35	TOR	Petr Svoboda	Havlickuv Brod, CZE	D	Signed w/ Leafs in July, 2000				
36	NYI	Chris Nielsen	Calgary	C	69PTS – WHL Calgary 99-00				
37	N.J.	Christian Berglund	Farjestad Karlstad Jr., SWE	RW	Played w/ Farjestads 99-00				
38	COL	Phillipe Sauve	Rimouski	G	16 wins w/ Rimouski 99-00				
39	DAL	John Erskine	London	D	43PTS – OHL London 99-00				
40	NYR	Randy Copley	Cape Breton	RW	34G, 81PTS w.Mtl-Rockets				
41	ST.L.	Maxim Linnik	Sokol Kiev, RUS	D	61GP – OHL London 99-00				
42	PHI	Jason Beckett	Seattle	D	183PIM – WHL Seattle 99-00				
43	PHX	Ossi Vaananen	Jokerit Helsinki Jr., FIN	D	w/ Jokerit Helsinki in 99-00				
44	OTT	Mike Fisher	Sudbury	C	32	4	5	9	15
45	MTL	Mike Ribeiro	Rouyn-Noranda	C	19	1	1	2	2
46	L.A.	Justin Papineau	Belleville	C	Re-entered Draft in 2000				
47	BUF	Norman Milley	Laval	RW	52G, 112PTS – Sudbury 99-00				
48	BOS	Jonathan Girard	Laval	D	26	1	2	3	2
49	WSH	Jomar Cruz	Brandon	G	3.84 GAA – WHL Tri-City 99-00				
50	BUF	Jaroslav Kristek	ZPS Zlin, CZE	RW	51PTS – WHL Tri-City 99-00				
51	PHI	Ian Forbes	Guelph	D	143PIM – OHL Guelph 99-00				
52	BOS	Bobby Allen	Boston College	D	27PTS – Boston College 99-00				
53	COL	Steve Moore	Harvard	C	26PTS – Harvard 99-00				
54	PIT	Alexander Zevakhin	CSKA Moscow, RUS	RW	w/ CSKA Moscow in 99-00				
55	DET	Ryan Barnes	Sudbury	LW	98PTS – Barrie Colts 99-00				

PICK	TEAM	NAME	DRAFTED FROM	NHL PLAYERS: POS NHL GOALTENDERS: POS	GP GP	G W	A GA	PTS SO	PIM AVG
56	DET	Tomek Valtonen	Ilves Tampere Jr., FIN	LW	w/ Jokerit Helsinki in 99-00				
57	DAL	Tyler Bouck	Prince George	RW	30G, 63PTS – Prince George				
58	OTT	Chris Bala	Harvard	LW	24PTS w/ Harvard in 99-00				

OTHER ROUNDS

PICK	TEAM	NAME	DRAFTED FROM	POS	GP	G	A	PTS	PIM
59	WSH	Todd Hornung	Portland	C					
60	NSH	Denis Arkhipov	Ak Bars Kazan	RW					
61	FLA	Joe DiPenta	Boston U.	D					
62	CGY	Paul Manning	Colorado College	D					
63	FLA	Lance Ward	Red Deer	D					
64	T.B.	Brad Richards	Rimouski	LW					
65	S.J.	Eric Laplante	Halifax	LW					
66	NYR	Jason Labarbera	Portland	G					
67	EDM	Alex Henry	London	D					
68	VAN	Jarkko Ruutu	HIFK Helsinki, FIN	LW	8	0	1	1	6
69	TOR	Jamie Hodson	Brandon	G					
70	CAR	Kevin Holdridge	Plymouth	D					
71	CAR	Erik Cole	Clarkson	LW					
72	T.B.	Dmitri Afanasenkov	Torpedo-2 Yaroslavl, RUS	LW					
73	PHX	Pat O'Leary	Robbinsdale-Armstrong H.S.	C					
74	OTT	Julien Vauclair	Lugano, SUI	D					
75	MTL	Francois Beauchemin	Laval	D					
76	L.A.	Alexey Volkov	Krylja Sovetov-2, RUS	G					
77	BUF	Mike Pandolfo	St. Sebastian's H.S.	LW					
78	BOS	Peter Nordstrom	Farjestad Karlstad Jr., SWE	C	2	0	0	0	0
79	COL	Yevgeny Lazarev	Kitchener Jr. B	RW					
80	PIT	David Cameron	Prince Albert	C					
81	VAN	Justin Morrison	Colorado College	RW					
82	N.J.	Brian Gionta	Boston College	RW					
83	ST.L.	Matt Walker	Portland	D					
84	DET	Jake McCracken	Sault Ste. Marie	G					
85	NSH	Geoff Koch	U. of Michigan	LW					
86	DAL	Gabriel Karlsson	HV 71 Jonkoping Jr., SWE	C					
87	TOR	Alexei Ponikarovsky	Dynamo-2 Moscow, RUS	RW					
88	NSH	Kent Sauer	North Iowa Jr. A	D					
89	FLA	Ryan Jardine	Sault Ste. Marie	LW					
90	VAN	Regan Darby	Tri-City	D					
91	CAR	Josef Vasicek	Slavia Praha Jr., CZE	C					
92	T.B.	Eric Beaudoin	Guelph	LW					
93	CAR	Tommy Westlund	Brynas Gavle, SWE	RW	81	4	8	12	19
94	CHI	Matthias Trattnig	U. of Maine	C					
95	NYI	Andy Burnham	Windsor	RW					
96	N.J.	Mikko Jokela	HIFK Helsinki, FIN	D					
97	CAR	Chris Madden	Guelph	G					
98	S.J.	Rob Davison	North Bay	D					
99	EDM	Shawn Horcoff	Michigan State	C					
100	PHX	Ryan Vanbuskirk	Sarnia	D	Re-entered Draft in 2000				
101	OTT	Petr Schastlivy	Torpedo Yaroslavl, RUS	LW	13	2	5	7	2
102	CGY	Shaun Sutter	Lethbridge	C					
103	L.A.	Kip Brennan	Sudbury	LW					
104	S.J.	Miroslav Zalesak	HC Plastika Nitra, SVK	RW					
105	N.J.	Pierre Dagenais	Rouyn-Noranda	LW					
106	WSH	Krys Barch	London	LW					
107	WSH	Chris Corrinet	Princeton	RW					
108	CGY	Dany Sabourin	Sherbrooke	G					
109	PHI	Jean-Philippe Morin	Drummondville	D					
110	PIT	Scott Myers	Prince George	G					
111	DET	Brent Hobday	Moose Jaw	C					
112	ANA	Viktor Wallin	HV 71 Jonkoping Jr., SWE	D					
113	EDM	Kristian Antila	Ilves Tampere, FIN	G					
114	NYR	Boyd Kane	Regina	LW					
115	PHX	Jay Leach	Providence	D					
116	PHX	Josh Blackburn	Lincoln Jr. A	G					
117	FLA	Jaroslav Spacek	Farjestad Karlstad, SWE	D	145	13	38	51	81
118	WSH	Mike Siklenka	Lloydminster	D					
119	N.J.	Anton But	Torpedo Yaroslavl 2, RUS	LW					
120	CGY	Brent Gauvreau	Oshawa	RW	Re-entered Draft in 2000				
121	T.B.	Curtis Rich	Calgary	D					
122	NYR	Patrick Leahy	Miami of Ohio	RW					
123	NYI	Jiri Dopita	DS Olomouc, CZE	C					
124	PHI	Francis Belanger	Rimouski	LW					
125	WSH	Erik Wendell	Maple Grove H.S.	C					
126	TOR	Morgan Warren	Moncton	RW					
127	S.J.	Brandon Coalter	Oshawa	LW					
128	EDM	Paul Elliott	Medicine Hat	D					
129	PHX	Robert Schnabel	Slavia Praha, CZE	D					
130	OTT	Gavin McLeod	Kelowna	D					
131	NYR	Tomas Kloucek	Slavia Praha Jr., CZE	D					
132	MTL	Andrei Bashkirov	Fort Wayne/Las Vegas IHL	LW	12	0	0	0	0
133	L.A.	Joe Rullier	Rimouski	D					
134	PIT	Robert Scuderi	Boston College	D					
135	BOS	Andrew Raycroft	Sudbury	G					
136	VAN	David Ytfeldt	Leksand, SWE	D					
137	BUF	Aaron Goldade	Brandon	C					
138	NSH	Martin Beauchesne	Sherbrooke	D					
139	PHI	Garrett Prosofsky	Saskatoon	C					
140	VAN	Rick Bertran	Kitchener	D					
141	COL	K.C. Timmons	Tri-City	LW					
142	DET	Calle Steen	Hammarby Stockholm, SWE	RW					
143	N.J.	Ryan Flinn	Laval	LW					
144	EDM	Oleg Smirnov	Kristall Elektrostal, CIS	LW					
145	S.J.	Mikael Samuelsson	Sodertalje, SWE	RW					
146	T.B.	Sergei Kuznetsov	Torpedo Yaroslavl 2, RUS	C					
147	NSH	Craig Brunel	Prince Albert	RW	Re-entered Draft in 1999				
148	FLA	Chris Ovington	Red Deer	D					
149	VAN	Paul Cabana	Fort McMurray	RW					
150	ANA	Trent Hunter	Prince George	RW					
151	DET	Adam DeLeeuw	Barrie	LW					
152	MTL	Gordie Dwyer	Beauport	LW	24	0	1	1	135
153	DAL	Pavel Patera	AIK Solna, SWE	C	12	1	4	5	4
154	TOR	Allan Rourke	Kitchener	D					
155	NYI	Kevin Clauson	Western Michigan	D					
156	CHI	Kent Huskins	Clarkson	D					
157	ST.L.	Brad Voth	Medicine Hat	D					
158	CHI	Jari Viuhkola	Karpat Oulu, FIN	C					
159	EDM	Trevor Ettinger	Cape Breton	D					
160	PHX	Rickard Wallin	Farjestad Karlstad Jr., SWE	C					
161	OTT	Christopher Neil	North Bay	RW					
162	MTL	Andrei Markov	Khimik Voskresensk, RUS	D					
163	L.A.	Tomas Zizka	ZPS Zlin, CZE	D					
164	BUF	Ales Kotalik	Ceske Budejovice Jr., CZE	RW					
165	BOS	Ryan Milanovic	Kitchener	LW					
166	CHI	Jonathan Pelletier	Drummondville	G					
167	COL	Alexander Ryazantsev	Victoriaville	D					
168	PHI	Antero Niittymaki	TPS Turku Jr., FIN	G					
169	PIT	Jan Fadrny	Slavia Praha, CZE	C					
170	ST.L.	Andrei Trochinsky	Ust-Kamenogorsk, RUS	C					
171	DET	Pavel Datsyuk	Dynamo-E. Yeka'burg, RUS	C					
172	N.J.	Jacques Lariviere	Moncton	LW					
173	DAL	Niko Kapanen	HPK Hameenlinna, FIN	C					
174	T.B.	Brett Allan	Swift Current	C					
175	PHI	Cam Ondrik	Medicine Hat	G					
176	FLA	B.J. Ketcheson	Peterborough	D					
177	VAN	Vincent Malts	Hull	RW					
178	ANA	Jesse Fibiger	Minnesota-Duluth	D					
179	WSH	Nathan Forster	Seattle	D					
180	NYR	Stefan Lundqvist	Brynas Gavle, SWE	RW					
181	TOR	Jonathan Gagnon	Cape Breton	C					
182	NYI	Evgeny Korolev	London	D	17	1	2	3	8
183	CHI	Tyler Arnason	St. Cloud St.	C					
184	CAR	Donald Smith	Clarkson	C					
185	S.J.	Robert Mulick	Sault Ste. Marie	D					
186	EDM	Michael Morrison	U. of Maine	G					
187	PHX	Erik Westrum	U. of Minnesota	C					
188	OTT	Michael Periard	Shawinigan	D					
189	MTL	Andrei Kruchinin	Lada Togliatti, RUS	D					
190	L.A.	Tommi Hannus	TPS Turku Jr., FIN	C					
191	BUF	Brad Moran	Calgary	C					
192	CGY	Radek Duda	Sparta Praha, CZE	RW					
193	WSH	Ratislav Stana	HC Kosice, SVK	G					
194	T.B.	Oak Hewer	North Bay	C					
195	PHI	Tomas Divisek	Slavia Praha, CZE	LW					
196	PIT	Joel Scherban	London	C					
197	ST.L.	Brad Twordik	Brandon	C					
198	DET	Jeremy Goetzinger	Prince Albert	D					
199	N.J.	Erik Jensen	Des Moines Jr. A	RW					
200	DAL	Scott Perry	Boston U.	C					
201	MTL	Craig Murray	U. of Michigan	C					
202	NSH	Martin Bartek	Sherbrooke	C					
203	FLA	Ian Jacobs	Ottawa	RW					
204	VAN	Graig Mischler	Northeastern	C					
205	ANA	David Bernier	Quebec	RW					
206	CGY	Jonas Frogren	Farjestad	D					
207	NYR	Johan Witehall	Leksand, SWE	LW	13	1	1	2	2
208	CAR	Jaroslav Svoboda	HC Olomouc, CZE	LW					
209	NYI	Frederik Brindamour	Sherbrooke	G					
210	CHI	Sean Griffin	Kingston	D					
211	CAR	Mark Kosick	U. of Michigan	C					
212	S.J.	Jim Fahey	Northeastern	D					
213	EDM	Christian Lefebvre	Granby	D					
214	PHX	Justin Hansen	Prince George	RW					
215	TOR	Dwight Wolfe	Halifax	D					
216	MTL	Michael Ryder	Hull	C					
217	L.A.	Jim Henkel	Ottawa	C					
218	BUF	David Moravec	HC Vitkovice, CZE	RW	1	0	0	0	0
219	VAN	Curtis Valentine	Bowling Green	LW					
220	WSH	Michael Farrell	Providence	D					
221	T.B.	Daniel Hulak	Swift Current	D					
222	PHI	Lubomir Pistek	Kelowna	RW					
223	OTT	Sergei Verenikin	Torpedo Yaroslavl, RUS	RW					
224	PIT	Mika Lehto	Assat Pori	G					
225	ST.L.	Yevgeny Pastukh	Khimik Voskresensk, RUS	LW					
226	DET	David Petrasek	HV 71 Jonkoping, SWE	D					
227	N.J.	Marko Ahosilta	KalPa Kuopio, FIN	C					

PICK	TEAM	NAME	DRAFTED FROM	NHL PLAYERS: POS / NHL GOALTENDERS: POS	GP / GP	G / W	A / GA	PTS / SO	PIM / AVG
228	TOR	Mihail Travnicek	Chemopetrol Litvinov, CZE	RW					
229	T.B.	Chris Lyness	Cape Breton	D					
230	NSH	Karlis Skrastins	TPS Turku, FIN	D	61	5	7	12	20
231	FLA	Adrian Wichser	EHC Kloten, SUI	C					
232	VAN	Jason Metcalfe	London	D					
233	ANA	Pelle Prestberg	Farjestad Karlstad, SWE	LW					
234	CGY	Kevin Mitchell	Guelph	D					
235	NYR	Jan Mertzig	Lulea, SWE	D	23	0	2	2	8
236	TOR	Sergei Rostov	Dynamo-2 Moscow, RUS	D					
237	NYI	Ben Blais	Walpole H.S.	D					
238	CHI	Alexandre Couture	Sherbrooke	LW					
239	CAR	Brent McDonald	Prince George	C					
240	CHI	Andrei Yershov	Khimik Voskresensk, RUS	D					
241	EDM	Maxim Spiridonov	London	LW					
242	NYI	Jason Doyle	Sault Ste. Marie	RW					
243	PHI	Petr Hubacek	Kometa Brno	C					
244	PIT	Toby Peterson	Colorado College	C					
245	ANA	Andreas Andersson	HV 71 Jonkoping, SWE	G					
246	OTT	Rastisla Pavlikovsky	Dukla Trencin, SVK	C					
247	MTL	Darcy Harris	Kitchener	RW					
248	L.A.	Matthew Yeats	Olds Jr. A	G					
249	BUF	Edo Terglav	Baie-Comeau	RW					
250	NYI	Radek Matejovsky	Slavia Praha, CZE	RW					
251	WSH	Blake Evans	Tri-City	C					
252	T.B.	Martin Cibak	Medicine Hat	C					
253	PHI	Bruno St. Jacques	Baie-Comeau	D					
254	PIT	Matt Hussey	Avon Old Farms H.S.	C					
255	ST.L.	John Pohl	U. of Minnesota	C					
256	DET	Petja Pietilainen	Saskatoon	LW					
257	N.J.	Ryan Held	Kitchener	C					
258	PHI	Sergei Skrobot	Dynamo-2 Moscow, RUS	D					

1999

PICK	TEAM	NAME	DRAFTED FROM	NHL PLAYERS: POS / NHL GOALTENDERS: POS	GP / GP	G / W	A / GA	PTS / SO	PIM / AVG
FIRST ROUND									
1	ATL	Patrik Stefan	Long Beach, IHL	C	72	5	20	25	30
2	VAN	Daniel Sedin	MoDo Ornskoldsvik, SWE	LW	19G, 45PTS w/ MoDo 99-00				
3	VAN	Henrik Sedin	MoDo Ornskoldsvik, SWE	C	38A, 47PTS w/ MoDo 99-00				
4	NYR	Pavel Brendl	Calgary	RW	59G, 111PTS w/ Calgary Jrs.				
5	NYI	Tim Connolly	Erie	C	81	14	20	34	44
6	NSH	Brian Finley	Barrie	G	36 wins, 2.66 w/ Barrie Jrs.				
7	WSH	Kris Beech	Calgary	C	32G, 86PTS w/ Calgary Jrs.				
8	NYI	Taylor Pyatt	Sudbury	LW	40G, 89PTS w/ Sudbury 99-00				
9	NYR	Jamie Lundmark	Moose Jaw	C	21G, 48PTS w/ Moose Jaw				
10	NYI	Branislav Mezei	Belleville	D	21A, 28PTS w/ Belleville 99-00				
11	CGY	Oleg Saprykin	Seattle	C	4	0	1	1	2
12	FLA	Denis Shvidki	Barrie	RW	41G, 106PTS w/ Barrie 99-00				
13	EDM	Jani Rita	Jokerit Helsinki, FIN	RW	Played – Jokerit Helsinki 99-00				
14	S.J.	Jeff Jillson	U. of Michigan	D	34PTS w/ U-Michigan 99-00				
15	PHX	Scott Kelman	Seattle	C	13G, 55PTS w/ Seattle 99-00				
16	CAR	David Tanabe	Wisconsin	D	31	4	0	4	14
17	ST.L.	Barret Jackman	Regina	D	Made pro debut – AHL playoffs				
18	PIT	Konstantin Koltsov	Severstal Cherepovets, RUS	RW	7PTS w/ Novokuznetsk 99-00				
19	PHX	Kirill Safronov	St. Petersburg	D	11G, 43PTS w/ Quebec Jrs.				
20	BUF	Barrett Heisten	U. of Maine	LW	13G, 37PTS w/ U-Maine 99-00				
21	BOS	Nick Boynton	Ottawa	D	5	0	0	0	0
22	PHI	Maxime Ouellet	Quebec	G	40-12-6, 3 SO – Quebec Jrs.				
23	CHI	Steve McCarthy	Kootenay	D	5	1	1	2	4
24	TOR	Luca Cereda	Ambri-Piotta, SUI	C	Signed 3-year deal w/ Leafs				
25	COL	Mikhail Kuleshov	Severstal Cherepovets, RUS	LW	Play 8 games – Cherepovets				
26	OTT	Martin Havlat	HC Zelezarny Trinec, CZE	C	13G, 42PTS w/ HC Trinec				
27	N.J.	Ari Ahonen	JYP HT Jyvaskyla Jr., FIN	G	Played 99-00 w/ HIFK Helsinki				
28	NYI	Kristian Kudroc	Michalovce, CZE	D	22A,31PTS w/ Quebec Jrs.				
SECOND ROUND									
29	WSH	Michal Sivek	HC Velvana Kladno, CZE	C	23G, 60PTS w/ Prince Albert				
30	ATL	Luke Sellars	Ottawa	D	34A,42PTS w/ Ottawa Jrs.				
31	WSH	Charlie Stephens	Guelph	C/RW	34A,50PTS w/ Guelph 99-00				
32	DAL	Michael Ryan	Boston College H.S.	C	13PTS w/ Northeastern 99-00				
33	NSH	Jonas Andersson	AIK Solna Jr.	RW	Scored 1st pro goal in IHL				
34	WSH	Ross Lupaschuk	Prince Albert	D	56PTS – 2 WHL teams in 99-00				
35	BUF	Milan Bartovic	Dukla Trencin Jr., SVK	RW	57PTS – 2 WHL teams in 99-00				
36	EDM	Alexei Semenov	Sudbury	D	Pro debut in AHL playoffs				
37	WSH	Nolan Yonkman	Kelowna	D	12PTS, 153PIM w/ Kelowna				
38	CGY	Dan Cavanaugh	Boston U.	C	9G, 34PTS w/ Boston-U 99-00				
39	MTL	Alexander Buturlin	CSKA Moscow, RUS	RW	20G, 47PTS w/ Sarnia 99-00				
40	FLA	Alexander Auld	North Bay	G	3.36 GAA w/ North Bay 99-00				
41	EDM	Tony Salmelainen	HIFK Helsinki, FIN	LW	Scored goal in Finn-Elite debut				
42	N.J.	Mike Commodore	North Dakota	D	5G, 12PTS w/ N-Dakota 99-00				
43	L.A.	Andrei Shefer	Severstal Cherepovets, RUS	RW	34G, 76PTS w/ Halifax 99-00				
44	ANA	Jordan Leopold	U. of Minnesota	D	18A, 24PTS w/ U-Minnesota				
45	COL	Martin Grenier	Quebec	D	35A, 46PTS w/ Quebec Jrs.				
46	CHI	Dmitri Levinski	Severstal Cherepovets, RUS	RW	w/ HC St-Petersburg 99-00				
47	T.B.	Sheldon Keefe	Barrie	RW	48G, 121PTS w/ Barrie 99-00				
48	OTT	Simon Lajeunesse	Moncton	G	18 wins, 2.94 GAA in Moncton				
49	CAR	Brett Lysak	Regina	C	38G, 78PTS w/ Regina 99-00				
50	N.J.	Brett Clouthier	Kingston	LW	26A,39PTS in Kingston 99-00				
51	PIT	Matt Murley	RPI	LW	29A,38PTS w/ RPI in 99-00				
52	NSH	Adam Hall	Michigan State	RW	26G, 39PTS w/ Mich-State				
53	PHX	Brad Ralph	Oshawa	LW	28G, 63PTS – Oshawa 99-00				
54	NSH	Andrew Hutchinson	Michigan State	D	17PTS w/ Mich-State 99-00				
55	BUF	Doug Janik	U. of Maine	D	19PTS w/ U-Maine 99-00				
56	BOS	Matt Zultek	Ottawa	C	Injured w/ 28 games in 99-00				
57	PIT	Jeremy Van Hoof	Ottawa	D	Plugger w/ 18PTS in Ottawa				
58	MTL	Matt Carkner	Peterborough	D	177PIM w/ Peterborough Jrs.				
59	NYR	David Inman	U. of Notre Dame	C	20PTS w/ Notre Dame 99-00				
60	TOR	Peter Reynolds	London	D	32PTS w/.London in 99-00				
61	NSH	Ed Hill	Barrie	D	19PTS w/ Barrie Jrs. in 99-00				
62	OTT	Teemu Sainomaa	Jokerit Helsinki Jr., FIN	LW	w/ Jokerit Helsinki in 99-00				
63	CHI	Stepan Mokhov	Severstal Cherepovets, RUS	D	w/ SK Novokuznetsk in 99-00				
64	BUF	Michael Zigomanis	Kingston	C	40G, 94PTS in Kingston 99-00				
65	NSH	Jan Lasak	HKM Zvolen, SVK	G	36 wins, 2.55 GAA in ECHL				
66	DAL	Dan Jancevski	London	D	15A, 23PTS w/ London 99-00				
OTHER ROUNDS									
67	T.B.	Yevgeny Konstantinov	Ital Kazan 2, RUS	G					
68	ATL	Zdenek Blatny	Seattle	C					
69	VAN	Rene Vydareny	Bratislava Jr., SVK	D					
70	FLA	Niklas Hagman	HIFK Helsinki, FIN	LW					
71	PHX	Jason Jaspers	Sudbury	C/LW					
72	NSH	Brett Angel	North Bay	D					
73	BUF	Tim Preston	Seattle	LW					
74	L.A.	Jason Crain	Ohio State	D					
75	T.B.	Brett Scheffelmaier	Medicine Hat	D					
76	L.A.	Frantisek Kaberle	MoDo Ornskoldsvik, SWE	D	51	1	15	16	10
77	CGY	Craig Andersson	Guelph	G					
78	NYI	Mattias Weinhandl	Troja-Ljungby, SWE	RW					
79	NYR	Johan Asplund	Brynas Gavle, SWE	G					
80	FLA	Jean-Francois Laniel	Shawinigan	G					
81	EDM	Adam Hauser	U. of Minnesota	G					
82	S.J.	Mark Concannon	Winchendon H.S.	LW					
83	ANA	Niclas Havelid	Malmo, SWE	D	50	2	7	9	20
84	CAR	Brad Fast	Prince George - TII	D					
85	ST.L.	Peter Smrek	Des Moines Jr. A	D					
86	PIT	Sebastian Caron	Rimouski	G					
87	NYI	Brian Collins	St. John's H.S.	C					
88	T.B.	Jimmie Olvestad	Djurgarden Stockholm, SWE	LW					
89	BOS	Kyle Wanvig	Kootenay	RW					
90	NYR	Patrick Aufiero	Boston U.	D					
91	EDM	Mike Comrie	Michigan	C					
92	L.A.	Cory Campbell	Belleville	G					
93	COL	Branko Radivojevic	Belleville	RW					
94	OTT	Chris Kelly	London	C/LW					
95	N.J.	Andre Lakos	Barrie	D					
96	DAL	Mathias Tjarnqvist	Rogle Angelholm, SWE	RW					
97	MTL	Chris Dyment	Boston U.	D					
98	ATL	David Kaczowka	Seattle	LW					
99	ATL	Rob Zepp	Plymouth	G					
100	N.J.	Teemu Kesa	Ilves Jr.	D					
101	NYI	Juraj Kolnik	Rimouski	RW					
102	NYI	Johan Halvardsson	HV 71 Jonkoping, SWE	D					
103	FLA	Morgan McCormick	Kingston	RW					
104	L.A.	Brian McGrattan	Sudbury	RW					
105	ANA	Alexander Chagodayev	CSKA Moscow, RUS	C					
106	CGY	Rail Rozakov	Lada Togliatti 2, RUS	D					
107	MTL	Evan Lindsay	Prince Albert	G					
108	TOR	Mirko Murovic	Moncton	LW					
109	FLA	Rod Sarich	Calgary	D					
110	TOR	Jonathon Zion	Ottawa	D					
111	S.J.	Willie Levesque	Northeastern	RW					
112	COL	Sanny Lindstrom	Huddinge, SWE	D					
113	CAR	Ryan Murphy	Bowling Green	LW					
114	ST.L.	Chad Starling	Kamloops	D					
115	PIT	Ryan Malone	Omaha Jr. A	LW					
116	PHX	Ryan Lauzon	Hull	C					
117	BUF	Karel Mosovsky	Regina	LW					
118	BOS	Jaakko Harikkala	Lukko Rauma, FIN	D					
119	PHI	Jeff Feniak	Calgary	D					
120	DET	Jari Toulsa	Vastra Frolunda Jr., SWE	C					
121	NSH	Yevgeny Pavlov	Lada Togliatti, RUS	LW					
122	COL	Kristian Kovac	HC Kosice Jr., SVK	RW					
123	PHX	Preston Mizzi	Peterborough	C					
124	NSH	Alexander Krevsun	CSK VVS Samara, RUS	RW					
125	L.A.	Daniel Johansson	MoDo Ornskoldsvik Jr., SWE	C					
126	DAL	Jeff Bateman	Brampton	C					
127	T.B.	Kaspars Astashenko	Cincinnati IHL	D	8	0	1	1	4
128	ATL	Derek MacKenzie	Sudbury	C					
129	VAN	Ryan Thorpe	Spokane	LW					
130	NYI	Justin Mapletoft	Red Deer	C					
131	NSH	Konstantin Panov	Kamloops	RW					
132	WSH	Roman Tvrdon	Dukla Trencin Jr., SVK	C					

PICK	TEAM	NAME	DRAFTED FROM	NHL PLAYERS: POS / NHL GOALTENDERS: POS	GP / GP	G / W	A / GA	PTS / SO	PIM / AVG
133	L.A.	Jean-Francois Nogues	Victoriaville	G					
134	CHI	Michael Jacobsen	Belleville	D					
135	CGY	Matt Doman	U. of Wisconsin	RW					
136	MTL	Dustin Jamieson	Sarnia	LW					
137	NYR	Garrett Bembridge	Saskatoon	RW					
138	BUF	Ryan Miller	Soo Indians	G					
139	EDM	Jonathan Fauteux	Val d'Or	D					
140	NYI	Adam Johnson	Greenway H.S.	D					
141	ANA	Maxim Rybin	Spartak Moscow, RUS	LW					
142	COL	William Magnuson	Lake Superior State	D					
143	ST.L.	Trevor Byrne	Deerfield Academy	D					
144	PIT	Tomas Skvaridlo	HKM Zvolen Jr., SVK	LW					
145	MTL	Marc-Andre Thinel	Victoriaville	RW					
146	BUF	Matthew Kinch	Calgary	D					
147	BOS	Seamus Kotyk	Ottawa	G					
148	T.B.	Michal Lanicek	Slavia Praha Jr., CZE	G					
149	DET	Andrei Maximenko	Soviet Wings	LW					
150	MTL	Matt Shasby	Des Moines Jr. A	D					
151	TOR	Vaclav Zavoral	HC Chemopetrol Litvinov Jr., CZE	D					
152	COL	Jordan Krestanovich	Calgary	LW					
153	CGY	Jesse Cook	U. of Denver	D					
154	OTT	Andrew Ianiero	Kingston	LW					
155	S.J.	Nicholas Dimitrakos	U. of Maine	RW					
156	DAL	Gregor Baumgartner	Acadie-Bathurst	LW					
157	PIT	Vladimir Malenkykh	Lada Togliatti, RUS	D					
158	COL	Anders Lovdahl	HV 71 Jonkoping Jr., SWE	C					
159	ATL	Yuri Dobryshkin	Soviet Wings	LW					
160	PHI	Konstantin Rudenko	Severstal Cherepovets 2, RUS	LW					
161	TOR	Jan Sochor	Slavia Praha, CZE	LW					
162	NSH	Timo Helbling	Davos, SUI	D					
163	NYI	Bjorn Melin	HV 71 Jonkoping Jr., SWE	RW					
164	OTT	Martin Prusek	HC Vitkovice, CZE	G					
165	CHI	Michael Leighton	Windsor	G					
166	CGY	Cory Pecker	Sault Ste. Marie	C					
167	MTL	Sean Dixon	Erie	D					
168	PHX	Erik Lewerstrom	Grums, SWE	D					
169	FLA	Brad Woods	Brampton	D					
170	CGY	Matt Underhill	Cornell	G					
171	EDM	Chris Legg	London, Jr. B	C					
172	VAN	Josh Reed	Vernon	D					
173	ANA	Jan Sandstrom	AIK Solna, SWE	D					
174	CAR	Damian Surma	Plymouth	LW					
175	WSH	Kyle Clark	Harvard	RW					
176	PIT	Doug Meyer	U. of Minnesota	LW					
177	NYR	Jay Dardis	Proctor H.S.	C					
178	BUF	Seneque Hyacinthe	Val d'Or	LW					
179	BOS	Donald Choukalos	Regina	G					
180	ST.L.	Tore Vikingstad	Farjestad Karlstad, SWE	C					
181	DET	Kent McDonell	Guelph	RW					
182	T.B.	Fedor Fedorov	Port Huron	C					
183	COL	Riku Hahl	HPK Hameenlinna, FIN	C					
184	DAL	Justin Cox	Prince George	RW					
185	N.J.	Scott Cameron	Barrie	C					
186	DAL	Brett Draney	Kamloops	LW					
187	T.B.	Ivan Rachunek	ZPS Zlin Jr., CZE	RW					
188	ATL	Stephan Baby	Green Bay	RW					
189	VAN	Kevin Swanson	Kelowna	G					
190	CGY	Blair Stayzer	Windsor	LW					
191	NSH	Martin Erat	ZPS Zlin Jr., CZE	LW					
192	WSH	David Johansson	AIK Solna Jr.	D					
193	L.A.	Kevin Baker	Belleville	RW					
194	CHI	Mattias Wennerberg	MoDo Ornskoldsvik Jr., SWE	C					
195	CHI	Yorick Treille	U. of Mass-Lowell	RW					
196	MTL	Vadim Tarasov	Metallurg Novokuznetsk, RUS	G					
197	NYR	Arto Laatikainen	Kiekko-Espoo, FIN	D					
198	FLA	Travis Eagles	Prince George	RW					
199	EDM	Christian Chartier	Saskatoon	D					
200	PHI	Pavel Kasparik	IHC Pisek, CZE	C					
201	OTT	Mikko Ruutu	HIFK Helsinki, FIN	LW					
202	CAR	Jim Baxter	Oshawa	D					
203	ST.L.	Phil Osaer	Ferris State	G					
204	PIT	Tom Kostopoulos	London	RW					
205	NSH	Kyle Kettles	Neepawa	G					
206	BUF	Bret Dececco	Seattle	RW					
207	BOS	Greg Barber	Victoria	RW					
208	PHI	Vaclav Pletka	HC Zelezarny Trinec, CZE	RW					
209	OTT	Layne Ulmer	Swift Current	C					
210	DET	Henrik Zetterberg	Timra, SWE	LW					
211	TOR	Vladimir Kulikov	CSKA Moscow, RUS	G					
212	COL	Radim Vrbata	Hull	RW					
213	OTT	Alexandre Giroux	Hull	C					
214	N.J.	Chris Hartsburg	Colorado College	C					
215	DAL	Jeff MacMillan	Oshawa	D					
216	T.B.	Erkki Rajamaki	HIFK Helsinki, FIN	LW					
217	ATL	Garnet Exelby	Saskatoon	D					
218	VAN	Markus Kankaanpera	JyP HT Jyvaskyla, FIN	D					
219	WSH	Maxim Orlov	CSKA Moscow, RUS	C					

PICK	TEAM	NAME	DRAFTED FROM	NHL PLAYERS: POS / NHL GOALTENDERS: POS	GP / GP	G / W	A / GA	PTS / SO	PIM / AVG
220	NSH	Miroslav Durak	Bratislava Jr., SVK	D					
221	ST.L.	Colin Hemingway	Surrey	RW					
222	L.A.	George Parros	Chicago Jr.	RW					
223	CHI	Andrew Carver	Hull	D					
224	PHI	David Nystrom	Vastra Frolunda Jr., SWE	RW					
225	MTL	Mikko Hyytia	JYP HT Jyvaskyla Jr., FIN	C					
226	NYR	Evgeny Gusakov	Lada Togliatti 2, RUS	RW					
227	FLA	Jonathon Charron	Val d'Or	G					
228	NYI	Radek Martinek	Budejovice, CZE	D					
229	S.J.	Eric Betournay	Acadie-Bathurst	C					
230	ANA	Petr Tenkrat	HC Velvana Kladno, CZE	RW					
231	CAR	David Evans	Clarkson	C					
232	ST.L.	Alexander Khavanov	Dynamo Moscow, RUS	D					
233	PIT	Darcy Robinson	Saskatoon	D					
234	PHX	Goran Bezina	Fribourg	D					
235	BUF	Brad Self	Peterborough	C					
236	BOS	John Cronin	Boston U.	D					
237	CAR	Antti Jokela	Lukko Rauma Jr., FIN	G					
238	DET	Anton Borodkin	Kamloops	LW					
239	TOR	Pierre Hedin	MoDo Ornskoldsvik, SWE	D					
240	COL	Jeff Finger	Green Bay	D					
241	S.J.	Doug Murray	Applecore	D					
242	N.J.	Justin Dziama	Nobles Prep.	RW					
243	DAL	Brian Sullivan	Thayer Academy	D					
244	T.B.	Mikko Kuparinen	Grand Rapids	D					
245	ATL	Tommi Santala	Jokerit Helsinki, FIN	C					
246	ATL	Ray DiLauro	St. Lawrence U.	D					
247	BOS	Mikko Eloranta	TPS Turku, FIN	LW	50	6	12	18	36
248	NSH	Darren Haydar	New Hampshire	RW					
249	WSH	Igor Schadilov	Dynamo Moscow, RUS	D					
250	L.A.	Noah Clarke	Des Moines Jr. A	LW					
251	NYR	Petter Henning	MoDo Ornskoldsvik, SWE	RW					
252	CGY	Dmitri Kirilenko	CSKA Moscow, RUS	C					
253	MTL	Jerome Marois	Quebec	LW					
254	NYR	Alexei Bulatov	Avtomo. Yekaterinburg, RUS	RW					
255	NYI	Brett Henning	U. of Notre Dame	C					
256	EDM	Tamas Groschl	UTE Budapest, HUN	RW					
257	S.J.	Hannes Hyvonen	Kiekko-Espoo, FIN	RW					
258	ANA	Brian Gornick	Air Force	C					
259	CAR	Yevgeny Kurilin	Anchorage	C					
260	ST.L.	Brian McMeekin	Cornell	D					
261	PIT	Andrew McPherson	RPI	LW					
262	PHX	Alexei Litvinenko	Ust-Kamenogorsk, RUS	D					
263	BUF	Craig Brunel	Prince Albert	RW					
264	BOS	Georgijs Pujacs	Dynamo-81 Riga, LAT	D					
265	DAL	Jamie Chamberlain	Peterborough	RW					
266	DET	Ken Davis	Portland	RW					
267	TOR	Peter Metcalf	U. of Maine	D					
268	NYI	Tyler Scott	Upper Canada College	D					
269	OTT	Konstantin Gorovikov	St. Petersburg	C					
270	ST.L.	James Desmarais	Rouyn Noranda	C					
271	VAN	Darrell Hay	Tri-City	D					
272	DAL	Mikhail Donika	Torpedo Yaroslavl, RUS	D					

2000

FIRST ROUND

PICK	TEAM	NAME	DRAFTED FROM	NHL PLAYERS: POS / NHL GOALTENDERS: POS	GP / GP	G / W	A / GA	PTS / SO	PIM / AVG
1	NYI	Rick DiPietro	Boston U.	G	First goalie drafted #1				
2	ATL	Dany Heatley	U. of Wisconsin	LW	52pts in WCHA				
3	MIN	Marian Gaborik	Dukla Trencin, SVK	LW	25g in 50gp w/ Dukla				
4	CBJ	Rostislav Klesla	Brampton	D	Brampton's top rookie				
5	NYI	Raffi Torres	Brampton	LW	Played in OHL All-Star Game				
6	NSH	Scott Hartnell	Prince Albert	RW	All-rounder w/ 82pts in 99-00				
7	BOS	Lars Jonsson	Leksand, SWE	D	Mobile tough scorer				
8	T.B.	Nikita Alexev	Erie	RW	Fastest skater at Top Prospects				
9	CGY	Brent Krahn	Calgary	G	33-6-0 in 99-00				
10	CHI	Mikhail Yakubov	Lada Togliatti, RUS	C	6pts & silver at U-18 WJC				
11	CHI	Pavel Vorobjev	Torpedo Yaroslavl, RUS	RW	8pts & silver at U-18 WJC				
12	ANA	Alexei Smirnov	Dynamo Moscow, RUS	LW	Highly skilled, fast scorer				
13	MTL	Ron Hainsey	U. of Mass-Lowell	D	Played for U.S. at 2000 WJC				
14	COL	Vaclav Nedorost	Budejovice, CZE	C	Gold for Csech-Rep at WJC				
15	BUF	Artem Kryukov	Torpedo Yaroslavl, RUS	C	Injured for much of 99-00				
16	MTL	Marcel Hossa	Portland	C	Played in WHL All-Star Game				
17	EDM	Alexei Mikhnov	Torpedo Yaroslavl, RUS	W	6'5" playmaker and passer				
18	PIT	Brooks Orpik	Boston College	D	Runner-up as NCAA champ				
19	PHX	Krystofer Kolanos	Boston College	C	Two hat tricks in 99-00				
20	L.A.	Alexander Frolov	Torpedo Yaroslavl 2, RUS	LW	Two-way player with finesse				
21	OTT	Anton Volchenkov	CSKA Moscow, RUS	D	2nd ranked Euro defenseman				
22	N.J.	David Hale	Sioux City Jr. A	D	Top U.S. junior in 2000 draft				
23	VAN	Nathan Smith	Swift Current	C	2g in Top Prospects Game				
24	TOR	Brad Boyes	Erie	C	36g, 46a in OHL				
25	DAL	Steve Ott	Windsor	C	62pts 131pim in OHL				
26	WSH	Brian Sutherby	Moose Jaw	C	Poised, good snap shot				
27	BOS	Martin Samuelsson	MoDo Ornskoldsvik, SWE	RW	8pts in 6gp at U-18 WJC				

PICK	TEAM	NAME	DRAFTED FROM	NHL PLAYERS: POS / NHL GOALTENDERS: POS	GP / GP	G / W	A / GA	PTS / SO	PIM / AVG
28	PHI	Justin Williams	Plymouth	RW	Top team scorer with 83PTS				
29	DET	Niklas Kronwall	Djurgarden Stockholm, SWE	D	All-Star at U-18 WJC				
30	ST.L.	Jeff Taffe	U. of Minnesota	C	State champion shortstop				

SECOND ROUND

PICK	TEAM	NAME	DRAFTED FROM	POS	GP	G	A	PTS	PIM
31	ATL	Ilya Nikulin	Tver, RUS	D	U-18 WJC in 99 and 00				
32	CAR	Tomas Kurka	Plymouth	LW	OHL First All-Rookie Team				
33	MIN	Nick Schultz	Prince Albert	D	44PTS in 72GP in WHL				
34	T.B.	Ruslan Zainullin	Ak Bars Kazan	RW	Junior and Senior in 99-00				
35	EDM	Brad Winchester	U. of Wisconsin	LW	Grad of U.S. U-18 program				
36	NSH	Daniel Widing	Leksand, SWE	RW	Bronze at U-18 WJC				
37	BOS	Andy Hilbert	U. of Michigan	C	Team USA at 99 and 00 WJC				
38	DET	Tomas Kopecky	Dukla Trencin, SVK	C	2000 WJC w/ Slovakia				
39	N.J.	Teemu Laine	Jokerit Helsinki, FIN	RW	Gold at U-18 WJC				
40	CGY	Kurtis Foster	Peterborough	D	3-time scholastic player				
41	S.J.	Tero Maatta	Jokerit Helsinki, FIN	D	Won Finnish junior title				
42	ATL	Libor Ustrnul	Plymouth	D	Czech all-star in 97-98				
43	WSH	Matt Pettinger	Calgary	LW	Played for U. of Denver and Cgy.				
44	ANA	Ilja Bryzgalov	Lada Togliatti, RUS	G	Top Euro goalie in 2000 draft				
45	OTT	Mathieu Chouinard	Shawinigan	G	3.34 GAA and 4SO in 99-00				
46	CGY	Jarret Stoll	Kootenay	C	Gold at 99 Four Nations				
47	COL	Jared Aulin	Kamloops	C	WHL top player for October				
48	BUF	Gerard Dicaire	Seattle	D	35PTS in WHL in 99-00				
49	CHI	Jonas Nordqvist	Leksand, SWE	C	39PTS top Leksand Jrs.				
50	COL	Sergei Soin	Krylja Sovetov Mosc., RUS	C	U-18 WJC in 99 and 00				
51	TOR	Kris Vernarsky	Plymouth	C	Excellent penalty killer				
52	PIT	Shane Endicott	Seattle	C	23G in 70 games in 99-00				
53	PHX	Alexander Tatarinov	Torpedo Yaroslavl, RUS	RW	Captain of Russian U-18 team				
54	L.A.	Andreas Lilja	Malmo, SWE	D	6'3", 220 lb w/ 8G & 88PIM				
55	OTT	Antoine Vermette	Victoriaville	C	Shot clocked at 95.8 mph				
56	N.J.	Aleksander Suglobov	Torpedo Yaroslavl, RUS	RW	23G, 10A in 99-00				
57	N.J.	Matt DeMarchi	U. of Minnesota	D	Smooth skater with grit				
58	FLA	Vladimir Sapozhnikov	Metallurg Novokuznetsk, RUS	D	Hard working stay-at-home D				
59	BOS	Ivan Huml	Langley	LW	104PTS 6th in BCHL				
60	DAL	Dan Ellis	Omaha Jr. A	G	USHL record 11SO in 99-00				
61	WSH	Jacob Cutta	Swift Current	D	Agile with hard point shop				
62	N.J.	Paul Martin	Elk River H.S.	D	Top hi-schooler in 2000 draft				
63	COL	Agris Saviels	Owen Sound	D	Team's top rookie in 99-00				
64	NYR	Filip Novak	Regina	D	Team's top rookie in 99-00				
65	ST.L.	David Morisset	Seattle	RW	WHL West's top player in March				

OTHER ROUNDS

PICK	TEAM	NAME	DRAFTED FROM	POS	GP	G	A	PTS	PIM
66	BOS	Tuukka Makela	HIFK Helsinki, FIN	D					
67	N.J.	Max Birbraer	Newmarket	LW					
68	DAL	Joel Lundqvist	Vastra Frolunda, SWE	C					
69	CBJ	Ben Knopp	Moose Jaw	RW					
70	TOR	Mikael Tellqvist	Djurgarden Stockholm, SWE	G					
71	VAN	Thatcher Bell	Rimouski	C					
72	NSH	Mattias Nilsson	MoDo Ornskoldsvik, SWE	D					
73	BOS	Sergei Zinovjev	Metallurg Novokuznetsk, RUS	RW					
74	CHI	Igor Radulov	Torpedo Yaroslavl, RUS	LW					
75	ST.L.	Justin Papineau	Belleville	C					
76	N.J.	Michael Rupp	Erie	LW					
77	FLA	Robert Fried	Deerfield Academy	RW					
78	MTL	Jozef Balej	Portland	RW					
79	MTL	Tyler Hanchuk	Brampton	D					
80	CAR	Ryan Bayda	North Dakota	LW					
81	T.B.	Alexader Kharitonov	Dynamo Moscow, RUS	LW					
82	FLA	Sean O'Connor	Moose Jaw	RW					
83	EDM	Alexander Lyubimov	Lada Togliatti, RUS	D					
84	PIT	Peter Hamerlik	HK 36 Skalica, SVK	G					
85	PHX	Ramzi Abid	Halifax	LW					
86	L.A.	Yanick Lehoux	Baie-Comeau	C					
87	OTT	Jan Bohac	Slavia Praha, CZE	C					
88	COL	Kurt Sauer	Spokane	D					
89	NSH	Libor Pivko	HC Femex Havirov, CZE	LW					
90	TOR	Jean-Francois Racine	Drummondville	G					
91	DAL	Alexei Terechenko	Dynamo Moscow, RUS	C					
92	COL	Sergei Klyazmin	Dynamo Moscow, RUS	LW					
93	VAN	Tim Branham	Barrie	D					
94	PHI	Alexander Drozdetsky	St. Petersburg	RW					
95	NYR	Dominic Moore	Harvard	C					
96	ST.L.	Antoine Bergeron	Val D'Or	D					
97	CAR	Niclas Wallin	Brynas	D					
98	ANA	Jonas Ronnqvist	Lulea, SWE	LW					
99	MIN	Marc Cavosie	RPI	LW					
100	TOR	Miguel Delisle	Ottawa	RW					
101	NYI	Arto Tukio	Ilves Tampere, FIN	D					
102	DET	Stefan Liv	HV 71 Jonkoping, SWE	G					
102	BOS	Brett Nowak	Harvard	C					
104	S.J.	Jon Disalvatore	Providence	RW					
105	NYI	Vladimir Gorbunov	CSKA Moscow, RUS	C					
106	CHI	Scott Balan	Regina	D					
107	ATL	Carl Mallette	Victoriaville	C					
108	ATL	Blake Robson	Portland	C					
109	MTL	Johan Enegvist	Leksand, SWE	LW					
110	CAR	Jared Newman	Plymouth	D					
111	BUF	Ghyslain Rousseau	Baie-Comeau	G					

PICK	TEAM	NAME	DRAFTED FROM	NHL PLAYERS: POS / NHL GOALTENDERS: POS	GP / GP	G / W	A / GA	PTS / SO	PIM / AVG
112	NYR	Premysl Duben	Dukla Jihlava, CZE	D					
113	EDM	Lou Dickenson	Mississauga	C					
114	MTL	Christian Larrivee	Chicoutimi	C					
115	FLA	Chris Eade	North Bay	D					
116	CGY	Levente Szuper	Ottawa	G					
117	CHI	Olli Malmivaara	Jokerit Helsinki, FIN	D					
118	L.A.	Lubomir Visnovsky	Bratislava	D					
119	COL	Brian Fahey	U. of Wisconsin	D					
120	FLA	Davis Parley	Kamloops	G					
121	WSH	Ryan Vanbuskirk	Sarnia	D					
122	OTT	Derrick Byfuglien	Fargo	D					
123	DAL	Vadim Khomitsky	HC Moscow, RUS	D					
124	PIT	Michel Ouellet	Rimouski	RW					
125	N.J.	Phil Cole	Lethbridge	D					
126	T.B.	Johan Hagglund	MoDo Ornskoldsvik, SWE	C					
127	DET	Dmitri Semenov	Dynamo Moscow, RUS	RW					
128	DET	Alexander Seluyanov	Salavat Yulayev Ufa, CIS	D					
129	ST.L.	Troy Riddle	Des Moines Jr. A	C					
130	DET	Aaron Van Leusen	Brampton	C					
131	NSH	Matt Hendricks	Blaine H.S.	C					
132	MIN	Maxim Sushinsky	Avangard Omsk, RUS	RW					
133	CBJ	Petteri Nummelin	Davos, SUI	D					
134	ANA	Peter Podhradsky	Bratislava	D					
135	N.J.	Mike Jefferson	Barrie	C					
136	NYI	Dmitri Upper	Torpedo Nizhny Novgorod, RUS	C					
137	NSH	Mike Stuart	Colorado College	D					
138	CBJ	Scott Heffernan	Sarnia	D					
139	DAL	Ruslan Bernikov	Amur	RW					
140	NYR	Nathan Martz	Chilliwack Jr. A	C					
141	CGY	Wade Davis	Calgary	D					
142	S.J.	Michal Pinc	Rouyn-Noranda	C					
143	NYR	Brandon Snee	Union College	G					
144	VAN	Pavel Duma	Neftekhimik Nizhnekamsk, RUS	C					
145	MTL	Ryan Glenn	Walpole H.S.	D					
146	PIT	David Prague	Sparta Praha, CZE	D					
147	ATL	Matt McRae	Cornell	C					
148	NYI	Kristofer Ottosson	Djurgarden Stockholm, SWE	RW					
149	BUF	Dennis Denisov	HC Moscow, RUS	D					
150	CBJ	Tyler Kolarik	Deerfield Academy	C					
151	CHI	Alexander Barkunov	Torpedo Yaroslavl, RUS	D					
152	ANA	Bill Cass	Boston College	D					
152	EDM	Paul Flache	Brampton	D					
154	NSH	Matt Koalska	Twin Cities	C					
155	CGY	Travis Moen	Kelowna	LW					
156	OTT	Greg Zanon	U. Nebraska-Omaha	D					
157	OTT	Grant Potulny	Lincoln H.S.	C					
158	OTT	Sean Connolly	Northern Michigan	D					
159	COL	John-Michael Liles	Michigan State	D					
160	PHX	Nate Kiser	Plymouth	D					
161	T.B.	Pavel Sedov	Khimik Voskresensk, RUS	LW					
162	DAL	Artem Chernov	Metallurg Novokuznetsk, RUS	C					
163	WSH	Ivan Nepryayev	Torpedo Yaroslavl, RUS	C					
164	N.J.	Matus Kostur	HKM Zvolen, SVK	G					
165	L.A.	Nathan Marsters	Chilliwack Jr. A	G					
166	S.J.	Nolan Schaefer	Providence	G					
167	ST.L.	Craig Weller	Calgary	D					
168	ATL	Zdenek Smid	Karlovy Vary, CZE	G					
169	CBJ	Shane Bendera	Red Deer	G					
170	MIN	Erik Reitz	Barrie	D					
171	PHI	Roman Cechmanek	HC Slovnaft Vsetin, CZE	G					
172	MTL	Scott Selig	Thayer Academy	C					
173	NSH	Tomas Harant	Zilina Jr., SVK	D					
174	BOS	Jarno Kultanen	HIFK Helsinki, FIN	D					
175	NYR	Sven Helfenstein	EHC Kloten Jr., SUI	LW					
176	CGY	Jukka Hentunen	HPK Hameenlinna, FIN	RW					
177	CHI	Michael Ayers	Dubuque Jr. A	G					
178	ATL	Jeff Dwyer	Choate	D					
179	TOR	Vadim Sozinov	Metallurg Novokuznetsk 2, RUS	C					
180	ATL	Darcy Hordichuk	Saskatoon	LW					
181	CAR	Justin Forrest	U.S. Nationals	D					
182	MTL	Petr Chvojka	HC Keramika Plzen, CZE	D					
183	S.J.	Michal Macho	Martin	C					
184	EDM	Shaun Norrie	Calgary	RW					
185	PIT	Patrick Foley	U. of New Hampshire	LW					
186	PHX	Brent Gauvreau	Oshawa	RW					
187	DET	Per Backer	Grums, SWE	RW					
188	OTT	Jason Maleyko	Brampton	D					
189	COL	Chris Bahen	Clarkson	D					
190	FLA	Josh Olson	Omaha Jr. A	LW					
191	T.B.	Aaron Gionet	Kamloops	D					
192	DAL	Ladislav Vlcek	HC Velvana Kladno, CZE	RW					
193	CHI	Joey Martin	Omaha Jr. A	D					
194	N.J.	Deryk Engelland	Moose Jaw	D					
195	PHI	Colin Shields	Cleveland	RW					
196	DET	Paul Ballantyne	Sault Ste. Marie	D					
197	NSH	Zybynek Irgl	HC Vitkovice, CZE	C					
198	N.J.	Ken Magowan	Vernon	LW					

PICK	TEAM	NAME	DRAFTED FROM	POS	GP	G / W	A / GA	PTS / SO	PIM / AVG
199	MIN	Brian Passmore	Oshawa	C					
200	CBJ	Janne Jokila	TPS Turku, FIN	LW					
201	L.A.	Yevgeny Fedorov	Molot Perm, RUS	C					
202	NYI	Ryan Caldwell	Thunder Bay Jr. A	D					
203	NSH	Jure Penko	Green Bay	G					
204	BOS	Chris Berti	Sarnia	C					
205	NYR	Henrik Lundqvist	Vastra Frolunda, SWE	G					
206	L.A.	Tim Eriksson	Vastra Frolunda, SWE	C					
207	CHI	Cliff Loya	U. of Maine	D					
208	VAN	Brandon Reid	Halifax	C					
209	TOR	Markus Seikola	TPS Turku, FIN	D					
210	PHI	John Eichelberger	Green Bay	C					
211	EDM	Joe Cullen	Colorado College	C					
212	CAR	Magnus Kahnberg	Vastra Frolunda, SWE	LW					
213	BUF	Vasili Bizyayev	CSKA Moscow, Jr. RUS	RW					
214	MIN	Peter Bartos	Budejovice, CZE	LW					
215	EDM	Matthew Lombardi	Victoriaville	C					
216	PIT	Jim Abbott	New Hampshire	LW					
217	PHX	Igor Samoilov	Torpedo Yaroslavl, RUS	D					
218	L.A.	Craig Olynick	Seattle	D					
219	DAL	Marco Tuokko	TPS Turku, FIN	C					
220	BUF	Paul Gaustad	Portland	C					
221	COL	Aaron Molnar	London	G					
222	T.B.	Marek Priechodsky	Trnava, SVK	D					
223	TOR	Lubos Velebny	HKM Zvolen, SVK	D					
224	DAL	Antti Miettinen	HPK Hameenlinna, FIN	C					
225	CHI	Vladislav Luchkin	Severstal Cherepovets, RUS	C					
226	T.B.	Brian Eklund	Brown University	G					
227	PHI	Guillaume Lefebvre	Rouyn Noranda	C					
228	DET	Jimmie Svensson	Vasteras	C					
229	ST.L.	Brett Lutes	Montreal	LW					
230	ATL	Samu Isosalo	North Bay	RW					
231	CBJ	Peter Zingoni	New England	C					
232	MIN	Lubomir Sekeras	HC Zelezarny Trinec, CZE	D					
233	T.B.	Alexander Polukeyev	St. Petersburg	G					
234	FLA	Janis Sprukts	Lukko Rauma, FIN	C					
235	CAR	Craig Kowalski	Compuware	G					
236	NSH	Mats Christeen	Sodertalje, SWE	D					
237	BOS	Zdenek Kutlak	Budejovice, CZE	D					
238	NYR	Dan Eberly	RPI	D					
239	CGY	David Hajek	Chomutov, CZE	D					
240	CHI	Adam Berkhoel	Twin Cities	G					
241	VAN	Nathan Barrett	Lethbridge	C					
242	ATL	Evan Nielsen	U. of Notre Dame	D					
243	MTL	Joni Puurula	Hermes	G					
244	ATL	Eric Bowen	Portland	RW					
245	L.A.	Dan Welch	U. of Minnesota	RW					
246	S.J.	Chad Wiseman	Mississauga	LW					
247	EDM	Jason Platt	Omaha Jr. A	D					
248	PIT	Steven Crampton	Moose Jaw	RW					
249	PHX	Sami Venalainen	Tappara Tampere, FIN	RW					
250	L.A.	Flavien Conne	Fribourg, SUI	C					
251	DET	Todd Jackson	U.S. Nationals	RW					
252	COL	Darryl Bootland	St. Michael's	RW					
253	FLA	Mathew Sommerfeld	Swift Current	LW					
254	TOR	Alexander Shinkar	Severstal Cherepovets, RUS	RW					
255	MIN	Eric Johansson	Tri-City	C					
256	S.J.	Pasi Saarinen	Ilves Tampere, FIN	D					
257	N.J.	Warren McCutcheon	Lethbridge	C					
258	BUF	Sean McMorrow	Kitchener	D					
259	PHI	Regan Kelly	Nipawin	D					
260	DET	Yevgeny Bumagin	Lada Togliatti, RUS	C					
261	ST.L.	Reinhard Divis	Leksand, SWE	G					
262	CHI	Peter Flache	Guelph	C					
263	T.B.	Thomas Ziegler	Ambri-Piotta, SUI	RW					
264	NYI	Dmitri Altarev	Dizelist Penza, RUS	LW					
265	TOR	Jean-Philippe Cote	Cape Breton	D					
266	COL	Sean Kotary	Northwood Prep	C					
267	NYI	Tomi Pettinen	Ilves Tampere, FIN	D					
268	BOS	Pavel Kolarik	Slavia Praha, CZE	D					
269	NYR	Martin Richter	SaiPa Lappeenranta, FIN	D					
270	CGY	Micki Dupont	Kamloops	D					
271	CHI	Reto Von Arx	Davos, SUI	C					
272	VAN	Tim Smith	Spokane	C					
273	PIT	Roman Simicek	HPK Hameenlinna, FIN	C					
274	EDM	Yevgeny Muratov	Neftekhimik Nizhnekamsk, RUS	LW					
275	MTL	Jonathan Gauthier	Rouyn Noranda	D					
276	CAR	Troy Ferguson	Michigan State	W					
277	BUF	Ryan Courtney	Windsor	LW					
278	CBJ	Martin Paroulek	HC Slovnaft Vsetin, CZE	RW					
279	BOS	Andreas Lindstrom	Lulea, SWE	RW					
280	PIT	Nick Boucher	Dartmouth	G					
281	PHX	Peter Fabus	Dukla Trencin, SVK	C					
282	L.A.	Carl Grahn	KalPa Kuopio, FIN	G					
283	OTT	James Demone	Portland	D					
284	NSH	Martin Hohener	EHC Kloten, SUI	D					
285	COL	Blake Ward	Tri-City	G					
286	CBJ	Andrej Nedorost	Essen, GER	C					
287	PHI	Milan Kopecky	Slavia Praha, CZE	LW					
288	ATL	Mark McRae	Cornell	D					
289	WSH	Bjorn Nord	Djurgarden Stockholm, SWE	D					
290	ATL	Simon Gamache	Val D'Or	C					
291	CHI	Arne Ramholt	EHC Kloten, SUI	D					
292	CBJ	Louis Mandeville	Rouyn Noranda	D					
293	ST.L.	Lauri Kinos	Montreal	D					

Column headers: NHL PLAYERS: POS, GP, G, A, PTS, PIM; NHL GOALTENDERS: POS, GP, W, GA, SO, AVG

CHAPTER 34

Keepers of the Stanley Cup

The Document that Entrusts the Trophy to the NHL

When Lord Stanley of Preston announced his intention to donate a hockey cup in 1892, he wished for it to be emblematic of the championship of the Dominion of Canada. As such, even though it would first be presented to the hockey club of the Montreal Amateur Athletic Association in recognition of winning the Amateur Hockey Association of Canada, the Stanley Cup could not belong to just one league. In order to make the trophy available to teams from all across the country, Lord Stanley appointed two trustees to devise a system of rules for challenges and to govern the Cup's presentation.

Modern hockey was not even 20 years old when Lord Stanley's trophy was first presented in 1893. As the sport evolved during the early years of the 20th century, the Stanley Cup trustees proved more than able to adapt to the changing times. When Canada's best hockey clubs began paying their players, the trustees announced that the Stanley Cup would be emblematic of professional hockey supremacy. When the pro game eventually provided two recognizable major leagues, the trustees agreed to abandon the challenge system in favor of an annual playoff between the two league champions. When those leagues began expanding into the United States, the trustees declared the Stanley Cup symbolic of the world's professional hockey championship. By doing these things, the trustees ensured that the former Governor-General's trophy remained the top prize in the game.

By the 1926–27 season, the National Hockey League was the game's only major professional league. The competition for the game's top prize became an expanded playoff within the league. Twenty years later, the Stanley Cup trustees formally turned over control of the trophy to the NHL. However, as you shall see, the agreement signed on June 30, 1947, did not simply give the Stanley Cup to the NHL. It merely granted the league the right to amend the conditions of competition and the responsibility of the care and custody of the trophy. The NHL has the right to return control of the Stanley Cup to the trustees at any time. Similarly, if the NHL should disband, or if a new league were to replace it as the game's top professional organization, control of the the Stanley Cup would revert to the trustees. The current trustees are former NHL vice president Brian O'Neill and former Supreme Court of Canada Justice Willard Estey.

MEMORANDUM OF AGREEMENT made in triplicate this Thirtieth day of June, 1947.

B E T W E E N:

PHILIP DANSKEN ROSS, Publisher, of Ottawa, Ontario, and J. COOPER SMEATON, Insurance Manager, of Montreal, Quebec, Trustees of the Stanley Cup, hereinafter called the "Trustees"

OF THE FIRST PART

– and –

NATIONAL HOCKEY LEAGUE, hereinafter called the League

OF THE SECOND PART.

W H E R E A S by Deed of Gift executed in 1893 the Earl of Derby, then Governor-General of Canada, donated a challenge cup known as the Stanley Cup to be held from year to year by the champion hockey club of the Dominion of Canada, and appointed Mr. Philip Dansken Ross and Sheriff Sweetland (later succeeded by William Foran and more recently by J. Cooper Smeaton) to act as trustees of the cup and maintain rules to govern the competitions.

AND WHEREAS the original purpose of the donor in presenting the Stanley Cup was primarily the development of hockey in Canada, and to advance this purpose he appointed two Canadian citizens as trustees and provided for the appointment of further trustees by the surviving trustees whenever a vacancy occurs.

AND WHEREAS it is desirable to make provision for cases of default of appointment of trustees.

AND WHEREAS the original conditions of competition as set out by the donor have been amended from time to time to meet the changing conditions brought about by the expansion of the game of hockey, and its popularity both in the Dominion of Canada and the United States of America.

AND WHEREAS the Stanley Cup has been emblematic of the World's Professional Hockey Championship since 1907.

AND WHEREAS the competition for the trophy from 1916 [sic] to 1926 was conducted between the winners of the National Hockey League and the Pacific Coast Hockey League [sic] (since dissolved).

AND WHEREAS the competition for the trophy since 1926 has been conducted between teams of the National Hockey League only and the trophy has been awarded annually to the winner of the "Stanley Cup Series" conducted by the National Hockey League upon rules and regulations made and amended by the League from time to time

AND WHEREAS it is recognized that the National Hockey League is the world's leading professional hockey league and the winners of its Annual Play-Off Series are recognized as the World's Professional Hockey Champions.

AND WHEREAS it is acknowledged that the right and title to the original trophy and the collars added down to 1926 are the property of the Trustees.

AND WHEREAS the care and custody and the determination of the conditions of competition for the trophy have been under the direction of the National Hockey League for twenty years.

AND WHEREAS it is desirable to reduce to writing the rights and responsibilities of the parties hereto in connection with the trophy.

NOW, THEREFORE, THIS AGREEMENT WITNESSETH that for and in consideration of the premises and the covenants hereinafter set out, the parties hereto agree as follows:

1. The Trustees hereby delegate the League full authority to determine and amend from time to time the conditions of competition for the Stanley Cup, including the qualifications of challengers, the appointment of officials, the appointment and distributions of all gate receipts, provided always that the winners of the trophy shall be the acknowledged World's Professional Hockey Champions.

2. The Trustees agree that during the currency of this agreement they will not acknowledge or accept any challenge for the Stanley Cup unless such challenge is in conformity with the conditions specified in paragraph one (1) hereof.

3. The League undertakes the responsibility for the care and safe custody of the Stanley Cup including all necessary repairs and alterations to the cup and sub-structure as may by required from time to time, and further undertakes to insure and keep insured the Stanley Cup for its full insurable value.

4. The League hereby acknowledges itself to be bound to the Trustees in the sum of One Thousand Dollars which bond is conditioned upon the safe return of the Stanley Cup to the Trustees in accordance with the terms of this Agreement, and it is agreed that the League shall have the right to return the trophy to the Trustees at any time.

5. This agreement shall remain in force so long as the League continues to be the world's leading professional hockey league as determined by its playing calibre, and in the event of dissolution or other termination of the National Hockey League, the Stanley Cup shall revert to the custody of the trustees.

6. In the event of default in the appointment of a new trustee by the surviving trustee the "Trustees" hereby delegate and appoint the Governors of the International Hockey Hall of Fame in Kingston, Ontario, to name two Canadian trustees to carry on under the terms of the original trust, and in conformity with this agreement.

7. And it is further mutually agreed that any disputes arising as to the interpretation of this Agreement or the facts upon which such interpretation is to be made, shall be settled by an Arbitration Board of three, one member to be appointed by each of the parties, and the third to be selected by the two appointees. The decisions of the Arbitration Board shall be final.

(Sgd) P. D. ROSS
Philip Dansken Ross, Trustee

(Sgd) J. COOPER SMEATON
J. Cooper Smeaton, Trustee

NATIONAL HOCKEY LEAGUE

(Sgd) Per. C. S. CAMPBELL
President

CHAPTER 35

The Stanley Cup Playoffs

Outstanding Moments and Significant Series, 1893-2000

FOUR PLAYOFF MOMENTS

Milt Dunnell

THIS IS AN UNSOLICITED AND UNABASHED PLEA for somebody to form an association for the preservation and propogandism of Stanley Cup legends that are in danger of being overlooked or forgotten.

Herewith, a few that might complement the old reliables of Lester Patrick's gig in goal or Bobby Baun's busted ankle.

April 3, 1933: A Goal That Identified a Career

It just seemed there always had to be a special reason for having Ken Doraty, nicknamed "Cagie," in the National Hockey League.

The Chicago Black Hawks (used to be two words) found him among the assets when they purchased the franchise of the Portland Rosebuds. They soon passed him along to the Minneapolis Millers of the old American Association. The Millers relayed him to the Kitchener club of the Can-Pro League—for mere money.

Being sold for cash was about as bad as it could get, but Doraty, born in Stittsville, Ontario, was the one person who didn't seem to know that at 5'7" and 133 pounds he was too small for the big league of hockey. He was with Syracuse in 1932. Other stops during his career were with clubs such as the Cleveland Indians, the New Haven Eagles and the Buffalo Bisons. If there seemed to be a message there, Doraty didn't read it.

And on the night of April 3, 1933, Doraty knew he had it right. Here he was, warming up for a playoff gig with the Toronto Maple Leafs against the Boston Bruins. The Sliver from Stittsville was on the same page as King Clancy, Charlie Conacher, Eddie Shore and the nobles of the hockey empire. Granted, there had to be the usual special reason for his being among the elite. This time there were two reasons. Ace Bailey had been badly injured and the Leafs, having returned Frank Finnigan to Ottawa, were a trifle short on offense. In search of help, Toronto had sent Doraty to Syracuse for somebody named Dave Downie. But they didn't like Downie, so they brought Doraty back. Lucky Leafs.

For Doraty, it was a terrific psychological boost. A big club was telling him: "You're our man." The way he responded became more than just local history in Stittsville at 1:48 in the morning of April 4. After 164 minutes and 46 seconds of gut-wrenching hockey—the longest playoff battle up to that time, and still the second-longest—the only goal that counted was scored by the little man that no one had wanted.

Some of the game's top stars had been turned back by the goaltending wizardry of Tiny Thompson in the Boston net and Lorne Chabot in the opposite cage. Each team had a goal disallowed by referee Odie Cleghorn. The big break in the game came when Eddie Shore lost control of the puck while trying to create an intentional offside in order to make a line change. Andy Blair of the Leafs pounced on the loose puck and passed to his right side. Doraty fired the shot that may not have been heard around the world, but it did rattle windows in North America.

Frank Selke used to claim that this Toronto victory was the greatest playoff game he ever saw. (He may have changed his rating later when he became manager of the Montreal Canadiens, who were involved in many a nail-biter.) But after the game, Doraty and the Leafs had no time for a champagne shower. Within hours they were due on the ice at Madison Square Garden to begin the Stanley Cup final. The New York Rangers were waiting.

April 5, 1938: Smythe wins the skirmish; Stewart wins the war

Bill Stewart and Conn Smythe were worthy opponents—like Muhammad Ali and Joe Frazier. Stewart was a big league umpire in the National League and had been a hard-nosed referee in the NHL. He never hesitated to make tough decisions. He and colorful Tommy Gorman, then the coach of the Chicago Black Hawks, actually exchanged punches during a riotous game at Boston. Stewart finally ordered the police to escort Tommy out of the rink. When Chicago players followed Gorman, Stewart awarded the game to Boston.

Conn Smythe was … well, he was the fiery owner of the Toronto Maple Leafs. Builder of Maple Leaf Gardens. The American press called him "Puck's Bad Boy" and he gloried in the label.

Smythe never liked referees and he wasn't forgetting that Stewart, now coaching the Black Hawks against the Leafs in the final round for the Stanley Cup, had made a few calls that still irritated. So, he wasn't inclined to be generous this day when Stewart needed a favor—a tremendous favor. The Black Hawks were ready for game one except for the little matter of having no goaltender.

Mike Karakas, Chicago's regular goalie, had suffered a broken toe in the previous round with the New York Americans and couldn't get his foot into his skate. The club was carrying no backup netminder. Such a situation was not exactly unique in those early days of the NHL when a second goaltender was considered a luxury. Stewart asked for permission to use Dave Kerr of the New York Rangers, merely the shutout leader in the league that season. Might as well go for the max, as they say in the casino.

Stewart and Smythe may well have duked it out when Smythe stopped laughing. The Toronto boss then countered by offering the services of Alfie Moore, a local boy and the goaltender for the Leafs' farm team at Pittsburgh.

"Alfie's an experienced goalie," Smythe assured, without

expounding on the experience. During a lengthy career in the nets, Alfie had a grand total of only 24 NHL games to his credit—all with the sadsack Americans.

When Smythe refused to budge, Stewart called a team meeting at the club's hotel. Did any of the players know Alfie Moore, the experienced goalie? A couple of them did, and they were told to go out and find him, which they did—at the second tap room they scouted. Alfie welcomed them. He hoped they could come up with a couple of tickets for that night's game.

"You're going to be at the game," they assured him, leading him back to Stewart. The coach quietly spread the word among his players: "Take it easy in the warmup. I don't want him hurt before the face-off."

Alfie was rinsed out with numerous cups of coffee before taking his place between the pipes at Maple Leaf Gardens. He might have looked a bit weak on the first shot, which was fired past him by the Leafs' Gordie Drillon. After that, though, he became Mister Zero. The Leafs couldn't have pelted a collar button by him. The Hawks won 3–1.

Alfie Moore was every Chicago fan's pinup boy, although he got no further chances to play. Smythe had seen enough. So had Frank Calder, then president of the NHL. He denied the Hawks permission to use him. After farmhand Paul Goodman was summoned for game two (a 5–1 Leafs victory), Karakas was fitted with a special skate boot that allowed him to play. Chicago went on to win the Stanley Cup with two victories at home in the best-of-five playoff.

"How much do we owe you?" the Hawks asked Alfie Moore.

"Would $150 be reasonable?" he wondered.

They gave him $300.

And they put his name on the Stanley Cup.

Try to put a price on that.

March 27, 1952: Spitting Against the Wind

In December, 1951, there had been an honor night for Turk Broda, Canada's favorite fatman and the goaltender of the Toronto Maple Leafs. This was a break with tradition in Toronto where the club had a policy of pretending that all men were equal—especially at contract time.

Broda had earned himself an international fan club several years earlier when he was ordered to shed weight within a given period or turn in his gear. Sympathy seeped from every fan's pores while Turk was pictured broiling in hot tubs, pumping iron and dining on spinach. The newspapers printed diets offered by people who assured Turk he would become skinnier than a rink rat if he listened to them. Others wrote poems and sonnets dedicated to his deadline. None of them seemed to realize the whole uproar was the result of club owner Conn Smythe's campaign to cut into the space which pro football was getting on the sports pages.

Broda was obviously nearing the end of his career by 1951 and the club was forced to relax its rule against gift nights. Fans lined up and paraded through Maple Leaf Gardens admiring the loot, which included a new car. There was only one tear in the outpouring of eulogy. Turk had been in 99 Stanley Cup playoff games as a Leaf. How nice it would have been if he could have made it to 100.

Come March 27, 1952, the Leafs were in Detroit and one game down to the rampaging Red Wings after the opener of the semifinal series for the Stanley Cup. There was no reason for Leaf optimism. They had been blanked 3–0 in a chippy contest that produced 15 penalties in the second period alone.

"Disgraceful," snorted Jack Adams, general manager of the Detroit club. "The dirty play was inspired by Toronto's management level [Smythe] in an attempt to injure our top line."

"The Wings started it," Smythe retorted. "They know our guy Fern Flaman has a broken jaw [actually a broken cheekbone] and they are trying to eliminate him from the series."

Ignoring the fact the Leafs had failed to score, Smythe confided to a newsman: "What we need is inspiration. I'm bringing Broda in from Toronto for the second game. It will be Turk's 100th playoff game. He's the best money goalie in hockey. The team will go all-out for Turk. We'll turn this thing around."

Coach Joe Primeau couldn't believe what he was hearing. Broda, he reminded Smythe, had played only 30 *minutes* of hockey all season. He considered himself retired. But Smythe, as usual, had it right—for awhile. Turk arrived for the second game and was sensational. Unfortunately, the Leafs didn't rise to his heights. They didn't score. Johnny Wilson, a rookie on Detroit's third line, scored the only goal of the game. Broda was the story, but the Red Wings still had the Leafs by the throat.

Unfortunately, Turk didn't halt at playoff game #100. He was back in the net for the third game in Toronto and was blasted 6–2. Headlines in the Detroit papers gloated: "Smythe Opens Flood Gates with Broda Boner."

But it didn't matter who played against the Red Wings that spring. They were unbeatable. After finishing off the Leafs in four straight, they swept the Canadiens for the Stanley Cup. And get this: in the entire playoffs, they didn't have a goal scored against them on Detroit ice.

April 18, 1963: For Imlach, Litz Meant Luck

Punch Imlach, one of the most controversial—and successful—coaches in NHL history, had two pet peeves. One was two-dollar bills. The other was referees.

Imlach couldn't do much about referees, but he could do something about two-dollar bills. He tore them up—especially on the day of a game.Then he would wander down the corridor to the Maple Leafs dressing room, tapping on doorknobs which had proved to have magical powers in the past, and beating his trademark felt hats out of shape. It worked. How else to explain why his team of oldsters seemed to have a lock on the Stanley Cup?

Punch's guys were high on the list of candidates for old age security, and for hockey purposes many of them were supposed to be past tense. His goalie, for instance. Johnny Bower had spent a career in the minors before he got a chance in the bigs. And how about Red Kelly? He had actually retired in Detroit. Tim Horton, Al Arbour (yes, later to be the Islanders' skipper) and Larry Hillman had big mileage on them. And there was one secret weapon that also fit the mold.

When Imlach took Ed Litzenberger from the Red Wings on waivers in December, 1961, the move was seen as just one more reminder of Punch's confidence in his old sweats. Conn Smythe had sold his stock in the club by this time, but was still around to comment on the scene: "That Imlach must be a genius," he observed, "because he does so many wrong things that turn out right."

Smythe refrained from saying what he really thought of the Litzenberger deal, but comment wasn't necessary. The evidence was there. Chicago had dumped the big guy from

Saskatchewan while he and his Black Hawk teammates were still being wined and dined for winning the 1961 Stanley Cup. That was in June. The Red Wings kept him until December before placing him on waivers. But what Imlach saw in Litzenberger was a hockey player who never seemed to live up to what others expected of him. No matter what he did, it was never enough.

Litzenberger's track record was actually quite good. He had won the Northey Trophy as the best rookie in the Quebec junior league. Later, with the Montreal Canadiens, even though he was having an excellent rookie season—he would win the Calder Trophy—his reward was being sold to the last-place Chicago Black Hawks for cash.

With the Black Hawks, Litzenberger had three successive seasons in which he scored more than 30 goals. But the media always wondered how many he could score if he ever pulled out all the stops. That question seemed to be kept in standing type. The final putdown came when he was traded within weeks of winning the Cup. The explanation was supposed to be that big Litz had lost his legs. With Imlach and the Toronto oldsters, he found new ones.

Litzenberger helped Toronto win the Stanley Cup in the spring of 1962. On April 18, 1963, he was accepting compliments of the Red Wings on what was his third consecutive Stanley Cup title. (He would make it four in a row in 1964.) Pumping his hand in the traditional postgame ritual, Gordie Howe told him: "We hear you're using the Stanley Cup for cheese dip at your house."

Montreal and Winnipeg 1896

Eric Zweig

Although the actual game rarely lives up to its overblown hype, it is almost impossible to conceive of a time when the Super Bowl might have been in trouble. Yet such was the case in January, 1969. The National Football League's Green Bay Packers had romped to victory over upstarts from the American Football League in each of the first two championship games. Now the Baltimore Colts were expected to do the same against the New York Jets.

Johnny Unitas and his flat-top crewcut perfectly embodied the old guard of the NFL, just as the flamboyantly long-haired Joe Namath symbolized the AFL. People laughed when Namath guaranteed a victory for his team, but come the NFL-AFL Championship Game it was the Jets over the Colts, 16–7, and suddenly the "Super Bowl" meant something. It took the Stanley Cup four years to come into its own in a similar fashion, but then life moved more slowly back in the 1890s.

When the Stanley Cup first was presented in 1893, it merely was awarded to the Montreal Amateur Athletic Association by virtue of its first-place finish in the Amateur Hockey Association of Canada. The first Stanley Cup playoffs one year later resulted only from the need to break a tie atop the AHAC standings. Not until 1895 was the first formal Stanley Cup challenge accepted, yet it was more likely to hold the young trophy up to ridicule than to see it held up in awe.

The trustees of the Stanley Cup had arranged for the challenge to take place on March 9, 1895—one day after the AHAC season ended. Unfortunately, they had arranged for Queen's University to play the Montreal AAA, who just had been unseated as league champions by the Montreal Victorias. Thus, the situation was that in order for the Vics to claim the Stanley Cup, the AAA had to beat Queen's—which they did, 5–1.

Though they were now champions, the first time the Montreal Victorias actually got a chance to play for the Stanley Cup was February 14, 1896. In a one-game challenge against the Winnipeg Victorias, the Montreal squad was blanked 2–0 by netminder Whitey Merritt, whose white cricket pads marked the first time a goaltender had so protected his legs in championship play. With Winnipeg's upset victory taking the Stanley Cup out west, the young trophy suddenly was national news. When the Montreal team traveled to Manitoba to take on its rivals in a rematch in December, hockey's championship game became a national passion.

The Montreal Victorias arrived in Winnipeg on Sunday evening, December 27, 1896. "As the train pulled in, a ringing cheer went up from the large crowd of hockeyists who had assembled to do honor to the visitors." Upwards of 700 people crowded into the McIntyre rink to watch the team practice on Monday morning. Meanwhile, the *Winnipeg Tribune* reported that $1 reserved tickets to Wednesday's championship game were already being sold for as much as $5 "and chances are that by the night of the match the price will reach $10." In fact, they would go for as much as $12.

Meanwhile, in Montreal, the *Daily Star* newspaper made special arrangements to announce bulletins from the game received by telegraph. An enormous crowd gathered in the streets to receive the updates.

In December, 1896, Cyclone Taylor was a 13-year-old boy living in Listowel, Ontario. In another 13 years he would win his first Stanley Cup title, yet he never forgot the excitement of those early era games.

"Hundreds would gather to get the latest bulletins," he told biographer Eric Whitehead. "The mobs would hang around at night in sub-zero weather just waiting for the operator to leave his key and come dashing out with an announcement. He'd appear ... and there'd be a sudden hush as he'd clear his throat and cry out something like: '[Montreal] has just scored and the game is now tied...' and there'd be a loud cheering. He'd chalk the score up on a blackboard and then go back into his office, and we'd just stand there and talk hockey and wait for the next bulletin."

It was 22 minutes past eight o'clock in Winnipeg on the evening of December 30, 1896, when the two Victorias hockey teams faced-off. The bulletins must have come fast and furious.

Ernie McLea of Montreal beat Jack Armytage to the draw, but the puck went back and forth for the first few minutes until McLea set up Robert McDougall for what appeared to be the game's first goal. However, referee Weldy Young of Ottawa ruled the play offside and the game remained scoreless until 6:30 of the first half when Dan Bain put the home team in front. Five minutes later the lead was up to 3–0. Winnipeg continued to pour it on until Toate Campbell received a five-minute penalty for kicking the puck. "This nerved the Montrealers up, and McLea and McDougall made matters tough for [Winnipeg defensemen Roddy] Flett and [Charlie] Johnstone." McLea finally put Montreal on the scoreboard. Six minutes later, Shirley Davidson cut the Winnipeg lead to 3–2, but Attie Howard restored the two-goal advantage just moments before halftime.

The ice was swept during the interval, and play resumed at 9:31 p.m. Winnipeg had the better of the play to begin the second half, but it was Montreal's Shirley Davidson who scored the first goal. Playing for the tie, McLea and McDougall pressed the attack, aided by teammates Graham Drinkwater and Mike Grant. McLea evened matters at 4–4. Armytage, Bain and Howard then went to work for the home side, but Gordon Lewis was not about to let the puck slide between his posts. When Bain finally beat him, it was not until after Montreal had already taken the lead. "One simultaneous yell of delight went up from 1,500 throats as the puck went through, but the note of joy was turned to one of sorrow when two minutes later McLea successfully obtained the puck on a pass from Drinkwater … and eluding all before him arrived in front of the Winnipeg goal and shot and scored."

McLea's third goal of the night deflated the western champions. "Winnipeg Victorias then felt that they were defeated and the last couple of minutes of the game was dead compared to what had passed before. The seconds passed and when the timekeepers rang their bell, the Victorias of Montreal were champions of Canada."

"We have never fought a harder game," said captain Mike Grant after the 6–5 victory. "It was a case of work for all we got." Winnipeg captain Jack Armytage echoed the sentiments. "We did our best and the best team won. We have never had a harder game and I can heartily congratulate the victors."

As should hockey fans everywhere. The battle between these two great rivals may well have saved the Stanley Cup.

WANDERERS AND OTTAWA 1906

Eric Zweig

LIKE THE MONTREAL CANADIENS versus the Philadelphia Flyers in 1976 or the Edmonton Oilers and New York Islanders in 1984, the Stanley Cup series that pitted the Montreal Wanderers against the Ottawa Silver Seven in 1906 marked a clash of styles and a changing of the guard.

Similar to the Islanders—and even more like the Flyers—the Silver Seven were a team that could beat its opponents any way they wanted to play. In a match of skills, Frank McGee and Harry Smith could outscore anyone, but if teams wanted to get tough, the Silver Seven were even happier to beat them like that. Either way, no one worked harder. Since first claiming the Stanley Cup with a win over the Montreal Victorias in 1903, the Ottawa squad had turned back nine more challengers, including two in the previous two weeks, by the time they took on the Montreal Wanderers in 1906.

To call the Wanderers a finesse team in the mold of the Canadiens or the Oilers would be to understate the violent nature of early hockey, still they were a stylish squad—and one that was much younger than the aging champions. Their clash with the Silver Seven was not a true Stanley Cup challenge of the type generally associated with the early era, meaning it was not a meeting of rival champions from two different leagues. The Wanderers faced the Silver Seven in a two-game, total-goals series to determine first place in the Eastern Canada Amateur Hockey Association. Since the Silver Seven were the current holders of the Stanley Cup, the winner of this playoff would not only claim the league title but also the former Governor-General's famous prize.

The Silver Seven and the Wanderers had finished the 1905–06 ECAHA season with identical 9–1 records. Their only losses had come against each other. Knowing that the league title might be on the line on the final night of the season (March 10), the Wanderers had crushed the Montreal Shamrocks, 15–1, but the Silver Seven kept pace with a 12–5 victory over Quebec. That the teams were both talented cannot be denied. Of the 15 players who took part in the two-game series, eight later would become members of the Hockey Hall of Fame.

The series opened in Montreal on March 14. Ottawa took control of the play early, particularly during a three-minute penalty to Moose Johnson for tripping Frank McGee, but Wanderers goaltender Henri Menard kept the Silver Seven off the scoreboard and slowly the game turned in the home team's favor. Pud Glass scored the first goal, and the Wanderers found the net twice more in the next eight minutes to take a 3–0 lead. Play then raced from end to end as the Silver Seven tried desperately to score the next goal, but the Ottawa players were clearly tired. With their two recent Stanley Cup matches in addition to finishing up the ECAHA schedule, Ottawa had played six games in the last two weeks while the Wanderers had played just twice in 11 days. Unable to keep up with their younger and better rested opponents, the Silver Seven became more physical. The strategy backfired when the Wanderers scored a fourth goal before halftime while Harvey Pulford was serving a penalty for cross-checking.

The Silver Seven came out strong to start the second half, but an early save by Menard on Harry Smith took away their momentum. The Montrealers poured in five more goals en route to a 9–1 victory. Though Ernie Russell had scored four times and Pud Glass three, 22-year-old rover Lester Patrick was considered the game's top star.

The teams had two days off before the series resumed at Ottawa's Dey Rink on March 17. With their heroes trailing by eight in the total-goals set, Silver Seven fans could have been forgiven for being downhearted yet interest in the game was at a fever pitch. Tickets sold out well before game day, and when temporary bleachers were added behind each net, a riot almost broke out as hundreds of fans—many of whom had camped out all night—jammed the box office trying to buy any ticket they could. Just 200 tickets had been allotted for Montreal fans, yet more than 1,000 descended on Ottawa in special trains scheduled for the series. Scalpers had a field day selling two-dollar tickets for up to 10 dollars—with no guarantee they were the real thing! Among the more than 5,400 fans who jammed an arena designed to seat 3,000 were the Earl and Lady Grey, Canada's then-Governor-General and his wife.

The Silver Seven made one change to their lineup for game two of the series, replacing goaltender Billy Hague with former Smith's Falls netminder Percy LeSueur. While the Wanderers would have been within their rights to do so, they did not protest the presence of the late addition to the

Ottawa roster. The change hardly appeared to matter, particularly when an early goal by Moose Johnson upped the lead to 10–1 on the round. But Ottawa refused to back down. Frank McGee got the Silver Seven on the scoreboard with a rink-long rush. After a goal by Harry Smith, McGee scored again and the Silver Seven took a 3–1 lead into half-time. Though they still trailed the series by six goals, the margin was cut in half just minutes after intermission when Smith, his brother Alf, and then Rat Westwick all scored. When Harry Smith scored twice more, the Wanderers' seemingly insurmountable lead had slipped to 10–9 with 10 minutes still to play.

The Ottawa squad sensed the kill and bore down on the beleaguered Montreal outfit. Harry Smith once again charged into the Wanderers zone, only to be met by a vicious cross-check from Rod Kennedy. The indignant roars of the Ottawa faithful soon turned to cheers when Smith slid into the net with the puck underneath him and the referee signalled a goal. Years later, in a *MacLean's* magazine interview in 1950, Lester Patrick would point to the Wanderers' collapse as proof of how hockey had improved over time. "No modern team," Lester argued, "would let nine goals past it in about 30 minutes."

Victory now was within Ottawa's grasp, and the Silver Seven poured on the pressure. But they pressed too hard. With two minutes to play, the Ottawa defensemen crept too far into the Montreal zone. When Patrick pounced on a loose puck, he flipped it across to Moose Johnson, who had a clear path into the Ottawa end. Johnson sped towards LeSueur in the Silver Seven goal, then dropped a return pass to Patrick, who rammed the puck home. With 90 seconds to play, the incredible comeback had fallen short. Patrick scored again just before the final bell and, despite a 9–3 loss on the evening, the Wanderers escaped with a 12–10 total-goal victory. The Stanley Cup reign of the Ottawa Silver Seven was over. Hockey had a brand new champion.

ROSEBUDS AND CANADIENS 1916

Eric Zweig

FROM THE TIME THAT BROTHERS FRANK AND LESTER PATRICK announced the formation of the Pacific Coast Hockey Association on December 7, 1911, relations with the eastern-based National Hockey Association were stormy at best. Yet despite the turmoil that resulted from constant player raids, the NHA and the PCHA soon agreed that their respective champions should meet to determine the winner of the Stanley Cup. In this era of train travel, the "World Series of Hockey" would alternate yearly between east and west. In the first series, the PCHA's Victoria Aristocrats came east to Toronto in 1914 only to be swept by the hometown Blueshirts in the best-of-five series. In 1915, the Vancouver Millionaires hosted the Ottawa Senators and destroyed them by scores of 6–2, 8–3 and 12–3. So dominant were the new PCHA champions that many hockey writers speculated that the Stanley Cup might remain the possession of western teams for years to come.

The 1914–15 PCHA season had seen the league's New Westminster Royals franchise head south to Oregon and become the Portland Rosebuds. This marked the first time an American-based team had played in a league that competed for the Stanley Cup—a trophy originally donated to recognize Canada's champion. When the PCHA expanded into Seattle the following season, Stanley Cup trustee William Foran announced that he considered hockey's top prize to be emblematic of the world championship and therefore open to be won by either Portland or Seattle. Thus when the Rosebuds finished atop the PCHA standings in 1915–16, they became the first American team to compete for the Stanley Cup.

Though the PCHA season had concluded on February 25, the Rosebuds did not arrive in Montreal until the day before the Stanley Cup series was to commence on March 20, 1916. They had not played a meaningful game in almost four weeks, though their train from Portland had stopped in Houghton, Michigan, for an exhibition contest against a local all-star team. There would be time for a pregame skate in Montreal, but not a full practice. The Canadiens, on the other hand, had just played their final game of the NHA season on March 18 and were on a roll with seven straight wins.

The general consensus heading into game one of the Stanley Cup series was that the Portland players could not possibly be expected to show at their best form after their long train trip. The Rosebuds roster only contained nine players, including goalie Tom Murray (Montreal carried 11 players) and it would be hard to stay fresh. Adding to Portland's problems would be the team's unfamiliarity with the NHA rules that would be in force for the first game; the PCHA still used the rover, but had modernized the game to allow forward passing and made teams play a man short when their players took penalties—features not yet adopted in the east. But the supposedly train-weary Rosebuds skated the Canadiens dizzy. Goals by Smokey Harris and Charles Uksila (the first Stanley Cup combatant born, raised and trained in the United States) paced Portland to a 2–0 victory. Only the stellar play of Georges Vezina kept the Canadiens close. As the *Ottawa Citizen* said of Montreal's play: "After the first five minutes they were a beaten team." It was the first time a home team had been defeated in the NHA-PCHA World Series.

With memories still fresh of the previous season's romp by Vancouver, and with game two to be played under western rules, talk turned to a Portland sweep. Matters were made worse for Montreal when it was learned that neither Newsy Lalonde nor Jack Laviolette would suit up for game two. Laviolette had suffered a broken nose and Lalonde was bothered by a bad cold that had rendered him ineffectual in the opener. But this time it was the Canadiens who upset the experts with a 2–1 victory to even the series on March 22. Game three, under NHA rules three nights later, was hard fought. Literally. Lalonde and Laviolette were back in action, and helped linemate and fellow future Hall of Famer Didier Pitre score three goals in a 6–3 victory, but the most noteworthy feature of this game was a third-period brawl that broke out while the Canadiens were clinging to a one-goal lead. Trouble began when Portland defenseman Moose Johnson attacked Newsy Lalonde, and it did not end until policemen broke up the ensuing scrap. Johnson and Lalonde both were given match penalties, while Portland's Eddie Oatman earned an additional major. During the first of two off days that followed, Chief Moffat of the Westmount police announced that no charges would be filed, but did warn of future arrests if the violence continued.

Game four of the series proved to be much more wide open than the previous three. Montreal now was favored despite the use of PCHA rules, but Portland struck first on a goal by Smokey Harris. Uksila and Harris again scored early in the second period before the Canadiens came to life. Goals by Goldie Prodgers, Newsy Lalonde, Didier Pitre and Amos Arbour had them ahead 4–3 after 40 minutes, but Eddie Oatman evened matters five minutes into the third. Then Harris scored another and Oatman fired his second, all within a 60-second span. Lalonde cut the lead to 6–5 late in the third period, but Portland held on to win.

For the first time in the brief history of the best-of-five format, a Stanley Cup series had been stretched to the limit. In fact, outside of a few one-sided one-game challenge matches, the 1916 final marked the first time since the Ottawa Silver Seven beat Rat Portage in a best-of-three affair in 1905 that a series had come down to winner-take-all. With so much on the line, the two teams went at it hard in the March 30 finalé. Fifteen minor penalties and two majors were handed out during the opening 20 minutes but, with the referees demonstrating they were prepared to call everything, play continued rough but relatively clean.

Skene Ronan had put the Canadiens out front late in the first period when he swatted the puck past Tom Murray directly from a face-off. After a scoreless second, Portland came out hard to open the third period. Just over six minutes later, Tommy Dunderdale tied it up. "This," remarked the *Ottawa Citizen*, "was the commencement of even more grueling play than had been shown in either of the two periods previous." Both teams had chances to score before Lalonde set up Prodgers for the winning goal on a rink-long rush with under four minutes remaining.

"Pandemonium broke loose among 5,000 people, [and when] the whistle finally blew, hundreds stormed down and literally carried Newsy Lalonde and his teammates to their dressing quarters." For the Montreal Canadiens and their fans, it was the first of 24 Stanley Cup championships.

MAROONS AND CANADIENS 1928

Eric Zweig

THE RIVALRY BETWEEN THE MONTREAL MAROONS and the Montreal Canadiens lasted just a few seasons, but it marked one of the most intense periods for a city long inflamed by its passion for hockey. During this era, the NHL housed between six and 10 teams, and schedules ranged from 30 to 48 games, meaning the two clubs met a minimum of six times per season. And the hockey they played was top-notch. The Canadiens were defending Stanley Cup champions when the Maroons entered the league in 1924–25. One year later, the Maroons themselves were champions. By 1926–27, the two teams shared the same building—the Montreal Forum. Add to this mix the French-English element—the Maroons were English Montreal's team, while Habs fans were French Canadian—and all the pieces were in place for a bitter rivalry. Indeed, their games were often described as "classics of hockey hate."

The Montreal teams first met in the playoffs in 1927, with the Canadiens winning the two-game, total-goals quarterfinal series, 2–1, on an overtime tally by Howie Morenz. One year later, the two were at it again—this time with a berth in the Stanley Cup finals on the line.

The Canadiens and Maroons had finished 1–2 atop the Canadian Division in 1927–28 with the two best records in the NHL. Led by Morenz and Aurel Joliat, who finished first and second in the league both in goals and points, the Canadiens boasted the best offense with 116 goals in 44 games. The Maroons were second-best with 96 goals, Nels Stewart's 27 trailing only Morenz (33) and Joliat (28) among the NHL leaders. The Canadiens had a distinct advantage in goals-against, with George Hainsworth beaten by opposition shooters only 48 times while recording a 1.05 average. In this defensively oriented era, the Maroons' 77 goals against was only fifth-best in the 10-team league, as was Clint Benedict's 1.70 average.

By virtue of winning their division, the Canadiens received a bye through the first round of the playoffs. The Maroons had to take on the Ottawa Senators, but they disposed of the defending Stanley Cup champions by scores of 1–0 and 2–1 in the total-goals series. "Playoff fever was definitely in the air," wrote William Brown in his book *The Montreal Maroons*. "Hundreds of people gathered in front of Morgan's department store on St. Catherine Street (later The Bay) to hear news of [the second] game broadcast over loudspeakers. A few days later, when the Maroons and the Canadiens started their two-game series to decide the winner of the Canadian Division, the crowd outside Morgan's was so big that a mounted policeman was assigned to keep order."

The matchup of the Maroons and Canadiens got under way on March 31, 1928. The series opener was considered a Canadiens home game, so the crowd of nearly 13,000 that jammed the Forum was dominated by their supporters. They saw their well-rested team come out quickly, though action soon slowed as a parade of players made its way to the penalty box. Most of the period's 13 penalties were levied against the Canadiens, though at one point the Maroons found themselves three men short. (Not until 1943–44 did the NHL add rules to remedy such situations.) They managed to kill off Red Dutton's penalty, but were still down two players when Battleship Leduc stuffed the puck past Clint Benedict, who had lost his stick making an earlier save. The Maroons appeared to be in real trouble when Art Gagne upped the lead to 2–0 early in the second, but then the Flying Frenchmen were finally done in by their own penalties.

With the Canadiens playing two men short—and Battleship Leduc trapped deep in the Maroons end—Dunc Munro and Jimmy Ward combined on a play that cut the lead to 2–1. The Canadiens still had two men in the box (players did not return to the ice after a goal was scored until 1956–57) when Nels Stewart won the ensuing face-off and rushed in on the depleted defense. He passed to Hooley Smith, whose quick shot fooled George Hainsworth and tied the score just 20 seconds after the Maroons' first goal. Stellar work by Hainsworth and Benedict in the third period saw the game end 2–2 and meant that the winner of the next game would advance to the Stanley Cup final.

Babe Siebert, who'd been moved to defense that season by Maroons coach Eddie Gerard, was hospitalized after the opening game with a case of the flu, but with two days off before the teams resumed action on April 3, he would be back in uniform for game two. So was Pit Lepine of the Canadiens, who had been out of action for six weeks with a broken collarbone.

Another sellout crowd filled the Forum for the finalé, but this time the majority of fans were Maroons supporters. Among those on hand was Montreal's newly elected mayor Camillien Houde who dropped the ceremonial face-off. Once the game faced off for real, the fans were treated to a much more wide-open affair than the penalty-filled first contest—though Howie Morenz did lose a couple of teeth in an altercation with Red Dutton. The goaltenders were the stars of the game and the two teams were scoreless after regulation time.

"During the brief rest before the first extra period, the Maroons struck some observers as being the fresher of the two teams," wrote William Brown. "It seemed that Eddie Gerard's two-line, short-shift strategy had begun to take its toll on the Canadiens" whose coach, Cecil Hart, relied heavily on his top line of Morenz, Joliat and Gagne. Indeed, it was one of the Maroons' superior second-line players who would make the difference. With just over eight minutes of overtime played, Russell Oatman took off on an end-to-end rush. Though George Hainsworth stopped his initial drive, Oatman continued hard toward the net and drilled the rebound between the goaltender's legs. The game was over.

For winning the series, the Montreal Maroons earned the George Kennedy Memorial Cup honoring the former owner of the Canadiens, but the big prize—the Stanley Cup—would elude them. Though all five games of the Stanley Cup final were played at the Forum due to a circus at Madison Square Garden, the New York Rangers beat the Maroons, three games to two. This was the series in which Lester Patrick made his legendary appearance in goal after Lorne Chabot suffered a serious eye injury in game two. Two years later, the Canadiens would win the first of consecutive Stanley Cup titles, and in 1935 the Maroons won their second NHL championship, but the two great Montreal rivals never again faced each other in the heat of playoff competition after 1928.

Rangers and Boston 1939

Stan Fischler

In establishing themselves among the National Hockey League's elite teams, the pre-World War II Boston Bruins had everything a dynasty requires, from offense to defense to goaltending and coaching.

Boston's success began with Frank Brimsek's airtight work in goal and ended with the awesome attacking unit of Milt Schmidt, Bobby Bauer and Woody Dumart, which operated under several pseudonyms but was mostly known as "the Kraut Line." In between, there was a healthy sprinkling of defensive aces such as Eddie Shore, Flash Hollett and Jack Portland, not to mention a wise, old coach named Art Ross. For added fillips the Bruins boasted Bill Cowley, a creative playmaking center of considerable repute, and 1938–39's goal-scoring leader, Roy Conacher.

The Bruins' excellence during this era was reflected in the standings. They produced the NHL's best record in 1937–38, 1938–39, 1939–40 and 1940–41. But it was during the 1939 playoffs that Boston's claim to greatness was firmly established. Until that year, the Bruins had won only a single Stanley Cup title (1929) since entering the league in 1924. In 1939, they would face the New York Rangers in the opening round. It was considered a superb playoff matchup because the Rangers had been runners-up to Boston—though they were 16 points behind in the standings. Added to the mix was the animosity between the teams. Art chided his New York counterpart Lester Patrick for his team's "streamline" passing plays, while the Rangers coach labeled the Bruins a roughhouse outfit.

In discussing the upcoming playoff set, nobody mentioned Mel Hill, a right wing out of Glenboro, Manitoba. Why should they? Hill hardly had distinguished himself in his first full season with Boston, collecting 10 goals and 10 assists in 46 games while playing in the shadow of The Krauts and Cowley. Hill remained obscure as the best-of-seven series opened at Madison Square Garden on March 21. The game was tied 1–1 at the end of regulation time and remained that way through two sudden-death periods until Ross decided to alter his strategy for the third.

"They're covering Conacher too well," said the Bruins coach. "Instead of feeding Roy, it would be better to feed Hill."

The plan did not work immediately, but late in the third overtime session, Cowley crossed into the New York zone. He lured defenseman Muzz Patrick toward him while skating for the corner. Hill camped in front of goalie Dave Kerr and converted Cowley's perfect pass at 1:10 a.m.

Game two at Boston Garden was a replica of the opener except that the teams were tied 2–2 after 60 minutes and minor league goalie Bert Gardiner had replaced Kerr in goal for the Rangers. What had not changed was the Ross game plan. His Cowley-Hill tandem was now a key unit and its value was underlined at 8:24 of the first overtime. Once again Cowley had challenged the New York defense sufficiently to distract them before dishing the puck to his unobtrusive sidekick. Hill then drove a 40-foot shot past Gardiner and the Bruins led two games to nothing.

The series appeared decided after Boston coasted to a 4–1 victory in game three, but the Rangers would not be dispatched so easily. In a bloody match, highlighted by a bout in which Muzz Patrick knocked out Eddie Shore, the Rangers rallied for a 2–1 win. They followed up with another 2–1 victory in game five and a 3–1 margin to tie the series after six. Gardiner had won all three games for New York, matching Brimsek save for save.

No team ever had come back from a three-game deficit to win a playoff series and now, with the score tied 1–1 after regulation, the Rangers had that opportunity. From the first overtime, game seven at Boston Garden on April 2, 1939, took on all aspects of a gem among clinchers.

Neither team had scored after two sudden-death periods and with more than seven minutes of the third overtime expired, the excruciatingly close match remained deadlocked. Finally, grizzled defenseman Eddie Shore launched an attack, moving the puck to sharpshooter Roy Conacher, whose shot the Rangers justifiably had feared. Conacher wristed a hard drive that Gardiner accepted with ease but then the goaltender's radar failed him.

Presuming that a friendly defenseman was near his net, Gardiner tossed the puck to the corner of the rink but

Cowley was there first and skimmed a pass toward the fellow wearing the brown-and-yellow jersey with number 18 who was camped in front of the New York net. The embattled goalie sensed disaster the moment he saw Hill but it was too late. The young Bruin had slammed the puck into the webbing and it was over.

Mel Hill's third overtime goal had won the game and the series. For his heroics, he instantly earned the nickname "Sudden Death" Hill, which would last forever. It is interesting to note, however, that Mel Hill would never have had the opportunity to score the first of this three overtime goals had not an errant bodycheck sent referee Mickey Ion over the boards. Ion's tumble meant he missed seeing a goal by Bobby Bauer, which would have given the Bruins the win earlier in game one.

After beating the Rangers, Boston dismissed the Toronto Maple Leafs in five games to win the Stanley Cup while Lester Patrick returned to New York believing that his club could have won it all had he not misjudged one chunky, 175-pound athlete from Glenboro, Manitoba.

"I could have had Mel Hill," Patrick recalled, "but I turned him down because he was too small. I didn't think he could stand the strain of a full season and the tough playoffs. I was wrong."

After winning the Stanley Cup in 1939, the Bruins finished first overall again in 1939–40. Schmidt led the NHL in scoring, with Dumart and Bauer tied for second place. It was a toss-up as to which of the three was most important to the Bruins' success. Dumart was invaluable as a checking forward and Schmidt was the master playmaker. Bauer was equally indispensible, once described by Schmidt as "my right arm."

The Rangers got their revenge on Boston with a first-round playoff victory in 1940, though the Bruins won the Cup again in 1941. But as the winds of war blew across Europe, many Canadians enlisted in the armed forces. Among the first to go was the Kraut Line. In February, 1942, the Boston dynasty came to an end when Schmidt, Bauer and Dumart enlisted together in the Royal Canadian Air Force. As for Mel Hill, his career with the Bruins had ended one year earlier when he was demoted to the American Hockey League during the 1940–41 campaign. He soon returned to the NHL with the Brooklyn Americans and later won the Stanley Cup again with Toronto in 1945.

TORONTO AND DETROIT 1942

Stan Fischler

As WORLD WAR II RAGED ON, it was clear that the 1942 Stanley Cup playoffs would be the last in which many star performers would participate before entering the armed forces of Canada and the United States.

The Toronto Maple Leafs, who had last won the championship in 1932, had a formidable sextet built around Turk Broda's clutch goaltending, the scoring of Syl Apps, Gordie Drillon and Sweeney Schriner, and a hard-hitting defensive corps anchored by Bucko McDonald. Former Leafs defenseman Clarence "Hap" Day was behind the bench on a team whose patriarch, Conn Smythe, already had enlisted for military duty and was now Major Smythe of the 30th Light Antiaircraft Battery, which he had mobilized.

By any standards, the Detroit team that met the Maple Leafs in the 1942 Stanley Cup final was an underdog. The Red Wings had finished fifth in the seven-team NHL, 15 points behind second-place Toronto, and barely had edged the Montreal Canadiens to reach the semifinals. They then upset the defending champion Boston Bruins and entered the Cup round with their coach's words ringing in their ears.

"We may not be the greatest hockey club in the world," said Jack Adams, "but we're loaded with fighting heart."

"Don't underestimate the Detroit club," Major Smythe warned his troops from his army camp in Petawawa, Ontario. "They can skate and they're going to run at us. Unless we match them check for check and stride for stride, we're going to be in trouble."

He was right.

Until that point in hockey history, conventional attacking strategy was based on a forward line passing or stickhandling its way past the enemy defenses which lined up to repel them. Suddenly—and unexpectedly—Adams changed all that. His forwards would toss the puck into Toronto territory, outrace the slow defensemen and forecheck them into errors. Artistic, it was not; effective it was as the new strategy caught the Leafs flatfooted.

While Torontonians got a collective case of lockjaw, Detroit hammered out three straight victories. Even more humiliating, the first pair of wins were at Maple Leaf Gardens. "You got the idea," wrote Vern DeGeer in the *Toronto Globe and Mail*, "that it was all over but the shouting."

Hap Day did little shouting. Instead, he quietly executed one of the most daring plans ever tried in a championship sports series. The coach benched his leading scorer, Drillon, and veteran defenseman McDonald, replacing them with little-known Don Metz up front and rookie Ernie Dickens on defense. He also read a letter from a 14-year-old girl who expressed her conviction that the Leafs could still win.

Nevertheless, it looked hopeless when the Red Wings opened a 2–0 lead in game four at Olympia Stadium and Toronto still had not put a shot past goalie John Mowers half way through the match. The Leafs did rally, but still trailed 3–2 after six minutes of the third period. It was then that Captain Apps organized the grand comeback. He tied the score at 6:15 and then—along with fill-in Don Metz—set up Nick Metz for the winner at 12:45.

The 4–3 victory did not conclude without incident. Furious over Mel Harwood's officiating, Adams leaped over the boards following the final buzzer and hurled blows at the official. When the dust had cleared, Adams was suspended indefinitely by NHL President Frank Calder and replaced behind the bench by aging forward Ebbie Goodfellow. Day not only retained Don Metz in the lineup but gambled further with youth by adding 19-year-old left wing Gaye Stewart.

Game five at Maple Leaf Gardens on April 14 was the contest that eternally sealed Don Metz's name among unlikely heroes. The Wilcox, Saskatchewan, wheat farmer went wild that night, scoring three goals and chipping in an assist, during the 9–3 drubbing of Detroit. Suddenly, it was a series.

Leading three games to two, the Red Wings hoped to put the lid on matters once and for all on home ice. Detroit's shooters opened game six by firing everything at Broda, but the score was 0–0 at the end of one and all signs suggested that the first goal would prove to be the winner. And it was.

Only 14 seconds into the second period Don Metz did it again, beating Mowers unassisted. A pair of third-period insurance goals by Schriner not only upped the final score to 3–0 but cast a pall over the Olympia. Nothing said it better than the sight of a flounder hurled on to the ice late in the third period. "That dead fish," said Leafs publicist Ed Fitkin, "seemed to be symbolic of Detroit fans' reaction to the collapse of their Red Wings."

Except for one thing; the Red Wings weren't dead yet.

Detroit showed up ready for the final game at Maple Leaf Gardens on April 18, 1942, and so did the largest crowd to that point in Canadian hockey history—16,240 fans, including Major Conn Smythe, on leave from the Canadian army. Smythe saw his team fall behind 1–0 on Syd Howe's second-period goal and watched Detroit maintain its slim lead through seven minutes of the third frame.

The Leafs needed a break, and they got it early in the third period when referee Bill Chadwick whistled Jimmy Orlando into the penalty box for two minutes. Coach Day sent the Schriner line out for the power-play instead of Apps and the Metz brothers and Schriner responded with the tying goal. The Leafs were alive again!

It appeared as if the next goal would be the Cup-clincher and just after the nine-minute mark, Day gambled by sending out a line comprising young center Pete Langelle with veteran left wing Bob Davidson and Johnny McCreedy on the right side. Immediately they stormed into Red Wing ice, McCreedy leading the way with a shot on Mowers. The Detroit goalie moved far out of his cage to deflect the drive, but the puck rebounded back into play and Mowers was stranded away from the gaping net. In a desperate lunge the Detroit defense tried to cover Mowers's abandoned net, but Langelle pounced on the puck and smacked it into the cage.

For the next six minutes the Red Wings desperately sought the equalizer but Schriner delivered his second goal of the game at 16:13 and Detroit was finished.

When the bell sounded to end the game, Maple Leaf Gardens thundered to its foundations as every player on the Toronto bench leaped over the boards to celebrate. Blood streaming from a cut down the side of his nose, Syl Apps dashed back to the bench and grabbed Major Smythe. "C'mon, Connie," he yelled, "and get the Cup!"

Never before and never again has a team lost the first three games of the Stanley Cup finals and then pulled itself together to win the next four and the championship. Canada's legendary broadcaster Foster Hewitt summed it up best when he said, "This was a team with the fight to turn a rout into a triumph."

CANADIENS AND DETROIT 1954

Ken Campbell

IT WAS THE SPRING OF 1954 AND THE HOCKEY WORLD—like the real one—was ripe for change. With conflicts escalating in Indo-China, fear and loathing of the Communist menace began to spread throughout the United States. The fear was fueled by a Wisconsin senator named Joe McCarthy who said the USA "may well die" because of an 18-month delay in hydrogen bomb research he claimed was caused by "Communists in the government of former President Truman."

In the hockey world, Jean Beliveau and Jacques Plante were finishing up the NHL season after making indelible marks on the game. Beliveau, a former star with the Quebec Aces, had signed a five-year contract worth $100,000 that was the richest in NHL history at the time. Plante—not yet a fulltime NHL netminder—was already baffling shooters and teammates alike with his wandering ways and ability to handle the puck. Elsewhere, Red Kelly was the first to win the Norris Trophy, a new award to recognize the NHL's best defenseman. Detroit Red Wings executive Marguerite Norris would become the first woman to have her name engraved on the Stanley Cup. Meanwhile, the Soviet Union had served notice of its future dominance on the international scene with its first World Championship in a 7–2 win over Canada in Stockholm.

And for the first time in his life, Terrible Ted Lindsay kissed a man.

The man Lindsay kissed was Tony Leswick, an unheralded left wing who scored 4:29 into overtime in game seven of the Stanley Cup finals to give the Wings their first of two straight Cup triumphs over the Canadiens. Leswick, who played on the Wings' checking line with Glen Skov and Marty Pavelich, took a shot from 30 feet out that hit the glove of Canadiens defenseman Doug Harvey and caromed over the shoulder of Habs goalie Gerry McNeil.

"You little toad," Lindsay said to Leswick before kissing him twice.

You can forgive Lindsay for his actions. One of the fiercest competitors in NHL history was simply caught up in the moment of exhilaration that capped one of the most memorable pre-expansion series in NHL history.

The Wings were in the midst of a dynasty that saw them finish first in the regular season an NHL-record seven straight times while taking the Stanley Cup three times in a four-year span. The Canadiens, with 10 future Hall of Famers in the lineup, were on the cusp of winning five straight Stanley Cup titles and establishing the dynasty by which all others are measured. It's little wonder the 1954 series was marked by two glaring characteristics: the razor-thin margin of victory and the utter disdain the teams had for one another.

"They were a great team, but we were even better," Lindsay said. "We had a hatred for one another and it was a wonderful way to play hockey. Every game was a war."

Gerry McNeil, who had to skate the length of the rink past the delirious Red Wings in order to get off the ice after giving up the winning goal, said it was the longest skate of his life. Many of the 15,791 fans who jammed the Detroit Olympia were trying to scale the screen at the end of the rink to get on the ice and celebrate with their heroes. The Canadiens were so disgusted, they refused to abide by the time-honored tradition of shaking hands after a series.

"I was a young guy and I was following our leaders," said Canadiens left wing Dickie Moore. "Doug Harvey was a great leader, and when he left the ice we followed him. Why would you want to shake the hand of a guy who just beat you anyway? We didn't want to give them any more satisfaction because we hated them and they hated us."

The series had begun 12 days earlier on April 4. The Red Wings had taken game one 3–1 on the strength of a goal and an assist by Dutch Reibel, who had been exiled from the Production Line in favor of Alex Delvecchio. Game two saw the Canadiens win by the same score. All three Montreal goals came within 56 seconds on a two-man advantage after Leswick and Gordie Howe had taken minor penalties 19 seconds apart. Detroit general manager Jack Adams was furious and co-owner Bruce Norris filed a protest with the league saying referee Red Storey, a Montreal resident, was on the Canadiens' payroll. Adams said Canadiens general manager Frank Selke had admitted it during a league meeting.

"I thought Adams was kidding," Selke said. "I certainly was kidding. I merely went along with the joke." Meanwhile, Selke had a battle of his own when he ran into the crowd to take on a fan who held up a sign which read: "Rocket Richard Stinks."

With both Harvey and Jean Beliveau injured for the Canadiens, the Red Wings easily took the third game by a 5–2 score. "Irvin should appreciate Harvey now," said Adams after the game, referring to Canadiens coach Dick Irvin and insinuating that the coach and his teammates gave Harvey too much abuse. Irvin responded by saying that the Wings had abandoned goalie Terry Sawchuk at the end of the season as he battled Harry Lumley of the Toronto Maple Leafs for the Vezina Trophy. "We beat them 6–1 at the end of the year and every time we scored, their defensemen were laughing," said Irvin.

After the Red Wings took the fourth game, 2–0, Irvin made the bold move of replacing Plante with McNeil. Plante had been spectacular since being called up from Buffalo and McNeil hadn't played a game since February 11. Still, he blanked the Red Wings, 2–0, in game five and beat them, 4–1, in game six ... only to allow Leswick's winning goal to bounce past him in game seven.

Not only did the Leswick-Skov-Pavelich line produce the Stanley Cup-winning goal for Detroit, it also had kept Montreal's big shooters at bay. Rocket Richard was frustrated throughout the series, jumping from line to line in an effort to break out. He had just one even-strength goal during the 1954 final.

"We always figured those guys put us up by a half-a-goal a game because they checked the best lines in the league," Lindsay said. "Marty Pavelich was a great player who never got the recognition he deserved. He had an understanding for the game that was beyond most people."

As for McNeil, he gave way to Plante again the next season and, with the exception of a short stint with the Canadiens when they won the Cup in 1957, spent the rest of his career in the minors.

"Doug Harvey apologized to me lots of times after that goal," McNeil said. "But he didn't have to. You could see it in his face."

CHICAGO AND TORONTO 1967

Stephen Cole

WE REMEMBER THE MAPLE LEAFS' 1967 playoff upset of the Chicago Black Hawks not because it was so unlikely, but because it offers a dramatically satisfying instance of a magnificent, flawed sporting hero's last triumphant stand.

The Hawks that year established 12 regular-season scoring records. The Scooter Line—Stan Mikita, Kenny Wharram and Doug Mohns—was an unmatched blend of speed, finesse and daring. The club's best attacker was Bobby Hull, who could shoot a puck harder (128 miles per hour) than any hockey player who lived. The opening-round goalie who stood in Chicago's way that playoff season was Toronto's Terry Sawchuk, arguably the best netminder in NHL history, but at age 37, a diminished warrior whose body ached from three decades of hard winters.

A difficult life punctuated by a car crash, mental breakdown, family problems and the pounding of two generations of hockey shooters had whittled Sawchuk down to 150 pounds. One arm was crooked and his back throbbed from two recent operations. Three times that season he had tried to retire, only to be talked back into the barrel by Leafs coach Punch Imlach.

Sawchuk seemed lost in a 5–2 Hawks victory in the playoff opener, but his fierce professionalism and peerless technique—he could play forwards as if they were drawn to him on a string—prevented him from going into slumps. In the next two games, which Leafs won by identical 3–1 scores, the Hawks found shooting at Sawchuk was like trying to beat a brick wall.

While Sawchuk messed with opponents' minds, teammates worked their bodies. The Leafs' best line—Jim Pappin, Bob Pulford, and Pete Stemkowski—threw its weight around with murderous aplomb. And defenders Allan Stanley, Tim Horton, Marcel Pronovost and Larry Hillman extracted bumps and bruises from any Hawk who entered the corners or goal crease. Still, this was a great, resourceful Hawks team. The fourth game, in Toronto, saw Chicago expertly deploy all its weapons, jumping to a 4–2 lead. The Leafs intensified their attack late in the contest, with Punch pulling Sawchuk (with four minutes left!) to help create a Mike Walton goal, but the Hawks escaped with a thrilling 4–3 win.

Now the series returned to Chicago, with Toronto reeling. Not only had the Hawks regained home-ice advantage, but Sawchuk appeared dead on his skates at the end of game four. Imlach turned to Johnny Bower for the fifth match, but the veteran netminder was hurt and hadn't played in weeks. The rust was apparent in an early stretch that saw Johnny misplay a clearing shot and leave a fat rebound for Hull. The Leafs hung on like a boxer in trouble trying to make it to the bell and the first 20 minutes ended in a 2–2 tie.

Toronto seemed old and tired when Sawchuk entered the game to begin the second period. He was hurt, having re-injured a shoulder that had given him trouble all year.

When the puck was dropped to begin a Hawks power-play early in the second period, Mikita pulled it back to

Pierre Pilote. Number 21 got the puck back, circled and then spotted Hull charging from the point.

"Hull was 30 feet out when he took the big swing," Red Kelly remembers. "That puck got off the ice so fast, it was like a golfer using a sand wedge. You wouldn't have thought a hockey stick could make a shot like that. Well, that was that danged curved stick. Anyway, Ukie probably never saw the ... rocket that caught him high in the shoulder. He went down like someone shot him."

Coming to, Sawchuk lifted himself to one elbow and gave his head a shake. "Stay down, Ukie," a grinning Pilote said, passing through the crease. The goalie shot him a murderous glare, then climbed back into position.

For the rest of the period, Chicago rained rubber on Sawchuk. Always it was the same men shooting: Mikita, Wharram, Mohns, Pilote and Hull. Especially Hull. Five times he tested the Leaf goalie with his best shot. On each occasion, Sawchuk took a hard shot somewhere to the body. The Scooters tried to overwhelm the Leaf goalie with guile, throwing the puck around in search of their favorite equation—an open man and an empty net. A man was sometimes open, but the net, never.

"Terry put on a clinic that afternoon," sportswriter Milt Dunnell recalls. "In [the second period] the Hawks must've had 15 quality chances. Hull could've scored three or four goals. Yes, I'd seen goaltending like that before—from Sawchuk in the early 1950s. After Hull hit him with that shot, he somehow reached back 15 years. It was the most remarkable demonstration of goaltending I've ever seen."

As was often the case with this Leaf team, Toronto took advantage of a lull in the Hawk attack for a swift, deadly counter-attack, with Stemkowski ramming in a rebound early in the third period. Now facing defeat in a pivotal matchup, Chicago took control of the game for 10 minutes. After standing Sawchuk up with high blasts all game, Hull blazed a low 30-footer that the locked-in-a-crouch Leaf goalie toed aside. During a power-play, brawny Ken Hodge got all his weight into a slapshot that hit the advancing Sawchuk in the arm, spinning him around. Seconds later, Mohns was in free. Sweeping across the front of the net, he tried a series of moves, but Sawchuk kept with him. For Mohns it was like trying to deke your image in a mirror. The finalé finally threw a weak backhand into the goalie's pads. Exhausted and out of ideas, the Chicago Black Hawks threw in what was by now a bloody towel.

"Sawchuk and all our hitting finally took its toll," Brian Conacher recalled.

The Leafs scored another goal late and won, 4–2. "I'll always remember Sawchuk after that game," Ron Ellis recalls. "He had ugly bruises up his arms and shoulders. He could barely move. It looked like he'd been badly beaten in a fight. Players saw that. They knew what it took to stand up to Bobby Hull's shot time and again. We were determined to go out next game and give him the support he deserved."

Indeed, in the sixth and final game back in Toronto, the determined Leafs protected Sawchuk as if he were fine china, taking the game, 3–1. The goalie was almost as heroic in games five and six of the triumphant Stanley Cup-winning series over Montreal that followed. Though Sawchuk would bounce around for three seasons after expansion and would die tragically in 1970, he will forever be remembered for what has justly been called one of the greatest, and certainly most dramatic, goaltending performances of all time.

CANADIENS AND BOSTON 1971

Dick Irvin

ON THE FINAL DAY OF THE NHL'S 1970–71 SEASON the Boston Bruins defeated the Montreal Canadiens 7–2 at the Boston Garden. The Bruins thus ended the 78-game campaign with 57 wins, 121 points and 399 goals scored—all new league records. Phil Esposito, Boston's brilliant center, captured the scoring title with a record 152 points, tallying a then-unimaginable total of 76 goals, 18 more than Bobby Hull's previous record. Esposito's teammate, Bobby Orr, was second in scoring with 139 points—including a record 102 assists. Johnny Bucyk and Ken Hodge ranked third and fourth in the league with 116 and 105 points respectively. The Bruins had finished the regular season 24 points ahead of the third-place Canadiens, who stayed in Boston to open the playoffs two nights later. Esposito's 152 points were exactly twice that of Montreal's scoring leader, Jean Beliveau, and the defending Stanley Cup champion Bruins appeared to be a lock to repeat.

Montreal coach Al MacNeil raised a few eyebrows by naming rookie goaltender Ken Dryden to start the series ahead of Rogatien Vachon. Originally a Boston draft choice back in 1964, Dryden had opted to attend Cornell University instead. He had not played in the NHL until March of the 1970–71 season and had appeared in only six games. While he had won them all, MacNeil's choice was still a surprise. "Our other goalers, Vachon and [Phil] Myre, were inconsistent," the coach would later explain. "Dryden had the hot hand."

The Bruins didn't overpower Dryden in the opener, but they did control the game and won 3–1. MacNeil stuck with Dryden two nights later, a decision that seemed headed for serious controversy when the Bruins took a 5–1 lead in the second period. Late in that frame, Montreal's Henri Richard swept around Orr to score on Boston goalie Eddie Johnston. It was 5–2 Bruins after two. Richard's goal seemed inconsequential, but it started the Canadiens on one of the biggest single-game comebacks in the long history of the franchise.

Early in the third period Jean Beliveau pinned a Bruin on the boards behind the Boston net, stole the puck and passed to John Ferguson whose quick shot beat Johnston to make the score 5–3. A couple of minutes later, Beliveau, who by then was turning back his hockey calendar and totally dominating the ice, beat Johnston with a beautiful backhand shot; 5–4.

Midway through the period Orr misplayed a pass at the Canadiens blue line allowing Jacques Lemaire to take off on a breakaway and beat the now-beleaguered Johnston with a vicious slap shot from just inside the Bruins blue line. Tie game.

The Bruins were floundering. With five minutes left in the period Beliveau made yet another brilliant play and again set up Ferguson, who scored to give the Canadiens a 6–5 lead. Frank Mahovlich added the clincher a minute later. The final score of 7–5, and the memories of how it got that way, are still indelibly etched in the minds of Canadiens fans from that era.

Boston coach Tom Johnson had alternated goaltenders all

season, and Gerry Cheevers was in the net for the third game in Montreal. It would be the Bruins' old pro against the Canadiens' raw rookie for the balance of the series. The teams split the next two games at the Forum, 3–2 Montreal and 5–2 Boston. The Bruins were only one win away from their expected series victory when they followed up with an easy 7–3 victory on home ice in game five.

With Dryden having been scored on 12 times in two games it seemed time for MacNeil to turn to the more experienced Vachon for game six in Montreal. But he stayed with Dryden who made a brilliant glove save on Orr early in the game and lit a spark under his team and the home crowd at the Forum. The Canadiens won big that night, 8–3. When Dryden's name was announced as receiving an assist on a goal late in the game, the fans gave the rookie netminder a standing ovation.

Game seven was played at the Boston Garden on Sunday afternoon, April 18. The Bruins took an early 1–0 lead on a goal by Ken Hodge. They were dominating the game early, but Dryden was brilliant against the team that had shattered so many scoring records during the regular season. One save in particular has been replayed many times on television. After Dryden dropped to the ice to make a big stop on Phil Esposito (who was limited to just three goals in the series), the Bruins superstar vented his frustration by smashing his stick against the glass behind the fallen Montreal goalie.

The Canadiens won the game 4–2 with Frank Mahovlich setting up Jacques Lemaire on a perfectly executed two-on-one break for the winning goal in the third period. When the team returned home to Montreal that evening, some 5,000 fans were on hand to greet them at Dorval airport. "Even if the Canadiens had come back from Boston with the Stanley Cup, they hardly could have expected a greater reception," reported *The Hockey News*. Exactly one month later, after victories over Minnesota and Chicago, the Montreal Canadiens had won a Stanley Cup title almost everyone had conceded to the runaway league champions from Boston. Dryden had played every game in goal for Montreal throughout the playoffs and was rewarded with the Conn Smythe Trophy as most valuable player.

The Canadiens victories over the North Stars and Black Hawks were hard-fought affairs, but the series against the Bruins is the one that seems to have remained uppermost in the minds of hockey fans. It was called an "upset," but should the victory really be considered that much of a surprise? Before the series, Canadiens defenseman Terry Harper had boasted that Montreal had the better team. There were eight future Hall of Famers on the Canadiens roster. The Bruins only had four. Certainly Phil Esposito and Bobby Orr had been the greatest players in the game that season, but the Canadiens lineup featured legendary names such as Jean Beliveau, Frank Mahovlich, Yvan Cournoyer, Jacques Lemaire, Jacques Laperriere, Guy Lapointe and Henri Richard. And of course, there was that unknown rookie goaltender, Ken Dryden, who took the first giant step toward his place in the Hockey Hall of Fame by standing tall against the greatest scoring team the game had ever seen. So perhaps it wasn't such an "upset" after all when the Montreal Canadiens eliminated the Boston Bruins back in the spring of 1971.

EDMONTON AND CALGARY 1986

Mark Paddock

THE CALGARY FLAMES may have had the second-ranked offense in 1985–86, but so did the Edmonton Oilers—second all-time that is, with 426 goals. Who could skate, shoot or score with the two-time defending champions? Their forward tandems of Mark Messier-Glenn Anderson and Wayne Gretzky-Jari Kurri were unmatched, and, in Paul Coffey, their blue line had a 138-point facsimile of Bobby Orr. It seemed every Oiler could make creative plays at top speed, and no opponent could think or move fast enough to stop them.

However, Calgary had been built especially to stop Edmonton through size, strength and toughness. Complementing a raft of skilled 20-goal scorers, players like Jim Peplinski, Neil Sheehy, Tim Hunter, Doug Risebrough and Paul Baxter had lots of penalty minutes and even more desire. Still, it wouldn't be enough to try to intimidate the Oilers in their quarterfinal playoff series. Calgary coach Bob Johnson had to come up with a defensive plan and his players had to implement it perfectly.

Studying videotape of the Oilers until his eyes turned red, Johnson created a seven-point program to defeat them. Normally, Johnson was the most affable, outgoing coach in the league, but he made sure no one spoke about the program. He ordered his players not to utter any revealing words to the media. But as the series progressed, the elements of his strategy became clear.

The Flames sent one forechecker deep and closed off the neutral zone with the other skaters. Rather than concentrate on Gretzky—a tactic which had failed them in the past—the Flames played man-to-man, trying to limit his passing options by covering both him and his teammates. Finally, the Flames defensemen made sure they didn't give Edmonton space to skate at the Calgary blueline. Ironically, despite the defensive strategy, the series is remembered for its deeply exciting, up-tempo play. Edmonton could not be stopped from playing its game, it could only be slowed down as Calgary's style created turnovers and rapid counterattacks for the Flames.

The one element that couldn't be planned was goaltending. Edmonton's Grant Fuhr was the world's best. At the other end, Calgary relied on rookie Mike Vernon, who hadn't lost for over a month and who had gained Johnson's trust with his controlled, unemotional style.

Edmonton looked unfocused in game one, taking silly penalties and missing prime scoring chances. Calgary won, 4–1. Key defenseman Al MacInnis and netminder Vernon both missed game two with minor injuries, allowing Edmonton to capitalize offensively. The Flames helped out by abandoning their game plan in the third period. Still, a late goal by Joe Mullen allowed Calgary to force overtime. In the extra frame, Glenn Anderson grabbed a lucky bounce, skated in on Rejean Lemelin and scored the winner.

Calgary's fans sensed the Flames were a different team this year, and they welcomed them home raucously for game three. The Flames responded with a dominating performance, making life easy for the returning Vernon. Still, the score was only 3–2. Coming off a subpar game, Fuhr had been outstanding—though he guessed incorrectly on the winner, committing to Jamie Macoun on a 2-on-1 break. Macoun passed to a trailing forward, Joel Otto, and the rookie no one had wanted to sign (he was practically forced on the Flames by agent Brian Burke) popped it into the net. Afterwards, Edmonton coach Glen Sather said he was disappointed in his players. In his view, they weren't making the extra effort to find space. Paul Coffey responded that when he rushed the puck, five men converged on him, making him feel like he was on the small ice of the Boston Garden.

Facing the prospect of falling behind 3–1 in games, Wayne Gretzky responded with a masterful show for Canadian viewers on CBC and Americans who watched game four on ESPN. Skating, controlling the puck and setting up plays as only he could, The Great One was on the ice for every goal and finished the night with three of his own plus two assists as Edmonton whipped Calgary, 7–4.

Game five in Edmonton started at a fast pace, and Vernon repelled Anderson on a breakaway in the second minute. The Flames took the lead, but the Oilers fought back though they could not put the puck past Vernon. Neil Sheehy helped by checking Gretzky into the ice and Calgary skated away with a 4–1 victory.

Lee Fogolin, a leader on Edmonton's defense, was lost for the series in the fifth game and Sather replaced him with rookie Steve Smith. In game six, Smith speared Carey Wilson, sending him to emergency surgery in order to remove a ruptured spleen. Smith didn't know what had happened, but the Flames took his number. Meanwhile, a concerned Sather switched Anderson to Gretzky's line and sent Kurri to Messier's line. The Oilers received the message, bouncing back from a two-goal deficit to win, 5–2. Anderson, one of the few Oilers to shine throughout the series, one-timed the winner through Vernon's legs. Fuhr performed his usual daily miracle by stopping Wilson on a four-on-one rush.

Game seven promised to be a classic. By this time, all of Canada had become so captivated by the series, that CBC unofficially elevated its coverage from regional to nationwide, using its parliamentary channel to bring the game to viewers in the east. The Flames showed no fear by racing to a 2–0 lead on goals by Hakan Loob and Jim Peplinski, but they became nervous and retreated into a defense-only posture. Gretzky and Anderson combined to score on a two-on-one before Messier, fighting off a pulled groin, tied the match on a breakaway. Midway through the third period, the decisive play occurred. Smith circled behind his net to pick up a dump-in by Perry Berezan. Trying a high-risk, cross-ice pass, Smith bounced the puck off Fuhr's leg and into his own net. Some Flames, thinking of Wilson, thought it was poetic justice.

There still was time for a comeback, but Vernon rose to the occasion and refused to let Edmonton tie it. After the final whistle, the Flames leaped from the bench to embrace their rookie star. The Oilers watched in shock. Exhausted by the effort, Calgary managed to edge St. Louis in the semifinals before crashing against Montreal in the championship round. For many Flames, beating the Oilers had been their only goal, their own version of the Stanley Cup. It would take them three more years to finish the job properly.

New York and Vancouver 1994

Stan Fischler

"1940! 1940!"For two decades, the sound reverberated through the ears of New York Rangers fans. It was a chant uttered by their New York Islanders counterparts, mocking the fact that the Broadway Blueshirts had not won the Stanley Cup since the early months of World War II. To some New Yorkers, it seemed the day of redemption would never come. But in the fifth year of Neil Smith's reign as general manager, the Rangers were reorganized into a formidable force. Powerful leadership came from center Mark Messier, while Brian Leetch proved the quintessential two-way defenseman. Anchored by the acrobatic goaltending of Mike Richter, the Rangers finished first overall in 1993–94 and won the Presidents' Trophy for the second time in three years. But the road to the Stanley Cup was strewn with thorns.

The Rangers opened the playoffs with decisive victories over the Islanders and Washington Capitals, only to be confronted with a spunky New Jersey Devils squad in the Conference Finals. It shouldn't have been as hard as it was. New York was favored to win the Stanley Cup. What's more, the Blueshirts had won all six of the games played with the Devils during the regular campaign. "But," noted Devils captain Scott Stevens, "that was one season and this is a new one."

The Rangers' domination of the Devils stopped at 15:23 of the first overtime in game one, when Stephane Richer beat Richter for a 4–3 decision. It was the start of an intense series in which the Rangers rebounded with two straight triumphs—including a Stephane Matteau sudden-death winner—followed by another New Jersey victory. Then came the surprise in game five. With a roaring, sellout Madison Square Garden crowd behind them, the Rangers fell apart. From start to finish, New Jersey coach Jacques Lemaire's squad was in control. They took a 4–0 lead and won 4–1.

Game six at the Meadowlands was a media circus with the Rangers—given the combative nature of Mike Keenan—dominating the headlines. Captain Messier captured the imagination of New Yorkers when he turned the focus on himself with a daring ploy. He went on record guaranteeing a Rangers victory. Meanwhile, Jacques Lemaire lobbied for his Devils. "I want my players to get the recognition they deserve," he argued.

The argument on the ice on May 25, 1994, tilted in the Devils' favor in the first period as they took a 2–0 lead on goals by Scott Niedermayer and Claude Lemieux. Every aspect of Lemaire's game plan was working, a fact not overlooked by the New Yorkers. They were a dispirited lot heading to their dressing room and it was reflected in the first half of the second period. The Rangers appeared on the brink of elimination, but Messier was as good as his word. He scored three goals in the third and the Blueshirts took the game 4–2.

With the teams now tied at three games apiece, the series returned to the Garden for the curtain-closer. The Devils were regarded as too deflated to win and fell behind 1–0 early in the game. They remained behind until Valeri

Zelepukin tipped the puck past Richter to tie the game with just seven seconds remaining in the third period. The series would be decided in overtime.

Neither team scored in the first extra session and the game went into a second heart-throbbing overtime. As the Devils mounted an attack, a clearing pass was intercepted by Stephane Matteau. He moved down the left side and swerved behind the net where he tried to wrap the puck around the right post. For a split second the puck was lost but then it showed up inside the goal, somehow sneaking between the post and Martin Brodeur's pads. The Rangers had won a classic. The Garden crowd erupted. But the best was yet to come.

The Rangers had reached the Stanley Cup finals for the first time since 1979 and just the third time since 1950. Their opponent would be the upstart Vancouver Canucks who, despite the presence of superstar Pavel Bure and dynamic leader Trevor Linden, seemed less threatening than the Devils. Yet when the series opened in New York, Vancouver rallied to tie the score 2–2 late in the third period. Canuck goalie Kirk McLean was stupendous throughout and, to the utter deflation of the Garden crowd, Greg Adams beat Mike Richter in overtime to give Vancouver a one-game lead.

The Rangers rebounded for a 3–1 win in game two, and then swept both games in Vancouver for a three-games-to-one series lead. If ever there was a case of premature rejoicing, this was it. While the Mayor's office talked of parade plans, the New York City Police Department prepared for a jubilant riot.

The riot was not to come. Nor was the Ranger victory. The Canucks won game five 6–3 and sent the series back to Vancouver. On top of that, a report had surfaced that Mike Keenan had agreed to become coach and general manager of the Detroit Red Wings after the season. No such deal had been made, but the rumor was enough to set off a chain reaction of assertions and denials that would last through the rest of the series and beyond.

As for game six, the Canucks won, 4–1, and it was back to the Big Apple for the finalé. "If they beat us three straight they deserve to win the Stanley Cup," said Messier.

Before game seven Mike Keenan delivered what some consider his most arresting speech. The Rangers then took to the Garden ice and took the game in their hands. They jumped into an early lead and built on it. New York was up 2–0 entering the second period and the situation seemed well in hand until Trevor Linden scored a shorthand goal at 5:21. After Messier restored the two-goal lead the Rangers took the ice to start the third period with what appeared to be a comfortable cushion. However, the ubiquitous Linden scored on the power-play at 4:50 of the third, sending the Rangers into a defensive shell.

New York's lead remained intact as the clock ticked down below the five-minute mark. At that point, Canucks youngster Nathan LaFayette came within an inch of bursting the balloon, but his shot struck the post behind Mike Richter and bounced harmlessly away.

As those in the overflow crowd bit fingernails, held their breath and prayed, the Rangers held on through four face-offs in their own end before the clock ran down to 37 seconds. There were 28 seconds left after two more face-offs. Once again, the puck was iced and a final face-off was held between Craig MacTavish and Pavel Bure. The Ranger pivot won the draw, and pushed the puck into the corner where Steve Larmer pinned it against the boards.

The game—and the decades of waiting—was over. The Rangers had won their first Stanley Cup in 54 years. The chant of "1940!" from their Islander counterparts was forever silenced.

CHAPTER 36

The Evolution of Hockey Strategy

Stu Hackel, editor

Recent Developments

Pierre McGuire

One of the most popular features of the first edition of Total Hockey *was Stu Hackel's discussion about the evolution of hockey strategy with Roger Neilson and Harry Neale. For this edition, Hackel discussed strategic innovations since 1998 with Pierre McGuire, a former coach of the Hartford Whalers and, currently, a radio broadcaster with the Montreal Canadiens. McGuire's insights appear here as a lead-in to the original Neilson/Neale discussion.*

Perhaps the biggest change in the NHL game in the past two years has been the move to four-on-four in overtime. How did coaches adapt to this new situation?

McGUIRE: Some teams tried to play very defensively at first, but that didn't really work because attacking players had too much time and space. That's the beauty of four-on-four: The better players can really utilize their skills. It really gives the game an element of excitement in this era of dominant defensive hockey. Four-on-four also adds an element of athleticism to the game. Instead of teams merely trying to survive in overtime, now they go for the win. If you ask the players, I would guess that 90 percent of them love four-on-four because it gives them a chance to go out and really play, to let their hair down, so to speak. The only way to try playing four-on-four safely is to play a puck-control game, to deny the other team the puck. But that is also the way to win at four-on-four. The key is to dictate the pace, rather than react to it.

Some teams put three forward and one defenseman on in overtime, especially later in the year when they needed points. Another four-on-four coaching development we saw was defensemen being totally turned loose and allowed to jump in and join the rush. That creates lots of odd-man opportunities. I noticed some teams always tried to have a speed defenseman on the ice all the time during four-on-fours —a Scott Niedermayer, a Brian Leetch or a Paul Coffey— to jump in to the rush, and also be quick enough to get back in case the rush is stopped.

The rules governing players in the goal crease were modified for the 1999–2000 season, reverting to the "no-harm, no-foul" standard employed previously. How has this affected tactics?

McGUIRE: As Roger and Harry noted in the original essay, coaches have long told players to drive to the net and create goalmouth confrontations. Players today will go in fearlessly because first, they know they won't get injured since the nets come off their pegs far more easily than they did, say 15 or 20 years ago; and second, goaltenders have become so good that it's pretty tough to score if there is no traffic in front of them. The change in the crease rule has meant more goals off the rush and also greater offensive zone presence. Now, defensemen have to stay closer to the net to clear the crease and, consequently, you see more play with the puck in the offensive zone. The defensemen are afraid to over-commit, and there is more activity by the offense away from the net.

Today, a coach has to preach fundamental defensive zone coverage. You want your player to stay between the man he is covering and the net. And the defensive team wants to encourage the offensive team to shoot the puck in. With shoot-ins, the goalie can get the puck and that's a turnover without confrontation.

One thing you see the better defensive teams do—New Jersey, Dallas, St. Louis— is get in the shooting lanes when the puck is at the point. Their players will step in front of the offensive player to block the shot. It's called "fronting" the offensive player. The Devils won the Stanley Cup doing that.

Today, good defending teams are more aggressive at the blue line. They try to capitalize on, or even force, a turnover on a pinch. So the offensive team is safer if one of their other players comes back to help out the guy at the blue line. Roger described the defending team doing this—"counter pinching"—in the original essay. He wants his forward to fight the battle—it's also called "skating the guy off"—at the offensive blue line rather than at the offensive circle or the hashmark, which is deeper in the zone and closer to the goal. Some coaches would rather you fight the battle at the circle, because you might get more puck support. There are guys there for the breakout. Your defense will not be as stretched out. Different coaches have different thoughts on that.

There has been a dramatic increase in penalty killing effectiveness. Five years ago, the best power-plays clicked at better than 25 percent. Now the best are around 20 percent. What developments have contributed to this?

McGUIRE: Roger certainly can take a bow for helping introduce video scouting into hockey a long time ago. Videotape reveals all the tendencies teams have on their power-play set-ups and makes it much easier to draw up a plan to counteract the power-play. Every team has someone on staff breaking down video, and studying various aspects of the game. Power-plays are chief among them.

Harry pointed out two early developments in penalty killing strategy that have both continued to have an impact. One started when Edmonton began using Gretzky and Kurri to kill penalties. Now that so many teams are playing a four-line game, some of the best players are on the penalty killing units. He also talked about penalty killing specialists, and they haven't disappeared. Those players who have clearly defined penalty killing roles take real pride in it.

I also think that shot blocking is probably at an all-time high, because players are better equipped and are not as reticent to get in the shooting lanes. And there's a different approach to shot blocking than before: Coaches no longer tell players to line up their body with the shooter's body; now they are instructed to line up their body against the puck—the stick and the puck—so more shots are directed into the defender.

Up-ice pressure has changed and it's even more aggressive than before, especially if your penalty killers have good speed and anticipation. You try to keep teams out of your zone, but if they do gain the zone, they often run into a very aggressive down-low rotation. Harry talked about how teams "switch off" their defensive zone coverage at even strength and this is one way it works when you are killing a penalty: Let's say the puck is in the defensive team's right corner. The right defenseman, (who is called "the strong side defenseman" because the puck is on his side of the ice) pursues the puck very aggressively. If the offense moves the puck down below the goal line, the weak side defenseman (the defenseman on the side where the puck isn't) goes down to cover the second puck carrier and the left wing collapses down. Strong-side rotation and weak-side rotation have become a very significant part of penalty killing. The whole idea is to take away time and space for the attacking team.

In recent years, we've seen puckhandling goaltenders become an integral part of their teams' offenses. How has this worked and why has it happened?

McGUIRE: First of all, goaltenders have become much better skaters. In the earliest days of the game, and even into the Original Six era, goaltenders were not always great skaters, but that has changed. Plus their equipment has improved dramatically: it's much lighter, which makes goaltenders more mobile and able to get to the puck easier.

Another factor since the mid-1980s has been the advent of goaltending coaches who are fully integrated into the coaching staff when game plans are devised. Coaches used to just throw the goalie in the net and hope he'd stop the puck. Anything else was a bonus. A guy like Plante was a big leap ahead of his contemporaries in using his stick and he had Doug Harvey to give the puck to, which made his stickwork more effective.

When teams became very adept at bottling up offenses in the neutral zone, the attacking team was forced to dump the puck into the zone and try to recover it. But goalies began intercepting the shoot-ins behind the net as the puck ringed the boards and the offense was short-circuited. The better goalies not only cut off the shoot-in, they began moving the puck to teammates to jump start the break out the other way.

In 1998–99, the amount of space behind the net was increased from 11 feet to 13. Theoretically, this would make it more difficult for the goalies to handle the puck because they had to travel a bit further to stop it. But it hasn't slowed down the best guys. And that's why against guys like Brodeur and Eddie Belfour, goalies who handle shoot-ins so well, you don't see the opposition spending a lot of time in the other team's zone. It is a major factor in the success of those teams. And, on the penalty kill, if you can get the offense to shoot the puck in, they can shoot it right back out again. The top goalies today have added this dimension to the game far and above stopping shots.

Today, especially in Canada, you see more of the better young athletes playing goal than before. Kids want to be goalies. They like the position. They think the masks are cool and they are drawn to the celebrity status achieved, first, by Patrick Roy and, more recently, by Brodeur and Curtis Joseph. Roy, for example, developed an identity with his superstitions: his talking to the goal posts and his twitching. He made it different—in a good way—to be a goalie. He made the position more appealing. And he also had success early, winning the Stanley Cup and the Conn Smythe Trophy in 1985–86, his first season.

The following season, 1986-87, Ron Hextall was a rookie. For years, he was considered the premier puck handler. Barrasso was just as good, but Hextall had made a big splash early on, going to the finals and winning the Conn Smythe Trophy in his first year, so he got the recognition. The next year, Sean Burke had a big run for New Jersey, and that made it three years in a row that new goalies had come into the NHL and gotten lots of attention in the playoffs. And, interestingly, Burke was Brodeur's biggest hero.

I recruited Marty to come to St. Lawrence when I coached there. I spent a lot of time with him and I got a lot of good insights into his character. He comes from a tremendously gifted athletic family; his father Denis was one of Canada's Olympic goalies in the 1950s. If you give Marty a regular player's stick, he can shoot the puck as hard as most forwards. A lot of comes from his training, and he has a great goalie coach in Jacques Caron. He's also tremendously strong.

Marty recognizes his outlets so well because he's a student of the game. He knows how to break down opposition forechecks and move the puck to the open outlet. He not only will pass the puck to his defenders, he can hit forwards right on the tape further up the ice. It's a very important weapon for the Devils.

The Devils have been one of the NHL's best teams in the last eight years or so. What exactly have they done?

McGUIRE: Contrary to what some observers said during the playoffs, I think the Devils still trap a good amount. But what they changed in 1999–2000 was they didn't hold up when they had a chance to forecheck. In the past, if they didn't have clear possession, they'd trap right away, but now they don't hold up if they have a chance to pressure the puck carrier. They go right into a 2-1-2 and they'll pinch their strong side defenseman along the boards, which is something they didn't do before. The Devils have the most underrated speed in the NHL, and it's their speed that makes this work effectively. It was a big reason Scott Niedermayer became such a factor in the 2000 playoffs.

One thing the Devils, and a few other teams—such as Ottawa—do well, is that they don't necessarily move the puck to a person when they are coming out of the zone. They move it to an area. They create a race for the puck and if your team has the speed, you win the race. Like New Jersey, the Senators are also an excellent skating team.

The Devils are also very strong on things called "chip-outs," which Roger alluded to in the original discussion. You get the puck, protect it on the boards, then bang it off the boards or flip it high in the air, past the initial pressure. Dallas is so good at pressuring the puck carrier, but everyone on the Devils was on the same page, so they know if the puck is on the right boards, it's either going to the middle of the zone or along the right boards. And they were going to win the race to the puck. They don't even bother worrying about a pass.

Another part of the Devils' success was how they broke down the trap of the teams they faced, including Dallas. They had a very unique situation where they made short little chip passes, four to six feet, and they supported the puck. They came out like a wedge. Instead of giving the puck up against the Dallas 1-2-2 trap, they held on to it, kept possession and broke down the trap with their short passes. You see that in soccer a lot, with regroups—another thing Roger spoke about two years ago. The Devils didn't try to force the puck through. They showed great patience with the puck.

The Changing Modern Game

Harry Neale and Roger Neilson

"COACHES ALWAYS USED TO WRITE on the rink diagram board, 'Pass' in your zone, 'Skate' in the neutral zone and 'Shoot' in the offensive zone," smiles Neilson. "You get the puck in your end and make a pass, you skate through the neutral zone and shoot in the offensive zone. In some ways, that's not bad."

"When I played, and for years afterward," recalls Neale, "a wing was in trouble with his coach if he came off the boards 10 or 15 feet. In fact, some North American coaches would draw lines on the ice down the length of the rink and the wingers were never to go inside those lines."

No single force changed hockey more profoundly than the injection of European play. Today's hybrid of North American and European styles began taking shape in 1972, the moment Team Canada encountered the swirling Soviet Nationals—whose own style was adapted from the firewagon hockey of the 1950s Montreal Canadiens, filtered though soccer and developed in relative isolation. Neale can delineate the elements of the cross-pollination.

"Beginning in 1972, we saw the European clubs—especially the Soviets—turn a lost puck in the neutral zone into a play. We'd get caught with the three forwards going the wrong way and the defensemen standing still. They'd just blow right by. Today, the ability to regroup on a turnover in the neutral zone is a part of any successful NHL team's game plan. We call it 'the transition game.' NHL teams today practice what to do if they get the puck from their opponent on a bad pass or giveaway in the neutral zone. You didn't practice that 25 years ago. There was no plan."

"Another thing the Europeans taught us was for our forwards to not be so structured staying on their side of the ice. Their wingers criss-crossed, skated to the open ice, and hopefully, they'd get a pass. We painfully learned that was a difficult tactic to defend against."

"I watched European teams practice at a much higher tempo than we did. Our drills were specific—we'd do a three-on-two rush for 10 minutes, then we'd do a two-on-one. But they incorporated three, four or five things that we had separate drills for into one drill. The old 90 minute practice is a rarity now; today it's 45 or 55 minutes and the players don't stand around very much. We picked up from them that you play the game at a high tempo and you try to practice that way."

"Puck control has always been more important to Europeans than giving it up and trying to get it back. Don't shoot it in, turn it back if you don't like the looks of the rush. Control it in the offensive zone. I think cycling, which used to be called 'offensive puck control,' is a tactic we took directly from playing against Europeans—especially the Russians. We were confused by their puck control and cycling tactics. They'd control the puck in our end, often outside the scoring area, and then—bang!— it's in the scoring area. All the NHL coaches buy into it now, but we dump it in to get it back before we start cycling."

"Europeans were first in using the neutral zone as an offensive area of the rink. In North America, we used to think of it as a dead area. Now, more teams practice neutral zone play, trying to answer the question, 'What are we going to do going through the neutral zone to confuse the defensemen or make them make a wrong decision?' If we just come though the neutral zone in a straight line, the opposition doesn't have to be very bright to figure out who to cover. So neutral zone play has become vital to creating goal-scoring chances."

"The neutral zone trap is a European tactic—especially in Sweden and Finland. The Swedish teams trap better than anyone. I think it's a product of their bigger ice surface, which eliminates effective forechecking. Their coaches want their teams to play strong defensively and wait for turnovers, because other teams will get frustrated and try low percentage plays and you can pounce on the puck."

"I used to keep a stat in the early North American versus European series. They would pass the puck about 35 percent more than we did. The theory was that the puck is the fastest thing on the ice and if you move it quickly, you'll look like a faster team. If you watch a tape of most NHL games in the 1950s and now look at a game from the 1990s, there are many more passes today. The exception was the old Montreal Canadiens, who passed more often. You wonder whether the wider ice made it an even better tactic for Europeans."

And how has North American hockey influenced the Europeans?

"Toughness," Neale explains. "I remember speaking about the 1972 Summit Series with Anatoli Tarasov, who said, 'We had more skill than the Canadian team, we had more speed, we were in better shape, we had better teamwork. But we could not equal their tenacity or grit or do-what-you-have-to-do-to-win spirit.' That's one big area the Europeans have improved immensely. They are far more successful in one-on-one fights for the puck, where hockey skills are less important than desire. I'm not saying that the North Americans don't have the advantage in that department today, but it is not an automatic advantage."

"The European goaltenders are much better than they used to be. They've learned the angles, which are different over here because of the smaller ice surface. They also come out of the net and handle the puck, which they never did previously. The European goalies were always quick but they were never part of the play and now they are far more adventurous."

"I don't know if it's because losing a face-off is of less consequence on the big ice, but North American teams used to have a tremendous advantage on face-offs against European competition. I don't think that's true anymore. It didn't seem as if face-offs were so important for Europeans but it seems to have become a priority there. It's always been a priority here."

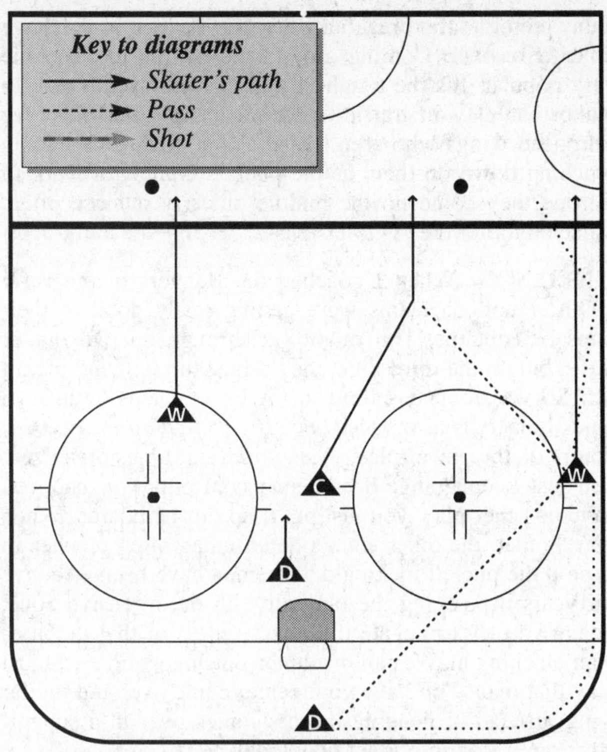

1950s Breakout

"It's harder to have good defensive zone coverage on Europe's wider rinks, but they play much better in their own zone now than they used to. I can't remember any Darius Kasparaitis or Ulf Samuelsson types from Europe 25 years ago. These two and Vladimir Konstantinov, when he played, have been among the best in the NHL. The Europeans produced more Fetisov and Ragulin types—big and strong, you couldn't push them around, good with the puck and they had good feet so you couldn't beat them—but they weren't robust and didn't aggressively go after the opposition. There are more hard-nosed European defensemen today who take you out with some enthusiasm. European coaches admired that in our defensemen and now encourage their own to play that way."

"It's harder to adopt an aggressive forechecking style on Europe's larger rinks than the smaller NHL rinks, and it has taken Europeans a bit longer to adapt to that part of the game. I don't think North American coaches have gotten their European players to dump-and-chase as often as North American forwards do today, and probably do too often, but now European forwards do use their speed to come up with loose pucks."

Apart from importing influences, the modern game has been shaped by the increased sophistication of coaching. Neilson's own development as a career coach is instructive: "For a guy like me, who was a junior B goalie, the way you learn about the game is from players, asking if they can try certain things, or from video—watching the teams' forechecking, breakout, the power play, whatever. You watch the video and something clicks in. I was watching video and it hit me—and I'm sure it hit others, too—that on the power play, the best way to score was point shots. Then everyone realized if they take away the points, it forces you to go down low. Today everyone has access to video immediately. If you come up with a new play and put it in, if it works, in two weeks everyone will be using it."

And that is how it goes: innovation breed imitation, then calculation, then innovation again. It is a constant theme when Neale and Neilson discuss the various aspects of hockey's evolution.

Breakouts may be the most underappreciated aspect of the game. What is the key and how have they changed over time?

NEALE: Making that first pass is the secret to a good breakout. When I played in the Leafs organization in the 1950s, the common form of breakout was up to the wing at the hashmarks, or a little further. His job was to get the pass and either skate with it or move it to center. If he was checked he'd just tip it out. *(see 1950s Breakout diagram)*

NEILSON: The key was always to stop behind the net; we'd always say, "Get the net." Some teams then had their center circle back and some would have a defenseman in front and the guy would bring it out and the defenseman would pick for him. You might try to hit the wing, but there were many different set plays—D to D or up the middle. *(see Middle Breakout to Winger diagram)*

NEALE: The better puckhandling defensemen back then—Red Kelly, Doug Harvey—would occasionally pass the puck up the middle to their center. *(see Middle Breakout to Center diagram)* It allows a team to break out with speed. That play is actually more common today than it used to be.

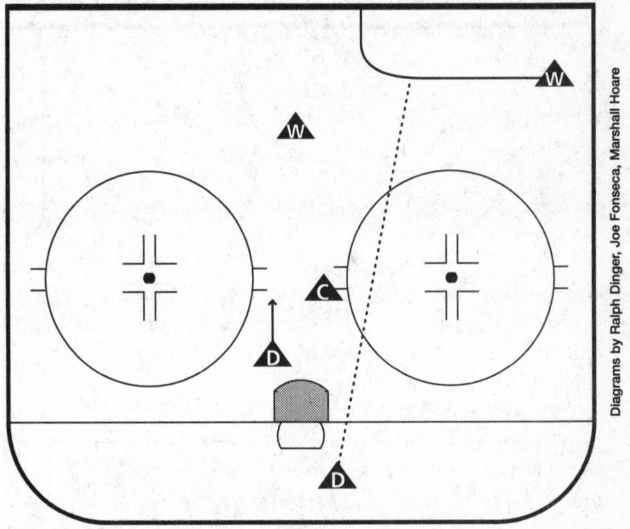

Middle Breakout to Winger

Diagrams by Ralph Dinger, Joe Fonseca, Marshall Hoare

Even today, if you make a mistake on that play, you're in an awful spot in your zone. Today, most defensemen make that pass to a wing cutting across. It's difficult to defend when people are moving into the holes. The defenders can't plug all the holes no matter what system they use. If the wing cuts across for a pass and someone fills his spot on the boards that he vacated, it gives the passer some options. *(see Modern Middle Breakout to Winger diagram)*

Was the idea of these breakouts to get an odd-man situation in the neutral zone or just gain the offensive zone?

NEILSON: You were hoping to bring the puck out, get it up and then get it in, but it's a good question. What are you trying to do? If you're just trying to get it out, why don't you just blast it out instead of wasting all that time? And I think that's basically what people are gradually realizing.

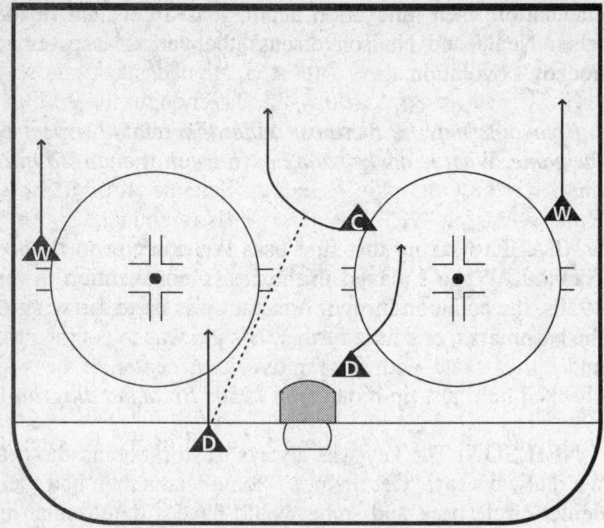

Middle Breakout to Center

Now there are a lot of players who really want to work it out. But I tell them, if you lose it one out of four times, you're in trouble.

NEALE: If you're an NHL defenseman, you're going to get hit after you pass the puck. If it bothers you, either you're going to pass it sooner, which will cause problems, or you're not going to go get it. A lot of times there just isn't a play, and the best thing you can do is just whack it off the boards into center or into the offensive zone. The purpose of the forecheck is to close off the options but European players are taught there are always options. Over here, because the players are faster, the rinks are smaller and the hits are harder, the options sometimes disappear. You don't have to be European to have problems reacting to the forecheck but it's probably more disconcerting for Europeans to admit to themselves, "I just have to get this thing out of here," because they are used to having options. It's one of the things a European defenseman has to learn: He's going to be confronted sooner when he gets the puck. The good ones adapt. Of course, for a lot of North American defensemen, if they took the boards away, they'd be out of work. But even the good ones who can handle the puck well have to use the boards in the NHL. Coaches today prefer a safer breakout where, if you miss it, you have time to recover. Coming around the boards has become very popular. It's the toughest thing a wing has to do—to make that play in traffic—and it's a big adjustment for European wings who aren't used to big NHL defensemen pinching down on them as the puck is coming around. In Europe they come up the middle or carry it more often, especially after the "D to D" pass.

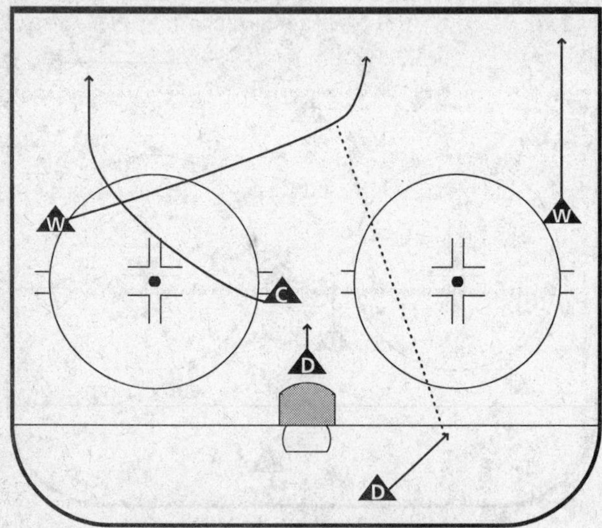

Modern Middle Breakout to Winger

NEILSON: When I coached the Rangers in the early 1990s, I noticed teams were getting really good in their traps or contains. You might get through on two out of three, but on the third time, they'd bust through and pick it off. So we stopped setting up. A lot of teams believe in quick breakouts now. *(see Quick Breakout diagram)* Unless you're on the power-play, when you want things organized, you just keep going. If someone confronts you and you have no other play, you just put it up off the boards. When you do that, the other team's defenseman often pinches in to stop the puck. Pinching defensemen have been effective for years in keeping the play alive in the offensive zone. Today you try to negate the effectiveness of that defenseman pinching in. We call it counter-pinching where you just play that man. You have your center come over and the far wing, instead of heading up ice, comes over in a support position. It's an important play today. We even do drills for it. We practice that once a week. Once you get over the blue line, then your skaters fan out. If the defenseman is circling the net and he's confronted by a forechecker, he can just reverse it to his partner. But you really don't want guys to stop and let the trap set.

What is your reaction after the trap has been set?

NEILSON: Teams want you to try a pass through the

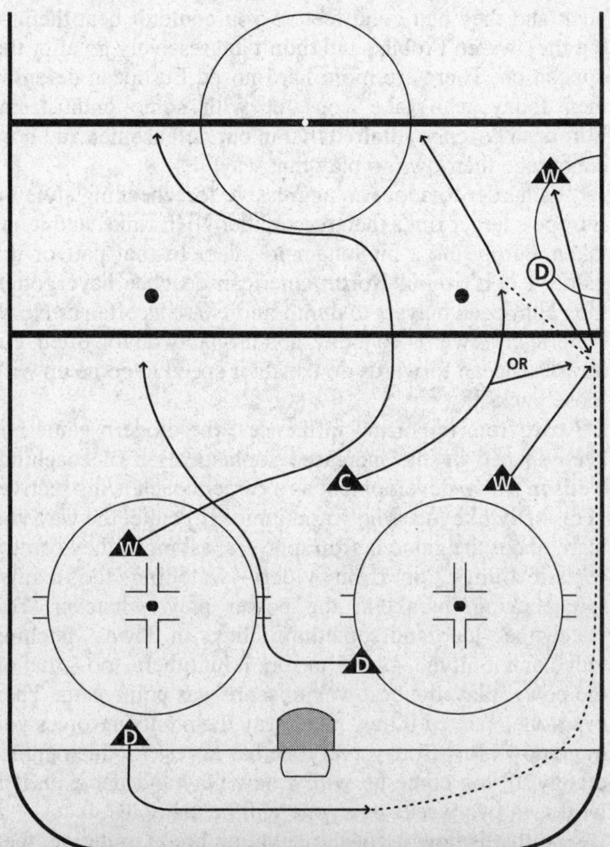

Quick Breakout with Counter-Pinching

middle, so instead your defenseman flips it high into the other team's end. It's not a bad play because their defenseman may have difficulty playing a bouncing puck with forwards bearing down on him.

NEALE: One of the ways to break the trap is to start out like you're going into it. You pass to the defenseman back on the far side and, if he can skate, he ought to be able to get into the neutral zone or to the red line without being seriously opposed and have the wing on his side of the rink

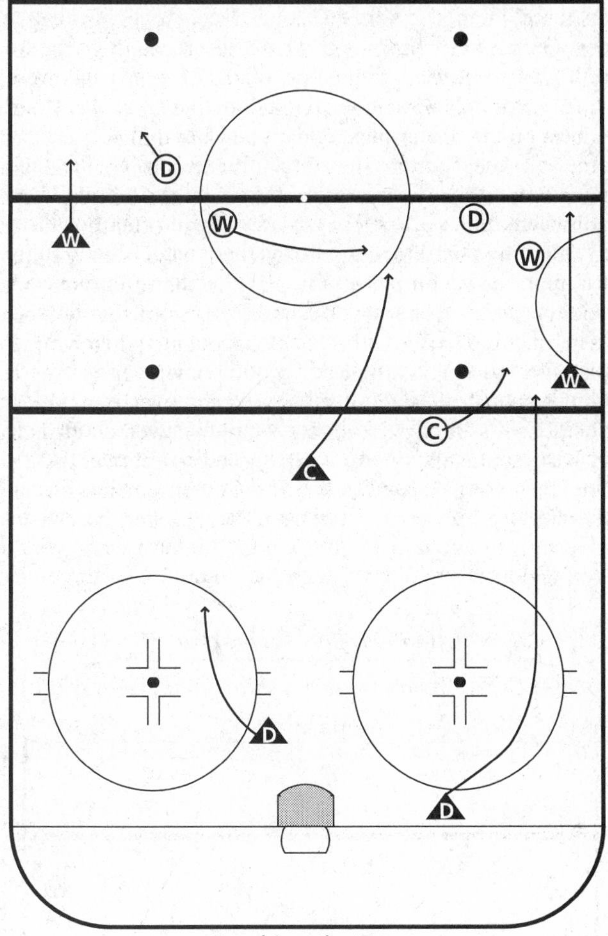

Breaking the Trap

to dump it to if he has to. You're not gaining the zone with any danger, but least you're out of your end. *(see Breaking the Trap diagram)*

To break the left wing lock, a defenseman has to join the rush to create an odd man situation in the neutral zone, jump past one of the two forecheckers to be the extra man. The first two forecheckers in the lock also have to pick up the defenseman on the rush, so they have a tough assignment—they're trying to forecheck and you can get knocked down forechecking, but to do their job properly, they can't afford to get knocked down. *(see Breaking the Left Wing Lock diagram)*

Gaining the offensive zone by dumping it in used to be a sin. Now it's almost standard.

NEALE: The main way teams used to gain the zone was to carry it in. Each team had at least one good stickhandler on every line. Their job was to beat people with that skill. It was more of a one-on-one game. Bobby Hull, Gordie Howe, Rocket Richard and Guy Lafleur all fought off more checkers than anyone today. It was part of the game and they accepted it. They challenged the opposing defenseman and took their chances. The stars all had speed and big shots. If you weren't backing up fast enough, they'd blow right by you—and if you backed up too much because of their speed, they'd shoot it by you. Even though lots has changed, the good players today—Selanne, Kariya, Bure, Bondra, Sundin—all have those skills in abundance. They are fast and can handle the puck. We don't see as much stickhandling today because there's more emphasis on passing and, since players are bigger and faster, there is less time and space to be fancy.

NEILSON: In the old days teams played two-line hockey. The 1940s Leafs might have been the first team to play four lines and one of the first to shoot it in and go after it. That was a new kind of game, where you'd forecheck hard all the time. Hap Day, the Leaf coach, was a conditioning maniac, and he would drive those guys until they were sick at practice. You had to be tough, but it really helped the Leafs win Cups.

NEALE: But generally, until 20 or 30 years ago, the shoot-in was the last resort as opposed to one of the first. The Leafs may have been the exception. They played you wing-on-wing coming back and had the two defensemen standing up on the blue line. Their job was to bodycheck, block shots and take guys out. So the puck carrier had both his wings covered and two big defensemen waiting to meet him. His best option was to pass it or dump it at the blue line. He could try to beat a defenseman into the zone, but that was like taking your life in your hands.

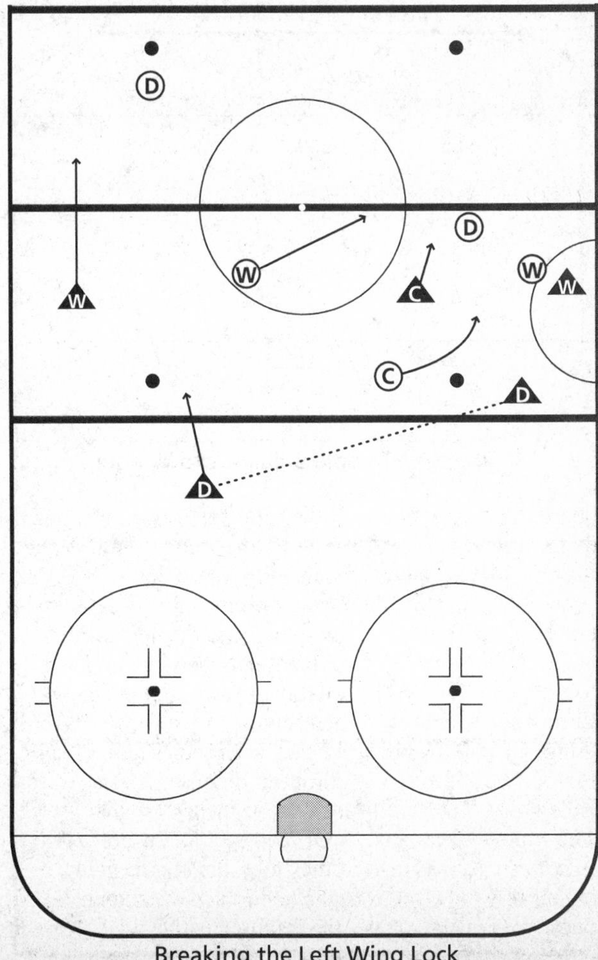

Breaking the Left Wing Lock

The theory on the shoot-in is that you're playing to dump the puck into a corner or hard around the boards so it ends up in the far corner, then you go in to forecheck and cause a giveaway. Coaches also like the shoot-in because it's a safe play, as opposed to stickhandling. If you lose it stickhandling, they could have all three forwards going the other way—four if a defenseman has joined.

NEILSON: There's so much emphasis today on counterattack that, conversely, there's a big emphasis on entries, making good decisions, sensing danger. Turnovers at the blue line are killers. The whole idea is that the puck must get in deep. You don't want to enter down the middle, because that's where everybody on the other team is. You want to pass wide, carry it wide, chip it through or shoot it in. *(see Wide Entry Even Strength diagram)* You want to bring it down the side and work it to the middle—even on the power-play. *(see Wide Entry on Power-Play diagram)* Teams used to come down the middle on the power-play, because the defensemen stood up at the blue line and the wings stayed with the offensive wings so they backed in. But now the penalty-killing wings stay high and the defensemen back off the line. So you don't want to go down the middle because the penalty killers are all there.

NEALE: The shoot-in is far less common in Europe. They can't forecheck as well on the big rinks, so they cross the blue line with the puck and then cause problems. We see NHL players now shoot it in when they're three-on-three or two-on-two. If you did that in Europe, you'd be in trouble with your coach for not trying to cross over and confuse the defensemen, go wide to beat him, turn back and regroup, or look for a late man coming in hoping to beat the backcheckers into the zone. The most skilled NHL players—Gretzky, Kariya, Selanne—only shoot it in when they're tired, want a change or it's two against four and you wouldn't try to make a play.

In the last 15 years, the neutral zone has become an area where you try things offensively, instead of just a space you have to go though before you try them. When I coached in the WHA against touring European teams, I used to say, "They look like they pass it to nobody, but when the puck gets there, their guy is there." And, of course, that's always been Gretzky's feeling—go where the puck is going to, don't wait for it to go there. The WHA Winnipeg Jets were the first North American team to adopt that style. They had the best group of European players and Bobby Hull. They'd come into the neutral zone three abreast and by the time they got into the offensive zone, they'd be in different lanes than where they started. They produced all sorts of chances because it was hard to sort out who's got who. They'd jump into the holes, get a pass on the fly and cause tremendous problems for the defenders. The backcheckers wondered, "What do I do? Do chase that guy all over the ice? We'll have one hell of a traffic jam." We had to learn first how to defend against it—if you're backchecking and your wing cuts in the middle, you'd better wait and stay in your lane because somebody's coming there, and that's going to be your guy—then we found out it was a pretty good tactic and started using it ourselves. You now see wings cut across, the defenseman jump up and go wide, the forwards criss-cross. Even if you're rushing through the neutral zone three-on-

Wide Entry Even Strength

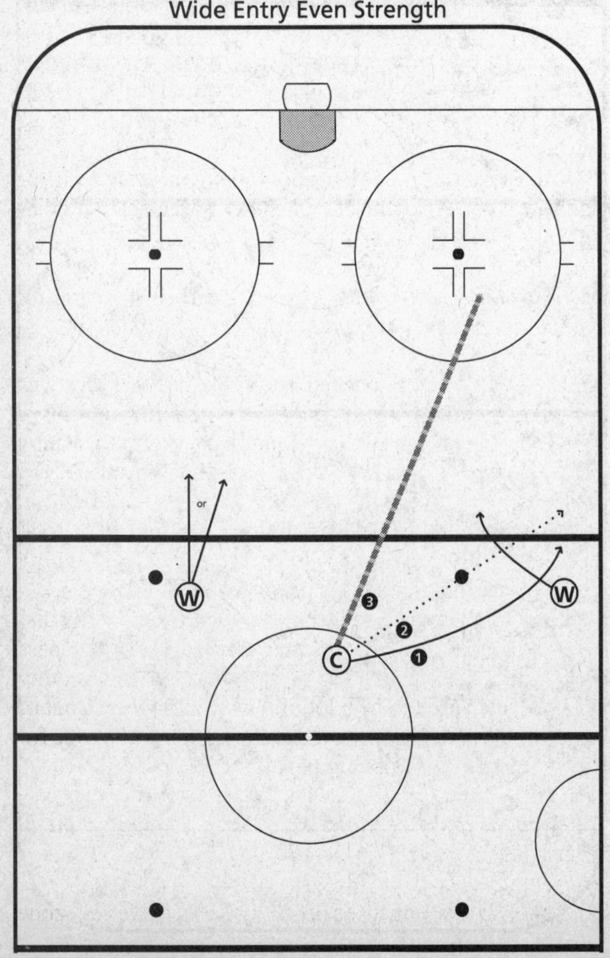

Wide Entry on Power-Play

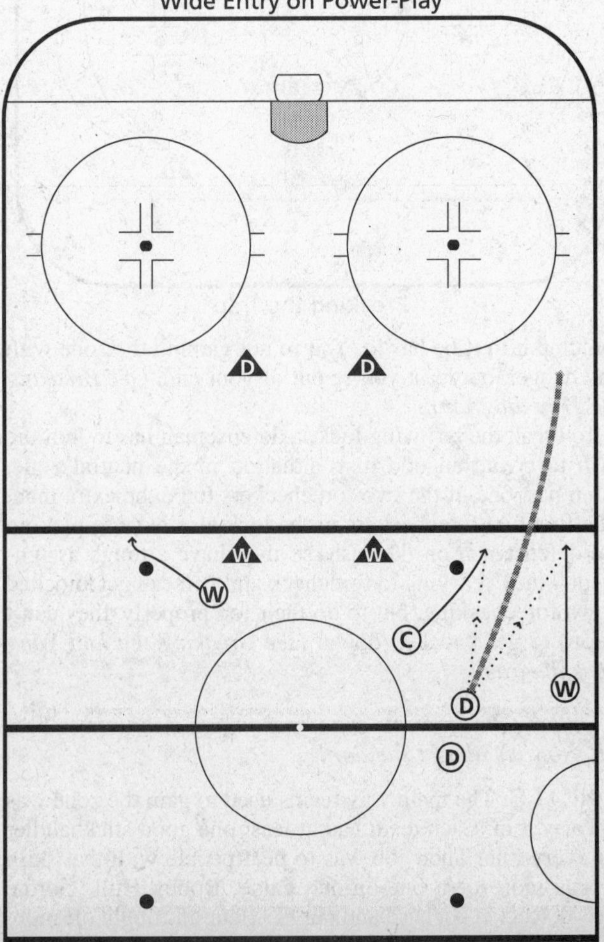

three, which is often the case, it's stupid to just be three across. You'd better cross over. Same thing two-on-two: do something to make the defensemen decide what to do, because some of them will make the wrong decision or be confused for a second, allowing you not only to get into the zone but toward the net.

NEILSON: The Europeans also brought regroups to the neutral zone. I don't think anyone in North America did that, where if you didn't like a play you turned back, or if you're changing on the go, you turned back until everybody got off. The Europeans were so good at it that you had to come up with a defense against it. That's where the traps, the Swedish one-three-one and all that came from. The fact that their rinks were so big was important because once they started to regroup, you couldn't chase them around. So you had to get into a zone defense.

Once you gain the zone, you go to the net.

NEILSON: Going to the net means two things: the guy without the puck goes to the net, and the guy with the puck puts it at the net. You used to see a lot of drop passes, where the puck carrier would leave it for a trailer and then either screen for him or go to the net for the rebound or a pass. That was great with two-line hockey, when you didn't have hard pressure from behind like today. Now coaches discourage that because you can drop it and a backchecker's there ready to take it the other way. Teams like New Jersey are very quick defensively coming back into the slot, so you can't afford to be putting the puck in there. Instead, you put the puck wide to bring it back in again. In the Middle Drive, a guy coming down the middle passes wide and goes through right to the middle of the net. The third guy can circle in behind him. *(see Middle Drive diagram)*

NEALE: North American hockey players are taught from Day 1—good things can happen if you go to the net.

Middle Drive

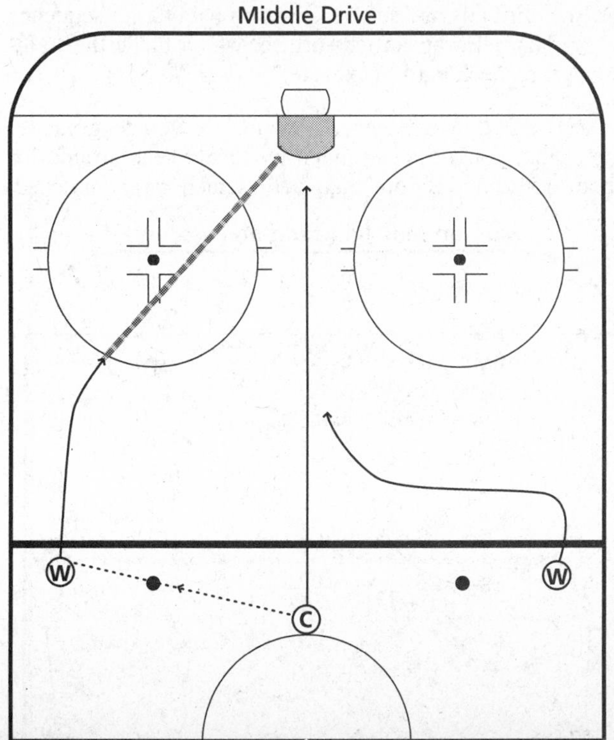

You can screen the shot, tip it in, grab the rebound. We used to call them "garbage goals." It seems like a derogatory term, but lots of big players score lots of goals because they go to the net without the puck. And you don't always have to be big—Dino Ciccarelli isn't big, but he plays big. It's a thankless task because you often have to get by someone from the other team. Once you get to the net, you have to stay there and take the pounding. Then the puck arrives and the question is, are your hands good enough to do something when you get them on the puck? Phil Esposito had the knack; often he was perfectly covered, but he got his hands free and could get the puck on net. Cam Neely, Clark Gillies, John LeClair—they somehow got impossible shots off while being held, tugged and grabbed.

And getting the puck on net has changed. In films from the 1950s and early 1960s, you don't see many slapshots from the outside. Most player wristed it toward the goal. Then everyone started to use the slapshot.

NEILSON: For years the slapshot was the only shot taken from the point. It was so much faster than the wrist shot. But now, more guys on the point take the wrist shot because there's no wind-up so it's easier to get it through when the opposition tries to take the point shots away. Against teams that wrist it in a lot, you can tell your defensemen, "Forget the guy parked in front of the net, you can play the puck. You can just step out and block the puck like a goalie."

NEALE: If going to the net for North Americans means going without the puck, for Europeans it means going there with the puck. Europeans want to make plays in the offensive zone involving multiple passes so at the end, when you go to the net, you're by yourself. You don't see them getting "garbage goals." Their idea is get the same chance without encountering all the physical resistance. There seem to be fewer European power forwards. They are the artists on the line, and when you pair them with a power forward you get a good result. One goes to the net, the other and gets them the puck.

Bobby Clarke is the first player I recall who regularly made the play to the net from behind the goal line.

NEILSON: When I coached Toronto, Darryl Sittler was also great at getting the puck behind the goal line off to one side of the net and making a quick pass out to Lanny McDonald going to the net. It concerned me because if the pass didn't work, the turnover would hurt us. I thought at first they were blind passes, but those two were pretty good at reading off each other. Then Gretzky started going behind the net and that was a pretty good play because all the defenders face the wrong way. Now most coaches discourage that play because it's too dangerous. If the pass doesn't work, you're looking at a three-on-two the other way. There also used to be a lot of pick plays coming out of the corner, where a player would almost run interference for the puck carrier. That's being penalized a lot today.

A recent tactic is cycling, which is quite important in today's game.

NEILSON: Cycling used to be called "offensive zone

play." The purpose is to test the other team's coverage in the defensive zone. You try to get a guy open, get someone to lose their check, or sneak a defenseman in. Having your defensemen join the cycle has recently become a pretty important part of the game. To execute it properly, you have to get someone following up the puck carrier so he can hand off the puck to him. He can either come in from behind so the players are actually skating in a circle, or sort of like football, with reversals or misdirection plays. Your players have to read each other and know that it's starting so they can jump in. The whole idea of cycling is to always make safe passes, so you always put your passes toward the boards. You never turn around and throw it away from the boards into traffic. Hopefully you have a guy coming out of the cycle to get open and you just keep moving it around until someone does. If a guy on the other team reads it, and moves in to cut you off, you just put it off the boards. Teams practice cycling quite often today and you even see players do it on the power-play now, because if they can get a defenseman to chase the cycle, they can move the puck in and get a quick three-on-two.

Cycling may result from good forechecking, but there are different types of forechecking.

NEALE: A one-man forecheck is a defensive play and a two-man forecheck is an offensive play. The lines a coach sends out to execute a two-man forecheck can change the atmosphere of a game. If things aren't going too well and you're lulled into a kind of calm, that line may go out three out of six shifts. It gets the crowd and your team going. It's always a lot easier to go out on the ice after your teammates have had a good shift than if they've been in trouble the whole minute.

The traditional view of forechecking is it's a physical part of the game. We're going to run in, our first forechecker is going to take the puck carrier with the body and our second man gets the puck. It sounds good—except you have to get your two guys there before their second guy arrives. With the safe game coaches play today, there is often a second guy back with the puck carrier. So if you only use the old style, you won't get much forechecking done. *(see Two-Man Forecheck diagram)*

One-Man Forecheck

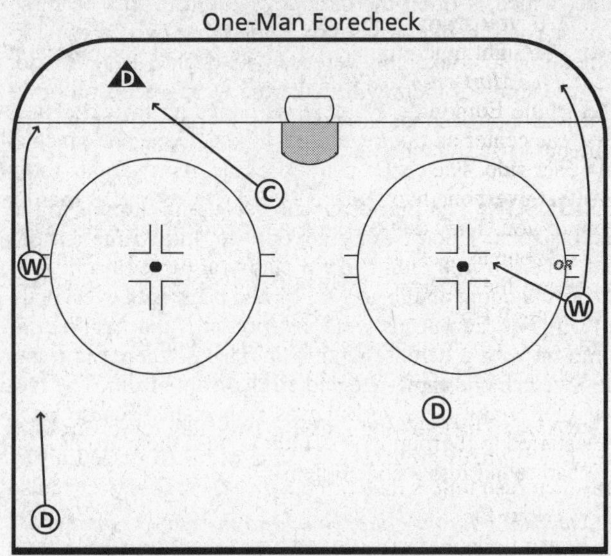

NEILSON: When you dump it in, the first thing you want is to pressure the puck carrier. *(see One-Man Forecheck diagram)* The other two guys must take away the boards, particularly the second guy, who is on the short boards so they can't use short corner reverse. The third guy is on the weak side and he's ready if it comes around the boards, or ready to move over into the slot and be the third man. That first guy denies them the net and flushes them out to the support and, if the defenseman pinches in, the third guy can back him up.

NEALE: Europeans use the "hurry principle" of forechecking. We'll hurry them into making a play and, because they can't take as much time as they'd like to survey all their options, they'll make a bad play. It's really a five-man exercise. The first man goes after the puck carrier and the second man has got to anticipate: if the puck squirts free, he gets it, or if the first pass was made, he hurries the second guy or tries to intercept. And the third forward hurries the third guy and so on. This is probably a consequence of the larger European ice surface, which made the traditional forecheck hard to execute.

NEILSON: Most teams now feel if you're going to forecheck, you've got to pinch in. That's been around for about 15 years. Before that, defensemen rarely pinched,

Two-Man Forecheck

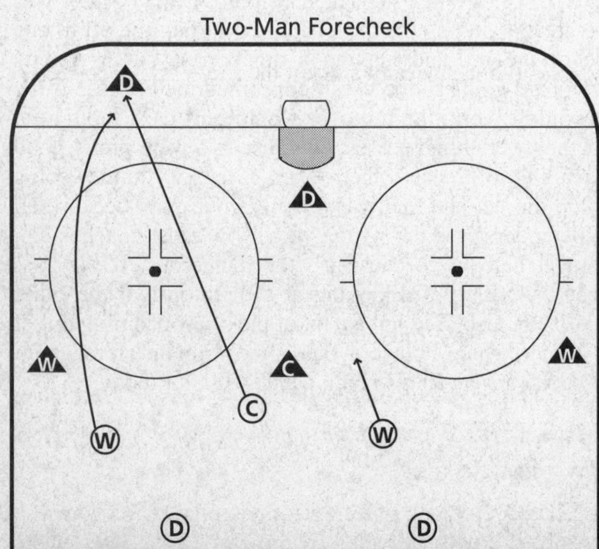

Man-on-Man (Pinching-in) Forecheck

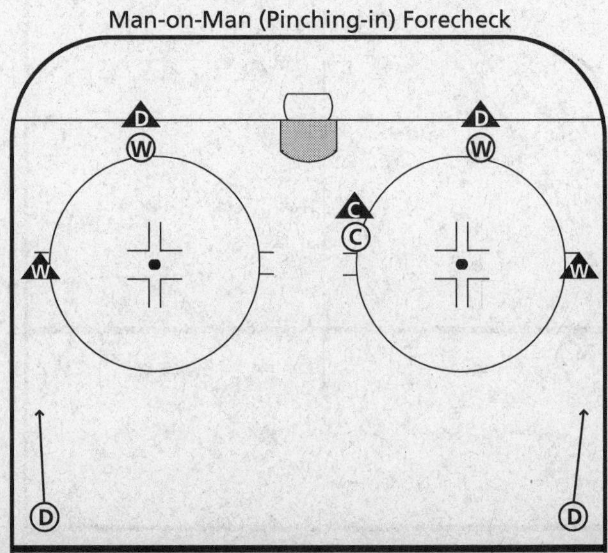

except if you were losing and had to take a chance. The Oilers brought pinching into the game on a more consistent basis. *(see Man-on-Man {Pinching-In} Forecheck diagram)* The whole Edmonton system was wings on their defensemen, the center on their center and the defensemen pinched on either side. The center could back up, but the main thing was that everyone had their man and you kept your man in front of you. They did that all the way down the rink, in the neutral zone as well. It was a wide-open system. I remember doing the video for them during the playoffs for their first Stanley Cup and there were many scoring chances for both sides. You had to have good skaters and lots of skill to execute that style. It was an exciting way to play.

NEALE: The left wing lock is a two-man forecheck with one guy high. It prevents the other team from getting an odd-man rush unless they bring a defenseman into it. It also allows your far side defenseman to pinch knowing he's got another guy back there. But it's just a way to keep a third guy high. The left wing is designated to stay high in the zone and seal off a breakout pass, although sometimes it's the center if the left wing is the first guy up the ice. They can get out of their end against that, but the best they can get is a three-on-three in the neutral zone. It's effective when you're protecting a lead. *(see Left Wing Lock diagram)*

These more complex offensive schemes have drastically changed defending in your zone.

NEILSON: The three-on-three down low coverage used to be strictly a man-on-man system; however, in today's game of cycling, picks and penalty calls, the man-on-man is too difficult to execute. The keys are—one: get to your man quickly; two: keep your stick in the passing lane; three: finish the check; four: the second man looks for puck; and, five: be sure to beat your man back to the net.

NEALE: The desired NHL style has long been to be physical in your own zone. When I take a guy in my own zone, I'm going to hit him, pin him against the glass or knock him down. Most defensemen were hitters 25–30 years ago. Teams still seem to want that, but with cycling and passing more prevalent, and forwards much quicker, it's harder to hit guys. So most teams now want one or two physical defensemen while the others play more of a European containment style. It combines both man-on-man and zone philosophies. You get to the forward quickly and under control. You may bump into him, but it's not to pin him, it's to tie him up so he can't go anywhere. If he passes the puck, you go with him. You don't give yourself up to make the hit, you seal off opportunities. On the "give and go," the approach was to take the play away by hitting the passer—if he gets the pass off and you knock him down, he can't get the return. But, if you go full out to hit him and miss, he can get around you for the return pass. In the containment approach, you take that away by having the defender stay with the man. They might execute the "give," but you can eliminate the "go." It's tough to do properly. With cycling, teams are willing to control the puck outside of the scoring area. So the defensive players have to be able to switch. They've got to talk to each other, yell "Switch!" or "I got him!" If not, when they cross over, they'll run into a traffic jam. The optimum today may be to split the difference. If you rely too much on containment, you may have trouble, because NHL teams love to play against defenses that never take you out.

Left Wing Lock

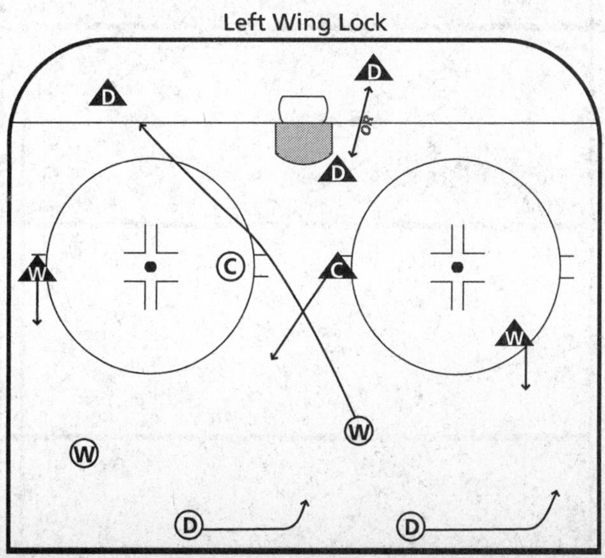

One of the biggest changes in the defending has been on the two-on-one.

NEALE: The old theory was the goalie takes the shooter, the defenseman takes away the pass and the goalie cuts down the angle.

NEILSON: But today's shooters are way too good for that. Actually, when I coached junior, we always told the defenseman to force a pass, force them to make another play and we'd take our chances with it. I didn't like the guy just walking in, letting him shoot. Occasionally, the pass was made and the goalie looked bad. But in the traditional theory, you always wanted the defenseman to stand up in the middle.

NEALE: The only exception was if the shooter cut across the net, the defenseman had to chop him down. But the newest theory is the slide.

NEILSON: The purpose of the slide on the two-on-one is to take the pass away. You slide on the ice toward the puck and the only way the guy can get it through is if he flips it or dekes or tries to go around—and if he does any of those things, you've got a good chance of stopping him. And usually the guy can't shoot if the slide is done correctly.

Another recent development is the neutral zone trap.

NEALE: Today's neutral zone trap is a variation of the old one-man forecheck. When I was growing up in the Leaf organization, if you were a wing for the Leafs and had three forwards coming down and you got caught not being in front of one of them, you were sent to Pittsburgh. It was called a "one-man forecheck." The media called it "Kitty-Bar-The-Door," and the Leafs won Stanley Cups doing it. Executing the one-man forecheck was easier back then because so few wings crossed; it was easy to sort out who your man was. Now it's not so easy.

NEILSON: Punch Imlach was one of those coaches who drew lines down the sides of the rink. That was where wings were supposed to go. When he coached in Montreal in the 1970s, Scotty Bowman was one of the first tell wings something different defensively, to lock the middle. I remember watching one game. Bob Gainey was backchecking his man and Scotty was screaming, "The middle! The middle!" A wing used to go back with his man, but Scotty wanted him to come over into the middle of the neutral zone and lock the middle to take away that pass. The defenseman's job became to watch the wide guys. It took the puck carrier's passing option away and so he'd be coming up facing four guys. *(see Backchecking – Locking the Middle diagram)* But that idea became obsolete. Back then, the defensemen tried to stay up at the blue line and the wings came back, so the other team would dump it in the end and the wing would have to come back and get the puck, making a breakout very difficult. It took another 10 years, but the next stage of that strategy was the trap. Not only did you lock the middle but you deny the puck carrier the red line. *(see Neutral Zone Trap diagram.)*

NEALE: Your first forechecker angles the puck carrier toward the boards and moves to cut him off before he gets out of the zone.

NEILSON: Your center has to mirror the movement of the far wing to force the puck carrier toward the boards. The near wing, who has backed off on the one-two-two, then jumps the puck carrier before center.

NEALE: The puck carrier's only options are—one: to beat you in a foot race, before you can cut him off at the blue line; two: chip it off the boards to his wing; or, three: pass it back into the middle to his center. If he beats you, your wing is there to jump him so he can't get to the blue line to dump it in; if he can't beat you and tries to chip it ahead, that same wing is there to intercept it; and if he tries to pass it back in the middle to his center…

NEILSON: …That can be picked off by the locking wing or the defenseman and lead to the counter-attack.

NEALE: The trap is designed to make the puck carrier think he can make one of those plays and then he can't make any of them. They get caught in the transition with their guys going to their net and four of your guys with the puck going the other way.

Some believe line matching is the biggest factor in a game's outcome.

NEILSON: My first year in Vancouver, Harry was coaching and I was an assistant. We hadn't been scoring. One night, we were playing Boston. I got the lineup, brought it back to Harry and I said, "Looks like they're starting their checking line." Harry brightens up and says,

Backchecking – Locking The Middle

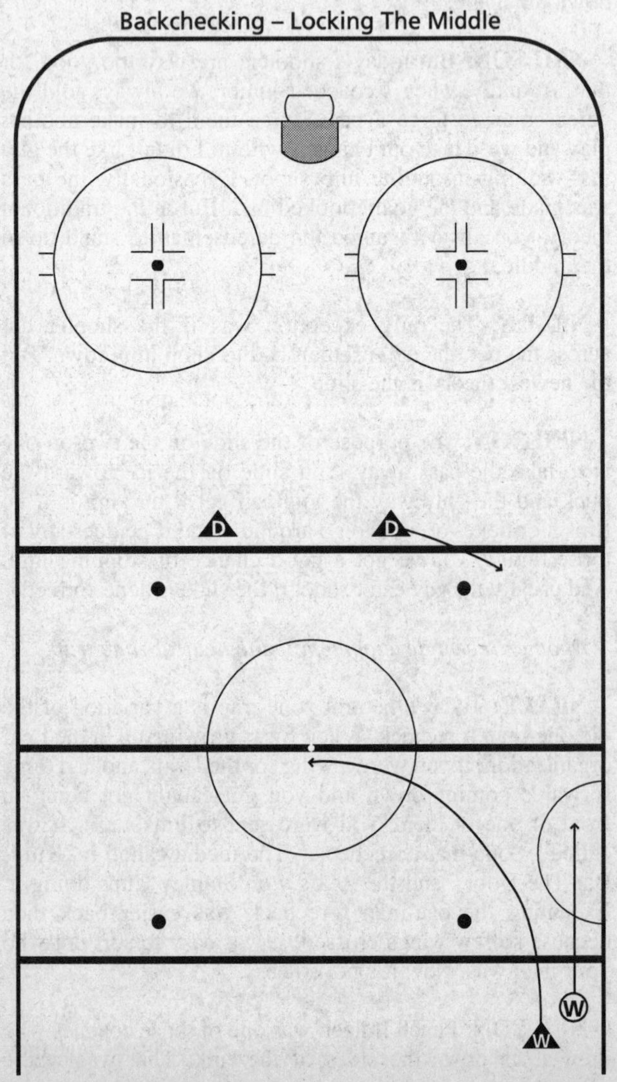

Neutral Zone Trap

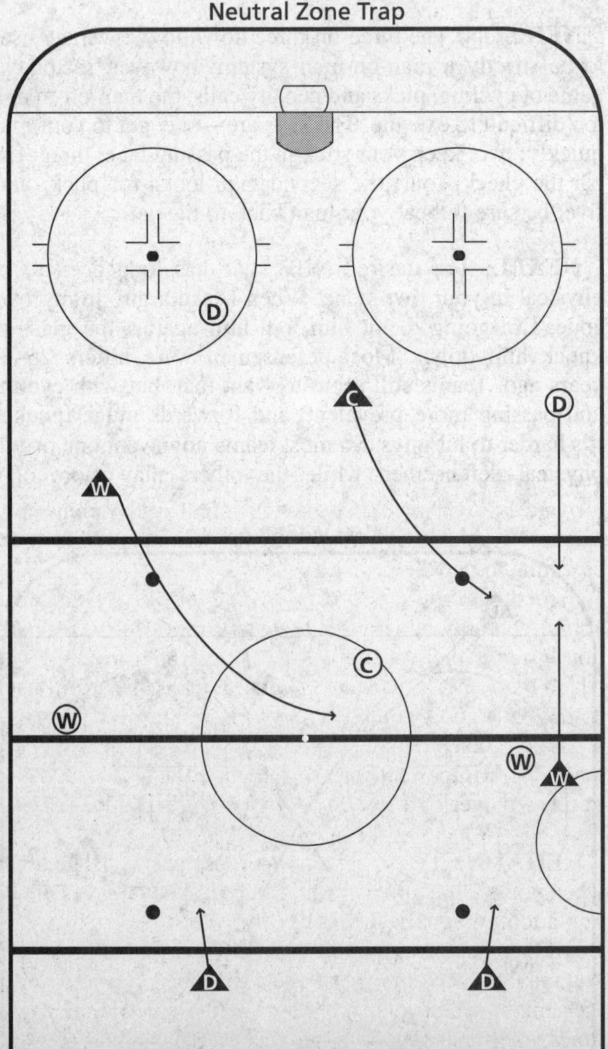

"Well, we can fool them. We'll start a line that can't score."

NEALE: When I began in hockey, the first lines played against each other, the second lines played against each other and so on. That was probably accidental. Both teams would start their best lines and they only had three. Shadowing, or matching certain individuals against others, is not new, however. For example, in the 1940s, the Leafs would send Bob Davidson out to check Maurice Richard. In the 1960s, Montreal used Claude Provost to shadow Bobby Hull. Chicago always used Eric Nesterenko against top forwards. Even recently, when Joel Otto played for Calgary, he always went against Mark Messier. But line matching has become more prevalent than shadowing in the last two decades. When I started to coach there was no rule giving the home team the last change. I think that was a product of all kinds of jockeying to get the match-up. That rule is a product of line matching.

Changing on the Go

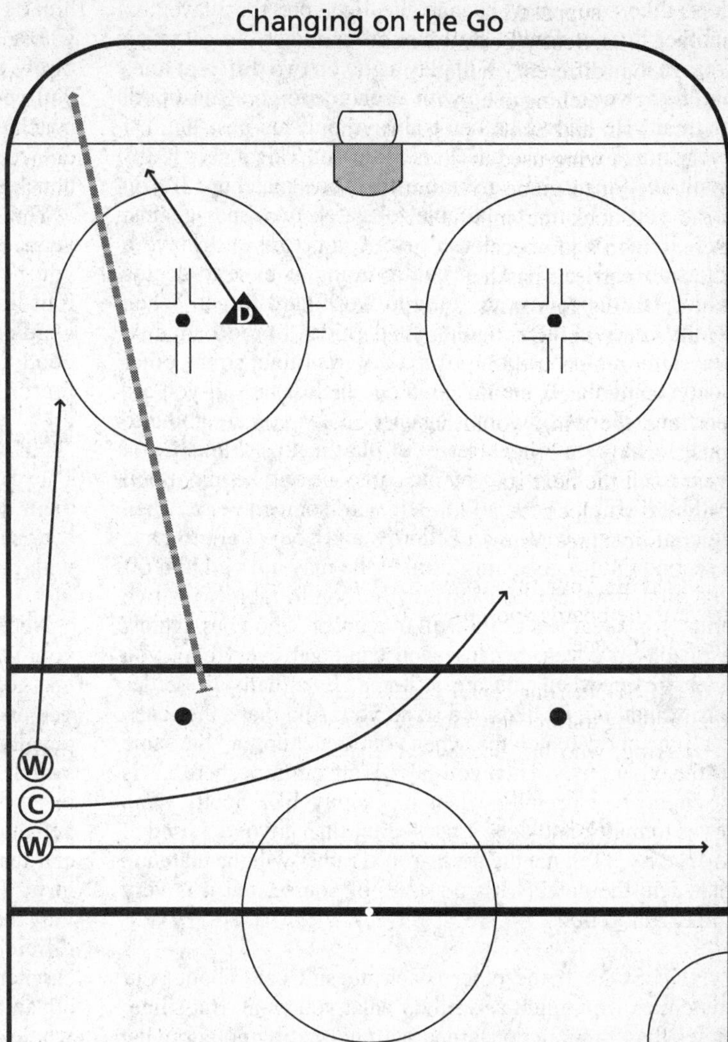

NEILSON: Changing on the go has become more of an art than it used to be. Previously, teams just changed. Now teams have plays for it and they change every 40 seconds. When they're killing penalties, they change every 20 seconds. It's become very important because the game has gotten so fast and intense. You've got to have good shoot-ins when you're changing on the go—especially in the second period when it's a long way back to your bench. You've always got to put it in on your bench side. If you put it in the far corner, they'll come up the other side and you're done. Teams have that long play they'll use to burn you. One tactic you see is that the first guy coming on goes directly to the far side to prevent that long play. That turns them back into the middle and second guy goes after the puck carrier and the third guy locks the middle. *(see Changing on the Go diagram)*

NEALE: Most often, matching involves putting out a defensive unit against an offensive line. Quite often now, you also see a certain defense pair matched against the top forward line, or matching your fifth and sixth defensemen against the opposition's weaker lines, figuring that is the best time to use them.

Sometimes you'll see a team put its best line against yours. You may take a little offense away from the opposition because their coach warns them to be careful. I love when the best players go against each other because it makes for a good game. Effective matchups are really more possible when you are familiar with the opposition, and never more important than in the playoffs. If you can neutralize a player or a line, it may give you a chance to win.

NEILSON: There are some important considerations when you are matching. There can be big advantages in getting a top line out against a line that doesn't check so well. But if they have a tough line and you have a tough line also, you may not want his tough line out against your top line—they might rough your guys up. On the other hand, sometimes you may want them out because your line is so much better than theirs. You've got to keep in mind the players don't really like matching. Let's say you send your top line out for a face-off and then the other team changes on the fly and gets their checkers out. If you're trying to keep your top guys away from their checkers and your guys just got out there, it's hard for them to come off. So you've got to weigh how important it is to get away from that checking line. And sometimes your matchups at the beginning of the game might be completely different than at the end of the game. You might want to go power against power but then, if you get a lead, you might want checkers against their power. And if you're ahead and you can get them to put their checkers on against your power, that's good, because it keeps their scorers off the ice. But if the matches aren't working or it's costing your team momentum, no matter what your plan was, a coach has to be ready to say, "It's not working, we're not going to match any more." I don't think you can be stubborn about that. Matching can be overrated, but it seems to me if you can get your guys on against the other team because of size or skill or whatever—without disrupting your team—you should do it.

Ken Dryden wrote in The Game *that he asked Habs coach Scotty Bowman what a coach's most important job was, and Scotty replied: "To get the right players on the ice."*

NEALE: The minute some coaches see a matchup they

don't like, they may change the line, put the player on another line, or double-shift him on two lines. To get away from matchups, Scotty will play a guy on two different lines and force you to come up with a scheme to go against both of them. He knows he can't always pull his best line off every time he sees the checkers come out. This makes it difficult for you to get any more than one matchup. If you think you're going to be able to match two lines against two, if the other guy doesn't want you to, you'll have a tough time doing it. Then you're going to have to decide which is the one you're going to work hard to get. When Scotty coached the Penguins, he'd "hide" Mario Lemieux, play him out of position or on a different line, so the other coach couldn't get the matchup out against him. If you are going to try matching lines against Scotty, you are going to have to have two lines ready to play against him. If you want to check Fedorov, you put someone out, he might pull Fedorov off and your guy is left with someone else. Then he comes right back with Fedorov, and you've got to have a second unit to go against him. Or he may not pull him off that first time. So you have to be comfortable with two units. It's a real test of the will of a coach who goes against a match-up coach, because you can't get everything you want—even when you are at home. Eventually he settles into something he likes and so do you. And that's the scariest thing about matchups, when your matchups are the same as the other guy's. Then you say, "Wait a minute, here ... Is he right?'—especially when it's a guy like Scotty, who loves to match and does it way better than anyone. I used to kid Scotty, "Tell me the truth. You'd rather win the matchup than win the game." It's not true, of course, but it is very important to him.

NEILSON: If the other coach doesn't care about your matchups, you might as well do what you want. But sometimes they're more concerned with not letting you do what you want, rather than trying to get what they want. So when the game begins, especially when you're on the road and the other team has last change, you can make it look like you're trying to get a certain matchup, but you're just pretending to want that. They'll take a line off to keep them away from your guys and put them on again later and you can put out who you really want against them.

NEALE: I've often thought that the matchup some coaches want is not the line that starts after a whistle, it's the one coming out. Roger is a matchup coach if there ever was one, and in 1982 when he coached us to the finals in Vancouver, he drove Chicago nuts in the Conference championships. He faked the matchup he wanted. He put a line out against Denis Savard's line and Bob Pulford thought that was the line Roger wanted. So he changed Savard's line and put him out on the next shift, or changed him on the fly and Roger would have the line out there that he actually wanted all along. But to do that, he had to have two lines he trusted. And if have that, the other guy simply can't get away from two lines.

NEILSON: When you're matching on the road, you can usually only get one matchup you want. If you try for more than one, you're just going to screw yourself up. One coach last year came into Philly and changed after every face-off to get his matchups. So our feeling was, we're going to make him change all the time because we're going to catch him on one of those changes. Still, it can favor a lesser team whose coach has convinced them that by matching we'll throw the other team off. If you can sell your team on that, you've got something in your favor. If you can get the other coach to take off his scorers when you put on your checkers, you'll see the faces of his players as they skate by to the bench and they're all put off.

You don't see a lot of double-shifting guys in recent years. It's a faster game with a lot of three-line hockey and you need four lines to double-shift a guy. You don't see four-line hockey now because often the fourth line isn't good enough. You have to have tough guys who are really good checkers on your fourth line. If you have a good fourth line, you can do it.

NEALE: European teams never engaged in matchups. They put their three five-man units out and you coped with them any way you wanted. The Russians were the first I ever saw employing complete units of five and they stuck with them.

NEILSON: You knew who was coming on, you'd put your guys out and they didn't care. I think they felt, "We're just going to worry about ourselves." I'd watch them practice and they'd have a power-play unit at each end against penalty killers and after a few minutes they would just switch and the penalty-killing unit would add a guy and go on the power-play and the power-play unit would kill penalties. Each group of five was capable playing both special teams. That was pretty good. They had a lot of skilled guys. They had great chemistry within their units and that's why they wanted to use them all. They composed their lines differently, each one having a checker, a playmaker and a shooter, each group was complete within itself and I can see advantages to that. We do it completely differently, having whole lines who are offensive or defensive. Who knows which method is best?

NEALE: North American coaches recently have begun using five-man units sporadically. Most notable was Detroit's "Russian Five" in 1997. The difference is, when you played against Russia's five-man units, although one was better than the others, they were all trying to play the same way. When you played Detroit and you are trying to check "the Russian Five," you face a group that plays a completely different style than Scotty's other groups. There have been others in the NHL: Kevin Constantine did it in 1994 when he had Larionov, Makarov and Ozolinsh on the Sharks and again at times with Pittsburgh in 1997–98. When the Rangers won the Cup in 1994, Mike Keenan used a five-man unit with Messier's line and Leetch's defense tandem. These units are allowed to play a different style and coaches want that weapon, although injuries, penalties, guys playing below their capability can prevent it. But first, you have to believe in that theory before you assemble five-man units that you really like and want to use.

Winning face-offs always has been important, but the execution has changed.

NEILSON: Teeder Kennedy of the 1940s Leafs was one of the first great face-off artists and I once asked him to help the Leafs with face-offs in the 1970s. But the game was different. He had all these little plays based on how the other

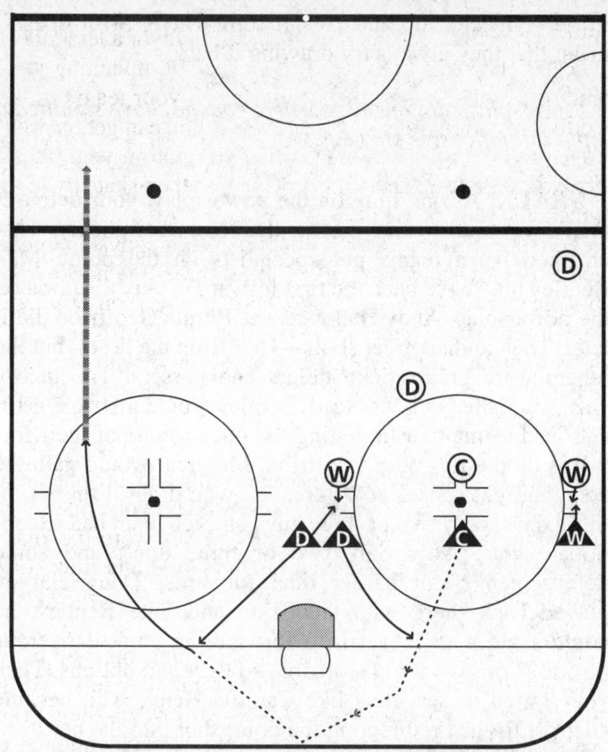

Penalty-Killing Defensive Zone Face-off Strategy

team was lined up. He might tell his wing on the boards to jump through and he'd flip it ahead to him right off the draw. Back then, wings lined up along the boards in the defensive zone. By the time he worked with us, big shots from the point meant you had to get out quickly to block that shot so we had stopped lining up that way.

NEALE: One of the first strategic plays I recall on face-offs was the defenseman taking the draw in the defensive zone. He'd draw it back to a more skilled guy who could use his imagination to get the puck out of the zone. Until the early 1960s, you'd also see the defenseman taking the face-off just run through the opposition center on the drop. His own center would be behind him and he'd come up and get the puck. Then face-off interference became a minor penalty and they put the lines in and made them line up.

NEILSON: There's a lot more strategy on penalty-killing face-offs today. *(see Penalty-Killing – Defensive Zone Face-off Strategy diagram)* Teams are putting their defensemen on the slot side of the circle and the wing on the boards side. As soon as the puck is dropped, the forwards start moving toward the puck, and if the penalty-killing center can draw it back, one of the defensemen comes back and grabs the puck while the others block the forwards and he'll bang it off the boards. Sometime the guy blocking in the slot will just hold the forward up to allow the guy with the puck some time, then come over to get the puck off the boards so he can clear it.

NEALE: Every team has a set of rules if they lose it in their zone. The strategy for the defense has long been to try to take away the point shot. The defensive wings charge the point men. For a long time, the offensive team would try to make them fight their way through, using football-style blocks. But today, we see a lot of obstruction-interference penalties for that.

Coaches have developed many set offensive plays if they win the draw. The first—and simplest—was probably just drawing it back to the point for a shot.

NEILSON: When I was in Chicago, we had Doug Wilson on the point and he had a big shot. So we'd put two men in the slot and get the puck back to him and he'd fire. The two guys would go to the net for a rebound. *(see Power-Play – Offensive Zone Face-off Strategy diagram)*

NEALE: Roger had an offensive play when he coached the Leafs where Lanny McDonald would be on his off wing along the boards. Darryl Sittler would tie up the other center and get the puck behind him. Lanny would come over and just slap it or take a step and shoot it. It was impossible for the guy lined up with McDonald to stay with him. The only way to stop him was with your defenseman lined up in the slot, who was going to go out to block the point shot. He had to take Lanny on the way out to the point. But Tiger Williams was there to try to tie that guy up. It became known as "the Lanny McDonald face-off play" and is still used today. *(see Lanny McDonald Face-off Play diagram)*

NEILSON: Wayne Gretzky still does this one: in the offensive zone, his team won't put anyone along the boards

Power-Play Offensive Zone Face-off Strategy

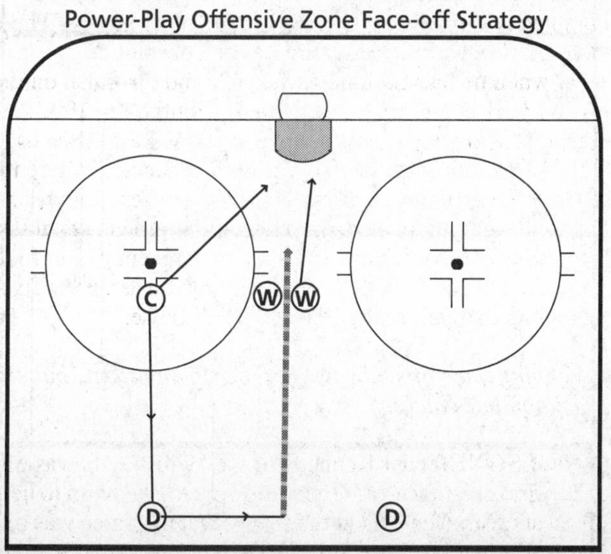

Lanny McDonald Face-off Play

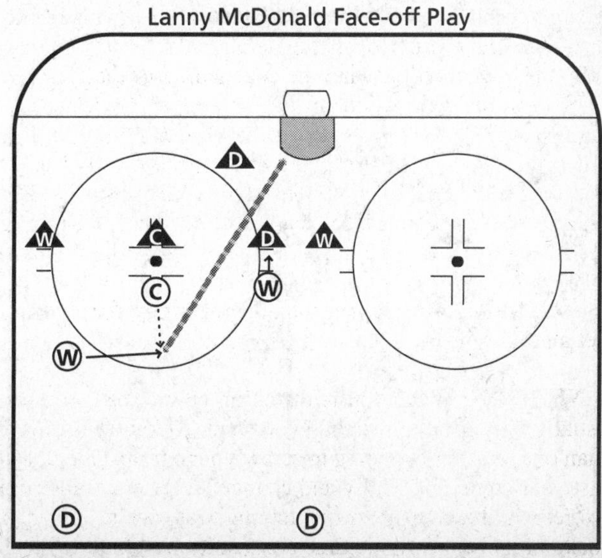

Wayne Gretzky Face-off Play

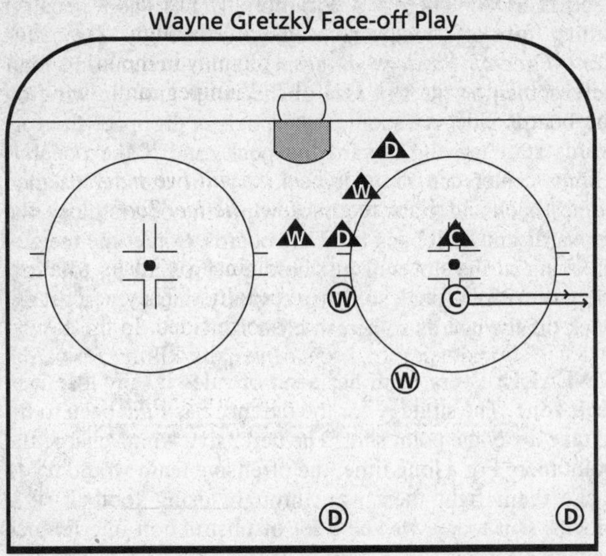

and if no one from the other team is there either, he'll put it there and then go get it himself and make a play. Most teams now put someone on the boards when Gretzky's facing off, but once in a while he'll get that play. *(see Wayne Gretzky Face-off Play diagram)*

NEALE: In the four-men-up face-off, you bring one defenseman up and put him about three or four feet off the line and usually on the outside. The other defenseman is inside the blue line in the middle of the zone. It gives you more guys to recover the puck if the draw is not cleanly won. If the face-off is scrambled and it's on the board side, the "up" defenseman steps in and gets it back to the "back" defenseman for the shot. If it goes to the other side, he hustles back to his position. This has become very popular on the power-play. *(see Four-Men-Up Face-off diagram)*

In the neutral zone we see plays after a draw where one defenseman throws it to the other defenseman while the wings cross over and look for a pass. At the end of periods, you'll see teams sending out two centers and then they'll try to get the other team's centerman thrown out by cheating on the face-off. Turning the bottom hand over is a new tactic, the theory being you get more leverage. The downside is the other team knows where you are going with it. But some guys do it all the time—although sometimes their tactic is

Four-Men-Up Faceoff

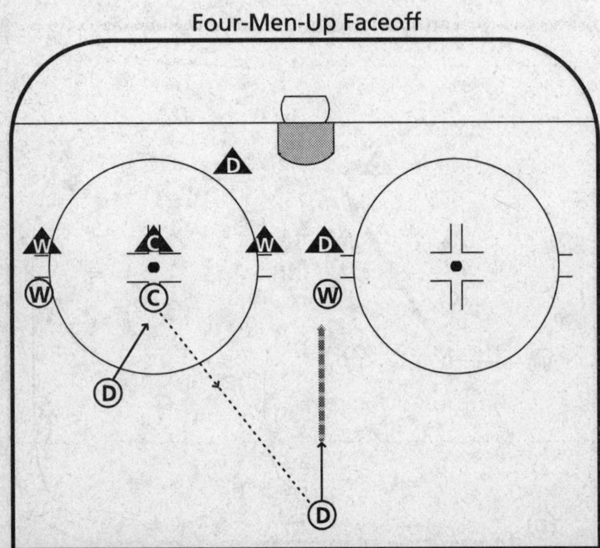

to tie your stick up and kick it somewhere. So it doesn't mean that they always try drawing it back.

Power-plays are one area where coaches have significant input into offensive strategy.

NEALE: At one time on the power-play, your defenseman's job was to move it to the forwards quickly. That changed when teams put specialists on the point. Max Bentley may have been the first forward to play the point on the power-play. Andy Bathgate and Bernie Geoffrion did it later. They all had great shots—Geoffrion the best—but the others were great stickhandlers and passers. The theory was, when the puck was iced, Bentley would go back, get it and lead a smart rush, getting the puck to one of their forwards on the fly. With Geoffrion, Montreal would gain the zone and get it back to "Boomer," who'd get it on net. In those days, only two or three guys on each team had exceptional shots. Now only two or three don't and some defensemen shoot harder than forwards. Doug Harvey played back there with Geoffrion and, like Bentley, he could skate with it, get it to forwards in more dangerous positions or give it to Geoffrion, so they had options. Then you started to see guys like Camille Henry who became adept at tip-ins, redirecting the point shot into the net.

Since Bobby Orr's time, teams want a strong skater and passer to quarterback the power-play, making good passes

1970s Power-Play Entry

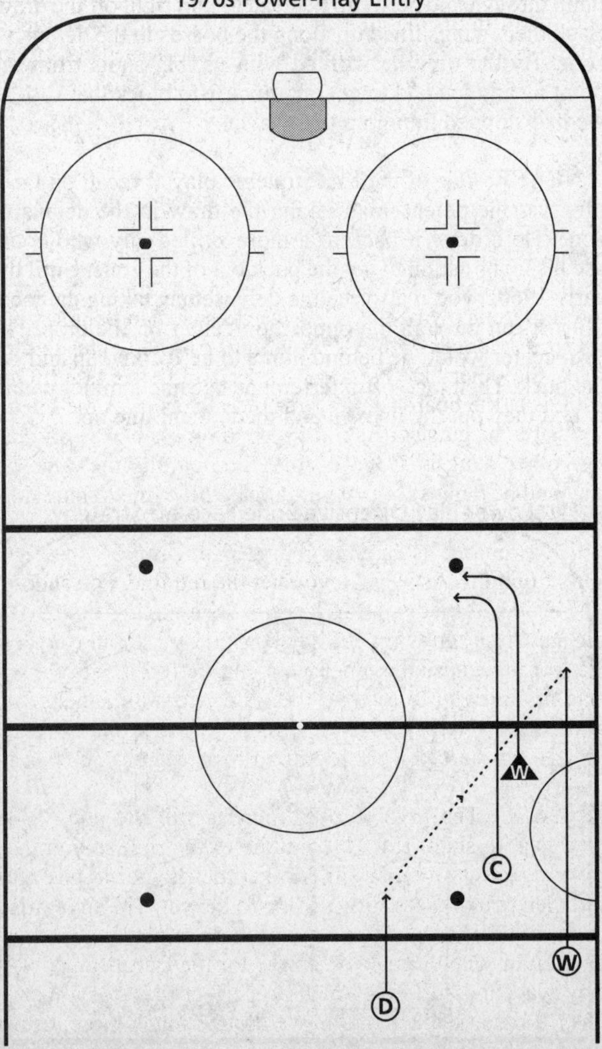

to the forwards and joining the play as a fourth forward. He, or someone on the power-play, has a big shot when the team sets up. Traditionally, it came from the point, but it can be from wherever your trigger man works best. The Orr-era Bruins worked the puck to Phil Esposito in the slot. He was big, hard to move, had a great release and the ability to move around and find the opening in the middle of the box. Mike Bossy and Jari Kurri had that same ability. Brett Hull has it, too. He gets on the off wing between the dot and the top of the circle, looks for the one-time pass from the other side and just wires it.

NEILSON: Going back 15 or 20 years, we never used shoot-ins on the power-play. One entry on the power-play *(see 1970s Power-Play Entry diagram)* was you'd have your breakout and you'd end up with a guy coming down the boards with another guy trailing him and the puck carrier would cut in toward the middle and the penalty killer would go with him. The trailer would be open and you'd pass to him. Then teams started to clog up that area around the blue line. They'd pounce right on you. The way to beat that was to shoot it in. But today you've got to be careful because some goalies shoot it out like a third penalty-killing defenseman.

When goalies started to stop the shoot-in behind the net, teams countered with various things to keep it away from the goalie. Al MacInnis and Brent Severyn could fake the ring-around and put the puck on net. That kept the goalie anchored in the crease. Teams tried other things. The diagonal shoot-in off the glass was a bit risky because it comes off the boards bouncing and its easier for the penalty killers to recover and ice it. The softer cross-corner dump-ins were also a problem because it's the furthest point away from where the puck is, so its hard to recover unless you've got a guy going hard to that corner. It's much better to dump it into your corner because you keep yourself in the play.

Some skilled players still don't like dumping it in, but coaches like it because you recover a high percentage. Today's standard power-play involves shooting it in, but it starts in your own zone, with the defenseman behind your net. *(see Modern Power-Play diagram)* The center circles back, the other "D" is in the corner and he starts up. One wing is at the boards at the near blue line and as the breakout starts, he cuts across for a potential pass up the middle. The other wing is at the far blue line cutting the opposite way and he delays for a potential pass blue line to blue line. The timing is important here. As the defenseman moves out, if everyone is running their routes properly, he's got lots of options. As soon as you get the red line, you shoot it in. The idea is that you ring it around behind the net and you can get three guys on the puck. And you should always recover it because the other team can't afford to send more than two men in to recover it, so they're outmanned. And often, if they've sent two men in, they're in a bad position. So you can start to work it around for the shot you want.

NEALE: The favored NHL play is still the point shot. You want to shoot from the middle of the rink so you may have to pass it around a little to get the shooter in position, and then two or three forwards go to the net. The shot might go in, be screened, be tipped in or there might be a rebound to put it in. The ultimate objective for the European power-play was, and still is, to make a perfect play for a tap-in. They'll pass the puck and move around much more, trying to get a goalmouth pass where the guy just taps it in. The theory is if we pass the puck quickly enough, those four guys can't be five places. It was a big play in the WHA with Nilsson, Hedberg and Hull in Winnipeg and then the Stastnys in Quebec.

Penalty killers once stayed on the full two minutes, ragging the puck and hoisting it down the ice. Today they are on for 20 seconds.

NEALE: Going back to the "Original Six" days, you had guys whose main job was to kill penalties. They might only see the ice when their team was shorthanded. In the 1960s, coaches started using two sets of penalty-killing forwards,

Modern Power-Play Breakout and Entry

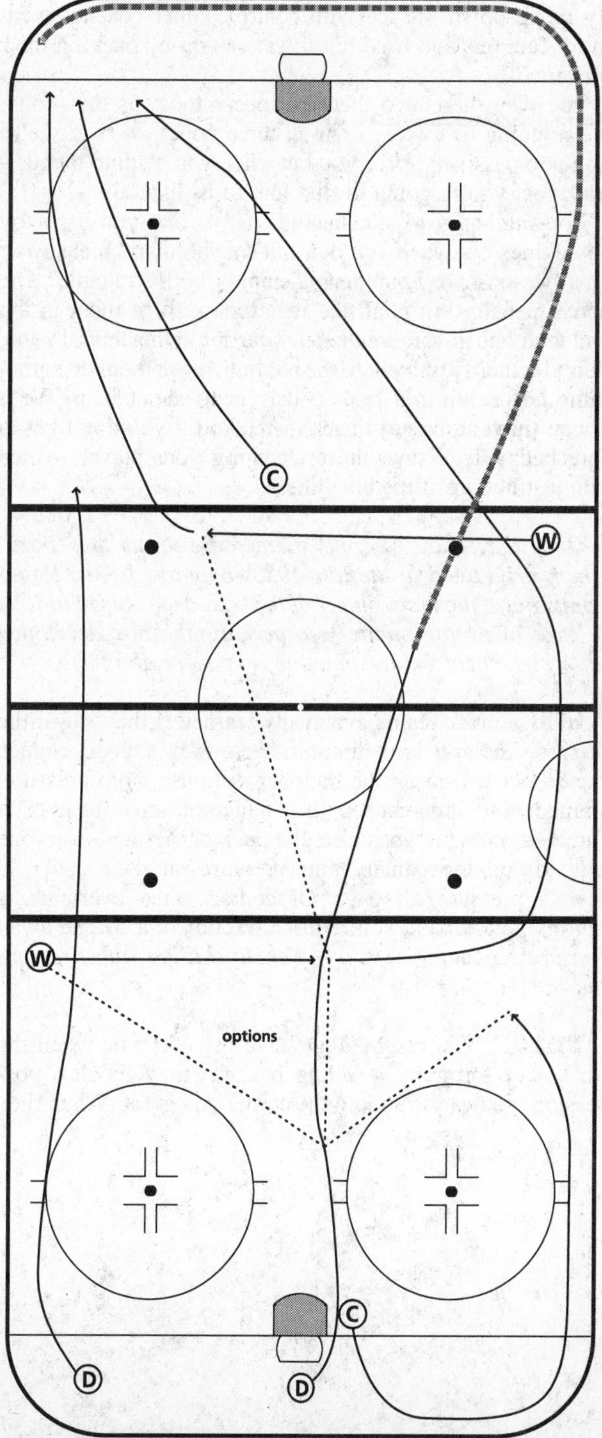

changing them midway through the kill. As coaches started to play more of their bench, these guys also had defensive responsibilities at even strength. Today, you sometimes see three sets, taking 20-second shifts.

Gretzky and Kurri may have been the first big offensive stars to be part of the penalty-killing. The last thing I'd say to my forwards when we saw them out there was "Be careful of the shorthand goal"—and already I'd be taking the edge off the power-play. There have always been different theories about penalty-killing. Some coaches have liked the penalty killers to forecheck, to keep the puck out the offensive zone as long as possible. But they had to be careful not to get caught. The first guy would circle and come back and the second guy would circle, but if you could beat the first guy, you had three or four against their three and could easily move down the ice with control. Other coaches were more cautious and tried not to get caught by backing their players off.

The way these two theories appear today is this—one: we're going to force you in all three zones, or two: we're going to passively force you but when you get into the neutral zone, you're going to find four of us lined up.

You might try to stickhandle past us and you'll get by sometimes but when you don't, it's a shorthand breakaway or a two-on-one. Some teams employ both strategies. The active penalty kill is all the rage today: force them in the end with one guy, force the puck carrier in the neutral zone, don't let them just walk to the red line, make them do something before the red line so they can't shoot it in. We'll always have three guys back there. And if you don't get to forecheck—let's say you're changing your players—then you just line up at the blue line.

Once they gain the zone, the defense forms the "box," which originated in the late 1950s or early 1960s. Roger points out, "the main object of the box, once you're in it, is to take away the points," so perhaps the box developed after big shots from the point became more of a factor.

NEILSON: Teams eventually learned if they sat in the box for the full two minutes, there was a good chance they'd get scored on. So they began to use more pressure. Immediately upon entry or after a face-off, or if the puck is fumbled, one guy goes after the puck carrier and everyone else killing the penalty puts pressure on their man. So there's pressure all over. Of course when everyone is putting pressure on, you're just a fraction of a second away from being caught at it. *(see Penalty-Killing with Pressure diagram)*

NEALE: You can be aggressive in your zone when the puck is up for grabs or rolling, but once they get clear possession, you can't run into the corner and get it. When they get clear possession, you're a bit less aggressive. Your emphasis then is to take away the point shot. When they've got a big point shooter like Al MacInnis on the point, you key on him. You want one guy always within a stick's length of him. You want to make it hard to get the puck to him or make it hard to get his shot through. If he passes it, then you've done the job because you've made the best shooter pass it. Scotty had another approach he began using in Montreal. If the big shooter gets the shot off, even if it's challenged, the other guys get back and he's got to get that shot through a forest of skates, sticks and legs. The goalie's job is to get the high shots and the other guys stop the low shots from getting through.

European teams rarely forecheck on penalty-killing. They put four guys in the neutral zone, force a play or pass, wait for a mistake and ice it and make you start over again. They weren't very aggressive in the box, their theory being that the rink is so wide that if you get beaten being aggressive, you've got a mile and a half to get back to where you're supposed to be.

But really, the best penalty killer on any team is the goalie. If a team is sitting at the top of the penalty-killing list, it's not just the penalty killers, it's also the goalie, who has taken some goals away from the offense.

Among this dialogue's lessons is that, like a shark, the game cannot remain still. Where will hockey go from here? Will the convergence of North American and European styles continue? Will the complex sophistication of coaching methods advance even further? Will the future demand more speed, making a game that is fast already somehow faster? It's a long way from rugby on ice.

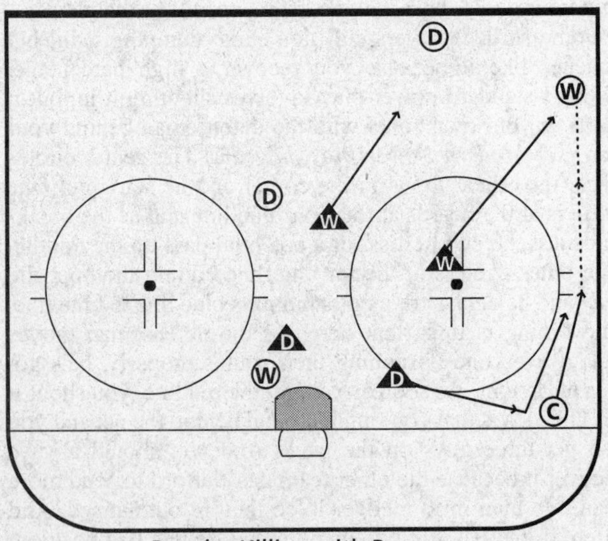

Penalty-Killing with Pressure

IV

Junior and Other Pro Hockey

Coach Charlie Conacher (wearing the hat) and the Oshawa Generals celebrate their Memorial Cup victory over the Trail Smoke Eaters in 1944. David Bauer (later Father Bauer) is directly in front of Conacher. Gus Mortson is to the coach's left. Future Hall of Famer Ted Lindsay is top row, right.

CHAPTER 37

The Evolution of Junior Hockey

The Changing Structure of Junior Leagues, 1946-1969

Dave Clamen

CANADIAN JUNIOR HOCKEY experienced a tremendous decline from the end of World War II until the beginnings of the three major junior leagues in 1970.

Before the present setup of three major leagues competing for the Memorial Cup, the country had ten districts (five in the East and five in the West). Each of these districts had one or more leagues whose winners would play off. The district champions would then play off against each other in elimination series to name the eastern and western winners who would then play off for the Memorial Cup. The ten districts were: (West) British Columbia, Alberta, Saskatchewan, Manitoba, and Thunder Bay; (East) Northern Ontario, (southern) Ontario, Ottawa (eastern Ontario and western Quebec), Quebec, and the Maritimes. With the exception of British Columbia, all these districts traditionally had good junior teams.

During the 1930s, most small towns across Canada had their own junior clubs and it was not uncommon for over one hundred teams to compete for the Memorial Cup. To use but one example, the district of Ottawa in 1935–36 had a seven-team league and two six-team leagues, all based in the city of Ottawa. Their winners played off for the city championship. Then, there were six other leagues totaling over 25 teams in the surrounding countryside who competed for the *Ottawa Citizen* Shield. The Shield and city winners then played off for the right to enter the Eastern Canada Memorial Cup playoffs. In 1936, the Shield winner, Pembroke, upset the city winner, University of Ottawa, by 7–6 in an exciting two-game, total-goals series.

Twenty years later, in 1955–56, there was one four-team league in the city. Its winner, the Ottawa Shamrocks, played off against the only junior hockey team in the surrounding area, Brockville. The Shamrocks won the series four games to none.

From nine leagues to five teams in twenty years!

The first step in the great decline came in the late 1930s when junior hockey began to be divided into A and B divisions. Invariably, the bigger cities got the A teams, which continued to compete for the Memorial Cup, while the smaller centers with B teams had less for which to play.

Next, came a concentration of the best junior talent in certain cities. In the Maritimes, the Halifax St. Mary's team was so dominant that not only did its junior opponents regularly default playoff games, but senior teams were beaten consistently. Yet, as powerful as they were locally, St. Mary's won only one Memorial Cup playoff in the seven years that it won the Maritime championship.

In the Ottawa region, the Inkerman Rockets were the local powerhouse in the late 1940s and early 1950s. Based in a small village in Eastern Ontario, the local arena attracted junior players from all over the region (including the later famous writer and broadcaster Brian McFarlane). Rather than the six leagues in the eastern Ontario countryside as in years gone by, the Rockets soon became the only team left. They regularly won the Ottawa district title, though they rarely advanced in the Memorial Cup playoffs. The other teams in the Ottawa countryside were relegated to Junior B status. They despaired of losing to the Rockets and would rather play among themselves and win sometimes—a self-defeating philosophy as the better players flocked to the Rockets to play at a higher level.

On the Prairies in the 1930s, each of the provinces had had their own playoffs before sending their champions on to the western Memorial Cup playdowns. But starting in 1948–49, the larger centers of Alberta and Saskatchewan combined to form the Western Canada League. This virtually eliminated the smaller towns from competition.

Only southern Ontario had the proper-sized towns and cities to expand its junior leagues. In 1945, there were six junior teams in the Ontario Hockey Association, three of them in Toronto. By 1955, there were eight teams, of which only two played in Toronto. Because of this broad base, the OHA became the darling of the NHL teams. They set up their main junior farm teams there and, more importantly, transferred players there from all parts of Canada. Saskatchewan's Gordie Howe and northern Ontario's Frank Mahovlich were but two of the more important examples. This led to a further strengthening of the OHA to the point where its champions took six straight Memorial Cup titles from 1951 to 1956.

Quebec, on the other hand, suffered a disastrous decline in junior hockey. Its teams had had little success in the Memorial Cup playoffs in the 1930s. But in the late 1940s the Quebec clubs took off. The Montreal Junior Royals won the Memorial Cup in 1949, while the Junior Canadiens took it in 1950. Players like Jean Beliveau, Dickie Moore, Bernie Geoffrion and Jacques Plante wowed the fans in the Quebec Junior Hockey League. The Montreal Canadiens and New York Rangers helped support the circuit.

But the provincial junior league had an Achilles' heel. The Montreal Canadiens were extremely successful in the NHL. The Quebec Senior Hockey League offered top-notch games at reasonable prices. Most important of all, there were very few towns outside of Montreal that could support junior hockey teams—and most of these had a QSHL franchise. The decline was steep. From nine teams in 1947–48 (six in Montreal) there were only three left in 1954–55 (one in Montreal). In a bid to arrest this decline, Ontario and Quebec started playing a partially interlocking schedule in 1952–53. This move might have saved Quebec junior hockey—had not other circumstances dealt it a terrible blow.

In 1950 two players from the Quebec Senior League, Larry Zeidel and Bill Heindl, jumped to the Western Senior League. The Quebec Amateur Hockey Association protested bitterly but to no avail—the Canadian Amateur Hockey Association upheld the transfers.

A more serious situation arose in 1952–53.

Ron Atwell had been drafted by the OHA junior Waterloo Hurricanes in 1951. Atwell instead went to Montreal. He stayed out of hockey for a year, which according to the QAHA made him a free agent. In 1952–53, Atwell started playing for the Montreal Junior Canadiens. The QAHA, remembering the Heindl–Zeidel problem, figured that Atwell's transfer was more legitimate.

The CAHA had other ideas. At a meeting on February 25, 1953—when the junior and senior teams were just winding down their regular seasons and getting ready for the playoffs—the CAHA suspended the QAHA and all its junior and senior leagues. The offer was made to all Quebec teams that if they withdrew from the QAHA they would then be eligible for the Allan, Memorial and Alexander cup playoffs.

The QAHA, in view of the lateness of the season, had offered to put off the dispute until the regular meeting of the CAHA after the season was over. In view of the harshness and suddenness of the ruling, almost all the Quebec teams stood firm with the QAHA. The QSHL withdrew from the Alexander Cup and the senior leagues pulled out of the Allan Cup. Of the four Quebec junior teams, only the Quebec Citadelles took up the CAHA's offer. They withdrew from the QJHL finals, which they were losing to the Junior Canadiens two games to one, and entered the Memorial Cup playoffs. They would lose the eastern final to the Barrie Flyers of the OHA.

The suspension of Quebec leagues was lifted following the season but problems remained. Frank Byrne, the owner of the Citadelles, moved the team into the OHA. A new team, the Frontenacs, replaced them in the Quebec junior loop. The competition for fans in Quebec City hurt both teams.

Then a problem arose in Ontario. The Kitchener Greenshirts, a Montreal farm team, were in deep financial trouble. The Canadiens agreed to buy the team and then sent the better players to other teams, most of them in Quebec. The OHA cried foul again. The Canadiens backed down, agreeing to sell the team to other local interests and to keep the players in Kitchener.

But as part of this deal, the OHA had to make peace with the Quebec Junior League. The Citadelles were bought by the Frontenacs and the OHA franchise was folded. Interlocking games were again started. The Montreal Canadiens were eager to stabilize their junior farm teams in Quebec so they themselves paid the OHA some compensation for the collapse of its Quebec City franchise.

Even these peace moves could not save Quebec junior hockey. Attendance was at an all-time low. Frank Selke even contemplated bringing back the NHL Maroons, saying that Montreal fans wanted only first-class hockey, not the junior variety. In 1955, the Quebec Junior League folded, replaced by a single team—the Montreal Junior Canadiens. Made up of the elite of Quebec junior players, they played exhibition games all over the country before entering the Memorial Cup playoffs as the Quebec representative. Junior hockey went from a thriving league of nine teams in 1947–48 to just one team in 1955–56.

A similar pattern occurred in the West. The Saskatchewan teams of the Western Junior League decided to form their own provincial league in 1956–57. This left the Edmonton Oil Kings without a league in which to play. They decided to go the way of the Montreal Junior Canadiens and pulled in all the elite players in Alberta and played all exhibition games. This didn't hurt their Memorial Cup aspirations, as they won every Western title from 1960 to 1967 and won the Cup itself in 1963 and 1966.

The national junior situation was very different in the late 1950s than it had been in the late 1940s. Only in Ontario and Saskatchewan were there strong leagues. Alberta and Quebec each had a single, elite team. British Columbia still had no decent junior program. The Maritimes, Thunder Bay and northern Ontario lacked the population bases to compete with the larger provinces. Manitoba had a decent program but was hampered by the lack of large towns outside of Winnipeg. The Ottawa region was hurt, ironically, by the basing of the Junior Canadiens in the city, which hampered the development of either a good junior league or a team in the OHA.

For Canadian junior players the options were few. In Alberta and Quebec, one could play for the Oil Kings or Junior Canadiens or move out of the province. Rod Gilbert and Jean Ratelle, who should have been stars in the Quebec Junior League, instead went to the OHA. Players from Ontario and Saskatchewan had their own leagues but had to compete with players from other parts of the country for positions. Juniors from the rest of Canada had to move where the good teams were or not play at the junior level.

In 1956, during a playoff series between the Junior Canadiens and the Toronto Marlboros, Frank Selke and Harold Ballard gave their views on the situation in junior hockey. At that time, the eastern teams (especially the OHA) had won seven straight Memorial Cup championships.

Selke said "The West must win the Memorial Cup in the near future and I wouldn't mind sending some of my best men out there. I'll probably get shouted down by my confreres in the NHL, but I'd like to see the players better distributed."

He said that junior teams would have to be satisfied with only two or three good players per team. "It would mean wonderful competition—but no packed teams. We'd get just as many pros in the long run, but at a lot less expense. You could [blame] us—and the Junior Canadiens—if you like."

Harold Ballard was in agreement with Selke and added: "If the pros would leave them [the west] alone for three years, they'd give us [the east] a real battle."

By the way, the Marlboros beat the Junior Canadiens four games to three with one tie to get the Eastern berth in the Memorial Cup that year. The Marlies won the final over the Regina Pats four games to none with one tie.

CHAPTER 38

The Memorial Cup

A Year-by-Year Review of Junior Hockey's Top Prize

Gregg Drinnan and Eric Zweig

THE MEMORIAL CUP has been junior hockey's most sought-after honor since the spring of 1919. As author Scott Young recounts it, in his book *100 Years of Dropping the Puck: A History of the OHA*, the trophy was born at the annual meeting of the Ontario Hockey Association in December 1918.

"One of the most lasting decisions of that annual meeting, however, was not concerned with playing rules," Young wrote. "This was an agreement that the OHA should establish a memorial 'of some enduring character, to OHA members who have fallen on the fields of war.' This, done immediately, was called the OHA Memorial Cup, for Canada-wide competition among junior teams."

The OHA Memorial Cup was awarded annually to Canada's junior hockey champion through 1933. In 1934, junior hockey split into A and B divisions. From that point through 1970, the Memorial Cup went to the junior A champion. By 1971, another level of junior hockey—major junior—had evolved. Since then, the Memorial Cup has gone to the major junior champion, which is crowned by the Canadian Hockey League, the organization that oversees the Quebec Major Junior Hockey League, the Ontario Hockey League and the Western Hockey League.

From 1919 through 1971, the Memorial Cup was awarded through an east-versus-west format—it began with two teams meeting in a two-game, total-goals series and then moved through best-of-three, best-of-five and best-of-seven championship formats. A round-robin format was introduced for the 1972 tournament. The Memorial Cup has been decided in that fashion, in one form or another, since then.

Summaries of each year's Memorial Cup competition follow. The Memorial Cup champion is listed in **bold.**

Regina Patricias vs. **University of Toronto Schools**
at Toronto (Arena Gardens)
March 19 and 22, 1919

The Regina Patricias earned the right to represent the west in the first Memorial Cup finals by beating Winnipeg 5–2 and 3–1 to win the Abbott Memorial Cup (named for Saskatchewan athlete Lyman "Hick" Abbott, who had been killed in World War I). The University of Toronto Schools team had won the eastern Canadian championship with an 8–2 win over the Montreal Melvilles.

"Toronto fans are greatly worked up over their juniors," reported *Winnipeg Free Press* sports editor W.J. Finlay, "and they are just a little afraid that their favorites are going to get beaten." They needn't have worried. UTS won the opener, 14–3, then scored a 15–5 victory three nights later. *Toronto Star* sportswriter Lou Marsh officiated both games.

The victorious Toronto team featured Joe Sullivan in goal. He would play later for the 1928 Olympic champion Varsity Grads and go on to become a well-known physician and Canadian senator. Sullivan's son, Frank, played briefly in the NHL. Frank's son, Peter, starred with the Winnipeg Jets in the WHA and the NHL.

Selkirk Juniors vs. **Toronto Canoe Club Paddlers**
at Toronto (Arena Gardens)
March 23 and 25, 1920

The Toronto Canoe Club recruited several star players in order to ice a competitive hockey team. Among them were future Hockey Hall of Famers Billy Burch, Roy Worters and Lionel Conacher. The Paddlers had dropped a 6–5 decision to Howie Morenz and the Stratford Midgets in game one of the OHA finals, but roared back for a 10–2 victory to win the series, 15–8. They then defeated the Quebec-champion Loyola College of Montreal, 16–4, and beat the Fort William Beavers, 16–1, to advance to the Memorial Cup.

Meanwhile, Selkirk played games all across western Canada, from their home in Manitoba to Victoria, B.C., as tuneups for the Memorial Cup. However, Bullet Joe Simpson and his Fishtown teammates proved no match for the Toronto Canoe Club. The Paddlers scored a 10–1 victory in game one, but even on home ice, the one-sided score didn't impress the fans. "They are very unpopular here," wrote *Winnipeg Free Press* sports editor W.J. Finlay, "owing to the fact that they were picked up from different parts of the country and molded into one strong aggregation."

Up nine goals on the round, the Toronto Canoe Club coasted to the Memorial Cup title with a 5–4 win in game two.

Winnipeg Falcons vs. Stratford Midgets
at Toronto (Arena Gardens)
March 24 and 27, 1921

Formed from the Young Men's Lutheran Club of the Icelandic Lutheran Church, the Winnipeg Falcons became junior champions of Canada one year after the Winnipeg Falcons senior team had won the Allan Cup and Olympic championship. The Falcons were led by Harry Neil, who later gained fame as coach of the Winnipeg Monarchs, and boasted a substitute player named Art Somers who would go on to play in the NHL.

The Falcons beat the Regina Vics, then trounced the Fort William YMCA 9–3 and 11–4 to win the western Canada championship. While the Falcons were dominating the west, the Stratford Midgets were romping to the eastern title, an honor they wrapped up on March 19 by beating Lower Canada College, the Quebec champions, 13–5, in a one-game playoff.

Winnipeg opened the Memorial Cup finals with a 9–2 victory, but almost let the seven-goal advantage slip away in game two. "From the commencement of the game, the Midgets forced the pace," read one report. "By close back-checking and heavy bodychecking they stopped the rushes of the speedy westerners and ... backed them into defensive tactics." Howie Morenz scored three goals to lead Stratford to a 7–2 victory, but the Falcons won the series 11–9 in total.

Regina Patricias vs. **Fort William War Veterans**
at Winnipeg (the Auditorium)
March 20 and 22, 1922

The Regina Patricias played the University of Manitoba for the Abbott Cup in 1922. The Patricias dropped the series opener, 4–1, but scored a 3–0 victory in game two. With the two-game total-goals series now tied, 4–4, Harry Naismith and Sil Acaster both scored during a full overtime period to give Regina the western Canada championship. The Patricias stayed in Winnipeg, where they played the Fort William War Veterans (who had ousted the Toronto-based Aura Lees in the eastern final) for the Memorial Cup.

The series opened with Fort William posting a 5–4 victory. The War Veterans led 3–1 after the first period, but trailed 4–3 going into the third after Acaster struck for three consecutive goals to end the second. But Clark Whyte, a speedy wing, provided Fort William with the victory by scoring the tying and winning goals, his second and third of the game. Regina actually thought it had scored a tying goal late in the third period. The goal umpire ruled the puck had entered the Fort William goal; however, the referee overruled him. It proved to be a huge ruling, as a 3–3 tie in game two gave Fort William the Memorial Cup title by a single goal.

University of Manitoba Bisons vs. Kitchener Greenshirts
at Toronto (Arena Gardens)
March 22 and 26, 1923

The University of Manitoba defeated Brandon, Calgary and Fort William in the playoffs en route to Toronto for a Memorial Cup date with Kitchener. The Greenshirts had downed Iroquois Falls and the Montreal AAA.

Manitoba showed what was called "superior speed, and courage, uncanny checking and resourcefulness," in whipping Kitchener 7–3 in game one. The referee was Lionel Conacher. The teams were tied, 2–2, after one period, but the varsity boys banged in five straight goals in the second period to put it away. Murray Murdoch scored four of those goals for Manitoba.

Murdoch followed up his four-goal opening game by scoring five times and setting up another in game two. Manitoba wrapped up the Memorial Cup with a second consecutive 7–3 victory that gave it the round by a 14–6 aggregate.

"The westerners were superior in all departments and Siebert was the only Kitchener player to hold his opponents in check," read one report. Albert Charles "Babe" Siebert would go on to star in the NHL with the Montreal Maroons, New York Rangers, Boston Bruins and Montreal Canadiens. Murray Murdoch would play 11 years with the Rangers, adding Stanley Cup victories to his Memorial Cup title in 1928 and 1933.

Calgary Canadians vs. **Owen Sound Greys**
at Winnipeg (Amphitheatre)
March 26 and 28, 1924

After lengthy negotiations, the Canadian Amateur Hockey Association ordered the Regina Pats to play the Winnipeg Tammany Tigers, the Manitoba champions, with the winner to face the Alberta-champion Calgary Canadians for the Abbott Cup. Regina beat Winnipeg, but then lost to Calgary, who advanced to play Owen Sound for the Memorial Cup.

The Greys reached the national junior final by splitting a two-game series with Kenora. They won the first, 11–7, and lost the second, 5–4, but still won it all 15–12 on goals.

Scoring three times on rebounds, Owen Sound led 1–0 and 3–2 at the period breaks en route to a 5–3 victory over Calgary in the first game of the Memorial Cup finals. Butch Keeling and Cooney Weiland scored two goals each for the Greys. When the second game ended in a 2–2 tie, Owen Sound went home with the Memorial Cup on a 7–5 two-game score.

A lot of the credit for Owen Sound's championship was given to Hedley Smith, the Greys' 16-year-old goalkeeper. "This young lad staved off what looked like certain defeat by his marvellous stops," newspapers reported. It doesn't seem that shots on goal were counted in game two, but one report credits Smith with 24 stops in the third period alone.

Regina Pats vs. Toronto Aura Lees
at Toronto (Arena Gardens)
March 23 to 25, 1925

By the spring of 1925, the CAHA had announced that the Memorial Cup would now be a best-of-three series. The Toronto Aura Lees advanced to the first final under the new format by beating the defending champions from Owen Sound in the eastern Canada final. Regina reached the final with a win over Fort William.

Game one was played before about 3,000 fans. The teams were scoreless through two periods before Sil Acaster scored at 4:05 of the third. It appeared Regina had it wrapped up, but, according to the *Regina Leader*, Johnny McPherson "dribbled a mean shot at [goaltender Jack] Cunning. The rubber bounced and jumbled over his feet." The Pats went on to win, 2–1, on Frank Ingram's goal just 37 seconds into overtime. Regina won it all two nights later when they downed the Aura Lees 5–2 in a game marred by a second-period brawl.

The donnybrook started when Toronto's Shrimp McPherson and Regina's Ken Doraty began fighting. "Before it was over every player on both teams including the subs was out on the ice ... exchanging blows.

"The police finally went into the affair and when it was all over Shrimp McPherson and Doraty were in the penalty box, having a good laugh and apologizing to each other."

Calgary Canadians vs. Queen's University
at Winnipeg (Amphitheatre)
March 23 to 26, 1926

The Calgary Canadians were back in the Memorial Cup finals in 1926, but they just made it, beating the hometown Winnipeg Tammany Tigers, 3–2, on Paul Thompson's overtime goal to take the two-game, total-goals Abbott Cup series 6–5. In the meantime, the visiting Queen's University team from Kingston was tying, 3–3, and winning, 2–1, to take the eastern final, 5–4, over Fort William.

Future Chicago Black Hawks star Paul Thompson reportedly was the best man on the ice in the opening game of the Memorial Cup finals, but Calgary "passed up numerous opportunities to score and found an almost insurmountable barrier in [Bill] Taugher in the Kingston nets." Queen's won the game, 4–2. Calgary won game two 3–2, setting up a sudden-death showdown for the championship the following evening.

"Tonight's game was lightning fast," one reporter wrote of the deciding contest. "Calgary opened with a burst of speed which netted a goal in the opening session and two in the second. The Canadians completely dominated the play until Kingston put up their characteristic fighting finish in the last period." Calgary held on for a 3–2 victory. Paul Thompson had scored twice for the new Memorial Cup champions.

Port Arthur West End Juniors vs. **Owen Sound Greys**
at Toronto (Arena Gardens)
March 25 to 28, 1927

The Port Arthur West End Juniors' trek to the Memorial Cup finals started to get serious in mid-March, just about the time the ice in their home facility turned to slush. As such, it was ruled that the West Ends, champions of the Thunder Bay Hockey League, would journey to Winnipeg to face the winner of a series between the Regina Pats and the Elmwood Millionaires.

Regina won the series with Elmwood, then beat the West Ends—or Westies as their fans called them—by a 2–1 score to open their set. Port Arthur rallied for a 4–1 victory in game two to take the series, 5–3, on the round. Meanwhile, Owen Sound had won the eastern Canadian championship with a 5–1 victory over the Montreal Amateur Athletic Association in a sudden-death game in Toronto on March 17.

Owen Sound won the opener of the Memorial Cup finals 5–4, with Port Arthur coming from behind three times before Martin Lauer scored the winner with 4:30 to play. The series ended with Owen Sound posting a 5–3 victory after 10 minutes of overtime before about 8,000 fans in game two. The Greys outscored the Westies, 3–1, in the full-length extra session.

Regina Monarchs vs. Ottawa Gunners
at Toronto (Arena Gardens and Varsity Arena)
March 21 to 26, 1928

The city of Regina, known throughout the Dominion for its Pats, sent another team to the Memorial Cup in the spring of 1928. This team was the Monarchs—formed from the ashes of two junior teams, the Pats and Falcons—and it was coached by Howie Milne, who had starred as a player with the Pats in the 1922 Memorial Cup playoffs. The Regina squad proved to be fan favorites in Toronto, because Ottawa had knocked off the Marlboros en route to the eastern title.

Regina led game one 4–1 in the third, with all four goals scored by future Chicago Black Hawks star Harold "Mush" March. Syd Howe, who also would go on to NHL stardom, scored two late goals for the Gunners, but Regina held on for a 4–3 victory. March scored his fifth goal of the series in game two, but it proved to be the only Monarchs marker as Ottawa evened the series with a 2–1 victory in front of 4,500 fans at Varsity Arena.

A crowd of about 9,000 jammed the Arena Gardens for game three. They witnessed two more goals from Mush March as Regina took the Memorial Cup back west with a 7–1 victory.

Elmwood Millionaires vs. **Toronto Marlboros**
at Toronto (Arena Gardens)
March 29 to 31, 1929

The Winnipeg-based Elmwood Millionaires had a difficult route to the 1929 Memorial Cup finals, needing overtime to defeat the Kenora Thistles and then a late three-goal rally to defeat the Calgary Canadian-Falcons for the Abbott Cup title. Billy Kendall was the hero in both series.

Toronto also needed to come from behind to advance to the Memorial Cup. After dropping the opener of the eastern final, 4–3, to the Ottawa Shamrocks, the Marlboros rallied for a 3–1 victory in game two and took the total-goals series, 6–5. Charlie Conacher scored all three Marlies goals in the second game.

The Marlies' big line of Conacher, Busher Jackson and Eddie Convey (known as the Three Musketeers) led Toronto to a 4–2 victory over Elmwood in game one. The score had been tied 2–2 after regulation time before Conacher set up Jackson twice in overtime. Coach Frank Selke saw his Marlboros sweep the series with another 4–2 victory in front of 8,000 fans in game two. Charlie Conacher had two goals for the winners.

Regina Pats vs. West Toronto
at Winnipeg (Amphitheatre)
March 27 to 29, 1930

While the West Toronto Athletic Club juniors were scraping by the Ottawa Rideaus to earn eastern Canada's berth in the Memorial Cup finals, the Regina Pats were running amuck in the west.

In Toronto, the Rideaus won the first game of the east's two-game, total-goals final, 4–3. But West Toronto won the second game, 3–1, to take the series by a combined score of 6–5. Meanwhile, Regina had outdistanced the Calgary Canadians and the Elmwood Millionaires by a combined score of 14–0 in a pair of two-game series. Pats goaltender Kenny Campbell went into the Memorial Cup finals having posted five straight shutouts.

Regina had a 2–0 lead in the opening game against West Toronto, and Campbell appeared well on his way to another shutout until Bob Gracie scored late in the third period. The final score was 3–1.

Over 5,000 fans saw a tense second game. "Forty seconds to go and the score tied," reported the *Regina Leader*. "To one team a goal would mean the Dominion junior hockey championship; to the other an opportunity to force another contest before the holders of the Memorial Cup for 1930 could be decided." The goal went to Ken Moore of Regina, and it gave the Pats a 3–2 victory.

Elmwood Millionaires vs. Ottawa Primroses
at Toronto (Arena Gardens) and Ottawa (Auditorium)
March 23 to 27, 1931

The Regina Pats were favored to repeat as Memorial Cup champions when they entered the 1931 Abbott Cup finals without having been scored on in six consecutive games. Ken Campbell made it seven straight shutouts with a 1–0 win over the Elmwood Millionaires. The Pats had a 1–0 lead late in the Abbott Cup finalé, but two quick goals allowed Elmwood to tie the total-goals series, 2–2. A full 10-minute overtime period was played. Regina scored early, but Elmwood tied it again when Kitson Massey scored with just 15 seconds to play. Spunk Duncanson eventually gave Elmwood a stunning upset with the winning goal in a second 10-minute overtime session.

The Millionaires advanced to face the Ottawa Primroses, who had qualified for the Memorial Cup finals with a victory over Niagara Falls. Brothers Dan and Bill Cowley gave Ottawa a 2–0 victory over Elmwood in the series opener, but the Millionaires forced a third and deciding game with a 2–1 victory in the second contest. The final game was moved to Ottawa, but despite a crowd of 9,000 fans the Winnipeg-based team claimed the Memorial Cup with a 3–0 victory. Elmwood's victory meant that the Memorial Cup had been won by the west seven times in the past 13 seasons.

Winnipeg Monarchs vs. **Sudbury Cub Wolves**
at Winnipeg (Amphitheatre)
March 31 to April 4, 1932

The Winnipeg Monarchs were coached by Harry Neil and Fred "Steamer" Maxwell. Neil had played for the Winnipeg Falcons when they beat the Stratford Midgets to win the 1921 Memorial Cup. Maxwell was a future member of the Hockey Hall of Fame.

The Sudbury Cub Wolves featured several future NHL players, most notably Toe Blake (though he would see action only as a substitute in the Memorial Cup finals). Sudbury tied the Montreal AAA, 1–1, in the opener in the eastern final, then scored a 3–0 victory in game two in front of 11,000 fans at Toronto's new Maple Leaf Gardens.

The Monarchs had defeated the Saskatoon Wesleys for the western title and were favored to win the Memorial Cup. They won the series opener, 4–3, but the Cub Wolves rallied to win the series with 2–1 and 1–0 victories.

And how did the folks of Sudbury handle all of this?

According to one report: "There was a hot time in the home town when word was flashed from Winnipeg that Sudbury had triumphed .... Scenes reminiscent of Armistice Day were enacted as the entire populace thronged into the downtown section to shout acclaim to the courageous little hockey band."

Regina Pats vs. **Newmarket Redmen**
at Toronto (Maple Leaf Gardens)
April 4 to 6, 1933

For the fourth time in eight years, Regina was represented in the Memorial Cup finals, Al Ritchie's Pats having won the Abbott Cup in a thrilling three-game series with the Brandon Native Sons. The first two games were ties before Regina won the series with a 2–1 victory in front of a sold-out crowd of 5,025 at the Winnipeg Amphitheatre.

In the east, the Newmarket Redmen and Montreal Royals played to a 2–2 tie in front of 11,000 fans at the Montreal Forum. Two nights later, 8,000 fans in Toronto saw Newmarket win the two-game, total-goals series with a 1–0 victory on Normie Mann's long-shot goal early in the second period.

Newmarket goaltender Randall Forder received rave reviews for his work in the Memorial Cup opener, especially in the second and third periods when the Pats owned a wide territorial edge. Newmarket won the game, 2–1, on goals by Mann and Pep Kelly. A 2–1 overtime victory in game two gave the Redmen the Memorial Cup. Regina blamed the loss on what widely was perceived as poor officiating. Pats captain Curly Kerr was suspended for the first six weeks of the following season after several Regina players scuffled with referee Johnny Mitchell.

Edmonton Athletics vs. **Toronto St. Michael's Majors**
at Winnipeg (Amphitheatre)
April 3 to 5, 1934

The 1934 St. Michael's Majors were a junior hockey powerhouse. St. Mike's featured the likes of future NHLers Bobby Bauer, Reg Hamilton, Art Jackson, Pep Kelly, Nick Metz, Don Wilson, Mickey Drouillard and goaltender Harvey Teno. Kelly and Wilson had come over from the Newmarket Redmen, the 1933 Memorial Cup champions. The Majors romped to the Memorial Cup finals in 1934, crushing the Ottawa Shamrocks, 8–2 and 9–3, and destroying the Charlottetown Abegweits, 12–2 and 7–2.

Out west, the Edmonton Athletic Club had been almost as dominant. Featuring captain Dan Carrigan, brothers Neil and Mac Colville, and Bill Carse, the Athletics beat Trail, 10–0 and 7–0, then downed the Saskatoon Wesleys, 10–5, on total goals. (Saskatoon had boasted Doug Bentley, Peter Leswick and Mel Hill.) In the western final, Edmonton beat the Port Arthur Westies, 7–3 and 4–0. Fred Layetzke earned the shutout with a 47-save effort.

Arriving in Winnipeg, St. Michael's borrowed Winnipeg Monarchs goalie Turk Broda for their practice sessions. Broda was impressed enough to predict a two-game sweep. The Majors won the opener, 5–0, behind two goals apiece from Pep Kelly and Johnny Acheson. Kelly scored two more in game two, including the clincher in overtime, as St. Mike's captured the Memorial Cup with a 6–4 victory.

Winnipeg Monarchs vs. Sudbury Cub Wolves
at Winnipeg (Amphitheatre)
April 9 to 13, 1935

The Memorial Cup of 1935 was a rematch of the 1932 series. This time around, Sudbury featured future NHLers Chuck Shannon, Dutch Hiller and Don Grosso. Coach Max Silverman had been the manager in 1932.

Though the Cub Wolves had gone undefeated through the playoffs, the Ottawa Rideaus were favored in the eastern final but fell to Sudbury 3–0 and 7–4. In the west, the Saskatoon Wesleys defeated the Vancouver King Georges and the Edmonton Canadians to set up a western final with the Winnipeg Monarchs, who had defeated the Fort William Maroons. Each game of the best-of-three western final was close, before Winnipeg emerged with a 3–2 victory in game three.

The Memorial Cup finals opened with a thriller, won 7–6 by Winnipeg. Sudbury evened matters with a convincing 7–2 win in game two. Art Stuart scored four times for the Cub Wolves. As for game three: "The mantle of dominion junior hockey supremacy today was draped around the slim shoulders of [the] Winnipeg Monarchs," wrote Herbert A. Honey of the *Canadian Press*. "A flying band of skating youth, the western champions joined a host of amateur hockey greats by defeating (the) Sudbury Cub Wolves 4-1."

Saskatoon Wesleys vs. **West Toronto Nationals**
at Toronto (Maple Leaf Gardens)
April 10 to 13, 1936

Coached by Hap Day and managed by Harold Ballard, the West Toronto Nationals did some heavy damage on the way to the Memorial Cup finals, including a 16–4 rout of the visiting Quebec Aces in an eastern semifinal game on March 31. West Toronto next bounced the Pembroke Little Lumber Kings to qualify for the Memorial Cup.

Out west, coach Hobb Wilson's Saskatoon Wesleys swept the Winnipeg-Elmwood Maple Leafs in a best-of-three series for the Abbott Cup. "I think our team is just as good as any western outfit in the past years," Wilson said. "We have a big, fast team and we're going to try awfully hard to take the mug back west."

It was not to be.

Following a 5–1 victory by West Toronto in the opener of the Memorial Cup the *Canadian Press* reported that "[the] Wesleys, not as polished as the eastern Canada titlists, lacked finish around the net." Red Hall, who had spent the previous summer tending goal for the Canadian senior lacrosse champion Orillia Terriers, turned aside Saskatoon's most dangerous drives. In game two, third-period goals by Peanuts O'Flaherty and Roy Conacher gave West Toronto a 4–2 victory and the Memorial Cup title.

Winnipeg Monarchs vs. Copper Cliff Redmen
at Toronto (Maple Leaf Gardens)
April 10 to 17, 1937

Coach Harry Neil's Winnipeg Monarchs capped off a stretch of nine games in 15 days by ousting Port Arthur, 8–2 and 8–0, to set up a best-of-three western final with the Saskatoon Wesleys. The Wesleys featured goaltender Charlie Rayner and center Sid Abel, but lost the Abbott Cup to the Monarchs.

In the meantime, the Copper Cliff Redmen defeated Timmins to win the Copeland Cup as champions of the Northern Ontario Hockey Association. They then ousted St. Michael's College of Toronto, the Montreal Victorias and the Ottawa Rideaus to reach the Memorial Cup finals. Led by their big line of Pat McReavy, Red Hamill and Roy Heximer, Copper Cliff had outscored its playoff opponents, 67–19.

In the opening game of the newly expanded best-of-five Memorial Cup series, Winnipeg led, 3–0, with 2:21 to play before Copper Cliff scored three late goals. The Redmen won, 4–3, in overtime. Down, but not out, the Monarchs rallied to win the next three games. "Climaxing one of the most spectacular junior series in history," the *Canadian Press* reported, "the Winnipeggers whitewashed [the] Copper Cliff Redmen 7-0." Copper Cliff had held a distinct edge in play in the first period, but wasn't able to score. Johnny McCreedy then went on to net four goals for the winners.

St. Boniface Seals vs. Oshawa Generals
at Toronto (Maple Leaf Gardens)
April 9 to 19, 1938

In the 1940s, Billy Taylor and Wally Stanowski would be teammates with the Toronto Maple Leafs. But this was 1938. Wally Stanowski was a star defenseman with the St. Boniface Seals. Billy Taylor was a scoring machine with the Oshawa Generals. Taylor led Oshawa past the Toronto Marlboros and Sudbury Cub Wolves, and went into the eastern final against the Perth Blue Wings with 15 goals in his last 12 games. He added five as Oshawa advanced to the Memorial Cup finals with 6–2 and 7–5 victories. Stanowski's Seals moved on with an Abbott Cup victory over the Edmonton Athletic Club.

Oshawa won the Memorial Cup opener, 3–2. Taylor had a goal and two assists, but "most of the huzzahs that burst from the throats of the 9,500 present were evoked by whirling Wally Stanowski," reported the *Canadian Press*. His play was compared to that of Eddie Shore.

The series see-sawed back and forth before St. Boniface wrapped it up with a 7–1 victory in game five. The crowd of 15,617 marked the largest attendance for any hockey game in Canada to that time. With four goals and seven assists, Taylor had figured in 11 of Oshawa's 12 goals in a losing cause. Still, the hockey world hadn't seen anything yet from him.

Edmonton Athletic Club Roamers vs. **Oshawa Generals**
at Toronto (Maple Leaf Gardens)
April 10 to 17, 1939

Billy Taylor and the Oshawa Generals were back in 1939, this time facing future Montreal Canadiens great Ken Reardon and the Edmonton Roamers. Oshawa had swept the North Bay Trappers, St. Michael's Majors and Toronto Native Sons before downing the Perth Blue Wings in the eastern Canadian final for the second straight year. Out west, Edmonton ran roughshod over the Trail Smoke Eaters, Moose Jaw Canucks and Brandon Elks.

The Roamers arrived in Toronto with an injury-riddled roster, but it was the humid conditions inside Maple Leaf Gardens, more than their injuries, that bothered Edmonton in game one. "I could hardly breathe after I had been on the ice a minute or so," said George Agar. "Whew, it was hot." Billy Taylor scored five times as Oshawa won the opener, 9–4. In game two, Billy the Kid had four goals and five assists in a 12–4 rout. "The way Taylor passes is incredible," said Lester Patrick, general manager of the New York Rangers. "I will venture to say there aren't more than half a dozen centers in the NHL who lay down passes as well as he does."

Edmonton used Elmer Kreller to shadow Taylor for the rest of the series, but the Generals won it in four. Taylor finished with nine goals and six assists.

Kenora Thistles vs. **Oshawa Generals**
at Winnipeg (Amphitheatre)
April 16 to 22, 1940

Billy Taylor was gone, but Buddy Hellyer, Dinny McManus and brothers Norm and Jud McAtee were back as the Oshawa Generals reached the Memorial Cup finals for the third straight year. The Generals beat the Toronto Young Rangers, the Toronto Marlboros and then the South Porcupine Dome Miners before downing the Verdun Maple Leafs in the eastern Canadian final.

Led by goaltender Chuck Rayner and defenseman Bill Juzda, the Kenora Thistles reached the Memorial Cup finals for the first time in 1940, defeating the Port Arthur Juniors and the Edmonton Athletic Club to win the west.

Oshawa won the series opener, 1–0, behind the netminding of McManus and a goal by center Roy Sawyer only 31 seconds before the end of the second period. The Generals went up 2–0 with a 4–1 victory in the second game, scoring twice with Juzda in the penalty box. But Kenora wasn't dead yet. The Thistles posted a 4–3 victory in game three to cut the Generals' lead to 2–1. However, the Thistles' dream ended when Oshawa posted a 4–2 victory in front of fewer than 3,000 fans, far short of the capacity crowds of at least 4,500 that had watched each of the first three games. With the victory, the Generals became the first team to win the Memorial Cup in consecutive seasons.

Winnipeg Rangers vs. Montreal Royals
at Toronto (Maple Leaf Gardens) and Montreal (Forum)
April 21 to 30, 1941

The Montreal Royals became the first team from Quebec to reach the Memorial Cup finals, dethroning the Oshawa Generals in the eastern final. Montreal suffered three injuries in the fifth game against Oshawa—Bob MacFarlane was left with a badly bruised side, Bruce Ward twisted a knee and Buddy Farmer was scheduled for surgery to repair a broken cheekbone. The Royals had also won the east despite having four players writing exams at McGill University during the series. Those players flew between Montreal and Toronto after each game. Because of that situation, the Royals hoped to have the entire Memorial Cup finals played in Montreal. Instead, the series rotated between Toronto and the Forum.

The Winnipeg Rangers needed seven games to defeat the Saskatoon Quakers for the Abbott Cup. They arrived in Toronto by train just 12 hours before the Memorial Cup series was to open but were still able to win game one, 4–2. The Royals had all of their student athletes back for game two in Montreal and won, 5–3. In the end, the Royals won both games in Montreal, while Winnipeg won all three in Toronto, including a 7–4 victory in the fifth and final game.

Portage la Prairie Terriers vs. Oshawa Generals
at Winnipeg (Amphitheatre)
April 14 to 21, 1942

The Oshawa Generals were back in the Memorial Cup finals for the fourth time in five years. This time, the Generals were under the guidance of manager Matt Leyden with coaching help from Charlie Conacher. The Generals featured veterans like Red Tilson, Ron Wilson, Ron Nelson and Floyd Curry. They swept the Montreal Royals in four games in the best-of-seven eastern final.

The Generals were not strangers to Memorial Cup play, but their opponents were. The Portage la Prairie Terriers, under coach Staff-Sgt. Addie Bell and manager Jack P. Bend, emerged as champions of Manitoba and then all of western Canada. The Terriers featured goaltender Gordon Bell and forward Joe Bell—both sons of Addie. Bend's son, Lin, had set a Manitoba junior scoring record with 57 regular-season points.

The Terriers took a 22-game winning streak into the Memorial Cup series, but Oshawa's experience made them slight favorites. Still, Portage la Prairie won the opener, 5–1, then took game two, 8–7 behind five goals and two assists from Bill Gooden. The Terriers' 24-game winning streak ended in game three, but an 8–2 romp in game four gave them the Memorial Cup.

"A great hockey team won," said Charlie Conacher. "They were really flying out there."

Winnipeg Rangers vs. Oshawa Generals
at Toronto (Maple Leaf Gardens)
April 17 to 28, 1943

Charlie Conacher had taken on full-time coaching duties in Oshawa in 1942-43, and he led the Generals to their fifth Memorial Cup appearance in six years. Oshawa had only the victories of 1939 and 1940 to show for their troubles. Their opponent this time would be the Winnipeg Rangers, who had beaten the Montreal Royals for the Memorial Cup title in 1941.

Red Tilson and Ken Smith combined with Floyd Curry on Oshawa's top line. (One year later, Tilson would be killed while serving in World War II—the Red Tilson Memorial Trophy has been presented to Ontario's best junior hockey player since 1945.) Winnipeg was led by captain Bill Boorman and Cal Gardner. Seven Rangers were in the navy—Church Russell, Ritchie McDonald, Bill Vickers, Joe Peterson, Smiley Irvine, Doug Jackson and Boorman. Eddie Coleman was awaiting his call from the RCAF.

The Memorial Cup finals were expanded to a best-of-seven affair in 1943. Oshawa manager Matt Leyden called his club the best-balanced team the Generals had ever had, but Winnipeg won the series in six games. The finalé was a 6–3 victory played in front of 14,485 fans. Paid attendance for the six games was 73,867—an average of 12,311, which was a record for amateur hockey in Canada.

Trail Smoke Eaters vs. **Oshawa Generals**
at Toronto (Maple Leaf Gardens)
April 15 to 22, 1944

Bob Kinnear, who had coached the Winnipeg Rangers to the 1943 Memorial Cup title, didn't mince any words prior to the 1944 event.

"Oshawa by a mile," Kinnear said. "Junior hockey in western Canada is not what it used to be. Most junior teams of previous years would have beaten either one of the two teams, Trail or Port Arthur, who have just concluded the western Canada playoffs."

Coached by Charlie Conacher, the 1943-44 Generals team was loaded with talent. Among those who would go on to play in the NHL were Floyd Curry, Bill Ezinicki and goaltenders Harvey Bennett and John Marois. The Generals also added Ted Lindsay, Gus Mortson and David Bauer (later known as Father David Bauer of the Canadian national team) from St. Michael's College after defeating the Majors in the playoffs.

Bill Ezinicki scored for Oshawa just seven seconds into the Memorial Cup opener with Trail. The fast start set the tone for the series, as the Generals swept the Smoke Eaters by scores of 9–2, 5–2, 15–4 and 11–4. Oshawa became the first team to win the Memorial Cup three times, but the dynasty was over. The Generals would not return to the Memorial Cup finals until 1966. They would not win it again until 1990.

Moose Jaw Canucks vs. **Toronto St. Michael's Majors**
at Toronto (Maple Leaf Gardens)
April 14 to 23, 1945

Two famous names were behind the bench during the 1945 Memorial Cup finals. Former Maple Leafs star Joe Primeau guided the St. Michael's Majors, while Reg Bentley, (older brother of Max and Doug, coached the Moose Jaw Canucks. There were also plenty of big names on the rosters. St. Michael's boasted future Maple Leafs like Gus Mortson, Jimmy Thomson and Tod Sloan. Moose Jaw featured Bert Olmstead in its lineup.

One player who would not suit up was Moose Jaw's their best player, Gerry Couture. A medical student at the University of Saskatchewan, it was thought he would have to stay behind to write his exams. Instead, Couture showed up in Toronto as a member of the Detroit Red Wings, who were battling the Maple Leafs for the Stanley Cup at the same time as the Memorial Cup finals were taking place.

St. Michael's opened the series with a 3–1 victory. Moose Jaw evened things with a 5–3 win in game two, but St. Mike's went on to take the next three, including a convincing 7–2 victory in game five. Leo Gravelle scored three for the Majors, who won the Memorial Cup for the first time in 11 years. Paid attendance for the series was 65,437, setting a record for a five-game junior series.

Winnipeg Monarchs vs. Toronto St. Michael's Majors
at Toronto (Maple Leaf Gardens)
April 13 to 27, 1946

Canada had lost a lot of young men on the battlefields of Europe. As the 1945-46 hockey season wound down, it was as though the country had decided to rediscover itself in its arenas. A crowd of 15,065 saw St. Michael's and the Guelph Biltmores close out the regular season at Maple Leaf Gardens. In Regina, a western Canadian record 6,672 fans saw the Edmonton Canadians defeat the Moose Jaw Canucks. Edmonton then lost the Abbott Cup finals to the Winnipeg Monarchs. St. Michael's, led by Tod Sloan, Red Kelly and Fleming Mackell, would again represent the east in the Memorial Cup series.

More than 30,000 ticket applications were received for the Memorial Cup opener, and a crowd of more than 14,000 was on hand as the Monarchs earned a 3–2 victory. St. Michael's, often being referred to as the Saints, rallied to win the next two games. They held a 3–2 series lead after five games when Tod Sloan scored five times in a 7–4 victory. After Winnipeg evened the series in game six, a record crowd of 15,803 saw the Monarchs win the series with a 4–2 victory in game seven. George Robertson scored two third-period goals to win it for Winnipeg.

All told, the 1946 Memorial Cup series drew 102,575 fans, a record for a seven-game amateur series in Canada.

Moose Jaw Canucks vs. **Toronto St. Michael's Majors**
at Winnipeg (Amphitheatre), Moose Jaw (Arena)
and Regina (Queen City Gardens)
April 15 to 22, 1947

The 1947 Memorial Cup finals were a rematch of the 1945 series, only this time it was played in the west. Joe Primeau was still the coach at St. Michael's, but this year the Moose Jaw Canucks were guided by Primeau's former Maple Leaf teammate and ex-Regina Pats star Ken Doraty.

The Canucks earned their Memorial Cup berth by winning a thrilling Abbott Cup final from the Brandon Elks. Because of a tie, an eighth game was necessary to determine a winner. St. Michael's outscored the Montreal Junior Canadiens 37–4, including 21–0 in game three, to sweep the Richardson Trophy series and win the east.

The best-of-seven Memorial Cup finals opened in Winnipeg.

"Heralded as the smoothest team to come out of the east in years," wrote Scotty Melville in the *Regina Leader-Post*, "Toronto St. Mike's lived up to all the nice words said about them by waltzing to a 12–3 triumph." Game two in Moose Jaw ended 6–1. The third game was played in Regina and the Majors had an 8–1 lead when the game was halted because of a bottle-throwing incident in the stands. The bad publicity over that incident limited the crowd to just 2,186 as St. Mike's wrapped up the series with a 3-2 victory.

Port Arthur West End Bruins vs. Barrie Flyers
at Toronto (Maple Leaf Gardens)
April 24 to May 1, 1948

It was a powerful Port Arthur West End Bruins team that qualified for the 1948 Memorial Cup finals. The Bruins were sparked by two players who had spent the 1946–47 season with the Memorial Cup-champion Toronto St. Michael's Majors—Rudy Migay and Benny Woit. Also in the Port Arthur lineup was flashy Danny Lewicki, who had been added to the roster from the Fort William Columbus club. And the Bruins featured goaltender Lorne Chabot, son of the former NHL great of the same name.

The Bruins reached the Memorial Cup finals by knocking off the Lethbridge Native Sons in the Abbott Cup. Lethbridge featured Eddie Dorohoy, who had 86 assists in 63 total games, and Bill Ramsden, who scored 107 goals! The last game of the Western final was played at Maple Leaf Gardens three days before the Memorial Cup series opened.

The experts were picking the Barrie Flyers and were surprised when Port Arthur opened the Memorial Cup finals with a 10–8 victory. Flyers coach Hap Emms blamed the many injuries his team faced. After two more Barrie losses, Emms turned his complaints toward the referees. The series was over in four games when Port Arthur scored a 9–8 victory in overtime to sweep it.

Brandon Wheat Kings vs. **Montreal Royals**
at Winnipeg (Amphitheatre) and Brandon (Wheat City Arena)
April 28 to May 16, 1949

Led by their top line of Gordie Knutson, Matt Benoit and Dickie Moore, the Montreal Royals reached the Memorial Cup finals on the strength of 16 wins in 17 playoff games, the last 13 in a row. The Brandon Wheat Kings featured captain Frank King, goaltender Ray Frederick, Joe Crozier and Glen Sonmor. Brandon defeated the defending champion Port Arthur West End Bruins for the Abbott Cup.

The best-of-seven Memorial Cup finals opened in Winnipeg, and before it was done it had turned into one of the greatest series in hockey history. The teams would end up playing eight games (one ended in a tie), and four were decided by a single goal. Games two, five, six, and seven were played in Brandon, but the deciding game was played on neutral ice in Winnipeg.

Brandon led the final game, 4–2, early in the third period, but Montreal scored the last four goals and won, 6–4. Quebec had its first Memorial Cup champion in the 31 years the trophy had been contested.

The Wheat Kings wouldn't make it back to the Memorial Cup finals for 30 years. When they returned in the spring of 1979, they would lose another close one—2–1 in overtime to the Peterborough Petes.

Regina Pats vs. **Montreal Junior Canadiens**
at Montreal (Forum) and Toronto (Maple Leaf Gardens)
April 27 to May 6, 1950

The Regina Pats ousted the Port Arthur West End Bruins in five games in the Abbott Cup finals and headed east to meet the Montreal Junior Canadiens for the Memorial Cup. The Pats, featuring Eddie Litzenberger, had won 14 of 18 playoff games.

Montreal, coached by Sam Pollock and Billy Reay, had finished off the Guelph Biltmores in six games to earn a spot in the Memorial Cup finals. The Canadiens started the series with an 8–7 victory at the Forum that featured 10 third-period goals. Dickie Moore, Art Rose and Don Marshall had two goals each for Montreal. Regina took a 2–1 lead into the third period of game two before the Canadiens rallied for a 5–2 victory. After a game-three victory in Toronto, the Canadiens seemed poised to sweep the series back in Montreal, but the Pats were able to save some face with a 7–4 victory.

Still at the Forum for game five, the Canadiens raced to a 6–1 lead and held on for a 6–3 victory. The media noted that on the same day as the Kentucky Derby, also known as the Run for the Roses, Art Rose had sparked Montreal with two goals six seconds apart in the second period. Rose was the leading scorer in the series with eight goals in five games.

Winnipeg Monarchs vs. **Barrie Flyers**
at Winnipeg (Amphitheatre) and Brandon (Wheat City Arena)
May 2 to May 8, 1951

In the spring of 1951, the Regina Pats and the Winnipeg Monarchs hooked up in an Abbott Cup finals that took eight games to decide. Game four of the series was notable in that it marked the junior debut of Gerry James, who later would win the Grey Cup with the Winnipeg Blue Bombers and the Stanley Cup with the Toronto Maple Leafs. James's Monarchs went on to take the Abbott Cup with an 8–4 victory in game eight.

The Monarchs knew they'd be in tough against the Barrie Flyers in the Memorial Cup finals. Barrie was coached by the legendary Hap Emms and featured the likes of Real Chevrefils, Jerry Toppazzini and Leo Labine, all of whom would go on to play in the NHL.

The final opened with Barrie winning 5–1. *CP* reported: "The well-conditioned Barrie club passed the Monarchs dizzy for the first two periods and only in the last session did the Regals show any resemblance to the form which carried them to the western title." The Flyers were now in the catbird seat, as the team that won the first game had gone on to win the Memorial Cup in every year since 1938. Barrie went on to sweep the series and win the national junior championship for the first time.

Regina Pats vs. **Guelph Biltmore Mad Hatters**
at Guelph (Arena) and Toronto (Maple Leaf Gardens)
April 25 to May 2, 1952

The Regina Pats advanced to the Memorial Cup finals on April 19 with a 2–1 victory over the Fort William Hurricanes. Eddie Litzenberger scored both goals as the Pats wrapped up the series in six games.

Regina's opposition in the Memorial Cup would be supplied by the Guelph Biltmore Mad Hatters of coach Alf Pike. Guelph's roster featured eight players who would go on to play in the NHL. Two of them—team captain Andy Bathgate and Harry Howell—would end up in the Hockey Hall of Fame. Their top scorer, however, was Ken Laufman, who totalled 53 goals and 86 assists in 54 games to set what was then an Ontario junior scoring record with 139 points in the regular season.

The Memorial Cup series opened in Guelph's new 4,247-seat arena, with tickets going for what was then the steep price of three dollars. "The Biltmores' edge on the scoreboard, 8–2, was a good indication of the play," admitted the *Regina Leader-Post*. "The number of shots on goal told a much more detailed story." Guelph outshot Regina, 46–10. The remainder of the series was played at Maple Leaf Gardens, but the results were the same as Guelph went on to sweep it by scores of 4–2, 8–2 and 10–2.

St. Boniface Canadiens vs. **Barrie Flyers**
at Winnipeg (Amphitheatre) and Brandon (Wheat City Arena)
April 27 to May 6, 1953

In the spring of 1953, Don Cherry was a defenseman with the Barrie Flyers. Among his teammates were Doug Mohns, Orval Tessier, Skip Teal, goaltender Marv Edwards (who was picked up from the St. Catharines Teepees) and captain Don McKenney. The Flyers, coached by Hap Emms, eliminated the Quebec Citadels in the eastern Canadian final to advance to the Memorial Cup series.

The Flyers traveled west to meet coach Bryan Hextall's St. Boniface Canadiens, who won the Abbott Cup with a seven-game series victory over the Lethbridge Native Sons. It was St. Boniface's first western junior title since 1938 when the Seals won the Memorial Cup.

The 1953 Memorial Cup finals would be played in Winnipeg, with the exception of game two, which was scheduled for Brandon. Eastern teams had won the last four titles and the Flyers, winners in 1951, went in as 8-to-5 favorites. Barrie overcame St. Boniface leads in each of the first two games as they raced out to a 3–0 series lead. Most people were now predicting a sweep, but the Canadiens stayed alive with a 7–4 victory that broke the east's 12-game Memorial Cup winning streak. The west hadn't won a game since game four of the 1950 final. Barrie then wrapped up the series with a 6–1 win in game five.

A Note on Don Cherry

FOR THE RECORD, Don Cherry had one assist in game one of the 1953 Memorial Cup. He was kept off the scoresheet in game two, picked up one minor penalty in game three, had a goal in game four (one report said he was "a standout"), and scored once in game five during which he also picked up a fighting major and a minor.

The Cherry legend includes—or doesn't include, depending upon to whom you are speaking—an incident from game five that included Gary Blaine, a St. Boniface defenseman of immense potential whose career would fall victim to the demon rum, and Cherry.

Legend has it that Blaine actually chased Cherry around the Winnipeg Amphitheatre in an attempt to get him to fight.

As *Winnipeg Free Press* columnist Hal Sigurdson recounted in June, 1996, "Blaine's teammate, Ab McDonald ... says it was Cherry. So does former provincial cabinet minister Larry Desjardins, who was general manager of Blaine's St. Boniface Canadiens at the time."

As for Blaine....

"To be honest," he told Sigurdson, "I'm not sure. Orval Tessier had just slashed our goaltender, Hal Dalkie, and I drilled him. When he went down I tried to pick him up, but he turtled. I'd never seen a guy do that before. Anyway, I heard another of their players chirping so I went after him. He took off and I chased him. When I asked our guys who it was they told me his name was Don Cherry."

Edmonton Oil Kings vs. **St. Catharines Teepees**
at Toronto (Maple Leaf Gardens)
May 9 to 16, 1954

When the Edmonton Oil Kings journeyed east for the best-of-seven Memorial Cup finals they didn't leave anything to chance—they even brought their own water. "The players claimed they suffered cramps in out-of-town games from drinking other water," claimed coach Ken McAuley. The likes of Norm Ullman and John Bucyk "didn't want to take any chances."

While the Oil Kings were sequestered in a Toronto motel, the Quebec Frontenacs and St. Catharines Teepees struggled to declare a winner in a bitterly contested eastern final. St. Catharines won the series in six games.

Rudy Pilous's Teepees had now played 91 games on the year. The Oil Kings, with an amazing 61 victories in 65 games, hadn't played in 16 days by the time the Memorial Cup series opened, and the Teepees rolled to an 8–2 victory over the rusty Oilers.

Edmonton played better in game two, but it still wasn't enough as they lost 5–3. St. Catharines' top line of Brian Cullen, Hughie Barlow and Barry Cullen combined for all four goals in a 4–1 victory in game three. After a 3–3 tie in game four, the Teepees wrapped up the series with a 6–2 victory. It marked the sixth straight season in which an eastern team had won the Memorial Cup.

Regina Pats vs. **Toronto Marlboros**
at Regina (Exhibition Stadium)
April 21 to 29, 1955

It was a talented group of Toronto Marlboros that took on the Regina Pats for the Memorial Cup in 1955. Coached by Turk Broda, the Marlies featured the likes of captain Al MacNeil, Bob Baun, Billy Harris and Bob Pulford. Toronto had dumped the St. Catharines Teepees in a six-game eastern final, then headed west to face Regina, who had knocked off the Winnipeg Monarchs.

Included on the Regina roster were Bill Hicke and Bill Hay. Murray Balfour would miss the first two games as he recovered from a cracked kneecap suffered seven weeks previously. Regina had also added Lionel Repka from the Edmonton Oil Kings, and Earl Ingarfield and Les Colwill from the Lethbridge Native Sons.

Prior to the Memorial Cup opener, Turk Broda said: "I haven't seen the Regina Pats in action ... [but] if we don't win the series in five games I might be looking for a new job. The pattern lately has been the east in five and I might get thrown out if I let the side down."

History shows that Broda didn't let the side down. Regina was the winner of game one by a score of 3–1, but the Marlies stormed back to take four in a row. Billy Harris was the hero, scoring the winning goal in overtime in each of the last two games.

Regina Pats vs. **Toronto Marlboros**
at Toronto (Maple Leaf Gardens)
April 27 to May 6, 1956

The Toronto Marlboros needed eight games to eliminate the Montreal Junior Canadiens and reach the Memorial Cup finals for the second straight year in 1956. The team again was coached by Turk Broda and featured the likes of Bob Nevin, Carl Brewer, Bob Pulford, Bobby Baun, Al MacNeil and Harry Neale. Len Broderick provided the goaltending.

The Regina Pats once again were the opposition for the Marlies. This year the Pats roster boasted Bill Hicke, Murray Balfour, captain Harry Ottenbreit and goaltender Hank Metcalf. It was bolstered by Len Lunde (Edmonton Oil Kings), Johnny Kowalchuk (Fort William Canadians) and Stewart McNeill (Port Arthur North Stars).

The Pats were coming off a 13-day layoff when the Memorial Cup started. Still they led game one, 4–2, late in the third period before settling for a 4–4 overtime tie. Playoff scoring star Bob Pulford was shut out that game. He went on to score 10 goals as the Marlboros won the next four games and claimed the Memorial Cup once again.

Maple Leafs president Conn Smythe had not been impressed with the type of hockey played by the Regina Pats. "That's why [the western teams] keep losing the Memorial Cup," Smythe said. "The Marlies play it like the pros and that's why they're winning."

Flin Flon Bombers vs. Ottawa Canadiens
at Flin Flon (Community Arena)
and Regina (Exhibition Stadium)
April 26 to May 8, 1957

Hockey had been part of the history of the mining town of Flin Flon, Manitoba—situated on the Saskatchewan border—since its beginnings in 1929. The junior Bombers began play in 1949 and had won six Saskatchewan Junior Hockey League titles. Until the spring of 1957, the Bombers had never gotten any further than that along the Memorial Cup trail.

SJHL scoring leader Ted Hampson (48 goals and 118 points) and league MVP George Konik led a group of Bombers that had mostly been brought up through the minor hockey system in Flin Flon. For the Memorial Cup series, Orland Kurtenbach was added from Prince Albert.

The Ottawa Canadiens—coached by Sam Pollock and Scotty Bowman, and featuring Ralph Backstrom, Murray Balfour and Claude Richard (brother of Maurice and Henri)—won two of the first three games in Flin Flon before the Memorial Cup series moved to Regina. Flin Flon won the next two games, but Ottawa won again to force game seven.

One of the greatest Memorial Cup finals in history ended with Flin Flon on top, 3–2, thanks to Hampson's winning goal at 10:30 of the third period. It was the Bombers' 88th game of the season—and their 72nd win. This victory put Flin Flon on the map.

Regina Pats vs. **Hull-Ottawa Canadiens**
at Ottawa (Auditorium) and Hull (Arena)
April 25 to May 6, 1958

Because the Montreal Canadiens did not want their junior squad playing in Quebec, where the junior competition was weak, the Hull-Ottawa Canadiens played against senior teams in the Eastern Ontario Hockey League and played exhibition games against OHA junior teams. Come the Memorial Cup playoffs, the Baby Habs proved they were ready for top-notch junior competition. With captain Ralph Backstrom, Claude Richard, Bobby Rousseau and J.C. Tremblay—plus goalie Bruce Gamble on loan from Guelph—Hull-Ottawa crushed the Cape Breton All-Stars, 18–3 and 12–2, before the rest of the series was called off. They then defeated the Toronto Marlboros in five games for the eastern Canadian championship.

The Regina Pats also were sponsored by the Montreal Canadiens. They were led by the high-scoring line of Billy Hicke, Red Berenson and Joe Lunghamer. Also in the lineup were Terry Harper and Aut Erickson. Regina defeated the Edmonton Oil Kings and St. Boniface to become western champions.

"The Habs are a free-wheeling bunch," said Regina coach Frank Mario. "We're going to have to skate and check like mad if we hope to keep them in tow." Regina won the opener and kept the series close through five games, but Hull-Ottawa won it all with a 6–1 victory in game six.

Winnipeg Braves vs. Peterborough TPT Petes
at Winnipeg (Arena) and Brandon (Wheat City Arena)
April 24 to May 1, 1959

Scotty Bowman, who would go on to become the winningest coach in NHL history, made his third straight appearance in the Memorial Cup finals in 1959. After two years as an assistant coach to Sam Pollock, Bowman had graduated to a head coaching position with the Peterborough TPT Petes. The Petes were in their third season in Peterborough, having moved over from Kitchener. They finished seventh in a seven-team league their first season there, then moved up to fifth the following year. Under Bowman, they finished second.

The Petes were captained by Bill Mahoney and featured a tough defenseman in Barclay Plager. His 252 penalty minutes in 1958-59 would remain an OHA record until broken by Bob Neely in 1972-73. The Petes upset the St. Michael's Majors in an eight-game OHA final, then defeated the Hull-Ottawa Canadiens for the eastern Canada title.

Out of the west rode the Winnipeg Braves, featuring Laurie Langrell, their leading scorer with 42 goals (including six in one game) and goaltender Ernie Wakely. Defenseman Ted Green was an addition from the St. Boniface Canadiens. The Braves dropped the Memorial Cup opener to Peterborough on home ice, then roared back to win three in a row before wrapping up the series with a 6–2 victory in game five at Brandon.

Edmonton Oil Kings vs. **St. Catharines Teepees**
at St. Catharines (Garden City Arena)
and Toronto (Maple Leaf Gardens)
April 27 to May 8, 1960

The St. Catharines Teepees had been in last place in their league at Christmas. They rallied to finish fourth. Featuring the likes of goaltender Roger Crozier, captain Chico Maki and Vic Hadfield, the Teepees went on to sideline the Brockville Canadians in an eight-game eastern Canada final.

The Edmonton Oil Kings took seven games to sideline the Brandon Wheat Kings in the western final. They were led by Ed Joyal and Bruce MacGregor, and picked up Cliff Pennington and Dunc McCallum for the Memorial Cup finals. Still, Oil Kings manager Leo LeClerc was concerned.

"In order to win at the other end of the country you've got to have a powerhouse," LeClerc said. "I figure we have to be 25 percent better, at least, and after watching St. Catharines … I'm very doubtful."

Edmonton won game one 5–3 in St. Catharines behind a 35-save effort from Russ Gillow, who was cut for eight stitches above his left eye during the game. Gillow was unable to play game two when the series moved to Toronto. He returned to face a 54-shot barrage in game three as the Teepees scored a 9–1 victory. Gillow faced 56 shots in a 9–6 loss in game five. St. Catharines wrapped up the series with a 7–3 win in game six.

Edmonton Oil Kings vs. **Toronto St. Michael's Majors**
at Edmonton (Gardens)
April 25 to May 5, 1961

Coached by Father David Bauer, the St. Michael's Majors featured the Draper twins, Bruce and Dave, along with the likes of Larry Keenan, Arnie Brown, Billy MacMillan, Terry Clancy, Terry O'Malley and Barry MacKenzie. In the nets, Dave Dryden shared playing time with Gerry Cheevers. During the regular season, Cheevers had spent eight games playing left wing! He didn't score, but did pick up one assist.

The Edmonton Oil Kings had won 16 of 19 playoff games against the Lethbridge Native Sons, Trail Smoke Eaters, Regina Pats and Winnipeg Rangers en route to the Memorial Cup finals. They were led by Don Chiz, who had scored 29 goals in the playoffs.

Despite their high-powered offense, Edmonton fired just 17 shots at Gerry Cheevers in game one of the Memorial Cup series. St. Michael's was an easy 4–0 winner. Edmonton manager Leo LeClerc assured all who would listen that the Oil Kings "could not be that bad again." He was right. The next time out, the Oil Kings scored a goal. It came at 13:25 of the third period, ending Cheevers' shutout string at 113 minutes and 25 seconds. Still, St. Michael's won 4–1. It was 4–2 Majors in game three before Edmonton kept the series alive with a pair of wins. Another 4–2 victory in game six gave the series to St. Mike's.

Edmonton Oil Kings vs. **Hamilton Red Wings**
at Hamilton (Forum), Guelph (Memorial Gardens) and
Kitchener (Auditorium)
April 29 to May 8, 1962

The Edmonton Oil Kings were led by captain Wayne

Muloin, Roger Bourbonnais, Larry Hale and Glen Sather. They needed seven games to finish off the Brandon Wheat Kings in the Abbott Cup finals, then headed east to meet the Hamilton Red Wings—featuring Paul Henderson, Lowell MacDonald and Pit Martin. Both Hamilton and Edmonton were affiliated with the NHL's Detroit Red Wings.

The fighting began before the Oil Kings arrived in the east. Originally scheduled to be played in Toronto, the CAHA announced the first game would be played in Hamilton, with the next three in Guelph. The rest of the series, if needed, would be played in Kitchener. All this was because of a hassle over television rights involving Hamilton and Toronto stations. Edmonton manager Leo LeClerc was not happy. He wanted to play all the games in Maple Leaf Gardens. As he said: "You don't play the Grey Cup in a cow pasture."

The Red Wings won the opener, 5–2, on home ice. The teams split the first two games in Guelph, before Hamilton moved into a 3–1 series lead with a 3–0 win in game four. There were 7,071 fans in the Kitchener Arena for game five as Hamilton posted a 7–4 victory to win the Memorial Cup.

Edmonton Oil Kings vs. Niagara Falls Flyers
at Edmonton (Gardens)
May 2 to 11, 1963

The Edmonton Oil Kings were back in the national final for a fourth consecutive year. This time coach Buster Brayshaw was all but guaranteeing victory over the Niagara Falls Flyers. This, he said, was the best team he had brought to the championship, and they had been taught to employ "the eastern style of play."

The Oil Kings had made it to the Memorial Cup finals with playoff victories over the Estevan Bruins, then the Brandon Wheat Kings in the Abbott Cup finals. Included on the Edmonton roster were Bert Marshall, Pat Quinn, Glen Sather and captain Roger Bourbonnais.

Niagara Falls, managed by the legendary Hap Emms, had eliminated the Neil McNeil Maroons and Espanola Eagles in Ontario playoffs, then dumped Montreal's Notre Dame de Grace Monarchs to reach the Memorial Cup finals. The Flyers were led by Bill Goldsworthy, Gary Dornhoefer, Don Awrey and Terry Crisp. They romped to an 8–2 victory in game one, but Edmonton won the next three in a row. The Flyers stayed alive with a 5–2 victory in game five. The Oil Kings led 4–0 early in the third period of game six, but had to hang on for a 4–3 victory. Russ Kirk made the game's biggest save on Wayne Maxner with about five minutes to play as Edmonton claimed the Memorial Cup.

Edmonton Oil Kings vs. **Toronto Marlboros**
at Toronto (Maple Leaf Gardens)
May 3 to 9, 1964

The Edmonton Oil Kings were in the Memorial Cup finals for the fifth consecutive season, but they were defending champions for the first time. This year, they added Fran Huck (Regina Pats), Larry Mickey (Moose Jaw Canucks) and Ron Boehm (Estevan Bruins) to their roster as they prepared to face the Toronto Marlboros.

The Marlies, run by Harold Ballard and coached by Jim Gregory, featured Gary Smith in goal, Rod Seiling and Jim McKenny on defense and the likes of Peter Stemkowski, Mike Walton, Wayne Carleton, Ron Ellis and Brit Selby up front. They had romped through the eastern playoffs, downing the Niagara Falls Flyers, the Montreal Junior Canadiens and Scotty Bowman's Notre Dame de Grace Monarchs to reach the Memorial Cup finals.

Toronto beat Edmonton, 5–2 and 3–2, to start the series, but the Marlies' Jim Gregory predicted that "[Game 3] will be a real tough one. It will take until tomorrow until the Kings are accustomed to Toronto." But the Oil Kings' top line of Butch Paul, Max Mestinsek and Glen Sather was on the limp. The Marlies won game three 5–2, then swept the series with a 7–2 romp. Despite their powerhouse squad, only a total of 10,000 Toronto fans had attended the Marlboros' sweep.

Edmonton Oil Kings vs. **Niagara Falls Flyers**
at Edmonton (Gardens)
May 4 to 14, 1965

When the Edmonton Oil Kings bounced the Winnipeg Braves to win the Abbott Cup, they earned their sixth consecutive berth in the Memorial Cup finals. It was an incredible streak of success, but the Oil Kings went into this final with just one championship in those five previous trips.

As in 1963, Edmonton's opposition for the Memorial Cup would be the Niagara Falls Flyers. This year's Flyers featured captain Dave Woodley, Gilles Marotte, Don Marcotte, Jean Pronovost, Derek Sanderson, Bill Goldsworthy, Jim Lorentz, Rosaire Paiement, 15-year-old defenseman Rick Ley and goaltenders Bernie Parent and Doug Favell.

The Oil Kings went into the 1965 Memorial Cup finals with their goaltending situation uncertain. Gary Simmons had suffered an eight-stitch cut on his right kneecap late in the regular season. It never healed properly and he was on crutches on the eve of game one. Edmonton added goaltender Wayne Stephenson from Winnipeg and he went the distance in the series. He outplayed future NHL teammate Bernie Parent in the opener, but Niagara Falls won, 3–2. Fran Huck was added to the Oil Kings lineup in game two, but the Flyers scored a 5–1 victory. Edmonton then scored a 5–1 win of its own, but Niagara Falls stormed back with 8–2 and 8–1 victories to wrap up the series.

Edmonton Oil Kings vs. Oshawa Generals
at Toronto (Maple Leaf Gardens)
May 4 to 16, 1966

The Edmonton Oil Kings made it seven Memorial Cup finals in a row when they beat the Estevan Bruins for the Abbott Cup. (This was the last Abbott Cup finals before major junior hockey came to the Prairies in the form of what would become the Western Hockey League.) Following the series, the Oil Kings, who featured the likes of Garnet "Ace" Bailey, Al Hamilton, Bob Falkenberg and goaltender Smokey McLeod, announced they would add three Bruins to their roster for the national final—Jim Harrison, Ross Lonsberry and Ted Hodgson.

Edmonton's opposition this time around was provided by the Oshawa Generals, featuring Bobby Orr, Wayne Cashman, Danny O'Shea and Nick Beverley. The Generals were coached by Bep Guidolin and managed by Wren Blair. Oshawa had only finished fourth in the Ontario Junior Hockey League, but went on to beat the Shawinigan Falls Bruins in the eastern Canada final.

The Oil Kings tested Orr repeatedly during a 7–2 victory in game one, but the young defenseman proved as tough as he was talented. Unfortunately he aggravated a groin injury that hampered him through the rest of the series, which the Oil Kings went on to win in six games.

The Memorial Cup finals of 1966 marked the last time the junior championship was held at Maple Leaf Gardens.

Port Arthur Marrs vs. **Toronto Marlboros**
at Fort William (Gardens)
May 7 to 14, 1967

The world of junior hockey began to change in 1966–67. No longer would the only junior hockey in western Canada be played in the provincial junior leagues; now there was something called the Canadian Major Junior Hockey League. In its first season, it featured the Edmonton Oil Kings, Estevan Bruins, Regina Pats, Moose Jaw Canucks, Saskatoon Blades, Weyburn Red Wings and Calgary Buffaloes. The CMJHL operated outside the CAHA's jurisdiction, which meant that member teams weren't eligible to compete for the Memorial Cup. As a result it was the Port Arthur Marrs carrying the west's colors in 1967. Under the CAHA's equalization rules, Port Arthur could add six players for the final. Among the pickups were Juha Widing and Bill Fairbairn from the Brandon Wheat Kings.

Representing the east was the Toronto Marlboros, coached by Gus Bodnar and featuring captain Brian Glennie, Gerry Meehan, Brad Park and Mike Pelyk. Paced by the line of Doug Acomb, Frank Hamill and Mike Byers, the Marlies posted a 6–3 victory to open the Memorial Cup finals. Toronto won game two, 8–4, behind three goals apiece from Meehan and Acomb. Port Arthur won game three, but the Marlies wrapped up the series in five.

"This is the best hockey club I've ever played with," said Brian Glennie as he accepted the Memorial Cup.

Estevan Bruins vs. **Niagara Falls Flyers**
at Niagara Falls (Memorial Arena) and Montreal (Forum)
May 6 to 15, 1968

The Canadian Major Junior Hockey League was replaced by the Western Canada Junior Hockey League in 1967–68. Though little but the name had changed, the league was mostly back in the good graces of the CAHA, meaning its teams were eligible for the Memorial Cup.

The Estevan Bruins finished second in the WCJHL standings, but knocked off the first-place Flin Flon Bombers (who featured Bobby Clarke and Reggie Leach) in the playoffs. By the time Jim Harrison led Estevan to an Abbott Cup victory over the Penticton Broncos, the Bruins had played 23 playoff games—winning 20 and losing only one.

In the East, the Niagara Falls Flyers survived three Ontario Junior Hockey League playoff series before beating the Verdun Maple Leafs for a Memorial Cup berth. Both Niagara Falls and Estevan wore Boston Bruins-style uniforms, which presented a problem in game one, won 7–4 by the Flyers. Niagara Falls dressed in Junior Canadiens jerseys when the series shifted to Montreal for game two. Only 1,849 fans saw Estevan even the series. The Flyers sported St. Catharines Teepees uniforms when the scene shifted back to Niagara Falls for the next three games. The home team won them all to wrap up the series, and captain Rick Ley accepted the Memorial Cup.

Regina Pats vs. **Montreal Junior Canadiens**
at Montreal (Forum) and Regina (Exhibition Stadium)
April 30 to May 6, 1969

The Western Canada Junior Hockey League became the WCHL in 1968–69 and broke away once again from the CAHA. Three teams—the Regina Pats, Moose Jaw Canucks and Weyburn Red Wings—didn't agree with the decision and returned to the security of the Saskatchewan Junior Hockey League. Regina would go on to represent the west in the Memorial Cup after beating Manitoba's Dauphin Kings in the Abbott Cup series. The Pats featured forwards Laurie Yaworski, Ron Garwasiuk, Larry Wright and Don Saleski, and borrowed three Dauphin players—including Butch Goring—before heading east.

The Pats met up with a powerhouse Montreal Junior Canadiens team that boasted such future NHL stars as Gil Perreault, Richard Martin, Marc Tardif, Rejean Houle and Jocelyn Guevremont, among others. Montreal defeated Hamilton, Peterborough and St. Catharines for the OJHL title before beating the Sorel Eperviers for the Richardson Trophy as eastern Canadian champions.

Guy Charron scored a hat trick as Montreal opened the Memorial Cup at home with a 5–3 victory. After a 7–2 win in game two, the series moved to Regina where the Canadiens completed the sweep with 5–2 and 8–6 victories. The Pats led game four, 5–1, before Montreal stormed back to tie it 6–6 and win it with a pair of overtime goals.

Weyburn Red Wings vs. **Montreal Junior Canadiens**
at Montreal (Forum)
May 6 to 12, 1970

The Montreal Junior Canadiens, featuring Gilbert Perreault, Richard Martin, Ian Turnbull and Paulin Bordeleau, finished atop the Ontario Junior Hockey League standings with a 37–12–5 record. Montreal then sidelined the Ottawa 67's and St. Catharines Black Hawks before being forced to go seven games with the Toronto Marlboros.

After beating Toronto, Montreal faced the Sault Ste. Marie Greyhounds, champions of the Northern Ontario Junior Hockey League. "The Soo" surprised visiting Montreal by winning the first game, 5–4. The Junior Canadiens then went out and won four straight, including a 20–3 romp in the fifth and final game. Turnbull and Perreault had four goals each in that victory. Next up were Guy Lafleur's Quebec Remparts, who were swept by Montreal in the best-of-five eastern final.

Out west, the breakaway WCHL was still ineligible for the Memorial Cup. The Weyburn Red Wings would advance to the national final, winning their first Saskatchewan junior title, then ousting the Vernon Essos, the Red Deer Rustlers and the Westfort (Thunder Bay) Hurricanes.

Richard Martin scored four goals as Montreal opened the Memorial Cup finals with a 9–4 victory. The Baby Habs took game two, 6–2. After 4–3 and 6–5 victories, the Junior Canadiens had their second straight championship sweep. It was the ninth time in 11 seasons that the Ontario Hockey Association representative won the Memorial Cup.

Edmonton Oil Kings vs. **Quebec Remparts**
at Quebec City (Le Colisée)
May 17 to 19, 1971

The Western Canada Hockey League sent its first representative to the Memorial Cup in 1971, but the Edmonton Oil Kings had to issue a challenge to the eastern champion before it could happen. Meanwhile, there were problems determining the eastern winner.

Guy Lafleur's Quebec Remparts had romped through the Quebec league playoffs, setting up a much-anticipated Richardson Trophy eastern final with Marcel Dionne's St. Catharines Black Hawks. After winning two of the first three games, the Remparts won game four 4–1 on home ice. It was a victory interrupted by a couple of third-period brawls, and marred by postgame incidents that saw Quebec fans attack Black Hawks players.

After winning game five in St. Catharines, the Black Hawks refused to return to Quebec City. Parents were concerned for the players' safety, and the Hawks were also unhappy about talk of the eastern winner facing the western champions for the Memorial Cup. With St. Catharines determined to stand its ground, CAHA president Earl Dawson declared the Remparts the eastern champs and arranged a best-of-three series against Edmonton.

Lafleur had scored 130 goals during the 1970–71 season. He had a goal and three assists in a 5–1 win over Edmonton in game one. Lafleur was shut out in game two, but Quebec still scored a 5–2 victory.

Edmonton Oil Kings, Peterborough Petes
and **Cornwall Royals**
at Ottawa (Civic Centre)
May 8 to 14, 1972

Junior hockey split into two distinct groups in 1971–72: Major Junior and Junior A. The premiere group formed three leagues, one in Ontario, one in Quebec and another in Western Canada. These three major junior leagues would continue to compete for the Memorial Cup, but now their champions would meet in a round-robin tournament at a pre-determined site. The two teams emerging with the best records would then play for the title. A formula based on the ratio of goals-for to goals-against would break any ties.

The Peterborough Petes knocked off the Ottawa 67's to win the OHA championship, then opened the Memorial Cup tournament with a 4–2 win over Cornwall. Ron Lalonde scored twice. Peterborough clinched a spot in the final when Doug Gibson had two goals and two assists in a 6–4 win over the WCJHL champs from Edmonton. The Oil Kings then dropped a 5–0 decision to the Quebec Major Junior Hockey League titlists.

Cornwall, in the Memorial Cup finals for the first time, edged the Petes 2–1 in front of 10,155 fans to win the championship. Gary McGregor scored the winner at 2:01 of the third period. Peterborough outshot Cornwall 47–38, but couldn't put more than one puck past the Royals' Richard Brodeur, who was selected the tournament's most outstanding player.

Medicine Hat Tigers, **Toronto Marlboros**
and Quebec Remparts
at Montreal (Forum)
May 7 to 12, 1973

The Medicine Hat Tigers won the Western Canada Hockey League championship in only their third season of existence. Some called them the Mad Hatters, but the Tigers were perhaps best known as the Gassoff Gang—Bob Gassoff was the league's toughest player, and brothers Brad and Ken were no slouches, either. But the Tigers were also talented. Tom Lysiak topped the WCHL with 96 assists and 154 points in 67 regular-season games as he won his second straight scoring title. Lanny McDonald was third, behind Dennis Sobchuk of the Regina Pats, with 62 goals and 139 points in 68 games.

Boasting the likes of Mike Palmateer, Wayne Dillon, Mark and Marty Howe and Paulin Bordeleau, the Toronto Marlboros had become the first OHA team to reach 100 points with a record of 47–7–9. Two days after eliminating the Peterborough Petes in the OHA finals, the Marlies opened the Memorial Cup tournament with a 5–2 win over the Quebec Remparts. Medicine Hat then beat the Marlies 3–2, but after a 7–3 loss to the Remparts it was Quebec and Toronto that advanced to the final.

The Marlies didn't leave any doubt in the championship game, scoring four times on the power-play and winning 9–1. Mark Howe had two goals and three assists. Glenn Goldup and Peter Marrin also had two goals apiece.

Regina Pats, St. Catharines Black Hawks
and Quebec Remparts
at Calgary (Corral)
May 5 to 12, 1974

The 1973–74 junior hockey season was dominated by talk of money. In early June 1973, 18-year-old Dennis Sobchuk was negotiating for a four-year, $350,000 contract with the World Hockey Association's Los Angeles Sharks. He later would sign a 10-year, $1.7-million deal with the WHA's Cincinnati Stingers. Sobchuk was 19 when he signed for what at the time was the most money ever given to a junior hockey player.

Sobchuk led the Regina Pats to first place in the WCHL with a 43–14–11 record. They then defeated the Saskatoon Blades, Swift Current Broncos and Calgary Centennials to reach the Memorial Cup tournament.

The Ontario champions were the St. Catharines Black Hawks, who had finished second to the Kitchener Rangers in the regular season, but then went unbeaten in the post-season (winning 12 and tying two) to take the OHA crown. The Black Hawks opened the Memorial Cup tournament with a 4–1 win over Quebec, then dropped a 4–0 decision to the Pats. The Remparts beat Regina 5–3, but the Pats still clinched a spot in the final. When St. Catharines and Quebec met again in the semifinals, the Remparts advanced with an 11–3 romp.

The Remparts raced to a 3–0 lead in the Memorial Cup finals, but Sobchuk had three goals and an assist as Regina rallied for a 7–4 victory.

New Westminster Bruins, **Toronto Marlboros**
and Sherbrooke Castors
at Kitchener (Memorial Auditorium)
May 3 to 11, 1975

Led by Bruce Boudreau, Mark Napier and John Tonelli, who would sit out the entire playoffs because taking part might jeopardize his chances of playing pro with the WHA's Houston Aeros the following season, the Toronto Marlboros scored an astounding 469 goals in 70 OHA games and posted a 48–13–8 record. Still they struggled in the postseason and ended up playing 23 games in 35 days en route to the Memorial Cup. The Sherbrooke Castors had rolled through the Quebec Major Junior Hockey League with 51 wins, then coasted through the playoffs with just one loss.

Out west, the Estevan Bruins relocated to the Vancouver suburb of New Westminster, where they would turn the Queen's Park Arena into the most intimidating facility in junior hockey. The Bruins made the first of four straight Memorial Cup appearances in the spring of 1975. They scored 7–5 and 6–2 wins over the Sherbrooke Castors and the Marlies to reach the tournament final. Toronto had opened with a 7–4 win over Sherbrooke, then beat them 10–4 in the semifinal.

In the title game, Toronto rallied from a 2–0 first-period deficit to score a 7–3 Memorial Cup victory. John Anderson and Mike Kaszycki scored twice each for the Marlies. Despite the loss, New Westminster captain Barry Smith won the Stafford Smythe Memorial Trophy as the tournament's most valuable player.

New Westminster Bruins, **Hamilton Fincups**
and Quebec Remparts
at Montreal (Forum)
May 9 to 16, 1976

Led by captain Dale McCourt, Ric Seiling and Joe Contini, the Hamilton Fincups advanced to the Memorial Cup tournament by ousting the Sudbury Wolves in five games from the Ontario final. Prior to that, they had coasted past the Kitchener Rangers and Toronto Marlboros. By the time they opened the Memorial Cup tournament, Hamilton hadn't played a game in 11 days.

Without a top-10 scorer, the Quebec Remparts had been the third-best regular-season team in the QMJHL. In the playoffs they eliminated both teams that had finished in front of them (the Cornwall Royals, then the Sherbrooke Castors) en route to the league title.

The big, bad and burly Bruins of New Westminster came east with a roster featuring eight players with more than 145 penalty minutes, including defenseman Barry Beck, at 325. But the team also had four players with more than 100 points: Fred Berry (146), Rick Shinske (143), Steve Clippingdale (117) and Mark Lofthouse (116). Defensemen Brad Maxwell and Beck each came in with 99 points.

Hamilton dropped the series opener, 4–3, to Quebec, but clinched a spot in the final with an 8–4 win over New Westminster. The two teams met again in the final after the Bruins downed Quebec, 10–3. Dale McCourt was selected the MVP after the Fincups won the Memorial Cup with a 5–2 victory.

New Westminster Bruins, Ottawa 67's
and Sherbrooke Castors
at Vancouver (Pacific Coliseum)
May 8 to 14, 1977

Defense was the key when the New Westminster Bruins won their third consecutive western championship in 1976–77. Coach Punch McLean called defensemen Barry Beck, Brad Maxwell, Brian Young and Miles Zaharko "the best group of four guys I've ever seen in junior hockey in Western Canada." In the playoffs, New Westminster silenced the highest-scoring line in junior hockey—Brandon's combination of Bill Derlago, Ray Allison and Brian Propp—to advance to the Memorial Cup tournament.

Led by Jere Gillis, Ron Carter, Rick Vaive and goalie Richard Sevigny, the Sherbrooke Castors won the QMJHL championship for the second time in three seasons. With captain Doug Wilson, goaltender Jay O'Connor, and sniper Bobby Smith leading the way, Brian Kilrea's Ottawa 67's claimed the OHA title.

This was the first Memorial Cup tournament to feature three teams playing a double round-robin format. After everyone had played everyone else twice, the top two teams would move into the one-game final. Playing at home in Vancouver, New Westminster's only loss during the round-robin portion was in a 4–3 overtime win by Ottawa. The Bruins got their revenge with a 6–5 victory in the final. Brad Maxwell was the hero, scoring the winner on a great individual effort at 14:06 of the third period after New Westminster had blown a 5–2 lead.

New Westminster Bruins, Peterborough Petes
and Trois-Rivieres Draveurs
at Sault Ste. Marie (Memorial Gardens) and Sudbury (Arena)
May 6 to 13, 1978

Veteran coach Punch McLean had his New Westminster Bruins back in the Memorial Cup tournament for the fourth straight year, this time as defending champions. He would be opposed by a new breed of coaches this year—Trois-Rivieres's Michel Bergeron and Peterborough bench boss Gary Green.

Despite 59 goals from John Ogrodnick, New Westminster was a team of grinders led by Stan Smyl. With a record of 33–28–11, the Bruins were only third in the WHL's four-team West Division, but came alive in the playoffs to take the title. The Trois-Rivieres Draveurs were led by Denis Pomerleau's 75 goals and 148 points. They topped the QMJHL standings with a 47–18–7 record and went on to take the playoff title as well. In Peterborough, the likes of Bill Gardner, Tim Trimper, Keith Crowder, Steve Larmer and Keith Acton could score, but the Petes preferred to check teams to a standstill en route to the Memorial Cup tournament.

The Petes took both games from New Westminster in the double round robin, including a 4–3 overtime thriller that put them in the final. The Bruins earned another shot at Peterborough when they beat the Draveurs, 6–3. New Westminster then won its second straight Memorial Cup title, dumping the Petes, 7–4, behind three goals and an assist from Scott MacLeod.

Brandon Wheat Kings, **Peterborough Petes**
and Trois-Rivieres Draveurs
at Sherbrooke (Le Palais de Sports), Trois-Rivieres (Colisee) and Verdun (Auditorium)
May 6 to 13, 1979

After two straight brilliant regular seasons had ended in playoff defeats, the Brandon Wheat Kings finally reached the Memorial Cup tournament in 1979. Bill Derlago had graduated to the NHL, but Laurie Boschman moved onto Brandon's top line. Brian Propp, Ray Allison and Boschman finished 1–2–3 in WHL scoring and led the Wheat Kings to a 58–5–9 record. They then breezed through the playoffs.

Trois-Rivieres was also a scoring machine, netting 527 goals en route to a 58–8–6 record in the QMJHL. Their offensive leader was Jean-Francois Sauve, who won the league scoring title with 176 points, including 111 assists. Behind Jacques Cloutier's superb goaltending, the Draveurs romped through the playoffs with a 12–1–0 record. The OHA champion Peterborough Petes succeeded by throwing a checking blanket over teams and scoring just enough to win. They had 11 players back from the team that had lost to New Westminster in the 1978 final.

Trois-Rivieres opened the Memorial Cup with wins over Peterborough and Brandon, but the two latter teams recovered to emerge from the double round robin with better scoring ratios after all three teams finished 2–2. In a thrilling final, the Petes beat Brandon 2–1 on Bob Attwell's goal at 2:38 of overtime.

"I've dreamed of doing something like this plenty of times," said Attwell. "It's unreal."

Regina Pats, Peterborough Petes and **Cornwall Royals**
at Brandon (Keystone Centre) and Regina (Agridome)
May 4 to 11, 1980

The Peterborough Petes became the first Ontario team since the St. Michael's Majors of 1945 to 1947 to make three straight Memorial Cup appearances. This year, under new head coach Mike Keenan, the Petes set a club record with 47 wins, and carried an 11-game playoff winning streak into the Memorial Cup tournament. Dale Hawerchuk, Dan Daoust and the Cornwall Royals would represent the QMJHL. Cornwall, situated near the Ontario-Quebec border, had been considering a move to the OHA, but felt there was too much travel involved there.

Out west, the Regina Pats rebounded from their second-worst season in franchise history to win the WHL in 1979–80. Doug Wickenheiser was the centerpiece of the Pats' rebuilding program. He had led the WHL with 89 goals and 170 points.

Though winning just once during the double round robin, Regina still had a chance to reach the Memorial Cup finals until Cornwall rallied to beat the Petes in the last game. Regina fans littered the rink with debris, as people speculated that Peterborough had thrown the game. It proved to be something of an anticlimax when the Royals went on to beat the Petes, 3–2 in overtime, to win the Memorial Cup on Robert Savard's only goal of the tournament. It was just his fifth goal of the season.

Victoria Cougars, Kitchener Rangers and **Cornwall Royals**
at Windsor (Arena)
May 3 to 10, 1981

A change was made in the Memorial Cup format in 1981 to prevent a repeat of the problems from the previous season. It was decided that if one team had clinched a berth in the final after the first four games of the double round robin, the other two teams would play a two-game, total-goals series. If one team clinched a spot in the final after five games, the other two would play a sudden-death semifinal.

For the second year in a row, the Cornwall Royals represented Quebec in the Memorial Cup tournament. (They would move to the Ontario league the next season.) The defending champions were again sparked by Dale Hawerchuk.

Just one year earlier, the Kitchener Rangers had finished 17–51–0 for the worst record in the OHA. In 1980–81, they doubled their regular-season points total, finishing 34–33–1. Led by Jeff Larmer and Brian Bellows, Kitchener won 13 of their last 14 games and rode that hot streak throughout the playoffs.

Grant Fuhr's Victoria Cougars were the western representative in the Memorial Cup tournament after winning a record 60 games, but Cornwall and Kitchener went through to the final. The Royals became the fourth team to win consecutive championships when they dumped the Rangers, 5–2, behind three goals from Scott Arniel. Doug Gilmour and Roy Russell also scored for Cornwall.

Portland Winter Hawks, **Kitchener Rangers**
and Sherbrooke Castors
at Hull (Robert Guertin Arena)
May 8 to 15, 1982

An American team qualified for the Canadian junior hockey championship for the first time in 1982. Before moving to Portland in 1976–77, the Winter Hawks had been the Edmonton Oil Kings, one of western hockey's most storied franchises. Unfortunately it had become apparent that Edmonton wasn't big enough for the WHA's Oilers and the junior Oil Kings. Offensively, Portland was led by center Ken Yaremchuk, who totaled 58 goals and 99 assists in 72 regular-season games. Gary Nylund anchored the defense.

Kitchener was back to represent Ontario for the second straight season. Captain Brian Bellows was the team's undisputed leader. Defensively, the star was Al MacInnis, who was becoming a legend thanks to his booming slapshot. Center John Chabot was the star of the QMJHL-champion Sherbrooke Castors. He finished third in the league scoring race with 143 points, including a league-high 109 assists. Also on this team were Gerard Gallant, Sean McKenna and Michel Petit.

Sherbrooke beat Kitchener, 10–4, to open the tournament, but the Rangers rebounded with a 9–2 win over Portland. The Winter Hawks' Memorial Cup dreams ended with a 7–3 loss to the Castors to close out the round-robin portion. In the final, Brian Bellows had three goals and two assists as Kitchener claimed its first Memorial Cup title with a 7–4 victory.

Portland Winter Hawks, Lethbridge Broncos,
Oshawa Generals and Verdun Juniors
at Portland (Memorial Coliseum)
May 7 to 14, 1983

The decision was made in 1983 to expand the Memorial Cup tournament to a four-team round robin and to reintroduce a semifinal game. To reach four teams, officials decided to allow the host team an automatic entry. Portland had that right in 1983, but the Winter Hawks were no lame ducks.

Seven Portland players (including Ken Yaremchuk and Cam Neely) topped 100 points in 1983–84, and the Winter Hawks had reached the WHL finals before losing to Lethbridge. Goaltender Mike Vernon was borrowed for the Memorial Cup tournament to address the team's lone weakness.

Led by Doug Kyle and twins Rich and Ron Sutter, the Lethbridge Broncos were a team that came alive in the playoffs after a strong second half of the regular season. Oshawa also enjoyed a strong playoff run, giving the Generals their first Ontario title since the days of Bobby Orr. Oshawa was led by Dave Andreychuk, Tony Tanti and Joe Cirella, though both Tanti and Andreychuk ended the season in the NHL.

Pat LaFontaine, an 18-year-old from Detroit, had led the QMJHL with an incredible 104 goals, 130 assists and 234 points. He also led the Verdun Juniors to the league championship. During Memorial Cup week, LaFontaine became the first American to be named Canadian Hockey League player of the year. The all-American theme continued when Portland beat Oshawa, 8–6, for the Memorial Cup title and Holt, Michigan, native Alfie Turcotte was named the tournament MVP.

Kamloops Junior Oilers, Kitchener Rangers,
Ottawa 67's and Laval Voisins
at Kitchener (Memorial Auditorium)
May 12 to 19, 1984

Mario Lemieux had rewritten the QMJHL record book during the 1983–84 regular season with 133 goals, 149 assists and 282 points in 70 games. In only 14 playoff games he added 29 goals and 23 assists, giving him a grand total of 334 points on the year. "It will be the 66th Memorial Cup and I hope our number 66 will continue his output," said Laval Voisins coach Jean Begin.

Out west, the Kamloops Junior Oilers had posted the best regular-season record in the WHL en route to the league championship. Kamloops led the loop with 467 goals (Laval had scored 527 in Quebec) and had 10 20-goal scorers, though none had more than Dean Evason's 49.

The Ottawa 67's rode a 13-game unbeaten streak into the Memorial Cup tournament, defeating the Kitchener Rangers in the OHL final. Still, both teams advanced because Kitchener had been named the host city after posting the best regular-season record in Ontario.

The Rangers opened the Memorial Cup with an 8–2 win over Laval, holding Lemieux pointless for just the third time all season. Lemieux wound up with just a goal and two assists as the Voisins went winless. Kitchener advanced to the finals, where they would take on Ottawa after the 67's eliminated Kamloops in the semifinal.

Kitchener and Ottawa already had met 10 times before the Memorial Cup finals. Each team sported four wins and two ties. Still, the 67's romped to a 7–2 victory behind two goals apiece from Bruce Cassidy and Phil Patterson. Adam Creighton was named the tournament MVP.

Prince Albert Raiders, Sault Ste. Marie Greyhounds,
Verdun Junior Canadiens and Shawinigan Cataractes
at Shawinigan (Municipal Auditorium) and
Drummondville (Marcel Dionne Arena)
May 11 to 18, 1985

Under g.m. and coach Terry Simpson, the Prince Albert Raiders had been a Canadian Junior A hockey dynasty. With nothing left to prove at that level, the Saskatchewan city entered the Western Hockey League in 1981–82. By 1984–85, the Raiders were WHL champions. Prince Albert was paced by Dan Hodgson's league-leading 112 assists. Linemates Dave Pasin and Tony Grenier scored 64 and 62 goals respectively.

In the OHL, Sault Ste. Marie set new league records with 54 wins and 109 points in 66 games. Center Wayne Groulx was second in the OHL with 144 points. Right wing Graeme Bonar led the team with 66 goals. The line's left wing was Bob Probert.

For the second year in a row, a high-scoring Lemieux reached the Memorial Cup tournament from Quebec. Claude (no relation to Mario) led the Verdun Junior Canadiens to the league championship. With the top regular-season record in the QMJHL, Shawinigan had won the right to play as the host city and would advance to the final.

Prince Albert beat Sault Ste. Marie in the semifinal and earned the right to meet the host team, though the title game would be played in Drummondville. Prince Albert won it 6–1. Dan Hodgson had turned in one of the best performances in Memorial Cup history, setting a record for most assists (13) in a series and in one game (five). His 15 points were one short of the record set by Kitchener's Jeff Larmer in 1982 as Hodgson was named the tournament's MVP.

Portland Winter Hawks, Kamloops Blazers,
Guelph Platers and Hull Olympiques
at Portland (Memorial Coliseum)
May 10 to 17, 1986

One year earlier, the Prince Albert Raiders had won the Memorial Cup in only their third season of play at the major junior level. In 1985–86, the Guelph Platers almost tore a page from that same book. The Platers had entered the Ontario Hockey League in 1982–83. They went 7–63–0 that season. Three years later, they were in the Memorial Cup tournament.

Under OHL coach of the year Jacques Martin, Guelph went 41–23–2 in the regular season, then went 15–3–2 through the playoffs to claim the league title. Guelph was sparked by left wing Gary Roberts, who had been acquired from the Ottawa 67's in a midseason deal.

The QMJHL-champion Hull Olympiques were owned by Wayne Gretzky and coached by former policeman Pat Burns. Led by Guy Rouleau and Luc Robitaille, who both led the league with 191 points, the Olympiques had easily been the QMJHL's leader with a 54–18–0 record, then cruised through the playoffs.

In the WHL, Ken Hitchcock's Kamloops Blazers had made it two straight West Division titles en route to a league championship. Kamloops and the host Portland Winter

Hawks were forced to play a tiebreaker after the round robin before the Blazers moved on to the semifinal. Hull then defeated them and advanced to face Guelph for the Memorial Cup. The Platers won, 6–2.

"This whole thing is a dream," said Guelph's Steve Chiasson, who was named the tournament's most valuable player. "I don't think we expected this. We've been surprising ourselves all season and we gave ourselves a real shock this week."

Medicine Hat Tigers, Oshawa Generals
and Longueuil Chevaliers
at Oshawa (Civic Auditorium)
May 9 to 15, 1987

The OHL chose to allow its two regular-season division winners to play a best-of-seven Super Series to determine who would host the Memorial Cup. It was also decided that should one team win both the Super Series and the league championship, the OHL would only send one representative.

The Oshawa Generals, who set a club record with 101 points, were led by Scott McCrory, who won the OHL scoring title with a team-record 99 assists and 150 points. The Generals defeated North Bay in a seven-game thriller to win the right to host the Memorial Cup. They later defeated the Centennials again in the OHL championship series.

Though they were coached by former NHL 50-goal scorer Guy Chouinard, the QMJHL-champion Longueuil Chevaliers were built around defense. With 259 goals against, Longueuil was the only QMJHL team to allow fewer than 300 goals in the regular season. Their goalie was Robert Desjardins, the 5'5" wonder who would be in the Memorial Cup for the third straight year with his third different team. In the WHL, goaltender Mark Fitzpatrick and center Trevor Linden led the Medicine Hat Tigers to the three-team Memorial Cup tournament.

When Oshawa clinched a spot in the final with three straight wins, the double round robin was abandoned and Medicine Hat and Longueuil played a two-game, total-goals semifinal. The Tigers won, 6–0 and 3–1. On a roll, Trevor Linden beat Jeff Hackett just 1:47 into the title game and Medicine Hat went on to win the Memorial Cup with a 6–2 victory.

Medicine Hat Tigers, Windsor Spitfires,
Drummondville Voltigeurs and Hull Olympiques
at Chicoutimi (Georges Vezina Arena)
May 7 to 14, 1988

After winning the Memorial Cup in 1987, Medicine Hat Tigers coach Bryan Maxwell left to become an assistant coach with the Los Angeles Kings. Tigers g.m. Russ Farwell hired Barry Melrose to take over a team loaded with returning talent. Players like Trevor Linden, Scott McCrady and Wayne McBean would lead Medicine Hat to its second straight WHL title. But "how can anybody say we're favored [to win the Memorial Cup]?" asked Melrose. "I think the Windsor Spitfires are the team everyone is talking about."

Led by Adam Graves, Glen Featherstone and goalie Pat Jablonski, Windsor had set seven club records, including most wins (50) and most points (102) en route to winning their first OHL championship. Windsor went 40–4–0 after Christmas!

Though the Memorial Cup tournament was being held in Chicoutimi, the QMJHL's two representatives were the Hull Olympiques, who were the league champions, and the Drummondville Voltigeurs, who had lost to Hull in the final. Coach Alain Vigneault's Olympiques were an offensive force led by Marc Saumier, Benoit Brunet and Martin Gelinas. They would reach the Memorial Cup semifinal, but were stopped there with a 5–3 loss to Medicine Hat.

Windsor had gone undefeated throughout the round robin. They raced to a 3–0 lead 12 minutes into the Memorial Cup finals, but Medicine Hat rallied for a 7–6 victory. Mark Pederson scored the game winner with 2:43 remaining. Longtime WHL and Canadian Hockey League president Ed Chynoweth presented the Memorial Cup to his son Dean, the Tigers captain.

Swift Current Broncos, Saskatoon Blades,
Peterborough Petes and Laval Titan
at Saskatoon (Saskatchewan Place)
May 6 to 13, 1989

The Saskatoon Blades were the only original members of the Western Hockey League to play every season since the first one, 1966–67. They finally found themselves in the Memorial Cup in 1989, albeit as the host team. The Swift Current Broncos were there as the WHL champions.

Less than three years after a bus crash had killed four of their players, Swift Current had posted the best record in Canadian junior hockey. Led by Tim Tisdale, Peter Kasowski, Sheldon Kennedy and Brian Sakic, the Broncos went 55–16–1. In the east, the Laval Titan emerged as QMJHL champions. They were led by Donald Audette and Patrice Brisebois. In the OHL, the goaltending tandem of John Tanner and Todd Bojcun led the Peterborough Petes to the title. The Petes roster also included Mike Ricci and the OHL's toughest player: Tie Domi.

Swift Current opened the Memorial Cup tournament with a 6–4 win over Peterborough. They next downed Laval 6–5, but a 5–4 loss to Saskatoon put the Blades in the final while the Broncos had to settle for a semifinal berth. Peterborough and Laval had to play a tiebreaker before the Petes reached the semifinal with a 5–4 victory. Swift Current then eliminated them with a 6–2 win.

The first all-western Memorial Cup final was a thriller, with Swift Current jumping to a 2–0 lead, but later having to rally to tie the game 3–3. In overtime, Broncos goalie Trevor Kruger made five straight saves before Tim Tisdale scored the game winner on the only shot Swift Current would need.

Kamloops Blazers, **Oshawa Generals,**
Kitchener Rangers and Laval Titan
at Hamilton (Copps Coliseum)
May 5 to 13, 1990

At just 17 years of age, Eric Lindros was already being called "The Next One" by those who touted him as a future NHL superstar. The Generals had acquired Lindros from Sault Ste. Marie (the Greyhounds had drafted him, but he refused to report) in time for him to play 25 games, during which he totaled 17 goals, 19 assists and 61 penalty minutes.

Because the Hamilton Steelhawks had been a dismal 11–49–6 in 1989-90, the decision was made to replace the Memorial Cup host team with the OHL runners-up, the Kitchener Rangers. Filling out the four-team field were the Laval Titan and the Kamloops Blazers. Led by Len Barrie's league-leading 85 goals and 100 assists, Kamloops was hoping to become the fourth straight WHL team to take the title. That dream was all but over after just two days of the tournament, as the Blazers were beaten by both Kitchener and Oshawa.

With four overtime games, including two double overtime thrillers, the 1990 Memorial Cup tournament is considered by many to be the best of all time. The first double overtime game came when Kitchener met Oshawa in the round-robin finalé. The winner would advance to the final, while the loser would face Laval in the semifinal. Dale Craigwell finally gave the Generals a 5–4 victory at 4:16 of the second overtime period. After the Rangers downed Laval, 5–4, Kitchener and Oshawa went into double overtime again to decide a champion. This time Bill Armstrong scored to give the Generals a 4–3 Memorial Cup victory in front of 17,383 fans.

Spokane Chiefs, Sault Ste. Marie Greyhounds,
Drummondville Voltigeurs and Chicoutimi Sagueneens
at Quebec City (Le Colisée)
May 11 to 19, 1991

A lot of people were anxiously awaiting the 1991 Memorial Cup tournament. Eric Lindros would be leading the defending-champion Oshawa Generals into Quebec City, where the Nordiques would have the first selection in the NHL's upcoming Entry Draft. Lindros was certain to be the first pick, though he was making noises about not wanting to play for Quebec. One year earlier, Lindros had balked at joining the Sault Ste. Marie Greyhounds. That team took its revenge against "The Next One" in 1991 when they eliminated Oshawa from Memorial Cup contention in a six-game OHL final. Coach Ted Nolan's Greyhounds had obtained five players when they had dealt the rights to Lindros to Oshawa. Among them was goaltender Mike Lenarduzzi, who had the OHL's best goals-against average in 1990–91.

While the Greyhounds upset the Generals, the QMJHL was deciding its championship. Felix Potvin's Chicoutimi Sagueneens knocked off the Drummondville Voltigeurs in four straight, but with the Memorial Cup in Quebec City, both teams advanced.

The Spokane Chiefs posted a 14–1 playoff record to emerge as the WHL representative. They opened the Memorial Cup with three straight wins to reach the final. Drummondville earned the right to meet Spokane for the title by avenging their playoff loss to Chicoutimi with a 2–1 overtime victory. A 5–1 win over Drummondville then made Spokane the second American team to win the Memorial Cup. Ray Whitney was the MVP, though teammate Pat Falloon had scored eight goals to tie the tournament record held by Dale Hawerchuk (1981) and Luc Robitaille (1986).

Seattle Thunderbirds, **Kamloops Blazers,**
Sault Ste. Marie Greyhounds and Verdun College-Francais
at Seattle (Coliseum and Center Ice Arena)
May 9 to 17, 1992

The Sault Ste. Marie Greyhounds hadn't won a single game at the 1991 Memorial Cup tournament. They were back to try again in 1992 after becoming the first OHL team to capture consecutive titles since the Kitchener Rangers did it in 1981 and 1982. Amazingly, not a single member of coach Ted Nolan's team was chosen to any of the three postseason OHL all-star teams. Kevin Hodson did win the Dave Pinkney Trophy as the goaltender on the team allowing the fewest goals.

With 101 points (48–17–5) the Verdun College-Francais was easily the best team in the QMJHL. Trois-Rivieres had been the second best, but Verdun beat the Draveurs in a tight seven-game playoff championship. In the west, observers of the WHL were beginning to recognize the Kamloops Blazers as something of a dynasty as they won the West Division for the third straight time with their third consecutive 50-win season (51–17–4). Seattle, meanwhile, had had a poor year and had not played a game in three weeks by the time the Memorial Cup tournament started.

Sault Ste. Marie won all three games during the round robin to clinch a spot in the final. Kamloops and Seattle reached the semifinal, where the Blazers bounced the Thunderbirds 8–3. Mike Mathers tied a tournament record with six points in the game (three goals, three assists). In the championship game, Zac Boyer's goal with 14.6 seconds left in the third period gave Kamloops a 5–4 victory over the Greyhounds and its first Memorial Cup championship.

Swift Current Broncos, Peterborough Petes,
Sault Ste. Marie Greyhounds and Laval Titan
at Sault Ste. Marie (Memorial Gardens)
May 15 to 23, 1993

As in 1987, the OHL had its division winners meet in a best-of-seven series to determine the Memorial Cup's host city. Peterborough had set a franchise record with 97 points to win the Emms Division, but the Petes were swept in the Super Series by Sault Ste. Marie. The Greyhounds became the first team to reach the national final three years in a row since the Petes of 1978 to 1980. Peterborough got its revenge in the OHL final, when Chris Pronger and Jason Dawe led the Petes past the Greyhounds in five games.

Out west, WHL scoring leader Jason Krywuluak (81 goals, 162 points) led Swift Current to the league's best regular-season record. Andy Schneider had 13 goals and 26 assists in 17 playoff games as the Broncos took the WHL championship. In the QMJHL, Martin Lapointe returned to Laval from the NHL's Detroit Red Wings at Christmas and led the Titan to the league title.

Laval lost two games to open the Memorial Cup tournament, but then beat Swift Current, 4–3. Laval beat the Broncos 4–3 again in a tiebreaker to advance to the semifinal. Patrick Cassin scored with 34.1 seconds left in the third period. Peterborough then beat Laval 3–1 to reach the final for a record fifth time.

The night before the Memorial Cup finals, Ralph Intranuovo was in hospital passing a kidney stone. He recovered, and had a goal and an assist to lead Sault Ste. Marie to a 4–2 victory. Intranuovo was one of eight Greyhounds appearing in their third straight Memorial Cup tournament.

Kamloops Blazers, North Bay Centennials,
Chicoutimi Sagueneens and Laval Titan
at Laval (Colisée)
May 14 to 22, 1994

The North Bay Centennials set a franchise record with 97 points in 1993-94 and went on to win their first OHL title. Out west, the Kamloops Blazers had the WHL's best regular-season record en route to the league championship. The Laval Titan would be the Memorial Cup's host team in 1994, having won that right by finishing with the QMJHL's best regular-season record. Laval was led by scoring leader Yannick Dube (66 goals, 141 points).

In the playoffs, the Titan rattled off 14 victories in their first 17 games. The last two of those victories were in the championship final against Chicoutimi. Incredibly, the Sagueneens turned it around and beat the Titan in each of the next four games. Chicoutimi was led by goaltender Eric Fichaud. Unfortunately, a dispute with the referees during the QMJHL final would spill over into the Memorial Cup tournament. Luc Lachapelle was injured in an altercation in the parking lot that led to the resignation of Laval g.m. and co-owner Jean-Claude Morrissette. Attendance at the tournament also was a disappointment, with crowds of less than 3,000 for most games.

Laval overcame the off-ice issues to reach the Memorial Cup finals with a 4–2 win over Chicoutimi in the semifinal. Michel Gaul led the way with two goals. Kamloops had gone undefeated throughout the round robin to clinch a spot in the final, and the Blazers maintained their winning ways with a 5–3 victory. Darcy Tucker scored the goal that held up as the game winner and was named the tournament MVP.

Kamloops Blazers, Brandon Wheat Kings,
Detroit Jr. Red Wings and Hull Olympiques
at Kamloops (Riverside Coliseum)
May 13 to 21, 1995

The Kamloops Blazers were 52–14–6 in 1994-95, topping the WHL standings with 110 points. Darcy Tucker led the team with 64 goals and 137 points. Hnat Domenichelli also broke the 100-point barrier, his 114 points including 52 goals.

In the playoffs, Kamloops reached the West Division final for the 12th straight year, advancing to the league final for the seventh time. The Blazers defeated the Brandon Wheat Kings for their sixth WHL championship in 12 years. Kamloops had already been chosen to host the Memorial Cup, so Brandon was added to the tournament as the league's runner-up. Wheat Kings star Marty Murray was the WHL's MVP.

The Detroit Jr. Red Wings had joined the OHL in 1990–91. They were already competitive by 1992–93 and had reached the league final in 1993–94. Goalie Jason Saal, defenseman Bryan Berard and center Bill McCauley led the Red Wings to the OHL title in 1994–95. Sebastien Bordeleau and goalie Jose Theodore led the Hull Olympiques to the QMJHL championship. In the Memorial Cup tournament, Hull dropped the opener 9–2 to Kamloops. The Olympiques went on to lose all three games, while Kamloops won three straight to reach the final. Detroit beat Brandon, 2–1, in the semifinal.

The Kamloops lineup included three players—Tucker, Ryan Huska and Tyson Nash—with a chance to win three Memorial Cup rings. Each of them scored a goal as the Blazers crushed the Red Wings 8–2. Kamloops became just the seventh team to win consecutive championships. No team ever had won three Memorial Cup titles in four seasons.

Brandon Wheat Kings, Guelph Storm,
Peterborough Petes and **Granby Predateurs**
at Peterborough (Memorial Centre)
May 11 to 19, 1996

The Petes had made more Memorial Cup appearances than any Canadian Hockey League team, but the city of Peterborough did not host the tournament until 1996. Led by Cameron Mann and goalie Zac Bierk, the Petes had a good season, but a great playoff. They downed the Guelph Storm in a seven-game OHL final, winning the deciding game, 8–7 in overtime. "None of this back-door stuff for us," said Mike Martone, who had scored the winning goal. Since Peterborough was the host team, Guelph also advanced to the Memorial Cup.

Out west, the Brandon Wheat Kings had won their first WHL championship since 1978–79. A defense led by Justin Kurtz and Wade Redden was the key to success. The QMJHL-champion Granby Predateurs had four 100-point players, including Daniel Goneau and Benoit Gratton—two of five teammates acquired from Laval. Granby was also solid defensively, and beat Guelph, 8–0, to open the Memorial Cup tournament. Despite a 6–3 loss to Peterborough, Granby went on to earn a spot in the final. The Petes advanced when they downed Brandon, 4–3, in the semifinal.

Humid conditions marred the championship game, as action had to be halted 10 times in the final period to allow players to skate around the ice in an attempt to disperse the fog. The disruptions took the hometown fans out of the game. Granby scored three times in the third period en route to a 4–0 victory. It was the first time since Guy Lafleur's Quebec Remparts in 1971 that a Quebec team had won the Memorial Cup.

Lethbridge Hurricanes, Oshawa Generals,
Hull Olympiques and Chicoutimi Sagueneens
at Hull (Robert Guertin Arena)
May 10 to 18, 1997

Hull had been designated as the host city of the Memorial Cup at the start of the 1996–97 season, but, not satisfied to go in merely as the host team, the Olympiques won the QMJHL championship. Chicoutimi also would represent Quebec after the Sagueneens dropped the league final to Hull.

Trades were the key to success in Hull, as Christian Dube and Mathieu Descoteaux were added to the roster. Hull went 30–4–1 after sending $50,000 and two draft choices to the Sherbrooke Faucons to obtain Dube's rights. A blockbuster trade also helped Lethbridge win the WHL. The Hurricanes went 33–8–2 after obtaining defenseman Chris Phillips and three others from the Prince Albert Raiders.

It had been expected that Ottawa would represent the OHL at the Memorial Cup, and the cross-river rivalry was much anticipated in Hull. However, though the 67's were the Canadian Hockey League's top-ranked team for more than 20 weeks during the regular season, they were knocked off by the Oshawa Generals in the OHL final. Marc Savard's overtime goal in game six gave Oshawa the series victory.

The Generals opened the Memorial Cup with a 5–3 win

over Chicoutimi, but then were crushed, 8–0, by Hull. The Olympiques went on to clinch a spot in the final, while Oshawa recovered to face Lethbridge in the semifinal. The Hurricanes won it, beating the Generals, 5–4 in overtime, on Byron Ritchie's third goal of the evening. The championship game saw Dube set up three goals as Hull won the Memorial Cup with a 5–1 victory.

Spokane Chiefs, **Portland Winter Hawks**, Guelph Storm and Val d'Or Foreurs at Spokane (Veterans' Memorial Arena) May 9 to 17, 1998

An unlikely representative hoped to win the QMJHL's third consecutive Memorial Cup title in 1998. The Val d'Or Foreurs had finished fourth in their division, but went on to sweep Vincent Lecavalier and the Rimouski Oceanic in the playoff final. Jean-Pierre Dumont had led the team with 57 goals and 99 points in the regular season. In the playoffs he collected 31 goals in just 19 games to break Mario Lemieux's postseason record of 29 set in 1984. Val d'Or got great goaltending from Roberto Luongo.

Great goaltending was also the key to success elsewhere. In Guelph, Chris Madden helped the Storm edge Ottawa by a single point as the top OHL team in the regular season. Consecutive game-winning goals by Brian Willsie gave the Storm another victory over the 67's in a five-game OHL final. Portland's Brent Belecki was the best in the west, backstopping the Winter Hawks to a league-leading 53–14–5 record, then a playoff championship. Portland had knocked off Spokane in the West Division championship, meaning the Chiefs were idle for 18 days before hosting the Memorial Cup tournament. Still, they opened with a 5–4 victory over Val d'Or, and went on to the semifinal where Guelph eliminated them, 2–1, in overtime.

Portland had gone undefeated through the round robin to earn a berth in the final. Though they outshot Guelph 56–32, the Winter Hawks needed Bobby Russell's goal at 6:21 of overtime to take the Memorial Cup with a 4–3 victory. Despite the loss, Guelph goalie Chris Madden was named tournament MVP.

Calgary Hitmen, Belleville Bulls, **Ottawa 67's** and Acadie-Bathurst Titan at Ottawa (Civic Centre) May 15 to 23, 1999

The Ottawa 67's were tabbed as the OHL's Memorial Cup host city in February, but Ottawa, along with Plymouth and Barrie (the top three teams in the OHL), was eliminated in the second round of the playoffs. The Belleville Bulls, who beat the 67's, went on to defeat the London Knights in the OHL final. Jonathan Cheechoo had five goals in a 9–2 win in game seven. Justin Papineau, who had 52 goals in the regular season, added 21 goals and 30 assists in 21 playoff games to win the inaugural Wayne Gretzky Trophy as OHL playoff MVP.

In the QMJHL, Acadie-Bathurst claimed the league title after numerous trades and a late-season coaching change. In the WHL, scoring leader Pavel Brendl (73 goals, 134 points) and playoff MVP Brad Moran led the first-place Calgary Hitmen past the second-overall Kamloops Blazers in a five-game final. Both Calgary and Belleville reached the Memorial Cup tournament for the first time. Acadie-Bathurst was the first team to make it from the Maritimes.

The 67's had not played in five weeks, but they fired five pucks past Roberto Luongo for a 5–1 victory over the Titan to open the Memorial Cup. By week's end Ottawa, Calgary and Belleville each sported records of 2–1 (Acadie-Bathurst was 0–3), but it was Calgary that earned the bye into the final after the Bulls beat the 67's, 5–4, in double overtime. Ottawa finally got its revenge in the semifinals, beating Belleville, 4–2. In the final, Ottawa had leads of 4–1 and 6–5, but it took Matt Zultek's goal at 1:58 of overtime to give the 67's a 7–6 win over the Hitmen.

Kootenay Ice, Barrie Colts, Halifax Moosehead and **Rimouski Oceanic** at Halifax (Metro Centre) May 20 to 28, 2000

For the first time in its 82-year history, the Memorial Cup tournament was held in the Maritimes. Ramzi Abid had 67 goals and 158 points for the Halifax Moosehead in 1999–2000, but the host-city team only lasted to the second round of the QMJHL playoffs before being beaten by Rimouski. The Oceanic had posted the league's best regular-season record and had defeated Hull in the QMJHL final.

In the OHL, scoring leader Sheldon Keefe and teammate Denis Shvidki gave the Barrie Colts the league's best offense, but it was goaltender Brian Finley who won the Wayne Gretzky Trophy as playoff MVP after Barrie knocked off the Plymouth Whalers in a thrilling seven-game OHL final. Out west, the Kootenay Ice reached the WHL final after knocking off the Calgary Hitmen, who had approached a Canadian Hockey League record with 58 wins in the regular season. The Spokane Chiefs rode a 53-point improvement over 1998–99 to post 100 points in 1999–2000, but the Ice cooled their hot run.

The Barrie Colts qualified for the semifinals when they beat Kootenay, 3–2, at 5:34 of double overtime in the longest game in Memorial Cup history. Barrie then beat Halifax and advanced to the final to take on Rimouski. The Oceanic had gone through the round robin undefeated and kept their perfect record intact with a 6–2 victory over the Colts in the final. "We had our game plan and everybody put it down all year," said tournament MVP Brad Richards, who had led the QMJHL with 71 goals and 115 assists. "Nobody gave us a chance, [but] it worked for us."

CHAPTER 39

Early Professional, Early Senior, WHA and Modern Minor Professional League Standings

Ernie Fitzsimmons

1893

Amateur Hockey Association

	GP	W	L	T	GF	GA	Pts
*Montreal AAA	8	7	1	1	38	18	14
Ottawa HC	8	6	2	0	49	22	12
Montreal Crystals	8	3	5	0	25	34	6
Quebec HC	8	2	5	1	23	46	5
Montreal Victorias	8	1	6	1	20	35	3

1894

	GP	W	L	T	GF	GA	Pts
*Montreal AAA	8	5	3	0	25	15	10
Ottawa HC	8	5	3	0	24	16	10
Montreal Victorias	8	5	3	0	36	20	10
Quebec HC	8	5	3	0	26	27	10
Montreal Crystals	8	0	8	0	10	43	0

1895

Amateur Hockey Association

	GP	W	L	T	GF	GA	Pts
*Montreal Victorias	8	6	2	0	35	20	12
Montreal AAA	8	4	4	0	33	22	8
Ottawa HC	8	4	4	0	25	24	8
Montreal Crystals	7	3	4	0	21	39	6
Quebec HC	7	2	5	0	18	27	4

1896

Amateur Hockey Association

	GP	W	L	T	GF	GA	Pts
*Montreal Victorias	8	7	1	0	41	24	14
Ottawa HC	8	6	2	0	22	16	12
Quebec HC	8	4	4	0	23	23	8
Montreal AAA	8	2	6	0	24	33	4
Montreal Shamrocks	8	1	7	0	16	30	2

1897

Amateur Hockey Association

	GP	W	L	T	GF	GA	Pts
*Montreal Victorias	8	7	1	0	48	26	14
Ottawa HC	8	5	3	0	25	18	10
Montreal AAA	8	5	3	0	31	26	10
Quebec HC	8	2	6	0	22	46	4
Montreal Shamrocks	8	1	7	0	27	37	2

1898

Amateur Hockey Association

	GP	W	L	T	GF	GA	Pts
*Montreal Victorias	8	8	0	0	53	33	16
Montreal AAA	8	5	3	0	34	21	10
Montreal Shamrocks	8	3	5	0	25	36	6
Quebec HC	8	2	6	0	29	35	4
Ottawa HC	8	2	6	0	28	44	4

1899

Canadian Amateur Hockey League

	GP	W	L	T	GF	GA	Pts
*Montreal Shamrocks	8	7	1	0	40	21	14
Montreal Victorias	8	6	2	0	44	23	12
Ottawa HC	8	4	4	0	21	43	8
Montreal AAA	8	3	5	0	30	29	6
Quebec HC	8	0	8	0	12	31	0

1900

Canadian Amateur Hockey League

	GP	W	L	T	GF	GA	Pts
*Montreal Shamrocks	8	7	1	0	49	26	14
Montreal AAA	8	5	3	0	34	36	10
Ottawa HC	8	4	4	0	28	19	8
Montreal Victorias	8	2	6	0	44	55	4
Quebec HC	8	2	6	0	33	52	4

1901

Canadian Amateur Hockey League

	GP	W	L	T	GF	GA	Pts
*Ottawa HC	8	7	0	1	33	20	15
Montreal Victorias	8	4	3	1	45	32	9
Montreal Shamrocks	8	4	4	0	30	25	8
Montreal AAA	8	3	5	0	28	37	6
Quebec HC	8	1	7	0	21	43	2

1901–02

Canadian Amateur Hockey League

	GP	W	L	T	GF	GA	Pts
*Montreal AAA	8	6	2	0	39	15	12
Ottawa HC	8	5	3	0	35	15	10
Montreal Victorias	8	4	4	0	36	25	8
Quebec HC	8	4	4	0	26	34	8
Montreal Shamrocks	8	1	7	0	15	62	2

Western Pennsylvania Hockey League

	GP	W	L	T	GF	GA	Pts
*Pittsburgh Keystones	14	9	5	0	42	32	18
Pittsburgh Athletic Club	14	8	6	0	46	28	16
Pittsburgh Bankers	14	4	10	0	27	55	8

1902–03

Canadian Amateur Hockey League

	GP	W	L	T	GF	GA	Pts
*Ottawa HC	8	6	2	0	47	26	12
Montreal Victorias	8	6	2	0	48	33	12
Montreal AAA	7	4	3	0	34	19	8
Quebec HC	7	3	4	0	30	46	6
Montreal Shamrocks	8	0	8	0	21	56	0

Western Pennsylvania Hockey League

	GP	W	L	T	GF	GA	Pts
*Pittsburgh Bankers	14	10	3	1	58	18	19
Pittsburgh Athletic Club	13	7	5	1	36	32	15
Pittsburgh Victorias	14	7	7	0	47	40	14
Pittsburgh Keystones	13	2	11	0	19	71	4

**Bankers lost to Portage Lakes for U.S. Pro title. Portage Lakes played exhibitions (12–0) until the playoffs*

1903–04

Canadian Amateur Hockey League

	GP	W	L	T	GF	GA	Pts
*Quebec HC	8	7	1	0	50	37	14
Montreal Victorias	8	5	3	0	74	48	10
Montreal AAA	8	3	5	0	34	49	6
Montreal Shamrocks	8	1	7	0	32	75	2
Ottawa HC	8	4	4	0	32	15	8

** Ottawa resigned 02/08/04 • Results not counted in final standings*

Federal Amateur Hockey League

	GP	W	L	T	GF	GA	Pts
*Montreal Wanderers	6	6	0	0	38	18	12
Montreal Nationals	6	3	3	0	27	27	6
Cornwall HC	6	2	4	0	20	27	4
Ottawa Capitals	6	1	5	0	28	41	2

Western Pennsylvania Hockey League

	GP	W	L	T	GF	GA	Pts
*Pittsburgh Victorias	13	10	3	0	56	23	20
Pittsburgh Bankers	15	8	7	0	45	45	16
Pittsburgh Athletic Club	14	4	10	0	44	62	8
Pittsburgh Keystones §	6	2	4	0	15	30	4

§ Withdrew January 17, 1904

• Victorias lost to Portage Lakes for US Pro title. Portage Lakes played exhibitions (13–1–0) until the playoffs. Portage Lakes beat Montreal Wanderers 2–0 in World Series

1904–05

Canadian Amateur Hockey League

	GP	W	L	T	GF	GA	Pts
*Montreal Victorias	10	9	1	0	64	32	18
Quebec HC	10	8	2	0	78	45	16
Montreal AAA	10	7	3	0	54	42	14
Montreal Shamrocks	10	3	7	0	41	62	6
Montreal Westmount	10	3	7	0	55	75	6
Montreal Nationals	10	0	10	0	6	42	0

Federal Amateur Hockey League

	GP	W	L	T	GF	GA	Pts
*Ottawa HC	8	7	1	0	60	19	14
Montreal Wanderers	8	6	2	0	44	27	12
Brockville HC	8	4	4	0	34	30	8
Cornwall HC	8	3	5	0	18	37	6
Ottawa Montagnards	8	0	8	0	19	62	0

International Pro Hockey League

	GP	W	L	T	GF	GA	Pts
*Calumet-Larium Miners	24	18	5	1	131	75	37
Houghton-Portage Lakes	24	15	7	2	98	81	32
Michigan Soo Indians	24	10	13	1	81	79	21
Pittsburgh Pros	24	8	15	1	82	114	17
Canadian Soo	24	6	17	1	97	140	13

Western Pennsylvania Hockey League

• WPHL did not operate from 1904 to 1907

1905–06

Eastern Canada Amateur Hockey Association

	GP	W	L	T	GF	GA	Pts
*Ottawa Silver Seven	10	9	1	0	90	42	18
Montreal Wanderers	10	9	1	0	74	38	18
Montreal Victorias	10	6	4	0	76	73	12
Quebec HC	10	3	7	0	57	70	6
Montreal AAA	10	3	7	0	49	63	6
Montreal Shamrocks	10	0	10	0	30	90	0

Federal Amateur Hockey League

	GP	W	L	T	GF	GA	Pts
*Smiths Falls HC	7	7	0	0	35	13	14
Ottawa Victorias	8	4	4	0	48	42	8
Brockville HC	7	3	4	0	55	32	6
Cornwall HC	6	2	4	0	16	30	4
Ottawa Montagnards	4	0	4	0	2	39	0

International Pro Hockey League

	GP	W	L	T	GF	GA	Pts
*Houghton-Portage Lakes	24	19	5	0	105	70	38
Michigan Soo Indians	24	18	6	0	126	57	36
Pittsburgh Pros	24	15	9	0	121	84	30
Calumet Miners	24	7	17	0	48	108	14
Canadian Soo	24	1	23	0	56	137	2

1906–07

Eastern Canada Amateur Hockey Association.

	GP	W	L	T	GF	GA	Pts
*Montreal Wanderers	10	10	0	...	105	39	20
Ottawa Silver Seven	10	7	3	...	76	54	14
Montreal Victorias	10	6	4	...	101	70	12
Montreal AAA	10	3	7	...	58	83	6
Quebec HC	10	2	8	...	62	88	4
Montreal Shamrocks	10	2	8	...	52	120	4

MANITOBA PROFESSIONAL HOCKEY LEAGUE

	GP	W	L	T	GF	GA	Pts
Brandon Wheat Kings	9	5	2	2	50	39	12
Portage-la-Prairie	9	5	3	1	35	33	11
*Kenora Thistles	6	4	2	0	38	19	8
Winnipeg Strathconas	10	1	8	1	38	70	3

INTERNATIONAL PRO HOCKEY LEAGUE

	GP	W	L	T	GF	GA	Pts
*Houghton-Portage Lakes	24	16	8	0	102	102	32
Canadian Soo	24	13	11	0	124	123	26
Pittsburgh Pros	25	12	12	1	94	82	25
Michigan Soo Indians	24	11	13	0	103	88	22
Calumet Wanderers	25	8	16	1	96	124	17

1907–08

EASTERN CANADA AMATEUR HOCKEY ASSOCIATION

	GP	W	L	T	GF	GA	Pts
*Montreal Wanderers	10	8	2	...	63	52	16
Ottawa Silver Seven	10	7	3	...	86	51	14
Quebec HC	10	5	5	...	81	74	10
Montreal Shamrocks	10	5	5	...	53	49	10
Montreal Victorias	10	4	6	...	73	78	8
Montreal AAA	10	1	9	...	53	105	2

ONTARIO PROFESSIONAL HOCKEY LEAGUE

	GP	W	L	T	GF	GA	Pts
*Toronto Professionals	12	10	2	...	88	55	20
Berlin Dutchmen	12	7	5	...	57	49	14
Brantford Indians	12	5	7	...	65	79	10
Guelph Professionals	12	2	10	...	33	60	4

FEDERAL HOCKEY LEAGUE

	GP	W	L	T	GF	GA	Pts
*Ottawa Victorias	4	2	2	0	32	22	4
Cornwall	5	2	3	0	22	44	4
Brockville §	1	1	0	0	12	0	0

§ Expelled for using imports from other leagues

UPPER OTTAWA VALLEY HOCKEY LEAGUE

	GP	W	L	T	GF	GA	Pts
*Renfrew Creamery Kings	4	4	0	0	33	16	8
Pembroke	4	2	2	0	20	22	4
Arnprior	4	0	4	0	15	30	0

• Second half of schedule cancelled • Renfrew awarded title

NEW ONTARIO HOCKEY LEAGUE

	GP	W	L	T	GF	GA	Pts
*Fort William Wanderers	11	8	3	0	47	29	16
Port Arthur Lake City	9	4	5	0	47	38	8
Port Arthur Thunder Bays	9	4	5	0	35	39	8
Fort William Arenas §	5	1	4	0	6	29	2

§ Withdrew 01/28/08

TEMISKAMING PRO HOCKEY LEAGUE

	GP	W	L	T	GF	GA	Pts
*New Liskeard	8	6	2	0			8
Haileybury	8	6	2	0			8
Cobalt §	8	0	8	0			0

§ Defaulted two games to each of other teams
• New Liskeard won total-goals first-place playoff 12–11

MANITOBA PROFESSIONAL HOCKEY LEAGUE

	GP	W	L	T	GF	GA	Pts
Winnipeg Maple Leafs	16	10	6	0	107	89	20
Portage-la-Prairie	15	8	7	0	76	73	16
Winnipeg Strathconas	15	5	10	0	92	113	10
Kenora Thistles §	...	...	...	...	...	...	...
Brandon Wheat Kings ¶	...	...	...	...	...	...	...

§ folded 01/01/08 ¶ folded 01/03/08

ALBERTA PROFESSIONAL HOCKEY LEAGUE

	GP	W	L	T	GF	GA	Pts
*Edmonton Pros	10	7	2	1	70	51	15
Strathcona Shamrocks	9	4	4	1	43	48	9
North Battleford	9	2	7	0	53	67	4

WESTERN PENNSYLVANIA HOCKEY LEAGUE

	GP	W	L	T	GF	GA	Pts
*Pittsburgh Bankers	19	12	4	3	81	59	24
Pittsburgh Lyceum	17	11	5	1	77	49	22
Pittsburgh Pirates	17	5	10	2	59	70	10
Pittsburgh Athletic Club	17	3	12	2	41	80	6

• Tie games were replayed and do not count in total points
• Bankers lost World Series two games to one to Montreal Wanderers

1908–09

EASTERN CANADA AMATEUR HOCKEY ASSOCIATION

	GP	W	L	T	GF	GA	Pts
*Ottawa Senators	12	10	2	...	117	63	20
Montreal Wanderers	12	9	3	...	82	61	18
Quebec Bulldogs	12	3	9	...	78	106	6
Montreal Shamrocks	12	2	10	...	56	103	4

ONTARIO PROFESSIONAL HOCKEY LEAGUE

	GP	W	L	T	GF	GA	Pts
*Galt Professionals	16	11	4	1	114	92	23
Brantford Indians	16	10	5	1	124	107	21
Berlin Dutchmen	15	9	6	0	96	72	18
Toronto Professionals	15	5	10	0	105	111	10
Guelph Professionals	6	1	5	0	28	56	2
St. Catharines Pros	6	0	6	0	29	58	0

• Galt beat Brantford 7-1 on 02/25/09 in replay of tied game

FEDERAL HOCKEY LEAGUE

	GP	W	L	T	GF	GA	Pts
*Renfrew Creamery Kings	6	6	0	0	93	25	12
Ottawa Victorias	6	3	3	0	37	38	6
Smiths Falls	6	2	4	0	34	71	4
Cornwall	6	1	5	0	30	60	2

NEW ONTARIO HOCKEY LEAGUE

	GP	W	L	T	GF	GA	Pts
*Port Arthur Thunder Bays	12	8	4	0	55	42	16
Fort William Forts	12	7	4	1	54	42	15
Fort William Wanderers	12	6	5	1	44	40	13
Port Arthur Hockey Club	12	2	10	0	36	65	4

TEMISKAMING PRO HOCKEY LEAGUE

	GP	W	L	T	GF	GA	Pts
*Cobalt	8	6	2	0	64	32	12
Haileybury	8	5	2	1	53	42	11
New Liskeard	8	0	7	1	24	67	1

MANITOBA PROFESSIONAL HOCKEY LEAGUE

First Half	GP	W	L	T	GF	GA	Pts
Winnipeg Maple Leafs	4	4	0	0	37	21	8
Winnipeg Shamrocks	4	1	3	0	22	29	2
Winnipeg Winnipegs §	2	0	2	0	13	22	0
§ folded 01/09/09							
Second Half							
*Winnipeg Shamrocks	5	4	1	0	48	35	8
Winnipeg Maple Leafs	5	1	4	0	35	48	2

ALBERTA PROFESSIONAL HOCKEY LEAGUE

	GP	W	L	T	GF	GA
Edmonton Pros	10	10	0	0	95	37

• Edmonton played exhibition games only. They won the Fit-Reform Trophy as Western Champs• Lost Stanley Cup to Montreal Wanderers

WESTERN PENNSYLVANIA HOCKEY LEAGUE

	GP	W	L	T	GF	GA	Pts
*Pittsburgh Bankers	15	9	4	2	56	49	20
Duquesne Athletic Club	15	9	5	1	63	48	19
Pittsburgh Athletic Club	14	2	12	0	46	74	2
Pittsburgh Lyceum §	8	4	3	1	31	25	9

§ Withdrew 12/23/08

1909–10

CANADIAN HOCKEY ASSOCIATION

	GP	W	L	T	GF	GA	Pts
Ottawa Senators	2	2	0	0	29	9	4
All-Montreal HC	4	2	2	0	20	24	4
Quebec Bulldogs	3	2	1	0	20	22	4
Montreal Shamrocks	3	2	1	0	29	18	4
Montreal Nationals	4	0	4	0	25	50	0

• CHA folded on 01/15/10 • No champion determined

NATIONAL HOCKEY ASSOCIATION

	GP	W	L	T	GF	GA	Pts
*Montreal Wanderers	12	11	1	0	91	41	22
Ottawa Senators	12	9	3	0	89	66	18
Renfrew Creamery Kings	12	8	3	1	96	54	17
Cobalt Silver Kings	12	4	8	0	79	104	8
Haileybury HC	12	4	8	0	77	83	8
Montreal Shamrocks	12	3	8	1	52	95	7
Montreal Canadiens	12	2	10	0	59	100	4

ONTARIO PROFESSIONAL HOCKEY LEAGUE

	GP	W	L	T	GF	GA	Pts
Berlin Dutchmen	17	11	6	...	103	74	22
*Waterloo Professionals	15	8	7	...	77	70	16
Brantford Indians	14	7	7	...	79	76	14
Galt Professionals	16	5	11	...	63	102	10

NEW ONTARIO HOCKEY LEAGUE

	GP	W	L	T	GF	GA	Pts
*Port Arthur Lake City	12	8	4	0	73	56	16
Port Thunder Bays	13	7	6	0	66	59	14
Fort William Forts	12	5	7	0	54	67	10
Fort William North Stars	13	5	8	0	52	63	10

• Thunder Bays vs North Stars game replayed 02/15/10

SASKATCHEWAN PROFESSIONAL HOCKEY LEAGUE

Saskatoon Strathconas — *Standings unavailable*
Moose Jaw
Prince Albert Mintos
Moosomin
Davidson
Regina

• Prince Albert declared champion when Saskatoon used ineligible players. Prince Albert lost Fit-Reform Trophy to Edmonton

ALBERTA PROFESSIONAL HOCKEY LEAGUE

Edmonton Pros

• Played only for Stanley Cup (lost 21–8) to Ottawa. Won Fit-Reform Trophy (3–1) over Prince Albert

1910–11

NATIONAL HOCKEY ASSOCIATION

	GP	W	L	T	GF	GA	Pts
*Ottawa Senators	16	13	3	...	122	69	26
Montreal Canadiens	16	8	8	...	66	62	16
Renfrew Creamery Kings	16	8	8	...	91	101	16
Montreal Wanderers	16	7	9	...	73	88	14
Quebec Bulldogs	16	4	12	...	65	97	8

ONTARIO PROFESSIONAL HOCKEY LEAGUE

	GP	W	L	T	GF	GA	Pts
*Galt Professionals	19	13	6	...	134	99	26
Waterloo Professionals	19	13	6	...	85	78	26
Berlin Dutchmen	18	10	8	...	93	87	20
Brantford Indians	18	1	17	...	59	107	2

EASTERN ONTARIO PROFESSIONAL HOCKEY LEAGUE

	GP	W	L	T	GF	GA	Pts
Port Hope	4	3	1	0	30	13	6
Picton Pirates	4	3	1	0	21	19	6
Trenton	4	0	2	2	18	22	2
Belleville	4	0	2	2	39	71	2

• Belleville moved to start a new OPHL team in Brantford 01/18/11 and league restarted. Trenton moved to Belleville

	GP	W	L	T	GF	GA	Pts
*Port Hope	6	5	1	0	51	28	10
Picton Pirates	3	1	2	0	8	9	2
Belleville	5	1	4	0	28	50	2

• Port Hope lost to Galt (OPHL) 12–8 in Stanley Cup playoffs

NEW ONTARIO HOCKEY LEAGUE

	GP	W	L	T	GF	GA	Pts
*Port Arthur Lake City	15	15	0	0	130	43	30
Fort William Forts	16	9	6	1	83	80	19
Port Arthur Thunder Bays	15	7	8	0	68	77	14
Fort William North Stars	14	5	8	1	61	57	11
Schreiber Colts	16	1	15	0	45	130	2

• Schreiber/Thunder Bays game replayed 01/12/11. Both games counted in standings
• Port Arthur beat Prince Albert (Saskatchewan) 12–6 but lost to Ottawa 13–4 in Stanley Cup Playoffs

INTERPROVINCIAL PROFESSIONAL HOCKEY LEAGUE

	GP	W	L	T	GF	GA	Pts
*Moncton Victorias	8	6	2	0	35	12	12
Halifax Crescents	8	5	3	0	45	41	10
New Glasgow Cubs	8	1	7	0	35	66	2

SASKATCHEWAN PROFESSIONAL HOCKEY LEAGUE

	GP	W	L	T	GF	GA	PTS
*Prince Albert Mintos	8	8	0	0	74	36	16
Regina Shamrocks	11	4	7	0	66	90	8
Saskatoon Westerns	8	3	5	0	49	44	6
Moose Jaw	9	3	6	0	48	67	6

• Prince Albert beat Saskatoon in playoff, but lost Stanley Cup playoff to Port Arthur 12–6

1911–12

NATIONAL HOCKEY ASSOCIATION

	GP	W	L	T	GF	GA	Pts
*Quebec Bulldogs	18	10	8	...	81	79	20
Ottawa Senators	18	9	9	...	99	93	18
Montreal Wanderers	18	9	9	...	95	96	18
Montreal Canadiens	18	8	10	...	59	66	16

PACIFIC COAST HOCKEY ASSOCIATION

	GP	W	L	T	GF	GA	Pts
*New Westm'ster Royals	15	9	6	...	78	77	18
Vancouver Millionaires	15	7	8	...	102	94	14
Victoria Aristocrats	16	7	9	...	81	90	14

MARITIME PROFESSIONAL HOCKEY LEAGUE

	GP	W	L	T	GF	GA	Pts
*Moncton Victorias	18	12	6	0	106	80	24
New Glasgow Cubs	18	10	8	0	108	80	20
Halifax Crescents	18	7	11	0	94	122	14
Halifax Socials	18	7	11	0	100	126	14

NEW ONTARIO HOCKEY LEAGUE

	GP	W	L	T	GF	GA	Pts
*Port Arthur Lake City	16	10	6	0	83	60	20
Ft-William North Stars §	15	9	6	0	52	46	18
Schreiber Colts	15	4	11	0	57	86	8

§ Dropped out of league 02/15/12
• Only games between Port Arthur and Schreiber counted for championship. • Port Arthur defeated Saskatoon 12-6 in Stanley Cup elimination series but declined invitation to play for championship.

Saskatchewan Professional Hockey League

	GP	W	L	T	GF	GA	Pts
*Saskatoon Hoo-Hoos	8	4	2	2	39	41	10
Moose Jaw Brewers	8	3	3	2	48	35	8
Saskatoon Wholesalers	7	2	5	0	30	44	4
Saskatoon Empires §	5	3	2	0	23	20	

§ Withdrew 02/11/12
- *Hoo-Hoos declined to play for Stanley Cup*
- *Wholesalers faced Port Arthur in playoff and lost 12–6*

1912–13

National Hockey Association

	GP	W	L	T	GF	GA	Pts
*Quebec Bulldogs	20	16	4	...	112	75	32
Montreal Wanderers	20	10	10	...	93	90	20
Ottawa Senators	20	9	11	...	87	81	18
Toronto Blueshirts	20	9	11	...	86	95	18
Montreal Canadiens	20	9	11	...	83	81	18
Toronto Tecumsehs	20	7	13	...	59	98	14

Pacific Coast Hockey Association

	GP	W	L	T	GF	GA	Pts
*Victoria Aristocrats	15	10	5	...	68	56	20
Vancouver Millionaires	16	7	9	...	84	89	14
New Westm'ster Royals	15	6	9	...	67	74	12

Maritime Professional Hockey League

	GP	W	L	T	GF	GA	Pts
*Sydney Millionaires	16	11	5	0	71	60	22
New Glasgow Cubs	16	10	6	0	89	58	20
Moncton Victorias	16	9	7	0	73	63	18
Halifax Socials	16	8	8	0	66	67	16
Halifax Crescents	16	2	14	0	44	95	4

1913–14

National Hockey Association

	GP	W	L	T	GF	GA	Pts
Montreal Canadiens	20	13	7	...	85	65	26
*Toronto Blueshirts	20	13	7	...	93	65	26
Quebec Bulldogs	20	12	8	...	111	73	24
Ottawa Senators	20	11	9	...	65	71	22
Montreal Wanderers	20	7	13	...	102	125	14
Toronto Ontarios	20	4	16	...	61	118	8

Pacific Coast Hockey Association

	GP	W	L	T	GF	GA	Pts
*Victoria Aristocrats	15	10	5	...	80	67	20
New Westm'ster Royals	16	7	9	...	75	81	14
Vancouver Millionaires	15	6	9	...	76	83	12

Maritime Professional Hockey League

	GP	W	L	T	GF	GA	Pts
*Sydney Millionaires	24	16	8	0	131	113	32
New Glasgow Foxes	24	16	8	0	162	117	32
Halifax Crescents	24	12	12	0	108	107	24
Halifax Socials	24	4	20	0	97	161	8

1914–15

National Hockey Association

	GP	W	L	T	GF	GA	Pts
*Ottawa Senators	20	14	6	...	74	65	28
Montreal Wanderers	20	14	6	...	127	82	28
Quebec Bulldogs	20	11	9	...	85	85	22
Toronto Blueshirts	20	8	12	...	66	84	16
Tor-Ontarios/Shamrocks	20	7	13	...	76	96	14
Montreal Canadiens	20	6	14	...	65	81	12

Pacific Coast Hockey Association

	GP	W	L	T	GF	GA	Pts
*Vancouver Millionaires	17	13	4	...	115	71	26
Portland Rosebuds	18	9	9	...	91	83	18
Victoria Aristocrats	17	4	13	...	64	116	8

Eastern Professional Hockey League

	GP	W	L	T	GF	GA	Pts
Glace Bay Miners	7	5	2	0	37	24	10
New Glasgow Foxes §	7	3	4	0	32	46	6
Sydney Millionaires	8	3	5	0	46	45	6

§ folded 01/31/15
- *EPHL folded 02/07/15 • No champion determined*

1915–16

National Hockey Association

	GP	W	L	T	GF	GA	Pts
*Montreal Canadiens	24	16	7	1	104	76	33
Ottawa Senators	24	13	11	0	78	72	26
Quebec Bulldogs	24	10	12	2	91	98	22
Montreal Wanderers	24	10	14	0	90	116	20
Toronto Blueshirts	24	9	14	1	97	98	19

Pacific Coast Hockey Association

	GP	W	L	T	GF	GA	Pts
*Portland Rosebuds	18	13	5	...	71	50	26
Vancouver Millionaires	18	9	9	...	75	69	18
Seattle Metropolitans	18	9	9	...	68	67	18
Victoria Aristocrats	18	5	13	...	74	102	10

1916–17

National Hockey Association

First Half

	GP	W	L	T	GF	GA	Pts
*Montreal Canadiens	10	7	3	...	58	38	14
Ottawa Senators	10	7	3	...	56	41	14
Toronto 228th	10	6	4	...	70	57	12
Toronto Blueshirts	10	5	5	...	50	45	10
Montreal Wanderers	10	3	7	...	56	72	6
Quebec Bulldogs	10	2	8	...	43	80	4

Second Half

	GP	W	L	T	GF	GA	Pts
Ottawa Senators	10	8	2	...	63	22	16
Quebec Bulldogs	10	8	2	...	54	46	16
Montreal Canadiens	10	3	7	...	31	42	6
Montreal Wanderers	10	2	8	...	38	65	4
Toronto Blueshirts ¶	4	2	2	...	14	16	4
Toronto 228th §	2	0	2	...	3	12	0

§ called overseas 02/10/17 ¶ dropped from league 02/11/17

Pacific Coast Hockey Association

	GP	W	L	T	GF	GA	Pts
*Seattle Metropolitans	24	16	8	...	125	80	32
Vancouver Millionaires	23	14	9	...	131	124	28
Portland Rosebuds	24	9	15	...	114	112	18
Spokane Canaries	23	8	15	...	89	143	16

1917–18

Pacific Coast Hockey Association

	GP	W	L	T	GF	GA	Pts
Seattle Metropolitans	18	11	7	...	67	65	22
*Vancouver Millionaires	18	9	9	...	70	60	18
Portland Rosebuds	18	7	11	...	63	75	14

1918–19

Pacific Coast Hockey Association

	GP	W	L	T	GF	GA	Pts
Vancouver Millionaires	20	12	8	...	72	55	24
*Seattle Metropolitans	20	11	9	...	66	46	22
Victoria Aristocrats	20	7	13	...	44	81	14

1919–20

Pacific Coast Hockey Association

	GP	W	L	T	GF	GA	Pts
*Seattle Metropolitans	22	12	10	...	59	55	24
Vancouver Millionaires	22	11	11	...	75	65	22
Victoria Aristocrats	22	10	12	...	57	71	20

1920–21

Pacific Coast Hockey Association

	GP	W	L	T	GF	GA	Pts
*Vancouver Millionaires	24	13	11	0	86	78	26
Seattle Metropolitans	24	12	11	1	77	68	25
Victoria Aristocrats	24	10	13	1	71	88	21

1921–22

Pacific Coast Hockey Association

	GP	W	L	T	GF	GA	Pts
Seattle Metropolitans	24	12	11	1	65	64	25
*Vancouver Millionaires	24	12	12	0	77	68	24
Victoria Aristocrats	24	11	12	1	61	71	23

Western Canada Hockey League

	GP	W	L	T	GF	GA	Pts
Edmonton Eskimos	24	15	9	...	117	76	30
*Regina Capitals	24	14	10	...	94	78	28
Calgary Tigers	24	14	10	...	75	62	28
Sask-Moose Jaw	24	5	19	...	67	137	10

1922–23

Pacific Coast Hockey Association

	GP	W	L	T	GF	GA	Pts
*Vancouver Maroons	30	17	12	1	116	88	35
Victoria Cougars	30	16	14	0	94	85	32
Seattle Metropolitans	30	15	15	0	100	106	30

- *Played interlocking schedule with WCHL*

Western Canada Hockey League

	GP	W	L	T	GF	GA	Pts
Edmonton Eskimos	30	19	10	1	112	90	39
*Regina Capitals	30	16	14	0	93	97	32
Calgary Tigers	30	12	18	0	91	106	24
Saskatoon Sheiks	30	8	20	2	91	125	18

- *Played interlocking schedule with PCHA*

1923–24

Pacific Coast Hockey Association

	GP	W	L	T	GF	GA	Pts
Seattle Metropolitans	30	14	16	0	84	99	28
*Vancouver Maroons	30	13	16	1	87	80	27
Victoria Cougars	30	11	18	1	78	103	23

- *Played interlocking schedule with WCHL*

Western Canada Hockey League

	GP	W	L	T	GF	GA	Pts
*Calgary Tigers	30	18	11	1	83	72	37
Regina Capitals	30	17	11	2	83	67	36
Saskatoon Crescents	30	15	12	3	91	73	33
Edmonton Eskimos	30	11	15	4	69	81	26

- *Played interlocking schedule with PCHA*

1924–25

Western Canada Hockey League

	GP	W	L	T	GF	GA	Pts
Calgary Tigers	28	17	11	0	96	80	34
Saskatoon Crescents	28	16	11	1	102	75	33
*Victoria Cougars	28	16	12	0	84	63	32
Edmonton Eskimos	28	14	13	1	97	109	29
Vancouver Maroons	28	12	16	0	91	102	24
Regina Capitals	28	8	20	0	82	123	16

1925–26

Western Hockey League

	GP	W	L	T	GF	GA	Pts
Edmonton Eskimos	30	19	11	0	94	77	38
Saskatoon Crescents	30	18	11	1	93	64	37
*Victoria Cougars	30	15	11	4	68	53	34
Portland Rosebuds	30	12	16	2	84	110	26
Calgary Tigers	30	10	17	3	71	80	23
Vancouver Maroons	30	10	18	2	64	90	22

California Professional Hockey League

	GP	W	L	T	GF	GA	Pts
*Palais-De-Glace	12	8	4	0	62	51	16
Richfield Oil	12	5	5	2	40	49	12
Culver City	12	3	7	2	40	52	8

- *All teams based in Los Angeles*

1926–27

Canadian-American Hockey League

	GP	W	L	T	GF	GA	Pts
New Haven Eagles	32	18	14	0	73	66	36
*Springfield Indians	32	14	13	5	59	53	33
Quebec Castors	32	15	14	3	69	67	33
Boston Tigers	32	14	15	3	48	46	31
Providence Reds	32	12	17	3	50	67	27

American Hockey Association

	GP	W	L	T	GF	GA	Pts
*Duluth Hornets	38	20	10	8	90	46	48
Minneapolis Millers	38	17	11	10	60	51	44
Winnipeg Maroons	38	19	14	5	83	77	43
St. Paul Saints	38	18	15	5	46	67	39
Chicago Cardinals¶	34	11	21	2	51	73	24
Detroit Greyhounds §	10	0	10	0	5	22	0

§ folded 12/11/26 ¶ renamed Americans 03/08/27, folded 3/21/27
- *Winnipeg and St. Paul given two wins each when Detroit folded Minneapolis and St. Paul given two wins each when Chicago folded*

Canadian Professional Hockey League

	GP	W	L	T	GF	GA	Pts
Stratford Nationals	32	20	12	0	92	80	40
*London Panthers	32	16	15	1	89	78	33
Hamilton Tigers	32	16	15	1	81	78	33
Windsor Hornets	32	14	17	1	72	95	29
Niagara Falls Cataracts	32	12	19	1	78	81	25

California Professional Hockey League

Richfield Oil — *Standings unavailable*
Palais-De-Glace
Globe Ice Cream
Wintergarden
Union Oil

- *All teams based in Los Angeles*

NORTHEASTERN HOCKEY LEAGUE

	GP	W	L	T	GF	GA	Pts
*Waterville-Maine	35	20	15	0	127	107	40
Lewiston St. Doms	33	13	15	5			31
Nashua Nationals	30	12	13	5			29
Berlin Mountaineers	31	11	16	4			16

1927–28

CANADIAN-AMERICAN HOCKEY LEAGUE

	GP	W	L	T	GF	GA	Pts
*Springfield Indians	40	24	13	3	90	71	51
Boston Tigers	40	21	14	5	80	71	47
Quebec Castors	40	18	14	8	70	68	44
New Haven Eagles	40	16	20	4	81	90	36
Providence Reds	40	13	19	8	88	83	34
Philadelphia Arrows	40	13	25	2	79	105	28

CANADIAN PROFESSIONAL HOCKEY LEAGUE

	GP	W	L	T	GF	GA	Pts
*Stratford Nationals	42	25	12	5	104	53	55
Detroit Olympics	42	24	14	4	99	75	52
Toronto Ravinas	42	20	18	4	93	95	44
Kitchener Millionaires	42	19	17	6	105	110	44
Hamilton Tigers	42	18	18	6	99	89	44
Niagara Falls Cataracts	42	13	17	12	89	90	38
Windsor Hornets	42	13	24	5	113	141	31
London Panthers	42	14	26	2	102	151	30

AMERICAN HOCKEY ASSOCIATION

	GP	W	L	T	GF	GA	Pts
Duluth Hornets	40	18	9	13	63	49	49
Kansas City Pla-Mors	40	18	14	8	61	53	44
*Minneapolis Millers	40	18	17	5	64	50	41
St. Paul Saints	40	14	17	9	76	87	37
Winnipeg Maroons	40	11	22	7	68	93	29

NORTHEASTERN HOCKEY LEAGUE

	GP	W	L	T	GF	GA	Pts
Waterville-Maine	24	13	7	4	67	54	30
*Nashua Nationals	24	11	8	5	54	37	27
Lewiston St. Doms ¶	22	8	12	2	26	42	18
Berlin Mountaineers §	22	8	13	1	42	56	17

§ Withdrew 02/08/28
¶ Lewiston suspended for using two Berlin players 02/12/28

CALIFORNIA PROFESSIONAL HOCKEY LEAGUE

Richfield Oilers — *Standings unavailable*
Los Angeles Maroons
Hollywood Millionaires

1928–29

CANADIAN-AMERICAN HOCKEY LEAGUE

	GP	W	L	T	GF	GA	Pts
*Boston Tigers	40	21	11	8	72	56	50
Providence Reds	40	18	12	10	64	58	46
New Haven Eagles	40	15	15	10	73	68	40
Springfield Indians	40	13	14	13	60	58	39
Newark Bulldogs	40	14	20	6	65	81	34
Philadelphia Arrows	40	12	21	7	60	73	31

AMERICAN HOCKEY ASSOCIATION

	GP	W	L	T	GF	GA	Pts
*Tulsa Oilers	40	23	9	8	125	63	54
Minneapolis Millers	40	18	12	10	77	51	46
St. Paul Saints	40	20	17	3	88	98	43
Kansas City Pla-Mors	40	17	16	7	66	75	41
Duluth Hornets	40	15	21	4	60	70	34
St. Louis Flyers	40	10	28	2	73	138	22

CANADIAN PROFESSIONAL HOCKEY LEAGUE

	GP	W	L	T	GF	GA	Pts
Detroit Olympics	42	27	10	5	131	67	59
*Windsor Bulldogs	42	25	12	5	114	76	55
Toronto Millionaires	42	19	16	7	94	88	45
Kitchener Dutchmen	42	19	19	4	105	113	42
Buffalo Bisons	42	17	18	7	89	72	41
London Panthers	42	16	22	4	86	113	36
Hamilton Tigers	42	14	24	4	83	115	32
Niagara Falls Cataracts	42	12	28	2	70	128	26

PACIFIC COAST HOCKEY LEAGUE

	GP	W	L	T	GF	GA	Pts
*Vancouver Lions	36	25	8	3	87	54	54
Seattle Eskimos	36	17	17	2	75	76	36
Portland Buckaroos	36	14	17	5	64	72	33
Victoria Cubs	36	8	22	6	68	91	22

PROVINCIAL INDEPENDENT HOCKEY LEAGUE

	GP	W	L	T	GF	GA	Pts
*La Tuques Loups-Nord	24	17	4	3	70	28	37
Grand'Mere Maroons	24	11	8	5	52	44	27
Quebec Citadelle	24	9	9	6	51	47	24
Trois-Rivieres Millionaires	24	9	13	2	51	72	20

CALIFORNIA HOCKEY LEAGUE

	GP	W	L	T	GF	GA	Pts
*Oakland Sheiks	36	18	13	5	67	64	41
San Francisco Seals	36	15	15	6	83	89	36
Los Angeles Richfields	36	15	17	4	56	60	34
Hollywood Millionaires	36	14	17	5	73	66	33

1929–30

CANADIAN-AMERICAN HOCKEY LEAGUE

	GP	W	L	T	GF	GA	Pts
*Providence Reds	40	24	11	5	120	98	53
Philadelphia Arrows	40	20	18	2	120	121	42
Boston Tigers	40	17	18	5	136	126	39
New Haven Eagles	40	14	20	6	94	101	34
Springfield Indians	40	15	23	2	96	120	32

INTERNATIONAL HOCKEY LEAGUE

	GP	W	L	T	GF	GA	Pts
*Cleveland Indians	42	24	9	9	125	78	57
Buffalo Bisons	42	26	12	4	102	67	56
London Panthers	42	24	13	5	117	93	53
Detroit Olympics	42	21	12	9	120	74	51
Windsor Bulldogs	42	20	14	8	123	93	48
Hamilton Tigers	42	9	25	8	95	128	26
Toronto Millionaires	42	10	28	4	84	172	24
Niagara Falls Cataracts	42	7	28	7	72	133	21

AMERICAN HOCKEY ASSOCIATION

	GP	W	L	T	GF	GA	Pts
*Kansas City Pla-Mors	48	21	13	14	75	65	56
Duluth Hornets	48	18	13	17	87	83	53
Tulsa Oilers	48	18	14	16	94	79	52
St. Paul Saints	48	18	16	14	93	90	50
Minneapolis Millers	48	15	21	12	82	83	42
St. Louis Flyers	48	12	25	11	98	129	35

CANADIAN PROFESSIONAL HOCKEY LEAGUE

	GP	W	L	T	GF	GA	Pts
*Guelph Maple Leafs	30	17	10	3	109	81	37
Galt Terriers	30	15	12	3	82	100	33
Kitchener Dutchmen	30	13	16	1	76	76	27
Brantford Indians	30	10	17	3	65	75	23

EASTERN CANADA HOCKEY ASSOCIATION

	GP	W	L	T	GF	GA	Pts
*Quebec Castors	24	16	6	2	77	59	34
La Tuque Loups-Nord	24	13	8	3	106	68	29
Shawinigan Cataracts	24	9	15	0	59	87	18
Trois-Rivieres Renards	24	6	15	3	74	102	15

PACIFIC COAST HOCKEY LEAGUE

	GP	W	L	T	GF	GA	Pts
*Vancouver Lions	36	20	8	8	86	46	48
Portland Buckaroos	36	20	10	6	64	34	46
Seattle Eskimos	36	15	13	8	77	58	38
Victoria Cubs	36	5	29	2	43	132	12

CALIFORNIA HOCKEY LEAGUE

	GP	W	L	T	GF	GA	Pts
*Oakland Sheiks	42	24	12	6	121	72	54
San Francisco Tigers	42	15	16	11	98	109	41
Los Angeles Richfields	42	17	19	6	91	122	40
Hollywood Millionaires	42	13	22	7	100	107	33

1930–31

CANADIAN-AMERICAN HOCKEY LEAGUE

	GP	W	L	T	GF	GA	Pts
*Springfield Indians	40	29	9	2	167	99	60
Providence Reds	40	23	11	6	132	96	52
Boston Tigers	40	14	22	4	96	114	32
Philadelphia Arrows	40	12	22	6	84	108	30
New Haven Eagles	40	9	23	8	78	140	26

INTERNATIONAL HOCKEY LEAGUE

	GP	W	L	T	GF	GA	Pts
Buffalo Bisons	48	30	13	5	115	76	65
*Windsor Bulldogs	48	25	16	7	141	114	57
Cleveland Indians	48	24	18	6	131	112	54
Pittsburgh Yelo Jackets	48	21	18	9	101	108	51
London Tecumsehs	48	21	21	6	89	83	48
Detroit Olympics	48	18	28	2	100	127	38
Syracuse Stars	48	9	34	5	114	171	23

AMERICAN HOCKEY ASSOCIATION

	GP	W	L	T	GF	GA	Pts
*Tulsa Oilers	48	30	15	3	152	112	60
Kansas City Pla-Mors	48	28	16	4	99	63	56
Duluth Hornets	48	28	19	1	118	92	56
Buffalo Majors	46	25	17	4	116	90	50
Chicago Shamrocks	47	24	21	2	118	97	48
Minneapolis Millers	46	11	33	2	65	136	22
St. Louis Flyers	47	11	36	0	84	162	22

• No points awarded for ties.

ONTARIO PROFESSIONAL HOCKEY LEAGUE

	GP	W	L	T	GF	GA	Pts
Guelph Maple Leafs	30	16	12	2	107	86	34
*Niagara Falls Cataracts	30	14	12	4	82	66	32
Stratford Nationals	30	14	14	2	98	93	30
Galt Terriers	30	13	15	2	84	103	28
Oshawa Patricias	30	12	14	4	94	86	28
Kitchener Silverwoods	30	13	15	2	70	101	28

EASTERN CANADA HOCKEY ASSOCIATION

	GP	W	L	T	GF	GA	Pts
Trois-Rivieres Renards	18	13	5	0	63	44	26
*La Tuques Loups-Nord	18	10	7	1	48	39	21
Quebec Castors	18	9	9	0	33	43	18
Shawinigan Cataracts §	18	3	14	1	31	49	7

§ Forfeited two games to Quebec and one to La Tuque

PACIFIC COAST HOCKEY LEAGUE

	GP	W	L	T	GF	GA	Pts
Seattle Eskimos	34	16	9	9	64	51	41
*Vancouver Lions	35	14	13	8	61	61	36
Portland Buckaroos	35	12	15	8	60	61	32
Tacoma Tigers §	10	2	7	1	12	24	5

§ folded 01/31

CALIFORNIA HOCKEY LEAGUE

	GP	W	L	T	GF	GA	Pts
*Oakland Sheiks	40	25	14	1	117	79	51
Oakland Checkers	41	20	17	4	109	117	44
Los Angeles Millionaires	39	16	17	6	93	91	38
San Francisco Tigers §	27	12	14	1	73	75	25
San-Fran Blackhawks¶	31	9	20	2	69	99	20

§ folded 02/12/31 • ¶ folded 02/23/31

1931–32

CANADIAN-AMERICAN HOCKEY LEAGUE

	GP	W	L	T	GF	GA	Pts
*Providence Reds	40	23	11	6	138	108	52
Boston Cubs	40	21	16	3	116	108	45
New Haven Eagles	40	19	15	6	113	75	44
Bronx Tigers	40	18	15	7	94	90	43
Philadelphia Arrows	40	13	22	5	85	114	31
Springfield Indians	40	10	25	5	85	136	25

INTERNATIONAL HOCKEY LEAGUE

	GP	W	L	T	GF	GA	Pts
*Buffalo Bisons	48	25	14	9	106	80	59
London Tecumsehs	48	21	15	12	92	70	54
Windsor Bulldogs	48	21	16	11	123	104	53
Detroit Olympics	48	19	19	10	96	97	48
Pittsburgh Y-Jackets	48	17	22	9	91	118	43
Syracuse Stars	48	16	23	9	111	118	41
Cleveland Indians	48	15	25	8	110	142	38

AMERICAN HOCKEY ASSOCIATION

	GP	W	L	T	GF	GA	Pts
*Chicago Shamrocks	48	30	13	5	121	72	60
Kansas City Pla-Mors	48	28	18	2	95	62	56
Duluth Hornets	48	21	24	3	97	97	42
St. Louis Flyers	48	18	22	8	80	97	36
Tulsa Oilers	48	16	29	3	85	121	32
Buffalo Majors §	24	7	14	3	28	57	14

• No points awarded for ties • § folded 01/30/32

CENTRAL HOCKEY LEAGUE

	GP	W	L	T	GF	GA	Pts
*Eveleth Rangers	33	23	10	0	97	70	50
Minneapolis Millers	36	22	11	3	113	67	44
St. Paul Saints	35	16	17	2	84	99	34
Hibbing Maroons	36	16	18	2	81	70	32
Virginia Rockets §	32	5	26	1	64	133	10

§ Played three 4-point games • No points awarded for ties.

EASTERN CANADA HOCKEY ASSOCIATION

	GP	W	L	T	GF	GA	Pts
*Quebec Castors	24	14	6	4	82	49	32
Chicoutimi Carabins	24	11	7	6	62	56	28
Trois-Rivieres Renards	24	8	11	5	57	58	21
La Tuque Loups-Nord	24	4	13	7	51	89	15

CALIFORNIA HOCKEY LEAGUE

	GP	W	L	T	GF	GA	Pts
*Hollywood Stars	31	20	7	4	134	86	44
San Francisco Rangers	30	12	12	6	100	110	30
Oakland Sheiks	30	11	12	7	99	95	29
Los Angeles Angels	31	9	21	1	112	154	19

1932–33

CANADIAN-AMERICAN HOCKEY LEAGUE

	GP	W	L	T	GF	GA	Pts
Philadelphia Arrows	48	29	12	7	153	95	65
Providence Reds	48	26	16	6	129	117	58
*Boston Cubs	48	21	18	9	136	119	51
New Haven Eagles	48	16	27	5	100	137	37
Quebec Castors	48	11	30	7	106	156	29
Springfield Indians §	13	6	5	2	29	29	14

§ folded, results did not count

International Hockey League

	GP	W	L	T	GF	GA	Pts
London Tecumsehs	44	27	9	8	111	66	62
* Buffalo Bisons	44	26	12	6	128	70	58
Syracuse Stars	44	23	15	6	136	119	52
Windsor Bulldogs	44	16	22	6	87	120	38
Detroit Olympics	42	10	27	5	100	147	25
Cleveland Indians	42	10	27	5	75	115	25

American Hockey Association

First Half	GP	W	L	T	GF	GA	Pts
* K.C. Pla-Mors	22	14	8	0	48	46	28
St. Louis Flyers	21	11	9	1	48	43	22
St. Paul Greyhounds	21	8	12	1	46	51	16
Duluth Hornets	18	7	11	0	42	44	14
Second Half							
Tulsa Oilers	24	13	11	0	68	69	26
St. Louis Flyers	24	13	11	0	64	47	26
* K.C. Pla-Mors	24	11	12	1	58	58	22
Wichita Blue Jays	24	10	13	1	70	86	20

• Duluth relocated to Wichita • St. Paul relocated to Tulsa
• No points awarded for ties

Central Hockey League

	GP	W	L	T	GF	GA	Pts
* Eveleth Rangers	40	26	12	2	114	83	54
Minneapolis Millers	40	25	13	2	99	78	52
St. Paul Saints	40	13	24	3	83	112	29
Hibbing Maroons	40	11	26	3	79	102	25
Duluth Natives §	9	1	8	0	10	28	

§ folded 01/02/33 • Duluth results not counted in standings

Western Canada Hockey League

	GP	W	L	T	GF	GA	Pts
* Calgary Tigers	30	16	10	4	70	61	36
Regina/Vancouver	30	15	13	2	110	97	32
Edmonton Eskimos	30	11	14	5	81	86	27
Saskatoon Crescents	30	11	16	3	82	99	25

California Hockey League

	GP	W	L	T	GF	GA	Pts
* Oakland Sheiks	29	16	11	2	100	92	34
Hollywood Millionaires§	34	15	16	3	151	161	33
San Francisco Rangers	29	11	15	3	118	116	25

§ folded 01/28/33

Tri-State Hockey League

	GP	W	L	T	GF	GA	Pts
Atlantic City Seagulls	18	15	1	2	100	27	32
Baltimore Orioles	18	12	5	1	43	33	25
Hershey B'Ars	18	6	11	1	69	58	13
Philadelphia Comets	16	0	16	0	25	119	0

1933–34

Canadian-American Hockey League

	GP	W	L	T	GF	GA	Pts
* Providence Reds	40	19	12	9	91	92	47
Boston Cubs	40	18	16	6	112	104	42
Philadelphia Arrows	40	17	15	8	121	101	42
Quebec Castors §	40	16	15	9	96	88	41
New Haven Eagles	40	12	24	4	72	107	28

§ played five 1-point games

International Hockey League

	GP	W	L	T	GF	GA	Pts
Detroit Olympics	44	23	16	5	104	98	51
Buffalo Bisons	44	20	13	11	90	66	51
* London Tecumsehs	44	18	17	9	92	80	45
Syracuse Stars	44	19	21	4	114	120	42
Windsor Bulldogs	44	18	23	3	84	103	39
Cleveland Falcons	44	16	24	4	104	121	36

American Hockey Association

	GP	W	L	T	GF	GA	Pts
* K.C. Greyhounds	48	26	18	4	106	87	52
St. Louis Flyers	48	26	18	4	97	84	52
Tulsa Oilers	48	23	25	0	107	110	46
Oklahoma City Warriors	48	16	30	2	86	115	32
Wichita Vikings §	3	0	3	0	3	9	0

• No points awarded for ties
§ folded 12/04/33 • Wichita results not counted in standings

North West Hockey League

	GP	W	L	T	GF	GA	Pts
* Calgary Tigers	34	17	11	6	117	76	40
Edmonton Eskimos	34	18	12	4	98	91	40
Vancouver Lions	34	17	16	1	95	111	35
Seattle Seahawks	34	15	17	2	99	95	32
Portland Buckaroos	34	10	21	3	80	116	23

Eastern Amateur Hockey League

	GP	W	L	T	GF	GA	Pts
* Baltimore Orioles	24	18	4	2	98	52	38
Atlantic City Seagulls	20	15	4	1	109	39	31
Hershey B'ars	26	14	11	1	77	63	29
Bronx Tigers	20	8	9	3	51	54	19
NY-Hamilton Crescents	20	6	14	0	28	76	12
New York Athletic Club	15	4	9	2	32	65	10
St. Nicholas HC	17	0	14	3	28	74	3

Central Hockey League

	GP	W	L	T	GF	GA	Pts
* Minneapolis Millers	44	28	11	5	129	86	56
Eveleth Rangers	44	26	14	4	117	91	52
Hibbing Miners	44	22	18	4	129	119	44
Duluth Hornets	44	12	27	5	79	119	24
St. Paul Saints	44	12	30	2	86	125	24

• No points awarded for ties

1934–35

Canadian-American Hockey League

	GP	W	L	T	GF	GA	Pts
* Boston Bruin Cubs	48	29	13	6	185	125	64
Quebec Castors	48	23	19	6	141	123	52
Providence Reds	48	19	17	12	124	144	50
New Haven Eagles	48	16	23	9	125	145	41
Philadelphia Arrows	48	15	30	3	122	160	33

International Hockey League

	GP	W	L	T	GF	GA	Pts
* Detroit Olympics	44	21	15	8	116	88	42
London Tecumsehs	44	21	17	6	98	110	42
Syracuse Stars	44	20	20	4	128	118	40
Cleveland Falcons	44	20	23	1	115	132	40
Buffalo Bisons	44	20	18	6	113	100	40
Windsor Bulldogs	44	14	23	7	94	116	28

• No points awarded for ties

American Hockey Association

	GP	W	L	T	GF	GA	Pts
* St. Louis Flyers	48	29	15	4	151	102	58
Tulsa Oilers	48	23	21	4	111	98	46
K.C. Greyhounds	48	23	25	0	82	102	46
Oklahoma City Warriors	48	15	28	5	88	133	30

• No points awarded for ties. • Played interlocking schedule with CHL

North West Hockey League

	GP	W	L	T	GF	GA	Pts
Seattle Seahawks	32	20	9	3	98	69	43
Portland Buckaroos	32	15	10	7	83	72	37
* Vancouver Lions	32	15	11	6	105	81	36
Edmonton Eskimos	26	7	15	4	77	101	18
Calgary Tigers	26	3	15	8	60	104	14

Eastern Hockey League

	GP	W	L	T	GF	GA	Pts
* NY-Hamilton Crescents	21	15	5	1	67	35	31
Hershey B'ars	21	10	9	2	60	56	22
Atlantic City Seagulls	21	8	10	3	44	64	19
Baltimore Orioles	21	4	13	4	41	57	12

Central Hockey League

	GP	W	L	T	GF	GA	Pts
* St. Paul Saints	47	28	10	9	137	88	56
Minneapolis Millers	48	21	19	8	108	105	42
Eveleth Rangers	47	9	30	8	88	137	18

• No points awarded for ties. • Played interlocking schedule with AHA

Eastern Amateur Hockey League

	GP	W	L	T	GF	GA	Pts
Hershey B'ars	40	27	11	2	119	78	56
Pittsburgh Y-Jackets	40	22	16	2	108	74	46
Atlantic City Seagulls	40	21	18	1	101	111	43
New York Rovers	40	16	21	3	108	110	35
* Baltimore Orioles	40	9	29	2	78	141	20

1935–36

Canadian-American Hockey League

	GP	W	L	T	GF	GA	Pts
* Philadelphia Ramblers	48	27	18	3	151	106	57
Providence Reds	47	21	20	6	106	127	48
Springfield Indians	48	21	22	5	131	129	47
Boston Bruins	47	20	23	4	128	127	44
New Haven Eagles	48	19	25	4	122	149	42

International Hockey League

Western Division	GP	W	L	T	GF	GA	Pts
* Detroit Olympics	47	26	18	3	127	101	55
Cleveland Falcons	48	25	19	4	149	146	54
Windsor Bulldogs	48	18	19	11	121	120	47
Pittsburgh Shamrocks	46	18	27	1	137	170	37
Eastern Division							
Syracuse Stars	48	26	19	3	167	130	55
Buffalo Bisons	48	22	20	6	109	101	50
London Tecumsehs	48	23	22	3	116	125	49
Rochester Cardinals	47	15	29	3	104	137	33

American Hockey Association

	GP	W	L	T	GF	GA	Pts
St. Paul Saints	48	32	13	3	153	99	64
* St. Louis Flyers	48	27	17	4	115	90	54
OK City Warriors§	48	21	22	5	92	86	42
Tulsa Oilers	48	21	27	0	99	140	42
K.C. Greyhounds	48	20	26	2	94	105	40
Wichita Skyhawks	48	16	32	0	81	114	32

• No points awarded for ties
§ Oklahoma City relocated to Minneapolis 03/12/36

North West Hockey League

	GP	W	L	T	GF	GA	Pts
* Seattle Seahawks	39	19	14	6	100	86	44
Portland Buckaroos	40	18	14	8	88	67	44
Vancouver Lions	40	18	17	5	125	117	41
Edmonton Eskimos	39	14	18	7	97	105	35
Calgary Tigers	40	15	21	4	107	141	34

1936–37

• IHL and Can-Am amalgamate to form IAHL

International-American Hockey League

Eastern Division	GP	W	L	T	GF	GA	Pts
Philadelphia Ramblers	48	26	14	8	152	106	60
Springfield Indians	48	22	17	9	118	127	53
Providence Reds	48	21	20	7	136	132	49
New Haven Eagles	48	14	28	6	106	143	34
Western Division							
* Syracuse Stars	48	27	16	5	182	135	59
Pittsburgh Hornets	48	22	23	3	125	131	47
Cleveland Barons	48	13	27	8	114	152	34
Buffalo Bisons §	11	3	8	0	23	30	6

§ folded 12/09/36 • Buffalo results not counted in standings

American Hockey Association

	GP	W	L	T	GF	GA	Pts
St. Louis Flyers	48	32	13	3	143	90	64
* Minneapolis Millers	48	23	21	4	102	105	46
K.C. Greyhounds	48	21	23	4	78	95	42
St. Paul Saints	48	21	24	3	90	102	42
Wichita Skyhawks	48	18	27	3	84	87	36
Tulsa Oilers	48	17	24	7	67	85	34

• No points awarded for ties

Pacific Coast Hockey League

	GP	W	L	T	GF	GA	Pts
* Portland Buckaroos	39	21	13	5	95	72	47
Vancouver Lions	36	16	12	8	111	86	40
Oakland-Spokane	39	14	18	7	85	96	35
Seattle Seahawks	38	13	21	4	78	115	30

Eastern Amateur Hockey League

	GP	W	L	T	GF	GA	Pts
Hershey B'ars	48	25	15	8	133	105	58
* Atlantic City Sea Gulls	48	27	19	2	148	120	56
Pittsburgh Y-Jackets	48	19	24	5	119	147	43
New York Rovers	48	18	23	7	130	144	43
Baltimore Orioles	48	16	24	8	121	135	40

1937–38

International-American Hockey League

Eastern Division	GP	W	L	T	GF	GA	Pts
* Providence Reds	48	25	16	7	114	86	57
Philadelphia Ramblers	48	26	18	4	134	108	56
New Haven Eagles	48	13	28	7	93	131	33
Springfield Indians	48	10	30	8	96	140	28
Western Division							
Cleveland Barons	48	25	12	11	126	114	61
Pittsburgh Hornets	48	22	18	8	100	104	52
Syracuse Stars	48	21	20	7	142	122	49

American Hockey Association

	GP	W	L	T	GF	GA	Pts
* St. Louis Flyers	48	29	14	5	143	102	58
Minneapolis Millers	48	24	15	9	140	100	48
Wichita Skyhawks	48	23	21	4	125	133	46
Tulsa Oilers	48	22	21	5	111	93	44
K.C. Greyhounds	48	21	22	5	120	120	42
St. Paul Saints	48	10	36	2	87	178	20

• No points awarded for ties

Pacific Coast Hockey League

	GP	W	L	T	GF	GA	Pts
* Seattle Seahawks	42	20	14	8	123	100	48
Vancouver Lions	42	19	18	5	87	91	43
Portland Buckaroos	42	16	18	8	88	84	40
Spokane Clippers	42	16	21	5	90	113	37

Eastern Amateur Hockey League

	GP	W	L	T	GF	GA	Pts
Hershey B'ars	58	32	15	11	197	136	75
* Atlantic City Seagulls	58	31	16	11	199	169	73
New York Rovers	58	29	23	6	193	179	64
Baltimore Orioles	58	21	29	8	177	195	50
Bronx Tigers	40	2	32	6	54	141	10

1938–39

International-American Hockey League

Eastern Division	GP	W	L	T	GF	GA	Pts
Philadelphia Ramblers	54	32	17	5	214	161	69
Providence Reds	54	21	22	11	136	153	53
Springfield Indians	54	16	29	9	121	179	41
New Haven Eagles	54	14	30	10	114	174	38
Western Division							
Hershey Bears	54	31	18	5	140	110	67
Syracuse Stars	54	26	19	9	152	117	61
* Cleveland Barons	54	23	22	9	145	138	55
Pittsburgh Hornets	54	22	28	4	176	166	48

AMERICAN HOCKEY ASSOCIATION

Team	GP	W	L	T	GF	GA	Pts
*St. Louis Flyers	48	36	12	0	183	95	72
Minneapolis Millers	48	31	17	0	214	139	62
Tulsa Oilers	48	25	23	0	137	153	50
St. Paul Saints	48	24	24	0	149	142	48
K.C. Greyhounds	48	15	33	0	133	225	30
Wichita Skyhawks	48	13	35	0	113	175	26

PACIFIC COAST HOCKEY LEAGUE

Team	GP	W	L	T	GF	GA	Pts
*Portland Buckaroos	48	31	9	8	180	114	70
Seattle Seahawks	48	21	21	6	168	167	48
Vancouver Lions	48	15	24	9	139	195	39
Spokane Clippers	48	14	27	7	144	155	35

TROPICAL HOCKEY LEAGUE

Team	GP	W	L	T	GF	GA	Pts
*Coral Gables Seminoles	14	12	2	0	85	53	24
Miami Clippers	14	7	7	0	55	62	14
Miami Beach Pirates	15	6	9	0	61	71	12
Havana Sugar Kings	15	4	11	0	69	84	8

• All teams based in Miami

EASTERN AMATEUR HOCKEY LEAGUE

Team	GP	W	L	T	GF	GA	Pts
*New York Rovers	53	31	13	9	196	121	71
Baltimore Orioles	53	26	22	5	180	165	57
Atlantic City Seagulls	53	22	25	6	166	180	50
Hershey Cubs	53	19	29	5	156	187	43
Canada	20	4	13	3	47	92	11

• Games played against Canada in Wills Trophy Tournament counted in standings

1939–40

INTERNATIONAL-AMERICAN HOCKEY LEAGUE

Eastern Division	GP	W	L	T	GF	GA	Pts
*Providence Reds	54	27	19	8	162	157	62
New Haven Eagles	54	27	24	3	176	183	57
Springfield Indians	54	24	24	6	165	149	54
Philadelphia Ramblers	54	15	31	8	133	170	38
Western Division							
Indianapolis Capitols	56	26	20	10	174	144	62
Pittsburgh Hornets	56	27	24	5	153	156	59
Hershey Bears	56	25	22	9	152	133	59
Cleveland Barons	56	24	24	8	125	128	56
Syracuse Stars	56	20	27	9	147	169	49

AMERICAN HOCKEY ASSOCIATION

Team	GP	W	L	T	GF	GA	Pts
St. Louis Flyers	48	37	11	0	195	99	74
St. Paul Saints •	47	29	18	0	159	121	60
Minneapolis Millers	48	26	22	0	170	140	52
*Omaha Knights	48	25	23	0	149	131	50
K.C. Greyhounds	48	20	28	0	129	175	40
Tulsa Oilers	46	16	30	0	141	180	32
Wichita Skyhawks •	45	12	33	0	97	194	24

• played one 4-point game

PACIFIC COAST HOCKEY LEAGUE

Team	GP	W	L	T	GF	GA	Pts
*Vancouver Lions	40	22	16	2	134	126	46
Portland Buckaroos	40	17	18	5	96	99	39
Seattle Seahawks	40	16	21	3	120	125	35

EASTERN AMATEUR HOCKEY LEAGUE

Team	GP	W	L	T	GF	GA	Pts
*Baltimore Orioles	61	37	22	2	263	185	78
Washington Eagles	61	32	25	4	259	229	68
New York Rovers	61	31	26	4	274	247	66
Atlantic City Seagulls	61	25	31	5	207	242	55
Rivervale Skeeters	61	16	38	7	173	267	39
Canadian teams	25	12	11	2	89	89	26

1940-41

AMERICAN HOCKEY LEAGUE

Eastern Division	GP	W	L	T	GF	GA	Pts
Providence Reds	56	31	21	4	196	171	66
New Haven Eagles	56	27	21	8	179	153	62
Springfield Indians	56	26	21	9	157	149	61
Philadelphia Rockets	56	25	25	6	166	167	56
Western Division							
*Cleveland Barons	56	26	21	9	177	162	61
Hershey Bears	56	24	23	9	193	189	57
Pittsburgh Hornets	56	21	29	6	156	170	48
Buffalo Bisons	56	19	27	10	148	176	48
Indianapolis Capitols	56	17	28	11	133	168	45

AMERICAN HOCKEY ASSOCIATION

Team	GP	W	L	T	GF	GA	Pts
*St. Louis Flyers	48	31	17	0	139	99	62
Kansas City Americans	48	25	23	0	150	152	50
Minneapolis Millers	48	25	23	0	136	106	50
St. Paul Saints	48	25	23	0	113	116	50
Omaha Knights	48	24	24	0	138	130	48
Tulsa Oilers	48	14	34	0	121	194	28

PACIFIC COAST HOCKEY LEAGUE

Team	GP	W	L	T	GF	GA	Pts
Spokane Bombers	48	25	18	5	146	127	55
*Vancouver Lions	48	22	21	5	163	145	49
Seattle Olympics	48	20	21	7	158	167	47
Portland Buckaroos	48	20	27	1	130	158	41

EASTERN AMATEUR HOCKEY LEAGUE

Team	GP	W	L	T	GF	GA	Pts
Washington Eagles	65	42	15	8	280	196	92
Baltimore Orioles	65	36	23	6	240	194	78
*Atlantic City Seagulls	65	32	28	5	253	256	69
Rivervale Skeeters	65	29	34	2	217	240	60
Boston Olympics	65	23	36	6	203	242	52
New York Rovers	65	19	45	1	218	283	39

1941–42

AMERICAN HOCKEY LEAGUE

Eastern Division	GP	W	L	T	GF	GA	Pts
Springfield Indians	56	31	20	5	213	167	67
New Haven Eagles	56	26	26	4	182	219	56
Washington Lions	56	20	30	6	160	172	46
Providence Reds	56	17	32	7	205	237	41
Philadelphia Rockets	56	11	41	4	157	254	26
Western Division							
*Indianapolis Capitols	56	34	15	7	204	144	75
Hershey Bears	56	33	17	6	207	169	72
Cleveland Barons	56	33	19	4	174	152	70
Buffalo Bisons	56	25	25	6	182	157	56
Pittsburgh Hornets	56	23	28	5	210	223	51

AMERICAN HOCKEY ASSOCIATION

Northern Division	GP	W	L	T	GF	GA	Pts
St. Louis Flyers	50	30	15	5	141	103	65
St. Paul Saints	50	28	17	5	141	99	61
*Omaha Knights	50	24	20	6	171	149	54
Minneapolis Millers	50	22	25	3	141	158	47
Southern Division							
Kansas City Americans	50	31	17	2	185	157	64
Fort Worth Rangers	50	25	23	2	190	176	52
Tulsa Oilers	50	13	34	3	120	188	29
Dallas Texans	50	12	34	4	131	190	28

EASTERN AMATEUR HOCKEY LEAGUE

Team	GP	W	L	T	GF	GA	Pts
*New York Rovers	60	34	20	6	272	197	74
Boston Olympics	60	34	20	6	263	218	74
Johnstown Bluebirds	60	34	20	6	248	215	74
Washington Eagles	60	28	27	5	261	253	61
Baltimore Orioles	60	26	30	4	252	262	56
Atlantic City Seagulls	60	20	39	1	239	316	41
Rivervale Skeeters	60	18	38	4	191	265	40

1942–43

AMERICAN HOCKEY LEAGUE

Team	GP	W	L	T	GF	GA	Pts
Hershey Bears	56	35	13	8	240	166	78
*Buffalo Bisons	56	28	21	7	189	143	63
Indianapolis Capitols	56	29	23	4	211	181	62
Pittsburgh Hornets	56	26	24	6	183	203	58
Providence Reds	56	27	27	2	211	216	56
Cleveland Barons	56	21	29	6	190	196	48
Washington Lions	56	14	34	8	184	272	36
New Haven Eagles §	32	9	18	5	85	116	23

§ folded 01/18/43

EASTERN AMATEUR HOCKEY LEAGUE

Team	GP	W	L	T	GF	GA	Pts
*Coast Guard Clippers	46	32	13	1	224	138	65
New York Rovers	46	24	20	2	197	158	50
Philadelphia Falcons	46	24	21	1	186	184	49
Boston Olympics	46	17	27	2	164	195	36

1943–44

AMERICAN HOCKEY LEAGUE

Eastern Division	GP	W	L	T	GF	GA	Pts
Hershey Bears	54	30	16	8	181	133	68
*Buffalo Bisons	54	25	16	13	201	168	63
Providence Reds	52	11	36	5	126	214	27
Western Division							
Cleveland Barons	54	33	14	7	224	176	73
Indianapolis Capitols	54	20	18	16	156	156	56
Pittsburgh Hornets	52	12	31	9	140	181	33

EASTERN AMATEUR HOCKEY LEAGUE

Team	GP	W	L	T	GF	GA	Pts
*Boston Olympics	45	39	4	2	250	93	80
New York Rovers	45	20	20	5	210	222	45
Philadelphia Falcons	45	17	23	5	185	207	39
New Haven Crescents	45	5	34	6	179	302	16

• U.S. Coast Guard folded 11/28/43. Played exhibitions only.

1944–45

AMERICAN HOCKEY LEAGUE

Eastern Division	GP	W	L	T	GF	GA	Pts
Buffalo Bisons	60	31	21	8	200	182	70
Hershey Bears	60	28	24	8	197	186	64
Providence Reds	60	23	31	6	241	249	52
Western Division							
*Cleveland Barons	60	34	16	10	256	199	78
Indianapolis Capitols	60	25	24	11	169	167	61
Pittsburgh Hornets	60	26	27	7	267	247	59
St. Louis Flyers	60	14	38	8	157	257	36

EASTERN AMATEUR HOCKEY LEAGUE

Team	GP	W	L	T	GF	GA	Pts
*Boston Olympics	48	32	13	3	295	178	67
Baltimore Orioles	48	28	19	1	228	177	57
Philadelphia Falcons	48	23	21	4	242	232	50
Washington Lions	48	15	28	5	212	310	35
New York Rovers	48	12	29	7	176	256	31

PACIFIC COAST HOCKEY LEAGUE

Central Division	GP	W	L	T	GF	GA	Pts
Oakland Oaks	19	12	7	0	112	100	24
San-Fran Shamrocks	20	7	12	1	102	142	15
Northern Division							
*Seattle Ironmen	27	20	6	1	161	84	43
Portland Eagles	27	19	7	1	150	104	39
Seattle Stars	27	12	14	1	140	148	25
Vancouver Vanguards	15	8	16	1	107	169	17
Southern Division							
*San Diego Skyhawks	18	11	7	0	106	80	22
Los Angeles Monarchs	18	11	7	0	94	84	19
Hollywood Wolves	18	9	8	1	86	103	19
Pasadena Panthers	18	4	13	1	95	111	9

1945–46

AMERICAN HOCKEY LEAGUE

Eastern Division	GP	W	L	T	GF	GA	Pts
*Buffalo Bisons	62	38	16	8	270	196	84
Hershey Bears	62	26	26	10	213	221	62
Providence Reds	62	23	33	6	221	254	52
New Haven Eagles	62	14	38	10	199	263	38
Western Division							
Indianapolis Capitols	62	33	20	9	286	238	75
Pittsburgh Hornets	62	30	22	10	262	226	70
Cleveland Barons	62	28	26	8	269	254	64
St. Louis Flyers	62	21	32	9	198	266	51

UNITED STATES HOCKEY LEAGUE

Team	GP	W	L	T	GF	GA	Pts
*Kansas City Pla-Mors	56	35	17	4	271	185	74
Omaha Knights	56	31	22	3	210	190	65
St. Paul Saints	56	28	26	2	208	186	58
Tulsa Oilers	56	27	25	4	269	230	58
Fort Worth Rangers	56	24	31	1	186	238	49
Dallas Texans	56	21	32	3	218	259	45
Minneapolis Millers	56	20	33	3	192	262	43

PACIFIC COAST HOCKEY LEAGUE

North Division	GP	W	L	T	GF	GA	Pts
*Vancouver Canucks	58	37	21	0	308	247	74
Portland Eagles	58	29	29	0	257	261	58
Seattle Ironmen	58	29	29	0	251	214	58
New Westm'ster Royals	58	26	32	0	228	268	52
South Division							
Oakland Oaks	40	25	15	0	188	159	50
Hollywood Wolves	40	21	19	0	157	157	42
San Diego Skyhawks	40	21	19	0	145	139	42
Los Angeles Monarchs	40	17	23	0	189	208	34
San-Fran Shamrocks	40	11	29	0	159	229	22

QUEBEC SENIOR HOCKEY LEAGUE

Team	GP	W	L	T	GF	GA	Pts
*Montreal Royals	40	30	8	2	209	131	62
Ottawa Senators	40	24	14	2	212	157	50
Shawinigan Cataracts	40	18	20	2	158	193	38
Quebec Aces	40	17	20	3	149	169	37
Valleyfield Braves	40	15	22	3	163	184	33
Hull Volants	40	9	29	2	158	211	20

INTERNATIONAL HOCKEY LEAGUE

Team	GP	W	L	T	GF	GA	Pts
Det-Bright's Goodyears	15	9	3	3	90	70	21
Windsor Gotfredsons	15	8	4	3	90	72	19
*Detroit Auto Club	15	8	7	0	82	81	16
Windsor Spitfires	15	1	12	2	50	89	4

EASTERN AMATEUR HOCKEY LEAGUE

Team	GP	W	L	T	GF	GA	Pts
*Boston Olympics	52	32	12	8	258	162	72
Philadelphia Falcons	52	26	21	5	180	186	57
New York Rovers	52	25	20	7	240	181	57
Baltimore Clippers	52	19	25	8	164	205	46
Washington Lions	52	8	32	12	128	236	28

WESTERN CANADA SENIOR HOCKEY LEAGUE

Team	GP	W	L	T	GF	GA	Pts
*Calgary Stampeders	36	28	7	1	219	95	57
Edmonton Flyers	36	24	10	2	181	130	50
Saskatoon Elks	35	14	19	2	104	147	30
Regina Caps	35	2	32	1	95	227	5

1946–47

American Hockey League

Eastern Division	GP	W	L	T	GF	GA	Pts
*Hershey Bears	64	36	16	12	276	174	84
Springfield Indians	64	24	29	11	202	220	59
New Haven Ramblers	64	23	31	10	199	218	56
Providence Reds	64	21	33	10	226	281	52
Philadelphia Rockets	64	5	52	7	188	400	17
Western Division							
Cleveland Barons	64	38	18	8	272	215	84
Buffalo Bisons	64	36	17	11	257	173	83
Pittsburgh Hornets	64	35	19	10	260	188	80
Indianapolis Capitols	64	33	18	13	285	215	79
St. Louis Flyers	64	17	35	12	211	292	46

United States Hockey League

North Division	GP	W	L	T	GF	GA	Pts
Omaha Knights	60	29	16	15	225	181	73
*Kansas City Pla-Mors	60	29	20	11	264	197	69
Minneapolis Millers	60	28	22	10	214	197	66
St. Paul Saints	60	27	27	6	216	234	60
South Division							
Dallas Texans	60	27	18	15	232	218	69
Fort Worth Rangers	60	22	27	11	195	214	55
Tulsa Oilers	60	17	31	12	203	259	46
Houston Huskies	60	14	32	14	210	259	42

Pacific Coast Hockey League

North Division	GP	W	L	T	GF	GA	Pts
Portland Eagles	60	39	21	0	281	216	78
Seattle Ironmen	60	34	25	1	263	195	69
Vancouver Canucks	60	30	29	1	267	287	61
New Westm'ster Royals	60	29	29	2	257	270	60
Tacoma Rockets	60	16	42	2	223	324	34
South Division							
Hollywood Wolves	60	43	16	1	238	138	87
*Los Angeles Monarchs	60	36	24	0	308	260	72
San Diego Skyhawks	60	33	26	1	194	160	67
Fresno Falcons	60	26	33	1	236	252	53
Oakland Oaks	60	22	38	0	253	306	44
San-Fran Shamrocks	60	17	42	1	217	329	35

Quebec Senior Hockey League

	GP	W	L	T	GF	GA	Pts
Ottawa Senators	40	26	10	4	206	148	56
*Montreal Royals	40	25	13	2	173	124	52
Quebec Aces	40	19	15	6	159	158	44
Shawinigan Cataracts	40	14	23	3	135	175	31
Valleyfield Braves	40	8	31	1	142	210	17

International Hockey League

	GP	W	L	T	GF	GA	Pts
Windsor Staffords	28	17	8	3	167	138	37
*Windsor Spitfires	28	14	10	4	162	141	32
Det-Bright's Goodyears	28	13	9	6	154	128	32
Det-Metal Mouldings	28	9	13	6	89	122	24
Detroit Auto Club	28	7	20	1	113	156	15

Eastern Amateur Hockey League

	GP	W	L	T	GF	GA	Pts
New York Rovers	56	30	22	4	232	202	64
Washington Lions	56	24	24	8	235	252	56
*Boston Olympics	56	25	26	5	284	273	55
Baltimore Clippers	56	18	30	8	203	253	44
Quebec Sr. League	32	15	10	7	167	141	37

• Played interlocking schedule with Quebec Senior League teams

Western Canada Senior Hockey League

	GP	W	L	T	GF	GA	Pts
*Calgary Stampeders	40	27	9	4	187	105	58
Edmonton Flyers	40	22	16	2	174	139	46
Lethbridge Maple Leafs	40	20	17	3	177	159	43
Saskatoon Elks	40	15	23	2	151	210	32
Regina Caps	40	10	29	1	125	201	21

1947–48

American Hockey League

Eastern Division	GP	W	L	T	GF	GA	Pts
Providence Reds	68	41	23	4	342	277	86
New Haven Ramblers	68	31	30	7	254	242	69
Hershey Bears	68	25	30	13	240	273	63
Philadelphia Rockets	68	22	41	5	260	331	49
Springfield Indians	68	19	42	7	237	308	45
Washington Lions	68	17	45	6	241	369	40
Western Division							
*Cleveland Barons	68	43	13	12	332	197	98
Pittsburgh Hornets	68	38	18	12	238	170	88
Buffalo Bisons	68	41	23	4	277	238	86
Indianapolis Capitols	68	32	30	6	293	260	70
St. Louis Flyers	68	22	36	10	242	291	54

United States Hockey League

North Division	GP	W	L	T	GF	GA	Pts
Kansas City Pla-Mors	66	35	27	4	274	244	74
Minneapolis Millers	66	34	26	6	259	228	74
Omaha Knights	66	32	27	7	275	252	71
St. Paul Saints	66	30	30	6	236	245	66
South Division							
*Houston Huskies	66	36	27	3	317	267	75
Fort Worth Rangers	66	30	31	5	230	234	65
Tulsa Oilers	66	23	34	9	222	275	55
Dallas Texans	66	21	39	6	208	276	48

Pacific Coast Hockey League

North Division	GP	W	L	T	GF	GA	Pts
Seattle Ironmen	66	42	21	3	311	239	87
Tacoma Rockets	66	34	28	4	294	281	72
*Vancouver Canucks	66	34	29	3	284	264	71
New Westm'ster Royals	66	27	38	1	293	322	55
Portland Eagles	66	17	46	3	256	345	37
South Division							
Los Angeles Monarchs	66	36	26	4	306	270	76
San-Fran Shamrocks	66	35	29	2	243	227	72
San Diego Skyhawks	66	32	31	3	242	258	67
Fresno Falcons	66	30	32	4	229	236	64
Oakland Oaks	66	29	36	1	236	252	59

Quebec Senior Hockey League

	GP	W	L	T	GF	GA	Pts
*Ottawa Senators	48	35	11	2	271	139	72
Montreal Royals	48	34	14	0	241	159	68
Shawinigan Cataracts	48	26	17	5	206	189	57
Quebec Aces	48	23	20	5	175	185	51
Valleyfield Braves	48	16	31	1	207	251	33
New York Rovers §	48	14	33	1	150	220	29
Boston Olympics §	48	13	35	0	173	287	26

§ Results of games between these teams counted in EAHL and QSHL

International Hockey League

	GP	W	L	T	GF	GA	Pts
Windsor Spitfires	30	19	10	1	151	105	39
*Toledo Mercurys	30	15	10	5	113	98	35
Det-Metal Mouldings	30	15	12	3	135	139	33
Det-Bright's Goodyears	30	13	14	3	157	149	29
Detroit Auto Club	30	13	16	1	161	155	27
Windsor Staffords	30	8	21	1	117	188	17

Eastern Amateur Hockey League

	GP	W	L	T	GF	GA	Pts
*Baltimore Clippers	48	31	16	1	246	154	63
New York Rovers §	48	27	19	2	125	150	56
Atlantic City Seagulls	48	17	25	6	167	196	40
Boston Olympics §	48	14	29	5	139	177	33

§ Results of games between these teams counted in EAHL and QSHL
• All teams played a series of 4-point games, each recorded as 2 games played

Western Canada Senior Hockey League

	GP	W	L	T	GF	GA	Pts
Calgary Stampeders	48	28	19	1	225	191	57
Regina Caps	48	26	21	1	225	226	53
*Edmonton Flyers	48	24	22	2	231	184	50
Lethbridge Maple Leafs	48	20	28	0	200	228	40
Saskatoon Quakers	48	19	27	2	187	239	40

1948–49

American Hockey League

Eastern Division	GP	W	L	T	GF	GA	Pts
*Providence Reds	68	44	18	6	347	219	94
Hershey Bears	68	28	35	5	256	261	61
Springfield Indians	68	22	37	9	240	276	53
New Haven Ramblers	68	20	40	8	223	286	48
Philadelphia Rockets	68	15	48	5	230	407	35
Washington Lions	68	11	53	4	179	401	26
Western Division							
Cleveland Barons	68	41	18	9	294	192	91
Pittsburgh Hornets	68	39	17	12	288	209	90
Buffalo Bisons	68	41	21	6	286	251	88
Indianapolis Capitols	68	39	19	10	301	175	88
St. Louis Flyers	68	33	27	8	246	213	74

Eastern Amateur Hockey League

• EAHL did not operate in 1948–49

United States Hockey League

North Division	GP	W	L	T	GF	GA	Pts
*St. Paul Saints	66	36	20	10	284	210	82
Kansas City Pla-Mors	66	30	23	13	261	206	73
Omaha Knights	66	28	25	13	226	220	69
Minneapolis Millers	66	27	24	15	223	211	69
South Division							
Tulsa Oilers	66	33	23	10	281	216	76
Dallas Texans	66	24	27	15	246	251	63
Fort Worth Rangers	66	24	35	7	217	298	55
Houston Huskies	66	17	42	7	200	326	41

Pacific Coast Hockey League

Northern Division	GP	W	L	T	GF	GA	Pts
New Westm'ster Royals	70	39	26	5	285	229	83
Tacoma Rockets	70	34	31	5	239	262	73
Vancouver Canucks	70	33	31	6	262	256	72
Portland Penguins	70	32	31	7	246	236	71
Seattle Ironmen	70	29	36	5	225	246	63
Southern Division							
Fresno Falcons	70	33	30	7	213	211	73
Oakland Oaks	70	33	33	4	241	222	70
*San Diego Skyhawks	70	32	35	3	249	275	67
Los Angeles Monarchs	70	28	33	9	246	271	65
San-Fran Shamrocks	70	29	36	5	273	271	63

Quebec Senior Hockey League

	GP	W	L	T	GF	GA	Pts
*Ottawa Senators	60	44	15	1	341	207	89
Sherbrook Red Raiders	60	41	16	3	263	176	85
Montreal Royals §	59	35	19	5	216	178	77
Valleyfield Braves	60	29	30	1	265	270	59
Quebec Aces	60	22	32	6	186	213	50
Shawinigan Cataracts	60	18	40	2	201	292	38
New York Rovers §	59	10	47	2	191	328	22

§ played one 4-point game

International Hockey League

North Division	GP	W	L	T	GF	GA	Pts
Toledo Mercurys	35	20	7	8	185	140	48
Detroit Jerry Lynch	31	16	6	9	163	125	44a
Detroit Auto Club	31	17	11	3	146	130	39b
*Windsor Sr. Spitfires	31	15	11	5	152	144	39c
Det-Bright's Goodyears	31	8	16	7	135	154	28d
Windsor Ryancretes	31	0	25	6	89	177	6

• All teams except Toledo played 4-point games

South Division	GP	W	L	T	GF	GA	Pts
Louisville Blades	32	21	5	6	192	127	48
Toledo Mercurys	32	21	7	4	173	93	46
Milwaukee Clarks	32	16	15	1	148	139	33
Muncie Flyers	32	9	19	4	103	168	22
Akron Americans	32	4	25	3	111	200	11

Western Canada Senior Hockey League

	GP	W	L	T	GF	GA	Pts
*Regina Capitals	48	33	13	2	214	150	68
Edmonton Flyers	48	30	17	1	262	172	61
Calgary Stampeders	48	23	22	3	220	177	49
Lethbridge Maple Leafs	48	20	24	4	175	209	44
Saskatoon Quakers	48	8	38	2	144	307	18

1949–50

American Hockey League

Eastern Division	GP	W	L	T	GF	GA	Pts
Buffalo Bisons	70	32	29	9	226	208	73
Providence Reds	70	34	33	3	268	267	71
Springfield Indians	70	28	34	8	245	258	64
New Haven Ramblers	70	24	36	10	196	250	58
Hershey Bears	70	21	39	10	229	310	52
Western Division							
Cleveland Barons	70	45	15	10	357	230	100
*Indianapolis Capitols	70	35	24	11	267	231	81
St. Louis Flyers	70	34	28	8	258	250	76
Pittsburgh Hornets	70	29	26	15	215	185	73
Cincinnati Mohawks	70	19	37	14	185	257	52

United States Hockey League

	GP	W	L	T	GF	GA	Pts
Omaha Knights	70	41	22	7	313	240	89
*Minneapolis Millers	70	33	28	9	297	257	75
Kansas City Mohawks	70	30	28	12	293	267	72
St. Paul Saints	70	29	30	11	253	289	69
Tulsa Oilers	70	25	33	12	276	302	62
Louisville Blades	70	22	39	9	256	333	53

Pacific Coast Hockey League

Northern Division	GP	W	L	T	GF	GA	Pts
*New Westm'ster Royals	71	36	19	16	291	233	88
Tacoma Rockets	70	34	27	9	302	238	77
Vancouver Canucks	70	33	28	9	300	263	75
Seattle Ironmen	70	32	27	11	212	237	75
Portland Penguins	71	32	30	9	237	229	73
Victoria Cougars	70	22	42	6	218	307	50
Southern Division							
San-Fran Shamrocks	71	35	27	9	266	233	79
Los Angeles Monarchs	70	30	30	10	259	247	70
San Diego Skyhawks	70	27	33	10	211	236	64
Fresno Falcons	70	21	35	14	197	239	56
Oakland Oaks §	29	10	14	5	78	109	25

§ folded 12/16/49

Quebec Senior Hockey League

	GP	W	L	T	GF	GA	Pts
*Sherbrooke Saints	60	39	20	1	246	173	79
Quebec Aces	60	35	22	3	207	175	73
Ottawa Senators	60	31	25	4	251	240	66
Montreal Royals	60	27	24	9	206	188	63
Valleyfield Braves	60	25	26	9	216	200	59
Chicoutimi Sagueneens	60	22	35	3	172	236	47
Shawinigan Cataracts	60	15	42	3	184	270	33

International Hockey League

	GP	W	L	T	GF	GA	Pts
Sarnia Sailors	40	26	11	3	219	136	55
Detroit Auto Club	40	19	14	7	170	139	45
*Chatham Maroons	40	19	18	3	152	148	41
Detroit Hettche	40	15	21	4	157	191	34
Windsor Ryancretes	40	10	25	5	152	236	25

EASTERN AMATEUR HOCKEY LEAGUE

	GP	W	L	T	GF	GA	Pts
Toledo Buckeyes	51	26	13	12	188	142	64
*New York Rovers	47	25	17	7	195	133	57
Grand Rapids Rockets	61	26	21	14	230	225	66
Boston Olympics	43	16	20	7	146	169	39
Milwaukee Clarks	51	19	24	8	191	210	46
Atlantic City Seagulls	47	14	31	2	122	193	30
Cleveland Knights §	18	4	10	4	....	....	12
Baltimore Clippers §	12	5	7	0	....	....	10

§ folded 12/20/49

WESTERN CANADA SENIOR HOCKEY LEAGUE

	GP	W	L	T	GF	GA	Pts
Edmonton Flyers	50	27	18	5	238	174	59
*Calgary Stampeders	50	22	23	5	176	163	49
Saskatoon Quakers	50	24	25	1	190	227	49
Regina Capitals	50	19	26	5	171	211	43

1950-51

AMERICAN HOCKEY LEAGUE

Eastern Division	GP	W	L	T	GF	GA	Pts
Buffalo Bisons	70	40	26	4	309	284	84
Hershey Bears	70	38	28	4	256	242	80
Springfield Indians	70	27	37	6	268	254	60
Providence Reds	70	24	41	5	247	303	53
New Haven Ramblers §	28	5	23	0	74	154	10
§ folded 12/10/51							
Western Division							
*Cleveland Barons	71	44	22	5	281	221	93
Indianapolis Capitols	70	38	29	3	287	255	79
Pittsburgh Hornets	71	31	33	7	212	177	69
St. Louis Flyers	70	32	34	4	233	252	68
Cincinnati Mohawks	70	28	34	8	203	228	64

UNITED STATES HOCKEY LEAGUE

	GP	W	L	T	GF	GA	Pts
*Omaha Knights	64	43	17	4	306	211	90
St. Paul Saints	64	33	26	5	213	186	71
Denver Falcons	64	31	31	2	233	232	64
Tulsa Oilers	64	30	31	3	248	237	63
Kansas City Royals	64	22	36	6	231	287	50
Milwaukee Seagulls	64	20	38	6	202	280	46

PACIFIC COAST HOCKEY LEAGUE

	GP	W	L	T	GF	GA	Pts
*Victoria Cougars	70	35	20	15	250	216	85
New Westm'ster Royals	70	38	24	8	267	205	84
Tacoma Rockets	70	27	26	17	219	222	71
Portland Eagles	70	30	32	8	266	255	68
Seattle Ironmen	70	23	36	11	214	249	57
Vancouver Canucks	70	19	34	17	216	285	55

QUEBEC MAJOR HOCKEY LEAGUE

	GP	W	L	T	GF	GA	Pts
*Valleyfield Braves	60	37	19	4	227	178	78
Quebec Aces	60	31	22	7	228	195	69
Ottawa Senators	60	29	23	8	214	189	66
Chicoutimi Sagueneens	60	28	29	3	200	203	59
Montreal Royals	60	27	28	5	220	216	59
Sherbrooke Saints	60	24	30	6	193	209	54
Shawinigan Cataracts	60	15	40	5	181	273	35

ONTARIO MAJOR HOCKEY LEAGUE

	GP	W	L	T	GF	GA	Pts
*St. Michael's Monarchs §	33	20	13	3	139	108	58
Hamilton Tigers §§	40	18	19	3	159	164	43
Toronto Marlboros ¶	32	19	12	1	137	109	42
Kitchener Dutchmen ¶¶	41	11	27	3	141	195	25

§ Played six 4-point games (also played 8-point game vs. Marlies)
§§ Played two 4-point games
¶ Played seven 4-point games (also played 8-point game vs. St. Mike's)
¶¶ Played one-4 point game
• St. Mike's beat Saskatoon 4–0 • Lost Alexander Cup to Valleyfield

INTERNATIONAL HOCKEY LEAGUE

	GP	W	L	T	GF	GA	Pts
Grand Rapids Rockets	56	39	11	6	274	165	84
Toledo Mercurys	56	35	15	6	290	174	76
*Chatham Maroons	52	25	23	4	211	215	59
Sarnia Sailors	52	24	19	9	226	191	59
Detroit Auto Club	52	10	32	10	136	238	31
Detroit Hettche	52	6	39	7	112	226	19

• Chatham, Sarnia, Detroit Auto and Detroit Hettche played 4-pt. games

EASTERN AMATEUR HOCKEY LEAGUE

	GP	W	L	T	GF	GA	Pts
Johnstown Jets	54	26	25	3	195	194	55
Boston Olympics	54	25	24	5	187	191	55
*Atlantic City Seagulls	54	23	24	7	231	218	53
New York Rovers	54	22	23	9	168	178	53

WESTERN CANADA SENIOR HOCKEY LEAGUE

	GP	W	L	T	GF	GA	Pts
Calgary Stampeders	60	38	21	1	282	202	77
Edmonton Flyers	60	34	25	1	242	198	69
*Saskatoon Quakers	59	31	27	1	246	234	63
Regina Caps	59	14	44	1	173	309	29

MARITIME MAJOR HOCKEY LEAGUE

	GP	W	L	T	GF	GA	Pts
*Charlottetown Islanders	77	49	23	5	340	216	103
Halifax St. Mary's	78	42	33	3	328	294	87
Saint John Beavers	78	36	39	3	293	310	75
Moncton Hawks	77	20	52	5	251	392	45

1951–52

AMERICAN HOCKEY LEAGUE

Eastern Division	GP	W	L	T	GF	GA	Pts
Hershey Bears	68	35	28	5	256	215	75
Providence Reds	68	32	33	3	263	270	67
Buffalo Bisons	68	28	36	4	230	298	60
Syracuse Warriors	68	25	42	1	211	272	51
Western Division							
*Pittsburgh Hornets	68	46	19	3	267	179	95
Cleveland Barons	68	44	19	5	265	166	93
Cincinnati Mohawks	68	29	33	6	183	228	64
St. Louis Flyers	68	28	39	1	256	262	57
Indianapolis Capitols	68	22	40	6	232	273	50

PACIFIC COAST HOCKEY LEAGUE

	GP	W	L	T	GF	GA	Pts
New Westm'ster Royals	70	40	19	11	286	200	91
*Saskatoon Quakers	70	35	21	14	273	225	84
Tacoma Rockets	70	34	25	11	293	244	79
Seattle Ironmen	70	30	31	9	252	280	69
Edmonton Flyers	70	30	32	8	244	246	68
Victoria Cougars	70	25	38	7	242	296	57
Calgary Stampeders	70	24	37	9	278	320	57
Vancouver Canucks	70	23	38	9	226	283	55

QUEBEC MAJOR HOCKEY LEAGUE

	GP	W	L	T	GF	GA	Pts
*Quebec Aces	60	37	16	7	230	168	81
Montreal Royals	60	30	24	6	219	204	66
Chicoutimi Sagueneens	60	26	25	9	210	179	61
Ottawa Senators	60	26	28	6	177	195	58
Sherbrooke Saints	60	24	29	7	155	183	55
Valleyfield Braves	60	24	30	6	169	178	54
Shawinigan Cataracts	60	19	34	7	147	200	45

INTERNATIONAL HOCKEY LEAGUE

	GP	W	L	T	GF	GA	Pts
Grand Rapids Rockets	48	29	13	6	213	156	64
*Toledo Mercurys	48	24	18	6	210	192	54
Troy Bruins	48	23	19	6	211	180	52
Chatham Maroons	48	22	23	3	206	218	47
Detroit Hettche	48	10	35	3	138	232	23

EASTERN AMATEUR HOCKEY LEAGUE

	GP	W	L	T	GF	GA	Pts
*Johnstown Jets	65	39	21	5	264	186	83
Boston Olympics	66	38	27	1	246	240	77
N-Haven Tomahawks	66	37	27	2	256	241	76
Springfield Indians	66	33	29	4	247	235	70
Atlantic City Seagulls	65	26	36	3	255	281	55
New York Rovers	61	25	34	2	233	231	52
Washington Lions §	36	9	24	3	124	155	21
Philadelphia Falcons ¶	25	8	17	0	68	124	16

§ folded 01/25/52 ¶ folded 12/17/52

MARITIME MAJOR HOCKEY LEAGUE

	GP	W	L	T	GF	GA	Pts
*Saint John Beavers	90	53	24	13	360	231	119
Charlottetown Islanders	90	42	39	9	317	316	93
Halifax St.Mary's	90	41	41	8	333	339	90
Glace Bay Miners	90	37	43	10	320	342	84
Sydney Millionaires	90	35	43	12	285	326	82
Moncton Hawks	90	30	48	12	268	329	72

1952–53

AMERICAN HOCKEY LEAGUE

	GP	W	L	T	GF	GA	Pts
*Cleveland Barons	64	42	20	2	248	164	86
Pittsburgh Hornets	64	37	21	6	223	149	80
Syracuse Warriors	64	31	31	2	213	201	64
Hershey Bears	64	31	32	1	208	217	63
Providence Reds	64	27	36	1	215	254	55
St. Louis Flyers	64	26	37	1	212	258	53
Buffalo Bisons	64	22	39	3	160	236	47

QUEBEC MAJOR HOCKEY LEAGUE

	GP	W	L	T	GF	GA	Pts
*Chicoutimi Sagueneens	60	33	15	12	213	149	78
Montreal Royals	60	32	22	6	201	162	70
Valleyfield Braves	60	27	25	8	175	178	62
Ottawa Senators	60	27	26	7	171	191	61
Sherbrooke Saints	60	26	27	7	184	175	57
Quebec Aces	60	22	26	12	178	197	56
Shawinigan Cataracts	60	15	39	6	171	241	36

INTERNATIONAL HOCKEY LEAGUE

	GP	W	L	T	GF	GA	Pts
*Cincinnati Mohawks	60	43	13	4	310	152	90
Troy Bruins	60	34	21	5	264	221	73
Toledo Mercurys	60	32	25	3	210	207	67
Grand Rapids Rockets	60	27	32	1	231	257	55
Fort Wayne Komets	60	20	38	2	182	244	42
Milwaukee Chiefs	60	15	42	3	234	350	33

EASTERN AMATEUR HOCKEY LEAGUE

	GP	W	L	T	GF	GA	Pts
Springfield Indians	60	39	19	2	296	234	80
*Johnstown Jets	60	28	29	3	226	244	59
New Haven Nutmegs	60	28	31	1	251	223	57
Washington Lions	60	26	31	3	201	215	55
Troy Uncle Sam Trojans	60	23	34	3	220	278	49

WESTERN HOCKEY LEAGUE

• PCHL and WCSHL amalgamate to form WHL

	GP	W	L	T	GF	GA	Pts
Saskatoon Quakers	70	35	26	9	268	240	79
Vancouver Canucks	70	32	28	10	222	216	74
Calgary Stampeders	70	31	27	12	254	252	74
*Edmonton Flyers	70	31	28	11	263	227	73
Seattle Bombers	70	30	32	8	222	225	68
New Westm'ster Royals	70	29	33	8	217	254	66
Tacoma Rockets	70	27	31	12	246	249	66
Victoria Cougars	70	26	36	8	244	273	60

MARITIME MAJOR HOCKEY LEAGUE

	GP	W	L	T	GF	GA	Pts
*Halifax Atlantics	84	47	33	4	350	308	98
Charlottetown Islanders	84	45	35	4	307	261	94
Glace Bay Miners	84	40	40	4	278	280	84
Sydney Millionaires	84	28	52	4	228	314	60

1953–54

AMERICAN HOCKEY LEAGUE

	GP	W	L	T	GF	GA	Pts
Buffalo Bisons	70	39	24	7	283	217	85
Hershey Bears	70	37	29	4	274	243	78
*Cleveland Barons	70	38	32	0	269	227	76
Pittsburgh Hornets	70	34	31	5	250	222	73
Providence Reds	70	26	40	4	211	276	56
Syracuse Warriors	70	24	42	4	215	317	52

QUEBEC HOCKEY LEAGUE

	GP	W	L	T	GF	GA	Pts
Chicoutimi Sagueneens	72	40	25	7	261	197	87
Montreal Royals	72	40	25	7	257	203	87
Ottawa Senators	72	34	32	6	223	212	74
*Quebec Aces	72	30	34	8	216	212	68
Sherbrooke Saints	72	30	36	6	223	244	66
Valleyfield Braves	72	31	38	3	207	252	65
Springfield Indians	72	25	40	7	222	289	57

INTERNATIONAL HOCKEY LEAGUE

	GP	W	L	T	GF	GA	Pts
*Cincinnati Mohawks	64	47	15	2	325	153	96
Marion Barons	64	40	24	0	279	207	80
Johnstown Jets	64	35	26	3	254	221	73
Toledo Mercurys	64	33	26	5	221	157	71
Troy Bruins	64	31	32	1	241	258	63
Fort Wayne Komets	64	29	30	5	203	220	63
Grand Rapids Rockets	64	29	32	3	252	274	61
Louisville Shooting Stars	64	18	42	4	202	331	40
Milwaukee Chiefs	64	13	48	3	187	343	29

WESTERN HOCKEY LEAGUE

	GP	W	L	T	GF	GA	Pts
Vancouver Canucks	70	39	24	7	218	174	85
*Calgary Stampeders	70	38	25	7	266	206	83
Saskatoon Quakers	70	32	29	9	226	214	73
Edmonton Flyers	70	29	30	11	246	260	69
Victoria Cougars	70	27	32	11	203	223	65
New Westm'ster Royals	70	28	34	8	218	261	64
Seattle Bombers	70	22	41	7	209	248	51

MARITIME MAJOR HOCKEY LEAGUE

	GP	W	L	T	GF	GA	Pts
*Halifax Atlantics	78	42	33	3	361	314	87
Sydney Millionaires	78	40	35	3	262	257	83
Glace Bay Miners	75	34	39	2	286	304	70
Charlottetown Islanders	75	33	42	0	290	324	66

EASTERN AMATEUR HOCKEY LEAGUE

• EAHL did not operate in 1953–54

1954–55

AMERICAN HOCKEY LEAGUE

	GP	W	L	T	GF	GA	Pts
*Pittsburgh Hornets	64	31	25	8	187	180	70
Cleveland Barons	64	32	29	3	254	222	67
Springfield Indians	64	32	29	3	251	233	67
Buffalo Bisons	64	31	28	5	248	228	67
Hershey Bears	64	29	28	7	217	225	65
Providence Reds	64	21	37	6	194	263	48

QUEBEC HOCKEY LEAGUE

	GP	W	L	T	GF	GA	Pts
*Shawinigan Cataracts	62	39	20	3	228	145	81
Quebec Aces	60	31	27	2	206	208	64
Montreal Royals	62	30	28	4	232	207	64
Chicoutimi Sagueneens	61	29	29	3	216	212	61
Valleyfield Braves	62	21	39	2	178	261	44
Ottawa Senators §	27	10	17	0	63	90	20

§ folded 12/21/54

International Hockey League

	GP	W	L	T	GF	GA	Pts
*Cincinnati Mohawks	60	40	19	1	268	164	81
Troy Bruins	60	31	27	2	190	180	64
Toledo Mercurys	60	31	29	0	183	196	62
Grand Rapids Rockets	60	28	31	1	199	215	57
Johnstown Jets	60	25	34	1	188	215	51
Fort Wayne Komets	60	22	37	1	181	235	45

Eastern Hockey League

	GP	W	L	T	GF	GA	Pts
Washington Lions	49	26	21	2	204	175	54
*New Haven Blades	46	23	21	2	201	199	48
Baltimore Clippers	47	22	23	2	208	180	46
Clinton Comets §	22	15	7	0	111	75	30
Worcester Warriors §	20	3	17	0	59	154	6

§ played partial schedule

Western Hockey League

	GP	W	L	T	GF	GA	Pts
*Edmonton Flyers	70	39	20	11	273	204	89
Victoria Cougars	70	33	29	8	237	199	74
Vancouver Canucks	70	31	30	9	207	202	71
Calgary Stampeders	70	29	29	12	262	258	70
New Westm'ster Royals	70	29	32	9	249	299	67
Saskatoon Quakers	70	19	40	11	207	273	49

1955–56

American Hockey League

	GP	W	L	T	GF	GA	Pts
*Providence Reds	64	45	17	2	263	193	92
Pittsburgh Hornets	64	43	17	4	271	186	90
Buffalo Bisons	64	29	30	5	239	250	63
Cleveland Barons	64	26	31	7	225	231	59
Hershey Bears	64	19	39	6	218	271	44
Springfield Indians	64	17	45	2	212	297	36

Quebec Hockey League

	GP	W	L	T	GF	GA	Pts
Shawinigan Cataracts	64	43	18	3	243	166	89
*Montreal Royals	64	34	23	7	192	162	75
Chicoutimi Sagueneens	64	32	28	4	212	188	68
Quebec Aces	64	23	37	4	190	230	50
Trois-Rivieres Lions	64	18	44	2	159	250	38

International Hockey League

	GP	W	L	T	GF	GA	Pts
*Cincinnati Mohawks	60	45	13	2	336	159	92
Troy Bruins	60	39	20	1	216	152	79
Fort Wayne Komets	60	29	29	2	272	219	60
Toledo-Marion Mercurys	60	25	30	5	178	229	55
Grand Rapids Rockets	60	24	33	3	198	237	51
Indianapolis Chiefs	60	11	48	1	126	330	23

Eastern Hockey League

	GP	W	L	T	GF	GA	Pts
*New Haven Blades	64	43	18	3	318	206	89
Clinton Comets	64	33	28	3	298	269	69
Washington Lions	64	33	28	3	258	267	69
Johnstown Jets	64	32	32	0	312	298	64
Baltimore Clippers	64	23	40	1	236	327	47
Philadelphia Ramblers	64	23	41	0	246	301	46

Western Hockey League

Prairie Division	GP	W	L	T	GF	GA	Pts
*Winnipeg Warriors	70	40	28	2	248	212	82
Calgary Stampeders	70	40	30	0	292	242	80
Edmonton Flyers	70	33	34	3	236	256	69
Saskatoon Quakers	70	27	35	8	208	249	62
Regina-Brandon Regals	70	23	39	8	199	243	54
Coast Division							
Vancouver Canucks	70	38	28	4	252	181	80
Victoria Cougars	70	35	30	5	206	196	75
New Westm'ster Royals	70	31	37	2	238	258	64
Seattle Americans	70	31	37	2	201	243	64

1956–57

American Hockey League

	GP	W	L	T	GF	GA	Pts
Providence Reds	64	34	22	8	236	168	76
*Cleveland Barons	64	35	26	3	249	210	73
Rochester Americans	64	34	25	5	224	199	73
Hershey Bears	64	32	28	4	223	237	68
Buffalo Bisons	64	25	37	2	209	270	52
Springfield Indians	64	19	41	4	217	274	42

Quebec Hockey League

	GP	W	L	T	GF	GA	Pts
*Quebec Aces	68	40	21	7	226	175	87
Chicoutimi Sagueneens	68	34	28	6	225	199	74
Trois-Rivieres Lions	68	29	32	7	168	197	65
Montreal Royals	68	28	34	6	191	211	62
Shawinigan Cataracts	68	24	35	9	202	213	57
Hull-Ottawa Canadiens	20	7	12	1	57	74	15

• Hull-Ottawa played 20-game exhibition schedule that counted in standings for QHL teams only

International Hockey League

	GP	W	L	T	GF	GA	Pts
*Cincinnati Mohawks	60	50	9	1	245	113	101
Indianapolis Chiefs	60	26	29	5	168	177	57
Huntington Hornets	60	26	30	4	180	188	56
Toledo Mercurys	60	26	30	4	166	186	56
Fort Wayne Komets	60	25	29	6	170	177	56
Troy Bruins	60	15	41	4	135	223	34

Eastern Hockey League

	GP	W	L	T	GF	GA	Pts
*Charlotte Checkers	64	50	13	1	364	239	101
Philadelphia Ramblers	64	34	27	3	277	233	71
New Haven Blades	64	31	30	3	276	263	65
Johnstown Jets	64	31	33	0	320	290	62
Clinton Comets	64	23	39	2	254	325	48
Washington Lions	64	18	45	1	256	397	37

Western Hockey League

Prairie Division	GP	W	L	T	GF	GA	Pts
*Brandon Regals	70	44	22	4	250	186	92
Edmonton Flyers	70	39	27	4	239	212	82
Calgary Stampeders	70	29	37	4	220	230	62
Winnipeg Warriors	70	23	45	2	198	273	48
Coast Division							
Seattle Americans	70	36	28	6	263	225	78
New Westm'ster Royals	70	34	31	5	215	235	73
Victoria Cougars	70	29	34	7	208	204	65
Vancouver Canucks	70	27	37	6	203	231	60

1957–58

American Hockey League

	GP	W	L	T	GF	GA	Pts
*Hershey Bears	70	39	24	7	241	198	85
Cleveland Barons	70	39	28	3	232	163	81
Providence Reds	70	33	32	5	237	220	71
Springfield Indians	70	29	33	8	231	246	66
Rochester Americans	70	29	35	6	205	242	64
Buffalo Bisons	70	25	42	3	224	301	53

Quebec Hockey League

	GP	W	L	T	GF	GA	Pts
Chicoutimi Sagueneens	64	35	24	5	241	209	75
*Shawinigan Cataracts	64	31	28	5	243	235	67
Montreal Royals	64	29	30	5	227	219	63
Quebec Aces	64	29	31	4	224	233	62
Trois-Rivieres Lions	64	24	35	5	176	215	53

International Hockey League

	GP	W	L	T	GF	GA	Pts
Cincinnati Mohawks	64	43	16	5	303	176	91
Fort Wayne Komets	64	28	28	8	213	224	64
Louisville Rebels	64	30	31	3	239	263	63
*Indianapolis Chiefs	64	28	30	6	209	208	62
Toledo Mercurys	64	26	32	6	214	248	58
Troy Bruins	64	20	38	6	192	251	46

Eastern Hockey League

	GP	W	L	T	GF	GA	Pts
Charlotte Clippers	64	38	25	1	275	243	77
*Washington Presidents	64	36	24	4	221	195	76
New Haven Blades	64	33	26	5	204	180	71
Johnstown Jets	64	31	30	3	228	225	65
Philadelphia Ramblers	64	30	31	3	210	211	63
Clinton Comets	64	15	47	2	186	270	32

Western Hockey League

Coast Division	GP	W	L	T	GF	GA	Pts
*Vancouver Canucks	70	44	21	5	238	174	93
New Westm'ster Royals	70	39	28	3	254	224	81
Seattle Americans	70	32	32	6	244	231	70
Victoria Cougars	70	18	50	2	226	313	38
Prairie Division							
Winnipeg Warriors	70	39	26	5	262	211	83
Edmonton Flyers	70	38	28	4	264	225	80
Calgary Stampeders	70	30	35	5	222	223	65
Sask-St. Paul Regals	70	25	45	0	214	323	50

1958–59

American Hockey League

	GP	W	L	T	GF	GA	Pts
Buffalo Bisons	70	38	28	4	233	201	80
Cleveland Indians	70	37	30	3	261	252	77
Rochester Americans	70	34	31	5	242	209	73
*Hershey Bears	70	32	32	6	200	202	70
Springfield Indians	70	30	38	2	253	282	62
Providence Reds	70	28	40	2	222	265	58

Quebec Hockey League

	GP	W	L	T	GF	GA	Pts
*Montreal Royals	62	34	22	6	206	162	74
Trois-Rivieres Lions	62	30	29	3	194	184	63
Chicoutimi Sagueneens	62	30	31	1	238	236	61
Quebec Aces	62	21	33	8	176	232	50

International Hockey League

	GP	W	L	T	GF	GA	Pts
*Louisville Rebels	60	35	24	1	280	197	71
Fort Wayne Komets	60	32	27	1	236	213	65
Troy Bruins	60	30	28	2	245	283	62
Indianapolis Chiefs	60	26	30	4	231	247	56
Toledo Mercurys	60	22	36	2	196	248	46

Eastern Hockey League

	GP	W	L	T	GF	GA	Pts
*Clinton Comets	64	41	21	2	291	180	84
Johnstown Jets	64	33	28	3	252	223	69
New Haven Blades	64	29	31	4	201	216	62
Philadelphia Ramblers	64	30	33	1	215	237	61
Washington Presidents	64	29	35	0	242	271	58
Charlotte Checkers	64	24	38	2	209	283	50

Western Hockey League

Coast Division	GP	W	L	T	GF	GA	Pts
*Seattle Totems	70	40	27	3	277	225	83
Vancouver Canucks	70	31	28	11	219	214	73
Victoria Cougars	70	30	36	4	219	254	64
Spokane Spokes	70	26	38	6	217	275	58
New Westm'ster Royals	70	23	45	2	237	301	48
Prairie Division							
Calgary Stampeders	64	42	21	1	263	196	85
Edmonton Flyers	64	33	28	3	205	206	69
Winnipeg Warriors	64	31	31	2	256	229	64
Saskatoon Quakers	64	29	31	4	208	201	62

1959–60

American Hockey League

	GP	W	L	T	GF	GA	Pts
*Springfield Indians	72	43	23	6	280	219	92
Rochester Americans	72	40	27	5	285	211	85
Providence Reds	72	38	32	2	251	237	78
Cleveland Barons	72	34	30	8	267	229	76
Buffalo Bisons	72	33	35	4	251	271	70
Hershey Bears	72	28	37	7	226	238	63
Quebec Aces	72	19	51	2	178	333	40

Eastern Professional Hockey League

	GP	W	L	T	GF	GA	Pts
Sudbury Wolves	70	36	26	8	310	283	80
*Montreal Royals	70	30	26	14	215	198	74
Hull-Ottawa Canadiens	70	31	28	11	249	241	73
Trois-Rivieres Lions	70	30	31	9	226	235	69
Soo Thunderbirds	70	27	32	11	248	262	65
Kingston Frontenacs	70	28	39	3	297	326	59

International Hockey League

East Division	GP	W	L	T	GF	GA	Pts
Fort Wayne Komets	68	50	16	2	312	187	102
Louisville Rebels	68	37	30	1	303	276	75
Toledo-St. Louis	68	28	36	4	266	298	60
Indianapolis Chiefs	68	25	40	3	234	322	53
West Division							
*St. Paul Saints	68	41	21	6	261	188	88
Minneapolis Millers	68	39	27	2	297	233	80
Milwaukee Falcons	67	24	42	1	251	314	49
Omaha Knights	67	15	47	5	198	303	35

Eastern Hockey League

North Division	GP	W	L	T	GF	GA	Pts
Clinton Comets	64	35	27	2	244	202	72
New Haven Blades	64	32	29	3	217	189	67
Philadelphia Ramblers	64	31	30	3	226	219	65
New York Rovers	64	19	44	1	205	294	39
South Division							
*Johnstown Jets	64	45	18	1	255	176	91
Charlotte Clippers	64	31	29	4	243	244	66
Greensboro Generals	64	26	33	5	229	250	57
Washington Presidents	64	25	34	5	207	252	55

Western Hockey League

	GP	W	L	T	GF	GA	Pts
*Vancouver Canucks	70	44	20	6	230	177	94
Seattle Totems	70	38	28	4	270	219	80
Edmonton Flyers	70	37	29	4	246	240	78
Victoria Cougars	70	37	29	4	227	194	78
Calgary Stampeders	70	32	36	2	245	227	66
Winnipeg Warriors	70	25	42	3	224	262	53
Spokane Comets	70	19	48	3	201	324	41

1960-61

American Hockey League

	GP	W	L	T	GF	GA	Pts
*Springfield Indians	72	49	22	1	344	206	99
Hershey Bears	72	36	32	4	218	210	76
Cleveland Barons	72	36	35	1	231	234	73
Buffalo Bisons	72	35	34	3	259	261	73
Rochester Americans	72	32	36	4	261	244	68
Quebec Aces	72	30	39	3	217	267	63
Providence Reds	72	26	46	0	225	333	52

EASTERN PROFESSIONAL HOCKEY LEAGUE

	GP	W	L	T	GF	GA	Pts
*Hull-Ottawa Canadiens	70	41	20	9	268	187	91
Soo Thunderbirds	70	32	29	9	236	234	73
Kitchener Dutchmen	70	31	28	11	220	215	73
Kingston Frontenacs	70	29	33	8	259	269	66
Sudbury Wolves	70	28	33	9	236	257	65
Montreal Royals	70	19	37	14	167	224	52

INTERNATIONAL HOCKEY LEAGUE

East Division	GP	W	L	T	GF	GA	Pts
Toledo Mercurys	70	36	33	1	274	260	73
Fort Wayne Komets	69	31	35	3	304	265	65
Muskegon Zephyrs	70	25	41	4	243	319	54
Indianapolis Chiefs	70	20	46	4	217	313	44
West Division							
Minneapolis Millers	72	50	20	2	323	229	102
*St. Paul Saints	72	46	22	4	309	233	96
Omaha Knights	70	35	32	3	254	235	73
Milwaukee Falcons §	17	1	15	1	45	115	3

§ folded 11/26/60

EASTERN HOCKEY LEAGUE

North Division	GP	W	L	T	GF	GA	Pts
New Haven Blades	64	38	25	1	278	221	77
Clinton Comets	64	30	32	2	267	228	62
Jersey Devils	64	24	39	1	215	254	49
New York Rovers	64	18	45	1	196	293	37
South Division							
Greensboro Generals	64	40	22	2	339	257	82
*Johnstown Jets	64	40	22	2	273	215	82
Philadelphia Ramblers	64	32	28	4	227	278	68
Charlotte Checkers	64	25	34	5	221	265	55

WESTERN HOCKEY LEAGUE

	GP	W	L	T	GF	GA	Pts
Calgary Stampeders	70	44	22	4	300	215	92
*Portland Buckaroos	70	38	23	9	242	192	85
Vancouver Canucks	70	38	29	3	208	191	79
Seattle Totems	70	37	28	5	262	222	79
Spokane Comets	70	33	34	3	247	258	69
Victoria Cougars	70	27	41	2	220	267	56
Edmonton Flyers	70	27	43	0	229	295	54
Winnipeg Warriors	70	21	45	4	191	259	46

1961–62

AMERICAN HOCKEY LEAGUE

Eastern Division	GP	W	L	T	GF	GA	Pts
*Springfield Indians	70	45	22	3	292	194	93
Hershey Bears	70	37	28	5	236	213	79
Providence Reds	70	36	32	2	261	267	74
Quebec Aces	70	30	36	4	208	207	64
Western Division							
Cleveland Barons	70	39	28	3	255	203	81
Buffalo Bisons	70	36	31	3	247	219	75
Rochester Americans	70	33	31	6	234	240	72
Pittsburgh Hornets	70	10	58	2	177	367	22

EASTERN PROFESSIONAL HOCKEY LEAGUE

	GP	W	L	T	GF	GA	Pts
*Hull-Ottawa Canadiens	70	38	21	11	233	172	87
Kingston Frontenacs	70	38	24	8	274	224	84
Kitchener Beavers	70	36	24	10	263	217	82
Sudbury Wolves	70	27	31	12	235	271	66
North Bay Trappers	70	23	37	10	186	229	56
Soo Greyhounds	70	17	42	11	207	285	45

INTERNATIONAL HOCKEY LEAGUE

	GP	W	L	T	GF	GA	Pts
*Muskegon Zephyrs	68	43	23	2	334	242	88
St. Paul Saints	68	42	25	1	291	209	85
Minneapolis Millers	68	41	26	1	261	234	83
Omaha Knights	68	37	28	3	264	227	77
Fort Wayne Komets	68	33	31	4	265	245	70
Indianapolis Chiefs	68	19	49	0	220	348	38
Toledo Mercurys	68	17	50	1	222	352	35

EASTERN HOCKEY LEAGUE

North Division	GP	W	L	T	GF	GA	Pts
Clinton Comets	68	45	22	1	314	204	91
*Johnstown Jets	68	41	26	1	296	255	83
New Haven Blades	68	34	34	0	239	224	68
Long Island Ducks	68	26	41	1	234	266	53
Southern Division							
Greensboro Generals	68	36	30	2	284	258	74
Knoxville Knights	68	30	35	3	216	256	63
Philadelphia Ramblers	68	28	38	2	265	341	58
Charlotte Checkers	68	26	40	2	226	270	54

WESTERN HOCKEY LEAGUE

North Division	GP	W	L	T	GF	GA	Pts
*Edmonton Flyers	70	39	27	4	296	245	82
Calgary Stampeders	70	36	29	5	292	271	77
Seattle Totems	70	36	29	5	244	222	77
Vancouver Canucks	70	18	48	4	223	324	40
South Division							
Portland Buckaroos	70	42	23	5	265	203	89
Spokane Comets	70	37	28	5	272	242	79
San Francisco Seals	70	29	39	2	229	270	60
Los Angeles Blades	70	25	39	6	265	309	56

1962–63

AMERICAN HOCKEY LEAGUE

East Division	GP	W	L	T	GF	GA	Pts
Providence Reds	72	38	29	5	239	203	81
Hershey Bears	72	36	28	8	262	231	80
Baltimore Clippers	72	35	30	7	226	244	77
Quebec Aces	72	33	28	11	206	210	77
Springfield Indians	72	33	31	8	282	236	74
West Division							
*Buffalo Bisons	72	41	24	7	237	199	89
Cleveland Barons	72	31	34	7	270	253	69
Rochester Americans	72	24	39	9	241	270	57
Pittsburgh Hornets	72	20	48	4	200	317	44

EASTERN PROFESSIONAL HOCKEY LEAGUE

	GP	W	L	T	GF	GA	Pts
Kingston Frontenacs	72	42	19	11	300	229	95
*Hull-Ottawa Canadiens	72	40	25	7	279	224	87
Sudbury Wolves	72	27	32	13	294	305	67
St. Louis Braves	72	26	37	9	275	304	61

INTERNATIONAL HOCKEY LEAGUE

	GP	W	L	T	GF	GA	Pts
*Fort Wayne Komets	70	35	30	5	283	255	75
Minneapolis Millers	70	36	32	2	296	301	74
Muskegon Zephyrs	70	34	31	5	328	326	73
Omaha Knights	70	30	35	5	252	248	65
Port Huron Flags	70	28	26	6	246	273	62
St. Paul Saints	70	23	44	3	241	328	49

EASTERN HOCKEY LEAGUE

Northern Division	GP	W	L	T	GF	GA	Pts
Clinton Comets	68	38	24	6	289	186	82
Long Island Ducks	68	36	28	4	287	261	76
Johnstown Jets	68	34	31	3	254	309	71
Philadelphia Ramblers	68	29	36	3	287	304	61
New Haven Blades	68	27	40	1	249	293	55
Southern Division							
*Greensboro Generals	68	40	26	2	305	263	82
Knoxville Knights	68	37	28	3	295	245	77
Charlotte Checkers	68	35	31	2	242	264	72
Nashville Dixie Flyers	68	16	48	4	181	264	36

WESTERN HOCKEY LEAGUE

North Division	GP	W	L	T	GF	GA	Pts
Vancouver Canucks	70	35	31	4	243	234	74
Seattle Totems	70	35	33	2	239	237	72
Edmonton Flyers	70	24	44	2	215	309	50
Calgary Stampeders	70	23	45	2	227	284	48
South Division							
Portland Buckaroos	70	43	21	6	279	184	92
*San Francisco Seals	70	44	25	1	288	219	89
Los Angeles Blades	70	35	32	3	235	226	73
Spokane Comets	70	30	38	2	219	252	62

1963–64

AMERICAN HOCKEY LEAGUE

East Division	GP	W	L	T	GF	GA	Pts
Quebec Aces	72	41	30	1	258	225	83
Hershey Bears	72	36	31	5	236	249	77
Providence Reds	72	32	35	5	248	239	69
Baltimore Clippers	72	32	37	3	200	220	67
Springfield Indians	72	23	44	5	238	292	51
West Division							
Pittsburgh Hornets	72	40	29	3	242	196	83
Rochester Americans	72	40	30	2	256	223	82
*Cleveland Barons	72	37	30	5	239	207	79
Buffalo Bisons	72	25	40	7	194	260	57

WESTERN HOCKEY LEAGUE

	GP	W	L	T	GF	GA	Pts
Denver Invaders	70	44	23	3	271	202	91
Portland Buckaroos	70	33	30	7	229	228	73
Los Angeles Blades	70	31	31	8	218	244	70
*San Francisco Seals	70	32	35	3	228	262	67
Seattle Totems	70	29	35	6	247	228	64
Vancouver Canucks	70	26	41	3	229	258	55

CENTRAL PROFESSIONAL HOCKEY LEAGUE

	GP	W	L	T	GF	GA	Pts
*Omaha Knights	72	44	19	9	311	218	97
St. Paul Rangers	72	38	30	4	259	230	80
Minneapolis Bruins	72	36	29	7	294	270	79
St. Louis Braves	72	33	32	7	316	275	73
Cincinnati Wings	72	12	53	7	207	394	31

INTERNATIONAL HOCKEY LEAGUE

	GP	W	L	T	GF	GA	Pts
*Toledo Blades	70	41	25	4	278	207	86
Fort Wayne Komets	70	41	28	1	322	264	83
Port Huron Flags	70	37	31	2	279	279	76
Windsor Bulldogs	70	32	35	3	226	280	67
Des Moines Oak Leafs	70	31	35	4	272	266	66
Muskegon Zephyrs	70	31	36	3	298	312	65
Chatham Maroons	70	21	44	5	211	278	47

EASTERN HOCKEY LEAGUE

Northern Division	GP	W	L	T	GF	GA	Pts
Johnstown Jets	72	41	26	5	297	245	87
*Clinton Comets	72	37	28	7	289	215	81
Long Island Ducks	72	32	34	6	245	263	70
New Haven Blades	72	27	42	3	252	296	57
Philadelphia Ramblers	72	21	44	7	261	374	49
Southern Division							
Greensboro Generals	72	41	29	2	294	257	84
Knoxville Knights	72	40	31	1	340	289	81
Nashville Dixie Flyers	72	37	31	4	231	242	78
Charlotte Checkers	72	30	41	1	276	304	61

1964–65

AMERICAN HOCKEY LEAGUE

East Division	GP	W	L	T	GF	GA	Pts
Quebec Aces	72	44	26	2	280	223	90
Hershey Bears	72	36	32	4	246	243	76
Baltimore Clippers	72	35	32	5	275	249	75
Springfield Indians	72	29	39	4	237	273	62
Providence Reds	72	20	50	2	193	312	42
West Division							
*Rochester Americans	72	48	21	3	310	199	99
Buffalo Bisons	72	40	26	6	261	218	86
Pittsburgh Hornets	72	29	36	7	228	256	65
Cleveland Barons	72	24	43	5	228	285	53

WESTERN HOCKEY LEAGUE

	GP	W	L	T	GF	GA	Pts
*Portland Buckaroos	70	42	23	5	267	216	89
Seattle Totems	70	36	30	4	204	198	76
Vancouver Canucks	70	32	32	6	262	243	70
Victoria Cougars	70	32	36	2	246	242	66
San Francisco Seals	70	31	37	2	255	283	64
Los Angeles Blades	70	26	41	3	217	269	55

CENTRAL PROFESSIONAL HOCKEY LEAGUE

	GP	W	L	T	GF	GA	Pts
*St. Paul Rangers	70	41	23	6	281	223	88
Omaha Knights	70	37	25	8	246	238	82
Minneapolis Bruins	70	36	27	7	239	193	79
Tulsa Oilers	70	35	27	8	254	224	78
Memphis Wings	70	26	35	9	243	245	61
St. Louis Braves	70	13	51	6	189	329	32

INTERNATIONAL HOCKEY LEAGUE

	GP	W	L	T	GF	GA	Pts
Port Huron Flags	70	43	22	5	336	258	91
*Fort Wayne Komets	70	40	25	5	344	240	85
Des Moines Oak Leafs	70	39	26	5	303	277	83
Toledo Blades	70	32	36	2	297	327	66
Dayton Gems	70	23	45	2	283	396	48
Muskegon Zephyrs	70	22	45	3	320	385	47

EASTERN HOCKEY LEAGUE

North Division	GP	W	L	T	GF	GA	Pts
*Long Island Ducks	72	50	20	2	336	182	102
Clinton Comets	72	42	29	1	279	233	85
Johnstown Jets	72	41	31	0	330	294	82
New Jersey Devils	72	34	34	4	297	312	72
New York Rovers	72	25	39	8	206	270	58
New Haven Blades	72	19	52	1	238	379	39
South Division							
Nashville Dixie Flyers	72	54	18	0	349	296	108
Greensboro Generals	72	37	33	2	333	301	76
Charlotte Checkers	72	35	35	2	262	286	72
Knoxville Knights	72	34	36	2	281	284	70
Jacksonville Rockets	72	13	57	2	211	385	28

1965–66

AMERICAN HOCKEY LEAGUE

East Division	GP	W	L	T	GF	GA	Pts
Quebec Aces	72	47	21	4	337	226	98
Hershey Bears	72	37	30	5	268	232	79
Springfield Indians	72	31	38	3	207	235	65
Baltimore Clippers	72	27	43	2	212	254	56
Providence Reds	72	20	49	3	184	310	43
West Division							
*Rochester Americans	72	46	21	5	288	221	97
Cleveland Barons	72	38	32	2	243	217	78
Pittsburgh Hornets	72	38	33	1	236	218	77
Buffalo Bisons	72	29	40	3	215	243	61

• Played interlocking schedule with WHL

WESTERN HOCKEY LEAGUE

	GP	W	L	T	GF	GA	Pts
Portland Buckaroos	72	43	24	5	271	218	91
*Victoria Cougars	72	40	28	4	260	243	84
Vancouver Canucks	72	33	35	4	252	233	70
San Francisco Seals	72	32	36	4	243	248	68
Seattle Totems	72	32	37	3	231	256	67
Los Angeles Blades	72	22	48	2	236	329	46

• Played interlocking schedule with AHL

Central Professional Hockey League

	GP	W	L	T	GF	GA	Pts
Minnesota Rangers	70	34	25	11	229	197	79
*Oklahoma City Blazers	70	31	26	13	188	203	75
Tulsa Oilers	70	29	29	12	218	198	70
St. Louis Braves	70	30	31	9	226	217	69
Houston Apollos	70	27	32	11	221	244	65
Memphis Wings	70	25	33	12	200	223	62

International Hockey League

	GP	W	L	T	GF	GA	Pts
Muskegon Mohawks	70	46	19	5	376	314	97
Fort Wayne Komets	70	38	26	6	312	259	82
*Port Huron Flags	70	34	32	4	308	274	72
Dayton Gems	70	33	35	2	347	322	68
Des Moines Oak Leafs	70	29	40	1	263	319	59
Toledo Blades	70	20	48	2	248	366	42

Eastern Hockey League

North Division	GP	W	L	T	GF	GA	Pts
Long Island Ducks	72	46	23	3	292	208	95
Clinton Comets	72	41	28	3	276	212	85
Johnstown Jets	72	39	31	2	303	267	80
New Haven Blades	72	27	43	2	283	353	56
New Jersey Devils	72	25	43	4	239	311	54
South Division							
*Nashville Dixie Flyers	72	42	23	7	277	179	91
Charlotte Checkers	72	42	30	0	300	251	84
Greensboro Generals	72	37	31	4	291	263	78
Knoxville Knights	72	34	36	2	278	261	70
Jacksonville Rockets	72	12	57	3	207	441	27

1966–67

American Hockey League

East Division	GP	W	L	T	GF	GA	Pts
Hershey Bears	72	38	24	10	273	216	86
Baltimore Clippers	72	35	27	10	252	247	80
Quebec Aces	72	35	30	7	275	249	77
Springfield Indians	72	32	31	9	267	261	73
Providence Reds	72	13	46	13	210	329	39
West Division							
*Pittsburgh Hornets	72	41	21	10	282	209	92
Rochester Americans	72	38	25	9	300	223	85
Cleveland Barons	72	36	27	9	284	230	81
Buffalo Bisons	72	14	51	7	207	386	35

Western Hockey League

	GP	W	L	T	GF	GA	Pts
Portland Buckaroos	72	41	24	7	255	209	89
*Seattle Totems	72	39	26	7	228	195	85
Vancouver Canucks	72	38	32	2	228	215	78
California Seals	72	32	30	10	228	242	74
Victoria Cougars	72	30	34	8	224	232	68
Los Angeles Blades	72	29	38	5	260	286	63
San Diego Gulls	72	22	47	3	222	266	47

Central Professional Hockey League

	GP	W	L	T	GF	GA	Pts
*Oklahoma City Blazers	70	38	23	9	233	196	85
Omaha Knights	70	36	24	10	262	203	82
Houston Apollos	70	32	28	10	255	229	74
Memphis Wings	70	30	32	8	230	259	68
St. Louis Braves	70	24	26	20	229	236	68
Tulsa Oilers	70	14	41	15	183	269	43

International Hockey League

	GP	W	L	T	GF	GA	Pts
Dayton Gems	72	44	25	3	315	282	91
Fort Wayne Komets	72	40	31	1	274	234	81
*Toledo Blades	72	39	31	2	284	247	80
Des Moines Oak Leafs	72	36	32	4	256	264	76
Port Huron Flags	72	34	33	5	314	300	73
Muskegon Mohawks	72	27	43	2	262	299	56
Columbus Checkers	72	23	48	1	294	373	47

Eastern Hockey League

North Division	GP	W	L	T	GF	GA	Pts
Clinton Comets	72	44	26	2	285	202	90
New Jersey Devils	72	39	30	3	292	210	81
Johnstown Jets	72	34	36	2	267	290	70
Long Island Ducks	72	29	39	4	198	233	62
New Haven Blades	72	27	44	1	241	346	55
South Division							
*Nashville Dixie Flyers	72	51	19	2	287	169	104
Charlotte Checkers	72	36	33	3	259	235	75
Greensboro Generals	72	35	37	0	265	279	70
Knoxville Knights	72	27	42	3	232	268	57
Florida Rockets	72	27	43	2	222	315	56

1967–68

American Hockey League

Eastern Division	GP	W	L	T	GF	GA	Pts
Hershey Bears	72	34	30	8	276	248	76
Springfield Kings	72	31	33	8	247	276	70
Providence Reds	72	30	33	9	235	272	69
Baltimore Clippers	72	28	34	10	235	255	66
Western Division							
*Rochester Americans	72	38	25	9	273	233	85
Quebec Aces	72	33	28	11	277	240	77
Buffalo Bisons	72	32	28	12	239	224	76
Cleveland Barons	72	28	30	14	236	255	70

• *Played interlocking schedule with WHL*

Western Hockey League

	GP	W	L	T	GF	GA	Pts
Portland Buckaroos	72	40	26	6	246	168	86
*Seattle Totems	72	35	30	7	207	199	77
San Diego Gulls	72	31	36	5	241	236	67
Phoenix Roadrunners	72	28	40	4	215	276	60
Vancouver Canucks	72	26	41	5	213	258	57

• *Played interlocking schedule with AHL*

Central Professional Hockey League

Northern Division	GP	W	L	T	GF	GA	Pts
*Tulsa Oilers	70	37	22	11	278	241	85
Kansas City Blues	70	31	29	10	249	243	72
Memphis South Stars	70	24	34	12	206	244	60
Omaha Knights	70	14	46	10	167	272	38
Southern Division							
Oklahoma City Blazers	70	38	20	12	245	174	88
Fort Worth Wings	70	34	25	11	245	199	79
Dallas Black Hawks	70	30	29	11	230	251	71
Houston Apollos	70	28	31	11	220	216	67

International Hockey League

	GP	W	L	T	GF	GA	Pts
*Muskegon Mohawks	72	43	17	12	305	216	98
Dayton Gems	72	33	27	12	332	275	78
Columbus Checkers	72	32	30	10	312	300	74
Fort Wayne Komets	72	30	29	13	282	272	73
Toledo Blades	72	29	29	14	261	307	72
Port Huron Flags	72	25	36	11	269	343	61
Des Moines Oak Leafs	72	19	43	10	244	292	48

Eastern Hockey League

Northern Division	GP	W	L	T	GF	GA	Pts
*Clinton Comets	72	57	5	10	436	185	124
New Haven Blades	72	43	22	7	387	242	93
Johnstown Jets	72	38	25	9	386	273	85
Long Island Ducks	72	29	36	7	333	329	65
New Jersey Devils	72	17	51	4	251	458	38
Syracuse Blazers	72	12	57	3	277	583	27
Southern Division							
Greensboro Generals	72	46	20	6	364	248	98
Charlotte Checkers	72	42	21	9	333	243	93
Nashville Dixie Flyers	72	42	23	7	341	256	91
Florida Rockets	72	30	34	8	262	288	68
Knoxville Knights	72	23	43	6	250	294	52
Salem Rebels	72	11	53	8	211	432	30

1968–69

American Hockey League

Eastern Division	GP	W	L	T	GF	GA	Pts
*Hershey Bears	74	41	27	6	307	234	88
Baltimore Clippers	74	33	34	7	266	257	73
Providence Reds	74	32	36	6	242	284	70
Springfield Kings	74	27	36	11	257	274	65
Western Division							
Buffalo Bisons	74	41	18	15	282	192	97
Cleveland Barons	74	30	32	12	213	245	72
Quebec Aces	74	26	34	14	235	258	66
Rochester Americans	74	25	38	11	237	295	61

Western Hockey League

	GP	W	L	T	GF	GA	Pts
Portland Buckaroos	74	40	18	16	291	201	96
*Vancouver Canucks	74	36	24	14	259	223	86
San Diego Gulls	74	33	29	12	273	260	78
Seattle Totems	74	33	30	11	236	238	77
Phoenix Roadrunners	74	21	41	12	199	282	54
Denver Spurs	74	23	44	7	254	308	53

Central Hockey League

Northern Division	GP	W	L	T	GF	GA	Pts
Tulsa Oilers	72	28	28	16	248	238	72
Kansas City Blues	72	26	28	18	236	242	70
Omaha Knights	72	29	32	11	249	252	69
Memphis South Stars	72	14	41	17	206	302	45
Southern Division							
Oklahoma City Blazers	72	40	19	13	295	225	93
*Dallas Black Hawks	72	37	25	10	264	218	84
Houston Apollos	72	34	26	12	224	204	80
Amarillo Wranglers	72	29	32	11	237	259	69
Fort Worth Wings	72	23	29	20	213	232	66

International Hockey League

	GP	W	L	T	GF	GA	Pts
*Dayton Gems	72	40	21	11	313	227	91
Toledo Blades	72	41	23	8	282	235	90
Muskegon Mohawks	72	34	29	9	332	287	77
Port Huron Flags	72	28	30	14	285	289	70
Fort Wayne Komets	72	24	33	15	235	262	63
Columbus Checkers	72	26	37	9	286	333	61
Des Moines Oak Leafs	72	21	41	10	226	326	52

Eastern Hockey League

Northern Division	GP	W	L	T	GF	GA	Pts
*Clinton Comets	72	44	18	10	284	181	98
Johnstown Jets	72	42	23	7	358	230	91
New Haven Blades	72	39	23	10	343	271	88
Long Island Ducks	72	27	37	8	256	318	62
New Jersey Devils	72	26	39	7	245	301	59
Syracuse Blazers	72	9	59	4	178	401	22
Southern Division							
Greensboro Generals	72	41	22	9	350	279	91
Nashville Dixie Flyers	72	41	25	6	336	253	88
Charlotte Checkers	72	37	29	6	274	281	80
Jacksonville Rockets	72	27	37	8	267	295	62
Salem Rebels	72	24	45	3	240	321	51

1969–70

American Hockey League

Eastern Division	GP	W	L	T	GF	GA	Pts
Montreal Voyageurs	72	43	15	14	327	195	100
Springfield Kings	72	38	29	5	287	287	81
Quebec Aces	72	27	39	6	221	272	60
Providence Reds	72	23	36	13	218	267	59
Western Division							
*Buffalo Bisons	72	40	17	15	280	193	95
Hershey Bears	72	28	28	16	247	249	72
Baltimore Clippers	72	25	30	17	230	252	67
Cleveland Barons	72	23	33	16	222	255	62
Rochester Americans	72	18	38	16	253	315	52

Western Hockey League

	GP	W	L	T	GF	GA	Pts
*Vancouver Canucks	72	47	17	8	334	219	102
Portland Buckaroos	72	42	23	7	322	241	91
San Diego Gulls	72	33	29	10	263	242	76
Seattle Totems	73	30	35	8	240	260	68
Phoenix Roadrunners	73	27	34	12	252	257	66
Denver Spurs	72	24	37	11	250	316	59
Salt Lake Golden Eagles	72	15	43	14	240	366	44

• *Seattle & Phoenix played extra game to decide fourth place*

Central Hockey League

	GP	W	L	T	GF	GA	Pts
*Omaha Knights	72	36	26	10	247	212	82
Iowa Stars	72	35	26	11	252	232	81
Tulsa Oilers	72	35	27	10	230	202	80
Fort Worth Wings	72	31	25	16	217	206	78
Dallas Black Hawks	72	30	37	5	236	241	65
Oklahoma City Blazers	72	26	39	7	233	291	59
Kansas City Blues	72	24	37	11	228	259	59

International Hockey League

Northern Division	GP	W	L	T	GF	GA	Pts
Muskegon Mohawks	72	46	18	8	356	271	100
Port Huron Flags	72	37	28	7	272	270	81
Fort Wayne Komets	72	26	38	8	241	266	60
Flint Generals	72	21	39	12	218	270	54
Southern Division							
*Dayton Gems	72	38	30	4	296	271	80
Toledo Blades	72	32	33	7	241	265	71
Des Moines Oak Leafs	72	31	33	8	261	254	70
Columbus Checkers	72	24	36	12	289	307	60

Eastern Hockey League

Northern Division	GP	W	L	T	GF	GA	Pts
*Clinton Comets	74	50	16	8	394	222	108
New Haven Blades	74	39	20	15	377	244	93
Johnstown Jets	74	27	33	14	318	344	68
Syracuse Blazers	74	23	37	14	292	350	60
Long Island Ducks	74	24	44	6	261	364	54
New Jersey Devils	74	20	48	6	278	440	46
Southern Division							
Greensboro Generals	74	45	22	7	333	241	97
Salem Rebels	74	37	27	10	279	266	84
Charlotte Checkers	74	34	31	9	284	266	77
Jacksonville Rockets	74	27	37	10	282	355	64
Nashville Dixie Flyers	74	27	38	9	279	305	63

1970-71

American Hockey League

East Division	GP	W	L	T	GF	GA	Pts
Providence Reds	72	28	31	13	257	270	69
Montreal Voyageurs	72	27	31	14	215	239	68
*Springfield Kings	72	29	35	8	244	281	66
Quebec Aces	72	25	31	16	211	240	66
West Division							
Baltimore Clippers	72	40	23	9	263	224	89
Cleveland Barons	72	39	26	7	272	208	85
Hershey Bears	72	31	31	10	238	212	72
Rochester Americans	72	25	36	11	222	248	61

WESTERN HOCKEY LEAGUE

	GP	W	L	T	GF	GA	Pts
*Portland Buckaroos	72	48	17	7	306	210	103
Phoenix Roadrunners	72	36	27	9	271	234	81
San Diego Gulls	72	33	27	12	248	223	78
Denver Spurs	72	25	31	16	242	253	66
Seattle Totems	72	27	36	9	223	260	63
Salt Lake Golden Eagles	72	18	49	5	217	327	41

CENTRAL HOCKEY LEAGUE

	GP	W	L	T	GF	GA	Pts
*Omaha Knights	72	45	16	11	312	216	101
Dallas Black Hawks	72	36	28	8	276	246	80
Fort Worth Wings	72	35	28	9	232	198	79
Oklahoma City Blazers	72	30	30	12	258	273	72
Kansas City Blues	72	30	31	11	214	223	71
Tulsa Oilers	72	27	37	8	252	275	62
Amarillo Wranglers	72	14	47	11	216	329	39

INTERNATIONAL HOCKEY LEAGUE

	GP	W	L	T	GF	GA	Pts
Muskegon Mohawks	72	43	24	5	300	212	91
Des Moines Oak Leafs	72	38	23	11	286	233	87
Dayton Gems	72	36	29	7	263	263	79
Flint Generals	72	33	32	7	247	224	73
Fort Wayne Komets	72	28	32	12	221	233	68
*Port Huron Flags	72	25	36	11	248	292	61
Toledo Hornets	72	17	44	11	211	319	45

EASTERN HOCKEY LEAGUE

Northern Division	GP	W	L	T	GF	GA	Pts
New Haven Blades	74	38	21	15	339	244	91
Syracuse Blazers	74	36	30	8	302	284	80
Johnstown Jets	74	30	29	15	273	297	75
Clinton Comets	74	31	32	11	257	233	73
Long Island Ducks	74	29	35	10	283	296	68
New Jersey Devils	74	22	39	13	282	353	57
Southern Division							
*Charlotte Checkers	74	55	12	7	383	153	117
Greensboro Generals	73	44	21	8	340	234	96
Salem Rebels	74	31	34	9	257	303	71
Nashville Dixie Flyers	73	26	42	5	270	342	57
Jacksonville Rockets	74	11	58	5	206	453	27

1971–72

AMERICAN HOCKEY LEAGUE

Eastern Division	GP	W	L	T	GF	GA	Pts
Boston Braves	76	41	21	14	260	191	96
*Nova Scotia Voyageurs	76	41	21	14	274	202	96
Springfield Kings	76	31	30	15	273	266	77
Providence Reds	76	28	37	11	250	274	67
Rochester Americans	76	28	38	10	242	311	66
Western Division							
Baltimore Clippers	76	34	31	11	240	249	79
Hershey Bears	76	33	30	13	266	253	79
Cincinnati Swords	76	30	28	18	252	258	78
Cleveland Barons	76	32	34	10	269	263	74
Richmond Robins	76	29	34	13	237	218	71
Tidewater Wings	76	22	45	9	197	275	53

WESTERN HOCKEY LEAGUE

	GP	W	L	T	GF	GA	Pts
*Denver Spurs	72	44	20	8	293	209	96
Phoenix Roadrunners	72	40	27	5	283	235	85
Portland Buckaroos	72	38	31	3	301	271	79
San Diego Gulls	72	32	31	9	241	243	73
Salt Lake Golden Eagles	72	29	33	10	250	254	68
Seattle Totems	72	12	53	7	175	331	31

CENTRAL PROFESSIONAL HOCKEY LEAGUE

	GP	W	L	T	GF	GA	Pts
*Dallas Black Hawks	72	43	22	7	317	232	93
Tulsa Oilers	72	34	30	8	256	243	76
Fort Worth Wings	72	30	30	12	238	246	72
Oklahoma City Blazers	72	29	34	9	235	273	67
Omaha Knights	72	29	35	8	241	260	66
Kansas City Blues	72	21	35	16	244	277	58

INTERNATIONAL HOCKEY LEAGUE

Northern Division	GP	W	L	T	GF	GA	Pts
Muskegon Mohawks	72	49	21	2	328	231	100
*Port Huron Wings	72	37	31	4	276	262	78
Flint Generals	72	31	36	5	253	259	67
Toledo Hornets	72	26	46	0	270	371	52
Southern Division							
Dayton Gems	72	49	23	0	319	243	98
Fort Wayne Komets	72	37	33	2	291	244	76
Des Moines Oak Leafs	72	35	34	3	296	278	73
Columbus Seals	72	15	55	2	220	365	32

EASTERN HOCKEY LEAGUE

Northern Division	GP	W	L	T	GF	GA	Pts
Syracuse Blazers	75	38	27	10	340	276	86
Johnstown Jets	75	33	28	14	290	269	80
Clinton Comets	75	30	32	13	272	278	73
New Haven Blades	75	30	35	10	307	333	70
Long Island Ducks	75	29	35	11	279	310	69
Jersey Devils	75	25	40	10	237	294	60
Southern Division							
*Charlotte Checkers	73	47	18	8	330	180	102
Greensboro Generals	73	34	27	12	284	252	80
Roanoke Valley Rebels	73	30	33	10	241	266	70
St. Petersburg Suns	73	27	34	12	248	291	66
Jacksonville Rockets §	28	6	20	2	81	160	14

§ folded 12/13/72

1972–73

WORLD HOCKEY ASSOCIATION

Eastern Division	GP	W	L	T	GF	GA	Pts
*New England Whalers	78	46	30	2	318	263	94
Cleveland Crusaders	78	43	32	3	287	239	89
Philadelphia Blazers	78	38	40	0	288	305	76
Ottawa Nationals	78	35	39	4	279	301	74
Quebec Nordiques	78	33	40	5	276	313	71
New York Raiders	78	33	43	2	303	334	68
Western Division							
Winnipeg Jets	78	43	31	4	285	249	90
Houston Aeros	78	39	35	4	284	269	82
Los Angeles Sharks	78	37	35	6	259	250	80
Minn. Fighting Saints	78	38	37	3	250	269	79
Alberta Oilers	78	38	37	3	269	256	79
Chicago Cougars	78	26	50	2	245	295	54

AMERICAN HOCKEY LEAGUE

Eastern Division	GP	W	L	T	GF	GA	Pts
Nova Scotia Voyageurs	76	43	18	15	316	191	101
Boston Braves	76	34	29	13	248	256	81
Rochester Americans	76	33	31	12	239	276	78
Providence Reds	76	32	30	14	253	255	78
Springfield Kings	76	18	42	16	265	344	52
N-Haven Nighthawks	76	16	40	20	246	331	52
Western Division							
*Cincinnati Swords	76	54	17	5	351	206	113
Hershey Bears	76	42	23	11	326	231	95
Virginia Wings	76	38	22	16	258	221	92
Richmond Robins	76	30	36	10	272	280	70
Jacksonville Barons	76	23	44	9	251	329	55
Baltimore Clippers	76	17	48	11	210	315	45

WESTERN HOCKEY LEAGUE

	GP	W	L	T	GF	GA	Pts
*Phoenix Roadrunners	72	37	26	9	310	250	83
Salt Lake Golden Eagles	72	32	25	15	288	259	79
San Diego Gulls	72	32	29	11	239	223	75
Denver Spurs	72	27	32	13	264	275	67
Seattle Totems	72	26	32	14	270	286	66
Portland Buckaroos	72	21	39	12	226	287	54

CENTRAL HOCKEY LEAGUE

	GP	W	L	T	GF	GA	Pts
Dallas Black Hawks	72	38	23	11	256	208	87
*Omaha Knights	72	35	27	10	262	263	80
Fort Worth Wings	72	31	35	6	254	267	68
Tulsa Oilers	72	26	37	9	259	308	61

INTERNATIONAL HOCKEY LEAGUE

North Division	GP	W	L	T	GF	GA	Pts
Flint Generals	74	44	29	1	347	281	89
Port Huron Wings	73	41	31	1	266	237	83
Toledo Hornets	74	36	33	5	257	261	77
Muskegon Mohawks	74	36	34	4	302	259	76
Saginaw Gears	74	30	41	3	305	304	63
South Division							
*Fort Wayne Komets	74	48	23	3	308	219	99
Dayton Gems	73	44	25	4	308	235	92
Des Moines Capitols	74	30	41	3	279	360	63
Columbus Seals	74	10	62	2	177	393	22

EASTERN HOCKEY LEAGUE

Central Division	GP	W	L	T	GF	GA	Pts
Cape Cod Cubs	76	36	29	11	338	314	83
Rhode Island Eagles	76	32	35	9	320	307	73
Long Island Ducks	76	26	43	7	287	386	59
Jersey Devils	76	23	41	12	239	300	58
Northern Division							
*Syracuse Blazers	76	63	9	4	453	190	130
Johnstown Jets	76	36	28	12	283	255	84
Clinton Comets	76	18	51	7	256	415	43
New England Blades §	24	9	13	2	91	109	20
§ folded 12/06/73							
Southern Division							
Roanoke Valley Rebels	76	40	25	11	345	276	91
Greensboro Generals	76	40	28	8	391	315	88
Suncoast Suns	76	30	37	9	301	365	69
Charlotte Checkers	76	26	40	10	241	313	62

1973–74

WORLD HOCKEY ASSOCIATION

Eastern Division	GP	W	L	T	GF	GA	Pts
New England Whalers	78	43	31	4	291	260	90
Toronto Toros	78	41	33	4	304	272	86
Cleveland Crusaders	78	37	32	9	266	264	83
Chicago Cougars	78	38	35	5	271	273	81
Quebec Nordiques	78	38	36	4	306	280	80
NY-Jersey Knights	78	32	42	4	268	313	68
Western Division							
*Houston Aeros	78	48	25	5	318	219	101
Minn. Fighting Saints	78	44	32	2	332	275	90
Edmonton Oilers	78	38	37	3	268	269	79
Winnipeg Jets	78	34	39	5	264	296	73
Vancouver Blazers	78	27	50	1	278	345	55
Los Angeles Sharks	78	25	53	0	239	339	50

AMERICAN HOCKEY LEAGUE

Northern Division	GP	W	L	T	GF	GA	Pts
Rochester Americans	76	42	21	13	296	248	97
Providence Reds	76	38	26	12	330	244	88
Nova Scotia Voyageurs	76	37	27	12	263	223	86
N-Haven Nighthawks	76	35	31	10	291	275	80
Boston Braves	76	23	40	13	239	297	59
Springfield Kings	76	21	40	15	251	327	57
Southern Division							
Baltimore Clippers	76	42	24	10	310	232	94
*Hershey Bears	76	39	23	14	320	241	92
Cincinnati Swords	76	40	25	11	273	233	91
Richmond Robins	76	22	40	14	248	320	58
Jacksonville Barons	76	24	44	8	244	334	56
Virginia Wings	76	22	44	10	216	307	54

WESTERN HOCKEY LEAGUE

	GP	W	L	T	GF	GA	Pts
*Phoenix Roadrunners	78	43	32	3	300	273	89
Salt Lake Golden Eagles	78	41	33	4	356	297	86
San Diego Gulls	78	40	33	5	278	281	85
Portland Buckaroos	78	39	33	6	292	258	84
Seattle Totems	78	32	42	4	288	319	68
Denver Spurs	78	28	50	0	249	335	56

CENTRAL HOCKEY LEAGUE

	GP	W	L	T	GF	GA	Pts
Oklahoma City Blazers	72	36	25	11	280	230	83
Omaha Knights	72	34	23	15	259	217	83
*Dallas Black Hawks	72	29	26	17	220	227	75
Fort Worth Wings	72	30	28	14	237	241	74
Tulsa Oilers	72	28	31	13	233	239	69
Albuquerque 6-Guns	72	16	40	16	188	263	48

INTERNATIONAL HOCKEY LEAGUE

North Division	GP	W	L	T	GF	GA	Pts
Muskegon Mohawks	76	44	26	6	272	234	94
Saginaw Gears	76	38	34	4	310	282	80
Toledo Hornets	76	33	42	1	260	302	67
Flint Generals	76	30	43	3	251	288	63
Port Huron Wings	76	29	44	3	229	268	61
South Division							
*Des Moines Capitols	76	45	25	6	316	247	96
Columbus Owls	76	40	34	2	288	270	82
Dayton Gems	76	38	35	3	272	247	79
Fort Wayne Komets	76	31	45	0	245	305	62

EASTERN HOCKEY LEAGUE

- *EHL folds to become NAHL and SHL*

NORTH AMERICAN HOCKEY LEAGUE

	GP	W	L	T	GF	GA	Pts
*Syracuse Blazers	74	54	16	4	358	218	112
Maine Nordiques	74	45	26	3	393	339	93
Long Island Cougars	74	35	36	3	310	274	73
Cape Cod Cubs	74	34	39	1	338	345	69
Johnstown Jets	74	32	38	4	267	302	68
Binghamton Dusters	74	28	41	5	275	356	61
Mohawk Valley Comets	74	20	52	2	238	367	42

SOUTHERN HOCKEY LEAGUE

	GP	W	L	T	GF	GA	Pts
*Roanoke Valley Rebels	72	53	19	0	366	244	106
Charlotte Checkers	72	44	27	1	309	227	89
Greensboro Generals	71	33	37	1	285	310	67
Winston-Salem P-Bears	72	26	44	2	283	363	54
Macon Whoopees §	62	22	38	2	244	290	46
Suncoast Suns ¶	31	9	22	0	123	176	18

§ folded 02/15/74 ¶ folded 12/19/73

1974–75

World Hockey Association

Eastern Division	GP	W	L	T	GF	GA	Pts
New England Whalers	78	43	30	5	274	279	91
Cleveland Crusaders	78	35	40	3	236	258	73
Chicago Cougars	78	30	47	1	261	312	61
Indianapolis Racers	78	18	57	3	216	338	39
Western Division							
* Houston Aeros	78	53	25	0	369	247	106
San Diego Mariners	78	43	31	4	326	268	90
Minn. Fighting Saints	78	42	33	3	308	279	87
Phoenix Roadrunners	78	39	31	8	300	265	86
Michigan-Baltimore	78	21	53	4	205	341	46
Canadian Division							
Quebec Nordiques	78	46	32	0	331	299	92
Toronto Toros	78	43	33	2	349	304	88
Winnipeg Jets	78	38	35	5	322	293	81
Vancouver Blazers	78	37	39	2	256	270	76
Edmonton Oilers	78	36	38	4	279	279	76

American Hockey League

Northern Division	GP	W	L	T	GF	GA	Pts
Providence Reds	76	43	21	12	317	263	98
Rochester Americans	76	42	25	9	317	243	93
Nova Scotia Voyageurs	75	40	26	9	270	227	89
* Springfield Indians	75	33	30	12	299	256	78
N-Haven Nighthawks	76	30	35	11	282	302	71
Southern Division							
Virginia Wings	75	31	31	13	254	250	75
Richmond Robins	75	29	39	7	261	293	65
Hershey Bears	75	27	38	10	259	303	64
Syracuse Eagles	75	21	43	11	254	332	53
Baltimore Clippers §	46	14	22	10	136	180	38

§ folded 01/23/75

Central Hockey League

North Division	GP	W	L	T	GF	GA	Pts
* Salt Lake Golden Eagles	78	43	24	11	317	245	97
Denver Spurs	78	36	29	13	285	263	85
Omaha Knights	78	34	33	11	254	268	79
Seattle Totems	78	29	38	11	258	296	69
South Division							
Dallas Black Hawks	78	40	30	8	302	259	88
Oklahoma City Blazers	78	33	33	12	267	267	78
Tulsa Oilers	78	27	41	10	262	289	64
Fort Worth Texans	78	26	40	12	264	322	64

International Hockey League

North Division	GP	W	L	T	GF	GA	Pts
Muskegon Mohawks	75	48	24	3	325	240	99
Flint Generals	75	44	26	5	287	220	93
Saginaw Gears	75	43	29	3	302	259	89
Port Huron Flags	76	35	38	3	255	270	73
Kalamazoo Wings	75	17	53	5	203	318	39
Lansing Lancers §	41	12	28	1	145	216	25
§ folded 01/16/75							
South Division							
Dayton Gems	75	46	26	3	297	256	95
Columbus Owls	76	40	32	4	307	275	84
* Toledo Goaldiggers	76	34	38	4	285	275	72
Des Moines Capitols	76	31	38	7	253	264	69
Fort Wayne Komets	76	26	44	6	247	313	58

North American Hockey League

	GP	W	L	T	GF	GA	Pts
Syracuse Blazers	74	46	25	3	345	232	95
Philadelphia Firebirds	74	40	31	3	310	289	83
Binghamton Dusters	74	39	32	3	293	285	81
* Johnstown Jets	74	38	32	4	274	255	80
Cape Cod Codders	74	32	38	4	319	310	68
Mohawk Valley Comets	74	31	38	5	312	345	67
Long Island Cougars	74	29	40	5	271	280	63
Maine Nordiques	74	27	46	1	266	394	55

Southern Hockey League

	GP	W	L	T	GF	GA	Pts
* Charlotte Checkers	72	50	21	1	370	256	101
Hampton Gulls	72	43	28	1	323	262	87
Winston-Salem P-Bears	72	32	40	0	300	345	64
Roanoke Valley Rebels	72	29	41	2	296	304	60
Greensboro Generals	72	23	47	2	262	384	48

1975–76

World Hockey Association

Eastern Division	GP	W	L	T	GF	GA	Pts
Indianapolis Racers	80	35	39	6	245	247	76
Cleveland Crusaders	80	35	40	5	273	279	75
New England Whalers	80	33	40	7	255	290	73
Cincinnati Stingers	80	35	44	1	285	340	71
Western Division							
Houston Aeros	80	53	27	0	341	263	106
Phoenix Roadrunners	80	39	35	6	302	287	84
San Diego Mariners	80	36	38	6	303	290	78
Minn. Fighting Saints §	59	30	25	4	211	212	64
Denver-Ottawa ¶	41	14	26	1	134	172	29
§ folded 02/27/76 ¶ folded 01/17/76							
Canadian Division							
* Winnipeg Jets	81	52	27	2	345	254	106
Quebec Nordiques	81	50	27	4	371	316	104
Calgary Cowboys	80	41	35	4	307	282	86
Edmonton Oilers	81	27	49	5	268	345	59
Toronto Toros	81	24	52	5	335	398	53

American Hockey League

Northern Division	GP	W	L	T	GF	GA	Pts
* Nova Scotia Voyageurs	76	48	20	8	326	209	104
Rochester Americans	76	42	25	9	304	243	93
Providence Reds	76	34	34	8	294	300	76
Springfield Indians	76	33	39	4	267	321	70
Southern Division							
Hershey Bears	76	39	31	6	304	275	84
Richmond Robins	76	29	39	8	262	297	66
N-Haven Nighthawks	76	29	39	8	261	295	66
Baltimore Clippers	76	21	48	7	238	316	49

Central Hockey League

	GP	W	L	T	GF	GA	Pts
* Tulsa Oilers	76	45	21	10	301	228	100
Dallas Black Hawks	76	41	24	11	282	211	93
Salt Lake Golden Eagles	76	37	35	4	300	299	78
Oklahoma City Blazers	76	32	34	10	256	263	74
Fort Worth Texans	76	29	31	16	287	271	74
Tucson Mavericks	76	14	53	9	242	396	37

International Hockey League

North Division	GP	W	L	T	GF	GA	Pts
Saginaw Gears	78	43	26	9	339	293	95
Port Huron Flags	78	36	31	11	304	291	83
Flint Generals	78	34	30	14	285	254	82
Muskegon Mohawks	78	34	31	13	260	238	81
Kalamazoo Wings	78	27	41	10	273	326	64
South Division							
* Dayton Gems	78	47	21	10	340	240	104
Fort Wayne Komets	78	28	36	14	289	309	70
Toledo Goaldiggers	78	27	37	14	269	293	68
Columbus Owls	78	24	47	7	251	366	55

North American Hockey League

Eastern Division	GP	W	L	T	GF	GA	Pts
Beauce Jaros	74	54	18	2	462	306	110
Syracuse Blazers	74	38	33	3	284	278	79
Mohawk Valley Comets	74	30	40	4	306	354	64
Cape Cod Codders §	52	24	25	3	244	227	51
Maine Nordiques	74	18	55	1	295	450	37
§ folded 02/13/76							
Western Division							
Johnstown Jets	74	47	25	2	346	257	96
* Philadelphia Firebirds	74	45	29	0	373	319	90
Erie Blades	74	37	36	1	310	298	75
Buffalo Norsemen	74	30	44	0	323	375	60
Binghamton Dusters	74	27	45	2	258	337	56

Southern Hockey League

	GP	W	L	T	GF	GA	Pts
* Charlotte Checkers	72	42	20	10	302	206	94
Hampton Gulls	72	33	23	16	262	234	82
Winston-Salem P-Bears	72	30	29	13	252	251	73
Roanoke Valley Rebels	72	29	28	15	239	238	73
Tidewater Sharks	72	24	34	14	230	260	62
Greensboro Generals	72	18	42	12	221	317	48

1976–77

World Hockey Association

Eastern Division	GP	W	L	T	GF	GA	Pts
* Quebec Nordiques	81	47	31	3	353	295	97
Cincinnati Stingers	81	39	37	5	354	303	83
Indianapolis Racers	81	36	37	8	276	305	80
New England Whalers	81	35	40	6	275	290	76
Birmingham Bulls	81	31	46	4	289	309	66
Minny Fighting Saints §	42	19	18	5	136	129	43
§ folded 01/17/76							
Western Division							
Houston Aeros	80	50	24	6	320	241	106
Winnipeg Jets	80	46	32	2	366	291	94
San Diego Mariners	81	40	37	4	284	283	84
Edmonton Oilers	81	34	43	4	243	304	72
Calgary Cowboys	81	31	43	7	252	296	69
Phoenix Roadrunners	80	28	48	4	281	383	60

American Hockey League

	GP	W	L	T	GF	GA	Pts
* Nova Scotia Voyageurs	80	52	22	6	308	225	110
N-Haven Nighthawks	80	43	31	6	333	287	92
Rochester Americans	80	42	33	5	320	273	89
Hershey Bears	80	36	38	6	282	293	78
Springfield Indians	80	28	51	1	302	390	57
Rhode Island Reds	80	25	51	4	282	359	54

Central Hockey League

	GP	W	L	T	GF	GA	Pts
* Kansas City Blues	76	46	21	9	322	225	101
Dallas Black Hawks	76	35	25	16	281	231	86
Tulsa Oilers	76	37	29	10	314	289	84
Fort Worth Texans	76	35	32	9	272	261	79
Salt Lake Golden Eagles	76	31	39	6	276	288	68
Oklahoma City Blazers	76	15	53	8	245	416	38

International Hockey League

North Division	GP	W	L	T	GF	GA	Pts
* Saginaw Gears	78	40	27	11	338	292	91
Kalamazoo Wings	78	38	27	13	325	290	89
Flint Generals	78	35	33	10	342	306	80
Muskegon Mohawks	78	31	36	11	294	322	73
Port Huron Flags	78	27	43	8	268	328	62
South Division							
Toledo Goaldiggers	78	40	31	7	321	317	87
Dayton Gems	78	35	38	5	304	312	75
Fort Wayne Komets	78	32	36	10	301	311	74
Columbus Owls	78	28	35	15	294	309	71

North American Hockey League

	GP	W	L	T	GF	GA	Pts
Syracuse Blazers	73	48	22	3	372	261	99
Maine Nordiques	74	40	29	5	311	284	85
Binghamton Dusters	74	41	31	2	363	324	84
Philadelphia Firebirds	74	38	33	3	319	294	79
Erie Blades	74	37	33	4	257	251	78
Mohawk Valley Comets	74	29	42	3	316	387	61
Johnstown Jets	73	22	49	2	253	334	46
Beauce Jaros §	30	6	22	2	109	165	14

§ folded 12/22/76

Southern Hockey League

	GP	W	L	T	GF	GA	Pts
Hampton Gulls	50	32	16	2	198	152	66
Tidewater Sharks §	41	26	13	2	158	131	54
Charlotte Checkers	50	22	25	3	180	186	47
Baltimore Clippers	47	21	24	2	182	169	44
Richmond Wildcats §	38	21	16	1	160	144	43
Greensboro Generals §	40	15	24	1	140	173	31
Winston-Salem P-Twins	42	11	30	1	130	193	23

§ folded 01/07/77
• SHL folded 01/31/77 • No champion crowned

1977–78

World Hockey Association

	GP	W	L	T	GF	GA	Pts
* Winnipeg Jets	80	50	28	2	381	270	102
New England Whalers	80	44	31	5	335	269	93
Houston Aeros	80	42	34	4	296	302	88
Quebec Nordiques	80	40	37	3	349	347	83
Edmonton Oilers	80	38	39	3	309	307	79
Birmingham Bulls	80	36	41	3	287	314	75
Cincinnati Stingers	80	35	42	3	298	332	73
Indianapolis Racers	80	24	51	5	267	353	53
Soviet All-Stars	8	3	4	1	27	36	7
Czechoslovakia	8	1	6	1	21	40	3

• Games vs. Soviet All-Stars and Czechoslovakia counted in standings

American Hockey League

Northern Division	GP	W	L	T	GF	GA	Pts
* Maine Mariners	80	43	28	9	305	256	95
Nova Scotia Voyageurs	81	37	28	16	304	250	90
Springfield Indians	81	39	33	9	348	350	87
Binghamton Whalers	81	27	46	8	287	377	62
Southern Division							
Rochester Americans	81	43	31	7	332	296	93
N-Haven Nighthawks	80	38	31	11	313	292	87
Philadelphia Firebirds	81	35	35	11	294	290	81
Hershey Bears	81	27	44	10	281	324	64
Hampton Gulls	46	15	28	3	142	171	33

§ folded 02/02/78

Central Hockey League

	GP	W	L	T	GF	GA	Pts
* Fort Worth Texans	76	44	29	3	262	251	91
Salt Lake Golden Eagles	76	42	31	3	283	238	87
Dallas Black Hawks	77	38	36	3	284	281	79
Tulsa Oilers	76	34	39	3	264	273	71
K.C. Red Wings	76	33	40	3	266	257	69
Phoenix Roadrunners §	27	4	20	3	75	134	11

§ folded 12/13/77

International Hockey League

North Division	GP	W	L	T	GF	GA	Pts
Saginaw Gears	80	40	28	12	360	278	92
Kalamazoo Wings	80	35	31	14	315	288	84
Flint Generals	80	36	34	10	364	381	82
Port Huron Flags	80	33	32	15	322	331	81
Muskegon Mohawks	80	27	42	11	290	322	65
South Division							
Fort Wayne Komets	80	40	23	17	305	287	97
* Toledo Goaldiggers	80	34	28	18	331	316	86
Milwaukee Admirals	80	27	38	15	257	299	69
Grand Rapids Owls	80	27	43	10	290	332	64

• Dayton relocated to Grand Rapids

Pacific Hockey League

	GP	W	L	T	GF	GA	Pts
* San-Fran Shamrocks	42	24	17	1	186	156	49
Phoenix Roadrunners	42	24	17	1	196	168	49
San Diego Mariners	42	20	22	0	171	175	40
Long Beach Monarchs	42	15	27	0	163	217	30

• Long Beach changed name from Sharks to Monarchs

1978–79

WORLD HOCKEY ASSOCIATION

	GP	W	L	T	GF	GA	Pts
Edmonton Oilers	80	48	30	2	340	266	98
Quebec Nordiques	80	41	34	5	288	271	87
*Winnipeg Jets	80	39	35	6	307	306	84
New England Whalers	80	37	34	9	298	287	83
Cincinnati Stingers	80	33	41	6	274	284	72
Birmingham Bulls	80	32	42	6	286	311	70
Indianapolis Racers §	25	5	18	2	78	130	12
Soviet All Stars	6	4	1	1	27	20	9
Czechoslovakia	6	1	4	1	14	33	3
Finland	1	0	1	0	4	8	0

• Soviet All Stars, Czechoslovakia and Finland games counted in standings § folded 12/15/78

AMERICAN HOCKEY LEAGUE

Northern Division	GP	W	L	T	GF	GA	Pts
*Maine Mariners	80	45	22	13	350	252	103
New Brunswick Hawks	80	41	29	10	315	288	92
Nova Scotia Voyageurs	80	39	37	4	313	302	82
Springfield Indians	80	33	38	9	289	290	75
Southern Division							
N-Haven Nighthawks	80	46	25	9	346	271	101
Hershey Bears	79	35	36	8	311	324	78
Binghamton Whalers	79	32	42	5	300	320	69
Rochester Americans	80	26	42	12	289	349	64
Philadelphia Firebirds	80	23	49	8	230	347	54

CENTRAL HOCKEY LEAGUE

	GP	W	L	T	GF	GA	Pts
Salt Lake Golden Eagles	76	47	22	7	314	209	101
*Dallas Black Hawks	76	45	28	3	339	289	93
Kansas City Red Wings	76	37	36	3	301	306	77
Fort Worth Texans	76	33	39	4	260	277	70
Oklahoma City Stars	76	34	41	1	277	311	69
Tulsa Oilers	76	21	51	4	258	357	46

INTERNATIONAL HOCKEY LEAGUE

North Division	GP	W	L	T	GF	GA	Pts
Port Huron Flags	80	44	29	7	393	292	95
*Kalamazoo Wings	80	40	28	12	368	327	92
Saginaw Gears	80	35	35	10	326	322	80
Flint Generals	80	35	40	5	356	349	75
Muskegon Mohawks	80	15	58	7	275	475	37
South Division							
Grand Rapids Owls	80	50	21	9	368	267	109
Fort Wayne Komets	80	45	29	6	386	327	96
Toledo Goaldiggers	80	35	32	13	320	302	83
Milwaukee Admirals	80	21	48	11	260	391	53

PACIFIC HOCKEY LEAGUE

	GP	W	L	T	GF	GA	Pts
Phoenix Roadrunners	60	37	20	3	234	206	77
San Diego Hawks	58	34	22	2	270	192	70
Spokane Flyers	55	32	22	1	246	198	65
Tucson Rustlers	58	20	38	0	215	305	40
Los Angeles Blades §	22	7	14	1	84	109	15
San-Fran Shamrocks¶	23	4	18	1	68	107	9

§ folded 01/03/79 ¶ folded 01/03/79
• League folded after regular season • No champion crowned

NORTHEASTERN HOCKEY LEAGUE

	GP	W	L	T	GF	GA	Pts
Erie Blades	69	47	19	3	344	260	97
Jersey/Hampton Aces	69	37	29	3	330	286	77
Cape Cod Freedom*	70	33	36	1	292	309	67
Utica Mohawks	70	27	43	0	308	355	54
Johnston Wings	70	25	42	3	251	315	53

** relocated from New Hampshire*

1979–80

AMERICAN HOCKEY LEAGUE

Northern Division	GP	W	L	T	GF	GA	Pts
New Brunswick Hawks	79	44	27	8	325	271	96
Nova Scotia Voyageurs	79	43	29	7	331	271	93
Maine Mariners	80	41	28	11	307	266	93
Adirondack Wings	80	32	37	11	297	309	75
Springfield Indians	80	31	37	12	292	302	74
Southern Division							
N-Haven Nighthawks	80	46	25	9	350	305	101
*Hershey Bears	80	35	39	6	289	273	76
Syracuse Firebirds	80	31	42	7	303	364	69
Rochester Americans	80	28	42	10	260	327	66
Binghamton Whalers	80	24	49	7	268	334	55

CENTRAL HOCKEY LEAGUE

	GP	W	L	T	GF	GA	Pts
*Salt Lake Golden Eagles	80	49	24	7	342	259	105
Indianapolis Checkers	79	40	32	7	275	238	87
Fort Worth Texans	80	37	34	9	312	298	83
Birmingham Bulls	80	36	39	5	260	295	77
Tulsa Oilers	80	34	37	9	241	256	77
Houston Apollos	80	32	38	10	300	310	74
Oklahoma City Stars	80	33	44	3	261	268	69
Dallas Black Hawks	80	29	43	8	291	334	66
U.S. Olympic team	18	14	3	1	85	57	29
Cincinnati Stingers §	33	11	21	1	108	151	23

§ folded 12/17/80 • Games vs. Olympic team counted in standings

INTERNATIONAL HOCKEY LEAGUE

North Division	GP	W	L	T	GF	GA	Pts
*Kalamazoo Wings	80	45	26	9	366	274	99
Saginaw Gears	80	43	27	10	349	306	96
Port Huron Flags	80	38	26	16	352	300	92
Flint Generals	80	35	32	13	298	316	83
Muskegon Mohawks	80	29	43	8	317	330	66
South Division							
Fort Wayne Komets	80	40	27	13	343	311	93
Toledo Goaldiggers	80	28	34	18	293	345	74
Milwaukee Admirals	80	29	41	10	327	402	68
Grand Rapids Owls	80	27	41	12	327	340	66
Dayton Gems	80	28	45	7	307	355	63

EASTERN HOCKEY LEAGUE

	GP	W	L	T	GF	GA	Pts
*Erie Blades	70	46	21	3	349	241	95
Richmond Rifles	70	40	24	6	315	240	86
Baltimore Clippers	70	41	25	4	308	225	86
Utica Mohawks	70	30	34	6	274	287	66
Johnstown Red Wings	70	24	45	1	281	384	49
Hampton Aces	70	17	49	4	214	364	38

1980-81

AMERICAN HOCKEY LEAGUE

Northern Division	GP	W	L	T	GF	GA	Pts
Maine Mariners	80	45	28	7	319	292	97
New Brunswick Hawks	80	37	33	10	317	298	84
Nova Scotia Voyageurs	80	38	37	5	335	298	81
Springfield Indians	80	34	41	5	312	343	73
Southern Division							
Hershey Bears	80	47	24	9	357	299	103
*Adirondack Wings	80	35	40	5	305	328	75
Binghamton Whalers	80	32	42	6	296	336	70
N-Haven Nighthawks	80	29	40	11	295	321	69
Rochester Americans	80	30	42	8	295	316	68

CENTRAL HOCKEY LEAGUE

	GP	W	L	T	GF	GA	Pts
Dallas Black Hawks	79	56	16	7	356	233	119
*Salt Lake Golden Eagles	80	46	29	5	368	295	97
Indianapolis Checkers	80	44	30	6	306	238	94
Oklahoma City Stars	79	39	38	2	312	328	80
Tulsa Oilers	79	33	42	4	285	312	70
Wichita Wind	80	32	45	3	307	346	67
Fort Worth Texans	80	24	53	3	201	309	51
Birmingham Bulls §	58	17	37	4	204	277	38
Houston Apollos ¶	33	12	13	8	97	98	32

§ folded 02/24/81 • ¶ folded 01/08/81

INTERNATIONAL HOCKEY LEAGUE

East Division	GP	W	L	T	GF	GA	Pts
*Saginaw Gears	82	45	29	8	392	289	98
Port Huron Flags	82	31	35	16	337	377	78
Flint Generals	82	32	42	8	324	363	72
Toledo Goaldiggers	82	26	47	9	303	392	61
West Division							
Kalamazoo Wings	82	52	20	10	369	244	114
Fort Wayne Komets	82	37	30	15	337	303	89
Milwaukee Admirals	82	32	35	15	354	371	79
Muskegon Mohawks	82	28	45	9	274	351	65

EASTERN HOCKEY LEAGUE

	GP	W	L	T	GF	GA	Pts
Erie Blades*	72	52	14	6	407	252	110
Richmond Rifles	72	38	29	5	331	295	81
Salem Raiders	72	32	31	9	272	289	73
Baltimore Clippers	72	29	36	7	278	286	65
Hampton Aces	72	17	49	6	282	385	40
Syracuse Hornets §	10	0	9	1	36	99	1

§ folded 11/13/80

1981–82

AMERICAN HOCKEY LEAGUE

Northern Division	GP	W	L	T	GF	GA	Pts
*New Brunswick Hawks	80	48	21	11	338	338	107
Maine Mariners	80	47	26	7	325	325	101
Nova Scotia Voyageurs	80	35	35	10	330	330	80
Springfield Indians	80	32	43	5	278	278	69
Fredericton Express	80	20	55	5	275	275	45
Southern Division							
Binghamton Whalers	80	46	28	6	329	266	98
Rochester Americans	80	40	31	9	325	286	89
N-Haven Nighthawks	80	39	33	8	292	276	86
Hershey Bears	80	36	38	6	316	347	78
Adirondack Wings	80	34	37	9	299	285	77
Erie Blades	80	22	52	6	317	425	50

CENTRAL HOCKEY LEAGUE

North Division	GP	W	L	T	GF	GA	Pts
Salt Lake Golden Eagles	80	47	30	3	368	329	97
Cincinnati Tigers	80	46	30	4	375	340	96
*Indianapolis Checkers	80	42	33	5	319	259	89
Nashville South Stars	80	41	35	4	313	319	86
South Division							
Wichita Wind	80	44	33	3	343	289	91
Tulsa Oilers	80	43	36	1	355	324	87
Dallas Black Hawks	80	37	37	6	394	382	80
Oklahoma City Stars	80	25	54	1	300	397	51
Fort Worth Texans	80	20	57	3	273	401	43

INTERNATIONAL HOCKEY LEAGUE

	GP	W	L	OTL	T	GF	GA	Pts
*Toledo Goaldiggers	82	53	25	1	4	407	320	111
Milwaukee Admirals	82	41	34	2	7	385	351	91
Kalamazoo Wings	82	41	36	2	5	355	333	89
Fort Wayne Komets	82	35	41	5	6	368	375	81
Saginaw Gears	82	36	38	0	8	401	402	80
Flint Generals	82	32	45	5	5	310	353	74
Muskegon Mohawks	82	30	49	1	3	319	411	64

• Teams receive one point for overtime tie and overtime loss

ATLANTIC COAST HOCKEY LEAGUE

	GP	W	L	T	GF	GA	Pts
Salem Raiders	47	32	15	0	246	161	64
*Mohawk Valley Stars	47	28	18	1	225	198	57
Baltimore Skipjacks	48	22	23	3	204	189	47
Winston-Salem T'birds	50	14	33	3	179	265	31
Cape Cod Buccaneers §	39	17	21	1	130	158	35
Schenectady Chiefs ¶	9	4	5	0	38	45	8
Fitchburg Trappers #	6	2	4	0	26	32	4

§ folded 02/01/82 • ¶ folded 11/16/81 • # folded 11/06/81

1982–83

AMERICAN HOCKEY LEAGUE

Northern Division	GP	W	L	T	GF	GA	Pts
Fredericton Express	80	45	27	8	348	284	98
Nova Scotia Voyageurs	80	41	34	5	378	333	87
Maine Mariners	80	39	33	8	342	309	86
Adirondack Wings	80	36	39	5	329	343	77
Moncton Alpines	80	34	39	7	304	315	75
Sherbrooke Jets	80	22	54	4	288	390	48
Southern Division							
*Rochester Americans	80	46	25	9	389	325	101
Hershey Bears	80	40	35	5	313	308	85
N-Haven Nighthawks	80	38	34	8	337	329	84
Binghamton Whalers	80	36	36	8	320	333	80
Baltimore Skipjacks	80	35	36	9	362	366	79
St. Catharines Saints	80	33	41	6	335	368	72
Springfield Indians	80	31	43	6	282	324	68

CENTRAL HOCKEY LEAGUE

	GP	W	L	T	GF	GA	Pts
*Indianapolis Checkers	80	50	28	2	335	242	102
Colorado Flames	80	41	36	3	322	322	85
Birmingham S. Stars	80	41	37	2	297	297	84
Salt Lake Golden Eagles	80	41	38	1	318	312	83
Tulsa Oilers	80	32	47	1	282	321	65
Wichita Wind	80	29	48	3	286	346	61

INTERNATIONAL HOCKEY LEAGUE

East Division	GP	W	L	OTL	T	GF	GA	Pts
*Toledo Goaldiggers	82	51	21	1	10	362	269	113
Fort Wayne Komets	82	45	26	2	11	377	344	103
Flint Generals	82	35	36	1	11	317	340	82
Saginaw Gears	82	29	44	4	9	332	376	71
West Division								
Milwaukee Admirals	82	43	30	3	9	407	312	98
Kalamazoo Wings	82	32	44	6	6	311	341	76
Muskegon Mohawks	82	29	41	1	12	335	354	71
Peoria Prancers	82	25	47	2	10	330	435	62

ATLANTIC COAST HOCKEY LEAGUE

	GP	W	L	OTL	T	GF	GA	Pts
*Carolina Thunderbirds	68	51	10	2	7	376	208	111
Erie Golden Blades	64	39	21	1	4	345	276	83
Mohawk Valley Stars	65	30	33	2	2	311	306	64
Virginia Raiders	65	20	36	2	9	257	306	51
Hampton Rds. Gulls§	42	16	24	1	2	170	213	35
Nashville South Stars	58	11	43	2	4	239	389	28

• Teams receive one point for overtime loss
§ folded 02/02/83

1983–84

AMERICAN HOCKEY LEAGUE

Northern Division	GP	W	L	T	GF	GA	Pts
Fredericton Express	80	45	30	5	340	262	95
Adirondack Wings	80	37	29	14	344	330	88
*Maine Mariners	80	33	36	11	310	312	77
Nova Scotia Voyageurs	80	32	37	11	277	288	75
Moncton Alpines	80	32	40	8	251	278	72
Sherbrooke Jets	80	22	53	5	301	419	49
Southern Division							
Baltimore Skipjacks	80	46	24	10	384	304	102
Rochester Americans	80	46	32	2	363	300	94
St. Catharines Saints	80	43	31	6	364	346	92
Springfield Indians	80	39	35	6	344	340	84
N-Haven Nighthawks	80	36	40	4	365	371	76
Binghamton Whalers	80	33	43	4	359	388	70
Hershey Bears	80	28	42	10	320	384	66

INTERNATIONAL HOCKEY LEAGUE

	GP	W	L	OTL	T	GF	GA	Pts
Fort Wayne Komets	82	52	23	1	7	371	273	112
Milwaukee Admirals	82	46	30	3	6	403	335	101
Flint Generals	82	41	32	2	9	375	319	93
*Toledo Goaldiggers	82	41	36	4	5	326	318	91
Kalamazoo Wings	82	37	38	2	7	333	316	83
Peoria Prancers	82	29	48	3	5	298	392	66
Muskegon Mohawks	82	19	58	3	5	282	435	46

CENTRAL HOCKEY LEAGUE

	GP	W	L	T	GF	GA	Pts
Colorado Flames	76	48	25	3	343	287	99
Tulsa Oilers	68	36	27	5	252	248	77
Salt Lake Golden Eagles	72	35	35	2	334	330	72
Indianapolis Checkers	72	34	36	2	308	289	70
Montana Magic	76	20	52	4	276	381	44

ATLANTIC COAST HOCKEY LEAGUE

	GP	W	L	OTL	T	GF	GA	Pts
Carolina Thunderbirds	72	43	24	1	5	381	300	92
*Erie Golden Blades	72	42	26	3	4	371	310	91
Virginia Lancers	73	34	37	1	2	384	400	71
Mohawk Valley Stars	74	28	39	5	7	322	370	60
Pinebridge Bucks	72	25	47	2	0	329	422	52
Birmingham Bulls §	3	2	1	0	0	17	8	4

• Teams receive one point for overtime loss • § folded 10/26/84

1984–85

AMERICAN HOCKEY LEAGUE

Northern Division	GP	W	L	T	GF	GA	Pts
Maine Mariners	80	38	32	10	296	266	86
Fredericton Express	80	36	36	8	279	301	80
*Sherbrooke Canadiens	80	37	38	5	323	329	79
Nova Scotia Oilers	80	36	37	7	292	295	79
Adirondack Wings	80	35	37	8	290	336	78
Moncton Golden Flames	80	32	40	8	291	300	72
Southern Division							
Binghamton Whalers	80	52	20	8	388	265	112
Baltimore Skipjacks	80	45	27	8	326	252	98
Rochester Americans	80	40	27	13	333	301	93
Springfield Indians	80	36	40	4	322	326	76
N-Haven Nighthawks	80	31	41	8	315	341	70
Hershey Bears	80	26	43	11	315	339	63
St. Catharines Saints	80	24	50	6	272	391	54

INTERNATIONAL HOCKEY LEAGUE

East Division	GP	W	L	OTL	T	GF	GA	Pts
Muskegon Mohawks	82	50	29	0	3	374	291	103
Flint Generals	82	43	35	3	4	349	340	93
Kalamazoo Wings	82	40	35	2	7	323	297	89
Toledo Goaldiggers	82	32	45	3	5	292	362	72
West Division								
*Peoria Rivermen	82	48	25	0	9	357	275	105
Fort Wayne Komets	82	37	34	5	11	339	327	90
Salt Lake Golden Eagles	82	35	39	4	8	332	323	82
Indianapolis Checkers	82	31	47	3	4	264	318	69
Milwaukee Admirals	82	25	52	5	5	292	389	60

ATLANTIC COAST HOCKEY LEAGUE

	GP	W	L	SOL	GF	GA	Pts
*Carolina Thunderbirds	64	53	11	1	374	220	107
Erie Golden Blades	64	41	23	1	362	261	83
Pinebridge Bucks	64	33	31	6	306	298	72
Virginia Lancers	64	19	45	4	248	434	42
Mohawk Valley Stars	64	14	50	5	290	417	33

1985–86

AMERICAN HOCKEY LEAGUE

Northern Division	GP	W	L	T	GF	GA	Pts
*Adirondack Wings	80	41	31	8	339	298	90
Maine Mariners	80	40	31	9	274	285	89
Moncton Gold. Flames	80	34	34	12	294	307	80
Fredericton Express	80	35	37	8	319	311	78
Sherbrooke Canadiens	80	33	38	9	340	341	75
Nova Scotia Oilers	80	29	43	8	314	353	66
Southern Division							
Hershey Bears	80	48	29	3	346	292	99
Binghamton Whalers	80	41	34	5	316	290	87
St. Catharines Saints	80	38	37	5	304	308	81
N-Haven Nighthawks	80	36	37	7	340	343	79
Springfield Indians	80	36	39	5	301	309	77
Rochester Americans	80	34	39	7	320	337	75
Baltimore Skipjacks	80	28	44	8	271	304	64

INTERNATIONAL HOCKEY LEAGUE

East Division	GP	W	L	OTL	T	GF	GA	Pts
*Muskegon Lumberjacks	82	50	32	5	0	378	294	105
Kalamazoo Wings	82	47	35	6	0	345	314	100
Saginaw Generals	82	41	41	8	0	322	290	90
Toledo Goaldiggers	82	24	58	10	0	305	427	58
Flint Spirits	82	16	66	6	0	271	497	38
West Division								
Fort Wayne Komets	82	52	30	8	0	350	266	112
Milwaukee Admirals	82	48	33	5	1	371	310	102
Peoria Rivermen	82	46	36	5	0	339	300	97
Salt Lake Golden Eagles	82	44	38	2	0	347	326	90
Indianapolis Checkers	82	41	40	5	1	302	306	88

ATLANTIC COAST HOCKEY LEAGUE

	GP	W	L	SOL	GF	GA	Pts
Carolina Thunderbirds	62	49	13	6	395	220	104
*Erie Golden Blades	64	34	30	6	371	321	74
Virginia Lancers	61	27	34	7	293	338	61
Mohawk Valley Comets	62	23	39	3	259	332	49
New York Slapshots	59	21	38	1	260	367	43

1986–87

AMERICAN HOCKEY LEAGUE

Northern Division	GP	W	L	T	GF	GA	Pts
Sherbrooke Canadiens	80	50	28	2	328	257	102
Adirondack Wings	80	44	31	5	329	296	93
Moncton Gold. Flames	80	43	31	6	338	315	92
Nova Scotia Oilers	80	38	39	3	318	315	79
Maine Mariners	80	35	40	5	272	298	75
Fredericton Express	80	32	43	5	292	357	69
Southern Division							
*Rochester Americans	80	47	26	7	315	263	101
Binghamton Whalers	80	47	26	7	309	259	101
N-Haven Nighthawks	80	44	25	11	331	315	99
Hershey Bears	80	43	36	1	329	309	87
Baltimore Skipjacks	80	35	37	8	277	295	78
Springfield Indians	80	34	40	6	296	344	74
Newmarket Saints	80	28	48	4	226	337	60

INTERNATIONAL HOCKEY LEAGUE

East Division	GP	W	L	OTL	GF	GA	Pts
Muskegon Lumberjacks	82	47	30	5	366	286	99
Saginaw Generals	82	44	32	6	383	344	94
Flint Spirits	82	42	33	7	343	361	91
Kalamazoo Wings	82	36	38	8	331	353	80
West Division							
Fort Wayne Komets	82	48	26	8	343	284	104
*Salt Lake Golden Eagles	82	39	31	12	360	357	90
Milwaukee Admirals	82	41	37	4	342	358	86
Indianapolis Checkers	82	37	38	7	360	387	81
Peoria Rivermen	82	31	42	9	264	362	71

ATLANTIC COAST HOCKEY LEAGUE

	GP	W	L	SOL	GF	GA	Pts
*Virginia Lancers	55	36	19	3	288	218	75
Erie Golden Blades	55	28	27	2	250	246	58
Mohawk Valley Comets	54	23	31	3	260	292	49
Carolina Thunderbirds	54	23	31	2	252	278	48
Troy Slapshots §	6	2	4	0	20	36	4

• Teams receive one point for overtime loss
§ folded 11/17/87

1987–88

AMERICAN HOCKEY LEAGUE

Northern Division	GP	W	L	OTL	T	GF	GA	Pts
Maine Mariners	80	44	29	4	7	308	284	99
Fredericton Express	80	42	30	3	8	370	318	95
Sherbrke Canadiens	80	42	34	1	4	316	243	89
Nova Scotia Oilers	80	35	36	2	9	323	343	81
N-Haven Nighthawks	80	33	40	3	7	288	307	76
Moncton Hawks	80	27	45	2	8	286	358	64
Springfield Indians	80	27	45	1	8	269	333	63
Southern Division								
*Hershey Bears	80	50	27	2	3	343	256	105
Rochester Americans	80	46	27	1	7	328	272	100
Adirondack Wings	80	42	27	4	11	306	275	99
Binghamton Whalers	80	38	34	3	8	353	300	87
Utica Devils	80	34	35	2	11	318	307	81
Newmarket Saints	80	33	39	6	8	282	328	80
Baltimore Skipjacks	80	13	58	6	9	268	434	41

• Teams receive one point for an overtime loss

INTERNATIONAL HOCKEY LEAGUE

East Division	GP	W	L	OTL	GF	GA	Pts
Muskegon Lumberjacks	82	58	14	10	415	269	126
Fort Wayne Komets	82	48	30	4	343	310	100
Saginaw Hawks	82	45	30	7	325	294	97
Flint Spirits	82	42	31	9	395	389	93
Kalamazoo Wings	82	37	33	12	328	360	86
West Division							
Colorado Rangers	82	44	35	3	344	354	91
*Salt Lake Golden Eagles	82	40	34	8	308	303	88
Peoria Rivermen	82	34	41	7	301	338	75
Milwaukee Admirals	82	21	54	7	288	430	49

• Teams receive one point for an overtime loss

ALL-AMERICAN HOCKEY LEAGUE

	GP	W	L	OTL	GF	GA	Pts
Virginia Lancers	43	37	5	1	321	129	75
*Carolina Thunderbirds	49	34	15	0	355	182	68
Johnstown Chiefs §	26	13	13	0	157	115	26
Miami Valley Sabres	37	17	19	1	217	260	35
Danville Fighting Saints	35	15	20	0	240	317	30
Jackson All-Americans	40	14	21	5	227	318	33
Port Huron Clippers	38	9	28	1	212	347	19
Michigan Stars¶	14	2	12	0	68	130	4

• Miami, Danville, Jackson and Port Huron folded after regular season
§ Played 2nd half of season only • ¶ folded 11/30/87

1988–89

AMERICAN HOCKEY LEAGUE

Northern Division	GP	W	L	T	GF	GA	Pts
Sherbrooke Canadiens	80	47	24	9	348	261	103
Halifax Citadels	80	42	30	8	345	300	92
Moncton Hawks	80	37	34	9	320	313	83
N-Haven Nighthawks	80	35	35	10	325	309	80
Maine Mariners	80	32	40	8	262	317	72
Springfield Indians	80	32	44	4	287	341	68
Cape Breton Oilers	80	27	47	6	308	388	60
Southern Division							
*Adirondack Wings	80	47	27	6	369	294	100
Hershey Bears	80	40	30	10	361	309	90
Utica Devils	80	37	34	9	309	295	83
Newmarket Saints	80	38	36	6	339	334	82
Rochester Americans	80	38	37	5	305	302	81
Baltimore Skipjacks	80	30	46	4	317	347	64
Binghamton Whalers	80	28	46	6	307	392	62

INTERNATIONAL HOCKEY LEAGUE

East Division	GP	W	L	OTL	GF	GA	Pts
*Muskegon Lumberjacks	82	57	18	7	433	308	121
Saginaw Hawks	82	46	26	10	378	294	102
Fort Wayne Komets	82	46	30	6	293	274	98
Kalamazoo Wings	82	39	36	7	345	350	85
Flint Spirits	82	22	54	6	287	428	50
West Division							
Salt Lake Golden Eagles	82	56	22	4	369	294	116
Milwaukee Admirals	82	54	23	5	399	323	113
Denver Rangers	82	33	42	7	323	394	73
Peoria Rivermen	82	31	42	9	339	383	71
Indianapolis Ice	82	26	54	2	312	430	54

EAST COAST HOCKEY LEAGUE

	GP	W	L	OTL	GF	GA	Pts
Erie Panthers	60	37	20	3	327	256	77
Johnstown Chiefs	60	32	22	6	295	251	70
Knoxville Cherokees	60	32	27	1	266	286	65
*Carolina Thunderbirds	60	27	32	1	266	329	55
Virginia Lancers	60	22	30	8	266	298	52

1989–90

AMERICAN HOCKEY LEAGUE

Northern Division	GP	W	L	T	GF	GA	Pts
Sherbrooke Canadiens	80	45	23	12	301	247	102
Cape Breton Oilers	80	39	34	7	317	306	85
*Springfield Indians	80	38	38	4	317	310	80
Halifax Citadels	80	37	37	6	317	300	80
Maine Mariners	80	31	38	11	294	317	73
Moncton Hawks	80	33	42	5	265	303	71
N-Haven Nighthawks	80	32	41	7	283	316	71
Southern Division							
Rochester Americans	80	43	28	9	337	286	95
Adirondack Wings	80	42	27	11	330	304	95
Baltimore Skipjacks	80	43	30	7	302	265	93
Utica Devils	80	44	32	4	354	315	92
Newmarket Saints	80	31	33	16	305	318	78
Hershey Bears	80	32	38	10	298	296	74
Binghamton Whalers	80	11	60	9	229	366	31

INTERNATIONAL HOCKEY LEAGUE

East Division	GP	W	L	OTL	GF	GA	Pts
Muskegon Lumberjacks	82	55	21	6	389	304	116
Kalamazoo Wings	82	53	23	6	389	311	112
Flint Spirits	82	40	36	6	326	358	86
Fort Wayne Komets	82	37	34	11	316	345	85
West Division							
*Indianapolis Ice	82	53	21	8	315	237	114
Salt Lake Golden Eagles	82	37	36	9	326	311	83
Milwaukee Admirals	82	36	39	7	316	370	79
Peoria Rivermen	82	31	38	13	317	378	75
Phoenix Roadrunners	82	27	44	11	314	394	65

EAST COAST HOCKEY LEAGUE

	GP	W	L	OTL	GF	GA	Pts
Winston-Salem T-Birds	60	38	16	6	312	257	82
Erie Panthers	60	38	16	6	357	251	82
Virginia Lancers	60	36	18	6	261	218	78
*Greensboro Monarchs	60	29	27	4	263	283	62
Hampton Rds Admirals	60	29	29	2	252	267	60
Nashville Knights	60	26	30	4	248	289	56
Johnstown Chiefs	60	23	31	6	233	291	52
Knoxville Cherokees	60	21	33	6	230	300	48

1990-91

AMERICAN HOCKEY LEAGUE

Northern Division	GP	W	L	T	GF	GA	Pts
*Springfield Indians	80	43	27	10	348	281	96
Cape Breton Oilers	80	41	31	8	306	301	90
Moncton Hawks	80	36	32	12	270	267	84
Fredericton Canadiens	80	36	35	9	295	292	81
Maine Mariners	80	34	34	12	269	284	80
Halifax Citadels	80	33	35	12	338	340	78
N-Haven Nighthawks	80	24	45	11	246	324	59
Southern Division							
Rochester Americans	80	45	26	9	326	253	99
Binghamton Rangers	80	44	30	6	318	274	94
Baltimore Skipjacks	80	39	34	7	325	289	85
Hershey Bears	80	33	35	12	313	324	78
Adirondack Wings	80	33	37	10	320	346	76
Utica Devils	80	36	42	2	325	346	74
Capital Dist. Islanders	80	28	43	9	284	323	65
Newmarket Saints	80	26	45	9	278	317	61

INTERNATIONAL HOCKEY LEAGUE

East Division	GP	W	L	OTL	GF	GA	Pts
Kalamazoo Wings	82	52	29	1	354	302	105
Indianapolis Ice	82	48	29	5	342	264	101
Fort Wayne Komets	83	43	35	5	369	335	91
Muskegon Lumberjacks	83	38	40	5	305	352	81
Albany Choppers §	55	22	30	3	191	232	47
§ folded 02/15/91							
West Division							
*Peoria Rivermen	82	58	19	5	405	261	121
Salt Lake Golden Eagles	83	50	28	5	353	296	105
Phoenix Roadrunners	83	38	36	9	326	343	85
Milwaukee Admirals	82	36	43	3	275	316	75
San Diego Gulls	83	30	45	8	273	362	68
Kansas City Blades	82	25	53	4	255	385	54

EAST COAST HOCKEY LEAGUE

East Division	GP	W	L	OTL	GF	GA	Pts
*Hampton Rds Admirals	64	38	20	6	300	248	82
Johnstown Chiefs	64	32	29	3	324	287	67
Erie Panthers	64	31	30	3	302	302	65
Richmond Renegades	64	29	29	6	300	307	64
Roanoke Valley Rebels	64	25	32	7	218	295	57
West Division							
Knoxville Cherokees	64	46	13	5	377	230	97
Cincinnati Cyclones	64	37	24	3	285	281	77
Greensboro Monarchs	64	34	27	3	275	268	71
Louisville IceHawks	64	31	29	4	251	309	66
Nashville Knights	64	29	31	4	307	317	62
Winston-Salem T-Birds	64	20	41	3	228	323	43

1991-92

AMERICAN HOCKEY LEAGUE

Atlantic Division	GP	W	L	T	GF	GA	Pts
Fredericton Canadiens	80	43	27	10	314	254	96
St. John's Maple Leafs	80	39	29	12	325	285	90
Cape Breton Oilers	80	36	34	10	336	330	82
Moncton Hawks	80	32	38	10	285	299	74
Halifax Citadels	80	25	38	17	280	324	67
Northern Division							
Springfield Indians	80	43	29	8	308	277	94
*Adirondack Wings	80	40	36	4	335	309	84
N-Haven Nighthawks	80	39	37	4	305	309	82
Capital District Islanders	80	32	37	11	261	289	75
Maine Mariners	80	23	47	10	296	352	56
Southern Division							
Binghamton Rangers	80	41	30	9	318	277	91
Rochester Americans	80	37	31	12	292	248	86
Hershey Bears	80	36	33	11	313	337	83
Utica Devils	80	34	40	6	268	313	74
Baltimore Skipjacks	80	28	42	10	287	320	66

INTERNATIONAL HOCKEY LEAGUE

East Division	GP	W	L	OTL	GF	GA	Pts
Fort Wayne Komets	82	52	22	8	340	287	112
Muskegon Lumberjacks	82	41	28	13	306	293	95
Milwaukee Admirals	82	38	36	8	306	309	84
Kalamazoo Wings	82	37	35	10	292	312	84
Indianapolis Ice	82	31	41	10	272	329	72
West Division							
*Kansas City Blades	82	56	22	4	302	248	116
Peoria Rivermen	82	48	25	9	333	300	105
San Diego Gulls	82	45	28	9	340	298	99
Salt Lake Golden Eagles	82	33	40	9	252	304	75
Phoenix Roadrunners	82	29	46	7	275	338	65

EAST COAST HOCKEY LEAGUE

East Division	GP	W	L	OTL	GF	GA	Pts
Greensboro Monarchs	64	43	17	4	297	252	90
*Hampton Rds Admirals	64	42	20	2	298	220	86
Winston-Salem T-Birds	64	36	24	4	270	245	76
Richmond Renegades	64	30	27	7	263	263	67
Raleigh IceCaps	64	25	33	6	228	284	56
Roanoke Valley Rebels	64	21	36	7	236	313	49
Knoxville Cherokees	64	20	36	8	265	355	48
West Division							
Toledo Storm	64	46	15	3	367	240	95
Cincinnati Cyclones	64	36	20	8	329	284	80
Johnstown Chiefs	64	36	23	5	294	248	77
Erie Panthers	64	33	27	4	284	309	70
Dayton Bombers	64	32	26	6	305	300	70
Louisville IceHawks	64	31	25	8	315	306	70
Columbus Chill	64	25	30	9	298	341	59
Nashville Knights	64	24	36	4	246	335	52

COLONIAL HOCKEY LEAGUE

	GP	W	L	OTL	T	GF	GA	Pts
Michigan Falcons	60	34	22	3	4	296	257	75
Brantford Smoke	60	34	22	0	4	327	265	72
*T-Bay Thunder Hawks	60	26	28	4	6	309	289	62
St. Thomas Wildcats	60	24	29	2	7	263	288	57
Flint Bulldogs	60	20	37	2	3	272	368	45

• *Teams receive one point for overtime tie and one point for overtime loss*

1992-93

AMERICAN HOCKEY LEAGUE

Atlantic Division	GP	W	L	T	GF	GA	Pts
St. John's Maple Leafs	80	41	26	13	351	308	95
Fredericton Canadiens	80	38	31	11	314	278	87
*Cape Breton Oilers	80	36	32	12	356	336	84
Moncton Hawks	80	31	33	16	292	306	78
Halifax Citadels	80	33	37	10	312	348	76
Northern Division							
Providence Bruins	80	46	32	2	384	348	94
Adirondack Wings	80	36	35	9	331	308	81
Capital Dist. Islanders	80	34	34	12	280	285	80
Springfield Indians	80	25	41	14	282	336	64
N-Haven Nighthawks	80	22	47	11	262	343	55
Southern Division							
Binghamton Rangers	80	57	13	10	392	246	124
Rochester Americans	80	40	33	7	348	332	87
Utica Devils	80	33	36	11	325	354	77
Baltimore Skipjacks	80	28	40	12	318	353	68
Hershey Bears	80	27	41	12	316	339	66
Hamilton Canucks	80	29	45	6	284	327	64

INTERNATIONAL HOCKEY LEAGUE

Atlantic Division	GP	W	L	OTL	GF	GA	Pts
Atlanta Knights	82	52	23	7	333	291	111
Cleveland Lumberjacks	82	39	34	9	329	330	87
Cincinnati Cyclones	82	27	48	7	305	364	61
Central Division							
*Fort Wayne Komets	82	49	27	6	339	294	104
Indianapolis Ice	82	34	39	9	324	347	77
Kalamazoo Wings	82	29	42	11	291	367	69
Midwest Division							
Milwaukee Admirals	82	49	23	10	329	280	108
Kansas City Blades	82	46	26	10	318	288	102
Peoria Rivermen	82	41	33	8	297	307	90
Pacific Division							
San Diego Gulls	82	62	12	8	381	229	132
Salt Lake Golden Eagles	82	38	39	5	269	305	81
Phoenix Roadrunners	82	26	50	6	248	361	58

EAST COAST HOCKEY LEAGUE

East Division	GP	W	L	OTL	GF	GA	Pts
Wheeling Thunderbirds	64	40	16	8	314	223	88
Hampton Rds Admirals	64	37	21	6	294	235	80
Raleigh IceCaps	64	37	22	5	289	262	79
Johnstown Chiefs	64	34	23	7	281	264	75
Richmond Renegades	64	34	28	2	292	292	70
Greensboro Monarchs	64	33	29	2	256	261	68
Roanoke Val. Rampage	64	14	49	1	227	387	29
West Division							
*Toledo Storm	64	36	17	11	316	238	83
Dayton Bombers	64	35	23	6	282	270	76
Nashville Knights	64	36	25	3	312	305	75
Erie Panthers	64	35	25	4	305	307	74
Louisville IceHawks	64	30	27	7	302	293	67
Birmingham Bulls	64	30	29	5	290	313	65
Columbus Chill	64	30	30	4	257	256	64
Knoxville Cherokees	64	19	39	6	212	323	44

CENTRAL HOCKEY LEAGUE

	GP	W	L	OTL	GF	GA	Pts
Oklahoma City Blazers	60	39	18	3	291	232	81
*Tulsa Oilers	60	35	22	3	270	230	73
Dallas Freeze	60	31	25	4	276	242	66
Memphis RiverKings	60	26	27	7	253	272	59
Fort Worth Fire	60	24	29	7	252	288	55
Wichita Thunder	60	25	33	2	242	320	52

• *Teams receive one point for an overtime loss*

COLONIAL HOCKEY LEAGUE

	GP	W	L	SOL	GF	GA	Pts
*Brantford Smoke	60	39	18	3	308	264	81
Detroit Falcons	60	36	20	4	239	239	76
T-Bay Thunder Hawks	60	32	24	4	271	271	68
Muskegon Fury	60	28	27	5	278	278	61
St. Thomas Wildcats	60	27	27	6	322	322	60
Flint Generals	60	27	29	4	296	296	58
Chatham Wheels	60	21	35	4	344	344	46

• *Teams receive one point for a shootout loss*

SUNSHINE HOCKEY LEAGUE

	GP	W	L	OTL	GF	GA	Pts
West Palm Beach Blaze	45	38	6	1	275	166	77
*Jacksonville Bullets	47	22	23	2	228	218	46
Daytona Sun Devils	48	18	25	5	226	258	41
Lakeland Ice Warriors	52	18	30	4	202	287	40
St. Petersburg Renegades	20	10	6	4	100	102	34

1993-94

AMERICAN HOCKEY LEAGUE

Atlantic Division	GP	W	L	T	GF	GA	Pts
St. John's Maple Leafs	80	45	23	12	360	287	102
Saint John Flames	80	37	33	10	304	305	84
Moncton Hawks	80	37	36	7	310	303	81
Cape Breton Oilers	80	32	35	13	316	339	77
Fredericton Canadiens	80	31	42	7	294	296	69
PEI Senators	80	23	49	8	269	356	54
Northern Division							
Adirondack Wings	80	45	27	8	333	273	98
*Portland Pirates	80	43	27	10	328	269	96
Albany River Rats	80	38	34	8	312	315	84
Springfield Indians	80	29	38	13	309	327	71
Providence Bruins	80	28	39	13	283	319	69
Southern Division							
Hershey Bears	80	38	31	11	306	298	87
Hamilton Canucks	80	36	37	7	302	305	79
Cornwall Aces	80	33	36	11	294	295	77
Rochester Americans	80	31	34	15	277	300	77
Binghamton Rangers	80	33	38	9	312	322	75

INTERNATIONAL HOCKEY LEAGUE

Atlantic Division	GP	W	L	SOL	GF	GA	Pts
Kalamazoo Wings	81	48	26	7	337	297	103
Fort Wayne Komets	81	41	29	11	347	297	93
Cleveland Lumberjacks	81	31	36	14	278	344	76
Central Division							
Peoria Rivermen	81	51	24	6	327	294	108
Cincinnati Cyclones	81	49	23	9	336	282	107
Indianapolis Ice	81	28	46	7	257	329	63
Midwest Division							
*Atlanta Knights	81	45	22	14	321	282	104
Milwaukee Admirals	81	40	24	17	338	302	97
Kansas City Blades	81	40	31	10	326	327	90
Russian Penguins	13	2	9	2	35	64	6
Pacific Division							
Las Vegas Thunder	81	52	18	11	319	282	115
San Diego Gulls	81	42	28	11	311	302	95
Phoenix Roadrunners	81	40	36	5	313	309	85
Salt Lake Golden Eagles	81	24	52	5	243	377	53

• *Teams receive one point for a shootout loss*
• *Games vs. touring Russian Penguins counted in standings*

EAST COAST HOCKEY LEAGUE

East Division	GP	W	L	OTL	GF	GA	Pts
Hampton Rds Admirals	68	41	19	8	298	246	90
Raleigh IceCaps	68	41	20	7	296	221	89
Greensboro Monarchs	68	41	21	6	319	262	88
Charlotte Checkers	68	39	25	4	281	271	82
Roanoke Express	68	37	28	3	300	290	77
S-Carolina Stingrays	68	33	26	9	294	291	75
Richmond Renegades	68	34	29	5	286	293	73
West Division							
Knoxville Cherokees	68	44	18	6	325	246	94
Birmingham Bulls	68	44	20	4	340	268	92
Nashville Knights	68	26	36	6	255	289	58
Huntsville Blast	68	20	39	9	241	315	49
Louisville IceHawks	68	16	44	8	236	356	40
Huntington Blizzard	68	14	49	5	191	413	33
North Division							
*Toledo Storm	68	44	20	4	338	289	92
Columbus Chill	68	41	20	7	344	285	89
Wheeling Thunderbirds	68	38	23	7	327	289	83
Johnstown Chiefs	68	37	27	4	323	308	78
Dayton Bombers	68	29	31	8	316	308	66
Erie Panthers	68	27	36	5	264	334	59

CENTRAL HOCKEY LEAGUE

	GP	W	L	OTL	GF	GA	Pts
*Wichita Thunder	64	40	18	6	309	275	86
Tulsa Oilers	64	36	24	4	347	281	76
Oklahoma City Blazers	64	35	23	6	260	246	76
Dallas Freeze	64	31	25	8	304	309	70
Memphis RiverKings	64	25	34	5	243	294	55
Fort Worth Fire	64	25	37	2	253	311	52

Colonial Hockey League

East Division	GP	W	L	SOL	GF	GA	Pts
*Thunder Bay Senators	64	45	15	4	331	236	94
Brantford Smoke	64	28	26	10	308	348	66
St. Thomas Wildcats	64	22	34	8	284	343	52
Utica Bulldogs	64	21	39	4	226	330	46
West Division							
Chatham Wheels	64	39	18	7	336	281	85
Muskegon Fury	64	35	24	5	319	301	75
Detroit Falcons	64	34	25	5	296	275	73
Flint Generals	64	32	23	9	328	314	73

Sunshine Hockey League

	GP	W	L	OTL	GF	GA	Pts
West Palm Beach Blaze	54	37	14	3	282	205	77
*Jacksonville Bullets	54	32	21	1	290	229	65
Lakeland Warriors	54	23	28	3	280	301	49
Daytona Sun Devils	54	16	35	3	210	327	35

1994–95

American Hockey League

Atlantic Division	GP	W	L	T	GF	GA	Pts
PEI Senators	80	41	31	8	305	271	90
St. John's Maple Leafs	80	33	37	10	263	263	76
Fredericton Canadiens	80	35	40	5	274	288	75
Saint John Flames	80	27	40	13	250	286	67
Cape Breton Oilers	80	27	44	9	298	342	63
Northern Division							
*Albany River Rats	80	46	17	17	293	219	109
Portland Pirates	80	46	22	12	333	233	104
Providence Bruins	80	39	30	11	300	268	89
Adirondack Wings	80	32	38	10	271	294	74
Springfield Falcons	80	31	37	12	269	289	74
Worcester Icecats	80	24	45	11	234	300	59
Southern Division							
Binghamton Rangers	80	43	30	7	302	261	93
Cornwall Aces	80	38	33	9	236	248	85
Hershey Bears	80	34	36	10	275	300	78
Rochester Americans	80	35	38	7	300	304	77
Syracuse Crunch	80	29	42	9	288	325	67

International Hockey League

North Division	GP	W	L	SOL	GF	GA	Pts
Detroit Vipers	81	48	27	6	311	273	102
Kalamazoo Wings	81	43	24	14	288	249	100
Chicago Wolves	81	34	33	13	261	306	82
Cleveland Lumberjacks	81	34	37	10	306	339	78
Midwest Division							
Peoria Rivermen	81	51	19	11	311	245	113
Cincinnati Cyclones	81	49	22	10	305	272	108
Fort Wayne Komets	81	34	39	8	296	324	76
Indianapolis Ice	81	32	41	8	273	330	72
Central Division							
Milwaukee Admirals	81	44	27	10	317	298	98
Houston Aeros	81	38	35	8	272	283	84
Atlanta Knights	81	39	38	5	279	296	83
Minnesota Moose	81	34	35	12	271	336	80
Kansas City Blades	81	35	40	6	277	300	76
Southwest Division							
*Denver Grizzlies	81	57	18	6	339	235	120
Las Vegas Thunder	81	46	30	5	328	278	97
Phoenix Roadrunners	81	41	26	14	325	310	96
San Diego Gulls	81	37	36	8	268	301	82
Soviet Wings	16	1	14	2	37	89	4

• Games vs. touring Soviet Wings counted in standings

East Coast Hockey League

East Division	GP	W	L	OTL	GF	GA	Pts
*Richmond Renegades	68	41	20	7	271	232	89
Roanoke Express	68	39	19	10	255	223	88
Charlotte Checkers	68	37	22	9	274	261	83
Hampton Rds Admirals	68	37	23	8	255	239	82
Greensboro Monarchs	68	31	28	9	277	293	71
Raleigh IceCaps	68	23	39	6	239	295	52
North Division							
Wheeling Thunderbirds	68	46	17	5	313	243	97
Dayton Bombers	68	42	17	9	307	224	93
Toledo Storm	68	41	22	5	287	230	87
Columbus Chill	68	31	32	5	282	315	67
Johnstown Chiefs	68	31	32	5	256	297	67
Erie Panthers	68	18	46	4	256	356	40
South Division							
S-Carolina Stingrays	68	42	19	7	255	215	91
Tallahassee T-Sharks	68	36	25	7	268	227	79
Nashville Knights	68	32	30	6	263	279	70
Knoxville Cherokees	68	30	30	8	241	267	68
Huntington Blizzard	68	28	37	3	224	275	59
Birmingham Bulls	68	26	38	4	273	325	56

Central Hockey League

	GP	W	L	SOL	GF	GA	Pts
*Wichita Thunder	66	44	18	4	320	268	92
San Antonio Iguanas	66	37	22	7	336	281	81
Tulsa Oilers	66	36	24	6	307	281	78
Oklahoma City Blazers	66	34	23	9	274	267	77
Fort Worth Fire	66	32	26	8	314	288	72
Memphis Riverkings	66	24	35	7	259	327	55
Dallas Freeze	66	24	36	6	266	364	54

• Teams receive one point for a shootout loss

Colonial Hockey League

East Division	GP	W	L	SOL	GF	GA	Pts
*Thunder Bay Senators	74	48	22	4	341	279	100
London Wildcats	74	34	38	2	341	380	70
Utica Blizzard	74	31	38	5	299	349	67
Brantford Smoke	74	26	36	12	299	357	64
West Division							
Detroit Falcons	74	45	27	2	329	273	92
Muskegon Fury	74	42	27	5	333	286	89
Saginaw Wheels	74	36	31	7	306	321	79
Flint Generals	74	34	34	6	350	353	74

Sunshine Hockey League

	GP	W	L	OTL	GF	GA	Pts
West Palm Beach Blaze	57	38	15	4	322	244	80
*Jacksonville Bullets	57	33	23	1	291	255	67
Fresno Falcons	16	9	7	0	76	75	50
Lakeland Warriors	56	23	32	1	240	299	47
Daytona Sun Devils	56	18	37	1	264	320	37

• Fresno received 5.6 points for a win and 2.8 points for an overtime loss

1995–96

American Hockey League

Atlantic Division	GP	W	L	OTL	T	GF	GA	Pts
PEI Senators	80	38	36	3	6	303	313	85
Saint John Flames	80	35	34	4	11	272	264	85
St. John's Maple Leafs	80	31	35	4	14	248	274	80
Fredericton Canadiens	80	34	35	0	11	307	308	79
Cape Breton Oilers	80	33	44	4	3	290	323	73
Northern Division								
Springfield Falcons	80	42	27	5	11	272	215	100
Worcester Icecats	80	36	32	4	12	242	244	88
Portland Pirates	80	32	38	4	10	282	283	78
Providence Bruins	80	30	40	4	10	249	280	74
Central Division								
Albany River Rats	80	54	19	0	7	322	218	115
Adirondack Wings	80	38	34	2	8	271	247	86
*Rochester Americans	80	37	38	4	5	294	297	83
Cornwall Aces	80	34	39	5	7	249	251	80
Syracuse Crunch	80	31	44	7	5	257	307	74
Southern Division								
Binghamton Rangers	80	39	34	3	7	333	331	88
Hershey Bears	80	36	33	3	11	301	287	86
Baltimore Bandits	80	33	38	2	9	279	299	77
Carolina Monarchs	80	28	41	3	11	313	343	70

• Teams receive one point for an overtime loss

International Hockey League

East Division	GP	W	L	SOL	GF	GA	Pts
Cincinnati Cyclones	82	51	22	9	318	247	111
Michigan K-Wings	82	40	24	18	290	272	98
Indianapolis Ice	82	43	33	6	304	295	92
Fort Wayne Komets	82	39	35	8	276	296	86
Central Division							
Orlando Solar Bears	82	52	24	6	352	307	110
Detroit Vipers	82	48	28	6	310	274	102
Cleveland Lumberjacks	82	43	27	12	334	330	98
Atlanta Knights	82	32	41	9	282	348	73
Houston Aeros	82	29	45	8	262	328	66
Midwest Division							
Milwaukee Admirals	82	40	32	10	290	307	90
Chicago Wolves	82	40	34	8	288	310	88
Peoria Rivermen	82	39	38	5	274	290	83
Kansas City Blades	82	39	38	5	288	326	83
Minnesota Moose	82	30	45	7	254	332	67
Southwest Division							
Las Vegas Thunder	82	57	17	8	380	249	122
*Utah Grizzlies	82	49	29	4	291	232	102
San Francisco Spiders	82	40	32	10	278	283	90
Phoenix Roadrunners	82	36	35	11	267	281	83
Los Angeles Ice Dogs	82	32	36	14	305	336	78

East Coast Hockey League

East Division	GP	W	L	OTL	GF	GA	Pts
Richmond Renegades	70	46	11	13	314	225	105
*Charlotte Checkers	70	45	21	4	294	250	94
S-Carolina Stingrays	70	40	22	8	284	251	88
Roanoke Express	70	36	28	6	231	260	78
Hampton Rds Admirals	70	32	25	13	278	265	77
Raleigh IceCaps	70	23	34	13	215	266	59
North Division							
Toledo Storm	70	48	14	8	301	240	104
Wheeling Thunderbirds	70	42	23	5	289	261	89
Louisville RiverFrogs	70	39	24	7	266	237	85
Columbus Chill	70	37	28	5	285	268	79
Dayton Bombers	70	35	28	7	247	237	77
Erie Panthers	70	25	40	5	227	293	55
Johnstown Chiefs	70	21	38	11	249	322	53
Huntington Blizzard	70	21	39	10	232	309	52
South Division							
Louisiana Ice Gators	70	43	21	6	312	261	92
Nashville Knights	70	42	22	6	368	307	90
Tallahassee T-Sharks	70	42	22	6	283	260	90
Knoxville Cherokees	70	37	29	4	323	303	78
Jacksonville Liz-Kings	70	33	29	8	267	288	74
Birmingham Bulls	70	26	39	5	258	360	57
Mobile Mysticks	70	22	37	11	265	325	55

Central Hockey League

	GP	W	L	SOL	GF	GA	Pts
*Oklahoma City Blazers	64	47	13	4	327	224	98
San Antonio Iguanas	64	39	17	8	313	240	86
Memphis Riverkings	64	34	24	6	308	271	74
Tulsa Oilers	64	26	33	5	244	302	57
Fort Worth Fire	64	24	34	6	244	289	54
Wichita Thunder	64	22	39	3	270	380	47

Colonial Hockey League

East Division	GP	W	L	SOL	GF	GA	Pts
*Flint Generals	74	51	18	5	347	248	107
Brantford Smoke	74	45	24	5	336	283	95
Detroit Falcons	74	33	32	9	275	310	75
Saginaw Wheels	74	32	35	7	299	341	71
Utica Blizzard	74	29	39	6	285	339	64
West Division							
Muskegon Fury	74	40	27	7	273	248	87
Thunder Bay Senators	74	36	26	12	302	289	84
Madison Monsters	74	37	30	7	267	284	81
Quad City Mallards	74	30	39	5	269	311	65

West Coast Hockey League

	GP	W	L	OTL	GF	GA	Pts
*San Diego Gulls	58	49	7	2	350	232	100
Fresno Falcons	58	30	21	7	270	232	67
Reno Renegades	58	26	24	8	271	283	60
Alaska Gold Kings	58	23	25	10	256	307	56
Anchorage Aces	58	24	29	5	271	299	53
Bakersfield Fog	58	24	29	5	271	323	53
CSKA Moscow	12	4	6	2	50	63	10

• Games vs. touring CSKA Moscow team counted in standings

Southern Hockey League

	GP	W	L	OTL	GF	GA	Pts
Lakeland Prowlers	60	41	13	6	342	229	88
Daytona Breakers	60	33	20	7	297	251	73
Win-Salem Mammoths	60	30	23	7	273	274	67
*Huntsville Channel Cats	60	27	31	2	274	294	56
W-Palm Barracudas	60	26	32	2	251	319	54
Jacksonville Bullets	60	23	33	4	282	352	50

1996–97

American Hockey League

Canadian Division	GP	W	L	OTL	T	GF	GA	Pts
St. John's Maple Leafs	80	36	28	6	10	265	264	88
Saint John Flames	80	28	36	3	13	237	269	72
Hamilton Bulldogs	80	28	39	4	9	220	276	69
Fredericton Canadiens	80	26	44	2	8	234	283	62
Empire State Division								
Rochester Americans	80	40	30	1	9	298	257	90
Albany River Rats	80	38	28	2	12	258	249	90
Adirondack Wings	80	38	28	5	9	269	231	90
Syracuse Crunch	80	32	38	0	10	241	265	74
Binghamton Rangers	80	27	38	2	13	245	300	69
New England Division								
Worcester Icecats	80	43	23	5	9	256	234	100
Springfield Falcons	80	41	25	2	12	268	229	96
Portland Pirates	80	37	26	7	10	279	264	91
Providence Bruins	80	35	40	2	3	262	289	75
Mid-Atlantic Division								
Philadelphia Phantoms	80	49	18	3	10	325	230	111
*Hershey Bears	80	43	22	5	10	273	220	101
KY Thoroughblades	80	36	35	0	9	278	284	81
Baltimore Bandits	80	30	37	3	10	251	285	73
Carolina Monarchs	80	28	43	5	4	273	303	65

International Hockey League

Northeast Division	GP	W	L	SOL	GF	GA	Pts
Detroit Vipers	82	57	17	8	280	188	122
Orlando Solar Bears	82	53	24	5	305	232	111
Cincinnati Cyclones	82	43	29	10	254	248	96
Quebec Rafales	82	41	30	11	267	248	93
Grand Rapids Griffins	82	40	30	12	244	246	92
Central Division							
Indianapolis Ice	82	44	29	9	289	230	97
Cleveland Lumberjacks	82	40	32	10	286	280	90
Michigan K-Wings	82	31	44	7	208	272	69
Fort Wayne Komets	82	28	47	7	223	318	63
Midwest Division							
San Antonio Dragons	82	45	30	7	276	278	97
Kansas City Blades	82	38	29	15	271	270	91
Chicago Wolves	82	40	36	6	276	290	86
Milwaukee Admirals	82	38	36	8	253	298	84
Manitoba Moose	82	32	40	10	262	300	74
Southwest Division							
Long Beach Ice Dogs	82	54	19	9	309	247	117
Houston Aeros	82	44	30	8	247	228	96
Utah Grizzlies	82	43	33	6	259	254	92
Las Vegas Thunder	82	41	34	7	287	299	89
Phoenix Roadrunners	82	27	42	13	239	309	67

EAST COAST HOCKEY LEAGUE

East Division	GP	W	L	SOL	GF	GA	Pts
*S-Carolina Stingrays	70	45	15	10	345	253	100
Hampton Rds Admirals	70	46	19	5	286	223	97
Richmond Renegades	70	41	25	4	252	235	86
Roanoke Express	70	38	26	6	262	250	82
Charlotte Checkers	70	35	28	7	27	267	77
Raleigh Icecaps	70	30	33	7	256	293	67
Knoxville Cherokees	70	24	43	3	260	343	51
North Division							
Columbus Chill	70	44	21	5	257	208	93
Peoria Rivermen	70	43	21	6	219	208	92
Daytona Bombers	70	36	26	8	258	208	80
Wheeling Thunderbirds	70	36	29	5	291	208	77
Toledo Storm	70	32	28	10	248	208	74
Huntington Blizzard	70	33	33	4	296	208	70
Louisville RiverFrogs	70	29	31	10	290	208	68
Johnstown Chiefs	70	24	39	7	354	208	55
South Division							
Tallahassee T-Sharks	70	39	23	8	263	236	86
Birmingham Bulls	70	36	25	9	291	296	81
Louisiana Ice Gators	70	38	28	4	292	244	80
Mobile Mysticks	70	34	25	11	257	263	79
Mississippi Sea Wolves	70	34	26	10	241	245	78
Pensacola Ice Pilots	70	36	31	3	275	275	75
Baton Rouge Kingfish	70	31	33	6	222	238	68
Jacksonville Liz-Kings	70	21	37	12	220	299	54

• Teams receive one point for a shootout loss

CENTRAL HOCKEY LEAGUE

Eastern Division	GP	W	L	SOL	GF	GA	Pts
Huntsville Channel Cats	66	39	24	3	311	297	81
Macon Whoopee	66	38	24	4	276	237	80
Memphis RiverKings	66	35	27	4	278	260	74
Columbus C-mouths	66	32	28	6	292	291	70
Nashville Nighthawks	66	12	52	2	219	359	26
Western Division							
Oklahoma City Blazers	66	48	12	6	307	200	102
*Fort Worth Fire	66	45	16	5	279	210	95
Tulsa Oilers	66	30	32	4	286	284	64
Wichita Thunder	66	25	31	10	279	324	60
San Antonio Iguanas	66	26	36	4	261	326	56

COLONIAL HOCKEY LEAGUE

East Division	GP	W	L	SOL	GF	GA	Pts
Flint Generals	74	55	18	1	371	232	111
Brantford Smoke	74	42	25	7	321	286	91
Port Huron Border Cats	74	38	31	5	280	288	81
Utica Blizzard	74	22	42	10	278	385	54
Saginaw Lumber Kings	74	21	48	5	263	399	47
West Division							
*Quad City Mallards	74	51	20	3	384	245	105
Madison Monsters	74	46	21	7	315	259	99
Thunder Bay Senators	74	43	23	8	333	266	94
Muskegon Fury	74	39	29	6	268	257	84
Dayton Ice Bandits	74	13	53	8	216	412	34

WEST COAST HOCKEY LEAGUE

	GP	W	L	SOL	GF	GA	Pts
*San Diego Gulls	64	50	12	2	400	210	102
Anchorage Aces	64	41	18	5	349	260	87
Fresno Falcons	64	38	20	6	313	254	82
Bakersfield Fog	64	33	26	5	345	325	71
Reno Renegades	64	16	43	5	252	418	37
Alaska Gold Kings	64	13	47	4	230	423	30
CSKA Moscow	12	7	4	1	56	55	15

• Games vs. touring CSKA Moscow team counted in standings

WESTERN PROFESSIONAL HOCKEY LEAGUE

	GP	W	L	SOL	GF	GA	Pts
New Mexico Scorpions	64	42	20	2	323	258	86
Austin Ice-Bats	64	35	22	7	271	249	77
*El Paso Buzzards	64	33	23	8	284	272	74
Central Tex. Stampede	64	35	27	2	243	229	72
Waco Wizards	64	30	30	4	220	249	64
Amarillo Rattlers	64	17	39	8	239	323	42

1997–98

AMERICAN HOCKEY LEAGUE

Atlantic Division	GP	W	L	OTL	T	GF	GA	Pts
Saint John Flames	80	43	24	0	13	231	201	99
Fredericton Canadiens	80	33	32	5	10	245	244	81
Portland Pirates	80	33	33	2	12	241	247	80
St. John's Maple Leafs	80	25	32	5	18	233	254	73
New England Division								
Springfield Falcons	80	45	26	2	7	278	248	99
Hartford Wolf Pack	80	43	24	1	12	272	227	99
New Haven Beasts	80	38	33	2	7	256	239	85
Worcester Icecats	80	34	31	6	9	267	268	83
Providence Bruins	80	19	49	5	7	211	301	50
Empire Division								
Albany River Rats	80	43	20	6	11	290	223	103
Hamilton Bulldogs	80	36	22	5	17	264	242	94
Syracuse Crunch	80	35	32	2	11	272	285	83
Adirondack Wings	80	31	37	3	9	245	275	74
Rochester Americans	80	30	38	0	12	238	260	72
Mid-Atlantic Division								
*Philadelphia Phantoms	80	47	21	2	10	314	249	106
Hershey Bears	80	36	31	6	7	238	235	85
KY Thoroughblades	80	29	39	3	9	241	278	70
Cincinnati M-Ducks	80	23	37	7	13	243	303	66

INTERNATIONAL HOCKEY LEAGUE

Northeast Division	GP	W	L	SOL	GF	GA	Pts
Detroit Vipers	82	47	20	15	267	232	109
Orlando Solar Bears	82	42	30	10	258	251	94
Grand Rapids Griffins	82	38	31	13	225	242	89
Quebec Rafales	82	27	48	7	211	292	61
Central Division							
Fort Wayne Komets	82	47	29	6	270	243	100
Cincinnati Cyclones	82	40	30	12	275	254	92
Indianapolis Ice	82	40	36	6	245	261	86
Cleveland Lumberjacks	82	35	37	10	228	262	80
Michigan K-Wings	82	36	39	7	223	261	79
Midwest Division							
*Chicago Wolves	82	55	24	3	301	258	113
Kansas City Blades	82	41	29	12	269	258	94
Milwaukee Admirals	82	43	34	5	267	262	91
Manitoba Moose	82	39	36	7	269	254	85
Southwest Division							
Long Beach Ice Dogs	82	53	20	9	282	210	115
Houston Aeros	82	50	22	10	268	214	110
Utah Grizzlies	82	47	27	8	276	234	102
Las Vegas Thunder	82	33	39	10	260	305	76
San Antonio Dragons	82	25	49	8	233	334	58

EAST COAST HOCKEY LEAGUE

Northeast Division	GP	W	L	SOL	GF	GA	Pts
Roanoke Express	70	42	21	7	235	208	91
Wheeling Nailers	70	37	24	9	255	255	83
Chesapk Icebreakers	70	34	28	8	252	239	76
*Hampton Rds Admirals	70	32	28	10	222	225	74
Richmond Renegades	70	30	33	7	218	277	67
Johnstown Chiefs	70	23	41	6	219	297	52
Northwest Division							
Peoria Rivermen	70	44	19	7	296	213	95
Toledo Storm	70	41	21	8	251	210	90
Daytona Bombers	70	36	26	8	255	256	80
Huntington Blizzard	70	34	29	7	230	259	75
Columbus Chill	70	33	30	7	221	220	73
Louisville RiverFrogs	70	32	31	7	228	257	71
Southeast Division							
S-Carolina Stingrays	70	41	23	6	246	218	88
Charlotte Checkers	70	35	24	11	251	237	81
Pee Dee Pride	70	34	25	11	214	215	79
Jacksonville Liz-Kings	70	35	29	6	243	239	76
Raleigh Icecaps	70	32	33	5	236	254	69
Tallahassee T-Sharks	70	24	44	2	210	320	50
Southwest Division							
Louisiana Icegators	70	43	17	10	298	232	96
Birmingham Bulls	70	39	23	8	293	257	86
Pensacola Ice Pilots	70	36	24	10	276	262	82
New Orleans Brass	70	36	24	10	278	263	82
Mobile Mysticks	70	35	27	8	236	233	78
Mississippi Sea Wolves	70	34	27	9	225	224	77
Baton Rouge Kingfish	70	33	27	10	220	238	76

CENTRAL HOCKEY LEAGUE

Eastern Division	GP	W	L	SOL	GF	GA	Pts
*Columbus C-mouths	70	51	13	6	341	219	108
Nashville Ice Flyers	70	41	19	10	274	246	92
Huntsville Channel Cats	70	40	22	8	333	281	88
Macon Whoopee	70	38	25	7	249	234	83
Fayetteville Force	70	25	42	3	247	348	53
Western Division							
Oklahoma City Blazers	70	48	19	3	319	237	99
Wichita Thunder	70	35	31	4	302	303	74
Tulsa Oilers	70	34	31	5	308	274	73
Memphis RiverKings	70	25	40	5	239	287	55
Fort Worth Fire	70	13	53	4	214	397	30

UNITED HOCKEY LEAGUE

East Division	GP	W	L	SOL	GF	GA	Pts
Flint Generals	74	46	22	6	371	278	98
Brantford Smoke	74	33	27	14	312	307	80
Port Huron Border Cats	74	31	33	10	256	303	72
Binghamton Icemen	74	25	40	9	237	339	59
Saginaw Lumber Kings	74	23	46	5	231	342	51
West Division							
*Quad City Mallards	74	55	18	1	360	257	111
Muskegon Fury	74	43	23	8	341	244	94
T-Bay Thunder Cats	74	42	26	6	337	304	90
Madison Monsters	74	39	24	11	271	265	89
Winston-Salem IceHawks	74	33	38	3	228	305	69

WEST COAST HOCKEY LEAGUE

North Division	GP	W	L	SOL	GF	GA	Pts
Tacoma Sabercats	64	42	19	3	300	214	87
Anchorage Aces	64	36	20	8	308	261	80
Idaho Steelheads	64	27	30	7	253	275	61
Reno Rage	64	23	39	2	219	297	48
South Division							
*San Diego Gulls	64	53	10	1	347	198	107
Phoenix Mustangs	64	36	25	3	267	235	75
Fresno Fighting Falcons	64	33	29	2	273	262	68
Bakersfield Fog	64	22	37	5	226	330	49
Tucson Gila Monsters	64	16	43	5	213	334	37

WESTERN PROFESSIONAL HOCKEY LEAGUE

Eastern Division	GP	W	L	SOL	GF	GA	Pts
Fort Worth Bulls	69	41	17	11	296	219	93
Shreveport Mudbugs	69	42	20	7	308	228	91
Central Tex. Stampede	69	40	23	6	258	251	86
Austin Ice-Bats	69	35	23	11	247	255	81
Lake Charles Ice Pirates	69	35	28	6	273	280	76
Monroe Moccasins	69	35	32	2	225	223	72
Waco Wizards	69	18	48	3	203	319	39
Western Division							
*El Paso Buzzards	69	43	20	6	338	252	92
New Mexico Scorpions	69	42	20	7	324	236	91
San Angelo Outlaws	69	29	34	6	280	326	64
Amarillo Rattlers	69	25	32	12	228	300	62
Odessa Jackalopes	69	26	37	6	262	360	58

1998–99

AMERICAN HOCKEY LEAGUE

Atlantic Division	GP	W	L	OTL	T	GF	GA	Pts
Lowell Lock Monsters	80	33	32	2	13	219	237	81
St. John's Maple Leafs	80	34	35	4	7	246	270	79
Fredericton Canadiens	80	33	36	5	6	246	246	77
Saint John Flames	80	31	40	1	8	238	296	71
Portland Pirates	80	23	48	2	7	214	273	55
New England Division								
*Providence Bruins	80	56	16	4	4	321	223	120
Hartford Wolf Pack	80	38	31	6	5	256	256	87
Springfield Falcons	80	35	35	1	9	245	232	80
Worcester IceCats	80	34	36	2	8	237	260	78
Beast of New Haven	80	33	35	5	7	240	250	78
Empire Division								
Rochester Americans	80	52	21	1	6	287	176	111
Albany River Rats	80	46	26	2	6	275	230	100
Hamilton Bulldogs	80	40	29	4	7	229	206	91
Adirondack Red Wings	80	21	48	3	8	184	280	53
Syracuse Crunch	80	18	50	3	9	220	327	48
Mid-Atlantic Division								
Philadelphia Phantoms	80	47	22	2	9	272	221	105
KY Thoroughblades	80	44	26	3	7	272	214	98
Hershey Bears	80	37	32	1	10	242	224	85
Cincinnati M-Ducks	80	35	39	2	4	227	249	76

INTERNATIONAL HOCKEY LEAGUE

Northeast Division	GP	W	L	SOL	GF	GA	Pts
Detroit Vipers	82	50	21	11	259	195	111
Orlando Solar Bears	82	45	33	4	264	253	94
Cincinnati Cyclones	82	44	32	6	269	270	94
Grand Rapids Griffins	82	34	40	8	256	281	76
Central Division							
Michigan K-Wings	82	35	34	13	232	253	83
Fort Wayne Komets	82	33	33	16	250	280	82
Indianapolis Ice	82	33	37	12	243	277	78
Cleveland Lumberjacks	82	28	47	7	248	310	63
Midwest Division							
Chicago Wolves	82	49	21	12	285	246	110
Manitoba Moose	82	47	21	14	269	236	108
Kansas City Blades	82	44	31	7	256	270	95
Milwaukee Admirals	82	38	28	16	254	265	92
Southwest Division							
*Houston Aeros	82	54	15	13	307	209	121
Long Beach Ice Dogs	82	48	28	6	260	237	102
Utah Grizzlies	82	39	43	9	244	254	87
Las Vegas Thunder	82	35	39	8	247	307	87

EAST COAST HOCKEY LEAGUE

Northeast Division	GP	W	L	T	GF	GA	Pts
Roanoke Express	70	38	22	10	224	201	86
Hampton Rds Admirals	70	38	24	8	215	213	84
Richmond Renegades	70	40	27	3	239	196	83
Chesapk Icebreakers	70	34	25	11	229	206	79
Johnstown Chiefs	70	27	34	9	218	265	63
Northwest Division							
Columbus Chill	70	39	24	7	257	242	85
Peoria Rivermen	70	39	25	6	243	230	84
Toledo Storm	70	39	26	5	256	246	83
Dayton Bombers	70	34	27	9	239	241	77
Huntington Blizzard	70	31	33	6	221	253	68
Wheeling Nailers	70	27	37	6	206	249	60
Southeast Division							
Pee Dee Pride	70	51	15	4	289	191	106
Florida Everblades	70	45	20	5	253	180	95
S-Carolina Stingrays	70	40	20	10	235	216	90
Augusta Lynx	70	38	27	5	235	233	81
Jacksonville Liz-Kings	70	35	33	2	235	255	72
Charlotte Checkers	70	29	30	11	221	262	69
Miami Matadors	70	28	32	10	208	266	66
Greenville Growl	70	26	33	11	208	241	63
Southwest Division							
Louisiana Icegators	70	46	18	6	297	205	98
*Mississippi Sea Wolves	70	41	22	7	251	215	89
Birmingham Bulls	70	37	29	4	251	267	78
New Orleans Brass	70	30	27	13	244	261	73
Mobile Mysticks	70	31	31	8	231	259	70
Baton Rouge Kingfish	70	30	30	10	222	228	70
Tallahassee T-Sharks	70	27	34	9	212	250	63
Pensacola Ice Pilots	70	25	41	4	199	267	54

CENTRAL HOCKEY LEAGUE

Eastern Division	GP	W	L	SOL	GF	GA	Pts
*Huntsville Channel Cats	70	47	19	4	310	251	98
Columbus C-mouths	70	42	21	7	277	209	91
Memphis RiverKings	70	36	27	7	313	307	79
Macon Whoopee	70	35	26	9	240	234	79
Fayetteville Force	70	35	27	8	267	285	78
Western Division							
Oklahoma City Blazers	70	49	19	2	322	203	100
San Antonio Iguanas	70	37	26	7	286	283	81
Wichita Thunder	70	34	26	10	257	262	78
Topeka Scare Crows	70	28	38	4	189	251	60
Fort Worth Fire	70	22	43	5	245	322	49
Tulsa Oilers	70	20	41	9	261	360	49

UNITED HOCKEY LEAGUE

Central Division	GP	W	L	SOL	GF	GA	Pts
*Muskegon Fury	74	50	18	6	304	208	106
Port Huron Border Cats	74	41	26	7	261	239	89
Flint Generals	74	37	32	5	318	299	79
Saginaw Gears	74	20	46	8	212	332	48
Eastern Division							
Binghamton Icemen	74	39	30	5	280	238	83
Asheville Smoke	74	36	35	3	292	331	75
Winston-Salem IceHawks	74	31	40	3	245	311	65
Mohawk Valley Prowlers	74	27	39	8	214	300	62
West Division							
Quad City Mallards	74	50	19	5	364	253	105
Thunder Bay T-Cats	74	47	20	7	325	247	101
Madison Monsters	74	29	40	5	237	294	63

WEST COAST HOCKEY LEAGUE

North Division	GP	W	L	OTL	GF	GA	Pts
*Tacoma Sabercats	70	44	18	8	278	234	96
Anchorage Aces	71	46	22	3	332	260	95
Colorado Gold Kings	71	32	33	6	270	288	70
Idaho Steelheads	71	32	33	6	260	284	70
South Division							
San Diego Gulls	71	45	19	7	342	242	97
Fresno Fighting Falcons	70	35	31	4	257	296	74
Phoenix Mustangs	71	32	33	6	260	284	70
Bakersfield Condors	70	21	40	9	213	308	75

• *Tucson Gila Monsters withdrew after 21 games*

WESTERN PROFESSIONAL HOCKEY LEAGUE

Central Division	GP	W	L	OTL	GF	GA	Pts
Waco Wizards	69	40	22	7	275	232	87
Corpus Christi Icerays	69	40	23	6	253	210	86
Central Texas Stampede	69	33	24	12	286	266	78
Fort Worth Brahmas	69	34	26	9	227	235	77
Austin Ice Bats	69	26	33	10	211	287	54
Eastern Division							
*Shreveport Mudbugs	69	47	17	5	315	234	99
Lake Charles Ice Pirates	69	40	25	4	275	232	84
Monroe Moccasins	69	37	26	6	252	248	80
Arkansas GlacierCats	69	37	27	5	272	247	79
Alexandria Warthogs	69	25	30	14	264	310	64
Tupelo T-Rex	69	20	45	4	195	316	44
Western Division							
Abilene Aviators	69	43	23	3	261	230	89
San Angelo Outlaws	69	39	25	5	284	253	83
El Paso Buzzards	69	36	27	6	246	231	78
Odessa Jackalopes	69	35	29	5	233	221	75
Amarillo Rattlers	69	31	30	8	246	271	70
New Mexico Scorpions	69	27	34	8	245	293	62
Touring Russian Clubs							
Kristall Elektrostal	8	3	4	1	23	35	7
Traktor Chelyabinsk	9	2	6	1	26	38	5

• *Games vs. touring Russian clubs counted in standings*

1999–2000

AMERICAN HOCKEY LEAGUE

Atlantic Division	GP	W	L	T	RT	GF	GA	Pts
Quebec Citadelles	80	37	34	5	4	227	238	83
Saint John Flames	80	32	32	11	5	267	283	80
Lowell Lock Monsters	80	33	36	7	4	228	240	77
St. John's Maple Leafs	80	23	45	8	4	202	277	58
New England Division								
*Hartford Wolf Pack	80	49	22	7	2	249	198	103
Portland Pirates	80	46	23	10	1	256	202	103
Worcester IceCats	80	34	31	11	4	249	250	83
Springfield Falcons	80	33	35	11	1	272	252	78
Providence Bruins	80	33	38	6	3	231	269	75
Empire Division								
Rochester Americans	80	46	22	9	3	247	201	104
Syracuse Crunch	80	35	35	9	1	290	294	80
Hamilton Bulldogs	80	27	34	13	6	225	262	73
Albany River Rats	80	30	40	7	3	225	250	70
Wilkes-Barre/Scranton	80	23	43	9	5	236	306	60
Mid-Atlantic Division								
KY Thoroughblades	80	42	25	9	4	250	211	97
Hershey Bears	80	43	29	5	3	297	267	94
Philadelphia Phantoms	80	44	31	3	2	281	239	93
Louisville Panthers	80	42	30	7	1	278	254	92
Cincinnati M-Ducks	80	30	37	9	4	227	244	73

INTERNATIONAL HOCKEY LEAGUE

East Division	GP	W	L	SOP	GF	GA	Pts
Grand Rapids Griffins	82	51	22	9	254	200	111
Orlando Solar Bears	82	47	23	12	250	202	106
Cincinnati Cyclones	82	44	30	8	244	246	96
Cleveland Lumberjacks	82	40	30	12	225	238	92
Milwaukee Admirals	82	37	36	9	222	246	83
Michigan K-Wings	82	33	37	12	178	223	78
Detroit Vipers	82	22	52	8	163	277	52
West Division							
*Chicago Wolves	82	53	21	8	270	228	114
Utah Grizzlies	82	45	25	12	265	220	102
Houston Aeros	82	44	29	9	219	197	97
Long Beach Ice Dogs	82	44	31	7	234	216	95
Manitoba Moose	82	37	31	14	227	237	88
Kansas City Blades	82	36	37	9	249	270	81

EAST COAST HOCKEY LEAGUE

Northeast Division	GP	W	L	T	GF	GA	Pts
Roanoke Express	70	44	20	6	221	181	94
Richmond Renegades	70	44	21	5	258	205	93
Hampton Rds Admirals	70	44	22	4	241	198	92
Trenton Titans	70	37	29	4	233	199	78
Charlotte Checkers	70	25	38	7	186	254	57
Greensboro Generals	70	20	43	7	229	337	47
Northwest Division							
*Peoria Rivermen	70	45	20	5	273	216	95
Huntington Blizzard	70	35	25	10	230	238	80
Johnstown Chiefs	70	33	28	9	235	234	75
Dayton Bombers	70	32	28	10	230	226	74
Wheeling Nailers	70	25	40	5	202	246	55
Toledo Storm	70	22	41	7	214	306	51
Southeast Division							
Florida Everblades	70	53	15	2	277	181	108
Pee Dee Pride	70	47	18	5	233	175	99
Greenville Growl	70	46	18	6	277	198	98
S-Carolina Stingrays	70	35	25	10	253	242	80
Augusta Lynx	70	34	31	5	243	248	73
Tallahassee T-Sharks	70	31	33	6	256	261	73
Jacksonville Liz-Kings	70	27	34	9	246	291	63
Southwest Division							
Louisiana Icegators	70	43	18	9	281	241	95
Mobile Mysticks	70	40	28	2	275	230	82
New Orleans Brass	70	36	27	7	230	219	79
Mississippi Sea Wolves	70	35	27	8	241	221	78
Pensacola Ice Pilots	70	35	29	6	215	216	78
Baton Rouge Kingfish	70	33	32	5	253	277	71
Jackson Bandits	70	32	32	6	201	227	70
Birmingham Bulls	70	29	37	4	255	297	62
Arkansas RiverBlades	70	18	49	3	192	316	39

CENTRAL HOCKEY LEAGUE

Eastern Division	GP	W	L	SOL	GF	GA	Pts
Fayetteville Force	70	45	22	3	255	202	93
Columbus C-mouths	70	39	20	11	233	203	89
Huntsville Channel Cats	70	37	27	6	242	244	80
Macon Whoopee	70	34	26	10	259	237	78
Memphis RiverKings	70	9	57	4	175	341	22
Western Division							
Oklahoma City Blazers	70	39	24	7	248	220	85
*Indianapolis Ice	70	39	28	3	290	244	81
Tulsa Oilers	70	38	27	5	251	244	81
Wichita Thunder	70	37	26	7	245	231	81
Topeka Scare Crows	70	35	27	8	245	243	78
San Antonio Iguanas	70	33	32	5	229	263	71

UNITED HOCKEY LEAGUE

Central Division	GP	W	L	SOL	GF	GA	Pts
*Flint Generals	74	51	14	9	379	250	111
Port Huron Border Cats	74	47	21	6	269	202	100
Muskegon Fury	74	43	26	5	266	250	91
Fort Wayne Komets	74	40	27	7	281	251	87
Ohio Gears	74	12	57	5	198	370	29
Eastern Division							
Binghamton Icemen	74	47	20	7	279	222	101
Mohawk Valley Prowlers	74	28	31	15	254	295	71
Asheville Smoke	74	34	38	2	279	315	70
Adirondack IceHawks	74	28	34	12	260	308	68
Knoxville Speed	74	29	41	4	236	314	62
West Division							
Quad City Mallards	74	53	16	5	369	264	111
Missouri River Otters	74	39	29	6	275	252	84
Madison Monsters	74	35	33	6	254	276	76
Rockford IceHogs	74	32	34	8	238	258	72

WEST COAST HOCKEY LEAGUE

North Division	GP	W	L	OTL	GF	GA	Pts
Tacoma Sabercats	72	51	12	9	297	193	111
Colorado Gold Kings	72	37	31	4	264	276	78
Anchorage Aces	74	31	34	9	272	334	71
Idaho Steelheads	72	31	36	5	287	300	67
South Division							
San Diego Gulls	70	46	16	8	297	221	100
Bakersfield Condors	72	34	29	9	244	272	77
*Phoenix Mustangs	72	31	35	6	264	284	68
Fresno Fighting Falcons	72	27	38	7	262	307	61

WESTERN PROFESSIONAL HOCKEY LEAGUE

Western Division	GP	W	L	SOL	GF	GA	Pts
New Mexico Scorpions	70	49	18	3	315	225	101
Lubbock Cotton Kings	70	42	24	4	320	267	88
El Paso Buzzards	70	39	24	7	287	250	85
Odessa Jackalopes	70	30	32	8	249	287	68
San Angelo Outlaws	70	26	41	3	225	297	55
Amarillo Rattlers	70	21	41	8	216	296	50
Central Division							
Central Texas Stampede	70	50	17	3	282	187	103
Austin Ice Bats	71	42	23	6	279	245	90
Corpus Christi IceRays	71	36	26	9	306	302	81
Fort Worth Brahmas	70	28	38	4	238	287	60
Eastern Division							
*Shreveport Mudbugs	70	44	19	7	272	198	95
Lake Charles Ice Pirates	70	41	25	4	285	222	86
Monroe Moccasins	70	39	25	6	240	211	84
Arkansas GlacierCats	70	32	29	9	241	281	73
Tupelo T-Rex	70	31	28	11	241	281	73
Alexandria Warthogs	70	21	40	10	211	307	52

• *Waco Wizards and Abilene Aviators folded 12/15/99*

2000–01 • NEW FRANCHISES

AMERICAN HOCKEY LEAGUE

Norfolk Admirals *(formerly Hampton Roads of ECHL)*

WEST COAST HOCKEY LEAGUE

Long Beach Ice Dogs *(formerly in IHL)*

WESTERN PROFESSIONAL HOCKEY LEAGUE

Tucson Scorch

CHAPTER 40

The Big-League Alternative

A Brief History of the World Hockey Association

Scott Surgent

THE WORLD HOCKEY ASSOCIATION was founded in January, 1971, and played its first games in October 1972. For seven eventful and often tumultuous seasons, it survived alongside the established National Hockey League as a second "major league," creating controversy every step of the way with its inauspicious origins, brazen raiding of the NHL for talent, unstable franchises and colorful players. The enormous popularity of hockey, and a perceived absence of the pro game in many parts of North America, created a situation in which a second major league could form and gain a foothold in the sport.

The WHA was not the first league to go up against the NHL's supremacy, but it was arguably the most successful for the simple reason that its legacy still is readily evident in the current-day NHL. The WHA was the first league to actively pursue and import European talent to North America during a time in which NHL rosters were almost exclusively Canadian. The WHA also heavily scouted the collegiate ranks and United States-born players. It was a wide-open league that adopted rule variations that promoted scoring (including overtime periods and a limited offside pass allowance). It offered players an opportunity to seek their value in a competitive market, and it moved the enormous mantle of power away from the owners, to be shared with the players. The WHA was ahead of its time, predating practices that became commonplace in the NHL during the 1980s and beyond.

The NHL was formed in 1917 as an offshoot of the National Hockey Association. During this time, the NHL competed for talent with the Pacific Coast Hockey Association, which eventually merged into the Western Canada Hockey League. By the time of the demise of the Western league in 1926, the NHL had grown from three teams to 10 before contracting to six teams in 1942. The NHL remained a six-team league for 25 years, staving off attempts at expansion (Cleveland and Buffalo were among the candidates during the 1950s) despite the high skill level of the league and the popularity of the sport across Canada and large regions of the United States. However, population shifts away from the east (the NHL's domain) to the midwest and west over the years made it evident to the NHL that it no longer could ignore the need to move into these areas. Finally, after much internal wrangling, the NHL radically expanded, adding eight new teams between 1967 and 1970. Teams in St. Louis and Minneapolis established the NHL in the American midwest, while teams in Los Angeles, Oakland and Vancouver gave the NHL a western presence and also served to cripple the rising Western Hockey League by moving into its prime territories. Nevertheless, many felt slighted and bemused by the NHL's choice of expansion sites; in particular, Canadian fans noted that only one of the eight new teams was based in Canada.

Concurrently, the NHL employed a reserve clause in its player contracts, an item which the fledgling WHA would neatly exploit for its own gain. The reserve clause allowed a team to renew a player's contract at the previous year's terms (an automatic "self-renewal" mechanism). The clause gave the players no bargaining power, and as such, hockey players were relatively underpaid compared to their counterparts in other sports. But with no alternative, players had little choice but to accept the clause as *fait accompli*.

In view of these conditions, two Californians—Dennis Murphy and Gary Davidson—formed the World Hockey Association in January, 1971, incorporating the league in Delaware but running it from Orange County, California. Both men knew little about hockey, but their strengths were as astute businessmen with a keen sense for opportunity. In 1967, Murphy had co-founded the American Basketball Association as a competitor to the National Basketball Association, and Davidson had been its first president. From this knowledge base, they established the framework of the WHA, and set about making it a reality.

Early 1971 was devoted to courting prospective ownership groups. In April 1971, Murphy and Davidson were introduced to William "Wild Bill" Hunter of Edmonton, through Walter Marlow, a columnist for the *Los Angeles Herald-Examiner*. Hunter ran a series of junior league teams in Saskatoon and Edmonton and was one of the most powerful men in Canadian hockey not affiliated with the NHL. Edmonton was considered an unlikely site for NHL expansion and Hunter was quite happy to turn his attentions to the WHA. Bill Hunter lobbied the support of other powerful men to join up with the new league: Ben Hatskin in Winnipeg and Bob Brownridge in Calgary. The WHA, barely six months old, already had a solid foothold in three of Canada's largest cities. The first-year WHA would number four teams in Canada, compared to three in the NHL. Later, it would operate an all-Canadian division.

To attract players, the WHA announced on October 20, 1971, that it would not employ the reserve clause in its contracts, nor would it honor the same in NHL player contracts. Most players in the NHL had been signed for one or two years, meaning that a considerable number of players would be available in 1972 when their contracts expired. Word of the new league had circulated around the NHL, and players were being told not to lock into new contracts without first considering offers from the WHA. Players were excited about the new league; long-time "loyalties" evaporated when a contract offering twice or more their previous salary was tendered.

In November 1971, the WHA announced its lineup. The 12-team league would consist of the Chicago Cougars, Los Angeles Sharks, New York Raiders, Minnesota (St. Paul) Fighting Saints, Winnipeg Jets, Edmonton Oilers, Calgary

Broncos, Miami Screaming Eagles, Dayton Aeros, New England (Boston) Whalers, an Ontario franchise that would eventually land in Ottawa as the Nationals, and a San Francisco entrant. At this time the WHA received another dose of good luck: the NHL stood still. A bold move on the part of the NHL—abandoning the reserve clause, for instance—would have likely spelled doom to the WHA. However, the NHL chose not to act, believing instead the WHA would collapse before ever starting play. It was an early game of bluffing that the NHL ultimately would lose.

The first half of 1972 was a busy time for the WHA. To stock its teams, a General Player Draft was held in February in which over 1,000 players from all levels (including Europe) were selected. Franchises were moving, as well. Days before the player draft, the San Francisco team, held by Gary Davidson and unlikely to ever play in the Bay Area, was sold to a Quebec City contingent and named the Nordiques. The Aeros transferred to Houston in April when a suitable arena could not be found in Dayton. Arena troubles also forced Miami to withdraw in April, while an illness to Bob Brownridge prompted Calgary's withdrawal that same month. In June, the Philadelphia Blazers and Cleveland Crusaders were formed to replace the Miami and Calgary franchises, respectively. Then the NHL finally acted, adding expansion franchises in Atlanta and Long Island. The Long Island expansion precluded the WHA from placing its New York team in the new Nassau Coliseum, a pivotal factor in the rapid demise of the WHA in New York and a rare victory for the NHL during this time.

By June, 1972, the WHA had signed a few dozen players to contracts. Bernie Parent was the first major star to make the move, signing with Miami-Philadelphia in April. However, the bulk of signees were fringe NHL players, minor leaguers and college players. The WHA landed its biggest star and gained instant viability in June, when Bobby Hull inked a five-year, $1-million contract with a $1-million signing bonus with the Winnipeg Jets. Hull, who admits he considered the Jets offer initially as a leverage tool to negotiate with the Black Hawks, could not help but be interested when these figures were presented to him. The signing of Hull virtually guaranteed the league's existence for that first season. In short order, many established NHL stars jumped to the new league, including John McKenzie, Derek Sanderson, J.C. Tremblay and Gerry Cheevers.

The WHA finally made its on-ice debut on October 11, 1972 in Ottawa, as the Nationals hosted the Alberta (Edmonton) Oilers. Five thousand fans half-filled the Ottawa Civic Centre as the Oilers defeated the Nats, 7–4. The hockey was a noticeable notch or two below the NHL, but the league had parity and showcased a number of players who previously had been buried on NHL depth charts. Andre Lacroix and Ron Ward broke through for 100-point seasons after having done little the previous year in the NHL. Tom Webster, Christian Bordeleau, Gary Veneruzzo and Danny Lawson also found a home in the WHA. The star players shined as well, acting as ambassadors for the league and helping draw crowds in the various arenas. The New England Whalers were the league's first champions and winners of the World Trophy (later named the Avco Cup when the Avco Financial Services Corporation subsidized the trophy).

The league was evolving as expected: some teams had strong leadership and good financial backing, other teams foundered on the edge of bankruptcy for much of the season. After the first year, Ottawa lost the Nationals to Toronto where the team was renamed the Toros. Philadelphia's Blazers left the substandard Philadelphia Civic Center for Vancouver's new Pacific Coliseum. The New York Raiders, perhaps the weakest financially of all the teams, were sold to an equally bereft set of owners and renamed the Golden Blades, only to fold partway into the following season. The Golden Blades were replaced by a temporary franchise, the Jersey Knights, that played its home games in an arena in Cherry Hill, New Jersey, that lacked a visitor's locker room.

Meanwhile, the two leagues had no correspondence except through the courts. A lawsuit filed by John McKenzie, attempting to fight the Boston Bruins' attempt to bind him to his NHL contract via the reserve clause, was acted upon on November 8, 1972, in Philadelphia. Judge Leon Higginbotham opined that the NHL could not use the option clause to bind its players, effectively rendering useless the reserve clause. Among other things, the opinion freed Bobby Hull to play, as he had sat out the first three weeks of the WHA's initial season awaiting results of the suit. With NHL president Clarence Campbell openly disavowing the WHA, and heavyweight owners such as Toronto's Harold Ballard and Jack Kent Cooke of Los Angeles absolutely unyielding in their enmity, no thawing in the icy relationship between the two leagues would be forthcoming. Still, many NHL players continued to jump to the new league, with stars Marc Tardif and Pat Stapleton joining up in 1973.

The biggest coup that year was the signing of hockey great Gordie Howe to a player contract with Houston in June, 1973. The Aeros, coached by Gordie's old Detroit teammate Bill Dineen, had drafted Gordie's sons Mark and Marty out of junior hockey in Toronto in May, 1973, by successfully arguing that they were professionals and thereby avoiding the policy of not drafting an amateur player before his 20th birthday (Mark was 19, Marty 18). Dineen approached Gordie about coming out of retirement and playing alongside his sons. Forty-five-year-old Gordie, fit as most men half his age and disenchanted in his figurehead role as vice president of the Red Wings, happily agreed. The move was met with derision by many in the hockey world, but Gordie proved them wrong. The rejuvenated elder Howe scored 100 points, threw some mean elbows and led the Aeros to the Avco Cup Championship in 1974.

Two new teams were added in 1974–75: the Indianapolis Racers and the Phoenix Roadrunners. Los Angeles moved to Detroit (later to move to Baltimore in a midseason flight) and the Jersey Knights became the San Diego Mariners. Frank Mahovlich, the third-leading goal scorer in NHL history at the time (behind Howe and Hull), was the biggest NHL star to move to the WHA in 1974 when he signed with the Toronto Toros. Also that year, the WHA began scouting and signing European stars. Previously the common belief was that the European players were too "soft" to survive the North American physical game. Winnipeg made the boldest moves, signing Swedes Anders Hedberg and Ulf Nilsson, and Finnish star Heikki Riihiranta. New England landed the Abrahamsson twins, Christer and Thommie, while Toronto signed the great Czechoslovakian star (and recent defector) Vaclav Nedomansky. The Europeans performed quite well, and in some cases were elite players in the league.

Houston dominated the 1974–75 season, easily winning its second Avco Cup title in May, 1975. However, there was much turnover in the league rolls. Chicago and Baltimore folded at the close of 1974–75 and were replaced by two expansion teams, the Denver Spurs and Cincinnati Stingers. Vancouver lost the Blazers to Calgary, with the team becoming the Cowboys and playing in the small Stampede Corral. The weakest of the franchises was a drain on the league, and when Denver folded after a brief sojourn to Ottawa in January, 1976, and Minnesota folded six weeks later, no replacement franchises were created. The league would never expand again. Winnipeg won its first of three Avco Cup titles in 1976, defeating Houston.

The 1976–77 season began with two franchise shifts: the Crusaders to St. Paul as the new Fighting Saints, and the Toros to Birmingham as the Bulls. Unfortunately, the new Fighting Saints folded quickly, lasting only 42 games, and other clubs such as Phoenix, San Diego and Calgary were in deep financial trouble. Only upon the ascendancy of John Ziegler to the NHL presidency in 1977 did the two leagues begin a dialogue for some sort of resolution. In the bidding war for talent, the two leagues were simply pricing themselves out of existence, and many teams in both leagues were struggling financially. New England's Howard Baldwin assumed the WHA's presidency in 1977 and toiled long hours to negotiate a merger with the NHL. The 1976–77 season ended with the Nordiques as champions, the loss of three more teams (Phoenix, San Diego and Calgary), and a strong sense of instability.

Merger was almost realized on two occasions. In May, 1977, an agreement that would have absorbed six of the WHA's eight teams into a fourth NHL division had majority support among NHL owners, but not the necessary three-quarters approval. In 1978, a less ambitious plan would have permitted Edmonton and New England to join the NHL immediately, followed by Winnipeg a year later. The exclusion of Quebec was a sore point: Montreal was unwilling to allow the Nordiques into its territory. The unpopular plan fell through with little overall support. In the meantime, the WHA played on, its existence a little more precarious each succeeding year.

The final two seasons were highlighted by a crop of young superstars and lowlighted by franchise failures. Houston folded and sold most of its players to Winnipeg in July, 1978, while Indianapolis staggered partway into the final season before bowing out in December, 1978. Winnipeg dominated the WHA in 1977–78, breezing to its second Avco Cup win behind the remarkable Hull-Nilsson-Hedberg line. The arrival of Wayne Gretzky to Edmonton by way of Indianapolis in 1978 catapulted the Oilers to the league's best record in 1978–79, but a more experienced Jets club defeated the Oilers for the final Avco Cup championship in 1979. Also debuting in the WHA during 1977–78 and 1978–79 were Rob Ramage, Rod Langway, Ken Linseman, Mike Liut, Mike Gartner, Rick Vaive, Mark Messier and Michel Goulet.

The two leagues finally came to an agreement on March 22, 1979, when the NHL approved the acceptance of four WHA teams by a 14–3 vote, effective for 1979–80. The four teams admitted were Edmonton, Winnipeg, New England and Quebec, while Birmingham and Cincinnati were given cash settlements to fold. Prior to the successful vote was an unsuccessful 12–5 vote that didn't meet the required three-quarters majority. Two of the nay votes were by Montreal and Vancouver, incensing Canadian fans who could not believe two of their own cities would deny entrance to three more Canadian franchises to the NHL (Toronto also voted no, but Harold Ballard's long-time opposition to any resolution was not unexpected). Vancouver was assured its legitimate scheduling concerns would be dealt with in order to gain its yes vote to the merger. Montreal, on the other hand, was steadfast in its refusal to permit Quebec to join. Canadian fans responded with the famous "beer boycott." The Canadiens, owned by Molson Breweries, changed their vote and avoided a public relations nightmare. The WHA ceased business at the end of the 1978–79 season.

The World Hockey Association was an exciting, brash and shamelessly self-promoting circuit that functioned on the continual brink of collapse, sometimes not sure of its own existence beyond the next round of paychecks. It demonstrated that two major hockey leagues were not feasible in the long term, took advantage of untapped European and American-born talent, brought big-league hockey to new cities and boosted players' salaries.

WHA Career Totals

Scott Surgent

KEY TO WHA TEAMS: Alb: Alberta Oilers (72-73); Bir: Birmingham Bulls (76-79); Chi: Chicago Cougars (72-75); Cgy: Calgary Cowboys (75-77); Cin: Cincinnati Stingers (75-79); Cle: Cleveland Crusaders (72-76); D-O: Denver Spurs-Ottawa Civics (75-76); Edm: Edmonton Oilers (73-79); Hou: Houston Aeros (72-78); Ind: Indianapolis Racers (74-79); LA: Los Angeles Sharks (72-74); M-B: Michigan Stags / Baltimore Blades (74-75); Min: Minnesota Fighting Saints (72-77, both versions); NE: New England Whalers (72-79); NY: New York Raiders (72-73); NY-J: New York Golden Blades / Jersey Knights (73-74); Ott: Ottawa Nationals (72-73); Phi: Philadelphia Blazers (72-73); Phx: Phoenix Roadrunners (74-77); Que: Quebec Nordiques (72-79); SD: San Diego Mariners (74-77); Tor: Toronto Toros (73-76); Van: Vancouver Blazers (73-75); Wpg: Winnipeg Jets (72-79). (G) = goaltender.

Scoring

			Regular Season					Playoffs				
Name	**Seasons**	**Team(s)**	**GP**	**G**	**A**	**Pts.**	**PIM**	**GP**	**G**	**A**	**Pts.**	**PIM**
— A —												
Bruce Abbey	75-76	Cincinnati	17	1	0	1	12	...	...	...	...	...
Dennis Abgrall	76-68	Cincinnati	145	36	50	86	35	4	2	0	2	5
Thommie Abrahamsson	74-77	New England	203	28	67	95	126	22	2	7	9	15
Christer Abrahamsson (G)	74-77	New England	101	0	1	1	6	3	0	0	0	0
Jim Adair	73-74	Vancouver	70	12	17	29	10	...	...	...	...	...
Ray Adduono	73-78	Cle, SD, Min, Ind	221	45	152	197	67	28	12	18	30	38
Rick Adduono	78-79	Birmingham	80	20	33	53	67	...	...	...	...	...
Kevin Ahearn	72-73	New England	78	20	22	42	18	14	1	2	3	9
Chris Ahrens	77-78	Edmonton	4	0	0	0	15	...	...	...	...	...
Claire Alexander	78-79	Edmonton	54	8	23	31	16	...	...	...	...	...
Jeff Allen	77-78	Cincinnati	2	0	0	0	0	...	...	...	...	...
Steve Alley	77-79	Birmingham	105	25	36	61	47	5	1	0	1	10
Mike Amodeo	72-79	Ott, Tor, Wpg	300	11	65	76	273	27	1	7	8	59
Ron C. Anderson	72-74	Alb, Edm	92	19	17	36	49	...	...	...	...	...
Ron F. Anderson	72-75	Chicago	114	3	35	38	44	...	...	...	...	...
Steve Andrascik	74-76	Ind, M-B, Cin	97	9	13	22	79	...	...	...	...	...
Paul Andrea	72-74	Cleveland	135	36	48	84	26	14	3	8	11	4
Lou Angotti	74-75	Chicago	26	2	5	7	9	...	...	...	...	...
Mike Antonovich	72-79	Min, Edm, NE	486	182	188	370	191	57	21	20	41	28
John Arbour	72-77	Min, D-O, Cgy	335	30	164	194	568	28	3	13	16	62
Michel Archambault	72-73	Quebec	57	12	25	37	36	...	...	...	...	...
Yves Archambault (G)	72-74	Phi, Van	11	0	1	1	0	3	0	0	0	0
Danny Arndt	75-78	NE, Edm, Bir	120	16	23	39	21	8	0	0	0	0
Bob Ash	72-75	Wpg, Ind	199	6	46	52	88	17	1	4	5	6
Ron Ashton	74-75	Winnipeg	36	1	3	4	66	...	...	...	...	...
Freeman "Duke" Asmundson	72-76	Winnipeg	260	16	54	70	211	29	4	6	10	17
Steve Atkinson	75-76	Toronto	52	2	6	8	22	...	...	...	...	...
Serge Aubry (G)	72-77	Que, Cin	142	0	4	4	88	3	0	0	0	0
— B —												
Ralph Backstrom	73-77	Chi, D-O, NE	304	100	153	253	104	38	10	18	28	12
Ken Baird	72-78	Alb, Edm, Cgy, Wpg	333	91	99	190	498	16	4	6	10	30
Blake Ball	73	Cleveland	0	0	0	0	0	2	0	0	0	2
Terry Ball	72-77	Min, Cle, Cin, Bir	305	28	134	162	174	28	5	8	13	14
Garnet "Ace" Bailey	78-79	Edmonton	38	5	4	9	22	2	0	0	0	4
Dave Balon	73-74	Quebec	9	0	0	0	2	...	...	...	...	...
Bryon Baltimore	74-79	Chi, D-O, Ind, Cin	331	18	72	90	390	...	...	...	...	...
Butch Barber	72-74	Chi, NY-J	78	4	19	23	41	...	...	...	...	...
Bob Barlow	74-75	Phoenix	51	6	20	26	8	...	...	...	...	...
Doug Barrie	72-77	Alb, Edm	351	37	122	159	620	12	1	1	2	22
Jamie Bateman	74-76	San Diego	31	1	3	4	100	...	...	...	...	...
Andy Bathgate	74-75	Vancouver	11	1	6	7	2	...	...	...	...	...
Paul Baxter	74-79	Cle, Que	290	25	88	113	962	30	6	11	17	84
Frank Beaton	75-78	Cin, Edm, Bir	153	12	21	33	614	10	2	2	4	31
Norm Beaudin	72-76	Winnipeg	309	97	155	252	69	31	18	19	37	14
Serge Beaudoin	73-79	Van, Phx, Cin, Bir	332	20	103	123	519	10	2	0	2	56
Alain Beaule	73-75	Que, Wpg	154	8	57	65	136	...	...	...	...	...
John Bennett	72-73	Philadelphia	34	4	6	10	18	...	...	...	...	...
Wendell Bennett	74-75	Phoenix	67	4	15	19	92	...	...	...	...	...
Jim Benzelock	72-76	Alb, Chi, Que	166	18	27	45	72	21	2	2	4	36
Yves Bergeron	72-73	Quebec	65	14	19	33	32	...	...	...	...	...

Name	Seasons	Team(s)	Regular Season GP	G	A	Pts.	PIM	Playoffs GP	G	A	Pts.	PIM
Thommie Bergman	74-78	Winnipeg	237	22	97	119	261	13	3	10	13	8
Bill Berglund (G)	73-75	New England	5	0	0	0	0	...	...	...	...	...
Jean Bernier	74-78	Quebec	261	17	84	101	50	32	3	8	11	4
Serge Bernier	73-79	Quebec	417	230	336	566	486	50	28	46	74	41
Doug Berry	78-79	Edmonton	29	6	3	9	4	...	...	...	...	...
Larry Bignell	75-76	Denver/Ottawa	41	5	5	10	43	...	...	...	...	...
Gilles Bilodeau	75-79	Tor, Bir, Que	143	7	15	22	570	6	0	0	0	52
Yvon Bilodeau	75-76	Calgary	4	0	0	0	2	...	...	...	...	...
Les Binkley (G)	72-76	Ott, Tor	81	0	0	0	0	10	0	0	0	0
Milt Black	72-75	Winnipeg	189	28	31	59	55	18	2	4	6	2
Don Blackburn	72-75	New England	146	40	74	114	40	12	3	6	9	6
Bill Blackwood	77-78	Indianapolis	3	0	0	0	0	...	...	...	...	...
Jacques Blain	72-73	Quebec	70	1	10	11	78	...	...	...	...	...
Bob Blanchet (G)	74-76	San Diego	4	0	0	0	0	...	...	...	...	...
Bernie Blanchette	72-73	Chi, Alb	47	7	7	14	10	...	...	...	...	...
Ken Block	72-79	NY, NY-J, SD, Ind	455	16	187	203	192	9	0	2	2	6
Frank Blum (G)	72-74	Ott, Tor, Wpg	7	0	0	0	0	2	0	0	0	0
Greg Boddy	76-77	SD, Edm	64	2	19	21	60	4	1	2	3	14
Mike Boland	72-73	Ott	41	1	15	16	44	1	0	0	0	12
Dan Bolduc	75-78	New England	88	15	13	28	51	30	3	10	13	8
J.Kerry Bond	74-76	Indianapolis	86	24	15	39	32	7	1	0	1	11
Christian Bordeleau	72-79	Wpg, Que	412	179	325	504	162	53	16	34	50	16
Paulin Bordeleau	76-79	Quebec	234	101	76	177	125	31	17	15	32	14
Don Borgeson	74-76	Phx, D-O, NE	145	59	52	111	68	8	1	2	3	2
Henry Boucha	75-76	Minnesota	36	15	20	35	47	...	...	...	...	...
Bruce Boudreau	75-76	Minnesota	30	3	6	9	4	...	...	...	...	...
Michel Boudreau	72-74	Phi, Van	36	8	7	15	4	2	0	0	0	0
Andre Boudrias	76-78	Quebec	140	22	48	70	34	28	3	14	17	10
Brian Bowles	75-76	Cleveland	3	0	0	0	0	...	...	...	...	...
Kirk Bowman	73-74	Los Angeles	10	0	2	2	0	...	...	...	...	...
Bob Boyd	73-75	Minnesota	54	1	14	15	35	7	0	0	0	4
Jim Boyd	74-77	Phx, Cgy	169	49	80	129	68	10	4	3	7	4
Wally Boyer	72-73	Winnipeg	69	6	28	34	27	14	4	2	6	4
Dean Boylan	73-75	NY-J, SD	64	1	5	6	122	...	...	...	...	...
Curt Brackenbury	73-79	Chi, Min, Que	265	41	50	91	753	...	...	...	...	...
Brian Bradley	72-75	NY, NY-J, SD	180	41	61	102	38	6	0	1	1	2
Duane Bray	76-77	Phoenix	46	2	6	8	62	...	...	...	...	...
Gary Bredin	74-76	Ind, M-B, D-O, SD	143	26	31	57	49	...	...	...	...	...
Carl Brewer	73-74	Toronto	77	2	23	25	42	12	0	4	4	11
Doug Brindley	72-74	Cleveland	103	28	20	48	19	14	0	1	1	2
Ken Broderick (G)	76-78	Que, Edm	73	0	3	3	2	5	0	0	0	0
Richard Brodeur (G)	72-79	Quebec	300	0	10	10	9	51	0	2	2	0
Gary Bromley (G)	76-78	Cgy, Wpg	67	0	1	1	2	5	0	0	0	2
Andy Brown (G)	74-77	Indianapolis	86	0	4	4	92	...	...	...	...	...
Arnie Brown	74-75	M-B, Van	60	3	5	8	40	...	...	...	...	...
Bob Brown	72-74	Phi, NY, NY-J	80	7	17	24	46	...	...	...	...	...
Ken Brown (G)	72-75	Alb, Edm	52	0	1	1	4	...	...	...	...	...
Jeff Brubaker	78-79	New England	12	0	0	0	19	3	0	0	0	12
Ron Buchanan	72-76	Cle, Edm, Ind	205	83	102	185	48	14	7	3	10	2
Brad Buetow	73-74	Cleveland	25	0	0	0	4	...	...	...	...	...
Randy Burchell (G)	76-77	Indianapolis	5	0	1	1	0	...	...	...	...	...
Don Burgess	72-79	Phi, Van, SD, Ind	446	107	122	229	87	22	4	9	13	4
Ron Busniuk	74-78	Min, NE, Edm	283	9	64	73	762	39	2	5	7	132
Bill Butters	74-78	Min, Hoe, Edm, NE	217	4	51	55	530	34	1	6	7	87
Brian Bye	75-76	San Diego	1	0	0	0	0	...	...	...	...	...
Mike Byers	72-76	LA, NE, SD	266	83	74	157	40	25	10	11	21	20
— C —												
Brian Cadle	72-73	Winnipeg	56	4	4	8	39	3	0	0	0	0
Terry Caffery	72-76	NE, Cgy	164	59	111	170	30	8	3	7	10	0
Larry Cahan	72-74	Chicago	78	1	10	11	46	...	...	...	...	...
Brett Callighen	76-79	NE, Edm	213	66	95	161	280	23	9	13	22	38
Bryan Campbell	72-78	Phi, Van, Cin, Ind, Edm	433	123	253	376	219	16	6	4	10	16
Colin Campbell	73-74	Vancouver	78	3	20	23	191	...	...	...	...	...
Scott Campbell	77-79	Hou, Wpg	149	11	44	55	364	16	1	3	4	33
Rychard Campeau	72-74	Phi, Van	82	1	18	19	74	4	1	0	1	17
Jim Cardiff	72-75	Phi, Van	200	4	47	51	398	4	0	0	0	11
Steve Cardwell	73-75	Min, Cle	152	32	36	68	227	15	0	1	1	34
Wayne Carleton	72-77	Ott, Tor, NE, Edm, Bir	290	132	180	312	135	25	8	21	29	24
Brian Carlin	72-74	Alb, Edm	70	13	22	35	6	...	...	...	...	...
Jack Carlson	74-79	Min, Edm, NE	272	36	51	87	694	28	3	4	7	68
Jeff Carlson	75-76	Minnesota	7	0	1	1	14	...	...	...	...	...

Name	Seasons	Team(s)	Regular Season					Playoffs				
			GP	G	A	Pts.	PIM	GP	G	A	Pts.	PIM
Steve Carlson	75-79	Min, NE, Edm	173	33	47	80	132	29	3	8	11	23
Steve Carlyle	72-76	Alb, Edm	218	13	59	72	109	5	0	1	1	4
Alain Caron	72-75	Que, M-B	195	82	50	132	30	...	...	...	...	...
Jacques Caron (G)	75-77	Cle, Cin	26	0	2	2	0	1	0	0	0	0
Greg Carroll	76-78	Cin, NE	151	30	66	96	116	4	1	2	3	0
Jean Yves Cartier	72-73	Quebec	15	0	3	3	8	...	...	...	...	...
Tony Cassolato	76-79	SD, Bir	184	44	44	88	137	7	0	0	0	8
Bob Charlebois	72-76	Ott, NE	188	32	50	82	34	16	2	1	3	8
Claude Chartre	72-75	NY, NY-J, M-B	18	2	3	5	0	...	...	...	...	...
Gerry Cheevers (G)	72-76	Cleveland	191	0	1	1	134	19	0	0	0	0
Mike Chernoff	73-75	Vancouver	39	11	10	21	4	...	...	...	...	...
Jack Chipchase	72-73	Philadelphia	3	0	0	0	2	...	...	...	...	...
Ron Chipperfield	74-79	Van, Cgy, Edm	369	153	177	330	189	28	15	15	30	14
Keith Christianson	72-74	Minnesota	138	23	55	78	60	15	1	1	2	2
Kim Clackson	75-79	Ind, Wpg	271	6	39	45	932	33	0	6	6	138
Gordie Clark	78-79	Cincinnati	21	3	3	6	2	...	...	...	...	...
Jim Clarke	75-76	Phoenix	59	1	9	10	57	...	...	...	...	...
Ray Clearwater	72-77	Cle, Min	214	27	77	104	141	18	2	3	5	10
Ron Climie	72-77	Ott, Edm, NE	249	98	106	204	68	15	4	0	4	4
Real "Buddy" Cloutier	74-79	Quebec	369	283	283	566	169	48	33	30	63	25
Brian Coates	73-78	Chi, Ind, Cin	202	42	43	85	85	21	0	3	3	41
Howie Colborne	73-74	Edmonton	2	0	0	0	0	...	...	...	...	...
Jim Cole	76-77	Winnipeg	2	0	1	1	0	...	...	...	...	...
Brian Conacher	72-73	Ott	69	8	19	27	32	5	1	3	4	4
Gary Connelly	73-74	Chicago	4	0	1	1	2	...	...	...	...	...
Wayne Connelly	72-77	Min, Cle, Cgy, Edm	366	167	162	329	93	36	16	15	31	16
Cam Connor	74-78	Phx, Hou	274	83	88	171	904	23	5	4	9	92
Mike Conroy	75-76	Cleveland	4	0	1	1	0	...	...	...	...	...
Charles Constantin	74-78	Que, Ind	192	28	35	63	229	20	0	2	2	19
Gaye Cooley (G)	76	New England	0	0	0	0	0	1	0	0	0	0
Michel Cormier	74-77	Phoenix	182	70	69	139	52	5	1	0	1	2
Jim Corsi (G)	77-79	Quebec	63	0	1	1	2	2	0	0	0	0
Alain Cote	77-79	Quebec	106	17	18	35	31	15	1	2	3	2
Roger Cote	72-75	Alb, Edm, Ind	156	3	14	17	104	2	0	0	0	0
Tom Cottringer (G)	72-73	Philadelphia	2	0	0	0	0	...	...	...	...	...
Norm Cournoyer	73-77	Cle, SD	32	4	7	11	14	...	...	...	...	...
Rich Coutu (G)	73-76	Chi, Cin	24	0	0	0	0	...	...	...	...	...
Bart Crashley	72-74	Los Angeles	148	22	53	75	26	6	0	2	2	2
Glen Critch	75-76	Indianapolis	3	0	0	0	0	...	...	...	...	...
Jim Cross	77-78	Edmonton	2	0	0	0	0	...	...	...	...	...
Keith Crowder	78-79	Birmingham	5	1	0	1	17	...	...	...	...	...
Paul Crowley	75-76	Toronto	4	0	0	0	0	...	...	...	...	...
Steve Cuddie	72-75	Wpg, Tor	221	17	47	64	235	26	1	9	10	32
John Cunniff	72-76	NE, Que	64	10	10	20	35	18	2	2	4	8
Gary Cunningham	73-74	Edmonton	2	0	0	0	0	...	...	...	...	...
Rick Cunningham	72-77	Ott, Tor, Bir	323	23	91	114	458	21	1	6	7	33
Mike Curran (G)	72-77	Minnesota	130	0	1	1	60	7	0	0	0	0
Paul Curtis	74-75	M-B	76	4	15	19	32	...	...	...	...	...
— D —												
Bob D'Alvise	75-76	Toronto	59	5	8	13	10	...	...	...	...	...
Joe Daley (G)	72-79	Winnipeg	308	0	10	10	45	49	0	1	1	20
John Danby	72-76	New England	150	16	25	41	16	19	1	1	2	0
Richard David	78-79	Quebec	14	0	4	4	4	...	...	...	...	...
Blair Davidson	76-77	Phoenix	2	0	0	0	2	...	...	...	...	...
Bill Davis	77-79	Winnipeg	17	1	2	3	2	...	...	...	...	...
Kelly Davis	78-79	Cincinnati	18	0	1	1	20	...	...	...	...	...
Ernest "Butch" Deadmarsh	74-78	Van, Cgy, Min, Edm, Cin	255	63	66	129	570	8	0	1	1	14
Barry Dean	76-77	Phoenix	71	9	25	34	110	...	...	...	...	...
Dave Debol	77-79	Cincinnati	68	13	29	42	11	...	...	...	...	...
Michel Deguise (G)	73-76	Quebec	50	0	2	2	0	...	...	...	...	...
Ray Delorenzi	74-76	Van, Cgy	42	8	12	20	4	...	...	...	...	...
Ron Delorme	75-76	Denver/Ottawa	22	1	3	4	28	...	...	...	...	...
Ab DeMarco	77-78	Edmonton	47	6	8	14	20	1	0	0	0	0
Brian Derksen	73-74	Los Angeles	1	0	0	0	2	...	...	...	...	...
Andre Deschamps	76-77	Calgary	9	1	2	3	19	...	...	...	...	...
Norm Descoteaux	72-74	Quebec	37	1	7	8	6	...	...	...	...	...
Ken Desjardine	72-76	Que, Ind, Cgy	174	4	24	28	148	...	...	...	...	...
Gerry Desjardins (G)	74-75	M-B	41	0	1	1	13	...	...	...	...	...
Kevin Devine	74-79	SD, Ind, Que	288	74	81	155	411	28	5	4	9	64
Bob Dillabough	72-73	Cleveland	72	8	8	16	8	9	1	0	1	0
Wayne Dillon	73-79	Tor, Bir	212	71	128	199	78	18	9	10	19	13

Name	Seasons	Team(s)	Regular Season GP	G	A	Pts.	PIM	Playoffs GP	G	A	Pts.	PIM
Michel Dion (G)	74-79	Ind, Cin	149	0	0	0	30	7	0	0	0	0
Bob Dobek	75-77	San Diego	72	10	18	28	19	16	1	2	3	4
Gary Donaldson	76-77	Houston	5	0	0	0	6	...	...	...	...	...
John Donnelly	72-73	Ott	15	1	1	2	44	...	...	...	...	...
Pat Donnelly	75-76	Cincinnati	23	5	7	12	4	...	...	...	...	...
Peter Donnelly (G)	72-76	NY, Van, Que	100	0	1	1	11	...	...	...	...	...
Jim Dorey	72-79	NE, Tor, Que	431	52	232	284	617	51	5	33	38	131
Dave Dornseif	77-79	Ind, Cin	4	0	1	1	0	...	...	...	...	...
Kent Douglas	72-73	NY	60	3	15	18	74	...	...	...	...	...
Jordy Douglas	78-79	New England	51	6	10	16	15	10	4	0	4	23
Gary Doyle (G)	73-74	Edmonton	1	0	0	0	0	...	...	...	...	...
Peter Driscoll	74-79	Van, Cgy, Que, Ind, Edm	326	90	101	191	577	23	3	11	14	49
Dave Dryden (G)	74-79	Chi, Edm	242	0	14	14	6	18	0	0	0	0
Norm Dube	76-79	Quebec	148	33	62	95	29	24	5	14	19	17
Michel Dubois	75-77	Ind, Que	59	2	5	7	127	2	0	1	1	0
Rick Dudley	75-79	Cincinnati	270	131	146	277	516	4	0	1	1	7
Guy Dufour	72-74	Quebec	83	30	25	55	32	...	...	...	...	...
Rich Dumas (G)	74-75	Chicago	1	0	0	0	0	...	...	...	...	...
David Dunn	76-78	Winnipeg	106	9	31	40	218	29	5	6	11	23
Steve Durbano	77-78	Birmingham	45	6	4	10	284	4	0	2	2	16
Ed Dyck (G)	74-75	Indianapolis	32	0	0	0	6	...	...	...	...	...
— E —												
Tom Earl	72-77	New England	346	40	56	96	116	46	3	11	14	28
Tom Edur	73-76	Cleveland	217	17	79	96	116	13	3	4	7	0
Grant Erickson	72-76	Cle, Phx	266	54	75	129	79	19	2	5	7	2
Bengt "Rollie" Eriksson	78-79	Winnipeg	33	5	10	15	2	10	1	4	5	0
Chris Evans	75-78	Cgy, Bir, Que	204	11	51	62	138	10	5	5	10	4
Bill Evo	74-76	M-B, Edm, Cle	97	14	18	32	64	...	...	...	...	...
— F —												
Bob Falkenberg	72-78	Alb, Edm, SD	377	14	74	88	183	29	1	5	6	24
Craig Falkman	72-73	Minnesota	44	1	5	6	12	...	...	...	...	...
Richard Farda	74-77	Tor, Bir	177	34	86	120	12	...	...	...	...	...
Tony Featherstone	74-76	Toronto	108	29	45	74	31	6	2	1	3	2
Mike Fedorko	76-77	Houston	4	0	0	0	0	...	...	...	...	...
Norm Ferguson	72-78	NY, NY-J, SD, Edm	436	181	184	365	45	26	10	9	19	9
John Fisher	72-73	Alberta	39	0	5	5	0	...	...	...	...	...
Bob Fitchner	73-79	Ind, Edm, Que	414	68	139	207	501	37	6	12	18	34
Reg Fleming	72-74	Chicago	119	25	57	82	144	12	0	4	4	12
Bill Flett	76-79	Edmonton	195	103	84	187	68	15	5	4	9	4
Peter Folco	75-77	Tor, Bir	21	1	8	9	15	...	...	...	...	...
Rick Foley	75-76	Toronto	11	1	2	3	6	...	...	...	...	...
Len Fontaine	74-75	M-B	21	1	8	9	6	...	...	...	...	...
Val Fonteyne	72-74	Alb, Edm	149	16	45	61	4	5	1	0	1	0
Dave Forbes	78-79	Cincinnati	73	6	5	11	83	3	0	1	1	7
Mike Ford	74-78	Wpg, Cgy	233	33	99	132	172	34	5	25	30	20
Connie Forey	73-74	Chicago	1	0	0	0	0	...	...	...	...	...
Dave Fortier	77-78	Indianapolis	51	1	15	16	86	...	...	...	...	...
Florent Fortier	75-76	Quebec	4	1	1	2	0	1	0	0	0	0
Joe Fortunato	76-77	Edmonton	1	0	0	0	0	...	...	...	...	...
Nick Fotiu	74-76	New England	110	5	4	9	238	20	5	2	7	84
Rick Fraser	74-75	Indianapolis	4	0	0	0	2	...	...	...	...	...
John French	72-78	NE, ED, Ind	420	108	192	300	130	44	14	25	39	6
Robbie Ftorek	74-79	Phx, Cin	373	216	307	523	365	13	6	10	16	10
— G —												
Gord Gallant	73-77	Min, Que, Bir	273	31	59	90	849	414	2	2	4	98
Gary Gambucci	74-76	Minnesota	112	29	24	53	33	12	4	0	4	6
George Gardner (G)	72-74	LA, Van	79	0	0	0	0	3	0	0	0	0
J. C. Garneau	74-75	Quebec	17	0	5	5	27	...	...	...	...	...
John Garrett (G)	73-79	Min, Tor, Bir, NE	323	0	7	7	75	32	0	0	0	0
Mike Gartner	78-79	Cincinnati	78	27	25	52	123	3	0	0	0	2
Ron Garwasiuk	73-74	Los Angeles	51	6	13	19	100	...	...	...	...	...
J. Marty Gateman	75-76	New England	12	0	1	1	6	...	...	...	...	...
Andre Gaudette	72-75	Quebec	221	61	105	166	34	9	0	1	1	0
Jean Gauthier	72-73	NY	31	2	1	3	21	...	...	...	...	...
Sam Gellard	72-74	Phi, Van	28	7	4	11	15	...	...	...	...	...
Jean-Guy Gendron	72-74	Quebec	127	28	41	69	155	...	...	...	...	...
Daniel Geoffrion	78-79	Quebec	77	12	14	26	74	4	1	2	3	2
Wes George	78-79	Ind, Edm	12	4	2	6	34	...	...	...	...	...
Brian Gibbons	72-76	Ott, Tor, D-O	226	15	88	103	251	17	3	7	10	22
Gerard Gibbons	73-76	Toronto	31	2	4	6	30	1	0	0	0	0

Name	Seasons	Team(s)	Regular Season GP	G	A	Pts.	PIM	Playoffs GP	G	A	Pts.	PIM
Jack Gibson	72-76	Ott, Tor	122	38	21	59	108	13	2	3	5	16
John Gibson	78-79	Winnipeg	9	0	1	1	5	...	...	...	...	...
Ed Gilbert	78-79	Cincinnati	29	3	3	6	40	...	...	...	...	...
Jeannot Gilbert	73-75	Quebec	133	24	60	84	32	11	3	6	9	2
Andre Gill (G)	72-74	Chicago	46	0	0	0	6	11	0	0	0	0
Bill Gilligan	77-79	Cincinnati	128	27	40	67	113	3	1	0	1	0
Russ Gillow (G)	72-76	LA, SD	109	0	1	1	12	9	0	0	0	0
Tom Gilmore	72-75	LA, Edm	201	48	60	108	439	10	2	7	9	17
Dave Gilmour	75-76	Calgary	1	0	0	0	0	...	...	...	...	...
Gaston Gingras	78-79	Birmingham	60	13	21	34	35	...	...	...	...	...
Rejean Giroux	72-74	Quebec	71	15	18	33	55	...	...	...	...	...
David Given	74-75	Vancouver	1	0	0	0	0	...	...	...	...	...
Brian Glenwright	72-74	Chicago	63	5	7	12	0	...	...	...	...	...
Alan Globensky	72-76	Quebec	43	1	2	3	18	...	...	...	...	...
Bill Goldsworthy	77-79	Ind, Edm	49	12	12	24	24	4	1	1	2	11
Bill Goldthorpe	73-76	Min, M-B, SD, D-O	33	1	0	1	87	3	0	0	0	25
Frank Golembrosky	72-73	Phi, Que	60	8	12	20	44	...	...	...	...	...
Don Gordon	73-75	LA, Chi	94	17	15	32	43	18	4	8	12	4
Dave Gorman	74-79	Phx, Bir	260	56	83	139	187	9	1	3	4	24
Rich Gosselin	78-79	Winnipeg	3	0	0	0	0	...	...	...	...	...
Michel Goulet	78-79	Birmingham	78	28	30	58	65	...	...	...	...	...
Ron Grahame (G)	73-77	Houston	143	0	3	3	2	36	0	2	2	0
Bill Gratton	75-76	Calgary	6	0	1	1	2	...	...	...	...	...
Gilles Gratton (G)	72-75	Ott, Tor	161	0	9	9	46	13	0	0	0	0
Jean-Guy Gratton	72-75	Winnipeg	188	31	41	72	52	14	1	1	2	4
John Gravel	72-73	Philadelphia	8	1	3	4	0	...	...	...	...	...
John Gray	74-79	Phx, Hou, Wpg	363	146	146	292	458	23	3	8	11	37
Ted Green	72-79	NE, Wpg	452	42	138	180	304	58	2	16	18	62
Bruce Greig	76-79	Cgy, Cin, Ind	60	7	9	16	131	...	...	...	...	...
Richard Grenier	76-77	Quebec	34	11	9	20	4	...	...	...	...	...
Gary Gresdal	75-76	Quebec	2	0	1	1	5	1	0	0	0	14
Wayne Gretzky	78-79	Ind, Edm	80	46	64	110	19	13	10	10	20	2
Don Grierson	72-74	Houston	143	33	40	73	128	17	1	5	6	29
Chris Grigg (G)	75-76	Denver/Ottawa	2	0	0	0	0	...	...	...	...	...
Danny Gruen	74-77	M-B, Wpg, Cle, Min, Cgy	181	56	61	117	185	3	2	0	2	0
Robert Guindon	72-79	Que, Wpg	461	112	145	257	156	65	24	19	43	33
Pierre Guite	72-79	Que, M-B, Edm, Cin	377	92	105	197	585	22	6	1	7	29
Walter "Bud" Gulka	74-75	Vancouver	5	1	0	1	10	...	...	...	...	...
Bengt-Ake Gustafsson	79	Edmonton	0	0	0	0	0	2	1	2	3	0

—H—

Name	Seasons	Team(s)	Regular Season GP	G	A	Pts.	PIM	Playoffs GP	G	A	Pts.	PIM
Derek Haas	75-76	Calgary	30	5	9	14	6	1	0	0	0	0
Matti Hagman	77-78	Quebec	53	25	31	56	16	...	...	...	...	...
Larry Hale	72-78	Houston	413	11	97	108	216	65	4	15	19	22
Del Hall	75-78	Phx, Cin, Edm	186	89	88	177	44	5	2	3	5	0
Murray Hall	72-76	Houston	312	96	125	221	155	54	21	17	38	32
Al Hamilton	72-79	Alb, Edm	454	53	258	311	492	26	5	11	16	29
Ted Hampson	72-76	Min, Que	305	60	144	204	51	33	8	14	22	18
Alf Handrahan	77-78	Cincinnati	14	1	3	4	42	...	...	...	...	...
Merv Haney	72-73	Ott	7	0	1	1	4	...	...	...	...	...
Alan Hangsleben	74-79	New England	334	36	73	109	437	47	4	12	16	97
Craig Hanmer	74-75	Indianapolis	27	1	0	1	15	...	...	...	...	...
John Hanna	72-73	Cleveland	65	6	20	26	68	...	...	...	...	...
Ron Hansis	76-78	Houston	100	17	12	29	57	14	2	2	4	8
Dave Hanson	76-79	Min, NE, Bir	103	13	40	53	497	6	0	1	1	48
Nick Harbaruk	74-77	Indianapolis	181	45	44	89	80	13	3	1	4	10
Joe Hardy	72-75	Cle, Chi, Ind, SD	210	46	94	140	201	24	4	10	14	13
Jim Hargreaves	73-76	Wpg, Ind, SD	174	12	20	32	151	15	1	0	1	8
Ted Hargreaves	73-74	Winnipeg	74	7	12	19	15	4	0	1	1	10
Derek Harker	72-73	Alb, Phi	28	0	5	5	46	...	...	...	...	...
George "Duke" Harris	72-75	Hou, Chi	193	53	47	100	52	28	7	7	14	6
Hugh Harris	73-78	NE, Phx, Van, Cgy, Ind, Cin	336	107	174	281	241	9	2	5	7	8
Jim Harrison	72-76	Alb, Edm, Cle	231	117	152	269	360	8	1	3	4	13
Richard Hart	76-77	Birmingham	4	0	0	0	0	...	...	...	...	...
Craig Hartsburg	78-79	Birmingham	77	9	40	49	73	...	...	...	...	...
Michel Harvey	72-73	Quebec	40	6	13	19	14	...	...	...	...	...
Ed Hatoum	72-74	Phi, Van	52	4	13	17	10	...	...	...	...	...
Murray Heatley	73-76	Min, Ind	156	48	54	102	86	10	1	0	1	2
Paul Heaver	75-77	Tor, Bir	71	2	12	14	83	...	...	...	...	...
Clay Hebenton (G)	75-77	Phoenix	58	0	0	0	2	...	...	...	...	...
Anders Hedberg	74-78	Winnipeg	286	236	222	458	201	42	35	28	63	30
Howie Heggedal	72-73	Los Angeles	8	2	1	3	0	1	0	0	0	0

Name	Seasons	Team(s)	Regular Season GP	G	A	Pts.	PIM	Playoffs GP	G	A	Pts.	PIM
Bill Heindl	73-74	Cleveland	67	4	14	18	4	5	0	1	1	2
Earl Heiskala	72-74	Los Angeles	94	14	23	37	195	...	...	...	...	...
Paul Henderson	74-79	Tor, Bir	360	140	143	283	112	5	1	1	2	0
Pierre Henry	72-73	Philadelphia	19	2	3	5	13	...	...	...	...	...
Don Herriman	72-75	Phi, NY-J, Edm	155	36	71	107	143	4	1	0	1	14
Bill Hicke	72-73	Alberta	72	14	24	38	16	...	...	...	...	...
Pat Hickey	73-75	Toronto	152	61	63	124	102	17	3	4	7	16
Glenn Hicks	78-79	Winnipeg	69	6	10	16	48	7	1	1	2	4
Larry Hillman	73-76	Cle, Wpg	192	6	49	55	182	17	1	5	6	40
Wayne Hillman	73-75	Cleveland	126	3	16	19	88	10	0	2	2	18
Andre Hinse	73-77	Hou, Phx	256	102	151	253	69	42	15	16	31	28
Jamie Hislop	76-79	Cincinnati	206	61	102	163	68	7	2	5	7	5
Mike Hobin	75-77	Phoenix	77	18	19	37	16	...	...	...	...	...
Ted Hodgson	72-74	Cle, LA	107	18	34	52	121	9	1	3	4	13
Ed Hoekstra	72-74	Houston	97	13	28	41	12	9	1	2	3	0
Dale Hoganson	73-79	Que, Bir	378	30	161	191	186	27	2	6	8	15
Paul Hoganson (G)	73-78	LA, M-B, NE, Cin, Ind	143	0	2	2	18	5	0	0	0	0
Terry Holbrook	74-76	Cleveland	93	11	15	26	13	8	0	1	1	0
Bill Holden (G)	73-74	Wpg, Tor	2	0	0	0	0	...	...	...	...	...
Jerry Holland	77-78	Edmonton	22	2	1	3	14	...	...	...	...	...
Paul Holmgren	75-76	Minnesota	51	14	16	30	121	...	...	...	...	...
Leif Holmquist (G)	75-76	Indianapolis	19	0	0	0	4	...	...	...	...	...
Ralph Hopiavuori	72-75	Cle, Ind	72	6	15	21	71	12	0	2	2	6
Larry Hornung	72-78	Wpg, Edm, SD	371	34	121	155	103	37	2	12	14	6
Bill Horton	72-75	Cle, LA, Ind	192	4	35	39	131	9	0	1	1	10
Rejean Houle	73-76	Quebec	204	118	139	257	115	20	12	6	18	10
Gordie Howe	73-79	Hou, NE	415	174	334	508	399	78	28	43	71	115
Mark Howe	73-79	Hou, NE	426	208	296	504	198	75	41	51	92	48
Marty Howe	73-79	Hou, NE	449	67	117	184	460	75	9	14	23	85
Harry Howell	73-76	NY-J, SD, Cgy	170	7	36	43	58	7	1	0	1	12
Fran Huck	73-78	Min, Wpg	228	67	127	194	133	23	3	15	18	14
Bill Hughes (G)	72-73	Houston	3	0	0	0	2	...	...	...	...	...
Brent Hughes	75-79	SD, Bir	268	23	79	102	180	22	1	9	10	18
Frank Hughes	72-78	Hou, Phx	385	173	180	353	173	54	24	16	40	33
John Hughes	74-79	Phx, Cin, Hou, Ind, Edm	372	18	130	148	778	23	2	1	3	49
Bobby Hull	72-79	Winnipeg	411	303	335	638	183	60	43	37	80	38
Steve Hull	75-77	Calgary	60	11	17	28	6	...	...	...	...	...
Ed Humphreys (G)	75-77	Cgy, Que	30	0	1	1	0	1	0	0	0	0
Dave Hunter	78-79	Edmonton	72	7	25	32	134	13	2	3	5	42
Paul Hurley	72-77	NE, Edm, Cgy	311	10	76	86	181	25	0	8	8	18
Ron Huston	75-77	Phoenix	159	42	83	125	14	5	1	1	2	0
Dave Hutchison	72-74	Phi, Van	97	0	15	15	185	3	0	0	0	2
Mike Hyndman	72-74	NE, LA	86	12	22	34	32	...	...	...	...	...
David Hynes	76-77	New England	22	5	4	9	4	...	...	...	...	...
— I —												
Lee Inglis	73-75	NY-J, SD	10	0	2	2	0	...	...	...	...	...
Dave Inkpen	75-79	Cin, Ind, Que, Edm, NE	293	13	76	89	273	14	0	3	3	12
Gary Inness (G)	77-79	Indianapolis	63	0	0	0	51	...	...	...	...	...
Glenn Irwin	74-79	Hou, Ind	233	7	24	31	633	18	0	2	2	17
Larry Israelson	74-77	Van, Cgy	105	22	31	53	36	3	0	0	0	0
— J —												
Jeff Jacques	74-77	Tor, Bir	199	50	68	118	231	6	0	4	4	2
Gary Jacquith	75-76	San Diego	2	0	0	0	0	...	...	...	...	...
Mike Jakubo	72-73	Los Angeles	7	0	0	0	0	...	...	...	...	...
Gary Jarrett	72-76	Cleveland	298	104	118	222	239	22	9	8	17	34
Pierre Jarry	77-78	Edmonton	18	4	10	14	4	5	1	0	1	4
Rick Jodzio	74-77	Van, Cgy	137	15	16	31	357	2	0	0	0	14
Bob Johnson (G)	75-76	D-O, Cle	42	0	0	0	0	2	0	0	0	0
Danny Johnson	72-75	Winnipeg	232	53	58	111	62	18	5	1	6	5
Jim Johnson	72-75	Min, Ind	157	32	71	103	54	16	3	5	8	6
Larry Johnston	74-75	M-B	49	0	9	9	93	...	...	...	...	...
Eddie Johnstone	74-75	M-B	23	4	4	8	43	...	...	...	...	...
Bob Jones	72-76	LA, NY, NY-J, M-B, Ind	161	30	48	78	60	...	...	...	...	...
James H. "Jimmy" Jones	73-75	Vancouver	81	14	9	23	62	...	...	...	...	...
James W. Jones	73-74	Chicago	1	0	0	0	0	...	...	...	...	...
Ric Jordan	72-77	NE, Que, Cgy	183	11	23	34	180	7	0	0	0	6
Eddie Joyal	72-76	Alb, Edm	239	57	55	112	26	5	2	0	2	4
Joe Junkin (G)	73-75	NY-J, SD	69	0	2	2	9	...	...	...	...	...
Dan Justin	75-77	Cincinnati	23	0	2	2	6	...	...	...	...	...

Name	Seasons	Team(s)	Regular Season GP	G	A	Pts.	PIM	Playoffs GP	G	A	Pts.	PIM
— K —												
Hannu Kampurri (G)	78-79	Edmonton	2	0	0	0	0	...	...	...	...	...
Gord Kannegiesser	72-75	Hou, Ind	127	1	34	35	62	12	0	3	3	13
Al Karlander	73-77	NE, Ind	269	60	111	171	107	21	3	7	10	6
Dennis Kassian	72-73	Alberta	50	6	7	13	14	...	...	...	...	...
Mike Keeler	73-74	New England	1	0	0	0	0	1	0	0	0	0
Jamie Kennedy	72-73	NY	52	4	6	10	11	...	...	...	...	...
Murray Kennett	74-76	Ind, Edm	106	8	21	29	39	...	...	...	...	...
Murray Keogan	74-76	Phx, Cgy	124	42	42	84	91	5	0	1	1	0
Dave Keon	75-79	Min, Ind, NE	301	102	189	291	20	36	13	23	36	8
Doug Kerslake	74-76	Edmonton	23	5	1	6	14	...	...	...	...	...
Veli-Pekka Ketola	74-77	Wpg, Cgy	235	94	99	183	118	13	7	5	12	2
Kerry Ketter	75-76	Edmonton	48	1	9	10	20	...	...	...	...	...
John Kiely (G)	75-76	Cincinnati	22	0	1	1	6	...	...	...	...	...
Steve King	72-74	Ott, Tor	136	32	56	88	54	17	0	4	4	18
Gavin Kirk	72-79	Ott, Tor, Edm, Cgy, Bir	422	117	243	360	279	38	14	19	33	41
Billy Klatt	72-74	Minnesota	143	50	28	78	34	16	4	5	9	23
Darrel Knibbs	72-73	Chicago	41	3	8	11	0	...	...	...	...	...
Keith Kokkola	74-77	Chi, D-O, Bir	54	0	5	5	130	...	...	...	...	...
George Konik	72-73	Minnesota	54	4	12	46	34	...	...	...	...	...
Skip Krake	72-76	Cle, Edm	207	52	77	129	318	19	2	4	6	66
Reg Krezanski	74-75	San Diego	2	0	0	0	2	...	...	...	...	...
Jarda Krupicka	72-73	LA, NY	36	2	2	4	6	...	...	...	...	...
Dave Kryskow	76-78	Cgy, Wpg	116	36	38	74	63	9	4	4	8	2
Gary Kurt (G)	72-77	NY, NY-J, Phx	176	0	11	11	16	4	0	0	0	0
George Kuzmicz	74-76	Toronto	35	0	12	12	22	...	...	...	...	...
— L —												
Gord Labossiere	72-76	Houston	300	102	162	264	144	50	16	28	44	46
Dan Labraaten	76-78	Winnipeg	111	42	43	85	51	24	8	18	26	23
Francois Lacombe	72-79	Que, Cgy	440	38	139	177	422	54	5	10	15	26
Andre Lacroix	72-79	Phi, NY-J, SD, Hou, NE	551	251	547	798	412	48	14	29	43	30
Peter Laframboise	76-77	Edmonton	17	0	5	5	12	...	...	...	...	...
Jean-Guy Lagace	76-77	Birmingham	78	2	25	27	110	...	...	...	...	...
Pierre Lagace	77-79	Quebec	38	2	5	7	24	4	0	1	1	2
Floyd Lahache	77-78	Cincinnati	11	0	3	3	13	...	...	...	...	...
Bill Laing	74-76	Edmonton	97	10	16	26	99	...	...	...	...	...
Rick Lalonde	75-76	San Diego	2	0	0	0	0	...	...	...	...	...
Bruce Landon (G)	72-77	New England	122	0	2	2	36	8	0	0	0	0
Dave Langevin	76-79	Edmonton	216	19	59	78	260	23	2	4	6	44
Rod Langway	77-78	Birmingham	52	3	18	21	52	4	0	0	0	9
Camille Lapierre	72-74	Phi, Van	33	5	12	17	2	4	0	2	2	0
Norm Lapointe (G)	75-78	Cincinnati	77	0	1	1	6	4	0	0	0	0
Garry Lariviere	74-79	Phx, Que	289	26	126	152	316	38	3	15	18	18
Claude Larose	75-79	Cin, Ind	252	88	114	202	45	4	2	1	3	0
Paul Larose	72-75	Que, M-B	33	1	8	9	9	...	...	...	...	...
Ray Larose	72-74	Hou, NY-J	86	1	11	12	45	8	0	0	0	2
Curt Larsson (G)	74-77	Winnipeg	68	0	3	3	14	3	0	0	0	0
Don Larway	74-79	Hou, Ind	323	95	92	187	318	38	12	8	20	33
Mike Laughton	72-75	NY, NY-J, SD	203	44	47	91	100	10	4	1	5	0
Brian Lavender	75-76	Denver/Ottawa	31	5	6	11	26	...	...	...	...	...
Danny Lawson	72-77	Phi, Van, Cgy, Wpg	392	218	204	422	142	26	6	9	15	25
J. P. Leblanc	72-76	LA, M-B, D-O	248	56	134	190	232	6	0	5	5	2
Rene Leclerc	72-79	Que, Ind	445	134	177	311	461	34	10	13	23	52
Bob Leduc	72-75	Ott, Tor	158	47	66	113	109	17	4	8	12	46
Rich Leduc	74-79	Cle, Cin, Ind, Que	394	195	195	390	399	16	3	8	11	20
Barry Legge	74-79	M-B, D-O, Cle, Min, Cin	345	26	80	106	341	10	0	5	5	12
Randy Legge	74-77	M-B, Wpg, Cle, SD	192	3	31	34	166	10	0	0	0	18
Bob Leiter	75-76	Calgary	51	17	17	34	8	3	2	0	2	0
Jacques Lemelin (G)	72-73	Quebec	9	0	0	0	0	...	...	...	...	...
Richard Lemieux	76-77	Calgary	33	6	11	17	9	...	...	...	...	...
Gerry Leroux	78-79	Indianapolis	10	0	3	3	2	...	...	...	...	...
Bill Lesuk	75-79	Winnipeg	318	55	81	136	269	50	7	11	18	48
Louis Levasseur	75-79	Min, Edm, NE, Que	85	0	1	1	6	15	0	1	1	4
Rick Ley	72-79	New England	478	35	210	245	716	73	7	33	40	142
Bob Liddington	72-77	Chi, D-O, Hou, Phx	346	96	82	178	115	18	6	5	11	11
Len Lilyholm	72-73	Minnesota	77	8	13	21	37	5	1	0	1	0
Mats Lindh	75-77	Winnipeg	138	33	32	65	14	33	4	9	13	6
Doug Lindskog	76-77	Calgary	2	0	0	0	2	...	...	...	...	...
Willy Lindstrom	75-79	Winnipeg	316	123	138	261	133	49	26	22	48	50
Ken Linseman	77-78	Birmingham	71	38	38	76	126	5	2	2	4	15
Mike Liut (G)	77-79	Cincinnati	81	0	3	3	9	3	0	0	0	0

Name	Seasons	Team(s)	GP	G	A	Pts.	PIM	GP	G	A	Pts.	PIM
			Regular Season					Playoffs				
Owen Lloyd	77-78	Edmonton	3	0	1	1	4	...	...	...	...	...
Jacques Locas	74-78	M-B, Ind, Cin, Cgy	187	49	70	119	111	...	...	...	...	...
Dan Lodboa	72-73	Chicago	59	15	18	33	16	...	...	...	...	...
Ken Lockett (G)	76-77	San Diego	45	0	0	0	0	5	0	0	0	0
Mark Lomenda	74-77	Chi, D-O, Ind	164	31	61	92	46	9	3	1	4	17
Barry Long	74-79	Edm, Wpg	386	51	171	222	322	43	3	13	16	20
Ted Long	76-77	Cincinnati	1	0	0	0	0	...	...	...	...	...
Bernie Lukowich	75-77	Calgary	21	5	3	8	18	10	4	3	7	8
Morris Lukowich	76-79	Hou, Wpg	222	132	87	219	317	27	15	13	28	57
Chuck Luksa	78-79	Cincinnati	78	8	12	20	116	3	0	0	0	7
Larry Lund	72-78	Houston	459	149	277	426	419	59	20	45	65	116
Len Lunde	73-74	Edmonton	71	26	22	48	8	5	0	1	1	0
George Lyle	76-79	New England	202	86	75	161	190	26	6	6	12	42
— M —												
Blair "B.J." MacDonald	73-79	Edm, Ind	476	171	165	336	153	39	20	21	41	12
Bruce MacGregor	74-76	Edmonton	135	37	38	75	23	...	...	...	...	...
Gary MacGregor	74-79	Chi, D-O, Cle, Ind, NE, Edm	251	90	70	160	87	3	0	0	0	4
Al MacKenzie	74-75	Chicago	2	0	0	0	0	...	...	...	...	...
Paul MacKinnon	78-79	Winnipeg	73	2	15	17	70	10	2	5	7	4
Bob MacMillan	72-74	Minnesota	153	27	61	88	129	16	2	6	8	4
Bernie MacNeil	72-76	LA, Cin	119	19	19	38	131	3	0	0	0	4
Ralph MacSweyn	72-74	LA, Van	147	2	44	46	97	6	1	2	3	4
Dean Magee	78-79	Indianapolis	5	0	1	1	10	...	...	...	...	...
Darryl Maggs	73-79	Chi, D-O, Ind, Cin	402	51	177	228	540	34	5	9	14	95
Frank Mahovlich	74-78	Tor, Bir	237	89	143	232	75	9	4	1	5	2
Peter Mara	74-76	Chi, D-O	97	20	28	48	24	...	...	...	...	...
Gilles Marotte	77-78	Cin, Ind	73	3	20	23	76	...	...	...	...	...
Peter Marrin	73-79	Tor, Bir	278	81	112	193	127	14	0	8	8	6
Jim Marsh	76-77	Birmingham	1	0	0	0	0	...	...	...	...	...
Peter Marsh	76-79	Cincinnati	227	91	76	167	270	7	3	0	3	0
Tom Martin	72-75	Ott, Tor	213	59	76	135	59	22	8	13	21	4
Markus Mattsson (G)	77-79	Wpg, Que	68	0	1	1	6	...	...	...	...	...
Larry Mavety	72-77	LA, Phi, Chi, Tor, D-O, Ind	248	37	113	150	418	24	4	11	15	52
Bryan Maxwell	75-78	Cle, Cin, NE	124	6	23	29	217	6	0	1	1	33
Jim Mayer	76-79	Cgy, NE, Edm	74	13	12	25	21	...	...	...	...	...
John Mazur	77-78	Houston	1	0	0	0	0	...	...	...	...	...
Bob McAneeley	72-76	Alb, Edm	174	29	34	63	134	7	2	0	2	0
Ted McAneeley	75-76	Edmonton	79	2	17	19	71	4	0	0	0	0
Dunc McCallum	72-75	Hou, Chi	100	9	30	39	136	10	2	3	5	6
Jack McCartan (G)	72-75	Minnesota	42	0	0	0	19	4	0	1	1	0
Ted McCaskill	72-74	Los Angeles	91	13	13	26	213	6	2	3	5	12
Jim McCrimmon	73-76	Edm, Cgy	114	3	8	11	158	...	...	...	...	...
Don McCulloch	74-75	Vancouver	51	1	9	10	42	...	...	...	...	...
Peter McDuffe (G)	77-78	Indianapolis	12	0	0	0	0	...	...	...	...	...
Ab McDonald	72-74	Winnipeg	147	29	41	70	24	18	2	6	8	4
Brian McDonald	72-77	Hou, LA, M-B, Ind	304	90	101	191	268	26	6	5	11	61
Al McDonough	74-77	Cle, Min	200	66	73	139	52	8	3	1	4	4
Dick McGlynn	72-73	Chicago	30	0	0	0	12	...	...	...	...	...
Ray McKay	74-78	Edm, Cle, Min, Bir	212	14	44	58	134	7	0	1	1	8
Brian McKenzie	73-75	Edm, Ind	87	19	20	39	72	5	0	1	1	0
John "Pie" McKenzie	72-79	Phi, Van, Min, Cin, NE	477	163	250	413	619	29	11	14	25	24
Al McLeod	74-79	Phx, Hou, Ind	342	15	93	108	311	26	2	9	11	19
Don "Smokey" McLeod (G)	72-78	Hou, Van, Cgy, Edm, Que	332	0	43	43	28	31	0	1	1	4
Jim McLeod (G)	72-75	Chi, NY-J, LA, M-B	97	0	1	1	4	...	...	...	...	...
Mike McMahon	72-76	Min, SD	269	29	101	130	249	32	1	14	15	13
Rob McManama	75-76	New England	37	3	10	13	28	12	4	3	7	4
Jim McMasters	72-74	Cleveland	85	1	7	8	41	...	...	...	...	...
Dale McMullen	77-78	Edmonton	1	0	0	0	0	...	...	...	...	...
Mike McNamara	72-73	Quebec	19	0	0	0	5	...	...	...	...	...
Pete McNamee	73-77	Van, Phx, SD	175	17	31	48	189	18	1	1	2	32
Gerry Meehan	78-79	Cincinnati	2	0	0	0	0	...	...	...	...	...
Denis Meloche	72-74	Phi, Van	45	7	14	21	18	...	...	...	...	...
Chris Meloff	72-73	Ott	28	1	6	7	40	...	...	...	...	...
Barry Melrose	76-79	Cincinnati	178	5	27	32	343	5	0	1	1	10
Paul Menard (G)	72-73	Chicago	1	0	0	0	0	...	...	...	...	...
Vic Mercredi	75-76	Calgary	3	0	0	0	29	...	...	...	...	...
Barry Merrell	76-77	Edmonton	10	1	3	4	0	...	...	...	...	...
Mark Messier	78-79	Ind, Cin	52	1	10	11	58	...	...	...	...	...
Garry Methe	74-75	New England	5	0	1	1	4	...	...	...	...	...
Joe Micheletti	76-79	Cgy, Edm	142	31	70	101	151	18	0	11	11	6
John "J.C." Migneault	72-76	Phi, Van, Phx	258	49	61	110	107	8	0	0	0	0

Name	Seasons	Team(s)	Regular Season GP	G	A	Pts.	PIM	Playoffs GP	G	A	Pts.	PIM
Tom Milani	76-77	Minnesota	2	0	0	0	0	...	...	...	...	...
Perry Miller	74-77	Wpg, Min	201	31	60	91	309	20	4	6	10	27
Warren Miller	75-79	Cgy, Edm, Que, NE	238	65	83	148	163	31	1	10	11	56
Ed Mio (G)	77-79	Ind, Edm	44	0	2	2	4	...	...	...	...	...
John Miszuk	74-77	M-B, Cgy	214	6	66	72	179	10	0	1	1	10
Lyle Moffatt	75-79	Cle, Wpg	276	53	61	114	244	49	13	11	24	46
Lauri Mononen	75-77	Phoenix	142	36	50	86	29	5	1	3	4	2
Brian Morenz	72-76	NY, NY-J, SD	225	53	57	110	165	21	2	4	6	17
Angelo Moretto	78-79	Indianapolis	18	3	1	4	2	...	...	...	...	...
Ron Morgan	73-74	Cleveland	4	0	1	1	7	2	1	0	1	0
Wayne Morin	76-77	Calgary	13	2	0	2	25	...	...	...	...	...
Bill Morris	74-75	Edmonton	36	4	8	12	6	...	...	...	...	...
Pete Morris	75-77	Edmonton	78	7	14	21	41	3	0	1	1	7
Rick Morris	72-78	Chi, D-O, Edm, Que	412	102	90	192	567	22	4	4	8	46
George Morrison	72-77	Min, Cgy	361	123	142	265	110	38	14	17	31	14
Kevin Morrison	73-79	NY-J, SD, Ind, Que	418	93	224	317	462	28	2	15	17	22
Dave Morrow	78-79	Indianapolis	10	2	10	12	29	...	...	...	...	...
Cleland "Keke" Mortson	72-78	Houston	75	13	17	30	102	12	0	4	4	16
Wayne Mosdell	72-73	Philadelphia	9	0	1	1	12	...	...	...	...	...
Darwin Mott	72-73	Philadelphia	1	0	0	0	0	...	...	...	...	...
Morris Mott	76-77	Winnipeg	2	0	1	1	5	...	...	...	...	...
Bob Mowat	74-75	Phoenix	53	9	10	19	34	3	0	0	0	0
Wayne Muloin	72-76	Cle, Edm	261	10	43	53	180	20	2	4	6	18
Murray Myers	72-76	Phi, Van, Cin	148	37	36	73	44	...	...	...	...	...

— N —

Name	Seasons	Team(s)	Regular Season GP	G	A	Pts.	PIM	Playoffs GP	G	A	Pts.	PIM
Mark Napier	75-78	Tor, Bir	237	136	118	254	53	5	0	2	2	14
Robbie Neale	73-75	Cle, Wpg	59	9	14	23	38	5	0	0	0	4
Vaclav Nedomansky	74-78	Tor, Bir	252	135	118	253	43	6	3	4	1	9
Greg Neeld	75-76	Toronto	17	0	1	1	18	...	...	...	...	...
Jim Neilson	78-79	Edmonton	35	0	5	5	18	...	...	...	...	...
Eric Nesterenko	73-74	Chicago	29	2	5	7	8	...	...	...	...	...
Bob Nevin	76-77	Edmonton	13	3	2	5	0	...	...	...	...	...
Rick Newell	74-75	Phoenix	25	0	4	4	39	5	0	1	1	2
Cam Newton (G)	73-76	Chi, D-O, Cle	102	0	2	2	0	11	0	0	0	0
Jim Niekamp	72-77	LA, Phx	383	16	96	112	484	11	2	2	4	10
Kent Nilsson	77-79	Winnipeg	158	81	133	214	16	19	5	19	24	14
Ulf Nilsson	74-78	Winnipeg	300	140	344	484	341	42	14	53	67	51
Lou Nistico	73-77	Tor, Bir	186	44	72	116	375	6	6	1	7	19
Joe Noris	75-78	SD, Bir	198	72	116	188	60	18	4	5	9	12
Jack Norris (G)	72-76	Alb, Edm, Phx	191	0	9	9	10	10	0	0	0	0
Craig Norwich	77-79	Cincinnati	145	13	74	87	121	3	0	1	1	4
Kevin Nugent	78-79	Indianapolis	25	2	5	8	20	...	...	...	...	...

— O —

Name	Seasons	Team(s)	Regular Season GP	G	A	Pts.	PIM	Playoffs GP	G	A	Pts.	PIM
Tim O'Connell	76-77	San Diego	16	0	3	3	4	...	...	...	...	...
Fred O'Donnell	74-76	New England	155	32	26	58	165	17	2	5	7	20
Don O'Donoghue	72-76	Phi, Van, Cin	147	25	37	62	63	4	0	1	1	0
Gerry Odrowski	72-76	LA, Phx, Min, Wpg	282	16	114	130	230	11	1	4	5	6
Wally Olds	72-76	NY, Cgy	89	5	12	17	10	9	0	2	2	4
Paul O'Neill	78-79	Birmingham	1	0	0	0	0	...	...	...	...	...
Bill Orr	73-74	Toronto	46	3	9	12	16	12	1	0	1	6
Danny O'Shea	74-75	Minnesota	76	16	25	41	47	...	...	...	...	...
Kevin O'Shea	74-75	Minnesota	68	10	10	20	42	...	...	...	...	...
Francois Ouimet	75-77	Min, Cin	25	1	10	11	12	...	...	...	...	...
Ted Ouimet (G)	74-75	New England	1	0	0	0	0	...	...	...	...	...

— PQ —

Name	Seasons	Team(s)	Regular Season GP	G	A	Pts.	PIM	Playoffs GP	G	A	Pts.	PIM
Pierre Paiement	72-73	Philadelphia	8	1	0	1	18	...	...	...	...	...
Rosaire Paiement	72-78	Chi, NE, Ind	455	146	221	367	602	44	13	22	35	72
Marcel Paille (G)	72-73	Philadelphia	15	0	0	0	0	1	0	0	0	0
Dick Paradise	72-74	Minnesota	144	5	22	27	260	12	0	1	1	8
Bernie Parent (G)	72-73	Philadelphia	63	0	1	1	36	1	0	0	0	0
Michel Parizeau	72-79	Que, Ind, Cin	509	142	252	394	320	33	10	14	24	24
Jim Park (G)	75-78	Indianapolis	54	0	2	2	14	6	0	0	0	0
Edgar "Rusty" Patenaude	72-78	Alb, Edm, Ind	428	159	131	290	368	10	1	6	7	22
Craig Patrick	76-77	Minnesota	30	6	11	17	6	...	...	...	...	...
Glenn Patrick	76-77	Edmonton	23	0	4	4	62	2	0	0	0	0
Denis Patry	74-75	Quebec	3	1	2	3	2	...	...	...	...	...
Dennis Patterson	76-77	Edmonton	23	0	2	2	2	...	...	...	...	...
Jean Payette	72-74	Quebec	112	19	40	59	52	...	...	...	...	...
Gene Peacosh	72-77	NY, NY-J, SD, Edm, Ind	367	165	165	330	134	30	12	9	21	27
Mel Pearson	72-73	Minnesota	70	8	12	20	12	5	2	0	2	0

Name	Seasons	Team(s)	Regular Season GP	G	A	Pts.	PIM	Playoffs GP	G	A	Pts.	PIM
Andre Peloffy	77-78	New England	10	2	0	2	2	2	0	0	0	0
Mike Pelyk	74-76	Van, Cin	150	24	49	73	238	…	…	…	…	…
Dwayne Pentland	76-77	Houston	29	1	2	3	6	2	0	0	0	0
Ross Perkins	72-75	Alb, Edm	225	44	93	137	95	5	1	3	4	2
Bob Perreault (G)	72-73	Los Angeles	1	0	0	0	0	…	…	…	…	…
Brian Perry	72-74	NY, NY-J, SD	145	33	31	64	49	6	1	2	3	6
George Pesut	76-77	Calgary	17	2	0	2	2	…	…	…	…	…
Garry Peters	72-74	NY, NY-J	57	4	12	16	42	…	…	…	…	…
Jean-Luc Phaneuf	75-77	Tor, Bir	78	10	15	25	6	…	…	…	…	…
Gerry Pinder	72-78	Cle, SD, Edm	353	93	141	234	336	18	5	10	15	40
Ed Pizunski	75-76	Denver/Ottawa	1	0	0	0	0	…	…	…	…	…
Jacques Plante (G)	74-75	Edmonton	31	0	1	1	2	…	…	…	…	…
Michel Plante	72-74	Phi, Van	92	16	14	30	37	4	0	0	0	2
Larry Pleau	72-79	New England	468	157	215	372	180	66	29	22	51	37
Ron Plumb	72-79	Phi, Van, SD, Cin, NE	549	65	262	327	341	41	5	15	20	40
Nick Polano	72-73	Philadelphia	17	0	3	3	24	…	…	…	…	…
Jan Popiel	72-77	Chi, D-O, Hou, Phx	296	78	82	160	256	26	9	6	15	16
Poul Popiel	72-78	Houston	468	62	265	327	517	71	7	47	54	118
Lynn Powis	75-78	Cgy, Ind, Wpg	153	50	65	115	66	13	7	5	12	19
Kelly Pratt	73-74	Winnipeg	46	4	6	10	50	…	…	…	…	…
Bill Prentice	72-78	Hou, Ind, Que, Edm	208	8	14	22	265	15	0	0	0	22
Rich Preston	74-79	Hou, Wpg	388	133	152	285	237	51	16	22	38	39
Pat Price	74-75	Vancouver	68	5	29	34	15	…	…	…	…	…
Kevin Primeau	77-78	Edmonton	7	0	1	1	0	2	0	0	0	2
Jim Pritchard	74-75	Chicago	2	0	0	0	0	…	…	…	…	…
Dick Proceviat	72-77	Chi, Ind	324	16	90	106	265	20	0	4	4	12
Rich Pumple	72-74	Cle, Ind	129	27	30	57	90	9	3	5	8	11

— R —

Name	Seasons	Team(s)	Regular Season GP	G	A	Pts.	PIM	Playoffs GP	G	A	Pts.	PIM
Robert "Cap" Raeder	75-77	New England	29	0	0	0	2	15	0	0	0	0
Rob Ramage	78-79	Birmingham	80	12	36	48	165	…	…	…	…	…
Pekka Rautakallio	75-77	Phoenix	151	15	70	85	16	5	0	2	2	0
Bill Reed	74-76	M-B, Cgy	40	0	5	5	26	…	…	…	…	…
Craig Reichmuth	72-75	NY, NY-J, SD, M-B	189	25	25	50	322	…	…	…	…	…
Seppo Repo	76-77	Phoenix	80	29	31	60	10	…	…	…	…	…
Brad Rhiness	76-78	SD, Ind	70	12	17	29	26	…	…	…	…	…
Steve Richardson	74-76	Ind, M-B, NE	72	9	22	31	74	…	…	…	…	…
Pat Riggin (G)	78-79	Birmingham	46	0	3	3	22	…	…	…	…	…
Heikki Riihiranta	74-77	Winnipeg	187	10	38	48	84	4	0	4	4	5
Ron Riley	72-73	Ott	22	0	5	5	2	2	0	0	0	0
Wayne Rivers	72-77	NY, NY-J, SD	357	158	176	334	183	23	8	6	14	14
Garth Rizzuto	72-74	Winnipeg	102	13	14	17	40	14	0	1	1	14
Phil Roberto	77-78	Birmingham	53	8	20	28	91	4	1	0	1	20
Doug Roberts	75-77	New England	140	7	31	38	84	19	1	1	2	8
Gordie Roberts	75-79	New England	311	42	144	186	502	46	4	20	24	81
Joe Robertson	74-75	Ind, Min	29	5	8	13	27	…	…	…	…	…
Francois Rochon	73-77	Chi, D-O, Ind	267	71	60	131	95	14	2	2	4	0
John Rogers	75-76	Edmonton	77	9	8	17	34	…	…	…	…	…
Mike Rogers	74-79	Edm, NE	396	145	222	367	109	46	13	21	34	14
Jerry Rollins	75-79	Tor, Bir, Phx, Ind	130	9	18	27	378	…	…	…	…	…
Lorne Rombough	73-74	Chicago	3	1	2	3	0	…	…	…	…	…
Bob Roselle	75-76	Indianapolis	1	0	0	0	0	…	…	…	…	…
Randy Rota	76-78	Edmonton	93	17	28	45	20	10	4	3	7	4
Michel Rouleau	72-75	Phi, Que, SD, M-B	115	13	35	48	289	…	…	…	…	…
Dunc Rousseau	72-74	Winnipeg	135	26	25	51	114	18	3	2	5	2
Pierre Roy	72-79	Que, Cin, NE	316	22	84	106	864	23	1	12	13	76
Kent Ruhnke	76-78	Winnipeg	72	19	20	39	4	5	2	0	2	0
Duane Rupp	74-76	Van, Cgy	114	3	42	45	78	7	0	2	2	8
Terry Ruskowski	74-79	Hou, Wpg	369	83	254	337	761	52	18	36	54	174
Bob Russell	75-77	Edmonton	115	20	24	44	60	5	1	0	1	0
Wayne Rutledge (G)	72-78	Houston	175	0	4	4	96	16	0	0	0	2
Terry Ryan	72-73	Minnesota	76	13	6	19	13	5	0	2	2	0
Al Rycroft	72-73	Cleveland	7	0	2	2	0	…	…	…	…	…
Blaine Rydman	72-74	NY, Min	39	0	1	1	90	1	0	0	0	0

— S —

Name	Seasons	Team(s)	Regular Season GP	G	A	Pts.	PIM	Playoffs GP	G	A	Pts.	PIM
Larry Sacharuk	78-79	Indianapolis	15	2	9	11	25	…	…	…	…	…
Claude St. Sauveur	72-79	Phi, Van, Cgy, Edm, Ind, Cin	285	112	112	224	131	5	1	0	1	0
Cal Sandbeck	77-79	Edmonton	17	1	2	3	41	5	0	0	0	10
Frank Sanders	72-73	Minnesota	78	8	8	16	94	4	0	1	1	0
Derek Sanderson	72-73	Philadelphia	8	3	3	6	69	…	…	…	…	…
Nick Sanza (G)	75-76	Denver/Ottawa	1	0	0	0	0	…	…	…	…	…
Craig Sarner	75-76	Minnesota	1	0	0	0	0	…	…	…	…	…

Name	Seasons	Team(s)	Regular Season GP	G	A	Pts.	PIM	Playoffs GP	G	A	Pts.	PIM
Dick Sarrazin	72-73	NE, Chi	68	7	15	22	2	...	...	...	...	...
Glen "Slats" Sather	76-77	Edmonton	81	19	34	53	77	5	1	1	2	2
Ted Scharf	72-77	NY, NY-J, SD, Ind, Edm	238	16	20	36	343	7	0	0	0	5
John Schella	72-78	Houston	385	39	143	182	844	66	4	25	29	143
William "Buzz" Schneider	76-77	Birmingham	4	0	0	0	2	...	...	...	...	...
Jim Schraefel	73-74	Edmonton	34	1	1	2	0	5	0	3	3	0
Brit Selby	72-75	Que, NE, Tor	153	23	51	74	73	23	4	7	11	15
Brad Selwood	72-79	New England	431	42	143	185	556	63	6	12	18	81
Dave Semenko	77-79	Edmonton	142	16	20	36	298	16	4	2	6	37
Dick Sentes	72-77	Ott, Tor, SD, Cgy	337	137	143	280	233	40	14	8	22	41
Ron Serafini	75-76	Cincinnati	16	0	2	2	15	...	...	...	...	...
Tom Serviss	72-76	LA, M-B, Que, Cgy	287	38	78	116	101	11	0	0	0	0
Sean Shanahan	78-79	Cincinnati	4	0	0	0	7	...	...	...	...	...
Jim Shaw (G)	74-76	Toronto	37	0	0	0	0	5	0	0	0	0
Bobby Sheehan	72-78	NY, NY-J, Edm, Ind	241	75	110	185	45	5	1	3	4	0
Tim Sheehy	72-78	NE, Edm, Bir	433	178	173	351	156	39	16	21	37	26
John Sheridan	74-76	Indianapolis	69	18	13	31	20	...	...	...	...	...
Jim Sherrit	73-76	Hou, D-O	193	63	72	135	59	27	8	10	18	8
Glen Shirton	73-74	Cleveland	4	0	0	0	0	...	...	...	...	...
John Shmyr	72-75	Wpg, Chi, Van	89	2	8	10	58	3	0	1	1	2
Paul Shmyr	72-79	Cle, SD, Edm	511	61	248	309	860	43	5	18	23	107
Byron Shutt	78-79	Cincinnati	65	10	7	17	115	3	1	1	2	14
Bob Sicinski	72-77	Chi, Ind	353	76	184	260	56	34	6	11	17	6
Risto Siltanen	78-79	Edmonton	20	3	4	7	4	11	0	9	9	4
Tom Simpson	72-77	Ott, Tor, Bir, Edm	314	125	84	209	160	22	6	2	8	5
Gary Sittler	74-75	M-B	5	1	1	2	14	...	...	...	...	...
Lars-Erik Sjoberg	74-79	Winnipeg	295	25	169	194	147	52	1	21	22	32
Peter Slater	72-74	Los Angeles	91	13	13	26	89	6	0	0	0	2
Mike Sleep	75-77	Phoenix	22	4	2	6	6	...	...	...	...	...
Louis Sleigher	78-79	Birmingham	62	26	12	38	46	...	...	...	...	...
Dale Smedsmo	75-78	Cin, NE, Ind	110	10	22	32	291	2	0	1	1	0
Al Smith (G)	72-79	New England	260	0	12	12	129	35	0	1	1	2
Brian Smith	72-73	Houston	48	7	6	13	19	10	0	2	2	0
Gary Smith (G)	78-79	Ind, Wpg	22	0	3	3	0	10	0	0	0	0
Guy Smith	72-74	New England	38	4	8	12	31	11	2	0	2	4
Rick Smith	73-76	Minnesota	200	20	89	109	260	23	2	8	10	28
Ross Smith	74-75	Indianapolis	15	1	6	7	19	...	...	...	...	...
Ron Snell	73-75	Winnipeg	90	24	25	49	40	4	0	0	0	0
Dennis Sobchuk	74-79	Phx, Cin, Edm	348	145	186	331	205	25	11	8	19	12
Gene Sobchuk	74-76	Phx, Cin	81	24	18	42	37	5	0	0	0	0
Fred Spezck	72-75	Min, LA, M-B	123	22	42	64	96	6	3	2	5	2
Bill Speer	72-74	NY, NY-J	135	4	26	30	70	...	...	...	...	...
Irv Spencer	72-74	Phi, Van	73	2	28	30	49	4	0	0	0	4
Dan Spring	73-76	Wpg, Edm	201	39	51	90	38	6	1	2	3	0
Jack Stanfield	72-74	Houston	112	9	15	24	10	16	1	0	1	2
Pat Stapleton	73-78	Chi, Ind, Cin	372	27	212	239	187	34	2	21	23	38
Billy Steele	75-77	Cincinnati	84	11	22	33	21	2	0	0	0	0
Ken Stephanson	72-74	Ott, Wpg	106	3	23	26	167	8	1	3	4	18
Bob Stephenson	77-79	Birmingham	117	30	30	60	105	...	...	...	...	...
Mike Stevens	74-76	Phx, Hou	76	2	16	18	71	5	0	1	1	0
John A. Stewart	75-77	Cle, Min, Bir	95	15	24	39	44	3	0	0	0	0
John C. "JC" Stewart	74-79	Cle, Bir	271	60	92	152	213	6	1	1	2	6
Paul Stewart	76-79	Edm, Cin	65	3	6	9	288	3	0	0	0	0
Blaine Stoughton	76-79	Cin, Ind, NE	219	89	90	179	121	11	4	6	10	6
Danny Sullivan (G)	72-74	Phi, Van	2	0	0	0	0	...	...	...	...	...
Peter Sullivan	75-79	Winnipeg	313	125	170	295	107	52	20	32	52	8
Bill Sutherland	72-74	Winnipeg	60	10	21	31	40	18	5	9	14	13
Steve Sutherland	72-78	LA, M-B, Que	378	97	76	173	805	51	9	6	15	112
Garry Swain	74-77	New England	171	22	33	55	70	25	3	5	8	56
Cal Swenson	72-74	Winnipeg	100	12	25	37	21	15	1	5	6	7
Dave Syvret	75-77	Tor, Bir	58	1	11	12	14	...	...	...	...	...
Joe Szura	72-74	LA, Hou	114	21	39	60	29	12	0	0	0	0
—T—												
Rudy Tajcnar	78-79	Edmonton	2	0	0	0	0	...	...	...	...	...
Juhani Tamminen	75-77	Cle, Phx	130	17	43	60	84	1	0	0	0	0
Don Tannahill	74-77	Min, Cgy	227	58	76	134	34	20	4	9	13	8
Marc Tardif	73-79	LA, M-B, Que	446	316	350	666	418	44	27	32	59	35
Dave Tataryn (G)	75-76	Toronto	23	0	0	0	0	...	...	...	...	...
Ted Taylor	72-78	Houston	420	123	164	287	598	63	18	21	39	217
Greg Tebbutt	78-79	Birmingham	38	2	5	7	83	...	...	...	...	...
Paul Terbenche	74-79	Van, Cgy, Bir, Hou, Wpg	277	18	64	82	74	26	2	8	10	10

Name	Seasons	Team(s)	Regular Season GP	G	A	Pts.	PIM	Playoffs GP	G	A	Pts.	PIM
Jean Tetreault	73-76	Van, Min	9	1	1	2	0	...	...	...	...	...
Reg Thomas	73-79	LA, M-B, Ind, Cin	433	121	138	159	199	19	9	10	19	8
Alex Tidey	75-76	San Diego	74	16	11	27	46	11	3	6	9	10
Gord Titcomb	74-75	Toronto	2	0	1	1	0	...	...	...	...	...
John Tonelli	75-78	Houston	224	64	86	150	278	34	11	14	25	28
Craig Topolnisky	77-78	Edmonton	10	0	2	2	4	...	...	...	...	...
J. C. Tremblay	72-79	Quebec	451	66	358	424	216	34	2	23	25	4
Tom Trevelyn	74-75	San Diego	20	0	2	2	4	...	...	...	...	...
Willie Trognitz	77-78	Cincinnati	29	2	1	3	94	...	...	...	...	...
Jerry Trooien	72-73	Chicago	2	0	0	0	0	...	...	...	...	...
Guy Trottier	72-75	Ott, Tor, M-B	166	60	73	133	87	17	6	7	13	4
Jim Troy	75-78	NE, Edm	68	2	0	2	174	4	0	0	0	29
Gord Tumilson (G)	72-73	Winnipeg	3	0	0	0	0	...	...	...	...	...
Jim Turkiewicz	74-79	Tor, Bir	392	24	119	143	234	11	1	3	4	6
Frank Turnbull (G)	75-78	Edmonton	4	0	0	0	0	...	...	...	...	...
— UV —												
Norm Ullman	75-77	Edmonton	144	47	83	130	40	9	1	6	7	2
Rick Vaive	78-79	Birmingham	75	26	33	59	248	...	...	...	...	...
John Van Horlick	75-76	Toronto	2	0	0	0	12	...	...	...	...	...
Gary Veneruzzo	72-77	LA, M-B, Cin, Phx, SD	348	151	123	274	212	18	5	0	5	11
Pierre Viau	72-73	Chicago	4	0	0	0	0	...	...	...	...	...
Mario Vien (G)	75-76	Toronto	26	0	0	0	0	...	...	...	...	...
Doug Volmar	74-75	San Diego	10	0	1	1	4	...	...	...	...	...
— W —												
Ernie Wakely (G)	72-79	Wpg, SD, Cin, Hou, Bir	334	0	0	0	0	31	0	0	0	0
Russ Walker	73-76	Cleveland	214	52	40	92	319	13	2	0	2	42
Bob Wall	72-76	Alb, Edm, SD	253	23	89	112	113	21	1	6	7	6
Brian Walsh	75-76	Calgary	5	0	2	2	12	...	...	...	...	...
Ed Walsh (G)	78-79	Edmonton	3	0	0	0	0	...	...	...	...	...
Dave Walter	73-76	Chi, SD	26	2	3	5	10	...	...	...	...	...
Ron Walters	72-74	Alb, LA, Ind	166	44	41	85	74	...	...	...	...	...
Mike Walton	73-76	Minnesota	211	136	145	281	148	23	20	15	35	26
Rob Walton	73-76	Min, Van, Cgy	150	40	71	111	54	...	...	...	...	...
Ron Ward	72-77	NY, Van, LA, Cle, Min, Cgy, Wpg	359	170	210	380	103	13	3	4	7	4
Jim Warner	78-79	New England	41	6	9	15	20	1	0	0	0	0
Steve Warr	72-74	Ott, Tor	72	3	8	11	79	4	0	0	0	0
Bryan Watson	78-79	Cincinnati	21	0	2	2	56	3	0	1	1	2
Jim Watson	72-76	LA, Chi, Que	211	7	33	40	228	22	2	4	6	20
Tom Webster	72-78	New England	352	220	205	425	241	43	28	26	54	19
Stan Weir	78-79	Edmonton	68	31	30	61	20	13	2	5	7	2
Wally Weir	76-79	Quebec	150	5	24	29	407	32	2	8	10	6
Steve West	74-79	M-B, Hou, Wpg	142	29	50	79	35	25	3	4	7	2
Pat Westrum	74-78	Min, Cgy, Bir	237	7	45	52	356	9	0	2	2	19
Carl Wtezel (G)	72-73	Minnesota	1	0	0	0	0	...	...	...	...	...
Bob Whidden (G)	72-76	Cleveland	98	0	1	1	11	...	...	...	...	...
Alton White	72-75	NY, LA, M-B	145	38	46	84	45	6	1	0	1	0
Bobby Whitlock	72-76	Chi, LA, Ind	244	81	98	179	173	...	...	...	...	...
Juha Widing	77-78	Edmonton	71	18	24	42	8	5	0	1	1	0
Ian Wilkie (G)	72-74	NY, LA, Edm	33	0	0	0	2	1	0	0	0	0
Barry Wilkins	76-78	Edm, Ind	130	6	45	51	154	4	0	1	1	2
Tommy Williams	72-74	New England	139	31	58	89	20	19	6	14	20	12
Warren "Butch" Williams	76-77	Edmonton	29	3	10	13	16	...	...	...	...	...
Gary Williamson	73-74	Houston	9	2	6	8	0	12	0	0	0	0
Hal Willis	72-74	NY, LA	92	4	23	27	183	...	...	...	...	...
Bob Winograd	72-77	NY, NY-J, SD	60	1	12	13	23	...	...	...	...	...
Jim Wiste	72-76	Cle, Ind	228	64	108	172	80	14	3	9	12	13
Wayne Wood (G)	74-79	Van, Cgy, Tor, Bir	104	0	4	4	32	1	0	0	0	0
Chris Worthy (G)	73-76	Edmonton	82	0	0	0	14	4	0	0	0	0
Bob Woytowich	72-76	Wpg, Ind	242	9	51	60	140	18	1	1	2	4
Randy Wyrozub	75-76	Indianapolis	55	11	14	25	8	...	...	...	...	...
— XYZ —												
Dale Yakiwchuk	78-79	Winnipeg	4	0	0	0	0	...	...	...	...	...
Bill Young	72-74	LA, Min, Cle	142	28	30	58	143	5	1	1	2	4
Howie Young	74-76	Phx, Wpg	98	17	25	42	109	...	...	...	...	...
Rod Zaine	72-75	Chicago	220	11	33	44	58	18	2	1	3	2
Joe Zanussi	72-74	Winnipeg	149	7	43	50	106	18	2	5	7	6
Lynn Zimmerman (G)	75-78	D-O, Hou	28	0	0	0	0	4	0	0	0	6
Jerry Zrymiak	72-77	LA, M-B, Min, Tor	156	7	40	47	112	2	1	0	1	0
Wayne Zuk	73-74	Edmonton	2	0	0	0	0	...	...	...	...	...
Mike Zuke	76-78	Ind, Edm	86	26	38	64	49	5	2	3	5	0

WHA GOALTENDERS

Name	Seasons	Team(s)	GP	MIN	GA	SO	W	L	T	GAA	GP	MIN	GA	SO	W	L	GAA
			Regular Season								Playoffs						
Christer Abrahamsson	74-77	New England	101	5739	342	3	41	46	7	3.58	3	91	5	0	0	1	3.30
Yves Archambault	72-74	Phi, Van	11	523	44	0	2	7	0	5.05	3	153	11	0	0	2	4.31
Serge Aubry	72-77	Que, Cin	142	7511	470	4	65	56	4	3.75	3	18	1	0	0	0	3.33
Shared shutout with Richard Brodeur, 7 Feb 1973																	
Bill Berglund	73-75	New England	5	216	13	0	2	1	0	3.61	...	...	...	...	...	...	...
Les Binkley	72-76	Ott, Tor	81	4228	262	1	30	36	2	3.72	10	464	39	0	3	6	5.17
Shared shutout with Gilles Gratton, 16 Oct 1973																	
Bob Blanchet	74-76	San Diego	4	211	11	1	2	2	0	3.13	...	...	...	...	...	...	...
Frank Blum	72-74	Ott, Tor, Wpg	7	158	8	0	1	0	0	3.02	2	120	15	0	0	2	7.50
Ken Broderick	76-78	Edm, Que	73	3938	259	4	29	31	2	3.95	5	227	12	0	1	3	3.17
Richard Brodeur	72-79	Quebec	300	17101	1037	8	165	114	12	3.64	51	2948	177	3	26	23	3.60
Shared shutout with Serge Aubry, 7 Feb 1973																	
Gary Bromley	76-78	Cgy, Wpg	67	3487	203	1	31	21	3	3.49	5	268	7	0	4	0	1.57
Andy Brown	74-77	Indianapolis	86	4777	314	3	25	50	3	3.55	...	...	...	...	...	...	...
Ken Brown	72-75	Alb, Edm	52	2500	149	3	20	19	0	3.55	...	...	...	...	...	...	...
Randy Burchell	76-77	Indianapolis	5	136	8	0	1	0	0	3.53	...	...	...	...	...	...	...
Jacques Caron	75-77	Cle, Cin	26	1422	69	3	14	6	3	2.91	1	14	2	0	0	1	12.86
Gerry Cheevers	72-76	Cleveland	191	11352	591	14	99	78	9	3.12	19	1151	63	0	7	12	3.28
Gaye Cooley	76	New England	0	0	0	0	0	0	0	-	1	1	0	0	0	0	0.00
Jim Corsi	77-79	Quebec	63	3380	208	3	26	27	1	3.69	2	66	7	0	0	1	6.36
Tom Cottringer	72-73	Philadelphia	2	122	8	0	1	1	0	3.93	...	...	...	...	...	...	...
Rich Coutu	73-76	Chi, Cin	24	1416	97	0	9	13	1	4.11	...	...	...	...	...	...	...
Mike Curran	72-77	Minnesota	130	7377	423	9	63	50	8	3.44	7	379	23	0	2	5	3.64
Joe Daley	72-79	Winnipeg	308	17835	1002	12	167	113	13	3.37	49	2706	149	2	30	15	3.30
Michel Deguise	73-76	Quebec	50	2585	156	1	18	18	3	3.62	...	...	...	...	...	...	...
Gerry Desjardins	74-75	M-B	41	2282	162	0	9	28	1	4.26	...	...	...	...	...	...	...
Michel Dion	74-79	Ind, Cin	149	8242	450	5	62	66	7	3.28	7	371	22	0	2	4	3.56
Peter Donnelly	72-75	NY, Van, Que	100	5559	344	5	44	44	2	3.71	...	...	...	...	...	...	...
Gary Doyle	73-74	Edmonton	1	60	4	0	1	0	0	4.00	...	...	...	...	...	...	...
Dave Dryden	74-79	Chi, Edm	242	13820	808	8	112	113	10	3.51	18	958	63	0	6	11	3.95
Rich Dumas	74-75	Chicago	1	1	0	0	0	0	0	0.00	...	...	...	...	...	...	...
Ed Dyck	74-75	Indianapolis	32	1692	123	0	3	21	3	4.36	...	...	...	...	...	...	...
George Gardner	72-74	LA, Van	79	4423	287	1	23	45	5	3.89	3	116	11	0	1	2	5.69
John Garrett	73-79	Min, Tor, Bir, NE	323	18919	1110	14	148	151	15	3.52	32	1816	124	1	15	15	4.10
Andre Gill	72-74	Chicago	46	2512	164	0	8	31	2	3.92	11	614	38	0	6	5	3.71
Russ Gillow	72-76	LA, SD	109	5713	333	4	37	47	6	3.50	9	346	17	0	1	2	2.95
Ron Grahame	73-77	Houston	143	8528	425	12	102	37	3	2.99	36	2158	116	4	22	14	3.23
Gilles Gratton	72-75	Ott, Tor	161	9102	560	4	81	66	7	3.69	13	662	37	1	5	5	3.35
Shared shutout with Les Binkley, 16 Oct 1973																	
Chris Grigg	75-76	Denver/Ottawa	2	80	13	0	0	0	0	9.75	...	...	...	...	...	...	...
Clay Hebenton	75-77	Phoenix	58	3209	229	0	17	30	3	4.28	...	...	...	...	...	...	...
Paul Hoganson	73-78	LA, M-B, NE, Cin, Ind	143	7244	496	5	44	71	4	4.11	5	348	17	1	3	2	2.93
Bill Holden	73-74	Tor, Wpg	2	70	4	0	0	1	0	3.43	...	...	...	...	...	...	...
Leif Holmquist	75-76	Indianapolis	19	1079	54	0	6	9	3	3.00	...	...	...	...	...	...	...
Bill Hughes	72-73	Houston	3	170	11	0	0	1	1	3.88	...	...	...	...	...	...	...
Ed Humphreys	75-77	Cgy, Que	30	1681	101	1	14	13	1	3.60	1	20	0	0	0	0	0.00
Gary Inness	77-79	Indianapolis	63	3459	251	0	17	36	5	4.35	...	...	...	...	...	...	...
Bob Johnson	75-76	D-O, Cle	42	2377	144	1	17	22	1	3.63	2	120	8	0	0	2	4.00
Joe Junkin	73-75	NY-J, SD	69	3961	243	2	27	32	4	3.68	...	...	...	...	...	...	...
Hannu Kampurri	78-79	Edmonton	2	90	10	0	0	1	0	6.67	...	...	...	...	...	...	...
John Kiely	75-76	Cincinnati	22	1087	78	0	6	8	1	4.31	...	...	...	...	...	...	...
Gary Kurt	72-77	NY, NY-J, Phx	176	9932	690	3	72	86	7	4.17	4	207	12	0	1	2	3.48
Bruce Landon	72-77	New England	122	6695	386	2	50	50	9	3.46	8	389	21	0	4	2	3.24
Norm Lapointe	75-78	Cincinnati	77	4105	280	2	30	37	3	4.09	4	273	16	0	0	3	3.52
Curt Larsson	74-77	Winnipeg	68	3820	265	1	30	30	2	4.16	3	130	7	0	2	0	3.23
Jacques Lemelin	72-73	Quebec	9	435	29	0	3	4	1	4.00	...	...	...	...	...	...	...
Louis Levasseur	75-79	Min, Edm, NE, Que	85	4916	281	5	37	36	8	3.43	15	911	49	0	8	7	3.23
Mike Liut	77-79	Cincinnati	81	4396	270	3	31	39	4	3.69	3	179	10	0	1	2	3.35
Ken Lockett	76-77	San Diego	45	2397	148	1	18	19	1	3.70	5	260	19	0	1	3	4.38
Markus Mattsson	77-79	Que, Wpg	68	3767	241	0	30	29	3	3.84	...	...	...	...	...	...	...
Jack McCartan	72-75	Minnesota	42	2263	139	1	16	19	1	3.69	4	213	14	0	1	2	3.94
Peter McDuffe	77-78	Indianapolis	12	539	39	0	1	6	1	4.34	...	...	...	...	...	...	...
Don McLeod	72-78	Hou, Van, Cgy, Que, Edm	332	18926	1051	11	157	143	15	3.33	31	1806	96	1	18	13	3.19
Jim McLeod	72-75	Chi, NY-J, LA, M-B	97	5176	324	2	32	51	3	3.76	...	...	...	...	...	...	...
Paul Menard	72-73	Chicago	1	45	5	0	0	1	0	6.67	...	...	...	...	...	...	...
Ed Mio	77-79	Ind, Edm	44	2210	148	2	15	20	1	4.02	...	...	...	...	...	...	...
Cam Newton	73-76	Chi, D-O, Cle	102	6106	352	2	48	51	3	3.46	11	546	40	0	2	6	4.39

Name	Seasons	Team(s)	GP	MIN	GA	SO	W	L	T	GAA	GP	MIN	GA	SO	W	L	GAA
			Regular Season								Playoffs						
Jack Norris	72-76	Alb, Edm, Phx	191	11030	582	5	86	82	12	3.16	10	509	36	0	2	7	4.24
Ted Ouimet	74-75	New England	1	20	3	0	0	0	0	9.00	...	...	...	...	...	...	...
Marcel Paille	72-73	Philadelphia	15	611	49	0	2	8	0	4.81	1	26	5	0	0	1	11.54
Bernie Parent	72-73	Philadelphia	63	3653	220	2	33	28	0	3.61	1	70	3	0	0	1	2.57
Jim Park	75-78	Indianapolis	54	2888	178	1	23	23	4	3.70	6	293	12	2	3	2	2.45
Bob "Miche" Perreault	72-73	Los Angeles	1	60	2	0	1	0	0	2.00	...	...	...	...	...	...	...
Jacques Plante	74-75	Edmonton	31	1592	88	1	15	14	1	3.32	...	...	...	...	...	...	...
Robert "Cap" Raeder	75-77	New England	29	1428	77	2	12	11	1	3.24	15	879	38	2	7	8	3.24
Pat Riggin	78-79	Birmingham	46	2511	158	1	16	22	5	3.78	...	...	...	...	...	...	...
Wayne Rutledge	72-78	Houston	175	10372	563	6	93	72	7	3.25	16	873	42	0	9	6	2.89
Nick Sanza	75-76	Denver/Ottawa	1	20	5	0	0	1	0	15.00	...	...	...	...	...	...	...
Jim Shaw	74-76	Toronto	37	1832	133	0	11	16	2	4.36	5	262	18	0	2	2	4.12
Al Smith	72-79	New England	260	15389	834	10	141	98	15	3.25	35	1947	124	1	18	15	3.82
Gary Smith	78-79	Ind, Wpg	22	1293	92	0	7	13	1	4.28	10	563	35	0	8	2	3.73
Danny Sullivan	72-74	Phi, Van	2	120	10	0	1	1	0	5.00	...	...	...	...	...	...	...
Dave Tataryn	75-76	Toronto	23	1261	100	0	7	12	1	4.76	...	...	...	...	...	...	...
Gord Tumilson	72-73	Winnipeg	3	106	10	0	0	2	0	5.66	...	...	...	...	...	...	...
Frank Turnbull	75-78	Edmonton	4	166	15	0	0	2	0	5.42	...	...	...	...	...	...	...
Mario Vien	75-76	Toronto	26	1228	105	0	4	14	3	5.13	...	...	...	...	...	...	...
Ernie Wakely	72-79	Wpg, SD, Cin, Hou, Bir	334	19331	1064	16	164	137	21	3.30	31	1740	109	2	15	16	3.76
Ed Walsh	78-79	Edmonton	3	144	9	0	0	2	0	3.75	...	...	...	...	...	...	...
Carl Wetzel	72-73	Minnesota	1	60	3	0	0	1	0	3.00	...	...	...	...	...	...	...
Bob Whidden	72-76	Cleveland	98	5725	327	2	34	51	9	3.43	...	...	...	...	...	...	...
Ian Wilkie	72-74	NY, LA, Edm	33	1766	118	1	15	13	1	4.01	1	41	4	0	0	1	5.85
Wayne Wood	74-79	Van, Cgy, Tor, Bir	104	5167	335	2	27	39	4	3.97	1	29	3	0	0	0	6.21
Chris Worthy	73-76	Edmonton	82	4368	289	2	27	39	4	3.97	4	206	15	0	1	2	4.37
Lynn Zimmermann	75-78	D-O, Hou	28	1661	115	0	12	14	0	4.15	4	239	21	0	1	2	5.27

CHAPTER 41

Significant Others

Nine Little-known and "Forgotten" Teams

St. Nicholas Hockey Club

Shirley Fischler

THE LONGEST-LIVED AMATEUR HOCKEY TEAM in the United States, the St. Nicholas Hockey Club, missed being the first U.S.-based amateur ice hockey club to play on indoor ice by little more than a season. The St. Nicholas rink opened in Manhattan at 66th Street and Columbus Avenue in 1895. It was the second major indoor rink opened in New York City in the waning years of the 19th century. Organized amateur ice hockey had come to big-city America the year before, when the Ice Palace opened December 14, 1894, at 101st Street and Lexington Avenue on Manhattan's upper East Side. Just a few days later, the city of Baltimore opened its North Avenue Rink with an ice hockey game between the Baltimore Athletic Club and Johns Hopkins University (December 26, 1894). The New York Hockey Club began playing at the Ice Palace in 1894, while the St. Nick's club started up in 1896.

With such notable patrons as Cornelius Vanderbilt, Mr. and Mrs. John Jacob Astor and Mr. and Mrs. J. Pierpont Morgan gliding across the ice, the St. Nicholas rink promised to be one of the greatest in the world—complete with lounges for club members. It also would have a grill room and restaurant "where luncheons and suppers will be served, it is promised, in a well-appointed manner," glowed *The New York Times*. The arena boasted one of the first state-of-the-art artificial ice plants in the world, enabling hockey to be played long after the arrival of spring. On April 11, 1896, for instance, the St. Paul's School varsity team and its alumni played a match at St. Nick's, with the grads winning 3–1. This game, incidentally, began a 70-year tradition whereby the Concord, New Hampshire, school would send a hockey team to New York City for an annual game.

In November, 1896, the first U.S. amateur hockey league was formed, with the official moniker of the American Amateur Hockey League (AAHL). In its inaugural season, the member clubs of the AAHL were the St. Nicholas Hockey Club, the New York Athletic Club, the Crescent Athletic Club and the Skating Club of Brooklyn (which played its games in the third new indoor rink to open in New York City, the Brooklyn Ice Palace, on Atlantic Avenue near Bedford). Although "amateur" would remain the second word in the title of the AAHL throughout its 21-year life, it didn't take long for the distinction between amateur and professional to become seriously blurred.

By the early 1900s, professional ice hockey was being played throughout Canada and the northern United States, and it wasn't long before the AAHL began to encourage professionals to join their ranks. How? By getting them jobs off the ice that supplied the ex-pros with an income while allowing them to maintain "amateur" status as players.

The New York Wanderers were an AAHL team after the turn of the 20th century, and one that was certainly not above luring professional talent from Canada. The Wanderers invited future NHL stars the Cleghorn brothers, Sprague and Odie, as well as Cooper Smeaton, to play for them in the eight-game 1907 season. Smeaton, who would later become a distinguished NHL referee and trustee of the Stanley Cup, explained how it all worked in a 1968 interview:

"The deal was an attractive one," Smeaton recalled. "In addition to playing hockey we were given jobs. I worked for the Spalding Sporting Goods Company. Odie was at a stock brokerage concern and Sprague went with the telephone company. We weren't considered professionals because our salaries were paid by the companies we worked for and we just played hockey at off-time .... We played at the St. Nicholas Rink near Central Park. It also had a riding academy, a bar and restaurant. If memory serves me, the rink was on the second floor."

While the Cleghorns and Smeaton raised the level of AAHL play, they also introduced a frontier-like, brawling style that had previously been unknown in the genteel, college-bred ranks of the early AAHL. The March 14, 1914, issue of the *Brooklyn Daily Eagle* described a game which St. Nick's managed to win 5–3 despite the violent tendencies of the Wanderers: "... The match was fairly clean until well along toward the end of the struggle. Then Ford, Aumond and Kinsella [Wanderers] started to show their true colors, and instead of playing hockey they began to 'lay' for the St. Nicholas players. 'Cupid' Ellis and Turrell [both of St. Nick's] were the men that the Wanderers trio were most anxious to 'get.' "

Kinsella finally did "get" Turrell, giving him a vicious but unpenalized check right in front of the Wanderers net. Although the Wanderers lost, outraged St. Nick's fans took issue with the Wanderers' play as they filed off the ice. Kinsella, the culprit who administered the nasty check to Turrell, didn't like the fans' jibes. Before leaving the ice, he called on his hecklers to join him, which they did.

"Inside of a second," continued the *Brooklyn Daily Eagle* report, "there were a half-dozen spectators on the playing surface, including one woman. Then the fun began. It was a small riot while it lasted. However, players and spectators were soon pushed off the ice and the incident was ended."

Still, for the most part, the AAHL teams would be composed of true amateurs who had come from the Ivy League. When the Intercollegiate Hockey League formed in the winter of 1900, with Columbia, Dartmouth, Harvard, Princeton and Yale as its founding members (Cornell would join for the 1910 season), it immediately became a veritable incubator or "farm" system for AAHL teams, among them St. Nick's.

The original St. Nicholas Hockey Club was organized by Kenneth Gordon of West Orange, New Jersey, a gifted amateur player who led the club until 1924, when it was taken over by Anton "Pop" von Bernuth. Von Bernuth, one of the best hockey players to come from Columbia University, remained honorary chairman of the St. Nick's club until his death in 1968. More importantly, von Bernuth coached and played with the St. Nicholas Hockey Club during the tragically short era of the team's most legendary star, Hobey Baker.

Hobey Baker was the St. Nick's rover back in the days when ice hockey was a seven-man game. The rover didn't play a set position, but was free to roam the ice, taking any role that was needed. Sometimes, the rover acted as a fourth forward, leading the rush or forechecking in the opponent's defensive zone. Just as often, the rover might act as a third defenseman. (Defensemen at the time were usually called the "point" and "cover point.") Most of all, the rover was always "on patrol." Hobey Baker was a superlative rover and was considered the first world-class hockey player born in the United States. In fact, in 1913, the *Boston Journal* said of Baker that he was "without doubt the greatest amateur hockey player ever developed in this country or in Canada. No player has ever been able to weave in or out of a defense and change his pace and direction with the uncanny skill and generalship of Baker. He is the wonder player of hockey. Above all, he is extremely clean in his work on the ice. He believes that rough stuff has no place in the game."

Born in Wissahickon, Pennsylvania, in 1892, Hobart Amory Hare Baker played his first organized ice hockey at the St. Paul's School in Concord, New Hampshire. From there, he went to Princeton, where he captained the varsity hockey team to two intercollegiate titles. After graduation, Baker immediately joined the St. Nicholas Hockey Club.

Although Baker had played at the St. Nick's rink with both St. Paul's and Princeton, his stint in the St. Nicholas jersey would be all too brief. In his first of just two seasons with the club in 1914–15, St. Nick's would be the AAHL champion. They also faced off against the University of Toronto, the Argonauts of Toronto and Queen's University of Kingston, Ontario, and defeated them all. On that team with Baker was Pop von Bernuth, Russell Ellis, Wendell Kohn, Walton Cox, Bill Willetts, Gouvy Carnochan (the goaltender, ex of Harvard), Rufus Trimble, Eric Kilner and Tunnicliff Fox.

The championship in Baker's first season with St. Nick's actually marked the fourth straight year in which the St. Nicholas Hockey Club had won the national senior amateur hockey title. But the Great War would soon intercede, and by the 1917–18 season, hockey operations were suspended for St. Nick's and the entire AAHL. Hobey Baker became an aviator and joined the 103rd Aero Squadron (formerly the famed Lafayette Esquadrille Flying Corps), exhibiting the same incredible ability and drive he had shown as a hockey player. Baker was awarded the French *Croix de Guerre* for exceptional valor under fire during the summer of 1918.

But after receiving his discharge papers on the morning of December 21, 1918, the 26-year-old Baker decided to test fly a recently repaired plane before departing the Continent for good. As Baker soared about 500 meters above the airfield, the plane's engine suddenly sputtered and died. The greatest amateur hockey player in the United States crashed and was killed in the French countryside.

Despite the death of the country's star player, hockey in the United States underwent a postwar renaissance, with amateur and professional leagues and teams sprouting all over the country. However, shortly after the end of World War I, the St. Nick's Hockey Club had been forced to leave the old St. Nicholas arena. For a couple of seasons, the team played in various rinks in Westchester County, mostly in the town of White Plains, New York. The old AAHL never resumed play after the war, so St. Nick's became part of the Eastern Amateur Hockey League, which later morphed into the Metropolitan Amateur Hockey Association (MAHA). In the meantime, professional hockey in the form of the National Hockey League soon came to New York City—first in the form of the New York Americans (1925) and then as the New York Rangers (1926). With the opening of the new Madison Square Garden at 8th Avenue between 49th and 50th Streets in 1925, the St. Nicholas Hockey Club moved back to Manhattan.

St. Nick's played Sunday nights at the Garden, competing with the other teams of the Metropolitan League. In 1926, for instance, St. Nick's joined five other New York-area clubs as they inaugurated the MAHA season with a tripleheader at the Garden. St. Nick's faced-off against the Canadian Club of New York, the Knickerbockers Hockey Club played the New York Athletic Club and the new Seventh Regiment team faced-off against the Crescent AC.

By 1935, the St. Nick's Hockey Club was taken over by player John Thomas (Yale, Class of 1933). Thomas would run the club until it was again disbanded because of world conflict in 1942, but before the Second World War forced the team to shutdown, Thomas distinguished himself with St. Nick's in more ways than on the ice. He had purchased the old Brooklyn Ice Palace and converted the old rink into a clubhouse for St. Nick's, complete with team pictures of every season and the likeness of handsome Hobey Baker over the fireplace. Before suspending operations, St. Nick's added another national championship in 1939.

After World War II, the reins of the St. Nicholas Hockey Club were assumed by S. Kip Farrington, Jr., a late-blooming goaltender who served as president of the club through 1950. During this time, St. Nick's played in a rink in Norwalk, Connecticut. Team captain "Junie" Merriam then took over the club until 1952, when the Korean War caused the third break in the life of St. Nick's. In 1956, another ex-Yale player named Danny Lufkin brought St. Nick's to life yet again. Lufkin passed the baton to Pete Bostwick of Middlebury, Vermont, in 1958. Bostwick still served as president of the hockey club as St. Nick's entered the new millennium and its third century of existence.

Practicing weekly at the Westchester Skating Academy rink in Elmsford, New York, St. Nick's plays at least 20 elite-level senior games per season. The under-35 elite senior team won the USA Hockey-sponsored national championship in 1996 and 1998. The club's 35-and-over (non-checking) team was even more successful, winning the nationals in three consecutive seasons from 1997 to 1999.

Terry Morris (Princeton, 1989) captained the St. Nick's under-35 team in 2000. Typical of most members over the decades, the former East Coast Division I collegiate player worked days in New York City's financial community, then strapped on the skates at night.

"We play at least six games a season versus various colleges in the Northeast," explained Morris. "Schools such as Yale, Trinity College, Quinnipiac College and Connecticut College. We played Army a couple of seasons ago. Colleges like to play St. Nick's early in October, using us as a primer before starting league games. I remember after an exhibition game at Yale, these kids were shaking their heads, saying to each other, 'How did these old guys beat us 6–2?'

"Most of us played Division I college; some tried the NHL. Now, we each pay our own way—ice time, travel, equipment—but we also get great support from team alumni. I send our annual alumni letter to former players who are in their late 90s, even a few who're 100 or more."

The St. Nicholas Hockey Club, the oldest amateur sports organization in the world (the Leander Boat Club in England is second), is still going strong.

PITTSBURGH YELLOW JACKETS

Bob Grove

AS THE MASTERMIND behind several successful mayoral campaigns, Roy D. Schooley was one of the most influential members of the Republican party in Pittsburgh in the 1920s and no stranger to rhetoric. But the claim he made to reporters in April 1925 had nothing to do with politics or, it could be argued, pretentiousness.

A native of Welland, Ontario, Schooley at this time also enjoyed a measure of notoriety in the hockey world. He was secretary-treasurer of the United States Amateur Hockey Association; manager of Duquesne Garden, the sprawling ice rink and showplace located in the Oakland section of the city; and the proud owner-manager of the defending USAHA champion Pittsburgh Yellow Jackets.

"The Yellow Jackets are not only a good team—they are the greatest amateur team in the world," Schooley said on the eve of his club's USAHA championship series with the rival Fort Pitt Hornets. It was a difficult statement to dispute—before or after it was issued.

Schooley had arrived in Pittsburgh in 1901, gaining acclaim as a hockey referee. He later gravitated toward administrative roles with various Pittsburgh teams. By the mid-1920s, he was respected and had the means and the vision to assemble an amateur team of remarkable quality.

Although a Pittsburgh team had competed in the Central Division of the USAHA in 1921–22, it wasn't until the following season that the entry became known as the Yellow Jackets. Moved to the Western Division, the 1922–23 team finished 10–10 for Rennison "Dinny" Manners, who served as player, coach and manager.

On behalf of the USAHA, Schooley invited 21-year-old Canadian Lionel Conacher to serve as referee for the Yellow Jackets' final two league games that season against Duluth. Conacher was a more noteworthy attraction than the game itself when he skated onto the Garden ice on March 9, 1923. The *Pittsburgh Gazette-Times* noted the Toronto native's accomplishments as a champion of hockey, wrestling, lacrosse, rugby, boxing, football, baseball and just about any other game Canada could conjure up.

Conacher's boxing skills were the first to manifest themselves in Pittsburgh. During his second game as a referee on March 10, Conacher's work prompted repeated criticism from Duluth player Sandy Seaborn. Seaborn suggested he would set Conacher straight once they were off the ice, and he renewed his criticism near a dressing room following the game. Conacher's reply was a right hand that knocked out Seaborn for 15 minutes.

The Yellow Jackets invited Conacher and Ottawa native Rodger Smith to play defense during the exhibition games that closed out the season. Conacher and Smith, who completed scoring rushes at one end of the ice almost as routinely as they broke them up at the other, made their Pittsburgh debut on March 16 at the Garden. The hulking Conacher, 6'2" and 195 pounds, scored the winning goal in a 5–2 victory over his former Toronto Aura Lee club and thus embarked on a brief but memorable career with the Yellow Jackets.

Schooley headed a group of businessmen who assumed management of the Garden for the 1923–24 season. Adding the title of Yellow Jackets president, he remade the team's roster.

Aware of Conacher's hockey skills and desire to play American football, Schooley suggested the former Toronto Argonauts halfback try the college game in Pittsburgh. This, of course, would leave him available to play hockey when the USAHA season began in late December.

Conacher failed to gain entrance to the University of Pittsburgh in 1923, although the Grey Cup hero was given a brief introduction to the American game that fall at Bellefonte Academy, a prep school near the Pennsylvania State University. Conacher later earned a spot in the backfield of Duquesne University's 1924 football team, by which time he was better known in Pittsburgh as a hockey player.

Schooley also brought back the 6', 175-pound Smith, spare defenseman Manners and forwards Paddy Sullivan, Terry McGovern and Herb Drury for the 1923–24 season while adding five new players. Foremost among that group, which included forwards Francis "Duke" McCurry, Wilfred "Tex" White, Harold "Baldy" Cotton and Alex McKinnon, was goaltender Roy "Shrimp" Worters.

Worters stood only 5'3" tall but compensated with great agility, quickness and anticipation. Worters was an interesting sight playing behind his two huge defensemen, but he was every bit as challenging for opponents as Conacher and Smith. He recorded 30 shutouts for the Yellow Jackets between 1923 and 1925, during which time Pittsburgh played 80 regular-season and playoff games in the USAHA. He allowed more than three goals in a game only twice.

Schooley went one step further toward shaping a winning team in the fall of 1923. As his coach, he hired Dick Carroll, who in 1918 had led the Toronto Arenas to the first Stanley Cup championship won by a National Hockey League team, and in 1920 had coached the Toronto Canoe Club to the Memorial Cup with a roster that included Conacher, Worters, McCurry and White.

Herb Drury, whose speed and stickhandling ability made him a favorite of the Pittsburgh fans, scored a goal in each of the first two games of the season. He didn't rejoin the lineup until the playoffs, however, as the naturalized American citizen was busy leading the United States to a silver medal in the 1924 Olympic Games by scoring 22 goals in five games. He had also helped the U.S. to the silver medal in the 1920 Games.

So deep were the Yellow Jackets that they didn't even miss Drury. They went 15–5–0 in a six-team Western Division that included Cleveland's Nels Stewart, Minneapolis's Ching Johnson and St. Paul's Moose Goheen—all future Hall of Famers. Captain Conacher scored a team-high 12 goals, and White fired home nine of his 11 goals in the first five games. The Yellow Jackets were a perfect 10–0 at home, where they lost only four games over two seasons.

Among the notable games that season was a 2–0 loss at Eveleth on January 11 in a match played with the temperature at 27 degrees below zero, and a 3–2 home win over Eveleth on February 2. The Yellow Jackets tied the latter game on a disputed goal with four minutes to play when the puck appeared inside the net, which had been toppled during a goal-mouth scramble. Rangers manager Tom Monroe pulled his team off the ice in protest, and when Schooley was unable to persuade him to continue the game, referee Jack Carmichael ordered Pittsburgh to line up and score the decisive goal. Paddy Sullivan carried the puck down the ice and allowed Worters to tap it home.

Pittsburgh played four games each against St. Paul and Cleveland in the Western Division playoffs, the scheduling of which drew howls of protest from St. Paul manager Eddie Fitzgerald. When he expressed his dismay with the USAHA forcing his team to play eight games in 14 days, an angered Schooley drew up a new schedule—giving St. Paul 13 days instead.

Worters allowed only two goals in the first six playoff games, including a scoreless tie at St. Paul on March 8 that lasted four overtimes and was the longest game in USAHA history to that point. (Pittsburgh fans had been invited to Duquesne Garden to hear reports of the March 7 and March 8 games in St. Paul via a special wire, not an uncommon practice at the time.) But because those two goals resulted in a pair of 1–0 victories by rival Cleveland, the Yellow Jackets needed heroics from Conacher to reach the championship series. He recorded a hat trick in a 6–0 home win over Cleveland on March 20 and scored the overtime goal at Cleveland on March 24 that produced a 2–1 victory and eliminated the Indians.

"If you were to ask the players on the opposing team who is likely to be the first man to break through their defense," Schooley said, "they would quickly reply, 'Connie.' He's a great hockey player and a leader of men. He proved this time and again this season."

Herb Drury, who aside from his skills, was always noticeable because he played with a cap on his bald head, scored four goals in the best-of-seven championship series against Boston AA, the Eastern Division champion. The oldest player on the team at 29, Drury scored twice in the 6–1 game five home victory that clinched the USAHA championship on April 4.

Alex McKinnon turned pro for the 1924–25 season, while Dinny Manners and Paddy Sullivan left the Yellow Jackets for the Fort Pitt Hornets, who were entered in the USAHA's Eastern Division and shared the Garden with their city rivals. Schooley replaced them with forwards Dalton Meeking, Harold Darragh and Hubert "Hib" Milks, the latter two having skated for the Yellow Jackets during the 1922–23 season.

Thus, Pittsburgh's depth and defensive prowess remained intact. After the Yellow Jackets opened the season with a pair of shutout victories over Eveleth, the Rangers' Eddie Rodden admitted, "Beating the Yellow Jackets is a mighty hard thing to do because they have strong players and they can shift forwards on you. The one line coming on is just as good as the one going to take the bench."

Worters recorded 12 shutouts in the first half of the 40-game schedule, during which the Yellow Jackets were beaten only three times. Newcomers Darragh and Milks accounted for 16 goals over the first 20 games, and they became even more important players during a lackluster second half.

In mid-February, Herb Drury suffered a badly cut thumb, Rodger Smith injured his knee and Duke McCurry missed games due to midterm examinations at Pitt. As a result, the Yellow Jackets scored only five goals during a 1–5–1 stretch and Eveleth took the second half title, forcing a playoff for the division championship.

Pittsburgh opened the series with a pair of home victories, then eliminated Eveleth with a 2–1 victory on March 31 in Duluth, where the series was moved because Eveleth's natural ice surface had melted. The Yellow Jackets had luck on their side in game three, as the winning goal resulted from an attempted Eveleth clear that bounced off Rodden's skate and into the net.

The victory over Eveleth set up a showdown between the Yellow Jackets and the Hornets, who featured the USAHA's leading scorer in John McKinnon. The first three games of the series each went to overtime as the Hornets, led not by McKinnon but by Paddy Sullivan, gave the Yellow Jackets all they could handle.

Conacher scored at 3:50 of the 10-minute overtime period in game one, stealing the puck from McKinnon behind his own goal and rushing the length of the ice to beat Fort Pitt goaltender Joe Miller for a 2–1 victory. Conacher's third-period goal in game two forced overtime, where Drury and McCurry scored for a 3–1 win before a record 8,000 fans at the Garden.

McCurry's goal with 2:24 to play in the third period forced overtime in game three, which ended in a 2–2 tie. Sullivan scored for the fourth consecutive game on April 11, but Conacher and Cotton answered for the Yellow Jackets, who thus retained their title.

So talented were the 1925 Yellow Jackets that every member of the team except Meeking turned pro that fall when Schooley sold the team to Duquesne Garden owner Henry Townsend and attorney James F. Callahan, who renamed it the Pirates and entered it in the NHL. Conacher and Worters went on to the Hockey Hall of Fame, while Conacher, Cotton and Darragh later played for Stanley Cup champions.

When the Pirates franchise was transferred to Philadelphia in 1930, Schooley revived the Yellow Jackets in the seven-team professional International-American Hockey League for the 1930–31 and 1931–32 seasons.

Coach Charley Reid's team finished fourth in its first season and was swept out of the playoffs, then finished fifth and missed the playoffs the following season. Those teams featured former Stanley Cup winners Eddie Rodden, Gord Fraser, Fred Lowry and Milt Halliday, as well as future Cup winners Earl Miller and Doc Romnes.

Schooley died in 1933 at the age of 53, two years after leaving his position as city treasurer amid an embezzlement scandal. Theater magnate John Harris assumed management of Duquesne Garden and in January 1935 revived the Yellow Jackets name for his unaffiliated amateur team. Coached by Dinny Manners, it won 15 of 21 exhibitions and by season's end featured a 19-year-old American goaltender named Frank Brimsek. He made his Pittsburgh debut on February 20, 1935, in a victory over Niagara Falls AC.

Harris put the Yellow Jackets in the Eastern Amateur Hockey League for the next two seasons, and Brimsek was often the team's best player. Gordie Drillon, who like Brimsek would later have his name engraved on the Stanley Cup and be enshrined in the Hall of Fame, registered a team-high 34 points to help Pittsburgh reach the Hershey Cup playoffs in 1935–36. Future United States Hockey Hall of Fame member Pete Bessone played defense for the 1936–37 team, which missed the playoffs.

Thus, there were three incarnations of the Pittsburgh Yellow Jackets in 15 years. The first, at least, lived up to Schooley's claim and, however briefly, carved out a special place in hockey history.

TORONTO CANADAS

Eric Zweig

TO COMMEMORATE ITS 70TH ANNIVERSARY in 1978, the International Ice Hockey Federation published a book about the history of the international game. In its chapter on the origins of the World Championship tournament, which first was held independent of the Olympic Games in 1930, the book states: "Canada won the world championship ahead of Germany, Switzerland and Austria, with the European crown going to Germany followed by Switzerland, Austria and Poland. In the world final, Germany went down to the Canadians of Port Arthur by a margin of only 6–1."

The Canadians of Port Arthur.

Books by writers from Canada also have credited the 1930 victory to Port Arthur, but at the time of the World Championships, the Bearcats were at home defending their Allan Cup title against Fort Francis, the Winnipeg Elmwoods and the Trail Smoke Eaters in the western playoffs. They eventually would be defeated by the Montreal Amateur Athletic Association in the national final. So why would they later be given credit for the 1930 victory in Europe? Likely because Canada had previously sent the defending Allan Cup champions to the Olympic tournaments in 1920, 1924 and 1928 and almost always would continue to do so at subsequent world events until the establishment of a Canadian national team in 1964. But if the Port Arthur Bearcats didn't travel to Europe in the winter of 1929–30, who did? The answer is a Toronto-area team made up of senior-aged hockey players who had chosen to continue playing the game they loved in a local industrial league.

The Weston, Ontario-based Canada Cycle and Motor company had sponsored a team in the Toronto and York Mercantile League since 1923–24. In 1928–29, the CCM team finished in first place during the regular season, beat out the second-place club from Imperial Oil in the playoffs, and went on to face the champion Stobie-Forlong team of the Mining and Brokers League for the Toronto industrial title. On Saturday, March 2, 1929, the Cycles, as city newspapers called them, won the one-game, winner-take-all series by a score of 4–3. It is interesting to note that one did not necessarily have to work for CCM to play for its hockey team. Gordie Grant, for example, actually worked at Stobie-Forlong. He played both for their team and the Cycles in 1929, suiting up for Stobie in the championship game. On the other hand, such players as Don Hutchinson and Wally Adams would continue to hold jobs at CCM long after their playing days were over. But how did a Toronto industrial league team come to represent all of Canada?

CCM executive George S. Braden traveled to Vienna on business in the late fall of 1929. While there, he decided that the growing number of hockey teams playing throughout Europe would benefit from increased exposure to Canadian clubs. No doubt he also saw a potentially lucrative new market for CCM merchandise. Upon his return to Canada, Braden lobbied the Canadian Amateur Hockey Association for permission to send his company team on a European tour. It was granted, and since the IIHF had decided to expand its European Championship into an annual World Championships, the Toronto team, wearing a white maple leaf on red sweaters and with the name 'Canadas' emblazoned beneath, also would represent the country at the tournament in Chamonix, France.

Nine of the 11 men who had played for CCM's championship team gathered at Toronto's Union Station on December 5, 1929, to begin their European adventure. One day later, goaltender Percy Timpson, defensemen Joe Griffin and Fred Radke, and forwards Grant, Adams, Hutchinson, Bert Clayton, Alex Park and Harold "Red" Armstrong, along with Braden and manager Les Grant, boarded the Canadian Pacific liner *Duchess of Atholi* at Saint John, New Brunswick, for the eight-day Atlantic crossing to England. They arrived in London on Saturday, December 14, and played their first game three nights later. Facing a team of British all-stars at the Westminster Ice Club, the Canadas won, 6–2.

"The score is of little importance," wrote the *London Times*. "The Canadas could have doubled it, had they been so inclined." What was important, the *Times* thought, were the lessons in teamwork that British hockey players could take from the game. "One of the chief troubles of ice hockey as it is played in Great Britain is the lack of understanding and cohesive team work on the part of the players; they so often become selfish individualists .... If anything is required to prove the truth of this all too obvious remark, the play of the Canadas provides this thing." In praise of their teamwork, the *Times* pointed out that "the fact that no Canadian player scored two goals suggests that the Canadas have brought their combination to a fine art." It might have been more accurate to suggest that the diversity of goal scorers pointed out the vast superiority of Canadian hockey—even Canadian industrial league hockey—over what was being played in Europe at the time.

One day after their victory in London, the Toronto Canadas left for Berlin, where they won a pair of games over the next three days. Then it was on to Sweden, but, as the *London Times* pointed out, "the situation with regard to this match is very curious: Sweden has no artificial ice rinks, hockey being played always in the open air, and for the fist time since records have been kept, which is for over a hundred years, there is as yet no ice in the country." Indeed, the game slated for Stockholm had to be rescheduled for an indoor artificial ice surface in Berlin on January 2, 1930. The Canadas beat the Swedish national team, 2–0, and then were off to Vienna for three games in the next four nights. On January 4, they faced Vienna Eislaufverein and beat them, 6–1. A day later, they took on the Prague Lawn Tennis Club, who were Continental champions in 1928, Spengler Cup champions in 1929 "and the strongest Continental team [the Canadas] are likely to encounter." The Canadian squad beat them, 15–0.

After a night off, the Canadas scored a 5–2 victory over a combined squad of Prague and Vienna players. On the morning of January 8, 1930, they took the train to Switzerland, where they posted a 12–0 win over the Rosey Club of Gstaad that same evening.

Among the many more games they played before the start of the World Championships, which was scheduled for January 27, the Canadas beat the national teams of France, Switzerland and Italy. Yet despite their hectic schedule there was some time for the players to simply be tourists. Among the small collection of photographs of the team that has survived to this day are pictures of the players on a ski vacation in the Alps. However, by the time they arrived in Chamonix the weather had turned decidedly un-winterlike.

Because the mountain town of Chamonix was relying on natural ice rinks for the world tournament, the start was delayed for four days until the weather finally became cold enough to play. The delay meant a change to the World Championship format, with the round-robin pool system being abandoned in favor of the single-game knockout method. The Canadas were given a bye into the finals, where they would face the champions from Europe in a one-game playoff for the world title. To stay sharp, the Canadian squad faced the British national team on February 1—one day after the Brits had been eliminated from the tournament by Germany. The Canadas won, 6–1. They were scheduled to take on the winner of the European final between Germany and Switzerland two days later, but once again warm weather played havoc with the plans. The Germany–Switzerland game was moved to Berlin, where it was rescheduled for Sunday, February 9. Canada would take on the winner on Monday night.

The Canadas traveled from Chamonix to Berlin via Vienna, which took them out of their way but allowed them to squeeze in three more games prior to the World Championship final. The first was played on February 6. They beat the national team of Poland, 5–0, that night. The next morning, the players awoke to a steady rain that lasted all day. Though it left the outdoor ice surface slushy and waterlogged the game that night went on as scheduled. Not surprisingly, the pace was slow. Only one goal was scored. It came in the second period when a player named Sell ("Vienna's best forward") slipped the puck past Percy Timpson. The Canadas were beaten, 1–0, but there was no time to sulk over the first loss of their European tour because on February 8, the Canadas were back on the ice for their third game in three nights. They got back on the winning track with a 6–0 victory over the Vienna Skating Club. Later that same evening, they boarded the train for Berlin—where they would arrive in time to see the German national team beat Switzerland 2–1 the next day. The following evening, the Germans would take on Canada for the world championship on home ice.

A crowd of 8,000 attended the title game. They saw the German team set a fast pace, perhaps hoping to wear down the travel-weary Canadian crew. But the Canadas kept up, and the play went from end to end with both Timpson and German goaltender Leinweber making several brilliant saves. Germany got on the scoreboard first with a goal by Gustav Jaenecke, but Gordie Grant retaliated right away after a fine solo rush. Play then became rough as the two teams pressed for the advantage. Jaenecke suffered a fractured collarbone in a fall to the ice and was forced to leave the game. A few minutes later, Alex Park put the Canadas in front. Both Grant and Park scored again in the second period as the Canadian team began to assert control. Red Armstrong and Joe Griffin completed the scoring in the third period with "the German team plainly becoming tired from their vigorous exertions, while the Canadians, thoroughly inured as they are to strenuous struggles, failed to show the least sign of fatigue." After the game, the Canadas were presented with a trophy. Later the two teams sat down to supper together.

Having won the world championship, the Canadian team flew back to London and wrapped up its tour with two more lopsided victories. On February 20, they sailed home from Southampton aboard the *Metagama*. They landed in Saint John four days later and immediately boarded a train for Toronto, which arrived at Union Station on the evening of February 25. In the 83 days since they had left, the Canadas had traveled a total of 14,000 miles. They had played 32 games and won 31 of them, outscoring their opponents 304 to 26 for an average score of better than 9–1. Yet after a small civic reception, the first Canadian hockey team to win a world championship independent from the Olympics faded into obscurity. As impressive as their accomplishments seem today, it really isn't very hard to understand why.

International hockey involving Europe and North America (Japan also was at the first World Championships) was still in its infancy in 1930. As such, the tournament at Chamonix and the title won in Berlin did not elicit much excitement in Canada where people knew there were dozens—if not hundreds—of teams playing the game at a higher level of competition than a CCM company team. *Toronto Star* sports editor W.A. Hewitt, secretary of the Ontario Hockey Association and father of Foster, summed up the prevailing attitude when he wrote:

> *"So far as Europe is concerned the Canadas team of Toronto are the 'world hockey champions' because the touring local team defeated Germany, which won the European championship. The title is an empty one, of course, and the Canadas will make no such pretensions when they come home. To their credit, however, they have played good hockey on their trip and plenty of it and have done much to educate Europeans in the fastest of all sports."*

As hockey becomes increasingly global, we might do well to remember one of the pioneering teams that helped spread the gospel overseas.

MINNESOTA'S TEAM: 1935–36 ST. PAUL SAINTS

Roger A. Godin

THE UNIVERSITY OF MINNESOTA GOLDEN GOPHERS hockey team has historically regarded itself as the state's team. The program, except for a brief period immediately after the Second World War, has recruited almost exclusively in the state. But there was another team, a minor-league professional club, that could lay claim to that title, albeit for one season. The 1935–36 St. Paul Saints of the American Hockey Association (AHA) were composed entirely of players with ties to Minnesota. The Saints won the association's regular season championship and took the St. Louis Flyers to a full five games before losing the playoff title.

The AHA was formed in 1927 as a professional league that evolved out of the once powerful United States Amateur Hockey Association (USAHA) that had folded after the 1924–25 season. The USAHA's demise was heightened by the defection of many of its key players to the NHL, which was then expanding into key American cities. The AHA existed until 1942. In the 1935–36 season, its membership consisted—in addition to St. Paul—of the St. Louis Flyers, Minneapolis Warriors (transferred from Oklahoma City in March), Tulsa Oilers, Kansas City Greyhounds and Wichita Skyhawks.

The Saints were led by league scoring champion Oscar Hansen, who had recorded 30 goals and 30 assists, and Carl "Cully" Dahlstrom's 20 goals and 23 assists. Hansen's brothers, Emory and Emil, were also on the team, with the latter serving as coach. The Hansen brothers were products of Augsburg College in Minneapolis, though two of the three were born in Centerville, South Dakota. They had grown up largely in Camrose, Alberta, where their parents had moved to farm. Other key forwards were Hodge Johnson and Jack Flood, while Virgil Johnson and Beef Munson were stalwarts on defense. Johnson was a rushing defenseman who scored nine goals and 20 assists while Oscar Almquist was superb in goal. Remaining team members are listed at the end of this essay, along with other American players who performed in the AHA that season. American players made up approximately 35 percent of the league's personnel.

St. Paul won the 48-game regular season with a record of 32–13–3, which was good for 64 points (no points were awarded for ties) to St. Louis's 54. Minneapolis and Tulsa tied for third with 42 points, while Kansas City was fifth with 40 and Wichita last with 32. The tie between Minneapolis and Tulsa was resolved by a special playoff game in Tulsa on March 21 in which the Oilers defeated the Warriors 2–1 in double overtime. That set the stage for a best-of-three series between St. Louis and Tulsa. The winner would go on to face the Saints in the best-of-five finals.

The semifinal series began on March 22 in St. Louis. The teams fought to a 1–1 overtime tie. Joe Matte of the Flyers and Sonny Wakeford of the Oilers traded goals in the second and third periods respectively. There was no provision for playing overtime. Two nights later, St. Louis, with borrowed goaltender Hub Nelson in the nets, shut out Tulsa 4–0. Fido Purpur, Pete Palangio, Harold Johnson and Johnny McKinnon got the Flyers goals. St. Louis's regular netminder Mickey Murray had been injured in the tie game and the Flyers got league permission to use Minneapolis's Nelson. He was to be a critical factor in their ultimate success.

The series shifted to Tulsa on March 25 as St. Louis advanced to the finals with a 2–1 victory. Ray Burmeister got the winning goal at 18:34 of the third period when he knocked in a rebound of Palangio's long shot past goalie Frank Ceryance. The final series was scheduled to begin in St. Paul on March 30. The second game would be played on April 1 in the Minnesota capital with all remaining games slated for St. Louis.

On March 27, the Saints traveled 200 miles to Hibbing to both practice and play an exhibition game. This was necessary as their home arena, the St. Paul Auditorium, was being used for an automobile show and the ice had been removed from the nearby Hippodrome. Their opponents in the exhibition game were billed as the Hibbing Independents and included future NHL players John Mariucci, Joe Papike, Paul Schaeffer and Al Suomi (all Eveleth, Minnesota natives), as well as some players from teams eliminated from the AHA playoffs. St. Paul won 7–4 as Oscar and Emory Hansen each had two goals.

Just before the finals opened, the *St. Paul Pioneer Press* announced its All-AHA team. Perhaps to no one's surprise the Saints garnered seven of the 13 spots on the team as three players each were named at center, left wing, right wing and defense plus one goaltender. St. Paul players Oscar Hansen and Cully Dahlstrom were at center, Jack Flood at left wing, Hodge Johnson and Emory Hansen at right wing, and Emil Hansen, along with Virgil Johnson, was on defense. St. Louis placed Peter Palangio at left wing and Leo Carbol on defense.

The St. Paul-St. Louis series actually marked a replay from 1934–35. That season, the Saints, as champions of the now defunct Central League, had defeated the Flyers three games to none to claim the mythical Midwest championship. St. Louis coach Alex "Shrimp" McPherson was confident of reversing the previous result as he told the *Pioneer Press*:

> *Remember that this club is a lot different than the one St. Paul whipped last spring. Then the boys were pretty low because several weeks of salaries were unpaid and we had to play the entire series here instead of having a couple of games at home. There's nothing like that this year. We've had a great financial season at St. Louis and the boys want to show the fans at home they can win the championship. I think we can win, and in four games, too.*

St. Paul jumped out to a 2–0 lead within the first 10 minutes of the opening game on two goals by Oscar Hansen. The teams then battled evenly until Pete Palangio ruined Oscar Almquist's shutout bid with five seconds to go in the game. The 2–1 victory wasn't without its costs. Julie Matschke left the game early because of the flu and Virgil Johnson was forced out after being slashed in the neck by Palangio. Both Emory Hansen and Hodge Johnson were playing hurt. Coach Emil Hansen later told the *Pioneer Press*:

> *We want to win that first game, and we did. Every one we can win at home is doubly important in the playoff, for we haven't had much success at St. Louis. I still don't believe either team will win in three straight games, but I do believe that we'll be champions for the second time after next Sunday night.*

When the puck was dropped for game two, Matschke, Johnson, Emory Hansen and Hodge Johnson were ready, but Matschke played only a few minutes and Johnson was below form. The Flyers were without right wing Gord Teel who was sent back to St. Louis with a severe case of the flu. The visitors took a 2–0 first-period lead on goals by Paddy Paddon and Palangio, the latter a shorthand effort. Future Hall of Famer Moose Goheen officiated this game and was responsible for the Flyers' shorthand situation. When he called St. Louis's Joe Matte for slashing Cully Dahlstrom, Matte cursed him and Moose gave him a five-minute major. The Saints finally scored at the 15:41 mark of the third period as Jack Flood scored from Bill McGlone and Oscar Hansen to make the score 2–1. The game was rough and Virgil Johnson was knocked out for five minutes when Matte charged him.

The series moved to St. Louis for the remainder of the games and the Flyers were thought to have a distinct advantage there because of the narrower ice surface. St. Paul had won only once there during the regular season, but they would win again on April 3 to go up two games to one in the series. Coach Emil Hansen got the game's only goal in the first period when he moved from behind his own blue line, cut down the right side, first feigned defenseman Leo Carbol before slipping the puck between his legs and then beat Nelson. It was another rough game as Dahlstrom was slashed across his left hand and was unable to shoot during the last period. Jack Flood was cut over his right eye and coach Hansen suffered a severely bruised leg.

The injury to Dahlstrom proved critical as it turned out to be a fractured left thumb and put him out of the series. With Dahlstrom gone, Hansen moved Flood to center between Pete Plegan and Hodge Johnson. The Saints coach still evoked confidence:

> *... Even with Dahlstrom out I think we can win Sunday but I hate to lose him because he has the courage as well as the hockey ability to help a team a lot in a series that has seen as much dirty hockey as this one.*

Game four on April 5 continued the chippy trend when soon after play began Oscar Hansen and St. Louis's Fido Purpur slashed at each other. While neither drew a penalty at this time, referees Fred Gordon and Ed Rodden handed out 15 in the game including three minors and a major to St. Paul's Bill McGlone. The Minnesotans sorely missed Dahlstrom, not only for his scoring touch but also for his effective backchecking. The Flyers' Gordon Teel returned to action but was too weak to continue after the first period.

St. Louis struck for three goals in the first period with Harold Johnson, Joe Carbol and Pete Palangio scoring. The latter had missed an earlier open net, but made up for it with a near rink-length dash that gave the home team a 3–0 lead at 17:10 of the first period. The Saints fought back and played their best hockey early in the middle session following a penalty to Carbol, but could not score. The Flyers went on to win 5–0 as playing coach Shrimp McPherson got two third-period goals.

> *We did very few things right. The Flyers did things right in that first period when they scored three times and were right enough through the rest of the game that we didn't score.*

So summed up coach Emil Hansen to the *St. Paul Dispatch* after St. Louis had evened the series at two games each. Unfortunately, while they started very well in the deciding game on April 6, St. Paul continued to do "very few things right." The game was held up for a half hour when the Flyers refused to take the ice while they debated with league president William Grant why they should have a larger cut of the gate receipts. Play got underway after the locals were held to the original agreement.

The Saints pressed very hard in the first period after Joe Carbol went off for tripping Hodge Johnson, but Hub Nelson came up with two brilliant stops. Shortly after Carbol returned to the ice, Paddon scored for St. Louis and they were never headed. Johnny McKinnon made it 2–0 before the end of the period when he eluded Bill McGlone and Virgil Johnson, the St. Paul defensemen, and beat Almquist. Pete Palangio, who would be the playoff scoring leader, made it 3–0 late in the third period with both Emil and Emory Hansen in the penalty box. Early in the final period, Paddon got his second goal when he stole the puck in the Saints end and hit the upper corner of the net. The visitors finally got one past Hub Nelson, who had played seven consecutive shutout periods, when Julie Matschke took a pass from Emory Hansen in front of the Flyers goal. It was the classic too little, too late as St. Louis took the game 4–1 and the championship three games to two.

Minnesota's team had been done in to a large extent by the brilliant goaltending of another Minnesotan, Hub Nelson. He was not only a Minnesotan, but a native of Minneapolis—St. Paul's rival city. In addition to Nelson's play, St. Paul also suffered from the lost of Dahlstrom and injuries that curtailed high-scoring defenseman Virgil Johnson. He had to leave the final game in the second period with a severe skate cut to his right foot. The Flyers played an aggressive game and effectively shut down league scoring leader Oscar Hansen.

Three Saints would go on to play in the NHL. The most notable was Dahlstrom who was the Calder Trophy winner for the Stanley Cup winning 1937–38 Chicago Black Hawks. Dahlstrom had an eight-year NHL career and Virgil Johnson served a two-year stint with Chicago. Oscar Hansen had "a cup of coffee" with the same team. His brother Emil had an earlier cup with the Detroit Red Wings. Dahlstrom was a 1973 inductee of the United States Hockey Hall of Fame. Johnson joined in 1974. Oscar Almquist was elected as a high school coach in 1983.

AMERICAN HOCKEY ASSOCIATION 1935–36 SEASON

St. Paul Saints • Regular Season Champions, Roster of Playing Personnel

Player	Hometown
Oscar Almquist	Eveleth, Minnesota
Cully Dahlstrom	Minneapolis, Minnesota
Jack Flood	Minneapolis, Minnesota
Emory Hansen	Minneapolis, Minnesota
Emil Hansen	Minneapolis, Minnesota
Oscar Hansen	Minneapolis, Minnesota
Hodge Johnson	Eveleth, Minnesota
Virgil Johnson	Minneapolis, Minnesota
Julie Matschke	St. Paul, Minnesota
Bill McGlone	Minneapolis, Minnesota
Beef Munson	St. Paul, Minnesota
Pete Belban	Eveleth, Minnesota

Other American Players

Player	Hometown
Rudy Ahlin, KC	Eveleth, Minnesota
Tony Anderson, KC	Duluth, Minnesota
Ted Breckheimer, St. L.	Minneapolis, Minnesota
Milt Brink, KC	Eveleth, Minnesota
Frank Ceryance, Tul	Eveleth, Minnesota
Tony Christello, Wic	Duluth, Minnesota
Billy DePaul, OC	Eveleth, Minnesota
Vic DesJardins, Tul	Sault Ste. Marie, Michigan
Art Erickson, Wic	Eveleth, Minnesota
Don Hoekstra, Wic	Duluth, Minnesota
Glee Jagunich, OC/Mpls	Eveleth, Minnesota
Bun LaPrairie, KC	Sault Ste. Marie, Michigan
Leroy Lilly, KC	Duluth, Minnesota
Hub Nelson, OC/Mpls	Minneapolis, Minnesota
Don Olson, OC/Mpls	Minneapolis, Minnesota
Joe Papike, Wic	Eveleth, Minnesota
John Phillips, Wic	Eveleth, Minnesota
Tony Prelesnik, OC/Mpls	Eveleth, Minnesota
Fido Purpur, St.L	Grand Forks, North Dakota
Pat Shea, KC	White Bear Lake, Minnesota
Louis Swenson, St.L	Minneapolis, Minnesota

BERWICK BRUINS

Dave Clamen

ONE OF THE NICER ASPECTS OF SENIOR HOCKEY in Canada was the sense of civic pride that it evoked. Each year many cities, towns and even villages competed for league, provincial, regional and national honors in the race for the Allan Cup. A victory in any of these areas would often be a cause for celebration in many communities across the country.

The Maritime provinces started to compete for the Allan Cup in 1927–28. The geography of the area dictated regional league play followed by provincial and then Maritime playoffs. The most important leagues were Cape Breton, Halifax City, Central Valley, Central, Southern New Brunswick and Northern New Brunswick. In the first 10 years, the champions came from Truro, Halifax and Moncton, all of which were the powerhouses of Maritime hockey. Moncton even won two Allan Cup titles. Halifax won one.

At the start of the 1936–37 season, the Central Valley League had only once produced a Nova Scotia champion. The town of Berwick had never won a league title. The odds against either happening were formidable.

In this era, amateur teams could only be made up of local residents, and they had to be in residence from November 18. Berwick put together a lineup of 10 players. Six of them were from the valley area—Willie Kyte, Ralph Boyle and George Warden from Kentville, Sonny Keith from Waterville, Bill Foster from Middleton and Orlay Bligh from Berwick itself. Four imports rounded out the squad—Jim White and Charles Silliker from Port Elgin, Walter Lawlor from Prince Edward Island and Buzz Saarinen from Ontario. Two reserves, Glen Dakin and Bernie Leblanc, were also from Berwick. In this age of widespread importing of players, the fact that there were only four imports (and three of these from the Maritimes region) was noteworthy.

At the beginning of the season in January, Berwick's prospects were rated highly in the local paper. Player-coach Walter Lawlor had a formidable aggregation to work with. New additions Kyte and Warden had experience with the Kentville Wildcats, while Foster had played with the Middleton Maple Leafs. Three crack rookies—Bligh, LeBlanc and Dakin, had come from the local junior team. But the Bruins were in a very tough, well balanced league.

The opening game of the season against the Bridgetown Hawks was played in Berwick on January 9, 1937. Soft, slushy ice (artificial ice was too expensive for most small towns then) made offensive play difficult. The game degenerated into a battle royal with the Bruins winning 1–0 on Jim White's goal. A fight between Orlay Bligh and Frank Finlay caused spectators to rush onto the ice, but no damage was done.

In the second game at Annapolis, the Bruins seemed to play a defensive game and let the hometown Tigers carry most of the play. Newspaper accounts do not mention this, but goalie Willie Kyte must have saved the Bruins in this one. The final score (in overtime) was 2–2 with White and Bligh scoring for Berwick.

Kyte got more credit for his efforts in the third game, a return match against the Tigers in Berwick. This outing was much rougher, with a brawl near the end and two penalty shots called earlier. The Bruins won 2–0 on goals by Lawlor and Bill Foster.

Great ice conditions enabled the Bruins to show their stuff in the next game against the Maple Leafs at Middleton. Kyte again got a great deal of credit for keeping his team in the game. The Bruins led 2–0 after the first period but could not quite hold on and were tied 3–3 at the end of regulation. The Leafs scored first in the overtime but the Bruins tied it and 4–4 was the score. One item of note: player-coach Walter Lawlor got a major penalty in overtime for roughing the referee—an indication of the intensity of the competition.

Despite the preseason boasts, by the end of the fifth game the local newspaper had labeled the Bruins' success "surprising." Their 1–1 home-ice tie with Annapolis had made them the only undefeated team in the league. Though the game was played on soft ice, it was reported as being "fast, furious, and exciting," with Berwick holding an edge in most of the play. Sensational goaltending by Kyte provided some of the highlights, as the goal by Annapolis came during a two-man advantage. A good sign for the home team was the fact that the game attracted the largest crowd of the season.

The Bruins' bubble burst in their sixth game played at Bridgetown. The Hawks came out roaring with two goals in the first minute and another later before Berwick could score on a nice individual effort by Lawlor. At the end of the first, the score was 4–2. Several fights enlivened a scoreless second period before the teams exchanged penalty-shot goals in the third. Final score: Bridgetown 5, Berwick 3.

The Bruins bounced back from their defeat to tie the Maple Leafs in Middleton 4–4. Lawlor and Kyte again turned in great performances. The visitors did blow a 3–1 lead in this one, but then came back from a 4–3 deficit. The return game in Berwick resulted in a 2–0 win for the Bruins on the strength of great goaltending by Kyte and goals from White and Charles Silliker. This victory clinched first place for the team.

Berwick won the season title with a record of 5–2–5 for 15 points, two ahead of the Middleton Maple Leafs and three points ahead of Bridgetown. In the league semifinal, Middleton defeated Bridgetown to qualify for the final against Berwick.

The Central Valley championship was to be a two-game, total-goals affair. In the first game in Middleton, the Leafs won by a score of 4–1. The Bruins got the first goal halfway through the opening period, but Middleton quickly tied it and then got three more in the second. The Leafs kept up a good pace throughout the game while the Bruins seemed to tire out.

A three-goal lead was considered pretty good in a two-game series, but with their backs to the wall, the Bruins took advantage of the good ice at home to score two quick goals in the second game and put the series within reach. The Leafs came back with two goals of their own, one at the end of the first and one at the beginning of the second, to seemingly clinch the final. The Bruins, however, were not to be outdone. They scored four unanswered goals to take the series by one at 7–6.

A record crowd of more than 800 fans had attended the game. Lawlor (with two goals and two assists) and Bill Foster (with the hat trick) were the offensive stars as the Bruins outshot the Leafs, 39–21. Yet, this victory was only the first step.

In the Maritime senior setup of the time, the various

regional league champions played off against each other. Next up for the Bruins would be the Bridgewater Hawks of the South Shore League. In a penalty-free game, the Bruins won 7–1 at home with Foster scoring another hat trick. The return match was also penalty free, ending in a 2–2 tie and a 9–3 series win for Berwick. Foster netted another goal in that game.

The next opponent was the Halifax Blue Sunocos of the powerful City League. Because of the superior ice conditions available and the larger seating capacity, the first game, scheduled for Berwick, was played at the arena in Kentville. Bruins fans were out in force to see their team beat the boys from the big city, 5–2. Berwick won the return match in Halifax 5–3 to take the series, 10–5. Buzz Saarinen accomplished the unusual with a hat trick in both games.

The next series was the Nova Scotia finals and it was against the defending champion Antigonish Bulldogs. Again, the first game was in Kentville and again the Bruins won, this time by a score of 2–1 on goals by Saarinen and Lawlor. The return match was more decisive with a 5–2 Berwick win in which Saarinen and Lawlor scored two goals each. The Berwick Bruins were the Nova Scotia champions! And the fans loved it, greeting their heroes at the train station upon their return.

It would be nice to end this Cinderella story with another playoff win, but it was not to be. The Moncton Maroons won the first game of the Maritime final, 2–1, on a long shot in the last second of the game. Walter Lawlor got the Bruins goal. The second game ended in a 1–1 tie as Buzz Saarinen accidentally scored on his own net. Foster got the Bruins goal, but Berwick's great season had come to an end.

Defending a championship in senior hockey was always hard. Players were not under contract, since they were unpaid amateurs, and could always jump teams to a certain extent. The Bruins lost five of their 10 regulars, including goalie Willie Kyte and scoring star Saarinen. Also, they entered a stronger league—the Eastern Nova Scotia, with teams from Kentville, Halifax and Dartmouth. The Bruins finished a distant third in the regular-season standings, but did grab the last playoff spot. Once in the postseason, they beat the Kentville Wildcats and then the Halifax Wolverines to take the league title. This time, though, they went no further. They lost to New Glasgow in the first provincial playoff round.

The 1937–38 season proved to be the last year of senior hockey competition in the town of Berwick, but the record was a fine one. Two league championships and one provincial title in the last two years of play was something of which to be proud. The town is still proud of the team's achievements, enshrining the Bruins in the Berwick sports hall of fame and happily providing the author with much of this material.

It's impossible to unring the bell. We cannot go back to the heyday of the Allan Cup, with its numerous playoffs and opportunities for small-town glory. But we can and should remember the Berwick Bruins—for giving a Nova Scotia town a moment of glory and the rest of us a lesson in what hockey is all about.

Nova Scotia League Champions 1936–37

League	Team
Valley	Wolfville Sunocos
Cape Breton	Sydney Telephones
Pictou County	All-Stars
Halifax City	Halifax Blue Sunocos
South Shore	Bridgewater Hawks
Central Valley	Berwick Bruins
unaffiliated	Truro Bearcats
unaffiliated	Antigonish Bulldogs

Playoffs all rounds two-game, total goals

First Round			
Truro	12	Pictou All-Stars	7
Berwick	9	Bridgewater	6
Halifax	18	Wolfville	12
Second Round			
Antigonish	9	Truro	5
Semifinals			
Antigonish	6	Sydney	5
Berwick	10	Halifax	5
Final			
Berwick	7	Antigonish	3
Maritime Final			
Moncton	3	Berwick	2

Eastern Nova Scotia League 1937–38

Team	W	L	T	Pts	GF	GA
Halifax Wolverines	8	2	3	19	63	37
Kentville Wildcats	8	3	1	17	42	38
Berwick Bruins	2	5	2	6	24	31
Dartmouth AOH	1	9	0	2	24	47

Semifinal: Berwick defeats Kentville two games to nothing (plus two ties)
Final: Berwick defeats Halifax two games to one (plus one tie)
Nova Scotia playoffs: New Glasgow 9 Berwick 7 (two-game, total-goals)

BROOKLYN AMERICANS

Stan Fischler

THE BROOKLYN AMERICANS were the most unlikely club ever to grace the National Hockey League for the pure and simple reason that they never played a single game within the confines of Brooklyn, although many other top local teams did.

How can a big-league team represent an area and yet not be a part of it?

To better obtain the answer one must first understand the uniqueness of Brooklyn, as well as its sporting history.

Alternately known as the Borough of Churches or County of Kings, Brooklyn was a bustling metropolis unto itself until it amalgamated with New York City in 1898 as one of the Big Apple's five boroughs. Even then, Brooklyn was a sporting hub best known for its professional baseball club—later to be called the Dodgers—and also for its hockey teams and two major indoor rinks, the Brooklyn Ice Palace and the Clermont Rink. The latter still stands in the shadows of the downtown area.

As early as 1896, Brooklyn was represented by the formidable Crescent Athletic Club which competed in the American Amateur Hockey League (AAHL) against such opponents as the New York Athletic Club and St. Nick's. In 1898, the Brooklyn Ice Palace sponsored a cup presented by the Skating Club of Brooklyn. This focused on intercollegiate play. Columbia, the local host team, competed against Yale and Brown, the latter of which won the tournament. Brooklyn's place in the hockey firmament was secured within the first few years after the turn of the 20th century, by which time the Crescent Athletic Club had won seven AAHL titles.

Hockey remained a staple in Brooklyn in the decades to come, both at the high school and high-class amateur level. In the amateur game, Brooklyn continued to be represented by the Crescents who, in the early 1930s, competed in the Eastern Amateur Hockey League against teams from Baltimore, Hershey, Atlantic City and the Bronx.

Playing at the Ice Palace, the Crescents soon became a New York Rangers farm team but became so popular they abandoned the bandbox Brooklyn rink and moved to Madison Square Garden, where their name was changed to New York Rovers. At that time the Garden's two NHL tenants were the Rangers and the Americans, whose 1925 entry into the NHL predated the Rangers by one year.

Competition between the Rangers and "Amerks," as they were affectionately known, was beyond keen. Owned by the Garden and considerably wealthier than their rivals, the Rangers were thought of as the patricians, much like the New York Yankees in baseball both then and now. By contrast, the Americans—originally owned by jailed bootlegger William "Big Bill" Dwyer—had fallen on bad times during The Great Depression of the 1930s. They were overseen by Mervyn "Red" Dutton, a former star defenseman who had become coach, manager and at least partial financier of the near-bankrupt Amerks.

Because his family had amassed a fortune from the construction business in Western Canada, Dutton was able to funnel some of that money to New York. The family finances kept the Americans afloat while other NHL clubs, such as the Montreal Maroons, folded before the 1930s had ended. For a time, Dutton was even able to keep the Amerks competitive and the New York-New York competition reached its peak when the teams collided in a best-of-three playoff round in the spring of 1938. All three games were played at Madison Square Garden. Dutton's sextet won the opener, 2–1, on Johnny Sorrell's overtime goal. The Rangers rebounded, winning the second match, 4–3, and setting the stage for the climactic finalé on March 28, 1938. The Americans won in the fourth overtime. Time of the game: 123 minutes and 40 seconds!

"That," said Dutton, "was the greatest thrill I ever got in hockey. The Rangers had a high-priced team then and beating them was like winning the Stanley Cup to us."

Dutton not only appreciated the quality of the New York-New York competition but believed it could still be improved. His inspiration was major league baseball.

At the time no fewer than three New York teams—one American, two National—competed on the diamond. Manhattan had the Giants playing at the Polo Grounds in Harlem. The Bronx had the Yankees playing at the Stadium across the East River from the Giants. Brooklyn boasted its Dodgers, who called Ebbets Field home.

Although the Yankees and Giants were regular pennant winners, Dutton felt a kinship to the Dodgers. One reason was that they reminded him of his endlessly underdog Americans. Another was that Brooklyn's manager, Leo Durocher, was an American version of Dutton—ebullient, excitable and entertaining.

Brooklyn, a hotbed of baseball at the end of the 1930s, also had become a popular source of American culture. "Brooklynese" was a language all its own for a borough that, with a population in excess of two million, was one of the continent's largest urban hubs.

"I've always regarded Brooklyn as one of the finest sports centers in the world," Dutton said. "The way the fans support the baseball and football Dodgers convinced me that they would be just as rabid for hockey."

Dutton realized that Kings County lacked a major league hockey arena to complement its major league baseball park and decided that the time had come for a new arena to be built on the east side of the East River. Having his own arena would not only free Dutton from the onerous lease at Madison Square Garden (which burdened his hockey club to the point of bankruptcy) but would also enable the Americans to generate their own revenues. Unfortunately, the outbreak of World War II in September, 1939, put a crimp in Dutton's plans. As the conflagration spread across Europe, the necessary steel required for his proposed hockey venue became unavailable and the idea for a Brooklyn Arena was put on hold for the duration of the war.

Nevertheless, Dutton was so invigorated by the Brooklyn concept that he chose to pursue it even without an arena. At the NHL's semiannual meeting in Toronto on September 12, 1941, Dutton requested that the league accept the name change from New York Americans to Brooklyn Americans. The request was accepted, although the club continued playing its home games at Madison Square Garden in Manhattan.

Dutton's idea was to capitalize on the Brooklyn-New York rivalry, which had reached an apotheosis in the fall of 1941 when the Yankees defeated the Dodgers in a highly controversial World Series. The underdog club from Ebbets Field put up a good fight before going down to the hated Bombers from the Bronx. Not surprisingly, Dutton likened his Brooklyn Americans to the Dodgers.

"The response that has greeted our decision to have the Americans represent Brooklyn in major league hockey has been tremendous," Dutton said. "I hope to make the Americans a team of which Brooklyn can be justly proud. And if we don't win, or come near winning, the Stanley Cup this [1941–42] season, I'll prove myself a real Brooklynite by shouting 'Wait'll next year!' "

Dutton did everything possible to legitimize the Brooklyn aspect of his Americans. He insisted that his players take up residence in Kings County and he and his wife, Phyllis, found a home in Flatbush, not far from the Dodgers' ballpark. What's more, he junked the once-popular star-spangled New York Americans uniform and replaced it with new colors and a sweater with the letters B R O O K L Y N running from right to left diagonally down the jersey. But when it came to winning, Dutton still faced difficult obstacles. Stuck with an exceptionally tight budget, he dealt one of his aces, Lorne Carr, to the Toronto Maple Leafs and loaded up with young, inexpensive players such as Harry Watson and Ken Mosdell. His farm team was the Springfield Indians of the American Hockey League, owned by Eddie Shore.

The veteran Earl Robertson was the Americans' starting goaltender, but when he was injured, Dutton imported youthful Chuck Rayner from Springfield. "Because of our youth," Rayner recalled, "we had some problems but some of our players later matured into excellent NHL players." Both Rayner and Watson eventually were inducted into the Hockey Hall of Fame, while Mosdell—later a Montreal Canadien—was named by the immortal Maurice Richard as "the most underrated player I ever skated with."

Perhaps the most surprising Brooklyn player of all was defenseman Tommy "Cowboy" Anderson, who scored 12 goals and 29 assists for 41 points in 48 games. Anderson was named to the NHL's First All-Star Team and won the Hart Trophy as well. Unfortunately, there were not enough Andersons on the team—although Dutton did his best to create them. One of his pet projects was rookie defenseman Pat Egan. "If he were a ball player," said Dutton, "they would love him at Ebbets Field."

The underdog Brooklyn Americans also managed to capture the imagination of the media. *New York Sun* columnist Frank Graham, one of the city's most respected sportswriters, took a keen liking to Egan. One day Graham engaged Dutton in conversation about Egan. Part of Graham's column read as follows:

> *Pat is big, fast, wild and tough, a throwback to the days when Dutton, Eddie Shore, Lionel Hitchman and the rest of that old mauling crew were at their peak.*
>
> *'He operates differently than we did, though,' Red pointed out. 'He doesn't hit them on the back line the way we used to. When he is backchecking, he heads the puck carrier off and flattens him against the boards.'*

The New York Rangers-Brooklyn Americans rivalry was sustained off the ice by their publicists. If one could rib the other's club, he would do so at the drop of a quote and often did. Jersey Jones, the Rangers' press agent during the pre-World War II years, dropped one of the best lines when Dutton first announced that the Amerks would hold practices in Brooklyn and change their name. At the time, the Brooklyn Dodgers baseball team had commonly been known as "Da Bums." This moved Jones to observe, "The Americans have been bums for years, but this is the first time they've made it official!"

In response, the *Herald-Tribune*'s scholarly hockey writer Kerr N. Petrie wrote, "He [Jones] could not have hit upon a happier choice for a nasty crack that will rally Brooklyn support around the Americans. If there is anything a Brooklynite resents, it is usurpation of his prior rights in calling a bum, a bum. As long as the Americans bear the Brooklyn name, then the Flatbush trade will fight to the end any outsider referring to them as Bums. It is a privilege which Brooklyn prefers to reserve for itself."

When the Americans carried the New York label, headline writers referred to them as the Amerks. But as soon as they became the Brooklyn Americans, the headline writers changed it to "Amoiks," which was a play on the Brooklynese dialect.

In their one and only season as the Brooklyn Americans, Dutton's sextet was less than an artistic success although the Amoiks did defeat Toronto, 6–3, on March 15, 1942. It was the club's final appearance at Madison Square Garden. Two days later, the Bruins routed the Americans by a score of 8–3 in Boston.

It was the last game the Americans played. The Brooklyn team that never played in Brooklyn had finished last in the seven-team NHL with a 16–29–3 record. On September 28, 1942, at the NHL's semiannual meeting in Toronto, President Frank Calder announced that Madison Square Garden had declined to renew its lease with the Americans and the club had suspended operations for the season.

When Calder died in 1943, Dutton succeeded him as president but vowed to build his dream arena in Brooklyn at War's end. When Clarence Campbell succeeded Dutton as NHL president in 1946, Red renewed his bid to build the Kings County rink.

"I've talked to people in Brooklyn," said Dutton. "They've got a site and they're ready to put up a $7-million building as soon as I get word from the league."

Dutton got the word, all right, but it was not what he wanted to hear. The owners rejected his bid and, as a result, the Brooklyn Americans never got to play hockey in Brooklyn.

SUNDRIDGE BEAVERS

Jim Proudfoot

IN SMALL-TOWN CANADA, the worries of World War II had begun to recede by the winter of 1946. Life was getting back to normal. The young men were coming home from the army, the navy and the air force and picking up their lives where they'd been disrupted by the conflict overseas. And in Sundridge, Ontario, the dominant concern once more had to do with hockey

More specifically: Why can't we ever beat Powassan?

All this, remember, was long before television and this sort of municipal hockey rivalry raged all over the country. In Parry Sound District, nothing was bigger than the annual doubleheader pitting Powassan and its customary powerhouse against tiny Sundridge 25 miles down the main north-south highway. Bragging rights for a dozen long months were at stake, and the folks from Powassan extracted maximum mileage from them year after year while some 700 Sundridge burghers squirmed in frustration.

But now something new had been added to the Sundridge shinny equation. Wilfred Kennedy "Bucko" McDonald had retired after a distinguished 11-year career on NHL defenses with two Stanley Cup championships in Detroit and a third while skating for Toronto. And while Bucko was in for busy stretches as the newly elected member of Canada's Parliament representing Parry Sound, he was only 31 years old and anxious to remain active in hockey.

So with McDonald as playing coach, the legendary Sundridge Beavers were assembled around a nucleus of eight young men freshly returned from military duty. Only one objective mattered at first, and it was accomplished with flair. Sundridge defeated Powassan so emphatically in game one of their annual series that for the return match the hated northerners recruited an NHL alumnus of their own—ex-Leaf Normie Mann. But the outcome was the same.

"We enjoyed that little taste of triumph so much we decided to carry on from there and see what else we could accomplish," related Sam Rennie, another charter member of that storied Sundridge roster. "But definitely we were just a pickup club at the outset, put together for that one little series."

The 1946–47 Beavers competed all winter and at the end entered the Ontario Intermediate B playoffs for the first time. On just their second try in 1948, they won the provincial championship. Before they were done, they would participate in 10 Ontario finals and win a remarkable six—

three of these victories being registered during a marvelous nine-year stretch when Sundridge's renown extended to all of the province's frontiers. The Beavers contested all-Ontario finals in six of those nine springs.

"But I'll tell you something funny," said Rennie, reminiscing at 86 in the kitchen of his Main Street home. "We had some great teams and won some terrific victories over that period but I don't think there was ever a celebration—right out there on the street—like the one in 1946 after we finally whipped Powassan. I'm talking about the whole town, just so happy and not wanting ever to go home because, see, that would be the end of the party. We were still at it when the sun came up.

"When I think back to those days, I realize the story of the Beavers was the story of hockey at a certain time in Canadian history. We followed the Leafs on radio, of course, and the odd guy even got to see them play in Toronto. But really, hockey in those days was the Beavers and in a town like ours, it was our whole life."

That initial successful lineup was simply a classic of Canadian rural mythology.

There were three Hill brothers—Cletus, the goalie, Lawrence, an occasional defenseman, and Harold, the Beavers' most skillful player from his postwar beginnings until retirement when he was 41.

On defense were Bucko McDonald, M.P., exploiting every ounce of his accumulated NHL wisdom together with fearsome bodychecking, and Gordon "Sam" Rennie, principal of the public school. They worked almost 60 minutes of every match until the natural ice would melt at the minuscule Sundridge arena. On faster footing in borrowed rinks, McDonald and Rennie would be relieved regularly by Aubrey Percival, a teenager who, with two brothers at war, had left school to help his father run the family hotel in neighboring South River.

The forwards: Keith and Harold "Archie" Kidd, hardware merchants; lumberman Harold "Nobby" Hill; Less Summers, a teacher at the local high school; Borden Wheeler, Canadian National Railway agent at the Sundridge station; George Russell, clerk of Strong Township; trucker Hugh Christie; Mye Sedore, later an area scout for the Maple Leafs; and Dave Christie, a delivery man for a local gas and oil dealership.

"As I mentioned, our original idea was to rustle up a club to beat Powassan," said Rennie. "Bucko and Willard Lang, the butcher, figured out how we could carry it on. And I must say the Beavers really put Sundridge on the map while doing a lot for the townspeople. Those were wonderful times to live in Sundridge.

"Willard Lang once organized a special train to go to a playoff match against Penetang in Midland. It would come down from North Bay, making stops along the way, and we guaranteed $600 (can you imagine?) worth of tickets. In Sundridge, 180 people got on the train—nearly a third the total population. What I recall about that trip is the conductor was persuaded to hold the train in Huntsville long enough for some fans to grab taxis and rush over to the liquor store to replenish their supplies."

The Beavers played a disciplined positional game far beyond anything one would expect at the Intermediate B level. The Ontario Hockey Association had three higher divisions, after all. Senior A teams were aiming for the Allan Cup as Canadian amateur titlists. Lesser competition was termed Senior B. Intermediate A fit in another classification below, but was still a distinct improvement on Intermediate B.

The Sundridge side grew famous for surprising skill, even as veterans were replaced. Once it became clear that McDonald's leadership was responsible, he was tapped to coach in professional leagues. At the end of his career, he headed the minor program in the town of Parry Sound and, over paternal objections, transformed a talented young center named Bobby Orr into a defenseman.

"The thing was, we all looked up so much to Bucko," said Rennie, who'd started out as a slick young attacker with Durham's Ontario Intermediate B titlists of 1936 before taking a teaching post in Sundridge. "I mean, he'd been a star in the NHL, eh? We worshiped him. So what he told us was gospel. We were prepared to obey his orders where we'd never have held still for the same stuff from somebody else."

Herb Anderson, long-time team captain, supplements Rennie's opinion of Bucko McDonald: "He showed us how to win and once we understood that, we were prepared to follow him anywhere.

"He skated the hell out of us, like stops and starts every night, and we always had a huge edge in conditioning. Don't forget, our opponents were all people with day jobs. So were we, of course, but on account of Bucko, we'd outskate and outlast everybody we faced.

"One year, the OHA decreed 12-man rosters for Intermediate B. What you'd expect, of course, was a goalie, two defense pairs, two forward lines and a swing guy. Bucko's idea was two defensemen—Ivan O'Shell and I were on almost all the time—and three forward lines. So our opponents were always dead in the third period, or sooner. Nobody could keep up with us, see?"

Educated by McDonald, the Beavers were incredibly consistent, with accurate passing in their own zone and tenacious forechecking on the far side of center. Gerry Odrowski, a regular at 17, ended up in the NHL with Detroit, Oakland and St. Louis without adding much to what Bucko McDonald had taught him.

"I've watched pro hockey for 50 years," Anderson said, "and never saw a team play a system the way we did."

After the championship campaigns of 1948 and 1949, Sundridge was beaten in the Ontario finals in 1950, 1954 and 1955—by Georgetown, Durham and then Walkerton with future NHLer Les Binkley in the nets. Then came the great adventure.

Down the road in Huntsville, the folks were constructing a new arena. The Beavers bought the vaulted roof from the old building and trucked it north to the Sundridge fairgrounds. No longer would they compete in their cramped rink where the tiny ice surface measured only 165 feet by 65 and the proximity of 500 hostile spectators intimidated every visitor. Now they ventured into more challenging Intermediate A competition, entering the tough Georgian Bay League.

With imports like goaltender Alex Dagenais from Callander and Thessaslon product Lloyd Boyer, Sundridge iced a truly imposing roster. Other first stringers included NHL-stalwart-to-be Gerry Odrowski, Tim Horton's brother Gerry, and Aub Percival, Archie Kidd and Harold Hill from the old Beavers.

"That was by far the best club Sundridge ever had," said Hill of the 1955–56 team. "Boyer centered for me and Johnny Woods, back from Junior A hockey down south.

Ross Johnstone was another Junior A graduate we had. In the provincial final we beat the Meaford Knights, who were packed with tough oldtimers, many of them ex-pros. Nobody lost a home game and we took the seventh, 5–2.

"But as much as I enjoyed playing on that club, which won 34 of 54 games over the season, there's no comparison with the thrill of our first championship in 1948 when we had no idea what we were getting into."

By 1963, the Beavers had dropped back to Intermediate C ranks and won Ontario championships that season and again in 1964. In all, Harold Hill collected six of the gold medals provincial titles entailed, and then a seventh during a year with Huntsville. By all accounts a remarkable player, Hill had been off skates throughout five years of military service before joining his fellow citizens in the Beavers project.

"I think I might have gone somewhere in hockey, but the war came along at the worst possible time—something that was true for lots of NHL stars," Hill said. "But I don't care. I absolutely loved all those years at home. I'll tell you though, they had a tough time peeling the uniform off me."

During five of the Beavers' peak campaigns, Hill worked as a ranger in nearby Algonquin Park. To get out for games and practices involved eight miles on foot each way, often on snowshoes. "My legs were in wonderful shape," he said, "and you know something? In all that time, I missed the first period once."

Regrets? Only one.

"I was suspended an entire calendar year once, for supposedly striking a referee. I didn't do it. The worst I was guilty of was threatening him because, this night in Bracebridge, he was really giving it to us—or so I felt. I'm not too proud of the fact he went over the boards to get away from me."

Hill then laughed.

"The year I sat out, the Little NHL asked me to be referee-in-chief for their big provincial tournament," he reported. "I accepted and always got a kick out of the memory, considering the circumstances."

In retirement at Huntsville, Aub Percival claims there's never a day when he doesn't think of the Beavers and what he learned from Bucko McDonald.

"He never singled out a player in front of others. He banned bad language. He opposed dirty play," said Percival. "We'd grown up in tough Depression times and gone through a World War, but what Bucko showed us was how these lessons could work in your favor.

"Many a team would drive around little Sundridge and kill themselves laughing. Then we'd get them on the ice and they'd sing a different tune. The Beavers had plenty of pride and lots of class. We carried ourselves like pros.

"It was something that can't be duplicated today. That was a different era. All you can do, if you were a player or a fan, is cling tightly to the memories.

"The Beavers, hey, we'll never see the like."

Long Island Ducks

Stan Fischler

WHEN THE FILM *SLAPSHOT* HAD ITS PREMIERE in the late 1970s, it was hailed as the ultimate satire on minor-league hockey.

Paul Newman starred as the playing coach of a fictional team called the Charlestown Chiefs, whose exploits were considered too Hollywood to be true. But in this case, fiction was as strange as hockey truth, for the Charlestown Chiefs were merely a cinematic version of a real minor-league hockey club called the Long Island Ducks. Every character in the film version—including the oddball owner—could be matched by an equally implausible or hilarious counterpart on the Ducks. Sometimes the characters on the real team were even more unlikely than those on the screen. And the character portrayed by Newman bore a striking resemblance to Ducks player-coach John Brophy.

The Ducks weren't meant to be crazy when they were originally conceived by Thomas F. Lockhart, who wore many hats as a hockey executive in the United States. Tommy Lockhart's claims to fame included the fact that he successfully introduced big-time amateur hockey to Madison Square Garden in the early 1930s and created a New York Rangers farm team in the Eastern Amateur Hockey League (EAHL) called the New York Rovers.

Lockhart was EAHL president as well as guiding force behind the Amateur Hockey Association of the United States. In his spare time, he doubled as business manager for the Rangers and also presided over the Metropolitan Amateur Hockey League, which played games prior to those of the Rovers on Sunday afternoons at the old Garden on Eighth Avenue between 49th and 50th Streets in Manhattan.

By the early 1950s, Lockhart observed two significant trends. First, pro basketball was becoming very popular at the Garden, which meant that the New York Knicks would soon be taking up more home dates. Second, a population explosion was taking place in suburban Nassau and Suffolk counties on Long Island where there were no professional sports teams.

"Tommy's idea was to capitalize on this virgin sports territory," said Herb Goren, then publicist for the Rangers. "He envisioned an arena built strictly for Long Island sports fans with a minor-league hockey team as its prime tenant."

Lockhart and his colleagues scoured both Nassau and Suffolk counties for a rink site and finally settled on a remote area of Suffolk called Commack. Unknown to most New Yorkers, Commack had two advantages for Lockhart: there was plenty of available land for an arena, and it was adjacent to a new superhighway called the Long Island Expressway. This meant that hockey fans from any part of the island could drive to his new rink.

At a cost of $800,000, the 4,500-seat rink was completed by 1957. Constructed with wood-laminated arches, Long Island Arena had no pillars, just a sweeping, curved ceiling—the second-largest of its type in the country. Lockhart did not actually move the Rovers to the Arena until the 1959–60 campaign, but when he did, he used Rangers prospects to fill out the roster. Among the more famous were future Hall of Famer Ed Giacomin (1959–60 and 1961–62) and Gilles Villemure (1960–61 and 1961–62), both goaltenders who eventually made it to the NHL club. By 1960–61 the Rovers were right at home in Commack and, slowly but surely, Long Islanders took to their new team.

Following the 1960–61 season, Lockhart decided that his job was done. His dream rink was up and thriving, but it was a good two-hour drive from his Upper East Side apartment in Manhattan. Since Lockhart had been involved in hockey for more than three decades, he decided it was time to call it a career. But what to do about the Rovers?

A Long Island electrical-supply magnate had the answer. Al Baron and his wife, Renee, were dedicated sports fans who had taken a liking to the Commack-based Rovers. "I always wanted my own team," said Baron, "and here was one for sale right in my own backyard."

After making the purchase, his first order of business was to give his new toy a more appropriate name. Since Suffolk County was renowned for its ducklings, and since the team was playing right in the heart of the island, Baron renamed the team the Long Island Ducks.

Baron was more than just an owner. He was a fan. He and Renee would sit in the first row along the boards at center ice. As the Long Island Arena had neither protective glass along the sideboards nor chicken wire, Renee was able to carry on running conversations with the players—when she wasn't gabbing with the many fans that had befriended her.

Although the Ducks' home was relatively new, it was minor league in every way.

"It looked like an airplane hanger from the outside," recalled Russ McClenaghan, a Ducks star in the 1960s. The visitors dressing room was just a tad larger than a closet and was located in a section of the Arena that forced the visitors to walk through the hostile crowd at the end of each period. This caused considerable tension and not a few fights between the spectators and foreign team.

Still, Baron did everything he could to give his club a big-league feel. While most Eastern League teams traveled by bus (alias "The Iron Lung"), the Ducks had their own plane for a time—although it was a vintage Douglas DC-3 twin prop model the flying capabilities of which were always questioned by the players.

Long Island fans were extremely passionate about their Ducks. At the time, their games were considered *the* event in Suffolk County. Even when a game was delayed several hours because the visiting team was late arriving, the stands would still be full when the clubs took to the ice. To ensure that the fans had a competitive club to watch, Baron stocked his squad with the best available talent. He obtained Rangers defensive prospect Ray Crew and another big, young backliner named Don Perry. Both men were enormous in relation to most Eastern Leaguers, and Crew and Perry immediately became the scourge of the circuit.

A Toronto Maple Leafs prospect, Norm Ryder, was also added to the Ducks defense along with John Muckler, who would later have a lengthy career as a National Hockey League coach and general manager. Up front, Baron featured top forwards such as Gene Achtymichuk, whose lengthy professional career had included NHL stints with the Montreal Canadiens and Detroit Red Wings. By the time Achtymichuk came to Commack, his big-league years were behind him—but not his talent. In both the 1964–65 and 1965–66 seasons, he led the Eastern League with 83 assists. Achtymichuk became one of the most popular players on Long Island at a time when the Ducks had become a household word in both Nassau and Suffolk counties.

By the time John Brophy arrived on the scene, Long Island Arena had already earned a reputation as the Animal House of minor-league hockey. In some regards, it may have more closely resembled a House of Horrors. The surface beneath the ice was dark—ranging from a deep brown to black—giving the ice a brackish complexion that complemented the dimly lit arena and the Ducks' blackish home uniforms. If the scene was not imposing enough visually, the team saw to it that visitors were intimidated physically. One of the team's most colorful characters, Brophy was a grinding rearguard whose competitive spirit and penchant for throwing brutal checks instilled fear in the hearts of opposing skaters and earned the respect of fellow Ducks.

A quiet man off the ice, Brophy changed the instant a game began. "Broph would wear down the opposition to the point where they'd say to themselves, 'I'm going to take a beating ... or this guy is going to follow me home,' " recalled teammate Buzz Deschamps.

"One thing about John," added Russ McClenaghan, "it didn't matter if we were on the road or at home, he played the first and last minutes of the game the same way. When it came down to giving his all, he gave it. Bobby Orr, he wasn't. But he never backed down. He wasn't a big man, but he knew how to get the most out of what he had."

Gilles Villemure was one who appreciated Long Island's hardnosed defense. "Ryder and Brophy in particular were really rough and there were fights all the time," said the goalie. "When an opposing player crossed our blue line, he took his life into his hands."

Sellouts were commonplace in an arena where every seat had a good view of the ice. And the flow of good players—Deschamps, Sam Gregory and Don Atamanchuk, among others—continued to keep the club competitive. Players were paid $150 per week, with the chance to earn performance-based incentives such as $500 for reaching the 20-goal plateau in a season, and another $500 for every five goals scored thereafter.

What set the Ducks apart was the off-the-wall antics of their players and coaches. One former Duck remembered a scam involving the players' daily meal-money allowance on the road. "We were supposed to get $4," the ex-player said, "but the coach pocketed a dollar from each of us for himself. None of us realized we were supposed to get $4 instead of three."

The Ducks often enlivened long, boring road trips with bizarre behavior. On one excursion along dangerously winding roads through the Smoky Mountains of North Carolina, a bunch of players decided it would be fun to try and tip the team bus over a cliff as it made S-turns en route to Charlotte.

"This was in 1968," recalled Barry Landers, who was the Ducks broadcaster at the time. "Suddenly, as we were making the curve, all the players got up and moved to the left side of the bus. That left me and the coach on the right side fighting for our lives to keep the vehicle from going over the cliff!"

A team legend relates to one of John Muckler's most significant of many contributions to the Ducks. The so-called "Pastrami Sandwich Luncheon" with Al Baron came at a time when it appeared that the team might fold. Desperate to save the club, Muckler invited Baron to a Long Island delicatessen where they worked out a fiscal formula to keep the Ducks alive.

Thanks to the Ducks, hockey had become so popular on Long Island by the late 1960s that Nassau County decided to build a big-league rink in Uniondale in hopes of attracting an NHL club. "I truly believed that I could be a part of it," said Baron, "but the NHL awarded the [Islanders] franchise to Roy Boe and that was the end of my chances to get up to the bigs." It was also the end of the Ducks, who played their final season in 1972–73.

While many journalistic observers of the Long Island hockey scene have credited Al Baron for paving the way for the NHL Islanders, the Ducks' owner and his pioneering puck work in Suffolk County was soon overlooked. From 1972 through 1975, he was seen at Nassau Coliseum attending Islanders games, but quickly became a forgotten figure. Ironically, the Ducks remained in the public eye even as Baron faded. As recently as the summer of 2000, members of the team's alumni—headed by Buzz Deschamps—held a reunion on the Island.

Like the movie *Slapshot*, the Long Island Ducks keep coming back like a song!

LONDON LIONS: PROFESSIONAL HOCKEY IN ENGLAND

Norman de Mesquita

IN 1973, BRUCE NORRIS, owner of the Detroit Red Wings, thought the time was ripe for a professional ice hockey league in Europe. He envisaged club teams based in London, Berlin, Prague, Helsinki, Stockholm, Moscow, Berne, Rome, Amsterdam and Brussels, made up mainly of Canadians and Americans but with a liberal sprinkling of native-born players. Ideally, each team would have a working agreement with an NHL club. To this end, Detroit's 1972–73 farm club that played in Port Huron (Michigan) was shifted to England to play as the London Lions for 1973–74. Their home rink was the Empire Pool Wembley. Wembley had been a force in British ice hockey since the mid-1930s, with the Wembley Lions, who had last played in November, 1968, a famous and respected name in the sport. So the venue was right and there could be no other team nickname. In addition, there was a ready-made fan base that had been starved of the sport for nearly five years.

The London Lions were run by a board of directors that included Bruce Norris, John Ziegler (at that time a Red Wings vice president), Joseph Besch (a Red Wings director) and Alan Weeks (a leading BBC television commentator who was very much at the forefront of bringing the team to Great Britain). After several years without British league hockey, the Lions were seen as a great boost to the sport and the team had the full backing of J.F. "Bunny" Ahearne, president of the British Ice Hockey Association and also a leading light in the International Ice Hockey Federation. (Ahearne was elected to the Builders section of the Hockey Hall of Fame in 1977.)

The London Lions were a mixture of veterans and young hopefuls, coached by Doug Barkley, a former Red Wing whose career was cut short at age 29 when, in January, 1966, he suffered an injury in a game against Chicago that resulted in the loss of an eye. The Lions' trainer was Al Coates, who had played and coached in Holland during the previous two seasons and who would later serve as general manager of the Calgary Flames. The Lions were captained by 29-year-old Rick McCann, a player in the Detroit organization for six years who had played only a handful of NHL games while spending most of his time with the Fort Worth Wings of the Central Hockey League and various American Hockey League clubs.

Other veterans with the Lions included Terry Clancy, previously with the Oakland Seals and Toronto Maple Leafs in the NHL, and two Swedes: Ulf Sterner and Leif Holmqvist. A third Swedish player, Tord Lundstrom, joined in midseason, having been sent down from the Red Wings. Sterner had played four games for the New York Rangers in the 1964–65 season, nine years before Borje Salming burst upon the scene with the Toronto Maple Leafs and became the first Swedish-born and trained player to star in the NHL. Holmqvist, a 31-year-old goaltender, shared the duties for the first two games with Bill McKenzie, who then had to return to Detroit. Tom McQuiston took over for a few weeks, but the backup goalie for the rest of the season was Terry Richardson, who subsequently saw limited NHL action over five seasons with Detroit and St. Louis. McQuiston did not make it to major-league level. London Lions who did included Nelson Pyatt (Red Wings, Capitals and Colorado Rockies), Mike Korney (Red Wings and Rangers), Earl Anderson (Red Wings and Bruins), Tom Mellor (Red Wings), Brian McCutcheon (Red Wings) and Murray Wing who played just one game for Detroit.

Besides the London Lions who graduated to the NHL, several visiting players made it. The Finnish Under-23 side that played in London included Mikko Leinonen (New York Rangers and Washington Capitals during a four-year NHL career), while the Prague team had Milan Novy (one season with the Capitals), Milan Chalupa (a few games with the Red Wings) and Frantisek Cernik (one season in Detroit).

Of course the one London Lions player who made an impact on the NHL was tough-guy Dennis Polonich, who played in 390 games for the Red Wings and scored 59 goals while amassing 1,242 penalty minutes. In 63 games for the London Lions, he scored just 15 goals and earned 55 minutes in penalties, which meant that he was not particularly popular with the Wembley public.

The British game before and after World War II was based on imported Canadians and was accepted as the best amateur hockey outside Canada. It featured high-speed skating, stickhandling and passing. But it took time and money to bring over a player so, to help reduce the likelihood of injury, bodychecking was allowed only on the side of the red line closest to each team's goal. In addition, there was no icing the puck when shorthanded; so forward lines were able to develop plays and "ragging the puck" to kill penalties became an art form. There was some bodychecking but the average British hockey fan of the postwar years was brought up on a game with minimal body contact and little or no fighting. While not the most productive member of the London Lions, the one player the Wembley fans took to was Mike Jakubo, a smooth-skating forward who scored only eight goals in 20 games but, most importantly, spent only four minutes in the penalty box.

The 1973–74 season at Wembley was to be a sounding board to test what sort of support the team might expect. The Detroit organization was pleasantly surprised at how many people turned up and Bruce Norris described himself as impressed by the strength of support. Although the price of admission was high by contemporary standards, the average crowd in the 8,000-seat arena was somewhere around the 5,000 mark, which was indeed surprising because there was no actual hockey league—just a succession of European teams coming into London for long weekends. They usually played the Lions on Thursday, Saturday and Sunday. A Supporters' Club was formed by fans of the team and some

200 people attended its first general meeting at which officers and a committee were elected. In the program for the season's final group of games, it was announced that those fans on the mailing list would be kept informed as to the progress in the formation of a European League.

Canadians and Americans are always surprised at the fervent support shown by British fans. While the excesses of hooliganism that mar football (soccer) happily are not present at hockey, there is no doubting the British hockey fan's enthusiasm and knowledge of the game. But the fans were not used to quite as much body contact as the Lions employed. Because of the more physical type of hockey and the tendency to play dump-and-chase, many fans were unimpressed. "They can't string two passes together," was a frequent complaint. "Far too physical; all they want to do is fight," was another. Still, at a time when the European game was far less physical than its Canadian counterpart, the contrast in styles—the in-your-face play of the Lions and the emphasis on skill and speed of the Europeans—made for entertaining contests.

Officiating was a problem. The two-man system was used in Britain and, in most games, a local referee shared the duties with one who had traveled with the visiting team. Because the Lions played a completely different type of game than anything they had experienced before, and played it much faster, the British referees had trouble keeping up. In addition, the fact that ice hockey had become very much a part-time, weekend-only sport in Great Britain meant that the referees lacked experience. One or two of them were not as good on their skates as they should have been, which was a shade embarrassing. On the whole, the players showed amazing self-control.

After a 1–0 loss to the Toledo Hornets in Detroit, the Lions started their Wembley season with 5–4 and 8–2 wins over a team of Austrian Internationals, most of whom were Eastern Europeans playing in the Austrian League. Then there was a three-game trip to Holland, Luxembourg and Belgium which brought three wins. The Lions then returned to London to face stronger opposition in a team called Finnish Olympics which was, in fact, the national Under-23 squad. The Finns were beaten 7–2 and 3–1 before holding the Lions to a 6–6 tie in the third game.

League hockey in Great Britain had died in the early 1960s, principally because of the cost of importing players. The smaller clubs wanted to cut down on the number of imports but the teams playing out of larger rinks insisted they were necessary to maintain standards. They also felt the Canadians added glamour to the game. For a while, the larger rinks subsidized the smaller ones to enable them to continue bringing over Canadians, but that policy proved financially disastrous. Another reason for the death of British league hockey was the introduction of an annual circus at Harringay Arena, which closed the building to hockey for a month. Even worse, an ice show at Wembley led to several temporary but major alterations to the arena that made it impossible to stage hockey games for three months from early December until early March.

Though Wembley had been without hockey for five years, the ice show still existed, which meant that from November 25 to March 7 the Lions embarked on one of the longest road trips in the history of sport. It featured 41 games in nine countries: Scotland, the northeast of England, Finland, Holland, Belgium, Austria, Czechoslovakia, Switzerland and West Germany. Only five of those 41 games were lost. When finally back at Wembley for 11 more games in March, the team lost the first two to Dynamo Moscow, who included two members of the Soviet national team—Vladimir Vikulov and Victor Zinger. The season ended with three games against Djurgarden. The leading Swedish club carried 10 players who were current Swedish internationals. Another player, Leif Svensson, was later to spend two seasons with the Washington Capitals.

In all, the London Lions played 70 games and had a 52–12–6 record. So, was the experiment a success? As far as the team was concerned, there was no doubt that it was. However, on two counts, the venture was not what Bruce Norris had hoped for.

The Wembley Pool had opened in the mid-1930s. While advanced for its time (flying buttress construction, no indoor pillars), it was too small. Norris wanted to build a 16,000-seat multipurpose arena at the back of the Pool but it was an unfortunate time for construction. A miners' strike had caused industrial chaos in the country and Norris's leading financial adviser warned that it was not a good idea to make such an investment. Norris regretted to his dying day that he accepted that advice. Wembley is still waiting for a new building and, nearly 30 years on, still does not have a hockey team.

And Europe is still waiting for its professional hockey league. The main stumbling block in 1973 concerned the availability of players for the World Championships, which were played in March and April when such a league would be approaching the playoffs and teams would want to be at full strength. The various European hockey federations were not prepared to allow international players to stay with their clubs at such a time and, for that reason, turned down any proposed league unless they could have uncontested call on their international players. Since then, of course, many European countries have sent so many players to the NHL that it is now something of a lottery as to who will be available for the World Championships. So much depends on whether a player's NHL team makes it to the Stanley Cup playoffs.

Could a European league affiliated with the NHL work today? As ever, there would be many issues to resolve, but air travel is now so easy that such a development is not beyond the bounds of possibility. If it ever did happen, remember, Bruce Norris was thinking about it almost 30 years ago.

V

The International Game

Dave Silk of Team USA covers Soviet superstar Valeri Kharlamov during a game at Madison Square Garden in which the Soviet Union defeated the Americans 10–3 prior to the start of the 1980 Lake Placid Olympics and Team USA's "Miracle on Ice."
Bruce Bennett photo

CHAPTER 42

Team Building for the 2002 Olympics

Nagano as Teacher; Salt Lake City as Clean Slate

Canada 2002

Alan Adams

It was a snowy day in the first April of the new millennium and a white-out was keeping people away from the semifinal round of the Women's World Championships in Mississauga, Ontario. But the last thing on Bob Nicholson's mind was snow. He was worrying where dinner would be two years hence.

"I'm trying to book restaurants in Salt Lake City and they are having a hard time understanding why I'm trying to book two years in advance," says Nicholson, president of the Canadian Hockey Association.

Granted, it seems a little obsessive to want to know where you are going to dine on any particular night some 24 months or so before you actually sit down at the table and break bread. But when you're feeding the best hockey players Canada can assemble for the Winter Olympics, it pays to make sure every little detail is covered well in advance. Top players deserve the best service available to them, so you make the reservations and hope the *maitre d'* remembers your name.

What is the moral of this story?

Take care of the people you want to take care of you.

In this case, Nicholson hopes that taking care of business translates into mining Olympic gold, not tin.

Let's face it. In Canada—the number-one hockey nation in the world, or so the beer commercial says—gold *is* the only color that shines, and Canadians want their hockey heroes to sparkle on the Olympic stage in Salt Lake City, Utah, in 2002. Nicholson's job is to make sure everything is as hassle-free as possible so everything can go as smoothly as possible.

In soccer, there is a kind of understanding that the two best nations in the world are the team that wins the World Cup and Brazil. If Brazil wins the World Cup, there is only one best. A similar measuring stick applies in hockey—at least for rabid Canadians. The two best hockey nations in the world are Canada and Canada. Whoever wins the World Cup of Hockey or the World Championships or the Olympics is a distant third.

But if there is one thing the 1998 Winter Olympics taught Canadians, it is that even with the best players wearing the maple leaf proudly on their chests, Team Canada is beatable. Your lineup can include Wayne Gretzky, and Eric Lindros, and Steve Yzerman, and Ray Bourque and everybody and anybody who's who in the NHL ... and you can still finish second ... or third ... or, as Canadians witnessed in Nagano, fourth, which is three rocks past the moon by any measuring stick in the land of the frozen north.

On a sunny February day in Big Hat—the name of the oddly shaped arena in Nagano—Gretzky, Yzerman, Lindros, Bourque *et al* ran into an obsessed, possessed and extraordinarily well-coached Czech Republic team that played a near-flawless game and got perfect goaltending in moments of truth in a thrilling sudden-death quarterfinal. The way Dominik Hasek's imposing shadow spread across the ice, maybe not even the addition of Mario Lemieux would have changed the outcome.

Even though the Canadians lost in a shootout—and some people still hang onto the notion that Canada did not lose the game, they lost a skills competition—they had as many shots to win the game as the Czechs.

So what did they—Canada's best NHL players—do wrong?

Nothing, really.

"Normally when you lose in hockey, you stand there and say, 'We didn't do this well' or 'We did that poorly,' " said Wayne Gretzky afterwards. "But we can't say that tonight. I honestly can't tell you what we did wrong. I mean it hasn't been a great couple of years for Canadian hockey so we were really focused on coming in here and re-establishing hockey for Canada." Gretzky added that despite the loss, "I think this team got the train back on track with how hard we worked as a group. I don't think there's anything wrong with hockey in Canada."

Simply put, what the hockey gods served up in Nagano was the greatest hockey tournament ever played. There was not a bad game, and that includes some of the opening-round matches between lesser lights such as Germany, Japan and Latvia. For the fans glued to their television sets back in North America, there were some games they were not all that crazy about watching; games where two teams had players they did not really know, and who, by NHL standards, were not very good. But because it was the Olympics, because it is and was a gathering of the best athletes in the world, the fact that Belarus was playing Kazakhstan or Japan was up against Norway in the shadow of the Olympic rings and the warmth of the Olympic flame, these so-called "bad games" were enhanced.

In other words, there are no real bad games in the Olympics, just some that are not as good as others. The pleasure of the Olympic tournament is mostly associated with the drama of it; with how much it matters to the people who are in the competition, with how well they are playing, and how much the size of the prize means to them. The 1998 Olympic tournament left much to be reflected on, and much to look forward to, going into Salt Lake City.

When it got down to the medal round in Nagano—when Canada, the United States, Russia, Czech Republic, Sweden, Finland, Belarus and Kazakhstan took the stage—the hockey was fabulous and the players were ecstatic about the pace of the games. The games were quick and the momentum swung like a pendulum. One minute a team was on the attack. The next, it was in full panic mode. One bad minute and you could be gone. One brilliant move and you could advance.

Olympic hockey is never boring. When the difference in the competitive level of teams is wafer-thin, the pressure is on to perform.

The Olympic tournament is one in which there are no excuses.

While it would have helped to have sensational offensive talents such as Joe Sakic and Paul Kariya available for the medal round in Nagano (Sakic was in the stands with an ailing knee, Kariya never made the trip because of a concussion), they weren't, and Team Canada can't use injuries as a crutch.

In Nagano, the hockey was remarkably entertaining. Great drama, heart-stopping play, brilliant hockey and tons of national pride were evident throughout the competition. The whole word was watching—and enjoying the tournament, which concluded with a wild celebration in the streets of Prague after the Czechs, behind Hasek's all-world performance, beat the Russians in the gold medal final.

While losing hurt back on the home front, Canadians understood that the Olympics are a very short tournament with a one-game gold medal showdown, and that there is always a way to lose. Yet, the expectations were, and remain, the same: any time a Canadian team enters a competition, they go in as the favorite.

But if Nagano taught Canadians anything, it is that the sense of invincibility has gone. Canadians know Team Canada can lose. In 1972, Canadians found out that their summer-softened pros had not cornered the market on world-class hockey. In Nagano, they found out that NHL players in midseason form were beatable by a team that had a dozen players who weren't even in the NHL.

Nagano put an end to any foregone conclusions about who is best.

And on that February day, Canada wasn't.

"I think our expectations were high and we found out in that format how competitive it [the Olympics] really is," says Pat Quinn, the thinking-man's general manager of the Toronto Maple Leafs. "It is so different than the NHL, and talented players can go over there and not succeed. The Czechs showed us how a group that plays a lot can focus on one thing and that is to win, regardless of the odds."

In Nagano, Canadians discovered a newfound respect for European hockey.

Prior to the decision to send the pros to the Winter Games, the only time Canadians saw their best against someone else's best was in the Canada Cup and its successor, the World Cup of Hockey. And while the Canada Cup and World Cup provided some lasting memories, there was still an emptiness because these were tournaments without a true meaning; an event void of significance.

The bottom line is that Canadians have always wanted NHLers in the Olympics, but NHL owners, putting their interests ahead of nationhood, held their dream captive.

But the feeling was mutual. As much as the NHL wasn't interested in the Olympics, the International Olympic Committee was not interested in the NHL. Canada used to send senior teams to the Winter Games, and for the longest while they dominated. But eventually the Europeans caught up and once they did, they never looked back. The historic Summit Series in 1972 changed perceptions; it showed that the Europeans had made real progress. Today, more than ever, nobody takes Europe for granted.

"Everybody knows the European players and how good they are," says Toronto goalie Curtis Joseph. "It is not a mystery anymore. Hockey is becoming bigger in other countries. We should not feel bad about our program. Canadians love to play, and we still have great players. It would not be any fun if it was a given for Canada."

Which brings us to Salt Lake City and the 2002 Winter Games.

What lessons were learned in Nagano?

What, if anything, does Team Canada have to do differently?

Going to Nagano, the braintrust behind Team Canada knew the big ice would have its profound impact on the hockey played there. Hockey on the bigger ice is about speed and puck control; the Europeans had an edge on puck control. In the end, however, what hurt most was that the Canadians didn't "finish." A 40-goal scorer is only effective if he buries the shot. They had their chances but did not put them away. Going into Salt Lake City, everyone knows a better job must be done on that front.

Of the lessons learned in Nagano, perhaps the most important is this: You can forget that notion about the Europeans lacking "heart." Their hearts are every bit as big as anyone in Canada. How else can you explain how a team with 12 players with unfamiliar names who never played in the NHL could win the gold medal? They don't lack heart, it's just that perhaps they don't wear it on their sleeves like Canadians do.

As for skill, the Europeans more than match whomever Canada puts on the ice. Let's face it. Canada lost fair and square in Nagano, and it's worth noting that when the medals were handed out, it was the Czechs, Russians and Finns who were on the podium.

At least when it came time to assume their roles as ambassadors, the Canadians were perfect role models. Team Canada thrived on the Olympic experience. The NHLers, initially criticized for being millionaires, lived in the Olympic Village and rubbed shoulders and shared the breakfast table with the *crème de la crème* of other sports.

They had an impact, too. Just go to any office of an organization representing a winter sport and your are likely to see a photograph somewhere on a wall of Gretzky or Yzerman or whoever playing cards with other athletes.

"At first, there were some false ideas and people thought we had satellite dishes in our room and other special treatment," says Rob Zamuner. "But we didn't. Once all the athletes got together and mingled and got to know each other, we realized we were all in it together. We were all members of Team Canada."

After Canada lost in the bronze medal game to Finland, the players were given the option to go home. It was an offer they easily refused. Canada's Olympic hockey players wanted to march in the closing ceremonies with the rest of the nation's athletes. They did their country proud.

"I still get chills when I recall the closing ceremony," says Zamuner.

From a logistical point of view, Nagano had as many pros as cons for Nicholson and his support staff at Canadian Hockey. Because it was Japan, there were some cultural differences to overcome. But patience and perseverance paid dividends.

On the other hand, because it was Japan, the public at large didn't have any idea who Steve Yzerman or Eric Lindros or Joe Sakic were—though they did know "The

Great One." The anonymity was welcomed.

It won't be the same in Salt Lake City, and it's Nicholson's job to provide as comfortable an environment as possible for the members of Team Canada. Canadian Hockey, which manages the Olympic hockey team, prides itself on working out the logistics well in advance of any event. They are making a push to make Canada's preparations for 2002 the envy of other hockey nations.

"Our job on the administrative side is to really clearly identify what the IOC and other regulations are and, around all that, make sure we have areas where the players can get away and relax and see their families and enjoy the Olympic experience," says Nicholson.

So instead of worrying about snow, Nicholson was mulling over a restaurant guide. "A reservation for 60, please," he said in jest.

"We want the players to experience the Olympic feeling and the Olympic dream, but they have to be able to get away from it at times and enjoy their families in a way that they are protected from the general public. Our challenge is to get the logistical things done in an Olympic city, which is difficult.

"That includes making sure we can get restaurants, and getting transportation in place for family members. You do not want your players worrying about their mom, or wife, and how they are going to get to the game."

It's taking care of the little details like these that make for hassle-free games.

Zamuner, for one, appreciated the effort in Japan.

"The only thing I would change is the result,"he says.

So would a hockey-mad nation of 28 million people.

WHAT KIND OF TEAM CANADA 2002?

Mike Brophy

IMAGINE, IF YOU WILL, that you have been put in charge of shaping Canada's entry at the 2002 Winter Olympic Games in Salt Lake City. It's a lofty position with a hefty weight attached to it. Win the gold medal, which of course, is what all Canadians expect, and you're the king. Come back empty-handed and you're, well ... the 1998 Canadian Olympic team.

So, how to build the team? Do you go only with veterans? What about sending a bunch of young legs to Utah? Or, how about paying tribute to all those who have served their country with distinction at the World Junior Championships? Then again, what about trying some new blood, players who developed later and didn't get a shot at playing for their country as juniors?

So many players; so many decisions.

The conventual wisdom is this: When you build a team with designs on gold, you want a little of everything. That includes experience, youth, grit, intelligence, leadership, size and speed. What makes Canada's 2002 entry so intriguing is that, for the first time in decades, many of the players the country has come to depend on in international battles—Wayne Gretzky, Paul Coffey, Larry Murphy and Mark Messier among them—have either retired or are too long in the tooth to be seriously considered for the squad. No matter which way Canada's general manager decides to go, you can rest assured there will be some new blood on the 2002 Olympic team.

Here are five examples of how Team Canada might look in Salt Lake City. Even these five examples are subject to infinite variations. Injuries have a way of forcing modification to the best-laid plans. No one conceived of Team Canada at Nagano without Paul Kariya, but reality intruded. Similarly, Eric Lindros is central to many visions of Team Canada 2002, but will he be able to play?

Team WJC Gold

The following players—listed alphabetically—have all represented Canada on international ponds as juniors.

Goal: Jeff Hackett, Roberto Luongo, Jose Theodore

Defense: Eric Desjardins, Scott Niedermayer, Chris Pronger, Wade Redden, Jason Smith, Darryl Sydor, Rhett Warriner

Forwards: Anson Carter, Theoren Fleury, Jeff Friesen, Jarome Iginla, Paul Kariya, Eric Lindros, Jeff O'Neill, Mark Recchi, Mike Ricci, Joe Sakic, Brendan Shanahan, Ryan Smyth, Joe Thornton

Does this team know a thing or two about winning on the world stage? You bet! The three goalies and 20 skaters have a total of 23 gold medals at the World Junior Championships. Not bad. In fact, center Eric Lindros is Canada's all-time leading scorer at the tournament with 31 points during the three years he competed. That includes getting 10 points in 1992, his third and final World Junior appearance, despite the fact he was quite sick with the flu and probably shouldn't have been playing.

Lindros, provided he is healthy, and defenseman Chris Pronger are the two key players for this particular grouping, though the supporting cast offers plenty of speed along with an abundance of experience.

All these players are graduates of Canada's Program of Excellence. That means they have experience on the international stage at various levels and shouldn't be intimidated by facing the best from other nations. The ultra-competitive Pronger is a workhorse on defense and will log many valuable minutes each game in both defensive and offensive situations—just as he does for the St. Louis Blues. He has proven beyond a shadow of a doubt he can comfortably play half the game and still be very effective where others would wilt from exhaustion.

The beauty of this defense is, with the likes of Jason Smith and Wade Redden, both of whom are solid in their own zone, Pronger would have the freedom to join in the rush, something he has started to do more often with the Blues. Aside from possessing the best outlet pass in the game, a skill he uses frequently to conserve energy, he is a slick skater with soft hands who likes to infiltrate the other team's slot on occasion. In fact, the Blues have been known to stick him in front of the other team's net on the power-play and have used the ploy effectively. Once thought to be mostly a defensive specialist, Pronger was second in scoring among defensemen in the 1999–2000 season with career highs in goals (14), assists (48) and points (62).

Imagine Pronger and Niedermayer, one of the fastest skaters in the NHL, on the point during a power-play with Lindros, Mark Recchi and Paul Kariya up front. Recchi led the NHL in power-play points in 1999–2000 with 39 in 82 games. A second unit with Joe Sakic, Brendan Shanahan and Theo Fleury or Ryan Smyth wouldn't be too shabby either.

Goal is something of a question mark for this team. Although there are plenty of Canadian goaltenders who have played in the World Junior Championships, including Stephane Fiset, Jamie Storr, Jose Theodore and Marc Denis who were all named top goalie in the event, none has established himself as a clear-cut number-one goalie in the NHL. Felix Potvin came the closest, helping the Toronto Maple Leafs make consecutive appearances in the Conference finals in the early 1990s, but his play fell off in Toronto and again in New York with the Islanders. He did finally appear to be recapturing some of his lost form in Vancouver last season.

Of the goalies available with World Junior experience, Jeff Hackett seems like the logical choice to be the team's number-one starter. That's based on his recent NHL play, not anything he did as a junior, and could change before 2002. His partner in Montreal, Theodore, has made tremendous strides and was solid with Canada at the 2000 World Championships—although it was a weak goal that cost Team Canada a victory in the semifinal. Roberto Luongo is the wild card in this scenario. While clearly on his way to a successful professional career, is 2002 too soon to expect him to lead a nation to gold?

Team No WJC

The following players did not represent Canada as juniors.

Goal: Fred Brathwaite, Martin Brodeur, Curtis Joseph

Defense: Rob Blake, Paul Coffey, Adam Foote, Dan McGillis, Kyle McLaren, Jason Wooley, Jason York

Forwards: Todd Bertuzzi, Mike Eastwood, Simon Gagne, Travis Green, Mike Johnson, Steve Larouche, John Madden, Darren McCarty, Michael Peca, Keith Primeau, Steve Rucchin, Brian Savage, Chris Simon

Admittedly, the talent on this team is not as deep as that on the team that experienced the World Junior Championships. Not even close, really. But be honest. Did you really believe the Czech Republic was as deep as either Canada or the United States, not to mention Russia, at the last Olympics? It was Dominik Hasek and Jaromir Jagr with a strong, but otherwise nameless, supporting cast against the world. And the Czechs took home gold.

In other words, how much does front-line talent mean in the big scheme of things when you have chemistry and determination?

"A team like this one definitely has some grit and guys that you win with, there's no question about that," said Ottawa Senators defenseman Jason York. (York attended the summer camp for the 1991 Canadian national junior team but didn't make the final camp the following December.) "This is a team that would have a great work ethic, and if you take a look at the teams that are successful in the Stanley Cup playoffs, that's what they have. This is a team of guys who would not be outworked."

And this team's strength starts with fabulous goaltending. Imagine having the option of starting Fred Brathwaite, Martin Brodeur or Curtis Joseph. Brodeur has won two Stanley Cup titles and all three are bona fide number-one goalies. This team unquestionably has better goaltending than the collection of ex-World Junior players. And it is not without star skaters, either. Rob Blake has a Norris Trophy in his resumé; Adam Foote played in the last Olympics and Paul Coffey, who would be a power-play specialist on this team, is the NHL's all-time leading scorer among defensemen.

What this team has, more than anything else, is character. Defensemen Jason York and Chris Therien are dependable in their own zone, while Jason Wooley and Dan McGillis are solid at both ends. Keith Primeau is the first-line center and then you can take your choice between Steve Rucchin, Michael Peca and John Madden. All three are strong two-way performers who would be as comfortable and effective in the number-two slot as they would be at number four. And pity the opposing center who has to go up against any of them on any given night.

The wings are also filled with grinders, although Todd Bertuzzi, Mike Johnson, Mike Eastwood and Simon Gagne might take exception to that classification. One thing is for certain, if you came up against this team, you'd know you were in a game.

You may have noticed the name Steve Larouche on the team. He has played in the NHL for the Ottawa Senators (eight goals and 15 points in just 18 games in 1994–95), the New York Rangers and the Los Angeles Kings, but has mostly been a minor leaguer. The reason he makes this team, however, is because he's so proficient in the shootout. In fact, of all the Canadian-born players in the International Hockey League in the 1999–2000 season, Larouche, who played for the Chicago Wolves, was the very best in the shootout with 16 goals on 24 attempts (67 percent). Considering that Canada bombed out in the shootout in Nagano, wouldn't it be nice to have somebody on board with a good track record?

Team Under 30

Goal: Martin Biron, Jamie Storr, Jose Theodore

Defense: Adrian Aucoin, Ed Jovanovski, Kyle McLaren, Scott Niedermayer, Chris Pronger, Wade Redden, Darryl Sydor

Forwards: Todd Bertuzzi, Curtis Brown, Anson Carter, Jeff Friesen, Jarome Iginla, Paul Kariya, Vincent Lecavalier, Eric Lindros, Owen Nolan, Jeff O'Neill, Michael Peca, Keith Primeau, Ryan Smyth

Could a team of "kids" mine gold? Well, the ice is bigger so it certainly wouldn't hurt to have young legs. Also, by the time the 2002 Olympics arrive, many of the Canadian players who are under the age of 30 will have secured plenty of NHL experience.

"With this type of team you'd have a little more speed and size," said Florida Panthers general manager Bryan Murray. "And you'd have fairly good leadership in the 28- and 29-year-old category."

That's for sure. With the likes of Pronger, Nolan, Lindros and Primeau, there would be no shortage of leadership.

The team obviously lacks the maturity and life experience of the over-30 squad that follows, but is that really necessary in a short tournament? Players such as Todd Bertuzzi, Jeff Friesen, Owen Nolan and Paul Kariya have demonstrated that when they get hot, they're awfully hard to contain. Primeau, O'Neill and Lecavalier can play center and the wing, which makes them that much more valuable.

Theodore seems to be on the right path to be the starting goalie, though, in time, Biron also looks like he would be capable of handling the number-one chore.

"Obviously most of the guys who played in the last Olympics were the older guys," said 24-year-old Carolina Hurricanes center/winger Jeff O'Neill. "But if you look at the U.S. team, you see they're using a lot of younger players ... bigger and younger guys. We have to do the same thing. For the most part, NHL players live for the Stanley Cup. But to be an Olympic athlete is quite an honor. Canada wants to get back on the hockey map. The World Junior Championships, Olympics and World Championships have been dominated by European teams and we want to get back on top."

Team Over 30

Goal: Martin Brodeur, Curtis Joseph, Chris Osgood

Defense: Rob Blake, Patrice Brisebois, Eric Desjardins, Adam Foote, Al MacInnis, Jason Wooley, Jason York

Forwards: Rod Brind'Amour, Vincent Damphousse, Mike Eastwood, Theoren Fleury, Adam Graves, Keith Jones, Darren McCarty, Yanic Perrault, Mark Recchi, Steve Rucchin, Joe Sakic, Brian Savage, Pierre Turgeon.

Thirty isn't as old as it used to be. Or so says longtime NHL coach Roger Neilson.

"Players train much better these days," said Neilson. "And they eat better so many of them remain productive through their 30s." All you had to do was watch Guy Carbonneau, the NHL's oldest player at 40, perform during the 1999–2000 playoffs to know that is true. But could a group of graybeards win at the Olympics?

Let's face it, they'd be up against speedy European and American legs. It's one thing to bring experience to the table, and this team has plenty of that, but quite another to be able to keep up on the big ice surface.

Take a close look at this team and it is not inconceivable to imagine it banding together. There's a nice balance of speed and scoring, which will be equally important in a two-week tournament. There is plenty of scoring potential from the likes of Fleury, Damphousse, Perrault, Sakic and Savage. Rucchin, Graves and Eastwood are responsible defensive players and the job of some of the forwards would simply be to slow down the opposition or make their lives miserable. Players such as Darren McCarty and Keith Jones have proven quite capable of doing that in the NHL.

"I think if you look at our league, there are plenty of players 30 and over who could be successful on a team like this," said Murray. "The guys on this team have a tremendous amount of experience. They would be hard to rattle."

Team Ultimate

Goal: Ed Belfour, Martin Brodeur, Curtis Joseph

Defense: Rob Blake, Eric Desjardins, Adam Foote, Richard Matvichuk, Scott Niedermayer, Chris Pronger, Wade Redden

Forwards: Anson Carter, Jeff Friesen, Jarome Iginla, Paul Kariya, Vincent Lecavalier, Eric Lindros, John Madden, Owen Nolan, Jeff O'Neill, Michael Peca, Keith Primeau, Mark Recchi, Brian Savage

On the bubble: Martin Lapointe, Joe Thornton

There is no formula for cooking up the perfect team. Putting together Team Canada for Salt Lake City involves much more than just bringing together the three hottest goalies and the top-scoring players at every position. For nearly every name on this team, you'll find 10 people who will say, "Yeah, but what about … "

That being said, young players such as John Madden, an NHL rookie in 1999–2000 who led the league in shorthand goals and displayed scintillating speed with the New Jersey Devils, and Jeff O'Neill of the Carolina Hurricanes, who has emerged as a disciplined player at both ends, are prime examples of youngsters who deserve the chance. Ditto Anson Carter of the Boston Bruins, who brings speed and tenacity to the mix.

At the same time, there will be a veteran presence. Foote, Desjardins and Blake are all experienced international performers on the blue line. Recchi, Lindros and Kariya understand the importance of performing under pressure. The question is, does Canada simply come back with the same old names and go with the players who are "next in line," or is it time to break in some fresh, new talent? Considering that the Canadian team came back from Nagano with no medal, the answer seems obvious. Combine these veterans with these kids and it could add up to gold in 2002.

U.S. Olympic Hockey in 2002

Rich Chere

THE DISAPPOINTING PERFORMANCE of Team USA in Nagano, Japan, during the 1998 Winter Olympics has spurred the next class of American Olympians to pursue the kind of magic that has been missing since Herb Brooks and his players pulled off the "Miracle on Ice" at the 1980 Games in Lake Placid.

While it is unlikely that National Hockey League players could ever recapture the stunning emotional impact Neal Broten, Mark Johnson, Jim Craig and their teammates had on the nation when they overcame the heavily favored Soviet Union in upstate New York more than two decades ago, there is the belief that both a medal and a return to glory is possible at Salt Lake City, Utah, in 2002.

"I think so," said Edmonton Oilers right wing Bill Guerin, a Wilbraham, Massachusetts, native who played on the team in Nagano. "I think we can win a medal. The core of top players is still around and there is a group of talented young guys who have a chance to make the team."

One of those young guys is New Jersey Devils center Scott Gomez, from Anchorage, Alaska, who won the Calder Trophy as the NHL's top rookie in 1999-2000.

"Your dream is to play in the NHL," Gomez said, "but before that it's the Olympics. That's always been a main goal for hockey players growing up in the United States. The Olympics are big with my family and in my house. It's my goal to play for Team USA in the Olympics and to be with all those great athletes. The Olympics are really the big-time."

In a sense, the dissatisfying performance in Nagano has injected new incentive into the U.S. Olympic program. After failing in its first try with NHL players, Team USA now has a target at which to shoot in Salt Lake City—to bring respect back to the program.

"I'm not bitter that we didn't win a medal, probably more disappointed for our country," said 1998 Team USA general manager Lou Lamoriello. "I thought we had the players to win a medal and we didn't. There are things that can be done to change that."

One of the changes will almost certainly be a different type of team to represent the U.S. in Salt Lake City. It will be more similar to the squad that won the gold medal in the 1996 World Cup of Hockey.

Instead of picking an all-star team of American-born players, as they did for the 1998 Olympics, U.S. officials will concentrate more on a building a team that can win.

"We might have needed a few more plumbers instead of skill players in Japan," Lamoriello said. "There was a lot of pressure to pick a team early, which is against my beliefs. I believe you should use time.

"I would have waited until the last second to pick the team. Some guys who made the team would not have been picked because of the way they played just before the break in the NHL season."

Guerin, who played at both the World Cup and the Olympics, agrees that the team must be chosen with a gold medal in mind. Politics and marketing should be removed from the process.

"If it were me, I'd pick a team that can play together, not an all-star team," Guerin explained. "You can almost have the best of both worlds, but you have to be honest with guys about their roles on the team. Even if guys are used to playing 20 minutes a game in the NHL, they have to be told their roles in the Olympics. You always want the best players, but you need chemistry, too. Our chemistry in Nagano was good, but not as good as it was in the World Cup."

Some might dispute Lamoriello's theory that Team USA could have used a few more plumbers. After all, wasn't the Czech Republic, which captured the gold medal, the most skilled team in the tournament?

"I don't think it was," Lamoriello said. "Look at the Czech team closely. They weren't the most talented team. No one was more skilled than Canada or Russia. But the Czechs were a team."

Although Europeans have dominated the NHL for the past few seasons, ranking among the top scorers and goaltenders in the league, the U.S. and Canada still have the deepest talent pools from which to assemble Olympics teams.

"There are so many good players in the United States now," Guerin said. "Behind Canada, there is the U.S. We definitely have enough players. I think we can be very good. We can compete with anybody in the world, including Canada, the team which is always the favorite."

Lamoriello, who has been involved in U.S. hockey since his days as a coach and athletic director at Providence College in Rhode Island, feels the U.S. has enough talent to assemble a winner.

"The Canadians are always going to have more quantity. And when you have more quantity, you're going to have more quality," he said. "In America, we have quality, but maybe not four deep. The U.S. should be able to put a team together that has a chance to win."

Guerin ranks among the power forwards that Lamoriello and USA Hockey officials covet. The others are a pair of Phoenix Coyotes stars, Keith Tkachuk (Melrose, Mass.) and Jeremy Roenick (Boston, Mass.), along with Colorado Avalanche forward Adam Deadmarsh.

Speed is just as important to the mix and that would include Mike Modano (Livonia, Mich.) and Jamie Langenbrunner (Duluth, Minn.) of the Dallas Stars. Also Boston Bruins wing Brian Rolston (Flint, Mich.). Top scorers John LeClair (St. Albans, Vt.) of the Philadelphia Flyers, Chicago Blackhawks right wing Tony Amonte (Hingham, Mass.), Edmonton Oilers veteran Doug Weight (Warren, Mich.) and Dallas Stars sniper Brett Hull also fit into the picture.

But it's the next generation of players that has U.S. officials so excited. They include playmaking center Gomez, Colorado center Chris Drury (Trumbull, Conn.), New York Islanders left wing Mark Parrish (Edina, Minn.), Nashville Predators center David Legwand (Detroit, Mich.) and New York Rangers center Michael York (Pontiac, Mich.).

Undoubtedly, Dallas Stars captain Derian Hatcher (Sterling Heights, Mich.) will anchor Team USA's defense. Lamoriello credits Hatcher with turning around the World Cup in 1996. "I thought he was the key. He was on a wrecking mission for about three weeks," Lamoriello recalled. "You need that kind of player."

Says Hatcher: "I remember that Lou came up to me after we played Canada and told me he thought my hits turned the tournament around. Canada had a reputation for being bullies."

Colorado's Aaron Miller (Buffalo, N.Y.) is also a top candidate to join Hatcher on the defense, while the size of young blueliners like Josh DeWolf, a New Jersey Devils prospect, may figure into the selection process. Of course speed on defense is also vital. That is where veterans like Brian Leetch (Corpus Christi, Texas) of the Rangers come in, along with Devils defenseman Brian Rafalski (Dearborn, Mich.). Rafalski spent four seasons in Sweden and Finland, so his experience on international ice surfaces would be invaluable. The remaining spot on the U.S. blue line likely will be filled by a veteran such as Chris Chelios (Chicago, Ill.), Phil Housley (St. Paul, Minn.) or Gary Suter (Madison, Wisc.). Bryan Berard (Woonsocket, R.I.) will also receive consideration if he has recovered from a serious eye injury sustained late in the 1999–2000 NHL season.

Rangers netminder Mike Richter (Abington, Penn.) was in goal during the World Cup and is the leading candidate to be the number-one goalie again in Salt Lake City. However, the play of Philadelphia Flyers rookie Brian Boucher (Woonsocket, R.I.) will make him a possible choice for the starting job. Another candidate is Nashville Predators goalie Mike Dunham (Johnson City, N.Y.).

It is a shame that some of the heroes from the 1980 gold medal team never had an opportunity to participate in the Olympics again after joining the NHL. Neal Broten, Ken Morrow and Mark Johnson might have given the U.S. a chance to win gold again. All were either too old or had retired by the time NHL players were allowed to compete in the Olympics.

"I think it's really good that they're sticking with NHL players for the 2002 Olympics," Guerin said. "The way everything is going, with the Dream Teams in basketball, we should be playing in the Olympics."

There really is no way to turn back the clock to 1980.

"You can never compare," Lamoriello said. "In 1980, you had the availability of the best amateurs because college players weren't able to play in the NHL. Today, your best potential college players are professionals. They've left college and turned pro."

Though it was generally assumed that NHL players would take part in the Olympics for the second time when the Winter Games are held in Salt Lake City, the official decision was not actually announced until May 9, 2000, in St. Petersburg, Russia. On that day, the International Ice Hockey Federation finalized an agreement with the NHL and NHL Players' Association. The agreement was approved by the NHL Board of Governors.

"We are pleased that the IIHF appears to have been able to work out all the final details of our Olympic participation," NHL commissioner Gary Bettman said. "We look forward to having the best hockey players in the world participate at Salt Lake City."

NHL Players' Association executive director Bob Goodenow echoed Bettman's feelings.

"It is always exciting for the fans to watch the world's best hockey players exhibit their skills on an international stage. The players are looking forward to participating in Salt Lake City in 2002 and at the World Cup of Hockey in 2004," Goodenow said.

With gold medals on home ice at Lake Placid in 1980 and Squaw Valley, California, in 1960, hopes will be high once again at Salt Lake City in 2002.

TEAM USA 2002 OLYMPIC ROSTER

Position	Name	Age in 2002
F	Tony Amonte	31
F	Adam Deadmarsh	26
F	Scott Gomez	22
F	Bill Guerin	31
F	Brett Hull	37
F	Jamie Langenbrunner	26
F	John LeClair	32
F	Mike Modano	31
F	Jeremy Roenick	32
F	Brian Rolston	28
F	Keith Tkachuk	29
F	Doug Weight	31
D	Josh DeWolf	24
D	Derian Hatcher	29
D	Sean Hill	31
D	Brian Leetch	33
D	Aaron Miller	30
D	Brian Rafalski	28
and one of...		
D	Bryan Berard	24
D	Chris Chelios	40
D	Phil Housley	37
D	Gary Suter	37
G	Brian Boucher	25
G	Mike Dunham	29
G	Mike Richter	35

CZECH REPUBLIC 2002

Pavel Barta and Ivan Filippov

THERE ARE NO EXPECTATIONS that Dominik Hasek will be in net for the Czech Republic at Salt Lake City in 2002. Hasek will be 37 by then. Most athletes at that age are already enjoying their pensions. But netminders have always been considered different. Maybe Hasek will change his mind.

Many players from the 1998 Czech team, including Jaromir Jagr and Robert Reichel, will be in their early 30s by the next Olympics. The burden of defending the gold medal will be placed on the shoulders of younger players who did not participate in Nagano but who have helped lead the Czechs to first-place finishes at the World Championships in 1999 and 2000. This next generation will have taken over by 2002. They may add yet another chapter to the Czech hockey dynasty if they are able to click as a team like the underdog squad of 1998.

The philosophy of Czech coaches always has been to rely on players who really wanted to dress for the national team. There is little reason to change this approach after the success of recent years. While some NHL players did not show much interest in joining the Czech squad before the 2000 World Championships in St. Petersburg, Russia, there will likely be many patriots among the NHLers when their country calls on them before the next Olympics. The Czechs have demonstrated on several occasions, including St. Petersburg, that they can survive without top stars, but having a good mix of NHL players and elite European-league talent has always been a trademark of Czech teams. It will likely be more necessary than ever to go with players with North American experience in Salt Lake City. Veteran European star Jiri Dopita was critical of his fellow Czechs in the NHL who refused to take part in the 2000 World Championships. Ironically, it is unlikely that Dopita would get the call in 2002. At age 34, this ultimate warrior likely will be seen as an over-the-hill veteran playing out his career with Eisbaeren Berlin in Germany.

Replacing Hasek will be the key to repeating as gold medal champions in 2002. That job likely will fall to Roman Turek. He is a gold medalist from the 1996 World Championships and his NHL history is similar to that of Hasek. Turek graduated from backup role to superstar and Vezina Trophy candidate in 1999–2000. He will be only 32 years old in 2002 and will have six years of NHL experience. He should be ready to step in as the number-one netminder. Milan Hnilicka and Roman Cechmanek, both backups to Hasek in Nagano, are expected to be the other candidates for the job in the Czech crease.

The defense in 2002 will be led by 1998 gold medal team members Jiri Slegr (who will be 31) and Roman Hamrlik, who, at 28, should be at the peak of his career. The rest of the blue-line crew could be built around proven international players such as Petr Buzek, who miraculously returned to top-level hockey after a life-threatening car accident in 1995, Jaroslav Spacek and Pavel Kubina. There will also be the first teaming of the defensive pair of Michal Sykora and Stanislav Neckar since the 1996 World Championships in Vienna and the World Cup of Hockey.

Up front, Robert Reichel should be called upon as a penalty-shot specialist if the shootout survives into the new millennium. He will be the heart and soul of the Czech team, as he always is when representing his country at a big tournament. Jaromir Jagr probably will ponder his Olympic invitation until the last moment, but he won't turn it down if he stays injury-free.

A healthy Jagr would make a big difference to the Czech team. The same applies to Patrik Elias and Petr Sykora (no relation to defenseman Michal), who starred on the New Jersey Devils 2000 Stanley Cup team. Elias brings more scoring touch, while Sykora supplies playmaking finesse and on-ice smarts. The Czech offense, balanced as it seems, will rely heavily on these two. Roman Simicek should be counted on to fill the role Jiri Dopita served for the gold medal winners in 1998—that of the team's top power forward. Simicek proved his worth in this regard at the 1999 World Championships.

Vaclav Prospal, who lost his spot on the 1998 team due to a broken hand, will be a part of the core troop in 2002. Radek Dvorak and Jan Hlavac will bring added speed and scoring touch. Grinders Vaclav Varada and Petr Cajanek will help in the corners and in front of the opponents' net. Bright new stars will emerge in Patrik Stefan, a potential franchise player with the Atlanta Thrashers, and flashy skater Martin Havlat, who won both junior and senior World Championships in 2000. They are willing to sacrifice their individual talents for a teamwork approach and are almost assured of spots on the Czech Olympic team. Other youngsters such as Jan Bulis, Michal Sivek or Milan Kraft should battle for the final spots.

Some will raise doubts about the lack of size or defensive depth on the Czech team, but these should not be issues. The only real concern could be coaching.

Ivan Hlinka led the Czechs to Olympic gold in 1998. He was hired by the Pittsburgh Penguins as an associate coach during the 1999–2000 season and was later named head coach. If his national team successor, Josef Augusta, doesn't remain on the bench until the 2002 Olympics, Marek Sykora and Vaclav Sykora (no relation to each other or either player named Sykora) will be the favorites to succeed him. But former national team defenseman and 1986 Calgary Flames draft pick Antonin Stavjana should act as a dark horse in the head coaching race. If Stavjana lands the job, his lack of international experience could see Ivan Hlinka join the team as a consultant or as the national team's first associate coach.

Czech Republic 2002 Olympic Roster

Position	Name	Age in 2002
G	Roman Turek	32
G	Roman Cechmanek	31
G	Milan Hnilicka	28
D	Jiri Slegr	31
D	Roman Hamrlik	28
D	Jaroslav Spacek	28
D	Michal Sykora	29
D	Petr Buzek	25
D	Stanislav Neckar	27
D	Pavel Kubina	25
F	Jaromir Jagr	30
F	Robert Reichel	31
F	Vaclav Prospal	27
F	Radek Dvorak	25
F	Vaclav Varada	26
F	Petr Sykora	26
F	Patrik Elias	26
F	Patrik Stefan	22
F	Jan Hlavac	25
F	Roman Simicek	30
F	Petr Cajanek	26
F	Martin Havlat	20

Slovakia 2002

Pavel Barta and Ivan Filippov

Despite winning a silver medal at the 2000 World Championships in St. Petersburg, Russia, the nation of Slovakia is not yet considered a major hockey power. This being the case, the Slovak team will have to begin play at the 2002 Salt Lake City Olympic tournament before the NHL takes its scheduled break—just as it had to in 1998 when Slovakia failed to make it out of the preliminary round. Without receiving a bye into the championship round like Canada, Russia, Sweden, Finland, the Czech Republic and the United States, the national team coaches from Slovakia will face difficult decisions.

Jan Filc coached Slovakia to its silver medal at the 2000 World Championships. It was the first trip to the medal podium in senior competition for the country since the former Czechoslovakia was split up in 1993. Filc had won bronze with the Under-20 junior national team just one year before. He likely will guide Slovakia through the 2002 Olympics, though Peter Stastny has indicated that he might take an interest in coaching. It is likely Stastny will end up working with Filc as an assistant. Many say that Filc reminds them of charismatic coach Ivan Hlinka, the former star of the Czechoslovakian national team who guided the Czech Republic to gold in Nagano. Stastny, however, is even more like Hlinka in terms of his status as a national icon. Both men are legends who used to be heroes for everybody in their countries. Unlike those two, Filc seemingly appeared from nowhere.

The biggest question for those running the 2002 Slovak Olympic team will be how many NHLers to add once the team gets past the preliminary round. (The whole country will have to hope that a team without NHL players will be good enough to top its preliminary group in 2002. At Nagano, Slovakia could not get past Kazakhstan.) If the team can advance in Salt Lake City, the influx of NHL talent will make the Slovaks very confident and dangerous. Clearing roster spots for the NHLers might be unfair to the players who have worked hard to get the team through, but Slovakia must add NHL stars to make good in the championship round.

With the success of players such as Miroslav Satan, Zigmund Palffy and the line of Pavol Demitra, Michal Handzus and Lubos Bartecko in St. Louis, the number of Slovaks in the NHL will have increased dramatically since the last Olympic tournament. Slovakia has always produced mobile and skilled forwards. Satan, Demitra, Palffy, Marian Hossa and Peter Bondra all have proven they can score. Along with them and other experienced playmakers such as Jozef Stumpel and Robert Petrovicky, there is a terrific core of young offensive talent with players such as Marian Gaborik (selected third overall by the Minnesota Wild in the 2000 NHL Entry Draft) and Marian Hossa's younger brother Marcel. Slovakia should be well equipped to create very fast and explosive firepower up front.

With the depth of talent available, coach Filc can afford to look at personalities when filling out his roster and likely won't have to worry about pushing people to joining the team. Not that this has been much of a problem; Slovaks are generally very proud patriots. At the same time, Filc does not have to guarantee a spot to anyone and could cut players that nobody would have imagined a Slovak national team doing without. Peter Bondra, for example, will be 34 years old in 2002. Perhaps his slump in 1999–2000 indicates that he is losing his speed and scoring touch. If this is the case, his best chance to make the team might be as a defensive forward—a role he has rarely, if ever, played in his career.

On the other hand, Filc has shown a talent for developing underrated players that nobody would have expected to flourish. Lubomir Hurtaj is one of these players. Maybe there are other young Slovaks playing in Europe who will follow him. These players seem more motivated by international experience than some of the veterans back home. By opening the team to anybody, both players and coaches feel pushed to achieve more.

Defense wins championships and this has been a traditional weakness for Slovak teams. Classy veterans such as Robert Svehla, Lubomir Sekeras and Ivan Droppa should be cornerstones of a defense that will be active in the attack and on power-plays, but will be lacking depth, consistency and mobility. At 6'8", Zdeno Chara and 6'4" Branislav Mezei might be too big to be effective on the larger ice surface, while Lubomir Visnovsky may be too small. At 5'8", he will at least form a visibly interesting pair with Chara—a hockey version of David and Goliath.

There will be many questions about goaltending too, as there long has been in Slovakian hockey. Members of the younger generation such as Jan Lasak and Martin Hamerlik have shown that they might be ready to improve the image of Slovak goaltending, but there is still the fear of too many red lights. Lasak and Hamerlik may be too young to handle an event as big as the 2002 Olympics, and besides, they might not be unavailable when Slovakia starts the tournament because they will be playing in North American leagues. Igor Murin would be the selection, although he almost quit hockey after the disaster at the 1998 Nagano Olympics and has not played in international competition since then. Miroslav Simonovic also comes to mind, but he hasn't shown much since surprising at the 1999 World Championships in Norway.

In the past, Slovak national teams have had problems playing disciplined hockey. Such was not the case in St. Petersburg, where the Slovaks showed they can play with both heart and hockey smarts. The Slovakian team did not display its typical offensive-minded, careless hockey at the 2000 World Championships, but there are no guarantees for 2002. With so many snipers on the roster, the defensive part of the game could again be a shortcoming at Salt Lake City, and the rough style of less-skilled opponents could prove to be a problem for the Slovaks in the preliminary round.

The winning attitude of the Slovaks always has been great, but the self-confidence has its limits. No player from this country has won the Stanley Cup, and this may be more significant than it seems. If everything is going right, the Slovaks can beat anybody. If it isn't, the team does not handle adversity well. Likely, the Slovakian national team will be as unpredictable as ever in 2002. Will they be the silver medal-winning team that showed up in St. Petersburg or the tenth-place finishers that played in Nagano? It all will depend on the beginning of the tournament.

SLOVAKIAN 2002 OLYMPIC ROSTER

Position	Name	Age in 2002
G	Igor Murin	28
G	Jan Lasak	21
G	Peter Hamerlik	20
D	Robert Svehla	33
D	Zdeno Chara	24
D	Ivan Droppa	30
D	Radoslav Suchy	25
D	Lubomir Visnovsky	27
D	Lubomir Sekeras	33
D	Branislav Mezei	21
F	Zigmund Palffy	29
F	Miroslav Satan	27
F	Pavol Demitra	27
F	Jozef Stumpel	29
F	Michal Handzus	24
F	Lubos Bartecko	25
F	Lubomir Hurtaj	26
F	Marian Hossa	23
F	Marcel Hossa	20
F	Marian Gaborik	20
F	Robert Petrovicky	28
F	Ladislav Nagy	21
F	Richard Zednik	26

RUSSIA 2002

New Century, Same Gold Ambitions

Igor Kuperman

A DECADE AGO, IN THE 1990S, waves of Russian hockey players started to land on North American shores. These Russian players came with something to brag about. Most of them were well-decorated champions of many major international tournaments, such as the Olympics, World Championships and World Junior Championships. Even among former Iron Curtain countrymen, there was a silent "ranking code" among those who had played for the mighty Soviet national team and those who had not. This type of separation is almost gone now for the very simple reason that the Russian national team has not won gold since the 1993 World Championships.

For many, the Olympic silver at Nagano in 1998 was seen as a ray of hope that the Russian team can still be a very powerful force. However, Viacheslav Fetisov, former Soviet superstar and assistant coach of the 2000 Stanley Cup-champion New Jersey Devils, wasn't impressed. "The team got so much credit for a silver medal that I was shocked," Fetisov said. "Since when have we started to celebrate the fact that we are second to somebody? For almost five decades anything less than gold was considered a failure." Even Russian Olympic coach Vladimir Yurzinov didn't allow himself to get too excited by the silver medal. After the Games, he mentioned how difficult is was to remind the players how to play under the old Soviet system of hockey. "They tried painfully to recall how to play our original style," Yurzinov said.

Nevertheless, Russians have reason to be optimistic about the 2002 Olympics. The team, at least on paper, looks very strong and should be a top contender for the gold. Nikolai Khabibulin is a top goaltender. Among Russian netminders, he is probably closer to Vladislav Tretiak's level of play than anybody else. But goalies are a difficult breed. Khabibulin still refuses to forget that he wasn't even dressed for the final two games of the World Cup of Hockey back in 1996. Since then, he has repeatedly refused to play for the Russian national team. But the Olympics are special and it won't take a lot of effort to convince him to play at Salt Lake City.

The Russian corps of rearguards for 2002 looks very impressive. Like all Russian defensemen, they are very skilled and have good shots, but what is surprising is that they can compete with the North Americans in terms of toughness. These Russian defensemen enjoy the physical part of the game as much as anyone else!

During the 1998 Olympics in Nagano, both Boris Mironov and Alexei Zhitnik delivered huge hits on Jaromir Jagr. Mironov has emerged as one of the best defencemen in the NHL. He is a powerful offensive and defensive force for the Chicago Blackhawks. Darius Kasparaitis is still feared by every forward, and Toronto's Dmitri Yushkevich has improved his physical game to become the Maple Leafs' most feared defenseman. The newest addition to this breed of tough Russian defensemen is Vitali Vishnevsky. The best defenseman at the 1999 World Junior Championships in Winnipeg, Vishnevsky played his first NHL game against the Dallas Stars after being called up to Anaheim during the 1999–2000 season. He immediately started to hit Mike Modano and Brett Hull and wasn't afraid of the Stars' intimidation.

"Our Hockey Thrives on Attack," was the most famous slogan of the Soviet game in the 1960s and 1970s, and the number of brilliant Russian forwards is still overwhelming. Pavel Bure, "The Russian Rocket," has recovered from knee injuries and is as good as ever. His blazing speed still amazes his opponents. Bure has become a real icon back in Russia, where his popularity is probably the widest among all Russian athletes. Younger brother Valeri finally emerged from Pavel's shadow in 1999–2000 and became a real offensive threat. Though he hadn't visited Russia since he left in the summer of 1991 (he was afraid that he could be taken to fulfill his mandatory army service), it was Valeri who expressed his patriotic feelings prior to the 1998 Nagano Olympics: "I think that everybody should put aside their millionaire's ambitions and play for the country that taught them how to play hockey," he said in response to the refusal of some players to play for the Russian national team.

Newcomer Maxim Afinogenov should be in his prime by 2002. His unmistakable resemblance to Pavel Bure—the way he skates, stickhandles and shoots—has amazed his NHL teammates. After one of his first practices with the Buffalo Sabres at the beginning of 1999–2000 season, team captain Michael Peca said: "As soon as he got the puck, he accelerates and he is gone…"

Afinogenov is one of the brightest stars among the new generation of Russian hockey players, a generation which has begun to win medals, including gold at the World Junior Championships level. Another young star, Sergei Samsonov, should finally show his true potential in Salt Lake City. His three years with the Boston Bruins haven't been as successful as expected, but the talent is still there. At 24, Samsonov could be one of the offensive leaders on the Russian Olympic team.

Roman Lyashenko proved to be a pleasant surprise during the 1999–2000 season. Originally penciled in to spend the season in the minors, the rash of injuries in Dallas brought Lyashenko to the NHL sooner than expected. He helped the Stars return to the Stanley Cup finals despite playing out of position (he is a natural center) and a lack of English. Lyashenko is a typical defensive-oriented Russian center, which made him a perfect fit in the Dallas system.

The poor showing of the Russian team at recent World Championships, including the shocking 11th-place finish on home ice in St. Petersburg in 2000, has convinced Russian hockey authorities that the Olympic team should consist of patriots. Alexei Yashin, whose contract dispute in Ottawa became notorious, is still a hero in Russia for his unending commitment to playing for the national team. He will undoubtably be one of the leaders of the 2002 Russian Olympic team. In fact, it will likely be between Yashin and Pavel Bure as to who will be the captain of the team.

Though relations between the Russian Hockey Federation and Russian players were strained over the past decade, both sides could usually overcome their off-ice problems when it came to international competition. The 2002 Olympics should once again bring everybody together. We may not see the familiar Russian style of play, but the golden ambitions will be the same.

RUSSIAN 2002 OLYMPIC ROSTER

Position	Name	Age in 2002
G	Nikolai Khabibulin	29
G	Alexei Volkov	22
G	Ilja Bryzgalov	22
D	Alexei Zhitnik	30
D	Sergei Zubov	32
D	Boris Mironov	30
D	Sergei Gonchar	28
D	Darius Kasparaitis	30
D	Dmitri Yushkevich	31
D	Oleg Tverdovsky	26
D	Vitali Vishnevsky	22
F	Sergei Berezin	31
F	Sergei Brylin	28
F	Roman Lyashenko	23
F	Sergei Fedorov	33
F	Sergei Samsonov	24
F	Alexei Kovalev	29
F	Alexei Yashin	29
F	Alexei Morozov	25
F	Valeri Bure	28
F	Pavel Bure	31
F	Andre Nikolishin	29
F	Maxim Afinogenov	23

SWEDEN 2002

Janne Stark

THE FIRST INTERNATIONAL TOURNAMENT of the new millennium was a big disappointment for the Three Crowns, Sweden's national team. General manager Peter Wallin was forced to leave office after the disastrous showing at the World Championships in St. Petersburg, Russia. The Swedes went out in the quarterfinals, losing to archrival Finland, en route to a seventh-place finish. It was the worst Swedish performance at the World Championships since 1937.

The new man in charge as Sweden prepares for the 2002 Winter Olympic Games in Salt Lake City will be Anders Hedberg, the former star player who became the leading European front-office man in the NHL. Hedberg will be general manager of the Olympic team, working together with coach Hardy Nilsson who led Djurgarden to the Swedish championship in 1999–2000.

Nilsson is a man with vision who introduced a whole new approach to the game with his club last season. His idea, in short, was to attack as much as possible and put a lot of pressure on the opponents in their zone. In other words, the best defense is a good offense. Nilsson's new approach meant wide-open games with a lot of scoring chances. It also meant that he changed the alignment of his team away from the traditional setup of two defensemen and three forwards to one defenseman and four forwards. The new lineup looked odd at first but proved to be successful.

Nilsson and Hedberg seem to have the same ideas about the game, meaning future national teams will have a different look from those we have seen in the past.

Goaltenders: Tommy Salo will remain in the number-one spot. His ability is well known to the hockey world and he has emerged as an all-star in North America. The backup position is a two-man race that will see Johan Holmqvist of Brynas fight it out with Mikael Tellqvist, the sensation of the 1999–2000 Swedish hockey season. Tellqvist took over from veteran Tommy Soderstrom in Djurgarden in November and remained the team's top netminder throughout the season. He is a tremendous prospect with a stand-up style and an exceptional glove hand.

Defensemen: Nicklas Lidstrom will be counted on to anchor the blue line as well as power-play and shorthand situations. The veteran rearguard is the most important player on the Swedish defense, even though he will be 32 when the Olympic Games begin. Hopefully, Mattias Ohlund will recover well from his eye injury and will strengthen the defensive corps with Kim Johnsson, Mattias Norstrom and Daniel Tjarnqvist. Johnsson is an offensive minded blueliner with good hands, while Tjarnqvist is a strong presence in his own end of the rink. Norstrom is the policeman. As for the last two positions on the Swedish defense, Jonas Elofsson has not emerged as expected and will be out of the picture. The same is true of Anders Eriksson. Replacements will be found in either Dick Tarnstrom of AIK, Jan Huokko of Leksand or Pierre Hedin of MoDo. Hedin and Huokko seem a better fit with the team's offensive strategy and will hopefully emerge from prospects to dependable international players.

Forwards: Mats Sundin will captain the Swedish Olympic team and center the first line with goal-scoring wing Fredrik Modin and strong backchecker Jorgen Jonsson. Sundin is a complete player with incredible wrists and a tremendous hockey sense. Peter Forsberg will have to be satisfied with centering the second line. His wingers will be Niklas Sundstrom and Kristoffer Ottosson. Sundstrom has the ability to cover for Forsberg's offensive adventures while also setting up scoring chances for Ottosson. (Ottosson was a star on Nilsson's Djurgarden team in 1999–2000, scoring 32 goals in 60 league and playoff games.) Forsberg, of course, creates havoc as soon as he touches the puck and will be a constant threat whenever he is on the ice.

Sweden's third line will be the most interesting. It should see twins Henrik and Daniel Sedin together with Mattias Weinhandl, last year's rookie sensation in the Swedish league. Weinhandl is a righthand shot who knows his way around the front of the enemy net, and if the Sedins continue to develop their skills at the same rate as over the last couple of season's, this line will be the sensation of the Salt Lake City Games.

With four roster spots left to fill, Hedberg and Nilsson will turn to Samuel Pahlsson, Mats Lindgren, Johan Davidsson and Marcus Nilson. Pahlsson is a strong, gifted center/forward who was drafted by the Colorado Avalanche in 1996 but traded to Boston in the spring of 2000. He should center the fourth line with Lindgren (a two-way wing with a good shot) and Davidsson. Marcus Nilson, who, like Davidsson, is a prospect with a lot of North American experience, can dig in the corners and take on anybody, which should make him useful in tight situations.

SWEDISH 2002 OLYMPIC ROSTER

Position	Name	Age in 2002
G	Tommy Salo	31
G	Johan Holmqvist	24
G	Mikael Tellqvist	23
D	Nicklas Lidstrom	32
D	Mattias Ohlund	26
D	Kim Johnsson	26
D	Mattias Norstrom	30
D	Daniel Tjarnqvist	26
D	Jan Huokko	28
D	Pierre Hedin	24
F	Mats Sundin	31
F	Fredrik Modin	28
F	Jorgen Jonsson	30
F	Peter Forsberg	29
F	Niklas Sundstrom	27
F	Kristoffer Ottosson	26
F	Henrik Sedin	22
F	Daniel Sedin	22
F	Mattias Weinhandl	22
F	Samuel Pahlsson	25
F	Johan Davidsson	26
F	Mats Lindgren	28
F	Marcus Nilson	24

FINLAND 2002

Tom Ratschunas

FINLAND HAD LITTLE SUCCESS in the first eight Olympic tournaments, never finishing higher than fourth, until things changed dramatically in Calgary. The blue-and-white defeated the Soviets in 1988 en route to a silver medal. It was not only the first Olympic medal for Finland, but the first medal of any sort for the senior national team. Coach Pentti Matikainen became a national idol. Though Finland fell to seventh at the 1992 Albertville Olympics, the Finnish squad played extraordinary hockey, exhibiting fluidity and motion, as well as great discipline, under coach Curt Lindstrom at Lillehammer in 1994. However, the surprise selection of Jukka Tammi in goal did not pay off as Finland suffered a 5–3 loss to Canada in the semifinals and had to settle for a bronze medal. Still, Lindstrom led the Finnish team to gold one year later at the World Championships in Stockholm, Sweden.

Four years after the bronze medal in Lillehammer, Finland again claimed bronze at Nagano. This result, even more than the gold medal victory in 1995, became a milestone in the history of Finnish hockey. That's because the opponent in the bronze medal game was the Dream Team of Canada, the cream of Canadian talent in the NHL in the first Olympic tournament to feature the full participation of the North American professionals. Coach Hannu Aravirta and his skaters were led by the great Jari Kurri in his last outing with the national team.

The stage is now set for the 2002 Olympic hockey tournament in Salt Lake City, as the International Ice Hockey Federation, the National Hockey League and the NHL Players' Association have again come to terms. This means that the bulk of Olympic players will again come from the ranks of the NHL, and this time the North Americans will have the advantage of playing on their own continent at the height of the season. Canada and the United States are also forewarned as to the determination of the Europeans based on the results of Nagano. So coach Hannu Aravirta, under contract through the 2002 event, must first make an inventory of all the Finns in the NHL.

One of Finland's strengths has been its top-class goalies, though sometimes this also has been a weakness. Key goaltenders on the national team also play important roles for their club teams and sometimes have found it difficult to recharge their batteries following a gruelling season.

The 1999–2000 season saw two young Finnish goalies establish themselves in minor-league hockey in North America. Both Mika Noronen and Jani Hurme led their respective teams (Rochester Americans, American Hockey League and Grand Rapids Griffins, International Hockey League) to the playoff finals in their leagues. Miikka Kiprusoff of the Kentucky Thoroughblades (AHL) also had a solid season. They could receive Olympic consideration by 2002. By then it's possible that Vesa Toskala and Pasi Nurminen also will have moved across the Atlantic, and they will be worthy of consideration. Antero Niitymaki, the rookie sensation as a junior in the 1999–2000 Finnish League, also will be one of the candidates.

Jarmo Myllys has played for all three of Finland's Olympic hockey medal winners, but did not pass muster for the 2000 World Championships in St. Petersburg. Ari Sulander made it to the tournament in Russia but did not enhance his chances for continued selection to the national team despite a great season in Switzerland that saw him lead the Zurich Lions to the national title. If any two of the younger goalies mentioned above are playing in the NHL on a regular basis by 2002, then they will be Aravirta's best selections. Of course, former NHLers who have returned to Finland—netminders like Myllys, Kari Takko and Hannu Kamppuri—have put together excellent careers back home and will deserve consideration.

Based on the type of opposition that will be faced in the important games at Salt Lake City, the Finnish blueliners will have to be players that are at home against NHL-type forwards. Among the favorites when Aravirta is making his selections will be Janne Laukkanen, Kimmo Timonen, Jere Karalahti, Toni Lydman and Antti-Jussi Niemi—who will join the Anaheim organization in the fall of 2000. Not far behind are the tough Sami Salo, Janne Niinimaa, Aki-Petteri Berg and Teppo Numminen, who will be 33 by then.

Of these nine players named, five (Numminen, Laukkanen, Timonen, Berg and Niinimaa) played at Nagano. Of these, the most interesting name is Teppo Numminen, who also was a member of the 1988 team at Calgary. Janne Laukkanen also has two bronze medals, earned at the last two Olympics.

With this contingent on call, it will be very tough for current juniors like Under-18 World Champion Tero Maattaa to steal a place on the 2002 Olympic squad. Of the other Finnish defenders who are Maattaa's age or a year older, nobody has the size to gain respect on the international stage despite their high skill level. Those like Olli Malmivaara, who do have the size, will require a lot of work to improve their strength.

Of European-based veterans, the top names for Olympic consideration will be Petteri Nummelin and Marko Kiprusoff. Both of these ex-Turku players will be at the top of their game as 30-year-olds, but playing in Switzerland will not be a strong recommendation for Aravirta and his defense-orientated style of play. However, Nummelin belongs to the absolute elite in Europe both as a quarterback on the power-play and as one of the top-paid defensemen on the continent. He finally made his mark internationally when he was selected to the first all-star team while playing a leading role for the Finnish team at the 2000 World Championships.

There is no doubt that if they are healthy, the offensive punch for the Finnish team at the 2002 Olympics will be provided by Teemu Selanne and Saku Koivu. They were the top scoring duo at Nagano and also at the 1999 World Championships in Lillehammer, which was their last outing with the Finnish Lions. A key role also will befall Jere Lehtinen, who is the type of two-way player that coach Aravirta likes. Next on the list of available forwards are Sami Kapanen, Juha Ylonen and Juha Lind, who all are adaptable to several types of roles. Ville Peltonen, a gold medal hero from the 1995 World Championships, has struggled offensively in recent years, but is another role player who will get a shot if all goes well for him in the Olympic year. It is hoped that by 2002 Olli Jokinen will have matured enough to earn a roster spot on merit instead of his previous selections, all of which were designed to help him improve as a player for the future rather than as a major asset at the time.

Other Finnish players currently in the NHL are not significantly better than those on the domestic scene. Antti Aalto, Mika Alatalo, Mikko Eloranta, Antti Laaksonen, Marko Tuomainen, Miika Elomo, Ville Nieminen and Jarkko Ruutu fill out the current legion of Finns in the NHL or on top minor pro teams, but this group will be lucky if more than one of them earn a trip to Salt Lake City. Of the major nations with player pools in the NHL, Finland has the poorest representation as far as absolute franchise forwards are concerned, but this may not cause coach Hannu Aravirta any undue concern or lack of sleep during Olympics preparations. He has very specific ideas about how to formulate his forward trios for prowess in international hockey.

Raimo Helminen, Finland's all-time leading scorer on the national team and a three-time Olympic medalist, will not pass the grade in two years time. Sadly, the same will also be the true of a couple of other legendary centers: Janne Ojanen and Mika Nieminen. The new generation of the Finnish national team has its leaders in the HPK Hameenlinna first line of left wing Timo Parssinen, center Niko Kapanen and right wing Jukka Hentunen. One truly outstanding player with a bright future is TPS forward Tomi Kallio, who's NHL rights belong to the Atlanta Thrashers. By the looks of it, he is a certainty for Salt Lake City.

One of the big surprises with Finland's team for the 2000 World Championships was the fact that the top-scoring Finnish players in Europe were not deemed suitable for the team. In fact, Juha Riihijarvi of the Malmo Red Hawks in Sweden and Kai Nurminen from Finnish champions TPS Turku were never even contacted. The Finnish media was all over Aravirta about the exclusion of Nurminen, who won five individual trophies, including the scoring crown for both the regular season and the playoffs as well as the regular-season plus-minus title. Nurminen was being held responsible for mistakes made years ago, and was apparently not yet forgiven despite his career year. However, the Minnesota Wild have invited the one-time Los Angeles Kings player back to the NHL, and a good showing there could make Nurminen an important addition to the 2002 Olympic team. Junior graduates such as Teemu Laine and Jani Rita from Jokerit Helsinki, Jani Vaananen of TPS Turku, diminutive Marko Ahosilta and others will have to improve by leaps and bounds to upset the pecking order for the 2002 Games.

Finnish 2002 Olympic Roster

Position	Name	Age in 2002
G	Mika Noronen	22
G	Jani Hurme	22
G	Ari Sulander	33
D	Janne Laukkanen	31
D	Kimmo Timonen	26
D	Jere Karalahti	26
D	Toni Lydman	24
D	Antti-Jussi Niemi	24
and two of...		
D	Sami Salo	27
D	Janne Niinimaa	26
D	Aki-Petteri Berg	24
D	Teppo Numminen	33
D	Petteri Nummelin	29
F	Teemu Selanne	31
F	Saku Koivu	27
F	Jere Lehtinen	28
F	Sami Kapanen	28
F	Juha Ylonen	30
F	Juha Lind	28
F	Ville Peltonen	28
F	Timo Parssinen	25
F	Niko Kapanen	23
F	Jukka Hentunen	28
F	Tomi Kallio	25
F	Kai Nurminen	32

CHAPTER 43

Olympic, World and European Championships

Olympic Games

The International Olympic Committee, together with the International Ice Hockey Federation, is responsible for Olympic hockey tournaments. The first tournament was held during the 1920 (Summer) Olympic Games. Later, in 1983, the IIHF decided to designate this tournament as a World Championship. The first Winter Olympic tournament took place in 1924.

Since 1924, hockey has been part of every Winter Olympic Games. Until 1992, the IIHF World Championships were combined with the Olympics (with the exception of 1972 and 1976). Beginning in 1992, a separate World Championship tournament has been held in Olympic years. In 1988, the IIHF allowed professional athletes to play at the Olympic hockey tournament. Women's hockey made its debut as an accredited medal sport at the 1998 Winter Olympics in Nagano, Japan.

There have been 18 Olympic tournaments between 1924 and 1998 (The 1920 tournament is officially considered to be the first World Championship rather than an Olympic competition). Here are the winning teams:

USSR/Unified Team - 8 1956, 1964, 1968, 1972, 1976, 1984, 1988, 1992
Canada - 5 1924, 1928, 1932, 1948, 1952
USA - 2 1960, 1980
Great Britain - 1 1936
Sweden - 1 1994
Czech Republic - 1 1998

European Championships

The first European Championships took place in 1910 organized by the *Ligue Internationale de Hockey sur Glace* that later became the International Ice Hockey Federation. Fourteen European Championships were staged as separate events from World Championships or the Olympic Games. The last separate European Championship tournament took place in 1932.

Beginning in 1933, the European Championships became part of the IIHF World Championships. Through 1970, the formula for determining European rankings was simple—the highest ranked European team at the World Championships become the European champion, the second-highest ranked European team the European silver medalist, etc. All games played by European teams were counted.

Beginning in 1971, games between European and North American teams weren't counted in calculating European standings. From 1982 to 1991, the system for determining the European Champion changed again, with only the results of the round-robin portion of the World Championships being employed to rank teams in contention for the European title. The last European Championship was held in conjunction with the World Championships in 1991.

The winners of the European Championships were presented with a substantial silver trophy. Prior to 1930, the players of the winning teams were awarded IIHF diplomas. From 1930 to 1991, players on the top three European teams were awarded gold, silver and bronze medals separate from those given to World winners.

There were 66 European Championships held between 1910 and 1991 (the results of the 1912 tournament were annulled). Here is the list of European Champions:

USSR - 27 1954, 1955, 1956, 1958, 1959, 1960, 1963, 1964, 1965, 1966, 1967, 1968, 1969, 1970, 1973, 1974, 1975, 1978, 1979, 1981, 1982 1983, 1985, 1986, 1987, 1989, 1991
Bohemia/Czechoslovakia - 14 1911, 1914, 1922, 1925, 1929, 1933, 1947, 1948, 1949, 1961, 1971, 1972, 1976, 1977
Sweden - 10 1921, 1923, 1928, 1932, 1951, 1952, 1953, 1957, 1962, 1990
Great Britain - 4 1910, 1936, 1937, 1938
Switzerland - 4 1926, 1935, 1939, 1950
Germany - 2 1930, 1934
Austria - 2 1927, 1931
France - 1 1924
Belgium –1 1913

World Championships

The first World Championships took place in 1920, during the (Summer) Olympics in Antwerp, Belgium. Prior to 1982, this 1920 tournament was considered an Olympic event, but in 1983 the International Ice Hockey Federation declared that this tournament was the first World Championship event. The decision was based on the fact that the 1920 event was an "exhibition" tournament held prior to the Olympic Games.

At the IIHF Congress in 1930, it was decided that the 1924 and 1928 Olympic tournaments would also gain the status of World Championships. At the same congress, the decision was made to hold the World Championships every year if at least one non-European country was represented. (There were no World Championships during the years of World War II).

Until 1972, Olympic tournaments incorporated the World Championships, but in 1972 and 1976 separate World and Olympic events were held for the first time. In 1980, 1984 and 1988, there were no World Championships apart from the Olympic Games, but since 1992, there have again been both World and Olympic tournaments held in Olympic years. Since 1976, the World Championships have been "open" to professional athletes.

There are four pools at the World Championships—A, B, C and D, with Pool A comprised of the world's top hockey nations. After every year, the last-place team from Pools A, B and C is relegated to the group below, while the first-place team from Pools B, C and D is promoted to the group above. The team winning each pool of the World Championships receives a Cup, while players from the top three teams in each Pool receive gold, silver and bronze medals.

Beginning in 1998, the IIHF increased the number of teams in Pool A from 12 to 16. These 16 teams are divided into four groups. Each group plays a round-robin preliminary, with the top two teams from each group advancing to another round robin before the semifinals and finals are held. Pools B, C and D each consist of eight teams.

There have been 64 World Championships from 1920 to 2000. Here is the list of World Champions:

USSR/Russia - 23 1954, 1956, 1963, 1964, 1965, 1966, 1967, 1968, 1969, 1970, 1971, 1973, 1974, 1975, 1978, 1979, 1981, 1982, 1983, 1986, 1989, 1990, 1993
Canada - 21 1920, 1924, 1928, 1930, 1931, 1932, 1934, 1935, 1937, 1938, 1939, 1948, 1950, 1951, 1952, 1955, 1958, 1959, 1961, 1994, 1997
Czechoslovakia/Czech Republlic - 7 1947, 1949, 1972, 1976, 1977, 1985, 1996, 1999, 2000
Sweden - 7 1953, 1957, 1962, 1987, 1991, 1992, 1998
USA - 2 1933, 1960
Great Britain - 1 1936
Finland - 1 1995

Year-by-Year Summaries

1910 European Championships The decision to hold a European Championship was made as early as 1908, and one year later the first unofficial international tournament sponsored by the *Ligue Internationale de Hockey sur Glace* took place. The games were played in Chamonix, France during the second congress of the LIGH. The host nation began the tournament with a 4–2 victory over Germany and a 6–0 win against Belgium, but was beaten in the finals by the team from London, England.

The third LIGH Congress opened in Montreux, Switzerland on January 9, 1910 and it was here that the first official European Championships were held. As proposed by a Swiss delegate, the Oxford Canadians, a club made up of Canadian players attending the prestigious university, was admitted to the Ligue (and would be admitted as an autonomous association on November 20, 1911). Another team that featured many Canadian players represented Great Britain and claimed the European title, beating Germany 1–0, Switzerland 5–1 and tying Belgium 1–1, but the new European champions refused to play the Oxford club. France, which had done so well in 1909, did not compete at the 1910 tournament.

The games of the first official European Championships were played on natural ice on frozen Lake Geneva in the Swiss Alps and consisted of two 30-minute periods. The rink was surrounded by low boards and was smaller than required by the rules. It was not surprising that Great Britain proved the winner in 1910, as England was the first European country to develop hockey. The game was already being played in England by 1894, and Europe's first electrically refrigerated rink was build in London in 1903. That same year, the first national championship ever held in a European country was won by the London Canadians. The unofficial European Championship of 1909 had been won by the London Princes Club, which, like the Oxford Canadians, was made up mostly of students from Canada plus British military officer Major B.M. Patton. Four years later, Patton would become president of the *Ligue Internationale de Hockey sur Glace*. Another future federation president, Max Sillig, played for Switzerland at the 1910 tournament.

1911 EUROPEAN CHAMPIONSHIPS were held indoors on artificial ice for the first time when Berlin hosted the event. Berlin boasted three artificial ice rinks at the time and the tournament was staged at the Eistpalast. The Belgian team had also been practicing on artificial ice at the Antwerp Palais de Glace, while the Swiss had excellent natural rinks. In Bohemia, temperatures dropped below freezing in January, enabling the players from the country that would one day be known as the Czech Republic to get in three weeks of practice prior to making the trip to Germany. Money was raised in Bohemia to finance the team's journey to the European Championships, though the players were forced to contribute a large share of the finances.

The Bohemian players arrived in Berlin in a third-class coach on a special night train and played their first game at 4 p.m. on the day of their arrival. They scored a 13–0 win over Switzerland, then defeated their favored German hosts 4–1 that same evening. After a 3–0 win over Belgium, they were Europe's new champions. The surprise win by Bohemia was something of a sensation in the European hockey community, which numbered about 300 to 400 players at the time. LIGH president Louis Magnus praised the teamwork of the Bohemian players when he wrote in *Les Sports d'Hiver* that "It was especially interesting to see the game of a team and not that of individual players." On their homecoming in Prague, the Bohemian team was met at the railway station by hundreds of enthusiastic fans.

The LIGH Congress was held in Berlin on February 16–17 at the same time the championships were played. Russia was admitted as the Ligue's seventh member. The Russian delegation, however, arrived in Berlin without a clear idea of what type of hockey was being played. Bandy was still the game of choice in Russia and it was not surprising when the country was dropped from the LIGH membership on September 25, 1911 due to inactivity.

1912 EUROPEAN CHAMPIONSHIPS On March 14, 1911, the *Ligue Internationale de Hockey sur Glace* (LIGH) was renamed the International Ice Hockey Federation (IIHF) and officially adopted the Canadian rules for amateur play. All subsequent championships would be held according to those rules. Bohemia, the new European Champion in 1911, was awarded the honor of hosting the 1912 tournament in Prague.

When only Germany and the host nation confirmed their participation for the 1912 European Championships, it was decided to invite a team of German-born players from the DEHG Prague club as representatives of Austria. At the IIHF Congress, which was held concurrently with the tournament, Austria's membership was formalized, though this decision would soon have repercussions

The games of the 1912 European Championships were well-attended with about 5,000 people jamming the small stadium of the Slavia club on Letna Street. (The arena was located near a water tower, which made it convenient to flood the rink). The teams featured seven-man lineups—a goaltender, two defencemen, a rover and three forwards—and countries were permitted to carry only two substitutes.

As in 1911, Bohemia emerged victorious, but their 1912 victory would be short-lived. Three days after the tournament ended, the German hockey club filed an unsuccessful protest against a goal scored by the champions. Since the decision of the panel of judges, which also acted as the IIHF Directorate, could not be appealed, another pretext was found to strip Bohemia of the title. Referring to the fact that Austria had not been eligible to enter the European Championships because it had not been made a member of the IIHF prior to the games, the Directorate canceled the results of the 1912 tournament.

1913 EUROPEAN CHAMPIONSHIPS Germany filed a protest against the participation of Bohemia prior to the 1913 European Championships in Munich. The protest was based on the fact that Austria was now a member of the IIHF and since Bohemia was a part of the Austro-Hungarian Empire, the inclusion of its team would in fact be giving Austria two spots in the tournament. Because only four teams were taking part in the event, and the former champions from Bohemia elicited great fan interest, Germany was convinced to withdraw its protest.

The games of the European Championships were played on a tiny ice surface this year, and, as a result, scores were very high. Both Bohemia and Belgium posted two wins and a tie, but Belgium was declared the winner based on a better goal differential. Of note, the 1913 tournament marked the first time teams wore numbers on their backs at the European Championships.

1914 EUROPEAN CHAMPIONSHIPS Prior to World War I, no European Championship event ever attracted more than four participants or lasted longer than three days. During this period, the players of Bohemia did not lose a single game, and in 1914 they celebrated their second official European Championship win, defeating both Belgium and Germany, the only other nations in the competition.

1920 WORLD CHAMPIONSHIPS A hockey tournament was held in Antwerp, Belgium in April, 1920 as a demonstration of winter sports in conjunction with the Olympic Games which would be staged later that summer. The Congress of the International Ice Hockey Federation used the occasion of this tournament to admit Canada and the United States as members, as the two North American countries would be participating in this event. Sixty-three years later, at the meetings of the IIHF Congress in the spring of 1983, this tournament was accorded the status of the first hockey World Championship.

The participation of teams from Canada and the U.S. helped to adjust the rules of both the IIHF and the Canadian game. There would be six players per side (the rover having been dropped at the IIHF Congress in March, 1912) and players could only be changed when the action was stopped. This tournament was played on a rink that was different in size from that prescribed by the IIHF rules. Seven nations were represented, but the first face-to-face confrontation of hockey players from the old and new worlds showed the overwhelming superiority of experienced North American players.

Canada was represented at the Olympic tournament by a club team (the Winnipeg Falcons) instead of a national squad, as would become the country's custom, and the Falcons won the tournament with three straight wins. Captain Frank Fredrickson later went on to fame in the Pacific Coast Hockey Association and the NHL and was inducted into the Hockey Hall of Fame. Moose Goheen of the American squad would also be accorded that honor in addition to winning a spot in the U.S. Hockey Hall of Fame.

The three teams beaten by Canada played for second and third place. The United States finished second and Czechoslovakia (formerly Bohemia) finished third despite scoring only one goal in three games. The tournament's format was flawed: Sweden played six games and won three, as many as Canada and the United States, but still finished out of the medals because of its loss to Czechoslovakia.

Playing for Switzerland at the tournament was IIHF president Max Sillig, the only president in the history of the sport to have taken part in the World Championships while holding office.

1921 EUROPEAN CHAMPIONSHIPS The impressive play of Sweden, which had ranked fourth in Antwerp in 1920 in the nation's first foray into international hockey, resulted in the a decision by the IIHF to award Stockholm the honor of hosting the European Championships in 1921.

Teams would now be permitted to carry 11 players on their rosters. Games would still consist of two 30-minute periods.

Because only two nations participated at the 1921 European Championships, this event is the only tournament not to award a third prize. The sole game of the tournament was held on an open rink with electrical lighting and attracted some 6,000 spectators. The Swedish fans cheered enthusiastically as their team defeated Czechoslovakia 6–4 to win the European title.

1922 EUROPEAN CHAMPIONSHIPS Sweden and Czechoslovakia were joined by Switzerland when the European Championships were held in St. Moritz in 1922. The Czechoslovaks avenged their loss in 1921 with a pair of victories.

1923 EUROPEAN CHAMPIONSHIPS For the first time, five nations attended the European Championships with France competing for the first time since the unofficial tournament of 1909. The debutantes played well, losing only to the champions from Sweden. Czechoslovakia finished in third place.

1924 WINTER OLYMPICS AND WORLD CHAMPIONSHIPS This competition was played according to new rules that divided the game into three 20-minute periods. Matches were held in late January and early February during the International Week of Winter Sport that one year later was renamed the Winter Olympic Games by the Congress of the International Olympic Committee.

The tournament was split into two groups with four teams in each. The top two ranking teams from each group went to the playoffs, thus the final standings included only the four playoff teams. A total of 255 goals were scored in the 16 games of the tournament, for an average of almost 16 goals per game. This level of output has never been matched.

The four years between this championship and the games in Antwerp in 1920 had done nothing to alter the balance of power between North America and Europe. Canada (represented by the Toronto Granites) established a record that has never been beaten by scoring 110 goals in five games. Included in this total is an Olympic record 33–0 win over Switzerland that featured 18 goals in the first period. The United States was almost as dominant, sweeping its European opponents before dropping a 6–1 decision to Canada in the gold medal game.

1924 EUROPEAN CHAMPIONSHIPS For the first time, six nations entered the competition for the European Championships in 1924, including newcomers Spain and Italy. Still, only six games were played in total as Spain did not show up for its game with Sweden. The tournament was held in two stages, with Sweden, the winner of Group A, facing Group B winner France for the championship. France emerged with a 2–1 victory to earn IIHF diplomas awarded to the winners for the first time.

1925 EUROPEAN CHAMPIONSHIPS Prepar-ations for the 1925 European Championships in Czechoslovakia began as early as November, 1924, with several options developed in the event of warm weather. It was believed that holding the games on the Slavia rink at Letna would have the greatest financial and publicity impact, but despite the fact that it had been sufficiently cold in Prague before the New Year, the beginning of January was marked by a deep thaw. A stand-by rink was located, but, at the last moment, it too was covered by water.

Thus the Championships moved to a region in the Vysoke Tatry Mountains. The snow was removed from the ice of a small mountain lake, several benches were built on a bank and the resulting rink had markings painted on it. No posters or tickets were issued for the games and so attendance was sparse. Snowstorms repeatedly forced the stoppage of play for snow removal.

The host Czechoslovaks did not allow a single goal in beating their three opponents and won the European Championship for the fourth time. Austria, which had entered the tournament for the first time in 12 years, finished second. The third-place Swiss team featured Carl Spengler, who had recently commissioned the Spengler Cup, a hockey trophy and tournament played annually in Davos, Switzerland in the last week of December.

1926 EUROPEAN CHAMPIONSHIPS In 1925, the International Ice Hockey Federation Congress established a minimum rink size of 18 meters (58 feet) wide by 50 meters (163.5 feet) long, with regulation size being 26 meters (85 feet) by 56 meters (184 feet). Body checking was introduced in the defensive zone. These new rules were applied at the 1926 European Championships which saw a record nine national teams in attendance. Poland made its first appearance. Sweden was the sole former champion not present this year, as Britain finally returned to the Championships 16 years after its success at the first official tournament in 1910.

The 1926 event in Davos, Switzerland was a true hockey marathon, with the favorites playing seven games each and, on several occasions, two games in a day. While the nine teams were split into three groups of three, insufficient experience in organizing large tournaments resulted in standings only being determined for the four best teams. The playoffs were made up of the three group winners, with the fourth finalist determined in a series of games involving the runners-up of the three groups. Two playoff rounds were needed after the first round robin ended in a three-way tie. Switzerland eventually emerged as the champion, which was a surprise because in the previous 15 years, the Swiss had only won one game in official tournaments.

Experts were unanimous in noting a higher standard of play among the top teams in 1926 when compared to previous years. Improved defensive play was noted in particular.

1927 EUROPEAN CHAMPIONSHIPS The host nation won the European Championships for the third year in a row, as Austria emerged victorious for the first time in a six-nation round-robin tournament. Belgium ranked second and added to its achievement with the Fair Play Cup established for the team with the fewest penalty minutes. Hungary made its first appearance at the European Championships in 1927, but did not score a goal in losing all five games.

1928 WINTER OLYMPICS, WORLD AND EUROPEAN CHAMPIONSHIPS At the time, the 1928 tournament at the Winter Games in St. Moritz, Switzerland contested only the Olympic Championship, but two years later the IIHF Congress awarded it the status of both the World and European Championships, thus making it the first tournament to contest three championship titles.

The United States was not present in 1928 and Canada was exempted from the preliminary games and awarded a bye directly into the medal round. The 10 European teams were split into three divisions, with the winner of each group also advancing to the medal round. Games were much closer than at previous Olympic tournaments, as warm weather often turned the natural ice surface to slush and thus reduced the advantage for strong skating teams.

Nevertheless, Canada's domination of international competition continued. The Toronto Varsity Grads cruised to the gold by outscoring its European opponents 38–0 in three games.

1929 EUROPEAN CHAMPIONSHIPS Eight national teams competed at the 1929 European Championships, which marked the last time that games were played in two periods of 30 minutes. Czechoslovakia won its fifth European title with a team comprised mainly of a new generation of players, though veteran goalie Jan Peka played just as confidently as he had in 1913. Peka had been the national team goalie for nearly a quarter of a century. This latest win by Czechoslovakia inspired the construction of the country's first artificial ice rink in Prague, which was opened on January 17, 1931.

Second place at the 1929 event in Budapest went to Poland, who also won the Fair Play Cup. Third place was determined in a playoff game for the first time this year, as semifinal losers Austria and Italy battled in a game won 4–2 by the Austrians.

1930 WORLD & EUROPEAN CHAMPIONSHIPS The International Ice Hockey Federation decided in 1930 to hold World and European Championships every year, if possible. It was ruled that in order for a tournament to gain World Championship status, at least one non-European team—Canada, the United States, or Japan—must be present. If such a World Championship was held in Europe, the highest-ranking European team would be declared European Champion.

The decision to play a World Championship in 1930 that was independent of the Winter Olympic Games marked a new stage in the development of hockey. The tournament broke all existing records with 12 countries taking part, including the first team from Japan. Canada was represented by a Toronto-based team sponsored by the C.C.M. sporting goods company that was touring Europe at the time. The Canadian team was once again exempt from preliminary competition and would play only in the finals.

The tournament began in Chamonix, but warm weather and poor ice conditions made it necessary to move the final games to Berlin. Germany scored a 2–1 victory over Switzerland on home ice to claim the 1930 European Championship, but dropped a 6–1 decision to Canada in the World Championship game. Austria beat Poland 2–0 in a game to determine third place among the European contestants. That game was played in Vienna, making this tournament the only one of its kind to be played in three different countries. The IIHF presented medals to the winners this year instead of the diplomas it had handed out in the past. Other firsts at this event included forward passing in the defensive zone and a new rule calling for three 15-minute periods.

1931 WORLD & EUROPEAN CHAMPIONSHIPS The World Championships now began to be held annually and each tournament marked a new stage in the search for an optimum system of determining the best team.

This time, the round-robin playoffs were preceded by a complex set of preliminary games which involved all 10 countries including Canada (the Manitoba Grads), the United States national squad (which had not played games in Europe since 1924) and Romania, which was making its initial appearance in international hockey. This system produced the first four contenders for the medals: Canada, the U.S., Sweden and Czechoslovakia.

To increase the medal-round field to six teams, Austria, which had a win in the preliminaries, France, Romania and Poland (as the host nation) were given a second chance to qualify for the round-robin playoffs. Poland advanced with a 2–1 win over France, while Austria beat Romania 7–0.

The six-team final round of the 1931 World Championships saw Sweden play Canada to a 0–0 tie, which marked the first time a European team did not lose to the Canadian squad in international tournament play. Still, with four wins and a tie, Canada won the gold medal and did not allow a single goal in the tournament. The United States finished second.

As in all combined World and European Championship events played before 1971, the European rankings were determined by the standings of European teams that had competed at the World Championships. Austria, third overall behind Canada and the U.S., was declared the European Champion for the second time in its history. Austria also won the Fair Play Cup, which was sponsored by the U.S. Ambassador in Poland.

1932 WINTER OLYMPICS AND WORLD CHAMPIONSHIPS Many countries had applied to participate in the first major international ice hockey tournament to be held on the American continent, but the economics of the Great Depression prevented many national teams from traveling to the Winter Olympics in Lake Placid, New York. As a result, the four-nation hockey tournament would be the smallest field in Olympic history. Poland was the only nation to finish without a medal.

It was decided that the four Olympic hockey teams would compete in a double round robin, meaning each team would face its opponents twice. In addition to those 12 games, the IOC ruled that five exhibition games would be played on the days in which no official matches were scheduled. Among the participants in the exhibition games was a team from McGill University in Montreal, whose students had played in the first "modern" hockey game on March 3, 1875.

Two rinks were used to play the Olympic Games at Lake Placid, one indoors and one outdoors, which made it necessary for the players to keep adjusting from artificial to natural ice. All 12 games of the Olympic tournament were officiated by the same two referees, Lou Marsh of Canada and Donald P. Sands of the United States. In the first-round game between the U.S. and Germany, the audience decided that Sands was prejudiced against the visitors and forced the American referee to leave the ice. Lou Marsh conducted the rest of the game alone to the satisfaction of all.

Canada and the U.S. were evenly matched and well ahead of their European opponents. Overtime was required in both Canada–U.S. games, with Victor Lindqvist scoring the winning goal for a 2–1 victory by Canada's Winnipeg Hockey Club in the first game. (He later become a prominent international referee, officiating games at the 1962 and 1963 World Championships.) The second game ended in a 2–2 tie after three overtime periods. Attendance for that game was 7,000 in a rink that had just 3,000 seats. "We will never give away the Olympic gold to anybody," wrote Canadian newspapers after the tie with the U.S. clinched first place for Canada.

1932 European Championships The last independent European Championship tournament drew nine national squads to Berlin in 1932, including Latvia which had joined the IIHF the year before.

Five teams advanced to the medal round. Sweden posted an undefeated record in final round play, finishing with two wins and two ties in four games. Games were low scoring, as Sweden tied 0–0 with second-place finisher Austria and 1–1 with the bronze medalists from Switzerland. Gustaf Johansson and Karl-Erik Furst were Sweden's top scorers with five and three goals respectively.

1933 World & European Championships Prague, with its considerable experience in organizing European Championships, hosted its first World Championship on the artificial ice of the new Stvanice winter stadium in 1933. The seventh World Championship tournament was the first to feature forward passing in any zone on the ice and ended in a surprise of historical importance, as a new champion emerged.

After winning six consecutive international tournaments (a record that would stand until 1969), Canada suffered its first lost in a World Championship game, as the Toronto National "Sea Fleas" were defeated 2–1 in overtime by the United States in the final game of the tournament. The victory gave the Americans first place, while Canada settled for second.

Czechoslovakia's Jan Krasl (1899–1980) made his debut as a referee at this tournament. He had played 17 games for his national team at the World and European Championships between 1924 and 1930, and would finish his refereeing career at the 1955 World Championships.

1934 World & European Championships The 1934 World Championships were held in Milan, which had hosted the European Championships 10 years earlier. The same 12 nations that had competed in 1933 were present and played through a complex system of preliminary games and playoff rounds to establish the champion.

The medal round was made up from teams that had won the three different divisions from the second round of play, plus Germany (who had won a special playoff among the second-place teams). Canada, represented by the Saskatoon Quakers, regained its position as World Champions by beating the United States 2–1 in the final game.

1935 World & European Championships attracted a record field of 15 nations to Davos, Switzerland, though the United States was not among them. Holland made its first appearance on the international stage and won the Fair Play Cup which was sponsored by Bucharest's daily *Universul* newspaper. Only European teams were eligible for this award. The tournament involved 51 games played over nine days.

As in past years, the World Championships began with a series of preliminary games, though this year all teams took part regardless of their past success. The two top-ranking teams from each of the four subgroups then advanced to the next round. This format resembled the one adopted by the IIHF in 1979.

The eight top teams were divided into two groups and played a separate series of round-robin games. The two top teams from each group moved on to play for the medals, while the four bottom teams (two from each division) took part in a consolation round. The two semifinal games in the medal round matched the first-place team from one division against the second-place team from the other, with the winners playing for the gold medal. Canada emerged victorious for the eighth time, represented this year by the Winnipeg Monarchs whose roster included many players from the Olympic championship squad of 1932. The Swiss settled for the silver medal after losing to Canada in the final, and were crowned European champions for the first time since 1926.

During the tournament, Czechoslovakia played a very competitive game against Canada, losing 2–1. Matej Buckna, of Czech origin, from the Canadian town of Trail, British Columbia, was a consultant for Czechoslovakia's team and a playing coach on contract for many years with LTC Prague. In 1948 He would take his club team to Moscow for the first series of games ever played between Czechoslovakia and the Soviet Union.

1936 Winter Olympics, World and European Championships Teams from 15 countries competed at the 1936 Winter Olympics, including Italy, Japan and Latvia, who were all making their Olympic debut. Japan's goaltender, Teiji Honma, wore a face mask for the first time in the history of World Championship play. Also for the first time, both the Canadians and Americans were defeated by European teams, as Canada failed to win the Olympic gold medal. Great Britain was the new hockey champion.

Coached by future IIHF president John "Bunny" Ahearne, the British team featured only one player (defenseman Carl Erhardt) who was a true Englishman. All his teammates were of British origin but had been raised and trained in Canada, as had the players who formed the core of the French team. Canada's delegation used this fact to argue for the disqualification of both France and England. After long negotiations, Canada withdrew its protest against Great Britain but not against France. The French team was permitted to take part, but almost refused to do so in its anger over the Canadian protest.

The games of the 1936 Olympics were played outdoors on natural ice. Snowstorms often forced the stoppage of play. The format of the tournament reflected past experience in planning World Championships. The first stage included four preliminary games. The two top-ranking teams from each subgroup then entered the semifinal round and formed two groups of four. Finally the two best teams from each semifinal played for the medals, counting the points won by the finalists during the previous stage. The loss by the U.S. to Italy in the elimination round was the biggest upset of the tournament, with the Italians scoring a 2–1 victory in overtime. The most important and surprising upset was Canada's loss to Great Britain during the semifinal round, as the 2–1 British victory over the Port Arthur Bearcats gave the team from the United Kingdom the gold medal.

The British players returned home in triumph, carrying not only their gold medals but the puck used to score the gold medal-winning goal against Canada. According to newspaper reports, it was bought by a London sports patron for a large sum of money.

1937 World & European Championships were held in Great Britain for the first time. The British had won the first European Championships in 1910 in addition to the 1936 Olympic tournament. The 1937 event in London featured 11 teams, including the debut of Norway. Teams were now permitted to use 14 players on their rosters and lineups usually included two goaltenders, three defenseman and three forward lines.

The format of the 1937 World tournament was virtually the same as it had been in 1935 except that results in the semifinal round would not be counted towards the final medal round. Canada (the Kimberly Dynamiters) returned to the top spot in the world by going undefeated at the tournament. Great Britain slipped to second. Switzerland finished third and won the Fair Play Cup. This prize to the team with the fewest penalties had been awarded since the early 1930s.

1938 World & European Championships In connection with the approaching 30th anniversary of the International Ice Hockey Federation, the Organizing Committee sent invitations for the 1938 World Championships to all 22 IIHF member countries. Teams from 15 nations attended the games in Prague, including newcomer Lithuania.

The host nation turned the World Championships into a festive occasion unequaled to that point in hockey history. Famous hockey players and organizers of the game came to the Czechoslovakian capital as guests of honor of the IIHF. A special yearbook was issued for the 25th Congress, informing readers that Czechoslovakia had the most ice hockey clubs in Europe with 361, while Sweden had 116 and Poland 92. The greatest number of rinks with artificial ice had been built in Great Britain (21) and Germany (14).

"I played my first games at the World Championships in 1938," recalled Harijs Vitolinsh, a well-known Latvian player who was among the best defensemen during ice hockey's early years in the USSR. "I remember most our game with Norway. After regulation time the score was tied and Klavs, who was to become a referee after the war, scored two goals in the overtime period."

The organizing committee did not always act consistently when it came to ties. A game between Czechoslovakia and Sweden was not declared a tie until a period of overtime was played, while a game between Sweden and Austria was declared a tie after just three periods of regulation time.

Canada, Great Britain, Germany and the host Czechoslovaks all reached the final medal round, with Canada (the Sudbury Wolves) again claiming the World title. The Fair Play Cup was awarded to Austria.

1939 WORLD & EUROPEAN CHAMPIONSHIPS Finland and Yugoslavia made their first appearance at the World Hockey Championships in 1939, the last such event prior to World War II. Team rosters were expanded to include 15 players. Canada was represented by the Trail Smoke Eaters, who breezed through the tournament with eight straight victories while allowing just one goal against.

The 1939 tournament was patterned on the format of the 1935 event, with the only difference being that results from the semifinal round would not be carried over into the final medal round. Canada, the United States, Switzerland and Czechoslovakia advanced to the final round, with the Czechoslovaks having to settle for the Fair Play Cup after finishing out of the medals.

As the two top contenders for the title of top European team, Switzerland and Czechoslovakia played to a scoreless tie in the medal round. An additional match was played between the two nations on March 5 in Basel, Switzerland, with the home team winning 2–0.

1947 WORLD & EUROPEAN CHAMPIONSHIPS The first postwar congress of the IIHF was held in Brussels in April, 1946 and dates were set to resume the World Championships in 1947. Great Britain, Czechoslovakia and Switzerland all expressed a desire to host the tournament, but by early October, 1946 both Britain and Switzerland had abandoned the idea. With Czechoslovakia now confirmed as the host country, invitations to attend the 1947 World Championships were sent out from Prague on November 14, 1946.

The Congress in Brussels introduced some very important rule changes to international hockey. Three periods of 20 minutes, which had been introduced in Europe in 1945, were approved at the meetings in 1946 (35 years later than in Canada). Also approved was the modern size of 183 centimeters (6') by 122 centimeters (4') for the goalie net, plus a goal line and center-ice red line. One- and three-minute penalties were omitted from the rules and a penalty shot was introduced.

The 1947 tournament marked the first time that Canada did not attend the IIHF World Championships, and a split among organizing committees in the United States doomed the American team to fifth place, leaving only European teams to contend for the medals. Sweden's victory over Czechoslovakia was marked by a telegram of congratulations from Swedish King Gustav, but the team had hardly finished celebrating when they were upset by Austria in a loss that ultimately handed the gold medal back to the host nation.

Meanwhile, amateur hockey in the United States had developed a rift due to competition for control of the game between the Amateur Athletic Union and the Amateur Hockey Association of the United States. A mixed team had come to Prague for the 1947 World Championships, but in the middle of the tournament the IIHF passed a decision to break ties with Avery Brundage and the AAU in favor of AHAUS headed up by well-known hockey personality Walter Brown, who would later serve as president of the International Ice Hockey Federation. This demoralized an already divided U.S. team and resulted in the first finish out of the medals for an American team at the World Championships.

Canada's decision not to send a team to the World Championships in 1947 highlighted a growing rift between the Canadian Amateur Hockey Association and the International Ice Hockey Federation over IIHF policy. The dispute was solved later in the year when the IIHF agreed to alternate presidential terms between European and North American representatives.

1948 WINTER OLYMPICS, WORLD AND EUROPEAN CHAMPIONSHIPS Because of the Second World War, there had been a 12-year break between Winter Olympic competitions. The Games at St. Moritz marked Canada's return to international competition for the first time since before the war, represented by the RCAF Flyers of Ottawa, a team made up of servicemen from the Royal Canadian Air Force.

The problems that had plagued the Americans at the 1947 World Championships produced grave complications in 1948, as two American teams arrived in Switzerland. One team was sent by AHAUS and was supported by the IIHF, while the other was sent by the AAU, which had represented the United States at all previous Winter Games and now used its old connections to gain support from the International Olympic Committee. Both American teams appeared on the ice for the opening ceremonies and police assistance was required to restore order. The IOC decided to disqualify both American teams, but passions later calmed down and the AAU team left for home, allowing the IOC to withdraw its suspension and let the AHAUS team play. In the end, the United States entry was "outlawed" by the IOC and was not counted in the final Olympic hockey standings (though it remained in the World Championships).

Problems also plagued the Olympic tournament on the ice, where warm weather played havoc with the schedule and made it necessary to begin some games at 7 a.m. Many games saw the winning team scoring in double digits, highlighting the differences in strength among the competing countries, but for the first time in a championship in which Canada competed, the winner was not decided until the final game. Because of a scoreless tie between Canada and Czechoslovakia, the two top medal contenders both finished the tournament without a loss. Canada ultimately claimed the Olympic title on the basis of goal differential. The results in 1948 proved that Czechoslovakia's World Championship in 1947 could not solely be attributed to Canada's absence, as it was generally agreed in St. Moritz that the Czechoslovak team was no weaker than Canada's and boasted a much stronger offense. Czechoslovakia's captain Vladimir Zabrodsky, who scored 27 goals in the tournament, was recognized as the Olympics' best forward.

The bronze medal in 1948 went to Switzerland, just as it had 20 years earlier when the Winter Olympics had also been staged in St. Moritz. Richard Torriani of Switzerland became the first hockey player to read the Olympic oath at the opening ceremony in 1948 on behalf of all the competitors.

1949 WORLD & EUROPEAN CHAMPIONSHIPS were held in Sweden for the first time and ended in great success for Europe, particularly Czechoslovakia. The Czechoslovaks had won the world title with Canada absent in 1947, and tied the Canadian team at the 1948 Olympics before settling for the silver medal. Finally, in 1949, Czechoslovakia beat Canada for the first time with Stanislav Konopasek scoring the winning goal in a 3–2 victory. By capitalizing on goals by Josef Trousilek, Vaclav Rozinak and Konopasek, Czechoslovakia was a 3–0 winner in the decisive game with Sweden and became undisputed World Champions, while also winning the European title for the third time in a row.

The victory by Czechoslovakia was all the more significant due to the fact that a much younger team had come to Stockholm after a tragic plane crash on November 8, 1948 had taken the lives of the players who had won the 1947 title and the silver medal in St. Moritz. The entire team had been killed in the accident, including the outstanding Czechoslovak stars Ladislav Trojak, Vilibald Stovik, Miloslav Pokorny, Karel Stibor and Zdenek Jarkovsky.

Canada, which had lost to the United States at the 1933 World Championships and been beaten by a British team stocked with Canadian players at the 1936 Olympics, had now lost the world title to a European team for the first time. However, the Sudbury Wolves established a record that is not likely to be beaten at this level of competition when they defeated Denmark 47–0 in the first round of the tournament. Denmark was making its first appearance at the World Championships. The lopsided victory was accomplished despite a system that was designed to avoid unnecessary games between teams of clearly different calibers. Using a set-up that was an exact replica of the 1932 European Championships, organizers split the competition into three divisions with the two top teams from each group advancing to a round-robin final.

Finishing behind Czechoslovakia and Canada at this tournament was the United States, though it was learned during the IIHF Congress held in conjunction with the World Championships that the International Olympic Committee had broken relations with the IIHF as a direct result of the squabbling at the 1948 Olympics. Meanwhile, Sweden finished fourth behind the U.S. at the 1949 tournament and Swedish player Ake Andersson was named unanimously as the best player by a special panel of judges and awarded a gold watch by the *Dagens Nyheter* newspaper.

1950 WORLD & EUROPEAN CHAMPIONSHIPS The defending World Champions from Czechoslovakia did not appear at the 1950 tournament in London. As a result, the number of competitors declined as did interest in the event. Canada, represented by the Edmonton Mercurys, won by going undefeated throughout the tournament. The United States lost only to Canada and finished in second place. Norway finished last among the six teams that reached the medal round, but took home the Fair Play Cup. Belgium received a consolation prize by winning the playoff among the three nations ranked seventh to ninth.

Although it was not widely reported at the time, Czechoslovakia was absent from the 1950 World Championships because its entire team had been arrested by the Czechoslovakian KGB at the airport in Prague prior its scheduled departure for London. It was suspected that the players planned to defect, and all were given jail sentences of varying lengths. Czechoslovakia did not return to world play until the Olympics in 1952.

1951 World & European Championships were split into two separate pools for the first time, with the weaker countries separated from the traditional powers. Czechoslovakia was again absent and because the American team sent to Paris wasn't first-rate, Canada had no trouble winning the world title once again. The Lethbridge Maple Leafs outscored their opposition 62–6 in winning all six of their games. Sweden claimed its fifth European Championship by finishing second overall behind Canada, though only edged out Switzerland based on a better goal differential.

In a Congress held at the same time as the World Championships, the IIHF decided to withdraw from participation in the Winter Olympics as a result of the ongoing feud that had started in 1948. This decision did not last long however and in August of the same year the IIHF made peace with the IOC at its Congress in Romania.

1952 Winter Olympics, World and European Championships As in 1948, the Olympic hockey tournament was staged as a single round-robin tournament with each team playing every other country once. With nine nations taking part, this meant each team played eight games. As in 1950, Canada was represented by the Edmonton Mercurys who won the gold medal with seven victories and a tie.

Only Sweden and the U.S. provided much opposition for Canada, as the Mercurys needed a goal with 20 seconds remaining to beat the Swedes 3–2. This proved to be the decisive victory in the tournament after Canada could only manage a 3–3 tie with the Americans despite outshooting them 58–13. The Olympic gold medal in 1952 was the fifth for Canada, an achievement not to be surpassed until 1984 by the USSR. No Canadian team has won the Olympic title since.

Czechoslovakia returned to international competition in 1952 and appeared to have won a bronze medal (and the European Championship) after a 4–0 victory over Sweden in their final game gave them the same record and goal differential as the Swedes. Newspapers had already reported Czechoslovakia's third-place finish when the organizing committee changed the European format and decided to hold an additional game to break the tie. Sweden then claimed the Olympic bronze medal and European title with a 5–3 victory.

1953 World & European Championships The 1953 tournament was the only World Championship to be attended solely by European teams. Canada's decision not to participate was explained this way by Canadian Amateur Hockey Association President W.B. George:"Every year we spend $10,000 to send a Canadian team over to Europe to play 40 exhibition games (plus the World Championships). All of these games are played to packed houses that only enrich European hockey coffers. In return we are subjected to constant, unnecessary abuse over our Canadian style of play."

With Canada and the United States absent, only four nations were included in the main group of the tournament, which copied the double round-robin format of the 1932 Olympics. Sweden won the World Championship for the first time, followed by West Germany (whose second place finish this year remains the best German finish ever). West Germany earned the silver medal despite a record of just one win and three losses because Czechoslovakia's players returned home without finishing the tournament as a gesture of mourning over the death of Czechoslovakian President Klement Gotvald. Third-place Switzerland was awarded the Fair Play Cup.

There was some talk that the Soviet Union would make its international hockey debut at the 1953 World Championships. Instead, hockey experts from the USSR—including legendary coach Anatoli Tarasov—were in Switzerland as observers. The Soviets would join IIHF competition in Stockholm in 1954.

1954 World & European Championships The Soviet Union made an outstanding debut at the World Championships in 1954, winning the tournament handily. The only blemish on their undefeated record was a 1–1 tie with the host team from Sweden. Canada was represented by the East York Lyndhursts, a club that was not as strong as the Senior A amateur champions that had represented Canada in previous seasons. Still, the Lyndhursts had easily handled their opponents until meeting the Soviet Union's national team in the final game.

The day of the Canada–USSR game began with the sale of tickets for an additional match the following day, because if Canada beat the Soviets—a result that practically no one doubted—the team would be required to play off against Sweden to decide the European Championship. But the USSR Nationals surprised everyone. Their style of play was unfamiliar to the Canadians, as the Soviets appeared to pass too much, check too little, and skate too fast. They were thoroughly dominating in a 7–2 victory. An audience of 16,000 watched the historic game, including a correspondent for *Sport-Informations Dienst* named Gunther Sabetzki, future president of the International Ice Hockey Federation.

The 1954 World Championships marked the first time that the Directorate of the IIHF awarded prizes to the best players. The first winners were goaltender Don Lockhart (Canada), defenseman Lars Bjorn (Sweden) and forward Vsevolod Bobrov (USSR). An IIHF All-Star Team was also selected and, in addition to the player award winners, included; defencemen Vaclav Bubnik (Czechoslovakia), Tom Jamieson, Thomas Campbell, and Doug Chapman (all Canada): forwards Bill Shill, Eric Unger, Maurice Galand (all Canada), Vlastimil Bubnik, Vladimir Zabrodsky, Bronislav Danda (all Czechoslovakia),Victor Shuvalov (USSR) and Sven Johansson (Sweden).

1955 World & European Championships were rotated between four cities and featured nine teams in the main pool. Canada was represented by the Penticton Vees, but the loss to the Soviets the previous year resulted in the addition of several players from other Canadian clubs. A problem arose before the championships when a passport check showed that 10 Canadian players listed hockey as their occupation. Vees president Clem Bird was quick to point out that all of these players had resumed their amateur status two years before.

Canada refused to take the Soviets lightly this year, studying the style of their play and sending scouts to observe the USSR's exhibition games. As a result, the Canadians went through the tournament without a loss in eight games, including a 5–0 win over the Soviets, to reclaim the World Championship. The USSR, whose players appeared to take the tournament a little too lightly, finished second with a record of 7–1.

1956 Winter Olympics, World and European Championships A special four-level Olympic Stadium was built at the Italian alpine resort of Cortina which would allow 12,000 spectators to view hockey action. IIHF president Bunny Ahearne declared the 1956 Olympic tournament the most representative in history, also serving to determine the Pool A World champion and the champion of Europe. The organizers returned to the two-stage formula and copied the format of the 1949 World Championships, with the two top teams from each of the three subgroups advancing to the round-robin final, while the remaining teams played in the consolation group.

West Germany's team was, in fact, a combined East–West squad.

The USSR was determined not to repeat the mistakes of 1955, and the Soviets swept through their first Olympic tournament without a defeat to win the gold medal. The United States took the silver, while the Kitchener-Waterloo Dutchmen of Canada lost to both the U.S. and USSR and settled for the bronze.

"There is one area," wrote the *New York Times*, "where the Russians have shown results bordering on the impossible and that area is ice hockey."

1957 World & European Championships The decision to hold the 1957 World Championships in Moscow was in recognition of the achievements of Soviet hockey. When it was learned that Canada and the United States would be boycotting the tournament over Soviet involvement in Hungary, the USSR Nationals were unanimously declared the tournament favorite. The Soviet team, however, was attempting to integrate younger players onto its aging roster and this hurt its performance. While not losing a single game, the USSR could manage only ties against their main rivals (Sweden and Czechoslovakia) and watched the gold medal go to the Swedes while settling for second place.

The 1957 tournament was the last World Championship to be played on natural ice. Most games were held in the new Luzhniki Sports Palace, but the decisive USSR–Sweden game was played at the nearby Grand Sports Arena where some 50,000 spectators were in attendance. This remains the largest audience in hockey history.

1958 World & European Championships All 28 games of the 1958 World Championships were held on the artificial ice of a rink set up at the Jordal Amfi Stadium in Oslo, Norway. Canada was represented by the Whitby Dunlops, a strong Ontario senior club that had defeated the Soviet Union 7–2 in December, 1957 during a Canadian tour by the USSR national team.

The roster of the Whitby Dunlops was reinforced for the World Championships by adding six former professional players. Some had finished their pro careers one year before, while others had played pro hockey right up to the IIHF tournament. A dozen players already had previous experience playing against the USSR, including Jack McKenzie who had played for the Kitchener/Waterloo Dutchmen at the 1956 Olympics. Whitby's captain was Harry Sinden, who later gained fame as coach and general manager of the Boston Bruins. Sinden coached the Canadian team in the historic Canada-Russia Summit Series of 1972.

The Canadians in Oslo had little trouble taking the gold medal in 1958, winning all seven games and outscoring their opponents 82–6. Only the Soviets provided much opposition in a 4–2 victory for Canada.

1959 WORLD & EUROPEAN CHAMPIONSHIPS in Czechoslovakia coincided with the 50th anniversary of hockey in that country. An unprecedented eight towns hosted the tournament, which was attended by 15 countries. This would be the last time that a championship played separately from the Olympics would be organized in two stages.

Canada was represented this year by the Belleville (Ontario) McFarlands and once again finished as World champions, losing only to the Czechs. The USSR took the silver medal. Czechoslovakia took the bronze.

1960 WINTER OLYMPICS, WORLD AND EUROPEAN CHAMPIONSHIPS It had been 28 years since the Winter Olympics had last been staged in the United States, and the host nation's hockey team would capture its first Olympic gold medal and second World Championship with a victory in Squaw Valley, California. The Americans had been gradually building towards this victory by bringing good teams to the recent World Championships and had been quite open about their goal of winning at home in 1960. Five players on the gold medal team had won silver medals in 1956, and 10 had had previous experience at the World Championships.

Canada, represented by the Kitchener-Waterloo Dutchmen, lost only to the Americans in California and claimed the silver medal, but had now gone two Olympic Games in a row without winning gold. The Soviets claimed the European Championship for the third year in a row, but were forced to settle for the bronze medal overall for the first time since their debut on the world stage in 1954.

Australia competed for the first time and finished last among the nine nations.

1961 WORLD & EUROPEAN CHAMPIONSHIPS marked the last time that games were held in the open air. A swimming pool in Lausanne provided the outdoor venue, with powerful freezing plants turning the water to ice. Diving platforms rose above the playing surface and proved an attractive perch for photographers. The warm March sun was a nuisance for players, who had to protect their eyes from the glare. The indoor rink in Geneva was also unusual, as it featured boards made of transparent plastic.

Beginning in 1961, the World Championships were played in three groups, which significantly increased the number of participating nations. A record 20 teams took part in Switzerland, including the first team from South Africa. The tournament was preceded by qualification games to determine the final berths in Pool A and Pool B. Wins by both East and West Germany put each country in the A Pool, which resulted in a forfeit when the West Germans refused to play the East.

Canada was represented by the Trail Smoke Eaters, who were reinforced with six players from other teams. Trail had won the World Championship for Canada in 1939 and did so again with an undefeated record in 1961, though a tie with Czechoslovakia meant that first place was awarded only on the basis of a better goal differential. This was Canada's 19th win at the World Championships (a record that would be equaled by the Soviets in 1983). It would also prove to be the last win by a Canadian amateur team. Canada would not win the World Championships again until 1994.

The Soviet Union recorded its poorest finish to date in 1961, claiming the bronze medal as it had in 1960 but losing the European title when Czechoslovakia finished second. Despite losing the European title, the Soviet rebuilding program was nearing completion and the USSR national team that competed in Switzerland in 1961 had seven future World Champions on its roster.

1962 WORLD & EUROPEAN CHAMPIONSHIPS In retaliation for the politically motivated boycott by the Canadians and Americans in 1957, the Soviet Union, Czechoslovakia and other Communist countries refused to participate in the 1962 IIHF World Championships at Colorado Springs, citing the American government's refusal to grant entry visas to East Germany's players and team management.

Canada, represented by the Galt Terriers, was upset by Sweden and finished in second place. The win marked Sweden's third gold medal. The United States took the bronze.

It was during these World Championships that Father David Bauer conceived the idea of establishing a permanent amateur Canadian national team to compete in the Olympics and World Championships.

1963 WORLD & EUROPEAN CHAMPIONSHIPS Stockholm hosted the World Championships in 1963, nine years after the USSR had first triumphed in the Swedish city. Tournament games would be broadcast on Soviet television for the first time. There were 21 nations competing in three groups over 10 days in Sweden in 1963, including Bulgaria which was making its debut on the world stage. The tournament involved 64 games, a record at the time.

The 1963 World Championships produced one of the most dramatic tournaments on record, with the final outcome still in doubt for the four medal contenders heading into the final day. Both the USSR and Sweden were in contention for the gold medal. Canada could finish no higher than second.

The first game of the day featured the United States and East Germany, and while both were out of contention for the top prize, an East German win would make it easier for the Soviets to claim the gold, while an American win would mean the Soviets would have to beat Canada by 9–0 or better in their final game. A tie would mean that the USSR would have to beat Canada 1–0 or by a margin of two goals. The game did end 3–3, but no matter how the Soviets did against Canada, Sweden would still claim the gold medal with either a win or tie against Czechoslovakia.

A silver medal was on the line for Canada if it could beat the Soviets in the final game, but the USSR was clearly the better team and held a 4–0 lead into the final minute. Canada (again represented by the Trail Smoke Eaters) managed to score two late goals, but the Soviets held on for the two-goal margin they needed in a 4–2 victory. When Czechoslovakia beat Sweden 3–2, the gold medal went to the USSR. The Swedes had to settle for the silver, while the Czechoslovaks took the bronze. Canada finished fourth and out of the medals for the first time. It was clear now that Canadian amateur club teams could no longer compete with the best Europeans. A permanent Canadian national team would wear the maple leaf in competition beginning in 1964.

Despite the fourth-place finish in 1963, Canadian goalie Seth Martin was among those selected as the best players at the World Championships. Swedish defenseman Roland Stolz and forward Miroslav Vlach of Czechoslovakia received similar honors.

1964 WINTER OLYMPICS, WORLD AND EUROPEAN CHAMPIONSHIPS For the first time in international play, Canada was represented by a true national team at the 1964 Olympics in Innsbruck, Austria. Though many players would come and go, Canada would be represented by this national team for six years. Canada finished the 1964 Olympics with a 5–2 record, as did Czechoslovakia and Sweden, and the national team believed it had claimed the bronze over Sweden on the basis of a better goal differential. But 10 minutes before the medal presentations, IIHF president Bunny Ahearne overruled the pre-arranged IOC tie-breaking formula and announced a change that dropped Canada into fourth place. The Soviet Union won gold.

The Olympic tournament began with a qualification round designed to seed the teams into groups and resulted in several one-sided blowouts. West Germany had earned the right to represent the combined German team with a win over East Germany in a qualification series.

The best players honored at the tournament by the IIHF were goalie Seth Martin of Canada, defenseman Frantisek Tikal of Czechoslovakia and forward Boris Mayorov of the USSR. The coaches of the USSR team reversed the IIHF's selection of Mayorov and instead presented the award for best forward to Eduard Ivanov despite the fact that he was a defenseman. Ivanov was accepted as the official winner of the award in the IIHF record book.

1965 WORLD & EUROPEAN CHAMPIONSHIPS Tampere, the second largest city in Finland, became the first Finnish city to host the World Championships in 1965. National teams from 15 countries played in the beautiful Gaahalli Ice Palace, Finland's first artificial rink.

Because the close competition in recent years had created situations whereby medal distribution depended only on how many goals had been scored, a new tie-breaking procedure was introduced in Tampere. It was decided that if two teams had an equal number of points, priority would be given to the winner of the game between the two. Only if two medal contenders played a tie game, or if there were more than two contenders would goal differential come into play.

In the event that goal differential was employed, the only games that would be counted would be those involving "the Big Quartet," as the teams from the USSR, Czechoslovakia, Sweden and Canada had begun to be known. This eliminated any advantage from running up lopsided scores against weak opponents as these games would not be factored into any goal differential calculation.

However, no complex arithmetic was needed to crown a World Champion in 1965. The Soviets did not lose a single game and became the first European team to win the World Championships three years in a row. As a result, the Soviets were permitted to keep the World Championship Cup.

1966 WORLD & EUROPEAN CHAMPIONSHIPS The USSR, Czechoslovakia and Canada finished 1–2–3 at the 1966 World Championships held in Lubljana, Yugoslavia. Mild weather make hockey feel like a year-round sport with only the snow-capped peaks of the Alps in the distance serving as a reminder of winter.

In an attempt to increase audiences, tournament organizers decided to hold three separate tournaments for each of Pool A, Pool B and Pool C in the three Yugoslavian towns where hockey was most popular.

As had been decided in Tampere the year before, results of head-to-head games between two tied teams would be used to break any ties, but only when medals were at stake. In all other cases, goal differential would be used as it was when the United States was ranked ahead of Finland in the final standings.

The Soviet Union won the gold, finishing 6–0–1. Czechoslovakia finished second (6–1–0) while Canada ws third (5–2–0). The Soviet's one tie game came against fourth-place Sweden.

1967 WORLD & EUROPEAN CHAMPIONSHIPS National teams from 21 countries assembled in Vienna for the 1967 World Championships, and the 66 games played set a new record. Rosters were increased to 18 players and tournament organizers had to cope with enormous logistical difficulties in providing accommodations and training facilities for the visiting teams. Proceeds from the games would only cover the expenses for the Pool A tournament, but dropping Pool B and Pool C would almost certainly result in severe setbacks for the game in a number of lesser hockey nations. The only logical option—and one suggested ten years earlier by then IIHF president Bunny Ahearne—was to organize three separate tournaments. This IIHF directors agreed to this new format in 1969.

The Soviet Union won its fifth consecutive World Championship in Vienna in 1967, claiming the title by the largest margin of victory (five points) in history. Canada's national team was bolstered by ex-pros Carl Brewer and Jack Bownass and had an excellent tournament before losing 6–0 to Sweden in the final game and settling for the bronze medal.

1968 WINTER OLYMPICS, WORLD AND EUROPEAN CHAMPIONSHIPS marked the last time in which the Olympic, World, and European titles would all be decided in one event. Heading into the final game at Grenoble, Czechoslovakia needed a win against Sweden to claim the Olympic title, but had to settle for the silver medal after a 2–2 tie. Because the regulations stated that if a team from Europe won the Olympic title it would also be crowned European Champion, the tie with Sweden cost Czechoslovakia a unique opportunity to capture the Olympic, World and European crowns.

The Soviets won the Olympic gold medal for the second time in a row in 1968 and claimed their sixth consecutive World title, equaling Canada's record achievement of 1920 to 1932. The USSR had also gone 39 straight games without a loss dating back to 1963, matching another record set by Canada between 1936 and 1948. The Canadian national team won the bronze medal at Grenoble.

1969 WORLD & EUROPEAN CHAMPIONSHIPS As proposed by the Swedish Hockey Union, the 1969 World Championships at Stockholm were played in two rounds. The top six countries would compete in a double round robin instead of the eight-team, single-round format of previous years, meaning each team would play 10 games instead of seven. The IIHF Council hoped the new format would increase competition, as the world title had been won by the Soviet Union for six straight years. Soviet coach Anatoli Tarasov disagreed. "I think our team will look better in the second round," he said. "As a matter of fact, the two-round system is to our advantage—our players rehabilitate faster and they know how to play with injuries. For this reason, it would be to our advantage if we had entry lists not for 19, but for 18 or even 17 players."

Despite Tarasov's talk, the USSR was lucky to win the gold medal in 1969. The Soviets, Sweden and Czechoslovakia all finished with identical 8–2 records and goal differential was needed to break the tie. If the Swedes had scored another goal in their 1–0 victory over Czechoslovakia in the final game, they would have been World Champions. Czechoslovakia would have claimed the gold if they could have tied the game. As it was, the Soviets, with an unprecedented seven rookies on the roster, won their seventh straight world title to establish a new international hockey record.

1970 WORLD & EUROPEAN CHAMPIONSHIPS were scheduled for Canada, with games set for Winnipeg and Montreal. It was to be the first time that the tournament would be played in the country where hockey was born. In March, 1969, representatives of a new organization called Hockey Canada gathered in Toronto to select the best possible team to play at home.

Meanwhile, Canadian hockey officials were becoming more and more convinced that their top amateurs, even reinforced by ex-professionals, were unable to compete with the leading European national teams. Having won just three bronze medals with their own national team since 1964, Canadian representatives at the IIHF Congress in Stockholm in March, 1969 opened a discussion about the joint participation of amateurs and professionals. At the IIHF's summer congress in Switzerland in July, NHL president Clarence Campbell was among a 15-member Canadian delegation. He invited the six best players from teams in Pool B and Pool C to come to Canada and watch NHL games at the NHL's expense. A film about professional hockey was also shown with Canada's Prime Minister proposing to make the World Championships an open event.

Canada's emissaries were very successful. The IIHF agreed to make the rules of amateur hockey more consistent with those of the pro game and to allow nine professionals to play as an experiment for one year. It was also decided that amateur status would be given to any player who had left the pro game within six weeks of the World Championships instead of the previous standard of six months. However, meetings held in Geneva in January, 1970 produced so many reciprocal claims between the IIHF leadership and the Canadian organizing committee that the Canadians were finally prohibited from using professional players altogether. IOC president Avery Brundage was also strongly opposed to amateurs and professionals playing on the same sheet of ice. The Canadians reacted by withdrawing from all international hockey competition. Canada would not return to the IIHF World Championships until 1977.

As a result of the Canadian decision, the 1970 World Championships were hastily relocated to Stockholm, making the Swedish capital the first city to host the event two years in a row. Poland was brought up from Pool B to replace Canada, but managed just one tie in 10 games. The Soviet Union ran up a 9–1 record in winning the world title for the eighth year in a row.

1971 WORLD & EUROPEAN CHAMPIONSHIPS A record-setting number of participants—22—competed in three World Pools in 1971. The main Pool A World Championships were held in Switzerland. Beginning with this year, points were counted separately for the World and European Championships. The results of games between European and North American teams at the World Championships would no longer count towards the European title. The Soviet Union won its ninth straight World title, but when games against the United States were eliminated, Czechoslovakia had the better record and so claimed the European gold for the 11th time. It was the first time since 1962 that a nation other than the USSR was crowned European Champion.

After playing in Pool B in 1970, the U.S. was back in Pool A at this tournament, but it turned out to be for only one year. By scoring just one goal in a 5–1 loss to West Germany in their final game, the Americans were relegated to Pool B again for the 1972 World Championships.

1972 WINTER OLYMPICS The 1972 Olympics in Sapporo, marked the first major international hockey event to be held in Japan. The 1940 Winter Games had been scheduled for Sapporo, but were canceled due to World War II. The Soviet Union was triumphant once again in 1972 with four wins and a tie in five games. The surprise of the Olympics was the United States team. Seeded sixth in the tournament, and already relegated to Pool B for the upcoming World Championships, the Americans won the silver medal. The U.S. team featured two players who would go on fine professional careers in the World Hockey Association and the NHL: Robbie Ftorek and Mark Howe.

1972 WORLD & EUROPEAN CHAMPIONSHIPS The 1972 tournament in Czechoslovakia was held in April and marked the first time the World and European Championships were conducted independently of the Olympics. This was a first step in bringing Canada back to the World Championships, as the separation from the Olympics made it possible to consider the participation of professional players. Allowing pros to play at the World Championships would now no longer have an impact on the Olympic movement, in much the same way soccer's World Cup did not affect the Olympics.

Twenty-five years after its first victory in Prague, Czechoslovakia once again used home-ice advantage to win the gold medal. Czechoslovakia's third World Championship equaled Sweden in this regard and snapped a Soviet winning streak that had reached 10 consecutive World and/or Olympic victories. The 1972 World Championships marked the first time that the Soviet squad was not led by long-time coaches Arkady Chernyshov and Anatoli Tarasov, as Vsevolod Bobrov made his international coaching debut.

It was at the 1972 tournament in Prague that final arrangements were made for the September series between the USSR and Canada's NHL professionals. Canadians had long believed their best pros would easily defeat Europe's amateur champions, but Team Canada was hard pressed to defeat the Soviets and had to rally to win the last three games in Moscow to take the eight-game series 4–3–1. Paul Henderson scored the decisive goal with 34 seconds left in the final game to give Canada a 6–5 victory.

1973 WORLD & EUROPEAN CHAMPIONSHIPS were held in Moscow, and the USSR easily recaptured the title it had lost in Prague the year before. The tournament marked the first time since the European Championships in 1927 that the host nation won all of its games. The Soviets finished with a perfect record of 10–0.

Poland had made impressive strides by the 1973 World Championships. Under the guidance of Soviet coach Anatoli Yegorov, Poland had managed to land a place in Pool A but only recorded one win and one tie in 10 games played.

1974 WORLD & EUROPEAN CHAMPIONSHIPS A drug-testing policy was introduced by the International Ice Hockey Federation at its congress in July, 1969 and first implemented at the Winter Olympics in Sapporo in 1972. Two years later, this drug testing suddenly made headlines at the Pool A tournament of the World Championships.

Drug testing required that two players were selected at random from each team after each game. A random test on the first day of the 1974 tournament in Helsinki following Sweden's 4–1 win over Poland showed that Ulf Nilsson from Sweden had used ephedrine, which was on the IOC's list of banned substances.

As a result, Poland was awarded the victory by a score of 5–0. This "win" ultimately allowed Poland to remain in Pool A. Later in the tournament, it was discovered the Finland's goalie Stig Wetzell had also taken ephedrine and the host nation's 5–2 upset of Czechoslovakia was reversed to a 5–0 defeat.

Once again in 1974, it was the Soviet Union that emerged as World Champions with nine wins in 10 games.

1975 WORLD & EUROPEAN CHAMPIONSHIPS The format for the 1975 World Championships in Germany remained unchanged for the seventh consecutive year, but by this time the formula was satisfying neither spectators nor participants. The IIHF had become convinced that the results in the A Pool had become predictable, thereby hurting attendance.

Since the Canadians had withdrawn from the World tournament, the Soviets, Czechoslovaks and Swedes controlled the top places in the standings. The bottom teams in Pool A had managed very few victories. Poland, however, was showing noticeable improvement and finished fifth for the third year in a row in 1975 to once again avoid demotion to Pool B.

1976 WINTER OLYMPICS marked the second time the Games were held in Innsbruck, Austria. The event had originally been awarded to Denver, Colorado, but was moved after disgruntled taxpayers protested the cost of staging an Olympics. Canada and Sweden did not take part.

The first round of competition served to divide the field into medal and consolation events. Influenza would prove to have a great effect on the outcome of the tournament as most of the players on the Czechoslovakian team took sick. Frantisek Pospisil tested positive for a prohibited substance after traces of codeine were detected following a game between Poland and Czechoslovakia. Because of this positive test, the results of the game were reversed and entered into the records as a 1–0 win for Poland.

Despite these distractions, the last game of the tournament between the Soviet Union and Czechoslovakia proved to be a gem. The USSR trailed 2–0 midway through the second period when a pair of penalties left them two men short for two minutes. The Soviet penalty killers smothered the Czechoslovak attack, not allowing a single dangerous shot on goal during the two-man disadvantage.

The USSR eventually came from behind to tie the game 2–2 before the Czechoslovaks scored a go-ahead goal with nine minutes remaining in the third period. Taking advantage of a power-play, the Soviets tied the game with less than five minutes to play and then scored the eventual winner 24 seconds later.

The Soviet Union's gold medal represented the first time in Olympic hockey history that a team had won four consecutive Winter Games titles. Czechoslovakia took the silver medal while the West Germans were surprise winners of the bronze.

1976 WORLD & EUROPEAN CHAMPIONSHIPS The appointment of Dr. Gunther Sabetzki to the position of president of the IIHF its July 1975 congress in Switzerland led to a declaration that professional players would be allowed to compete at the 1976 World Championships. This move was made to entice Canada back into the international fold, and Canada did return, but not until the following year.

The 1976 World Championships were held in Katowice, in recognition of Poland's improved play in recent years. Pool A was expanded to eight teams, which allowed the United States to avoid relegation to Pool B after a last-place finish in 1975. The second opening had been offered to Canada, but went instead to Pool B runner-up West Germany.

With eight teams in Pool A, a new format was devised that would split the competing nations into two groups of four after an opening round-robin series. The top two nations from each of the two groups of four would then play a round-robin final, while the bottom four countries held a separate playoff. The United States used the new rules to advantage, employing seven pros from the NHL and World Hockey Association to break into the top four for the first time since 1962. The gold medal went to Czechoslovakia, who comfortably outdistanced the USSR with a record of 9–1.

1977 WORLD & EUROPEAN CHAMPIONSHIPS Canada returned to the World Championships in 1977 after an eight-year absence. The tournament in Austria began two weeks later than other World Championships, but the April dates still meant the best Canadian professional players in both the NHL and WHA were competing in their league playoffs. Canada's team in 1977 was selected only from players on six NHL clubs that had failed to qualify for postseason play. Canada finished out of the medals in fourth place, but did beat the eventual champions from Czechoslovakia 8–2, which was the worst loss ever suffered by a gold medal-winning team.

The Soviet Union was able to beat Canada twice, but a loss to Czechoslovakia and two losses to the silver medalists from Sweden meant the that for the first time the USSR had to settle for the bronze medal in both the World and European Championships. Czechoslovakia's victory gave them consecutive world titles for the first time in history.

1978 WORLD & EUROPEAN CHAMPIONSHIPS in Prague were staged from late April to early May, latest start date in the history of the event. This delayed start allowed the Canadian team to draw on players whose NHL clubs had been eliminated during the first round of the playoffs. Though the 20-man roster was assembled just nine days before the World Championships, Canada managed to win the bronze medal.

After two years of disappointment, the Soviet Union unveiled a roster that included nine newcomers. The Soviets managed to win the gold medal despite playing on the home ice of Czechoslovakia, the two-time defending World champions. The Soviet victory required a clutch 3–1 win over the host nation in the final game of the tournament.

Since the admittance of pro players to the World Championships, members of the same club team began to find themselves representing opposing national squads. This year in Prague, for example, two NHL players from the Minnesota North Stars defended Canada's colors, three played for Sweden and four were members of the United States team. Circumstances such as these had only previously been encountered in soccer's World Cup.

1979 WORLD & EUROPEAN CHAMPIONSHIPS Over the preceding decade, the IIHF, seeking to further perfect the game, did much to make the amateur and professional rules more consistent. This included the termination of a two-minute penalty as soon as the team on the power-play scored, the elimination of icing for teams playing short-handed, and the introduction of delayed penalties. Other decisions adopted during the May 1978 congress that went into effect at the 1979 World Championships included making it necessary for the defending team to touch the puck before icing was called, abandoning the change of ends in the middle of the third period when games were played indoors, and increasing the rosters to 22.

A record 26 nations competed at the World Championships in 1979, with the eight teams in Pool A playing in Moscow. At the suggestion of the USSR Ice Hockey Federation, these eight teams were split into two groups of four based on the standings from the previous year. After a round-robin series for each group, the top two teams from each side would advance to the medal round with the points they gained in the first round counting towards the final standings. The format was, in fact, the same as it had been at the World Championships in 1935, and allowed for the tournament to be played in 14 days instead of 19.

Because the Soviets wanted the tournament concluded in time for May Day celebrations, the World Championships began one week earlier than the year before. As a result, Canada began the tournament with only a 19-man roster made up of young players whose teams had missed the NHL playoffs. The Canadians played poorly and finished fourth. As in 1973, the host Soviets won every game en route to the gold medal with the second-place Czechoslovakian team finishing well behind in the standings.

1980 WINTER OLYMPICS No World and European Championships were played in this Olympic year. Unlike 1972 and 1976, no separate World Championships would be played following the Winter Games.

The gold medal victory by the United States was quickly dubbed a "Miracle on Ice." Professionals were still not allowed to compete at the Olympics, and so Canada and the U.S. once again had to rely on amateur national teams. Canada would finish sixth, while the Americans became champions. Coach Herb Brooks, who had been the last player cut from the 1960 gold medal team, stocked his American team with an assortment of unknown college players who played a pre-Olympic schedule of 60 games. The team was 42–14–3 over 59 games, before being crushed 10–3 by the Soviet Union just three days before their first game in Lake Placid.

The USA began the Olympic tournament with a 2–2 tie against Sweden on defenseman Bill Baker's goal with 27 seconds remaining. Jim Craig starred in net, as he would throughout the tournament. The Americans then downed Czechoslovakia 7–3 and followed up with easy victories over Norway and Romania. In the final game of the round-robin division series, the U.S. fell behind West Germany 2–0 after one period, but rebounded for a 4–2 victory. Both the U.S. and Sweden finished the round robin with 4–0–1 records, but the Swedes were ranked on top due to a better goal differential. As a result, the Americans would have to take on the undefeated Soviets in the first game of the medal round just 13 days after their humiliating pre-Olympic defeat.

On February 22, 1980 a crowd of 10,000 jammed the Olympic Arena, while millions more Americans, turned on by their team's surprising success, tuned in at home. The Soviets built up leads of 1–0 and 2–1 during the first period, but a Mark Johnson goal as time expired sent the teams to the dressing room tied 2–2. Soviet coach Victor Tikhonov replaced legendary goaltender Vladislav Tretiak with backup Vladimir Myshkin to start the second period. After 40 minutes, the Soviets led 3–2 and had outshot the Americans 30–10. In the third period, Johnson tied the game and captain Mark Eruzione put the U.S. ahead 4–3 with 10 minutes to go. Jim Craig made the lead hold up and an entire nation celebrated. The Americans faced Finland in the final game two days after the victory over the Soviet Union. A loss would have meant a silver medal, but the United States won gold with a 4–2 victory.

1981 WORLD & EUROPEAN CHAMPIONSHIPS After settling for the silver medal at the 1980 Olympics, the Soviet Union returned to top spot at the 1981 World Championships, winning the title for the third time running. Sweden, enthusiastically cheered by their fans at home, won the silver medal for the eleventh time. The Netherlands achieved a record of sorts, as the team from Holland had jumped from Pool C to Pool A in just two seasons.

1982 WORLD & EUROPEAN CHAMPIONSHIPS The format of the Pool A World Championships was changed again in 1982. All eight teams would play a round-robin series with the top four teams advancing to a medal round. As had been the case prior to 1979, teams would be credited with all the points they had accumulated in the first round, not just those gained against the other medal-round opponents. Only the results of the first round-robin series would be used to determine the European Champion.

By initially sending over a team stocked with junior players, Canada was able to wait until the first round of the NHL playoffs was finished before finalizing its roster. Wayne Gretzky, Bobby Clarke and Darryl Sittler helped give Canada its strongest team since returning to international competition in 1977, though the team only had time to practice once before play began.

The Soviet Union easily won the gold medal in Finland in 1982, and Czechoslovakia claimed the silver after tying the USSR 0–0 in the final game. The tie dropped Canada into third place, and resulted in protests by the Canadians that the Soviets had conspired to deny them a silver medal.

1983 WORLD & EUROPEAN CHAMPIONSHIPS Unlike the preceding year's tournament, medal-round contenders at the World Championships in 1983 would only count the points they earned in the final round in order to determine medal standings. The four bottom teams that did not qualify for the medal round after the opening round robin would count all of their points in determining the ranking from fifth to eighth place. The IIHF congress also ruled that teams must provide a preliminary entry list of not less than 19 players, with the remaining three roster spots eligible to be filled during the course of the championships. These new rules were introduced in order to better balance the competition for medals. As in 1982, only the results of the initial round-robin series would be used to crown the European Champion.

In winning the 1983 World Championships, the Soviets claimed their 19th title, equaling Canada's record.

1984 WINTER OLYMPICS The hockey competition at the 1984 Winter Olympics in Sarajevo comprised 12 teams competing in two separate divisions. Canada's Olympic team had posted a dismal 2–17–3 record in its last 22 exhibition games, and had seen players Mark Morrison and Don Dietrich disqualified after the Americans protested their former professional status. However, Russ Courtnall and Kirk Muller were added to the roster a week before the Olympics to boost the team's sagging offense.

Canada defeated the defending Olympic champions from the United States in the first game of the tournament and ran up four straight wins before losing to Czechoslovakia in the final game of their first-round schedule. Both nations advanced to the medal round, as did the Soviets and Swedes. Canada's weak offense eventually doomed the team to fourth place, while the USSR clinched the gold medal with a win over Czechoslovakia in the final game.

No World and European Championships were played in this Olympic year.

1985 WORLD & EUROPEAN CHAMPIONSHIPS By winning the initial round-robin portion of the tournament, the Soviet Union was once again European Champion, but because results of the first round were no longer carried over into the medal round of play, losses to Canada and Czechoslovakia saw the USSR fall to third place overall. The Soviet team was playing without legendary goalie Vladislav Tretiak for the first time since 1969.

Czechoslovakia won the World Championship for the sixth time in 1985, making this their third victory on home ice. Canada finished second for the first time since 1962. The talented Canadian team still had a chance for the gold medal entering the final game of the tournament against the host nation, but was beaten 5–3.

Sweden's poor play was a surprising feature of the 1985 World Championships. The sixth-place finish of the Tre Kronor was the worst result for the Swedes since 1931.

1986 WORLD & EUROPEAN CHAMPIONSHIPS were held in Moscow for the fourth time, and for the third time at home the Soviet Union won every game en route to the gold medal. However, the USSR did not clinch the title until the third period of the last game, when they beat Sweden 3–2. The Swedes were forced to play without star Peter Lindmark, the best goaltender of the tournament, who had been injured in a previous game.

The biggest surprise of the tournament was the poor showing of Czechoslovakia. The 1985 World Champions did not even qualify for the medal round and finished fifth. It was the first time since 1967 that Czechoslovakia finished out of the medals.

Canada finished third at the 1986 World Championships with a roster that included established NHL stars Denis Potvin and Brent Sutter, who made the tournament's second all-star team. Brett Hull made his international debut for the United States.

1987 WORLD & EUROPEAN CHAMPIONSHIPS Sweden won the World Championships in Vienna in 1987, 25 years after its last world title. Both Sweden and the Soviet Union had one win and two ties during the medal round, but the Swedes claimed the gold medal with a better goal differential largely achieved in a 9–0 win over Canada on the last day of the tournament.

The 1987 World Championships were marred by a scandal relating to the eligibility of West Germany's Miroslav Sikora. The West Germans had been playing well and appeared to have a chance to reach the medal round after scoring victories over Canada and Finland. However, the Finns filed a protest because Sikora had played for Poland at the 1976 European Junior Championships. International Ice Hockey Federation rules at that time prohibited players from representing more than one country in official tournaments, but the Germans stated that they had obtained permission from the IIHF for Sikora to play.

The IIHF Directorate suspended Sikora after the Finnish protest and stripped West Germany of its two wins. The Germans protested this decision and filed a lawsuit in a Vienna court, which eventually ruled in favor of Germany and ordered the IIHF to reinstate the two victories or pay a substantial fine. The IIHF Directorate voted 11–2 to accept the court's decision regarding the West German victories, but Sikora remained suspended for the rest of the tournament. Meanwhile, the distracted West German team lost its three remaining games and failed to make the medal round.

Pool D made its debut on the World and European hockey scene in 1987.

1988 WINTER OLYMPICS Several months before the start of the 1988 Olympic hockey tournament in Calgary, the decision was made to allowed teams to include professional players on their rosters. This made it possible for goalie Andy Moog, who was involved in a contract dispute with the Edmonton Oilers, to join the Canadian Olympic team. Oilers teammate Randy Gregg also joined the team, as did Brian Bradley of the Calgary Flames and Ken Yaremchuk of the Toronto Maple Leafs. Just a few days before the Olympics began, Tim Watters (Winnipeg Jets), Steve Tambellini (Vancouver Canucks) and Jim Peplinski (Calgary Flames) were also added to the roster. Despite these reinforcements, Canada wound up out of the medals with a fourth-place finish.

The Soviet Union dominated the tournament in Calgary, clinching the Olympic gold medal even before the last game (which they lost 2–1 to Finland). The Soviet team featured a 19-year-old rookie named Alexander Mogilny, who later went on to NHL stardom. The Finns took the silver in Calgary for their first Olympic medal.

No World and European Championships were played in this Olympic year.

1989 WORLD & EUROPEAN CHAMPIONSHIPS Sweden, who had won the last World Championships in 1987, were denied the title on home ice in 1989 by a Soviet team that was a perfect 10–0 during the tournament. The Swedes finished fourth. This year marked the last appearance together of the USSR's famous "Green Unit" of Viacheslav Fetisov, Alexei Kasatonov, Sergei Makarov, Igor Larionov and Vladimir Krutov. All five players joined NHL clubs the following season.

Canada won its fifth medal in the last six World Championships with a silver in Stockholm in 1989. In the middle of the tournament, a random drug test showed a positive result for Canadian defenseman Randy Carlyle. However, IIHF rules called for two samples to be taken from each player and a check of Carlyle's second sample 24 hours later cleared him of any wrongdoing.

The Americans weren't as lucky as Canada when it came to drug testing. The high levels of testosterone (a banned substance) found in the body of Corey Millen resulted in his suspension. Team USA officials tried to prove that this level was normal for Millen, but the IIHF did not reverse its decision.

1990 WORLD & EUROPEAN CHAMPIONSHIPS The USSR won the World Championships once again in Switzerland in 1990. The tournament featured great performances by two goaltenders. Arturs Irbe, who was named the tournament's best goalie, led the Soviets to the title while Czechoslovakia took the bronze medal on the strength of Dominik Hasek's play. Hasek was named to the tournament all-star team for the third year in a row. He moved to the NHL's Chicago Blackhawks the following year.

Norway returned to Pool A at the 1990 World Championships for the first time since 1965.

1991 WORLD & EUROPEAN CHAMPIONSHIPS in Finland marked the last time that eight nations competed in Pool A, as the decision was made to include 12 teams in subsequent years. More importantly, the IIHF decided that beginning in 1992, it would no longer award a separate European title as part of the World Championships.

Perhaps most significantly, the 1991 World Championships marked the last time Soviet players would wear the famous letters "CCCP" on their chests. The political breakup of the Soviet Union meant that the longtime hockey power would play as Russia after 1991. Political changes also saw the merging of East Germany and West Germany into one nation, and a new German team now appeared on the hockey scene.

Sweden won the World Championship in 1991, with Canada taking the silver medal. The USSR departed with a bronze medal.

1992 WINTER OLYMPICS After the breakup of the Soviet Union in January, 1992, the former Soviet Olympic committee decided to call its delegation to the Albertville Winter Games the "Unified Team" due to the fact that several athletes in various sports were from former Soviet republics. Though the hockey team was comprised only of ethnic Russian players, it was known as the Unified Team as well and played with no logo on its uniform. No national anthem was played when the former Soviets won the gold medal in hockey. The Olympic anthem was played instead.

The 1992 Olympic hockey tournament used a playoff system for the first time in the postwar era. The one-game elimination playoff system included eight teams in the quarterfinals and saw the four teams with the best records in the preliminary round reach the semifinals. Led by Joe Juneau and Eric Lindros, Canada advanced to the finals, but a 3–1 victory by the Unified Team denied the country its first Olympic hockey gold medal since 1952. Still, a silver medal represented Canada's best finish since winning the bronze in 1968.

1992 WORLD CHAMPIONSHIPS Like the Olympics, the World Championships introduced a one-game elimination playoff system in 1992. After a preliminary round involving two groups of six teams, the top four teams from each group advanced to the playoffs. Canada and Russia were both victims of the new system, as hockey's two historic powers were knocked out in the quarterfinals.

Sweden advanced through the playoffs to clinch the World Championships for the second year in a row, marking the first time consecutive wins had been recorded by a team other than the Soviet Union since Czechoslovakia won in 1976 and 1977.

Greece, Israel, Luxembourg and Turkey each made their debut at the World Championships in 1992, appearing in Pool C, Group 2.

1993 WORLD CHAMPIONSHIPS Former international star Boris Mikhailov took over as coach of the Russian team, replacing Viktor Tikhonov who had ruled the Soviet/Russian squad for 15 years. Mikhailov's World Championship coaching debut was a success as Russia won the gold medal. The Russians defeated Sweden in the final game, denying the Swedes a third straight World Championship.

Though Canada finished fourth after losing the bronze medal game to Czechoslovakia, the tournament was dominated by the brilliant performance of 20-year-old Canadian center Eric Lindros. Lindros led the tournament in both goals and points. He was named best forward and voted to the all-star team.

The Czech Republic made its first appearance at the World Championships in 1993 (replacing Czechoslovakia), while national teams from Slovenia and three former Soviet republics—Latvia, Ukraine and Kazakhstan—made their first appearances in Pool C. Latvia, which took part in World and European Championships before World War II, returned to the international hockey scene for the first time in more than half a century.

1994 WINTER OLYMPICS The International Olympic Committee decided to have stage its Winter and Summer Games in different years, so the Winter Olympics in Lillehammer, Norway took place just two years after the previous competition in Albertville, France.

Russia, Slovakia and the Czech Republic each made their Olympic hockey debut in Norway.

The exciting tournament had a thrilling conclusion with a shootout in the final game between Sweden and Canada. The winning goal by Peter Forsberg gave the Swedes their first Olympic championship. Three players on the Swedish team—Tomas Jonsson, Hakan Loob, and Mats Naslund—became the first players to win World, Olympic, and Stanley Cup titles in separate tournaments.

The loss to Sweden in the finals gave Canada its second consecutive Olympic silver medal. Russia lost to Finland in the third-place game and finished out of the medals for the first time in the history of Soviet/Russian Olympic hockey.

1994 WORLD CHAMPIONSHIPS For the first time since the Trail Smoke Eaters' victory in 1961, Canada won the World Championships in 1994. Avenging their loss to Sweden at the Olympics, the Canadians defeated Finland in a shoot-out when Luc Robitaille scored the winning goal. Canada's win was truly a team effort, as only Paul Kariya ranked among the top–10 leading scorers at the World Championships. Bill Ranford was spectacular in goal for Canada.

Great Britain returned to Pool A in 1994 for the first time since 1951. Slovakia, Belarus, Estonia and Croatia all made their debut in the Pool C World Championships.

1995 WORLD CHAMPIONSHIPS Finland won the World Championships for the first time in 1995, beating their rivals from Sweden in the gold-medal game. The Finns were led by the line of Jere Lehtinen, Saku Koivu and Ville Peltonen, all of whom were named to the tournament all-star team. For the second year in a row, Russia lost in the quarterfinals and did not have an opportunity to play for a medal.

For the first time in 20 years, the 1995 World Championships were played without the participation of NHL players. Because a long lockout delayed the start of their 1994–95 season, NHL teams were still playing and were unable to release their players go to represent their respective countries. Team Canada and the United States suffered the most from this situation.

Lithuania returned to the World tournament this year for the first time since 1938, competing in Pool C.

1996 WORLD CHAMPIONSHIPS A different team was crowned World champion for the fifth year in a row when the Czech Republic beat Canada in the gold medal game in Vienna in 1996. It was the first world title for players representing the Czech Republic. (Czechoslovakia last won in 1985).

The Czech Republic's victory came in the year in which Slovakia made its first appearance in Pool A. Like the Czech Republic, Slovakia was formerly a part of Czechoslovakia.

The growth of hockey on a world level and the changing political landscape saw 36 national teams play in Pools A, B, C and D in 1996.

1997 WORLD CHAMPIONSHIPS A new system was introduced for the World tournament in Finland in 1997. In the preliminaries, two groups of six teams each played round robins with the top three teams from each side advancing to a final group to play for the medals. The six remaining teams played off to determine rankings from seventh to 12th place.

The top six teams in the final group carried their points forward from the preliminary round. Each final-round team then played the three nations that had qualified for the finals from the other preliminary round group. The top two final-round teams then advanced to play in a best-of-three final, while the third- and fourth-place teams played one game for the bronze.

Sweden beat Canada in the first game of the finals, before the Canadians rallied to win two in a row and claim their 21st World Championship. Geoff Sanderson and Rob Blake had also been members of Canada's gold medal-winning team in 1994.

Latvia qualified for Pool A in 1997, returning to play with the world's top hockey nations for the first time since before World War II.

1998 WINTER OLYMPICS Qualification for the 1998 Olympics began in the fall of 1995. Hockey's six major nations (Canada, the Czech Republic, Finland, Russia, Sweden and the USA) were accorded six of eight berths in the final round at Nagano.

Based on the results of the 1995 Pool A World Championships, Italy and France were also admitted to the Olympics. Japan automatically qualified as the host country. These three nations were placed in an eight-team preliminary round.

To determine the five other preliminary round participants in Nagano, teams from 18 nations were put into four qualifying groups. The four winners of these groups were placed in two final qualifying groups along with the three teams that finished at the bottom of the standings at the Pool A World Championships in 1995 and the winner of 1995's Pool B tournament.

The first- and second-place finishers from each final qualifying group (Germany, Slovakia, Kazakhstan and Belarus) were promoted to take part in the Nagano Olympic tournament along with Austria, which won a playoff game between third-place teams.

The Olympic hockey tournament was played in two phases: a preliminary round and a final round. In the preliminary round Austria, Italy, Kazakhstan and Slovakia competed in Group A; Belarus, France, Germany and Japan competed in Group B. The winners of each group (Kazakhstan and Belarus) advanced to the final round to compete with Canada, the Czech Republic, Finland, Russia, Sweden and the United States.

Again divided into two groups of four, the eight top countries played a round robin to determine seedings for the quarterfinals. The quarterfinals, semifinals and finals were all single-game playoffs.

Beginning with the quarterfinals, the story of the Nagano Olympics was the sensational play of Czech goaltender Dominik Hasek. Despite being badly outshot, the defense held around Hasek and the entire Czech team gathered strength as the tournament progressed. They defeated the U.S. in the quarterfinals 4–1, got past Canada in the semifinals when Hasek stopped all five shots in a tie-breaking shootout and finally defeated Russia 1–0 to win the gold. Finland defeated Canada 4–2 to win the bronze medal.

1998 WORLD CHAMPIONSHIPS were expanded to include 16 countries. The teams were split into four groups of four, with a preliminary round robin played within each group to determine which eight nations would advance to play for the medals and which eight would be relegated to a consolation round.

The traditional hockey countries all advanced to the medal round with one exception. Though the Americans beat Switzerland 5–2 in their head-to-head matchup, both had identical records and Switzerland had a better goal-differential so the host nation moved on while the United States missed the medal round and eventually finished 12th. Switzerland continued its upset trend in the quarterfinal round, beating the Russians 4–2. Sweden, Finland and the Czech Republic also advanced, while Canada joined Russia, Belarus and Slovakia on the sidelines after dropping a must-win game 7–1 to a powerful Swedish team led by Peter Forsberg and Mats Sundin.

The semifinals were played in a two-game, total-goals format with Finland beating the Czech Republic 6–3 on the round and Sweden downing the Swiss team 11–3. Hopes of a medal for the host nation were dashed when the Czechs beat Switzerland 4–0 to take third place. Sweden edged Finland 1–0 on a goal by Johan Tornberg in game one of a two-game, total-goals final to win its first World Championship since 1992.

1999 WORLD CHAMPIONSHIPS For 1999 the IIHF introduced a new method of determining the winner in playoff rounds. Unlike previous years, if after a two-game semifinal or final series, both teams have an equal number of points, the winner is determined not by goal differential, but by means of a tie-breaker. This tie-breaker consists of a sudden death, 20-minute mini-game. If neither team scores in the tie-breaker, a shoot-out is used to determine the winner.

Canada, Sweden, the Czech Republic and Finland finished first in their preliminary groups and, after a second round of play, advanced to the final four. Russia failed to advance to the semifinal round despite a brilliant performance by Alexei Yashin (the only NHLer on the team), who scored eight goals in six games.

The semifinal between the Czech Republic and Canada mirrored their Olympic battle in Nagano. Both teams won one game and played a scoreless tie-breaker before the Czechs won in a shoot-out. A tie-breaker determined the winner in the other semifinal, and later, in the final as well where the Czech Republic beat the Finns. The Czechs won the first game 3–1 while Finland won game two 4–1. In the resulting tie-breaker, Jan Hlavac scored the sudden-death gold medal-winner.

2000 WORLD CHAMPIONSHIPS were staged in a new arena constructed for the tournament in St. Petersburg, Russia. Expectations were high for the home team that had been reinforced with 14 NHL players including Pavel Bure, Alexei Zhamnov, Alexei Zhitnik, Valeri Kamensky and Alexei Yashin. Despite playing in their home country, the Russian team never performed well, finishing in 11th place, by far the poorest showing by a Russian or Soviet team in the history of the tournament.

The Czech Republic won its second consecutive World Championship despite dressing few NHLers and despite the fact that their coach, Ivan Hlinka, could not attend because he was coaching Pittsburgh in the NHL playoffs. The Slovaks finished a strong second to record the best result in their nation's history.

Canada lost its semifinal game to the Czech Republic and then lost the bronze medal game to Finland, after being victimized by soft goals late in the third period in both encounters.

Miroslav Satan led the tournament with ten goals for Slovakia.

IIHF COUNTRY ABBREVIATIONS

Includes countries that were later renamed:
Bohemia
Commonwealth of Independent States,
Czechoslovakia,
East Germany,
Soviet Union,
West Germany

Andorra	AND
Australia	AUS
Austria	AUT
Azerbaijan	AZE
Belarus	BLR
Belgium	BEL
Bohemia	BOH
Brazil	BRA
Bulgaria	BUL
Commonwealth of Independent States	CIS
Canada	CAN
China	PRC
Chinese Taipei	TPE
Croatia	CRO
Czech Republic	CZE
Czechoslovakia	TCH
Denmark	DEN
East Germany	GDR
Estonia	EST
Finland	FIN
France	FRA
Germany	GER
Great Britain	GBR
Greece	GRE
Hong Kong	HKG
Hungary	HUN
Iceland	ISL
India	IND
Israel	ISR
Italy	ITA
Japan	JAP
Kazakhstan	KAZ
Korea, North	PRK
Korea, South	KOR
Kuweit	KUW
Latvia	LAT
Lithuania	LIT
Luxembourg	LUX
Mexico	MEX
Netherlands	HOL
New Zealand	NZL
Norway	NOR
Poland	POL
Romania	ROM
Russia	RUS
Slovakia	SVK
Slovenia	SLO
South Africa	SAF
Soviet Union	URS
Spain	ESP
Sweden	SWE
Switzerland	SUI
Thailand	THA
Turkey	TUR
U.S.A.	USA
Ukraine	UKR
West Germany	FRG
Yugoslavia	YUG

WINTER OLYMPIC STANDINGS, RANKINGS, MEDAL ROUND GAME RESULTS, AND LEADING SCORERS

Cumulative Medal Rankings, 1924–1998

	G	S	B	Total	Last Medal
1. USSR/Russia*	8	2	1	11	**Silver 98**
2. Canada	5	4	2	11	Silver 94
3. USA	2	5	1	8	Gold 80
4. Sweden	1	2	4	7	Gold 94
5. Czechoslovakia/ Czech Republic	1	4	3	8	**Gold 98**
6. Great Britain	1	0	1	2	Gold 36
7. Finland	0	1	1	2	Bronze 94
8. W. Germany	0	0	2	2	Bronze 76
9. Switzerland	0	0	2	2	Bronze 48
10. Finland	0	0	1	1	**Bronze 98**

* Soviet Union/Russia played as the Unified Team in 1992.

Antwerp, Belgium • 1920
(unofficial)

Hockey was played at the 1920 Summer Olympics in Antwerp, Belgium. This tournament is not counted in cumulative Winter Olympic Hockey statistics. The IIHF has declared it the first World Championship. Standings can be found on page 513.

1920 Final Rankings
1. Canada
2. USA
3. Czechoslovakia
4. Sweden
5. Switzerland

Chamonix, France • 1924

Group A

Team	GP	W	L	T	GF	GA	PTS
Canada	3	3	0	0	85	0	6
Sweden	3	2	1	0	18	25	4
Czech.	3	1	2	0	14	41	2
Switzerland	3	0	3	0	2	53	0

Group B

Team	GP	W	L	T	GF	GA	PTS
USA	3	3	0	0	52	0	6
Great Britain	3	2	1	0	34	16	4
France	3	1	2	0	9	42	2
Belgium	3	0	3	0	8	35	0

Final Round

Team	GP	W	L	T	GF	GA	PTS
Canada	3	3	0	0	47	3	6
USA	3	2	1	0	32	6	4
Great Britain	3	1	2	0	6	33	2
Sweden	3	0	3	0	3	46	0

1924 Final Rankings
1. Canada
2. USA
3. Great Britain
4. Sweden
5. Czechoslovakia
5. France
7. Switzerland
7. Belgium

St. Moritz, Switzerland • 1928

Group A

Team	GP	W	L	T	GF	GA	PTS
Great Britain	3	2	1	0	10	6	4
France	3	2	1	0	6	5	4
Belgium	3	2	1	0	9	10	4
Hungary	3	0	3	0	2	6	0

Group B

Team	GP	W	L	T	GF	GA	PTS
Sweden	2	1	0	1	5	2	3
Czech.	2	1	1	0	3	5	2
Poland	2	0	0	1	4	5	1

Group C

Team	GP	W	L	T	GF	GA	PTS
Switzerland	2	1	0	1	5	4	3
Austria	2	0	0	2	4	4	2
Germany	2	0	0	1	0	1	1

Final Round

Team	GP	W	L	T	GF	GA	PTS
Canada	3	3	0	0	38	0	6
Sweden	3	2	1	0	7	12	4
Switzerland	3	1	2	0	4	17	2
Great Britain	3	0	3	0	1	21	0

1928 Final Rankings
1. Canada
2. Sweden
3. Switzerland
4. Great Britain
5. France
5. Czechoslovakia
5. Austria
8. Belgium
8. Poland
8. Germany
11. Hungary

Lake Placid, New York, USA • 1932

Team	GP	W	L	T	GF	GA	PTS
Canada	6	5	0	1	32	4	11
USA	6	4	1	1	27	5	9
Germany	6	2	4	0	7	26	4
Poland	6	0	6	0	3	34	0

1932 Final Rankings
1. Canada
2. USA
3. Germany
4. Poland

Garmisch-Partenkirchen, Germany • 1936

Group A

Team	GP	W	L	T	GF	GA	PTS
Canada	3	3	0	0	24	3	6
Austria	3	2	1	0	11	7	4
Poland	3	1	2	0	11	12	2
Latvia	3	0	0	3	3	27	0

Group B

Team	GP	W	L	T	GF	GA	PTS
Germany	3	2	1	0	5	1	4
USA	3	2	1	0	5	2	4
Italy	3	1	2	0	2	5	2
Switzerland	3	1	2	0	1	5	2

Group C

Team	GP	W	L	T	GF	GA	PTS
Czech.	3	3	0	0	10	0	6
Hungary	3	2	1	0	14	5	4
France	3	1	2	0	4	7	2
Belgium	3	0	3	0	4	20	6

Group D

Team	GP	W	L	T	GF	GA	PTS
Great Britain	2	2	0	0	4	0	4
Sweden	2	1	1	0	2	1	2
Japan	2	0	2	0	0	5	0

Group A Semifinal Round

Team	GP	W	L	T	GF	GA	PTS
Great Britain	3	2	0	1	8	3	5
Canada	3	2	1	0	22	4	4
Germany	3	1	1	1	5	8	3
Hungary	3	0	0	3	2	22	0

Group B Semifinal Round

Team	GP	W	L	T	GF	GA	PTS
USA	3	3	0	0	5	1	6
Czech.	3	2	1	0	6	4	4
Sweden	3	1	2	0	3	6	2
Austria	3	0	3	0	1	4	0

Final Round

Team	GP	W	L	T	GF	GA	PTS
Great Britain	3	2	0	1	7	1	5
Canada	3	2	1	0	9	2	4
USA	3	1	1	1	2	1	3
Czech.	3	0	3	0	0	14	0

1936 Final Rankings
1. Great Britain
2. Canada
3. USA
4. Czechoslovakia
5. Germany
5. Sweden
7. Hungary
7. Austria

St. Moritz, Switzerland • 1948

Team	GP	W	L	T	GF	GA	PTS
Canada	7	6	0	1	57	2	13
Czech.	7	6	0	1	76	15	13
Switzerland	7	5	2	0	62	17	10
Sweden	7	4	3	0	53	23	8
Great Britain	7	3	4	0	36	43	6
Poland	7	2	5	0	25	74	4
Austria	7	1	6	0	31	64	2
Italy	7	0	7	0	23	125	0

1948 Final Rankings
1. Canada
2. Czechoslovakia
3. Switzerland
4. Sweden
5. Great Britain
6. Poland
7. Austria
8. Italy

Oslo, Norway • 1952

Team	GP	W	L	T	GF	GA	PTS
Canada	8	7	0	1	71	1	15
USA	8	6	1	1	43	21	13
Sweden	8	6	2	0	48	19	12
Czech.	8	6	2	0	47	18	12
Switzerland	8	4	4	0	40	40	8
Poland	8	2	5	1	21	56	5
Finland	8	2	6	0	21	60	4
W. Germany	8	1	6	1	21	53	3
Norway	8	0	8	0	15	46	0

1952 Final Rankings
1. Canada
2. USA
3. Sweden
4. Czechoslovakia
5. Switzerland
6. Poland
7. Finland
8. W. Germany
9. Norway

Cortina d'Ampezzo, Italy • 1956

Group A

Team	GP	W	L	T	GF	GA	PTS
Canada	3	3	0	0	30	1	6
W. Germany	3	1	1	1	9	6	3
Italy	3	0	1	2	5	7	2
Austria	3	0	2	1	2	32	1

Group B

Team	GP	W	L	T	GF	GA	PTS
Czech.	2	2	0	0	12	6	4
USA	2	1	1	0	7	4	2
Poland	2	0	2	0	3	12	0

Group C

Team	GP	W	L	T	GF	GA	PTS
Soviet Union	2	2	0	0	15	4	4
Sweden	2	1	1	0	7	10	2
Switzerland	2	0	2	0	8	16	0

Final Round

Team	GP	W	L	T	GF	GA	PTS
Soviet Union	5	5	0	0	25	5	10
USA	5	4	1	0	26	12	8
Canada	5	3	2	0	23	11	6
Sweden	5	1	3	1	10	17	3
Czech.	5	1	4	0	20	30	2
W. Germany	5	0	4	1	6	35	1

Consolation Round

Team	GP	W	L	T	GF	GA	PTS
Italy	3	3	0	0	21	7	6
Poland	3	2	1	0	12	10	4
Switzerland	3	1	2	0	12	8	2
Austria	3	0	3	0	9	19	0

1956 Final Rankings
1. Soviet Union
2. USA
3. Canada
4. Sweden
5. Czechoslovakia
6. W. Germany
7. Italy
8. Poland
9. Switzerland
10. Austria

1956 Scoring Leaders

Player	Team	GP	G	A	PTS	PIM
Jim Logan	Canada	8	7	5	12	2
Paul Knox	Canada	8	7	5	12	2
Vsevolod Bobrov	Soviet Union	7	9	2	11	4
Gerry Theberge	Canada	8	9	2	11	8
Jack McKenzie	Canada	8	7	4	11	4
John Mayasich	USA	7	7	3	10	2
Alexei Guryshev	Soviet Union	7	7	2	9	0
Vlastimil Bubnik	Czech.	7	5	4	9	14
George Scholes	Canada	8	5	3	8	2

Squaw Valley, California, USA • 1960

Group A

Team	GP	W	L	T	GF	GA	PTS
Canada	2	2	0	0	24	3	4
Sweden	2	1	1	0	21	5	2
Japan	2	0	2	0	1	38	0

Group B

Team	GP	W	L	T	GF	GA	PTS
Soviet Union	2	2	0	0	16	4	4
W. Germany	2	1	1	0	4	9	2
Finland	2	0	2	0	5	12	0

Group C

Team	GP	W	L	T	GF	GA	PTS
USA	2	2	0	0	19	6	4
Czech.	2	1	1	0	23	6	2
Austria	2	0	2	0	2	30	0

Final Round

Team	GP	W	L	T	GF	GA	PTS
USA	5	5	0	0	29	11	10
Canada	5	4	1	0	31	12	8
Soviet Union	5	2	2	1	24	19	5
Czech.	5	2	3	0	21	23	4
Sweden	5	1	3	1	19	19	3
W. Germany	5	0	5	0	5	45	0

Consolation Round

Team	GP	W	L	T	GF	GA	PTS
Finland	4	3	0	1	50	11	7
Japan	4	2	1	1	32	22	5
Austria	4	0	4	0	8	57	0

1960 Final Rankings

1. USA
2. Canada
3. Soviet Union
4. Czechoslovakia
5. Sweden
6. W. Germany
7. Finland
8. Japan
9. Austria

1960 Scoring Leaders

Player	Team	GP	G	A	PTS	PIM
Fred Etcher	Canada	7	9	12	21	0
Bobby Attersley	Canada	7	6	12	18	4
Bill Cleary	USA	7	7	7	14	2
Bill Christian	USA	7	2	11	13	2
G. Samolenko	Canada	7	8	4	12	0
Lars E. Lundvall	Sweden	7	8	4	12	2
Vaclav Panucek	Czech.	7	7	5	12	0
John Mayasich	USA	7	7	5	12	2
Nisse Nilsson	Sweden	7	7	5	12	4
V. Alexandrov	Soviet Union	7	7	5	12	8
Butch Martin	Canada	7	6	6	12	14
Ronald Petersson	Sweden	7	4	8	12	2

Innsbruck, Austria • 1964

Group A

Team	GP	W	L	T	GF	GA	PTS
Soviet Union	7	7	0	0	54	10	14
Sweden	7	5	2	0	47	16	10
Czech.	7	5	2	0	38	19	10
Canada	7	5	2	0	32	17	10
USA	7	2	5	0	29	33	4
Finland	7	2	5	0	10	31	4
W. Germany	7	2	5	0	13	49	4
Switzerland	7	0	7	0	9	57	0

Group B

Team	GP	W	L	T	GF	GA	PTS
Poland	7	6	1	0	40	13	12
Norway	7	5	2	0	40	19	10
Japan	7	4	2	1	35	31	9
Romania	7	3	3	1	31	28	7
Austria	7	3	3	1	24	28	7
Yugoslavia	7	3	3	1	29	37	7
Italy	7	2	5	0	24	42	4
Hungary	7	0	7	0	14	39	0

1964 Final Rankings

1. Soviet Union
2. Sweden
3. Czechoslovakia
4. Canada
5. USA
6. Finland
7. W. Germany
8. Switzerland
9. Poland
10. Norway
11. Japan
12. Romania
13. Austria
14. Yugoslavia
15. Italy
16. Hungary

1964 Scoring Leaders

Player	Team	GP	G	A	PTS	PIM
Sven Tumba	Sweden	7	8	3	11	0
Ulf Sterner	Sweden	7	6	5	11	0
Victor Yakushev	Soviet Union	7	7	3	10	0
Boris Mayorov	Soviet Union	7	7	3	10	0
Jiri Dolana	Czech.	7	7	3	10	0
Vy. Starshinov	Soviet Union	7	7	3	10	6
Josef Cerny	Czech.	7	5	5	10	2
A. Andersson	Sweden	7	7	2	9	8
K. Loktev	Soviet Union	7	4	5	9	8
Gary Dineen	Canada	7	3	6	9	10

Grenoble, France • 1968

Group A

Team	GP	W	L	T	GF	GA	PTS
Soviet Union	7	6	1	0	48	10	12
Czech.	7	5	1	1	33	17	11
Canada	7	5	2	0	28	15	10
Sweden	7	4	2	1	23	18	9
Finland	7	3	3	1	17	23	7
USA	7	2	4	1	23	28	5
W. Germany	7	1	6	0	13	39	2
E. Germany	7	0	7	0	13	48	0

Group B

Team	GP	W	L	T	GF	GA	PTS
Yugoslavia	5	5	0	0	33	9	10
Japan	5	4	1	0	27	12	8
Norway	5	3	2	0	15	15	6
Romania	5	2	3	0	22	23	4
Austria	5	1	4	0	12	27	2
France	5	0	5	0	9	32	0

1968 Final Rankings

1. Soviet Union
2. Czechoslovakia
3. Canada
4. Sweden
5. Finland
6. USA
7. W. Germany
8. E. Germany
9. Yugoslavia
10. Japan
11. Norway
12. Romania
13. Austria
14. France

1968 Scoring Leaders

Player	Team	GP	G	A	PTS	PIM
Anatoli Firsov	Soviet Union	7	12	4	16	4
Vladimir Vikulov	Soviet Union	7	2	10	12	2
Vyatch. Starshinov	Soviet Union	7	6	6	12	2
Victor Populanov	Soviet Union	7	6	6	12	10
Josef Golonka	Czech.	7	4	6	10	8
Jan Hrbaty	Czech.	7	2	7	9	2
Fran Huck	Canada	7	4	5	9	10
Marshall Johnston	Canada	7	2	6	8	4
Jack Morrison	USA	7	2	6	8	10
V. Nedomansky	Czech.	7	5	2	7	4

Sapporo, Japan • 1972

Group A

Team	GP	W	L	T	GF	GA	PTS
Soviet Union	5	4	0	1	33	13	9
USA	5	3	2	0	18	15	6
Czech.	5	3	2	0	26	13	6
Sweden	5	2	2	1	17	13	5
Finland	5	2	3	0	14	24	4
Poland	5	0	5	0	9	39	0

Group B

Team	GP	W	L	T	GF	GA	PTS
W. Germany	4	3	1	0	22	10	6
Norway	4	3	1	0	16	14	6
Japan	4	2	1	1	17	16	5
Switzerland	4	0	2	2	9	16	2
Yugoslavia	4	0	3	1	9	17	1

1972 Final Rankings

1. Soviet Union
2. USA
3. Czechoslovakia
4. Sweden
5. Finland
6. Poland
7. W. Germany
8. Norway
9. Japan
10. Switzerland
11. Yugoslavia

1972 Scoring Leaders

Player	Team	GP	G	A	PTS	PIM
Valeri Kharlamov	Soviet Union	5	9	6	15	2
V. Nedomansky	Czech.	5	6	3	9	0
Vladimir Vikulov	Soviet Union	5	5	4	9	0
Craig Sarner	USA	5	4	5	9	0
Kevin Ahearn	USA	5	4	3	7	0
Alexander Maltsev	Soviet Union	5	4	3	7	0
Anatoli Firsov	Soviet Union	5	2	5	7	0
Yuri Blinov	Soviet Union	5	3	3	6	0
Jiri Kochta	Czech.	5	3	3	6	0
Richard Farda	Czech.	5	1	5	6	0

Innsbruck, Austria • 1976

Group A

Team	GP	W	L	T	GF	GA	PTS
Soviet Union	5	5	0	0	40	11	10
Czech.	5	3	2	0	17	10	6
W. Germany	5	2	3	0	21	24	4
Finland	5	2	3	0	19	18	4
USA	5	2	3	0	15	21	4
Poland	5	0	5	0	9	37	0

Group B

Team	GP	W	L	T	GF	GA	PTS
Romania	5	4	1	0	23	15	8
Austria	5	3	2	0	18	14	6
Japan	5	3	2	0	20	18	6
Yugoslavia	5	3	2	0	22	19	6
Switzerland	5	2	3	0	24	22	4
Bulgaria	5	0	5	0	19	38	0

1976 Final Rankings

1. Soviet Union
2. Czechoslovakia
3. W. Germany
4. Finland
5. USA
6. Poland
7. Romania
8. Austria
9. Japan
10. Yugoslavia
11. Switzerland
12. Bulgaria

1976 Scoring Leaders

Player	Team	GP	G	A	PTS	PIM
Vladimir Shadrin	Soviet Union	5	6	4	10	0
Alexander Maltsev	Soviet Union	5	5	5	10	0
Victor Shalimov	Soviet Union	5	5	5	10	2
Erich Kuhnhackl	W. Germany	5	5	5	10	10
Valeri Kharlamov	Soviet Union	5	3	6	9	6
Ernst Kopf	W. Germany	5	3	5	8	2
Vladimir Petrov	Soviet Union	5	4	3	7	8
A. Yakushev	Soviet Union	5	3	4	7	2
Bob Dobek	USA	5	3	4	7	4
Lorenz Funk	W. Germany	5	2	5	7	4
Victor Zhluktov	Soviet Union	5	1	6	7	2

Lake Placid, New York, USA • 1980

Red Division

Team	GP	W	L	T	GF	GA	PTS
Soviet Union	5	5	0	0	51	11	10
Finland	5	3	2	0	26	18	6
Canada	5	3	2	0	28	12	6
Poland	5	2	3	0	15	23	4
Holland	5	1	3	1	16	43	3
Japan	5	0	4	1	7	36	1

Blue Division

Team	GP	W	L	T	GF	GA	PTS
Sweden	5	4	0	1	26	7	9
USA	5	4	0	1	25	10	9
Czech.	5	3	2	0	34	16	6
Romania	5	1	3	1	13	29	3
W. Germany	5	1	4	0	21	30	2
Norway	5	0	4	1	9	36	1

Final Round

Team	GP	W	L	T	GF	GA	PTS
USA	3	2	0	1	10	7	5
Soviet Union	3	2	1	0	16	8	4
Sweden	3	0	1	2	7	14	2
Finland	3	0	2	1	7	11	1

1980 Final Rankings

1. USA
2. Soviet Union
3. Sweden
4. Finland
5. Czechoslovakia
6. Canada
7. Poland
8. Holland
9. Romania
10. W. Germany
11. Norway
12. Japan

1980 Scoring Leaders

Player	Team	GP	G	A	PTS	PIM
Milan Novy	Czech.	6	7	8	15	0
Peter Stastny	Czech.	6	7	7	14	6
Jaroslav Pouzar	Czech.	6	8	5	13	8
Alexander Golikov	Soviet Union	7	7	6	13	6
Jukka Porvari	Finland	7	7	4	11	4
Boris Mikhailov	Soviet Union	7	6	5	11	2
Vladimir Krutov	Soviet Union	7	6	5	11	4
Sergei Makarov	Soviet Union	7	5	6	11	2
Marian Stastny	Czech.	6	5	6	11	4
Mark Johnson	USA	7	5	6	11	6

Sarajevo, Yugoslavia • 1984

Group A

Team	GP	W	L	T	GF	GA	PTS
Soviet Union	5	5	0	0	42	5	10
Sweden	5	3	1	1	34	15	7
W. Germany	5	3	1	1	27	17	7
Poland	5	1	4	0	16	37	2
Italy	5	1	4	0	15	31	2
Yugoslavia	5	1	4	0	8	37	2

Group B

Team	GP	W	L	T	GF	GA	PTS
Czech.	5	5	0	0	38	7	10
Canada	5	4	1	0	24	10	8
Finland	5	2	2	1	27	19	5
USA	5	1	2	2	16	17	4
Austria	5	1	4	0	13	37	2
Norway	5	0	4	1	15	43	1

Final Round

Team	GP	W	L	T	GF	GA	PTS
Soviet Union	3	3	0	0	16	1	6
Czech.	3	2	1	0	6	2	4
Sweden	3	1	2	0	3	12	2
Canada	3	0	3	0	0	10	0

Consolation Round

Team	GP	W	L	T	GF	GA	PTS
W. Germany	1	1	0	0	7	4	2
USA	1	1	0	0	7	4	2
Finland	1	0	1	0	4	7	0
Poland	1	0	1	0	4	7	0

1984 Final Rankings

1. Soviet Union
2. Czechoslovakia
3. Sweden
4. Canada
5. W. Germany
6. Finland
7. USA
8. Poland

1984 Scoring Leaders

Player	Team	GP	G	A	PTS	PIM
Erich Kuhnhackl	W. Germany	6	8	6	14	12
Peter Gradin	Sweden	7	9	4	13	6
N. Drozdetski	Soviet Union	7	10	2	12	2
V. Fetisov	Soviet Union	7	3	8	11	8
Petri Skriko	Finland	6	6	4	10	8
Vladimir Ruzicka	Czech.	7	4	6	10	0
R. Summanen	Finland	6	4	6	10	4
Darius Rusnak	Czech.	7	4	6	10	6
Jiri Hrdina	Czech.	7	4	6	10	10
Vincent Lukac	Czech.	7	4	5	9	2
Viktor Tjumenev	Soviet Union	6	0	9	9	2

Calgary, Canada • 1988

Group A

Team	GP	W	L	T	GF	GA	PTS
Finland	5	3	1	1	22	8	7
Sweden	5	2	0	3	23	10	7
Canada	5	3	1	1	17	12	7
Switzerland	5	3	2	0	19	10	6
Poland	5	0	4	1	3	13	1
France	5	1	4	0	10	41	0

Group B

Team	GP	W	L	T	GF	GA	PTS
Soviet Union	5	5	0	0	32	10	10
W. Germany	5	4	1	0	19	12	8
Czech.	5	3	2	0	23	14	6
USA	5	2	3	0	27	27	4
Austria	5	0	4	1	12	29	1
Norway	5	0	4	1	11	32	1

Final Round

Team	GP	W	L	T	GF	GA	PTS
Soviet Union	5	4	1	0	25	7	8
Finland	5	3	1	1	18	10	7
Sweden	5	2	1	2	15	16	6
Canada	5	2	2	1	17	14	5
W. Germany	5	1	4	0	8	26	2
Czech.	5	1	4	0	12	22	2

1988 Final Rankings

1. Soviet Union
2. Finland
3. Sweden
4. Canada
5. W. Germany
6. Czechoslovakia
7. USA
8. Switzerland
9. Austria
10. Poland
11. France
12. Norway

1988 Scoring Leaders

Player	Team	GP	G	A	PTS	PIM
Vladimir Krutov	Soviet Union	8	6	9	15	0
Igor Larionov	Soviet Union	8	4	9	13	4
V. Fetisov	Soviet Union	8	4	9	13	6
Corey Millen	USA	6	6	5	11	4
Dusan Pasek	Czech.	8	6	5	11	8
Sergei Makarov	Soviet Union	8	3	8	11	10
Erkki Lehtonen	Finland	8	4	6	10	2
Anders Eldebrink	Sweden	8	4	6	10	4
Igor Liba	Czech.	8	4	6	10	8
Gerd Truntschka	W. Germany	8	3	7	10	10
Raimo Helminen	Finland	7	2	8	10	4

Albertville, France • 1992

Group A

Team	GP	W	L	T	GF	GA	PTS
USA	5	4	0	1	18	7	9
Sweden	5	3	0	2	22	11	8
Finland	5	3	0	1	22	11	7
Germany	5	2	3	0	11	12	4
Italy	5	1	4	0	18	24	2
Poland	5	0	5	0	4	30	0

Group B

Team	GP	W	L	T	GF	GA	PTS
Canada	5	4	1	0	28	9	8
Unified Team*	5	4	1	0	32	10	8
Czechoslovakia	5	4	1	0	25	15	8
France	5	2	3	0	14	22	4
Switzerland	5	1	4	0	13	25	2
Norway	5	0	5	0	7	38	0

* Soviet Union/Russia played as Unified Team in 1992.

Medal Round

Canada	4	Germany	3
Czechoslovakia	3	Sweden	1
USA	4	France	1
Unified Team	6	Finland	1

Semifinals

Canada	4	Czechoslovakia	2
Unified Team	5	USA	2

Bronze Medal Game

Czechoslovakia	6	USA	1

Gold Medal Game

Unified Team	3	Canada	1

1992 Final Rankings

1. Unified Team
2. Canada
3. Czechoslovakia
4. USA
5. Sweden
6. Germany
7. Finland
8. France
9. Norway
10. Switzerland
11. Poland
12. Italy

1992 Scoring Leaders

Player PIM?	Team	GP	G	A	PTS
Joe Juneau	Canada	8	6	9	15
Andrei Khomutov	Unified	8	7	7	14
Robert Lang	Czech.	8	5	8	13
Teemu Selanne	Finland	8	7	4	11
Eric Lindros	Canada	8	5	6	11
H. Jarvenpaa	Finland	8	5	6	11
V. Bykov	Unified	8	4	7	11
Yuri Khmylev	Unified	8	4	6	10
Mika Nieminen	Finland	8	4	6	10
N. Borschevsky	Unified	8	7	2	9

Lillehammer, Norway • 1994

Group A

Team	GP	W	L	T	GF	GA	PTS
Finland	5	5	0	0	25	4	10
Germany	5	3	2	0	11	14	6
Czech Rep.	5	3	2	0	16	11	6
Russia	5	3	2	0	20	14	6
Austria	5	1	4	0	13	28	2
Norway	5	0	5	0	5	19	0

Group B

Team	GP	W	L	T	GF	GA	PTS
Slovakia	5	3	0	2	26	14	8
Canada	5	3	1	1	17	11	7
Sweden	5	3	1	1	23	13	7
USA	5	1	1	3	21	17	5
Italy	5	1	4	0	15	31	2
France	5	0	4	1	11	27	1

Quarterfinals

Canada	3	Czech Rep.	2
Finland	6	USA	1
Sweden	3	Germany	0
Russia	3	Slovakia	2

Semifinals

Canada	5	Finland	3
Sweden	4	Russia	3

Bronze Medal Game

Finland	4	Russia	0

Gold Medal Game

Sweden	3	Canada	2

1994 Final Standings

1. Sweden
2. Canada
3. Finland
4. Russia
5. Czech Republic
6. Slovakia
7. Germany
8. USA
9. Italy
10. France
11. Norway
12. Austria

1994 Scoring Leaders

Player	Team	GP	G	A	PTS	PIM
Zigmund Palffy	Slovakia	8	3	7	10	8
Miroslav Satan	Slovakia	8	9	0	9	0
Peter Stastny	Slovakia	8	5	4	9	9
Hakan Loob	Sweden	8	4	5	9	2
Gates Orlando	Italy	7	3	6	9	41
Patrik Juhlin	Sweden	8	7	1	8	16
Jiri Kucera	Czech Rep.	8	6	2	8	4
Marty Dallman	Austria	7	4	4	8	8
Mika Nieminen	Finland	8	3	5	8	0
David Sacco	USA	8	3	5	8	12
Peter Forsberg	Sweden	8	2	6	8	6

Nagano, Japan • 1998 • Men

Preliminary Round

Group A

Team	GP	W	L	T	GF	GA	Pts
Kazakhstan	3	2	0	1	14	11	5
Slovakia	3	1	1	1	9	9	3
Italy	3	1	2	0	11	11	2
Austria	3	0	1	2	9	12	2

Group B

Team	GP	W	L	T	GF	GA	Pts
Belarus	3	2	0	1	14	4	5
Germany	3	2	1	0	7	9	4
France	3	1	2	0	5	8	2
Japan	3	0	2	1	5	10	1

Final Round

Group A

Team	GP	W	L	T	GF	GA	Pts
Canada	3	3	0	0	12	3	6
Sweden	3	2	1	0	11	7	4
USA	3	1	2	0	8	10	2
Belarus	3	0	3	0	4	15	0

Group B

Team	GP	W	L	T	GF	GA	Pts
Russia	3	3	0	0	15	6	6
Czech Rep.	3	2	1	0	12	4	4
Finland	3	1	2	0	11	9	2
Kazakhstan	3	0	3	0	6	25	0

Quarterfinals

Canada	4	Kazakhstan	1
Czech Republic	4	USA	1
Finland	2	Sweden	1
Russia	4	Belarus	1

Semifinals

Czech Republic	2	Canada	1
Russia	7	Finland	4

Bronze Medal game

Finland	3	Canada	2

Gold Medal game

Czech Republic	1	Russia	0

1998 Final Rankings, Men

1	Czech Republic
2	Russia
3	Finland
4	Canada
5–8	USA
5–8	Sweden
5–8	Belarus
5–8	Kazakhstan
9	Germany
10	Slovakia
11	France
12	Italy
13	Japan
14	Austria

1998 Scoring Leaders

Player	Team	GP	G	A	PTS	PIM
Teemu Selanne	Finland	5	4	6	10	8
Saku Koivu	Finland	6	2	8	10	4
Pavel Bure	Russia	6	9	0	9	2
Alex. Koreshkov	Kazakhstan	7	3	6	9	2
Phillipe Bozon	France	4	5	2	7	4
K. Shafranov	Kazakhstan	7	4	3	7	6
Dominik Lavoie	Austria	4	5	1	6	8
Jere Lehtinen	Finland	6	4	2	6	2
Alexei Yashin	Russia	6	3	3	6	0
Serge Poudrier	France	6	2	4	6	4
Sergei Fedorov	Russia	6	1	5	6	8

Women's Olympic results are found on page 115

World and European Championships, Pool A Final Standings 1910–2000

European Championships

1910

Rank	Team	GP	W	L	T	GF	GA	Pts
1	Great Britain	3	2	0	1	7	2	5
2	Germany	3	2	1	0	14	6	4
3	Belgium	3	1	1	1	6	6	3
4	Switzerland	3	0	3	0	2	15	0

1911

Rank	Team	GP	W	L	T	GF	GA	Pts
1	Bohemia	3	3	0	0	20	1	6
2	Germany	3	2	1	0	17	4	4
3	Belgium	3	1	2	0	5	13	2
4	Switzerland	3	0	3	0	4	28	0

1912

Rank	Team	GP	W	L	T	GF	GA	Pts
1	Bohemia	2	1	0	1	7	2	3
2	Germany	2	1	0	1	6	3	3
3	Austria	2	0	2	0	1	9	0

1913

Rank	Team	GP	W	L	T	GF	GA	Pts
1	Belgium	3	2	0	1	25	7	5
2	Bohemia	3	2	0	1	15	6	5
3	Germany	3	1	2	0	18	16	2
4	Austria	3	0	3	0	5	34	0

1914

Rank	Team	GP	W	L	T	GF	GA	Pts
1	Bohemia	2	2	0	0	11	1	4
2	Germany	2	1	1	0	4	3	2
3	Belgium	2	0	2	0	2	13	0

1921

Rank	Team	GP	W	L	T	GF	GA	Pts
1	Sweden	1	1	0	0	6	4	2
2	Czechoslovakia	1	0	1	0	4	6	0

1922

Rank	Team	GP	W	L	T	GF	GA	Pts
1	Czechoslovakia	2	2	0	0	11	3	4
2	Sweden	2	1	1	0	9	3	2
3	Switzerland	2	0	2	0	1	15	0

1923

Rank	Team	GP	W	L	T	GF	GA	Pts
1	Sweden	4	4	0	0	23	6	8
2	France	4	3	1	0	13	8	6
3	Czechoslovakia	4	2	2	0	16	9	4
4	Belgium	4	1	3	0	5	18	2
5	Switzerland	4	0	4	0	7	23	0

1924

Rank	Team	GP	W	L	T	GF	GA	Pts
1	France	3	3	0	0	17	1	6
2	Sweden	3	2	1	0	8	4	4
3	Switzerland	2	1	1	0	14	6	2
4	Belgium	2	1	1	0	4	3	2
5	Spain	2	0	2	0	0	13	0
6	Italy	2	0	2	0	0	16	0

1925

Rank	Team	GP	W	L	T	GF	GA	Pts
1	Czechoslovakia	3	3	0	0	10	0	6
2	Austria	3	1	1	1	4	5	3
3	Switzerland	3	0	1	2	3	4	2
4	Belgium	3	0	2	1	1	9	1

1926

Rank	Team	GP	W	L	T	GF	GA	Pts
1	Switzerland	7	5	1	1	35	15	11
2	Czechoslovakia	7	5	2	0	18	8	10
3	Austria	7	4	2	1	14	13	9
4	Great Britain	7	3	4	0	26	19	6
5	France	4	2	2	0	5	6	4
6	Belgium	4	1	3	0	5	8	2
7	Poland	4	2	2	0	9	5	4
8	Italy	4	0	3	1	3	26	1
8	Spain	4	0	3	1	5	20	1

1927

Rank	Team	GP	W	L	T	GF	GA	Pts
1	Austria	5	5	0	0	13	2	10
2	Belgium	5	3	1	1	13	3	7
3	Germany	5	3	2	0	10	7	6
4	Poland	5	1	2	2	11	8	4
5	Czechoslovakia	5	1	3	1	7	6	3
6	Hungary	5	0	5	0	0	28	0

1929

Rank	Team	GP	W	L	T	GF	GA	Pts
1	Czechoslovakia	4	4	0	0	8	3	8
2	Poland	3	2	1	0	6	3	4
3	Austria	6	4	2	0	13	9	8
4	Italy	4	2	2	0	5	6	4
NR	Switzerland	3	1	2	0	2	5	2
NR	Hungary	4	0	3	1	2	7	1
NR	Germany	2	0	2	0	1	3	0
NR	Belgium	2	0	1	1	1	2	1

1932

Rank	Team	GP	W	L	T	GF	GA	Pts
1	Sweden	6	4	0	2	12	2	10
2	Austria	6	1	0	5	9	6	7
3	Switzerland	6	1	0	5	10	9	7
4	Germany	6	1	1	4	5	5	6
5	Czechoslovakia	6	1	4	1	10	10	3
6	France	5	3	0	2	11	4	8
7	Great Britain	5	3	1	1	11	9	7
8	Latvia	5	1	4	0	5	14	2
9	Romania	5	0	5	0	0	14	0

World Championships

Note: WR – World Ranking; ER – European Ranking

For events that had separate preliminary and medal rounds, the results of all games are combined in these standings.

1920

WR	ER	Team	GP	W	L	T	GF	GA	Pts
1		Canada	3	3	0	0	29	1	6
2		USA	4	3	1	0	52	2	6
3		Czechoslovakia	3	1	2	0	1	31	2
4		Sweden	6	3	3	0	17	20	6
5		Switzerland	2	0	2	0	0	33	0

1930

WR	ER	Team	GP	W	L	T	GF	GA	Pts
1		Canada	1	1	0	0	6	1	2
2	1	Germany	5	4	1	0	14	11	8
3	2	Switzerland	3	2	1	0	6	4	4
4	3	Austria	3	2	1	0	5	3	4
5	4	Poland	3	1	2	0	6	5	2

1931

WR	ER	Team	GP	W	L	T	GF	GA	Pts
1		Canada	6	5	0	1	24	0	11
2		USA	6	5	1	0	22	3	10
3	1	Austria	8	4	4	0	14	16	8
4	2	Poland	7	2	4	1	6	11	5
5	3	Czechoslovakia	7	3	3	1	10	7	7
6	4	Sweden	6	2	3	1	4	7	5
7	5	Hungary	4	3	1	0	14	6	6
8	6	Great Britain	4	2	2	0	14	5	4
9	7	France	5	1	4	0	9	15	2
10	8	Romania	5	0	5	0	2	49	0

1933

WR	ER	Team	GP	W	L	T	GF	GA	Pts
1		USA	5	5	0	0	23	1	10
2		Canada	5	4	1	0	17	3	8
3	1	Czechoslovakia	8	6	2	0	17	12	12
4	2	Austria	8	4	4	0	14	13	8
5	3	Germany	6	3	2	1	13	8	7
5	3	Switzerland	6	3	2	1	10	11	7
7	5	Hungary	5	0	4	1	2	10	1
7	5	Poland	6	1	4	1	3	11	3
9	7	Romania	5	2	3	0	5	19	4

1934

WR	ER	Team	GP	W	L	T	GF	GA	Pts
1		Canada	4	4	0	0	19	2	8
2		USA	4	3	1	0	6	2	6
3	1	Germany	8	5	3	0	12	14	10
4	2	Switzerland	7	5	2	0	36	7	10
5	3	Czechoslovakia	6	3	3	0	8	4	6
6	4	Hungary	6	1	4	1	2	5	3
7	5	Austria	7	3	3	1	9	10	7
8	6	Great Britain	5	3	2	0	9	7	6
9	7	France	7	2	3	2	9	12	6
10	8	Romania	6	1	5	0	7	21	2
11	9	Belgium	3	1	2	0	5	23	2
12	10	France	5	1	4	0	4	19	2

1935

WR	ER	Team	GP	W	L	T	GF	GA	Pts
1		Canada	7	6	0	1	35	6	13
2	1	Switzerland	8	6	1	1	33	9	13
3	2	Great Britain	7	4	3	0	17	16	8
4	3	Czechoslovakia	8	5	3	0	34	11	10
5	4	Sweden	8	5	2	1	21	14	11
6	5	Austria	8	3	4	1	16	16	7
7	6	France	8	2	3	3	9	21	7
8	7	France	8	1	4	3	7	14	5
9	8	Germany	7	4	3	0	18	9	8
10	9	Poland	6	2	2	2	20	13	6

1937

WR	ER	Team	GP	W	L	T	GF	GA	Pts
1		Canada	9	9	0	0	60	4	18
2	1	Great Britain	9	8	1	0	50	3	16
3	2	Switzerland	8	4	3	1	27	13	9
4	3	Germany	9	3	5	1	13	32	7
5	4	Hungary	9	3	4	2	14	24	8
6	5	Czechoslovakia	8	4	2	2	22	9	10
7	6	France	9	2	7	0	8	54	4
8	7	Poland	9	3	6	0	16	24	6

1938

WR	ER	Team	GP	W	L	T	GF	GA	Pts
1		Canada	7	6	0	1	17	6	13
2	1	Great Britain	8	6	1	1	27	8	13
3	2	Czechoslovakia	7	4	2	1	9	6	9
4	3	Germany	8	3	5	0	12	9	6
5	4	Sweden	6	2	2	2	8	7	6
6	5	Switzerland	7	5	2	0	34	7	10

1939

WR	ER	Team	GP	W	L	T	GF	GA	Pts
1		Canada	8	8	0	0	42	1	16
2		USA	9	7	2	0	25	8	14
3	1	Switzerland	10	7	2	1	51	13	15
4	2	Czechoslovakia	10	3	5	2	37	11	8
5	3	Germany	10	6	2	2	32	22	14
6	4	Poland	7	3	4	0	17	19	6
7	5	Hungary	7	1	6	0	15	24	2
8	6	Great Britain	3	0	3	0	0	7	0
9	7	France	6	4	1	1	15	14	9
10	8	Latvia	6	3	3	0	16	24	6
11	9	Netherlands	4	1	3	0	3	20	2
12	10	Belgium	4	0	3	1	6	19	1
13	11	Yugoslavia	5	0	4	1	3	60	1
14	12	Finland	5	0	5	0	5	25	0

1947

WR	ER	Team	GP	W	L	T	GF	GA	Pts
1	1	Czechoslovakia	7	6	1	0	85	10	12
2	2	Sweden	7	5	1	1	55	15	11
3	3	Austria	7	5	2	0	49	32	10
4	4	Switzerland	7	4	2	1	47	22	9
5		USA	7	4	3	0	42	26	8
6	5	Poland	7	2	5	0	27	40	4
7	6	Romania	7	1	6	0	17	88	2
8	7	Belgium	7	0	7	0	15	104	0

1949

WR	ER	Team	GP	W	L	T	GF	GA	Pts
1	1	Czechoslovakia	7	5	2	0	42	12	10
2		Canada	7	4	1	2	74	10	10
3		USA	8	6	2	0	59	22	12
4	2	Sweden	7	4	2	1	42	15	9
5	3	Switzerland	8	4	3	1	48	32	9
6	4	Austria	7	1	6	0	30	60	2
7	5	Finland	4	2	2	0	27	36	4
8	6	Norway	5	2	3	0	22	27	4
9	7	Belgium	6	1	5	0	13	67	2
10	8	Denmark	3	0	3	0	4	80	0

1950

WR	ER	Team	GP	W	L	T	GF	GA	Pts
1		Canada	7	7	0	0	88	5	14
2		USA	7	5	2	0	49	29	10
3	1	Switzerland	7	4	3	0	57	46	8
4	2	Great Britain	7	4	3	0	25	32	8
5	3	Sweden	7	3	4	0	33	19	6
6	4	Norway	7	1	6	0	26	47	2
7	5	Belgium	4	2	2	0	15	60	4
8	6	Netherlands	4	1	3	0	7	33	2
9	7	France	4	0	4	0	3	32	0

1951

WR	ER	Team	GP	W	L	T	GF	GA	Pts
1		Canada	6	6	0	0	62	6	12
2	1	Sweden	6	4	1	1	33	14	9
3	2	Switzerland	6	4	1	1	28	12	9
4	3	Norway	6	2	4	0	10	27	4
5	4	Great Britain	6	1	4	1	18	42	3
6		USA	6	1	4	1	14	42	3
7	5	Finland	6	1	5	0	15	37	2

1953

WR	ER	Team	GP	W	L	T	GF	GA	Pts
1	1	Sweden	5	5	0	0	43	14	10
2	2	West Germany	6	1	5	0	23	46	2
3	3	Switzerland	5	1	4	0	13	36	2
NR		Czechoslovakia	4	3	1	0	32	15	6

1954

WR	ER	Team	GP	W	L	T	GF	GA	Pts
1	1	Soviet Union	7	6	0	1	37	10	13
2		Canada	7	6	1	0	59	12	12
3	2	Sweden	7	5	1	1	30	18	11
4	3	Czechoslovakia	7	4	3	0	41	21	8
5	4	West Germany	7	2	4	1	22	32	5
6	5	Finland	7	1	5	1	12	52	3
7	6	Switzerland	7	0	5	2	15	34	2
8	7	Norway	7	1	6	0	6	43	2

1955

WR	ER	Team	GP	W	L	T	GF	GA	Pts
1		Canada	8	8	0	0	66	6	16
2	1	Soviet Union	8	7	1	0	39	13	14
3	2	Czechoslovakia	8	5	2	1	63	22	11
4		USA	8	4	2	2	43	29	10
5	3	Sweden	8	3	3	2	31	16	8
6	4	West Germany	8	2	6	0	28	43	4
7	5	Poland	8	2	5	1	19	50	5
8	6	Switzerland	8	1	7	0	15	69	2
9	7	Finland	8	1	7	0	16	72	2

1957

WR	ER	Team	GP	W	L	T	GF	GA	Pts
1	1	Sweden	7	6	0	1	62	11	13
2	2	Soviet Union	7	5	0	2	77	9	12
3	3	Czechoslovakia	7	5	1	1	66	9	11
4	4	Finland	7	4	3	0	28	33	8
5	5	East Germany	7	3	4	0	23	48	6
6	6	Poland	7	2	5	0	25	45	4
7	7	Austria	7	0	6	1	8	61	1
8		Japan	7	0	6	1	11	84	1

1958

WR	ER	Team	GP	W	L	T	GF	GA	Pts
1		Canada	7	7	0	0	82	6	14
2	1	Soviet Union	7	5	1	1	44	15	11
3	2	Sweden	7	5	2	0	46	22	10
4	3	Czechoslovakia	7	3	2	2	21	21	8
5		USA	7	3	3	1	29	33	7
6	4	Finland	7	1	5	1	9	51	3
7	5	Norway	7	1	6	0	12	44	2
8	6	Poland	7	0	6	1	14	65	1

1959

WR	ER	Team	GP	W	L	T	GF	GA	Pts
1		Canada	8	7	1	0	60	9	14
2	1	Soviet Union	8	7	1	0	44	15	14
3	2	Czechoslovakia	8	5	3	0	46	22	10
4		USA	8	5	3	0	45	25	10
5	3	Sweden	8	3	4	1	27	26	7
6	4	Finland	8	1	6	1	20	44	3

1961

WR	ER	Team	GP	W	L	T	GF	GA	Pts
1		Canada	7	6	0	1	45	11	13
2	1	Czechoslovakia	7	6	0	1	33	9	13
3	2	Soviet Union	7	5	2	0	51	20	10
4	3	Sweden	7	4	3	0	33	27	8
5	4	East Germany	8	3	5	0	27	36	6
6		USA	7	1	5	1	24	43	3
7	5	Finland	7	1	5	1	19	43	3
8	6	West Germany	8	1	5	2	16	55	4

1962

WR	ER	Team	GP	W	L	T	GF	GA	Pts
1	1	Sweden	7	7	0	0	67	10	14
2		Canada	7	6	1	0	58	12	12
3		USA	7	5	2	0	54	23	10
4	2	Finland	7	3	4	0	32	42	6
5	3	Norway	7	3	4	0	32	54	6
6	4	West Germany	7	2	5	0	27	36	4
7	5	Switzerland	7	1	6	0	21	60	2
8	6	Great Britain	7	1	6	0	19	73	2

1963

WR	ER	Team	GP	W	L	T	GF	GA	Pts
1	1	Soviet Union	7	6	1	0	50	9	12
2	2	Sweden	7	6	1	0	44	10	12
3	3	Czechoslovakia	7	5	1	1	41	16	11
4		Canada	7	4	2	1	46	23	9
5	4	Finland	7	1	5	1	20	35	3
6	5	East Germany	7	1	5	1	16	43	3
7	6	West Germany	7	1	5	1	18	56	3
8		USA	7	1	5	1	21	64	3

1965

WR	ER	Team	GP	W	L	T	GF	GA	Pts
1	1	Soviet Union	7	7	0	0	51	13	14
2	2	Czechoslovakia	7	6	1	0	43	10	12
3	3	Sweden	7	4	2	1	33	17	9
4		Canada	7	4	3	0	28	21	8
5	4	East Germany	7	3	4	0	18	33	6
6		USA	7	2	5	0	22	44	4
7	5	Finland	7	1	5	1	14	27	3
8	6	Norway	8	1	7	0	17	60	2

1966

WR	ER	Team	GP	W	L	T	GF	GA	Pts
1	1	Soviet Union	7	6	0	1	55	7	13
2	2	Czechoslovakia	7	6	1	0	32	15	12
3		Canada	7	5	2	0	33	10	10
4	3	Sweden	7	3	3	1	26	17	7
5	4	East Germany	7	3	4	0	12	30	6
6		USA	7	2	5	0	18	39	4
7	5	Finland	7	2	5	0	18	43	4
8	6	Poland	7	0	7	0	11	44	0

1967

WR	ER	Team	GP	W	L	T	GF	GA	Pts
1	1	Soviet Union	7	7	0	0	58	9	14
2	2	Sweden	7	4	2	1	31	22	9
3		Canada	7	4	2	1	28	15	9
4	3	Czechoslovakia	7	3	2	2	29	18	8
5		USA	7	3	3	1	20	23	7
6	4	Finland	7	2	4	1	14	24	5
7	5	East Germany	7	1	5	1	14	38	3
8	6	West Germany	7	0	6	1	11	56	1

1969

WR	ER	Team	GP	W	L	T	GF	GA	Pts
1	1	Soviet Union	10	8	2	0	59	23	16
2	2	Sweden	10	8	2	0	45	19	16
3	3	Czechoslovakia	10	8	2	0	40	20	16
4		Canada	10	4	6	0	26	31	8
5	4	Finland	10	2	8	0	26	52	4
6		USA	10	0	10	0	23	74	0

1970

WR	ER	Team	GP	W	L	T	GF	GA	Pts
1	1	Soviet Union	10	9	1	0	68	11	18
2	2	Sweden	10	7	2	1	45	21	15
3	3	Czechoslovakia	10	5	4	1	47	30	11
4	4	Finland	10	5	5	0	31	40	10
5	5	East Germany	10	2	7	1	20	50	5
6	6	Poland	10	0	9	1	11	70	1

1971

WR	ER	Team	GP	W	L	T	GF	GA	Pts
1	1	Soviet Union	10	8	1	1	77	24	17
2	2	Czechoslovakia	10	7	2	1	44	20	15
3	3	Sweden	10	5	4	1	29	33	11
4	4	Finland	10	4	5	1	31	42	9
5	5	West Germany	12	3	8	1	32	69	7
6		USA	10	2	8	0	31	53	4

1972

WR	ER	Team	GP	W	L	T	GF	GA	Pts
1	1	Czechoslovakia	10	9	0	1	72	16	19
2	2	Soviet Union	10	7	1	2	78	17	16
3	3	Sweden	10	5	4	1	49	33	11
4	4	Finland	10	4	6	0	47	48	8
5	5	West Germany	10	2	8	0	21	76	4
6	6	Switzerland	10	1	9	0	19	96	2

1973

WR	ER	Team	GP	W	L	T	GF	GA	Pts
1	1	Soviet Union	10	10	0	0	100	18	20
2	2	Sweden	10	7	2	1	53	23	15
3	3	Czechoslovakia	10	6	3	1	48	20	13
4	4	Finland	10	3	6	1	24	39	7
5	5	Poland	10	1	8	1	14	76	3
6	6	West Germany	10	1	9	0	19	82	2

1974

WR	ER	Team	GP	W	L	T	GF	GA	Pts
1	1	Soviet Union	10	9	1	0	64	18	18
2	2	Czechoslovakia	10	7	3	0	57	20	14
3	3	Sweden	10	5	4	1	38	24	11
4	4	Finland	10	4	4	2	34	39	10
5	5	Poland	10	1	7	2	22	64	4
6	6	East Germany	10	1	8	1	21	71	3

1975

WR	ER	Team	GP	W	L	T	GF	GA	Pts
1	1	Soviet Union	10	10	0	0	90	23	20
2	2	Czechoslovakia	10	8	2	0	55	19	16
3	3	Sweden	10	5	5	0	51	34	10
4	4	Finland	10	5	5	0	36	34	10
5	5	Poland	10	2	8	0	18	78	4
6		USA	10	0	10	0	22	84	0

1976

WR	ER	Team	GP	W	L	T	GF	GA	Pts
1	1	Czechoslovakia	10	9	0	1	72	15	19
2	3	Soviet Union	10	6	3	1	50	23	13
3	2	Sweden	10	6	4	0	36	29	12
4		USA	10	3	6	1	25	47	7
5	4	Finland	10	3	4	3	40	38	9
6	5	West Germany	10	3	6	1	23	46	7
7	6	Poland	10	3	5	2	33	47	8
8	7	East Germany	10	2	7	1	19	53	5

1977

WR	ER	Team	GP	W	L	T	GF	GA	Pts
1	1	Czechoslovakia	10	7	2	1	54	32	15
2	2	Sweden	10	7	3	0	43	19	14
3	3	Soviet Union	10	7	3	0	77	24	14
4		Canada	10	6	3	1	47	35	13
5	4	Finland	10	5	5	0	45	43	10
6		USA	10	3	6	1	29	43	7
7	5	West Germany	10	2	7	1	23	58	5
8	6	Romania	10	1	9	0	20	84	2

1978

WR	ER	Team	GP	W	L	T	GF	GA	Pts
1	1	Soviet Union	10	9	1	0	61	26	18
2	2	Czechoslovakia	10	9	1	0	54	21	18
3		Canada	10	5	5	0	38	36	10
4	3	Sweden	10	4	6	0	39	37	8
5	4	West Germany	10	3	4	3	35	43	9
6		USA	10	2	6	2	38	58	6
7	5	Finland	10	2	6	2	37	44	6
8	6	East Germany	10	1	6	3	20	57	5

1979

WR	ER	Team	GP	W	L	T	GF	GA	Pts
1	1	Soviet Union	8	8	0	0	61	14	16
2	2	Czechoslovakia	8	4	2	2	32	32	10
3	3	Sweden	8	3	4	1	33	46	7
4		Canada	8	3	5	0	31	43	6
5	4	Finland	8	4	3	1	27	27	9
6	5	West Germany	8	3	4	1	32	31	7
7		USA	8	2	3	3	27	28	7
8	6	Poland	8	0	6	2	20	42	2

1981

WR	ER	Team	GP	W	L	T	GF	GA	Pts
1	1	Soviet Union	8	6	0	2	55	14	14
2	2	Sweden	8	5	2	1	24	30	11
3	3	Czechoslovakia	8	4	2	2	37	26	10
4		Canada	8	2	5	1	28	34	5
5		USA	8	4	3	1	39	43	9
6	4	Finland	8	3	3	2	37	32	8
7	5	West Germany	8	3	4	1	44	40	7
8	6	Netherlands	8	0	8	0	24	69	0

1982

WR	ER	Team	GP	W	L	T	GF	GA	Pts
1	1	Soviet Union	10	9	0	1	58	20	19
2	2	Czechoslovakia	10	5	3	2	38	20	12
3		Canada	10	5	3	2	46	30	12
4	3	Sweden	10	3	4	3	26	35	9
5	4	Finland	7	3	3	1	21	31	7
6	5	West Germany	7	2	4	1	19	30	5
7	6	France	7	1	5	1	20	44	3
8		USA	7	0	6	1	21	39	1

1983

WR	ER	Team	GP	W	L	T	GF	GA	Pts
1	1	Soviet Union	10	9	0	1	54	10	19
2	2	Czechoslovakia	10	6	2	2	40	21	14
3		Canada	10	6	4	0	35	30	12
4	3	Sweden	10	4	5	1	28	32	9
5	4	West Germany	10	5	4	1	31	34	11
6	5	East Germany	10	3	7	0	29	40	6
7	6	Finland	10	2	6	2	30	40	6
8	7	France	10	1	8	1	16	56	3

1985

WR	ER	Team	GP	W	L	T	GF	GA	Pts
1	2	Czechoslovakia	10	7	2	1	48	22	15
2		Canada	10	6	3	1	42	31	13
3	1	Soviet Union	10	8	2	0	64	16	16
4		USA	10	4	5	1	31	58	9
5	3	Finland	10	4	4	2	39	33	10
6	4	Sweden	10	4	6	0	37	40	8
7	5	West Germany	10	3	6	1	28	41	7
8	6	East Germany	10	0	8	2	16	64	2

1986

WR	ER	Team	GP	W	L	T	GF	GA	Pts
1	1	Soviet Union	10	10	0	0	50	15	20
2	2	Sweden	10	6	2	2	46	30	14
3		Canada	10	4	6	0	37	38	8
4	3	Finland	10	4	3	3	35	34	11
5	4	Czechoslovakia	10	5	4	1	38	21	11
6		USA	10	4	6	0	41	43	8
7	5	West Germany	10	2	7	1	23	52	5
8	6	Poland	10	1	8	1	26	63	3

1987

WR	ER	Team	GP	W	L	T	GF	GA	Pts
1	1	Sweden	10	5	3	2	44	22	12
2	2	Soviet Union	10	8	0	2	49	15	18
3	3	Czechoslovakia	10	6	2	2	32	24	14
4		Canada	10	3	5	2	25	29	8
5	4	Finland	10	5	4	1	32	31	11
6	5	West Germany	10	4	5	1	31	37	9
7		USA	10	4	6	0	38	49	8
8	6	Switzerland	10	0	10	0	25	69	0

1989

WR	ER	Team	GP	W	L	T	GF	GA	Pts
1	1	Soviet Union	10	10	0	0	47	16	20
2		Canada	10	7	3	0	57	29	14
3	2	Czechoslovakia	10	4	4	2	38	21	10
4	3	Sweden	10	4	4	2	34	32	10
5	4	Finland	10	5	4	1	35	27	11
6		USA	10	4	5	1	37	40	9
7	5	West Germany	10	1	7	2	22	41	4
8	6	Poland	10	1	9	0	12	76	2

1990

WR	ER	Team	GP	W	L	T	GF	GA	Pts
1	1	Soviet Union	10	8	1	1	53	13	17
2	2	Sweden	10	7	2	1	40	23	15
3	3	Czechoslovakia	10	5	4	1	36	30	11
4		Canada	10	6	3	1	43	32	13
5		USA	10	6	4	0	35	43	12
6	4	Finland	10	2	6	2	29	32	6
7	5	West Germany	10	1	8	1	19	42	3
8	6	Norway	10	1	8	1	21	61	3

1991

WR	ER	Team	GP	W	L	T	GF	GA	Pts
1	1	Sweden	10	5	0	5	43	29	15
2		Canada	10	5	2	3	39	30	13
3	2	Soviet Union	10	7	1	2	51	25	16
4		USA	10	3	5	2	35	51	8
5	3	Finland	10	6	3	1	35	21	13
6	4	Czechoslovakia	10	4	6	0	28	27	8
7	5	Switzerland	10	2	7	1	22	38	5
8	6	Germany	10	0	8	2	19	51	2

1992

Rank	Team	GP	W	L	T	GF	GA	Pts
1	Sweden	8	4	2	2	25	15	10
2	Finland	8	7	1	0	41	18	14
3	Czechoslovakia	8	6	2	0	33	13	12
4	Switzerland	8	3	3	2	18	21	8
5	Russia	6	4	1	1	23	12	9
6	Germany	6	4	2	0	31	17	8
7	USA	6	2	3	1	15	23	5
8	Canada	6	2	3	1	18	22	5
9	France	5	1	3	1	10	18	3
10	Norway	5	1	4	0	8	16	2
11	France	6	1	5	0	11	23	2
12	Poland	6	0	6	0	9	44	0

1993

Rank	Team	GP	W	L	T	GF	GA	Pts
1	Russia	8	5	2	1	27	16	11
2	Sweden	8	5	3	0	27	22	10
3	Czech Republic	8	6	1	1	33	10	13
4	Canada	8	6	2	0	41	17	12
5	Germany	6	4	2	0	21	17	8
6	USA	6	2	2	2	16	15	6
7	Finland	6	2	3	1	8	12	5
8	France	6	1	3	2	9	28	4
9	Austria	6	1	4	1	8	21	3
10	France	6	1	5	0	13	25	2
11	Norway	7	2	5	0	13	25	4
12	Switzerland	7	2	5	0	14	22	4

1994

Rank	Team	GP	W	L	T	GF	GA	Pts
1	Canada	8	7	1	0	35	19	14
2	Finland	8	6	1	1	48	11	13
3	Sweden	8	6	1	1	45	21	13
4	USA	8	4	4	0	24	35	8
5	Russia	6	4	2	0	31	10	8
6	France	6	3	3	0	19	22	6
7	Czech Republic	6	1	3	2	17	20	4
8	Austria	6	1	4	1	15	25	3
9	Germany	5	1	3	1	9	14	3
10	France	5	1	4	0	8	25	2
11	Norway	6	1	3	2	14	23	4
12	Great Britain	6	0	6	0	9	49	0

1995

Rank	Team	GP	W	L	T	GF	GA	Pts
1	Finland	8	6	1	1	34	15	13
2	Sweden	8	5	2	1	28	15	11
3	Canada	8	4	3	1	27	21	9
4	Czech Republic	8	4	4	0	17	16	8
5	Russia	5	4	1	0	18	12	8
6	USA	6	3	1	2	18	15	8
7	France	6	3	2	1	14	18	7
8	France	7	4	3	0	22	16	8
9	Germany	5	1	4	0	11	20	2
10	Norway	5	1	4	0	9	18	2
11	Austria	7	1	5	1	17	31	3
12	Switzerland	7	0	6	1	14	32	1

1996

Rank	Team	GP	W	L	T	GF	GA	Pts
1	Czech Republic	8	7	0	1	42	15	15
2	Canada	8	4	3	1	25	22	9
3	USA	8	5	2	1	22	22	11
4	Russia	8	5	2	1	31	17	11
5	Finland	6	2	2	2	24	18	6
6	Sweden	6	2	2	2	16	15	6
7	France	6	2	3	1	22	31	5
8	Germany	6	2	4	0	13	17	4
9	Norway	5	1	2	2	6	11	4
10	Slovakia	5	1	3	1	13	16	3
11	France	7	2	5	0	24	32	4
12	Austria	7	1	6	0	9	31	2

1997

Rank	Team	GP	W	L	T	GF	GA	Pts
1	Canada	11	7	3	1	36	22	15
2	Sweden	11	7	3	1	32	21	15
3	Czech Republic	9	6	3	0	30	20	12
4	Russia	9	4	3	2	28	24	10
5	Finland	8	5	3	0	29	15	10
6	USA	8	4	3	1	19	21	9
7	Latvia	8	4	2	2	37	23	10
8	France	8	3	4	1	28	28	7
9	Slovakia	8	3	4	1	20	23	7
10	France	8	2	6	0	20	43	4
11	Germany	8	2	6	0	10	30	4
12	Norway	8	0	7	1	13	32	1

1998

Rank	Team	GP	W	L	T	GF	GA	Pts
1	Sweden	10	9	0	1	38	9	19
2	Finland	10	4	3	3	26	14	11
3	Czech Republic	9	6	1	1	33	14	13
4	Switzerland	9	2	6	1	18	32	5
5–8	Russia	6	4	1	1	29	18	9
5–8	Canada	5	3	1	2	22	17	8
5–8	Slovakia	6	2	2	2	11	12	6
5–8	Belarus	6	2	4	0	17	23	4
9	Latvia	6	3	2	1	21	18	7
10	Italy	6	2	2	2	17	13	6
11	Germany	6	1	3	2	13	23	4
12	USA	6	1	4	1	10	19	3
13–16	France	3	1	2	0	5	12	2
13–16	Japan	3	0	3	0	7	19	0
13–16	Austria	3	0	3	0	3	15	0
13–16	Kazakhstan	3	0	3	0	6	19	0

1999

Rank	Team	GP	W	L	T	GF	GA	Pts
1	Czech Republic	10	7	3	0	47	24	14
2	Finland	10	7	2	1	33	19	15
3	Sweden	9	7	2	0	26	16	14
4	Canada	9	6	3	0	34	24	12
5-8	Russia	6	2	1	3	18	13	7
5-8	USA	6	3	3	0	22	15	6
5-8	Slovakia	6	2	3	1	22	21	5
5-8	Switzerland	6	2	4	0	15	25	4
9	Belarus	6	4	1	1	16	10	9
10	Austria	6	3	3	0	16	19	6
11	Latvia	6	2	4	0	24	22	4
12	Norway	6	1	5	0	10	26	2
13-16	Italy	3	0	3	0	8	17	0
13-16	Ukraine	3	0	3	0	3	13	0
13-16	France	3	0	3	0	6	18	0
13-16	Japan	3	0	3	0	5	23	0

2000

Rank	Team	GP	W	L	T	GF	GA	Pts
1	Czech Republic	8	8	0	0	28	10	16
2	Slovakia	8	5	1	2	28	15	12
3	Finland	8	4	1	3	24	12	11
4	Canada	8	2	6	0	16	16	4
5-8	USA	6	3	1	2	16	12	8
5-8	Switzerland	6	2	2	2	17	19	6
5-8	Sweden	6	5	1	0	28	6	10
5-8	Latvia	6	3	3	0	17	16	6
9-12	Belarus	5	1	4	0	13	29	2
9-12	Norway	5	3	2	0	22	17	6
9-12	Russia	5	1	4	0	12	13	2
9-12	Italy	5	1	4	0	7	24	2
13	Austria	6	2	2	2	14	16	6
14	Ukraine	6	2	4	0	15	21	4
15	France	6	2	3	1	19	21	5
16	Japan	6	0	6	0	8	37	0

CHAPTER 44

World Junior Championships

The Elite International Showcase for 18- and 19-year-old Players

IN 1973, THE SOVIET HOCKEY FEDERATION and the Czechoslovakian Ice Hockey Union proposed the creation of a World Junior Championship for players under the age of 20. The International Ice Hockey Federation supported the idea and, as a test, held an unofficial World Junior Championship tournament during the 1973–74 season. Three more unofficial tournaments took place before the first officially sanctioned World Junior Championship was held in 1976–77. A World Junior B Pool was created in 1979, then a C Pool in 1983 and a D Pool in 1996. The promotion-relegation system between the pools generally sees the winning team from B, C and D promoted up to the next level while the last-place team in A, B and C is dropped down.

Throughout the years, Canada and the former Soviet Union have been the most successful countries at the World Junior Championships, which are held annually in late December and early January. Beginning in 1996, the A Pool at the World Junior Championships was expanded to include 10 teams divided into two groups of five. After round-robin games within each group, the top four teams advance to a playoff round while the two last-place teams play a two-game, total-goals series to determine which team will be demoted to play in the B Pool the following year.

In the playoffs, the first-place team from each group crosses over to play the fourth-place team from the other group in the quarterfinals while the teams that finish second play the third-place team from the opposite group. The losers of the quarterfinals are paired off for one game each. The winners of these games then meet to determine fifth and sixth place, while the losers play off for seventh and eighth. Meanwhile, quarterfinals winners advance to the semifinals, with the winners advancing to the finals. The losers in the semifinals are paired to determine third and fourth place.

In the B Pool of the IIHF's World Junior Championships, eight teams are divided into two groups. After a round robin within these groups, the two last-place teams meet in a best-of-three series to determine which team will be relegated to the C Pool. Meanwhile, the three top teams from each group keep the points they've attained against the other advancing teams from their group and cross over to play another round-robin set with the teams of the other group. The winner of the tournament is determined by the team with the most total points after the second round robin.

The C Pool of the IIHF's World Junior Championships also comprises eight teams split into two divisions. After round-robin games within each group, teams are paired for a set of one-game playoffs to determine the final standings. The top teams from each group meet to establish first and second place, while the next two teams from each group play for third and fourth place, and so on. The same system applies to the D Pool.

Summaries of each Pool A World Junior Championship tournament follow:

1974 (UNOFFICIAL)

The first unofficial World Junior Championship was held in Leningrad, USSR in 1974 and marked the first contact for European teams with Canadian amateur hockey since 1969, when Canada severed its relationship with the International Ice Hockey Federation. The Peterborough Petes of the Ontario Hockey League represented Canada at the tournament, where the hosts were unstoppable. Seven future World and Olympic champions played for the Soviets as they cruised to the gold medal. Finland took silver while Canada finished third to claim the bronze. Viktor Khatulev of the USSR was the tournament's top scorer with three goals and six assists, though it was Sweden's Mats Ulander (seven goals, one assist) who was named best forward. Best defenseman was the Soviets' Vladimir Kucherenko while Canada's Frank Salive was best goaltender.

1975 (UNOFFICIAL)

For the first time ever, a world hockey championship was held on Canadian soil when Winnipeg and Brandon, Manitoba played host to the second edition of the unofficial World Junior Championships in 1975. The gold medal was not decided until the final game of the tournament when the Soviets beat Canada 4–3 and won the title again. Bryan Trottier (five goals and two assists) starred for the Canadian junior team, though the top scorer was Dale McMullin, who had three goals and five assists and was named to the tournament all-star team at forward along with Soviet players Boris Alexandrov and Viktor Khatulev (who was also named best player). Following the Soviets and Canada on the medal trail was Sweden, who won the bronze.

1976 (UNOFFICIAL)

The last unofficial World Junior Championship was held in Finland without the participation of the United States. The Soviets won again, making it three in a row. Canada finished second for the second straight year while Czechoslovakia earned a bronze medal. It was now obvious that this tournament had become a very important event on the international calendar. It was decided that the first IIHF-sanctioned World Junior Championships would take place the next year.

The Soviet Union was the top team at the first official World Junior Championships in Banske, Czechoslovakia, finishing the 1977 tournament with a perfect record of 7–0. The Soviets scored 51 goals to set a record which would not be beaten until the Canadian junior team scored 54 goals in 1986. Still, it was Dale McCourt of the second-place Canadians who led the tournament with 18 points (10 goals and eight assists). Viacheslav Fetisov began his brilliant career by being named best defenseman. The host Czechs were bronze medal winners.

1978

Though it was not the final game, the main attraction at the 1978 World Junior Championships in Montreal was the game between Canada and the Soviet Union. Soviet defenseman Viacheslav Fetisov was matched against 16-year-old phenomenon Wayne Gretzky. The two would be named tournament all-stars. Gretzky would top the scoring parade with 17 points (eight goals and nine assists), but it was Fetisov and the Soviets who emerged as 3–2 winners. The Soviets later beat Sweden in the gold medal game, while Canada had to settle for a bronze medal on home ice.

1979

The 1979 World Junior Championships in Karlstad, Sweden brought together a large collection of future international and NHL stars. Soviets Alexei Kasatonov, Vladimir Krutov and Igor Larionov, Canadians Brian Propp and Brad McCrimmon, Americans Mike Ramsey, Neal Broten and Dave Christian, Finns Reijo Ruotsalainen and Jari Kurri, Swedes Pelle Lindbergh, Tomas Jonsson, Mats Naslund, Hakan Loob and Thomas Steen and Czechoslovakians Anton Stastny, Darius Rusnak, Jiri Lala, Dusan Pasek and Igor Liba all showed the promise of great futures at the top levels of the game. The Soviet Union made it three straight championships (and six in a row dating back to 1974) this year, with the Czechoslovakians taking the silver and the host Swedes the bronze. Canada tumbled into fifth place behind Finland. Vladimir Krutov of the USSR was the tournament's top scorer with eight goals and six assists and was named best forward while Soviet teammate Alexei Kasatonov was best defenseman. Best goaltender honors went to Sweden's Pelle Lindbergh who would later star in the NHL with the Philadelphia Flyers.

1980

The Soviet junior team won its fourth straight official World Junior Championship (and seventh in total, if the three unofficial championships in 1974, 1975 and 1976 are included) at Helsinki in 1980, with very difficult one-goal wins over Finland and Sweden. The Soviets' incredible winning run has been beaten only by Canada in the 1990s. In 1980, however, Canada would settle for a fifth-place finish. Finland (silver) and Sweden (bronze) rounded out the medal winners, while Czechoslovakia finished fourth. The United States finished seventh in its first appearance at the official tournament. For the second year in a row, Vladimir Krutov was the tournament's top scorer with seven goals and four assists. Finland's Jari Kurri also had 11 points (four goals and seven assists), but it was Krutov who was named best forward. Finns Reijo Ruotsalainen and Jari Paavola were selected as the tournament's best defenseman and best goaltender respectively.

1981

The Soviet domination of the World Junior Championships finally stopped in Bavaria, West Germany in 1981. The Swedes won the title behind the all-star performances of goaltender Lars Eriksson, defenseman Hakan Nordin and forwards Jan Erixon and Patrik Sundstrom. Eriksson was chosen as best goaltender while Sundstrom was tabbed as best forward. The tournament had very high scores, with an average of 10.3 goals scored in every game. The Czechoslovakians beat Austria by a record score of 21–4. Six players tied for the tournament scoring lead with nine points, Germany's Dieter Hegen leading the parade with eight goals. Ranking behind the Swedes at the tournament were the silver medal-winning Finns followed by the Soviet Union.

1982

Canada climbed on the world junior hockey throne in 1982, taking the gold medal with a record of 6–0–1 at the World Junior Championships in Minnesota. The team, coached by Dave King and Mike Keenan, beat the Soviets 7–0 en route to winning Canadian hockey's first world championship of any kind since the 1961 World Championship was won by the Trail Smoke Eaters. The Soviets slumped to fourth place this year, with Czechoslovakia (silver) and Finland (bronze) following Canada on the medal podium. The host Americans finished sixth. Defense made the difference for Canada, as Mike Moffat was named best goaltender and Gord Kluzak was tabbed as best defenseman. Mike Moller joined his teammates on the tournament all-star team after leading Canada with 14 points (five goals and nine assists). Leading the tournament was Finland's Raimo Summanen, who had seven goals and nine assists.

1983

After two years off of the top spot on the podium, the Soviet Union again won the gold medal at the World Junior Championships in 1983. The Soviet Juniors won all seven games on home ice in Leningrad, where the first unofficial version of the tournament had been staged nine years before. The Soviets scored 50 goals while allowing only 13, as Ilja Byakin was named the tournament's best defenseman and earned a spot on the all-star team. Matti Rautiainen of Finland was named best goaltender, though Dominik Hasek earned the berth on the all-star team after helping Czechoslovakia to earn the silver medal. Canada, led by Mario Lemieux, Dave Andreychuk and Steve Yzerman, finished third under the coaching of Dave King. Andreychuk (11 points) and Lemieux (10) each ranked among the scoring leaders, though the tournament's top scorer was Vladimir Ruzicka of Czechoslovakia with 12 goals and eight assists. However, Tomas Sandstrom of the fourth-place Swedes was tabbed as the tournament's best forward.

1984

The Soviet Union won the 1984 tournament in Nykoping, Sweden with a record of 6–0–1. The only team that did not lose to the Soviets was Canada, who managed a 3–3 tie but could finish no better than fourth with a record of 4–1–2. Following the USSR along the medal trail was Finland (silver) and Czechoslovakia (bronze). The Finns had a really good run for the title, but finished one point behind the Soviets with a record of 6–1–0. Finnish center Raimo Helminen set a World Junior Championship record that would last for many years when he recorded 11 goals and 13 assists for 24 points in seven games. Not surprisingly, Helminen was named best forward and earned a berth on the tournament all-star team. Allan Perry became the first American to claim a Directorate Honor at the World Junior Championships when he was named the tournament's best goaltender despite his country's sixth-place finish.

1985

Canada won the World Junior Championships for just the second time in 1985 at a tournament held in Helsinki, Finland. As in 1982, the Canadians soundly defeated the Soviets (5–0) en route to the gold medal. The team was coached by Terry Simpson and consisted of many future NHLers such as Jeff Beukeboom, Brian Bradley, Adam Creighton, Stephane Richer, Wendel Clark, Shayne Corson, Bob Bassen and Claude Lemieux. The Canadians claimed top prize with a record of 5–0–2. Czechoslovakia was also 5–0–2 but settled for silver. The bronze medal went to the USSR. Craig Billington of Canada was named best goaltender, while Michal Pivonka of Czechoslovakia was best forward, though the tournament scoring leader was Esa Keskinen of Finland with 20 points (six goals, 14 assists). Fellow Finn Esa Tikkanen had 19 points. Honors for best defenseman went to Vesa Salo of Finland.

1986

The 1986 World Junior Championships, held in many cities across Southern Ontario, came to its dramatic peak in the final game. The Soviet Union beat Canada 4–1 to finish the tournament with a perfect record of 7–0 and reclaim the global title. The game attracted a lot of interest in Europe and was televised to the Soviet Union. Canada settled for a silver medal on home ice despite establishing a new scoring record with 54 goals. Two Canadians topped the tournament scoring parade, as Shayne Corson (seven goals, seven assists) and Joe Murphy (four goals, 10 assists) each had 14 points. Best forward at the tournament was another Canadian, Jim Sandlak, who had five goals and seven assists, the same totals as fellow Canadian Joe Nieuwendyk. The Soviets had the best defensive record, allowing just 14 goals against in seven games. Yevgeny Belosheikin was named best goaltender, while Mikhail Tatarinov was best defenseman.

1987

The last game of the 1987 World Junior Championships in Piestany, Czechoslovakia could have brought Canada the title. However, the game against the Soviet Union was halted prematurely due to a bench-clearing brawl. At the height of the on-ice melee, tournament officials doused all the lights in the arena, plunging the rink into darkness. The International Ice Hockey Federation suspended both teams. As a result, Finland won its first world junior title. Czechoslovakia finished second, while the United States claimed the bronze for its first medal in tournament history. Ulf Dahlen of Sweden was the top scorer with seven goals and eight assists, but it was Czechoslovakia's Robert Kron who was chosen as best forward. Finland's Markus Ketterer was best goaltender and Calle Johansson of Sweden was best defenseman.

1988

Canada rebounded from a disappointing finish in 1987, when a brawl with the Soviet Union cost them a chance at a gold medal, to win the 1988 World Junior Championships on Soviet ice in Moscow. In a dramatic game versus the host nation on January 1, 1988, the Canadians were outshot 40–16, but the brilliant goaltending of Jimmy Waite saved the day. Team Canada won the game 3–2 and later claimed the world title with a record of 6–0–1. The Soviets lost only to Canada and settled for a silver medal after posting a 6–1–0 record. The bronze medal went to Finland. Jimmy Waite was tabbed as the tournament's best goaltender. Teppo Numminen of Finland was best defenseman. Alexander Mogilny of the Soviet Union was named best forward after topping the scoring list with 18 points (eight goals and 10 assists). Canada's top scorer was Greg Hawgood, who just cracked the top 10 with a goal and eight assists.

1989

After failing to win gold on home ice in 1988, the Soviet Union took revenge at the World Junior Championships in Anchorage, Alaska in 1989. With a gold medal on the line on the last day of the tournament, the Soviets crushed Canada 7–2. The line of Pavel Bure, Sergei Fedorov (one goal) and Alexander Mogilny (three goals) was unstoppable against Team Canada. Canada fell into fourth place behind Sweden (silver) and Czechoslovakia (bronze). The United States could finish no better than fifth despite the fact that Jeremy Roenick (16 points) and Mike Modano (15) finished first and second in tournament scoring. Still, Pavel Bure (eight goals, six assists) was named best forward, while teammate Alexei Ivashkin was best goaltender. Rickard Persson of Sweden was selected as best defenseman.

1990

Once again, the Soviet Union and Canada collided for the title, which was not decided until the final game in Helsinki. Canada previously had rallied to beat the Soviets 6–4, but the USSR could win the gold medal with a win over Sweden on the last day. However, a Soviet lineup packed with future NHL stars could manage only a 3–3 tie. Both Canada and the Soviets finished the tournament with records of 5–1–1, but the gold went to the Canadians because of their head-to-head victory. Czechoslovakia finished third. The Czech team dominated the tournament awards with Robert Reichel winning the scoring title with 11 goals and 10 assists and earning a selection to the all-star team as well as the honor of best forward. Jaromir Jagr was second in scoring with 18 points and joined Reichel on the tournament all-star team. Canadian Dave Chyzowski (who was third in scoring with 13 points) rounded out the all-star forward line. Czechoslovakia's Jiri Slegr and the USSR's Alexander Godynyuk were the all-star defensemen, with Godynyuk tabbed as the tournament's best defenseman. Canada's Stephane Fiset was named best goaltender and chosen as an all-star.

1991

Eric Lindros led Team Canada to a gold medal on home ice in Saskatchewan at the World Junior Championships in 1991. He topped the team with six goals and 11 assists, but it was a goal by John Slaney that proved to be the key to victory. Slaney's goal gave Canada a 3–2 win over the Soviet Union. Both countries finished the tournament with identical records of 5–1–1 for the second year in a row, but Canada earned the gold because of its head-to-head victory over the Soviets. Czechoslovakia finished just one point behind both countries with a 5–2–0 record to claim the bronze. Doug Weight of the fourth-place United States team topped the scoring parade with 19 points (five goals and 14 assists), while Pavel Bure of the Soviet Union led the tournament with 12 goals, but it was Eric Lindros who was picked as best forward. Jiri Slegr of Czechoslovakia was selected as best defenseman, while Switzerland's Pauli Jaks was best goaltender.

1992

A unique situation occurred during the 1992 World Junior Championships in Fussen, Germany. The Soviet team started the tournament under the name of the Soviet Union, but due to the official breakup of the country on January 1, 1992, finished the tournament under the name of the Commonwealth of Independent States. However, political upheaval did not prevent the hockey team from winning the title for the ninth time. Ten players from the winning team had great NHL careers ahead of them, while another five players would make the NHL as well. Sweden earned the silver medal, as Swedish players ranked 1–2–3–4 atop the tournament's scoring list. Michael Nylander led the way with 17 points and was chosen as best forward. Peter Forsberg (11 points) Markus Naslund (10) and Mikael Renberg (10) rounded out the top four scoring positions. American Mike Dunham was named best goaltender after leading the United States to a bronze medal. Canada's Scott Niedermayer was selected as best defenseman, although the two-time defending champion Canadians plummeted to sixth place at the tournament.

1993

Team Canada began its incredible run of five straight victories at the World Junior Championships with a gold medal at the 1993 tournament in Gavle, Sweden. Led by Paul Kariya and Chris Pronger, Canada had to defeat the host Swedes to claim gold. The silver medalists from Sweden received superb performances from two of their forwards. Peter Forsberg set a new tournament scoring record by registering seven goals and 24 assists for 31 points in just seven games. Markus Naslund accumulated 13 goals and 11 assists for 24 points. Forsberg was named best forward and was joined by Naslund and Kariya on the tournament all-star team. Janne Gronvall of Finland earned honors as best defenseman. Canada's Manny Legace was best goaltender as the Canadians claimed the gold medal despite placing no players among the top 10 in scoring.

1994

As in 1993, the Swedes competed hard against Canada at the World Junior Championships in the Czech Republic but had to settle for a second-place finish in 1994 at 6–1–0. The gold medal went to Canada with a record of 6–0–1. The only team that did not lose to Team Canada was Russia, who managed a 3–3 tie. It was a real team effort by Canada, as no one from the country made the all-star team despite the fact that four Canadians cracked the top 10 in scoring, including Martin Gendron, who led the low-scoring tournament with six goals. Niklas Sundstrom of Sweden, who led with 11 points (four goals, seven assists), was named best forward, while teammate Kenny Jonsson was best defenseman. Russia's Yevgeny Ryabchikov made the all-star team in goal, but it was Canada's Jamie Storr who was named best goaltender.

1995

On home ice in Red Deer, Alberta, Canada made it three gold medals in a row at the 1995 World Junior Championships. For the first time in tournament history, Canada ran up a perfect record of 7–0. Due to a labor dispute in the NHL, the regular season did not start until mid-January and several junior-aged players who normally might have been unavailable were able to join the Canadian team. Canadian players grabbed the top three spots in tournament scoring, with Marty Murray leading the pack with 15 points (six goals and nine assists). Jason Allison also had 15 points on three goals and 12 assists, while Bryan McCabe had three goals and nine assists. McCabe was named the tournament's best defenseman, with Murray selected as best forward. Yevgeny Tarasov of the silver medal-winning Russians was named best goaltender. The bronze medal went to Sweden.

1996

Ten teams took part at the 1996 World Junior Championships in Boston (up from the traditional eight) and for the first time the teams were split into two groups. Canada finished with a 4–0 record to top Group A, then won its two playoff games, including a 4–1 victory over Sweden in the gold medal game. Canada's fourth straight tournament victory and ninth in all tied two records previously held by the former Soviet Union. Sweden settled for the silver medal, while Russia took the bronze. Canada had brilliant performances at the tournament from Jose Theodore, who was named best goaltender, and Jarome Iginla, who was the scoring leader with five goals and seven assists (Germany's Florian Keller also had 12 points) and was named best forward. Honors for best defenseman went to Sweden's Mattias Ohlund.

1997

The road to a record-breaking fifth win in a row and tenth title overall was not an easy one for the Canadian team playing at the 1997 World Junior Championships in Geneva. Canada finished second behind the United States in its preliminary group with two ties and two wins. After victories in the quarterfinals and semifinals, the Canadian team faced the United States in the first all-North American final in the history of the World Junior Championships. Canada beat Team USA 2–0 to claim the gold while the Americans settled for silver. Russia earned the bronze medal. The tournament was low-scoring. Slovakia's Radoslav Pavlikovsky, USA's Erik Rasmussen and Finland's Tommi Kallio sharing the lead with nine points apiece, though it was Russia's Alexei Morozov (one of four players to finish with eight points) who was tabbed as the tournament's best forward. Best defenseman was Joseph Corvo of the United States, while Canada's Marc Denis was best goaltender.

1998

The 1998 World Junior Championship was held in Helsinki and was dominated by the hosts from Finland. In the preliminary round, they went 3–0–1 to top Group A. After victories in the quarterfinals and semifinals, the Finns played Russia, who were undefeated with just one tie in the tournament. For the first time in the history of World Junior Championships, the final game went into overtime with Finland emerging with a 2–1 victory and just its second world junior title in history. Russia settled for the silver, with the bronze medal going to the surprising team from Switzerland. The five-time defending champions from Canada had trouble scoring throughout the tournament. After going 2–2 during the preliminaries, Team Canada dropped three straight playoff games, including a 6–3 loss to Kazakhstan that dropped the team into eighth place for its worst finish in tournament history. Olli Jokinen of Finland was named best forward of the tournament after he and American Jeff Farkas tied atop the scoring list with 10 points apiece. Best defenseman was Pavel Skrbek of the Czech Republic. Switzerland's David Aebischer was best goaltender.

1999

The province of Manitoba hosted an outstanding event, beating all attendance records of previous World Junior Championships. Almost all games were sold out and the pro-Canada crowd in the Winnipeg Arena created a "white out" during Canadian games, continuing a tradition that began in the days of the Winnipeg Jets, when everybody wore white during the NHL playoffs.

The host team, led by the superb goaltending of Roberto Luongo, reached the finals. Their opponents, the Russians, didn't impress in the early stages of the tournament but saved their best for last. The final game was dominated by the Russians, led by skilled wings Maxim Afinogenov and Maxim Balmochnykh. The thrilling gold-medal game was decided in overtime on a shot by Artem Chubarov. The Russians won the title for the first time since 1992. Six players from this strong club were signed by NHL teams later in the year.

2000

For the third year in a row, the Russians reached the finals of the World Junior Championship, and for the third year in a row the gold medal game went into overtime. For the first time the title game went to a shootout after 20 minutes of extended play failed to break a scoreless tie between Russia and the Czech Republic. After turning back 35 Russian shots, Zdenek Smid stopped four of five breakaways to give the Czechs their first tournament victory. Milan Kraft, who had already been named the tournament's best forward, scored the goal that proved the winner. The Russians had to settle for silver despite that fact that goalies Alexei Volkov and Ilia Bryzgalov allowed only six goals in seven games. Canada's 3–2 loss to Russia in the semifinals marked the third year in a row that the Russians had defeated the Canadian team by a single goal. Canada rallied to defeat the Americans in the bronze medal game, winning in a shootout after overtime failed to break a 3–3 tie. Maxime Ouellet had provided Canada with solid goaltending throughout the tournament, but it was Brian Finley who backstopped the team past the United States. Though Henrik Sedin (13 points) and twin brother Daniel (10) finished first and third in tournament scoring (Kraft was second with 12 points), the play of the host Swedes was a disappointment. Considered potential gold medalists, the Swedes had to settle for second place in Group B after a 5–1 loss to the Russians, then were knocked into the relegation round with a 5–1 loss to the Americans in the quarterfinals. They finished fifth. Equally disappointing was the attendance in the northern Swedish towns of Skelleftea and Umea. Until the playoffs, crowds failed to top even 1,000 fans for any non-Sweden games.

WORLD JUNIOR CHAMPIONSHIPS POOL A STANDINGS AND RANKINGS

1974

Rank	Team	GP	W	L	T	GF	GA	Pts
1	Soviet Union	5	5	0	0	36	12	10
2	Finland	5	3	2	0	21	23	6
3	Canada	5	3	2	0	17	23	6
4	Sweden	5	2	3	0	32	21	4
5	USA	5	1	4	0	10	32	2
6	Czechoslovakia	5	1	4	0	19	24	2

1975

Rank	Team	GP	W	L	T	GF	GA	Pts
1	Soviet Union	5	5	0	0	22	8	10
2	Canada	5	4	1	0	27	10	8
3	Sweden	5	2	2	1	18	24	5
4	Czechoslovakia	5	1	2	2	9	11	4
5	Finland	5	1	3	1	10	14	3
6	USA	5	0	5	0	9	28	0

1976

Rank	Team	GP	W	L	T	GF	GA	Pts
1	Soviet Union	4	4	0	0	19	10	8
2	Canada	4	2	2	0	12	27	4
3	Czechoslovakia	4	2	2	0	12	10	4
4	Finland	4	1	3	0	12	14	2
5	Sweden	4	1	3	0	23	17	2

1977

Rank	Team	GP	W	L	T	GF	GA	Pts
1	Soviet Union	7	7	0	0	51	19	14
2	Canada	7	5	1	1	50	20	11
3	Czechoslovakia	7	4	2	1	32	17	9
4	Finland	7	4	3	0	35	29	8
5	Sweden	7	3	4	0	28	30	6
6	W. Germany	7	2	5	0	18	33	4
7	USA	7	1	5	1	25	45	3
8	Poland	7	0	6	1	12	58	1

1978

Rank	Team	GP	W	L	T	GF	GA	Pts
1	Soviet Union	7	6	1	0	50	16	12
2	Sweden	7	3	2	2	27	24	8
3	Canada	6	4	2	0	36	18	8
4	Czechoslovakia	6	2	3	1	21	31	5
5	USA	5	4	1	0	36	22	8
6	Finland	6	3	2	1	45	25	7
7	W. Germany	7	1	6	0	25	41	2
8	Switzerland	6	0	6	0	7	70	0

1979

Rank	Team	GP	W	L	T	GF	GA	Pts
1	Soviet Union	6	5	0	1	46	11	11
2	Czechoslovakia	6	3	1	2	19	23	8
3	Sweden	6	4	1	1	19	13	9
4	Finland	6	2	4	0	20	19	4
5	Canada	5	3	2	0	23	10	6
6	USA	5	2	3	0	21	23	4
7	W. Germany	5	1	4	0	17	26	2
8	Norway	5	0	5	0	6	46	0

1980

Rank	Team	GP	W	L	T	GF	GA	Pts
1	Soviet Union	5	5	0	0	24	9	10
2	Finland	5	4	1	0	29	8	8
3	Sweden	5	2	2	1	23	15	5
4	Czechoslovakia	5	2	3	0	28	27	4
5	Canada	5	3	2	0	25	18	6
6	W. Germany	5	2	3	0	15	28	4
7	USA	5	1	3	1	21	26	3
8	Switzerland	5	0	5	0	13	47	0

Note: For events that had separate preliminary and medal rounds, the results of all games are combined in these standings.

1981

Rank	Team	GP	W	L	T	GF	GA	Pts
1	Sweden	5	4	0	1	25	11	9
2	Finland	5	3	1	1	29	18	7
3	Soviet Union	5	3	2	0	36	14	6
4	Czechoslovakia	5	1	1	3	34	21	5
5	W. Germany	5	3	2	0	29	24	6
6	USA	5	2	3	0	19	27	4
7	Canada	5	1	3	1	26	25	3
8	Austria	5	0	5	0	9	67	0

1982

Rank	Team	GP	W	L	T	GF	GA	Pts
1	Canada	7	6	0	1	45	14	13
2	Czechoslovakia	7	5	1	1	44	17	11
3	Finland	7	5	2	0	47	29	10
4	Soviet Union	6	3	3	0	31	21	6
5	Sweden	7	4	3	0	42	26	8
6	USA	8	3	5	0	39	38	6
7	W. Germany	7	1	6	0	19	56	2
8	Switzerland	7	0	7	0	15	81	0

1983

Rank	Team	GP	W	L	T	GF	GA	Pts
1	Soviet Union	7	7	0	0	50	13	14
2	Czechoslovakia	7	5	1	1	43	22	11
3	Canada	7	4	2	1	39	24	9
4	Sweden	7	4	3	0	35	23	8
5	USA	7	3	4	0	28	29	6
6	Finland	7	3	4	0	35	29	6
7	W. Germany	7	1	6	0	12	46	2
8	Norway	7	0	7	0	13	69	0

1984

Rank	Team	GP	W	L	T	GF	GA	Pts
1	Soviet Union	7	6	0	1	47	17	13
2	Finland	7	6	1	0	44	21	12
3	Czechoslovakia	7	5	2	0	51	24	10
4	Canada	7	4	2	1	39	17	9
5	Sweden	7	3	4	0	27	25	6
6	USA	7	2	5	0	32	38	4
7	W. Germany	7	1	6	0	12	54	2
8	Switzerland	7	0	7	0	16	72	0

1985

Rank	Team	GP	W	L	T	GF	GA	Pts
1	Canada	7	5	0	2	44	14	12
2	Czechoslovakia	7	5	0	2	32	13	12
3	Soviet Union	7	5	2	0	38	17	10
4	Finland	7	4	1	2	42	20	10
5	Sweden	7	3	4	0	32	26	6
6	USA	7	2	5	0	23	37	4
7	W. Germany	7	0	6	1	9	44	1
8	Poland	7	0	6	1	10	59	1

1986

Rank	Team	GP	W	L	T	GF	GA	Pts
1	Soviet Union	7	7	0	0	42	14	14
2	Canada	7	5	2	0	54	22	10
3	USA	7	4	3	0	36	25	8
4	Czechoslovakia	7	4	3	0	30	20	8
5	Sweden	7	4	3	0	26	23	8
6	Finland	7	3	4	0	30	23	6
7	Switzerland	7	1	6	0	19	54	2
8	W. Germany	7	0	7	0	9	65	0

1987

Rank	Team	GP	W	L	T	GF	GA	Pts
1	Finland	7	5	1	1	45	23	11
2	Czechoslovakia	7	5	2	0	36	23	10
3	Sweden	7	4	2	1	45	11	9
4	USA	7	4	3	0	42	30	8
5	Poland	7	1	6	0	21	80	2
6	Switzerland	7	0	7	0	15	62	0
DQ	Canada	6	4	1	1	41	23	9
DQ	Soviet Union	6	2	3	1	27	20	5

1988

Rank	Team	GP	W	L	T	GF	GA	Pts
1	Canada	7	6	0	1	37	16	13
2	Soviet Union	7	6	1	0	44	18	12
3	Finland	7	5	1	1	36	20	11
4	Czechoslovakia	7	3	3	1	36	23	7
5	Sweden	7	3	3	1	36	24	7
6	USA	7	1	6	0	28	46	2
7	W. Germany	7	1	6	0	18	47	2
8	Poland	7	1	6	0	12	53	2

1989

Rank	Team	GP	W	L	T	GF	GA	Pts
1	Soviet Union	7	6	1	0	51	14	12
2	Sweden	7	6	1	0	39	14	12
3	Czechoslovakia	7	4	2	1	36	19	9
4	Canada	7	4	2	1	31	23	9
5	USA	7	3	3	1	41	25	7
6	Finland	7	2	4	1	29	37	5
7	Norway	7	1	6	0	14	56	2
8	W. Germany	7	0	7	0	13	66	0

1990

Rank	Team	GP	W	L	T	GF	GA	Pts
1	Canada	7	5	1	1	36	18	11
2	Soviet Union	7	5	1	1	50	23	11
3	Czechoslovakia	7	5	2	0	51	17	10
4	Finland	7	4	2	1	32	21	9
5	Sweden	7	4	2	1	38	29	9
6	Norway	7	2	5	0	25	51	4
7	USA	7	1	6	0	22	37	2
8	Poland	7	0	7	0	7	65	0

1991

Rank	Team	GP	W	L	T	GF	GA	Pts
1	Canada	7	5	1	1	40	18	11
2	Soviet Union	7	5	1	1	44	15	11
3	Czechoslovakia	7	5	2	0	44	19	10
4	USA	7	4	2	1	45	19	9
5	Finland	7	3	3	1	35	30	7
6	Sweden	7	3	4	0	32	29	6
7	Switzerland	7	1	6	0	5	48	2
8	Norway	7	0	7	0	8	75	0

1992

Rank	Team	GP	W	L	T	GF	GA	Pts
1	Russia	7	6	1	0	39	11	12
2	Sweden	7	5	1	1	41	24	11
3	USA	7	5	2	0	30	22	10
4	Finland	7	3	3	1	21	21	7
5	Czechoslovakia	6	3	3	0	26	20	6
6	Canada	7	2	3	2	19	30	6
7	Germany	7	1	6	0	15	42	2
8	Switzerland	8	1	7	0	23	44	2

1993

Rank	Team	GP	W	L	T	GF	GA	Pts
1	Canada	7	6	1	0	39	18	12
2	Sweden	7	6	1	0	53	15	12
3	Czech Republic	7	4	2	1	38	27	9
4	USA	7	4	3	0	32	23	8
5	Finland	7	3	3	1	32	22	7
6	Russia	7	2	3	2	26	20	6
7	Germany	7	1	6	0	16	37	2
8	Japan	7	0	7	0	9	83	0

1994

Rank	Team	GP	W	L	T	GF	GA	Pts
1	Canada	7	6	0	1	39	20	13
2	Sweden	7	6	1	0	35	16	12
3	Russia	7	5	1	1	23	17	11
4	Finland	7	3	4	0	24	24	6
5	Czech Republic	7	3	4	0	31	29	6
6	USA	7	1	5	1	20	33	3
7	Germany	7	1	6	0	10	26	2
8	Switzerland	7	1	5	1	10	27	3

1995

Rank	Team	GP	W	L	T	GF	GA	Pts
1	Canada	7	7	0	0	51	22	14
2	Russia	7	5	2	0	38	24	10
3	Sweden	7	4	2	1	35	21	9
4	Finland	7	3	3	1	31	30	7
5	USA	7	3	4	0	28	33	6
6	Czech Republic	7	3	4	0	43	26	6
7	Germany	7	1	6	0	17	55	2
8	Ukraine	7	1	6	0	12	44	2

1996

Rank	Team	GP	W	L	T	GF	GA	Pts
1	Canada	6	6	0	0	27	8	12
2	Sweden	7	4	2	1	26	13	9
3	Russia	7	4	2	1	32	19	9
4	Czech Republic	6	2	2	2	18	22	6
5	Finland	6	2	4	0	23	24	4
6	USA	6	3	3	0	21	27	6
7	Slovakia	6	2	1	3	24	23	7
8	Germany	6	1	3	2	19	27	4
9	Switzerland	6	1	4	1	16	24	3
10	Ukraine	6	1	5	0	12	31	2

1997

Rank	Team	GP	W	L	T	GF	GA	Pts
1	Canada	7	5	0	2	27	13	12
2	USA	6	4	1	1	23	9	9
3	Russia	6	4	1	1	26	9	9
4	Czech Republic	7	2	3	2	21	20	6
5	Finland	6	4	2	0	26	18	8
6	Slovakia	6	2	4	0	23	26	4
7	Switzerland	6	3	2	1	20	14	7
8	Sweden	6	2	3	1	20	18	5
9	Germany	6	1	5	0	14	34	2
10	Poland	6	0	6	0	7	46	0

1998

Rank	Team	GP	W	L	T	GF	GA	Pts
1	Finland	7	6	0	1	35	13	13
2	Russia	7	5	1	1	30	10	11
3	Switzerland	7	4	2	1	21	14	9
4	Czech Republic	7	3	3	1	24	22	7
5	USA	7	4	3	0	25	19	8
6	Sweden	7	3	4	0	25	13	6
7	Kazakhstan	7	2	5	0	16	51	4
8	Canada	7	2	5	0	13	18	4
9	Slovakia	6	3	3	0	26	18	6
10	Germany	6	0	6	0	4	41	0

1998

Rank	Team	GP	W	L	T	GF	GA	Pts
1	Russia	7	6	1	0	34	10	12
2	Canada	7	4	2	1	30	15	9
3	Slovakia	6	4	1	1	17	14	9
4	Sweden	6	4	2	0	30	22	8
5	Finland	6	3	3	0	25	20	6
6	Kazakhstan	6	1	4	1	12	38	3
7	Czech Republic	6	3	3	0	26	18	6
8	USA	6	3	3	0	25	23	6
9	Switzerland	6	1	5	0	13	27	2
10	Belarus	6	0	5	1	13	38	1

2000

Rank	Team	GP	W	L	T	GF	GA	Pts
1	Czech Republic	7	5	0	2	23	11	12
2	Russia	7	6	1	0	37	7	12
3	Canada	7	4	1	2	23	14	10
4	USA	7	2	3	2	14	15	6
5	Sweden	7	5	2	0	45	17	10
6	Switzerland	7	3	4	0	23	31	6
7	Finland	7	2	4	1	19	19	5
8	Kazakhstan	7	1	6	0	13	61	2
9	Slovakia	7	2	4	1	11	15	5
10	Ukraine	7	1	6	0	10	28	2

CANADA CUP AND WORLD CUP OF HOCKEY
STANDINGS AND RANKINGS

Canada Cup

1976

Rank	Team	GP	W	L	T	GF	GA	Pts
1	Canada	7	6	1	0	33	10	11
2	Czechoslovakia	7	3	3	1	23	20	7
3	Soviet Union	5	2	2	1	23	14	5
4	Sweden	5	2	2	1	16	18	6
5	USA	5	1	3	1	14	21	3
6	Finland	5	1	4	0	16	42	2

1981

Rank	Team	GP	W	L	T	GF	GA	Pts
1	Soviet Union	7	5	1	1	32	15	11
2	Canada	7	5	1	1	37	22	11
3	Czechoslovakia	6	2	2	2	22	17	6
4	USA	6	2	3	1	18	23	5
5	Sweden	5	1	4	0	13	20	2
6	Finland	5	0	4	1	6	31	1

1984

Rank	Team	GP	W	L	T	GF	GA	Pts
1	Canada	8	5	2	1	37	27	11
2	Sweden	8	4	4	0	31	29	8
3	Soviet Union	6	5	1	0	24	10	10
4	USA	6	3	2	1	23	22	7
5	Czechoslovakia	5	0	4	1	10	21	1
6	W. Germany	5	0	4	1	13	29	1

1987

Rank	Team	GP	W	L	T	GF	GA	Pts
1	Canada	9	6	1	2	41	32	14
2	Soviet Union	9	5	3	1	42	32	11
3	Sweden	6	3	3	0	19	18	6
4	Czechoslovakia	6	2	3	1	15	20	5
5	USA	5	2	3	0	13	14	4
6	Finland	5	0	5	0	9	23	0

1991

Rank	Team	GP	W	L	T	GF	GA	Pts
1	Canada	8	6	0	2	33	14	14
2	USA	8	5	3	0	29	26	10
3	Finland	6	2	3	1	13	20	5
4	Sweden	6	2	4	0	13	21	4
5	Soviet Union	5	1	3	1	14	14	3
6	Czechoslovakia	5	1	4	0	11	18	2

World Cup of Hockey

1996

Rank	Team	GP	W	L	T	GF	GA	Pts
1	USA	7	6	1	0	37	18	12
2	Canada	8	5	3	0	26	26	10
3	Sweden	4	3	1	0	16	6	6
4	Russia	5	2	3	0	19	19	4
5	Finland	4	2	2	0	17	16	4
6	Germany	4	1	3	0	12	19	2
7	Slovakia	3	0	3	0	9	19	0
8	Czech Republic	3	0	3	0	4	17	0

Note: For events that had separate preliminary and medal rounds, the results of all games are combined in these standings.

CHAPTER 45

International "Open" Events

NHL Players and Teams versus European Opponents since 1972

BEGINNING WITH THE 1972 SUMMIT SERIES between Team Canada and the Soviet national team, a variety of events were staged in either pre- or midseason that saw NHLers—playing either with their regular club teams or as part of national or all-star squads—playing their European counterparts.

Statistics for each of the events described here are included in player and goaltender data panels found in the Modern Player Register (Chapter 68) and the Goaltender Register (Chapter 69).

CANADA–RUSSIA 1972

For years, the best amateur teams in Canada were easily able to win World Championships and Olympic gold medals, but by the 1960s this was no longer true. Canada's top amateur clubs found themselves unable to compete with the Soviet Union and other top European countries and, denied the use of professional players by the International Ice Hockey Federation, Canada withdrew from international competition in 1970. Canadian fans were longing to see a series that would pit their best professionals against the best the Soviets had to offer. In September, 1972, they got their wish.

Most Canadians expected the 1972 Canada-Russia series to be a one-sided win for the NHL's best professionals. Certainly the Soviets had dominated World and Olympic play since 1962, but they were only amateurs! When Canadian hockey officials got a first-hand look at the Soviets' strange practice rituals and shabby equipment, the talk of a rout only increased. When Canada scored twice in the opening 6:32 of game one at the Montreal Forum on September 2, 1972 it appeared that Canadians had been correct.

"Until then," recalled Team Canada assistant coach John Ferguson, "NHL players never worked on their upper-body strength and seldom used off-ice training. Sure, a few jogged in the summer, but, mostly, players came to training camp and skated themselves into condition." This wasn't enough against the supremely fit Soviets. Team Canada wilted on that hot September night and the resulting 7–3 victory by the USSR sent shockwaves across Canada. Valeri Kharlamov scored twice that night, Vladimir Petrov, Boris Mikhailov and Alexander Yakushev had singles. A young goaltender named Vladislav Tretiak made 29 saves. Few Canadians knew those names at the start of September. By the end of the month they were as familiar as Esposito, Henderson, Cournoyer and Dryden.

Coach Harry Sinden shuffled his lineup for game two in Toronto and the result was a 4–1 Canadian victory, but Tretiak was magnificent in a 4–4 tie in game three at Winnipeg. Game four saw Team Canada take several careless penalties en route to a 5–3 loss. Canada's rugged style appeared graceless next to the smooth skating and slick passing of the Soviets and fans in Vancouver booed the Canadians loudly, inspiring Phil Esposito to deliver an impassioned speech in a postgame television interview: "To people across Canada, we tried. We gave it our best and for the people that boo us, I am—all of us—are really disheartened and we're disillusioned and we're disappointed in some of the people. We cannot believe the ... booing we've gotten in our own building . We know we're trying [but] they've got a good team—let's face facts—but it doesn't mean we're not giving 150%. We certainly are. If the Russians boo their players like some of our Canadian fans—not all, just some—then I'll come back and apologize."

Esposito's speech marked a turning point in the Canadian squad's evolution as a team. "It was a war," Esposito would later say, "and yes, hell for us whether we wanted it or not."

Canada trailed 2–1–1 in the eight-game series and played two games in Sweden en route to Moscow in order to get familiar with the larger European ice surface. The games were rough, and much scorn was heaped on Team Canada for its rowdy tactics. Further controversy erupted after the team's arrival in Moscow when little-used players Vic Hadfield, Gilbert Perreault, Rick Martin and Jocelyn Guevremont elected to return home for their NHL training camps. But 3,200 Canadian fans had arrived in Moscow by then and they helped boost team morale. Especially after game five on September 22 when Team Canada let a 4–1 lead slip away in a 5–4 defeat.

"We were having a rough time in Moscow with the defections, lousy hotels, phone calls to the players' rooms in the middle of the night, the Russians snatching much of the food we had sent over for the team, especially the steaks and beer, and the terrible officiating by the European officials," recalls Harry Sinden. "But a long cheer at the end of the first game in Moscow by the Canadian fans was a big lift for our spirits."

Game six produced three goals within a span of 1:23 of the second period, with Paul Henderson's holding up as the game winner in a match that saw Team Canada overcome more blatantly pro-Soviet officiating for a 3–2 victory. This game contained the most controversial incident of the series when Bobby Clarke slashed Valeri Kharlamov on an already tender ankle and handicapped the star player's performance for the rest of the series. Henderson was again the hero in game seven when his goal at 17:54 of the third period gave Canada a 4–3 victory that evened the series at 3–3–1.

Few Canadians who were alive on September 28, 1972 missed game eight, as it was carried live on TV and radio in the mid-afternoon. Absenteeism was high at work places across the country and schools suspended classes to allow students to watch the game, many of them assembled in auditoriums or gymnasiums. The game started badly for Team Canada, with referee Josef Kompalla issuing cheap penalties that allowed the Soviets to score a pair of first-period power-play goals and build up a 5–3 lead through two. Goals by Phil Esposito and Yvan Cournoyer allowed Team Canada to tie the game midway through the third. In the dying moments, Paul Henderson corralled the rebound from a Phil Esposito shot, but his own shot was stopped by Tretiak. With 34 seconds left, Henderson slipped his own rebound past the Soviet netminder. Team Canada had a thrilling 6–5 victory. An entire nation rejoiced.

"The Canadians battled with the ferocity of a cornered animal," marveled Anatoli Tarasov, godfather of Soviet hockey. "They believed the stories of their hockey superiority, which were not quite correct. Our players were better conditioned physically and stronger in skills than the Canadian professionals. But we could not match them in heart and desire."

CANADA–RUSSIA 1974

Most Canadians knew little about the opposition when Team Canada faced the Soviet Union in 1972. Many predicted an eight-game sweep for the Canadians. The country was shocked when the Soviets outclassed Canada in a 7–3 victory to open the series and the feeling was as much one of relief as of joy when Paul Henderson scored his winning goal with 34 seconds remaining in the final game. No one would be taking the Russians lightly in 1974. Back were many of the familiar names that had so impressed Canadian fans two years earlier: Tretiak, Yakushev, Maltsev, Mikhailov, Petrov and Kharlamov. Many in Canada knew these players better than the ones who would be representing them this time.

Team Canada 1974 was stocked with players from the World Hockey Association, the rival league which had sprung up to battle the NHL in 1972–73. Many had played in the NHL, but nobody was about to confuse Ralph Backstrom or Mike Walton with Phil Esposito. Bobby Hull—barred from playing for Canada in 1972 after his departure to the rival league—would be on hand this time, as would Gordie Howe, who had retired prior to the 1972 series but then returned to hockey in the WHA in order to play with sons Mark and Marty. Three members of Team Canada 1972 would be back to face the Soviets a second time: Pat Stapleton, Frank Mahovlich and Paul Henderson.

Canadian hockey fans had not entirely warmed to the World Hockey Association during its first two seasons, and the 1974 series was played as much to lend credibility to the WHA as it was to pit Canada against the Soviet Union. As such, the series did not elicit the same excitement, but Canadians did come around. The series opened in Quebec City on September 17 and Bobby Hull's goal with 5:42 remaining lifted Team Canada to a 3–3 tie. "I thought this would be just another game," said Gordie Howe afterwards, "but you put on a Canadian sweater and realize that it's not just another game. Too many Canadians are counting on it." Game two in Toronto resulted in a 4–1 Canadian victory (just as it had in 1972). The third game in Winnipeg was won 8–5 by the Soviets and a 5–5 tie in Vancouver meant that the two teams headed to Moscow with a win, a loss, and two ties apiece.

Tempers were on edge when the series resumed with game five on October 1 and the Soviets were 3–2 winners in a chippy game. "Oh, the Russians trip and hook, all right," commented Gordie Howe. "But we're not angels, are we?" Two nights later the Soviets won 5–2 in a contest marred by a postgame punch-up that saw Rick Ley bloody the face of Valeri Kharlamov. The players were able to maintain their cool in game six, a contest Canada needed to win in order to salvage a tie in the series. Bobby Hull scored a late goal that appeared to give Canada a 5–4 victory, but the referee (Canadian Tom Brown) ruled that time had expired. Though Canada had received only two minor penalties in game seven, the Soviets announced that they would pull their team off the ice in game eight if the WHA players persisted in their dirty play. As it was, the Soviets rested several of their stars (including Vladislav Tretiak and Vladimir Petrov) and still beat a dispirited Canadian squad 3–2.

As had been the case in 1972, Alexander Yakushev was the Soviets' top scorer, netting five goals and adding three assists in seven games played. Vladimir Petrov (two goals, five assists) and Valeri Kharlamov (one and six) each contributed seven points. Bobby Hull was the series leader with seven goals and two assists and Andre Lacroix's six assists led the Canadians. The ageless Gordie Howe had three goals and four assists. Gerry Cheevers handled the bulk of Canada's goaltending, allowing 24 goals in seven games for a 3.43 goals-against average. He actually outperformed Vladislav Tretiak, who surrendered 25 goals in seven games for a 3.57 mark.

"My first idols," said Yakushev when the games were done, "were Boris Mayorov and Anatoli Firsov. When I was growing up, they were big in our game. After this series, I have another hero. Bobby Hull." Hull signed a photograph for his newest admirer and requested an autograph in return. "If I could," Hull admitted, "what I'd really like Yakushev to do is sign a contract with Winnipeg. God, but he's good."

SUPER SERIES

Various Super Series of midseason exhibition games were played North American arenas between Soviet and NHL teams were staged between 1975–76 and 1990–91.

The Soviet Union was represented by two teams, Central Red Army and the Soviet Wings in the first Super Series that took place during the 1975–76 NHL season. In subsequent years, the USSR sent over Spartak (1977–78), Soviet Wings (1978–79), the Red Army and Dynamo Moscow (1979–80), the Soviet national team (1982–83), Red Army and Dynamo Moscow (1985–86), Red Army and Dynamo Riga (1988–89), Khimik, Soviet Wings, Red Army and Dynamo Moscow (1989–90), and Khimik, Dynamo Moscow and Red Army (1990–91).

CANADA CUP

The Canada Cup was created in 1976 as an initiative of the NHL, the NHLPA and Hockey Canada. Staged before the start of the NHL regular season, the tournament offered hockey fans their first chance to see top NHL players representing their respective countries. All games were held in North America. The Canada Cup was held five times in total: 1976, 1981, 1984, 1987 and 1991. In four of the five tournaments, the six competing nations were Canada, Czechoslovakia, Finland, Sweden, USA and USSR. In 1984 Germany replaced Finland because of a higher finish in the previous IIHF World Championships. Canada won the event on each occasion except for 1981 when the USSR national team finished on top.

Summaries of each tournament follow.

CANADA CUP '76 Created by the NHL, the NHLPA and Hockey Canada in 1976, the Canada Cup heralded Canada's official return to international hockey after a boycott that had begun in 1970. The tournament included Canada, the United States and the top four hockey nations in Europe (the USSR, Czechoslovakia, Sweden and Finland) and gave NHL players a chance to represent their respective countries.

Team Canada's roster was built by Montreal Canadiens general manager Sam Pollock and coached by Scotty Bowman. It boasted one of the strongest lineups ever assembled, including Bobby Orr and Bobby Hull, who had missed the 1972 Canada-Russia Summit Series (Orr due to injuries and Hull because he had left the NHL for the World Hockey Association and thus had been ruled ineligible). The roster also included Phil Esposito, Guy Lafleur, Gilbert Perreault and Darryl Sittler. The Soviet Union, on the other hand, was a team in transition after losing to Czechoslovakia at the 1976 World tournament. Many familiar names from 1972 were gone, including long-time stars such as Valeri Kharlamov and Vladimir Petrov.

The tournament opened in Ottawa on September 2 with Team Canada scoring an easy 11–2 victory over Finland. Victories followed against the United States (4–2) and Sweden (4–0), but Canada's hopes of an undefeated tournament were dashed on September 9 with a 1–0 loss to Czechoslovakia. Vladimir Dzurilla earned the shutout, while Milan Novy scored the lone goal. Canada rebounded for a 3–1 win over the Soviets two nights later and finished the round-robin portion of the tournament in first place with a record of 4–1–0. The Czechs had dropped a surprising 2–1 decision to Sweden, but still advanced to face Canada in the finals on the strength of a 3–1–1 record.

Despite Dzurilla's initial success against Canada, he was pulled after allowing four goals in the first period in game one of the best-of-three finals. Jiri Holecek finished up in a 6–0 Canadian victory. Dzurilla then replaced Holecek after he surrendered two early goals in game two and was brilliant in a 4–4 tie through regulation time. At 11:03 of overtime, Darryl Sittler streaked down the left side of the Montreal Forum ice and, with a slight deke, slipped the puck past Dzurilla for the Canada Cup-winning goal.

The star of the tournament for Team Canada was Bobby Orr, who enjoyed a final turn in the spotlight before repeated knee injuries ended his brilliant career. Orr had two goals and seven assists for nine points in seven games (tying Viktor Zhluktov of the Soviet Union and teammate Denis Potvin for the scoring lead) and was named the tournament's Most Valuable Player.

CANADA CUP '81 After a five-year hiatus, the Canada Cup competition resumed in 1981 with Canada, the United States, Sweden, Finland, Czechoslovakia and the Soviet Union once again vying for international hockey supremacy. A total of 60 NHL players (22 Canadians, 22 Americans, 12 Swedes and four Finns) participated for their homelands.

As in 1976, the Soviet Union was in a rebuilding mode (after their Olympic loss to the United States in 1980). Only eight players remained from their 1976 Canada Cup squad, and just 11 players were back from the team that had defeated a group of NHL All-Stars at the Challenge Cup in 1979. Among the talented crop of Soviet newcomers were 21-year-olds Alexei Kasatonov, Igor Larionov and Vladimir Krutov. Viacheslav Fetisov made his Canada Cup debut, while veteran Vladislav Tretiak once again tended goal.

Meanwhile, Team Canada had a young phenom of its own in Wayne Gretzky, who had set an NHL scoring record with 164 points in 1980–81. Gretzky headed up a Canadian roster that also featured Mike Bossy, Bryan Trottier, Clark Gillies and Denis Potvin of the two-time defending Stanley Cup champion New York Islanders. Goaltending duties were handled by Mike Liut. Canada waltzed through the round-robin portion of the tournament with only a 4–4 tie against Czechoslovakia blemishing a record that included a 7–3 victory over the Soviets in the final game on September 9. Despite the loss, the USSR held down second place with a record of 3–1–1. The Canada Cup format had been expanded to include a semifinals round this year, and Canada defeated the fourth-place United States 4–1 while the Soviets bounced the Czechs by the same score.

The one-game 1981 Canada Cup final took place in Montreal on September 13 and saw the Soviet Union destroy Team Canada by a final score of 8–1. The Soviets frustrated Wayne Gretzky throughout and kept the tournament's leading scorer (12 points on five goals and seven assists) off the scoresheet, while Sergei Shepelev beat Mike Liut three times and Igor Larionov added two goals. Despite their victory, the Soviet team was not permitted to take home the Canada Cup trophy in a decision by Alan Eagleson that nearly sparked an international incident.

Vladislav Tretiak was named the Most Valuable Player of the Canada Cup tournament after the Soviets allowed just 15 goals in seven games. Behind Wayne Gretzky on the scoring list were Mike Bossy, Bryan Trottier, Guy Lafleur and Alexei Kasatonov, who all had 11 points. Bossy's eight goals topped the tournament, as did Kasatonov's 10 assists.

CANADA CUP '84 Though the 1984 Canada Cup took place just three years after the previous event, it featured a number of differences both on the ice and in its format. Among them was the debut of the West German squad, who replaced Finland by virtue of a fifth-place finish at the most recent World Championships. (Finland had finished seventh.) Another change saw Bryan Trottier jump the border, switching from Team Canada to the United States. Trottier's presence, along with Bob Carpenter, Joe Mullen, Rod Langway and Tom Barrasso (all bona fide NHL stars) gave the Americans their strongest lineup in Canada Cup history. The USA finished second behind the Soviet Union in the round robin with a record of 3–1–1.

In addition to the loss of Trottier, Team Canada had only five players return from its 1981 roster. Newcomers included Michel Goulet and Paul Coffey (who tied for second behind Wayne Gretzky in scoring with 11 points) and John Tonelli, whose gritty two-way play earned him the tournament's Most Valuable Player award. However, the Canadian team limped through the round robin with a record of 2–2–1 and finished fourth behind the USSR, the USA and Sweden (3–2–0).

As was the case in the first two Canada Cup tournaments, the USSR used the event to experiment with its roster. Soviet coach Viktor Tikhonov added 11 fresh faces to his club, including goaltender Alexander Tyzhnykh, who shared netminding duties with Vladimir Myshkin in the first post-Tretiak Canada Cup. Even without Viacheslav Fetisov, who was out with an injury, the Soviets became the first team in tournament history to emerge from the round robin with a perfect record, capping off their 5–0–0 run with a 6–3 win over Canada on September 10. Three nights later, the two bitter rivals met in a one-game semifinals.

With Pete Peeters replacing Reggie Lemelin in goal, Canada battled the Soviets to a 2–2 tie through 60 minutes. At 12:29 of overtime, Mike Bossy tipped in a Paul Coffey shot and Canada had a 3–2 victory. One night before, the Swedes had crushed the Americans 9–2 to set up a Canada-Sweden final. As in 1976, the final of the 1984 Canada Cup was a best-of-three affair, though the series proved to be an anti-climax after the thrilling Canada–Russia game. Sweden featured such NHL stars as Kent Nilsson, Mats Naslund, Thomas Steen and Hakan Loob, but Team Canada swept the series with two victories by 5–2 and 6–5 scores.

CANADA CUP '87 The 1987 Canada Cup featured the emergence of Mario Lemieux as a true superstar. Teamed with Wayne Gretzky, Lemieux finally developed a work ethic to match his immense talent and the combination of hockey's two most gifted offensive players resulted in some of the most exciting games in the game's history.

Wayne Gretzky was late in accepting his invitation to join Team Canada after his Edmonton Oilers team won the Stanley Cup during the longest season in NHL history, but he arrived at training camp in the best shape of his life. Thirty-four other players also arrived at training camp and the reduction to a 23-man roster left such stars as Patrick Roy, Steve Yzerman, Cam Neely and Wendel Clark off the team.

The Soviet Union brought a veteran-laden lineup to the 1987 Canada Cup and was eager to regain its championship form after losing the most recent world title to Sweden. The Swedish squad would see eight national team members replaced by nine NHL stars during the Canada Cup, which only figured to make the team stronger. However, the 1984 Canada Cup finalists would not make it past the semifinals this year. The Americans were hurt by injuries to Mark Howe, Bryan Trottier and Neal Broten. Despite strong goaltending from John Vanbiesbrouck, the USA finished just 2–3–0 and was spared last place only by the 0–5–0 record of Finland, who had returned to the Canada Cup this year.

Canada was undefeated in the round robin, but only had managed a 4–4 tie with Czechoslovakia to open the tournament and a 3–3 tie with the Soviets in the final game. Canada faced the Czechs again in the semifinals and fell behind 2–0 after one period before rallying for a 5–3 victory. The USSR had lost 5–3 to Sweden during the round robin, but avenged that defeat with a 4–2 victory in the semifinals. Canada and the Soviets would meet for the Canada Cup championship.

Game one in the best-of-three finals was played at the Montreal Forum on September 11 and saw the Soviets defeat Canada 6–5 on Alexander Semak's overtime goal. Two nights later at Copps Coliseum in Hamilton, Mario Lemieux ended a classic game on a feed from Wayne Gretzky at 10:06 of the second overtime period for a 6–5 Canadian victory. With 1:26 remaining in the third and final game on September 15, Lemieux again converted a Gretzky pass for a 6–5 Canada Cup-winning victory. Lemieux had scored a tournament-leading 11 goals in nine games (including four game winners), while his 18 points were second behind Wayne Gretzky's tournament-record 21 points (on three goals and 18 assists).

CANADA CUP '91 "Anything less than winning is not acceptable," said Wayne Gretzky prior to the 1991 Canada Cup. The Great One would be back to help his country defend its 1987 championship, but he would not have his brilliant partner from that series. The back injury that had kept Mario Lemieux out for more than half the 1990–91 season sidelined him for the Canada Cup as well. However, hockey's next anointed superstar would be a member of Team Canada this year. Though he had refused to report to the Quebec Nordiques and was not yet a member of the NHL, 18-year-old Eric Lindros would contribute three goals and a tough, physical presence to Team Canada.

The 1991 Canada Cup witnessed a partial changing of the guard atop the hockey hierarchy, as Czechoslovakia fell to last place with a 1–4–0 record in the round robin (despite the presence of young Dominik Hasek) and the Soviet Union failed to reach the playoffs after going 1–3–1. The USSR had been on the decline since its last Olympic gold medal victory in 1988. With veteran national team members Vladimir Krutov and Igor Larionov allowed to join the NHL in 1989–90 and the subsequent defections of Alexander Mogilny and Sergei Fedorov, the Soviets no longer had complete access to their finest hockey resources.

Sweden edged the Soviet Union for fourth place in the round robin behind Mats Sundin's six points (two goals, four assists) before losing 4–0 to Canada in the semifinals. Christian Ruuttu, Petri Skriko and Esa Tikkanen led Finland into the playoffs for the first time in Canada Cup history before they lost 7–3 to the United States.

"There is no doubt this will be the best U.S. team ever," said American general manager Craig Patrick before the tournament. Led by Mike Modano, Brett Hull, Brian Leetch and Pat LaFontaine, and featuring solid goaltending by Mike Richter, Team USA lost only to Canada during the round robin, and it was looking for revenge in the playoffs. Canada scored a 4–1 victory over the Americans in game one of the finals, but the victory proved costly when a Gary Suter cross-check put Wayne Gretzky out of action. Gretzky watched game two in civilian clothes and saw Mark Messier and Steve Larmer give Team Canada an early 2–0 lead. Jeremy Roenick and Kevin Miller evened the game 2–2 after two periods, but a shorthand goal by Larmer at 12:13 of the third and an empty-netter from Dirk Graham capped a 4–2 clinching victory. Despite missing the final game, Wayne Gretzky earned his fourth consecutive Canada Cup scoring title with 12 points in seven games on four goals and eight assists.

CHALLENGE CUP

In February, 1979, the Soviet national team played a three-game series against the NHL All-Star Team at Madison Square Garden in New York. This one-time series replaced the NHL All-Star Game that season. The winner of the series, the Soviets, was awarded a trophy named the NHL Challenge Cup.

RENDEZ-VOUS '87

In February, 1987, the NHL All-Star Game was replaced by a series in Quebec City that pitted the Soviet national team against a squad of NHL All-Stars. There was no winner of the two-game Rendez-Vous '87 series after each team won one game.

FRIENDSHIP TOUR

In September of both 1989 and 1990, two NHL teams traveled to the Soviet Union where they played a series of exhibition games against Soviet club teams. The Calgary Flames and Washington Capitals made the initial tour, while the Montreal Canadiens and Minnesota North Stars visited in 1990. Each NHL team played four different Soviet opponents.

WORLD CUP OF HOCKEY

The World Cup of Hockey was staged in August and September, 1996. The tournament was a successor to the Canada Cup and was organized by the NHL, the NHLPA and the IIHF. Like the Canada Cup, it was played before the NHL's regular season began, allowing top professional players to represent their countries. The eight best national teams in the world—Canada, USA, Russia, Czech Republic, Slovakia, Sweden, Finland and Germany—were divided into two groups, one playing in North America and the other in Europe. After a round robin within both groups, the top three teams from each advanced to the playoffs. All playoff games took place in North America. The teams that finished first in their groups received a bye in the first playoff round, advancing to the semifinals. Second and third-place teams played one game each, the winners advancing. Canada and the USA won their semifinals and met in a three-game finals won by Team USA two games to one. Goaltender Mike Richter was a standout for Team USA, receiving MVP honors.

CHAPTER 46

Other International Tournaments and Leagues

INTERNATIONAL HOCKEY places great emphasis on tournament play. National teams and club teams participate in a variety of annual events, some recently organized and some, like the Spengler Cup and the Izvestia/Baltica Cup, long established.

International leagues involving club teams are a relatively recent addition to the hockey scene. (Historically, league play had been confined to within each country.)

All are profiled here.

Also described is the European Junior Championships. This event acquires World Championship status in 1999. It is of particular interest because it is Europe's leading showcase for players under the age of 18. As a result, it is thoroughly scouted by NHL clubs looking to find talent in next year's Entry Draft.

Alpenliga

The Alpenliga operated from 1991 to 2000 with the exception of 1994 when no games were played. The tournament included participants from Austria, Italy and Slovenia and generally concluded in the first part of the season.

Teams in the Alpenliga played a quadruple round-robin schedule. The top eight teams then advanced to the final round, where they were split into two groups of four. After a round robin within each group, the top teams from each group advanced to play a two-game, total-goals final. The Alpenliga was succeeded by the International Eishockey League in 1999–2000.

Asian Cup

The International Ice Hockey Federation created the Asian Cup competition to broaden the scope of international hockey and to assist Asian nations in the staging of international games. The first tournament for Asian national teams took place in 1990 and was held annually until 1996 (except for 1991, when the tournament was canceled due to the Gulf War). The final tournament in January, 1996 matched the national teams of Kazakhstan, Japan, China and Korea in a round-robin series and was won by Kazakhstan.

Asia-Oceania Junior Championship

The Asia-Oceania Junior Championship for players under the age of 18 was held for the first time in 1983–84. The event was known as the Asian Junior Championships for its first two years, it acquired its current name in 1986. Tournaments generally are held in March. Currently, six nations take part play a round-robin series to determine a champion as well as silver and bronze medal winners.

Atlantic League

In 1995–96, six club teams from France, Denmark and the Netherlands met in a new tournament called the Atlantic League. A winner was declared after a double round-robin schedule of games.

Balkan League

The first Balkan League tournament was held in 1994–95 and has become an annual event. Club teams from Romania, Yugoslavia and Bulgaria compete, with four teams playing a double round-robin schedule to determine the winner.

Calgary Cup

The Calgary Cup took place in December 1986–January 1987 during the Pre-Olympic Week tournament in Calgary one year before the 1988 Winter Olympic Games. National teams from Canada, the United States, Czechoslovakia and the Soviet Union met in a round-robin series, with the two top teams playing off to decide a winner while the two bottom finishers met to determine third and fourth place. The event was won by Czechoslovakia.

Cup of Low Countries

The first tournament of the Cup of Low Countries was held in 1995–96 with the participation of clubs from the Netherlands and Belgium. Currently, the tournament involves 12 teams divided into two groups. After a double round robin within the groups, the teams from each group are paired for a one-game playoff to determine the final standings. The two first-place teams meet to determine top spot, the second-best teams meet to decide third place and so on.

Deutschland Cup

Created in 1987 as a national team tournament by the German Ice Hockey Union, the Deutschland Cup usually is played in Stuttgart at the beginning of November. No tournament was held in 1989.

East European Hockey League

The East European Hockey League was created in 1995–96 to allow club teams from the newly independent former Soviet republics to have full-time competition. The EEHL was strengthened in 1996–97 when the creation of the new Russian Hockey League excluded the top clubs from the Ukraine and Belarus. The EEHL is made up of teams from the Ukraine, Belarus, Latvia, Lithuania and a team from Poland.

Nine teams play a quadruple round-robin schedule to begin the EEHL, with the top eight clubs advancing to the playoffs. Quarterfinals and semifinals employ a best-of-three format while the finals and the series for third place are played as a best-of-five.

European Cup

The European Cup (or European Champions Cup) was created by the International Ice Hockey Federation in 1965 through the efforts of the German Ice Hockey Union—particularly those of future IIHF president Gunther Sabetzki. The object of the tournament was to determine the best club team in Europe. The first three tournaments, however, were held without the participation of the Soviet Union, whose teams later would dominate the event.

In the first two years of the European Cup tournament, the teams world play a four-game total-goals series. Until 1978–79, the event was played in a two-game, total-goals format. After 1978–79, only the preliminary rounds used the total-goal format. The creation of the European Hockey League for the top clubs on the continent replaced the European Cup, which was held for the last time in 1996–97.

European/World Junior Championships

The idea of a European Junior Championships for players under the age of 19 was proposed by the Soviet Hockey Federation and the Czechoslovakian Ice Hockey Union. An initial unofficial tournament was held in 1967, with the tournament gaining official status the following year. (After the creation of the World Junior Championships for players under 20 in 1976–77, the age limit for participation in the European Junior Championships was lowered to 18. This lower age limit has resulted in the event being intensely scouted by representatives of NHL clubs looking to draft talented 18-year-old Europeans.) Team USA participated for the first time in 1999. Pool B was created in 1969, with a C Pool added in 1978 and a D Pool in 1996. The promotion-relegation system between the pools generally sees the winning team from B, C and D promoted up to the next level while the last-place team in A, B and C is dropped down.

The European Junior Championships are held in March and April. Currently, the format of the A Pool sees eight countries divided into two groups. After an initial round robin within the groups, the teams that have finished last play a best-of-three series to determine the team that will be demoted to the B Pool.

The three top finishers from each group keep the points they have attained against the other advancing teams from their group and cross over to play a round-robin series against each of teams from the other group. The winner of the tournament is the team with the most total points after the second round robin. The same format is also employed in the B Pool.

The C Pool of the European Junior Championships also is comprised of eight teams split into two divisions. After round-robin games within each group, teams are paired for a set of one-game playoffs to determine the final standings. The top teams from each group meet to establish first and second place, while the next two teams from each group play for third and fourth place, and so on.

In the D Pool, eight teams are divided into two groups to play a round-robin series within each group. The top two teams from each group then advance (keeping any points they have gained against the other advancing team) to form a final group of four. After another round-robin series, the team with the most points is declared the winner. The two bottom teams from each group play a similar series to round out the final standings.

EUROPEAN HOCKEY LEAGUE

The International Ice Hockey Federation created a new tournament called the European Hockey League in 1996–97. The EHL is made up of the best clubs on the continent, including the national champions of European countries.

In 1997–98, the EHL included 24 clubs from 12 countries. Teams are divided into six divisions and play a double round-robin series (home-and-home games) within their divisions. After that, the six division winners and the two second-place teams with the best records advance to the playoffs. Teams play each other twice (home and away) in a total-goal quarterfinals with the four winners advancing to the final stage. At this stage in the tournament, teams play one-game semifinals with the winners advancing to a one-game final and the losers playing one game to determine third place.

FOUR NATION TOURNAMENT

The Four Nation Tournament was created by the International Ice Hockey Federation and originally allowed the best junior players from Europe's top hockey countries—the USSR (now Russia), Czechoslovakia (now represented by the Czech Republic), Sweden and Finland—to compete in tournaments for various age groups.

In 1977, the first Four Nation Tournament was held for players under the age of 20. The tournaments are held in late August/early September in order to help the country's national teams prepare for the upcoming season. The Four Nation Tournament for players under 18 was created in 1979 and is held annually at the beginning of February to serve as the last test before the European Junior Championships. A tournament for players under 16 was created in 1978, with an under–17 bracket added in 1990. These tourneys are played in early February. All Four Nation Tournaments are made up of round-robin games.

Since 1996, the Four Nation events have been transformed into Five and Six Nation tournaments with the participation of junior national teams of different ages from Slovakia, Germany, Canada and the United States.

GOODWILL GAMES

The Goodwill Games hockey tournament took place only once, in July-August, 1990 in the Tri-Cities area of Washington state. The top six national teams from Europe played together with Canadian and U.S. teams. The eight teams were divided into two groups, with the winner declared after a series of playoff games. The tournament was won by the Soviet Union despite the defection of Sergei Fedorov prior to the event.

INTERNATIOPNAL EISHOCKEY LEAGUE

See Alpenliga. Began operations in 1999–2000.

IZVESTIA CUP

Created by the Soviet Hockey Federation in 1967, the Izvestia Cup was known as the Moscow International Tournament for its first two years. In 1969, it became known as the Izvestia Cup after its sponsor, a Soviet national newspaper. The tournament is played annually (except for 1991) in the middle of December. National teams from a variety of countries have participated, though in the mid-1970s, the WHA's Winnipeg Jets and Quebec Nordiques each played once. A team called the NHL Future Stars played in 1978.

In 1997, the *Izvestia* newspaper gave up its patronage of the tournament, which is now known as the Baltica Cup after the Baltica brewing company that sponsors the event.

JAPAN CUP

Created by the Japan Ice Hockey Federation, the Japan Cup was played in 1989 and 1990. Both tournaments were held in Tokyo in May. Three national teams (two from Europe and the hosts from Japan) played a double round-robin format to determine a winner. In 1989, the Soviet Union and Czechoslovakia were declared co-winners. Both teams had earned the same number of points and the organizing committee declined to count goal differential. The Soviets were sole winners in 1990.

KRAJALA CUP

Created by the Finnish Ice Hockey Union, the first Krajala Cup tournament was held in December, 1995. Since 1996, the event has been held in November. The Krajala Cup pits Europe's top four national teams in a round-robin tournament.

NISSAN CUP

The Nissan Cup was created by the Swiss Ice Hockey Union in 1988. The tournament is held in Switzerland in November or February and generally sees four top European national teams meet in a round-robin series.

PRAGOBANKA CUP

A round-robin tournament created by the Czech Republic's Ice Hockey Union in 1994, the Pragobanka Cup is an annual event for top European national teams. It is played in the Czech Republic in late August and early September.

RUDE PRAVO CUP

The Czechoslovak Ice Hockey Union created the Rude Pravo Cup in 1977. The first three tournaments (1977, 1978 and 1979) were played in September and involved the top national teams of Europe. The inaugural tournament of 1977 also included the Cincinnati Stingers of the World Hockey Association. In 1981–82 and 1982–83, the format of the Rude Pravo Cup was changed. The four best European teams—the Soviet Union, Czechoslovakia, Sweden and Finland—met throughout the season in a double round-robin (home-and-home) series. Both tournaments were won by the Soviets.

ST. PETERSBURG GRAND PRIX

The St. Petersburg Grand Prix was created by the Soviet Hockey Federation in 1975 when it was known as the International B-Team Tournament. The first tournament took place in Riga but has been held in St. Petersburg (previously known as Leningrad) since 1976. In 1982, the event was named the Leningradskaya Pravda Tournament due to the sponsorship of the *Leningradskaya Pravda* newspapers. It has been known as the St. Petersburg Grand Prix since 1992.

Europe's national B-teams usually have gathered for this tournament in April, with teams from Russia, the Czech Republic, Sweden and Finland having participated the most. A champion is declared through a round-robin format.

SPENGLER CUP

The Spengler Cup is the oldest European tournament for club teams. The cup was donated by Dr. Carl Spengler of Davos, Switzerland in 1923 with the understanding that Germany and Austria would represent themselves internationally with their best club teams. (At the time, those countries were banned from official International Ice Hockey Federation competitions in the wake of World War I.)

The Spengler Cup is played every year in Davos between Christmas and the New Year. Five teams participate in the tournament, with a select team from Canada usually included. Canada first competed at the Spengler Cup in 1984, though Canadians studying at Oxford University in England played in the tournament's early years. Canada's modern Spengler roster is built around Canadians playing professionally in European national leagues.

Each team at the Spengler plays a round-robin series after which the top two teams meet in the final game. The Rochester Americans of the American Hockey League were the first North American professional team to compete at the tournament when they took part in 1996.

SWEDEN CUP

The Sweden Cup was created by the Swedish Ice Hockey Association and was only held twice—in the Olympic years of 1980 and 1984. Top national teams played a round-robin tournament in Sweden in April. The 1980 tournament was won by the Soviet Union. Czechoslovakia won in 1984.

SWEDEN HOCKEY GAMES

The Sweden Hockey Games tournament was created by the Swedish Ice Hockey Union in 1991. Since then, top national teams have met annually in Sweden in February. Usually, the top European national teams (Russia, the Czech Republic, Sweden and Finland) plus Canada play this round-robin event in Stockholm.

VIKING CUP

Organized in 1981 by Camrose Lutheran College (now Augustana University College), this tournament has been known as the Viking Cup since its inception and is named after the host team—the Augustana University College Vikings. It is held ever second year in late December and early January in the city of Camrose, Alberta, Canada.

The Viking Cup features national teams from Europe and the United States, junior all-star teams from Western Canada and the host Vikings. In the most recent tournament, 10 teams were divided into two pools. After the round robin portion of the tournament, the top four teams from each pool advanced to a playoff round, The quarterfinal winners met in semifinal action with the winners proceeding to the championship final and the losers going to the bronze medal game.

WORLD HOCKEY CHALLENGE

The Quebec Esso Cup began in 1985–86 for teams of players under 17 years old. The tournament generally was held every second year in late December/early January. Canada was represented by five all-star teams—Ontario, Quebec, Atlantic, Western and Pacific—which participated along with an American team and three European national junior teams.

In 1992, the Quebec Esso Cup was replaced by the World Hockey Challenge. The format, however, remained the same. Ten junior teams are divided into two groups of five each. After a round robin within the groups, the top two teams from each group advance to the semifinals. Winners move on to the finals while the semifinals losers play to determine third place. The teams that finished third in the two round-robin groups meet to determine fifth and sixth place. The fourth and fifth-place finishers from the round robin also play off to round out the final standings.

CHAPTER 47

Other IIHF Championships

World Senior and Junior B–C–D Pools plus European and Asian Junior Championships

Teams are listed by final ranking. W–L–T–Pts are calculated from all games played including preliminary, medal and consolation rounds. Often teams with superior W–L–T marks finish with inferior rankings due to early tournament losses that seed them in a lower bracket.

Ranking in Senior or Junior B, C or D events is sequential. As an example, if there are eight teams in Pool A, the top team in Pool B is ranked ninth.

Some final standings are missing. Research is ongoing to obtain them. In those instances, only rankings are published here.

IIHF three-letter abbreviations are use for country names. A list of these abbreviations is found on page 492.

World Championships, Pool B

1951

Rank	Team	GP	W	L	T	GF	GA	Pts
8	ITA	5	4	0	1	26	11	9
9	FRA	5	4	1	0	35	15	8
10	HOL	5	3	2	0	17	16	6
11	AUT	5	1	4	0	20	25	2
12	BEL	5	1	3	1	23	30	3
13	YUG	5	1	4	0	13	37	2

1952

Rank	Team	GP	W	L	T	GF	GA	Pts
10	GBR	5	4	1	0	28	10	8
11	AUT	5	3	1	1	32	19	7
12	ITA	5	3	2	0	26	21	6
13	HOL	5	1	3	1	19	26	3
14	BEL	5	1	3	1	17	24	3
15	FRA	5	1	3	1	19	41	3

1953

Rank	Team	GP	W	L	T	GF	GA	Pts
4	ITA	4	4	0	0	24	9	8
5	GBR	4	3	1	0	21	10	6
6	AUT	4	2	2	0	18	16	4
7	HOL	4	1	3	0	13	26	2
8	FRA	4	0	4	0	11	26	0

1955

Rank	Team	GP	W	L	T	GF	GA	Pts
10	ITA	4	4	0	0	50	4	8
11	AUT	4	3	1	0	15	9	6
12	HOL	4	2	2	0	18	20	4
13	YUG	4	1	3	0	9	23	2
14	BEL	4	0	4	0	8	44	0

1956

Rank	Team	GP	W	L	T	GF	GA	Pts
11	GDR	2	2	0	0	18	8	4
12	NOR	2	1	1	0	8	9	2
13	BEL	2	0	2	0	12	21	0

1959

Rank	Team	GP	W	L	T	GF	GA	Pts
13	ROM	2	2	0	0	12	4	4
14	HUN	2	1	1	0	5	9	2
15	AUT	2	0	2	0	4	8	0

1961

Rank	Team	GP	W	L	T	GF	GA	Pts
9	NOR	5	4	1	0	27	9	8
10	GBR	5	3	0	2	21	11	8
11	SUI	5	2	2	1	17	15	5
12	ITA	5	2	2	1	19	20	5
13	POL	5	1	4	0	13	17	2
14	AUT	5	1	4	0	10	35	2

1962

Rank	Team	GP	W	L	T	GF	GA	Pts
9	JAP	5	5	0	0	63	16	10
10	AUT	5	4	1	0	49	9	8
11	FRA	5	3	2	0	35	25	6
12	HOL	5	2	3	0	20	46	4
13	AUS	5	1	4	0	13	51	2
14	DEN	5	0	5	0	9	42	0

1963

Rank	Team	GP	W	L	T	GF	GA	Pts
9	NOR	6	5	1	0	35	15	10
10	SUI	6	4	1	1	28	10	9
11	ROM	6	4	1	1	29	17	9
12	POL	6	4	2	0	52	13	8
13	YUG	6	2	4	0	23	49	4
14	FRA	6	1	5	0	14	38	2
15	GBR	6	0	6	0	8	47	0

1964

Rank	Team	GP	W	L	T	GF	GA	Pts
9	POL	7	6	1	0	40	13	12
10	NOR	7	5	2	0	40	19	10
11	JAP	7	4	2	1	35	31	9
12	ROM	7	3	3	1	31	28	7
13	AUT	7	3	3	1	24	28	7
14	YUG	7	3	3	1	29	37	7
15	ITA	7	2	5	0	24	42	4
16	HUN	7	0	7	0	14	39	0

1965

Rank	Team	GP	W	L	T	GF	GA	Pts
9	POL	6	5	0	1	35	15	11
10	SUI	6	4	1	1	27	15	9
11	FRG	6	3	1	2	30	20	8
12	HUN	6	2	3	1	19	24	5
13	AUT	6	2	4	0	21	28	4
14	GBR	6	1	4	1	24	41	3
15	YUG	6	0	4	2	16	29	2
16	ITA	2	0	1	1	4	5	1
17	FRA	2	1	1	0	5	10	2

1966

Rank	Team	GP	W	L	T	GF	GA	Pts
9	FRG	7	7	0	0	34	12	14
10	ROM	7	5	1	1	29	16	11
11	YUG	7	4	1	2	25	23	10
12	NOR	7	4	3	0	28	17	8
13	AUT	7	3	4	0	25	30	6
14	SUI	7	2	5	0	24	26	4
15	HUN	7	1	6	0	19	30	2
16	GBR	7	0	6	1	15	45	1

1967

Rank	Team	GP	W	L	T	GF	GA	Pts
9	POL	7	5	0	2	32	13	12
10	ROM	7	5	0	2	34	18	12
11	NOR	7	0	2	5	35	38	5
12	YUG	7	2	1	4	36	31	8
13	ITA	7	2	3	2	26	31	6
14	AUT	6	2	3	1	21	29	5
15	SUI	7	1	4	2	25	37	4
16	HUN	7	0	4	3	28	40	3

1968

Rank	Team	GP	W	L	T	GF	GA	Pts
9	YUG	5	5	0	0	33	9	10
10	JAP	5	4	1	0	27	12	8
11	NOR	5	3	2	0	15	15	6
12	ROM	5	2	3	0	22	23	4
13	AUT	5	1	4	0	12	27	2
14	FRA	5	0	5	0	9	32	0

1969

Rank	Team	GP	W	L	T	GF	GA	Pts
7	GDR	7	7	0	0	62	13	14
8	POL	7	6	1	0	31	13	12
9	YUG	7	3	2	2	17	20	8
10	FRG	7	4	3	0	28	16	8
11	NOR	7	2	3	2	26	35	6
12	ROM	7	2	4	1	24	36	5
13	AUT	6	1	4	1	12	28	3
14	ITA	7	0	7	0	10	41	0

1970

Rank	Team	GP	W	L	T	GF	GA	Pts
7	USA	7	7	0	0	70	11	14
8	FRG	7	6	1	0	34	13	12
9	NOR	7	3	2	2	26	28	8
10	YUG	7	3	3	1	30	23	7
11	JAP	7	3	3	1	31	34	7
12	SUI	7	2	5	0	22	31	4
13	ROM	7	2	5	0	21	38	4
14	BUL	7	0	7	0	11	67	0

1971

Rank	Team	GP	W	L	T	GF	GA	Pts
7	SUI	7	6	0	1	31	14	13
8	POL	7	5	1	1	36	19	11
9	GDR	7	5	2	0	49	24	10
10	NOR	7	4	3	0	37	32	8
11	YUG	7	2	4	1	25	34	5
12	JAP	7	2	4	1	33	40	5
13	AUT	7	1	6	0	17	34	2
14	ITA	7	0	5	2	12	43	2

1972

Rank	Team	GP	W	L	T	GF	GA	Pts
7	POL	6	6	0	0	41	12	12
8	USA	6	5	1	0	39	22	10
9	GDR	6	4	2	0	31	18	8
10	ROM	6	3	3	0	25	26	6
11	JAP	6	1	4	1	20	49	3
12	YUG	6	1	5	0	25	28	2
13	NOR	6	0	5	1	15	41	1

1973

Rank	Team	GP	W	L	T	GF	GA	Pts
7	GDR	7	7	0	0	56	21	14
8	USA	7	5	1	1	52	23	11
9	YUG	7	4	1	2	36	22	10
10	ROM	7	4	2	1	24	20	9
11	JAP	7	2	5	0	23	28	4
12	AUT	7	2	5	0	21	44	4
13	SUI	7	2	5	0	26	44	4
14	ITA	7	0	7	0	18	54	0

1974

Rank	Team	GP	W	L	T	GF	GA	Pts
7	USA	7	7	0	0	40	14	14
8	YUG	7	4	1	2	41	27	10
9	FRG	7	5	2	0	34	28	10
10	JAP	7	4	3	0	31	31	8
11	HOL	7	2	4	1	33	37	5
12	ROM	7	2	4	1	30	29	5
13	NOR	7	1	5	1	18	31	3
14	AUT	7	0	6	1	12	42	1

1975

Rank	Team	GP	W	L	T	GF	GA	Pts
7	GDR	7	6	1	0	41	18	12
8	FRG	7	6	1	0	34	17	12
9	SUI	7	4	3	0	31	33	8
10	YUG	7	3	3	1	30	23	7
11	ROM	7	2	3	2	26	26	6
12	JAP	7	2	3	2	21	24	6
13	ITA	7	2	5	0	22	40	4
14	HOL	7	0	6	1	11	35	1

1976

Rank	Team	GP	W	L	T	GF	GA	Pts
9	ROM	7	5	1	1	40	23	11
10	JAP	7	5	2	0	34	17	10
11	NOR	7	4	3	0	29	21	8
12	SUI	7	4	3	0	25	28	8
13	YUG	7	4	3	0	37	26	8
14	HOL	7	3	4	0	22	30	6
15	ITA	7	2	4	1	23	41	5
16	BUL	7	0	7	0	23	47	0

1977

Rank	Team	GP	W	L	T	GF	GA	Pts
9	GDR	8	8	0	0	57	16	16
10	POL	8	6	2	0	39	22	12
11	JAP	8	5	2	1	30	21	11
12	NOR	8	3	2	3	28	30	9
13	SUI	8	4	4	0	35	33	8
14	HUN	8	3	5	0	27	46	6
15	YUG	8	2	5	1	30	36	5
16	HOL	8	1	5	2	23	39	4
17	AUT	8	0	7	1	19	45	1

1978

Rank	Team	GP	W	L	T	GF	GA	Pts
9	POL	7	6	0	1	51	19	13
10	JAP	7	5	1	1	26	17	11
11	SUI	7	4	2	1	42	32	9
12	ROM	7	3	3	1	41	29	7
13	HUN	7	3	4	0	21	36	6
14	NOR	7	2	4	1	29	34	5
15	ITA	7	1	5	1	32	41	3
16	YUG	7	1	6	0	14	48	2

1979

Rank	Team	GP	W	L	T	GF	GA	Pts
9	HOL	6	6	0	0	36	13	12
10	GDR	6	5	1	0	42	12	10
11	ROM	6	3	2	1	27	21	7
12	NOR	6	3	3	0	17	25	6
13	SUI	6	4	2	0	23	20	8
14	JAP	7	3	4	0	36	30	6
15	AUT	5	2	2	1	17	23	5
16	DEN	6	1	5	0	13	32	2
17	HUN	4	0	4	0	10	25	0
18	PRC	4	0	4	0	8	28	0

1981

Rank	Team	GP	W	L	T	GF	GA	Pts
9	ITA	7	6	0	1	38	18	13
10	POL	7	5	1	1	49	25	11
11	SUI	7	4	1	2	28	20	10
12	GDR	7	4	2	1	37	25	9
13	ROM	7	2	5	0	25	30	4
14	NOR	7	2	5	0	21	39	4
15	YUG	7	1	5	1	23	44	3
16	JAP	7	1	6	0	18	38	2

1982

Rank	Team	GP	W	L	T	GF	GA	Pts
9	GDR	7	6	0	1	48	25	13
10	AUT	7	4	2	1	33	26	9
11	POL	7	4	2	1	42	23	9
12	NOR	7	3	4	0	24	43	6
13	ROM	7	2	4	1	27	30	5
14	SUI	7	1	3	3	20	27	5
15	PRC	7	2	4	1	32	47	5
16	HOL	7	2	5	0	22	27	4

1983

Rank	Team	GP	W	L	T	GF	GA	Pts
9	USA	7	6	0	1	53	14	13
10	POL	7	5	1	1	43	19	11
11	AUT	7	3	0	4	41	27	10
12	NOR	7	4	3	0	29	28	8
13	JAP	7	2	3	2	23	31	6
14	SUI	7	1	4	2	25	35	4
15	ROM	7	1	5	1	20	48	3
16	YUG	7	0	6	1	18	50	1

1985

Rank	Team	GP	W	L	T	GF	GA	Pts
9	POL	7	6	0	1	37	13	13
10	SUI	7	5	1	1	29	13	11
11	ITA	7	5	2	0	29	22	10
12	AUT	7	3	4	0	18	24	6
13	JAP	7	3	4	0	31	36	6
14	HOL	7	3	4	0	36	25	6
15	NOR	7	2	5	0	28	38	4
16	HUN	7	0	7	0	17	54	0

Rank	Team	GP	W	L	T	GF	GA	Pts
1986								
9	SUI	7	6	1	0	38	20	12
10	ITA	7	4	3	0	21	18	8
11	GDR	7	4	3	0	25	21	8
12	FRA	7	3	4	0	22	25	6
13	HOL	7	3	4	0	25	32	6
14	AUT	7	3	4	0	24	27	6
15	YUG	7	3	4	0	24	25	6
16	JAP	7	2	5	0	15	26	4
1987								
9	POL	7	6	1	0	39	11	12
10	NOR	7	5	1	1	33	25	11
11	AUT	7	5	2	0	41	27	10
12	FRA	7	4	2	1	37	26	9
13	GDR	7	2	3	2	25	31	6
14	ITA	7	2	4	1	28	30	5
15	HOL	7	1	5	1	30	37	3
16	PRC	7	0	7	0	14	60	0
1989								
9	NOR	7	5	1	1	28	16	11
10	ITA	7	5	1	1	37	16	11
11	FRA	7	4	1	2	29	18	10
12	SUI	7	5	2	0	40	21	10
13	GDR	7	3	4	0	22	29	6
14	AUT	7	2	5	0	25	32	4
15	JAP	7	2	5	0	20	34	4
16	DEN	7	0	7	0	9	44	0
1990								
9	SUI	7	5	0	2	30	14	12
10	ITA	7	3	2	2	29	18	8
11	AUT	7	4	1	2	30	14	10
12	FRA	7	4	1	2	19	17	10
13	GDR	7	2	3	2	22	19	6
14	POL	7	3	2	2	25	16	8
15	JAP	7	0	6	1	13	41	1
16	HOL	7	0	6	1	14	43	1
1991								
9	ITA	7	7	0	0	49	10	14
10	NOR	7	5	2	0	26	13	10
11	FRA	7	5	2	0	28	18	10
12	POL	7	4	3	0	25	15	8
13	AUT	7	3	3	1	21	18	7
14	YUG	7	2	5	0	18	36	4
15	HOL	7	1	6	0	9	40	2
16	JAP	7	0	6	1	9	35	1
1992								
13	AUT	7	7	0	0	73	4	14
14	HOL	7	5	1	1	53	16	11
15	JAP	7	4	3	0	30	24	8
16	DEN	7	4	3	0	23	24	8
17	BUL	7	3	4	0	14	38	6
18	ROM	7	1	3	3	13	26	5
19	PRC	7	1	5	1	15	50	3
20	YUG	7	0	6	1	7	46	1
1993								
13	GBR	7	7	0	0	50	13	14
14	POL	7	6	1	0	71	12	12
15	HOL	7	5	2	0	47	20	10
16	DEN	7	4	3	0	38	24	8
17	JAP	7	3	4	0	34	31	6
18	ROM	7	2	5	0	20	44	4
19	PRC	7	1	6	0	12	79	2
20	BUL	7	0	7	0	9	58	0
1994								
13	SUI	7	6	0	1	52	9	13
14	LAT	7	6	1	0	61	9	12
15	POL	7	5	1	1	45	21	11
16	JAP	7	3	3	1	37	38	7
17	DEN	7	3	4	0	31	27	6
18	HOL	7	2	4	1	23	33	5
19	ROM	7	1	6	0	18	43	2
20	PRC	7	0	7	0	11	98	0
1995								
13	SVK	7	7	0	0	60	15	14
14	LAT	7	6	1	0	65	16	12
15	POL	7	4	3	0	29	30	8
16	HOL	8	3	5	0	22	41	6
17	DEN	6	3	3	0	28	25	6
18	JAP	7	2	5	0	26	45	4
19	GBR	7	2	5	0	19	35	4
20	ROM	7	1	6	0	15	57	2
1996								
13	LAT	7	6	0	1	41	16	13
14	SUI	7	5	1	1	37	13	11
15	BLR	7	5	2	0	29	18	10
16	GBR	7	4	2	1	29	23	9
17	POL	7	1	4	2	18	27	4
18	DEN	7	1	5	1	14	32	3
19	HOL	7	1	5	1	12	35	3
20	JAP	7	0	4	3	14	30	3
1997								
13	BLR	7	7	0	0	48	21	14
14	KAZ	7	5	1	1	31	21	11
15	SUI	7	3	2	2	26	22	8
16	AUT	7	2	2	3	22	22	7
17	POL	7	2	3	2	19	24	6
18	GBR	7	2	4	1	28	22	5
19	HOL	7	2	4	1	21	38	5
20	DEN	7	0	7	0	19	44	0
1998								
17	UKR	7	7	0	0	38	13	14
18	SLO	7	5	1	1	28	15	11
19	EST	7	3	3	1	15	19	7
20	DEN	7	2	2	3	18	24	7
21	NOR	7	3	4	0	21	19	6
22	GBR	7	3	4	0	32	27	6
23	POL	7	2	4	1	21	28	5
24	HOL	7	0	7	0	12	40	0
1999								
17	DEN	7	6	0	1	30	12	13
18	GBR	7	5	1	1	24	16	11
19	KAZ	7	5	2	0	25	11	10
20	GER	7	5	2	0	19	17	10
21	SLO	7	2	4	1	14	17	5
22	EST	7	2	4	1	17	25	5
23	POL	7	1	6	0	15	23	2
24	HUN	7	0	7	0	10	33	0
2000								
17	GER	7	6	1	0	30	15	12
18	KAZ	7	5	2	0	30	22	10
19	GBR	7	4	2	1	31	23	9
20	POL	7	4	2	1	28	19	9
21	DEN	7	2	3	2	22	19	6
22	EST	7	3	4	0	19	27	6
23	SLO	7	0	5	2	16	31	2
24	HOL	7	0	5	2	13	33	2

World Championships, Pool C

Rank	Team	GP	W	L	T	GF	GA	Pts
1961								
15	ROM	5	5	0	0	69	5	10
16	FRA	5	4	1	0	34	16	8
17	YUG	5	3	2	0	34	22	6
18	HOL	5	2	3	0	18	36	4
19	SAF	5	1	4	0	18	47	2
20	BEL	5	0	5	0	9	56	0
1963								
16	AUT	5	5	0	0	62	7	10
17	HUN	5	4	1	0	57	12	8
18	DEN	5	3	2	0	22	31	6
19	BUL	5	1	3	1	19	22	3
20	HOL	5	1	3	1	21	34	3
21	BEL	5	0	5	0	8	83	0
1966								
17	ITA	4	4	0	0	54	8	8
18	DEN	4	2	2	0	21	21	4
19	SAF	4	0	4	0	4	50	0
20	FRA							
1967								
17	JAP	4	4	0	0	46	8	8
18	BUL	4	2	2	0	17	17	4
19	DEN	4	2	2	0	18	23	4
20	FRA	4	1	3	0	18	21	2
21	HOL	4	1	3	0	19	49	2
1969								
15	JAP	5	4	1	0	36	10	8
16	SUI	5	4	1	0	41	9	8
17	HUN	5	0	2	3	26	39	3
18	HOL	5	2	2	1	24	40	5
19	BUL	5	2	2	1	21	28	5
20	DEN	5	0	4	1	10	32	1
1970								
15	AUT	6	5	0	1	44	9	11
16	ITA	6	0	0	6	27	27	6
17	HUN	6	3	2	1	35	15	7
18	FRA	6	4	1	1	32	15	9
19	DEN	6	1	3	2	21	27	4
20	HOL	6	1	3	2	19	37	4
21	BEL	6	0	5	1	15	63	1
1971								
15	ROM	7	6	0	1	70	12	13
16	FRA	7	6	1	0	45	19	12
17	HUN	7	5	1	1	58	27	11
18	GBR	7	3	3	1	47	39	7
19	BUL	7	2	4	1	36	32	5
20	DEN	7	2	5	0	33	30	4
21	HOL	7	2	5	0	31	30	4
22	BEL	7	0	7	0	7	138	0
1972								
14	AUT	6	5	0	1	21	12	11
15	ITA	6	4	1	1	31	13	9
16	HUN	6	2	2	2	31	24	6
17	BUL	6	3	3	0	20	19	6
18	PRC	6	2	2	2	19	20	6
19	HOL	6	1	5	0	13	25	2
20	DEN	6	1	5	0	11	33	2
1973								
15	NOR	7	7	0	0	53	14	14
16	HOL	7	5	2	0	52	21	10
17	HUN	7	5	2	0	44	24	10
18	BUL	7	3	3	1	29	28	7
19	PRC	7	2	3	2	21	28	6
20	FRA	7	3	4	0	23	29	6
21	DEN	7	0	5	2	22	58	2
22	GBR	7	0	6	1	18	60	1
1974								
15	SUI	7	6	1	0	63	4	12
16	ITA	7	5	1	1	42	14	11
17	BUL	7	4	2	1	39	18	9
18	HUN	7	3	1	3	38	22	9
19	FRA	7	4	3	0	37	25	8
20	PRC	7	1	4	2	16	38	4
21	AUS	7	1	6	0	13	74	2
22	PRK	7	0	6	1	12	65	1
1975								
15	NOR	6	5	0	1	43	3	11
16	BUL	6	4	1	1	40	17	9
17	AUT	6	3	2	1	32	16	7
18	HUN	6	3	2	1	44	21	7
19	FRA	6	2	2	2	32	22	6
20	DEN	6	1	5	0	26	32	2
21	BEL	6	0	6	0	5	111	0
1976								
17	AUT	10	7	2	1	70	25	15
18	HUN	10	6	3	1	74	30	13
19	FRA	10	4	4	2	46	40	10
20	DEN	10	2	8	0	42	56	4
21	GBR	4	0	4	0	6	44	0
1977								
18	ITA	6	5	0	1	64	6	11
19	DEN	6	5	0	1	61	15	11
20	BUL	6	4	2	0	47	25	8
21	FRA	6	3	3	0	37	24	6
22	ESP	6	1	5	0	17	61	2
23	BEL	6	1	5	0	24	89	2
24	GBR	6	1	5	0	17	47	2
1978								
17	HOL	7	6	0	1	74	17	13
18	AUT	7	5	1	1	65	31	11
19	DEN	7	4	2	1	59	25	9
20	PRC	7	4	3	0	47	30	8
21	BUL	7	3	3	1	27	30	7
22	FRA	7	3	4	0	46	39	6
23	ESP	7	1	6	0	26	84	2
24	BEL	7	0	7	0	13	101	0
1979								
19	YUG	7	7	0	0	83	10	14
20	ITA	7	6	1	0	64	17	12
21	FRA	7	5	2	0	59	27	10
22	BUL	7	4	3	0	35	28	8
23	ESP	7	2	5	0	25	48	4
24	GBR	7	2	5	0	23	68	4
25	KOR	7	1	5	1	16	67	3
26	AUS	7	0	6	1	13	53	1
1981								
17	AUT	7	7	0	0	43	5	14
18	PRC	7	6	1	0	46	14	12
19	HUN	7	4	2	1	38	22	9
20	DEN	7	3	3	1	36	27	7
21	FRA	7	3	4	0	48	36	6
22	BUL	7	3	4	0	22	32	6
23	PRK	7	1	6	0	18	66	2
24	GBR	7	0	7	0	11	60	0
1982								
17	JAP	7	7	0	0	70	14	14
18	YUG	7	5	2	0	59	20	10
19	DEN	7	4	2	1	35	20	9
20	FRA	7	4	3	0	56	30	8
21	HUN	7	4	3	0	43	29	8
22	BUL	7	2	4	1	29	30	5
23	ESP	7	1	6	0	26	50	2
24	KOR	7	0	7	0	11	136	0
1983								
17	HOL	7	7	0	0	78	11	14
18	HUN	7	5	2	0	50	25	10
19	PRC	7	4	2	1	28	23	9
20	DEN	7	4	3	0	24	26	8
21	FRA	7	3	3	1	41	25	7
22	BUL	7	1	5	1	20	36	3
23	ESP	7	1	5	1	17	55	3
24	PRK	7	1	6	0	15	72	2
1985								
17	FRA	7	6	0	1	54	13	13
18	YUG	7	6	1	0	36	13	12
19	PRC	7	5	1	1	45	22	11
20	ROM	7	4	3	0	51	29	8
21	DEN	7	3	4	0	16	23	6
22	BUL	7	2	5	0	27	45	4
23	PRK	7	1	6	0	18	56	2
24	ESP	7	0	7	0	9	55	0
1986								
17	NOR	6	5	0	1	55	11	11
18	PRC	6	4	0	2	42	10	10
19	BUL	6	4	2	0	21	30	8
20	ROM	6	3	3	0	33	20	6
21	DEN	6	4	2	0	32	18	8
22	HUN	6	2	3	1	31	27	5
23	PRK	6	1	4	1	14	27	3
24	ESP	6	1	4	1	19	47	3
1987								
17	JAP	7	5	1	1	61	13	11
18	DEN	7	5	1	1	47	23	11
19	ROM	7	5	1	1	48	22	11
20	YUG	7	3	0	4	60	23	10
21	HUN	7	3	4	0	33	28	6
22	PRK	7	2	5	0	13	45	4
23	BUL	7	1	5	1	21	40	3
24	BEL	7	0	7	0	8	97	0

1989

Rank	Team	GP	W	L	T	GF	GA	Pts
17	HOL	7	7	0	0	48	15	14
18	YUG	7	6	1	0	55	14	12
19	PRC	7	4	2	1	31	29	9
20	HUN	7	3	3	1	32	30	7
21	BUL	7	3	3	1	35	35	7
22	PRK	7	2	5	0	26	40	4
23	KOR	7	1	5	1	26	46	3
24	AUS	7	0	7	0	14	58	0

1990

Rank	Team	GP	W	L	T	GF	GA	Pts
17	YUG	8	7	0	1	57	16	15
18	DEN	8	7	1	0	55	14	14
19	PRC	8	4	3	1	34	29	9
20	ROM	8	4	3	1	36	27	9
21	PRK	8	5	3	0	28	34	10
22	BUL	8	4	4	0	31	38	8
23	HUN	8	2	5	1	33	28	5
24	BEL	8	1	7	0	16	67	2
25	KOR	8	0	8	0	21	58	0

1991

Rank	Team	GP	W	L	T	GF	GA	Pts
17	DEN	8	7	0	1	71	13	15
18	PRC	8	6	1	1	44	24	13
19	ROM	8	6	2	0	51	22	12
20	BUL	8	4	3	1	35	26	9
21	GBR	8	4	3	1	45	25	9
22	HUN	8	3	4	1	37	32	7
23	PRK	8	2	5	1	29	35	5
24	KOR	8	1	7	0	19	64	2
25	BEL	8	0	8	0	11	101	0

1992

Rank	Team	GP	W	L	T	GF	GA	Pts
13	GBR	5	5	0	0	62	10	10
14	PRK	5	3	2	0	22	28	6
15	AUS	5	2	2	1	24	23	5
16	HUN	5	2	3	0	18	33	4
17	BEL	5	2	3	0	17	24	4
18	KOR	5	0	4	1	18	43	1
19	ESP	5	5	0	0	114	5	10
20	SAF	5	4	1	0	49	17	8
21	GRE	5	3	2	0	36	31	6
22	ISR	5	1	3	1	22	42	3
23	LUX	5	1	3	1	20	73	3
24	TUR	5	0	5	0	10	83	0

1993

Rank	Team	GP	W	L	T	GF	GA	Pts
17	LAT	9	8	0	1	120	14	17
18	UKR	9	6	2	1	113	20	13
19	KAZ	9	6	3	0	91	19	12
20	SLO	9	7	2	0	100	19	14
21	HUN	5	3	2	0	36	31	6
22	PRK	5	3	2	0	30	26	6
23	AUS	5	2	3	0	19	51	4
24	BEL	5	2	3	0	19	74	4
25	KOR	6	2	4	0	23	63	4
26	ESP	6	1	5	0	21	46	2
27	ISR	7	2	5	0	30	97	4
28	SAF	5	0	5	0	8	100	0

1994

Rank	Team	GP	W	L	T	GF	GA	Pts
21	SVK	6	4	0	2	43	3	10
22	BLR	6	5	1	0	35	11	10
23	UKR	6	3	1	2	49	7	8
24	KAZ	6	3	1	2	52	12	8
25	SLO	6	2	4	0	26	27	4
26	HUN	6	1	5	0	14	47	2
27	BUL	6	0	6	0	3	115	0
28	EST	7	7	0	0	77	5	14
29	ESP	5	3	1	1	30	16	7
30	KOR	5	3	1	1	13	16	7
31	CRO	7	4	3	0	65	17	8
32	BEL	5	3	2	0	25	21	6
33	AUS	5	2	3	0	20	16	4
34	ISR	5	1	4	0	15	31	2
35	SAF	5	0	5	0	8	62	0

1995

Rank	Team	GP	W	L	T	GF	GA	Pts
21	BLR	4	3	1	0	14	8	6
22	KAZ	4	3	0	1	23	3	7
23	UKR	4	2	1	1	28	9	5
24	EST	4	3	1	0	22	16	6
25	PRC	4	2	2	0	13	26	4
26	HUN	4	1	3	0	15	20	2
27	SLO	4	2	2	0	28	15	4
28	YUG	4	1	3	0	13	31	2
29	BUL	4	0	4	0	4	32	0
30	CRO	6	5	0	1	50	17	11
31	LIT	6	5	0	1	48	13	11
32	ESP	6	4	2	0	42	19	8
33	KOR	6	3	3	0	42	19	6
34	BEL	6	2	3	1	30	27	5
35	ISR	6	3	3	0	31	22	6
36	AUS	6	3	3	0	31	31	6
37	SAF	6	1	5	0	14	47	2
38	GRE	4	0	3	1	9	56	1
39	NZL	4	0	4	0	7	53	0

1996

Rank	Team	GP	W	L	T	GF	GA	Pts
21	KAZ	7	6	1	0	51	10	12
22	UKR	7	6	1	0	40	13	12
23	SLO	7	5	2	0	41	19	10
24	HUN	7	2	3	2	34	31	6
25	EST	7	3	3	1	36	29	7
26	ROM	7	3	4	0	32	27	6
27	PRC	7	1	5	1	23	68	3
28	CRO	7	0	7	0	11	71	0

1997

Rank	Team	GP	W	L	T	GF	GA	Pts
21	UKR	5	4	0	1	21	6	9
22	SLO	5	3	2	0	25	13	6
23	EST	5	2	1	2	27	17	6
24	JAP	5	2	1	2	14	9	6
25	ROM	5	3	2	0	15	20	6
26	HUN	5	2	2	1	18	16	5
27	PRC	5	1	4	0	16	34	2
28	LIT	5	0	5	0	11	32	0

1998

Rank	Team	GP	W	L	T	GF	GA	Pts
25	HUN	5	5	0	0	36	4	10
26	ROM	5	4	1	0	31	13	8
27	LIT	5	3	2	0	13	29	6
28	PRC	5	2	3	0	21	25	4
29	CRO	5	1	2	2	11	15	4
30	YUG	5	1	2	2	10	13	4
31	KOR	5	1	4	0	4	18	2
32	ESP	5	0	3	2	12	21	2

1999

Rank	Team	GP	W	L	T	GF	GA	Pts
25	HOL	5	5	0	0	43	3	10
26	ROM	4	3	1	0	24	16	6
27	LIT	4	0	2	2	11	19	2
28	PRC	5	2	2	1	16	26	5
29	CRO	4	1	2	1	20	18	3
30	KOR	4	1	1	2	18	22	4
31	BUL	4	0	4	0	7	35	0

2000

Rank	Team	GP	W	L	T	GF	GA	Pts
25	HUN	4	4	0	0	32	9	8
26	PRC	4	3	1	0	25	5	6
27	CRO	4	1	2	1	18	22	3
28	LIT	4	2	1	1	23	16	5
29	KOR	4	2	2	0	19	23	4
30	ROM	4	1	1	2	21	14	4
31	ESP	4	1	2	1	11	21	3
32	YUG	4	0	2	2	4	22	2
33	BUL	4	0	3	1	7	28	1

World Championships, Pool D

1987

Rank	Team	GP	W	L	T	GF	GA	Pts
25	AUS	6	5	0	1	176	6	11
26	KOR	6	4	1	1	130	16	9
27	NZL	6	2	4	0	42	142	4
28	HKG	6	0	6	0	1	185	0

1989

Rank	Team	GP	W	L	T	GF	GA	Pts
25	BEL	4	3	0	1	35	9	7
26	ROM	4	2	0	2	69	7	6
27	GBR	4	1	1	2	19	16	4
28	ESP	4	1	3	0	29	27	2
29	NZL	4	0	3	1	3	96	1

1990

Rank	Team	GP	W	L	T	GF	GA	Pts
26	GBR	4	4	0	0	57	7	8
27	AUS	4	0	2	2	10	34	2
28	ESP	4	0	2	2	11	37	2

1996

Rank	Team	GP	W	L	T	GF	GA	Pts
29	LIT	5	5	0	0	33	4	10
30	YUG	5	4	1	0	20	10	8
31	ESP	5	2	2	1	22	18	5
32	BEL	5	2	3	0	10	24	4
33	KOR	5	2	1	2	24	17	6
34	BUL	5	2	3	0	16	16	4
35	ISR	7	2	4	1	30	21	5
36	AUS	5	0	5	0	14	43	0

1997

Rank	Team	GP	W	L	T	GF	GA	Pts
29	CRO	5	3	1	1	16	9	7
30	KOR	5	4	1	0	19	9	8
31	ESP	5	2	3	0	21	19	4
32	YUG	5	1	2	2	13	18	4
33	ISR	5	2	3	0	18	25	4
34	AUS	5	1	3	1	20	25	3
35	BUL	5	2	1	2	17	15	6
36	BEL	5	2	3	0	12	16	4

1998

Rank	Team	GP	W	L	T	GF	GA	Pts
33	BUL	5	4	0	1	50	7	9
34	AUS	5	3	1	1	35	15	7
35	ISR	5	3	2	0	34	16	6
36	BEL	5	3	2	0	28	15	6
37	RSA	5	3	2	0	32	20	6
38	NZL	5	1	4	0	15	39	2
39	TUR	5	1	4	0	12	56	2
40	GRE	5	1	4	0	15	53	2

1999

Rank	Team	GP	W	L	T	GF	GA	Pts
32	ESP	4	3	0	1	38	7	7
33	ISR	4	3	0	1	22	5	7
34	AUS	4	2	2	0	29	9	4
35	BEL	4	3	1	0	32	9	6
36	RSA	4	2	2	0	24	14	4
37	NZL	4	1	3	0	7	39	2
38	TUR	4	1	3	0	7	42	2
39	GRE	4	1	3	0	10	18	2
40	ISL	4	1	3	0	9	35	2

2000

Rank	Team	GP	W	L	T	GF	GA	Pts
34	ISR	4	3	0	1	31	7	7
35	BEL	4	3	0	1	23	5	7
36	AUS	4	2	2	0	23	16	4
37	SAF	4	3	1	0	26	19	6
38	ISL	4	2	2	0	22	18	4
39	NZL	4	1	3	0	9	24	2
40	MEX	4	2	2	0	16	17	4
41	LUX	4	1	3	0	9	23	2
42	TUR	4	0	4	0	7	37	0

World Junior Championships, Pool B

1979

Rank	Team	GP	W	L	T	GF	GA	Pts
9	SUI	4	4	0	0	32	11	8
10	FRA	4	3	1	0	26	13	6
11	POL	4	3	1	0	43	17	6
12	DEN	4	2	2	0	13	14	4
13	AUT	4	2	2	0	17	20	4
14	HOL	4	1	3	0	16	23	2
15	ITA	4	1	3	0	22	21	2
16	BEL	4	0	4	0	9	59	0

1980

Rank	Team	GP	W	L	T	GF	GA	Pts
9	AUT	4	4	0	0	33	9	8
10	POL	4	3	1	0	30	10	6
11	NOR	4	3	1	0	28	10	6
12	HOL	4	2	2	0	19	16	4
13	DEN	4	2	2	0	18	19	4
14	ITA	4	1	3	0	12	20	2
15	FRA	4	1	3	0	19	31	2
16	HUN	4	0	4	0	11	55	0

1981

Rank	Team	GP	W	L	T	GF	GA	Pts
9	SUI	5	4	0	1	34	10	9
10	NOR	5	3	0	2	32	18	8
11	POL	5	3	2	0	34	16	6
12	HOL	5	2	3	0	10	28	4
13	DEN	5	3	2	0	22	22	6
14	YUG	5	1	3	1	20	27	3
15	ITA	5	1	3	1	17	33	3
16	FRA	5	0	4	1	20	35	1

1982

Rank	Team	GP	W	L	T	GF	GA	Pts
9	NOR	4	4	0	0	18	9	8
10	AUT	4	3	1	0	21	13	6
11	JAP	4	3	1	0	23	13	6
12	DEN	4	2	2	0	22	18	4
13	FRA	4	2	2	0	18	16	4
14	ITA	4	0	3	1	9	19	1
15	HOL	4	1	2	1	12	19	3
16	YUG	4	0	4	0	12	28	0
9	SUI	5	4	1	0	29	14	8

1983

Rank	Team	GP	W	L	T	GF	GA	Pts
10	JAP	5	3	2	0	30	19	6
11	POL	5	4	1	0	29	17	8
12	AUT	5	2	3	0	23	25	4
13	FRA	5	2	2	1	32	21	5
14	HOL	5	2	2	1	32	35	5
15	DEN	5	1	3	1	17	41	3
16	ITA	5	0	4	1	18	38	1

1984

Rank	Team	GP	W	L	T	GF	GA	Pts
9	POL	5	4	0	1	29	18	9
10	AUT	5	4	1	0	22	17	8
11	JAP	5	2	1	2	30	21	6
12	NOR	5	2	3	0	29	21	4
13	HOL	5	3	1	1	22	20	7
14	FRA	5	2	3	0	28	25	4
15	ROM	5	1	4	0	15	33	2
16	DEN	5	0	5	0	9	29	0

1985

Rank	Team	GP	W	L	T	GF	GA	Pts
9	SUI	7	7	0	0	58	22	14
10	HOL	7	5	1	1	47	14	11
11	JAP	7	4	2	1	34	23	9
12	AUT	7	3	3	1	30	53	7
13	NOR	7	2	4	1	23	28	5
14	ITA	7	2	5	0	14	28	4
15	ROM	7	1	5	1	27	42	3
16	FRA	7	1	5	1	19	42	3

1986

Rank	Team	GP	W	L	T	GF	GA	Pts
9	POL	7	6	1	0	46	17	12
10	NOR	7	5	1	1	54	18	11
11	AUT	7	5	2	0	42	35	10
12	ROM	7	3	2	2	32	28	8
13	JAP	7	3	4	0	35	31	6
14	HOL	7	3	4	0	30	43	6
15	ITA	7	1	5	1	26	40	3
16	BUL	7	0	7	0	9	62	0

1987

Rank	Team	GP	W	L	T	GF	GA	Pts
9	FRG	5	4	0	1	48	11	9
10	NOR	5	3	1	1	38	25	7
11	JAP	5	3	2	0	28	24	6
12	AUT	5	1	3	1	14	36	3
13	FRA	5	3	1	1	21	16	7
14	ROM	5	2	3	0	25	36	4
15	HOL	5	1	3	1	25	30	3
16	ITA	5	0	4	1	14	35	1

Rank	Team	GP	W	L	T	GF	GA	Pts
1988								
9	NOR	7	5	2	0	38	18	10
10	ROM	7	5	2	0	24	27	10
11	SUI	7	4	2	1	34	23	9
12	JAP	7	3	2	2	34	27	8
13	FRA	7	4	3	0	31	36	8
14	YUG	7	3	3	1	37	36	7
15	HOL	7	0	4	3	20	35	3
16	AUT	7	0	6	1	26	42	1
1989								
9	POL	7	7	0	0	48	20	14
10	SUI	7	6	1	0	45	19	12
11	ROM	7	4	3	0	32	31	8
12	JAP	7	4	3	0	32	34	8
13	YUG	7	4	3	0	42	40	8
14	FRA	7	1	5	1	23	31	3
15	DEN	9	3	5	1	31	46	7
16	HOL	7	0	7	0	17	47	0
DNQ	ITA	2	0	2	0	4	6	0
1990								
9	SUI	7	6	1	0	48	14	12
10	FRG	7	6	1	0	35	12	12
11	JAP	7	4	2	1	38	33	9
12	DEN	7	2	3	2	26	31	6
13	FRA	7	3	4	0	39	30	6
14	AUT	7	2	4	1	20	43	5
15	ROM	7	2	5	0	26	39	4
16	YUG	7	0	5	2	25	55	2
1991								
9	GER	7	6	0	1	47	15	13
10	POL	7	6	1	0	53	17	12
11	FRA	7	4	1	2	42	19	10
12	JAP	7	4	2	1	34	22	9
13	ROM	7	2	4	1	23	43	5
14	HOL	7	1	5	1	16	41	3
15	AUT	7	1	6	0	13	48	2
16	DEN	7	1	6	0	22	45	2
1992								
9	JAP	7	5	2	0	32	17	10
10	POL	7	5	2	0	42	19	10
11	NOR	7	5	2	0	45	17	10
12	FRA	7	5	2	0	31	15	10
13	ROM	7	4	3	0	23	26	8
14	HOL	7	2	5	0	14	38	4
15	AUT	7	2	5	0	16	29	4
16	PRK	7	0	7	0	12	54	0
1993								
9	SUI	7	6	0	1	39	13	13
10	NOR	7	6	1	0	49	11	12
11	ITA	7	4	2	1	23	18	9
12	AUT	7	4	3	0	26	23	8
13	FRA	7	3	4	0	26	30	6
14	POL	7	1	5	1	17	28	3
15	ROM	7	1	5	1	16	37	3
16	HOL	7	1	6	0	10	46	2
1994								
9	UKR	7	7	0	0	35	8	14
10	NOR	7	5	1	1	26	15	11
11	FRA	7	3	3	1	23	23	7
12	POL	7	3	4	0	15	26	6
13	ITA	7	2	4	1	20	22	5
14	AUT	7	1	3	3	21	27	5
15	JAP	7	2	5	0	19	27	4
16	ROM	7	1	4	2	21	32	4
1995								
9	SUI	7	5	0	2	40	12	12
10	SVK	7	5	2	0	33	16	10
11	POL	7	4	2	1	26	22	9
12	FRA	7	5	2	0	25	14	10
13	NOR	7	2	4	1	26	27	5
14	AUT	7	2	4	1	20	31	5
15	JAP	7	1	5	1	17	44	3
16	ITA	7	1	6	0	16	37	2
1996								
11	POL	6	6	0	0	47	7	12
12	LAT	6	5	1	0	27	20	10
13	NOR	6	3	3	0	18	16	6
14	HUN	6	3	3	0	24	20	6
15	ITA	6	2	4	0	13	27	4
16	JAP	6	1	5	0	13	31	2
NR	FRA	5	3	2	0	18	14	6
NR	AUT	5	0	5	0	10	35	0
1997								
11	KAZ	7	6	0	1	39	15	13
12	LAT	7	5	1	1	28	19	11
13	FRA	7	4	1	2	22	16	10
14	NOR	7	2	2	3	33	23	7
15	UKR	7	3	3	1	26	18	7
16	JAP	7	2	3	2	24	17	6
17	HUN	7	1	6	0	14	44	2
18	ITA	7	0	7	0	12	46	0
1998								
11	BLR	6	4	1	1	22	11	9
12	UKR	6	4	1	1	31	13	9
13	POL	6	4	2	0	29	17	8
14	LAT	6	3	3	0	20	20	6
15	HUN	6	1	3	2	11	29	4
16	FRA	6	1	4	1	20	29	3
17	NOR	6	3	3	0	21	22	6
18	JAP	6	1	4	1	21	34	3
1999								
11	UKR	6	5	0	1	30	13	11
12	POL	6	3	1	2	20	16	8
13	DEN	6	3	2	1	18	18	7
14	GER	6	2	4	0	19	14	4
15	LAT	6	2	4	0	12	17	4
16	NOR	6	2	4	0	17	25	4
17	FRA	5	3	2	0	22	16	6
18	HUN	5	1	4	0	5	24	2
2000								
11	BLR	5	4	0	1	20	10	9
12	GER	5	4	1	0	15	7	8
13	FRA	5	2	2	1	15	21	5
14	NOR	5	2	3	0	18	14	4
15	POL	5	2	1	2	17	15	6
16	ITA	5	1	2	2	6	10	4
17	LAT	5	1	4	0	8	14	2
18	DEN	5	1	4	0	17	25	2

World Junior Championships, Pool C

Rank	Team	GP	W	L	T	GF	GA	Pts
1983								
17	ROM	6	6	0	0	49	9	12
18	BUL	6	3	3	0	16	18	6
19	HUN	6	3	3	0	21	30	6
20	AUS	6	0	6	0	12	41	0
1984								
17	ITA	5	4	0	1	41	14	9
18	BUL	5	3	1	1	24	12	7
19	HUN	5	3	1	1	34	18	7
20	ESP	5	2	2	1	21	29	5
21	BEL	5	3	2	0	26	18	6
22	GBR	5	2	3	0	22	36	4
23	AUS	5	1	4	0	19	37	2
NR	ITA–2	5	0	5	0	7	30	0
1985								
17	BUL	5	5	0	0	28	17	10
18	HUN	5	4	1	0	35	12	8
19	BEL	5	2	2	1	32	27	5
20	DEN	5	2	2	1	20	24	5
21	GBR	5	1	4	0	10	37	2
22	ESP	5	0	5	0	18	26	0
1986								
17	FRA	5	4	0	1	52	13	9
18	DEN	5	3	0	2	29	16	8
19	GBR	5	3	2	0	20	32	6
20	PRC	5	2	3	0	23	27	4
21	HUN	5	1	4	0	16	32	2
22	BEL	5	0	4	1	14	34	1
1987								
17	YUG	5	5	0	0	56	12	10
18	DEN	5	4	1	0	44	24	8
19	GBR	5	3	2	0	25	21	6
20	BUL	5	2	3	0	21	23	4
21	ESP	5	1	4	0	19	34	2
22	AUS	5	0	5	0	5	56	0
1988								
17	DEN	7	7	0	0	59	11	14
18	ITA	7	6	1	0	27	17	12
19	BUL	7	5	2	0	39	16	10
20	GBR	7	3	3	1	21	27	7
21	ESP	7	2	4	1	19	45	5
22	HUN	7	2	5	0	14	28	4
23	PRK	7	1	4	2	20	29	4
24	BEL	7	0	7	0	8	34	0
1989								
17	AUT	4	3	0	1	21	14	7
18	ITA	4	2	0	2	22	14	6
19	PRK	4	2	2	0	17	20	4
20	GBR	4	0	2	2	15	19	2
21	BUL	4	0	3	1	12	20	1
1990								
17	HOL	6	5	1	0	40	17	10
18	PRK	6	4	1	1	27	14	9
19	ITA	6	5	1	0	35	10	10
20	BUL	6	2	3	1	25	31	5
21	KOR	6	3	3	0	25	39	6
22	GBR	6	1	5	0	17	31	2
23	HUN	6	0	6	0	19	46	0
1991								
17	PRK	7	6	1	0	50	18	12
18	ITA	7	6	1	0	57	11	12
19	YUG	7	5	1	1	77	21	11
20	GBR	7	4	3	0	45	20	8
21	KOR	7	3	3	1	55	28	7
22	BUL	7	2	5	0	34	48	4
23	HUN	7	1	6	0	28	46	2
24	GRE	7	0	7	0	4	158	0
1992								
17	ITA	3	3	0	0	17	6	6
18	DEN	4	3	1	0	30	9	6
19	GBR	4	1	3	0	22	19	2
20	ESP	4	3	1	0	19	15	6
21	HUN	4	2	2	0	13	18	4
22	KOR	3	0	3	0	8	18	0
23	YUG	3	1	1	1	11	16	3
24	BUL	3	0	2	1	2	21	1
25	GRE	DISQUALIFIED						
1993								
17	UKR	4	4	0	0	46	6	8
18	DEN	4	2	1	1	26	18	5
19	HUN	4	2	1	1	30	19	5
20	BUL	4	1	2	1	16	32	3
21	GBR	4	2	1	1	19	14	5
22	PRK	4	0	2	2	11	28	2
23	ESP	4	1	2	1	17	26	3
24	KOR	4	0	3	1	12	34	1
1994								
17	SVK	4	4	0	0	55	3	8
18	LAT	4	3	1	0	56	9	6
19	DEN	4	3	1	0	15	31	6
20	GBR	4	2	2	0	21	27	4
21	HUN	4	2	2	0	25	19	4
22	HOL	4	1	3	0	8	33	2
23	ESP	4	1	3	0	7	30	2
24	BUL	4	0	4	0	10	45	0
1995								
17	LAT	4	4	0	0	34	8	8
18	HUN	4	3	1	0	24	8	6
19	DEN	4	3	1	0	18	13	6
20	BLR	4	2	2	0	15	12	4
21	ESP	4	2	2	0	9	19	4
22	ROM	4	1	3	0	8	20	2
23	HOL	4	1	3	0	10	25	2
24	GBR	4	0	4	0	9	22	0
25	KAZ	5	3	0	2	47	10	8
26	SLO	5	3	0	2	40	15	8
27	EST	5	2	1	2	24	25	6
28	LIT	5	2	3	0	29	30	4
29	CRO	5	0	2	3	10	21	3
30	YUG	5	0	4	1	13	62	1
1996								
17	KAZ	4	4	0	0	31	16	8
18	SLO	4	3	1	0	27	11	6
19	DEN	4	3	1	0	23	9	6
20	BLR	4	2	2	0	27	16	4
21	GBR	4	2	2	0	17	16	4
22	ROM	4	1	3	0	12	29	2
23	HOL	4	1	3	0	10	21	2
24	ESP	4	0	4	0	5	34	0
1997								
19	BLR	4	4	0	0	34	4	8
20	SLO	4	3	1	0	24	14	6
21	DEN	4	3	1	0	32	12	6
22	GBR	4	2	2	0	17	14	4
23	AUT	4	2	2	0	9	13	4
24	ROM	4	1	3	0	9	21	2
25	CRO	4	1	3	0	5	25	2
26	HOL	4	0	4	0	10	37	0
1998								
19	DEN	4	4	0	0	32	12	8
20	ITA	4	2	1	1	24	12	5
21	SLO	4	3	1	0	19	10	6
22	AUT	4	2	1	1	20	10	5
23	CRO	4	2	2	0	9	16	4
24	EST	4	1	3	0	7	23	2
25	GBR	4	1	3	0	10	19	2
26	ROM	4	0	4	0	12	31	0
1999								
19	ITA	4	3	1	0	10	6	6
20	JAP	4	3	1	0	16	5	6
21	SLO	4	3	1	0	19	11	6
22	AUT	4	2	2	0	17	17	4
23	EST	4	2	1	1	13	11	5
24	LIT	4	0	3	1	11	18	1
25	GBR	4	1	2	1	9	15	3
26	CRO	4	0	3	1	10	22	1
2000								
19	AUT	4	4	0	0	37	7	8
20	SLO	4	2	1	1	14	13	5
21	GBR	4	2	0	2	16	9	6
22	HUN	4	2	2	0	16	25	4
23	JAP	4	2	1	1	20	10	5
24	EST	4	0	3	1	11	28	1
25	LIT	4	1	3	0	11	16	2
26	YUG	4	0	3	1	8	25	1

World Junior Championships, Pool D

Rank	Team	GP	W	L	T	GF	GA	Pts
1996								
25	CRO	3	3	0	0	22	4	6
26	EST	3	2	1	0	24	5	4
27	YUG	3	2	1	0	15	9	4
28	LIT	3	1	2	0	25	12	2
29	BUL	3	1	2	0	14	35	2
30	SAF	3	0	3	0	3	38	0

1997

Rank	Team	GP	W	L	T	GF	GA	Pts
27	EST	4	4	0	0	46	11	8
28	LIT	4	3	1	0	49	12	6
29	YUG	4	3	1	0	26	13	6
30	ESP	4	2	2	0	18	16	4
31	ISR	4	2	2	0	20	26	4
32	BUL	4	1	3	0	12	27	2
33	SAF	4	1	3	0	8	37	2
34	MEX	4	0	4	0	8	45	0

1998

Rank	Team	GP	W	L	T	GF	GA	Pts
27	LIT	4	4	0	0	39	5	8
28	HOL	4	3	1	0	61	10	6
29	YUG	4	3	1	0	32	7	6
30	ESP	4	2	2	0	18	18	4
31	MEX	4	2	2	0	9	32	4
32	BUL	4	1	3	0	21	35	2
33	RSA	4	1	3	0	15	26	2
34	TUR	4	0	4	0	5	67	0

1999

Rank	Team	GP	W	L	T	GF	GA	Pts
27	YUG	4	4	0	0	30	4	8
28	HOL	4	3	1	0	51	9	6
29	ROM	4	2	2	0	33	11	4
30	ESP	4	2	1	1	16	15	5
31	MEX	4	2	2	0	40	13	4
32	RSA	4	1	3	0	13	22	2
33	BUL	4	2	2	0	25	37	4
34	ISL	4	1	2	1	24	29	3
35	TUR	4	0	4	0	1	93	0

2000

Rank	Team	GP	W	L	T	GF	GA	Pts
27	CRO	4	4	0	0	47	10	8
28	ROM	4	3	1	0	33	13	6
29	HOL	4	2	2	0	30	12	4
30	ESP	4	3	1	0	24	15	6
31	MEX	4	2	2	0	13	24	4
32	SAF	4	1	3	0	18	23	2
33	AUS	4	2	2	0	21	29	4
34	BUL	4	1	3	0	11	43	2
37	ISL	4	0	4	0	9	37	0

European Junior Championships, (Under 18) Pool A

1968

Rank	Team	GP	W	L	T	GF	GA	Pts
1	TCH	6	6	0	0	47	14	12
2	URS	7	6	1	0	52	15	12
3	SWE	7	4	2	1	71	20	9
4	FIN	5	2	3	0	26	21	4
5	POL	7	2	3	2	41	53	6
6	GDR	7	2	5	0	21	62	4
NR	FRG	1	0	1	0	0	1	0
NR	NOR	2	0	2	0	1	35	0
NR	BUL	2	0	2	0	1	13	0
NR	SUI	2	0	2	0	2	13	0
NR	FRA	2	0	1	1	7	22	1

1969

Rank	Team	GP	W	L	T	GF	GA	Pts
1	URS	5	4	0	1	46	12	9
2	SWE	5	4	1	0	37	17	8
3	TCH	5	3	1	1	28	8	7
4	FRG	5	1	4	0	15	33	2
5	FIN	5	1	4	0	18	32	2
6	POL	5	1	4	0	11	53	2

1970

Rank	Team	GP	W	L	T	GF	GA	Pts
1	URS	5	5	0	0	41	11	10
2	TCH	5	4	1	0	26	12	8
3	SWE	5	3	2	0	44	10	6
4	FIN	5	2	3	0	13	19	4
5	FRG	5	1	4	0	11	33	2
6	SUI	5	0	5	0	8	58	0

1971

Rank	Team	GP	W	L	T	GF	GA	Pts
1	URS	5	5	0	0	46	5	10
2	SWE	5	3	1	1	46	15	7
3	TCH	5	3	1	1	40	19	7
4	FIN	5	2	3	0	30	31	4
5	FRG	5	1	4	0	10	45	2
6	NOR	5	0	5	0	7	64	0

1972

Rank	Team	GP	W	L	T	GF	GA	Pts
1	SWE	5	5	0	0	32	10	10
2	URS	5	4	1	0	30	14	8
3	TCH	5	3	2	0	37	14	6
4	FIN	5	2	3	0	19	24	4
5	FRG	5	1	4	0	19	42	2
6	NOR	5	0	5	0	11	44	0

1973

Rank	Team	GP	W	L	T	GF	GA	Pts
1	URS	5	5	0	0	53	8	10
2	SWE	5	3	1	1	45	16	7
3	TCH	5	3	1	1	27	19	7
4	FIN	5	2	3	0	18	35	4
5	SUI	5	1	4	0	12	47	2
6	FRG	5	0	5	0	14	44	0

1974

Rank	Team	GP	W	L	T	GF	GA	Pts
1	SWE	5	5	0	0	56	9	10
2	URS	5	4	1	0	45	11	8
3	FIN	5	3	2	0	23	25	6
4	TCH	5	2	3	0	27	26	4
5	POL	5	1	4	0	15	44	2
6	SUI	5	0	5	0	10	61	0

1975

Rank	Team	GP	W	L	T	GF	GA	Pts
1	URS	5	4	1	0	32	8	8
2	TCH	5	4	1	0	25	13	8
3	SWE	5	4	1	0	36	17	8
4	FIN	5	1	3	1	10	19	3
5	POL	5	1	4	0	14	34	2
6	FRG	5	0	4	1	13	39	1

1976

Rank	Team	GP	W	L	T	GF	GA	Pts
1	URS	6	5	0	1	34	12	11
2	SWE	6	3	2	1	28	14	7
3	FIN	5	2	3	0	14	22	4
4	TCH	6	4	2	0	28	23	8
5	FRG	5	2	3	0	24	35	4
6	POL	5	1	4	0	22	40	2
7	SUI	5	0	5	0	13	47	0

1977

Rank	Team	GP	W	L	T	GF	GA	Pts
1	SWE	6	6	0	0	58	7	12
2	TCH	6	5	1	0	49	13	10
3	URS	6	4	2	0	49	19	8
4	FIN	6	3	3	0	31	38	6
5	SUI	6	1	4	1	21	52	3
6	FRG	6	1	4	1	14	45	3
7	POL	6	0	6	0	11	59	0
8	ROM							

1978

Rank	Team	GP	W	L	T	GF	GA	Pts
1	FIN	6	6	0	0	37	17	12
2	URS	6	5	1	0	37	11	10
3	SWE	6	3	3	0	30	13	6
4	TCH	6	2	4	0	25	19	4
5	POL	6	4	2	0	23	28	8
6	SUI	6	3	3	0	34	38	6
7	FRG	6	1	5	0	17	47	2
8	NOR	6	0	6	0	15	45	0

1979

Rank	Team	GP	W	L	T	GF	GA	Pts
1	TCH	5	5	0	0	33	7	10
2	FIN	5	4	1	0	45	8	8
3	URS	5	3	2	0	25	11	6
4	SWE	5	2	3	0	19	17	4
5	POL	5	3	2	0	19	12	6
6	SUI	5	2	3	0	21	21	4
7	FRG	5	1	4	0	14	32	2
8	ITA	5	0	5	0	0	68	0

1980

Rank	Team	GP	W	L	T	GF	GA	Pts
1	URS	5	5	0	0	42	9	10
2	TCH	5	4	1	0	35	12	8
3	SWE	5	3	2	0	18	15	6
4	FIN	5	2	3	0	20	23	4
5	FRG	5	3	2	0	26	30	6
6	POL	5	2	3	0	18	30	4
7	SUI	5	1	4	0	16	30	2
8	NOR	5	0	5	0	13	39	0

1981

Rank	Team	GP	W	L	T	GF	GA	Pts
1	URS	5	4	0	1	56	8	9
2	TCH	5	3	0	2	45	10	8
3	SWE	5	3	1	1	39	20	7
4	FIN	5	2	3	0	26	21	4
5	SUI	5	2	2	1	18	28	5
6	POL	5	2	3	0	13	50	4
7	FRG	5	1	3	1	9	33	3
8	AUT	5	0	5	0	4	40	0

1982

Rank	Team	GP	W	L	T	GF	GA	Pts
1	SWE	5	5	0	0	44	12	10
2	TCH	5	4	1	0	46	12	8
3	URS	5	3	2	0	28	19	6
4	FIN	5	2	3	0	20	27	4
5	SUI	5	1	3	1	16	26	3
6	FRG	5	0	3	2	9	23	2
7	FRA	5	0	4	1	11	79	1
8	POL	Did Not Play						

1983

Rank	Team	GP	W	L	T	GF	GA	Pts
1	URS	5	5	0	0	44	13	10
2	FIN	5	4	1	0	30	10	8
3	TCH	5	3	2	0	33	14	6
4	SWE	5	2	3	0	29	20	4
5	FRG	5	3	2	0	27	28	6
6	FRA	5	1	3	1	16	43	3
7	SUI	5	1	4	0	12	35	2
8	NOR	5	0	4	1	14	42	1

1984

Rank	Team	GP	W	L	T	GF	GA	Pts
1	URS	5	5	0	0	50	11	10
2	TCH	5	4	1	0	35	9	8
3	SWE	5	3	2	0	41	13	6
4	FIN	5	2	3	0	18	22	4
5	FRG	5	3	2	0	29	33	6
6	SUI	5	2	3	0	23	34	4
7	FRA	5	1	4	0	11	30	2
8	HOL	5	0	5	0	9	64	0

1985

Rank	Team	GP	W	L	T	GF	GA	Pts
1	SWE	5	4	0	1	39	5	9
2	URS	5	4	0	1	21	5	9
3	TCH	5	3	2	0	38	15	6
4	NOR	5	1	3	1	11	31	3
5	FIN	5	2	2	1	34	23	5
6	FRG	5	2	2	1	20	16	5
7	SUI	5	1	3	1	15	26	3
8	FRA	5	0	5	0	10	67	0

1986

Rank	Team	GP	W	L	T	GF	GA	Pts
1	FIN	5	4	0	1	51	14	9
2	SWE	5	2	1	2	34	17	6
3	TCH	5	2	1	2	28	14	6
4	URS	5	1	1	3	27	23	5
5	FRG	5	3	2	0	19	26	6
6	SUI	5	2	2	1	21	27	5
7	NOR	5	1	3	1	19	28	3
8	ROM	5	0	5	0	12	62	0

1987

Rank	Team	GP	W	L	T	GF	GA	Pts
1	SWE	7	6	1	0	51	5	12
2	TCH	7	6	1	0	48	16	12
3	URS	7	6	1	0	43	16	12
4	FIN	7	4	3	0	41	21	8
5	SUI	7	1	4	2	14	46	4
6	POL	7	1	4	2	13	55	4
7	NOR	7	1	5	1	13	37	3
8	FRG	7	0	6	1	13	40	1

1988

Rank	Team	GP	W	L	T	GF	GA	Pts
1	TCH	6	5	1	0	42	13	10
2	FIN	6	5	1	0	49	12	10
3	URS	6	4	1	1	44	11	9
4	SWE	6	3	2	1	46	22	7
5	NOR	6	2	4	0	22	40	4
6	SUI	6	1	5	0	13	55	2
7	ROM	6	1	4	1	12	54	3
8	POL	6	1	4	1	14	35	3

1989

Rank	Team	GP	W	L	T	GF	GA	Pts
1	URS	6	6	0	0	45	7	12
2	TCH	6	5	1	0	61	18	10
3	FIN	6	3	2	1	50	14	7
4	SWE	6	3	2	1	39	25	7
5	FRG	6	2	4	0	18	42	4
6	SUI	6	1	5	0	14	69	2
7	NOR	3	0	3	0	11	33	0
8	ROM	3	0	3	0	2	32	0

1990

Rank	Team	GP	W	L	T	GF	GA	Pts
1	SWE	8	7	0	1	49	16	15
2	URS	8	6	2	0	56	15	12
3	TCH	8	6	1	1	57	16	13
4	FIN	8	4	4	0	34	33	8
5	NOR	8	2	6	0	31	57	4
6	POL	8	1	7	0	24	75	2
7	FRG	6	2	4	0	19	40	4
8	SUI	6	1	5	0	13	31	2

1991

Rank	Team	GP	W	L	T	GF	GA	Pts
1	TCH	6	5	0	1	50	8	11
2	URS	6	5	0	1	42	13	11
3	FIN	6	4	2	0	47	15	8
4	SWE	6	3	3	0	53	22	6
5	GER	6	2	4	0	18	60	4
6	NOR	6	1	5	0	19	65	2
7	POL	5	2	3	0	23	33	4
8	FRA	5	0	5	0	7	43	0

1992

Rank	Team	GP	W	L	T	GF	GA	Pts
1	TCH	6	6	0	0	39	13	12
2	SWE	6	3	1	2	23	12	8
3	RUS	6	4	2	0	28	11	8
4	FIN	6	3	2	1	38	10	7
5	GER	6	1	3	2	16	28	4
6	POL	6	1	5	0	11	58	2
7	NOR	6	2	4	0	19	29	4
8	SUI	6	1	4	1	18	31	3

1993

Rank	Team	GP	W	L	T	GF	GA	Pts
1	SWE	8	8	0	0	69	13	16
2	RUS	8	5	2	1	50	21	11
3	CZE	8	6	2	0	97	12	12
4	FIN	8	4	3	1	27	27	9
5	NOR	8	1	6	1	16	74	3
6	GER	8	0	7	1	5	64	1
7	POL	6	2	3	1	32	45	5
8	ITA	6	1	4	1	23	63	3

1994

Rank	Team	GP	W	L	T	GF	GA	Pts
1	SWE	5	4	0	1	38	11	9
2	RUS	5	3	0	2	25	15	8
3	CZE	5	3	1	1	31	11	7
4	FIN	5	2	3	0	19	21	4
5	SUI	5	2	2	1	20	20	5
6	GER	5	2	3	0	26	25	4
7	NOR	5	0	3	2	12	33	2
8	POL	5	0	4	1	10	45	1

1995

Rank	Team	GP	W	L	T	GF	GA	Pts
1	FIN	5	4	1	0	24	11	8
2	GER	5	2	1	2	17	15	6
3	SWE	5	3	1	1	22	17	7
4	RUS	5	3	2	0	20	13	6
5	CZE	5	3	1	1	37	11	7
6	SUI	5	2	3	0	15	16	4
7	BLR	5	0	4	1	11	36	1
8	NOR	5	0	4	1	8	35	1

1996

Rank	Team	GP	W	L	T	GF	GA	Pts
1	RUS	5	3	0	2	26	12	8
2	FIN	5	4	0	1	17	9	9
3	SWE	5	3	2	0	23	12	6
4	SUI	5	2	3	0	16	22	4
5	CZE	5	3	1	1	25	8	7
6	GER	5	2	3	0	14	26	4
7	SVK	5	1	4	0	17	24	2
8	BLR	5	0	5	0	12	37	0

1997

Rank	Team	GP	W	L	T	GF	GA	Pts
1	FIN	6	5	0	1	31	8	11
2	SWE	6	4	0	2	27	15	10
3	SUI	6	3	3	0	18	21	6
4	RUS	6	2	2	2	28	23	6
5	CZE	6	2	3	1	22	23	5
6	SVK	6	1	5	0	14	28	2
7	UKR	6	3	3	0	13	25	6
8	GER	6	1	5	0	12	22	2
1	SWE	6	4	1	1	35	13	9
2	FIN	6	4	1	1	25	12	9
3	RUS	6	4	1	1	18	10	9
4	CZE	6	4	1	1	33	18	9
5	SUI	6	2	4	0	12	21	4
6	SVK	6	1	5	0	15	21	2
7	NOR	6	2	4	0	12	32	4
8	UKR	6	1	5	0	10	33	2

World Junior Championships, (Under 18) Pool B

1999

Rank	Team	GP	W	L	T	GF	GA	Pts
1	FIN	7	5	1	1	27	14	11
2	SWE	7	4	1	2	30	14	10
3	SVK	7	5	2	0	26	17	10
4	SUI	7	5	2	0	23	14	10
5	CZE	7	3	3	1	22	16	7
6	RUS	7	3	4	0	19	20	6
7	USA	6	3	3	0	28	15	6
8	UKR	6	2	4	0	11	26	4
9	GER	6	1	5	0	8	24	2
10	NOR	6	0	6	0	8	42	0

2000

Rank	Team	GP	W	L	T	GF	GA	Pts
1	FIN	7	6	1	0	29	12	12
2	RUS	6	5	1	0	38	8	10
3	SWE	6	5	1	0	30	10	10
4	SUI	7	4	3	0	23	23	8
5	SVK	6	3	3	0	16	16	6
6	CZE	6	2	4	0	18	19	4
7	GER	6	2	3	1	21	16	5
8	USA	6	2	4	0	20	16	4
9	UKR	6	1	4	1	14	33	3
10	BLR	6	0	6	0	7	63	0

European Junior Championships, (Under 18) Pool B

1969

Rank	Team
7	SUI
8	HUN
9	YUG
10	AUT

1970

Rank	Team
7	NOR
8	HOL
9	POL
10	ROM
11	AUT
12	YUG
13	HUN

1971

Rank	Team
7	ROM
8	POL
9	DEN
10	HUN
11	BUL
7	SUI

1972

Rank	Team
8	POL
9	YUG
10	ROM
11	ITA
12	HUN
13	AUT
14	DEN
15	HOL
16	FRA

1973

Rank	Team	GP	W	L	T	GF	GA	Pts
7	POL	5	5	0	0	53	12	10
8	ITA	5	3	1	1	28	26	7
9	YUG	5	2	0	3	26	19	7
10	ROM	5	3	2	0	33	20	6
11	FRA	5	2	3	0	21	31	4
12	AUT	5	1	2	2	19	24	4
13	NOR	5	1	1	3	27	19	5
14	DEN	5	1	4	0	14	41	2
15	BUL	4	1	3	0	7	26	2
16	HOL	4	0	3	1	8	18	1

1974

Rank	Team
7	FRG
8	ROM
9	BUL
10	NOR
11	DEN
12	YUG
13	AUT
14	FRA
15	HUN
16	ITA

1975

Rank	Team	GP	W	L	T	GF	GA	Pts
7	SUI	4	4	0	0	45	11	8
8	BUL	4	2	1	1	26	16	5
9	YUG	4	2	1	1	18	23	5
10	ROM	4	0	1	3	17	18	3
11	NOR	4	2	1	1	12	13	5
12	DEN	4	1	3	0	12	24	2
13	AUT	4	1	2	1	13	27	3
14	FRA	4	0	3	1	15	26	1

1976

Rank	Team
8	ROM
9	YUG
10	AUT
11	NOR
12	DEN
13	FRA
14	ITA
15	HUN
16	ESP

1977

Rank	Team
8	NOR
9	YUG
10	DEN
11	AUT
12	ITA
13	FRA
14	HOL
15	ESP

1978

Rank	Team	GP	W	L	T	GF	GA	Pts
9	ITA	5	3	1	1	21	16	7
10	FRA	5	2	1	2	23	13	6
11	ROM	4	2	0	2	28	15	6
12	YUG	4	2	2	0	14	13	4
13	AUT	4	2	1	1	27	14	5
14	HOL	4	1	3	0	11	14	2
15	DEN	4	2	2	0	23	13	4
16	BEL	4	0	4	0	4	53	0

1979

Rank	Team	GP	W	L	T	GF	GA	Pts
9	NOR	4	4	0	0	21	5	8
10	ROM	4	3	1	0	29	9	6
11	YUG	4	3	1	0	16	16	6
12	FRA	4	2	2	0	15	12	4
13	HOL	4	2	2	0	19	19	4
14	HUN	4	0	3	1	15	25	1
15	AUT	4	1	2	1	19	20	3
16	DEN	4	0	4	0	5	33	0

1980

Rank	Team	GP	W	L	T	GF	GA	Pts
9	AUT	4	3	1	0	22	18	6
10	YUG	4	2	1	1	18	18	5
11	BUL	4	3	1	0	19	14	6
12	ROM	4	1	3	0	21	17	2
13	FRA	4	3	1	0	24	20	6
14	ITA	4	1	2	1	15	19	3
15	HUN	4	1	3	0	25	22	2
16	HOL	4	1	3	0	17	33	2

1981

Rank	Team	GP	W	L	T	GF	GA	Pts
9	FRA	5	5	0	0	28	14	10
10	NOR	5	4	1	0	34	12	8
11	YUG	5	3	2	0	22	21	6
12	ITA	5	2	3	0	23	21	4
13	ROM	5	3	2	0	35	23	6
14	DEN	5	2	3	0	44	29	4
15	BUL	5	1	4	0	22	37	2
16	HUN	5	0	5	0	10	61	0

1982

Rank	Team	GP	W	L	T	GF	GA	Pts
9	NOR	5	5	0	0	45	8	10
10	AUT	5	3	2	0	27	18	6
11	HOL	5	3	2	0	24	18	6
12	DEN	5	1	3	1	8	18	3
13	ROM	5	3	2	0	27	23	6
14	BUL	5	1	2	2	16	21	4
15	ITA	5	2	2	1	25	28	5
16	YUG	5	0	5	0	10	48	0

1983

Rank	Team	GP	W	L	T	GF	GA	Pts
9	HOL	5	5	0	0	36	14	10
10	DEN	5	4	1	0	34	15	8
11	ROM	5	3	2	0	33	33	6
12	ITA	5	1	3	1	22	35	3
13	AUT	5	3	2	0	34	23	6
14	POL	5	2	3	0	37	24	4
15	BUL	5	1	3	1	12	31	3
16	HUN	5	0	5	0	16	49	0

1984

Rank	Team	GP	W	L	T	GF	GA	Pts
9	NOR	6	5	0	1	36	15	11
10	POL	6	5	1	0	50	20	10
11	AUT	6	3	3	0	29	36	6
12	ROM	6	2	4	0	36	52	4
13	DEN	6	4	2	0	38	26	8
14	BUL	6	1	4	1	20	33	3
15	YUG	6	2	4	0	21	34	4
16	ITA	6	0	4	2	19	33	2

1985

Rank	Team	GP	W	L	T	GF	GA	Pts
9	ROM	5	5	0	0	29	10	10
10	POL	5	4	1	0	27	16	8
11	BUL	5	3	2	0	23	18	6
12	HOL	5	2	3	0	19	27	4
13	DEN	5	3	2	0	25	24	6
14	AUT	5	2	3	0	20	21	4
15	YUG	5	1	4	0	16	25	2
16	HUN	5	0	5	0	12	30	0

1986

Rank	Team	GP	W	L	T	GF	GA	Pts
9	POL	5	5	0	0	52	9	10
10	DEN	5	4	1	0	27	27	8
11	FRA	5	2	3	0	18	25	4
12	BUL	5	2	3	0	23	26	4
13	ITA	5	2	2	1	16	20	5
14	YUG	5	2	3	0	22	31	4
15	AUT	5	1	3	1	13	25	3
16	HOL	5	1	4	0	17	25	2

1987

Rank	Team	GP	W	L	T	GF	GA	Pts
9	ROM	6	5	1	0	40	20	10
10	DEN	6	4	2	0	35	22	8
11	ITA	6	3	3	0	26	22	6
12	FRA	6	2	4	0	23	33	4
13	YUG	5	4	1	0	31	18	8
14	AUT	5	1	4	0	11	27	2
15	GBR	5	0	5	0	11	42	0
NR	BUL	3	2	1	0	15	8	4

1988

Rank	Team	GP	W	L	T	GF	GA	Pts
9	FRG	6	6	0	0	35	9	12
10	AUT	6	4	1	1	25	10	9
11	YUG	6	3	2	1	25	27	7
12	DEN	6	2	4	0	16	23	4
13	ITA	6	2	2	2	22	24	6
14	FRA	6	3	3	0	38	20	6
15	HOL	6	1	5	0	18	46	2
16	GBR	6	0	4	2	17	37	2

1989

Rank	Team	GP	W	L	T	GF	GA	Pts
9	POL	5	5	0	0	44	7	10
10	FRA	5	4	1	0	29	15	8
11	AUT	5	2	2	1	24	18	5
12	DEN	5	2	2	1	18	19	5
13	HOL	5	2	2	1	20	26	5
14	ITA	5	2	3	0	21	26	4
15	YUG	5	1	3	1	18	31	3
16	BUL	5	0	5	0	11	43	0

1990

Rank	Team	GP	W	L	T	GF	GA	Pts
9	FRA	7	5	0	2	51	16	12
10	ITA	7	5	1	1	45	20	11
11	ROM	7	4	0	3	34	21	11
12	YUG	7	3	2	2	26	31	8
13	AUT	7	3	4	0	25	26	6
14	DEN	7	2	4	1	34	33	5
15	HOL	7	1	5	1	16	40	3
16	ESP	7	0	7	0	21	65	0

1991

Rank	Team	GP	W	L	T	GF	GA	Pts
9	SUI	5	5	0	0	34	6	10
10	YUG	5	3	2	0	24	17	6
11	DEN	5	3	2	0	23	17	6
12	ITA	5	3	2	0	20	17	6
13	AUT	5	3	2	0	29	21	6
14	ROM	5	2	3	0	18	24	4
15	ESP	5	1	4	0	10	28	2
16	HOL	5	0	5	0	13	41	0

1992

Rank	Team	GP	W	L	T	GF	GA	Pts
9	ITA	6	4	0	2	20	12	10
10	DEN	6	5	1	0	36	25	10
11	AUT	6	3	3	0	22	14	6
12	ROM	6	2	4	0	32	31	4
13	FRA	6	4	1	1	49	16	9
14	ESP	6	1	5	0	13	34	2
15	GBR	6	1	4	1	19	37	3
16	YUG	6	2	4	0	24	46	4

1993

Rank	Team	GP	W	L	T	GF	GA	Pts
9	SUI	7	7	0	0	58	8	14
10	HUN	7	6	1	0	40	14	12
11	FRA	7	5	2	0	39	13	10
12	AUT	7	3	3	1	22	30	7
13	ROM	7	2	5	0	23	39	4
14	DEN	7	2	5	0	13	26	4
15	ESP	7	1	5	1	18	48	3
16	GBR	7	1	6	0	17	52	2

1994

Rank	Team	GP	W	L	T	GF	GA	Pts
9	BLR	5	3	1	1	27	18	7
10	HUN	5	4	1	0	35	12	8
11	DEN	5	3	2	0	31	17	6
12	AUT	5	3	2	0	21	21	6
13	ITA	5	3	1	1	17	9	7
14	ROM	5	1	3	1	13	22	3
15	FRA	5	1	3	1	19	24	3
16	ESP	5	0	5	0	7	47	0

1995

Rank	Team	GP	W	L	T	GF	GA	Pts
9	SVK	5	5	0	0	58	3	10
10	POL	5	4	1	0	30	21	8
11	DEN	5	3	2	0	26	27	6
12	HUN	5	1	3	1	16	38	3
13	ITA	5	3	2	0	21	25	6
14	FRA	5	2	2	1	19	19	5
15	ROM	5	1	4	0	11	28	2
16	AUT	5	0	5	0	13	33	0

Rank	Team	GP	W	L	T	GF	GA	Pts
1996								
9	UKR	5	5	0	0	26	12	10
10	DEN	5	4	1	0	32	19	8
11	FRA	5	3	2	0	25	17	6
12	NOR	5	2	3	0	17	18	4
13	POL	5	3	2	0	41	18	6
14	ITA	5	2	3	0	16	22	4
15	HUN	5	1	4	0	15	21	2
16	ROM	5	0	5	0	11	56	0
1997								
9	NOR	6	3	1	2	20	15	8
10	POL	6	4	1	1	27	19	9
11	HUN	7	3	1	3	27	23	9
12	BLR	6	3	2	1	23	25	7
13	DEN	6	3	3	0	25	21	6
14	FRA	7	1	5	1	25	34	3
15	ITA	5	2	3	0	24	23	4
16	SLO	5	1	4	0	15	26	2
1998								
9	GER	6	6	0	0	26	8	12
10	ITA	6	4	2	0	21	12	8
11	POL	6	3	2	1	22	24	7
12	HUN	6	3	3	0	25	24	6
13	BLR	6	3	3	0	21	16	6
14	DEN	6	1	4	1	27	38	3
15	FRA	5	2	3	0	19	13	4
16	GBR	5	0	5	0	4	30	0

World Junior Championships, (Under 18) Pool B

Rank	Team	GP	W	L	T	GF	GA	Pts
1999								
11	BLR	5	3	0	2	28	11	8
12	AUT	5	2	1	2	28	12	6
13	POL	5	3	1	1	19	16	7
14	DEN	5	2	2	1	23	22	5
15	ITA	5	3	1	1	22	13	7
16	FRA	5	2	2	1	21	15	5
17	HUN	5	1	4	0	11	41	2
18	GBR	5	0	5	0	9	31	0
2000								
11	NOR	5	4	1	0	27	12	8
12	AUT	5	3	1	1	21	13	7
13	LAT	5	2	1	2	19	17	6
14	JAP	5	2	2	1	13	15	5
15	DEN	5	2	3	0	22	24	4
16	ITA	5	2	2	1	15	19	5
17	POL	5	2	2	1	20	24	5
18	FRA	5	0	5	0	12	25	0

European Junior Championships, (Under 18) Pool C

Rank	Team	GP	W	L	T	GF	GA	Pts
1978								
17	HUN	4	2	0	2	21	13	6
18	BUL	4	1	2	1	17	13	3
19	ESP	4	1	2	1	11	23	3
1979								
17	BUL	4	4	0	0	33	6	8
18	ESP	4	2	2	0	16	23	4
19	GBR	4	0	4	0	6	26	0
1980								
17	DEN	4	4	0	0	51	5	8
18	BEL	4	1	3	0	13	30	2
19	GBR	4	1	3	0	12	41	2
1981								
17	HOL	4	4	0	0	44	8	8
18	GBR	4	1	2	1	18	26	3
19	BEL	4	0	3	1	8	36	1
1982								
17	HUN	4	2	1	1	29	22	5
18	ESP	4	2	2	0	22	25	4
19	GBR	4	1	2	1	20	24	3
1983								
17	YUG							
18	GBR							
19	BEL							
20	ESP							
1984								
17	HUN	6	5	1	0	44	28	10
18	GBR	6	4	2	0	45	34	8
19	BEL	6	3	3	0	39	30	6
20	ESP	6	0	6	0	17	53	0
1985								
17	ITA	4	3	1	0	20	14	6
18	BEL	4	2	2	0	14	12	4
19	GBR	4	1	3	0	17	25	2
1986								
17	GBR	4	3	1	0	17	11	6
18	HUN	4	2	2	0	9	12	4
19	ESP	4	1	3	0	12	15	2
1987								
17	HOL	4	4	0	0	30	7	8
18	HUN	4	2	2	0	20	14	4
19	BEL	4	0	4	0	4	33	0
1988								
17	BUL	3	3	0	0	15	5	6
18	ESP	3	2	1	0	22	11	4
19	HUN	3	1	2	0	14	11	2
20	BEL	3	0	3	0	9	33	0
1989								
17	ESP	4	3	0	1	19	13	7
18	GBR	4	2	1	1	15	10	5
19	HUN	4	0	4	0	12	23	0
1990								
17	GDR	3	3	0	0	35	4	6
18	HUN	3	2	1	0	16	14	4
19	GBR	3	1	2	0	7	20	2
20	BUL	3	0	3	0	7	27	0
1991								
17	GBR	3	3	0	0	28	5	6
18	BUL	3	2	1	0	29	9	4
19	HUN	3	1	2	0	18	16	2
20	BEL	3	0	3	0	2	47	0
1992								
17	HUN	3	3	0	0	34	1	6
18	HOL	3	2	1	0	17	17	4
19	BUL	3	1	2	0	9	18	2
20	BEL	3	0	3	0	6	30	0
1993								
17	BLR	4	3	0	1	16	9	7
18	SVK	4	3	1	0	54	6	6
19	SLO	4	2	1	1	18	13	5
20	UKR	4	3	1	0	56	11	6
21	LAT	4	2	2	0	21	14	4
22	LIT	4	1	3	0	10	35	2
23	EST	4	2	2	0	38	20	4
24	HOL	4	1	3	0	14	24	2
25	BUL	4	0	4	0	4	99	0
1994								
17	SVK	6	6	0	0	111	14	12
18	LAT	6	5	1	0	85	15	10
19	SLO	6	4	2	0	39	22	8
20	UKR	6	3	3	0	67	16	6
21	EST	6	4	2	0	27	56	8
22	GBR	6	3	3	0	29	55	6
23	LIT	6	2	4	0	25	50	4
24	CRO	6	1	5	0	23	46	2
25	HOL	4	0	4	0	9	57	0
26	BUL	4	0	4	0	2	86	0
1995								
17	UKR	5	4	1	0	51	12	8
18	LAT	5	4	1	0	33	7	8
19	SLO	5	4	1	0	38	11	8
20	GBR	5	2	3	0	22	21	4
21	EST	5	1	4	0	9	38	2
22	ESP	5	0	5	0	2	66	0
23	LIT	5	5	0	0	69	10	10
24	CRO	5	4	1	0	61	9	8
25	HOL	4	2	2	0	16	14	4
26	YUG	4	1	3	0	17	25	2
27	ISR	4	2	2	0	22	26	4
28	BUL	4	1	3	0	27	20	2
29	TUR	4	0	4	0	3	111	0
1996								
17	SLO	4	4	0	0	36	6	8
18	AUT	4	2	1	1	17	9	5
19	LAT	4	3	1	0	34	8	6
20	EST	4	1	1	2	12	17	4
21	GBR	4	2	1	1	28	12	5
22	LIT	4	1	3	0	20	40	2
23	CRO	4	1	3	0	17	27	2
24	ESP	4	0	4	0	2	47	0
1997								
17	GBR	4	4	0	0	20	6	8
18	LAT	4	2	1	1	21	10	5
19	EST	4	3	1	0	15	17	6
20	AUT	4	2	1	1	13	8	5
21	ROM	4	2	2	0	13	10	4
22	LIT	4	1	3	0	10	22	2
23	CRO	4	1	3	0	5	12	2
24	HOL	4	0	4	0	6	18	0
1998								
17	AUT	4	4	0	0	37	10	8
18	LAT	4	3	1	0	26	9	6
19	LIT	4	3	1	0	15	15	6
20	SLO	4	2	2	0	24	9	4
21	ROM	4	2	2	0	15	27	4
22	EST	4	1	3	0	5	18	2
23	CRO	4	1	3	0	17	24	2
24	YUG	4	0	4	0	7	34	0

European Junior Championships, (Under 18) Div. I

Rank	Team	GP	W	L	T	GF	GA	Pts
1999								
19	LAT	4	4	0	0	46	6	8
20	SLO	4	3	1	0	23	14	6
21	LIT	4	3	1	0	23	10	6
22	EST	4	2	2	0	22	18	4
23	KAZ	4	2	2	0	27	13	4
24	ROM	4	1	3	0	11	38	2
25	CRO	4	1	3	0	22	26	2
26	YUG	4	0	4	0	7	56	0
2000								
1	KAZ	4	4	0	0	36	7	8
2	EST	4	3	1	0	23	11	6
3	SLO	4	3	1	0	34	9	6
4	HUN	4	2	2	0	24	26	4
5	GBR	4	2	2	0	15	22	4
6	LIT	4	1	3	0	18	28	2
7	ROM	4	1	3	0	10	36	2
8	ESP	4	0	4	0	14	35	0

European Junior Championships, (Under 18) Pool D

Rank	Team	GP	W	L	T	GF	GA	Pts
1996								
25	HOL	3	3	0	0	62	4	6
26	YUG	2	1	1	0	10	8	2
27	ISR	2	1	1	0	6	9	2
28	BUL	3	1	2	0	26	21	2
29	TUR	2	0	2	0	1	63	0
1997								
25	YUG	5	5	0	0	114	5	10
26	ESP	5	3	1	1	39	26	7
27	BUL	5	3	2	0	22	26	6
28	ISR	5	2	2	1	30	27	5
29	ISL	5	1	4	0	17	48	2
30	TUR	5	0	5	0	6	96	0
1998								
25	KAZ	5	5	0	0	155	4	10
26	HOL	5	4	1	0	36	18	8
27	BEL	5	3	2	0	29	31	6
28	ESP	5	2	3	0	27	31	4
29	BUL	5	3	2	0	18	30	6
30	ISR	5	1	3	1	10	28	3
31	ISL	5	1	3	1	11	82	3
32	LUX	5	0	5	0	7	69	0

European Junior Championships, (Under 18) Div. II

Rank	Team	GP	W	L	T	GF	GA	Pts
1999								
27	ESP	5	4	0	1	37	9	9
28	HOL	5	3	0	2	68	6	8
29	BEL	5	3	1	1	35	8	7
30	ISR	5	2	3	0	32	39	4
31	LUX	5	2	3	0	19	21	4
32	BUL	5	2	3	0	22	32	4
33	ISL	5	2	3	0	21	27	4
34	IRL	5	0	5	0	3	95	0
2000								
9	CRO	4	4	0	0	57	6	8
10	HOL	4	3	1	0	22	12	6
11	YUG	4	2	2	0	18	29	4
12	BEL	4	3	1	0	21	7	6
13	ISR	4	2	2	0	20	19	4
14	BUL	4	1	3	0	7	35	2
15	SAF	4	1	2	1	9	20	3
16	LUX	4	1	3	0	11	31	2
17	ISL	4	0	3	1	14	20	1

Asian Junior Championships

Rank	Team	GP	W	L	T	GF	GA	Pts
1984								
1	JAP	6	6	0	0	64	9	12
2	PRC	6	4	2	0	48	24	8
3	KOR	4	0	4	0	5	36	0
4	AUS	4	0	4	0	2	50	0
1985								
1	JAP	4	4	0	0	34	8	8
2	KOR	4	1	2	1	23	23	3
3	AUS	4	0	3	1	6	32	1

Asian-Oceanic Junior Championships

Rank	Team	GP	W	L	T	GF	GA	Pts
1986								
1	JAP	6	5	1	0	65	14	10
2	PRC	6	4	1	1	25	26	9
3	KOR	6	1	4	1	15	43	3
4	AUS	6	1	5	0	18	40	2
1987								
1	PRK	4	3	1	0	31	9	6
2	PRC	4	3	1	0	17	9	6
3	JAP	4	3	1	0	22	8	6
4	AUS	4	1	3	0	14	35	2
5	KOR	4	0	4	0	9	32	0

1988

Rank	Team	GP	W	L	T	GF	GA	Pts
1	PRC	6	5	0	1	50	13	11
2	JAP	6	4	1	1	59	19	9
3	KOR	6	2	4	0	42	53	4
4	AUS	6	0	6	0	14	80	0

1989

Rank	Team	GP	W	L	T	GF	GA	Pts
1	JAP	4	3	0	1	32	14	7
2	KOR	4	2	2	0	19	26	4
3	PRC	4	0	3	1	16	27	1

1990

Rank	Team	GP	W	L	T	GF	GA	Pts
1	JAP	6	6	0	0	86	4	12
2	PRC	6	4	2	0	48	19	8
3	KOR	6	2	4	0	42	35	4
4	AUS	6	0	6	0	5	123	0

1991

Rank	Team	GP	W	L	T	GF	GA	Pts
1	JAP	4	3	0	1	62	6	7
2	PRC	4	3	0	1	49	11	7
3	PRK	4	2	2	0	18	11	4
4	KOR	4	1	3	0	31	20	2
5	MEX	4	0	4	0	3	115	0

1992

Rank	Team	GP	W	L	T	GF	GA	Pts
1	JAP	4	3	0	1	36	3	7
2	PRC	4	2	2	0	20	16	4
3	PRK	4	3	0	1	22	6	7
4	KOR	4	1	3	0	12	25	2
5	AUS	4	0	4	0	11	51	0

1993

Rank	Team	GP	W	L	T	GF	GA	Pts
1	KAZ	4	4	0	0	88	0	8
2	JAP	4	3	1	0	65	9	6
3	KOR	4	2	2	0	31	24	4
4	PRC	4	1	3	0	26	27	2
5	AUS	4	0	4	0	1	151	0

1994

Rank	Team	GP	W	L	T	GF	GA	Pts
1	KAZ	4	4	0	0	66	3	8
2	KOR	4	2	1	1	42	16	5
3	JAP	4	2	1	1	42	23	5
4	PRC	4	1	3	0	26	20	2
5	AUS	4	0	4	0	0	114	0

1995

Rank	Team	GP	W	L	T	GF	GA	Pts
1	JAP	3	2	1	0	14	7	4
2	KAZ	3	2	1	0	15	10	4
3	PRC	3	1	2	0	6	16	2
4	KOR	3	1	2	0	12	14	2

1996

Rank	Team	GP	W	L	T	GF	GA	Pts
1	KAZ	3	3	0	0	32	8	6
2	KOR	3	2	1	0	13	14	4
3	JAP	3	1	2	0	11	13	2
4	PRC	3	0	3	0	4	25	0

1997

Rank	Team	GP	W	L	T	GF	GA	Pts
1	JAP	3	3	0	0	20	8	6
2	KAZ	3	2	1	0	15	11	4
3	KOR	3	1	2	0	18	15	2
4	PRC	3	0	3	0	7	26	0

1998

Rank	Team	GP	W	L	T	GF	GA	Pts
1	KOR	5	4	0	1	148	4	9
2	JAP	5	4	0	1	130	3	9
3	PRC	5	3	2	0	69	12	6
4	AUS	5	2	3	0	42	60	4
5	NZL	5	1	4	0	14	110	2
6	THA	5	0	5	0	3	217	0

Asian-Oceanic Junior Championships, Division I

1999

Rank	Team	GP	W	L	T	GF	GA	Pts
1	JAP	3	3	0	0	36	5	6
2	KOR	3	2	1	0	24	11	4
3	PRC	3	1	2	0	15	19	2
4	AUS	3	0	3	0	0	40	0

2000

Rank	Team	GP	W	L	T	GF	GA	Pts
1	PRK	3	3	0	0	16	3	6
2	KOR	3	2	1	0	15	7	4
3	PRC	3	1	2	0	13	9	2
4	AUS	3	0	3	0	2	27	0

Asian-Oceanic Junior Championships, Division II

1999

Rank	Team	GP	W	L	T	GF	GA	Pts
5	PRK	5	5	0	0	94	4	10
6	RSA	5	3	2	0	54	19	6
7	NZL	5	2	3	0	46	46	4
8	TPE	5	0	5	0	8	133	0

2000

Rank	Team	GP	W	L	T	GF	GA	Pts
5	NZL	3	2	0	1	15	6	5
6	TPE	3	2	0	1	12	6	5
7	THA	3	0	2	1	7	14	1
8	MGL	3	0	2	1	7	15	1

CHAPTER 48

Leading National Leagues

Final Standings, 1994–95 to 1999–2000, for Major European and Japanese National Leagues

INTERNATIONAL HOCKEY usually evokes images of players wearing the uniforms of their national teams, but in almost all hockey countries, a national league also flourishes. Club teams are supported in Europe and Asia in the same way that NHL clubs are followed by their fans in North America.

European leagues often consist of two or more division, with promotion and relegation between these divisions determined by results each season.

Top division standings are provided here for the following 16 countries: Austria, Czech Republic, Denmark, Finland, France, Germany, Great Britain, the Netherlands, Italy, Japan, Norway, Poland, Russia, Slovakia, Sweden and Switzerland

AUSTRIA

1994–95

1st to 6th place

Team	GP	W	L	T	GF	GA	PTS
VEU Feldkirch	10	9	0	1	55	20	20
Klagenfurter AC	10	7	2	1	64	34	18
VSV Villach	10	5	4	1	45	31	15
ECO Graz	10	5	4	1	42	33	13
EC Ehrwald	10	1	9	0	26	62	2
EHC Lustenau	10	1	9	0	21	73	2

Bonus points included

7th to 10th place

Team	GP	W	L	T	GF	GA	PTS
SV Kapfenberg	12	6	5	1	60	51	14
CE Wien	12	5	5	2	65	63	14
EV Zeltweg	12	6	5	1	62	70	13
Pinzgauer Eisbaren	12	4	6	2	54	57	10

1995–96

Team	GP	W	L	T	GF	GA	PTS
VEU Feldkirch	28	23	2	3	170	63	49
Klagenfurter AC	28	17	6	5	137	78	39
VSV Villach	28	15	5	8	149	82	38
CE Wien	28	12	8	8	130	97	32
EHC Lustenau	28	11	15	2	106	116	24
SV Kapfenberg	28	7	15	6	80	124	20
ECO Graz	28	4	19	5	67	162	13
EV Zeltweg	28	3	22	3	75	192	9

1996–97

Team	GP	W	L	T	GF	GA	PTS
EC P. Kapfenberg	4	3	1	0	20	13	6
CE Wien	4	3	1	0	29	14	6
EC Graz	4	0	4	0	14	36	0

1997–98

Team	GP	W	L	T	GF	GA	PTS
VEU Feldkirch	18	10	5	3	65	46	27
Klagenfurter AC	18	10	5	3	74	66	26
VSV Villach	18	10	6	2	74	62	23
EV Wien	18	9	8	1	83	68	21
EC Graz	18	5	12	1	59	87	11
EC P. Kapfenberg	10	1	9	0	22	48	2

Note: Alpenliga bonus points included

1998–99

Team	GP	W	L	T	GF	GA	B	PTS
SV Villach	12	8	4	1	43	33	4	21
AC Klagenfurt	12	7	5	0	43	33	3	17
EV Wien	12	5	7	2	35	46	2	14
VEU Feldkirch	12	4	8	0	41	50	1	9

B – bonus points from Alpenliga

1999–2000

Team	GP	W	L	OTL	GF	GA	PTS
Villacher SV	6	6	0	0	35	5	12
AC Klagenfurt	6	3	3	0	24	22	6
EV Wien	6	2	4	1	15	29	5
VEU Feldkirch	6	1	5	0	11	29	2

Overtime loss :1 point

CZECH REPUBLIC

1994–95

Team	GP	W	L	T	GF	GA	PTS
HC Vsetin	44	23	13	8	141	107	54
HC Kladno	44	24	14	6	178	142	54
HC Olomouc	44	19	15	10	130	124	48
AC ZPS Zlin	44	20	16	8	158	149	48
HC Skoda Plzen	44	16	14	14	118	112	46
HC Ceske Budejovice	44	20	18	6	142	124	46
HC Slavia Praha	44	18	19	7	133	164	43
HC CHP Litvinov	44	18	20	6	149	143	42
HC Sparta Praha	44	16	19	9	123	129	41
HC Vitkovice	44	18	21	5	144	156	41
HC Pardubice	44	13	20	11	134	151	37
HC Dukla Jihlava	44	12	28	4	117	166	28

1995–96

Team	GP	W	L	T	GF	GA	PTS
HC Sparta Praha	40	27	10	3	152	108	57
HC Petra Vsetin	40	24	9	7	149	85	55
HC Ceske Budejovice	40	20	11	9	120	85	49
Chemopetrol Litvinov	40	21	12	7	155	117	49
AC ZPS Zlin	40	20	14	6	126	111	46
Slavia Praha	40	18	17	5	148	140	41
HC Olomouc	40	16	16	8	112	109	40
HC Kladno	40	17	18	5	127	131	39
HC Vitkovice	40	13	16	11	105	121	37
HC Dukla Jihlava	40	13	18	9	115	142	35
ZKZ Plzen	40	12	21	7	103	134	31
HC Zelezarny Trinec	40	12	22	6	128	162	30
Pojistovna Pardubice	40	12	24	4	103	128	28
Kometa BVV Brno	40	9	26	5	95	165	23

1996–97

Team	GP	W	L	T	GF	GA	PTS
HC Petra Vsetin	52	34	11	7	198	120	75
HC Sparta Praha	52	28	13	11	227	168	67
HC Vitkovice	52	25	15	12	160	120	62
HC Zelezarny Trinec	52	23	19	10	175	152	56
Pojistovna Pardubice	52	25	22	5	170	164	55
Poldi Kladno	52	21	19	12	132	152	54
HC Ceske Budejovice	52	20	20	12	149	145	52
HC Slavia Praha	52	21	21	10	166	167	52
Chemopetrol Litvinov	52	20	20	12	171	185	52
ZRS Zlin	52	22	24	6	179	179	50
ZKZ Plzen	52	19	24	9	155	172	47
HC Olomouc	52	16	25	11	122	155	43
HC Dukla Jihlava	52	13	29	10	140	187	36
Slezan Opava	52	10	35	7	125	203	27

1997–98

Team	GP	W	L	T	GF	GA	PTS
HC Petra Vsetin	52	33	13	6	181	116	72
HC Vitkovice	52	31	14	7	174	142	69
HC Zelezarny Trinec	52	29	12	11	189	156	69
HC Sparta Praha	52	27	15	10	176	117	64
HC ZKZ Plzen	52	24	17	11	160	146	59
HC Slavia Praha	52	22	18	12	152	132	56
HC Chemo. Litvinov	52	22	18	12	167	128	56
HC IPB Poj. Pardubice	52	22	22	8	158	149	52
HC Dukla Jihlava	52	21	22	9	137	139	51
HC Ceske Budejovice	52	19	23	10	149	149	48
HC ZPS-Barum Zlin	52	20	24	8	166	183	48
HC Velvana Kladno	52	11	31	10	124	194	32
HC Bech. Karlovy Vary	52	9	31	12	130	202	30
HC B. Trade Opava	52	7	37	8	101	211	22

1998–99

Team	GP	W	L	T	GF	GA	PTS
HC Slovnaft Vsetin	52	33	7	12	184	92	78
HC ZPS-Barum Zlin	52	26	9	17	180	138	69
HC Zelezarny Trinec	52	28	16	8	174	140	64
HC Sparta Praha	52	27	16	9	186	123	63
HC Ceske Budejovice	52	23	15	14	173	129	60
HC Keramika Plzen	52	23	15	14	148	136	60
HC IPB Poj. Pardubice	52	20	19	13	128	126	53
HC Vitkovice	52	21	23	8	147	140	50
HC Chemo. Litvinov	52	19	23	10	130	144	48
HC Slavia Praha	52	17	24	11	152	166	45
HC Bech. Karlovy Vary	52	14	28	10	130	181	38
HC Opava	52	15	29	8	97	158	38
HC Velvana Kladno	52	11	26	15	119	175	37
HC Dukla Jihlava	52	7	34	11	88	188	25

1999–2000

Team	GP	W	L	T	GF	GA	PTS
HC Sparta Praha	52	34	10	8	193	112	76
HC Barum Zlin	52	27	14	11	166	116	65
HC Slovnaft Vsetin	52	28	15	9	160	140	65
HC Ocelari Trinec	52	29	17	6	192	154	64
HC Keramika Plzen	52	26	15	11	151	113	63
HC Ceske Budejovice	52	25	16	11	163	152	61
HC Chemo. Litvinov	52	22	19	11	151	140	55
HC IPB Poj. Pardubice	52	18	25	9	153	173	45
HC Znojemsti Orli	52	16	25	11	140	169	43
HC Slavia Praha	52	14	25	13	100	138	41
HC Bech. Karlovy Vary	52	14	26	12	153	185	40
HC Velvana Kladno	52	13	27	12	121	164	38
HC Femax Havirov	52	14	28	10	130	173	38
HC Vitkovice	52	10	28	14	117	161	34

DENMARK

1994–95

1st to 6th place

Team	GP	W	L	T	GF	GA	PTS
Herning IK	36	31	2	3	281	104	49
Esbjerg IK	36	26	6	4	218	109	42
Rungsted IK	36	21	10	5	207	139	34
AAB Aalborg	36	16	11	9	159	138	32
Fredrikshavn IK	36	14	17	5	143	171	25
Vojens IK	36	15	20	1	183	198	23

7th to 10th place

Team	GP	W	L	T	GF	GA	PTS
Odense IK	36	13	19	4	157	169	23
Hellerup IK	36	11	17	8	110	134	22
Rodovre SIK	36	7	22	7	109	225	17
Hvidovre IK	36	1	31	4	79	254	5

Note: Special count of points in effect after double round robin

1995–96

Team	GP	W	L	T	GF	GA	PTS
Esbjerg IK	36	26	5	5	205	103	44
Herning IK	36	26	7	3	200	115	43
Rungsted IK	36	17	12	7	171	145	32
Hvidovre IK	36	19	13	4	178	165	31
Vojens IK	36	17	16	3	178	170	28
Odense IK	36	12	15	9	146	165	25
Rodovre SIK	36	11	18	7	118	145	22
Fredrikshavn IK	36	10	19	7	133	173	20
Hellerup IK	36	9	22	5	119	184	16
AAB Aalborg	36	5	27	4	111	197	11

Note: Special count of points in effect after double round robin

1996–97

Team	GP	W	L	T	GF	GA	PTS
Herning IK	27	18	6	3	144	74	39
Esbjerg IK	27	17	9	1	134	103	35
Rungsted IK	27	16	9	2	135	98	34
Vojens IK	27	16	9	2	131	107	34
Rodovre SIK	27	11	9	7	100	99	29
Hvidovre IK	27	13	12	2	94	96	28
Gentofte IC	27	11	14	2	121	137	24
AAB Aalborg	27	10	16	1	82	128	21
Fredrikshavn IK	27	8	17	2	92	121	18
Odense IK	27	4	23	0	75	145	8

1st to 6th place

Team	GP	W	L	T	GF	GA	PTS
Herning IK	15	12	2	1	94	36	25
Vojens IK	15	8	4	3	67	72	19
Esbjerg IK	15	8	5	2	82	57	18
Rundsted IK	15	6	8	1	68	70	13
Rodovre SIK	15	4	11	0	60	91	8
Hvidovre IK	15	3	11	1	46	91	7

7th to 14th place

Team	GP	W	L	T	GF	GA	PTS
Gentofte IC	14	12	2	0	97	37	27
Fredrikshavn IK	14	11	2	1	90	34	26
Odense IK	14	11	2	1	85	42	24
AAB Aalberg	14	10	4	0	84	41	21
KSF Kobnhavn	14	4	9	1	41	71	12
Arhus IK	14	3	9	2	55	117	8
Gladaxe SF	14	2	12	0	37	83	6
Herlev IK	14	1	12	1	36	99	4

Note: Bonus points included

1997–98

Team	GP	W	L	T	GF	GA	PTS
Herning	10	6	1	3	51	27	15
Esbjerg	10	7	2	1	45	35	15
Rungsted	10	5	4	1	38	40	11
Frederikshavn	10	4	6	0	41	43	8
Vojens	10	3	6	1	38	45	7
Rodovre	10	2	8	0	25	48	4

1998–99

Regular season – part one

Team	GP	W	L	OTW	T	OTL	GF	GA	PTS
Fredrikshavn IK	36	25	7	0	2	2	182	95	54
Rungsted IK	36	21	8	3	3	1	205	149	52
Vojens IK	36	22	10	1	2	1	176	144	49
Esbjerg IK	36	20	9	0	4	3	179	115	47
Herning IK	36	20	11	2	2	1	187	115	47
Rodorve IK Kobenhavn	36	16	15	3	2	0	149	120	40
Odense IK	36	13	18	1	3	1	138	159	32
Hvidovre Kobenhavn	36	11	24	0	0	1	117	170	23
AAB Aalborg	36	8	24	0	3	1	114	191	20
Gentofte IK	36	2	32	0	2	0	89	278	6

Overtime win – 2 pts; overtime loss – 1 pt.

Regular season – part two

Group A

Team	GP	W	L	OTW	T	OTL	GF	GA	PTS	B
Fredrikshavn IK	6	5	0	0	0	1	24	11	13	2
Esbjerg IK	6	2	2	1	1	0	33	19	8	1
Herning IK	6	3	2	0	1	0	29	24	7	
Hvidovre Kobenhavn	6	0	6	0	0	0	12	44	0	
Group B										
Rodorve IK Kobenhavn	6	4	1	0	0	1	25	15	9	
Vojens IK	6	3	2	1	0	0	25	24	9	1
Rungsted IK	6	3	2	0	0	1	28	21	9	2
Odense IK	6	0	5	1	0	0	10	28	2	

B – bonus point carried forward from part one

1999–2000

Team	GP	W	L	T	B	GF	GA	PTS
Fredrikshavn IK	36	27	4	5	0	175	90	59
Esbjerg IK	36	24	8	4	0	184	105	52
Herning IK	36	22	10	4	2	170	99	50
Rungsted IK	36	19	10	7	2	140	99	47
Vojens IK	36	20	13	3	0	139	107	43
Rodorve IK Kobenhavn	36	17	15	4	0	153	149	38
AAB Aalborg	36	14	19	3	1	135	143	32
Odense IK	36	13	22	1	0	148	151	27
Herlev	36	5	28	3	1	105	205	14
Gladsaxe	36	1	33	2	0	80	281	4

B – 1 bonus point awarded for overtime win

FINLAND

1994–95

Team	GP	W	L	T	GF	GA	PTS
Jokerit Helsinki	50	34	10	6	202	122	74
Lukko Rauma	50	29	12	9	210	134	67
IFK Helsinki	50	32	15	3	203	141	67
TPS Turku	50	30	17	3	219	149	63
JyP HT Jyvaskyla	50	22	20	8	164	181	52
Assat Pori	50	20	19	11	164	166	51
Kiekko-Espoo	50	20	26	4	154	169	44
KalPa Kuopio	50	17	25	8	154	195	42
HPK Hameenlinna	50	16	27	7	170	197	39
Tappara Tampere	50	16	30	4	154	221	36
TuTo Turku	50	18	32	0	152	227	36
Ilves Tampere	50	12	33	5	152	196	29

1995–96

Team	GP	W	L	T	GF	GA	PTS
Jokerit Helsinki	50	31	8	11	190	91	73
TPS Turku	50	33	12	5	216	141	71
Lukko Rauma	50	25	16	9	205	177	59
Tappara Tampere	50	24	19	7	172	131	55
HPK Hameenlinna	50	23	20	7	160	151	53
IFK Helsinki	50	21	19	10	142	158	52
Assat Pori	50	22	23	5	140	160	49
Ilves Tampere	50	18	25	7	153	183	43
Kiekko-Espoo	50	18	26	6	131	164	42
Jyp HT Jyvaskyla	50	13	26	11	132	155	37
KalPa Kuopio	50	13	27	10	126	162	36
TuTo Hockey Turku	50	12	32	6	140	204	30

1996–97

Team	GP	W	L	T	GF	GA	PTS
Jokerit Helsinki	50	35	11	4	192	116	74
TPS Turku	50	32	11	7	191	105	71
HPK Hameenlinna	50	28	15	7	191	143	63
Ilves Tampere	50	26	17	7	183	147	59
JyP HT Jyvaskyla	50	25	19	6	163	136	56
Kiekko-Espoo	50	21	20	9	154	163	51
Assat Pori	50	19	21	10	171	182	48
Tappara Tampere	50	18	24	8	139	171	44
IFK Helsinki	50	17	25	8	159	171	42
Lukko Rauma	50	16	29	5	136	170	37
SaiPa Lapeenranta	50	13	29	8	118	181	34
KalPa Kuopio	50	8	37	5	116	228	21

1997–98

Team	GP	W	L	T	GF	GA	PTS
TPS Turku	48	30	12	6	162	111	66
IFK Helsinki	48	29	14	5	179	115	63
Ilves Tampere	48	27	15	6	184	138	60
Jokerit Helsinki	48	24	19	5	139	137	53
Tappara Tampere	48	22	19	7	157	147	51
SaiPa Lapeenranta	48	21	20	7	135	142	49
Assat Pori	48	20	20	8	163	156	48
Kiekko-Espoo	48	20	22	6	153	139	46
Lukko Rauma	48	20	22	6	131	143	46
HPK Hameenlinna	48	18	25	5	148	181	41
JyP HT Jyvaskyla	48	17	28	3	135	167	37
KalPa Kuopio	48	6	38	4	91	201	16

1998–99

Team	GP	W	L	T	GF	GA	PTS
TPS Turku	54	37	10	7	179	107	81
HIFK Helsinki	54	34	14	6	209	104	74
Jokerit Helsinki	54	31	20	3	171	140	65
HPK Hameenlinna	54	27	21	6	192	152	60
Ilves Tampere	54	30	24	0	180	143	60
SaiPa Lappeenranta	54	25	25	4	141	153	54
Blues Espoo	54	21	26	7	146	183	49
JyP HT Jyvaskyla	54	22	28	4	137	157	48
Tappara Tampere	54	21	27	6	148	196	48
Assat Pori	54	20	28	6	152	178	46
Lukko Rauma	54	16	31	7	126	176	39
KalPa Kuopio	54	9	39	6	95	187	24

1999–2000

Team	GP	W	L	T	GF	GA	PTS
TPS Turku	54	39	10	5	232	118	83
HPK Hameenlinna	54	32	15	7	209	161	71
Tappara Tampere	54	31	15	8	187	148	70
Lukko Rauma	54	28	17	9	159	125	65
Jokerit Helsinki	54	27	18	9	147	131	63
HIFK Helsinki	54	23	21	10	171	162	56
Blues Espoo	54	19	25	10	163	165	48
Ilves Tampere	54	19	26	9	151	190	47
SaiPa Lappeenranta	54	16	25	13	154	185	45
JyP Jyvaskyla	54	13	28	13	158	211	39
Assat Pori	54	14	31	9	171	217	37
Pelicans Lahti	54	8	38	8	108	197	24

FRANCE

1994–95

Team	GP	W	L	T	GF	GA	PTS
HC Rouen	28	22	4	2	159	66	46
HGA Brest	28	16	8	4	147	82	36
HC Chamonix	28	15	10	3	106	107	33
CSG Grenoble	28	15	10	3	89	90	33
HCFB Reims	28	12	11	5	104	92	29
HCS Amiens	28	11	14	3	103	108	25
ASGA Angers	28	5	19	4	81	141	14
OHC Viry	28	3	23	2	81	184	8

1995–96

Team	GP	W	L	T	GF	GA	PTS
HC Rouen	28	22	5	1	172	77	45
HG Brest	28	19	5	4	142	70	42
HCS Amiens	28	13	10	5	108	101	31
HC Reims	28	10	9	9	111	105	29
CSG Grenoble	28	10	13	5	101	109	25
HC Chamonix	28	10	13	5	101	97	25
ASG Angers	28	8	15	5	84	112	21
OHC Viry	28	2	24	2	78	226	6

1996–97

1st to 6th place

Team	GP	W	L	T	GF	GA	PTS
Les Albatros Brest	10	6	2	2	43	29	14
HCS Amiens	10	6	3	1	36	35	13
HC Reims	10	5	4	1	30	32	11
Rouen HC	10	4	4	2	36	28	10
CSG Grenoble	10	3	4	3	32	31	9
ASG Angers	10	1	8	1	26	48	3

7th to 12th place

Team	GP	W	L	T	GF	GA	PTS
OHC Viry	10	8	2	0	49	29	16
HC Bordeaux	10	7	3	0	69	31	14
HC Lyon	10	6	4	0	51	40	12
HC Gap	10	4	4	2	41	45	10
HC Megeve	10	2	6	2	47	57	6
Epinal	10	1	9	0	36	91	2

1997–98

Team	GP	W	L	T	GF	GA	PTS
CSG Grenoble	18	17	1	0	86	47	44
HCS Amiens	18	12	4	2	102	51	35
HC Lyon	18	13	4	1	87	64	34
Rouen HC	18	10	7	1	78	60	27
HC Reims	18	8	8	2	62	53	26
HC Chamonix	18	9	8	1	73	62	24
ASGA Angers	18	10	8	0	84	64	23
HC Bordeaux	18	5	12	1	64	108	12
OHC Viry-Essonne	18	3	14	1	47	105	11
HC Anglet	18	2	15	1	50	119	5

Note: Includes bonus points from stage one

1998–99

Regular season – part one

Team	GP	W	L	OTW	T	OTL	GF	GA	PTS
Flammes Bleues Reims	18	12	2	1	3	0	55	35	29
Gothiques Amiens	18	10	3	2	3	0	84	40	27
Bruleurs de Loups Grenoble	17	10	5	1	1	0	80	48	23
Caen Leopards	18	8	6	0	2	2	65	61	20
Ducs Angers	18	7	6	1	1	3	52	52	20
Orques Anglet	18	7	8	1	1	1	64	68	18
Dragons Rouen	18	7	8	0	3	0	64	69	17
Lions Lyon	18	8	9	0	0	1	43	47	16
Huskies Chamonix	18	4	11	1	2	0	44	73	12
Jets Viry-Essone	17	1	16	0	0	0	26	87	2

One game (Grenoble-Viry) not played. Lyon had one point deducted. Dogues Bordeau folded. Overtime win – 2 pts; overtime loss – 1 pt.

Regular season – part two

Team	GP	W	L	OTW	T	OTL	GF	GA	PTS	B
Flammes Bleues Reims	18	12	3	1	2	0	79	37	38	10
Gothiques Amiens	18	14	3	0	1	0	101	38	38	9
Bruleurs de Loups Grenoble	18	11	5	0	1	1	66	56	32	8
Ducs Angers	18	9	6	1	1	1	89	65	28	6
Lions Lyon	18	11	5	0	1	1	80	53	27	3
Caen Leopards	18	7	9	1	1	0	71	71	24	7
Orques Anglet	18	8	9	0	1	0	49	82	22	5
Dragons Rouen	18	5	9	1	3	0	54	55	19	4
Huskies Chamonix	18	3	13	0	1	1	44	78	10	2
Jets Viry-Essone	18	0	18	0	0	0	38	136	1	1

B – bonus points carried forward from part one

1999–2000

Team	GP	W	L	OTW	T	OTL	GF	GA	PTS
Flammes Bleues Reims	32	20	8	0	2	2	138	98	44
Caen Leopards	32	17	9	3	1	2	127	97	43
Dragons Rouen	32	16	8	1	6	1	139	94	41
Gothiques Amiens	32	18	11	1	1	1	117	97	40
Ducs Angers	32	17	11	0	3	1	128	94	38
Orques Anglet	32	15	13	0	2	2	134	118	34
Lions Lyon	32	10	19	1	1	1	81	121	24
Huskies Chamonix	32	9	21	1	1	0	91	140	21
Jets Viry-Essone	32	3	25	3	1	0	89	185	13

OTW – 2 points; OTL – 1 point

GERMANY

1994–95

Team	GP	W	L	T	GF	GA	PTS
Berliner SC Preussen	44	33	11	0	228	127	66
EV Landshut	44	31	10	3	187	98	64
Adler Mannheim	44	29	9	6	164	108	64
Dusseldorfer EG	44	29	11	4	196	128	62
Krefelder EV	44	29	12	3	203	127	61
Kolner Haie	44	28	14	2	185	125	58
EC Kassel Huskies	44	22	18	4	145	138	48
Star Bulls Rosenheim	44	20	17	7	131	124	47
SERC Wild Wings	44	18	19	7	174	148	43
Frankfurt Lions	44	16	23	5	110	140	37
Kaufbeurer Adler	44	12	25	7	138	181	31
EHC 80 Nurnberg	44	11	24	9	151	187	31
Augsburg EV	44	12	25	7	137	189	31
EC Hannover	44	13	27	4	120	177	30
Ratingen Lowen	44	9	30	5	102	214	23
Fuchse Sachsen	44	8	31	5	89	182	21
EHC Eisbaren Berlin	44	10	32	2	136	229	22

1995–96

Team	GP	W	L	OTL	T	GF	GA	PTS
Koln Sharks	50	37	9	1	4	261	129	79
Preussen Berlin Devils	50	35	8	2	7	219	107	79
Dusseldorf	50	36	10	1	4	228	127	77
Landschut	50	38	11	0	1	222	127	77
Schwenningen Wild Wings	50	30	14	2	6	214	150	68
Mannheim Eagles	50	29	14	2	7	195	163	67
Krefeld Penguins	50	26	19	1	5	169	154	58
Frankfurt Lions	50	22	23	3	5	189	182	52
Kassel Huskies	50	19	19	2	12	149	148	52
Ratingen Lions	50	21	26	3	3	181	195	48
Nurnberger Ice Tigers	50	16	26	2	8	143	179	42
Augsburg Panthers	50	17	27	2	6	163	180	42
Rosenheim Star Bulls	50	16	28	3	6	158	195	41
Riessersee	50	16	30	1	4	147	213	37
Kaufbeuren Eagles	50	13	31	1	6	145	228	33
EC Hannover	50	12	34	0	4	138	251	28
Eisbaren Berlin	50	11	36	2	3	125	236	27
Saxonia Foxes	50	9	38	0	3	126	236	21

Note: one point awarded for an Overtime Loss (OTL)

1996–97

Team	GP	W	L	OTL	T	GF	GA	PTS
Adler Mannheim	50	35	10	1	5	212	123	76
Kolner Haie	50	36	12	2	2	235	142	76
Kassel Huskies	50	27	19	1	4	190	167	59
Eisbaren Berlin	50	26	20	1	4	177	163	57
Berlin Capitals	50	23	21	3	6	162	149	55
Star Bulls Rosenheim	50	20	28	5	2	171	209	47
Landshut	48	29	16	3	3	202	122	64
Krefeld Pinguine	48	28	18	3	2	198	166	61
Dusseldorf	48	28	18	0	2	164	138	58
Schwenningen Wild Wings	48	23	24	5	1	200	191	52
Augsburg Panthers	48	21	22	1	5	176	181	48
Frankfurt Lions	48	21	23	1	4	136	142	47
Kaufbeurer Adler	48	17	28	3	3	166	252	40
Wedemark Scorpions	48	12	35	3	1	150	231	28
Nurnberg Ice Tigers	48	9	33	1	6	149	229	25
Ratinger Lowen	48	9	37	2	2	136	219	22

Note: one point awarded for an Overtime Loss (OTL)

1997–98

Team	GP	W	L	OTL	T	GF	GA	PTS
EHC Eisbaren Berlin	48	27	15	1	6	179	139	61
Frankfurt Lions	48	27	15	1	6	160	126	61
Kolner Haie	48	26	16	2	6	160	147	60
Adler Mannheim	48	26	19	3	3	170	145	58
Dusseldorfer EG	48	27	20	2	1	166	164	57
EV Landshut	48	25	19	2	4	148	118	56
Hannover Scorpions	44	22	16	2	6	160	142	52
Berlin Capitals	44	19	18	4	7	136	119	49
Schwenningen Wild Wings	44	19	20	3	5	157	148	46
Kassel Huskies	44	19	22	4	3	140	128	45
Krefeld Pinguine	44	18	20	1	6	126	141	43
Nurnberg Ice Tigers	44	18	22	2	4	158	154	42
Augsburger Panther	44	16	26	2	2	122	160	36
ECR Revier Lowen	44	14	26	1	4	132	184	33
Star Bulls Rosenheim	44	6	35	0	3	105	204	15

Note: one point awarded for an Overtime Loss (OTL)

1998–99

Team	GP	W	OTW	OTL	L	GF	GA	PTS
Nurnberg Ice Tigers	52	30	7	2	13	199	141	106
EHC Eisbaren Berlin	52	26	4	5	17	210	163	91
Adler Mannheim	52	24	5	7	16	208	182	89
Frankfurt Lions	52	25	5	4	18	184	168	89
Kolner Haie	52	21	9	7	15	182	159	88
EV Landshut	52	21	8	9	14	163	140	88
Krefeld Pinguine	52	23	7	4	18	183	159	87
Augsburger Panther	52	22	8	3	19	169	155	85
Kassel Huskies	52	24	4	4	20	165	145	84
Schwenninger W. Wings	52	19	4	7	22	195	217	72
Hannover Scorpions	52	18	3	6	25	175	195	66
Star Bulls Rosenheim	52	15	6	5	26	169	213	62
Berlin Capitals	52	12	4	8	28	146	205	52
Revier Lowen	52	10	0	3	39	148	254	33

Note: W – 3 pts., OTW – 2 pts., OTL – 1 pt.

1999–2000

Team	GP	W	L	PSW	PSL	GF	GA	PTS
1st to 8th place								
Kolner Haie	56	33	10	2	11	217	144	114
Munchen Barons	56	31	14	5	6	203	158	106
Krefeld Pinguine	56	28	17	6	5	213	171	101
Kassel Huskies	56	28	17	2	9	168	137	97
Adler Mannheim	56	27	19	6	4	196	182	97
Berlin Capitals	56	24	16	9	7	183	172	97
Frankfurt Lions	56	24	20	8	4	190	175	92
Augsburger Panther	56	25	24	5	2	178	161	90
9th to 15th place								
Hannover Scorpions	68	26	29	9	4	257	245	100
Nurnberg Ice Tigers	68	29	33	3	3	214	209	96
Schwenninger W. Wings	68	24	30	5	9	199	232	91
Star Bulls Rosenheim	68	24	31	5	8	213	244	90
EHC Eisbaren Berlin	68	25	37	2	4	230	256	83
Revier Lowen	68	16	37	11	4	174	234	74
ESC Moskitos Essen	68	15	45	5	3	167	282	58

Note: W – 3 pts., Penalty Shootout Win (PSW) – 2 pts., Penalty Shootout Loss (PSL) – 1 pt.

GREAT BRITAIN

1994–95

Team	GP	W	L	T	GF	GA	PTS
Sheffield Steelers	44	35	5	4	334	183	74
Cardiff Devils	44	32	8	4	366	217	68
Nottingham Panthers	44	32	8	4	372	213	68
Edinburgh Racers	44	25	14	5	335	289	55
Durham Wasps	44	22	19	3	264	242	47
Fife Flyers	44	20	20	4	271	242	44
Basingstoke Beavers	44	20	22	2	271	279	42
Humberside Hawks	44	17	21	6	331	330	40
Peterborough Pirates	44	12	27	5	248	368	29
Whitley Warriors	44	10	30	4	242	372	24
Miton Keynes Kings	44	9	31	4	248	363	22
Bracknell Bees	44	6	35	3	189	373	15

Group A

Team	GP	W	L	T	GF	GA	PTS
Sheffield Steelers	6	4	2	0	35	24	8
Nottingham Panthers	6	3	3	0	36	25	6
Fife Flyers	6	3	3	0	29	37	6
Humberside Hawks	6	2	4	0	28	42	4

Group B

Team	GP	W	L	T	GF	GA	PTS
Edinburgh Racers	6	4	1	1	42	37	9
Cardiff Devils	6	3	1	2	46	30	8
Basingstoke Beavers	6	2	3	1	33	38	5
Durham Wasps	6	0	4	2	23	39	2

1995–96

Team	GP	W	L	T	GF	GA	PTS
Sheffield Steelers	36	27	4	5	268	122	59
Cardiff Devils	36	26	7	3	271	140	55
Durham Wasps	36	22	10	4	213	158	48
Nottingham Panthers	36	19	12	5	214	174	43
Humberside Hawks	36	16	16	4	202	235	36
Fife Flayers	36	14	16	6	209	238	34
Basingstoke Biston	36	11	20	5	146	190	27
Newcastle Warriors	36	10	22	4	167	256	24
Milton Keynes Kings	36	7	22	7	186	237	21
Slough Jets	36	5	28	3	172	298	13

1996–97

Team	GP	W	L	OTL	T	GF	GA	PTS
Cardiff Devils	42	30	8	1	3	208	130	64
Sheffield Steelers	42	27	9	2	4	168	127	60
Ayr Scottish Eagles	42	21	15	0	6	171	157	48
Nottingham Panthers	42	21	18	2	1	160	147	45
Newcastle Cobras	42	17	18	5	2	158	172	41
Bracknell Bees	42	15	24	1	2	169	202	33
Manchester Storm	42	14	24	1	3	142	191	32
Basingstoke Bisons	42	11	25	3	3	152	202	28

Note: one point awarded for an Overtime Loss (OTL)

1997–98

Team	GP	W	L	OTL		GF	GA	PTS
Ayr Scottish Eagles	28	20	5	1	2	117	69	43
Manchester Storm	28	18	6	3	1	123	80	40
Cardiff Devils	28	15	9	2	2	99	79	34
Nottingham Panthers	28	14	11	3	0	95	99	31
Bracknell Bees	28	14	12	1	1	95	115	30
Sheffield Steelers	28	11	12	2	3	103	101	27
Basington Bisons	28	5	13	4	6	80	116	20
Newcastle Cobras	28	6	19	2	1	66	119	15

1998–99

Regular Season

Team	GP	W	L	OTL	T	GF	GA	PTS
Manchester Storm	42	30	7	4	1	155	86	65
Cardiff Devils	42	27	10	5	0	144	102	59
Nottingham Panthers	42	25	14	2	1	140	134	53
Bracknell Bees	42	19	17	4	2	144	149	44
Ayr Scottish Eagles	42	18	18	3	3	136	140	42
Sheffield Steelers	42	17	19	2	4	135	141	40
Newcastle Riverkings	42	14	24	2	2	117	150	32
London Knights	42	10	25	4	3	114	183	27
Group A								
Manchester Storm	6	5	1	0	0	22	9	10
Bracknell Bees	6	5	1	0	0	25	19	10
Sheffield Steelers	6	2	4	0	0	20	23	4
London Knights	6	0	5	1	0	14	30	1
Group B								
Nottingham Panthers	6	5	1	0	0	20	16	10
Cardiff Devils	6	3	2	0	1	20	16	7
Ayr Scottish Eagles	6	2	3	0	1	21	20	5
Newcastle Riverkings	6	1	3	2	0	14	23	4

Overtime loss – 1 pt.

1999–2000

Regular Season

Team	GP	W	L	OTL	T	GF	GA	PTS
Bracknell Bees	42	24	15	5	3	181	138	56
Sheffield Steelers	42	24	16	2	2	188	155	52
Manchester Storm	42	23	17	3	2	155	138	51
London Knights	42	23	16	1	3	135	125	50
Ayr Scottish Eagles	42	17	20	4	5	144	147	43
Nottingham Panthers	42	18	21	1	3	140	165	40
Cardiff Devils	42	17	21	2	4	138	149	40
Newcastle Riverkings	42	11	31	2	0	113	177	24

Overtime loss – 1 pt.

ITALY

1994–95

Team	GP	W	L	T	GF	GA	PTS
HC Bolzano Wurth	36	26	9	1	215	115	53
Shimano Varese	36	23	10	3	169	111	49
HC Courmaosta	36	17	12	7	139	120	41
Saima Milano	36	16	16	4	141	149	36
Hockey Devils Milano	36	14	16	6	156	165	34
HC Gardena	36	15	17	4	158	166	34
HC Alleghe	36	15	17	4	110	130	34
SG Brunico	36	15	19	2	143	176	32
HC Fassa Wuber	36	13	21	2	162	183	28
HC Asiago	36	8	25	3	117	195	19

1995–96

Team	GP	W	L	T	GF	GA	PTS
HC Bolzano	32	26	3	3	214	105	55
HC 24 Milano	32	19	9	4	171	123	42
HC Gardena	32	19	9	4	154	114	42
Varese Hockey	32	19	10	3	138	94	41
HC Fassa	32	12	17	3	126	163	27
HC Asiago	32	12	19	1	111	144	25
SG Brunico	32	10	18	4	120	140	24
HC Alleghe	32	11	19	2	101	148	24
Devils Milano	32	4	28	0	110	214	8

1996–97

Team	GP	W	L	T	GF	GA	PTS
HC 24 Milano	10	8	2	0	84	31	16
HC Bolzano	10	8	2	0	70	45	16
SHC Fassa	10	6	3	1	53	44	13
HC Merano	10	4	6	0	34	34	8
SG Brunico	10	3	6	1	40	65	7
HC Gardena	10	0	10	0	26	88	0

1997–98

Team	GP	W	L	OTL	OTW	GF	GA	PTS
HC Bolzano	20	16	4	0	1	114	63	79
HC Asiago	20	13	7	1	0	84	63	68
SHC Fassa	20	11	9	1	0	78	89	60
HC Merano	20	10	10	0	1	97	91	54
HC Gardena	20	8	12	0	0	84	93	48
SG Brunico	20	2	18	0	0	55	113	34

W – 3 pts., OTW – 2 pts., OTL–1 pt.
Note: Includes bonus points from stage one

1998–99

Team	GP	W	L	T	GF	GA	PTS
HC Bolzano	16	12	4	0	94	58	37
HC Merano	16	12	4	0	95	58	36
SG Saima Cortina/Milano	16	11	5	0	65	47	33
Supermercati A&O Asiago	16	9	7	0	92	66	32
SSI Vipiteno Erdinger	16	9	7	0	79	65	30
SHC Fassa Levoni	16	9	7	0	69	59	25
HC Alleghe Stop Mods	16	5	11	0	58	90	17
SG Brunico	16	3	13	0	55	101	13
HC Lions Courmaosta	16	2	14	0	45	108	8

Three points for a win. Note: Includes bonus points from Alpenliga.

1999–2000

Team	GP	W	L	T	OTL	GF	GA	PTS
Supermercati Asiago	28	27	1	1	0	204	38	80
HC Merano	28	23	5	2	0	129	73	67
SHC Fassa Levoni	28	21	7	0	2	145	67	65
Forst Bolzano Foxes	28	21	7	2	3	168	63	64
Sterzing-Vipiteno	28	21	7	3	0	130	93	59
HC Alleghe Teg. Can.	28	19	9	2	1	140	78	56
SG Bruneck Brunico	28	17	11	0	1	129	108	53
HC Valpellice	28	14	14	2	2	93	88	42
Como Promolinea	28	12	16	0	2	95	120	38
SV Renon/Ritten	28	11	17	2	0	96	132	31
Auronzo di Cadore	28	9	19	1	0	107	171	26
HC Eppan/Appiano	28	7	21	1	3	84	144	23
AS Mastini Varese	28	3	25	0	2	66	142	11
LSC Val Venosta	28	3	25	1	1	57	188	9
USG Zoldo	28	2	26	0	0	72	210	6

W – 3 pts., OTW – 2 pts., OTL–1 pt.
Wins and Overtime Wins combined in W column

JAPAN

1994–95

Stage one

Team	GP	W	L	T	GF	GA	PTS
Kokudo Tokyo	15	13	1	1	59	25	27
New Oji Tomakomai	15	8	5	2	67	47	18
Seibu Tetsudo Tokyo	15	8	6	1	56	42	17
Nippon Paper Kushiro	15	7	7	1	52	50	15
Yukijrushi Sapporo	15	6	8	1	36	48	13
Furukawa Denko Nikko	15	0	15	0	23	81	0

Stage two

Team	GP	W	L	T	GF	GA	PTS
Seibu Tetsudo Tokyo	15	12	3	0	76	38	24
New Oji Tomakomai	15	12	3	0	72	42	24
Kokudo Tokyo	15	9	6	0	68	48	18
Nippon Paper Kushiro	15	7	8	0	51	59	14
Yukijrushi Sapporo	15	4	10	1	35	70	9
Furukawa Denko Nikko	15	0	14	1	27	72	1

1995–96

Stage one

Team	GP	W	L	T	GF	GA	PTS
New Oji Tamakomai	20	15	3	2	101	55	32
Kokudo Keikadu Tokyo	20	12	4	4	76	54	28
Seibu Tetsudo Tokyo	20	13	7	0	88	76	26
Furukawa Denko Nikko	20	7	12	1	60	85	15
Yukijrushi Sapporo	20	4	13	3	59	99	11
Nippon Paper Kushiro	20	3	15	2	70	85	8

Stage two

Team	GP	W	L	T	GF	GA	PTS
Seibu Tetsudo Tokyo	20	17	2	1	95	48	35
Kokudo Keikadu Tokyo	20	16	3	1	109	58	33
New Oji Tamakomai	20	10	10	0	84	76	20
Furukawa Denko Nikko	20	7	13	0	63	98	14
Nippon Paper Kushiro	20	6	14	0	70	86	12
Yukijrushi Sapporo	20	3	17	0	52	107	6

1996–97

Team	GP	W	L	T	GF	GA	PTS
New Oji Tomakomai	30	22	4	4	152	92	48
Seibu Tetsudo Tokyo	30	16	9	5	128	102	37
Kokudo Kaikadu Tokyo	30	18	12	0	105	72	36
Yukijushi Sapporo	30	10	18	2	78	116	22
Nippon Paper Kushiro	30	8	19	3	83	125	19
Furukawa Denko Nikko	30	8	20	2	71	110	18

1997–98

Team	GP	W	L	T	GF	GA	PTS
Kokudo Tokyo	40	24	12	4	149	119	52
Oji Tomakomai	40	22	14	4	165	129	48
Snow Brand	40	19	15	6	125	124	44
Seibu Tetsudo Tokyo	40	18	19	3	160	151	39
Furukawa Denko Nikko	40	16	23	1	110	139	33
Cranes Kushiro	40	11	27	2	120	167	24

1998–99

Team	GP	W	L	T	GF	GA	PTS
Kokudo Tokyo	40	31	8	1	182	93	63
Seibu Tetsudo Tokyo	40	26	12	2	165	122	54
New Oji Tomakomai	40	21	18	1	147	142	43
Cranes Kushiro	40	18	18	4	138	147	40
Snow Brand Sapporo	40	11	26	3	120	162	25
Furukawa Denko Nikko	40	6	31	3	100	186	15

1999–2000

Team	GP	W	L	T	GF	GA	PTS
Kokudo Tokyo	30	22	5	3	130	75	47
Seibu Tetsudo Tokyo	30	20	9	1	104	79	41
Cranes Kushiro	30	14	13	3	94	88	31
New Oji Tomakomai	30	13	15	2	103	97	28
Snow Brand Sapporo	30	9	17	4	79	110	22
HC Nikko Icebucks	30	3	22	5	45	106	11

NETHERLANDS

1994–95

Team	GP	W	L	T	GF	GA	PTS
Tilberg Trappers	24	22	1	1	220	52	45
Smoke Eaters Geleen	24	17	5	2	189	74	36
Fulda Tigers Nijmegen	24	17	6	1	118	92	35
CP & A Eindhoven	24	13	10	1	124	136	27
Pandas Rotterdam	24	7	17	0	98	151	14
Heerenveen Flyers	24	2	20	2	70	159	6
Dordrecht Lions	24	2	21	1	68	223	5

1995–96

Team	GP	W	L	T	GF	GA	PTS
Tilburg Trappers	20	16	1	3	123	36	35
Fulda Tigers Nijmegen	20	16	3	1	145	58	33
Flyers Heerenveen	20	8	9	3	71	78	19
Smoke Eaters Geleen	20	6	8	6	72	66	18
Kemphanen Eindhoven	20	3	12	5	57	139	11
Loons Dordrecht	20	2	18	0	48	139	4

1996–97

Team	GP	W	L	T	GF	GA	PTS
Flyers Heerenveen	14	13	1	0	84	24	26
Fulda Tigers Nijmegen	14	11	3	0	100	33	22
Tilburg Trappers	14	10	3	1	74	34	21
Smoke Eaters Geleen*	14	6	7	1	59	64	11
Kemphanen Eindhoven	14	5	9	0	52	59	10
Phantoms Deume	14	5	9	0	38	89	10
MBB Builders Utrecht	14	4	10	0	54	81	8
Jordens Lions Dordrecht	14	1	13	0	43	120	2

1st to 4th place

Team	GP	W	L	T	GF	GA	PTS
Fulda Tigers Nijmegen	6	5	1	0	37	19	10
Tilburg Trappers	6	3	2	1	27	22	7
Flyers Heerenveen	6	2	3	1	11	18	5
Smoke Eaters Geleen	6	1	5	0	21	37	2

** – two points deducted*

1997–98

Team	GP	W	L	T	GF	GA	PTS
Tilburg Trappers	24	21	3	0	200	48	42
Tigers Nijmegen	24	19	4	1	162	85	39
Flyers Heerenveen	24	16	7	1	178	64	33
MBB Builders Utrecht	24	13	8	3	107	104	29
Wolves Den Haag	24	6	17	1	85	194	13
C.M./IJCK Eindhoven	24	5	19	0	70	188	10
H'wood Phantoms Deume	24	1	23	0	72	191	2

1998–99

Team	GP	W	L	OTW	OTL	GF	GA	PTS
Tigers Nijmegen	20	16	3	1	0	105	58	50
Tigers Amsterdam	20	13	3	1	3	96	59	44
Trappers Tilburg	20	12	6	2	0	96	63	40
Flyers Heerenveen	20	8	10	1	1	72	72	27
Phantoms Deurne	20	3	16	0	1	69	120	10
Wolves Den Haag	20	2	16	1	1	72	138	9

Group A

Team	GP	W	L	OTW	OTL	GF	GA	PTS	B
Tigers Nijmegen	6	4	1	1	0	33	21	17	3
Trappers Tilburg	6	3	1	1	1	22	21	13	1
Tigers Amsterdam	6	1	2	1	2	18	23	9	2
Flyers Heerenveen	6	1	5	0	0	14	22	3	0

Bonus points from part one

Group B

Team	GP	W	L	OTW	OTL	GF	GA	PTS
Wolves Den Haag	6	5	1	0	0	32	24	15
Phantoms Deurne	6	4	1	0	1	39	23	13
Cema Eatars Geleen	6	1	3	2	0	30	32	7
Red Eagles Den Bosch	6	0	5	0	1	14	36	1

W – 3 pts.; OTW – 2 pts; OTL – 1 pt.

1999–2000

Team	GP	W	OTW	L	OTL	GF	GA	PTS
Tigers Nijmegen	18	11	2	5	0	86	63	37
Trappers Tilburg	18	9	2	4	3	90	57	34
Flyers Heerenveen	18	10	2	3	2	78	56	33
Tigers Amsterdam	18	7	2	6	3	70	73	28
Geleen	18	7	1	9	1	81	85	24
s-Hertogenbosch	18	3	3	11	1	56	91	16
Wolves Den Haag	18	4	0	12	2	61	97	14

1st to 4th place

Team	GP	W	OTW	L	OTL	GF	GA	PTS
Tigers Nijmegen	6	4	0	2	0	26	15	15
Trappers Tilburg	6	3	0	3	0	19	16	11
Flyers Heerenveen	6	3	0	2	1	22	27	11
Tigers Amsterdam	6	1	1	4	0	18	27	5

5th to 7th place

Team	GP	W	OTW	L	OTL	GF	GA	PTS
s-Hertogenbosch	8	5	1	2	0	39	28	17
Wolves Den Haag	8	3	0	3	2	34	38	11
Geleen	8	2	1	5	0	25	32	8

Win – 3 pts.; overtime win – 2 pts; overtime loss – 1 pt.

NORWAY

1994–95

Team	GP	W	L	T	GF	GA	PTS
Storhamar IL Hamar	28	21	2	5	195	52	47
VIF Hockey Oslo	28	18	6	4	134	91	40
Lillehammer IK	28	17	7	4	117	97	38
Spektrum Flyers Oslo	28	15	10	3	118	87	33
Stjermen Fredrikstad	28	13	12	3	134	125	29
Viking Stavanger	28	7	19	2	88	128	16
Trondheim IK	28	7	20	1	79	138	15
Sparta Sarpsborg	28	2	24	2	70	217	6

1995–96

Team	GP	W	L	T	GF	GA	PTS
VIF Hockey Oslo	28	21	7	0	135	86	42
Stjernen Fredrikstad	28	19	7	2	140	94	40
Storhamar Hamar	28	20	8	0	128	56	40
Spektrum Flyers Oslo	28	18	9	1	132	90	37
Lillehammer IHK	28	13	13	2	101	101	28
TIK Trondheim	28	8	18	2	87	108	18
Frisk Asker	28	5	21	1	69	154	11
Viking Stavanger	28	3	23	2	90	193	8

Group A

Team	GP	W	L	T	GF	GA	PTS
Storhamar Hamar	4	4	0	0	19	8	8
VIF Hockey Oslo	4	2	2	0	15	15	4
TIK Trondheim	4	0	4	0	9	20	0

Group B

Team	GP	W	L	T	GF	GA	PTS
Stjernen Fredrikstad	4	3	1	0	18	16	6
Lillehammer IHK	4	2	2	0	16	17	4
Spektrum Flyers Oslo	4	1	3	0	14	15	2

1996–97

Team	GP	W	L	T	GF	GA	PTS
Storhamar Hamar	36	33	1	2	252	58	68
Valerenga Oslo	36	27	9	0	214	99	54
TIK Trondheim	36	22	12	2	144	107	46
Frisk Asker	36	21	14	1	170	123	43
Stjernen Fredrikstad	36	20	14	2	153	133	42
Lillehammer IHK	36	17	16	3	158	160	37
Manglerud Star Oslo	36	13	21	2	127	179	28
Lorenskog	36	8	27	1	115	216	17
Furuset Oslo	36	6	27	3	96	211	15
Hasle Loren Oslo	36	5	31	0	88	231	10

1997–98

Team	GP	W	L	T	GF	GA	PTS
Valerengen Oslo	44	34	8	2	240	94	70
Storhamar Hamar	44	32	9	3	213	92	67
IL Stjernen	44	23	17	4	172	149	50
Sparta Sarpsborg	44	23	18	3	165	152	49
Frisk Asker	44	21	16	7	183	147	49
Lillehammer IHK	44	22	17	5	163	139	49
Manglerud Star Oslo	44	18	23	3	172	179	39
TIK Trondheim	44	15	24	5	159	181	35.
Furuset Oslo	44	13	28	3	155	218	29
Lorenskog IHK	44	1	42	1	79	350	3

1998–99

Team	GP	W	L	T	GF	GA	PTS
Vaalerega IF Oslo	44	34	3	7	219	93	74*
Storhamar IL Hamar	44	30	8	6	196	104	66
Stjernen IL Fredrikstad	44	27	14	3	190	112	57
Trondheim IK	44	20	17	7	153	136	46*
Frisk Asker	44	20	21	3	171	145	43
Sparta Sarpsborg	44	20	21	3	141	138	42*
Lillehammer IHK	44	19	22	3	154	185	40*
Manglerud/Star Oslo	44	15	24	5	140	159	35
Viking Stavanger	44	8	34	2	98	254	18
Furuset IL Oslo	44	6	35	3	97	233	15

** – one point deduction*

1999–2000

Team	GP	W	L	T	GF	GA	PTS
Valerenga IF Oslo	38	32	5	1	219	75	65
Storhamar IL Hamar	38	27	10	1	167	81	55
Frisk Asker	38	27	11	0	172	109	54
Sparta Sarpsborg	38	20	17	1	123	117	41
Trondheim IK	38	19	17	2	119	134	40
Stjernen IL Fredrikstad	38	15	19	4	99	119	34
Manglerud/Star Oslo	38	12	25	1	105	155	25
Lillehammer IHK	38	7	29	2	84	157	16
Lornshog	38	5	31	2	63	204	12

POLAND

1994–95

Team	GP	W	L	T	GF	GA	PTS
Podhale Nowy Targ	32	25	2	5	196	77	55
KS Unia Oswiecim	32	23	6	3	202	78	49
KKH Katowice	32	21	8	3	182	86	45
Naprzod Janow	32	16	9	7	152	95	39
TTH Metron Torun	32	15	11	6	131	121	36
MHKS Polonia Bytom	32	11	18	3	97	167	25
Stoczniowec Gdansk	32	16	11	5	138	131	37
MkH Tysovia	32	16	14	2	122	101	34
STS Autosan Sanok	32	16	14	2	140	122	34
SMS PZHL Sosnowiec	32	8	23	1	77	159	17
BTH Bydgoszcz	32	4	27	1	65	165	9
Cracowia Krakow	32	1	29	2	85	285	4

1995–96

1st to 6th place

Team	GP	W	L	T	GF	GA	PTS
KS Unia Oswiecin	20	19	1	0	109	50	38
Podhale Nowy Targ	20	16	4	0	114	66	32
KKH Katowice	20	8	11	1	77	73	17
TTH Metrom Torun	20	7	12	1	59	73	15
STS Autosan Sanok	20	6	14	0	76	105	12
SMS PZHL Sosnowiec	20	3	17	0	48	116	6

7th to 13th place

Team	GP	W	L	T	GF	GA	PTS
Naprzod Janow	20	16	1	3	122	44	35
Stoczniowec Gdansk	20	15	4	1	106	59	31
MKH Tysovia Tychy	20	11	9	0	87	81	22
Cracowia Krakow	20	4	12	4	48	96	12
Polisa Bydgoszcz	20	5	14	1	60	95	11
MHKS Polonia Bytom	20	3	14	3	59	107	9

1996–97

1st to 6th place

Team	GP	W	L	T	GF	GA	PTS
Podhale Nowy Targ	40	31	9	0	215	99	62
KKH Katowice	40	28	10	2	168	120	58
KS Unia Oswiecim	40	26	13	1	186	105	53
STS Autosan Sanok	40	14	23	3	134	166	31
TTH Metron Torun	40	11	26	3	99	193	25
Naprzod Katowice	40	5	34	1	99	218	11

7th to 13th place

Team	GP	W	L	T	GF	GA	PTS
Stoczniowiec Danzig	24	20	3	1	147	73	41
KS Cracovia Krakow	24	19	4	1	132	60	39
MHKS Polonia Bytom	24	16	8	0	110	80	32
MKH Tysovia Tychy	24	8	15	1	91	161	17
Polisa Bydgozcz	24	8	16	0	79	99	16
Optimus Krynica	24	7	16	1	92	111	15
SMS PZHL Sosnowiec	24	3	19	2	78	145	8

1997–98

1st to 6th place

Team	GP	W	L	T	GF	GA	PTS
Podhale Nowy Targ	30	22	5	3	106	70	47
Unia Oswiecim	30	17	10	3	106	78	37
STS Autosan Sanok	30	16	12	2	118	92	34
Hortex Katowice	30	15	14	1	103	83	31
Optimus Krynica	30	10	20	0	91	122	20
Stoczniowiec Gdansk	30	5	24	1	83	162	11

7th to 13th place

Team	GP	W	L	T	GF	GA	PTS
Cracowia Krakow	24	21	3	0	129	72	42
TTH Metron Torun	24	18	6	0	118	75	36
TTS Tychy	24	16	7	1	137	90	33
SMS Sosnowiec 1	24	12	12	0	137	95	24
Naprzod Janow	24	9	13	2	93	83	20
Polonia Bytom	24	6	17	1	83	134	13
SMS Sosnowiec 2	24	0	24	0	43	191	0

1998–99

Team	GP	W	L	GF	GA	PTS
Unia Dwory Oswencim	26	24	2	139	41	48
Podhale Nowy Targ	26	23	3	187	61	46
KKH Hortex Katowice	26	20	6	120	60	40
SMS Warszawa	26	19	7	172	59	38
KTH PZU Krynica	26	19	7	119	53	38
Stoczniowiec Gdansk	26	15	11	101	82	30
STS Autosan Sanok	26	12	14	96	88	24
TTS Tychy	26	12	14	100	112	24
Polonia Bytom	26	11	15	77	95	22
Cracovia Krakow	26	10	16	81	89	20
TTH Filmar Torun	26	9	17	89	121	18
STH Zaglebie Sosnowiec	26	5	21	75	149	10
BTH Micronel Bydgoszaz	26	2	24	47	197	4
SMS II Sosnowiec	26	1	25	28	224	2

Group A

Team	GP	W	L	GF	GA	PTS
Podhale Nowy Targ	46	39	7	281	120	78
Unia Dwory Oswencim	46	34	12	206	98	68
SMS Warszawa	46	33	13	254	101	66
KTH PZU Krynica	46	28	18	173	132	56
KKH Hortex Katowice	46	27	19	175	128	54
Stoczniiiowiec Gdansk	46	19	27	151	180	38

Group B

Team	GP	W	L	GF	GA	PTS
STS Autosan Sanok	40	25	15	181	122	50
TTS Tychy	40	23	17	187	170	46
Cracovia Krakow	40	20	20	154	126	40
Polonia Bytom	40	19	21	136	141	38
TTH Filmar Torun	40	15	25	149	171	30
STH Zaglebie Sosnowiec	40	9	31	132	227	18
SMS II Sosnowiec	40	5	35	66	298	10
BTH Micronel Bydgoszaz	40	2	38	82	313	4

1999–2000

Team	GP	W	L	GF	GA	PTS
Unia Dwory Oswencim	42	36	6	198	71	72
Podhale Nowy Targ	42	27	15	178	122	55
PZU S.A. KTH Krynica	42	27	15	160	94	55
GKS Tychy	42	25	17	153	108	51
STH Sanok	42	22	20	130	131	44
Stoczniowiec Gdansk	42	14	28	116	175	29
KKH 100% Hortex Katowice	42	13	29	119	139	28
Cracovia Krakow	42	4	38	81	295	9

Note: 1 pt. for overtime loss. OTLs included in Loss column

RUSSIA/C.I.S.

1994–95

Western Division

Team	GP	W	L	T	GF	GA	pts
Torpedo Yaroslavl	52	33	15	4	152	96	70
Krylja Sovetov Moscow	52	30	14	8	173	120	68
Dynamo Moscow	52	30	16	6	172	107	66
Nizhny Novgorod	52	26	16	10	137	111	62
Itil Kazan	52	27	18	7	150	123	61
CSKA Moscow	52	25	20	7	158	114	57
SKA St.Petersburg	52	26	21	5	127	122	57
Khimik Voskresensk	52	23	21	8	122	125	54
Spartak Moscow	52	23	24	5	132	154	51
Severstal Cherepovets	52	20	28	4	11	151	44
Kristall Elektrostal	52	17	31	4	112	157	38
Tivali Minsk	52	13	31	8	102	151	34
Sokol Kiev	52	12	30	10	104	142	34
Paradaugava Riga	52	14	34	4	99	168	32

Eastern Division

Team	GP	W	L	T	GF	GA	PTS
Lada Togliatti	52	41	7	4	229	83	86
Avangard Omsk	52	36	8	8	220	100	80
Metallurg Magnitogorsk	52	37	12	3	260	134	77
Salavat Yulayev Ufa	52	31	10	11	219	126	73
Traktor Chelyabinsk	52	26	21	5	177	146	57
Molot Perm	52	27	22	3	144	140	57
Ust-Kamenogorsk	52	24	24	4	173	171	52
Avto. Yekaterinburg	52	18	22	12	126	137	48
CSK VVS Samara	52	19	26	7	161	169	45
Kristall Saratov	52	19	28	5	134	173	43
Rubin Tyumen	52	18	30	4	155	205	40
Sibir Novosibirsk	52	14	35	3	158	273	31
Metallurg Novokuznetsk	52	11	33	8	125	185	30
Stroitel Karaganda	52	3	46	3	99	338	9

1995–96

1st to 14th place

Team	GP	W	L	T	GF	GA	PTS
Lada Togliatti	26	21	3	2	122	50	48
Dynamo Moscow	26	18	5	3	79	53	46
Avangard Omsk	26	16	6	4	87	54	42
Salavat Yzlayev Ufa	26	17	6	3	80	46	42
Metallurg Magnitogorsk	26	14	10	2	70	55	37
Torpedo Yaroslavl	26	15	10	1	70	55	37
AK Bars Kazan	26	14	8	4	68	56	36
Kristall Elektrostal	26	10	12	4	73	76	27
Severstal Cherepovets	26	7	16	3	62	83	22
SKA St.Petersburg	26	9	15	2	64	67	22
Rubin Tyumen	26	7	16	3	63	104	18
Molot Perm	26	6	18	2	74	95	17
Kristall Saratov	26	6	19	1	55	127	15
Spartak Moscow	26	5	21	0	69	117	11

15th to 28th place

Team	GP	W	L	T	GF	GA	PTS
CSKA Moscow	26	19	4	3	85	32	45
Nizhny Novgorod	26	17	5	4	74	43	44
Krylja Sovetov Moscow	26	18	8	0	89	41	43
Khimik Voskresensk	26	15	9	2	74	66	37
Avto. Yekaterinburg	26	15	10	1	70	55	36
Metallurg Novokuznetsk	26	13	11	2	67	64	35
Sokol Kiev	26	11	8	7	59	59	32
Ust-Kamenogorsk	26	11	12	3	84	84	31
Traktor Chelyabinsk	26	10	12	4	49	42	27
Sibir Novosibirsk	26	12	13	1	70	72	26
Neftekhimik Nizhnekamsk	26	10	13	3	58	65	25
CSK VVS Samara	26	9	16	1	50	77	23
Bulat Karaganda	26	4	22	0	62	124	10
Tivali Minsk	26	2	23	1	39	106	6

Bonus points included

1996–97

Western Division

Team	GP	W	L	T	GF	GA	PTS
AK Bars Kazan	24	17	4	3	77	40	37
Torpedo Yaroslavl	24	16	4	4	65	31	36
HC CSKA Moscow	24	12	7	5	58	58	29
Krylja Sovetov Moscow	24	12	9	3	83	61	27
Dynamo Moscow	24	12	9	3	60	55	27
Spartak Moscow	24	11	10	3	62	63	25
Khimik Voskresensk	24	9	9	6	65	63	24
Neftekhimik Nizhnekamsk	24	10	10	4	47	49	24
Severstal Cherepovets	24	6	8	10	56	59	22
SKA St.Petersburg	24	7	12	5	46	59	19
Nizhny Novgorod	24	6	14	4	47	64	16
Dizelist Penza	24	6	15	3	52	81	15
Kristall Elektrostal	24	4	17	3	44	79	11

Eastern Division

Team	GP	W	L	T	GF	GA	PTS
Lada Togliatti	24	20	2	2	116	43	42
Rubin Tyumen	24	15	6	3	81	61	33
Metallurg Magnitogorsk	24	15	6	3	81	50	33
Avangard Omsk	24	14	7	3	75	47	31
Salavat Yzlayev Ufa	24	14	9	1	83	58	29
Traktor Chelyabinsk	24	10	8	6	60	56	26
Kristal Saratov	24	10	13	1	76	87	21
Metallurg Novokuznetsk	24	8	12	4	65	81	20
CSK VVS Samara	24	9	14	1	65	72	19
Sibir Novosibirsk	24	8	14	2	62	106	18
SKA Amur	24	6	13	5	62	84	17
Spartak Yekaterinburg	24	6	17	1	68	104	13
Molot Perm	24	5	19	0	50	95	10

Second Half

Team	GP	W	L	T	GF	GA	PTS
Lada Togliatti	38	30	5	3	146	63	63
AK Bars Kazan	38	25	8	5	113	78	55
Torpedo Yaroslavl	38	24	8	6	120	62	54
Metallurg Magnitogorsk	38	23	11	4	134	91	50
Avangard Omsk	38	19	12	7	126	84	45
Dynamo Moscow	38	17	14	7	105	88	41
Salavat Yulayev Ufa	38	17	15	6	116	97	40
Rubin Tyumen	38	17	16	5	114	106	39
Krylja Sovetov Moscow	38	17	17	4	112	105	38
Severstal Cherepovets	38	14	14	10	95	92	38
Traktor Chelyabinsk	38	13	16	9	82	95	35
Chimik Voskresensk	38	13	17	8	97	114	34
HC CSKA Moscow	38	12	16	10	83	104	34
Neftekhimik Nizhnekamsk	38	12	17	9	65	85	33
Kristall Saratov	38	14	20	4	102	125	32
CSK VVS Samara	38	14	20	4	85	114	32
Spartak Moscow	38	13	20	5	95	119	31
SKA St.Petersburg	38	8	23	7	85	116	23
Metallurg Novokuznetsk	38	7	23	8	77	122	22
Sibir Novosibirsk	38	8	25	5	78	170	21

1997–98

Western Division

Team	GP	W	L	T	GF	GA	PTS
Torpedo Yaroslavl	26	19	4	3	74	37	41
Dynamo Moscow	26	17	4	5	83	40	39
Lada Togliatti	26	16	4	6	75	42	38
Severstal Cherepovets	26	16	6	4	60	43	36
Spartak Moscow	26	13	8	5	81	61	31
SKA St. Petersburg	26	12	10	4	55	52	28
Neftekhimik Nizhnekamsk	26	10	12	4	64	61	24
CSKA Moscow	26	11	14	1	57	67	23
Krylja Sovetov Moscow	26	11	14	1	57	66	23
Khimik Voskresensk	26	8	12	6	60	72	22
Nizhny Novgorod	26	9	13	4	48	57	22
HC CSKA Moscow	26	6	17	3	44	82	15
Kristall Elektrostal	26	6	18	2	47	78	14
Dizelist Penza	26	2	20	4	43	90	8

Eastern Division

Team	GP	W	L	T	GF	GA	PTS
Ak Bars Kazan	26	22	3	1	96	40	45
Metallurg Magnitogorsk	26	19	2	5	109	42	43
Avangard Omsk	26	14	7	5	78	50	33
Molot-Prikamje Perm	26	12	7	7	82	71	31
CSK VVS Samara	26	12	11	3	59	60	27
Rubin Tyumen	26	11	10	5	85	79	27
Salavat Yulayev Ufa	26	11	11	4	70	63	26
Mechel Chelyabinsk	26	9	10	7	51	57	25
Traktor Chelyabinsk	26	8	11	7	60	68	23
SKA-Amur Khabarovsk	26	8	13	5	64	78	21
Metallurg Novokuznetsk	26	7	13	6	56	76	20
Kristall Saratov	26	6	14	6	54	78	18
Dynamo-E. Yekaterinburg	26	6	19	1	40	88	13
Sibir Novosibirsk	26	4	18	4	41	95	12

Second Half

Team	GP	W	L	T	GF	GA	PTS
Ak Bars Kazan	46	36	7	3	158	79	75
Metallurg Magnitogorsk	46	31	5	10	173	82	72
Torpedo Yaroslavl	46	33	7	6	130	60	72
Lada Togliatti	46	32	7	7	165	71	71
Dynamo Moscow	46	30	10	6	151	91	66
Avangard Omsk	46	28	13	5	139	86	61
Severstal Cherepovets	46	27	12	7	110	81	61
Molot-Prikamje Perm	46	21	18	7	150	130	49
Spartak Moscow	46	20	17	9	128	115	49
SKA St.Petersburg	46	20	19	7	107	105	47
Neftekhimik Nizhnekamsk	46	19	22	5	126	121	43
Rubin Tyumen	46	17	22	7	137	152	41
SKA-Amur Khabarovsk	46	17	22	7	112	138	41
Khimik Voskresensk	46	16	23	7	101	126	39
CSK VVS Samara	46	16	24	6	92	117	38
Traktor Chelyabinsk	46	14	22	10	99	129	38
CSKA Moscow	46	17	26	3	107	137	37
Krylja Sovetov Moscow	46	17	27	2	99	132	36
Salavat Yulayev Ufa	46	15	25	6	108	128	36
Mechel Chelyabinsk	46	13	25	8	84	125	34

1998–99

Team	GP	W	L	T	GF	GA	PTS
Metallurg Magnitogorsk	42	34	2	6	180	80	74
Metallurg Novokuznetsk	42	32	8	2	133	64	66
Dynamo Moscow	42	26	5	11	127	63	63
Avangard Omsk	42	28	7	7	118	71	63
Torpedo Yaroslavl	42	26	11	5	99	61	57
Lada Togliatti	42	20	10	12	122	83	52
Ak Bars Kazan	42	20	12	10	105	75	50
Molot-Prikamje Perm	42	16	16	10	110	102	42
Salavat Yulayev Ufa	42	14	17	11	98	113	39
Amur Khabarovsk	42	16	20	6	85	100	38
HC Lipetsk	42	13	18	11	82	120	37
CSKA Moscow	42	14	19	9	91	85	37
Neftekhimik Nizhnekamsk	42	13	18	11	109	122	37
Mechel Chelyabinsk	42	14	19	9	98	117	37
Severstal Cherepovets	42	14	20	8	98	112	36
CSK VVS Samara	42	17	23	2	85	114	36
Krylja Sovetov Moscow	42	12	20	10	83	114	34
Traktor Chelyabinsk	42	13	23	6	80	118	32
Spartak Moscow	42	14	24	4	84	107	32
SKA St. Petersburg	42	10	20	12	100	111	32
Khimik Voskresensk	42	8	32	2	68	140	18
Rubin Tyumen	42	4	34	4	86	169	12

1999–2000

Team	GP	W	OTW	L	OTL	T	GF	GA	PTS
Ak Bars Kazan	38	25	1	8	1	3	144	82	81
Metallurg Magnitogorsk	38	24	1	9	1	3	132	96	78
Torpedo Yaroslavl	38	21	2	10	0	5	91	59	72
Metallurg Novokuznetsk	38	20	3	12	1	2	122	98	69
Avangard Omsk	38	20	1	11	0	6	116	96	68
Severstal Cherepovets	38	19	1	10	1	7	101	66	67
Molot-Prikamje Perm	38	19	1	11	0	7	107	78	66
Lada Togliatti	38	20	0	13	1	4	113	71	65
CSKA Moscow	38	17	1	15	1	4	81	88	58
Amur Khabarovsk	38	13	4	15	3	3	84	85	53
SKA St. Petersburg	38	14	2	15	3	4	72	76	53
Torpedo Nizhny Novgorod	38	15	2	18	0	3	86	98	52
Neftekhimik Nizhnekamsk	38	12	2	14	3	7	114	119	50
Mechel Chelyabinsk	38	13	1	20	2	2	85	113	45
Dynamo Yekaterinburg	38	11	0	18	3	6	73	101	42
Salavat Yulayev Ufa	38	6	2	22	2	6	78	107	30
CSK VVS Samara	38	9	0	26	1	2	60	109	30
HC Lipetsk	38	3	1	28	1	5	50	146	17
Kristall Elektrostal	38	3	2	29	1	3	70	150	17

SLOVAKIA

1994–95

Team	GP	W	L	T	GF	GA	PTS
HK Dukla Trencin	36	27	4	5	188	82	86
HC Kosice	36	26	5	5	188	96	83
HC Slovan Bratislava	36	23	11	2	167	117	71
SKP PS Poprad	36	19	13	4	128	106	61
HK Liptovsky Mikulas	36	14	18	4	107	130	46
Martimex Martin	36	12	18	6	94	110	42
HC Dragon Presov	36	9	16	11	92	131	38
HK Spartak Dubnica	36	9	23	4	83	153	31
HC Nitra	36	8	22	6	87	147	30
HK Spisska Nova Ves	36	7	24	5	83	145	26

Win – 3 pts.

1995–96

Team	GP	W	L	T	GF	GA	PTS
HC Kosice	36	25	6	5	173	88	55
HK Dukla Trencin	36	20	10	6	139	94	46
HC Martimex Martin	36	18	11	7	112	95	43
PS SKP Poprad	36	18	13	5	127	98	41
HC Slovan Bratislava	36	18	13	5	127	123	41
AC Nitra	36	14	17	5	98	101	33
HK Sparta Dubnica	36	12	17	7	96	121	31
HC Liptovsky Mikulas	36	12	19	5	111	130	29
Iskra Banska Bystrica	36	9	21	6	80	124	24
HC Dragon Presov	36	7	26	3	75	164	17

1996–97

Team	GP	W	L	T	GF	GA	PTS
HK Dukla Trencin	36	27	6	3	151	100	57
HC Kosice	36	24	10	2	154	112	50
HC Slovan Bratislava	36	21	10	5	150	108	47
SKP PS Poprad	36	18	10	8	146	112	44
Martimex Martin	36	19	11	6	111	92	44
HK Liptovsky Mikulas	36	12	20	4	117	144	28
VTJ Spisska Nova Ves	36	12	20	4	111	140	28
Spartak Dubnica	36	9	21	6	116	161	24
Plastika Nitra	36	8	24	4	106	143	20
Iskra Banska Bystrica	36	6	24	6	97	147	18

1997–98

Team	GP	W	L	T	GF	GA	PTS
HC Slovan Bratislava	36	28	6	2	170	72	58
HC Kosice	36	27	7	2	174	87	56
HC SKP PS Poprad	36	18	11	7	122	106	43
HK Dukla Trencin	36	19	13	4	117	103	42
HKM Zvolen	36	15	19	2	92	112	32
HK 36 Skalica	36	13	18	5	100	124	31
Martimex ZTS Martin	36	12	18	6	112	120	30
VTJ Spisska Nova Ves	36	10	20	6	93	121	26
MHC Plastika Nitra	36	8	20	6	81	144	24
HK Liptovsky Mikulas	36	7	25	4	87	159	18

1998–99

1st to 6th place

Team	GP	W	L	T	GF	GA	PTS
HC Slovan Bratislava	42	32	5	5	245	102	69
HK 36 Skalica	42	20	16	6	135	118	46
Dukla Trencin	42	20	16	6	125	114	46
HK Liptovsky Mikulas	42	20	16	6	140	134	46
HC VSZ Kosice	42	18	16	8	146	136	44
HKm Zvolen	42	12	18	12	117	144	36
7th to 14th place							
HC SKP Poprad	28	18	5	5	132	71	41
VTJ Spisska Nova Ves	28	17	4	7	110	71	41
SK I.B. Bystrica	28	17	6	5	95	62	39
HC Mart. ZTS Martin	28	11	7	10	85	77	32
MHC Plastika Nitra	28	8	11	9	91	95	25
HK SKP PChZ Zilina	28	8	16	4	66	98	20
HK VTJ Presov	28	5	18	5	78	121	15
HK Spartak ZTS Dubnica	28	3	20	5	63	125	11

1999–2000

Team	GP	W	L	T	GF	GA	PTS
HC Slovan Bratislava	56	34	15	7	233	133	75
HKm Zvolen	56	31	16	9	218	160	71
HC SKP Poprad	56	29	19	8	182	162	66
Dukla Trencin	56	27	20	9	207	151	63
HK 36 Skalica	56	23	22	11	158	175	57
Liptovsky Mikulas	56	20	20	16	157	183	56
HC VSZ Kosice	56	12	33	11	142	235	35
HK Spisska Nova Ves	56	9	40	7	114	212	25

SWEDEN

1994–95

Team	GP	W	L	T	GF	GA	PTS
Djurgardens Stockholm	40	24	9	7	139	96	55
Malmo IF	40	20	7	13	130	105	53
Lulea HF	40	21	9	10	164	116	52
Leksand IF	40	21	13	6	155	132	48
Brynas Gavle	40	17	15	8	119	127	42
Farjestad Karlstad	40	17	17	6	128	135	40
Vasteras IK	40	15	18	7	145	137	37
HV 71 Jonkoping	40	12	19	9	117	143	33
AIK Solna Stockholm	40	11	21	8	111	146	30
MoDo Domsjo	40	8	22	10	121	140	26
Vastra Frolunda	22	6	11	5	63	70	17
Rogle Angelholm	22	5	16	1	49	93	11

1995–96

Team	GP	W	L	T	GF	GA	PTS
Lulea HF	40	22	12	6	153	109	50
Vastra Frolunda Goteborg	40	20	10	10	130	95	50
Farjestad BK Karlstad	40	20	14	6	150	117	46
HV 71 Jonkoping	40	18	14	8	156	132	44
Djurgardens Stockholm	40	17	14	9	122	119	43
MoDo Ornskoldsvik	40	15	13	12	127	133	42
Leksands IF	40	15	15	10	123	117	40
Malmo IF	40	15	18	7	129	147	37
AIK Solna Stockholm	40	11	18	11	96	126	33
Vasteras IK	40	12	22	6	123	163	30

1996–97

Team	GP	W	L	T	GF	GA	PTS
Leksands IF	50	28	15	7	166	132	63
Lulea HF	50	26	16	8	150	121	60
Farjestad BK Karlstad	50	26	16	8	148	132	60
Djurgardens Stockholm	50	27	18	5	186	135	59
AIK Solna Stockholm	50	23	17	10	149	131	56
HV 71 Jonkoping	50	22	19	9	178	159	53
Vastra Frolunda Goteborg	50	17	16	17	134	133	51
Malmo IF	50	20	20	10	171	154	50
Brynas Gavle	50	21	21	8	155	144	50
MoDo Ornskoldsvik	50	17	27	6	136	167	40
Sodertalje SK	50	15	28	7	122	179	37
Vasteras IK	50	5	34	11	133	241	21

1997–98

Team	GP	W	L	T	GF	GA	PTS
Djurgardens Stockholm	46	27	13	6	148	110	60
Farjestads BK Karlstad	46	24	12	10	154	112	58
Leksands IF	46	24	14	8	165	143	56
Frolunda HC Goteborg	46	17	14	15	136	107	49
Brynas Gavle	46	21	19	6	138	131	48
Modo Ornskoldsvik	46	20	20	6	129	123	46
HV 71 Jonkoping	46	19	19	8	127	145	46
Lulea HF	46	15	18	13	112	125	43
Malmo IF	46	17	21	8	134	121	42
Vasteras IK	46	15	22	9	102	146	39
AIK Solna Stockholm	46	13	26	7	93	134	33
Sodertalje SK	46	10	24	12	110	151	32

1998–99

Team	GP	W	OTW	L	OTL	T	GF	GA	PTS
MoDo Ornskoldsvik	50	30	3	10	2	5	168	100	103
Farjestads BK Karlstad	50	23	0	15	3	9	147	137	81
Djurgardens IF Stockholm	50	22	3	16	5	4	143	144	81
Leksands IF	50	20	2	16	3	9	174	152	76
Brynas IF Gavle	50	21	4	20	3	2	167	152	76
Lulea HF	50	22	1	20	2	5	148	143	75
V. Frolunda HC Goteborg	50	19	5	23	0	3	148	136	70
Malmo IF	50	18	5	23	1	3	140	144	68
HV 71 Jonkoping	50	18	1	20	4	7	133	148	67
AIK Solna	50	18	1	21	4	6	150	159	66
Vasteras IK	50	19	1	24	2	4	139	176	65
IF Bjorkloven Umea	50	9	4	31	1	5	101	167	41

W – 3 pts; OTW – 2 pts; OTL – 1 pt; T – 1 pt; L – 0 pts.

1999–2000

Team	GP	W	L	T	OW	OL	PW	PL	GF	GA	PTS
Djurgardens IF Stockholm	50	23	12	15	2	1	7	5	180	127	93
Brynas IF Gavle	50	28	15	7	1	1	0	5	165	134	92
Vastra Frolunda	50	25	15	10	2	1	2	5	155	131	89
Lulea HF	50	25	17	8	1	1	5	1	158	140	89
Malmo IF	50	22	14	14	2	1	6	5	170	131	88
MoDo Ornskoldsvik	50	24	19	7	2	1	2	2	149	134	83
Farjestads BK Karlstad	50	22	18	10	3	3	2	2	168	142	81
HV 71 Jonkoping	50	18	19	13	1	0	7	5	144	131	75
AIK Solna	50	19	19	12	2	4	3	3	151	155	74
Leksands IF	50	14	24	12	1	2	4	5	150	174	59
Vasteras IK	50	9	31	10	2	3	4	1	103	196	43
Linkopings HC	50	9	35	6	0	1	1	4	107	205	34

win – 3 pts.; overtime win – 1 pt.; overtime loss – 0 pts.; postseason win – 1 pt.; postseason loss – 0 pts.

SWITZERLAND

1994–95

Team	GP	W	L	T	GF	GA	PTS
EV Zug	36	22	10	4	152	125	48
HC Lugano	36	21	10	5	147	102	47
HC Ambri-Piotta	36	19	12	5	151	136	43
HC Davos	36	19	13	4	139	125	42
Fribourg-Gotteron	36	18	13	5	177	140	41
SC Bern	36	18	15	3	146	123	39
EHC Kloten	36	15	13	8	116	119	38
Zurcher SC	36	12	21	3	129	152	27
SC Rapperswil-Jona	36	8	25	3	102	165	19
EHC Biel	36	7	27	2	108	170	16

1995–96

Team	GP	W	L	T	GF	GA	PTS
SC Bern	36	21	11	4	139	98	46
EHC Kloten	36	20	10	6	109	83	46
SC Rapperswil-Jona	36	18	13	5	137	127	41
EV Zug	36	18	15	3	149	129	39
HC Davos	36	15	12	9	140	124	39
HC Ambri-Piotta	36	16	14	6	142	139	38
HC Lugano	36	16	16	4	129	114	36
Zurcher SC	36	16	17	3	119	140	35
Fribourg-Gotteron	36	11	17	8	114	116	30
HC Lausanne	36	4	30	2	71	179	10

1996–97

Team	GP	W	L	T	GF	GA	PTS
SC Bern	46	29	15	2	205	140	60
EV Zug	46	26	15	5	188	142	57
HC Davos	46	24	20	2	187	181	50
EHC Kloten	46	21	18	7	152	131	49
HC Lugano	46	22	19	5	166	153	49
Fribourg-Gotteron	46	20	19	7	167	154	47
SC Rapperswil-Jona	45	21	22	2	156	163	44
Zuricher SC	45	19	24	2	155	188	40
HC Ambri-Piotta	45	17	25	3	153	165	37
HC La Chaux-de-Fonds	45	11	33	1	131	243	23

1997–98

Team	GP	W	L	T	GF	GA	PTS
EV Zug	40	24	10	6	151	109	54
Fribourg-Gotteron	40	23	12	5	142	111	51
HC Davos	40	24	14	2	150	119	50
HC Ambri-Piotta	40	23	15	2	156	116	48
SC Bern	40	19	14	7	139	131	45
HC Lugano	40	17	16	7	140	127	41
EHC Kloten	40	16	17	7	125	120	39
SC Rapperswil-Jona	40	15	22	3	118	142	33
HC La Chaux-de-Fonds	40	12	22	6	128	164	30
Zuricher SC	40	12	23	5	109	141	29
SC Herisau	40	9	29	2	94	172	20

1998–99

Team	GP	W	L	T	GF	GA	PTS
HC Ambri-Piotta	45	33	7	5	188	104	71
ZSC Lions Zurich	45	27	11	7	170	115	61
HC Lugano	45	27	13	5	155	114	59
SC Bern	45	22	18	5	162	157	49
EV Zug	45	20	19	6	157	130	46
HC Davos	45	19	19	7	166	156	45
EHC Kloten	45	12	20	13	134	145	37
SC Rapperswil-Jona	45	15	25	5	128	177	35
HC Fribourg-Gotteron	45	13	29	3	112	165	29
SC Langnau	45	7	34	4	112	221	18

1999–2000

Team	GP	W	L	T	GF	GA	PTS
HC Lugano	45	29	7	9	164	83	67
ZSC Lions Zurich	45	26	15	4	143	99	56
EV Zug	45	24	15	6	154	148	54
HC Ambri-Piotta	45	24	17	4	147	116	52
SC Bern	45	19	19	7	134	130	45
EHC Kloten	45	19	21	5	116	129	43
HC Davos	45	15	24	6	123	147	36
HC Fribourg-Gotteron	45	14	25	6	132	153	34
SC Rapperswil-Jona	45	13	26	6	127	173	32
SC Langnau	45	12	26	7	102	164	31

CHAPTER 49

League Champions around the Globe

From New Zealand to Iceland, an All-time List of National Champions

Australia

1992–93	New South Wales
1993–94	New South Wales
1994–95	New South Wales
1995–96	South Australia
1996–97	New South Wales
1997–98	New South Wales
1998-99	Aust. Capital Territory
1999-2000	New South Wales

Austria

1922–23	Wiener EV
1923–24	Wiener EV
1924–25	Wiener EV
1925–26	Wiener EV
1926–27	Wiener EV
1927–28	Wiener EV
1928–29	Wiener EV
1929–30	Wiener EV
1930–31	Wiener EV
1931–32	Potzleinsdorfer SK
1932–33	Wiener EV
1933–34	Klagenfurter AC
1934–35	Klagenfurter AC
1935–36	No championship
1936–37	Wiener EV
1937–38	EK Engelmann Wien
1938–39 to 1944–45	No championship
1945–46	EK Engelmann Wien
1946–47	Wiener EV
1947–48	Wiener EV
1948–49	Wiener EG
1949–50	Wiener EG
1950–51	Wiener EG
1951–52	Klagenfurter AC
1952–53	EV Innsbruck
1953–54	EV Innsbruck
1954–55	Klagenfurter AC
1955–56	EK Engelmann Wien
1956–57	EK Engelmann Wien
1957–58	EV Innsbruck
1958–59	EV Innsbruck
1959–60	Klagenfurter AC
1960–61	EV Innsbruck
1961–62	Wiener EVg
1962–63	EV Innsbruck
1963–64	Klagenfurter AC
1964–65	Klagenfurter AC
1965–66	Klagenfurter AC
1966–67	Klagenfurter AC
1967–68	Klagenfurter AC
1968–69	Klagenfurter AC
1969–70	Klagenfurter AC
1970–71	Klagenfurter AC
1971–72	Klagenfurter AC
1972–73	Klagenfurter AC
1973–74	Klagenfurter AC
1974–75	ATSE Graz
1975–76	Klagenfurter AC
1976–77	Klagenfurter AC
1977–78	ATSE Graz
1978–79	Klagenfurter AC
1979–80	Klagenfurter AC
1980–81	EC Villach
1981–82	VEU Feldkirch
1982–83	VEU Feldkirch
1983–84	VEU Feldkirch
1984–85	Klagenfurter AC
1985–86	Klagenfurter AC
1986–87	Klagenfurter AC
1987–88	Klagenfurter AC
1988–89	GEV Innsbruck
1989–90	VEU Feldkirch
1990–91	Klagenfurter AC
1991–92	EC BIC Villach
1992–93	EC BIC Villach
1993–94	VEU Feldkirch
1994–95	VEU Feldkirch
1995–96	VEU Feldkirch
1996–97	VEU Feldkirch
1997–98	VEU Feldkirch
1998–99	EC Villach
1999–2000	Klagenfurter AC

Belarus

1992–93	Dynamo Minsk
1993–94	Tivali Minsk
1994–95	Tivali Minsk
1995–96	Polimir Novopolotsk
1996–97	Polimir Novopolotsk
1997–98	Neman Grodno
1998–99	Neman Grodno
1999–2000	Tivali Minsk

Belgium

1911–12	Brussels IHSC
1912–13	Brussels IHSC
1913–14	CdP Bruxelles
1914–15 to 1918–19	No championship
1919–20	CdP Bruxelles
1920–21	CdP Bruxelles
1921–22	Brussels IHSC
1922–23	Brussels IHSC
1923–24	Le Puck Anvers
1924–25	Le Puck Anvers
1925–26	Le Puck Anvers
1926–27	Le Puck Anvers
1927–28	Le Puck Anvers
1928–29	CdP Anvers
1929–30 to 1932–33	No championship
1933–34	CdP Anvers
1934–35	CdP Anvers
1935–36	CdP Anvers
1936–37	CdP Anvers
1937–38	Brussels IHSC
1938–39	Brussels IHSC
1939–40	Brussels IHSC
1940–41	Brussels IHSC
1941–42	Brussels IHSC
1942–43	Brussels IHSC
1943–44	No championship
1944–45	Brussels IHSC
1945–46	Brussels IHSC
1946–47	Brussels IHSC
1947–48	Brussels IHSC
1948–49	Brussels IHSC
1949–50	Brabo Antwerpen
1950–51	No championship
1951–52	No championship
1952–53	No championship
1953–54	Brabo Antwerpen
1954–55 to 1958–59	No championship
1959–60	CPL Liege
1960–61	CPL Liege
1961–62	Brussels IHSC
1962–63	Brussels IHSC
1963–64	Brussels IHSC
1964–65	No championship
1965–66	No championship
1966–67	Brussels IHSC
1967–68	Brussels IHSC
1968–69	No championship
1969–70	Brussels IHSC
1970–71	Brussels IHSC
1971–72	Brussels IHSC
1972–73	No championship
1973–74	No championship
1974–75	Brussels IHSC
1975–76	Brussels IHSC
1976–77	Brussels IHSC
1977–78	Brussels IHSC
1978–79	Olympia Heist-op-den-Berg
1979–80	Olympia Heist-op-den-Berg
1980–81	HYC Herentals
1981–82	Brussels IHSC
1982–83	Olympia Heist-op-den-Berg
1983–84	HYC Herentals
1984–85	HYC Herentals
1985–86	Olympia Heist-op-den-Berg
1986–87	Olympia Heist-op-den-Berg
1987–88	Phantoms Deurne
1988–89	Olympia Heist-op-den-Berg
1989–90	Olympia Heist-op-den-Berg
1990–91	Olympia Heist-op-den-Berg
1991–92	Olympia Heist-op-den-Berg
1992–93	HYC Herentals
1993–94	HYC Herentals
1994–95	No championship
1995–96	HYC Herentals
1996–97	HYC Herentals
1997–98	HYC Herentals
1998–99	Olympia Heist-op-den-Berg
1999–2000	Hollywood Phantoms Deurne

Bulgaria

1951–52	Cerveno zname Sofia
1952–53	Udarnik Sofia
1953–54	Udarnik Sofia
1954–55	Torpedo Sofia
1955–56	Cerveno zname Sofia
1956–57	Cerveno zname Sofia
1957–58	No championship
1958–59	Cerveno zname Sofia
1959–60	Cerveno zname Sofia
1960–61	Cerveno zname Sofia
1961–62	Cerveno zname Sofia
1962–63	Cerveno zname Sofia
1963–64	CDNA Sofia
1964–65	CSKA Cerveno zname Sofia
1965–66	CSKA Cerveno zname Sofia
1966–67	CSKA Cerveno zname Sofia
1967–68	Metallurg Pernik
1968–69	CSKA Septemvriisko zname S
1969–70	Krakra Pernik
1970–71	CSKA Septemvriisko zname S
1971–72	CSKA Septemvriisko zname S

1972–73	CSKA Septemvriisko zname S
1973–74	CSKA Septemvriisko zname S
1974–75	CSKA Septemvriisko zname S
1975–76	Levski-Spartak Sofia
1976–77	Levski-Spartak Sofia
1977–78	Levski-Spartak Sofia
1978–79	Levski-Spartak Sofia
1979–80	Levski-Spartak Sofia
1980–81	Levski-Spartak Sofia
1981–82	Levski-Spartak Sofia
1982–83	CSKA Septemvriisko zname S
1983–84	CSKA Septemvriisko zname S
1984–85	Slavia Sofia
1985–86	CSKA Septemvriisko zname S
1986–87	Slavia Sofia
1987–88	Slavia Sofia
1988–89	Levski-Spartak Sofia
1989–90	Levski-Spartak Sofia
1990–91	Slavia Sofia
1991–92	DFS Levski-Spartak Sofia
1992–93	DFS Slavia Sofia
1993–94	DFS Slavia Sofia
1994–95	HC Levski Sofia
1995–96	Slavia SF Sofia
1996–97	Slavia SF Sofia
1997–98	Slavia SF Sofia
1998–99	HC Levski Sofia
1999–2000	Slavia Sofia

China

1987–88	Changchun
1988–89	Harbin
1989–90	No championship
1990–91	Nei Menggol
1991–92	No championship
1992–93	Qiqihar
1993–94	Qiqihar
1994–95	Qiqihar
1995–96	Qiqihar A
1996–97	Qiqihar A
1997–98	Qiqihar A
1998–99	Harbin A
1999–2000	Qiqihar A

Chinese Taipei

1999–2000	Max Club Taipei

Croatia

1991–92	HK Zagreb
1992–93	HK Zagreb
1993–94	HK Zagreb
1994–95	Medvescak Zagreb
1995–96	HK Zagreb
1996–97	Medvescak Zagreb
1997–98	Medvescak Zagreb
1998–99	Medvescak Zagreb
1999–2000	Medvescak Zagreb

Czechoslovakia

1936–37	LTC Praha
1937–38	LTC Praha
1938–39 to 1944–45	No championship
1945–46	LTC Praha
1946–47	LTC Praha
1947–48	LTC Praha
1948–49	LTC Praha
1949–50	ATK Praha
1950–51	SKP Ceske Budejovice
1951–52	VZKG Ostrava
1952–53	Spartak Praha Sokolovo
1953–54	Spartak Praha Sokolovo
1954–55	RH Brno
1955–56	RH Brno
1956–57	RH Brno
1957–58	RH Brno
1958–59	SONP Kladno
1959–60	RH Brno
1960–61	RH Brno
1961–62	ZKL Brno
1962–63	ZKL Brno
1963–64	ZKL Brno
1964–65	ZKL Brno
1965–66	ZKL Brno
1966–67	Dukla Jihlava
1967–68	Dukla Jihlava
1968–69	Dukla Jihlava
1969–70	Dukla Jihlava
1970–71	Dukla Jihlava
1971–72	Dukla Jihlava
1972–73	Tesla Pardubice
1973–74	Dukla Jihlava
1974–75	SONP Kladno
1975–76	SONP Kladno
1976–77	Poldi SONP Kladno
1977–78	Poldi SONP Kladno
1978–79	Slovan Bratislava
1979–80	Poldi SONP Kladno
1980–81	TJ Vitkovice
1981–82	Dukla Jihlava
1982–83	Dukla Jihlava
1983–84	Dukla Jihlava
1984–85	Dukla Jihlava
1985–86	VSZ Kosice
1986–87	Tesla Pardubice
1987–88	VSZ Kosice
1988–89	Tesla Pardubice
1989–90	Sparta Praha
1990–91	Dukla Jihlava
1991–92	Dukla Trencin
1991–92	Dukla Trencin

Czech Republic

1992–93	HC Sparta Praha
1993–94	HC Olomouc
1994–95	HC Dadak Vsetin
1995–96	HC Petra Vsetin
1996–97	HC Petra Vsetin
1997–98	HC Petra Vsetin
1998–99	HC Slovnaft Vsetin
1999–2000	HC Sparta Praha

Denmark

1954–55	Rungsted IK
1955–56	Kobenhavns SF
1956–57	No championship
1957–58	No championship
1958–59	No championship
1959–60	Kobenhavns SF
1960–61	Kobenhavns SF
1961–62	Kobenhavns SF
1962–63	Rungsted IK
1963–64	Kobenhavns SF
1964–65	Kobenhavns SF
1965–66	Kobenhavns SF
1966–67	Gladsaxe SF
1967–68	Gladsaxe SF
1968–69	Esbjerg IK
1969–70	Kobenhavns SF
1970–71	Gladsaxe SF
1971–72	Kobenhavns SF
1972–73	Herning IK
1973–74	Gladsaxe SF
1974–75	Gladsaxe SF
1975–76	Kobenhavns SF
1976–77	Herning IK
1977–78	Rodovre SIK
1978–79	Vojens IK
1979–80	Vojens IK
1980–81	Aalborg BK
1981–82	Vojens IK
1982–83	Rodovre SIK
1983–84	Herlev IK
1984–85	Rodovre SIK
1985–86	Rodovre SIK
1986–87	Herning IK
1987–88	Esbjerg IK
1988–89	Fredrikshavn IK
1989–90	Rodovre SIK
1990–91	Herning IK
1991–92	Herning IK
1992–93	Esbjerg IK
1993–94	Herning IK
1994–95	Herning IK
1995–96	Esbjerg IK
1996–97	Herning IK
1997–98	Herning IK
1998–99	Rodovre SIK
1999–2000	Fredrikshavn IK

Estonia

1933–34	Kalev Tallinn
1934–35	No championship
1935–36	ASC Tartu
1936–37	Kalev Tallinn
1937–38	No championship
1938–39	ASC Tartu
1939–40	Sport Tallinn
1940–41 to 1991–92	No championship
1992–93	Kreenholm Narva
1993–94	Kreenholm Narva
1994–95	Kreenholm Narva
1995–96	Kreenholm Narva
1996–97	Valk–494 Tartu
1997–98	Kreenholm Narva
1998–99	Valk–494 Tartu
1999–2000	Valk–494 Tartu

Finland

1927–28	Viipurin Reipas
1928–29	HJK Helsinki
1929–30	No championship
1930–31	TaPa Tampere
1931–32	HJK Helsinki
1932–33	HSK Helsinki
1933–34	HSK Helsinki
1934–35	HJK Helsinki
1935–36	Ilves Tampere
1936–37	Ilves Tampere
1937–38	Ilves Tampere
1938–39	KIF Helsinki
1939–40	No championship
1940–41	KIF Helsinki
1941–42	No championship
1942–43	KIF Helsinki
1943–44	No championship
1944–45	Ilves Tampere
1945–46	Ilves Tampere
1946–47	Ilves Tampere
1947–48	Tarmo Hameenlinna
1948–49	Tarmo Hameenlinna
1949–50	Ilves Tampere
1950–51	Ilves Tampere
1951–52	Ilves Tampere
1952–53	TBK Tampere
1953–54	TBK Tampere
1954–55	TBK Tampere
1955–56	TPS Turku
1956–57	Ilves Tampere
1957–58	Ilves Tampere
1958–59	Tappara Tampere
1959–60	Ilves Tampere
1960–61	Tappara Tampere
1961–62	Ilves Tampere
1962–63	Lukko Rauma
1963–64	Tappara Tampere
1964–65	Karhut Pori
1965–66	Ilves Tampere
1966–67	RU–38 Pori
1967–68	KooVee Tampere
1968–69	HIFK Helsinki
1969–70	HIFK Helsinki
1970–71	Assat Pori
1971–72	Ilves Tampere
1972–73	Jokerit Helsinki
1973–74	HIFK Helsinki
1974–75	Tappara Tampere
1975–76	TPS Turku
1976–77	Tappara Tampere
1977–78	Assat Pori
1978–79	Tappara Tampere
1979–80	HIFK Helsinki
1980–81	Karpat Oulu
1981–82	Tappara Tampere
1982–83	HIFK Helsinki
1983–84	Tappara Tampere
1984–85	Ilves Tampere
1985–86	Tappara Tampere
1986–87	Tappara Tampere

1987–88 Tappara Tampere
1988–89 TPS Turku
1989–90 TPS Turku
1990–91 TPS Turku
1991–92 Jokerit Helsinki
1992–93 TPS Turku
1993–94 Jokerit Helsinki
1994–95 TPS Turku
1995–96 Jokerit Helsinki
1996–97 Jokerit Helsinki
1997–98 HIFK Helsinki
1998–99 TPS Turku
1999–2000 TPS Turku

FRANCE

1903–04 Patineurs de Paris
1904–05 Patineurs de Paris
1905–06 Patineurs de Paris
1906–07 Sporting Club Lyon
1907–08 Patineurs de Paris
1908–09 No championship
1909–10 No championship
1910–11 No championship
1911–12 Patineurs de Paris
1912–13 Patineurs de Paris
1913–14 Patineurs de Paris
1914–15 to 1918–19 No championship
1919–20 Ice Skating Club Paris
1920–21 Sports D'Hiver Paris
1921–22 Sports D'Hiver Paris
1922–23 HC Chamonix
1923–24 No championship
1924–25 HC Chamonix
1925–26 HC Chamonix
1926–27 HC Chamonix
1927–28 No championship
1928–29 HC Chamonix
1929–30 HC Chamonix
1930–31 HC Chamonix
1931–32 Stade Francais Paris
1932–33 Stade Francais Paris
1933–34 Rapides de Paris
1934–35 Stade Francais Paris
1935–36 Francais Volants de Paris
1936–37 Francais Volants de Paris
1937–38 Francais Volants de Paris
1938–39 HC Chamonix
1939–40 No championship
1940–41 No championship
1941–42 HC Chamonix
1942–43 No championship
1943–44 HC Chamonix
1944–45 No championship
1945–46 HC Chamonix
1946–47 No championship
1947–48 No championship
1948–49 HC Chamonix
1949–50 Racing Club de Paris
1950–51 Racing Club de Paris
1951–52 HC Chamonix
1952–53 Paris Universite Club
1953–54 HC Chamonix
1954–55 HC Chamonix
1955–56 Patineurs de Lyon
1956–57 ACBB Paris
1957–58 HC Chamonix
1958–59 HC Chamonix
1959–60 ACBB Paris
1960–61 HC Chamonix
1961–62 ACBB Paris
1962–63 HC Chamonix
1963–64 HC Chamonix
1964–65 HC Chamonix
1965–66 HC Chamonix
1966–67 HC Chamonix
1967–68 HC Chamonix
1968–69 HC Saint-Gervais
1969–70 HC Chamonix
1970–71 HC Chamonix
1971–72 HC Chamonix
1972–73 HC Chamonix
1973–74 HC Saint-Gervais
1974–75 HC Saint-Gervais
1975–76 HC Chamonix
1976–77 HC Gap
1977–78 HC Gap
1978–79 HC Chamonix
1979–80 ASG Tours
1980–81 CSG Grenoble
1981–82 CSG Grenoble
1982–83 HC Saint-Gervais
1983–84 CS Megeve
1984–85 HC Saint-Gervais
1985–86 HC Saint-Gervais
1986–87 HC Mont Blanc Megeve
1987–88 HC Mont Blanc Megeve
1988–89 Francais Volants de Paris
1989–90 HC Rouen
1990–91 CSG Grenoble
1991–92 HC Rouen
1992–93 HC Rouen
1993–94 HC Rouen
1994–95 HC Rouen
1995–96 SP Brest
1996–97 SP Brest
1997–98 CSG Grenoble
1998–99 Les Gothiques Amiens-Somme
1999–2000 Flammes Bleues Reims

GERMANY

1911–12 Berliner SC
1912–13 Berliner SC
1913–14 Berliner SC
1914–15 to 1918–19 No championship
1919–20 Berliner SC
1920–21 Berliner SC
1921–22 MTV Munchen
1922–23 Berliner SC
1923–24 Berliner SC
1924–25 Berliner SC
1925–26 Berliner SC
1926–27 SC Riessersee Garmisch-Partenkirchen
1927–28 Berliner SC
1928–29 Berliner SC
1929–30 Berliner SC
1930–31 Berliner SC
1931–32 Berliner SC
1932–33 Berliner SC
1933–34 SC Brandenburg Berlin
1934–35 SC Riessersee Garmisch-Partenkirchen
1935–36 Berliner SC
1936–37 Berliner SC
1937–38 SC Riessersee Garmisch-Partenkirchen
1938–39 Engelmann Wien
1939–40 Wiener EG
1940–41 SC Riessersee Garmisch-Partenkirchen
1941–42 No championship
1942–43 No championship
1943–44 Berliner SC/SC Brandenburg
1944–45 No championship
1945–46 No championship
1946–47 SC Riessersee Garmisch-Partenkirchen
1947–48 SC Riessersee Garmisch-Partenkirchen
1948–49 EV Fussen
1949–50 SC Riessersee Garmisch-Partenkirchen
1950–51 Preussen Krefeld
1951–52 Krefelder EV
1952–53 EV Fussen
1953–54 EV Fussen
1954–55 EV Fussen
1955–56 EV Fussen
1956–57 EV Fussen
1957–58 EV Fussen
1958–59 EV Fussen
1959–60 SC Riessersee Garmisch-Partenkirchen
1960–61 EV Fussen
1961–62 EC Bad Tolz
1962–63 EV Fussen
1963–64 EV Fussen
1964–65 EV Fussen
1965–66 EC Bad Tolz
1966–67 Dusseldorfer EG
1967–68 EV Fussen
1968–69 EV Fussen
1969–70 EV Landshut
1970–71 EV Fussen
1971–72 Dusseldorfer EG
1972–73 EV Fussen
1973–74 Berliner SC
1974–75 Dusseldorfer EG
1975–76 Berliner SC
1976–77 Kolner EC
1977–78 SC Riessersee Garmisch-Partenkirchen
1978–79 Kolner EC
1979–80 Mannheimer ERC
1980–81 SC Riessersee Garmisch-Partenkirchen
1981–82 SB Rosenheim
1982–83 EV Landshut
1983–84 Kolner EC
1984–85 SB Rosenheim
1985–86 Kolner EC
1986–87 Kolner EC
1987–88 Kolner EC
1988–89 SB Rosenheim
1989–90 Dusseldorfer EG
1990–91 Dusseldorfer EG
1991–92 Dusseldorfer EG
1992–93 Dusseldorfer EG
1993–94 Hedos Munchen
1994–95 Kolner EC
1995–96 Dusseldorfer EG
1996–97 Adler Mannheim
1997–98 Adler Mannheim
1998–99 Munich Barons
1999–2000 Munich Barons

GREAT BRITAIN

1897–98 Niagara
1898–99 Princes' Skating Club London
1899–00 Princes' Skating Club London
1900–01 Princes' Skating Club London
1901–02 Cambridge University
1902–03 London Canadians
1903–04 London Canadians
1904–05 Princes' Skating Club London
1905–06 Princes' Skating Club London
1906–07 Oxford Canadians
1907–08 Princes' Skating Club London
1908–09 Princes' Skating Club London
1909–10 Oxford Canadians
1910–11 Oxford Canadians
1911–12 Princes' Skating Club London
1912–13 Oxford Canadians
1913–14 Princes' Skating Club London
1914–15 to 1926–27 No championship
1927–28 United Services
1928–29 United Services
1929–30 London Lions
1930–31 London Lions
1931–32 Oxford University
1932–33 Oxford University
1933–34 Grosvenor House Canadians
1934–35 Streatham
1935–36 Wembley Lions
1936–37 Wembley Lions
1937–38 Harringay Racers
1938–39 Harringay Greyhounds
1939–40 Harringay Greyhounds

1940–41 to 1945–46 No championship
1946–47 Brighton Tigers
1947–48 Brighton Tigers
1948–49 Harringay Racers
1949–50 Streatham
1950–51 Nottingham Panthers
1951–52 Wembley Lions
1952–53 Streatham
1953–54 Nottingham Panthers
1954–55 Harringay Racers
1955–56 Nottingham Panthers
1956–57 Wembley Lions
1957–58 Brighton Tigers
1958–59 Paisley Pirates
1959–60 Brighton Tigers
1960–61 to 1974–75 No championship
1975–76 Ayr Bruins
1976–77 Fife Flyers
1977–78 Fife Flyers
1978–79 Murrayfield Racers
1979–80 Murrayfield Racers
1980–81 Murrayfield Racers
1981–82 Dundee Rockets
1982–83 Dundee Rockets
1983–84 Dundee Rockets
1984–85 Fife Flyers
1985–86 Murrayfield Racers
1986–87 Durham Wasps
1987–88 Durham Wasps
1988–89 Nottingham Panthers
1989–90 Cardiff Devils
1990–91 Durham Wasps
1991–92 Durham Wasps
1992–93 Cardiff Devils
1993–94 Cardiff Devils
1994–95 Sheffield Steelers
1995–96 Sheffield Steelers
1996–97 Sheffield Steelers
1997–98 Ayr Scottish Eagles
1998–99 Cardiff Devils
1999–2000 London Knights

GREECE

1988–89 Aris Thessaloniki
1989–90 Aris Thessaloniki
1990–91 Aris Thessaloniki
1991–92 Aris Thessaloniki
1992–93 Ice Flyers Athens
1993–94 to 1998–99 No championship
1999–2000 Iptamenoi Pagodromoi Athens

HONG KONG

1995–96 Planet Hollywood
1996–97 Drahmala Jets
1997–98 Drahmala Jets
1998–99 Drahmala Jets
1999–2000 Nike Jets

HUNGARY

1936–37 BKE Budapest
1937–38 BKE Budapest
1938–39 BKE Budapest
1939–40 BKE Budapest
1940–41 BBTE Budapest
1941–42 BKE Budapest
1942–43 BBTE Budapest
1943–44 BKE Budapest
1944–45 No championship
1945–46 BKE Budapest
1946–47 MTK Budapest
1947–48 MTK Budapest
1948–49 MTK Budapest
1949–50 BVM Budapest
1950–51 Budapesti Kinizsi
1951–52 BVM Budapest
1952–53 Budapesti Postas
1953–54 Budapesti Postas
1954–55 Budapesti Kinizsi
1955–56 Budapesti Kinizsi
1956–57 BVM Budapest
1957–58 Ujpesti Dozsa Budapest
1958–59 BVM Budapest
1959–60 Ujpesti Dozsa Budapest
1960–61 Ferencvarosi TC Budapest
1961–62 Ferencvarosi TC Budapest
1962–63 BVM Budapest
1963–64 Ferencvarosi TC Budapest
1964–65 Ujpesti Dozsa Budapest
1965–66 Ujpesti Dozsa Budapest
1966–67 Ujpesti Dozsa Budapest
1967–68 Ujpesti Dozsa Budapest
1968–69 Ujpesti Dozsa Budapest
1969–70 Ujpesti Dozsa Budapest
1970–71 Ferencvarosi TC Budapest
1971–72 Ferencvarosi TC Budapest
1972–73 Ferencvarosi TC Budapest
1973–74 Ferencvarosi TC Budapest
1974–75 Ferencvarosi TC Budapest
1975–76 Ferencvarosi TC Budapest
1976–77 Ferencvarosi TC Budapest
1977–78 Ferencvarosi TC Budapest
1978–79 Ferencvarosi TC Budapest
1979–80 Ferencvarosi TC Budapest
1980–81 Volan Szekesfehervar
1981–82 Ujpesti Dozsa Budapest
1982–83 Ujpesti Dozsa Budapest
1983–84 Ferencvarosi TC Budapest
1984–85 Ujpesti Dozsa Budapest
1985–86 Ujpesti Dozsa Budapest
1986–87 Ujpesti Dozsa Budapest
1987–88 Ujpesti Dozsa Budapest
1988–89 Ferencvarosi TC Budapest
1989–90 Lehel Jaszberenyi
1990–91 Ferencvarosi TC Budapest
1991–92 Ferencvarosi TC Budapest
1992–93 Ferencvarosi TC Budapest
1993–94 Ferencvarosi TC Budapest
1994–95 Ferencvarosi TC Budapest
1995–96 Dunaferr SE Dunaujvaros
1996–97 Ferencvarosi TC Budapest
1997–98 Dunaferr SE Dunaujvaros
1998–99 Alba Volan SC Szekesfehervar
1999–2000 Dunaferr SE Dunaujvaros

ICELAND

1967–68 Skautafelag Akureyrar
1968–69 Skautafelag Akureyrar
1969–70 Skautafelag Reykjavikur
1970–71 to 1977–78 No championship
1978–79 Skautafelag Reykjavikur
1979–80 Skautafelag Akureyrar
1980–81 No championship
1981–82 Skautafelag Akureyrar
1982–83 Skautafelag Akureyrar
1983–84 Skautafelag Akureyrar
1984–85 Skautafelag Reykjavikur
1985–86 No championship
1986–87 Skautafelag Akureyrar
1987–88 Skautafelag Akureyrar
1988–89 No championship
1989–90 No championship
1990–91 No championship
1991–92 Skautafelag Akureyrar
1992–93 Skautafelag Akureyrar
1993–94 Skautafelag Akureyrar
1994–95 Skautafelag Akureyrar
1995–96 Skautafelag Akureyrar
1996–97 Skautafelag Akureyrar
1997–98 Skautafelag Akureyrar
1998–99 Skautafelag Reykjavikur
1999–2000 Skautafelag Reykjavikur

IRELAND

1999–2000 No championship

ISRAEL

1989–90 HC Haifa
1990–91 HC Haifa
1991–92 No championship
1992–93 No championship
1993–94 HC Haifa
1994–95 HC Bat Yam
1995–96 Lions Jerusalem
1996–97 Lions Jerusalem
1997–98 Macabi Lod
1998–99 SC Metulla
1999–2000 HC Maalot

ITALY

1924–25 HC Milano
1925–26 HC Milano
1926–27 HC Milano
1927–28 No championship
1928–29 No championship
1929–30 HC Milano
1930–31 HC Milano
1931–32 SG Cortina
1932–33 HC Milano
1933–34 HC Milano
1934–35 HC Diavoli Rosso-Neri
1935–36 HC Diavoli Rosso-Neri
1936–37 AMDG Milano
1937–38 AMDG Milano
1938–39 No championship
1939–40 No championship
1940–41 AMDG Milano
1941–42 to 1945–46 No championship
1946–47 HC Milano
1947–48 HC Milano
1948–49 HC Diavoli Rosso-Neri
1949–50 HC Milano
1950–51 HC Milano-Inter
1951–52 HC Milano-Inter
1952–53 HC Diavoli Rosso-Neri
1953–54 HC Milano-Inter
1954–55 HC Milano-Inter
1955–56 No championship
1956–57 SG Cortina
1957–58 Milan-Inter HC
1958–59 SG Cortina
1959–60 Diavoli HC Milano
1960–61 SG Cortina Rex

1961–62 SG Cortina Rex
1962–63 HC Bolzano Ozo
1963–64 SG Cortina Rex
1964–65 SG Cortina Rex
1965–66 SG Cortina Rex
1966–67 SG Cortina Rex
1967–68 SG Cortina Rex
1968–69 HC Val Gardena Recoaro
1969–70 SG Cortina Doria
1970–71 SG Cortina Doria
1971–72 SG Cortina Doria
1972–73 HC Bolzano Coca-Cola
1973–74 SG Cortina Doria
1974–75 SG Cortina Doria
1975–76 HC Gardena Cinzano Vermouth
1976–77 HC Bolzano Coca-Cola
1977–78 HC Bolzano Henkel
1978–79 HC Bolzano Despar
1979–80 HC Gardena Recoaro
1980–81 HC Gardena Finstral
1981–82 HC Bolzano Wurth
1982–83 HC Bolzano Wurth
1983–84 HC Bolzano Wurth
1984–85 HC Bolzano Wurth
1985–86 HC Merano Lancia
1986–87 AS Kronenburg Varese Hockey
1987–88 HC Bolzano Dival
1988–89 AS Kronenburg Varese Hockey
1989–90 HC Bolzano Lancia
1990–91 HC Saima Milano
1991–92 HC Devils Milan
1992–93 HC Devils Milan
1993–94 HC Devils Milan
1994–95 HC Bolzano Wurth
1995–96 HC Bolzano
1996–97 HC Bolzano
1997–98 HC Bolzano
1998–99 HC Merano
1999–2000 HC Forst Bolzano Foxes

JAPAN

1974–75 Kokudo Keikaku Tokyo
1975–76 Oji Seishi Tomakomai
1976–77 Oji Seishi Tomakomai
1977–78 Seibu Tetsudo Tokyo
1978–79 Seibu Tetsudo Tokyo
1979–80 Oji Seishi Tomakomai
1980–81 Oji Seishi Tomakomai
1981–82 Kokudo Keikaku Tokyo
1982–83 Oji Seishi Tomakomai
1983–84 Oji Seishi Tomakomai
1984–85 Oji Seishi Tomakomai
1985–86 Oji Seishi Tomakomai
1986–87 Oji Seishi Tomakomai
1987–88 Kokudo Keikaku Tokyo
1988–89 Oji Seishi Tomakomai
1989–90 Oji Seishi Tomakomai
1990–91 Oji Seishi Tomakomai
1991–92 Kokudo Keikaku Tokyo
1992–93 Kokudo Tokyo
1993–94 New Oji Tomakomai
1994–95 Kokudo Tokyo
1995–96 Seibu Tetsudo Tokyo
1996–97 Seibu Tetsudo Tokyo
1997–98 Kokudo Tokyo
1998–99 Kokudo Tokyo
1999–2000 Seibu Tetsudo Tokyo

KAZAKHSTAN

1992–93 Torpedo Ust-Kamenogorsk
1993–94 Torpedo Ust-Kamenogorsk
1994–95 Torpedo Ust-Kamenogorsk
1995–96 Torpedo Ust-Kamenogorsk
1996–97 Torpedo Ust-Kamenogorsk
1997–98 Torpedo Ust-Kamenogorsk
1998–99 Bulat Temirtau
1999–2000 Torpedo Ust-Kamenogorsk

LATVIA

1931–32 Union Riga
1932–33 Union Riga
1933–34 ASK Riga
1934–35 ASK Riga
1935–36 ASK Riga
1936–37 Universitates Sports Riga
1937–38 ASK Riga
1938–39 ASK Riga
1939–40 Universitates Sports Riga
1940–41 No championship
1941–42 Universitates Sports Riga
1942–43 No championship
1943–44 Universitates Sports Riga
1944–45 to 1991–92 No championship
1992–93 Pardaugava Riga
1993–94 Hokeja Centrs Riga
1994–95 HK Nik's-Brih Riga
1995–96 HK Nik's-Brih Riga
1996–97 LB/Essamika Ogre
1997–98 HK Nik's-Brih Riga
1998–99 HK Nik's-Brih Riga
1999–2000 Liepajas Metalurgs

LITHUANIA

1925–26 LFLS Kaunas
1926–27 LFLS Kaunas
1927–28 LFLS Kaunas
1928–29 STSK Kaunas
1929–30 No championship
1930–31 LFLS Kaunas
1931–32 LGSF Kaunas
1932–33 LGSF Kaunas
1933–34 LFLS Kaunas
1934–35 No championship
1935–36 No championship
1936–37 LGSF Kaunas
1937–38 Tauras Kaunas
1938–39 KJK Kaunas
1939–40 Tauras Kaunas
1940–41 Spartakus
1941–42 Tauras Kaunas
1942–43 to 1991–92 No championship
1992–93 Energija Elektrenai
1993–94 Energija Elektrenai
1994–95 Energija Elektrenai
1995–96 Energija Elektrenai
1996–97 Energija Elektrenai
1997–98 Energija Elektrenai
1998–99 Energija Elektrenai
1999–2000 Viltis Kaunas

LUXEMBOURG

1993–94 Tornado Luxembourg
1994–95 No championship
1995–96 Tornado Luxembourg
1996–97 Tornado Luxembourg
1997–98 Tornado Luxembourg
1998–99 Tornado Luxembourg
1999–2000 Tornado Luxembourg

MONGOLIA

1999–2000 Baganuurg

NETHERLANDS

1937–38 HIJC den Haag
1938–39 HIJC den Haag
1939–40 to 1944–45 No championship
1945–46 HIJC den Haag
1946–47 TIJSC Tilburg
1947–48 HIJC den Haag
1948–49 No championship
1949–50 Ijsvogels Amsterdam
1950–51 to 1963–64 No championship
1964–65 HIJS Hokij den Haag
1965–66 HIJS Hokij den Haag
1966–67 HIJS Hokij den Haag
1967–68 HIJS Hokij den Haag
1968–69 HIJS Hokij den Haag
1969–70 SIJ den Bosch
1970–71 Tilburg Trappers
1971–72 Tilburg Trappers
1972–73 Tilburg Trappers
1973–74 Tilburg Trappers
1974–75 Tilburg Trappers
1975–76 Tilburg Trappers
1976–77 Feenstra Flyers Heerenveen
1977–78 Feenstra Flyers Heerenveen
1978–79 Feenstra Flyers Heerenveen
1979–80 Feenstra Flyers Heerenveen
1980–81 Feenstra Flyers Heerenveen
1981–82 Feenstra Flyers Heerenveen
1982–83 Feenstra Flyers Heerenveen
1983–84 Vissers Nijmegen
1984–85 Deko Builders Amsterdam
1985–86 Noorder Stores GIJS Gronin
1986–87 Pandas Rotterdam
1987–88 Spitman Nijmegen
1988–89 Turbana Pandas Rotterdam
1989–90 Gunco Pandas Rotterdam
1990–91 Peter Langhout Utrecht
1991–92 Pro Badge Utrecht
1992–93 Flame Guards Nijmegen
1993–94 Couwenberg Trappers Tilburg
1994–95 CVT Tilburg Trappers
1995–96 CVT Tilburg Trappers
1996–97 Fulda Tigers Nijmegen
1997–98 Van Heumen Tigers Nijmegen
1998–99 Agio Huys Tigers Nijmegen
1999–2000 Agio Huys Tigers Nijmegen

NEW ZEALAND

1989–90 Auckland
1990–91 Auckland
1991–92 Auckland
1992–93 Auckland
1993–94 Auckland
1994–95 North Island

1995–96 North Island
1996–97 North Island
1997–98 Auckland
1998–99 Southern
1999–2000 Auckland

NORWAY

1934–35 SFK Trygg Oslo
1935–36 SK Grane Sandvika
1936–37 SK Grane Sandvika
1937–38 SFK Trygg Oslo
1938–39 SK Grane Sandvika
1939–40 SK Grane Sandvika
1940–41 to 1944–45 No championship
1945–46 Forward Oslo
1946–47 Stabaek IF Baerum
1947–48 SK Strong Oslo
1948–49 Furuset IF Oslo
1949–50 Gamlebyen IF Oslo
1950–51 Furuset IF Oslo
1951–52 Furuset IF Oslo
1952–53 Gamlebyen IF Oslo
1953–54 Furuset IF Oslo
1954–55 Gamlebyen IF Oslo
1955–56 Gamlebyen IF Oslo
1956–57 IK Tigrene Oslo
1957–58 Gamlebyen IF Oslo
1958–59 Gamlebyen IF Oslo
1959–60 Valerengens IF Oslo
1960–61 IK Tigrene Oslo
1961–62 Valerengens IF Oslo
1962–63 Valerengens IF Oslo
1963–64 Gamlebyen IF Oslo
1964–65 Valerengens IF Oslo
1965–66 Valerengens IF Oslo
1966–67 Valerengens IF Oslo
1967–68 Valerengens IF Oslo
1968–69 Valerengens IF Oslo
1969–70 Valerengens IF Oslo
1970–71 Valerengens IF Oslo
1971–72 Hasle/Loren IL Oslo
1972–73 Valerengens IF Oslo
1973–74 Hasle/Loren IL Oslo
1974–75 Frisk Asker
1975–76 Hasle/Loren IL Oslo
1976–77 IL Manglerud/Star Oslo
1977–78 IL Manglerud/Star Oslo
1978–79 Frisk Asker
1979–80 Furuset IF Oslo
1980–81 IL Stjernen Fredrikstad
1981–82 Valerengens IF Oslo
1982–83 Furuset IF Oslo
1983–84 IL Sparta Sarpsborg
1984–85 Valerengens IF Oslo
1985–86 IL Stjernen Fredrikstad
1986–87 Valerengens IF Oslo
1987–88 Valerengens IF Oslo
1988–89 IL Sparta Sarpsborg
1989–90 Furuset IF Oslo
1990–91 Valerengens IF Oslo
1991–92 Valerengens IF Oslo
1992–93 Valerengens IF Oslo
1993–94 Lillehammer IK
1994–95 Storhamar IL Hamar
1995–96 Storhamar IL Hamar
1996–97 Storhamar IL Hamar
1997–98 Valerengens IF Oslo
1998–99 Valerengens IF Oslo
1999–2000 Storhamar IL Hamar

POLAND

1926–27 AZS Warszawa
1927–28 AZS Warszawa
1928–29 AZS Warszawa
1929–30 AZS Warszawa
1930–31 AZS Warszawa
1931–32 No championship
1932–33 Legia Warszawa & Pogon Lwo
1933–34 AZS Poznan
1934–35 Czarni Lwow
1935–36 No championship
1936–37 Cracovia Krakow
1937–38 No championship
1938–39 Dab Katowice
1939–40 to 1944–45 No championship
1945–46 Cracovia Krakow
1946–47 Cracovia Krakow
1947–48 No championship
1948–49 Cracovia Krakow
1949–50 KTH Krynica
1950–51 CWKS Warszawa
1951–52 CWKS Warszawa
1952–53 CWKS Warszawa
1953–54 CWKS Warszawa
1954–55 Legia Warszawa
1955–56 Legia Warszawa
1956–57 Legia Warszawa
1957–58 Gornik Katowice
1958–59 Legia Warszawa
1959–60 Gornik Katowice
1960–61 Legia Warszawa
1961–62 Gornik Katowice
1962–63 Legia Warszawa
1963–64 Legia Warszawa
1964–65 GKS Katowice
1965–66 Podhale Nowy Targ
1966–67 Legia Warszawa
1967–68 GKS Katowice
1968–69 Podhale Nowy Targ
1969–70 GKS Katowice
1970–71 Podhale Nowy Targ
1971–72 Podhale Nowy Targ
1972–73 Podhale Nowy Targ
1973–74 Podhale Nowy Targ
1974–75 Podhale Nowy Targ
1975–76 Podhale Nowy Targ
1976–77 Podhale Nowy Targ
1977–78 Podhale Nowy Targ
1978–79 Podhale Nowy Targ
1979–80 GKS Zaglebie Sosnowiec
1980–81 GKS Zaglebie Sosnowiec
1981–82 GKS Zaglebie Sosnowiec
1982–83 GKS Zaglebie Sosnowiec
1983–84 Polonia Bytom
1984–85 GKS Zaglebie Sosnowiec
1985–86 Polonia Bytom
1986–87 Podhale Nowy Targ
1987–88 Polonia Bytom
1988–89 Polonia Bytom
1989–90 Polonia Bytom
1990–91 Polonia Bytom
1991–92 Unia Oswiecim
1992–93 Podhale Nowy Targ
1993–94 Podhale Nowy Targ
1994–95 Podhale Nowy Targ
1995–96 Podhale Nowy Targ
1996–97 Podhale Nowy Targ
1997–98 Podhale Nowy Targ
1998–99 Unia Dwory Oswiecim
1999–2000 Dwory S.A. Unia Oswiecim

ROMANIA

1924–25 Brasovia Brasov
1925–26 No championship
1926–27 HC Roman Bucuresti
1927–28 HC Roman Bucuresti
1928–29 HC Roman Bucuresti
1929–30 TC Roman Bucuresti
1930–31 TC Roman Bucuresti
1931–32 TC Roman Bucuresti
1932–33 TC Roman Bucuresti
1933–34 TC Roman Bucuresti
1934–35 TC Bucuresti
1935–36 HC Bragadiru Bucuresti
1936–37 TC Bucuresti
1937–38 Dragos Voda Cernauti
1938–39 No championship
1939–40 HC Rapid Bucuresti
1940–41 HC Juventus Bucuresti
1941–42 HC Rapid Bucuresti
1942–43 No championship
1943–44 Venus Bucuresti
1944–45 HC Juventus Bucuresti
1945–46 HC Juventus Bucuresti
1946–47 HC Ciocanul Bucuresti
1947–48 No championship
1948–49 Avintul Meircurea Ciuc
1949–50 Locomotiva RTA Tirgu Mures
1950–51 Locomotiva RTA Tirgu Mures
1951–52 Avintul Meircurea Ciuc
1952–53 CCA Bucuresti
1953–54 Stiinta Kluz
1954–55 CCA Bucuresti
1955–56 CCA Bucuresti
1956–57 Recolta Miercurea Ciuc
1957–58 CCA Bucuresti
1958–59 CCA Bucuresti
1959–60 Vointa Miercurea Ciuc
1960–61 CCA Bucuresti
1961–62 CCA Bucuresti
1962–63 Vointa Miercurea Ciuc
1963–64 Steaua Bucuresti
1964–65 Steaua Bucuresti
1965–66 Steaua Bucuresti
1966–67 Steaua Bucuresti
1967–68 Dinamo Bucuresti
1968–69 Steaua Bucuresti
1969–70 Dinamo Bucuresti
1970–71 Steaua Bucuresti
1971–72 Dinamo Bucuresti
1972–73 Dinamo Bucuresti
1973–74 Steaua Bucuresti
1974–75 Steaua Bucuresti
1975–76 Steaua Bucuresti
1976–77 Steaua Bucuresti
1977–78 Steaua Bucuresti
1978–79 Dinamo Bucuresti
1979–80 Steaua Bucuresti
1980–81 Dinamo Bucuresti
1981–82 Steaua Bucuresti
1982–83 Steaua Bucuresti
1983–84 Steaua Bucuresti
1984–85 Steaua Bucuresti
1985–86 Steaua Bucuresti
1986–87 Steaua Bucuresti
1987–88 Steaua Bucuresti
1988–89 Steaua Bucuresti
1989–90 Steaua Bucuresti
1990–91 Steaua Bucuresti
1991–92 Steaua Bucuresti
1992–93 Steaua Bucuresti
1993–94 Steaua Bucuresti
1994–95 Steaua Bucuresti
1995–96 Steaua Bucuresti
1996–97 SC Miercurea Ciuc
1997–98 Steaua Bucuresti
1998–99 Steaua Bucuresti
1999–2000 SC Miercurea Ciuc

RUSSIA/C.I.S

see also Soviet Union

1992–93 Dynamo Moscow
1993–94 Lada Togliatti
1994–95 Dynamo Moscow
1995–96 Lada Togliatti
1996–97 Torpedo Yaroslavl
1997–98 Ak Bars Kazan
1998–99 Metallurg Magnitogorsk
1999–2000 Dynamo Moscow

SLOVAKIA

1993–94	Dukla Trencin
1994–95	HC Kosice
1995–96	HC Kosice
1996–97	Dukla Trencin
1997–98	HC Slovan Harvard Bratislava
1998–99	HC VSZ Kosice
1999–2000	HC Slovan Bratislava

SLOVENIA

1991–92	Acroni Jesenice
1992–93	Acroni Jesenice
1993–94	Acroni Jesenice
1994–95	Olimpija Hertz Ljubljana
1995–96	Olimpija Hertz Ljubljana
1996–97	Olimpija Hertz Ljubljana
1997–98	Olimpija Hertz Ljubljana
1998–99	Olimpija Hertz Ljubljana
1999–2000	Olimpija Ljubljana

SOUTH AFRICA

1991–92	Flyers Roodenpoort
1992–93	Flyers Roodenpoort
1993–94	Flyers Roodenpoort
1994–95	Can-Ams Johannesburg
1995–96	Can-Ams Johannesburg
1996–97	Can-Ams Johannesburg
1997–98	Pretoria Capitals
1998–99	Pretoria Capitals
1999–2000	Wildcats Krugersdorp

SOUTH KOREA

1986–87	Yonsei University
1987–88	Yonsei University
1988–89	Korea University
1989–90	Yonsei University
1990–91	Yonsei University
1991–92	Yonsei University
1992–93	Yonsei University
1993–94	Yonsei University
1994–95	Seoktop Seoul
1995–96	Seoktop Seoul
1996–97	Yonsei University
1997–98	Halla Winia
1998–99	Yonsei University
1999–2000	Halla Winia

SOVIET UNION

1946–47	Dynamo Moscow
1947–48	CDKA Moscow
1948–49	CDKA Moscow
1949–50	CDKA Moscow
1950–51	VVS MVO Moscow
1951–52	VVS MVO Moscow
1952–53	VVS MVO Moscow
1953–54	Dynamo Moscow
1954–55	CSK MO Moscow
1955–56	CSK MO Moscow
1956–57	Krylja Sovetov Moscow
1957–58	CSK MO Moscow
1958–59	CSK MO Moscow
1959–60	CSKA Moscow
1960–61	CSKA Moscow
1961–62	Spartak Moscow
1962–63	CSKA Moscow
1963–64	CSKA Moscow
1964–65	CSKA Moscow
1965–66	CSKA Moscow
1966–67	Spartak Moscow
1967–68	CSKA Moscow
1968–69	Spartak Moscow
1969–70	CSKA Moscow
1970–71	CSKA Moscow
1971–72	CSKA Moscow
1972–73	CSKA Moscow
1973–74	Krylja Sovetov Moscow
1974–75	CSKA Moscow
1975–76	Spartak Moscow
1976–77	CSKA Moscow
1977–78	CSKA Moscow
1978–79	CSKA Moscow
1979–80	CSKA Moscow
1980–81	CSKA Moscow
1981–82	CSKA Moscow
1982–83	CSKA Moscow
1983–84	CSKA Moscow
1984–85	CSKA Moscow
1985–86	CSKA Moscow
1986–87	CSKA Moscow
1987–88	CSKA Moscow
1988–89	CSKA Moscow
1989–90	Dynamo Moscow
1990–91	Dynamo Moscow
1991–92	Dynamo Moscow

SPAIN

1952–53	Atletico Madrid
1953–54	Club Alpine Nurin
1954–55 to 1971–72	No championship
1972–73	Real Sosiedad San Sebastia
1973–74	Real Sosiedad San Sebastia
1974–75	Txuri Urdin San Sebastian
1975–76	Txuri Urdin San Sebastian
1976–77	Casco Viejo Bolbao
1977–78	Casco Viejo Bolbao
1978–79	Casco Viejo Bolbao
1979–80	Txuri Urdin San Sebastian
1980–81	Casco Viejo Bolbao
1981–82	Vizcaya Bilbao
1982–83	CH Jaca
1983–84	CH Jaca
1984–85	Txuri Urdin San Sebastian
1985–86	HC Puigcerda
1986–87	No championship
1987–88	FC Barcelona
1988–89	HC Puigcerda
1989–90	Txuri Urdin San Sebastian
1990–91	CH Jaca
1991–92	Txuri Urdin San Sebastian
1992–93	Txuri Urdin San Sebastian
1993–94	CH Jaca
1994–95	Txuri Urdin San Sebastian
1995–96	CH Jaca
1996–97	FC Barcelona
1997–98	CH Majadahonda
1998–99	Txuri Urdin San Sebastian
1999–2000	Txuri Urdin San Sebastian

SWEDEN

1921–22	IK Gota Stockholm
1922–23	IK Gota Stockholm
1923–24	IK Gota Stockholm
1924–25	Sodertalje SK
1925–26	Djurgardens IF Stockholm
1926–27	IK Gota Stockholm
1927–28	IK Gota Stockholm
1928–29	IK Gota Stockholm
1929–30	IK Gota Stockholm
1930–31	Sodertalje SK
1931–32	Hammarby IF Stockholm
1932–33	Hammarby IF Stockholm
1933–34	AIK Solna
1934–35	AIK Solna
1935–36	Hammarby IF Stockholm
1936–37	Hammarby IF Stockholm
1937–38	AIK Solna
1938–39	No championship
1939–40	IK Gota Stockholm
1940–41	Sodertalje SK
1941–42	Hammarby IF Stockholm
1942–43	Hammarby IF Stockholm
1943–44	Sodertalje SK
1944–45	Hammarby IF Stockholm
1945–46	AIK Solna
1946–47	AIK Solna
1947–48	IK Gota Stockholm
1948–49	No championship
1949–50	Djurgardens IF Stockholm
1950–51	Hammarby IF Stockholm
1951–52	No championship
1952–53	Sodertalje SK
1953–54	Djurgardens IF Stockholm
1954–55	Djurgardens IF Stockholm
1955–56	Sodertalje SK
1956–57	Gavle GIK
1957–58	Djurgardens IF Stockholm
1958–59	Djurgardens IF Stockholm
1959–60	Djurgardens IF Stockholm
1960–61	Djurgardens IF Stockholm
1961–62	Djurgardens IF Stockholm
1962–63	Djurgardens IF Stockholm
1963–64	Brynas IF Gavle
1964–65	Vastra Frolunda IF Goteborg
1965–66	Brynas IF Gavle
1966–67	Brynas IF Gavle
1967–68	Brynas IF Gavle
1968–69	Leksands IF
1969–70	Brynas IF Gavle
1970–71	Brynas IF Gavle
1971–72	Brynas IF Gavle
1972–73	Leksands IF
1973–74	Leksands IF
1974–75	Leksands IF
1975–76	Brynas IF Gavle
1976–77	Brynas IF Gavle
1977–78	Skelleftea AIK
1978–79	MoDo AIK Orskoldsvik
1979–80	Brynas IF Gavle
1980–81	Farjestads BK Karlstad
1981–82	AIK Solna
1982–83	Djurgardens IF Stockholm
1983–84	AIK Solna
1984–85	Sodertalje SK
1985–86	Farjestads BK Karlstad
1986–87	IF Bjorkloven Umea
1987–88	Farjestads BK Karlstad
1988–89	Djurgardens IF Stockholm
1989–90	Djurgardens IF Stockholm
1990–91	Djurgardens IF Stockholm
1991–92	Malmo IF
1992–93	Brynas IF Gavle
1993–94	Malmo IF
1994–95	HV 71 Jonkoping
1995–96	Lulea HF
1996–97	Farjestads BK Karlstad
1997–98	Farjestads BK Karlstad
1998–99	Brynas IF Gavle
1999–2000	Djurgardens IF Stockholm

SWITZERERLAND

1915–16	HC Bern
1916–17	HC Bern
1917–18	HC Bern
1918–19	HC Bellerive Vevey
1919–20	HC Bellerive Vevey
1920–21	HC Rosey Gstaad
1921–22	EHC St. Moritz
1922–23	EHC St. Moritz
1923–24	HC Rosey Gstaad

1924–25 HC Rosey Gstaad
1925–26 HC Davos
1926–27 HC Davos
1927–28 EHC St. Moritz
1928–29 HC Davos
1929–30 HC Davos
1930–31 HC Davos
1931–32 HC Davos
1932–33 HC Davos
1933–34 HC Davos
1934–35 HC Davos
1935–36 Zurcher SC
1936–37 HC Davos
1937–38 HC Davos
1938–39 HC Davos
1939–40 No championship
1940–41 HC Davos
1941–42 HC Davos
1942–43 HC Davos
1943–44 HC Davos
1944–45 HC Davos
1945–46 HC Davos
1946–47 HC Davos
1947–48 HC Davos
1948–49 Zurcher SC
1949–50 HC Davos
1950–51 EHC Arosa
1951–52 EHC Arosa
1952–53 EHC Arosa
1953–54 EHC Arosa
1954–55 EHC Arosa
1955–56 EHC Arosa
1956–57 EHC Arosa
1957–58 HC Davos
1958–59 SC Bern
1959–60 HC Davos
1960–61 Zurcher SC
1961–62 EHC Visp
1962–63 HC Villars
1963–64 HC Villars
1964–65 SC Bern
1965–66 GC Zurich
1966–67 EHC Kloten
1967–68 HC La Chaux-de-Fonds
1968–69 HC La Chaux-de-Fonds
1969–70 HC La Chaux-de-Fonds
1970–71 HC La Chaux-de-Fonds
1971–72 HC La Chaux-de-Fonds
1972–73 HC La Chaux-de-Fonds
1973–74 SC Bern
1974–75 SC Bern
1975–76 SC Langnau
1976–77 SC Bern
1977–78 EHC Biel
1978–79 SC Bern
1979–80 EHC Arosa
1980–81 EHC Biel
1981–82 EHC Arosa
1982–83 EHC Biel
1983–84 HC Davos
1984–85 HC Davos
1985–86 HC Lugano
1986–87 HC Lugano
1987–88 HC Lugano
1988–89 SC Bern
1989–90 HC Lugano
1990–91 SC Bern
1991–92 SC Bern
1992–93 EHC Kloten
1993–94 EHC Kloten
1994–95 EHC Kloten
1995–96 EHC Kloten
1996–97 SC Bern
1997–98 EV Zug
1998–99 HC Lugano
1999–2000 ZSC Lions Zurich

THAILAND

1999–2000 Blue Wave Bangkok

TURKEY

1991–92 Belpa Ankara
1992–93 Ankara Buyuksehir Belediye
1993–94 Ankara Buyuksehir Belediye
1994–95 Ankara Buyuksehir Belediye
1995–96 Kavaklidere Ankara
1996–97 Ankara Buyuksehir Belediye
1997–98 Istanbul Paten Kulubu
1998–99 Gumus Patenler Spor Kulubu Ankara
1999–2000 Ankara Buyuksehir Belediye

UKRAINE

1992–93 Sokol Kiev
1993–94 ShVSM Kiev
1994–95 Sokol Kiev
1995–96 No championship
1996–97 Sokol Kiev
1997–98 Sokol Kiev
1998–99 Sokol Kiev
1999–2000 Berkut-PVO Kiev

UNITED ARAB EMIRATES

1999–2000 Desert Snake Abu Dhabi

YUGOSLAVIA

1938–39 Ilirija Ljubljana
1939–40 Ilirija Ljubljana
1940–41 to 1945–46 No championship
1946–47 Mladost Zagreb
1947–48 Partizan Belgrad
1948–49 Mladost Zagreb
1949–50 No championship
1950–51 Partizan Belgrad
1951–52 Partizan Belgrad
1952–53 Partizan Belgrad
1953–54 Partizan Belgrad
1954–55 Partizan Belgrad
1955–56 Zagreb
1956–57 HK Jesenice
1957–58 HK Jesenice
1958–59 HK Jesenice
1959–60 HK Jesenice
1960–61 HK Jesenice
1961–62 HK Jesenice
1962–63 HK Jesenice
1963–64 HK Jesenice
1964–65 HK Jesenice
1965–66 HK Jesenice
1966–67 HK Jesenice
1967–68 HK Jesenice
1968–69 HK Jesenice
1969–70 HK Jesenice
1970–71 HK Jesenice
1971–72 Olimpija Ljubljana
1972–73 HK Jesenice
1973–74 Olimpija Ljubljana
1974–75 Olimpija Ljubljana
1975–76 Olimpija Ljubljana
1976–77 HK Jesenice
1977–78 HK Jesenice
1978–79 Olimpija Ljubljana
1979–80 Olimpija Ljubljana
1980–81 HK Jesenice
1981–82 HK Jesenice
1982–83 Olimpija Ljubljana
1983–84 Olimpija Ljubljana
1984–85 HK Jesenice
1985–86 Partizan Belgrad
1986–87 HK Jesenice
1987–88 HK Jesenice
1988–89 Medvescak Zagreb
1989–90 Medvescak Zagreb
1990–91 Medvescak Zagreb
1991–92 Crvena Zvezda Belgrad
1992–93 Crvena Zvezda Belgrad
1993–94 Partizan BLP Belgrad
1994–95 Partizan BLP Belgrad
1995–96 Crvena Zve. Belgrad
1996–97 Crvena Zve. Belgrad
1997–98 Vojvodina Novi Sad
1998–99 Vojvodina Novi Sad
1999–2000 Vojvodina Novi Sad

CHAPTER 50

From Andorra to Yugoslavia

The History of Hockey and Its Structure Today in Each IIHF Nation

Igor Kuperman

EACH IIHF MEMBER NATION is listed here in alphabetical order. Each country's name is followed by the formal name of its national hockey federation.

ANDORRA

Federacion Andorrana d'Esports de Gel
Ice Hockey Committee

HISTORY: Ice hockey did not begin in Andorra until the 1990s. The lack of ice and equipment has slowed the development of the game in the country, but a major step towards popularizing hockey was made in 1996–97 when the city of Canillo hosted the D Pool World Championships.

HOCKEY TODAY: Teams from Andorra currently play exhibition games only.

AUSTRALIA

Australian Ice Hockey Federation

HISTORY: The history of Australian ice hockey began in 1907 when a group of young skaters from Melbourne issued a challenge to the crew of the American battleship Baltimore. The game drew a capacity crowd to the Melbourne Glaciarium and attracted considerable attention in the press. Though the home team was defeated by the Americans, the game had found its feet in Australia. In 1908, games were played in the country's two artificial indoor ice rinks in Sydney and Melbourne. By 1909, there were four hockey clubs in the province of Victoria and two more in New South Wales. The first inter-provincial games in Australia were played that year, with Melbourne (Victoria) defeating Sydney (New South Wales) two games to one. This early chapter in Australian hockey history came to a close with the outbreak of the First World War in 1914. It was many years before the game was played again.

Hockey in Australia experienced a revival during the 1950s. The country joined the International Ice Hockey Federation in 1950, though the Australian Ice Hockey Federation was not founded until 1954. The popularity of the game declined during the late 1950s and early 1960s due to the shortage of rinks in the country, though Australia did compete in hockey at the 1960 Winter Olympics in Squaw Valley, California. This marked the Australian national team's international debut (their first game was a 12–1 loss to the United States on February 18, 1960). In later years, the arrival of Eastern Bloc immigrants to Australia helped to boost the number of hockey players in the country to around 3,500.

HOCKEY TODAY: Because of the huge distances between settlements in Australia, there is no national league competition. Australia's most prestigious hockey trophy is the Goodall Cup, which was presented by Melbourne player John Goodall in 1921. Since 1991–92, selected teams have been playing off for the Goodall Cup. In 1999–2000, four teams representing different areas of the country played a round-robin tournament to decide the Goodall Cup champion.

The different states across Australia have teams playing in their own leagues. The Superleague, with teams from New South Wales and the Australian Capital Territory, is the country's most important league and attracts the largest audience. The best of this league's 14 arenas is the Macquarie (with a capacity of 3,500) which is located in a shopping mall in suburban Sydney. In addition to the Eastcoast Superleague, there are leagues in Queensland and Victoria. Each league has playoffs to determine a regional championship.

In recent years, the national emphasis has been on developing junior hockey with seasonal clinics and top overseas and local coaches hosting provincial clinics. Players under 21 compete for the Brown Trophy, while those under 16 play for the Tange Trophy. The President's Cup has been inaugurated by the Australian Ice Hockey Federation for boys and girls under age 13 as an introduction to the sport in a fun and less competitive atmosphere.

AUSTRIA

Osterreichischer Eishockeyverband

HISTORY: The first mention of hockey in Austria occurred on January 12, 1896, when the Vienna newspaper *Allgemeine Sport-Zeitung* printed an article called "Hockey Game," which was, in fact, about bandy (field hockey on ice). The article described the game as being played on a surface measuring 60 x 100 meters and involving seven players per team. It was mentioned that the game was already popular in Prague (which was, at the time, a part of the Austro-Hungarian Empire).

Bandy arrived in Austria in 1899 when the first game was played in Vienna. The sport spread quickly across the country and teams soon were organized in other cities. The first international bandy game involving Austria took place in 1901 when a team from Vienna was defeated, 17–3, by Slavia Praha. Around the same time, three Austrian clubs organized an ice hockey committee, and though the new sport could not yet match the popularity of bandy, it had made huge strides by 1911 when almost all bandy players began to play hockey. The first artificial ice rink had opened in Vienna on November 10, 1909, and this did much to increase the popularity of hockey.

The Austrian Hockey Union was created on January 15, 1912, and Austria was admitted into the International Ice Hockey Federation on March 18, 1912. Austria played its first international game on February 2, 1912, at the European Championships and lost to Bohemia, 5–0. Austria was represented at the European Championships in 1913, though at this time the only national championship that existed in Austria was for bandy. Still, the popularity of hockey grew quickly and regional hockey unions started to form. Canadian Blake Watson (who also helped to coach in Germany) did much to advance the game in Austria. In 1922, the country held its first national ice hockey championship.

The development of hockey slowed in Austria during the 1930s and 1940s, with the decline attributed to financial difficulties, a lack of coaches and a shrinking player base. However, by the end of the 1950s, Austrian clubs began recruiting coaches and players from abroad—particularly from Czechoslovakia and Canada, and later from the Soviet Union. The level of competition in Austria increased and in 1965 the Bundesliga was created.

HOCKEY TODAY: In 1999–2000, the best clubs in Austria began the season in the International Ice Hockey League, (formerly the Alpenliga) along with teams from Italy and Slovenia. After playing a quadruple round-robin schedule, the Austrian clubs are ranked according to their standings and the four top teams move on to the Austrian League-Division 1. They play a quadruple round-robin schedule and all four team advance to the playoffs. Best-of-seven series are played in the semifinals and finals.

Austrian League-Division 2 is divided into East (eight teams) and West (seven teams) with teams playing a double round-robin schedule within these groups. The top three teams from each group then play a double round robin among themselves, while the remaining teams play a separate double round robin in the East and West. The two teams that win the East and West series then join the top six teams in the playoffs. Quarterfinals, semifinals and finals are all a best-of-three. There is no promotion after the playoffs.

The next level of competition in Austria below Division 2 is in the regional leagues. There are also national championships for junior, midget and other age groups broken down into under 20, under 16, under 14, under 12 and under 10.

AZERBAIJAN

Azerbaidzhanskaya Federatsiya Hokkeya

HISTORY: The Ice Hockey Federation of the Republic of Azerbaijan was founded in 1991 as a part of the Soviet Ice Hockey Federation. After the breakup of the Soviet Union, Azerbaijan became an independent country in 1992. The federation joined the International Ice Hockey Federation on May 6, 1992.

HOCKEY TODAY: There is no national championship in Azerbaijan.

BELARUS
Federatsiya Hokkeya Belarusi

HISTORY: Hockey in the Soviet Republic of Belorussia (now the independent country Belarus) became very popular right after World War II when ice hockey made its first inroads in the Soviet Union. In 1946, Torpedo Minsk (later Dynamo Minsk and now Tivali Minsk) was formed and began to play in the top Soviet division. After the breakup of the Soviet Union, the team from Minsk played in the Inter-State Hockey League. Since 1996, Tivali Minsk and three other Belarus clubs (Polimir Novopolotsk, Yunost Minsk and Neman Grodno) have played in the East European Hockey League along with teams from the Ukraine, Latvia, Lithuania and a team from Poland.

The Ice Hockey Federation of the Belarus Republic became independent in 1992 after the breakup of the Soviet Union. Belarus became a member of the International Ice Hockey Federation on May 6, 1992, and staged its first independent national championship in 1992–93. Dynamo Minsk was the winner. Belarus played its first international game against the Ukraine in 1992. The Belarus national team made its debut at the World Championships in the C Pool in 1994 and has progressed rapidly since. In 1998, Belarus played at the Olympics and in the A Pool of the World Championships.

Oleg Mikulchik (formerly of Winnipeg and Anaheim), Vladimir Tsyplakov (Los Angeles and Buffalo) and Ruslan Salei (Anaheim) are Belarus natives who have reached the NHL. Andrei Kovalev was under contract in the Washington Capitals organization.

HOCKEY TODAY: In 1999–2000, the top four clubs in Belarus played a six-part round-robin tournament to declare the country's champion.

BELGIUM
Koninklijke Belgische Ijshockey Federatie

HISTORY: Bandy (field hockey on ice) was first played in Belgium in Brussels and Antwerp in 1899. Soon, bandy players began learning to play ice hockey and in 1908 the Royal Belgian Ice Hockey Federation was founded. Belgians were very active in the roots of ice hockey in Europe and on December 8, 1908, Belgium joined France, Bohemia, England and Switzerland as the fifth member of the *Ligue Internationale de Hockey sur Glace* (which became the IIHF in 1911).

Hockey quickly became a popular sport in Belgium and the first national championship was held in 1912. It was won by Brussels IHSC. Belgians also had great success on the European scene, beating France 6–2 in their first international game in 1906. At the first official European Championships in 1910, Belgium tied gold medal-winning Great Britain 1–1 and earned a bronze medal, doing so again in 1911 and 1914. Belgium won the European Championship in Munich in 1913 and earned a silver medal in 1927. The first Olympic hockey tournament (which would later be recognized by the IIHF as the first World Championships) was held in Antwerp in April, 1920, in conjunction with the upcoming Summer Olympic Games.

Paul Loicq, who was president of the IIHF for 25 years (1922 to 1947), is the most famous Belgian in the history of international hockey, but the country's most legendary hockey player is Jef Lekens of Antwerp. He played in nine World and/or European championships between 1929 and 1955 and was also an international referee during the 1950s. From 1961 through 1966, he coached the Belgian national team.

HOCKEY TODAY: In 1999–2000, the top six Belgian clubs played a double round-robin schedule with the top four teams advancing to the playoffs. The top four teams then played a double round-robin. Semifinals and finals are played in a best-of-three format while third place is decided with a two-game, total-goals series between the two losers of the semifinals. Belgium also has a second division with 10 teams, a reserve division and junior leagues for players under 18, 16 and 14 years old.

BRAZIL
Confederacao Brasileira de Desportos Terrestres

HISTORY: The first ice hockey games in Brazil were played in 1967 in the ice hall (which used to be a casino) of the hotel Quitandinha in Petropolis (40 miles from Rio de Janeiro). Games took place there for eight years until the hotel was closed. During that time, the CCEG Rio de Janeiro team was the best in Brazil.

Hockey resumed in Brazil in 1978 with teams playing on a rink used for performances of the ice show Holiday on Ice. The revival of hockey in Brazil is attributed to businessman Erwin Dietenhofer of Munich, Germany. His efforts made possible the creation of the Brazil Ice Sport Union and the organization Brazil Hockey as part of the sports union. Dietenhofer served as the first president of both Brazil Hockey and the Brazil Ice Sport Union.

Brazil joined the International Ice Hockey Federation in November, 1984. In 1985, the country had five senior teams and five junior clubs, 180 senior and 130 junior players and five arenas with artificial ice. However, only one rink with a regulation-sized ice surface existed (in Rio de Janeiro).

HOCKEY TODAY: Currently, there are four regulation-size hockey arenas in Brazil located in Rio de Janeiro, Sao Paulo, Brasilia and Riberao Preto. Generally, these arenas are located in the so-called "play centers" of large supermarkets. There are also temporary ice facilities located in Belo Horizonte, Recife and Petropolis. There is no national hockey championship in Brazil.

BULGARIA
Bulgarska Federatsiya po Hokej na Led

HISTORY: The history of hockey in Bulgaria began in 1929 when the Bulgarian Skating Club was created. A handful of players took part in a few intra-squad games and later played against each other on newly created teams: AS–23 and FC–13. Sources indicate the Bulgarian national team played its first international game against Yugoslavia on January 17, 1942, and won, 4–2.

Hockey was revived in Bulgaria after World War II and in 1946 the Bulgarian Skating and Ice Hockey Federation (now the Bulgarian Ice Hockey Federation) was founded. In Sofia, the old Yunak sports arena was converted into a hockey rink and the country's first tournament was held in 1949. Four teams participated—Spartak, Slavia, Levski and Sredec—with Spartak emerging victorious. Also that year, Akademik won the first Sofia championship.

Hockey became popular in Bulgaria and in 1950 five new sports clubs were founded, each with their own hockey team. In 1952, the country's first national championship took place on the ice of a frozen lake near the Musala mountains. The first national junior tournament also was held that year. Bulgaria's first artificial ice rink opened in Sofia in 1960. After joining the International Ice Hockey Federation on July 25, 1963, Bulgaria began to play regularly at the World and European Championships.

HOCKEY TODAY: In 1999–2000, the top four clubs in Bulgaria played a quadruple round-robin schedule with no playoffs. A national junior championship is held annually and a national midget competition began in 1971.

CANADA
Canadian Hockey

HISTORY: The game of hockey was born in Canada. Conflicting claims surround the origins of the game, but it is accepted generally that antecedents of hockey were played in various garrison towns and in Montreal, where the sport first flourished. A hockey game first was advertised in a Montreal newspaper in 1875. The game rapidly took root in Ottawa, Toronto and soon after, throughout the young country.

In 1893, Canada's Governor-General, Lord Stanley of Preston, donated a silver bowl to be awarded to the top senior amateur team in the country. This Dominion Hockey Challenge Cup soon came to be known by the name of its patron.

By the turn of the century, hockey was played in every part of Canada. Even before 1910, openly professional players were competing for the Stanley Cup. Accounts of the exploits of storied teams such as the Ottawa Silver Seven, Montreal Wanderers and Renfrew Millionaires filled newspapers of the day. The National Hockey League was established in 1917 and by the end of its first decade, it stood alone as the game's number one professional circuit.

As the game in Canada became increasingly professionalized, the Allan Cup was donated in 1908 to honor Canada's senior amateur champions. In 1914, the Canadian Amateur Hockey Association was created and in 1920 the CAHA was accepted by the International Ice Hockey Federation as Canada's representative in international hockey. Canada competed at the 1920 Olympics in Antwerp, Belgium, and was represented by the Allan Cup-champion Winnipeg Falcons, who easily won the gold medal at the event later considered to be the first World Championships. The Toronto Granites won gold as well at the first Winter Olympics in 1924, outscoring their opponents 110–3. Hockey Hall of Fame member Harry Watson scored 36 goals at that tournament. Canada's gold medal streak came to an end in 1933 when the National Sea Fleas, managed by future Toronto Maple Leafs owner Harold Ballard, lost, 2–1, to the United States at the World Championships in Prague.

By using top amateur club teams, Canada was able to remain the dominant nation in international hockey until 1954. That year, the Senior B East York Lyndhursts were defeated by the Soviet national team when the USSR made its debut at the World Championships. Senior clubs continued to carry Canada's colors into the early 1960s, with teams like the Penticton Vees and Whitby Dunlops still able to defeat the Soviets.

However, the Trail Smoke Eaters would prove to be the last Canadian senior amateur club to win the World Championship when they captured the title in 1961.

In the early 1960s, Father David Bauer, coach of the 1961 Memorial Cup-winning St. Michael's junior team in Toronto, presented a plan to develop a Canadian national hockey team. The CAHA accepted Bauer's proposal and the "Nats" were launched at the University of British Columbia.

The Nats were a good club, but the Soviet hockey system was in full flower during the 1960s. The best finishes managed by Father Bauer's squad were third-place bronze medals at the 1966 and 1967 World Championships and at the 1968 Olympics.

Canada withdrew from international competition after 1969. Hockey Canada was created that year to improve Canada's performance in international play. Beginning with the famed eight-game series against the Soviet Union's superb national team in 1972, professional players started to participate in some international events. Canada dominated play throughout the history of the Canada Cup tournament from 1976 to 1991. This event always saw Team Canada employ its very best professional skaters and goaltenders.

Hockey Canada and its successor, Canadian Hockey, have operated successful national junior and national/Olympic team programs. Canada has won 10 World Junior Championships since 1982 and Team Canada earned silver medals at the Olympics in 1992 and 1994.

A team stocked mainly with National Hockey League players brought Canada its first world championship title since 1961 at the IIHF 1994 World Championships. Canada won the world title again in 1997. However, the loss to the United States at the World Cup of Hockey in 1996 and the disappointing performance of the 1998 Olympic team have stung Canadian fans' pride in their country's hockey prowess.

Canadian Hockey has supported the development of women's hockey in the country and has operated a national women's team that won six consecutive gold medals at the IIHF Women's World Championships. The Canadian team finished second behind the United States when women's hockey made its Olympic debut in 1998.

HOCKEY TODAY: Though Canadian teams are struggling to survive in the economics of sports since the 1990s, and there are only six teams from Canada currently playing in the NHL, the National Hockey League remains the top league in Canada as it has since its formation in 1917.

Canadian cities also are represented in the biggest minor professional leagues of North America. While many more players from the United States and Europe are playing professional hockey in North America, Canada still provides more players than any other country.

More Canadian prospects are beginning to play at American universities, but the top junior hockey players in Canada mainly continue to play in the three major junior leagues that make up the Canadian Hockey League—the Ontario Hockey League, the Quebec Major Junior Hockey League and the Western Hockey League. All three leagues are mainly Canadian-based, though both the OHL and the WHL have American franchises. An increasing number of European and American players are entering the ranks of Canadian junior hockey, though the overwhelming number of players are still growing up in Canada.

Below the top junior leagues, Canadian players can compete at several different levels in many different age groups. Canada's recent disappointments at the international level have caused Canadian Hockey to take a serious look at its youth programs, but it remains true that more young people are playing hockey in Canada than in any other major hockey nation.

CHINA

Ice Hockey Association of the People's Republic of China

HISTORY: The roots of Chinese ice hockey date back to 1915 when a few games took place in Sen Jan (Mugden). The next mention of hockey in China does not occur until January 26, 1935, when the country's first tournament took place as part of the First Winter Spartakaide Games.

The Ice Hockey Association of the People's Republic of China was founded in 1951. Two years later, the first national championship was held. In 1956, the National Winter Sports Federation was founded and in March of that year the Chinese national team made its international debut at the Universiade in Wroclaw, Poland. China joined the International Ice Hockey Federation on July 25, 1963, and played its first game in the C Pool of the World and European Championships in Miercurea Ciuc, Romania, on March 3, 1972. China beat Bulgaria, 4–3.

HOCKEY TODAY: In 1999–2000, the best six clubs in China (a group made up of two teams each from Qiqihar, Harbin and Jiamusi) played for the national title. After playing a round-robin schedule, the top four teams advance to the national league championship where they play a quadruple round-robin format followed by the final and a game for third place. China also has a second division with six teams. Due to a lack of indoor rinks, many teams in China still play on natural ice in the country's mountain region.

CHINESE TAIPEI

Chinese Taipei Skating Association

HISTORY: The Chinese Taipei Skating Association was founded in 1980. Two years later, in 1982, the first national championship took place. In 1983, Chinese Taipei became a member of the International Ice Hockey Federation.

The debut of the Chinese Taipei national team took place in 1987 in Perth, Australia, when the team played at the D Pool World Championships. (Due to Asian political considerations, results with Chinese Taipei didn't count in the final standings.) The national team tied its first game, 2–2, versus Hong Kong on March 13, 1987.

HOCKEY TODAY: A national championship is held almost every year. Polar Bears Taipei is the most successful team.

CROATIA

Hrvatski Savez Hokeja na Ledu

HISTORY: The roots of ice hockey in Croatia go back to 1906 when the first hockey team in Yugoslavia (HASK—the Croatian Academic Sports Club) was formed in the city of Zagreb. The first official hockey games also took place in Zagreb in 1916–17 when HASK played a two-game series against I.HSK (I. Croatian Sports Club). HASK won the first game, 2–0, but lost the second, 6–0. In 1930, the Yugoslav Ice Hockey Federation was founded in Zagreb. Not surprisingly, clubs from Zagreb were among the best in Yugoslavia for many years.

The Croatian Ice Hockey Association was founded in 1991 and the first Croatian national championship was won by HK Zagreb in 1992. The newly independent nation joined the International Ice Hockey Federation on May 6, 1992, and the Croatian national team made its debut in the C2 Pool of the IIHF World Championships in Barcelona, Spain, in 1994.

HOCKEY TODAY: In 1999–2000, there were about 400 hockey players in Croatia playing on two indoor and two outdoor rinks. Croatia's top four teams play a triple round-robin schedule with all four teams then advancing to the playoffs. Semifinals and the third-place series use a best-of-three format, while the finals are a best-of-five series.

CZECH REPUBLIC

Cesky Svaz Ledniho Hokeje

HISTORY: The game of bandy (field hockey on ice) was introduced to Czechoslovakia by Josef Rossler-Orovsky in 1890 when the country was known as Bohemia. Orovsky brought sticks and a ball to Bohemia from Paris and translated rules that had been brought into the country from England. When the game of ice hockey first was demonstrated in Prague in 1905 by Canadian Ruck Anderson, the country's bandy background provided players with a solid basis for the new game. As a result, hockey's growth here occurred much sooner than in countries like Sweden and Finland, whose climates were better suited to the game.

The spread of hockey in the future Czechoslovakia was largely due to the efforts of Josef Gruss, a professor at Karlov University, who made the first translation of Canadian rules into Czech. In the summer of 1908, Gruss began establishing the first hockey clubs in Prague (I. CLTK, Slavia, AC Sparta, ASK and others) which led to the formation in principle of a Czech Hockey Union (Cesky Svaz Hokejovi) on November 6, 1908. Because Gruss was well-connected with the founder of the *Ligue Internationale de Hockey sur Glace* (which became the International Ice Hockey Federation in 1911), Bohemia joined France as the second member of the LIHG on November 15, 1908. (When Bohemia became Czechoslovakia after World War I, it was readmitted to the IIHF under its new name on April 26, 1920.)

The constituent meeting of the Czech Hockey Union actually was not held until December 11, 1908. Speed skating champion Jaroslav Potucek was elected as the first chairman of the ice hockey union, which included 12 member clubs. An invitation was extended to the Czech players to attend the upcoming inaugural international hockey tournament in Chamonix and seven Prague players went to France with their bandy equipment. Although they lost all four games they played, the experience proved invaluable. In 1911, the Bohemian national team won the European Championship. Their victory in 1912 was annulled later due to a technicality, but Bohemia won again in 1914. After World War I, the Czechoslovakian national team continued to rank as one of the top squads in Europe, winning the European championships again in 1922, 1925, 1929 and 1933.

Czechoslovakian hockey progressed rapidly during the 1930s. The first artificial ice rink opened in Prague on January 17, 1931, with the University of Manitoba playing LTC Prague in the inaugural game en route to representing Canada at the World Championships in Poland. Also in 1931, Slovakia's Hockey Union merged with the Czech Hockey Union to form the Czechoslovakian Hockey Union. Prior to that, there had been separate national Czech championships (since 1910) and Slovak Championships (since 1930). National championships have been held regularly since 1936–37.

Czechoslovakian hockey continued to flourish after World War II despite two tragic events. The Czechs had won the World Championships with Canada absent in 1947, and tied the Canadian team at the 1948 Olympics before settling for the silver medal, but five national team members were killed in a plane crash in November, 1948. Still, Czechoslovakia was able to beat Canada to win the World Championship in 1949. The Czechs would be denied a chance to repeat in 1950 when the entire team was arrested prior to the tournament amid accusations the players planned to defect. The Soviet Union would emerge as a world power in 1954, but Czechoslovakia would continue to rank among the best teams in Europe. After the fall of Communism, the Czech Republic succeeded Czechoslovakia in the IIHF in 1993 and won the World Championship in 1996, 1999 and 2000 as well as an Olympic gold medal in 1998.

HOCKEY TODAY: In 1999–2000, the Czech Republic Extraleague comprised 14 teams that played a quadruple round-robin, 52-game regular season. The top eight teams advance to the playoffs, where series are a best-of-five. In a promotion/relegation round, the bottom team from the Extraleague play a set of best-of-seven series against the top team from the First League. The First League also has 14 teams playing a quadruple round-robin schedule. The Second League has two divisions with 16 teams in each. The top juniors in the Czech Republic play in the Junior Extraleague, which consists of two divisions with 10 teams in each.

DENMARK

Danmarks Ishockey Union

HISTORY: The first mention of hockey (bandy) in Denmark dates back to the beginning of the 20th century when the members of KSF Copenhagen (Copenhagen Skating Club, founded in 1869) tried the new game. The growth of hockey proceeded slowly in the country and did not begin in earnest until the creation of the Dansk (now Danmarks) Ishockey Union on November 27, 1949. Prior to that date, the only ice hockey association in Denmark had been a branch of the Danish Winter Sports Federation. Through that organization, Denmark had become a member of the International Ice Hockey Federation on April 27, 1946.

The first appearance of Danish hockey players on the world stage resulted in what remains the worst defeat in international hockey at its highest level. On February 12, 1949, Denmark was defeated 47–0 by Canada at the World and European Championships in Stockholm, Sweden. Nevertheless, Denmark kept sending its national teams to the World and European tournaments and the development of hockey in the country progressed. Danish clubs began to extend invitations to coaches from North America, and in 1954–55 the first national championship was held. Since 1960, all games have been played on indoor rinks. By the 1970s, Danish teams began employing talented coaches from other European nations, particularly Czechoslovakia.

HOCKEY TODAY: In 1999–2000, the top 10 clubs in Denmark played in the Elitserien. After a quadruple round-robin schedule, the top eight teams advance to the next round, where they are put into two groups of four and play each of the other teams twice. The top two teams from these two new groups then advance to the playoffs. Semifinals and finals are five-game series, while the two losers in the semifinals play a three-game series to determine third place. Junior and midget clubs in Denmark have competed for national titles since 1962.

ESTONIA

Eesti Jaahoki Federatsiooni

HISTORY: Like so many European nations, hockey in Estonia developed out of the game of bandy (field hockey on ice) which was played in Tallinn prior to World War I. By the 1930s, there were many hockey clubs in Estonia, with most of the teams concentrated in Revel (now Tallinn) and the university town of Dorpat (now Tartu). The first national championship took place in 1934 and was won by Kalev Tallinn. Later, Kalev, the Tartu academic sport club, and Sport Tallinn dominated competition in Estonia.

The Estonian Ice Hockey Federation was founded in 1921 when Estonia was an independent country and was re-established in 1991 as a part of the Soviet Ice Hockey Federation. Estonia originally joined the International Ice Hockey Federation on February 17, 1937, but was excluded from the IIHF after World War II (on April 27, 1946). During this time, Estonia never sent its national team to the World and European Championships and restricted its play to exhibition games against other Baltic countries and Finland. Estonia was represented at the World Championships in Prague in 1938—by referee Raoul Saue. The Estonian national team played its first game on February 20, 1937, losing 2–1 to Finland in Helsinki. Estonia won the second game of the series, 2–1, but dropped the final game, 9–1. The country's last international game was a 3–0 victory over Lithuania in February, 1941. The most famous Estonian player in prewar Europe was a 6'7" giant known as Tipner, who later became well-known as a soccer goalkeeper. Another internationally known Estonian player was Juha Sevo, who played for the HC Augsburg team in Germany after World War II. After becoming part of the Soviet Union, the best Estonian club (Dynamo Tallinn) played in the top division of the Soviet league from 1946 to 1953. After 1955, Dynamo Tallinn played only for the Estonian Republic Championship.

The newly independent nation of Estonia again became a member of the IIHF on May 6, 1992, and played in the C2 Pool World Championships in 1994.

HOCKEY TODAY: The four best Estonian clubs played in the country's top league in 1999–2000 with the winner of the national title determined after a 24-game season (each club plays the others eight times). There are no playoffs.

FINLAND

Suomen Jaakiekkoliitto

HISTORY: The first attempt to introduce hockey to Finland was made by professor Leonard Borgstrom at the end of the 19th century. Training sessions were held in the early mornings in the North Harbour area (Pohjoisranta) in Helsinki and were reported by the press. "The new ice sport is called hockey," the Finnish sports newspaper *Suomen Urheilulehti* told its readers in 1899. "The players divided into two groups of skaters on ice and hit the puck with sticks trying to get it into their opponent's goal, two poles over one meter high set one and a half meters from each other. The game is very entertaining and requires strong arms and legs, as well as nerves, determination, and speed."

Interest in the new sport waned, however, and the second coming of hockey to Finland did not occur until 1927 under the instigation of the Finnish Skating Union. Skaters long had been unhappy with bandy because the huge surface that this game required resulted in competition for ice time with speed skaters. The Finnish speed skating organization had seen "Canadian" hockey in Sweden and at the Olympic Games in Antwerp in 1920 and had come to the conclusion that this game could be played without interfering with their skating competitions. As a result, hockey was added to the program of the Finnish Skating Union. The skating union published the first set of rules for hockey in Finland based on the rules of the International Ice Hockey Federation. The first club game was played in Tampere on January 15, 1928. Finland was admitted to the IIHF through the efforts of the skating union on February 10, 1928.

A year after the Finnish Skating Union had become involved with hockey, the country's soccer union added hockey to its program in 1928 and published its own set of rules based on those of the Canadian Amateur Hockey Association. The soccer union initially restricted its participation to organizing tournaments. The first national championship was held in 1928 and won by Viipurin Reipas. The soccer union also entered the international scene by inviting the Swedish champions (IK Gota of Stockholm) to play in Helsinki on January 29, 1928. The game received widespread publicity and resulted in an 8–1 victory by the Swedish team.

Recognizing the need for cooperation, representatives from both the Finnish Skating Union and the Finnish Soccer Union formed the Finnish Ice Hockey Association on January 20, 1929. The new group organized an expanded national championship and found resources to pay visiting Swedish coaches. The lack of coaches in Finland limited the work of the new hockey association to the Helsinki-Tampere-Turku area during the 1930s, but this approach made it possible to keep the teams' traveling expenses at a minimum.

Interest in hockey grew rapidly in Finland and even the national team's 0–5–0 record at its World Championship debut in 1939 was accepted as a useful step in gaining experience and knowledge of the game. However, Finland soon was seen to be losing ground to the other European countries due to its inadequate training facilities. While the best players in Europe had been practicing on artificial ice rinks, Finnish players were still totally dependent on the weather. Though Finland's first artificial rink did not open until November 22, 1955, in Tampere, the country had by that time experienced a great hockey boom because of the development of a hockey equipment manufacturing industry that had made Finland one of Europe's leading equipment exporters. The result of that had seen an unprecedented interest in hockey among Finnish youth.

Finally, by the 1960s, the Finnish national team arrived as a real force at the international level. The Finns won their first medal (a silver) at the European Championships in 1962, but their greatest successes came at the junior level, winning a silver medal at the World Junior Championships in 1974 and gold in 1978. In 1988, the Finnish national team earned a silver medal at the Olympics and in 1992 they finished in second place behind Sweden at the World Championships. In 1995, Finland beat Sweden to win its first World Championship. The Finns have added bronze medals at the Olympics in 1994 and 1998.

HOCKEY TODAY: The top league in Finland, the SM-Liiga, was founded in 1975. There were 12 teams playing a 54-game schedule in this league in 1999–2000. The eight top teams advance to the playoffs, which are played in a best-of-five format (plus a one-game series to decide third place among the two losers in the semifinals).

Finland's Division 1 comprises 12 teams who play a quadruple round-robin regular season. Six teams advance to the playoffs with the three winners from these best-of-five series moving on to play with the worst team from SM-Liiga in the semifinals and finals.

Division 2 is made up of seven different groups containing between eight and 10 teams. Each group plays a double round robin with the best team in each group qualifying for a promotional pool. Winners from this pool are advanced to Division 1 for the next season. Finland also has regional divisions 3, 4, 5 and 6.

Junior hockey is very well-organized in Finland, with the country's top junior players (aged 18–21) playing in three leagues: SM-Liiga, Division 1 and Division 2. Players under 17 play in Junior B competitions with their own SM-Liiga and Division 1. Junior C players (under 16) also have their own SM-Liiga and Division 1.

FRANCE

Federation Francaise des Sports de Glace
Comite National de Hockey sur Glace

HISTORY: France is one of a few European countries which has been playing hockey since the end of the 19th century. The game was introduced in France by Canadian George Meagher, who brought a rule book and coaching instructions to Paris in 1894. Meagher began running practices to teach the elements of hockey to the French, but the first official game did not take place until 1903 when a team from Paris beat a Lyon team, 2–1. It was also in 1903 that Europe's first official hockey club, the Patineurs de Paris, was formed. They played their first international game against a team from London.

France held its first national hockey championship in 1904, making it the second country in Europe (behind Great Britain) to stage one. Patineurs de Paris were France's first champions. The French national team played its first game against Belgium in 1906. In 1907, an ice hockey association was founded as part of the French Federation of Ice Sports. One year later, France, England, Belgium and Switzerland founded the *Ligue Internationale de Hockey sur Glace*, forerunner of the International Ice Hockey Federation. On October 20, 1908, France became the first member of the new organization and Frenchman Louis Magnus became its first president. The first international tournament took place in 1908 in Chamonix, France, with teams from Paris, London, Lausanne, Brussels and Prague taking part. Paris finished second behind London. The French national team competed at the first World Championships, held in conjunction with the Antwerp Olympics in 1920, losing its first game, 4–0, to Sweden on April 25. Still, France would rank among the top countries in Europe during the 1920s and 1930s, winning a silver medal at the European Championships in 1923 and a gold medal the following year.

HOCKEY TODAY: In 1999–2000, the 10 teams of the Ligue Nationale play an initial double round-robin schedule before playing another similar schedule with bonus points included. The top eight team advance to the playoffs. Quarterfinals use a best-of-seven format, while the semifinals and finals are played under a best-of-five format. The teams that lose in the semifinals play a best-of-five series to decide third place. The champions of France receive the Magnus Cup, though the best teams also compete for the French Cup.

French hockey also has a Nationale 1 League, with eight teams in the East and eight in the West playing a double round-robin schedule. Nationale 2 League has three six-team divisions: South, Northeast and Northwest. There is a Division 3 league.

Junior and midget teams in France began competing for the French national title in their age categories during the 1950s. Later, four other age groups began playing for national titles.

GERMANY

Deutscher Eishockey Bund E.V.

HISTORY: The beginning of ice sports in Germany date back to 1888 when the German National Skating Union was founded in Berlin. Among its other duties, the union was in charge of the country's bandy players. The first game of hockey took place on Lake Halensee in Berlin on February 4, 1897. By 1901, the first hockey team had been created with players practicing at a rink on the grounds of the Berlin Zoo. Germany's first indoor arena opened in Berlin in 1909, and by 1910 hockey had become so popular that Berlin held its first city championship. Ten teams took part, with the tournament being won by the Berliner Schlittschuh-Club. The Berliner SC had helped to christen Germany's first indoor arena the year before in an international tournament with teams from London and Paris. In 1912, Berliner SC would win Germany's first national championship.

On September 19, 1909, Germany had become the sixth nation in the world, after Belgium, Bohemia, England, Switzerland and France, to join the *Ligue Internationale de Hockey sur Glace* (forerunner of the International Ice Hockey Federation). In 1910, the Germans won the silver medal at the first official European Championships. German hockey players quickly became among the best in Europe and never failed to win a medal at the European Championships through 1914. So popular was hockey in Germany at this time that the European tournament was held in Berlin in both 1911 and 1914 and in Munich in 1913. After World War I, Germany was excluded from the IIHF from 1920 until January 11, 1926. However, even during this period of time, German teams continued to play internationally at the Spengler Cup. Berliner SC won that tournament in 1924, and again in 1926 and 1928.

The success of Berliner SC on the international scene was not a surprise to the European hockey community. The team was coached by two Canadians—Dr. Blake Watson and Dr. Roche—who also coached the German national team to great success. Stocked mainly with players from the roster of Berliner SC, the German national team finished third, earning a bronze medal in its return to the European Championships in 1927. Before the outbreak of World War II, the German national team would win two European Championships, while earning three silver medals and seven bronze medals. Germany also won a silver medal at the 1930 World Championships, a bronze medal at the 1932 Olympics and a bronze medal at the World Championships in 1934.

After World War II, Germany was excluded from the IIHF again but reinstated as the Federal Republic of Germany (West Germany) on March 10, 1951. During its absence from the world scene, the Germans created the Oberliga in 1947–48 as the top league in the country. Eleven years later, the Oberliga was replaced by the Bundesliga. Other steps toward strengthening ice hockey in Germany were made on June 16, 1963, when the Germany Hockey Union was founded. It consisted of 32 teams in eight provincial associations. Dr. Gunther Sabetzki of Dusseldorf was elected as one of the first two presidents of the union. He would serve as president of the IIHF from 1975 to 1994.

German hockey authorities always have attempted to boost the popularity of the game in their country by inviting foreign players. Traditionally, German club teams usually carried two or three foreign players per team, but those numbers have increased greatly since the creation of the Deutsche Eishockey League—Germany's first professional league—in 1994.

HOCKEY TODAY: In 1999–2000, the Deutsche Eishockey League was made up of 15 teams. A quadruple round-robin schedule is played with the top eight teams advancing to playoffs. Meanwhile, the teams finishing ninth to 15th play a double round robin with points added to their first-stage total. All playoff series prior to the finals are a best-of-five. Finals are a best-of-seven format. The two last teams face the two best teams from 1.Liga in a best-of-three playoff with the winners of this series promoted to the DEL the following season.

The lower divisions in Germany hockey are 1.Liga and 2.Liga, both with groups in the north and south. There are also seven regional leagues. The junior Bundesliga is also divided into North and South divisions. There are national competitions among junior and boys teams of different age groups.

GREAT BRITAIN

British Ice Hockey Association

HISTORY: The roots of British ice hockey go far back into history. In about 1600, skates equipped with metal blades were introduced to Britain from Holland and in 1642 the Edinburgh Skating Club (believed to be Britain's oldest skating organization) was formed. Skating became a very popular sport in Great Britain under the reign of Charles II and the *Art of Skating* by Robert Jones was published in 1772. Many sketches and paintings during the 18th and 19th centuries depict people skating on frozen lakes and rivers, often using sticks and a ball or some other object. In 1876, the world's first artificial ice rinks were opened in London.

The first official ice hockey game played outside of Canada is said to have been Cambridge University versus Oxford University at St. Moritz, Switzerland, in 1885. Oxford won, 6–0. What was played in that match, however, was probably not ice hockey as the game is known today. A very important part in popularizing hockey in Britain belongs to the Stanley brothers. The Honorable Arthur Stanley, son of Lord Stanley of Preston (then Governor-General of Canada) formed the Rideau Rebels hockey club in Ottawa in 1888. Five year later, in 1893, he and his hockey-playing brothers helped to persuade their father to present the Stanley Cup. In the same year, A.C.A.Wade, one of Britain's first hockey writers, recalled playing the game at Gravenhurst in Bedfordshire.

After their return to England, the Stanley brothers continued their efforts to popularize ice hockey in Great Britain. During the hard winter of 1895, the lake of Buckingham Palace was frozen over and a palace team which included the Prince of Wales (later King Edward VII), the Duke of York (the future King George V), Lord Mildmay, Sir Francis Astley-Corbett, Sir William Bromley Davenport and Mr. Ronald Moncrieff played the Stanley team led by Arthur Stanley and four of his brothers. The Palace team was beaten easily by the experienced Stanley squad. However, it remains unclear as to whether or not the game played was truly ice hockey—both sides were using bandy sticks. The Stanley family continued its missionary work and in 1896–97 Arthur Stanley and five of his brothers played the Niagara Hall ice rink team and defeated them easily. Two Stanley brothers, A.F. and F.W., also played for an Old Wellingtonians team which lost to Niagara, 2–0, on January 1, 1899.

Despite the importance of the Stanley family in the history of British ice hockey, the "Founding Father" of the sport in the United Kingdom is considered to be Major B.M. "Peter" Patton. It was he who approached Admiral Maxe, founder of the Princes' Skating Club in London, and asked for permission to form a hockey team at the rink. Permission was granted and the first game took place in February, 1897. Patton was 21 at the time and did not retire from the game until 1931, when he was 55. Over the years, the team he formed often represented England abroad. The Princes played and won an international bandy tournament in Davos, Switzerland, in 1904 and also beat France in Lyon that same year. In 1908, the Princes gave England victory in the first indoor international ice hockey tournament when they defeated Germany and France in Berlin. The first official European Championship was held in Switzerland in 1910 and Peter Patton was on hand to captain England to victory. In 1913, he founded the British Ice Hockey Association (BIHA). He revived it in 1923 after it had been disbanded during the First World War.

The first English Ice Hockey League was formed in 1903–04 with five teams participating: the Princes club, the London Canadians, Cambridge University and two teams from Henglers Circus Ice Rink (also known as the National Ice Palace)—Argyll and the Amateur Skating Club. The London Canadians won the first championship.

In 1908, England joined France, Belgium and Switzerland in the founding of the *Ligue Internationale de Hockey sur Glace*, forerunner of the International Ice Hockey Federation. That same year, the first hockey games played in Scotland took place in Glasgow. The Scottish Ice Hockey Association was formed in 1929. Britain remained a European hockey power until World War II, culminating in Olympic, World and European championships at Garmisch-Partenkirchen, Germany, in 1936.

HOCKEY TODAY: The British League folded at the end of the 1995–96 season and the leading 23 teams split into three leagues running independently of each other and the governing BIHA. League membership depended heavily upon how many overseas players a club was willing to sign as well as a club's geographical location. Beginning in 1997–98, the eight-team Superleague comprised most of the clubs who were formerly members of the Premier Division in the British League. The winner of the Superleague is considered to be the national champion. The eight teams play a 42-game schedule after which all of them advance to the playoffs. The teams finishing first, fourth, sixth and eighth are then placed in Group A, with the four other teams in Group B. After a double round robin within each group, the two best teams from each group advance to the semifinals. Both the semifinals and finals consist of a single game.

The eight teams playing in Britain's Premier League and the seven clubs in the Northern Premier League are mainly members of the old Division 1. In the Premier League, the eight teams play each other eight times (for a 56-game schedule per team) with the top six qualifying for the playoffs. Those teams then play a double round-robin series with the top two teams competing in a two-game, total-goals finals. The winner then meets the Northern Premier League playoff champion in the Premier Leagues Championship finals.

The seven teams of the Northern Premier League play each other six times for a 36-game schedule. Afterwards, all seven teams are split into two groups for a double round-robin playoff round. The top two teams from each group then advance to play in a final four-team, double round robin with the top team emerging as the Northern Premier League champion and qualifying to play against the Premier League champion.

Superleague teams are permitted to employ overseas players without any restrictions. Premier League clubs have an agreement to allow three per team. The Northern Premier League has the toughest eligibility rules, allowing only three players who require an International Transfer Card (ITC) regardless of passport. In addition, the Northern Premier League imposes a salary cap of £75,000 compared to £250,000 in the Premier League. The Superleague has no salary cap. The Superleague and the Premier League have formed companies to operate and administer their organizations—Ice Hockey Superleague Ltd. and the Premier Ice Hockey League Ltd.

The 20-team English League (with 12 teams in the Southern Conference and eight in the Northern) is run by the English Ice Hockey Association for teams with smaller budgets. These teams rely mostly on players born and trained in Britain. The junior English Under-19 League has nine teams in its North Conference and seven teams in the South.

GREECE

Elliniki Omospondia Pagodromion

HISTORY: Ice hockey in Greece was introduced in Thessaloniki by Czechoslovakian emigrants in the early 1980s. Romanians and Canadians built ice rinks in Greece, but most of them were not of standard hockey size. A regulation-sized facility did exist at the sports stadium at Neo Faliro but it was used generally for basketball. Ice was only available for about two or three weeks in November.

Despite the difficulties, Greece joined the International Ice Hockey Federation in April, 1987. By then, Greece had four different hockey clubs. The Flying Ice Skaters in Athens had a senior and junior team as well as a beginners club with 32 children between the age of six and 10. Albatros Athens had a senior team. The Chalkis Ice Hockey Club (based about 50 miles outside of Athens) had a senior and a junior team, as did Aris Thessaloniki. The first Greek national hockey championship took place in 1988–89 and was won by Aris Thessaloniki. There has been no national championship in Greece since 1992.

In 1989, Greece's ice hockey association became a section of the Hellenic Ice Sports Federation. Three years later, the Greek national team made its first international appearance at the C2 Pool of the World Championships. Greece was a winner in its national team debut, defeating Turkey, 15–3, on March 21, 1992, in Johannesburg, South Africa.

HOCKEY TODAY: Greek teams played in the C and D Pools of the World Championships and the World Junior Championships on several occasions throughout the 1990s.

HONG KONG

Hong Kong Ice Hockey Association

HISTORY: The Hong Kong Ice Hockey Association was founded on August 8, 1980. Hong Kong joined the International Ice Hockey Federation on March 31, 1983, and made its debut on the world stage at the D Pool World Championships in Perth, Australia, in 1987. Hong Kong tied Taiwan, 2–2, in its first international game on March 13, 1987 and went on to win the Fair Play Cup at the world tournament.

Although there was plenty of hockey activity in Hong Kong, local teams (usually stocked with Canadian and American players) did not compete for a national championship until 1995–96. The first title was won by a team sponsored by Planet Hollywood.

HOCKEY TODAY: In 1999–2000, six teams played in the Hong Kong league. A triple round-robin schedule sees each team play 18 games. After that, the top four teams meet in a one-game playoff semifinals and final for the national title.

HUNGARY

Magyar Jegkorong Szovetseg

HISTORY: The roots of hockey in Hungary begin with the sport of bandy (field hockey on ice). The country's first bandy team was formed in 1905 and the first public bandy game was held in Budapest two years later. In 1914, the BKE Budapest team, representing the Budapest Skating Union, won international bandy competitions in St. Moritz and Prague and was thus considered to be the best bandy team in Europe. The appeal of bandy was stopped, however, by the introduction of a new game—"Canadian" ice hockey. Hockey was introduced to Hungary by Englishman John Dunlop in 1925 and the first real hockey game in Hungary was staged on December 26 of that year between BKE and a team from Vienna. Vienna won the game, 1–0.

The Hungarian Winter Sports Federation had been founded in 1908 and ice hockey was given a division within the federation. (Today, hockey in Hungary is represented by the Hungarian Ice Hockey Federation). Hungary joined the International Ice Hockey Federation on January 24, 1927, and that same day the Hungarian national team played its first game, losing 6–0 to Austria.

Hungary had gotten its first artificial ice rink (an outdoor facility) in Budapest in 1926, but the Hungarians still had a lot to learn about hockey. At the European Championships in Vienna in 1927, Hungary's national team finished last.

Two years later, Hungary hosted the tournament during the bitterly cold winter of 1929 and by the 1930s the Hungarians had become one of the top teams in Europe. In 1934, a touring Canadian team could only manage a scoreless tie against the Hungarian national team at an exhibition match in Budapest. In 1937, Hungary held its first national championship (won by the BKE Budapest hockey club) and at the IIHF World Championships in Prague in 1938, the Hungarians managed a 1–1 tie against the gold medal-winning Canadian team. The big hero of the Hungarian team was goaltender Istvan Hircsak, who was considered one of the best in Europe at the time.

World War II stopped the development of hockey in Hungary for nearly 10 years, but interest in the game rose again by the late 1940s. In later years, training methods were significantly improved by Czechoslovakian coach Vladimir Kominek, who led the Hungarian national team between 1959 and 1964.

HOCKEY TODAY: In 1999–2000, the top four clubs in Hungary played each other 10 times for a 30-game schedule. The national championship is determined after a best-of-seven playoff between the top two teams in the league. The remaining two treams played a best-of-three series for the third place. The top four teams compete for the Hungarian Medicor Cup, playing one-game semifinals and finals. Some games in the league are played on outdoor rinks. Ten clubs play in Hungary's second division. Junior teams have been competing for a national title since 1954, midget teams since 1961.

ICELAND

Icelandic Skating Association

HISTORY: Hockey was first played in Iceland in 1937. The first national championship was held in 1968–69 and won by Skautefelag Akureyri. However, after two years of national competition, the development of hockey in Iceland slowed down. The Icelandic national championship was revived in 1978–79 but it did not take place every year. Skautefelag Akureyri is still the country's best hockey team.

The Icelandic Skating Association, as a part of the of Ithrottasambaud Islands (Sports Union of Iceland), was created in 1987 and included an Ice Hockey Division. Iceland joined the International Ice Hockey Federation on May 6, 1992, and made its debut on the world stage in 1997 when the Icelandic national junior team (under-18) played at the D Pool of the European Junior Championships. In 1998, Iceland had a junior team (under 20) at the D Pool of the World Junior Championships.

HOCKEY TODAY: In 1999–2000, Iceland had 360 registered players (including 130 senior players) and two outdoor hockey arenas. Three teams compete in the national league, playing a double round-robin schedule. The top two teams then meet in a best-of-five finals for the Icelandic national title.

INDIA

Winter Games Federation of India

HISTORY: The Winter Games Federation of India was founded in 1979 and became a member of the International Ice Hockey Federation in 1989. The first two clubs to play hockey in India were Bombay IHC and Madras IHC, though the majority of hockey in the country has been played by two other clubs: the Shimla Ice Skating Club in the Himalayan Mountains and the Ladakh Ice Skating Club in Leh near the Tibet border. The distance between these two hockey cities is about 1,000 miles and the teams travel by plane to play one another. However, because Leh in located in a valley in the Himalayan Mountains, heavy clouds often make air travel difficult. The teams only travel when clear skies permit, so they often will continue to play games against one another until improved weather conditions allow a return flight.

HOCKEY TODAY: There are about 100 hockey players in India. Many more are interested in playing but the lack of facilities has slowed hockey's development. Currently, there are no national competitions.

IRELAND

Irish Ice Hockey Association

HISTORY: Ice hockey in Ireland did not gain popularity until the 1980s when the game's supporters began to form new teams. Much of the activity took place in Dublin. The first official game took place on April 21, 1982, between the Dublin Stags and the Liverpool Leopards of England. Dublin won, 11–7.

HOCKEY TODAY: There is no national championship in Ireland yet and the country has not been active on the international scene.

ISRAEL

Ice Hockey Federation of Israel

HISTORY: The first ice skating rink in Israel opened in January, 1986. It is located in Kiryat Motzkin, a suburb of Haifa in northern Israel. Hockey practices began in April, 1986, with former Canadian players as instructors. Shortly after formal instruction began, "shinny" hockey started and attracted many players who formerly lived in Canada, the United States, the Soviet Union and other traditional hockey countries.

In May, 1988, a new and larger skating rink opened in the city of Bat Yam near Tel Aviv. That same year, the Israel Ice Hockey and Figure Skating Association was founded. One of the first hockey games played in Israel was an exhibition game in July, 1988, between teams representing the rinks in Kiryat Motzkin and Bat Yam. Bat Yam won the game, 8–5, before 200 spectators. Marcus Silverberg scored a hat trick and was the hero of the game.

Israel's national team played its first game in 1989–90 against a team made up of Canadian UN peacekeepers posted in the Golan Heights. Although the Israeli team featured several immigrant Jewish players from North America and the USSR, it was a native Israeli (18-year-old Gal Assa of Bat Yam) who scored the country's first goal. The first Israeli championship was played in the summer of 1990 with HC Haifa defeating Jerusalem in the playoffs. Because most of the rinks in Israel were too small for a normal hockey game, teams played with only four skaters per side.

Israel joined the International Ice Hockey Federation on May 2, 1991. Israel's national team made its debut at the World Championships in the C2 Pool in 1992, losing its first game versus Spain by a score of 23–4 in Johannesburg, South Africa, on March 22. Israeli hockey has received a major boost in recent years with the opening of an almost Olympic-sized skating rink at the Canada Centre in Metulla in 1995. Israel won the D Pool in 2000.

HOCKEY TODAY: In 1999–2000, the four best Israeli clubs played a double round-robin as the first stage of the national championship. Next, the teams play two playoffs rounds. The semifinals consist of one game only, while the finals are a best-of-three series.

ITALY

Federazione Italiana Sport del Ghiaccio

HISTORY: The first attempts to introduce ice hockey to Italy were made in Torino in 1911 when a skating club called Circolo Pattinatori Valentino organized Italy's first hockey team. After playing a series of scrimmage games, Circolo Pattinatori Valentino played its first official game later in the year against a team from Lyon, France. Soon, hockey was gaining popularity in Italy—particularly in the north where winter mountain resorts had lots of natural ice.

The first hockey teams started to appear in Italy during the early 1920s and the country's first indoor ice rink opened in Milan on December 28, 1923. The Hockey Club Milano (which had played roller hockey) soon was playing ice hockey in the new arena. Italy's first hockey association was created in 1924 and later was admitted into the International Ice Hockey Federation. In 1925, the Italian Federation of Winter Sports was founded. The hockey association became a part of the Federation in 1926.

Italy had staged its first national hockey championship in 1924–25 but it was not until 1935 that the first national league was formed. It was made up of seven teams. From the very beginning, Italian clubs have relied heavily on Canadians of Italian descent and the eligibility of these Canadians to play for the national team helped to make it strong. By the 1970s, Italian-Canadian players helped to boost hockey in the northern part of the country, producing such strong club teams as Val Gardena, Bolzano, Brunico and Merano.

HOCKEY TODAY: In 1999–2000, the Serie A league (Italy's top league) comprised nine teams. The teams play a double round-robin schedule in the first stage. Eight teams then advance to the playoffs. All series are best-of-five. In addition to the Serie A league, a few of Italy's top teams also compete in the International Ice Hockey League (formerly known as the Alpenliga).

The next level of hockey in Italy below Serie A is Serie B1 and B2. Serie B1 has 10 teams playing a quadruple round-robin with the top eight teams advancing to the playoffs. Best-of-three series are played in the quarterfinals, with the semifinals and finals both being best-of-five. Serie B2 is divided into two groups—Group A (eight teams) and Group B (nine teams). The Serie C league has four teams.

Italian juniors (under 20) have been playing for a national championship since 1962. In 1997–98, seven teams battled for Italy's national junior title. There are also national competitions for those under 18 (11 teams), under 16 (16 teams in two groups), under 14 (eight teams), under 12 and under 10-years-old.

JAPAN

Japan Ice Hockey Federation

HISTORY: Ice hockey was brought to Japan by the English at the beginning of the 20th century. The new game quickly became popular (particularly in the northern regions of the country) and in 1929 teams located in from Tokyo, Waseda and Tomakomai founded the Japan Ice Hockey Federation.

The Japan Ice Hockey Federation became a member of the International Ice Hockey Federation on January 26, 1930. That same year, the IIHF made a decision to hold its World Hockey Championships in conjunction with the European Championships if a team was present from either Canada, the United States or Japan. The Japanese national team played its first international game at the World Championships in Davos, Switzerland, in 1930, losing to England, 3–0. Japan's national team continued to participate in major tournaments. At the 1936 Winter Olympics in Garmisch-Partenkirchen, Germany, Japanese goaltender Teiji Honma surprised everyone by wearing a mask. After World War II, Japan was barred from the IIHF on April 27, 1946. The Japan Ice Hockey Federation was not reinstated until March 10, 1951.

Traditionally, Japanese teams had quite a few foreign players on their rosters, especially from Canada and Russia. In 1984, the Japan Ice Hockey Federation banned the use of foreign players (though foreigners could continue to coach). This ruling was overturned during the 1990s and foreign players have returned.

HOCKEY TODAY: In 1999–2000, Japan's national league comprised six teams. Each team plays the others eight times for a 40-game schedule, after which the top four clubs qualify for the playoffs. Semifinals and finals are played in a best-of-five format. Japan's national champion receives the National Cup. The country's second division is made up of regional leagues.

KAZAKHSTAN

Federatsiya Hokkeya Kazakhstana

HISTORY: Hockey in Kazakhstan dates back to the 1950s when the first teams were created in what was then known as the Soviet Republic of Kazakhstan. Torpedo Ust-Kamenogorsk became Kazakhstan's best team and in 1987–88 it made its debut in the top Soviet league after playing in lower divisions for many years.

The Kazakhstan Ice Hockey Federation was created as part of the Soviet Ice Hockey Federation in 1991. It became a separate organization when Kazakhstan gained its independence in 1992, uniting the region's four teams—Torpedo Ust-Kamenogorsk, ShVSM Ust-Kamenogorsk, Bulat Temirtau and Avtomobilist Karaganda (later Bulat Karaganda). The Kazakhstan national team made its debut at the St. Petersburg Grand Prix tournament on April 14, 1992, and beat the Ukrainian national team, 5–1. On May 6, 1992, Kazakhstan became a member of the International Ice Hockey Federation and in 1993 the national team made its World Championship debut in the C Pool. Torpedo Ust-Kamenogorsk became the first Kazakh champion in 1993, though all four Kazakhstan teams continued to compete among the Russian teams after the breakup of the Soviet Union. Until 1996, Torpedo Ust-Kamenogorsk and Bulat Karaganda played in the Inter-State Hockey League.

The best hockey player developed in Kazakhstan to date is Boris Alexandrov, who played for the Moscow Central Red Army and the Soviet national team in the late 1970s. Alexandrov won an Olympic gold medal with the Soviet team in 1976. Kazakh native Yevgeny Poladjev played for Spartak and the Soviet national team in the late 1960s and early 1970s. Andrei Raisky of Kazakhstan was signed by the Winnipeg Jets in 1992 and played in the club's farm system. Konstantin Shafranov made his NHL debut with the St. Louis Blues in 1996–97. The Toronto Maple Leafs selected Nikolai Antropov 10th overall in the 1998 NHL Entry Draft and he enterd the league in 1999–2000.

HOCKEY TODAY: In 1999–2000, five teams from Kazakhstan battled for the national title. The champion was determined after a double round-robin schedule and a one-game playoff final. There is also a third-place game. In addition to the five-team competition, Kazakhstan's best team, Torpedo Ust-Kamenogorsk, also played in the third division of the Russian league.

LATVIA

Latvijas Hokeja Federacija

HISTORY: Like most other European countries, hockey in Latvia developed from the traditional game of bandy (field hockey on ice). Bandy championships were taking place in Riga prior to World War I and the city later became the center of hockey in Latvia. Three Riga-based teams—the German Club Union, the university sport club US (Universitates Sports) and the army sports club ASK—were among the best-known teams in Europe by the 1930s. Latvia held its first championship in 1931–32, with nine teams taking part. The national championship of the Republic of Latvia (as a part of the Soviet Union) began in 1946 and was held every year until the breakup of the USSR.

The Latvian Ice Hockey Federation was founded on January 5, 1923, and became a member of the International Ice Hockey Federation on February 22, 1931. The Latvian national team played its first international game on February 27, 1932, and beat Lithuania, 3–0. Its first international tournament was the 1932 European Championships in Berlin. Prior to World War II, Latvia took part in five World Championships, including the 1936 Olympic Games in Garmisch-Partenkirchen, Germany. The most successful Latvian player of this time period was Leonid Vedejs, who played in 34 out of 36 international games for Latvia between 1932 and 1940. Latvia's final international match was a 2–1 victory over Estonia in Riga on March 10, 1940. On April 27, 1946, Latvia was ejected from the IIHF after becoming a part of the Soviet Union.

Following its incorporation into the Soviet Union after World War II, the best Latvian teams began to play for the USSR championship and Latvian players often acted as coaches for other Soviet players. The most successful Latvian team was Dynamo Riga, which produced the legendary Soviet national team coach Viktor Tikhonov. (Tikhonov worked for Dynamo Riga from 1971 to 1977.) The three most outstanding Latvian players are Helmut Balderis, who starred for the Soviet national team from 1976 to 1983, and current NHLers Arturs Irbe and Sandis Ozolinsh.

After regaining its independence following the breakup of the Soviet Union, Latvia again held a national championship in 1991–92. On May 6, 1992, Latvia rejoined the International Ice Hockey Federation.

HOCKEY TODAY: In 1999–2000, seven clubs played in the top Latvian league. Teams play a double round robin in the league's first stage, with the top four teams then advancing to play in quadruple round robin to determine a champion. The teams that finish fifth through seventh in stage one play a consolation quadruple round-robin. Latvian teams also play in the East European Hockey League with teams from the Ukraine, Belarus, Lithuania and Poland.

LITHUANIA

Lietuvos Ledo Ritulio Federacija

HISTORY: Hockey in Lithuania was developed from the traditional game of bandy, as it was in most other European countries. The first ice hockey activity in Lithuania took place in the 1920s. Teams were formed in the cities of Kaunas and Memel (now Klaipeda) and the first national championship was held in 1926. LFLS Kaunas won Lithuania's first title. The Lithuanian Ice Hockey Federation was founded on October 14, 1932, and Lithuania joined the International Ice Hockey Federation in 1932. It was expelled on April 26, 1946, after becoming a part of the Soviet Union following World War II. The newly independent Lithuania had its hockey federation reinstated in 1991 and rejoined the IIHF on May 6, 1992.

The Lithuanian national team played its first international game on February 27, 1932, when it was beaten, 3–0, by Latvia. Lithuania made its debut at the World Championships in Prague in 1938 and beat Romania, 1–0, for its only victory in its first game of the tournament. Lithuania played its last international game in Kaunus in 1941 and suffered a 3–0 loss to Estonia. After the country became a part of the Soviet Union, Spartak Kaunus (later Zalgiris Kaunas) played in either the first or second division of the Soviet league. After 1955, the team played only in the Lithuanian Republican Championship.

Lithuania finally returned to the world stage in 1995, playing in the C2 Pool of the IIHF World Championships. Two Lithuanians—Darius Kasparaitis and Dainius Zubrus—are currently playing in the NHL.

HOCKEY TODAY: In 1999–2000, the best Lithuanian team (Energija Elektrenai) played in the East European Hockey League along with teams representing the Ukraine, Belarus and Latvia. Four other Lithuanian teams play in the country's top division. Each team plays the other three six times for an 18-game schedule. The teams that finish second and third play a two-game, total-goals series to determine the league's third-best team. The first-place team plays a two-game, total-goals series against Energija Elektrenai to determine the Lithuanian national champion.

LUXEMBOURG

Federation Luxembourgeoise de Hockey sur Glace

HISTORY: Luxembourg's Ice Hockey Federation is one of the oldest in Europe, having been formed in 1912. Luxembourg joined the International Ice Hockey Federation on March 23, 1912, but the popularity of hockey in the country grew slowly. Luxembourg did not hold its first national championship until 1978. Only two hockey teams existed in the country at that time and Hiversport Luxembourg defeated Beaufort Echternach for the championship. In 1984, financial difficulties forced the two teams to merge into one new club called HC Luxembourg. For two years, HC Luxembourg played exhibition games against teams from West Germany, France, the Netherlands, Belgium, Switzerland and Canada and also participated in the European Champions Cup. All home games for HC Luxembourg took place at either the indoor arena of Luxembourg-Stadt or the outdoor rink in Echternach. In 1986–87, HC Luxembourg changed its name to Tornado and played in the Rheinland-Pfalz regional league in West Germany.

The Luxembourg national team made its debut on the international scene at the C2 Pool of the World Championships in 1992. The team lost its first game to the Republic of South Africa by a lopsided score of 23–0 on March 21, 1992, in Johannesburg. In 1998, Luxembourg iced a national junior team (under 18) in the D Pool of the European Junior Championships.

HOCKEY TODAY: In 1999–2000, the national champion of Luxembourg was determined in a playoff for the Luxembourg Cup. Four teams from Luxembourg, as well as teams from Germany, Belgium and France, take part in the tournament. Seven teams in total play a double round robin. The top Luxembourg team is declared the national champion.

MEXICO

Federacion Mexicana de Deportes Invernales A.C.

HISTORY: The earliest mention of ice hockey in Mexico dates back to 1964; however, the Mexican Federation of Winter Sports was not founded until 1984. Mexico joined the International Ice Hockey Federation in 1985. At the time, Mexico boasted two indoor rinks (one in Mexico City and one in Guadalajara) and six hockey teams. The first national championship was held in 1988–89 and was won by the Association del Estado de Mexico.

HOCKEY TODAY: Currently, there is no Mexican championship. Mexico competed internationally for the first time in 1997 when a national junior team (under 20) competed in the D Pool of the World Junior Championships.

NETHERLANDS

Nederlandse Ijshockey Bond

HISTORY: The history of ice hockey in the Netherlands can be traced back to the 16th century, as artists from that period have depicted people playing "hockey" on frozen ponds with sticks and a ball. These pictures are the oldest in Europe showing people playing with sticks and, as such, it is safe to say that bandy, as an early form of hockey, likely developed in the Netherlands. Despite this early start, hockey was not introduced in the Netherlands until the early 1930s. The country's first artificial ice rink was build in the Hague in 1937, though the first indoor arena did not appear until 1961 in Amsterdam.

The Dutch Ice Hockey Union was founded on September 6, 1934, and the Netherlands joined the International Ice Hockey Federation on January 20, 1935. The best teams in the country began competing for a national championship in 1937, but no championship was held from 1950 to 1963 because of a lack of teams. The 1960s saw Dutch clubs begin to invite players and coaches from Canada and the United States, with personnel from other European countries added later. All Dutch hockey clubs are sponsored by different companies, with the names of those companies included in the name of the team.

The Dutch national team made its debut on the international scene with a 4–0 loss to Belgium in Amsterdam on January 5, 1935. Two weeks later, the Netherlands made its first appearance at the World and European Championships in Davos, Switzerland. The Netherlands lost their first game, 6–0, to Hungary on January 19, but went on to win the Fair Play Cup at the 1935 tournament. After playing in the lower levels of international hockey following the introduction of the pool system, the Dutch team made its A Pool debut in 1981.

HOCKEY TODAY: In 1999–2000, the top division in the Netherlands was the six-team Eredivisie. After a quadruple round-robin schedule, the top four teams play a double round-robin series to determine the standings for the playoffs. Semifinals and finals are played in a best-of-seven format. Meanwhile, the teams ranked fifth and sixth join with the top two teams from Division 1 to play their own new double round robin and playoff games to determine places from fifth to eighth. After the national championship, the top two clubs play one game for the Netherlands Cup. The next levels of hockey in the country are Division 1 (six teams) and Division 2 (eight teams). National junior competitions began in 1968.

NEW ZEALAND

New Zealand Ice Hockey Federation

HISTORY: Ice hockey has been played in New Zealand for over 60 years. Many of the early games were played on the frozen ponds in the South Canterbury mountains and teams were made up of local farm workers who had regular access to the ice. The first organized hockey tournament in New Zealand was held at Opawa, near Albury, in 1937. Teams competed for the Erewhon Cup, which had been presented by Wyndham Barker to the Mt. Harper club before being turned over to the newly formed New Zealand Ice Skating Association in 1937. This new association was formed at a meeting following the inaugural tournament in Opawa and though it was established for the organization of hockey, it soon became more concerned with speed skating and figure skating. Despite this fact, hockey continued to be played in an organized fashion in New Zealand except during the war years of 1939 to 1945 and from 1978 to 1982 when poor winters caused a lack of ice. In the early days of hockey in New Zealand, teams from Mt. Harper, Windwhistle, Tekapo, Irishman Creek, Fairlie, Opawa, Mt. Hull and Canterbury were regular competitors.

In 1954, the New Zealand Ice Skating Association formed an Ice Hockey Committee to administer the game. Vic Hahn was appointed chairman and the Erewhon Cup series was divided into three sections (Otago, South Canterbury and Canterbury) to cut down on travel. It was decided later that all Erewhon Cup competitions would be played on outdoor rinks. In 1957, a new competition confined to South Canterbury provided additional interest in the game. The McKerrow Memorial Cup had been donated in the memory of Graham McKerrow, a prominent New Zealand hockey player who drowned in Saltwater Creek at Timaru after going through the ice during hockey practice.

Another notable year in New Zealand hockey history is 1963, when a team from the Hakoah Club in Melbourne, Australia, made the first international visit to New Zealand by a hockey team, for a series of games at Christchurch and Tekapo. The Australian visit also marked the first time a hockey game was televised in New Zealand when Hakoah played the Hawks of Christchurch and beat them, 8–6.

New Zealand became a member of the International Ice Hockey Federation on May 2, 1977. On September 14, 1986, all 19 ice hockey associations and clubs of New Zealand met at Tekapo in order to form a new federation to help develop and coordinate the game throughout the country. Thus, the New Zealand Ice Hockey Federation was created. The inaugural national club championship games for the Norm Hawker Shield were held at the Big Apple rink in Christchurch over the weekend of June 19–21, 1987. Ten teams entered the competition with the Manuwai Warriors of Auckland winning the title. That same year, a national competition for Provincial Select teams was held and won by Canterbury. Also in 1987, the New Zealand national team made its debut in the D Pool of the World Championships. The first official game took place in Perth, Australia, on March 13, 1987, and resulted in a 35–2 loss to South Korea.

HOCKEY TODAY: New Zealand has several ice hockey associations which hold their own regional championships: Canterbury, Southern Districts, Queen City, Auckland, Albury, Oturehua, Alexandra, Queenstown, Gore and Ranfurly.

NORWAY

Norges Ishockeyforbund

HISTORY: The roots of hockey in Norway go back to the late 1920s when the game first began to be played in the northern part of the country. Like many other European countries, the first ice hockey players in Norway had a great deal of previous experience playing bandy. The first hockey teams in Norway were created in 1932 in Trondheim, Sandviken and Tromso. The first Norwegian national championship was played in 1934–35 and was won by the Trygg SFK club of Oslo. The 1934–35 season also saw the formation of the Norwegian Ice Hockey Union on September 18, 1934, and the inclusion of Norway in the International Ice Hockey Federation on January 20, 1935.

The Norwegian national team began its official history on February 13, 1937, when Norway was defeated, 13–2, by Switzerland in the opening game of the IIHF World and European Championships. However, Norway would make its mark on the international scene by winning a bronze medal at the European Championships in 1951 and 1962. Norway's performance in 1951 also saw them finish fourth in the World Championship tournament—the highest placing ever for the team.

HOCKEY TODAY: In 1999–2000, Norwegian hockey's top division—the Eliteserien—was made up of 10 teams. After a 44-game season, the top four teams advance to the playoffs where the semifinals and finals are played in a best-of-five format. The team that finishes last in the Eliteserien is relegated to Division 1 for the following year while the top team in Division 1 is promoted to the Eliteserien. In addition, the team that finishes second-last in the Eliteserien plays a best-of-three series with the second-best team in Division 1 to determine the final team in the Eliteserien the following season.

Division 1 consists of eight teams who play a quadruple round-robin season. Division 2 also has eight teams playing a quadruple round-robin schedule. Division 3 is divided into groups based on geographic region.

Since the late 1950s, junior and midget teams in Norway have played for a national title in their age category. The top division in junior hockey features eight teams, while the top midget division has seven teams. Both leagues play a quadruple round-robin tournament.

NORTH KOREA

Ice Hockey Association of the Democratic People's Republic of Korea

HISTORY: The game of ice hockey in the People's Democratic Republic of Korea (North Korea) became popular during the 1950s when Soviet and Chinese workers taught the game and its rules in the capital city of Pyongyang. The Ice Hockey Association of the Democratic People's Republic of Korea was founded in 1955. North Korea became a member of the IIHF on August 8, 1964.

North Korea's first national championship was held in 1956 and was won by Amnokang Pyongyang. However, the North Korean national team did not make its debut until 1974 when it competed in the C Pool of the World Championships. The team lost its first official game to Italy, 11–2, on March 8, 1974, but rebounded for surprising victories over China and Australia.

HOCKEY TODAY: North Korea's only indoor arena is in Pyongyang. It has a seating capacity of 8,000. Eight teams play in the country's top division while a second division consisting of four teams also plays a league schedule.

POLAND

Polski Zwiazek Hokeja na Lodzie

HISTORY: Ice hockey has a long history in Poland. Two hockey teams (Polonia and AZS) were formed in Warsaw in 1922, playing their first game (a 3–0 win by AZS) on February 17. Students at the Warsaw Academic Sports Union (AZS) soon were promoting the game, but hockey in Poland did not really begin to advance until 1924 when Canadian immigrant Wilhelm Rybak began demonstrating the rules and techniques of the game.

Four clubs in Warsaw established the Polish Ice Hockey Union in January, 1925, and the Union joined the International Ice Hockey Federation on January 11, 1926. Six teams took part in the first Polish national championship in 1927. In 1931, an outdoor hockey arena was built in Katowice.

Poland first participated in international tournaments in 1926 and has been entering the World Championships ever since. Polish hockey flourished during the late 1920s and early 1930s with the national team bolstered by the use of Polish-Canadians who had returned to their native country.

Among these players was Polish national team captain Tadeusz Adamowski. Brothers Adam and Aleksander Kowalski also returned from Canada and were among the best players in Europe prior to World War II. Aleksander Kowalski lost his life in the war, as did goaltender Jozef Stogowski, who had participated in 11 World and European Championships for Poland. A hockey rink in his hometown of Kopernik bears his name in tribute.

Polish hockey was slow to recover after World War II, but the sport slowly began to take root again. The construction of the country's first indoor artificial ice rinks in the early 1950s helped to spur a rebirth of the game.

HOCKEY TODAY: In 1999–2000, the top division of Polish hockey comprised 14 teams. During the first stage, the teams played a double round robin. The six best teams advance to play in Group A and face each other four times for a 46-game season (including stage one). The eight clubs in Group B play a double round-robin schedule. All six teams from Group A and the top two teams from Group B qualify for the playoffs. Quarterfinals and semifinals are played in a best-of-five format, and the finals are a best-of-seven. The two semifinal losers meet in a best-of-five series to decide third place, while losers from the quarterfinals play a consolation round to determine fifth through eighth place. The four top Group B teams that failed to qualify for the playoffs play their own series to decide ninth through 12th place. National junior and midget competitions have been held in Poland since 1955.

ROMANIA

Federatia Romana de Hochei pe Gheata

HISTORY: Ice hockey began in Romania in 1921 when the first games took place in Miercurea Cuic. They quickly proved popular and, in 1924, the Romania Ice Hockey Association was founded. On January 24, 1924, Romania joined the International Ice Hockey Federation. Until 1927, Romania's hockey association was a part of the Romanian Winter Sports Committee. In 1927, this group was renamed the Romanian Ice Sports Committee. Four years later, it became the Romanian Winter Sports Federation. Today, the Romanian Ice Hockey Federation is in charge of the sport.

Romania's first national hockey championship was held in 1925 and won by Brasovia Brasov. The popularity of the sport increased after the country's first artificial ice rink was built in 1931, though many games continued to be played on natural ice surfaces in the country's mountain areas. Major steps towards developing the game took place in the 1940s and 1950s, including the construction of new ice rinks in Bucharest, Galati and Miercurea Ciuc in 1958. Coaches from Czechoslovakia and the Soviet Union also helped to develop hockey in Romania.

Romania made its international debut at the World and European Championships in Poland in 1931, losing its first game to the United States, 15–0, on February 2 in Krynica.

HOCKEY TODAY: In 1999–2000, six teams played in Romania's top division. The country's national champion is determined after a quadruple round-robin (20-game) schedule. The top two teams then play a best-of-five final series, while the third and fourth teams play a best-of-five series for third place. There is also a second division in the country. Junior and midget teams have been playing for a national championship since 1960.

RUSSIA

Federatsiya Hokkeya Rossii

HISTORY: "Canadian" hockey was first demonstrated in the former Soviet Union in Moscow in March, 1932, shortly after that year's Olympic hockey tournament in Lake Placid. A German trade union team called Fichte played a series of exhibition games against the Central Red Army Sports Club and the Moscow Selects. The games attracted a small number of spectators to an outdoor rink and resulted in a 3–0 win by the Red Army and 6–0 and 8–0 victories by the Selects. The Soviet teams were made up of bandy players (field hockey on ice) and neither the players nor the spectators were impressed with the new game. (Among the players was Alexander Igumnov, a future Soviet hockey coach who would later develop such world-class players as Vyacheslav Starshinov, Anatoli Firsov, Alexander Yakushev, Vladimir Shadrin and brothers Boris and Yevgeny Mayorov, as well as several others.)

The *Fizkultura i Sport* magazine gave a detailed report on the first hockey games in Russia, explaining that the rules were not to its liking: "With the rules such as they are, hockey appears to be purely individualistic and primitive," the article stated, stressing that forward passing was not permitted, which forced players to carry the puck (rather than pass it) almost all the time. "The game is very poor in combinations [passing] and in this regard cannot be favorably compared to bandy. From the viewpoint of its technique, the game is also quite primitive. The question of whether there is any need to cultivate Canadian hockey in our country should be answered negatively."

Even before the *Fizkultura* article, the Soviet sports press had derided what was called "Western hockey," describing it as a bourgeois game and therefore unacceptable to proletarian athletes. In addition, the foreign game had a strong native rival in bandy—or Russian hockey—which had been widespread in the country since the 1890s. However, despite its overall unpopularity, hockey had its supporters. "An advantage of Canadian hockey," stated the Leningrad magazine *Spartak* in its November, 1931, issue, "is in the size of the ice fields. It would be possible to set up a hockey ground on any skating rink." In 1933, an attempt was made to start hockey in Moscow. The regulations of the Moscow bandy championship stipulated that five clubs—Central Army Sports Club, Promkooperatsiya, Dukat, Serp i Molot and Dynamo—were each to be represented by a hockey team as well, with the results of those games to count towards the championship. However, a shortage of proper sticks meant the hockey plans never materialized.

The next serious attempt to introduce hockey to the Soviet Union was undertaken in 1935 following a letter by K. Kvashnin, captain of the Moscow Bandy Selects, to the newspaper *Krasnyi Sport*. Kvashnin proposed to start playing the new game "as soon as possible," but plans for the game were not implemented until the winter of 1938 when the Moscow Sports Committee made it mandatory for top league clubs playing bandy in the Moscow championship to have a team of "Canadians" as well. Efforts to manufacture equipment with no competent advisors proved unsuccessful and so this attempt to start hockey also failed.

Nevertheless, the development of Soviet hockey did not stop. In 1939, the game was introduced into the curriculum of the Physical Culture Institute in Moscow. Arrangements were made to stage demonstrations of games, seminars were planned for players to share their experiences and experts in the manufacturing of hockey equipment were invited to Moscow from the Soviet Baltic republics of Latvia, Estonia and Lithuania. (The three formerly independent republics would remain members of the International Ice Hockey Federation until 1946.)

World War II interrupted the development of hockey in the Soviet Union, but training resumed as soon as the war was over. The opening games of the first official Soviet championship were played on December 22, 1946, and the first goal was scored by Arkady Chernyshev—future coach of the Soviet national team. A major turning point in Soviet hockey occurred in February, 1948, with the historic visit of the LTC Prague team of Czechoslovakia. Almost every player on the Prague team had been a member of the Czech national squad which had received a silver medal at the recently concluded Olympic Games in St. Moritz, Switzerland. The results of the three-game series (the Moscow Selects won 6–3, lost 5–3 and tied 2–2) surprised everyone, but even more surprising was the success of the Soviet national team when it entered the World Championships for the first time in 1954. The USSR defeated Canada 7–2 in the gold medal game and would remain a power in international hockey until the breakup of the Soviet Union in 1992. Since then, Russia has become the successor to the former USSR, though the Russians struggled on the international hockey stage before earning a silver medal at the Olympics in Nagano in 1998 with a team of players with NHL experience.

HOCKEY TODAY: In 1999–2000, Russian hockey consisted of three leagues: the Superleague, the Top League and the Regional League. The Superleague comprises 20 teams. Each team plays a double round robin. The top 16 teams then advance to the playoffs. The first three rounds of the playoffs see teams playing best-of-five series, with the finals being a best-of-seven.

Beneath the Superleague is the Top League, which is made up of 23 teams (11 in the East and 12 in the West). Each team plays a quadruple round robin within its division. The top two teams from each division and four teams from the Superleague (the four bottom teams after the first stage) are then placed in a promotion pool. The eight teams then play a double round robin, with the two winning teams to join the Superleague the following season.

The Regional League consists of five regional divisions. Regional competitions also are held every year for youth teams aged 13 to 18 with the winners taking part in the All-Russian finals. These national finals help to determine the top youth and junior teams in the country and identify prospects for the upper leagues. All aspects of hockey development in Russia are managed by the Russian Hockey Federation.

SINGAPORE
Skating Federation of Singapore

HISTORY: After initial efforts by the Touras and Marine teams to establish hockey in Singapore in the 1970s, students at the University of Singapore have begun taking up the game in recent years.

HOCKEY TODAY: So far no league has been formed, with student teams playing only exhibition games.

SLOVAKIA
Slovensky Zvaz Ladoveho Hokeja

HISTORY: The roots of hockey in Slovakia date back to the end of the 19th century when skating associations first began to appear in Bratislava (1871), Presov (1872), Poprad (1881) and Banska Bystrica (1889). Bandy was being played in Slovakia by 1902, but the first organized game of hockey did not take place until January, 1921, in the Petrzalka area of Bratislava. CSSK Bratislava defeated SK Velke Mezirici 9–2. Three years later, in 1924, CSSK Bratislava played Slovakia's first international game, losing to Wiener EV of Austria, 6–1.

Hockey in Slovakia received a major boost in popularity after the European Championships of 1925 were held in Stary Smokovec and won by the host Czechoslovakians. In 1929, the Tatra Cup was held in Czechoslovakia for the first time. (Today, it is the second-oldest hockey tournament in Europe after the Spengler Cup in Switzerland.) Just one year later, the Slovakia Hockey Union organized its first official competition—the Slovak national championship. In 1931, however, the Slovak Union joined with the Czech Union to form the Czechoslovakian Hockey Union. The Slovakian Union would remain in charge of teams in Slovakia, and by 1932 the union was organized into three divisions: West, Central and East. In 1940, the union was renamed the Championship of the Slovak Republic and a new league—the Slovakian Hockey League—was formed. Also in 1940, the first artificial ice rink was opened in the city of Bratislava. Prior to this, all hockey games had been played outdoors.

After World War II, the clubs from Slovakia started to play permanently in the Czechoslovakian League. Three Slovak teams became national champions: Slovan Bratislava (1979), VSZ Kosice (1986 and 1988) and Dukla Trencin (1992). These clubs produced international stars like Vladimir Dzurilla, Jozef Golonka, Vaclav Nedomansky, Peter, Marian and Anton Stastny, Vincent Lukac, Darius Rusnak, Igor Liba, Dusan Pasek, Robert Svehla, Peter Bondra, Zigmund Palffy and others.

Shortly after the separation of Czechoslovakia into two independent countries in 1993, Slovakia qualified for its first Olympics by winning a qualification tournament held in Sheffield, England. Peter Stastny (who had represented Czechoslovakia at the Lake Placid Olympics in 1980) carried his new nation's flag in Lillehammer, Norway, in 1994. Slovakia finished in sixth place at the tournament. Later the same year, Slovakia made its debut at the World Championships in the C Pool. It took only two years (and two tournament victories) to earn a promotion to the A Pool in 1996.

HOCKEY TODAY: In 1999–2000, the Slovak Extraleague was made up of eight teams playing an eight-tier round-robin series. At the completion of the regular schedule, the top four teams qualify for the playoffs, which are played in a best-of-five format.

Slovakia's First League has existed since 1963 as a part of the Czechoslovakian League under the name of the Slovak National Hockey League. It comprises 12 clubs playing a quadruple round-robin schedule. The Second League is divided into three divisions. The East Division consists of six teams; the West Division has five teams; and the Central Division has four. Two sets of junior leagues, divided by age, each consist of 16 teams.

SLOVENIA
Hokejska Zveza Slovenije

HISTORY: The history of hockey in Slovenia officially began on February 7, 1929, when the new hockey section of the Ilirija Sports Club in Ljubljana played against a team from Kamnik, a small town near the Slovenian capital. Ilirija won the game, 15–1. The team in Kamnik only had been formed at the urging of Ilirija and it fell apart after the game.

Credit for introducing hockey to Slovenia is given to Stanko Bloudek, who brought the first hockey equipment to Ljubljana from Vienna in 1928 and founded the Ilirija hockey club with Viktor Vodisek. After the demise of Kamnik, the Ilirija team had to find opponents in Austria and would play games against KAC of Klagenfurt and VSV of Villach. During the 1930s, new hockey teams were formed in Croatia and Serbia but this still provided little competition for Ilirija. The team was considered so strong that it was proclaimed the national champion of Yugoslavia by the Skating and Ice Hockey Federation in both 1937 and 1938 without playing a single game. In 1939, Irilija was again the national champion after winning a tournament in Zagreb.

The development of hockey continued in Yugoslavia after World War II, with Slovenia figuring prominently. The Slovenian club Jesenice was the champion of Yugoslavia 15 years in a row from 1957 to 1971 and players from Slovenia made up the majority of the Yugoslav national team.

The Ice Hockey Federation of Slovenia was founded in 1991 and the newly independent nation of Slovenia joined the International Ice Hockey Federation on May 6, 1992. Slovenia had held its first national championship (won by Acroni Jesenice) that year and the Slovenian national team had played its first international game on March 20, 1992, losing to Austria, 1–0, in Klagenfurt. The country's debut in the C Pool of the IIHF World Championships took place on home ice in Ljubljana and Bled in 1993.

HOCKEY TODAY: In 1999–2000, the top Slovenian teams began play in the International Ice Hockey League (formerly the Alpenliga) with teams from Austria and Italy. After that, the top four Slovenian clubs played a triple round robin. On the next stage, these four clubs played a double round robin with bonus points after stage one. The two top teams qualify for the playoffs. Finals are best-of-five format.

SOUTH AFRICA
South African Ice Hockey Association

HISTORY: Ice hockey as an organized sport has been played in South Africa for more than 60 years. Its origins date back to the construction of an ice rink at Wembley Stadium which was built during for the British Empire Exhibition staged in Johannesburg during the mid-1930s. The sport reached the peak of its popularity in the late 1960s and early 1970s when a semi-professional league was run at the old Wembley rink. The high level of immigration into South Africa had brought many people who had been familiar with hockey in their home countries. The majority of players in South Africa's first semi-pro league formed ethnically-based teams of Canadians, Germans, Austrians and Swiss with some South African players included. By the 1970s, though, attendance for games dropped and the importation of overseas players became more expensive. There was also a scarcity of ice and little time for young players to learn to skate and practice.

In recent years, the construction of additional rinks in Johannesburg, as well as new facilities in Pretoria and Cresta, has seen an increase in the number of people learning to skate and becoming involved in hockey. Presently, there are nine ice rinks in South Africa, including three that are of international size. The center of hockey in South Africa is the province of Transvaal. Almost 80 percent of the approximately 1,000 players in South Africa come from this area.

The South African Ice Hockey Association was founded in 1936 and became a member of the International Ice Hockey Federation on February 25, 1937. In 1938, South Africa's hockey players played their first international game when they took on a team from Toronto. The South African national team played its first official game in the C Pool of the World and European Championships in Lausanne, Switzerland, on March 3, 1961, losing 12–3 to Yugoslavia. National championships have been held in the country since 1992 when the Roodenpoort Flyers became South Africa's first national champions.

HOCKEY TODAY: In 1999–2000, four clubs played nine games each in South Africa's top division (the Transvaal League) to determine the country's national champion. Six teams play in the second division, including three B-teams of the top division clubs.

SOUTH KOREA

Korean Ice Hockey Association

HISTORY: Although the Korean Ice Hockey Association was founded in 1928 and the first national champion (Yonsei University) was crowned in 1930, the modern history of South Korea's national championship began in 1946. Since then, university teams mainly located in the capital city of Seoul have competed annually for the South Korean championship. Korea joined the International Ice Hockey Federation on July 25, 1963.

In recent years, attendance for hockey games in South Korea has averaged about 4,000 fans, particularly when Yonsei University and Korea University (the dominant teams of the 1990s) are playing. The Korean army and some major corporations also have their own hockey teams.

HOCKEY TODAY: Currently, there are two indoor rinks of international standards in Seoul—Tae Reung and Mok Dong. In 1999–2000, the Korean league was made up of eight teams (five of which represent universities). The teams play a double round-robin schedule with three points awarded for a win. The top four team qualify for the playoffs. The semifinals are played in a best-of-three format, while the finals are the best of five.

SPAIN

Federacion Espanola Deportes de Invierno

HISTORY: In the early days of Spanish ice hockey, the game was played on natural rinks in the Pyrenees Mountains and in the capital city of Madrid. The game first made an impact in the country at the beginning of the 20th century with a series of exhibition games featuring Canadian and British players. Spain's first indoor rink with artificial ice was built in Madrid in the 1930s. Four clubs created a hockey association in the early 1920s as a division of the Spanish Field Hockey Federation. The Spanish Winter Sports Federation was founded in 1923. On March 10 of that year, Spain joined the International Ice Hockey Federation. The country participated at the 1924 European Championships in Madrid but lost, 12–0, to Switzerland in its first international game on March 12, 1924. Spain also played at the 1926 European Championships.

For the next 25 years, ice hockey was rarely played in Spain, though roller hockey was very popular. The game was revived in the 1950s, but with only a few games played among the country's three hockey teams. During the 1970s, some of the country's top soccer clubs (such as FC Barcelona) began to sponsor hockey teams as well. In 1971, Spain's first modern indoor arena opened in San Sebastian and in 1972–73 the Real Sociedad team of San Sebastian won Spain's first official championship.

HOCKEY TODAY: The best six teams in Spain played a triple round-robin schedule in 1999–2000, with the top four clubs advancing to the playoffs. After the best-of-three semifinals, the winners meet for the championship in another best-of-three series. The top two teams in Spain also play one game for the prestigious King's Cup trophy. There is a national junior championship as well.

SWEDEN

Svenska Ishockeyforbundet

HISTORY: American Roul La Mat is credited with introducing the game of hockey to Sweden. La Mat was a movie distributor who arrived in Stockholm in 1919. Already familiar with "Canadian" hockey, La Mat became fascinated by the game of bandy, which had been played in Sweden since 1895. He was impressed with the talent of the local players and believed their excellent skating skills would make them successful in hockey. It was La Mat's idea to enter Sweden in the Olympic hockey tournament in 1920 (this tournament was recognized later as the first World Championships), though it is unclear as to how he managed to convince the Swedish Olympic Committee to send a hockey team to Antwerp, considering no one in the country really understood the game at this time. Still, the committee did agree, though it granted only third-class travel expenses.

Picking Sweden's first national hockey team was not easy. The country had only one experienced player at that time. He was Nils Molander, who had been living in Germany since 1908 and played hockey for the team operated by Berliner SC. Eventually, the decision was made to send Molander to the Olympics along with the 10 best bandy players from the cities of Stockholm, Uppsala and Gavle. They received jerseys from the Swedish national soccer team. The rest of their equipment was bandy-style, but, once they arrived in Antwerp, the Swedes received proper hockey sticks from the American team as a gesture of generosity towards their compatriot La Mat, who served as coach of the Swedish team. Despite their newcomer status, Sweden made an impressive showing at the Olympics, finishing fourth behind Canada, the U.S. and Czechoslovakia. The gold medal-winning Winnipeg Falcons were so impressed by the Swedish team, they decided to let them score a goal. (Sweden's goal in the 12–1 defeat was the only one Canada allowed in the tournament.)

Hockey found many supporters in Sweden after the Olympic tournament. As a reward for its team's strong showing, Sweden was named the host city of the European Championships in 1921 and won the event after only one other nation (Czechoslovakia) showed up. This success, however modest, gave a real boost to the development of hockey in Sweden and on November 17, 1922, seven teams from Stockholm founded the Swedish Ice Hockey Union. In 1923, the Swedish hockey union was admitted to the Royal Sports Union of Sweden. Isaac Westergren served as the first chairman of the hockey union, to be replaced two years later by Anton Johansson, who occupied the post for 24 years.

National championships have been held in Sweden since 1922, with the first title being won by IK Gota, whose team included several players from the 1920 national team. By 1925, the game had begun to spread across the country from its roots in Stockholm, and by 1927, interest in Swedish hockey brought the first visit of a Canadian team to the country with the arrival of the Victoria Hockey Club of Montreal. The first artificial ice rink in Sweden was built into an airplane hangar in 1931 and it remained the country's only indoor arena until 1938, hosting 1,032 games over that time.

The Swedish Ice Hockey Union was instrumental in establishing hockey as one of the most popular sports in the country. It also has been responsible for maintaining a unique list of the greatest players in the country's history. The "Stor Grabb" (Great Men) are determined according to a special system of points. Fittingly, the list is headed by Swedish hockey pioneer Nils Molander of the 1920 national team, who is accorded the title of Stor Grabb #1. Over the years, Sweden's national team has come to be known as Tre Kronor (Three Crowns) for the emblem on its uniform. To date, Sweden has won the World Championships in 1953, 1957, 1962, 1987, 1991, 1992 and 1998. They also won an Olympic gold medal in 1994.

HOCKEY TODAY: Sweden's Elite League (Elitserien) was created in 1975. In 1999–2000, the Elitserien featured 12 teams playing a 50-game schedule. The eight best teams qualify for the playoffs, which are played in best-of-five format. The next level in Swedish hockey is the Allsvenska with 10 teams in each of two groups (North and South).

Division 1 has four groups (North, South, East, West) consisting of eight to 10 teams. After a double round-robin regular season, the two best teams from each group advance to play in another round-robin series to determine which four teams will move up to the promotion/relegation series. Division 2 has eight groups (two each in the North, South, East and West) with 10 to 12 teams in each group.

Top junior players in Sweden played in the Junior Elitserien, which is broken up into age groups of under 20, under 18, under 16 and under 14.

SWITZERLAND

Schweizerischer Eishockeyverband

HISTORY: Bandy was being played in Switzerland by the late 19th century, but British tourists and students later convinced Swiss bandy players to switch to hockey due to the lack of large ice surfaces in the country. The first hockey games were played in Switzerland in 1902, and soon eight clubs in the French part of Switzerland created the country's first hockey league. After the incorporation of the Swiss Hockey Union on September 27, 1908, this league officially was designated as the Swiss League. However, union officials chose to make the Swiss League an open league with clubs from other countries invited to battle for the championship. These open championships took place for five years between 1909 and 1913. Since 1916, Switzerland has held tournaments for Swiss clubs only.

Swiss players began playing games abroad shorty after the sport was taken up, with the first game taking place on December 19, 1904, in Lyon, France. One of the Swiss players in the two-game series against the Hockey Club Lyon was Max Sillig—future president of the International Ice Hockey Federation. The games consisted of two 20-minute periods. Switzerland lost the first game, 3–1, but rebounded to win game two by the same score. Through the initiative of Sillig and Louis Dufour, Switzerland joined France, Bohemia and England as the fourth member of the *Ligue Internationale de Hockey sur Glace* (forerunner of the IIHF) on November 23, 1908.

Switzerland took part in the first international hockey tournament, along with teams from England, France, Belgium and Bohemia, in Chamonix, France, in 1909. The Swiss national team played its first game on January 23, 1909, and lost, 3–0, to Great Britain, who went on to win the tournament. Switzerland finished third. A year later, Switzerland hosted the first official European Championships with games played on the natural ice of a frozen lake in the Alps near Montreux. Games at this tournament consisted of two 30-minute halves.

Hockey now was becoming popular in all parts of Switzerland, with the Akademischer Sports Club of Zurich having become the first team from the German part of the country to join the Swiss Hockey Union in 1910. In 1926, the first indoor artificial ice rink was built in Davos. Three years earlier, Dr. Carl Spengler of Davos created what has become the longest-running event for European club teams when he originated the tournament for the Spengler Cup. Over the years, Swiss hockey players would become among the best in Europe as Switzerland won four European Championships, while adding six silver and seven bronze medals. Swiss teams also won one silver and eight bronze medals at the World Championships, including bronze medals at the Olympics in 1928 and 1948.

HOCKEY TODAY: By 1977, the top teams in Switzerland were playing in the Nationalliga A. In 1999–2000, Nationalliga A had 10 teams playing a five-tier round-robin schedule. The top eight teams advance to the playoffs, which are played in a best-of-seven format. Switzerland's other national league, Nationalliga B, contains 12 teams split into East and West Conferences. A double round-robin schedule is played to determine the top three teams in each conference who advance to play in another double round-robin series. Meanwhile, the lower three teams in each conference play their own double round robin and the two top teams from this group join the six best clubs in the best-of-five league playoffs. The winner of the Nationalliga B playoffs is promoted to Nationalliga A.

Lower levels of Swiss hockey include the 1.Liga (with three groups containing 36 teams), the 2.Liga (with six groups comprising 57 teams) and the 3.Liga (with 12 groups and 99 teams). Top juniors in Switzerland play in the Elite A League, which has eight teams. There is also an Elite B League with eight teams each in the East and West Division.

THAILAND

Thailand Ice Skating Association

HISTORY: The Thailand Ice Skating Association was founded in 1986. Three years later, in April, 1989, the association joined the International Ice Hockey Federation.

HOCKEY TODAY: There is no national championship in the country, but the game is very popular among students at the University of Bangkok. Thailand participated in the 1998 Asia-Oceania Junior Championship.

TURKEY

Turkiye Buz Sporlari Federasyonu

HISTORY: The Turkish Ice Sports Federation, formerly known as the Turkish Skating and Skiing Union, was created in 1991. It governs ice hockey in Turkey. In May, 1991, Turkey became a member of the International Ice Hockey Federation and in 1992 the Turkish national team made its debut in the C2 Pool of the World Championships. Turkey's first hockey club was Eagologlu Istanbul and a national championship was played for the first time in 1992–93. In 1995, Turkey's national junior team (under 18) made its debut at the C2 Pool of the European Junior Championships. By 1997, more than 300 hockey players were registered in Turkey, playing on three indoor arenas and one outdoor rink. In 1997–98, the Turkish national team played in the D Pool at the World Championships and a junior team competed in the D Pool of the World Junior Championships.

HOCKEY TODAY: In 1999–2000, eight Turkish clubs played a double round-robin schedule in the country's top league. The top four teams advance to the playoffs. The semifinals, the series for third place and the final all consist of one game only.

UKRAINE

Federatsiya Hokkeya Ukrainy

HISTORY: Hockey has a long history in the Ukraine, dating back to 1912 when two teams from Kharkov (Gelferikh and Feniks) played a series of exhibition games. The real development of Ukrainian hockey, however, began in 1946 when the game started to catch on in the Soviet Union. Spartak Uzhgorod played games against Vodnik Arkhangelsk in the Dynamo soccer stadium in Kiev and the team was invited to participate in the first Soviet championship in 1946–47. Prior to World War II, Uzhgorod had been part of Czechoslovakia, a country with a long hockey heritage. Players from Uzhgorod had excellent equipment and could compete well against other Soviet clubs during the first championship.

The first championship of the Ukrainian Republic took place in 1949 and was won by Lokomotiv Kharkov. In 1963, Dynamo Kiev (later Sokol Kiev) was created. It would become the best team in the Ukraine and participate in the top division of the Soviet League. In 1985, Sokol Kiev won the bronze medal in the Soviet Championship. After the breakup of the USSR, Sokol Kiev played in the Inter-State Hockey League. Since 1996, Sokol Kiev has played in the East European Hockey League with Ldinka Kiev of the Ukraine and teams from Belarus, Latvia, Lithuania and a team from Poland. Sokol Kiev also won the first Ukrainian national championship in 1992.

Before the breakup of the Soviet Union, the Ukrainian Ice Hockey Federation was a part of the Soviet federation. It became an independent body in 1992 and joined the International Ice Hockey Federation on May 6 of that year. The Ukrainian national team had made its debut at the St. Petersburg Grand Prix on April 13, 1992, tying the Russian national B-team, 3–3. The Ukraine made its first appearance at the World Championships in the C Pool in 1993.

While many Canadian-born players of Ukrainian descent have played in the NHL, the first Ukrainian-trained player to reach the NHL was Alexander Godynyuk, who made his debut with the Toronto Maple Leafs in 1990–91. Dimitri Khristich (Washington, Los Angeles, Boston and Toronto), Alexei Zhitnik (Los Angeles and Buffalo) and Oleg Tverdovsky (Anaheim and Phoenix) are among the others who have followed.

HOCKEY TODAY: In 1999–2000, the eight best Ukrainian clubs played for the national title. They play a double round-robin schedule with the top four teams advancing to the playoffs. The semifinals and third-place series consist of a best of three, while the final is played as a best-of-five series.

UNITED STATES

USA Hockey

HISTORY: Hockey's origins in the United States are almost as old as they are in Canada, though it was not until Canadian teams began to tour the northeastern United States in the late 19th century that the game really caught on. Canadians were paid to play in the U.S. as part of hockey's first professional league in the early 1900s. The United States did not meet teams from outside North America until 1920. That year, the Americans made their international debut at the Antwerp Olympics. Led by Hall of Fame member Moose Goheen, they took the silver medal, losing only to Canada.

Until the creation of the United States Amateur Hockey Association in 1920, amateur hockey had been controlled by the International Skating Union. In 1924, the Americans repeated as silver medalists at the Chamonix Olympics. In 1924–25, the Boston Bruins became the first team based in the United States to play in the National Hockey League.

At the end of the 1925–26 season, the USAHA disbanded and left amateur hockey in the United States without a governing body until 1930, when the Amateur Athletic Union took over. In the meantime, the U.S. missed the 1928 Olympics and 1930 World Championships.

The first entirely American team to represent the country internationally was the Boston Olympics, a squad composed of Massachusetts-born players. The team placed second behind Canada in the 1931 World Championships and won another silver medal at the 1932 Olympics in Lake Placid. The USA finally upset Canada in 1933 to win its first and only World Championship in a non-Olympic year.

The growth of the game in the 1930s was sporadic. Canadian imports were taking most college hockey scholarships and there was no clear policy to develop young American players. More emphasis was placed on developing home-grown players after the Amateur Hockey Association of the United States was formed in

1937. Still, squabbles between AHAUS and the Amateur Athletic Union hampered American hockey and were not resolved until after the 1948 Olympics. With AHAUS fully in control, Olympic silver medals were won in 1952 and 1956. Notable members of the U.S. national team included Jack Riley, John Mayasich and Bill Cleary.

The 1960 Winter Olympics, staged in Squaw Valley, California, were a spectacular success for American hockey. Led by goaltender Jack McCartan, the Americans defeated Canada and the Soviet Union en route to the gold medal. This triumph spurred interest in hockey and U.S. college programs began to see more American talent. High school hockey programs in Minnesota, Massachusetts and other states began to feed increasingly skilled players into the college hockey system.

The U.S. won a surprising silver medal at the 1972 Olympics with a team that included Mark Howe and Robbie Ftorek on its roster, but the late 1960s and 1970s were not a good time for American hockey. In 1969, the United States sent more men to the moon than it did to the National Hockey League. Internationally, using a team built around a nucleus of college players, Team USA was relegated to the IIHF's B Pool in the early to mid-1970s. Coached by Canadian Bob Pulford, Team USA finished fifth among six teams at the inaugural Canada Cup tournament in 1976.

Another Olympic triumph—widely known as the "Miracle on Ice"—took place in 1980 in Lake Placid. Many of the players on this team went on to enjoy successful careers in the NHL and the upstart squad helped to spur renewed interest in hockey in the United States. With more Americans going on to NHL careers, the late NHL and NCAA coach "Badger" Bob Johnson revamped the national team program in 1987, making greater use of NHL players. By 1991, Team USA finished runner-up at the 1991 Canada Cup. A bronze medal at the 1996 World Championships was followed with a win over Canada at the World Cup of Hockey. While the Americans were a disappointment in men's hockey at the 1998 Olympics in Nagano, the women's team that had finished second behind Canada at four consecutive World Championships finally beat its arch-rival to win the gold medal.

HOCKEY TODAY: Twenty-four of 30 National Hockey League franchises are based in the United States. While most players in the NHL are still Canadians, the number of Americans in the league has increased significantly in the years since the U.S. Olympic gold medal victory in 1980. Many of the NHL's top stars today are American-born.

More American players are finding their way onto the rosters of the top major junior teams in the Canadian Hockey League and American cities are represented in both the Ontario Hockey League and the Western Hockey League. Junior hockey programs are growing in the United States, though most American prospects continue to find their way to the NHL from university teams in the National Collegiate Athletic Association.

In terms of youth hockey, USA Hockey is the national governing body that oversees the development of the sport. USA Hockey is divided into 11 districts throughout the United States. Each district has a registrar, referee-in-chief, coach-in-chief and an administrator who facilitates learn-to-play programs for youth players and their parents. Hockey registration has increased rapidly in recent years. USA Hockey is responsible for organizing and training American teams for international competitions.

YUGOSLAVIA

Savez Hokeja na Ledu Jugoslavije

HISTORY: The origins of ice hockey in Yugoslavia date back to the early 20th century. The first team—HASK (Croatian Academic Sports Club)—was founded in Zagreb in 1906. The first official hockey games in Yugoslavia were not played until 1916–17 when HASK and another Zagreb club (I.HSK) played each other in a two-game series. HASK won the first game, 2–0, while I.HSK won the second, 6–0. In 1921, the Yugoslav Winter Sports Union was created in Ljubljana. In 1930, the Yugoslav Ice Hockey Union was created out of the Winter Sports Union. The Yugoslavian national team played its first game on January 30, 1934, in Ljubljana and lost, 1–0, to Romania.

Yugoslavia became a member of the International Ice Hockey Federation in February, 1939. Earlier that year, the country held its first national championship. Four teams competed in the tournament on January 6, 1939, with Ilirija Ljubljana emerging as champion. The first rinks with artificial ice were opened in Ljubljana and Jesenice in 1954.

Hockey has always enjoyed great popularity in the northern regions of the country, especially in the area that is now Slovenia. Since 1991, Slovenia and Croatia have had their own independent hockey associations.

HOCKEY TODAY: In 1999–2000, the top three Yugoslavian teams played a quadruple round-robin schedule (eight games each) with the top two clubs qualifying for the playoffs. The finals are then played in a best-of-three format. National championships for boys and juniors are held in four different age groups. A championship playdown for junior teams was first played in 1962. The corresponding boys event has been staged since 1972.

VI

Other Facets of the Game

Bill Cook, Frank Boucher and Bun Cook formed the NHL's first great forward line when they joined the New York Rangers for the club's inaugural season, 1926–27. These three future Hall of Famers changed the way the game was played with their precision passing.
Hockey Hall of Fame photo

CHAPTER 51

110 Percent until the Fat Lady Sings

An Interview with Sports Scribe Rene Cliché

Jack Falla

In 1949 The New Yorker *magazine published Frank Sullivan's "The Cliché Expert Testifies on Baseball," a piece of casual humor still available in several anthologies including the first edition of* The Fireside Book of Baseball *(Simon and Schuster) where I read it many years ago. Inspired by Sullivan's story, I went to great pains and personal expense to track down sportswriter Rene Cliché, the world's foremost expert on hockey clichés. Mr. Cliché graciously agreed to an interview designed to help readers make sense out of the hackneyed hockey phrases we will read and hear throughout the coming season.*

– Jack Falla

WELCOME TO ANOTHER HOCKEY SEASON, the time of year players and coaches have to dance with who brung them, take it one shift at a time, step it up, go to the next level, dig deep and stay focused. They must do this with an eye to reaching the playoffs where they then need remember only two things: 1) what got us here and 2) that there's no tomorrow.

But if you think players and coaches have it tough, what about hockey writers, those ink-stained wretches, scribes, laptop dancers and knights of the keyboard who have to come up with a story or two every day from training camp in September to the Stanley Cup finals in June? When a writer is up against a tight deadline, or when his Muse hasn't answered the wake-up call, there's nothing like a cliché—a stock phrase hastily grabbed out of inventory—to speed a story along. Herein we are pleased to be joined by veteran hockey writer Rene Cliché, who has agreed to provide us with insight and thesauretical enlightenment in the matter of hockey clichés.

Total Hockey: *Mr. Cliché, what is the key to hockey coverage?*

Rene Cliché: The key is key. From September to June you'll see a steady increase in key games, key players, key faceoffs, key matchups, key injuries and key statistics. I go into a season with more keys than the Sheriff of Nottingham. I also like the Key Lime pie in the press room at the Florida Panthers' rink.

TH: *But doesn't a game deserved to be called "key" if it determines a playoff spot or a Stanley Cup champion?*

RC: The playoffs? Oh, you mean the Dance? The Second Season? Well, Scribe, teams aren't really playing for the Stanley Cup. They're playing for hockey's Holy Grail, the Silver Chalice, Lord Stanley's Mug, His Lordship's Ceremonial Beaker and the oldest trophy competed for by professional athletes in North America. They're also playing for next year's contract.

TH: *And who wins the Cup?*

RC: The Cup is won by the team that wants it the most and stays focused. Which, coincidentally, is the team that lights the lamp, roofs the rubber, puts the biscuit in the basket and finds the back of the net most often.

TH: *The biscuit in the basket? You mean score a goal?*

RC: You're catching on, Scribe.

TH: *And how does one put the biscuit in the basket?*

RC: With a wickedslapshot (it's all one word) to the top shelf, the short side or the five-hole.

TH: *The five-hole?*

RC: Through the wickets.

TH: *You mean between the goalie's legs?*

RC: You've got to be quicker, Scribe.

TH: *And the team that finds the back of the net the most will win?*

RC: Assuming they take their game to the next level, kick it up a notch, are willing to pay the price, to take away the neutral zone, to grind along the wall and to push their opponents to the brink.

TH: *The brink of what?*

RC: Elimination, of course.

TH: *And what happens to eliminated teams?*

RC: Players get early tee times and management reevaluates personnel.

TH: *And what fates await reevaluated personnel?*

RC: They often get put on the trading block, banished to the minors, placed on the bubble or nailed to the pine.

TH: *But what about the players management likes?*

RC: Those players ink new pacts in renegotiated contracts for fair market value. Then they get flushed with success and the nearest they get to the boards is Home Depot.

TH: *So life is good for the stars?*

RC: There are no stars in hockey, Scribe. There are superstars, megastars, sure-fire Future Hall-of-Famers, all-stars and even potential stars.

TH: *And what kind of pacts do those players sign?*

RC: They sign multi-year deals for undisclosed amounts.

TH: *OK, that nails it right down. Do the big scorers get all the money?*

RC: No, Scribe. Some of it goes to steady blueliners, stay-at-home defensemen, acrobatic goaltenders, grinding wings, defensive forwards and hard-nosed, two-fisted enforcers—the job market being somewhat weak these days for soft-nosed, one-fisted enforcers.

TH: *And what is the enforcer's job?*

RC: Enforcers answer the bell, stand up for their teammates, get up and dance, and instigate altercations.

TH: *And what happens to enforcers who instigate altercations?*

RC: They are sent to the sin bin, banished from the contest and sometimes called on the carpet.

TH: *What happens on the carpet?*

RC: The offender gets slapped and hit by Colin Campbell, the NHL disciplinarian.

TH: *Slapped and hit? That's terrible.*

RC: Slapped with a fine and hit with a suspension, Scribe. It only hurts them in the pocketbook.

TH: *So that makes Colin Campbell the top enforcer.*

RC: You catch on fast.

TH: *Don't passing skills also count for something in hockey?*

RC: Pros don't simply pass the puck, Scribe. They feather it, saucer it, dish it, go tape-to-tape, and hit the home run. Except of course when they take a wickedslapshot.

TH: *You haven't told us anything about goalies. How do they play?*

RC: Goalies like to make the first save, act as a third defenseman, keep their team in the game, clear loose rubber, take away the angle and make phenomenal saves—except in games ESPN's Barry Melrose is watching, in which case a goalie only makes "unbelievable" saves. And remember, Scribe, a hot goaltender can win you the Stanley Cup.

TH: *And what do defensemen—excuse me, I mean "blue-liners"—do?*

RC: They play the body, stand 'em up at the blue line, finish their checks, avoid the odd-man rush, dominate down low, bang in the corners, give up their bodies and stay out of the penalty box. And remember, Scribe, offense wins games but defense wins championships. I think the 1984 Oilers said that.

TH: *And how do you describe what the offense does?*

RC: They create the odd-man rush, work the puck down low, find the open man, take a check to make a play, take the high-percentage shots, pay the price in front of the cage and win key face-offs. Remember, Scribe, one hundred percent of the shots you don't take don't go in.

TH: *And do injuries play a big role in the hockey season?*

RC: Be specific, Scribe. What kind of injuries? Injuries are reported as nagging, chronic, career-threatening and recurring—except in the playoffs. Then there are only undisclosed injuries to undisclosed parts of the body. Any player so afflicted is listed as "day to day" whether or not the player is dead or alive.

TH: *You've enlightened us about the players and the game, Mr. Cliché, but what's going on up in those press boxes? What's most important to you as a writer?*

RC: Originality is key.

CHAPTER 52

The Hockey Hall of Fame

Tangibles, Intangibles and Honoured Members

David Spaner

THE NHL WASN'T THE ONLY HOCKEY INSTITUTION to undergo major expansion in the 1990s. The Hockey Hall of Fame grew to 51,000 square feet from 7,000 when it moved out of its cramped quarters at Toronto's Canadian National Exhibition. The new Hall of Fame opened in June, 1993, in a renovated Bank of Montreal building in downtown Toronto that had been constructed in 1885. Though many of its exhibits and interactive displays were actually housed in modern constructions, it was somehow fitting that the Hockey Hall of Fame's "new" building, like the game itself, is considerably older than the NHL. This is a hall of fame for all of hockey, and its artifacts reach back to the 1800s.

The roots of the Hockey Hall of Fame reach back to a meeting in 1943. Baseball's Hall of Fame had opened to success seven years earlier in Cooperstown, New York, and other sports were now beginning to consider the notion. In 1945, James T. Sutherland, who had long been active in Canadian amateur hockey, announced plans to construct a Hall of Fame in his hometown of Kingston, Ontario. The first players were inducted that year: Hobey Baker, Dan Bain, Dubbie Bowie, Charlie Gardiner, Eddie Gerard, Frank McGee, Howie Morenz, Tom Phillips, Harvey Pulford, Art Ross, Hod Stuart and Georges Vezina.

Along with the players, there were two builders: Sir H. Montagu Allan and Lord Stanley of Preston. Frank Calder, W.A. Hewitt, Francis Nelson, William Northey, John Ross Robertson, Claude Robinson and James Sutherland himself were inducted two years later. The players also inducted in 1947 were Dit Clapper, Aurel Joliat, Frank Nighbor, Lester, Patrick, Eddie Shore and Cyclone Taylor.

These two original sets of inductees were fairly lonely during the next few years, as they would be joined by others only sporadically. For instance, following the class of 1952, there were no new inductees until 1958.

"The whole concept was dying in the 1950s," says the Hall's current curator Phil Pritchard. It wasn't until an actual Hall of Fame building opened in 1961 that there was any consistency to the process.

The Kingston building had never gotten off the ground, and when Sutherland died in 1955, the focus shifted to Maple Leafs owner Conn Smythe and the grounds of Toronto's Canadian National Exhibition, where artifacts were stored starting in 1958. Smythe personally supervised construction of the small, utilitarian Hall, which was completed on May 1, 1961. The $500,000 cost was borne by the National Hockey League and the City of Toronto. Prime Minister John Diefenbaker officially opened the site at a ceremony on August 26. Hockey shared the space with Canada's Sports Hall of Fame.

The Hockey Hall of Fame would become a Toronto landmark and a popular stop for CNE patrons. Generations of Canadian children looked up in awe at its displays. But the Hall didn't just wait for visitors to come to it. There were traveling exhibitions, sometimes in a Greyhound bus, that toured small-town Canada.

The first curators, Bobby Hewitson (1961 to 1967) and Lefty Reid (1967 to 1988), acquired a huge collection of memorabilia, and the original building soon was too small to house the artifacts or any modern interactive displays. In addition, there was a disagreement with the CNE Association, which refused to let the cash-strapped Hall charge admission during the annual summer Exhibition (which attracted 75 percent of the Hall's visitors). In 1986, former NHL referee-in-chief Scotty Morrison was named the Hall's chairman. His mandate: Find a new venue for the Hockey Hall of Fame.

"Not only will I miss seeing the people come through and seeing their excited reactions to the displays," said longtime employee Ray Paquet of the plan to leave the CNE, "but this was such a focal point of the grounds. If you were going to a concert next door, you would always say, 'Meet me at the Hockey Hall of Fame building.'"

The new Hockey Hall of Fame would cost $24.2 million, financed by corporate sponsors and a loan from the NHL. As for the NHL's relationship to the Hall, the league does choose seven of the Hall's 18 board of directors, but "we run our own business," says chairman of the board Bill Hay. "It's not a National Hockey League Hall of Fame, but they are a good partner."

Hay says the Hall is an independent money-making operation, although it is non-profit. And the Hall is paying off the NHL's start-up loan.

More than 500,000 people attended the new Hockey Hall of Fame the year it opened. Since then, between 325,000 and 350,000 visit annually. Exhibits include a remarkable re-creation of the Canadiens' Forum dressing room and a Canadian living room scene from the 1950s with Tim Horton, Ralph Backstrom and others from the era playing in black-and-white television matchups described by Foster Hewitt. There are exhibits from pre-NHL days, the minor leagues, international hockey, and much more.

"In the 1990s," said Scotty Morrison, "the Hall of Fame had to be an entertainment center. The days are gone when you could hang up a pair of old skates. You need as many interactive exhibits as possible. You can live out these fantasies if you want."

Interactive technologies enable visitors to try their voice at play-by-play or try to score on video goaltenders. During construction, Hall-of-Famer Darryl Sittler was asked to test the slap shot exhibit and his shot destroyed the computerized goalie target.

"It was a year's work down the drain," said Nick DeSante, president of Technovision, the company that designed it.

But not everything in the Hall was brand new. Legend says a woman by the name of Dorothy committed suicide in the Bank of Montreal building and that her ghost is responsible for shrieks and a cold wind. "But she's a friendly ghost," said Christine Simpson, the Hall's first marketing manager.

The new Hockey Hall of Fame has areas for banquets and meetings, along with a library and resource center complete with photos and clippings and practically every hockey book ever published. The Hall's glass cases offer glimpses of Gordie Howe's skates or Guy Lafleur's first NHL stick or Jacques Plante's mask or a California Golden Seals jersey. The old bank's vault holds the original Stanley Cup, while the Great Hall in the bank houses more than 300 plaques of the Hall of Fame's Honoured Members. (The Canadian spelling is always used for "Honoured.")

So how do the players get here?

They are elected by the Player Selection Committee, whose 18 members are ex-players, media representatives and hockey executives. Up to four players, officials or builders are elected each year. To be eligible, a player must be retired three years—though both Gordie Howe and Guy Lafleur unretired after being elected to the Hall and actually played in the NHL as active Hockey Hall of Famers.

Over the years, 10 star players have been exempted from the three-year waiting period: Dit Clapper, Maurice Richard, Ted Lindsay, Red Kelly, Terry Sawchuk, Jean Beliveau, Gordie Howe, Bobby Orr, Mario Lemieux and Wayne Gretzky. Gretzky will be the last player to be so honored.

"It gives you two classes," says Bill Hay, "and I don't think that's fair."

Hay says the Player Selection Committee meets in June at the Hall of Fame building for a lively meeting to select new members. Committee members nominate players earlier, and by the time of the meeting have looked over material that has been prepared on each nominee. The Hall's board of directors appoints members of the selection committee, which includes everyone from former players (Pat Quinn, Bobby Orr) to media figures (Red Fisher, Dick Irvin) to a former prime minister (John Turner).

"Not only are there experts from different categories, they're from different eras too," says Hay.

Each committee member speaks on each nominee and the top four vote-getters are elected, provided they receive at least 75 percent of the vote.

"There was one year when no one went in," says Hay.

That year was 1994, when only veterans committee nominees Lionel Conacher and Harry Watson were inducted. In 2000, the Hall eliminated its veterans committee, which had been responsible for electing players who had been retired for more than 25 years. All of the oldtime stars had been recognized, says Hay.

Some say the selection process of other professional sports' halls of fame—those that use a sportswriting association's vote, for example—are more fair, but Hay argues for his Hall's system.

"It's cleaner and more direct and more organized and better controlled," he says.

Still, the Hockey Hall of Fame selection process has not been without controversy. In one instance, Gil Stein, who had briefly served as NHL president, left the Hall after improprieties in the election process were revealed.

Prior to the Stein incident, the board of directors elected builders. The uproar over his selection resulted in an investigation which led to changes in the selection process. Now, everyone is elected by the selection committee.

Over the years, there had been concerns that a disproportionate number of builders were being selected, and suggestions that hockey brass had an inordinate amount of power over the process. Players who had never come close to leading the league in anything were being elected while others were overlooked. Toronto Maple Leafs' five-time all-star left wing Harvey "Busher" Jackson—who was disliked by Conn Smythe—was kept out of the Hall for years, while Smythe favorites such as brawler Red Horner, who was never even a Second-Team All-Star, were inducted.

"Today, that could never happen," says Morrison. "There's no interference from anybody."

Still, some of the Hall's practices remain a mystery. Why, for instance, was Soviet goalie Vladimir Tretiak elected in 1989, only to have no other Soviet stars follow him? Perhaps the Hall must decide whether or not it's an international hall of fame. If it is, it should start inducting Europe's best, circa 1960 to 1990, when they didn't play in the NHL. As well, will the Hockey Hall of Fame open its doors to women players as the Basketball Hall of Fame has?

Despite these questions, the Hockey Hall of Fame does represent hockey at its best. Every hockey fan has an opinion about who belongs in a hall of fame, but the qualifications of the overwhelming majority of inducted players are beyond question and the Hall itself is magic for fans who visit.

They waited, a thousand people, to get inside the Hall on opening day. Thousands more lined Front Street for a look at one of the greatest collections of hockey players ever assembled, maybe the last great assembly of pre-expansion stars.

As the Hall of Famers open-car parade made its way from the Royal York Hotel to the new Hall of Fame, the onlookers roared their approval. "It just gave me goose pimples," said Dickie Moore, in a car with Ken Dryden and Bob Gainey.

Local heroes such as Maple Leafs' Dave Keon, Ted Kennedy, Red Kelly and Darryl Sittler shared the spotlight with former rivals such as Glenn Hall, Guy Lafleur, Stan Mikita and Jean Beliveau. "I feel like a kid again," said Lanny McDonald after speaking with Frank Mahovlich and Johnny Bower.

"To be back with all these great people, to see guys like Charlie Rayner and Bill Mosienko, it was just so great I can't describe it," said Gump Worsley. "This is the best thing to happen to hockey in 100 years. This is the best Hall of Fame there is in any sport. I think the people in the street are going to appreciate this."

The Hockey Hall of Fame had traveled a long road to the corner of Yonge and Front streets in Toronto. In the 1950s, the original CNE site had barely beaten out Montreal. This time, six American cities (Chicago, Washington, New York, Bloomington, Hartford and Buffalo) and five other Canadian cities (Winnipeg, Calgary, Edmonton, Montreal and Quebec) all made bids for the Hall. There were also applications from two smaller Canadian cities, Peterborough and Kingston, and the town of Niagara-on-the-Lake. The finalists came down to Toronto, Montreal (offering to house it in Olympic Park) and Peterborough (boosted by such hometown hockey luminaries as Bob Gainey, Red Sullivan and Gary Green). The Hall eventually became part of a huge downtown redevelopment in

Toronto that included office towers, a half-acre garden and other refurbished historic buildings.

"It's the most significant historic site in Toronto, and it will assure the Hall of a classic interior, including its cathedral-like center," Morrison gushed after the Bank of Montreal site was approved by Toronto's land-use committee in 1988. "It will become a cathedral for the icons of hockey and its history."

It's not a static one.

From the beginning, the Hockey Hall of Fame was committed to being interactive and multimedia-focused. A Web site (www.hhof.com) was launched in January, 1997, and has continued to expand since. In 1998, the Hall itself expanded to 62,000 square feet, including an interactive world of hockey exhibit with tributes to women's hockey, the Olympics and other highlights of the international game.

In 1999, the first annual Hockey Hall of Fame Game was held, featuring the Toronto Maple Leafs and the New York Rangers, at Air Canada Centre. Unlike the Hall of Fame games of other sports, this one counted as part of the NHL regular-season schedule. It was part of the Hall's induction weekend and included a tribute to the 1999 inductees: Wayne Gretzky, Scotty Morrison and referee Andy Van Hellemond. A Gretzky exhibit, the largest ever dedicated to one player, also opened in 1999, displaying the mounds of material Walter Gretzky had accumulated from his son's life.

Morrison says: "When it opened, I said to Bill Hay, 'This is, by far, the finest display we've ever had.' He agreed it was and said, 'There are only two things missing.' I thought, what the hell could be missing? Then Bill said, 'One of Wayne Gretzky's soothers and a dirty diaper.' And that's about it. Everything else is there."

In the works is NHL Odyssey, an interactive history of the league. Further in the future, curator Phil Pritchard sees satellite Halls, with archives and other resources, located around the world. "At least 55 countries are playing hockey. It's not fair to have it all in Toronto," says Pritchard.

Hockey fans pay almost as much attention to statistics as baseball fans and here are some opening-day Hall of Fame numbers: photos on display – 850; players profiled – 1,000; words of text in exhibits – 379,350.

But the Hockey Hall of Fame is about more than numbers or high-tech displays. It's even more than a physical place. It is also something intangible, an honor Hall of Famers carry wherever they go. Even people who will never get to Toronto and have no idea what the Hall of Fame looks like know that its Honoured Members have a special place in the game.

CHAPTER 53

The Evolution of the Hockey Arena

Building Better Hockey Barns: 1860 to 2000

Howard Shubert

HOCKEY WAS FIRST PLAYED INDOORS BY 1875, in buildings originally constructed for skating and curling. Today, NHL hockey is played in multipurpose entertainment centers where it shares the auditorium with basketball and soccer, Pavarotti and the Smashing Pumpkins. In the intervening 125 years, hockey buildings, whether major-league arenas in metropolitan centers or anonymous, Quonset hut rinks in tiny hamlets, have played a remarkable role in the lives of Canadians and Americans. The sites of intense shared experiences and civic pride, they have also served as true cultural centers, the glue that binds many small communities together. Arenas have even been accorded the status of secular shrines. When Montreal Canadiens great Howie Morenz died in 1937, his funeral service was held at the Montreal Forum before 15,000 faithful fans. When, after 72 years of continuous operation, the venerable Forum closed in 1996, the event was attended with all the pomp, ceremony and symbolism typically associated with the de-consecration of a major religious building—a vivid acknowledgement of the mythic status this building had achieved.

What follows is a brief outline and table charting the development of the architectural form and function of buildings in which hockey has been played. Five chronological periods have been identified; each corresponds to major changes in these buildings with respect to siting, design, use and technology. The important influences of economics and the media are highlighted, as are the ways in which architecture in turn has affected the game.

Curling and Skating Rinks: 1852 to 1907

Architecture is not a requirement for playing sports. Hockey was first played, in various forms, on frozen lakes and rivers before moving indoors by the last quarter of the 19th century. Canada's long, cold winters made it a natural site for the popularization of curling, ice skating and hockey. Covered rinks allowed patrons to escape the coldest weather and enabled them to participate in evening competition and social events. Indoor rinks for curling first appeared in Canada as early as 1837, although many of these were probably no more than rinks laid down within existing barns or sheds. This practice continued even later in the century.

By 1870, purpose-built skating and curling rinks already were quite common throughout eastern Canada and the northeastern United States. These early rinks, constructed of wood and sometimes fronted by a brick- or stone-faced clubhouse, were in fact multifunctional buildings. Used for ice skating, curling, and later hockey, they often incorporated bowling alleys and archery ranges, as well. Many rinks included reception rooms for the comfort of private members who had the wealth and leisure to indulge in such activities. Whether for private curling or public skating, these buildings were sites of participation, where people came to exercise or meet friends.

Indoor hockey first was played in these skating and curling rinks. Montreal's Victoria Skating Rink, the premiere example of its kind, was internationally renowned, described in both newspaper engravings and tourist guidebooks. The building opened for skating daily at 8 o'clock in the morning and didn't close its doors until 10 at night. On March 3, 1875, it hosted the first hockey game played according to rules resembling today's. The Victoria Skating Rink's 200' x 85' ice surface also provided the model for today's NHL arenas. The more restricted indoor ice surfaces, as compared to frozen streams and lakes, obliged a decrease in the number of players per team, from eight or nine in 1875 to six by 1913. The change from rubber ball to puck and the introduction of boards to protect spectators from flying bodies and objects equally affected the evolution of hockey as innovative players introduced puck control, sliding passes and carom passes off the boards. These developments further distinguished hockey from those games out of which it is reputed to have developed: shinty, bandy, hurling and field hockey.

A second type of covered ice-skating rink with a circular skating surface was popular in eastern Canada during the 19th century. Frequently built by civic or provincial governments to house annual agricultural or cattle fairs, they could also be transformed into skating rinks for the winter months. The Victoria Skating Rink at Saint John, New Brunswick, may be the most spectacular example of this model. More than 160 feet in diameter and some 80 feet high, the building's interior featured a conical wooden structure that descended in a tapering spiral from the center of the roof down to the ice surface. It contained viewing platforms and a stage for musicians, who regularly accompanied skaters in 19th- and early-20th-century skating rinks. Circular rinks did not proliferate, however, likely owing to their hopelessness as hockey venues.

The First Spectator Arenas: 1898 to 1915

By the end of the 19th century, hockey had become a spectator sport. While still officially amateur, matches between leading senior teams were staged regularly by promoters. Admission was charged and a cut of the gate split between the teams. But rink surfaces at that time could be of widely varying dimensions. Artificial ice was the exception, and new ice was rarely provided for matches. Worse yet for fans of the game, the skating rinks that had been constructed earlier in the century could accommodate as many as 3,000 standing spectators, but the cramped spaces of the promenades that encircled the ice of these early rinks afforded limited views. Lighting often left large portions of the rink in semidarkness and ventilation was non-existent.

Steam and cigarette smoke soon filled these buildings, further impeding the view.

The Westmount Arena in Montreal was the first purpose-built hockey arena in the world. It combined seating for 6,000 in a continuous graded grandstand around an ice surface enclosed by four-foot high boards. It was purpose-built also in the sense that its owner, the Montreal Arena Company, had been formed specifically in order to profit from the growing interest in amateur hockey by constructing a proper venue for such games. The Westmount facility was the first "Arena." All subsequent buildings on this model, whether in Toronto or Vancouver, St. Louis or Seattle, would be named arenas. Equipment for making artificial ice had been installed in rinks in the United States as early as the 1860s but was only introduced to Canada when Frank and Lester Patrick built their two new arenas in Victoria and Vancouver in 1911.

Hockey Arenas of the Golden Era: 1920 to 1931

The post-World War I era, often referred to as the Golden Age of Sport, witnessed a boom in sports architecture to match the growing numbers of urban spectators. Larger arenas and stadiums, designed by architects and built of permanent materials, resulted. Earlier arenas had been constructed mainly of wood and burned with alarming regularity. (In Montreal alone, during 1918 and 1919, fire destroyed the Jubilee and Ontario rinks and Westmount Arena.)

Nine new NHL arenas in eight cities were constructed during this period. All provided seating for more than 10,000 fans packed tightly into steeply graded grandstands. The buildings were centrally located on downtown streets served by bus or trolley lines, and often incorporated other attractions such as bowling alleys, restaurants and ground floor shops. All were specifically designed to be multi-functional, adaptable to boxing, wrestling, the circus and conventions; they typically included space for property storage and the stabling of animals. Toronto's Maple Leaf Gardens is noteworthy for its early accommodation of the media. Foster Hewitt's national radio broadcasts of Maple Leaf games originated from a booth (named after the gondolas that hung beneath dirigibles), suspended 56 feet above the ice, and which had been planned as an integral part of the building from an early date. Other technological advancements, including heating and air conditioning, electric timing devices and sound systems, improved the spectator's experience and led to a broadening of the fan base.

Two classes of buildings for skating and hockey now existed: community rinks—usually erected at public expense, beyond the city's central business district, with minimal seating capacity, and meant for public skating, amateur hockey and other events; and commercial recreational arenas—initially built at private expense and intended for professional sport and mass entertainment. Arenas for the NHL's Original Six teams benefited from periodic renovations, including increases in seating capacity, which allowed them to continue in operation for between 40 and 70 years. This longevity is partly responsible for the iconic status these buildings have been accorded. For generations of fans, the shared collective memories of historic moments and emotionally intense encounters—with athletes, musicians, or politicians—become inseparable from the physical places in which they were experienced. The iconic status of these arenas has virtually nothing to do with architecture and everything to do with myth, memory, and culture.

Expansion Era/Suburban Arenas: 1960 to 1983

The proliferation of sports franchises and new leagues beginning in the 1960s led to a second great surge in the construction of hockey arenas, with some 20 new NHL facilities built. Following a North American-wide trend, most of these arenas were located in the suburbs, closer to their middle-class patrons who prized easy access by car and ample parking. These stand-alone buildings were typically situated in the middle of a vast parking lot. Currently reviled for their apparent cookie-cutter sameness, they include some of the most architecturally accomplished arenas yet constructed, such as Oakland-Alameda County Coliseum and Kansas City's Kemper Arena.

The new Madison Square Garden in New York pointed to the hockey arena's future as a site of spectacle. It was planned as a vast entertainment complex encompassing an auditorium, theaters, bowling alleys and its own television studio in addition to an arena that serves many team sports and events.

Corporate Entertainment Centers: 1990 to 2000

The sports architecture boom of the past 10 years has been spurred by franchise expansion and economics. Twenty-two of 30 NHL teams now play in buildings no more than 10 years old, while three others have new arenas either in the planning stages or under construction. Many of these new buildings replace existing facilities whose primary defect lay in their inability to generate the greater income levels possible with private boxes, executive seating, more concessions and interior advertising. These new multipurpose entertainment venues are adaptable to many functions, feature superior acoustics, and are among the first arenas designed to maximize the sightlines of spectators and the television camera. They have grown in size, sophistication, and comfort, in step with the growing popularity and commercialization of professional sport, and in order to better accommodate an increasing variety of events, further blurring the line between sport and entertainment. The buildings' names reflect their indeterminacy of function; they are now called Centers or Places. Most also have corporate sponsors.

Critics charge that these new arenas are fundamentally different from the idiosyncratic, fan-driven buildings they replace. The new buildings, they claim, are not built for the loyal and knowledgeable fan but for a mobile and affluent consumer (often, one who can't skate). The homogeneity of experience that they find in these new buildings is, for them, symptomatic of a more general detachment of sport from both place and civic history.

More and more cities are being defined by the sports palaces they build. Economic and urban historians have noted that the presence of a professional sports franchise, and its requisite arena or stadium, has become the hallmark of every major North American city. The real or imagined economic "spin-off" to the host community resulting from the operation of a major-league facility has become a central argument used by team owners in lobbying governments to divert public funds to the construction of new buildings. Recent arenas reflect their new "public" roles architecturally through the use of large expanses of transparent glass—suggesting openness and accessibility—towers, sculpture, and spotlighting, as well as direct access to public buildings, transportation, and commercial shopping.

CHRONOLOGICAL LIST OF SELECTED NORTH AMERICAN RINKS AND HOCKEY ARENAS

CURLING AND SKATING RINKS (1852 – 1907)

BUILDING	CITY	BUILT	HOCKEY USE	DESTROYED	HOCKEY TENANT(S)	ARCHITECT
Quebec Skating Club Rink	Quebec City	1852				
Montreal Skating Club Rink	Montreal	1860				Mr. Simpson (contractor)
Victoria Ice Rink	Montreal	1862		1937	Montreal Victorias	Lawford & Nelson
King Street Skating Rink	Kingston	1862		1872		
Halifax Skating Rink	Halifax	1862-63				
Victoria Skating Rink	Saint John, N.B.	1864-65				Charles Walker
Royal Skating Rink	Ottawa	1868				
Boston Skating Rink	Boston	1868				
Toronto Curling and Skating Rink	Toronto	1877		ca. 1887		
Quebec Skating Club Rink	Quebec City	1877		1888	Quebec Bulldogs	William Tutin Thomas
Yarmouth Skating Rink	Yarmouth, N.S.	1878		1893		
Granite Club Ice Rink	Toronto	1880		1913		Norman B. Dick
Singer Rink	Saint John	1880s				
Dey's Skating Rink I	Ottawa	1884		1895		
Crystal Skating Rink I	Montreal	ca. 1878		1888	Mtl. Crystals, Mtl. AAA	
Caledonian Rink	Toronto	1885		ca. 1911		
Victoria Rink	Toronto	1887		1962		Norman B. Dick
Rideau Rink	Ottawa	pre-1888	1889-96		Ottawa Senators	
Duquesne Gardens	Pittsburgh	1890	1925-30	1956	Pittsburgh Pirates	
Quebec Skating Club Rink	Quebec City	1891			Quebec Bulldogs	Harry Staveley
McIntyre Rink	Winnipeg	1893	? - 1898		Winnipeg Victorias	
Casino Rink	Pittsburgh	early 1890s		1896		
Crystal Skating Rink II	Montreal	ca. 1893		1907		
St. Nicholas Arena	New York	1895				
Dey's Skating Rink II	Ottawa		1896, 1897-1907	1920	Ottawa Senators	
Windsor Skating Rink I	Windsor, N.S.	pre-1897		1897		
Winnipeg Auditorium	Winnipeg	1898		1926	Winnipeg Victorias	
Windsor Skating Rink II	Windsor, N.S.	1899				
Montagnard Skating Rink	Montreal	1898				Gamelin & Huout
Chicago Coliseum	Chicago	1900	1926-29	1974	Chicago Black Hawks	
Thistle Rink I	Edmonton	pre-1902				
Sherman Rink	Calgary	1904		1915		
Coliseum Skating Rink	Montreal	1907		1950		

THE FIRST SPECTATOR ARENAS (1898 – 1915)

BUILDING	CITY	BUILT	HOCKEY USE	DESTROYED	HOCKEY TENANT(S)	ARCHITECT
Westmount Arena	Montreal	1898	1912-18	1918	Montreal AAA, Shamrocks, Wanderers, Canadiens	
Amphidrome	Houghton, Mich.	1902	1902-07		Portage Lakes Hockey Club	
Thistle Rink II	Edmonton	1902	1902-13		Edmonton Eskimos	H.B. Johnson
Palestra	Calumet, Mich.	1904	1904-07		Calumet Miners	
St. Paul Hippodrome	St. Paul, Minn.	1906	1926-29	1946	St. Paul Saints	
Dey's (Laurier) Arena	Ottawa	1907	1907-23	n/a	Ottawa Senators	
Jubilee Ice Rink	Montreal	1910	1910-12, 1918-19	1919	Montreal Canadiens, Wanderers	
Elysium Rink	Cleveland	pre-1911				
Boston Arena	Boston	1911	1924-28		Boston Bruins	Funk & Wilcox
Denman Street Arena	Vancouver	1911	1911-26	1936	Vancouver Millionaires	Thomas Hooper
Victoria Arena orig. Willows Arena	Victoria	1911	1911-26	1929	Victoria Aristocrats, Cougars	Thomas Hooper
Ravina Ice Arena	Toronto	1911		1925		
Mutual Street Arena orig. Arena Gardens	Toronto	1911-12	1912-31	1990	Toronto Blueshirts, Arenas, St. Pats, Maple Leafs	Ross & MacFarlane with F.H. Herberts
Edmonton Gardens orig. Edmonton Arena	Edmonton	1913	1921-26		Edmonton Eskimos	
Portland Hippodrome	Portland	1914	1914-19, 1926		Portland Rosebuds	
Regina Amphitheatre	Regina	pre-1914	1921-25		Regina Victorias, Capitals	Storey & Van Edmond (?)
Seattle Arena	Seattle	1915	1915-24	ca. 1961	Seattle Metropolitans	Grant Smith & Co.,General Contractors
Spokane Arena	Spokane	1916	1916-17		Spokane Canaries	
Victoria Arena orig. Horse Show Building	Calgary	1911	1919, 1921-26	1961	Calgary Tigers	
Saskatoon Arena	Saskatoon	pre-1920	1921-26		Saskatoon Crescents, Sheiks	
Winnipeg Amphitheatre	Winnipeg	pre-1923				

ARENAS OF THE GOLDEN ERA (1920 – 1931)

BUILDING	CITY	BUILT	HOCKEY USE	DESTROYED	HOCKEY TENANT(S)	ARCHITECT
Mount Royal Arena	Montreal	1920	1920-26	2000	Montreal Canadiens	
Ottawa Auditorium	Ottawa	1923	1923-31		Ottawa Senators	
Ravina Gardens	Toronto	1925	1928	1961	Toronto Ravinas	A. W. Connor Co.
Madison Square Garden II	New York	1925	1925-66	1969	New York Rangers, Americans	Thomas Lamb
Border City Arena	Windsor		1926-27		Detroit Cougars	
Varsity Arena	Toronto	1926	1973-74		Toronto Toros (WHA)	Prof. T.R. Loudon
Montreal Forum	Montreal	1926	1926-96	1996	Montreal Maroons, Canadiens	John S. Archibald
The Olympia	Detroit	1927	1927-79	1979	Detroit Red Wings	C. Howard Crane
Boston Garden	Boston	1928	1928-95	1995	Boston Bruins, New England Whalers (WHA)	Funk & Wilcox
Chicago Stadium	Chicago	1929	1929-94	1995	Chicago Black Hawks	Eric Hall
St. Louis Arena	St. Louis	1929	1934-35, 1967-94	1999	St. Louis Eagles, Blues	Gustell R. Kiewitt, Herman Max Sohrmann
Vancouver Forum	Vancouver	1930				
Maple Leaf Gardens	Toronto	1931	1931-99		Toronto Maple Leafs, Toros (WHA 1974-76)	Ross & MacDonald
Cow Palace	Daly City, Calif.	ca 1937	1991-93		San Jose Sharks	
Memorial Auditorium	Buffalo	1940	1970-96		Buffalo Sabres	
Le Colisee	Quebec City	1954	1972-79		Quebec Nordiques	Robert Blatter

EXPANSION ERA ARENAS (1960 – 1983)

BUILDING	CITY	BUILT	HOCKEY USE	DESTROYED	HOCKEY TENANT(S)	ARCHITECT
Winnipeg Arena	Winnipeg	1954	1972-96		Winnipeg Jets	
Greensboro Coliseum orig. War Memorial Coliseum	Greensboro, N.C.	1959	1997-99		Carolina Hurricanes	
Los Angeles Sports Arena	Los Angeles	1960	1967, 1972-74		Los Angeles Kings (1967), L.A. Sharks (WHA 1972-74)	Welton Becket & Associates
Mellon Arena orig. Civic Arena	Pittsburgh	1961	1967-		Pittsburgh Penguins	Mitchell & Ritchey
Calgary Corral	Calgary	1949-50	1975-83		Calgary Cowboys (WHA), Calgary Flames (79-83)	J.M. Stevenson
Oakland-Alameda County Coliseum	Oakland	1966	1967-76		Oakland/California Seals/Golden Seals	Skidmore, Owings & Merril (Myron Goldsmith)

EXPANSION ERA ARENAS (1960 – 1983)

continued

BUILDING	CITY	BUILT	HOCKEY USE	DESTROYED	HOCKEY TENANT(S)	ARCHITECT
Pacific Coliseum	Vancouver	1966	1970-95		Vancouver Canucks	W.K. Noppe
Metropolitan Sports Center	Bloomington, Minn.	1967	1967-93	1994	Minnesota North Stars, Fighting Saints (WHA)	Haarstrick, Lundgren & Associates
Civic Centre Arena	Ottawa	1967	1972-73, 1992-95		Ottawa Nationals (WHA), Ottawa Senators	Gerald Hamilton and Assoc., Craig & Kohler
The Great Western Forum orig. The Forum	Los Angeles	1967	1967-99		Los Angeles Kings	Charles Luckman
The Spectrum	Philadelphia	1968	1968-96		Philadelphia Flyers	Skidmore, Owings & Merril (Myron Goldsmith)
Madison Square Garden Center	New York	1968	1968-		NY Rangers, NY/NJ Raiders/ Golden Blades (WHA)	Charles Luckman Associates
The Omni	Atlanta	1968	1972-80	1997	Atlanta Flames	Thompson, Ventulett and Stainback, Architects
Nassau Veterans Memorial (County) Coliseum	Long Island N.Y.	1972	1972-		New York Islanders	Welton Beckett & Associates
Saint Paul Civic Center	Saint Paul, Minn.	1972-73	1973-75, 1976-77		Minnesota Fighting Saints (WHA)	
US Air Arena orig. Capital Centre	Landover, Maryland	1973	1974-97		Washington Capitals	
Skyreach Centre orig. Northlands Coliseum	Edmonton	1974	1974-		Edmonton Oilers	W.K. Noppe
Kemper Arena	Kansas City	1974	1974-76		Kansas City Scouts	Helmut Jahn, C.F. Murphy Associates
McNichols Sports Arena	Denver	1975	1975-76, 1976-82, 1995-98		Denver Spurs (WHA), Colorado Rockies, Avalanche	Sink/Combs Architects
Hartford Civic Center	Hartford	1975	1975-76, 1979-97		New England Whlaers (WHA), Hartford Whalers	
Joe Louis Arena	Detroit	1979	1979-		Detroit Red Wings	Sith, Hinchmen and Gylls
Reunion Arena	Dallas	1980	1993-		Dallas Stars	Harwood K. Smith & Partners
Continental Airlines Arena orig. Brendan Byrne Arena	New Jersey	1981	1982-		New Jersey Devils	The Grad Partnership, DiLullo, Claus Ostroski & Partners

CORPORATE ENTERTAINMENT CENTERS

BUILDING	CITY	BUILT	HOCKEY USE	DESTROYED	HOCKEY TENANT(S)	ARCHITECT
Olympic Saddledome	Calgary	1983	1983-		Calgary Flames	Graham McCourt
Miami	Miami Arena	1988	1994-98		Florida Panthers	
Thunderdome	Tampa	1990	1993-96		Tampa Bay Lightning	HOK
orig. Suncoast Dome						
America West Arena	Phoenix	1991-92	1996-		Phoenix Coyotes	Ellerbe Beckett
Arrowhead Pond of Anaheim	Anaheim	1993	1993-		Anaheim Mighty Ducks	HOK
San Jose Arena	San Jose	1990-93	1993-		San Jose Sharks	Sink Combs Dethlefs
Greensboro Coliseum *(renovation)*	Greensboro, N.C.	1993	1997-99		Carolina Hurricanes	
United Center	Chicago	1994	1994-		Chicago Blackhawks	HOK
Kiel Center	St. Louis	1994	1994-		St. Louis Blues	Ellerbe Becket
FleetCenter	Boston	1993-95	1995-		Boston Bruins	Ellerbe Becket
General Motors Place	Vancouver	1995	1995-		Vancouver Canucks	Brisbin Brook Banyon Architects
HSBC Arena	Buffalo	1994-96	1996-		Buffalo Sabres	Ellerbe Becket
orig. Marine Midland Arena						
Centre Molson	Montreal	1993-96	1996-		Montreal Canadiens	Lemay et associés/LeMoyne Lapointe Magne
Corel Centre	Ottawa	1994-96	1996-		Ottawa Senators	Rosetti Architects
orig. The Palladium						
First Union Center	Philadelphia	1996	1996-		Philadelphia Flyers	Ellerbe Becket
orig. Corestates Center						
Ice Palace	Tampa	1996	1996-		Tampa Bay Lightning	Ellerbe Becket
Gaylord Entertainment Center	Nashville	1994-96	1998-		Nashville Predators	HOK
orig. Nashville Arena						
MCI Center	Washington, D.C.	1995-97	1997-		Washington Capitals	Ellerbe Becket
National Car Rental Center	Miami	1996-98	1998-		Florida Panthers	Ellerbe Becket
Air Canada Centre	Toronto	1997-99	1999-		Toronto Maple Leafs	Brisbin, Brook, Banyon
Pepsi Center	Denver	1997-99	1999-		Colorado Avalanche	HOK
Raleigh Arena	Raleigh, N.C.	1997-99	1999-		Carolina Hurricanes	
Philips Arena	Atlanta	1997-99	1999-		Atlanta Thrashers	HOK / Arquitectonica
Staples Center	Los Angeles	1998-99	1999-		Los Angeles Kings	NBBJ
Xcel Energy Center	Saint Paul, Minn.	1998-2000	2000-		Minnesota Wild	HOK
Nationwide Arena	Columbus, Ohio	1999-2000	2000-		Columbus Blue Jackets	Heinlein & Schrock
American Airlines Arena	Dallas	2001			Dallas Stars	HOK / David Schwartz
New Arizona Arena	Scottsdale	...			Phoenix Coyotes	

CHAPTER 54

The Oakland Seals Two Decades Later

Boosters Keep the Faith

Scott Surgent

EVERY COUPLE OF MONTHS in the San Francisco Bay Area, a group of approximately 65 hockey fans get together to enjoy each other's company, put up their feet, and talk hockey. The Sharks of San Jose are a hot topic, and the San Francisco Spiders of the International Hockey League drew some interest during 1995-96, but invariably, the talk returns to their first love: the late, great California Golden Seals.

The who?

Older fans might recall there was once a National Hockey League franchise in the Bay Area—Oakland to be exact—from 1967 through 1976. The team was known variously during those years as the Oakland Seals, the California Seals, the California Golden Seals, and finally the California Seals once again. No matter the name, the team was most famous for playing bad hockey in front of empty houses while wearing garish kelly green and California gold uniforms and white skates. In most seasons, the Seals had clinched last place by mid-February. April was reserved for family, golf and relaxing. The Seals were, in a word, awful. But to Ty Toki and many others, the Seals were the glue that bound friendships together and helped form one of the most supportive booster clubs in the league—both then and now.

Today, Ty Toki is an energetic man enjoying his 70s. He has been associated with the Seals Booster Club since its creation back in the early 1960s in support of the old Western Hockey League Seals. The Boosters made the transition to the NHL with the Seals in 1967. In its heyday during the 1970s, the Booster Club counted more than 1,000 members.

"Win or lose, most of us were die-hard fans," recalls Toki. "We supported them 100 percent. We even made road trips to show [the Seals] that we were 'all the way' with them."

Most remarkable is the fact that nearly 25 years after the Seals were uprooted and moved to Cleveland, the Seals Boosters are still going strong. The lack of a hockey team was no excuse to stop meeting, these friends thought, and continue to meet they did. The Seals Boosters currently consist of 65 members, most of whom joined after the last Seals edition of 1976.

"Many of our current members never saw the Seals play," admits Toki. "They became members through friends in the Seals Booster Club. There are very few old Seals Boosters left. After all, most of us are past 70!"

Ty Toki ran a dry-cleaning business, from which he is retired. His company was the official Seals cleaners, specializing in cleaning and repairing uniforms and supplying towels. He also did cleaning for many of the Seals players and staff. His association with the team was deep, and very good. To this day he can recall with fondness his friendships with such luminaries as Bud Poile, Bill Torrey, Craig Patrick, Terry Murray and Charlie Simmer, among many others. Even the late Charles Finley, controversial owner of baseball's Athletics and one-time owner of the Seals, gets high praise from Toki.

"I have nothing but good things to say about him," Toki says. "The majority of people that talk bad about [Finley] never met the man. [When] I ran into him in the team's locker room, he always stopped to say hello to me."

For their entire nine seasons the Seals were in constant financial duress, shuttling from one owner to another with the NHL stepping in on more than one occasion to prop up the franchise. Mel Swig, owner of the Western League Seals, came aboard again in 1975 but could do little to save the franchise. By the time brothers George and Gordon Gund bought into the team in 1976, the NHL had all but given up on the Oakland franchise. A move was imminent, especially when the Richfield Coliseum outside of Cleveland became available after the World Hockey Association's Crusaders folded that same year. From the NHL's point of view, a franchise relocation to Cleveland was an obvious solution to a persistent problem. The California Seals became the Cleveland Barons. The cadre of die-hard Seals fans did not greet the move warmly.

"When the month of July (1976) came by, we found that the team was moving to Cleveland," says Toki. "We and the players were shocked to hear that the team was going. Anyone knows that things like this don't happen overnight. It really left a bitter taste for all the hockey fans in the Bay Area."

So, you're a rabid hockey fan in the Bay Area and all of a sudden your team is gone. Left town. No more. What are you going to do? Over the years, Ty and the Boosters kept vigil by meeting regularly, organizing get-togethers, and—when the need for a hockey fix grew too large to ignore—making the odd road trip to see the closest NHL team, the Los Angeles Kings. Even trips to Vancouver were not unknown.

For 11 years, Ty served as Booster Club president (a position he no longer holds, though he is still active as a member of the board of directors). He helped to organize the 1994 NHL Booster Club Convention, which the Seals Boosters hosted. In attendance at these conventions are booster club members from all of the NHL teams, including some from the defunct Atlanta Flames and even the old Kansas City Scouts. The Seals Boosters are regular attendees at the yearly conventions, making a lot of hay for a team that hasn't been around since 1976.

The Seals Boosters are still very visible in the Bay Area hockey scene. Every July they attend the Snoopy's Senior World Hockey Tournament at the Redwood Empire Ice Arena in Santa Rosa, about an hour's drive north of the Bay Area. (The event was organized by another avid Seals fan of note, the late Charles Schulz, creator of the *Peanuts* comic strip and adjoining empire.) Teams compete from all over Canada and the United States, as well as from as far away as Japan and Australia. Former Seals players such as Ernie Hicke and Bert Marshall join in the fun, along with other ex-NHLers and those who just enjoy the experience.

As the years pass, the Seals will recede further into oblivion and there will come a day when virtually no one will remember them in all their glory. But not Ty. He has converted one of the rooms at his home into a virtual shrine devoted almost entirely to his beloved Seals. There are patches, pins, buttons, bumper stickers, trophies, pucks, photos, and over 50 individual hockey sticks—many of them autographed by Seals players. But the most precious items in Ty's collection are his memories.

"Back in the WHL days, Bud Poile was the general manager and coach of the Seals," Ty recalls. "He once invited me to travel with him and the team (to Seattle and Los Angeles). At both games, I realized I didn't have a ticket, so I asked Bud. I was shocked when he told me to sit on the bench with him and the players. At Los Angeles, Howie Young (of L.A.) leaned over and told Bud 'Watch me skate through your entire team and score.' He almost accomplished the feat except that the puck glanced over the crossbar! I'll never forget watching a hockey game sitting on the players' bench."

Another time, Ty traveled with the team to Sacramento for an exhibition game and the team picked him to sit in as an honorary coach! He won his only game behind the bench.

Today, Ty and his wife Mary spend their time following the San Jose Sharks, where they hold season tickets. In 1995, he helped form the IHL's San Francisco Spiders Fan Club, an entity totally separate from the Seals Boosters. Although a few Seals Boosters members held membership in the Spiders Fan Club and/or the San Jose Sharks Boosters, Ty was the only one to hold memberships in all three. The Spiders have since departed town, allowing Ty to follow the Sharks more closely.

The Sharks present a curious closure to the 15 years during which there was no big league hockey in the Bay Area. In 1978, after two unsuccessful seasons in Cleveland, the Barons were merged with the Minnesota North Stars, and the Gunds became owners of the new North Stars team. As time passed, the Gunds grew impatient with the money-losing team in suburban Bloomington. Very desirous of relocating the team, particularly to the Bay Area, the Gunds were convinced otherwise by the NHL. In an agreement, the Gunds sold the North Stars and were granted an expansion franchise of their own, the San Jose Sharks. The Sharks began play in 1991 and have become wildly successful at the gate. As an interesting footnote, the North Stars eventually were moved to Dallas in 1993.

At first, Ty and his fellow Seals supporters were wary of the Gunds in view of the previous history, but those feelings quickly subsided as the Sharks established themselves as a prime attraction in the Bay Area. Ty assisted with the initial formation of the San Jose Sharks Hammerhead Booster Club during the team's two seasons at the Cow Palace just south of San Francisco. Currently, about 15 Seals Boosters belong to the Sharks Boosters, although Ty has no official connection to the Sharks other than as an avid fan.

Almost 25 years have passed since the Seals last graced the ice. Seals alumni are scattered around the NHL in various management positions, as coaches, scouts, television analysts, or just happy retirees. The Seals are dead, long live the Seals Booster Club. And their sprightly leader, Ty Toki—happily retired businessman, 11-year Booster Club president, and the coach with the best winning percentage in Seals history.

CHAPTER 55

Hockey Benefit Games

Philanthropy on Ice

Glen R. Goodhand

THE FIRST NHL ALL-STAR GAME was billed as "The Game Of The Century." Even though the selectors had only five teams from which to draw the lineup to oppose the champion Toronto Maple Leafs, those decked out in the special red, white and blue sweaters looked like a preview of a conglomerate of Hockey Hall Of Fame inductions. The starting six were Ken Reardon, Elmer Lach, Bill Quackenbush, Frank Brimsek, Rocket Richard and Ted Lindsay. The All-Stars squeaked past the ruling Stanley Cup holders, 4–3.

Reports stressed that the 1947 All-Star Game was a "bruising battle, a rip-roaring struggle from the word go, with the bodychecking fierce, and frequent tempers flaring." The excitement was tempered only by Bill Mosienko breaking his leg. After $17,000 was deposited in an account for the players' pension fund, the remainder of the $25,000 gate was distributed to various charities.

But this first NHL All-Star contest was not the first such game to be played at the major-league level. Back on Thursday, January 2, 1908, the current world champions—the Eastern Canada Amateur Hockey Association's Montreal Wanderers—were pitted against selected skaters from five other league teams. The match, known as the Hod Stuart Memorial Game, was arranged to raise money for the widow of the brilliant coverpoint (defenseman) who had drowned in Belleville, Ontario, the previous July. The *Montreal Herald* billed the game as "unique in the history of hockey in Montreal, if not in the whole of Canada."

Percy LeSueur stood between the pipes; Rod Kennedy (Victorias) played point (defense) with Frank Patrick as his partner; Joe Power and Ed Hogan represented Quebec; Jack Marshall (Shamrocks) and Grover Sargent (Montreal AAA), rounded out the all-star roster. The Wanderers managed one more tally than the selects, winning, 8–7. Some $2,000 from the gate receipts were turned over to Mrs. Stuart.

Three factors of the Hod Stuart Game, including the high score, smack of the stuff of which more recent NHL All-Star contests are made. Another was the fact that fans were invited to mail in their choices for the all-star squad, a foretaste of big league practice now. The contest winners were awarded with two free tickets for the sold-out challenge. A third factor relating this all-star game to modern times was that it was cleanly played. In an era when rough play was the norm, the judge of play remarked afterwards: "If all hockey games were played as this one was there would never be any talk of police in connection with hockey."

During the First World War, there were a rash of contests tagged as "Patriotic Games." In one way or another, they were intended to benefit the war effort. On December 14, 1914, the National Hockey Association champion Toronto Blueshirts took on a combined sextet from the Ottawa Senators and the Toronto Ontarios. The hockey players offered their services gratis and the arena forfeited its take. As a result, $1,700 was collected for the unemployed in the Queen City.

A similar effort saw the Montreal Wanderers challenge their crosstown rivals, *les Canadiens*, who were bolstered by Quebec Bulldogs players. A total of $1,000 was realized through this benefit. Two weeks later, the amateur Toronto Victorias donated $40 to the Sick Children's Hospital from their exhibition tilt with Berlin (Kitchener). On the Pacific coast, the Vancouver Arena hosted a tripleheader in the spring of 1917 with the British Columbia amateur championship on the line. More important was the $500 raised for soldiers returning from the front lines. The management of the Quebec Bulldogs voted to make every contest of the 1916–17 NHA season a Patriotic Game. A percentage of the gate was to be donated to the Canadian Red Cross.

Fifteen years before the outbreak of World War I, in October, 1899, Canada had answered Britain's call for troops to fight in South Africa. In March, 1900, a group of prominent residents in Hawkesbury, Ontario, established a grassroots campaign to help pay for the Boer War effort. On March 21, 1900, a benefit hockey game was played between a Hawkesbury team and the Canadian Pacific Railway intermediate hockey club from nearby Ottawa. After expenses were covered, the game raised $120 for families of Canadian soldiers. What makes this game noteworthy is the fact that one of the Ottawa players was struck in the eye during the contest. That player was Frank McGee, who would go on to become the "one-eyed" scoring star of the famed Ottawa Silver Seven.

Three later benefit games—games in which the NHL was directly involved—can be seen as forerunners of the 1947 All-Star Game. These games are a well-known part of shinny lore. On Valentine's Day, 1934, the host Maple Leafs faced off against All-Stars from the eight opposing NHL teams. The hometown favorites won 7–3, but Ace Bailey, the injured Leafs star for whom the contest was played, was the real winner. His portion of the gate was over $20,000. Another game between the Bruins and the Maroons netted him an additional $6,000. Bailey commented later: "I bought a house with the money and had plenty left over."

In memory of the late Howie Morenz, his team, the Montreal Canadiens, combined with the Maroons to challenge another team of NHL selects in November, 1937. The score, 6–5 for the All-Stars, once more took second place to the cause. The $12,000 gate receipts, combined with other donations, totalled some $26,000 for the family of "The Stratford Streak." A little-publicized counterpart was the Canadiens' intersquad contest staged in Morenz's hometown. In that game, Howie Jr. centered the forward line with whom his famous dad had skated.

In 1939, Babe Siebert, who had been appointed coach of the Canadiens during the summer, drowned while attempting to catch up to one of his children's flotation devices. His former mates were defeated 5–2 by the NHL All-Stars, but the event produced $15,000 worth of "insurance" for his family. It is an eerie coincidence that at the Morenz Memorial two years earlier Siebert had been presented with the Hart Trophy prior to the opening face-off.

The only other charity game directly connected with an NHL competitor also related to a 1939 incident. On March 4, George Parsons was playing left wing for the Maple Leafs, having been called up from the Syracuse Stars. The game was against Chicago, and in the course of the action Earl Robinson tried to lift Parsons' stick. Unfortunately, it slipped and the blade tore the retina of Parsons' left eye. NHL president Frank Calder informed him that because of the possibility of losing the other eye, he would not be allowed to play in the league any more. His benefit game produced $20,000.

Outside the NHL, there have been more than a dozen games staged at various levels of hockey to raise money for individuals or groups with special needs. One of the first indicated the ongoing fraternal spirit connected with Canada's national sport.

On February 28, 1928, John Brackenbury of the Hamilton senior club suffered an eye injury as the result of a high stick. The next day, the eye was removed by specialists in Toronto. Immediately, friend and foe from far and wide, responded. There were two benefit games held within a week—one in Hamilton and another in Toronto. A total of $15,000 was gathered for Brackenbury before he was even released from hospital!

A little-publicized contest in March, 1948, saw the 1928–29 Pacific Coast Hockey League champion Vancouver Lions reunited to take on an aggregation called "Cyclone Taylor's Old Timers." The lineups read like a Who's Who of hockey's early era. Taylor himself, Duke Keats, Frank Fredrickson and Busher Jackson were pitted against former stars such as Porky Levine, Paul Thompson and Mac Colville. Jimmy Ward and Johnny Sheppard were standouts in the 1–1 tie that raised $2,000 for the Food For British Athlete's Fund.

That same July, the Trail Smoke Eaters, bolstered by former Canadien Joe Benoit, and the Nelson Maple Leafs, who added Doug Bentley and his brother Wyatt (known as "Scoop") to their roster, attracted a crowd of 2,000, who watched the teams skate to a 5–5 standoff. Lester Patrick was the referee and he gained more attention than all the rest put together. The game was sponsored by the local Kinsmen Club. It was a charity affair for the benefit of flood victims.

Aldege "Baz" Bastien looked like he was headed for a promising career in pro hockey until he was injured. Bastien had already played five games for the Toronto Maple Leafs in 1945–46 and had settled in as goal guardian with their farm team in Pittsburgh. But in training camp in the fall of 1949, he was hit with an errant shot and suffered the loss of an eye. On October 17, his former mates with the Hornets bravely faced off against the Stanley Cup-champion Leafs in an exhibition contest to raise funds for their wounded comrade. Although the Steel Town was suffering economically at the time, 3,225 fans turned out to pool a kitty of $5,212. Ushers, timers, referees and players all paid their way in, keeping expenses to a minimum. The home squad was whipped, 4–0, but Bastien's tear-filled response to this act of generosity made up for the loss.

Five months after leading the Montreal Royals to victory in the 1949 Memorial Cup marathon, Tag Miller passed away as a result of a rare blood disease. Seldom has there been a tribute to compare with the one organized by Frank Selke at the Forum in February, 1950. The event featured a broomball game between the firemen and local policemen; a contest between the Junior Canadiens and the Quebec junior league all-stars; a similar match featured the senior Royals and the Quebec League selects; plus an additional tilt, which saw the NHL Canadiens face-off against some hand-picked senior and junior stars. A puck-carrying race featuring Bill Mosienko, Max McNab, Floyd Curry and Tony Leswick capped off the evening, which turned over $10,000 to Miller's young widow and small son, Jimmy. Maple Leaf Gardens had hosted a similar event back on January 30, 1942, when $11,500 was raised for the family of Robert "Moose" Ecclestone. The longtime manager of the powerhouse Toronto Goodyears senior team had been killed in a car accident.

Charity events of this kind have not always warranted national attention, nor raised stacks of greenbacks. In 1950, the small town of Dryden, Ontario, staged a local benefit game for Maurice Lobreau. A total of $1,400 represented the community's efforts to help with brain surgery and the removal of an eye following a critical on-ice accident. The loss of sight has fostered the inspiration for several duels on ice away from the main shinny thoroughfare, but when the Omaha Knights arranged a benefit game for Gordon Petrie on March 1, 1953, the recipient of this effort was already in an iron lung. He had been struck down with polio the previous July. The Petrie All Stars, coached by Mud Bruneteau, added players from Hershey, Tulsa, Kansas City and St. Louis, to face Wichita at the local arena.

Crippled children were the beneficiaries of an Oldtimer's joust in early 1954. Several former NHLers dug their skates and equipment out of moth balls to form opposing teams from Ontario and Quebec. Although skaters such as Dit Clapper, Sylvio Mantha, Johnny "Black Cat" Gagnon and Lionel Conacher moved at a slower pace than they had 20 years before, it was a wide-open affair with the Quebecers prevailing by a score of 11–9. Four Conachers strutted their stuff for Ontario, with one-eyed Burt, Roy's twin brother, gaining an assist. Jake Forbes and Roy Worters each took their turn in the nets for Ontario, while Bill Durnan tended the twine for the bulk of the game for the Quebec team. Bill Cowley, 41 years young, tallied six assists. Over $10,000 was raised for the cause.

Like so many others, Glen Sonmor found himself finished as a pro puckchaser after he was hit in the eye with a puck on February 27, 1955. Shortly after the accident, Marguerite Norris, president of the Detroit Red Wings, authorized manager Jack Adams to offer the Motor City club as a drawing card in an exhibition match with Sonmor's Cleveland Barons to raise money for the stricken forward. Shortage of time to make suitable arrangements aborted this plan, but the regular-season American Hockey League game between Cleveland and Pittsburgh on March 16 was set aside for the same purpose. Over $8,000 was realized that evening. Added to that would be $5,000 from the Cleveland team's insurance and $4,000 from a state fund. The fiery Sonmor was later appointed coach of the Minnesota North Stars, where he was bench boss for six-plus seasons beginning in 1979–80.

Some rare sights greeted the 15,000 fans who crammed the Winnipeg Arena for a benefit game on April 25, 1980. The contest marked the only time that Bobby Orr and Wayne Gretzky ever played together. The recently retired Orr was also joined by former goaltending great Ken Dryden—who skated as a forward—in the Bill Heindl Benefit game. The former North Star and Ranger battled depression and had been left paralyzed after a suicide attempt. A squad of 1960s vintage Canadian national team players led by Fran Huck, Gerry Pinder and Bill Lesuk lined up against several present and past NHLers, including Bobby Leiter, Peter Sullivan and Morris Lukowich—as well as Orr and Gretzky. The Nats defeated the NHL stars 8–6, and $80,000 was realized for the guest of honor.

Retired players who were not finding post-NHL life easy also attracted journalist Bill Fleischman's attention in March, 1982. *The Hockey News* guest writer profiled a benefit game for pucksters no longer drawing paychecks for playing shinny and who instead might be earning enough to keep body and soul together "as watchmen or lunch vendors." A crowd of 15,000 gathered in Madison Square Garden for the Masters of Hockey contest, featuring many of the game's legends: Yvan Cournoyer, Jean Ratelle and Gordie Howe. The take was estimated to be between $75,000 and $100,000, to be put toward medical funds, insurance and counselling for those in need.

A different type of on-ice contest had taken place in October, 1971. During a break in an AHL game between Providence and the Boston Braves, a best-of-seven penalty shot contest was held pitting Vic Hadfield against Ed Giacomin. The Vezina Trophy winner bettered his Rangers teammate and accepted the $1,000 prize, which he immediately turned over to the local United Fund.

But the most unusual benefit scenario of all must be the help given to Jerry Cotnoir of the 1948 Tacoma Rockets. The PCHL twinetender had recently lost $750 when thieves broke into his car during a road trip. Between periods of a Rockets-Vancouver tilt, fans showered $500 on the ice to help relieve the sting of his loss. The stake was waiting for Cotnoir in a box in the goal mouth when he skated back on the ice following intermission!

Benefit games of the aforementioned kind are virtually a thing of the past. There are still Oldtimers games for charity held at local levels; but the demanding schedules of modern day pro hockey makes it almost impossible for such exhibitions to be squeezed in. But this is not say that today's millionaires on skates have no spirit of philanthropy. Annually, the King Clancy Memorial Trophy is awarded to NHLers who have "made a noteworthy humanitarian contribution to the community." Recent winners such as Kelly Chase, Trevor Linden and Rob Ray have given of their time to visit children in hospitals, raised funds for Ronald McDonald House, supported the Canadian Cancer Society and sponsored programs providing toys, clothing and food for needy families. Chivalry may be dead … but not among those in the hockey fraternity.

CHAPTER 56

Company Teams in Senior Hockey

Some of the Best Hockey Outside the Six-Team NHL

Dave Clamen

NOW PLAYING IN THE STANLEY CUP PLAYOFFS—the Toronto Air Canadas vs. Vancouver General Motors. Far-fetched? Maybe. But such matchups became quite common in Allan Cup competitions during the days when this Canadian senior amateur trophy meant so much to hockey fans across the country.

For the first 20-plus years of its competition, which began in 1908, the Allan Cup was usually won by university teams (Toronto, Queen's and Manitoba) or by amateur sports organizations such as the Toronto Granite Club or the Montreal Amateur Athletic Association. Community-based teams such as the Port Arthur Bearcats and the Sault Ste. Marie Greyhounds also won the national senior championship. During this time, the staunchly amateur Ontario Hockey Association in particular shunned the so-called "commercial teams." The logic behind this move was that players on company teams could be transferred by their employers to whatever city team most needed their help. That was one step toward professionalism! Even so, Toronto Eaton's did manage to sneak away with a couple of OHA senior titles.

But the hockey climate began to change in the late 1920s.

The first change was the growing national interest in the Allan Cup. Formerly a competition mostly restricted to Manitoba and southern Ontario, the senior amateur trophy soon attracted teams from all over the country—which led to more and expensive travel for the players. Also, beginning in 1930, the Allan Cup winner would qualify for the annual World Championships in Europe—which meant spending even more money for travel.

The rising interest in senior hockey came at a time of increased competition. The collapse of major league hockey out west in 1926 had actually hurt the senior game as it spawned a new level of play—the minor pros. Since the popular notion was that professional players were better than amateurs, senior hockey faded out in the larger western cities. Minor pro hockey also hurt the seniors in Ontario. And then came the Great Depression, which of course, cut down on fan support—and the ability of players to support themselves.

In order to survive, senior hockey turned to corporate sponsorship by private sector companies.

The two best places in Canada for company sponsorship proved to be interior British Columbia and northeastern Ontario. Minor pro teams were far away, but even more importantly, these relatively isolated areas were both dominated by large mining companies who were willing to subsidize hockey teams as an entertainment outlet for their workers. But no one could forget who was paying the bill! Just look at the final standings of the Nickel Belt (Sudbury) Hockey League of 1936–37:

Nickel Belt (Sudbury) Hockey League, 1936–37

Team	Record
Frood Mines Tigers	13–1–1
Falconbridge Falcons	9–5–0
Ontario Refinery	8–6–1
Creighton Mines	8–6–1
Conniston Blues	2–11–0

This league was certainly not just a local organization of limited importance, as the Tigers went on to win the Allan Cup that year. They are in the record books as the Sudbury Tigers. Of course, even the local Sudbury paper had to defend the team against charges of "corralling all available star material from the length and breadth of the provinces." In depressed times, company teams had the powerful incentive of a full-time job.

But the Sudbury team was not alone in the corporate hockey game. The Tigers had some serious company competition en route to the Allan Cup. In Saskatoon, the Quaker Oats Company lent its name to the local team—the Quakers. The Senior League in Manitoba was made up of Great West Life, Canada Packers, the Canadian National Railroad and the Canadian Pacific Railway. The Goodyears, Dominion Brewers, British Consols and the Oshawa G-Men (General Motors) played off for the Ontario title. In the Maritimes, there were no fewer than three senior teams with Sunoco in their names. The Quebec title was won by the Quebec Aces (Anglo Canadian Employees). The best playoff series of 1937 was between the Tigers and the Port Colborne Sailors. It was billed as a contest between the mining and refining operations of International Nickel.

The area around the town of Timmins, a northern Ontario mining town like Sudbury, had a six-team league in 1936–37 of which four had company names. One of those Timmins-area teams would win the Allan Cup in 1940. Known to the record books as the Kirkland Lake Blue Devils, it was more commonly known at the time as the Lake Shore (Mines) Blue Devils.

Interior British Columbia was able to keep pace with northern Ontario. Tiny Trail, B.C., the home of Cominco Mines, for a long time boasted one of the only artificial ice surface between Winnipeg and Vancouver. Subsidized by the mining companies, the local league produced several champions, including the 1936 Kimberley Dynamiters and the 1938 Trail Smoke Eaters.

When World War II broke out, it of course changed the face of senior hockey. Many men enlisted in the military, thus lowering the available pool for sports. This led to a different form of "company" sponsorship. Military teams sprung up all over the country to compete for the Allan Cup and to provide diversion from the war. Many NHL stars who had enlisted found themselves on these clubs.

The Depression had devastated senior hockey in the bigger cities, but now these cities had seen the talented war-era teams and wanted more of the same. With more money to spend in the postwar economy, three senior leagues—Western Canada, Quebec and Ontario—based largely in the big cities—dominated the Allan Cup from 1946 to 1950. The company teams from northern Ontario and British Columbia fell by the wayside. But these "Big Three" leagues soon fell victim to their own success. Inspired, in part, by the boom in minor pro baseball, the Quebec and Western Leagues soon went professional. Ironically these leagues would not be felled by an economic depression, but by prosperity. The rise of television allowed Canadians to see the apex of hockey, the NHL, and minor pro seemed well … minor in comparison.

Again, company teams filled the vacuum. Teams such as the Owen Sound Mercurys and the Edmonton Mercurys (sponsored by car dealers) won senior amateur titles. The British Columbia leagues that had suffered in the late 1940s came into their own again during the 1950s with teams such as the Penticton Vees. Northern Ontario started up again, but one of the best examples of a company league was begun in, of all places, southern Ontario.

The Eastern Ontario league, led by Wren Blair, realized the need for sponsorship. The result was team names like the Whitby Dunlops (after the tire company), the Belleville McFarlands (after the mayor and local car dealer), and the Kingston CKLCs (after a radio station). This southern Ontario league vied with the B.C. leagues for the Allan Cup.

But like the successful senior leagues of the 1940s, this loop also became a victim of its own success. It turned pro, merging into the Eastern Professional Hockey League in 1959. And like its cousins, this league, too, faded away to the south.

Senior hockey's hold on the country faded in the 1960s as the rise of minor pro and NHL hockey in the United States pulled players away from Canadian amateur teams. Though the senior amateur game remains a part of the hockey scene today, it is a very small part indeed and a far cry from the time the Allan Cup rivaled the Stanley Cup.

CHAPTER 57

The Odd and the Unusual

Hockey's Allotment of Flamboyant and Rambunctious Characters

Bob Duff

THE INCREDIBLE FIVE CONSECUTIVE STANLEY CUP championships won by the Montreal Canadiens. Wayne Gretzky's amazing 50 goals in 39 games. The astonishing 35-game unbeaten run of the Philadelphia Flyers.

Hockey is rich with tradition, filled with great players and teams and the magical moments they perform. But alongside the fabulous, room must be made for the foibles, the follies and the foolishness which often pervades this great game. The goalie who went to Maple Leaf Gardens in search of a ticket to a Stanley Cup game and ended up on the hot seat. The players who entertained a sellout crowd by rolling the dice. Two guys who scored game-tying goals in sudden-death overtime. The live game that was tape delayed. And the player who took his coach literally and literally brought about an end to his stay in the NHL.

Dan Belisle's NHL playing career was short-lived, but his exit was unforgettable. When the New York Rangers were hit with a rash of injuries during the 1960–61 season, the right wing was summoned from Vancouver of the Western Hockey League and got off to an impressive start, netting two goals in four games. Belisle was busily putting on his gear before what was to be his fifth appearance in an NHL contest when he was summoned to coach Alf Pike's office. He was told to change back into his civvies. One of the injured players would be able to go and Belisle's services were not required. Glumly, he began doffing his gear. Then he received another message—suit up, the other player's injury wasn't sufficiently healed. He happily returned to lacing up his skates, but this on-again off-again relationship would be played out a few more times before Belisle was finally told to stay half dressed in case he was needed. A few minutes later, when Pike came to tell Belisle he'd been scratched from the lineup, he found the player wearing a dress shirt, tie and sport coat with hockey pants, socks, shin pads and skates. While the other players burst out laughing, Pike didn't see the humor. Belisle was shipped to the minors, never to play in the NHL again.

One night in Montreal, New York Americans goalie Roy Worters stopped the puck with his glove, but then things got a little hairy. Seeking to toss the puck to a teammate behind the net, Worters instead heaved the biscuit into the top shelf, snapping a 1–1 tie and giving the Canadiens the victory. Worters had a hand in Montreal's win, but at least his assistance was accidental. Boston goalie Hec Fowler purposely engineered a Bruins defeat during the club's inaugural season of 1924–25 and also engineered the end of his big-league career in the process. Boston manager Art Ross became so enraged with Fowler's lackluster netminding in a 10–1 loss to Toronto that he replaced him with defenseman George Redding. The next day, Fowler admitted he'd deliberately allowed some of the goals in the hopes the Bruins would be embarrassed enough to pursue better players. Ross heeded Fowler's wish—sort of. He got a new goalie.

Fowler gambled and lost, but Toronto's Harry Cameron and Reg Noble and Ottawa's Frank Nighbor gambled purely for the purpose of amusing the paying spectators during a St. Patricks-Senators game at Ottawa in 1921. When a power outage halted play, candles were ringed around the boards to illuminate the building. As the crowd grew restless, the three players emerged from the dressing room with a pair of dice. They circled some candles near the boards at center ice and entertained the fans with an impromptu game of craps. No money exchanged hands during this game, but Montreal Maroons captain Dunc Munro didn't mind making a Hamilton fan's pocketbook a little lighter prior to a 1925 game. Munro wore a black-and-gold necktie—Hamilton Tigers' colors—during the pregame warmup after a Hamilton fan wagered he wouldn't.

There were no tigers on the ice when Ottawa battled Vancouver for the Stanley Cup in 1922, but there was one wild man—Vancouver rookie forward Syd "Wildman" Desireau. Desireau earned his nickname through his out-of-control playing style. He also had a temper and Senators defenseman Eddie Gerard decided to test Desireau's self-control. After laying out the Vancouver player with a body-check, Gerard hovered over his fallen foe, barking at Desireau like a dog. Desireau responded by punching Gerard in the face. Referee Mickey Ion assessed minor penalties against both players—Desireau's for roughing and Gerard's, apparently, for barking up the wrong tree.

Another colorful character was Jean-Baptiste Pusie, a defenseman who had brief flings with the Canadiens, Rangers and Bruins in the 1930s, Pusie was always stirring up something, but at the NHL level seldom created anything more than havoc. Once, while on a breakaway, his attention was gained by a heckling fan. Pusie disregarded the puck, dropped his stick and hurdled the boards. On another occasion, Pusie was the only player back on a five-on-one break. Instead of attempting to defend, he screamed in horror, threw his stick skyward and covered his eyes with his glove. The distracted puck carrier shot wide. Pusie had unsuccessful cameos as a prizefighter and a wrestler, and he often brought antics from these sports to the ice. One such incident resulted in a suspension from the Pacific Coast League, leading Pusie to announce, "I have been kicked out of much better leagues than this."

Tommy Dunderdale was another who terrorized the Pacific Coast back in the days when the PCHA was a major league competing for the Stanley Cup.

In 1919–20, Dunderdale established a unique record

when he led the Pacific Coast Hockey Association in scoring with 33 points and also topped the penalty parade with 52 minutes in 22 games for Victoria. Playing for Portland in 1918, Dunderdale assumed a familiar position—in the penalty box, serving 10 minutes for a double-major foul during a game against Vancouver. Under PCHA rules of the day, a team played shorthanded for only the first three minutes of a double-major foul, but when their three minutes were up, the Rosebuds had no replacement to put on the ice because Charley Uksila, their only substitute, had been injured earlier in the game. Referee George Irvine permitted Dunderdale to return to the ice, allowing him to be playing and serving a penalty simultaneously.

A couple of seasons earlier, Blunderdale would have been a more appropriate name for the future Hall of Famer. Playing for Victoria, Dunderdale swiped the puck from Vancouver's Cyclone Taylor, then stunned everyone—including Victoria goalie Bert Lindsay—by whipping a shot into his own net. Luckily for Dunderdale, he scored at the right end later and the game finished in a 1–1 tie.

Montreal's Newsy Lalonde one-upped Dunderdale's recovery skills during a 1920 game with Quebec. With the Canadiens maintaining a 3–2 lead late in the contest, Lalonde thought the referee's bell had sounded to halt play and playfully fired the puck into the Montreal net. Whatever was ringing, it was all in Newsy's head because he'd just tied the score. The game headed into overtime and wouldn't you know it, Lalonde won it, beating Quebec goalie Frank Brophy with a spectacular tally six minutes into the extra session.

Howie Morenz replaced Lalonde as the heartthrob of Habs fans in the mid 1920s. "The Stratford Streak" scored just one Stanley Cup overtime goal in his career and it wasn't even a game winner. Montreal led its 1930 two-game, total-goals quarterfinal series with Chicago 1–0 heading into game two, but Chicago fashioned a 2–1 decision in this contest, sending the series into overtime. Morenz scored after 51:43 of extra time, evening the count for the game at 2–2, but winning the series for Montreal. The Black Hawks might have been fit to be tied by this result, but four years later found a tie fit quite nicely into their plans when the two clubs clashed again in quarterfinal play. After a 3–2 Chicago win in the opener, Montreal took a 1–0 verdict in game two and once again OT was necessary. This time, Chicago's Mush March scored the game-tying goal and the series winner 11:05 into the extra period.

Interestingly, both Morenz and March went on to score Stanley Cup-winning goals for their teams, but only Bob Errey can boast that he once scored a Cup-tying goal, earning Detroit a 3–3 tie in a 1996 contest against Dallas when Dino Ciccarelli's shot banked off him past Stars goalie Andy Moog. "It went in off my athletic supporter," Errey said with a grimace. Overhearing this jock talk, Ciccarelli chuckled. "If it had been anybody but me shooting the puck, he'd be in the hospital," Ciccarelli said.

Errey probably needed taping up after that one, but nobody felt they needed a tape when Kingston played at Windsor in a 1995 Ontario Hockey League game. As fans entered the arena, each received a souvenir videotape. With Kingston comfortably ahead 6–3 late in the game, a fight broke out. When a Kingston player sucker-punched a Windsor player, angry fans littered the ice with their free videos, creating the first tape delay in a game that wasn't televised. "Unless it's Nerf balls, I don't think that they should be giving fans anything when they come in the doors," offered Kingston coach Gary Agnew. The videotape fans used to create this not-so-great moment in sports? *The Not So Great Moments In Sports.*

According to the cantankerous Conn Smythe, who never met a battle he wasn't willing to fight, another not-so-great moment in sports occurred in 1954 when the Soviet Union beat Canada to win the world hockey title for the first time. A veteran of both World Wars, Smythe was so incensed that hockey's international crown was now worn by Communists that he demanded permission from NHL president Clarence Campbell to take the Leafs to Russia and restore Canada's lost pride—a suggestion met with concern in league circles. "If Canada wants to take responsibility for starting World War III, I can see no surer way then to send Smythe to Moscow with a hockey team," suggested New York Rangers manager Frank Boucher.

CHAPTER 58

The Lighter Side of Hockey

Moments when the Game Seems to be Played for Laughs

Stan Fischler

TO THE AVERAGE FAN, COACH, MANAGER AND CLUB OWNER, there's nothing funny about hockey. It is the most emotion-filled sport and a business to be taken seriously, if not fanatically.

Yet somewhere near the fury of referee-baiting, replay disputes and salary arbitration, there is a corner of comedy in which the lighter side of hockey can be found. It was there in the earliest years when Charlie Conacher hung Toronto Maple Leafs teammate Harold Cotton upside-down outside a New York hotel window (because Cotton didn't pass to him the night before!) and it remains a part of the game today.

One of the earliest, most competent and zaniest teams of all time was the Stanley Cup champion Maple Leafs of 1932. Otherwise known as hockey's Gashouse Gang—not unlike the St. Louis Cardinals Gashouse Gang of the same era in baseball—this Toronto edition featured a number of characters. The protagonists were minuscule defenseman Frank "King" Clancy, who was often abetted by Conacher—a full-blown super scorer when he wasn't fooling around—and defenseman Clarence "Happy" Day.

A typical caper occurred in the early 1930s when the Leafs were in Boston for a game with the Bruins. In those days, the likeable Clancy was often the butt of the practical jokes. This day, when Clancy and Day were rooming together, was no exception.

On road trips the players usually convened for their pregame meal in the afternoon and then retired to their rooms to rest. At that time, Bruins games started at 8:30 p.m., so it was customary for Clancy to get up around 6:30, enabling him to get to the rink about an hour before game time. Little to his knowledge, Conacher and Day huddled after the pregame meal and agreed that it was time for another joke on Clancy.

When King and Hap retired to their room, Clancy set his alarm and soon fell into a deep sleep. Day remained awake and, when he saw that Clancy was well into slumber land, tiptoed out of the room, met Conacher in the hall, and the two of them took the elevator to the lobby. The pair then persuaded the room clerk to ring Clancy's room. The hotel employee was advised to inform Clancy that he was working for Boston Garden, it was game time, and the two teams were on the ice ready for the opening face-off.

With their plans intact, the culprits returned to their floor and huddled outside Clancy's room. They listened as the phone rang and King screamed in horror. A moment later, Clancy ran out the door, dashed downstairs and sprinted for the nearest taxicab. He found one and advised the astonished driver that he was King Clancy of the Maple Leafs and he was late for his hockey game. The driver happened to be a hockey fan and knew very well the game wouldn't start for more than two hours. He asked what Clancy's rush was all about since it was only 6:00 p.m.

As the truth dawned on King, he ordered the driver to stop. He slowly climbed out and walked back to the hotel, where Day and Conacher were waiting for him in the lobby. There is no official record of what Clancy said to them, but it probably could not be printed here anyway.

Friends of Clancy—and they number in the thousands—often are hard-pressed to decide whether King was funnier as a player, a referee or a coach. Those who knew King best generally lean toward his playing days. One reason is that when Clancy was playing, he was surrounded by other jesters such as Day, Conacher and Cotton.

King always had a very wholesome ability to laugh at himself and his shortcomings. His one-liners were to hockey enthusiasts what Henny Youngman's were to show business people. After one of his more amusing scraps, King snapped: "I don't finish fights, I just start 'em."

Clancy's most famous bout took place against Montreal Maroons defenseman Harold Starr. At that time, the Maple Leafs were the classiest team in the NHL and the Maroons were regarded as one of the toughest sextets in the business. Most players instinctively shied away from big, burly Starr because of his size and the fact that he was known to have tried his hand at professional wrestling before joining the Maroons. But Clancy treated Starr as if he were a 98-pound weakling.

On that historic night at the Maple Leaf Gardens, the Maroons were giving Toronto a substantial pasting and Toronto's tempers were becoming edgy. Finally, in the last minute of play, a brawl erupted involving most members of both teams. Normally these mass hockey fights break into two skirmishes: the instigators fight their battle while the other players go at it mildly or just hold each other until the main event is over. Somehow, more than a few serious fights developed this time and, to everyone's amazement, Clancy was taking on the huge Harold Starr.

The David-and-Goliath bout between Clancy and Starr so arrested the attention of the other battlers that they cut short their own fights to see whether the King would come out alive. Some observers had grave doubts about Clancy's ability to survive the clash. Starr embraced the King with his huge arms, dropped the little Leaf to the ice and pushed him around the rink as if he was playing broomball with Clancy as the ball. But that wasn't enough. Next he lifted Clancy over his head like a lumberjack would pick up a log and hurled King about 40 feet across the rink. Still that wasn't enough.

Starr skated over to his crumpled foe and concluded the bout by sitting on top of Clancy. Bellowing like a bull moose, Clancy demanded that Starr release him immediately. Being the good sport that he was, the Maroon finally rose to his skates and looked down at the King. As a final insult, Starr said, "That just about took care of you tonight, my friend."

Surrendering never came easily to Clancy. He adjusted his disheveled jersey, clambered to his feet, skated directly at his tormentor and said: "Starr, you never saw the day you could lay a hand on me!"

Some of the game's best lines have come about from fisticuffs and tough checking. One such episode involved a youthful French-Canadian center named Phillipe Henri Watson of the New York Rangers (better known as Phil) and Toronto's rugged veteran defenseman Wilfred "Bucko" McDonald.

In the late 1930s, when the episode took place, Watson's command of the English language was minimal, to say the least, but he did have a light grasp of some idioms. On this particular night, the larger McDonald had singled out Watson for some heavy hits, saving the best for the third period. As Watson thudded to the ice, he instantly searched his mind for the ultimate put-down and decided that McDonald's advanced age was the best bet. "Bucko," the embattled Ranger yelled from his horizontal position, "you're nutting but a *been-has*!"

The Rangers were responsible for a bizarre publicity stunt when they entered the NHL in November, 1926. At the time, Madison Square Garden employed a pair of press agents—Bruno and Blythe—who knew little about hockey but plenty about publicity. The public relations pair scanned the Rangers' training camp lineup before the inaugural home game and noticed that there was neither a player of Italian nor Jewish extraction among the regulars. This was not good news to them, since New York at the time had very significant Jewish and Italian neighborhoods where sports was king.

Bruno and Blythe decided that since there was no Jew or Italian on the roster, they would have to do something to ensure that there was. They decided that the Jew would be the Rangers' French-Canadian goalie, Lorne Chabot. Bruno changed his name to Chabotsky. Blythe then went to work on forward Oliver Reinikka and converted him to Ollie Rocco. Poof! You're Italian! Unfortunately, neither player enjoyed his *nom de glace*. What's more the Canadian hockey writers knew Chabot and Reinikka for what they really were and lampooned Bruno and Blythe. As a result the two press agents became ex-press agents faster than Chabot could clear the puck to Rocco … rather Reinikka.

Another case of mistaken identity of sorts involved Rangers rookie defenseman Myles Lane, who played for New York in the late 1920s. At the time, Eddie Shore of the Boston Bruins was one of the NHL's best defensemen. Although a Shore for Lane deal seemed preposterous, Rangers president John Hammond insisted that manager Lester Patrick try to wangle Shore from the Bruins. Patrick obliged by sending a wire to his Boston counterpart Art Ross. The Ross reply has gone down in NHL annals for its pithy accuracy:

"You're so many Myles from the Shore, you need a life preserver!"

After reaching the seventh game of the 1950 Stanley Cup finals, the Rangers suffered through hard times. During the 1950–51 season, the Broadway Blueshirts hit a terrible slump that even depressed Times Square restaurateur Gene Leone, who hosted the weekly New York Hockey Writers' Association luncheons. To cure the slump, Leone concocted what he called a "magic elixir." Just before Christmas, he poured it into a large black bottle three times the size of a normal whiskey bottle. He then collected such Rangers as Don Raleigh, Neil Colville, Frankie Eddolls and Pentti Lund for a sip of the brew.

Suddenly, the slumping Rangers turned into winners. By early January, 1951, they had become the NHL's hottest team. Still, cynics insisted the real test would come when the Blueshirts visited Toronto, where they hadn't had a victory for ages.

Now the fun started. Leone demanded that the "magic elixir," whose formula was so secret that he wouldn't even trust it to paper, be prepared at the last possible moment. This was done on Saturday afternoon. When the elixir was ready, he turned it over to *New York World-Telegram* hockey writer Jim Burchard, who boarded a plane for Toronto. The plan was for Jim to arrive just before game time and present the potion to the Rangers.

Unknown to the Ranger strategists, the Maple Leaf organization was arranging for the Canadian customs agent to seize the black bottle at the Toronto airport, denying its use to the New Yorkers. But a Toronto photographer named Harold Robinson saved the Rangers by slipping through security. Robinson then pushed Burchard into a car and set several Ontario speed records driving him to Maple Leaf Gardens just in time for the quaffing. The Rangers, who enjoyed the joke more than the elixir itself, had their laughs and then went out on the ice and performed like supermen. Within seven minutes of the first period they scored three goals and coasted to a 4–2 win.

Two weeks later, Burchard arrived in Toronto without the bottle and the Rangers lost. The papers attributed the loss to the missing elixir. Leone soon produced more. Though it seemed to keep the Rangers in contention for a while longer, the psychological value of the elixir had run its course and the Blueshirts faded into fifth place at the end of the season.

Scotty Bowman's teams rarely suffered situations such as those that faced the Rangers, and the NHL's winningest coach rarely was known for his humor. But, when Bowman's Canadiens were winning four straight Stanley Cup titles between 1976 and 1979, one of his disciplinary tactics drew a few laughs.

Montreal had beaten the Kings at the Forum in Inglewood, California, and were looking forward to celebrating with a night on the town in Los Angeles. Although there was no game scheduled the next day, Bowman imposed a curfew on the club. Several players were vexed over Scotty's decision. Feeling unjustly confined, a group of them took off for the bright lights and watering holes.

Many hours later—long after curfew—the entourage returned to the hotel and was greeted by an enthusiastic doorman who seemed like an avid hockey fan. Armed with an authentic Canadiens hockey stick, the doorman asked each of the incoming players if they would be good enough to autograph his stick. Feeling no pain, the Habs were glad to oblige and each put his John Hancock on the stick shaft.

Little did they realize that their signatures would incriminate them.

At breakfast the next morning, Bowman singled out of every one of the curfew-breakers and doled out fines.

How did Bowman know which players were guilty?

Simple. It was the coach who had given the stick to the doorman, asking him to get the postmidnight players to sign their names—and inadvertently admit their guilt.

CHAPTER 59

Equipment and Safety

From Masks to Sticks to Elbow Pads, Equipment and Injuries Closely Linked

The Hockey Stick

Bruce Dowbiggin

ANDREAS DACKELL WAS IN A RUT. The Ottawa Senators forward had only two goals in the first half of the 1999-2000 season, and the man who had 15 goals the previous season was an unimpressive plus-minus rating of -9. Shots that had produced goals in the past were suddenly missing the net or getting buried in the goalie's pads. Some said he missed his former linemate, holdout center Alexei Yashin. Others claimed he was only fit for the fourth line. The usually sunny Dackell didn't know what to think.

When the Swedish native went 26 games without a goal, he finally went looking for salvation. He found it in a bundle of Joe Sakic-model sticks brought to the Corel Centre. Dackell spied the composite stick, liked what he saw and felt, and had the Easton representative convert Sakic's righthanded sticks to lefthanded for him. Then, he gave the new stick a shot. Make that hundreds of shots. In practice. In games.

Using the Sakic model, Dackell's season suddenly turned around; he scored eight goals in the second half of the 1999-2000 season. His skating and overall game picked up with the added confidence of the Sakic stick. A personal testimonial to the power of a new stick—a graphite composite one at that—was born.

Did the stick make Dackell a better player or was it simply the change of habit? The symbiotic relationship between a hockey player and his stick is so shrouded in myth and legend that the answer to both questions could be yes. But there's no question that hockey sticks have always been part security blanket, part Excalibur to the men who use them for a living. What has changed is the look of the stick that Dackell used to save his season. Any Victorian-era hockey player looking at the hockey stick as the 21st century began would be amazed to see the sleek model that rescued Dackell. What was this artificial material in the shaft? Who bent the blade out of shape? Where did all the bright colors come from? It costs how much?

The hockey stick, with its long wooden shaft and thin, narrow blade, is thought to have been modeled on the hurley—the weapon used in the traditional Irish game of hurling. Immigrants brought the field game to Canada and simply adapted the sport, and the hurley, to the ice of their frozen playing grounds at the start of the 1800s. The innovations that followed, however, were purely Canadian.

Looking down at the lumber the pioneer player carried in 1900, he would have seen a well-oiled, one-piece Hilborn or Starr stick carved from yellow birch, hornbeam, rock elm or white ash. The weightiness of the stick and its relative lack of flexibility would have made it good for passing and sliding the puck; but any attempt at a slap shot with this solid specimen would have touched off reverberations though a player's cranium.

As the 20th century dawned, most of the best sticks were either hand-carved by the Mi'kmaq Indians in Nova Scotia or lathed from rock elm or ash in Ontario sawmills that usually produced axe handles or wagon wheels. In the latter, hockey-stick production was often an afterthought. (Ironically, these afterthoughts would long outlive the primary products of those same factories.) The Mi'kmaq stick was sought after for its sturdy yellow-birch construction. When a suitable tree was found, it was uprooted and the stick was carved from the lower tree and root system. The roots—which had the toughest wood—formed the blade, while the shaft was carved from the trunk. Mi'kmaq sticks were shipped under the Starr or Rex labels as far as Ontario and the northeast United States into the 1920s at a price of 45 cents a dozen. (Today's best wooden sticks can cost well upwards of $30 apiece.)

The best sticks at the turn of the last century had tight, long grains that ran without knots or flaws right into the blade. This gave them a natural toughness that guaranteed longevity. They were also oiled for hardness and this durability made some sticks last two or three seasons if properly stored and treated. To provide grip on these smooth sticks, the shafts contained serrations that ran the length of the stick. Blades were double grooved for better shooting accuracy.

From the dawn of the 20th century until World War II, refinements in the basic stick-manufacturing process were directed toward lightness, flexibility and adding velocity to the shot. This involved finding better wood with high-quality grain cut from white ash, hickory or rock elm stands in Ontario, Quebec, the Maritimes or the northeast U.S. In the 1920s, St. Marys Wood Specialty Products in St. Marys, Ontario, introduced the first two-piece sticks, with the blade now being wedged into the heel of the shaft and glued. This eliminated the need for steam-bending and other complicated processes to bend the wood into the traditional shape. And it removed the time-consuming searching for perfect wood. Lighter blades allowed for harder, faster shots.

St. Marys was joined by Hespeler, Hilborn, Pirate and Starr as preeminent names in the stick business before World War II. Many other sticks were manufactured under the labels of oil companies, department stores and hardware stores as promotions or giveaways. Following World War II, new names emerged: Northland, Victoriaville, Louisville and CCM, among others. But the center of the hockey-stick industry shifted to Quebec's Eastern Townships where Leo Drolet used a $600 loan to start the Sher-Wood factory in Sherbrooke. Using the powerful Montreal Canadiens teams of the 1950s as a springboard, Drolet came to dominate the pro market for wood sticks—a position that continued into the last decade of the century.

Sher-Wood was to usher in a remarkable era of change for the stick. Even if Drolet didn't innovate something, he was quick to copy and refine the best ideas, such as three-piece sticks in the 1950s, curved blades and fibreglass wrapping in the 1960s, layered shafts in the 1970s and insertable blades in the 1980s. Each was a remarkable transformation in its day, but no innovation was as visible or controversial as the curved blade that overtook hockey—and goalies—in the 1960s.

As far back as the 1940s, future NHL star Andy Bathgate of the Rangers had been fooling around with the blade of his stick in his hometown of Winnipeg, adding a banana-like curve by soaking, then heating the blade to shape it under a door or in a chair. He and his brother discovered that the curved blade gave their shot a slingshot quality, a marked increase in speed and a marked decrease in accuracy. In short, the curved blade scared the daylights out of goalies.

While Bathgate's coach in New York, Alf Pike, went around breaking the novelty blades, Chicago's Stan Mikita found only acceptance from coach Billy Reay when he started bending blades in the early 1960s. When his Black Hawk teammate Bobby Hull adopted the banana blade, a new era in scoring was inaugurated. Married to the powerful slap shot, the curved blade sent records tumbling. Hull soon shattered the single-season record of 50 goals set by Rocket Richard in 1944–45 and equaled by Bernie Geoffrion in 1960–61. Within a decade, the new record was 76 goals in a season. Such was the power and unpredictability of the curved blade that NHL owners imposed severe limits on the size of the curve in the belief that some goalie or fan was going to be killed by the erratic path of a slap shot. In very short order, however, the straight hockey blade became extinct in the NHL.

Sher-Wood kept pace with the changing tastes and its overall dominance of the market might have grown larger had it not been for two factors: European competition and artificial materials. They cut into Sher-wood's mighty market share in the final decades of the 20th century.

The first European sticks came to North America from Finland in the late 1960s and early 1970s, thanks in part to former NHL All-Star Carl Brewer, who played in that country and brought the Koho brand back to Canada with him. The Finnish sticks were considered exceptionally light for their time—18 or 19 ounces compared to 22 or 23 for Canadian sticks.

Because proper hardwood was scarce in Finland, Koho had glued together many thin layers of birch to form the shaft, producing a lighter stick with similar flex points to a North American model. Koho also pioneered the use of colorful graphics on the previously staid stick. Soon, all the companies were following Koho's lead, using as many as 18 or 20 layers in their pro-model sticks and searching out bold color schemes. To create even lighter sticks, manufacturers now drill holes in these layered shafts, creating a honeycomb effect. Today, European sticks such as Koho, Titan and Canadian comprise an estimated 25 percent of the world market.

The other stick revolution has come in synthetic materials. As tennis and golf showed how aluminum and graphite could dramatically increase power and speed in their sport, hockey followed suit. The first sticks made of aluminum were introduced in 1979. While they were dramatically lighter and fired the puck with greater velocity, they lacked "feel" and emitted a strange pinging noise when struck. Metal fatigue was also a problem. The next move in artificial sticks was in the direction of composite or graphite sticks. Mike Bossy of the New York Islanders introduced the Titan Turbo in 1984, a fibreglass/graphite shaft with a laminated wooden blade. In one form or another, all the succeeding composite sticks sprang from this model. Today, Easton is producing a one-piece graphite stick with matching blade.

Composite sticks have superior weight and feel, and they are easier for manufacturers to reproduce to precise specifications than wooden sticks. But they have been prone to snapping following a sharp blow on the shaft. After a surge among NHLers toward graphite in the early 1990s, this fragility caused a number of pros to return to wooden sticks later in the decade.

While a number of veteran stars such as Al MacInnis of St. Louis and Teemu Selanne of Anaheim remained loyal to lumber as the new century dawned, most of the top young stars such as Paul Kariya of Anaheim and Pavel Bure of Florida were employing composite sticks. As Andreas Dackell illustrates, one thing hasn't changed in all the innovations during the 20th century: most players are very finicky about their sticks. Go into the dressing room before a game and you're likely to see players lovingly shaping, filing and wrapping their game sticks for that contest. Talcum, tape and blow torches are still used in this time-honored ritual.

Taping styles have gone in and out of fashion. For a time, everyone taped their blades from heel to toe to produce friction with the ice and control of the puck. Then fibreglass-wrapped sticks produced their own friction and so Bobby Orr inaugurated an era of minimal tape on the blade. Now, with the smooth composite blades in style, players are again taping their blades almost completely.

Players know their sticks, too. Most can sort through a batch from the factory and pick out samples that are a quarter ounce too light or too heavy, or that have the flex points in the shaft misaligned. Paul Kariya is said to be able to identify most opponents' sticks simply by their look and feel. And they treat those sticks like treasured objects. The Phoenix Coyotes' Jeremy Roenick, for instance, is phobic about having a teammate's stick fall over into his stall in the dressing room for fear it might touch his stick. If anyone or anything comes into contact with one of his, the Phoenix center throws it away.

Derek Plante is similarly superstitious about friends and foes getting their prints on his game sticks, discarding ones that have been "polluted" by strangers. Former NHLer Petr Klima believed there was only one goal in every stick. So, he broke them after he'd scored. That policy would have emptied several forests in the case of Wayne Gretzky. Thankfully for the environment, the NHL's all-time scoring champ broke very few of his sticks in games. That didn't stop him from going through about 700 sticks a season, most of which ended up as souvenirs. At the 1998 Winter Olympics, for instance, Gretzky brought 48 sticks to Japan—four for each day of his stay in Nagano. He left with none.

No one is predicting the death of the wooden stick just yet. Still, wooden sticks will need to be constantly refined if they are to deliver the performance now delivered by composites. If the wooden stick does go the way of the tube skate, it will mark the end of a tradition that has its roots in the forests of early Canada, and the people who tamed them.

HOCKEY EQUIPMENT

Peter Wilton

IN THE EARLY DAYS OF HOCKEY, little thought was given to the equipment. The skate blade was forged from the kiln of the blacksmith and strapped onto the shoe or boot of the player. The stick could be literally a branch from a tree shaped to hit the puck. At best, it might be an adapted field hockey stick. The puck itself was an India rubber ball—with or without the sides cut off—or a piece of tin, a block of wood or a lump of coal. Sometimes it was just a frozen piece of horse dung. The ice surface was the frozen lakes and ponds that dotted the winter landscape of Canada. The games were played by both men and women as social outings.

When hockey started to be played by set teams, it became necessary to have team sweaters for identification. Not only did the sweaters provide a uniformity of appearance amongst the players, it also helped them keep warm in games that were played either outside or in unheated arenas. The toque was also part of the uniform, not because it offered any protection against a blow to the head, but because the knitted hats offered added protection against the cold. Like their counterparts in soccer, hockey goalies often wore a cap to protect their eyes against the glare of the sun.

The story of the innovations surrounding the development of the equipment used to play hockey is a story of individuals who, tired of being hurt, invented a way to protect themselves from the rough-and-tumble aspects of the game. The equipment was not developed all at once, but came about over a century, each generation of hockey players improving and adding to the equipment bag for the next generation.

It's not surprising to learn that the first area early players of the game of hockey tried to protect was their shins. In the 1880s, players started using strips of leather or felt, reinforced with thin lengths of cane, to protect their shins from errant sticks and pucks. It would take another decade before players began to design protection for their knees. The original knee pad consisted of a large square of leather or canvas, reinforced with felt. By the 1920s, knee and shin pads were attached together. The material flexibility of the knee and shin pads improved greatly with the development of plastics and velcro after World War II.

Despite the greater vulnerability of the goalie to being injured, those who played this position in the early days of hockey did not wear any more protective equipment than the other members of their team. George "Whitey" Merritt, the goaltender with the Winnipeg Victorias hockey team, sought to improve upon the protection offered by cane and felt shin pads when he took the ice prior to a February 14, 1896, game wearing cricket pads. Although Merritt is often credited with introducing these pads to hockey, both the goalie of the Queen's University team and of the Toronto Granites had been wearing cricket pads back in 1893. There is no question, however, that Merritt wearing them during a Stanley Cup game, brought the issue to the forefront. When it was determined that there was no rule preventing the wearing of such pads, other goalies followed Merritt's lead.

In the early 1920s, a Hamilton, Ontario, harness maker named Emil "Pop" Kenesky made an observation while watching a Catholic league hockey game. Kenesky noted that the cricket pads worn by the goaltenders—pads which followed the curvature of the goalies' leg—were allowing pucks to ricochet into the net. He decided to modify the cricket pads using material from the harness making trade: tanned horse leather stuffed with deer hair. By doing so, he widened the leg protectors to 12 inches per pad.

During the 1923–24 season, Kenesky was approached by the coach of the Hamilton Tigers. The team had been suffering through a lengthy losing streak, and it was hoped that the Kenesky pads could help them. Again using cricket pads as the base, Kenesky modified his design and the new pads he came up with were credited with bringing an end to the losing streak. When the NHL ruled in 1925-26 that the Kenesky pads did not violate any rule, goalies began to beat a path to Hamilton and to Kenesky. For the next 50 years, a goalie proved himself in two ways: by stopping pucks and by wearing Kenesky pads.

There was only one major shortcoming to Kenesky's pads. They would sponge up water from the ice. A pair of Kenesky pads that started off weighing roughly 17 pounds (better materials have today's goalie pads weighing about 11 pounds each) would get heavier and heavier over the course of the game. Naturally, this would slow down the goalie. To combat this problem, goalies by the 1930s had developed the habit of smacking their pads with their stick as a ways of trying to get rid of some excess moisture. A side advantage to using their sticks this way was that in thumping their pads they would get a little wider. (The NHL had ruled prior to the 1927-28 season that goalie pads could not exceed 10 inches in width. This rule held until the 1989-90 season, when the 12-inch pads were once again okayed by the league.)

In the early days of hockey, scars, missing teeth, and stitches were a badge of honor. Many players looked upon hockey as a rough-and-tumble game, and the lack of equipment added to this image. But slowly, better equipment began to creep into the game. One example of this is the development of players' gloves.

Initially, all that the glove protected a player against was the cold. Old pictures of teams such as the Rideau Rebels show players wearing gloves that look similar to what a modern oil-rigger might wear, with the long gauntlet running up the arm. Around the 1900 season, players began to wear padded leather gloves, the padding made up of animal hair and felt. Some gloves included rattan reeds over the wrist portion to add extra protection. Big Bill O'Brien, trainer for both the Montreal Maroons and the Montreal Canadiens, claims to have invented the reinforced thumb which is now standard on hockey gloves. According to O'Brien, the development came about after Babe Siebert broke his thumb in 1931. Unable to play without some form of added protection, the Maroons were scrambling to find something to safeguard Siebert's damaged digit. They settled on a shoe horn. The reinforced protection of this shoe horn was the impetus for the reinforced fibre thumb, which shortly thereafter became an integral part of the hockey glove.

Goalies' gloves at first followed the same basic design as those worn by other players, but as early as 1915 gloves with extra padding were being developed for goalies. However, the only other concession made to the role that the goalie played was a leather web between the thumb and index finger which could be used to help stop the puck. It would take over 30 years before the catching glove was developed. It was the innovation of one player, Emile Francis, goalie with the Chicago Black Hawks, who showed up for a game against the Detroit Red Wings in

1948 after having sewn a first baseman's mitt to his goalie glove. Despite protests from the opposing team's coach, there was no rule against such a glove. Soon, other goalies were following his example and modifying their own gloves to include a baseball mitt. Over the years, the pocket had been extended and the material has been improved. The basic idea of attaching a first baseman's glove to the end of the leather gauntlet has now become a very specialized piece of equipment.

The stick hand of a goalie is particularly vulnerable to injury, as the back of the hand faces the shooter. The trend towards protection in this area accelerated in 1925, and continued into the 1930s. It was during this time period that the design for the modern blocker developed. The main material for the blocker remained a firm sheet of harness leather until the late 1960s and early 1970s when a hard sheet of lexan, a shatter-proof form of plexiglass, was developed. This was placed inside the blocker, cushioned by styrene and covered with a hard leather shell. In more recent years, the changes in both goalie gloves and pads have consisted mainly of changes in material. Plastics, polyethylene absorbing foams, waterproof nylons and synthetic leather have all improved the quality and lessened the weight of goaltending equipment. Chest protectors have followed a similar pattern of evolution.

If asked, most hockey fans would identify Jacques Plante, the Montreal Canadiens netminder, as the man behind the goalie mask. His battle for the right to be able to wear the mask after suffering a serious injury is the stuff of legend. But Plante was not the first NHL goalkeeper to wear a mask. That honor belongs to Clint Benedict, who suffered a smashed nose from a blistering shot fired by Howie Morenz on January 7, 1930. Benedict, who played for the Montreal Maroons, took to wearing a leather facemask after this injury. He wore the mask for only two games because the design was not practical. He was unable to see around the nose pad.

But even Benedict may not have been the first netminder to cover his face. Stewart Bell, writing for the *Queen's Alumni Review*, claims it was his grandmother who first wore a hockey mask. Elizabeth Graham, goaltender of the Queen's University women's hockey team, started to wear a fencing mask to protect her features when she was playing back in 1927. Graham was wearing a mode of facial protection three years before Benedict donned his, and 32 years prior to Jacques Plante donning his modified mask! Today, there are a wide variety of masks worn by goalies. Some also wear a neck protector, which dangles below the mask to protect the netminder from skates or pucks to the throat. This, too, was an innovation that developed outside the NHL.

In the late 1970s, Kim Crouch was playing goal at Chesswood arena in suburban Toronto. There was a lot of traffic in front of his net as the 18-year-old went down to cover the puck. When play ended, it was apparent that there was something seriously wrong. Blood was pooling around Crouch, who had taken a skate blade to his neck. There was a nasty six-inch wound that had severed his jugular vein. Had it had not been for the quick thinking of 22-year-old coach Joe Piccininni, who managed to stem the flow of blood, Crouch might have died on the ice.

After his injury, Crouch was anxious to get back to the game. His father, a fireman with the North York Fire Department, was determined to prevent a similar injury from occurring—not just to his own son but to other goaltenders as well. He designed the "Crouch Collar" that has become standard equipment for most goaltenders.

As with goaltenders, it was the harness maker that originally provided clues as to how other players could protect their shoulders and back against injury. One of the alltime greats of the game, Fred "Cyclone" Taylor, was said to be in a harness shop in Renfrew, Ontario, in 1910 when he noticed how the harness makers were using felt to protect the horses from the weight of the harnesses. Taylor took some scraps of felt from the shop and sewed them into his undershirt around the shoulders and down his back. Although other players may have teased Cyclone about not being tough enough to play the game, it was not long before all the players were wearing felt shoulder pads in their undergarments. Another Taylor legend claims that his mother had begun sewing felt and corset supports into his sweater and undergarments when he played junior hockey in Listowel, Ontario.

Felt and leather continued to be the main material used to make shoulder pads until after World War II, which saw the creation of such materials as plastic and fiberglass. These new materials proved to be more practical and efficient, and different styles of shoulder pads began to be developed depending on the position of the player. Defensemen, for example, needed greater protection in the chest and biceps area, since their position would sometimes require them to drop to the ice and block a shot. The shoulder pads were also extended around and down to provide protection to the vulnerable back area. The development of velcro allowed for a better fit.

Elbow pads were first used by hockey players in 1910. The original pads were simplistic in design, consisting of an elastic bandage for support with strips of felt to protect against bruising. They were worn on the outside of the uniform until the 1940s, when too many injuries were resulting from elbows to the face. Even after they were required to be worn inside the sweater, there was an effort to ensure that pads met certain criteria and were not simply brass knuckles worn on the elbows. This led the to the NHL passing a rule prior to the 1958–59 hockey season that became known as the "dangerous equipment rule." The idea behind it was to force manufacturers to design pads with the idea of absorbing impact and not inflicting pain. Toward this end, the new ruling made illegal any equipment containing metal. Any such equipment would have to be replaced with equipment made of plastics and fiberglass. Suspicions ran high that some teams were not complying with this ruling, so in order to alleviate these fears, a referee was ordered to check all the equipment of all the teams to ensure that they complied with the new standards.

For the past century, Canadian women have been playing competitive hockey. Of course, the numbers have increased dramatically over the past decade, and only since then have equipment manufacturers begun to reflect this reality by designing hockey gear with the fit, comfort and protection of women in mind. Some examples of the modifications for women include hockey pants with narrower legs and tapered hips, and gloves with narrower fingers and palms. Shoulder pads are designed to protect the chests of female athletes. The pelvic area is protected by a piece of equipment known, informally, as the "Jill."

The most basic piece of equipment for any hockey player, male or female, is the skate. Until 1901, hockey players wore skates which were similar in design to modern figure skates in that the blade was attached directly to the boot. Tube skates were invented in Norway and brought to Canada in the early 1900s. They featured a sharp steel blade welded to a steel tube. In turn, this steel tube—not the blade—had supports that were riveted to the heel and toe of the skate boot. With the blade beneath the tube, skaters had better balance and could turn more quickly. It was the Winnipeg Victorias who introduced tube skates to hockey when they wore them in a Stanley Cup challenge in 1901.

Early hockey skates, whether they were tube skates or not, offered very little protection around the ankle area. To combat this problem, Russell Bowie began wearing horse hobbles (wooden blocks used to impede a horse's movement) over his skates in 1903. A rudimentary tendon guard later was sewn to the back of the skates to try and protect that area, though it was not until World War II, and the development of nylon, that real tendon protection was developed.

Another concern regarding tube skates was the sharp edge at the back of the skates. The worry was that the sharp edge could cut the Achilles tendon. The risk of this happening was particularly strong when two players became entangled and had to scramble to get back in the game. Maurice Richard was injured in just this way on November 13, 1958, causing him to miss 42 games. This injury was the impetus for equipment manufacturer CCM to develop a plastic heel which fit over the end of the skate blade. The so-called "safety heel" protected players from injuries such as the one that Richard had suffered.

The Canadian Cycle and Motor company (CCM) had been heavily into the manufacturing of bicycles at the turn of the century, but, being aware of the cyclical nature of the bicycle business, sought to offset the slow winter season by manufacturing skates. CCM's brand were called "automobile skates." Though it would take almost two decades, CCM had an active role in combating another problem found in early hockey skates—the fact that they were hard on the muscles in the front of the skater's legs.

It took a number of years to discover that the design of the skate and the way that people naturally skated (by pushing off on the toe) had the same result on the legs as climbing up a hill. When this observation was made, skate manufacturers began to add an elevated heel piece to the skates to prevent this muscle strain. (It is interesting to note that while CCM was among the early innovators, and is still known to this day for the protective equipment which they manufacture, it was Spalding Canada that was in fact the first sporting goods company to get into the hockey equipment market.)

In 1978, a completely new look in skates was introduced. First used by members of the Montreal Canadiens like Guy Lafleur, Steve Shutt, Jacques Lemaire and Jim Roberts, the futuristic-looking skates with plastic moldings to hold the blade to the boot offered better protection and stability to the player. The Tuuk blade these skates featured was the next revolution in skate design, and became the standard for the last quarter of the 20th century.

The new Tuuk blade was lighter, stylish and easy to replace. However, there were some initial shortcomings. The main complaint was that they broke easily, which was an irritant in that it could take weeks to receive a replacement blade (particularly if one was not an NHL player) and a safety concern, as the broken blade could become a razor sharp point at the back of the skate. These problems were dealt with quickly, as the blades were made stronger and safety edges were reinforced at the back of the skate. Tuuk also made changes to the pigmentation in the blade holder and in so doing strengthened the plastic, which had had the tendency to crack and break in the early models. With these changes complete, the new style of molded skate soon captured the imagination of a new generation of hockey players much as the tube skate had some 75 years before.

Despite the development of safety equipment over the last 125 years of hockey history, one of the most vulnerable areas of the player was, for a long time, left surprisingly bare. There were spurts in which players would don a helmet, such as after the Eddie Shore and Ace Bailey incident that saw Shore upend the star of the Maple Leafs in a game in 1933. Bailey struck his head against the ice and suffered through three brain operations before it was known that the injury would end only his career and not his life. Shore, who suffered a concussion after a retaliation hit, wore a helmet for the rest of his playing days. Though he was one of the game's greatest players, very few others would follow Shore's lead until another tragedy more than 34 years later.

On January 13, 1968, a mere two weeks after suffering a serious concussion, Bill Masterton of the Minnesota North Stars suffered another blow to his head. He spent the next 30 hours in the hospital before dying from his injuries. Following his death, a number of players did begin to wear helmets. By this time, plastic and foam had replaced the leather which traditionally had been used to make hockey helmets, but there were no standards regarding the safety requirements surrounding hockey headgear. After Masterton's death, standards were set in Canada to establish minimum requirements that a helmet had to meet before being acceptable. During the 1970s, helmets became mandatory for players in the college and junior ranks, and NHL legislation was passed making helmets mandatory for any player who signed a contract after June 1, 1979. Though an exemption was passed in 1992 to allow players to go without a helmet if they signed a waiver, by the 1995–96 season Craig MacTavish was the last bareheaded player in the NHL. Though helmet use was universal, many players wore helmets that had been modified for comfort usually by reducing the amount of padding. These helmets did not meet the same safety standards as those helmets approved for use in youth and minor hockey associations. Beginning in 1997, NHL regulations required that safety-certified helmets be worn by all players who already wore a certified model or were 25 or younger. The number of older players wearing helmets that aren't certified declines each year.

Since the adoption of mandatory helmet rules in hockey, eye and neck protection has been instituted for all junior and youth players. Young hockey players no longer have toothless smiles and scarred faces, but increased protection cuts both ways. Some say that improved equipment adds to the increase in injuries, that players feel so well-protected that they no longer believe that they can be hurt and no longer have the proper concern about the well-being of the others on the ice. On the other hand, with the risks of injury inherent in the sport, there is no question that effective protective equipment should be mandatory.

We have come a long way since the toques and cardigan sweaters of the last century. Light, effective equipment has only improved the game. The magic and speed remain.

The Year of the Mask

Fred Addis

In April, 1959, Don Spencer wrote a letter to Montreal Canadiens goaltender Jacques Plante. He had read of Plante's interest in developing face protection for goalies and wanted to tell the Habs netminder about a form-fitting fiberglass mask designed by his college trainer Gene Long.

Spencer hoped his letter might net him a couple of tickets to a future Canadiens game. He never received a reply but his letter would provide the missing link for Plante to fast-track the introduction of his goalie mask to the NHL.

In four years of tending goal for Hamilton College in Clinton, New York, Spencer had totaled more than 50 stitches to the head from sticks and pucks. Long, the athletics trainer at Hamilton College, had been experimenting with fiberglass insert pads for football and hockey. Long made a fiberglass pad that Spencer inserted in the boot of his skate to protect his inside ankle when making kick saves. When Spencer had his nose broken in 1958 he tried a plexiglas shield, similar to a welding mask, which was already in broad circulation. Goaltenders used these shields in practice only. They were not perfect and were noted for heat build-up, fogging and excessive weight. In addition they hampered a goalie's vision because of the glare from arena lights.

Using Spencer as his prototype, Gene Long determined to adapt his fiberglass expertise to create a form-fitting mask for his Hamilton College goalies. He made two, which were used only in practice beginning in 1958. Although Spencer graduated before he could wear his mask in college competition, he did use it in senior amateur play and even made masks himself for goalies he later coached in youth hockey.

Long's mask-making process involved laying two- to three-inch strips of gauze soaked in plaster on the goalie's face, much the same as preparing a cast for an arm or a leg. When dry, this "cast" provided a negative mold into which dental rock (a quick-setting plaster used by dentists to make an impression of one's teeth) was poured. A positive dental rock impression was then lifted from the negative mold. With a perfect plaster model of the goalie's face resulting, the plaster was covered with Vaseline, and strips of fiberglass, impregnated with resin, were laid over the positive form. When the fiberglass had set it was released from the form and the custom work began. Gene Long used a saber saw to cut holes for the eyes, nose and mouth as well as some additional holes for ventilation. Liquid fiberglass was then added to smooth out the surface, especially around the openings. Finally, suspender straps, similar to those used for a baseball catcher's mask, were attached and the job was finished. Long estimated the cost at $5.00 for materials plus a lot of labor.

The mask reduced cuts, and the impact of direct hits from pucks and sticks was distributed across the face. It still hurt, but the possibility of having one's appearance altered was greatly reduced. It is somewhat ironic that dental rock would prove essential in the preparation of form-fitting fiberglass facemasks for goalies, as a goaltender's only previous experience with the material was invariably when being fitted for false teeth. A gap in a goalie's smile was a fact of life and a visible badge of office. Few goalies sported a full set of their own choppers.

Among his early successes, Gene Long had fashioned a fiberglass mask for Spider Brown, a forward for the Clinton Comets of the Eastern Hockey League. With Long's mask, Brown was able to resume playing before his broken jaw had completely mended. Long would later produce one of his masks for Comets goalie Norm DeFelice. (It should be noted, however, that DeFelice was not the first goalie to wear a protective mask in the EHL. New York Rovers netminder Don Rich wore a helmet with a removable clear bubble visor, much like a fighter pilot's headgear, during league games in the fall of 1959.)

Don Spencer never received a reply from Jacques Plante but the Habs goalie did visit Hamilton College during the summer of 1959. He met with Gene Long, who explained his fiberglass mask technology and showed some samples. However Long's pioneering fiberglass creations in upstate New York were quickly upstaged when Plante made NHL history on November 1, 1959.

After being cut by a shot from Andy Bathgate of the New York Rangers, the Montreal netminder went off to be stitched up. (The nasty gash on his nose and mouth required seven sutures to close.) When Plante returned to the ice he was wearing a form fitting fiberglass mask. The notoriety Plante received for doing this spread to every corner of the hockey world, if only for its novelty. W.A. "Bill" Burchmore, a Montreal-based fiberglass salesman, had produced several prototype designs from his basement workshop. He first contacted Plante in August, 1958, and offered to produce a fiberglass mask molded from Plante's face. How much the 1959 product introduced to the NHL was influenced by Plante's visit to Long is open to conjecture.

When initial media and public reaction showed disdain toward the other-worldly appearance of the innovation, Burchmore was prompted to point out that "I designed it for protection, not for good looks.

"Besides," he added, "the mask has all of Jacques Plante's facial features. If it was made for Clark Gable it would look like Clark Gable." Burchmore valued the Plante-style mask at $300—considerably more than Long's appraisal.

The National Hockey League had approved masks for goaltenders as early as the 1958–59 season. League President Clarence Campbell stated, "It's completely ridiculous for anyone to think a goalie who wants to wear a mask is chicken because anyone who would stand up to a 100-mile-an-hour projectile is no coward.

"No goalie has to play without a mask to prove his courage as far as I'm concerned." the president added.

However, few of his NHL brethren seemed ready to follow Plante's lead. Suggesting that the mask would go the same way as the Charleston, the zoot suit, the hula hoop and other fads, future Hall of Famer Terry Sawchuk of Detroit stated, "Plante is a good goalie … and not because of a mask. I've been a pro goalie for more than a dozen years and I've never worn a mask in a game. I don't see any reason for starting now."

Rangers goalie Gump Worsley was similarly unimpressed. "My objection to the mask is that it's not necessary. Why, all of a sudden, after hockey has been played for 70 years do they decide we should wear masks?"

Ranger general manager Muzz Patrick offered criticism from a different perspective. "Our game has a greater percentage of women fans than any team sport I know," he was quoted as saying. "And I'm talking about real fans—ones who can give you the scoring averages and the all star lineups.

"Those women fans want to see men—not masks. They want to see the blondes, the redheads... and the bald spots. That's why I'm against helmets and masks. They rob the players of their individuality."

Patrick would do an about face later that season when he ordered that all juvenile and junior goaltenders in the Rangers system be fitted for facemasks. By that time, Gump Worsley had been demoted to Springfield and Marcel Paille was promoted to the big club. "I saw Paille get hit in the head twice in successive games recently." Patrick pointed out. "The second time the puck caromed into the goal. If he had the mask he'd have stopped the shot."

Paille experimented with a Plante-style mask in practice. He complained of perspiration from his forehead dripping into his eyes and impairing his vision. He described the effect as like wearing someone else's glasses. Paille threatened to ship the mask back to the manufacturer and is not known to have worn it in NHL play.

Meanwhile, Plante and his mask had made their first visit to Toronto on November 21, 1959. The Habs goalie backstopped Montreal to a 2–1 victory and the newspapers reported that "the game presented an argument in favor of Plante's grotesque but effective fibre glass face mask. The bare-faced Bower had to retire to the hospital to have a badly gashed mouth repaired." A deflection by the Habs' Donnie Marshall had knocked out a bottom tooth, loosened three others and cut Bower for three stitches. But, the report added, "Bower still insists he wants no part of a mask."

At Boston, goalie Don Simmons had been given lots of opportunity to see Jacques Plante's work first hand. Simmons and his Bruins mates had been runners-up to Plante and the Canadiens in the 1957 and 1958 Stanley Cup Finals. When coach Milt Schmidt benched Simmons in favor of Harry Lumley in mid-November, 1959, Simmons had plenty of time to mull over his next move. When he was called upon to re-enter the nets for the Bruins against the Rangers at New York on December 13, 1959, he did so wearing a fiberglass mask. However, Simmons lost the game 4–3 and credited at least one Ranger score to adjusting to the new mask.

When Plante was introducing the goalie mask to the NHL in the fall of 1959, a quick survey of the hockey world reveals that goaltenders in other leagues were being felled by pucks and sticks at an alarming rate. Inspired by Plante's example, they began wearing masks upon their return to action.

The University of Toronto Varsity Blues were preparing to begin defense of their university hockey title in mid-October. But during a preseason practice goalie Bob Giroux sustained a fractured cheekbone and the Blues' hopes seemed to rest on how soon he would recover. On December 1, 1959, Giroux returned to action sporting a new molded plastic mask designed by sports equipment retailer Doug Laurie. After losses to the University of Michigan and the Senior A Kitchener-Waterloo Dutchmen in exhibition play, Giroux shut out the University of Montreal Carabins 8–0. Backstopped by Giroux, the University of Toronto team then entered the Sixth Annual Boston Arena Christmas Tournament. The Blues defeated Harvard University 7–2 in the final.

In the American Hockey League the Cleveland Barons were practicing on the morning of October 29, 1959, when Eddie Mazur let go a drive that struck goalie Gil Mayer in the face. X-rays revealed a broken lower jaw.

Using a new medical technique developed at Walter Reed Hospital in Washington, D.C., Mayer's lower jaw was wired together across the break. With the addition of a splint to maintain rigidity, the injured goaltender was eating normal food in eight days and was soon back working out with the Barons with a specially developed aluminum mask.

While recuperating Mayer traveled to Montreal, where a mask similar to Plante's was made for him. He returned to league play wearing the mask on December 30 when the Barons tied the Rochester Americans, 2–2. Two days later Mayer shut out the same Americans by a 2–0 score on New Year's Day.

On the very same day that Mayer had been injured, the reigning world champion Belleville McFarlands were playing the Whitby Dunlops in their fourth game of the Ontario Hockey Association Senior A season. At 4:41 of the third period, Belleville goalie Gordie Bell was dropped by a shot which struck him flush under the eye and resulted in a lacerated eyeball. The rival Kitchener-Waterloo Dutchmen loaned backup goalie Cesare Maniago to Belleville while Bell recuperated. A week later, on November 7, 1959, Maniago was facing Whitby when he, too, was struck in the face. The game was delayed 20 minutes before Maniago returned to finish the contest with eight stitches and one fewer teeth. Whitby marksmen continued their assault on league goalies when "Boat" Hurley, Kitchener's regular backstop, was cut for six stitches to the forehead after stopping a rising shot by the Dunlops' Eric Pogue on November 12.

Meanwhile, as Gordie Bell convalesced, he made a trip to Montreal for a Plante-style mask. When he returned to play against Whitby on December 2, he did so as the first goaltender in OHA Senior A play to don facial protection. The first facemask was introduced to the OHA Junior A league two weeks later after Peterborough Petes goalie John Chandick suffered a cut over the eye during practice on December 16, 1959. With Chandick unavailable for a scheduled contest against the Barrie Flyers the following night, George Holmes subbed for him wearing a protective mask. He shut out the Flyers, 3–0.

The mask was introduced to the Pacific Coast Hockey League the same day that Holmes wore his in Peterborough, albeit in a somewhat backhanded manner.

After Spokane goalie Emile "The Cat" Francis had separated his shoulder, the team trainer had developed a special harness for him. Fearing that he would not be able to raise his arms quickly enough to protect his face, Francis was also provided with a mask. He wore it on December 17 in a 4–3 loss to the Seattle Totems.

It seems that by the 1959-60 season goaltenders all across hockey were just waiting for someone to make the first move. At the start of that season, in what must have then seemed like a very unusual development, the minor hockey association in the Toronto suburb of Don Mills had passed a bylaw making facemasks compulsory for all goalies up to age 14. Masks were optional for those aged 14 to 17. The association bought two masks and had the referee collect them from the departing goaltenders at the end of each game. The masks were then passed to the goalies who were taking the ice for the next game. Organizers noted the marked improvement in goaltending and described the goalies' acceptance of the masks as enthusiastic.

As the New Year turned and ushered in the new decade of the 1960s, Jacques Plante was being fitted with a bar-type fiberglass mask that resembled a spider's web. Plante would continue to refine mask designs. Don Simmons would have an on-again/off-again relationship with the mask over the rest of his career, but he would also be something of an innovator, widening eye holes for better vision and increasing ventilation holes to reduce perspiration. He too would convert to the spider-web style mask and would later make his fortune selling goaltending equipment worldwide. The role of men like Don Spencer and Gene Long in the saga of the mask has become lost in the Plante legend, but truly it was the determination and pioneering efforts of all of hockey's early masked men that improved the lot of goaltenders wherever the world's fastest game is played.

Sports Injuries and Safety in the NHL

Jay Greenberg and Peter Wilton

ALMOST EVERY YEAR, the padding gets ever sturdier. So does the backbone of NHL referees and administrators in protecting players who, having grown an average of 16 pounds and two inches in the last 27 years, should be built more durably than ever.

Nevertheless, the participants have also become more dangerous to opponents and themselves, leaving today's NHL more safe and more threatening than ever. The advances only seem to run alongside the peril, as what the game has learned about itself races the growing G-forces and perhaps inadvertently accelerates them.

"I don't believe there is much difference in the level of safety from 15 or 20 years ago," said Lou Lamoriello, general manager of the New Jersey Devils since 1987. "For all the new rules we've put in, the injuries are very similar to the ones in the past. If it looks worse, it's because of video exposure, more games, more highlights. Image has become reality and I think that's tied to the players having less respect for the risk because of a false sense of safety with the newer equipment.

"Goalies survived well for decades without face masks because players didn't raise their shots in practice. But, players now feel so protected that they raise sticks higher than they should. There is a reckless abandon," said Lamoriello.

In fact, in 1997–98, teams reported 1,404 game-related injuries for a total of 3,992 regular-season man-games lost. In 1999–2000, 1,148 injuries resulted in 2,949 missed contests.

It's too early to call that a trend, only a hopeful sign. The numbers can't tell you how much worse the danger would be if the NHL went back to a lower standard of protection that long-time participants and administrators of the game insist served the players at least as well as today's synthetics.

"The protection is so good that you don't hurt yourself even when you hit them wrong," said Bob Clarke, Philadelphia's Hall of Fame player from 1969 to 1984 and now the Flyers' general manager. "There used to be a price to be paid for not lining up a guy correctly but now they can just tee off.

"They come through youth hockey wearing facial covering and helmets, so hitting with your stick is not such a big deal. When they get to the NHL and take off their shields, it's hard to be careful all of a sudden," Clarke added.

"The glass around the rink is higher to protect the fans, but as a result, it has to be braced real hard and no longer moves with your body to take some of the shock. Another thing is, we've had the same height for the boards for 75 years and now players are two inches taller. Their hips aren't hitting the boards, but the glass," said Clarke.

In other words, the protection itself may have become as dangerous as the false sense of security it inspires. "Pads used to have a soft leather feel," said Lamoriello. "Now, they are almost like steel."

Nevertheless, according to Colin Campbell, the NHL's executive vice president and director of hockey operations, equipment manufacturers are satisfied through their own tests that harder shells on shoulders and elbow pads do not constitute an additional hazard for head injuries.

Because years ago the only data kept on concussions was deposited by players into a bucket by the bench before they foolishly climbed back over the boards with symptoms that would now keep them out of uniform for weeks, number crunching on the head crunching is relatively new and ongoing. The number of concussions declined from 94 during the 1997–98 season to 87 in 1998–99, but rose to 104 in 1999–2000.

"I don't think we're years away from [answers]," said Dr. Charles Burke, the Pittsburgh Penguins doctor, who has been chairing the NHL's Post Concussion Syndrome Project for three years. "It's hopefully sooner." But, as he collects data, here is the summary of knowledge he imparts on the players for his team: "I tell them there is no evidence that [helmets, mouth guards and visors] prevent injuries and none that there isn't," said Dr. Burke, "The choice is theirs."

Almost no one was wearing helmets back in 1962 when Jean Beliveau hit his head during a Stanley Cup semifinal game between the Montreal Canadiens and the Chicago Black Hawks. Beliveau stayed on the bench for the remainder of that game. He dressed for the rest of the series but did not play. He was diagnosed by the team doctor as having suffered a minor concussion. The following September, Beliveau returned to training camp. Despite the respite over the summer, his head still hurt.

Fearing that he had suffered a fractured skull, Beliveau arranged to get a second opinion about the severity of the injury. The second doctor confirmed that he had suffered a concussion, not a fractured skull. Despite his nagging headaches, Beliveau was expected to suit up and play for the Canadiens—and he did even though "My head hurt for two years."

It has been four decades since the Beliveau injury and neurologists have yet to agree upon the definitive terms of what constitutes a concussion. The American Academy of Neurology, however, does agree that a concussion "involves a trauma induced alteration in mental status that may or may not be accompanied by a loss of consciousness."

Today, roughly one million Americans suffer head injuries each year. Of these, 300,000 are sports injuries. In recent years, the NHL has made a concerted effort to better understand how to deal with players who have suffered a concussion. Every team in the NHL now has an affiliation with a neurologist. There are different guidelines available for the use of coaches and medical personnel that provide a loose framework for the rating and treatment of concussions. They range from a Grade One concussion in which there is no loss of consciousness and any confusion regarding date, name, address, clears up within 15 minutes. A Grade Two concussion involves no loss of consciousness, but confusion remains for longer than 15 minutes. Vomiting may also occur. Grade Three involves a loss of consciousness. While the various guidelines agree on the three-grade rating system, the treatment of the concussion varies depending upon which guidelines are followed.

Dr. Burke and the Post Concussion Syndrome Project (PCSP) aim to address some of the issues surrounding head injuries. There still is not a set criteria from which to accurately rank the severity of a concussion. Neurologists still don't know which of the many and varying symptoms surrounding a concussion are most important. There is still conflicting information surrounding the number of brain injuries a player can sustain before risking permanent damage. There is little information surrounding the long-term implications of a head injury. Are athletes putting themselves at greater risk of developing Parkinson's or Alzheimer's or other neurological diseases in their old age?

Though he works for the Penguins, Dr. Burke's study involves all NHL teams. Prior to the start of the season, every player now is required to undergo a battery of neurological tests. The purpose of these tests is to establish a baseline to better gauge the length of time it takes the player to recover from a head injury. After a concussion, the athlete is required to retake the same set of tests. If there is a discrepancy, the tests will be retaken every week until the results match. Dr. Burke will keep track of the statistics surrounding the length of time it takes for players to return to baseline. This information will be compiled through the Post Concussion Syndrome Project, the purpose being to better understand how a blow to the head affects the brain waves and how long it takes them to return to normal.

Unquestionably, doctors have acquired a healthier understanding of the warning signs of concussions, the exponential danger of multiple ones, and the perils of returning from them too soon. But the baseline neurological testing that the NHL has instituted during training camps is mostly aimed towards reducing the number and severity of repeat concussions, not preventing the first and second, many of which occur before a player reaches the NHL level.

"The athletes themselves are reporting more symptoms and media attention has improved dramatically," said Dr. Karen Johnston, an associate professor in the Division of Neurological Studies and the Director of the Neurological Trauma Unit at Montreal General Hospital. But, as a McGill University researcher and clinician who has worked with pros from the Canadiens and the Canadian Football League's Alouettes and with the amateur sports community, she also says it can't be proven that the danger is increasing or decreasing.

Meanwhile, not even those who blame new standards of protection for creating new standards of recklessness suggest helmets should come off. "I don't know how you are going to reduce the amount of protection without causing other problems," says Colin Campbell.

Thanks to grandfathered legislation passed before the 1979–80 season, every NHL player now wears a helmet. Some players, however, continue to use ones that are flimsy and many more wear helmets that are not fastened correctly. And even headgear tested to standards is of far more use in saving fractured skulls and lacerations than concussions, which are caused by the brain slamming against the skull before the skull bangs against the helmet. A more practical preventative for some hockey concussions probably is mouth guards, because they can absorb the shock of a hit on the jaw.

"We're talking about a Type 3 guard, fitted by a dentist from a mold, that goes right to the back molars," said Dr. Johnston. "But, that is impractical for kids, and kids hockey is where many first concussions are suffered.

"We need more studies. Meanwhile, it is probably fair to say that a mouth guard will only prevent the concussion you get from a specific type of hit. For one on the back of the head, it wouldn't do you any good. And there is some thought that helmet technology might have reached its limits.

"An appropriately fastened, properly maintained, helmet does offer protection against direct hits. But rotational forces create the majority of concussions. You can get one from a whiplash effect from a blow to the neck or to the face, so visors can be useful in that regard as well as to protect eyes," Dr. Johnston said.

"Meanwhile, anything that can prevent contact with the head probably is prevention at its best. From studies of CT scans, new imaging techniques, brain wave studies, the most important thing we have learned is when it is safe to send players back out there."

The list of players known to have had careers prematurely ended because of head trauma—Dave Taylor, Brett Lindros, Michel Goulet, Dennis Vaske, Pat LaFontaine, Russ Courtnall, Nick Kypreos, Jeff Beukeboom—is sobering. A number of top NHLers have suffered at least one concussion: Sergei Fedorov, Mark Recchi, Paul Kariya, Mike Modano, Mark Messier, Teemu Selanne, Pavol Demitra, Peter Forsberg, Eric Lindros, Keith Primeau, Rob Blake, Sami Kapanen, Doug Weight, Larry Murphy, Owen Nolan, Mattias Ohlund, Richard Zednik, Kenny Jonsson and Darius Kasparaitis.

Most baffling is the newly identified phenomenon of post-concussion syndrome—months of depression and inability to focus.

"I saw lots of guys get knocked out while I was playing," said Clarke, "and we never heard one player saying he had yellow vision or disorientation. If they had it, they couldn't have played with it for long. I don't understand why we never saw it."

Toronto defenseman Bryan Berard never saw the stick of Ottawa's Marian Hossa in a game played in March, 2000. The resulting injury renewed the call for visors to become mandatory.

According to Dr. Tom Pashby, the Toronto ophthalmologist who has tracked such accidents and pioneered facial protection for players, 40 NHL players since 1972 have been forced into retirement because of an injury to an eye. In half those cases, the damage was caused by pucks, which, of course, change direction without enforcement of any rules. Still, the National Hockey League Players' Association adamantly insists shields should be a matter of personal choice.

"There are 132 NHL players [out of 700-plus who dressed for an NHL game during the 1999–2000 season] wearing facial protection," said Dr. Pashby. "That's up 12 to 15 percent. Like helmets, it will come."

What has come so far are new rules and more aggressive enforcement of them. For the three seasons from 1979 to 1982, an average of 13 NHL players were suspended each year, reflecting an average of 54 games per campaign lost to league discipline. From 1977 to 2000, suspensions were handed out an average of 37 times a year, which cooled players heels for an average 129 games per season.

"Players are suspended for things they never were before," said Campbell, who hands out the penalties. "There used to be a [collective bargaining agreement] maximum of $1,000 you could fine a player. Now, they lose salary in the games they miss."

Fighting still is argued to have an escape-valve value and, for better or worse, remains part of the game. But, if the sight of two fighters seeking each other out to transfer courage to teammates offends the principles of those who do not understand the psyche of the game, such dances have become more ritual than serious hazard. Mass brawling is long gone, instigator penalties have raised the stakes for living by the sword, and certain types of hitting are policed like never before.

"One thing they've done a really good job of taking out is the submarine hit from underneath," said Clarke. "Hip on hip is okay, but when guys get too low, it becomes butt against knee."

Knees are more repairable than ever and can return to action in shorter periods of time. The career-ending orthopedic injury practically no longer exists. Degenerative arthritic conditions in joints, which were inevitable with old surgical techniques, have been reduced. "Bobby Orr would have had a much longer career now, no question," said Lamoriello.

In November, 1978, Bobby Orr retired from hockey—his career cut short by a series of chronic injuries to his left knee. These injuries became as important in defining the career of Bobby Orr as the speed and stickhandling skill that allowed him to play like an extra forward on the rush. It was this style that Orr brought to the game that revolutionized the role of the defense. However, the image of Orr doubled over on the ice, his knee once again failing him, is etched into the memory of a generation of hockey fans.

Throughout Orr's career, the only option available to doctors such as Carter Rowe, Orthopedic Specialist and Orr's surgeon with the Massachusetts General Hospital, was surgery. This entailed a general anesthetic, a large surgical incision, extensive tissue damage and muscle loss due to the six weeks required in a cast. The risk of osteoarthritis and the wear and tear on the knee increased with each operation. In fact, by the time major technological advancements came along, Orr's knee was too far gone to benefit.

Dr. John Palmer and Dr. John Kostiuk of Toronto General Hospital performed the sixth operation on the famous knee on April 19, 1977. Dr. Kostiuk, in a press conference after the operation, gave some insight into what was involved:

"Putting Bobby back on ice as a big league hockey player was not a major part of the decision in this operation, although I'm sure Bobby is hoping for that one-in-ten chance that he will be able to play again. This was a pretty major operation on the knee. We opened it up quite widely to remove bone chips and loose articular cartilage. Bobby understands that he must not even think of hockey for the coming season. He has agreed to one whole year of treatment for that knee. What we want is free movement and muscle development. As I said, Bobby will not be able to bear weight on that knee in the next four months, he will, however, be using a cycle...."

Dr. Jim Murray, team physician to Team Canada in 1972 (when the effects of a previous surgery kept Orr out of the series with the Soviets), described the toll of the operations on Orr's knee to Trent Frayne of the *Toronto Sun* : "He has osteoarthritis," Murray explained. "When you get osteoarthritis, it sort of perpetuates itself. I don't know how long he'll last as a hockey player but, whatever it is, he'd have gone 10 years longer without this problem. When you look at X-rays you'd think you were looking at the knees of a man of 65 [years old]; the surface of the joints are very ragged. Now he has to get all of his skating power from the quadriceps, the big muscles in the thighs. They get small after an operation and he has to work very hard to keep them built up. It's a thing that gets worse with time...."

When Orr finally hung up his skates for the last time as a professional hockey player in 1978, he had undergone six operations, had his cartilage removed, his joints scraped and, as a result of the repeated trauma to the knee, arthritis had set into the joint. But what if, instead of entering the NHL in 1966, Orr had broken in 10 years later as a dynamic young player with an injury-prone knee? Would that have made a difference? Dr. Charles Burke feels that without a doubt Orr's knee would have been treated very differently because of the development of one diagnostic and surgical aide—the arthroscopy, which came into widespread use in 1976.

The arthroscopy is a tube and fiberoptic equipment that is inserted into the knee. An image of the inside of the knee is then carried back, and the doctor is able to see the workings of the knee on a monitor. Small problems such as cartilage damage or bone chips can be removed with the arthroscopy. The incision necessary to insert this piece of equipment is very small and usually does not even require stitches to close. The procedure is done under local anesthetic and on an out-patient basis. It is recommended that the patient takes it easy for a few days before getting back to regular activity. There is no muscle loss associated with the procedure. In addition, the arthroscopy has provided a window into the inner workings of the knee. The information gathered by looking through this window has allowed for better diagnosis and treatment of knee injury prior to even having to take the step of any type of surgical procedure. There are three main advantages to the arthroscopy—the diagnosis, procedure, and recovery time.

One of the concerns that remains is the prevention of further injury to the knee. This is usually handled prior to the player returning to the ice through a stint of physiotherapy that strengthens the knee to the level required to face the vigor of professional hockey. It is this therapy that can keep a player out for six to eight weeks after suffering a knee injury.

"I see what our doctors do with an arthroscope and it's just incredible," said Lamoriello. At the same time, he believes the operating rooms are busier today because of the additional stress participants put on their joints. "We never had physical training the way they do now," Lamoriello said. "We are making ourselves more vulnerable by overtaxing muscles with weights and machine [workouts]. It will catch up with knees and shoulders because they start training at an early age. The Good Lord made the body for certain reasons, not to carry more weight in certain areas."

The counter argument is how many knees are saved and careers prolonged by the built-up strength of muscles surrounding joints? Players add bulk to survive. For the same purpose, they use their sticks and elbows to ward off checks.

A significant part of the solution is simple according to Lamoriello. "The stick shouldn't be carried above the waist. If it wasn't, accidents would be greatly reduced."

"I have tried to increase the toll paid for dirty play," said the NHL's Colin Campbell. "We're looking into everything: medical care, equipment, enforcement and education."

CHAPTER 60

Two Minutes for Booking So Good

A Century of Hockey Books Surveyed

Mark Brender

THE FIRST KNOWN HOCKEY BOOK, WRITTEN by Art Farrell in 1899, includes a section explaining why snowshoeing and tobogganing would prove no match for hockey's exploding popularity. That hockey did soon surpass its snowy competition—just as Farrell predicted—shows that the sport has come far indeed since its origins more than a century ago. With no disrespect intended to Farrell, the same can be said for the works of hundreds of writers who have contributed to our enjoyment of the game since then by transferring hockey's mystique from the ice to the written page.

Appropriately enough, given the legions of players who would much later follow his creative path (many with ghostwriters, mind you), Farrell was a hockey player by trade. A member of the 1898–99 Stanley Cup champion Montreal Shamrocks, he decided to try his hand at writing about hockey simply because no one else had. Hockey had been played in Montreal in a recognizable form for at least 20 years, but the sole permanent accounts were found in newspapers or journal entries. Farrell saw a void in the libraries of the nation and felt duty's call.

In the introduction to his book, *Hockey: Canada's Royal Winter Game*, Farrell points out that his new vocation was born more of the necessity for a hockey book "than by any impression of confidence in [my] ability to do justice to the subject." Adds the player-turned-author: "That a book on our national winter sport in Canada has not yet appeared is a marvel. If hockey were a novelty to us, then we might not reproach ourselves for our tardiness in this respect, but it is our most popular winter game, long established, thoroughly appreciated, and it certainly deserves a place with the other athletic pastimes that boast of a hand-book."

Farrell's pocket-sized, 121-page hockey manual is complete with sketches and photographs of leading teams of the day such as the Shamrocks and Montreal Victorias. The book contains a short history of the birth and development of the game, its rules, hints on training, practice and specific plays. Of note today are Farrell's warnings against the "foolish, dangerous practice" of wearing short pants that provide no protection for the knees; his advice to eschew heavy weights for training purposes in favor of aerobic workouts with a skipping rope or punching bag; and his suggestion that "it is better to think more and rush less, than to rush more and think less." Also dealing with strategy, the captain of the Shamrocks, forward Harry Trihey, advises players not to waste too much energy fighting for the puck behind the goal line in the offensive zone since more goals are scored off the rush.

Farrell's pioneering work did not set off a rush to the printers. It took until the1940s and beyond before the appearance of books that chronicled the lives of hockey heroes. One of the first was Ed Fitkin's *Max Bentley: Hockey's Dipsy Doodle Dandy.*

Fitkin's opening scene is taken from the 1938 Boston Bruins training camp in Hershey, Pennsylvania. Bentley, a rookie, was trying to crack the Bruins lineup. Fitkin writes that as Bentley looked around the room, the star-struck future Hall of Famer couldn't believe his eyes.

"Here in the same room were some of the greatest stars in hockey. The one and only Eddie Shore; the evergreen Dit Clapper with his slick black hair parted, razor-like, in the middle; the famous Kraut Line from Kitchener, Milt Schmidt, Woody Dumart, Bobby Bauer. Almost self-consciously, Max bent down and started to tug at the laces of his skates. For the first time, he started to wonder how he had ever had the audacity to hope that he could become one of these men."

Only the names in Fitkin's description of Bentley's awe vary from what a biographer might write today.

Many of the other early hockey works were instructional in nature, but no less inspirational than Fitkin's for an audience starved for books on the subject. Stan Fischler, hockey's most prolific author with some 80-plus books to his credit, remembers heading to the Tompkins Park library in Brooklyn and being enthralled the first time he actually found a hockey book on its shelves. The book was called *Hockey: The Fastest Game on Earth*. It was written by New York Americans playing coach Red Dutton.

"I can remember to this day that he had a line he kept stressing," Fischler recalls. "It was, 'Remember, keep punching,' meaning never quit. It was the kind of book that enhanced my love of hockey and also made me want to write about it."

Thirteen years after Dutton, Canadian amateur hockey coach and sport researcher Lloyd Percival released what remains the most influential and comprehensive instructional hockey book ever written. *The Hockey Handbook* began as a research project funded by Sports College, a Canadian public service organization dedicated to raising fitness and sports standards. In a massive six-year undertaking, Percival and colleagues sent surveys to every country where hockey was played, interviewed hundreds of players and coaches, watched hundreds of games, analyzed more than 500 scoring chances from the 1949–50 NHL season, and charted in detail the shooting habits of 70 NHL players. Most of the players were surprised to learn they had predictable "hot spots" or favorite areas they tried to reach before shooting.

Using data collected on scoring chances, Percival concluded that there were times that called for a shot and others that called for a deke. Players had to learn to get it right by honing their instincts through practice. He also said players should always stickhandle before shooting, because the physiology of the human eye causes a short blackout time whenever a goalie has to refocus after puck movement.

In its day, *The Hockey Handbook* was roundly dismissed

by the likes of Montreal Canadiens coach Dick Irvin and other professional hockey men who were scornful of its scientific approach. But Percival was ahead of his time. He voiced many of the same concerns over aerobic fitness and skill development in Canadian hockey that others repeated after the 1972 Summit Series and continue to spout today. Legendary Russian coach Anatoli Tarasov was one of the few who gave the book any notice. After reading it, Tarasov sent Percival a note thanking him for all the helpful information.

Among his perceptive insights, Percival hinted at the possible value of using five-man units and—in a particularly prescient passage that the Russians must have taken to heart—speculated that a game plan built around strong passing was hockey's great undiscovered art. "The ultimate effectiveness of passing has not yet been demonstrated," he wrote. "However, to judge from the results gained by teams developing it to a fairly high level, the possibilities are great."

Percival also asked hockey fans across Canada what kind of hockey they most liked to watch. Seventy percent favored a finesse game, which led Percival to conclude hockey's popularity would grow faster if rules allowed a skill game to flourish. "The professional hockey executive may take issue with this argument and point to the gate receipts to prove that people like to watch rugged, scrambly hockey. However, according to the results of the survey, it is quite possible that the gate receipts would climb even higher if the emphasis were shifted to a smooth, smart, passing game."

From the 1950s through the early 1980s, writers such as Fitkin, Fischler, Trent Frayne, Scott Young, Frank Orr and Brian McFarlane gave a boost to the space hockey took up on library shelves. Through them and others, the careers of all the great stars were chronicled, often in irreverent, first-person "as told to" accounts. As an example, take Lorne Worsley's no-holds-barred autobiography *They Call Me Gump*, written with Tim Moriarity. Commenting on the fact that some of his best friends were members of the media, Worsley wrote: "One was Jim Burchard of the *New York World-Telegram*. He's dead now and so is the newspaper. We called him Whisky Jim. If he walked up to you while your back was turned, you knew who it was without turning around."

Former Montreal Canadiens goalie Ken Dryden chose to reflect on his fame and the sport that created it in a subtler fashion in his 1983 book *The Game*. No reliable figures are available, but many publishers believe *The Game* is the best-selling non-statistical hockey book of all time.

Dryden's position as the backbone of one of hockey's greatest dynasties provided him with a unique insider's perspective on the most storied franchise in pro sports and the cast of characters who made winning a way of life. His writing ability and intellectual pedigree—he earned a law degree from Cornell—allowed him to express himself with a clarity few full-time writers can match. *The Game* is the kind of book whose images keep their power years later: Dryden's feeling of warm satisfaction upon seeing his neighbors the morning after a win; his wariness of defenseman Rick Chartraw's penchant for uncontrollable, unpredictable wipeouts in practice; his fear that Larry Robinson's granite reputation might one day crumble; the boyish glee of a busload of Montreal Canadiens, idols of a nation, making faces at the man caught picking his nose in the car below.

The decade of the 1980s was a good one for hockey books. Other top sellers include: *The Game of Our Lives*, Peter Gzowski's chronicle of the young, pre-Stanley Cup Edmonton Oilers, and *Lions in Winter*, a sociological exploration of the Canadiens' history of success, by Alan Turowetz and Chrys Goyens. How many times have you read about Habs architect Frank Selke without anyone else pointing out that he was only 5'2" and 150 pounds?

The 1990s brought strikes and lockouts and southward expansion to the NHL. For the book market that meant dozens of volumes taking a nostalgic look back at hockey's glory days. Books about the Original Six teams and original buildings, ancient heroes and long-fought battles clamored for attention. Some of the best work came in the form of pictorial coffee table books put out by the NHL and Dan Diamond, and the Hockey Hall of Fame and Toronto author Andrew Podnieks. Together they presented some of hockey's most historically significant photographs from the likes of Nat and Lou Turofsky and Lewis Portnoy. Podnieks's book on Portnoy (*Shooting Stars: Photographs from the Portnoy Collection at the Hockey Hall of Fame*) contains a fascinating account of Portnoy's pioneering experimentation with strobe lighting at the St. Louis Arena in the 1970s. Before strobes, arenas didn't provide enough light to take the kind of close-up action shots, ice chips flying, beads of sweat pouring down a player's face, that capture hockey's gritty essence.

The 1990s were also about the fall from grace of NHL Players' Association executive director Alan Eagleson. No one is more responsible for dismantling Eagleson's empire than Russ Conway, a reporter with the small-town *Eagle Tribune* in Lawrence, Massachusetts. Conway's *Eagle Tribune* series in 1991 is hockey's equivalent to Woodward and Bernstein's Watergate chronicles. His subsequent book, *Game Misconduct: Alan Eagleson and the Corruption of Hockey*, remains the most damning condemnation of Eagleson's tenure and should be at the top of any hockey reading list. *Net Worth: Exploding the Myths of Pro Hockey*, by David Cruise and Alison Griffiths, and *The Defense Never Rests* by Bruce Dowbiggin look into the NHL-NHLPA pension dispute and other player-league labor issues.

No book list would be complete without the requisite number of Wayne Gretzky titles. If Gretzky wasn't the most written-about hockey player in history before his retirement, he certainly is today. There are a handful of worthy tribute titles to choose from, but, from a publishing perspective, perhaps none offers as good a story as the 1984 collaboration between Walter Gretzky and Vancouver writer Jim Taylor. One story has it that Walter wanted to call the book *My Son Wayne*. Eventually, editors at McClelland & Stewart won him over to calling it *Gretzky*, and it became a top seller in hardcover and paperback.

The one book category that hasn't seen much hockey activity over the years is fiction. The best-selling fictions have been children's books, led by Roch Carrier's famed picture book *The Hockey Sweater* and Roy MacGregor's *Screech Owls* series. But other works such as Paul Quarrington's *King Leary* and MacGregor's *The Last Season* have gone largely unnoticed.

There are a couple of theories for the dearth of hockey fiction. Peter Gzowski has suggested that hockey is a curious pursuit for a writer's mind. The leisurely pace of baseball and golf provide ample time for reflection, but in hockey everything happens so fast that it leaves little time for writers to reflect or readers to absorb. There may also be cultural differences at work. Canadians have tended to mythologize hockey by reporting actual stories of small-town rinks, fathers and sons, and oldtimers having too much fun to quit.

"Why nobody has taken hockey fiction seriously [until recently] probably says more about us as Canadians than anything else," says Rob Sanders, publisher of Vancouver-based Greystone Books. "We tend to live our sport as a cultural endeavor more than stand back and feel it's worth writing about."

The growth of women's hockey has captured the attention of book publishers in the past decade. Prior to the 1990s, it was almost impossible to find a women's hockey book. Today, the published works could easily fill a shelf. Following the American victory at the 1998 Olympics, U.S. players Tricia Dunn and Katie King wrote an instructional book titled *Gold Medal Ice Hockey for Women and Girls*. While women's hockey is officially a non-contact sport, Dunn and King advise all players to be prepared and to make collisions work to their advantage, "'cause either way they're going to happen."

Looking back to Farrell's day, this women's instruction manual is another measure of how hockey, and writing about hockey, has grown for the better. Farrell himself believed the clinching proof of hockey's popularity was that even "the gentler sex" was beginning to take up the game "by bravely lining up to meet, in gentle combat, their tender adversaries." Once again, Farrell may have been right, but we can only guess what hockey's first author would have to say about the less-than-gentle tactics of Dunn and King.

FAVORITE HOCKEY BOOKS

IT SHOULDN'T COME AS SURPRISE TO ANYONE that some of the most memorable books are those we read as children. The best hockey books have the ability to take the reader onto the ice, into the dressing room, inside the places where a player's dreams are dashed or destroyed or delayed for another day. That part has never changed, whether the subject is the history of the National Hockey League, Max Bentley, Wayne Gretzky or anyone else.

Inspiration is shaped early in the young mind. First impressions, those priceless snippets and sharply defined images that linger years after the words are read and the pictures studied, are the ones that stay for a lifetime. No matter the era, the books of our youth become the basis for how we understand the game and its history. This can be seen in some of the responses of four hockey personalities when asked for their favorite hockey books of all time.

TOP FIVE HOCKEY BOOKS

Harry Sinden, president and general manager, Boston Bruins

1. *Hockey Showdown*, by Harry Sinden and Will McDonough (1972)
2. *Boston Bruins Celebrating 75 Years*, published by Tehabi (1999)
3. *The Patricks: Hockey's Royal Family*, by Eric Whitehead (1980)
4. *NHL Official Guide and Record Book*
5. *The Game*, by Ken Dryden (1983)

Stan Fischler, hockey author

1. *When the Rangers Were Young*, by Frank Boucher and Trent Frayne (1973)
2. *The Habs*, by Dick Irvin (1991)
3. *Hockey: The Fastest Game on Earth*, by Mervyn "Red" Dutton (1938)
4. *The Patricks: Hockey's Royal Family*, by Eric Whitehead (1980)
5. *The Hockey Book*, by Bill Roche (1953)

Bob Goodenow, executive director, NHL Players' Association

1. *The Hockey Handbook*, by Lloyd Percival (1965)
2. *Hockey...Here's Howe*, by Gordie Howe (1963)
3. *Hockey is My Game*, by Bobby Hull (1967)
4. *Game Misconduct: Alan Eagleson & the Corruption of Hockey*, by Russ Conway (1995)
5. *Puck is a Four Letter Word*, by Frank Orr (1983)

Steve Dryden, editor in chief, *The Hockey News*

1. *Boy on Defense*, by Scott Young (1985-reprint)
2. *The Jean Beliveau Story*, by Hugh Hood (1970)
3. *Death of a Legend*, by Henk Hoppener
4. *The Game*, by Ken Dryden (1983)
5. *Total Hockey*, by Dan Diamond (ed) *et al*

SELECTED HOCKEY BOOK LIST

This list presents a cross-section of books about hockey published from the late 19th century up to and including the year 2000. Books are listed alphabetically by author within each category. Many books could be listed under more than one category—e.g., *The Official NHL 75th Anniversary Commemorative Book* could be listed under both History and Illustrated Books. In these instances, the compilers have selected one category and entered the title there.

Activity Books

Author	Title
	Hockey Night in Canada TV Game Book
	The New Hockey Action Digest TV Game Book

Annuals

Author	Title
	Arets Ishockey (Sweden)
	Charlton Standard Catalogue of Hockey Cards
	Hockey Yearbook 1923
	Jaakiekkokirja (Finland)
	The National Hockey League Official Rules
	NHL Rulebook and Casebook
	National Hockey League Sourcebook
	Swedish Icehockey Federation Official Calender
Abbott, Scott and John Epstein	Hockey Pool Fever
Andrews, Ron (ed)	NHL Official Guide (to 1983)
Berger, Michael A., Frank Brown and Sherry Ross	Hockey Scouting Report
Carter, Craig and George Puro (ed)	The Sporting News: Complete Hockey Book
Diamond, Dan (ed)	NHL Official Guide and Record Book (1984-)
Eckert, Horst	Eishockey Almanahc IIHF Yearbook (Germany)
Fischler, Stan	Hockey Stars of (Various Years)
Fischler, Stan and Shirley	Breakaway
Hendy, Jim (ed)	Hendy's Hockey Guide
Hendy Jim (ed)	Who's Who in Hockey
Hollander, Zander	Inside Sports Magazine Hockey
Hollander, Zander (ed)	The Complete Handbook of Pro Hockey
Keegan, Tom	Hockey Camp Guide
Keegan, Tom	Junior Hockey Guide
Keegan, Tom	Men's College Hockey Guide
Keegan, Tom	Prep School Hockey Guide
Keegan, Tom	Junior Hockey Guide
Klein, Gunter	Eishockey (Germany)
MacKinnon, John	NHL Hockey: The Official Fan's Guide
Martin, William J. (ed)	The Hockey Review
Martin, William J. (ed)	The Hockey Herald
McFarlane, Brian	Hockey 76
McKenzie, Bob	Bob McKenzie's Hockey Annual
Montgomery, Ted	Pro Hockey Play by Play
Mulvoy, Mark	Sports Illustrated Ice Hockey
Ratschunas, Tom (ed)	IIHF International Hockey Guide
Roberts, Stewart (ed)	The Ice Hockey Annual (Great Britain)
Sadowski, Rick	Los Angeles Kings Annual
Sandler, Corey	Inside NHL '94
Schettino, Tom	Ice Pages: Minor Professional Hockey Guide
Stewart, Robert	Ice Hockey Annual
The Hockey News	IIHF International Hockey Guide
Townsend, Murray	The Hockey Annual

Anthologies

Author	Title
Beardsley, Doug	The Rocket the Flower the Hammer and Me
Beardsley, Doug (ed)	Our Game: An All Star Collection of Hockey Fiction
Benedict, Michael and D'Arcy Jenish (eds.)	Canada on Ice: Fifty Years of Great Hockey
Brehl, Robert	The Best of Milt Dunnell
Brook, Kevin and Sean (ed)	Poetry Thru the Smoky End Boards
Cuthbert, Chris & Scott Russell	The Rink: Stories from Hockey's Home Towns
Douglas, Thom J.	The Hockey Bibliography
Gowdy, David	Riding On the Roar of The Crowd
Green, Jeremiah Lawrence	Above The Olympian Hill: Three Hockey Stories
Harrison, Richard	Hero of The Play
LaSalle, Peter	Hockey Sur Glace
Lee, John B	Hockey Player Sonnets
Lee, John B. (ed)	That Sign of Perfection
MacGregor, Roy	The Seven A.M. Practice
McCrae, Earl	Requiem For Reggie and Other Great Stories
McInnes, John and Emily Hearn	Hockey Cards & Hopscoth
Roche, Bill	The Hockey Book
Safarik, Allan (ed)	Quotations on the Great One: The Little Book of Wayne Gretzky
Scriver, Stephen	More! All Star Poet
Scriver, Stephen	Between The Lines
Society for Int'l Hockey Research	The SIHR Journal, (Vol. 1-4)
Wimmer, Dick (ed)	Fastest Game: Anthology of Hockey Writings

Autobiographies

Author	Title
Beliveau, Jean	My Life in Hockey
Bossy, Mike and Barry Meisel	Boss: The Mike Bossy Story
Boucher, Frank and Trent Frayne	When The Rangers Were Young
Bucyk, Johnny	Hockey in My Blood
Buffy, Vern	Black & White and Never Right
Carnegie, Herb	A Fly in a Pail Of Milk: The Herb Carnegie Story
Chadwick, Bill and Hal Bock	The Big Whistle
Cheevers, Gerry	Goaltender
Cherry, Don with Stan Fischler	Grapes: A Vintage View of Hockey
Eagleson, Alan with Scott Young	Power Play
Esposito, Phil and Tony with Tim Moriarty	The Brothers Esposito
Esposito, Phil with Gerald Eskenazi	Hockey Is My Life
Ferguson, John	Thunder and Lightning
Finn, Ron	On The Lines
Geoffrion, Bernard and Stan Fischler	Boom Boom: The Life and Times of Bernard Geoffrion
Gilbert, Rod with Stan Fischler and Hal Bock	Goal! My Life on Ice
Gooding, Cuba, Michael McKinley and Willie O'Ree	The Autobiography of Willie O'Ree: Hockey's Black Pioneer
Gretzky, Walter and Jim Taylor	Gretzky
Gretzky, Wayne	Gretzky: An Autobiography
Hart, Gene and Buzz Ringe	Score: My 25 Years With the Broad Street Bullies
Henderson, Paul with Mike Leonetti	Shooting For Glory
Hewitt, Foster	His Own Story
Hewitt, Foster	Hockey Night In Canada
Hewitt, Foster	He Shoots, He Scores
Hodge, Charlie and Howie Meeker	Stop It There, Back It Up! 50 Years of Hockey
Hodge, Charlie and Howie Meeker	Golly Gee, It's Me: The Howie Meeker Story
Hood, Bruce and Murray Townsend	Calling the Shots
Howe, Gordie	Gordie Howe: My Hockey Memories
Howe, Gordie and Colleen with Tom Delisle	And Howe!
Hull, Bobby	Hockey Is My Game
Hull, Brett and Kevin Allen	Brett: Shootin' and Smilin'
Imlach, Punch with Scott Young	Hockey Is A Battle
Imlach, Punch with Scott Young	Heaven and Hell in the NHL: Punch Imlach's Own Story
Irvin, Dick	Now Back to You Dick
Larionov, Igor	Larionov
Michel, Doug as told to Bob Mellor	Left Wing and a Prayer
Mikita, Stan	I Play To Win
Orr, Bobby with Dick Grace	Orr on Ice
Parent, Bernie with Bill Fleischman and Sonny Schwarts	Bernie, Bernie, Bernie
Park, Brad with Stan Fischler	Play the Man
Potvin, Denis	Power on Ice
Rheaume, Manon with Chantal Gilbert	Manon: Alone in Front of the Net
Robinson, Larry	Robinson For The Defense
Salming, Borje	Blood, Sweat And Hockey
Sanderson, Derek with Stan Fischler	I've Got to Be Me
Schultz, Dave	The Hammer
Selke, Frank J. and Gordon Gree	Behind The Cheering
Semenko, Dave	Looking Out for Number One
Shero, Fred	Shero: The Man Behind The System
Sittler, Darryl	Sittler at Centre
Smythe, Conn with Scott Young	Conn Smythe: If You Can't Beat 'Em In The Alley
Storey, Red and Brodie Snyder	Red's Story
Tarasov, Anatoli	Tarasov: The Father of Russian Hockey
Tretiak, Vladislav	Tretiak
Williams, Tiger with James Lawton	Tiger: A Hockey Story
Worsley, Lorne and Tim Moriarty	They Call Me Gump
Young, Scott	A Writer's Life

Biographies

Banks, Kerry ....Pavel Bure: The Riddle of the Russian Rocket
Beckett Publications Staff ....Wayne Gretzky (Beckett Great Sports Heroes)
Beddoes, Dick ....Pal Hal
Bock, Hal ....Dynamite on Ice: The Bobby Orr Story
Brewitt, Ross ....Clear the Track: The Eddie Shack Story
Burchard, Marshall and Sue ....Bobby Orr
Burchard, S.H. ....Brad Park
Clayton, Diedra ....Eagle
Cohen, Tom ....Roger Crozier Daredevil Goalie
Conway, Russ ....Game Misconduct: Alan Eagleson and the Corruption of Hockey
Davidson, Gary ....Breaking the Game Wide Open
Davidson, James ....Killer: The Brian Kilrea Story
Davies, John ....The Legend of Hobey Baker
Devaney, John ....The Bobby Orr Story
Dolan, Edward F. Jr. and Richard B. Lyttle...Bobby Clarke
Dryden, Steve (ed) ....Total Gretzky: The Magic, The Legend, The Numbers
Dupuis, David ....Sawchuk: The Troubles and Triumphs of the World's Greatest Goalie
Eskenazi, Gerald ....The Derek Sanderson Nobody Knows
Falls, Joem and Vartan Kupelian, Cynthia Lambert, John Bacon, Terry Foster....................Steve Yzerman: Heart of a Champion
Fischler, Stan ....Gordie Howe
Fischler, Stan and Maurice Richard ....The Flying Frenchman
Fisher, Red ....Hockey, Heroes and Me
Fitkin, Ed ....Maurice Richard
Fitkin, Ed ....Max Bentley
Fitkin, Ed ....Come On, Teeder!
Fitkin, Ed ....Turk Broda of the Leafs
Germain, Georges-Herbert ....Overtime: The Legend of Guy Lafleur
Goyens, Chrys and Allan Turowetz ....Jean Beliveau, My Life In Hockey
Green, Ted with Al Hirshberg ....High Stick
Hartje, Tod ....From Behind the Red Line
Hirshberg, Albert ....Bobby Orr: Fire on Ice
Hood, Hugh ....Strength Down Centre: The Jean Beliveau Story
Horton, Lori and Tim Griggs ....In Loving Memory: A Tribute to Tim Horton
Houston, Willam ....Ballard
Hunt, Jim ....Bobby Hull
Hunter, Douglas ....Scotty Bowman: A Life in Hockey
Hunter, Douglas ....Open Ice: The Tim Horton Story
Jackson, Robert B. ....Here Comes Bobby Orr
Kendall, Brian ....Shutout: The Legend of Terry Sawchuk
Larochelle, Claude ....Guy Lafleur - Hockey's #1
Libby, Bill ....Phil Esposito
Libby, Bill ....Rookie Goalie Gerry Desjardins
Liss, Howard ....Bobby Orr: Lightning on Ice
Logan, Anne M. ....Rare Jewel For A King
Loranger, Phil ....If They Played Hockey In Heaven
Loranger, Phil ....Cowboy On Ice: The Howie Young Story
MacSkimming, Roy ....Gordie: A Hockey Legend
Magnuson, Keith and Robert Bradford ....None Against!
Mahovlich, Ted ....The Big M: The Frank Mahovlich Story
Malcolm, Andrew H. ....Fury: Inside the Life of Theoren Fleury
Martin, Lawrence ....Mario
May, Julian ....Bobby Orr: Star on Ice
McAdam, Robert ....Bull on Ice
McDonald Lanny with Steve Simmons ....Lanny
McFarlane, Brian ....The King Clancy Story
Melady, John ....Overtime, Overdue: The Bill Barilko Story
Molinari, Dave *et al* ....Mario Lemieux: Best There Ever Was
Morrison, Scott ....Wayne Gretzky: The Great Goodbye
O'Brien, Andy ....Rocket Richard
O'Brien, Andy and Jacques Plante ....The Jacques Plante Story
O'Malley, Martin ....Gross Misconduct
O'Reilly, Dan ....Mr. Hockey: The World of Gordie Howe
Obodiac, Stan ....Red Kelly
Page, N.H. ....Bobby Orr - Number Four
Pellerin, Jean-Marie ....Maurice Richard: L'Idole d'un peuple (French)
Podnieks, Andrew ....The Great One: The Life and Times of Wayne Gretzky
Poulin, Daniel ....Lindros: Doing What's Right for Eric
Rainbolt, Richard and Ralph Turtinen ....The Goldy Shuffle: The Bill Goldsworthy Story
Redmond, Gerald ....Wayne Gretzky: The Great One
Richards, David Adam ....Hockey Dreams (Memories of a Man Who Couldn't Play)
Robinson, Dean ....Howie Morenz: Hockey's First Superstar
Rossiter, Sean ....Hockey Heroes: Dominik Hasek
Rozens, Aleksandrs ....Wayne Gretzky: Magician on the Ice
Sheppard, Chess ....Heaven on Ice: Ray Sheppard's Life in Hockey
Sonmor, Jean ....Mario Lemieux: Hockey's Gentle Giant
Spiros, Dean ....Six Shooters: Hockey's Sutter Brothers
Starkman, Randy ....Fire on Ice: Eric Lindros
Stellick, Gord and Jim O'Leary ....Hockey Heartaches And Hal
Tretiak, Vladislav ....The Hockey I Love
Vipond, Jim ....Gordie Howe Number 9
Whitehead, Eric ....The Patricks: Hockey's Royal Family
Whitehead, Eric ....Cyclone Taylor: A Hockey Legend
Wilheim, John Jay ....Hockey's Golden Jet
Young, Scott ....Hello Canada! The Life and Times of Foster Hewitt
Young, Scott ....O'Brien
Zwolinski, Mark ....The John Kordic Story

Biographies for Children

Banks, Kerry ....Teemu Selanne
Banks, Kerry ....Mats Sundin
Brenner, Richard ....Mario Lemeiux
Brenner, Richard ....Wayne Gretzky
Brophy, Mike ....Curtis Joseph: The Acrobat
Christopher, Matt ....On the Ice with Wayne Gretzky
Ferguson, Ted ....Superkid: Wayne Gretzky
Friedman, Lou ....Brett Hull
Goldstein, M. ....Brett Hull: Hockey's Top Gun
Hughes, Morgan ....Mario Lemieux: Beating the Odds
Hughes, Morgan ....Patrick Roy: Champion Goalie
Johnson, Ann Donegan ....The Value of Tenacity: The Story of Maurice Richard
Kramer, S.A. ....Great Gretzky
Kreisler, John ....Eric Lindros
Leder, Jane Mersky ....Wayne Gretzky
McFadden, Fred ....Bobby Clarke
McFadden, Fred ....Ken Dryden
McFadden, Fred ....Wayne Gretzky
Raber, Tom ....Wayne Gretzky: Hockey Great
Rappoport, Ken ....Eric Lindros
Rappoport, Ken ....Wayne Gretzky
Rombeck, Richard ....Wayne Gretzky
Savage, Jeff ....Paul Kariya: Hockey Magician
Schabner, Dean ....Jaromir Jagr
Tarcy, Brian ....Mario Lemieux
Wilner, Barry ....Mark Messier
Wilner, Josh ....Wayne Gretzky
Wolff, Craig Thomas ....Wayne Gretzky

Biographies – Reference

Diamond, Dan (ed) ....Hockey Hall of Fame: The Official Registry of the Game's Honour Roll
Diamond, Dan and Joseph Romain ....Hockey Hall Of Fame
Duplacey, James and Eric Zweig ....A Century of Hockey Heroes
Fischler, Stan ....Hockey's 100
Fischler, Stan ....The All-New Hockey's 100
Fischler, Stan and Shirley ....Heroes and History: Voices from the NHL's Past!
The Hockey News ....The Top 50 NHL Players of All Time

Coaching

AHAUS ....Hockey Coaching
American Sports Education Program ....Coaching Youth Hockey
Andjelic, Alex and Doug Hearns ....European Hockey Drill Book
Brothers, Kam ....Hockey Drills for Skill Development
Brothers, Kam ....Practice to Play at a High Tempo
Canadian Amateur Hockey Association ....IIHF Coaches Manual
Canadian Amateur Hockey Association ....On the Attack Drill Manual
Canadian National Coaching Certificate Program....................Advanced II Proceedings
Chambers, Dave ....Complete Hockey Instructions: Skills and Strategies for Coaches and Players
Chambers, Dave ....The Incredible Hockey Drill Book
Chambers, Dave ....Winning Strategies for Every Level of Play
Cielo, Bob ....Winning Hockey: Systems & Strategies for all Three Zones
Czech Ice Hockey Federation ....Czechoslovakian Youth Hockey Training
Dussiaume, Ron ....Mitron High Performance, High Tempo Hockey Practice and Drill Manual for Junior & Pro
Dussiaume, Ron ....Mitron Hockey High Tempo, High Flow Half Ice Drills
Dussiaume, Ron ....Mitron Hockey System Curriculum Sets
Fullerton, James ....Ice Hockey: Playing and Coaching
Gare, Danny ....BCAHA Coach's Drill Manual
Gibson, Dave ....Coach's Yearly Pratice Planner

Gregg, Randy .... Hockey: The Technical, the Physical and the Mental Game
Gregus, Gary and Val Belmonte .... Half-Ice Drill Book
Gwozdecky, George and Vern Stenlund .... Hockey Drills for Passing & Receiving
MacDonald, Leo .... Perfect Practice: The Coaching Edge
Mooley, Tom .... Hockey Coaching: The ABC's of International Hockey
Percival, Lloyd .... The Hockey Handbook
Shero, Fred and Andre Beaulieu .... Hockey For The Coach, The Player and The Fan
Smith, Michael A .... The Hockey Play Book
Smith, Michael A. .... The Hockey Coach's Manual
Smith, Michael A. .... The Hockey Drill Book
Smith, Ron .... Hockey Practice Drills
Smith, Ron .... Hockey Systems
Stenlund, Vern and Tom Webster .... Hockey Drills for Puck Control
Trimble, Richard M. .... The Ultimate Hockey Drill Book (Vol 1-2)
Trumble, Hal .... Coaching Youth Ice Hockey
Vernacchia, Ralph, Rick McGuire and David Cook .... Coaching Mental Excellence
Walford, Dr. Gerald A. and Gerald E. .... Coaching Hockey
Walford, Dr. Gerald A. and Gerald E. .... Hockey Skills
Walford, Gerald A. .... Ice Hockey: An Illustrated Guide for Coaches
Westerlund, Erkka .... Transition: From Game to Practice
Zulewski, Richard .... A Parent's Guide to Coaching Hockey

Commentary

Cruise, David and Alison Griffiths .... Net Worth: Exploding the Myths of Pro Hockey
Dryden, Ken .... The Game
Heinz, Rick .... Many Are Called, Few Are Signed
Jenkins, Sandy .... Yellow Sunday
Klein, Jeff Z. and Karl-Eric Reif .... Death of Hockey
Lapp, Richard and Silas White .... Local Heroes: A History of the Western Hockey League
Silver, Jim .... Thin Ice: Money Politics and the Demise of an NHL Franchise
Stein, Gil .... Power Plays: An Inside Look at the Big Business of the National Hockey League

Evolution of Hockey

Dimetrio, Steve .... History of Hockey
Duplacey, James et al. .... 20th Century Hockey Guide
Farrell, Arthur .... Hockey: Canada's Royal Winter Game
McFarlane, Brian .... Brian McFarlane's History of Hockey
McFarlane, Brian .... One Hundred Years Of Hockey
McFarlane, Brian .... 60 Years Of Hockey
O'Brien, Andy .... Headline Hockey
Strachan, Al (ed) .... 100 Years of Hockey
Tremblay, Jack .... The Birth Of Hockey
Weiles, L.J. Sparky .... Hockey Then and Now

Fans'/Parents' Guides

.... A Basic Guide to Ice Hockey
.... Ice Hockey: A Guide for Parents and Coaches
Arlott, John .... The Oxford Companion to Sports and Games
Ayres, Tom .... The Illustrated Rules of Ice Hockey
Brannen, Jack .... Spalding's First Standard Guide to Hockey
Brown, Michael .... Hockey Rules in Pictures
Davidson, John .... Hockey for Dummies
Eskenazi, Gerald .... A Thinking Man's Guide to Pro Hockey
Ferguson, Will, Bruce Spencer, Teena Spencer .... The Girlfriend's Guide to Hockey
Harari, P.J. and Dave Ominsky .... Ice Hockey Made Simple: A Spectator's Guide
Keegan, Tom .... Hockey Desk Top Reference
Liss, Howard .... Hockey Talk
Neely, Cam and Bobby Orr .... Hockey for Everybody
Nicol, Eric .... The Joy Of Hockey
Poteet, Lewis J. and Aaron C. .... Hockey Talk
Poteet, Lewis J. and Aaron C. .... The Hockey Phrase Book
Scharff, Robert .... Ice Hockey Rules in Pictures
Shorley, John .... Hockey Made Easy
Smushkin, Dr. Yasha .... From Zero to Hockey Hero: Guide for Parents
Sullivan, George .... Face-Off: A Guide to Modern Ice Hockey
USA Hockey .... The Official Rules of Ice Hockey
Whitehead, Eric .... Ice Hockey
Wilson, Dave and Bill McLean .... Simply Hockey
Wolfe, Bernie and Mitch Henkin .... How to Watch Ice Hockey

Fiction

Alguire, Judith .... Iced!
Birdwell, Cleo .... Amazons: An Intimate Memoir by the First Woman Ever to Play in the NHL
Jacobs, Dale (ed) .... Ice: New Writing on Hockey
MacGregor, Roy .... The Last Season
McCormack, Pete .... Understanding Ken
Orr, Frank .... Puck Is a Four Letter Word
Quarrington, Paul .... Logan In Overtime
Quarrington, Paul .... King Leary
Quarrington, Paul (ed) .... Original Six: True Stories from Hockey's Classic Era
Reddick, Don .... Dawson City Seven
Robertson, George and Scott Young .... Face-Off
Salutin, Rick .... Les Canadiens
Robertson, Ray .... Heroes
Wake, Bob .... Level Ice
Woodley, Richard .... Slap Shot
Wright, Richard B. .... The Age of Longing
Zweig, Eric .... Hockey Night in the Dominion of Canada

Fiction for Children

Alger, Horatio .... Making His Way
Alger, Horatio .... Wait and Hope
Ayoub, Susan and Katie Nguyen .... Hockey Pups
Barwin, Steven & Gabriel David Tick .... Roller Hockey Blues
Belisle, David .... There's a Shark in My Hockey Pool
Bianci, J. .... Bungalo Boys, Champions of Hockey
Bilson, Geoffrey .... Hockey Bat Harris
Blair, L.E. .... Face-Off!
Bowman, Crystal .... Ivan and the Dynamos
Brooks, Bruce .... The Wolfbay Wings #1: Woodsie
Brooks, Bruce .... The Wolfbay Wings #2: Zip
Brooks, Bruce .... The Wolfbay Wings #3: Cody
Brouwer, Sigmund .... Thunderbird Spirit (Lightning on Ice series)
Brouwer, Sigmund .... Winter Hawk Star (Lightning on Ice series)
Brownridge, William Roy .... The Moccasin Goalie
Brownridge, William Roy .... The Final Game: Further Adventures of the Moccasin Goalie
Carrier, Roch .... The Hockey Sweater
Childerhose, R.J. .... Hockey Fever in Goganne
Childerhose, R.J. .... Winter Racehorse
Christopher, Matt .... Wingman on Ice
Christopher, Matt .... Ice Monster
Christopher, Matt .... Ice Magic
Christopher, Matt .... Face-Off
Christopher, Matt .... Penalty Shot
Christopher, Matt .... The Hockey Machine
Connors, Stompin' Tom .... Hockey Night Tonight
Corbett, Scott .... The Hockey Trick
Danakas, John .... Hockey Night in Transcona
Dumtra, Stacy .... Face-Off
Ferguson, Donald .... Scranton High Chums
Ferguson, Donald .... Scranton High Chums at Ice Hockey
Ferguson, Donald .... Scranton High Chums on the Cinder Path
Filare, Cosimo .... You Can't Win Them All
Fishel, Dick and Ken Hay .... Terry and Bunky Play Hockey
Fisher, Lois I. .... Sarah Dunes, Weird Person
Flood, Richard T. .... Pass That Puck
Gault, Clare .... Norman Plays Ice Hockey
Godfrey, Martyn .... Please Remove Your Elbow from My Ear
Horowitz, Jordan .... D2: The Mighty Ducks Are Back!
Jackson, C.P. and O.B. .... Puck Grabber
Korman, Gordon .... The Chicken Doesn't Skate
Leblanc, Louise .... Maddie in Goal
Leonetti, Mike .... My Leafs Sweater
Lewis, Maggie and Michael Chessworth (ill.) .... Morgy Makes His Move
Longstreth, T. Morris .... The Calgary Challengers
Lunemann, Evelyn .... Face-off
Lynch, Chris .... Iceman
MacGregor, Roy .... The Quebec City Crisis
MacGregor, Roy .... The Screech Owls' Home Loss
MacGregor, Roy .... Kidnapped in Sweden
MacGregor, Roy .... Murder at Hockey Camp
MacGregor, Roy .... Mystery at Lake Placid
MacGregor, Roy .... The Night They Stole the Stanley Cup
MacGregor, Roy .... The Screech Owls' Northern Adventure
MacMillan, Don .... Rink Rat
Maloney, Peter and Felicia Zekauskas .... The Magic Hockey Stick
McFarlane, Brian .... The Youngest Goalie
McFarlane, Brian .... Peter Puck and the Stolen Stanley Cup
McFarlane, Brian .... Peter Puck's Great Moments in Hockey
McFarlane, Leslie .... McGonigle Scores
McFarlane, Leslie .... The Dynamite Flynns
Morgan, Allen and Michael Marchenko .... The Magic Hockey Skates
Muller, Charles Geoffrey .... Puck Chasers, Incorporated
Myers, Bill .... My Life as a Human Hockey Puck

Neigoff, Mike ....Terror on Ice
O'Brien, Andy..................................Hockey Wingman
O'Connor, Jim ....Call Me Gretzky! (The No Stars Series)
O'Connor, Jim ....Let's Hear It For The Shrumps! (The No Stars Series)
O'Connor, Jim ....Sticking It Out (The No Stars Series)
O'Keefe, Frank ....It's Only a Game
Orr, Frank ....Buck Martin: Take Centre Ice
Palmer, Bernard..................................Danny Orlis Plays Hockey
Porter, Mark ....Slashing Blades
Rathjen, Carl Henry ....Shadow On The Ice
Riddell, Jacqueline S..................................Face-Off at Center Ice
Rodriguez, K.S. ....Are You Afraid of the Dark: The Tale of the Horrifying Hockey Team
Romain, Joseph..................................Two Minutes for Roughing
Salata, Estelle ....Mice at Center Ice
Scott, Morgan ....Boys of Oakdale Academy
Sherman, Harold M. ....Down The Ice
Smith, Helen ....Echoes of Hockey
Standish, Bert L. ....Frank Merriwell on Top
Stokes, Bill ....Slap Shot
Verral, Charles Spain ....Captains of the Ice
Walsh, Ann ....Shabash!
Wolfe, L.E...................................The Case of the Screaming Skates
Wright, Jack ....Champs on Ice
Young, Scott ....A Boy at the Leafs Camp
Young, Scott ....Boy On Defense
Young, Scott ....Scrubs on Skates
Young, Scott ....That Old Gang of Mine

Great Moments

Beddoes, Dick ....Greatest Hockey Stories
Camelli, Allen..................................Great Moments in Pro Hockey
Fischler, Stan..................................Strange But True Hockey Stories
Fischler, Stan..................................The Zany World of Hockey
Gitler, Ira ....Blood on the Ice: Hockey's Most Violent Moments
Kendall, Brian ....100 Great Moments In Hockey
Liss, Howard ....Strange But True Hockey Stories
McKinley, Michael ....Etched in Ice: Hockey's Defining Moments

History

..................................History of British Colombia Hockey
Allen, Kevin ....Crunch: A History of Fighting in the NHL
Bartlett, R. Paul ....Raising the Rafters: A History of Hockey in Tavistock
Beardsley, Doug..................................Country On Ice
Beddoes, Dick, Stan Fischler, and Ira Gitler ....Hockey!
Beer, Anthony..................................It's Funny When You Win Everything
Berger, Howard and Bruce Bennett ....Sticks and Pucks
Boyd, Bill ....Hockey Towns: Stories of Small Town Hockey in Canada
Brewitt, Ross ....Into The Empty Net
Brewitt, Ross ....Last Minute Of Play
Brunt, Stephen ....The New Ice Age: A Year in the Life of the NHL
Bull, Wm. Perkins ....From Rattlesnake Hunt to Hockey
Cole, Stephen ....The Last Hurrah: A Celebration of Hockey's Greatest Season 66-67
Conacher, Brian ....Hockey In Canada: The Way It Is!
Diamond, Dan (ed) ....Hockey: The Official Book of the Game
Diamond, Dan (ed) ....The Official NHL Stanley Cup Centennial Book
Diamond, Dan (ed) ....The Official NHL 75th Anniversary Commemorative Book
Diamond, Dan (ed) ....Years of Glory 1942-1967: The NHL's Official Book of the Six-Team Era
Diamond, Dan and Lew Stubbs ....Hockey: Twenty Years
Dion, Jacques ....La petite histoire d'un grand tournoi (French)
Dolan, Edward F. Jr. ....The National Hockey League
Dryden, Ken and Roy MacGregor ....Home Game
Duplacey, James and Dan Diamond (ed) ......The (Annotated) Rules of Hockey
Dutton, Mervyn ....Hockey: The Fastest Game On Earth
Eksteins, Modris ....Rites of Spring: The Great War and the Birth of the Modern Age
Eskenazi, Gerald ....Hockey
Finnigan, Joan ....Some of the Stories I Told You Were True
Fischler, Stan..................................Cracked Ice
Fischler, Stan..................................Golden Ice
Fischler, Stan..................................Hockey's Greatest Rivalries
Fischler, Stan..................................Hockey's Greatest Teams
Fischler, Stan..................................Off Side: Hockey From The Inside
Fischler, Stan..................................Power Play!
Fischler, Stan..................................Slashing!
Fischler, Stan and Shirley ....Everybody's Hockey Book
Fischler, Stan and Shirley ....Great Book of Hockey
Fischler, Stan and Shirley ....Up From the Minor Leagues Of Hockey
Fischler, Stan and Dan Baliotti ....This Is Hockey
Fitsell, J.W..................................Hockey's Captains, Colonels & Kings
Frayne, Trent ....Hockey
Frayne, Trent ....It's Easy—All You Have To Do Is Win
Freeberg, Lloyd ....In The Bin
Garton, Harold ....Hockey Town Canada
Greenberg, Jay ....NHL: The World of Professional Ice Hockey
Greig, Murry ....Big Bucks and Blue Bucks: An Anecdotal History of the Late, Great WHA
Gruneau, Richard and David Whitson ......Hockey Night In Canada
Guay, Donald ....L'histoire du Hockey au Quebec (French)
Guttmann, Allen ....Sports Spectators
Hood, Bruce and Murray Townsend ....The Good of the Game: Recapturing Hockey's Greatness
Hoppener, Henk W. ....Death of a Legend
Houston, William and David Shoalts ......Greed & Glory
Hughes, Morgan..................................The Best of Hockey
Isaacs, Neil D. ....Checking Back: A History of the NHL
Kidd, Bruce and John Macfarlane ....The Death of Hockey
Lablanc, Michael L. and Mary K. Ruby (ed)...Professional Sports Team Histories: Hockey
Lautier, Jack and Frank Polnesek ....Same Game, Different Name
Leah, Vince ....Manitoba's Hockey History
MacAulay, Alex et al ....The Memorial Cup: Canada's National Junior Hockey Championship
MacGregor, Roy ....Road Games
MacGregor, Roy ....The Home Team: Fathers, Sons & Hockey
Mason, Daniel Scott ....A History of The International Hockey League 1904-1907
McFarlane, Brian ....Everything You've Always Wanted to Know About Hockey
McFarlane, Brian ....The Lively World of Hockey
McFarlane, Brian ....The Story of the National Hockey League
Mickoski, Howard ....Hockeyology: Digging up Hockey's Past
Miles, Gary ....Inside Hockey
Moriarty, Tim ....Hockey's Hall of Fame
Morrison, Scott ....Fire on Ice
Morrow, Don, Mary Keyes, Wayne Simpson, Frank Cosentino and Ron Lappage......A Concise History of Sport In Canada
Olney, Ross R. ....This Game Called Hockey
Olney, Ross R. ....Winners! Super Champions of Ice Hockey
Orr, Frank ....Hockey Scrapbook
Orr, Frank ....The Story Of Hockey
Patton, Major ....Ice Hockey
Quarrington, Paul ....Hometown Heroes
Revelin, Jaques ....Pee Wee
Ronberg, Gary ....The Violent Game
Roper, Jim (ed) ....From Pond to Pro: A History of Hockey in the Moncton Region
Ross, Alan ....Hooked on Hockey
Roxbourough, Henry ....Great Days in Canadian Sport
Roxbourough, Henry ....One Hundred-Not Out
Tatomyr, George..................................Beyond the Uke Line: Ukrainians in the National Hockey League
Vaughn, Garth ....The Puck Starts Here
Vaz, Edmund ....The Professionalization of Young Hockey Players
York, Holcomb and Richard F. Vaughn ....Hockey
Young, Scott ....100 Years of Dropping the Puck: A History of the OHA
Young, Scott ....The Boys of Saturday Night
Zeman, Brenda ....Hockey Heritage: 88 Years of Puck-Chasing In Saskatchewan
Zeman, Gary W. ....Alberta On Ice

History – Team

..................................Boston Bruins Celebrating 75 Years
..................................Boston Garden: Banner Years 1928-1995
..................................Dallas Stars: '99 NHL Champs
..................................The New York Rangers: Millennium Memories
Albert, Marv with Stan Fischler ....Ranger Fever
Aretha, David..................................The Montreal Canadiens Hockey Team
Bailey, Budd ....Celebrate the Tradition: The History of the Buffalo Sabres
Baldwin, Gary, Don Barrie, Kevin Varrin.........Five Decades with the Petes
Barris, Ted, George Hanson, John Short, Bob Mummery, Davis Strong............Positive Power: The Story of the Edmonton Oilers

Batten, Jack ....The Leafs, An Anecdotal History
Batten, Jack ....Hockey Dynasty
Batten, Jack ....The Leafs in Autumn
Berger, Howard ....On The Road
Berger, Howard ....Maple Leaf Moments
Boyd, Denny ....The Vancouver Canucks Story
Brewitt, Ross ....A Spin of The Wheel
Brewitt, Ross ....Sabres: 26 Seasons in Buffalo's Memorial Aud
Brogan, John ....We're #1: The Story of the Flyers' Skate to the Stanley Cup
Brown, Babe, Bobby Attersley, Bill Kurelo......A History of the Oshawa Generals
Brown, Frank ....New York Rangers: Broadway Blues
Buckley, Steve and Augie Favazza ....Mariners Mania
Cameron, Steve ....Feeding Frenzy: The Wild New World of the San Jose Sharks
Chadwin, Dean ....Rocking the Pond (Mighty Ducks 1993-94)
Chadwin, Dean ....Taking the Ice: The Mighty Ducks of Anaheim
Chevalier, Jack ....The Broad Street Bullies
Cosentino, Frank ....The Renfrew Millionaires
Detroit Free Press ....Stanleytown
Diamond, Dan (ed) ....Maple Leaf Gardens: Memories and Dreams
Dinger, Ralph ....Shadows on Thin Ice
Duhatschek, Eric and Steve Simmon ......On Fire – Calgary Flames
Duplacey, James ....Maple Leaf Magic
Duplacey, James and Charles Wilkins ......Forever Rivals
Durso, Joseph ....Madison Square Garden: 100 Years of History
Eskenazi, Gerald ....A Year on Ice
Falls, Joe, Jerry Green and Vartan Kupelian ....Greatest Moments in Detroit Red Wing History
Finnigan, Joan ....Old Scores, New Goals
Fischler, Stan ....Boston Bruins: Greatest Moments and Players
Fischler, Stan ....The Greatest Players and Moments of the Philadelphia Flyers
Fischler, Stan ....Motor City Muscle
Fischler, Stan ....The Rivalry
Fischler, Stan ....Bobby Clarke and the Ferocious Flyers
Fischler, Stan ....Blazing North Stars
Fischler, Stan ....Bobby Orr and the Big, Bad Bruins
Fischler, Stan ....Garry Unger and the Battling Blues
Fischler, Stan ....Go Leafs Go
Fischler, Stan ....Make Way for the Leafs
Fischler, Stan ....New York's Rangers
Fischler, Stan ....Saga of the St. Louis Blues
Fischler, Stan ....The Buffalo Sabres: Swashbucklers of the Ice
Fischler, Stan ....The Burly Bruins
Fischler, Stan ....The Fast-Flying Wings
Fischler, Stan ....The Roaring Rangers and the Emile Francis Years
Fischler, Stan and Chris Botta ....Pride and Passion: 25 Years of the New York Islanders
Fitkin, Ed ....The Gashouse Gang of Hockey
Gallagher, Tony and Mike Gasher ....Towels, Triumph and Tears
Godber, Sid ....Go-Vees-Go: The Incredible Saga of the Pentiction Vees 1951-1955
Gottselig, Johnny ....30 Memorable Games Played by Chicago's Blackhawks
Goyens, Chrys ....The Montreal Forum: 1924-1996
Goyens, Chrys and Allan Turowetz ....Lions In Winter
Greenberg, Jay ....Full Spectrum: The Complete History of the Philadelphia Flyers
Greenland, Paul R. ....Wings Of Fire
Greenland, Paul R. ....Hockey Chicago Style, The History of the Chicago Blackhawks
Grove, Bob ....Pittsburgh Penguins: The Official History of the First 30 Years
Gurba, Andy ....History of the Brandon Wheat Kings
Gzowski, Peter ....The Game of Our Lives
Hackel, Stu ....1994: The Official Book of the New York Rangers Stanley Cup Championship
Harris, Billy ....The Glory Years
Haynes, Don and Tom McNamee...........The Stadium: 1929-1994 The Official Commemorative History of the Chicago Stadium
Hollander, Zander (ed) ....Madison Square Garden
Hornby, Lance ....The Story of Maple Leaf Gardens: 100 Memories at Church and Carlton
Houston, William ....Pride & Glory
Houston, William ....Inside Maple Leaf Gardens
Irvin, Dick ....The Habs
Kane, Mike ....Minor in Name Only: The History of the Adirondack Red Wings
Kent, Geoffrey, W. ....Here Come the Vees
Kiczek, Gene ....Forgotten Glory, The Cleveland Barons
Kreiser, John and Lou Friedman ....The New York Rangers: Broadway's Longest Running Hit
Lambert, Cynthia et al ....Quest For the Cup: The Detroit Red Wings' Unforgettable Journey to the 1997 Stanley Cup
Larochelle, Claude ....Les Nordiques (French)
Lautier, Jack ....15 Years of Whalers Hockey
Lautier, Jack ....Forever Whalers
Maher, Peter with John Iaboni..............The Eternal Flames
Martin, Lawrence ....The Red Machine
McFarlane, Brian ....The Red Wings: Brian McFarlane's Original Six
McFarlane, Brian ....The Rangers: Brian McFarlane's Original Six
McFarlane, Brian ....The Habs: Brian McFarlane's Original Six
McFarlane, Brian ....The Leafs: Brian McFarlane's Original Six
McMillan, Tom ....The Penguins: Cellar to Summit
Meisel, Barry ....Losing the Edge: The Rise and Fall of the Stanley Cup Champion New York Rangers
Moriarty, Tim ....The Dynamic Islanders
Moriarty, Tim ....The Incredible Islanders
Morrison, John and Doug McClatchy ......Chicago Black Hawks: 1960-61
Morrison, John and Doug McClatchy ......Boston Bruins: 1969-70
Morrison, John and Doug McClatchy ......Detroit Red Wings: 1951-52
Morrison, John and Doug McClatchy ......Montreal Canadiens: 1959-60
Morrison, John and Doug McClatchy ......New York Rangers: 1939-40
Morrison, John and Doug McClatchy ......Toronto Blue Shirts (a.k.a. the Torontos): 1917-18
Morrison, John and Doug McClatchy ......Toronto Maple Leafs: 1961-62
Mummery, Bob ....Countdown to the Stanley Cup: An Illustrated History of the Calgary Flames
Mummery, Bob and Davis Strong ....The Amazing Oilers
O'Brien, Andy ....Les Canadiens
O'Brien, Andy ....Fire Wagon Hockey
Obodiac, Stan ....Maple Leaf Gardens
Obodiac, Stan ....The First 50 Years
Obodiac, Stan ....The Toronto Maple Leafs 1979/80
Pfeiffer, Gerald L. ....The Chicago Blackhawks: A Sixty Year History 1926-1986
Podnieks, Andrew ....The Blue & White Book: 1997
Podnieks, Andrew ....The Red Wing Book: 1997
Podnieks, Andrew ....Return to Glory
Reid, M.H. (Lefty) ....The First 50 Years: Peterborough and the OHA
Rocky Mountain News ....Avalanche
Rosenbaum, Dave ....Miami Ice: Winning the NHL Rat Race with the Florida Panthers
Rossiter, Sean ....Vancouver Canucks: The Silver Edition
Sadowski, Rick ....Los Angeles Kings: Hollywood
Simons, Dave ....Blue Fire: A Season Inside the St. Louis Blues
Sloman, Larry ....Thin Ice: A Season in Hell with the New York Rangers
Sterling, Chandler, W. ....The Icehouse Gang
Sullivan, Michael John ....The New York Rangers Hockey Team
Swanson, Jim ....Saskatoon Blades History Book
Tedesco, Theresa ....Offside
Ulmer, Michael ....Captains: Nine Great Toronto Maple Leafs
Ulmer, Michael ....Canadiens Captains
Vass, George ....The Chicago Blackhawks Story
Vautour, Kevin ....The Bruins Book 1997-1998
Wendel, Tim ....Going for Gold: How the U.S. Won at Lake Placid
Young, Scott ....The Leafs I Knew

History – Team – for Children

Babineau, Jeff ....Florida Panthers
Babineau, Jeff ....Tampa Bay Lightning
Brothers, Bruce ....St. Louis Blues
Everson, Mark ....New York Islanders
Everson, Mark ....New York Rangers
Gilbert, John ....Buffalo Sabres
Gilbert, John ....Dallas Stars
Gilbert, John ....Philadelphia Flyers
Gilbert, John ....Pittsburgh Penguins
Goodman, Michael ....Mighty Ducks of Anaheim
Goyens, Chrys ....Montreal Canadiens
Goyens, Chrys ....Toronto Maple Leafs
Jones, Terry ....Calgary Flames
Jones, Terry ....Edmonton Oilers
Kupelian, Vartan ....Boston Bruins
Kupelian, Vartan ....Chicago Blackhawks
Kupelian, Vartan ....Detroit Red Wings
MacGregor, Roy ....Ottawa Senators
MacIntyre, Iain ....Vancouver Canucks

Myers, Jess ....Winnipeg Jets
Olson, Gary ....Colorado Avalanche
Olson, Gary ....Hartford Whalers
Rennie, Ross ....Boston Bruins
Rennie, Ross ....Buffalo Sabres
Rennie, Ross ....Calgary Flames
Rennie, Ross ....Chicago Blackhawks
Rennie, Ross ....Detroit Red Wings
Rennie, Ross ....Edmonton Oilers
Rennie, Ross ....Hartford Whalers
Rennie, Ross ....Los Angeles Kings
Rennie, Ross ....Minnesota North Stars
Rennie, Ross ....Montreal Canadiens
Rennie, Ross ....New Jersey Devils
Rennie, Ross ....New York Islanders
Rennie, Ross ....New York Rangers
Rennie, Ross ....Philadelphia Flyers
Rennie, Ross ....Pittsburgh Penguins
Rennie, Ross ....Quebec Nordiques
Rennie, Ross ....St. Louis Blues
Rennie, Ross ....Toronto Maple Leafs
Rennie, Ross ....Vancouver Canucks
Rennie, Ross ....Washington Capitals
Rennie, Ross ....Winnipeg Jets
Smerle, David ....Washington Capitals
St. Peter, Joan ....Los Angeles Kings
St. Peter, Joan ....San Jose Sharks
Yannis, Alex ....New Jersey Devils

Illustrated Books

................................Our Goal is Gold: A Pictorial Profile of the 1998 USA Hockey Team
Bak, Richard ....Detroit Red Wings: The Illustrated History
Barrett, Norman ....Ice Sports (Picture Library)
Berger, Michael A. ....Hockey: The World of the Pros
Brodeur, Denis ....30 Ans de Photos de Hockey (French)
Brown, Frank and Roy Cummings, Lisa Dillman, Pat Hickey, Len Hochberg, Tom McMillan, Nancy Marrapease, Scott Morrison, Brian Scrivener, Jim Taylor ....A Day in the Life of the NHL
Chadwick, Bill ....Illustrated Ice Hockey Rules
Devaney, John and Burt Goldblatt ....The Stanley Cup
Diamond, Dan (ed) ....The Spirit of The Game
Diamond, Dan and Charles Wilkins ....Hockey: The Illustrated History
Duplacey, James and Joseph Romain ....Images of Glory
Elston, Dave ....The Evolution of Hockey
Fischler, Stan ....Fischler's Illustrated History of Hockey
Goyens, Chrys and Frank Orr ....Blades on Ice
Gretzky, Wayne, John Davidson and Dan Diamond (ed) ....99: My Life in Pictures
Hunter, Douglas ....A Breed Apart: An Illustrated History of Goaltending
Leonetti, Mike ....Hockey's Golden Era: Stars of the Original Six
Leonetti, Mike and Harold Barkley ....Hockey in the Seventies: The Game We Knew
Leonetti, Mike and Harold Barkley ....The Game We Knew: Hockey in the Sixties
Leonetti, Mike and Harold Barkley ....The Game We Knew: Hockey in the Fifties
McDonell, Chris ....La Passion du Hockey (French)
McKinley, Michael ....Hockey Hall of Fame Legends
Mouton, Claude ....The Montreal Canadiens: An Illustrated History of a Hockey Dynasty
Pincus, Arthur ....The Official Illustrated NHL History
Podnieks, Andrew ....Shooting Stars: Photographs from the Portnoy Collection at the Hockey Hall of Fame
Podnieks, Andrew ....Portraits of the Game
Romain, Joseph ....The Pictorial History Of Hockey
Romain, Joseph and Dan Diamond ....The Pictorial History Of Hockey
Taylor, Jim ....Wayne Gretzky
Turofsky, Lou and Nat................................Sports Seen

Instructional

................................Fun and Games: Canadian Hockey
................................Hockey Equipment
................................The Professional Hockey Handbook
Allaire, Francois ....Hockey Goaltending for Young Players
Alter, Michael J. ....Sports Stretch
Awrey, Don and Ken Hodge ....Power Hockey
Bakewell, Audrey ....Get the Edge: Audrey Bakewell's Power Skating Technique
Bathgate, Andy and Bob Wolff................................Andy Bathgate's Hockey Secrets
Bertagna, Joe ....Goaltending: A Complete Handbook
Brace, Ian ....Ice Hockey: Play The Game
Brown, Newell et al ....Hockey Drills for Scoring
Cady, Steve and Vern Stenlund ....High-Performance Skating for Hockey
Castaldi, C.R. and Earl F. Hoerner (ed) ....Safety in Ice Hockey
Chu, Donald A. ....Jumping into Plyometrics
Coombs, Charles Ira ....Be a Winner in Ice Hockey
Croce, Bruce C. ....Conditioning for Ice Hockey: Year Round
Daccord, Brian ....Hockey Goaltending
Dolan, John ....How to Develop Hockey Speed, Power & Strength
Dreayer, Barry ....Teach Me Sports: Hockey/Join the Fun by Learning the Game
Esposito, Phil and Tony ....We Can Teach You to Play Hockey
Falla, Jack ....Sports Illustrated Hockey: Learn to Play the Modern Way
Francis, Emile and Tim Moriarty ....The Secrets of Winning Hockey
Fuhr, Grant and Bob Mummery ....Fuhr on Goaltending
Gutman, Bill ....Ice Hockey: Start Right and Play Well (Go for It)
Harris, Lisa et al................................Hockey (How to Play the All-Star Way)
Hodge, Melville ....The Technique of Ice Hockey
Howe, Gordie................................Hockey ... Here's Howe!
Hull, Bobby and Roy G. Nelson ....Bobby Hull's Hockey Made Easy
Jeremiah, Eddie................................Ice Hockey
Kalb, Jonah ....The Easy Hockey Book
Kalchman, Lois ....Safe Hockey: How to Survive the Game Intact
Keegan, Tom ....Opportunities in Hockey
Korn, Mitch ....Goaltender's Manual
Lariviere, Georges ....Beginner's Program
Lariviere, Georges ....Physical Fitness and Technical Skill Appraisal of Ice Hockey Players
Lener, Slavomire ....Transition: Defense to Offense
MacAdam, Don and Gail Reynolds ....How To Make Best Use of Your Ice Time
MacAdam, Don et al ....Hockey Fitness: Year Round Conditioning on and Off the Ice
May, Dr. Robert H. ....The Hockey Road
McDougall, Shannon ....Progressive Psychological Performance for Hockey
McLean, Norman ....Hockey Basics
Meeker, Howie ....Meeker's Hockey Basics
Odums, R.I. and O.G. Allen ....Career Guide to Officiating Ice Hockey
Patrick, Lynn and D. Leo Monahan ....Let's Play Hockey
Paulsen ....Facing Off, Checking and Goaltending
Perron, Jean ....Shooting To Win
Plante, Jacques ....Jacques Plante on Goaltending
Quistgard, Fred ....Controlling the Crease
Riley, Jack................................Ice Hockey
Rossiter, Sean ....Hockey the NHL Way: The Basics
Rossiter, Sean ....Hockey the NHL Way: Goal Scoring
Rossiter, Sean ....Hockey the NHL Way: Goaltending
Sayles, Alexander and Gerard Hallock ....Ice Hockey: How To Play and Understand The Game
Smushkin, Dr. Yasha and Dr. Elena ....Hockey Agility
Solomon, Chuck................................Playing Hockey
Stamm, Laura ....Power Skating: A Pro Coach's Secrets
Stamm, Laura ....Power Skating the Hockey Way
Stark, Jerome ....Goaltender's Handbook
Taylor, Joe ....Lloyd Percival's Total Conditioning For Hockey
Thom, Douglas and Donald Ward ....The Total Hockey Player
Twist, Peter and Pavel Bure ....Complete Conditioning for Ice Hockey
Walford, Dr. Gerald A. and Gerald E. ....Youth Hockey for Parents & Players
Wark, Laurie and Scot Ritchie................................Basics for Beginners
Watt, Tom ....How to Play Hockey
Wenger, Howie PhD ....Fitness for High Performance Hockey
Williams, Barbara ....More Power to Your Skating
Young, Ian and Chris Gudeon ....Beyond the Mask
Young, Ian and Terry Walker ....Lords of the Rink

Instructional for Children

................................Better Ice Hockey for Boys
Etter, Les ....The Game of Hockey
McFarlane, Brian ....Hockey For Kids: Heroes, Tips & Facts
McFarlane, Brian ....Hockey Annual

International Hockey

Beddoes, Dick and John Roberts................................Summit 74: The Canada/Russia Hockey Series
Boyce, Trevor................................British Ice Hockey Players from the Golden Days
Cameron, James M. ....The Last Time We Won Hockey
Coleman, Jim................................Hockey Is Our Game
Drackett, Phil................................Flashing Blades – The Story of British Ice Hockey
Dryden, Ken with Mark Mulvoy ....Face-off at the Summit
Fischler, Stan and Shirley ....Red Line: The Soviets in the NHL
Frayne, Trent ....Canada-Russia '74
Gault, John ....The Fans Go Wild
Giddens, Robert ....Ice Hockey: The International Game

Ice Skating Institute of America	Olympic Ice Hockey
Lonetto, Richard	Russian Hockey Packet
Ludwig, Jack	Hockey Night in Moscow
MacFarlane, John	Twenty-seven Days in September
MacSkimming, Roy	Cold War: The Amazing Canada-Soviet Hockey Series of 1972
McFarlane, Brian	Canada Cup '81
Morrison, Scott	The Day Canada Stood Still
Podnieks, Andrew	Canada's Olympic Hockey Teams: The Complete History 1920-1998
Sinden, Harry with Will McDonough	Hockey Showdown
Sluyter, Liam	Seasons to be Cheerful: British Ice Hockey's Arena Era
Tarasov, Anatoli	Hockey Russian Style
Tarasov, Anatoli	Russian Hockey Secrets
Young, Scott	War on Ice

Miscellaneous

Barbour, Ralph Henry	The Crimson Sweater
Barris, Ted	Playing Overtime: Oldtimers' Hockey
Brodrick, Doc	Ice Hockey
Curtis, Richard	The Pro #2
Farrington, S. Kip Jr.	Skates, Sticks and Men
Fisher, Thomas Knight	Ice Hockey
Fitzsimmons, Cortland	Crimson Ice
Gault, William Campbell	Thin Ice
Hallock, Sayles	Ice Hockey
Hayes, Dan	Ice Hockey
Plimpton, George	Open Net
Sproxton, Birk	Hockey Fan Came Riding
Thieda, Shirley Ann	Fast Ice

Miscellaneous for Children

Halescroft, David	Hot Shot on Ice
Halescroft, David	Power Play
Harkins, Philip	Center Ice
Harkins, Philip	Lightning on Ice
Hewitt, Foster	Hello Canada!
Hewitt, Foster	Down The Ice
Hewitt, Foster	Along Olympic Road
Hill, John A.	Stories of the Railroad
Ilowite, Sheldon A.	Fury on Ice: An American-Canadian Hockey Story
Jennings, Jay	Teamwork: United in Victory
Kalman, Bobbie	Hockey In Action
Kelley, Ture, Dave Marzollo and Jean Marzollo	Hockey Hero
Klassen, Dale	I Love to Play Hockey
Leonetti, Mike and Dan Hamilton	Hockey Now
Martel, Suzanne	Pi-Oui
Renick, Marion	Five Points for Hockey

Player Profiles

Aaseng, Nathan	Hockey's Fearless Goalies
Bazunov, B.	Knights of the Rink
Bock, Hal	Save! Hockey's Brave Goalies
Bowlsby, Craig	Ice Age Memoirs
Brodeur, Denis and Daniel Daignault	Goalies: Guardians of The Net
Bylsma, Dan and Jay Bylsma	So Your Son Wants to Play in the NHL
Devaney, John	Tough Guys of Pro Hockey
Dowbiggin, Bruce	Of Ice and Men
Dowbiggin, Bruce	The Defense Never Rests
Dryden, Murray with Jim Hunt	Playing The Shots at Both Ends
Duplacey, James and Mark Paddock	The NHL: Today's Stars Tomorrow's Legends
Dwyer, Eric	Hockey's Young Superstars
Fischler, Stan	Bad Boys: Legends of Hockey's Toughest Men
Fischler, Stan	Bad Boys II
Fischler, Stan	Coaches
Fischler, Stan	Fire on Ice: Hockey Superstars
Fischler, Stan	Goalies: Legends from the NHL's Toughest Job
Fischler, Stan	Heroes of Pro Hockey
Fischler, Stan	Hockey Stars Speak
Fischler, Stan	Hockey's Toughest Ten
Fischler, Stan	Hockey: The New Champions
Fischler, Stan	More Bad Boys
Fischler, Stan	The Flakes of Winter
Fischler, Stan	The New Breed: Hockey's Hot Young Superstars
Fischler, Stan	Those Were The Days
Fischler, Stan	Ultimate Bad Boys: Hockey's Greatest Fighters
Fischler, Stan with Chico Resch	Hot Goalies
Frayne, Trent	Famous Hockey Players
Frayne, Trent	The Mad Men of Hockey
Gilbert, John	Shooters
Gretzky, Walter, Gordie Howe, Brett Hull, Mark Messier et al	Wayne Gretzky: The Making of the Great One
Gutman, Bill	Great Hockey Players #1: Park, Clarke, Mikita, Cournoyer
Gutman, Bill	Modern Hockey Superstars
Heit, Robert	Hockey: The Men Who Made it Great
Heit, Robert	The Name of the Game
Hewitt, W.A.	Down the Stretch
Howe, Colleen	My Three Hockey Players
Howe, Gordie and Colleen with Charles Wilkins	After The Applause
Hughes, Morgan and Joseph Romain, consultant	Hockey Legends of All Time
Hull, Dennis and Robert Thompson	The Third Best Hull
Hunt, Jim	The Men In The Nets
Hunter, Douglas	War Games: Conn Smythe & Hockey's Fighting Men
Irvin, Dick	Behind The Bench
Irvin, Dick	In The Crease
Irvin, Dick	Tough Calls: NHL Referees and Linesmen Tell Their Story
Jacobs, Jeff	Hockey Legends
Kariher, Harry C.	Who's Who In Hockey
Kaz, George	Hockey Legends
Klein, Jeff Z. and Karl-Eric Reif	The Coolest Guys On Ice
Larry Bortstein (ed)	My Greatest Day in Hockey
Libby, Bill	Hockey Heroes of Today
Liss, Howard	Hockey's Greatest All-Stars
Lowe, Kevin and Stan and Shirley Fischler	Champions
MacPeek, Walt	Hot Shots of Pro Hockey
McAllister, Ron	Hockey Heroes
McAllister, Ron	Hockey Stars Today and Yesterday
McDonell, Chris	For the Love of Hockey: Hockey Star's Personal Stories
McDonell, Chris	Hockey's Greatest Stars: Legends and Young Lions
McFarlane, Brian	NHL Hockey
Molinari, Dave	Best in the Game
Newhouse, Dave	After The Glory
O'Brien, Andy	Superstars: Hockey's Greatest Players
O'Brien, Andy	Young Hockey Champions
O'Brien, Jim	Penguins Profiles: Pittsburgh's Boys of Winter
Olney, Ross R.	Super Champions of Ice Hockey
Olver, Robert	The Making of Champions
Orr, Frank	Great Goalies of Pro Hockey
Orr, Frank	Hockey Superstars of the '70s
Orr, Frank	Hockey's Greatest Superstars
Pagnucco, Frank	Heroes: Stars of Hockey's Golden Era
Ronberg, Gary	The Ice Men
Smith, Don	Hockey: Rookie on Ice
Smith, Michael A.	Life After Hockey
Spiros, Dean	Top 10 Hockey Goalies
Sullivan, George	Hockey Heroes: The Game's Greatest Players
Swift, E.M.	Eleven Seconds: A Story of Tragedy, Courage, & Triumph
Tarasov, Anatoli	Road To Olympus
Thurn, Walter R.	The Famous Bentleys
Wayne, Bennett (ed)	Hockey Hotshots
Weiler, Diana	Bad Boy
Wilkins, Charles	Breakaway

Player Profiles for Children

Beeles, Richard	Hockey Heroes
Duplacey, James	Hockey's Hottest Centers
Duplacey, James	Hockey's Hottest Defensemen
Duplacey, James	Hockey's Hottest Wingers
Duplacey, James	The Stanley Cup: 100 Years of Hockey
Duplacey, James	Hockey Superstars: 1000 Point Players
Duplacey, James	Hockey Superstars: Amazing Forwards
Duplacey, James	Hockey Superstars: Champion Defensemen
Duplacey, James	Hockey Superstars: Great Goaltenders
Duplacey, James	Hockey Superstars: The Leafs vs. The Canadiens
Duplacey, James	Hockey Superstars: Top Rookies
Duplacey, James	Hockey's Hottest Goalies
Italia, Bob	Hockey's Heroes
Knapp, Ron	Top 10 Hockey Heroes
Kramer, S.A.	Hockey's Greatest Players
Kramer, S.A.	Hockey Stars: Gretzky, Lemieux, Roy and Lindros
McGuire, William	The Stanley Cup

Morse, Charles and Ann ....Phil and Tony Esposito
Rockwell, Bart ....World's Strangest Hockey Stories
Rockwell, Bart ....World's Greatest Hockey Stories
Romanuk, Paul ....Tough Guys of Hockey: 16 Players Who Beat the Odds
Romanuk, Paul ....Hockey Superstars 1999-2000
Zweig, Eric ....Goals!
Zweig, Eric ....Saves!

Reference

....Stats Hockey Handbook
Bonavita, Mark and Sean Stewart (ed) ......Hockey Register
Carter, Craig (ed) ....The Sporting News Hockey Guide
Chapman, Jeff, Travis Weir, Glen Weir ......Ultimate Hockey
Coleman, Charles L. ....The Trail of the Stanley Cup. Vol (1-3)
Diamond, Dan (ed) et al ....Total Hockey II
Diamond, Dan (ed) et al ....Total Hockey
Diamond, Dan (ed) ....Stanley Cup Playoff Fact Guide
Diamond, Dan (ed) ....Total Stanley Cup
Diamond, Dan (ed) ....World Cup of Hockey Media Guide
Diamond, Dan (ed) ....NHL Stanley Cup Playoffs Guide
Fischler, Stan and Shirley ....The Hockey Encyclopedia
Gitler, Ira ....Ice Hockey A to Z
Hollander, Zander ....The Hockey News Hockey Almanac
Hollander, Zander and Hal Bock (ed) ......The Complete Encyclopedia of Hockey
Klein, Jeff Z. and Karl-Eric Reif ....The Hockey Compendium
Ronberg, Gary ....The Hockey Encyclopedia
Sporting News ....The Sporting News Hockey Guide
Sporting News ....The Sporting News Hockey Register
Styler, Robert A. ....The Encyclopedia of Hockey
Surgent, Scott Adam ....The Complete Historical and Statistical Reference to the WHA, 1972-1979
The Hockey News ....The Hockey News Yearbook

Stanley Cup

Bortstein, Larry ....Stanley Cup
Devaney, John ....Great Upsets of Stanley Cup Hockey
Hunter, Douglas ....Champions: The Illustrated History of Hockey's Greatest Dynasties
Jenish, D'Arcy ....The Stanley Cup
Libby, Bill ....Great Stanley Cup Playoffs
Liss, Howard ....Goal! Hockey's Stanley Cup Playoffs
McFarlane, Brian ....Stanley Cup Fever
McFarlane, Brian ....The Stanley Cup
Romain, Joseph and James Duplacey ......The Stanley Cup
Roxbourough, Henry ....The Stanley Cup Story

Trivia and Collectibles

....Zap Hockey
Cole, Stephen ....Slapshots: The Best & Worst of 100 Years of Hockey
Cole, Stephen ....More Slapshots: The Best & Worst of 100 Years of Hockey
Davis, Jefferson and Andrew Podnieks ......Hello Hockey Fans from Coast to Coast
Diamond, Dan (ed) ....The Official NHL 1980s Quiz Book
Diamond, Dan (ed) ....The Official NHL Toronto Maple Leafs Quiz Book
Diamond, Dan (ed) ....The Official NHL 1970s Quiz Book
Diamond, Dan (ed) ....The Official NHL Philadelphia Flyers Quiz Book
Elston, Dave ....Back to the Drawing Board
Elston, Dave ....Elston Shorthanded
Elston, Dave ....Elston's Hat Trick
Leibman, Glen ....Hockey Shorts: 1001 Funniest One Liners
Mackenzie, Floyd ....101 Ways to Recycle a Hockey Stick
Maguire, Liam ....Liam Maguire's Hockey Trivia
Magus, Merv ....Hockey is a Funny Game
McAllister, Ron ....More Hockey Stories
McFarlane, Brian ....The Ultimate Hockey Quiz Book
McFarlane, Brian ....It Happened In Hockey
McFarlane, Brian ....More It Happened In Hockey
McFarlane, Brian ....Still More It Happened In Hockey
McFarlane, Brian ....The Best of It Happened In Hockey
Nelson, Kevin ....Slap Shots: Hockey's Greatest Insults
Polnaszek, Frank ....505 Hockey Questions Your Friends Can't Answer
Pywowarczuk, Andrew ....Hockey Card Checklist and Price Guide
Weekes, Don ....Extreme Hockey Trivia
Weekes, Don ....Awesome Hockey Trivia
Weekes, Don ....Old Time Hockey Trivia
Weekes, Don ....Hockey: The Official Trivia Handbook
Weekes, Don ....The Hockey Trivia Quiz Book
Weekes, Don ....Classic Hockey Trivia
Weekes, Don ....Hockey Trivia
Weekes, Don ....Hockey, Hockey, Hockey: The All-New Trivia Book
Weekes, Don ....Montreal Canadiens: The Hockey Trivia Handbook
Weekes, Don ....The Goal Scorers: Old Time Hockey Trivia
Weekes, Don ....The Stanley Cup: Old Time Hockey Trivia
Weekes, Don ....Ultimate Hockey Trivia

USA

Allen, Kevin ....USA Hockey: A Celebration of A Great Tradition
Eskenazi, Gerald et al ....Victory for America: Miracle on Ice
Fischler, Stan with Tom Sarro ....Metro Ice: A Century of Hockey in Greater New York
Fischler, Stan and Kevin Hubbard ....Hockey America: The Ice Game's History, Growth and Bright Future in the U.S
Prisuta, Mike ....Awe Inspiring: The Storied History of Spartan Hockey
Williamson, Murray ....The Great American Hockey Dilemma

Women's Hockey

Avery, Joanna and Julie Stevens...........Too Many Men on the Ice: Women's Hockey in North America
Dunn, Tricia and Katie King ....Gold Medal Ice Hockey for Women and Girls
Etu, Elizabeth and Megan K. Williams ......On the Edge: Women Making Hockey History
Keegan, Tom ....Women's College Hockey Guide
McFarlane, Brian ....Proud Past, Bright Future: One Hundred Years of Canadian Women's Hockey
Stewart, Barbara ....She Shoots, She Scores: A Complete Guide to Women's Hockey
Targ Brill, Marlene ....Winning Women in Ice Hockey
Turco, Mary ....Crashing the Net: The U.S. Women's Olympic Ice Hockey Team and the Road to Gold

CHAPTER 61

Hockey and the Tube

The Early Years of Hockey on Television

Paul Patskou

"WHAT A GREAT, GREAT FEELING, what a wonderful sense..." These were the opening words of the nostalgic "Esso Happy Motoring Song" that preceded the telecasts of hockey games in the 1950s and 1960s. And it was a great feeling. Millions of Canadians and Americans tuned in on their black-and-white TV sets every Saturday night during the hockey season to watch the Leafs or Canadiens battle it out with one of the four other NHL teams in the "Original Six" league.

On October 11, 1952, the Canadian Broadcasting Corporation (CBC) began televising NHL games from the Forum in Montreal. The renowned Rene Lecavalier described the play in French. Broadcasts began three weeks later from Maple Leaf Gardens in Toronto with the legendary Foster Hewitt calling the action. At that time, viewers were joining the game in progress around the middle of the second period. By the 1963–64 season the telecasts began to air a half-hour earlier, thereby allowing anxious viewers to see what play in the first period looked like. It was not until the 1968–69 season that the entire game was televised by the CBC.

Although hockey fans at the dawn of the TV era were only allowed to observe the last half of a game, it did add a suspenseful element to the evening. What would the score be? Would the graphic show the Leafs or Canadiens ahead or behind? Usually, Toronto or Montreal, each having great teams in that era, would be leading when Bill Hewitt or Danny Gallivan signed on. But that wasn't always the case.

There was one game that is forever etched in the memory of a generation of fans of that era. On January 18, 1964, the Stanley Cup champion Leafs were playing the perennial last place, pre-Bobby Orr, Boston Bruins. The Toronto team and their fans expected another easy Leaf victory. But on this night, Bill Hewitt revealed the score at the moment the plain graphic appeared—Boston 6 Toronto 0. Hewitt repeated, "yes, its Boston 6 and Toronto 0!" as if he couldn't believe the one-sided score. The game ended up 11 to 0 for Boston and it was truly a shocker in the hockey world at the time. Fortunately for the beleaguered Leaf goalie Don Simmons, the instant replay was still a year away from being a regular feature on *Hockey Night in Canada*.

As a youngster growing up in Toronto in the early 1960s, it seemed like an eternity waiting for 9 o'clock on Saturday nights to arrive and to hear the familiar Esso opening and Bill Hewitt's "Hello Canada and hockey fans in the United States." After watching *Rin Tin Tin* and *Zorro*, we then played with our hockey bubble gum cards while waiting for *Perry Mason* (and later *The Jackie Gleason* show or *The Saint)* to end before the game came on in glorious black and white. When the game ended and *Juliette* was joined in progress, we would go to bed dreaming about the day when we would play in the NHL.

In addition to game action, the intermissions on early hockey broadcasts also bring back fond memories. In December, 1955, Lorne Greene, not yet known as Ben Cartwright on *Bonanza*, would recite a Christmas poem. Yogi Berra, Phil Rizzuto and even the Cisco Kid all showed up as unlikely intermission guests. In the early 1960s, after Ed Fitkin would present highlights of the first period, Ward Cornell would conduct player interviews. One such interview in 1968 was especially memorable. The great Leaf defenseman Tim Horton managed to get in a plug for his burgeoning donut business, which today is one of the largest in Canada.

Other gems from those intermissions included Johnny Bower, the superb Leaf goalie, who, when asked what his favorite moment in his hockey career was, replied seriously, "the day Rocket Richard retired." Or when the rotund New York goalie Gump Worsley, asked which team gave him the most trouble, replied with a straight face, "the Rangers." And then there was the intermission feature on a skinny little 11-year-old from Brantford who was setting all kinds of scoring records. We would, of course, see this young phenom again when Wayne Gretzky grew up to dominate the game.

From 1959 to 1972, Ward Cornell was the foremost intermission host on *Hockey Night in Canada*. His on-air career, however, almost was terminated on April 14, 1960. After the Canadiens had just won their record fifth Stanley Cup title in a row, the postgame coverage had Cornell interviewing a number of players and executives that were thrust in his direction. In one instance, he turned to interview an already dejected Stafford Smythe, then an executive of the Maple Leafs, and erroneously announced him as Frank Selke Jr., the son of the general manager of the hated rival *les Canadiens*. Realizing his mistake—and undoubtedly remembering the enmity between the Smythe and Selke families—the horrified Cornell immediately apologized—with Smythe quickly countering, "you should be sorry." But the usually unflappable Cornell survived the incident and became a fixture on the broadcasts.

Another recognizable face on hockey telecasts was a Canadian actor named Murray Westgate. Westgate would appear dressed as an Esso gas station attendant and would extol the virtues of Esso gasoline. He closed off the telecast with his famous line, "Always look to Imperial for the best." He was so believable in his role that visitors to Toronto would actually drive around the city looking for his Esso station!

A long-standing tradition of the hockey telecasts was the Imperial Oil "Three-Star" selection. After the game ended, and following the Esso commercial break, the three stars of the game would skate onto the ice separately to a chorus of cheers or boos. Johnny Bower was frequently one of those three stars during the 1960s. Bower would skate out, stop at center ice, look at the crowd and wave with his left hand. He would always wave and because he was the only player doing so, it made the gesture more apparent. But to whom was Bower waving? The venerable goalie explained that the acknowledgement was originally intended for the mother of his wife Nancy, but that later the wave was for all the grandmothers watching him play.

One night, when Bower was chosen as one of the game's three stars, he felt that he did not deserve the honor. When he skated out to center, he did not perform his customary wave. Big mistake. It seems that in the following week John and Nancy received numerous letters, including many from angry grandmothers, admonishing him for neglecting his usual wave.

CBC began televising *Hockey Night in Canada* in color at the start of the 1966–67 season. Stronger lighting was installed in the Forum and at Maple Leaf Gardens in preparation for the color broadcasts. The players on the ice had to adjust to this new, brighter lighting. Kent Douglas of the Leafs would apply burnt cork under his eyes to dull the glare, much in the way football and baseball players used to combat the sun. Terry Sawchuk actually sat on the end of the Leafs bench wearing sunglasses! But the viewers could now distinguish why Leonard Kelly was called "Red" and observe Punch Imlach's face turn different shades of the color when his Leafs received a penalty.

Then as now, hockey broadcasts were even more thrilling come the playoffs. Prior to the start of each playoff game during the early TV era, a commentator would thank "the makers of Pepsodent toothpaste, the sponsors of *The Ed Sullivan Show* [or any other show or sponsor that was preempted] for relinquishing their time" so that the playoff game could be televised that night. Then came the drum roll and the voice-over, "Direct from the Forum in Montreal..." Danny Gallivan would eloquently describe the play as only he could with his "enormous saves," "spin-a-ramas" and "cannonading shots." Oh, those games between the Leafs and Canadiens were battles, played with much passion and frequent brawling. The two rivals met in the playoffs seven times between 1959 and 1967.

The playoffs were generally the only time that "away" games would be shown on television, but there were two long-forgotten, but astonishingly farsighted, experiments in Toronto beginning in the fall of 1962 that permitted hockey enthusiasts the chance to observe the Maple Leafs in out-of-town games. One was "Telemeter" hockey, which enabled fans to watch the road games in Toronto movie theaters. Ads in Maple Leafs game programs read: "Thrill to NHL hockey on giant screens of nine theaters exactly as they are being played through the magic of EIDOPHOR"—a new type of large screen.

The second experiment in road game broadcasts was an early form of pay-TV. In the Toronto suburb of Etobicoke, certain homes had their TV sets equipped with an electronic box and slot. Residents would deposit coins into the slot in order to watch the Leafs play on the road.

The televising of hockey was not exclusively a Canadian production in the era when the CBC began its broadcasts. From 1957 to 1960, the Columbia Broadcasting System (CBS) would cover NHL games in the United States on Saturday afternoons—the first time hockey was broadcast nationally in the States. CBS aired the "Game of the Week" from the four American cities, with Bud Palmer providing the play-by-play. The CBS effort proved innovative, televising the entire game more than a decade before the CBC did so.

A regular feature of these CBS broadcasts had a former minor league goaltender named Julian Klymkiw facing NHL shooters in a sort of "Showdown" contest. Julian, a Red Wings assistant trainer who usually wore a Detroit uniform, often did quite well in these competitions and we all wondered why Terry Sawchuk was in net for the Wings when young Julian was available.

CBS intermissions also included player interviews, which were conducted on the ice surface by one of the broadcast crew while dodging the Zamboni ice-resurfacing machine. In the 1959–60 season, Brian McFarlane, who later spent many years on *Hockey Night in Canada*, was hired to do these on-ice interviews. One of the reasons McFarlane got the job was because he could skate!

Advertisements for CBS telecasts appeared in newspapers and magazines—"Snappa Cappa Red Cap while you watch Carling's NHL Hockey Telecasts." And who could forget the commercials by Carling: "Hey Mabel, Black Label." Yet the CBS Game of the Week was not the first effort to televise hockey in the United States. Remarkably, KTLA in Los Angeles began televising games from the Pacific Coast Hockey League commencing in November, 1946, when television was in its infancy. Apparently, the production chief was one of the most rabid hockey fans in the Los Angeles area. The New York Rangers also began broadcasting games on television during the 1946–47 season. Bud Palmer began calling Rangers games on television station WPIX in the early 1950s.

Another significant moment in hockey broadcast history in the United States was the coverage of the 1960 Winter Olympics from Squaw Valley, California. (Viewers may remember Walter Cronkite of CBS shivering in a blizzard during the opening ceremonies.) The celebrated hockey game in which the U.S. Olympic team upset the Russians was played on an outdoor rink with shadows and sunshine and the reflection of Olympic symbols on the ice. An unforgettable scene had Jack McCartan, the U.S. goalie, racing out of his net to embrace his teammates after a slightly hysterical Bud Palmer had counted down the seconds as the USA clung to its tenuous one-goal lead. It was comparable to the scenario in Lake Placid 20 years later.

But the world of 1960 was not like the one of 1980. After Walter Cronkite read off the Olympic standings—with the Russians capturing the majority of the medals—the Schlitz commercial about "the beer that made Milwaukee famous" that usually aired was instead replaced by a public service announcement asking people to give their "support for 'Radio Free Europe' and to give towards assistance to those behind the 'Iron Curtain' and help defeat Communism." Apparently, at the height of the Cold War in 1960, sports and politics did mix.

Televised hockey has indeed changed over the years. Undoubtedly, today's product is technically superior, but there was something magical about the early days of hockey on TV. Many fans at that time could identify a majority of the NHL players. And players like Gordie Howe, Jean Beliveau, Frank Mahovlich and Bobby Hull seemed to have a special aura about them. In addition to the players, the Hewitts, Danny Gallivan, Brian McFarlane, Dick Irvin, Ward Cornell, Murray Westgate, Bud Palmer and other broadcasters always will be remembered fondly for the pleasure they provided on those cold, wintry Saturdays.

As the Esso song said, it was a "great, great feeling."

CHAPTER 62

Hockey and the Moving Image

Hockey as Depicted in Newsreels and Documentary Films

Paul Patskou

THERE IS MUCH WRITTEN MATERIAL documenting the history of hockey. Additionally, the game's past has long been preserved in still images thanks to the extensive photographic collections of the Turofsky brothers, Harold Barkley and others. Less well-known is the fact that the history of the game has also been impressively captured as a "moving image."

Various types of films on hockey have been preserved dating back to the late 1890s, when renowned inventor Thomas Edison filmed a short sequence called *Hockey Match on the Ice* in 1898. This footage, which is the earliest moving image of hockey, was shot using a stationary camera. It shows men on a frozen pond playing an early form of the game.

The next earliest known footage of hockey is the 1903 film *Hockey on Skates,* depicting ice hockey being played in the Swiss Alps. There also are clips of a four-team tournament between Britain, Germany, Switzerland and France in Les Aveniers, France, in 1910. And there is an extensive collection of hockey footage shot in Europe in the 1920s—primarily from the 1924 Olympics and of the long-forgotten Oxford University team touring the Continent.

A clear indication of how hockey appeared in its formative years in North America is revealed from footage shot in the early 1920s. An item entitled *Canadian National Pictorial Hockey in the West* has film of the Calgary Tigers and the Moose Jaw Maple Leafs of the old Western Canada Hockey League. This clip shows the referee carrying a bell and a goal judge wearing a fur coat on the ice behind the net.

Newsreel companies using 35-millimeter and 16-millimeter cameras were the primary source of early footage. Film companies such as Fox Movietone News, Universal News, British Pathe and other newsreel outfits were covering current events of the time to be shown in movie theaters. Patrons at the theater could view events of the week, including hockey and other sports, between feature films. Much of this newsreel hockey footage includes clips from Stanley Cup games from the 1930s and never has been shown since the original screening.

In some cases, the sound has been preserved, usually with crowd noise, sometimes with commentary, and on occasion with music of the era that adds a sense of time and authenticity to the footage. These newsreels capture long-forgotten aspects of the game and moments not generally known to the modern day hockey fan. For instance, there is footage of a New York Rangers player scoring a goal on a penalty shot from the penalty shot circle that existed in the NHL between 1934 and 1940. We also can see face-offs with the players facing the boards instead of the opposing nets. As well, by viewing vintage film, we can watch long-defunct teams such as the original Ottawa Senators, the Cougars and Falcons of Detroit, and the New York Americans.

Prior to the 1930s, hockey footage was shot outdoors. But on March 2, 1931, the *Toronto Star* reported that the first hockey game ever filmed indoors was played at the Mutual Street Arena in Toronto and produced by the Leiter Flicker Company. The game, played on February 28, featured such legends as Howie Morenz, Aurel Joliet, Joe Primeau and Ace Bailey as the Montreal Canadiens faced off against the Toronto Maple Leafs. According to the *Star*, the game was "about the craziest contest in the history of big league hockey, as the Kleig lights went to the boys' heads." There were fights on the ice and altercations with Toronto police. This film may be the only known footage of the old Mutual Street Arena in existence. Nine months later, Universal News cameramen were on hand at the new Maple Leaf Gardens to capture for posterity the opening ceremonies and game action.

By the 1940s, newsreel companies were routinely sending cameramen to Stanley Cup-clinching games to capture the game action and celebrations. On April 12, 1942, the Detroit Red Wings had a commanding 3–0 lead in games and were expected to clinch the Stanley Cup with a victory on home ice in the fourth game of the finals. Opportunely, film crews were on hand at the Olympia to capture the Leafs coming from behind and winning the game to stay alive in the series. The Leaf team then went on to win the next three games and miraculously win the series. Aside from the rarity and the historical importance of this footage, the film is notable for the close-up, ice-level action and bright lighting which was unusual for that era of filming. The footage also illustrates the artistry and skating style of Toronto great Syl Apps in particular and other stars of that era.

Newsreel footage also exists of off-ice action including views of the Stanley Cup parade in Ottawa after the original Senators won the championship in 1921. Clips also exist of the Toronto Maple Leafs Stanley Cup parade in 1948, with players in a motorcade driving past the current site of the Hockey Hall of Fame in downtown Toronto. Cameras also were present to record the disturbing images of the mob scene at St. Catherine Street in downtown Montreal during the "Richard Riot."

There also is an extraordinary preserved bit of hockey footage that was not taken by a newsreel company but by an individual situated behind the rail seats at Maple Leaf Gardens. On April 3, 1933, the Maple Leafs and Boston Bruins would play in what was then the longest playoff game in history before the diminutive Ken Doraty of the Leafs scored on Boston goalie Tiny Thompson in the sixth overtime period. This amazing footage has Bruin legends Eddie Shore and Dit Clapper, as well as King Clancy of the Leafs and others, in action leading rushes during the game. All of it is captured in close-up shots from ice level.

In the 1930s, movie theaters were beginning to screen

hockey movies such as Warner Brothers' *King of Hockey* with Dick Purcell as Gabby Dugan of the New York Violets. John Wayne starred (but skated poorly) in *Idol of the Crowds*. Actual game footage from the original Madison Square Garden in New York augmented the hockey "action" in the latter film.

Some excellent documentary-style hockey films were produced in the 1930s and 1940s. In *Hockey Champions of 1933*, a young Foster Hewitt describes play by play of the final Stanley Cup match between the New York Rangers and the Toronto Maple Leafs. The legendary broadcaster also interviews players and coaches from the two teams in their dressing rooms. *The Battered Mug* is a depiction of the General Motors Hockey Broadcast from coast to coast on radio in 1936. Foster Hewitt describes the action as the Montreal Maroons with Lionel Conacher competing against his brother, Charlie, and the Maple Leafs. This film also explains the history of broadcasting, detailing how radio broadcasts are transmitted across Canada. The opening scene has youngsters on a makeshift rink passing the puck and possessing "the hopes of every Canadian boy to go from the cradle of hockey [the frozen pond] to its throne [the then new Maple Leaf Gardens]."

In 1940, Morley Callaghan narrated a superb hockey documentary film called *Hot Ice—The Anatomy of Hockey*. Callaghan explains why hockey is "the national folk dance" of Canada and that Canadian youth "learn to skate as they learn to walk." Legendary figures such as Frank Nighbor are shown instructing Canadian youth on the intricacies of the game. The film also shows boys playing shinny on the frozen ponds and schoolyards with the aspiring hockey players shouting: "I'm Syl Apps" ... "I'm Eddie Shore." Callaghan further explains that the popular "shinny is hockey before it grew up" and that the game of hockey "is ours, it's us." Well said.

An editorial of *The Hockey News,* in an edition dated December 1, 1948, states that the "latest hockey achievement—a pictorial record of the history of hockey—has at last appeared on film." This documentary, *Hockey Cavalcade*, not only has sound but also is filmed in color—which was extremely rare for this era. The editorial added that it was "hoped that it is the forerunner of a series of such celluloid subjects—that will bring big-time hockey virtually within reach of all the fans." Films of this type were the only method of allowing fans that were not able to attend NHL games the chance to view the stars of the day as described by the legendary Foster Hewitt on his far-reaching radio broadcasts.

The Toronto Maple Leafs hockey club was one of the first teams to use footage of their home games for the purpose of training and scouting. From the mid-1940s to the early 1960s, the building superintendent of the Gardens, Don "Shanty" Mackenzie, filmed all Leaf home games from the stands with a 16-millimeter camera. On days following the games, Leaf coaches would screen the footage for their players as a teaching tool. Many remarkable moments in Toronto Maple Leaf history have been preserved on these films, including action from playoff series in the 1940s and Bill Barilko's famous overtime marker in the finals of 1951. This collection also has footage of the 1947 Chicago and Toronto match where Howie Meeker scored five goals. Where there may have been doubts about the accuracy of who actually scored the goals—as in this instance—there is an opportunity to correct certain historical accounts. Memories may fade but the camera doesn't lie.

With the advent of television, hockey followers who could not attend games were now able to see NHL hockey—provided they could afford TV sets in the late 1940s and early 1950s. Among the few to have the opportunity to see hockey live on a small black and white set was a young Gordie Howe, who was recuperating from a head injury suffered in the opening game of the bitter 1950 semifinal between Detroit and Toronto. The star Red Wing was able to view the seventh game of that series on Detroit television, much to the surprise of his teammates who visited him after the game to celebrate the victory.

In the years prior to the use of videotape, the method of retaining television broadcasts was referred to as the "kinescope" process. A 16-millimeter film camera was placed against the face of the television screen and the game was actually filmed right off the screen. Each 16-millimeter reel, or "kine," was approximately a half-hour long. Many of these black and white kinescopes still exist. They date from the first year that hockey was broadcast on the CBC in 1952 until the early 1970s, when broadcasts could be videotaped and preserved in color.

With the advent and use of videotape in Canada in the early 1970s, other methods of film retention were used, including two-inch, one-inch and Betacam tapes as well as modern digital storage media. Today, almost every game is not only telecast but retained. Every notable moment is now captured for future generations of hockey fans to reflect upon for historical purposes or simply to enjoy and re-live fond memories.

Hockey has indeed changed a great deal since its formative years, and the "moving image" is an important method of preserving hockey's history and providing a tool for understanding the game and its many changes. Fortunately, there exists an archive of vintage footage to do just that.

CHAPTER 63

Hockey on the Internet

A World of Icy Information Just a Few Clicks Away

Surveying the Web

John McCauley

The Internet has come to the forefront in hockey information. Injury reports, pregame reports, postgame reports, reports on the postgame reports—hockey information flows over your telephone or cable connection like a tidal wave 24 hours a day.

When the Internet first started, it was a new way for a few intellectual elite to exchange information via computer. Then it became a new way to keep in touch with friends and relatives around the world. Now it is a way to give your business venture a great deal of exposure and, of course, money. The Internet has become an integral part of sports media promotion and it continues to grow. An uncountable number of Web pages are already posted on the Internet with more and more added every day.

The Internet has become the land of opportunity for the NHL, sports publications, and thousands of entrepreneurs trying to capitalize on the emerging e-commerce marketplace. There are still fans creating sites for the love of the game.

The NHL has taken the lead in Internet promotion. in order to bring the game to a worldwide audience. NHL.com (www.nhl.com), the most obvious destination for NHL fans, gives a lot to its viewers. There is up-to-the-minute information on every NHL team and player, along with an interesting feature that allows you to hear analysis from various prominent hockey commentators. The site also provides video and audio clips that can be downloaded onto your computer.

NHL.com is a great start for any new fan of the game, especially someone that is trying to learn the rules or strategy. In the Hockey University section, beginners can learn about everything from an offside to an icing.

Despite the success of NHL.com, the league revamped the entire site last summer in order to stay at the forefront of website design.

Finding alternate sources of hockey information can be confusing to the Internet rookie—not because it's difficult to use the Internet itself, but because there is so much information available.

One of the best ways to learn about something is to look at the past, and the Hockey Hall of Fame (www.hhof.com) is a great place for historical information. The site not only offers information about all of the inducted members, it also has developed a new time capsule section that gives interesting facts and trends about hockey during different eras. HHOF has already opened the 1970s section, with the 1960s and 1980s soon to follow.

The Hockey Hall of Fame integrates the museum and its Web site, but has been able to make the site more than just an extension of the museum. Their philosophy has paid off. Just two years ago, the site had 800 visitors a day. Now there are well over 2,500.

Peter Jagla, an executive with the Hockey Hall of Fame's Internet division, believes the key to his site is making it fun for the visitor.

"Our goal is to be star-based," said Jagla. "Rather than all of them [hockey stars] having sites, we want to bring them together. We just want to promote hockey."

The Hockey Hall of Fame has not ignored the technical side of site development. Visitors are able to take virtual tours of the museum, and will be able to do so with 3-D technology in the near future. Scanning the Stanley Cup for your favorite player's name at your computer will be the next best thing to being there. The Hall has also developed a partnership with TSN (The Sports Network) for the rights to induction ceremonies so fans can see their favorite player inducted any time they want. Another new partnership is with NTN Trivia. Visitors can be linked with their network and test their knowledge.

E-commerce is in such demand on the Internet that the Hockey Hall of Fame could not ignore the trend. Any profits made through hhof.com go back into getting more exhibits for the museum and creating new features for the site. Along with cyber-store, HHOF has created the Legends Line E-store. Because the intermediary has been eliminated, fans can be confident of the authenticity of memorabilia they purchase. Players give the collectors' items directly to the Hockey Hall of Fame which ships it directly to the consumer. At the same time, the Hall has given its members a free avenue to promote themselves and created more on-line traffic for themselves.

A relative newcomer to the Internet scene—but one that can not be taken lightly—is Faceoff.com (www.faceoff.com). Owned by Hollinger Inc. and Wayne Gretzky, this site has taken advantage of a massive editorial base. Owning a chain of newspapers and aligning with the biggest name in hockey is a surefire way to create a buzz about a Web site. The site has only been running since February 28, 2000, but has quickly been able to carve a niche in the industry.

Executive director Tim Doyle plans to concentrate not just on the NHL but on a number of other leagues. as well. European leagues, minor pros, the Canadian juniors and many other leagues are being made part of the experience.

With a site that is editorial based, the company had to create something different. Enter Wayne Gretzky and MVP.com (www.mvp.com), of which he is part owner. Visitors can make purchases through MVP.com via a link on Faceoff.com. That means people can read an article by "The Great One" and then, in a few short clicks, buy a jersey from his Web site.

"E-commerce is an essential part of the experience," said Doyle. "It is boundless; television, video, there is great potential."

Faceoff.com has not focused on innovative technology

just yet, but has come up with little things that impress. Viewers are able to post reactions to the articles placed on the site. If you do not agree with Number 99, tell him so in the sound-off feature. Visitors also can register for pregame reports, an option that will e-mail you information on games free of charge.

Another Web site that has just been overhauled is *The Hockey News* (www.thehockeynews.com). On April 27, 2000, they released their first daily Internet publication. Readers gain all the regular features of the hockey newspaper along with daily league reports and a feature called Rink Rat Insider. Readers will also have the opportunity to purchase material distributed by *The Hockey News*.

Not every site has to be a multimillion dollar investment or have a name synonymous within the hockey industry to be of value to fans. People who just want the game to reach more people are building Web sites all over the world.

Phil Stamp, who has loved hockey his entire life, lives in the United Kingdom, where soccer and rugby reign supreme. Stamp and Stewart Roberts, who has been editor of the *British Ice Hockey Annual* for the past 25 years, decided that they wanted to create an A to Z encyclopedia of ice hockey (www.azhockey.com) that dedicated itself to the history of the game.

"We set out for the A to Z to be an historic site, not a news site," said Stamp. "We wanted it to be free access for hockey fans across the globe and encourage visitors to suggest new entries or correct our mistakes and/or omissions."

The site gives details about players, teams, leagues, competitions, awards, events, rinks, books and magazines. Information is added on a daily basis, but the focus is not statistically based. The site is trying to be a reference point for people interested in hockey on a global scale.

One of the most informative Web sites for players and their worried parents is www.hockeyinjuries.com. The site contains information on a number of injuries that are common to hockey players. It gives coaches, parents and players an opportunity to learn more about diagnosis, treatment and prevention of common ailments. It is a valuable asset for any hockey family.

For people interested in statistical information, the Internet Hockey Database (www.hockeydb.com) can help fans find players in almost any league. Creator Ralph Slate has filled a gap other Web masters have missed.

In addition to information, there are sites that are specifically in place to sell hockey merchandise. Don Lee of the Hockey Mart Mall (www.hockeymart.com) started his merchandise site because he knew what it was like to live in an area where hockey equipment was very rare. Another good site for purchasing equipment online is Hockey Gear.com (www.hockeygear.com).

As the lines between print, visual and audio media merge, the Internet is acting as the road connecting them. Editorial content and commercialism are closer than they have ever been with the onset of e-commerce and the rules surrounding it are constantly changing. Is there anything wrong with authors selling merchandise on the very same pages that they are basing opinions? Purists would say yes, but ultimately the public will decide. Are we able to recognize which Web sites are blowing smoke to take advantage of the rapidly changing Internet environment? The answer is just a mouse click away.

How the Internet has Revolutioned Hockey Coverage

Stu Hackel

Advances in information dissemination on the Internet have revolutionized the way fans are able to follow sports. The World Wide Web has explosively increased the amount of hockey information available, not just from official sources but, first and foremost, from newspaper sites (Slam! Hockey being a leader among them) and sites connected to television (ESPN.com, Foxsports.com, CNN/SI.com—which marries CNN coverage with *Sports Illustrated* content—and CBC.ca). The Hockey Night in Canada section of the CBC website allows fans to download Don Cherry's weekly Coach's Corner segment, the Satellite Hot Stove, interviews by Scott Oakes, etc. This is especially useful for fans outside of Canada who are unable to receive Hockey Night In Canada.

Newspaper and television Web sites are updated so frequently that the Internet can be like having a news service wire on your desktop. This immediacy has rendered the old method of learning about what's going on in the game—waiting for the morning newspaper—almost obsolete. In addition, all newspapers have space limitations, whereas Websites can publish everything that's relevant. The Web can provide a breadth and depth of information that no one newspaper could ever publish.

The Web also allows hockey fans to transcend geographical limitations. You can read coverage from newspapers in virtually every hockey market (NHL, minor pro, college, junior, Europe, etc.) and you can read them from anywhere in the world where you have access to a computer. A good place to find links to newspaper Web sites is the Ecola Newsstand (http://www.ecola.com/). Bruce Bennett Studios has a site that provides links to top hockey sites and NHL newspapers (http://www.bbshockey.com/linkage.htm). Scotty Bowman, a tireless consumer of hockey information and minutiae, likes to use Carole's No Frills Hockey Media Links (http://www.geocities.com/Colosseum/Track/7342/).

Another bonus for hockey fans on the Web is that radio broadcasts of every NHL game are available through www.broadcast.com. Fans can now follow their favorite teams no matter where they live. Montreal Canadiens Webcasts are so popular around the world that radio voices Pierre McGuire and Dino Sisto get e-mail from virtually everywhere: Europe, Asia, Africa.

In addition, every NHL team has its own Web site, most of which are very attractive and informative. While some teams are better than others when it comes to keeping their information up to date, most—if not all teams—post media game notes on their site in advance of every game. Team Web sites generally include a history section, team records, photos and the like. These sites are better than having the team media guide and are updated when trades are made. Most junior and minor-pro teams also have their own Web sites.

From a statistical standpoint, Ralph Slate's hockey database (http://www.hockeydb.com) has a remarkable assemblage of historical statistics, including those from virtually every minor hockey league past and present. Several newspaper and television-based sites also provide access to searchable data. Faceoff.com (www.faceoff.com/nhl/historicalstats/) and Fox Sports (http://www.foxsports.com/

nhl/history/) offer access to databases that can be queried by name, birthplace, birth date, team and season. The quality and ease of use of these sites are improving steadily.

In addition to these more formal Web sites, there are also a plethora of fan sites, many of them related to NHL teams. many are listed at http://www.rivals.com/default.asp?sid=0&p=26&c=10. There are sites about every aspect of hockey from high school leagues in Minnesota to second division teams in France and defunct teams like the Quebec Nordiques, Winnipeg Jets and the Atlanta Flames.

And to think that when the last century began, fans were content to gather in the cold outside the telegraph office to read scoring updates from big chalkboards set up in the street.

HOCKEY WEB SITES

LEAGUE AND TEAM SITES

National Hockey League ....www.nhl.com
Hockey Hall of Fame ....www.hhof.com
International Ice Hockey Federation ...www.iihf.com
NHL games on radio ....www.broadcast.com
NHL Site for Kids ....www.nhl.com/kids
NHL Players' Association..............www.nhlpa.com
Various fan/team Web sites ....www.rivals.com
Official NHL team Web sites:
Anaheim ....www.mightyducks.com
Atlanta ....www.atlantathrashers.com
Boston ....www.bostonbruins.com
Buffalo ....www.sabres.com
Calgary ....www.calgaryflames.com
Carolina ....www.caneshockey.com
Chicago ....www.chicagoblackhawks.com
Colorado ....www.coloradoavalanche.com
Columbus ....www.columbusbluejackets.com
Dallas ....www.dallasstars.com
Detroit ....www.detroitredwings.com
Edmonton...........................www.edmontonoilers.com
Florida ....www.flpanthers.com
Los Angeles ....www.lakings.com
Minnesota ....www.wild.com
Montreal ....www.canadiens.com
Nashville ....www.nashvillepredators.com
New Jersey ....www.newjerseydevils.com
NY Islanders........................www.newyorkislanders.com
NY Rangers ....www.newyorkrangers.com
Ottawa..............................www.ottawasenators.com
Philadelphia ....www.philadelphiaflyers.com
Phoenix ....www.phoenixcoyotes.com
Pittsburgh ....www.nhlpenguins.com
St. Louis ....www.stlouisblues.com
San Jose ....www.sj-sharks.com
Tampa Bay ....www.tampabaylightning.com
Toronto..............................www.torontomapleleafs.com
Vancouver ....www.vancouvercanucks.com
Washington ....www.washingtoncaps.com

NEWSPAPER AND TELEVISION SITES

Bennett Studio's top hockey sites ...www.bbshockey.com/linkage
Canadian Broadcasting Corporation ...cbc.ca/sports/hockey
Carole's No Frills Hockey Media Links www.geocities.com/Colosseum/Track/7342
CNN/Sports Illustrated.................www.sportsillustrated.cnn.com
CTV SportsNet ....www.ctvsportsnet.com
The Ecola Newsstand ....www.ecola.com
ESPN ....espn.go.com/NHL/index/html
Faceoff/Southam/Wayne Gretzky ......www.faceoff.com
FOXSports ....foxsports.com/NHL/index.sml
Headline Sports (The Score) ....www.headlinesports.com
Slam! Hockey ....www.canoe.ca/Hockey/home.html
The Sports Network ....tsn.ca/NHL

OTHER SITES

Links to European Hockey Sites ......www.eurohockey.cz
A to Z Encyclopedia of Hockey ......www.azhockey.com
Coaching Site ....www.hockeycoach.com
Encyclopedia site about Ice hockey ...proicehockey.about.com
The Internet Hockey Database.........hockeydb.com
Equipment site ....www.pagekraft.com/hockeymart.htm
Equipment site ....www.HockeyGear.com

CHAPTER 64

Hockey Video Games

Realism Rockets Upward in New Generation Games

Tom Hoffarth

THE TWO RESIDENT VIDEO GAME EXPERTS of the Los Angeles Kings are in the players-only lounge at the team's practice facility after a recent workout, intently focused on the giant video screen. Ian Laperriere and Jamie Storr aren't watching game film as the NHL playoffs approach. They're in awe of themselves—or rather, cyber versions of themselves.

Laperriere was uncharacteristically speechless as he watched how Sega Sports's NHL 2K hockey video game was performing on the popular Sega Dreamcast player.

"When they first started coming out with these games, everyone skated the same... Looked the same..." said Laperriere, the aggressive centerman who has over 100 games for his video players and computer system. "But now it's getting scary. I can recognize myself in the game, all the little details like how I skate. I'm not like Luc Robitaille—I'm not the fastest guy—and that's how I am in this game."

Laperriere shook his head and looked at Storr, the team's goalie, who was also in disbelief.

"What are they going to do to improve these games in five years?"

They might not have long to wait to find out.

One of the most popular sports genres with so-called "gamers" across the globe, computer and video hockey games continue to lead the way in technological advancement. It might be because hockey game players, more than those who play any other sports-themed video games, demand more than just the standard bells and whistles.

It helps that the technology continues to improve at a fast-forward rate in all aspects of computers and platforms, allowing hockey games to become more realistic. In the evolution—and revolution—of the hockey video game, it's all about increased realism down to every minute detail. The NHL 2K game, for example, has more than 1,400 polygons per model for each player to make their movements more fluid. There are more than 1,000 motion-captured movements built in that each player can use. This means players get upset when they're sent to the penalty box. The body checks sound real. Even the ice becomes more scraped up as the game goes along.

Artificial intelligence is the key element. It's what the two dozen or so computer-game companies such as Sony, Electronic Arts, Konami, Acclaim and Midway commit more hours to research and development of for games on such platforms as the Dreamcast, Nintendo 64 and Sony Playstation (plus its soon-to-be-released Playstation2), as well as desktop computers. Both computer and video game systems have advanced to the level of offering a modem to transfer information across the Internet to play with other gamers online (such as the Video Hockey League that has a home on the Net at www.geocities.com/Colosseum/Arena/6996).

The genesis for video hockey goes beyond the Sega Genesis many grew up with, so let's back up a bit to what seems like prehistoric times.

The video game boom of the early 1980s did not include many hockey titles, per se. Advancing past table hockey or Strat-o-matic dice games to the age of Atari 2600, Pong was about as close to hockey on the video screen as one could get for awhile. Mattel's Intellivision can be credited with introducing hockey in a video form. Atari's first hockey try was a two-on-two version. Sega then came out with games such as Blades of Steel and Mutant Hockey League—each more of a home arcade version of games available in public amusement facilities.

Finally, Electronic Art's NHL '93 raised the bar in terms of realism and entertainment. These have become the criteria that everyone—including EA's own game designers—has been using as the measuring stick in the years since then. To date, more than a half-dozen NHL-licensed and approved games are on the market, rotating in and out as the years go by, updated not only with current rosters of current teams but with the latest development in gamesmanship. Keeping the games priced in the $50 range keeps them competitive with all other video games, sports and non-sports.

Although most hockey video games have become sophisticated enough to offer many of the same options on the controllers, the difference is in the philosophy of those who produce and program each game, which can take more than a year to develop. With the trend toward using actual NHL players (although gamers can "create" their own players by other means), the task for the programmer in charge of the artificial intelligence is how to break down each and every player's game and assign values to the different parts. Each player will have as many as 40 attributes—such as skating speed, stickhandling, shot accuracy, offensive and defensive awareness—and each quality is assigned a numerical value between 1 and 100. Players are also programmed to their actual height and weight, and bodychecks are calculated in this 3D animated world as they are in real physical life—meaning smaller guys aren't going to knock down bigger guys so easily. Game producers can pour over statistics to help determine a player's numerical values, but they've also been keen to use input from current NHL coaches and players for the last few years.

Then Colorado Avalanche coach Marc Crawford was the consultant for EA's version of NHL '98 along with Avs star Peter Forsberg. "When playing hockey, the keys to victory depend on how well teams change their offensive and defensive strategy, depending on what type of situation they're up against," said Crawford, who is currently coaching the Vancouver Canucks. "Teams play a different strategy when they are down by a goal or up by a goal. On the power play or when killing a penalty, teams need to recognize their opponents' strengths and weaknesses and take advantage of them. Working with the EA Sports people, we got to a point where it was possible to have complete control over what type of strategy a team utilizes. It is amazing to think that interactive sports games have come so far as to simulate exactly what happens on the real ice."

Once the information is compiled, the video game lead programmer orchestrates the game. During the course of play with a typical video game, the computer platform will make hundreds of split-second decisions about the players on the ice. The game controllers are making decisions as well. That's where the fun begins.

A Sony Dreamcast controller will let the user make dozens of specific decisions. Press one button and the player on the screen tries a wrist shot (if he's on offense), a hook and knee-sliding block (if he's on defense), or a save-and-smother action (if he's the goalie with the puck). The longer a player holds onto the puck, the more chance he'll have to be checked—just like in a real game. But unlike a real game, each rule can be modified or turned off to suit the player. The modes of play can also be altered to do a complete regular season, playoff-quality action, or an exhibition which allows the players to create their own style of play. And, yes, there is fighting. The NHL and NHLPA monitor fighting elements in video games, insist the makers, and in no way endorse fighting. But it is included as an option in the name of realism.

Control buttons allow fighters to duck, jab or throw hard punches, but taking on-ice brawls to an extreme can have a backlash. When the NHL and NHLPA licensed a video game to EA Sports called NHL Rock the Rink—which included fights where players practically went into a World Wrestling Federation routine of piledriving, clotheslining etc.—the league was quick to point out that while it seemed to reinforce the game's worst stereotypes, it was not a replication of an NHL game. "The violence is actually very cartoonish," said NHL Group Vice President Bernadette Mansur. "You don't look at the game and think you're sitting in Montreal watching the Canadiens."

In that vein, there are several game makers who design their games to have an arcade-like effect. NHL Open Ice by Midway Games for GT Interactive created a game that allowed for some spectacular moves, such as Pavel Bure spinning three times in the air about 30 feet above the ice then launching a shot so powerful the net caught fire. Some games have option buttons where the players can have oversized heads. A popular version of Wayne Gretzky 3D Hockey series for Nintendo 64 has graphics that take on a life of their own.

Because of television's impact on hockey, video games try to recreate much of that feel. Camera angles can be changed from overhead (best for strategy) to ice level (to get a closer feel). Instant replay is available on every play. *Hockey Night In Canada* broadcaster Bob Cole does the call on NHL 2K with commentary from former NHL coach Harry Neale.

Each year, the cost of making a hockey video game increases as companies hire the top programmers and audio people from around the world to improve the product. Developers are always keeping their ears open to what the public wants, whether it be more realism or more fanfare. For Electronic Arts and its annual version of NHL games—the latest being NHL 2000—it's just a matter of tweaking since their product continues to be the most popular for PlayStation.

Some in the industry predict future games will include virtual reality wrap goggles to make the player feel as if he's on the ice with everyone else. Others have the sense that as younger hockey fans learn the Xs and Os of the game via the video player, it will be used as a learning tool for actual players as a way to reinforce strategy.

Regardless of changes, the most popular players will continue to be the ones featured on the box covers. The early morning after a Pittsburgh Penguins night game in Los Angeles, Jaromir Jagr stayed behind while the rest of the team went off to San Jose. He found himself in a near-deserted ice rink dressed in a costume with dozens of large white dots. He stood surrounded by a circle of about two dozen cameras and was asked to start and stop over and over while different shots and skating motions were captured on several computer screens by a Hollywood company that specialized in music videos. This was for the latest hockey video game—with his picture on the front—that would be part of Konami's new line of games with the Sony PlayStation2 platform. At least Jagr had decided to cut the flowing locks of hair that had been his trademark in previous seasons. As one programmer noted: "I don't know how we'd be able to duplicate that in a video game."

But knowing how games rely on realism, it's most likely they'd have figured out a way.

CHAPTER 65

Exotic Hockey

A Worldwide Survey of Hockey's Backwaters Lands in Hong Kong

Dave Bidini

It was Richard Harrison, the talented Calgary poet, who helped me see that hockey existed outside of North America and Europe. On a trip to the Ivory Coast, Richard discovered hockey being played on a rink built for Scandinavian tourists in the 1950s. The story goes that he was sitting in the lobby of the Hotel D'Ivoire when one of the hotel employees strode across the floor decked out in a Chicago Blackhawks jersey. Fearful that this was the first deadly stage of some malarial dementia, Richard moved in for a closer look until he found himself face to face with this backwoods Magnuson, pointing vigorously at the player's crest, to which the fellow responded:

"Bobby Hull."

Now, if you were to walk up to a stranger in a big North American city and gesture wordlessly at his midriff, chances are he'd snap off your finger like a tea biscuit. But lucky for Richard, there was no such antagonism and he was able to get to the bottom of this Blackhawk-in-the-Ivory Coast hockey mystery. As it turned out, a tournament was staged once a year (the temperature and dust storms made it impossible to maintain ice in other months of the year) using players from neighboring hotels who'd learned the game using equipment the Scandinavians had left behind.

At first glance, this story may seem unlikely. "Africans playing hockey?" you can hear them scoff in alumni rooms across the land. "Pshaw!" But sport, like dandelion spores sown on the wind, has the tendency to settle where you least expect it. All it takes is one or more freaks in love with their sport, and presto, the Jamaican bobsled team. Igor Kuperman, a Russian who has worked with the Winnipeg Jets and Phoenix Coyotes, wrote of a two-team Indian hockey league made up of players from cities on either side of a mountain range. He described a rink in the shadows of the Himalayas and games that would last for days whenever the fog was too thick for the visiting team's plane to leave.

Stories like this piqued my curiosity, and so it was that I spent the spring and autumn of 1999 skirting the globe in search of hockey in unlikely places. On my day of departure—March 1, 1999—I arrived at the airport carrying my Winnwell hockey bag and three Koho hockey sticks. A few days before the trip, I weeded out my bag. The challenge of lugging an equipment duffel around the world was daunting enough, let alone one sagging with wet socks, cruddy T-shirts and used tape clods. As I cleaned it, I found the bottom to be too damp and malodorous to inflict upon the world; its foul stench had the potential to defeat whatever measures we'd taken to comport ourselves like touring diplomats. I envisioned my gear being held at the border and searched by an unlucky customs official with a hanky pressed to his face who would have no choice but to drag it out back against a wall and blast holes into its fetid carcass.

Upon arrival in Hong Kong 14 hours after departure, I was met by a strange man in glasses who took me to his apartment. That actually sounds more like a scene from a Bond caper than it was because, the truth is, this was a man with whom I was vaguely familiar. I'd communicated with Herb Shoveller—a journalist for the *London Free Press* who was on sabbatical in Hong Kong with his family—after reading an article he'd written for the *National Post* about hockey in Mongolia. He'd visited Ulan Bator in December, 1998 with a Chinese ex-patriot team for a round-robin tourney against a local Mongol club, and wrote of natural ice and players with newspaper pads. He told of sitting in his hotel watching CNN, then looking out his window to see men riding horses through the snow. Herb had arranged for me to play on a team in the Hong Kong 5's Hockey Tournament—which I'd read about while researching Chinese hockey on the Web. The full name of the tournament was The Sunday Ice Hockey Five's 99, Sunday being a communications company that was at war over the lucrative Hong Kong market. There were 44 teams entered in the tournament, making it unquestionably the largest ice hockey contest held in Asia. In total, there were 16 nationalities represented among international mens and kids teams, as well as domestic North American mens and womens sides. The tournament had grown to include the likes of the Singapore Winter Flames, Japanese Tomy Monsters, St. Lucia Saints, United Arab Emirate Nationals, Bud Americans, Manila Knights, Dubai Mighty Camels, Al-Ma Pee Wee, Can Tai Dragons, Toronto Tigers and the Bangkok Flying Farangs—names that seemed pulled from some exotic sports league of the future.

The HK 5's (named for the number of players allowed on the ice per side, one fewer than in typical hockey) was run by Tom Barnes, an employee of Asiasports, a company that also helps organize hockey tournaments in Thailand and Manila. The 5's was in its seventh year. Barnes also organized Hong Kong's domestic league—the Budweiser South China Ice Hockey League—a year-round recreational division with upwards of 12 teams, including all-Asian clubs. Barnes estimated that the league consisted of 40 percent Canadians, 30 percent locals from Hong Kong, 15 percent Americans and 15 percent Europeans. The fee to play in the Bud League was 1800 HK dollars—about 350 Canadian—per season, a sum comparable to recreational hockey in my hometown of Toronto. There was also a junior league with upwards of 90 kids (aged 4 to 16) and a womens' division that had grown more popular each year.

My initial journey to the tournament's main rink—SkyRink—was certainly not what I was used to back home in Toronto. The road into town was trimmed with long-armed trees cupping orange and pink blossoms like altar boys holding candles. The blossoms hung in bunches over the road and whipped against the flank of the bus, which curled along the road gripping the edge of the cliffside. The bus tilted and tipped as it fought corners, and with each turn, little squares of the city were revealed: knots of blue and white high-rises, the shimmering green track of the Happy Valley raceway, a white-washed mansion with guard dogs and gold gates, a regatta of iron ships floating in the bay, the stone shelves of an old terraced graveyard rising over the city and a procession of checker-skirted schoolgirls, whose faces rounded into focus as I sloped into Hong Kong.

I stood in front of Dragon Centre mall—a huge, shadow-casting building which loomed arms-crossed over the market. The entrance to the mall was filled with a circus of laughing children being scooped up by an escalator, which we rode upwards into the building against a floor-to-ceiling glass facade. The ride was spectacular. I stared out across Kowloon looking at acres of high-rises pressed shoulder to shoulder, their sides thistled with television antennae sticking out of apartment windows like bony fingers reaching through the bars of a cell. Laundry waved in a parade of colored flags. Beyond that lay smokestacks, the sea and the red horizon.

We floated higher.

Finally, on the eighth floor of the mall, I could hear it—the honking of the score-clock, the concussive sound of the puck against the boards, the referee's whistle, skates chopping snow. I could smell the chemicals of the ice and the Zamboni diesel and then I saw it —a rink small enough to fit in your palm: a sprite's pond, a place of Tom Thumb, or Gabby Boudreau. It could have been drawn from a child's imagination. It looked like a proper rink that had shrunk or was malnourished. To best describe it would be to use a word not often associated with some of the greatest sporting structures of our time: cute.

It was a play rink.

It's hard to imagine a pad of ice more unusual than SkyRink. It was a fifth the size of an NHL oval—18' x 42', to be exact. One thought of a home-sick architect from Trois Rivieres being left with a narrow lane of concrete and deciding to fill it with ice. It was maybe the width of three bowling lanes. I suspected that bigger puddles had been left by the monsoon. Every element of SkyRink was odd. Since it was located eight stories high, you could look out and see clouds rolling in off the South China Sea and forecast the weather. There was a mezzanine with an arcade that hung over the rink—pinball machines, toy cars, and robotic clowns—and which filled the air with the sound of bells and horns and the voices of children crying out to each other. Below that, a yellow roller coaster track curved over the ice like long strips of pulled toffee. It was close enough that you could reach up with your hockey stick and tap it. The front car was painted in the image of a flame-tongued turquoise dragon and it hurtled over the ice at high speeds, a frightful vision for even the most steel-nerved goaltender. The layout suggested that SkyRink had been designed with the idea of marrying amusement park folly to hockey, and while the NHL has experimented with this theme before—San Jose's shark blimp and Anaheim's daredevil duck come to mind, as do the barrel jumping and dog sled races that were part of intermissions in the 1920s—at least those novelties were kept at a relatively safe distance from the action. But at SkyRink, it was possible to load your pockets with eggs and pelt the players as you careened over them. There was no barrier nor railing to prevent this, and it did nothing to allay my fears of becoming the first hockey fan killed by a large porcelain lizard.

At both ends of the ice, loose white netting—the kind used to catch trapeze artists—was strung up behind the goals. It reminded me of the mesh in those old Soviet rinks, which Team Canada used to complain about for the way the puck whipped back to the ice. The SkyRink netting served two purposes: to catch pucks that flew out of the rink and to act as a curtain for the dressing area which lay just behind the end boards. It did neither job well. Behind it, players changed in and out of their clothes freely. The scene was like something out of a rogue health club: fellows in towels striding to and from the bathrooms. While not every player flashed skin—some used a series of towels like semaphores to guard their parts—many treated the area like a Roman bath.

SkyRink had a Zamboni. It was old and dented and was something you might have found at a Used Zamboni Sale. It had "South China Ice Hockey League" written in Chinese and English on the side and was driven by a young Chinese man in yellow sweats who was far too slender to bring any credibility to his job.

SkyRink had other problems, too. Frankly, it didn't smell bad enough. As you may have gathered from the description of my hockey bag, I believe that in order to make players feel at home, arenas should have a foul air. But SkyRink smelled strangely like jasmine. (I should be grateful, I know.) The source of this fragrance, I believe, was Kathy K's Pro Shop, which was stocked with a surprising complement of top of the line hockey gear. Unlike many skate-sharpening depots—which tend to smell of plugged plumbing and are operated by large, unshaven men—Kathy K's carried the scent of blossoms, and if that wasn't strange enough, Kathy thanked you for your business and offered a bowl of candies by the cash register, allowing you to take to the ice chewing a gumball, spitting rainbow trails of purple, blue and red across the white pond.

There was also the food problem. Although again, it wasn't so much a problem as, well … a treat. There was no snack bar at SkyRink, unless you counted the Jack in the Box, which I only saw used by ex-pats teary-eyed for a taste of pressed snout. Instead, there was a food court opposite the rink where women with faces carved by the knife of time spooned sea snails the size of silver dollars and braised aubergine and double-cooked pork onto plastic plates, the aroma of garlic and soya and sesame oil mingling with the faint odor of hockey. There were kiosks selling blackened grouper, lemon chicken, bean curd seared in garlic and peppers, sushi, and hot soup with prawns—atypical hockey cuisine to be sure. (Where I come from, you were lucky if you could get the coffee machine to spit black muck into your paper cup!)

The crowd at SkyRink was also its own. It was mostly seniors who'd come over from the food court (proving that, no matter where you go in the world, you'll find the same people hanging out in malls). It was a rare treat, however, to skate along the boards and have your eyes meet a group of old men who could have been extras from the film *The Last Emperor*. After a few days, I discovered that these men were not drawn to athletic grace and beauty but rather to pratfalls and gaffes. If someone scored an end-to-end goal they'd get little reaction, but if they tripped over the net, were slew-footed or slashed in the eye, the old men would laugh and pantomime their fall. It became clear to me that the less able you were on your skates, the more you were liked by the gallery. Before the tournament ended, there was a real chance that I'd be a star.

CHAPTER 66

Bandy

The Least Known On-Ice Game

Janne Stark

BANDY IS A WINTER SPORT played on an ice-covered field the size of a soccer pitch. Like soccer, there are 11 players on each side and the playing time is 90 minutes divided into two halves of 45 minutes each. The game is played mainly in the Nordic countries, Finland, Norway and Sweden, as well as in Russia and Kazakhstan. There have been attempts made to introduce the game in the United States and Canada, but without much success. The World Championship of bandy, which is held every second year, was played in Minnesota in 1995.

A bandy playing field is between 90 and 110 meters long (approximately 290 to 350 feet) and between 45 and 65 meters wide (145 to 210 feet). All players wear skates similar to the ones used in ice hockey and all players except the goalkeeper use curved wooden sticks similar to those in field hockey. The ball is hard, usually red or orange, and six centimeters (two-plus inches) in diameter. The goals are 2.1 meters high and 3.5 meters wide (7' x 11').

The object of bandy, like that of so many sports, is to put the ball into the opponent's goal. This must be done with the stick, which may not be raised higher than the level of the shoulders. The ball may be stopped with the skate but kicking, except by the goaltender, is allowed only to position the ball so that the player himself may strike it. The only player that can touch the ball with his hands is the goalkeeper. Restrictions as to impeding an opponent are similar to those in ice hockey.

Freestrokes are awarded for infringements of the rules and serious infringements within the penalty area are punished with a penalty stroke taken 12 meters (39 feet) from the center of the goal line. The referee may send off a player who is guilty of infringements for either five or 10 minutes, or for the rest of the game.

Bandy was born in England at the beginning of the 19th century, around the same time that other ball-and-stick games became popular throughout the British Isles. The exact date of bandy's birth is impossible to determine since precious few records of the game remain in its country of origin, where it has not been played since the early years of the last century. It is known that by 1865, the game had reached the town of Nottingham in the English midlands where the Nottingham Forest Football and Bandy Club was founded. There are records of a game in the Netherlands in the 1890s and the first rules of the game were published in 1891. Bandy came to Sweden in 1895, where it was known as hockey during its early years.

The game of bandy soon became very popular in Sweden, Finland and Russia. For many years, it was considered the national winter sport in these three countries. The first international game between two countries was played in 1919 when Finland faced Sweden in Helsinki and won 4–1. The first World Championship was played in Finland in 1957 and has been decided every second year since 1961. The Soviet Union won the first 11 tournaments and the Soviet Union/Russia has won 15 of the 21 championships played through 1999. Sweden was champion for the first time in 1981 and has won five more times since then.

Bandy is still immensely popular in Russia and in Sweden but there is no way for it to compete with the popularity of hockey. There are two main reasons for this: the game of bandy is played outdoors instead of in nice, warm indoor rinks (though an indoor version of the game has become very popular in Sweden) and there is no chance to make a living out of bandy, since there are no professional bandy players.

But the tradition of bandy remains strong and the game lives on—even though it is hard to recruit young players.

BANDY WORLD CHAMPIONSHIP STANDINGS

Year	Gold	Silver	Bronze
1957	Soviet Union	Finland	Sweden
1961	Soviet Union	Sweden	Finland
1963	Soviet Union	Finland	Sweden
1965	Soviet Union	Norway	Sweden
1967	Soviet Union	Finland	Sweden
1969	Soviet Union	Sweden	Finland
1971	Soviet Union	Sweden	Finland
1973	Soviet Union	Sweden	Finland
1975	Soviet Union	Sweden	Finland
1977	Soviet Union	Sweden	Finland
1979	Soviet Union	Sweden	Finland
1981	Sweden	Soviet Union	Finland
1983	Sweden	Soviet Union	Finland
1985	Soviet Union	Sweden	Finland
1987	Sweden	Finland	Soviet Union
1989	Soviet Union	Finland	Sweden
1991	Soviet Union	Sweden	Finland
1993	Sweden	Russia	Norway
1995	Sweden	Russia	Finland
1997	Sweden	Russia	Finland
1999	Russia	Finland	Sweden

CHAPTER 67

It's All in the Family

Cousins, Uncles, Grandsons, In-laws, Parents and Spouses

Patrick Houda

FOR YEARS HOCKEY FANS HAVE READ ABOUT BROTHER ACTS and fathers and sons in the NHL. We all recognize the Hulls, the Mahovlichs, the Gretzkys, the Howes, the Stastnys, the Bures etc. More than 70 father and son combinations and over 200 brothers have appeared in the NHL over the years. A complete list was published in the first edition of *Total Hockey*, while this volume includes notes about family connections in the appropriate statistical panels. But what about the numerous other NHL-related family connections? What about the grandfathers, cousins and uncles that we've never heard about? There have also been fathers- and brothers-in-law, famous marriages and other connections.

COUSINS

The hard-nosed trio of cousins Wendel Clark, Joey Kocur and Barry Melrose has collected over 5,000 penalty minutes in the NHL. Clark, who had his third stint with the Toronto Maple Leafs in 1999–2000, was the oldest active first overall draft pick still playing in the league at season's end. Joey Kocur holds the distinction of having won the Stanley Cup with the two teams that had the longest championship droughts in NHL history. In 1994, Kocur won with the New York Rangers who hadn't won the Cup in 54 years. In 1997, he helped the Detroit Red Wings win their first Stanley Cup title in 42 years. Barry Melrose, who now is an ESPN hockey analyst, coached the Los Angeles Kings and Wayne Gretzky to the Stanley Cup finals in 1993. Melrose and Gretzky's paths had crossed earlier on many occasions while they both were players. Once, in the World Hockey Association, Melrose was in the penalty box when Gretzky completed his first pro career hat trick (December 12, 1978).

Ron Francis, the sixth-highest scorer in NHL history, a Lady Byng and Selke Trophy winner, is the cousin of Mike Liut who was the Hart Trophy runner-up behind Wayne Gretzky in 1981.

Skilled center Barry Pederson still holds several Boston Bruins scoring records. Cousin Brian Skrudland, a 15-year NHL veteran, doesn't have Barry's offensive flair but has won the Stanley Cup in both Montreal and Dallas. Barry won only once, with the Pittsburgh Penguins.

Jerry Korab, another 15-year NHL veteran, once held the Buffalo Sabres club record for most points by a defenseman in one season. Korab's cousin, Lou Nanne, played 11 NHL seasons for Minnesota and then spent another 11 as the North Stars' general manager. Nanne is in the U.S. Hockey Hall of Fame.

Gerry O'Flaherty began his NHL career in Toronto. Exactly 10 years later, cousin Craig Muni debuted with the Maple Leafs. He went on to win the Stanley Cup three times as a member of the Edmonton Oilers during his 16-year NHL career.

Joe Nieuwendyk, the 1988 Calder Trophy winner, had a great season in 1998–99 as he won the Stanley Cup and the Conn Smythe Trophy. Cousin Jeff Beukeboom had to retire due to a concussion that season. Not only that, but their uncle Ed Kea, the NHL's only Dutch-born player, drowned that season.

Anders Eldebrink had only a brief NHL career but was a vital cog on the Swedish national team for almost a decade. Together with his cousin Robert Nordmark, he patrolled the blue line when Sweden became world champions in 1987. They also played for the Vancouver Canucks.

Another Swedish cousin combo in the NHL was Thomas Steen and Dan Labraaten. Steen played more years and games for the Winnipeg Jets than any other player in franchise history. Labraaten only played for Winnipeg in the WHA, but the two played together back in Sweden for Leksands IF and they also represented Sweden in the 1986 World Championships where they won a silver medal.

Bill McCreary Jr. played only 12 games in the NHL, but he made one of them memorable by delivering perhaps the most devastating check Wayne Gretzky ever received during his long NHL career. McCreary's cousin Bob Atwell saw limited action in the NHL as well. (In addition to being cousins, both McCreary and Atwell had fathers who played in the NHL. Bill's uncle Keith was also an NHLer.)

Todd Sloan won three Stanley Cup titles (two with Toronto and one with Chicago) in his career. In 1958–59, he centered the league's highest-scoring line with wings Ted Lindsay and Ed Litzenberger. During Sloan's final NHL season of 1960–61, his cousin Dave Keon broke into the league. Keon enjoyed an 18-year NHL career and won the Stanley Cup on four occasions. In 1,388 NHL games, he only had one fighting major (against Greg Sheppard of Boston).

Ed Harrison and Ed Sandford were cousins who played together in juniors for the St. Michael Majors between 1945 and 1947 and then with Boston in the NHL between 1947 and 1950. Sandford played in the NHL All-Star Game five straight years and was a Second Team All-Star in 1954.

Dennis Kearns was the first Vancouver Canuck to play 500 games and retired as the Canucks' all-time leader in games (677) and points among Canuck defensemen (321). Kearns's cousin Shawn Evans played only nine career NHL games, scoring one goal.

Don Jackson was a big, aggressive defenseman who patrolled the blue line in Edmonton during their heyday and won the Stanley Cup twice. Cousin Brett Hauer followed in his footsteps. Brett was also a defenseman who played for Edmonton and, like Jackson, he represented the United States in the World Championships twice.

Jimmy Peters Jr. was born in Montreal where his father Jimmy Sr. played, but moved to Detroit when he was four. The younger Peters started his NHL career in Detroit and was eventually traded to Los Angeles for Hall of Fame goalie Terry Sawchuk. Cousin Glenn Currie was also born in Montreal. He began his NHL career in Washington, where he was a vital cog on their checking line. He was Washington's first winner of the Emery Edge team award for best plus-minus rating in 1983.

Keith Tkachuk is one of only four players in NHL history to have scored 50 goals and accumulated 200 penalty minutes in the same season. This power forward who led the league in goals in 1996–97 is the cousin of Tom Fitzgerald, a reliable defensive player who was the first player in NHL history to score two shorthand goals on the same minor penalty in the Stanley Cup playoffs.

Guy Leveque was a center who played 17 NHL games for Los Angeles. He grew up idolizing Wayne Gretzky, who was his teammate in L.A. Leveque scored only two goals in his NHL career. One came against Gretzky's old team, Edmonton, which was also the team he made his NHL debut against. The other goal came against Toronto, the same team that he later was traded to. Leveque's cousin Marty Murray was a great prospect who only played 19 NHL games for Calgary. He led Canada to a gold medal in the 1994 World Junior Championships. Murray was the tournament's leading scorer and was selected as the best forward.

Other cousin combinations in the NHL have been: Dale and Paul Hoganson; Wes and Doug Jarvis; Allan and Reg Kerr; Morris and Bernie Lukowich; Mark, Joby and Mitch Messier; Gilbert and Bob Perreault; Craig, Mickey and Dick Redmond; Darcy and Randy Rota; Joe and Scott Thornton; Randy and Perry Turnbull; Matthew Barnaby and Ray Sheppard (distant cousins); Adam and Butch Deadmarsh (second cousins); Bob Errey and Ted Lindsay (third cousins); Al Iafrate and Dino Ciccarelli (distant cousins); Denis, Jean and Marc Potvin (second cousins); Bob Sullivan and Wayne Connelly (second cousins); Ed and Darren Van Impe (second cousins); and Jack and Stephen Valiquette (first cousins, once removed).

NEPHEWS AND UNCLES

Larry Hillman is one of only five players in NHL history (the others being Bronco Horvath, Vic Lynn, Dave Creighton and Forbes Kennedy to have been the property of every Original Six team. Nephew Brian Savage became only the second player in Montreal Canadiens history to register a six-point game on the road on January 8, 1998, against the New York Islanders. The only other Canadiens player to accomplish that feat was the legendary Joe Malone back in 1917—a year before Montreal entered the NHL.

Jim McFadden won the Calder Trophy in 1948 and the Stanley Cup in 1950. Unfortunately, nephew Bill Mikkelson holds the record for the worst plus-minus rating in NHL history. His not-so-flattering record of -82 was set with the first-year Washington Capitals (1974–75). Two seasons earlier, Mikkelson had "led" another first-year team (the New York Islanders) in the plus-minus department with a rating of -54.

Larry Aurie played on some great lines with guys such as Cooney Weiland, Marty Barry and Herb Lewis. Aurie was the NHL's leading playoff scorer in 1934. He also tied for the league lead in goals during the 1936–37 season and was a First Team All-Star. Nephew Cummy Burton also played in Detroit and wore number six like his uncle—though his NHL career lasted only 43 games plus three in the playoffs.

Jacques Lemaire won the Stanley Cup eight times in 12 seasons as a player and earned a ninth title as a coach in 1995. He was inducted into the Hockey Hall of Fame in 1984. Lemaire's nephew Emanuel Fernandez has been in goal sporadically for Dallas over the past six years. Dick and Barrie Meissner both had solid junior careers but never really caught on in the NHL. So far, their nephew Landon Wilson seems to be going that same route.

The Conacher family used to be one of the most prominent in hockey. Lionel Conacher was voted Canada's male athlete of the half-century in 1950. His brother Charlie was the NHL's leading goal scorer five times and led the league in points twice. Their youngest brother Roy led the league in goals and points once. All three are in the Hockey Hall of Fame. Their nephew Murray Henderson didn't have the charisma and flair of his uncles. He was an unspectacular but steady defenseman who played over 400 NHL games for Boston.

George Armstrong played 21 years and 1,187 regular-season games for Toronto, more than any other player in Maple Leafs history. "The Chief" was almost 40 years and nine months old when he played his last NHL game, making him the oldest Maple Leafs forward ever. His nephew Dale McCourt was the first overall NHL pick in the 1977 Amateur Draft. He enjoyed a splendid junior career. He was voted the Canadian Major Junior Player of the Year in 1977. Dale's older brother Dan McCourt has been an NHL linesman since 1980, and has worked in well over 1,000 games.

Earl Miller made his NHL debut for the second-year Chicago Black Hawks in 1927–28. He played over 100 games in the league. Nephew Bill Hay won the Calder Memorial Trophy in 1960 and played his entire NHL career for Chicago. Hay's mother, Florence Miller, was one of Canada's outstanding track and field stars. Father Charlie was a goalie for the Regina team that lost the 1923 Allan Cup finals to the Toronto Granites team which went on to win an Olympic gold medal in 1924.

Bob Gracie was a speedy wing who played for six different NHL teams in the 1930s. His grandnephew Graeme Nicolson was a tough and aggressive defenseman who played only one NHL game for Boston. He then spent some time in the minors before retiring from hockey to attend the University of Guelph. After a one-year layoff, he got contract offers from several teams and went on to play another two NHL seasons for Colorado and the New York Rangers.

Some other nephew/uncle combinations worth mentioning include: Mike and Harry Meeker; Mark, Marty and Vic Howe; Kevin and Blair MacDonald; Denis and Jean Savard; Robert and Noel Picard; Sebastien and Christian Bordeleau; John and Randy Bucyk; Allan and Barney Stanley; Rick and Moose Vasko; Don and Roy Edwards; Gordie and Dave Roberts; Andre and Dollard St.Laurent; Ron and Johnny Wilson; Normand and Leon Rochefort; John, Brian and Ray Cullen; and Brett and Dennis Hull.

GRANDSONS

Hall of Famer Aubrey "Dit" Clapper was the first NHLer to play 20 seasons in the league. When Clapper's grandson Greg Theberge was drafted by Washington in 1979 (109th overall), Capitals management had high hopes for him. Theberge had a good junior career, winning the Max Kaminsky Award as the best defenseman in the OHL in 1979. He was also a unanimous choice for the first all-star team. Theberge was Washington's highest scoring defenseman in 1981–82 and still holds the team record for most points in a game by a rookie (five). But soon he was out of the NHL and he finished his playing career in Europe.

Bill Stewart coached the Chicago Black Hawks to the Stanley Cup title in 1938. He was also an NHL referee and a National League baseball umpire. He was inducted into the U.S. Hockey Hall of Fame in 1982. But Paul Stewart, Bill's grandson, had more guts than skills. He played in both the WHA and NHL, but his NHL stint lasted for only 21 games. His NHL debut with the Quebec Nordiques on November 22, 1979, was a memorable one, as he fought three of the toughest guys in the league—Terry O'Reilly, Stan Jonathan and Al Secord of the Bruins. Fittingly enough, Paul himself was born in Boston. Today, he is one of the most respected referees in the business.

Sammy McManus was born in Belfast, Northern Ireland, but his parents moved to Toronto in 1912 when he was barely two years old. Sammy had a long career and won the Allan Cup, the Willis Cup (for the North American amateur championship) and the Stanley Cup. Grandson Scott Pellerin had an excellent junior career. He won the Centennial Cup, gold in the World Junior Championships and the Hobey Baker Award as the top U.S. college player. As a pro, Pellerin has won the Calder Cup and has been a valuable member of the St. Louis Blues for the last few years.

Jean Pusie played for the Montreal Canadiens, the New York Rangers and the Boston Bruins. During the summers, he was a professional wrestler. Grandson Pierre-Claude Drouin, better known as P.C. Drouin, played only three games in the NHL before moving to England. Like his grandfather, Drouin played for Boston Bruins.

Hal Janvrin played major league baseball between 1911 and 1922. He won the World Series in 1916 as a second baseman with the Boston Red Sox. One of his teammates that year was a young pitcher named Babe Ruth. Janvrin still holds the World Series record for most at bats in a five game series. Grandson Dave Silk was a member of the heroic 1980 U.S. Olympic team. Silk played for the New York Rangers, Boston, Detroit and Winnipeg between 1980 and 1986. His cousin Mike Milbury, a 12-year veteran with Boston, is currently the New York Islanders general manager.

Other grandfather/grandson combos include Fred "Cyclone" Taylor and Mark Taylor. Cyclone was a swift-skating future Hall of Famer who never played in the NHL but was one of the game's first true superstars. Mark, who started to play hockey as a five year old, played five seasons in the NHL for Philadelphia, Pittsburgh and Washington.

Both the Hextall family (Bryan–Bryan Jr. and Dennis–Ron) and the Patricks (Lester–Lynn and Muzz–Craig) had three generations of players in the NHL.

In-Laws

Some of the current and former brothers- or fathers-in-law in the NHL over the years have included:

Brothers-in-law: Shayne Corson and Darcy Tucker; Luc Dufour and Alain Cote; Danny Geoffrion and Hartland Monahan; Bobby Holik and Frantisek Musil; Harry Howell and Ron Murphy; Kerry Huffman and Mike Posavad; Rick Lapointe and Brad Maxwell; Don Lever and Rick Ley; Don Luce and Mike A. Boland; Mark Messier and John Blum; Mark Napier and Pat Hughes; Wayne Rutledge and Dale Rolfe; Larry Sacharuk and Greg Holst; Doug Risebrough and referee Don Koharski.

Fathers-in-law: Bernie Geoffrion and Hartland Monahan; Howie Morenz and Bernie Geoffrion; George Swarbrick and Greg Adams; Phil Esposito and Alexander Selivanov; Howie Menard and Darren Eliot; Bobby Clarke and Peter White.

Parents and Other Relatives

It's not uncommon that parents and other relatives of NHL players have, in one way or another, been involved in sports. Naturally, a lot of them have been involved with hockey where they've participated in the Olympics, World Championships, etc.

Martin Brodeur's father Denis was the goalie for Canada in the 1956 Olympics where he won a bronze medal. He's also been the official photographer of the Montreal Expos and Montreal Canadiens. Another NHL team photographer was John Hartman, Mike Hartman's father. He took pictures for the Detroit Red Wings. Like Brodeur, Gary Sampson's father Ed played in the 1956 Olympics, winning a silver medal while representing the USA. Dave Christian's uncle Gord also won a silver in 1956. Dave's father Bill and uncle Ron won the gold for the United States in the 1960 Olympics. Rob Gaudreau's father Bob represented America in the 1968 Olympics. Gerald Diduck's sister Judy and Pascal Rheaume's sister Manon have both won the Women's World Championship title for Canada. They were also silver medalists in the 1998 Olympics. So was the late Doug Wickenheiser's cousin Hayley. Their team was beaten in the finals at Nagano by an American team captained by Tony Granato's sister Cammi.

Andy Moog's father Don was a member of the Canadian world champion Penticton Vees in 1955. Mickey and Dick Redmond's father Ed (who was later president of the Peterborough Petes) won the 1958 world championship for Canada with the Whitby Dunlops. Marc Crawford's father Floyd captained the Belleville McFarlands to a world title for Canada in 1959. The Trail Smoke Eaters team that won the 1961 world championship had several players whose sons later played in the NHL. Bobby Kromm, the father of Rick Kromm, was one of them. Another one was Ed Christofoli Sr. A third player was Addie Tambellini, the father of Steve Tambellini.

Some European players' fathers were also successful on the international hockey scene.

Jiri Bubla and Jiri Slegr are the only European father-and-son combo to have played in the NHL. Bubla played 230 games for the national team of Czechoslovakia. He was a three-time world champion and he also played in two Olympic tournaments as well as the inaugural 1976 Canada Cup. Bobby Holik's father Jaroslav was a world champion once and participated in the Olympics once. Bobby's uncle Jiri spent 319 games with the Czechoslovakian national team, which for a long time was a world record. He was a three-time world champion and played at the Olympics four times. He also played in one Canada Cup tournament. Patrik Augusta's father, Josef, played 100 games for Czechoslovakia, including four World Championship tournaments, one Olympic tournament and one Canada Cup tournament. Tomas and Frantisek Kaberle's father Frantisek Sr. played 104 games for Czechoslovakia. He won two world championships and played in one Olympic and one Canada Cup tournament.

Sami Kapanen's father Hannu played in one World Championships, one Olympic tournament and one Canada Cup. Peter Forsberg's father Kent coached the Swedish national team between 1995 and 1998. Borje Salming's brother Stig represented Sweden 94 times in national team play. Robert Reichel's brother Martin has represented Germany in four World Championships. Steve Rucchin's brother Larry has represented Italy in three World Championships and one Olympic tournament.

Aside from the Olympics and World Championships, there has been involvement on the hockey scene on all kind of levels. Adam Brown's father Andy used to be the chief Ontario scout for the New York Rangers. Ken Gernander's father Bob was the chief scout for Dallas. Dean Chynoweth's father Ed was a longtime president of the Western Hockey League. Steve Durbano's father Nick was the owner of the Hamilton Red Wings of the Ontario Hockey Association. Carey Wilson's father Gerry was vice president and team doctor of the Winnipeg Jets during their WHA days. Jeff Madill's father Greg was an NHL referee for 11 years. Glenn Skov's brother Art was also an NHL referee. Marty Pavelich's brother Matt was an NHL referee and linesman between 1956 and 1979 and was inducted into the Hockey Hall of Fame in 1987. Kelly, Kevin and Kip Miller didn't have any trouble with their ice time as kids since their father Lyle was a part owner of the Lansing, Michigan Arena.

A lot of hockey relatives have been involved with football, both in the CFL and NFL. Some who played in the CFL include: Jeff Christian's father Gord, who played for the Hamilton Tiger-Cats between 1967 and 1972; Nathan Lafayette's father David (British Columbia Lions); and Dan Quinn's father Peter (Ottawa Rough Riders).

Bruce Racine's father Maurice played 17 seasons in the CFL. Grant Ledyard's father Hal used to be a quarterback for the Winnipeg Blue Bombers and the Saskatchewan Roughriders. James and Steve Patrick's father Stephen played for the Winnipeg Blue Bombers and later became a member of Manitoba's legislature. Mickey Volcan's father Mike was a 10-year standout with the Edmonton Eskimos, winning the Grey Cup three years in a row between 1954 and 1956. Rocky Dundas's father Ron played in the CFL as well.

Paul DiPietro's cousin Rocky DiPietro was elected into the Canadian Football Hall of Fame in 1997. He played his entire CFL career with the Hamilton Tiger-Cats (1978 to 1991) and won numerous individual awards. He became the CFL's all-time pass reception leader in 1989.

John Tucker's nephew, Whit Tucker, was elected to the Hall of Fame in 1993. He played for the Ottawa Rough Riders between 1962 and 1970 and was a three-time CFL East Division all-star. Rich Preston's father, Ken, is in the Canadian Football Hall of fame as a builder. He was the general manager of the Saskatchewan Roughriders between 1958 and 1977. During that time the Roughriders compiled more wins than any other CFL club and made the playoffs 15 times in 20 seasons.

The NHL has also had its share of NFL relatives. Ben Hankinson's father, John, used to play with the Philadelphia Eagles and Minnesota Vikings. Barry Richter's father, Pat, played for the Washington Redskins and once held the record for most receptions in the Rose Bowl. Mike O'Connell's father, Tommy, used to be a quarterback for the Cleveland Browns. Jim Niekamp's cousin, Bill Simpson, played in the NFL for the Los Angeles Rams, among other teams. Mike Grier's father, Bobby, is the director of player personnel for the New England Patriots. Shane Churla is the second cousin of former quarterback Mark Rypien, a 10-year NFL veteran who was the most valuable player of Super Bowl XXVI in 1991.

Neil and Tim Sheehy's uncle, Bronislaw "Bronco" Nagurski, was a football star with the Chicago Bears in the 1930s. (He also had a wrestling career.) Nagurski was inducted into the Pro Football Hall of Fame in 1963. This bone-crushing linebacker/fullback of Ukrainian descent helped Chicago win the first official NFL championship title in 1933.

Lacrosse, of course, is another sport with a strong hockey connection. Doug Favell's father, Doug Sr., was one of Canada's better lacrosse goalies. He won the Mann Cup (Canadian senior lacrosse championship) in 1950 and is in the Canadian Lacrosse Hall of Fame. Another member of the Canadian Lacrosse Hall of Fame is Gord Hammond, the father of Ken Hammond. Eddie Sandford's father was once the president of the Ontario Lacrosse Association.

A lot of the relatives who came over from Europe used to play soccer. Iain Duncan's father played pro soccer in England. Glen Featherstone's father, Roy, played professionally in Ireland. Another one who played pro soccer in Ireland was Bobby Orr's grandfather. Mike Ricci's father played pro soccer in Italy. Tony Tanti's father was a pro soccer player in Malta. Adrien Plavsic's uncle Drago represented the Yugoslavian national soccer team. John and Dan Kordic's uncle played pro soccer in Yugoslavia. Dominik Hasek's younger brother, Martin, was one of the best players in the Czech Republic, representing the national team several times.

There have been some hockey relatives in the wrestling business as well. Todd Okerlund's father is "Mean" Gene Okerlund, a World Wrestling Federation announcer. Denis Dupere's cousin was the popular wrestler Maurice "Mad Dog" Vachon. His wrestling career spanned for an incredible 44 years and close to 13,000 matches and included a gold medal at the British Empire Games and a seventh-place finish at the 1948 Olympics. Ted Irvine's son is the famous wrestler Chris Jericho. Denis Gauthier's uncle is Jacques Rougeau, one of the wrestlers of the famous Rougeau family.

Several other sports have been represented by hockey relatives as well. Both Jere Gillis's father and mother were selected to compete in the Winter Olympic Games in skiing. Mark Hardy's mother competed in the 1952 Winter Olympics. She represented England in figure skating and finished seventh. That same year, another NHLer's mother participated in the Summer Olympics. Craig Simpson's mother Marion was a member of the Canadian women's track team.

Pavel Bure's father, Vladimir, swam in three Olympic Games for the Soviet Union (1968, 1972 and 1976). He won a bronze medal in 1968 (4x200-meter freestyle relay), and added two bronze medals (4x200-meter freestyle relay and 100-meter freestyle) and one silver (4x100-meter freestyle relay) in 1972. Andre Hidi's father never swam in the Olympics, but he was a Hungarian swimming champion before he defected to North America in 1956.

Paul Kariya's father, Tetsuhiko Kariya, used to play with the Canadian national rugby team. Kevin Weekes's father was a member of the national cricket team of Barbados. Morris Lukowich's brother, Ed, was a two-time Canadian curling champion who led Canada to a world championship title in 1986. He represented Canada in the 1988 Olympics and was inducted into the Alberta Sports Hall of Fame in 1998. Basil McRae's cousin, Walter Henry, was a Commonwealth Games flyweight boxing champion.

Jeff Lazaro's uncle, Joe, was a famous blind golf champion after losing his eyesight while he worked on an Army mine detection team as a 26-year-old on a World War II battlefield in Italy. He was a seven-time national champion of the U.S. Blind Golfers Association and also served as the UBGA's president. Joe was named Massachusetts Athlete of the 1960s, beating out legends John Havlicek and Carl Yastrzemski. Tony Leswick's nephew (and Pete Leswick's grandson) Len Dykstra played major league baseball for the New York Mets and the Philadelphia Phillies.

Scott Mellanby's father, Ralph, didn't participate actively as an athlete in the Olympics, but he was an executive producer for television coverage of the 1988 Olympics in Calgary and was also involved in the 1996 Atlanta Olympics. He was also the executive producer for *Hockey Night In Canada*.

Outside the sports world, Zac Bierk's brother Sebastian Bach was the lead singer for Skid Row. Their debut album sold over three million copies. Zac's sister Heather has appeared on the cover of *Vogue* and *Elle*. General Major Charles Sweeney, uncle of Tim and Bob Sweeney, was the pilot on the plane "Fifi" that dropped the atomic bomb on Nagasaki during World War II.

MARRIAGES

Russ Anderson, Terry Ruskowski and Charlie Simmer were all teammates in Los Angeles. Russ married Dorothy Benham, Miss America 1977. Terry's wife, Carol, was a former Miss Texas and Charlie's wife, Terri Welles, was *Playboy*'s Playmate of the Year in 1981. Wayne Gretzky married actress Janet Jones. Ron Duguay's wife was well-known model Kim Alexis and Ron Greschner was married to model/actress Carol Alt. Mariusz Czerkawski's wife was Polish-born model and James Bond girl Isabella Scorupco. Valeri Bure's wife Candace Cameron starred in the comedy *Full House*. Russ Courtnall's wife, actress Paris Vaughn, is the daughter of famous jazz singer Sarah Vaughn.

A lot of hockey players have married other athletes. Paul Cavallini married Tracy Smith, who was a Canadian Olympic track star. Kevin Lowe's wife, Karen Percy, won a bronze medal for Canada in downhill skiing at the 1988 Calgary Olympics. Kevin's teammate Randy Gregg married Kathy Vogt, who used to be a member of the Canadian speed skating team. Gord Labossiere's wife, Claire, was once a member of the Canadian ski team. Brad Selwood married Bonnie Murdison, a former Canadian Olympic water skier. Paul Ranheim's wife, Kathy, used to play for the Canadian national soccer team.

Bret Hedican married figure skater Kristi Yamaguchi in the summer of 2000. Yamaguchi won an Olympic gold medal in 1992. She was also a two-time world champion and a four-time pro figure skating champion. She was inducted into both the U.S. Figure Skating Hall of Fame and the World Figure Skating Hall of Fame in 1999. Bob Barlow's wife, Marilyn, is also a former gold medalist in figure skating. Igor Larionov is married to figure skater Elena Botanova, who used to represent the Soviet Union. Larionov's longtime teammate Doug Brown married the granddaughter of New York Giants owner Wellington Mara. Wayne Mulloin's wife Maxine is the sister of former major league pitcher Bill Monbouquette.

A few other "hockey marriages" are worth mentioning.

Frantisek Musil is married to Andrea Holikova, Bobby Holik's sister. At one time, she was one of the top-ranked tennis players in the world. Al Smith married Nancy Keon, Dave Keon's cousin. Mike Foligno is married to Ed Giacomin's niece Janice. Mike Murphy's wife Yvon Hanat is the sister of the wife of Mike's former teammate Vic Venasky. Alexei Zhamnov's wife is the daughter of legendary Soviet defenseman Valeri Vasiliev who represented his country 284 times in national team play. He was an eight-time world champion and a two-time Olympic gold medalist. Vasiliev played in the classic 1972 Summit Series, the 1976 and 1981 Canada Cup tournaments and the 1979 Challenge Cup series between the Soviet national team and the NHL All-Stars.

VII

Statistical Registers

Maurice "Rocket" Richard poses with Wayne Gretzky after the young superstar shattered the NHL's single-season assists and points records to win the Art Ross and Hart trophies in 1981. Richard won the Hart as the League's MVP in 1947 but, despite recording the NHL's first 50-goal season, never won the Art Ross awarded to the top point scorer. The NHL's newest trophy is named after Richard and is awarded to the NHL player with the most goals each season.
Canadian Press

CHAPTER 68

Introduction to the Player Registers

James Duplacey

THE PLAYER REGISTER in *Total Hockey* has been divided into five sections that reflect both the availability of statistics through the 80-year history of the National Hockey League and the global growth of the league and the sport.

The Pre-Expansion Register *(Chapter 76, page 647)* is set in two columns. It contains the complete statistical history of every player who concluded his NHL career between 1917–18 and 1966–67, the year before the league's first major expansion.

The Modern Register *(Chapter 78, page 833)* contains the complete statistical history of every player who played in the NHL after 1966–67, up to and including the 1999–2000 season. Players whose careers spanned the two eras, beginning before and ending after 1966–67, are entered in both registers. Their complete data panels are located in the Modern Register, while their names and the page where their statistical information can be found are listed alphabetically in the Pre-Expansion Register.

The Goaltender Register *(Chapter 80, page 1783)* contains the complete statistical record for every goaltender who played in the NHL from 1917–18 to 1999–2000. Painstaking research by the *Total Hockey* staff and historians Ernie Fitzsimmons and Patrick Houda corrected numerous statistical errors and compiled the most thorough record of wins, losses and ties ever assembled. There are some very interesting twists and turns in the Goaltender Register. From 1917–18 to 1964–65, NHL rules permitted teams to dress only one goaltender for a game. If that goalie was injured and was unable to resume play, a replacement goaltender was used in his place. The home team was responsible for ensuring that a substitute goaltender was on hand. Often these goalies were minor league, senior or junior league netminders and this chance-of-a-lifetime opportunity would prove to be their only NHL appearance. This explains the one-game NHL careers of such well-traveled goalies as Claude Cyr, Nick Damore and Mickey Murray.

Other teams preferred to have their trainer serve as the substitute goaltender, accounting for the NHL careers of Lefty Wilson, Julian Klymkiw and Dan Olesevich. Another interesting addition to the Goaltender Register is the inclusion of all forwards and defensemen, who were forced by circumstances to take a turn in the crease. Until the 1941–42 season, goaltenders served their own penalties, requiring a position player to take his place. This accounts for famous hockey names such as Charlie Conacher, King Clancy and Sprague Cleghorn finding their way into both the Player and Goaltender registers. Injuries to Frank Brophy forced Quebec Bulldogs' defenseman Harry Mummery to don the pads three times in a single season. All of these players, with detailed notes and complete statistics, can be found in the Goaltender Register.

In the early years of the game, statistics were not recorded with the same accuracy and thoroughness that they are today. Even core stats such as games played, assists and penalty minutes were rarely accurate. Adding to the confusion were wildly differing accounts of the statistics that were tabulated. Game sheets for the first four seasons of league play weren't kept reliably, creating confusion as to the accuracy of early statistics. Bob Duff, a reporter for the *Windsor Star,* was hired to research the early years of the NHL. Duff's research included reading newspaper game summaries from every NHL city and cross-checking them with other source material. Using the resulting data, Duff was able to compile an entirely new set of statistics for the first four years of the NHL, including the awarding of assists for every player who participated in the league's inaugural season.

Using the recommendations from our readers as a starting point, we have added numerous new features and improvements.

Notable North American Non-NHL Players *(page 616)* and Notable North American Non-NHL Goaltenders *(page 627)* were compiled by Ernie Fitzsimmons. These contain complete career statistical panels for many members of the Hockey Hall of Fame—familiar names such as Punch Imlach, Harry Sinden and Cyclone Taylor—as well as less well-known players such as Georges Roy and Herb Carnegie. These players share one common bond other then their athletic ability: they had long and illustrious careers but never ascended the ladder to the NHL, be it by choice or by circumstance.

This section also includes the top 10 WHA players never to appear in an NHL game as compiled by Ernie Fitzsimmons and Scott Surgent.

Notable European Non-NHL Players are found on page 631 and Notable European Non-NHL Goaltenders on page 642. Compiled and selected by Igor Kuperman, this section features complete career statistical panels for the best European-born players who never donned NHL jerseys. It honors names like Tretiak, Kharlamov and Bobrov, men who are familiar to hockey fans throughout the world because of their participation in the Olympic and World Championship tournaments. At the same time, it praises players such as Jiri Kralik and Leif Holmqvist, who are not as well-known as their contemporaries.

Since the first *Total Hockey* encyclopedia was published in September, 1998, we have spent two years rebuilding, refining and polishing the data panels of the Player Registers. We have added more than 30,000 new lines of statistics for those players who were in the first edition. Many of these additions came from the hundreds of contributors who mailed, e-mailed and even telephoned in additions, corrections and suggestions.

During the course of our preparation for the first *Total Hockey* encyclopedia, we determined that nine players thought to have played in the NHL actually did not. Over the past 24 months, we have reinstated Tom Coulter. A number of researchers and *Total Hockey* readers delivered concrete proof that Coulter did indeed play in the NHL and his name and record have been reinserted in the active player database (*see page 685*). We were also provided irrefutable proof that Vic Lynn played one game with the New York Rangers during the 1942-43 season, making him the only player in NHL history to play for each of the "original six" franchises (*see page 753*).

NHL playoff statistics from 1918 to 1926 have been completely revised in this edition. During these years, the Stanley Cup was not an exclusive, all-NHL affair. The champion of the NHL would play the champions of the PCHA or WCHL/WHL for the right to carry home the Stanley Cup. For those NHL players who participated in these Stanley Cup championship rounds, their individual goals, assists and points statistics were always included as part of their NHL playoff totals. We determined that these Stanley Cup totals should stand on their own, thereby separating NHL playoff stats from Stanley Cup numbers. This same treatment also has been applied to those players from the western pro leagues who also played in the NHL. For Stanley Cup playoff totals between 1918 to 1926, you will find these numbers in their own separate line designated "**St-Cup**." Let the debate begin!

In total, more than 25 innovations have been introduced into the individual player panels, including the one most requested by our readers: the addition of Stanley Cup "diamonds" (♦) to designate players who have played on a Stanley Cup winner from 1893 to 2000. This symbol supplements the asterisk (*) which continues to be used to indicate league- or tournament-leading statistics.

Specialty statistical categories were researched and inserted. The player panels now include Allan Cup (Canadian Senior Hockey Championship) statistics from 1909 to 1962; Memorial Cup (Canadian Major Junior Championship) statistics from 1919 to 2000 and Centennial Cup (Canadian Junior "A" Championship) statistics (where available) from 1967 to 1984 for those players who participated in these important tournaments.

We did not neglect Europe's specialty tournaments. Statistics from the European Junior Tournament (1960 to 2000), European Hockey League (1995 to 2000), Alpenliga (1994 to 1999) and International Eishockey League (1999 to 2000) have been included for each NHL player who participated in these tournaments and competitions.

We have also continued to include tournament totals for events such as the DN-Cup, a preseason Swedish exhibition that featured two NHL teams and two Swedish Elite teams playing a four-game round-robin series. You'll have the surprise of a hockey lifetime when you discover the hard-shooting NHL superstar who completed his illustrious career playing in this tournament! *(page 1207)*

Since Britain was the first European country to welcome former and future NHLers into its league in large numbers, we have also included specialty tournament statistics for England's major competitions. In the pre-1960 era—when imports played in significant numbers—we have included the London Cup, Autumn Cup and National Tournament statistics from the 1930s and 1940s, as researched by Martin C. Harris. In the post-1980 era when Britain again opened its doors to imports, readers will discover Benson and Hedges Cup, Autumn Trophy and Union Cup statistics for all former NHLers who continued their careers in Britain. These statistics have never been previously published in North America. In subsequent editions, we will afford the rest of Europe the same courtesy and hope to include Continental Cup, Izvestia Cup and Spengler Cup totals.

Many readers requested we include proper and middle names, and we have been able to find that information for more than 70 percent of North American-born NHL players. These names can be found on each player's biographical line. If a player's proper name is the one he is commonly known by (**William**), both it and his middle name are included (**William Joseph**). If the player goes by his common name (**Bill**), then both his proper name and his middle name (**William Joseph**) are included. The players "nickname" follows his proper and middle names in quotation marks (William Joseph **"Skippy"**).

Considerable work has been done to the trade notes field in the statistical panel. Father, son, and brother designations for all related players can be found directly under the NHL and Other Major League career-total line. We have tried to include notes for all current players who missed more than half-a-season due to injury; we have updated notes concerning retirement dates; coaching appointments and details of career-ending injuries. The trade notes field is also home to condensed statistics (teams played for and year-by-year totals) for all those NHL players and goaltenders who spent their summer vacations playing in the *Roller Hockey International League* from 1990 to 1999.

In the Modern Players register, we have compiled the most extensive collection of pre-NHL bantam, midget, high school, tier-2 junior, junior B, C and D and Canadian College statistics ever collected. For instance, we have been able to add pre-NHL stats for most players who competed in junior A, B, C and D leagues in Ontario from 1979-2000. See Curtis Joseph's career panel (*page 1852*) for an example of this addition.

All NHLers who competed in the Quebec *AAA* Major Midget League from 1978 to 1999 can find their statistics in this edition.

Where statistics could not be found, the player's previous team and league have been included.

Total Hockey now includes extensive European statistics for former and current NHL players. North American-born players such as Eric Calder *(page 947)*, Michel Galarneau *(page 1097)*, Larry Huras *(page 1210)*, Moe Lemay *(page 1325)* and goaltender Jim Corsi *(page 1808)*, now have statistical panels that document their extensive European playing careers.

Pioneer European-born NHLers who opened the door for other European players imports in the NHL have been thoroughly documented for the first time as well. See Udo Kiessling *(page 1258)*, Jaroslav Jirik *(page 1226)* and Ulf Sterner *(page 814)*.

Of the 5,195 players to appear in the NHL since 1917–18, more than 26 percent (1,367) also played in Europe. A tip of the helmet-and-visor must be given to contributing statistician Patrick Houda, whose research in this area proved invaluable.

The Pre-Expansion Player Register has been enhanced as well. American Hockey League yearly totals for most, if not all, traded players from 1940 to 1970 have now been separated to reflect games played and points earned with each team. These numbers have never been published before.

As well, complete World War II-era hockey statistics for all National Defense Hockey Leagues located in cities such as Vancouver, Calgary, Winnipeg, Toronto, Ottawa, Montreal and Halifax have also been published for the first time. Hundreds of NHL players participated in these leagues, formed to boost morale on the home front as war was waged in Europe.

Other new features include "Little" World Series statistics for tournaments between "outlaw" pro leagues such as the IHL and WPHL in the early 1900s and PCHA-NHA All-Star series statistics from 1912 to 1918.

We have added additional league designations for City Senior, Junior, Industrial and Intermediate teams. We also corrected the names of a number of pro leagues to reflect what they were called and when they operated. The EHL is now the EAHL between 1933–34 and 1952–53 and the EHL from 1954–55 to 1972–73. The CHL is now the CPHL between 1963–64 and 1967–68 and the CHL from 1968–69 to 1983–84. The IAHL is now the IHL from 1929–30 to 1935–36 and the AHL is now the IAHL from 1936–37 to 1939–40.

Other updated league designations include the Ontario Junior Leagues: OHA-Jr. (1909–10 to 1970–71); OMJHL (1971–72 to 1980–81) and the OHL (1981–82 to present); Quebec Junior Leagues: QJHL (1920–21 to 1970–71) and QMJHL (1971–72 to present; Western Junior Leagues: CMJHL (1966–67), WCJHL (1968–69 to 1977–78) and WHL (1978–79 to present).

The final league re-designation concerns the top four Senior leagues in Canada. In the 1950s, the Ontario Senior Hockey League, Quebec Senior Hockey League, Western Canada Senior Hockey League and the Maritime Senior Hockey League became the OMHL, QMHL, WCMHL and MMHL, "major" Senior leagues who competed for a new nation-wide championship trophy called the Alexander Cup. The concept was short-lived. The Western Senior league and the Ontario Senior league dropped out after only one year and returned to Allan Cup competition. The Maritime Senior league and the Quebec Senior league continued to compete as "major" senior leagues until 1953.

The group of leagues included in the "Other Major Leagues" total line that appears at the end of some stat panels now includes the following: (League abbreviations are listed on pages 1973 and 1974.)

League	Start	End	
CHA	1909–10	same year	
ECHA	1908-09	same year	
ECAHA	all years		
IHL	1903-04	1906-07	
MHL Sr/Man-Pro	1906-07	1908-09	New in this edition
MPHL	all years		
NHA	all years		
NOHL	1907-08	1911-12	New in this edition
OPHL	1908-09	1910-11	
PCHA	all years		
WCHL	1920-21	1924-25	
WHA	all years		
WHL	1925-26		
WPHL	1901-02	1903-04	New in this edition

All the other "firsts" found in the first edition of *Total Hockey* remain in place. We welcome all your comments, concerns, corrections and, hopefully, congratulations. To contact *Total Hockey*, see page 1974.

ADJUSTED SCORING

Single-Season and Career Leaders

ADJUSTED GOALS

SINGLE SEASON

Name	Season	AG
Brett Hull	1990-91	80
Phil Esposito	1970-71	76
Mario Lemieux	1988-89	73
Wayne Gretzky	1981-82	73
Babe Dye	1924-25	70
Wayne Gretzky	1983-84	70
Howie Morenz	1927-28	69
Mario Lemieux	1995-96	68
Phil Esposito	1971-72	67
Gordie Howe	1952-53	67
Jean Beliveau	1955-56	66
Phil Esposito	1973-74	66
Pavel Bure	1999-00	66
Ace Bailey	1928-29	65
Brett Hull	1991-92	64
Alexander Mogilny	1992-93	64
Teemu Selanne	1992-93	64
Charlie Conacher	1930-31	64
Gordie Howe	1951-52	64
Bobby Hull	1965-66	63
Cooney Weiland	1929-30	62
Bobby Hull	1966-67	62
Bobby Hull	1968-69	62
Brett Hull	1989-90	62
Nels Stewart	1928-29	62
Bill Cook	1930-31	62
Peter Bondra	1997-98	61
Teemu Selanne	1997-98	61
Jaromir Jagr	1995-96	61
Joe Malone	1917-18	61
Nels Stewart	1925-26	61

CAREER

Name	AG
Gordie Howe	988
Wayne Gretzky	779
Phil Esposito	708
Bobby Hull	699
Maurice Richard	677
Marcel Dionne	627
Mike Gartner	623
Jean Beliveau	615
Brett Hull	602
John Bucyk	595
Nels Stewart	594
Frank Mahovlich	593
Steve Yzerman	583
Stan Mikita	577
Mark Messier	572

ADJUSTED ASSISTS

SINGLE SEASON

Name	Season	AA
Wayne Gretzky	1985-86	111
Frank Boucher	1928-29	110
Howie Morenz	1927-28	105
Andy Blair	1928-29	103
Joe Primeau	1930-31	99
Dick Irvin	1926-27	97
Wayne Gretzky	1990-91	94
Wayne Gretzky	1984-85	93
Wayne Gretzky	1986-87	89
Frank Nighbor	1925-26	88
Wayne Gretzky	1982-83	87
Frank Boucher	1929-30	87
Bobby Orr	1970-71	86
Joe Primeau	1931-32	84
Frank Boucher	1930-31	83
Bobby Orr	1969-70	83
Mario Lemieux	1988-89	81
Wayne Gretzky	1983-84	81
Bun Cook	1927-28	81
Wayne Gretzky	1988-89	81
Frank Boucher	1926-27	80
Wayne Gretzky	1981-82	80
Cy Denneny	1925-26	80
Jaromir Jagr	1998-99	80

CAREER

Name	AA
Wayne Gretzky	1480
Gordie Howe	1121
Ron Francis	869
Paul Coffey	863
Ray Bourque	861
Mark Messier	847
Stan Mikita	834
Alex Delvecchio	825
Marcel Dionne	760
Steve Yzerman	741
John Bucyk	740
Adam Oates	737
Phil Esposito	736
Frank Boucher	734
Jean Beliveau	722

ADJUSTED POINTS

SINGLE SEASON

Name	Season	APts
Howie Morenz	1927-28	174
Mario Lemieux	1988-89	154
Wayne Gretzky	1984-85	153
Wayne Gretzky	1985-86	153
Wayne Gretzky	1981-82	153
Wayne Gretzky	1983-84	151
Wayne Gretzky	1982-83	146
Mario Lemieux	1995-96	144
Wayne Gretzky	1986-87	143
Phil Esposito	1970-71	140
Frank Boucher	1928-29	139
Andy Blair	1928-29	138
Cooney Weiland	1929-30	134
Jaromir Jagr	1995-96	133
Ace Bailey	1928-29	133
Wayne Gretzky	1990-91	132
Jaromir Jagr	1998-99	132
Mario Lemieux	1987-88	131
Phil Esposito	1973-74	130
Dick Irvin	1926-27	129
Howie Morenz	1930-31	128
Wayne Gretzky	1988-89	127
Phil Esposito	1971-72	125
Frank Boucher	1929-30	124
Gordie Howe	1952-53	124
Bobby Orr	1970-71	123
Ebbie Goodfellow	1930-31	122
Cy Denneny	1925-26	122
Mario Lemieux	1992-93	121
Phil Esposito	1968-69	121
Aurel Joliat	1927-28	121

CAREER

Name	APts
Wayne Gretzky	2259
Gordie Howe	2109
Phil Esposito	1444
Mark Messier	1419
Stan Mikita	1411
Marcel Dionne	1387
Alex Delvecchio	1363
Jean Beliveau	1337
John Bucyk	1335
Steve Yzerman	1324
Ron Francis	1311
Norm Ullman	1254
Bobby Hull	1234
Ray Bourque	1229
Paul Coffey	1214

CHAPTER 69

Adjusted Scoring

Further Refinement to Total Hockey's Cross-Era Statistical Categories

Dan Diamond

IT IS A RARE PRIVILEGE FOR A FAN to have followed the game long enough and closely enough to have naked-eye comparisons of superstars from different eras clearly fixed in his or her mind. Most of us don't have the benefit of sufficient years following the sport to be able to do this on our own. Instead we rely on written accounts and statistics, but how accurate are these as a basis for comparison? The game of hockey has undergone an unending series of fundamental changes. The length of the season, the size of players, the equipment they wear, the ice they skate on and the rules of hockey continue to evolve, making cross-era comparison chancy at best.

In preparing *Total Hockey* we set out to create a reliable method of comparing players from disparate eras. These resulting new statistical categories have been named Adjusted Scoring. In the player registers that follow, three Adjusted Scoring statistics are included: Adjusted Goals (**AG**), Adjusted Assists (**AA**) and Adjusted Points (**APts**).

Adjusted Average (**AAvg**) is a similar comparative statistic that has been created to evaluate goaltenders. *(See page 1782.)*

In each of these new statistical categories the object is the same: to place every NHL player's numbers on an equalized footing to facilitate comparison from season to season and era to era. Adjusted Scoring statistics have been calculated for each season in a player's NHL career. These, in turn, have been totaled to provide career Adjusted Goals, Adjusted Assists and Adjusted Points.

Adjusted Scoring statistics account for the following: 1) the average number of goals scored per game in each season, 2) the length of the NHL regular-season schedule and 3) the maximum number of skaters allowed to dress for each game.

The same method is used to calculate all three.

Using Adjusted Goals as an example, since the NHL began play in the 1917–18 season, 224,938 goals have been scored in 35,020 games, for an average of 6.423 goals per game. The average number of goals scored per game has also been calculated for each of the NHL's 83 seasons. The average of these individual season averages is 6.11213 goals per game. We have chosen to use this average-of-the-averages figure, rather than the higher grand total average because we feel it removes an unfair weighting toward recent seasons when the number of games on the NHL schedule has been at an all-time high.

Each season's average number of goals scored per game is then factored against the overall average of individual season averages (6.11213). If the individual season average is less than this figure, goals that season were, in fact, harder to come by than the overall figure. Therefore each goal scored is more valuable (i.e., worth more than 1.00) than the baseline overall average. Conversely, in seasons in which goals are plentiful, each goal scored is worth less than 1.00.

Some concrete examples: Defense was king in 1952–53. Only 4.7905 goals were scored per game. Therefore each goal scored that year has been factored to represent 1.2759 Adjusted Goals. By comparison, goals were plentiful in 1981–82 with 8.0095 scored per game. Each goal scored this season represents .7631 Adjusted Goals. (These two sample seasons are of particular interest. In 1952–53 Gordie Howe scored 49 goals; in 1981–82 Wayne Gretzky scored 92. Both are single-season career highs for these two great scorers. Howe' 49 goals adjust to 67; Gretzky's 92 become 73.)

To further remove bias from our formula, we subtract each player's individual goals scored total from the calculation of the average number of goals per game in the season being adjusted. In the modern era, with so many players and so many goals scored, an individual total has little impact on the factoring, but in the early years a top scorers' output can skew the numbers. (In 1917–18, Joe Malone scored almost 13 percent of the goals in the NHL.)

The result of all of this number crunching is a factoring that is unique to each player for each season.

What about length of schedule? The NHL has played schedules ranging in length from 18 to 84 games. We have factored every player's scoring stats to today's standard of 82 games. This is done by expressing each individual's games played as a percentage of a full schedule. This percentage is applied to the 82-game baseline, resulting in an equivalent number of games played out of 82. The actual number of games played is then factored against the out-of-82 number, resulting in a multiplier that is applied to the factored scoring total.

The newest addition to the Adjusted Scoring formula accounts for roster size. Since 1982–83, teams have dressed a maximum of 18 skaters. This number has been modified on numerous occasions since the NHL's first season, growing from a maximum of 11 in the 1920s. Smaller rosters require more ice time per player, yielding more opportunities to score. *Total Hockey*'s Adjusted Scoring factors every scoring line to reflect the modern roster size of 18 skaters. As an example, in 1942–43, teams were allowed to dress 13 skaters. Each scoring point recorded in 1942–43 is factored by .7222 to take into account the increased opportunities to score that come from sharing ice time with fewer teammates. Factoring for roster size enables accurate comparison between modern hockey and the small-roster game of the 1920s NHL. Without it, the adjusted scoring numbers for the NHL's top scorers don't make for effective cross-era comparison as those of the early era would be miles higher than those of any other. *(See tables on page 612.)*

Combining these factors of weighted goals and schedule length results in a powerful new statistical tool. Does it clearly decide who's number one? Of course not, but it provides plenty of ammunition for the discussion.

CHAPTER 70

Giveaways, Blocks and Time-on-Ice

The Story Behind the NHL Real-Time Scoring System

Dan Diamond

For 80 years, National Hockey League official scorers recorded game statistics by hand. The NHL office contains files filled with hand-written game sheets from almost every game played between 1917 and 1997. This system of recording statistics changed in 1997 when the NHL introduced its computer-based Real-Time Scoring System.

This scoring system was born in chilly small-town Ontario arenas and came of age in NHL buildings across North America. It is an interesting story worth recounting because of the effort by so many people to make it happen.

In the early 1990s, the NHL was evaluating its procedure for gathering and distributing game statistics. The desktop computing revolution was in full swing while at the same time, club personnel and statistical hobbyists were exploring new and more elaborate ways to track the high-speed action of NHL hockey. The Internet explosion hadn't arrived, but its rumblings were on the horizon.

About the same time, a new concept in computer-based scoring was being invented in the small Ontario town of Huntsville that would become the foundation for today's modern NHL scoring system.

The germ of this concept started one bitterly cold Saturday morning in January, 1988, in the Huntsville arena where Stuart Reid was watching his son play hockey—and keeping warm. The "scorers" for this game were two young girls who used a piece of brown paper bag to write down the goals and penalties. It inspired the observation that there must be a better way for minor hockey teams to gather and report their stats.

A year and a half later, Reid got together with Terry Clarke to explore the concept. During one of their sessions, they realized that the computer screen had to be the hockey rink. Instead of writing the stats on a piece of paper and, later, entering them into the computer, the key to a real-time scoring system was immediately capturing the events into the computer and placing them on a map of the ice.

Simultaneously, Toronto hockey fan Paul Bruno had devised a pen-and-paper system of stats keeping that tracked much more than just goals, assists, points and penalty minutes. In 1991, he convinced the public relations department of the Toronto Maple Leafs that his system could yield useful information. He gained permission to view games and record stats from the press box in Maple Leaf Gardens where he met Reid and Clarke. By the end of that season, they had joined forces under the company name SQRA (an acronymn for the Latin phrase *scientia quaestus res athleta*—"the athlete's quest for knowledge") with the goal of developing a computer program that tracked traditional and new hockey statistics.

Months of development and design ensued. Brad Scott, a University of Waterloo undergraduate, joined the team to write the computer code to put the concept into an application. By the fall of 1992, the first working prototype was used to score midget hockey games. It still had a long way to go, but the concept was proven.

The new stats-gathering program was operated by a series of mouse clicks. A full-scale version of the hockey rink occupied most of the computer screen. The program recorded the location of any mouse clicks on the "rink." A clock was added to attach a time to everything that occurred. Just add players, drop the puck and start scoring.

At that time, hockey stats had consisted mainly of goals, shots and penalties. The SQRA system rounded out this menu by adding shoot-ins, missed shots, face-offs, blocked shots, giveaways/takeaways and hits—nine items in total. In the jargon of Real-Time scoring, each of these items is known as an event.

The result was a quick visual breakdown of accumulated events, where these events were represented by recognizable icons which were color coded and contained the sweater number of the key player. In addition, a new broader range of statistics was numerically displayed, also in real time. Any portion of the game could now be replayed on a computer screen at varying speeds, both graphically and statistically, to provide immediate situational analysis. The system also included the ability to isolate the activity of any player during any portion of the game, creating a personalized game summary, where every event involving that player could be presented on one screen.

Before this system was devised, statisticians recorded about 40 to 50 shots a game plus the usual complement of penalties. With Real-Time Scoring tracking nine events, the number of items recorded in a game grew to more than 400.

Time-on-ice is a major factor in evaluating hockey players but, until 1997, was recorded by the home team and not released to the public. In a typical NHL game there can be 800 to 1,000 player changes. It's a Herculean task to record all of these activities. The Real-Time system tracks time on ice and ensures no time is lost while the scorer "changes" players.

Like a young prospect working his way up to the NHL, the Real-Time system was dragged from arena to arena from local midget and juvenile teams to junior hockey in nearby North Bay, Ontario. In March, 1993, the Toronto Maple Leafs allocated three seats in the press box to try out the system in an NHL game. Contact with other NHL organizations followed and a demonstration was arranged for Commissioner Gary Bettman at a Buffalo-New Jersey playoff game in April, 1994. The system performed well. NHL statistician Benny Ercolani determined that existing staff could be trained to operate the system.

By 1994, Internet use was exploding. Sports content was some of the first information on the Web, leading the NHL to realize that a scoring and stats capturing system was only part of a larger technology requirement. The marketplace and its technology was evolving so quickly that the league decided to seek a partner who could build an overall package.

After months of discussions with major computer firms, a deal was struck with IBM Corporation during the winter of 1995–96. The NHL directed IBM to implement an overall technology solution that would include the SQRA system as the foundation of the NHL's real-time scoring and statistics gathering apparatus.

The next step saw NHL off-ice officials testing the system in live game situations. Tests were set up in New Jersey, Vancouver and Los Angles.

Dick Trimble and his off-ice staff in New Jersey agreed to start the ball rolling. After an evening training session, the team scored its first game in December, 1995. By midway through the first period, the crew was relaxed and enjoying the process. A second game was almost redundant—the scorers were comfortable and didn't want to go back to pad and paper. On to Vancouver, where the off-ice officials were given a training session and had similar success in their games. The Los Angles test was cancelled since the viability had been proven.

On Labor Day weekend 1996, Commissioner Bettman and Bill Moses of IBM announced their joint venture at Madison Square Garden following a World Cup of Hockey game. The starting gun had sounded.

All NHL arenas had to be outfitted with hardware and arena clocks had to be connected to the computers. The NHL's host computer system had to be upgraded and expanded to facilitate the new format and exponential growth in data. Programs had to be written to automate the data display on the Web. Almost 270 off-ice officials had to be trained. From top to bottom, the SQRA system had to be integrated in IBM's overall data processing solution for the NHL.

Responsibilities were divided as follows: SQRA assisted in the integration of software, developed documents, prepared drawings and specs for arena installations and for setup and training in use the program itself. IBM provided money, advertising, credibility, resources, and people.

IBM's project manager, Bill Sangrey, commented that this was the first project in his career where the deadline could not be moved; such was the importance of this venture.

Twelve short months later, the first preseason games were being scored in NHL arenas. By October 1, 1997—Commissioner Bettman's original deadline—all 11 games on the first night of the regular season were scored using the new system.

There were still lots of bugs and technical issues to work out, but the league had accomplished its goal, stepping straight from the pen and paper of the 19th century to digital input and output of the 21st century, all before the millennium arrived!

The resulting statistical output was considered to be complete and accurate for 1998–99. The data was added to player data panels in the *NHL Official Guide & Record Book.* By the 2000 Stanley Cup playoffs, broadcasters were making regular references to time-on-ice, face-off percentage, hits and blocked shots.

Some of the new information being presented to viewers identifies players generating the most scoring opportunities, how ice time is divided among the defense corps and how much attack zone offense is generated on the power-play. All of these statistics are accumulated by team officials in every NHL arena and allow for a more informative game summary both for the team and for the individual player.

CHAPTER 71

Notable North American Non-NHL Players

Early Era, Minor Professional and WHA Players

Compiled By Ernie Fitzsimmons

• ADDUONO, Ray
Raymond Peter
C – L. 5′9″, 160 lbs. b: Fort William, Ont., 1/21/1947.

Season	Club	League	REGULAR SEASON GP	G	A	Pts	PIM	PLAYOFFS GP	G	A	Pts	PIM
1962-63	Port Arthur North Stars	TBJHL	28	11	21	32	4	8	2	4	6	2
1963-64	Port Arthur North Stars	TBJHL	28	*25	15	*40	21	7	1	8	9	8
	Fort William Canadiens	M-Cup	5	5	1	6	0	....	....	....	....	....
1964-65	Port Arthur North Stars	TBJHL	24	27	*29	56	41	10	*10	*10	*20	17
	Port Arthur North Stars	M-Cup	5	4	6	10	4	....	....	....	....	....
1965-66	Port Arthur Marrs	TBJHL	30	36	*55	*91	49	8	*9	*12	*21	13
1966-67	Port Arthur Marrs	TBJHL	28	32	49	*81	44	5	4	5	9	4
1967-68	Syracuse Blazers	EHL	72	45	101	146	43	....	....	....	....	....
	Oklahoma City Blazers	CPHL	1	0	1	1	0	....	....	....	....	....
1968-69	Hershey Bears	AHL	12	1	2	3	4	....	....	....	....	....
	Amarillo Wranglers	CHL	59	16	41	57	41	....	....	....	....	....
1969-70	Syracuse Blazers	EHL	74	42	*92	*134	55	4	2	0	2	2
1970-71	Syracuse Blazers	EHL	63	31	70	101	50	6	4	11	15	9
1971-72	Syracuse Blazers	EHL	75	43	122	*165	133	17	8	*20	28	36
1972-73	Syracuse Blazers	EHL	76	54	116	170	138	14	9	26	35	19
1973-74	**Cleveland Crusaders**	**WHA**	**2**	**0**	**0**	**0**	**0**	....	....	....	....	....
	Macon Whoopees	SHL	40	14	38	52	95	....	....	....	....	....
	Syracuse Blazers	EHL	20	7	20	27	10	15	8	*20	*28	14
1974-75	**San Diego Mariners**	**WHA**	**78**	**15**	**59**	**74**	**23**	**10**	**5**	**9**	**14**	**13**
1975-76	**San Diego Mariners**	**WHA**	**80**	**23**	**67**	**90**	**22**	**11**	**4**	**7**	**11**	**6**
1976-77	**Minnesota Fighting Saints**	**WHA**	**40**	**4**	**19**	**23**	**17**	....	....	....	....	....
	San Diego Mariners	**WHA**	**13**	**2**	**5**	**7**	**5**	**7**	**3**	**2**	**5**	**19**
1977-78	**Indianapolis Racers**	**WHA**	**8**	**1**	**2**	**3**	**0**	....	....	....	....	....
	Thunder Bay Twins	OHA-Sr.	20	5	23	28	31	....	....	....	....	....
1978-79	San Diego Hawks	PHL	56	14	61	75	73	....	....	....	....	....
	Major League Totals		**221**	**45**	**152**	**197**	**67**	**28**	**12**	**18**	**30**	**38**

• TBJHL Rookie-of-the-Year (1963) • TBJHL First All-Star Team (1964) • TBJHL MVP (1964) • EHL Rookie-of-the-Year (1968) • EHL First All-Star Team (1972, 1973)

• BAIN, Dan
Donald Henderson — HHOF
C. b: Belleville, Ont., 2/14/1874 d: 8/15/1962.

Season	Club	League	GP	G	A	Pts	PIM	GP	G	A	Pts	PIM
1894-95	Winnipeg Victorias	MNWHL	STATISTICS NOT AVAILABLE									
1895-96	Winnipeg Victorias	MNWHL	STATISTICS NOT AVAILABLE									
♦	Winnipeg Victorias	St-Cup	2	3	0	3	....	....	....	....	....	....
1896-97	Winnipeg Victorias	MNWHL	STATISTICS NOT AVAILABLE									
1897-98	Winnipeg Victorias	MHL-Sr.	STATISTICS NOT AVAILABLE									
1898-99	Winnipeg Victorias	MHL-Sr.	STATISTICS NOT AVAILABLE									
	Winnipeg Victorias	St-Cup	1	0	0	0	....	....	....	....	....	....
99-1900	Winnipeg Victorias	MHL-Sr.	STATISTICS NOT AVAILABLE									
	Winnipeg Victorias	St-Cup	3	4	0	4	....	....	....	....	....	....
1900-01	Winnipeg Victorias	MHL-Sr.	STATISTICS NOT AVAILABLE									
♦	Winnipeg Victorias	St-Cup	2	3	0	3	....	....	....	....	....	....
1901-02	Winnipeg Victorias	MHL-Sr.	STATISTICS NOT AVAILABLE									
♦	Winnipeg Victorias	St-Cup	3	0	0	0	....	....	....	....	....	....

• BAKER, Hobey
Hobart Amory Hare — USHOF HHOF
Rover – R. 5′9″, 160 lbs. b: Wisahicton, PA, 1/15/1892 d: 12/21/1918.

Season	Club	League	GP	G	A	Pts	PIM	GP	G	A	Pts	PIM
1906/10	Concord St. Paul's	H.S.	STATISTICS NOT AVAILABLE									
1910/13	Princeton University	Ivy	STATISTICS NOT AVAILABLE									
1913-14	Princeton University	Ivy	11	12	0	12	2	....	....	....	....	....
1914-15	St. Nicholas Club	AAHL	8	*17	0	*17	....	....	....	....	....	....
1915-16	St. Nicholas Club	AAHL	7	9	0	9	....	3	1	0	1	....

AAHL First All-Star Team (1915, 1916)

• BOON, Dickie
HHOF
Point. 5′5″, 130 lbs. b: Belleville, Ont., 2/14/1874 d: 5/3/1961.

Season	Club	League	GP	G	A	Pts	PIM	GP	G	A	Pts	PIM
99-1900	Montreal AAA	CAHL	8	2	0	2	....	....	....	....	....	....
1900-01	Montreal AAA	CAHL	7	3	0	3	....	....	....	....	....	....
1901-02	Montreal AAA	CAHL	8	2	0	2	6	....	....	....	....	....
♦	Montreal AAA	St-Cup	3	0	0	0	3	....	....	....	....	....
1902-03	Montreal AAA	CAHL	7	3	0	3	6	....	....	....	....	....
♦	Montreal AAA	St-Cup	4	0	0	0	10	....	....	....	....	....
1903-04	Montreal Wanderers	FAHL	4	0	0	0	0	....	....	....	....	....
1904-05	Montreal Wanderers	FAHL	8	0	0	0	6	....	....	....	....	....
1905-06	**Montreal Wanderers**	**ECAHA**	DID NOT PLAY – COACHING									

• BURGESS, Don
LW – L. 6′, 170 lbs. b: Port Edward, Ont., 6/8/1946.

Season	Club	League	GP	G	A	Pts	PIM	GP	G	A	Pts	PIM
1965-66	Sarnia Legionaires	OHA-B	STATISTICS NOT AVAILABLE									
1966-67	St. Catharines Blackhawks	OHA-Jr.	42	6	11	17	30	6	0	1	1	4
1967-68	Greensboro Generals	EHL	72	30	37	67	59	11	5	8	13	5
1968-69	Greensboro Generals	EHL	72	44	51	95	18	8	1	7	8	0
1969-70	Greensboro Generals	EHL	74	36	49	85	26	16	11	*17	*28	0
1970-71	Greensboro Generals	EHL	72	41	76	117	18	9	4	1	5	0
1971-72	Greensboro Generals	EHL	73	39	58	97	29	11	7	8	15	11
1972-73	**Philadelphia Blazers**	**WHA**	**74**	**20**	**22**	**42**	**15**	**4**	**1**	**0**	**1**	**0**
1973-74	**Vancouver Blazers**	**WHA**	**78**	**30**	**36**	**66**	**8**	....	....	....	....	....
1974-75	**Vancouver Blazers**	**WHA**	**62**	**11**	**18**	**29**	**19**	....	....	....	....	....
	Tulsa Oilers	CHL	12	6	5	11	4	....	....	....	....	....
1975-76	**San Diego Mariners**	**WHA**	**73**	**14**	**11**	**25**	**35**	**11**	**1**	**7**	**8**	**4**
1976-77	**San Diego Mariners**	**WHA**	**77**	**20**	**22**	**42**	**8**	**7**	**2**	**2**	**4**	**0**
1977-78	**Indianapolis Racers**	**WHA**	**79**	**11**	**12**	**23**	**2**	....	....	....	....	....
1978-79	**Indianapolis Racers**	**WHA**	**3**	**1**	**1**	**2**	**0**	....	....	....	....	....
	San Diego Hawks	PHL	52	22	24	46	17	....	....	....	....	....
1979-80	Spokane Jets	WIHL	STATISTICS NOT AVAILABLE									
	Major League Totals		**446**	**107**	**122**	**229**	**87**	**22**	**4**	**9**	**13**	**4**

• CAMPBELL, Lorne
C – L. b: Ottawa, Ont., Deceased.

Season	Club	League	GP	G	A	Pts	PIM	GP	G	A	Pts	PIM
99-1900	Montreal AAA-2	CAHL-I	STATISTICS NOT AVAILABLE									
1900-01	Montreal AAA-2	CAHL-I	STATISTICS NOT AVAILABLE									
	Montreal AAA	CAHL	7	10	0	10	....	....	....	....	....	....
1901-02	**Pittsburgh Bankers**	**WPHL**	**13**	**6**	**6**	**12**	**19**	....	....	....	....	....
	Pittsburgh Bankers	X-Games	5	6	3	9	6	....	....	....	....	....
1902-03	**Pittsburgh Bankers**	**WPHL**	**14**	**14**	**8**	**22**	**22**	**4**	***4**	**1**	***5**	**4**
1903-04	**Pittsburgh Bankers**	**WPHL**	**15**	**21**	***8**	***29**	**25**	**2**	***5**	***2**	***7**	**0**
1904-05	**Pittsburgh Pros**	**IHL**	**24**	**29**	**0**	**29**	**9**	....	....	....	....	....
	Portage Lakes	**IHL**	**4**	**6**	**0**	**6**	**0**	....	....	....	....	....
1905-06	**Pittsburgh Pros**	**IHL**	**24**	**35**	**0**	**35**	**28**	....	....	....	....	....
	Calumet Wanderers	**IHL**	**1**	**3**	**0**	**3**	**1**	....	....	....	....	....
1906-07	**Pittsburgh Pros**	**IHL**	**24**	**35**	***25**	**60**	**40**	....	....	....	....	....
1907-08	**Winnipeg Maple Leafs**	**Man-Pro**	**15**	***29**	**0**	***29**	....	....	....	....	....	....
	Winnipeg Maple Leafs	St-Cup	2	0	0	0	*25	....	....	....	....	....
1908-09	**Winnipeg Strathconas**	**Man-Pro**	**1**	**0**	**0**	**0**	**0**	....	....	....	....	....
	Pittsburgh Professionals	WPHL	14	11	0	11	....	....	....	....	....	....
1909-10	**Cobalt Silver Kings**	**NHA**	**3**	**2**	**0**	**2**	**28**	....	....	....	....	....
	Cobalt Silver Kings	**NHA**	**2**	**4**	**0**	**4**	**8**	....	....	....	....	....
	Major League Totals		**140**	**184**	**47**	**231**	**180**	**6**	**9**	**3**	**12**	**4**

WPHL First All-Star Team (1903, 1904) • IHL Second All-Star Team (1906) • IHL First All-Star Team (1907)

• CARNEGIE, Herb
C – L. 5′9″, 170 lbs. b: Toronto, Ont., 11/8/1919.

Season	Club	League	GP	G	A	Pts	PIM	GP	G	A	Pts	PIM
1933-34	Toronto Observers	OHA	STATISTICS NOT AVAILABLE									
1934-35	Earl Haig Collegiate	H.S.	STATISTICS NOT AVAILABLE									
1935/38	Toronto Vocational	OHA-B	STATISTICS NOT AVAILABLE									
1938-39	Toronto Young Rangers	OHA-Jr.	13	10	6	16	10	5	3	2	5	14
	Toronto Port Office	TIHL	2	1	1	2	0	....	....	....	....	....
1939-40	Noranda Flyers	NOHA	STATISTICS NOT AVAILABLE									
1940-41	Timmins Ankerites	GBHL	24	9	7	16	20	3	4	4	*8	2
	Timmins Ankerites	Al-Cup	3	0	1	1	0	....	....	....	....	....
1941-42	Timmins Ankerites	GBHL	9	6	7	13	4	4	0	3	3	0
	Timmins Ankerites	Al-Cup	3	1	1	2	4	....	....	....	....	....
1942-43	Timmins Ankerites	GBHL	STATISTICS NOT AVAILABLE									
1943-44	Porcupine All-Stars	X-Games	STATISTICS NOT AVAILABLE									
1944-45	Shawinigan Cataracts	QPHL	33	24	30	54	36	....	....	....	....	....
1945-46	Sherbrooke Randies	QPHL	40	45	30	75	57	10	5	*6	*11	8
	Toronto Mahers	TMHL	2	3	2	5	0	....	....	....	....	....
1946-47	Sherbrooke St. Francois	QPHL	50	33	50	83	25	10	8	8	16	6
1947-48	Sherbrooke St. Francois	QPHL	56	48	*79	*127	51	10	2	9	11	8
1948-49	Sherbrooke Saints	QSHL	63	35	36	71	52	12	7	8	*15	10
1949-50	Quebec Aces	QSHL	59	26	33	59	32	13	2	8	10	16
1950-51	Quebec Aces	QMHL	57	18	40	58	35	19	3	10	13	23
1951-52	Quebec Aces	QMHL	56	22	30	52	16	15	4	12	16	8
	Quebec Aces	Alx-Cup	5	0	0	0	16	....	....	....	....	....
1952-53	Quebec Aces	QMHL	52	11	18	29	10	22	8	9	17	2
1953-54	Owen Sound Mercuries	OHA-Sr.	54	20	35	55	22	10	5	6	11	8

Named QPHL MVP (1946, 1947, 1948) • QSHL Second All-Star Team (1950) • QMHL Second All-Star Team (1951)

• COCHRANE, George
"Goldie"
Rover. 5′7″, 150 lbs. b: Berlin, Ont., 1883 Deceased.

Season	Club	League	GP	G	A	Pts	PIM	GP	G	A	Pts	PIM
99-1900	Berlin Athletics	WOHA	8	*17	0	*17	0	....	....	....	....	....
1900-01	Berlin Athletics	WOHA	6	*15	0	*15	0	....	....	....	....	....
1901-02	Berlin Athletics	WOHA	8	12	0	12	0	....	....	....	....	....
1902-03	Berlin Athletics	WOHA	6	15	0	15	....	1	2	0	2	....
1903-04	Berlin Athletics	WOHA	6	14	0	14	....	....	....	....	....	....
1904-05	Berlin Athletics	OHA-I	8	*14	0	*14	30	8	*13	0	*13	....
1905-06	Berlin Athletics	OHA-Sr.	8	*17	0	*17	30	2	1	0	1	0
1906-07	**Portage Lakes**	**IHL**	**17**	**15**	**5**	**20**	**12**	....	....	....	....	....
1907-08	**Berlin Athletics**	**OPHL**	**12**	**8**	**0**	**8**	**3**	....	....	....	....	....
1908-09	**Galt Professionals**	**OPHL**	**17**	**20**	**0**	**20**	**31**	....	....	....	....	....

Season	Club	League	GP	G	A	Pts	PIM	GP	G	A	Pts	PIM
			REGULAR SEASON					PLAYOFFS				
1909-10	Galt Professionals	X-Games	3	1	0	1	3	....	....	....	....	....
	Montreal All-Montreal	CHA	1	0	0	0	0	....	....	....	....	....
	Galt Professionals	OPHL	12	3	0	3	15	....	....	....	....	....
	Galt Professionals	St-Cup	1	0	0	0	0	....	....	....	....	....
1910-11	Belleville Professionals	EOPHL	1	0	0	0	....	....	....	....	....	....
	Major League Totals		59	46	5	51	61	....	....	....	....	....

OPHL Second All-Star Team (1909)

• DAVIDSON, Allan "Scotty" HHOF

RW – R. 6'1", 195 lbs. b: Kingston, Ont., 3/6/1892 d: 6/6/1915.

Season	Club	League	GP	G	A	Pts	PIM	GP	G	A	Pts	PIM
1908-09	Kingston 14th Army	OSrBL	4	*8	0	*8	11	4	4	0	4	6
1909-10	Kingston Frontenacs	OHA-Jr.	STATISTICS NOT AVAILABLE									
1910-11	Kingston Frontenacs	OHA-Jr.	STATISTICS NOT AVAILABLE									
1911-12	Calgary Athletics	CCSHL	....	....	....	....	....	3	3	0	3	6
1912-13	Toronto Blueshirts	NHA	20	19	0	19	69	....	....	....	....	....
	Toronto Tecumsehs	X-Games	2	0	0	0	0	....	....	....	....	....
1913-14	Toronto Blueshirts	NHA	20	23	13	36	64	2	2	0	2	*11
♦	Toronto Blueshirts	St-Cup	2	1	0	1	0	....	....	....	....	....
	Major League Totals		40	42	13	55	133	2	2	0	2	11

• DRINKWATER, Graham Charles Graham HHOF

Rover – R. 5'11", 165 lbs. b: Montreal, Que., 2/22/1875 d: 9/26/1946.

Season	Club	League	GP	G	A	Pts	PIM	GP	G	A	Pts	PIM
1892-93	Montreal Victorias	AHAC	3	1	0	1	....	....	....	....	....	....
1893-94			STATISTICS NOT AVAILABLE									
1894-95	Montreal Victorias	AHAC	8	9	0	9	....	....	....	....	....	....
1895-96	Montreal Victorias	AHAC	8	7	0	7	....	....	....	....	....	....
♦	Montreal Victorias	St-Cup	1	1	0	1	....	....	....	....	....	....
1896-97	Montreal Victorias	AHAC	4	3	0	3	....	....	....	....	....	....
♦	Montreal Victorias	St-Cup	1	0	0	0	....	....	....	....	....	....
♦1897-98	Montreal Victorias	AHAC	8	10	0	10	....	....	....	....	....	....
1898-99	Montreal Victorias	CAHL	6	0	0	0	....	....	....	....	....	....
♦	Montreal Victorias	St-Cup	2	1	0	1	....	....	....	....	....	....

• DUNDERDALE, Tommy HHOF

C – R. 5'8", 160 lbs. b: Benella, Australia, 5/6/1887 d: 12/15/1960.

Season	Club	League	GP	G	A	Pts	PIM	GP	G	A	Pts	PIM
1905-06	Winnipeg Ramblers	MAHA-I	STATISTICS NOT AVAILABLE									
1906-07	Winnipeg Strathconas	Man-Pro	10	8	0	8	....	....	....	....	....	....
1907-08	Winnipeg Maple Leafs	Man-Pro	3	1	0	1	....	....	....	....	....	....
	Strathcona-Alberta	Man-Pro	5	11	1	12	17	3	6	1	7	3
1908-09	Winnipeg Shamrocks	Man-Pro	5	12	*6	*18	6	3	3	0	3	6
	Winnipeg Shamrocks	Man-Pro	4	5	1	6	3	....	....	....	....	....
1909-10	Montreal Shamrocks	CHA	3	7	0	7	5	....	....	....	....	....
	Montreal Shamrocks	NHA	12	14	0	14	19	....	....	....	....	....
1910-11	Quebec Bulldogs	NHA	9	13	0	13	25	....	....	....	....	....
1911-12	Victoria Aristocrats	PCHA	16	24	0	24	25	....	....	....	....	....
	PCHA All-Stars	X-Games	3	*6	0	*6	3	....	....	....	....	....
1912-13	Victoria Aristocrats	PCHA	15	*24	5	*29	36	....	....	....	....	....
	Victoria Aristocrats	St-Cup	3	3	0	3	8	....	....	....	....	....
1913-14	Victoria Aristocrats	PCHA	16	*24	4	28	34	....	....	....	....	....
	Victoria Aristocrats	St-Cup	3	2	0	2	11	....	....	....	....	....
1914-15	Victoria Aristocrats	PCHA	17	17	10	27	22	....	....	....	....	....
	PCHA All-Stars	X-Games	2	0	0	0	0	....	....	....	....	....
1915-16	Portland Rosebuds	PCHA	18	14	3	17	45	....	....	....	....	....
	Portland Rosebuds	St-Cup	5	1	1	2	9	....	....	....	....	....
	PCHA All-Stars	X-Games	3	3	2	5	0	....	....	....	....	....
1916-17	Portland Rosebuds	PCHA	24	22	4	26	*141	....	....	....	....	....
1917-18	Portland Rosebuds	PCHA	18	14	6	20	*57	....	....	....	....	....
1918-19	Victoria Cougars	PCHA	20	5	4	9	28	....	....	....	....	....
1919-20	Victoria Cougars	PCHA	22	*26	7	*33	35	....	....	....	....	....
1920-21	Victoria Cougars	PCHA	24	9	11	20	18	....	....	....	....	....
1921-22	Victoria Cougars	PCHA	24	13	6	19	*37	....	....	....	....	....
1922-23	Victoria Cougars	PCHA	27	2	0	2	16	....	....	....	....	....
1923-24	Saskatoon Crescents	WCHL	6	1	0	1	4	....	....	....	....	....
	Edmonton Eskimos	WCHL	11	1	1	2	5	....	....	....	....	....
	Major League Totals		309	267	69	336	578	6	9	1	10	9

PCHA First All-Star Team (1912, 1913, 1914, 1915, 1920, 1922)

• FRENCH, John John George

LW – L. 5'11", 165 lbs. b: Orillia, Ont., 8/25/1950.
Montreal's 5th, 52nd overall in 1970.

Season	Club	League	GP	G	A	Pts	PIM	GP	G	A	Pts	PIM
1967-68	York Steel	OHA-B	35	23	37	60	....	....	....	....	....	....
1968-69	Toronto Marlboros	OHA-Jr.	54	17	25	42	62	6	3	3	6	12
1969-70	Toronto Marlboros	OHA-Jr.	52	23	25	48	92	8	1	2	3	2
1970-71	Montreal Voyageurs	AHL	65	15	22	37	14	1	0	0	0	0
1971-72	Baltimore Clippers	AHL	69	17	29	46	14	15	9	10	19	7
1972-73	New England Whalers	WHA	74	24	35	59	43	15	3	11	14	2
1973-74	New England Whalers	WHA	77	24	48	72	31	7	4	2	6	2
1974-75	New England Whalers	WHA	75	12	41	53	28	4	1	2	3	0
1975-76	San Diego Mariners	WHA	76	25	39	64	16	11	4	7	11	0
1976-77	San Diego Mariners	WHA	44	14	21	35	6	7	2	3	5	2
1977-78	Indianapolis Racers	WHA	74	9	8	17	6	....	....	....	....	....
1978-79	Springfield Indians	AHL	18	4	6	10	0	....	....	....	....	....
	Major League Totals		420	108	192	300	130	44	14	25	39	6

• GARDNER, Jimmy Jimmy Henry HHOF

LW – L. 5'9", 180 lbs. b: Montreal, Que., 5/21/1881 d: 11/7/1940.

Season	Club	League	GP	G	A	Pts	PIM	GP	G	A	Pts	PIM
99-1900	Montreal AAA-2	CAHL-I	STATISTICS NOT AVAILABLE									
1900-01	Montreal AAA-2	CAHL-I	STATISTICS NOT AVAILABLE									
	Montreal AAA	CAHL	1	0	0	0	0	....	....	....	....	....
1901-02	Montreal AAA	CAHL	8	1	0	1	16	....	....	....	....	....
♦	Montreal AAA	St-Cup	3	0	0	0	*12	....	....	....	....	....
1902-03	Montreal AAA	CAHL	3	3	0	3	9	....	....	....	....	....
♦	Montreal AAA	St-Cup	2	1	0	1	6	....	....	....	....	....
1903-04	Montreal Wanderers	FAHL	6	5	0	5	12	....	....	....	....	....
	Montreal Wanderers	St-Cup	1	1	0	1	0	....	....	....	....	....
1904-05	Calumet Wanderers	IHL	23	16	0	16	33	....	....	....	....	....
1905-06	Calumet Wanderers	IHL	19	3	0	3	30	....	....	....	....	....
1906-07	Pittsburgh Pros	IHL	20	10	8	18	61	....	....	....	....	....
1907-08	Montreal Shamrocks	ECAHA	10	7	0	7	*42	....	....	....	....	....
1908-09	Montreal Wanderers	ECHA	12	11	0	11	51	....	....	....	....	....
♦	Montreal Wanderers	St-Cup	2	0	0	0	*13	....	....	....	....	....
1909-10	Montreal Wanderers	NHA	1	3	0	3	9	....	....	....	....	....
	Montreal Wanderers	NHA	12	10	0	10	*58	....	....	....	....	....
♦	Montreal Wanderers	St-Cup	1	0	0	0	6	....	....	....	....	....
1910-11	Montreal Wanderers	NHA	14	5	0	5	35	....	....	....	....	....
1911-12	New Westminster Royals	PCHA	15	8	0	8	50	....	....	....	....	....
1912-13	New Westminster Royals	PCHA	13	3	4	7	21	....	....	....	....	....
1913-14	Montreal Canadiens	NHA	15	10	9	19	12	....	....	....	....	....
1914-15	Montreal Canadiens	NHA	2	0	0	0	0	....	....	....	....	....
	Major League Totals		156	86	21	107	402	....	....	....	....	....

IHL Second All-Star Team (1905)

• GIBSON, Jack John Liddell MacDonald "Doc" HHOF

Point. 6', 185 lbs. b: Glen Allen, Ont., 1880 d: 1950.

Season	Club	League	GP	G	A	Pts	PIM	GP	G	A	Pts	PIM
1894-95	Pickering College	H.S.	STATISTICS NOT AVAILABLE									
1895-96	Berlin Hockey Club	OHA-I	STATISTICS NOT AVAILABLE									
1896-97	Berlin Hockey Club	OHA-I	4	1	0	1	....	4	1	0	1	....
1897-98	Berlin Hockey Club	OHA-I	2	1	0	1	....	....	....	....	....	....
	Detroit College	MCAA	STATISTICS NOT AVAILABLE									
1898-99	Berlin Hockey Club	X-Games	STATISTICS NOT AVAILABLE									
	Detroit College	MCAA	STATISTICS NOT AVAILABLE									
99-1900	Berlin Hockey Club	OHA-Sr.	7	4	0	4	....	....	....	....	....	....
	Detroit College	MCAA	STATISTICS NOT AVAILABLE									
1900/02	Portage Lakes	X-Games	STATISTICS NOT AVAILABLE									
1902-03	Portage Lakes	X-Games	10	8	0	8	....	3	0	0	0	....
1903-04	Portage Lakes	X-Games	12	10	0	10	2	9	0	0	0	....
	Portage Lakes	W-S	2	0	0	0	....	....	....	....	....	....
1904-05	Portage Lakes	IHL	24	2	0	2	49	....	....	....	....	....
1906-07	Portage Lakes	IHL	4	0	0	0	0	....	....	....	....	....
	Major League Totals		28	2	0	2	49	....	....	....	....	....

• GILMOUR, Billy Hamilton Livingston HHOF

RW. b: Ottawa, Ont., 3/21/1885 d: 1959.

Season	Club	League	GP	G	A	Pts	PIM	GP	G	A	Pts	PIM
1900-01	Ottawa Aberdeens	CAHL-I	STATISTICS NOT AVAILABLE									
1901-02	Ottawa Aberdeens	CAHL-I	STATISTICS NOT AVAILABLE									
1902-03	Ottawa Silver Seven	CAHL	7	10	0	10	3	....	....	....	....	....
♦	Ottawa Silver Seven	St-Cup	4	5	0	5	3	....	....	....	....	....
♦1903-04	McGill University	MCHL	4	5	0	5	12	....	....	....	....	....
	Ottawa Silver Seven	St-Cup	3	1	0	1	0	....	....	....	....	....
1904-05	McGill University	MCHL	4	5	0	5	12	....	....	....	....	....
	Ottawa Silver Seven	FAHL	1	0	0	0	0	....	....	....	....	....
♦	Ottawa Silver Seven	St-Cup	2	1	0	1	8	....	....	....	....	....
1905-06	Ottawa Senators	ECAHA	1	0	0	0	0	....	....	....	....	....
	McGill University	MCHL	4	5	0	5	21	....	....	....	....	....
1906-07	McGill University	MCHL	3	2	0	2	8	....	....	....	....	....
1907-08	Montreal Victorias	ECAHA	10	5	0	5	33	....	....	....	....	....
1908-09	Ottawa Senators	ECHA	11	9	0	9	*74	....	....	....	....	....
1909-10			STATISTICS NOT AVAILABLE									
1910-11	Ottawa New Edinburgh	X-Games	STATISTICS NOT AVAILABLE									
1911-12	Ottawa Senators	NHA	2	1	0	1	0	....	....	....	....	....
	Major League Totals		24	15	0	15	107	....	....	....	....	....

MCHL First All-Star Team (1907) • ECAHA First All-Star Team (1908)

• GLASS, Pud Frank

LW – L. 5'10", 190 lbs. b: Kirk's Ferry, Scotland, 2/10/1884 d: 3/2/1965.

Season	Club	League	GP	G	A	Pts	PIM	GP	G	A	Pts	PIM
1902-03	Montreal St. Lawrence	MCSHL	STATISTICS NOT AVAILABLE									
1903-04	Montreal St. Charles	MCJHL	STATISTICS NOT AVAILABLE									
1904-05	Montreal Wanderers	FAHL	6	9	0	9	6	....	....	....	....	....
1905-06	Montreal Wanderers	ECAHA	10	10	0	10	12	....	....	....	....	....
♦	Montreal Wanderers	St-Cup	2	3	0	3	6	....	....	....	....	....
1906-07	Montreal Wanderers	ECAHA	10	14	0	14	11	....	....	....	....	....
♦	Montreal Wanderers	St-Cup	6	8	0	8	21	....	....	....	....	....
1907-08	Montreal Wanderers	ECAHA	9	3	0	3	23	....	....	....	....	....
♦	Montreal Wanderers	St-Cup	5	6	0	6	13	....	....	....	....	....
1908-09	Montreal Wanderers	ECHA	12	18	0	18	29	....	....	....	....	....
♦	Montreal Wanderers	St-Cup	2	*5	0	*5	11	....	....	....	....	....
1909-10	Montreal Wanderers	NHA	1	0	0	0	8	....	....	....	....	....
	Montreal Wanderers	NHA	12	15	0	15	38	....	....	....	....	....
♦	Montreal Wanderers	St-Cup	1	0	0	0	0	....	....	....	....	....
1910-11	Montreal Wanderers	NHA	16	17	0	17	31	....	....	....	....	....
1911-12	Montreal Canadiens	NHA	16	8	0	8	10	....	....	....	....	....
	Major League Totals		86	85	0	85	162	....	....	....	....	....

ECAHA Second All-Star Team (1908)

• GLAUDE, Gerry

D – L. 6'2", 225 lbs. b: Valleyfield, Que., 11/10/1927.

Season	Club	League	GP	G	A	Pts	PIM	GP	G	A	Pts	PIM
1946-47	Valleyfield Athletics	QAHA-I	STATISTICS NOT AVAILABLE									
	Valleyfield Braves	QSHL	2	0	0	0	0	....	....	....	....	....
1947-48	New York Rovers	QSHL	46	4	3	7	31	4	1	0	1	2
	New York Rovers	EAHL	17	2	4	6	17	....	....	....	....	....
1948-49	New Haven Ramblers	AHL	64	6	18	24	25	....	....	....	....	....
1949-50	Chicoutimi Sagueneens	QSHL	54	3	13	16	56	5	0	1	1	6
1950-51	Chicoutimi Sagueneens	QMHL	59	9	31	40	40	6	2	1	3	6
1951-52	Chicoutimi Sagueneens	QMHL	54	10	25	35	32	18	1	3	4	11
1952-53	Chicoutimi Sagueneens	QMHL	56	4	10	14	39	20	3	3	6	8
1953-54	Chicoutimi Sagueneens	QHL	65	12	30	42	28	7	1	1	2	2
1954-55	Chicoutimi Sagueneens	QHL	61	10	35	45	44	7	2	3	5	0
1955-56	Chicoutimi Sagueneens	QHL	51	8	32	40	58	5	0	3	3	0
1956-57	Chicoutimi Sagueneens	QHL	64	11	21	32	32	10	0	9	9	8
1957-58	Chicoutimi Sagueneens	QHL	35	8	13	21	23	6	0	1	1	4
1958-59	Chicoutimi Sagueneens	QHL	58	13	36	49	26	....	....	....	....	....
1959-60	Quebec Aces	AHL	64	5	19	24	27	....	....	....	....	....

Season	Club	League	GP	G	A	Pts	PIM	GP	G	A	Pts	PIM
			REGULAR SEASON					PLAYOFFS				
1960-61	Muskegon Zephyrs	IHL	70	12	47	59	28	13	3	7	10	4
1961-62	Muskegon Zephyrs	IHL	64	18	67	85	48	9	5	13	18	6
1962-63	Muskegon Zephyrs	IHL	70	15	*86	101	60	6	1	6	7	2

IHL First All-Star Team (1961, 1962, 1963)

• GOHEEN, Moose — Francis Xavier — USHOF HHOF

LW – L. 6', 220 lbs. b: White Bear Lake, MN, 2/8/1894 d: 11/13/1979.

Season	Club	League	GP	G	A	Pts	PIM	GP	G	A	Pts	PIM
1914-15	St. Paul A.C.	NMHL	STATISTICS NOT AVAILABLE									
1915-16	St. Paul A.C.	NMHL	STATISTICS NOT AVAILABLE									
1916-17	White Bear Lake Bears	NMHL	STATISTICS NOT AVAILABLE									
	St. Paul A.C.	X-Games	STATISTICS NOT AVAILABLE									
1917/19			STATISTICS NOT AVAILABLE									
1919-20	St. Paul A.C.	NMHL	STATISTICS NOT AVAILABLE									
	United States	Olympics	3	0	0	0	....	....				
1920-21	St. Paul A.C.	NMHL	STATISTICS NOT AVAILABLE									
1921-22	St. Paul A.C.	USAHA	STATISTICS NOT AVAILABLE									
1922-23	St. Paul Saints	USAHA	20	11	0	11	....	4	3	0	3	....
1923-24	St. Paul Saints	USAHA	20	10	4	14	....	8	1	*3	4	....
1924-25	St. Paul Saints	USAHA	32	6	0	6	....	....				
1925-26	St. Paul Saints	CHL	36	13	10	23	87	....				
1926-27	St. Paul Saints	AHA	27	2	7	9	40	....				
1927-28	St. Paul Saints	AHA	39	19	5	24	96	....				
1928-29	St. Paul Saints	AHA	28	7	4	11	39	8	2	0	2	*20
1929-30	St. Paul Saints	AHA	35	9	6	15	47	....				
1930-31	Buffalo Majors	AHA	2	0	0	0	0	....				
1931-32	St. Paul Saints	CHL	20	2	7	9	17	....				

• GRANT, Mike — HHOF

Point. b: Montreal, Que., 1874 Deceased.

Season	Club	League	GP	G	A	Pts	PIM	GP	G	A	Pts	PIM
1893-94	Montreal Maples	MCJHL	STATISTICS NOT AVAILABLE									
	Montreal Victorias	AHAC	5	0	0	0	....	1	0	0	0	....
1894-95	Montreal Victorias	AHAC	8	1	0	1	....	....				
1895-96	Montreal Victorias	AHAC	8	3	0	3	....	....				
♦	Montreal Victorias	St-Cup	2	0	0	0	....	....				
1896-97	Montreal Victorias	AHAC	8	3	0	3	....	....				
♦	Montreal Victorias	St-Cup	1	0	0	0	....	....				
♦1897-98	Montreal Victorias	AHAC	8	1	0	1	....	....				
1898-99	Montreal Victorias	CAHL	7	2	0	2	....	....				
♦	Montreal Victorias	St-Cup	2	0	0	0	....	....				
99-1900	Montreal Victorias	CAHL	2	0	0	0	....	....				
1900-01	Montreal Shamrocks	CAHL	2	0	0	0	....	....				
	Montreal Shamrocks	St-Cup	2	0	0	0	....	....				
1901-02	Montreal Victorias	CAHL	7	0	0	0	....	....				

• GRAY, John — John Gordon

RW – L. 5'10", 180 lbs. b: Little Current, Ont., 8/13/1949.

Season	Club	League	GP	G	A	Pts	PIM	GP	G	A	Pts	PIM
1970-71	U. of New Hampshire	ECAC	20	30	20	50	39	....				
1971-72	U. of New Hampshire	ECAC	30	*29	33	62	44	....				
1972-73	Tulsa Oilers	CHL	68	15	25	40	147	....				
1973-74	Oklahoma City Blazers	CHL	59	25	35	60	155	....				
1974-75	**Phoenix Roadrunners**	WHA	75	35	33	68	107	5	2	3	5	12
1975-76	**Phoenix Roadrunners**	WHA	79	35	45	80	136	5	1	1	2	7
1976-77	**Phoenix Roadrunners**	WHA	28	10	10	20	59	....				
	Houston Aeros	WHA	47	21	20	41	25	6	0	1	1	8
1977-78	**Houston Aeros**	WHA	77	35	23	58	80	6	0	3	3	10
1978-79	**Winnipeg Jets**	WHA	57	10	15	25	51	1	0	0	0	0
	Major League Totals		363	146	146	292	458	23	3	8	11	37

CHL Second All-Star Team (1974)

• GRIFFIS, Si — Silas Seth — HHOF

Point – L. 6'1", 195 lbs. b: Onega, KA, 9/22/1883 d: 7/9/1950.

Season	Club	League	GP	G	A	Pts	PIM	GP	G	A	Pts	PIM
1902-03	Rat Portage Thistles	MHL-Sr.	STATISTICS NOT AVAILABLE									
	Rat Portage Thistles	St-Cup	2	0	0	0	....					
1903-04	Rat Portage Thistles	MHL-Sr.	STATISTICS NOT AVAILABLE									
1904-05	Rat Portage Thistles	MHL-Sr.	8	15	0	15	3					
	Rat Portage Thistles	St-Cup	3	3	0	3	3					
1905-06	Kenora Thistles	MHL-Sr.	9	9	0	9	....					
1906-07	**Kenora Thistles**	Man-Pro	6	5	0	5	....					
♦	Kenora Thistles	St-Cup	4	1	0	1	6					
1907-09			DID NOT PLAY									
1909-10	Nelson Hockey Club	WKHL	STATISTICS NOT AVAILABLE									
1910-11			DID NOT PLAY									
1911-12	**Vancouver Millionaires**	PCHA	15	8	0	8	18	....				
1912-13	**Vancouver Millionaires**	PCHA	14	10	3	13	30	....				
1913-14	**Vancouver Millionaires**	PCHA	13	2	3	5	21	....				
♦1914-15	**Vancouver Millionaires**	PCHA	17	2	3	5	32	....				
	PCHA All-Stars	X-Games	2	0	0	0	0	....				
1915-16	**Vancouver Millionaires**	PCHA	18	7	5	12	12	....				
1916-17	**Vancouver Millionaires**	PCHA	23	7	4	11	34	....				
1917-18	**Vancouver Millionaires**	PCHA	8	2	6	8	0	7	1	0	1	9
1918-19	**Vancouver Millionaires**	PCHA	2	0	2	2	0	2	1	1	2	0
	Major League Totals		116	43	26	69	147	9	2	1	3	9

• HOLDEN, Barney

D – R. 6', 200 lbs. b: Winnipeg, Man., Deceased.

Season	Club	League	GP	G	A	Pts	PIM	GP	G	A	Pts	PIM
1904-05	**Portage Lakes**	IHL	24	9	0	9	47	....				
1905-06	**Portage Lakes**	IHL	20	9	0	9	31	....				
1906-07	**Winnipeg Strathconas**	Man-Pro	1	1	0	1	....	....				
	Portage Lakes	IHL	20	4	3	7	35	....				
1907-08	**Winnipeg Maple Leafs**	Man-Pro	15	4	0	4	....	....				
	Winnipeg Maple Leafs	St-Cup	2	0	0	0	2	....				
1908-09	**Winnipeg Maple Leafs**	Man-Pro	4	1	2	3	6	....				
	Winnipeg Maple Leafs	Man-Pro	5	2	2	4	3	2	1	0	1	0
1909-10	**Montreal Shamrocks**	CHA	3	1	0	1	....	....				
	Montreal Shamrocks	NHA	12	5	0	5	23	....				
1910-11	**Quebec Bulldogs**	NHA	16	4	0	4	40	....				
1911-12	Saskatoon Wholesalers	Ssk-Pro	7	6	0	6	....	....				
	Saskatoon Wholesalers	St-Cup	1	0	0	0	*12	....				
	Major League Totals		120	40	7	47	185	2	1	0	1	0

IHL Second All-Star Team (1905, 1906) • IHL First All-Star Team (1907)

• HOOPER, Tom — Charles Thomas — HHOF

Rover. 5'10", 175 lbs. b: Rat Portage, Ont., 11/24/1883 d: 3/23/1960.

Season	Club	League	GP	G	A	Pts	PIM	GP	G	A	Pts	PIM
1902-03	Rat Portage Thistles	MHL-Sr.	STATISTICS NOT AVAILABLE									
1903-04	Rat Portage Thistles	MHL-Sr.	STATISTICS NOT AVAILABLE									
1904-05	Kenora Thistles	MHL-Sr.	8	9	0	9	....	3	2	0	2	12
1905-06	Kenora Thistles	MHL-Sr.	9	4	0	4	....	....				
1906-07	**Kenora Thistles**	Man-Pro	3	4	0	4	....	....				
♦	Kenora Thistles	St-Cup	3	3	0	3	0	....				
1907-08	**Montreal AAA**	ECAHA	7	9	0	9	5	....				
	Pembroke Lumber	UOVHL	1	0	0	0	0	....				
	Montreal Wanderers	ECAHA	2	1	0	1	0	....				
♦	Montreal Wanderers	St-Cup	2	0	0	0	3	....				
	Major League Totals		12	14	0	14	5	....				

• HUCUL, Sandy — Alexander Kenneth

D – R. 6', 190 lbs. b: Eston, Sask., 12/5/1933.

Season	Club	League	GP	G	A	Pts	PIM	GP	G	A	Pts	PIM
1951-52	Moose Jaw Canucks	WCJHL	33	1	7	8	43	....				
1952-53	Moose Jaw Canucks	WCJHL	25	4	5	9	39	9	1	2	3	21
1953-54	Moose Jaw Canucks	WCJHL	36	6	16	22	68	5	0	0	0	2
1954-55	Kamloops Elks	OSHL	15	1	1	2	8	....				
	Calgary Stampeders	WHL	49	3	8	11	33	9	0	0	0	2
1955-56	Calgary Stampeders	WHL	70	5	20	25	110	8	0	0	0	8
1956-57	Calgary Stampeders	WHL	36	3	14	17	58	....				
	Buffalo Bisons	AHL	28	2	4	6	47	....				
1957-58	Calgary Stampeders	WHL	62	4	21	25	100	14	1	4	5	26
1958-59	Saskatoon Quakers	WHL	63	4	16	20	41	....				
1959-60	Vancouver Canucks	WHL	67	6	20	26	62	11	1	3	4	4
1960-61	Spokane Comets	WHL	62	6	24	30	83	4	2	1	3	2
1961-62	Spokane Comets	WHL	61	6	21	27	100	6	0	4	4	15
1962-63	Spokane Comets	WHL	68	7	24	31	85	....				
1963-64	Denver Invaders	WHL	66	7	23	30	85	6	1	2	3	10
1964-65	Victoria Maple Leafs	WHL	70	4	26	30	106	11	1	2	3	20
1965-66	Victoria Maple Leafs	WHL	68	5	22	27	92	14	1	4	5	28
1966-67	Victoria Maple Leafs	WHL	69	1	27	28	87	....				
1967-68	Phoenix Roadrunners	WHL	71	6	26	32	67	4	0	0	0	2
1968-69	Phoenix Roadrunners	WHL	49	2	17	19	46	....				
1969-70	Phoenix Roadrunners	WHL	63	8	21	29	38	....				
1970-71	Phoenix Roadrunners	WHL	56	3	17	20	46	10	1	2	3	8
1971-72	Phoenix Roadrunners	WHL	69	5	23	28	91	6	0	4	4	4
1972-73	Phoenix Roadrunners	WHL	DID NOT PLAY – COACHING									

WCJHL Second All-Star Team (1954) • WHL Second All-Star Team (1962, 1965, 1966) • WHL First All-Star Team (1964, 1968, 1972)

• IMLACH, Punch — George — HHOF

C – R. 5'8", 160 lbs. b: Toronto, Ont., 3/15/1918 d: 12/1/1987.

Season	Club	League	GP	G	A	Pts	PIM	GP	G	A	Pts	PIM
1935-36	Toronto Young Rangers	OHA-Jr.	8	0	0	0	2	2	0	0	0	0
1936-37	Toronto Young Rangers	OHA-Jr.	12	15	3	18	6	3	2	3	5	7
1937-38	Toronto Young Rangers	OHA-Jr.	11	4	4	8	4	3	6	0	6	0
1938-39	Toronto Goodyears	OHA-Sr.	17	14	13	27	8	1	2	0	2	0
	Toronto Goodyears	Al-Cup	1	0	0	0	0					
1939-40	Toronto Goodyears	OHA-Sr.	24	25	23	48	23	7	6	*6	12	6
	Toronto Goodyears	Al-Cup	4	1	4	5	2					
1940-41	Toronto Marlboros	OHA-Sr.	21	5	9	14	19	11	2	2	4	2
	Toronto Marlboros	Al-Cup	7	4	2	6	0					
	Toronto RCAF	TMHL	3	2	1	3	0	5	3	1	4	2
	Toronto Donnell-Mudge	TMHL	....	....	....	....	....	4	*5	3	*8	2
1941-42	Cornwall Flyers	QSHL	37	25	17	42	11	5	4	1	5	0
1942-43	Cornwall Army	QSHL	34	*24	23	*47	6	6	5	0	5	2
1943-45			MILITARY SERVICE									
1945-46	Quebec Aces	QSHL	40	19	21	40	14	6	2	2	4	2
1946-47	Quebec Aces	QSHL	33	10	28	38	20	1	0	0	0	0
1947-48	Quebec Aces	QSHL	42	21	20	41	44	10	2	6	8	8
1948-49	Quebec Aces	QSHL	50	26	26	52	32	3	3	1	4	0
1949-50	Quebec Aces	QMHL	DID NOT PLAY – COACHING									

• JOHNSON, Moose — Thomas Ernest — HHOF

D – L. 5'11", 185 lbs. b: Montreal, Que., 2/26/1886 d: 3/24/1963.

Season	Club	League	GP	G	A	Pts	PIM	GP	G	A	Pts	PIM
1902-03	Montreal St. Lawrence	MCHL	STATISTICS NOT AVAILABLE									
1903-04	Montreal AAA	CAHL	2	1	0	1	....	....				
	Montreal AAA-2	CAHL-I	STATISTICS NOT AVAILABLE									
1904-05	Montreal AAA	CAHL	9	8	0	8	9	....				
♦1905-06	**Montreal Wanderers**	ECAHA	10	12	0	12	44	2	1	0	1	3
♦1906-07	**Montreal Wanderers**	ECAHA	10	15	0	15	42	6	5	0	5	8
♦1907-08	**Montreal Wanderers**	ECAHA	10	9	0	9	33	5	*11	0	*11	*28
♦1908-09	**Montreal Wanderers**	ECHA	10	10	0	10	34	2	1	0	1	6
1909-10	**Montreal Wanderers**	NHA	1	0	0	0	6	....				
♦	**Montreal Wanderers**	NHA	12	7	0	7	41	1	0	0	0	9
1910-11	**Montreal Wanderers**	NHA	16	6	0	6	60	....				
1911-12	**New Westminster Royals**	PCHA	14	9	0	9	13	....				
	PCHA All-Stars	X-Games	3	1	0	1	10	....				
1912-13	**New Westminster Royals**	PCHA	13	7	3	10	15	....				
1913-14	**New Westminster Royals**	PCHA	16	3	5	8	27	....				
1914-15	**Portland Rosebuds**	PCHA	18	6	4	10	21	....				
	PCHA All-Stars	X-Games	2	0	0	0	0	....				
1915-16	**Portland Rosebuds**	PCHA	18	6	3	9	62	5	1	0	1	9
	PCHA All-Stars	X-Games	3	0	1	1	3	....				
1916-17	**Portland Rosebuds**	PCHA	24	12	9	21	54	....				
1917-18	**Portland Rosebuds**	PCHA	15	3	2	5	3	....				
1918-19	**Victoria Cougars**	PCHA	15	3	3	6	0	....				
1919-20	**Victoria Cougars**	PCHA	21	0	5	5	22	....				
1920-21	**Victoria Cougars**	PCHA	24	5	2	7	26	....				
1921-22	**Victoria Cougars**	PCHA	13	1	1	2	12	....				

Season	Club	League	REGULAR SEASON GP	G	A	Pts	PIM	PLAYOFFS GP	G	A	Pts	PIM
1922-25			OUT OF HOCKEY – RETIRED									
1925-26	L.A. Palais-de-Glace	Cal-Pro	STATISTICS NOT AVAILABLE									
1926-27	Minneapolis Millers	AHA	30	1	2	3	43	5	0	0	0	12
1927-28			OUT OF HOCKEY – RETIRED									
1928-29	Portland Buckaroos	PCHL	28	1	0	1	27	1	0	0	0	0
1929-30	Hollywood Millionaires	Cal-Pro	....	1	2	3	....	....	....	....	....	....
1930-31	San Francisco Tigers	Cal-Pro	....	10	6	16	....	....	....	....	....	....
	Major League Totals		**260**	**114**	**37**	**151**	**515**	**21**	**19**	**0**	**19**	**63**

ECAHA Second All-Star Team (1908) • PCHA First All-Star Team (1912, 1913, 1915, 1916, 1917, 1918, 1919, 1921)

• JONES, Art Art George

C – L. 5'10", 165 lbs. b: Bangor, Sask., 1/31/1935.

Season	Club	League	GP	G	A	Pts	PIM	GP	G	A	Pts	PIM
1954-55	Saskatoon Wesleys	SJHL	48	29	36	65	56	5	7	2	9	2
1955-56	Spokane Flyers	WIHL	50	*44	34	78	33	10	9	8	17	6
1956-57	Spokane Flyers	WIHL	48	*50	46	*96	55	9	6	7	13	2
1957-58	New Westminster Royals	WHL	69	29	37	66	26	4	2	2	4	6
1958-59	New Westminster Royals	WHL	60	22	52	74	34	....	....	....	....	....
1959-60	Victoria Cougars	WHL	70	35	44	79	30	11	4	4	8	4
1960-61	Portland Buckaroos	WHL	69	36	64	*100	22	14	*8	*10	*18	0
1961-62	Portland Buckaroos	WHL	70	38	48	86	12	7	2	5	7	0
1962-63	Portland Buckaroos	WHL	70	25	48	73	18	7	1	3	4	0
1963-64	Portland Buckaroos	WHL	67	36	51	87	10	5	2	4	6	0
1964-65	Portland Buckaroos	WHL	70	34	56	90	32	10	3	*9	12	6
1965-66	Portland Buckaroos	WHL	70	35	67	102	40	14	*10	9	19	16
1966-67	Portland Buckaroos	WHL	65	38	51	89	26	4	0	0	0	2
1967-68	Portland Buckaroos	WHL	70	34	53	*87	12	12	*7	*10	*17	12
1968-69	Portland Buckaroos	WHL	74	38	*76	*114	29	11	5	*9	*14	2
1969-70	Portland Buckaroos	WHL	71	43	*84	*127	16	9	7	8	15	8
1970-71	Portland Buckaroos	WHL	71	44	*70	*114	43	11	4	7	11	22
1971-72	Portland Buckaroos	WHL	70	38	*86	*124	34	11	3	6	9	0
1972-73	Portland Buckaroos	WHL	66	34	55	89	42	....	....	....	....	....
1973-74	Portland Buckaroos	WHL	78	19	60	79	32	10	1	4	5	18
1974-75	Seattle Totems	CHL	16	4	9	13	6	....	....	....	....	....
1975-76	Portland Buckaroos	WIHL	....	7	18	25	18	....	....	....	....	....

WHL Second All-Star Team (1960, 1961, 1964, 1967, 1970) • WHL First All-Star Team (1968, 1969, 1971, 1972) Won Leader Trophy as WHL MVP 1968, 1971)

• KILBURN, Colin David Colin

LW – L. 5'9", 178 lbs. b: Wilkie, Sask., 12/26/1927.

Season	Club	League	GP	G	A	Pts	PIM	GP	G	A	Pts	PIM
1945-46	Edmonton All-Stars	AAHA-I	STATISTICS NOT AVAILABLE									
1946-47	Edmonton Capitals	EJrHL	7	3	6	9	15	3	2	0	2	9
1948-49	Edmonton Flyers	WCSHL	47	24	37	61	85	9	2	3	5	12
1949-50	Edmonton Flyers	WCSHL	50	*51	29	*80	114	6	3	1	4	10
1950-51	Edmonton Flyers	WCMHL	57	32	42	74	122	8	4	4	8	4
1951-52	Edmonton Flyers	PCHL	63	31	37	68	73	4	2	1	3	12
1952-53	Victoria Cougars	WHL	67	34	40	74	106	....	....	....	....	....
1953-54	Victoria Cougars	WHL	70	22	36	58	45	5	1	3	4	10
1954-55	Victoria Cougars	WHL	70	23	47	70	73	5	1	2	3	4
1955-56	Victoria Cougars	WHL	70	43	38	81	86	9	2	5	7	21
1956-57	Victoria Cougars	WHL	70	32	39	71	76	3	0	1	1	4
1957-58	Victoria-Edmonton	WHL	70	28	54	82	108	....	....	....	....	....
1958-59	Springfield Indians	AHL	70	28	34	62	88	....	....	....	....	....
1959-60	Vancouver Canucks	WHL	70	23	47	70	79	11	5	6	11	11
1960-61	Spokane Comets	WHL	70	21	39	60	103	4	0	3	3	0
1961-62	Spokane Comets	WHL	68	20	41	61	88	16	5	10	15	38
1962/65	Spokane Comets	WHL	DID NOT PLAY – COACHING									
1965-66	Spokane Jets	WIHL	11	2	6	8	4	6	0	2	2	2
1966-67	Spokane Jets	WIHL	DID NOT PLAY – COACHING									
1967-68	Spokane Jets	WIHL	12	3	8	11	6	....	....	....	....	....
1968-69			OUT OF HOCKEY – RETIRED									
1969-70	Salem Rebels	EHL	2	0	1	1	2	....	....	....	....	....
1970-71	Salem Rebels	EHL	6	1	2	3	23	....	....	....	....	....

Named WCSHL Rookie-of-the-Year (1949) • Named WCSHL MVP (1950) • WCMHL First All-Star Team (1951)

• KING, Connie Conway Bertram

C – L. 5'8", 160 lbs. b: Provost, Alta., 1/16/1910.

Season	Club	League	GP	G	A	Pts	PIM	GP	G	A	Pts	PIM
1926-27	Asquith Juniors	N-SJHL	STATISTICS NOT AVAILABLE									
1927-28	Saskatoon Tigers	N-SJHL	3	4	0	4	0	....	....	....	....	....
	Saskatoon Tigers	N-SSHL	1	0	0	0	0	....	....	....	....	....
	Saskatoon Wesleys	M-Cup	4	3	0	3	2	....	....	....	....	....
1928-29	Drumheller Miners	ASHL	STATISTICS NOT AVAILABLE									
1929-30	Drumheller Miners	ASHL	16	9	5	14	3	2	1	0	1	2
1930-31	Philadelphia Arrows	Can-Am	38	8	4	12	34	....	....	....	....	....
1931-32	Philadelphia Arrows	Can-Am	38	14	11	25	31	....	....	....	....	....
1932-33	Boston Cubs	Can-Am	25	6	8	14	22	....	....	....	....	....
	New Haven Eagles	Can-Am	20	2	6	8	12	....	....	....	....	....
1933-34	Philadelphia Arrows	Can-Am	40	*30	15	*45	30	2	2	0	2	4
1934-35	Detroit Olympics	IHL	44	11	16	27	6	5	2	*4	6	0
1935-36	Windsor Bulldogs	IHL	48	11	18	29	9	8	2	2	4	0
1936-37	Spokane Clippers	PCHL	39	13	14	27	25	6	0	0	0	0
1937-38	Spokane Clippers	PCHL	42	*24	17	*41	16	....	....	....	....	....
1938-39	Spokane Clippers	PCHL	47	21	*41	62	13	....	....	....	....	....
1939-40	Seattle Seahawks	PCHL	39	22	18	40	11	....	....	....	....	....
1940-41	Tulsa Oilers	AHA	48	15	24	39	2	....	....	....	....	....
1941-42	Fort Worth Rangers	AHA	50	34	*44	*78	11	5	5	5	10	0
1942-43	Nanaimo Clippers	NWIHL	16	27	13	40	0	3	0	1	1	0
1943-44	New Westminster Royals	NWIHL	19	25	11	36	10	2	0	2	2	0
	Portland Decleros	NNDHL	2	2	3	5	7	....	....	....	....	....
	New Westminster Royals	Al-Cup	10	13	9	22	0	....	....	....	....	....

• KIRK, Gavin

C – L. 5'10", 165 lbs. b: London, England, 12/6/1951.
Toronto's 3rd, 37th overall in 1971.

Season	Club	League	GP	G	A	Pts	PIM	GP	G	A	Pts	PIM
1968-69	Markham Waxers	OHA-B	27	24	22	46	....	....	....	....	....	....
1969-70	Toronto Marlboros	OHA-Jr.	53	17	33	50	40	18	6	12	18	28
1970-71	Toronto Marlboros	OHA-Jr.	62	38	69	107	101	13	5	14	19	8
1971-72	Loyola College	QUAA	29	24	41	65	48	....	....	....	....	....
	Phoenix Roadrunners	WHL	3	1	2	3	2	....	....	....	....	....
1972-73	**Ottawa Nationals**	**WHA**	**78**	**28**	**40**	**68**	**54**	**5**	**2**	**3**	**5**	**12**
1973-74	**Toronto Toros**	**WHA**	**78**	**20**	**48**	**68**	**44**	**12**	**2**	**4**	**6**	**4**
1974-75	**Toronto Toros**	**WHA**	**78**	**15**	**58**	**73**	**69**	**6**	**5**	**6**	**11**	**2**
1975-76	**Toronto Toros**	**WHA**	**62**	**29**	**38**	**67**	**32**	....	....	....	....	....
	Calgary Cowboys	**WHA**	**15**	**7**	**8**	**15**	**14**	**10**	**4**	**6**	**10**	**19**
1976-77	**Birmingham Bulls**	**WHA**	**29**	**9**	**18**	**27**	**34**	....	....	....	....	....
	Edmonton Oilers	**WHA**	**52**	**8**	**28**	**36**	**16**	**5**	**1**	**0**	**1**	**4**
1977-78	Philadelphia Firebirds	AHL	59	21	26	47	32	4	0	1	1	2
1978-79	**Birmingham Bulls**	**WHA**	**30**	**1**	**5**	**6**	**27**	....	....	....	....	....
	Major League Totals		**422**	**117**	**243**	**360**	**290**	**38**	**14**	**19**	**33**	**41**

QUAA First All-Star Team (1972)

• LAKE, Fred Fred Edgar

LW/D – R. 5'7", 175 lbs. b: Moosomin, Sask., 1882 d: 12/1/1937.

Season	Club	League	GP	G	A	Pts	PIM	GP	G	A	Pts	PIM
1901-02	Winnipeg Winnipegs	WSrHL	STATISTICS NOT AVAILABLE									
1902-03	**Pittsburgh Keystones**	**WPHL**	**5**	**1**	**1**	**2**	**4**	....	....	....	....	....
	Portage Lakes	X-Games	2	8	0	8	....	2	1	0	1	....
1903-04	American Soo	X-Games	20	27	0	27	....	3	1	0	1	2
1904-05	**Portage Lakes**	**IHL**	**24**	**14**	**0**	**14**	**16**	....	....	....	....	....
1905-06	**Portage Lakes**	**IHL**	**20**	**25**	**0**	**25**	**13**	....	....	....	....	....
1906-07	**Portage Lakes**	**IHL**	**23**	**27**	**6**	**33**	**40**	....	....	....	....	....
1907-08	**Winnipeg Strathconas**	**Man-Pro**	**14**	**23**	**0**	**23**	....	....	....	....	....	....
	Winnipeg Maple Leafs	**Man-Pro**	**1**	**0**	**0**	**0**	**0**	....	....	....	....	....
	Winnipeg Maple Leafs	St-Cup	2	2	0	2	5	....	....	....	....	....
1908-09	Pittsburgh Professionals	WPHL	3	3	0	3	....	....	....	....	....	....
	Ottawa Senators	**ECHA**	**12**	**6**	**0**	**6**	**33**	....	....	....	....	....
♦	Ottawa Senators	St-Cup	2	0	0	0	5	....	....	....	....	....
1909-10	**Ottawa Senators**	**CHA**	**2**	**3**	**0**	**3**	**4**	....	....	....	....	....
	Ottawa Senators	**NHA**	**11**	**6**	**0**	**6**	**18**	....	....	....	....	....
♦	Ottawa Senators	St-Cup	4	2	0	2	0	....	....	....	....	....
1910-11	**Ottawa Senators**	**NHA**	**16**	**5**	**0**	**5**	**12**	....	....	....	....	....
♦	Ottawa Senators	St-Cup	2	1	0	1	0	....	....	....	....	....
1911-12	**Ottawa Senators**	**NHA**	**18**	**7**	**0**	**7**	**0**	....	....	....	....	....
1912-13	**Ottawa Senators**	**NHA**	**13**	**4**	**0**	**4**	**13**	....	....	....	....	....
1913-14	**Toronto Ontarios**	**NHA**	**20**	**4**	**4**	**8**	**23**	....	....	....	....	....
1914-15	**Ottawa Senators**	**NHA**	**2**	**0**	**0**	**0**	**0**	....	....	....	....	....
	Major League Totals		**181**	**125**	**11**	**136**	**176**	....	....	....	....	....

IHL First All-Star Team (1906, 1907)

• LUND, Larry

C – R. 6', 190 lbs. b: Penticton, B.C., 9/9/1940.

Season	Club	League	GP	G	A	Pts	PIM	GP	G	A	Pts	PIM
1960-61	Edmonton Oil Kings	CAHL	STATISTICS NOT AVAILABLE									
1961-62	Muskegon Zephyrs	IHL	64	29	26	55	92	9	2	3	5	6
1962-63	Muskegon Zephyrs	IHL	70	13	38	51	69	6	3	2	5	12
1963-64	San Francisco Seals	WHL	67	2	11	13	19	11	1	0	1	4
1964-65	San Francisco Seals	WHL	37	8	12	20	28	....	....	....	....	....
	Minneapolis Bruins	CPHL	37	30	17	47	26	....	....	....	....	....
1965-66	Seattle Totems	WHL	69	24	31	55	56	....	....	....	....	....
1966-67	Seattle Totems	WHL	72	34	38	72	74	10	5	6	*11	4
1967-68	Seattle Totems	WHL	68	16	37	53	96	9	2	5	7	15
1968-69	Quebec Aces	AHL	9	1	2	3	2	....	....	....	....	....
	Seattle Totems	WHL	58	7	14	21	49	4	0	1	1	4
1969-70	Phoenix Roadrunners	WHL	68	33	40	73	54	....	....	....	....	....
1970-71	Phoenix Roadrunners	WHL	69	29	63	92	147	10	*8	6	*14	16
1971-72	Phoenix Roadrunners	WHL	66	30	66	96	149	6	3	3	6	4
1972-73	**Houston Aeros**	**WHA**	**77**	**21**	**45**	**66**	**120**	**10**	**3**	**7**	**10**	**24**
1973-74	**Houston Aeros**	**WHA**	**75**	**33**	**53**	**86**	**109**	**14**	**9**	***14**	***23**	**56**
1974-75	**Houston Aeros**	**WHA**	**78**	**33**	**75**	**108**	**68**	**13**	**5**	***13**	**18**	**13**
1975-76	**Houston Aeros**	**WHA**	**73**	**24**	**49**	**73**	**50**	**5**	**1**	**1**	**2**	**4**
1976-77	**Houston Aeros**	**WHA**	**80**	**29**	**38**	**67**	**36**	**11**	**2**	**8**	**10**	**17**
1977-78	**Houston Aeros**	**WHA**	**76**	**9**	**17**	**26**	**36**	**6**	**0**	**2**	**2**	**2**
	Major League Totals		**459**	**149**	**277**	**426**	**419**	**59**	**20**	**45**	**65**	**116**

• MACFARLAND, Bill William Herbert

LW – L. 6'1", 190 lbs. b: Toronto, Ont., 4/4/1932.

Season	Club	League	GP	G	A	Pts	PIM	GP	G	A	Pts	PIM
1950-51	Toronto Marlboros	OHA-Jr.	47	17	24	41	30	13	1	6	7	8
1951-52	Toronto Marlboros	OHA-Jr.	41	12	14	26	18	2	0	0	0	0
1952-53	U. of Michigan	WCHA	DID NOT PLAY – FRESHMAN									
	Sarnia Sailors	OHA-Sr.	18	9	13	22	4	....	....	....	....	....
1953-54	U. of Michigan	WCHA	....	26	17	43	40	....	....	....	....	....
1954-55	U. of Michigan	WCHA	....	33	24	57	63	....	....	....	....	....
1955-56	U. of Michigan	WCHA	....	19	*28	47	45	....	....	....	....	....
1956-57	Edmonton Flyers	WHL	70	16	33	49	39	6	0	0	0	0
1957-58	Seattle Totems	WHL	70	31	28	59	57	9	2	5	7	9
1958-59	Seattle Totems	WHL	68	35	40	75	43	12	6	*11	17	4
1959-60	Seattle Totems	WHL	70	35	51	86	36	4	2	1	3	0
1960-61	Seattle Totems	WHL	70	40	55	95	24	11	6	8	14	10
1961-62	Seattle Totems	WHL	70	*46	35	81	60	2	1	0	1	0
1962-63	Seattle Totems	WHL	66	26	32	58	40	17	6	16	*22	34
1963-64	Seattle Totems	WHL	69	34	37	71	25	....	....	....	....	....
1964-65	Seattle Totems	WHL	70	21	31	52	33	7	2	2	4	4
1965-66	Seattle Totems	WHL	72	31	35	66	22	....	....	....	....	....
1966-67	Seattle Totems	WHL	1	0	0	0	0	....	....	....	....	....

WCHA Second All-Star Team (1955) • WCHA First All-Star Team (1956) • WHL Second All-Star Team (1960, 1964) • Won Leader Trophy (WHL - MVP) (1962)

• MacPHERSON, Alex "Shrimp"

C – L. 5'4", 155 lbs. b: Inverness, Scotland, 3/14/1908.

Season	Club	League	GP	G	A	Pts	PIM	GP	G	A	Pts	PIM
			REGULAR SEASON					PLAYOFFS				
1923-24	Toronto Aura Lee	OHA-Jr.	9	7	*5	12	2	3	1	1	2	2
	Toronto Aura Lee	OHA-Sr.	1	0	0	0	0	....	....	....	....	....
1924-25	Toronto Aura Lee	OHA-Jr.	7	*11	7	18	....	2	*2	*2	*4	....
	Toronto Aura Lee	M-Cup	13	25	11	36	....	....	....	....	....	....
1925-26	London Ravens	OHA-Sr.	20	15	6	21	2	2	2	0	2	0
1926-27	Toronto Stockyards	TMHL	STATISTICS NOT AVAILABLE									
1927-28	Toronto Marlboros	OHA-Jr.	6	7	*9	*16	....	2	*3	1	*4	....
	Toronto Marlboros	OHA-Sr.	1	1	1	2	0	....	....	....	....	....
1928-29	Willowdale Willows	OHA-I	STATISTICS NOT AVAILABLE									
1929-30	Tulsa Oilers	AHA	31	14	5	19	18	9	1	1	2	2
1930-31	Detroit Olympics	IHL	45	8	4	12	18	....	....	....	....	....
1931-32	St. Louis Flyers	AHA	48	*21	5	26	14	....	....	....	....	....
1932-33	St. Louis Flyers	AHA	43	20	8	28	23	4	2	*3	*5	4
1933-34	St. Louis Flyers	AHA	47	18	*15	33	29	7	1	*3	*4	2
1934-35	St. Louis Flyers	AHA	48	21	*34	*55	21	3	3	4	*7	0
1935-36	St. Louis Flyers	AHA	48	17	18	35	18	8	2	*3	5	9
1936-37	Tulsa Oilers	AHA	29	1	7	8	2	....	....	....	....	....
	Wichita Skyhawks	AHA	17	6	7	13	0	....	....	....	....	....
1937-38	Wichita Skyhawks	AHA	48	14	*37	51	4	4	1	0	1	2
1938-39	Wichita Skyhawks	AHA	7	0	6	6	0	....	....	....	....	....
	Kansas City Greyhounds	AHA	8	0	1	1	0	....	....	....	....	....
1939-40	Kansas City Greyhounds	AHA	23	6	13	19	0	....	....	....	....	....

AHA Second All-Star Team (1935)

• MALLEN, Ken

RW – L. 5'8", 160 lbs. b: Morrisburg, Ont., 10/4/1884 d: 4/23/1930.

Season	Club	League	GP	G	A	Pts	PIM	GP	G	A	Pts	PIM
1903-04	Cornwall Kolts	FAHL	4	9	0	9	0	....	....	....	....	....
	Montreal Wanderers	FAHL	2	1	0	1	0	1	1	0	1	0
1904-05	**Calumet Wanderers**	**IHL**	**24**	**38**	**0**	**38**	**8**	....	....	....	....	....
1905-06	**Calumet Wanderers**	**IHL**	**5**	**4**	**0**	**4**	**7**	....	....	....	....	....
1906-07	Morrisburg Athletics	FAHL	5	6	0	6	6	....	....	....	....	....
	Calumet Wanderers	**IHL**	**11**	**13**	**2**	**15**	**12**	....	....	....	....	....
1907-08	Toronto Professionals	OPHL	3	2	0	2	0	....	....	....	....	....
	Montreal AAA	**ECAHA**	**7**	**10**	**0**	**10**	**8**	....	....	....	....	....
1908-09	Pittsburgh PAC	WPHL	10	12	0	12	....	....	....	....	....	....
	Renfrew Creamery Kings	FAHL	3	4	0	4	2	....	....	....	....	....
1909-10	**Ottawa Senators**	**CHA**	**1**	**2**	**0**	**2**	**0**	....	....	....	....	....
♦	**Ottawa Senators**	**NHA**	**1**	**2**	**0**	**2**	**3**	**2**	**0**	**0**	**0**	**3**
1910-11	**Quebec Bulldogs**	**NHA**	**12**	**13**	**0**	**13**	**15**	....	....	....	....	....
1911-12	**New Westminster Royals**	**PCHA**	**13**	**14**	**0**	**14**	**30**	....	....	....	....	....
1912-13	**New Westminster Royals**	**PCHA**	**10**	**4**	**3**	**7**	**28**	....	....	....	....	....
1913-14	**New Westminster Royals**	**PCHA**	**16**	**20**	**6**	**26**	**46**	....	....	....	....	....
1914-15	**Vancouver Millionaires**	**PCHA**	**14**	**9**	**5**	**14**	**45**	....	....	....	....	....
♦	Vancouver Millionaires	St-Cup	2	0	0	0	0	....	....	....	....	....
1915-16	**Victoria Aristocrats**	**PCHA**	**18**	**7**	**5**	**12**	**31**	....	....	....	....	....
1916-17	**Spokane Canaries**	**PCHA**	**23**	**10**	**3**	**13**	**24**	....	....	....	....	....
	Major League Totals		**155**	**146**	**24**	**170**	**257**	**2**	**0**	**0**	**0**	**3**

IHL First All-Star Team (1905)

• MANTHA, Moe Sr. Maurice Roland

D – R. 6'1", 185 lbs. b: North Bay, Ont., 12/13/1933.

Season	Club	League	GP	G	A	Pts	PIM	GP	G	A	Pts	PIM
1952-53	Galt Black Hawks	OHA-Jr.	54	9	10	19	78	11	0	4	4	15
1953-54	Galt Black Hawks	OHA-Jr.	13	1	2	3	14	....	....	....	....	....
	Quebec Frontenacs	QJHL	42	6	19	25	137	3	1	0	1	10
1954-55	Cincinnati Mohawks	IHL	60	10	22	32	88	10	2	2	4	18
1955-56	Cincinnati Mohawks	IHL	60	12	29	41	104	8	0	1	1	2
1956-57	Cincinnati Mohawks	IHL	54	6	19	25	59	7	4	2	6	8
	Hull-Ottawa Canadiens	QHL	2	0	0	0	2	....	....	....	....	....
1957-58	Montreal Royals	QHL	53	3	18	21	90	6	0	2	2	4
1958-59	Montreal Royals	QHL	61	12	32	44	80	8	1	4	5	15
1959-60	Montreal Royals	EPHL	57	10	29	39	69	14	1	5	6	4
1960-61	Cleveland Barons	AHL	72	7	20	27	88	4	0	1	1	9
1961-62	Quebec Aces	AHL	52	7	16	23	56	....	....	....	....	....
1962-63	San Francisco Seals	WHL	66	19	30	49	58	16	5	7	12	28
1963-64	San Francisco Seals	WHL	70	13	32	45	59	11	3	9	12	12
1964-65	Seattle Totems	WHL	57	7	19	26	50	7	1	2	3	10
1965-66	Vancouver Canucks	WHL	43	1	8	9	28	....	....	....	....	....
1966-67	California Seals	WHL	68	8	24	32	43	3	0	0	0	0
1967-68	Providence Reds	AHL	70	8	27	35	56	7	2	1	3	8
1968-69	Providence Reds	AHL	74	4	18	22	42	9	0	8	8	12
1969-70	Columbus Owls	IHL	55	12	33	45	93	....	....	....	....	....

IHL First All-Star Team (1957) • QHL Second All-Star Team (1959)• EPHL First All-Star Team (1960) • WHL Second All-Star Team (1963)

• MARRIN, Peter

C – R. 5'10", b: Toronto, Ont., 8/8/1953.
Montreal's 3rd, 22nd overall in 1973.

Season	Club	League	GP	G	A	Pts	PIM	GP	G	A	Pts	PIM
1970-71	Markham Waxers	OHA-B	STATISTICS NOT AVAILABLE									
	Toronto Marlboros	OHA-Jr.	14	2	2	4	2	....	....	....	....	....
1971-72	Toronto Marlboros	OHA-Jr.	43	14	29	43	21	10	3	3	6	2
1972-73	Toronto Marlboros	OHA-Jr.	59	42	64	106	26	....	....	....	....	....
1973-74	**Toronto Toros**	**WHA**	**31**	**1**	**4**	**5**	**4**	**3**	**0**	**1**	**1**	**0**
	Mohawk Valley Comets	NAHL	24	7	16	23	2	....	....	....	....	....
1974-75	Mohawk Valley Comets	NAHL	54	33	45	78	36	....	....	....	....	....
	Toronto Toros	**WHA**	**4**	**3**	**1**	**4**	**0**	**6**	**0**	**4**	**4**	**2**
1975-76	**Toronto Toros**	**WHA**	**64**	**22**	**16**	**38**	**16**	....	....	....	....	....
1976-77	**Birmingham Bulls**	**WHA**	**79**	**23**	**37**	**60**	**36**	....	....	....	....	....
1977-78	**Birmingham Bulls**	**WHA**	**80**	**28**	**43**	**71**	**53**	**5**	**0**	**3**	**3**	**2**
1978-79	**Birmingham Bulls**	**WHA**	**20**	**4**	**11**	**15**	**18**	....	....	....	....	....
1979-80	Syracuse Firebirds	AHL	5	0	2	2	4	....	....	....	....	....
	Birmingham Bulls	CHL	25	3	5	8	4	4	1	0	1	0
1980-81	Hershey Bears	AHL	67	16	39	55	24	9	3	1	4	4
1981-82	Fredericton Express	AHL	54	5	29	34	18	....	....	....	....	....
	Major League Totals		**278**	**81**	**112**	**193**	**127**	**14**	**0**	**8**	**8**	**4**

• MARSHALL, Jack Jack Calder HHOF

C. 5'9", 160 lbs. b: Vallier, Que., 3/14/1877 d: 8/7/1965.

Season	Club	League	GP	G	A	Pts	PIM	GP	G	A	Pts	PIM
1894-98	Montreal Pointe Charles	H.S.	STATISTICS NOT AVAILABLE									
1898-99	Winnipeg Victorias	WPSHL	STATISTICS NOT AVAILABLE									
99-1900	Winnipeg Victorias	WPSHL	STATISTICS NOT AVAILABLE									
1900-01	Winnipeg Victorias	WPSHL	STATISTICS NOT AVAILABLE									
♦	Winnipeg Victorias	St-Cup	2	0	0	0	....					
1901-02	Montreal AAA	CAHL	8	11	0	11	8	....	....	....	....	....
♦	Montreal AAA	St-Cup	3	2	0	2	8	....	....	....	....	....
1902-03	Montreal AAA	CAHL	2	8	0	8	3	....	....	....	....	....
♦	Montreal AAA	St-Cup	4	7	0	7	2	....	....	....	....	....
1903-04	Montreal Wanderers	FAHL	4	*11	0	*11	6	....	....	....	....	....
	Montreal Wanderers	St-Cup	1	1	0	1	0	....	....	....	....	....
1904-05	Montreal Wanderers	FAHL	8	*17	0	*17	9	....	....	....	....	....
1905-06	Toronto Pros	X-Games	STATISTICS NOT AVAILABLE									
1906-07	Ottawa Montagnards	FAHL	3	6	0	6	....	....	....	....	....	....
	Montreal Wanderers	**ECAHA**	**3**	**6**	**0**	**6**	**0**	....	....	....	....	....
♦	Montreal Wanderers	St-Cup	1	1	0	1	0	....	....	....	....	....
1907-08	**Montreal Shamrocks**	**ECAHA**	**9**	**20**	**0**	**20**	**13**	....	....	....	....	....
1908-09	**Montreal Shamrocks**	**ECHA**	**12**	**10**	**0**	**10**	**14**	....	....	....	....	....
1909-10	**Montreal Wanderers**	**NHA**	**1**	**0**	**0**	**0**	**0**	....	....	....	....	....
	Montreal Wanderers	**NHA**	**11**	**2**	**0**	**2**	**8**	....	....	....	....	....
♦	Montreal Wanderers	St-Cup	1	0	0	0	0	....	....	....	....	....
1910-11	**Montreal Wanderers**	**NHA**	**5**	**1**	**0**	**1**	**2**	....	....	....	....	....
1911-12	**Montreal Wanderers**	**NHA**	**3**	**0**	**0**	**0**	**0**	....	....	....	....	....
1912-13	**Toronto Blueshirts**	**NHA**	**13**	**3**	**0**	**3**	**8**	....	....	....	....	....
1913-14	**Toronto Blueshirts**	**NHA**	**20**	**3**	**3**	**6**	**16**	**2**	**0**	**0**	**0**	**0**
♦	Toronto Blueshirts	St-Cup	3	1	0	1	0	....	....	....	....	....
1914-15	**Toronto Blueshirts**	**NHA**	**4**	**0**	**1**	**1**	**8**	....	....	....	....	....
1915-16	**Montreal Wanderers**	**NHA**	**15**	**1**	**0**	**1**	**2**	....	....	....	....	....
1916-17	**Montreal Wanderers**	**NHA**	**8**	**0**	**0**	**0**	**3**	....	....	....	....	....
	Major League Totals		**104**	**46**	**4**	**50**	**74**	**2**	**0**	**0**	**0**	**0**

• MATTHEWS, Ron Ronald Otto "Laddy"

D – R. 5'11", 175 lbs. b: Winnipeg, Man., 1/9/1927.

Season	Club	League	GP	G	A	Pts	PIM	GP	G	A	Pts	PIM
1943-44	Stratford Kroehlers	OHA-Jr.	1	0	1	1	2	....	....	....	....	....
	Toronto Marlboros	OHA-Jr.	22	5	3	8	20	....	....	....	....	....
1944-45	Oshawa Generals	OHA-Jr.	20	0	9	9	15	3	3	1	4	2
	St. Catharines Teepees	OHA-Jr.	....	....	....	....	....	3	0	0	0	0
1945-46	Edmonton Canadians	EJrHL	STATISTICS NOT AVAILABLE									
1946-47	Edmonton Canadians	EJrHL	6	4	3	7	14	3	1	1	2	2
1947-48	Hershey Bears	AHL	16	0	0	0	2	....	....	....	....	....
	Tulsa Oilers	USHL	43	0	2	2	18	2	0	0	0	0
1948-49	Oakland Oaks	PCHL	62	4	8	12	32	3	0	1	1	0
1949-50	Sydney Millionaires	CBSHL	72	14	21	35	60	5	3	3	6	0
	North Sydney Victorias	CBSHL	1	0	0	0	0	....	....	....	....	....
	Sydney Millionaires	Al-Cup	9	2	4	6	12	....	....	....	....	....
1950-51	Sydney Millionaires	CBMHL	74	18	30	48	81	3	0	3	3	2
	Sydney Millionaires	Alx-Cup	12	2	4	6	19	....	....	....	....	....
1951-52	Sydney Millionaires	MMHL	70	18	20	38	20	....	....	....	....	....
	Moncton Hawks	MMHL	17	6	5	11	16	....	....	....	....	....
1952-53	Sherbrooke Saints	QMHL	59	7	23	30	22	7	2	3	5	8
1953-54	New Westminster Royals	WHL	69	9	25	34	30	7	2	1	3	4
1954-55	New Westminster Royals	WHL	59	13	16	29	20	....	....	....	....	....
1955-56	New Westminster Royals	WHL	69	9	32	41	38	4	0	1	1	4
1956-57	New Westminster Royals	WHL	60	9	20	29	40	13	1	6	7	23
1957-58	New Westminster Royals	WHL	70	11	40	51	46	4	0	2	2	4
1958-59	New Westminster Royals	WHL	68	9	35	44	44	....	....	....	....	....
1959-60	Victoria Cougars	WHL	70	11	36	47	40	11	2	3	5	4
1960-61	Portland Buckaroos	WHL	70	15	36	51	22	14	1	8	9	2
1961-62	Portland Buckaroos	WHL	70	14	40	54	22	7	2	3	5	2
1962-63	Vancouver Canucks	WHL	70	8	35	43	53	7	1	4	5	2
1963-64	Vancouver Canucks	WHL	70	7	31	38	60	....	....	....	....	....
1964-65	Vancouver Canucks	WHL	70	15	35	50	42	5	2	1	3	6
1965-66	Vancouver Canucks	WHL	70	5	13	18	107	7	1	6	7	0

CBSHL First All-Star Team (1950) • WHL First All-Star Team (1958) WHL Second All-Star Team • (1961, 1962, 1963)

• MAVETY, Larry Lawrence Douglas

D – R. 5'11", 185 lbs. b: Woodstock, Ont., 5/29/1942.

Season	Club	League	GP	G	A	Pts	PIM	GP	G	A	Pts	PIM
1960-61	St. Catharines Blackhawks	OHA-Jr.	6	0	0	0	4	....	....	....	....	....
1961-62	Belleville Bobcats	OHA-B	34	14	30	44	132	....	....	....	....	....
1962-63	Timmins Flyers	NOHA	5	0	3	3	8	....	....	....	....	....
1963-64	Toledo Blades	IHL	70	6	14	20	133	13	1	1	2	16
1964-65	Syracuse Stars	X-Games	STATISTICS NOT AVAILABLE									
	Port Huron Flags	IHL	23	4	14	18	61	7	0	1	1	6
1965-66	Port Huron Flags	IHL	69	19	43	62	141	9	3	9	12	28
1966-67	Port Huron Flags	IHL	71	25	48	73	169	....	....	....	....	....
1967-68	Vancouver Canucks	WHL	72	2	23	25	148	....	....	....	....	....
1968-69	Denver Spurs	WHL	74	5	28	33	142	....	....	....	....	....
1969-70	Denver Spurs	WHL	72	10	47	57	123	....	....	....	....	....
1970-71	Denver Spurs	WHL	71	18	45	63	100	5	0	4	4	2
1971-72	Salt Lake Golden Eagles	WHL	62	15	38	53	114	....	....	....	....	....
1972-73	**Los Angeles Sharks**	**WHA**	**2**	**1**	**0**	**1**	**2**	....	....	....	....	....
	Philadelphia Blazers	**WHA**	**4**	**0**	**0**	**0**	**14**	....	....	....	....	....
	Chicago Cougars	**WHA**	**67**	**9**	**40**	**49**	**73**	....	....	....	....	....
1973-74	**Chicago Cougars**	**WHA**	**77**	**15**	**36**	**51**	**157**	**18**	**4**	**8**	**12**	**46**
1974-75	**Chicago Cougars**	**WHA**	**57**	**10**	**22**	**32**	**126**	....	....	....	....	....
	Long Island Cougars	NAHL	4	2	0	2	4	....	....	....	....	....
	Toronto Toros	**WHA**	**17**	**0**	**9**	**9**	**24**	**6**	**0**	**3**	**3**	**6**
1975-76	**Denver Spurs**	**WHA**	**14**	**0**	**4**	**4**	**14**	....	....	....	....	....
	Erie Blades	NAHL	24	7	17	24	30	....	....	....	....	....
	Binghamton Dusters	NAHL	31	14	22	36	50	....	....	....	....	....
1976-77	**Indianapolis Racers**	**WHA**	**10**	**2**	**2**	**4**	**8**	....	....	....	....	....
	Binghamton Dusters	NAHL	59	16	51	67	83	10	1	9	10	4
1977-78	Brantford Redmen	OHA-Sr.	39	9	31	40	36	....	....	....	....	....
	Major League Totals		**248**	**37**	**113**	**150**	**418**	**24**	**4**	**11**	**15**	**52**

IHL Second All-Star Team (1966) • IHL First All-Star Team (1967) • WHL Second All-Star Team (1970, 1971)

• McDONALD, Ran Ranald J.

RW – R. 5'8", 170 lbs. b: Cashion's Glen, Ont., 11/21/1889 d: 1950.

Season	Club	League	GP	G	A	Pts	PIM	GP	G	A	Pts	PIM
			REGULAR SEASON					PLAYOFFS				
1907-08	Port Arthur Royals	TBSHL	....	....	....	....	....	....	....	....	....	....
	Fort William Arenas	NOHL	1	0	0	0	0	....	....	....	....	....
1908-09	Fort William Forts	NOHL	12	6	0	6	....	2	0	0	0	....
1909-10	Fort William Forts	NOHL	10	12	0	12	50	....	....	....	....	....
	Rossland Rockies	WKHL	STATISTICS NOT AVAILABLE									
1910-11	Rossland Rockies	WKHL	STATISTICS NOT AVAILABLE									
	Port Arthur North Stars	NOHL	7	8	0	8	6	....	....	....	....	....
1911-12	New Westminster Royals	PCHA	15	16	0	16	56	....	....	....	....	....
	PCHA All-Stars	X-Games	3	3	0	3	0	....	....	....	....	....
1912-13	New Westminster Royals	PCHA	12	11	3	14	29	....	....	....	....	....
1913-14	New Westminster Royals	PCHA	16	15	5	20	34	....	....	....	....	....
1914-15	Portland Rosebuds	PCHA	18	22	7	29	24	....	....	....	....	....
	PCHA All-Stars	X-Games	1	2	0	2	0	....	....	....	....	....
1915-16	Victoria Aristocrats	PCHA	16	10	3	13	32	....	....	....	....	....
1916-17	Spokane Canaries	PCHA	23	13	9	22	23	....	....	....	....	....
1917-18	Vancouver Millionaires	PCHA	11	2	1	3	6	....	....	....	....	....
	Vancouver Millionaires	St-Cup	3	2	1	3	9	....	....	....	....	....
1918-19	Seattle Metropolitans	PCHA	11	2	1	3	6	2	1	1	2	3
	Seattle Metropolitans	St-Cup	5	1	1	2	3	....	....	....	....	....
1919-20			DID NOT PLAY									
1920-21	Edmonton Dominions	Big-4	4	2	1	3	2	....	....	....	....	....
	Major League Totals		152	117	29	146	266	4	1	1	2	3

PCHA First All-Star Team (1912, 1913, 1914) • PCHA Second All-Star Team (1916)

• McGEE, Frank

Rover/Center. 5'6", 150 lbs. b: Ottawa, Ont., 11/4/1892 d: 9/16/1916.

Season	Club	League	GP	G	A	Pts	PIM	GP	G	A	Pts	PIM
99-1900	Ottawa Seconds	CAHL-I	....	....	....	....	....	....	....	....	....	....
1900-01	Ottawa Aberdeens	OCJHL	....	....	....	....	....	....	....	....	....	....
1901-02	Ottawa Aberdeens	CAHL-I	....	....	....	....	....	....	....	....	....	....
♦1902-03	Ottawa Silver Seven	CAHL	6	14	0	14	9	2	3	0	3	3
♦1903-04	Ottawa Silver Seven	CAHL	4	12	0	12	9	....	....	....	....	....
♦1904-05	Ottawa Senators	FAHL	6	17	0	17	14	....	....	....	....	....
♦1905-06	Ottawa Senators	ECAHA	7	28	0	28	18	2	3	0	3	9
	Major League Totals		7	28	0	28	18	2	3	0	3	9

• McGIMSIE, Billie Billie George HHOF

C. 5'8", 145 lbs. b: Woodsville, Ont., 6/7/1880 Deceased.

Season	Club	League	GP	G	A	Pts	PIM	GP	G	A	Pts	PIM
1902-03	Rat Portage Thistles	MHL-Sr.	STATISTICS NOT AVAILABLE									
	Rat Portage Thistles	St-Cup	2	3	0	3	....	....	....	....	....	....
1903-04	Rat Portage Thistles	MHL-Sr.	STATISTICS NOT AVAILABLE									
1904-05	Rat Portage Thistles	MHL-Sr.	8	*28	0	*28	3	....	....	....	....	....
	Rat Portage Thistles	St-Cup	3	0	0	0	....	....	....	....	....	....
1905-06	Kenora Thistles	MHL-Sr.	9	21	0	21	....	....	....	....	....	....
1906-07	Kenora Thistles	Man-Pro	2	2	0	2	....	....	....	....	....	....
♦	Kenora Thistles	St-Cup	2	1	0	1	8	....	....	....	....	....
	Major League Totals		2	2	0	2	....	....	....	....	....	....

• McNAMARA, George George Andrew HHOF

D – L. 6'1", 220 lbs. b: Penetaguishene, Ont., 8/26/1886 d: 3/10/1952.

Season	Club	League	GP	G	A	Pts	PIM	GP	G	A	Pts	PIM
1904/06	S.S. Marie Marlboros	NOHA	STATISTICS NOT AVAILABLE									
1906-07	Canadian Soo	IHL	3	0	0	0	0					
	Cobalt Hockey Club	TPHL	STATISTICS NOT AVAILABLE									
1907-08	Canadian Soo	X-Games	STATISTICS NOT AVAILABLE									
	Michigan Soo	X-Games	STATISTICS NOT AVAILABLE									
	Montreal Shamrocks	ECAHA	10	3	0	3	34	....	....	....	....	....
1908-09	Montreal Shamrocks	ECHA	12	4	0	4	60	....	....	....	....	....
1909-10			STATISTICS NOT AVAILABLE									
1910-11	Waterloo Colts	OPHL	16	15	0	15	....	....	....	....	....	....
1911-12	Halifax Crescents	MPHL	10	2	0	2	24	....	....	....	....	....
1912-13	Toronto Tecumsehs	NHA	20	4	0	4	23	....	....	....	....	....
	Toronto Tecumsehs	X-Games	2	2	0	2	0	....	....	....	....	....
1913-14	Toronto Ontarios	NHA	9	0	1	1	0	....	....	....	....	....
	Toronto Blueshirts	NHA	9	0	1	1	2	....	....	....	....	....
♦	Toronto Blueshirts	St-Cup	3	2	0	2	0	....	....	....	....	....
1914-15	Toronto Shamrocks	NHA	18	4	8	12	67	....	....	....	....	....
1915-16	Toronto Blueshirts	NHA	23	5	2	7	74	....	....	....	....	....
1916-17	Toronto 228th	NHA	11	2	1	3	15	....	....	....	....	....
	Major League Totals		141	39	13	52	299	....	....	....	....	....

• McVIE, Tom Tom Ballentine

LW – L. 5'9", 162 lbs. b: Trail, B.C., 6/6/1935.

Season	Club	League	GP	G	A	Pts	PIM	GP	G	A	Pts	PIM
1953-54	Medicine Hat Tigers	WCJHL	2	0	0	0	0	....	....	....	....	....
1954-55	Prince Albert Mintos	SJHL	41	17	28	45	48	10	3	1	4	10
1955-56	Nanaimo Clippers	RMSHL	STATISTICS NOT AVAILABLE									
1956-57	Toledo Mercurys	IHL	60	17	26	43	43	5	0	1	1	4
1957-58	Toledo Mercurys	IHL	64	34	31	65	31	....	....	....	....	....
	Seattle Totems	WHL	3	0	2	2	0	....	....	....	....	....
1958-59	Seattle Totems	WHL	50	26	23	49	43	12	1	10	11	2
1959-60	Seattle Totems	WHL	70	27	44	71	34	4	0	2	2	0
1960-61	Seattle Totems	WHL	70	33	32	65	79	11	1	2	3	12
1961-62	Portland Buckaroos	WHL	67	45	40	85	80	7	4	2	6	9
1962-63	Portland Buckaroos	WHL	68	37	35	72	65	7	3	3	6	6
1963-64	Portland Buckaroos	WHL	69	36	38	74	26	5	1	4	5	22
1964-65	Portland Buckaroos	WHL	70	37	29	66	59	10	3	6	9	16
1965-66	Portland Buckaroos	WHL	35	13	10	23	21	23	2	4	6	4
1966-67	Los Angeles Blades	WHL	70	24	30	54	48	13	2	4	6	4
1967-68	Phoenix Roadrunners	WHL	71	29	31	60	34	4	0	3	3	4
1968-69	Phoenix Roadrunners	WHL	73	25	31	56	28	....	....	....	....	....
1969-70	Seattle Totems	WHL	73	19	33	52	63	6	1	1	2	0
1970-71	Seattle Totems	WHL	58	10	21	31	60	....	....	....	....	....
1971-72	Seattle Totems	WHL	10	1	2	3	12	....	....	....	....	....
	Fort Wayne Komets	IHL	50	21	36	57	28	8	7	4	11	8
1972-73	Portland Buckaroos	WHL	1	0	1	1	0	....	....	....	....	....
	Johnstown Jets	EHL	30	13	12	25	64	....	....	....	....	....
1973-74	Dayton Gems	IHL	10	0	1	1	4	....	....	....	....	....
1974-75	Dayton Gems	IHL	DID NOT PLAY – COACHING									

WHL First All-Star Team (1962) • WHL Second All-Star Team (1968)

• MILFORD, Jake John Caverley HHOF

LW – L. 5'9", 198 lbs. b: Charlottetown, P.E.I., 7/29/1916 d: 12/24/1984.

Season	Club	League	GP	G	A	Pts	PIM	GP	G	A	Pts	PIM
1932-33	Winnipeg Columbus	MJHL	11	5	3	8	23	3	1	0	1	8
1933-34	Kenora Thistles	MJHL	16	18	4	22	18	9	4	0	4	*20
1934-35	Wembley Canadians	Britain	STATISTICS NOT AVAILABLE									
1935-36	Wembley Canadians	Britain	....	15	9	24	23	....	....	....	....	....
1936-37	Wembley Monarchs	Britain	....	19	6	25	36	....	....	....	....	....
1937-38	Wembley Monarchs	Britain	....	16	11	27	....	....	....	....	....	....
1938-39	Lethbridge Maple Leafs	ASHL	31	15	12	27	37	6	3	4	7	8
	Lethbridge Maple Leafs	Al-Cup	3	0	1	1	*4	....	....	....	....	....
1939-40	Turner Valley Oilers	ASHL	32	16	15	31	29	7	2	2	4	14
1940-41	Cleveland Barons	AHL	51	13	14	27	19	9	3	2	5	2
1941-42	Cleveland Barons	AHL	48	6	15	21	16	3	0	0	0	2
1942-43	Saskatoon RCAF	SSHL	7	1	0	1	6	....	....	....	....	....
	Lethbridge Bombers	ASHL	2	0	1	1	2	2	1	0	1	2
1943-45			MILITARY SERVICE									
1945-46	New Haven Eagles	AHL	31	5	7	12	36	....	....	....	....	....
	Dallas Texans	USHL	18	2	2	4	2	....	....	....	....	....
1946-47	Dallas Texans	USHL	47	2	8	10	18	6	0	3	3	0
1947-48	Dallas Texans	USHL	64	4	15	19	24	....	....	....	....	....

• MORRIS, Rick

LW – L. 5'10", 175 lbs. b: Hamilton, Ont., .

Season	Club	League	GP	G	A	Pts	PIM	GP	G	A	Pts	PIM
1964-65	Hamilton Red Wings	OHA-Jr.	4	0	1	1	0	....	....	....	....	....
1965-66	Hamilton Red Wings	OHA-Jr.	6	2	0	2	10	....	....	....	....	....
1966-67	Hamilton Red Wings	OHA-Jr.	48	7	14	21	83	17	1	6	7	29
1967-68	Greensboro Generals	EHL	58	34	38	72	71	11	7	6	13	15
1968-69	Dallas Black Hawks	CHL	64	7	19	26	48	11	2	2	4	18
1969-70	Dallas Black Hawks	CHL	58	9	13	22	77	....	....	....	....	....
	Laurentian University	OUAA	9	12	8	20	....	....	....	....	....	....
1970-71	Laurentian University	OUAA	16	17	27	44	....	....	....	....	....	....
1971-72	Laurentian University	OUAA	17	18	28	46	44	....	....	....	....	....
1972-73	Chicago Cougars	WHA	78	31	17	48	84	....	....	....	....	....
1973-74	Chicago Cougars	WHA	76	17	16	33	140	18	4	3	7	42
1974-75	Chicago Cougars	WHA	78	15	13	28	110	....	....	....	....	....
1975-76	Denver Spurs	WHA	40	9	16	25	58	....	....	....	....	....
	Edmonton Oilers	WHA	33	11	15	26	52	4	0	1	1	6
1976-77	Edmonton Oilers	WHA	79	18	17	35	76	5	0	1	1	4
1977-78	Edmonton Oilers	WHA	5	1	1	2	7	....	....	....	....	....
	Quebec Nordiques	WHA	25	0	5	5	40	....	....	....	....	....
1978-80			OUT OF HOCKEY – RETIRED									
1980-81	Dundas Real McCoys	OHA-Sr.	....	28	27	55	....	....	....	....	....	....
	Major League Totals		414	102	100	202	567	27	4	5	9	52

Named EHL Rookie-of-the-Year (1968)

• MORTSON, Keke Cleland Lindsay

C – R. 5'10", 165 lbs. b: Arnfield, Que., 3/29/1934.

Season	Club	League	GP	G	A	Pts	PIM	GP	G	A	Pts	PIM
1951-52	Porcupine Combines	NOJHA	STATISTICS NOT AVAILABLE									
	Kitchener Greenshirts	OHA-Jr.	3	0	0	0	4	....	....	....	....	....
1952-53	New Haven Blades	EAHL	58	17	52	69	55	....	....	....	....	....
1953-54	Barrie Flyers	OHA-Jr.	59	28	50	78	137	....	....	....	....	....
	Cleveland Barons	AHL	3	0	1	1	0	....	....	....	....	....
1954-55	Troy Bruins	IHL	60	25	23	48	108	11	3	0	3	*39
1955-56	S.S. Marie Greyhounds	NOHA	60	27	33	60	82	5	2	2	4	14
1956-57	S.S. Marie Greyhounds	NOHA	57	24	30	54	130	10	3	5	8	21
1957-58	S.S. Marie Greyhounds	NOHA	23	7	12	19	18	....	....	....	....	....
	North Bay Trappers	NOHA	33	9	20	29	64	....	....	....	....	....
1958-59	North Bay Trappers	NOHA	53	35	42	77	69	....	....	....	....	....
1959-60	Sudbury Wolves	EPHL	58	25	55	80	70	14	4	5	9	25
1960-61	Sudbury Wolves	EPHL	64	25	45	70	94	....	....	....	....	....
	Hershey Bears	AHL	....	....	....	....	....	1	0	0	0	0
1961-62	Sudbury Wolves	EPHL	42	18	31	49	75	....	....	....	....	....
	Hershey Bears	AHL	24	13	11	24	34	7	1	2	3	15
1962-63	Hershey Bears	AHL	72	32	54	86	97	15	4	11	15	42
1963-64	Quebec Aces	AHL	71	28	55	83	122	9	7	6	13	13
1964-65	Quebec Aces	AHL	70	29	43	72	77	5	1	2	3	4
1965-66	Quebec Aces	AHL	65	33	*62	95	56	6	1	3	4	0
1966-67	Quebec Aces	AHL	58	13	34	47	78	4	1	2	3	0
1967-68	Seattle Totems	WHL	72	11	21	32	58	9	1	2	3	0
1968-69	Baltimore Clippers	AHL	74	20	49	69	141	4	0	1	1	6
1969-70	Baltimore Clippers	AHL	4	2	4	6	2	....	....	....	....	....
	Vancouver Canucks	WHL	55	5	12	17	39	11	0	1	1	34
1970-71	Rochester Americans	AHL	44	6	21	27	84	....	....	....	....	....
	Dallas Black Hawks	CHL	10	2	13	15	6	10	4	7	11	11
1971-72	Cincinnati Swords	AHL	76	17	50	67	133	10	4	7	11	59
1972-73	Houston Aeros	WHA	69	13	16	29	95	10	0	3	3	16
1973-74	Jacksonville Barons	AHL	14	5	16	21	18	....	....	....	....	....
	Macon Whoopees	SHL	59	24	51	75	135	....	....	....	....	....
1974-75			OUT OF HOCKEY – RETIRED									
1975-76	Buffalo Norsemen	NAHL	12	8	9	17	29	4	3	2	5	2
1976-77			OUT OF HOCKEY – RETIRED									
1977-78	Houston Aeros	WHA	6	0	1	1	7	2	0	1	1	0
	Major League Totals		75	13	17	30	102	12	0	4	4	16

NOHA First All-Star Team (1956) • EPHL First All-Star Team (1960) • EPHL Second All-Star Team (1961)

• NEEDHAM, Bill Bill Eric

D – L. 5'10", 190 lbs. b: Kirkland Lake, Ont., 1/12/1932.

Season	Club	League	GP	G	A	Pts	PIM	GP	G	A	Pts	PIM
1949-50	Porcupine Combines	NOJHA	STATISTICS NOT AVAILABLE									
	Porcupine Combines	M-Cup	5	0	1	1	6	....	....	....	....	....
1950-51	Porcupine Combines	NOJHA	STATISTICS NOT AVAILABLE									
1951-52	Porcupine Combines	NOJHA	STATISTICS NOT AVAILABLE									
1952-53	Grand Rapids Rockets	IHL	49	7	10	17	85	10	0	4	4	10

Season	Club	League	GP	G	A	Pts	PIM	GP	G	A	Pts	PIM
			REGULAR SEASON					PLAYOFFS				
1953-54	Glace Bay Miners	MMHL	44	6	8	14	83	....	....	....	....	....
	Valleyfield Braves	QHL	31	3	3	6	65	7	0	1	1	8
1954-55	New Westminster Royals	WHL	5	0	0	0	2	....	....	....	....	....
	Valleyfield Braves	QHL	46	5	3	8	30	....	....	....	....	....
1955-56	North Bay Trappers	NOHA	60	4	13	17	63	10	1	3	4	20
1956-57	North Bay Trappers	NOHA	58	8	11	19	61	13	1	1	2	8
	Cleveland Barons	AHL	2	0	0	0	2	....	....	....	....	....
1957-58	Cleveland Barons	AHL	69	4	11	15	35	7	0	3	3	6
1958-59	Cleveland Barons	AHL	70	5	11	16	59	7	0	0	0	10
1959-60	Cleveland Barons	AHL	72	5	16	21	79	7	0	1	1	4
1960-61	Cleveland Barons	AHL	72	2	16	18	79	4	0	0	0	0
1961-62	Cleveland Barons	AHL	70	6	17	23	62	6	0	1	1	4
1962-63	Cleveland Barons	AHL	72	8	25	33	76	7	0	2	2	2
1963-64	Cleveland Barons	AHL	72	3	22	25	74	9	0	2	2	*24
1964-65	Cleveland Barons	AHL	63	4	15	19	70	....	....	....	....	....
1965-66	Cleveland Barons	AHL	72	8	17	25	48	12	0	1	1	10
1966-67	Cleveland Barons	AHL	72	5	33	38	59	5	0	1	1	0
1967-68	Cleveland Barons	AHL	72	5	27	32	80	....	....	....	....	....
1968-69	Cleveland Barons	AHL	67	3	11	14	50	5	0	2	2	4
1969-70	Cleveland Barons	AHL	72	2	19	21	46	....	....	....	....	....
1970-71	Cleveland Barons	AHL	64	2	6	8	40	7	0	0	0	2
1971-72	Toledo Hornets	IHL	32	0	5	5	29	....	....	....	....	....

• NICHOL, Sibby John Sebastian

C/LW. 5'8", 150 lbs. b: Montreal, Que., 1889 Deceased.

Season	Club	League	GP	G	A	Pts	PIM	GP	G	A	Pts	PIM
1904-05	Montreal St. Pats	MCJHL	STATISTICS NOT AVAILABLE									
1905/07	Montreal Shamrocks-3	MCJHL	STATISTICS NOT AVAILABLE									
1907-08	Montreal Shamrocks-2	CAHL-I	STATISTICS NOT AVAILABLE									
	Montreal Shamrocks-2	CAHL-I	STATISTICS NOT AVAILABLE									
1908-09	**Montreal Shamrocks**	**ECHA**	**2**	**0**	**0**	**0**	**3**	....	....	....	....	....
	Montreal Power	MCIHL	10	11	0	11	7	1	1	0	1	0
1909-10	Montreal Shamrocks-2	CAHL-I	STATISTICS NOT AVAILABLE									
	Montreal Shamrocks	**CHA**	**1**	**1**	**0**	**1**	**0**	....	....	....	....	....
	Montreal Power	MIHL	9	11	0	11	....	....	....	....	....	....
1910-11	Montreal Astor	MIHL	2	2	0	2	2	....	....	....	....	....
	Belleville Bulls	EOPHL	2	3	0	3	....	....	....	....	....	....
	Moncton Victorias	**MPHL**	**5**	**13**	**0**	**13**	**4**	**4**	***14**	**0**	***14**	**0**
1911-12	**Vancouver Millionaires**	**PCHA**	**15**	**19**	**0**	**19**	**35**	....	....	....	....	....
1912-13	**Vancouver Millionaires**	**PCHA**	**1**	**0**	**0**	**0**	**0**	....	....	....	....	....
1913-14	**Vancouver Millionaires**	**PCHA**	**12**	**14**	**6**	**20**	**21**	....	....	....	....	....
1914-15			STATISTICS NOT AVAILABLE									
1915-16	**Vancouver Millionaires**	**PCHA**	**1**	**0**	**0**	**0**	**0**	....	....	....	....	....
	Victoria Aristocrats	**PCHA**	**11**	**12**	**10**	**22**	**3**	....	....	....	....	....
	PCHA All-Stars	X-Games	2	2	0	2	0	....	....	....	....	....
1916-17	**Spokane Canaries**	**PCHA**	**23**	**10**	**11**	**21**	**68**	....	....	....	....	....
1917/19			MILITARY SERVICE									
1919-20	**Seattle Metropolitans**	**PCHA**	**4**	**0**	**0**	**0**	**3**	**2**	**0**	**0**	**0**	**0**
	Seattle Metropolitans	St-Cup	4	0	0	0	0	....	....	....	....	....
	Major League Totals		**75**	**69**	**27**	**96**	**137**	**6**	**14**	**0**	**14**	**0**

MTMHL First All-Star Team (1909)

• O'NEIL, Tip Charles

RW – R. 5'9", 160 lbs. b: Clonnell, Ireland, 7/26/1910.

Season	Club	League	GP	G	A	Pts	PIM	GP	G	A	Pts	PIM
1929-30	High River Flyers	ASHL	16	*17	4	*21	8	2	1	0	1	0
1930-31	Boston Tigers	Can-Am	1	0	0	0	0	....	....	....	....	....
	Chicago Shamrocks	AHA	1	0	0	0	0	....	....	....	....	....
	St. Louis Flyers	AHA	16	3	1	4	4	....	....	....	....	....
	Minneapolis Millers	AHA	24	3	3	6	7	....	....	....	....	....
1931-32	Chicago Shamrocks	AHA	44	10	3	13	18	4	1	1	2	0
1932-33	Detroit Olympics	IHL	32	6	10	16	10	....	....	....	....	....
1933-34	Buffalo-Windsor	IHL	12	0	0	0	2	....	....	....	....	....
	Calgary Tigers	NWHL	14	12	5	17	2	5	3	1	4	4
1934-35	Vancouver Lions	NWHL	32	11	8	19	12	8	*6	0	6	2
1935-36	Vancouver Lions	NWHL	35	23	10	33	4	7	*4	1	5	9
1936-37	Vancouver Lions	PCHL	36	17	11	28	7	6	2	0	2	0
1937-38	Vancouver Lions	PCHL	42	13	12	25	9	6	1	*5	*6	4
1938-39	Vancouver Lions	PCHL	48	34	24	58	14	2	0	1	1	0
1939-40	Vancouver Lions	PCHL	40	18	15	33	8	5	0	2	2	0
1940-41	Vancouver Lions	PCHL	48	*33	26	59	6	6	*4	1	5	0
1941-42	Vancouver Norvans	NWIHL	4	2	1	3	0	1	0	0	0	0

• PADDON, Paddy Hillis Baird

LW – L. 5'11", 157 lbs. b: Dryden, Ont., 5/26/2007 d: 1/29/1963.

Season	Club	League	GP	G	A	Pts	PIM	GP	G	A	Pts	PIM
1924/26	Milverton Mites	OHA-Jr.	STATISTICS NOT AVAILABLE									
1926-27	Owen Sound Greys	X-Games	16	8	12	20	....	....	....	....	....	....
1927-28	London Panthers	Can-Pro	20	1	0	1	0	....	....	....	....	....
1928-29	Hamilton Tigers	Can-Pro	28	3	3	6	10	....	....	....	....	....
1929-30	Hamilton Tigers	IHL	40	6	7	13	14	....	....	....	....	....
1930-31	Syracuse Stars	IHL	46	6	5	11	27	....	....	....	....	....
1931-32	Syracuse Stars	IHL	13	0	0	0	0	....	....	....	....	....
	New Haven Eagles	Can-Am	25	10	8	18	4	2	0	1	1	0
1932-33	New Haven Eagles	Can-Am	44	8	4	12	16	....	....	....	....	....
1933-34	St. Louis Flyers	AHA	48	22	14	*36	21	7	*3	1	*4	2
1934-35	St. Louis Flyers	AHA	48	*34	19	53	8	3	3	4	7	2
1935-36	St. Louis Flyers	AHA	48	17	14	31	21	8	3	1	4	6
1936-37	Kansas City Greyhounds	AHA	14	0	2	2	0	....	....	....	....	....
1937-38	Wichita Skyhawks	AHA	48	*27	26	53	6	4	0	1	1	2
1938-39	Wichita Skyhawks	AHA	7	2	3	5	0	....	....	....	....	....
	Kansas City Greyhounds	AHA	34	12	10	22	0	....	....	....	....	....

AHA Second All-Star Team (1935)

• PATENAUDE, Ed Edgar "Rusty"

RW – R. 5'9", 175 lbs. b: Williams Lake, B.C., 10/17/1949.
Pittsburgh's 4th, 50th overall in 1969.

Season	Club	League	GP	G	A	Pts	PIM	GP	G	A	Pts	PIM
1966-67	Moose Jaw Canucks	CMJHL	55	11	13	24	21	14	0	3	3	4
1967-68	Moose Jaw Canucks	WCJHL	59	46	31	77	103	....	....	....	....	....
1968-69	Calgary Centennials	WCJHL	53	21	41	62	74	....	....	....	....	....
1969-70	Calgary Centennials	WCJHL	51	37	36	73	72	....	....	....	....	....
	Baltimore Clippers	AHL	1	0	0	0	0	....	....	....	....	....
1970-71	Amarillo Wranglers	CHL	72	13	24	37	39	....	....	....	....	....
1971-72	Fort Wayne Komets	IHL	70	35	41	76	109	8	3	2	5	8
1972-73	**Alberta Oilers**	**WHA**	**78**	**29**	**27**	**56**	**59**	....	....	....	....	....
1973-74	**Edmonton Oilers**	**WHA**	**71**	**20**	**23**	**43**	**55**	**4**	**0**	**2**	**2**	**2**
1974-75	**Edmonton Oilers**	**WHA**	**56**	**20**	**16**	**36**	**38**	....	....	....	....	....
1975-76	**Edmonton Oilers**	**WHA**	**77**	**42**	**30**	**72**	**88**	**4**	**1**	**4**	**5**	**12**
1976-77	**Edmonton Oilers**	**WHA**	**73**	**25**	**16**	**41**	**57**	**2**	**0**	**0**	**0**	**8**
1977-78	**Indianapolis Racers**	**WHA**	**76**	**23**	**19**	**42**	**71**	....	....	....	....	....
	Major League Totals		**431**	**159**	**131**	**290**	**368**	**10**	**1**	**6**	**7**	**22**

• PATRICK, Frank Francis Alexis HHOF

D – L. 5'11", 185 lbs. b: Ottawa, Ont., 12/21/1885 d: 6/29/1960.

Season	Club	League	GP	G	A	Pts	PIM	GP	G	A	Pts	PIM
1901-02	Westmount Academy	QAHA-I	STATISTICS NOT AVAILABLE									
1902-03	Westmount Academy	H.S.	STATISTICS NOT AVAILABLE									
	Westmount Academy	MCJHL	STATISTICS NOT AVAILABLE									
1903-04	Westmount Academy-2	CAHL-I	STATISTICS NOT AVAILABLE									
	Montreal Victorias	CAHL	5	4	0	4	....	....	....	....	....	....
1904-05	Westmount Academy	CAHL	2	4	0	4	0	....	....	....	....	....
1905-06	McGill University	MCHL	3	6	0	6	0	....	....	....	....	....
1906-07	McGill University	MCHL	4	6	0	6	12	....	....	....	....	....
1907-08	**Montreal Victorias**	**ECAHA**	**8**	**8**	**0**	**8**	**6**	....	....	....	....	....
1908-09	Nelson Hockey Club	WKHL	STATISTICS NOT AVAILABLE									
1909-10	**Renfrew Creamery Kings**	**NHA**	**11**	**8**	**0**	**8**	**23**	....	....	....	....	....
1910-11	Nelson Hockey Club	WKHL	STATISTICS NOT AVAILABLE									
1911-12	**Vancouver Millionaires**	**PCHA**	**15**	**23**	**0**	**23**	**0**	....	....	....	....	....
	PCHA All-Stars	X-Games	2	2	0	2	0	....	....	....	....	....
1912-13	**Vancouver Millionaires**	**PCHA**	**14**	**12**	***8**	**20**	**17**	....	....	....	....	....
1913-14	**Vancouver Millionaires**	**PCHA**	**16**	**11**	**9**	**20**	**3**	....	....	....	....	....
1914-15	**Vancouver Millionaires**	**PCHA**	**4**	**2**	**2**	**4**	**6**	....	....	....	....	....
♦	Vancouver Millionaires	St-Cup	3	2	1	3	8	....	....	....	....	....
	PCHA All-Stars	X-Games	2	2	0	2	0	....	....	....	....	....
1915-16	**Vancouver Millionaires**	**PCHA**	**8**	**3**	**1**	**4**	**3**	....	....	....	....	....
1916-17	**Vancouver Millionaires**	**PCHA**	**23**	**13**	**13**	**26**	**30**	....	....	....	....	....
1917-18	**Vancouver Millionaires**	**PCHA**	**1**	**1**	**1**	**2**	**0**	....	....	....	....	....
1918/22			OUT OF HOCKEY – RETIRED									
1922-23	**Vancouver Maroons**	**PCHA**	**2**	**0**	**1**	**1**	**0**	....	....	....	....	....
1923-24	**Vancouver Maroons**	**WCHL**	**4**	**0**	**1**	**1**	**0**	....	....	....	....	....
	Major League Totals		**106**	**81**	**36**	**117**	**88**	....	....	....	....	....

MCHL First All-Star Team (1907) • PCHA First All-Star Team (1912, 1914) • PCHA Second All-Star Team (1917)

• PEACOSH, Gene Eugene Michael

LW – L. 5'11", 180 lbs. b: Sheridan, Man., 9/28/1948.

Season	Club	League	GP	G	A	Pts	PIM	GP	G	A	Pts	PIM
1965-66	Edmonton Jr. Oil Kings	ASHL	....	12	8	20	31	....	....	....	....	....
1966-67	Penticton Broncos	BCJHL	40	*51	43	*94	34	....	....	....	....	....
	Edmonton Jr. Oil Kings	CMJHL	6	2	0	2	8	....	....	....	....	....
1967-68	Swift Current Broncos	WCJHL	53	52	48	100	60	....	....	....	....	....
1968-69	Johnstown Jets	EHL	71	44	43	87	38	3	0	1	1	0
1969-70	Johnstown Jets	EHL	74	49	66	115	42	4	1	0	1	2
1970-71	Johnstown Jets	EHL	74	51	66	117	34	10	9	4	13	20
1971-72	Johnstown Jets	EHL	75	43	64	107	28	11	11	6	17	9
1972-73	**New York Raiders**	**WHA**	**67**	**37**	**34**	**71**	**23**	....	....	....	....	....
1973-74	**NY-Jersey Blades**	**WHA**	**68**	**21**	**32**	**53**	**17**	....	....	....	....	....
1974-75	**San Diego Mariners**	**WHA**	**78**	**43**	**36**	**79**	**22**	**10**	**7**	**5**	**12**	**4**
1975-76	**San Diego Mariners**	**WHA**	**79**	**37**	**33**	**70**	**35**	**11**	**2**	**1**	**3**	**21**
1976-77	**Edmonton Oilers**	**WHA**	**11**	**5**	**4**	**9**	**14**	....	....	....	....	....
	Indianapolis Racers	**WHA**	**64**	**22**	**26**	**48**	**21**	**9**	**3**	**3**	**6**	**2**
	Major League Totals		**367**	**165**	**165**	**330**	**132**	**30**	**12**	**9**	**21**	**27**

BCJHL First All-Star Team (1967)

• PHILLIPS, Tommy Thomas Neil "Nibs" HHOF

LW – L. 5'9", 168 lbs. b: Toronto, Ont., 5/22/1883 d: 11/30/1923.

Season	Club	League	GP	G	A	Pts	PIM	GP	G	A	Pts	PIM
1901-02	Montreal Shamrocks	MCSHL	STATISTICS NOT AVAILABLE									
1902-03	Montreal AAA	CAHL	4	6	0	6	....	....	....	....	....	....
♦	Montreal AAA	St-Cup	4	3	0	3	....	....	....	....	....	....
1903-04	Toronto Marlboros	OHA-Sr.	4	5	0	5	21	....	....	....	....	....
	Toronto Marlboros	St-Cup	4	7	*8	15	*15	....	....	....	....	....
1904-05	Rat Portage Thistles	MHL-Sr.	8	26	0	26	....	....	....	....	....	....
	Rat Portage Thistles	St-Cup	3	8	0	8	....	....	....	....	....	....
1905-06	Kenora Thistles	MHL-Sr.	9	24	0	24	....	....	....	....	....	....
1906-07	**Kenora Thistles**	**Man-Pro**	**6**	***18**	**0**	***18**	....	....	....	....	....	....
♦	Kenora Thistles	St-Cup	4	*9	0	*9	*16	....	....	....	....	....
1907-08	**Ottawa Senators**	**ECAHA**	**10**	**26**	**0**	**26**	**40**	....	....	....	....	....
1908-09	Edmonton Professionals	X-Games	1	0	2	2	3	....	....	....	....	....
	Edmonton Professionals	St-Cup	1	1	0	1	0	....	....	....	....	....
1909-10	Nelson Hockey Club	WKHL	STATISTICS NOT AVAILABLE									
1910-11			OUT OF HOCKEY – RETIRED									
1911-12	**Vancouver Millionaires**	**PCHA**	**17**	**17**	**0**	**17**	**38**	....	....	....	....	....
	Major League Totals		**33**	**61**	**0**	**61**	**78**					

• PILOUS, Rudy HHOF

LW – L. b: Winnipeg, Man., 8/11/1914 d: 12/3/1995.

Season	Club	League	GP	G	A	Pts	PIM	GP	G	A	Pts	PIM
1929-30	Winnipeg Rangers	MAHA	STATISTICS NOT AVAILABLE									
1930-32	Winnipeg JV Rangers	MAHA	STATISTICS NOT AVAILABLE									
1932-33	Winnipeg Monarchs	MJHL	4	0	0	0	2	....	....	....	....	....
1933-34	Portage Terriers	MJHL	14	5	7	12	6	2	0	0	0	0
1934-35	Selkirk Fishermen	MHL-Sr.	2	0	0	0	2	....	....	....	....	....
	Nelson Maple Leafs	WKHL	STATISTICS NOT AVAILABLE									
1935-36	Nelson Maple Leafs	WKHL	10	2	5	7	5	....	....	....	....	....
1936-37	Richmond Hawks	Britain	....	8	3	11	16	....	....	....	....	....
1937-38	New York Rovers	EAHL	56	2	10	12	58	....	....	....	....	....
1938-39	St. Catharines Chiefs	OHA-Sr.	19	5	7	12	10	4	1	2	3	2
1939-40	St. Catharines Saints	OHA-Sr.	24	19	20	39	25	8	1	5	6	4
1940-41	St. Catharines Saints	OHA-Sr.	12	0	3	3	4	....	....	....	....	....

• POULIN, Skinner George Vincent
W. 5'6", 155 lbs. b: Smiths Falls, Ont., 9/17/1887 d: 5/3/1971.

Season	Club	League	GP	G	A	Pts	PIM	GP	G	A	Pts	PIM
			REGULAR SEASON					PLAYOFFS				
1904-05	Smiths Falls Mic-Macs	OHA-Jr.	STATISTICS NOT AVAILABLE									
1905-06	Smiths Falls Mic-Macs	OHA-I	STATISTICS NOT AVAILABLE									
1906-07	Smiths Falls Mic-Macs	OHA-I	4	*19	0	*19	....	3	4	0	4	....
1907-08	Portage-La-Prairie	Man-Pro	15	14	0	14	....	....	....	....	....	....
1908-09	Winnipeg Maple Leafs	Man-Pro	4	7	3	10	*18	....	....	....	....	....
	Winnipeg Maple Leafs	Man-Pro	4	5	1	6	0	....	....	....	....	....
1909-10	Montreal Canadiens	NHA	12	8	0	8	53	....	....	....	....	....
	Galt Professionals	OPHL	2	2	0	2	3	....	....	....	....	....
1910-11	Montreal Canadiens	NHA	13	3	0	3	59	....	....	....	....	....
1911-12	Victoria Aristocrats	PCHA	16	9	0	9	48	....	....	....	....	....
1912-13	Victoria Aristocrats	PCHA	15	5	4	9	*64	....	....	....	....	....
	Victoria Aristocrats	St-Cup	3	2	0	2	....	....	....	....	....	....
1913-14	Victoria Aristocrats	PCHA	15	9	9	18	*47	....	....	....	....	....
	Victoria Aristocrats	St-Cup	3	2	0	2	....	....	....	....	....	....
1914-15	Victoria Aristocrats	PCHA	16	4	4	8	*47	....	....	....	....	....
	PCHA All-Stars	X-Games	2	0	0	0	0	....	....	....	....	....
1915-16	Montreal Canadiens	NHA	16	5	1	6	43	....	....	....	....	....
♦	Montreal Canadiens	St-Cup	3	1	0	1	9	....	....	....	....	....
1916-17	Montreal Canadiens	NHA	4	0	0	0	8	....	....	....	....	....
	Montreal Wanderers	NHA	9	3	0	3	8	....	....	....	....	....
1917-18			DID NOT PLAY									
1918-19	Victoria Cougars	PCHA	1	0	0	0	0	....	....	....	....	....
1919-20	Saskatoon Crescents	N-SSHL	12	4	2	6	*31	....	....	....	....	....
1920-21	Saskatoon Crescents	N-SSHL	4	1	1	2	11	4	0	0	0	3
1921-22		WCHL	DID NOT PLAY – REFEREE									
	Major League Totals		142	74	22	96	398	....	....	....	....	....

• PULFORD, Harvey HHOF
Point. b: Toronto, Ont., 4/22/1875 d: 1940.

Season	Club	League	GP	G	A	Pts	PIM	GP	G	A	Pts	PIM
1893-94	Ottawa Hockey Club	AHA-Sr.	6	0	0	0	....	....	....	....	....	....
	Ottawa Hockey Club	St-Cup	1	0	0	0	....	....	....	....	....	....
1894-95	Ottawa Hockey Club	AHA-Sr.	7	0	0	0	....	....	....	....	....	....
1895-96	Ottawa Hockey Club	AHA-Sr.	8	0	0	0	....	....	....	....	....	....
1896-97	Ottawa Hockey Club	AHA-Sr.	8	0	0	0	....	....	....	....	....	....
1897-98	Ottawa Silver Seven	AHA-Sr.	7	0	0	0	....	....	....	....	....	....
1898-99	Ottawa Silver Seven	AHA-Sr.	5	0	0	0	....	....	....	....	....	....
99-1900	Ottawa Silver Seven	CAHL	6	1	0	1	....	....	....	....	....	....
	Ottawa Aberdeens	CAHL-I	1	0	0	0	....	....	....	....	....	....
1900-01	Ottawa Silver Seven	CAHL	5	0	0	0	....	....	....	....	....	....
	Ottawa Silver Seven	St-Cup	2	3	0	3	....	....	....	....	....	....
1901-02			STATISTICS NOT AVAILABLE									
1902-03	Ottawa Silver Seven	CAHL	7	0	0	0	15	....	....	....	....	....
♦	Ottawa Silver Seven	St-Cup	4	0	0	0	9	....	....	....	....	....
1903-04	Ottawa Silver Seven	CAHL	2	0	0	0	3	....	....	....	....	....
♦	Ottawa Silver Seven	St-Cup	7	1	0	1	12	....	....	....	....	....
1904-05	Ottawa Silver Seven	FAHL	6	1	0	1	6	....	....	....	....	....
♦	Ottawa Silver Seven	St-Cup	4	0	0	0	6	....	....	....	....	....
1905-06	Ottawa Senators	ECAHA	10	3	0	3	27	....	....	....	....	....
♦	Ottawa Senators	St-Cup	6	1	0	1	*36	....	....	....	....	....
1906-07	Ottawa Senators	ECAHA	10	0	0	0	31	....	....	....	....	....
1907-08	Ottawa Senators	ECAHA	9	1	0	1	32	....	....	....	....	....
	Major League Totals		29	4	0	4	90	....	....	....	....	....

• RANKIN, Frank HHOF
Rover. 5'5", 145 lbs. b: Stratford, Ont., 4/1/1884 Deceased.

Season	Club	League	GP	G	A	Pts	PIM	GP	G	A	Pts	PIM
1904-09	Stratford Hockey Club	OHA-Sr.	STATISTICS NOT AVAILABLE									
1909-10	Stratford Hockey Club	X-Games	....	....	....	....	....	2	*4	0	*4	....
1910-11	Toronto Eaton's	OHA-Sr.	4	*15	0	*15	....	2	*4	0	*4	....
1911-12	Toronto Eaton's	OHA-Sr.	6	6	0	6	....	4	3	0	3	12
1912-13	Toronto St. Michael's	OHA-Sr.	5	*22	0	*22	....	4	4	0	4	....
1913-14	Toronto St. Michael's	OHA-Sr.	2	10	0	10	....	2	3	0	3	....

• RIDPATH, Bruce
W– R. b: Toronto, Ont., d: 6/4/1925.

Season	Club	League	GP	G	A	Pts	PIM	GP	G	A	Pts	PIM
1903-04	Toronto Western Canoe	OHA-Jr.	4	5	0	5	3	1	3	0	3	0
1904-05	Toronto Marlboros	OHA-Sr.	6	9	0	9	17	8	9	0	9	17
1905-06	Toronto Marlboros	OHA-Sr.	6	14	0	14	9	2	*8	0	*8	*12
1906-07	Toronto Professionals	X-Games	8	*20	0	*20	10	....	....	....	....	....
	Cobalt Silver Kings	TPHL	STATISTICS NOT AVAILABLE									
1907-08	Toronto Professionals	OPHL	12	8	0	8	32	1	1	0	1	0
1908-09	Toronto Professionals	OPHL	11	21	0	21	11	....	....	....	....	....
	Cobalt Silver Kings	TPHL	2	6	0	6	4	2	*3	0	*3	3
1909-10	Ottawa Senators	CHA	2	3	0	3	....	....	....	....	....	....
	Ottawa Senators	NHA	12	16	0	16	32	....	....	....	....	....
♦	Ottawa Senators	St-Cup	4	6	0	6	*16	....	....	....	....	....
1910-11	Ottawa Senators	NHA	16	23	0	23	54	....	....	....	....	....
♦	Ottawa Senators	St-Cup	2	4	0	4	3	....	....	....	....	....
	Major League Totals		53	71	0	71	129	1	1	0	1	0

OPHL Second All-Star Team (1908, 1909)

• ROBERTS, Gord Gordon William "Doc"
LW – L. 5'11", 180 lbs. b: Ottawa, Ont., 9/5/1891 d: 9/2/1966.

Season	Club	League	GP	G	A	Pts	PIM	GP	G	A	Pts	PIM
1906-07	Stratford Hockey Club	OHA-Jr.	STATISTICS NOT AVAILABLE									
1908-09	Ottawa Emmetts	OCHL	6	*19	0	*19	8	2	2	0	2	0
1909-10	Ottawa Senators	CHA	1	3	0	3	6	....	....	....	....	....
	Ottawa Senators	NHA	9	13	0	13	34	....	....	....	....	....
♦	Ottawa Senators	St-Cup	2	7	0	7	0	....	....	....	....	....
	Ottawa Seconds	OCHL	1	3	0	3	5	....	....	....	....	....
1910-11	Montreal Wanderers	NHA	4	1	0	1	3	....	....	....	....	....
1911-12	Montreal Wanderers	NHA	18	16	0	16	0	....	....	....	....	....
1912-13	Montreal Wanderers	NHA	16	16	0	16	22	....	....	....	....	....
1913-14	Montreal Wanderers	NHA	20	31	13	44	15	....	....	....	....	....
1914-15	Montreal Wanderers	NHA	19	29	5	34	74	....	....	....	....	....
	Montreal Wanderers	St-Cup	2	0	0	0	15	....	....	....	....	....
1915-16	Montreal Wanderers	NHA	21	18	7	25	64	....	....	....	....	....
1916-17	Vancouver Millionaires	PCHA	23	*43	10	53	42	....	....	....	....	....
1917-18	Seattle Metropolitans	PCHA	18	20	3	23	24	....	....	....	....	....
	Seattle Metropolitans	St-Cup	2	0	0	0	3	....	....	....	....	....
1918-19			DID NOT PLAY									
1919-20	Vancouver Millionaires	PCHA	22	16	3	19	13	....	....	....	....	....
	Vancouver Millionaires	St-Cup	2	1	0	1	0	....	....	....	....	....
	Major League Totals		171	206	41	247	297	....	....	....	....	....

PCHA First All-Star Team (1917)

• ROY, Georges
D – R. 5'8", 190 lbs. b: Quebec City, Que., 9/28/1927.

Season	Club	League	GP	G	A	Pts	PIM	GP	G	A	Pts	PIM
1947-48	Victoriaville Tigers	QPHL	....	7	13	20	108	12	4	2	6	6
	Victoriaville Tigers	Al-Cup	3	0	0	0	11	....	....	....	....	....
1948-49	Sherbrooke Saints	QSHL	54	9	10	19	84	11	0	2	2	12
1949-50	Chicoutimi Sagueneens	QSHL	50	7	16	23	66	5	1	2	3	14
1950-51	Chicoutimi Sagueneens	QMHL	58	17	24	41	109	6	1	0	1	13
1951-52	Chicoutimi Sagueneens	QMHL	57	10	23	33	123	18	3	1	4	40
1952-53	Chicoutimi Sagueneens	QMHL	54	5	27	32	73	16	3	6	9	22
1953-54	Chicoutimi Sagueneens	QHL	72	13	45	58	121	7	0	0	0	8
1954-55	Chicoutimi Sagueneens	QHL	59	11	28	39	130	7	0	6	6	2
1955-56	Chicoutimi Sagueneens	QHL	64	14	27	41	132	5	0	1	1	21
1956-57	Chicoutimi Sagueneens	QHL	67	14	33	47	*159	10	3	5	8	15
1957-58	Chicoutimi Sagueneens	QHL	64	12	43	55	102	6	2	1	3	11
1958-59	Chicoutimi Sagueneens	QHL	62	11	45	56	104	....	....	....	....	....
1959-60	Quebec Aces	AHL	63	6	13	19	161	....	....	....	....	....
1960-61	S.S. Marie Thunderbirds	EPHL	13	0	2	2	25	....	....	....	....	....
	Victoria Cougars	WHL	4	0	2	2	2	....	....	....	....	....
1961-62	Charlotte Checkers	EHL	68	10	51	61	73	....	....	....	....	....
1962-63	Windsor Maple Leafs	NSSHL	....	5	15	20	59	7	1	7	8	6
	Moncton Hawks	Al-Cup	12	2	4	6	23	....	....	....	....	....
1963-64	Windsor Maple Leafs	NSSHL	65	22	85	107	220	6	0	7	7	14
	Windsor Maple Leafs	Al-Cup	11	4	11	15	*50	....	....	....	....	....
1964-65	Sherbrooke Castors	QSHL	STATISTICS NOT AVAILABLE									
	Sherbrooke Castors	Al-Cup	STATISTICS NOT AVAILABLE									
1965-66	Sherbrooke Castors	QSHL	39	4	25	29	57	12	0	6	6	36
	Sherbrooke Castors	Al-Cup	19	2	11	13	13	....	....	....	....	....
1966-67	Sherbrooke Castors	QSHL	52	5	27	32	54	10	3	4	7	18
1967-68	Sherbrooke Castors	QSHL	45	3	12	15	39	5	1	1	2	7

• RUSSELL, Blair HHOF
LW – L. b: Montreal, Que., 9/17/1890 Deceased.

Season	Club	League	GP	G	A	Pts	PIM	GP	G	A	Pts	PIM
1894-96	Montreal Victorias	MCJHL	STATISTICS NOT AVAILABLE									
1896-97	Montreal Victorias	QAHA-I	STATISTICS NOT AVAILABLE									
1897-98	Montreal Rotal-Queen	QAHA-I	STATISTICS NOT AVAILABLE									
1898-99	Montreal Victorias	CAHL-I	STATISTICS NOT AVAILABLE									
	Montreal Victorias	MCJHL	STATISTICS NOT AVAILABLE									
	Montreal Rotal-Queen	QAHA-I	STATISTICS NOT AVAILABLE									
99-1900	Montreal Victorias	CAHL-I	STATISTICS NOT AVAILABLE									
	Montreal Victorias	CAHL	7	9	0	9	....	....	....	....	....	....
1900-01	Montreal Victorias	CAHL	8	8	0	8	....	....	....	....	....	....
	Montreal Victorias	CAHL-I	STATISTICS NOT AVAILABLE									
1901-02	Montreal Victorias	CAHL	8	9	0	9	3	....	....	....	....	....
1902-03	Montreal Victorias	CAHL	8	7	0	7	6	....	....	....	....	....
	Montreal Victorias	St-Cup	2	0	0	0	6	....	....	....	....	....
1903-04	Montreal Victorias	CAHL	8	17	0	17	15	....	....	....	....	....
1904-05	Montreal Victorias	CAHL	8	19	0	19	6	....	....	....	....	....
1905-06	Montreal Victorias	ECAHA	4	7	0	7	....	....	....	....	....	....
1906-07	Montreal Victorias	ECAHA	10	25	0	25	6	....	....	....	....	....
1907-08	Montreal Victorias	ECAHA	6	8	0	8	26	....	....	....	....	....
1908-09	Montreal Victorias	IPAHU	1	2	0	2	1	....	....	....	....	....
1909-10	Montreal Victorias	IPAHU	1	2	0	2	2	....	....	....	....	....
	Major League Totals		20	40	0	40	32	....	....	....	....	....

• RUSSELL, Ernie HHOF
C – R. b: Montreal, Que., 10/21/1883 Deceased.

Season	Club	League	GP	G	A	Pts	PIM	GP	G	A	Pts	PIM
1902-03	Stirling Athletics	MCJHL	STATISTICS NOT AVAILABLE									
	Stirling Athletics	FAHL-I	STATISTICS NOT AVAILABLE									
1903-04	Stirling Athletics	FAHL-I	STATISTICS NOT AVAILABLE									
1904-05	Montreal AAA	CAHL	8	11	0	11	....	....	....	....	....	....
1905-06	Montreal Wanderers	ECAHA	6	21	0	21	13	....	....	....	....	....
♦	Montreal Wanderers	St-Cup	2	4	0	4	6	....	....	....	....	....
1906-07	Montreal Wanderers	ECAHA	9	*43	0	*43	26	....	....	....	....	....
♦	Montreal Wanderers	St-Cup	5	12	0	12	*35	....	....	....	....	....
1907-08	Montreal Wanderers	ECHA	9	20	0	20	37	....	....	....	....	....
♦	Montreal Wanderers	St-Cup	3	11	0	11	7	....	....	....	....	....
1908-09			OUT OF HOCKEY – RETIRED									
1909-10	Montreal Wanderers	NHA	12	32	0	32	51	....	....	....	....	....
♦	Montreal Wanderers	St-Cup	1	4	0	4	3	....	....	....	....	....
1910-11	Montreal Wanderers	NHA	11	18	0	18	56	....	....	....	....	....
1911-12	Montreal Wanderers	NHA	18	27	0	27	*110	....	....	....	....	....
1912-13	Montreal Wanderers	NHA	15	7	0	7	48	....	....	....	....	....
1913-14	Montreal Wanderers	NHA	12	2	4	6	21	....	....	....	....	....
	Major League Totals		92	170	4	174	362	....	....	....	....	....

• SAUNDERS, Bill Bill George
LW – L. 5'9", 170 lbs. b: Winnipeg, Man., 11/22/1937.

Season	Club	League	GP	G	A	Pts	PIM	GP	G	A	Pts	PIM
1955-56	St. Boniface Canadiens	MJHL	15	5	7	12	14	3	1	0	1	0
1956-57	Winnipeg Monarchs	MJHL	27	24	12	36	21	11	9	7	16	16
	Winnipeg Monarchs	M-Cup	8	5	1	6	4	....	....	....	....	....
1957-58	Winnipeg Monarchs	MJHL	30	32	44	76	34	7	5	6	11	8
	St. Boniface Canadiens	M-Cup	11	11	8	19	12	....	....	....	....	....
1958-59	Kitchener Dutchmen	OHA-Sr.	53	45	26	71	50	11	*8	4	12	12
1959-60	Rochester Americans	AHL	72	24	28	52	38	11	1	0	1	0
1960-61	Rochester Americans	AHL	10	2	2	4	0	....	....	....	....	....
	Victoria Cougars	WHL	60	33	43	76	13	5	1	2	3	0
1961-62	Portland Buckaroos	WHL	68	34	45	79	30	7	1	3	4	0
1962-63	Portland Buckaroos	WHL	69	37	26	63	37	7	1	2	3	0
1963-64	Portland Buckaroos	WHL	70	17	23	40	2	5	0	0	0	0
1964-65	Portland Buckaroos	WHL	68	15	27	42	6	7	2	0	2	0

Season	Club	League	GP	G	A	Pts	PIM	GP	G	A	Pts	PIM
			REGULAR SEASON					PLAYOFFS				
1965-66	Portland Buckaroos	WHL	71	26	41	67	42	12	1	7	8	14
1966-67	Portland Buckaroos	WHL	72	34	36	70	58	4	0	0	0	7
1967-68	Portland Buckaroos	WHL	72	38	26	64	31	11	5	0	5	8
1968-69	Portland Buckaroos	WHL	74	*53	59	112	38	11	1	5	6	2
1969-70	Portland Buckaroos	WHL	69	39	52	91	16	7	4	1	5	0
1970-71	Portland Buckaroos	WHL	65	39	44	83	33	10	8	2	10	2
1971-72	Portland Buckaroos	WHL	70	37	46	83	21	11	5	4	9	10
1972-73	Portland Buckaroos	WHL	68	23	39	62	38	....	....	....	....	....
1973-74			OUT OF HOCKEY – RETIRED									
1974-75	Portland Buckaroos	WHL	....	6	11	17	2	....	....	....	....	....

• SCOTT, Harry — Harry Duncan

C – R. 5'10", 180 lbs. b: Moncton, N.B., 1887 d: 10/22/1954.

Season	Club	League	GP	G	A	Pts	PIM	GP	G	A	Pts	PIM
1905-06	Ft-William Rowing Club	NOHL	STATISTICS NOT AVAILABLE									
1906-07	**Portage-La-Prairie**	**Man-Pro**	**2**	**1**	**0**	**1**	....	....	....	....	....	....
	Winnipeg Strathconas	**Man-Pro**	**1**	**1**	**0**	**1**	....	....	....	....	....	....
	Pembroke Lumber Kings	UOVHL	STATISTICS NOT AVAILABLE									
1907-08	**Fort William Wanderers**	**NOHL**	**10**	***18**	**0**	***18**	....	**4**	**5**	**0**	**5**	....
1908-09	**Fort William Wanderers**	**NOHL**	**12**	**21**	**0**	**21**	....	**2**	**1**	**0**	**1**	....
	Winnipeg Maple Leafs	**Man-Pro**	STATISTICS NOT AVAILABLE									
1909-10	**Fort William Forts**	**NOHL**	**11**	**10**	**0**	**10**	**26**	....	....	....	....	....
1910-11	**Fort William Forts**	**NOHL**	**1**	**1**	**0**	**1**	**0**	....	....	....	....	....
	Moncton Victorias	**MPHL**	**8**	***20**	**0**	***20**	**16**	**4**	**6**	**0**	**6**	**6**
1911-12	**New Glasgow Cubs**	**MPHL**	**18**	***54**	**0**	***54**	**21**	....	....	....	....	....
1912-13	**Sydney Millionaires**	**MPHL**	**1**	**2**	**0**	**2**	**0**	....	....	....	....	....
	Halifax Crescents	**MPHL**	**9**	**6**	**0**	**6**	**25**	....	....	....	....	....
	Moncton Victorias	**MPHL**	**3**	**4**	**0**	**4**	**4**	....	....	....	....	....
1913-14	**Toronto Ontarios**	**NHA**	**7**	**4**	**1**	**5**	**2**	....	....	....	....	....
	Montreal Canadiens	**NHA**	**11**	**9**	**2**	**11**	**44**	**2**	**1**	**0**	**1**	**6**
1914-15	**Montreal Canadiens**	**NHA**	**16**	**9**	**0**	**9**	**35**	....	....	....	....	....
1915-17			MILITARY SERVICE									
1917-18	Winnipeg Vimy	MHL-Sr.	7	18	1	19	6	....	....	....	....	....
	Major League Totals		**110**	**160**	**3**	**163**	**173**	**12**	**13**	**0**	**13**	**12**

NOHL First All-Star Team (1909) • MPHL First All-Star Team (1911)

• SEIBERT, Oliver — Oliver Levi — HHOF

C. b: Berlin, Ont., 3/18/1881 d: 3/15/1944.

Season	Club	League	GP	G	A	Pts	PIM	GP	G	A	Pts	PIM
99-1900	Berlin Hockey Club	WOHA	8	10	0	10	....	....	....	....	....	....
1900-01	Berlin Hockey Club	WOHA	6	13	0	13	....	....	....	....	....	....
1901-02	Berlin Hockey Club	WOHA	8	*17	0	*17	....	....	....	....	....	....
1902-03	Guelph O.A.C.	WOHA	STATISTICS NOT AVAILABLE									
1903-04	Berlin Hockey Club	WOHA	STATISTICS NOT AVAILABLE									
1904-05	**Canadian Soo**	**IHL**	**1**	**0**	**0**	**0**	**0**	....	....	....	....	....
1905-06	Suspended ex-Pro		DID NOT PLAY – SUSPENDED									
1906-07	Berlin Hockey Club	X-Games	DID NOT PLAY – SPARE GOALTENDER									
	Major League Totals		**1**	**0**	**0**	**0**	**0**	....	....	....	....	....

• SENTES, Rick — Richard James

LW – L. 6', 185 lbs. b: Regina, Sask., 1/10/1947.

Season	Club	League	GP	G	A	Pts	PIM	GP	G	A	Pts	PIM
1963-64	Regina Pats	SJHL	61	8	11	19	23	19	0	0	0	8
1964-65	Regina Pats	SJHL	7	1	0	1	2	12	2	1	3	4
1965-66	Regina Pats	SJHL	60	41	59	100	152	5	2	1	3	10
1966-67	Regina Pats	CMJHL	56	66	61	127	101	16	15	10	25	32
1967-68	Houston Apollos	CPHL	69	22	33	55	58	....	....	....	....	....
1968-69	Vancouver Canucks	WHL	8	0	0	0	4	....	....	....	....	....
	Cleveland Barons	AHL	67	16	13	29	40	2	1	0	1	0
1969-70	Denver Spurs	WHL	15	7	5	12	8	....	....	....	....	....
	Iowa Stars	CHL	42	14	10	24	40	....	....	....	....	....
1970-71	Denver Spurs	WHL	69	20	27	47	102	5	0	2	2	12
1971-72	Tidewater Wings	AHL	74	32	21	53	104	....	....	....	....	....
1972-73	**Ottawa Nationals**	**WHA**	**74**	**22**	**19**	**41**	**75**	**5**	**3**	**1**	**4**	**2**
1973-74	**Toronto Toros**	**WHA**	**64**	**26**	**30**	**56**	**46**	**12**	**7**	**4**	**11**	**19**
1974-75	**San Diego Mariners**	**WHA**	**74**	**44**	**41**	**85**	**52**	**10**	**0**	**2**	**2**	**0**
1975-76	**Calgary Cowboys**	**WHA**	**72**	**25**	**24**	**49**	**33**	**8**	**0**	**1**	**1**	**8**
1976-77	**Calgary Cowboys**	**WHA**	**29**	**10**	**14**	**24**	**8**	....	....	....	....	....
	San Diego Mariners	**WHA**	**24**	**10**	**11**	**21**	**16**	**5**	**4**	**0**	**4**	**12**
	Major League Totals		**337**	**137**	**139**	**276**	**230**	**40**	**14**	**8**	**22**	**41**

• SICKINSKI, Bob — Robert Stanley

C – R. 5'9", 175 lbs. b: Toronto, Ont., 11/13/1946.

Season	Club	League	GP	G	A	Pts	PIM	GP	G	A	Pts	PIM
1963-64	Dixie Beehives	OHA-B	41	24	38	62	12	....	....	....	....	....
1964-65	St. Catharines Blackhawks	OHA-Jr.	47	10	26	36	12	5	1	5	6	0
1965-66	St. Catharines Blackhawks	OHA-Jr.	48	17	32	49	24	7	2	0	2	2
1966-67	St. Catharines Blackhawks	OHA-Jr.	46	10	25	35	12	5	2	4	6	8
1967-68	Greensboro Generals	EHL	69	29	63	92	4	11	3	6	9	2
1968-69	Greensboro Generals	EHL	72	38	72	110	10	8	0	4	4	0
1969-70	Dallas Black Hawks	CHL	3	1	3	4	0	....	....	....	....	....
	Greensboro Generals	EHL	72	40	75	115	30	16	3	2	5	7
1970-71	Dallas Black Hawks	CHL	20	3	5	8	4	....	....	....	....	....
1971-72	Dallas Black Hawks	CHL	67	23	61	84	14	12	1	*9	10	4
1972-73	**Chicago Cougars**	**WHA**	**77**	**25**	**63**	**88**	**18**	....	....	....	....	....
1973-74	**Chicago Cougars**	**WHA**	**69**	**11**	**29**	**40**	**8**	**18**	**6**	**8**	**14**	**0**
1974-75	**Indianapolis Racers**	**WHA**	**77**	**19**	**34**	**53**	**12**	....	....	....	....	....
1975-76	**Indianapolis Racers**	**WHA**	**70**	**9**	**34**	**43**	**4**	**7**	**0**	**0**	**0**	**2**
1976-77	Oklahoma City Blazers	CHL	12	8	14	22	6	....	....	....	....	....
	Indianapolis Racers	**WHA**	**60**	**12**	**24**	**36**	**14**	**9**	**0**	**3**	**3**	**4**
1977-78	San Diego Mariners	PHL	42	17	36	53	12	....	....	....	....	....
	Brantford Redmen	OHA-Sr.	13	6	8	14	12	....	....	....	....	....
	Major League Totals		**353**	**76**	**184**	**260**	**56**	**34**	**6**	**11**	**17**	**6**

EHL First All-Star Team (1970)

• SIMPSON, Tom — Thomas Phillip "Shot Gun"

RW – R. 5'9", 190 lbs. b: Bowmanville, Ont., 8/15/1952.
St. Louis' 5th, 89th overall in 1972.

Season	Club	League	GP	G	A	Pts	PIM	GP	G	A	Pts	PIM
1968-69	Oshawa Generals	OHA-Jr.	2	1	0	1	0	....	....	....	....	....
1969-70	Oshawa Generals	OHA-Jr.	53	28	26	54	44	6	1	6	7	8
1970-71	Oshawa Generals	OHA-Jr.	59	42	20	62	82	....	....	....	....	....
1971-72	Oshawa Generals	OHA-Jr.	44	29	18	47	53	12	10	9	19	19
1972-73	**Ottawa Nationals**	**WHA**	**57**	**10**	**7**	**17**	**45**	**5**	**1**	**0**	**1**	**0**
1973-74	**Toronto Toros**	**WHA**	**74**	**33**	**20**	**53**	**27**	**12**	**4**	**1**	**5**	**5**
1974-75	**Toronto Toros**	**WHA**	**70**	**52**	**28**	**80**	**48**	**5**	**1**	**1**	**2**	**0**
1975-76	**Toronto Toros**	**WHA**	**73**	**20**	**21**	**41**	**15**	....	....	....	....	....
1976-77	**Birmingham Bulls**	**WHA**	**25**	**7**	**6**	**13**	**10**	....	....	....	....	....
	Edmonton Oilers	**WHA**	**15**	**3**	**2**	**5**	**16**	....	....	....	....	....
	Springfield Indians	AHL	12	1	8	9	14	....	....	....	....	....
1977-78	Binghamton Dusters	AHL	10	2	3	5	2	....	....	....	....	....
	Whitby Warriors	OHA-Sr.	13	13	2	15	6	....	....	....	....	....
	Major League Totals		**314**	**125**	**84**	**209**	**161**	**22**	**6**	**2**	**8**	**5**

• SINCLAIR, Gord — John Gordon

D – R. 5'10", 155 lbs. b: Vancouver, B.C., 9/30/1932.

Season	Club	League	GP	G	A	Pts	PIM	GP	G	A	Pts	PIM
1950-51	Trail Smoke Eaters	WIHL	34	11	14	25	29	9	7	5	12	8
1951-52	Trail Smoke Eaters	WIHL	43	15	21	36	40	8	1	3	4	0
1952-53	Trail Smoke Eaters	WIHL	46	10	19	29	59	9	4	1	5	8
1953-54	Trail Smoke Eaters	WIHL	31	10	14	24	46	4	0	3	3	4
1954-55	New Westminster Royals	WHL	59	5	12	17	34	....	....	....	....	....
1955-56	Seattle Americans	WHL	70	13	12	25	83	....	....	....	....	....
1956-57	Seattle Americans	WHL	70	14	34	48	66	10	2	6	8	10
1957-58	Seattle Totems	WHL	70	11	32	43	78	9	0	4	4	10
1958-59	Seattle Totems	WHL	69	14	31	45	80	12	1	4	5	4
1959-60	Seattle Totems	WHL	67	6	33	39	34	4	0	0	0	2
1960-61	Seattle Totems	WHL	62	6	31	37	26	11	2	4	6	6
1961-62	Seattle Totems	WHL	70	10	38	48	48	2	0	1	1	0
1962-63	Seattle Totems	WHL	70	10	43	53	44	17	4	4	8	6
1963-64	Seattle Totems	WHL	69	14	42	56	62	....	....	....	....	....
1964-65	Seattle Totems	WHL	61	9	26	35	52	7	0	4	4	10
1965-66	Seattle Totems	WHL	66	7	36	43	42	....	....	....	....	....
1966-67	San Diego Gulls	WHL	69	4	29	33	44	....	....	....	....	....
1967-68	San Diego Gulls	WHL	72	10	33	43	22	7	0	0	0	8
1968-69	San Diego Gulls	WHL	74	5	34	39	32	6	1	7	8	2
1969-70	San Diego Gulls	WHL	36	3	8	11	8	6	0	4	4	4

WHL First All-Star Team • (1957, 1959, 1960, 1963, 1965) • WHL Second All-Star Team (1958, 1964, 1968)

• SINDEN, Harry — Harry James — HHOF

D – L. 5'10", 180 lbs. b: Collins Bay, Ont., 9/14/1932.

Season	Club	League	GP	G	A	Pts	PIM	GP	G	A	Pts	PIM
1949-50	Oshawa Generals	OHA-Jr.	37	1	5	6	28	....	....	....	....	....
1950-51	Oshawa Generals	OHA-Jr.	53	9	28	37	71	5	1	3	4	8
1951-52	Oshawa Generals	OHA-Jr.	43	3	24	27	35	....	....	....	....	....
1952-53	Oshawa Generals	OHA-Jr.	55	12	34	46	49	5	1	1	2	6
1953-54	Oshawa Truckmen	OSrBL	STATISTICS NOT AVAILABLE									
1954-55	Whitby Dunlops	EOHL	STATISTICS NOT AVAILABLE									
1955-56	Whitby Dunlops	EOHL	40	20	47	67	83	9	1	*13	14	11
1956-57	Whitby Dunlops	EOHL	47	11	33	44	82	9	1	2	3	6
	Whitby Dunlops	Al-Cup	8	1	9	10	22	....	....	....	....	....
1957-58	Whitby Dunlops	EOHL	33	6	16	22	44	....	....	....	....	....
	Canada	WEC-A	7	4	3	7	4	....	....	....	....	....
1958-59	Whitby Dunlops	EOHL	52	13	34	47	38	10	2	5	7	12
	Whitby Dunlops	Al-Cup	12	3	10	13	8	....	....	....	....	....
1959-60	Whitby Dunlops	OHA-Sr.	38	7	14	21	30	11	0	5	5	0
	Canada	WEC-A	STATISTICS NOT AVAILABLE									
	Hull-Ottawa Canadiens	EPHL	....	....	....	....	....	5	0	2	2	2
1960-61	Kingston Frontenacs	EPHL	54	3	36	39	24	5	1	5	6	4
1961-62	Kingston Frontenacs	EPHL	68	11	61	72	98	1	1	10	11	11
1962-63	Kingston Frontenacs	EPHL	71	10	56	66	74	5	2	2	4	9
1963-64	Minneapolis Bruins	CPHL	57	6	25	31	64	5	0	2	2	0
	Providence Reds	AHL	1	0	0	0	0	....	....	....	....	....
1964-65	Minneapolis Bruins	CPHL	62	5	5	10	42	....	....	....	....	....
1965-66	Oklahoma City Blazers	CPHL	59	3	10	13	16	9	1	7	8	4

EPHL First All-Star Team (1962, 1963) • Named EPHL Top Defenseman (with Jean Gauthier) (1962) • Named EPHL MVP (1963) • Named EPHL Top Defenseman (1963)

• SMAILL, Walter — Walter Sydney

D – L. 5'10", 180 lbs. b: Montreal, Que., 12/18/1884 d: 1971.

Season	Club	League	GP	G	A	Pts	PIM	GP	G	A	Pts	PIM
1897/03	Westmount Academy	MCJHL	STATISTICS NOT AVAILABLE									
1903-04	Westmount Academy	MCSHL	STATISTICS NOT AVAILABLE									
	Westmount Academy-2	CAHL-I	STATISTICS NOT AVAILABLE									
1904-05	Westmount Academy	CAHL	2	1	0	1	....	....	....	....	....	....
1905-06	**Montreal AAA**	**ECAHA**	**10**	**19**	**0**	**19**	**15**	....	....	....	....	....
1906-07	**Montreal AAA**	**ECAHA**	**10**	**15**	**0**	**15**	**2**	....	....	....	....	....
1907-08	**Montreal Wanderers**	**ECAHA**	**5**	**8**	**0**	**8**	**5**	....	....	....	....	....
♦	Montreal Wanderers	St-Cup	4	3	0	3	8	....	....	....	....	....
	Grand'Mere A.C.C.	CAHL-I	STATISTICS NOT AVAILABLE									
1908-09	**Montreal Wanderers**	**ECHA**	**11**	**9**	**0**	**9**	**36**	....	....	....	....	....
♦	Montreal Wanderers	St-Cup	2	1	0	1	3	....	....	....	....	....
	Cobalt Silver Kings	TPHL	2	1	0	1	2	....	....	....	....	....
1909-10	**Cobalt Silver Kings**	**NHA**	**3**	**1**	**0**	**1**	**21**	....	....	....	....	....
	Cobalt Silver Kings	**NHA**	**4**	**1**	**0**	**1**	**12**	....	....	....	....	....
	Ottawa Senators	**NHA**	**5**	**5**	**0**	**5**	**22**	....	....	....	....	....
1910-11	**Montreal Wanderers**	**NHA**	**13**	**7**	**0**	**7**	**36**	....	....	....	....	....
1911-12	**Victoria Aristocrats**	**PCHA**	**16**	**9**	**0**	**9**	**34**	....	....	....	....	....
1912-13	**Victoria Aristocrats**	**PCHA**	**10**	**7**	**5**	**12**	**9**	....	....	....	....	....
	PCHA All-Stars	X-Games	2	1	0	1	....	....	....	....	....	....
1913-14	**Victoria Aristocrats**	**PCHA**	**16**	**9**	**5**	**14**	**8**	....	....	....	....	....
	Victoria Aristocrats	St-Cup	3	1	0	1	....	....	....	....	....	....
1914-15	**Victoria Aristocrats**	**PCHA**	**13**	**3**	**1**	**4**	**6**	....	....	....	....	....
1915-16	**Montreal Wanderers**	**NHA**	**21**	**6**	**1**	**7**	**37**	....	....	....	....	....

Season	Club	League	REGULAR SEASON GP	G	A	Pts	PIM	PLAYOFFS GP	G	A	Pts	PIM
1916-17			MILITARY SERVICE									
1917-18	Winnipeg Sommes	WSrHL	9	9	5	14	8	....	....	....	....	....
	Winnipeg Ypres	WSrHL	1	0	0	0	0	....	....	....	....	....
	Major League Totals		**137**	**99**	**12**	**111**	**243**	....	....	....	....	....

PCHA First All-Star Team (1914)

• SMITH, Alf — Alfred Edward — HHOF

RW – R. 5'7", 165 lbs. b: Ottawa, Ont., 6/3/1873 d: 8/21/1953.

Season	Club	League	GP	G	A	Pts	PIM	GP	G	A	Pts	PIM
1894-95	Ottawa Hockey Club	AHA-Sr.	8	5	0	5	....	....	....	....	....	....
1895-96	Ottawa Hockey Club	AHA-Sr.	8	7	0	7	....	....	....	....	....	....
1896-97	Ottawa Hockey Club	AHA-Sr.	8	*12	0	*12	....	....	....	....	....	....
1897-99			STATISTICS NOT AVAILABLE									
99-1900	Ottawa Capitals	AHA-Sr.	....	....	....	....	....	....	....	....	....	....
1900-01			STATISTICS NOT AVAILABLE									
1901-02	**Pittsburgh PAC**	**WPHL**	**14**	**11**	***9**	***20**	**17**	....	....	....	....	....
	Pittsburgh PAC	X-Games	8	*17	*8	*25	*14	....	....	....	....	....
1902-03	Ottawa Silver Seven	CAHL	STATISTICS NOT AVAILABLE									
1903-04	Ottawa Silver Seven	CAHL	4	8	0	8	6	....	....	....	....	....
♦	Ottawa Silver Seven	St-Cup	7	13	0	13	20	....	....	....	....	....
1904-05	Ottawa Silver Seven	FAHL	8	13	0	13	30	....	....	....	....	....
♦	Ottawa Silver Seven	St-Cup	5	11	0	11	9	....	....	....	....	....
1905-06	**Ottawa Senators**	**ECAHA**	**10**	**13**	**0**	**13**	**36**	....	....	....	....	....
♦	Ottawa Senators	St-Cup	6	8	0	8	6	....	....	....	....	....
1906-07	**Ottawa Senators**	**ECAHA**	**9**	**17**	**0**	**17**	**19**	....	....	....	....	....
	Kenora Thistles	**Man-Pro**	**1**	**2**	**0**	**2**	....	....	....	....	....	....
	Kenora Thistles	St-Cup	2	2	0	2	3	....	....	....	....	....
1907-08	**Ottawa Senators**	**ECAHA**	**9**	**12**	**0**	**12**	**20**	....	....	....	....	....
1908-09	Ottawa Senators	FAHL	1	1	0	1	0	....	....	....	....	....
	Pittsburgh Duquesne	WPHL	2	3	0	3	....	....	....	....	....	....
	Pittsburgh Bankers	WPHL	3	2	0	2	....	....	....	....	....	....
1909-10	Renfrew Rivers	FAHL	DID NOT PLAY – COACHING									
	Major League Totals		**43**	**55**	**9**	**64**	**92**	....	....	....	....	....

WPHL First All-Star Team (1902) • FAHL Second All-Star Team (1905)

• SMITH, Harry — Harry Henry

C – L. b: Ottawa, Ont., 12/29/1883 d: 1953.

Season	Club	League	GP	G	A	Pts	PIM	GP	G	A	Pts	PIM
1902-03	Ottawa Aberdeens	CAHL-I	STATISTICS NOT AVAILABLE									
1903-04	Arnprior Hockey Club	UOVHL	6	23	0	23	....	....	....	....	....	....
1904-05	Smiths Falls Seniors	OHA-Sr.	5	12	0	12	....	3	5	0	5	19
1905-06	**Ottawa Senators**	**ECAHA**	**8**	***31**	**0**	***31**	**29**	....	....	....	....	....
♦	Ottawa Senators	St-Cup	5	16	0	16	21	....	....	....	....	....
1906-07	**Ottawa Senators**	**ECAHA**	**9**	**23**	**0**	**23**	***56**	....	....	....	....	....
1907-08	**Winnipeg Maple Leafs**	**Man-Pro**	STATISTICS NOT AVAILABLE									
	Pittsburgh Bankers	WPHL	16	*44	0	*44	....	....	....	....	....	....
	Pittsburgh Bankers	W-S	3	*4	0	*4	....	....	....	....	....	....
1908-09	Pittsburgh Bankers	WPHL	7	14	0	14	....	....	....	....	....	....
	Montreal Wanderers	**ECHA**	**4**	**9**	**0**	**9**	**29**	....	....	....	....	....
♦	Montreal Wanderers	St-Cup	2	*5	0	*5	3	....	....	....	....	....
	Montreal Rubber	MIHL	1	1	0	1	8	....	....	....	....	....
	Haileybury Hawks	TPHL	5	18	0	18	8	2	2	0	2	15
1909-10	**Haileybury Hawks**	**NHA**	**3**	**4**	**0**	**4**	**0**	....	....	....	....	....
	Cobalt Silver Kings	**NHA**	**10**	**28**	**0**	**28**	**26**	....	....	....	....	....
1910-11	Cobalt Silver Kings	TPHL	1	1	0	1	0	....	....	....	....	....
	Waterloo Colts	**OPHL**	**13**	**20**	**0**	**20**	....	....	....	....	....	....
1911-12	**Schreiber Colts**	**NOHL**	**13**	***32**	**0**	***32**	**48**	....	....	....	....	....
1912-13	**Toronto Tecumsehs**	**NHA**	**15**	**14**	**0**	**14**	**40**	....	....	....	....	....
1913-14	**Ottawa Senators**	**NHA**	**3**	**1**	**0**	**1**	**7**	....	....	....	....	....
	Halifax Crescents	**MPHL**	**20**	**26**	**0**	**26**	**40**	....	....	....	....	....
	Major League Totals		**98**	**188**	**0**	**188**	**275**	....	....	....	....	....

• STUART, Bruce — HHOF

C – L. 6'2", 180 lbs. b: Ottawa, Ont., d: 10/28/1961.

Season	Club	League	GP	G	A	Pts	PIM	GP	G	A	Pts	PIM
1898-99	Ottawa Silver Seven	CAHL	1	1	0	1	....	....	....	....	....	....
99-1900	Ottawa Silver Seven	CAHL	5	11	0	11	....	....	....	....	....	....
	Ottawa Aberdeens	OHA-I	STATISTICS NOT AVAILABLE									
1900-01	Quebec Bulldogs	CAHL	6	5	0	5	....	....	....	....	....	....
1901-02	Ottawa Silver Seven	CAHL	8	9	0	9	....	....	....	....	....	....
1902-03	**Pittsburgh Victorias**	**WPHL**	**10**	***16**	**6**	***22**	**20**	....	....	....	....	....
1903-04	Portage Lakes	X-Games	14	44	0	44	6	9	*28	0	28	13
	Portage Lakes	W-S	2	3	0	3	*10	....	....	....	....	....
1904-05	**Portage Lakes**	**IHL**	**22**	**33**	**0**	**33**	***59**	....	....	....	....	....
1905-06	**Portage Lakes**	**IHL**	**20**	**15**	**0**	**15**	**22**	....	....	....	....	....
1906-07	**Portage Lakes**	**IHL**	**23**	**20**	**9**	**29**	***81**	....	....	....	....	....
1907-08	**Montreal Wanderers**	**ECAHA**	**3**	**3**	**0**	**3**	**18**	....	....	....	....	....
♦	Montreal Wanderers	St-Cup	3	8	0	8	18	....	....	....	....	....
♦**1908-09**	**Ottawa Senators**	**ECHA**	**11**	**22**	**0**	**22**	**30**	....	....	....	....	....
1909-10	**Ottawa Senators**	**CHA**	**2**	**4**	**0**	**4**	**0**	....	....	....	....	....
	Ottawa Senators	**NHA**	**7**	**14**	**0**	**14**	**17**	....	....	....	....	....
♦	Ottawa Senators	St-Cup	4	*10	0	*10	6	....	....	....	....	....
1910-11	**Ottawa Senators**	**NHA**	**3**	**0**	**0**	**0**	**0**	....	....	....	....	....
1911-12	Ottawa Stewartons	IPAHU	DID NOT PLAY – COACHING									
	Major League Totals		**101**	**127**	**15**	**142**	**247**	....	....	....	....	....

WPHL First All-Star Team (1903) • IHL Second All-Star Team (1905) • IHL First All-Star Team (1906)

• STUART, Hod — William Hodgeson — HHOF

Point. 6', 190 lbs. b: Ottawa, Ont., 1879 d: 6/23/1907.

Season	Club	League	GP	G	A	Pts	PIM	GP	G	A	Pts	PIM
1895-96	Rat Portage Thistles	MHL-Sr.	STATISTICS NOT AVAILABLE									
1896-98			STATISTICS NOT AVAILABLE									
1898-99	Ottawa Silver Seven	CAHL	3	1	0	1	....	....	....	....	....	....
99-1900	Ottawa Silver Seven	CAHL	7	5	0	5	....	....	....	....	....	....
1900-01	Quebec Bulldogs	CAHL	7	2	0	2	....	....	....	....	....	....
1901-02	Quebec Bulldogs	CAHL	8	5	0	5	....	....	....	....	....	....
1902-03	**Pittsburgh Bankers**	**WPHL**	**13**	**7**	**8**	**15**	**29**	**4**	**1**	**2**	**3**	**2**
1903-04	Portage Lakes	X-Games	14	13	0	13	*23	9	4	0	4	12
	Portage Lakes	W-S	2	0	0	0	0	....	....	....	....	....
1904-05	**Calumet Miners**	**IHL**	**22**	**18**	**0**	**18**	**19**	....	....	....	....	....
1905-06	**Pittsburgh Pros**	**IHL**	**20**	**11**	**0**	**11**	**50**	....	....	....	....	....
	Calumet Miners	**IHL**	**1**	**0**	**0**	**0**	**0**	....	....	....	....	....
1906-07	**Pittsburgh Pros**	**IHL**	**4**	**1**	**3**	**4**	**19**	....	....	....	....	....
	Montreal Wanderers	**ECAHA**	**8**	**3**	**0**	**3**	**21**	....	....	....	....	....
♦	Montreal Wanderers	St-Cup	4	0	0	0	8	....	....	....	....	....
	Major League Totals		**68**	**40**	**11**	**51**	**138**	**4**	**1**	**2**	**3**	**2**

WPHL First All-Star Team (1903) • IHL First All-Star Team (1905, 1906)

• TABOR, Harold

RW – R. 5'9", 160 lbs. b: Ottawa, Ont., 1/26/1910.

Season	Club	League	GP	G	A	Pts	PIM	GP	G	A	Pts	PIM
1927/29	Ottawa Gunners	OCJHL	STATISTICS NOT AVAILABLE									
1929-30	Ottawa Shamrocks	OCHL	20	*11	5	*16	23	4	2	0	2	2
	Ottawa Shamrocks	Al-Cup	2	1	1	2	2	....	....	....	....	....
1930-31	Guelph Maple Leafs	OPHL	2	1	0	1	0	....	....	....	....	....
	Detroit Olympics	IHL	25	0	0	0	2	....	....	....	....	....
1931-32	Detroit Olympics	IHL	1	0	0	0	0	....	....	....	....	....
	Syracuse Stars	IHL	1	0	0	0	0	....	....	....	....	....
1932-33	St. Louis Flyers	AHA	45	13	9	22	49	4	2	0	2	4
1933-34	Seattle Seahawks	NWHL	34	19	6	25	15	....	....	....	....	....
1934-35	Seattle Seahawks	NWHL	36	22	16	38	32	5	4	1	5	0
1935-36	Seattle Seahawks	NWHL	39	25	12	37	16	4	2	1	3	0
1936-37	Seattle Seahawks	PCHL	40	12	11	23	38	....	....	....	....	....
1937-38	Seattle Seahawks	PCHL	41	18	14	32	30	4	3	0	3	4
1938-39	Seattle Seahawks	PCHL	48	31	29	60	22	7	*5	3	*8	10
1939-40	Seattle Seahawks	PCHL	39	17	21	38	24	....	....	....	....	....
1940-41	Seattle Olympics	PCHL	48	27	30	57	58	2	0	0	0	0
1941-42	St. Paul Saints	AHA	49	23	12	35	12	2	0	1	1	5
1942-43	New Haven Eagles	AHL	8	1	0	1	2	....	....	....	....	....
1943-44	Seattle Shipyards	MWIHL	STATISTICS NOT AVAILABLE									
1944-45	Seattle Stars	PCHL	STATISTICS NOT AVAILABLE									

NWHL Second All-Star Team (1935)

• TAYLOR, Cyclone — Frederick Wellington — HHOF

Rover – L. 5'8", 165 lbs. b: Tara, Ont., 6/23/1885.

Season	Club	League	GP	G	A	Pts	PIM	GP	G	A	Pts	PIM
1902-03	Listowel Hockey Club	OHA-Jr.	STATISTICS NOT AVAILABLE									
1903-04	Listowel Hockey Club	OHA-I	STATISTICS NOT AVAILABLE									
1905-06	Portage-La-Prairie	MHL	4	4	0	4	....	....	....	....	....	....
	Portage Lakes	**IHL**	**6**	**11**	**0**	**11**	**4**	....	....	....	....	....
1906-07	Portage Lakes	IHL	23	18	7	25	31	....	....	....	....	....
1907-08	**Ottawa Senators**	**ECAHA**	**10**	**9**	**0**	**9**	**40**	....	....	....	....	....
1908-09	Pittsburgh Pros	WPHL	3	0	0	0	....	....	....	....	....	....
♦	**Ottawa Senators**	**ECHA**	**11**	**9**	**0**	**9**	**28**	....	....	....	....	....
1909-10	**Renfrew Creamery Kings**	**NHA**	**1**	**1**	**0**	**1**	**5**	....	....	....	....	....
	Renfrew Creamery Kings	**NHA**	**12**	**9**	**0**	**9**	**14**	....	....	....	....	....
1910-11	**Renfrew Creamery Kings**	**NHA**	**16**	**12**	**0**	**12**	**21**	....	....	....	....	....
1911-12			DID NOT PLAY									
	East All-Stars	X-Games	3	0	0	0	3	....	....	....	....	....
1912-13	**Vancouver Millionaires**	**PCHA**	**14**	**10**	***8**	**18**	**5**	....	....	....	....	....
1913-14	**Vancouver Millionaires**	**PCHA**	**16**	***24**	***15**	***39**	**18**	....	....	....	....	....
1914-15	**Vancouver Millionaires**	**PCHA**	**16**	**23**	***22**	***45**	**9**	**3**	***8**	**2**	***10**	**3**
♦	Vancouver Millionaires	St-Cup	3	*8	2	*10	....	....	....	....	*....	....
1915-16	**Vancouver Millionaires**	**PCHA**	**18**	**22**	***13**	***35**	**9**	....	....	....	....	....
1916-17	**Vancouver Millionaires**	**PCHA**	**11**	**14**	**15**	**29**	**12**	....	....	....	....	....
1917-18	**Vancouver Millionaires**	**PCHA**	**18**	***32**	**11**	***43**	**0**	**7**	**9**	**2**	**11**	**15**
1918-19	**Vancouver Millionaires**	**PCHA**	**20**	***23**	***13**	***36**	**12**	**2**	**1**	**0**	**1**	**0**
1919-20	**Vancouver Millionaires**	**PCHA**	**10**	**6**	**6**	**12**	**0**	**1**	**0**	**0**	**0**	**0**
1920-21	**Vancouver Millionaires**	**PCHA**	**6**	**5**	**1**	**6**	**0**	**3**	**0**	**1**	**1**	**0**
1921-22			DID NOT PLAY									
1922-23	**Vancouver Maroons**	**PCHA**	**1**	**0**	**0**	**0**	**0**	....	....	....	....	....
1943-44	Vancouver St. Regis	NWIHL	DID NOT PLAY – GENERAL MANAGER									
	Major League Totals		**186**	**210**	**104**	**314**	**177**	**16**	**18**	**5**	**23**	**18**

• TAYLOR, William — "Lady"

C. b: Brantford, Ont.

Season	Club	League	GP	G	A	Pts	PIM	GP	G	A	Pts	PIM
1901/03	Brantford Redmen	OHA-Sr.	STATISTICS NOT AVAILABLE									
1903-04	Brantford Redmen-2	OHA-I	STATISTICS NOT AVAILABLE									
1904-05	**Canadian Soo**	**IHL**	**24**	**35**	**0**	**35**	....	....	....	....	....	....
1905-06	**Canadian Soo**	**IHL**	**10**	**13**	**0**	**13**	**22**	....	....	....	....	....
	American Soo	**IHL**	**4**	**5**	**0**	**5**	**12**	....	....	....	....	....
1906-07	**Canadian Soo**	**IHL**	**24**	***46**	**18**	***64**	**50**	....	....	....	....	....
	Cobalt Silver Kings	TPHL	3	7	0	7	3	....	....	....	....	....
1907-08	**Brantford Athletics**	**OPHL**	**12**	**28**	**0**	**28**	**12**	....	....	....	....	....
1908-09	**St. Catharines Legion**	**OPHL**	**1**	**0**	**0**	**0**	**0**	....	....	....	....	....
	Pittsburgh Professionals	WPHL	2	1	0	1	0	....	....	....	....	....
	Berlin Athletics	**OPHL**	**2**	**4**	**0**	**4**	**7**	....	....	....	....	....
	New Liskeard A.C.C.	TPHL	2	1	0	1	0	....	....	....	....	....
1909-10			DID NOT PLAY									
1910-11	**Port Arthur T-Bays**	**NOHL**	**5**	**4**	**0**	**4**	**3**	....	....	....	....	....
	Port Arthur Athletics	EOPHL	1	0	0	0	0	....	....	....	....	....
	Major League Totals		**82**	**135**	**18**	**153**	**106**	....	....	....	....	....

IPHL Second All-Star Team (1905, 1907) • OPHL First All-Star Team (1908)

• TOBIN, Charles — Charles Stuart

RW – R. 5'10", 160 lbs. b: Winnipeg, Man., 11/24/1885 d: 5/30/1924.

Season	Club	League	GP	G	A	Pts	PIM	GP	G	A	Pts	PIM
1906-07	Winnipeg Shamrocks	WCAHA	1	3	0	3	....	....	....	....	....	....
	North Battleford Pros	APHL	STATISTICS NOT AVAILABLE									
1907-08	North Battleford Pros	APHL	9	19	9	28	11	....	....	....	....	....
1908-09	**Winnipeg Shamrocks**	**Man-Pro**	**1**	**1**	**0**	**1**	**0**	....	....	....	....	....
1909-10	Manitoba Varsity	MHL-Sr.	2	6	0	6	....	....	....	....	....	....
1910-11	Winnipeg Monarchs	MHL-Sr.	3	4	0	4	....	....	....	....	....	....
	Saskatoon Pros	Sk-Pro	6	9	0	9	....	....	....	....	....	....
	Prince Albert Mintos	Sk-Pro	2	*8	0	*8	....	....	....	....	....	....
	Prince Albert Mintos	St-Cup	2	4	0	4	9	....	....	....	....	....
1911-12	Moose Jaw Athletics	Sk-Pro	2	4	0	4	12	....	....	....	....	....
1912-13	**New Westminster Royals**	**PCHA**	**13**	**11**	**3**	**14**	**20**	....	....	....	....	....
1913-14	**New Westminster Royals**	**PCHA**	**14**	**5**	**2**	**7**	**12**	....	....	....	....	....
1914-15	**Portland Rosebuds**	**PCHA**	**18**	**11**	**2**	**13**	**15**	....	....	....	....	....
	PCHA All-Stars	X-Games	2	3	0	3	0	....	....	....	....	....

Season	Club	League	GP	G	A	Pts	PIM	GP	G	A	Pts	PIM
			REGULAR SEASON					PLAYOFFS				
1915-16	**Portland Rosebuds**	**PCHA**	**18**	**20**	**8**	**28**	**22**	**5**	**2**	**0**	**2**	**12**
	PCHA All-Stars	X-Games	3	2	0	2	0	....	....	....	....	....
1916-17	**Portland Rosebuds**	**PCHA**	**24**	**15**	**7**	**22**	**45**	....	....	....	....	....
1917-18	**Portland Rosebuds**	**PCHA**	**18**	**13**	**3**	**16**	**0**	....	....	....	....	....
1918-19	**Victoria Cougars**	**PCHA**	**20**	**10**	**1**	**11**	**3**	....	....	....	....	....
1919-20	**Seattle Metropolitans**	**PCHA**	**19**	**10**	**4**	**14**	**3**	**2**	**0**	**0**	**0**	**0**
	Seattle Metropolitans	St-Cup	5	0	0	0	0	....	....	....	....	....
1920-21	**Seattle Metropolitans**	**PCHA**	**21**	**4**	**0**	**4**	**6**	**2**	**0**	**0**	**0**	**0**
1921-22	**Vancouver Millionaires**	**PCHA**	**9**	**1**	**0**	**1**	**0**	**2**	**0**	**0**	**0**	**0**
	Vancouver Millionaires	St-Cup	5	0	0	0	0	....	....	....	....	....
	Major League Totals		**175**	**101**	**30**	**131**	**126**	**11**	**2**	**0**	**2**	**12**

• TRIHEY, Harry Henry Judah HHOF

C. b: Montreal, Que., 12/25/1877 d: 12/9/1942.

Season	Club	League	GP	G	A	Pts	PIM	GP	G	A	Pts	PIM
1893/96	Montreal St. Mary's	H.S.	STATISTICS NOT AVAILABLE									
1895-96	Montreal Orioles	QAHA-I	STATISTICS NOT AVAILABLE									
1896-97	Montreal Shamrocks	QAHA-I	STATISTICS NOT AVAILABLE									
	Montreal Shamrocks	MCSHL	1	0	0	0	....	....	....	....	....	....
1897-98	Montreal Shamrocks	AHA-Sr.	8	3	0	3	....	....	....	....	....	....
1898-99	Montreal Shamrocks	CAHL	7	*19	0	*19	....	....	....	....	....	....
♦	Montreal Shamrocks	St-Cup	1	3	0	3	....	....	....	....	....	....
99-1900	Montreal Shamrocks	CAHL	7	*17	0	*17	....	....	....	....	....	....
♦	Montreal Shamrocks	St-Cup	5	12	0	12	....	....	....	....	....	....
1900-01	Montreal Shamrocks	CAHL	7	7	0	7	....	....	....	....	....	....
	Montreal Shamrocks	St-Cup	2	1	0	1	....	....	....	....	....	....

• WALSH, Marty HHOF

C – L. b: Kingston, Ont., 1883 d: 1915.

Season	Club	League	GP	G	A	Pts	PIM	GP	G	A	Pts	PIM
1902-03	Queen's University	LOVHL	STATISTICS NOT AVAILABLE									
1903-04	Queen's University	LOVHL	4	*9	0	*9	*30	....	....	....	....	....
	Kingston A.C.	OHA-I	STATISTICS NOT AVAILABLE									
1904-05	Queen's University	LOVHL	4	9	0	9	15	....	....	....	....	....
1905-06	Queen's University	OHA-Sr.	STATISTICS NOT AVAILABLE									
	Queen's University	St-Cup	2	4	0	4	....	....	....	....	....	....
1906-07	**Canadian Soo**	**IHL**	**7**	**4**	**5**	**9**	**0**	....	....	....	....	....
1907-08	**Ottawa Senators**	**ECAHA**	**9**	***27**	**0**	***27**	**30**	....	....	....	....	....
♦**1908-09**	**Ottawa Senators**	**ECHA**	**12**	***42**	**0**	***42**	**41**	....	....	....	....	....
1909-10	**Ottawa Senators**	**CHA**	**2**	**9**	**0**	**9**	**14**	....	....	....	....	....
	Ottawa Senators	**NHA**	**11**	**19**	**0**	**19**	**44**	....	....	....	....	....
♦	Ottawa Senators	St-Cup	4	8	0	8	12	....	....	....	....	....
1910-11	**Ottawa Senators**	**NHA**	**16**	***35**	**0**	***35**	**51**	....	....	....	....	....
♦	Ottawa Senators	St-Cup	2	*13	0	*13	0	....	....	....	....	....
1911-12	**Ottawa Senators**	**NHA**	**12**	**9**	**0**	**9**	**0**	....	....	....	....	....
	Major League Totals		**69**	**145**	**5**	**150**	**180**	....	....	....	....	....

• WATSON, Harry Henry Ellis HHOF

LW – L. 165 lbs. b: St. John's, Nfld., 7/14/1898 d: 9/11/1957.

Season	Club	League	GP	G	A	Pts	PIM	GP	G	A	Pts	PIM
1913-14	Whitby Athletics	OHA-I	STATISTICS NOT AVAILABLE									
1914-15	Toronto St. Andrews	OHA-Jr.	STATISTICS NOT AVAILABLE									
1915-16	Toronto Aura Lee	OHA-Jr.	STATISTICS NOT AVAILABLE									
1916-17	Toronto Aura Lee	OHA-Sr.	8	*18	0	*18	....	....	....	....	....	....
1917-18			MILITARY SERVICE									
1918-19	Toronto Dentals	OHA-Sr.	....	....	....	....	....	1	1	0	1	....
1919-20	Toronto Granites	OHA-Sr.	8	17	4	21	....	5	4	1	5	....
	Toronto Granites	Al-Cup	2	1	0	1	....	....	....	....	....	....
1920-21	Toronto Granites	OHA-Sr.	9	10	4	14	....	2	2	0	2	....
1921-22	Toronto Granites	OHA-Sr.	10	18	4	22	....	2	*5	0	*5	....
	Toronto Granites	Al-Cup	5	13	2	15	....	....	....	....	....	....
1922-23	Toronto Granites	OHA-Sr.	12	*21	4	25	....	2	*3	0	*3	0
	Toronto Granites	Al-Cup	6	*11	4	*15	2	....	....	....	....	....
1923-24	Canada	X-Games	14	*24	6	*30	....	....	....	....	....	....
	Canada	Olympics	5	*37	9	*46	....	....	....	....	....	....
1924-25	Parkdale Canoe Club	OHA-Sr.	6	6	2	8	....	....	....	....	....	....
1925-26	Parkdale Canoe Club	OHA-Sr.	1	1	1	2	....	2	0	0	0	....
1926-27	Parkdale Canoe Club	OHA-Sr.	1	2	0	2	....	....	....	....	....	....
1927-28	Toronto Marlboros	OHA-Sr.	2	1	1	2	2	....	....	....	....	....
1928-29			DID NOT PLAY									
1929-30	Toronto Nationals	OHA-Sr.	1	0	0	0	0	....	....	....	....	....
1930-31			DID NOT PLAY									
1931-32	Toronto Nationals	OHA-Sr.	2	0	0	0	0	....	....	....	....	....

OHA-Jr. First All-Star Team (1915) • OHA-Sr. Second All-Star Team (1920) • OHA-Sr. First All-Star Team (1922, 1923) • Named OHA-Sr. MVP (1922, 1923)

• WESTWICK, Harry "Rat" HHOF

Rover. b: Ottawa, Ont., 4/23/1876 d: 4/3/1957.

Season	Club	League	GP	G	A	Pts	PIM	GP	G	A	Pts	PIM
1893-94	Ottawa Aberdeens	AHA-Sr.	STATISTICS NOT AVAILABLE									
1894-95	Ottawa Silver Seven	AHA-Sr.	5	1	0	1	....	....	....	....	....	....
1895-96	Ottawa Silver Seven	AHA-Sr.	8	8	0	8	....	....	....	....	....	....
1896-97	Ottawa Silver Seven	AHA-Sr.	8	6	0	6	....	....	....	....	....	....
1897-98	Ottawa Silver Seven	AHA-Sr.	5	1	0	1	....	....	....	....	....	....
1898-99			STATISTICS NOT AVAILABLE									
99-1900	Ottawa Capitals	OHA-Sr.	STATISTICS NOT AVAILABLE									
1900-01	Ottawa Silver Seven	CAHL	7	6	0	6	....	....	....	....	....	....
1901-02	Ottawa Silver Seven	CAHL	8	11	0	11	6	....	....	....	....	....
1902-03	Ottawa Silver Seven	CAHL	6	6	0	6	9	....	....	....	....	....
♦	Ottawa Silver Seven	St-Cup	1	0	0	0	0	....	....	....	....	....
1903-04	Ottawa Silver Seven	CAHL	2	5	0	5	0	....	....	....	....	....
♦	Ottawa Silver Seven	St-Cup	8	6	0	6	6	....	....	....	....	....
1904-05	Ottawa Silver Seven	FAHL	8	15	0	15	9	....	....	....	....	....
♦	Ottawa Silver Seven	St-Cup	5	9	0	9	3	....	....	....	....	....
1905-06	**Ottawa Senators**	**ECAHA**	**8**	**6**	**0**	**6**	**15**	....	....	....	....	....
♦	Ottawa Senators	St-Cup	6	8	0	8	9	....	....	....	....	....
1906-07	**Ottawa Senators**	**ECAHA**	**9**	**14**	**0**	**14**	**12**	....	....	....	....	....
	Kenora Thistles	**Man-Pro**	**1**	**0**	**0**	**0**	**0**	**2**	**2**	**0**	**2**	**6**
	Kenora Thistles	St-Cup	2	0	0	0	6	....	....	....	....	....
1907-08	**Ottawa Senators**	**ECAHA**	**10**	**10**	**0**	**10**	**20**	....	....	....	....	....
1908-09	**Ottawa Senators**	**ECHA**	**10**	**8**	**0**	**8**	....	....	....	....	....	....
	Major League Totals		**38**	**38**	**0**	**38**	**47**	**2**	**2**	**0**	**2**	**6**

FAHL Second All-Star Team (1905)

• WHITCROFT, Fred HHOF

Rover – R. 5'10", 165 lbs. b: Port Perry, Ont., 1883 d: 1931.

Season	Club	League	GP	G	A	Pts	PIM	GP	G	A	Pts	PIM
1899/02	Peterborough Colts	OHA-Jr.	STATISTICS NOT AVAILABLE									
1902/04	Peterborough Colts	OHA-I	STATISTICS NOT AVAILABLE									
1904-05	Midland Club	OHA-I	STATISTICS NOT AVAILABLE									
1905-06	Peterborough Colts	OHA-I	STATISTICS NOT AVAILABLE									
1906-07	Peterborough Colts	OHA-I	5	13	0	13	33	....	....	....	....	....
	Kenora Thistles	**Man-Pro**	**4**	**3**	**0**	**3**	....	**2**	***5**	**0**	***5**	**0**
	Kenora Thistles	St-Cup	2	2	0	2	3	....	....	....	....	....
1907-08	Edmonton Professionals	APHL	10	*35	*7	*42	12	8	*24	7	*31	12
1908-09	Edmonton Professionals	X-Games	10	*27	0	*27	12	....	....	....	....	....
	Edmonton Professionals	St-Cup	9	21	0	21	*32	....	....	....	....	....
1909-10	Edmonton Professionals	St-Cup	2	5	0	5	2	....	....	....	....	....
	Renfrew Creamery Kings	**NHA**	**5**	**3**	**0**	**3**	**13**	....	....	....	....	....
	Major League Totals		**9**	**6**	**0**	**6**	**13**	**2**	**5**	**0**	**5**	**0**

• WHITLOCK, Buck Roy Nelson

C – L. 5'7", 170 lbs. b: Charlottetown, P.E.I., 1/5/2024.

Season	Club	League	GP	G	A	Pts	PIM	GP	G	A	Pts	PIM
1938-39	Charlottetown Primroses	PEI-I	2	3	0	3	0	....	....	....	....	....
	Charlottetown Abbies	PEI-Jr.	....	....	....	....	....	1	2	0	2	0
1939-40	Charlottetown Royals	PEI-Jr.	6	4	2	6	0	....	....	....	....	....
	Charlottetown Royals	M-Cup	6	2	2	4	0	....	....	....	....	....
1940-41	Charlottetown Royals	PEI-Jr.	2	1	0	1	2	5	*11	5	*16	5
	Charlottetown Abbies	PEI-Jr.	2	4	1	5	0	....	....	....	....	....
1941-42	Charlottetown Royals	PEI-Jr.	1	3	3	6	0	2	*8	0	*8	0
	Charlottetown Holmans	PEI-Sr.	2	4	2	6	0	....	....	....	....	....
1942-43	Charlottetown Navy	PEI-Sr.	9	*20	13	*33	20	3	4	*6	*10	4
	Charlottetown Abbies	Al-Cup	4	11	4	15	9	....	....	....	....	....
1943-44	Charlottetown Navy	PEI-Sr.	4	6	3	9	2	....	....	....	....	....
1944-45			MILITARY SERVICE									
1945-46	New Glasgow Bombers	NSAPC	15	19	21	40	17	2	3	1	4	0
1946-47	Moncton Hawks	MSHL	40	25	35	60	25	9	3	10	13	7
	Moncton Hawks	Al-Cup	10	5	10	15	6	....	....	....	....	....
1947-48	Moncton Hawks	MSHL	46	*59	35	*94	37	11	*10	7	*17	9
	Moncton Hawks	Al-Cup	4	1	3	4	2	....	....	....	....	....
1948-49	Moncton Hawks	MSHL	48	18	30	48	33	7	5	2	7	0
1949-50	Saint John Beavers	MSHL	64	*64	49	*113	26	11	*12	*9	*21	7
1950-51	Saint John Beavers	MMHL	78	*57	69	*126	20	5	0	3	3	2
1951-52	Charlottetown Islanders	MMHL	86	33	57	90	48	4	1	0	1	2
1952-53	Charlottetown Islanders	MMHL	80	*55	73	*128	29	17	5	10	15	6
1953-54	Charlottetown Islanders	MMHL	54	51	63	114	45	7	6	4	10	8
1954-55	Charlottetwon Islanders	ACSHL	59	36	*58	*94	51	11	2	8	10	16
1955-56	Fredericton Capitals	ACSHL	67	31	58	89	55	9	3	5	8	6
1956-57	Miramichi Beavers	NBNHL	15	8	9	17	8	....	....	....	....	....
	Charlottetown B.Y.C.	PEI-Sr.	15	18	*42	60	14	11	11	13	24	6
1957-58	Parkdale Sandy's Royals	PEI-Sr.	20	28	32	60	44	....	....	....	....	....
1958-59	Parkdale Sandy's Royals	PEI-Sr.	9	6	14	20	14	8	2	10	12	4
1959-60	Parkdale Sandy's Royals	PEI-Sr.	27	48	67	115	34	12	13	21	34	4
1960-61	Parkdale Sandy's Royals	PEI-Sr.	20	17	*27	*44	15	6	1	11	12	4
1961-62	Parkdale Sandy's Royals	PEI-Sr.	18	24	26	50	24	9	8	9	17	10
	Parkdale Sandy's Royals	Al-Cup	6	8	3	11	4	....	....	....	....	....
1962-63	Parkdale Sandy's Royals	PEI-Sr.	24	*27	*38	*65	46	10	7	13	20	6
	Parkdale Sandy's Royals	Al-Cup	1	0	1	1	0	....	....	....	....	....

MSHL First All-Star Team (1948, 1950) • MMHL First All-Star Team (1951, 1953, 1954) • ACSHL First All-Star Team (1955)

CHAPTER 72

Notable North American Non-NHL Goaltenders

Early Era, Minor Professional and WHA Goaltenders

Compiled by Ernie Fitzsimmons

Season	Club	League	REGULAR SEASON GP	W	L	T	Mins	GA	SO	Avg	PLAYOFFS GP	W	L	T	Mins	GA	SO	Avg
• AUBRY, Serge	G. 5'7", 165 lbs. b: Montreal, Que., 1/2/1942.																	
1959-60	Montreal Jr. Canadiens	QJHL	STATISTICS NOT AVAILABLE															
	Brockville Jr. Canadiens	Mem-Cup	13	7	5	1	790	38	2	2.89	....	....	....	....	....	....	....	....
1960-61	Verdun Maple Leafs	QJHL	STATISTICS NOT AVAILABLE															
1961-62	Montreal Jr. Canadiens	QJHL	STATISTICS NOT AVAILABLE															
1962-63	Quebec Aces	AHL	DID NOT PLAY – SPARE GOALTENDER															
1963-64	Windsor Maple Leafs	NSSHL	70	*58	9	3	4200	233	*5	*3.33	8	*8	0	0	480	13	*3	*1.63
	Windsor Maple Leafs	Al-Cup	11	8	3	0	668	35	1	3.14	....	....	....	....	....	....	....	....
1964-65	Sherbrooke Castors	QSHL	STATISTICS NOT AVAILABLE															
	Sherbrooke Castors	Al-Cup	15	14	1	0	900	34	2	2.27	....	....	....	....	....	....	....	....
1965-66	Sherbrooke Castors	QSHL	42	26	15	1	2520	154	0	3.67	12	8	4	0	752	36	0	2.87
1966-67	Sherbrooke Castors	QSHL	42	27	15	1	2520	148	0	3.00	10	5	5	0	32	32	0	3.06
1967-68	Tulsa Oilers	CPHL	32	....	....	....	1922	115	0	3.59	7	5	2	0	420	17	0	2.45
1968-69	Des Moines Oak Leafs	IHL	6	....	....	....	305	20	0	3.92	....	....	....	....	....	....	....	....
	Tulsa Oilers	CHL	31	....	....	....	1741	104	0	3.58	7	3	4	0	433	23	0	3.21
1969-70	Tulsa Oilers	CHL	37	....	....	....	2180	92	2	2.53	5	2	3	0	306	18	*1	3.17
1970-71	Rochester Americans	AHL	51	....	....	....	2787	149	2	3.20	....	....	....	....	....	....	....	....
1971-72	Rochester Americans	AHL	37	....	....	....	1813	137	0	4.53	....	....	....	....	....	....	....	....
1972-73	**Quebec Nordiques**	**WHA**	**52**	**25**	**22**	**2**	**3036**	**182**	**2**	**3.59**	....	....	....	....	....	....	....	....
1973-74	**Quebec Nordiques**	**WHA**	**26**	**11**	**11**	**2**	**1395**	**90**	**1**	**3.87**	....	....	....	....	....	....	....	....
1974-75	**Quebec Nordiques**	**WHA**	**31**	**17**	**11**	**0**	**1762**	**109**	**0**	**3.71**	....	....	....	....	....	....	....	....
1975-76	**Cincinnati Stingers**	**WHA**	**12**	**6**	**4**	**0**	**549**	**38**	**1**	**4.15**	....	....	....	....	....	....	....	....
1976-77	**Quebec Nordiques**	**WHA**	**21**	**6**	**5**	**0**	**769**	**51**	**1**	**3.98**	**3**	**0**	**1**	**0**	**18**	**1**	**0**	**3.33**
	Quebec Nordiques	**WHA**	DID NOT PLAY															
1977-1979	**Quebec Nordiques**	**WHA**	DID NOT PLAY – SCOUTING															
1979-1979	Quebec Nordiques	NHL	DID NOT PLAY – SCOUTING															
1991-1995	Los Angeles Kings	NHL	DID NOT PLAY – SCOUTING															
	Major League Totals		**142**	**65**	**53**	**4**	**7511**	**470**	**5**	**3.75**	**3**	**0**	**1**	....	**18**	**1**	**0**	**3.33**
• BENTLEY, Bev	Beverly G. 5'10", 175 lbs. b: Delisle, Sask., 6/8/1927.																	
1943-44	Trail Smoke Eaters	BCJHL	17	11	6	0	1039	68	1	3.93	....	....	....	....	....	....	....	....
1944-45	Moose Jaw Canucks	SJHL	16	*14	2	0	960	960	41	2.56	4	*4	0	0	240	5	*1	*1.25
	Moose Jaw Canucks	Mem-Cup	17	12	5	0	1020	63	0	3.71	....	....	....	....	....	....	....	....
1946-47	Moose Jaw Canucks	SJHL	22	....	....	....	1320	88	0	4.00	6	5	1	0	360	20	0	*3.33
	Moose Jaw Canucks	Mem-Cup	15	7	7	1	910	69	0	4.55	....	....	....	....	....	....	....	....
1947-48	Oakland-LA Blades	PCHL	44	....	....	....	2640	162	3	3.68	4	....	....	....	240	17	0	4.25
1948-49	Regina Caps	WCSHL	48	*33	13	2	2880	150	*6	*3.13	8	*7	1	0	490	20	0	*2.45
	Regina Caps	Al-Cup	14	8	6	0	850	44	1	3.11	....	....	....	....	....	....	....	....
1949-50	Kitchener-Waterloo Dutchmen	OHA-Sr.	42	20	20	2	2520	149	2	3.54	14	7	7	0	840	43	2	3.07
1950-51	Regina Caps	WCMHL	54	....	....	....	3240	293	1	5.43	....	....	....	....	....	....	....	....
1951-52	Spokane Flyers	WIHL	66	*37	23	6	3960	247	1	*3.74	5	2	3	0	300	24	0	4.80
1952-53	Saskatoon Quakers	WHL	58	30	19	8	3480	192	2	3.31	13	6	*7	0	780	42	1	3.23
1953-54			STATISTICS NOT AVAILABLE															
1954-55	Saskatoon Quakers	WHL	45	14	24	7	2700	175	4	3.88	....	....	....	....	....	....	....	....
	Vancouver Canucks	WHL	6	0	5	1	360	24	0	4.00	....	....	....	....	....	....	....	....
	New Westminster Royals	WHL	2	0	1	1	119	7	0	3.50	....	....	....	....	....	....	....	....
	Victoria Cougars	WHL	....	....	....	....	....	....	....	....	1	0	1	0	60	7	0	7.00
1955-56	New Westminster Royals	WHL	61	29	30	2	3700	201	6	3.29	4	1	3	0	240	14	0	3.50
1956-57	New Westminster Royals	WHL	51	28	18	4	3089	153	*7	2.97	11	6	*5	0	660	33	*1	3.00
1957-58	New Westminster Royals	WHL	70	39	28	3	4200	222	3	3.17	4	1	3	0	240	14	0	3.50
1958-59	New Westminster Royals	WHL	7	1	5	1	420	16	0	2.28	....	....	....	....	....	....	....	....
	Seattle Totems	WHL	64	35	26	3	3840	233	2	3.65	12	*11	1	0	734	20	*2	*1.64
1959-60	Seattle Totems	WHL	68	38	26	4	4080	206	3	3.02	4	0	4	0	249	12	0	2.89
1960-61	Seattle Totems	WHL	63	32	26	5	3780	197	1	3.12	11	6	*5	0	666	32	0	2.88
1961-62	San Francisco Seals	WHL	60	27	32	1	3618	230	*4	3.81	2	0	2	0	120	11	0	5.50
1962-1965			STATISTICS NOT AVAILABLE															
1965-66	Knoxville Knights	EHL	5	....	....	....	300	11	0	2.20	....	....	....	....	....	....	....	....
1966-67	Knoxville Knights	EHL	9	....	....	....	540	27	0	3.00	....	....	....	....	....	....	....	....

• Son of Roy • PCHL First All-Star Team (1948-49

Season	Club	League	REGULAR SEASON GP	W	L	T	Mins	GA	SO	Avg	PLAYOFFS GP	W	L	T	Mins	GA	SO	Avg
• DECHENE, Lucien	G. 5'10", 200 lbs. b: Quebec City, Que., 8/17/1925.																	
1945-46	Valleyfield Braves	QSHL	9	....	....	....	540	41	0	4.56	....	....	....	....	....	....	....	....
1946-47	Valleyfield Braves	QSHL	40	8	*31	1	2400	211	2	5.27	....	....	....	....	....	....	....	....
1947-48	Victoriaville Tigers	QPHL	59	*42	10	7	3540	157	*4	*2.66	12	*9	3	0	720	36	1	3.00
	Victoriaville Tigers	Al-Cup	3	1	2	0	180	21	0	7.00	....	....	....	....	....	....	....	....
1948-49	New Westminster Royals	PCHL	70	*39	26	5	4200	229	2	3.27	12	8	4	0	722	33	0	2.74
1949-50	Vancouver Canucks	PCHL	69	33	27	9	4140	258	4	3.74	12	6	6	0	760	32	0	2.53
1950-51	New Westminster Royals	PCHL	70	*38	24	8	4200	198	*5	*2.82	11	5	6	0	666	29	2	2.61
1951-52	New Westminster Royals	PCHL	70	*40	19	11	4200	199	*5	*2.84	7	3	4	0	472	18	0	2.29
1952-53	New Westminster Royals	WHL	70	29	33	8	4200	252	*6	3.60	6	3	3	0	348	17	0	*2.93
1953-54	New Westminster Royals	WHL	70	28	34	8	4200	258	2	3.68	7	2	5	0	424	26	0	3.68
	Vancouver Canucks	WHL	....	....	....	....	....	....	....	....	2	0	2	0	77	5	0	3.90
1954-55	New Westminster Royals	WHL	59	25	27	6	3485	253	5	4.36	....	....	....	....	....	....	....	....
1955-56	Brandon Regals	WHL	68	23	37	8	4195	230	4	3.29	....	....	....	....	....	....	....	....
1956-57	Brandon Regals	WHL	67	*41	*21	4	4013	173	3	*2.59	9	8	4	0	542	18	1	*1.99
1957-58	Saskatoon-St. Paul Regals	WHL	61	24	37	0	3660	259	2	4.24	....	....	....	....	....	....	....	....
	Cleveland Barons	AHL	5	2	3	0	320	16	0	3.00	7	3	4	0	430	15	0	2.09

Season	Club	League	REGULAR SEASON								PLAYOFFS							
			GP	W	L	T	Mins	GA	SO	Avg	GP	W	L	T	Mins	GA	SO	Avg
1958-59	Saskatoon Quakers	WHL	56	26	27	3	3381	169	4	*3.00	....	....	....	....	....	....	....	....
	Vancouver Canucks	WHL	....	....	....	....	....	....	....	....	4	2	2	0	258	9	1	*2.09
1959-60	Calgary Stampeders	WHL	28	15	12	1	1704	77	1	2.71	....	....	....	....	....	....	....	....
	Quebec Aces	AHL	10	3	7	0	600	45	0	4.50	....	....	....	....	....	....	....	....
1960-61	Calgary Stampeders	WHL	42	28	12	2	2513	120	4	2.86	5	1	4	0	300	17	0	3.40

First All-Star Team (1948-49, 50-51, 51-52, 56-57) MVP 1951-52) Prairie Division MVP 1956-57)

• FOSTER, Jimmy James G. 140 lbs. b: Glasgow, Scotland, 9/13/1907.

Season	Club	League	GP	W	L	T	Mins	GA	SO	Avg	GP	W	L	T	Mins	GA	SO	Avg
1925-26	Brandon Legion	S-SSHL	16	8	7	1	990	54	0	*3.27	....	....	....	....	....	....	....	....
1926-27	Winnipeg Winnipegs	MHL-Sr.	8	*7	1	0	480	10	*3	*1.25	5	3	1	2	300	9	1	1.80
	Winnipeg CNR	WSrHL	STATISTICS NOT AVAILABLE															
1927-28	University of Manitoba	WSrHL	2	2	0	0	120	7	0	3.50	....	....	....	....	....	....	....	....
	Winnipeg CNR	WSrHL	9	4	*5	0	580	21	2	2.33	....	....	....	....	....	....	....	....
1928-29	Winnipeg CPR	WSrHL	5	....	....	....	300	9	0	*1.80	....	....	....	....	....	....	....	....
1929-30	Elmwood Millionaires	MHL-Sr.	8	5	2	1	520	12	0	*1.50	2	*2	0	0	130	1	*1	*0.46
	Elmwood Millionaires	Al-Cup	5	2	2	1	330	7	2	1.27	....	....	....	....	....	....	....	....
	Winnipeg Harris-Abatoir	WSrHL	STATISTICS NOT AVAILABLE															
1930-31	Elmwood Millionaires	MHL-Sr.	11	*6	5	0	660	21	1	1.91	2	....	....	....	120	5	0	2.50
1931-32	Moncton Hawks	X-Games	4	2	0	2	250	9	0	2.16	....	....	....	....	....	....	....	....
	Moncton Hawks	MSHL	24	*16	6	2	1530	36	6	1.40	5	2	3	0	310	16	0	3.10
	Moncton Hawks	Al-Cup	5	1	2	2	360	9	1	1.50	....	....	....	....	....	....	....	....
1932-33	Moncton Hawks	X-Games	3	2	1	0	180	2	1	0.67	....	....	....	....	....	....	....	....
	Moncton Hawks	MSHL	26	*14	10	0	1690	31	11	*1.10	5	*3	1	2	330	6	1	*1.20
	Moncton Hawks	Al-Cup	8	7	1	0	480	6	4	0.75	....	....	....	....	....	....	....	....
1933-34	Moncton Hawks	X-Games	4	1	3	0	240	6	2	1.50	....	....	....	....	....	....	....	....
	Moncton Hawks	MSHL	41	*28	8	5	2550	60	10	*1.41	3	*3	0	0	180	4	*1	*1.30
	Moncton Hawks	Al-Cup	12	8	3	1	730	19	1	....	....	....	....	....	....	....	....	1.56
1934-35	Moncton Hawks	MSHL	20	9	7	3	1190	49	2	2.47	....	....	....	....	....	....	....	....
	Moncton Hawks	Big-3	4	1	*3	0	240	6	2	1.50	....	....	....	....	....	....	....	....
	Saint John Beavers	X-Games	6	2	4	0	370	49	0	7.95	12	*7	4	2	730	53	1	4.36
1935-36	Richmond Hawks	Britain	STATISTICS NOT AVAILABLE															
	Britain	Olympics	7	5	0	2	330	3	*4	*0.55	....	....	....	....	....	....	....	....
1936-37	Harringay Greyhounds	Britain	STATISTICS NOT AVAILABLE															
1937-38	Harringay Greyhounds	Britain	48	24	16	8	2880	109	....	2.27	....	....	....	....	....	....	....	....
1938-39	Harringay Greyhounds	Britain	30	*16	8	6	1800	78	8	2.60	....	....	....	....	....	....	....	....
	Britain	WEC-A	....	....	....	....	....	....	....	....	....	....	....	....	....	....	7	....
1939-40	Quebec Aces	QSHL	29	10	13	6	1740	81	0	*2.79	....	....	....	....	....	....	....	....
1940-41	Glace Bay Miners	CBSHL	38	21	15	2	2280	128	*3	3.37	....	....	....	....	....	....	....	....
1941-42	North Sydney Victorias	CBSHL	37	....	....	....	2220	159	1	4.30	7	3	4	0	420	26	0	3.71

• GILLOW, Russ Russ Howard G. b: Hespeler, Ont., 9/2/1940.

Season	Club	League	GP	W	L	T	Mins	GA	SO	Avg	GP	W	L	T	Mins	GA	SO	Avg
1959-60	Edmonton Oil Kings	CAHL	26	....	....	....	1560	139	0	5.35	....	....	....	....	....	....	....	....
	Edmonton Oil Kings	Mem-Cup	21	12	9	0	1260	99	0	4.71	....	....	....	....	....	....	....	....
1961-62	Lacombe Rockets	CAHL	STATISTICS NOT AVAILABLE															
1962-63	Lacombe Rockets	CAHL	STATISTICS NOT AVAILABLE															
1963-64	Lacombe Rockets	CAHL	18	....	....	....	1080	63	0	3.50	5	4	1	0	310	17	0	3.29
1964-65	Lacombe Rockets	CAHL	STATISTICS NOT AVAILABLE															
1965-66	Lacombe Rockets	CAHL	34	....	....	....	2040	192	0	5.65	4	0	4	0	250	23	0	5.52
1966-67	Des Moines Oak Leafs	IHL	72	32	36	4	4320	263	*4	3.65	7	3	4	0	420	26	0	3.71
1967-68	Oklahoma City Blazers	CPHL	43	25	8	10	2524	91	*8	*2.16	7	3	4	0	420	24	0	3.43
1968-69	Oklahoma City Blazers	CHL	49	....	....	....	2870	143	4	2.99	10	4	6	0	522	26	0	2.99
1969-70	Salt Lake City Golden Eagles	WHL	32	....	....	....	1899	143	1	4.52	....	....	....	....	....	....	....	....
	Seattle Totems	WHL	14	....	....	....	790	39	0	2.96	5	....	....	....	247	12	0	3.93
1970-71	Seattle Totems	WHL	3	....	....	....	140	11	0	4.72	....	....	....	....	....	....	....	....
	Drumheller Miners	ASHL	22	....	....	....	1320	83	0	3.77	....	....	....	....	....	....	....	....
1971-72	Spokane Jets	WIHL	29	....	....	....	1740	98	1	*3.38	....	....	....	....	....	....	....	....
1972-73	**Los Angeles Sharks**	**WHA**	**38**	**17**	**13**	**2**	**1982**	**96**	**2**	**2.88**	**5**	**1**	**2**	**0**	**260**	**17**	....	....
1973-74	**Los Angeles Sharks**	**WHA**	**18**	**4**	**13**	**0**	**1041**	**69**	**1**	**3.98**	....	....	....	....	....	....	....	....
	Greensboro Generals	SHL	2	1	1	0	100	7	0	4.20	....	....	....	....	....	....	....	....
	Syracuse Blazers	NAHL	9	....	....	....	550	26	1	2.84	9	....	....	....	540	19	*1	*2.11
1974-75	**San Diego Mariners**	**WHA**	**30**	**15**	**11**	**2**	**1653**	**94**	**1**	**3.41**	**3**	**0**	**0**	**0**	**79**	**5**	**0**	**3.80**
	Syracuse Blazers	NAHL	2	....	....	....	129	4	0	2.00	....	....	....	....	....	....	....	....
1975-76	**San Diego Mariners**	**WHA**	**23**	**1**	**10**	**2**	**1037**	**74**	**0**	**4.28**	....	....	....	....	....	....	....	....
	Calgary Cowboys	**WHA**	....	....	....	....	....	....	....	....	**1**	**0**	**0**	**0**	**20**	**0**	**0**	**0.00**
	Major League Totals		**109**	**37**	**47**	**6**	**5713**	**333**	**4**	**3.50**	**9**	**1**	**2**	....	**359**	**22**	**0**	**3.68**

Named CAHL MVP (1966)

• HERN, Riley William Milton G. 5′9″, 170 lbs. b: St. Mary's, Ont., 12/5/1880 d: 6/24/1929. HHOF

Season	Club	League	GP	W	L	T	Mins	GA	SO	Avg	GP	W	L	T	Mins	GA	SO	Avg
1898-1901	Stratford Legionaires	OHA-Sr.	STATISTICS NOT AVAILABLE															
1901-02	**Pittsburgh Keystones**	**WPHL**	**14**	***9**	**5**	**0**	**580**	**32**	**1**	**2.21**	**1**	***1**	**0**	**0**	**40**	**1**	**1**	***1.00**
	Pittsburgh Keystones	X-Games	5	5	0	0	200	8	1	1.60	....	....	....	....	....	....	....	....
1902-03	**Pittsburgh Keystones**	**WPHL**	**12**	**1**	***10**	**0**	**460**	**61**	**0**	**5.30**	....	....	....	....	....	....	....	....
1903-04	Portage Lakes	X-Games	14	13	1	0	840	21	4	1.50	....	....	....	....	....	....	....	....
	Portage Lakes	W-S	2	*2	0	0	120	6	0	*3.00	....	....	....	....	....	....	....	....
1904-05	**Portage Lakes**	**IHL**	**24**	**15**	**7**	**2**	**1374**	**81**	***2**	***3.54**	....	....	....	....	....	....	....	....
1905-06	**Portage Lakes**	**IHL**	**20**	**15**	**5**	**0**	**1215**	**70**	**1**	**3.46**	....	....	....	....	....	....	....	....
1906-07	**Montreal Wanderers**	**ECAHA**	**10**	***10**	**0**	**0**	**610**	**39**	**0**	**3.84**	....	....	....	....	....	....	....	....
♦	Montreal Wanderers	St-Cup	6	3	3	0	360	25	0	4.17	....	....	....	....	....	....	....	....
1907-08	**Montreal Wanderers**	**ECAHA**	**10**	***8**	**2**	**0**	**610**	**52**	**0**	**5.12**	....	....	....	....	....	....	....	....
♦	Montreal Wanderers	St-Cup	5	*5	0	0	300	16	0	3.20	....	....	....	....	....	....	....	....
1908-09	**Montreal Wanderers**	**ECHA**	**12**	**9**	**3**	**0**	**728**	**61**	**0**	**5.03**	....	....	....	....	....	....	....	....
♦	Montreal Wanderers	St-Cup	2	1	1	0	120	10	0	5.00	....	....	....	....	....	....	....	....
1909-10	**Montreal Wanderers**	**NHA**	**12**	***11**	**1**	**0**	**720**	**41**	**1**	**3.42**	....	....	....	....	....	....	....	....
♦	Montreal Wanderers	St-Cup	1	1	0	0	60	3	0	3.00								
1910-11	**Montreal Wanderers**	**NHA**	**16**	**7**	**9**	**0**	**973**	**88**	**0**	**5.43**	....	....	....	....	....	....	....	....
	Major League Totals		**130**	**85**	**42**	**2**	**7270**	**525**	**5**	**4.33**	**1**	**1**	**0**	....	**40**	**1**	**1**	**1.50**

WPHL First All-Star Team (1902) • IHL First All-Star Team (1905) • IHL Second All-Star Team (1906)

• HUTTON, Bowse John Bower G. b: Ottawa, Ont., 10/24/1877 d: 10/27/1962. HHOF

Season	Club	League	GP	W	L	T	Mins	GA	SO	Avg	GP	W	L	T	Mins	GA	SO	Avg
1898-99	Ottawa Silver Seven	CAHL	2	....	....	....	120	11	0	5.50	....	....	....	....	....	....	....	....
99-1900	Ottawa Silver Seven	CAHL	7	4	3	0	420	19	0	2.70	....	....	....	....	....	....	....	....
1900-01	Ottawa Silver Seven	CAHL	7	7	0	1	480	20	0	2.50	....	....	....	....	....	....	....	....
1901-02	Ottawa Silver Seven	CAHL	8	5	3	0	480	15	2	1.70	....	....	....	....	....	....	....	....
1902-03	Ottawa Silver Seven	CAHL	8	*6	2	0	480	26	0	3.80	....	....	....	....	....	....	....	....
♦	Ottawa Silver Seven	St-Cup	4	3	0	1	240	5	1	*1.30	....	....	....	....	....	....	....	....
1903-04	Ottawa Silver Seven	CAHL	4	4	0	0	240	15	0	3.82	....	....	....	....	....	....	....	....
♦	Ottawa Silver Seven	St-Cup	8	*6	1	1	480	23	1	2.90	....	....	....	....	....	....	....	....

• JONES, Chief Joseph G. 6′, 205 lbs. b: Renfrew, Ont., 1880.

			REGULAR SEASON								PLAYOFFS							
Season	Club	League	GP	W	L	T	Mins	GA	SO	Avg	GP	W	L	T	Mins	GA	SO	Avg
1902-03	Portage Lakes Lakers	X-Games	10	10	0	0	600	16	2	1.60	4	2	1	1	240	11	1	2.75
1903-04	Michigan Soo Indians	X-Games	20	13	6	1	1200	67	3	3.35	4	0	4	0	240	31	0	7.75
1904-05	**Michigan Soo Indians**	**IHL**	**24**	**10**	**13**	**1**	**1428**	**79**	**1**	**3.32**	....	....	....	....	....	....	....	....
1905-06	**Michigan Soo Indians**	**IHL**	**22**	***16**	**6**	**0**	**1340**	**57**	***2**	***2.55**	....	....	....	....	....	....	....	....
1906-07	**Michigan Soo Indians**	**IHL**	**23**	**10**	**13**	**0**	**1358**	**88**	**0**	**3.80**	....	....	....	....	....	....	....	....
	Cobalt Silver Kings	TPHL	STATISTICS NOT AVAILABLE															
1907-08	Michigan Soo Indians	X-Games	4	1	3	0	240	20	0	5.00	....	....	....	....	....	....	....	....
1908-09	Cobalt Silver Kings	TPHL	8	*6	2	0	484	32	0	3.97	2	1	0	1	120	6	0	*3.00
1909-10	**Cobalt Silver Kings**	**NHA**	**3**	**1**	**2**	**0**	**186**	**26**	**0**	**8.39**	....	....	....	....	....	....	....	....
	Cobalt Silver Kings	**NHA**	**12**	**4**	**8**	**0**	**724**	**104**	**0**	**8.60**	....	....	....	....	....	....	....	....
1910-11	Cobalt Silver Kings	TPHL	....	....	....	....	....	....	....	....	....	....	....	....	....	....	....	....
	Waterloo Colts	**OPHL**	**16**	**9**	**7**	**0**	**1035**	**83**	**0**	**4.81**	....	....	....	....	....	....	....	....
1911-12			DID NOT PLAY															
1912-13	Cochrane Colts	X-Games	4	0	4	0	240	24	0	6.00	....	....	....	....	....	....	....	....
1913-14	Detroit Manufacturers	X-Games	DID NOT PLAY – COACHING															
	Major League Totals		**100**	**50**	**49**	**1**	**6071**	**437**	**3**	**4.32**	....	....	....	....	....	....	....	....

IHL First All-Star Team (1906) • IHL Second All-Star Team (1907) • TPHL Second All-Star Team (1908)

• LAIRD, Bill William C. G. 5′10″, 180 lbs. b: Cobourg, Ont., 10/29/1892 d: 2/16/1953.

Season	Club	League	GP	W	L	T	Mins	GA	SO	Avg	GP	W	L	T	Mins	GA	SO	Avg
1907/10	Regina Greys	S-SSHL	STATISTICS NOT AVAILABLE															
1910-11	University of Toronto	OHA Jr.	STATISTICS NOT AVAILABLE															
1911-12	University of Toronto	OHA-Sr.	DID NOT PLAY – INJURED															
	Toronto Canoe Club	OHA Jr.	....	....	....	....	....	....	....	....	7	5	1	2	420	14	1	2.00
1912-13	University of Toronto	OHA-Sr.	4	2	2	0	240	21	0	5.25	....	....	....	....	....	....	....	....
1913-14			STATISTICS NOT AVAILABLE															
1914-15	Regina Victorias	S-SSHL	1	0	1	0	60	6	0	6.00	....	....	....	....	....	....	....	....
1915-16	Regina Victorias	S-SSHL	15	10	4	1	920	56	*1	3.65	....	....	....	....	....	....	....	....
	Regina Victorias	Al-Cup	4	2	2	0	240	21	0	5.25	....	....	....	....	....	....	....	....
1916-17	Regina Victorias	SSHL-S	DID NOT PLAY – COACHING															
1917-18	Regina 77th Battery	Al-Cup	2	0	1	1	120	8	0	4.00	....	....	....	....	....	....	....	....
1918-19			MILITARY SERVICE															
1919-20	Regina Victorias	S-SSHL	DID NOT PLAY – COACHING															
1920-21	Regina Victorias	S-SSHL	8	7	1	0	480	19	1	*2.38	4	*4	0	0	240	10	0	2.50
1921-22	**Regina Capitals**	**WCHL**	**25**	***14**	**10**	**1**	**1500**	**78**	**0**	**3.12**	**4**	***4**	**0**	**0**	**240**	**3**	***1**	***0.75**
	Regina Capitals	St-Cup	2	1	1	0	120	5	0	2.50	....	....	....	....	....	....	....	....
1922-23	**Regina Capitals**	**WCHL**	**28**	**16**	**12**	**0**	**1702**	**83**	***3**	***2.93**	**2**	**0**	**1**	**1**	**150**	**4**	**0**	**1.60**
	Major League Totals		**53**	**30**	**22**	**1**	**3202**	**161**	**3**	**3.02**	**6**	**4**	**1**	....	**390**	**7**	**1**	**1.08**

OHA-Jr. First All-Star Team (1911) • WCHL Second All-Star Team (1922, 1923)

• LeSUEUR, Percy Percy Helier G. 5′7″, 150 lbs. b: Quebec City, Que., 11/21/1881 d: 1/27/1962. HHOF

Season	Club	League	GP	W	L	T	Mins	GA	SO	Avg	GP	W	L	T	Mins	GA	SO	Avg
1903-04	Smiths Falls Seniors	OHA-Sr.	6	3	3	0	370	13	*2	2.11	....	....	....	....	....	....	....	....
1904-05	Smiths Falls Seniors	OHA-Sr.	STATISTICS NOT AVAILABLE															
1905-06	Smiths Falls Seniors	FAHL	7	*7	0	0	420	16	*1	*2.30	....	....	....	....	....	....	....	....
	Smiths Falls Seniors	St-Cup	2	0	*2	0	120	14	0	7.00	....	....	....	....	....	....	....	....
	Ottawa Senators	St-Cup	1	1	0	0	60	3	0	3.00	....	....	....	....	....	....	....	....
1906-07	**Ottawa Senators**	**ECAHA**	**10**	**7**	**3**	**0**	**602**	**54**	**0**	**5.38**	....	....	....	....	....	....	....	....
1907-08	**Ottawa Senators**	**ECAHA**	**10**	**7**	**3**	**0**	**630**	**51**	**0**	**4.86**	....	....	....	....	....	....	....	....
1908-09♦	**Ottawa Senators**	**ECHA**	**12**	***10**	**2**	**0**	**728**	**63**	**0**	**5.19**	....	....	....	....	....	....	....	....
1909-10	**Ottawa Senators**	**CHA**	**2**	**2**	**0**	**0**	**120**	**9**	**0**	**4.50**	....	....	....	....	....	....	....	....
	Ottawa Senators	**NHA**	**12**	**9**	**3**	**0**	**730**	**66**	**0**	**5.41**	....	....	....	....	....	....	....	....
♦	Ottawa Senators	St-Cup	4	*4	0	0	240	15	0	3.75	....	....	....	....	....	....	....	....
1910-11	**Ottawa Senators**	**NHA**	**16**	***13**	**3**	**0**	**990**	**69**	**1**	**4.18**	....	....	....	....	....	....	....	....
♦	Ottawa Senators	St-Cup	2	*2	0	0	120	8	0	4.00	....	....	....	....	....	....	....	....
1911-12	**Ottawa Senators**	**NHA**	**18**	**9**	**9**	**0**	**1126**	**91**	**0**	**4.84**	....	....	....	....	....	....	....	....
1912-13	**Ottawa Senators**	**NHA**	**18**	**7**	**10**	**0**	**934**	**65**	**0**	**4.18**	....	....	....	....	....	....	....	....
1913-14	**Ottawa Senators**	**NHA**	**13**	**6**	**6**	**0**	**773**	**42**	***1**	**3.26**	....	....	....	....	....	....	....	....
1914-15	**Toronto Shamrocks**	**NHA**	**19**	**8**	**11**	**0**	**1145**	**96**	**0**	**5.03**	....	....	....	....	....	....	....	....
1915-16	**Toronto Blueshirts**	**NHA**	**23**	**9**	**13**	**0**	**1416**	**92**	**1**	**3.90**	....	....	....	....	....	....	....	....
	Major League Totals		**153**	**87**	**63**	**0**	**9194**	**698**	**3**	**4.56**	....	....	....	....	....	....	....	....

• McCUSKER, Hugh Hugh Albert "Red" G. 5′10″, 180 lbs. b: unknown.

Season	Club	League	GP	W	L	T	Mins	GA	SO	Avg	GP	W	L	T	Mins	GA	SO	Avg
1911-12	Regina Bankers	S-SSHL	STATISTICS NOT AVAILABLE															
1912-13			STATISTICS NOT AVAILABLE															
1913-14	Edmonton Athletics	ESrHL	STATISTICS NOT AVAILABLE															
1914-15			STATISTICS NOT AVAILABLE															
1915-16	Regina 68th Battalion	S-SSHL	15	*11	3	1	930	53	0	*3.42	1	0	1	0	60	13	0	13.00
1916/19			MILITARY SERVICE															
1919-20	Regina Braves	S-SSHL	7	3	4	0	420	54	0	7.71	....	....	....	....	....	....	....	....
1920-21	Regina Victorias	S-SSHL	STATISTICS NOT AVAILABLE															
1921-22	Regina Victorias	S-SSHL	11	5	6	0	660	47	1	4.27	1	1	0	0	60	2	0	2.00
1922-23	**Regina Capitals**	**WCHL**	**2**	**0**	**2**	**0**	**120**	**14**	**0**	**7.00**	....	....	....	....	....	....	....	....
1923-24	**Regina Capitals**	**WCHL**	**30**	**17**	**11**	**2**	**1861**	**67**	***4**	***2.16**	**2**	**0**	**2**	**0**	**120**	**4**	**0**	**2.00**
1924-25	**Regina Capitals**	**WCHL**	**28**	**8**	**20**	**0**	**1680**	**123**	**0**	**4.39**	....	....	....	....	....	....	....	....
1925-26	**Portland Rosebuds**	**WHL**	**30**	**12**	**16**	**2**	**1825**	**110**	**0**	**3.62**	....	....	....	....	....	....	....	....
1926-27	Windsor Hornets	Can-Pro	18	....	....	....	1080	53	*3	2.95	....	....	....	....	....	....	....	....
1927-28	St. Paul Saints	AHA	40	14	17	9	2519	87	5	2.07	....	....	....	....	....	....	....	....
1928-29	Tulsa Oilers	AHA	40	*23	9	8	2458	63	12	1.52	4	2	0	2	260	5	1	*1.15
1929-30	Tulsa Oilers	AHA	48	18	14	6	2880	79	1	1.39	9	4	3	2	560	11	*3	0.96
1930-31	Tulsa Oilers	AHA	44	26	15	2	2660	105	7	2.42	4	3	1	0	240	6	0	1.49
1931-32	Tulsa Oilers	AHA	46	16	*26	4	2826	114	6	2.42	....	....	....	....	....	....	....	....
1932-33	Calgary Tigers	WCHL	30	*16	10	4	1800	61	3	*2.03	6	....	....	....	360	9	0	*1.50
1933-34	Calgary Tigers	NWHL	34	17	11	6	2040	76	*5	*2.24	5	3	2	0	300	14	0	*2.80
	Edmonton Eskimos	NWHL	1	1	0	0	60	2	0	2.00	....	....	....	....	....	....	....	....
1934-35	Edmonton Eskimos	PCHL	7	....	....	....	420	27	0	3.86	....	....	....	....	....	....	....	....
	Portland Buckaroos	PCHL	11	....	....	....	660	33	1	3.00	....	....	....	....	....	....	....	....
1935-36	Edmonton Eskimos	PCHL	40	14	19	7	2400	114	3	2.85	....	....	....	....	....	....	....	....
	Major League Totals		**90**	**37**	**49**	**4**	**5486**	**314**	**4**	**3.43**	**2**	**0**	**2**	....	**120**	**4**	**0**	**2.00**

WCHL First All-Star Team (1924)

• MORAN, Paddy Patrick Joseph G. 5′11″, 180 lbs. b: Quebec City, Que., 3/11/1877 d: 1966. HHOF

Season	Club	League	GP	W	L	T	Mins	GA	SO	Avg	GP	W	L	T	Mins	GA	SO	Avg
1899-1901	Quebec Crescents	CAHL-I	STATISTICS NOT AVAILABLE															
1901-02	Quebec Athletics	CAHL	8	4	4	0	480	34	0	4.25	....	....	....	....	....	....	....	....
1902-03	Quebec Athletics	CAHL	7	3	4	0	420	46	0	6.57	....	....	....	....	....	....	....	....
1903-04	Quebec Athletics	CAHL	6	*5	1	0	360	37	0	6.17	....	....	....	....	....	....	....	....
1904-05	Quebec Athletics	CAHL	9	*7	2	0	540	45	0	5.00	....	....	....	....	....	....	....	....
1905-06	**Quebec Bulldogs**	**ECAHA**	**10**	**3**	**7**	**0**	**619**	**70**	**0**	**6.79**	....	....	....	....	....	....	....	....
1906-07	**Quebec Bulldogs**	**ECAHA**	**6**	**0**	**6**	**0**	**362**	**58**	**0**	**9.61**	....	....	....	....	....	....	....	....

Season	Club	League	REGULAR SEASON GP	W	L	T	Mins	GA	SO	Avg	PLAYOFFS GP	W	L	T	Mins	GA	SO	Avg
1907-08	**Quebec Bulldogs**	**ECAHA**	**10**	**5**	**5**	**0**	**602**	**74**	**0**	**7.38**	....	....	....	....	....	....	....	....
1908-09	**Quebec Bulldogs**	**ECHA**	**12**	**3**	**9**	**0**	**720**	**106**	**0**	**8.83**	....	....	....	....	....	....	....	....
1909-10	**All-Montreal**	**CHA**	**4**	**2**	**2**	**0**	**240**	**24**	**0**	**6.00**	....	....	....	....	....	....	....	....
	Haileybury Hockey Club	**NHA**	**11**	**3**	**8**	**0**	**665**	**80**	**0**	**7.21**	....	....	....	....	....	....	....	....
1910-11	**Quebec Bulldogs**	**NHA**	**16**	**4**	***12**	**0**	**983**	**97**	**0**	**5.91**	....	....	....	....	....	....	....	....
1911-12	**Quebec Bulldogs**	**NHA**	**18**	***10**	**8**	**0**	**1099**	**78**	**0**	**4.26**	....	....	....	....	....	....	....	....
♦	Quebec Bulldogs	St-Cup	2	*2	0	0	120	3	1	1.50	....	....	....	....	....	....	....	....
	NHA All-Stars	X-Games	3	1	*2	0	180	23	0	7.67	....	....	....	....	....	....	....	....
1912-13	**Quebec Bulldogs**	**NHA**	**20**	***16**	**4**	**0**	**1215**	**75**	***1**	***3.70**	....	....	....	....	....	....	....	....
♦	Quebec Bulldogs	St-Cup	5	3	2	0	300	21	0	4.20	....	....	....	....	....	....	....	....
1913-14	**Quebec Bulldogs**	**NHA**	**20**	**12**	**8**	**0**	**1225**	**73**	***1**	**3.58**	....	....	....	....	....	....	....	....
1914-15	**Quebec Bulldogs**	**NHA**	**20**	**11**	**9**	**0**	**1305**	**85**	**0**	**3.91**	....	....	....	....	....	....	....	....
1915-16	**Quebec Bulldogs**	**NHA**	**22**	**10**	**10**	**0**	**1391**	**82**	**0**	**3.54**	....	....	....	....	....	....	....	....
1916-17	**Quebec Bulldogs**	**NHA**	**7**	**1**	**5**	**0**	**307**	**35**	**0**	**6.84**	....	....	....	....	....	....	....	....
	Major League Totals		**176**	**80**	**93**	**0**	**10733**	**937**	**2**	**5.24**	....	....	....	....	....	....	....	....

● NELSON, Hub Hubert J. G. 5'10", 180 lbs. b: Minneapolis, MN, 8/14/1912 d: 5/10/1981.

Season	Club	League	GP	W	L	T	Mins	GA	SO	Avg	GP	W	L	T	Mins	GA	SO	Avg
1931-32	Minneapolis Millers	CHL	35	*21	11	3	2159	65	4	*1.18	....	....	....	....	....	....	....	....
1932-33	Minneapolis Millers	CHL	40	25	13	2	2505	78	*6	*1.87	7	*3	4	0	441	12	*2	1.63
1933-34	Minneapolis Millers	CHL	42	*26	11	5	2520	85	6	*2.02	3	*3	0	0	180	5	*1	*1.67
1934-35	Oklahoma City Warriors	AHA	37	13	20	4	2240	99	6	2.65	....	....	....	....	....	....	....	....
1935-36	Oklahoma City Warriors	AHA	48	21	22	5	3031	86	8	*1.70	....	....	....	....	....	....	....	....
	St. Louis Flyers	AHA	....	....	....	....	....	....	....	....	7	5	2	0	420	6	2	*0.86
1936-37	St. Louis Flyers	AHA	48	*32	13	3	2935	90	6	1.84	6	3	3	0	408	14	*1	2.06
1937-38	St. Louis Flyers	AHA	46	*29	12	5	2877	88	*12	*1.84	7	*5	2	0	425	4	*4	*0.57
1938-39	St. Louis Flyers	AHA	48	*36	12	0	2983	95	*8	*2.43	7	*6	1	0	420	17	0	2.43
1939-40	St. Louis Flyers	AHA	48	*37	11	0	2912	99	*9	*2.04	5	2	3	0	370	12	1	1.95
1940-41	Minneapolis Millers	AHA	47	25	22	0	2912	101	*7	2.08	3	0	3	0	180	12	0	4.00
1941-42	Minneapolis Millers	AHA	50	22	25	3	3070	158	4	3.09	....	....	....	....	....	....	....	....
1942-43	Coast Guard Clippers	EAHL	35	....	....	....	2100	107	1	3.66	6	*6	0	0	360	13	0	*2.17
1943-44	Coast Guard Clippers	X-Games	7	....	....	....	420	24	0	3.43	7	*7	0	0	420	14	1	2.00

AHA First All-Star Team (1939) • EAHL First All-Star Team (1943)

● NICHOLSON, Bill William G. 5'10", 220 lbs. b: Montreal, Que., 1878 Deceased.

Season	Club	League	GP	W	L	T	Mins	GA	SO	Avg	GP	W	L	T	Mins	GA	SO	Avg
1897-98	Montreal Shamrocks	CAHL	7	....	....	....	420	19	1	2.71	4	....	....	....	240	8	0	2.00
1898-99	Montreal Shamrocks	CAHL-I	STATISTICS NOT AVAILABLE															
99-1900	Montreal AAA	CAHL	4	3	1	0	240	11	*1	2.75	....	....	....	....	....	....	....	....
	Montreal AAA	CAHL-I	5	3	2	0	300	13	0	*2.89	....	....	....	....	....	....	....	....
1900-01	Montreal AAA	CAHL	8	3	5	0	488	37	*1	4.55	....	....	....	....	....	....	....	....
1901-02	Montreal AAA	CAHL	8	*6	2	0	480	15	2	1.88	....	....	....	....	....	....	....	....
♦	Montreal AAA	St-Cup	3	*2	1	0	180	2	*1	*0.67	....	....	....	....	....	....	....	....
1902-03	Montreal AAA	CAHL	7	4	3	0	420	19	1	2.71	....	....	....	....	....	....	....	....
	Montreal AAA	St-Cup	4	2	1	1	240	8	0	2.00	....	....	....	....	....	....	....	....
1903-04	Montreal Wanderers	FAHL	6	*6	0	0	360	18	0	3.00	....	....	....	....	....	....	....	....
	Montreal Wanderers	St-Cup	1	0	0	1	60	5	0	5.00	....	....	....	....	....	....	....	....
1904-05	**Calumet Wanderers**	**IHL**	**24**	***18**	**5**	**1**	**1419**	**75**	**1**	***3.17**	....	....	....	....	....	....	....	....
1905-06	**Calumet Wanderers**	**IHL**	**21**	**4**	***17**	**0**	**1281**	**107**	**0**	**5.01**	....	....	....	....	....	....	....	....
1906-07	**Calumet Wanderers**	**IHL**	**25**	**8**	***16**	**0**	**1510**	**124**	***3**	**4.93**	....	....	....	....	....	....	....	....
1907-08	**Montreal Shamrocks**	**ECAHA**	**10**	**5**	**5**	**0**	**630**	**49**	**0**	**4.67**	....	....	....	....	....	....	....	....
1908-09	Edmonton Professionals	X-Games	1	1	0	0	60	3	0	3.00	2	2	0	0	120	7	0	3.50
	Haileybury Hockey Club	TPHL	5	5	0	0	364	15	*1	2.47	2	0	1	1	120	12	0	6.00
1909-10	**Haileybury Hockey Club**	**NHA**	**1**	**1**	**0**	**0**	**60**	**3**	**0**	**3.00**	....	....	....	....	....	....	....	....
1910-11	Haileybury Hockey Club	TPHL	STATISTICS NOT AVAILABLE															
1911-12			DID NOT PLAY															
1912-13	**Toronto Tecumsehs**	**NHA**	**20**	**7**	***13**	**0**	**1238**	**98**	**0**	**4.75**	....	....	....	....	....	....	....	....
1913-14	**Montreal Wanderers**	**NHA**	**11**	**4**	**5**	**0**	**544**	**41**	**0**	**4.78**	....	....	....	....	....	....	....	....
1914/16			DID NOT PLAY															
1916-17	**Toronto Blueshirts**	**NHA**	**10**	**5**	**5**	**0**	**560**	**41**	**0**	**4.39**	....	....	....	....	....	....	....	....
	Major League Totals		**122**	**52**	**66**	**1**	**7242**	**538**	**4**	**4.46**	....	....	....	....	....	....	....	....

● WINCHESTER, Jack "Bill" G. 5'8", 155 lbs. b: Belleville, Ont., 1882 Deceased.

Season	Club	League	GP	W	L	T	Mins	GA	SO	Avg	GP	W	L	T	Mins	GA	SO	Avg
99-1900	Belleville Hockey Club	OHA-I	STATISTICS NOT AVAILABLE															
1900-01	Belleville Hockey Club	OHA-Sr.	STATISTICS NOT AVAILABLE															
1901-02	Belleville Hockey Club	OHA-Sr.	STATISTICS NOT AVAILABLE															
	Toronto Dominion Bank	TMHL	STATISTICS NOT AVAILABLE															
1902-03	Belleville Hockey Club	OHA-I	STATISTICS NOT AVAILABLE															
1903-04	Belleville Hockey Club	OHA-I	STATISTICS NOT AVAILABLE															
1904-05	Lindsay Muskies	OHA-I	STATISTICS NOT AVAILABLE															
	Pittsburgh Professionals	**IHL**	**15**	**7**	**8**	**0**	**908**	**60**	**2**	**3.96**	....	....	....	....	....	....	....	....
1905-06	**Pittsburgh Professionals**	**IHL**	**24**	**15**	**9**	**0**	**1448**	**85**	**2**	**3.52**	....	....	....	....	....	....	....	....
1906-07	**Pittsburgh Professionals**	**IHL**	**24**	**12**	**12**	**0**	**1448**	**82**	**1**	***3.40**	....	....	....	....	....	....	....	....
1907-08	**Winnipeg Strathconas**	**Man-Pro**	**15**	**5**	**10**	**0**	**900**	**113**	**0**	**7.53**	....	....	....	....	....	....	....	....
	Winnipeg Maple Leafs	**Man-Pro**	**1**	**1**	**0**	**0**	**60**	**3**	**0**	**3.00**	....	....	....	....	....	....	....	....
	Winnipeg Maple Leafs	St-Cup	2	0	*2	0	120	23	0	11.50	....	....	....	....	....	....	....	....
1908-09	Edmonton Professionals	X-Games	3	3	0	0	180	8	1	2.67	3	3	0	0	180	17	0	5.67
	Winnipeg Maple Leafs	**Man-Pro**	**4**	***4**	**0**	**0**	**240**	**21**	**0**	***5.25**	....	....	....	....	....	....	....	....
	Winnipeg Maple Leafs	**Man-Pro**	**5**	**4**	***4**	**0**	**300**	**47**	**0**	**9.20**	**2**	**0**	***2**	**0**	**120**	**16**	**0**	**8.00**
1909-10	Edmonton Professionals	St-Cup	4	1	2	1	240	22	1	5.50	....	....	....	....	....	....	....	....
	Montreal Shamrocks	**NHA**	**5**	**2**	**2**	**1**	**301**	**26**	**0**	**5.18**	....	....	....	....	....	....	....	....
1910-11	Edmonton Professionals	F-R	2	0	1	1	120	5	0	2.50	....	....	....	....	....	....	....	....
	Major League Totals		**93**	**50**	**45**	**1**	**5605**	**437**	**5**	**4.68**	**2**	**0**	**2**	....	**120**	**16**	**0**	**8.00**

IHL First All-Star Team (1907)

CHAPTER 73

Notable European Non-NHL Players

Club Team Statistics for Top International Players

Compiled by Igor Kuperman

• AHLBERG, Mats SWE
C – L. 5'10", 178 lbs. b: Avesta, Sweden, 5/16/1947.

Season	Club	League	GP	G	A	Pts	PIM	GP	G	A	Pts	PIM
			REGULAR SEASON					PLAYOFFS				
1963-64	Avesta BK	Sweden-2	18	11	....	11	....	....	....	....	....	....
1964-65	Avesta BK	Sweden-2	18	23	....	23	....	....	....	....	....	....
1965-66	Avesta BK	Sweden-2	18	34	....	34	....	....	....	....	....	....
1966-67	Leksands IF	Sweden	....	6	6	12	6	2	0	0	0	0
1967-68	Leksands IF	Sweden	28	20	8	28	4	....	....	....	....	....
1968-69	Leksands IF	Sweden	27	14	14	28	2	....	....	....	....	....
1969-70	Leksands IF	Sweden	28	13	14	27	....	....	....	....	....	....
1970-71	Leksands IF	Sweden	28	21	18	39	8	....	....	....	....	....
1971-72	Leksands IF	Sweden	25	18	10	28	4	....	....	....	....	....
1972-73	Leksands IF	Sweden	27	12	28	40	32	....	....	....	....	....
1973-74	Leksands IF	Sweden	35	28	26	54	30	....	....	....	....	....
1974-75	Leksands IF	Sweden	30	27	24	51	14	5	0	1	1	2
1975-76	Leksands IF	Sweden	35	22	19	41	24	4	4	1	5	0
1976-77	Leksands IF	Sweden	35	39	25	64	26	5	3	0	3	2
1977-78	Leksands IF	Sweden	36	30	13	43	15	....	....	....	....	....
1978-79	Leksands IF	Sweden	36	28	15	43	18	3	0	0	0	2
1979-80	Leksands IF	Sweden	35	21	15	36	22	2	1	1	2	0
1980-81	Leksands IF	Sweden	26	10	12	22	8	....	....	....	....	....

Olympics 1972, 1980. Six World Championships, 1973 to 1978. Canada Cup in 1976.

• ALEXANDROV, Veniamin URS
LW – L. 5'11", 178 lbs. b: Moscow, USSR, 4/18/1937 d: 11/12/1991.

Season	Club	League	GP	G	A	Pts	PIM	GP	G	A	Pts	PIM
1955-56	CSK Moscow	USSR	....	18	....	18	....	....	....	....	....	....
1956-57	CSK Moscow	USSR	....	18	....	18	....	....	....	....	....	....
1957-58	CSK Moscow	USSR	....	32	....	32	....	....	....	....	....	....
1958-59	CSK Moscow	USSR	....	14	....	14	....	....	....	....	....	....
1959-60	CSKA Moscow	USSR	....	19	....	19	....	....	....	....	....	....
1960-61	CSKA Moscow	USSR	....	19	....	19	....	....	....	....	....	....
1961-62	CSKA Moscow	USSR	....	21	....	21	....	....	....	....	....	....
1962-63	CSKA Moscow	USSR	38	53	....	53	....	....	....	....	....	....
1963-64	CSKA Moscow	USSR	....	39	....	39	....	....	....	....	....	....
1964-65	CSKA Moscow	USSR	....	25	....	25	....	....	....	....	....	....
1965-66	CSKA Moscow	USSR	....	31	....	31	....	....	....	....	....	....
1966-67	CSKA Moscow	USSR	....	27	....	27	....	....	....	....	....	....
1967-68	CSKA Moscow	USSR	40	23	....	23	....	....	....	....	....	....
1968-69	CSKA Moscow	USSR	24	12	....	12	....	....	....	....	....	....

Olympics in 1960, 1964 and 1968. Played at 11 World Championships from 1957 to 1968.

• ALMETOV, Alexander URS
C – R. 5'10", 185 lbs. b: Moscow, USSR, 1/18/1940 d: 1992.

Season	Club	League	GP	G	A	Pts	PIM	GP	G	A	Pts	PIM
1958-59	CSK Moscow	USSR	....	8	....	8	....	....	....	....	....	....
1959-60	CSKA Moscow	USSR	....	16	....	16	....	....	....	....	....	....
1960-61	CSKA Moscow	USSR	....	21	....	21	....	....	....	....	....	....
1961-62	CSKA Moscow	USSR	....	29	....	29	....	....	....	....	....	....
1962-63	CSKA Moscow	USSR	....	23	....	23	....	....	....	....	....	....
1963-64	CSKA Moscow	USSR	....	40	....	40	....	....	....	....	....	....
1964-65	CSKA Moscow	USSR	....	26	....	26	....	....	....	....	....	....
1965-66	CSKA Moscow	USSR	....	24	....	24	....	....	....	....	....	....
1966-67	CSKA Moscow	USSR	....	1	....	1	....	....	....	....	....	....

Olympics in 1960 and 1964. Seven World Championships, winning from 1963 to 1967.

• BABINOV, Sergei URS
D – L. 5'11", 183 lbs. b: Chelyabinsk, USSR, 7/11/1955.

Season	Club	League	GP	G	A	Pts	PIM	GP	G	A	Pts	PIM
1972-73	Traktor Chelyabinsk	USSR	4	0	0	0	2	....	....	....	....	....
1973-74	Traktor Chelyabinsk	USSR	8	0	0	0	8	....	....	....	....	....
1974-75	Traktor Chelyabinsk	USSR	35	5	0	5	35	....	....	....	....	....
1975-76	Krylja Sovetov Moscow	USSR	34	0	2	2	18	....	....	....	....	....
1976-77	Krylja Sovetov Moscow	USSR	36	4	8	12	26	....	....	....	....	....
1977-78	CSKA Moscow	USSR	29	2	7	9	22	....	....	....	....	....
1978-79	CSKA Moscow	USSR	41	1	16	17	40	....	....	....	....	....
1979-80	CSKA Moscow	USSR	41	9	11	20	31	....	....	....	....	....
1980-81	CSKA Moscow	USSR	49	11	14	25	40	....	....	....	....	....
1981-82	CSKA Moscow	USSR	47	5	4	9	25	....	....	....	....	....
1982-83	CSKA Moscow	USSR	18	1	2	3	8	....	....	....	....	....
1983-84	CSKA Moscow	USSR	42	0	10	10	4	....	....	....	....	....
1984-85	CSKA Moscow	USSR	28	0	2	2	6	....	....	....	....	....
1985-86	CSKA Moscow	USSR	40	1	4	5	8	....	....	....	....	....

Winner 1976 Olympics, 1981 Canada Cup. Six World Championships, 1976 to 1983.

• BILYALETDINOV, Zinetula URS
D – L. 5'11", 191 lbs. b: Moscow, USSR, 3/13/1955.

Season	Club	League	GP	G	A	Pts	PIM	GP	G	A	Pts	PIM
1973-74	Dynamo Moscow	USSR	22	0	1	1	2	....	....	....	....	....
1974-75	Dynamo Moscow	USSR	36	2	1	3	6	....	....	....	....	....
1975-76	Dynamo Moscow	USSR	34	1	2	3	13	....	....	....	....	....
1976-77	Dynamo Moscow	USSR	33	1	4	5	18	....	....	....	....	....
1977-78	Dynamo Moscow	USSR	35	2	3	5	27	....	....	....	....	....
1978-79	Dynamo Moscow	USSR	43	6	4	10	55	....	....	....	....	....
1979-80	Dynamo Moscow	USSR	43	14	8	22	44	....	....	....	....	....
1980-81	Dynamo Moscow	USSR	49	6	5	11	54	....	....	....	....	....
1981-82	Dynamo Moscow	USSR	47	6	9	15	28	....	....	....	....	....
1982-83	Dynamo Moscow	USSR	42	1	8	9	20	....	....	....	....	....
1983-84	Dynamo Moscow	USSR	42	2	6	8	36	....	....	....	....	....
1984-85	Dynamo Moscow	USSR	36	4	8	12	24	....	....	....	....	....
1985-86	Dynamo Moscow	USSR	40	11	14	25	38	....	....	....	....	....
1986-87	Dynamo Moscow	USSR	40	6	5	11	12	....	....	....	....	....
1987-88	Dynamo Moscow	USSR	46	1	10	11	20	....	....	....	....	....

Olympics in 1980, 1984. Eight World Championships. Canada Cup in 1976, 1981 and 1984.

• BJORN, Lars SWE
D – L. 6'2", 191 lbs. b: Stockholm, Sweden, 12/16/1931.

Season	Club	League	GP	G	A	Pts	PIM	GP	G	A	Pts	PIM
1949-50	Djurgardens IF	Sweden	STATISTICS NOT AVAILABLE									
1950-51	Djurgardens IF	Sweden	STATISTICS NOT AVAILABLE									
1951-52	Djurgardens IF	Sweden	STATISTICS NOT AVAILABLE									
1952-53	Djurgardens IF	Sweden	STATISTICS NOT AVAILABLE									
1953-54	Djurgardens IF	Sweden	....	....	....	....	....	2	0	....	0	....
1954-55	Djurgardens IF	Sweden	....	....	....	....	....	2	1	....	1	....
1955-56	Djurgardens IF	Sweden	STATISTICS NOT AVAILABLE									
1956-57	Djurgardens IF	Sweden	STATISTICS NOT AVAILABLE									
1957-58	Djurgardens IF	Sweden	STATISTICS NOT AVAILABLE									
1958-59	Djurgardens IF	Sweden	STATISTICS NOT AVAILABLE									
1959-60	Djurgardens IF	Sweden	STATISTICS NOT AVAILABLE									
1960-61	Djurgardens IF	Sweden	....	3	....	3	....	....	....	....	....	....
1961-62	Djurgardens IF	Sweden	....	5	....	5	....	....	....	....	....	....
1962-63	Djurgardens IF	Sweden	21	1	2	3	14	....	....	....	....	....
1963-64	Djurgardens IF	Sweden	....	3	7	10	8	....	....	....	....	....
1964-65	Djurgardens IF	Sweden	12	1	0	1	6	....	....	....	....	....
1965-66	Djurgardens IF	Sweden	20	0	4	4	10	6	0	1	1	15

Three Olympics and 10 World Championships. Won world title in 1953 and 1957.

• BOBROV, Vsevolod URS
LW – R. 5'11", 176 lbs. b: Sestroretsk, USSR, 12/1/1922 d: 7/1/1979.

Season	Club	League	GP	G	A	Pts	PIM	GP	G	A	Pts	PIM
1946-47	CDKA Moscow	USSR	1	3	....	3	....	....	....	....	....	....
1947-48	CDKA Moscow	USSR	18	52	....	52	....	....	....	....	....	....
1948-49	CDKA Moscow	USSR	....	27	....	27	....	....	....	....	....	....
1949-50	VVS Moscow	USSR	13	29	....	29	....	....	....	....	....	....
1950-51	VVS Moscow	USSR	15	43	....	43	....	....	....	....	....	....
1951-52	VVS Moscow	USSR	16	37	....	37	....	....	....	....	....	....
1952-53	VVS Moscow	USSR	....	7	....	7	....	....	....	....	....	....
1953-54	CDSA Moscow	USSR	7	15	....	15	....	....	....	....	....	....
1954-55	CSK Moscow	USSR	....	25	....	25	....	....	....	....	....	....
1955-56			DID NOT PLAY									
1956-57	CSK Moscow	USSR	....	17	....	17	....	....	....	....	....	....

First Soviet national team captain. Olympics in 1956. World Championships from 1954 to 1957.

• BRANDL, Thomas GER
C – L. 5'11", 183 lbs. b: Bad Tolz, W.Germany, 2/9/1969.

Season	Club	League	GP	G	A	Pts	PIM	GP	G	A	Pts	PIM
1986-87	EC Bad Tolz	German-2	40	36	54	90	95	....	....	....	....	....
1987-88	Kolner EC	Germany	35	2	6	8	14	11	2	2	4	14
1988-89	Kolner EC	Germany	25	4	10	14	34	7	1	3	4	4
1989-90	Kolner EC	Germany	33	8	16	24	54	5	1	4	5	12
1990-91	Kolner EC	Germany	44	16	34	50	80	14	5	6	11	32
1991-92	Kolner EC	Germany	30	3	15	18	92	4	3	1	4	2
1992-93	Kolner EC	Germany	43	19	23	42	45	12	6	12	18	6
1993-94	Kolner EC	Germany	44	16	25	41	53	9	0	3	3	2
1994-95	Kolner Haie	Germany	38	18	35	53	48	15	8	13	21	16
1995-96	Kolner Haie	Germany	41	19	46	65	44	5	0	5	5	0
1996-97	Dusseldorfer EG	Germany	44	16	29	45	73	2	0	2	2	2
1997-98	Dusseldorfer EG	Germany	29	9	17	26	14	2	0	0	0	0
1998-99	Krefeld Pinguine	Germany	42	12	23	35	73	4	1	4	5	4
99-2000	Krefeld Pinguine	Germany	47	17	33	50	72	3	0	1	1	27

Olympics in 1992, 1994 and 1998. World Championships five times. Pool B champion in 1987.

• BYKOV, Vyacheslav URS
C – L. 5'8", 161 lbs. b: Chelyabinsk, USSR, 7/24/1960.
Quebec's 10th, 169th overall in 1989.

Season	Club	League	GP	G	A	Pts	PIM	GP	G	A	Pts	PIM
1979-80	Traktor Chelyabinsk	USSR	3	2	0	2	0	....	....	....	....	....
1980-81	Traktor Chelyabinsk	USSR	48	26	16	42	4	....	....	....	....	....
1981-82	Traktor Chelyabinsk	USSR	44	20	16	36	14	....	....	....	....	....
1982-83	CSKA Moscow	USSR	44	22	22	44	10	....	....	....	....	....
1983-84	CSKA Moscow	USSR	44	22	11	33	12	....	....	....	....	....
1984-85	CSKA Moscow	USSR	36	21	14	35	4	....	....	....	....	....
1985-86	CSKA Moscow	USSR	36	10	10	20	6	....	....	....	....	....
1986-87	CSKA Moscow	USSR	40	18	15	33	10	....	....	....	....	....

Season	Club	League	GP	G	A	Pts	PIM	GP	G	A	Pts	PIM
			REGULAR SEASON					PLAYOFFS				
1987-88	CSKA Moscow	USSR	47	17	30	47	26	....	....	....	....	....
1988-89	CSKA Moscow	USSR	40	16	20	36	10	....	....	....	....	....
1989-90	CSKA Moscow	USSR	48	21	16	37	12	....	....	....	....	....
1990-91	HC Fribourg-Gotteron	Switz.	36	35	49	84	18	8	7	16	23	8
1991-92	HC Fribourg-Gotteron	Switz.	34	39	48	87	24	14	4	16	20	10
1992-93	HC Fribourg-Gotteron	Switz.	35	25	51	76	14	9	10	12	22	4
1993-94	HC Fribourg-Gotteron	Switz.	36	30	43	73	2	11	11	21	32	2
1994-95	HC Fribourg-Gotteron	Switz.	30	24	51	75	35	8	7	4	11	4
1995-96	HC Fribourg-Gotteron	Switz.	28	10	25	35	8	4	2	1	3	0
1996-97	HC Fribourg-Gotteron	Switz.	46	23	45	68	18	3	0	3	3	2
1997-98	HC Fribourg-Gotteron	Switz.	18	14	18	32	4	12	2	6	8	6
1998-99	HC Lausanne	Switz-2	24	19	20	39	38	3	2	4	6	2
99-2000	HC Lausanne	Switz-2	6	2	9	11	2	....	....	....	....	....

Olympic gold 1988, 1992. Nine World Championships from 1983. Canada Cup in 1987.

• CARLSSON, Arne — SWE

D – L. 6'2", 189 lbs. b: Uppsala, Sweden, 1/5/1943.

Season	Club	League	GP	G	A	Pts	PIM	GP	G	A	Pts	PIM
1960-61	Almtuna Uppsala	Sweden-2	STATISTICS NOT AVAILABLE									
1961-62	Almtuna Uppsala	Sweden-2	STATISTICS NOT AVAILABLE									
1962-63	Almtuna Uppsala	Sweden	21	4	5	9	22	....	....	....	....	....
1963-64	Almtuna Uppsala	Sweden-2	STATISTICS NOT AVAILABLE									
1964-65	Vastra Frolunda	Sweden	28	7	7	14	12	....	....	....	....	....
1965-66	Vastra Frolunda	Sweden	21	2	6	8	8	8	0	3	3	4
1966-67	Vastra Frolunda	Sweden	....	6	3	9	12	7	2	4	6	4
1967-68	Vastra Frolunda	Sweden	25	5	9	14	....	....	....	....	....	....
1968-69	Vastra Frolunda	Sweden	28	7	17	24	8	....	....	....	....	....
1969-70	Sodertalje SK	Sweden	26	9	9	18	....	....	....	....	....	....
1970-71	Sodertalje SK	Sweden	28	6	3	9	22	....	....	....	....	....
1971-72	Sodertalje SK	Sweden	28	9	5	14	18	....	....	....	....	....
1972-73	Sodertalje SK	Sweden	28	4	7	11	8	....	....	....	....	....
1973-74	Sodertalje SK	Sweden	34	4	11	15	12	....	....	....	....	....
1974-75	Sodertalje SK	Sweden	30	4	5	9	12	....	....	....	....	....
	Sodertalje SK	Sweden-Q	6	1	1	2	8	....	....	....	....	....
1975-76	Sodertalje SK	Sweden	34	7	4	11	16	....	....	....	....	....
1976-77	Sodertalje SK	Sweden	30	4	6	10	12	....	....	....	....	....

Olympics 1968. Seven World Championships, 1967 to 1974. Played 142 int'l games.

• CERNY, Josef — TCH

LW – L. 5'8", 165 lbs. b: Rozmital, Czechoslovakia, 10/18/1930.

Season	Club	League	GP	G	A	Pts	PIM	GP	G	A	Pts	PIM
1957-58	Spartak Plzen	Czech.	STATISTICS NOT AVAILABLE									
1958-59	RH Brno	Czech.	STATISTICS NOT AVAILABLE									
1959-60	RH Brno	Czech.	STATISTICS NOT AVAILABLE									
1960-61	RH Brno	Czech.	STATISTICS NOT AVAILABLE									
1961-62	RH Brno	Czech.	STATISTICS NOT AVAILABLE									
1962-63	ZKL Brno	Czech.	STATISTICS NOT AVAILABLE									
1963-64	ZKL Brno	Czech.	....	43	....	43	....	....	....	....	....	....
1964-65	ZKL Brno	Czech.	STATISTICS NOT AVAILABLE									
1965-66	ZKL Brno	Czech.	....	34	....	34	....	....	....	....	....	....
1966-67	ZKL Brno	Czech.	....	21	....	21	....	....	....	....	....	....
1967-68	ZKL Brno	Czech.	....	16	19	35	....	....	....	....	....	....
1968-69	ZKL Brno	Czech.	....	29	14	43	....	....	....	....	....	....
1969-70	ZKL Brno	Czech.	....	32	14	46	12	....	....	....	....	....
1970-71	ZKL Brno	Czech.	....	18	26	44	....	....	....	....	....	....
1971-72	ZKL Brno	Czech.	....	20	15	35	....	....	....	....	....	....
1972-73	ZKL Brno	Czech.	....	17	13	30	....	....	....	....	....	....
1973-74	ZKL Brno	Czech.	....	23	9	32	....	....	....	....	....	....
1974-75	ZKL Brno	Czech.	....	18	9	27	....	....	....	....	....	....
1975-76	ZKL Brno	Czech.	32	10	6	16	18	....	....	....	....	....
1976-77	Zetor Brno	Czech.	STATISTICS NOT AVAILABLE									
1977-78	Zetor Brno	Czech.	28	2	0	2	14	....	....	....	....	....
1978-79	ATSE Graz	Austria	32	12	21	33	6	....	....	....	....	....

Four Olympics and 12 World Championships between 1959 and 1972. Longtime team captain.

• DAVYDOV, Vitali — URS

D – L. 5'8", 158 lbs. b: Moscow, USSR, 4/1/1939.

Season	Club	League	GP	G	A	Pts	PIM	GP	G	A	Pts	PIM
1957-58	Dynamo Moscow	USSR	17	1	....	1	....	....	....	....	....	....
1958-59	Dynamo Moscow	USSR	27	1	....	1	....	....	....	....	....	....
1959-60	Dynamo Moscow	USSR	33	3	....	3	....	....	....	....	....	....
1960-61	Dynamo Moscow	USSR	29	3	....	3	....	....	....	....	....	....
1961-62	Dynamo Moscow	USSR	29	3	3	6	10	....	....	....	....	....
1962-63	Dynamo Moscow	USSR	28	2	1	3	12	....	....	....	....	....
1963-64	Dynamo Moscow	USSR	35	7	....	7	....	....	....	....	....	....
1964-65	Dynamo Moscow	USSR	23	1	2	3	4	....	....	....	....	....
1965-66	Dynamo Moscow	USSR	35	1	2	3	20	....	....	....	....	....
1966-67	Dynamo Moscow	USSR	41	3	1	4	18	....	....	....	....	....
1967-68	Dynamo Moscow	USSR	41	5	3	8	14	....	....	....	....	....
1968-69	Dynamo Moscow	USSR	42	0	....	0	....	....	....	....	....	....
1969-70	Dynamo Moscow	USSR	38	3	....	3	....	....	....	....	....	....
1970-71	Dynamo Moscow	USSR	40	1	6	7	6	....	....	....	....	....
1971-72	Dynamo Moscow	USSR	30	0	0	0	0	....	....	....	....	....
1972-73	Dynamo Moscow	USSR	31	3	0	3	8	....	....	....	....	....

Olympic gold 1964, 1968, 1972. World champion nine times in a row from 1963 to 1971.

• DROZDETSKY, Nikolai — URS

RW – L. 6'1", 187 lbs. b: Kolpino, USSR, 6/14/1957 d: 1995.

Season	Club	League	GP	G	A	Pts	PIM	GP	G	A	Pts	PIM
1974-75	SKA Leningrad	USSR	6	1	1	2	2	....	....	....	....	....
	SKA Leningrad	USSR-Q	2	2	2	4	0	....	....	....	....	....
1975-76	SKA Leningrad	USSR	31	6	7	13	4	....	....	....	....	....
	SKA Leningrad	USSR-Q	2	2	0	2	0	....	....	....	....	....
1976-77	SKA Leningrad	USSR	16	3	3	6	20	....	....	....	....	....
1977-78	SKA Leningrad	USSR	27	15	14	29	21	....	....	....	....	....
1978-79	SKA Leningrad	USSR	41	27	17	44	72	....	....	....	....	....
	SKA Leningrad	USSR-Q	5	8	6	14	10	....	....	....	....	....
1979-80	CSKA Moscow	USSR	41	31	18	49	22	....	....	....	....	....
1980-81	CSKA Moscow	USSR	44	30	28	58	21	....	....	....	....	....
1981-82	CSKA Moscow	USSR	46	28	16	44	25	....	....	....	....	....
1982-83	CSKA Moscow	USSR	42	17	18	35	16	....	....	....	....	....
1983-84	CSKA Moscow	USSR	44	31	20	51	34	....	....	....	....	....
1984-85	CSKA Moscow	USSR	39	12	11	23	28	....	....	....	....	....
1985-86	CSKA Moscow	USSR	31	12	8	20	20	....	....	....	....	....
1986-87	CSKA Moscow	USSR	7	3	2	5	2	....	....	....	....	....
	SKA Leningrad	USSR	14	13	1	14	4	....	....	....	....	....
1987-88	SKA Leningrad	USSR	30	8	9	17	20	....	....	....	....	....
1988-89	SKA Leningrad	USSR	42	13	17	30	20	....	....	....	....	....
1989-90	Boras HC	Sweden-3	34	41	42	83	152	....	....	....	....	....
1990-91	Boras HC	Sweden-3	34	42	46	88	104	....	....	....	....	....
1991-92	Boras HC	Sweden-2	28	24	20	44	80	....	....	....	....	....
1992-93	Boras HC	Sweden-2	26	12	33	45	56	....	....	....	....	....
1993-94	Boras HC	Sweden-2	32	13	28	41	60	....	....	....	....	....
1994-95	Boras HC	Sweden-2	31	8	17	25	69	....	....	....	....	....

Winner 1981 Canada Cup, 1984 Olympics. Three World Championships.

• EBERMANN, Bohuslav — TCH

LW – L. 6', 180 lbs. b: Vochov, Czechoslovakia, 9/19/1948.

Season	Club	League	GP	G	A	Pts	PIM	GP	G	A	Pts	PIM
1967-68	Skoda Plzen	Czech-2	STATISTICS NOT AVAILABLE									
1968-69	Dukla Jihlava	Czech.	STATISTICS NOT AVAILABLE									
1969-70	Dukla Jihlava	Czech.	....	15	16	31	24	....	....	....	....	....
1970-71	Skoda Plzen	Czech.	STATISTICS NOT AVAILABLE									
1971-72	Skoda Plzen	Czech.	STATISTICS NOT AVAILABLE									
1972-73	Skoda Plzen	Czech.	....	12	16	28	....	....	....	....	....	....
1973-74	Skoda Plzen	Czech.	....	24	15	39	38	....	....	....	....	....
1974-75	Skoda Plzen	Czech.	....	23	14	37	....	....	....	....	....	....
1975-76	Skoda Plzen	Czech.	31	19	16	35	20	....	....	....	....	....
1976-77	Skoda Plzen	Czech.	....	31	29	60	....	....	....	....	....	....
1977-78	Skoda Plzen	Czech.	43	27	9	36	46	....	....	....	....	....
1978-79	Skoda Plzen	Czech-2	....	36	....	36	....	....	....	....	....	....
1979-80	Skoda Plzen	Czech.	43	19	0	19	30	....	....	....	....	....
1980-81	Skoda Plzen	Czech.	38	14	16	30	33	....	....	....	....	....
1981-82	HC Lausanne	Switz-2	38	39	36	75	....	....	....	....	....	....
1982-83	HC Lausanne	Switz-2	37	28	30	58	....	....	....	....	....	....
1983-84	CSG Grenoble	France	STATISTICS NOT AVAILABLE									
1984-85	CSG Grenoble	France	....	44	16	60	....	....	....	....	....	....
1985-86	CSG Grenoble	France	STATISTICS NOT AVAILABLE									
1986-87	CSG Grenoble	France	35	35	32	67	32	....	....	....	....	....
1987-88	CSG Grenoble	France	17	8	14	22	24	....	....	....	....	....

Olympics in 1976 and 1980. Six World Championships beginning in 1974. Canada Cup in 1976.

• FARDA, Richard — TCH

C – L. 5'9", 175 lbs. b: Brno, Czechoslovakia, 11/8/1945.

Season	Club	League	GP	G	A	Pts	PIM	GP	G	A	Pts	PIM
1962-63	Spartak Brno	Czech.	STATISTICS NOT AVAILABLE									
1963-64	Dukla Jihlava	Czech.	STATISTICS NOT AVAILABLE									
1964-65	Dukla Jihlava	Czech.	STATISTICS NOT AVAILABLE									
1965-66	ZKL Brno	Czech.	STATISTICS NOT AVAILABLE									
1966-67	ZKL Brno	Czech.	....	17	....	17	....	....	....	....	....	....
1967-68	ZKL Brno	Czech.	....	25	19	44	....	....	....	....	....	....
1968-69	ZKL Brno	Czech.	....	22	....	22	....	....	....	....	....	....
1969-70	ZKL Brno	Czech.	....	12	19	31	12	....	....	....	....	....
1970-71	ZKL Brno	Czech.	....	30	24	54	....	....	....	....	....	....
1971-72	ZKL Brno	Czech.	....	13	16	29	....	....	....	....	....	....
1972-73	ZKL Brno	Czech.	....	14	20	34	....	....	....	....	....	....
1973-74	ZKL Brno	Czech.	....	21	22	43	....	....	....	....	....	....
1974-75	**Toronto Toros**	**WHA**	**66**	**6**	**25**	**31**	**2**	**1**	**0**	**0**	**0**	**0**
1975-76	**Toronto Toros**	**WHA**	**63**	**19**	**35**	**54**	**8**	....	....	....	....	....
1976-77	**Birmingham Bulls**	**WHA**	**48**	**9**	**26**	**35**	**2**	....	....	....	....	....
1977-78	HC Geneve-Servette	Switz-2	28	26	12	38	....	....	....	....	....	....
1978-79	ZSC Zurich	Switz-2	30	37	27	64	....	....	....	....	....	....
1979-80	ZSC Zurich	Switz-2	34	34	25	59	....	....	....	....	....	....
1980-81	ZSC Zurich	Switz-2	18	24	18	42	....	....	....	....	....	....
1981-82	ZSC Zurich	Switz-2	18	20	14	34	....	....	....	....	....	....
1982-83	HC Ascona	Switz-2	16	12	9	21	....	....	....	....	....	....
	Major League Totals		**177**	**34**	**86**	**120**	**12**	**1**	**0**	**0**	**0**	**0**

Olympics in 1972. Six World Championships from 1969 to 1974. Champion in 1972.

• FIRSOV, Anatoli — URS

LW – R. 5'9", 154 lbs. b: Moscow, USSR, 2/1/1941 d: 7/24/2000.

Season	Club	League	GP	G	A	Pts	PIM	GP	G	A	Pts	PIM
1958-59	Spartak Moscow	USSR	....	0	....	0	....	....	....	....	....	....
1959-60	Spartak Moscow	USSR	....	6	....	6	....	....	....	....	....	....
1960-61	Spartak Moscow	USSR	....	10	....	10	....	....	....	....	....	....
1961-62	Spartak Moscow	USSR	....	1	....	1	....	....	....	....	....	....
	CSKA Moscow	USSR	....	17	....	17	....	....	....	....	....	....
1962-63	CSKA Moscow	USSR	....	20	....	20	....	....	....	....	....	....
1963-64	CSKA Moscow	USSR	....	34	....	34	....	....	....	....	....	....
1964-65	CSKA Moscow	USSR	....	21	....	21	....	....	....	....	....	....
1965-66	CSKA Moscow	USSR	....	40	....	40	....	....	....	....	....	....
1966-67	CSKA Moscow	USSR	....	41	....	41	....	....	....	....	....	....
1967-68	CSKA Moscow	USSR	43	33	....	33	....	....	....	....	....	....
1968-69	CSKA Moscow	USSR	38	28	....	28	....	....	....	....	....	....
1969-70	CSKA Moscow	USSR	38	33	....	33	....	....	....	....	....	....
1970-71	CSKA Moscow	USSR	33	17	....	17	....	....	....	....	....	....
1971-72	CSKA Moscow	USSR	29	18	10	28	....	....	....	....	....	....
1972-73	CSKA Moscow	USSR	32	25	8	33	....	....	....	....	....	....
1973-74	CSKA Moscow	USSR	4	1	2	3	2	....	....	....	....	....

Olympic gold 1964, 1968, 1972. Won world title from 1964 to 1971. Four-time WC all-star.

• FRANZ, Georg — GER

LW – R. 5'9", 172 lbs. b: Rosenheim, W.Germany, 1/9/1965.

Season	Club	League	GP	G	A	Pts	PIM	GP	G	A	Pts	PIM
1982-83	EHC Straubing	German-2	31	24	9	33	6	....	....	....	....	....
1983-84	SB Rosenheim	Germany	26	5	5	10	12	....	....	....	....	....
1984-85	SB Rosenheim	Germany	33	22	15	37	12	9	5	2	7	4
1985-86	SB Rosenheim	Germany	33	15	13	28	12	9	6	4	10	0
1986-87	SB Rosenheim	Germany	35	12	11	23	27	9	3	4	7	2
1987-88	SB Rosenheim	Germany	35	24	19	43	26	14	9	5	14	22
1988-89	SB Rosenheim	Germany	36	29	16	45	28	11	6	8	14	12
1989-90	SB Rosenheim	Germany	26	20	17	37	10	11	8	2	10	8
1990-91	SB Rosenheim	Germany	33	29	15	44	12	11	3	4	7	10
1991-92	SB Rosenheim	Germany	42	21	20	41	22	10	3	3	6	4
1992-93	EC Hedos Munchen	Germany	44	15	13	28	28	4	0	1	1	2
1993-94	EC Hedos Munchen	Germany	44	11	7	18	10	10	3	1	4	6
1994-95	EV Landshut	Germany	40	21	15	36	83	18	9	7	16	12

Season	Club	League	REGULAR SEASON GP	G	A	Pts	PIM	PLAYOFFS GP	G	A	Pts	PIM
1995-96	EV Landshut	Germany	39	16	15	31	24	....	....	....	....	....
1996-97	EV Landshut	Germany	48	7	16	23	16	7	1	2	3	4
1997-98	ERC Sonthofen	German-2	54	29	27	56	38	....	....	....	....	....
1998-99	EHC Straubing	German-3	38	11	16	27	24	....	....	....	....	....
99-2000	EHC Straubing	German-2	61	24	21	45	40	....	....	....	....	....

Olympics in 1988, 1994. Seven World Championships. World Juniors in 1983 and 1985.

• GOLONKA, Jozef TCH

C – L. 5'8", 169 lbs. b: Bratislava, Czechoslovakia, 1/6/1938.

Season	Club	League	REGULAR SEASON GP	G	A	Pts	PIM	PLAYOFFS GP	G	A	Pts	PIM
1955-56	Slovan Bratislava	Czech.	STATISTICS NOT AVAILABLE									
1956-57	Slovan Bratislava	Czech.	STATISTICS NOT AVAILABLE									
1957-58	Dukla Jihlava	Czech.	....	8	....	8	....	....	....	....	....	....
1958-59	Dukla Jihlava	Czech.	....	9	....	9	....	....	....	....	....	....
1959-60	Slovan Bratislava	Czech.	....	22	....	22	....	....	....	....	....	....
1960-61	Slovan Bratislava	Czech.	....	35	....	35	....	....	....	....	....	....
1961-62	Slovan Bratislava	Czech.	....	32	....	32	....	....	....	....	....	....
1962-63	Slovan Bratislava	Czech.	....	23	....	23	....	....	....	....	....	....
1963-64	Slovan Bratislava	Czech.	....	28	....	28	....	....	....	....	....	....
1964-65	Slovan Bratislava	Czech.	....	24	....	24	....	....	....	....	....	....
1965-66	Slovan Bratislava	Czech.	....	37	....	37	....	....	....	....	....	....
1966-67	Slovan Bratislava	Czech.	....	17	....	17	....	....	....	....	....	....
1967-68	Slovan Bratislava	Czech.	....	17	20	37	....	....	....	....	....	....
1968-69	Slovan Bratislava	Czech.	....	24	20	44	....	....	....	....	....	....
1969-70	SC Riessersee	Germany	STATISTICS NOT AVAILABLE									
1970-71	SC Riessersee	Germany	STATISTICS NOT AVAILABLE									
1971-72	SC Riessersee	Germany	STATISTICS NOT AVAILABLE									
1972-73	Bucina Zvolen	Czech-2	STATISTICS NOT AVAILABLE									
1973-74	Bucina Zvolen	Czech-2	STATISTICS NOT AVAILABLE									
1974-75	Bucina Zvolen	Czech-2	STATISTICS NOT AVAILABLE									

Three Olympics, eight World Championships from 1959. Had 82 goals in 134 int'l games.

• GURYSHEV, Alexei URS

C – L. 5'11", 183 lbs. b: Moscow, USSR, 3/14/1925.

Season	Club	League	REGULAR SEASON GP	G	A	Pts	PIM	PLAYOFFS GP	G	A	Pts	PIM
1947-48	Krylja Sovetov Moscow	USSR	....	21	....	21	....	....	....	....	....	....
1948-49	Krylja Sovetov Moscow	USSR	....	29	....	29	....	....	....	....	....	....
1949-50	Krylja Sovetov Moscow	USSR	....	27	....	27	....	....	....	....	....	....
1950-51	Krylja Sovetov Moscow	USSR	....	20	....	20	....	....	....	....	....	....
1951-52	Krylja Sovetov Moscow	USSR	....	21	....	21	....	....	....	....	....	....
1952-53	Krylja Sovetov Moscow	USSR	....	26	....	26	....	....	....	....	....	....
1953-54	Krylja Sovetov Moscow	USSR	16	30	....	30	....	....	....	....	....	....
1954-55	Krylja Sovetov Moscow	USSR	....	41	....	41	....	....	....	....	....	....
1955-56	Krylja Sovetov Moscow	USSR	....	36	....	36	....	....	....	....	....	....
1956-57	Krylja Sovetov Moscow	USSR	....	32	....	32	....	....	....	....	....	....
1957-58	Krylja Sovetov Moscow	USSR	....	40	....	40	....	....	....	....	....	....
1958-59	Krylja Sovetov Moscow	USSR	....	15	....	15	....	....	....	....	....	....
1959-60	Krylja Sovetov Moscow	USSR	....	22	....	22	....	....	....	....	....	....
1960-61	Krylja Sovetov Moscow	USSR	....	19	....	19	....	....	....	....	....	....

Olympic gold 1956. World champion in 1954. Six World Championships from 1954 to 1959.

• HEGEN, Dieter GER

LW – L. b: Kaufbeuren, W. Germany, 4/29/1962.
Montreal's 6th, 46th overall in 1981.

Season	Club	League	REGULAR SEASON GP	G	A	Pts	PIM	PLAYOFFS GP	G	A	Pts	PIM
1979-80	ESV Kaufbeuren-2	German-2	42	60	64	124	51	....	....	....	....	....
1980-81	ESV Kaufbeuren	Germany	43	54	35	89	34	....	....	....	....	....
1981-82	ESV Kaufbeuren	Germany	44	42	36	78	44	3	3	0	3	7
1982-83	ESV Kaufbeuren	Germany	36	38	15	53	60	7	8	7	15	18
1983-84	ESV Kaufbeuren	Germany	41	39	23	62	59	6	7	4	11	17
1984-85	ESV Kaufbeuren	Germany	33	31	23	54	40	9	7	4	11	25
1985-86	ESV Kaufbeuren	Germany	26	21	25	46	43	4	2	4	6	2
1986-87	Kolner EC	Germany	25	11	12	23	10	8	3	7	10	8
1987-88	Kolner EC	Germany	35	26	35	61	34	11	4	5	9	12
1988-89	Kolner EC	Germany	36	35	31	66	27	9	3	5	8	12
1989-90	Dusseldorfer EG	Germany	36	34	15	49	36	11	13	12	25	20
1990-91	Dusseldorfer EG	Germany	32	29	14	43	35	13	13	6	19	8
1991-92	Dusseldorfer EG	Germany	44	41	42	83	26	9	8	13	21	6
1992-93	EC Munchen	Germany	44	23	18	41	48	4	2	3	5	0
1993-94	EC Munchen	Germany	44	21	26	47	39	9	10	11	21	6
1994-95	Munich Mad Dogs	Germany	15	13	12	25	28	....	....	....	....	....
	Dusseldorfer EG	Germany	25	17	21	38	16	5	1	3	4	2
1995-96	Dusseldorfer EG	Germany	48	24	31	55	38	13	3	7	10	10
1996-97	Dusseldorfer EG	Germany	41	17	22	39	24	4	2	4	6	6
1997-98	Dusseldorfer EG	Germany	45	22	23	45	57	3	0	1	1	0
1998-99	Star Bulls Rosenheim	Germany	46	16	20	36	62	....	....	....	....	....
99-2000	Star Bulls Rosenheim	Germany	33	4	14	18	20	....	....	....	....	....

Five Olympics, 12 Worlds, 1984 Canada Cup, 1996 World Cup. Top scorer, 1981 World Jrs.

• HOLIK, Jaroslav TCH

C – R. 5'11", 180 lbs. b: Havlickuv Brod, Czechoslovakia, 8/3/1942.

Season	Club	League	REGULAR SEASON GP	G	A	Pts	PIM	PLAYOFFS GP	G	A	Pts	PIM
1959-60	Jiskra Havlickuv Brod	Czech-2	STATISTICS NOT AVAILABLE									
1960-61	Jiskra Havlickuv Brod	Czech-2	STATISTICS NOT AVAILABLE									
1961-62	Dukla Jihlava	Czech.	STATISTICS NOT AVAILABLE									
1962-63	Dukla Jihlava	Czech.	STATISTICS NOT AVAILABLE									
1963-64	Dukla Jihlava	Czech.	STATISTICS NOT AVAILABLE									
1964-65	Dukla Jihlava	Czech.	STATISTICS NOT AVAILABLE									
1965-66	Dukla Jihlava	Czech.	STATISTICS NOT AVAILABLE									
1966-67	Dukla Jihlava	Czech.	....	26	....	26	....	....	....	....	....	....
1967-68	Dukla Jihlava	Czech.	....	17	12	29	....	....	....	....	....	....
1968-69	Dukla Jihlava	Czech.	....	26	26	52	....	....	....	....	....	....
1969-70	Dukla Jihlava	Czech.	....	18	21	39	30	....	....	....	....	....
1970-71	Dukla Jihlava	Czech.	....	21	13	34	....	....	....	....	....	....
1971-72	Dukla Jihlava	Czech.	....	17	25	42	....	....	....	....	....	....
1972-73	Dukla Jihlava	Czech.	....	8	14	22	....	10	2	....	2	....
1973-74	Dukla Jihlava	Czech.	....	18	28	46	98	....	....	....	....	....
1974-75	Dukla Jihlava	Czech.	....	12	26	38	87	....	....	....	....	....
1975-76	Dukla Jihlava	Czech.	32	11	15	26	90	....	....	....	....	....
1976-77	Dukla Jihlava	Czech.	....	14	15	29	....	....	....	....	....	....
1977-78	Dukla Jihlava	Czech.	34	4	15	19	73	....	....	....	....	....
1978-79	Dukla Jihlava	Czech.	16	1	7	8	8	....	....	....	....	....

Olympics in 1972. Seven World Championships, 1965 to 1973. Won world title in 1972.

• HOLIK, Jiri TCH

LW – L. 5'10", 183 lbs. b: Havlickuv Brod, Czechoslovakia, 7/9/1944.

Season	Club	League	REGULAR SEASON GP	G	A	Pts	PIM	PLAYOFFS GP	G	A	Pts	PIM
1961-62	Jiskra Havlickuv Brod	Czech-2	STATISTICS NOT AVAILABLE									
1962-63	Jiskra Havlickuv Brod	Czech-2	STATISTICS NOT AVAILABLE									
1963-64	Dukla Jihlava	Czech.	STATISTICS NOT AVAILABLE									
1964-65	Dukla Jihlava	Czech.	STATISTICS NOT AVAILABLE									
1965-66	Dukla Jihlava	Czech.	STATISTICS NOT AVAILABLE									
1966-67	Dukla Jihlava	Czech.	....	21	....	21	....	....	....	....	....	....
1967-68	Dukla Jihlava	Czech.	....	20	10	30	....	....	....	....	....	....
1968-69	Dukla Jihlava	Czech.	....	28	11	39	....	....	....	....	....	....
1969-70	Dukla Jihlava	Czech.	....	23	17	40	21	....	....	....	....	....
1970-71	Dukla Jihlava	Czech.	....	23	14	37	....	....	....	....	....	....
1971-72	Dukla Jihlava	Czech.	....	15	17	32	....	....	....	....	....	....
1972-73	Dukla Jihlava	Czech.	....	21	16	37	....	10	4	....	4	....
1973-74	Dukla Jihlava	Czech.	....	21	18	39	....	....	....	....	....	....
1974-75	Dukla Jihlava	Czech.	....	16	12	28	....	....	....	....	....	....
1975-76	Dukla Jihlava	Czech.	32	8	12	20	13	....	....	....	....	....
1976-77	Dukla Jihlava	Czech.	....	14	9	23	....	....	....	....	....	....
1977-78	Dukla Jihlava	Czech.	42	15	13	28	28	....	....	....	....	....
1978-79	SB Rosenheim	Germany	48	28	31	59	14	....	....	....	....	....
1979-80	SB Rosenheim	Germany	51	21	28	49	32	....	....	....	....	....
1980-81	WAT Stadlau Wien	Austria	34	18	22	40	16	....	....	....	....	....
1981-82			DID NOT PLAY									
1982-83			DID NOT PLAY									
1983-84			DID NOT PLAY									
1984-85	WEV Wein	Austria-2	13	5	9	14	2	....	....	....	....	....

Four Olympics and 14 World Championships. Canada Cup in 1976. Won three world titles.

• HORESOVSKY, Josef TCH

D – L. 6'1", 202 lbs. b: Zilina u Kladna, Czechoslovakia, 7/18/1946.

Season	Club	League	REGULAR SEASON GP	G	A	Pts	PIM	PLAYOFFS GP	G	A	Pts	PIM
1964-65	SONP Kladno	Czech.	STATISTICS NOT AVAILABLE									
1965-66	Sparta CKD Praha	Czech.	STATISTICS NOT AVAILABLE									
1966-67	Sparta CKD Praha	Czech.	....	12	....	12	....	....	....	....	....	....
1967-68	Sparta CKD Praha	Czech.	....	3	7	10	....	....	....	....	....	....
1968-69	Sparta CKD Praha	Czech.	STATISTICS NOT AVAILABLE									
1969-70	Dukla Jihlava	Czech.	....	9	3	12	32	....	....	....	....	....
1970-71	Dukla Jihlava	Czech.	....	4	9	13	....	....	....	....	....	....
1971-72	Sparta Praha	Czech.	....	3	6	9	....	....	....	....	....	....
1972-73	Sparta Praha	Czech.	....	4	5	9	....	....	....	....	....	....
1973-74	Sparta Praha	Czech.	....	7	9	16	....	....	....	....	....	....
1974-75	Sparta Praha	Czech.	....	4	6	10	....	....	....	....	....	....
1975-76	Sparta Praha	Czech.	29	0	5	5	10	....	....	....	....	....
1976-77	Motor Ceske Budejovice	Czech.	STATISTICS NOT AVAILABLE									
1977-78	Motor Ceske Budejovice	Czech.	42	1	4	5	14	....	....	....	....	....

Olympics 1968, 1972. Six World Championships. Best defenseman, 1968. World title, 1972.

• JOHANSSON, Stig-Goran SWE

RW – L. 5'8", 158 lbs. b: Surahammar, Sweden, 7/18/1943.

Season	Club	League	REGULAR SEASON GP	G	A	Pts	PIM	PLAYOFFS GP	G	A	Pts	PIM
1960-61	Surahammars IF	Sweden-2	STATISTICS NOT AVAILABLE									
1961-62	Surahammars IF	Sweden-2	STATISTICS NOT AVAILABLE									
1962-63	Surahammars IF	Sweden-2	18	29	....	29	....	....	....	....	....	....
1963-64	Sodertalje SK	Sweden	21	10	8	18	14	....	....	....	....	....
1964-65	Sodertalje SK	Sweden	28	12	14	26	22	....	....	....	....	....
1965-66	Sodertalje SK	Sweden	21	9	12	21	8	3	0	1	1	4
1966-67	Sodertalje SK	Sweden	20	10	17	27	10	7	6	3	9	5
1967-68	Sodertalje SK	Sweden	28	27	15	42	14	....	....	....	....	....
1968-69	Sodertalje SK	Sweden	28	20	18	38	8	....	....	....	....	....
1969-70	Sodertalje SK	Sweden	28	8	17	25	....	....	....	....	....	....
1970-71	Sodertalje SK	Sweden	28	14	13	27	16	....	....	....	....	....
1971-72	Sodertalje SK	Sweden	28	17	14	31	4	....	....	....	....	....
1972-73	Sodertalje SK	Sweden	27	7	9	16	4	....	....	....	....	....
1973-74	Sodertalje SK	Sweden	34	12	11	23	13	....	....	....	....	....
1974-75	Sodertalje SK	Sweden	27	4	15	19	8	....	....	....	....	....
	Sodertalje SK	Sweden-Q	6	2	3	5	0	....	....	....	....	....
1975-76	Sodertalje SK	Sweden	36	8	14	22	4	....	....	....	....	....

Olympics in 1972. Six World Championships, 1967 to 1974. Played 113 int'l games.

• JOHANSSON, Tumba Sven SWE

C – L. 6'2", 191 lbs. b: Tumba, Sweden, 8/28/1931.

Season	Club	League	REGULAR SEASON GP	G	A	Pts	PIM	PLAYOFFS GP	G	A	Pts	PIM
1948-49	Djurgardens IF	Sweden	STATISTICS NOT AVAILABLE									
1950-51	Djurgardens IF	Sweden	STATISTICS NOT AVAILABLE									
1951-52	Djurgardens IF	Sweden	STATISTICS NOT AVAILABLE									
1952-53	Djurgardens IF	Sweden	STATISTICS NOT AVAILABLE									
1953-54	Djurgardens IF	Sweden	....	....	....	....	....	2	1	....	1	....
1954-55	Djurgardens IF	Sweden	....	....	....	....	....	2	3	....	3	....
1955-56	Djurgardens IF	Sweden	STATISTICS NOT AVAILABLE									
1956-57	Djurgardens IF	Sweden	....	27	....	27	....	....	....	....	....	....
1957-58	Djurgardens IF	Sweden	STATISTICS NOT AVAILABLE									
1958-59	Djurgardens IF	Sweden	20	27	12	39	....	....	....	....	....	....
1959-60	Djurgardens IF	Sweden	....	23	11	34	....	....	....	....	....	....
1960-61	Djurgardens IF	Sweden	....	28	....	28	....	....	....	....	....	....
1961-62	Djurgardens IF	Sweden	21	17	11	28	....	....	....	....	....	....
1962-63	Djurgardens IF	Sweden	16	18	10	28	4	....	....	....	....	....
1963-64	Djurgardens IF	Sweden	21	17	14	31	2	....	....	....	....	....
1964-65	Djurgardens IF	Sweden	15	15	10	25	0	....	....	....	....	....
1965-66	Djurgardens IF	Sweden	21	16	19	35	6	7	3	6	9	0

Four Olympics and 14 World Championships. Won three world titles. WC all-star 1954.

• KAPUSTIN, Sergei URS

LW – L. 5'11", 194 lbs. b: Ukhta, USSR, 2/13/1953 d: 1995.
NY Rangers' 6th, 141st overall in 1982.

Season	Club	League	REGULAR SEASON GP	G	A	Pts	PIM	PLAYOFFS GP	G	A	Pts	PIM
1969-70	Neftyanik Ukhta	USSR-4	STATISTICS NOT AVAILABLE									
1970-71	Neftyanik Ukhta	USSR-4	STATISTICS NOT AVAILABLE									
1971-72	Krylja Sovetov Moscow	USSR	30	10	....	10	....	....	....	....	....	....
1972-73	Krylja Sovetov Moscow	USSR	32	14	7	21	26	....	....	....	....	....
1973-74	Krylja Sovetov Moscow	USSR	32	12	8	20	26	....	....	....	....	....
1974-75	Krylja Sovetov Moscow	USSR	32	23	9	32	18	....	....	....	....	....
1975-76	Krylja Sovetov Moscow	USSR	36	25	13	38	34	....	....	....	....	....
1976-77	Krylja Sovetov Moscow	USSR	23	16	4	20	29	....	....	....	....	....

Season	Club	League	GP	G	A	Pts	PIM	GP	G	A	Pts	PIM
			REGULAR SEASON					PLAYOFFS				
1977-78	CSKA Moscow	USSR	33	9	11	20	16	....	....	....	....	....
1978-79	CSKA Moscow	USSR	42	21	15	36	28	....	....	....	....	....
1979-80	CSKA Moscow	USSR	30	18	14	32	12	....	....	....	....	....
1980-81	Spartak Moscow	USSR	44	36	25	61	18	....	....	....	....	....
1981-82	Spartak Moscow	USSR	38	30	22	52	53	....	....	....	....	....
1982-83	Spartak Moscow	USSR	44	12	8	20	38	....	....	....	....	....
1983-84	Spartak Moscow	USSR	41	22	21	43	26	....	....	....	....	....
1984-85	Spartak Moscow	USSR	19	5	1	6	10	....	....	....	....	....
1985-86	Spartak Moscow	USSR	38	23	13	36	50	....	....	....	....	....
1986-87	Spartak Moscow	USSR	3	1	0	1	10	....	....	....	....	....
	EC Innsbruck	Austria	31	28	29	57	20	6	5	3	8	0
1987-88	EC Salzburg	Austria	34	20	25	45	22	....	....	....	....	....

Olympic gold 1976. Nine World Championships; all-star in 1978, 1981. Canada Cup 1976, 1981.

• KARLSSON, Stefan SWE

RW – L. 5'9", 156 lbs. b: Gavle, Sweden, 9/11/1946.

Season	Club	League	GP	G	A	Pts	PIM	GP	G	A	Pts	PIM
1964-65	Brynas IF Gavle	Sweden	19	2	1	3	4	....	....	....	....	....
1965-66	Brynas IF Gavle	Sweden	19	18	11	29	8	7	3	4	7	2
1966-67	Brynas IF Gavle	Sweden	....	9	5	14	2	6	4	0	4	2
1967-68	Brynas IF Gavle	Sweden	28	17	14	31	8	....	....	....	....	....
1968-69	Brynas IF Gavle	Sweden	28	14	8	22	18	....	....	....	....	....
1969-70	Brynas IF Gavle	Sweden	28	15	10	25	....	....	....	....	....	....
1970-71	Brynas IF Gavle	Sweden	28	22	12	34	14	....	....	....	....	....
1971-72	Brynas IF Gavle	Sweden	28	15	7	22	10	....	....	....	....	....
1972-73	Brynas IF Gavle	Sweden	28	14	9	23	30	....	....	....	....	....
1973-74	Brynas IF Gavle	Sweden	34	33	15	48	18	....	....	....	....	....
1974-75	Brynas IF Gavle	Sweden	30	28	14	42	28	6	6	0	6	14
1975-76	Krefelder EV	Germany	29	20	16	36	28	....	....	....	....	....
1976-77	Brynas IF Gavle	Sweden	31	16	10	26	22	4	0	0	0	0
1977-78	Brynas IF Gavle	Sweden	35	15	9	24	28	2	0	0	0	0
1978-79	Brynas IF Gavle	Sweden	34	18	6	24	12	....	....	....	....	....
1979-80	Brynas IF Gavle	Sweden	36	13	8	21	36	7	1	2	3	12
1980-81	Brynas IF Gavle	Sweden	22	2	2	4	14	....	....	....	....	....

World Championships, 1969 to 1974. Played 143 games with the Swedish national team.

• KEINONEN, Matti FIN

LW – L. 5'9", 163 lbs. b: Tampere, Finland, 11/6/1941.

Season	Club	League	GP	G	A	Pts	PIM	GP	G	A	Pts	PIM
1960-61	Lukko Rauma	Finland	18	7	7	14	10	....	....	....	....	....
1961-62	Lukko Rauma	Finland	17	7	7	14	18	....	....	....	....	....
1962-63	Lukko Rauma	Finland	18	19	6	25	22	....	....	....	....	....
1963-64	Lukko Rauma	Finland	18	20	7	27	22	....	....	....	....	....
1964-65	Lukko Rauma	Finland	18	14	7	21	4	....	....	....	....	....
1965-66	RU-38 Pori	Finland	4	1	2	3	0	....	....	....	....	....
1966-67	RU-38 Pori	Finland	22	26	17	43	40	....	....	....	....	....
1967-68	Lukko Rauma	Finland-2	STATISTICS NOT AVAILABLE									
1968-69	Lukko Rauma	Finland	22	20	14	34	28	....	....	....	....	....
1969-70	Lukko Rauma	Finland	22	14	14	28	38	....	....	....	....	....
1970-71	HJK Helsinki	Finland	1	1	0	1	0	....	....	....	....	....
1971-72	HJK Helsinki	Finland	32	15	13	28	14	....	....	....	....	....
1972-73	HJK Helsinki	Finland	36	25	16	41	72	....	....	....	....	....
1973-74	Jokerit Helsinki	Finland	36	16	15	31	28	....	....	....	....	....
1974-75	Jokerit Helsinki	Finland	1	1	0	1	0	....	....	....	....	....
1975-76			DID NOT PLAY									
1976-77			DID NOT PLAY									
1977-78	TPS Turku	Finland	2	0	0	0	0	....	....	....	....	....

Two Olympics, 10 World Championships from 1962 to 1973. Had 71 goals in 196 int'l games.

• KESKINEN, Esa FIN

C – R. 5'9", 191 lbs. b: Ylojarvi, Finland, 2/3/1965.
Calgary's 6th, 101st overall in 1985.

Season	Club	League	GP	G	A	Pts	PIM	GP	G	A	Pts	PIM
1980-81	KooVee Tampere Jr.	Finn-Jr	32	46	20	66	35	....	....	....	....	....
1981-82	FoPS Forssa	Finland-2	27	14	18	32	8	....	....	....	....	....
1982-83	FoPS Forssa	Finland-2	19	9	20	29	8	....	....	....	....	....
1983-84	TPS Turku	Finland	31	10	25	35	0	6	0	0	0	0
1984-85	TPS Turku	Finland	35	11	22	33	6	10	2	3	5	0
1985-86	TPS Turku	Finland	36	18	28	46	4	7	2	0	2	0
1986-87	TPS Turku	Finland	44	25	36	61	4	5	1	1	2	0
1987-88	TPS Turku	Finland	44	14	55	69	14	....	....	....	....	....
1988-89	Lukko Rauma	Finland	41	24	46	70	12	....	....	....	....	....
1989-90	Lukko Rauma	Finland	44	25	26	51	16	....	....	....	....	....
1990-91	Lukko Rauma	Finland	44	17	51	68	14	....	....	....	....	....
	Lukko Rauma	Finland-Q	STATISTICS NOT AVAILABLE									
1991-92	TPS Turku	Finland	44	24	45	69	12	3	1	1	2	0
1992-93	TPS Turku	Finland	46	16	43	59	12	12	1	6	7	4
1993-94	TPS Turku	Finland	47	23	47	70	28	11	5	4	9	4
1994-95	HV-71 Jonkoping	Sweden	39	15	29	44	48	13	3	5	8	10
1995-96	HV-71 Jonkoping	Sweden	39	18	41	59	18	4	0	5	5	2
1996-97	HV-71 Jonkoping	Sweden	34	9	27	36	28	....	....	....	....	....
1997-98	HV-71 Jonkoping	Sweden	46	16	29	45	24	3	0	4	4	0
1998-99	HV-71 Jonkoping	Sweden	45	3	22	25	28	....	....	....	....	....
	HV-71 Jonkoping	Sweden	45	3	22	25	28	....	....	....	....	....
99-2000	TPS Turku	Finland	22	8	19	27	8	11	2	5	7	4
	TPS Turku	Finland	22	8	19	27	8	11	2	5	7	4

Olympics 1988, 1994. Six World Championships. Won world title in 1995.

• KHARLAMOV, Valeri URS

LW – L. 5'8", 165 lbs. b: Moscow, USSR, 1/14/1948 d: 8/27/1981.

Season	Club	League	GP	G	A	Pts	PIM	GP	G	A	Pts	PIM
1967-68	CSKA Moscow	USSR	15	2	3	5	6	....	....	....	....	....
	Zvezda Chebarkul	USSR-3	STATISTICS NOT AVAILABLE									
1968-69	CSKA Moscow	USSR	42	37	12	49	24	....	....	....	....	....
1969-70	CSKA Moscow	USSR	33	33	10	43	16	....	....	....	....	....
1970-71	CSKA Moscow	USSR	34	40	12	52	18	....	....	....	....	....
1971-72	CSKA Moscow	USSR	31	26	16	42	22	....	....	....	....	....
1972-73	CSKA Moscow	USSR	27	19	13	32	22	....	....	....	....	....
1973-74	CSKA Moscow	USSR	26	20	10	30	28	....	....	....	....	....
1974-75	CSKA Moscow	USSR	31	15	24	39	35	....	....	....	....	....
1975-76	CSKA Moscow	USSR	34	18	18	36	6	....	....	....	....	....
1976-77	CSKA Moscow	USSR	21	18	8	26	16	....	....	....	....	....
1977-78	CSKA Moscow	USSR	29	18	24	42	35	....	....	....	....	....
1978-79	CSKA Moscow	USSR	41	22	26	48	36	....	....	....	....	....
1979-80	CSKA Moscow	USSR	42	16	22	38	40	....	....	....	....	....
1980-81	CSKA Moscow	USSR	30	9	16	25	14	....	....	....	....	....

Three Olympics, 11 World Championships from 1969 to 1980. Canada-Russia series in 1972.

• KHUMUTOV, Andrei URS

RW – L. 5'9", 176 lbs. b: Yaroslavl, USSR, .
Quebec's 11th, 190th overall in 1989.

Season	Club	League	GP	G	A	Pts	PIM	GP	G	A	Pts	PIM
1979-80	CSKA Moscow	USSR	4	0	0	0	0	....	....	....	....	....
1980-81	CSKA Moscow	USSR	43	23	18	41	4	....	....	....	....	....
1981-82	CSKA Moscow	USSR	44	17	13	30	12	....	....	....	....	....
1982-83	CSKA Moscow	USSR	44	21	17	38	6	....	....	....	....	....
1983-84	CSKA Moscow	USSR	39	17	9	26	14	....	....	....	....	....
1984-85	CSKA Moscow	USSR	37	21	13	34	18	....	....	....	....	....
1985-86	CSKA Moscow	USSR	38	14	15	29	10	....	....	....	....	....
1986-87	CSKA Moscow	USSR	33	15	18	33	22	....	....	....	....	....
1987-88	CSKA Moscow	USSR	48	29	14	43	22	....	....	....	....	....
1988-89	CSKA Moscow	USSR	44	19	16	35	14	....	....	....	....	....
1989-90	CSKA Moscow	USSR	47	21	14	35	16	....	....	....	....	....
1990-91	HC Fribourg-Gotteron	Switz.	36	39	43	82	10	8	14	12	26	4
1991-92	HC Fribourg-Gotteron	Switz.	35	33	46	79	34	14	11	12	23	6
1992-93	HC Fribourg-Gotteron	Switz.	27	23	36	59	16	11	7	11	18	8
1993-94	HC Fribourg-Gotteron	Switz.	35	39	35	74	18	11	11	14	25	6
1994-95	HC Fribourg-Gotteron	Switz.	35	41	45	86	32	8	4	9	13	4
1995-96	HC Fribourg-Gotteron	Switz.	9	3	6	9	6	0	0	0	0	0
1996-97	HC Fribourg-Gotteron	Switz.	44	26	42	68	67	3	1	6	7	0
1997-98	HC Fribourg-Gotteron	Switz.	27	16	18	34	47	12	5	7	12	4

Olympic gold 1984, 1988, 1992. Won seven world titles to 1993. Canada Cup 1981, 1987.

• KILPIO, Raimo FIN

C – R. 5'9", 161 lbs. b: Parikkala, Finland, 2/2/1936.

Season	Club	League	GP	G	A	Pts	PIM	GP	G	A	Pts	PIM
1953-54	Ilves Tampere	Finland	3	0	0	0	0	....	....	....	....	....
1954-55	Ilves Tampere	Finland-2	STATISTICS NOT AVAILABLE									
1955-56	Ilves Tampere	Finland	10	7	3	10	2	....	....	....	....	....
1956-57	Ilves Tampere	Finland	10	9	6	15	4	....	....	....	....	....
1957-58	Ilves Tampere	Finland	11	14	7	21	6	....	....	....	....	....
1958-59	Ilves Tampere	Finland	18	13	15	28	14	....	....	....	....	....
1959-60	Ilves Tampere	Finland	18	23	21	44	0	....	....	....	....	....
1960-61	Ilves Tampere	Finland	18	16	11	27	4	....	....	....	....	....
1961-62	Ilves Tampere	Finland	18	20	10	30	10	....	....	....	....	....
1962-63	RU-38 Pori	Finland-2	STATISTICS NOT AVAILABLE									
1963-64	RU-38 Pori	Finland-2	15	12	10	22	0	....	....	....	....	....
1964-65	RU-38 Pori	Finland	18	10	5	15	9	....	....	....	....	....
1965-66	RU-38 Pori	Finland	20	6	9	15	4	....	....	....	....	....
1966-67	RU-38 Pori	Finland	22	20	15	35	2	....	....	....	....	....
1967-68	Assat Pori	Finland	20	10	13	23	4	....	....	....	....	....
1968-69	Assat Pori	Finland	21	8	10	18	14	....	....	....	....	....
1969-70	Assat Pori	Finland	12	6	6	12	4	....	....	....	....	....
1970-71	Assat Pori	Finland	32	17	22	39	8	....	....	....	....	....
1971-72	Assat Pori	Finland	32	8	12	20	4	....	....	....	....	....
1972-73	Assat Pori	Finland	36	15	14	29	10	....	....	....	....	....
1973-74	Assat Pori	Finland	36	19	12	31	14	....	....	....	....	....
1974-75	Assat Pori	Finland	36	12	12	24	24	....	....	....	....	....
1975-76	Assat Pori	Finland	36	22	18	40	6	4	0	1	1	2
1976-77	Assat Pori	Finland	32	6	10	16	4	....	....	....	....	....

Olympics in 1960, 1964. Played at 10 World Championships from 1957 to 1967.

• KOCHTA, Jiri TCH

C – L. 6', 183 lbs. b: Prague, Czechoslovakia, 10/11/1946.

Season	Club	League	GP	G	A	Pts	PIM	GP	G	A	Pts	PIM
1963-64	Bohemians Praha	Czech-3	STATISTICS NOT AVAILABLE									
1964-65	Bohemians Praha	Czech-3	STATISTICS NOT AVAILABLE									
1965-66	Dukla Jihlava	Czech.	STATISTICS NOT AVAILABLE									
1966-67	Dukla Jihlava	Czech.	STATISTICS NOT AVAILABLE									
1967-68	Dukla Jihlava	Czech.	....	....	....	44	....	....	....	....	....	....
1968-69	Sparta Praha	Czech.	STATISTICS NOT AVAILABLE									
1969-70	Sparta Praha	Czech.	....	25	27	52	6	....	....	....	....	....
1970-71	Sparta Praha	Czech.	STATISTICS NOT AVAILABLE									
1971-72	Sparta Praha	Czech.	....	14	10	24		....	....	....	....	....
1972-73	Sparta Praha	Czech.	....	11	16	27		....	....	....	....	....
1973-74	Sparta Praha	Czech.	....	16	16	32		....	....	....	....	....
1974-75	Sparta Praha	Czech.	....	18	18	36		....	....	....	....	....
1975-76	Sparta Praha	Czech.	20	2	6	8	6	....	....	....	....	....
1976-77	Sparta Praha	Czech.	STATISTICS NOT AVAILABLE									
1977-78	Sparta Praha	Czech.	36	9	12	21	10	....	....	....	....	....
1978-79	Sparta Praha	Czech.	38	9	7	16	10	....	....	....	....	....
1979-80	EV Landshut	Germany	48	63	81	144	23	....	....	....	....	....
1980-81	EV Landshut	Germany	44	37	54	91	20	5	1	5	6	2
1981-82	EHC 70 Munchen	German-2	42	51	58	109	50	....	....	....	....	....
1982-83	EC Hedos Munchen	German-5	STATISTICS NOT AVAILABLE									
1983-84	EC Hedos Munchen	German-5	STATISTICS NOT AVAILABLE									
1984-85	EC Hedos Munchen	German-5	STATISTICS NOT AVAILABLE									
1985-86	EC Hedos Munchen	German-4	STATISTICS NOT AVAILABLE									

Olympics in 1968, 1972. Eight World Championships. Won world title in 1972.

• KOSKELA, Ilpo FIN

D – L. 5'10", 165 lbs. b: Janakkala, Finland, 1/29/1945.

Season	Club	League	GP	G	A	Pts	PIM	GP	G	A	Pts	PIM
1963-64	Tarmo Hameenlinna	Finland-2	9	5	4	9	4	....	....	....	....	....
1964-65	Tarmo Hameenlinna	Finland-2	STATISTICS NOT AVAILABLE									
1965-66	Reipas Lahti	Finland	19	6	5	11	8	....	....	....	....	....
1966-67	Reipas Lahti	Finland	22	4	6	10	20	....	....	....	....	....
1967-68	Reipas Lahti	Finland	29	7	5	12	18	....	....	....	....	....
1968-69	Reipas Lahti	Finland	22	8	4	12	16	....	....	....	....	....
1969-70	Jokerit Helsinki	Finland	22	6	7	13	20	....	....	....	....	....
1970-71	Jokerit Helsinki	Finland	32	6	10	16	24	....	....	....	....	....
1971-72	Jokerit Helsinki	Finland	32	8	10	18	10	....	....	....	....	....
1972-73	Jokerit Helsinki	Finland	36	1	7	8	12	....	....	....	....	....
1973-74	Jokerit Helsinki	Finland	36	8	7	15	24	....	....	....	....	....

Season	Club	League	Regular Season GP	G	A	Pts	PIM	Playoffs GP	G	A	Pts	PIM
1974-75	Jokerit Helsinki	Finland	36	3	9	12	16	....	....	....	....	....
1975-76	Kiekkoreipas Lahti	Finland-2	42	19	27	46	48	....	....	....	....	....
1976-77	Kiekkoreipas Lahti	Finland	36	7	7	14	2	....	....	....	....	....
1977-78	Kiekkoreipas Lahti	Finland	36	3	5	8	6	....	....	....	....	....

Olympics 1968, 1972. Five World Championships, 1968 to 1973. Best Defenseman in 1971.

• KUHNHACKL, Erich GER

C – L. 6'5", 209 lbs. b: Citice, Czechoslovakia, 10/17/1950.

Season	Club	League	Regular Season GP	G	A	Pts	PIM	Playoffs GP	G	A	Pts	PIM
1967-68	Banik Sokolov	Czech-2	STATISTICS NOT AVAILABLE									
1968-69	EV Landhut	Germany	14	6	2	8	2	....	....	....	....	....
1969-70	EV Landhut	Germany	35	21	14	35	14	....	....	....	....	....
1970-71	EV Landhut	Germany	35	16	12	28	18	....	....	....	....	....
1971-72	EV Landhut	Germany	32	24	19	43	36	....	....	....	....	....
1972-73	EV Landhut	Germany	40	38	30	68	43	....	....	....	....	....
1973-74	EV Landhut	Germany	36	50	26	76	40	....	....	....	....	....
1974-75	EV Landhut	Germany	35	47	20	67	90	....	....	....	....	....
1975-76	EV Landhut	Germany	35	29	17	46	73	....	....	....	....	....
1976-77	Kolner EC	Germany	40	47	26	73	79	....	....	....	....	....
1977-78	Kolner EC	Germany	46	52	43	95	43	....	....	....	....	....
1978-79	Kolner EC	Germany	52	59	58	117	99	....	....	....	....	....
1979-80	EV Landshut	Germany	48	83	72	155	67	....	....	....	....	....
1980-81	EV Landshut	Germany	44	40	46	86	74	5	4	2	6	4
1981-82	EV Landshut	Germany	38	41	61	102	34	8	6	9	15	4
1982-83	EV Landshut	Germany	36	32	48	80	70	10	7	7	14	10
1983-84	EV Landshut	Germany	42	35	52	87	75	10	4	11	15	18
1984-85	EV Landshut	Germany	36	30	39	69	59	4	2	3	5	14
1985-86	EHC Olten	Switz.	35	22	23	45	88	....	....	....	....	....
1986-87	EHC Olten	Switz.	15	6	8	14	38	....	....	....	....	....
	EV Landshut	Germany	11	6	16	22	18	4	1	4	5	2
1987-88	EV Landshut	Germany	35	20	29	49	47	4	2	1	3	6
1988-89	EV Landshut	Germany	36	21	38	59	67	3	1	2	3	4

Three Olympics and 10 World Championships. German record 131 goals in 211 int'l games.

• KUZKIN, Viktor URS

D – L. 5'11", 194 lbs. b: Moscow, USSR, 7/6/1940.

Season	Club	League	Regular Season GP	G	A	Pts	PIM	Playoffs GP	G	A	Pts	PIM
1958-59	CSK Moscow	USSR	....	0	....	0	....	....	....	....	....	....
1959-60	CSKA Moscow	USSR	....	3	....	3	....	....	....	....	....	....
1960-61	CSKA Moscow	USSR	....	3	....	3	....	....	....	....	....	....
1961-62	CSKA Moscow	USSR	....	9	....	9	....	....	....	....	....	....
1962-63	CSKA Moscow	USSR	....	6	....	6	....	....	....	....	....	....
1963-64	CSKA Moscow	USSR	....	5	....	5	....	....	....	....	....	....
1964-65	CSKA Moscow	USSR	....	4	....	4	....	....	....	....	....	....
1965-66	CSKA Moscow	USSR	....	9	....	9	....	....	....	....	....	....
1966-67	CSKA Moscow	USSR	....	5	....	5	....	....	....	....	....	....
1967-68	CSKA Moscow	USSR	40	3	....	3	....	....	....	....	....	....
1968-69	CSKA Moscow	USSR	39	7	....	7	....	....	....	....	....	....
1969-70	CSKA Moscow	USSR	32	3	....	3	....	....	....	....	....	....
1970-71	CSKA Moscow	USSR	40	3	....	3	....	....	....	....	....	....
1971-72	CSKA Moscow	USSR	31	4	....	4	....	....	....	....	....	....
1972-73	CSKA Moscow	USSR	29	3	....	3	....	....	....	....	....	....
1973-74	CSKA Moscow	USSR	30	0	3	3	2	....	....	....	....	....
1974-75	CSKA Moscow	USSR	28	1	1	2	2	....	....	....	....	....
1975-76	CSKA Moscow	USSR	36	2	2	4	2	....	....	....	....	....

Olympic gold 1964, 1968, 1972. Eight world titles. Canada-Russia 1972. Long-time captain.

• LALA, Jiri TCH

RW – R. 5'10", 180 lbs. b: Tabor, Czechoslovakia, 8/21/1959.
Quebec's 4th, 76th overall in 1982.

Season	Club	League	Regular Season GP	G	A	Pts	PIM	Playoffs GP	G	A	Pts	PIM
1976-77	Motor Ceske Budejovice	Czech.	32	9	5	14	8	....	....	....	....	....
1977-78	Motor Ceske Budejovice	Czech.	27	9	4	13	10	....	....	....	....	....
1978-79	Motor Ceske Budejovice	Czech.	40	3	7	10	14	....	....	....	....	....
1979-80	Motor Ceske Budejovice	Czech.	44	22	18	40	18	....	....	....	....	....
1980-81	Dukla Jihlava	Czech.	44	40	22	62	10	....	....	....	....	....
1981-82	Dukla Jihlava	Czech.	42	25	26	51	26	....	....	....	....	....
1982-83	Motor Ceske Budejovice	Czech.	44	38	22	60	18	....	....	....	....	....
1983-84	Motor Ceske Budejovice	Czech.	44	26	24	50	12	....	....	....	....	....
1984-85	Motor Ceske Budejovice	Czech.	36	28	13	41	10	....	....	....	....	....
1985-86	Motor Ceske Budejovice	Czech.	35	18	25	43	28	....	....	....	....	....
1986-87	Motor Ceske Budejovice	Czech.	31	14	17	31	32	8	6	6	12	....
1987-88	Motor Ceske Budejovice	Czech.	38	30	38	68	40	....	....	....	....	....
1988-89	Motor Ceske Budejovice	Czech.	33	19	30	49	26	12	8	9	17	....
1989-90	Eintracht Frankfurt	Germany	35	36	39	75	12	3	1	2	3	4
1990-91	Eintracht Frankfurt	Germany	44	47	59	106	28	3	0	1	1	2
1991-92	Mannheimer ERC	Germany	28	27	27	54	41	7	6	5	11	6
	SC Bern	Switz.	STATISTICS NOT AVAILABLE									
1992-93	Mannheimer ERC	Germany	36	32	34	66	28	8	2	6	8	4
1993-94	Mannheimer ERC	Germany	41	21	29	50	18	4	4	1	5	4
	HC Ceske Budejovice	Cze-Rep.	STATISTICS NOT AVAILABLE									
1994-95	Frankfurt Lions	Germany	41	18	44	62	39	5	4	5	9	4
	ZSC Zurich	Switz-2	STATISTICS NOT AVAILABLE									
1995-96	Frankfurt Lions	Germany	50	36	48	84	18	3	0	3	3	0
1996-97	Ayr Scottish Eagles	Britain	40	24	20	44	10	7	11	4	15	0
1997-98	ERC Selb	German-2	52	32	52	84	30	....	....	....	....	....
1998-99	ERC Selb	German-3	43	46	42	88	22	....	....	....	....	....
99-2000	ERC Selb	German-3	34	22	33	55	8	....	....	....	....	....

Olympics in 1984 and 1988. Six World Championships. Canada Cup in 1981 and 1984.

• LINDSTROM, Seppo FIN

D – L. 5'11", 187 lbs. b: Turku, Finland, 5/16/1941.

Season	Club	League	Regular Season GP	G	A	Pts	PIM	Playoffs GP	G	A	Pts	PIM
1959-60	TuTo Turku	Finland-2	STATISTICS NOT AVAILABLE									
1960-61	TuTo Turku	Finland-2	STATISTICS NOT AVAILABLE									
1961-62	TuTo Turku	Finland-2	STATISTICS NOT AVAILABLE									
1962-63	TuTo Turku	Finland-2	STATISTICS NOT AVAILABLE									
1963-64	TuTo Turku	Finland-2	10	6	3	9	10	....	....	....	....	....
1964-65	TuTo Turku	Finland-2	STATISTICS NOT AVAILABLE									
1965-66	TuTo Turku	Finland	20	1	3	4	30	....	....	....	....	....
1966-67	TuTo Turku	Finland	22	3	2	5	20	....	....	....	....	....
1967-68	TuTo Turku	Finland	20	5	7	12	18	....	....	....	....	....
1968-69	TuTo Turku	Finland	22	3	5	8	20	....	....	....	....	....
1969-70	TuTo Turku	Finland	22	6	13	19	21	....	....	....	....	....
1970-71	KAC Klagenfurt	Austria	22	14	17	31	17	....	....	....	....	....
1971-72	TuTo Turku	Finland	32	4	10	14	34	....	....	....	....	....
1972-73	TuTo Turku	Finland	33	5	6	11	26	....	....	....	....	....
1973-74	TuTo Turku	Finland	33	5	7	12	20	....	....	....	....	....
1974-75	TuTo Turku	Finland	35	5	10	15	22	....	....	....	....	....
1975-76	TPS Turku	Finland	36	6	9	15	22	4	1	2	3	0
1976-77	TPS Turku	Finland	36	9	14	23	24	8	2	1	3	2
1977-78	Berliner SC	Germany	32	7	16	23	28	....	....	....	....	....
1978-79	Berliner SC	Germany	52	14	37	51	24	....	....	....	....	....
1979-80	Berliner SC	Germany	44	15	36	51	40	....	....	....	....	....
1980-81	Berliner SC	Germany	42	6	34	40	14	10	2	5	7	4
1981-82	TPS Turku	Finland	31	4	5	9	8	....	....	....	0	....

Olympics in 1968, 1972, 1976. Eight World Championships. Played 214 int'l games.

• LOKTEV, Konstantin URS

RW – L. 5'7", 165 lbs. b: Moscow, USSR, 4/16/1933 d: 1998.

Season	Club	League	Regular Season GP	G	A	Pts	PIM	Playoffs GP	G	A	Pts	PIM
1952-53	Spartak Moscow	USSR	....	11	....	11	....	....	....	....	....	....
1953-54	ODO Leningrad	USSR	6	4	....	4	....	....	....	....	....	....
1954-55	CSK Moscow	USSR	....	5	....	5	....	....	....	....	....	....
1955-56	CSK Moscow	USSR	....	17	....	17	....	....	....	....	....	....
1956-57	CSK Moscow	USSR	....	13	....	13	....	....	....	....	....	....
1957-58	CSK Moscow	USSR	....	28	....	28	....	....	....	....	....	....
1958-59	CSK Moscow	USSR	....	19	....	19	....	....	....	....	....	....
1959-60	CSKA Moscow	USSR	....	14	....	14	....	....	....	....	....	....
1960-61	CSKA Moscow	USSR	....	19	....	19	....	....	....	....	....	....
1961-62	CSKA Moscow	USSR	....	10	....	10	....	....	....	....	....	....
1962-63	CSKA Moscow	USSR	....	8	....	8	....	....	....	....	....	....
1963-64	CSKA Moscow	USSR	....	24	....	24	....	....	....	....	....	....
1964-65	CSKA Moscow	USSR	....	23	....	23	....	....	....	....	....	....
1965-66	CSKA Moscow	USSR	....	16	....	16	....	....	....	....	....	....
1966-67	CSKA Moscow	USSR	....	2	....	2	....	....	....	....	....	....

Two Olympics, eight World Championships from 1957 to 1966. WC all-star in 1965 and 1966.

• LUKAC, Vincent TCH

RW – L. 5'9", 172 lbs. b: Kosice, Czechoslovakia, .
Quebec's 8th, 202nd overall in 1982.

Season	Club	League	Regular Season GP	G	A	Pts	PIM	Playoffs GP	G	A	Pts	PIM
1971-72	VSZ Kosice	Czech.	STATISTICS NOT AVAILABLE									
1972-73	VSZ Kosice	Czech.	STATISTICS NOT AVAILABLE									
1973-74	VSZ Kosice	Czech.	....	27	11	38	....	....	....	....	....	....
1974-75	VSZ Kosice	Czech.	....	25	8	33	....	....	....	....	....	....
1975-76	VSZ Kosice	Czech.	28	17	11	28	12	....	....	....	....	....
1976-77	VSZ Kosice	Czech.	....	48	26	74	....	....	....	....	....	....
1977-78	VSZ Kosice	Czech.	42	36	25	61	51	....	....	....	....	....
1978-79	VSZ Kosice	Czech.	38	27	25	52	21	....	....	....	....	....
1979-80	VSZ Kosice	Czech.	41	43	24	67	36	....	....	....	....	....
1980-81	VSZ Kosice	Czech.	35	29	29	58	12	....	....	....	....	....
1981-82	Dukla Jihlava	Czech.	37	22	10	32	21	....	....	....	....	....
1982-83	VSZ Kosice	Czech.	42	49	19	68	46	....	....	....	....	....
1983-84	VSZ Kosice	Czech.	41	30	20	50	34	....	....	....	....	....
1984-85	VSZ Kosice	Czech.	38	28	19	47	18	....	....	....	....	....
1985-86	SB Rosenheim	Germany	32	22	17	39	4	9	10	7	17	0
1986-87	SB Rosenheim	Germany	29	19	23	42	2	9	4	6	10	0
1987-88	WEV Wein	Austria	31	31	24	55	2	....	....	....	....	....
1988-89	Fife Flyers	Britain	34	88	73	161	34	4	6	4	10	2
1989-90	Streatham Redskins	Britain	28	71	51	122	30	....	....	....	....	....

Olympics in 1980, 1984. Four World Championships; winning 1977, 1985. Canada Cup 1984.

• LUNDVALL, Lars-Erik SWE

LW – L. 5'11", 176 lbs. b: Karlskoga, Sweden, 4/3/1934.

Season	Club	League	Regular Season GP	G	A	Pts	PIM	Playoffs GP	G	A	Pts	PIM
1950-51	Bofors Karlskoga	Sweden-2	STATISTICS NOT AVAILABLE									
1951-52	Bofors Karlskoga	Sweden-2	STATISTICS NOT AVAILABLE									
1952-53	Bofors Karlskoga	Sweden	STATISTICS NOT AVAILABLE									
1953-54	Bofors Karlskoga	Sweden	STATISTICS NOT AVAILABLE									
1954-55	Bofors Karlskoga	Sweden	STATISTICS NOT AVAILABLE									
1955-56	Sodertalje SK	Sweden	STATISTICS NOT AVAILABLE									
1956-57	Sodertalje SK	Sweden	....	17	....	17	....	....	....	....	....	....
1957-58	Bofors Karlskoga	Sweden	STATISTICS NOT AVAILABLE									
1958-59	Sodertalje SK	Sweden	STATISTICS NOT AVAILABLE									
1959-60	Sodertalje SK	Sweden	....	24	10	34	....	....	....	....	....	....
1960-61	Vastra Frolunda	Sweden-2	14	32	....	32	....	....	....	....	....	....
1961-62	Vastra Frolunda	Sweden	21	32	11	43	....	....	....	....	....	....
1962-63	Vastra Frolunda	Sweden	21	27	12	39	10	....	....	....	....	....
1963-64	Vastra Frolunda	Sweden	21	16	14	30	4	....	....	....	....	....
1964-65	Vastra Frolunda	Sweden	28	27	14	41	8	....	....	....	....	....
1965-66	Vastra Frolunda	Sweden	21	23	9	32	2	8	5	4	9	2
1966-67	Vastra Frolunda	Sweden	21	17	18	35	2	7	2	3	5	0
1967-68	Vastra Frolunda	Sweden	26	6	6	12	....	....	....	....	....	....

Three Olympics and nine World Championships. Won world title in 1957 and 1962.

• LUTCHENKO, Vladimir URS

D – L. 6'1", 205 lbs. b: Ramenskoye, USSR, 1/2/1949.

Season	Club	League	Regular Season GP	G	A	Pts	PIM	Playoffs GP	G	A	Pts	PIM
1966-67	CSKA Moscow	USSR	....	0	....	0	....	....	....	....	....	....
1967-68	CSKA Moscow	USSR	38	5	....	5	....	....	....	....	....	....
1968-69	CSKA Moscow	USSR	34	1	....	1	....	....	....	....	....	....
1969-70	CSKA Moscow	USSR	39	2	....	2	....	....	....	....	....	....
1970-71	CSKA Moscow	USSR	40	4	....	4	....	....	....	....	....	....
1971-72	CSKA Moscow	USSR	26	1	....	1	....	....	....	....	....	....
1972-73	CSKA Moscow	USSR	32	5	....	5	....	....	....	....	....	....
1973-74	CSKA Moscow	USSR	32	10	5	15	20	....	....	....	....	....
1974-75	CSKA Moscow	USSR	33	10	5	15	32	....	....	....	....	....
1975-76	CSKA Moscow	USSR	33	4	7	11	16	....	....	....	....	....
1976-77	CSKA Moscow	USSR	35	6	4	10	22	....	....	....	....	....
1977-78	CSKA Moscow	USSR	34	5	3	8	22	....	....	....	....	....
1978-79	CSKA Moscow	USSR	36	2	4	6	20	....	....	....	....	....
1979-80	CSKA Moscow	USSR	38	3	9	12	22	....	....	....	....	....
1980-81	CSKA Moscow	USSR	9	0	0	0	2	....	....	....	....	....

Olympic gold 1972, 1976. Eight world titles. Canada-Russia 1972. Canada Cup 1976.

• MACHAC, Oldrich — TCH
D – L. 5'9", 198 lbs. b: Prostejov, Czechoslovakia, 4/18/1946.

			REGULAR SEASON					PLAYOFFS				
Season	Club	League	GP	G	A	Pts	PIM	GP	G	A	Pts	PIM
1963-64	Zelezarny Prostejov	Czech-2	STATISTICS NOT AVAILABLE									
1964-65	Zelezarny Prostejov	Czech-2	STATISTICS NOT AVAILABLE									
1965-66	Dukla Kosice	Czech.	STATISTICS NOT AVAILABLE									
1966-67	Dukla Kosice	Czech.	....	6	....	6	....	....	....	....	....	....
1967-68	ZKL Brno	Czech.	....	14	5	19	....	....	....	....	....	....
1968-69	ZKL Brno	Czech.	STATISTICS NOT AVAILABLE									
1969-70	ZKL Brno	Czech.	....	7	9	16	37	....	....	....	....	....
1970-71	ZKL Brno	Czech.	....	18	7	25	....	....	....	....	....	....
1971-72	ZKL Brno	Czech.	....	3	11	14	....	....	....	....	....	....
1972-73	ZKL Brno	Czech.	....	1	13	14	....	....	....	....	....	....
1973-74	ZKL Brno	Czech.	....	12	16	28	....	....	....	....	....	....
1974-75	ZKL Brno	Czech.	....	11	17	28	44	....	....	....	....	....
1975-76	ZKL Brno	Czech.	32	7	12	19	60	....	....	....	....	....
1976-77	Zetor Brno	Czech.	STATISTICS NOT AVAILABLE									
1977-78	Zetor Brno	Czech.	44	6	14	20	30	....	....	....	....	....
1978-79	SB Rosenheim	Germany	STATISTICS NOT AVAILABLE									
1979-80	SB Rosenheim	Germany	39	12	25	37	26	....	....	....	....	....
1980-81	SB Rosenheim	Germany	STATISTICS NOT AVAILABLE									
1981-82	SB Rosenheim	Germany	44	8	15	23	29	....	0	0	0	....

Three Olympics, 12 World Championships, 1976 Canada Cup. A three-time world champion.

• MALTSEV, Alexander — URS
RW – L. 5'9", 174 lbs. b: Kirovo-Chepetsk, USSR, 4/20/1949.

			REGULAR SEASON					PLAYOFFS				
Season	Club	League	GP	G	A	Pts	PIM	GP	G	A	Pts	PIM
1965-66	Kirovo-Chepetsk	USSR-3	STATISTICS NOT AVAILABLE									
1966-67	Kirovo-Chepetsk	USSR-4	STATISTICS NOT AVAILABLE									
1967-68	Dynamo Moscow	USSR	23	9	2	11	4	....	....	....	....	....
1968-69	Dynamo Moscow	USSR	42	26	....	26	....	....	....	....	....	....
1969-70	Dynamo Moscow	USSR	42	32	....	32	....	....	....	....	....	....
1970-71	Dynamo Moscow	USSR	37	36	20	56	8	....	....	....	....	....
1971-72	Dynamo Moscow	USSR	26	20	11	31	14	....	....	....	....	....
1972-73	Dynamo Moscow	USSR	27	20	16	36	30	....	....	....	....	....
1973-74	Dynamo Moscow	USSR	32	25	22	47	14	....	....	....	....	....
1974-75	Dynamo Moscow	USSR	32	18	16	34	28	....	....	....	....	....
1975-76	Dynamo Moscow	USSR	29	28	19	47	0	....	....	....	....	....
1976-77	Dynamo Moscow	USSR	33	31	27	58	4	....	....	....	....	....
1977-78	Dynamo Moscow	USSR	24	17	12	29	22	....	....	....	....	....
1978-79	Dynamo Moscow	USSR	8	2	3	5	0	....	....	....	....	....
1979-80	Dynamo Moscow	USSR	36	11	28	39	10	....	....	....	....	....
1980-81	Dynamo Moscow	USSR	38	14	28	42	8	....	....	....	....	....
1981-82	Dynamo Moscow	USSR	37	19	22	41	6	....	....	....	....	....
1982-83	Dynamo Moscow	USSR	32	14	15	29	0	....	....	....	....	....
1983-84	Dynamo Moscow	USSR	32	7	15	22	6	....	....	....	....	....
1984-85			DID NOT PLAY									
1985-86			DID NOT PLAY									
1986-87			DID NOT PLAY									
1987-88			DID NOT PLAY									
1988-89			DID NOT PLAY									
1989-90	Ujpesti Dozsa Budapest	Hungary	13	8	12	20	....	....	....	....	....	....

Two Olympic golds, one silver, nine world titles, 1969 to 1983. Canada-Russia series in 1972.

• MARJAMAKI, Pekka — FIN
D – L. 6'1", 198 lbs. b: Tampere, Finland, 12/18/1947.

			REGULAR SEASON					PLAYOFFS				
Season	Club	League	GP	G	A	Pts	PIM	GP	G	A	Pts	PIM
1964-65	Tappara Tampere	Finland	18	1	2	3	25	....	....	....	....	....
1965-66	Tappara Tampere	Finland-2	STATISTICS NOT AVAILABLE									
1966-67	Tappara Tampere	Finland	22	5	3	8	47	....	....	....	....	....
1967-68	Tappara Tampere	Finland	17	0	3	3	25	....	....	....	....	....
1968-69	Tappara Tampere	Finland	22	4	7	11	30	....	....	....	....	....
1969-70	Tappara Tampere	Finland	22	15	5	20	40	....	....	....	....	....
1970-71	Tappara Tampere	Finland	32	11	7	18	38	....	....	....	....	....
1971-72	Tappara Tampere	Finland	32	10	8	18	18	....	....	....	....	....
1972-73	Tappara Tampere	Finland	36	7	13	20	23	....	....	....	....	....
1973-74	Tappara Tampere	Finland	36	8	10	18	38	....	....	....	....	....
1974-75	Tappara Tampere	Finland	36	16	9	25	16	....	....	....	....	....
1975-76	Tappara Tampere	Finland	35	9	11	20	52	4	2	0	2	0
1976-77	Tappara Tampere	Finland	32	14	12	26	31	6	3	4	7	4
1977-78	Tappara Tampere	Finland	36	14	14	28	48	8	2	2	4	6
1978-79	Tappara Tampere	Finland	36	7	14	21	48	10	2	4	6	4
1979-80	HV-71 Jonkoping	Sweden	36	5	2	7	23	....	....	....	....	....
1980-81	HV-71 Jonkoping	Sweden-2	31	15	14	29	41	....	....	....	....	....
1981-82	Tappara Tampere	Finland	35	3	6	9	8	11	1	2	3	2
1982-83	Tappara Tampere	Finland	16	1	4	5	6	8	4	3	7	6
1983-84	Tappara Tampere	Finland	13	0	1	1	0	3	0	1	1	0

Two Olympics and 10 World Championships. Played 251 games for the Finnish national team.

• MARTINEC, Vladimir — TCH
RW – L. 5'8", 178 lbs. b: Lomnice nad Popelkou, Czechoslovakia, 12/22/1949.

			REGULAR SEASON					PLAYOFFS				
Season	Club	League	GP	G	A	Pts	PIM	GP	G	A	Pts	PIM
1967-68	Tesla Pardubice	Czech.	....	20	19	39	....	....	....	....	....	....
1968-69	Tesla Pardubice	Czech.	STATISTICS NOT AVAILABLE									
1969-70	Tesla Pardubice	Czech.	....	22	14	36	25	....	....	....	....	....
1970-71	Tesla Pardubice	Czech.	STATISTICS NOT AVAILABLE									
1971-72	Tesla Pardubice	Czech.	....	23	19	42	....	....	....	....	....	....
1972-73	Tesla Pardubice	Czech.	....	26	23	49	....	12	5	....	5	....
1973-74	Tesla Pardubice	Czech.	....	31	22	53	....	....	....	....	....	....
1974-75	Tesla Pardubice	Czech.	....	27	18	45	....	....	....	....	....	....
1975-76	Tesla Pardubice	Czech.	32	22	26	48	30	....	....	....	....	....
1976-77	Tesla Pardubice	Czech.	....	29	24	53	....	....	....	....	....	....
1977-78	Tesla Pardubice	Czech.	44	19	18	37	19	....	....	....	....	....
1978-79	Dukla Jihlava	Czech.	21	21	8	29	12	....	....	....	....	....
	Tesla Pardubice	Czech.	24	21	12	33	12	....	....	....	....	....
1979-80	Tesla Pardubice	Czech.	35	27	19	46	19	....	....	....	....	....
1980-81	Tesla Pardubice	Czech.	39	21	22	43	26	....	....	....	....	....
1981-82	ESV Kaufbeuren	Germany	44	38	29	67	10	3	1	2	3	0
1982-83	ESV Kaufbeuren	Germany	35	28	28	56	22	7	9	8	17	4
1983-84	ESV Kaufbeuren	Germany	41	24	24	48	4	7	6	6	12	8
1984-85	ESV Kaufbeuren	Germany	36	25	33	58	19	9	5	3	8	4

Three Olympics, 11 World Championships, 1976 Canada Cup. Three-time world champion.

• MAYOROV, Boris — URS
LW – R. 5'9", 158 lbs. b: Moscow, USSR, 2/11/1938.

			REGULAR SEASON					PLAYOFFS				
Season	Club	League	GP	G	A	Pts	PIM	GP	G	A	Pts	PIM
1955-56	Spartak Moscow	USSR	....	1	....	1	....	....	....	....	....	....
1956-57	Spartak Moscow	USSR	....	3	....	3	....	....	....	....	....	....
1957-58	Spartak Moscow	USSR	....	8	....	8	....	....	....	....	....	....
1958-59	Spartak Moscow	USSR	....	18	....	18	....	....	....	....	....	....
1959-60	Spartak Moscow	USSR	....	10	....	10	....	....	....	....	....	....
1960-61	Spartak Moscow	USSR	....	20	....	20	....	....	....	....	....	....
1961-62	Spartak Moscow	USSR	38	30	....	30	....	....	....	....	....	....
1962-63	Spartak Moscow	USSR	37	27	....	27	....	....	....	....	....	....
1963-64	Spartak Moscow	USSR	....	18	....	18	....	....	....	....	....	....
1964-65	Spartak Moscow	USSR	....	25	....	25	....	....	....	....	....	....
1965-66	Spartak Moscow	USSR	....	22	....	22	....	....	....	....	....	....
1966-67	Spartak Moscow	USSR	....	27	....	27	....	....	....	....	....	....
1967-68	Spartak Moscow	USSR	....	29	....	29	....	....	....	....	....	....
1968-69	Spartak Moscow	USSR	38	16	....	16	....	....	....	....	....	....
1969-70	Spartak Moscow	USSR	5	1	....	1	....	....	....	....	....	....

Olympic gold 1964, 1968. World champion, 1963 to 1968. WC all-star 1961. Soviet captain.

• MIKHAILOV, Boris — URS
RW – L. 5'9", 169 lbs. b: Moscow, USSR, 10/6/1944.

			REGULAR SEASON					PLAYOFFS				
Season	Club	League	GP	G	A	Pts	PIM	GP	G	A	Pts	PIM
1962-63	Avangard Saratov	USSR-2	STATISTICS NOT AVAILABLE									
1963-64	Avangard Saratov	USSR-3	STATISTICS NOT AVAILABLE									
1964-65	Avangard Saratov	USSR-2	....	23	....	23	....	....	....	....	....	....
1965-66	Lokomotiv Moscow	USSR	28	18	8	26	8	....	....	....	....	....
1966-67	Lokomotiv Moscow	USSR	44	20	7	27	16	....	....	....	....	....
1967-68	CSKA Moscow	USSR	43	29	16	45	16	....	....	....	....	....
1968-69	CSKA Moscow	USSR	42	36	14	50	14	....	....	....	....	....
1969-70	CSKA Moscow	USSR	44	40	15	55	22	....	....	....	....	....
1970-71	CSKA Moscow	USSR	40	32	15	47	16	....	....	....	....	....
1971-72	CSKA Moscow	USSR	31	20	13	33	18	....	....	....	....	....
1972-73	CSKA Moscow	USSR	30	24	13	37	20	....	....	....	....	....
1973-74	CSKA Moscow	USSR	31	18	9	27	12	....	....	....	....	....
1974-75	CSKA Moscow	USSR	35	40	11	51	30	....	....	....	....	....
1975-76	CSKA Moscow	USSR	36	31	7	38	43	....	....	....	....	....
1976-77	CSKA Moscow	USSR	34	28	23	51	10	....	....	....	....	....
1977-78	CSKA Moscow	USSR	35	32	20	52	18	....	....	....	....	....
1978-79	CSKA Moscow	USSR	43	30	24	54	23	....	....	....	....	....
1979-80	CSKA Moscow	USSR	41	27	23	50	19	....	....	....	....	....
1980-81	CSKA Moscow	USSR	15	4	5	9	4	....	....	....	....	....

Three Olympics and 11 World Championships from 1969 to 1980. Canada-Russia 1972.

• NIEMINEN, Mika — FIN
C – R. 6'1", 202 lbs. b: Tampere, Finland, 1/1/1966.

			REGULAR SEASON					PLAYOFFS				
Season	Club	League	GP	G	A	Pts	PIM	GP	G	A	Pts	PIM
1983-84	Ilves Tampere	Finn-Jr.	27	22	15	37	16	....	....	....	....	....
1984-85	Ilves Tampere	Finn-Jr.	27	23	17	40	28	....	....	....	....	....
1985-86	Kiekkoreipas Lahti	Finland-2	43	35	27	62	67	....	....	....	....	....
	Kiekkoreipas Lahti	Finn-Jr.	4	5	1	6	0	....	....	....	....	....
1986-87	Kiekkoreipas Lahti	Finland-2	44	31	32	63	34	....	....	....	....	....
1987-88	Ilves Tampere	Finland	41	21	20	41	2	4	2	3	5	0
1988-89	Ilves Tampere	Finland	23	10	21	31	14	5	3	6	9	4
1989-90	Ilves Tampere	Finland	25	12	34	46	12	9	2	6	8	4
1990-91	Ilves Tampere	Finland	44	20	42	62	20	....	....	....	....	....
1991-92	Lukko Rauma	Finland	44	17	38	55	16	2	0	0	0	2
1992-93	Lulea HF	Sweden	40	17	22	39	26	11	2	2	4	6
1993-94	Lulea HF	Sweden	40	14	38	52	24	....	....	....	....	....
1994-95	Lulea HF	Sweden	38	18	31	49	24	9	5	8	13	16
1995-96	ZSC Zurich	Switz-2	36	28	46	74	16	10	4	9	13	4
1996-97	ZSC Zurich	Switz-2	38	41	33	74	60	10	7	10	17	31
1997-98	Jokerit Helsinki	Finland	48	16	25	41	37	8	3	5	8	14
1998-99	HIFK Helsinki	Finland	53	20	28	48	12	11	4	7	11	0
99-2000	HIFK Helsinki	Finland	36	15	19	34	42	9	2	6	8	18

World Championship debut in 1991. Gold in 1995. Olympic bronze in 1994 and 1998.

• NILSSON, Lars-Goran — SWE
LW – L. 5'10", 161 lbs. b: Vuollerim, Sweden, 3/9/1944.

			REGULAR SEASON					PLAYOFFS				
Season	Club	League	GP	G	A	Pts	PIM	GP	G	A	Pts	PIM
1962-63	Kiruna AIF	Sweden-2	STATISTICS NOT AVAILABLE									
1963-64	Kiruna AIF	Sweden-2	18	20	....	20	....	....	....	....	....	....
1964-65	Brynas IF Gavle	Sweden	28	15	7	22	0	....	....	....	....	....
1965-66	Brynas IF Gavle	Sweden	20	11	6	17	8	7	2	6	8	0
1966-67	Brynas IF Gavle	Sweden	21	19	17	36	6	6	5	2	7	2
1967-68	Brynas IF Gavle	Sweden	27	14	16	30	22	....	....	....	....	....
1968-69	Brynas IF Gavle	Sweden	27	31	18	49	16	....	....	....	....	....
1969-70	Brynas IF Gavle	Sweden	28	20	24	44	....	....	....	....	....	....
1970-71	Brynas IF Gavle	Sweden	28	34	28	62	22	....	....	....	....	....
1971-72	Brynas IF Gavle	Sweden	28	15	12	27	49	....	....	....	....	....
1972-73	Brynas IF Gavle	Sweden	28	17	15	32	22	....	....	....	....	....
1973-74	Brynas IF Gavle	Sweden	35	26	28	54	52	....	....	....	....	....
1974-75	Brynas IF Gavle	Sweden	30	16	15	31	15	6	4	4	8	12
1975-76	Brynas IF Gavle	Sweden	35	15	21	36	30	4	1	3	4	6
1976-77	Brynas IF Gavle	Sweden	35	16	19	35	68	4	0	1	1	9
1977-78	Brynas IF Gavle	Sweden	35	17	25	42	40	2	0	0	0	0
1978-79	Brynas IF Gavle	Sweden	36	14	11	25	22	....	....	....	....	....

Olympics in 1968, 1972. Eight World Championships, 1966 to 1974. Canada Cup 1976.

• NILSSON, Nils — SWE
C – L. 5'11", 176 lbs. b: Forshaga, Sweden, 3/8/1936.

			REGULAR SEASON					PLAYOFFS				
Season	Club	League	GP	G	A	Pts	PIM	GP	G	A	Pts	PIM
1952-53	Forshaga IF	Sweden	STATISTICS NOT AVAILABLE									
1953-54	Forshaga IF	Sweden-2	STATISTICS NOT AVAILABLE									
1954-55	Forshaga IF	Sweden-2	STATISTICS NOT AVAILABLE									
1955-56	Forshaga IF	Sweden-2	STATISTICS NOT AVAILABLE									
1956-57	Forshaga IF	Sweden	....	18	....	18	....	....	....	....	....	....
1957-58	Forshaga IF	Sweden	....	21	6	27	....	....	....	....	....	....
1958-59	Forshaga IF	Sweden	12	17	4	21	....	....	....	....	....	....
1959-60	Forshaga IF	Sweden	....	20	15	35	....	....	....	....	....	....
1960-61	Forshaga IF	Sweden	13	25	....	25	....	....	....	....	....	....
1961-62	Forshaga IF	Sweden	21	32	11	43	....	....	....	....	....	....
1962-63	Leksands IF	Sweden	21	22	13	35	2	....	....	....	....	....
1963-64	Leksands IF	Sweden	21	18	6	24	2	....	....	....	....	....

Season	Club	League	GP	G	A	Pts	PIM	GP	G	A	Pts	PIM
			REGULAR SEASON					PLAYOFFS				
1964-65	Leksands IF	Sweden	26	19	12	31	6	....	....	....	....	....
1965-66	Leksands IF	Sweden	21	15	16	31	0	5	5	0	5	0
1966-67	Leksands IF	Sweden	21	17	9	26	2	2	1	2	3	2
1967-68	Leksands IF	Sweden	28	27	17	44	4	....	....	....	....	....
1968-69	Leksands IF	Sweden	25	21	14	35	0	....	....	....	....	....

Three Olympics and 10 World Championships. Won world title in 1957 and 1962.

• NORDLANDER, Bert-Ola SWE

D – L. 5'11", 178 lbs. b: Sundsvall, Sweden, 8/12/1938.

Season	Club	League	GP	G	A	Pts	PIM	GP	G	A	Pts	PIM
1956-57	Ostrands IF Timra	Sweden	STATISTICS NOT AVAILABLE									
1957-58	Ostrands IF Timra	Sweden	STATISTICS NOT AVAILABLE									
1958-59	Ostrands IF Timra	Sweden	STATISTICS NOT AVAILABLE									
1959-60	Ostrands IF Timra	Sweden	STATISTICS NOT AVAILABLE									
1960-61	Ostrands IF Timra	Sweden	....	1	....	1	....	....	....	....	....	....
1961-62	Ostrands IF Timra	Sweden	....	2	....	2	....	....	....	....	....	....
1962-63	Ostrands IF Timra	Sweden	21	4	0	4	12	....	....	....	....	....
1963-64	AIK Solna	Sweden	....	1	1	2	6	....	....	....	....	....
1964-65	AIK Solna	Sweden	27	4	4	8	2	....	....	....	....	....
1965-66	AIK Solna	Sweden	21	9	10	19	16	2	0	0	0	0
1966-67	AIK Solna	Sweden	....	3	4	7	2	....	....	....	....	....
1967-68	AIK Solna	Sweden	26	3	11	14	....	....	....	....	....	....
1968-69	AIK Solna	Sweden	28	7	9	16	4	....	....	....	....	....
1969-70	AIK Solna	Sweden	27	2	8	10	....	....	....	....	....	....
1970-71	AIK Solna	Sweden	28	4	4	8	20	....	....	....	....	....
1971-72	AIK Solna	Sweden	28	5	13	18	28	....	....	....	....	....
1972-73	AIK Solna	Sweden	22	5	4	9	4	....	....	....	....	....

Olympics in 1960, 1964, 1968, 1972. Ten World Championships. Won world title in 1962.

• NOVAK, Jiri TCH

C – L. 5'9", 165 lbs. b: Jaromer, Czechoslovakia, 6/6/1950.

Season	Club	League	GP	G	A	Pts	PIM	GP	G	A	Pts	PIM
1967-68	Tesla Pardubice	Czech.	STATISTICS NOT AVAILABLE									
1968-69	Tesla Pardubice	Czech.	STATISTICS NOT AVAILABLE									
1969-70	Tesla Pardubice	Czech.	....	14	11	25	24	....	....	....	....	....
1970-71	Dukla Jihlava	Czech.	....	16	9	25	....	....	....	....	....	....
1971-72	Dukla Jihlava	Czech.	....	22	9	31	....	....	....	....	....	....
1972-73	Tesla Pardubice	Czech.	....	18	18	36	....	11	4	....	4	....
1973-74	Tesla Pardubice	Czech.	....	12	9	21	....	....	....	....	....	....
1974-75	Tesla Pardubice	Czech.	....	24	29	53	....	....	....	....	....	....
1975-76	Tesla Pardubice	Czech.	28	19	10	29	17	....	....	....	....	....
1976-77	Tesla Pardubice	Czech.	....	30	21	51	....	....	....	....	....	....
1977-78	Tesla Pardubice	Czech.	44	23	14	37	45	....	....	....	....	....
1978-79	Tesla Pardubice	Czech.	36	16	15	31	22	....	....	....	....	....
1979-80	Tesla Pardubice	Czech.	40	26	27	53	42	....	....	....	....	....
1980-81	Tesla Pardubice	Czech.	32	20	21	41	28	....	....	....	....	....
1981-82	HC Lausanne	Switz-2	32	37	25	62	....	....	....	....	....	....
1982-83	HC Lausanne	Switz-2	38	37	30	67	....	....	....	....	....	....
1983-84	HC Villard-de-Lans	France	....	30	32	62	....	....	....	....	....	....
1984-85	SG Cortina	Italy	23	24	20	44	10	6	2	4	6	4

Olympics in 1976, 1980. Six World Championships, winning 1976, 1977. Canada Cup 1976.

• NUMMELIN, Timo FIN

D – L. 5'10", 194 lbs. b: Turku, Finland, 9/7/1948.

Season	Club	League	GP	G	A	Pts	PIM	GP	G	A	Pts	PIM
1964-65	TPS Turku	Finland	7	0	0	0	0	....	....	....	....	....
1965-66	TPS Turku	Finland	20	2	0	2	22	....	....	....	....	....
1966-67	TPS Turku	Finland	22	5	4	9	16	....	....	....	....	....
1967-68	TPS Turku	Finland	20	3	1	4	26	....	....	....	....	....
1968-69	TPS Turku	Finland-2	STATISTICS NOT AVAILABLE									
1969-70	TPS Turku	Finland	22	8	4	12	14	....	....	....	....	....
1970-71	TPS Turku	Finland	22	2	7	9	20	....	....	....	....	....
1971-72	TPS Turku	Finland	32	17	5	22	12	....	....	....	....	....
1972-73	TPS Turku	Finland	35	4	7	11	45	....	....	....	....	....
1973-74	TPS Turku	Finland	34	6	5	11	37	....	....	....	....	....
1974-75	TPS Turku	Finland	36	5	8	13	58	....	....	....	....	....
1975-76	TPS Turku	Finland	36	9	8	17	10	4	1	0	1	2
1976-77	TPS Turku	Finland	36	6	8	14	20	8	0	0	0	0
1977-78	TPS Turku	Finland	35	11	3	14	16	8	0	2	2	4
1978-79	TPS Turku	Finland	36	5	7	12	18	8	1	1	2	18
1979-80	TPS Turku	Finland	36	7	16	23	14	6	1	2	3	6
1980-81	TPS Turku	Finland	36	17	9	26	44	7	0	4	4	8
1981-82	TPS Turku	Finland	36	12	9	21	16	7	1	1	2	0
1982-83	TPS Turku	Finland	36	8	9	17	26	3	2	0	2	4
1983-84	TPS Turku	Finland	37	6	11	17	32	10	0	2	2	2
1984-85	TPS Turku	Finland	36	10	9	19	12	10	1	0	1	0
1985-86	TPS Turku	Finland	36	4	5	9	24	7	0	1	1	0
1986-87	TPS Turku	Finland	44	0	2	2	8	5	0	0	0	0
1987/93			OUT OF HOCKEY – RETIRED									
1993-94	TPS Turku	Finland	1	0	0	0	0	....	....	....	....	....

Olympics in 1976. Eight World Championships. Canada Cup in 1976 and 1981.

• OBERG, Carl-Goran SWE

LW – L. 6', 180 lbs. b: Valbo, Sweden, 12/24/1938.

Season	Club	League	GP	G	A	Pts	PIM	GP	G	A	Pts	PIM
1955-56	Gavle GIK	Sweden	STATISTICS NOT AVAILABLE									
1956-57	Gavle GIK	Sweden	....	10	....	10	....	....	....	....	....	....
1957-58	Gavle GIK	Sweden	....	21	9	30	....	....	....	....	....	....
1958-59	Gavle GIK	Sweden	20	19	7	26	....	....	....	....	....	....
1959-60	Gavle GIK	Sweden	....	23	18	41	....	....	....	....	....	....
1960-61	Djurgardens IF	Sweden	....	14	....	14	....	....	....	....	....	....
1961-62	Djurgardens IF	Sweden	21	22	13	35	....	....	....	....	....	....
1962-63	Djurgardens IF	Sweden	21	25	18	43	16	....	....	....	....	....
1963-64	Djurgardens IF	Sweden	21	11	14	25	20	....	....	....	....	....
1964-65	Djurgardens IF	Sweden	20	6	3	9	4	....	....	....	....	....
1965-66	Djurgardens IF	Sweden	21	12	9	21	13	7	7	5	12	2
1966-67	Djurgardens IF	Sweden	21	9	16	25	26	3	0	1	1	0
1967-68	Djurgardens IF	Sweden	27	9	13	22	....	....	....	....	....	....
1968-69	Tranas AIF	Sweden-2	22	17	6	23	....	....	....	....	....	....
1969-70	Tranas AIF	Sweden-2	16	14	7	21	....	....	....	....	....	....

Season	Club	League	GP	G	A	Pts	PIM	GP	G	A	Pts	PIM
			REGULAR SEASON					PLAYOFFS				
1970-71	Sodertalje SK	Sweden	28	8	7	15	29	....	....	....	....	....
1971-72	Sodertalje SK	Sweden	27	11	3	14	18	....	....	....	....	....
1972-73	Sodertalje SK	Sweden	26	5	11	16	0	....	....	....	....	....

Olympics in 1960, 1964, 1968. Nine World Championships from 1958 to 1968.

• OKSANEN, Lasse FIN

RW – R. 5'11", 180 lbs. b: Tampere, Finland, 12/7/1942.

Season	Club	League	GP	G	A	Pts	PIM	GP	G	A	Pts	PIM
1960-61	Ilves Tampere	Finland	2	1	0	1	0	....	....	....	....	....
1961-62	Ilves Tampere	Finland	17	3	4	7	0	....	....	....	....	....
1962-63	Ilves Tampere	Finland	18	5	7	12	9	....	....	....	....	....
1963-64	Ilves Tampere	Finland	17	13	10	23	12	....	....	....	....	....
1964-65	Ilves Tampere	Finland	18	13	7	20	8	....	....	....	....	....
1965-66	Ilves Tampere	Finland	19	8	13	21	12	....	....	....	....	....
1966-67	Ilves Tampere	Finland	21	23	14	37	6	....	....	....	....	....
1967-68	Ilves Tampere	Finland	19	15	11	26	4	....	....	....	....	....
1968-69	Ilves Tampere	Finland	22	21	15	36	10	....	....	....	....	....
1969-70	Ilves Tampere	Finland	22	32	19	51	6	....	....	....	....	....
1970-71	Ilves Tampere	Finland	32	17	20	37	12	....	....	....	....	....
1971-72	Ilves Tampere	Finland	26	18	19	37	10	....	....	....	....	....
1972-73	Ilves Tampere	Finland	36	12	13	25	12	....	....	....	....	....
1973-74	Ilves Tampere	Finland	36	23	20	43	16	....	....	....	....	....
1974-75	Ilves Tampere	Finland	30	15	11	26	16	....	....	....	....	....
1975-76	HC Val Gardena	Italy	....	27	....	27	....	....	....	....	....	....
1976-77	HC Val Gardena	Italy	....	23	....	23	....	....	....	....	....	....
1977-78	Ilves Tampere	Finland	35	13	16	29	4	7	2	4	6	0
1978-79	Ilves Tampere	Finland	36	18	10	28	10	....	....	....	....	....
1979-80	HC Asiago	Italy	....	24	37	61	6	....	....	....	....	....
1980-81	Ilves Tampere	Finland	35	13	8	21	6	2	0	0	0	0
1981-82	Ilves Tampere	Finland	36	5	13	18	2	....	....	....	....	....

Three Olympics, 13 World Championships. Record 282 games with Finnish national team.

• PALMQVIST, Bjorn SWE

C – L. 5'11", 180 lbs. b: Bjasta, Sweden, 3/15/1944.

Season	Club	League	GP	G	A	Pts	PIM	GP	G	A	Pts	PIM
1960-61	Bjasta IF	Sweden-3	STATISTICS NOT AVAILABLE									
1961-62	Alfredshems IK	Sweden-2	16	13	....	13	....	....	....	....	....	....
1962-63	Alfredshems IK	Sweden	21	16	5	21	8	....	....	....	....	....
1963-64	MoDo AIK	Sweden	21	16	3	19	0	....	....	....	....	....
1964-65	MoDo AIK	Sweden	28	24	16	40	6	....	....	....	....	....
1965-66	Djurgardens IF	Sweden	5	4	2	6	0	7	1	6	7	2
1966-67	Djurgardens IF	Sweden	20	19	10	29	9	3	0	0	0	0
1967-68	Djurgardens IF	Sweden	28	24	12	36	4	....	....	....	....	....
1968-69	Djurgardens IF	Sweden	16	13	12	25	0	....	....	....	....	....
1969-70	Djurgardens IF	Sweden	20	19	8	27	....	....	....	....	....	....
1970-71	Djurgardens IF	Sweden	17	10	11	21	2	....	....	....	....	....
1971-72	Djurgardens IF	Sweden	27	18	12	30	2	....	....	....	....	....
1972-73	Djurgardens IF	Sweden	28	17	11	28	6	....	....	....	....	....
1973-74	IF Bjorkloven	Sweden	33	8	10	18	14	....	....	....	....	....
1974-75	Djurgardens IF	Sweden	29	18	16	34	4	....	....	....	....	....
	Djurgardens IF	Sweden-Q	6	2	6	8	2	....	....	....	....	....
1975-76	Djurgardens IF	Sweden	32	14	14	28	4	....	....	....	....	....
1976-77	Djurgardens IF	Sweden-2	41	44	39	83	....	....	....	....	....	....
1977-78	Djurgardens IF	Sweden	35	17	9	26	26	....	....	....	....	....

Olympics in 1968, 1972. Played at seven straight World Championships from 1966 to 1972.

• PELTONEN, Esa FIN

LW – L. 5'9", 176 lbs. b: Oulu, Finland, 2/25/1947.

Season	Club	League	GP	G	A	Pts	PIM	GP	G	A	Pts	PIM
1963-64	Karpat Oulu	Finland-2	9	8	0	8	0	....	....	....	....	....
1964-65	Karpat Oulu	Finland-2	STATISTICS NOT AVAILABLE									
1965-66	Karpat Oulu	Finland	13	10	5	15	0	....	....	....	....	....
1966-67	Upon Pallo Lahti	Finland-2	STATISTICS NOT AVAILABLE									
1967-68	Upon Pallo Lahti	Finland	20	10	2	12	8	....	....	....	....	....
1968-69	Upon Pallo Lahti	Finland	22	13	4	17	18	....	....	....	....	....
1969-70	HJK Helsinki	Finland-2	STATISTICS NOT AVAILABLE									
1970-71	HJK Helsinki	Finland	27	17	13	30	14	....	....	....	....	....
1971-72	HJK Helsinki	Finland	32	31	13	44	30	....	....	....	....	....
1972-73	HIFK Helsinki	Finland	35	28	11	39	48	....	....	....	....	....
1973-74	HIFK Helsinki	Finland	36	20	22	42	17	....	....	....	....	....
1974-75	HIFK Helsinki	Finland	31	22	14	36	17	....	....	....	....	....
1975-76	HIFK Helsinki	Finland	34	29	13	42	12	4	2	1	3	2
1976-77	HIFK Helsinki	Finland	31	17	24	41	10	7	3	4	7	10
1977-78	HIFK Helsinki	Finland	36	24	12	36	22	....	....	....	....	....
1978-79	HIFK Helsinki	Finland	34	30	13	43	34	6	3	4	7	0
1979-80	HIFK Helsinki	Finland	36	27	19	46	10	7	7	3	10	4
1980-81	HIFK Helsinki	Finland	31	14	18	32	32	7	2	2	4	4
1981-82	HIFK Helsinki	Finland	30	15	12	27	18	8	3	1	4	6
1982-83	HIFK Helsinki	Finland	10	4	3	7	6	....	....	....	....	....
1983-84	Kiekkoreipas Lahti	Finland	30	6	12	18	14	....	....	....	....	....

Four Olympics, 11 World Championships, 1976 Canada Cup. Played 277 int'l games.

• PELTONEN, Jorma FIN

C – L. 5'10", 176 lbs. b: Messukyla, Finland, 1/11/1944.

Season	Club	League	GP	G	A	Pts	PIM	GP	G	A	Pts	PIM
1962-63	Ilves Tampere	Finland	18	7	4	11	12	....	....	....	....	....
1963-64	Ilves Tampere	Finland	18	14	14	28	12	....	....	....	....	....
1964-65	Ilves Tampere	Finland	5	1	5	6	0	....	....	....	....	....
1965-66	Ilves Tampere	Finland	20	28	11	39	14	....	....	....	....	....
1966-67	Ilves Tampere	Finland	20	11	20	31	16	....	....	....	....	....
1967-68	Ilves Tampere	Finland	20	18	20	38	10	....	....	....	....	....
1968-69	Ilves Tampere	Finland	22	23	35	58	8	....	....	....	....	....
1969-70	Ilves Tampere	Finland	21	18	41	59	13	....	....	....	....	....
1970-71	Ilves Tampere	Finland	31	21	18	39	21	....	....	....	....	....
1971-72	Ilves Tampere	Finland	31	28	35	63	12	....	....	....	....	....
1972-73	Ilves Tampere	Finland	36	19	24	43	34	....	....	....	....	....
1973-74	Ilves Tampere	Finland	35	26	27	53	24	....	....	....	....	....
1974-75	Ilves Tampere	Finland	36	21	27	48	20	....	....	....	....	....
1975-76	EV Zug	Switz-2	28	35	38	73	....	....	....	....	....	....
1976-77	EV Zug	Switz.	28	15	19	34	....	....	....	....	....	....
1977-78	SG Brunico	Italy	32	36	....	36	....	....	....	....	....	....
1978-79	EHC Visp	Switz-2	28	32	31	63	....	....	....	....	....	....
1979-80	EHC Visp	Switz-2	27	24	30	54	....	....	....	....	....	....

Season	Club	League	GP	G	A	Pts	PIM	GP	G	A	Pts	PIM
			REGULAR SEASON					PLAYOFFS				
1980-81	Jokerit Helsinki	Finland	13	4	9	13	2	....	....	....	....	....
	Jokerit Helsinki	Finland-Q	6	1	4	5	0	....	....	....	....	....
1981-82	Lukko Rauma	Finland	3	1	1	2	2	....	....	....	....	....

Olympics in 1964, 1968, 1972. Eight World Championships from 1964 to 1975.

• PERVUKHIN, Vasili URS

D – L. 5′11″, 194 lbs. b: Penza, USSR, 1/1/1956.

Season	Club	League	GP	G	A	Pts	PIM	GP	G	A	Pts	PIM
1974-75	Dizelist Penza	USSR-2	STATISTICS NOT AVAILABLE									
1975-76	Dizelist Penza	USSR-2	STATISTICS NOT AVAILABLE									
1976-77	Dynamo Moscow	USSR	35	2	6	8	2	....	....	....	....	....
1977-78	Dynamo Moscow	USSR	36	4	7	11	4	....	....	....	....	....
1978-79	Dynamo Moscow	USSR	44	3	19	22	6	....	....	....	....	....
1979-80	Dynamo Moscow	USSR	44	5	10	15	4	....	....	....	....	....
1980-81	Dynamo Moscow	USSR	49	11	4	15	6	....	....	....	....	....
1981-82	Dynamo Moscow	USSR	45	8	12	20	10	....	....	....	....	....
1982-83	Dynamo Moscow	USSR	42	6	11	17	8	....	....	....	....	....
1983-84	Dynamo Moscow	USSR	43	6	9	15	4	....	....	....	....	....
1984-85	Dynamo Moscow	USSR	40	8	13	21	6	....	....	....	....	....
1985-86	Dynamo Moscow	USSR	40	7	8	15	8	....	....	....	....	....
1986-87	Dynamo Moscow	USSR	39	11	13	24	14	....	....	....	....	....
1987-88	Dynamo Moscow	USSR	47	5	4	9	10	....	....	....	....	....
1988-89	Dynamo Moscow	USSR	44	8	10	18	6	....	....	....	....	....
1989-90			DID NOT PLAY									
1990-91			DID NOT PLAY									
1991-92			DID NOT PLAY									
1992-93			DID NOT PLAY									
1993-94			DID NOT PLAY									
1994-95			DID NOT PLAY									
1995-96	Krylja Sovetov Moscow	CIS	29	2	5	7	8	....	....	....	....	....
1996-97	Krylja Sovetov Moscow	Russia	25	2	3	5	4	....	....	....	....	....
	Severstal Cherepovets	Russia	16	2	2	4	0	3	0	0	0	0
1997-98	Molot-Prikamje Perm	Russia	43	3	12	15	6	....	....	....	....	....
1998-99	Molot-Prikamje Perm	Russia	35	0	10	10	2	4	0	0	0	0

Olympics in 1980, 1984. Nine World Championships. Canada Cup in 1981, 1984 and 1987.

• PETROV, Vladimir URS

C – R. 6′, 198 lbs. b: Krasnogorsk, USSR, 6/30/1947.

Season	Club	League	GP	G	A	Pts	PIM	GP	G	A	Pts	PIM
1965-66	Krylja Sovetov Moscow	USSR	23	1	8	9	....	....	....	....	....	....
1966-67	Krylja Sovetov Moscow	USSR	44	15	9	24	....	....	....	....	....	....
1967-68	CSKA Moscow	USSR	38	21	19	40	....	....	....	....	....	....
1968-69	CSKA Moscow	USSR	39	27	18	45	....	....	....	....	....	....
1969-70	CSKA Moscow	USSR	43	51	21	72	....	....	....	....	....	....
1970-71	CSKA Moscow	USSR	37	16	16	32	....	....	....	....	....	....
1971-72	CSKA Moscow	USSR	32	21	16	37	....	....	....	....	....	....
1972-73	CSKA Moscow	USSR	30	27	22	49	....	....	....	....	....	....
1973-74	CSKA Moscow	USSR	28	14	14	28	34	....	....	....	....	....
1974-75	CSKA Moscow	USSR	34	27	26	53	58	....	....	....	....	....
1975-76	CSKA Moscow	USSR	34	22	22	44	46	....	....	....	....	....
1976-77	CSKA Moscow	USSR	35	26	36	62	57	....	....	....	....	....
1977-78	CSKA Moscow	USSR	31	28	28	56	41	....	....	....	....	....
1978-79	CSKA Moscow	USSR	43	26	37	63	54	....	....	....	....	....
1979-80	CSKA Moscow	USSR	32	21	20	41	28	....	....	....	....	....
1980-81	CSKA Moscow	USSR	40	19	24	43	42	....	....	....	....	....
1981-82	SKA Leningrad	USSR	20	4	3	7	24	....	....	....	....	....
1982-83	SKA Leningrad	USSR	12	4	4	8	18	....	....	....	....	....

Three Olympic medals, nine-time world champion, 1969 to 1981. Canada-Russia 1972.

• PETTERSSON, Ronald SWE

RW – L. 6′, 183 lbs. b: Surahammar, Sweden, 4/16/1935.

Season	Club	League	GP	G	A	Pts	PIM	GP	G	A	Pts	PIM
1951-52	Surahammars IF	Sweden-2	STATISTICS NOT AVAILABLE									
1952-53	Surahammars IF	Sweden	STATISTICS NOT AVAILABLE									
1953-54	Surahammars IF	Sweden	STATISTICS NOT AVAILABLE									
1954-55	Surahammars IF	Sweden-2	STATISTICS NOT AVAILABLE									
1955-56	Sodertalje SK	Sweden	STATISTICS NOT AVAILABLE									
1956-57	Sodertalje SK	Sweden	....	12	....	12	....	....	....	....	....	....
1957-58	Sodertalje SK	Sweden	....	25	9	34	....	....	....	....	....	....
1958-59	Sodertalje SK	Sweden	14	15	7	22	....	....	....	....	....	....
1959-60	Sodertalje SK	Sweden	....	27	16	43	....	....	....	....	....	....
1960-61	Vastra Frolunda IF	Sweden-2	20	44	....	44	....	....	....	....	....	....
1961-62	Vastra Frolunda IF	Sweden	21	13	17	30	....	....	....	....	....	....
1962-63	Vastra Frolunda IF	Sweden	20	26	13	39	22	....	....	....	....	....
1963-64	Vastra Frolunda IF	Sweden	21	20	10	30	20	....	....	....	....	....
1964-65	Vastra Frolunda IF	Sweden	28	17	8	25	14	....	....	....	....	....
1965-66	Vastra Frolunda IF	Sweden	21	12	17	29	18	8	8	3	11	6
1966-67	Vastra Frolunda IF	Sweden	20	16	13	29	14	7	4	3	7	0
1967-68	Vastra Frolunda IF	Sweden	14	11	5	16	....	....	....	....	....	....

Three Olympics and 13 World Championships. Played 252 games for Swedish national team.

• POSPISIL, Frantisek TCH

D – L. 5′11″, 198 lbs. b: Unhost, Czechoslovakia, 4/2/1944.

Season	Club	League	GP	G	A	Pts	PIM	GP	G	A	Pts	PIM
1961-62	SONP Kladno	Czech.	STATISTICS NOT AVAILABLE									
1962-63	SONP Kladno	Czech.	STATISTICS NOT AVAILABLE									
1963-64	SONP Kladno	Czech.	STATISTICS NOT AVAILABLE									
1964-65	SONP Kladno	Czech.	STATISTICS NOT AVAILABLE									
1965-66	SONP Kladno	Czech.	STATISTICS NOT AVAILABLE									
1966-67	SONP Kladno	Czech.	....	7	....	7	....	....	....	....	....	....
1967-68	SONP Kladno	Czech.	....	10	32	42	....	....	....	....	....	....
1968-69	SONP Kladno	Czech.	STATISTICS NOT AVAILABLE									
1969-70	SONP Kladno	Czech.	....	13	25	38	32	....	....	....	....	....
1970-71	SONP Kladno	Czech.	....	12	37	49	....	....	....	....	....	....
1971-72	SONP Kladno	Czech.	....	14	26	40	....	....	....	....	....	....
1972-73	SONP Kladno	Czech.	....	7	17	24	....	9	2	....	....	....
1973-74	SONP Kladno	Czech.	....	6	23	29	....	....	....	....	....	....
1974-75	SONP Kladno	Czech.	....	5	29	34	....	....	....	....	....	....
1975-76	SONP Kladno	Czech.	32	7	9	16	14	....	....	....	....	....
1976-77	SONP Kladno	Czech.	....	6	25	31	....	....	....	....	....	....
1977-78	SONP Kladno	Czech.	44	11	31	42	37	....	....	....	....	....
1978-79	EV Landshut	Germany	49	11	24	35	20	....	....	....	....	....

Three Olympics and 11 World Championships, 1976 Canada Cup. Three-time world champion.

• RAGULIN, Alexander URS

D – L. 6′1″, 220 lbs. b: Moscow, USSR, 5/5/1941.

Season	Club	League	GP	G	A	Pts	PIM	GP	G	A	Pts	PIM
			REGULAR SEASON					PLAYOFFS				
1957-58	Khimik Voskresensk	USSR	....	0	....	0	....	....	....	....	....	....
1958-59	Khimik Voskresensk	USSR	....	2	....	2	....	....	....	....	....	....
1959-60	Khimik Voskresensk	USSR	....	2	....	2	....	....	....	....	....	....
1960-61	Khimik Voskresensk	USSR	....	4	....	4	....	....	....	....	....	....
1961-62	Khimik Voskresensk	USSR	....	5	....	5	....	....	....	....	....	....
1962-63	CSKA Moscow	USSR	....	2	....	2	....	....	....	....	....	....
1963-64	CSKA Moscow	USSR	....	9	....	9	....	....	....	....	....	....
1964-65	CSKA Moscow	USSR	....	4	....	4	....	....	....	....	....	....
1965-66	CSKA Moscow	USSR	....	6	....	6	....	....	....	....	....	....
1966-67	CSKA Moscow	USSR	....	8	....	8	....	....	....	....	....	....
1967-68	CSKA Moscow	USSR	40	5	....	5	....	....	....	....	....	....
1968-69	CSKA Moscow	USSR	40	6	....	6	....	....	....	....	....	....
1969-70	CSKA Moscow	USSR	41	3	....	3	....	....	....	....	....	....
1970-71	CSKA Moscow	USSR	36	4	....	4	....	....	....	....	....	....
1971-72	CSKA Moscow	USSR	28	0	....	0	....	....	....	....	....	....
1972-73	CSKA Moscow	USSR	28	0	....	0	....	....	....	....	....	....

Three Olympic golds, nine straight world titles, between 1961 and 1973. Canada-Russia 1972.

• RANTASILA, Juha FIN

D – R. 6′, 189 lbs. b: Pori, Finland, 6/5/1945.

Season	Club	League	GP	G	A	Pts	PIM	GP	G	A	Pts	PIM
1961-62	Karhut Pori	Finland	13	0	0	0	2	....	....	....	....	....
1962-63	Karhut Pori	Finn-Jr.	STATISTICS NOT AVAILABLE									
1963-64	Karhut Pori	Finland	18	4	0	4	4	....	....	....	....	....
1964-65	Karhut Pori	Finland	18	4	1	5	18	....	....	....	....	....
1965-66	Karhut Pori	Finland	20	7	0	7	12	....	....	....	....	....
1966-67	Karhut Pori	Finland	22	5	2	7	26	....	....	....	....	....
1967-68	HIFK Helsinki	Finland	20	13	7	20	18	....	....	....	....	....
1968-69	HIFK Helsinki	Finland	21	17	5	22	26	....	....	....	....	....
1969-70	HIFK Helsinki	Finland	22	15	10	25	28	....	....	....	....	....
1970-71	HIFK Helsinki	Finland	32	30	8	38	42	....	....	....	....	....
1971-72	HIFK Helsinki	Finland	32	17	12	29	51	....	....	....	....	....
1972-73	HIFK Helsinki	Finland	36	14	17	31	71	....	....	....	....	....
1973-74	HIFK Helsinki	Finland	36	22	28	50	71	....	....	....	....	....
1974-75	HIFK Helsinki	Finland	36	13	13	26	69	....	....	....	....	....
1975-76	HC Lugano	Switz-2	27	5	7	12	....	....	....	....	....	....
1976-77	SC Luzern	Switz-2	28	20	8	28	....	....	....	....	....	....
1977-78	SC Luzern	Switz-2	27	24	30	54	....	....	....	....	....	....

Olympics in 1968, 1972. Six World Championships, 1966 to 1974. Played 116 intl games.

• REINDL, Franz GER

RW – L. 5′10″, 172 lbs. b: Garmisch-Partenkirchen, W.Germany, 11/24/1954.

Season	Club	League	GP	G	A	Pts	PIM	GP	G	A	Pts	PIM
1972-73	SC Riessersee	Germany	40	9	6	15	14	....	....	....	....	....
1973-74	SC Riessersee	Germany	36	10	10	20	26	....	....	....	....	....
1974-75	SC Riessersee	Germany	36	16	8	24	62	....	....	....	....	....
1975-76	SC Riessersee	Germany	36	23	12	35	58	....	....	....	....	....
1976-77	SC Riessersee	Germany	48	28	14	42	69	....	....	....	....	....
1977-78	SC Riessersee	Germany	46	28	19	47	70	....	....	....	....	....
1978-79	SC Riessersee	Germany	50	32	30	62	103	....	....	....	....	....
1979-80	SC Riessersee	Germany	48	40	29	69	93	....	....	....	....	....
1980-81	SC Riessersee	Germany	44	47	31	78	92	10	9	12	21	24
1981-82	SC Riessersee	Germany	43	49	53	102	71	2	1	2	3	2
1982-83	SC Riessersee	Germany	31	20	27	47	54	7	6	6	12	6
1983-84	SC Riessersee	Germany	36	12	28	40	69	....	....	....	....	....
1984-85	SB Rosenheim	Germany	36	28	38	66	58	9	5	7	12	14
1985-86	SB Rosenheim	Germany	35	24	28	52	69	9	5	6	11	0
1986-87	SB Rosenheim	Germany	16	8	10	18	18	9	8	3	11	7
1987-88	SB Rosenheim	Germany	35	13	18	31	46	14	4	4	8	28

Three Olympics, one Canada Cup, eight World Championships. Olympic bronze medal in 1976.

• RIIHIRANTA, Heikki FIN

D – L. 5′10″, 191 lbs. b: Helsinki, Finland, 10/4/1948.

Season	Club	League	GP	G	A	Pts	PIM	GP	G	A	Pts	PIM
1967-68	HIFK Helsinki	Finland	20	3	2	5	6	....	....	....	....	....
1968-69	HIFK Helsinki	Finland	20	3	7	10	26	....	....	....	....	....
1969-70	HIFK Helsinki	Finland	21	6	15	21	16	....	....	....	....	....
1970-71	HIFK Helsinki	Finland	30	2	15	17	29	....	....	....	....	....
1971-72	HIFK Helsinki	Finland	32	1	8	9	32	....	....	....	....	....
1972-73	HIFK Helsinki	Finland	35	3	8	11	63	....	....	....	....	....
1973-74	HIFK Helsinki	Finland	36	10	22	32	50	....	....	....	....	....
1974-75	**Winnipeg Jets**	**WHA**	**64**	**8**	**14**	**22**	**30**	....	....	....	....	....
1975-76	**Winnipeg Jets**	**WHA**	**70**	**1**	**8**	**9**	**26**	**4**	**0**	**4**	**4**	**6**
1976-77	**Winnipeg Jets**	**WHA**	**53**	**1**	**16**	**17**	**28**	....	....	....	....	....
1977-78	HIFK Helsinki	Finland	32	5	12	17	54	....	....	....	....	....
1978-79	HIFK Helsinki	Finland	36	5	8	13	82	6	0	5	5	25
1979-80	HIFK Helsinki	Finland	32	5	6	11	41	7	3	1	4	12
1980-81	HIFK Helsinki	Finland	35	4	8	12	54	7	2	0	2	12
1981-82	HIFK Helsinki	Finland	31	3	4	7	71	5	0	2	2	2
1982-83	HIFK Helsinki	Finland	33	0	4	4	17	9	1	0	1	13
	Major League Totals		**187**	**10**	**38**	**48**	**84**	**4**	**0**	**4**	**4**	**6**

Olympics in 1972. Four World Championships from 1970 to 1974. Canada Cup 1976.

• RUSNAK, Darius TCH

C – R. 6′1″, 187 lbs. b: Ruzomberck, Czechoslovakia, 12/2/1959.
Philadelphia's 11th, 230th overall in 1987.

Season	Club	League	GP	G	A	Pts	PIM	GP	G	A	Pts	PIM
1976-77	Slovan Bratislava	Czech.	42	18	8	26	20	....	....	....	....	....
1977-78	Slovan Bratislava	Czech.	44	4	11	15	24	....	....	....	....	....
1978-79	Slovan Bratislava	Czech.	28	7	6	13	16	....	....	....	....	....
1979-80	Slovan Bratislava	Czech.	42	16	14	30	40	....	....	....	....	....
1980-81	Slovan Bratislava	Czech.	44	32	26	58	54	....	....	....	....	....
1981-82	Slovan Bratislava	Czech-2	....	31	29	60	....	....	....	....	....	....
1982-83	Slovan Bratislava	Czech.	42	19	14	33	52	....	....	....	....	....
1983-84	Slovan Bratislava	Czech.	40	23	22	45	90	....	....	....	....	....
1984-85	Slovan Bratislava	Czech.	37	16	15	31	56	....	....	....	....	....
1985-86	Slovan Bratislava	Czech.	39	18	22	40	22	....	....	....	....	....
1986-87	Slovan Bratislava	Czech.	32	15	13	28	62	8	3	7	10	....
1987-88	Dukla Jihlava	Czech.	44	17	34	51	33	....	....	....	....	....
1988-89	Slovan Bratislava	Czech.	31	16	15	31	44	....	....	....	....	....

Season	Club	League	Regular Season GP	G	A	Pts	PIM	Playoffs GP	G	A	Pts	PIM
1989-90	KalPa Kuopio	Finland	44	29	24	53	77	1	0	1	1	0
1990-91	KalPa Kuopio	Finland	44	22	38	60	58	8	3	3	6	8
1991-92	KalPa Kuopio	Finland	38	8	24	32	57	....	....	....	....	....
1992-93	KalPa Kuopio	Finland	43	20	24	44	57	....	....	....	....	....

Olympics in 1984. Five World Championships. Won world title in 1985. Canada Cup in 1981.

• SAMUELSSON, Tommy — SWE

D – L. 5'9", 169 lbs. b: Mariestad, Sweden, 1/12/1960.

Season	Club	League	Regular Season GP	G	A	Pts	PIM	Playoffs GP	G	A	Pts	PIM
1976-77	Farjestads BK Karlstad	Sweden	1	0	0	0	0	....	....	....	....	....
1977-78	Farjestads BK Karlstad	Sweden	3	0	0	0	0	....	....	....	....	....
1978-79	Farjestads BK Karlstad	Sweden	34	3	2	5	16	3	0	0	0	0
1979-80	Farjestads BK Karlstad	Sweden	36	3	6	9	20	....	....	....	....	....
1980-81	Farjestads BK Karlstad	Sweden	36	2	7	9	18	7	1	0	1	6
1981-82	Farjestads BK Karlstad	Sweden	36	6	8	14	28	2	0	1	1	0
1982-83	Farjestads BK Karlstad	Sweden	36	6	18	24	22	8	3	5	8	6
1983-84	Farjestads BK Karlstad	Sweden	28	7	15	22	26	....	....	....	....	....
1984-85	Farjestads BK Karlstad	Sweden	36	0	10	10	26	3	0	1	1	2
1985-86	Farjestads BK Karlstad	Sweden	36	9	16	25	26	8	0	8	8	....
1986-87	Farjestads BK Karlstad	Sweden	36	7	15	22	16	7	1	4	5	0
1987-88	Farjestads BK Karlstad	Sweden	31	4	11	15	32	....	....	....	....	....
1988-89	Farjestads BK Karlstad	Sweden	36	6	19	25	18	2	0	1	1	2
1989-90	Farjestads BK Karlstad	Sweden	36	7	18	25	20	10	2	4	6	2
1990-91	Farjestads BK Karlstad	Sweden	39	4	11	15	44	8	1	3	4	2
1991-92	Farjestads BK Karlstad	Sweden	38	6	27	33	30	6	0	1	1	6
1992-93	Farjestads BK Karlstad	Sweden	39	7	9	16	28	3	0	2	2	6
1993-94	Farjestads BK Karlstad	Sweden	22	1	4	5	4	....	....	....	....	....
	Farjestads BK Karlstad	Sweden-Q	18	4	5	9	6	3	0	1	1	0
1994-95	Farjestads BK Karlstad	Sweden	38	2	8	10	20	4	0	0	0	2

Olympics in 1980, 1984, 1988. Eight World Championships; 1991 title. Canada Cup 1987.

• SCHLODER, Alois — GER

RW – L. 6', 180 lbs. b: Landshut, W.Germany, 8/11/1947.

Season	Club	League	Regular Season GP	G	A	Pts	PIM	Playoffs GP	G	A	Pts	PIM
1963-64	EV Landshut	Germany	20	12	7	19	14	....	....	....	....	....
1964-65	EV Landshut	Germany	20	13	9	22	18	....	....	....	....	....
1965-66	EV Landshut	Germany	26	11	8	19	14	....	....	....	....	....
1966-67	EV Landshut	Germany	27	28	15	43	22	....	....	....	....	....
1967-68	EV Landshut	Germany	28	23	6	29	14	....	....	....	....	....
1968-69	EV Landshut	Germany	30	35	14	49	22	....	....	....	....	....
1969-70	EV Landshut	Germany	36	35	7	42	26	....	....	....	....	....
1970-71	EV Landshut	Germany	36	36	17	53	20	....	....	....	....	....
1971-72	EV Landshut	Germany	31	27	22	49	26	....	....	....	....	....
1972-73	EV Landshut	Germany	40	34	28	62	34	....	....	....	....	....
1973-74	EV Landshut	Germany	27	29	11	40	49	....	....	....	....	....
1974-75	EV Landshut	Germany	35	33	18	51	30	....	....	....	....	....
1975-76	EV Landshut	Germany	36	31	20	51	36	....	....	....	....	....
1976-77	EV Landshut	Germany	25	14	21	35	32	....	....	....	....	....
1977-78	EV Landshut	Germany	46	27	32	59	46	....	....	....	....	....
1978-79	EV Landshut	Germany	50	30	46	76	62	....	....	....	....	....
1979-80	EV Landshut	Germany	44	19	43	62	49	....	....	....	....	....
1980-81	EV Landshut	Germany	25	14	20	34	30	5	1	2	3	4
1981-82	EV Landshut	Germany	44	21	38	59	45	8	4	5	9	4
1982-83	EV Landshut	Germany	32	3	14	17	30	8	2	4	6	2
1983-84	EV Landshut	Germany	51	5	20	25	52	....	....	....	....	....
1984-85	EV Landshut	Germany	35	3	17	20	43	4	0	1	1	0
1985-86	EV Landshut	Germany	33	3	12	15	46	3	3	0	3	12

Three Olympics, 13 World Championships (A and B). National team captain 1971 to 1978.

• SHADRIN, Vladimir — URS

C – L. 5'11", 189 lbs. b: Moscow, USSR, 6/6/1948.

Season	Club	League	Regular Season GP	G	A	Pts	PIM	Playoffs GP	G	A	Pts	PIM
1965-66	Spartak Moscow	USSR	STATISTICS NOT AVAILABLE									
1966-67	Spartak Moscow	USSR	STATISTICS NOT AVAILABLE									
1967-68	Spartak Moscow	USSR	....	10	....	10	....	....	....	....	....	....
1968-69	Spartak Moscow	USSR	42	12	....	12	....	....	....	....	....	....
1969-70	Spartak Moscow	USSR	31	28	....	28	....	....	....	....	....	....
1970-71	Spartak Moscow	USSR	37	22	11	33	....	....	....	....	....	....
1971-72	Spartak Moscow	USSR	31	14	....	14	....	....	....	....	....	....
1972-73	Spartak Moscow	USSR	31	24	15	39	16	....	....	....	....	....
1973-74	Spartak Moscow	USSR	32	18	11	29	14	....	....	....	....	....
1974-75	Spartak Moscow	USSR	36	14	14	28	14	....	....	....	....	....
1975-76	Spartak Moscow	USSR	35	17	18	35	20	....	....	....	....	....
1976-77	Spartak Moscow	USSR	29	14	17	31	14	....	....	....	....	....
1977-78	Spartak Moscow	USSR	20	7	14	21	12	....	....	....	....	....
1978-79	Spartak Moscow	USSR	22	9	8	17	6	....	....	....	....	....
1979-80	Oji Seishi Tomakomai	Japan	15	17	14	31	....	....	....	....	....	....
1980-81	Oji Seishi Tomakomai	Japan	20	16	23	39	....	....	....	....	....	....
1981-82	Oji Seishi Tomakomai	Japan	30	25	54	79	....	....	....	....	....	....
1982-83	Oji Seishi Tomakomai	Japan	30	20	49	69	....	....	....	....	....	....

Olympic gold 1972, 1976. Eight World Championships, 1970 to 1977. Canada-Russia 1972.

• SHALIMOV, Viktor — URS

RW – L. 5'10", 176 lbs. b: Solnechnogorsk, USSR, 4/20/1951.

Season	Club	League	Regular Season GP	G	A	Pts	PIM	Playoffs GP	G	A	Pts	PIM
1969-70	Spartak Moscow	USSR	2	1	....	1	....	....	....	....	....	....
1970-71	Spartak Moscow	USSR	15	6	....	6	....	....	....	....	....	....
1971-72	Spartak Moscow	USSR	32	13	....	13	....	....	....	....	....	....
1972-73	Spartak Moscow	USSR	30	16	....	16	....	....	....	....	....	....
1973-74	Spartak Moscow	USSR	32	17	10	27	18	....	....	....	....	....
1974-75	Spartak Moscow	USSR	36	20	11	31	6	....	....	....	....	....
1975-76	Spartak Moscow	USSR	36	28	25	53	8	....	....	....	....	....
1976-77	Spartak Moscow	USSR	36	18	17	35	10	....	....	....	....	....
1977-78	Spartak Moscow	USSR	36	26	11	37	10	....	....	....	....	....
1978-79	Spartak Moscow	USSR	42	12	17	29	18	....	....	....	....	....
1979-80	Spartak Moscow	USSR	44	34	19	53	12	....	....	....	....	....
1980-81	Spartak Moscow	USSR	47	21	32	53	12	....	....	....	....	....
1981-82	Spartak Moscow	USSR	47	27	32	59	34	....	....	....	....	....
1982-83	Spartak Moscow	USSR	44	14	16	30	18	....	....	....	....	....
1983-84	Spartak Moscow	USSR	44	24	21	45	4	....	....	....	....	....
1984-85	Spartak Moscow	USSR	49	16	22	38	30	....	....	....	....	....

Season	Club	League	Regular Season GP	G	A	Pts	PIM	Playoffs GP	G	A	Pts	PIM
1985-86	IEV Innsbruck	Austria	42	37	57	94	12	....	....	....	....	....
1986-87	IEV Innsbruck	Austria	34	37	36	73	10	6	6	5	11	0
1987-88	EC Salzburg	Austria	33	27	29	56	0	....	....	....	....	....

Olympic gold in 1976. Five World Championships. Top scorer in 1975. Best forward in 1982.

• SODERGREN, Hakan — SWE

LW – R. 5'9", 180 lbs. b: Rosersberg, Sweden, 6/14/1959.

Season	Club	League	Regular Season GP	G	A	Pts	PIM	Playoffs GP	G	A	Pts	PIM
1977-78	Djurgardens IF	Sweden	12	0	3	3	0	....	....	....	....	....
1978-79	Djurgardens IF	Sweden	15	4	3	7	6	....	....	....	....	....
1979-80	Djurgardens IF	Sweden	28	4	10	14	22	....	....	....	....	....
1980-81	Djurgardens IF	Sweden	35	12	10	22	46	....	....	....	....	....
1981-82	Djurgardens IF	Sweden	33	6	11	17	72	....	....	....	....	....
1982-83	Djurgardens IF	Sweden	35	14	22	36	64	7	4	5	9	22
1983-84	Djurgardens IF	Sweden	29	5	19	24	74	4	2	0	2	21
1984-85	Djurgardens IF	Sweden	35	11	16	27	42	8	3	5	8	10
1985-86	Djurgardens IF	Sweden	33	11	18	29	38	....	....	....	....	....
1986-87	Djurgardens IF	Sweden	32	14	19	33	52	2	0	2	2	2
1987-88	Djurgardens IF	Sweden	32	17	24	41	38	3	0	0	0	0
1988-89	Djurgardens IF	Sweden	29	13	11	24	36	8	4	5	9	6
1989-90	Djurgardens IF	Sweden	31	10	15	25	40	5	1	2	3	4
1990-91	Djurgardens IF	Sweden-2	40	9	13	22	26	7	0	0	0	0
1991-92	Huddinge IK	Sweden-2	33	13	24	37	52	4	2	3	5	0

Olympics in 1984, 1988. Five World Championships; 1987 title. Canada Cup in 1987.

• SODERSTROM, Dan — SWE

RW – L. 5'8", 167 lbs. b: Horndal, Sweden, 4/5/1948.

Season	Club	League	Regular Season GP	G	A	Pts	PIM	Playoffs GP	G	A	Pts	PIM
1966-67	Leksands IF	Sweden	....	6	1	7	0	2	0	0	0	0
1967-68	Leksands IF	Sweden	28	14	7	21	10	....	....	....	....	....
1968-69	Leksands IF	Sweden	28	20	7	27	6	....	....	....	....	....
1969-70	Leksands IF	Sweden	26	15	15	30	....	....	....	....	....	....
1970-71	Leksands IF	Sweden	28	12	19	31	6	....	....	....	....	....
1971-72	Leksands IF	Sweden	25	15	9	24	20	....	....	....	....	....
1972-73	Leksands IF	Sweden	28	20	15	35	18	....	....	....	....	....
1973-74	Leksands IF	Sweden	32	23	20	43	14	....	....	....	....	....
1974-75	Leksands IF	Sweden	29	24	33	57	2	5	2	0	2	0
1975-76	Leksands IF	Sweden	35	24	23	47	16	4	0	3	3	0
1976-77	Leksands IF	Sweden	35	18	29	47	9	5	0	0	0	6
1977-78	Leksands IF	Sweden	30	11	32	43	19	....	....	....	....	....
1978-79	Leksands IF	Sweden	9	1	2	3	9	....	....	....	....	....
1979-80	Leksands IF	Sweden	36	18	13	31	24	2	0	2	2	2
1980-81	Leksands IF	Sweden	35	10	20	30	18	....	....	....	....	....
1981-82	Leksands IF	Sweden	36	11	17	28	26	....	....	....	....	....
1982-83	Leksands IF	Sweden	32	2	19	21	10	....	....	....	....	....

Olympics in 1980. Five World Championships, 1973 to 1981. Captain of Swedish team.

• SOLOGUBOV, Nikolai — URS

D – L. 5'10", 180 lbs. b: Moscow, USSR, 3/8/1924 d: 1988.

Season	Club	League	Regular Season GP	G	A	Pts	PIM	Playoffs GP	G	A	Pts	PIM
1949-50	CDKA Moscow	USSR	....	7	....	7	....	....	....	....	....	....
1950-51	CDKA Moscow	USSR	....	5	....	5	....	....	....	....	....	....
1951-52	CDSA Moscow	USSR	....	15	....	15	....	....	....	....	....	....
1952-53	CDSA Moscow	USSR	....	13	....	13	....	....	....	....	....	....
1953-54	CDSA Moscow	USSR	16	12	....	12	....	....	....	....	....	....
1954-55	CSK Moscow	USSR	....	6	....	6	....	....	....	....	....	....
1955-56	CSK Moscow	USSR	....	5	....	5	....	....	....	....	....	....
1956-57	CSK Moscow	USSR	....	10	....	10	....	....	....	....	....	....
1957-58	CSK Moscow	USSR	....	12	....	12	....	....	....	....	....	....
1958-59	CSK Moscow	USSR	....	7	....	7	....	....	....	....	....	....
1959-60	CSKA Moscow	USSR	....	11	....	11	....	....	....	....	....	....
1960-61	CSKA Moscow	USSR	....	6	....	6	....	....	....	....	....	....
1961-62	CSKA Moscow	USSR	....	12	....	12	....	....	....	....	....	....
1962-63	CSKA Moscow	USSR	....	5	....	5	....	....	....	....	....	....
1963-64	CSKA Moscow	USSR	....	3	....	3	....	....	....	....	....	....
1964-65	SKA Kalinin	USSR-2	....	4	....	4	....	....	....	....	....	....

Two Olympics, eight World Championships. Best defenseman at WC in 1956, 1957 and 1960.

• STARSHINOV, Vyacheslav — URS

C – R. 5'8", 183 lbs. b: Moscow, USSR, 5/6/1940.

Season	Club	League	Regular Season GP	G	A	Pts	PIM	Playoffs GP	G	A	Pts	PIM
1957-58	Spartak Moscow	USSR	....	0	....	0	....	....	....	....	....	....
1958-59	Spartak Moscow	USSR	....	12	....	12	....	....	....	....	....	....
1959-60	Spartak Moscow	USSR	....	16	....	16	....	....	....	....	....	....
1960-61	Spartak Moscow	USSR	....	16	....	16	....	....	....	....	....	....
1961-62	Spartak Moscow	USSR	38	29	....	29	....	....	....	....	....	....
1962-63	Spartak Moscow	USSR	37	23	....	23	....	....	....	....	....	....
1963-64	Spartak Moscow	USSR	....	34	....	34	....	....	....	....	....	....
1964-65	Spartak Moscow	USSR	....	25	....	25	....	....	....	....	....	....
1965-66	Spartak Moscow	USSR	....	22	....	22	....	....	....	....	....	....
1966-67	Spartak Moscow	USSR	....	47	....	47	....	....	....	....	....	....
1967-68	Spartak Moscow	USSR	....	46	....	46	....	....	....	....	....	....
1968-69	Spartak Moscow	USSR	41	40	....	40	....	....	....	....	....	....
1969-70	Spartak Moscow	USSR	39	34	....	34	....	....	....	....	....	....
1970-71	Spartak Moscow	USSR	39	22	....	22	....	....	....	....	....	....
1971-72	Spartak Moscow	USSR	25	15	....	15	....	....	....	....	....	....
1972-73			DID NOT PLAY									
1973-74			DID NOT PLAY									
1974-75	Spartak Moscow	USSR	27	13	8	21	20	....	....	....	....	....
1975-76	Oji Seishi Tomakomai	Japan	15	20	12	32	....	....	....	....	....	....
1976-77	Oji Seishi Tomakomai	Japan	18	22	17	39	....	....	....	....	....	....
1977-78	Oji Seishi Tomakomai	Japan	15	13	11	24	....	....	....	....	....	....
1978-79	Spartak Moscow	USSR	37	11	7	18	30	....	....	....	....	....

Olympic gold 1964, 1968. Nine straight world titles, 1963 to 1971. Best forward at 1965 WC.

• STASTNY, Bohuslav — TCH

LW – L. 5'9", 180 lbs. b: Chotebor, Czechoslovakia, 4/23/1949.

Season	Club	League	Regular Season GP	G	A	Pts	PIM	Playoffs GP	G	A	Pts	PIM
1966-67	PS Pardubice	Czech-3	STATISTICS NOT AVAILABLE									
1967-68	Tesla Pardubice	Czech.	....	16	12	28	....	....	....	....	....	....
1968-69	Tesla Pardubice	Czech.	STATISTICS NOT AVAILABLE									
1969-70	Tesla Pardubice	Czech.	....	16	8	24	30	....	....	....	....	....
1970-71	Tesla Pardubice	Czech.	STATISTICS NOT AVAILABLE									

Season	Club	League	GP	G	A	Pts	PIM	GP	G	A	Pts	PIM
			REGULAR SEASON					PLAYOFFS				
1971-72	Tesla Pardubice	Czech.	....	22	11	33	....	....	....	....	....	....
1972-73	Tesla Pardubice	Czech.	....	26	8	34	....	11	6	....	6	....
1973-74	Tesla Pardubice	Czech.	....	31	9	40	....	....	....	....	....	....
1974-75	Tesla Pardubice	Czech.	STATISTICS NOT AVAILABLE									
1975-76	Tesla Pardubice	Czech.	32	16	9	25	18	....	....	....	....	....
1976-77	Tesla Pardubice	Czech.	....	17	16	33	....	....	....	....	....	....
1977-78	Tesla Pardubice	Czech.	44	14	9	23	32	....	....	....	....	....
1978-79	Tesla Pardubice	Czech.	38	16	14	30	14	....	....	....	....	....
1979-80	Tesla Pardubice	Czech.	43	19	11	30	26	....	....	....	....	....
1980-81	Tesla Pardubice	Czech.	41	15	20	35	31	....	....	....	....	....
1981-82	ESV Kaufbeuren	Germany	27	16	15	31	22	3	1	1	2	0
1982-83	ESV Kaufbeuren	Germany	36	14	24	38	34	7	3	3	6	4
1983-84	ESV Kaufbeuren	Germany	28	14	23	37	33	7	2	4	6	2
1984-85	ESV Kaufbeuren	Germany	33	25	19	44	16	8	2	1	3	19

Won world title in 1972, 1976. Also played in the 1976 Canada Cup and the 1976 Olympics.

• STAVJANA, Antonin — TCH

D – L. 6', 187 lbs. b: Gottwaldov, Czechoslovakia, 2/10/1963.
Calgary's 11th, 247th overall in 1986.

Season	Club	League	GP	G	A	Pts	PIM	GP	G	A	Pts	PIM
1980-81	TJ Gottwaldov	Czech.	41	1	3	4	14	....	....	....	....	....
1981-82	TJ Gottwaldov	Czech.	43	3	7	10	12	....	....	....	....	....
1982-83	Dukla Trencin	Czech-2	....	4	....	4	....	....	....	....	....	....
1983-84	Dukla Trencin	Czech.	38	3	10	13	12	....	....	....	....	....
	TJ Gottwaldov	Czech.	5	0	1	1	0	....	....	....	....	....
1984-85	TJ Gottwaldov	Czech.	43	5	6	11	10	....	....	....	....	....
1985-86	TJ Gottwaldov	Czech.	34	10	8	18	10	5	1	3	4	0
1986-87	TJ Gottwaldov	Czech.	33	11	7	18	10	7	1	2	3	....
1987-88	TJ Gottwaldov	Czech.	40	10	15	25	27	....	....	....	....	....
1988-89	TJ Gottwaldov	Czech.	43	11	12	23	10	....	....	....	....	....
1989-90	TJ Zlin	Czech.	39	6	12	18	....	7	1	2	3	....
1990-91	JoKP Joensuu	Finland-2	42	13	35	48	10	....	....	....	....	....
1991-92	JoKP Joensuu	Finland	44	9	11	20	24	....	....	....	....	....
1992-93	HV-71 Jonkoping	Sweden	39	2	11	13	14	....	....	....	....	....
1993-94	HV-71 Jonkoping	Sweden	39	4	13	17	20	....	....	....	....	....
1994-95	Dadak Vsetin	Cze-Rep.	41	1	15	16	20	11	4	4	8	4
1995-96	HC Petra Vsetin	Cze-Rep.	34	8	19	27	14	13	2	2	4	0
1996-97	HC Petra Vsetin	Cze-Rep.	44	9	9	18	10	10	0	5	5	2
1997-98	HC Petra Vsetin	Cze-Rep.	44	6	6	12	24	10	0	4	4	10

Two Olympics, two Canada Cup tournaments, eight World Championships. Word title in 1996.

• STOLTZ, Roland — SWE

D – R. 6'2", 189 lbs. b: Stockholm, Sweden, 8/1/1931.

Season	Club	League	GP	G	A	Pts	PIM	GP	G	A	Pts	PIM
1948-49	Atlas Diesels IF	Sweden-2	STATISTICS NOT AVAILABLE									
1949-50	Atlas Diesels IF	Sweden	STATISTICS NOT AVAILABLE									
1950-51	Atlas Diesels IF	Sweden-2	STATISTICS NOT AVAILABLE									
1951-52	Atlas Diesels IF	Sweden-2	STATISTICS NOT AVAILABLE									
1952-53	Atlas Diesels IF	Sweden	STATISTICS NOT AVAILABLE									
1953-54	Atlas Diesels IF	Sweden	STATISTICS NOT AVAILABLE									
1954-55	Atlas Diesels IF	Sweden-2	STATISTICS NOT AVAILABLE									
1955-56	Atlas Copco IF	Sweden-2	STATISTICS NOT AVAILABLE									
1956-57	Djurgardens IF	Sweden	STATISTICS NOT AVAILABLE									
1957-58	Djurgardens IF	Sweden	STATISTICS NOT AVAILABLE									
1958-59	Djurgardens IF	Sweden	STATISTICS NOT AVAILABLE									
1959-60	Djurgardens IF	Sweden	STATISTICS NOT AVAILABLE									
1960-61	Djurgardens IF	Sweden	....	5	....	5	....	....	....	....	....	....
1961-62	Djurgardens IF	Sweden	....	7	....	7	....	....	....	....	....	....
1962-63	Djurgardens IF	Sweden	21	9	8	17	20	....	....	....	....	....
1963-64	Djurgardens IF	Sweden	....	6	9	15	16	....	....	....	....	....
1964-65	Djurgardens IF	Sweden	19	2	6	8	16	....	....	....	....	....
1965-66	Djurgardens IF	Sweden	20	2	1	3	10	7	2	2	4	2
1966-67	Djurgardens IF	Sweden	....	3	6	9	10	3	0	1	1	6
1967-68	Djurgardens IF	Sweden	28	6	8	14	....	....	....	....	....	....
1968-69	Djurgardens IF	Sweden	21	3	7	10	12	....	....	....	....	....
1969-70	Djurgardens IF	Sweden	6	2	5	7	....	....	....	....	....	....

Three Olympics and 12 World Championships from 1957 to 1968. Never missed a tournament.

• SUCHY, Jan — TCH

D – L. 5'8", 161 lbs. b: Havlickuv Brod, Czechoslovakia, 10/10/1944.

Season	Club	League	GP	G	A	Pts	PIM	GP	G	A	Pts	PIM
1961-62	Jiskra Havlickuv	Czech-2	STATISTICS NOT AVAILABLE									
1962-63	Jiskra Havlickuv	Czech-2	STATISTICS NOT AVAILABLE									
1963-64	Dukla Jihlava	Czech.	STATISTICS NOT AVAILABLE									
1964-65	Dukla Jihlava	Czech.	STATISTICS NOT AVAILABLE									
1965-66	Dukla Jihlava	Czech.	STATISTICS NOT AVAILABLE									
1966-67	Dukla Jihlava	Czech.	....	11	....	11	....	....	....	....	....	....
1967-68	Dukla Jihlava	Czech.	....	7	20	27	....	....	....	....	....	....
1968-69	Dukla Jihlava	Czech.	....	28	26	54	....	....	....	....	....	....
1969-70	Dukla Jihlava	Czech.	....	21	23	44	35	....	....	....	....	....
1970-71	Dukla Jihlava	Czech.	....	9	20	29	....	....	....	....	....	....
1971-72	Dukla Jihlava	Czech.	....	6	14	20	....	....	....	....	....	....
1972-73	Dukla Jihlava	Czech.	STATISTICS NOT AVAILABLE									
1973-74	Dukla Jihlava	Czech.	....	5	18	23	....	....	....	....	....	....
1974-75	Dukla Jihlava	Czech.	....	4	11	15	....	....	....	....	....	....
1975-76	Dukla Jihlava	Czech.	32	2	7	9	14	....	....	....	....	....
1976-77	Dukla Jihlava	Czech.	....	7	13	20	....	....	....	....	....	....
1977-78	Dukla Jihlava	Czech.	39	3	7	10	10	....	....	....	....	....
1978-79	Dukla Jihlava	Czech.	40	1	4	5	12	....	....	....	....	....
1979-80	Stadlau Wien	Austria-2	STATISTICS NOT AVAILABLE									
1980-81	Stadlau Wien	Austria	33	9	16	25	31	....	....	....	....	....
1981-82	ESV Kaufbeuren	Germany	16	3	3	6	8	....	....	....	....	....
1982-83	EV Landsberg	German-3	33	18	23	41	42	....	....	....	....	....
1983-84	UEC Modling	Austria-2	STATISTICS NOT AVAILABLE									

National team 1965 to 1974. Best defenseman at WC in 1969, 1971. Three-time WC all-star.

• SVEDBERG, Lennart — SWE

D – R. 5'11", 165 lbs. b: Sundsvall, Sweden, 2/29/1944 d: 1972.

Season	Club	League	GP	G	A	Pts	PIM	GP	G	A	Pts	PIM
1960-61	Ostrands IF Timra	Sweden	....	3	....	3	....	....	....	....	....	....
1961-62	Ostrands IF Timra	Sweden	....	10	....	10	....	....	....	....	....	....
1962-63	Grums IK	Sweden	21	6	5	11	14	....	....	....	....	....
1963-64	Brynas IF Gavle	Sweden	....	6	10	16	6	....	....	....	....	....
1964-65	Brynas IF Gavle	Sweden	28	8	6	14	20	....	....	....	....	....
1965-66	Mora IK	Sweden-2	STATISTICS NOT AVAILABLE									
1966-67	Mora IK	Sweden	....	5	8	13	10	2	1	1	2	0
1967-68	Mora IK	Sweden	28	12	16	28	14	....	....	....	....	....
1968-69	Mora IK	Sweden	28	7	10	17	4	....	....	....	....	....
1969-70	Timra IK	Sweden	20	12	7	19	....	....	....	....	....	....
1970-71	Timra IK	Sweden	28	8	16	24	15	....	....	....	....	....
1971-72	Timra IK	Sweden	28	13	11	24	10	....	....	....	....	....

Olympics in 1968, six World Championships. Two-time WC all-star. Best defenseman in 1970.

• TREGUBOV, Ivan — URS

D – R. 5'11", 183 lbs. b: Komsomolsk-na-Amure, USSR, 1/19/1930. Deceased.

Season	Club	League	GP	G	A	Pts	PIM	GP	G	A	Pts	PIM
1951-52	CDSA Moscow	USSR	....	2	....	2	....	....	....	....	....	....
1952-53	CDSA Moscow	USSR	....	4	....	4	....	....	....	....	....	....
1953-54	CDSA Moscow	USSR	15	6	....	6	....	....	....	....	....	....
1954-55	CSK MO Moscow	USSR	....	4	....	4	....	....	....	....	....	....
1955-56	CSK MO Moscow	USSR	....	8	....	8	....	....	....	....	....	....
1956-57	CSK MO Moscow	USSR	....	7	....	7	....	....	....	....	....	....
1957-58	CSK MO Moscow	USSR	....	8	....	8	....	....	....	....	....	....
1958-59	CSK MO Moscow	USSR	....	5	....	5	....	....	....	....	....	....
1959-60	CSKA Moscow	USSR	....	5	....	5	....	....	....	....	....	....
1960-61	CSKA Moscow	USSR	....	6	....	6	....	....	....	....	....	....
1961-62	CSKA Moscow	USSR	....	2	....	2	....	....	....	....	....	....
1962-63	SKA Kuibyshev	USSR	....	2	....	2	....	....	....	....	....	....
1963-64	SKA Kuibyshev	USSR-2	....	2	....	2	....	....	....	....	....	....
1964-65	Khimik Voskresensk	USSR	....	1	....	1	....	....	....	....	....	....

Olympics in 1956, six World Championships. Best defenseman at WC in 1958 and 1961.

• TRUNTSCHKA, Gerd — GER

C/LW – L. 5'8", 170 lbs. b: Landshut, W. Germany, 9/10/1958.
St. Louis' 20th, 200th overall in 1978.

Season	Club	League	GP	G	A	Pts	PIM	GP	G	A	Pts	PIM
1975-76	EV Landshut	Germany	23	12	6	18	8	....	....	....	....	....
1976-77	EV Landshut	Germany	46	33	25	58	36	....	....	....	....	....
1977-78	EV Landshut	Germany	35	19	13	32	34	....	....	....	....	....
1978-79	EV Landshut	Germany	49	52	54	106	49	....	....	....	....	....
1979-80	Kolner EC	Germany	44	38	45	83	84	....	....	....	....	....
1980-81	Kolner EC	Germany	50	26	58	84	85	....	....	....	....	....
1981-82	Kolner EC	Germany	44	40	59	99	59	8	6	10	16	4
1982-83	Kolner EC	Germany	30	17	40	57	18	9	2	10	12	20
1983-84	Kolner EC	Germany	42	22	57	79	61	8	4	4	8	14
1984-85	Kolner EC	Germany	36	22	35	57	37	9	6	8	14	18
1985-86	Kolner EC	Germany	35	14	54	68	24	10	2	15	17	12
1986-87	Kolner EC	Germany	36	9	37	46	43	9	7	12	19	10
1987-88	Kolner EC	Germany	35	21	48	69	18	11	5	6	11	27
1988-89	Kolner EC	Germany	34	25	50	75	36	9	4	8	12	16
1989-90	Dusseldorfer EG	Germany	36	9	40	49	60	11	10	23	33	14
1990-91	Dusseldorfer EG	Germany	44	18	63	81	40	11	4	11	15	12
1991-92	Dusseldorfer EG	Germany	43	18	67	85	53	3	2	3	5	4
1992-93	EC Hedos Munchen	Germany	44	13	36	49	44	4	0	3	3	2
1993-94	EC Hedos Munchen	Germany	40	11	33	44	49	10	6	10	16	10

Four Olympics, nine World Championships, 1984 Canada Cup. National team, 1979 to 1993.

• TSYGANKOV, Gennady — URS

D – L. 5'11", 209 lbs. b: Vanino, USSR, 8/16/1947.

Season	Club	League	GP	G	A	Pts	PIM	GP	G	A	Pts	PIM
1966-67	SKA Khabarovsk	USSR-4	STATISTICS NOT AVAILABLE									
1967-68	SKA Khabarovsk	USSR-4	STATISTICS NOT AVAILABLE									
1968-69	CSKA Moscow	USSR	6	0	....	0	....	....	....	....	....	....
1969-70	CSKA Moscow	USSR	37	5	....	5	....	....	....	....	....	....
1970-71	CSKA Moscow	USSR	40	4	....	4	....	....	....	....	....	....
1971-72	CSKA Moscow	USSR	32	7	....	7	....	....	....	....	....	....
1972-73	CSKA Moscow	USSR	29	4	....	4	....	....	....	....	....	....
1973-74	CSKA Moscow	USSR	28	2	3	5	32	....	....	....	....	....
1974-75	CSKA Moscow	USSR	29	3	4	7	20	....	....	....	....	....
1975-76	CSKA Moscow	USSR	33	3	3	6	10	....	....	....	....	....
1976-77	CSKA Moscow	USSR	33	8	8	16	12	....	....	....	....	....
1977-78	CSKA Moscow	USSR	34	7	9	16	42	....	....	....	....	....
1978-79	CSKA Moscow	USSR	41	7	10	17	29	....	....	....	....	....
1979-80	CSKA Moscow	USSR	10	1	2	3	8	....	....	....	....	....
	SKA Leningrad	USSR	9	1	0	1	6	....	....	....	....	....
	SKA Leningrad	USSR-Q	6	0	0	0	2	....	....	....	....	....

Olympic gold 1972, 1976. Won six world titles, 1971 to 1979. Canada-Russia 1972.

• VASILIEV, Valeri — URS

D – L. 5'11", 187 lbs. b: Volkovo, USSR, 8/3/1949.

Season	Club	League	GP	G	A	Pts	PIM	GP	G	A	Pts	PIM
1966-67	Torpedo Gorky	USSR	2	0	0	0	0	....	....	....	....	....
1967-68	Dynamo Moscow	USSR	42	2	1	3	28	....	....	....	....	....
1968-69	Dynamo Moscow	USSR	34	2	1	3	34	....	....	....	....	....
1969-70	Dynamo Moscow	USSR	43	5	2	7	37	....	....	....	....	....
1970-71	Dynamo Moscow	USSR	40	2	4	6	36	....	....	....	....	....
1971-72	Dynamo Moscow	USSR	31	4	0	4	35	....	....	....	....	....
1972-73	Dynamo Moscow	USSR	29	3	1	4	59	....	....	....	....	....
1973-74	Dynamo Moscow	USSR	31	4	11	15	42	....	....	....	....	....
1974-75	Dynamo Moscow	USSR	34	7	5	12	34	....	....	....	....	....
1975-76	Dynamo Moscow	USSR	28	6	15	21	13	....	....	....	....	....
1976-77	Dynamo Moscow	USSR	34	3	12	15	21	....	....	....	....	....
1977-78	Dynamo Moscow	USSR	33	2	6	8	30	....	....	....	....	....
1978-79	Dynamo Moscow	USSR	42	6	14	20	26	....	....	....	....	....
1979-80	Dynamo Moscow	USSR	41	8	10	18	26	....	....	....	....	....
1980-81	Dynamo Moscow	USSR	43	6	7	13	16	....	....	....	....	....
1981-82	Dynamo Moscow	USSR	36	3	12	15	18	....	....	....	....	....
1982-83	Dynamo Moscow	USSR	32	5	7	12	16	....	....	....	....	....
1983-84	Dynamo Moscow	USSR	44	3	7	10	14	....	....	....	....	....
1984-85			DID NOT PLAY									
1985-86			DID NOT PLAY									
1986-87			DID NOT PLAY									
1987-88			DID NOT PLAY									
1988-89			DID NOT PLAY									
1989-90	Ujpesti Budapest	Hungary	15	3	5	8	....	....	....	....	....	....
1990-91	Bad Reichenhall	German-4	STATISTICS NOT AVAILABLE									

Three Olympics, 11 World Championships; three-time best defenseman. Canada-Russia 1972.

• VEHMANEN, Jorma — FIN

RW – R. 5'10", 176 lbs. b: Rauma, Finland, 9/18/1945.

Season	Club	League	GP	G	A	Pts	PIM	GP	G	A	Pts	PIM
			REGULAR SEASON					PLAYOFFS				
1963-64	Lukko Rauma	Finland	18	6	8	14	2	....	....	....	....	....
1964-65	Lukko Rauma	Finland	17	8	4	12	10	....	....	....	....	....
1965-66	Lukko Rauma	Finland	20	15	10	25	8	....	....	....	....	....
1966-67	Lukko Rauma	Finland	21	14	7	21	14	....	....	....	....	....
1967-68	Lukko Rauma	Finland-2	STATISTICS NOT AVAILABLE									
1968-69	Lukko Rauma	Finland	22	14	13	27	18	....	....	....	....	....
1969-70	Lukko Rauma	Finland	22	21	9	30	26	....	....	....	....	....
1970-71	HJK Helsinki	Finland	30	20	10	30	14	....	....	....	....	....
1971-72	HJK Helsinki	Finland	32	23	10	33	23	....	....	....	....	....
1972-73	HJK Helsinki	Finland	36	20	21	41	10	....	....	....	....	....
1973-74	Lukko Rauma	Finland	36	23	13	36	28	....	....	....	....	....
1974-75	Lukko Rauma	Finland	36	22	11	33	24	....	....	....	....	....
1975-76	Lukko Rauma	Finland	36	14	25	39	28	....	....	....	....	....
1976-77	Lukko Rauma	Finland	36	9	12	21	18	....	....	....	....	....
1977-78	Lukko Rauma	Finland	36	17	12	29	26	....	....	....	....	....
1978-79	Lukko Rauma	Finland	35	22	15	37	17	....	....	....	....	....
1979-80	Lukko Rauma	Finland	36	15	22	37	28	....	....	....	....	....
1980-81	Lukko Rauma	Finland	35	11	17	28	18	....	....	....	....	....
	Lukko Rauma	Finland-Q	6	4	2	6	0	....	....	....	....	....
1981-82	Lukko Rauma	Finland	31	18	11	29	12	....	....	....	....	....
	Lukko Rauma	Finland-Q	3	2	2	4	0	....	....	....	....	....
1982-83	Lukko Rauma	Finland	35	13	9	22	12	....	....	....	....	....

Olympics in 1972, 1976. Seven World Championships, 1966 to 1976. Canada Cup 1976.

• VIKULOV, Vladimir — URS

RW – L. 5'9", 176 lbs. b: Moscow, USSR, 7/20/1946.

Season	Club	League	GP	G	A	Pts	PIM	GP	G	A	Pts	PIM
1963-64	CSKA Moscow	USSR	....	2	....	2	....	....	....	....	....	....
1964-65	CSKA Moscow	USSR	....	1	....	1	....	....	....	....	....	....
1965-66	CSKA Moscow	USSR	....	12	....	12	....	....	....	....	....	....
1966-67	CSKA Moscow	USSR	....	27	....	27	....	....	....	....	....	....
1967-68	CSKA Moscow	USSR	43	29	....	29	....	....	....	....	....	....
1968-69	CSKA Moscow	USSR	40	13	....	13	....	....	....	....	....	....
1969-70	CSKA Moscow	USSR	43	25	....	25	....	....	....	....	....	....
1970-71	CSKA Moscow	USSR	39	19	....	19	....	....	....	....	....	....
1971-72	CSKA Moscow	USSR	31	34	8	42	....	....	....	....	....	....
1972-73	CSKA Moscow	USSR	32	21	19	40	....	....	....	....	....	....
1973-74	CSKA Moscow	USSR	32	14	19	33	18	....	....	....	....	....
1974-75	CSKA Moscow	USSR	36	17	23	40	26	....	....	....	....	....
1975-76	CSKA Moscow	USSR	35	19	17	36	18	....	....	....	....	....
1976-77	CSKA Moscow	USSR	35	22	18	40	12	....	....	....	....	....
1977-78	CSKA Moscow	USSR	34	12	22	34	12	....	....	....	....	....
1978-79	CSKA Moscow	USSR	33	12	10	22	14	....	....	....	....	....
	SKA Leningrad	USSR	8	3	4	7	2	....	....	....	....	....
	SKA Leningrad	USSR-Q	3	1	0	1	0	....	....	....	....	....

Olympic gold 1968, 1972. Eight World Championships. Canada-Russia 1972. Canada Cup.

• WALTIN, Mats — SWE

D – R. 5'11", 176 lbs. b: Stockholm, Sweden, 10/7/1953.

Season	Club	League	GP	G	A	Pts	PIM	GP	G	A	Pts	PIM
1970-71	IK Stockholm	Sweden-2	17	15	7	22	....	....	....	....	....	....
1971-72	IK Stockholm	Sweden-2	17	16	7	23	....	....	....	....	....	....
1972-73	Sodertalje SK	Sweden	28	5	6	11	6	....	....	....	....	....
1973-74	Sodertalje SK	Sweden	32	12	12	24	12	....	....	....	....	....
1974-75	Sodertalje SK	Sweden	27	2	10	12	14	....	....	....	....	....
	Sodertalje SK	Sweden-Q	6	4	5	9	0	....	....	....	....	....
1975-76	Sodertalje SK	Sweden	35	10	12	22	10	....	....	....	....	....
1976-77	Sodertalje SK	Sweden	33	5	8	13	26	....	....	....	....	....
1977-78	Sodertalje SK	Sweden	33	4	6	10	22	....	....	....	....	....
1978-79	Djurgardens IF	Sweden	36	12	25	37	22	6	4	2	6	2
1979-80	Djurgardens IF	Sweden	31	12	11	23	10	....	....	....	....	....
1980-81	Djurgardens IF	Sweden	35	11	9	20	12	....	....	....	....	....
1981-82	Djurgardens IF	Sweden	31	10	11	21	12	....	....	....	....	....
	Djurgardens IF	Sweden-Q	STATISTICS NOT AVAILABLE									
1982-83	Djurgardens IF	Sweden	15	5	5	10	8	8	0	4	4	8
1983-84	Djurgardens IF	Sweden	28	3	5	8	6	6	4	2	6	2
1984-85	HC Lugano	Switz.	35	12	27	39	....	....	....	....	....	....
1985-86	HC Lugano	Switz.	36	11	26	37	....	4	0	3	3	....
1986-87	HC Lugano	Switz.	30	7	9	16	....	6	4	4	8	....
1987-88	EV Zug	Switz.	34	7	12	19	....	....	....	....	....	....
1988-89	EV Zug	Switz.	35	7	17	24	....	3	0	0	0	....
1989-90	Djurgardens IF	Sweden	27	0	2	2	8	1	0	0	0	2
1990-91	Sodertalje SK	Sweden	40	3	4	7	26	2	0	0	0	0

Olympics in 1980, 1984. Nine World Championships. Canada Cup 1976, 1981.

• WICKBERG, Hakan — SWE

C – L. 5'8", 176 lbs. b: Sandviken, Sweden, 2/3/1943.

Season	Club	League	GP	G	A	Pts	PIM	GP	G	A	Pts	PIM
1958-59	Brynas IF Gavle	Sweden-2	STATISTICS NOT AVAILABLE									
1959-60	Brynas IF Gavle	Sweden-2	STATISTICS NOT AVAILABLE									
1960-61	Brynas IF Gavle	Sweden	....	16	....	16	....	....	....	....	....	....
1961-62	Brynas IF Gavle	Sweden	21	21	6	27	....	....	....	....	....	....
1962-63	Brynas IF Gavle	Sweden	20	22	5	27	2	....	....	....	....	....
1963-64	Brynas IF Gavle	Sweden	21	17	21	38	2	....	....	....	....	....
1964-65	Brynas IF Gavle	Sweden	28	21	27	48	7	....	....	....	....	....
1965-66	Brynas IF Gavle	Sweden	21	20	22	42	0	7	6	5	11	2
1966-67	Brynas IF Gavle	Sweden	21	14	21	35	0	6	5	7	12	0
1967-68	Brynas IF Gavle	Sweden	28	19	24	43	6	....	....	....	....	....
1968-69	Brynas IF Gavle	Sweden	23	16	11	27	2	....	....	....	....	....
1969-70	Brynas IF Gavle	Sweden	28	19	23	42	....	....	....	....	....	....
1970-71	Brynas IF Gavle	Sweden	28	20	24	44	10	....	....	....	....	....
1971-72	Brynas IF Gavle	Sweden	28	23	25	48	6	....	....	....	....	....
1972-73	Brynas IF Gavle	Sweden	28	9	17	26	4	....	....	....	....	....
1973-74	Brynas IF Gavle	Sweden	35	21	20	41	6	....	....	....	....	....
1974-75	Brynas IF Gavle	Sweden	5	0	0	0	0	....	....	....	....	....

Olympics in 1968, 1972. Seven World Championships, 1965 to 1974.

• YAKUSHEV, Alexander — URS

LW – L. 6'3", 198 lbs. b: Moscow, USSR, 1/2/1947.

Season	Club	League	GP	G	A	Pts	PIM	GP	G	A	Pts	PIM
1963-64	Spartak Moscow	USSR	....	1	....	1	....	....	....	....	....	....
1964-65	Spartak Moscow	USSR	....	5	....	5	....	....	....	....	....	....
1965-66	Spartak Moscow	USSR	....	7	....	7	....	....	....	....	....	....
1966-67	Spartak Moscow	USSR	44	34	....	34	....	....	....	....	....	....
1967-68	Spartak Moscow	USSR	44	17	....	17	....	....	....	....	....	....
1968-69	Spartak Moscow	USSR	42	50	....	50	....	....	....	....	....	....
1969-70	Spartak Moscow	USSR	43	33	....	33	....	....	....	....	....	....
1970-71	Spartak Moscow	USSR	40	13	....	13	....	....	....	....	....	....
1971-72	Spartak Moscow	USSR	32	17	....	17	....	....	....	....	....	....
1972-73	Spartak Moscow	USSR	29	26	10	36	....	....	....	....	....	....
1973-74	Spartak Moscow	USSR	32	26	11	37	12	....	....	....	....	....
1974-75	Spartak Moscow	USSR	35	16	18	34	34	....	....	....	....	....
1975-76	Spartak Moscow	USSR	36	31	20	51	15	....	....	....	....	....
1976-77	Spartak Moscow	USSR	31	17	11	28	24	....	....	....	....	....
1977-78	Spartak Moscow	USSR	32	10	9	19	12	....	....	....	....	....
1978-79	Spartak Moscow	USSR	44	19	20	39	44	....	....	....	....	....
1979-80	Spartak Moscow	USSR	43	17	12	29	20	....	....	....	....	....
1980-81	SV Kapfenberg	Austria	34	46	44	90	61	....	....	....	....	....
1981-82	SV Kapfenberg	Austria	37	29	43	72	....	....	....	....	....	....
1982-83	SV Kapfenberg	Austria	38	33	58	91	....	....	....	....	....	....

Two Olympic golds, seven world titles, 1967 to 1979. Top Soviet scorer at Canada-Russia 1972.

• ZHLUKTOV, Viktor — URS

LW – L. 6'2", 209 lbs. b: Inta, USSR, 1/26/1954.
Minnesota's 7th, 143rd overall in 1982.

Season	Club	League	GP	G	A	Pts	PIM	GP	G	A	Pts	PIM
1972-73	CSKA Moscow	USSR	5	2	0	2	0	....	....	....	....	....
1973-74	CSKA Moscow	USSR	28	8	3	11	10	....	....	....	....	....
1974-75	CSKA Moscow	USSR	35	19	11	30	20	....	....	....	....	....
1975-76	CSKA Moscow	USSR	36	23	13	36	25	....	....	....	....	....
1976-77	CSKA Moscow	USSR	36	17	20	37	2	....	....	....	....	....
1977-78	CSKA Moscow	USSR	24	11	6	17	8	....	....	....	....	....
1978-79	CSKA Moscow	USSR	44	20	24	44	12	....	....	....	....	....
1979-80	CSKA Moscow	USSR	36	17	13	30	8	....	....	....	....	....
1980-81	CSKA Moscow	USSR	49	29	26	55	18	....	....	....	....	....
1981-82	CSKA Moscow	USSR	47	19	24	43	16	....	....	....	....	....
1982-83	CSKA Moscow	USSR	39	12	7	19	16	....	....	....	....	....
1983-84	CSKA Moscow	USSR	42	12	11	23	8	....	....	....	....	....
1984-85	CSKA Moscow	USSR	34	9	10	19	8	....	....	....	....	....

Olympics in 1976, 1980. Seven World Championships. Top scorer at 1976 Canada Cup.

CHAPTER 74

Notable European Non-NHL Goaltenders

Club Team Statistics for Top International Goaltenders

Compiled by Igor Kuperman

• ABRAHAMSSON, Christer

G – L. 6′, 180 lbs. b: Umea, Sweden, 4/8/1947. SWE

			REGULAR SEASON								PLAYOFFS							
Season	Club	League	GP	W	L	T	Mins	GA	SO	Avg	GP	W	L	T	Mins	GA	SO	Avg
1965-66	Leksands IF	Sweden	20	13	4	3	1200	69	1	3.45	7	2	3	1	420	32	0	4.57
1966-67	Leksands IF	Sweden	21	11	8	2	1260	68	2	3.24	2	0	2	....	120	9	0	4.50
1967-68	Leksands IF	Sweden	27	19	6	2	1600	70	3	2.63	....	....	....	....	....	....	....	....
1968-69	Leksands IF	Sweden	26	17	4	5	1540	71	2	2.77	....	....	....	....	....	....	....	....
1969-70	Leksands IF	Sweden	28	15	12	1	1680	92	1	3.29	....	....	....	....	....	....	....	....
1970-71	Leksands IF	Sweden	28	17	6	5	1680	87	4	3.11	....	....	....	....	....	....	....	....
1971-72	Leksands IF	Sweden	28	17	6	5	1680	86	0	3.07	....	....	....	....	....	....	....	....
1972-73	Leksands IF	Sweden	28	20	5	3	1680	80	0	2.86	....	....	....	....	....	....	....	....
1973-74	Leksands IF	Sweden	35	....	....	....	2060	92	4	2.68	....	....	....	....	....	....	....	....
1974-75	**New England Whalers**	**WHA**	**15**	**8**	**6**	**1**	**870**	**47**	**1**	**3.24**	....	....	....	....	....	....	....	....
1975-76	**New England Whalers**	**WHA**	**41**	**18**	**18**	**2**	**2385**	**136**	**2**	**3.42**	**1**	**0**	**0**	....	**1**	**0**	**0**	**0.00**
1976-77	**New England Whalers**	**WHA**	**45**	**15**	**22**	**4**	**2484**	**159**	**0**	**3.84**	**2**	**0**	**1**	....	**90**	**5**	**0**	**3.33**
1977-78	Leksands IF	Sweden	34	14	14	6	1964	136	0	4.15	....	....	....	....	....	....	....	....
1978-79	Leksands IF	Sweden	25	....	....	....	1486	79	2	3.19	3	1	2	....	180	10	0	3.33
1979-80	Leksands IF	Sweden	33	....	....	....	1951	114	4	3.51	2	0	2	....	88	13	0	8.86
1980-81	Leksands IF	Sweden	30	....	....	....	1753	118	0	4.04	....	....	....	....	....	....	....	....
1981-82	Leksands IF	Sweden	19	....	....	....	1060	84	0	4.75	....	....	....	....	....	....	....	....
	Major League Totals		**101**	**41**	**46**	**7**	**5739**	**342**	**3**	**3.58**	**3**	**0**	**1**	....	**91**	**5**	**0**	**3.30**

CHRISTER ABRAHAMSSON became a regular goalie with the national team at the age of 23... Shared the duties with all-time great Leif Holmqvist... Made his debut at 1971 World and European Championships and played at tournament again in 1972, 1973, 1974 and 1981... Won silver medals in 1973 and 1981, bronze medals in 1971, 1972 and 1974 ... Saw action at the 1972 Sapporo Olympics ... Played in 106 games for the Swedish national team and has been named to the honorary list of top Swedish players (Stor Grabb).

• BRIZA, Petr

G – L. 6′, 176 lbs. b: Prague, Czechoslovakia, 12/9/1964. TCH

			REGULAR SEASON								PLAYOFFS							
Season	Club	League	GP	W	L	T	Mins	GA	SO	Avg	GP	W	L	T	Mins	GA	SO	Avg
1981-82	Slavia Praha	Czech-2	STATISTICS NOT AVAILABLE															
1982-83	Slavia Praha	Czech-2	STATISTICS NOT AVAILABLE															
1983-84	Motor Ceske Budejovice	Czech.	19	....	....	....	937	40	....	2.56	....	....	....	....	....	....	....	....
1984-85	Motor Ceske Budejovice	Czech.	16	....	....	....	785	40	....	3.06	....	....	....	....	....	....	....	....
1985-86	Dukla Jihlava	Czech.	35	....	....	....	2023	73	....	2.17	....	....	....	....	....	....	....	....
1986-87	Dukla Jihlava	Czech.	29	....	....	....	1724	77	....	2.68	9	6	3	....	551	21	1	2.29
1987-88	Motor Ceske Budejovice	Czech.	42	....	....	....	2265	98	....	2.60	....	....	....	....	....	....	....	....
1988-89	Motor Ceske Budejovice	Czech.	46	....	....	....	2692	150	....	3.34	....	....	....	....	....	....	....	....
1989-90	Sparta CKD Praha	Czech.	53	....	....	....	3108	137	....	2.64	....	....	....	....	....	....	....	....
1990-91	HC Sparta Praha	Czech.	32	....	....	....	1818	75	5	2.48	....	....	....	....	....	....	....	....
1991-92	Lukko Rauma	Finland	44	20	15	8	2660	120	4	2.71	2	0	2	....	120	8	0	4.00
1992-93	Lukko Rauma	Finland	47	22	17	7	2784	133	2	2.87	3	0	3	....	179	8	0	2.68
1993-94	EV Landshut	Germany	44	26	14	4	2583	108	5	2.51	7	3	4	....	422	19	0	2.70
1994-95	EV Landshut	Germany	40	27	8	3	2339	82	3	2.10	17	12	5	....	992	49	1	2.96
1995-96	EV Landshut	Germany	43	30	11	1	2407	111	5	2.77	9	7	2	....	551	24	1	2.61
1996-97	EV Landshut	Germany	48	29	16	3	2883	118	4	2.46	7	3	4	....	422	27	0	3.84
1997-98	EV Landshut	Germany	48	25	19	4	2708	109	5	2.42	6	3	3	....	368	17	0	2.77
1998-99	EV Landshut	Germany	35	18	17	0	2012	73	2	2.18	3	0	3	....	179	11	0	3.69
99-2000	HC Sparta Praha	Cze-Rep.	50	....	....	....	2870	99	....	2.07	9	....	....	....	550	10	....	1.09

PETR BRIZA was the backup goaltender for Czechoslovakia at the 1987 Canada Cup, 1988 Olympics and 1989 World Championships but never saw action... Won a bronze medal at the 1990, 1992 and 1993 World Championships and at the 1992 Albertville Olympics... Named the best goaltender and named to the all-star team at the 1993 World Championships... From 1992 to 1994 played in all but one game for the national team at Albertville and Lillehammer Olympics and at the World Championships... Played two games for Czech Republic at the 1996 World Cup of Hockey.

The only goalie in Czech hockey history to score a goal (1991 versus Steaua Bucharest from Romania)... Romanian goaltender was on the ice when goal was scored.

• DE RAAF, Helmut

G – L. 6′1″, 176 lbs. b: Neuss, W.Germany, 11/5/1961. GER

			REGULAR SEASON								PLAYOFFS							
Season	Club	League	GP	W	L	T	Mins	GA	SO	Avg	GP	W	L	T	Mins	GA	SO	Avg
1981-82	Dusseldorfer EG	Germany	28	....	....	....	1656	116	....	4.20	2	0	2	0	120	11	0	5.50
1982-83	Dusseldorfer EG	Germany	27	....	....	....	1568	139	0	5.32	1	0	0	0	40	6	0	9.00
1983-84	Kolner EC	Germany	21	....	....	....	1240	65	....	3.15	2	2	0	0	120	5	0	2.50
1984-85	Kolner EC	Germany	32	....	....	....	1829	85	3	2.79	9	4	3	0	440	20	1	2.73
1985-86	Kolner EC	Germany	30	....	....	....	1760	65	3	2.22	8	6	1	0	463	20	1	2.59
1986-87	Kolner EC	Germany	22	....	....	....	1320	54	....	2.45	9	9	0	0	543	15	2	1.66
1987-88	Kolner EC	Germany	18	....	....	....	930	44	....	2.84	11	9	2	0	660	29	0	2.64
1988-89	Dusseldorfer EG	Germany	34	....	....	....	1780	114	....	3.84	11	7	3	0	623	27	0	2.60
1989-90	Dusseldorfer EG	Germany	36	....	....	....	1782	88	....	2.96	11	8	3	0	655	32	0	2.93
1990-91	Dusseldorfer EG	Germany	44	....	....	....	2477	111	....	2.69	13	9	4	0	760	27	1	2.13
1991-92	Dusseldorfer EG	Germany	33	....	....	....	1960	74	....	2.27	9	9	0	0	495	12	0	1.45
1992-93	Dusseldorfer EG	Germany	34	....	....	....	2024	80	....	2.37	10	8	2	0	593	21	0	2.12
1993-94	Dusseldorfer EG	Germany	32	25	5	2	1920	65	4	2.03	11	6	5	0	660	26	1	2.36
1994-95	Dusseldorfer EG	Germany	35	20	9	4	2046	99	2	2.90	8	5	3	0	489	16	1	1.96
1995-96	Dusseldorfer EG	Germany	40	25	9	4	2319	94	5	2.43	13	11	1	0	745	32	2	2.58
1996-97			DID NOT PLAY															
1997-98	ESC Moskitos Essen	German-2	16	....	....	....	973	50	1	3.08	....	....	....	....	....	....	....	....
1998-99	Grefrather EV	German-2	25	....	....	....	1428	89	1	3.74	....	....	....	....	....	....	....	....
	Adler Mannheim	Germany	11	....	....	....	665	35	0	3.16	....	....	....	....	....	....	....	....
99-2000	Adler Mannheim	Germany	1	....	....	....	60	4	0	4.00	....	....	....	....	....	....	....	....

HELMUT DE RAAF played nine years for the German national team... Participated in three Olympics and seven World and European Championships... Played in 114 games for the national team.

• DZURILLA, Vladimir

G – L. 5'10", 205 lbs. b: Bratislava, Czechoslovakia, 8/2/1942. Deceased. TCH

			REGULAR SEASON								PLAYOFFS							
Season	Club	League	GP	W	L	T	Mins	GA	SO	Avg	GP	W	L	T	Mins	GA	SO	Avg
1959-60	Slovan Bratislava	Czech.	STATISTICS NOT AVAILABLE															
1960-61	Slovan Bratislava	Czech.	STATISTICS NOT AVAILABLE															
1961-62	Slovan Bratislava	Czech.	STATISTICS NOT AVAILABLE															
1962-63	Slovan Bratislava	Czech.	STATISTICS NOT AVAILABLE															
1963-64	Slovan Bratislava	Czech.	STATISTICS NOT AVAILABLE															
1964-65	Slovan Bratislava	Czech.	STATISTICS NOT AVAILABLE															
1965-66	Slovan Bratislava	Czech.	STATISTICS NOT AVAILABLE															
1966-67	Slovan Bratislava	Czech.	STATISTICS NOT AVAILABLE															
1967-68	Slovan Bratislava	Czech.	STATISTICS NOT AVAILABLE															
1968-69	Slovan Bratislava	Czech.	STATISTICS NOT AVAILABLE															
1969-70	Slovan Bratislava	Czech.	36	....	....	....	....	79	....	....	....	....	....	....	....	....	....	....
1970-71	Slovan Bratislava	Czech.	25	....	....	....	....	63	....	....	....	....	....	....	....	....	....	....
1971-72	Slovan Bratislava	Czech.	30	....	....	....	....	64	....	....	....	....	....	....	....	....	....	....
1972-73	Slovan Bratislava	Czech.	STATISTICS NOT AVAILABLE															
1973-74	ZKL Brno	Czech.	STATISTICS NOT AVAILABLE															
1974-75	ZKL Brno	Czech.	38	....	....	....	....	111	....	....	....	....	....	....	....	....	....	....
1975-76	ZKL Brno	Czech.	STATISTICS NOT AVAILABLE															
1976-77	Zetor Brno	Czech.	38	....	....	....	....	138	....	....								
1977-78	Zetor Brno	Czech.	39	....	....	....	2080	117	....	3.38	....	....	....	....	....	....	....	....
1978-79	Augsburger EV	Germany	14	9	2	3	840	31	2	2.21	....	....	....	....	....	....	....	....
1979-80	SC Riessersee	Germany	42	27	11	4	2500	126	3	3.02	....	....	....	....	....	....	....	....
1980-81	SC Riessersee	Germany	42	31	8	3	2381	121	3	3.05	8	6	2	....	480	24	0	3.00
1981-82	SC Riessersee	Germany	38	20	14	4	2168	110	2	3.04	2	0	2	....	130	6	0	2.77

VLADIMIR DZURILLA made his debut with the Czechoslovakian national team at the 1963 World and European Championships... Saw action in three Olympics, 10 World and European Championships, and the 1976 Canada Cup... World champion in 1972, 1976 and 1977, silver medalist in 1965, 1966 and 1968, bronze medalist in 1963, 1964, 1969 and 1970... Silver medalist at 1968 Grenoble Olympics, bronze medalist at the 1964 Innsbruck Games and the 1972 Sapporo Olympics... Finalist at the 1976 Canada Cup... Named the best goaltender of 1965 World and European Championships... Made the tournament all-star team in 1965 and 1969.

• HEISS, Josef

G – L. 5'11", 187 lbs. b: Garmisch-Partenkirchen, W.Germany, 6/13/1963. GER

			REGULAR SEASON								PLAYOFFS							
Season	Club	League	GP	W	L	T	Mins	GA	SO	Avg	GP	W	L	T	Mins	GA	SO	Avg
1981-82	SC Riessersee	Germany	8	....	....	....	472	27	....	3.43	....	....	....	....	....	....	....	....
1982-83	SC Riessersee	Germany	31	....	....	....	1837	122	1	3.98	3	1	2	0	180	12	0	4.00
1983-84	SC Riessersee	Germany	42	10	32	0	2440	162	0	3.98	....	....	....	....	....	....	....	....
1984-85	SC Riessersee	Germany	36	9	24	3	2127	188	0	5.30	....	....	....	....	....	....	....	....
	SC Riessersee	German-Q	18	12	6	0	1080	63	0	3.50	....	....	....	....	....	....	....	....
1985-86	SC Riessersee	Germany	36	9	24	3	2140	193	0	5.41	....	....	....	....	....	....	....	....
	SC Riessersee	German-Q	18	11	7	0	1080	61	0	3.39	....	....	....	....	....	....	....	....
1986-87	Dusseldorfer EG	Germany	36	....	....	....	2120	120	....	3.40	8	4	3	1	452	48	0	6.37
1987-88	Dusseldorfer EG	Germany	18	....	....	....	1018	62	....	3.65	9	4	4	1	520	27	0	3.12
1988-89	Kolner EC	Germany	35	....	....	....	1800	85	....	2.83	9	5	3	1	540	32	0	3.56
1989-90	Kolner EC	Germany	36	....	....	....	2160	101	....	2.81	8	4	4	0	503	27	0	3.22
1990-91	Kolner EC	Germany	43	....	....	....	2488	122	....	2.94	14	8	6	0	840	39	2	2.79
1991-92	Kolner EC	Germany	40	....	....	....	2354	103	....	2.63	4	1	3	0	240	19	0	4.75
1992-93	Kolner EC	Germany	44	....	....	....	2554	112	....	2.63	12	8	4	0	730	27	1	2.22
1993-94	Kolner EC	Germany	44	26	15	3	2652	109	2	2.47	10	4	6	0	602	32	1	3.19
1994-95	Kolner Haie	Germany	42	27	12	3	2481	121	1	2.93	18	14	4	0	1058	34	3	1.93
1995-96	Kolner Haie	Germany	45	33	8	3	2478	97	3	2.35	14	9	4	0	696	51	0	4.40
1996-97	Kolner Haie	Germany	31	22	5	2	1804	76	2	2.53	2	1	1	0	120	7	0	3.50
1997-98	Kolner Haie	Germany	29	....	....	....	1495	64	3	2.57	3	0	3	0	158	11	0	4.18
1998-99	Kolner Haie	Germany	30	....	....	....	1596	76	3	2.86	1	0	1	0	60	5	0	5.00
99-2000	Kolner Haie	Germany	25	....	....	....	1426	56	1	2.36	3	....	....	....	131	7	0	3.21

JOSEF HEISS played at the 1981 European Junior Championships and the 1981, 1982 and 1983 World Junior Championships... Joined the German national team after spending 10 years in the German League... Made his debut at the 1990 World Championships... Has seen action at the 1992, 1994 and 1998 Olympics and at eight World Championships... Played two games at the 1996 World Cup of Hockey.

• HOLECEK, Jiri

G – L. 5'11", 165 lbs. b: Prague, Czechoslovakia, 3/18/1944. TCH

			REGULAR SEASON								PLAYOFFS							
Season	Club	League	GP	W	L	T	Mins	GA	SO	Avg	GP	W	L	T	Mins	GA	SO	Avg
1962-63	Dynamo Praha	Czech-2	STATISTICS NOT AVAILABLE															
1963-64	Dukla Kosice	Czech-2	STATISTICS NOT AVAILABLE															
1964-65	Dukla Kosice	Czech.	STATISTICS NOT AVAILABLE															
1965-66	Dukla Kosice	Czech.	STATISTICS NOT AVAILABLE															
1966-67	Dukla Kosice	Czech.	STATISTICS NOT AVAILABLE															
1967-68	VSZ Kosice	Czech.	STATISTICS NOT AVAILABLE															
1968-69	VSZ Kosice	Czech.	STATISTICS NOT AVAILABLE															
1969-70	VSZ Kosice	Czech.	35	....	....	....	....	103	....	....	....	....	....	....	....	....	....	....
1970-71	VSZ Kosice	Czech.	STATISTICS NOT AVAILABLE															
1971-72	VSZ Kosice	Czech.	30	....	....	....	....	74	....	....	....	....	....	....	....	....	....	....
1972-73	VSZ Kosice	Czech.	STATISTICS NOT AVAILABLE															
1973-74	Sparta Praha	Czech.	STATISTICS NOT AVAILABLE															
1974-75	Sparta Praha	Czech.	40	....	....	....	....	98	....	....	....	....	....	....	....	....	....	....
1975-76	Sparta Praha	Czech.	STATISTICS NOT AVAILABLE															
1976-77	Sparta Praha	Czech.	38	....	....	....	....	99	....	....	....	....	....	....	....	....	....	....
1977-78	Sparta Praha	Czech.	44	....	....	....	2520	104	....	2.48	....	....	....	....	....	....	....	....
1978-79	EHC 70 Munchen	German-2	40	22	11	7	2284	111	3	2.92	....	....	....	....	....	....	....	....
1979-80	EHC 70 Munchen	German-2	42	31	2	9	2311	104	3	2.70	....	....	....	....	....	....	....	....
1980-81	EHC Essen-West	German-2	44	32	6	4	2240	91	2	2.44	....	....	....	....	....	....	....	....

JIRI HOLECEK began his international career in 1966 at the World and European Championships... Played at two Olympics and 10 World and European Championships from 1966 to 1978... World champion in 1972, 1976 and 1977, silver medalist in 1966, 1971, 1974, 1975 and 1978, bronze medalist in 1973... Winter Olympic silver medalist at Innsbruck in 1976, bronze medalist at Sapporo in 1972... Finalist at the 1976 Canada Cup... Named the best goaltender at the World and European Championships five times (1971, 1973, 1975, 1976 and 1978), voted to the all-star team five times (1971, 1972, 1973, 1976 and 1978).

• HOLMQVIST, Leif

G – L. 5'9", 175 lbs. b: Gavle, Sweden, 11/22/1942. SWE

			REGULAR SEASON								PLAYOFFS							
Season	Club	League	GP	W	L	T	Mins	GA	SO	Avg	GP	W	L	T	Mins	GA	SO	Avg
1958-59	Stromsbro IF Gavle	Sweden	STATISTICS NOT AVAILABLE															
1959-60	Stromsbro IF Gavle	Sweden	STATISTICS NOT AVAILABLE															
1960-61	Stromsbro IF Gavle	Sweden	STATISTICS NOT AVAILABLE															
1961-62	Stromsbro IF Gavle	Sweden	STATISTICS NOT AVAILABLE															
1962-63	Stromsbro IF Gavle	Sweden-2	STATISTICS NOT AVAILABLE															
1963-64	Stromsbro IF Gavle	Sweden	21	8	9	4	1260	92	0	4.38	....	....	....	....	....	....	....	....
1964-65	AIK Solna	Sweden	27	14	10	3	1620	106	0	3.93	....	....	....	....	....	....	....	....
1965-66	AIK Solna	Sweden	21	16	5	0	1260	63	0	3.00	2	0	2	0	120	13	0	6.50
1966-67	AIK Solna	Sweden	21	10	9	2	1260	51	3	2.43	....	....	....	....	....	....	....	....
1967-68	AIK Solna	Sweden	28	20	3	5	1680	62	4	2.21	....	....	....	....	....	....	....	....
1968-69	AIK Solna	Sweden	28	18	7	3	1680	69	2	2.46	....	....	....	....	....	....	....	....
1969-70	AIK Solna	Sweden	28	16	11	1	1680	84	0	3.00	....	....	....	....	....	....	....	....
1970-71	AIK Solna	Sweden	28	15	11	2	1680	83	2	2.96	....	....	....	....	....	....	....	....
1971-72	AIK Solna	Sweden	28	11	12	5	1680	91	4	3.25	....	....	....	....	....	....	....	....
1972-73	AIK Solna	Sweden	24	11	8	5	1410	94	1	4.00	....	....	....	....	....	....	....	....
1973-74	London Lions	Britain	48	....	....	....	2490	126	2	3.04	....	....	....	....	....	....	....	....
1974-75	AIK Solna	Sweden	28	16	10	2	1640	106	0	3.88	....	....	....	....	....	....	....	....
1975-76	**Indianapolis Racers**	**WHA**	**19**	**6**	**9**	**3**	**1079**	**54**	**0**	**3.00**	....	....	....	....	....	....	....	....
	Major League Totals		**19**	**6**	**9**	**3**	**1079**	**54**	**0**	**3.00**	....	....	....	....	....	....	....	....

LEIF HOLMQVIST was a member of the Swedish national team from 1962 to 1975... Played in 202 games for Sweden... Participated at the 1968 and 1972 Olympics and at nine World and European Championships... Silver medalist at the World Championships in 1967, 1969 and 1970, bronze medalist in 1965, 1971, 1972 and 1975... Named the best goaltender of the World and European Championships in 1969.

			REGULAR SEASON								PLAYOFFS							
Season	Club	League	GP	W	L	T	Mins	GA	SO	Avg	GP	W	L	T	Mins	GA	SO	Avg

• KONOVALENKO, Viktor

G – L. 5'6", 167 lbs. b: Gorky, USSR, 3/11/1938. d: 2/20/1996. URS

Season	Club	League	GP	W	L	T	Mins	GA	SO	Avg	GP	W	L	T	Mins	GA	SO	Avg
1956-57	Torpedo Gorky	USSR	30	....	....	....	....	....	....	....	....	....	....	....	....	....	....	....
1957-58	Torpedo Gorky	USSR	34	....	....	....	....	....	....	....	....	....	....	....	....	....	....	....
1958-59	Torpedo Gorky	USSR	27	....	....	....	....	....	....	....	....	....	....	....	....	....	....	....
1959-60	Torpedo Gorky	USSR	37	....	....	....	....	....	....	....	....	....	....	....	....	....	....	....
1960-61	Torpedo Gorky	USSR	33	....	....	....	....	....	....	....	....	....	....	....	....	....	....	....
1961-62	Torpedo Gorky	USSR	38	....	....	....	....	....	....	....	....	....	....	....	....	....	....	....
1962-63	Torpedo Gorky	USSR	37	....	....	....	....	....	....	....	....	....	....	....	....	....	....	....
1963-64	Torpedo Gorky	USSR	36	....	....	....	....	....	....	....	....	....	....	....	....	....	....	....
1964-65	Torpedo Gorky	USSR	36	....	....	....	....	....	....	....	....	....	....	....	....	....	....	....
1965-66	Torpedo Gorky	USSR	36	....	....	....	....	....	....	....	....	....	....	....	....	....	....	....
1966-67	Torpedo Gorky	USSR	44	....	....	....	....	....	....	....	....	....	....	....	....	....	....	....
1967-68	Torpedo Gorky	USSR	44	....	....	....	....	....	....	....	....	....	....	....	....	....	....	....
1968-69	Torpedo Gorky	USSR	22	....	....	....	....	....	....	....	....	....	....	....	....	....	....	....
1969-70	Torpedo Gorky	USSR	35	....	....	....	....	....	....	....	....	....	....	....	....	....	....	....
1970-71	Torpedo Gorky	USSR	29	....	....	....	....	....	....	....	....	....	....	....	....	....	....	....
1971-72	Torpedo Gorky	USSR	22	....	....	....	....	60	....	....	....	....	....	....	....	....	....	....

VIKTOR KONOVALENKO participated at the 1964 and 1968 Olympics and at nine World and European Championships from 1961 to 1971... Olympic champion at Innsbruck in 1964 and at Grenoble in 1968... World Champion from 1963 to 1968, 1970 and 1971... Voted to the all-star team at the World and European Championships in 1970... At the end of his career, played with Vladislav Tretiak on the national team and helped his development.

• KRALIK, Jiri

G – L. 5'9", 165 lbs. b: Gottwaldov, Czechoslovakia, 4/11/1952. TCH

Season	Club	League	GP	W	L	T	Mins	GA	SO	Avg	GP	W	L	T	Mins	GA	SO	Avg
1969-70	TJ Gottwaldov	Czech.	STATISTICS NOT AVAILABLE															
1970-71	TJ Gottwaldov	Czech-2	STATISTICS NOT AVAILABLE															
1971-72	TJ Gottwaldov	Czech.	STATISTICS NOT AVAILABLE															
1972-73	TJ Gottwaldov	Czech-2	STATISTICS NOT AVAILABLE															
1973-74	TJ Gottwaldov	Czech-2	STATISTICS NOT AVAILABLE															
1974-75	TJ Gottwaldov	Czech.	STATISTICS NOT AVAILABLE															
1975-76	TJ Gottwaldov	Czech-2	STATISTICS NOT AVAILABLE															
1976-77	Dukla Jihlava	Czech.	32	....	....	....	....	63	....	....	....	....	....	....	....	....	....	....
1977-78	Dukla Jihlava	Czech.	44	....	....	....	2540	107	....	2.53	....	....	....	....	....	....	....	....
1978-79	Dukla Jihlava	Czech.	33	....	....	....	1900	56	....	1.77	....	....	....	....	....	....	....	....
1979-80	Dukla Jihlava	Czech.	44	....	....	....	2600	111	....	2.56	....	....	....	....	....	....	....	....
1980-81	Dukla Jihlava	Czech.	33	....	....	....	1940	86	....	2.66	....	....	....	....	....	....	....	....
1981-82	Dukla Jihlava	Czech.	42	....	....	....	....	81	....	....	....	....	....	....	....	....	....	....
1982-83	Dukla Jihlava	Czech.	43	....	....	....	2413	90	....	2.24	....	....	....	....	....	....	....	....
1983-84	TJ Gottwaldov	Czech.	24	....	....	....	1300	74	....	3.42	....	....	....	....	....	....	....	....
1984-85	TJ Gottwaldov	Czech.	42	....	....	....	2427	89	....	2.20	....	....	....	....	....	....	....	....
1985-86	SB Rosenheim	Germany	36	20	12	4	2160	100	1	2.78	9	5	4	....	541	38	0	4.21
1986-87	SB Rosenheim	Germany	7	4	1	2	409	26	0	3.81	....	....	....	....	....	....	....	....

JIRI KRALIK began his international career in 1970, when he won a silver medal as a member of the Czechoslovakian junior team at the European Junior Championships... Made his debut with the Czechoslovak national team in 1978-79... Played at the World and European Championships in 1979, 1982, 1983 and 1985... Won the world title in 1985, silver medals in 1979, 1982 and 1983... Named best goaltender and voted to the all-star team in 1982 and 1985... Saw action at the 1980 and 1984 Olympics, winning silver medal at Sarajevo in 1984... Played at the 1981 Canada Cup... Played 99 games for the national team.

• LINDMARK, Peter

G – L. 5'11", 176 lbs. b: Kiruna, Sweden, 11/8/1956. SWE

Season	Club	League	GP	W	L	T	Mins	GA	SO	Avg	GP	W	L	T	Mins	GA	SO	Avg
1974-75	IFK Kiruna	Sweden-2	STATISTICS NOT AVAILABLE															
1975-76	IFK Kiruna	Sweden-2	STATISTICS NOT AVAILABLE															
1976-77	IFK Kiruna	Sweden-2	STATISTICS NOT AVAILABLE															
1977-78	IFK Kiruna	Sweden-2	STATISTICS NOT AVAILABLE															
1978-79	Timra IK	Sweden-2	STATISTICS NOT AVAILABLE															
1979-80	Timra IK	Sweden-2	STATISTICS NOT AVAILABLE															
1980-81	Timra IK	Sweden-2	STATISTICS NOT AVAILABLE															
1981-82	Timra IK	Sweden	34	....	....	....	2036	166	1	4.89	....	....	....	....	....	....	....	....
1982-83	Timra IK	Sweden-2	STATISTICS NOT AVAILABLE															
1983-84	Timra IK	Sweden-2	STATISTICS NOT AVAILABLE															
1984-85	Farjestads BK Karlstad	Sweden	32	....	....	....	1900	93	3	2.94	3	1	2	....	180	12	0	4.00
1985-86	Farjestads BK Karlstad	Sweden	28	....	....	....	1652	83	2	3.01	8	5	3	....	480	26	0	3.25
1986-87	Farjestads BK Karlstad	Sweden	32	....	....	....	....	95	0	....	7	3	4	....	425	32	0	4.52
1987-88	Farjestads BK Karlstad	Sweden	27	....	....	....	1650	87	3	3.16	9	7	2	....	542	21	1	2.32
1988-89	Malmo IF	Sweden-2	STATISTICS NOT AVAILABLE															
1989-90	Malmo IF	Sweden-2	STATISTICS NOT AVAILABLE															
1990-91	Malmo IF	Sweden	32	....	....	....	1860	97	2	3.13	2	0	2	....	121	7	0	3.47
1991-92	Malmo IF	Sweden	19	....	....	....	1120	59	1	3.16	10	7	3	....	622	23	1	2.22
1992-93	Malmo IF	Sweden	19	....	....	....	1140	60	0	3.16	3	1	2	....	182	15	0	4.95
1993-94	Malmo IF	Sweden	17	....	....	....	951	50	1	3.15	2	....	....	....	80	8	0	6.00
1994-95	Malmo IF	Sweden	14	....	....	....	840	34	1	2.43	2	1	1	....	128	5	0	2.34
1995-96	Malmo IF	Sweden	18	....	....	....	911	57	0	3.75	1	0	0	....	37	4	0	6.49
1996-97	Malmo IF	Sweden	16	....	....	....	886	39	1	2.64	4	1	3	....	237	12	0	3.04

PETER LINDMARK played in 174 games for the Swedish national team... Participated at the 1988 Calgary Olympics and at seven World and European Championships... Olympic bronze medalist in 1988... World Champion in 1987 and 1991, silver medalist in 1981 and 1986... Named the best goaltender of the World and European Championships in 1986... Voted to the all-star team at the World and European Championships in 1981 and 1986... Played at the 1981, 1984 and 1987 Canada Cup tournaments... A highlight of his career was an excellent performance when Sweden beat Team Canada 4-2 at the 1984 Canada Cup.

• PUCHKOV, Nikolai

G – R. 5'8", 165 lbs. b: Moscow, USSR, 1/30/1930. URS

Season	Club	League	GP	W	L	T	Mins	GA	SO	Avg	GP	W	L	T	Mins	GA	SO	Avg
1949-50	VVS MVO Moscow	USSR	22	....	....	....	....	....	....	....	....	....	....	....	....	....	....	....
1950-51	VVS MVO Moscow	USSR	15	....	....	....	....	....	....	....	....	....	....	....	....	....	....	....
1951-52	VVS MVO Moscow	USSR	16	....	....	....	....	....	....	....	....	....	....	....	....	....	....	....
1952-53	VVS MVO Moscow	USSR	21	....	....	....	....	....	....	....	....	....	....	....	....	....	....	....
1953-54	CDSA Moscow	USSR	9	....	....	....	....	....	....	....	....	....	....	....	....	....	....	....
1954-55	CSK MO Moscow	USSR	18	....	....	....	....	....	....	....	....	....	....	....	....	....	....	....
1955-56	CSK MO Moscow	USSR	28	....	....	....	....	....	....	....	....	....	....	....	....	....	....	....
1956-57	CSK MO Moscow	USSR	30	....	....	....	....	....	....	....	....	....	....	....	....	....	....	....
1957-58	CSK MO Moscow	USSR	34	....	....	....	....	....	....	....	....	....	....	....	....	....	....	....
1958-59	CSK MO Moscow	USSR	27	....	....	....	....	....	....	....	....	....	....	....	....	....	....	....
1959-60	CSKA Moscow	USSR	36	....	....	....	....	....	....	....	....	....	....	....	....	....	....	....
1960-61	CSKA Moscow	USSR	31	....	....	....	....	....	....	....	....	....	....	....	....	....	....	....
1961-62	CSKA Moscow	USSR	38	....	....	....	....	....	....	....	....	....	....	....	....	....	....	....
1962-63	SKA Leningrad	USSR	12	....	....	....	....	38	....	....	....	....	....	....	....	....	....	....

NIKOLAI PUCHKOV participated at two Olympics and at seven World and European Championships... Olympic gold medalist at Cortina d'Ampezzo in 1956, bronze medalist at Squaw Valley in 1960... World Champion in 1954... Named the best goaltender at the World and European Championships in 1959... Assistant coach of the silver medal-winning Soviet team at the 1972 World and European Championships.

• TAMMI, Jukka

G – L. 5'11", 176 lbs. b: Tampere, Finland, 4/10/1962. FIN

Season	Club	League	GP	W	L	T	Mins	GA	SO	Avg	GP	W	L	T	Mins	GA	SO	Avg
			REGULAR SEASON								PLAYOFFS							
1980-81	Ilves Tampere Jr.	Finn-Jr	STATISTICS NOT AVAILABLE															
1981-82	Ilves Tampere Jr.	Finn-Jr	STATISTICS NOT AVAILABLE															
	Ilves Tampere	Finland	4	....	....	....	....	12	....	....	....	....	....	....	....	....	....	....
1982-83	Ilves Tampere	Finland	25	....	....	....	....	79	2	....	7	....	....	....	393	21	0	3.21
1983-84	Ilves Tampere	Finland	28	....	....	....	....	114	1	....	2	0	2	....	120	9	0	4.50
1984-85	Ilves Tampere	Finland	30	....	....	....	....	107	0	....	7	....	....	....	....	22	0	....
1985-86	Ilves Tampere	Finland	20	....	....	....	....	79	....	....	....	....	....	....	....	....	....	....
1986-87	Ilves Tampere	Finland	44	21	18	5	2626	164	3	3.75	....	....	....	....	....	....	....	....
1987-88	Ilves Tampere	Finland	44	30	11	3	2655	142	3	3.21	4	0	4	....	236	20	0	5.08
1988-89	Ilves Tampere	Finland	41	26	11	4	2484	152	0	3.67	5	2	3	....	304	18	0	3.55
1989-90	Ilves Tampere	Finland	44	25	12	7	2649	137	2	3.10	9	5	4	....	538	34	0	3.79
1990-91	Ilves Tampere	Finland	43	15	21	6	2513	165	0	3.94	....	....	....	....	....	....	....	....
1991-92	Ilves Tampere	Finland	44	16	24	3	2590	145	0	3.36	....	....	....	....	....	....	....	....
1992-93	Ilves Tampere	Finland	40	14	17	7	2374	129	0	3.26	....	....	....	....	....	....	....	....
1993-94	Ilves Tampere	Finland	27	9	10	6	1513	73	0	2.89	3	1	2	....	179	12	0	4.02
1994-95	Ilves Tampere	Finland	31	7	21	2	1804	106	1	3.53	....	....	....	....	....	....	....	....
	Ilves Tampere	Finland-Q	STATISTICS NOT AVAILABLE															
1995-96	TuTo Turku	Finland	41	10	25	5	2315	148	1	3.84	....	....	....	....	....	....	....	....
	TuTo Turku	Finland-Q	STATISTICS NOT AVAILABLE															
1996-97	Frankfurt Lions	Germany	40	17	19	4	2277	107	2	2.82	5	2	3	....	253	18	0	4.27
1997-98	Frankfurt Lions	Germany	42	24	14	4	2422	100	0	2.48	5	2	3	....	287	17	0	3.55
1998-99	Frankfurt Lions	Germany	43	27	11	5	2560	130	2	3.05	8	3	5	....	507	24	0	2.84

JUKKA TAMMI made his debut on the international scene in 1980, as a member of the Finnish team at the European Junior Championships... Won bronze medal at the World Junior Championships in 1982 ... Made his debut with the Finnish national team in 1983-84 and became a regular the following season... Played at seven World and European Championships (1985, 1986, 1987, 1989, 1990, 1994 and 1995), winning gold in 1995 and silver in 1994... Four-time Olympian (1988, 1992, 1994 and 1998), winning silver in 1988 and bronze in 1994 and 1998... Played at the Canada Cup tournament in 1987 and 1991 ... His 213 games with the Finnish national team rank second all-time among goaltenders behind Jorma Valtonen.

• TRETIAK, Vladislav

G – L. 6'1", 202 lbs. b: Dmitrov, USSR, 4/25/1952. Montreal's 9th, 143rd overall in 1983. URS **HHOF**

Season	Club	League	GP	W	L	T	Mins	GA	SO	Avg	GP	W	L	T	Mins	GA	SO	Avg
1968-69	CSKA Moscow	USSR	3	....	....	....	....	2	....	....	....	....	....	....	....	....	....	....
1969-70	CSKA Moscow	USSR	34	....	....	....	....	76	....	....	....	....	....	....	....	....	....	....
1970-71	CSKA Moscow	USSR	40	....	....	....	....	81	....	....	....	....	....	....	....	....	....	....
1971-72	CSKA Moscow	USSR	30	....	....	....	....	78	....	....	....	....	....	....	....	....	....	....
1972-73	CSKA Moscow	USSR	30	....	....	....	....	80	....	....	....	....	....	....	....	....	....	....
1973-74	CSKA Moscow	USSR	27	....	....	....	....	94	....	....	....	....	....	....	....	....	....	....
1974-75	CSKA Moscow	USSR	35	....	....	....	....	104	....	....	....	....	....	....	....	....	....	....
1975-76	CSKA Moscow	USSR	33	....	....	....	....	100	....	....	....	....	....	....	....	....	....	....
1976-77	CSKA Moscow	USSR	35	....	....	....	....	98	....	....	....	....	....	....	....	....	....	....
1977-78	CSKA Moscow	USSR	29	....	....	....	....	72	....	....	....	....	....	....	....	....	....	....
1978-79	CSKA Moscow	USSR	40	....	....	....	....	111	....	....	....	....	....	....	....	....	....	....
1979-80	CSKA Moscow	USSR	36	....	....	....	....	85	....	....	....	....	....	....	....	....	....	....
1980-81	CSKA Moscow	USSR	18	....	....	....	....	32	....	....	....	....	....	....	....	....	....	....
1981-82	CSKA Moscow	USSR	41	34	4	3	2295	65	6	1.70	....	....	....	....	....	....	....	....
1982-83	CSKA Moscow	USSR	29	25	3	1	1641	40	6	1.46	....	....	....	....	....	....	....	....
1983-84	CSKA Moscow	USSR	22	22	0	0	1267	40	4	1.89	....	....	....	....	....	....	....	....

VLADISLAV TRETIAK came to prominence in North America after starring in the historic 1972 Summit Series between Team Canada and the Soviet Union... Participated at the 1972, 1976, 1980 and 1984 Olympics and at 13 World and European Championships from 1970 to 1984... Olympic gold medalist in 1972, 1976 and 1984, silver medalist at Lake Placid in 1980... World Champion in 1970, 1971, 1973 to 1975, 1978, 1979, and 1981 to 1983... Named the best goaltender at the World and European Championships in 1974, 1979, 1981 and 1983... Voted to the tournament all-star team in 1975, 1979 and 1983... Voted to the all-star team and named the tournament MVP after the Soviets won the 1981 Canada Cup... Became first European player elected to the Hockey Hall of Fame in 1989.

• VALTONEN, Jorma

G – L. 5'8", 150 lbs. b: Turku, Finland, 12/22/1946. FIN

Season	Club	League	GP	W	L	T	Mins	GA	SO	Avg	GP	W	L	T	Mins	GA	SO	Avg
1964-65	TPS Turku	Finland	18	....	....	....	....	....	....	....	....	....	....	....	....	....	....	....
1965-66	TPS Turku	Finland	20	....	....	....	....	....	....	....	....	....	....	....	....	....	....	....
1966-67	RU-38 Pori	Finland	22	....	....	....	....	....	....	....	....	....	....	....	....	....	....	....
1967-68	Assat Pori	Finland	20	....	....	....	....	....	....	....	....	....	....	....	....	....	....	....
1968-69	Assat Pori	Finland	22	....	....	....	....	....	....	....	....	....	....	....	....	....	....	....
1969-70	Assat Pori	Finland	22	....	....	....	....	....	....	....	....	....	....	....	....	....	....	....
1970-71	Assat Pori	Finland	32	....	....	....	....	....	....	....	....	....	....	....	....	....	....	....
1971-72	Assat Pori	Finland	32	....	....	....	....	....	....	....	....	....	....	....	....	....	....	....
1972-73	Jokerit Helsinki	Finland	36	....	....	....	....	....	....	....	....	....	....	....	....	....	....	....
1973-74	Jokerit Helsinki	Finland	33	....	....	....	....	....	....	....	....	....	....	....	....	....	....	....
1974-75	FoPS Forssa	Finland-2	23	....	....	....	....	....	....	....	....	....	....	....	....	....	....	....
1975-76	HC Val Gardena	Italy	STATISTICS NOT AVAILABLE															
1976-77	HC Val Gardena	Italy	STATISTICS NOT AVAILABLE															
1977-78	HC Alleghe	Italy	STATISTICS NOT AVAILABLE															
1978-79	TPS Turku	Finland	22	....	....	....	....	55	....	....	8	....	....	....	....	....	....	....
1979-80	TPS Turku	Finland	25	....	....	....	....	80	....	....	6	....	....	....	....	....	....	....
1980-81	EHC 70 Munchen	Germany	43	11	24	8	2580	204	....	4.74	....	....	....	....	....	....	....	....
1981-82	TPS Turku	Finland	8	....	....	....	....	25	....	....	7	....	....	....	....	....	....	....
1982-83	TPS Turku	Finland	33	....	....	....	....	115	1	....	3	....	....	....	143	15	0	6.29
1983-84	TPS Turku	Finland	29	....	....	....	....	92	1	....	5	....	....	....	....	16	0	....
1985-85	TPS Turku	Finland	21	....	....	....	....	66	2	....	5	....	....	....	....	21	0	....
1985-86	TPS Turku	Finland	25	....	....	....	....	69	....	....	6	....	....	....	359	20	0	3.34
1986-87	TPS Turku	Finland	25	12	9	4	1434	107	1	4.48	1	0	1	....	60	5	0	5.00

JORMA VALTONEN played at three Olympics and nine World and European Championships from 1970 to 1984... Was 38 years old when he played for the national team for the final time... Named the best goaltender at the World and European Championships in 1972... In total, played in 232 games for the Finnish national team-fifth position on the all-time list... Played 65 games for Finland at major international tournaments.

• YLONEN, Urpo

G – L. 5'8", 163 lbs. b: Kakisalmi, Finland, 5/25/1943. FIN

Season	Club	League	GP	W	L	T	Mins	GA	SO	Avg	GP	W	L	T	Mins	GA	SO	Avg
1961-62	HP-47 Heinola	Finland-2	STATISTICS NOT AVAILABLE															
1962-63	TuTo Turku	Finland-2	STATISTICS NOT AVAILABLE															
1963-64	TuTo Turku	Finland-2	STATISTICS NOT AVAILABLE															
1964-65	TuTo Turku	Finland-2	STATISTICS NOT AVAILABLE															
1965-66	TuTo Turku	Finland	20	....	....	....	....	....	....	....	....	....	....	....	....	....	....	....
1966-67	TuTo Turku	Finland	22	....	....	....	....	....	....	....	....	....	....	....	....	....	....	....
1967-68	TuTo Turku	Finland	20	....	....	....	....	....	....	....	....	....	....	....	....	....	....	....
1968-69	TuTo Turku	Finland	22	....	....	....	....	....	....	....	....	....	....	....	....	....	....	....
1969-70	TuTo Turku	Finland	22	....	....	....	....	....	....	....	....	....	....	....	....	....	....	....
1970-71	TuTo Turku	Finland	22	....	....	....	....	....	....	....	....	....	....	....	....	....	....	....
1971-72	TuTo Turku	Finland	31	....	....	....	....	....	....	....	....	....	....	....	....	....	....	....
1972-73	TuTo Turku	Finland	36	....	....	....	....	....	....	....	....	....	....	....	....	....	....	....
1973-74	TuTo Turku	Finland	36	....	....	....	....	....	....	....	....	....	....	....	....	....	....	....
1974-75	TuTo Turku	Finland	28	....	....	....	....	161	0	....	....	....	....	....	....	....	....	....
1975-76	TPS Turku	Finland	36	....	....	....	....	106	4	....	4	....	....	....	....	....	....	....
1976-77	TPS Turku	Finland	36	....	....	....	....	....	....	....	6	....	....	....	....	....	....	....
1977-78	TPS Turku	Finland	27	....	....	....	....	89	1	....	8	....	....	....	....	....	....	....
1978-79	TPS Turku	Finland	18	....	....	....	....	67	....	....	8	....	....	....	....	....	....	....
1979-80	ERC Freiburg	Germany	24	4	18	2	1440	126	....	5.25	....	....	....	....	....	....	....	....
	ERC Freiburg	German-Q	7	3	4	0	398	34	....	5.13	....	....	....	....	....	....	....	....
1980-81	ERC Freiburg	German-2	43	32	6	4	2580	72	....	1.67	....	....	....	....	....	....	....	....
1981-82	ERC Freiburg	Germany	42	6	31	5	2160	271	....	7.53	....	....	....	....	....	....	....	....

URPO YLONEN made his debut with the Finnish national team at the 1963 World and European Championships... Played for the nationals until 1978... Participated at three Olympics and 10 World and European Championships... Named the best goaltender of 1970 World and European Championships... In total, he played in 188 games for the national team.

CHAPTER 75

Using the Pre-Expansion Player Register

James Duplacey

THE PRE-EXPANSION REGISTER begins on the facing page. It contains the complete statistical history of every forward, defenseman and rover whose NHL careers concluded between 1917–18 to 1966–67, the year before the league's expansion from six to 12 teams. Players whose careers straddle the 1967–68 expansion are listed in full in the Modern Player Register. *(See page 833.)*

Here are notes on the various statistical categories used in the Pre-Expansion Player Register:

Biographical Information – The first line contains the player's last name and common name in bold type. That is followed by the player's proper name, middle name and nickname. If a player's proper name is the one he is commonly known by (**William**), both it and his middle name are included (**William Joseph**). If the player goes by his common name (**Bill**), then both his proper name and his middle name (**William Joseph**) are included. The players "nickname" follows his proper and middle names in quotation marks (William Joseph **"Soupy"**). The second line contains the player's position (**C** – center, **RW** – right wing, **LW** – left wing, **F** – forward, **W** – wing, **D** – defense, **R** – rover); shooting side (**R** – right, **L** – left), height in feet and inches, weight in pounds, date of birth (month/day/year), place of birth (city/town and province/state for North America, city/town and country for all others) and date of death. If only the birth year is known, it is included. If the death date is not known, the date is represented by "Deceased." If any other biographical information is not known, the appropriate field is left blank. If the player is a member of the Hockey Hall of Fame (**HHOF**) and/or the United States Hockey Hall of Fame (**USHOF**), it is noted here.

Season – From 1917–18 through 1966–67, the hockey season started in the fall and ended the following spring. It is represented as 1966–67. For players who retired or did not play for three or more seasons but later returned to the game, those years are represented by a four-digit date, a vertical slash (/) and final two years of the time period (1964/67).

Club – This field gives information as to which team or teams the player performed with during the season. If statistics for a particular team or season could not be located, the club name has been included with a Statistics not Available notation.

League – This field contains the league name or abbreviated league name for each team line. If a player was with his country's national team, "Nat-Team" is listed in the league column. If a player was with a team that played an exhibition season only, the league field designation is "X-Games." In the pre-expansion era, it was not uncommon for junior and senior teams to be formed for the purpose of winning the Memorial or Allan Cup championships. If a player took part in a championship competition such as the Allan Cup, the league field is where that information can be found. A new feature of the pre-expansion register in this edition is the inclusion of full statistical information for the Allan Cup (**Al-Cup**), Memorial Cup (**M-Cup**), Stanley Cup (**St-Cup**) and World Series (**W-S**); Alexander Cup (**Alx-Cup**); Edinburgh Trophy (**Ed-Cup**) championships in North America. The régister also features London Cup (**Ln-Cup**), Autumn Cup (**A-Cup**) and National Tournament (**Nat-Tmt**) statistics for those players who played in England and Scotland in the 1930s and 1940s *(See page 748)*. A full list of the leagues found in *Total Hockey* and their abbreviations can be found on pages 1973 and 1974.

GP – Games Played – Games in which a player appears on the ice during a game. Players who are dressed but do not step on the ice during play are not credited with a game played.

G – Goals scored – A goal is credited to the last player from the scoring team to touch the puck before it completely crosses the goal line. A player may not direct the puck into the net with a skate or deflect a puck into the net with his stick above the height of the crossbar of the goal net.

A – Assists – An assist is awarded to any player, or players, directly taking part in the play preceding a goal. From 1917–18 to 1926–27, only one assist was awarded. From 1930–31 to 1935–36, as many as three assists could be awarded. No more than two assists were awarded from 1936–37 to 1966–67.

Pts – Points – Any player or goaltender credited with a goal or an assist receives one point.

AG – Adjusted goals – *(See page 613)*

AA – Adjusted assists – *(See page 613)*

APts – Adjusted points – *(See page 613)*

PIM – Penalties in minutes – Number of minutes a player is penalized during a season. Before the NHL was established from 1903–04 to 1913–14, penalties were either two, three or five minutes long, charged at the discretion of the referee. From 1914–15 to 1916–17, all penalties were five minutes in duration. From 1917–18 to 1921–22 penalties were either three or five minutes in duration depending on the nature of the offense. In 1922–23, penalties were two, three or five minutes in duration, again depending on the infraction. Beginning in 1923–24, players were penalized two minutes for a minor penalty, five minutes for a major penalty and 10 minutes for major fouls. The 10-minute misconduct was introduced in 1937–38 and the game misconduct and gross misconduct penalty were introduced in ensuing years.

NHL Totals – The totals of a player's complete NHL career.

Other Major League Totals – This field includes the total of all the other major leagues a player performed in from 1893 to 1967. To be categorized as major a league must fall into one of the following three categories: it must have employed professional talent, challenged for the Stanley Cup and/or competed with other major leagues to sign the top hockey talent of the day. Refer to page 611 for a list of leagues we have designated to be of "major league" quality.

Award and All-Star Notes – This field details all-star selections, major trophy awards in the NHL and the minors, and appearances in the NHL All-Star Game.

Trade Notes – This field contains NHL trade notes for every player from 1917–18 to the end of their major professional careers. WHA trade notes are included for those players who played in the WHA, but not the NHL, after 1967. Trade notes and free agent signings for every NHL player who played in the PCHA, WCHL and the WHL have also been included. We have endeavored to include as many minor league transactions as we could find.

Special notes concerning injuries and other oddities and curiosities are indicated by a bullet (•). An asterisk (*) is used to indicate league- or tournament-leading statistics.

CHAPTER 76

Pre-Expansion Player Register

Career Records for Players whose Last NHL Appearance was Prior to 1967-68

• ABBOTT, Reg

C – L. 5′11″, 164 lbs. b: Winnipeg, Man., 2/4/1930.

Season	Club	League	GP	G	A	Pts	AG	AA	APts	PIM	Playoffs GP	G	A	Pts	PIM
1948-49	Brandon Wheat Kings	MJHL	39	16	16	32	....	....	....	6	7	5	1	6	4
	Brandon Wheat Kings	M-Cup	16	7	6	13	....	....	....	9	....	....	....	....	....
1949-50	Brandon Wheat Kings	MJHL	36	*27	27	*54	....	....	....	24	6	6	7	13	4
	Brandon Wheat Kings	M-Cup	6	6	1	7	....	....	....	2	....	....	....	....	....
1950-51	Victoria Cougars	PCHL	70	14	24	38	....	....	....	29	12	3	*9	12	8
1951-52	Victoria Cougars	PCHL	57	16	27	43	....	....	....	30	13	3	6	9	7
1952-53	**Montreal Canadiens**	**NHL**	**3**	**0**	**0**	**0**	**0**	**0**	**0**	**0**	....	....	....	....	....
	Victoria Cougars	WHL	65	22	22	44	....	....	....	18	....	....	....	....	....
1953-54	Victoria Cougars	WHL	69	7	17	24	....	....	....	24	3	0	2	2	2
1954-55	Pittsburgh Hornets	AHL	3	0	0	0	....	....	....	2	....	....	....	....	....
	Windsor Bulldogs	OHA-Sr.	48	22	34	56	....	....	....	20	12	7	4	11	2
1955-56	Windsor Bulldogs	OHA-Sr.	48	20	24	44	....	....	....	25	....	....	....	....	....
1956-57	Windsor Bulldogs	OHA-Sr.	52	21	26	47	....	....	....	18	8	3	1	4	2
1957-58	Windsor Bulldogs	NOHA	35	6	12	18	....	....	....	10	12	5	1	6	4
1958-59	Windsor Bulldogs	NOHA	8	1	1	2	....	....	....	4	....	....	....	....	....
1959-60			DID NOT PLAY												
1960-61	Winnipeg Maroons	X-Games	20	14	9	23	....	....	....	5	....	....	....	....	....
1961-62	Winnipeg Maroons	X-Games	STATISTICS NOT AVAILABLE												
	Winnipeg Maroons	Al-Cup	11	7	10	17	....	....	....	0	....	....	....	....	....
1962-63	Winnipeg Maroons	X-Games	11	5	21	26	....	....	....	4	....	....	....	....	....
	Winnipeg Maroons	Al-Cup	15	6	13	19	....	....	....	9	....	....	....	....	....
1963-64	Winnipeg Maroons	SSHL	11	9	10	19	....	....	....	2	....	....	....	....	....
	Clinton Comets	EHL	10	2	3	5	....	....	....	6	....	....	....	....	....
1964-65	Winnipeg Maroons	SSHL	6	6	6	12	....	....	....	2	....	....	....	....	....
	Canada	WEC-A	7	2	2	4	....	....	....	0	....	....	....	....	....
	NHL Totals		**3**	**0**	**0**	**0**	**0**	**0**	**0**	**0**	....	....	....	....	....

MJHL First All-Star Team (1950)

• ABEL, Clarence

Clarence John "Taffy" **USHOF**

D – L. 6′1″, 225 lbs. b: Sault Ste. Marie, MI, 5/28/1900 d: 8/1/1964.

Season	Club	League	GP	G	A	Pts	AG	AA	APts	PIM	Playoffs GP	G	A	Pts	PIM
1918-19	Michigan Soo Nationals	TBSHL	STATISTICS NOT AVAILABLE												
1919-20	Michigan Soo Wildcats	NMHL	8	3	1	4	....	....	....	26	....	....	....	....	....
1920-21	Michigan Soo Wildcats	NMHL	STATISTICS NOT AVAILABLE												
1921-22	Michigan Soo Wildcats	NMHL	STATISTICS NOT AVAILABLE												
1922-23	St. Paul Athletic Club	USAHA	18	3	0	3	....	....	....	....	4	0	0	0	....
1923-24	St. Paul Athletic Club	USAHA	3	1	0	1	....	....	....	....	8	0	0	0	....
	United States	Olympics	5	15	0	15	....	....	....	....	....	....	....	....	....
1924-25	St. Paul Atheltic Club	USAHA	39	8	0	8	....	....	....	....	....	....	....	....	....
1925-26	Minneapolis Millers	CHL	35	12	9	21	....	....	....	56	3	0	1	1	6
1926-27	**New York Rangers**	**NHL**	**44**	**8**	**4**	**12**	**14**	**21**	**35**	**78**	**2**	**0**	**1**	**1**	**8**
♦1927-28	**New York Rangers**	**NHL**	**23**	**0**	**1**	**1**	**0**	**6**	**6**	**28**	**9**	**1**	**0**	**1**	**14**
1928-29	**New York Rangers**	**NHL**	**44**	**3**	**1**	**4**	**9**	**7**	**16**	**41**	**6**	**0**	**0**	**0**	**8**
1929-30	**Chicago Black Hawks**	**NHL**	**38**	**3**	**3**	**6**	**4**	**7**	**11**	**42**	**2**	**0**	**0**	**0**	**10**
1930-31	**Chicago Black Hawks**	**NHL**	**43**	**0**	**1**	**1**	**0**	**3**	**3**	**45**	**9**	**0**	**0**	**0**	**8**
1931-32	**Chicago Black Hawks**	**NHL**	**48**	**3**	**3**	**6**	**5**	**7**	**12**	**34**	**2**	**0**	**0**	**0**	**2**
1932-33	**Chicago Black Hawks**	**NHL**	**47**	**0**	**4**	**4**	**0**	**8**	**8**	**63**	....	....	....	....	....
♦1933-34	**Chicago Black Hawks**	**NHL**	**46**	**2**	**1**	**3**	**3**	**2**	**5**	**28**	**8**	**0**	**0**	**0**	**8**
	NHL Totals		**333**	**19**	**18**	**37**	**35**	**61**	**96**	**359**	**38**	**1**	**1**	**2**	**58**

CHL First All-Star Team (1926)

Signed as a free agent by **NY Rangers**, August 14, 1926. Traded to **Chicago** by **NY Rangers** for $15,000, April 15, 1929.

• ABEL, Gerry

Gerald Scott

LW – L. 6′2″, 168 lbs. b: Detroit, MI, 12/25/1944.

Season	Club	League	GP	G	A	Pts	AG	AA	APts	PIM	Playoffs GP	G	A	Pts	PIM
1964-65	Hamilton Red Wings	OHA-Jr.	27	3	13	16	....	....	....	31	....	....	....	....	....
	Memphis Wings	CPHL	8	2	2	4	....	....	....	0	....	....	....	....	....
1965-66	Memphis Wings	CPHL	12	0	1	1	....	....	....	0	....	....	....	....	....
1966-67	**Detroit Red Wings**	**NHL**	**1**	**0**	**0**	**0**	**0**	**0**	**0**	**0**	....	....	....	....	....
	Memphis Wings	CPHL	44	2	9	11	....	....	....	20	6	0	1	1	2
	Pittsburgh Hornets	AHL	2	0	2	2	....	....	....	0	....	....	....	....	....
1967-68	Fort Worth Wings	CPHL	52	3	14	17	....	....	....	35	6	1	2	3	2
	NHL Totals		**1**	**0**	**0**	**0**	**0**	**0**	**0**	**0**	....	....	....	....	....

• Son of Sid

• ABEL, Sid

Sidney Gerald "Boot Nose" **HHOF**

C/LW – L. 5′11″, 170 lbs. b: Melville, Sask., 2/22/1918 d: 2/7/2000.

Season	Club	League	GP	G	A	Pts	AG	AA	APts	PIM	Playoffs GP	G	A	Pts	PIM
1936-37	Melville Millionaires	S-SJHL	STATISTICS NOT AVAILABLE												
	Saskatoon Wesleys	N-SJHL	....	....	....	....	....	....	....	....	3	6	2	8	2
	Saskatoon Wesleys	M-Cup	8	8	5	13	....	....	....	6	....	....	....	....	....
1937-38	Flin Flon Bombers	N-SJHL	23	12	16	28	....	....	....	13	8	4	*4	8	17
	Flin Flon Bombers	M-Cup	7	6	1	7	....	....	....	4	....	....	....	....	....
1938-39	**Detroit Red Wings**	**NHL**	**15**	**1**	**1**	**2**	**2**	**2**	**4**	**0**	**6**	**1**	**1**	**2**	**2**
	Pittsburgh Hornets	IAHL	41	22	24	46	....	....	....	27	....	....	....	....	....
1939-40	**Detroit Red Wings**	**NHL**	**24**	**1**	**5**	**6**	**2**	**8**	**10**	**4**	**5**	**0**	**3**	**3**	**21**
	Indianapolis Capitols	IAHL	21	7	11	18	....	....	....	10	....	....	....	....	....
1940-41	**Detroit Red Wings**	**NHL**	**47**	**11**	**22**	**33**	**17**	**32**	**49**	**29**	**9**	**2**	**2**	**4**	**2**
1941-42	**Detroit Red Wings**	**NHL**	**48**	**18**	**31**	**49**	**24**	**37**	**61**	**45**	**12**	**4**	**2**	**6**	**8**
♦1942-43	**Detroit Red Wings**	**NHL**	**49**	**18**	**24**	**42**	**18**	**22**	**40**	**33**	**10**	**5**	**8**	**13**	**4**
1943-44	Montreal RCAF	QSHL	7	5	4	9	....	....	....	12	....	....	....	....	....
	Montreal Canada Car	MCHL	2	1	0	1	....	....	....	4	....	....	....	....	....
1944-45	Montreal RCAF	MCHL	4	6	8	14	....	....	....	4	....	....	....	....	....
	Lachine Rapides	QPHL	2	2	2	4	....	....	....	0	....	....	....	....	....
	Kingston RCAF	X-Games	2	2	1	3	....	....	....	0	....	....	....	....	....
1945-46	**Detroit Red Wings**	**NHL**	**7**	**0**	**2**	**2**	**0**	**3**	**3**	**0**	**3**	**0**	**0**	**0**	**0**
1946-47	**Detroit Red Wings**	**NHL**	**60**	**19**	**29**	**48**	**21**	**35**	**56**	**29**	**3**	**1**	**1**	**2**	**2**
1947-48	**Detroit Red Wings**	**NHL**	**60**	**14**	**30**	**44**	**18**	**40**	**58**	**69**	**10**	**0**	**3**	**3**	**16**
1948-49	**Detroit Red Wings**	**NHL**	**60**	***28**	**26**	**54**	**40**	**37**	**77**	**49**	**11**	**3**	**3**	**6**	**6**
♦1949-50	**Detroit Red Wings**	**NHL**	**69**	**34**	**35**	**69**	**44**	**43**	**87**	**46**	**14**	***6**	**2**	**8**	**6**
1950-51	**Detroit Red Wings**	**NHL**	**69**	**23**	**38**	**61**	**29**	**47**	**76**	**30**	**6**	**4**	**3**	**7**	**0**
♦1951-52	**Detroit Red Wings**	**NHL**	**62**	**17**	**36**	**53**	**23**	**45**	**68**	**32**	**7**	**2**	**2**	**4**	**12**
1952-53	**Chicago Black Hawks**	**NHL**	**39**	**5**	**4**	**9**	**7**	**5**	**12**	**6**	**1**	**0**	**0**	**0**	**0**
1953-54	**Chicago Black Hawks**	**NHL**	**3**	**0**	**0**	**0**	**0**	**0**	**0**	**4**	....	....	....	....	....
	NHL Totals		**612**	**189**	**283**	**472**	**245**	**356**	**601**	**376**	**97**	**28**	**30**	**58**	**79**

• Father of Gerry • NHL Second All-Star Team (1942, 1951) • NHL First All-Star Team (1949, 1950) • Won Hart Trophy (1949) • Played in NHL All-Star Game (1949, 1950, 1951)

Traded to **Chicago** by **Detroit** for cash, July 22, 1952.

• ACHTYMICHUK, Gene

Eugene Edward "Acky"

C – L. 5′11″, 170 lbs. b: Lamont, Alta., 9/7/1932.

Season	Club	League	GP	G	A	Pts	AG	AA	APts	PIM	Playoffs GP	G	A	Pts	PIM
1949-50	Edmonton Canadians	EJrHL	40	*27	16	*43	....	....	....	2	....	....	....	....	....
1950-51	Crowsnest Pass Lions	WCJHL	40	37	27	64	....	....	....	22	14	10	*17	27	4
1951-52	Crowsnest Pass Lions	WCJHL	44	53	33	86	....	....	....	63	....	....	....	....	....
	Montreal Canadiens	**NHL**	**1**	**0**	**0**	**0**	**0**	**0**	**0**	**0**	....	....	....	....	....
1952-53	Buffalo Bisons	AHL	50	7	4	11	....	....	....	18	....	....	....	....	....
1953-54	Victoria Cougars	WHL	65	11	21	32	....	....	....	25	5	1	0	1	0
1954-55	Victoria Cougars	WHL	69	18	19	37	....	....	....	18	5	0	1	1	2
1955-56	Quebec Aces	QHL	64	22	28	50	....	....	....	34	7	0	5	5	2
1956-57	**Montreal Canadiens**	**NHL**	**3**	**0**	**0**	**0**	**0**	**0**	**0**	**0**	....	....	....	....	....
	Quebec Aces	QHL	62	16	41	57	....	....	....	40	10	2	4	6	4
	Quebec Aces	Ed-Cup	6	0	3	3	....	....	....	*12	....	....	....	....	....
1957-58	**Montreal Canadiens**	**NHL**	**16**	**3**	**5**	**8**	**4**	**5**	**9**	**2**	....	....	....	....	....
	Montreal Royals	QHL	54	14	38	52	....	....	....	28	....	....	....	....	....
1958-59	**Detroit Red Wings**	**NHL**	**12**	**0**	**0**	**0**	**0**	**0**	**0**	**0**	....	....	....	....	....
	Edmonton Flyers	WHL	39	16	17	33	....	....	....	30	3	0	1	1	6
1959-60	Edmonton Flyers	WHL	67	20	51	71	....	....	....	44	4	1	3	4	4
1960-61	Sudbury Wolves	EPHL	37	5	28	33	....	....	....	16	....	....	....	....	....
	Edmonton Flyers	WHL	25	6	14	20	....	....	....	2	....	....	....	....	....
1961-62	Portland Buckaroos	WHL	68	17	56	73	....	....	....	10	3	0	0	0	0
1962-63	Knoxville Knights	EHL	68	30	*96	126	....	....	....	29	5	1	5	6	4
1963-64	Knoxville Knights	EHL	72	30	*88	118	....	....	....	42	8	4	4	8	4
1964-65	Long Island Ducks	EHL	71	30	*83	113	....	....	....	28	15	3	9	12	8
1965-66	Long Island Ducks	EHL	72	34	*83	117	....	....	....	62	12	6	10	16	8
	Portland Buckaroos	WHL	....	....	....	....	....	....	....	....	2	0	0	0	0
1966-67	Long Island Ducks	EHL	71	13	45	58	....	....	....	82	3	0	0	0	2
1967-68	Long Island Ducks	EHL	35	6	12	18	....	....	....	24	....	....	....	....	....
1968-69	Edmonton Monarchs	ASHL	30	9	9	18	....	....	....	11	8	1	5	6	2
1969/72	Edmonton Monarchs	ASHL	PLAYER/COACH – STATISTICS UNAVAILABLE												
	NHL Totals		**32**	**3**	**5**	**8**	**4**	**5**	**9**	**2**	....	....	....	....	....

WCJHL First All-Star Team (1952) • EHL Second All-Star Team (1964) • EHL North First All-Star Team (1965, 1966)

Traded to **Detroit** by **Montreal** with Claude Laforge and Bud MacPherson for cash, June 3, 1958. Traded to **Boston** by **Detroit** for Gord Haworth, August, 1961. Traded to **Portland** (WHL) by **Boston** with Don Ward as part of transaction that sent Don Head to Boston (May, 1961), August, 1961.

• ADAM, Douglas

Douglas Patrick

LW – L. 5′11″, 165 lbs. b: Toronto, Ont., 9/7/1923.

Season	Club	League	GP	G	A	Pts	AG	AA	APts	PIM	Playoffs GP	G	A	Pts	PIM
1941-42	Toronto Marlboros	OHA-Jr.	17	6	1	7	....	....	....	6	2	0	0	0	2
	Toronto HMCS York	TNDHL	3	1	2	3	....	....	....	0	6	2	3	5	6
1942-43	Toronto Army Daggers	OHA-Sr.	3	0	1	1	....	....	....	4	2	0	1	1	2
1943-44			MILITARY SERVICE												
1944-45	Toronto Bowsers	TMHL	2	0	1	1	....	....	....	0	....	....	....	....	....
	Toronto Shamrocks	TIHL	2	0	2	2	....	....	....	0	....	....	....	....	....
	Toronto Uptown Tires	TMHL	18	20	19	39	....	....	....	7	....	....	....	....	....
	Toronto Peoples Credit	TIHL	....	....	....	....	....	....	....	....	3	1	3	4	0
1945-46	Toronto Dorst's	TMHL	3	2	3	5	....	....	....	4	....	....	....	....	....
	Hollywood Wolves	PCHL	10	0	4	4	....	....	....	8	4	1	0	1	0
1946-47	Toronto Peoples Credit	TIHL	28	27	16	43	....	....	....	14	5	1	3	4	13
1947-48	Tacoma Rockets	PCHL	57	34	25	59	....	....	....	57	5	6	1	7	4
1948-49	Tacoma Rockets	PCHL	68	24	30	54	....	....	....	45	6	5	1	6	4
1949-50	**New York Rangers**	**NHL**	**4**	**0**	**1**	**1**	**0**	**1**	**1**	**0**	....	....	....	....	....
	Tacoma Rockets	PCHL	63	*53	26	79	....	....	....	68	5	3	2	5	6
1950-51	Tacoma Rockets	PCHL	68	31	19	50	....	....	....	68	6	2	0	2	4
1951-52	Tacoma Rockets	PCHL	53	31	26	57	....	....	....	43	6	0	0	0	0
1952-53	Tacoma Rockets	WHL	70	*39	31	70	....	....	....	74	....	....	....	....	....
1953-54	Seattle Bombers	WHL	1	0	0	0	....	....	....	0	....	....	....	....	....
	Saskatoon–Vancouver	WHL	62	18	20	38	....	....	....	30	12	4	1	5	12

Season	Club	League	GP	G	A	Pts	AG	AA	APts	PIM	GP	G	A	Pts	PIM
			REGULAR SEASON								PLAYOFFS				
1954-55	Vancouver Canucks	WHL	29	14	7	21				20					
	New Westminster Royals	WHL	36	16	15	31				33					
1955-56	New Westminster Royals	WHL	55	16	20	36				36					
1956-57	Charlotte Clippers	EHL	63	*65	49	114				46	13	*11	7	18	16
1957-58	Charlotte Clippers	EHL	55	44	33	77				32	14	7	10	*17	8
1958-59	Philadelphia Ramblers	EHL	64	39	38	77				66					
1959-60	Philadelphia Ramblers	EHL	64	46	43	89				114	4	1	2	3	20
	Louisville Rebels	IHL									1	0	0	0	0
1960-61	Philadelphia Ramblers	EHL	41	16	23	39				24	3	1	0	1	2
	NHL Totals		**4**	**0**	**1**	**1**	**0**	**1**	**1**	**0**					

PCHL Northern First All-Star Team (1950) • WHL First All-Star Team (1953) • EHL First All-Star Team (1957, 1958, 1960) • EHL Second All-Star Team (1959)

Signed as a free agent by **Hollywood** (PCHL), January 25, 1946.

• ADAMS, Jack John James HHOF

C – R. 5'9", 175 lbs. b: Fort William, Ont., 6/14/1895 d: 5/1/1968.

Season	Club	League	GP	G	A	Pts	AG	AA	APts	PIM	GP	G	A	Pts	PIM
1914-15	Fort William Maple Leafs	NMHL									2	4	0	4	3
1915-16	Calumet Miners	NMHL	STATISTICS NOT AVAILABLE												
1916-17	Peterborough 247th	OIHA	STATISTICS NOT AVAILABLE												
1917-18	Sarnia Sailors	OHA-Sr.	6	15	0	15									
♦	**Toronto Arenas**	**NHL**	**8**	**0**	**0**	**0**	**0**	**0**	**0**	**31**	**2**	**0**	**0**	**0**	**6**
1918-19	**Toronto Arenas**	**NHL**	**17**	**3**	**3**	**6**	**5**	**16**	**21**	**35**					
1919-20	Vancouver Millionaires	PCHA	22	9	6	15				18	2	0	0	0	0
1920-21	Vancouver Millionaires	PCHA	24	17	12	29				*60	2	3	0	3	0
	Vancouver Millionaires	St-Cup	5	2	1	3				6					
1921-22	Vancouver Millionaires	PCHA	24	*26	4	*30				24	2	1	0	1	12
	Vancouver Millionaires	St-Cup	7	6	1	7				30					
1922-23	**Toronto St. Pats**	**NHL**	**23**	**19**	**9**	**28**	**33**	**35**	**68**	***64**					
1923-24	**Toronto St. Pats**	**NHL**	**22**	**14**	**4**	**18**	**29**	**23**	**52**	**51**					
1924-25	**Toronto St. Pats**	**NHL**	**27**	**21**	**10**	**31**	**37**	**42**	**79**	**67**	**2**	**1**	**0**	**1**	**7**
1925-26	**Toronto St. Pats**	**NHL**	**36**	**21**	**5**	**26**	**37**	**32**	**69**	**52**					
♦1926-27	**Ottawa Senators**	**NHL**	**40**	**5**	**1**	**6**	**9**	**5**	**14**	**66**	**6**	**0**	**0**	**0**	**0**
	NHL Totals		**173**	**83**	**32**	**115**	**150**	**153**	**303**	**366**	**10**	**1**	**0**	**1**	**13**
	Other Major League Totals		70	52	22	74				102	6	4	0	4	12

PCHA First All-Star Team (1921, 1922) • Won Lester Patrick Trophy (1966)

Signed as a free agent by **Toronto Arenas**, February 9, 1918. Traded to **Vancouver** (PCHA) by **Toronto** for cash, December 7, 1919. Traded to **Toronto** by **Vancouver** (PCHA) for the PCHA rights to Corb Denneny, December 18, 1922. Traded to **Ottawa** by **Toronto** for cash, August, 1926. • 1922 St-Cup totals include series vs. Regina.

• ADAMS, John John Ellis "Jack"

LW – L. 5'10", 163 lbs. b: Calgary, Alta., 5/5/1920.

Season	Club	League	GP	G	A	Pts	AG	AA	APts	PIM	GP	G	A	Pts	PIM
1936-37	Calgary Canadians	CCJHL	1	0	0	0				0					
1937-38	Calgary K. of C.	CCSHL	11	4	5	9				2	1	0	0	0	0
1938-39	Vancouver Lions	PCHL	29	5	13	18				16	2	0	1	1	2
1939-40	Vancouver Lions	PCHL	40	12	12	24				16	5	1	1	2	4
1940-41	**Montreal Canadiens**	**NHL**	**42**	**6**	**12**	**18**	**9**	**17**	**26**	**11**	**3**	**0**	**0**	**0**	**0**
1941-42			MILITARY SERVICE												
1942-43	Calgary RCAF	CNDHL	22	19	12	31				15	8	5	6	11	4
1943-44	Vancouver RCAF	NNDHL	9	4	3	7				11					
	Vancouver Seahawks	NNDHL									3	2	2	4	4
1944-45	Vancouver RCAF	NNDHL	DID NOT PLAY – INJURED												
1945-46	Montreal Royals	QSHL	4	2	1	3				5					
	Buffalo Bisons	AHL	19	2	2	4				0	9	4	4	8	4
1946-47	Houston Huskies	USHL	20	3	5	8				6					
1947-48	New Westminster Royals	PCHL	52	20	13	33				36	5	0	0	0	2
1948-49	New Westminster Royals	PCHL	41	8	8	16				21	12	1	2	3	8
	NHL Totals		**42**	**6**	**12**	**18**	**9**	**17**	**26**	**11**	**3**	**0**	**0**	**0**	**0**

Traded to **Montreal** by **Vancouver** (PCHL) for cash, May 13, 1940. • Missed entire 1944-45 season recovering from knee injury suffered in pre-season game vs. Vancouver All-Stars, October 30, 1944. Traded to **Buffalo** (AHL) by **Montreal** with Moe White for Murdo MacKay with Montreal holding right of recall, January 14, 1946.

• ADAMS, Stew Stewart Alexander

LW – L. 5'10", 165 lbs. b: Calgary, Alta., 10/16/1904 d: 5/18/1978.

Season	Club	League	GP	G	A	Pts	AG	AA	APts	PIM	GP	G	A	Pts	PIM
1921-22	Calgary Hustlers	CCJHL	STATISTICS NOT AVAILABLE												
	Calgary Hustlers	M-Cup	3	1	0	1				0					
1922-23	Calgary Canadians	CCJHL	12	3	5	8				8					
1923-24	Calgary Canadians	CCJHL	STATISTICS NOT AVAILABLE												
	Calgary Canadians	M-Cup	7	8	5	13				2					
1924-25	Calgary Canadians	CCJHL	STATISTICS NOT AVAILABLE												
	Calgary Canadians	M-Cup	2	0	0	0				6					
1925-26	Minneapolis Millers	CHL	5	1	0	1				3					
1926-27	Minneapolis Millers	AHA	32	2	4	6				15	6	1	0	1	2
1927-28	Minneapolis Millers	AHA	38	4	3	7				24	8	1	0	1	8
1928-29	Minneapolis Millers	AHA	40	11	8	19				41	4	0	0	0	4
1929-30	Minneapolis Millers	AHA	16	8	4	12				4					
	Chicago Black Hawks	**NHL**	**24**	**4**	**6**	**10**	**6**	**14**	**20**	**16**	**2**	**0**	**0**	**0**	**6**
1930-31	**Chicago Black Hawks**	**NHL**	**37**	**5**	**13**	**18**	**10**	**39**	**49**	**18**	**9**	**3**	**3**	**6**	**8**
	London Panthers	IHL	3	1	0	1				2					
1931-32	**Chicago Black Hawks**	**NHL**	**26**	**0**	**5**	**5**	**0**	**11**	**11**	**26**					
1932-33	**Toronto Maple Leafs**	**NHL**	**8**	**0**	**2**	**2**	**0**	**4**	**4**	**0**					
	Syracuse Stars	IHL	36	11	22	33				48	6	0	1	1	6
1933-34	Minneapolis Millers	CHL	43	*22	8	30				40	3	0	3	3	
1934-35	Calgary Tigers	NWHL	8	5	6	11				13					
1935-36	Calgary Tigers	NWHL	29	11	7	18				16					
	NHL Totals		**95**	**9**	**26**	**35**	**16**	**68**	**84**	**60**	**11**	**3**	**3**	**6**	**14**

Traded to **Chicago** by **Minneapolis** (AHA) for Tom Westwick and $15,000, January 4, 1930. Traded to **Toronto** by **Chicago** for cash, November 3, 1932. Traded to **Montreal Maroons** (Windsor-IHL) by **Toronto** (Syracuse-IHL) for Al Huggins, November 1, 1933.

• AHLIN, Tony Anthony Rudolph

LW – L. 5'11", 176 lbs. b: Eveleth, MN, 12/12/1914.

Season	Club	League	GP	G	A	Pts	AG	AA	APts	PIM	GP	G	A	Pts	PIM
1931-32	Eveleth Rangers	CHL	33	12	7	19				22					
1932-33	Eveleth Rangers	CHL	40	4	15	19				29	3	1	0	1	0
1933-34	Duluth Hornets	CHL	30	16	12	28				20					
1934-35	Eveleth Rangers	CHL	46	12	9	21				36					
1935-36	Kansas City Greyhounds	AHA	47	15	9	24				34					
1936-37	Kansas City Greyhounds	AHA	48	7	19	26				34	3	0	1	1	2
1937-38	**Chicago Black Hawks**	**NHL**	**1**	**0**	**0**	**0**	**0**	**0**	**0**	**0**					
	Kansas City Greyhounds	AHA	47	6	18	24				29					
1938-39	Kansas City Greyhounds	AHA	48	12	13	25				33					
1939-40	Kansas City Greyhounds	AHA	41	10	15	25				16					
1940-41	Kansas City Americans	AHA	1	0	0	0				2					
1941-42	Rivervale Skeeters	EAHL	56	20	13	33				45	7	1	4	5	0
	NHL Totals		**1**	**0**	**0**	**0**	**0**	**0**	**0**	**0**					

• AILSBY, Lloyd Harold Lloyd

D – L. 5'11", 194 lbs. b: Lac Pelletier, Sask., 5/11/1917.

Season	Club	League	GP	G	A	Pts	AG	AA	APts	PIM	GP	G	A	Pts	PIM
1934-35	Moose Jaw CPR	MJJHL	6	3	3	6				0					
	Moose Jaw Canucks	M-Cup	6	4	1	5				2					
1935-36	Regina Caps	S-SJHL	16	5	2	7				6	2	0	0	0	0
1936-37	New York Rovers	EAHL	47	11	21	32				8	3	2	5	7	2
1937-38	New York Rovers	EAHL	56	28	22	50				6					
1938-39	New York Rovers	EAHL	53	17	13	30				38					
1939-40	Philadelphia Ramblers	AHL	52	11	19	30				24					
1940-41	Philadelphia Rockets	AHL	56	8	13	21				28					
1941-42	Cornwall Flyers	QSHL	39	9	7	16				20	5	0	1	1	2
1942-43			MILITARY SERVICE												
1943-44	Moose Jaw Victorias	SSHL	9	3	5	8				0					
	Ottawa Commandos	QSHL	8	0	2	2				4	3	2	2	4	4
1944-45	Ottawa Senators	QSHL	18	6	8	14				26	2	0	0	0	4
1945-46	St. Paul Saints	USHL	53	4	19	23				23	6	0	3	3	0
1946-47	New Haven Ramblers	AHL	63	4	16	20				36	3	0	2	2	0
1947-48	St. Paul Saints	USHL	65	7	26	33				4					
1948-49	St. Paul Saints	USHL	66	5	32	37				14	7	0	3	3	0
1949-50	St. Paul Saints	USHL	68	5	32	37				32	3	0	3	3	0
1950-51	St. Paul Saints	USHL	47	8	17	25				8	4	0	1	1	4
1951-52	**New York Rangers**	**NHL**	**3**	**0**	**0**	**0**	**0**	**0**	**0**	**2**					
	New York Rovers	EAHL	27	1	12	13				14					
1952-53	Seattle Bombers	WHL	61	7	15	22				22	5	1	1	2	0
1953-54	Seattle Bombers	WHL	34	0	5	5				6					
	Nelson Maple Leafs	WIHL	18	4	12	16				4	8	3	5	8	6
	Nelson Maple Leafs	Al-Cup	8	0	3	3				10					
1954-55			DID NOT PLAY												
1955-56	Johnstown Jets	EHL	36	3	18	21				27	4	0	2	2	2
1956-57	Johnstown Jets	EHL	46	6	23	29				16	6	0	1	1	0
1957-58	Johnstown Jets	EHL									6	0	1	1	8
	NHL Totals		**3**	**0**	**0**	**0**	**0**	**0**	**0**	**2**					

USHL Second All-Star Team (1946, 1948, 1951) • USHL First All-Star Team (1949, 1950) • EHL First All-Star Team (1957)

Signed as a free agent by **NY Rangers**, October 21, 1940.

• ALBRIGHT, Clint Clint Howard "The Professor"

C – L. 6'2", 180 lbs. b: Winnipeg, Man., 2/28/1926 d: 12/30/1999.

Season	Club	League	GP	G	A	Pts	AG	AA	APts	PIM	GP	G	A	Pts	PIM
1944-45	Winnipeg Monarchs	MJHL	8	10	6	16				8	8	*9	6	*15	4
	Winnipeg Monarchs	M-Cup	9	5	3	8				18					
1945-46	Winnipeg Monarchs	MJHL	6	5	3	8				12	7	6	1	7	9
	Winnipeg Monarchs	M-Cup	15	6	5	11				10					
1946-47	University of Manitoba	WSrHL	4	*8	7	15				0					
	Winnipeg Flyers	MHL-Sr.	10	11	6	17				16	5	6	0	6	8
	Winnipeg Flyers	Al-Cup	7	3	2	5				7					
1947-48	Winnipeg Flyers	MHL-Sr.	16	17	12	29				21	7	2	3	5	16
	Winnipeg Flyers	Al-Cup	1	0	0	0				0					
1948-49	**New York Rangers**	**NHL**	**59**	**14**	**5**	**19**	**20**	**7**	**27**	**19**					
1949-50	Winnipeg Monarchs	MHL-Sr.	STATISTICS NOT AVAILABLE												
1950-51	St. Paul Saints	USHL	62	21	19	40				36	4	1	1	2	4
1951/53			OUT OF HOCKEY – RETIRED												
1953-54	Trail Smoke Eaters	WIHL	8	0	2	2				0					
	NHL Totals		**59**	**14**	**5**	**19**	**20**	**7**	**27**	**19**					

• ALDCORN, Gary Gary William

LW – L. 5'11", 170 lbs. b: Shaunavon, Sask., 3/7/1935.

Season	Club	League	GP	G	A	Pts	AG	AA	APts	PIM	GP	G	A	Pts	PIM
1951-52	Winnipeg Monarchs	MJHL	20	9	7	16									
1952-53	Winnipeg Monarchs	MJHL	35	18	24	42				16	4	2	0	2	2
1953-54	Winnipeg Monarchs	MJHL	36	23	14	37				37	5	4	2	6	2
	Winnipeg Maroons	Al-Cup	16	14	12	26				8					
1954-55	Toronto Marlboros	OHA-Jr.	47	27	22	49				57	13	5	6	11	*37
	Toronto Marlboros	M-Cup	11	4	1	5				4					
1955-56	Winnipeg Warriors	WHL	67	22	12	34				66	14	5	2	7	2
	Winnipeg Warriors	Ed-Cup	6	2	4	6				6					
1956-57	**Toronto Maple Leafs**	**NHL**	**22**	**5**	**1**	**6**	**6**	**1**	**7**	**4**					
	Rochester Americans	AHL	42	13	10	23				28	10	1	4	5	2
1957-58	**Toronto Maple Leafs**	**NHL**	**59**	**10**	**14**	**24**	**12**	**14**	**26**	**12**					
	Rochester Americans	AHL	11	2	10	12				22					
1958-59	**Toronto Maple Leafs**	**NHL**	**5**	**0**	**3**	**3**	**0**	**3**	**3**	**2**					
	Rochester Americans	AHL	66	37	42	79				52	5	0	2	2	0
1959-60	**Detroit Red Wings**	**NHL**	**70**	**22**	**29**	**51**	**26**	**28**	**54**	**32**	**6**	**1**	**2**	**3**	**4**
1960-61	**Detroit Red Wings**	**NHL**	**49**	**2**	**6**	**8**	**2**	**6**	**8**	**16**					
	Boston Bruins	**NHL**	**21**	**2**	**3**	**5**	**2**	**3**	**5**	**12**					
1961-62	Winnipeg Maroons	X-Games	STATISTICS NOT AVAILABLE												
1962-63	Winnipeg Maroons	SSHL	3	1	3	4				2					
1963-64	Winnipeg Maroons	SSHL	STATISTICS NOT AVAILABLE												
1964-65	Winnipeg Maroons	SSHL	4	5	3	8				2					
	Canada	WEC-A	7	4	2	6				8					
1965/68	St. Boniface Mohawks	SSHL	STATISTICS NOT AVAILABLE												
1967-68	St. Boniface Mohawks	Al-Cup	12	4	8	12				8					
	NHL Totals		**226**	**41**	**56**	**97**	**48**	**55**	**103**	**78**	**6**	**1**	**2**	**3**	**4**

AHL First All-Star Team (1959)

Claimed by **Toronto** from **Pittsburgh** (AHL) in Inter-League Draft, June 5, 1956. Claimed by **Detroit** from **Toronto** in Intra-League Draft, June 10, 1959. Traded to **Boston** by **Detroit** with Murray Oliver and Tom McCarthy for Vic Stasiuk and Leo Labine, January 23, 1961.

• ALEXANDRE, Art

LW – R. 5'5", 150 lbs. b: St. Jean, Que., 3/2/1909 d: 1976.

			REGULAR SEASON								PLAYOFFS				
Season	Club	League	GP	G	A	Pts	AG	AA	APts	PIM	GP	G	A	Pts	PIM
1930-31	Montreal St. Francois	MCHL	STATISTICS NOT AVAILABLE												
	Montreal CPR	MCHL	STATISTICS NOT AVAILABLE												
1931-32	**Montreal Canadiens**	**NHL**	**10**	**0**	**2**	**2**	**0**	**4**	**4**	**8**	**4**	**0**	**0**	**0**	**0**
	Montreal Sr. Canadiens	MCHL	11	6	2	8	....	....	....	2	2	0	1	1	0
1932-33	Providence Reds	Can-Am	47	10	24	34	....	....	....	18	2	0	0	0	0
	Montreal Canadiens	**NHL**	**1**	**0**	**0**	**0**	**0**	**0**	**0**	**0**	....	....	....	....	....
1933-34	Providence Reds	Can-Am	37	2	3	5	....	....	....	19	2	0	0	0	2
1934-35	Providence Reds	Can-Am	10	1	0	1	....	....	....	4	....	....	....	....	....
	Quebec Castors	Can-Am	32	5	8	13	....	....	....	15	3	0	0	0	8
1935-36	Springfield Indians	Can-Am	47	13	16	29	....	....	....	32	3	0	1	1	2
1936-37	Kansas City Greyhounds	AHA	1	0	0	0	....	....	....	0	....	....	....	....	....
1937-38	Montreal Concordia	QSHL	22	9	6	15	....	....	....	23	1	0	1	1	0
	NHL Totals		**11**	**0**	**2**	**2**	**0**	**4**	**4**	**8**	**4**	**0**	**0**	**0**	**0**

Traded to **Providence** (Can-Am) by **Montreal Canadiens** for cash, May 8, 1932. Traded to **Montreal Canadiens** by **Providence** (Can-Am) for cash, February 6, 1933. Loaned to **Providence** (Can-Am) by **Montreal Canadiens**, February, 1933.

• ALLEN, George George Trenholm

LW/D – L. 5'10", 162 lbs. b: Bayfield, N.B., 7/27/1914.

Season	Club	League	GP	G	A	Pts	AG	AA	APts	PIM	GP	G	A	Pts	PIM
1929/35	Kerrobert Tigers	SIHA	STATISTICS NOT AVAILABLE												
1934-35	North Battleford UCT	SAHA	....	....	....	....	....	....	....	....	2	0	0	0	0
1935-36	North Battleford Beavers	N-SSHL	21	10	5	15	....	....	....	10	3	2	1	*3	4
1936-37	North Battleford Beavers	N-SSHL	26	15	9	24	....	....	....	26	4	4	1	5	4
1937-38	Sudbury Frood Tigers	NOHA	4	2	0	2	....	....	....	8	....	....	....	....	....
	New Haven Eagles	IAHL	35	9	13	22	....	....	....	20	2	0	0	0	0
1938-39	**New York Rangers**	**NHL**	**19**	**6**	**6**	**12**	**10**	**9**	**19**	**10**	**7**	**0**	**0**	**0**	**4**
	Philadelphia Ramblers	IAHL	33	23	11	34	....	....	....	15	3	1	0	1	0
1939-40	**Chicago Black Hawks**	**NHL**	**48**	**10**	**12**	**22**	**17**	**19**	**36**	**26**	**2**	**0**	**0**	**0**	**0**
1940-41	**Chicago Black Hawks**	**NHL**	**44**	**14**	**17**	**31**	**22**	**24**	**46**	**22**	**5**	**2**	**2**	**4**	**10**
1941-42	**Chicago Black Hawks**	**NHL**	**43**	**7**	**13**	**20**	**9**	**15**	**24**	**31**	**3**	**1**	**1**	**2**	**0**
1942-43	**Chicago Black Hawks**	**NHL**	**47**	**10**	**14**	**24**	**10**	**13**	**23**	**26**	....	....	....	....	....
1943-44	**Chicago Black Hawks**	**NHL**	**45**	**17**	**24**	**41**	**15**	**21**	**36**	**36**	**9**	**5**	**4**	**9**	**8**
1944-45			MILITARY SERVICE												
1945-46	**Chicago Black Hawks**	**NHL**	**44**	**11**	**15**	**26**	**13**	**22**	**35**	**16**	**4**	**0**	**0**	**0**	**4**
1946-47	**Montreal Canadiens**	**NHL**	**49**	**7**	**14**	**21**	**8**	**17**	**25**	**12**	**11**	**1**	**3**	**4**	**6**
	Buffalo Bisons	AHL	3	1	1	2	....	....	....	4	....	....	....	....	....
1947-48	Cleveland Barons	AHL	68	15	34	49	....	....	....	30	9	2	5	7	6
1948-49	Cleveland Barons	AHL	28	2	3	5	....	....	....	26	....	....	....	....	....
	Minneapolis Millers	USHL	37	7	6	13	....	....	....	6	....	....	....	....	....
1949-50	Kerrobert Tigers	SIHL	STATISTICS NOT AVAILABLE												
1950-51	Regina Caps	WCSHL	50	9	18	27	....	....	....	26	....	....	....	....	....
1951/57	Kerrobert Tigers	SIHA	STATISTICS NOT AVAILABLE												
	NHL Totals		**339**	**82**	**115**	**197**	**104**	**140**	**244**	**179**	**41**	**9**	**10**	**19**	**32**

• Brother of Vivian • IAHL Second All-Star Team (1939)

Traded to **Chicago** by **NY Rangers** for cash, May 17, 1939. Traded to **Montreal** by **Chicago** for Paul Bibeault with both teams holding right of recall, September 23, 1946. Players returned to original teams, June 2, 1947. Traded to **Minneapolis** (USHL) by **Cleveland** (AHL) for Tom Williams, December 21, 1948. • Suffered eventual career-ending eye injury during the summer of 1949.

• ALLEN, Keith Courtney Keith "Bingo" HHOF

D – L. 5'10", 190 lbs. b: Saskatoon, Sask., 8/21/1923.

Season	Club	League	GP	G	A	Pts	AG	AA	APts	PIM	GP	G	A	Pts	PIM
1939-40	North Battleford Beavers	N-SJHL	STATISTICS NOT AVAILABLE												
1940-41	Saskatoon Quakers	N-SJHL	10	4	0	4	....	....	....	2	2	1	0	1	2
	Saskatoon Quakers	Al-Cup	14	3	3	6	....	....	....	8	....	....	....	....	....
1941-42	Washington Eagles	EAHL	60	13	11	24	....	....	....	27	8	0	1	1	0
1942-43	Buffalo Bisons	AHL	55	1	14	15	....	....	....	29	7	1	0	1	0
1943-44	Saskatoon Navy	N-SSHL	15	9	7	16	....	....	....	12	1	0	0	0	0
1944-45	Saskatoon Navy	N-SSHL	5	0	1	1	....	....	....	0	....	....	....	....	....
1945-46	Saskatoon Elks	N-SSHL	33	5	4	9	....	....	....	42	3	1	0	1	6
1946-47	Springfield Indians	AHL	61	2	8	10	....	....	....	23	2	0	0	0	0
1947-48	Springfield Indians	AHL	51	2	12	14	....	....	....	12	....	....	....	....	....
1948-49	Springfield Indians	AHL	68	3	28	31	....	....	....	28	3	1	0	1	4
1949-50	Springfield Indians	AHL	69	3	17	20	....	....	....	30	2	0	2	2	0
1950-51	Springfield Indians	AHL	70	8	34	42	....	....	....	18	3	0	0	0	0
1951-52	Syracuse Warriors	AHL	67	4	17	21	....	....	....	24	....	....	....	....	....
1952-53	Syracuse Warriors	AHL	64	1	18	19	....	....	....	24	2	0	0	0	0
1953-54	Syracuse Warriors	AHL	47	6	17	23	....	....	....	14	....	....	....	....	....
	Sherbrooke Saints	QHL	3	0	1	1	....	....	....	4	....	....	....	....	....
♦	**Detroit Red Wings**	**NHL**	**10**	**0**	**4**	**4**	**0**	**5**	**5**	**2**	**5**	**0**	**0**	**0**	**0**
1954-55	**Detroit Red Wings**	**NHL**	**18**	**0**	**0**	**0**	**0**	**0**	**0**	**6**	....	....	....	....	....
	Edmonton Flyers	WHL	34	4	12	16	....	....	....	10	9	0	2	2	6
	Edmonton Flyers	Ed-Cup	6	0	1	1	....	....	....	14	....	....	....	....	....
1955-56	Brandon Regals	WHL	69	0	13	13	....	....	....	40	....	....	....	....	....
1956-57	Seattle Americans	WHL	41	0	6	6	....	....	....	0	....	....	....	....	....
1957-58	Seattle Americans	WHL	DID NOT PLAY – COACHING												
	NHL Totals		**28**	**0**	**4**	**4**	**0**	**5**	**5**	**8**	**5**	**0**	**0**	**0**	**0**

AHL Second All-Star Team (1953) • WHL Second All-Star Team (1955) • Won Lester Patrick Trophy (1988) • Played in NHL All-Star Game (1954)

• Suspended by **Syracuse** (AHL) for refusing to report to **Springfield** (AHL), February 11, 1954. Traded to **Detroit** by **Syracuse** (AHL) for cash, February 26, 1954.

• ALLEN, Vivian Vivian Mariner "Squee"

RW – R. 5'6", 140 lbs. b: Bayfield, N.B., 9/9/1916 d: 1995.

Season	Club	League	GP	G	A	Pts	AG	AA	APts	PIM	GP	G	A	Pts	PIM
1934/36	Kerrobert Tigers	SIHA	STATISTICS NOT AVAILABLE												
1936-37	North Battleford Beavers	N-SSHL	21	5	3	8	....	....	....	9	4	1	1	2	0
1937-38	Creighton Eagles	NOHA	15	4	6	10	....	....	....	16	4	0	1	1	4
1938-39	Lethbridge Maple Leafs	ASHL	16	9	6	15	....	....	....	20	17	8	4	12	24
1939-40	Rivervale Skeeters	EAHL	60	26	47	73	....	....	....	28	....	....	....	....	....
1940-41	**New York Americans**	**NHL**	**6**	**0**	**1**	**1**	**0**	**1**	**1**	**0**	....	....	....	....	....
	Springfield Indians	AHL	29	5	7	12	....	....	....	6	3	0	3	3	0
1941-42	Pittsburgh Hornets	AHL	51	20	30	50	....	....	....	10	....	....	....	....	....
1942-43	Pittsburgh Hornets	AHL	47	6	32	38	....	....	....	22	2	0	1	1	0
	Washington Lions	AHL	1	0	0	0	....	....	....	0	....	....	....	....	....
1943-44	Pittsburgh Hornets	AHL	12	4	0	4	....	....	....	5	....	....	....	....	....
	Saskatoon HMCS Unicorn	SNDHL	8	3	6	9	....	....	....	4	4	5	2	7	2
	Philadelphia Falcons	EAHL	4	2	1	3	....	....	....	2	....	....	....	....	....
1944-45	Cornwallis Navy	NSDHL	7	1	2	3	....	....	....	2	....	....	....	....	....
1945-46	Pittsburgh Hornets	AHL	2	0	0	0	....	....	....	0	....	....	....	....	....
	Dallas Texans	USHL	34	21	17	38	....	....	....	10	....	....	....	....	....
1946-47	Dallas Texans	USHL	58	*34	18	52	....	....	....	14	6	0	0	0	4
1947-48	Dallas Texans	USHL	61	16	27	43	....	....	....	19	....	....	....	....	....
1948-49	Dallas Texans	USHL	24	7	6	13	....	....	....	6	4	0	1	1	0
1949-50	Saskatoon Quakers	WCSHL	13	2	6	8	....	....	....	4	....	....	....	....	....
	NHL Totals		**6**	**0**	**1**	**1**	**0**	**1**	**1**	**0**	....	....	....	....	....

• Brother of George

Signed as a free agent by **NY Americans**, October 15, 1940. Traded to **Toronto** (Pittsburgh-AHL) by **NY Americans** with Glenn Brydson for Phil McAtee and the return of Peanuts O'Flaherty (previously on loan), October 8, 1941. • Missed majority of 1948-49 season recovering from leg injury suffered in exhibition game vs. Montreal Royals, October 3, 1948.

• ALLUM, Bill William James Douglas

D – L. 5'11", 194 lbs. b: Winnipeg, Man., 10/9/1916 d: 3/14/1992.

Season	Club	League	GP	G	A	Pts	AG	AA	APts	PIM	GP	G	A	Pts	PIM
1934-35	Winnipeg Rangers	WJrHL	10	0	1	1	....	....	....	16	....	....	....	....	....
1935-36	Winnipeg Rangers	WJrHL	6	3	1	4	....	....	....	6	2	0	0	0	2
1936-37	Winnipeg Packers	WSrHL	11	1	1	2	....	....	....	12	3	1	1	2	0
	Winnipeg Packers	Al-Cup	3	0	0	0	....	....	....	2	....	....	....	....	....
1937-38	New York Rovers	EAHL	56	2	5	7	....	....	....	47	....	....	....	....	....
1938-39	New York Rovers	EAHL	51	6	14	20	....	....	....	59	....	....	....	....	....
	Philadelphia Ramblers	IAHL	2	0	0	0	....	....	....	0	9	0	1	1	2
1939-40	Philadelphia Rockets	IAHL	54	6	9	15	....	....	....	53	....	....	....	....	....
1940-41	**New York Rangers**	**NHL**	**1**	**0**	**1**	**1**	**0**	**1**	**1**	**0**	....	....	....	....	....
	Philadelphia Rockets	AHL	55	3	10	13	....	....	....	54	....	....	....	....	....
1941-42	Buffalo Bisons	AHL	56	2	11	13	....	....	....	53	....	....	....	....	....
	New Haven Eagles	AHL	....	....	....	....	....	....	....	....	2	1	0	1	2
1942-43	Buffalo Bisons	AHL	54	2	16	18	....	....	....	31	9	*5	2	7	2
1943-44	Winnipeg Navy	WNDHL	10	0	2	2	....	....	....	4	....	....	....	....	....
	Cornwallis Navy	NSDHL	1	0	1	1	....	....	....	....	....	....	....	....	....
	Cornwallis Navy	Al-Cup	6	2	0	2	....	....	....	6	....	....	....	....	....
1944-45	Winnipeg Navy	WNDHL	1	0	0	0	....	....	....	0	....	....	....	....	....
	Cornwallis Navy	NSDHL	10	0	4	4	....	....	....	0	....	....	....	....	....
1945-46	Buffalo Bisons	AHL	23	2	4	6	....	....	....	4	....	....	....	....	....
	St. Louis Flyers	AHL	35	3	9	12	....	....	....	6	....	....	....	....	....
1946-47	St. Louis Flyers	AHL	42	1	10	11	....	....	....	38	....	....	....	....	....
	Cleveland Barons	AHL	26	0	6	6	....	....	....	18	4	1	0	1	2
1947-48	Minneapolis Millers	USHL	63	0	13	13	....	....	....	34	10	0	1	1	2
1948-49	Owen Sound Mercurys	OHA-Sr.	DID NOT PLAY – COACHING												
1949-50	Owen Sound Mercurys	OHA-Sr.	42	3	12	15	....	....	....	47	....	....	....	....	....
1950-51	Owen Sound Mercurys	OHA-Sr.	DID NOT PLAY – COACHING												
	Owen Sound Mercurys	Al-Cup	16	1	4	5	....	....	....	11	....	....	....	....	....
1951-52	Owen Sound Mercurys	OHA-Sr.	48	9	18	27	....	....	....	35	12	1	9	10	6
1952-53	Owen Sound Mercurys	OHA-Sr.	46	5	23	28	....	....	....	30	11	2	4	6	4
	NHL Totals		**1**	**0**	**1**	**1**	**0**	**1**	**1**	**0**	....	....	....	....	....

EAHL First All-Star Team (1939) • USHL Second All-Star Team (1948)

Signed as a free agent by **NY Rangers**, October 12, 1937. Traded to **Buffalo** (AHL) by **NY Rangers** for cash, September 11, 1941.

• AMADIO, Dave — see page 841

• ANDERSON, Bill "Red"

D – R. 6', 190 lbs. b: Tillsonburg, Ont., 12/13/1912 Deceased.

Season	Club	League	GP	G	A	Pts	AG	AA	APts	PIM	GP	G	A	Pts	PIM
1933-34	Simcoe Travellers	OIHA	STATISTICS NOT AVAILABLE												
1934-35	London Tecumsehs	IHL	39	1	1	2	....	....	....	10	5	0	0	0	0
1935-36	London Tecumsehs	IHL	4	0	0	0	....	....	....	4	....	....	....	....	....
	Cleveland Falcons	IHL	16	1	1	2	....	....	....	15	2	0	0	0	0
	Pittsburgh Shamrocks	IHL	16	2	1	3	....	....	....	13	....	....	....	....	....
	Rochester Cardinals	IHL	8	0	1	1	....	....	....	17	....	....	....	....	....
1936-37	Cleveland Barons	IAHL	4	0	0	0	....	....	....	9	....	....	....	....	....
	Minneapolis Millers	AHA	15	1	0	1	....	....	....	23	....	....	....	....	....
	Pittsburgh Hornets	IAHL	15	1	1	2	....	....	....	12	5	0	0	0	2
1937-38	St. Paul Saints	AHA	34	4	8	12	....	....	....	72	....	....	....	....	....
1938-39	St. Paul Saints	AHA	48	6	9	15	....	....	....	85	3	0	1	1	10
1939-40	Tulsa Oilers	AHA	48	3	19	22	....	....	....	91	....	....	....	....	....
1940-41	Tulsa Oilers	AHA	14	0	0	0	....	....	....	22	....	....	....	....	....
	Detroit Holtzbaugh	MOHL	20	3	5	8	....	....	....	11	7	0	1	1	2
1941-42	Johnstown Bluebirds	EAHL	59	10	32	42	....	....	....	100	4	1	1	2	6
1942-43	Boston Olympics	EAHL	37	5	10	15	....	....	....	54	8	2	1	3	8
	Boston Bruins	**NHL**	....	....	....	....	....	....	....	....	**1**	**0**	**0**	**0**	**0**
	NHL Totals		....	....	....	....	....	....	....	....	**1**	**0**	**0**	**0**	**0**

EAHL First All-Star Team (1942)

Traded to **Cleveland** (IHL) by **London** (IHL) with Al Groh for Patsy Callighen, November 22, 1935. Loaned to **Pittsburgh** (IHL) by **Cleveland** (IHL), December 5, 1935. Recalled by **Cleveland** (IHL) on January 17, 1936 and loaned to **Rochester** (IHL), January 24, 1936. Recalled by **Cleveland** (IHL) from **Rochester** (IHL) for return of Harvey Rockburn, February 16, 1936.

• ANDERSON, Dale Dale Norman

D – L. 6'3", 190 lbs. b: Regina, Sask., 3/5/1932.

Season	Club	League	GP	G	A	Pts	AG	AA	APts	PIM	GP	G	A	Pts	PIM
1950-51	Prince Albert Mintos	SJHL	36	6	7	13	....	....	....	*129	6	0	4	4	*16
	Prince Albert Mintos	M-Cup	5	0	1	1	....	....	....	27	....	....	....	....	....
1951-52	Prince Albert Mintos	SJHL	49	13	38	51	....	....	....	217	5	3	4	7	24
1952-53	Vancouver Canucks	WHL	3	0	3	3	....	....	....	8	....	....	....	....	....
	Nelson Maple Leafs	WIHL	29	3	9	12	....	....	....	71	3	0	0	0	6
1953-54	Saskatoon Quakers	WHL	3	1	1	2	....	....	....	6	....	....	....	....	....
	Moose Jaw Millers	SSHL	33	3	20	23	....	....	....	*115	8	0	1	1	29
1954-55	Saskatoon Quakers	WHL	12	1	3	4	....	....	....	29	....	....	....	....	....
	Sault Ste. Marie Indians	NOHA	30	2	7	9	....	....	....	64	7	1	2	3	14
1955-56	Sault Ste. Marie Indians	NOHA	59	11	17	28	....	....	....	*184	7	0	5	5	26
1956-57	**Detroit Red Wings**	**NHL**	**13**	**0**	**0**	**0**	**0**	**0**	**0**	**6**	**2**	**0**	**0**	**0**	**0**
	Springfield Indians	AHL	40	4	16	20	....	....	....	121	....	....	....	....	....
1957-58	Springfield Indians	AHL	70	4	18	22	....	....	....	99	13	1	2	3	18

Season	Club	League	GP	G	A	Pts	AG	AA	APts	PIM	GP	G	A	Pts	PIM
			REGULAR SEASON								PLAYOFFS				
1958-59	Springfield Indians	AHL	18	2	4	6	....	....	....	36	....	....	....	....	....
1959-60	Vancouver Canucks	WHL	52	2	28	30	....	....	....	63	11	2	8	10	16
1960-61	Vancouver Canucks	WHL	61	1	17	18	....	....	....	105	9	0	0	0	10
1961-62	Vancouver Canucks	WHL	25	0	12	12	....	....	....	45	....	....	....	....	....
1962-63	Springfield Indians	AHL	52	3	5	8	....	....	....	42	....	....	....	....	....
1963-64	Vancouver Canucks	WHL	70	5	20	25	....	....	....	76	....	....	....	....	....
1964-65			REINSTATED AS AN AMATEUR												
1965-66	Saskatoon Quakers	SSHL	30	12	32	44	....	....	....	53	11	2	9	11	22
1966-67	Saskatoon Quakers	SSHL	33	17	22	39	....	....	....	45	14	3	9	12	*36
	Portland Buckaroos	WHL	....	....	....	....	....	....	....	....	1	0	0	0	0
1967-68	Saskatoon Quakers	SSHL	....	3	12	15	....	....	....	51	....	2	6	8	8
	NHL Totals		**13**	**0**	**0**	**0**	**0**	**0**	**0**	**6**	**2**	**0**	**0**	**0**	**0**

SJHL First All-Star Team (1952) • SSHL First All-Star Team (1964)

• ANDERSON, Doug Douglas "Andy"

C – L. 5'7", 157 lbs. b: Edmonton, Alta., 10/20/1927.

Season	Club	League	GP	G	A	Pts	AG	AA	APts	PIM	GP	G	A	Pts	PIM
1945-46	Edmonton Canadians	EJrHL	STATISTICS NOT AVAILABLE												
	Edmonton Canadians	M-Cup	10	3	4	7	....	....	....	0	....	....	....	....	....
1946-47	Edmonton Canadians	EJrHL	6	4	4	8	....	....	....	2	....	....	....	....	....
1947-48	Edmonton Flyers	WCSHL	40	15	35	50	....	....	....	10	10	5	10	*15	4
	Edmonton Flyers	Al-Cup	14	6	*19	25	....	....	....	2	....	....	....	....	....
1948-49	Edmonton Flyers	WCSHL	40	16	31	47	....	....	....	20	9	2	2	4	6
1949-50	Edmonton Flyers	WCSHL	45	18	44	62	....	....	....	28	6	1	5	6	7
1950-51	Edmonton Flyers	WCMHL	51	16	30	46	....	....	....	20	7	1	5	6	0
1951-52	Victoria Cougars	PCHL	67	14	33	47	....	....	....	10	13	4	4	8	10
1952-53	Victoria Cougars	WHL	70	18	50	68	....	....	....	14	....	....	....	....	....
♦	**Montreal Canadiens**	**NHL**	....	....	....	....	....	....	....	....	**2**	**0**	**0**	**0**	**0**
1953-54	Buffalo Bisons	AHL	7	0	2	2	....	....	....	4	....	....	....	....	....
	Victoria Cougars	WHL	60	7	15	22	....	....	....	10	....	....	....	....	....
1954-55	Victoria Cougars	WHL	51	15	28	43	....	....	....	4	3	0	0	0	0
1955-56	Victoria Cougars	WHL	62	23	40	63	....	....	....	24	9	3	2	5	4
1956-57	Victoria Cougars	WHL	70	22	42	64	....	....	....	22	3	1	0	1	0
1957-58	Victoria Cougars	WHL	26	4	9	13	....	....	....	2	....	....	....	....	....
1958-59	Victoria Cougars	WHL	67	16	32	48	....	....	....	12	3	0	2	2	0
1959-60	Victoria Cougars	WHL	70	10	22	32	....	....	....	2	11	2	2	4	0
1960-61	Victoria Cougars	WHL	70	6	30	36	....	....	....	12	5	1	4	5	0
1961-62	Portland Buckaroos	WHL	54	4	22	26	....	....	....	2	7	1	2	3	7
1962-63	Portland Buckaroos	WHL	60	5	6	11	....	....	....	0	....	....	....	....	....
	NHL Totals		....	....	....	....	....	....	....	....	**2**	**0**	**0**	**0**	**0**

• ANDERSON, Tom Thomas Linton "Cowboy"

LW/D – L. 5'10", 180 lbs. b: Edinburgh, Scotland, 7/9/1910 d: 9/15/1971.

Season	Club	League	GP	G	A	Pts	AG	AA	APts	PIM	GP	G	A	Pts	PIM
1929-30	Drumheller Miners	ASHL	16	6	3	9	....	....	....	18	2	0	0	0	0
1930-31	Philadelphia Arrows	Can-Am	38	7	8	15	....	....	....	89	....	....	....	....	....
1931-32	Philadelphia Arrows	Can-Am	25	5	6	11	....	....	....	36	....	....	....	....	....
1932-33	Philadelphia Arrows	Can-Am	45	11	24	35	....	....	....	49	5	2	*4	6	5
1933-34	Philadelphia Arrows	Can-Am	40	20	25	45	....	....	....	46	2	0	2	2	4
1934-35	**Detroit Red Wings**	**NHL**	**27**	**5**	**2**	**7**	**8**	**3**	**11**	**16**	....	....	....	....	....
	Detroit Olympics	IHL	15	5	8	13	....	....	....	14	5	1	0	1	2
	Detroit Olympics	L-W-S	5	1	1	2	....	....	....	18	....	....	....	....	....
1935-36	**New York Americans**	**NHL**	**24**	**3**	**2**	**5**	**6**	**4**	**10**	**20**	**5**	**0**	**0**	**0**	**6**
1936-37	**New York Americans**	**NHL**	**45**	**10**	**15**	**25**	**17**	**28**	**45**	**24**	....	....	....	....	....
	Cleveland Falcons	IAHL	4	1	1	2	....	....	....	17	....	....	....	....	....
1937-38	**New York Americans**	**NHL**	**45**	**4**	**21**	**25**	**6**	**34**	**40**	**22**	**6**	**1**	**4**	**5**	**2**
	New Haven Eagles	IAHL	6	0	0	0	....	....	....	15	....	....	....	....	....
1938-39	**New York Americans**	**NHL**	**47**	**13**	**27**	**40**	**23**	**43**	**66**	**14**	**2**	**0**	**0**	**0**	**0**
1939-40	**New York Americans**	**NHL**	**48**	**12**	**19**	**31**	**20**	**30**	**50**	**22**	**3**	**1**	**3**	**4**	**0**
1940-41	**New York Americans**	**NHL**	**35**	**3**	**12**	**15**	**5**	**17**	**22**	**8**	....	....	....	....	....
1941-42	**Brooklyn Americans**	**NHL**	**48**	**12**	**29**	**41**	**16**	**35**	**51**	**54**	....	....	....	....	....
1942-43	Calgary Currie Army	CNDHL	16	5	11	16	....	....	....	26	5	0	4	4	6
	Calgary Currie Army	Al-Cup	5	0	2	2	....	....	....	10	....	....	....	....	....
1943-44	Calgary Currie Army	CNDHL	16	2	6	8	....	....	....	21	2	0	2	2	2
1944-45	Calgary Currie Army	CNDHL	11	1	3	4	....	....	....	32	3	0	0	0	8
1945-46	Providence Reds	AHL	47	3	17	20	....	....	....	12	2	1	0	1	0
1946-47	Hollywood Wolves	PCHL	60	9	22	31	....	....	....	42	7	2	1	3	6
	NHL Totals		**319**	**62**	**127**	**189**	**101**	**194**	**295**	**180**	**16**	**2**	**7**	**9**	**8**

NHL First All-Star Team (1942) • Won Hart Trophy (1942) • CNDHL First All-Star Team (1943) • CNDHL Second All-Star Team (1944) • Played in NHL All-Star Game (1939)

Traded to **Detroit** by **Philadelphia** (Can-Am) with Irwin Boyd for cash, May 8, 1934. Traded to **NY Americans** by **Detroit** for cash, October 11, 1935. Rights transferred to **Chicago** from **Brooklyn** in Special Dispersal Draw, September 11, 1943.

• ANDREA, Paul — see page 848

• ANDREWS, Lloyd Lloyd Thomas "Shrimp"

LW – L., b: Tillsonburg, Ont., 1899 Deceased.

Season	Club	League	GP	G	A	Pts	AG	AA	APts	PIM	GP	G	A	Pts	PIM
1914/17	Dunville Mudcats	OIHA	STATISTICS NOT AVAILABLE												
1917-18			MILITARY SERVICE												
1918/21	Niagara Falls Cataracts	OHA-Sr.	STATISTICS NOT AVAILABLE												
1921-22	**Toronto St. Pats**	**NHL**	**11**	**0**	**0**	**0**	**0**	**0**	**0**	**0**	**2**	**0**	**0**	**0**	**0**
♦	Toronto St. Pats	St-Cup	5	2	0	2	....	....	....	3	....	....	....	....	....
1922-23	**Toronto St. Pats**	**NHL**	**23**	**5**	**4**	**9**	**8**	**15**	**23**	**10**	....	....	....	....	....
1923-24	**Toronto St. Pats**	**NHL**	**12**	**2**	**1**	**3**	**4**	**6**	**10**	**0**	....	....	....	....	....
1924-25	**Toronto St. Pats**	**NHL**	**7**	**1**	**0**	**1**	**2**	**0**	**2**	**0**	....	....	....	....	....
1925-26			DID NOT PLAY												
1926-27	New Haven Eagles	Can-Am	32	17	*11	28	....	....	....	11	4	*4	0	*4	4
1927-28	New Haven Eagles	Can-Am	39	15	9	24	....	....	....	25	....	....	....	....	....
1928-29	Philadelphia Arrows	Can-Am	39	10	4	14	....	....	....	12	....	....	....	....	....
1929-30	Philadelphia Arrows	Can-Am	40	24	19	43	....	....	....	30	2	1	0	1	2
1930-31	Philadelphia Arrows	Can-Am	40	15	14	29	....	....	....	24	....	....	....	....	....
1931-32	Philadelphia Arrows	Can-Am	39	8	15	23	....	....	....	16	....	....	....	....	....
1932-33	St. Paul-Tulsa	AHA	12	1	4	5	....	....	....	2	....	....	....	....	....
	Hibbing Maroons	CHL	34	13	16	29	....	....	....	10	....	....	....	....	....
1933-34	Hibbing Miners	CHL	43	18	16	34	....	....	....	28	6	*3	1	4	0
	NHL Totals		**53**	**8**	**5**	**13**	**14**	**21**	**35**	**10**	**2**	**0**	**0**	**0**	**0**

Signed as a free agent by **Toronto St. Pats**, January 23, 1922.

• ANGOTTI, Lou — see page 849

• ANSLOW, Hub Hubert Wallace

C – L. 6', 173 lbs. b: Pembroke, Ont., 3/23/1926.

Season	Club	League	GP	G	A	Pts	AG	AA	APts	PIM	GP	G	A	Pts	PIM
1939-40	Pembroke Lumber Kings	UOVHL	....	....	....	....	....	....	....	....	4	5	0	5	....
1940-41	Pembroke Dairy	UOVHL	4	4	0	4	....	....	....	....	....	....	....	....	....
1941-42	Pembroke Maple Leafs	UOVHL	....	....	....	....	....	....	....	....	5	6	1	7	....
1942-43	Pembroke All-Stars	UOVHL	....	....	....	....	....	....	....	....	3	4	0	4	....
1943-44	Pembroke All-Stars	UOVHL	....	....	....	....	....	....	....	....	5	7	4	11	....
1944-45			MILITARY SERVICE												
1945-46	Pembroke Lumber Kings	UOVHL	17	31	14	45	....	....	....	27	3	6	*6	12	2
	Pembroke Lumber Kings	Al-Cup	9	7	12	19	....	....	....	4	....	....	....	....	....
1946-47	New York Rovers	EAHL	49	24	13	37	....	....	....	36	9	1	1	2	5
1947-48	**New York Rangers**	**NHL**	**2**	**0**	**0**	**0**	**0**	**0**	**0**	**0**	....	....	....	....	....
	New Haven Ramblers	AHL	3	0	0	0	....	....	....	0	....	....	....	....	....
	New York Rovers	EAHL	16	17	15	32	....	....	....	32	....	....	....	....	....
	New York Rovers	QSHL	44	22	25	47	....	....	....	49	3	1	4	5	4
1948-49	Tacoma Rockets	PCHL	66	18	42	60	....	....	....	58	4	0	1	1	0
1949-50	St. Paul Saints	USHL	55	24	24	48	....	....	....	58	....	....	....	....	....
	New Haven Ramblers	AHL	14	3	3	6	....	....	....	6	....	....	....	....	....
1950-51	Kansas City Royals	USHL	26	5	8	13	....	....	....	18	....	....	....	....	....
	Calgary Stampeders	WCMHL	16	6	11	17	....	....	....	6	....	....	....	....	....
1951-52	Pembroke Lumber Kings	UOVHL	43	32	42	74	....	....	....	26	11	*9	7	*16	6
	Pembroke Lumber Kings	Al-Cup	13	9	3	12	....	....	....	10	....	....	....	....	....
1952-53	Pembroke Lumber Kings	UOVHL	35	22	32	54	....	....	....	32	1	0	1	1	0
1953-54	Hamilton Tigers	OHA-Sr.	42	17	15	32	....	....	....	56	....	....	....	....	....
1954-55	Pembroke Lumber Kings	UOVHL	48	10	19	29	....	....	....	10	6	0	1	1	4
1955-56	Petawawa Army	UOVHL	5	0	5	5	....	....	....	....	4	0	3	3	....
1956-57			DID NOT PLAY												
1957-58			DID NOT PLAY												
1958-59	Deep River Diggers	UOVHL	12	3	3	6	....	....	....	....	7	8	4	12	....
1959-60	Pembroke Cleaners	UOVHL	5	2	2	4	....	....	....	0	2	1	1	2	2
	NHL Totals		**2**	**0**	**0**	**0**	**0**	**0**	**0**	**0**	....	....	....	....	....

• APPS Sr., Syl Charles Joseph Svylvanus HHOF

C – L. 6', 185 lbs. b: Paris, Ont., 1/18/1915 d: 12/24/1998.

Season	Club	League	GP	G	A	Pts	AG	AA	APts	PIM	GP	G	A	Pts	PIM
1930-31	Paris Greens	OHA-Jr.	7	5	1	6	....	....	....	0	....	....	....	....	....
1931/35	McMaster University	OHA-Sr.	STATISTICS NOT AVAILABLE												
1935-36	Hamilton Tigers	OHA-Sr.	19	22	16	*38	....	....	....	10	9	12	*7	*19	4
	Toronto Dominions	OHA-Sr.	1	0	1	1	....	....	....	0	....	....	....	....	....
	Hamilton Tigers	Al-Cup	4	5	4	9	....	....	....	2	....	....	....	....	....
1936-37	**Toronto Maple Leafs**	**NHL**	**48**	**16**	***29**	**45**	**27**	**54**	**81**	**10**	**2**	**0**	**1**	**1**	**0**
1937-38	**Toronto Maple Leafs**	**NHL**	**47**	**21**	***29**	**50**	**35**	**47**	**82**	**9**	**7**	**1**	**4**	**5**	**0**
1938-39	**Toronto Maple Leafs**	**NHL**	**44**	**15**	**25**	**40**	**26**	**39**	**65**	**4**	**10**	**2**	**6**	**8**	**2**
1939-40	**Toronto Maple Leafs**	**NHL**	**27**	**13**	**17**	**30**	**22**	**27**	**49**	**5**	**10**	***5**	**2**	**7**	**2**
1940-41	**Toronto Maple Leafs**	**NHL**	**41**	**20**	**24**	**44**	**31**	**35**	**66**	**6**	**7**	**3**	**2**	**5**	**2**
♦1941-42	**Toronto Maple Leafs**	**NHL**	**38**	**18**	**23**	**41**	**24**	**27**	**51**	**0**	**13**	**5**	***9**	***14**	**2**
1942-43	**Toronto Maple Leafs**	**NHL**	**29**	**23**	**17**	**40**	**24**	**16**	**40**	**2**	....	....	....	....	....
1943-44	Toronto Army Daggers	OHA-Sr.	1	1	2	3	....	....	....	0	....	....	....	....	....
1944-45	Ottawa All-Stars	ONDHL	1	6	1	7	....	....	....	0	....	....	....	....	....
	Brockville Army	ONDHL	STATISTICS NOT AVAILABLE												
1945-46	**Toronto Maple Leafs**	**NHL**	**40**	**24**	**16**	**40**	**29**	**23**	**52**	**2**	....	....	....	....	....
♦1946-47	**Toronto Maple Leafs**	**NHL**	**54**	**25**	**24**	**49**	**28**	**29**	**57**	**6**	**11**	**5**	**1**	**6**	**0**
♦1947-48	**Toronto Maple Leafs**	**NHL**	**55**	**26**	**27**	**53**	**34**	**36**	**70**	**12**	**9**	**4**	**4**	**8**	**0**
	NHL Totals		**423**	**201**	**231**	**432**	**280**	**333**	**613**	**56**	**69**	**25**	**29**	**54**	**8**

• Father of Syl Jr. • Won Calder Trophy (1937) • NHL Second All-Star Team (1938, 1941, 1943) • NHL First All-Star Team (1939, 1942) • Won Lady Byng Trophy (1942) • Played in NHL All-Star Game (1939, 1947)

• Missed majority of 1942-43 season recovering from leg injury suffered in game vs. Boston, January 30, 1943.

• ARBOUR, Al — see page 851

• ARBOUR, Amos "Butch"

LW – L. 5'8", 160 lbs. b: Victoria Harbour, Ont., d: 11/4/1943.

Season	Club	League	GP	G	A	Pts	AG	AA	APts	PIM	GP	G	A	Pts	PIM
1914-15	Victoria Harbour Station	OHA-Jr.	STATISTICS NOT AVAILABLE												
♦1915-16	Montreal Canadiens	NHA	20	5	0	5	....	....	....	6	4	3	0	3	11
1916-17	Toronto 228th Battalion	NHA	10	14	3	17	....	....	....	6	....	....	....	....	....
1917-18			MILITARY SERVICE												
1918-19	**Montreal Canadiens**	**NHL**	**1**	**0**	**0**	**0**	**0**	**0**	**0**	**0**	....	....	....	....	....
1919-20	**Montreal Canadiens**	**NHL**	**22**	**21**	**5**	**26**	**24**	**17**	**41**	**13**	....	....	....	....	....
1920-21	**Montreal Canadiens**	**NHL**	**23**	**15**	**3**	**18**	**19**	**11**	**30**	**40**	....	....	....	....	....
1921-22	**Hamilton Tigers**	**NHL**	**23**	**9**	**6**	**15**	**12**	**19**	**31**	**8**	....	....	....	....	....
1922-23	**Hamilton Tigers**	**NHL**	**23**	**6**	**3**	**9**	**10**	**11**	**21**	**12**	....	....	....	....	....
1923-24	**Toronto St. Pats**	**NHL**	**21**	**1**	**3**	**4**	**2**	**17**	**19**	**4**	....	....	....	....	....
	NHL Totals		**113**	**52**	**20**	**72**	**67**	**75**	**142**	**77**	....	....	....	....	....
	Other Major League Totals		30	19	3	22	....	....	....	12	4	3	0	3	11

Signed as a free agent by **Montreal Canadiens**, January 23, 1919. Traded to **Hamilton** by **Montreal Canadiens** with Harry Mummery for Sprague Cleghorn, November 26, 1921. Traded to **Toronto** by **Hamilton** with Bert Corbeau and George Carey for Ken Randall, the NHL rights to Corb Denneny and cash, December 14, 1923.

• ARBOUR, Jack John Albert

D – L. 5'8", 172 lbs. b: Waubaushene, Ont., 3/7/1899 Deceased.

Season	Club	League	GP	G	A	Pts	AG	AA	APts	PIM	GP	G	A	Pts	PIM
1919-20	Calgary Wanderers	Big-4	12	3	0	3	....	....	....	17	1	0	0	0	0
1920-21	Calgary Tigers	Big-4	15	2	3	5	....	....	....	15	....	....	....	....	....
1921-22	Calgary Tigers	WCHL	14	2	2	4	....	....	....	8	....	....	....	....	....
1922-23	Calgary Tigers	WCHL	5	0	1	1	....	....	....	2	....	....	....	....	....
1923-24	Seattle Metropolitans	PCHA	28	3	2	5	....	....	....	16	2	1	0	1	0
1924-25	Calgary Tigers	WCHL	3	0	0	0	....	....	....	0	....	....	....	....	....
1925-26			STATISTICS NOT AVAILABLE												
1926-27	**Detroit Cougars**	**NHL**	**37**	**4**	**1**	**5**	**7**	**5**	**12**	**46**	....	....	....	....	....
1927-28	Detroit Olympics	Can-Pro	42	12	6	18	....	....	....	77	2	0	0	0	2

			REGULAR SEASON								PLAYOFFS				
Season	Club	League	GP	G	A	Pts	AG	AA	APts	PIM	GP	G	A	Pts	PIM
1928-29	**Toronto Maple Leafs**	**NHL**	**10**	**1**	**0**	**1**	**3**	**0**	**3**	**10**	....	....	....	....	....
	London Panthers	Can-Pro	9	0	0	0	....	....	....	8	....	....	....	....	....
	Windsor Bulldogs	Can-Pro	30	7	3	10	....	....	....	33	8	0	0	0	18
1929-30	Windsor Bulldogs	IHL	41	8	5	13	....	....	....	57	....	....	....	....	....
1930-31	Windsor Bulldogs	IHL	46	7	16	23	....	....	....	34	6	3	1	4	*13
1931-32	Windsor Bulldogs	IHL	45	9	9	18	....	....	....	74	6	0	0	0	2
1932-33	Windsor Bulldogs	IHL	43	5	9	14	....	....	....	39	6	0	0	0	4
1933-34	Seattle Seahawks	NWHL	34	5	4	9	....	....	....	24	....	....	....	....	....
1934-35	Portland Buckaroos	NWHL	32	11	9	20	....	....	....	12	3	0	0	0	2
1935-36	Portland Buckaroos	PCHL	39	6	4	10	....	....	....	41	3	0	1	1	6
1936-37	Spokane Clippers	PCHL	13	1	2	3	....	....	....	12	....	....	....	....	....
1937-38	Spokane Clippers	PCHL	9	0	1	1	....	....	....	2	....	....	....	....	....
1938-39	Spokane Clippers	PCHL	2	0	0	0	....	....	....	0	....	....	....	....	....
	NHL Totals		**47**	**5**	**1**	**6**	**10**	**5**	**15**	**56**	....	....	....	....	....
	Other Major League Totals		50	5	5	10	....	....	....	26	2	1	0	1	0

• Brother of Ty

Signed as a free agent by **Calgary** (WCHL), November 4, 1921. Traded to **Seattle** (PCHA) by **Calgary** (WCHL) with Ed Fisher for cash, August 21, 1923. Signed as a free agent by **Calgary** (WCHL), January 1, 1925. Traded to **Detroit** by **Calgary** (WHL) for cash, October 27, 1926. Rights traded to **Toronto** by **Detroit** with $12,500 for Jimmy Herbert, April 8, 1928. Traded to **London** (Can-Pro) by **Toronto** for cash, December 12, 1928. Traded to **Windsor** (Can-Pro) by **London** (Can-Pro) for Mickey McGuire and cash, January 15, 1929.

• ARBOUR, John — see page 851

• ARBOUR, Ty Ernest J.

LW – L. 5'7", 160 lbs. b: Waubaushene, Ont., 6/29/1896 Deceased.

Season	Club	League	GP	G	A	Pts	AG	AA	APts	PIM	GP	G	A	Pts	PIM
1913/15	Waubaushene A.C.	OHA-Jr.	STATISTICS NOT AVAILABLE												
1915/18			MILITARY SERVICE												
1918-19	Port Arthur Pascoes	TBSHL	6	8	1	9	....	....	....	4	....	....	....	....	....
1919-20	Midland Aces	OHA-Sr.	STATISTICS NOT AVAILABLE												
1920-21	Brandon Elks	MHL-Sr.	12	11	4	15	....	....	....	4	....	....	....	....	....
	Brandon Elks	Al-Cup	5	8	4	12	....	....	....	2	....	....	....	....	....
1921-22	Edmonton Eskimos	WCHL	24	27	6	33	....	....	....	22	2	0	0	0	0
1922-23	Edmonton Eskimos	WCHL	30	18	9	27	....	....	....	10	2	0	1	1	0
	Edmonton Eskimos	St-Cup	2	0	0	0	....	....	....	0	....	....	....	....	....
1923-24	Edmonton Eskimos	WCHL	30	13	5	18	....	....	....	12	....	....	....	....	....
1924-25	Vancouver Maroons	WCHL	27	15	5	20	....	....	....	12	....	....	....	....	....
1925-26	Vancouver Maroons	WCHL	30	10	6	16	....	....	....	6	....	....	....	....	....
1926-27	**Pittsburgh Pirates**	**NHL**	**41**	**7**	**8**	**15**	**12**	**42**	**54**	**10**	....	....	....	....	....
1927-28	**Pittsburgh Pirates**	**NHL**	**7**	**0**	**0**	**0**	**0**	**0**	**0**	**0**	....	....	....	....	....
	Chicago Black Hawks	**NHL**	**32**	**5**	**5**	**10**	**10**	**28**	**38**	**32**	....	....	....	....	....
1928-29	**Chicago Black Hawks**	**NHL**	**44**	**3**	**4**	**7**	**9**	**27**	**36**	**32**	....	....	....	....	....
1929-30	**Chicago Black Hawks**	**NHL**	**42**	**10**	**8**	**18**	**14**	**19**	**33**	**26**	**2**	**1**	**0**	**1**	**0**
1930-31	**Chicago Black Hawks**	**NHL**	**41**	**3**	**3**	**6**	**6**	**9**	**15**	**12**	**9**	**1**	**0**	**1**	**6**
1931-32	Pittsburgh Yellowjackets	IHL	47	13	3	16	....	....	....	10	....	....	....	....	....
1932-33	Buffalo Bisons	IHL	17	2	1	3	....	....	....	4	....	....	....	....	....
1933-34	Edmonton Eskimos	NWHL	33	18	8	26	....	....	....	2	1	0	0	0	0
	NHL Totals		**207**	**28**	**28**	**56**	**51**	**125**	**176**	**112**	**11**	**2**	**0**	**2**	**6**
	Other Major League Totals		111	73	25	98	....	....	....	56	4	0	1	1	0

• Brother of Jack • WCHL 2nd All-Star Team (1922)

Signed as a free agent by **Edmonton** (WCHL), November 23, 1921. Traded to **Vancouver** (WCHL) by **Edmonton** (WCHL) for cash, November 10, 1924. Traded to **Pittsburgh** by **Vancouver** (WHL) for cash, October 9, 1926. Traded to **Chicago** by **Pittsburgh** to complete three-team transaction that sent Bert McCaffrey to Pittsburgh and Ed Rodden to Toronto, December, 1927. Traded to **Pittsburgh** (IAHL) by **Chicago** for cash, October 21, 1931.

• ARMSTRONG, Bob Robert Richard

D – R. 6'1", 190 lbs. b: Toronto, Ont., 4/7/1931 d: 11/6/1990.

Season	Club	League	GP	G	A	Pts	AG	AA	APts	PIM	GP	G	A	Pts	PIM
1948-49	Stratford Kroehlers	OHA-Jr.	37	6	5	11	....	....	....	33	3	0	1	1	2
1949-50	Stratford Kroehlers	OHA-Jr.	46	10	12	22	....	....	....	50	....	....	....	....	....
1950-51	Stratford Kroehlers	OHA-Jr.	52	13	16	29	....	....	....	87	3	2	1	3	9
	Boston Bruins	**NHL**	**2**	**0**	**0**	**0**	**0**	**0**	**0**	**2**	....	....	....	....	....
1951-52	Hershey Bears	AHL	67	6	15	21	....	....	....	61	5	0	0	0	4
	Boston Bruins	**NHL**	....	....	....	....	....	....	....	....	**5**	**0**	**0**	**0**	**2**
1952-53	**Boston Bruins**	**NHL**	**55**	**0**	**8**	**8**	**0**	**10**	**10**	**45**	**11**	**1**	**1**	**2**	**10**
1953-54	**Boston Bruins**	**NHL**	**64**	**2**	**10**	**12**	**3**	**12**	**15**	**81**	**4**	**0**	**1**	**1**	**0**
1954-55	**Boston Bruins**	**NHL**	**57**	**1**	**3**	**4**	**1**	**3**	**4**	**38**	**5**	**0**	**0**	**0**	**2**
1955-56	**Boston Bruins**	**NHL**	**68**	**0**	**12**	**12**	**0**	**14**	**14**	**122**	....	....	....	....	....
1956-57	**Boston Bruins**	**NHL**	**57**	**1**	**15**	**16**	**1**	**16**	**17**	**79**	**10**	**0**	**3**	**3**	**10**
1957-58	**Boston Bruins**	**NHL**	**47**	**1**	**4**	**5**	**1**	**4**	**5**	**66**	....	....	....	....	....
	Springfield Indians	AHL	26	5	11	16	....	....	....	37	13	5	8	13	*31
1958-59	**Boston Bruins**	**NHL**	**60**	**1**	**9**	**10**	**1**	**9**	**10**	**50**	**7**	**0**	**2**	**2**	**4**
1959-60	**Boston Bruins**	**NHL**	**69**	**5**	**14**	**19**	**6**	**14**	**20**	**96**	....	....	....	....	....
1960-61	**Boston Bruins**	**NHL**	**54**	**0**	**10**	**10**	**0**	**10**	**10**	**72**	....	....	....	....	....
1961-62	**Boston Bruins**	**NHL**	**9**	**2**	**1**	**3**	**2**	**1**	**3**	**20**	....	....	....	....	....
	Hull-Ottawa Canadiens	EPHL	61	6	28	34	....	....	....	116	13	1	3	4	10
1962-63	Rochester Americans	AHL	70	1	28	29	....	....	....	89	2	1	0	1	4
	NHL Totals		**542**	**13**	**86**	**99**	**15**	**93**	**108**	**671**	**42**	**1**	**7**	**8**	**28**

Played in NHL All-Star Game (1960)

Loaned to **Montreal** (Hull-Ottawa-EPHL) by **Boston** with the loan of Dallas Smith and cash for Wayne Connelly, October 26, 1961.

• ARMSTRONG, George — see page 853

• ARMSTRONG, Murray Murray Alexander

C – L. 5'10", 170 lbs. b: Manor, Sask., 1/1/1916.

Season	Club	League	GP	G	A	Pts	AG	AA	APts	PIM	GP	G	A	Pts	PIM
1931-32	Regina Pats	S-SJHL	3	1	0	1	....	....	....	0	2	1	1	2	0
	Regina Pats	M-Cup	1	0	0	0	....	....	....	0	....	....	....	....	....
1932-33	Regina Pats	S-SJHL	3	0	0	0	....	....	....	7	2	0	0	0	10
	Regina Pats	M-Cup	13	9	2	11	....	....	....	29	....	....	....	....	....
1933-34	Regina Pats	S-SJHL	2	4	2	6	....	....	....	0	....	....	....	....	....
	Regina Pats	M-Cup	4	2	1	3	....	....	....	4	....	....	....	....	....
1934-35	Regina Vics	S-SSHL	22	9	6	15	....	....	....	15	6	2	1	3	2
1935-36	New York Rovers	EAHL	32	15	23	38	....	....	....	18	7	1	2	3	0
1936-37	Syracuse Stars	IAHL	43	14	21	35	....	....	....	8	8	*4	*6	*10	6
1937-38	**Toronto Maple Leafs**	**NHL**	**9**	**0**	**0**	**0**	**0**	**0**	**0**	**0**	**3**	**0**	**0**	**0**	**0**
	Syracuse Stars	IAHL	35	7	31	38	....	....	....	10	5	3	1	4	0
1938-39	**Toronto Maple Leafs**	**NHL**	**3**	**0**	**1**	**1**	**0**	**2**	**2**	**0**	....	....	....	....	....
	Syracuse Stars	IAHL	50	27	27	54	....	....	....	10	3	1	1	2	0
1939-40	**New York Americans**	**NHL**	**47**	**16**	**20**	**36**	**27**	**32**	**59**	**12**	**3**	**0**	**0**	**0**	**0**
1940-41	**New York Americans**	**NHL**	**48**	**10**	**14**	**24**	**15**	**20**	**35**	**6**	....	....	....	....	....
1941-42	**Brooklyn Americans**	**NHL**	**45**	**6**	**22**	**28**	**8**	**26**	**34**	**15**	....	....	....	....	....
1942-43	Regina Army Caps	RNDHL	24	29	32	61	....	....	....	36	5	5	*12	*17	4
	Regina Army Caps	Al-Cup	4	1	5	6	....	....	....	4	....	....	....	....	....
1943-44	**Detroit Red Wings**	**NHL**	**28**	**12**	**22**	**34**	**11**	**19**	**30**	**4**	**5**	**0**	**2**	**2**	**0**
1944-45	**Detroit Red Wings**	**NHL**	**50**	**15**	**24**	**39**	**15**	**28**	**43**	**31**	**14**	**4**	**2**	**6**	**2**
1945-46	**Detroit Red Wings**	**NHL**	**40**	**8**	**18**	**26**	**9**	**26**	**35**	**4**	**5**	**0**	**2**	**2**	**0**
1946-47	Buffalo Bisons	AHL	19	10	8	18	....	....	....	4	....	....	....	....	....
	Dallas Texans	USHL	42	15	31	46	....	....	....	10	6	0	3	3	0
1947-48	Regina Pats	SJHL	DID NOT PLAY – COACHING												
	NHL Totals		**270**	**67**	**121**	**188**	**85**	**153**	**238**	**72**	**30**	**4**	**6**	**10**	**2**

EAHL Second All-Star Team (1936) • Won Herman W. Paterson Cup (USHL - MVP) (1947) • Won Lester Patrick Trophy (1977)

Claimed by **Toronto** from **NY Rangers** (Philadelphia-Can-Am) in Inter-League Draft, May 7, 1936. Traded to **NY Americans** by **Toronto** with Buzz Boll, Busher Jackson, Jimmy Fowler and Doc Romnes for Sweeney Schriner, May 18, 1939. Rights transferred to **Detroit** from **Brooklyn** in Special Dispersal Draw, September 11, 1943.

• ARMSTRONG, Norm Norman Gerrard "Red"

D – L. 5'11", 205 lbs. b: Owen Sound, Ont., 10/17/1938 d: 7/23/1974.

Season	Club	League	GP	G	A	Pts	AG	AA	APts	PIM	GP	G	A	Pts	PIM
1958-59	Sarnia Legionaires	OHA-B	45	21	25	46	....	....	....	....	....	....	....	....	....
1959-60	Wallaceburg Hornets	OHA-Sr.	36	3	13	16	....	....	....	....	....	....	....	....	....
1960-61	Charlotte Checkers	EHL	64	8	13	21	....	....	....	192	....	....	....	....	....
1961-62	Charlotte Checkers	EHL	2	0	1	1	....	....	....	2	....	....	....	....	....
	Philadelphia Ramblers	EHL	66	17	30	47	....	....	....	212	3	0	1	1	6
1962-63	**Toronto Maple Leafs**	**NHL**	**7**	**1**	**1**	**2**	**1**	**1**	**2**	**2**	....	....	....	....	....
	Rochester Americans	AHL	18	1	6	7	....	....	....	30	....	....	....	....	....
	Sudbury Wolves	EPHL	44	14	23	37	....	....	....	144	8	2	3	5	21
1963-64	Rochester Americans	AHL	67	17	13	30	....	....	....	112	2	0	1	1	4
1964-65	Rochester Americans	AHL	70	32	14	46	....	....	....	123	10	2	3	5	17
1965-66	Rochester Americans	AHL	67	14	26	40	....	....	....	146	12	0	0	0	12
1966-67	Tulsa Oilers	CPHL	11	2	5	7	....	....	....	8	....	....	....	....	....
	Rochester Americans	AHL	57	13	34	47	....	....	....	77	....	....	....	....	....
1967-68	Rochester Americans	AHL	54	13	25	38	....	....	....	112	1	0	0	0	6
1968-69	Rochester Americans	AHL	74	29	40	69	....	....	....	133	....	....	....	....	....
1969-70	Rochester Americans	AHL	70	30	45	75	....	....	....	117	....	....	....	....	....
1970-71	Rochester Americans	AHL	44	13	17	30	....	....	....	101	....	....	....	....	....
	Springfield Kings	AHL	10	0	16	16	....	....	....	15	3	0	0	0	6
1971-72	Baltimore Clippers	AHL	68	9	15	24	....	....	....	61	18	2	2	4	19
1972-73	Rochester Americans	AHL	45	4	5	9	....	....	....	22	5	0	1	1	2
	NHL Totals		**7**	**1**	**1**	**2**	**1**	**1**	**2**	**2**	....	....	....	....	....

Traded to **LA Kings** (Springfield-AHL) by **Toronto** for Don Westbrooke, February, 1971. Claimed by **Baltimore** (AHL) from **LA Kings** in Reverse Draft, June 8, 1971. • Died of injuries suffered in industrial accident, July 23, 1974.

• ARUNDEL, John John O'Gorman

D – L. 5'11", 181 lbs. b: Winnipeg, Man., 11/4/1927.

Season	Club	League	GP	G	A	Pts	AG	AA	APts	PIM	GP	G	A	Pts	PIM
1944-45	St. Michael's Majors	OHA-Jr.	10	3	5	8	....	....	....	10	....	....	....	....	....
	St. Michael's Majors	M-Cup	1	0	1	1	....	....	....	0	....	....	....	....	....
1945-46	Oshawa Generals	OHA-Jr.	27	10	8	18	....	....	....	7	12	2	8	10	6
1946-47	Winnipeg Monarchs	MJHL	13	8	9	17	....	....	....	8	7	5	2	7	8
1947-48	Winnipeg Monarchs	MJHL	23	23	26	49	....	....	....	8	11	*13	8	*21	4
	Winnipeg Monarchs	M-Cup	6	2	3	5	....	....	....	0	....	....	....	....	....
1948-49	Sydney Millionaires	CBSHL	60	12	29	41	....	....	....	66	6	0	0	0	0
	Sydney Millionaires	Al-Cup	16	4	6	10	....	....	....	14	....	....	....	....	....
1949-50	**Toronto Maple Leafs**	**NHL**	**3**	**0**	**0**	**0**	**0**	**0**	**0**	**9**	....	....	....	....	....
	Pittsburgh Hornets	AHL	34	0	8	8	....	....	....	17	....	....	....	....	....
	Los Angeles Monarchs	PCHL	32	3	10	13	....	....	....	17	17	1	7	8	28
1950-51	St. Michael's Monarchs	OMHL	29	6	9	15	....	....	....	36	9	1	2	3	14
	St. Michael's Monarchs	Alx-Cup	6	0	1	1	....	....	....	14	....	....	....	....	....
1951-52	Saint John Beavers	MMHL	85	10	21	31	....	....	....	143	10	1	6	7	14
	Saint John Beavers	Alx-Cup	5	0	0	0	....	....	....	12	....	....	....	....	....
1952-53	Ottawa Senators	QMHL	55	5	14	19	....	....	....	87	11	2	5	7	6
1953-54	Ottawa Senators	QHL	58	4	4	8	....	....	....	44	22	3	4	7	18
1954-55	Ottawa Senators	QHL	25	1	5	6	....	....	....	18	....	....	....	....	....
	Sudbury Wolves	NOHA	21	2	7	9	....	....	....	2	....	....	....	....	....
	NHL Totals		**3**	**0**	**0**	**0**	**0**	**0**	**0**	**9**	....	....	....	....	....

MJHL First All-Star Team (1948)

• ASHBEE, Barry — see page 855

• ASHWORTH, Frank

C – L. 5'8", 155 lbs. b: Moose Jaw, Sask., 10/16/1927.

Season	Club	League	GP	G	A	Pts	AG	AA	APts	PIM	GP	G	A	Pts	PIM
1943-44	New York Rovers	EAHL	17	10	1	11	....	....	....	16	....	....	....	....	....
	Brooklyn Crescents	EAHL	30	15	19	34	....	....	....	7	11	3	6	9	10
1944-45	Moose Jaw Canucks	SJHL	16	*22	13	35	....	....	....	26	4	6	*5	11	8
	Moose Jaw Canucks	M-Cup	17	11	*22	*33	....	....	....	8	....	....	....	....	....
1945-46	Moose Jaw Canucks	SJHL	16	*30	20	*50	....	....	....	17	4	5	5	10	4
	Moose Jaw Canucks	M-Cup	8	8	8	16	....	....	....	2	....	....	....	....	....
1946-47	**Chicago Black Hawks**	**NHL**	**18**	**5**	**4**	**9**	**6**	**5**	**11**	**2**	....	....	....	....	....
	Kansas City Pla-Mors	USHL	47	17	23	40	....	....	....	47	....	....	....	....	....
1947-48	Kansas City Pla-Mors	USHL	66	19	27	46	....	....	....	40	7	3	1	4	4
1948-49	Hershey Bears	AHL	8	0	0	0	....	....	....	2	....	....	....	....	....
	Tulsa Oilers	USHL	58	36	60	96	....	....	....	27	7	3	5	8	14
1949-50	Tulsa Oilers	USHL	70	28	50	78	....	....	....	44	....	....	....	....	....
1950-51	Tulsa Oilers	USHL	DID NOT PLAY – SUSPENDED												
1951-52	Calgary Stampeders	PCHL	55	22	26	48	....	....	....	69	....	....	....	....	....
1952-53	Calgary Stampeders	WHL	70	15	26	41	....	....	....	66	5	3	3	6	0
1953-54	Calgary Stampeders	WHL	67	24	42	66	....	....	....	28	18	5	11	16	21
	Calgary Stampeders	Ed-Cup	7	1	1	2	....	....	....	7	....	....	....	....	....
1954-55	Calgary–Vancouver	WHL	51	5	7	12	....	....	....	20	5	0	1	1	2
1955-56	Olds Elks	AIHA	STATISTICS NOT AVAILABLE												
1956-57	Calgary Stampeders	WHL	48	11	20	31	....	....	....	33	3	0	1	1	0

Season	Club	League	GP	G	A	Pts	AG	AA	APts	PIM	GP	G	A	Pts	PIM
			REGULAR SEASON								PLAYOFFS				
1957-58	Olds Elks	AIHA	STATISTICS NOT AVAILABLE												
1958-59	Olds Elks	AIHA	STATISTICS NOT AVAILABLE												
1959-60	Olds Elks	AIHA	STATISTICS NOT AVAILABLE												
	Calgary Spurs	Al-Cup	3	1	1	2				0					
1960/65	Olds Elks	AIHA	STATISTICS NOT AVAILABLE												
1965-66	Calgary Spurs	WCSHL	27	8	13	21				6	3	2	1	3	2
	NHL Totals		18	5	4	9	6	5	11	2					

USHL 2nd All-Star Team (1949)

• Suspended for entire 1950-51 season by **Tulsa** (USHL) for refusing to report to team, September, 1950.

• ASMUNDSON, Oscar "Ossie"

C – R. 5'11", 170 lbs. b: Red Deer, Alta., 11/17/1908.

Season	Club	League	GP	G	A	Pts	AG	AA	APts	PIM	GP	G	A	Pts	PIM
1928-29	Victoria Cubs	PCHL	29	2	2	4				6					
1929-30	Victoria Cubs	PCHL	35	8	3	11				40					
1930-31	Tacoma–Vancouver	PCHL	30	10	2	12				36	4	1	0	1	4
1931-32	Bronx Tigers	Can-Am	40	15	16	31				61	1	0	0	0	0
♦1932-33	New York Rangers	NHL	48	5	10	15	9	21	30	20	8	0	2	2	4
1933-34	New York Rangers	NHL	46	2	6	8	3	13	16	8	1	0	0	0	0
1934-35	Detroit Red Wings	NHL	3	0	0	0	0	0	0	0					
	Detroit Olympics	IHL	18	8	8	16				20					
	St. Louis Eagles	NHL	11	4	7	11	7	12	19	2					
1935-36	New Haven Eagles	Can-Am	25	4	11	15				26					
1936-37	New York Americans	NHL	1	0	0	0	0	0	0	0					
	New Haven Eagles	IAHL	44	13	22	35				32					
1937-38	Montreal Canadiens	NHL	2	0	0	0	0	0	0	0					
	New Haven Eagles	IAHL	44	13	26	39				57	2	0	0	0	0
1938-39	Cleveland Barons	IAHL	22	1	4	5				2					
1939-40	Cleveland Barons	IAHL	39	14	18	32				34					
1940-41	Cleveland Barons	AHL	48	8	22	30				33	9	3	3	6	15
1941-42	Providence Reds	AHL	2	0	2	2				0					
	Philadelphia Rockets	AHL	54	13	33	46				48					
1942-43	Washington Lions	AHL	41	9	19	28				32					
1943-44	Coast Guard Cutters	X-Games	28	15	23	38				8	12	11	15	*26	2
1944-45	Hollywood Wolves	PCHL	15	15	20	35									
	NHL Totals		111	11	23	34	19	46	65	30	9	0	2	2	4

Traded to **NY Rangers** by **Vancouver** (PCHL) for cash, October 25, 1931. Traded to **Detroit** by **NY Rangers** for cash, October 1, 1934. Signed as a free agent by **St. Louis** after securing release from **Detroit**, February 6, 1935. Signed as a free agent by **NY Americans**, February 14, 1937. Traded to **Montreal Canadiens** by **NY Americans** for cash, October 28, 1937. Traded to **Cleveland** (IAHL) by **Montreal Canadiens** for cash, November, 1938.

• ATANAS, Walt Walter "Ants"

RW – R. 5'8", 174 lbs. b: Hamilton, Ont., 12/22/1923 d: 8/8/1991.

Season	Club	League	GP	G	A	Pts	AG	AA	APts	PIM	GP	G	A	Pts	PIM
1942-43	Hamilton Whizzers	OHA-Jr.	23	*37	12	49				21	5	1	1	2	10
1943-44	Buffalo Bisons	AHL	46	16	19	35				33	9	6	7	13	2
	Toronto Mahers	TIHL	1	2	0	2				0					
1944-45	New York Rangers	NHL	49	13	8	21	13	9	22	40					
	Toronto Maher Jewels	TIHL	1	2	0	2				0					
1945-46	Cleveland Barons	AHL	31	10	10	20				30					
	Minneapolis Millers	USHL	22	11	10	21				36					
1946-47	Minneapolis Millers	USHL	51	10	19	29				40	3	1	0	1	4
1947-48	Minneapolis Millers	USHL	66	25	38	63				59	10	6	2	8	8
1948-49	Minneapolis Millers	USHL	64	35	20	55				15					
1949-50	Minneapolis Millers	USHL	69	24	28	52				49	7	*7	4	11	10
1950-51	Buffalo Bisons	AHL	61	19	26	45				23	4	0	0	0	8
1951-52	Buffalo Bisons	AHL	11	2	2	4				4					
	Victoria Cougars	PCHL	36	21	8	29				32	13	3	6	9	11
1952-53	Vancouver Canucks	WHL	68	28	24	52				28	9	1	1	2	14
1953-54	Springfield Indians	QHL	18	7	15	22				24					
	Syracuse Warriors	AHL	28	9	19	28				14					
1954-55	Springfield Indians	AHL	62	29	45	74				66	4	0	1	1	2
1955-56	Springfield Indians	AHL	56	24	28	52				49					
1956-57	North Bay Trappers	NOHA	52	15	31	46				35	13	4	5	9	6
	NHL Totals		49	13	8	21	13	9	22	40					

Claimed by **NY Rangers** from **Buffalo** (AHL) in Inter-League Draft, May 12, 1944.

• AUBUCHON, Ossie Oscar

LW – L. 5'10", 175 lbs. b: St. Hyacinthe, Que., 1/1/1917.

Season	Club	League	GP	G	A	Pts	AG	AA	APts	PIM	GP	G	A	Pts	PIM
1934-35	Montreal Victorias	MCJHL									1	0	0	0	0
1935-36	Montreal Jr. Canadiens	MCJHL	1	1	0	1				0					
	Montreal Sr. Canadiens	MCHL	17	0	3	3				4					
1936-37	Montreal Sr. Canadiens	MCHL	17	7	2	9				16					
1937-38	Brighton Tigers	Ln-Cup	....	2	0	2									
	Brighton Tigers	Britain	....	13	8	21									
	Brighton Tigers	Nat-Tmt	....	4	4	8									
1938-39	Brighton Tigers	Ln-Cup	....	4	1	5									
	Brighton Tigers	Britain	....	19	12	31									
	Brighton Tigers		....	13	7	20									
1939-40	Pittsburgh Hornets	IAHL	37	4	19	23				6	9	1	2	3	4
1940-41	Cleveland Barons	AHL	47	7	11	18				14	8	1	1	2	2
	New Haven Eagles	AHL	1	0	1	1				0					
1941-42	Providence Reds	AHL	52	14	19	33				27					
1942-43	Boston Bruins	NHL	3	3	0	3	3	0	3	0	6	1	0	1	0
	Providence Reds	AHL	45	29	35	64				9					
1943-44	Boston Bruins	NHL	9	1	0	1	1	0	1	0					
	New York Rangers	NHL	38	16	12	28	14	10	24	4					
1944-45	Buffalo Bisons	AHL	57	13	17	30				9	2	0	0	0	0
1945-46	Hershey Bears	AHL	4	1	1	2				5					
	St. Louis Flyers	AHL	32	8	9	17				9					
1946-47	Shawinigan Cataracts	QSHL	10	6	1	7				2					
	St-Hyacinthe Gaulois	QPHL	37	26	32	58				10	4	0	2	2	0
	NHL Totals		50	20	12	32	18	10	28	4	6	1	0	1	0

Traded to **Boston** by **Providence** (AHL) with Norm Calladine and Ab DeMarco for cash, March 8, 1943. Traded to **NY Rangers** by **Boston** for cash, November, 1943.

• AURIE, Larry Harry Lawrence "Little Dempsey"

RW – R. 5'6", 148 lbs. b: Sudbury, Ont., 2/8/1905 d: 12/11/1952.

Season	Club	League	GP	G	A	Pts	AG	AA	APts	PIM	GP	G	A	Pts	PIM
1921-22	Sudbury Cub Wolves	NOJHA	4	5	2	7				2	2	2	1	3	0
1922-23	St. Michael's Majors	OHA-Jr.	7	*16	4	*20					3	2	0	2	
1923-24	Sudbury Wolves	NOHA	STATISTICS NOT AVAILABLE												
1924-25	Sudbury Wolves	NOHA	STATISTICS NOT AVAILABLE												
1925-26	Galt Terriers	OHA-Sr.	20	11	4	15				35	2	0	0	0	0
1926-27	London Panthers	Can-Pro	32	14	7	21				38	4	4	0	4	4
1927-28	Detroit Cougars	NHL	44	13	3	16	26	17	43	43					
1928-29	Detroit Cougars	NHL	35	1	1	2	3	7	10	26	2	1	0	1	2
1929-30	Detroit Cougars	NHL	43	14	5	19	20	12	32	28					
1930-31	Detroit Falcons	NHL	41	12	6	18	24	18	42	23					
1931-32	Detroit Falcons	NHL	48	12	8	20	20	18	38	18	2	0	0	0	0
1932-33	Detroit Red Wings	NHL	45	12	11	23	22	23	45	25	4	1	0	1	4
1933-34	Detroit Red Wings	NHL	48	16	19	35	28	40	68	36	9	3	*7	*10	2
1934-35	Detroit Red Wings	NHL	48	17	29	46	28	51	79	24					
♦1935-36	Detroit Red Wings	NHL	44	16	18	34	31	34	65	17	7	1	2	3	2
♦1936-37	Detroit Red Wings	NHL	45	*23	20	43	39	37	76	20					
1937-38	Detroit Red Wings	NHL	47	10	9	19	16	14	30	19					
1938-39	Detroit Red Wings	NHL	1	1	0	1	2	0	2	0					
	Pittsburgh Hornets	IAHL	39	8	19	27				16					
1939-40	Pittsburgh Hornets	IAHL	39	12	12	24				12	9	3	8	11	4
1940-41	Pittsburgh Hornets	AHL	6	0	3	3				2					
1941/43	Pittsburgh Hornets	AHL	DID NOT PLAY – COACHING												
1943-44	Pittsburgh Hornets	AHL	1	0	0	0				0					
	NHL Totals		489	147	129	276	259	271	530	279	24	6	9	15	10

NHL First All-Star Team (1937) • IAHL Second All-Star Team (1939) • Played in NHL All-Star Game (1934)

Signed as a free agent by **London** (Can-Pro), November 14, 1926. Claimed by **Detroit** from **London** (Can-Pro) in Inter-League Draft, September 26, 1927.

• AWREY, Don

— *see page 859*

• AYRES, Vern Thomas Vernon

D – L. 6'2", 220 lbs. b: Toronto, Ont., 4/27/1909 d: 2/18/1968.

Season	Club	League	GP	G	A	Pts	AG	AA	APts	PIM	GP	G	A	Pts	PIM
1927-28	Parkdale Canoe Club	OHA-Jr.	9	3	1	4					1	0	0	0	
1928-29	Parkdale Canoe Club	OHA-Jr.	8	4	1	5									
1929-30	Toronto Young Rangers	OHA-Jr.	STATISTICS NOT AVAILABLE												
	Toronto Stockyards	TMHL	5	1	0	1				4	1	1	0	1	2
1930-31	New York Americans	NHL	26	2	1	3	4	3	7	54					
	New Haven Eagles	Can-Am	8	1	0	1				22					
1931-32	New York Americans	NHL	45	2	4	6	3	9	12	82					
1932-33	New York Americans	NHL	48	0	0	0	0	0	0	97					
1933-34	Montreal Maroons	NHL	17	0	0	0	0	0	0	19					
	Quebec Castors	Can-Am	29	0	4	4				52					
1934-35	St. Louis Eagles	NHL	47	2	2	4	3	3	6	60					
1935-36	New York Rangers	NHL	28	0	4	4	0	8	8	38					
	Philadelphia Ramblers	Can-Am	20	4	6	10				26	4	0	0	0	8
1936-37	Philadelphia Ramblers	IAHL	49	4	7	11				44	6	0	0	0	2
1937-38	Philadelphia Ramblers	IAHL	44	1	11	12				34	5	0	1	1	2
1938-39	Hershey Bears	IAHL	52	3	5	8				19	5	0	1	1	0
1939-40	Pittsburgh Hornets	IAHL	54	0	10	10				37	1	0	0	0	0
1940-41	St. Louis Flyers	AHA	38	1	7	8				20	9	0	2	2	2
1941-42	St. Louis Flyers	AHA	45	2	9	11				36	3	1	0	1	6
	NHL Totals		211	6	11	17	10	23	33	350					

Signed as a free agent by **NY Americans**, October 22, 1930. Traded to **Montreal Maroons** by **NY Americans** for $6,000, June 1, 1933. Traded to **St. Louis** by **Montreal Maroons** with Normie Smith to complete transaction that sent Al Shields to Montreal Maroons (September 20, 1934), October 22, 1934. Claimed by **NY Rangers** from **St. Louis** in Dispersal Draft, October 15, 1935.

• BABANDO, Pete Peter Joseph

LW – L. 5'9", 187 lbs. b: Braeburn, PA, 5/10/1925.

Season	Club	League	GP	G	A	Pts	AG	AA	APts	PIM	GP	G	A	Pts	PIM
1942-43	Holman Pluggers	NOHA	STATISTICS NOT AVAILABLE												
1943-44	Galt Kists	OHA-Jr.	6	2	0	2				10	4	1	2	3	2
	South Porcupine Porkies	TMHL	STATISTICS NOT AVAILABLE												
1944-45	Galt Red Wings	OHA-Jr.	19	13	10	23				30					
1945-46	Boston Olympics	EAHL	32	25	10	35				50	12	8	8	16	10
1946-47	Hershey Bears	AHL	51	19	26	45				81	11	2	0	2	0
1947-48	Boston Bruins	NHL	60	23	11	34	30	14	44	52	5	1	1	2	2
1948-49	Boston Bruins	NHL	58	19	14	33	27	20	47	34	4	0	0	0	2
♦1949-50	Detroit Red Wings	NHL	56	6	6	12	8	7	15	25	8	2	2	4	2
1950-51	Chicago Black Hawks	NHL	70	18	19	37	23	23	46	36					
1951-52	Chicago Black Hawks	NHL	49	11	14	25	15	17	32	29					
1952-53	Chicago Black Hawks	NHL	29	5	5	10	7	6	13	14					
	New York Rangers	NHL	29	4	4	8	5	5	10	4					
1953-54	Buffalo Bisons	AHL	63	21	43	64				46	3	2	0	2	2
1954-55	Buffalo Bisons	AHL	59	20	30	50				61	10	5	6	11	6
1955-56	Buffalo Bisons	AHL	59	26	19	45				65	5	1	1	2	2
1956-57	Buffalo Bisons	AHL	33	7	9	16				30					
1957-58	North Bay Trappers	NOHA	16	9	8	17				44					
1958-59	Whitby Dunlops	OHA-Sr.	50	22	27	49				28	9	3	5	8	8
	Whitby Dunlops	Al-Cup	12	3	5	8				8					
1959-60	Whitby Dunlops	OHA-Sr.	53	28	34	62				48	10	8	3	11	12
1960-61	Clinton Comets	EHL	1	0	0	0				2					
1961-62	Clinton Comets	EHL	67	43	68	111				37	6	2	3	5	4
1962-63	Clinton Comets	EHL	66	55	83	138				26	13	9	*22	*31	16
1963-64	Clinton Comets	EHL	68	26	65	91				34	15	12	11	*23	34

Season	Club	League	REGULAR SEASON GP	G	A	Pts	AG	AA	APts	PIM	PLAYOFFS GP	G	A	Pts	PIM
1964-65	Clinton Comets	EHL	61	37	65	102				26	11	8	6	14	2
1965-66	Clinton Comets	EHL	1	1	0	1				0					
1966-67	Clinton Comets	EHL	71	39	49	88				101	9	2	4	6	4
	NHL Totals		**351**	**86**	**73**	**159**	**115**	**92**	**207**	**194**	**17**	**3**	**3**	**6**	**6**

EHL 2nd All-Star Team (1962) • EHL 1st All-Star Team (1963) • EHL North 2nd All-Star Team (1967)

Traded to **Detroit** by **Boston** with Claire Martin, Lloyd Durham and Jimmy Peters for Bill Quackenbush and Pete Horeck, August 16, 1949. Traded to **Chicago** by **Detroit** with Harry Lumley, Jack Stewart, Al Dewsbury and Don Morrison for Jim Henry, Bob Goldham, Gaye Stewart and Metro Prystai, July 13, 1950. Traded to **NY Rangers** by **Chicago** for cash, January 9, 1953. Traded to **Montreal** by **NY Rangers** with Eddie Slowinski for Ivan Irwin, August 8, 1953. Traded to **Buffalo** (AHL) by **Montreal** with Gaye Stewart and Eddie Slowinski for Jackie LeClair and cash, August 17, 1954.

• BACKOR, Pete

D – L. 6', 190 lbs. b: Fort William, Ont., 4/29/1919 Deceased.

Season	Club	League	GP	G	A	Pts	AG	AA	APts	PIM	GP	G	A	Pts	PIM
1938-39	Fort William Forts	TBSHL	23	9	6	15				6					
1939-40	St. Catharines Saints	OHA-Sr.	29	27	17	44				28	8	2	2	4	6
1940-41	St. Catharines Saints	OHA-Sr.	31	14	9	23				20	12	2	7	9	12
1941-42	St. Catharines Saints	OHA-Sr.	27	7	7	14				26	11	2	4	6	11
1942-43	St. Catharines Saints	OHA-Sr.	21	8	12	20				26	3	2	1	3	9
1943-44	St. Catharines Saints	OHA-Sr.	28	11	12	23				27	5	0	1	1	4
	Montreal Royals	QSHL									1	1	0	1	0
	Port Arthur Shipbuilders	TBSHL									9	1	1	2	4
♦1944-45	**Toronto Maple Leafs**	**NHL**	**36**	**4**	**5**	**9**	**4**	**6**	**10**	**6**					
1945-46	Pittsburgh Hornets	AHL	61	5	26	31				65	6	1	1	2	4
1946-47	Hollywood Wolves	PCHL	16	5	5	10				24					
	Pittsburgh Hornets	AHL	48	9	10	19				30	12	2	1	3	6
1947-48	Pittsburgh Hornets	AHL	68	14	39	53				63	2	0	0	0	0
1948-49	Pittsburgh Hornets	AHL	68	10	42	52				64					
1949-50	Pittsburgh Hornets	AHL	63	8	29	37				34					
1950-51	Pittsburgh Hornets	AHL	71	7	33	40				80	13	0	4	4	8
1951-52	Pittsburgh Hornets	AHL	57	3	18	21				49	11	0	0	0	10
1952-53	Pittsburgh Hornets	AHL	53	1	10	11				36	3	0	1	1	16
1953-54	Pittsburgh Hornets	AHL	45	3	11	14				21	5	0	0	0	4
1954-55	Sault Ste. Marie Indians	NOHA	34	6	8	14				24	6	3	0	3	6
1955-56	Sault Ste. Marie Indians	NOHA	2	0	1	1				0	2	0	0	0	2
	NHL Totals		**36**	**4**	**5**	**9**	**4**	**6**	**10**	**6**					

AHL First All-Star Team (1946, 1948, 1949, 1950, 1951)

• BACKSTROM, Ralph

— *see page 862*

• BAILEY, Ace

Irvine Wallace HHOF

RW – R. 5'10", 160 lbs. b: Bracebridge, Ont., 7/3/1903 d: 4/7/1992.

Season	Club	League	GP	G	A	Pts	AG	AA	APts	PIM	GP	G	A	Pts	PIM
1918/22	Bracebridge Bird Mill	OHA-Jr.	STATISTICS NOT AVAILABLE												
1922-23	Toronto St. Mary's	OHA-Jr.	4	2	1	3					4	2	1	3	
1923-24	Toronto St. Mary's	OHA-Jr.	8	10	0	10									
1924-25	Peterborough Seniors	OHA-Sr.	8	5	0	5					2	3	0	3	2
1925-26	Peterborough Seniors	OHA-Sr.	9	9	2	11				2	2	2	1	*3	
	Peterborough Seniors	Al-Cup	6	2	2	4									
1926-27	**Toronto Pats/Leafs**	**NHL**	**42**	**15**	**13**	**28**	**27**	**69**	**96**	**82**					
1927-28	**Toronto Maple Leafs**	**NHL**	**43**	**9**	**3**	**12**	**18**	**17**	**35**	**72**					
1928-29	**Toronto Maple Leafs**	**NHL**	**44**	***22**	**10**	***32**	**65**	**68**	**133**	**78**	**4**	**1**	***2**	***3**	**4**
1929-30	**Toronto Maple Leafs**	**NHL**	**43**	**22**	**21**	**43**	**31**	**50**	**81**	**69**					
1930-31	**Toronto Maple Leafs**	**NHL**	**40**	**23**	**19**	**42**	**47**	**58**	**105**	**46**	**2**	**1**	**1**	**2**	**0**
♦1931-32	**Toronto Maple Leafs**	**NHL**	**41**	**8**	**5**	**13**	**13**	**11**	**24**	**62**	**7**	**1**	**0**	**1**	**4**
1932-33	**Toronto Maple Leafs**	**NHL**	**47**	**10**	**8**	**18**	**18**	**17**	**35**	**52**	**8**	**0**	**1**	**1**	**4**
1933-34	**Toronto Maple Leafs**	**NHL**	**13**	**2**	**3**	**5**	**3**	**6**	**9**	**11**					
	NHL Totals		**313**	**111**	**82**	**193**	**222**	**296**	**518**	**472**	**21**	**3**	**4**	**7**	**12**

NHL Scoring Leader (1929)

Signed as a free agent by **Toronto**, November 3, 1926. • Suffered career-ending head injury in game vs. Boston, December 12, 1933.

• BAILEY, Bob

Robert Allan "Bashin' Bob"

RW – R. 5'11", 180 lbs. b: Kenora, Ont., 5/29/1931.

Season	Club	League	GP	G	A	Pts	AG	AA	APts	PIM	GP	G	A	Pts	PIM
1947-48	Detroit–Windsor	IHL	22	2	7	9				14	8	0	0	0	10
1948-49	Kenora Thistles	NOJHA	14	5	10	15				*51	5	2	3	5	8
1949-50	Windsor Spitfires	OHA-Jr.	48	10	17	27				66	11	1	5	6	20
1950-51	Stratford Kroehlers	OHA-Jr.	53	21	45	66				109	3	1	0	1	2
1951-52	Stratford Kroehlers	OHA-Jr.	DID NOT PLAY – INJURED												
	Toledo Mercurys	IHL	2	0	3	3				0					
1952-53	Cleveland Barons	AHL	54	11	35	46				*115	10	2	2	4	33
1953-54	**Toronto Maple Leafs**	**NHL**	**48**	**2**	**7**	**9**	**3**	**8**	**11**	**70**	**5**	**0**	**2**	**2**	**4**
	Ottawa Senators	QHL	2	0	0	0				12					
	Pittsburgh Hornets	AHL	7	2	3	5				19					
1954-55	**Toronto Maple Leafs**	**NHL**	**32**	**4**	**2**	**6**	**5**	**2**	**7**	**52**	**1**	**0**	**0**	**0**	**0**
	Pittsburgh Hornets	AHL	26	9	19	28				23	5	0	8	8	*24
1955-56	**Toronto Maple Leafs**	**NHL**	**6**	**0**	**0**	**0**	**0**	**0**	**0**	**6**					
	Pittsburgh Hornets	AHL	48	6	30	36				98	4	2	1	3	4
1956-57	Springfield Indians	AHL	40	11	33	44				83					
	Detroit Red Wings	**NHL**									**5**	**0**	**2**	**2**	**2**
1957-58	**Chicago Black Hawks**	**NHL**	**28**	**3**	**6**	**9**	**4**	**6**	**10**	**38**					
	Detroit Red Wings	**NHL**	**36**	**6**	**6**	**12**	**7**	**6**	**13**	**41**	**4**	**0**	**0**	**0**	**16**
1958-59	Cleveland Barons	AHL	64	28	41	69				153	7	4	3	7	16
1959-60	Cleveland Barons	AHL	5	0	3	3				13					
	Buffalo Bisons	AHL	29	6	24	30				54					
1960-61	Quebec Aces	AHL	38	6	11	17				91					
1961-62	Pittsburgh Hornets	AHL	27	3	17	20				91					
	San Francisco Seals	WHL	12	2	6	8				12	2	0	0	0	16
1962-63	San Francisco Seals	WHL	11	0	6	6				14					
	Philadelphia Ramblers	EHL	50	26	65	91				64	3	0	3	3	10
1963-64	Philadelphia Ramblers	EHL	7	2	4	6				67					
	Fort Wayne Komets	IHL	22	12	19	31				64					
1964-65	Dayton Gems	IHL	54	31	56	87				102					
1965-66	Dayton Gems	IHL	61	45	87	132				127	10	9	8	17	53
1966-67	Dayton Gems	IHL	35	13	36	49				59	4	3	1	4	8
1967-68	Dayton Gems	IHL	24	15	36	51				93					
	NHL Totals		**150**	**15**	**21**	**36**	**19**	**22**	**41**	**207**	**15**	**0**	**4**	**4**	**22**

• Missed majority of 1951-52 season recovering from knee injury suffered in training camp, September, 1951. Traded to **Cleveland** (AHL) by **Detroit** with John Bailey for the rights to Lou Jankowski and Bill Dineen, June, 1951. Traded to **Toronto** by **Cleveland** (AHL) with Gerry Foley for Chuck Blair and $30,000, May 30, 1953. • Suspended by AHL for remainder of 1955 AHL playoffs for assaulting referee Jerry Olinski, April 2, 1956. Traded to **Springfield** (AHL) by **Toronto** (Pittsburgh-AHL) with Bob Sabourin for $11,000, May 28, 1956. Traded to **Detroit** by **Springfield** (AHL) for cash, September 22, 1956. Loaned to **Springfield** (AHL) by **Detroit** for 1956-57 season, September, 1956. Claimed by **Chicago** from **Detroit** in Intra-League Draft, June 5, 1957. Traded to **Detroit** by **Chicago** with Jack McIntyre, Nick Mickoski and Hec Lalonde for Earl Reibel, Billy Dea, Lorne Ferguson and Bill Dineen, December 17, 1957. Traded to **Cleveland** (AHL) by **Detroit** for cash, July 31, 1958. Traded to **Buffalo** (AHL) by **Cleveland** (AHL) for Bill Dineen, October 20, 1959. Traded to **Montreal** by **Chicago** (Buffalo-AHL) with Glen Skov, the rights to Danny Lewicki, Terry Gray and Lorne Ferguson for Cec Hoekstra, Reggie Fleming, Ab McDonald and Bob Courcy, June 7, 1960. Traded to **San Francisco** (WHL) by **Pittsburgh** (AHL) for Gord Redahl, February 27, 1962. Traded to **Dayton** (IHL) by **Fort Wayne** (IHL) for Roger Maisonneuve, November, 1964.

• BALDWIN, Doug

Douglas Colin Roy

D – L. 6', 175 lbs. b: Winnipeg, Man., 11/2/1922.

Season	Club	League	GP	G	A	Pts	AG	AA	APts	PIM	GP	G	A	Pts	PIM
1939-40	Winnipeg Rangers	WJrHL	2	0	0	0				2					
1940-41	Winnipeg Rangers	WJrHL	17	12	5	17				35	6	3	2	5	6
	Winnipeg Rangers	M-Cup	7	0	1	1				4					
1941-42	Winnipeg Falcons	WJrHL	14	12	6	18				27	6	4	5	9	19
1942-43	Quebec Aces	QSHL	33	0	5	5				4	4	0	1	1	2
1943-44	Quebec Aces	QSHL	25	7	15	22				46	6	4	2	6	14
	Quebec Aces	Al-Cup	9	3	6	9				12					
1944-45	Quebec Aces	QSHL	17	5	18	23				44	5	2	2	4	0
	Quebec Aces	Al-Cup	3	1	1	2				8					
1945-46	**Toronto Maple Leafs**	**NHL**	**15**	**0**	**1**	**1**	**0**	**1**	**1**	**6**					
	Pittsburgh Hornets	AHL	4	2	2	4				4					
1946-47	**Detroit Red Wings**	**NHL**	**4**	**0**	**0**	**0**	**0**	**0**	**0**	**0**					
	Kansas City Pla-Mors	USHL	43	8	16	24				57	12	1	6	7	23
1947-48	**Chicago Black Hawks**	**NHL**	**5**	**0**	**0**	**0**	**0**	**0**	**0**	**2**					
	Kansas City Pla-Mors	USHL	58	21	42	63				70	4	0	0	0	0
1948-49	Kansas City Pla-Mors	USHL	38	10	27	37				28					
	Cleveland Barons	AHL	21	3	4	7				14					
1949-50	Kansas City Mohawks	USHL	70	12	36	48				58	3	1	0	1	2
1950/54			OUT OF HOCKEY – RETIRED												
1954-55	Grand Rapids Rockets	IHL	13	1	6	7				4					
1955-56	Windsor Bulldogs	OHA-Sr.	6	0	0	0				43					
	Chatham Maroons	OHA-Sr.	35	6	14	20				0	11	1	6	7	14
	Chatham Maroons	Al-Cup	17	0	2	2				20					
1956-57	Chatham Maroons	OHA-Sr.	39	5	18	23				40	6	1	3	4	6
1957-58	Toledo Mercurys	IHL	63	6	22	28				39					
1958-59	Toledo Mercurys	IHL	26	2	5	7				12					
	Washington Presidents	EHL	11	1	6	7				10					
	NHL Totals		**24**	**0**	**1**	**1**	**0**	**1**	**1**	**8**					

USHL First All-Star Team (1947, 1948) • USHL Second All-Star Team (1950)

Traded to **Detroit** by **Toronto** with Ray Powell for Gerry Brown, September 21, 1946. Traded to **Chicago** by **Detroit** for cash, June, 1947. Traded to **Cleveland** (AHL) by **Chicago** (Kansas City-USHL) for Ed Wares, January 28, 1949. Traded to **Chicago** (Kansas City-USHL) by **Cleveland** (AHL) with Bus Wycherley for Al Rollins, September 13, 1949.

• BALFOUR, Earl

Earl Frederick "Spider"

LW – L. 6'1", 180 lbs. b: Toronto, Ont., 1/4/1933.

Season	Club	League	GP	G	A	Pts	AG	AA	APts	PIM	GP	G	A	Pts	PIM
1949-50	Toronto Marlboros	OHA-Jr.	2	0	0	0				2					
1950-51	Toronto Marlboros	OHA-Jr.	53	10	16	26				53	13	6	4	10	16
1951-52	Toronto Marlboros	OHA-Jr.	51	10	29	39				75	6	3	3	6	8
	Toronto Maple Leafs	**NHL**	**3**	**0**	**0**	**0**	**0**	**0**	**0**	**2**	**1**	**0**	**0**	**0**	**0**
1952-53	Pittsburgh Hornets	AHL	63	14	30	44				33	10	0	4	4	14
1953-54	**Toronto Maple Leafs**	**NHL**	**17**	**0**	**1**	**1**	**0**	**1**	**1**	**6**					
	Pittsburgh Hornets	AHL	51	16	22	38				29	4	1	1	2	0
1954-55	Pittsburgh Hornets	AHL	63	17	31	48				42	10	2	*9	11	9
1955-56	**Toronto Maple Leafs**	**NHL**	**59**	**14**	**5**	**19**	**19**	**6**	**25**	**40**	**3**	**0**	**1**	**1**	**2**
1956-57	Rochester Americans	AHL	63	21	16	37				38	10	3	5	8	6
1957-58	**Toronto Maple Leafs**	**NHL**	**1**	**0**	**0**	**0**	**0**	**0**	**0**	**0**					
	Rochester Americans	AHL	70	27	31	58				58					
1958-59	**Chicago Black Hawks**	**NHL**	**70**	**10**	**8**	**18**	**12**	**8**	**20**	**10**	**6**	**0**	**2**	**2**	**0**
1959-60	**Chicago Black Hawks**	**NHL**	**70**	**3**	**5**	**8**	**3**	**5**	**8**	**16**	**4**	**0**	**0**	**0**	**0**
♦1960-61	**Chicago Black Hawks**	**NHL**	**68**	**3**	**3**	**6**	**3**	**3**	**6**	**4**	**12**	**0**	**0**	**0**	**2**
1961-62	Pittsburgh Hornets	AHL	64	19	19	38				28					
1962-63	Pittsburgh Hornets	AHL	71	7	15	22				30					
1963-64			REINSTATED AS AN AMATEUR												
1964-65	Galt Hornets	OHA-Sr.	34	19	23	42				18	4	4	6	10	6
1965-66	Galt Hornets	OHA-Sr.	42	22	28	50				33					
1966-67	Galt Hornets	OHA-Sr.	39	21	15	36				32					
1967-68	Toronto Marlboros	OHA-Sr.	36	22	22	44				12					
1968-69	Orillia Terriers	OHA-Sr.	37	4	13	17				10					
	NHL Totals		**288**	**30**	**22**	**52**	**37**	**23**	**60**	**78**	**26**	**0**	**3**	**3**	**4**

OHA-Sr. Second All-Star Team (1965, 1966, 1967)

Claimed by **Chicago** from **Toronto** in Intra-League Draft, June 3, 1958. Claimed by **Boston** from **Chicago** in Intra-League Draft, June 13, 1961.

• BALFOUR, Murray

Murray Lewis

RW – R. 5'9", 178 lbs. b: Regina, Sask., 8/24/1936 d: 5/30/1965.

Season	Club	League	GP	G	A	Pts	AG	AA	APts	PIM	GP	G	A	Pts	PIM
1952-53	Regina Pats	WCJHL	31	2	4	6				38	7	0	1	1	10
	Regina Capitals	Al-Cup	2	0	0	0				5					
1953-54	Regina Pats	WCJHL	35	7	5	12				*99	16	4	4	8	*45
1954-55	Regina Pats	WCJHL	38	10	16	26				*156	12	7	4	11	*30
	Regina Pats	M-Cup	3	1	2	3				4					
1955-56	Regina Pats	WCJHL	34	24	18	42				*104	10	7	5	12	20
	Regina Pats	M-Cup	19	15	4	19				65					

Season	Club	League	GP	G	A	Pts	AG	AA	APts	PIM	GP	G	A	Pts	PIM
			REGULAR SEASON								PLAYOFFS				
1956-57	Hull-Ottawa Canadiens	OHA-Jr.	19	12	7	19	....	....	....	76	....	....	....	....	....
	Hull-Ottawa Canadiens	QHL	18	2	6	8	....	....	....	15	....	....	....	....	....
	Hull-Ottawa Canadiens	EOHL	14	5	10	15	....	....	....	41	....	....	....	....	....
	Montreal Canadiens	**NHL**	**2**	**0**	**0**	**0**	**0**	**0**	**0**	**2**	....	....	....	....	....
	Hull-Ottawa Canadiens	M-Cup	15	5	12	17	....	....	....	35	....	....	....	....	....
1957-58	**Montreal Canadiens**	**NHL**	**3**	**1**	**1**	**2**	**1**	**1**	**2**	**4**	....	....	....	....	....
	Montreal Royals	QHL	62	23	25	48	....	....	....	107	7	1	2	3	20
1958-59	Rochester Americans	AHL	67	14	23	37	....	....	....	*181	1	0	0	0	0
1959-60	**Chicago Black Hawks**	**NHL**	**61**	**18**	**12**	**30**	**21**	**12**	**33**	**55**	**4**	**1**	**0**	**1**	**0**
♦1960-61	**Chicago Black Hawks**	**NHL**	**70**	**21**	**27**	**48**	**24**	**26**	**50**	**123**	**11**	**5**	**5**	**10**	**14**
1961-62	**Chicago Black Hawks**	**NHL**	**49**	**15**	**15**	**30**	**17**	**14**	**31**	**72**	**12**	**1**	**1**	**2**	**15**
1962-63	**Chicago Black Hawks**	**NHL**	**65**	**10**	**23**	**33**	**12**	**23**	**35**	**75**	**6**	**0**	**2**	**2**	**12**
1963-64	**Chicago Black Hawks**	**NHL**	**41**	**2**	**10**	**12**	**2**	**10**	**12**	**36**	**7**	**2**	**2**	**4**	**4**
1964-65	**Boston Bruins**	**NHL**	**15**	**0**	**2**	**2**	**0**	**2**	**2**	**26**	....	....	....	....	....
	Hershey Bears	AHL	31	10	8	18	....	....	....	36	....	....	....	....	....
	NHL Totals		**306**	**67**	**90**	**157**	**77**	**88**	**165**	**393**	**40**	**9**	**10**	**19**	**45**

• Hull-Ottawa played partial schedule against OHA-Jr. teams in 1956-57 and 1957-58 that counted for the opposition only. Traded to **Chicago** by **Montreal** for cash, June 9, 1959. Traded to **Boston** by **Chicago** with Mike Draper for Matt Ravlich and Jerry Toppazzini, June 9, 1964. • Missed remainder of the 1964-65 season after being diagnosed with lung cancer, February 5, 1965.

• BALON, Dave

— see page 865

• BALUIK, Stan

Stanley
C – L. 5'8", 160 lbs. b: Port Arthur, Ont., 10/5/1935.

Season	Club	League	GP	G	A	Pts	AG	AA	APts	PIM	GP	G	A	Pts	PIM
1950-51	Fort William Canadiens	NOJHA	12	4	3	7	....	....	....	8	3	0	2	2	0
1951-52	Fort William Canadiens	NOJHA	30	25	14	39	....	....	....	39	....	....	....	....	....
1952-53	Fort William Canadiens	NOJHA	30	27	*33	60	....	....	....	40	6	0	5	5	4
	Fort William Canadiens	M-Cup	2	1	0	1	....	....	....	0	....	....	....	....	....
1953-54	Fort William Canadiens	NOJHA	34	35	*50	*85	....	....	....	30	4	3	4	7	6
	Fort William Canadiens	M-Cup	13	7	7	14	....	....	....	8	....	....	....	....	....
1954-55	Kitchener Canucks	OHA-Jr.	49	20	*51	71	....	....	....	122	....	....	....	....	....
	Montreal Royals	QHL	2	0	0	0	....	....	....	0	....	....	....	....	....
1955-56	Kitchener Canucks	OHA-Jr.	48	31	*73	*104	....	....	....	46	8	2	10	12	30
1956-57	Chicoutimi Sagueneens	QHL	68	16	20	36	....	....	....	36	10	1	3	4	12
1957-58	Victoria Cougars	WHL	32	13	15	28	....	....	....	45	....	....	....	....	....
	Springfield Indians	AHL	5	2	0	2	....	....	....	8	....	....	....	....	....
1958-59	Victoria Cougars	WHL	55	28	26	54	....	....	....	57	3	1	1	2	0
1959-60	**Boston Bruins**	**NHL**	**7**	**0**	**0**	**0**	**0**	**0**	**0**	**2**	....	....	....	....	....
	Providence Reds	AHL	65	23	57	80	....	....	....	60	5	2	3	5	2
1960-61	Providence Reds	AHL	71	26	37	63	....	....	....	67	....	....	....	....	....
1961-62	Providence Reds	AHL	69	25	56	81	....	....	....	55	3	1	0	1	6
1962-63	Providence Reds	AHL	72	23	58	81	....	....	....	52	6	2	3	5	4
1963-64	Providence Reds	AHL	65	27	41	68	....	....	....	55	3	1	2	3	4
	NHL Totals		**7**	**0**	**0**	**0**	**0**	**0**	**0**	**2**	....	....	....	....	....

Won Dudley "Red" Garrett Memorial Award (Top Rookie - AHL) (1960)

Claimed by **Boston** from **Chicoutimi** (QHL) in Inter-League Draft, June 4, 1957.

• BARBE, Andy

Andrew Joseph
RW – R. 6', 170 lbs. b: Coniston, Ont., 7/27/1923.

Season	Club	League	GP	G	A	Pts	AG	AA	APts	PIM	GP	G	A	Pts	PIM
1941-42	Falconbridge Falcons	NOJHA	8	3	3	6	....	....	....	6	2	0	0	0	10
1942-43			MILITARY SERVICE												
1943-44			MILITARY SERVICE												
1944-45	Sudbury Open Pit Miners	NOHA	8	4	4	8	....	....	....	9	3	1	2	3	0
1945-46	Oakland Oaks	PCHL	40	11	11	22	....	....	....	76	2	1	0	1	0
1946-47	Los Angeles Monarchs	PCHL	54	55	39	94	....	....	....	55	11	*12	4	16	2
1947-48	Los Angeles Monarchs	PCHL	57	42	38	80	....	....	....	95	4	1	0	1	0
1948-49	Los Angeles Monarchs	PCHL	70	42	35	77	....	....	....	32	7	5	2	7	0
1949-50	Pittsburgh Hornets	AHL	64	25	8	33	....	....	....	12	....	....	....	....	....
1950-51	**Toronto Maple Leafs**	**NHL**	**1**	**0**	**0**	**0**	**0**	**0**	**0**	**2**	....	....	....	....	....
	Pittsburgh Hornets	AHL	67	23	28	51	....	....	....	20	13	9	5	14	0
1951-52	Pittsburgh Hornets	AHL	68	22	40	62	....	....	....	16	11	3	6	9	2
1952-53	Pittsburgh Hornets	AHL	29	14	21	35	....	....	....	4	6	2	3	5	14
1953-54	Pittsburgh Hornets	AHL	67	25	36	61	....	....	....	8	5	0	1	1	2
1954-55	Pittsburgh Hornets	AHL	57	19	20	39	....	....	....	10	7	0	2	2	2
	NHL Totals		**1**	**0**	**0**	**0**	**0**	**0**	**0**	**2**	....	....	....	....	....

PCHL Southern First All-Star Team (1949)

• BARILKO, Bill

William "Bashin' Bill"
D – R. 5'11", 180 lbs. b: Timmins, Ont., 3/25/1927 d: 8/26/1951.

Season	Club	League	GP	G	A	Pts	AG	AA	APts	PIM	GP	G	A	Pts	PIM
1942/44	Holman Pluggers	NOHA	STATISTICS NOT AVAILABLE												
1944-45	Timmins Canadians	NOHA	STATISTICS NOT AVAILABLE												
	Porcupine Combines	NOHA	....	3	2	5	....	....	....	8	....	....	....	....	....
1945-46	Hollywood Wolves	PCHL	38	4	5	9	....	....	....	103	12	2	3	5	26
♦1946-47	**Toronto Maple Leafs**	**NHL**	**18**	**3**	**7**	**10**	**3**	**8**	**11**	**33**	**11**	**0**	**3**	**3**	**18**
	Hollywood Wolves	PCHL	47	9	2	11	....	....	....	69	....	....	....	....	....
♦1947-48	**Toronto Maple Leafs**	**NHL**	**57**	**5**	**9**	**14**	**6**	**12**	**18**	***147**	**9**	**1**	**0**	**1**	**17**
♦1948-49	**Toronto Maple Leafs**	**NHL**	**60**	**5**	**4**	**9**	**7**	**6**	**13**	**95**	**9**	**0**	**1**	**1**	**20**
1949-50	**Toronto Maple Leafs**	**NHL**	**59**	**7**	**10**	**17**	**9**	**12**	**21**	**85**	**7**	**1**	**1**	**2**	**18**
♦1950-51	**Toronto Maple Leafs**	**NHL**	**58**	**6**	**6**	**12**	**8**	**7**	**15**	**96**	**11**	**3**	**2**	**5**	**31**
	NHL Totals		**252**	**26**	**36**	**62**	**33**	**45**	**78**	**456**	**47**	**5**	**7**	**12**	**104**

Played in NHL All-Star Game (1947, 1948, 1949) • Died of injuries suffered in airplane accident, August 26, 1951.

• BARKLEY, Doug

Norman Douglas
D – R. 6'2", 185 lbs. b: Lethbridge, Alta., 1/6/1937.

Season	Club	League	GP	G	A	Pts	AG	AA	APts	PIM	GP	G	A	Pts	PIM
1955-56	Medicine Hat Tigers	WCJHL	44	19	10	29	....	....	....	85	5	0	2	2	0
1956-57	Calgary Stampeders	WHL	63	4	8	12	....	....	....	112	3	0	0	0	0
1957-58	**Chicago Black Hawks**	**NHL**	**3**	**0**	**0**	**0**	**0**	**0**	**0**	**0**	....	....	....	....	....
	Calgary Stampeders	WHL	31	3	5	8	....	....	....	72	14	2	1	3	37
	Buffalo Bisons	AHL	27	0	3	3	....	....	....	22	....	....	....	....	....
1958-59	Buffalo Bisons	AHL	55	2	5	7	....	....	....	59	8	0	0	0	12
1959-60	**Chicago Black Hawks**	**NHL**	**3**	**0**	**0**	**0**	**0**	**0**	**0**	**2**	....	....	....	....	....
	Calgary Stampeders	WHL	55	7	18	25	....	....	....	82	....	....	....	....	....
1960-61	Buffalo Bisons	AHL	66	9	28	37	....	....	....	106	4	0	1	1	10
1961-62	Calgary Stampeders	WHL	70	25	49	74	....	....	....	82	7	2	3	5	17
1962-63	**Detroit Red Wings**	**NHL**	**70**	**3**	**24**	**27**	**3**	**24**	**27**	**78**	**11**	**0**	**3**	**3**	**16**
1963-64	**Detroit Red Wings**	**NHL**	**67**	**11**	**21**	**32**	**14**	**22**	**36**	**115**	**14**	**0**	**5**	**5**	**33**
1964-65	**Detroit Red Wings**	**NHL**	**67**	**5**	**20**	**25**	**6**	**20**	**26**	**122**	**5**	**0**	**1**	**1**	**14**
1965-66	**Detroit Red Wings**	**NHL**	**43**	**5**	**15**	**20**	**6**	**14**	**20**	**65**	....	....	....	....	....
1966-67	**Detroit Red Wings**	**NHL**	DID NOT PLAY – INJURED												
1967-68	**Detroit Red Wings**	**NHL**	DID NOT PLAY – INJURED												
1968-69	Fort Worth Wings	CHL	DID NOT PLAY – COACHING												
	NHL Totals		**253**	**24**	**80**	**104**	**29**	**80**	**109**	**382**	**30**	**0**	**9**	**9**	**63**

WHL First All-Star Team (1962)

Traded to **Detroit** by **Chicago** for Len Lunde and John McKenzie, June 5, 1962. • Suffered career-ending eye injury in game vs. Chicago, January 30, 1966.

• BARRY, Ed

Edward Thomas
LW – L. 5'10", 180 lbs. b: Wellesley, MA, 10/12/1919.

Season	Club	League	GP	G	A	Pts	AG	AA	APts	PIM	GP	G	A	Pts	PIM
1938/40	Northeastern University	WIAA	STATISTICS NOT AVAILABLE												
1940-41	Boston Olympics	EAHL	25	3	6	9	....	....	....	24	4	2	1	3	5
1941-42	Boston Olympics	EAHL	45	19	6	25	....	....	....	40	6	4	0	4	13
1942-43	Boston Olympics	EAHL	7	8	2	10	....	....	....	22	....	....	....	....	....
	Coast Guard Cutters	EAHL	31	20	17	37	....	....	....	17	12	8	6	14	13
1943-44	Coast Guard Cutters	X-Games	37	22	20	42	....	....	....	28	12	8	9	17	8
1944-45			MILITARY SERVICE												
1945-46	Boston Olympics	EAHL	48	26	25	51	....	....	....	57	8	4	7	11	4
1946-47	Boston Olympics	EAHL	32	21	15	36	....	....	....	61	....	....	....	....	....
	Boston Bruins	**NHL**	**19**	**1**	**3**	**4**	**1**	**4**	**5**	**2**	....	....	....	....	....
1947-48	Boston Olympics	EAHL	20	17	8	25	....	....	....	69	....	....	....	....	....
	Boston Olympics	QSHL	40	18	10	28	....	....	....	47	....	....	....	....	....
1948-49	Boston Olympics	QSHL	23	15	13	28	....	....	....	43	....	....	....	....	....
1949-50	Boston Olympics	EAHL	13	10	2	12	....	....	....	23	....	....	....	....	....
1950/52	Boston Olympics	EAHL	DID NOT PLAY – COACHING												
	NHL Totals		**19**	**1**	**3**	**4**	**1**	**4**	**5**	**2**	....	....	....	....	....

EAHL Second All-Star Team (1946)

Signed as a free agent by **Boston**, January 9, 1947. • Coached Boston University, 1953-1973.

• BARRY, Marty

Martin **HHOF**
C – L. 5'11", 175 lbs. b: Quebec City, Que., 12/8/1905 d: 8/20/1969.

Season	Club	League	GP	G	A	Pts	AG	AA	APts	PIM	GP	G	A	Pts	PIM
1924-25	Montreal St-Anthony	MCHL	STATISTICS NOT AVAILABLE												
	Montreal Ste-Anne's	ECHL	1	0	0	0	....	....	....	0	....	....	....	....	....
1925-26	Montreal St-Anthony	MCHL	STATISTICS NOT AVAILABLE												
1926-27	Montreal Bell Telephone	MCHL	STATISTICS NOT AVAILABLE												
1927-28	**New York Americans**	**NHL**	**9**	**1**	**0**	**1**	**2**	**0**	**2**	**2**	....	....	....	....	....
	Philadelphia Arrows	Can-Am	33	11	3	14	....	....	....	70	....	....	....	....	....
1928-29	New Haven Eagles	Can-Am	35	*19	10	*29	....	....	....	54	2	0	1	1	2
1929-30	**Boston Bruins**	**NHL**	**44**	**18**	**15**	**33**	**26**	**36**	**62**	**34**	**6**	**3**	**3**	***6**	**14**
1930-31	**Boston Bruins**	**NHL**	**44**	**20**	**11**	**31**	**41**	**33**	**74**	**26**	**5**	**1**	**1**	**2**	**4**
1931-32	**Boston Bruins**	**NHL**	**48**	**21**	**17**	**38**	**35**	**38**	**73**	**22**	....	....	....	....	....
1932-33	**Boston Bruins**	**NHL**	**47**	**24**	**13**	**37**	**44**	**27**	**71**	**40**	**5**	**2**	**2**	**4**	**6**
1933-34	**Boston Bruins**	**NHL**	**48**	**27**	**12**	**39**	**47**	**25**	**72**	**12**	....	....	....	....	....
1934-35	**Boston Bruins**	**NHL**	**48**	**20**	**20**	**40**	**33**	**35**	**68**	**33**	**4**	**0**	**0**	**0**	**2**
♦1935-36	**Detroit Red Wings**	**NHL**	**48**	**21**	**19**	**40**	**41**	**36**	**77**	**16**	**7**	**2**	**4**	**6**	**6**
♦1936-37	**Detroit Red Wings**	**NHL**	**47**	**17**	**27**	**44**	**29**	**50**	**79**	**6**	**10**	***4**	***7**	***11**	**2**
1937-38	**Detroit Red Wings**	**NHL**	**48**	**9**	**20**	**29**	**15**	**32**	**47**	**34**	....	....	....	....	....
1938-39	**Detroit Red Wings**	**NHL**	**48**	**13**	**28**	**41**	**23**	**44**	**67**	**4**	**6**	**3**	**1**	**4**	**0**
1939-40	**Montreal Canadiens**	**NHL**	**30**	**4**	**10**	**14**	**7**	**16**	**23**	**2**	....	....	....	....	....
	Pittsburgh Hornets	IAHL	6	2	0	2	....	....	....	0	7	2	1	3	4
1940-41	Minneapolis Millers	AHA	32	10	10	20	....	....	....	8	3	1	0	1	0
1941-42	Minneapolis Millers	AHA	DID NOT PLAY – COACHING												
	NHL Totals		**509**	**195**	**192**	**387**	**343**	**372**	**715**	**231**	**43**	**15**	**18**	**33**	**34**

NHL First All-Star Team (1937) • Won Lady Byng Trophy (1937) • Played in NHL All-Star Game (1937)

Signed as a free agent by **NY Americans**, October 27, 1927. Claimed by **Boston** from **NY Americans** (New Haven-Can-Am) in Inter-League Draft, May 13, 1929. Traded to **Detroit** by **Boston** with Art Giroux for Cooney Weiland and Walt Buswell, June 30, 1935. Signed as a free agent by **Montreal**, October 20, 1939. Signed as a free agent by **Pittsburgh** (IAHL), February 11, 1940.

• BARRY, Ray

William Raymond
C – L. 5'11", 170 lbs. b: Boston, MA, 10/4/1928.

Season	Club	League	GP	G	A	Pts	AG	AA	APts	PIM	GP	G	A	Pts	PIM
1945-46	Edmonton Maple Leafs	EJrHL	STATISTICS NOT AVAILABLE												
1946-47	Edmonton Caps	EJrHL	7	5	2	7	....	....	....	2	3	2	1	3	0
1947-48	St. Michael's Majors	OHA-Jr.	31	9	28	37	....	....	....	8	....	....	....	....	....
1948-49	Sherbrooke Saints	QSHL	63	18	61	79	....	....	....	18	12	2	*10	12	6
1949-50	Sherbrooke Saints	QSHL	59	21	40	61	....	....	....	47	11	2	2	4	8
	Sherbrooke Saints	Al-Cup	10	3	7	10	....	....	....	18	....	....	....	....	....
1950-51	Edmonton Flyers	WCMHL	60	28	40	68	....	....	....	38	8	5	5	10	0
1951-52	**Boston Bruins**	**NHL**	**18**	**1**	**2**	**3**	**1**	**2**	**3**	**6**	....	....	....	....	....
	Hershey Bears	AHL	49	17	29	46	....	....	....	20	4	1	1	2	2
1952-53	Calgary Stampeders	WHL	53	15	25	40	....	....	....	16	5	2	2	4	0
1953-54	Calgary Stampeders	WHL	70	17	24	41	....	....	....	20	18	4	10	14	12
	Calgary Stampeders	Ed-Cup	5	1	1	2	....	....	....	0	....	....	....	....	....
1954-55	Calgary Stampeders	WHL	68	25	28	53	....	....	....	17	9	1	4	5	0
1955-56	Calgary Stampeders	WHL	65	23	43	66	....	....	....	13	8	3	8	11	0
1956-57	Calgary Stampeders	WHL	61	11	37	48	....	....	....	26	3	1	2	3	0
1957-58	Red Deer Rustlers	ASHL	STATISTICS NOT AVAILABLE												
	NHL Totals		**18**	**1**	**2**	**3**	**1**	**2**	**3**	**6**	....	....	....	....	....

• WCMHL Second All-Star Team (1952)

Signed as a free agent by **Boston**, October 3, 1950.

• BARTLETT, Jim

James Baker "Rocky"
LW – L. 5'9", 165 lbs. b: Verdun, Que., 5/27/1932.

Season	Club	League	GP	G	A	Pts	AG	AA	APts	PIM	GP	G	A	Pts	PIM
1949-50	Verdun Maple Leafs	QJHL	6	0	0	0	....	....	....	4	1	0	0	0	0
1950-51	Verdun LaSalle	QJHL	38	8	8	16	....	....	....	67	3	1	0	1	7
1951-52	St-Jerome Eagles	QJHL	44	25	31	56	....	....	....	167	....	....	....	....	....
	Boston Olympics	EAHL	14	2	6	8	....	....	....	39	2	1	0	1	4
1952-53	Cincinnati Mohawks	IHL	49	32	30	62	....	....	....	122	9	4	5	9	22

Season	Club	League	REGULAR SEASON								PLAYOFFS				
Season	Club	League	GP	G	A	Pts	AG	AA	APts	PIM	GP	G	A	Pts	PIM
1953-54	Matane Red Rockets	QPHL	61	43	29	72	....	....	....	*139	....	....	....	....	....
	Matane Red Rockets	Al-Cup	16	*11	14	*25	....	....	....	*46	....	....	....	....	....
1954-55	Montreal Canadiens	NHL	2	0	0	0	0	0	0	4	2	0	0	0	0
	Chicoutimi Sagueneens	QHL	58	28	28	56	....	....	....	150	7	1	4	5	20
1955-56	New York Rangers	NHL	12	0	1	1	0	1	1	8	....	....	....	....	....
	Providence Reds	AHL	50	28	19	47	....	....	....	110	9	3	5	8	27
1956-57	Providence Reds	AHL	63	21	22	43	....	....	....	105	4	1	0	1	27
1957-58	Providence Reds	AHL	59	25	21	46	....	....	....	86	5	2	1	3	11
1958-59	New York Rangers	NHL	70	11	9	20	13	9	22	118	....	....	....	....	....
1959-60	New York Rangers	NHL	44	8	4	12	9	4	13	48	....	....	....	....	....
	Springfield Indians	AHL	21	7	3	10	....	....	....	12	8	5	3	8	15
1960-61	Boston Bruins	NHL	63	15	9	24	17	9	26	95	....	....	....	....	....
1961-62	Providence Reds	AHL	62	31	34	65	....	....	....	80	3	0	1	1	8
1962-63	Providence Reds	AHL	67	28	38	66	....	....	....	87	6	1	2	3	10
1963-64	Providence Reds	AHL	72	26	39	65	....	....	....	75	3	2	1	3	4
1964-65	Providence Reds	AHL	71	22	36	58	....	....	....	92	....	....	....	....	....
1965-66	Providence Reds	AHL	68	19	26	45	....	....	....	70	....	....	....	....	....
1966-67	Baltimore Clippers	AHL	67	30	21	51	....	....	....	24	13	3	3	6	10
1967-68	Baltimore Clippers	AHL	71	22	29	51	....	....	....	71	....	....	....	....	....
1968-69	Baltimore Clippers	AHL	73	25	23	48	....	....	....	40	4	1	0	1	10
1969-70	Baltimore Clippers	AHL	65	30	28	58	....	....	....	34	5	2	1	3	2
1970-71	Baltimore Clippers	AHL	63	14	25	39	....	....	....	51	6	0	1	1	4
1971-72	Columbus Seals	IHL	14	4	6	10	....	....	....	23	....	....	....	....	....
	Baltimore Clippers	AHL	11	8	2	10	....	....	....	12	18	6	5	11	14
1972-73	Baltimore Clippers	AHL	72	24	16	40	....	....	....	31	....	....	....	....	....
	NHL Totals		191	34	23	57	39	23	62	273	2	0	0	0	0

Claimed by **NY Rangers** from **Montreal** in Intra-League Draft, June, 1955. Claimed by **Boston** from **NY Rangers** in Intra-League Draft, June 8, 1960. Traded to **Providence** (AHL) by **Boston** for cash, August, 1961. Traded to **Baltimore** (AHL) by **Providence** (AHL) with Aldo Guidolin, Willie Marshall and Ian Anderson for Mike Corbett, Ed Lawson and Ken Stephanson, June, 1966.

• BARTON, Cliff Clifford John

RW – R. 5'7", 155 lbs. b: Sault Ste. Marie, MI, 9/3/1907 d: 9/14/1969.

Season	Club	League	GP	G	A	Pts	AG	AA	APts	PIM	GP	G	A	Pts	PIM
1923/26	Port Arthur Bruins	TBJHL	STATISTICS NOT AVAILABLE												
1926-27	Port Arthur Bruins	TBJHL	STATISTICS NOT AVAILABLE												
	Port Arthur Bruins	M-Cup	6	8	5	13	....	....	....	6	....	....	....	....	....
1927-28	Port Arthur Ports	TBSHL	21	13	6	19	....	....	....	15	....	....	....	....	....
1928-29	Port Arthur Ports	TBSHL	20	10	8	18	....	....	....	12	2	0	0	0	2
	Port Arthur Ports	Al-Cup	7	4	0	4	....	....	....	4	....	....	....	....	....
1929-30	Pittsburgh Pirates	NHL	39	4	2	6	6	5	11	4	....	....	....	....	....
1930-31	Philadelphia Quakers	NHL	43	6	7	13	12	21	33	18	....	....	....	....	....
1931-32	Pittsburgh Yellowjackets	IHL	39	2	3	5	....	....	....	39	....	....	....	....	....
	Springfield Indians	Can-Am	2	0	0	0	....	....	....	0	....	....	....	....	....
1932-33	Buffalo Bisons	IHL	40	1	2	3	....	....	....	12	5	0	0	0	0
1933-34	Buffalo Bisons	IHL	44	19	8	27	....	....	....	18	6	2	1	3	4
1934-35	Buffalo Bisons	IHL	44	18	8	26	....	....	....	43	....	....	....	....	....
1935-36	Buffalo Bisons	IHL	47	12	17	29	....	....	....	32	5	0	0	0	4
1936-37	Buffalo Bisons	IAHL	11	4	3	7	....	....	....	8	....	....	....	....	....
	Philadelphia Ramblers	IAHL	34	7	11	18	....	....	....	10	6	2	0	2	2
1937-38	Philadelphia Ramblers	IAHL	47	13	19	32	....	....	....	11	5	0	1	1	0
1938-39	Philadelphia Ramblers	IAHL	52	21	28	49	....	....	....	16	9	3	3	6	6
1939-40	New York Rangers	NHL	3	0	0	0	0	0	0	0	....	....	....	....	....
	Philadelphia Rockets	IAHL	51	9	19	28	....	....	....	6	....	....	....	....	....
1940-41	Hershey Bears	AHL	6	1	1	2	....	....	....	0	....	....	....	....	....
	St. Louis Flyers	AHA	43	6	8	14	....	....	....	12	9	3	3	6	0
1941-42	St. Louis Flyers	AHA	50	26	22	48	....	....	....	22	3	0	0	0	2
1942-43	New Haven Eagles	AHL	12	2	9	11	....	....	....	0	....	....	....	....	....
	Washington Lions	AHL	22	6	12	18	....	....	....	0	....	....	....	....	....
1943-44	Pittsburgh Hornets	AHL	41	6	15	21	....	....	....	6	....	....	....	....	....
	NHL Totals		85	10	9	19	18	26	44	22	....	....	....	....	....

Transferred to **Philadelphia** after **Pittsburgh** franchise relocated, September 27, 1930. Claimed by **NY Rangers** from **Philadelphia** in Dispersal Draft, September 26, 1931. Signed as a free agent by **Philadelphia** (IAHL) after Buffalo (IAHL) franchise folded, December 9, 1936. Traded to **Hershey** (IAHL) by **NY Rangers** for cash, April 4, 1940.

• BATHGATE, Andy *— see page 873*

• BATHGATE, Frank Frank Douglas

C – R. 5'10", 162 lbs. b: Winnipeg, Man., 2/14/1930.

Season	Club	League	GP	G	A	Pts	AG	AA	APts	PIM	GP	G	A	Pts	PIM
1947-48	Guelph Biltmores	OHA-Jr.	29	4	5	9	....	....	....	6	....	....	....	....	....
1948-49	Guelph Biltmores	OHA-Jr.	45	16	22	38	....	....	....	34	....	....	....	....	....
1949-50	Guelph Biltmores	OHA-Jr.	42	15	30	45	....	....	....	77	15	7	10	17	10
	Guelph Biltmores	M-Cup	11	3	7	10	....	....	....	11	....	....	....	....	....
1950-51	Charlottetown Islanders	MMHL	75	35	58	93	....	....	....	47	11	*9	*10	*19	22
	Charlottetown Islanders	Alx-Cup	4	0	0	0	....	....	....	4	....	....	....	....	....
1951-52	Vancouver Canucks	PCHL	13	0	3	3	....	....	....	2	....	....	....	....	....
	Sydney Millionaires	MMHL	68	25	40	65	....	....	....	46	....	....	....	....	....
1952-53	New York Rangers	NHL	2	0	0	0	0	0	0	2	....	....	....	....	....
	Shawinigan Cataracts	QMHL	54	22	31	53	....	....	....	10	....	....	....	....	....
1953-54	Vancouver Canucks	WHL	5	0	3	3	....	....	....	7	....	....	....	....	....
	Windsor Bulldogs	OHA-Sr.	42	20	39	59	....	....	....	81	3	0	1	1	4
1954-55	Windsor Bulldogs	OHA-Sr.	45	18	31	49	....	....	....	76	12	6	2	8	16
1955-56	Windsor Bulldogs	OHA-Sr.	48	23	30	53	....	....	....	82	....	....	....	....	....
1956-57	Windsor Bulldogs	OHA-Sr.	52	16	37	53	....	....	....	67	12	6	6	12	31
1957-58	Windsor Bulldogs	NOHA	59	33	37	70	....	....	....	99	13	3	11	14	20
1958-59	Windsor Bulldogs	NOHA	21	4	10	14	....	....	....	10	....	....	....	....	....
	Belleville McFarlands	OHA-Sr.	18	7	7	14	....	....	....	2	....	....	....	....	....
	Toledo Mercurys	IHL	25	9	18	27	....	....	....	34	....	....	....	....	....
1959-60	Chatham Maroons	OHA-Sr.	51	13	25	38	....	....	....	12	19	7	12	19	20
	Chatham Maroons	Al-Cup	13	6	21	27	....	....	....	33	....	....	....	....	....
1960-61	Chatham Maroons	OHA-Sr.	15	6	11	17	....	....	....	4	....	....	....	....	....
1961-62	Waterloo Tigers	OHA-Sr.	11	3	10	13	....	....	....	10	....	....	....	....	....
	NHL Totals		2	0	0	0	0	0	0	2	....	....	....	....	....

• Brother of Andy

Loaned to **Sydney** (MMHL) by **NY Rangers** for cash, November 7, 1951. Loaned to **Toledo** (IHL) by **Windsor** (NOHA) for cash, February 7, 1959.

• BAUER, Bobby Robert Theodore HHOF

RW – R. 5'6", 150 lbs. b: Waterloo, Ont., 2/16/1915 d: 9/16/1964.

Season	Club	League	GP	G	A	Pts	AG	AA	APts	PIM	GP	G	A	Pts	PIM
1930-31	St. Michael's Buzzers	OHA-B	STATISTICS NOT AVAILABLE												
1931/33	St. Michael's Majors	OHA-Jr.	STATISTICS NOT AVAILABLE												
1933-34	St. Michael's Majors	OHA-Jr.	10	4	2	6	....	....	....	0	2	0	1	1	0
	St. Michael's Majors	M-Cup	13	10	5	15	....	....	....	0	....	....	....	....	....
1934-35	Toronto British Consols	TMHL	6	2	0	2	....	....	....	0	4	2	3	5	2
	Kitchener Greenshirts	OHA-Jr.	11	12	6	18	....	....	....	0	3	1	2	3	2
1935-36	Boston Cubs	Can-Am	48	15	13	28	....	....	....	8	....	....	....	....	....
1936-37	Boston Bruins	NHL	1	1	0	1	2	0	2	0	1	0	0	0	0
	Providence Reds	IAHL	44	14	4	18	....	....	....	4	2	0	1	1	0
1937-38	Boston Bruins	NHL	48	20	14	34	33	23	56	9	3	0	0	0	2
♦1938-39	Boston Bruins	NHL	48	13	18	31	23	28	51	4	12	3	2	5	0
1939-40	Boston Bruins	NHL	48	17	26	43	28	41	69	2	6	1	0	1	2
♦1940-41	Boston Bruins	NHL	48	17	22	39	26	32	58	2	11	2	2	4	0
1941-42	Boston Bruins	NHL	36	13	22	35	17	26	43	11	....	....	....	....	....
	Ottawa RCAF	QSHL	....	....	....	....	....	....	....	....	6	7	6	13	4
	Ottawa RCAF	Al-Cup	5	3	6	9	....	....	....	0	....	....	....	....	....
1942-43	Halifax RCAF	NSDHL	7	*12	8	20	....	....	....	0	5	7	5	12	0
	Halifax RCAF	Al-Cup	7	2	5	7	....	....	....	0	....	....	....	....	....
1943-44			MILITARY SERVICE												
1944-45	Toronto Peoples Credit	TIHL	1	1	0	1	....	....	....	0	8	5	5	8	2
1945-46	Boston Bruins	NHL	39	11	10	21	13	14	27	4	10	4	3	7	2
1946-47	Boston Bruins	NHL	58	30	24	54	34	29	63	4	5	1	1	2	0
1947-48	Kitchener Dutchmen	OHA-Sr.	8	8	7	15	....	....	....	22	10	5	4	9	6
1948-49	Kitchener Dutchmen	OHA-Sr.	31	17	21	38	....	....	....	13	12	4	4	8	0
1949-50	Kitchener Dutchmen	OHA-Sr.	23	10	14	24	....	....	....	9	9	1	2	3	2
1950-51			OUT OF HOCKEY – RETIRED												
1951-52	Kitchener Dutchmen	OHA-Sr.	37	8	10	18	....	....	....	14	1	0	1	1	0
	Boston Bruins	NHL	1	1	1	2	1	1	2	0	....	....	....	....	....
	NHL Totals		327	123	137	260	177	194	371	36	48	11	8	19	6

NHL Second All-Star Team (1939, 1940, 1941, 1947) • Won Lady Byng Trophy (1940, 1941, 1947) • Played in NHL All-Star Game (1939, 1947)

Claimed by **Boston** from **Syracuse** (IHL) in Inter-League Draft, May 11, 1935. • Played in game that Kraut Line had their jersey numbers retired, Boston vs. Chicago, March 18, 1952.

• BAUN, Bob *— see page 874*

• BEATTIE, Red John

LW – L. 5'9", 170 lbs. b: Ibstock, England, 10/2/1907 Deceased.

Season	Club	League	GP	G	A	Pts	AG	AA	APts	PIM	GP	G	A	Pts	PIM
1925/28	Edmonton Superiors	ESrHL	STATISTICS NOT AVAILABLE												
1928-29	Vancouver Lions	PCHL	26	5	0	5	....	....	....	24	2	0	0	0	2
1929-30	Vancouver Lions	PCHL	36	12	9	21	....	....	....	30	4	2	0	2	2
1930-31	Springfield Indians	Can-Am	7	8	6	14	....	....	....	4	....	....	....	....	....
	Boston Bruins	NHL	32	10	11	21	20	33	53	25	4	0	0	0	0
1931-32	Boston Bruins	NHL	1	0	0	0	0	0	0	0	....	....	....	....	....
1932-33	Boston Bruins	NHL	48	8	12	20	14	25	39	12	5	0	0	0	2
1933-34	Boston Bruins	NHL	48	9	13	22	15	27	42	26	....	....	....	....	....
1934-35	Boston Bruins	NHL	48	9	18	27	15	31	46	27	4	1	0	1	2
1935-36	Boston Bruins	NHL	48	14	18	32	27	34	61	27	2	0	0	0	2
1936-37	Boston Bruins	NHL	48	8	7	15	13	13	26	10	3	1	0	1	0
1937-38	Boston Bruins	NHL	14	0	0	0	0	0	0	0	....	....	....	....	....
	Detroit Red Wings	NHL	11	1	2	3	2	3	5	0	....	....	....	....	....
	Pittsburgh Hornets	IAHL	2	0	0	0	....	....	....	0	....	....	....	....	....
	New York Americans	NHL	19	3	4	7	5	6	11	5	6	2	2	4	2
1938-39	New York Americans	NHL	17	0	0	0	0	0	0	5	....	....	....	....	....
	New Haven Eagles	IAHL	13	1	3	4	....	....	....	2	....	....	....	....	....
1939-40			DID NOT PLAY												
1940-41			DID NOT PLAY												
1941-42	Vancouver Norvans	PCHL	21	15	9	24	....	....	....	6	3	1	0	1	2
1942-43	Victoria VMD	NNDHL	16	6	1	7	....	....	....	11	....	....	....	....	....
	NHL Totals		334	62	85	147	111	172	283	137	24	4	2	6	8

Traded to **NY Rangers** by **Vancouver** (PCHL) with Joe Jerwa for $25,000, May 6, 1930. Rights awarded to **Boston** by NHL to settle contract dispute, December 12, 1930. Traded to **Detroit** by **Boston** for Gord Pettinger, December 19, 1937. Traded to **NY Americans** by **Detroit** for Joe Lamb, January 24, 1938.

• BECKETT, Bob Robert Owen

C – L. 6', 185 lbs. b: Unionville, Ont., 4/8/1936.

Season	Club	League	GP	G	A	Pts	AG	AA	APts	PIM	GP	G	A	Pts	PIM
1954-55	Galt Black Hawks	OHA-Jr.	49	16	22	38	....	....	....	18	4	0	3	3	0
1955-56	Barrie Flyers	OHA-Jr.	48	16	26	42	....	....	....	24	18	*16	8	*24	8
	Hershey Bears	AHL	1	0	1	1	....	....	....	0	....	....	....	....	....
1956-57	Boston Bruins	NHL	18	0	3	3	0	3	3	2	....	....	....	....	....
	Victoria Cougars	WHL	16	0	0	0	....	....	....	5	....	....	....	....	....
	Quebec Aces	QHL	26	9	15	24	....	....	....	6	10	4	3	7	11
	Quebec Aces	Ed-Cup	6	1	3	4	....	....	....	0	....	....	....	....	....
1957-58	Boston Bruins	NHL	9	0	0	0	0	0	0	2	....	....	....	....	....
	Springfield Indians	AHL	62	17	16	33	....	....	....	40	13	4	4	8	13
1958-59	Quebec Aces	QHL	25	6	5	11	....	....	....	5	....	....	....	....	....
	Providence Reds	AHL	32	5	10	15	....	....	....	4	....	....	....	....	....
1959-60	Providence Reds	AHL	57	11	31	42	....	....	....	12	5	1	3	4	2
1960-61	Providence Reds	AHL	72	22	34	56	....	....	....	28	....	....	....	....	....
1961-62	Boston Bruins	NHL	34	7	2	9	8	2	10	14	....	....	....	....	....
	Providence Reds	AHL	27	13	15	28	....	....	....	21	3	1	1	2	0
1962-63	Providence Reds	AHL	62	12	25	37	....	....	....	34	6	0	2	2	2
1963-64	Boston Bruins	NHL	7	0	1	1	0	1	1	0	....	....	....	....	....
	Providence Reds	AHL	33	14	15	29	....	....	....	4	....	....	....	....	....
	NHL Totals		68	7	6	13	8	6	14	18	....	....	....	....	....

• BEDARD, James James Leo

D – L. 6', 180 lbs. b: Admiral, Sask., 11/19/1927.

Season	Club	League	GP	G	A	Pts	AG	AA	APts	PIM	GP	G	A	Pts	PIM
1945-46	Moose Jaw Canucks	SJHL	10	0	3	3	....	....	....	20	4	0	1	1	8
	Moose Jaw Canucks	M-Cup	8	2	2	4	....	....	....	15	....	....	....	....	....
1946-47	Moose Jaw Canucks	SJHL	26	11	5	16	....	....	....	*82	6	0	1	1	*18
	Moose Jaw Canucks	M-Cup	6	0	1	1	....	....	....	50	....	....	....	....	....
1947-48	Moose Jaw Canucks	SJHL	25	12	5	17	....	....	....	60	5	0	0	0	*19
	Moose Jaw Canucks	M-Cup	4	1	1	2	....	....	....	10	....	....	....	....	....

			REGULAR SEASON								PLAYOFFS				
Season	Club	League	GP	G	A	Pts	AG	AA	APts	PIM	GP	G	A	Pts	PIM
1948-49	Kansas City Pla-Mors	USHL	63	5	6	11	....	....	....	2	1	1	2	3	0
1949-50	**Chicago Black Hawks**	**NHL**	**5**	**0**	**0**	**0**	**0**	**0**	**0**	**2**	....	....	....	....	....
	Kansas City Pla-Mors	USHL	56	3	15	18	....	....	....	43	3	0	0	0	4
1950-51	**Chicago Black Hawks**	**NHL**	**17**	**1**	**1**	**2**	**1**	**1**	**2**	**6**	....	....	....	....	....
	Milwaukee Seagulls	USHL	50	4	16	20	....	....	....	59	....	....	....	....	....
1951-52	New Westminster Royals	PCHL	66	4	12	16	....	....	....	104	7	1	1	2	14
1952-53	New Westminster Royals	WHL	70	4	15	19	....	....	....	116	....	....	....	....	....
1953-54	New Westminster Royals	WHL	58	1	12	13	....	....	....	77	7	0	2	2	19
1954-55	New Westminster Royals	WHL	60	1	7	8	....	....	....	70	....	....	....	....	....
1955-56	Seattle Americans	WHL	15	1	0	1	....	....	....	29	....	....	....	....	....
	Penticton Vees	OSHL	40	2	13	15	....	....	....	96	7	1	1	2	20
1956-57	Vancouver Canucks	WHL	16	1	1	2	....	....	....	23	....	....	....	....	....
	Kelowna Packers	OSHL	27	1	6	7	....	....	....	18	7	0	2	2	4
1957-58	New Westminster Royals	WHL	12	0	2	2	....	....	....	4	....	....	....	....	....
	NHL Totals		**22**	**1**	**1**	**2**	**1**	**1**	**2**	**8**	....	....	....	....	....

• BEHLING, Dick Clarence Richard

D – R. 6'1", 195 lbs. b: Berlin, Ont., 3/16/1916 Deceased.

Season	Club	League	GP	G	A	Pts	AG	AA	APts	PIM	GP	G	A	Pts	PIM
1934-35	Kitchener Greenshirts	OHA-Jr.	7	1	0	1	....	....	....	4	....	....	....	....	....
1935-36	Kitchener Greenshirts	OHA-Jr.	STATISTICS NOT AVAILABLE												
1936-37	Baltimore Orioles	EAHL	48	9	5	14	....	....	....	16	3	1	2	3	2
1937-38	Baltimore Orioles	EAHL	56	14	11	25	....	....	....	26	....	....	....	....	....
1938-39	Harringay Greyhounds	Ln-Cup	....	2	3	5	....	....	....	....	....	....	....	....	....
	Harringay Greyhounds	Britain	....	8	10	18	....	....	....	....	....	....	....	....	....
	Harringay Greyhounds	Nat-Tmt	....	9	4	13	....	....	....	....	....	....	....	....	....
1939-40	Detroit Holzbaugh	MOHL	35	9	7	16	....	....	....	22	1	0	0	0	0
1940-41	**Detroit Red Wings**	**NHL**	**3**	**0**	**0**	**0**	**0**	**0**	**0**	**0**	....	....	....	....	....
	Indianapolis Capitols	AHL	54	5	8	13	....	....	....	18	....	....	....	....	....
1941-42	Indianapolis Capitols	AHL	54	4	5	9	....	....	....	26	10	0	2	2	4
1942-43	**Detroit Red Wings**	**NHL**	**2**	**1**	**0**	**1**	**1**	**0**	**1**	**2**	....	....	....	....	....
	Indianapolis Capitols	AHL	22	1	4	5	....	....	....	10	....	....	....	....	....
1943-44			MILITARY SERVICE												
1944-45			MILITARY SERVICE												
1945-46	Indianapolis Capitols	AHL	17	0	3	3	....	....	....	4	5	0	0	0	0
1946-47	Hamilton Pats	OHA-Sr.	14	3	4	7	....	....	....	6	3	0	0	0	0
1947-48	Kitchener Dutchmen	OHA-Sr.	36	7	15	22	....	....	....	16	10	1	5	6	6
1948-49	Kitchener Dutchmen	OHA-Sr.	39	1	13	14	....	....	....	20	12	4	3	7	6
1949-50	Kitchener Dutchmen	OHA-Sr.	26	1	9	10	....	....	....	10	14	0	3	3	6
1950-51	Kitchener Dutchmen	OMHL	23	2	9	11	....	....	....	4	....	....	....	....	....
	NHL Totals		**5**	**1**	**0**	**1**	**1**	**0**	**1**	**2**	....	....	....	....	....

EAHL First All-Star Team (1938)

Signed as a free agent by **Detroit**, October 16, 1940.

• BEISLER, Frank

D – L. 6'2", 190 lbs. b: New Haven, CT, 10/18/1913.

Season	Club	League	GP	G	A	Pts	AG	AA	APts	PIM	GP	G	A	Pts	PIM
1930-31	New Haven Collegiate	H.S.	STATISTICS NOT AVAILABLE												
1931-32	Bronx Tigers	X-Games	STATISTICS NOT AVAILABLE												
1932-33	Bronx Tigers	X-Games	STATISTICS NOT AVAILABLE												
1933-34	Hershey B'ars	EAHL	25	3	1	4	....	....	....	23	6	1	0	1	8
1934-35	New Haven Eagles	Can-Am	41	3	1	4	....	....	....	32	....	....	....	....	....
1935-36	New Haven Eagles	Can-Am	46	4	5	9	....	....	....	38	....	....	....	....	....
1936-37	**New York Americans**	**NHL**	**1**	**0**	**0**	**0**	**0**	**0**	**0**	**0**	....	....	....	....	....
	New Haven Eagles	IAHL	44	3	2	5	....	....	....	50	....	....	....	....	....
1937-38	New Haven Eagles	IAHL	26	0	2	2	....	....	....	21	2	0	0	0	0
1938-39	Springfield Indians	IAHL	53	1	1	2	....	....	....	75	3	0	1	1	2
1939-40	**New York Americans**	**NHL**	**1**	**0**	**0**	**0**	**0**	**0**	**0**	**0**	....	....	....	....	....
	Springfield Indians	IAHL	50	3	8	11	....	....	....	37	3	0	2	2	2
1940-41	Springfield Indians	AHL	56	1	10	11	....	....	....	46	3	0	0	0	0
1941-42	Springfield Indians	AHL	42	2	6	8	....	....	....	35	5	0	0	0	0
1942-43	Buffalo Bisons	AHL	55	2	7	9	....	....	....	27	9	1	0	1	4
1943-44	Buffalo Bisons	AHL	25	3	4	7	....	....	....	15	....	....	....	....	....
1944-45			MILITARY SERVICE												
1945-46	Buffalo Bisons	AHL	4	0	1	1	....	....	....	0	....	....	....	....	....
1946-47	Buffalo Bisons	AHL	DID NOT PLAY – COACHING												
1947-48	Baltimore Clippers	EAHL	DID NOT PLAY – COACHING												
	NHL Totals		**2**	**0**	**0**	**0**	**0**	**0**	**0**	**0**	....	....	....	....	....

EAHL First All-Star Team (1934) • AHL Second All-Star Team (1941) • AHL First All-Star Team (1942, 1943)

• BELISLE, Danny Daniel George

RW – R. 5'10", 164 lbs. b: South Porcupine, Ont., 5/9/1937.

Season	Club	League	GP	G	A	Pts	AG	AA	APts	PIM	GP	G	A	Pts	PIM
1955-56	Guelph Biltmores	OHA-Jr.	48	25	25	50	....	....	....	25	3	1	0	1	0
1956-57	Guelph Biltmores	OHA-Jr.	52	36	30	66	....	....	....	70	10	6	10	16	21
	Guelph Biltmores	M-Cup	6	2	2	4	....	....	....	8	....	....	....	....	....
1957-58	Trois-Rivieres Lions	QHL	55	24	31	55	....	....	....	32	....	....	....	....	....
	Providence Reds	AHL	7	2	2	4	....	....	....	2	....	....	....	....	....
1958-59	Vancouver Canucks	WHL	70	31	31	62	....	....	....	41	9	4	1	5	13
1959-60	Vancouver Canucks	WHL	68	24	24	48	....	....	....	27	11	*6	7	13	0
1960-61	**New York Rangers**	**NHL**	**4**	**2**	**0**	**2**	**2**	**0**	**2**	**0**	....	....	....	....	....
	Kitchener Beavers	EPHL	16	8	7	15	....	....	....	14	....	....	....	....	....
	Vancouver Canucks	WHL	51	30	17	47	....	....	....	17	9	0	2	2	0
1961-62	Los Angeles Blades	WHL	61	30	38	68	....	....	....	27	....	....	....	....	....
1962-63	San Francisco Seals	WHL	63	29	41	70	....	....	....	14	17	8	7	15	2
1963-64	Baltimore Clippers	AHL	13	1	2	3	....	....	....	4	....	....	....	....	....
	Vancouver Canucks	WHL	52	22	22	44	....	....	....	22	....	....	....	....	....
1964-65	Omaha Knights	CPHL	6	2	6	8	....	....	....	2	....	....	....	....	....
	Quebec Aces	AHL	4	0	0	0	....	....	....	0	....	....	....	....	....
	Victoria Maple Leafs	WHL	53	23	24	47	....	....	....	40	12	2	5	7	6
1965-66	Memphis Wings	CPHL	65	16	30	46	....	....	....	39	....	....	....	....	....
1966-67	California Seals	WHL	62	25	22	47	....	....	....	22	1	0	0	0	0
1967-68	Vancouver Canucks	WHL	66	15	20	35	....	....	....	8	....	....	....	....	....
1968-69	Jacksonville Rockets	EHL	71	39	46	85	....	....	....	88	4	2	1	3	0
1969-70	Barrie Flyers	OHA-Sr.	7	1	2	3	....	....	....	16	....	....	....	....	....
	Columbus Checkers	IHL	58	32	43	75	....	....	....	21	....	....	....	....	....
1970-71	Des Moines Oak Leafs	IHL	41	8	21	29	....	....	....	10	....	....	....	....	....
1971-72	Des Moines Oak Leafs	IHL	DID NOT PLAY – COACHING												
	NHL Totals		**4**	**2**	**0**	**2**	**2**	**0**	**2**	**0**	....	....	....	....	....

Traded to **San Francisco** (WHL) by **NY Rangers** (LA Blades-WHL) for Bob Solinger with NY Rangers holding right of recall, July, 1962. Loaned to **Victoria** (WHL) by **NY Rangers** for remainder of 1964-65 season for cash, December 12, 1964. Claimed by **Detroit** (Pittsburgh (AHL) from **NY Rangers** in Reverse Draft, June 9, 1965. Claimed by **Springfield** (AHL) from **Detroit** in Reserve Draft, June 15, 1966. Signed as a free agent by **Columbus** (IHL), December, 1969. Traded to **Des Moines** (IHL) by **Port Huron** (IHL) with Nelson Neclair for Ken Knapton, October, 1970.

• BELIVEAU, Jean — see page 880

• BELL, Billy William Edward

C/RW – R. 5'10", 180 lbs. b: Lachine, Que., 6/10/1891 d: 6/3/1959.

Season	Club	League	GP	G	A	Pts	AG	AA	APts	PIM	GP	G	A	Pts	PIM
1909-10	Montreal Bell	MCMHL	1	0	0	0	....	....	....	3	....	....	....	....	....
1910-11	Lachine Eagles	MCHL	STATISTICS NOT AVAILABLE												
	Montreal Ranger Rustlers	MCJHL	STATISTICS NOT AVAILABLE												
1911-12	Montreal Baillargeon	MCHL	4	3	0	3	....	....	....	6	....	....	....	....	....
1912-13	Montreal Stars	MCHL	7	4	0	4	....	....	....	16	....	....	....	....	....
	Montreal Dominions	MCMHL	8	4	0	4	....	....	....	....	2	0	0	0	*14
1913-14	Montreal Wanderers	NHA	2	1	0	1	....	....	....	0	....	....	....	....	....
	Montreal AAA	MCHL	3	0	0	0	....	....	....	13	....	....	....	....	....
1914-15	Ottawa Senators	NHA	11	1	0	1	....	....	....	17	....	....	....	....	....
1915-16	Montreal Wanderers	NHA	22	8	2	10	....	....	....	78	....	....	....	....	....
1916-17	Montreal Wanderers	NHA	14	11	0	11	....	....	....	44	....	....	....	....	....
1917-18	**Montreal Wanderers**	**NHL**	**2**	**1**	**0**	**1**	**1**	**0**	**1**	**0**	....	....	....	....	....
	Montreal Canadiens	**NHL**	**6**	**0**	**0**	**0**	**0**	**0**	**0**	**6**	....	....	....	....	....
1918-19	**Montreal Canadiens**	**NHL**	**1**	**0**	**0**	**0**	**0**	**0**	**0**	**0**	....	....	....	....	....
1919-20			DID NOT PLAY												
1920-21	**Montreal Canadiens**	**NHL**	**4**	**0**	**0**	**0**	**0**	**0**	**0**	**2**	....	....	....	....	....
1921-22	**Montreal Canadiens**	**NHL**	**6**	**1**	**0**	**1**	**1**	**0**	**1**	**0**	....	....	....	....	....
	Ottawa Senators	**NHL**	**23**	**2**	**2**	**4**	**3**	**6**	**9**	**4**	**1**	**0**	**0**	**0**	**0**
1922-23	**Montreal Canadiens**	**NHL**	**19**	**0**	**0**	**0**	**0**	**0**	**0**	**2**	**2**	**0**	**0**	**0**	**0**
1923-24	**Montreal Canadiens**	**NHL**	**11**	**0**	**0**	**0**	**0**	**0**	**0**	**0**	**2**	**0**	**0**	**0**	**0**
♦	Montreal Canadiens	St-Cup	3	0	0	0	....	....	....	0	....	....	....	....	....
	NHL Totals		**72**	**4**	**2**	**6**	**5**	**6**	**11**	**14**	**5**	**0**	**0**	**0**	**0**
	Other Major League Totals		49	21	2	23	....	....	....	139					

Signed as a free agent by **Montreal Wanderers** (NHA), January 12, 1914. Rights retained by **Montreal Wanderers** after NHA folded, November 26, 1917. Claimed by **Montreal Canadiens** from **Montreal Wanderers** in Dispersal Draft, January 4, 1918. Transferred to **Ottawa** by **Montreal Canadiens** for the remainder of the 1921-22 season as compensation for Montreal acquiring the rights of Sprague Cleghorn (November 26, 1921), January 6, 1922. • 1923-24 Stanley Cup totals includes series with Calgary (WCHL) and Vancouver (PCHA).

• BELL, Harry

RW/D – R. 5'9", 176 lbs. b: Regina, Sask., 10/31/1925.

Season	Club	League	GP	G	A	Pts	AG	AA	APts	PIM	GP	G	A	Pts	PIM
1943-44	Regina Commandos	S-SSHL	16	4	5	9	....	....	....	8	5	2	0	2	6
	Regina Commandos	Al-Cup	10	0	0	0	....	....	....	4	....	....	....	....	....
1944-45			MILITARY SERVICE												
1945-46	New York Rovers	EAHL	35	9	11	20	....	....	....	16	....	....	....	....	....
1946-47	**New York Rangers**	**NHL**	**1**	**0**	**1**	**1**	**0**	**1**	**1**	**0**	....	....	....	....	....
	New York Rovers	EAHL	26	6	7	13	....	....	....	8	....	....	....	....	....
	New Haven Ramblers	AHL	28	3	5	8	....	....	....	10	3	0	1	1	2
1947-48	New Haven Ramblers	AHL	66	10	15	25	....	....	....	61	4	0	0	0	10
1948-49	St. Paul Saints	USHL	60	9	21	30	....	....	....	77	7	1	4	5	2
1949-50	St. Paul Saints	USHL	63	14	15	29	....	....	....	57	3	0	0	0	4
1950-51	Tacoma Rockets	PCHL	62	14	26	40	....	....	....	25	6	0	3	3	2
1951-52	New York Rovers	EAHL	34	11	10	21	....	....	....	28	....	....	....	....	....
1952-53	Regina Caps	SSHL	31	22	20	42	....	....	....	22	7	7	3	10	24
	Regina Caps	Al-Cup	13	9	5	14	....	....	....	19	....	....	....	....	....
	NHL Totals		**1**	**0**	**1**	**1**	**0**	**1**	**1**	**0**	....	....	....	....	....

SSHL First All-Star Team (1953) • Signed as a free agent by **NY Rangers**, October 10, 1944.

• BELL, Joe Joseph Alexander

LW – L. 5'9", 165 lbs. b: Portage la Prairie, Man., 11/27/1923.

Season	Club	League	GP	G	A	Pts	AG	AA	APts	PIM	GP	G	A	Pts	PIM
1939-40	Portage Terriers	MJHL	1	0	1	1	....	....	....	0	....	....	....	....	....
1940-41	Portage Terriers	MJHL	16	17	13	30	....	....	....	14	5	5	2	7	12
1941-42	Portage Terriers	MJHL	18	*36	19	55	....	....	....	21	12	*31	16	*47	6
1942-43	**New York Rangers**	**NHL**	**15**	**2**	**5**	**7**	**2**	**5**	**7**	**6**	....	....	....	....	....
	Winnipeg Navy	WNDHL	9	4	5	9	....	....	....	2	4	2	2	4	8
1943-44	Winnipeg Navy	WNDHL	10	*17	6	*23	....	....	....	14	....	....	....	....	....
	Cornwallis Navy	NSDHL	1	5	2	7	....	....	....	....	11	12	15	27	*29
1944-45	St. John's Navy	Nfld-Sr.	2	2	4	6	....	....	....	0	....	....	....	....	....
1945-46	New Haven Ramblers	AHL	45	*33	17	50	....	....	....	16	....	....	....	....	....
	Hershey Bears	AHL	17	*13	14	27	....	....	....	20	3	1	1	2	4
1946-47	**New York Rangers**	**NHL**	**47**	**6**	**4**	**10**	**7**	**5**	**12**	**12**	....	....	....	....	....
	New Haven Ramblers	AHL	13	10	4	14	....	....	....	10	....	....	....	....	....
1947-48	Buffalo Bisons	AHL	66	30	27	57	....	....	....	64	8	4	0	4	4
1948-49	Buffalo Bisons	AHL	3	0	0	0	....	....	....	0	....	....	....	....	....
	Dallas Texans	USHL	55	37	38	75	....	....	....	40	4	4	1	5	2
1949-50	Cincinnati Mohawks	AHL	7	1	2	3	....	....	....	0	....	....	....	....	....
	Louisville Blades	USHL	53	31	25	56	....	....	....	8	....	....	....	....	....
1950-51	Seattle Ironmen	PCHL	63	*46	32	78	....	....	....	32	....	....	....	....	....
1951-52	Seattle Ironmen	PCHL	66	38	31	69	....	....	....	24	4	0	3	3	0
1952-53	Seattle Bombers	WHL	59	25	28	53	....	....	....	20	5	1	3	4	2

Season	Club	League	GP	G	A	Pts	AG	AA	APts	PIM	GP	G	A	Pts	PIM
			REGULAR SEASON								PLAYOFFS				
1953-54	Seattle Bombers	WHL	70	24	23	47	....	....	....	22	....	....	....	....	....
1954-55	Nelson Maple Leafs	WIHL	38	29	49	*78	....	....	....	58	9	5	3	8	*24
1955-56	Nelson Maple Leafs	WIHL	42	19	31	50	....	....	....	42	5	1	1	2	14
	NHL Totals		**62**	**8**	**9**	**17**	**9**	**10**	**19**	**18**	....	....	....	....	....

• Brother of Gordie • AHL First All-Star Team (1946) • USHL Second All-Star Team (1949) • PCHL First All-Star Team (1951)

Signed as a free agent by **NY Rangers**, October 30, 1942. Traded to **Montreal** by **NY Rangers** with Hal Laycoe and George Robertson for Buddy O'Connor and Frank Eddolls, August 19, 1947.

• BELLEFEUILLE, Pete "The Fleeting Frenchman"

RW – R. 5'10", 180 lbs. b: Trois-Rivieres, Que., 10/19/1901 Deceased.

Season	Club	League	GP	G	A	Pts	AG	AA	APts	PIM	GP	G	A	Pts	PIM
1920-21	Quebec Voltigers	QCHL	11	*17	0	17	....	....	....	....	4	0	1	1	....
1921-22	Quebec Voltigers	QCHL	STATISTICS NOT AVAILABLE												
1922-23	Trois-Rivieres Volants	QPHL	4	7	0	7	....	....	....	....	....	....	....	....	....
	Trois-Rivieres Violettes	Big-4	7	9	0	9	....	....	....	....	3	*4	0	4	....
1923-24	Iroquois Papermakers	NOHA	8	*10	4	*14	....	....	....	12	....	....	....	....	....
1924-25	London AAA	OHA-Sr.	11	9	4	13	....	....	....	27	....	....	....	....	....
1925-26	**Toronto St. Pats**	**NHL**	**36**	**14**	**2**	**16**	**24**	**13**	**37**	**22**	....	....	....	....	....
1926-27	**Toronto St. Pats**	**NHL**	**13**	**0**	**0**	**0**	**0**	**0**	**0**	**12**	....	....	....	....	....
	London Panthers	Can-Pro	6	4	0	4	....	....	....	4	....	....	....	....	....
	Detroit Cougars	**NHL**	**18**	**6**	**0**	**6**	**11**	**0**	**11**	**14**	....	....	....	....	....
1927-28	Detroit Olympics	Can-Pro	42	20	6	26	....	....	....	75	2	1	0	1	12
1928-29	**Detroit Cougars**	**NHL**	**1**	**1**	**0**	**1**	**3**	**0**	**3**	**0**	....	....	....	....	....
	Detroit Olympics	Can-Pro	42	19	5	24	....	....	....	43	2	1	0	1	2
1929-30	**Detroit Cougars**	**NHL**	**24**	**5**	**2**	**7**	**7**	**5**	**12**	**10**	....	....	....	....	....
	Detroit Olympics	IHL	18	6	4	10	....	....	....	13	2	0	0	0	2
1930-31	Seattle Eskimos	PCHL	34	12	1	13	....	....	....	12	4	*2	0	2	6
1931-32	Syracuse Stars	IHL	6	1	1	2	....	....	....	4	....	....	....	....	....
	Trois-Rivieres Renards	QPHL	24	8	10	18	....	....	....	29	....	....	....	....	....
1932-33			DID NOT PLAY												
1933-34	Quebec Beavers	Can-Am	1	0	0	0	....	....	....	0	....	....	....	....	....
	NHL Totals		**92**	**26**	**4**	**30**	**45**	**18**	**63**	**58**	....	....	....	....	....

Signed as a free agent by **Toronto**, September 21, 1925. Traded to **Detroit** by **Toronto** for Harold Halderson, January 9, 1927. Traded to **Seattle** (PCHL) by **Detroit** with Bobby Connors for cash, September 12, 1930.

• BELLEMER, Andy Andrew Edward

D – L. 5'11", 185 lbs. b: Penetanguishene, Ont., 7/3/1903 d: 4/12/1960.

Season	Club	League	GP	G	A	Pts	AG	AA	APts	PIM	GP	G	A	Pts	PIM
1925-26	New Hamburg Sailors	OHA-Sr.	STATISTICS NOT AVAILABLE												
1926-27	Windsor Hornets	Can-Pro	32	4	0	4	....	....	....	*88	....	....	....	....	....
1927-28	Windsor Hornets	Can-Pro	38	5	3	8	....	....	....	110	....	....	....	....	....
1928-29	Windsor Bulldogs	Can-Pro	41	3	1	4	....	....	....	75	8	0	0	0	19
1929-30	Windsor Bulldogs	IHL	41	6	2	8	....	....	....	49	....	....	....	....	....
1930-31	Windsor Bulldogs	IHL	47	6	5	11	....	....	....	*114	6	0	2	2	6
1931-32	Windsor Bulldogs	IHL	21	0	2	2	....	....	....	59	....	....	....	....	....
	Cleveland Indians	IHL	20	2	3	5	....	....	....	49	....	....	....	....	....
1932-33	**Montreal Maroons**	**NHL**	**15**	**0**	**0**	**0**	**0**	**0**	**0**	**0**	....	....	....	....	....
	Cleveland Indians	IHL	26	0	1	1	....	....	....	78	5	0	0	0	12
1933-34	Windsor–Syracuse	IHL	42	2	3	5	....	....	....	79	6	1	0	1	*27
1934-35	Kansas City Greyhounds	AHA	41	4	4	8	....	....	....	59	2	0	0	0	2
1935-36	Rochester Cardinals	IHL	45	0	8	8	....	....	....	80	....	....	....	....	....
1936-37	Tulsa Oilers	AHA	46	9	6	15	....	....	....	64	....	....	....	....	....
1937-38	Tulsa Oilers	AHA	43	3	9	12	....	....	....	37	4	0	0	0	0
1938-39	Tulsa Oilers	AHA	48	2	13	15	....	....	....	65	8	1	0	1	10
1939-40	Tulsa Oilers	AHA	43	4	7	11	....	....	....	51	....	....	....	....	....
1940-41	Tulsa Oilers	AHA	48	3	7	10	....	....	....	67	....	....	....	....	....
1941-42	Tulsa Oilers	AHA	33	2	8	10	....	....	....	20	....	....	....	....	....
	Dallas Texans	AHA	15	2	5	7	....	....	....	24	....	....	....	....	....
1942-43	Toronto Research	OHA-Sr.	1	0	0	0	....	....	....	2	....	....	....	....	....
	Toronto Dehavilland	TMHL	14	2	5	7	....	....	....	32	4	0	0	0	12
	NHL Totals		**15**	**0**	**0**	**0**	**0**	**0**	**0**	**0**	....	....	....	....	....

AHA First All-Star Team (1937) • AHA Second All-Star Team (1938)

Signed as a free agent by **Windsor** (Can-Pro), October 14, 1926. Traded to **Montreal Maroons** by **Windsor** (IHL) for cash, November 28, 1932. Traded to **Syracuse** (IHL) by **Windsor** (IHL) for Gus Forslund and Sparky Vail, December, 1933. Signed as a free agent by **Rochester** (IHL), October 10, 1936.

• BEND, Lin John Linthwaite

C – L. 5'10", 165 lbs. b: Poplar Point, Man., 12/20/1922 d: 4/10/1978.

Season	Club	League	GP	G	A	Pts	AG	AA	APts	PIM	GP	G	A	Pts	PIM
1939-40	Portage Terriers	MJHL	1	0	0	0	....	....	....	0	....	....	....	....	....
1940-41	Portage Terriers	MJHL	19	16	15	31	....	....	....	10	6	4	2	6	2
1941-42	Portage Terriers	MJHL	17	27	*31	*58	....	....	....	24	5	9	7	16	8
	Portage Terriers	M-Cup	10	13	8	21	....	....	....	7	....	....	....	....	....
1942-43	**New York Rangers**	**NHL**	**8**	**3**	**1**	**4**	**3**	**1**	**4**	**2**	....	....	....	....	....
	Winnipeg Army	WNDHL	7	3	1	4	....	....	....	4	....	....	....	....	....
1943-44			MILITARY SERVICE												
1944-45	Winnipeg Army	WNDHL	16	16	14	30	....	....	....	17	2	2	0	2	2
1945-46	St. Paul Saints	USHL	56	18	25	43	....	....	....	25	6	2	2	4	4
1946-47	New Haven Ramblers	AHL	64	18	17	35	....	....	....	18	3	2	2	4	2
1947-48	St. Paul Saints	USHL	66	22	27	49	....	....	....	25	....	....	....	....	....
1948-49	St. Paul Saints	USHL	66	29	35	64	....	....	....	20	7	2	3	5	0
1949-50	St. Paul Saints	USHL	70	21	23	44	....	....	....	34	3	1	1	2	2
1950-51	Kansas City Royals	USHL	39	10	11	21	....	....	....	24	....	....	....	....	....
	NHL Totals		**8**	**3**	**1**	**4**	**3**	**1**	**4**	**2**	....	....	....	....	....

MJHL First All-Star Team (1942)

Signed as a free agent by **NY Rangers**, October 30, 1942. Traded to **St. Paul** (USHL) by **NY Rangers** for cash, October 7, 1947.

• BENNETT, Frank

LW/D – R. 5'11", 182 lbs. b: Toronto, Ont., 3/4/1922.

Season	Club	League	GP	G	A	Pts	AG	AA	APts	PIM	GP	G	A	Pts	PIM
1939-40	St. Michael's Buzzers	OHA-B	6	1	3	4	....	....	....	0	3	1	0	1	0
1940-41	St. Michael's Buzzers	OHA-B	STATISTICS NOT AVAILABLE												
1941-42	St. Michael's Majors	OHA-Jr.	17	9	11	20	....	....	....	10	2	1	1	2	0
	Toronto Kodaks	TMHL	8	5	2	7	....	....	....	7	7	1	6	7	0
1942-43	St. Michael's Majors	OHA-Jr.	20	7	10	17	....	....	....	8	6	3	4	7	4
	Toronto Staffords	TMHL	18	4	9	13	....	....	....	2	2	0	0	0	2
	Oshawa Generals	OHA-Jr.	....	....	....	....	....	....	....	....	9	1	5	6	8
1943-44	**Detroit Red Wings**	**NHL**	**7**	**0**	**1**	**1**	**0**	**1**	**1**	**2**	....	....	....	....	....
	Assumption College	MOHL	STATISTICS NOT AVAILABLE												
1944-45	Hershey Bears	AHL	3	1	0	1	....	....	....	4	....	....	....	....	....
	Providence Reds	AHL	49	6	23	29	....	....	....	0	....	....	....	....	....
1945-46	Providence Reds	AHL	3	0	2	2	....	....	....	2	....	....	....	....	....
	Shawinigan Cataracts	QSHL	38	1	11	12	....	....	....	15	4	0	0	0	2
1946-47	Shawinigan Cataracts	QSHL	40	2	5	7	....	....	....	25	4	1	1	2	0
1947-48	Shawinigan Cataracts	QSHL	19	0	7	7	....	....	....	9	....	....	....	....	....
	Dolbeau Castors	LSJHL	STATISTICS NOT AVAILABLE												
	NHL Totals		**7**	**0**	**1**	**1**	**0**	**1**	**1**	**2**	....	....	....	....	....

• BENNETT, Max

RW – R. 5'6", 157 lbs. b: Cobalt, Ont., 11/4/1912 d: 1/5/1972.

Season	Club	League	GP	G	A	Pts	AG	AA	APts	PIM	GP	G	A	Pts	PIM
1930-31	Iroquois Papermakers	NOJHA	STATISTICS NOT AVAILABLE												
1931-32	Falconbridge Falcons	NOHA	7	2	0	2	....	....	....	8	2	0	0	0	0
	Sudbury Wolves	NOHA	1	0	0	0	....	....	....	0	....	....	....	....	....
1932-33	Falconbridge Falcons	NOHA	6	4	*3	*7	....	....	....	0	2	0	1	1	0
	Falconbridge Falcons	Al-Cup	5	6	3	9	....	....	....	0	....	....	....	....	....
1933-34	Hamilton Tigers	OHA-Sr.	23	*20	12	32	....	....	....	34	4	*6	1	*7	6
	Hamilton Tigers	Al-Cup	8	5	2	7	....	....	....	2	....	....	....	....	....
1934-35	Hamilton Tigers	OHA-Sr.	18	19	7	26	....	....	....	17	6	0	1	1	2
1935-36	**Montreal Canadiens**	**NHL**	**1**	**0**	**0**	**0**	**0**	**0**	**0**	**0**	....	....	....	....	....
	Springfield Indians	Can-Am	44	6	9	15	....	....	....	25	3	1	0	1	0
1936-37	Springfield Indians	IAHL	1	0	0	0	....	....	....	2	....	....	....	....	....
	Cleveland Barons	IAHL	11	2	1	3	....	....	....	8	....	....	....	....	....
	Syracuse Stars	IAHL	21	7	8	15	....	....	....	8	9	3	4	7	6
1937-38	Syracuse Stars	IAHL	44	20	15	35	....	....	....	18	8	2	*6	8	0
1938-39	Syracuse Stars	IAHL	54	15	33	48	....	....	....	18	3	0	1	1	0
1939-40	Syracuse Stars	IAHL	56	25	31	56	....	....	....	10	....	....	....	....	....
1940-41	Buffalo Bisons	AHL	55	12	31	43	....	....	....	22	....	....	....	....	....
1941-42	Buffalo Bisons	AHL	52	19	29	48	....	....	....	14	....	....	....	....	....
1942-43	Buffalo Bisons	AHL	56	20	24	44	....	....	....	19	9	4	5	9	0
	Pittsburgh Hornets	AHL	1	0	1	1	....	....	....	0	....	....	....	....	....
	Washington Lions	AHL	1	0	0	0	....	....	....	0	....	....	....	....	....
1943-44	Buffalo Bisons	AHL	54	21	30	51	....	....	....	17	9	1	6	7	2
	Pittsburgh Hornets	AHL	1	1	0	1	....	....	....	0	....	....	....	....	....
1944-45	Pittsburgh Hornets	AHL	21	4	11	15	....	....	....	13	....	....	....	....	....
1945-46	Washington Lions	EAHL	DID NOT PLAY – COACHING												
	NHL Totals		**1**	**0**	**0**	**0**	**0**	**0**	**0**	**0**	....	....	....	....	....

Signed as a free agent by **Montreal Canadiens**, May 27, 1935.

• BENOIT, Joe

RW – R. 5'10", 160 lbs. b: St. Albert, Alta., 2/27/1916 d: 10/19/1981.

Season	Club	League	GP	G	A	Pts	AG	AA	APts	PIM	GP	G	A	Pts	PIM
1935-36	Edmonton Athletics	EJrHL	8	8	2	10	....	....	....	4	3	0	0	0	2
1936-37	Trail Canucks	WKHL	13	13	7	20	....	....	....	18	....	....	....	....	....
1937-38	Trail Smoke Eaters	WKHL	20	26	6	32	....	....	....	21	5	5	3	8	8
	Trail Smoke Eaters	Al-Cup	12	12	7	19	....	....	....	9	....	....	....	....	....
1938-39	Trail Smoke Eaters	X-Games	STATISTICS NOT AVAILABLE												
	Canada	WEC	7	6	3	9	....	....	....	....	....	....	....	....	....
1939-40	Trail Smoke Eaters	WKHL	24	26	17	43	....	....	....	49	4	2	*3	5	6
	Trail Smoke Eaters	Al-Cup	3	0	1	1	....	....	....	4	....	....	....	....	....
1940-41	**Montreal Canadiens**	**NHL**	**45**	**16**	**16**	**32**	**25**	**23**	**48**	**32**	**3**	**4**	**0**	**4**	**2**
1941-42	**Montreal Canadiens**	**NHL**	**46**	**20**	**16**	**36**	**27**	**19**	**46**	**27**	**3**	**1**	**0**	**1**	**5**
1942-43	**Montreal Canadiens**	**NHL**	**49**	**30**	**27**	**57**	**31**	**25**	**56**	**23**	**5**	**1**	**3**	**4**	**4**
1943-44			MILITARY SERVICE												
1944-45	Calgary Currie Army	CNDHL	13	7	3	10	....	....	....	8	2	1	0	1	2
♦1945-46	**Montreal Canadiens**	**NHL**	**39**	**9**	**10**	**19**	**11**	**14**	**25**	**8**	....	....	....	....	....
1946-47	**Montreal Canadiens**	**NHL**	**6**	**0**	**0**	**0**	**0**	**0**	**0**	**4**	....	....	....	....	....
	Springfield Indians	AHL	34	9	10	19	....	....	....	4	2	0	0	0	0
1947-48			DID NOT PLAY												
1948-49	Montreal Royals	QSHL	1	0	0	0	....	....	....	0	....	....	....	....	....
	Spokane Flyers	WIHL	DID NOT PLAY – COACHING												
	NHL Totals		**185**	**75**	**69**	**144**	**94**	**81**	**175**	**94**	**11**	**6**	**3**	**9**	**11**

Rights traded to **Montreal** by **Toronto** for the rights to Frank Eddolls, June 7, 1940.

• BENSON, Bill William Lloyd

C – L. 5'11", 165 lbs. b: Winnipeg, Man., 7/29/1920.

Season	Club	League	GP	G	A	Pts	AG	AA	APts	PIM	GP	G	A	Pts	PIM
1937-38	Winnipeg Monarchs	MJHL	20	7	10	17	....	....	....	2	5	1	3	4	0
1938-39	Winnipeg Monarchs	MJHL	21	18	12	30	....	....	....	2	7	6	3	9	2
1939-40	Winnipeg Monarchs	MJHL	24	19	*20	*39	....	....	....	16	7	5	4	9	2
1940-41	**New York Americans**	**NHL**	**22**	**3**	**4**	**7**	**5**	**6**	**11**	**4**	....	....	....	....	....
	Springfield Indians	AHL	22	3	6	9	....	....	....	4	....	....	....	....	....
1941-42	**Brooklyn Americans**	**NHL**	**45**	**8**	**21**	**29**	**11**	**25**	**36**	**31**	....	....	....	....	....
1942-43	Sydney Navy	NSDHL	3	3	4	7	....	....	....	0	....	....	....	....	....
	Winnipeg Navy	WNDHL	....	....	....	....	....	....	....	....	2	1	0	1	0
1943-44			MILITARY SERVICE												
1944-45			MILITARY SERVICE												
1945-46	Cleveland Barons	AHL	14	3	4	7	....	....	....	4	9	0	0	0	2
1946-47	Pittsburgh Hornets	AHL	64	20	22	42	....	....	....	26	12	4	3	7	4
1947-48	Pittsburgh Hornets	AHL	65	18	20	38	....	....	....	13	2	0	0	0	0
1948-49	Pittsburgh Hornets	AHL	67	18	22	40	....	....	....	24	....	....	....	....	....
1949-50	Pittsburgh Hornets	AHL	63	15	13	28	....	....	....	0	....	....	....	....	....
	NHL Totals		**67**	**11**	**25**	**36**	**16**	**31**	**47**	**35**	....	....	....	....	....

Signed as a free agent by **NY Americans**, October 11, 1940.

• BENSON, Bobby Robert John

D – L. 5'6", 135 lbs. b: Winnipeg, Man., 5/18/1894 d: 9/7/1965.

Season	Club	League	GP	G	A	Pts	AG	AA	APts	PIM	GP	G	A	Pts	PIM
1912-13	Winnipeg Strathconas	WSrHL	8	3	0	3	....	....	....	....	2	0	0	0	0
1913-14	Winnipeg Falcons	MHL-Sr.	12	2	0	2	....	....	....	....	....	....	....	....	....
1914-15	Winnipeg Falcons	MHL-Sr.	8	3	0	3	....	....	....	....	2	0	0	0	6
1915-16	Winnipeg Falcons	MHL-Sr.	7	2	0	2	....	....	....	12	....	....	....	....	....
1916-17	Winnipeg 223rd Battalion	MHL-Sr.	8	3	1	4	....	....	....	4	....	....	....	....	....
1917-18			MILITARY SERVICE												
1918-19			MILITARY SERVICE												

			REGULAR SEASON								PLAYOFFS				
Season	Club	League	GP	G	A	Pts	AG	AA	APts	PIM	GP	G	A	Pts	PIM
1919-20	Winnipeg Falcons	MHL-Sr.	9	2	1	3	....	....	....	*26	....	....	....	....	....
	Canada	WEC	3	0	1	1	....	....	....	....	....	....	....	....	....
	Winnipeg Falcons	Al-Cup	6	0	5	5	....	....	....	13	....	....	....	....	....
1920-21	Saskatoon Crescents	N-SSHL	16	12	1	13	....	....	....	39	4	2	1	3	*12
1921-22	Saskatoon Crescents	WCHL	23	9	4	13	....	....	....	21	....	....	....	....	....
1922-23	Calgary Tigers	WCHL	27	7	1	8	....	....	....	22	....	....	....	....	....
1923-24	Calgary Tigers	WCHL	26	5	5	10	....	....	....	24	2	0	0	0	4
	Calgary Tigers	St-Cup	2	0	1	1	....	....	....	0	....	....	....	....	....
1924-25	Calgary Tigers	WCHL	9	0	1	1	....	....	....	4	....	....	....	....	....
	Boston Bruins	**NHL**	**8**	**0**	**1**	**1**	**0**	**4**	**4**	**4**	....	....	....	....	....
1925-26	Saskatoon Crescents	WHL	12	0	0	0	....	....	....	0	....	....	....	....	....
	Edmonton Eskimos	WHL	12	0	0	0	....	....	....	0	2	0	0	0	2
1926-27	Moose Jaw Maroons	PrHL	32	6	4	10	....	....	....	65	....	....	....	....	....
1927-28	Winnipeg Maroons	AHA	2	0	0	0	....	....	....	0	....	....	....	....	....
	Minneapolis Millers	AHA	21	2	0	2	....	....	....	36	8	0	1	1	*23
1928-29	Minneapolis Millers	AHA	40	3	4	7	....	....	....	92	4	0	0	0	2
1929-30	Seattle Eskimos	PCHL	36	2	3	5	....	....	....	82	....	....	....	....	....
1930-31	Seattle Eskimos	PCHL	33	2	2	4	....	....	....	76	4	0	0	0	8
1931-32	Hollywood Stars	Cal-Pro	....	1	1	2	....	....	....	....	....	....	....	....	....
	NHL Totals		**8**	**0**	**1**	**1**	**0**	**4**	**4**	**4**	....	....	....	....	....
	Other Major League Totals		109	21	11	32	....	....	....	71	4	0	0	0	6

Signed as a free agent by **Saskatoon** (WCHL), November 14, 1921. Traded to **Calgary** (WCHL) by **Saskatoon** (WCHL) for Rube Brandow, November 27, 1922. Traded to **Montreal Maroons** by **Calgary** (WCHL) for cash, January 3, 1925. Traded to **Boston** by **Montreal Maroons** with Bernie Morris for Alf Skinner, January 3, 1925. Signed as a free agent by **Saskatoon** (WHL), October 27, 1925. Traded to **Edmonton** (WHL) by **Saskatoon** (WHL) for cash, January 17, 1926. Signed as a free agent by **Moose Jaw** (PrHL), November 15, 1926. Signed as a free agent by **Winnipeg** (AHA), December 29, 1927. Traded to **Minneapolis** (AHA) by **Winnipeg** (AHA) for cash, January 9, 1928.

• BENTLEY, Doug

Douglas Wagner HHOF

LW – L. 5'8", 145 lbs. b: Delisle, Sask., 9/3/1916 d: 11/24/1972.

Season	Club	League	GP	G	A	Pts	AG	AA	APts	PIM	GP	G	A	Pts	PIM
1932-33	Delisle Tigers	SIHA	STATISTICS NOT AVAILABLE												
	Delisle Tigers	Al-Cup	2	0	0	0	....	....	....	0	....	....	....	....	....
1933-34	Saskatoon Wesleys	N-SJHL	4	3	3	6	....	....	....	0	9	3	1	4	8
1934-35	Regina Vics	S-SSHL	19	10	4	14	....	....	....	21	6	0	0	0	13
1935-36	Moose Jaw Millers	S-SSHL	20	3	3	6	....	....	....	30	....	....	....	....	....
1936-37	Moose Jaw Millers	S-SSHL	24	18	19	37	....	....	....	49	3	3	0	3	4
1937-38	Moose Jaw Millers	S-SSHL	21	25	18	43	....	....	....	20	6	6	*8	*14	6
	Moose Jaw Millers	Al-Cup	4	3	2	5	....	....	....	8	....	....	....	....	....
1938-39	Drumheller Miners	ASHL	32	24	29	53	....	....	....	31	6	*7	0	7	6
1939-40	**Chicago Black Hawks**	**NHL**	**39**	**12**	**7**	**19**	**20**	**11**	**31**	**12**	**2**	**0**	**0**	**0**	**0**
1940-41	**Chicago Black Hawks**	**NHL**	**47**	**8**	**20**	**28**	**12**	**29**	**41**	**12**	**5**	**1**	**1**	**2**	**4**
1941-42	**Chicago Black Hawks**	**NHL**	**38**	**12**	**14**	**26**	**16**	**17**	**33**	**11**	**3**	**0**	**1**	**1**	**4**
1942-43	**Chicago Black Hawks**	**NHL**	**50**	***33**	**40**	***73**	**34**	**38**	**72**	**18**	....	....	....	....	....
	San Diego Skyhawks	X-Games	STATISTICS NOT AVAILABLE												
1943-44	**Chicago Black Hawks**	**NHL**	**50**	***38**	**39**	**77**	**35**	**35**	**70**	**22**	**9**	**8**	**4**	**12**	**4**
1944-45	Laura Beavers	AIHA	STATISTICS NOT AVAILABLE												
1945-46	**Chicago Black Hawks**	**NHL**	**36**	**19**	**21**	**40**	**23**	**31**	**54**	**16**	**4**	**0**	**2**	**2**	**0**
1946-47	**Chicago Black Hawks**	**NHL**	**52**	**21**	***34**	**55**	**24**	**41**	**65**	**18**	....	....	....	....	....
1947-48	**Chicago Black Hawks**	**NHL**	**60**	**20**	***37**	**57**	**26**	**49**	**75**	**16**	....	....	....	....	....
1948-49	**Chicago Black Hawks**	**NHL**	**58**	**23**	***43**	**66**	**32**	**62**	**94**	**38**	....	....	....	....	....
1949-50	**Chicago Black Hawks**	**NHL**	**64**	**20**	**33**	**53**	**25**	**40**	**65**	**28**	....	....	....	....	....
1950-51	**Chicago Black Hawks**	**NHL**	**44**	**9**	**23**	**32**	**11**	**28**	**39**	**20**	....	....	....	....	....
1951-52	**Chicago Black Hawks**	**NHL**	**8**	**2**	**3**	**5**	**3**	**4**	**7**	**4**	....	....	....	....	....
	Saskatoon Quakers	PCHL	35	11	14	25	....	....	....	12	13	6	6	12	4
1952-53	Saskatoon Quakers	WHL	70	22	23	45	....	....	....	37	13	6	3	9	14
1953-54	**New York Rangers**	**NHL**	**20**	**2**	**10**	**12**	**3**	**12**	**15**	**2**	....	....	....	....	....
	Saskatoon Quakers	WHL	42	8	13	21	....	....	....	18	....	....	....	....	....
1954-55	Saskatoon Quakers	WHL	61	14	23	37	....	....	....	52	....	....	....	....	....
1955-56	Saskatoon–Brandon	WHL	60	7	26	33	....	....	....	21	....	....	....	....	....
1956-57			DID NOT PLAY												
1957-58	Saskatoon-St. Paul	WHL	19	11	16	27	....	....	....	0	....	....	....	....	....
1958-59	Saskatoon Quakers	WHL	DID NOT PLAY – COACHING												
1959-60	Saskatoon Quakers	WHL	DID NOT PLAY – COACHING												
1960-61	Saskatoon Quakers	WHL	DID NOT PLAY – COACHING												
1961-62	Los Angeles Blades	WHL	8	0	2	2	....	....	....	2	....	....	....	....	....
	NHL Totals		**566**	**219**	**324**	**543**	**264**	**397**	**661**	**217**	**23**	**9**	**8**	**17**	**12**

• Brother of Reggie and Max • NHL First All-Star Team (1943, 1944, 1947) • NHL Scoring Leader (1943) • NHL Second All-Star Team (1949) • Played in NHL All-Star Game (1947, 1948, 1949, 1950, 1951)

• Missed entire 1944-45 NHL season after being given permission to stay home and tend family farm by Canadian Armed Forces officials, September, 1944. Traded to **NY Rangers** by **Chicago** for cash, June 30, 1953.

• BENTLEY, Max

Maxwell Herbert Lloyd "Dipsy-Doodle-Dandy" HHOF

C – L. 5'10", 155 lbs. b: Delisle, Sask., 3/1/1920 d: 1/19/1984.

Season	Club	League	GP	G	A	Pts	AG	AA	APts	PIM	GP	G	A	Pts	PIM
1935-36	Rosetown Red Wings	SIHA	STATISTICS NOT AVAILABLE												
1937-38	Drumheller Miners	ASHL	26	28	15	*43	....	....	....	10	5	*7	1	*8	2
1938-39	Drumheller Miners	ASHL	32	29	24	53	....	....	....	16	6	5	3	8	6
1939-40	Saskatoon Quakers	N-SSHL	31	*37	14	51	....	....	....	4	4	1	1	2	2
1940-41	Providence Reds	AHL	9	4	2	6	....	....	....	0	....	....	....	....	....
	Kansas City Americans	AHA	5	5	5	10	....	....	....	0	....	....	....	....	....
	Chicago Black Hawks	**NHL**	**36**	**7**	**10**	**17**	**11**	**14**	**25**	**6**	**4**	**1**	**3**	**4**	**2**
1941-42	**Chicago Black Hawks**	**NHL**	**39**	**13**	**17**	**30**	**17**	**20**	**37**	**2**	**3**	**2**	**0**	**2**	**0**
1942-43	**Chicago Black Hawks**	**NHL**	**47**	**26**	**44**	**70**	**27**	**42**	**69**	**2**	....	....	....	....	....
	Victoria Navy	NNDHL	STATISTICS NOT AVAILABLE												
	San Diego Skyhawks	X-Games	STATISTICS NOT AVAILABLE												
1943-44	Calgary Currie Army	CNDHL	15	*18	13	*31	....	....	....	*26	2	3	4	7	0
1944-45	Calgary Currie Army	CNDHL	12	14	14	28	....	....	....	24	3	3	2	*5	0
1945-46	**Chicago Black Hawks**	**NHL**	**47**	**31**	**30**	***61**	**38**	**44**	**82**	**6**	**4**	**1**	**0**	**1**	**4**
1946-47	**Chicago Black Hawks**	**NHL**	**60**	**29**	**43**	***72**	**33**	**52**	**85**	**12**	....	....	....	....	....
1947-48	**Chicago Black Hawks**	**NHL**	**6**	**3**	**3**	**6**	**4**	**4**	**8**	**4**	....	....	....	....	....
♦	**Toronto Maple Leafs**	**NHL**	**53**	**23**	**25**	**48**	**30**	**33**	**63**	**10**	**9**	**4**	***7**	**11**	**0**
♦1948-49	**Toronto Maple Leafs**	**NHL**	**60**	**19**	**22**	**41**	**27**	**31**	**58**	**18**	**9**	**4**	**3**	**7**	**2**
1949-50	**Toronto Maple Leafs**	**NHL**	**69**	**23**	**18**	**41**	**29**	**22**	**51**	**14**	**7**	**3**	**3**	**6**	**0**
♦1950-51	**Toronto Maple Leafs**	**NHL**	**67**	**21**	**41**	**62**	**27**	**51**	**78**	**34**	**11**	**2**	***11**	***13**	**4**
1951-52	**Toronto Maple Leafs**	**NHL**	**69**	**24**	**17**	**41**	**32**	**21**	**53**	**40**	**4**	**1**	**0**	**1**	**2**
1952-53	**Toronto Maple Leafs**	**NHL**	**36**	**12**	**11**	**23**	**16**	**13**	**29**	**16**	....	....	....	....	....
1953-54	**New York Rangers**	**NHL**	**57**	**14**	**18**	**32**	**19**	**22**	**41**	**15**	....	....	....	....	....
1954-55	Saskatoon Quakers	WHL	40	24	17	41	....	....	....	23	....	....	....	....	....
1955-56	Saskatoon Quakers	WHL	10	2	2	4	....	....	....	20	....	....	....	....	....
1956-57	Saskatoon Jr. Quakers	SJHL	DID NOT PLAY – COACHING												
1957-58	Saskatoon Jr. Quakers	SJHL	DID NOT PLAY – COACHING												
1958-59	Saskatoon Quakers	WHL	26	6	12	18	....	....	....	2	....	....	....	....	....
	NHL Totals		**646**	**245**	**299**	**544**	**310**	**369**	**679**	**179**	**51**	**18**	**27**	**45**	**14**

• Brother of Reggie and Doug • Won Lady Byng Trophy (1943) • NHL First All-Star Team (1946) • NHL Scoring Leader (1946, 1947) • Won Hart Trophy (1946) • NHL Second All-Star Team (1947) • Played in NHL All-Star Game (1947, 1948, 1949, 1951)

Traded to **Toronto** by **Chicago** with Cy Thomas for Gus Bodnar, Bud Poile, Gaye Stewart, Ernie Dickens and Bob Goldham, November 2, 1947. Traded to **NY Rangers** by **Toronto** for cash, August 11, 1953. • Officially announced retirement from NHL, November 16, 1955.

• BENTLEY, Reggie

LW – L. 5'8", 155 lbs. b: Delisle, Sask., 5/3/1914.

Season	Club	League	GP	G	A	Pts	AG	AA	APts	PIM	GP	G	A	Pts	PIM
1931-32	Delisle Tigers	S-SSHL	20	5	4	9	....	....	....	10	....	....	....	....	....
	Delisle Tigers	Al-Cup	2	0	0	0	....	....	....	2	....	....	....	....	....
1932-33	Delisle Tigers	S-SSHL	STATISTICS NOT AVAILABLE												
	Delisle Tigers	Al-Cup	2	0	0	0	....	....	....	2	....	....	....	....	....
1933/35	Kerrobert Tigers	AIHA	STATISTICS NOT AVAILABLE												
1935-36	Saskatoon Standards	SIHA	19	7	0	7	....	....	....	16	....	....	....	....	....
1936-37	Saskatoon Quakers	N-SSHL	20	7	2	9	....	....	....	4	....	....	....	....	....
1937-38	Moose Jaw Millers	S-SSHL	24	14	9	23	....	....	....	14	6	6	3	9	4
	Moose Jaw Millers	Al-Cup	4	4	1	5	....	....	....	4	....	....	....	....	....
1938-39	Drumheller Miners	ASHL	32	21	10	31	....	....	....	52	6	4	1	5	9
1939-40	Drumheller Miners	ASHL	32	23	8	31	....	....	....	27	....	....	....	....	....
1940-41	Saskatoon Quakers	S-SSHL	30	14	5	19	....	....	....	2	4	0	0	0	0
1941-42	Kansas City Americans	AHA	50	16	16	32	....	....	....	16	6	3	4	7	0
1942-43	**Chicago Black Hawks**	**NHL**	**11**	**1**	**2**	**3**	**1**	**2**	**3**	**2**	....	....	....	....	....
	Victoria Navy	NNDHL	STATISTICS NOT AVAILABLE												
	San Diego Skyhawks	X-Games	STATISTICS NOT AVAILABLE												
1943-44	Calgary Currie Army	CNDHL	14	7	2	9	....	....	....	6	2	0	0	0	0
	Moose Jaw Victorias	SSHL	2	2	3	5	....	....	....	0	....	....	....	....	....
1944-45	Calgary Currie Army	CNDHL	10	1	1	2	....	....	....	2	2	0	1	1	0
1945-46	New Westminster Royals	PCHL	57	30	27	57	....	....	....	18	....	....	....	....	....
1946-47	New Westminster Royals	PCHL	60	41	30	71	....	....	....	14	4	2	1	3	0
1947-48	Saskatoon Quakers	WCSHL	45	28	22	50	....	....	....	17	....	....	....	....	....
1948-49	Saskatoon Quakers	WCSHL	48	22	18	40	....	....	....	4	....	....	....	....	....
	Spokane Flyers	Al-Cup	4	4	3	7	....	....	....	0	....	....	....	....	....
1949-50	Saskatoon Quakers	WCSHL	50	15	14	29	....	....	....	14	4	1	0	1	0
1950-51	Saskatoon Quakers	WCMHL	40	12	13	25	....	....	....	8	8	2	1	3	0
	Saskatoon Quakers	Alx-Cup	4	0	0	0	....	....	....	0	....	....	....	....	....
1951-52	Yorkton Legionnaires	SSHL	30	20	23	43	....	....	....	4	7	3	5	8	0
	NHL Totals		**11**	**1**	**2**	**3**	**1**	**2**	**3**	**2**	....	....	....	....	....

• Brother of Doug and Max

• BERENSON, Red

— see page 885

• BERGDINON, Fred

RW – R. 6'1", 170 lbs. b: Parry Sound, Ontario, 1906 d: 1995.

Season	Club	League	GP	G	A	Pts	AG	AA	APts	PIM	GP	G	A	Pts	PIM
1922/24	Parry Sound	OHA-Jr.	STATISTICS NOT AVAILABLE												
1924-25			STATISTICS NOT AVAILABLE												
1925-26	**Boston Bruins**	**NHL**	**2**	**0**	**0**	**0**	**0**	**0**	**0**	**0**	....	....	....	....	....
	NHL Totals		**2**	**0**	**0**	**0**	**0**	**0**	**0**	**0**	....	....	....	....	....

Signed as a free agent by **Boston**, December 14, 1925.

• BERGMAN, Gary

— see page 889

• BERLINQUETTE, Louis

LW – L. 5'11", 175 lbs. b: Papineau, Que., 1887 d: 6/2/1959.

Season	Club	League	GP	G	A	Pts	AG	AA	APts	PIM	GP	G	A	Pts	PIM
1908-09	Haileybury Seniors	TPHL	8	9	0	9	....	....	....	19	....	....	....	....	....
1909-10	Haileybury Hockey Club	NHA	1	2	0	2	....	....	....	0	....	....	....	....	....
1910-11	Galt Professionals	OPHL	5	0	0	0	....	....	....	....	3	4	0	4	....
1911-12	Montreal Canadiens	NHA	4	0	0	0	....	....	....	5	....	....	....	....	....
	Moncton Victorias	MPHL	9	7	0	7	....	....	....	15	2	0	0	0	5
1912-13	Montreal Canadiens	NHA	16	4	0	4	....	....	....	14	....	....	....	....	....
1913-14	Montreal Canadiens	NHA	20	4	9	13	....	....	....	14	2	0	0	0	0
1914-15	Montreal Canadiens	NHA	20	2	1	3	....	....	....	40	....	....	....	....	....
♦1915-16	Montreal Canadiens	NHA	19	2	2	4	....	....	....	19	1	0	0	0	0
1916-17	Montreal Canadiens	NHA	20	8	4	12	....	....	....	36	5	0	0	0	8
1917-18	**Montreal Canadiens**	**NHL**	**20**	**2**	**1**	**3**	**2**	**4**	**6**	**12**	**2**	**0**	**0**	**0**	**0**
1918-19	**Montreal Canadiens**	**NHL**	**18**	**5**	**3**	**8**	**9**	**16**	**25**	**9**	**5**	**0**	**2**	**2**	**9**
	Montreal Canadiens	St-Cup	5	1	1	2	....	....	....	0	....	....	....	....	....
1919-20	**Montreal Canadiens**	**NHL**	**24**	**8**	**9**	**17**	**9**	**31**	**40**	**36**	....	....	....	....	....
1920-21	**Montreal Canadiens**	**NHL**	**24**	**11**	**9**	**20**	**14**	**35**	**49**	**28**	....	....	....	....	....
1921-22	**Montreal Canadiens**	**NHL**	**24**	**13**	**5**	**18**	**18**	**16**	**34**	**10**	....	....	....	....	....
1922-23	**Montreal Canadiens**	**NHL**	**24**	**2**	**4**	**6**	**3**	**15**	**18**	**4**	**2**	**0**	**2**	**2**	**0**
1923-24	Saskatoon Quakers	WCHL	29	9	6	15	....	....	....	9	....	....	....	....	....
1924-25	**Montreal Maroons**	**NHL**	**29**	**4**	**2**	**6**	**7**	**8**	**15**	**22**	....	....	....	....	....
1925-26	**Pittsburgh Pirates**	**NHL**	**30**	**0**	**0**	**0**	**0**	**0**	**0**	**8**	**2**	**0**	**0**	**0**	**0**
1926-27	Quebec Castors	Can-Am	19	3	3	6	....	....	....	31	....	....	....	....	....
	NHL Totals		**193**	**45**	**33**	**78**	**62**	**125**	**187**	**129**	**11**	**0**	**4**	**4**	**9**
	Other Major League Totals		143	38	22	60	....	....	....	152	13	4	0	4	13

Rights retained by **Montreal Canadiens** after NHA folded, November 26, 1917. Traded to **Saskatoon** (WCHL) by **Montreal Canadiens** for cash, November 1, 1923. Traded to **Montreal Maroons** by **Saskatoon** (WCHL) for cash, November 26, 1924. Signed as a free agent by **Pittsburgh**, November 10, 1925. Signed as a free agent by **Quebec** (Can-Am) and named player coach, October 28, 1926.

• BESLER, Phil

Philip Rudolph

RW – R. 5'11", 180 lbs. b: Melville, Sask., 12/9/1913 Deceased.

Season	Club	League	GP	G	A	Pts	AG	AA	APts	PIM	GP	G	A	Pts	PIM
1929-30	Melville Millionaires	S-SSHL	20	3	0	3	....	....	....	25	2	0	0	0	0
1930-31	Melville Millionaires	S-SSHL	20	4	2	6	....	....	....	37	....	....	....	....	....
1931-32			DID NOT PLAY												
1932-33	Humboldt Indians	N-SSHL	17	7	5	12	....	....	....	6	....	....	....	....	....
1933-34	Prince Albert Mintos	N-SSHL	21	*31	4	35	....	....	....	12	4	2	1	3	2
1934-35	Boston Cubs	Can-Am	38	6	3	9	....	....	....	30	3	*2	0	2	13

Season	Club	League	GP	G	A	Pts	AG	AA	APts	PIM	GP	G	A	Pts	PIM
			REGULAR SEASON								PLAYOFFS				
1935-36	**Boston Bruins**	**NHL**	**8**	**0**	**0**	**0**	**0**	**0**	**0**	**0**	....	....	....	....	....
	Boston Cubs	Can-Am	29	4	6	10	....	....	....	25	....	....	....	....	....
1936-37	Vancouver–Portland	PCHL	28	13	6	19	....	....	....	27	3	1	0	1	2
1937-38	Portland Buckaroos	PCHL	38	*24	3	27	....	....	....	26	2	0	1	1	6
1938-39	**Chicago Black Hawks**	**NHL**	**17**	**1**	**3**	**4**	**2**	**5**	**7**	**16**	....	....	....	....	....
	Providence Reds	IAHL	2	0	0	0	....	....	....	0	....	....	....	....	....
	Cleveland Barons	IAHL	1	0	0	0	....	....	....	0	....	....	....	....	....
	Detroit Red Wings	**NHL**	**5**	**0**	**1**	**1**	**0**	**2**	**2**	**2**	....	....	....	....	....
	Pittsburgh Hornets	IAHL	9	1	1	2	....	....	....	2	....	....	....	....	....
1939-40	Omaha Knights	AHA	48	20	16	36	....	....	....	57	9	3	2	5	*26
1940-41	Omaha Knights	AHA	47	15	15	30	....	....	....	26	....	....	....	....	....
1941-42	Omaha Knights	AHA	49	17	15	32	....	....	....	36	8	0	3	3	17
	NHL Totals		**30**	**1**	**4**	**5**	**2**	**7**	**9**	**18**	....	....	....	....	....

Signed as a free agent by **Chicago**, September 29, 1938. Traded to **Detroit** by **Chicago** for Charley Mason, January 27, 1939.

• BESSONE, Pete USHOF

D – L. 5'11", 200 lbs. b: New Bedford, MA, 1/13/1913 Deceased.

Season	Club	League	GP	G	A	Pts	AG	AA	APts	PIM	GP	G	A	Pts	PIM
1935-36	Paris Stade Francais	France	STATISTICS NOT AVAILABLE												
1936-37	Pittsburgh Yellowjackets	EAHL	47	6	4	10	....	....	....	53	....	....	....	....	....
1937-38	**Detroit Red Wings**	**NHL**	**6**	**0**	**1**	**1**	**0**	**2**	**2**	**6**	....	....	....	....	....
	Pittsburgh Hornets	AHL	16	1	1	2	....	....	....	4	1	0	0	0	0
	Detroit Pontiacs	MOHL	15	6	2	8	....	....	....	38	....	....	....	....	....
1938-39	Pittsburgh Hornets	IAHL	53	3	8	11	....	....	....	87	....	....	....	....	....
1939-40	Pittsburgh Hornets	IAHL	54	4	8	12	....	....	....	100	9	0	2	2	20
1940-41	Pittsburgh Hornets	AHL	17	0	3	3	....	....	....	22	....	....	....	....	....
1941-42	Pittsburgh Hornets	AHL	53	2	18	20	....	....	....	102	....	....	....	....	....
1942-43	Pittsburgh Hornets	AHL	54	10	16	26	....	....	....	92	2	0	0	0	4
	Cleveland Barons	AHL	1	0	0	0	....	....	....	0	....	....	....	....	....
1943-44	Cleveland Barons	AHL	50	6	20	26	....	....	....	119	11	0	1	1	6
1944-45	Cleveland Barons	AHL	60	6	26	32	....	....	....	100	12	1	2	3	18
1945-46	Cleveland Barons	AHL	50	2	14	16	....	....	....	88	8	0	0	0	9
1946-47	Providence Reds	AHL	54	4	9	13	....	....	....	94	....	....	....	....	....
1947-48	Paris Racing Club	France	DID NOT PLAY – COACHING												
1948-49	Paris Racing Club	France	DID NOT PLAY – COACHING												
1949-50	Springfield Indians	AHL	4	0	0	0	....	....	....	2	....	....	....	....	....
	NHL Totals		**6**	**0**	**1**	**1**	**0**	**2**	**2**	**6**	....	....	....	....	....

EAHL Second All-Star Team (1937)

Signed as a free agent by **Detroit**, January 15, 1938. Traded to **Pittsburgh** (AHL) by **Detroit** for cash, October 5, 1939. Traded to **Cleveland** (AHL) by **Pittsburgh** (AHL) for Fred Robertson, November 1, 1943.

• BETTIO, Sam Silvio Angelo

LW – L. 5'8", 175 lbs. b: Copper Cliff, Ont., 12/1/1928.

Season	Club	League	GP	G	A	Pts	AG	AA	APts	PIM	GP	G	A	Pts	PIM
1945-46	Copper Cliff Redmen	NOJHA	8	2	3	5	....	....	....	0	3	7	2	9	0
1946-47	Copper Cliff Redmen	NOJHA	9	*10	6	16	....	....	....	10	5	*7	*7	*14	8
	Timmins Combines	M-Cup	3	1	0	1	....	....	....	4	....	....	....	....	....
1947-48	Hershey Bears	AHL	21	3	3	6	....	....	....	8	....	....	....	....	....
	Boston Olympics	EAHL	8	8	5	13	....	....	....	10	....	....	....	....	....
	Boston Olympics	QSHL	22	11	14	25	....	....	....	31	....	....	....	....	....
1948-49	Hershey Bears	AHL	58	15	25	40	....	....	....	18	11	3	4	7	4
1949-50	**Boston Bruins**	**NHL**	**44**	**9**	**12**	**21**	**11**	**14**	**25**	**32**	....	....	....	....	....
	Hershey Bears	AHL	23	7	10	17	....	....	....	8	....	....	....	....	....
1950-51	Hershey Bears	AHL	57	19	42	61	....	....	....	28	6	2	4	6	0
1951-52	Hershey Bears	AHL	64	18	37	55	....	....	....	27	5	2	0	2	13
1952-53	Hershey Bears	AHL	63	21	43	64	....	....	....	24	3	2	1	3	2
1953-54	Victoria Cougars	WHL	68	24	39	63	....	....	....	49	5	1	1	2	2
1954-55	Buffalo Bisons	AHL	53	13	31	44	....	....	....	27	10	4	8	12	6
1955-56	Buffalo Bisons	AHL	61	14	17	31	....	....	....	37	2	1	1	2	0
1956-57	Buffalo Bisons	AHL	62	38	29	67	....	....	....	40	....	....	....	....	....
1957-58	Buffalo Bisons	AHL	70	19	34	53	....	....	....	39	....	....	....	....	....
1958-59	Sudbury Wolves	NOHA	19	13	15	28	....	....	....	0	5	4	0	4	4
1959-60	Sudbury Wolves	EPHL	67	45	56	101	....	....	....	39	14	7	7	14	23
1960-61	Sudbury Wolves	EPHL	65	37	50	87	....	....	....	99	....	....	....	....	....
1961-62	Sudbury Wolves	EPHL	35	12	22	34	....	....	....	41	6	1	7	8	2
	NHL Totals		**44**	**9**	**12**	**21**	**11**	**14**	**25**	**32**	....	....	....	....	....

Traded to **Victoria** (WHL) by **Boston** with Pentti Lund for cash, July 1, 1953.

• BEVERLEY, Nick — *see page 893*

• BIONDA, Jack John Arthur

D – L. 6', 180 lbs. b: Hunstville, Ont., 9/18/1933.

Season	Club	League	GP	G	A	Pts	AG	AA	APts	PIM	GP	G	A	Pts	PIM
1951-52	Toronto Marlboros	OHA-Jr.	13	1	1	2	....	....	....	20	2	1	1	2	2
1952-53	Toronto Marlboros	OHA-Jr.	50	2	11	13	....	....	....	116	7	0	1	1	8
1953-54	Toronto Marlboros	OHA-Jr.	56	16	19	35	....	....	....	107	15	2	2	4	32
1954-55	S.S. Marie Greyhounds	NOHA	20	1	5	6	....	....	....	30	....	....	....	....	....
1955-56	**Toronto Maple Leafs**	**NHL**	**13**	**0**	**1**	**1**	**0**	**1**	**1**	**18**	....	....	....	....	....
	Pittsburgh Hornets	AHL	46	7	9	16	....	....	....	*190	4	0	2	2	12
1956-57	**Boston Bruins**	**NHL**	**35**	**2**	**3**	**5**	**3**	**3**	**6**	**43**	**10**	**0**	**1**	**1**	**14**
	Springfield Indians	AHL	21	2	12	14	....	....	....	65	....	....	....	....	....
1957-58	**Boston Bruins**	**NHL**	**42**	**1**	**4**	**5**	**1**	**4**	**5**	**50**	....	....	....	....	....
	Springfield Indians	AHL	15	0	4	4	....	....	....	22	11	0	4	4	18
1958-59	**Boston Bruins**	**NHL**	**3**	**0**	**1**	**1**	**0**	**1**	**1**	**2**	**1**	**0**	**0**	**0**	**0**
	Providence Reds	AHL	66	9	17	26	....	....	....	144	....	....	....	....	....
1959-60	Victoria Cougars	WHL	68	6	19	25	....	....	....	85	11	0	3	3	10
1960-61	Portland Buckaroos	WHL	69	7	29	36	....	....	....	102	14	2	4	6	27
1961-62	Portland Buckaroos	WHL	70	2	25	27	....	....	....	121	7	1	3	4	25
1962-63	Portland Buckaroos	WHL	70	12	28	40	....	....	....	99	7	0	5	5	2
1963-64	Portland Buckaroos	WHL	63	5	14	19	....	....	....	79	5	0	1	1	6
1964-65	Portland Buckaroos	WHL	16	0	3	3	....	....	....	26	6	0	1	1	2
1965-66	Portland Buckaroos	WHL	72	3	24	27	....	....	....	109	14	1	6	7	14
1966-67	Portland Buckaroos	WHL	41	2	7	9	....	....	....	24	....	....	....	....	....
	NHL Totals		**93**	**3**	**9**	**12**	**4**	**9**	**13**	**113**	**11**	**0**	**1**	**1**	**14**

Claimed by **Boston** from **Toronto** in Intra-League Draft, June 6, 1956. Loaned to **Springfield** (AHL) by **Boston** with the trade of Norm Defelice and future considerations (Floyd Smith, June, 1957) for Don Simmons, January 22, 1957. Traded to **Portland** (WHL) by **Boston** for cash with Boston retaining right of recall, August 26, 1960. Traded to **Portland** (WHL) by **Boston** with future considerations (Gene Achtymichuk and Don Ward (August, 1961) and the loan of Bruce Gamble (September, 1961) for Don Head, May, 1961.

• BLACK, Stephen

LW – L. 6', 185 lbs. b: Fort William, Ont., 3/31/1927.

Season	Club	League	GP	G	A	Pts	AG	AA	APts	PIM	GP	G	A	Pts	PIM
1943-44	Port Arthur Flyers	TBJHL	10	4	2	6	....	....	....	8	6	3	6	9	0
	Port Arthur Flyers	M-Cup	9	6	2	8	....	....	....	6	....	....	....	....	....
1944-45	Port Arthur Flyers	TBJHL	11	17	8	25	....	....	....	4	3	2	0	2	0
	Port Arthur Bruins	M-Cup	10	2	4	6	....	....	....	6	....	....	....	....	....
1945-46	Port Arthur Flyers	TBJHL	6	11	10	21	....	....	....	0	5	7	5	12	4
1946-47	Oakland Oaks	PCHL	60	43	36	79	....	....	....	79	....	....	....	....	....
1947-48	St. Louis Flyers	AHL	58	11	18	29	....	....	....	29	....	....	....	....	....
1948-49	St. Louis Flyers	AHL	62	24	47	71	....	....	....	59	7	0	5	5	12
♦1949-50	**Detroit Red Wings**	**NHL**	**69**	**7**	**14**	**21**	**9**	**17**	**26**	**53**	**13**	**0**	**0**	**0**	**13**
1950-51	**Detroit Red Wings**	**NHL**	**5**	**0**	**0**	**0**	**0**	**0**	**0**	**2**	....	....	....	....	....
	Indianapolis Capitols	AHL	8	1	2	3	....	....	....	13	....	....	....	....	....
	Chicago Black Hawks	**NHL**	**39**	**4**	**6**	**10**	**5**	**7**	**12**	**22**	....	....	....	....	....
	Milwaukee Seagulls	USHL	9	4	6	10	....	....	....	11	....	....	....	....	....
1951-52	St. Louis Flyers	AHL	37	9	21	30	....	....	....	34	....	....	....	....	....
1952-53	Calgary Stampeders	WHL	45	21	16	37	....	....	....	61	5	4	3	7	2
1953-54	Calgary Stampeders	WHL	43	21	33	54	....	....	....	29	18	2	4	6	6
	Calgary Stampeders	Alx-Cup	7	2	3	5	....	....	....	0	....	....	....	....	....
	NHL Totals		**113**	**11**	**20**	**31**	**14**	**24**	**38**	**77**	**13**	**0**	**0**	**0**	**13**

Played in NHL All-Star Game (1950)

Traded to **Detroit** by **St. Louis** (AHL) with Bill Brennan for Fern Gauthier, Cliff Simpson, Ed Nicholson and future considerations, August 29, 1949. Traded to **Chicago** by **Detroit** with Lee Fogolin for Bert Olmstead and Vic Stasiuk, December 2, 1950.

• BLACKBURN, Don — *see page 897*

• BLADE, Hank

LW – L. 5'11", 190 lbs. b: Peterborough, Ont., 4/28/1920.

Season	Club	League	GP	G	A	Pts	AG	AA	APts	PIM	GP	G	A	Pts	PIM
1939-40	Ottawa Montagnards	OCHL	20	5	0	5	....	....	....	8	7	0	0	0	0
1940-41	Ottawa Montagnards	OCHL	20	12	5	17	....	....	....	2	....	....	....	....	....
	Ottawa Car Bombers	UOVHL	....	....	....	....	....	....	....	....	2	4	3	7	4
1941-42	Ottawa RCAF	OCHL	16	7	10	17	....	....	....	6	3	0	1	1	0
	Ottawa RCAF	Al-Cup	2	0	0	0	....	....	....	0	....	....	....	....	....
1942-43	Ottawa RCAF	OCHL	19	10	13	23	....	....	....	6	8	5	*1	6	6
	Vancouver RCAF	NNDHL	14	14	6	20	....	....	....	6	....	....	....	....	....
	Ottawa RCAF	Al-Cup	9	2	8	10	....	....	....	4	....	....	....	....	....
1943-44	Vancouver Seahawks	NNDHL	....	....	....	....	....	....	....	....	3	*4	2	6	4
1944-45	Ottawa Depot #17	OCHL	12	*22	21	*43	....	....	....	8	....	....	....	....	....
	Ottawa Senators	QSHL	2	1	3	4	....	....	....	0	....	....	....	....	....
1945-46	Kansas City Pla-Mors	USHL	46	29	36	65	....	....	....	16	12	7	8	15	4
	Ottawa Senators	QSHL	5	0	2	2	....	....	....	6	....	....	....	....	....
1946-47	**Chicago Black Hawks**	**NHL**	**18**	**1**	**3**	**4**	**1**	**4**	**5**	**2**	....	....	....	....	....
	Kansas City Pla-Mors	USHL	38	23	24	47	....	....	....	17	12	4	7	11	4
1947-48	**Chicago Black Hawks**	**NHL**	**6**	**1**	**0**	**1**	**1**	**0**	**1**	**0**	....	....	....	....	....
	Pittsburgh Hornets	AHL	7	1	2	3	....	....	....	6	....	....	....	....	....
	Kansas City Pla-Mors	USHL	51	29	41	70	....	....	....	32	7	0	3	3	0
1948-49	Kansas City Pla-Mors	USHL	54	27	36	63	....	....	....	19	2	0	0	0	0
1949-50	Kansas City Mohawks	USHL	66	27	48	75	....	....	....	27	3	0	0	0	0
1950-51	Milwaukee Seagulls	USHL	63	26	48	74	....	....	....	34	....	....	....	....	....
1951-52	Calgary Stampeders	PCHL	62	14	27	41	....	....	....	24	....	....	....	....	....
1952-53	Calgary Stampeders	WHL	22	3	6	9	....	....	....	32	....	....	....	....	....
1953-54	Simcoe Gunners	OHA-Sr.	DID NOT PLAY – COACHING												
	NHL Totals		**24**	**2**	**3**	**5**	**2**	**4**	**6**	**2**	....	....	....	....	....

Won Herman W. Paterson Cup (USHL - MVP) (1951)

• BLAINE, Garry Garry James

RW – R. 5'11", 190 lbs. b: St. Boniface, Man., 4/19/1933 d: 12/19/1998.

Season	Club	League	GP	G	A	Pts	AG	AA	APts	PIM	GP	G	A	Pts	PIM
1950-51	Winnipeg Canadians	MJHL	33	13	14	27	....	....	....	45	....	....	....	....	....
1951-52	St. Boniface Canadiens	MJHL	35	14	18	32	....	....	....	45	5	3	1	4	0
1952-53	St. Boniface Canadiens	MJHL	17	16	15	31	....	....	....	50	8	*6	6	*12	10
	St. Boniface Canadiens	M-Cup	17	17	10	27	....	....	....	21	....	....	....	....	....
1953-54	Montreal Royals	QHL	54	11	20	31	....	....	....	24	11	2	6	8	6
1954-55	**Montreal Canadiens**	**NHL**	**1**	**0**	**0**	**0**	**0**	**0**	**0**	**0**	....	....	....	....	....
	Montreal Royals	QHL	53	18	31	49	....	....	....	56	14	5	*11	*16	2
1955-56	Trois-Rivieres Lions	QHL	22	6	6	12	....	....	....	4	....	....	....	....	....
	Winnipeg Warriors	WHL	40	9	12	21	....	....	....	20	....	....	....	....	....
1956-57	Chicoutimi Sagueneens	QHL	12	2	6	8	....	....	....	2	....	....	....	....	....
	Buffalo Bisons	AHL	43	13	14	27	....	....	....	20	....	....	....	....	....
1957-58	Quebec Aces	QHL	62	23	38	61	....	....	....	28	13	3	5	8	12
1958-59	Vancouver Canucks	WHL	67	16	19	35	....	....	....	60	8	1	2	3	10
1959-60	S.S. Marie Thunderbirds	EPHL	70	20	37	57	....	....	....	54	....	....	....	....	....
	NHL Totals		**1**	**0**	**0**	**0**	**0**	**0**	**0**	**0**	....	....	....	....	....

• BLAIR, Andy Andrew Dryden

C – L. 6'1", 180 lbs. b: Winnipeg, Man., 2/27/1908 d: 12/27/1977.

Season	Club	League	GP	G	A	Pts	AG	AA	APts	PIM	GP	G	A	Pts	PIM
1923-24	University of Manitoba	MHL-Sr.	2	0	0	0	....	....	....	2	1	0	0	0	0
1924-25	University of Manitoba	WJrHL	9	14	4	18	....	....	....	4	8	10	1	11	6
	University of Manitoba	M-Cup	5	8	0	8	....	....	....	8	....	....	....	....	....
1925-26	University of Manitoba	MHL-Sr.	4	5	1	6	....	....	....	....	....	....	....	....	....
1926-27	University of Manitoba	X-Games	1	1	1	2	....	....	....	....	....	....	....	....	....
	Winnipeg Winnipegs	Al-Cup	2	0	0	0	....	....	....	8	....	....	....	....	....

Season	Club	League	GP	G	A	Pts	AG	AA	APts	PIM	GP	G	A	Pts	PIM
			REGULAR SEASON								PLAYOFFS				
1927-28	University of Manitoba	MHL-Sr.	10	11	8	19	....	....	....	16	2	0	0	0	*10
	Winnipeg CPR	WSrHL	4	3	2	5	....	....	....	2	....	....	....	....	....
	University of Manitoba	Al-Cup	5	3	2	5	....	....	....	10	....	....	....	....	....
1928-29	**Toronto Maple Leafs**	**NHL**	**44**	**12**	**15**	**27**	**35**	**103**	**138**	**41**	**4**	***3**	**0**	***3**	**2**
1929-30	**Toronto Maple Leafs**	**NHL**	**42**	**11**	**10**	**21**	**16**	**24**	**40**	**27**	....	....	....	....	....
1930-31	**Toronto Maple Leafs**	**NHL**	**44**	**11**	**8**	**19**	**22**	**24**	**46**	**32**	**2**	**1**	**0**	**1**	**0**
♦1931-32	**Toronto Maple Leafs**	**NHL**	**48**	**9**	**14**	**23**	**15**	**31**	**46**	**35**	**7**	**2**	**2**	**4**	**6**
1932-33	**Toronto Maple Leafs**	**NHL**	**43**	**6**	**9**	**15**	**11**	**19**	**30**	**38**	**9**	**0**	**2**	**2**	**4**
1933-34	**Toronto Maple Leafs**	**NHL**	**47**	**14**	**9**	**23**	**24**	**19**	**43**	**35**	**5**	**0**	**2**	**2**	**16**
1934-35	**Toronto Maple Leafs**	**NHL**	**45**	**6**	**14**	**20**	**10**	**24**	**34**	**22**	**2**	**0**	**0**	**0**	**2**
1935-36	**Toronto Maple Leafs**	**NHL**	**45**	**5**	**4**	**9**	**10**	**8**	**18**	**60**	**9**	**0**	**0**	**0**	**2**
1936-37	**Chicago Black Hawks**	**NHL**	**44**	**0**	**3**	**3**	**0**	**5**	**5**	**33**	....	....	....	....	....
	NHL Totals		**402**	**74**	**86**	**160**	**143**	**257**	**400**	**323**	**38**	**6**	**6**	**12**	**32**

Played in NHL All-Star Game (1934)

Traded to **Chicago** by **Toronto** for cash, May 7, 1936.

• BLAIR, Chuck Charles

RW – R. 5'10", 175 lbs. b: Edinburgh, Scotland, 7/23/1928.

Season	Club	League	GP	G	A	Pts	AG	AA	APts	PIM	GP	G	A	Pts	PIM
1946-47	Oshawa Generals	OHA-Jr.	28	19	22	41	....	....	....	6	....	....	....	....	....
1947-48	Oshawa Generals	OHA-Jr.	33	18	20	38	....	....	....	24	6	0	1	1	13
1948-49	**Toronto Maple Leafs**	**NHL**	**1**	**0**	**0**	**0**	**0**	**0**	**0**	**0**	....	....	....	....	....
	Toronto Marlboros	OHA-Sr.	36	21	14	35	....	....	....	47	10	6	5	11	6
	Toronto Marlboros	Al-Cup	13	4	5	9	....	....	....	10	....	....	....	....	....
1949-50	Toronto Marlboros	OHA-Sr.	39	21	23	44	....	....	....	36	14	5	4	9	4
	Toronto Marlboros	Al-Cup	17	8	9	17	....	....	....	17	....	....	....	....	....
1950-51	Pittsburgh Hornets	AHL	71	27	16	43	....	....	....	41	13	6	1	7	8
1951-52	Pittsburgh Hornets	AHL	57	13	25	38	....	....	....	22	11	1	2	3	6
1952-53	Pittsburgh Hornets	AHL	48	17	18	35	....	....	....	16	10	2	3	5	10
1953-54	Cleveland Barons	AHL	59	23	15	38	....	....	....	2	9	4	3	7	2
1954-55	Cleveland Barons	AHL	21	3	4	7	....	....	....	0	....	....	....	....	....
	Buffalo Bisons	AHL	38	9	13	22	....	....	....	8	10	5	0	5	0
1955-56	Buffalo Bisons	AHL	56	17	16	33	....	....	....	20	5	3	1	4	4
1956-57	Buffalo Bisons	AHL	64	19	18	37	....	....	....	22	....	....	....	....	....
1957-58	Calgary Stampeders	WHL	65	25	23	48	....	....	....	31	14	2	9	11	0
1958-59	Calgary Stampeders	WHL	35	19	15	34	....	....	....	6	8	4	0	4	4
1959-60	Quebec Aces	AHL	48	8	12	20	....	....	....	8	....	....	....	....	....
1960-61	Clinton Comets	EHL	61	21	41	62	....	....	....	12	4	0	1	1	0
1961-62	Fort Erie Meteors	OHA-Sr.	DID NOT PLAY – COACHING												
	NHL Totals		**1**	**0**	**0**	**0**	**0**	**0**	**0**	**0**	....	....	....	....	....

• Brother of Dusty (George)

Traded to **Cleveland** (AHL) by **Toronto** with $30,000 for Bob Bailey and Gerry Foley, May 30, 1953. Traded to **Buffalo** (AHL) by **Cleveland** (AHL) for Joe Lund, December 5, 1954.

• BLAIR, Dusty George

C – R. 5'8", 160 lbs. b: South Porcupine, Ont., 9/15/1929.

Season	Club	League	GP	G	A	Pts	AG	AA	APts	PIM	GP	G	A	Pts	PIM
1947-48	Oshawa Generals	OHA-Jr.	36	17	13	30	....	....	....	17	6	0	3	3	5
1948-49	Oshawa Generals	OHA-Jr.	46	23	26	49	....	....	....	15	2	1	1	2	0
1949-50	Los Angeles Monarchs	PCHL	44	18	14	32	....	....	....	10	....	....	....	....	....
	Pittsburgh Hornets	AHL	17	1	3	4	....	....	....	2	....	....	....	....	....
1950-51	**Toronto Maple Leafs**	**NHL**	**2**	**0**	**0**	**0**	**0**	**0**	**0**	**0**	....	....	....	....	....
	St. Michael's Monarchs	OMHL	23	11	13	24	....	....	....	4	9	4	2	6	4
	St. Michael's Monarchs	Alx-Cup	10	4	5	9	....	....	....	0	....	....	....	....	....
1951-52	Pittsburgh Hornets	AHL	4	0	0	0	....	....	....	0	....	....	....	....	....
	Saint John Beavers	MMHL	60	31	33	64	....	....	....	6	10	7	7	*14	0
	Saint John Beavers	Alx-Cup	5	2	2	4	....	....	....	2	....	....	....	....	....
1952-53	Ottawa Senators	QMHL	3	0	1	1	....	....	....	0	....	....	....	....	....
	Smiths Falls Rideaus	OHA-Sr.	45	22	*43	65	....	....	....	11	10	2	8	10	2
	Smiths Falls Rideaus	Al-Cup	11	3	9	12	....	....	....	0	....	....	....	....	....
1953-54	Ottawa Senators	QHL	71	28	43	71	....	....	....	0	22	*9	*12	*21	0
1954-55	Buffalo Bisons	AHL	64	18	31	49	....	....	....	6	10	3	1	4	0
1955-56	Providence Reds	AHL	55	18	16	34	....	....	....	6	9	1	12	13	0
1956-57	Providence Reds	AHL	59	9	24	33	....	....	....	4	5	1	1	2	2
1957-58	Calgary Stampeders	WHL	69	11	31	42	....	....	....	11	14	3	4	7	2
1958-59	Calgary Stampeders	WHL	53	14	13	27	....	....	....	4	8	3	1	4	0
1959-60	Calgary Stampeders	WHL	69	6	27	33	....	....	....	7	....	....	....	....	....
1960-61	S.S. Marie Thunderbirds	EPHL	66	11	23	34	....	....	....	20	10	1	1	2	0
1961-62	S.S. Marie Thunderbirds	EPHL	67	9	28	37	....	....	....	8	....	....	....	....	....
1962-63	Clinton Comets	EHL	65	17	44	61	....	....	....	4	13	2	9	11	0
1963-64	New Haven Blades	EHL	21	2	7	9	....	....	....	0	....	....	....	....	....
	Clinton Comets	EHL	15	1	3	4	....	....	....	0	....	....	....	....	....
1964-65	Nashville Dixie Flyers	EHL	66	13	42	55	....	....	....	14	13	4	8	12	0
	NHL Totals		**2**	**0**	**0**	**0**	**0**	**0**	**0**	**0**	....	....	....	....	....

• Brother of Chuck • MMHL Second All-Star Team (1952) • Won Byng of Vimy Trophy (MVP - QHL) (1954)

Traded to **Chicago** (Buffalo-AHL) by **Toronto** with Frank Sullivan and Jackie LeClair for Brian Cullen, May 4, 1954. Loaned to **NY Rangers** by **Buffalo** (AHL) with $10,000 and the loan of Gord Pennell for Pete Conacher, August 20, 1956.

• BLAKE, Bob Louis Robert

LW – L. 6', 200 lbs. b: Ashland, WI, 8/16/1914.

Season	Club	League	GP	G	A	Pts	AG	AA	APts	PIM	GP	G	A	Pts	PIM
1932-33	Hibbing Blue Jackets	H.S.	STATISTICS NOT AVAILABLE												
1933-34	Hibbing Miners	CHL	42	10	12	22	....	....	....	74	6	*3	1	4	8
1934-35	Boston Cubs	Can-Am	44	5	7	12	....	....	....	28	3	0	0	0	4
1935-36	**Boston Bruins**	**NHL**	**12**	**0**	**0**	**0**	**0**	**0**	**0**	**0**	....	....	....	....	....
	Boston Cubs	Can-Am	37	7	10	17	....	....	....	38	....	....	....	....	....
1936-37	Minneapolis Millers	AHA	48	13	24	37	....	....	....	13	6	2	*7	9	0
1937-38	Minneapolis Millers	AHA	48	17	26	43	....	....	....	40	7	2	*4	*6	0
1938-39	Cleveland Barons	IAHL	53	9	11	20	....	....	....	14	9	0	2	2	2
1939-40	Pittsburgh Hornets	IAHL	3	1	1	2	....	....	....	4	....	....	....	....	....
	Cleveland Barons	IAHL	46	8	8	16	....	....	....	8	....	....	....	....	....
1940-41	Minneapolis Millers	AHA	19	4	9	13	....	....	....	8	....	....	....	....	....
	Buffalo Bisons	AHL	33	1	6	7	....	....	....	20	....	....	....	....	....
1941-42	Buffalo Bisons	AHL	56	6	15	21	....	....	....	58	....	....	....	....	....
1942-43	Buffalo Bisons	AHL	42	3	14	17	....	....	....	28	9	1	3	4	2
1943-44			MILITARY SERVICE												
1944-45			MILITARY SERVICE												
1945-46	Buffalo Bisons	AHL	10	1	2	3	....	....	....	2	12	0	4	4	0
1946-47	Buffalo Bisons	AHL	63	6	11	17	....	....	....	57	4	0	2	2	0
1947-48	Buffalo Bisons	AHL	5	0	0	0	....	....	....	0	....	....	....	....	....
	Houston Huskies	USHL	49	12	20	32	....	....	....	29	12	2	2	4	10
1948-49	Buffalo Bisons	AHL	63	8	10	18	....	....	....	32	....	....	....	....	....
1949-50	Cincinnati Mohawks	AHL	49	4	15	19	....	....	....	33	....	....	....	....	....
1950-51	New Haven Eagles	AHL	27	3	6	9	....	....	....	16	....	....	....	....	....
	Buffalo Bisons	AHL	24	4	5	9	....	....	....	6	....	....	....	....	....
	Cincinnati Mohawks	AHL	2	0	0	0	....	....	....	0	....	....	....	....	....
	NHL Totals		**12**	**0**	**0**	**0**	**0**	**0**	**0**	**0**	....	....	....	....	....

Signed as a free agent by **Boston**, October, 1934. Traded to **Minneapolis** (AHA) (Cleveland-IAHL) by **Boston** for cash, September, 1936. Traded to **Buffalo** (AHL) by **Minneapolis** (AHA) for the loan of Paul Runge and cash, December 27, 1940. Traded to **Cincinnati** (AHL) by **Buffalo** (AHL) with Bob Thorpe for Les Hickey, October 27, 1949. Signed as a free agent by **Buffalo** (AHL) after **New Haven** (AHL) franchise folded, December 10, 1950.

• BLAKE, Mickey Francis Joseph

LW/D – L. 5'10", 186 lbs. b: Barriefield, Ont., 10/31/1912 Deceased.

Season	Club	League	GP	G	A	Pts	AG	AA	APts	PIM	GP	G	A	Pts	PIM
1931-32	Kingston Frontenacs	OHA-Sr.	STATISTICS NOT AVAILABLE												
1932-33	Windsor Bulldogs	IHL	38	3	2	5	....	....	....	26	6	2	0	2	6
	Montreal Maroons	**NHL**	**1**	**0**	**0**	**0**	**0**	**0**	**0**	**0**	....	....	....	....	....
1933-34	Quebec Beavers	Can-Am	40	6	3	9	....	....	....	36	....	....	....	....	....
1934-35	**St. Louis Eagles**	**NHL**	**8**	**1**	**1**	**2**	**2**	**2**	**4**	**2**	....	....	....	....	....
	Detroit Olympics	IHL	25	0	0	0	....	....	....	26	5	1	0	1	0
1935-36	**Toronto Maple Leafs**	**NHL**	**1**	**0**	**0**	**0**	**0**	**0**	**0**	**2**	....	....	....	....	....
	Syracuse Stars	IHL	43	17	17	34	....	....	....	27	3	0	0	0	0
1936-37	Syracuse Stars	IAHL	50	9	17	26	....	....	....	20	9	1	2	3	2
1937-38	Syracuse Stars	IAHL	25	2	4	6	....	....	....	14	8	0	0	0	2
1938-39	Cleveland Barons	IAHL	47	7	12	19	....	....	....	20	8	0	0	0	0
1939-40	Pittsburgh Hornets	IAHL	55	3	11	14	....	....	....	26	9	0	0	0	6
1940-41	Pittsburgh Hornets	AHL	56	18	14	32	....	....	....	28	6	0	2	2	0
1941-42	Pittsburgh Hornets	AHL	48	9	11	20	....	....	....	14	....	....	....	....	....
1942-43	Kingston Frontenacs	OHA-Sr.	16	6	3	9	....	....	....	2	4	1	0	1	2
	NHL Totals		**10**	**1**	**1**	**2**	**2**	**2**	**4**	**4**	....	....	....	....	....

IHL Second All-Star Team (1936)

Traded to **St. Louis** by **Montreal Maroons** for cash, October 12, 1934. Traded to **Detroit** by **St. Louis** with $3,500 for George Patterson, November 28, 1934. • Detroit held option on services and returned Blake to St. Louis after 1934-35 season. Claimed by **Toronto** from **St. Louis** in Dispersal Draft, October 15, 1935.

• BLAKE, Toe Hector HHOF

LW – L. 5'10", 165 lbs. b: Victoria Mines, Ont., 8/21/1912 d: 5/17/1995.

Season	Club	League	GP	G	A	Pts	AG	AA	APts	PIM	GP	G	A	Pts	PIM
1929-30	Cochrane Dunlops	NOJHA	7	3	0	3	....	....	....	4	....	....	....	....	....
1930-31	Sudbury Cub Wolves	NOJHA	6	3	1	4	....	....	....	12	2	0	0	0	6
	Sudbury Industries	NOHA	8	7	1	8	....	....	....	10	3	1	1	2	4
	Sudbury Cub Wolves	M-Cup	5	4	1	5	....	....	....	6	....	....	....	....	....
	Sudbury Wolves	Al-Cup	3	3	1	4	....	....	....	0	....	....	....	....	....
1931-32	Sudbury Cub Wolves	NOJHA	3	*5	0	5	....	....	....	4	....	....	....	....	....
	Falconbridge Falcons	NOHA	10	*8	1	9	....	....	....	18	2	1	0	1	2
1932-33	Hamilton Tigers	OHA-Sr.	22	9	4	13	....	....	....	26	2	0	0	0	2
1933-34	Hamilton Tigers	OHA-Sr.	23	19	14	33	....	....	....	28	4	3	4	7	4
	Hamilton Tigers	Al-Cup	8	5	2	7	....	....	....	4	....	....	....	....	....
1934-35	Hamilton Tigers	OHA-Sr.	18	15	11	26	....	....	....	48	....	....	....	....	....
♦	**Montreal Maroons**	**NHL**	**8**	**0**	**0**	**0**	**0**	**0**	**0**	**0**	**1**	**0**	**0**	**0**	**0**
1935-36	Providence Reds	Can-Am	33	12	11	23	....	....	....	65	7	2	3	5	2
	Montreal Canadiens	**NHL**	**11**	**1**	**2**	**3**	**2**	**4**	**6**	**28**	....	....	....	....	....
1936-37	**Montreal Canadiens**	**NHL**	**43**	**10**	**12**	**22**	**17**	**22**	**39**	**12**	**5**	**1**	**0**	**1**	**0**
1937-38	**Montreal Canadiens**	**NHL**	**43**	**17**	**16**	**33**	**28**	**26**	**54**	**33**	**3**	**3**	**1**	**4**	**2**
1938-39	**Montreal Canadiens**	**NHL**	**48**	**24**	**23**	***47**	**43**	**36**	**79**	**10**	**3**	**1**	**1**	**2**	**2**
1939-40	**Montreal Canadiens**	**NHL**	**48**	**17**	**19**	**36**	**28**	**30**	**58**	**48**	....	....	....	....	....
1940-41	**Montreal Canadiens**	**NHL**	**48**	**12**	**20**	**32**	**19**	**29**	**48**	**49**	**3**	**0**	**3**	**3**	**5**
1941-42	**Montreal Canadiens**	**NHL**	**48**	**17**	**28**	**45**	**23**	**33**	**56**	**19**	**3**	**0**	**3**	**3**	**2**
1942-43	**Montreal Canadiens**	**NHL**	**48**	**23**	**36**	**59**	**24**	**34**	**58**	**26**	**5**	**4**	**3**	**7**	**0**
♦1943-44	**Montreal Canadiens**	**NHL**	**41**	**26**	**33**	**59**	**24**	**29**	**53**	**10**	**9**	**7**	***11**	***18**	**2**
1944-45	**Montreal Canadiens**	**NHL**	**49**	**29**	**38**	**67**	**30**	**45**	**75**	**25**	**6**	**0**	**2**	**2**	**5**
♦1945-46	**Montreal Canadiens**	**NHL**	**50**	**29**	**21**	**50**	**35**	**31**	**66**	**2**	**9**	***7**	**6**	**13**	**5**
1946-47	**Montreal Canadiens**	**NHL**	**60**	**21**	**29**	**50**	**24**	**35**	**59**	**6**	**11**	**2**	***7**	**9**	**0**
1947-48	**Montreal Canadiens**	**NHL**	**32**	**9**	**15**	**24**	**12**	**20**	**32**	**4**	....	....	....	....	....
1948-49	Buffalo Bisons	AHL	18	1	3	4	....	....	....	0	....	....	....	....	....
1949-50	Valleyfield Braves	QSHL	43	12	15	27	....	....	....	15	3	0	1	1	0
1950-51	Valleyfield Braves	QMHL	DID NOT PLAY – COACHING												
	Valleyfield Braves	Alx-Cup	1	0	0	0	....	....	....	0	....	....	....	....	....
	NHL Totals		**577**	**235**	**292**	**527**	**309**	**374**	**683**	**272**	**58**	**25**	**37**	**62**	**23**

NHL Second All-Star Team (1938, 1946) • NHL First All-Star Team (1939, 1940, 1945) • NHL Scoring Leader (1939) • Won Hart Trophy (1939) • Won Lady Byng Trophy (1946) • Played in NHL All-Star Game (1937, 1939)

Signed as a free agent by **Montreal Maroons**, February 21, 1935. Traded to **Montreal Canadiens** by **Montreal Maroons** with Bill Miller and Ken Gravel for Lorne Chabot, February, 1936. • Missed remainder of 1947-48 season recovering from leg injury suffered in game vs. NY Rangers, January 10, 1948.

• BLINCO, Russ "Beaver"

C – L. 5'10", 171 lbs. b: Grand'Mere, Que., 3/12/1908 Deceased.

Season	Club	League	GP	G	A	Pts	AG	AA	APts	PIM	GP	G	A	Pts	PIM
1926-27	McGill Redmen	MCHL	9	0	1	1	....	....	....	0	....	....	....	....	....
1927-28	McGill University	OQAA	STATISTICS NOT AVAILABLE												
1928-29	Grand'Mere Maroons	ECHL	5	4	0	4	....	....	....	2	....	....	....	....	....
1929-30	Brooklyn Crescents	USAHA	STATISTICS NOT AVAILABLE												
1930-31	Brooklyn Crescents	USAHA	STATISTICS NOT AVAILABLE												
1931-32	Brooklyn Crescents	USAHA	STATISTICS NOT AVAILABLE												
1932-33	Springfield Indians	Can-Am	13	2	2	4	....	....	....	....	....	....	....	....	....
	Windsor Bulldogs	IHL	28	13	10	23	....	....	....	12	6	2	3	5	2
1933-34	**Montreal Maroons**	**NHL**	**31**	**14**	**9**	**23**	**24**	**19**	**43**	**2**	**4**	**0**	**1**	**1**	**0**
	Windsor Bulldogs	IHL	16	6	5	11	....	....	....	4	....	....	....	....	....
♦1934-35	**Montreal Maroons**	**NHL**	**48**	**13**	**14**	**27**	**21**	**24**	**45**	**4**	**7**	**2**	**2**	**4**	**2**
1935-36	**Montreal Maroons**	**NHL**	**46**	**13**	**10**	**23**	**25**	**19**	**44**	**10**	**3**	**0**	**0**	**0**	**0**

Season	Club	League	GP	G	A	Pts	AG	AA	APts	PIM	GP	G	A	Pts	PIM
			REGULAR SEASON								PLAYOFFS				
1936-37	Montreal Maroons	NHL	48	6	12	18	10	22	32	2	5	1	0	1	2
1937-38	Montreal Maroons	NHL	47	10	9	19	16	14	30	4	....	....	....	....	....
1938-39	Chicago Black Hawks	NHL	48	3	12	15	5	19	24	2	....	....	....	....	....
	NHL Totals		268	59	66	125	101	117	218	24	19	3	3	6	4

NHL Rookie of the Year (1934) • Played in NHL All-Star Game (1937)

Traded to **Montreal Maroons** (Windsor-IHL) by **NY Rangers** after Springfield (Can-Am) franchise folded, December 18, 1932. Traded to **Chicago** by **Montreal Maroons** with Baldy Northcott and Earl Robinson for $30,000, September 15, 1938.

• BODNAR, Gus August

C – R. 5'11", 160 lbs. b: Fort William, Ont., 4/24/1923.

Season	Club	League	GP	G	A	Pts	AG	AA	APts	PIM	GP	G	A	Pts	PIM
1940-41	Fort William Rangers	TBJHL	18	13	8	21	....	....	....	12	2	0	0	0	0
1941-42	Fort William Rangers	TBJHL	16	20	16	36	....	....	....	22	3	*5	4	9	2
	Fort William Rangers	M-Cup	3	2	5	7	....	....	....	*16	....	....	....	....	....
1942-43	Fort William Rangers	TBJHL	9	10	*29	*39	....	....	....	9	3	2	3	5	2
	Fort William Forts	M-Cup	3	2	1	3	....	....	....	2	....	....	....	....	....
1943-44	Toronto Maple Leafs	NHL	50	22	40	62	20	36	56	18	5	0	0	0	0
♦1944-45	Toronto Maple Leafs	NHL	49	8	36	44	8	42	50	18	13	3	1	4	4
1945-46	Toronto Maple Leafs	NHL	49	14	23	37	17	34	51	14	....	....	....	....	....
♦1946-47	Toronto Maple Leafs	NHL	39	4	6	10	4	7	11	10	1	0	0	0	0
	Pittsburgh Hornets	AHL	15	10	9	19	....	....	....	10	9	2	2	4	4
1947-48	Pittsburgh Hornets	AHL	6	2	3	5	....	....	....	0	....	....	....	....	....
	Chicago Black Hawks	NHL	46	13	22	35	17	29	46	23	....	....	....	....	....
1948-49	Chicago Black Hawks	NHL	59	19	26	45	27	37	64	14	....	....	....	....	....
1949-50	Chicago Black Hawks	NHL	70	11	28	39	14	34	48	6	....	....	....	....	....
1950-51	Chicago Black Hawks	NHL	44	8	12	20	10	15	25	8	....	....	....	....	....
1951-52	Chicago Black Hawks	NHL	69	14	26	40	19	32	51	26	....	....	....	....	....
1952-53	Chicago Black Hawks	NHL	66	16	13	29	21	16	37	26	7	1	1	2	2
1953-54	Chicago Black Hawks	NHL	45	6	15	21	8	18	26	20	....	....	....	....	....
	Boston Bruins	NHL	14	3	3	6	4	4	8	10	1	0	0	0	0
1954-55	Boston Bruins	NHL	67	4	4	8	5	5	10	14	5	0	1	1	4
	NHL Totals		667	142	254	396	174	309	483	207	32	4	3	7	10

Won Calder Memorial Trophy (1944) • Played in NHL All-Star Game (1951)

Traded to **Chicago** by **Toronto** with Bud Poile, Gaye Stewart, Ernie Dickens and Bob Goldham for Max Bentley and Cy Thomas, November 2, 1947. Traded to **Boston** by **Chicago** for Jerry Toppazzini, February 16, 1954.

• BOESCH, Garth Garth Vernon

D – R. 6', 180 lbs. b: Milestone, Sask., 10/7/1920 d: 5/14/1998.

Season	Club	League	GP	G	A	Pts	AG	AA	APts	PIM	GP	G	A	Pts	PIM
1937-38	Notre Dame Hounds	S-SJHL	6	5	0	5	....	....	....	4	2	0	0	0	0
1938-39	Notre Dame Hounds	S-SJHL	9	5	1	6	....	....	....	4	....	....	....	....	....
1939-40	Notre Dame Hounds	S-SJHL	12	7	4	11	....	....	....	12	....	....	....	....	....
1940-41	Regina Rangers	S-SSHL	32	10	7	17	....	....	....	26	8	1	2	3	10
	Regina Rangers	Al-Cup	14	6	2	8	....	....	....	16	....	....	....	....	....
1941-42	Regina Rangers	S-SSHL	31	12	8	20	....	....	....	36	3	0	0	0	6
	Lethbridge Maple Leafs	ASHL	....	....	....	....	....	....	....	....	9	2	2	4	2
	Lethbridge Maple Leafs	Al-Cup	5	1	1	2	....	....	....	8	....	....	....	....	....
1942-43	Lethbridge Bombers	ASHL	22	8	8	16	....	....	....	40	3	2	0	2	2
1943-44			MILITARY SERVICE												
1944-45	Winnipeg RCAF	WNDHL	1	0	1	1	....	....	....	0	4	2	1	3	13
1945-46	Pittsburgh Hornets	AHL	43	15	9	24	....	....	....	16	6	0	4	4	8
♦1946-47	Toronto Maple Leafs	NHL	35	4	5	9	4	6	10	47	11	0	2	2	6
♦1947-48	Toronto Maple Leafs	NHL	45	2	7	9	3	9	12	52	8	2	1	3	2
♦1948-49	Toronto Maple Leafs	NHL	59	1	10	11	1	14	15	43	9	0	2	2	6
1949-50	Toronto Maple Leafs	NHL	58	2	6	8	2	7	9	63	6	0	0	0	4
	NHL Totals		197	9	28	37	10	36	46	205	34	2	5	7	18

ASHL First All-Star Team (1943) • Played in NHL All-Star Game (1948, 1949)

Claimed by **NY Americans** from **Seattle** (PCHL) in Inter-League Draft, June 27, 1941. • Refused permission to leave Canada for NY Americans training camp because of war-time travel restrictions, September, 1941. Rights transferred to **Toronto** from **Brooklyn** in Special Dispersal Draw, September 11, 1943.

• BOILEAU, Marc Marc Claude

C – L. 5'11", 170 lbs. b: Pointe Claire, Que., 9/3/1932.

Season	Club	League	GP	G	A	Pts	AG	AA	APts	PIM	GP	G	A	Pts	PIM
1950-51	Verdun LaSalle	QJHL	45	5	8	13	....	....	....	6	3	0	1	1	0
1951-52	St-Jerome Eagles	QJHL	36	17	17	34	....	....	....	16	....	....	....	....	....
1952-53	Kitchener Greenshirts	OHA-Jr.	20	10	19	29	....	....	....	38	....	....	....	....	....
	Montreal Jr. Canadiens	QJHL	17	3	7	10	....	....	....	5	....	....	....	....	....
1953-54	Cincinnati Mohawks	IHL	38	12	21	33	....	....	....	13	11	1	1	2	0
1954-55	Fort Wayne Komets	IHL	DID NOT PLAY – SUSPENDED												
1955-56	Saint John Beavers	ACSHL	63	22	43	65	....	....	....	66	15	5	3	8	9
	Saint John Beavers	Al-Cup	5	1	0	1	....	....	....	9	....	....	....	....	....
1956-57	Indianapolis Chiefs	IHL	60	25	32	57	....	....	....	50	8	2	3	5	2
1957-58	Indianapolis Chiefs	IHL	63	26	*61	87	....	....	....	64	11	*8	5	13	7
1958-59	Seattle Totems	WHL	67	17	30	47	....	....	....	52	12	*10	7	17	10
1959-60	Seattle Totems	WHL	68	32	45	77	....	....	....	54	4	0	0	0	5
1960-61	Seattle Totems	WHL	70	42	31	73	....	....	....	49	11	5	4	9	14
1961-62	Detroit Red Wings	NHL	54	5	6	11	6	6	12	8	....	....	....	....	....
	Hershey Bears	AHL	14	7	8	15	....	....	....	6	....	....	....	....	....
1962-63	Los Angeles Blades	WHL	66	17	45	62	....	....	....	77	3	0	3	3	2
1963-64	Los Angeles Blades	WHL	69	12	32	44	....	....	....	35	12	3	3	6	33
1964-65	Los Angeles Blades	WHL	60	12	23	35	....	....	....	62	....	....	....	....	....
1965-66	Los Angeles Blades	WHL	72	10	29	39	....	....	....	48	....	....	....	....	....
1966-67			OUT OF HOCKEY – RETIRED												
1967-68	Seattle Totems	WHL	66	6	31	37	....	....	....	41	9	3	2	5	4
1968-69	Seattle Totems	WHL	73	14	30	44	....	....	....	42	2	0	0	0	0
1969-70	Seattle Totems	WHL	73	16	28	44	....	....	....	65	6	1	0	1	8
1970-71	Fort Wayne Komets	IHL	67	19	40	59	....	....	....	35	2	0	1	1	0
1971-72	Fort Wayne Komets	IHL	66	11	44	55	....	....	....	27	6	0	6	6	4
1972-73	Fort Wayne Komets	IHL	2	0	0	0	....	....	....	0	....	....	....	....	....
1973-74	Pittsburgh Penguins	NHL	DID NOT PLAY – COACHING												
	NHL Totals		54	5	6	11	6	6	12	8	....	....	....	....	....

• Son of Rene • IHL First All-Star Team (1958) • WHL Second All-Star Team (1960)

• Suspended by **Montreal** for refusing assignment to **Fort Wayne** (IHL), September, 1954. Traded to **Detroit** (Seattle-WHL) by **Indianapolis** (IHL) for cash, September, 1958. Traded to **LA Blades** (WHL) by **Seattle** (WHL) with Frank Arnett for Jim Powers, Terry Slater and Jim Hay, July, 1962. Traded to **Seattle** (WHL) by **Chicago** (LA Blades-WHL) with Bobby Schmautz for cash with Chicago retaining NHL rights, August 10, 1967.

• BOILEAU, Rene "Rainy Drinkwater"

C – L. 5'10", 160 lbs. b: Pointe Claire, Que., 5/18/1904.

Season	Club	League	GP	G	A	Pts	AG	AA	APts	PIM	GP	G	A	Pts	PIM
1923-24	Pointe Claire Maple Leafs	MCHL	STATISTICS NOT AVAILABLE												
1924-25	Montreal K of C	MCHL	STATISTICS NOT AVAILABLE												
1925-26	Montreal Columbus	MCHL	4	0	0	0	....	....	....	0	....	....	....	....	....
	New York Americans	NHL	7	0	0	0	0	0	0	0	....	....	....	....	....
	Montreal Bell-Telephone	MRTHL	3	7	0	7	....	....	....	0	....	....	....	....	....
1926-27	Niagara Falls Cataracts	Can-Pro	18	4	0	4	....	....	....	8	....	....	....	....	....
1927-28	New Haven Eagles	Can-Am	36	5	3	8	....	....	....	51	....	....	....	....	....
1928-29	St. Louis Flyers	AHA	36	4	0	4	....	....	....	28	....	....	....	....	....
1929-30	St. Louis Flyers	AHA	30	2	1	3	....	....	....	46	....	....	....	....	....
1930-31	St. Louis Flyers	AHA	37	3	0	3	....	....	....	43	....	....	....	....	....
1931-32	Trois-Rivieres Renards	ECHA	4	0	0	0	....	....	....	6	....	....	....	....	....
1932-33			DID NOT PLAY												
1933-34	Verdun Maple Leafs	MCHL	5	1	0	1	....	....	....	10	2	0	0	0	0
	NHL Totals		7	0	0	0	0	0	0	0	....	....	....	....	....

• Father of Marc

Signed as a free agent by **NY Americans** (Niagara Falls-Can-Pro), January 15, 1926.

• BOIVIN, Leo — *see page 904*

• BOLL, Buzz Frank Thurman

LW – L. 5'10", 166 lbs. b: Filmore, Sask., 3/6/1911 d: 1/1/1990.

Season	Club	League	GP	G	A	Pts	AG	AA	APts	PIM	GP	G	A	Pts	PIM
1928-29	Weyburn Wanderers	S-SJHL	STATISTICS NOT AVAILABLE												
	Weyburn Wanderers	M-Cup	3	0	2	2	....	....	....	0	....	....	....	....	....
1929-30	Regina Pats	S-SJHL	2	1	0	1	....	....	....	0	8	3	3	6	*12
	Regina Pats	M-Cup	5	3	3	6	....	....	....	12	....	....	....	....	....
1930-31	Weyburn Beavers	S-SSHL	20	12	4	16	....	....	....	16	....	....	....	....	....
1931-32	Toronto Marlboros	OHA-Sr.	20	14	4	18	....	....	....	17	2	1	1	2	2
	Syracuse Stars	IHL	9	3	0	3	....	....	....	4	....	....	....	....	....
1932-33	Syracuse Stars	IHL	38	9	6	15	....	....	....	16	6	1	2	3	2
	Toronto Maple Leafs	NHL	....	....	....	....	....	....	....	....	1	0	0	0	0
1933-34	Toronto Maple Leafs	NHL	42	12	8	20	21	17	38	21	5	0	0	0	9
1934-35	Toronto Maple Leafs	NHL	47	14	4	18	23	7	30	4	6	0	0	0	0
1935-36	Toronto Maple Leafs	NHL	44	15	13	28	29	25	54	14	9	*7	3	*10	2
1936-37	Toronto Maple Leafs	NHL	25	6	3	9	10	5	15	12	2	0	0	0	0
1937-38	Toronto Maple Leafs	NHL	44	14	11	25	23	18	41	18	7	0	0	0	2
1938-39	Toronto Maple Leafs	NHL	11	0	0	0	0	0	0	0	....	....	....	....	....
	Syracuse Stars	IAHL	7	2	2	4	....	....	....	6	....	....	....	....	....
1939-40	New York Americans	NHL	47	5	10	15	8	16	24	18	1	0	0	0	0
1940-41	New York Americans	NHL	47	12	14	26	19	20	39	16	....	....	....	....	....
1941-42	Brooklyn Americans	NHL	48	11	15	26	15	18	33	23	....	....	....	....	....
1942-43	Boston Bruins	NHL	43	25	27	52	26	25	51	20	....	....	....	....	....
1943-44	Boston Bruins	NHL	39	19	25	44	17	22	39	2	....	....	....	....	....
	NHL Totals		437	133	130	263	191	173	364	148	31	7	3	10	13

Played in NHL All-Star Game (1934)

Traded to **NY Americans** by **Toronto** with Busher Jackson, Doc Romnes, Jim Fowler and Murray Armstrong for Sweeney Schriner, May 18, 1939. Rights transferred to **Boston** from **Brooklyn** in Special Dispersal Draw, October 9, 1942.

• BOLTON, Hugh Hugh Edward "Yug"

D – L. 6'3", 186 lbs. b: Toronto, Ont., 4/15/1929 d: 10/17/1999.

Season	Club	League	GP	G	A	Pts	AG	AA	APts	PIM	GP	G	A	Pts	PIM
1945-46	Toronto Young Rangers	OHA-Jr.	24	5	5	10	....	....	....	6	1	0	0	0	0
1946-47	Toronto Young Rangers	OHA-Jr.	15	7	2	9	....	....	....	16	....	....	....	....	....
1947-48	Toronto Marlboros	OHA-Jr.	32	3	13	16	....	....	....	42	....	....	....	....	....
	Toronto Marlboros	OHA-Sr.	2	0	1	1	....	....	....	0	....	....	....	....	....
1948-49	Toronto Marlboros	OHA-Jr.	18	5	2	7	....	....	....	24	10	3	2	5	4
	Toronto Marlboros	OHA-Sr.	....	....	....	....	....	....	....	....	1	0	1	1	4
	Toronto Marlboros	Al-Cup	13	1	0	1	....	....	....	29	....	....	....	....	....
1949-50	Toronto Maple Leafs	NHL	2	0	0	0	0	0	0	2	....	....	....	....	....
	Toronto Marlboros	OHA-Sr.	38	9	31	40	....	....	....	35	2	0	0	0	2
	Toronto Marlboros	Al-Cup	15	6	14	20	....	....	....	22	....	....	....	....	....
1950-51	Toronto Maple Leafs	NHL	13	1	3	4	1	4	5	4	....	....	....	....	....
	Pittsburgh Hornets	AHL	9	2	4	6	....	....	....	6	13	1	3	4	6
1951-52	Toronto Maple Leafs	NHL	60	3	13	16	4	16	20	73	3	0	0	0	4
1952-53	Toronto Maple Leafs	NHL	9	0	0	0	0	0	0	10	....	....	....	....	....
	Pittsburgh Hornets	AHL	35	1	9	10	....	....	....	58	6	2	0	2	7
1953-54	Toronto Maple Leafs	NHL	9	0	0	0	0	0	0	10	5	0	1	1	4
	Ottawa Senators	QHL	24	2	15	17	....	....	....	30	....	....	....	....	....
1954-55	Toronto Maple Leafs	NHL	69	2	19	21	3	22	25	55	4	0	3	3	6
1955-56	Toronto Maple Leafs	NHL	67	4	16	20	5	19	24	65	5	0	1	1	0
1956-57	Toronto Maple Leafs	NHL	6	0	0	0	0	0	0	2	....	....	....	....	....
1957-58	Rochester Americans	AHL	5	0	1	1	....	....	....	2	....	....	....	....	....
	NHL Totals		235	10	51	61	13	61	74	221	17	0	5	5	14

Played in NHL All-Star Game (1956) • Missed majority of 1953-54 season recovering from shoulder injury suffered in game vs. Detroit, December 25, 1953. • Suffered eventual career-ending leg injury in exhibition game vs. Montreal, September 24, 1956.

• BONIN, Marcel Marcel Jacques

W – L. 5'10", 170 lbs. b: Montreal, Que., 9/12/1932.

Season	Club	League	GP	G	A	Pts	AG	AA	APts	PIM	GP	G	A	Pts	PIM
1949-50	Joliette Cyclones	QPHL	STATISTICS NOT AVAILABLE												
1950-51	Trois-Rivieres Flambeaux	QJHL	44	30	43	73	....	....	....	73	8	1	6	7	7
	Shawinigan Cataracts	QMHL	2	0	1	1	....	....	....	0	....	....	....	....	....
1951-52	Quebec Aces	QMHL	60	15	36	51	....	....	....	131	15	4	9	13	32
	Quebec Aces	Alx-Cup	5	0	5	5	....	....	....	18	....	....	....	....	....
1952-53	Quebec Aces	QMHL	4	0	2	2	....	....	....	9	....	....	....	....	....
	Detroit Red Wings	NHL	37	4	9	13	5	11	16	14	5	0	1	1	0
	St. Louis Flyers	AHL	24	7	23	30	....	....	....	4	....	....	....	....	....
1953-54	Detroit Red Wings	NHL	1	0	0	0	0	0	0	0	....	....	....	....	....
	Sherbrooke Saints	QHL	17	10	11	21	....	....	....	38	....	....	....	....	....
	Edmonton Flyers	WHL	43	16	33	49	....	....	....	53	13	5	6	11	30
♦1954-55	Detroit Red Wings	NHL	69	16	20	36	21	23	44	53	11	0	2	2	4
1955-56	Boston Bruins	NHL	67	9	9	18	12	11	23	49	....	....	....	....	....
1956-57	Quebec Aces	QHL	68	20	*60	80	....	....	....	88	10	5	9	*14	14
	Quebec Aces	Ed-Cup	6	3	*9	*12	....	....	....	4	....	....	....	....	....
♦1957-58	Montreal Canadiens	NHL	66	15	24	39	18	25	43	37	9	0	1	1	2

			REGULAR SEASON								PLAYOFFS				
Season	Club	League	GP	G	A	Pts	AG	AA	APts	PIM	GP	G	A	Pts	PIM
♦**1958-59**	**Montreal Canadiens**	**NHL**	**57**	**13**	**30**	**43**	**15**	**30**	**45**	**38**	**11**	***10**	**5**	**15**	**4**
	Rochester Americans	AHL	7	3	5	8	....	....	....	4	....	....	....	....	....
♦**1959-60**	**Montreal Canadiens**	**NHL**	**59**	**17**	**34**	**51**	**20**	**33**	**53**	**59**	**8**	**1**	**4**	**5**	**12**
1960-61	**Montreal Canadiens**	**NHL**	**65**	**16**	**35**	**51**	**18**	**34**	**52**	**45**	**6**	**0**	**1**	**1**	**29**
1961-62	**Montreal Canadiens**	**NHL**	**33**	**7**	**14**	**21**	**8**	**13**	**21**	**41**	....	....	....	....	....
	NHL Totals		**454**	**97**	**175**	**272**	**117**	**180**	**297**	**336**	**50**	**11**	**14**	**25**	**51**

QJHL Second All-Star Team (1951) • QHL First All-Star Team (1957) • Played in NHL All-Star Game (1954, 1957, 1958, 1959, 1960)

Traded to **Detroit** by **Quebec** (QMHL) for cash, October 22, 1952. Traded to **Boston** by **Detroit** with Lorne Davis, Terry Sawchuk and Vic Stasiuk for Gilles Boisvert, Real Chevrefils, Norm Corcoran, Warren Godfrey and Ed Sandford, June 3, 1955. Claimed by **Montreal** from **Boston** (Springfield-AHL) in Inter-League Draft, June 4, 1957. • Suffered eventual career-ending back injury in game vs. Detroit, February 9, 1962.

• BOONE, Buddy   Carl George

RW – R. 5'7", 158 lbs.   b: Kirkland Lake, Ont., 9/11/1932.

Season	Club	League	GP	G	A	Pts	AG	AA	APts	PIM	GP	G	A	Pts	PIM
1949-50	St. Catharines Teepees	OHA-Jr.	45	13	17	30	....	....	....	75	5	4	1	5	10
1950-51	St. Catharines Teepees	OHA-Jr.	53	28	27	55	....	....	....	94	9	7	4	11	8
1951-52	St. Catharines Teepees	OHA-Jr.	45	43	23	66	....	....	....	38	14	*8	4	12	4
1952-53	St. Louis Flyers	AHL	64	13	26	39	....	....	....	20	....	....	....	....	....
1953-54	Edmonton Flyers	WHL	28	3	5	8	....	....	....	22	....	....	....	....	....
	Quebec Aces	QHL	35	6	14	20	....	....	....	57	16	8	8	16	18
	Quebec Aces	Ed-Cup	7	2	1	3	....	....	....	2	....	....	....	....	....
1954-55	Springfield Indians	AHL	63	30	31	61	....	....	....	38	4	2	0	2	0
1955-56	Springfield Indians	AHL	31	11	12	23	....	....	....	24	....	....	....	....	....
1956-57	Springfield Indians	AHL	57	24	22	46	....	....	....	45	....	....	....	....	....
	Boston Bruins	**NHL**	....	....	....	....	....	....	....	....	**10**	**1**	**0**	**1**	**12**
1957-58	**Boston Bruins**	**NHL**	**34**	**5**	**3**	**8**	**6**	**3**	**9**	**28**	**12**	**1**	**1**	**2**	**13**
	Springfield Indians	AHL	33	13	16	29	....	....	....	34	....	....	....	....	....
1958-59	Quebec Aces	QHL	20	5	6	11	....	....	....	14	....	....	....	....	....
	Providence Reds	AHL	28	7	10	17	....	....	....	16	....	....	....	....	....
1959-60	Kingston Frontenacs	EPHL	69	25	29	54	....	....	....	33	....	....	....	....	....
1960-61	Kingston Frontenacs	EPHL	51	24	23	47	....	....	....	26	....	....	....	....	....
	Winnipeg Warriors	WHL	13	7	7	14	....	....	....	10	....	....	....	....	....
1961-62	San Francisco Seals	WHL	62	30	27	57	....	....	....	22	2	0	0	0	0
1962-63	Vancouver Canucks	WHL	69	44	36	80	....	....	....	24	7	3	0	3	4
1963-64	Vancouver Canucks	WHL	66	38	25	63	....	....	....	18	....	....	....	....	....
1964-65	Vancouver Canucks	WHL	54	22	24	46	....	....	....	29	5	2	0	2	2
1965-66	Los Angeles Blades	WHL	58	17	19	36	....	....	....	6	....	....	....	....	....
1966-67	Los Angeles Blades	WHL	45	14	13	27	....	....	....	16	....	....	....	....	....
1967-68			OUT OF HOCKEY – RETIRED												
1968-69	Des Moines Oak Leafs	IHL	59	20	22	42	....	....	....	20	....	....	....	....	....
1969-70	Des Moines Oak Leafs	IHL	8	1	1	2	....	....	....	2	....	....	....	....	....
	NHL Totals		**34**	**5**	**3**	**8**	**6**	**3**	**9**	**28**	**22**	**2**	**1**	**3**	**25**

WHL First All-Star Team (1963) • WHL Second All-Star Team (1964)

Signed as a free agent by **Winnipeg** (WHL) following release by **Kingston** (EPHL), February 27, 1961. Claimed by **NY Rangers** from **Vancouver** (WHL) in Inter-League Draft, June 9, 1965. Traded to **LA Blades** (WHL) by **NY Rangers** for Gord Vejprava, November, 1965. Signed as a free agent by **Des Moines** (IHL), January 27, 1970. • Suffered career-ending knee injury in game vs. Columbus (IHL), February 25, 1970.

• BOOTHMAN, George   George Edward

C/D – R. 6'2", 175 lbs.   b: Calgary, Alta., 9/25/1916.

Season	Club	League	GP	G	A	Pts	AG	AA	APts	PIM	GP	G	A	Pts	PIM
1938-39	Calgary Stampeders	ASHL	4	0	0	0	....	....	....	0	....	....	....	....	....
1939-40	Turner Valley Oilers	ASHL	9	0	1	1	....	....	....	0	....	....	....	....	....
1940-41	Nelson Maple Leafs	WKHL	29	6	11	17	....	....	....	30	2	0	1	1	0
1941-42	Sydney Millionaires	CBSHL	41	15	15	30	....	....	....	48	....	....	....	....	....
1942-43	**Toronto Maple Leafs**	**NHL**	**9**	**1**	**1**	**2**	**1**	**1**	**2**	**4**	....	....	....	....	....
	Providence Reds	AHL	35	7	18	25	....	....	....	18	2	0	1	1	2
1943-44	**Toronto Maple Leafs**	**NHL**	**49**	**16**	**18**	**34**	**14**	**16**	**30**	**14**	**5**	**2**	**1**	**3**	**2**
1944-45	Buffalo Bisons	AHL	41	12	29	41	....	....	....	25	6	4	0	4	2
1945-46	New Haven Ramblers	AHL	14	5	8	13	....	....	....	11	....	....	....	....	....
	Providence Reds	AHL	23	5	4	9	....	....	....	6	....	....	....	....	....
	Buffalo Bisons	AHL	15	2	3	5	....	....	....	4	12	5	6	11	0
1946-47	Dallas Texans	USHL	4	1	2	3	....	....	....	2	....	....	....	....	....
1947-48	San Diego Skyhawks	PCHL	56	18	18	36	....	....	....	17	14	3	3	6	14
1948-49	Milwaukee Clarks	IHL	32	13	20	33	....	....	....	26	8	4	4	8	17
1949-50	Milwaukee Clarks	EAHL	6	0	3	3	....	....	....	2	....	....	....	....	....
	NHL Totals		**58**	**17**	**19**	**36**	**15**	**17**	**32**	**18**	**5**	**2**	**1**	**3**	**2**

IHL Southern Division Second All-Star Team (1949)

Loaned to **Providence** (AHL) by **Toronto** with Jack Forsey for Buck Jones and the loan of Ab DeMarco, February 3, 1943. Traded to **Buffalo** (AHL) by **Toronto** with Don Webster for the rights to Bill Ezinicki, October 13, 1944. Traded to **NY Rangers** (Providence-AHL) by **New Haven** (AHL) with cash for Guy Labrie, Paul Courteau and Roland Forget, November 19, 1945.

• BOSTROM, Helge

D – L. 5'8", 185 lbs.   b: Gimli, Man., 1/9/1894.

Season	Club	League	GP	G	A	Pts	AG	AA	APts	PIM	GP	G	A	Pts	PIM
1916-17	Winnipeg Monarchs	WSrHL	3	0	0	0	....	....	....	4	....	....	....	....	....
1917-18	Winnipeg Ypres	WSrHL	9	0	0	0	....	....	....	12	1	0	0	0	2
	Winnipeg Ypres	Al-Cup	4	0	0	0	....	....	....	24	....	....	....	....	....
1918-19			MILITARY SERVICE												
1919-20	Moose Jaw Maple Leafs	S-SSHL	11	2	3	5	....	....	....	26	2	*2	*1	*3	4
1920-21	Moose Jaw Maple Leafs	S-SSHL	15	5	2	7	....	....	....	26	4	1	0	1	0
1921-22	Edmonton Eskimos	WCHL	1	0	0	0	....	....	....	0	2	0	0	0	0
1922-23	Edmonton Eskimos	WCHL	22	2	1	3	....	....	....	20	2	0	0	0	0
	Edmonton Eskimos	St-Cup	1	0	0	0	....	....	....	0	....	....	....	....	....
1923-24	Vancouver Maroons	PCHA	26	3	0	3	....	....	....	24	2	0	1	1	2
	Vancouver Maroons	St-Cup	2	2	0	2	....	....	....	0	....	....	....	....	....
1924-25	Vancouver Maroons	WCHL	28	7	4	11	....	....	....	18	....	....	....	....	....
1925-26	Vancouver Maroons	WHL	29	0	1	1	....	....	....	28	....	....	....	....	....
1926-27	Minneapolis Millers	AHA	35	4	2	6	....	....	....	45	6	0	0	0	6
1927-28	Minneapolis Millers	AHA	36	10	3	13	....	....	....	39	8	0	0	0	22
1928-29	Minneapolis Millers	AHA	39	5	3	8	....	....	....	74	4	1	0	1	8
1929-30	Minneapolis Millers	AHA	12	2	1	3	....	....	....	14	....	....	....	....	....
	Chicago Black Hawks	**NHL**	**20**	**0**	**1**	**1**	**0**	**2**	**2**	**8**	**2**	**0**	**0**	**0**	**0**
1930-31	**Chicago Black Hawks**	**NHL**	**42**	**2**	**2**	**4**	**4**	**6**	**10**	**32**	**9**	**0**	**0**	**0**	**16**
1931-32	**Chicago Black Hawks**	**NHL**	**14**	**0**	**0**	**0**	**0**	**0**	**0**	**4**	**2**	**0**	**0**	**0**	**0**
1932-33	**Chicago Black Hawks**	**NHL**	**20**	**1**	**0**	**1**	**2**	**0**	**2**	**14**	....	....	....	....	....
	St. Paul–Tulsa	AHA	22	2	6	8	....	....	....	10	4	0	1	1	6
1933-34	Oklahoma City Warriors	AHA	48	5	8	13	....	....	....	48	....	....	....	....	....
1934-35	Philadelphia Arrows	Can-Am	15	0	5	5	....	....	....	10	....	....	....	....	....
	Syracuse Stars	IHL	23	2	2	4	....	....	....	10	....	....	....	....	....
1935-36	Kansas City Greyhounds	AHA	25	0	1	1	....	....	....	18	....	....	....	....	....
	NHL Totals		**96**	**3**	**3**	**6**	**6**	**8**	**14**	**58**	**13**	**0**	**0**	**0**	**16**
	Other Major League Totals		106	12	6	18	....	....	....	90	6	0	1	1	2

Signed as a free agent by **Edmonton** (WCHL), January 8, 1922. Traded to **Vancouver** (PCHA) by **Edmonton** (WCHL) for cash, October 2, 1923. Traded to **Minneapolis** (AHA) by **Vancouver** (WHL) for cash, October 13, 1926. Traded to **Chicago** by **Minneapolis** (AHA) for Bobby Burns, January 15, 1930. Traded to **St. Paul** (AHA) by **Chicago** for Art Wiebe, December 29, 1932.

• BOUCHARD, Butch   Emile Joseph   HHOF

D – R. 6'2", 205 lbs.   b: Montreal, Que., 9/11/1920.

Season	Club	League	GP	G	A	Pts	AG	AA	APts	PIM	GP	G	A	Pts	PIM
1937-38	Verdun Jr. Maple Leafs	MCJHL	2	0	0	0	....	....	....	2	2	0	0	0	2
	Verdun Jr. Maple Leafs	M-Cup	5	2	1	3	....	....	....	*8	....	....	....	....	....
1938-39	Verdun Jr. Maple Leafs	MCJHL	9	1	1	2	....	....	....	20	3	0	0	0	0
	Verdun Jr. Maple Leafs	M-Cup	7	0	2	2	....	....	....	12	....	....	....	....	....
1939-40	Verdun Jr. Maple Leafs	MCJHL	STATISTICS NOT AVAILABLE												
1940-41	Montreal Jr. Canadiens	QJHL	31	2	8	10	....	....	....	60	....	....	....	....	....
	Providence Reds	AHL	12	3	1	4	....	....	....	8	3	0	1	1	8
1941-42	**Montreal Canadiens**	**NHL**	**44**	**0**	**6**	**6**	**0**	**7**	**7**	**38**	**3**	**1**	**1**	**2**	**0**
1942-43	**Montreal Canadiens**	**NHL**	**45**	**2**	**16**	**18**	**2**	**15**	**17**	**47**	**5**	**0**	**1**	**1**	**4**
♦**1943-44**	**Montreal Canadiens**	**NHL**	**39**	**5**	**14**	**19**	**4**	**12**	**16**	**52**	**9**	**1**	**3**	**4**	**4**
1944-45	**Montreal Canadiens**	**NHL**	**50**	**11**	**23**	**34**	**11**	**27**	**38**	**34**	**6**	**3**	**4**	**7**	**4**
♦**1945-46**	**Montreal Canadiens**	**NHL**	**45**	**7**	**10**	**17**	**8**	**14**	**22**	**52**	**9**	**2**	**1**	**3**	**17**
1946-47	**Montreal Canadiens**	**NHL**	**60**	**5**	**7**	**12**	**6**	**8**	**14**	**60**	**11**	**0**	**3**	**3**	**21**
1947-48	**Montreal Canadiens**	**NHL**	**60**	**4**	**6**	**10**	**5**	**8**	**13**	**78**	....	....	....	....	....
1948-49	**Montreal Canadiens**	**NHL**	**27**	**3**	**3**	**6**	**4**	**4**	**8**	**42**	**7**	**0**	**0**	**0**	**6**
1949-50	**Montreal Canadiens**	**NHL**	**69**	**1**	**7**	**8**	**1**	**8**	**9**	**88**	**5**	**0**	**2**	**2**	**2**
1950-51	**Montreal Canadiens**	**NHL**	**52**	**3**	**10**	**13**	**4**	**12**	**16**	**80**	**11**	**1**	**1**	**2**	**2**
1951-52	**Montreal Canadiens**	**NHL**	**60**	**3**	**9**	**12**	**4**	**11**	**15**	**45**	**11**	**0**	**2**	**2**	**14**
♦**1952-53**	**Montreal Canadiens**	**NHL**	**58**	**2**	**8**	**10**	**3**	**10**	**13**	**55**	**12**	**1**	**1**	**2**	**6**
1953-54	**Montreal Canadiens**	**NHL**	**70**	**1**	**10**	**11**	**1**	**12**	**13**	**89**	**11**	**2**	**1**	**3**	**4**
1954-55	**Montreal Canadiens**	**NHL**	**70**	**2**	**15**	**17**	**3**	**17**	**20**	**81**	**12**	**0**	**1**	**1**	**37**
♦**1955-56**	**Montreal Canadiens**	**NHL**	**36**	**0**	**0**	**0**	**0**	**0**	**0**	**22**	**1**	**0**	**0**	**0**	**0**
	NHL Totals		**785**	**49**	**144**	**193**	**56**	**165**	**221**	**863**	**113**	**11**	**21**	**32**	**121**

• Father of Pierre • NHL Second All-Star Team (1944) • NHL First All-Star Team (1945, 1946, 1947) • Played in NHL All-Star Game (1947, 1948, 1950, 1951, 1952, 1953)

Signed as a free agent by **Montreal**, February 21, 1941.

• BOUCHARD, Dick   Richard

RW – R. 5'8", 155 lbs.   b: Lettelier, Man., 12/2/1934.

Season	Club	League	GP	G	A	Pts	AG	AA	APts	PIM	GP	G	A	Pts	PIM
1953-54	Quebec Frontenacs	QJHL	63	21	29	50	....	....	....	43	8	9	8	17	4
	Quebec Frontenacs	M-Cup	8	6	7	13	....	....	....	8	....	....	....	....	....
1954-55	Quebec Frontenacs	QJHL	45	25	33	58	....	....	....	52	9	*8	3	11	14
	New York Rangers	**NHL**	**1**	**0**	**0**	**0**	**0**	**0**	**0**	**0**	....	....	....	....	....
	Quebec Frontenacs	M-Cup	9	3	8	11	....	....	....	4	....	....	....	....	....
1955-56	Winnipeg Warriors	WHL	2	0	0	0	....	....	....	0	....	....	....	....	....
	Shawinigan Cataracts	QHL	54	10	22	32	....	....	....	28	11	2	6	8	8
1956-57	Shawinigan Cataracts	QHL	65	15	30	45	....	....	....	27	....	....	....	....	....
1957-58	Shawinigan Cataracts	QHL	63	23	38	61	....	....	....	60	14	4	6	10	6
1958-59	Rochester Americans	AHL	43	2	11	13	....	....	....	19	....	....	....	....	....
1959-60			REINSTATED AS AN AMATEUR												
1960-61	St. Paul Saints	IHL	35	9	14	23	....	....	....	24	10	6	4	10	16
1961-62	St. Paul Saints	IHL	57	27	31	58	....	....	....	48	11	6	2	8	8
1962-63	St. Paul Saints	IHL	65	31	34	65	....	....	....	29	....	....	....	....	....
1963-64	St. Paul Rangers	CPHL	29	6	11	17	....	....	....	16	....	....	....	....	....
	NHL Totals		**1**	**0**	**0**	**0**	**0**	**0**	**0**	**0**	....	....	....	....	....

• BOUCHARD, Edmond

LW/D – L. 5'10", 185 lbs.   b: St. Etienne, Que., 5/24/1892   d: 7/18/1955.

Season	Club	League	GP	G	A	Pts	AG	AA	APts	PIM	GP	G	A	Pts	PIM
1914-15	Trois-Rivieres Leafs	QCHL	STATISTICS NOT AVAILABLE												
1915-16	Montreal Nationales	MCHL	10	3	0	3	....	....	....	14	....	....	....	....	....
1916-17	Quebec Montagnais	QCHL	9	16	5	21	....	....	....	....	....	....	....	....	....
1917-18	Quebec Montagnais	QCHL	11	*27	6	*33	....	....	....	....	....	....	....	....	....
1918-19	Quebec Montagnais	QCHL	6	*21	0	*21	....	....	....	....	4	*8	0	*8	3
1919-20	Quebec Crescents	QCHL	1	1	0	1	....	....	....	0	....	....	....	....	....
	Montreal Hochelaga	MCHL	10	12	*8	20	....	....	....	18	5	*10	*3	*13	9
1920-21	Quebec Voltigers	QCHL	5	6	0	6	....	....	....	....	4	*4	0	*4	....
1921-22	**Montreal Canadiens**	**NHL**	**18**	**1**	**5**	**6**	**1**	**16**	**17**	**4**	....	....	....	....	....
1922-23	**Montreal Canadiens**	**NHL**	**2**	**0**	**0**	**0**	**0**	**0**	**0**	**4**	....	....	....	....	....
	Hamilton Tigers	**NHL**	**22**	**5**	***12**	**17**	**8**	**47**	**55**	**40**	....	....	....	....	....
1923-24	**Hamilton Tigers**	**NHL**	**20**	**5**	**0**	**5**	**10**	**0**	**10**	**2**	....	....	....	....	....
1924-25	**Hamilton Tigers**	**NHL**	**24**	**2**	**2**	**4**	**3**	**8**	**11**	**14**	....	....	....	....	....
1925-26	**New York Americans**	**NHL**	**30**	**3**	**1**	**4**	**5**	**6**	**11**	**10**	....	....	....	....	....
1926-27	**New York Americans**	**NHL**	**38**	**2**	**1**	**3**	**4**	**5**	**9**	**12**	....	....	....	....	....
	Niagara Falls Cataracts	Can-Pro	4	2	1	3	....	....	....	19	....	....	....	....	....
1927-28	**New York Americans**	**NHL**	**39**	**1**	**0**	**1**	**2**	**0**	**2**	**27**	....	....	....	....	....
1928-29	**New York Americans**	**NHL**	**6**	**0**	**0**	**0**	**0**	**0**	**0**	**2**	....	....	....	....	....
	New Haven Eagles	Can-Am	25	5	4	9	....	....	....	45	....	....	....	....	....
	Pittsburgh Pirates	**NHL**	**12**	**0**	**0**	**0**	**0**	**0**	**0**	**2**	....	....	....	....	....
1929-30	New Haven Eagles	Can-Am	38	18	3	21	....	....	....	58	....	....	....	....	....
1930-31	Pittsburgh Yellowjackets	IHL	8	0	0	0	....	....	....	6	....	....	....	....	....
	Buffalo Majors	AHA	40	23	12	35	....	....	....	44	....	....	....	....	....
1931-32	Buffalo Majors	AHA	24	3	2	5	....	....	....	30	....	....	....	....	....
	St. Louis Flyers	AHA	3	1	0	1	....	....	....	2	....	....	....	....	....
	Duluth Hornets	AHA	18	2	1	3	....	....	....	20	8	1	1	2	10
	NHL Totals		**211**	**19**	**21**	**40**	**33**	**82**	**115**	**117**	....	....	....	....	....

Signed as a free agent by **Montreal Canadiens**, January 2, 1922. Traded to **Hamilton** by **Montreal Canadiens** for Joe Malone, December 22, 1922. Transferred to **NY Americans** after NHL club purchased **Hamilton** franchise, September 26, 1925. Loaned to **Pittsburgh** by **NY Americans** for remainder of 1928-29 season with trade of Jesse Spring for loan of Tex White for remainder of 1928-29 season, February 15, 1929. Signed as a free agent by **Pittsburgh** (IHL), November 28, 1930. Traded to **Buffalo** (AHA) by **Pittsburgh** (IHL) for cash, January 3, 1931.

• BOUCHER, Billy
William Martin
RW – R. 5'7", 155 lbs. b: Ottawa, Ont., 11/10/1899 d: 11/4/1958.

Season	Club	League	GP	G	A	Pts	AG	AA	APts	PIM	GP	G	A	Pts	PIM
			REGULAR SEASON								PLAYOFFS				
1915-16	Ottawa Creighton	H.S.	STATISTICS NOT AVAILABLE												
1916-17	Ottawa Munitions	OCJHL	10	1	0	1	....	....	....	6	....	....	....	....	....
1917-18	Ottawa Munitions	OCHL	6	*5	0	*5	....	....	....	24	1	1	0	1	0
1918-19	Ottawa Munitions	OCHL	8	6	*3	9	....	....	....	18	....	....	....	....	....
1919-20	Ottawa Munitions	OCHL	8	4	0	4	....	....	....	....	5	*11	4	*15	....
1920-21	Iroquois Papermakers	NOHA	5	5	0	5	....	....	....	....	....	....	....	....	....
1921-22	Montreal Canadiens	NHL	24	17	5	22	24	16	40	18	....	....	....	....	....
1922-23	Montreal Canadiens	NHL	24	24	7	31	42	27	69	55	2	1	0	1	2
1923-24	Montreal Canadiens	NHL	23	16	6	22	34	36	70	48	2	1	0	1	9
♦	Montreal Canadiens	St-Cup	4	5	1	6	....	....	....	6	....	....	....	....	....
1924-25	Montreal Canadiens	NHL	30	17	13	30	30	55	85	92	2	1	0	1	4
	Montreal Canadiens	St-Cup	4	1	1	2	....	....	....	13	....	....	....	....	....
1925-26	Montreal Canadiens	NHL	34	8	5	13	14	32	46	112	....	....	....	....	....
1926-27	Montreal Canadiens	NHL	21	4	0	4	7	0	7	14	....	....	....	....	....
	Boston Bruins	NHL	14	2	0	2	4	0	4	12	8	0	0	0	2
1927-28	New York Americans	NHL	43	5	2	7	10	11	21	58	....	....	....	....	....
1928-29	New Haven Eagles	Can-Am	38	11	1	12	....	....	....	117	2	0	0	0	4
1929-30	New Haven Eagles	Can-Am	32	8	7	15	....	....	....	54	....	....	....	....	....
1930-31	New Haven Eagles	Can-Am	38	20	8	28	....	....	....	98	....	....	....	....	....
1931-32	Bronx Tigers	Can-Am	39	3	4	7	....	....	....	25	1	0	0	0	0
1932-33	Quebec Granites	ECHA	DID NOT PLAY – COACHING												
	NHL Totals		213	93	38	131	165	177	342	409	14	3	0	3	17

• Brother of Georges, Frank and Bobby

Signed as a free agent by **Montreal Canadiens**, December 13, 1921. • 1923-24 Stanley Cup totals includes series with Calgary (WCHL) and Vancouver (PCHA). Traded to **Boston** by **Montreal Canadiens** for Carson Cooper with both teams holding right of recall, January 17, 1927. • Players returned to original teams, May 22, 1927. Traded to **NY Americans** by **Montreal Canadiens** for cash, October 17, 1927.

• BOUCHER, Bobby
Robert James "Shorty"
C – R. 5'8", 142 lbs. b: Ottawa, Ont., 2/14/1904 d: 6/10/1931.

Season	Club	League	GP	G	A	Pts	AG	AA	APts	PIM	GP	G	A	Pts	PIM
1916-17	Ottawa New Edinburghs	OCHL	9	1	0	1	....	....	....	....	2	0	0	0	....
1917-18	Ottawa Mutchmore	OMHA	STATISTICS NOT AVAILABLE												
	Ottawa New Edinburghs	OCJHL	1	0	0	0	....	....	....	0	....	....	....	....	....
1918-19	Ottawa Creighton	OMHA	STATISTICS NOT AVAILABLE												
1919-20	Ottawa New Edinburghs	OCHL	4	0	0	0	....	....	....	0	....	....	....	....	....
1920-21	Ottawa New Edinburghs	OCHL	1	1	0	1	....	....	....	....	....	....	....	....	....
	Iroquois Falls Eskimos	NOHA	STATISTICS NOT AVAILABLE												
1921-22	Ottawa New Edinburghs	OCHL	1	0	0	0	....	....	....	0	....	....	....	....	....
1922-23	Iroquois Falls Eskimos	NOHA	STATISTICS NOT AVAILABLE												
1923-24	Ottawa Gunners	OCHL	7	4	1	5	....	....	....	....	....	....	....	....	....
	Montreal Canadiens	NHL	11	1	0	1	2	0	2	0	2	0	0	0	0
♦	Montreal Canadiens	St-Cup	3	0	0	0	....	....	....	0	....	....	....	....	....
1924-25	Vancouver Maroons	WCHL	19	1	0	1	....	....	....	3	....	....	....	....	....
1925-26	Edmonton Eskimos	WHL	29	2	1	3	....	....	....	16	....	....	....	....	....
1926-27	London Panthers	Can-Pro	32	8	2	10	....	....	....	39	4	0	0	0	2
1927-28	Toronto Falcons	Can-Pro	1	0	0	0	....	....	....	2	....	....	....	....	....
	Quebec Castors	Can-Am	23	3	0	3	....	....	....	18	6	1	0	1	10
1928-29	Newark Bulldogs	Can-Am	5	0	0	0	....	....	....	2	....	....	....	....	....
	NHL Totals		11	1	0	1	2	0	2	0	2	0	0	0	0
	Other Major League Totals		48	3	1	4	....	....	....	19	....	....	....	....	....

• Brother of Georges, Billy and Frank

Signed as a free agent by **Montreal Canadiens**, January 25, 1924. • 1923-24 Stanley Cup totals includes series with Calgary (WCHL) and Vancouver (PCHA). Traded to **Vancouver** (PCHA) by **Montreal Canadiens** for Charlie Cotch, March 26, 1924. Traded to **Edmonton** (WHL) by **Vancouver** (WHL) for cash, November 16, 1925. Signed as a free agent by **London** (Can-Pro), November 2, 1926.

• BOUCHER, Clarence
Clarence a.k.a. Bowcher
D – L. 6'1", 195 lbs. b: North Bay, Ont., 11/1/1896 Deceased.

Season	Club	League	GP	G	A	Pts	AG	AA	APts	PIM	GP	G	A	Pts	PIM
1919-20	Sudbury Cub Wolves	NOJHA	STATISTICS NOT AVAILABLE												
	Sudbury Wolves	NOHA	6	3	1	4	....	....	....	6	7	1	2	3	*20
1920-21	Cleveland Indians	USAHA	STATISTICS NOT AVAILABLE												
	Sudbury Wolves	NOHA	9	7	3	10	....	....	....	40	....	....	....	....	....
1921-22	Sudbury Wolves	NOHA	9	9	5	14	....	....	....	*39	....	....	....	....	....
1922-23	Iroquois Papermakers	NOHA	STATISTICS NOT AVAILABLE												
1923-24	Iroquois Papermakers	NOHA	8	0	0	0	....	....	....	*22	....	....	....	....	....
1924-25	Sudbury Wolves	NOHA	STATISTICS NOT AVAILABLE												
1925-26	Galt Terriers	OHA-Sr.	16	4	3	7	....	....	....	*37	2	0	1	1	2
1926-27	New York Americans	NHL	11	0	1	1	0	5	5	4	....	....	....	....	....
	Niagara Falls Cataracts	Can-Pro	12	4	0	4	....	....	....	27	....	....	....	....	....
1927-28	New York Americans	NHL	36	2	1	3	4	6	10	129	....	....	....	....	....
	Niagara Falls Cataracts	Can-Pro	10	1	1	2	....	....	....	17	....	....	....	....	....
1928-29	New Haven Eagles	Can-Am	40	3	2	5	....	....	....	79	2	0	0	0	4
	NHL Totals		47	2	2	4	4	11	15	133	....	....	....	....	....

Signed as a free agent by **NY Americans**, July 14, 1926.

• BOUCHER, Frank
"Raffles" HHOF
C – L. 5'9", 185 lbs. b: Ottawa, Ont., 10/7/1901 d: 12/12/1977.

Season	Club	League	GP	G	A	Pts	AG	AA	APts	PIM	GP	G	A	Pts	PIM
1916-17	Ottawa New Edinburghs	OCJHL	9	11	0	11	....	....	....	....	2	*6	0	*6	....
1917-18	Ottawa New Edinburghs	OCJHL	4	1	0	1	....	....	....	0	....	....	....	....	....
	Ottawa Munitions	OCHL	1	0	0	0	....	....	....	0	1	0	0	0	0
1918-19	Ottawa New Edinburghs	OCHL	7	1	2	3	....	....	....	5	....	....	....	....	....
1919-20			MILITARY SERVICE												
1920-21	Lethbridge Vets	ASHL	STATISTICS NOT AVAILABLE												
1921-22	Ottawa Senators	NHL	24	8	2	10	11	6	17	4	1	0	0	0	0
1922-23	Vancouver Maroons	PCHA	29	11	9	20	....	....	....	2	2	0	1	1	2
	Vancouver Maroons	St-Cup	4	2	0	2	....	....	....	0	....	....	....	....	....
1923-24	Vancouver Maroons	PCHA	28	15	5	20	....	....	....	10	2	1	0	1	0
	Vancouver Maroons	St-Cup	2	2	1	3	....	....	....	2	....	....	....	....	....
1924-25	Vancouver Maroons	WCHL	27	16	12	28	....	....	....	6	....	....	....	....	....
1925-26	Vancouver Maroons	WHL	29	15	7	22	....	....	....	14	....	....	....	....	....
1926-27	New York Rangers	NHL	44	13	15	28	23	80	103	17	2	0	0	0	4
♦1927-28	New York Rangers	NHL	44	23	12	35	47	69	116	15	9	*7	3	*10	2
1928-29	New York Rangers	NHL	44	10	*16	26	29	110	139	8	6	1	0	1	0
1929-30	New York Rangers	NHL	42	26	*36	62	37	87	124	16	3	1	1	2	0
1930-31	New York Rangers	NHL	44	12	27	39	24	83	107	20	4	0	2	2	0
1931-32	New York Rangers	NHL	48	12	23	35	20	51	71	18	7	3	*6	*9	0
♦1932-33	New York Rangers	NHL	46	7	*28	35	13	59	72	4	8	2	2	4	6
1933-34	New York Rangers	NHL	48	14	30	44	24	64	88	4	2	0	0	0	0
1934-35	New York Rangers	NHL	48	13	32	45	21	56	77	2	4	0	3	3	0
1935-36	New York Rangers	NHL	48	11	18	29	21	34	55	2	....	....	....	....	....
1936-37	New York Rangers	NHL	44	7	13	20	12	24	36	5	9	2	3	5	0
1937-38	New York Rangers	NHL	18	0	1	1	0	2	2	2	....	....	....	....	....
1938-39	New York Rovers	EAHL	DID NOT PLAY – COACHING												
1939-40	New York Rangers	NHL	DID NOT PLAY – COACHING												
1940/43	New York Rangers	NHL	DID NOT PLAY – COACHING												
1943-44	New York Rangers	NHL	15	4	10	14	4	9	13	2	....	....	....	....	....
1944/49	New York Rangers	NHL	DID NOT PLAY – COACHING												
1949/55	New York Rangers	NHL	DID NOT PLAY – GENERAL MANAGER												
	NHL Totals		557	160	263	423	286	734	1020	119	55	16	20	36	12
	Other Major League Totals		113	57	33	90	....	....	....	32	4	1	1	2	2

• Brother of Georges, Billy and Bobby • PCHA First All-Star Team (1923) • PCHA All-Star Team (1924) • WCHL All-Star Team (1925) • Won Lady Byng Trophy (1928, 1929, 1930, 1931, 1933, 1934, 1935) • NHL Second All-Star Team (1931) • NHL First All-Star Team (1933, 1934, 1935) • Won Lester Patrick Trophy (1993) • Played in NHL All-Star Game (1937)

Signed as a free agent by **Ottawa**, December 6, 1921. Traded to **Vancouver** (PCHA) by **Ottawa** for cash, September 19, 1922. Traded to **NY Rangers** by **Vancouver** (WHL) for $15,000, September 28, 1926.

• BOUCHER, Georges
"Buck" HHOF
D – L. 5'9", 169 lbs. b: Ottawa, Ont., 8/19/1896 d: 10/17/1960.

Season	Club	League	GP	G	A	Pts	AG	AA	APts	PIM	GP	G	A	Pts	PIM
1913-14	Ottawa New Edinburghs	X-Games	5	1	0	1	....	....	....	....	....	....	....	....	....
1914-15	Ottawa New Edinburghs	OCHL	15	12	0	12	....	....	....	....	1	0	0	0	....
	Ottawa Royal Canadiens	OCHL	4	6	0	6	....	....	....	....	2	2	0	2	....
1915-16	Ottawa Royal Canadiens	OCHL	STATISTICS NOT AVAILABLE												
	Montreal La Casquette		1	1	0	1	....	....	....	0	....	....	....	....	....
	Ottawa Senators	NHA	19	9	1	10	....	....	....	62	....	....	....	....	....
1916-17	Ottawa Senators	NHA	18	10	5	15	....	....	....	27	2	1	0	1	8
1917-18	Ottawa Senators	NHL	21	9	8	17	11	34	45	46	....	....	....	....	....
1918-19	Ottawa Senators	NHL	17	3	2	5	5	11	16	29	5	2	0	2	9
1919-20	Ottawa Senators	NHL	22	9	8	17	10	27	37	55	....	....	....	....	....
♦	Ottawa Senators	St-Cup	5	2	0	2	....	....	....	2	....	....	....	....	....
1920-21	Ottawa Senators	NHL	23	11	8	19	14	31	45	53	2	3	0	3	10
♦	Ottawa Senators	St-Cup	5	2	0	2	....	....	....	9	....	....	....	....	....
1921-22	Ottawa Senators	NHL	23	13	12	25	18	39	57	12	2	0	0	0	4
1922-23	Ottawa Senators	NHL	24	14	9	23	24	35	59	58	2	0	1	1	2
♦	Ottawa Senators	St-Cup	6	2	1	3	....	....	....	6	....	....	....	....	....
1923-24	Ottawa Senators	NHL	21	13	10	23	27	61	88	38	2	0	1	1	4
1924-25	Ottawa Senators	NHL	28	15	5	20	26	21	47	*95	....	....	....	....	....
1925-26	Ottawa Senators	NHL	36	8	4	12	14	26	40	64	2	0	0	0	10
♦1926-27	Ottawa Senators	NHL	40	8	3	11	14	16	30	115	6	0	0	0	43
1927-28	Ottawa Senators	NHL	43	7	5	12	14	28	42	78	2	0	0	0	4
1928-29	Ottawa Senators	NHL	29	3	1	4	9	7	16	60	....	....	....	....	....
	Montreal Maroons	NHL	12	1	1	2	3	7	10	10	....	....	....	....	....
1929-30	Montreal Maroons	NHL	37	2	6	8	3	14	17	50	3	0	0	0	2
1930-31	Montreal Maroons	NHL	30	0	0	0	0	0	0	25	....	....	....	....	....
1931-32	Chicago Black Hawks	NHL	43	1	5	6	2	11	13	50	2	0	1	1	0
1932-33	Boston Cubs	Can-Am	9	0	0	0	....	....	....	8	....	....	....	....	....
1933-34	Ottawa Senators	NHL	DID NOT PLAY – COACHING												
	NHL Totals		449	117	87	204	194	368	562	838	28	5	3	8	88
	Other Major League Totals		37	19	6	25	....	....	....	89	2	1	0	1	8

• Brother of Billy, Frank and Bobby

Rights retained by **Ottawa** after NHA folded, November 26, 1917. • 1922-23 Stanley Cup totals includes series with Regina (WCHL) and Edmonton (PCHA). Traded to **Montreal Maroons** by **Ottawa** for Joe Lamb, February 14, 1929. Claimed on waivers by **Chicago** from **Montreal Maroons**, November 27, 1931.

• BOUDRIAS, Andre
— *see page 913*

• BOURCIER, Conrad
C – L. 5'6", 155 lbs. b: Montreal, Que., 5/28/1916 Deceased.

Season	Club	League	GP	G	A	Pts	AG	AA	APts	PIM	GP	G	A	Pts	PIM
1934-35	Verdun Maple Leafs	MCJHL	10	5	12	17	....	....	....	0	6	*6	4	*10	4
1935-36	Montreal Canadiens	NHL	6	0	0	0	0	0	0	0	....	....	....	....	....
	Pittsburgh Yellowjackets	IHL	9	2	2	4	....	....	....	2	....	....	....	....	....
	Verdun Maple Leafs	MCHL	10	5	1	6	....	....	....	4	....	....	....	....	....
1936-37	Verdun Maple Leafs	MCHL	STATISTICS NOT AVAILABLE												
1937-38	Verdun Maple Leafs	MCHL	21	4	6	10	....	....	....	8	8	4	*6	10	12
1938-39	Verdun Maple Leafs	MCHL	22	10	9	19	....	....	....	16	2	0	0	0	0
1939-40	Verdun Bulldogs	QPHL	41	21	32	53	....	....	....	30	2	1	0	1	2
1940-41	Verdun Maple Leafs	QSHL	32	12	12	24	....	....	....	17	....	....	....	....	....
1941-42	Montreal Cyclones	QPHL	7	8	4	12	....	....	....	12	....	....	....	....	....
1942-43			MILITARY SERVICE												
1943-44			MILITARY SERVICE												
1944-45	Montreal Cyclones	QPHL	....	14	11	25	....	....	....	....	....	....	....	....	....
	Cornwall Cookies	QPHL	1	0	0	0	....	....	....	0	....	....	....	....	....
1945-46	St-Hyacinthe Saints	QPHL	8	4	6	10	....	....	....	6	4	2	0	2	0
1946-47	Verdun Eagles	QPHL	47	40	28	68	....	....	....	24	....	....	....	....	....
1947-48			OUT OF HOCKEY – RETIRED												
1948-49	Montreal Hydro	MCHL	12	10	*13	*23	....	....	....	....	....	....	....	....	....
	NHL Totals		6	0	0	0	0	0	0	0	....	....	....	....	....

Brother of Jean

Signed as a free agent by **Montreal Canadiens**, December 18, 1935.

• BOURCIER, Jean
LW – L. 5'11", 175 lbs. b: Montreal, Que., 1/3/1911.

Season	Club	League	GP	G	A	Pts	AG	AA	APts	PIM	GP	G	A	Pts	PIM
1933-34	Verdun Maple Leafs	MCHL	16	15	6	21	....	....	....	2	2	0	1	1	0
1934-35	Verdun Maple Leafs	MCHL	20	*22	18	*40	....	....	....	4	....	....	....	....	....
1935-36	Montreal Canadiens	NHL	9	0	1	1	0	2	2	0	....	....	....	....	....
	Pittsburgh Yellowjackets	IHL	18	8	5	13	....	....	....	4	....	....	....	....	....
	Verdun Maple Leafs	MCHL	10	11	8	19	....	....	....	2	....	....	....	....	....
1936-37	Verdun Maple Leafs	MCHL	STATISTICS NOT AVAILABLE												
1937-38	Verdun Maple Leafs	MCHL	22	16	13	29	....	....	....	0	8	0	3	3	14

			REGULAR SEASON								PLAYOFFS				
Season	Club	League	GP	G	A	Pts	AG	AA	APts	PIM	GP	G	A	Pts	PIM
1938-39	Verdun Maple Leafs	MCHL	21	10	3	13	....	....	....	10	2	1	0	1	0
1939-40	Verdun Bulldogs	QPHL	39	22	20	42	....	....	....	8	2	2	2	4	0
1940-41	Verdun Maple Leafs	QSHL	13	5	4	9	....	....	....	0	....	....	....	....	....
	NHL Totals		9	0	1	1	0	2	2	0	....	....	....	....	....

• Brother of Conrad

Signed as a free agent by **Montreal Canadiens**, October 11, 1935.

• BOURGEAULT, Leo

D – L. 5'6", 165 lbs. b: Sturgeon Falls, Ont., 1/17/1903 Deceased.

Season	Club	League	GP	G	A	Pts	AG	AA	APts	PIM	GP	G	A	Pts	PIM
1921-22	North Bay Trappers	NOHA	4	4	1	5	....	....	....	....	8	6	3	9	....
1922-23	North Bay Trappers	NOHA	STATISTICS NOT AVAILABLE												
1923-24	Guelph Royals	OHA-Sr.	STATISTICS NOT AVAILABLE												
1924-25	Saskatoon Crescents	WCHL	19	3	0	3	....	....	....	8	....	....	....	....	....
1925-26	Saskatoon Crescents	WHL	30	5	2	7	....	....	....	18	2	0	0	0	8
1926-27	**Toronto St. Pats**	**NHL**	**22**	**0**	**0**	**0**	**0**	**0**	**0**	**44**	....	....	....	....	....
	New York Rangers	**NHL**	**20**	**2**	**1**	**3**	**4**	**5**	**9**	**28**	**2**	**0**	**0**	**0**	**4**
♦**1927-28**	**New York Rangers**	**NHL**	**37**	**7**	**0**	**7**	**14**	**0**	**14**	**7**	**9**	**0**	**0**	**0**	**8**
1928-29	**New York Rangers**	**NHL**	**44**	**2**	**3**	**5**	**6**	**20**	**26**	**59**	**6**	**0**	**0**	**0**	**0**
1929-30	**New York Rangers**	**NHL**	**44**	**7**	**6**	**13**	**10**	**14**	**24**	**54**	**3**	**1**	**1**	**2**	**6**
1930-31	**New York Rangers**	**NHL**	**10**	**0**	**1**	**1**	**0**	**3**	**3**	**12**	....	....	....	....	....
	Ottawa Senators	**NHL**	**28**	**0**	**4**	**4**	**0**	**12**	**12**	**28**	....	....	....	....	....
1931-32	Bronx Tigers	Can-Am	40	10	9	19	....	....	....	89	2	0	0	0	4
1932-33	**Ottawa Senators**	**NHL**	**35**	**1**	**1**	**2**	**2**	**2**	**4**	**18**	....	....	....	....	....
	Montreal Canadiens	**NHL**	**15**	**1**	**1**	**2**	**2**	**2**	**4**	**9**	**2**	**0**	**0**	**0**	**0**
1933-34	**Montreal Canadiens**	**NHL**	**48**	**4**	**3**	**7**	**7**	**6**	**13**	**10**	**2**	**0**	**0**	**0**	**0**
1934-35	**Montreal Canadiens**	**NHL**	**4**	**0**	**0**	**0**	**0**	**0**	**0**	**0**	....	....	....	....	....
	Quebec Castors	Can-Am	43	13	14	27	....	....	....	34	3	1	0	1	2
1935-36	Springfield Indians	Can-Am	2	1	0	1	....	....	....	0	2	0	2	2	0
	NHL Totals		**307**	**24**	**20**	**44**	**45**	**64**	**109**	**269**	**24**	**1**	**1**	**2**	**18**
	Other Major League Totals		49	8	2	10	....	....	....	26	2	0	0	0	8

Signed as a free agent by **Saskatoon** (WCHL), November 27, 1924. Traded to **Toronto St. Pats** by **Saskatoon** (PrHL) with Corb Denneny and Laurie Scott for cash, September 27, 1926. Traded to **NY Rangers** by **Toronto St. Pats** for cash, January, 1927. Traded to **Ottawa** by **NY Rangers** for cash, December 7, 1930. Traded to **Montreal Canadiens** by **Ottawa** with Harold Starr for Marty Burke and future considerations (Nick Wasnie, March 23, 1933), February 14, 1933.

• BOWMAN, Ralph "Scotty"

D – L. 5'11", 190 lbs. b: Winnipeg, Man., 6/20/1911 d: 10/17/1990.

Season	Club	League	GP	G	A	Pts	AG	AA	APts	PIM	GP	G	A	Pts	PIM
1929-30	Parkdale Canoe Club	OHA-Jr.	8	1	1	2	....	....	....	20	3	0	0	0	2
1930-31	Niagara Falls Cataracts	OHA-Jr.	7	10	1	11	....	....	....	2	2	1	0	1	0
1931-32	Niagara Falls Cataracts	OHA-Jr.	18	1	1	2	....	....	....	28	2	0	0	0	8
1932-33	Niagara Falls Cataracts	OHA-Jr.	19	3	0	3	....	....	....	49	5	1	0	1	2
	Niagara Falls Cataracts	M-Cup	6	0	1	1	....	....	....	4	....	....	....	....	....
1933-34	**Ottawa Senators**	**NHL**	**46**	**0**	**2**	**2**	**0**	**4**	**4**	**64**	....	....	....	....	....
1934-35	**St. Louis Eagles**	**NHL**	**31**	**2**	**2**	**4**	**3**	**3**	**6**	**51**	....	....	....	....	....
	Detroit Red Wings	**NHL**	**13**	**1**	**3**	**4**	**2**	**5**	**7**	**21**	....	....	....	....	....
♦**1935-36**	**Detroit Red Wings**	**NHL**	**48**	**3**	**2**	**5**	**6**	**4**	**10**	**44**	**7**	**2**	**1**	**3**	**2**
♦**1936-37**	**Detroit Red Wings**	**NHL**	**37**	**0**	**1**	**1**	**0**	**2**	**2**	**24**	**10**	**0**	**1**	**1**	**4**
1937-38	**Detroit Red Wings**	**NHL**	**45**	**0**	**2**	**2**	**0**	**3**	**3**	**26**	....	....	....	....	....
1938-39	**Detroit Red Wings**	**NHL**	**43**	**2**	**3**	**5**	**3**	**5**	**8**	**26**	**5**	**0**	**0**	**0**	**0**
1939-40	**Detroit Red Wings**	**NHL**	**11**	**0**	**2**	**2**	**0**	**3**	**3**	**4**	....	....	....	....	....
	Indianapolis Capitols	IAHL	12	1	2	3	....	....	....	8	5	0	0	0	0
1940-41	Pittsburgh Hornets	AHL	48	1	4	5	....	....	....	14	5	0	0	0	0
1941-42	Philadelphia Rockets	AHL	55	3	6	9	....	....	....	92	....	....	....	....	....
	Providence Reds	AHL	2	0	0	0	....	....	....	0	....	....	....	....	....
1942-43	Hershey Bears	AHL	11	0	3	3	....	....	....	2	....	....	....	....	....
	Washington Lions	AHL	36	1	11	12	....	....	....	12	....	....	....	....	....
	NHL Totals		**274**	**8**	**17**	**25**	**14**	**29**	**43**	**260**	**22**	**2**	**2**	**4**	**6**

Transferred to **St. Louis** after **Ottawa** franchise relocated, September 22, 1934. Traded to **Detroit** by **St. Louis** with Syd Howe for Ted Graham and $50,000, February 11, 1935. Traded to **Philadelphia** (AHL) by **Pittsburgh** (AHL) for cash, October 22, 1941.

• BOWNASS, Jack John

D – L. 6'1", 190 lbs. b: Winnipeg, Man., 7/27/1930.

Season	Club	League	GP	G	A	Pts	AG	AA	APts	PIM	GP	G	A	Pts	PIM
1946-47	Winnipeg Rangers	MAHA	STATISTICS NOT AVAILABLE												
1947-48	Winnipeg Black Hawks	MJHL	1	0	0	0	....	....	....	0	....	....	....	....	....
1948-49	Winnipeg Black Hawks	WJrHL	29	3	2	5	....	....	....	16	....	....	....	....	....
1949-50	Winnipeg Black Hawks	WJrHL	36	3	7	10	....	....	....	76	6	1	1	2	12
1950-51	Sarnia Sailors	IHL	3	0	0	0	....	....	....	0	....	....	....	....	....
	Detroit Hettche	IHL	43	6	7	13	....	....	....	101	3	0	0	0	4
1951-52	Shawinigan Cataracts	QMHL	49	0	3	3	....	....	....	84	....	....	....	....	....
1952-53	Chicoutimi Sagueneens	QMHL	38	2	4	6	....	....	....	59	....	....	....	....	....
1953-54	Sherbrooke Saints	QHL	71	9	17	26	....	....	....	111	5	1	0	1	4
1954-55	Montreal Royals	QHL	56	5	27	32	....	....	....	88	14	1	2	3	8
1955-56	Seattle Americans	WHL	65	10	22	32	....	....	....	131	....	....	....	....	....
1956-57	Trois-Rivieres Lions	QHL	62	7	16	23	....	....	....	75	4	0	4	4	4
1957-58	**Montreal Canadiens**	**NHL**	**4**	**0**	**1**	**1**	**0**	**1**	**1**	**0**	....	....	....	....	....
	Montreal Royals	QHL	61	3	31	34	....	....	....	120	7	0	6	6	21
1958-59	**New York Rangers**	**NHL**	**35**	**1**	**2**	**3**	**1**	**2**	**3**	**20**	....	....	....	....	....
	Buffalo Bisons	AHL	21	3	9	12	....	....	....	26	....	....	....	....	....
1959-60	**New York Rangers**	**NHL**	**37**	**2**	**5**	**7**	**2**	**5**	**7**	**34**	....	....	....	....	....
	Springfield Indians	AHL	16	0	0	0	....	....	....	37	....	....	....	....	....
1960-61	Kitchener Beavers	EPHL	70	1	36	37	....	....	....	110	7	0	4	4	12
1961-62	**New York Rangers**	**NHL**	**4**	**0**	**0**	**0**	**0**	**0**	**0**	**4**	....	....	....	....	....
	Kitchener Beavers	EPHL	62	6	40	46	....	....	....	119	7	2	0	2	0
1962-63	Los Angeles Blades	WHL	67	4	24	28	....	....	....	55	3	0	1	1	0
1963-64	Los Angeles Blades	WHL	53	2	19	21	....	....	....	65	....	....	....	....	....
	Baltimore Clippers	AHL	15	0	4	4	....	....	....	27	....	....	....	....	....
1964-65			DID NOT PLAY												
1965-66	Winnipeg Rangers	MJHL	DID NOT PLAY – COACHING												
1966-67	Canada	Nt-Team	STATISTICS NOT AVAILABLE												
	Canada	WEC-A	7	0	2	2	....	....	....	12	....	....	....	....	....
1967-68	Hull Nationals	QSHL	24	0	13	13	....	....	....	21	....	....	....	....	....
1968-69	Ottawa Nationals	OHA-Sr.	4	0	0	0	....	....	....	2	....	....	....	....	....
	Canada	WEC-A	4	0	0	0	....	....	....	4	....	....	....	....	....
1969-70	Canada	Nt-Team	STATISTICS NOT AVAILABLE												
1970-71	Jacksonville Rockets	EHL	8	0	0	0	....	....	....	2	....	....	....	....	....
	Canada	Nt-Team	DID NOT PLAY – COACHING												
	Omaha Knights	CHL	....	....	....	....	....	....	....	....	1	0	0	0	0
1971/73	Vastra Frolunda	Sweden	DID NOT PLAY – COACHING												
1973-74	Kingston Canadians	OMJHL	DID NOT PLAY – COACHING												
	NHL Totals		**80**	**3**	**8**	**11**	**3**	**8**	**11**	**58**	....	....	....	....	....

MJHL Second Team All-Star (1949) • IHL Second All-Star Team (1951) • QHL First All-Star Team (1958)

Signed as a free agent by **Montreal**, October 21, 1954. Loaned to **Seattle** (WHL) by **Montreal** for the 1955-56 season, November, 1955. Claimed by **NY Rangers** (Buffalo-AHL) from **Montreal** (Montreal Royals-QHL) in Inter-League Draft, June 3, 1958. Traded to **LA Blades** (WHL) by **NY Rangers** for cash, September, 1962. • Named player coach of **LA Blades** (WHL), September, 1962.

• BOYD, Bill

RW – R. 5'10", 185 lbs. b: Belleville, Ont., 5/15/1898 d: 11/17/1940.

Season	Club	League	GP	G	A	Pts	AG	AA	APts	PIM	GP	G	A	Pts	PIM
1916-17	Hamilton Tigers	OHA-Sr.	STATISTICS NOT AVAILABLE												
1917-18	Hamilton Tigers	OHA-Sr.	5	11	0	11	....	....	....	....	....	....	....	....	....
1918-19			MILITARY SERVICE												
1919-20	Hamilton Tigers	OHA-Sr.	6	9	1	10	....	....	....	....	2	0	2	2	....
1920-21	Halifax Wanderers	HCHL	6	6	1	7	....	....	....	16	2	0	0	0	6
1921-22	Hamilton Tigers	OHA-Sr.	9	8	8	16	....	....	....	....	....	....	....	....	....
1922-23	Milwaukee A.C.	USAHA	20	9	0	9	....	....	....	....	....	....	....	....	....
1923-24	Minneapolis Millers	USAHA	20	1	0	1	....	....	....	....	....	....	....	....	....
1924-25	Minneapolis Rockets	USAHA	39	4	0	4	....	....	....	....	....	....	....	....	....
1925-26	Minneapolis Millers	CHL	34	11	2	13	....	....	....	30	3	0	0	0	4
1926-27	**New York Rangers**	**NHL**	**41**	**4**	**1**	**5**	**7**	**5**	**12**	**40**	....	....	....	....	....
♦**1927-28**	**New York Rangers**	**NHL**	**43**	**4**	**0**	**4**	**8**	**0**	**8**	**11**	**9**	**0**	**0**	**0**	**4**
1928-29	**New York Rangers**	**NHL**	**11**	**0**	**0**	**0**	**0**	**0**	**0**	**5**	**1**	**0**	**0**	**0**	**0**
	Springfield Indians	Can-Am	30	3	2	5	....	....	....	16	....	....	....	....	....
1929-30	**New York Americans**	**NHL**	**43**	**7**	**6**	**13**	**10**	**14**	**24**	**16**	....	....	....	....	....
	NHL Totals		**138**	**15**	**7**	**22**	**25**	**19**	**44**	**72**	**10**	**0**	**0**	**0**	**4**

Signed as a free agent by **NY Rangers**, November 9, 1926. Claimed by **NY Americans** from **Springfield** (Can-Am) in Inter-League Draft, May 13, 1929.

• BOYD, Irvin "Yank"

RW – R. 5'10", 152 lbs. b: Ardmore, PA, 11/13/1908.

Season	Club	League	GP	G	A	Pts	AG	AA	APts	PIM	GP	G	A	Pts	PIM
1925-26	Toronto Canoe Club	OHA-Jr.	7	5	1	6	....	....	....	....	....	....	....	....	....
	Toronto Canoe Club	OHA-Sr.	2	3	0	3	....	....	....	....	....	....	....	....	....
1926-27	Toronto Marlboros	OHA-Sr.	4	0	2	2	....	....	....	0	....	....	....	....	....
1927-28	Toronto CCM	TMHL	STATISTICS NOT AVAILABLE												
1928-29	Toronto CCM	TMHL	STATISTICS NOT AVAILABLE												
1929-30	Boston Tigers	Can-Am	40	24	12	36	....	....	....	90	5	2	2	4	8
1930-31	Boston Tigers	Can-Am	39	17	14	31	....	....	....	71	9	1	4	5	6
1931-32	**Boston Bruins**	**NHL**	**29**	**2**	**1**	**3**	**3**	**2**	**5**	**10**	....	....	....	....	....
	Boston Cubs	Can-Am	20	10	10	20	....	....	....	31	....	....	....	....	....
1932-33	Philadelphia Arrows	Can-Am	48	21	22	43	....	....	....	43	5	2	3	5	0
1933-34	Philadelphia Arrows	Can-Am	40	14	20	34	....	....	....	26	2	0	1	1	2
1934-35	**Detroit Red Wings**	**NHL**	**42**	**2**	**3**	**5**	**3**	**5**	**8**	**14**	....	....	....	....	....
	Detroit Olympics	IHL	9	4	6	10	....	....	....	6	....	....	....	....	....
1935-36	Windsor Bulldogs	IHL	18	5	4	9	....	....	....	14	....	....	....	....	....
	London Tecumsehs	IHL	24	14	10	24	....	....	....	22	2	3	0	3	0
1936-37	New Haven Eagles	IAHL	42	13	13	26	....	....	....	24	....	....	....	....	....
1937-38	New Haven Eagles	IAHL	38	3	9	12	....	....	....	6	2	1	1	2	0
1938-39	St. Paul Saints	AHA	45	14	40	54	....	....	....	31	3	1	0	1	2
1939-40	St. Paul Saints	AHA	46	26	22	48	....	....	....	27	7	5	3	8	2
1940-41	St. Paul Saints	AHA	30	8	8	16	....	....	....	9	4	0	0	0	0
1941-42	St. Paul Saints	AHA	47	6	20	26	....	....	....	18	2	0	0	0	0
1942-43	**Boston Bruins**	**NHL**	**20**	**6**	**5**	**11**	**6**	**5**	**11**	**6**	**5**	**0**	**1**	**1**	**4**
1943-44	**Boston Bruins**	**NHL**	**5**	**0**	**1**	**1**	**0**	**1**	**1**	**0**	....	....	....	....	....
	Providence Reds	AHL	38	6	27	33	....	....	....	12	....	....	....	....	....
1944-45	Providence Reds	AHL	1	0	1	1	....	....	....	0	....	....	....	....	....
	NHL Totals		**96**	**10**	**10**	**20**	**12**	**13**	**25**	**30**	**5**	**0**	**1**	**1**	**4**

Can-Am Second All-Star Team (1930)

Traded to **Philadelphia** (Can-Am) by **Boston** for cash, October, 1932. Traded to **Detroit** by **Philadelphia** (Can-Am) with Tom Anderson for cash, May 8, 1934. Traded to **London** (IHL) by **Windsor** (IHL) for cash, January 15, 1936. Signed as a free agent by **Boston**, December 18, 1942.

• BOYER, Wally — *see page 918*

• BRACKENBOROUGH, John "Spider"

LW/C – L. 5'11", 170 lbs. b: Parry Sound, Ont., d: 7/8/1993.

Season	Club	League	GP	G	A	Pts	AG	AA	APts	PIM	GP	G	A	Pts	PIM
1915-16	Ottawa Grand Trunk	OCHL	4	2	0	2	....	....	....	....	....	....	....	....	....
1916-17			MILITARY SERVICE												
1917-18			MILITARY SERVICE												
1918-19			MILITARY SERVICE												
1919-20	Depot Harbour	NOHA	STATISTICS NOT AVAILABLE												
1920-21	North Bay Trappers	NOHA	6	6	5	11	....	....	....	4	....	....	....	....	....
1921-22	North Bay Trappers	NOHA	6	7	3	10	....	....	....	6	....	....	....	....	....
1922-23	Hamilton Tigers	OHA-Sr.	12	20	8	*28	....	....	....	....	2	1	*2	*3	....
1923-24	Hamilton Tigers	OHA-Sr.	10	13	*12	25	....	....	....	....	2	1	*2	3	....
1924-25	Galt Terriers	OHA-Sr.	DID NOT PLAY – SUSPENDED												
1925-26	**Boston Bruins**	**NHL**	**7**	**0**	**0**	**0**	**0**	**0**	**0**	**0**	....	....	....	....	....
	NHL Totals		**7**	**0**	**0**	**0**	**0**	**0**	**0**	**0**	....	....	....	....	....

• Lost sight and use of right eye in game vs. University of Toronto, February 28, 1924. • Missed entire 1924-25 season after OHA rejected transfer from Hamilton (OHA-Sr.) to Galt (OHA-Sr.). Signed as a free agent by **Boston**, November 16, 1925.

• BRADLEY, Bart Bart William

C – L. 5'8", 150 lbs. b: Fort William, Ont., 7/29/1930.

Season	Club	League	GP	G	A	Pts	AG	AA	APts	PIM	GP	G	A	Pts	PIM
1946-47	Port Arthur Bruins	TBJHL	6	5	6	11	....	....	....	7	7	5	4	9	4
1947-48	Port Arthur Bruins	TBJHL	9	9	9	18	....	....	....	7	5	4	3	7	2
	Port Arthur Bruins	M-Cup	17	10	18	28	....	....	....	12	....	....	....	....	....
1948-49	Port Arthur Bruins	TBJHL	12	10	*20	30	....	....	....	28	5	2	*9	*11	12
	Port Arthur Bruins	M-Cup	5	3	3	6	....	....	....	2	....	....	....	....	....

Season	Club	League	GP	G	A	Pts	AG	AA	APts	PIM	GP	G	A	Pts	PIM
			REGULAR SEASON								PLAYOFFS				
1949-50	**Boston Bruins**	**NHL**	**1**	**0**	**0**	**0**	**0**	**0**	**0**	**0**					
	Hershey Bears	AHL	61	16	19	35				8					
1950-51	Tulsa Oilers	USHL	64	27	37	64				32	9	3	3	6	30
1951-52	Tacoma Rockets	PCHL	70	37	39	76				28	7	2	8	10	2
1952-53	Tacoma Rockets	WHL	70	26	47	73				28					
1953-54	Seattle Bombers	WHL	27	7	19	26				8					
1954-55	Victoria–N-Westminster	WHL	47	12	15	27				9	1	0	0	0	0
1955-56	Seattle Americans	WHL	68	22	28	50				37					
1956-57	Seattle Americans	WHL	63	10	16	26				19	6	1	1	2	7
1957-58	Belleville McFarlands	EOHL	50	30	34	64				32	13	*9	11	20	
	Belleville McFarlands	Al-Cup	12	3	9	12				2					
1958-59	Belleville McFarlands	EOHL	48	21	29	50				18					
	Canada	WEC-A	8	5	5	10				8					
1959-60	Belleville McFarlands	EOHL	53	12	30	42				8	12	3	5	8	8
1960-61	Dryden Rockets	OMHL	DID NOT PLAY – COACHING												
1961-62	Port Arthur Bearcats	TBSHL	STATISTICS NOT AVAILABLE												
1962-63	Port Arthur Bearcats	TBSHL	STATISTICS NOT AVAILABLE												
1963-64	Port Arthur Bearcats	TBSHL	STATISTICS NOT AVAILABLE												
	Port Arthur Bearcats	Al-Cup	2	0	0	0				0					
1964-65	Port Arthur Bearcats	TBSHL	DID NOT PLAY – COACHING												
1965-66	Fort William Beavers	TBSHL	10	5	7	12				2					
	NHL Totals		**1**	**0**	**0**	**0**	**0**	**0**	**0**	**0**					

• BRANIGAN, Andy   Andrew John

D – L. 5'11", 190 lbs.   b: Winnipeg, Man., 4/11/1922   d: 4/13/1995.

Season	Club	League	GP	G	A	Pts	AG	AA	APts	PIM	GP	G	A	Pts	PIM
1938-39	East Kildonan Bisons	MAHA	STATISTICS NOT AVAILABLE												
1939-40	Winnipeg Monarchs	MJHL	23	0	1	1				38	7	5	0	5	14
1940-41	**New York Americans**	**NHL**	**6**	**1**	**0**	**1**	**2**	**0**	**2**	**5**					
	Springfield Indians	AHL	50	2	6	8				21	3	0	0	0	4
1941-42	**Brooklyn Americans**	**NHL**	**21**	**0**	**2**	**2**	**0**	**2**	**2**	**26**					
	Springfield Indians	AHL	1	0	0	0				0					
1942-43	Winnipeg RCAF	WNDHL	13	4	1	5				*26	5	1	0	1	*18
	Winnipeg RCAF	Al-Cup	12	3	3	6				20					
1943-44	Winnipeg RCAF	WNDHL	1	0	1	1				6					
1944-45	Winnipeg RCAF	WNDHL	9	2	1	3				18					
	Rockcliffe RCAF	OCHL	4	0	2	2				8					
1945-46	Indianapolis Capitols	AHL	62	4	17	21				71	5	0	1	1	0
1946-47	Hershey Bears	AHL	62	6	9	15				42	11	1	2	3	8
1947-48	Hershey Bears	AHL	63	1	11	12				91	2	0	0	0	6
1948-49	Hershey Bears	AHL	68	5	14	19				54	11	0	2	2	10
1949-50	Hershey Bears	AHL	66	1	15	16				73					
1950-51	Hershey Bears	AHL	64	6	9	15				114	6	0	0	0	8
1951-52	Hershey Bears	AHL	66	6	19	25				110	5	1	1	2	10
1952-53	Hershey Bears	AHL	51	5	4	9				71					
1953-54	Hershey Bears	AHL	68	3	22	25				124	11	0	1	1	10
1954-55	Providence Reds	AHL	61	2	12	14				114					
1955-56	Providence Reds	AHL	64	5	17	22				103	9	2	5	7	14
1956-57	Providence Reds	AHL	46	2	10	12				46	5	0	0	0	6
1957-58	Providence Reds	AHL	67	2	6	8				61	1	0	0	0	0
1958-59	Washington Presidents	EHL	63	5	16	21				82					
1959-60	New York Rovers	EHL	48	2	10	12				73					
	NHL Totals		**27**	**1**	**2**	**3**	**2**	**2**	**4**	**31**					

AHL Second All-Star Team (1956)

Signed as a free agent by **NY Americans**, October 15, 1940. Rights transferred to **Detroit** from **Brooklyn** in Special Dispersal Draw, September 11, 1943.

• BRAYSHAW, Russ   Russ Ambrose "Buster"

LW – L. 5'10", 170 lbs.   b: Saskatoon, Sask., 1/17/1918   d: 1996.

Season	Club	League	GP	G	A	Pts	AG	AA	APts	PIM	GP	G	A	Pts	PIM
1936-37	Noranda Cooper Kings	NOHA	....	11	8	19									
1937-38	Saskatoon Quakers	N-SSHL	16	2	1	3				4	5	0	0	0	0
1938-39	Moose Jaw Millers	S-SSHL	22	10	2	12				8	10	1	2	3	6
1939-40	Moose Jaw Millers	S-SSHL	32	9	8	17				40	7	1	1	2	4
	Moose Jaw Millers	Al-Cup	3	0	1	1				0					
1940-41	Moose Jaw Millers	S-SSHL	30	11	11	22				14					
1941-42	Moose Jaw Millers	S-SSHL	28	9	15	24				26	9	5	3	8	4
1942-43	Victoria VMD	NNDHL	18	16	15	31				16					
	New Westminster Spitfires	PCHL	1	0	0	0				2	6	4	5	9	8
1943-44	Seattle Ironmen	NNDHL	2	1	1	2				0					
	New Westminster Spitfires	PCHL	19	17	15	32				25	3	3	1	4	4
	New Westminster Spitfires	Al-Cup	15	*21	8	29				10					
1944-45	**Chicago Black Hawks**	**NHL**	**43**	**5**	**9**	**14**	**5**	**10**	**15**	**24**					
1945-46	Cleveland Barons	AHL	57	24	24	48				37	5	1	1	2	0
1946-47	Providence Reds	AHL	38	10	16	26				27					
	St. Louis Flyers	AHL	21	8	4	12				2					
1947-48	St. Louis Flyers	AHL	7	2	2	4				6					
	Tulsa Oilers	USHL	52	22	21	43				12	2	0	0	0	0
1948-49	Vancouver–Seattle	PCHL	20	5	11	16				20					
	Saskatoon Quakers	WCSHL	12	2	7	9				16					
	NHL Totals		**43**	**5**	**9**	**14**	**5**	**10**	**15**	**24**					

Traded to **St. Louis** (AHL) by **Providence** (AHL) with Bill McComb for Eddie Bush, Carl Liscombe, Roly Rossignol and cash, January 9, 1947. Traded to **Seattle** (PCHL) by **Vancouver** (PCHL) with Paul Waldner for Bill Shill and Ab Collings, November 8, 1948.

• BRENNAN, Doug   Douglas Richard

D – L. 5'11", 180 lbs.   b: Peterborough, Ont., 1/10/1905.

Season	Club	League	GP	G	A	Pts	AG	AA	APts	PIM	GP	G	A	Pts	PIM
1925-26	Peterborough Seniors	OHA-Sr.	STATISTICS NOT AVAILABLE												
1926-27	Winnipeg Maroons	AHA	7	2	0	2				10					
	Kenora Thistles	NOHA	18	9	1	10				21					
1927-28	Winnipeg Maroons	AHA	26	2	0	2				8					
1928-29	Vancouver Lions	PCHL	35	8	4	12				61	3	1	0	1	6
1929-30	Vancouver Lions	PCHL	32	11	4	15				58	4	1	0	1	*10
1930-31	Vancouver Lions	PCHL	29	8	1	9				93					
1931-32	**New York Rangers**	**NHL**	**38**	**4**	**3**	**7**	**7**	**7**	**14**	**40**	**7**	**1**	**0**	**1**	**10**
♦1932-33	**New York Rangers**	**NHL**	**48**	**5**	**4**	**9**	**9**	**8**	**17**	**94**	**8**	**0**	**0**	**0**	**11**
1933-34	**New York Rangers**	**NHL**	**37**	**0**	**0**	**0**	**0**	**0**	**0**	**18**	**1**	**0**	**0**	**0**	**0**
	Windsor Bulldogs	IHL	7	1	0	1				0					
1934-35	Philadelphia Arrows	Can-Am	22	3	3	6				14					
	Vancouver Lions	NWHL	12	1	4	5				10	8	0	1	1	4
1935-36	Springfield Indians	Can-Am	42	2	3	5				8	3	0	1	1	8
	NHL Totals		**123**	**9**	**7**	**16**	**16**	**15**	**31**	**152**	**16**	**1**	**0**	**1**	**21**

Traded to **NY Rangers** by **Vancouver** (PCHL) for cash, October 30, 1931. • Suspended for five games by Canadian-American Hockey League for assault on referee Norm Shay, January 20, 1936.

• BRENNAN, Tom   Thomas Ernest

RW – R. 5'9", 155 lbs.   b: Philadelphia, PA, 1/22/1922.

Season	Club	League	GP	G	A	Pts	AG	AA	APts	PIM	GP	G	A	Pts	PIM
1937-38	Montreal Victorias	MCJHL	STATISTICS NOT AVAILABLE												
1938-39	Montreal Victorias	MCJHL	12	11	7	18				15	2	1	1	2	14
1939-40	Montreal Westmount	MCHL	11	9	6	15				7	2	2	0	2	0
1940-41	Montreal Jr. Canadiens	QJHL	10	5	10	15				10	4	*6	1	*7	0
1941-42	Montreal Sr. Canadiens	QSHL	5	2	0	2				2					
1942-43	Philadelphia Falcons	EAHL	44	34	34	68				28	12	8	6	14	16
1943-44	**Boston Bruins**	**NHL**	**11**	**2**	**1**	**3**	**2**	**1**	**3**	**2**					
	Boston Olympics	EAHL	30	36	25	61				58	11	10	4	14	19
1944-45	**Boston Bruins**	**NHL**	**1**	**0**	**1**	**1**	**0**	**1**	**1**	**0**					
	Boston Olympics	EAHL	46	53	55	*108				42	10	13	17	30	15
1945-46	**Boston Bruins**	**NHL**	DID NOT PLAY – INJURED												
1946-47	Valleyfield Braves	QSHL	13	4	2	6				16					
	Boston Olympics	EAHL	32	15	21	36				35	6	3	3	6	0
1947-48	Boston Olympics	QSHL	13	3	4	7				4					
	Boston Olympics	EAHL	5	3	1	4				2					
1948-49	Halifax St. Mary's	MSHL	49	26	35	61				56	11	6	3	9	0
	Halifax St. Mary's	Al-Cup	5	1	3	4				12					
1949-50	Halifax St. Mary's	MSHL	61	23	34	57				12	12	7	8	15	12
	Boston Olympics	EAHL	1	0	0	0				0					
	Halifax St. Mary's	Al-Cup	5	0	6	6				4					
1950-51	Saint John Beavers	MMHL	53	24	42	66				78					
1951-52	Saint John Beavers	MMHL	1	0	0	0				0					
	Joliette Cyclones	QPHL	PLAYER/COACH – STATISTICS UNAVAILABLE												
1952-53	Ste-Therese Titans	QPHL	41	19	40	59									
	NHL Totals		**12**	**2**	**2**	**4**	**2**	**2**	**4**	**2**					

EAHL Second All-Star Team (1943) • EAHL First All-Star Team (1944, 1945) • Won John Carlin Trophy (Top Scorer - EAHL) (1945)

Signed as a free agent by **Boston**, November 27, 1943. • Missed entire 1945-46 season recovering from back surgery. • Suffered season-ending eye injury in game vs. St-Jerome (QPHL), November 29, 1951.

• BRENNEMAN, John   *— see page 923*

• BRETTO, Joe   "Brute"

D – L. 6'1", 248 lbs.   b: Hibbing, MN, 11/29/1913.

Season	Club	League	GP	G	A	Pts	AG	AA	APts	PIM	GP	G	A	Pts	PIM
1931-32	Hibbing Maroons	CHL	36	6	1	7				48					
1932-33	Hibbing Maroons	CHL	40	7	9	16				96					
1933-34	Hibbing Miners	CHL	29	10	5	15				*141	6	0	1	1	14
	Boston Cubs	Can-Am	4	0	0	0				2					
1934-35	Boston Cubs	Can-Am	7	0	0	0				8					
	Minneapolis Millers	CHL	42	3	4	7				*86	5	3	2	5	*8
1935-36	Detroit Olympics	IHL	4	1	0	1				0					
	Windsor Bulldogs	IHL	41	5	7	12				32	8	1	0	1	8
1936-37	Cleveland Barons	IAHL	47	2	8	10				41					
1937-38	Cleveland Barons	IAHL	1	0	0	0				15					
	Minneapolis Millers	AHA	38	8	11	19				70	7	2	2	4	*22
1938-39	St. Paul Saints	AHA	44	8	8	16				39	3	0	*6	6	0
1939-40	St. Paul Saints	AHA	46	14	12	26				66	7	1	6	7	8
1940-41	St. Paul Saints	AHA	48	5	10	15				64	4	1	0	1	2
1941-42	St. Paul Saints	AHA	29	6	5	11				44					
1942-43			OUT OF HOCKEY – RETIRED												
1943-44			OUT OF HOCKEY – RETIRED												
1944-45	**Chicago Black Hawks**	**NHL**	**3**	**0**	**0**	**0**	**0**	**0**	**0**	**4**					
1945-46	St. Paul Saints	USHL	3	0	1	1				0					
	NHL Totals		**3**	**0**	**0**	**0**	**0**	**0**	**0**	**4**					

AHA First All-Star Team (1938, 1940) • AHA Second All-Star Team (1939, 1941, 1942)

Signed as a free agent by **Detroit Olympics** (IHL), October, 1935. Loaned to **Windsor** (IHL) by **Detroit** (IHL), November 27, 1935. Traded to **Chicago** by **St. Paul** (AHA) for cash, October 15, 1944. Traded to **Cleveland** (AHL) by **Chicago** for cash, November 14, 1944. • Suspended for remainder of the 1944-45 season by **Cleveland** (AHL) for refusing to report, November 19, 1944.

• BREWER, Carl   *— see page 923*

• BRIDEN, Archie   Archie Edward "Bones"

LW – L. 5'8", 170 lbs.   b: Renfrew, Ont., 7/16/1898   Deceased.

Season	Club	League	GP	G	A	Pts	AG	AA	APts	PIM	GP	G	A	Pts	PIM
1912-13	Cobalt O'Brien Mines	CoMHL	3	1	0	1				0					
	Haileybury Rexalls	X-Games	3	1	0	1				3					
1913-14	Cobalt O'Brien Mines	CoMHL	STATISTICS NOT AVAILABLE												
1914-15	Haileybury Rexalls	NOHA	STATISTICS NOT AVAILABLE												
1915-16	Cleveland Indians	USAHA	STATISTICS NOT AVAILABLE												
1916-17	Toronto Blueshirts	NHA	13	4	2	6				12					
1917-18			MILITARY SERVICE												
1918-19			MILITARY SERVICE												
1919-20	Edmonton Eskimos	Big-4	12	10	8	18				21	2	*2	0	2	4
1920-21	Edmonton Eskimos	Big-4	15	18	7	25				12					
1921-22	Seattle Metropolitans	PCHA	24	1	2	3				12	2	0	0	0	3
1922-23	Seattle Metropolitans	PCHA	30	7	3	10				27					
1923-24	Seattle Metropolitans	PCHA	18	7	0	7				24					
	Victoria Cougars	PCHA	12	9	1	10				4					
1924-25	Edmonton Eskimos	WCHL	28	17	6	23				33					
1925-26	Calgary Tigers	WHL	26	14	2	16				10					
1926-27	**Boston Bruins**	**NHL**	**16**	**2**	**2**	**4**	**4**	**10**	**14**	**8**					
	Detroit Cougars	**NHL**	**26**	**3**	**0**	**3**	**5**	**0**	**5**	**28**					
1927-28	Philadelphia Arrows	Can-Am	37	13	3	16				26					
1928-29	Philadelphia Arrows	Can-Am	40	12	5	17				46					

			REGULAR SEASON								PLAYOFFS				
Season	Club	League	GP	G	A	Pts	AG	AA	APts	PIM	GP	G	A	Pts	PIM
1929-30	**Pittsburgh Pirates**	**NHL**	**29**	**4**	**3**	**7**	**6**	**7**	**13**	**20**	....	....	....	....	....
	London Panthers	IHL	16	3	0	3	....	....	....	14	2	0	0	0	2
1930-31	London Panthers	IHL	12	0	2	2	....	....	....	16	....	....	....	....	....
	Cleveland Indians	IHL	34	8	11	19	....	....	....	20	6	2	2	4	2
1931-32	Cleveland Indians	IHL	48	6	10	16	....	....	....	16	....	....	....	....	....
	NHL Totals		**71**	**9**	**5**	**14**	**15**	**17**	**32**	**56**	....	....	....	....	....
	Other Major League Totals		151	59	16	75	....	....	....	122	2	0	0	0	3

PCHA Second All-Star Team (1923, 1924)

Signed as a free agent by **Seattle** (PCHA), November 7, 1921. Traded to **Victoria** (PCHA) by **Seattle** (PCHA) for cash, January 17, 1924. Traded to **Edmonton** (WCHL) by **Victoria** (WCHL) with Roy Rickey for Ty Arbour, November 6, 1924. Signed as a free agent by **Calgary** (WHL), September 21, 1925. Traded to **Boston** by **Calgary** (WHL) for cash, August 30, 1926. Traded to **Detroit Cougars** by **Boston** with Duke Keats for Harry Meeking and Frank Fredrickson, January 7, 1927. Traded to **NY Rangers** by **Detroit Cougars** with Harry Meeking for Stan Brown, October 10, 1927. Traded to **Pittsburgh** by **NY Rangers** (Philadelphia—Can-Am) for cash, October 8, 1929. Traded to **London** (IHL) by **Pittsburgh** for cash, January 27, 1930. Traded to **Cleveland** (IHL) by **London** (IHL) for Don Goodwillie, Roy Colquhoun and future considerations (Ed Kuntz, January 11, 1931), December 12, 1930.

• BRINK, Milt "Curly"

C – R. 5'10", 165 lbs. b: Hibbing, MN, 11/26/1910 Deceased.

Season	Club	League	GP	G	A	Pts	AG	AA	APts	PIM	GP	G	A	Pts	PIM
1931-32	Boston Cubs	Can-Am	4	1	0	1	....	....	....	0	1	0	0	0	0
1932-33	Eveleth Rangers	CHL	38	9	14	23	....	....	....	6	3	0	1	1	7
1933-34	Eveleth Rangers	CHL	41	17	*17	34	....	....	....	10	3	2	1	3	2
1934-35	Eveleth Rangers	CHL	35	12	18	30	....	....	....	10	....	....	....	....	....
1935-36	Kansas City Greyhounds	AHA	45	9	20	29	....	....	....	4	....	....	....	....	....
1936-37	**Chicago Black Hawks**	**NHL**	**5**	**0**	**0**	**0**	**0**	**0**	**0**	**0**	....	....	....	....	....
	Kansas City Greyhounds	AHA	2	0	1	1	....	....	....	0	....	....	....	....	....
	Minneapolis Millers	AHA	11	0	2	2	....	....	....	4	....	....	....	....	....
1937-38	St. Paul Saints	AHA	48	8	26	34	....	....	....	6	....	....	....	....	....
1938-39	Wichita Skyhawks	AHA	5	0	1	1	....	....	....	0	....	....	....	....	....
1939-40	Portage Lakes Lakers	NMHL	24	19	11	30	....	....	....	....	....	....	....	....	....
	NHL Totals		**5**	**0**	**0**	**0**	**0**	**0**	**0**	**0**	....	....	....	....	....

• BRISSON, Gerry Gerald

RW – L. 5'9", 155 lbs. b: St. Boniface, Man., 9/3/1937.

Season	Club	League	GP	G	A	Pts	AG	AA	APts	PIM	GP	G	A	Pts	PIM
1951-52	Winnipeg Excelsiors	MAHA	....	8	*11	19	....	....	....	8	....	....	....	....	....
1952-53	Winnipeg Excelsiors	MAHA	STATISTICS NOT AVAILABLE												
1953-54	Winnipeg Canadians	MJHL	1	0	0	0	....	....	....	0	....	....	....	....	....
1954-55	Winnipeg Canadians	MJHL	29	20	21	41	....	....	....	14	....	....	....	....	....
1955-56	St. Boniface Canadiens	MJHL	21	*30	19	49	....	....	....	45	10	*12	3	*15	4
1956-57	St. Boniface Canadiens	MJHL	22	21	19	40	....	....	....	60	7	4	6	10	2
1957-58	Peterborough Petes	OHA-Jr.	52	28	23	51	....	....	....	34	5	3	0	3	2
	Winnipeg Warriors	WHL	1	1	0	1	....	....	....	0	....	....	....	....	....
	Montreal Royals	QHL	2	0	0	0	....	....	....	0	....	....	....	....	....
1958-59	Winnipeg Warriors	WHL	62	38	45	83	....	....	....	20	7	5	0	5	2
1959-60	Winnipeg Warriors	WHL	66	24	32	56	....	....	....	20	....	....	....	....	....
1960-61	Winnipeg Warriors	WHL	70	29	26	55	....	....	....	35	....	....	....	....	....
1961-62	Spokane Comets	WHL	70	44	39	83	....	....	....	60	16	7	9	16	16
1962-63	**Montreal Canadiens**	**NHL**	**4**	**0**	**2**	**2**	**0**	**2**	**2**	**4**	....	....	....	....	....
	Spokane Comets	WHL	66	26	21	47	....	....	....	44	....	....	....	....	....
1963-64	Quebec Aces	AHL	12	0	1	1	....	....	....	6	....	....	....	....	....
	San Francisco Seals	WHL	50	18	25	43	....	....	....	15	11	6	2	8	4
1964-65	Seattle Totems	WHL	63	19	19	38	....	....	....	35	7	0	1	1	2
1965-66	San Francisco Seals	WHL	65	22	15	37	....	....	....	23	3	0	0	0	0
1966-67	California Seals	WHL	7	1	1	2	....	....	....	2	....	....	....	....	....
1967/69			OUT OF HOCKEY – RETIRED												
1969-70	St. Boniface Mohawks	Al-Cup	13	6	3	9	....	....	....	0	....	....	....	....	....
	NHL Totals		**4**	**0**	**2**	**2**	**0**	**2**	**2**	**4**	....	....	....	....	....

WHL Prairie Division First All-Star Team (1959)

Claimed by **Cleveland** (AHL) (Montreal) from **Montreal** in Reverse Draft, June 9, 1965. Traded to **San Francisco** (WHL) by **Montreal** (Seattle-WHL) for Len Haley, October 22, 1965. Traded to **NY Rangers** (Vancouver-WHL) by **California** (WHL) for Bob Kabel with NY Rangers holding right of recall, October, 1966.

• BROADBENT, Punch Harold "Harry" HHOF

RW – R. 5'7", 183 lbs. b: Ottawa, Ont., 7/13/1892 d: 3/6/1971.

Season	Club	League	GP	G	A	Pts	AG	AA	APts	PIM	GP	G	A	Pts	PIM
1908-09	Ottawa Emmetts	OCHL	6	14	0	14	....	....	....	6	2	1	0	1	0
1909-10	Ottawa Seconds	OCHL	2	3	0	3	....	....	....	5	....	....	....	....	....
	Hull Volants	LOVHL	1	0	0	0	....	....	....	0	....	....	....	....	....
	Ottawa Cliffsides	IPAHU	....	....	....	....	....	....	....	....	3	1	0	1	6
1910-11	Ottawa Cliffsides	OCHL	2	2	0	2	....	....	....	6	....	....	....	....	....
	Ottawa Cliffsides	IPAHU	6	14	0	14	....	....	....	18	1	0	0	0	3
1911-12	Ottawa New Edinburghs	IPAHU	10	20	0	20	....	....	....	*39	4	7	0	7	0
1912-13	Ottawa Senators	NHA	20	20	0	20	....	....	....	15	....	....	....	....	....
1913-14	Ottawa Senators	NHA	17	6	7	13	....	....	....	61	....	....	....	....	....
1914-15	Ottawa Senators	NHA	20	24	3	27	....	....	....	115	5	3	0	3	....
1915-16			MILITARY SERVICE												
1916-17			MILITARY SERVICE												
1917-18			MILITARY SERVICE												
1918-19	**Ottawa Senators**	**NHL**	**8**	**4**	**3**	**7**	**7**	**16**	**23**	**12**	**5**	**2**	**1**	**3**	***18**
1919-20	**Ottawa Senators**	**NHL**	**21**	**19**	**6**	**25**	**22**	**20**	**42**	**40**	....	....	....	....	....
♦	Ottawa Senators	St-Cup	4	0	0	0	....	....	....	3	....	....	....	....	....
1920-21	**Ottawa Senators**	**NHL**	**9**	**4**	**1**	**5**	**5**	**4**	**9**	**10**	**2**	**0**	**2**	**2**	**4**
♦	Ottawa Senators	St-Cup	4	2	0	2	....	....	....	0	....	....	....	....	....
1921-22	**Ottawa Senators**	**NHL**	**24**	***32**	**14**	***46**	**46**	**46**	**92**	**28**	**2**	**0**	**1**	**1**	**8**
1922-23	**Ottawa Senators**	**NHL**	**24**	**14**	**1**	**15**	**24**	**4**	**28**	**34**	**2**	**0**	**0**	**0**	**2**
♦	Ottawa Senators	St-Cup	6	6	1	7	....	....	....	12	....	....	....	....	....
1923-24	**Ottawa Senators**	**NHL**	**22**	**9**	**4**	**13**	**18**	**23**	**41**	**44**	**2**	**0**	**0**	**0**	**2**
1924-25	**Montreal Maroons**	**NHL**	**30**	**14**	**6**	**20**	**24**	**25**	**49**	**75**	....	....	....	....	....
1925-26	**Montreal Maroons**	**NHL**	**36**	**12**	**5**	**17**	**21**	**32**	**53**	**112**	**4**	**2**	**1**	**3**	**14**
♦	Montreal Maroons	St-Cup	4	1	0	1	....	....	....	20	....	....	....	....	....
1926-27	**Montreal Maroons**	**NHL**	**42**	**9**	**5**	**14**	**16**	**26**	**42**	**88**	**2**	**0**	**0**	**0**	**0**
1927-28	**Ottawa Senators**	**NHL**	**43**	**3**	**2**	**5**	**6**	**11**	**17**	**62**	**2**	**0**	**0**	**0**	**0**
1928-29	**New York Americans**	**NHL**	**44**	**1**	**4**	**5**	**3**	**27**	**30**	**59**	**2**	**0**	**0**	**0**	**2**
	NHL Totals		**303**	**121**	**51**	**172**	**192**	**234**	**426**	**564**	**23**	**4**	**5**	**9**	**50**
	Other Major League Totals		57	50	10	60	....	....	....	191	5	3	0	3	....

NHL Scoring Leader (1922)

Signed as a free agent by **Ottawa**, January 21, 1919. Rights transferred to **Hamilton** by **NHL** with Sprague Cleghorn, December 30, 1920. • Broadbent and Cleghorn refused to report. Rights traded to **Montreal Canadiens** by **Hamilton** for cash, January 4, 1921. • Broadbent refused to report. Rights returned to **Ottawa** by **NHL**, February 21, 1921. • Scored at least one goal in 16 consecutive games (NHL record) from December 21, 1921 to February 15, 1922. • 1922-23 Stanley Cup totals includes series with Regina (WCHL) and Edmonton (PCHA). Traded to **Montreal Maroons** by **Ottawa** with Clint Benedict for cash, October 20, 1924. • 1925-26 Montreal Maroons playoff totals includes series against Ottawa and Pittsburgh. Traded to **Ottawa** by **Montreal Maroons** with $22,500 for Hooley Smith, October 7, 1927. Traded to **NY Americans** by **Ottawa** for cash, October 15, 1928.

• BRODEN, Connie Connell

C – L. 5'8", 160 lbs. b: Montreal, Que., 4/6/1932.

Season	Club	League	GP	G	A	Pts	AG	AA	APts	PIM	GP	G	A	Pts	PIM
1949-50	Montreal Jr. Royals	QJHL	36	7	19	26	....	....	....	14	3	0	1	1	0
1950-51	Montreal Jr. Royals	QJHL	29	15	12	27	....	....	....	15	....	....	....	....	....
	Montreal Royals	QMHL	1	0	0	0	....	....	....	0	....	....	....	....	....
1951-52	Montreal Jr. Canadiens	QJHL	39	16	24	40	....	....	....	18	10	5	2	7	8
	Montreal Jr. Canadiens	M-Cup	8	5	5	10	....	....	....	8	....	....	....	....	....
1952-53	Cincinnati Mohawks	IHL	57	29	38	67	....	....	....	39	9	4	3	7	8
1953-54	Cincinnati Mohawks	IHL	59	32	37	69	....	....	....	34	11	3	2	5	14
1954-55	Shawinigan Cataracts	QHL	62	27	35	62	....	....	....	25	13	5	7	12	15
	Shawinigan Cataracts	Ed-Cup	7	2	1	3	....	....	....	0	....	....	....	....	....
1955-56	**Montreal Canadiens**	**NHL**	**3**	**0**	**0**	**0**	**0**	**0**	**0**	**2**	....	....	....	....	....
	Shawinigan Cataracts	QHL	61	17	40	57	....	....	....	45	11	2	8	10	8
1956-57	Shawinigan Cataracts	QHL	68	20	29	49	....	....	....	32	....	....	....	....	....
♦	**Montreal Canadiens**	**NHL**	....	....	....	....	....	....	....	....	**6**	**0**	**1**	**1**	**0**
1957-58	Whitby Dunlops	EOHL	7	5	9	14	....	....	....	0	....	....	....	....	....
	Canada	WEC-A	7	12	7	*19	....	....	....	6	....	....	....	....	....
♦	**Montreal Canadiens**	**NHL**	**3**	**2**	**1**	**3**	**2**	**1**	**3**	**0**	**1**	**0**	**0**	**0**	**0**
1958-59	Hull-Ottawa Canadiens	EOHL	26	11	12	23	....	....	....	40	7	0	4	4	20
	NHL Totals		**6**	**2**	**1**	**3**	**2**	**1**	**3**	**2**	**7**	**0**	**1**	**1**	**0**

Won William Northey Trophy (Top Rookie - QHL) (1955)

Claimed by **Springfield** (AHL) from **Montreal** (Shawinigan-QHL) in Inter-League Draft, June 4, 1957.

• BROPHY, Bernie

LW – L. 5'8", 165 lbs. b: Collingwood, Ont., 8/9/1905 Deceased.

Season	Club	League	GP	G	A	Pts	AG	AA	APts	PIM	GP	G	A	Pts	PIM
1924-25	Fort Pitt Hornets	USAHA	17	4	0	4	....	....	....	....	5	0	0	0	....
1925-26	**Montreal Maroons**	**NHL**	**10**	**0**	**0**	**0**	**0**	**0**	**0**	**0**	....	....	....	....	....
1926-27	Providence Reds	Can-Am	10	3	0	3	....	....	....	8	....	....	....	....	....
	Detroit Greyhounds	AHA	1	0	0	0	....	....	....	0	....	....	....	....	....
	Duluth Hornets	AHA	1	0	0	0	....	....	....	0	....	....	....	....	....
1927-28	Providence Reds	Can-Am	33	9	2	11	....	....	....	31	....	....	....	....	....
1928-29	**Detroit Cougars**	**NHL**	**37**	**2**	**4**	**6**	**6**	**27**	**33**	**23**	**2**	**0**	**0**	**0**	**2**
	Detroit Olympics	Can-Pro	10	3	4	7	....	....	....	12	....	....	....	....	....
1929-30	**Detroit Cougars**	**NHL**	**15**	**2**	**0**	**2**	**3**	**0**	**3**	**2**	....	....	....	....	....
	Detroit Olympics	IHL	25	14	5	19	....	....	....	26	3	0	0	0	6
1930-31	Detroit Olympics	IHL	35	11	5	16	....	....	....	38	....	....	....	....	....
1931-32	Cleveland Indians	IHL	46	15	13	28	....	....	....	60	....	....	....	....	....
1932-33	Cleveland Indians	IHL	23	13	5	18	....	....	....	20	....	....	....	....	....
1933-34	London Tecumsehs	IHL	37	9	5	14	....	....	....	19	6	4	0	4	4
1934-35	London Tecumsehs	IHL	34	12	10	22	....	....	....	20	5	1	*4	5	0
1935-36	Windsor Bulldogs	IHL	41	6	6	12	....	....	....	11	5	0	1	1	0
1936/39	Collingwood Shippers	OIHA	STATISTICS NOT AVAILABLE												
	NHL Totals		**62**	**4**	**4**	**8**	**9**	**27**	**36**	**25**	**2**	**0**	**0**	**0**	**2**

Signed as a free agent by **Montreal Maroons**, January 4, 1926. Signed as a free agent by **Montreal Canadiens** after release by **Montreal Maroons**, February 10, 1927. Signed as a free agent by **Montreal Maroons**, September, 1928. Traded to **Detroit Cougars** by **Montreal Maroons** for cash, October 23, 1928. Traded to **Cleveland** (IHL) by **Detroit Falcons** for cash, November 3, 1931. • Suspended for life by IHL after leaving team during 1935-36 playoffs, March, 1936.

• BROWN, Adam "The Flying Scotsman"

LW – L. 5'9", 175 lbs. b: Johnstone, Scotland, 2/4/1920 d: 8/9/1960.

Season	Club	League	GP	G	A	Pts	AG	AA	APts	PIM	GP	G	A	Pts	PIM
1937-38	Hamilton Bengal Cubs	OHA-Jr.	8	5	1	6	....	....	....	24	....	....	....	....	....
1938-39	Stratford Majors	OHA-Sr.	25	11	4	15	....	....	....	45	2	1	1	2	2
1939-40	Guelph Biltmores	OHA-Jr.	20	21	7	28	....	....	....	22	3	2	5	7	2
1940-41	Omaha Knights	AHA	48	18	18	36	....	....	....	33	....	....	....	....	....
1941-42	**Detroit Red Wings**	**NHL**	**28**	**6**	**9**	**15**	**8**	**11**	**19**	**15**	**10**	**0**	**2**	**2**	**4**
	Indianapolis Capitols	AHL	29	11	19	30	....	....	....	22	....	....	....	....	....
1942-43	Indianapolis Capitols	AHL	55	34	51	85	....	....	....	47	4	3	2	5	4
♦	**Detroit Red Wings**	**NHL**	....	....	....	....	....	....	....	....	**6**	**1**	**1**	**2**	**2**
1943-44	**Detroit Red Wings**	**NHL**	**50**	**24**	**18**	**42**	**22**	**16**	**38**	**56**	**5**	**0**	**0**	**0**	**8**
1944-45	Barriefield Bears	OHA-Sr.	....	21	9	30	....	....	....	14	....	....	....	....	....
	Toronto Tip Tops	TIHL	1	0	3	3	....	....	....	0	....	....	....	....	....
	Toronto Uptown Tires	TMHL	3	4	0	4	....	....	....	9	2	2	1	3	0
	Toronto Bowsers	TMHL	....	....	....	....	....	....	....	....	4	6	3	9	0
1945-46	**Detroit Red Wings**	**NHL**	**48**	**20**	**11**	**31**	**24**	**16**	**40**	**27**	**5**	**1**	**1**	**2**	**0**
1946-47	**Detroit Red Wings**	**NHL**	**22**	**8**	**5**	**13**	**9**	**6**	**15**	**30**	....	....	....	....	....
	Chicago Black Hawks	**NHL**	**42**	**11**	**25**	**36**	**12**	**30**	**42**	**57**	....	....	....	....	....
1947-48	**Chicago Black Hawks**	**NHL**	**32**	**7**	**10**	**17**	**9**	**13**	**22**	**41**	....	....	....	....	....
1948-49	**Chicago Black Hawks**	**NHL**	**58**	**8**	**12**	**20**	**11**	**17**	**28**	**69**	....	....	....	....	....
1949-50	**Chicago Black Hawks**	**NHL**	**25**	**2**	**2**	**4**	**2**	**2**	**4**	**16**	....	....	....	....	....
	Kansas City Mohawks	USHL	5	2	8	10	....	....	....	0	....	....	....	....	....
	St. Louis Flyers	AHL	24	13	11	24	....	....	....	9	2	1	0	1	0
1950-51	**Chicago Black Hawks**	**NHL**	**53**	**10**	**12**	**22**	**13**	**15**	**28**	**61**	....	....	....	....	....
1951-52	**Boston Bruins**	**NHL**	**33**	**8**	**9**	**17**	**11**	**11**	**22**	**6**	....	....	....	....	....
	Hershey Bears	AHL	30	14	16	30	....	....	....	22	5	0	1	1	0
1952-53	Hershey Bears	AHL	62	11	25	36	....	....	....	23	3	0	0	0	0

Season	Club	League	GP	G	A	Pts	AG	AA	APts	PIM	GP	G	A	Pts	PIM
			REGULAR SEASON								PLAYOFFS				
1953-54	Quebec Aces	QHL	70	23	32	55	....	....	....	58	12	3	2	5	12
	Quebec Aces	Ed-Cup	7	1	2	3	....	....	....	0	....	....	....	....	....
1954-55	Sudbury Wolves	NOHA	29	15	13	28	....	....	....	8	....	....	....	....	....
	NHL Totals		**391**	**104**	**113**	**217**	**121**	**137**	**258**	**378**	**26**	**2**	**4**	**6**	**14**

• Father of Andy • AHL First All-Star Team (1943)

Signed as a free agent by **Detroit**, October 3, 1940. Traded to **Chicago** by **Detroit** with Ray Powell for Leo Reise and Pete Horeck, December 9, 1946. Traded to **Boston** by **Chicago** for cash, August 20, 1951.

• BROWN, Arnie

— *see page 928*

• BROWN, Connie

Cornelius
C – L. 5'7", 168 lbs. b: Vankleek Hill, Ont., 1/11/1917 d: 6/3/1966.

Season	Club	League	GP	G	A	Pts	AG	AA	APts	PIM	GP	G	A	Pts	PIM
1933-34	Ottawa St. Malachy's	OCJHL	16	11	9	20	....	....	....	17	....	....	....	....	....
1934-35	Ottawa Jr. Rideaus	OCJHL	12	11	*23	34	....	....	....	8	5	5	1	6	2
	Ottawa Rideaus	OCSHL	1	1	0	1	....	....	....	0	....	....	....	....	....
	Ottawa Jr. Rideaus	M-Cup	8	10	*9	19	....	....	....	0	....	....	....	....	....
1935-36	Ottawa Senators	OCHL	19	3	7	10	....	....	....	8	4	1	1	2	2
1936-37	Cornwall Flyers	OCHL	23	16	12	*28	....	....	....	21	6	0	2	2	4
1937-38	Cornwall Flyers	OCHL	24	14	*36	*50	....	....	....	14	6	6	5	11	0
	Cornwall Flyers	Al-Cup	11	6	*8	*14	....	....	....	8	....	....	....	....	....
1938-39	**Detroit Red Wings**	**NHL**	**2**	**1**	**0**	**1**	**2**	**0**	**2**	**0**	....	....	....	....	....
	Pittsburgh Hornets	IAHL	53	11	34	45	....	....	....	38	....	....	....	....	....
1939-40	**Detroit Red Wings**	**NHL**	**36**	**8**	**3**	**11**	**13**	**5**	**18**	**2**	**5**	**2**	**1**	**3**	**0**
	Indianapolis Capitols	IAHL	15	9	10	19	....	....	....	11	....	....	....	....	....
1940-41	**Detroit Red Wings**	**NHL**	**3**	**1**	**2**	**3**	**2**	**3**	**5**	**0**	**9**	**0**	**2**	**2**	**0**
	Indianapolis Capitols	AHL	50	16	28	44	....	....	....	17	....	....	....	....	....
1941-42	**Detroit Red Wings**	**NHL**	**9**	**0**	**3**	**3**	**0**	**4**	**4**	**4**	....	....	....	....	....
	Indianapolis Capitols	AHL	44	19	34	53	....	....	....	19	10	6	5	11	5
♦1942-43	**Detroit Red Wings**	**NHL**	**23**	**5**	**16**	**21**	**5**	**15**	**20**	**6**	....	....	....	....	....
	Indianapolis Capitols	AHL	38	12	25	37	....	....	....	6	7	2	6	8	2
1943-44	Petawawa Grenades	OVHL	1	0	4	4	....	....	....	0	....	....	....	....	....
1944-45	Ottawa Engineers	OCHL	....	....	....	....	....	....	....	....	3	2	2	4	4
1945-46	Ottawa Senators	QSHL	36	12	39	51	....	....	....	16	9	5	5	10	10
	Ottawa Quarter-Masters	OCHL	....	8	*20	*28	....	....	....	....	4	*8	8	16	....
1946-47	Ottawa Senators	QSHL	18	7	11	18	....	....	....	8	8	1	2	3	4
1947-48	Valleyfield Braves	QSHL	40	20	36	56	....	....	....	34	6	4	2	6	2
1948-49	Valleyfield Braves	QSHL	63	41	47	88	....	....	....	22	4	0	2	2	0
1949-50	Glace Bay Miners	CBSHL	70	31	47	78	....	....	....	38	10	6	*13	*19	0
1950-51	Ottawa Army	ECSHL	37	20	28	48	....	....	....	16	3	5	2	7	2
1951-52	Hull Volants	ECSHL	29	9	21	30	....	....	....	0	5	0	*10	10	0
	NHL Totals		**73**	**15**	**24**	**39**	**22**	**27**	**49**	**12**	**14**	**2**	**3**	**5**	**0**

• BROWN, Fred

"Baldy"
LW – L. 5'8", 155 lbs. b: Kingston, Ont., 9/15/1900 Deceased.

Season	Club	League	GP	G	A	Pts	AG	AA	APts	PIM	GP	G	A	Pts	PIM
1923-24	Brockville Indians	OHA-Jr.	STATISTICS NOT AVAILABLE												
1924-25	Hamilton Rowing Club	OHA-Sr.	8	*10	3	*13	....	....	....	....	....	....	....	....	....
1925-26	Windsor Hornets	OHA-Sr.	20	15	4	19	....	....	....	8	....	....	....	....	....
1926-27	Windsor Hornets	Can-Pro	29	9	3	12	....	....	....	16	....	....	....	....	....
1927-28	Stratford Nationals	Can-Pro	16	6	5	11	....	....	....	2	....	....	....	....	....
	Montreal Maroons	**NHL**	**19**	**1**	**0**	**1**	**2**	**0**	**2**	**0**	**9**	**0**	**0**	**0**	**0**
	Windsor Bulldogs	Can-Pro	13	5	2	7	....	....	....	9	....	....	....	....	....
1928-29	Kitchener Dutchmen	Can-Pro	40	15	6	21	....	....	....	56	3	0	0	0	2
1929-30	Niagara Falls Cataracts	IHL	16	2	0	2	....	....	....	25	....	....	....	....	....
	Windsor Bulldogs	IHL	24	3	3	6	....	....	....	18	....	....	....	....	....
1930-31	Syracuse Stars	IHL	48	15	7	22	....	....	....	39	....	....	....	....	....
	NHL Totals		**19**	**1**	**0**	**1**	**2**	**0**	**2**	**0**	**9**	**0**	**0**	**0**	**0**

Traded to **Montreal Maroons** by **Stratford** (Can-Pro) for Bill Touhey with Montreal holding right of recall, February 14, 1928. Traded to **Stratford** (Can-Pro) by **Montreal Maroons** for cash, April 23, 1928. Traded to **Windsor** (IHL) by **London** (IHL) with Ed Kuntz for Fred Elliot, November 21, 1929.

• BROWN, George

George Allan
C – L. 5'11", 185 lbs. b: Winnipeg, Man., 5/17/1912.

Season	Club	League	GP	G	A	Pts	AG	AA	APts	PIM	GP	G	A	Pts	PIM
1930-31	Elmwood Millionaires	WJrHL	10	5	0	5	....	....	....	22	3	1	*1	*2	6
	Elmwood Millionaires	M-Cup	9	3	0	3	....	....	....	*20	....	....	....	....	....
1931-32	Winnipeg Jr. Monarchs	WJrHL	12	5	1	6	....	....	....	*40	4	1	0	1	*15
	Winnipeg Jr. Monarchs	M-Cup	8	4	1	5	....	....	....	*25	....	....	....	....	....
1932-33	Winnipeg Monarchs	WSrHL	STATISTICS NOT AVAILABLE												
1933-34	Montreal Royals	MCHL	16	6	5	11	....	....	....	*36	2	0	0	0	4
1934-35	Verdun Maple Leafs	MCHL	20	18	19	37	....	....	....	22	....	....	....	....	....
1935-36	Verdun Maple Leafs	MCHL	22	19	*23	*42	....	....	....	48	7	4	4	8	22
1936-37	**Montreal Canadiens**	**NHL**	**27**	**4**	**6**	**10**	**7**	**11**	**18**	**10**	**4**	**0**	**0**	**0**	**0**
1937-38	**Montreal Canadiens**	**NHL**	**34**	**1**	**7**	**8**	**2**	**11**	**13**	**14**	**3**	**0**	**0**	**0**	**2**
	New Haven Eagles	IAHL	10	1	4	5	....	....	....	2	2	0	0	0	0
1938-39	**Montreal Canadiens**	**NHL**	**18**	**1**	**9**	**10**	**2**	**14**	**16**	**10**	....	....	....	....	....
	New Haven Eagles	IAHL	35	10	7	17	....	....	....	27	....	....	....	....	....
1939-40	Springfield Indians	IAHL	12	0	5	5	....	....	....	10	....	....	....	....	....
	Hershey Bears	IAHL	7	0	0	0	....	....	....	0	....	....	....	....	....
	Syracuse Stars	IAHL	11	1	2	3	....	....	....	2	....	....	....	....	....
1940-41	St-Jerome Papermakers	QPHL	13	8	7	15	....	....	....	12	....	....	....	....	....
	St-Jerome Papermakers	Al-Cup	4	1	0	1	....	....	....	6	....	....	....	....	....
1941-42	Montreal Sr. Canadiens	QSHL	38	3	6	9	....	....	....	83	6	0	1	1	16
1942-43	Montreal Sr. Canadiens	QSHL	24	3	5	8	....	....	....	32	4	1	0	1	8
	NHL Totals		**79**	**6**	**22**	**28**	**11**	**36**	**47**	**34**	**7**	**0**	**0**	**0**	**2**

Rights traded to **Montreal Maroons** by **NY Rangers** for Eddie Wares, October 30, 1935. Rights traded to **Montreal Canadiens** by **Montreal Maroons** for Gerry Carson, October 7, 1936. • Suspended by **Montreal** for refusing assignment to **New Haven** (IAHL), November 26, 1939. Traded to **Boston** by **Montreal** for cash, November 29, 1939.

• BROWN, Gerry

Gerald William Joseph
LW – L. 5'9", 170 lbs. b: Edmonton, Alta., 7/7/1917 d: 8/18/1998.

Season	Club	League	GP	G	A	Pts	AG	AA	APts	PIM	GP	G	A	Pts	PIM
1933-34	Edmonton Southsides	EJrHL	9	4	2	6	....	....	....	4	3	1	0	1	0
1934-35	Edmonton Southsides	EJrHL	11	10	3	*13	....	....	....	15	6	1	*3	4	4
1935-36	Edmonton Dominions	ESrHL	13	*13	5	*18	....	....	....	12	3	0	0	0	5
1936-37	Edmonton Dominions	ESrHL	26	21	18	39	....	....	....	28	6	3	3	6	2
	Edmonton Dominions	Al-Cup	8	6	1	7	....	....	....	13	....	....	....	....	....
1937-38	Earls Court Rangers	Ln-Cup	....	2	3	5	....	....	....	....	....	....	....	....	....
	Earls Court Rangers	Britain	....	7	15	22	....	....	....	....	....	....	....	....	....
	Earls Court Rangers	Nat-Tmt	....	9	4	13	....	....	....	....	....	....	....	....	....
1938-39	Earls Court Rangers	Ln-Cup	....	5	3	8	....	....	....	....	....	....	....	....	....
	Earls Court Rangers	Britain	....	21	9	30	....	....	....	....	....	....	....	....	....
	Earls Court Rangers	Nat-Tmt	....	9	3	12	....	....	....	....	....	....	....	....	....
1939-40	Cornwall Royals	QSHL	30	16	15	31	....	....	....	23	5	1	2	3	2
1940-41	Cornwall Flyers	QSHL	36	18	22	40	....	....	....	35	4	1	1	2	0
	Montreal Concordia	MCHL	2	0	0	0	....	....	....	0	....	....	....	....	....
1941-42	**Detroit Red Wings**	**NHL**	**13**	**4**	**4**	**8**	**5**	**5**	**10**	**0**	**12**	**2**	**1**	**3**	**4**
	Indianapolis Capitols	AHL	42	10	26	36	....	....	....	25	....	....	....	....	....
1942-43			MILITARY SERVICE												
1943-44			MILITARY SERVICE												
1944-45			MILITARY SERVICE												
1945-46	**Detroit Red Wings**	**NHL**	**10**	**0**	**1**	**1**	**0**	**1**	**1**	**2**	....	....	....	....	....
	Indianapolis Capitols	AHL	48	28	25	53	....	....	....	22	5	0	1	1	4
1946-47	Buffalo Bisons	AHL	64	29	30	59	....	....	....	48	4	1	1	2	0
1947-48	Buffalo Bisons	AHL	67	25	43	68	....	....	....	45	8	2	3	5	8
1948-49	Hershey Bears	AHL	68	16	36	52	....	....	....	31	11	3	6	9	2
1949-50	Hershey Bears	AHL	70	19	35	54	....	....	....	16	....	....	....	....	....
1950-51	Hershey Bears	AHL	67	21	36	57	....	....	....	31	6	4	0	4	2
1951-52	Hershey Bears	AHL	68	26	28	54	....	....	....	38	5	1	3	4	0
1952-53	Oshawa Generals	OHA-Jr.	DID NOT PLAY – COACHING												
	NHL Totals		**23**	**4**	**5**	**9**	**5**	**6**	**11**	**2**	**12**	**2**	**1**	**3**	**4**

Signed as a free agent by **Detroit**, October 14, 1941. Traded to **Toronto** by **Detroit** for Doug Baldwin and Ray Powell, September 21, 1946. Traded to **Montreal** (Buffalo-AHL) by **Toronto** (Pittsburgh-AHL) with John Mahaffy for Dutch Hiller and Vic Lynn, September 21, 1946. Traded to **Boston** (Hershey-AHL) by **Montreal** (Buffalo-AHL) with Hal Jackson for Jack McGill, June 30, 1948.

• BROWN, Harold

Harold Fraser "Hal"
RW – L. 5'10", 160 lbs. b: Brandon, Man., 9/14/1920.

Season	Club	League	GP	G	A	Pts	AG	AA	APts	PIM	GP	G	A	Pts	PIM
1938-39	Portage Terriers	MJHL	17	5	4	9	....	....	....	4	2	0	0	0	0
1939-40	Portage Terriers	MJHL	3	0	2	2	....	....	....	0	....	....	....	....	....
	Brandon Elks	MJHL	12	5	1	6	....	....	....	4	3	2	0	2	2
1940-41	Flin Flon Bombers	N-SSHL	32	25	20	45	....	....	....	12	3	0	1	1	0
1941-42	Flin Flon Bombers	N-SSHL	32	26	20	46	....	....	....	12	3	2	0	2	4
1942-43	Nanaimo Navy	NNDHL	19	*30	11	41	....	....	....	15	2	3	1	4	2
1943-44	Nanaimo Navy	NNDHL	19	*30	8	*38	....	....	....	6	....	....	....	....	....
1944-45	Calgary Navy	CNDHL	4	1	1	2	....	....	....	2	....	....	....	....	....
1945-46	**New York Rangers**	**NHL**	**13**	**2**	**1**	**3**	**2**	**1**	**3**	**2**	....	....	....	....	....
	St. Paul Saints	USHL	39	20	17	37	....	....	....	4	6	1	2	3	2
1946-47	New Haven Ramblers	AHL	14	8	4	12	....	....	....	0	....	....	....	....	....
	St. Paul Saints	USHL	48	28	18	46	....	....	....	4	....	....	....	....	....
1947-48	St. Paul Saints	USHL	66	43	24	67	....	....	....	10	....	....	....	....	....
1948-49	St. Paul Saints	USHL	65	38	39	77	....	....	....	8	7	*6	2	8	0
1949-50	St. Paul Saints	USHL	70	30	24	54	....	....	....	16	3	1	1	2	0
1950-51	Denver Falcons	USHL	56	16	17	33	....	....	....	2	5	2	0	2	0
1951-52	Calgary Stampeders	PCHL	32	20	8	28	....	....	....	2	....	....	....	....	....
	Kamloops Elks	OSHL	27	16	15	31	....	....	....	24	....	....	....	....	....
1952-53	Calgary Stampeders	WHL	19	5	4	9	....	....	....	0	....	....	....	....	....
	Kamloops Elks	OSHL	27	18	11	29	....	....	....	0	12	3	1	4	0
	NHL Totals		**13**	**2**	**1**	**3**	**2**	**1**	**3**	**2**	....	....	....	....	....

USHL Second All-Star Team (1947, 1949) • USHL First All-Star Team (1948)

Traded to **St. Paul** (USHL) by **NY Rangers** for cash, October 7, 1947.

• BROWN, Stan

D – L. 5'10", 150 lbs. b: North Bay, Ont., 5/9/1898 d: 7/6/1987.

Season	Club	League	GP	G	A	Pts	AG	AA	APts	PIM	GP	G	A	Pts	PIM
1914-15	North Bay Arena Stars	NBHL	STATISTICS NOT AVAILABLE												
1915-16	Berlin Union Jacks	OHA-Jr.	STATISTICS NOT AVAILABLE												
1916-17	Toronto St. Pats	OHA-Sr.	8	3	0	3	....	....	....	....	....	....	....	....	....
1917-18	St. Michael's Majors	OHA-Jr.	STATISTICS NOT AVAILABLE												
1918-19	Toronto Dentals	OHA-Sr.	7	10	6	16	....	....	....	....	2	0	0	0	0
1919-20	Toronto Dentals	OHA-Sr.	6	1	0	1	....	....	....	....	....	....	....	....	....
1920-21	University of Toronto	OHA-Sr.	9	5	3	8	....	....	....	....	2	3	*3	*6	....
	University of Toronto	Al-Cup	5	4	*4	8	....	....	....	....	....	....	....	....	....
1921-22	University of Toronto	OHA-Sr.	10	7	4	11	....	....	....	....	....	....	....	....	....
1922-23	S.S. Marie Greyhounds	NOHA	8	2	*5	7	....	....	....	6	2	0	0	0	4
	S.S. Marie Greyhounds	Al-Cup	5	4	3	7	....	....	....	4	....	....	....	....	....
1923-24	S.S. Marie Greyhounds	NOHA	8	4	5	9	....	....	....	6	7	1	1	2	8
1924-25	S.S. Marie Greyhounds	NOHA	STATISTICS NOT AVAILABLE												
1925-26	S.S. Marie Greyhounds	CHL	19	3	5	8	....	....	....	8	....	....	....	....	....
1926-27	Detroit Greyhounds	AHA	6	0	0	0	....	....	....	2	....	....	....	....	....
	New York Rangers	**NHL**	**24**	**6**	**2**	**8**	**11**	**10**	**21**	**14**	**2**	**0**	**0**	**0**	**0**
1927-28	**Detroit Cougars**	**NHL**	**24**	**2**	**0**	**2**	**4**	**0**	**4**	**4**	....	....	....	....	....
	Windsor Hornets	Can-Pro	10	3	1	4	....	....	....	2	....	....	....	....	....
1928-29	Windsor Bulldogs	Can-Pro	40	9	4	13	....	....	....	14	8	0	2	2	8
1929-30	Windsor Bulldogs	IHL	41	13	10	23	....	....	....	22	....	....	....	....	....
1930-31	Windsor Bulldogs	IHL	44	15	6	21	....	....	....	28	6	0	1	1	2
1931-32	Windsor Bulldogs	IHL	47	6	15	21	....	....	....	26	6	1	0	1	2
1932-33	Windsor Bulldogs	IHL	44	6	5	11	....	....	....	26	6	0	2	2	4
1933-34	Windsor Bulldogs	IHL	32	0	1	1	....	....	....	0	....	....	....	....	....
1934-35	Windsor Bulldogs	IHL	1	0	0	0	....	....	....	0	....	....	....	....	....
	NHL Totals		**48**	**8**	**2**	**10**	**15**	**10**	**25**	**18**	**2**	**0**	**0**	**0**	**0**

OHA-Jr. First All-Star Team (1916) • OHA-Sr. First All-Star Team (1919) • OHA-Sr. Second All-Star Team (1921)

Signed as a free agent by **Detroit** (AHA), November 10, 1926. Signed as a free agent by **NY Rangers** after **Detroit** (AHA) franchise folded, December 23, 1926. Traded to **Detroit** by **NY Rangers** for Harry Meeking and Archie Briden, October 10, 1927. Traded to **Montreal Canadiens** (Windsor-Can-Pro) by **Detroit** for cash and the loan of Pete Palangio, February 13, 1928.

• BROWN, Wayne

Wayne Hewitson "Weiner"
RW – L. 5'8", 150 lbs. b: Deloro, Ont., 11/16/1930.

Season	Club	League	GP	G	A	Pts	AG	AA	APts	PIM	GP	G	A	Pts	PIM
1948-49	St. Catharines Teepees	OHA-Jr.	46	9	13	22	....	....	....	35	5	0	1	1	0
1949-50	St. Catharines Teepees	OHA-Jr.	47	23	17	40	....	....	....	58	5	0	0	0	0
1950-51	St. Catharines Teepees	OHA-Jr.	51	29	23	52	....	....	....	80	9	5	3	8	12

			REGULAR SEASON								PLAYOFFS				
Season	Club	League	GP	G	A	Pts	AG	AA	APts	PIM	GP	G	A	Pts	PIM
1951-52	Tacoma Rockets	PCHL	70	28	30	58				36	6	1	0	1	2
1952-53	Tacoma Rockets	WHL	70	27	24	51				37					
1953-54	Seattle Bombers	WHL	70	*49	32	81				24					
	Boston Bruins	NHL									4	0	0	0	2
1954-55	Victoria Cougars	WHL	3	1	1	2				2					
1955-56	Victoria Cougars	WHL	70	21	26	47				25	9	3	2	5	0
1956-57	Victoria Cougars	WHL	70	27	30	57				14	3	1	1	2	2
1957-58	Belleville McFarlands	EOHL	48	26	24	50				22	13	10	7	17	14
	Belleville McFarlands	Al-Cup	14	*9	7	16				2					
1958-59	Belleville McFarlands	EOHL	46	24	29	53				46					
	Canada	WEC-A	5	2	1	3				7					
1959-60	Belleville McFarlands	EOHL	48	23	28	51				6	13	3	4	7	4
1960-61	Clinton Comets	EHL	53	30	46	76				14					
1961/63			OUT OF HOCKEY – RETIRED												
1963-64	Morrisburg Combines	OSLHL	STATISTICS NOT AVAILABLE												
1964-65	Syracuse Stars	X-Games	47	34	33	67									
1965-66	Syracuse Stars	X-Games	STATISTICS NOT AVAILABLE												
1966-67	Belleville Mohawks	OHA-Sr.	35	14	20	34				24					
1967-68	Belleville Mohawks	OHA-Sr.	39	14	24	38				2					
1968-69	Belleville Mohawks	OHA-Sr.	25	8	21	29				2					
1969-70	Belleville Mohawks	OHA-Sr.	20	2	9	11				12					
1970-71	Belleville Mohawks	OHA-Sr.	STATISTICS NOT AVAILABLE												
1971-72	Belleville Quintes	OHA-Sr.	6	0	2	2				0					
1972-73	Belleville Quintes	OHA-Sr.	1	0	0	0				0					
	NHL Totals										4	0	0	0	2

NHL rights traded to **Boston** by **Seattle** (WHL) for cash, October, 1953.

• BROWNE, Cecil

LW – L. 6', 165 lbs. b: St. James, Man., 2/13/1896 d: 8/13/1985.

Season	Club	League	GP	G	A	Pts	AG	AA	APts	PIM	GP	G	A	Pts	PIM
1914-15	Winnipeg Strathconas	WJrHL	5	15	5	20				6					
1915-16	Winnipeg Strathconas	WJrHL	6	12	4	16				8					
	Winnipeg Monarchs	MHL-Sr.	1	1	1	2				6					
1916-17	Winnipeg Monarchs	MHL-Sr.	8	9	*6	15				4					
1917-18	Winnipeg Vimy	MHL-Sr.	10	7	*9	16				10					
1918-19			MILITARY SERVICE												
1919-20	Moose Jaw Maple Leafs	S-SSHL	12	20	3	23				14	2	*2	0	2	4
1920-21	Regina Victorias	S-SSHL	15	14	3	17				15	4	2	*3	5	0
1921-22	Regina Victorias	S-SSHL	6	7	2	9				2	1	*2	0	2	0
	Regina Victorias	Al-Cup	5	8	3	11				2					
1922-23	Winnipeg Winnipegs	MHL-Sr.	10	9	2	11				14					
1923-24	Selkirk Fishermen	MHL-Sr.	11	5	4	9				4	10	8	3	11	16
1924-25	Selkirk Fishermen	MHL-Sr.	12	12	2	14				10	2	0	0	0	8
1925-26	Winnipeg Maroons	CHL	25	8	2	10				40	5	2	0	2	4
1926-27	Winnipeg Maroons	AHA	35	*24	6	*30				84	3	1	0	1	6
1927-28	Chicago Black Hawks	NHL	13	2	0	2	4	0	4	4					
1928-29	Seattle Eskimos	PCHL	33	23	6	29				22	5	2	2	4	12
1929-30	Seattle Eskimos	PCHL	33	12	10	*22				36					
	NHL Totals		13	2	0	2	4	0	4	4					

Traded to **Chicago** by **Winnipeg** (AHA) with Charlie Gardiner for cash, April 8, 1927.

• BRUCE, Gordie

Arthur Gordon
LW – L. 5'11", 190 lbs. b: Ottawa, Ont., 5/9/1919 Deceased.

Season	Club	League	GP	G	A	Pts	AG	AA	APts	PIM	GP	G	A	Pts	PIM
1936-37	Ottawa Glebe Collegiate	H.S.	STATISTICS NOT AVAILABLE												
1937-38	Sudbury Frood Tigers	NBHL	1	0	0	0				4					
	Sudbury Wolves	M-Cup	4	*8	1	*9				6					
	Canada	WEC	7	3	2	5									
1938-39	North Bay Trappers	NOJHA	45	23	44	*67									
	North Bay Trappers	M-Cup	2	4	3	7				6					
1939-40	Hershey Bears	IAHL	50	10	20	30				13	5	2	3	5	6
♦1940-41	Boston Bruins	NHL	8	0	1	1	0	1	1	2	2	0	0	0	0
	Hershey Bears	AHL	46	23	19	42				39	10	*4	5	*9	6
1941-42	Boston Bruins	NHL	15	4	8	12	5	9	14	11	5	2	3	5	4
	Hershey Bears	AHL	38	19	13	32				34					
1942-43	Montreal Army	QSHL	13	14	5	19				6					
	Ottawa Commandos	QSHL									8	1	1	2	2
	Ottawa Commandos	Al-Cup	2	0	0	0				0					
1943-44	Ottawa Commandos	QSHL	8	3	3	6				10					
1944-45			MILITARY SERVICE												
1945-46	Boston Bruins	NHL	5	0	0	0	0	0	0	0					
1946-47	Hershey Bears	AHL	57	35	28	63				44	10	6	9	15	0
1947-48	Hershey Bears	AHL	67	27	25	52				32	2	1	0	1	0
1948-49	Hershey Bears	AHL	62	22	23	45				34	11	*7	9	*16	2
1949-50	Hershey Bears	AHL	58	16	21	37				31					
1950-51	Glace Bay Miners	CBMHL	59	7	10	17				52	10	*7	2	9	16
	NHL Totals		28	4	9	13	5	10	15	13	7	2	3	5	4

Signed as a free agent by **Boston**, October 24, 1939. Signed as player coach by **Glace Bay** (CBMHL), October 16, 1950.

• BRUCE, Morley

Morley Callander
D/C – R. 5'9", 170 lbs. b: North Gower, Ont., 3/7/1894 d: 11/25/1959.

Season	Club	League	GP	G	A	Pts	AG	AA	APts	PIM	GP	G	A	Pts	PIM
1913-14	Ottawa New Edinburghs	X-Games	6	2	0	2									
1914-15	Ottawa Aberdeens	X-Games	2	2	0	2									
1915-16	Ottawa New Edinburghs	OCHL	8	6	0	6				18	1	0	0	0	0
1916-17	Ottawa Munitions	OCHL	10	7	0	7				52					
1917-18	Ottawa Senators	NHL	7	0	0	0	0	0	0	0					
1918-19			MILITARY SERVICE												
1919-20	Ottawa Senators	NHL	21	1	1	2	1	3	4	2					
♦	Ottawa Senators	St-Cup	5	0	0	0				0					
♦1920-21	Ottawa Senators	NHL	21	3	1	4	4	4	8	23	2	0	0	0	2
1921-22	Ottawa Senators	NHL	22	4	1	5	5	3	8	2	1	0	0	0	0
	NHL Totals		71	8	3	11	10	10	20	27	3	0	0	0	2

Signed as a free agent by **Ottawa**, December 7, 1917.

• BRUNETEAU, Eddie

Edward H.
RW – R. 5'9", 172 lbs. b: St. Boniface, Man., 8/1/1919.

Season	Club	League	GP	G	A	Pts	AG	AA	APts	PIM	GP	G	A	Pts	PIM
1936-37	Winnipeg Rangers	MJHL	16	17	6	23				6	1	1	0	1	5
1937-38	Duluth Zephyrs	IASHL	27	*26	11	37				10					
1938-39	Duluth Zephyrs	IASHL	10	7	1	8				6					
	Duluth Zephyrs	USHL	12	8	2	10				12					
1939-40	Omaha Knights	AHA	37	13	15	28				16	9	2	0	2	0
1940-41	Detroit Red Wings	NHL	11	1	1	2	2	1	3	2	3	0	0	0	0
	Omaha Knights	AHA	18	3	2	5				6					
	Indianapolis Capitols	AHL	13	3	4	7				6					
1941-42	Quebec Aces	QSHL	30	10	5	15				17	7	4	1	5	0
	Quebec Aces	Al-Cup	8	8	5	13				0					
1942-43	Quebec Aces	QSHL	31	20	17	37				0	6	1	2	3	0
	Quebec Aces	Al-Cup	9	9	*14	*23				4					
1943-44	Detroit Red Wings	NHL	2	0	1	1	0	1	1	0					
	Quebec Aces	QSHL	25	14	27	41				6	15	10	*16	*26	4
1944-45	Quebec Aces	QSHL	2	1	4	5				0					
	Detroit Red Wings	NHL	42	12	13	25	12	15	27	6	14	5	2	7	0
1945-46	Detroit Red Wings	NHL	46	17	12	29	20	17	37	11	4	1	0	1	0
1946-47	Detroit Red Wings	NHL	60	9	14	23	10	17	27	14	4	1	4	5	0
1947-48	Detroit Red Wings	NHL	18	1	1	2	1	1	2	2	6	0	0	0	0
	Indianapolis Capitols	AHL	42	19	19	38				16					
1948-49	Detroit Red Wings	NHL	1	0	0	0	0	0	0	0					
	Indianapolis Capitols	AHL	61	20	18	38				16	2	0	0	0	0
1949-50	Omaha Knights	USHL	69	43	40	83				16	7	5	3	8	0
1950-51	Omaha Knights	USHL	56	39	27	66				10	10	6	5	*11	0
1951-52	Indianapolis Capitols	AHL	56	20	21	41				0					
1952-53	Milwaukee Clarks	IHL	43	23	28	51				2					
1953-54	Sherbrooke Saints	QHL	71	4	35	39				4	5	2	3	5	0
	NHL Totals		180	40	42	82	45	52	97	35	31	7	6	13	0

• Brother of Mud • USHL Second All-Star Team (1950, 1951) • IHL Second All-Star Team (1953)

Traded to **Detroit** by **Duluth** (USHL) for cash, October 2, 1939. Signed as a free agent by **Quebec** (QSHL), November 13, 1941. Traded to **Detroit** by **Quebec** (QSHL) for Bob Thorpe, November 16, 1944.

• BRUNETEAU, Mud

Modere Fernand
RW – R. 5'11", 185 lbs. b: St. Boniface, Man., 11/28/1914 d: 4/15/1982.

Season	Club	League	GP	G	A	Pts	AG	AA	APts	PIM	GP	G	A	Pts	PIM
1931-32	Winnipeg K of C	WJrHL	9	2	2	4				4					
1932-33	Winnipeg K of C	WJrHL	11	4	4	8				10	3	3	0	3	2
1933-34	Winnipeg Falcons	MHL-Sr.	15	13	4	17				11	1	1	0	1	0
1934-35	Detroit Olympics	IHL	38	10	6	16				26	5	0	2	2	0
	Detroit Olympics	L-W-S	3	0	0	0				0					
♦1935-36	Detroit Red Wings	NHL	24	2	0	2	4	0	4	2	7	2	2	4	4
	Detroit Olympics	IHL	23	8	9	17				17					
♦1936-37	Detroit Red Wings	NHL	42	9	7	16	15	13	28	18	10	2	0	2	6
1937-38	Detroit Red Wings	NHL	24	3	6	9	5	10	15	16					
	Pittsburgh Hornets	IAHL	4	1	4	5				2	2	1	0	1	2
1938-39	Detroit Red Wings	NHL	20	3	7	10	5	11	16	0	6	0	0	0	0
1939-40	Detroit Red Wings	NHL	48	10	14	24	17	22	39	10	5	3	2	5	0
1940-41	Detroit Red Wings	NHL	45	11	17	28	17	24	41	12	9	2	1	3	2
	Pittsburgh Hornets	AHL	4	1	4	5				2					
1941-42	Detroit Red Wings	NHL	48	14	19	33	19	23	42	8	12	5	1	6	6
♦1942-43	Detroit Red Wings	NHL	50	23	22	45	24	21	45	2	9	5	4	9	0
1943-44	Detroit Red Wings	NHL	39	35	18	53	32	16	48	4	5	1	2	3	2
1944-45	Detroit Red Wings	NHL	43	23	24	47	23	28	51	6	14	3	2	5	2
1945-46	Detroit Red Wings	NHL	28	6	4	10	7	6	13	2					
	Indianapolis Capitols	AHL	14	6	10	16				0	5	1	2	3	0
1946-47	Omaha Knights	USHL	16	6	4	10				2	3	0	1	1	0
1947-48	Omaha Knights	USHL	6	4	2	6				2					
1948-49	Omaha Knights	USHL	DID NOT PLAY – COACHING												
	NHL Totals		411	139	138	277	168	174	342	80	77	23	14	37	22

• Brother of Eddie

• BRYDGE, Bill

D – R. 5'9", 195 lbs. b: Renfrew, Ont., 10/22/1901 d: 11/2/1949.

Season	Club	League	GP	G	A	Pts	AG	AA	APts	PIM	GP	G	A	Pts	PIM
1921-22	Iroquois Papermakers	NOHA									4	*4	2	*6	*12
1922-23	Iroquois Papermakers	NOHA	STATISTICS NOT AVAILABLE												
1923-24	Port Arthur Bearcats	MHL-Sr.	16	2	5	7				8	2	0	0	0	2
1924-25	Port Arthur Bearcats	MHL-Sr.	20	13	4	17				9	10	7	1	8	20
1925-26	Port Arthur Bearcats	MHL-Sr.	20	9	3	12				18	3	*2	0	*2	8
	Port Arthur Bearcats	Al-Cup	6	1	1	2				16					
1926-27	Toronto Pats/Leafs	NHL	41	6	3	9	11	16	27	76					
1927-28	Detroit Olympics	Can-Pro	41	5	4	9				91	2	0	0	0	8
1928-29	Detroit Cougars	NHL	31	2	2	4	6	13	19	59	2	0	0	0	4
	Detroit Olympics	Can-Pro	12	6	0	6				24					
1929-30	New York Americans	NHL	41	2	6	8	3	14	17	64					
1930-31	New York Americans	NHL	43	2	5	7	4	15	19	70					
1931-32	New York Americans	NHL	48	2	8	10	3	18	21	77					
1932-33	New York Americans	NHL	48	4	15	19	7	31	38	60					
1933-34	New York Americans	NHL	48	6	7	13	10	15	25	44					
1934-35	New York Americans	NHL	47	2	6	8	3	10	13	29					
1935-36	New York Americans	NHL	21	0	0	0	0	0	0	27					
	NHL Totals		368	26	52	78	47	132	179	506	2	0	0	0	4

• Regular season totals unavailable for Iroquois Falls (NOHA) in 1921-22. Signed as a free agent by **Toronto St. Pats**, October 13, 1926. Traded to **Detroit Cougars** by **Toronto** for Art Duncan, May 16, 1927. Traded to **NY Americans** by **Detroit** for $5,000, November 22, 1929.

• BRYDSON, Glenn

"Swampy"
RW – R. 5'10", 170 lbs. b: Swansea, Ont., 11/7/1910 Deceased.

Season	Club	League	GP	G	A	Pts	AG	AA	APts	PIM	GP	G	A	Pts	PIM
1926-27	Toronto Canoe Club	OHA-Jr.	2	1	0	1									
1927-28	Toronto Canoe Club	OHA-Jr.	9	3	0	3					3	*3	0	3	
1928-29	Toronto Canoe Club	OHA-Jr.	9	5	1	6					3	5	0	5	
1929-30	Montreal AAA	MCHL	10	3	0	3				12	2	0	0	0	4
1930-31	Montreal AAA	MCHL	11	5	*4	*9				22					
	Montreal Maroons	NHL	14	0	0	0	0	0	0	4	2	0	0	0	0
1931-32	Montreal Maroons	NHL	47	12	13	25	20	29	49	44	4	0	0	0	4

Season	Club	League	GP	G	A	Pts	AG	AA	APts	PIM	GP	G	A	Pts	PIM
			REGULAR SEASON								PLAYOFFS				
1932-33	**Montreal Maroons**	**NHL**	**48**	**11**	**17**	**28**	**20**	**35**	**55**	**26**	**2**	**0**	**0**	**0**	**0**
1933-34	**Montreal Maroons**	**NHL**	**37**	**4**	**5**	**9**	**7**	**10**	**17**	**19**	**1**	**0**	**0**	**0**	**0**
	Windsor Bulldogs	IHL	2	1	1	2	....	....	....	0	....	....	....	....	....
1934-35	**St. Louis Eagles**	**NHL**	**48**	**11**	**18**	**29**	**18**	**31**	**49**	**45**	....	....	....	....	....
1935-36	**New York Rangers**	**NHL**	**30**	**4**	**12**	**16**	**8**	**23**	**31**	**7**	....	....	....	....	....
	Chicago Black Hawks	**NHL**	**22**	**6**	**4**	**10**	**11**	**8**	**19**	**32**	**2**	**0**	**0**	**0**	**4**
1936-37	**Chicago Black Hawks**	**NHL**	**34**	**7**	**7**	**14**	**12**	**13**	**25**	**20**	....	....	....	....	....
1937-38	**Chicago Black Hawks**	**NHL**	**19**	**1**	**3**	**4**	**2**	**5**	**7**	**6**	....	....	....	....	....
	New Haven Eagles	IAHL	25	6	9	15	....	....	....	17	2	0	0	0	*12
1938-39	New Haven Eagles	IAHL	51	8	25	33	....	....	....	18	....	....	....	....	....
1939-40	New Haven Eagles	IAHL	34	5	14	19	....	....	....	17	....	....	....	....	....
	Indianapolis Capitols	IAHL	5	4	2	6	....	....	....	2	....	....	....	....	....
1940-41	Springfield Indians	AHL	54	20	36	56	....	....	....	28	3	1	2	3	0
1941-42	Pittsburgh Hornets	AHL	45	8	17	25	....	....	....	2	....	....	....	....	....
1942-43	Kingston Frontenacs	OHA-Sr.	2	1	3	4	....	....	....	0	4	1	3	4	2
	NHL Totals		**299**	**56**	**79**	**135**	**98**	**154**	**252**	**203**	**11**	**0**	**0**	**0**	**8**

• Brother of Gord

Signed as a free agent by **Montreal Maroons**, February 4, 1931. Traded to **Ottawa** by **Montreal Maroons** to complete transaction that sent Alex Connell to Montreal (October 2, 1934), October 22, 1934. Transferred to **St. Louis** after **Ottawa** franchise relocated, September 22, 1934. Claimed by **NY Rangers** from **St. Louis** in Dispersal Draft, October 15, 1935. Traded to **Chicago** by **NY Rangers** for Howie Morenz, January 26, 1936. Traded to **NY Americans** (New Haven-AHL) by **Chicago** for cash, January 9, 1938. Traded to **Toronto** (Pittsburgh-AHL) by **NY Americans** with Viv Allen for Phil McAtee and the return of Peanuts O'Flaherty (previously on loan), October 8, 1941.

• BRYDSON, Gord

C/RW – R. 5'7", 150 lbs. b: Toronto, Ont., 1/3/1907.

Season	Club	League	GP	G	A	Pts	AG	AA	APts	PIM	GP	G	A	Pts	PIM
1923-24	Toronto Canoe Club	OHA-Jr.	8	1	3	4	....	....	....	8	....	....	....	....	....
1924-25	Toronto Canoe Club	OHA-Jr.	8	*11	*8	*19	....	....	....	....	2	1	1	2	....
1925-26	Toronto Canoe Club	OHA-Jr.	9	13	2	15	....	....	....	....	....	....	....	....	....
	Toronto Canoe Club	OHA-Sr.	1	0	0	0	....	....	....	0	....	....	....	....	....
1926-27	Chicago Cardinals	AHA	32	10	3	13	....	....	....	23	....	....	....	....	....
1927-28	Hamilton Tigers	Can-Pro	42	30	3	33	....	....	....	59	....	....	....	....	....
1928-29	Buffalo Bisons	Can-Pro	42	18	5	23	....	....	....	42	....	....	....	....	....
1929-30	**Toronto Maple Leafs**	**NHL**	**8**	**2**	**0**	**2**	**3**	**0**	**3**	**8**	....	....	....	....	....
	London Panthers	IHL	32	18	8	26	....	....	....	8	2	1	0	1	2
1930-31	Chicago Shamrocks	AHA	47	*35	12	*47	....	....	....	54	....	....	....	....	....
1931-32	Chicago Shamrocks	AHA	46	9	9	18	....	....	....	35	3	2	1	3	0
1932-33	Detroit Olympics	IHL	41	4	14	18	....	....	....	57	....	....	....	....	....
	NHL Totals		**8**	**2**	**0**	**2**	**3**	**0**	**3**	**8**	....	....	....	....	....

• Brother of Glenn

Rights awarded to **Stratford** (Can-Pro) by NHL President Frank Calder, October 14, 1927. Traded to **Hamilton** (Can-Pro) by **Stratford** (Can-Pro) for Dutch Cain, October 27, 1927. Traded to **Buffalo** (Can-Pro) by **Hamilton** (Can-Pro) for cash, October 25, 1928. Traded to **Toronto** by **Buffalo** (IHL) for Carl Voss and Wes King, October 10, 1929. Traded to **London** (IHL) by **Toronto** for cash, December 6, 1929. Signed as a free agent by **Chicago** (AHA), November 4, 1930. Traded to **Detroit** (IHL) by **Chicago** (AHA) for cash, October 6, 1932.

• BUCHANAN, Al

Allaster William

LW – L. 5'8", 160 lbs. b: Winnipeg, Man., 5/17/1927 Deceased.

Season	Club	League	GP	G	A	Pts	AG	AA	APts	PIM	GP	G	A	Pts	PIM
1944-45	Winnipeg Monarchs	MJHL	6	5	5	10	....	....	....	0	6	5	2	7	4
	Winnipeg Monarchs	M-Cup	10	4	2	6	....	....	....	4	....	....	....	....	....
1945-46	Winnipeg Monarchs	MJHL	9	7	0	7	....	....	....	0	7	2	1	3	0
	Winnipeg Monarchs	M-Cup	17	6	4	10	....	....	....	14	....	....	....	....	....
1946-47	Winnipeg Monarchs	MJHL	15	16	9	25	....	....	....	11	6	1	4	5	7
1947-48	Toronto Marlboros	OHA-Jr.	34	22	24	46	....	....	....	0	5	0	0	0	0
1948-49	**Toronto Maple Leafs**	**NHL**	**3**	**0**	**1**	**1**	**0**	**1**	**1**	**2**	....	....	....	....	....
	Toronto Marlboros	OHA-Sr.	37	21	16	37	....	....	....	33	10	1	3	4	*26
	Toronto Marlboros	Al-Cup	13	3	8	11	....	....	....	15	....	....	....	....	....
1949-50	**Toronto Maple Leafs**	**NHL**	**1**	**0**	**0**	**0**	**0**	**0**	**0**	**0**	....	....	....	....	....
	Toronto Marlboros	OHA-Sr.	35	21	24	45	....	....	....	21	14	*7	4	11	4
	Toronto Marlboros	Al-Cup	16	10	11	21	....	....	....	2	....	....	....	....	....
1950-51	Toronto Marlboros	OMHL	32	14	19	33	....	....	....	25	3	1	1	2	2
1951-52	Saint John Beavers	MMHL	77	21	33	54	....	....	....	44	3	1	1	2	0
1952-53	Kitchener Dutchmen	OHA-Sr.	46	20	21	41	....	....	....	24	11	1	2	3	8
	Kitchener Dutchmen	Al-Cup	17	3	9	12	....	....	....	11	....	....	....	....	....
1953-54			OUT OF HOCKEY – RETIRED												
1954-55	Niagara Falls Cataracts	OHA-Sr.	36	8	10	18	....	....	....	10	....	....	....	....	....
	NHL Totals		**4**	**0**	**1**	**1**	**0**	**1**	**1**	**2**	....	....	....	....	....

Signed as a free agent by **Saint John** (MMHL), September 17, 1951.

• BUCHANAN, Bucky

Ralph Leonard

C/RW – R. 5'9", 172 lbs. b: Bout De L'Isle, Que., 12/28/1922.

Season	Club	League	GP	G	A	Pts	AG	AA	APts	PIM	GP	G	A	Pts	PIM
1940-41	Montreal Jr. Canadiens	QJHL	7	1	3	4	....	....	....	6	3	2	2	4	0
1941-42	Montreal Jr. Canadiens	QJHL	STATISTICS NOT AVAILABLE												
1942-43	Montreal Jr. Royals	QJHL	15	8	6	14	....	....	....	8	....	....	....	....	....
	Montreal Navy	MNDHL	10	4	7	11	....	....	....	11	5	3	2	5	2
	Toronto Navy	OHA-Sr.	....	....	....	....	....	....	....	....	2	0	2	2	2
1943-44	Montreal Navy	MNDHL	15	10	8	18	....	....	....	10	4	*7	4	11	4
1944-45	Montreal Navy	MNDHL	13	*17	13	30	....	....	....	10	5	4	6	10	2
1945-46	San Francisco Shamrocks	PCHL	40	*50	25	75	....	....	....	27	....	....	....	....	....
1946-47	San Francisco Shamrocks	PCHL	57	*66	27	93	....	....	....	45	....	....	....	....	....
1947-48	Shawinigan Cataracts	QSHL	47	43	35	78	....	....	....	23	7	4	1	5	2
1948-49	Shawinigan Cataracts	QSHL	33	21	25	46	....	....	....	8	7	2	3	5	12
	New York Rangers	**NHL**	**2**	**0**	**0**	**0**	**0**	**0**	**0**	**0**	....	....	....	....	....
1949-50	Shawinigan Cataracts	QSHL	60	36	49	85	....	....	....	2	....	....	....	....	....
1950-51	Shawinigan Cataracts	QMHL	52	28	36	64	....	....	....	30	....	....	....	....	....
1951-52	Shawinigan Cataracts	QMHL	59	23	33	56	....	....	....	0	....	....	....	....	....
1952-53	Chicoutimi Sagueneens	QMHL	60	31	42	73	....	....	....	33	20	9	6	15	4
1953-54	Chicoutimi Sagueneens	QHL	63	29	34	63	....	....	....	18	7	2	2	4	2
1954-55	Quebec Aces	QHL	55	11	31	42	....	....	....	12	8	1	5	6	8
1955-56	Quebec Aces	QHL	52	10	17	27	....	....	....	2	7	3	0	3	2
1956-57	Quebec Aces	QHL	17	1	6	7	....	....	....	8	....	....	....	....	....
	Kingston CKLC's	OHA-Sr.	30	26	22	48	....	....	....	12	5	2	2	4	0
1957-58	Pembroke Lumber Kings	EOHL	29	11	14	25	....	....	....	14	....	....	....	....	....
	NHL Totals		**2**	**0**	**0**	**0**	**0**	**0**	**0**	**0**	....	....	....	....	....

• Father of Ron • QSHL First All-Star Team (1948, 1950) • Won Vimy Trophy (MVP - QSHL) (1948, 1950) • QMHL First All-Star Team (1951) • QMHL Second All-Star Team (1952) • QHL First All-Star Team (1953)

Traded to **Chicoutimi** (QMHL) by **Shawinigan** (QMHL) for cash, September 25, 1952. Traded to **Quebec** (QHL) by **Chicoutimi** (QHL) for cash, September 3, 1954.

• BUCHANAN, Mike

D – L. 6'1", 185 lbs. b: Sault Ste. Marie, Ont., 3/1/1932.

Season	Club	League	GP	G	A	Pts	AG	AA	APts	PIM	GP	G	A	Pts	PIM
1947-48	Ottawa St. Pats	OCJHL	20	3	9	12	....	....	....	6	2	0	0	0	0
1948-49	St. Michael's Majors	OHA-Jr.	16	0	0	0	....	....	....	14	....	....	....	....	....
1949-50	Guelph–Galt	OHA-Jr.	42	2	4	6	....	....	....	65	....	....	....	....	....
1950-51	Galt Black Hawks	OHA-Jr.	52	6	15	21	....	....	....	86	3	0	3	3	7
1951-52	Galt Black Hawks	OHA-Jr.	46	15	25	40	....	....	....	98	3	0	1	1	4
	Chicago Black Hawks	**NHL**	**1**	**0**	**0**	**0**	**0**	**0**	**0**	**0**	....	....	....	....	....
	St. Louis Flyers	AHL	2	0	0	0	....	....	....	0	....	....	....	....	....
1952-53	Fort Wayne Komets	IHL	43	2	6	8	....	....	....	80	....	....	....	....	....
1953-54	Fort Wayne Komets	IHL	39	1	10	11	....	....	....	62	....	....	....	....	....
1954-55	University of Michigan	WCHA	....	3	7	10	....	....	....	48	....	....	....	....	....
1955-56	University of Michigan	WCHA	....	0	1	1	....	....	....	18	....	....	....	....	....
1956-57			DID NOT PLAY												
1957-58	Wembley Lions	Britain	22	2	7	9	....	....	....	32	....	....	....	....	....
	Wembley Lions	Nat-Tmt	2	1	0	1	....	....	....	0	....	....	....	....	....
	NHL Totals		**1**	**0**	**0**	**0**	**0**	**0**	**0**	**0**	....	....	....	....	....

NCAA West First All-American Team (1955)

• BUCHANAN, Ron

— see page 935

• BUCYK, John

— see page 936

• BUKOVICH, Tony

LW/C – L. 5'11", 160 lbs. b: Painesdale, MI, 8/30/1917.

Season	Club	League	GP	G	A	Pts	AG	AA	APts	PIM	GP	G	A	Pts	PIM
1939-40	Painesdale Pontiac Chiefs	MOHL	24	16	*17	33	....	....	....	....	....	....	....	....	....
1940-41	Painesdale Pontiac Chiefs	MOHL	STATISTICS NOT AVAILABLE												
1941-42	Fort Worth Rangers	AHA	47	1	4	5	....	....	....	6	5	0	0	0	0
1942-43	Windsor Colonial Tools	MOHL	7	10	6	16	....	....	....	2	7	10	*13	23	4
1943-44	**Detroit Red Wings**	**NHL**	**3**	**0**	**1**	**1**	**0**	**1**	**1**	**0**	....	....	....	....	....
	Indianapolis Capitols	AHL	6	1	0	1	....	....	....	5	....	....	....	....	....
1944-45	**Detroit Red Wings**	**NHL**	**14**	**7**	**2**	**9**	**7**	**2**	**9**	**6**	**6**	**0**	**1**	**1**	**0**
	Indianapolis Capitols	AHL	32	22	18	40	....	....	....	43	....	....	....	....	....
1945-46	Indianapolis Capitols	AHL	59	25	28	53	....	....	....	68	5	2	3	5	2
1946-47	Indianapolis Capitols	AHL	49	20	23	43	....	....	....	43	....	....	....	....	....
1947-48	Cleveland Barons	AHL	7	4	2	6	....	....	....	2	3	1	1	2	4
	Minneapolis Millers	USHL	10	4	4	8	....	....	....	11	....	....	....	....	....
	NHL Totals		**17**	**7**	**3**	**10**	**7**	**3**	**10**	**6**	**6**	**0**	**1**	**1**	**0**

• BULLER, Hy

"The Blueline Blaster"

D – L. 5'11", 183 lbs. b: Montreal, Que., 3/15/1926 Deceased.

Season	Club	League	GP	G	A	Pts	AG	AA	APts	PIM	GP	G	A	Pts	PIM
1941-42	Saskatoon Quakers	N-SJHL	8	3	5	8	....	....	....	*27	6	6	2	8	*28
	Saskatoon Quakers	M-Cup	3	1	1	2	....	....	....	*14	....	....	....	....	....
1942-43	New York Rovers	EAHL	41	11	14	25	....	....	....	61	9	1	2	3	14
1943-44	**Detroit Red Wings**	**NHL**	**7**	**0**	**3**	**3**	**0**	**3**	**3**	**4**	....	....	....	....	....
	Indianapolis Capitols	AHL	46	6	12	18	....	....	....	51	5	2	1	3	2
1944-45	**Detroit Red Wings**	**NHL**	**2**	**0**	**0**	**0**	**0**	**0**	**0**	**2**	....	....	....	....	....
	Hershey Bears	AHL	41	5	17	22	....	....	....	44	11	1	2	3	6
1945-46	Hershey Bears	AHL	59	8	19	27	....	....	....	61	3	0	0	0	2
1946-47	Hershey Bears	AHL	63	12	32	44	....	....	....	56	11	3	3	6	8
1947-48	Hershey Bears	AHL	31	5	12	17	....	....	....	31	....	....	....	....	....
	Cleveland Barons	AHL	36	10	21	31	....	....	....	55	8	1	2	3	2
1948-49	Cleveland Barons	AHL	62	7	30	37	....	....	....	44	5	0	7	7	6
1949-50	Cleveland Barons	AHL	43	10	19	29	....	....	....	32	9	0	3	3	10
1950-51	Cleveland Barons	AHL	66	16	41	57	....	....	....	31	11	1	4	5	11
1951-52	**New York Rangers**	**NHL**	**68**	**12**	**23**	**35**	**16**	**28**	**44**	**96**	....	....	....	....	....
1952-53	**New York Rangers**	**NHL**	**70**	**7**	**18**	**25**	**9**	**22**	**31**	**73**	....	....	....	....	....
1953-54	**New York Rangers**	**NHL**	**41**	**3**	**14**	**17**	**4**	**17**	**21**	**40**	....	....	....	....	....
	Saskatoon Quakers	WHL	27	4	10	14	....	....	....	36	6	0	3	3	2
	NHL Totals		**188**	**22**	**58**	**80**	**29**	**70**	**99**	**215**	....	....	....	....	....

EAHL Second All-Star Team (1943) • AHL First All-Star Team (1949, 1951) • NHL Second All-Star Team (1952) • Played in NHL All-Star Game (1952)

Claimed on waivers by **Hershey** (AHL) from **Detroit**, October 22, 1944. Traded to **Cleveland** (AHL) by **Hershey** (AHL) for Babe Pratt and Joe Cooper, December 24, 1947. Traded to **NY Rangers** by **Cleveland** (AHL) with Wally Hergesheimer for Ed Reigle, Jackie Gordon, Fred Shero, Fern Perreault and cash, May 14, 1951. Traded to **Montreal** (Victoria-WHL) by **NY Rangers** for Dick Gamble and the rights to Eddie Dorohoy, June 8, 1954. Transaction voided when Buller decided to retire.

• BURCH, Billy

Harry Wilfred HHOF

C/LW – L. 6', 200 lbs. b: Yonkers, N.Y., 11/20/1900 d: 11/30/1950.

Season	Club	League	GP	G	A	Pts	AG	AA	APts	PIM	GP	G	A	Pts	PIM
1919-20	Toronto Canoe Club	OHA-Jr.	....	....	....	....	....	....	....	....	12	*42	*12	*54	....
1920-21	Toronto Aura Lee	OHA-Jr.	10	12	2	14	....	....	....	....	....	....	....	....	....
1921-22	Toronto Aura Lee	OHA-Jr.	9	13	*10	*23	....	....	....	....	2	2	1	3	....
1922-23	New Haven Westminsters	USAHA	....	4	0	4	....	....	....	....	....	....	....	....	....
	Hamilton Tigers	**NHL**	**10**	**6**	**3**	**9**	**10**	**11**	**21**	**4**	....	....	....	....	....
1923-24	**Hamilton Tigers**	**NHL**	**24**	**16**	**6**	**22**	**34**	**36**	**70**	**6**	....	....	....	....	....
1924-25	**Hamilton Tigers**	**NHL**	**27**	**20**	**7**	**27**	**35**	**29**	**64**	**10**	....	....	....	....	....
1925-26	**New York Americans**	**NHL**	**36**	**22**	**3**	**25**	**39**	**19**	**58**	**33**	....	....	....	....	....
1926-27	**New York Americans**	**NHL**	**43**	**19**	**8**	**27**	**34**	**42**	**76**	**40**	....	....	....	....	....
1927-28	**New York Americans**	**NHL**	**32**	**10**	**2**	**12**	**20**	**11**	**31**	**34**	....	....	....	....	....
1928-29	**New York Americans**	**NHL**	**44**	**11**	**5**	**16**	**32**	**33**	**65**	**45**	**2**	**0**	**0**	**0**	**0**
1929-30	**New York Americans**	**NHL**	**35**	**7**	**3**	**10**	**10**	**7**	**17**	**22**	....	....	....	....	....
1930-31	**New York Americans**	**NHL**	**44**	**14**	**8**	**22**	**28**	**24**	**52**	**35**	....	....	....	....	....

			REGULAR SEASON								PLAYOFFS				
Season	Club	League	GP	G	A	Pts	AG	AA	APts	PIM	GP	G	A	Pts	PIM
1931-32	New York Americans	NHL	48	7	15	22	12	33	45	20					
1932-33	Boston Bruins	NHL	23	3	1	4	5	2	7	4					
	Chicago Black Hawks	NHL	24	2	0	2	4	0	4	2					
	NHL Totals		390	137	61	198	263	247	510	255	2	0	0	0	0

Won Hart Trophy (1925) • Won Lady Byng Trophy (1927)

Signed as a free agent by **Hamilton**, January 30, 1923. Transferred to **NY Americans** after NHL club purchased **Hamilton** franchise, September 25, 1925. Traded to **Boston** by **NY Americans** for cash, April 13, 1932. Traded to **Chicago** by **Boston** for Vic Ripley, January 17, 1933.

• BURCHELL, Fred Frederick "Skippy"

C – L. 5'6", 143 lbs. b: Montreal, Que., 1/9/1931 d: 6/4/1998.

Season	Club	League	GP	G	A	Pts	AG	AA	APts	PIM	GP	G	A	Pts	PIM
1947-48	Montreal Jr. Royals	QJHL	2	3	0	3				0	10	1	5	6	0
1948-49	Montreal Jr. Royals	QJHL	47	10	25	35				15	10	4	6	10	7
	Montreal Jr. Royals	M-Cup	15	4	8	12				12					
1949-50	Montreal Jr. Royals	QJHL	1	0	1	1				0					
	Montreal Royals	QSHL	2	0	0	0				0					
	Laval Nationals	QJHL	34	22	*54	76				47	7	4	5	9	4
1950-51	Montreal Nationales	QJHL	45	48	*76	*124				46	3	0	1	1	6
	Montreal Canadiens	NHL	2	0	0	0	0	0	0	0					
1951-52	Johnstown Jets	EAHL	56	37	56	93				71	8	2	*12	*14	12
1952-53	Montreal Royals	QMHL	52	18	38	56				41	11	0	0	0	9
1953-54	Montreal Canadiens	NHL	2	0	0	0	0	0	0	2					
	Montreal Royals	QHL	66	31	59	90				34	11	2	8	10	6
1954-55	Montreal Royals	QHL	61	19	41	60				50	13	2	2	4	6
1955-56	Montreal Royals	QHL	5	1	3	4				4					
	Winnipeg Warriors	WHL	61	11	47	58				48	14	7	*12	19	8
	Winnipeg Warriors	Ed-Cup	6	1	*10	*11				6					
1956-57	Winnipeg Warriors	WHL	66	17	40	57				22					
1957-58	Rochester Americans	AHL	70	20	40	60				65					
1958-59	Montreal Royals	QHL	59	11	41	52				31	8	*7	2	9	4
1959-60	Montreal Royals	EPHL	67	12	58	70				44	13	7	8	15	2
1960-61	Montreal Royals	EPHL	68	13	61	74				12					
1961-62	Quebec Aces	AHL	67	21	57	78				14					
1962-63	Quebec Aces	AHL	69	17	55	72				12					
1963-64	Quebec Aces	AHL	58	4	30	34				10	8	1	2	3	0
1964-65	Verdun Pirates	QSHL	STATISTICS NOT AVAILABLE												
	Sherbrooke Castors	Al-Cup	15	6	17	23				2					
1965-66	Jersey Devils	EHL	2	1	0	1				2					
	St-Hyacinthe Saints	QSHL	32	10	31	41				6	12	6	11	*17	2
	NHL Totals		4	0	0	0	0	0	0	2					

QJHL Second All-Star Team (1950, 1951) • EAHL First All-Star Team (1952) • QHL First All-Star Team (1954)

Traded to **Chicago** by **Montreal** for Max Quackenbush, July 3, 1955. Transaction voided when Quackenbush officially announced retirement, July 15, 1955.

• BUREGA, Bill William

D – L. 6', 195 lbs. b: Winnipeg, Man., 3/13/1932.

Season	Club	League	GP	G	A	Pts	AG	AA	APts	PIM	GP	G	A	Pts	PIM
1948-49	Winnipeg Cubs	MAHA	STATISTICS NOT AVAILABLE												
1949-50	Winnipeg Monarchs	MJHL	28	3	2	5				45	12	0	4	4	16
	Winnipeg Monarchs	M-Cup	19	2	3	5				52					
1950-51	Winnipeg Monarchs	MJHL	36	10	11	21				59	10	1	3	4	*27
	Winnipeg Monarchs	M-Cup	19	2	3	5				*52					
1951-52	Winnipeg Canadians	MJHL	36	4	8	12				111	5	1	1	2	17
	Winnipeg Canadians	M-Cup	6	0	0	0				16					
	Winnipeg Monarchs	M-Cup	6	0	0	0				16					
1952-53	Glace Bay Miners	MMHL	72	6	10	16				*163	8	0	1	1	16
1953-54	Pittsburgh Hornets	AHL	5	0	1	1				4					
	Ottawa–Quebec	QHL	41	0	5	5				115	7	0	0	0	0
	Quebec Aces	Alx-Cup	6	0	2	2				2					
1954-55	Pittsburgh Hornets	AHL	57	2	5	7				140	10	0	2	2	*24
1955-56	Toronto Maple Leafs	NHL	4	0	1	1	0	1	1	4					
	Winnipeg Warriors	WHL	67	2	18	20				151	14	2	4	6	*33
	Winnipeg Warriors	Ed-Cup	6	1	1	2				12					
1956-57	Winnipeg Warriors	WHL	70	1	14	15				197					
1957-58	Buffalo Bisons	AHL	56	0	7	7				136					
1958-59	Saskatoon Quakers	WHL	62	2	10	12				104					
1959-60	S.S. Marie Thunderbirds	EPHL	2	0	0	0				6					
	Spokane Comets	WHL	65	4	14	18				162					
1960-61	Calgary Stampeders	WHL	67	3	32	35				73	5	1	1	2	6
1961-62	Los Angeles Blades	WHL	70	1	14	15				142					
1962-63	Los Angeles Blades	WHL	70	1	11	12				142	3	0	2	2	6
1963-64	Los Angeles Blades	WHL	51	0	7	7				75	12	0	3	3	31
1964-65	Vancouver Canucks	WHL	70	3	10	13				161	5	0	1	1	10
1965-66	Kingston Aces	OHA-Sr.	12	1	10	11				49					
	Guelph Regals	Al-Cup	6	0	5	5				16					
1966-67	Kingston Aces	OHA-Sr.	38	4	19	23				84					
1967-68	Kingston Aces	OHA-Sr.	40	1	14	15				86					
1968-69	Kingston Aces	OHA-Sr.	1	0	0	0				6					
1969-70	Kingston Aces	OHA-Sr.	25	1	9	10				61					
	NHL Totals		4	0	1	1	0	1	1	4					

OHA-Sr. First All-Star Team (1967) • OHA-Sr. Second All-Star Team (1970)

Signed as a free agent by **Toronto** (Pittsburgh-AHL), September 28, 1953. Claimed by **Buffalo** (AHL) from **Toronto** (Winnipeg-WHL) in Inter-League Draft, June 4, 1957.

• BURKE, Eddie Edmund George "Shanty"

RW/C – R. 5'8", 175 lbs. b: Toronto, Ont., 6/3/1907 Deceased.

Season	Club	League	GP	G	A	Pts	AG	AA	APts	PIM	GP	G	A	Pts	PIM
1921-22	Toronto St. Mary's	OHA-Jr.	STATISTICS NOT AVAILABLE												
1922-23	Toronto St. Mary's	OHA-Jr.	6	5	*3	8					7	*7	1	*8	
1923-24	Toronto St. Mary's	OHA-Jr.	8	7	4	11				21					
1924-25	S.S. Marie Greyhounds	NOHA	STATISTICS NOT AVAILABLE												
1925-26	S.S. Marie Greyhounds	CHL	26	1	0	1				16					
1926-27	Toronto Marlboros	OHA-Sr.	STATISTICS NOT AVAILABLE												
1927-28	Boston Tigers	Can-Am	39	12	1	13				54	2	1	0	1	4
1928-29	Boston Tigers	Can-Am	34	3	3	6				55	4	1	0	1	4
1929-30	Boston Tigers	Can-Am	40	14	9	23				60	5	0	0	0	4
1930-31	Boston Tigers	Can-Am	40	20	18	38				60	9	4	3	7	12
1931-32	Boston Bruins	NHL	16	3	0	3	5	0	5	12					
	Boston Tigers	Can-Am	28	9	5	14				47	5	2	1	3	5
1932-33	Philadelphia Arrows	Can-Am	21	9	11	20				28					
	New York Americans	NHL	15	2	0	2	4	0	4	4					
1933-34	New York Americans	NHL	46	20	10	30	35	21	56	24					
1934-35	New York Americans	NHL	29	4	10	14	7	17	24	15					
1935-36	Syracuse Stars	IHL	47	11	32	43				18	3	1	1	2	2
1936-37	Buffalo Bisons	IAHL	1	0	0	0				2					
	Syracuse Stars	IAHL	21	0	7	7				9					
	NHL Totals		106	29	20	49	51	38	89	55					

Traded to **Boston** by **Boston** (Can-Am) for cash, November 4, 1931. Traded to **Philadelphia** (Can-Am) by **Boston** for Sheldon Buckles, Connie King and Frank Ingram, November, 1932. Traded to **NY Americans** by **Philadelphia** (Can-Am) for Hub Wilson and Norm Clooings, February 11, 1933.

• BURKE, Marty Marty Alphonsus

D – L. 5'8", 160 lbs. b: Toronto, Ont., 1/28/1905 d: 3/7/1968.

Season	Club	League	GP	G	A	Pts	AG	AA	APts	PIM	GP	G	A	Pts	PIM
1923-24	Toronto St. Mary's	OHA-Jr.	5	4	1	5				8					
	Toronto St. Mary's	OHA-Jr.	2	0	0	0									
1924-25	Stratford Indians	OHA-Sr.	18	1	4	5				*52	2	0	0	0	2
1925-26	Stratford Indians	OHA-Sr.	20	3	4	7				34					
1926-27	Port Arthur Ports	TBSHL	20	3	1	4				*65	2	1	0	1	*4
1927-28	Montreal Canadiens	NHL	11	0	0	0	0	0	0	10					
	Pittsburgh Pirates	NHL	35	2	1	3	4	6	10	51	2	1	0	1	2
1928-29	Montreal Canadiens	NHL	44	4	2	6	11	13	24	68	3	0	0	0	8
♦1929-30	Montreal Canadiens	NHL	44	2	11	13	3	26	29	71	6	0	1	1	6
♦1930-31	Montreal Canadiens	NHL	44	2	5	7	4	15	19	91	10	1	2	3	10
1931-32	Montreal Canadiens	NHL	48	3	6	9	5	13	18	50	4	0	0	0	12
1932-33	Montreal Canadiens	NHL	29	2	5	7	4	10	14	36					
	Ottawa Senators	NHL	16	0	0	0	0	0	0	10					
1933-34	Montreal Canadiens	NHL	45	1	4	5	2	8	10	28	2	0	1	1	2
1934-35	Chicago Black Hawks	NHL	47	2	2	4	3	3	6	29	2	0	0	0	2
1935-36	Chicago Black Hawks	NHL	40	0	3	3	0	6	6	49	2	0	0	0	2
1936-37	Chicago Black Hawks	NHL	41	1	3	4	2	5	7	28					
1937-38	Chicago Black Hawks	NHL	12	0	0	0	0	0	0	8					
	Montreal Canadiens	NHL	38	0	5	5	0	8	8	31					
1938-39	Saskatoon Quakers	N-SSHL	DID NOT PLAY – COACHING												
	NHL Totals		494	19	47	66	38	113	151	560	31	2	4	6	44

Loaned to **Pittsburgh** by **Montreal Canadiens** for remainder of 1927-28 season for the loan of Charlie Langlois, December 16, 1927. Traded to **Ottawa** by **Montreal Canadiens** with future considerations (Nick Wasnie, March 23, 1933) for Harold Starr and Leo Bourgeault, February 14, 1933. Traded to **Montreal Canadiens** by **Ottawa** for Nick Wasnie, March 23, 1933. Traded to **Chicago** by **Montreal Canadiens** with Lorne Chabot and Howie Morenz for Leroy Goldsworthy, Lionel Conacher and Roger Jenkins, October 3, 1934. Traded to **Montreal Canadiens** by **Chicago** for Bill MacKenzie, December 10, 1937.

• BURMEISTER, Roy

LW – L. 5'10", 155 lbs. b: Collingwood, Ont., 8/12/1906 Deceased.

Season	Club	League	GP	G	A	Pts	AG	AA	APts	PIM	GP	G	A	Pts	PIM
1924-25	Owen Sound Greys	X-Games	17	8	8	16									
	Owen Sound Greys	M-Cup	8	3	0	3				0					
1925-26	Niagara Falls Cataracts	OHA-Sr.	19	3	5	8				2					
1926-27	Niagara Falls Cataracts	Can-Pro	22	6	3	9				4					
1927-28	Niagara Falls Cataracts	Can-Pro	39	6	1	7				18					
1928-29	New Haven Eagles	Can-Am	35	1	1	2				8	2	0	0	0	0
1929-30	New York Americans	NHL	40	1	1	2	1	2	3	0					
	New Haven Eagles	Can-Am	6	1	1	2				40					
1930-31	New York Americans	NHL	11	0	0	0	0	0	0	0					
	New Haven Eagles	Can-Am	32	12	14	26				18					
1931-32	New Haven Eagles	Can-Am	26	9	7	16				16					
	New York Americans	NHL	16	3	2	5	5	4	9	2					
1932-33	New Haven Eagles	Can-Am	28	6	0	6				10					
	Boston Cubs	Can-Am	21	4	3	7				9	7	2	1	3	0
1933-34	Windsor–London	IHL	40	2	1	3				11					
1934-35	Philadelphia Arrows	Can-Am	48	12	22	34				13					
1935-36	St. Louis Flyers	AHA	48	14	19	33				11	8	1	*3	4	0
1936-37	St. Paul Saints	AHA	42	8	19	27				2	3	0	1	1	0
1937-38	St. Paul Saints	AHA	47	6	10	16				4					
1938-39	Kansas City Greyhounds	AHA	47	8	7	15				0					
	NHL Totals		67	4	3	7	6	6	12	2					

Traded to **Boston** (Boston-Can-Am) by **NY Americans** (New Haven-Can-Am) for Connie King, February 12, 1933. Traded to **NY Rangers** by **Boston** with Vic Ripley for Babe Siebert, December 18, 1933.

• BURNETT, Kelly James Kelvin

C – L. 5'10", 160 lbs. b: Lachine, Que., 6/16/1926.

Season	Club	League	GP	G	A	Pts	AG	AA	APts	PIM	GP	G	A	Pts	PIM
1943-44	Montreal Jr. Canadiens	QJHL	15	11	12	23				0	3	3	3	6	0
	Montreal Noordyn	MCHL	4	2	0	2				0					
1944-45	Montreal Jr. Canadiens	QJHL	13	*20	6	26				4	9	6	5	11	2
	Montreal Jr. Royals	M-Cup									6	2	2	4	0
1945-46	Barrie Flyers	OHA-Jr.	3	5	1	6				2					
	Montreal Jr. Canadiens	QJHL	12	10	6	16				2	6	4	7	11	2
	Montreal Jr. Canadiens	M-Cup	5	4	6	10				2					
1946-47	Victoriaville Tigers	QPHL	50	40	*75	*115				18	2	1	3	4	0
1947-48	Victoriaville Tigers	QPHL	50	36	*71	*107				8	11	*11	7	*18	0
	Victoriaville Tigers	Al-Cup	3	0	2	2				0					
1948-49	Sherbrooke Saints	QSHL	63	37	38	75				40	12	4	7	11	2
1949-50	Springfield Indians	AHL	67	27	49	76				14	2	0	1	1	0
1950-51	Springfield Indians	AHL	68	26	48	74				12	3	0	0	0	0
1951-52	Syracuse Warriors	AHL	68	25	43	68				12					
1952-53	Syracuse Warriors	AHL	56	23	53	76				16	4	1	3	4	0
	New York Rangers	NHL	3	1	0	1	1	0	1	0					
1953-54	Syracuse Warriors	AHL	45	8	29	37				12					
1954-55	Montreal Royals	QHL	62	30	46	*76				12	14	4	4	8	0
1955-56	Montreal Royals	QHL	58	25	40	65				22	12	3	2	5	4
	Montreal Royals	Ed-Cup	6	1	4	5				2					
1956-57	Montreal Royals	QHL	67	22	35	57				28	4	3	1	4	0
1957-58	Montreal Royals	QHL	55	32	36	68				14	7	2	6	8	0

			REGULAR SEASON								PLAYOFFS				
Season	Club	League	GP	G	A	Pts	AG	AA	APts	PIM	GP	G	A	Pts	PIM
1958-59	Montreal Royals	QHL	57	16	28	44	....	....	....	6	8	2	*5	7	2
1959-60	Montreal Royals	EPHL	66	23	30	53	....	....	....	26	7	3	4	7	2
1960-61	Montreal Royals	EPHL	3	0	1	1	....	....	....	0	....	....	....	....	....
	NHL Totals		**3**	**1**	**0**	**1**	**1**	**0**	**1**	**0**	....	....	....	....	....

AHL Second All-Star Team (1953) • QHL First All-Star Team (1955, 1957) • Won President's Cup (Scoring Champion - QHL) (1955) • Won Byng of Vimy Trophy (MVP - QHL) (1955)

Signed as a free agent by **Springfield** (AHL), September 28, 1949. Transferred to **Syracuse** (AHL) after **Springfield** (AHL) franchise relocated in time for 1951-52 season. Loaned to **NY Rangers** by **Syracuse** (AHL) for cash, November 22, 1952. Traded to **Springfield** (QHL) by **Syracuse** (AHL) for cash, February, 1954. • Suspended for remainder of 1953-54 season by **Springfield** (AHL) for refusing to report to club, February 11, 1954. Traded to **Montreal** by **Springfield** (AHL) for Bob McCord, September 12, 1954.

• BURNS, Bobby Robert Andrew

LW – L. 5'10", 155 lbs. b: Gore Bay, Ont., 4/4/1905.

Season	Club	League	GP	G	A	Pts	AG	AA	APts	PIM	GP	G	A	Pts	PIM
1924-25	Owen Sound Greys	OHA-Jr.	17	17	*11	28	....	....	....	....	9	2	3	5	4
1925-26	Preston Riversides	OHA-Sr.	20	8	0	8	....	....	....	8	....	....	....	....	....
1926-27	Chicago Cardinals	AHA	33	6	3	9	....	....	....	20	....	....	....	....	....
1927-28	**Chicago Black Hawks**	**NHL**	**1**	**0**	**0**	**0**	**0**	**0**	**0**	**0**	....	....	....	....	....
	Duluth Hornets	AHA	39	9	1	10	....	....	....	38	5	0	0	0	6
1928-29	**Chicago Black Hawks**	**NHL**	**7**	**0**	**0**	**0**	**0**	**0**	**0**	**6**	....	....	....	....	....
1929-30	**Chicago Black Hawks**	**NHL**	**12**	**1**	**0**	**1**	**1**	**0**	**1**	**2**	....	....	....	....	....
	Minneapolis Millers	AHA	25	7	4	11	....	....	....	25	....	....	....	....	....
1930-31	Chicago Shamrocks	AHA	46	16	10	26	....	....	....	54	....	....	....	....	....
1931-32	Chicago Shamrocks	AHA	29	7	2	9	....	....	....	30	....	....	....	....	....
	St. Louis Flyers	AHA	13	3	0	3	....	....	....	12	....	....	....	....	....
1932-33	Kansas City Pla-Mors	AHA	27	11	4	15	....	....	....	28	....	....	....	....	....
1933-34	Oklahoma City Warriors	AHA	47	16	12	28	....	....	....	30	....	....	....	....	....
1934-35	Oklahoma City Warriors	AHA	48	17	19	36	....	....	....	35	....	....	....	....	....
1935-36	Oklahoma–Minneapolis	AHA	48	20	20	40	....	....	....	33	....	....	....	....	....
1936-37	St. Louis Flyers	AHA	46	25	19	44	....	....	....	34	6	4	3	7	9
1937-38	St. Louis Flyers	AHA	43	11	22	33	....	....	....	24	7	0	1	1	5
1938-39	St. Louis Flyers	AHA	45	15	23	38	....	....	....	46	7	2	3	5	2
	NHL Totals		**20**	**1**	**0**	**1**	**1**	**0**	**1**	**8**	....	....	....	....	....

AHA Second All-Star Team (1936) • AHA First All-Star Team (1937)

Signed as a free agent by **Chicago** (AHA), October 20, 1926. Traded to **Minneapolis** (AHA) by **Chicago** for Helge Bostrum, January 15, 1930. NHL rights transferred to **Detroit** from **Chicago Shamrocks** (AHA) after AHA club owners purchased Detroit (NHL and IAHL) franchises, September 2, 1932.

• BURNS, Charlie *— see page 939*

• BURNS, Norm

C – R. 6', 195 lbs. b: Youngstown, Alta., 2/20/1918 d: 2/23/1995.

Season	Club	League	GP	G	A	Pts	AG	AA	APts	PIM	GP	G	A	Pts	PIM
1938-39	Sherbrooke Saints	QPHL	STATISTICS NOT AVAILABLE												
1939-40	Atlantic City Seagulls	EAHL	49	22	28	50	....	....	....	14	....	....	....	....	....
	Rivervale Skeeters	EAHL	14	10	8	18	....	....	....	0	....	....	....	....	....
1940-41	Washington Eagles	EAHL	64	*67	26	*93	....	....	....	35	2	3	0	3	4
1941-42	**New York Rangers**	**NHL**	**11**	**0**	**4**	**4**	**0**	**5**	**5**	**2**	....	....	....	....	....
	New Haven Eagles	AHL	35	27	32	59	....	....	....	13	2	0	0	0	0
1942-43	Montreal RCAF	QSHL	25	12	14	26	....	....	....	10	9	2	1	3	6
1943-44	Toronto RCAF	OHA-Sr.	11	3	5	8	....	....	....	4	....	....	....	....	....
	Toronto Fuels	TMHL	9	11	11	22	....	....	....	0	4	10	7	17	0
1944-45			MILITARY SERVICE												
1945-46	St. Paul Saints	USHL	54	30	22	52	....	....	....	28	5	0	0	0	0
1946-47	New Haven Ramblers	AHL	29	21	21	42	....	....	....	6	....	....	....	....	....
	Cleveland Barons	AHL	13	2	2	4	....	....	....	4	4	0	0	0	0
1947-48	Minneapolis Millers	USHL	57	23	27	50	....	....	....	8	10	1	2	3	0
1948-49	Springfield Indians	AHL	21	2	13	15	....	....	....	4	....	....	....	....	....
	Washington Lions	AHL	18	3	8	11	....	....	....	0	....	....	....	....	....
	NHL Totals		**11**	**0**	**4**	**4**	**0**	**5**	**5**	**2**	....	....	....	....	....

EAHL First All-Star Team (1941) • Won John Carlin Trophy (Top Scorer - EAHL) (1941)

Claimed by **NY Rangers** from **Minneapolis** (AHA) in Inter-League Draft, June 27, 1941. Traded to **Cleveland** (AHL) by **New Haven** (AHL) for cash, February 7, 1947. Traded to **Springfield** (AHL) by **Cleveland** (AHL) for cash, October 1, 1948.

• BURRY, Bert Berthold

D – L. 5'9", 180 lbs. b: Toronto, Ont., 1909 Deceased.

Season	Club	League	GP	G	A	Pts	AG	AA	APts	PIM	GP	G	A	Pts	PIM
1927-28	Toronto Marlboros	OHA-Jr.	2	0	0	0	....	....	....	....	....	....	....	....	....
1928/34			STATISTICS NOT AVAILABLE												
1931-32	Springfield Indians	Can-Am	19	0	1	1	....	....	....	20	....	....	....	....	....
1932-33	**Ottawa Senators**	**NHL**	**4**	**0**	**0**	**0**	**0**	**0**	**0**	**0**	....	....	....	....	....
	Hibbing Maroons	CHL	7	0	0	0	....	....	....	6	....	....	....	....	....
1934-35			STATISTICS NOT AVAILABLE												
1935-36			STATISTICS NOT AVAILABLE												
1936-37	Ottawa Senators	OCHL	8	0	0	0	....	....	....	2	....	....	....	....	....
	NHL Totals		**4**	**0**	**0**	**0**	**0**	**0**	**0**	**0**	....	....	....	....	....

• BURTON, Cummy Cumming Scott

RW – R. 5'10", 170 lbs. b: Sudbury, Ont., 5/12/1936.

Season	Club	League	GP	G	A	Pts	AG	AA	APts	PIM	GP	G	A	Pts	PIM
1952-53	Windsor Spitfires	OHA-Jr.	54	7	4	11	....	....	....	88	....	....	....	....	....
1953-54	Hamilton Tiger Cubs	OHA-Jr.	58	30	25	55	....	....	....	100	7	0	1	1	10
1954-55	Hamilton Tiger Cubs	OHA-Jr.	28	6	10	16	....	....	....	54	3	1	1	2	6
1955-56	Hamilton Tiger Cubs	OHA-Jr.	38	31	30	61	....	....	....	50	....	....	....	....	....
	Detroit Red Wings	**NHL**	**3**	**0**	**0**	**0**	**0**	**0**	**0**	**0**	**3**	**0**	**0**	**0**	**0**
1956-57	Edmonton Flyers	WHL	57	14	15	29	....	....	....	83	8	3	4	7	16
1957-58	**Detroit Red Wings**	**NHL**	**26**	**0**	**1**	**1**	**0**	**1**	**1**	**12**	....	....	....	....	....
	Edmonton Flyers	WHL	35	10	11	21	....	....	....	26	5	3	2	5	8
1958-59	**Detroit Red Wings**	**NHL**	**14**	**0**	**1**	**1**	**0**	**1**	**1**	**9**	....	....	....	....	....
	Seattle Totems	WHL	50	16	25	41	....	....	....	60	....	....	....	....	....
1959-60	Sudbury Wolves	EPHL	64	26	32	58	....	....	....	44	10	1	5	6	6
1960-61	Sudbury Wolves	EPHL	62	15	21	36	....	....	....	49	....	....	....	....	....
1961-62	Sudbury Wolves	EPHL	63	18	31	49	....	....	....	59	1	0	2	2	0
1962-63	Edmonton Flyers	WHL	42	4	10	14	....	....	....	24	3	0	0	0	7
	Pittsburgh Hornets	AHL	3	0	0	0	....	....	....	0	....	....	....	....	....

			REGULAR SEASON								PLAYOFFS				
Season	Club	League	GP	G	A	Pts	AG	AA	APts	PIM	GP	G	A	Pts	PIM
1963-64	Charlotte Checkers	EHL	35	15	31	46	....	....	....	28	3	0	1	1	0
1964/67			OUT OF HOCKEY – RETIRED												
1967-68	Florida Rockets	EHL	52	7	20	27	....	....	....	23	....	....	....	....	....
	NHL Totals		**43**	**0**	**2**	**2**	**0**	**2**	**2**	**21**	**3**	**0**	**0**	**0**	**0**

• BUSH, Eddie Edward Webster

D – R. 6'1", 195 lbs. b: Collingwood, Ont., 7/11/1918 d: 5/31/1984.

Season	Club	League	GP	G	A	Pts	AG	AA	APts	PIM	GP	G	A	Pts	PIM
1936-37	Guelph Indians	OHA-Jr.	10	7	3	10	....	....	....	24	5	2	1	3	8
1937-38	Guelph Indians	OHA-Jr.	14	8	4	12	....	....	....	41	9	7	*6	13	18
	Guelph Indians	M-Cup	3	1	0	1	....	....	....	6	....	....	....	....	....
1938-39	**Detroit Red Wings**	**NHL**	**8**	**0**	**0**	**0**	**0**	**0**	**0**	**0**	....	....	....	....	....
	Pittsburgh Hornets	IAHL	16	1	2	3	....	....	....	18	....	....	....	....	....
	Kansas City Greyhounds	AHA	25	4	13	17	....	....	....	69	....	....	....	....	....
1939-40	Indianapolis Capitols	IAHL	41	7	10	17	....	....	....	49	2	0	0	0	2
1940-41	Indianapolis Capitols	AHL	19	2	3	5	....	....	....	33	....	....	....	....	....
	Providence Reds	AHL	37	8	10	18	....	....	....	60	4	2	0	2	11
1941-42	Providence Reds	AHL	36	12	24	36	....	....	....	62	....	....	....	....	....
	Detroit Red Wings	**NHL**	**18**	**4**	**6**	**10**	**5**	**7**	**12**	**40**	**11**	**1**	**6**	**7**	**23**
1942-43	Toronto RCAF	OHA-Sr.	8	0	2	2	....	....	....	25	1	0	2	2	2
	Toronto RCAF	Al-Cup	2	0	1	1	....	....	....	38	....	....	....	....	....
1943-44	Dartmouth RCAF	NSDHL	3	1	3	4	....	....	....	4	....	....	....	....	....
1944-45	Dartmouth RCAF	NSDHL	4	1	1	2	....	....	....	6	....	....	....	....	....
1945-46			MILITARY SERVICE												
1946-47	St. Louis Flyers	AHL	34	5	14	19	....	....	....	71	....	....	....	....	....
	Providence Reds	AHL	26	7	11	18	....	....	....	*111	....	....	....	....	....
1947-48	Philadelphia Rockets	AHL	68	24	48	72	....	....	....	163	....	....	....	....	....
1948-49	Philadelphia Rockets	AHL	46	2	16	18	....	....	....	72	....	....	....	....	....
	Cleveland Barons	AHL	21	3	5	8	....	....	....	41	1	0	0	0	4
1949-50	Cincinnati Mohawks	AHL	8	0	2	2	....	....	....	12	....	....	....	....	....
	Louisville Blades	USHL	8	0	7	7	....	....	....	28	....	....	....	....	....
	Sherbrooke Saints	QSHL	31	7	18	25	....	....	....	89	8	4	2	6	16
	Sherbrooke Saints	Al-Cup	10	2	7	9	....	....	....	27	....	....	....	....	....
1950-51	Collingwood Shipbuilders	OHA-Sr.	DID NOT PLAY – COACHING												
	NHL Totals		**26**	**4**	**6**	**10**	**5**	**7**	**12**	**40**	**11**	**1**	**6**	**7**	**23**

AHL Second All-Star Team (1948)

Traded to **Providence** (AHL) by **Detroit** with Cecil Dillon for Harold Jackson, December 15, 1940. Traded to **Detroit** by **Providence** (AHL) with future considerations for Buck Jones and Bob Whitelaw, February 3, 1942. Traded to **St. Louis** (AHL) by **Detroit** for cash, August 17, 1946. Traded to **Providence** (AHL) by **St. Louis** (AHL) with Carl Liscombe, Roly Rossignol and cash for Bill McComb and Russ Brayshaw, January 9, 1947. Traded to **Cleveland** (AHL) by **Providence** (AHL) for cash, February 2, 1949.

• BUSWELL, Walt

D – L. 5'11", 170 lbs. b: Montreal, Que., 11/6/1907 d: 10/16/1991.

Season	Club	League	GP	G	A	Pts	AG	AA	APts	PIM	GP	G	A	Pts	PIM
1929-30	Montreal CPR	MRTHL	STATISTICS NOT AVAILABLE												
1930-31	St. Francis Xavier	MCHL	STATISTICS NOT AVAILABLE												
1931-32	Chicago Shamrocks	AHA	48	9	5	14	....	....	....	39	4	0	1	1	4
1932-33	**Detroit Red Wings**	**NHL**	**46**	**2**	**4**	**6**	**4**	**8**	**12**	**16**	**4**	**0**	**0**	**0**	**4**
1933-34	**Detroit Red Wings**	**NHL**	**47**	**1**	**2**	**3**	**2**	**4**	**6**	**8**	**9**	**0**	**1**	**1**	**2**
1934-35	**Detroit Red Wings**	**NHL**	**47**	**1**	**3**	**4**	**2**	**5**	**7**	**32**	....	....	....	....	....
	Detroit Olympics	IHL	2	0	0	0	....	....	....	0	....	....	....	....	....
1935-36	**Montreal Canadiens**	**NHL**	**44**	**0**	**2**	**2**	**0**	**4**	**4**	**34**	....	....	....	....	....
1936-37	**Montreal Canadiens**	**NHL**	**44**	**0**	**4**	**4**	**0**	**7**	**7**	**30**	**5**	**0**	**0**	**0**	**2**
1937-38	**Montreal Canadiens**	**NHL**	**48**	**2**	**15**	**17**	**3**	**24**	**27**	**24**	**3**	**0**	**0**	**0**	**0**
1938-39	**Montreal Canadiens**	**NHL**	**46**	**3**	**7**	**10**	**5**	**11**	**16**	**10**	**3**	**2**	**0**	**2**	**2**
1939-40	**Montreal Canadiens**	**NHL**	**46**	**1**	**3**	**4**	**2**	**5**	**7**	**10**	....	....	....	....	....
1940-41	Joliette Cyclones	QPHL	12	3	5	8	....	....	....	2	3	1	6	7	4
	NHL Totals		**368**	**10**	**40**	**50**	**18**	**68**	**86**	**164**	**24**	**2**	**1**	**3**	**10**

Played in NHL All-Star Game (1937, 1939)

NHL rights transferred to **Detroit** from **Chicago Shamrocks** (AHA) after AHA club owners purchased Detroit (NHL and IAHL) franchises, September 2, 1932. Traded to **Boston** by **Detroit** with Cooney Weiland for Marty Barry and Art Giroux, July 11, 1935. Traded to **Montreal Canadiens** by **Boston** with Jean Pusie and cash for Roger Jenkins, July 13, 1935.

• BUTLER, Dick John Richard

RW – R. 5'7", 175 lbs. b: Delisle, Sask., 6/2/1926.

Season	Club	League	GP	G	A	Pts	AG	AA	APts	PIM	GP	G	A	Pts	PIM
1943-44	Trail Smoke Eaters	WKJHL	STATISTICS NOT AVAILABLE												
	Trail Smoke Eaters	M-Cup	17	7	8	15	....	....	....	8	....	....	....	....	....
1944-45	Moose Jaw Canucks	S-SJHL	16	18	16	34	....	....	....	41	3	4	*5	9	6
	Moose Jaw Canucks	M-Cup	8	5	2	7	....	....	....	8	....	....	....	....	....
1945-46	Moose Jaw Canucks	S-SJHL	15	21	17	38	....	....	....	22	4	8	2	10	6
	Moose Jaw Canucks	M-Cup	8	*13	10	*23	....	....	....	12	....	....	....	....	....
1946-47	Kansas City Pla-Mors	USHL	59	19	39	58	....	....	....	48	12	7	1	8	13
1947-48	**Chicago Black Hawks**	**NHL**	**7**	**2**	**0**	**2**	**3**	**0**	**3**	**0**	....	....	....	....	....
	Kansas City Pla-Mors	USHL	49	16	22	38	....	....	....	26	7	1	2	3	2
1948-49	Hershey Bears	AHL	6	1	0	1	....	....	....	0	....	....	....	....	....
	Tulsa Oilers	USHL	57	42	41	83	....	....	....	35	7	2	5	7	0
1949-50	Tulsa Oilers	USHL	70	37	36	73	....	....	....	22	....	....	....	....	....
1950-51	Tulsa Oilers	USHL	61	23	27	50	....	....	....	13	9	0	5	5	6
1951-52	Calgary Stampeders	PCHL	13	2	2	4	....	....	....	21	....	....	....	....	....
1952-53	Spokane Flyers	WIHL	55	24	45	69	....	....	....	71	9	1	4	5	12
	Spokane Flyers	Al-Cup	7	5	4	9	....	....	....	10	....	....	....	....	....
1953-54	Vernon Canadians	OSHL	53	27	38	65	....	....	....	57	5	3	3	6	12
1954/58	Kindersley Klippers	SIHA	STATISTICS NOT AVAILABLE												
	NHL Totals		**7**	**2**	**0**	**2**	**3**	**0**	**3**	**0**	....	....	....	....	....

USHL First All-Star Team (1949)

• BUTTREY, Gord Gordon Roy

W – L. 6'1", 180 lbs. b: Regina, Sask., 3/17/1926.

Season	Club	League	GP	G	A	Pts	AG	AA	APts	PIM	GP	G	A	Pts	PIM
1941-42	Regina Abbotts	S-SJHL	3	0	0	0	....	....	....	0	5	0	0	0	0
	Regina Pats	M-Cup	7	0	1	1	....	....	....	0	....	....	....	....	....
1942-43	Regina Abbotts	S-SJHL	13	7	5	12	....	....	....	4	4	0	0	0	4
1943-44	**Chicago Black Hawks**	**NHL**	**10**	**0**	**0**	**0**	**0**	**0**	**0**	**0**	....	....	....	....	....
	Providence Reds	AHL	26	2	4	6	....	....	....	18	....	....	....	....	....
	Philadelphia Falcons	EAHL	....	....	....	....	....	....	....	....	9	1	1	2	0
1944-45	Saskatoon Navy	S-SSHL	9	9	10	19	....	....	....	8	5	*9	2	11	9

Season	Club	League	GP	G	A	Pts	AG	AA	APts	PIM	GP	G	A	Pts	PIM
			REGULAR SEASON								PLAYOFFS				
1945-46	Saskatoon Quakers	S-SSHL	23	3	3	6	....	....	....	2	3	1	0	1	0
	Portland Eagles	PCHL	5	1	1	2	....	....	....	0	....	....	....	....	....
1946-47	Saskatoon Quakers	WCSHL	37	7	14	21	....	....	....	27	3	0	0	0	0
1947-48	Edmonton Flyers	WCSHL	14	0	3	3	....	....	....	10	....	....	....	....	....
1948-49	Milwaukee Clarks	IHL	21	9	8	17	....	....	....	48	8	5	5	10	19
1949-50	Milwaukee Clarks	EAHL	51	20	22	42	....	....	....	62	14	3	1	4	15
1950-51	Atlantic City Seagulls	EAHL	54	26	40	66	....	....	....	25	13	1	4	5	2
1951-52	Atlantic City Seagulls	EAHL	65	33	38	71	....	....	....	33	....	....	....	....	....
1952-53	Troy Bruins	IHL	59	28	33	61	....	....	....	42	6	2	1	3	2
1953-54	Troy Bruins	IHL	64	29	34	63	....	....	....	23	3	4	1	5	0
1954-55	Troy Bruins	IHL	60	19	28	47	....	....	....	69	11	3	4	7	14
1955-56	Troy–Indianapolis	IHL	53	16	17	33	....	....	....	34	....	....	....	....	....
	NHL Totals		**10**	**0**	**0**	**0**	**0**	**0**	**0**	**0**	....	....	....	....	....

EAHL Second All-Star Team (1951)

Traded to **Providence** (AHL) by **Chicago** with Hec Highton and $10,000 for Mike Karakas, January 7, 1944.

• BYERS, Gord
Gordon Charles
D – R. 5'10", 182 lbs. b: Eganville, Ont., 3/11/1930.

Season	Club	League	GP	G	A	Pts	AG	AA	APts	PIM	GP	G	A	Pts	PIM
1947-48	Copper Cliff Jr. Redmen	NBHL	8	0	2	2	....	....	....	10	3	1	1	2	2
	Copper Cliff Redmen	M-Cup	7	2	2	4	....	....	....	12	....	....	....	....	....
1948-49	St. Catharines Teepees	OHA-Jr.	29	2	2	4	....	....	....	63	5	0	1	1	11
1949-50	St. Catharines Teepees	OHA-Jr.	41	5	17	22	....	....	....	102	5	0	1	1	8
	Boston Bruins	**NHL**	**1**	**0**	**1**	**1**	**0**	**1**	**1**	**0**	....	....	....	....	....
	Boston Olympics	EAHL	2	0	1	1	....	....	....	6	5	0	2	2	9
1950-51	Tulsa–Kansas City	USHL	61	6	7	13	....	....	....	67	....	....	....	....	....
1951-52	Boston Olympics	EAHL	50	0	5	5	....	....	....	100	....	....	....	....	....
1952-53	Troy Uncle Sam Trojans	EAHL	56	3	13	16	....	....	....	103	....	....	....	....	....
1953-54	Chatham–Niagara Falls	OHA-Sr.	43	1	10	11	....	....	....	133	6	2	1	3	18
1954-55	Sudbury Wolves	NOHA	14	0	1	1	....	....	....	20	....	....	....	....	....
1955-56			DID NOT PLAY												
1956-57	Sudbury Wolves	NOHA	5	1	0	1	....	....	....	10	....	....	....	....	....
	NHL Totals		**1**	**0**	**1**	**1**	**0**	**1**	**1**	**0**	....	....	....	....	....

Signed as a free agent by **Boston**, October 3, 1950.

• CAFFERY, Jack
C – R. 6', 165 lbs. b: Kingston, Ont., 6/30/1934 Deceased.

Season	Club	League	GP	G	A	Pts	AG	AA	APts	PIM	GP	G	A	Pts	PIM
1950-51	St. Michael's Buzzers	OHA-B	STATISTICS NOT AVAILABLE												
	St. Michael's Majors	OHA-Jr.	1	0	0	0	....	....	....	0	....	....	....	....	....
1951-52	St. Michael's Buzzers	OHA-B	STATISTICS NOT AVAILABLE												
	St. Michael's Majors	OHA-Jr.	1	2	1	3	....	....	....	0	1	0	0	0	0
1952-53	St. Michael's Majors	OHA-Jr.	56	37	39	76	....	....	....	38	17	7	10	17	9
1953-54	St. Michael's Majors	OHA-Jr.	54	25	34	59	....	....	....	40	8	5	8	13	11
1954-55	**Toronto Maple Leafs**	**NHL**	**3**	**0**	**0**	**0**	**0**	**0**	**0**	**0**	....	....	....	....	....
	Pittsburgh Hornets	AHL	55	15	11	26	....	....	....	52	9	2	2	4	4
1955-56	Pittsburgh Hornets	AHL	58	18	22	40	....	....	....	62	4	1	0	1	0
1956-57	**Boston Bruins**	**NHL**	**47**	**2**	**2**	**4**	**3**	**2**	**5**	**20**	**10**	**1**	**0**	**1**	**4**
1957-58	**Boston Bruins**	**NHL**	**7**	**1**	**0**	**1**	**1**	**0**	**1**	**2**	....	....	....	....	....
	Springfield Indians	AHL	46	13	22	35	....	....	....	22	13	2	3	5	10
1958-59			PLAYED PROFESSIONAL BASEBALL												
1959-60			PLAYED PROFESSIONAL BASEBALL												
1960-61	Springfield Indians	AHL	38	6	10	16	....	....	....	10	8	1	3	4	0
1961-62			PLAYED PROFESSIONAL BASEBALL												
1962-63			PLAYED PROFESSIONAL BASEBALL												
1963-64	Greensboro Generals	EHL	38	2	14	16	....	....	....	21	....	....	....	....	....
	NHL Totals		**57**	**3**	**2**	**5**	**4**	**2**	**6**	**22**	**10**	**1**	**0**	**1**	**4**

• Brother of Terry

Claimed by **Boston** from **Pittsburgh** (AHL) in Inter-League Draft, June 5, 1956. • Missed entire 1958-59, 1959-60, 1961-62, 1962-63 seasons playing professional baseball in the **Milwaukee Braves** farm system.

• CAHAN, Larry
— see page 946

• CAHILL, Charles
"Chuck"
RW – R. 5'10", 180 lbs. b: Summerside, PEI, 1/4/1904 d: 6/5/1954.

Season	Club	League	GP	G	A	Pts	AG	AA	APts	PIM	GP	G	A	Pts	PIM
1921-22	Summerside Pioneers	PEI-Sr.	STATISTICS NOT AVAILABLE												
1922-23	Summerside Crystals	NBPEI	6	*19	3	*22	....	....	....	12	....	....	....	....	....
1923-24	Summerside Crystals	PEI-Sr.	9	*16	2	*18	....	....	....	4	4	5	1	6	0
1924-25	Summerside Crystals	PEI-Sr.	5	*11	*6	*17	....	....	....	4	4	*4	*2	*6	4
1925-26	**Boston Bruins**	**NHL**	**31**	**0**	**1**	**1**	**0**	**6**	**6**	**4**	....	....	....	....	....
1926-27	**Boston Bruins**	**NHL**	**1**	**0**	**0**	**0**	**0**	**0**	**0**	**0**	....	....	....	....	....
	New Haven Eagles	Can-Am	26	10	1	11	....	....	....	35	4	0	0	0	15
1927-28	New Haven Eagles	Can-Am	28	8	1	9	....	....	....	24	....	....	....	....	....
1928-29	Philadelphia Arrows	Can-Am	36	9	1	10	....	....	....	38	....	....	....	....	....
1929-30	Philadelphia Arrows	Can-Am	39	18	13	31	....	....	....	60	2	0	0	0	2
1930-31	Buffalo Bisons	IHL	37	6	1	7	....	....	....	30	6	0	2	2	0
1931-32			DID NOT PLAY – REFEREE												
1932-33			DID NOT PLAY – REFEREE												
1933/35			DID NOT PLAY												
1935-36	Summerside Crystals	PEI-Sr.	5	4	6	10	....	....	....	2	4	*4	*5	*9	2
1936-37	Summerside Crystals	PEI-Sr.	9	5	1	6	....	....	....	8	4	2	1	3	10
1937-38	Summerside Crystals	PEI-Sr.	12	10	*12	22	....	....	....	16	6	3	4	7	6
	Summerside Crystals	Al-Cup	4	2	1	3	....	....	....	2	....	....	....	....	....
1938-39	Summerside Crystals	PEI-Sr.	4	4	4	8	....	....	....	0	5	3	3	6	2
	NHL Totals		**32**	**0**	**1**	**1**	**0**	**6**	**6**	**4**	....	....	....	....	....

Signed as a free agent by **Boston**, December 1, 1925. Traded to **New Haven** (Can-Am) by **Boston** for cash, January 31, 1927. Signed as a free agent by **Buffalo** (IHL), December 8, 1930. • Missed entire 1933-34 and 1934-35 seasons serving jail sentence for vehicular homicide. • Reinstated as an amateur, November 22, 1935.

• CAIN, Francis
"Dutch"
D – R. 5'8", 175 lbs. b: Newmarket, Ont., 3/22/1899 d: 1/13/1962.

Season	Club	League	GP	G	A	Pts	AG	AA	APts	PIM	GP	G	A	Pts	PIM
1920-21	Newmarket Redmen	OHA-Sr.	10	2	1	3	....	....	....	....	....	....	....	....	....
1921-22	Toronto St. Mary's	OHA-Jr.	STATISTICS NOT AVAILABLE												
1922-23	Toronto Aura Lee	OHA-Jr.	10	3	5	8	....	....	....	....	....	....	....	....	....
1923-24	Sault Ste. Marie Greyhounds	NOHA	4	3	0	3	....	....	....	2	6	1	1	2	6
1924-25	**Montreal Maroons**	**NHL**	**28**	**4**	**0**	**4**	**7**	**0**	**7**	**27**	....	....	....	....	....
1925-26	**Montreal Maroons**	**NHL**	**10**	**0**	**0**	**0**	**0**	**0**	**0**	**0**	....	....	....	....	....
	Toronto St. Pats	**NHL**	**23**	**0**	**0**	**0**	**0**	**0**	**0**	**8**	....	....	....	....	....
1926-27	Hamilton Tigers	Can-Pro	18	4	0	4	....	....	....	10	....	....	....	....	....
	Niagara Falls Cataracts	Can-Pro	14	2	4	6	....	....	....	4	....	....	....	....	....
1927-28	Toronto Falcons	IHL	20	3	2	5	....	....	....	25	2	0	0	0	0
1928-29	Niagara Falls Cataracts	Can-Pro	25	7	3	10	....	....	....	25	....	....	....	....	....
	Buffalo Bisons	Can-Pro	15	4	1	5	....	....	....	8	....	....	....	....	....
1929-30	Buffalo Bisons	IHL	41	3	7	10	....	....	....	22	7	2	*3	5	8
1930-31	Buffalo Bisons	IHL	42	3	6	9	....	....	....	18	6	1	0	1	0
1931-32	Buffalo Bisons	IHL	25	1	1	2	....	....	....	13	6	0	0	0	0
1932-33	St. Louis Flyers	AHA	23	1	1	2	....	....	....	16	....	....	....	....	....
	Tulsa Oilers	AHA	2	0	0	0	....	....	....	0	....	....	....	....	....
	NHL Totals		**61**	**4**	**0**	**4**	**7**	**0**	**7**	**35**	....	....	....	....	....

Signed as a free agent by **Montreal Maroons**, October 23, 1924. Claimed on waivers by **Toronto** from **Montreal Maroons**, January 7, 1926. Claimed on waivers by **Hamilton** (Can-Pro) from **Toronto**, October 18, 1926. Traded to **Niagara Falls** (Can-Pro) by **Hamilton** (Can-Pro) for Ken Randall, January 25, 1927. Signed as a free agent by **Hamilton** (Can-Pro), October, 1927. Traded to **Stratford** (Can-Pro) by **Hamilton** (Can-Pro) for Gord Brydson, October 27, 1927. Loaned to **Toronto** (IHL) by **Stratford** (Can-Pro), January, 1928. Signed as a free agent by **Niagara Falls** (Can-Pro), October 28, 1928. Traded to **Buffalo** (Can-Pro) by **Niagara Falls** (Can-Pro) for Harry Lott and Jim Smith, February 2, 1929.

• CAIN, Herb
Herbert Joseph
LW – L. 5'11", 180 lbs. b: Newmarket, Ont., 12/24/1912 d: 2/15/1982.

Season	Club	League	GP	G	A	Pts	AG	AA	APts	PIM	GP	G	A	Pts	PIM
1931-32	Newmarket Redmen	OHA-Jr.	7	*7	*2	*9	....	....	....	6	6	*11	0	11	....
1932-33	Hamilton Tigers	OHA-Sr.	22	14	5	19	....	....	....	20	5	3	3	6	2
1933-34	**Montreal Maroons**	**NHL**	**30**	**4**	**5**	**9**	**7**	**10**	**17**	**14**	**4**	**0**	**0**	**0**	**0**
	Hamilton Tigers	OHA-Sr.	11	4	2	6	....	....	....	17	....	....	....	....	....
♦1934-35	**Montreal Maroons**	**NHL**	**44**	**20**	**7**	**27**	**33**	**12**	**45**	**13**	**7**	**1**	**0**	**1**	**2**
	Windsor Bulldogs	IHL	6	1	3	4	....	....	....	6	....	....	....	....	....
1935-36	**Montreal Maroons**	**NHL**	**48**	**5**	**13**	**18**	**10**	**25**	**35**	**16**	**3**	**0**	**1**	**1**	**0**
1936-37	**Montreal Maroons**	**NHL**	**42**	**13**	**17**	**30**	**22**	**31**	**53**	**18**	**5**	**1**	**1**	**2**	**0**
1937-38	**Montreal Maroons**	**NHL**	**47**	**11**	**19**	**30**	**18**	**31**	**49**	**10**	....	....	....	....	....
1938-39	**Montreal Canadiens**	**NHL**	**45**	**13**	**14**	**27**	**23**	**22**	**45**	**26**	**3**	**0**	**0**	**0**	**2**
1939-40	**Boston Bruins**	**NHL**	**48**	**21**	**10**	**31**	**35**	**16**	**51**	**30**	**6**	**1**	**3**	**4**	**2**
♦1940-41	**Boston Bruins**	**NHL**	**41**	**8**	**10**	**18**	**12**	**14**	**26**	**6**	**11**	**3**	**2**	**5**	**5**
	Hershey Bears	AHL	1	1	0	1	....	....	....	0	....	....	....	....	....
1941-42	**Boston Bruins**	**NHL**	**34**	**8**	**10**	**18**	**11**	**12**	**23**	**2**	**5**	**1**	**0**	**1**	**0**
1942-43	**Boston Bruins**	**NHL**	**45**	**18**	**18**	**36**	**18**	**17**	**35**	**19**	**7**	**4**	**2**	**6**	**0**
1943-44	**Boston Bruins**	**NHL**	**48**	**36**	**46**	***82**	**33**	**41**	**74**	**4**	....	....	....	....	....
1944-45	**Boston Bruins**	**NHL**	**50**	**32**	**13**	**45**	**33**	**15**	**48**	**16**	**7**	**5**	**2**	**7**	**0**
1945-46	**Boston Bruins**	**NHL**	**48**	**17**	**12**	**29**	**20**	**17**	**37**	**4**	**9**	**0**	**2**	**2**	**2**
1946-47	Hershey Bears	AHL	59	36	30	66	....	....	....	19	11	*9	6	15	9
1947-48	Hershey Bears	AHL	49	19	19	38	....	....	....	25	2	0	1	1	0
1948-49	Hershey Bears	AHL	49	25	35	60	....	....	....	10	11	4	6	10	6
1949-50	Hershey Bears	AHL	41	12	14	26	....	....	....	8	....	....	....	....	....
	NHL Totals		**570**	**206**	**194**	**400**	**275**	**263**	**538**	**178**	**67**	**16**	**13**	**29**	**13**

NHL Second All-Star Team (1944) • NHL Scoring Leader (1944)

• **Montreal Canadiens** protested Cain's contract with **Montreal Maroons**, claiming they owned his rights, October 3, 1934. NHL rights transferred to **Montreal Canadiens** by **NHL** after ruling by NHL President Frank Calder, October 3, 1934. NHL rights traded to **Montreal Maroons** by **Montreal Canadiens** with Lionel Conacher for the rights to Nels Crutchfield, October 3, 1934. Traded to **Montreal Canadiens** by **Montreal Maroons** for cash, September 24, 1938. Traded to **Boston** by **Montreal** for Charlie Sands and Ray Getliffe, October 10, 1939.

• CALLADINE, Norm
C – R. 5'9", 155 lbs. b: Peterborough, Ont., 7/30/1916 Deceased.

Season	Club	League	GP	G	A	Pts	AG	AA	APts	PIM	GP	G	A	Pts	PIM
1938-39	Baltimore Orioles	EAHL	51	33	*41	74	....	....	....	4	....	....	....	....	....
1939-40	Baltimore Orioles	EAHL	61	*53	41	94	....	....	....	12	9	5	*7	*12	0
1940-41	Philadelphia Rockets	AHL	52	8	24	32	....	....	....	4	....	....	....	....	....
1941-42	Providence Reds	AHL	56	32	23	55	....	....	....	6	....	....	....	....	....
1942-43	Providence Reds	AHL	51	16	35	51	....	....	....	7	2	0	0	0	0
	Boston Bruins	**NHL**	**3**	**0**	**1**	**1**	**0**	**1**	**1**	**0**	....	....	....	....	....
1943-44	**Boston Bruins**	**NHL**	**49**	**16**	**27**	**43**	**14**	**24**	**38**	**8**	....	....	....	....	....
1944-45	**Boston Bruins**	**NHL**	**11**	**3**	**1**	**4**	**3**	**1**	**4**	**0**	....	....	....	....	....
	Boston Olympics	EAHL	2	0	3	3	....	....	....	0	....	....	....	....	....
	Hershey Bears	AHL	14	4	8	12	....	....	....	0	11	3	4	7	0
1945-46	Hershey Bears	AHL	5	0	2	2	....	....	....	0	....	....	....	....	....
	Washington Lions	EAHL	22	13	6	19	....	....	....	0	12	9	7	16	0
	NHL Totals		**63**	**19**	**29**	**48**	**17**	**26**	**43**	**8**	....	....	....	....	....

EAHL First All-Star Team (1939, 1940)

Traded to **Providence** (AHL) by **NY Rangers** for cash, September 11, 1941. Traded to **Boston** by **Providence** (AHL) with Oscar Aubuchon and Ab DeMarco for cash, March 8, 1943.

• CALLIGHEN, Patsy
Francis Charles Winslow
D – L. 5'6", 175 lbs. b: Toronto, Ont., 2/13/1906.

Season	Club	League	GP	G	A	Pts	AG	AA	APts	PIM	GP	G	A	Pts	PIM
1922-23	Toronto St. Andrews	OHA-Jr.	7	5	*5	10	....	....	....	....	....	....	....	....	....
1923-24	Toronto St. Mary's	OHA-Jr.	8	2	4	6	....	....	....	0	....	....	....	....	....
	Toronto St. Mary's	M-Cup	2	2	0	2	....	....	....	0	....	....	....	....	....
1924-25	Owen Sound Greys	X-Games	17	6	7	13	....	....	....	....	....	....	....	....	....
	Owen Sound Greys	M-Cup	9	4	4	8	....	....	....	23	....	....	....	....	....
1925-26	Owen Sound Greys	X-Games	11	9	4	13	....	....	....	....	....	....	....	....	....
	Owen Sound Greys	M-Cup	6	0	0	0	....	....	....	27	....	....	....	....	....
1926-27	Springfield Indians	Can-Am	31	5	2	7	....	....	....	*83	6	0	0	0	*27
♦1927-28	**New York Rangers**	**NHL**	**36**	**0**	**0**	**0**	**0**	**0**	**0**	**32**	**9**	**0**	**0**	**0**	**0**
	Springfield Indians	Can-Am	7	1	1	2	....	....	....	20	....	....	....	....	....
1928-29	Springfield Indians	Can-Am	39	2	2	4	....	....	....	*124	....	....	....	....	....
1929-30	Springfield Indians	Can-Am	37	10	6	16	....	....	....	63	....	....	....	....	....
1930-31	Springfield Indians	Can-Am	38	14	8	22	....	....	....	108	7	3	1	4	16
1931-32	Springfield Indians	Can-Am	40	1	5	6	....	....	....	74	....	....	....	....	....
1932-33	Quebec Castors	Can-Am	43	3	4	7	....	....	....	52	....	....	....	....	....
1933-34	Cleveland Indians	IHL	43	5	12	17	....	....	....	92	....	....	....	....	....
1934-35	Cleveland Falcons	IHL	44	3	4	7	....	....	....	67	2	1	0	1	2

Season	Club	League	GP	G	A	Pts	AG	AA	APts	PIM	GP	G	A	Pts	PIM
			REGULAR SEASON								PLAYOFFS				
1935-36	Cleveland Falcons	IHL	5	0	0	0	....	....	....	11	....	....	....	....	....
	Rochester Cardinals	IHL	13	2	1	3	....	....	....	8	....	....	....	....	....
	London Tecumsehs	IHL	28	0	5	5	....	....	....	51	2	0	1	1	2
	NHL Totals		**36**	**0**	**0**	**0**	**0**	**0**	**0**	**32**	**9**	**0**	**0**	**0**	**0**

Signed as a free agent by **NY Rangers**, August 22, 1926. Traded to **London** (IHL) by **Cleveland** with Bill Anderson (IHL) for Alvin Groh, November 22, 1935. Loaned to **Rochester** (IHL) by **London** (IHL), November 22, 1935 and recalled January 4, 1936.

• CAMERON, Billy William Alexander

RW – L. 5'11", 160 lbs. b: Timmins, Ont., 12/5/1896 Deceased.

Season	Club	League	GP	G	A	Pts	AG	AA	APts	PIM	GP	G	A	Pts	PIM
1914-15	Cleveland H.C.	USAHA	STATISTICS NOT AVAILABLE												
	Buckingham A.C.C.	LOVHL	7	3	0	3	....	....	....	....	5	5	0	5	....
1915-16	Buckingham A.C.C.	LOVHL	....	....	....	....	....	....	....	....	3	1	0	1	....
1916-17	Pittsburgh AA	USAHA	40	12	0	12	....	....	....	....	....	....	....	....	....
1917-18	Ottawa Ordinance Corps	OCHL	STATISTICS NOT AVAILABLE												
1918-19			MILITARY SERVICE												
1919-20			MILITARY SERVICE												
1920-21	Quebec Royal Rifles	QCHL	7	5	0	5	....	....	....	....	4	1	0	1	....
1921-22	Timmins Seniors	NOHA	STATISTICS NOT AVAILABLE												
1922-23	Porcupine Gold Miners	GBHL	....	....	....	....	....	....	....	....	1	1	0	1	....
1923-24	**Montreal Canadiens**	**NHL**	**18**	**0**	**0**	**0**	**0**	**0**	**0**	**2**	**2**	**0**	**0**	**0**	**0**
♦	Montreal Canadiens	St-Cup	4	0	0	0	....	....	....	0	....	....	....	....	....
1924-25			DID NOT PLAY – SUSPENDED												
1925-26	**New York Americans**	**NHL**	**21**	**0**	**0**	**0**	**0**	**0**	**0**	**0**	....	....	....	....	....
1926-27	St. Paul Saints	AHA	31	3	1	4	....	....	....	22	....	....	....	....	....
1927-28	Kitchener Millionaires	Can-Pro	25	1	0	1	....	....	....	34	4	0	0	0	18
1928-29	Toronto Millionaires	Can-Pro	32	3	1	4	....	....	....	39	2	0	0	0	2
1929-30	Hamilton Tigers	IHL	1	0	0	0	....	....	....	0	....	....	....	....	....
	Buffalo Bisons	IHL	1	0	0	0	....	....	....	0	....	....	....	....	....
	NHL Totals		**39**	**0**	**0**	**0**	**0**	**0**	**0**	**2**	**2**	**0**	**0**	**0**	**0**

Signed as a free agent by **Montreal Canadiens**, December 21, 1923. • 1923-24 Stanley Cup totals includes series with Calgary (WCHL) and Vancouver (PCHA). Traded to **Vancouver** (WCHL) by **Montreal** for cash, October 10, 1924. • Suspended for entire 1924-25 season by Montreal for refusing to report to Vancouver (WCHL), October 30, 1924. Signed as a free agent by **NY Americans**, November 1, 1925. Signed as a free agent by **St. Paul** (AHA), November 2, 1926. Traded to **Kitchener** (IHL) by **Cleveland** (IHL) with Clarence Wedgewood for Gord McFarlane, October 18, 1929. • Suffered career-ending shoulder injury, January 19, 1930.

• CAMERON, Craig *— see page 949*

• CAMERON, Harry Harold Hugh "Cammie" HHOF

D – R. 5'10", 155 lbs. b: Pembroke, Ont., 2/6/1890 d: 10/20/1953.

Season	Club	League	GP	G	A	Pts	AG	AA	APts	PIM	GP	G	A	Pts	PIM
1908-09	Pembroke Debaters	UOVHL	6	13	0	13	....	....	....	....	....	....	....	....	....
1909-10	Pembroke Debaters	UOVHL	8	17	0	17	....	....	....	....	....	....	....	....	....
1910-11	Pembroke Debaters	UOVHL	6	*9	1	*10	....	....	....	8	2	4	*4	*8	0
1911-12	Port Arthur Lake City	NOHL	15	6	0	6	....	....	....	48	2	2	0	2	0
1912-13	Toronto Blueshirts	NHA	20	9	0	9	....	....	....	20	....	....	....	....	....
♦1913-14	Toronto Blueshirts	NHA	19	15	4	19	....	....	....	22	5	1	2	3	6
1914-15	Toronto Blueshirts	NHA	17	12	8	20	....	....	....	43	....	....	....	....	....
1915-16	Toronto Blueshirts	NHA	24	8	3	11	....	....	....	70	....	....	....	....	....
1916-17	Toronto 228th Battalion	NHA	14	8	4	12	....	....	....	20	....	....	....	....	....
	Montreal Wanderers	NHA	6	1	1	2	....	....	....	9	....	....	....	....	....
1917-18	**Toronto Arenas**	**NHL**	**21**	**17**	***10**	**27**	**22**	**43**	**65**	**28**	**2**	**1**	**2**	**3**	**0**
♦	Toronto Arenas	St-Cup	5	3	1	4	....	....	....	0	....	....	....	....	....
1918-19	**Toronto Arenas**	**NHL**	**7**	**6**	**2**	**8**	**11**	**11**	**22**	**9**	....	....	....	....	....
	Ottawa Senators	**NHL**	**7**	**5**	**1**	**6**	**9**	**5**	**14**	**26**	**5**	**4**	**0**	**4**	**6**
1919-20	**Toronto St. Pats**	**NHL**	**7**	**3**	**0**	**3**	**3**	**0**	**3**	**6**	....	....	....	....	....
	Montreal Canadiens	**NHL**	**16**	**12**	**5**	**17**	**14**	**17**	**31**	**36**	....	....	....	....	....
1920-21	**Toronto St. Pats**	**NHL**	**24**	**18**	**9**	**27**	**23**	**35**	**58**	**35**	**2**	**0**	**0**	**0**	**2**
1921-22	**Toronto St. Pats**	**NHL**	**24**	**18**	***17**	**35**	**25**	**56**	**81**	**22**	**2**	**0**	**2**	**2**	**8**
♦	Toronto St. Pats	St-Cup	4	0	2	2	....	....	....	11	....	....	....	....	....
1922-23	**Toronto St. Pats**	**NHL**	**22**	**9**	**7**	**16**	**15**	**27**	**42**	**27**	....	....	....	....	....
1923-24	Saskatoon Crescents	WCHL	29	10	10	20	....	....	....	16	....	....	....	....	....
1924-25	Saskatoon Crescents	WCHL	28	13	7	20	....	....	....	21	2	1	0	1	0
1925-26	Saskatoon Crescents	WHL	30	9	3	12	....	....	....	12	2	0	0	0	0
1926-27	Saskatoon Sheiks	PrHL	31	26	19	45	....	....	....	20	4	1	0	1	4
1927-28	Minneapolis Millers	AHA	19	2	3	5	....	....	....	32	....	....	....	....	....
1928-29	St. Louis Flyers	AHA	34	14	3	17	....	....	....	30	....	....	....	....	....
1929-30	St. Louis Flyers	AHA	46	14	6	20	....	....	....	34	....	....	....	....	....
1930-31	St. Louis Flyers	AHA	37	4	3	7	....	....	....	30	....	....	....	....	....
1931-32			DID NOT PLAY												
1932-33	Saskatoon Crescents	NWHL	9	0	0	0	....	....	....	4	....	....	....	....	....
	NHL Totals		**128**	**88**	**51**	**139**	**122**	**194**	**316**	**189**	**11**	**5**	**4**	**9**	**16**
	Other Major League Totals		202	91	40	131	....	....	....	281	11	4	2	6	6

Signed as a free agent by **Toronto** (NHA), November 23, 1912. Assigned to **Montreal Wanderers** (NHA) by NHA in dispersal of Toronto 228th Battalion (NHA) players, February 11, 1917. Rights not retained by **Montreal Wanderers** after NHA folded, November 26, 1917. Signed as a free agent by **Toronto**, December 5, 1917. Loaned to **Ottawa** by **Toronto** to complete earlier transaction that sent Rusty Crawford to Toronto (December 14, 1918), January 19, 1919. Returned to **Toronto** by **Ottawa**, November 25, 1919. Traded to **Montreal Canadiens** by **Toronto** for Goldie Prodgers and Joe Matte, January 14, 1920. Traded to **Toronto** by **Montreal Canadiens** for Goldie Prodgers and Joe Matte, November 27, 1920. Claimed on waivers by **Saskatoon** (WCHL) from **Toronto**, November 9, 1923. • Named player coach of Saskatoon Sheiks (PrHL), November 4, 1926.

• CAMERON, Scotty Scott Angus

C – L. 6'2", 175 lbs. b: Prince Albert, Sask., 11/5/1921 d: 4/12/1993.

Season	Club	League	GP	G	A	Pts	AG	AA	APts	PIM	GP	G	A	Pts	PIM
1938-39	Regina Wares	RJrHL	STATISTICS NOT AVAILABLE												
1939-40	Regina Abbots	S-SJHL	11	6	5	11	....	....	....	16	2	*4	1	5	4
	Regina Abbots	M-Cup	6	2	1	3	....	....	....	6	....	....	....	....	....
1940-41	Regina Rangers	N-SSHL	32	20	20	40	....	....	....	9	8	3	5	8	8
	Regina Rangers	Al-Cup	14	5	8	13	....	....	....	0	....	....	....	....	....
1941-42	New York Rovers	EAHL	6	0	0	0	....	....	....	0	....	....	....	....	....
1942-43	**New York Rangers**	**NHL**	**35**	**8**	**11**	**19**	**8**	**10**	**18**	**0**	....	....	....	....	....
	Montreal RCAF	QSHL	....	....	....	....	....	....	....	....	2	0	2	2	0
1943-44	Montreal Canada Car	MCHL	5	3	1	4	....	....	....	0	....	....	....	....	....
	Montreal RCAF	QSHL	4	0	0	0	....	....	....	2	....	....	....	....	....
1944-45			MILITARY SERVICE												
1945-46			MILITARY SERVICE												
1946-47	New Haven Ramblers	AHL	64	11	18	29	....	....	....	16	3	0	1	1	0
1947-48	New Haven Ramblers	AHL	64	13	23	36	....	....	....	6	3	0	1	1	0
1948-49	St. Paul Saints	USHL	57	14	30	44	....	....	....	6	7	1	6	7	0
1949-50	St. Paul Saints	USHL	70	7	31	38	....	....	....	8	3	0	3	3	2
1950-51	Regina Caps	WCMHL	9	1	3	4	....	....	....	2	....	....	....	....	....
	Yorkton Legionnaires	SSHL	19	15	13	28	....	....	....	6	10	4	4	8	8
	NHL Totals		**35**	**8**	**11**	**19**	**8**	**10**	**18**	**0**	....	....	....	....	....

Claimed by **NY Rangers** from **Philadelphia** (AHA) in Inter-League Draft, June 27, 1941.

• CAMPBELL, Dave David Dewar

D – L. 6', 200 lbs. b: Lachute, Que., 4/27/1896 Deceased.

Season	Club	League	GP	G	A	Pts	AG	AA	APts	PIM	GP	G	A	Pts	PIM
1913-14	Montreal Northern Electric	MCHL	10	2	0	2	....	....	....	10	....	....	....	....	....
	Montreal La Casquette	MCHL	9	3	0	3	....	....	....	....	....	....	....	....	....
1914-15	Montreal La Casquette	MCHL	10	3	0	3	....	....	....	12	....	....	....	....	....
1915-16	Laval University	MCHL	9	2	0	2	....	....	....	20	1	0	0	0	0
1916-17			MILITARY SERVICE												
1917-18			MILITARY SERVICE												
1918-19	Montreal Nationale	MCHL	9	4	8	12	....	....	....	15	....	....	....	....	....
1919-20	Laval University	IPAHU	10	2	3	5	....	....	....	18	....	....	....	....	....
1920-21	**Montreal Canadiens**	**NHL**	**2**	**0**	**0**	**0**	**0**	**0**	**0**	**0**	....	....	....	....	....
1921-22			REINSTATED AS AN AMATEUR												
1922-23	Montreal Nationale	MCHL	5	0	0	0	....	....	....	0	....	....	....	....	....
1923-24	Montreal Nationale	MCHL	10	4	0	4	....	....	....	....	....	....	....	....	....
1924-25	Montreal Nationale	ECHL	14	2	0	2	....	....	....	....	....	....	....	....	....
1925-26	Montreal Nationale	MCHL	9	6	0	6	....	....	....	10	....	....	....	....	....
	Montreal Bell Telephone	MRTHL	7	2	1	3	....	....	....	12	....	....	....	....	....
1926-27	Montreal Victorias	QSHL	4	2	2	4	....	....	....	16	....	....	....	....	....
	Montreal Victorias	X-Games	15	26	0	26	....	....	....	....	....	....	....	....	....
1927-28	Philadelphia Arrows	Can-Am	19	0	0	0	....	....	....	30	....	....	....	....	....
	Montreal Northern Electric	MRTHL	STATISTICS NOT AVAILABLE												
1928-29	Montreal AAA	MCHL	DID NOT PLAY – COACHING												
	NHL Totals		**2**	**0**	**0**	**0**	**0**	**0**	**0**	**0**	....	....	....	....	....

Signed as a free agent by **Montreal Canadiens**, February 26, 1921. • Amateur status revoked by CAHA, February 21, 1923.

• CAMPBELL, Don Donald William

LW – L. 5'10", 175 lbs. b: Drumheller, Alta., 7/12/1925.

Season	Club	League	GP	G	A	Pts	AG	AA	APts	PIM	GP	G	A	Pts	PIM
1941-42	Portage Terriers	MJHL	14	2	0	2	....	....	....	2	4	0	1	1	0
	Portage Terriers	M-Cup	10	0	0	0	....	....	....	0	....	....	....	....	....
1942-43	Portage Terriers	MJHL	11	2	2	4	....	....	....	14	....	....	....	....	....
1943-44	Portage Terriers	MJHL	1	0	0	0	....	....	....	0	2	0	0	0	2
	Chicago Black Hawks	**NHL**	**17**	**1**	**3**	**4**	**1**	**3**	**4**	**8**	....	....	....	....	....
1944-45			MILITARY SERVICE												
1945-46	Vancouver–Seattle	PCHL	49	21	27	48	....	....	....	31	3	0	1	1	0
1946-47	Seattle Ironmen	PCHL	37	7	10	17	....	....	....	16	10	2	2	4	6
1947-48	Portland Eagles	PCHL	5	0	2	2	....	....	....	4	....	....	....	....	....
1948-49	Portland Penguins	PCHL	17	0	1	1	....	....	....	15	....	....	....	....	....
1949-50	Kamloops Elks	OSHL	45	24	28	52	....	....	....	61	7	2	4	6	4
1950-51	Calgary Stampeders	WCSHL	7	1	0	1	....	....	....	10	....	....	....	....	....
	Kamloops Elks	OSHL	41	24	27	51	....	....	....	24	6	6	4	10	6
1951-52	Kamloops Elks	OSHL	27	11	12	23	....	....	....	24	....	....	....	....	....
1952-53			DID NOT PLAY												
1953-54	Kimberley Dynamiters	WIHL	38	18	20	38	....	....	....	41	9	3	3	6	12
	NHL Totals		**17**	**1**	**3**	**4**	**1**	**3**	**4**	**8**	....	....	....	....	....

• CAMPBELL, Earl Robert Earl "Spiff"

D – L. 5'11", 166 lbs. b: Buckingham, Que., 7/23/1900 d: 2/11/1953.

Season	Club	League	GP	G	A	Pts	AG	AA	APts	PIM	GP	G	A	Pts	PIM
1918-19	Ottawa New Edinburghs	OCHL	3	0	0	0	....	....	....	0	....	....	....	....	....
	Ottawa Aberdeens	OCHL	5	0	1	1	....	....	....	3	....	....	....	....	....
1919-20	Hull Volants	OCHL	8	8	0	8	....	....	....	....	....	....	....	....	....
1920-21	Hull Volants	OCHL	STATISTICS NOT AVAILABLE												
1921-22	Saskatoon Quakers	WCHL	20	7	4	11	....	....	....	19	....	....	....	....	....
1922-23	Saskatoon Quakers	WCHL	10	2	2	4	....	....	....	8	....	....	....	....	....
	Edmonton Eskimos	WCHL	14	3	2	5	....	....	....	6	4	0	0	0	0
1923-24	Edmonton Eskimos	WCHL	5	0	2	2	....	....	....	4	....	....	....	....	....
	Ottawa Senators	**NHL**	**18**	**5**	**3**	**8**	**10**	**17**	**27**	**8**	**1**	**0**	**0**	**0**	**6**
1924-25	**Ottawa Senators**	**NHL**	**29**	**0**	**0**	**0**	**0**	**0**	**0**	**0**	....	....	....	....	....
1925-26	**New York Americans**	**NHL**	**29**	**1**	**0**	**1**	**2**	**0**	**2**	**6**	....	....	....	....	....
1926-27	Hamilton Tigers	Can-Pro	26	4	0	4	....	....	....	22	2	1	0	1	0
1927-28	Hamilton Tigers	Can-Pro	4	0	0	0	....	....	....	0	....	....	....	....	....
	Stratford Nationals	Can-Pro	12	1	0	1	....	....	....	4	....	....	....	....	....
1928-29	Kitchener Dutchmen	Can-Pro	29	4	2	6	....	....	....	37	....	....	....	....	....
	NHL Totals		**76**	**6**	**3**	**9**	**12**	**17**	**29**	**14**	**1**	**0**	**0**	**0**	**6**
	Other Major League Totals		49	12	10	22	....	....	....	37	4	0	0	0	0

WCHL All-Star Team (1923)

Signed as a free agent by **Saskatoon** (WCHL), November 28, 1921. Traded to **Edmonton** (WCHL) by **Saskatoon** (WCHL) for cash, January 30, 1923. Loaned to **Ottawa** by **Edmonton** (WCHL) for 1923-24 season, December 23, 1923. Traded to **Ottawa** by **Edmonton** (WCHL) for cash, November 19, 1924. Signed as a free agent by **NY Americans**, September 18, 1925. Signed as a free agent by **Stratford** (Can-Pro) after release by **Hamilton** (Can-Pro), November 29, 1927.

• CAMPEAU, Tod Jean-Claude

C – L. 5'11", 170 lbs. b: St. Jerome, Que., 6/4/1923.

Season	Club	League	GP	G	A	Pts	AG	AA	APts	PIM	GP	G	A	Pts	PIM
1940-41	Concordia College	MCHL	1	0	0	0	....	....	....	0	....	....	....	....	....
1941-42	Concordia College	MCHL	STATISTICS NOT AVAILABLE												
1942-43	Montreal Jr. Canadiens	QJHL	14	11	*21	32	....	....	....	0	7	6	5	11	17
	Montreal Sr. Canadiens	QSHL	1	0	0	0	....	....	....	0	....	....	....	....	....
	Montreal Jr. Canadiens	M-Cup	7	6	14	20	....	....	....	2	....	....	....	....	....
1943-44	**Montreal Canadiens**	**NHL**	**2**	**0**	**0**	**0**	**0**	**0**	**0**	**0**	....	....	....	....	....
	Montreal Vickers	MCHL	12	*13	13	26	....	....	....	7	....	....	....	....	....
	Montreal Royals	QSHL	20	18	12	30	....	....	....	8	7	3	5	8	2
1944-45	Pittsburgh Hornets	AHL	6	1	2	3	....	....	....	2	....	....	....	....	....
	Valleyfield Braves	IPHL	22	16	23	39	....	....	....	10	11	8	8	16	11
	Valleyfield Braves	Al-Cup	3	0	1	1	....	....	....	2	....	....	....	....	....
1945-46	Valleyfield Braves	QSHL	40	28	*50	*78	....	....	....	45	....	....	....	....	....

			REGULAR SEASON								PLAYOFFS				
Season	Club	League	GP	G	A	Pts	AG	AA	APts	PIM	GP	G	A	Pts	PIM
1946-47	Montreal Royals	QSHL	39	22	31	53	....	....	....	44	9	3	9	12	12
	Montreal Royals	Al-Cup	14	*14	11	*25	....	....	....	6	....	....	....	....	....
1947-48	**Montreal Canadiens**	**NHL**	**14**	**2**	**2**	**4**	**3**	**3**	**6**	**4**	....	....	....	....	....
	Buffalo Bisons	AHL	31	10	9	19	....	....	....	6	8	0	1	1	6
1948-49	**Montreal Canadiens**	**NHL**	**26**	**3**	**7**	**10**	**4**	**10**	**14**	**12**	**1**	**0**	**0**	**0**	**0**
	Dallas Texans	USHL	30	16	28	44	....	....	....	13	....	....	....	....	....
1949-50	Cincinnati Mohawks	AHL	68	22	41	63	....	....	....	53	....	....	....	....	....
1950-51	Cincinnati Mohawks	AHL	68	13	41	54	....	....	....	36	....	....	....	....	....
1951-52	Sherbrooke Saints	QMHL	51	20	29	49	....	....	....	32	11	2	9	11	14
1952-53	Sherbrooke Saints	QMHL	60	19	49	68	....	....	....	48	7	1	4	5	6
1953-54	Sherbrooke Saints	QHL	13	1	1	2	....	....	....	0	....	....	....	....	....
	Providence Reds	AHL	44	10	26	36	....	....	....	16	....	....	....	....	....
1954-55	Ottawa Senators	QHL	12	3	4	7	....	....	....	15	....	....	....	....	....
	Moncton Flyers	ACSHL	29	12	34	46	....	....	....	35	13	2	10	12	14
	Moncton Flyers	Al-Cup	13	3	19	22	....	....	....	20	....	....	....	....	....
1955-56	Chicoutimi Sagueneens	QHL	57	5	13	18	....	....	....	36	2	0	0	0	2
1956-57	Dalhousie Rangers	NNBHL	48	38	45	83	....	....	....	75	13	6	7	13	16
	Dalhousie Rangers	Al-Cup	8	8	10	18	....	....	....	6	....	....	....	....	....
	NHL Totals		**42**	**5**	**9**	**14**	**7**	**13**	**20**	**16**	**1**	**0**	**0**	**0**	**0**

Traded to **Pittsburgh** (AHL) by **Montreal** for cash, November 24, 1944. Signed as a free agent by **Valleyfield** (QSHL), September 19, 1945. Traded to **Sherbrooke** (QMHL) by **Montreal Royals** (QMHL) for cash, December 13, 1951.

• CARBOL, Leo

D – R. 5'11", 170 lbs. b: Ottawa, Ont., 6/5/1910.

Season	Club	League	GP	G	A	Pts	AG	AA	APts	PIM	GP	G	A	Pts	PIM
1929-30	Canmore Canadians	ASHL	STATISTICS NOT AVAILABLE												
	Seattle Eskimos	PCHL	1	0	0	0	....	....	....	0	....	....	....	....	....
1930-31	Minneapolis Millers	AHA	44	5	5	10	....	....	....	*110	....	....	....	....	....
1931-32	Buffalo Majors	AHA	19	2	0	2	....	....	....	30	....	....	....	....	....
	St. Louis Flyers	AHA	7	0	1	1	....	....	....	4	....	....	....	....	....
1932-33	Detroit Olympics	IHL	23	0	3	3	....	....	....	46	....	....	....	....	....
	St. Louis Flyers	AHA	19	2	2	4	....	....	....	40	4	0	0	0	8
1933-34	St. Louis Flyers	AHA	48	3	2	5	....	....	....	65	7	0	0	0	10
1934-35	St. Louis Flyers	AHA	48	6	7	13	....	....	....	69	6	0	1	1	*32
1935-36	St. Louis Flyers	AHA	46	2	5	7	....	....	....	63	8	1	0	1	8
1936-37	St. Louis Flyers	AHA	47	2	7	9	....	....	....	82	6	0	1	1	*16
1937-38	St. Louis Flyers	AHA	48	6	15	21	....	....	....	62	7	0	1	1	10
1938-39	St. Louis Flyers	AHA	48	3	15	18	....	....	....	67	7	1	2	3	10
1939-40	St. Louis Flyers	AHA	48	6	17	23	....	....	....	53	5	1	1	2	2
1940-41	St. Louis Flyers	AHA	43	3	19	22	....	....	....	58	9	1	*6	7	6
1941-42	St. Louis Flyers	AHA	48	5	11	16	....	....	....	69	2	0	0	0	10
1942-43	**Chicago Black Hawks**	**NHL**	**6**	**0**	**1**	**1**	**0**	**1**	**1**	**4**	....	....	....	....	....
1943-44			MILITARY SERVICE												
1944-45			MILITARY SERVICE												
1945-46	St. Louis Flyers	AHL	1	0	0	0	....	....	....	0	....	....	....	....	....
	NHL Totals		**6**	**0**	**1**	**1**	**0**	**1**	**1**	**4**	....	....	....	....	....

AHA First All-Star Team (1935, 1939, 1941, 1942) • AHA Second All-Star Team (1938)

NHL rights transferred to **Detroit** from **Chicago Shamrocks** (AHA) after AHA club owners purchased Detroit (IHL and NHL) franchises, September 2, 1932. Traded to **Chicago** by **St. Louis** (AHA) with Alex Wood for cash, October 9, 1942.

• CAREY, George

RW – R. 5'6", 140 lbs. b: unknown Deceased.

Season	Club	League	GP	G	A	Pts	AG	AA	APts	PIM	GP	G	A	Pts	PIM
1911-12	Quebec Crescents	QCHL	STATISTICS NOT AVAILABLE												
	Quebec Bulldogs	NHA	1	0	0	0	....	....	....	0	....	....	....	....	....
1912-13	Shawinigan Seniors	IPAHU	6	3	0	3	....	....	....	3	....	....	....	....	....
1913-14	Quebec St. Pats	IPAHU	7	7	0	7	....	....	....	....	....	....	....	....	....
1914-15	Quebec YMCA	QCHL	9	16	0	16	....	....	....	....	....	....	....	....	....
1915-16	Quebec Sons of Ireland	QCHL	8	17	0	17	....	....	....	....	2	*6	0	*6	....
1916-17	Quebec Bulldogs	NHA	19	8	13	21	....	....	....	11	....	....	....	....	....
1917-18	**Montreal Wanderers**	**NHL**	DID NOT PLAY – SUSPENDED												
1918-19			MILITARY SERVICE												
1919-20	**Quebec Bulldogs**	**NHL**	**20**	**11**	**9**	**20**	**12**	**31**	**43**	**6**	....	....	....	....	....
1920-21	**Hamilton Tigers**	**NHL**	**20**	**6**	**1**	**7**	**8**	**4**	**12**	**8**	....	....	....	....	....
1921-22	**Hamilton Tigers**	**NHL**	**23**	**3**	**2**	**5**	**4**	**6**	**10**	**6**	....	....	....	....	....
1922-23	**Hamilton Tigers**	**NHL**	**5**	**1**	**0**	**1**	**2**	**0**	**2**	**0**	....	....	....	....	....
	Calgary Tigers	WCHL	16	3	4	7	....	....	....	0	....	....	....	....	....
1923-24	**Toronto St. Pats**	**NHL**	**4**	**0**	**0**	**0**	**0**	**0**	**0**	**0**	....	....	....	....	....
	NHL Totals		**72**	**21**	**12**	**33**	**26**	**41**	**67**	**20**	....	....	....	....	....
	Other Major League Totals		36	11	17	28	....	....	....	11	....	....	....	....	....

Transferred to **Montreal Wanderers** from **Quebec** in Dispersal Draft, November 26, 1917. • Suspended by **Montreal Wanderers** for refusing to report to NHL club, November 29, 1917. Transferred to **Quebec** by **NHL** after Quebec franchise returned to NHL, November 25, 1919. Transferred to **Hamilton** after **Quebec** franchise relocated, November 2, 1920. Loaned to **Calgary** (WCHL) by **Hamilton**, January 16, 1923. Traded to **Toronto** by **Hamilton** with Amos Arbour and Bert Corbeau for Ken Randall, the NHL rights to Corb Denneny and cash, December 14, 1923.

• CARLETON, Wayne *— see page 953*

• CARPENTER, Ed

Everard Lorne

D – R. 6', 170 lbs. b: Hartford, MI, 6/15/1890 d: 4/30/1963.

Season	Club	League	GP	G	A	Pts	AG	AA	APts	PIM	GP	G	A	Pts	PIM
1909-10	Port Arthur Thunder Bays	NOHL	13	2	0	2	....	....	....	51	....	....	....	....	....
1910-11	Port Arthur Lake City	NOHL	14	6	0	6	....	....	....	54	3	1	0	1	*18
1911-12	Port Arthur Lake City	NOHA	15	2	0	2	....	....	....	39	2	0	0	0	3
1912-13	Moncton Victorias	MPHL	14	6	0	6	....	....	....	17	....	....	....	....	....
1913-14	New Glascow Black Foxes	MPHL	19	8	0	8	....	....	....	37	2	0	0	0	7
1914-15	Toronto Blueshirts	NHA	19	1	0	1	....	....	....	63	....	....	....	....	....
1915-16	Seattle Metropolitans	PCHA	18	6	4	10	....	....	....	17	....	....	....	....	....
	PCHA All-Stars	X-Games	3	0	0	0	....	....	....	3	....	....	....	....	....
♦1916-17	Seattle Metropolitans	PCHA	24	5	3	8	....	....	....	19	4	0	0	0	3
1917-18			MILITARY SERVICE												
1918-19			MILITARY SERVICE												
1919-20	**Quebec Bulldogs**	**NHL**	**24**	**8**	**4**	**12**	**9**	**13**	**22**	**24**	....	....	....	....	....
1920-21	**Hamilton Tigers**	**NHL**	**21**	**2**	**1**	**3**	**2**	**4**	**6**	**17**	....	....	....	....	....
	NHL Totals		**45**	**10**	**5**	**15**	**11**	**17**	**28**	**41**	....	....	....	....	....
	Other Major League Totals		121	34	7	41	....	....	....	258	9	1	0	1	28

Signed as a free agent by **Toronto Blueshirts** (NHA), December 9, 1914. Jumped contract with **Toronto Blueshirts** (NHA) and signed with **Seattle** (PCHA), November 12, 1915. Signed as a free agent by **Montreal Canadiens**, December 15, 1919. Traded to **Quebec** by **Montreal Canadiens** for Goldie Prodgers, December 21, 1919. Transferred to **Hamilton** after **Quebec** franchise relocated, November 2, 1920. Traded to **Toronto** by **Hamilton** for Cully Wilson, November 9, 1921.

• CARR, Lorne

Lorne William Bell

RW – R. 5'8", 161 lbs. b: Stoughton, Sask., 7/2/1910.

Season	Club	League	GP	G	A	Pts	AG	AA	APts	PIM	GP	G	A	Pts	PIM
1928-29	Calgary Canadians	CCJHL	3	4	2	6	....	....	....	0	4	6	0	6	0
	Calgary Canadians	M-Cup	9	*16	1	*17	....	....	....	4	....	....	....	....	....
1929-30	Calgary Canadians	CCJHL	....	....	....	....	....	....	....	....	2	0	0	0	0
	Calgary Canadians	M-Cup	7	7	3	10	....	....	....	2	....	....	....	....	....
1930-31	Vancouver Lions	PCHL	32	5	4	9	....	....	....	2	4	0	0	0	0
1931-32	Buffalo Bisons	IHL	40	5	9	14	....	....	....	10	6	2	0	2	4
1932-33	Buffalo Bisons	IHL	44	22	18	40	....	....	....	13	6	2	1	3	4
1933-34	**New York Rangers**	**NHL**	**14**	**0**	**0**	**0**	**0**	**0**	**0**	**0**	....	....	....	....	....
	Philadelphia Arrows	Can-Am	9	4	2	6	....	....	....	0	....	....	....	....	....
	Syracuse Stars	IHL	18	8	4	12	....	....	....	6	6	0	1	1	2
1934-35	**New York Americans**	**NHL**	**48**	**17**	**14**	**31**	**28**	**24**	**52**	**14**	....	....	....	....	....
1935-36	**New York Americans**	**NHL**	**44**	**8**	**10**	**18**	**15**	**19**	**34**	**4**	**5**	**1**	**1**	**2**	**0**
1936-37	**New York Americans**	**NHL**	**48**	**18**	**16**	**34**	**30**	**29**	**59**	**22**	....	....	....	....	....
1937-38	**New York Americans**	**NHL**	**48**	**16**	**7**	**23**	**26**	**11**	**37**	**12**	**6**	**3**	**1**	**4**	**2**
1938-39	**New York Americans**	**NHL**	**46**	**19**	**18**	**37**	**34**	**28**	**62**	**16**	**2**	**0**	**0**	**0**	**0**
1939-40	**New York Americans**	**NHL**	**48**	**8**	**17**	**25**	**13**	**27**	**40**	**17**	**3**	**0**	**0**	**0**	**0**
1940-41	**New York Americans**	**NHL**	**48**	**13**	**19**	**32**	**20**	**27**	**47**	**10**	....	....	....	....	....
♦1941-42	**Toronto Maple Leafs**	**NHL**	**47**	**16**	**17**	**33**	**21**	**20**	**41**	**4**	**13**	**3**	**2**	**5**	**6**
1942-43	**Toronto Maple Leafs**	**NHL**	**50**	**27**	**33**	**60**	**28**	**31**	**59**	**15**	**6**	**1**	**2**	**3**	**0**
1943-44	**Toronto Maple Leafs**	**NHL**	**50**	**36**	**38**	**74**	**33**	**34**	**67**	**9**	**5**	**0**	**1**	**1**	**0**
♦1944-45	**Toronto Maple Leafs**	**NHL**	**47**	**21**	**25**	**46**	**21**	**29**	**50**	**7**	**13**	**2**	**2**	**4**	**5**
1945-46	**Toronto Maple Leafs**	**NHL**	**42**	**5**	**8**	**13**	**6**	**12**	**18**	**2**	....	....	....	....	....
	NHL Totals		**580**	**204**	**222**	**426**	**275**	**291**	**566**	**132**	**53**	**10**	**9**	**19**	**13**

NHL First All-Star Team (1943, 1944)

Traded to **Buffalo** (IHL) by **NY Rangers** with $15,000 for Carl Voss, October 4, 1932. Traded to **NY Rangers** by **Buffalo** (IHL) for cash, April 8, 1933. Traded to **Syracuse** (IHL) by **NY Rangers** for cash, January 30, 1934. Traded to **NY Americans** by **Syracuse** (IHL) for Ron Martin and the loan of Walter Jackson for the 1934-35 season, November 5, 1934. Traded to **Toronto** by **Brooklyn** for the loan of Red Heron, Gus Marker, Nick Knott and future considerations (cash, February 2, 1942), October 30, 1941.

• CARR, Red

Alfred George Richard

LW – L. 5'8", 178 lbs. b: Winnipeg, Man., 12/29/1916.

Season	Club	League	GP	G	A	Pts	AG	AA	APts	PIM	GP	G	A	Pts	PIM
1931-32	Winnipeg Falcons	WJrHL	4	0	0	0	....	....	....	12	1	0	0	0	0
1932-33	Winnipeg Falcons	WJrHL	10	0	2	2	....	....	....	20	....	....	....	....	....
1933-34	Winnipeg Falcons	WJrHL	STATISTICS NOT AVAILABLE												
1934-35	Nelson Maple Leafs	WKHL	DID NOT PLAY – SUSPENDED												
1935-36	Trail Smoke Eaters	WKHL	14	5	1	6	....	....	....	11	8	*7	2	9	4
1936-37	Nelson Maple Leafs	WKHL	14	6	5	11	....	....	....	*20	3	1	0	1	*12
	Nelson Maple Leafs	Al-Cup	4	3	5	8	....	....	....	4	....	....	....	....	....
1937-38	Nelson Maple Leafs	WKHL	24	19	16	35	....	....	....	43	2	0	1	1	2
1938-39	Nelson Maple Leafs	WKHL	19	12	6	18	....	....	....	43	3	3	0	3	8
1939-40	Nelson Maple Leafs	WKHL	23	12	7	19	....	....	....	29	7	0	3	3	*14
1940-41	Bralorne Barons	BCIHA	STATISTICS NOT AVAILABLE												
1941-42	Nanaimo Clippers	BCIHA	27	20	16	36	....	....	....	*54	7	6	2	8	6
1942-43	Nanaimo Clippers	BCIHA	20	12	8	20	....	....	....	9	3	0	1	1	2
1943-44	**Toronto Maple Leafs**	**NHL**	**5**	**0**	**1**	**1**	**0**	**1**	**1**	**2**	....	....	....	....	....
	Providence Reds	AHL	2	0	0	0	....	....	....	0	....	....	....	....	....
	Toronto Staffords	TMHL	2	2	0	2	....	....	....	0	....	....	....	....	....
	Toronto CIL	TMHL	3	0	0	0	....	....	....	2	....	....	....	....	....
1944-45	Providence Reds	AHL	2	0	0	0	....	....	....	0	....	....	....	....	....
	Toronto Staffords	OHA-Sr.	4	3	7	10	....	....	....	0	....	....	....	....	....
	Toronto Auto Workers	TMHL	9	15	15	30	....	....	....	9	....	....	....	....	....
1945-46	Portland Eagles	PCHL	54	43	49	92	....	....	....	91	8	7	3	*10	15
1946-47	Portland /N-Westminster	PCHL	57	19	42	61	....	....	....	34	4	1	2	3	0
1947-48	N-Westminster/Tacoma	PCHL	33	7	14	21	....	....	....	22	....	....	....	....	....
1948-49	Milwaukee Clarks	IHL	32	19	27	46	....	....	....	39	4	0	1	1	0
1949-50	Nanaimo Clippers	BCIHA	31	14	31	45	....	....	....	33	8	2	2	4	6
1950-51	Nanaimo Clippers	BCIHA	45	18	41	59	....	....	....	42	9	3	*9	12	8
1951-52	Nanaimo Clippers	BCIHA	41	15	17	32	....	....	....	33	6	2	3	5	2
	Nanaimo Clippers	Al-Cup	5	0	1	1	....	....	....	6	....	....	....	....	....
	NHL Totals		**5**	**0**	**1**	**1**	**0**	**1**	**1**	**2**	....	....	....	....	....

• Father of Gene • Suspended for entire 1934-35 season by CAHA when transter from Manitoba to British Columbia was refused, October, 1934.

• CARRIGAN, Gene

Eugene

C – L. 6'1", 200 lbs. b: Edmonton, Alta., 7/5/1907 d: 3/15/1944.

Season	Club	League	GP	G	A	Pts	AG	AA	APts	PIM	GP	G	A	Pts	PIM
1923-24	Edmonton Eskimos	EJrHL	STATISTICS NOT AVAILABLE												
1924-25	Edmonton Eskimos	EJrHL	STATISTICS NOT AVAILABLE												
1925-26	Camrose Canadians	ASHL	STATISTICS NOT AVAILABLE												
1926-27	Edmonton Eskimos	PrHL	19	0	0	0	....	....	....	4	....	....	....	....	....
1927-28	Hollywood Millionaires	Cal-Pro	STATISTICS NOT AVAILABLE												
1928-29	Springfield Indians	Can-Am	39	10	1	11	....	....	....	23	....	....	....	....	....
	Portland Buckaroos	PCHL	10	0	0	0	....	....	....	0	....	....	....	....	....
	Victoria Cubs	PCHL	2	0	0	0	....	....	....	0	....	....	....	....	....
1929-30	Springfield Indians	Can-Am	38	*28	24	52	....	....	....	22	....	....	....	....	....
1930-31	**New York Rangers**	**NHL**	**33**	**2**	**0**	**2**	**4**	**0**	**4**	**13**	....	....	....	....	....
	Springfield Indians	Can-Am	13	5	10	15	....	....	....	10	7	4	4	8	2
1931-32	London Tecumsehs	IHL	48	19	9	28	....	....	....	27	6	0	0	0	5
1932-33	London Tecumsehs	IHL	41	19	14	33	....	....	....	23	6	2	3	5	2
1933-34	Detroit Olympics	IHL	43	17	18	35	....	....	....	19	4	2	3	5	0
	Detroit Red Wings	**NHL**	....	....	....	....	....	....	....	....	**4**	**0**	**0**	**0**	**0**
1934-35	Boston Cubs	Can-Am	42	19	*37	56	....	....	....	18	3	1	1	2	2
	St. Louis Eagles	**NHL**	**4**	**0**	**1**	**1**	**0**	**2**	**2**	**0**	....	....	....	....	....

Season	Club	League	GP	G	A	Pts	AG	AA	APts	PIM	GP	G	A	Pts	PIM
			REGULAR SEASON								PLAYOFFS				
1935-36	Boston Cubs	Can-Am	18	3	7	10				4					
	Detroit Olympics	IHL	28	5	13	18				11	6	0	4	4	2
1936-37	Springfield Indians	IAHL	47	6	11	17				22	5	0	0	0	0
1937-38	Springfield Indians	IAHL	14	1	7	8				0					
	New Haven Eagles	IAHL	24	1	2	3				17	2	0	0	0	0
1938-39	St. Paul Saints	AHA	47	28	26	54				13	3	1	0	1	0
1939-40	St. Paul Saints	AHA	47	16	36	52				19	7	2	3	5	2
1940-41	St. Paul Saints	AHA	48	5	15	20				18	4	0	0	0	0
1941-42	Fort Worth Rangers	AHA	43	11	11	22				19	5	0	3	3	4
	NHL Totals		**37**	**2**	**1**	**3**	**4**	**2**	**6**	**13**	**4**	**0**	**0**	**0**	**0**

Can-Am Second All-Star Team (1930) • AHA Second All-Star Team (1939)

Signed as a free agent by **Edmonton** (PrHL), November 7, 1926. Claimed by **NY Rangers** from **Hollywood** (Cal-Pro) in Inter-League Draft, May 14, 1928. Signed as a free agent by **Victoria** (PCHL) after release by **Portland** (PCHL), November 29, 1927. Traded to **Chicago** (London-IHL) by **NY Rangers** for cash, October 27, 1931. Traded to **Detroit** by **Chicago** (London-IHL) for Frank Waite and Leroy Goldsworthy, October 19, 1933. Traded to **Boston** by **Detroit** for George Patterson, May 12, 1934. Loaned to **St. Louis** by **Boston** to replace injured Frank Jerwa, January 18, 1935 and returned January 30, 1935. Traded to **Detroit** by **Boston** for Lorne Duguid, December 29, 1935. Signed as a free agent by **St. Paul** (AHA), Ocotber 23, 1939

• CARROLL, George

George Edward
D – R. 6'2", 210 lbs. b: Moncton, N.B., 6/3/1897 d: 8/1/1939.

Season	Club	League	GP	G	A	Pts	AG	AA	APts	PIM	GP	G	A	Pts	PIM
1912-13	Moncton CNR Machinists	MCSHL	STATISTICS NOT AVAILABLE												
1913-14	Moncton CNR Machinists	MCSHL	7	6	0	6					1	1	0	1	0
1914-15	Moncton St. Bernard's	MISSL	2	0	0	0									
1915-16	Moncton St. Bernard's	X-Games	2	1	0	1									
1916-17	Moncton St. Bernard's	X-Games	2	5	0	5									
1917-18			DID NOT PLAY												
1918-19	Moncton Victorias	X-Games	2	1	0	1									
1919-20	Moncton Victorias	MIHL	6	3	4	7				*27	11	16	6	22	*25
1920-21	Moncton Victorias	MIHL	9	5	0	5				*31	2	0	0	0	0
1921-22	Moncton Victorias	MIHL	13	12	0	12				*64					
1922-23	Moncton Victorias	MIHL	9	1	0	1				35	2	1	0	1	4
1923-24	Moncton Victorias	MIHL	16	10	0	10				*63					
1924-25	**Montreal Maroons**	**NHL**	**5**	**0**	**0**	**0**	**0**	**0**	**0**	**2**					
	Boston Bruins	**NHL**	**11**	**0**	**0**	**0**	**0**	**0**	**0**	**9**					
	Moncton Victorias	MIHL	3	1	1	2				2					
1925-26	Sunny Brae Rovers	NBCSL	DID NOT PLAY – COACHING												
	NHL Totals		**16**	**0**	**0**	**0**	**0**	**0**	**0**	**11**					

MIHL First All-Star Team (1921, 1922, 1924) • MIHL Second Team All-Star (1923)

Signed as a free agent by **Montreal Maroons**, November 13, 1924. Traded to **Boston** by **Montreal Maroons** for the rights to Ernie Parkes, December 19, 1924. Signed as a free agent by **Montreal Maroons** folowing release by **Boston**, February 22, 1925.

• CARRUTHERS, Dwight

— *see page 958*

• CARSE, Bill

Bill Alexander
C – L. 5'8", 165 lbs. b: Edmonton, Alta., 5/29/1914.

Season	Club	League	GP	G	A	Pts	AG	AA	APts	PIM	GP	G	A	Pts	PIM
1930-31	Edmonton Strathconas	EJrHL	1	1	0	1				0					
1931-32	Edmonton Canadians	EJrHL	12	2	1	3				3					
	Edmonton Strathconas	EJrHL	1	1	0	1				0					
1932-33	Edmonton Canadiens	EJrHL	12							16	3	*2	0	*2	6
	Edmonton Canadiens	M-Cup	3	2	1	3				12					
1933-34	Edmonton Athletic Club	EJrHL	9	6	2	8				12	2	*4	0	4	4
	Edmonton Athletic Club	M-Cup	13	21	11	32				16					
1934-35	Edmonton Eskimos	NWHL	28	19	13	32				27					
1935-36	Edmonton Eskimos	NWHL	24	10	7	17				27					
	Vancouver Lions	NWHL	15	7	1	8				6	5	0	0	0	4
1936-37	Vancouver Lions	PCHL	40	*29	9	*38				40	3	1	0	1	2
1937-38	Philadelphia Ramblers	IAHL	48	15	25	40				26	5	1	2	3	0
1938-39	**New York Rangers**	**NHL**	**1**	**0**	**1**	**1**	**0**	**2**	**2**	**0**	**6**	**1**	**1**	**2**	**0**
	Philadelphia Ramblers	IAHL	54	24	33	57				22	5	1	4	5	0
1939-40	**Chicago Black Hawks**	**NHL**	**48**	**10**	**13**	**23**	**17**	**20**	**37**	**10**	**2**	**1**	**0**	**1**	**0**
1940-41	**Chicago Black Hawks**	**NHL**	**32**	**5**	**15**	**20**	**8**	**21**	**29**	**12**	**2**	**0**	**0**	**0**	**0**
1941-42	**Chicago Black Hawks**	**NHL**	**43**	**13**	**14**	**27**	**17**	**17**	**34**	**16**	**3**	**1**	**1**	**2**	**0**
1942-43	Victoria Army	PCHL	20	21	*23	*44				8	5	4	6	10	0
	Victoria Army	Al-Cup	13	10	15	25				12					
1943-44	Nanaimo Army	PCHL	3	0	3	3				0					
1944-45			MILITARY SERVICE												
1945-46	Vancouver Canucks	PCHL	56	38	43	81				22	10	*6	7	13	2
1946-47			DID NOT PLAY												
1947-48	Vancouver Canucks	PCHL	63	19	40	59				44	13	4	10	14	4
1948-49	Vancouver Canucks	PCHL	70	29	*64	93				12	3	1	2	3	0
1949-50	Vancouver Canucks	PCHL	41	9	13	22				2					
1950-51	Vancouver Canucks	PCHL	DID NOT PLAY – COACHING												
	NHL Totals		**124**	**28**	**43**	**71**	**42**	**60**	**102**	**38**	**13**	**3**	**2**	**5**	**0**

• Brother of Bob • AHL Second All-Star Team (1939) • PCHL Northern First All-Star Team (1949)

• Only games played and penalty minute totals available for Edmonton (EJrHL) in 1932-33. Traded to **Vancouver** (NWHL) by **Edmonton** (NWHL) with Lorin Mercer for future considerations (loan of Henry Dyck and Norm Pridham, January 26, 1936) and cash, January 22, 1936. Traded to **NY Rangers** by **Vancouver** (PCHL) for cash, October 12, 1937. Traded to **Chicago** by **NY Rangers** for cash, May 17, 1939. Signed as a free agent by **Vancouver** (PCHL), October 6, 1947.

• CARSE, Bob

Robert Allison
LW – L. 5'9", 170 lbs. b: Edmonton, Alta., 7/19/1919.

Season	Club	League	GP	G	A	Pts	AG	AA	APts	PIM	GP	G	A	Pts	PIM
1935-36	Edmonton Athletic Club	EJrHL	12	1	6	7				9					
1936-37	Edmonton Athletic Club	EJrHL	11	8	6	14				25	3	1	1	2	2
1937-38	Edmonton Athletic Club	EJrHL	15	11	5	16				25	4	3	13	16	8
	Edmonton Athletic Club	M-Cup	11	13	2	15				20					
1938-39	Edmonton Athletic Club	EJrHL	7	12	9	21				8	2	3	0	3	5
	Edmonton Athletic Club	M-Cup	12	12	8	20				10					
1939-40	**Chicago Black Hawks**	**NHL**	**22**	**3**	**5**	**8**	**5**	**8**	**13**	**11**	**2**	**0**	**0**	**0**	**0**
	Providence Reds	IAHL	31	5	12	17				9	6	3	2	5	2
1940-41	**Chicago Black Hawks**	**NHL**	**43**	**9**	**9**	**18**	**14**	**13**	**27**	**9**	**5**	**0**	**0**	**0**	**2**
1941-42	**Chicago Black Hawks**	**NHL**	**33**	**7**	**16**	**23**	**9**	**19**	**28**	**10**	**3**	**0**	**2**	**2**	**0**
	Kansas City Americans	AHA	18	9	13	22				9					
1942-43	**Chicago Black Hawks**	**NHL**	**47**	**10**	**22**	**32**	**10**	**21**	**31**	**6**					
1943-44	Calgary Currie Army	CNDHL	16	8	12	20				16	2	0	5	5	0
1944-45			MILITARY SERVICE												
1945-46	Edmonton Flyers	WCSHL	36	32	46	78				18	8	5	5	*10	8
1946-47	Cleveland Barons	AHL	62	27	*61	88				16	4	0	0	0	0
1947-48	**Montreal Canadiens**	**NHL**	**22**	**3**	**3**	**6**	**4**	**4**	**8**	**16**					
	Cleveland Barons	AHL	43	21	33	54				14	9	4	5	9	4
1948-49	Cleveland Barons	AHL	65	18	47	65				28	5	1	3	4	4
1949-50	Cleveland Barons	AHL	69	30	52	82				23	9	3	4	7	4
	NHL Totals		**167**	**32**	**55**	**87**	**42**	**65**	**107**	**52**	**10**	**0**	**2**	**2**	**2**

• Brother of Bill • ASHL Second All-Star Team (1944) • WCSHL First All-Star Team (1946) • AHL First All-Star Team (1947, 1950)

Signed as a free agent by **Montreal**, October 14, 1947. Traded to **Cleveland** (AHL) by **Montreal** for future considerations, December 16, 1947.

• CARSON, Bill

William Joseph "Doc"
C – L. 5'8", 158 lbs. b: Bracebridge, Ont., 11/25/1900 d: 5/29/1967.

Season	Club	League	GP	G	A	Pts	AG	AA	APts	PIM	GP	G	A	Pts	PIM
1918-19	Woodstock Athletics	OHA-Jr.	STATISTICS NOT AVAILABLE												
1919-20	University of Toronto	OHA-Sr.	3	6	1	7									
	University of Toronto	Al-Cup	6	9	4	13									
1920-21	University of Toronto	OHA-Sr.	10	13	3	16					3	2	0	2	
	University of Toronto	Al-Cup	8	14	2	16									
1921-22	University of Toronto	OHA-Sr.	9	15	3	18									
1922-23	University of Toronto	OHA-Sr.	11	8	10	18									
1923-24	Grimsby Peach Kings	OHA-Sr.	STATISTICS NOT AVAILABLE												
	Toronto Granites	X-Games	5	9	2	11									
1924-25	Stratford Indians	OHA-Sr.	20	*29	8	*37				41	2	0	*2	2	3
1925-26	Stratford Indians	OHA-Sr.	17	19	3	22				23					
1926-27	**Toronto Pats/Leafs**	**NHL**	**40**	**16**	**6**	**22**	**29**	**31**	**60**	**41**					
1927-28	**Toronto Maple Leafs**	**NHL**	**32**	**20**	**6**	**26**	**41**	**34**	**75**	**36**					
1928-29	**Toronto Maple Leafs**	**NHL**	**24**	**7**	**6**	**13**	**20**	**40**	**60**	**45**					
♦	**Boston Bruins**	**NHL**	**19**	**4**	**2**	**6**	**11**	**13**	**24**	**10**	**5**	**2**	**0**	**2**	**8**
1929-30	**Boston Bruins**	**NHL**	**44**	**7**	**4**	**11**	**10**	**9**	**19**	**24**	**6**	**1**	**0**	**1**	**6**
1930-31	London Tecumsehs	IHL	7	0	1	1				2					
1931-32			OUT OF HOCKEY – RETIRED												
1932-33			OUT OF HOCKEY – RETIRED												
1933-34	New Haven Eagles	Can-Am	33	7	4	11				6					
	NHL Totals		**159**	**54**	**24**	**78**	**111**	**127**	**238**	**156**	**11**	**3**	**0**	**3**	**14**

• Brother of Frank and Gerry • OHA-Sr. Second All-Star Team (1920, 1922, 1923) • OHA-Sr. First All-Star Team (1921)

Signed as a free agent by **Toronto**, April 16, 1926. Traded to **Boston** by **Toronto** for cash, January 25, 1929. Traded to **London** (IHL) by **Boston** for cash, November 24, 1930.

• CARSON, Frank

Frank Reginald "Frosty"
RW – R. 5'7", 165 lbs. b: Bracebridge, Ont., 1/12/1902 d: 4/2/1957.

Season	Club	League	GP	G	A	Pts	AG	AA	APts	PIM	GP	G	A	Pts	PIM
1918-19	Woodstock Athletics	OHA-Jr.	STATISTICS NOT AVAILABLE												
1919-20	Stratford Midgets	OHA-Jr.	5	10	8	18					6	16	11	27	
1920-21	Stratford Midgets	OHA-Jr.	8	*20	9	29					13	33	15	48	
1921-22	Stratford Midgets	OHA-Jr.	4	10	5	15				6	4	9	3	12	
	Stratford Indians	OHA-Sr.	4	7	2	9				2	8	8	4	12	16
1922-23	Stratford Indians	OHA-Sr.	10	*21	9	*30				8	9	13	*10	23	20
1923-24	Stratford Indians	OHA-Sr.	12	19	10	*29				14	2	*3	*2	*5	0
1924-25	Stratford Indians	OHA-Sr.	20	18	8	26				38	2	*2	0	*2	*4
1925-26	Stratford Indians	OHA-Sr.	12	6	6	12				16					
	Montreal Maroons	**NHL**	**16**	**2**	**1**	**3**	**3**	**6**	**9**	**6**	**4**	**0**	**0**	**0**	**0**
♦	Montreal Maroons	St-Cup	4	0	0	0				0					
1926-27	**Montreal Maroons**	**NHL**	**44**	**2**	**3**	**5**	**4**	**16**	**20**	**12**	**2**	**0**	**0**	**0**	**2**
1927-28	**Montreal Maroons**	**NHL**	**21**	**0**	**1**	**1**	**0**	**6**	**6**	**10**	**9**	**0**	**0**	**0**	**0**
	Stratford Nationals	Can-Pro	13	6	1	7				18	5	3	*4	*7	4
1928-29	Windsor Bulldogs	Can-Pro	41	17	*12	29				60	8	4	1	5	18
1929-30	Windsor Bulldogs	IHL	41	*31	14	*45				65					
1930-31	**New York Americans**	**NHL**	**44**	**6**	**7**	**13**	**12**	**21**	**33**	**36**					
1931-32	New Haven Eagles	Can-Am	15	6	3	9				28					
	Detroit Falcons	**NHL**	**31**	**10**	**14**	**24**	**17**	**31**	**48**	**31**	**2**	**0**	**0**	**0**	**2**
1932-33	**Detroit Red Wings**	**NHL**	**45**	**12**	**13**	**25**	**22**	**27**	**49**	**35**	**4**	**0**	**1**	**1**	**0**
1933-34	**Detroit Red Wings**	**NHL**	**47**	**10**	**9**	**19**	**17**	**19**	**36**	**36**	**6**	**0**	**1**	**1**	**5**
1934-35	Windsor Mic-Macs	MIHL	DID NOT PLAY – COACHING												
	NHL Totals		**248**	**42**	**48**	**90**	**75**	**126**	**201**	**166**	**27**	**0**	**2**	**2**	**9**

• Brother of Bill and Gerry • IHL First All-Star Team (1930)

Signed as a free agent by **Montreal Maroons**, January 26, 1926. • 1925-26 Montreal Maroons playoff totals includes series against Ottawa and Pittsburgh. Traded to **NY Americans** by **Montreal Maroons** (Windsor-IHL) with Mike Neville, Hap Emms and Red Dutton for $35,000, May 14, 1930. Traded to **Detroit** by **NY Americans** with Hap Emms for Bert McInenly, Tommy Filmore, December 29, 1931. • Officially announced retirement, October 15, 1934. • Named coach of Windsor Mic-Macs (MIHL), November 4, 1934.

• CARSON, Gerry

Gerry George "Stub"
D – L. 5'10", 175 lbs. b: Parry Sound, Ont., 10/10/1905 d: 11/1/1956.

Season	Club	League	GP	G	A	Pts	AG	AA	APts	PIM	GP	G	A	Pts	PIM
1922-23	Woodstock Athletics	OHA-Jr.	STATISTICS NOT AVAILABLE												
1923/27	Grimsby Peach Kings	OHA-Sr.	STATISTICS NOT AVAILABLE												
1927-28	Philadelphia Arrows	Can-Am	37	7	4	11				38					
1928-29	**Montreal Canadiens**	**NHL**	**26**	**0**	**0**	**0**	**0**	**0**	**0**	**4**					
	New York Rangers	**NHL**	**14**	**0**	**0**	**0**	**0**	**0**	**0**	**5**	**5**	**0**	**0**	**0**	**0**
♦1929-30	**Montreal Canadiens**	**NHL**	**35**	**1**	**0**	**1**	**1**	**0**	**1**	**8**	**6**	**0**	**0**	**0**	**0**
	Providence Reds	Can-Am	6	1	0	1				19					
1930-31	Providence Reds	Can-Am	38	4	2	6				84	2	0	0	0	14
1931-32	Providence Reds	Can-Am	40	9	5	14				77	5	1	0	1	8
1932-33	**Montreal Canadiens**	**NHL**	**48**	**5**	**2**	**7**	**9**	**4**	**13**	**53**	**2**	**0**	**0**	**0**	**2**
1933-34	**Montreal Canadiens**	**NHL**	**48**	**5**	**1**	**6**	**9**	**2**	**11**	**51**	**2**	**0**	**0**	**0**	**2**

Season	Club	League	REGULAR SEASON GP	G	A	Pts	AG	AA	APts	PIM	PLAYOFFS GP	G	A	Pts	PIM
1934-35	Montreal Canadiens	NHL	48	0	5	5	0	9	9	56	2	0	0	0	4
1935-36	Montreal Canadiens	NHL	DID NOT PLAY – INJURED												
1936-37	Montreal Maroons	NHL	42	1	3	4	2	5	7	28	5	0	0	0	4
	NHL Totals		261	12	11	23	21	20	41	205	22	0	0	0	12

• Brother of Bill and Frank

Loaned to **NY Rangers** by **Montreal Canadiens** for remainder of 1929-30 season, February 15, 1929. Traded to **Providence** (Can-Am) by **Montreal Canadiens** with cash and the loan of Jean Pusie for Johnny Gagnon, October 21, 1930. • Missed entire 1935-36 season recovering from knee surgery, September, 1935. Traded to **Montreal Maroons** by **Montreal Canadiens** for the rights to George Brown, October 7, 1936.

• CARTER, Billy William Gordon

C – L. 5'11", 155 lbs. b: Cornwall, Ont., 12/2/1937.

Season	Club	League	GP	G	A	Pts	AG	AA	APts	PIM	GP	G	A	Pts	PIM
1954-55	Hochelaga Indians	QJHL	36	25	35	60	....	....	....	6	....	....	....	....	....
1955-56	Montreal Jr. Canadiens	QJHL	STATISTICS NOT AVAILABLE												
	Montreal Jr. Canadiens	M-Cup	1	0	0	0	....	....	....	2	....	....	....	....	....
1956-57	Hull-Ottawa Canadiens	OHA-Jr.	28	14	17	31	....	....	....	21	....	....	....	....	....
	Hull-Ottawa Canadiens	EOHL	16	7	7	14	....	....	....	6	....	....	....	....	....
	Rochester Americans	AHL	1	0	0	0	....	....	....	0	....	....	....	....	....
	Hull-Ottawa Canadiens	M-Cup	15	11	9	20	....	....	....	2	....	....	....	....	....
1957-58	Hull-Ottawa Canadiens	OHA-Jr.	27	15	29	44	....	....	....	26	....	....	....	....	....
	Hull-Ottawa Canadiens	EOHL	34	14	38	52	....	....	....	2	....	....	....	....	....
	Montreal Royals	QHL	1	0	0	0	....	....	....	0	....	....	....	....	....
	Montreal Canadiens	NHL	1	0	0	0	0	0	0	0	....	....	....	....	....
	Rochester Americans	AHL	1	0	0	0	....	....	....	0	....	....	....	....	....
	Hull-Ottawa Canadiens	M-Cup	13	15	15	30	....	....	....	4	....	....	....	....	....
1958-59	Rochester Americans	AHL	69	7	19	26	....	....	....	10	5	0	0	0	0
1959-60	Hull-Ottawa Canadiens	EPHL	70	42	60	102	....	....	....	2	7	1	4	5	2
1960-61	Boston Bruins	NHL	8	0	0	0	0	0	0	2	....	....	....	....	....
	Hull-Ottawa Canadiens	EPHL	60	27	32	59	....	....	....	6	14	4	5	9	6
1961-62	Montreal Canadiens	NHL	7	0	0	0	0	0	0	4	....	....	....	....	....
	Hull-Ottawa Canadiens	EPHL	62	26	47	73	....	....	....	17	13	6	8	14	0
1962-63	Hull-Ottawa Canadiens	EPHL	72	27	50	77	....	....	....	12	3	0	0	0	0
1963-64	Quebec Aces	AHL	36	2	9	11	....	....	....	2	....	....	....	....	....
	Seattle Totems	WHL	16	3	4	7	....	....	....	0	....	....	....	....	....
1964-65	Seattle Totems	WHL	16	0	2	2	....	....	....	0	....	....	....	....	....
	Memphis Wings	CPHL	41	6	20	26	....	....	....	0	6	1	4	5	0
1965-66	Buffalo Bisons	AHL	71	16	45	61	....	....	....	2	....	....	....	....	....
1966-67	Buffalo Bisons	AHL	71	14	38	52	....	....	....	8	....	....	....	....	....
1967-68	Omaha Knights	CPHL	67	9	30	39	....	....	....	6	....	....	....	....	....
	Buffalo Bisons	AHL	2	0	0	0	....	....	....	0	....	....	....	....	....
1968-69	Denver Spurs	WHL	74	16	49	65	....	....	....	4	....	....	....	....	....
	NHL Totals		16	0	0	0	0	0	0	6	....	....	....	....	....

EPHL Second All-Star Team (1960)

• Hull-Ottawa played partial schedule against OHA-Jr. teams in 1956-57 and 1957-58 that counted for the opposition only. Traded to **Boston** by **Montreal** for cash, June 6, 1960. Traded to **Montreal** by **Boston** for cash, November, 1961. Traded to **Detroit** (Pittsburgh-AHL) by **Montreal** (Seattle-WHL) for Chuck Holmes with Detroit holding right of recall, December, 1964.

• CARVETH, Joe Joseph Gordon

RW – R. 5'10", 180 lbs. b: Regina, Sask., 3/21/1918 d: 8/15/1985.

Season	Club	League	GP	G	A	Pts	AG	AA	APts	PIM	GP	G	A	Pts	PIM
1935-36	Regina Green Seals	RJrHL	6	*7	0	7	....	....	....	0	....	....	....	....	....
1936-37	Regina Jr. Aces	S-SSHL	6	6	*7	*13	....	....	....	2	2	2	1	3	0
	Regina Aces	S-SSHL	1	0	0	0	....	....	....	0	3	0	0	0	0
1937-38	Detroit Pontiacs	MOHL	27	9	16	25	....	....	....	57	3	0	0	0	0
1938-39	Detroit Pontiacs	MOHL	27	19	*25	44	....	....	....	25	7	3	5	8	4
1939-40	Indianapolis Capitols	IAHL	11	2	2	4	....	....	....	0	....	....	....	....	....
1940-41	Detroit Red Wings	NHL	19	2	1	3	3	1	4	2	....	....	....	....	....
1941-42	Detroit Red Wings	NHL	29	6	11	17	8	13	21	2	9	4	0	4	0
	Indianapolis Capitols	AHL	29	8	17	25	....	....	....	9	....	....	....	....	....
♦1942-43	Detroit Red Wings	NHL	43	18	18	36	18	17	35	6	10	*6	2	8	4
1943-44	Detroit Red Wings	NHL	46	21	35	56	19	31	50	6	5	2	1	3	8
	Indianapolis Capitols	AHL	1	1	1	2	....	....	....	2	....	....	....	....	....
1944-45	Detroit Red Wings	NHL	50	26	28	54	26	33	59	6	14	5	*6	*11	2
1945-46	Detroit Red Wings	NHL	48	17	18	35	20	26	46	10	5	0	1	1	0
1946-47	Boston Bruins	NHL	51	21	15	36	24	18	42	18	5	2	1	3	0
1947-48	Boston Bruins	NHL	22	8	9	17	10	12	22	2	....	....	....	....	....
	Montreal Canadiens	NHL	35	1	10	11	1	13	14	6	....	....	....	....	....
1948-49	Montreal Canadiens	NHL	60	15	22	37	21	31	52	8	7	0	1	1	8
1949-50	Montreal Canadiens	NHL	11	1	1	2	1	1	2	2	....	....	....	....	....
♦	Detroit Red Wings	NHL	60	13	17	30	16	20	36	13	14	2	4	6	6
1950-51	Detroit Red Wings	NHL	30	1	4	5	1	5	6	0	....	....	....	....	....
	Indianapolis Capitols	AHL	37	18	30	48	....	....	....	9	3	0	0	0	0
1951-52	Cleveland Barons	AHL	40	9	15	24	....	....	....	18	....	....	....	....	....
	Vancouver Canucks	PCHL	19	4	12	16	....	....	....	4	....	....	....	....	....
1952-53	Chatham Maroons	OHA-Sr.	47	45	39	84	....	....	....	38	....	....	....	....	....
	Toledo Mercurys	IHL	8	2	3	5	....	....	....	0	5	0	4	4	6
1953-54	Chatham Maroons	OHA-Sr.	55	16	26	42	....	....	....	105	6	3	1	4	4
	NHL Totals		504	150	189	339	168	221	389	81	69	21	16	37	28

Played in NHL All-Star Game (1950)

Signed as a free agent by **Detroit**, October 5, 1939. Traded to **Boston** by **Detroit** for Roy Conacher, August, 1946. Traded to **Montreal** by **Boston** for Jimmy Peters and John Quilty, December 16, 1947. Traded to **Detroit** by **Montreal** for Calum MacKay, November 11, 1949. Traded to **Cleveland** (AHL) by **Detroit** for cash, June 6, 1951.

• CASHMAN, Wayne — *see page 959*

• CERESINO, Ray

RW – R. 5'9", 160 lbs. b: Port Arthur, Ont., 4/24/1929.

Season	Club	League	GP	G	A	Pts	AG	AA	APts	PIM	GP	G	A	Pts	PIM
1944-45	Port Arthur Bruins	TBJHL	10	17	6	23	....	....	....	2	8	6	4	10	4
	Port Arthur Bruins	M-Cup	10	8	4	12	....	....	....	4	....	....	....	....	....
1945-46	Port Arthur Bruins	TBJHL	6	10	9	19	....	....	....	0	7	6	*11	*17	0
	Port Arthur Flyers	TBSHL	....	....	....	....	....	....	....	....	5	*7	1	*8	0
1946-47	Oshawa Generals	OHA-Jr.	28	24	29	53	....	....	....	4	5	0	6	6	2
1947-48	Oshawa Generals	OHA-Jr.	1	0	0	0	....	....	....	0	5	2	2	4	0

Season	Club	League	REGULAR SEASON GP	G	A	Pts	AG	AA	APts	PIM	PLAYOFFS GP	G	A	Pts	PIM
1948-49	Toronto Maple Leafs	NHL	12	1	1	2	1	1	2	2	....	....	....	....	....
	Pittsburgh Hornets	AHL	47	22	16	38	....	....	....	14	....	....	....	....	....
1949-50	Cleveland Barons	AHL	47	17	24	41	....	....	....	22	9	3	2	5	5
1950-51	Cleveland Barons	AHL	52	21	27	48	....	....	....	11	11	4	3	7	2
1951-52	Cleveland Barons	AHL	14	3	1	4	....	....	....	0	....	....	....	....	....
	Seattle Ironmen	PCHL	44	13	15	28	....	....	....	18	2	0	1	1	0
1952-53	Cleveland Barons	AHL	64	23	35	58	....	....	....	12	11	2	1	3	0
1953-54	Cleveland Barons	AHL	57	14	22	36	....	....	....	9	6	1	1	2	2
1954-55	Providence Reds	AHL	22	4	10	14	....	....	....	2	....	....	....	....	....
	Montreal Royals	QHL	3	0	0	0	....	....	....	0	....	....	....	....	....
1955-56	Victoria Cougars	WHL	21	1	4	5	....	....	....	2	....	....	....	....	....
1956-57	Sault Ste. Marie Indians	NOHA	43	9	20	29	....	....	....	4	....	....	....	....	....
	NHL Totals		12	1	1	2	1	1	2	2	....	....	....	....	....

Traded to **Cleveland** (AHL) by **Toronto** with Harry Taylor and the loan of Tod Sloan for the 1949-50 season for Bob Solinger, September 6, 1949. Traded to **Providence** (AHL) by **Cleveland** (AHL) for cash, June 19, 1954.

• CHAD, John

RW – R. 5'10", 167 lbs. b: Provost, Alta., 9/16/1919 d: 10/11/1970.

Season	Club	League	GP	G	A	Pts	AG	AA	APts	PIM	GP	G	A	Pts	PIM
1935-36	Prince Albert St. Marks	SAHA	....	....	....	....	....	....	....	....	2	2	0	2	0
1936-37	Prince Albert St. Marks	SAHA	....	....	....	....	....	....	....	....	2	3	0	3	0
1937-38	Saskatoon Chiefs	SCJHL	6	11	8	19	....	....	....	4	2	*4	*2	*6	9
	Saskatoon Chiefs	M-Cup	6	10	4	14	....	....	....	9	....	....	....	....	....
1938-39	Edmonton Athletic Club	EJrHL	7	*15	*15	*30	....	....	....	0	2	2	1	3	0
	Edmonton Athletic Club	M-Cup	14	26	15	41	....	....	....	16	....	....	....	....	....
1939-40	Chicago Black Hawks	NHL	22	8	3	11	13	5	18	11	2	0	0	0	0
	Providence Reds	IAHL	31	14	8	22	....	....	....	8	6	0	3	3	0
1940-41	Chicago Black Hawks	NHL	45	7	18	25	11	26	37	16	5	0	0	0	2
1941-42	Regina Rangers	S-SSHL	25	16	7	23	....	....	....	10	3	1	0	1	16
1942-43	Calgary RCAF	ASHL	23	20	21	41	....	....	....	32	7	7	4	11	*22
1943-44	Calgary Combines	CNDHL	9	2	1	3	....	....	....	4	....	....	....	....	....
1944-45	Calgary RCAF	CNDHL	9	5	6	11	....	....	....	6	....	....	....	....	....
1945-46	Wembley Lions	Britain	STATISTICS NOT AVAILABLE												
	Chicago Black Hawks	NHL	13	0	1	1	0	1	1	2	3	0	1	1	0
1946-47	Providence Reds	AHL	63	32	43	75	....	....	....	12	....	....	....	....	....
1947-48	Providence Reds	AHL	67	41	53	94	....	....	....	8	5	0	1	1	0
1948-49	Providence Reds	AHL	55	32	46	78	....	....	....	8	8	3	6	9	0
1949-50	Providence Reds	AHL	70	36	54	90	....	....	....	4	4	1	3	4	0
1950-51	Providence Reds	AHL	34	13	19	32	....	....	....	2	....	....	....	....	....
1951-52	Saskatoon Quakers	PCHL	67	35	47	82	....	....	....	6	13	7	10	17	0
1952-53	Saskatoon Quakers	WHL	70	26	34	60	....	....	....	20	13	7	4	11	0
	NHL Totals		80	15	22	37	24	32	56	29	10	0	1	1	2

ASHL Second All-Star Team (1943) • Named AHL's Most Gentlemanly Player (1950) • PCHL First All-Star Team (1952)

• Regular season totals unavailable for Prince Albert (SAHA) in 1935-36 and 1936-37 seasons. Signed as a free agent by **Chicago**, October 18, 1939.

• CHALMERS, Chick William

C – L. 6', 180 lbs. b: Stratford, Ont., 1/24/1934 d: 12/7/1994.

Season	Club	League	GP	G	A	Pts	AG	AA	APts	PIM	GP	G	A	Pts	PIM
1951-52	Guelph Biltmores	OHA-Jr.	53	11	17	28	....	....	....	12	11	2	2	4	2
	Guelph Biltmores	M-Cup	11	1	3	4	....	....	....	4	....	....	....	....	....
1952-53	Guelph Biltmores	OHA-Jr.	33	13	12	25	....	....	....	8	....	....	....	....	....
1953-54	Guelph Biltmores	OHA-Jr.	22	11	17	28	....	....	....	21	....	....	....	....	....
	Galt Black Hawks	OHA-Jr.	39	12	14	26	....	....	....	20	....	....	....	....	....
	New York Rangers	NHL	1	0	0	0	0	0	0	0	....	....	....	....	....
1954-55	Vancouver Canucks	WHL	17	2	3	5	....	....	....	4	....	....	....	....	....
	Kelowna Packers	OSHL	37	14	25	39	....	....	....	10	4	2	1	3	2
1955-56	Chatham Maroons	OHA-Sr.	45	13	12	25	....	....	....	29	11	3	6	9	8
	Chatham Maroons	Al-Cup	17	5	9	14	....	....	....	10	....	....	....	....	....
1956-57	Troy Bruins	IHL	1	0	0	0	....	....	....	0	....	....	....	....	....
	Chatham Maroons	OHA-Sr.	3	0	2	2	....	....	....	2	....	....	....	....	....
	S.S. Marie Greyhounds	NOHA	40	8	11	19	....	....	....	6	9	3	0	3	0
1957-58	Louisville Rebels	IHL	64	23	*58	81	....	....	....	4	11	2	4	6	0
1958-59	Louisville Rebels	IHL	53	34	49	83	....	....	....	14	11	3	7	10	4
1959-60	Louisville Rebels	IHL	68	41	*93	*134	....	....	....	4	6	3	0	3	0
1960-61	Omaha Knights	IHL	70	35	69	104	....	....	....	15	8	2	7	9	0
1961-62	Omaha Knights	IHL	68	29	73	102	....	....	....	18	7	3	5	8	2
1962-63	Omaha Knights	IHL	68	28	59	87	....	....	....	16	7	3	5	8	2
1963-64	Toledo Blades	IHL	70	32	62	94	....	....	....	20	13	2	*15	*17	2
1964-65	Toledo Blades	IHL	64	27	63	90	....	....	....	12	4	5	1	6	0
1965-66	Toledo Blades	IHL	70	28	65	93	....	....	....	31	....	....	....	....	....
1966-67	Toledo Blades	IHL	72	34	67	101	....	....	....	20	10	5	8	13	8
1967-68	Toledo Blades	IHL	70	22	45	67	....	....	....	14	....	....	....	....	....
1968-69	Des Moines Oak Leafs	IHL	64	6	32	38	....	....	....	12	....	....	....	....	....
1969-70	Toledo Blades	IHL	51	18	42	60	....	....	....	20	3	1	0	1	2
1970-71	Toledo Blades	IHL	35	6	14	20	....	....	....	12	....	....	....	....	....
	Greensboro Generals	EHL	20	2	17	19	....	....	....	0	9	1	3	4	2
	NHL Totals		1	0	0	0	0	0	0	0	....	....	....	....	....

IHL 2nd All-Star Team (1960, 1961, 1967) • Won George H. Wilkinson Trophy (Top Scorer - IHL) (1960) • IHL First All-Star Team (1962) • Won James Gatschene Memorial Trophy (MVP - IHL) (1965)

Traded to **Des Moines** (IHL) by **Toledo** (IHL) with Terry Kerr for John Annable, August, 1968. Traded to **Toledo** (IHL) by **Des Moines** (IHL) for Bob Regis, November, 1969. Traded to **Greensboro** (EHL) by **Toledo** (IHL) for cash, January, 1971.

• CHAMBERLAIN, Murph Erwin Groves "Old Hardrock"

LW – L. 5'11", 165 lbs. b: Shawville, Que., 2/14/1915 d: 5/8/1986.

Season	Club	League	GP	G	A	Pts	AG	AA	APts	PIM	GP	G	A	Pts	PIM
1932-33	Ottawa Primroses	OCJHL	11	7	2	9	....	....	....	19	4	3	1	4	6
1933-34	Ottawa New Edinburghs	OCHL	STATISTICS NOT AVAILABLE												
1934-35	Noranda Copper Kings	GBHL	13	6	5	11	....	....	....	10	....	....	....	....	....
1935-36	South Porcupine Porkies	NOHA	8	7	0	7	....	....	....	33	2	0	1	1	*11
1936-37	Sudbury Frood Miners	NBHL	15	12	3	15	....	....	....	38	2	0	0	0	2
	Sudbury Frood Miners	Al-Cup	13	17	3	20	....	....	....	37	....	....	....	....	....
1937-38	Toronto Maple Leafs	NHL	43	4	12	16	6	19	25	51	5	0	0	0	2
1938-39	Toronto Maple Leafs	NHL	48	10	16	26	17	25	42	32	10	2	5	7	4
1939-40	Toronto Maple Leafs	NHL	40	5	17	22	8	27	35	63	3	0	0	0	0
1940-41	Montreal Canadiens	NHL	45	10	15	25	15	21	36	75	3	0	2	2	11

Season	Club	League	GP	G	A	Pts	AG	AA	APts	PIM	GP	G	A	Pts	PIM
			REGULAR SEASON								PLAYOFFS				
1941-42	**Montreal Canadiens**	**NHL**	**26**	**6**	**3**	**9**	**8**	**4**	**12**	**30**	....	....	....	....	....
	Brooklyn Americans	**NHL**	**11**	**6**	**9**	**15**	**8**	**11**	**19**	**16**	....	....	....	....	....
	Springfield Indians	AHL	3	2	1	3	....	....	....	0	....	....	....	....	....
1942-43	**Boston Bruins**	**NHL**	**45**	**9**	**24**	**33**	**9**	**22**	**31**	**67**	**6**	**1**	**1**	**2**	**12**
♦1943-44	**Montreal Canadiens**	**NHL**	**47**	**15**	**32**	**47**	**14**	**28**	**42**	**85**	**9**	**5**	**3**	**8**	**12**
1944-45	**Montreal Canadiens**	**NHL**	**32**	**2**	**12**	**14**	**2**	**14**	**16**	**38**	**6**	**1**	**1**	**2**	**10**
♦1945-46	**Montreal Canadiens**	**NHL**	**40**	**12**	**14**	**26**	**14**	**20**	**34**	**42**	**9**	**4**	**2**	**6**	**18**
1946-47	**Montreal Canadiens**	**NHL**	**49**	**10**	**10**	**20**	**11**	**12**	**23**	**97**	**11**	**1**	**3**	**4**	**19**
1947-48	**Montreal Canadiens**	**NHL**	**30**	**6**	**3**	**9**	**8**	**4**	**12**	**62**	....	....	....	....	....
1948-49	**Montreal Canadiens**	**NHL**	**54**	**5**	**8**	**13**	**7**	**11**	**18**	**111**	**4**	**0**	**0**	**0**	**8**
1949-50	Sydney Millionaires	CBSHL	STATISTICS NOT AVAILABLE												
	NHL Totals		**510**	**100**	**175**	**275**	**127**	**218**	**345**	**769**	**66**	**14**	**17**	**31**	**96**

Traded to **Montreal** by **Toronto** for $7,500, May 10, 1940. Loaned to **Brooklyn** by **Montreal** for the loan of Red Heron, February 10, 1942. Loaned to **Boston** by **Montreal** for 1942-43 season for cash, September, 1942. • Missed majority of 1947-48 season recovering from leg injury suffered in game vs. Detroit, October 25, 1947. • Named player/coach of **Sydney Millionaires** (CBSHL), September 16, 1949.

• CHAMPAGNE, Andre
Andre Joseph Orius
LW – L. 6', 190 lbs. b: Ottawa, Ont., 9/19/1943.

Season	Club	League	GP	G	A	Pts	AG	AA	APts	PIM	GP	G	A	Pts	PIM
1959-60	St. Michael's Buzzers	OHA-B	STATISTICS NOT AVAILABLE												
	St. Michael's Majors	OHA-Jr.	1	0	0	0	....	....	....	0	....	....	....	....	....
1960-61	St. Michael's Majors	OHA-Jr.	47	11	12	23	....	....	....	59	18	7	2	9	22
	St. Michael's Majors	M-Cup	9	*10	*11	*21	....	....	....	6	....	....	....	....	....
1961-62	St. Michael's Majors	MTJHL	29	14	18	32	....	....	....	79	3	1	4	5	26
1962-63	Neil McNeil Maroons	MTJHL	24	16	32	48	....	....	....	61	10	8	12	20	*37
	Toronto Maple Leafs	**NHL**	**2**	**0**	**0**	**0**	**0**	**0**	**0**	**0**	....	....	....	....	....
	Rochester Americans	AHL	....	....	....	....	....	....	....	....	1	0	0	0	0
	Neil McNeil Maroons	M-Cup	6	3	2	5	....	....	....	30	....	....	....	....	....
1963-64	Toronto Marlboros	OHA-Jr.	47	31	40	71	....	....	....	105	9	6	10	16	38
	Rochester Americans	AHL	3	0	0	0	....	....	....	0	....	....	....	....	....
	Toronto Marlboros	M-Cup	12	7	11	18	....	....	....	61	....	....	....	....	....
1964-65	Tulsa Oilers	CPHL	60	24	41	65	....	....	....	118	12	3	4	7	*43
1965-66	Rochester Americans	AHL	1	0	0	0	....	....	....	0	....	....	....	....	....
	Tulsa Oilers	CPHL	65	16	49	65	....	....	....	38	11	1	5	6	4
1966-67	Tulsa Oilers	CPHL	10	1	2	3	....	....	....	6	....	....	....	....	....
1967-68	Rochester Americans	AHL	48	2	5	7	....	....	....	14	....	....	....	....	....
1968-69	Rochester Americans	AHL	69	7	12	19	....	....	....	78	....	....	....	....	....
1969-70	Rochester Americans	AHL	24	3	5	8	....	....	....	25	....	....	....	....	....
	NHL Totals		**2**	**0**	**0**	**0**	**0**	**0**	**0**	**0**	....	....	....	....	....

Rights transferred to **Vancouver** (WHL) after WHL club purchased **Rochester** (AHL) franchise, August 13, 1968. Rights transferred to **Vancouver** after NHL club purchased **Vancouver** (WHL) franchise, December 19, 1969.

• CHAPMAN, Art
Arthur John
C – L. 5'10", 170 lbs. b: Winnipeg, Man., 5/29/1906 d: 1/1/1963.

Season	Club	League	GP	G	A	Pts	AG	AA	APts	PIM	GP	G	A	Pts	PIM
1922-23	University of Manitoba	MHL-Sr.	8	8	2	10				2	....	....	....	....	....
1923-24	Winnipeg Tigers	WJrHL	STATISTICS NOT AVAILABLE												
	Winnipeg Tigers	MHL-Sr.	1	1	0	1	....	....	....	0	....	....	....	....	....
1924-25	Winnipeg Falcons	MHL-Sr.	8	5	0	5	....	....	....	0	....	....	....	....	....
1925-26	Port Arthur Ports	TBSHL	19	13	2	15	....	....	....	17	3	0	0	0	0
	Port Arthur Ports	Al-Cup	6	3	1	4	....	....	....	6	....	....	....	....	....
1926-27	Port Arthur Ports	TBSHL	20	19	10	29	....	....	....	16	2	0	0	0	0
1927-28	Springfield Indians	Can-Am	39	14	5	19	....	....	....	6	4	1	1	2	6
1928-29	Providence Reds	Can-Am	39	14	*14	28	....	....	....	5	6	0	1	1	4
1929-30	Providence Reds	Can-Am	39	*26	19	45	....	....	....	22	3	*5	0	5	6
1930-31	**Boston Bruins**	**NHL**	**44**	**7**	**7**	**14**	**14**	**21**	**35**	**22**	**5**	**0**	**1**	**1**	**7**
1931-32	**Boston Bruins**	**NHL**	**48**	**11**	**14**	**25**	**18**	**31**	**49**	**18**	....	....	....	....	....
1932-33	**Boston Bruins**	**NHL**	**46**	**3**	**6**	**9**	**5**	**12**	**17**	**19**	**5**	**0**	**0**	**0**	**2**
1933-34	**Boston Bruins**	**NHL**	**21**	**2**	**5**	**7**	**3**	**10**	**13**	**7**	....	....	....	....	....
	New York Americans	**NHL**	**25**	**3**	**7**	**10**	**5**	**15**	**20**	**8**	....	....	....	....	....
1934-35	**New York Americans**	**NHL**	**47**	**9**	***34**	**43**	**15**	**60**	**75**	**4**	....	....	....	....	....
1935-36	**New York Americans**	**NHL**	**48**	**10**	***28**	**38**	**19**	**54**	**73**	**14**	**5**	**0**	**3**	**3**	**0**
1936-37	**New York Americans**	**NHL**	**43**	**8**	**23**	**31**	**13**	**43**	**56**	**36**	....	....	....	....	....
1937-38	**New York Americans**	**NHL**	**45**	**2**	**27**	**29**	**3**	**44**	**47**	**8**	**6**	**0**	**1**	**1**	**0**
1938-39	**New York Americans**	**NHL**	**45**	**3**	**19**	**22**	**5**	**30**	**35**	**2**	**2**	**0**	**0**	**0**	**0**
1939-40	**New York Americans**	**NHL**	**26**	**4**	**6**	**10**	**7**	**9**	**16**	**2**	**3**	**1**	**0**	**1**	**0**
1940-41	**New York Americans**	**NHL**	DID NOT PLAY – COACHING												
1941-42	**Brooklyn Americans**	**NHL**	DID NOT PLAY – COACHING												
1942-43	Buffalo Bisons	AHL	45	9	19	28	....	....	....	12	....	....	....	....	....
1943-44	Buffalo Bisons	AHL	1	0	0	0	....	....	....	0	....	....	....	....	....
	NHL Totals		**438**	**62**	**176**	**238**	**107**	**329**	**436**	**140**	**26**	**1**	**5**	**6**	**9**

NHL Second All-Star Team (1937) • Played in NHL All-Star Game (1937)

Signed as a free agent by **Chicago** (AHA), October 31, 1926. Jumped contract with **Chicago** (AHA) and signed with **Port Arthur** (TBSHL), November 2, 1926. Signed as a free agent by **Windsor** (Can-Pro), September 22, 1927. Traded to **NY Rangers** by **Windsor** (Can-Pro) for cash, November 1, 1927. Traded to **Providence** (Can-Am) by **NY Rangers** for cash, October 18, 1928. Claimed by **Boston** from **Providence** (Can-Am) in Inter-League Draft, May 13, 1929. Traded to **NY Americans** by **Boston** with Bob Gracie for Lloyd Gross and George Patterson, January 11, 1934.

• CHECK, Lude
Ludic
LW – L. 5'10", 165 lbs. b: Brandon, Man., 5/22/1919.

Season	Club	League	GP	G	A	Pts	AG	AA	APts	PIM	GP	G	A	Pts	PIM
1936-37	Brandon Wheat Kings	MJHL	15	13	6	19	....	....	....	16	4	4	0	4	0
1937-38	Brandon Wheat Kings	MJHL	15	19	13	32	....	....	....	16	5	3	3	6	4
1938-39	Regina Aces	S-SSHL	39	19	6	25	....	....	....	12	....	....	....	....	....
1939-40	Regina Aces	S-SSHL	32	15	10	25	....	....	....	12	7	0	1	1	6
1940-41	New York Rovers	EAHL	64	21	20	41	....	....	....	10	3	1	0	1	0
1941-42	Sydney Millionaires	CBSHL	40	29	22	51	....	....	....	24	....	....	....	....	....
	North Sydney Victorias	CBSHL	....	....	....	....	....	....	....	....	7	5	4	9	12
1942-43	Quebec Aces	QSHL	34	20	13	33	....	....	....	26	4	1	1	2	2
1943-44	Quebec Aces	QSHL	25	*28	18	46	....	....	....	14	6	3	1	4	4
	Detroit Red Wings	**NHL**	**1**	**0**	**0**	**0**	**0**	**0**	**0**	**0**	....	....	....	....	....
	Quebec Aces	Al-Cup	9	12	9	21	....	....	....	2	....	....	....	....	....
1944-45	**Chicago Black Hawks**	**NHL**	**26**	**6**	**2**	**8**	**6**	**2**	**8**	**4**	....	....	....	....	....
1945-46	Ottawa Senators	QSHL	39	31	29	60	....	....	....	29	9	6	5	11	6
1946-47	Ottawa Senators	QSHL	40	22	19	41	....	....	....	36	11	5	2	7	4
1947-48	Ottawa Senators	QSHL	46	17	23	40	....	....	....	35	12	*8	8	16	13
	Ottawa Senators	Al-Cup	14	*8	3	11	....	....	....	2	....	....	....	....	....
1948-49	Ottawa Senators	QSHL	59	26	30	56	....	....	....	29	11	3	6	9	6
	Ottawa Senators	Al-Cup	12	5	4	9	....	....	....	2	....	....	....	....	....
1949-50	Ottawa Senators	QSHL	51	14	15	29	....	....	....	8	2	0	0	0	0
1950-51	Ottawa Senators	QMHL	38	11	9	20	....	....	....	16	11	2	4	6	4
	NHL Totals		**27**	**6**	**2**	**8**	**6**	**2**	**8**	**4**	....	....	....	....	....

Signed as a free agent by **Montreal**, October 24, 1944. Loaned to **Detroit** by **Montreal** (Quebec-QSHL) as an emergency injury replacement, March 11, 1944. Loaned to **Chicago** by **Montreal** for cash, October 25, 1944. Loaned to **Ottawa** (QSHL) by **Montreal** with Jim McFadden as compensation for Montreal's signing of Mike McMahon, October 24, 1945.

• CHERRY, Dick
— see page 968

• CHERRY, Don
Donald Stewart "Grapes"
D – L. 5'11", 180 lbs. b: Kingston, Ont., 2/5/1934.

Season	Club	League	GP	G	A	Pts	AG	AA	APts	PIM	GP	G	A	Pts	PIM
1951-52	Barrie Flyers	OHA-Jr.	18	2	3	5	....	....	....	30	....	....	....	....	....
	Windsor Spitfires	OHA-Jr.	18	0	3	3	....	....	....	30	....	....	....	....	....
1952-53	Barrie Flyers	OHA-Jr.	56	5	3	8	....	....	....	66	15	1	1	2	28
	Barrie Flyers	M-Cup	10	3	2	5	....	....	....	18	....	....	....	....	....
1953-54	Barrie Flyers	OHA-Jr.	55	10	14	24	....	....	....	61	....	....	....	....	....
1954-55	Hershey Bears	AHL	63	7	13	20	....	....	....	125	....	....	....	....	....
	Boston Bruins	**NHL**	....	....	....	....	....	....	....	....	**1**	**0**	**0**	**0**	**0**
1955-56	Hershey Bears	AHL	58	3	22	25	....	....	....	102	....	....	....	....	....
1956-57	Hershey Bears	AHL	64	5	20	25	....	....	....	197	7	2	0	2	27
1957-58	Springfield Indians	AHL	65	9	17	26	....	....	....	83	13	1	1	2	10
1958-59	Springfield Indians	AHL	70	6	22	28	....	....	....	118	....	....	....	....	....
1959-60	Trois-Rivieres Lions	EPHL	23	3	4	7	....	....	....	12	7	0	1	1	2
	Springfield Indians	AHL	46	2	11	13	....	....	....	45	1	0	0	0	2
1960-61	Kitchener Beavers	EPHL	70	13	26	39	....	....	....	78	7	0	3	3	23
1961-62	Springfield Indians	AHL	11	1	3	4	....	....	....	10	....	....	....	....	....
	Sudbury Wolves	EPHL	55	9	20	29	....	....	....	62	5	3	2	5	10
1962-63	Spokane Comets	WHL	68	9	13	22	....	....	....	68	....	....	....	....	....
1963-64	Rochester Americans	AHL	70	5	11	16	....	....	....	106	2	0	0	0	4
1964-65	Rochester Americans	AHL	62	4	8	12	....	....	....	56	10	0	1	1	34
1965-66	Tulsa Oilers	CPHL	17	1	2	3	....	....	....	28	....	....	....	....	....
	Rochester Americans	AHL	56	5	11	16	....	....	....	61	12	2	5	7	14
1966-67	Rochester Americans	AHL	72	6	24	30	....	....	....	61	13	1	2	3	16
1967-68	Rochester Americans	AHL	68	6	15	21	....	....	....	74	11	1	1	2	2
1968-69	Rochester Americans	AHL	43	7	11	18	....	....	....	20	....	....	....	....	....
	Vancouver Canucks	WHL	33	0	6	6	....	....	....	29	8	2	2	4	6
1969/71			OUT OF HOCKEY – RETIRED												
1971-72	Rochester Americans	AHL	19	1	4	5	....	....	....	8	....	....	....	....	....
	Rochester Americans	AHL	DID NOT PLAY – COACHING												
1972/74	Rochester Americans	AHL	DID NOT PLAY – COACHING												
1974/78	**Boston Bruins**	**NHL**	DID NOT PLAY – COACHING												
1978-79	**Colorado Rockies**	**NHL**	DID NOT PLAY – COACHING												
	NHL Totals		....	....	....	....	....	....	....	....	**1**	**0**	**0**	**0**	**0**

• Brother of Dick • Won Jack Adams Award (1976)

Traded to **Springfield** (AHL) by **Boston** for cash, September, 1957. Traded to **Detroit** by **Springfield** (AHL) for cash, November, 1961. Traded to **Montreal** by **Detroit** for cash, September 13, 1962. Rights transferred to **Toronto** after NHL club purchased **Spokane** (WHL) franchise, June 4, 1963. Rights transferred to **Vancouver** (WHL) after WHL club purchased **Rochester** (AHL) franchise, August 13, 1968.

• CHEVREFILS, Real
LW – L. 5'10", 180 lbs. b: Timmins, Ont., 5/2/1932 d: 8/1/1981.

Season	Club	League	GP	G	A	Pts	AG	AA	APts	PIM	GP	G	A	Pts	PIM
1948-49	Barrie Flyers	OHA-Jr.	43	13	13	26	....	....	....	36	8	6	7	13	16
	Barrie Flyers	M-Cup	7	8	2	10	....	....	....	8	....	....	....	....	....
1949-50	Barrie Flyers	OHA-Jr.	48	27	32	59	....	....	....	95	9	6	7	13	16
1950-51	Barrie Flyers	OHA-Jr.	54	52	51	103	....	....	....	104	12	*14	11	25	16
	Barrie Flyers	M-Cup	11	9	10	19	....	....	....	14	....	....	....	....	....
1951-52	**Boston Bruins**	**NHL**	**33**	**8**	**17**	**25**	**11**	**21**	**32**	**8**	**7**	**1**	**1**	**2**	**6**
	Hershey Bears	AHL	34	20	28	48	....	....	....	14	....	....	....	....	....
1952-53	**Boston Bruins**	**NHL**	**69**	**19**	**14**	**33**	**25**	**17**	**42**	**44**	**7**	**0**	**1**	**1**	**6**
1953-54	**Boston Bruins**	**NHL**	**14**	**4**	**1**	**5**	**5**	**1**	**6**	**2**	....	....	....	....	....
1954-55	**Boston Bruins**	**NHL**	**64**	**18**	**22**	**40**	**23**	**25**	**48**	**30**	**5**	**2**	**1**	**3**	**4**
1955-56	**Detroit Red Wings**	**NHL**	**38**	**3**	**4**	**7**	**4**	**5**	**9**	**24**	....	....	....	....	....
	Boston Bruins	**NHL**	**25**	**11**	**8**	**19**	**15**	**9**	**24**	**10**	....	....	....	....	....
1956-57	**Boston Bruins**	**NHL**	**70**	**31**	**17**	**48**	**40**	**19**	**59**	**38**	**10**	**2**	**1**	**3**	**4**
1957-58	**Boston Bruins**	**NHL**	**44**	**9**	**9**	**18**	**11**	**9**	**20**	**21**	**1**	**0**	**0**	**0**	**0**
	Springfield Indians	AHL	15	7	8	15	....	....	....	0	11	0	3	3	2
1958-59	**Boston Bruins**	**NHL**	**30**	**1**	**5**	**6**	**1**	**5**	**6**	**8**	....	....	....	....	....
	Providence Reds	AHL	6	1	1	2	....	....	....	0	....	....	....	....	....
	Quebec Aces	QHL	12	2	7	9	....	....	....	6	....	....	....	....	....
1959-60	Sudbury Wolves	EPHL	65	23	36	59	....	....	....	26	14	6	6	12	4
1960-61	Kingston Frontenacs	EPHL	37	16	20	36	....	....	....	16	....	....	....	....	....
	Winnipeg Warriors	WHL	19	6	7	13	....	....	....	2	....	....	....	....	....
1961-62	Los Angeles Blades	WHL	69	22	32	54	....	....	....	12	....	....	....	....	....
1962-63	San Francisco Seals	WHL	6	1	1	2	....	....	....	0	....	....	....	....	....
	Windsor Bulldogs	OHA-Sr.	42	25	48	73	....	....	....	18	10	0	11	11	7
	Windsor Bulldogs	AL-Cup	9	4	7	11	....	....	....	2	....	....	....	....	....
1963-64	Windsor Bulldogs	IHL	48	19	22	41	....	....	....	8	6	2	2	4	2
	NHL Totals		**387**	**104**	**97**	**201**	**135**	**111**	**246**	**185**	**30**	**5**	**4**	**9**	**20**

NHL Second All-Star Team (1957) • Played in NHL All-Star Game (1955, 1957)

Traded to **Detroit** by **Boston** with Ed Sandford, Norm Corcoran, Gilles Boisvert and Warren Godfrey for Marcel Bonin, Terry Sawchuk, Vic Stasiuk and Lorne Davis, June 3, 1955. Traded to **Boston** by **Detroit** with Jerry Toppazzini for Lorne Ferguson and Murray Costello, January 17, 1956.

• CHISHOLM, Art
Arthur Joseph
C/D – L. 5'9", 160 lbs. b: Arlington, MA, 11/11/1934.

Season	Club	League	GP	G	A	Pts	AG	AA	APts	PIM	GP	G	A	Pts	PIM
1951-52	Arlington North Shore	H.S.	13	0	0	0	....	....	....	16	2	0	0	0	0
1952/54			MILITARY SERVICE												
1954-55	Arlington Military Aces	MBSHL	8	8	4	12	....	....	....	....	....	....	....	....	....
1955/57			MILITARY SERVICE												
1957-58	Northeastern University	ECAC	DID NOT PLAY – FRESHMAN												

Season	Club	League	GP	G	A	Pts	AG	AA	APts	PIM	GP	G	A	Pts	PIM
			REGULAR SEASON								PLAYOFFS				
1958-59	Northeastern University	ECAC	24	*40	24	64				35					
1959-60	Northeastern University	ECAC	24	25	31	56				15					
1960-61	Northeastern University	ECAC	25	35	26	61				25					
	Boston Bruins	**NHL**	**3**	**0**	**0**	**0**	**0**	**0**	**0**	**0**					
1961/65			DID NOT PLAY – REFEREE												
1965-66	Framingham Falcons	MASHL	25	28	*36	*64									
	NHL Totals		**3**	**0**	**0**	**0**	**0**	**0**	**0**	**0**					

Signed as a free agent by **Boston** to a 3-game amateur try-out contract, March 15, 1961.

• CHISHOLM, Lex Alexander

C/RW – R. 5'11", 175 lbs. b: Galt, Ont., 4/1/1915 d: 8/6/1981.

Season	Club	League	GP	G	A	Pts	AG	AA	APts	PIM	GP	G	A	Pts	PIM
1932-33	Galt Terrier Pups	OHA-Jr.	14	14	1	15				22	2	0	0	0	6
1933-34	Galt Terrier Pups	OHA-Jr.	16	11	14	25				23	2	1	1	2	2
1934-35	Oshawa Generals	MTHL	12	14	5	19				17					
	Oshawa Chevies	TIHL	1	0	0	0				0					
1935-36	Oshawa Chevies	TIHL	12	2	5	7				19					
1936-37	Oshawa G-Men	OHA-Sr.	9	1	0	1				4					
1937-38	Oshawa G-Men	OHA-Sr.	13	9	10	19				10	2	1	0	1	4
1938-39	Syracuse Stars	IAHL	3	1	1	2				0	3	0	0	0	0
	Oshawa G-Men	OHA-Sr.	19	15	*28	*43				24	7	2	5	7	15
1939-40	**Toronto Maple Leafs**	**NHL**	**28**	**6**	**8**	**14**	**10**	**12**	**22**	**11**					
1940-41	**Toronto Maple Leafs**	**NHL**	**26**	**4**	**0**	**4**	**6**	**0**	**6**	**8**	**3**	**1**	**0**	**1**	**0**
	Pittsburgh Hornets	AHL	2	0	1	1				2					
1941-42	Halifax Army	NSDHL	STATISTICS NOT AVAILABLE												
1942-43	Toronto Army Daggers	OHA-Sr.	5	6	9	15				8	4	6	1	7	4
	NHL Totals		**54**	**10**	**8**	**18**	**16**	**12**	**28**	**19**	**3**	**1**	**0**	**1**	**0**

• CHOUINARD, Gene Eugene Vincent "Noisy"

D – L. 5'6", 160 lbs. b: Ottawa, Ont., 1/5/1907 d: 1/29/1951.

Season	Club	League	GP	G	A	Pts	AG	AA	APts	PIM	GP	G	A	Pts	PIM
1921-22	Ottawa Montagnards	OCHL	14	7	*9	16				14	7	2	4	6	3
1922-23	Ottawa Montagnards	OCHL	9	*8	3	*11				14	2	0	0	0	0
1923-24	Ottawa Montagnards	OCHL	10	2	1	3					2	0	0	0	0
	Ottawa Montagnards	Al-Cup	4	4	0	4									
1924-25	Ottawa Montagnards	OCHL	16	12	1	13					3	1	0	1	4
	Ottawa Montagnards	Al-Cup	4	0	1	1				14					
1925-26	Eveleth-Hibbing Rangers	CHL	19	0	0	0				0					
1926-27	Niagara Falls–Stratford	Can-Pro	27	3	3	6				16	1	0	0	0	0
1927-28	**Ottawa Senators**	**NHL**	**8**	**0**	**0**	**0**	**0**	**0**	**0**	**0**					
	Quebec Castors	Can-Am	2	0	0	0				0					
	Waterville Maine	NEHL	5	0	1	1				2	2	0	0	0	0
1928-29	New Haven Eagles	Can-Am	22	4	1	5				8	2	0	0	0	4
1929-30	New Haven Eagles	Can-Am	40	4	7	11				60					
1930-31	New Haven Eagles	Can-Am	40	7	11	18				56					
1931-32	Bronx Tigers	Can-Am	39	5	7	12				40	2	1	1	2	4
1932-33	Riviere-du-Loup Lancers	SLVHL	STATISTICS NOT AVAILABLE												
	Quebec Castors	Can-Am	20	3	5	8				16					
1933-34	New Haven Eagles	Can-Am	40	8	12	20				25					
1934-35	Tulsa Oilers	AHA	48	11	13	24				11	5	1	0	1	8
	London Tecumsehs	IHL	1	0	0	0				0					
1935-36	Tulsa Oilers	AHA	36	1	7	8				10	3	0	0	0	5
1936-37	Perth Blue Wings	OVHL	DID NOT PLAY – COACHING												
1937-38	Perth Crescents	OVHL	1	0	0	0				0					
	NHL Totals		**8**	**0**	**0**	**0**	**0**	**0**	**0**	**0**					

Signed as a free agent by **Minneapolis** (AHA), October 21, 1926. Traded to **Niagara Falls** (Can-Pro) by **Minneapolis** (AHA) for cash, November 14, 1926. Traded to **Stratford** (Can-Pro) by **Niagara Falls** (Can-Pro) for Herb Hamel, January 17, 1927. Signed as a free agent by **Ottawa**, December 19, 1927.

• CHRYSTAL, Bob Robert Harry

D – L. 6', 180 lbs. b: Winnipeg, Man., 4/3/1930.

Season	Club	League	GP	G	A	Pts	AG	AA	APts	PIM	GP	G	A	Pts	PIM
1947-48	Winnipeg Orioles	MAHA	STATISTICS NOT AVAILABLE												
1948-49	Brandon Wheat Kings	MJHL	30	2	10	12				72	7	1	0	1	8
	Brandon Wheat Kings	M-Cup	18	4	2	6				49					
1949-50	Brandon Wheat Kings	MJHL	36	9	13	22				*89	6	3	2	5	6
	Brandon Wheat Kings	M-Cup	6	1	2	3				11					
1950-51	Denver Falcons	USHL	64	7	13	20				71	5	0	5	5	10
1951-52	Cleveland Barons	AHL	68	3	16	19				109	5	0	0	0	6
1952-53	Cleveland Barons	AHL	63	5	17	22				87	11	4	4	8	24
1953-54	**New York Rangers**	**NHL**	**64**	**5**	**5**	**10**	**7**	**6**	**13**	**44**					
1954-55	**New York Rangers**	**NHL**	**68**	**6**	**9**	**15**	**8**	**10**	**18**	**68**					
1955-56	Saskatoon Quakers	WHL	48	5	5	10				67	3	0	2	2	8
1956-57	Brandon Regals	WHL	70	8	20	28				52	9	3	2	5	12
	Brandon Regals	Ed-Cup	6	0	2	2				8					
1957-58	Sask/St. Paul Regals	WHL	69	9	23	32				87					
1958-59	Winnipeg Warriors	WHL	59	14	17	31				54	7	0	1	1	7
	NHL Totals		**132**	**11**	**14**	**25**	**15**	**16**	**31**	**112**					

USHL Second All-Star Team (1951) • WHL Prairie Division First All-Star Team (1957, 1958)

Traded to **NY Rangers** by **Cleveland** (AHL) for Steve Kraftcheck and cash, June, 1953. Claimed by **Chicago** from **NY Rangers** (Brandon-WHL) in Inter-League Draft, June 4, 1957.

• CHURCH, Jack

D – R. 5'11", 180 lbs. b: Kamsack, Sask., 5/24/1915 d: 1/5/1996.

Season	Club	League	GP	G	A	Pts	AG	AA	APts	PIM	GP	G	A	Pts	PIM
1932-33	Regina Maple Leafs	S-SJHL	3	0	0	0				10	2	0	0	0	8
1933-34	Regina Maple Leafs	S-SJHL	3	0	0	0				*10	2	0	0	0	*10
	Regina Vics	S-SSHL	16	0	1	1				42	1	0	0	0	6
1934-35	Toronto Dominions	TIHL	16	2	2	4				*73	3	0	1	1	8
1935-36	Toronto Dominions	TIHL	16	0	*12	12				*78					
	Toronto Dukes	TIHL	16	3	1	4				*70	3	0	1	1	12
1936-37	Syracuse Stars	IAHL	50	2	4	6				*93	9	1	0	1	10
1937-38	Syracuse Stars	IAHL	43	3	2	5				47	8	0	0	0	8
1938-39	**Toronto Maple Leafs**	**NHL**	**3**	**0**	**2**	**2**	**0**	**3**	**3**	**2**	**1**	**0**	**0**	**0**	**0**
	Syracuse Stars	IAHL	52	3	12	15				45	3	0	0	0	5
1939-40	**Toronto Maple Leafs**	**NHL**	**31**	**1**	**4**	**5**	**2**	**6**	**8**	**62**	**10**	**1**	**1**	**2**	**6**
1940-41	**Toronto Maple Leafs**	**NHL**	**11**	**0**	**1**	**1**	**0**	**1**	**1**	**22**	**5**	**0**	**0**	**0**	**8**
1941-42	**Toronto Maple Leafs**	**NHL**	**27**	**0**	**3**	**3**	**0**	**4**	**4**	**30**					
	Brooklyn Americans	**NHL**	**15**	**1**	**3**	**4**	**1**	**4**	**5**	**10**					
1942-43	Cornwall Army	OHA-Sr.	33	6	12	18				*102	6	1	2	3	10
1943-44			MILITARY SERVICE												
1944-45			MILITARY SERVICE												
1945-46	**Boston Bruins**	**NHL**	**43**	**2**	**6**	**8**	**2**	**9**	**11**	**28**	**9**	**0**	**0**	**0**	**4**
1946-47	New Haven Ramblers	AHL	64	7	11	18				83	3	0	0	0	2
1947-48	Providence Reds	AHL	64	1	17	18				67	5	0	2	2	6
	NHL Totals		**130**	**4**	**19**	**23**	**5**	**27**	**32**	**154**	**25**	**1**	**1**	**2**	**18**

AHL First All-Star Team (1939)

Traded to **Brooklyn** by **Toronto** for cash, February 2, 1942. Rights transferred to **Boston** from **Brooklyn** in Special Dispersal Draw, September 11, 1943. Traded to **NY Rangers** by **Boston** for $5,000, September 17, 1946. Traded to **Providence** (AHL) by **NY Rangers** for cash, October 4, 1947.

• CIESLA, Hank Henry Edward

C – L. 6'2", 190 lbs. b: St. Catharines, Ont., 10/15/1934 d: 4/22/1976.

Season	Club	League	GP	G	A	Pts	AG	AA	APts	PIM	GP	G	A	Pts	PIM
1950-51	St. Catharines Teepees	OHA-Jr.	1	0	1	1				0	1	0	0	0	0
1951-52	St. Catharines Teepees	OHA-Jr.	41	14	25	39				27	14	5	7	12	14
1952-53	St. Catharines Teepees	OHA-Jr.	56	19	24	43				43	1	0	0	0	0
1953-54	St. Catharines Teepees	OHA-Jr.	59	39	30	69				66	15	6	7	13	8
	St. Catharines Teepees	M-Cup	11	5	8	13				29					
1954-55	St. Catharines Teepees	OHA-Jr.	45	*57	49	*106				36	11	7	8	15	23
1955-56	**Chicago Black Hawks**	**NHL**	**70**	**8**	**23**	**31**	**11**	**27**	**38**	**22**					
1956-57	**Chicago Black Hawks**	**NHL**	**70**	**10**	**8**	**18**	**13**	**9**	**22**	**28**					
1957-58	**New York Rangers**	**NHL**	**60**	**2**	**6**	**8**	**2**	**6**	**8**	**16**	**6**	**0**	**2**	**2**	**0**
1958-59	**New York Rangers**	**NHL**	**69**	**6**	**14**	**20**	**7**	**14**	**21**	**21**					
1959-60	Rochester Americans	AHL	64	27	44	71				31	11	3	7	10	14
1960-61	Rochester Americans	AHL	70	30	44	74				23					
1961-62	Cleveland Barons	AHL	70	25	38	63				22	6	4	3	7	6
1962-63	Cleveland Barons	AHL	72	*42	56	98				41	7	3	8	11	8
1963-64	Pittsburgh Hornets	AHL	69	18	38	56				46	5	1	3	4	8
1964-65	Buffalo Bisons	AHL	49	8	8	16				34					
	NHL Totals		**269**	**26**	**51**	**77**	**33**	**56**	**89**	**87**	**6**	**0**	**2**	**2**	**0**

AHL Second All-Star Team (1963)

• Rights claimed by both Montreal and Toronto out of junior. Rights traded to **Chicago** by **Buffalo** (AHL) for $15,000 with Montreal receiving Bob Duncan (Toronto/OHA-Jr.) and Toronto receiving Gary Collins (Kitchener/OHA-Jr.), September, 1955. Traded to **NY Rangers** by **Chicago** for Ron Murphy, June, 1957. Traded to **Toronto** by **NY Rangers** with Bill Kennedy and future considerations for Noel Price, October 3, 1959. Traded to **Cleveland** (AHL) by **Toronto** (Rochester-AHL) for Bill Dineen and cash, August, 1961. Claimed by **Detroit** (Pittsburgh-AHL) from **Cleveland** (AHL) in Inter-League Draft, June 4, 1963. Traded to **Chicago** (Buffalo-AHL) by **Detroit** (Pittsburgh-AHL) for Jerry Toppazzini, October 10, 1964.

• CLANCY, King Francis Michael HHOF

D – L. 5'7", 155 lbs. b: Ottawa, Ont., 2/25/1903 d: 11/8/1986.

Season	Club	League	GP	G	A	Pts	AG	AA	APts	PIM	GP	G	A	Pts	PIM
1916-17	Ottawa Sandy Hill	OCJHL	4	3	0	3									
	Ottawa St. Joseph's	H.S.									2	3	0	3	
1917-18	Ottawa Munitions	OCJHL	4	2	0	2									
	Ottawa Collegiate	H.S.									2	3	0	3	
1918-19	Ottawa St. Brigids	OCHL	8	0	1	1				3	1	0	0	0	6
1919-20	Ottawa St. Brigids	OCHL	8	1	0	1									
1920-21	Ottawa St. Brigids	OCHL	11	6	0	6					6	*5	1	*6	12
1921-22	**Ottawa Senators**	**NHL**	**24**	**4**	**6**	**10**	**5**	**19**	**24**	**21**	**2**	**0**	**0**	**0**	**2**
1922-23	**Ottawa Senators**	**NHL**	**24**	**3**	**2**	**5**	**5**	**7**	**12**	**20**	**2**	**0**	**0**	**0**	**0**
♦	Ottawa Senators	St-Cup	6	1	0	1				4					
1923-24	**Ottawa Senators**	**NHL**	**24**	**8**	***8**	**16**	**16**	**48**	**64**	**26**	**2**	**0**	**0**	**0**	**6**
1924-25	**Ottawa Senators**	**NHL**	**29**	**14**	**7**	**21**	**24**	**29**	**53**	**61**					
1925-26	**Ottawa Senators**	**NHL**	**35**	**8**	**4**	**12**	**14**	**26**	**40**	**80**	**2**	**1**	**0**	**1**	**8**
♦1926-27	**Ottawa Senators**	**NHL**	**43**	**9**	**10**	**19**	**16**	**53**	**69**	**78**	**6**	**1**	**1**	**2**	**14**
1927-28	**Ottawa Senators**	**NHL**	**39**	**8**	**7**	**15**	**16**	**40**	**56**	**73**	**2**	**0**	**0**	**0**	**6**
1928-29	**Ottawa Senators**	**NHL**	**44**	**13**	**2**	**15**	**38**	**13**	**51**	**89**					
1929-30	**Ottawa Senators**	**NHL**	**44**	**17**	**23**	**40**	**24**	**55**	**79**	**83**	**2**	**0**	**1**	**1**	**2**
1930-31	**Toronto Maple Leafs**	**NHL**	**44**	**7**	**14**	**21**	**14**	**43**	**57**	**63**	**2**	**1**	**0**	**1**	**0**
♦1931-32	**Toronto Maple Leafs**	**NHL**	**48**	**10**	**9**	**19**	**17**	**20**	**37**	**61**	**7**	**2**	**1**	**3**	**14**
1932-33	**Toronto Maple Leafs**	**NHL**	**48**	**13**	**12**	**25**	**24**	**25**	**49**	**79**	**9**	**0**	**3**	**3**	**14**
1933-34	**Toronto Maple Leafs**	**NHL**	**46**	**11**	**17**	**28**	**19**	**36**	**55**	**62**	**3**	**0**	**0**	**0**	**8**
1934-35	**Toronto Maple Leafs**	**NHL**	**47**	**5**	**16**	**21**	**8**	**28**	**36**	**53**	**7**	**1**	**0**	**1**	**8**
1935-36	**Toronto Maple Leafs**	**NHL**	**47**	**5**	**10**	**15**	**10**	**19**	**29**	**61**	**9**	**2**	**2**	**4**	**10**
1936-37	**Toronto Maple Leafs**	**NHL**	**6**	**1**	**0**	**1**	**2**	**0**	**2**	**4**					
1937-38	**Montreal Maroons**	**NHL**	DID NOT PLAY – COACHING												
1938-39			DID NOT PLAY – REFEREE												
	NHL Totals		**592**	**136**	**147**	**283**	**252**	**461**	**713**	**914**	**55**	**8**	**8**	**16**	**92**

• Father of Terry • NHL First All-Star Team (1931, 1934) • NHL Second All-Star Team (1932, 1933) • Played in NHL All-Star Game (1934, 1937)

Signed as a free agent by **Ottawa**, December 14, 1921. • 1922-23 Stanley Cup totals includes series with Regina (WCHL) and Edmonton (PCHA). Traded to **Toronto** by **Ottawa** for Art Smith, Eric Pettinger and $35,000, October 11, 1930. • Officially announced retirement, November 24, 1936. • Came out of retirement to play in Howie Morenz Memorial Game, November 2, 1937.

• CLAPPER, Dit Aubrey Victor HHOF

RW/D – R. 6'2", 195 lbs. b: Newmarket, Ont., 2/9/1907 d: 1/21/1978.

Season	Club	League	GP	G	A	Pts	AG	AA	APts	PIM	GP	G	A	Pts	PIM
1925-26	Toronto Parkdale	OHA-Jr.	2	0	0	0				0					
	Toronto Parkdale	M-Cup	5	1	0	1									
1926-27	Boston Tigers	Can-Am	29	6	1	7				57					
1927-28	**Boston Bruins**	**NHL**	**40**	**4**	**1**	**5**	**8**	**6**	**14**	**20**	**2**	**0**	**0**	**0**	**2**
♦1928-29	**Boston Bruins**	**NHL**	**40**	**9**	**2**	**11**	**26**	**13**	**39**	**48**	**5**	**1**	**0**	**1**	**0**
1929-30	**Boston Bruins**	**NHL**	**44**	**41**	**20**	**61**	**59**	**48**	**107**	**48**	**6**	**4**	**0**	**4**	**4**
1930-31	**Boston Bruins**	**NHL**	**43**	**22**	**8**	**30**	**45**	**24**	**69**	**50**	**5**	**2**	**4**	**6**	**4**
1931-32	**Boston Bruins**	**NHL**	**48**	**17**	**22**	**39**	**28**	**49**	**77**	**21**					
1932-33	**Boston Bruins**	**NHL**	**48**	**14**	**14**	**28**	**26**	**29**	**55**	**42**	**5**	**1**	**1**	**2**	**2**
1933-34	**Boston Bruins**	**NHL**	**48**	**10**	**12**	**22**	**17**	**25**	**42**	**6**					
1934-35	**Boston Bruins**	**NHL**	**48**	**21**	**16**	**37**	**35**	**28**	**63**	**21**	**3**	**1**	**0**	**1**	**0**
1935-36	**Boston Bruins**	**NHL**	**44**	**12**	**13**	**25**	**23**	**25**	**48**	**14**	**2**	**0**	**1**	**1**	**0**
1936-37	**Boston Bruins**	**NHL**	**48**	**17**	**8**	**25**	**29**	**15**	**44**	**25**	**3**	**2**	**0**	**2**	**5**
1937-38	**Boston Bruins**	**NHL**	**46**	**6**	**9**	**15**	**10**	**14**	**24**	**24**	**3**	**0**	**0**	**0**	**12**
♦1938-39	**Boston Bruins**	**NHL**	**42**	**13**	**13**	**26**	**23**	**20**	**43**	**22**	**12**	**0**	**1**	**1**	**6**
1939-40	**Boston Bruins**	**NHL**	**44**	**10**	**18**	**28**	**17**	**28**	**45**	**25**	**5**	**0**	**2**	**2**	**2**
♦1940-41	**Boston Bruins**	**NHL**	**48**	**8**	**18**	**26**	**12**	**26**	**38**	**24**	**11**	**0**	**5**	**5**	**4**
1941-42	**Boston Bruins**	**NHL**	**32**	**3**	**12**	**15**	**4**	**14**	**18**	**31**					
1942-43	**Boston Bruins**	**NHL**	**38**	**5**	**18**	**23**	**5**	**17**	**22**	**12**	**9**	**2**	**3**	**5**	**9**
1943-44	**Boston Bruins**	**NHL**	**50**	**6**	**25**	**31**	**5**	**22**	**27**	**13**					

Season	Club	League	GP	G	A	Pts	AG	AA	APts	PIM	GP	G	A	Pts	PIM
			REGULAR SEASON								PLAYOFFS				
1944-45	**Boston Bruins**	**NHL**	**46**	**8**	**14**	**22**	**8**	**16**	**24**	**16**	**7**	**0**	**0**	**0**	**0**
1945-46	**Boston Bruins**	**NHL**	**30**	**2**	**3**	**5**	**2**	**4**	**6**	**0**	**4**	**0**	**0**	**0**	**0**
1946-47	**Boston Bruins**	**NHL**	**6**	**0**	**0**	**0**	**0**	**0**	**0**	**0**	....	....	....	....	....
1947-48	**Boston Bruins**	**NHL**	DID NOT PLAY – COACHING												
	NHL Totals		**833**	**228**	**246**	**474**	**382**	**423**	**805**	**462**	**82**	**13**	**17**	**30**	**50**

NHL Second All-Star Team (1931, 1935, 1944) • NHL First All-Star Team (1939, 1940, 1941) • Played in NHL All-Star Game (1937, 1939)

Traded to **Boston** by **Boston Tigers** (Can-Am) for cash, October 25, 1927.

• CLARK, Nobby

Patrick Joseph
D – R. 6'1", 190 lbs. b: Orillia, Ont., 6/18/1897 Deceased.

Season	Club	League	GP	G	A	Pts	AG	AA	APts	PIM	GP	G	A	Pts	PIM
1920-21	Eveleth Rangers	NMHL	STATISTICS NOT AVAILABLE												
1921-22	Eveleth Rangers	NMHL	STATISTICS NOT AVAILABLE												
1922-23	Duluth Hornets	USAHA	20	6	0	6	....	....	....	....	....	....	....	....	....
1923-24	Eveleth Rangers	USAHA	11	1	0	1	....	....	....	....	....	....	....	....	....
1924-25	Eveleth Arrowheads	USAHA	38	6	0	6	....	....	....	....	4	0	0	0	....
1925-26	Eveleth-Hibbing Rangers	CHL	38	9	3	12	....	....	....	26	....	....	....	....	....
1926-27	Minneapolis Millers	AHA	36	7	5	12	....	....	....	46	6	0	0	0	4
1927-28	**Boston Bruins**	**NHL**	**5**	**0**	**0**	**0**	**0**	**0**	**0**	**0**	....	....	....	....	....
	New Haven Eagles	Can-Am	40	6	2	8	....	....	....	35	....	....	....	....	....
1928-29	Philadelphia Arrows	Can-Am	37	4	7	11	....	....	....	54	....	....	....	....	....
1929/32			OUT OF HOCKEY – RETIRED												
1932-33	Hibbing Maroons	CHL	12	1	6	7	....	....	....	4	....	....	....	....	....
	NHL Totals		**5**	**0**	**0**	**0**	**0**	**0**	**0**	**0**	....	....	....	....	....

Traded to **Boston** by **Minneapolis** (AHA) with Dutch Gainor for Red Stuart, cash and future considerations, October 24, 1927. Traded to **New Haven** (Can-Am) by **Boston** with Billy Coutu for cash, January 5, 1928

• CLEGHORN, Odie

James Ogilvie
RW/C – R. 5'9", 195 lbs. b: Montreal, Que., 9/19/1891 d: 7/13/1956.

Season	Club	League	GP	G	A	Pts	AG	AA	APts	PIM	GP	G	A	Pts	PIM
1908-09	Montreal Westmount	CAHL	STATISTICS NOT AVAILABLE												
1909-10	New York Wanderers	USAHA	8	*15	0	*15	....	....	....	....	....	....	....	....	....
1910-11	Renfrew Millionaires	NHA	16	20	0	20	....	....	....	66	....	....	....	....	....
1911-12	Montreal Wanderers	NHA	17	23	0	23	....	....	....	....	....	....	....	....	....
	East All-Stars	X-Games	3	1	0	1	....	....	....	5	....	....	....	....	....
1912-13	Montreal Wanderers	NHA	19	18	0	18	....	....	....	44	....	....	....	....	....
1913-14	Montreal Wanderers	NHA	13	9	7	16	....	....	....	19	....	....	....	....	....
1914-15	Montreal Wanderers	NHA	15	21	5	26	....	....	....	39	2	0	0	0	12
1915-16	Montreal Wanderers	NHA	21	16	7	23	....	....	....	51	....	....	....	....	....
1916-17	Montreal Wanderers	NHA	18	28	4	32	....	....	....	49	....	....	....	....	....
1917-18			DID NOT PLAY												
1918-19	**Montreal Canadiens**	**NHL**	**17**	**22**	**6**	**28**	**42**	**33**	**75**	**22**	**5**	**7**	**0**	**7**	**0**
	Montreal Canadiens	St-Cup	5	2	0	2	....	....	....	9	....	....	....	....	....
1919-20	**Montreal Canadiens**	**NHL**	**21**	**20**	**4**	**24**	**23**	**13**	**36**	**30**	....	....	....	....	....
1920-21	**Montreal Canadiens**	**NHL**	**21**	**6**	**6**	**12**	**8**	**23**	**31**	**8**	....	....	....	....	....
1921-22	**Montreal Canadiens**	**NHL**	**24**	**21**	**3**	**24**	**29**	**9**	**38**	**26**	....	....	....	....	....
1922-23	**Montreal Canadiens**	**NHL**	**24**	**19**	**6**	**25**	**33**	**23**	**56**	**18**	**2**	**0**	**0**	**0**	**2**
1923-24	**Montreal Canadiens**	**NHL**	**22**	**2**	**5**	**7**	**4**	**29**	**33**	**16**	**2**	**0**	**0**	**0**	**0**
♦	Montreal Canadiens	St-Cup	4	0	1	1	....	....	....	0	....	....	....	....	....
1924-25	**Montreal Canadiens**	**NHL**	**30**	**3**	**3**	**6**	**5**	**12**	**17**	**14**	**2**	**0**	**1**	**1**	**0**
	Montreal Canadiens	St-Cup	4	0	0	0	....	....	....	0	....	....	....	....	....
1925-26	**Pittsburgh Pirates**	**NHL**	**17**	**2**	**1**	**3**	**3**	**6**	**9**	**4**	**1**	**0**	**0**	**0**	**0**
1926-27	**Pittsburgh Pirates**	**NHL**	**3**	**0**	**0**	**0**	**0**	**0**	**0**	**0**	....	....	....	....	....
1927-28	**Pittsburgh Pirates**	**NHL**	**2**	**0**	**0**	**0**	**0**	**0**	**0**	**4**	....	....	....	....	....
	NHL Totals		**181**	**95**	**34**	**129**	**147**	**148**	**295**	**142**	**12**	**7**	**1**	**8**	**2**
	Other Major League Totals		119	135	23	158	....	....	....	268	2	0	0	0	12

• Brother of Sprague

Traded to **Montreal Wanderers** (NHA) by **Quebec** (NHA) for cash, January, 1911. • Granted wartime exemption on condition that he not play professional hockey in 1917-18. Retained by **Montreal Wanderers** after NHA folded, November 26, 1917. Signed as a free agent by **Montreal Canadiens**, December 9, 1918. • 1923-24 Stanley Cup totals includes series with Calgary (WCHL) and Vancouver (PCHA). • Released by **Montreal Canadiens**, September, 1925. Signed as a free agent by **Pittsburgh** and named player/coach, October 18, 1925.

• CLEGHORN, Sprague

Sprague Horace "Peg" **HHOF**
D – L. 5'10", 190 lbs. b: Montreal, Que., 3/11/1890 d: 7/11/1956.

Season	Club	League	GP	G	A	Pts	AG	AA	APts	PIM	GP	G	A	Pts	PIM
1908-09	Mtl-Canadian Rubber	MCHL	3	1	0	1	....	....	....	10	....	....	....	....	....
1909-10	New York Wanderers	USAHA	8	7	0	7	....	....	....	....	....	....	....	....	....
1910-11	Renfrew Millionaires	NHA	12	5	0	5	....	....	....	27	....	....	....	....	....
1911-12	Montreal Wanderers	NHA	18	9	0	9	....	....	....	40	....	....	....	....	....
	East All-Stars	X-Games	3	1	0	1	....	....	....	10	....	....	....	....	....
1912-13	Montreal Wanderers	NHA	19	12	0	12	....	....	....	46	....	....	....	....	....
1913-14	Montreal Wanderers	NHA	20	12	8	20	....	....	....	17	....	....	....	....	....
1914-15	Montreal Wanderers	NHA	19	21	*12	33	....	....	....	51	2	0	0	0	17
1915-16	Montreal Wanderers	NHA	8	9	4	13	....	....	....	22	....	....	....	....	....
1916-17	Montreal Wanderers	NHA	19	16	9	25	....	....	....	62	....	....	....	....	....
1917-18			DID NOT PLAY												
1918-19	**Ottawa Senators**	**NHL**	**18**	**7**	**6**	**13**	**12**	**33**	**45**	**27**	**5**	**2**	**0**	**2**	**11**
1919-20	**Ottawa Senators**	**NHL**	**21**	**16**	**5**	**21**	**18**	**17**	**35**	**85**	....	....	....	....	....
♦	Ottawa Senators	St-Cup	5	0	1	1	....	....	....	4	....	....	....	....	....
1920-21	**Toronto St. Pats**	**NHL**	**13**	**3**	**5**	**8**	**4**	**19**	**23**	**31**	**1**	**0**	**0**	**0**	**0**
♦	Ottawa Senators	St-Cup	5	1	2	3	....	....	....	0	....	....	....	....	....
1921-22	**Montreal Canadiens**	**NHL**	**24**	**17**	**9**	**26**	**24**	**29**	**53**	***80**	....	....	....	....	....
1922-23	**Montreal Canadiens**	**NHL**	**24**	**9**	**8**	**17**	**15**	**31**	**46**	**34**	**1**	**0**	**0**	**0**	**7**
1923-24	**Montreal Canadiens**	**NHL**	**23**	**8**	**4**	**12**	**16**	**23**	**39**	**45**	**2**	**0**	**0**	**0**	**0**
♦	Montreal Canadiens	St-Cup	4	2	2	4	....	....	....	2	....	....	....	....	....
1924-25	**Montreal Canadiens**	**NHL**	**27**	**8**	**10**	**18**	**14**	**42**	**56**	**89**	**2**	**1**	**2**	**3**	**2**
	Montreal Canadiens	St-Cup	4	0	0	0	....	....	....	2	....	....	....	....	....
1925-26	**Boston Bruins**	**NHL**	**28**	**6**	**5**	**11**	**10**	**32**	**42**	**49**	....	....	....	....	....
1926-27	**Boston Bruins**	**NHL**	**44**	**7**	**1**	**8**	**12**	**5**	**17**	**84**	**8**	**1**	**0**	**1**	**8**
1927-28	**Boston Bruins**	**NHL**	**37**	**2**	**2**	**4**	**4**	**11**	**15**	**14**	**2**	**0**	**0**	**0**	**0**
1928-29	Newark Bulldogs	Can-Am	3	0	0	0	....	....	....	0	....	....	....	....	....
1929-30	Providence Reds	Can-Am	DID NOT PLAY – COACHING												
	NHL Totals		**259**	**83**	**55**	**138**	**129**	**242**	**371**	**538**	**21**	**4**	**2**	**6**	**28**
	Other Major League Totals		115	84	33	117	....	....	....	265	2	0	0	0	17

• Brother of Odie

• Granted wartime exemption on condition that he not play professional hockey in 1917-18. Rights retained by **Montreal Wanderers** after NHA folded, November 26, 1917. Claimed by **Ottawa** from **Montreal Wanderers** in Dispersal Draft, January 4, 1918. Rights transferred to **Hamilton** by **NHL** with Punch Broadbent, December 30, 1920. • Broadbent and Cleghorn refused to report. Traded to **Toronto** by **Hamilton** for future considerations, January 25, 1921. Signed as a free agent by **Ottawa** after securing his release from **Toronto**, March 15, 1921. Rights transferred to **Hamilton** by **NHL**, April 6, 1921. Traded to **Montreal** by **Hamilton** for Harry Mummery and Amos Arbour, November 26, 1921. • 1923-24 Stanley Cup totals includes series with Calgary (WCHL) and Vancouver (PCHA). Traded to **Boston** by **Montreal** for $5,000, November 8, 1925.

• CLINE, Bruce

RW – R. 5'7", 137 lbs. b: Massawippi, Que., 11/14/1931.

Season	Club	League	GP	G	A	Pts	AG	AA	APts	PIM	GP	G	A	Pts	PIM
1950-51	Quebec Citadelle	QJHL	46	11	20	31	....	....	....	4	23	6	8	14	13
1951-52	Quebec Citadelle	QJHL	50	20	30	50	....	....	....	19	13	2	2	4	5
	Quebec Citadelle	M-Cup	10	4	6	10	....	....	....	8	....	....	....	....	....
1952-53	Valleyfield Braves	QSHL	59	15	9	24	....	....	....	10	4	1	2	3	0
1953-54	Valleyfield Braves	QHL	71	17	24	41	....	....	....	34	4	0	1	1	0
1954-55	Valleyfield Braves	QHL	62	13	42	55	....	....	....	2	....	....	....	....	....
1955-56	Providence Reds	AHL	64	27	30	57	....	....	....	18	9	3	3	6	9
1956-57	**New York Rangers**	**NHL**	**30**	**2**	**3**	**5**	**3**	**3**	**6**	**10**	....	....	....	....	....
	Providence Reds	AHL	36	14	21	35	....	....	....	13	5	2	1	3	2
1957-58	Providence Reds	AHL	70	19	40	59	....	....	....	27	5	0	7	7	4
1958-59	Buffalo Bisons	AHL	70	22	39	61	....	....	....	39	7	0	2	2	0
1959-60	Springfield Indians	AHL	70	25	50	75	....	....	....	9	10	5	5	10	0
1960-61	Springfield Indians	AHL	72	40	52	92	....	....	....	13	8	2	3	5	4
1961-62	Springfield Indians	AHL	70	38	40	78	....	....	....	21	11	5	2	7	6
1962-63	Springfield Indians	AHL	72	39	48	87	....	....	....	26	....	....	....	....	....
1963-64	Hershey Bears	AHL	64	26	20	46	....	....	....	6	6	0	3	3	2
1964-65	Hershey Bears	AHL	72	17	28	45	....	....	....	6	15	4	3	7	2
1965-66	Hershey Bears	AHL	53	19	26	45	....	....	....	2	3	0	1	1	0
1966-67	Hershey Bears	AHL	70	28	42	70	....	....	....	63	....	....	....	....	....
1967-68	Hershey Bears	AHL	40	7	16	23	....	....	....	17	5	2	3	5	2
	NHL Totals		**30**	**2**	**3**	**5**	**3**	**3**	**6**	**10**	....	....	....	....	....

Won Dudley "Red" Garrett Memorial Award (Top Rookie - AHL) (1956) • AHL First All-Star Team (1961) • AHL Second All-Star Team (1963)

Traded to **Montreal** by **Springfield** (AHL) with Ted Harris, Terry Gray, Wayne Larkin and John Chasczewski for the loan of Gary Bergman, Wayne Boddy, Fred Hilts, Brian D. Smith, John Rodger and Lorne O'Donnell, June, 1963.

• CLUNE, Wally

Walter James
D – R. 5'9", 150 lbs. b: Toronto, Ont., 2/20/1930 d: 2/3/1998.

Season	Club	League	GP	G	A	Pts	AG	AA	APts	PIM	GP	G	A	Pts	PIM
1947-48	St. Michael's Majors	OHA-Jr.	32	3	5	8	....	....	....	37	....	....	....	....	....
1948-49	St. Michael's Majors	OHA-Jr.	31	2	3	5	....	....	....	68	....	....	....	....	....
1949-50	Guelph Biltmores	OHA-Jr.	44	7	10	17	....	....	....	68	15	0	2	2	27
	Guelph Biltmores	M-Cup	11	2	4	6	....	....	....	12	....	....	....	....	....
1950-51	Montreal Royals	QMHL	8	0	0	0	....	....	....	6	....	....	....	....	....
	Boston Olympics	EAHL	50	10	19	29	....	....	....	112	6	0	1	1	16
1951-52	Montreal Royals	QMHL	57	3	11	14	....	....	....	84	7	0	2	2	6
1952-53	Montreal Royals	QMHL	43	1	13	14	....	....	....	67	16	0	3	3	21
1953-54	Victoria Cougars	WHL	64	8	6	14	....	....	....	69	5	1	0	1	2
1954-55	Victoria Cougars	WHL	69	7	17	24	....	....	....	85	5	0	2	2	8
1955-56	**Montreal Canadiens**	**NHL**	**5**	**0**	**0**	**0**	**0**	**0**	**0**	**6**	....	....	....	....	....
	Montreal Royals	QHL	53	2	9	11	....	....	....	110	13	0	3	3	*39
	Montreal Royals	Ed-Cup	6	0	0	0	....	....	....	*15	....	....	....	....	....
1956-57	Montreal Royals	QHL	54	1	6	7	....	....	....	105	3	0	0	0	0
1957-58	Montreal Royals	QHL	56	1	15	16	....	....	....	87	7	1	0	1	*30
1958-59	Montreal Royals	QHL	57	7	25	32	....	....	....	84	8	0	1	1	13
1959-60	Montreal Royals	EPHL	62	2	20	22	....	....	....	63	14	0	5	5	13
1960-61	Montreal Royals	EPHL	65	2	7	9	....	....	....	22	....	....	....	....	....
	NHL Totals		**5**	**0**	**0**	**0**	**0**	**0**	**0**	**6**	....	....	....	....	....

EAHL First All-Star Team (1951)

Claimed by **Montreal** from **Montreal Royals** (QMHL) in Intra-League Draft, June 10, 1953.

• COFLIN, Hugh

Hugh Alexander
D – L. 6', 190 lbs. b: Blaine Lake, Sask., 12/15/1928.

Season	Club	League	GP	G	A	Pts	AG	AA	APts	PIM	GP	G	A	Pts	PIM
1946-47	Humboldt Indians	SJHL	22	7	4	11	....	....	....	4	....	....	....	....	....
1947-48	Moose Jaw Canucks	SJHL	26	8	11	19	....	....	....	34	5	1	2	3	8
	Moose Jaw Canucks	M-Cup	5	2	0	2	....	....	....	4	....	....	....	....	....
1948-49	Moose Jaw Canucks	WCJHL	26	10	7	17	....	....	....	62	9	0	1	1	19
	Moose Jaw Canucks	M-Cup	7	2	1	3	....	....	....	11	....	....	....	....	....
1949-50	Calgary Stampeders	WCSHL	50	6	11	17	....	....	....	*133	10	0	4	4	*35
	Calgary Stampeders	Al-Cup	14	4	10	14	....	....	....	*42	....	....	....	....	....
1950-51	**Chicago Black Hawks**	**NHL**	**31**	**0**	**3**	**3**	**0**	**4**	**4**	**33**	....	....	....	....	....
	Milwaukee Seagulls	USHL	35	1	16	17	....	....	....	26	....	....	....	....	....
1951-52	Indianapolis Capitols	AHL	68	3	25	28	....	....	....	64	....	....	....	....	....
1952-53	Edmonton Flyers	WHL	23	1	4	5	....	....	....	55	....	....	....	....	....
1953-54	Edmonton Flyers	WHL	70	8	18	26	....	....	....	115	13	1	3	4	12
1954-55	Edmonton Flyers	WHL	44	5	25	30	....	....	....	78	9	0	2	2	18
	Edmonton Flyers	Ed-Cup	7	3	2	5	....	....	....	22	....	....	....	....	....
1955-56	Edmonton Flyers	WHL	67	9	14	23	....	....	....	109	3	0	0	0	2
1956-57	Edmonton Flyers	WHL	57	6	20	26	....	....	....	77	8	1	0	1	8
1957-58	Edmonton Flyers	WHL	70	12	32	44	....	....	....	61	5	1	1	2	10
1958-59	Edmonton Flyers	WHL	61	9	25	34	....	....	....	61	3	0	1	1	0
1959-60	Edmonton Flyers	WHL	65	7	20	27	....	....	....	18	4	0	0	0	0
	NHL Totals		**31**	**0**	**3**	**3**	**0**	**4**	**4**	**33**	....	....	....	....	....

WCSHL Rookie-of-the-Year (1950) • WHL Prairie Division First All-Star Team (1959)

Traded to **Detroit** by **Chicago** to complete transaction that sent George Gee, Jimmy Peters Sr., Clare Martin, Rags Raglan, Max McNab and Jim McFadden to Chicago (August 20, 1951), October, 1951. Claimed by **Hershey** (AHL) from **Edmonton** (WHL) in Inter-League Draft, June 1, 1955. Traded to **Detroit** (Edmonton-WHL) by **Hershey** (AHL) for Jimmy Uniac and Larry Zeidel, August 14, 1955.

• COLLINGS, Norm
Norman Edward "Dodger"
F – L. 6'2", 175 lbs. b: Bradford, Ont., 5/6/1910.

Season	Club	League	GP	G	A	Pts	AG	AA	APts	PIM	GP	G	A	Pts	PIM
			REGULAR SEASON								PLAYOFFS				
1927-28	Newmarket Redmen	OHA-Jr.	STATISTICS NOT AVAILABLE												
1928-29	West Toronto Redmen	OHA-Jr.	2	1	0	1	....	....	....	....	3	2	0	2	....
1929-30	West Toronto Nationals	OHA-Jr.	3	4	1	5	....	....	....	0	2	0	1	1	0
	West Toronto Nationals	M-Cup	12	8	7	15	....	....	....	6	....	....	....	....	....
1930-31	Minneapolis Millers	AHA	25	3	1	4	....	....	....	2	....	....	....	....	....
1931-32	New Haven Eagles	Can-Am	37	6	5	11	....	....	....	10	2	1	0	1	0
1932-33	New Haven Eagles	Can-Am	27	7	8	15	....	....	....	6	....	....	....	....	....
	Philadelphia Arrows	Can-Am	15	4	7	11	....	....	....	2	5	0	0	0	4
1933-34	Philadelphia Arrows	Can-Am	35	5	12	17	....	....	....	26	2	0	1	1	0
1934-35	**Montreal Canadiens**	**NHL**	**1**	**0**	**1**	**1**	**0**	**2**	**2**	**0**	....	....	....	....	....
	Philadelphia Arrows	Can-Am	44	7	15	22	....	....	....	29	....	....	....	....	....
1935-36	New Haven Eagles	Can-Am	34	3	9	12	....	....	....	15	....	....	....	....	....
1936-37			DID NOT PLAY												
1937-38	Tulsa Oilers	AHA	36	7	9	16	....	....	....	21	4	0	1	1	2
	NHL Totals		**1**	**0**	**1**	**1**	**0**	**2**	**2**	**0**	....	....	....	....	....

• COLLINS, Gary
Ranleigh Gary
C – L. 5'11", 185 lbs. b: Toronto, Ont., 9/27/1935.

Season	Club	League	GP	G	A	Pts	AG	AA	APts	PIM	GP	G	A	Pts	PIM
1951-52	Kitchener Greenshirts	OHA-Jr.	30	9	3	12	....	....	....	4	4	0	0	0	4
1952-53	Kitchener Greenshirts	OHA-Jr.	56	16	28	44	....	....	....	28	....	....	....	....	....
1953-54	Kitchener Greenshirts	OHA-Jr.	59	28	36	64	....	....	....	14	4	2	1	3	2
1954-55	Toronto Marlboros	OHA-Jr.	51	20	16	36	....	....	....	44	13	*10	2	12	*37
	Toronto Marlboros	M-Cup	11	5	5	10	....	....	....	14	....	....	....	....	....
1955-56	Toronto Marlboros	OHA-Jr.	48	16	45	61	....	....	....	55	11	2	10	12	22
	Toronto Marlboros	M-Cup	13	2	9	11	....	....	....	16	....	....	....	....	....
1956-57	Rochester Americans	AHL	33	6	17	23	....	....	....	6	....	....	....	....	....
1957-58	Rochester Americans	AHL	27	7	7	14	....	....	....	4	....	....	....	....	....
	Providence Reds	AHL	44	8	14	22	....	....	....	20	4	1	0	1	2
1958-59	New Westminster Royals	WHL	53	7	13	20	....	....	....	62	....	....	....	....	....
	Toronto Maple Leafs	**NHL**	....	....	....	....	....	....	....	....	**2**	**0**	**0**	**0**	**0**
1959-60	Rochester Americans	AHL	15	2	3	5	....	....	....	0	....	....	....	....	....
	Quebec Aces	AHL	49	7	16	23	....	....	....	12	....	....	....	....	....
1960-61	Quebec Aces	AHL	70	10	21	31	....	....	....	55	....	....	....	....	....
1961-62	Pittsburgh Hornets	AHL	36	2	9	11	....	....	....	25	....	....	....	....	....
	San Francisco Seals	WHL	16	0	2	2	....	....	....	10	....	....	....	....	....
1962-63	Trail Smoke Eaters	WIHL	DID NOT PLAY – COACHING												
1963-64			PLAYED PROFESSIONAL BASEBALL												
1964-65			PLAYED PROFESSIONAL BASEBALL												
1965-66	Galt Hornets	OHA-Sr.	31	5	12	17	....	....	....	26	....	....	....	....	....
1966-67	Collingwood Georgians	OHA-Sr.	32	2	13	15	....	....	....	12	....	....	....	....	....
1967-68	Collingwood Kings	OHA-Sr.	18	3	11	14	....	....	....	8	....	....	....	....	....
	NHL Totals		....	....	....	....	....	....	....	....	**2**	**0**	**0**	**0**	**0**

OHA-Sr. Second All-Star Team (1967)

Transferred to **Toronto** by **Chicago** as compensation for Chicago's signing of free agent Hank Ciesla, June, 1955. Loaned to **Providence** (AHL) by **Toronto** (Rochester-AHL) for loan of Ray Cyr for remainder of 1957-58 season, January 2, 1958. Traded to **Montreal** (Quebec-AHL) by **Toronto** (Rochester-AHL) for $10,000, November, 1959.

• COLVILLE, Mac
Matthew Lamont
RW/D – R. 5'9", 175 lbs. b: Edmonton, Alta., 1/8/1916.

Season	Club	League	GP	G	A	Pts	AG	AA	APts	PIM	GP	G	A	Pts	PIM
1930-31	Edmonton Poolers	EJrHL	3	0	0	0	....	....	....	0	....	....	....	....	....
1931-32	Edmonton Y's Men	AAHA	STATISTICS NOT AVAILABLE												
1932-33	Edmonton Poolers	EJrHL	11	....	....	....	....	....	....	14	3	0	0	0	0
1933-34	Edmonton Athletic Club	EJrHL	9	8	1	9	....	....	....	12	2	1	*2	3	0
	Edmonton Athletic Club	M-Cup	13	8	7	15	....	....	....	10	....	....	....	....	....
1934-35	Brooklyn Crescents	USAHA	21	5	10	15	....	....	....	26	8	4	5	9	8
1935-36	**New York Rangers**	**NHL**	**18**	**1**	**4**	**5**	**2**	**8**	**10**	**6**	....	....	....	....	....
	Philadelphia Ramblers	Can-Am	16	3	15	18	....	....	....	26	4	2	2	4	0
1936-37	**New York Rangers**	**NHL**	**46**	**7**	**12**	**19**	**12**	**22**	**34**	**10**	**9**	**1**	**2**	**3**	**2**
1937-38	**New York Rangers**	**NHL**	**48**	**14**	**14**	**28**	**23**	**23**	**46**	**18**	**3**	**0**	**2**	**2**	**0**
1938-39	**New York Rangers**	**NHL**	**48**	**7**	**21**	**28**	**12**	**33**	**45**	**24**	**7**	**1**	**2**	**3**	**4**
♦1939-40	**New York Rangers**	**NHL**	**47**	**7**	**14**	**21**	**12**	**22**	**34**	**12**	**12**	**3**	**2**	**5**	**6**
1940-41	**New York Rangers**	**NHL**	**47**	**14**	**17**	**31**	**22**	**24**	**46**	**18**	**3**	**1**	**1**	**2**	**2**
1941-42	**New York Rangers**	**NHL**	**46**	**14**	**16**	**30**	**19**	**19**	**38**	**26**	**6**	**3**	**1**	**4**	**0**
1942-43	Ottawa Commandos	QSHL	19	7	7	14	....	....	....	19	11	2	5	7	10
	Ottawa Army	OCHL	9	6	3	9	....	....	....	4	....	....	....	....	....
	Ottawa Commandos	Al-Cup	12	11	9	20	....	....	....	15	....	....	....	....	....
1943-44	Red Deer Wheelers	ASHL	16	4	9	13	....	....	....	17	5	0	3	3	*14
1944-45			MILITARY SERVICE												
1945-46	**New York Rangers**	**NHL**	**39**	**7**	**6**	**13**	**8**	**9**	**17**	**8**	....	....	....	....	....
1946-47	**New York Rangers**	**NHL**	**14**	**0**	**0**	**0**	**0**	**0**	**0**	**8**	....	....	....	....	....
	New Haven Ramblers	AHL	45	1	9	10	....	....	....	28	2	0	0	0	2
1947-48	Vancouver Canucks	PCHL	DID NOT PLAY – COACHING												
1948-49			DID NOT PLAY												
1949-50	New Haven Ramblers	AHL	DID NOT PLAY – COACHING												
1950-51	Edmonton Flyers	WCMHL	48	7	18	25	....	....	....	71	8	1	1	2	0
	NHL Totals		**353**	**71**	**104**	**175**	**110**	**160**	**270**	**130**	**40**	**9**	**10**	**19**	**14**

• Brother of Neil • EAHL First All-Star Team (1935)

• Only regular season games played and penalty minute totals available for Edmonton (EJrHL) in 1932-33. Signed as a free agent by **NY Rangers**, October 18, 1935.

• COLVILLE, Neil
Neil McNeil — HHOF
C/D – R. 5'11", 175 lbs. b: Edmonton, Alta., 8/4/1914 d: 12/26/1987.

Season	Club	League	GP	G	A	Pts	AG	AA	APts	PIM	GP	G	A	Pts	PIM
1929-30	Edmonton Enarcos	EJrHL	12	1	0	1	....	....	....	....	....	....	....	....	....
1930-31	Edmonton Canadians	EJrHL	13	2	0	2	....	....	....	8	....	....	....	....	....
1931-32	Edmonton Poolers	EJrHL	11	7	3	10	....	....	....	....	4	2	1	3	0
	Edmonton Poolers	M-Cup	5	2	0	2	....	....	....	2	....	....	....	....	....
1932-33	Edmonton Athletic Club	EJrHL	11	....	....	....	....	....	....	10	3	0	0	0	2
1933-34	Edmonton Athletic Club	EJrHL	9	*14	4	*18	....	....	....	13	2	*4	*2	*6	5
	Edmonton Athletic Club	M-Cup	12	15	6	21	....	....	....	4	....	....	....	....	....
1934-35	New York Crescents	EAHL	21	*24	11	*35	....	....	....	16	8	*8	4	12	2
1935-36	**New York Rangers**	**NHL**	**1**	**0**	**0**	**0**	**0**	**0**	**0**	**0**	....	....	....	....	....
	Philadelphia Ramblers	Can-Am	35	15	16	31	....	....	....	8	4	0	2	2	0
1936-37	**New York Rangers**	**NHL**	**45**	**10**	**18**	**28**	**17**	**33**	**50**	**33**	**9**	**3**	**3**	**6**	**0**
1937-38	**New York Rangers**	**NHL**	**45**	**17**	**19**	**36**	**28**	**31**	**59**	**11**	**3**	**0**	**1**	**1**	**0**
1938-39	**New York Rangers**	**NHL**	**47**	**18**	**19**	**37**	**32**	**30**	**62**	**12**	**7**	**0**	**2**	**2**	**2**
♦1939-40	**New York Rangers**	**NHL**	**48**	**19**	**19**	**38**	**32**	**30**	**62**	**22**	**12**	**2**	***7**	***9**	**18**
1940-41	**New York Rangers**	**NHL**	**48**	**14**	**28**	**42**	**22**	**40**	**62**	**28**	**3**	**1**	**1**	**2**	**0**
1941-42	**New York Rangers**	**NHL**	**48**	**8**	**25**	**33**	**11**	**30**	**41**	**37**	**6**	**0**	**5**	**5**	**6**
1942-43	Ottawa Commandos	QSHL	22	12	*30	42	....	....	....	32	....	....	....	....	....
	Ottawa Army	OCHL	12	11	12	23	....	....	....	6	....	....	....	....	....
	Ottawa Commandos	Al-Cup	12	14	14	28	....	....	....	17	....	....	....	....	....
1943-44			MILITARY SERVICE												
1944-45	**New York Rangers**	**NHL**	**4**	**0**	**1**	**1**	**0**	**1**	**1**	**2**	....	....	....	....	....
	Winnipeg RCAF	WNDHL	6	5	4	9	....	....	....	4	....	....	....	....	....
	Ottawa Commandos	QSHL	2	0	0	0	....	....	....	0	....	....	....	....	....
	Quebec Aces	QSHL	5	1	2	3	....	....	....	0	7	2	5	7	4
	Quebec Aces	Al-Cup	3	0	3	3	....	....	....	0	....	....	....	....	....
1945-46	**New York Rangers**	**NHL**	**49**	**5**	**4**	**9**	**6**	**6**	**12**	**25**	....	....	....	....	....
1946-47	**New York Rangers**	**NHL**	**60**	**4**	**16**	**20**	**4**	**19**	**23**	**16**	....	....	....	....	....
1947-48	**New York Rangers**	**NHL**	**55**	**4**	**12**	**16**	**5**	**16**	**21**	**25**	**6**	**1**	**0**	**1**	**6**
1948-49	**New York Rangers**	**NHL**	**14**	**0**	**5**	**5**	**0**	**7**	**7**	**2**	....	....	....	....	....
	New Haven Ramblers	AHL	11	0	3	3	....	....	....	8	....	....	....	....	....
1949-50	New Haven Ramblers	AHL	17	3	4	7	....	....	....	13	....	....	....	....	....
	NHL Totals		**464**	**99**	**166**	**265**	**157**	**243**	**400**	**213**	**46**	**7**	**19**	**26**	**32**

• Brother of Mac • EAHL First All-Star Team (1935) • Won John Carlin Trophy (Top Scorer - EAHL) (1935) • NHL Second All-Star Team (1939, 1940) • Played in NHL All-Star Game (1939, 1948)

• Only regular season games played and penalty minute totals available for Edmonton (EJrHL) in 1932-33. Signed as a free agent by **NY Rangers**, October 18, 1935.

• COLWILL, Les
Leslie John
RW – R. 5'11", 170 lbs. b: Diwide, Sask., 1/1/1935.

Season	Club	League	GP	G	A	Pts	AG	AA	APts	PIM	GP	G	A	Pts	PIM
1951-52	Lethbridge Native Sons	WCJHL	28	11	7	18	....	....	....	0	4	5	2	7	0
1952-53	Lethbridge Native Sons	WCJHL	28	15	10	25	....	....	....	8	13	4	6	10	0
	Lethbridge Native Sons	M-Cup	11	1	3	4	....	....	....	0	....	....	....	....	....
1953-54	Lethbridge Native Sons	WCJHL	36	37	35	72	....	....	....	4	4	1	1	2	4
1954-55	Lethbridge Native Sons	WCJHL	38	20	*32	52	....	....	....	23	11	4	*9	13	0
	Saskatoon Quakers	WHL	2	0	0	0	....	....	....	0	....	....	....	....	....
	Regina Pats	M-Cup	2	1	0	1	....	....	....	4	....	....	....	....	....
1955-56	Saskatoon Quakers	WHL	70	17	21	38	....	....	....	37	3	2	1	3	2
1956-57	Brandon Regals	WHL	68	29	26	55	....	....	....	23	9	4	3	7	6
	Brandon Regals	Ed-Cup	6	2	2	4	....	....	....	0	....	....	....	....	....
1957-58	Sask/St. Paul Regals	WHL	70	35	27	62	....	....	....	30	....	....	....	....	....
1958-59	**New York Rangers**	**NHL**	**69**	**7**	**6**	**13**	**8**	**6**	**14**	**16**	....	....	....	....	....
1959-60	Vancouver–Calgary	WHL	66	17	22	39	....	....	....	10	....	....	....	....	....
	NHL Totals		**69**	**7**	**6**	**13**	**8**	**6**	**14**	**16**	....	....	....	....	....

• CONACHER, Brian
— see page 984

• CONACHER, Charlie
Charles William "The Big Bomber" — HHOF
RW – R. 6'1", 195 lbs. b: Toronto, Ont., 12/20/1909 d: 12/30/1967.

Season	Club	League	GP	G	A	Pts	AG	AA	APts	PIM	GP	G	A	Pts	PIM
1926-27	North Toronto Juniors	OHA-Jr.	9	9	1	10	....	....	....	....	1	0	0	0	0
	North Toronto Seniors	OHA-Sr.	2	1	0	1	....	....	....	2	....	....	....	....	....
1927-28	Toronto Marlboros	OHA-Jr.	9	11	0	11	....	....	....	....	2	1	0	1	....
	Toronto Marlboros	OHA-Sr.	1	2	0	2	....	....	....	0	....	....	....	....	....
	Toronto Marlboros	M-Cup	11	15	3	18	....	....	....	....	....	....	....	....	....
1928-29	Toronto Marlboros	OHA-Jr.	8	*18	3	*21	....	....	....	....	2	*7	0	7	....
	Toronto Marlboros	M-Cup	15	*28	8	*36	....	....	....	12	....	....	....	....	....
1929-30	**Toronto Maple Leafs**	**NHL**	**38**	**20**	**9**	**29**	**29**	**21**	**50**	**48**	....	....	....	....	....
1930-31	**Toronto Maple Leafs**	**NHL**	**37**	***31**	**12**	**43**	**64**	**36**	**100**	**78**	**2**	**0**	**1**	**1**	**0**
♦1931-32	**Toronto Maple Leafs**	**NHL**	**44**	***34**	**14**	**48**	**58**	**31**	**89**	**66**	**7**	***6**	**2**	**8**	**6**
1932-33	**Toronto Maple Leafs**	**NHL**	**40**	**14**	**19**	**33**	**26**	**40**	**66**	**64**	**9**	**1**	**1**	**2**	**10**
1933-34	**Toronto Maple Leafs**	**NHL**	**42**	***32**	**20**	***52**	**56**	**42**	**98**	**38**	**5**	**3**	**2**	**5**	**0**
1934-35	**Toronto Maple Leafs**	**NHL**	**47**	***36**	**21**	***57**	**60**	**37**	**97**	**24**	**7**	**1**	***4**	***5**	**6**
1935-36	**Toronto Maple Leafs**	**NHL**	**44**	***23**	**15**	**38**	**45**	**28**	**73**	**74**	**9**	**3**	**2**	**5**	**12**
1936-37	**Toronto Maple Leafs**	**NHL**	**15**	**3**	**5**	**8**	**5**	**9**	**14**	**13**	**2**	**0**	**0**	**0**	**5**
1937-38	**Toronto Maple Leafs**	**NHL**	**19**	**7**	**9**	**16**	**11**	**14**	**25**	**6**	....	....	....	....	....
1938-39	**Detroit Red Wings**	**NHL**	**40**	**8**	**15**	**23**	**14**	**23**	**37**	**39**	**5**	**2**	**5**	**7**	**2**
1939-40	**New York Americans**	**NHL**	**47**	**10**	**18**	**28**	**17**	**28**	**45**	**41**	**3**	**1**	**1**	**2**	**8**
1940-41	**New York Americans**	**NHL**	**46**	**7**	**16**	**23**	**11**	**23**	**34**	**32**	....	....	....	....	....
	NHL Totals		**459**	**225**	**173**	**398**	**396**	**332**	**728**	**523**	**49**	**17**	**18**	**35**	**49**

• Father of Pete • Brother of Lionel and Roy • NHL Second All-Star Team (1932, 1933) • NHL First All-Star Team (1934, 1935, 1936) • NHL Scoring Leader (1934, 1935) • Played in NHL All-Star Game (1934, 1937)

Signed as a free agent by **Toronto**, October 7, 1929. • Missed majority of 1936-37 season recovering from wrist injury originally suffered in training camp and re-injured in game vs. NY Americans , December 17, 1936. Traded to **Detroit** by **Toronto** for $16,000 with Detroit holding option of contract renewal, October 12, 1938. • Rights returned to **Toronto** by **Detroit** after NHL club failed to renew contract, July 1, 1939. Traded to **NY Americans** by **Toronto** for future considerations (cash, May 21, 1940), September 22, 1939.

• CONACHER, Jim
James "Pencil"
C – L. 5'10", 155 lbs. b: Motherwell, Scotland, 5/5/1921.

Season	Club	League	GP	G	A	Pts	AG	AA	APts	PIM	GP	G	A	Pts	PIM
1938-39	Toronto Young Rangers	OHA-Jr.	8	2	1	3	....	....	....	0	3	0	1	1	0
1939-40	Toronto Young Rangers	OHA-Jr.	16	13	9	22	....	....	....	8	2	2	0	2	0
	Toronto CPR	TIHL	9	6	8	14	....	....	....	4	....	....	....	....	....
1940-41	Oshawa Generals	OHA-Jr.	16	17	15	32	....	....	....	8	12	6	8	14	10
	Toronto Donnell-Mudge	TMHL	....	....	....	....	....	....	....	....	1	1	0	1	0
	Oshawa Generals	M-Cup	5	2	5	7	....	....	....	2	....	....	....	....	....
1941-42	Omaha Knights	AHA	47	21	23	44	....	....	....	22	8	5	7	12	10
1942-43	Cornwall Army	QSHL	26	3	18	21	....	....	....	12	....	....	....	....	....
1943-44	Toronto Tip Tops	TIHL	3	1	4	5	....	....	....	0	....	....	....	....	....
1944-45	Toronto Tip Tops	TIHL	1	1	0	1	....	....	....	0	....	....	....	....	....
1945-46	**Detroit Red Wings**	**NHL**	**20**	**1**	**5**	**6**	**1**	**7**	**8**	**10**	**5**	**1**	**1**	**2**	**0**
	Indianapolis Capitols	AHL	32	17	30	47	....	....	....	6	....	....	....	....	....
1946-47	**Detroit Red Wings**	**NHL**	**33**	**16**	**13**	**29**	**18**	**16**	**34**	**2**	**5**	**2**	**1**	**3**	**2**
	Indianapolis Capitols	AHL	24	15	18	33	....	....	....	6	....	....	....	....	....
1947-48	**Detroit Red Wings**	**NHL**	**60**	**17**	**23**	**40**	**22**	**30**	**52**	**2**	**9**	**2**	**0**	**2**	**2**
1948-49	**Detroit Red Wings**	**NHL**	**4**	**1**	**0**	**1**	**1**	**0**	**1**	**2**	....	....	....	....	....
	Chicago Black Hawks	**NHL**	**55**	**25**	**23**	**48**	**35**	**33**	**68**	**41**	....	....	....	....	....
1949-50	**Chicago Black Hawks**	**NHL**	**66**	**13**	**20**	**33**	**16**	**24**	**40**	**14**	....	....	....	....	....

			REGULAR SEASON								PLAYOFFS				
Season	Club	League	GP	G	A	Pts	AG	AA	APts	PIM	GP	G	A	Pts	PIM
1950-51	**Chicago Black Hawks**	**NHL**	**52**	**10**	**27**	**37**	**13**	**33**	**46**	**16**					
	Milwaukee Seagulls	USHL	9	2	4	6				2					
1951-52	**Chicago Black Hawks**	**NHL**	**5**	**1**	**1**	**2**	**1**	**1**	**2**	**0**					
	New York Rangers	**NHL**	**16**	**0**	**1**	**1**	**0**	**1**	**1**	**2**					
1952-53	**New York Rangers**	**NHL**	**17**	**1**	**4**	**5**	**1**	**5**	**6**	**2**					
	Buffalo Bisons	AHL	34	6	21	27				19					
	NHL Totals		**328**	**85**	**117**	**202**	**108**	**150**	**258**	**91**	**19**	**5**	**2**	**7**	**4**

Signed as a free agent by **Detroit**, October 17, 1941. Traded to **Chicago** by **Detroit** with Bep Guidolin and Doug McCaig for George Gee and Bud Poile, October 25, 1948. Claimed on waivers by **NY Rangers** from **Chicago**, October 26, 1951. Traded to **Buffalo** (AHL) by **NY Rangers** for cash, December 31, 1952.

• CONACHER, Lionel

Lionel Pretoria "The Big Train" HHOF
D – L. 6'2", 195 lbs. b: Toronto, Ont., 5/24/1901 d: 5/26/1954.

Season	Club	League	GP	G	A	Pts	AG	AA	APts	PIM	GP	G	A	Pts	PIM
1916-17	Toronto Century Rovers	OMHA	STATISTICS NOT AVAILABLE												
1917-18	Toronto Aura Lee	OHA-Jr.	STATISTICS NOT AVAILABLE												
1918-19	Toronto Aura Lee	OHA-Jr.	STATISTICS NOT AVAILABLE												
1919-20	Toronto Canoe Club	OHA-Jr.									12	21	9	30	
1920-21	Toronto Aura Lee	OHA-Sr.	10	3	2	5									
1921-22	Toronto Aura Lee	OHA-Sr.	20	7	2	9					2	2	0	2	0
1922-23	North Toronto Seniors	OHA-Sr.									6	12	4	16	
1923-24	Pittsburgh Yellowjackets	USAHA	20	12	4	16					13	*6	3	*9	
1924-25	Pittsburgh Yellowjackets	USAHA	40	14	0	14					8	5	0	5	
1925-26	**Pittsburgh Pirates**	**NHL**	**33**	**9**	**4**	**13**	**15**	**26**	**41**	**64**	**2**	**0**	**0**	**0**	**0**
1926-27	**Pittsburgh Pirates**	**NHL**	**9**	**0**	**0**	**0**	**0**	**0**	**0**	**12**					
	New York Americans	**NHL**	**30**	**8**	**9**	**17**	**14**	**47**	**61**	**81**					
1927-28	**New York Americans**	**NHL**	**35**	**11**	**6**	**17**	**22**	**34**	**56**	**82**					
1928-29	**New York Americans**	**NHL**	**44**	**5**	**2**	**7**	**14**	**13**	**27**	**132**	**2**	**0**	**0**	**0**	**10**
1929-30	**New York Americans**	**NHL**	**40**	**4**	**6**	**10**	**6**	**14**	**20**	**73**					
1930-31	**Montreal Maroons**	**NHL**	**36**	**4**	**3**	**7**	**8**	**9**	**17**	**57**	**2**	**0**	**0**	**0**	**2**
1931-32	**Montreal Maroons**	**NHL**	**45**	**7**	**9**	**16**	**12**	**20**	**32**	**60**	**4**	**0**	**0**	**0**	**2**
1932-33	**Montreal Maroons**	**NHL**	**47**	**7**	**21**	**28**	**13**	**44**	**57**	**61**	**2**	**0**	**1**	**1**	**0**
♦**1933-34**	**Chicago Black Hawks**	**NHL**	**48**	**10**	**13**	**23**	**17**	**27**	**44**	**87**	**8**	**2**	**0**	**2**	**4**
♦**1934-35**	**Montreal Maroons**	**NHL**	**38**	**2**	**6**	**8**	**3**	**10**	**13**	**44**	**7**	**0**	**0**	**0**	**14**
1935-36	**Montreal Maroons**	**NHL**	**46**	**7**	**7**	**14**	**13**	**13**	**26**	**65**	**3**	**0**	**0**	**0**	**0**
1936-37	**Montreal Maroons**	**NHL**	**47**	**6**	**19**	**25**	**10**	**35**	**45**	**64**	**5**	**0**	**1**	**1**	**2**
	NHL Totals		**498**	**80**	**105**	**185**	**147**	**292**	**439**	**882**	**35**	**2**	**2**	**4**	**34**

• Father of Brian • Brother of Charlie and Roy • USAHA First Team All-Star (1924) • NHL Second All-Star Team (1933, 1937) • NHL First All-Star Team (1934) • Played in NHL All-Star Game (1934)

Signed as a free agent by **Pittsburgh**, November 11, 1925. Traded to **NY Americans** by **Pittsburgh** for Charlie Langlois and $2,000, December 16, 1926. Traded to **Montreal Maroons** by **NY Americans** for cash, November 5, 1930. Traded to **Chicago** by **Montreal Maroons** for Ted Graham, October 1, 1933. Traded to **Montreal Canadiens** by **Chicago** with Leroy Goldsworthy and Roger Jenkins for Lorne Chabot, Marty Burke and Howie Morenz, October 3, 1934. Traded to **Montreal Maroons** by **Montreal Canadiens** with the rights to Herb Cain for the rights to Nels Crutchfield, October 3, 1934.

• CONACHER, Pete

Charles William Jr.
LW – L. 5'10", 165 lbs. b: Toronto, Ont., 7/29/1932.

Season	Club	League	GP	G	A	Pts	AG	AA	APts	PIM	GP	G	A	Pts	PIM
1949-50	Galt Black Hawks	OHA-Jr.	48	25	27	52				22					
1950-51	Galt Black Hawks	OHA-Jr.	52	32	32	64				10	3	5	6	11	0
1951-52	Galt Black Hawks	OHA-Jr.	51	53	67	120				33	3	3	3	6	0
	Chicago Black Hawks	**NHL**	**2**	**0**	**1**	**1**	**0**	**1**	**1**	**0**					
1952-53	**Chicago Black Hawks**	**NHL**	**41**	**5**	**6**	**11**	**7**	**7**	**14**	**7**	**2**	**0**	**0**	**0**	**0**
	St. Louis Flyers	AHL	29	12	16	28				6					
1953-54	**Chicago Black Hawks**	**NHL**	**70**	**19**	**9**	**28**	**26**	**11**	**37**	**23**					
1954-55	**Chicago Black Hawks**	**NHL**	**18**	**2**	**4**	**6**	**3**	**5**	**8**	**2**					
	New York Rangers	**NHL**	**52**	**10**	**7**	**17**	**13**	**8**	**21**	**10**					
1955-56	**New York Rangers**	**NHL**	**41**	**11**	**11**	**22**	**15**	**13**	**28**	**10**	**5**	**0**	**0**	**0**	**0**
	Buffalo Bisons	AHL	18	17	15	32				6					
1956-57	Buffalo Bisons	AHL	60	26	29	55				16					
1957-58	**Toronto Maple Leafs**	**NHL**	**5**	**0**	**1**	**1**	**0**	**1**	**1**	**5**					
	Buffalo Bisons	AHL	48	12	32	44				2					
1958-59	Belleville McFarlands	EOHL	1	0	0	0				0					
	Canada	WEC-A	8	7	3	10				2					
1959-60	Buffalo Bisons	AHL	56	5	10	15				16					
1960-61	Hershey Bears	AHL	69	11	24	35				4	8	1	2	3	4
1961-62	Hershey Bears	AHL	70	27	29	56				16	7	2	0	2	5
1962-63	Hershey Bears	AHL	70	29	24	53				6	15	5	4	9	0
1963-64	Hershey Bears	AHL	72	34	26	60				12	6	0	3	3	2
1964-65	Hershey Bears	AHL	63	34	24	58				10	15	8	2	10	4
1965-66	Hershey Bears	AHL	60	14	20	34				4					
	NHL Totals		**229**	**47**	**39**	**86**	**64**	**46**	**110**	**57**	**7**	**0**	**0**	**0**	**0**

• Son of Charlie

Traded to **NY Rangers** by **Chicago** with Bill Gadsby for Rich Lamoureux, Allan Stanley and Nick Mickoski, November 23, 1954. Traded to **Buffalo** (AHL) by **NY Rangers** for $10,000 and the loan of Dusty Blair and Gord Pennell, August 20, 1956. Traded to **Toronto** by **NY Rangers** for $15,000, June 4, 1957. Traded to **NY Rangers** by **Toronto** for $15,000, November 18, 1957. Traded to **Detroit** by **NY Rangers** (Buffalo-AHL) for Barry Cullen, August, 1960. Traded to **Hershey** (AHL) by **Detroit** with Marc Reaume and Jack McIntyre for Howie Young, January, 1961.

• CONACHER, Roy

Roy Gordon HHOF
LW – L. 6'2", 175 lbs. b: Toronto, Ont., 10/5/1916 d: 12/29/1984.

Season	Club	League	GP	G	A	Pts	AG	AA	APts	PIM	GP	G	A	Pts	PIM
1933-34	West Toronto Nationals	OHA-Jr.	6	0	1	1				0					
1934-35	West Toronto Nationals	OHA-Jr.	9	4	3	7				8					
1935-36	West Toronto Nationals	OHA-Jr.	10	*12	3	15				11	5	4	2	6	4
	West Toronto Nationals	M-Cup	12	8	5	13				11					
1936-37	Toronto Dominions	OHA-Sr.	8	3	3	6				4	1	0	0	0	0
	Toronto Dominions	Al-Cup	3	3	0	3				2					
1937-38	Kirkland Lake Hargreaves	NOHA	14	12	11	23				2	1	1	0	1	0
♦**1938-39**	**Boston Bruins**	**NHL**	**47**	***26**	**11**	**37**	**46**	**17**	**63**	**12**	**12**	**6**	**4**	**10**	**12**
1939-40	**Boston Bruins**	**NHL**	**31**	**18**	**12**	**30**	**30**	**19**	**49**	**9**	**6**	**2**	**1**	**3**	**0**
♦**1940-41**	**Boston Bruins**	**NHL**	**41**	**24**	**14**	**38**	**38**	**20**	**58**	**7**	**11**	**1**	**5**	**6**	**0**
1941-42	**Boston Bruins**	**NHL**	**43**	**24**	**13**	**37**	**32**	**15**	**47**	**12**	**5**	**2**	**1**	**3**	**0**
1942-43	Saskatoon RCAF	N-SSHL	20	13	8	21				2	3	2	2	4	0
1943-44	Dartmouth RCAF	NSDHL	3	*9	2	11				4					
1944-45	Dartmouth RCAF	NSDHL	4	1	2	3				0					
	Millward-St. George RCAF	Britain	STATISTICS NOT AVAILABLE												
1945-46	**Boston Bruins**	**NHL**	**4**	**2**	**1**	**3**	**2**	**1**	**3**	**0**	**3**	**0**	**0**	**0**	**0**
1946-47	**Detroit Red Wings**	**NHL**	**60**	**30**	**24**	**54**	**34**	**29**	**63**	**6**	**5**	**4**	**4**	**8**	**2**
1947-48	**Chicago Black Hawks**	**NHL**	**52**	**22**	**27**	**49**	**29**	**36**	**65**	**4**					
1948-49	**Chicago Black Hawks**	**NHL**	**60**	**26**	**42**	***68**	**37**	**61**	**98**	**8**					
1949-50	**Chicago Black Hawks**	**NHL**	**70**	**25**	**31**	**56**	**32**	**38**	**70**	**16**					
1950-51	**Chicago Black Hawks**	**NHL**	**70**	**26**	**24**	**50**	**33**	**29**	**62**	**16**					
1951-52	**Chicago Black Hawks**	**NHL**	**12**	**3**	**1**	**4**	**4**	**1**	**5**	**0**					
	NHL Totals		**490**	**226**	**200**	**426**	**317**	**266**	**583**	**90**	**42**	**15**	**15**	**30**	**14**

• Brother of Lionel and Charlie • NHL First All-Star Team (1949) • Won Art Ross Trophy (1949) • Played in NHL All-Star Game (1949)

Traded to **Detroit** by **Boston** for Joe Carveth, August, 1946. Traded to **NY Rangers** by **Detroit** for Eddie Slowinski and future considerations, October 22, 1947. Conacher refused to report and transaction was voided. Traded to **Chicago** by **Detroit** for cash, November 1, 1947.

• CONN, Red

Hugh Maitland
LW – L. 5'11", 180 lbs. b: Hartney, Man., 10/25/1904 Deceased.

Season	Club	League	GP	G	A	Pts	AG	AA	APts	PIM	GP	G	A	Pts	PIM
1921-22	Melville Millionaires	N-SSHL	8	7	2	9				8					
1922-23	Saskatoon Collegiate	H.S.	STATISTICS NOT AVAILABLE												
1923-24	Saskatoon Civics	N-SSHL	5	4	0	4				4					
1924-25	Saskatoon Civics	N-SSHL	STATISTICS NOT AVAILABLE												
1925-26	Melville Millionaires	N-SSHL	17	8	*13	21				18					
1926-27	Regina Capitals	PrHL	17	3	1	4				26					
	Moose Jaw Maroons	PrHL	16	8	4	12				17					
1927-28	Moose Jaw Maroons	PrHL	28	14	7	21				36					
1928-29	Portland Buckaroos	PCHL	36	16	3	19				44	1	0	0	0	0
1929-30	Portland Buckaroos	PCHL	36	6	4	10				22	4	1	0	1	0
1930-31	Portland Buckaroos	PCHL	33	9	6	15				54					
1931-32	Boston Cubs	Can-Am	40	8	11	19				43	5	2	0	2	13
1932-33	Philadelphia Arrows	Can-Am	42	15	16	31				38	3	0	0	0	0
1933-34	**New York Americans**	**NHL**	**48**	**4**	**17**	**21**	**7**	**36**	**43**	**12**					
	Edmonton Eskimos	NWHL	1	0	0	0				0					
1934-35	**New York Americans**	**NHL**	**48**	**5**	**11**	**16**	**8**	**19**	**27**	**10**					
1935-36	Providence Reds	Can-Am	45	11	15	26				30	7	1	2	3	2
1936-37	Springfield Indians	IAHL	43	9	6	15				26	5	1	2	3	2
1937-38	Vancouver Lions	PCHL	41	10	14	24				20	6	1	4	5	2
1938-39	Portland Buckaroos	PCHL	43	9	26	35				58	5	1	1	2	10
1939-40	Portland Buckaroos	PCHL	32	3	3	6				20	5	0	0	0	8
1940-41	Portland Buckaroos	PCHL	48	11	10	21				91					
1941/44			OUT OF HOCKEY – RETIRED												
1944-45	Oakland Oaks	PCHL	STATISTICS NOT AVAILABLE												
	NHL Totals		**96**	**9**	**28**	**37**	**15**	**55**	**70**	**22**					

Signed as a free agent by **Regina** (PrHL), November 8, 1926. Traded to **Moose Jaw** (PrHL) by **Regina** (PrHL) for Lawrence Rose, January 27, 1927. Traded to **Montreal Canadiens** by **Springfield** (AHL) for Sammy Godin, September 30, 1937.

• CONNELLY, Bert

Albert Patrick
LW – L. 5'11", 174 lbs. b: Montreal, Que., 4/22/1909 Deceased.

Season	Club	League	GP	G	A	Pts	AG	AA	APts	PIM	GP	G	A	Pts	PIM
1928-29	Montreal Eurekas	MCHL		10	0	10									
	Montreal CNR	MCHL		7	0	7									
1929-30	Montreal Columbus	MCHL	10	0	0	0				11					
1930-31	Verdun CPR	MCHL	STATISTICS NOT AVAILABLE												
1931-32	Moncton Hawks	NBSHL	24	10	4	14				44	5	0	0	0	4
1932-33	Moncton Hawks	MSHL	26	6	3	9				37	5	2	0	2	8
	Moncton Hawks	Al-Cup	8	5	0	5				6					
1933-34	Moncton Hawks	NBSHL	29	14	11	25				31	3	*5	2	*7	2
	Moncton Hawks	Al-Cup	11	5	3	8				10					
1934-35	**New York Rangers**	**NHL**	**47**	**10**	**11**	**21**	**16**	**19**	**35**	**23**	**4**	**1**	**0**	**1**	**0**
1935-36	**New York Rangers**	**NHL**	**25**	**2**	**2**	**4**	**4**	**4**	**8**	**10**					
1936-37	Philadelphia Ramblers	IAHL	45	9	12	21				35	3	0	0	0	0
1937-38	Springfield Indians	IAHL	29	5	9	14				31					
♦	**Chicago Black Hawks**	**NHL**	**15**	**1**	**2**	**3**	**2**	**3**	**5**	**4**	**10**	**0**	**0**	**0**	**0**
1938-39	Springfield Indians	IAHL	45	15	12	27				30	3	0	0	0	0
1939-40	St. Paul Saints	AHA	46	24	25	49				53	7	4	2	6	21
1940-41	St. Paul Saints	AHA	46	16	11	27				31	4	0	0	0	4
1941-42	Fort Worth Rangers	AHA	49	27	32	59				36	5	3	0	3	6
1942-43	Montreal Royals	QSHL	14	3	5	8				2					
1943-44	Montreal Canada Car	MCHL	11	12	10	22				4					
1944-45	Valleyfield Braves	QSHL	35	23	23	46				26	11	7	4	11	6
	Valleyfield Braves	Al-Cup	3	2	0	2				2					
1945-46	St-Hyacinthe Saints	QPHL	17	13	10	23				33	4	1	2	3	2
	NHL Totals		**87**	**13**	**15**	**28**	**22**	**26**	**48**	**37**	**14**	**1**	**0**	**1**	**0**

AHA First All-Star Team (1942)

Signed as a free agent by **NY Rangers**, October 26, 1934. Signed as a free agent by **Chicago**, February 7, 1938.

• CONNELLY, Wayne

— see page 985

• CONNOR, Harry

Henry Alexander
LW – L. 6', 195 lbs. b: Ottawa, Ont., 12/3/1904 d: 3/2/1947.

Season	Club	League	GP	G	A	Pts	AG	AA	APts	PIM	GP	G	A	Pts	PIM
1923-24	Ottawa Munitions	OCHL	STATISTICS NOT AVAILABLE												
1924-25	Ottawa Rideaus	OCHL	15	8	1	9					3	0	0	0	0
1925-26	Guelph Royals	OHA-Sr.	STATISTICS NOT AVAILABLE												
1926-27	Saskatoon Crescents	PrHL	32	22	14	36				*73	3	1	0	1	4
1927-28	**Boston Bruins**	**NHL**	**42**	**9**	**1**	**10**	**18**	**6**	**24**	**36**	**2**	**0**	**0**	**0**	**0**
1928-29	**New York Americans**	**NHL**	**43**	**6**	**2**	**8**	**17**	**13**	**30**	**83**	**2**	**0**	**0**	**0**	**2**
1929-30	**Ottawa Senators**	**NHL**	**25**	**1**	**2**	**3**	**1**	**5**	**6**	**22**					
	Boston Bruins	**NHL**	**13**	**0**	**0**	**0**	**0**	**0**	**0**	**4**	**6**	**0**	**0**	**0**	**0**
1930-31	**Ottawa Senators**	**NHL**	**11**	**0**	**0**	**0**	**0**	**0**	**0**	**4**					
	London Tecumsehs	IHL	15	3	0	3				8					
1931-32	Providence Reds	Can-Am	29	12	13	25				18	5	0	1	1	2

Season	Club	League	REGULAR SEASON GP	G	A	Pts	AG	AA	APts	PIM	PLAYOFFS GP	G	A	Pts	PIM
1932-33	Providence Reds	Can-Am	36	8	7	15	....	....	....	30	....	....	....	....	....
	Quebec Castors	Can-Am	11	3	4	7	....	....	....	24	....	....	....	....	....
	NHL Totals		**134**	**16**	**5**	**21**	**36**	**24**	**60**	**149**	**10**	**0**	**0**	**0**	**2**

PrHL First Team All-Star (1927)

Signed as a free agent by **Saskatoon** (PrHL), November 10, 1926. Traded to **Boston** by **Saskatoon** (PrHL) for cash, October, 1927. Traded to **NY Americans** by **Boston** for Red Green, May 18, 1928. Claimed on waivers by **Ottawa** from **NY Americans** for $5,000, November 18, 1929. Traded to **Boston** by **Ottawa** for Bill Hutton, January 30, 1930. Traded to **Ottawa** by **Boston** for Bill Hutton, October 16, 1930.

• CONNORS, Bob Robert Allan

LW/D – L. 5'9", 165 lbs. b: Glasgow, Scotland, 10/19/1904 d: 7/27/1931.

Season	Club	League	GP	G	A	Pts	AG	AA	APts	PIM	GP	G	A	Pts	PIM
1921-22	Grand'Mere Maroons	QPHL	3	0	0	0	....	....	....	0	....	....	....	....	....
1922-23	Iroquois Papermakers	NOJHA	STATISTICS NOT AVAILABLE												
1923-24	Port Arthur Bearcats	TBSHL	16	4	1	5	....	....	....	5	2	0	0	0	0
1924-25	Port Arthur Bearcats	TBSHL	15	3	0	3	....	....	....	....	....	....	....	....	....
	Port Arthur Bearcats	Al-Cup	9	1	0	1	....	....	....	2	....	....	....	....	....
1925-26	Niagara Falls Cataracts	OHA-Sr.	18	12	6	18	....	....	....	26	....	....	....	....	....
1926-27	Niagara Falls Cataracts	Can-Pro	17	6	2	8	....	....	....	31	....	....	....	....	....
	New York Americans	**NHL**	**6**	**1**	**0**	**1**	**2**	**0**	**2**	**0**	....	....	....	....	....
1927-28	Detroit Olympics	IHL	38	14	10	24	....	....	....	*131	2	0	0	0	6
1928-29	**Detroit Cougars**	**NHL**	**41**	**13**	**3**	**16**	**38**	**20**	**58**	**68**	**2**	**0**	**0**	**0**	**10**
1929-30	**Detroit Cougars**	**NHL**	**31**	**3**	**7**	**10**	**4**	**16**	**20**	**42**	....	....	....	....	....
	Detroit Olympics	IHL	15	9	5	14	....	....	....	29	3	1	0	1	13
1930-31	Seattle Eskimos	PCHL	27	9	1	10	....	....	....	88	....	....	....	....	....
	NHL Totals		**78**	**17**	**10**	**27**	**44**	**36**	**80**	**110**	**2**	**0**	**0**	**0**	**10**

Signed as a free agent by **Niagara Falls** (Can-Pro), November 1, 1926. Traded to **NY Americans** by **Niagara Falls** (Can-Pro) for cash, February 1, 1927. Traded to **Detroit** by **NY Americans** for cash, September, 1928. Traded to **Seattle** (PCHL) by **Detroit** with Pete Bellefeuille for cash, September 12, 1930. • Suspended for remainder of 1930-31 season by PCHL for stick assault on Doug Brennan, March 10, 1931. • Drowned near Port Arthur, Ontario, July 27,1931.

• CONVEY, Eddie

LW/C – L. 5'11", 165 lbs. b: Toronto, Ont., 12/16/1910 Deceased.

Season	Club	League	GP	G	A	Pts	AG	AA	APts	PIM	GP	G	A	Pts	PIM
1926-27	St. Michael's Majors	OHA-Jr.	6	1	2	3	....	....	....	....	6	0	1	1	....
1927-28	St. Michael's Majors	OHA-Jr.	6	12	*6	18	....	....	....	....	6	*7	*6	*13	....
1928-29	St. Michael's Majors	OHA-Jr.	7	7	2	9	....	....	....	....	2	0	1	1	....
	St. Michael's Majors	M-Cup	13	8	*12	20	....	....	....	18	....	....	....	....	....
1929-30	Toronto Nationals	OHA-Sr.	9	2	2	4	....	....	....	*33	2	0	0	0	2
1930-31	**New York Americans**	**NHL**	**2**	**0**	**0**	**0**	**0**	**0**	**0**	**0**	....	....	....	....	....
	New Haven Eagles	Can-Am	32	7	6	13	....	....	....	98	....	....	....	....	....
1931-32	**New York Americans**	**NHL**	**21**	**1**	**0**	**1**	**2**	**0**	**2**	**21**	....	....	....	....	....
	New Haven Eagles	Can-Am	23	5	11	16	....	....	....	28	2	1	1	2	0
1932-33	**New York Americans**	**NHL**	**13**	**0**	**1**	**1**	**0**	**2**	**2**	**12**	....	....	....	....	....
	New Haven Eagles	Can-Am	38	8	6	14	....	....	....	81	....	....	....	....	....
1933-34	Buffalo Bisons	IHL	44	4	8	12	....	....	....	35	6	0	1	1	12
1934-35	Windsor Bulldogs	IHL	44	*24	17	41	....	....	....	54	....	....	....	....	....
1935-36	Syracuse Stars	IHL	45	20	19	39	....	....	....	58	2	2	0	2	0
1936-37	Syracuse Stars	IAHL	50	12	37	49	....	....	....	82	9	2	4	6	*19
1937-38	Syracuse Stars	IAHL	48	19	*33	52	....	....	....	42	8	2	3	5	0
1938-39	Syracuse Stars	IAHL	54	14	25	39	....	....	....	30	3	1	1	2	0
1939-40	Syracuse Stars	IAHL	53	17	33	50	....	....	....	24	....	....	....	....	....
1940-41	Pittsburgh Hornets	AHL	56	15	28	43	....	....	....	22	6	2	0	2	4
	NHL Totals		**36**	**1**	**1**	**2**	**2**	**2**	**4**	**33**	....	....	....	....	....

IAHL Second All-Star Team (1938)

• COOK, Bill William Osser HHOF

RW – R. 5'10", 170 lbs. b: Brantford, Ont., 10/9/1896 d: 4/6/1986.

Season	Club	League	GP	G	A	Pts	AG	AA	APts	PIM	GP	G	A	Pts	PIM
1913/15	Kingston Frontenacs	OHA-Jr.	STATISTICS NOT AVAILABLE												
1914-15	Kingston Frontenacs	OHA-Sr.	STATISTICS NOT AVAILABLE												
1915/19			MILITARY SERVICE												
1919-20	Kingston Frontenacs	OHA-Sr.	STATISTICS NOT AVAILABLE												
1920-21	S.S. Marie Greyhounds	NOHA	9	*12	7	*19	....	....	....	48	5	5	1	6	....
	S.S. Marie Greyhounds	NMHL	12	12	6	18	....	....	....	48	....	....	....	....	....
1921-22	S.S. Marie Greyhounds	AAHA	12	*20	8	*28	....	....	....	....	....	....	....	....	....
	S.S. Marie Greyhounds	NOHA	8	7	5	12	....	....	....	38	2	1	1	2	2
1922-23	Saskatoon Sheiks	WCHL	30	9	16	25	....	....	....	19	....	....	....	....	....
1923-24	Saskatoon Crescents	WCHL	30	*26	*14	*40	....	....	....	20	....	....	....	....	....
1924-25	Saskatoon Crescents	WCHL	27	22	10	32	....	....	....	79	2	0	0	0	4
1925-26	Saskatoon Crescents	WHL	30	*31	13	*44	....	....	....	26	2	2	0	2	26
1926-27	**New York Rangers**	**NHL**	**44**	***33**	**4**	***37**	**60**	**21**	**81**	**58**	**2**	**1**	**0**	**1**	**6**
♦1927-28	**New York Rangers**	**NHL**	**43**	**18**	**6**	**24**	**37**	**34**	**71**	**42**	**9**	**2**	**3**	**5**	**26**
1928-29	**New York Rangers**	**NHL**	**43**	**15**	**8**	**23**	**44**	**54**	**98**	**41**	**6**	**0**	**0**	**0**	**6**
1929-30	**New York Rangers**	**NHL**	**44**	**29**	**30**	**59**	**42**	**72**	**114**	**56**	**4**	**0**	**1**	**1**	**11**
1930-31	**New York Rangers**	**NHL**	**43**	**30**	**12**	**42**	**62**	**36**	**98**	**39**	**4**	**3**	**0**	**3**	**4**
1931-32	**New York Rangers**	**NHL**	**48**	***34**	**14**	**48**	**58**	**31**	**89**	**33**	**7**	**3**	**3**	**6**	**2**
♦1932-33	**New York Rangers**	**NHL**	**48**	***28**	**22**	***50**	**52**	**46**	**98**	**51**	**8**	**3**	**2**	**5**	**4**
1933-34	**New York Rangers**	**NHL**	**48**	**13**	**13**	**26**	**22**	**27**	**49**	**21**	**2**	**0**	**0**	**0**	**2**
1934-35	**New York Rangers**	**NHL**	**48**	**21**	**15**	**36**	**35**	**26**	**61**	**23**	**4**	**1**	**2**	**3**	**7**
1935-36	**New York Rangers**	**NHL**	**44**	**7**	**10**	**17**	**13**	**19**	**32**	**16**	....	....	....	....	....
1936-37	**New York Rangers**	**NHL**	**21**	**1**	**4**	**5**	**2**	**7**	**9**	**6**	....	....	....	....	....
1937-38	Cleveland Barons	IAHL	5	0	0	0	....	....	....	5	1	0	0	0	0
	NHL Totals		**474**	**229**	**138**	**367**	**427**	**373**	**800**	**386**	**46**	**13**	**11**	**24**	**68**
	Other Major League Totals		117	88	53	141	....	....	....	144	4	2	0	2	30

• Brother of Bun and Bud • WCHL All-Star Team (1924, 1925) • WHL All-Star Team (1926) • NHL Scoring Leader (1927, 1933) • NHL First All-Star Team (1931, 1932, 1933) • NHL Second All-Star Team (1934) • Played in NHL All-Star Game (1934)

Signed as a free agent by **Saskatoon** (WCHL), August 24, 1922. Traded to **NY Rangers** by **Saskatoon** (WHL) for cash, October 18, 1926.

• COOK, Bud Alexander Leone

C – L. 5'10", 160 lbs. b: Kingston, Ont., 11/20/1907 d: 11/13/1993.

Season	Club	League	GP	G	A	Pts	AG	AA	APts	PIM	GP	G	A	Pts	PIM
1924-25	Saskatoon Pats	N-SJHL	6	5	1	6	....	....	....	....	....	....	....	....	....
1925-26	Saskatoon Wesleys	N-SJHL	10	7	*2	9	....	....	....	....	....	....	....	....	....
1926-27	Toronto Imperial Oil	TIHL	STATISTICS NOT AVAILABLE												
1927-28	Saskatoon Collegiate	N-SJHL	3	1	0	1	....	....	....	0	....	....	....	....	....
1928-29	Oakland Sheiks	Cal-Pro	20	13	7	20	....	....	....	33	....	....	....	....	....
1929-30	Oakland Sheiks	Cal-Pro	24	24	*21	*45	....	....	....	34	....	....	....	....	....
1930-31	Providence Reds	Can-Am	33	16	11	27	....	....	....	61	2	0	1	1	4
1931-32	**Boston Bruins**	**NHL**	**28**	**4**	**4**	**8**	**7**	**9**	**16**	**14**	....	....	....	....	....
	Boston Cubs	Can-Am	7	1	2	3	....	....	....	9	....	....	....	....	....
1932-33	Boston Cubs	Can-Am	42	16	26	42	....	....	....	70	7	3	*4	*7	10
1933-34	**Ottawa Senators**	**NHL**	**18**	**1**	**0**	**1**	**2**	**0**	**2**	**8**	....	....	....	....	....
	Detroit Olympics	IHL	26	11	6	17	....	....	....	30	6	3	0	3	17
1934-35	**St. Louis Eagles**	**NHL**	**4**	**0**	**0**	**0**	**0**	**0**	**0**	**0**	....	....	....	....	....
	Cleveland Falcons	IHL	37	20	21	41	....	....	....	50	2	1	1	2	4
1935-36	Cleveland Falcons	IHL	44	27	19	46	....	....	....	29	2	1	0	1	0
1936-37	Cleveland Barons	IAHL	43	20	16	36	....	....	....	18	....	....	....	....	....
1937-38	Cleveland Barons	IAHL	43	13	27	40	....	....	....	46	2	0	0	0	2
1938-39	Cleveland Barons	IAHL	DID NOT PLAY – INJURED												
1939-40	Cleveland Barons	IAHL	54	14	15	29	....	....	....	27	....	....	....	....	....
1940-41	Cleveland Barons	AHL	54	9	22	31	....	....	....	26	9	1	5	6	13
1941-42	Cleveland Barons	AHL	54	8	32	40	....	....	....	32	5	0	2	2	4
1942-43	Cleveland Barons	AHL	51	5	21	26	....	....	....	28	4	0	1	1	0
1943-44	Cleveland Barons	AHL	4	2	3	5	....	....	....	2	....	....	....	....	....
	Coast Guard Cutters	X-Games	31	16	18	34	....	....	....	2	8	7	5	12	6
1944-45			MILITARY SERVICE												
1945-46	Oakland Oaks	PCHL	37	17	30	47	....	....	....	30	2	3	2	5	0
1946-47	Oakland Oaks	PCHL	....	....	....	....	....	....	....	....	....	....	....	....	....
	NHL Totals		**50**	**5**	**4**	**9**	**9**	**9**	**18**	**22**	....	....	....	....	....

• Brother of Bill and Bun • IAHL First All-Star Team (1938)

Traded to **Montreal Canadiens** by **Oakland** (Cal-Pro) for cash, February 18, 1930. Traded to **Boston** by **Montreal Canadiens** for cash, May 13, 1931. Traded to **Ottawa** by **Boston** with Percy Galbraith and Ted Saunders for Bob Gracie, October 4, 1933. Transferred to **St. Louis** after **Ottawa** franchise relocated, September 22, 1934. Traded to **Cleveland** (IHL) by **St. Louis** for cash, November 29, 1934. • Missed entire 1938-39 season recovering from injuries suffered in automobile accident, October 14, 1938.

• COOK, Bun Frederick Joseph HHOF

LW – L. 5'11", 180 lbs. b: Kingston, Ont., 9/18/1903 d: 3/19/1988.

Season	Club	League	GP	G	A	Pts	AG	AA	APts	PIM	GP	G	A	Pts	PIM
1921-22	S.S. Marie Greyhounds	NOHA	3	2	1	3	....	....	....	2	....	....	....	....	....
1922-23	S.S. Marie Greyhounds	NOHA	8	2	3	5	....	....	....	10	2	0	*2	2	0
	S.S. Marie Greyhounds	Al-Cup	3	2	0	2	....	....	....	4	....	....	....	....	....
1923-24	S.S. Marie Greyhounds	NOHA	8	3	3	6	....	....	....	10	7	1	0	1	8
1924-25	Saskatoon Crescents	WCHL	28	17	4	21	....	....	....	44	2	0	1	1	0
1925-26	Saskatoon Crescents	WHL	30	8	4	12	....	....	....	22	2	0	0	0	0
1926-27	**New York Rangers**	**NHL**	**44**	**14**	**9**	**23**	**25**	**47**	**72**	**42**	**2**	**0**	**0**	**0**	**6**
♦1927-28	**New York Rangers**	**NHL**	**44**	**14**	**14**	**28**	**29**	**81**	**110**	**45**	**9**	**2**	**1**	**3**	**10**
1928-29	**New York Rangers**	**NHL**	**43**	**13**	**5**	**18**	**38**	**33**	**71**	**70**	**6**	**1**	**0**	**1**	**12**
1929-30	**New York Rangers**	**NHL**	**43**	**24**	**18**	**42**	**34**	**43**	**77**	**55**	**4**	**2**	**0**	**2**	**2**
1930-31	**New York Rangers**	**NHL**	**44**	**18**	**17**	**35**	**36**	**52**	**88**	**72**	**4**	**0**	**0**	**0**	**2**
1931-32	**New York Rangers**	**NHL**	**45**	**14**	**20**	**34**	**23**	**44**	**67**	**43**	**7**	**6**	**2**	**8**	**12**
♦1932-33	**New York Rangers**	**NHL**	**48**	**22**	**15**	**37**	**40**	**31**	**71**	**35**	**8**	**2**	**0**	**2**	**4**
1933-34	**New York Rangers**	**NHL**	**48**	**18**	**15**	**33**	**31**	**32**	**63**	**36**	**2**	**0**	**0**	**0**	**2**
1934-35	**New York Rangers**	**NHL**	**48**	**13**	**21**	**34**	**21**	**37**	**58**	**26**	**4**	**2**	**0**	**2**	**0**
1935-36	**New York Rangers**	**NHL**	**26**	**4**	**5**	**9**	**8**	**9**	**17**	**12**	....	....	....	....	....
1936-37	**Boston Bruins**	**NHL**	**40**	**4**	**5**	**9**	**7**	**9**	**16**	**8**	....	....	....	....	....
1937-38	Providence Reds	IAHL	19	0	1	1	....	....	....	4	4	0	0	0	2
1938-39	Providence Reds	IAHL	11	1	3	4	....	....	....	4	....	....	....	....	....
1939-40	Providence Reds	IAHL	1	0	0	0	....	....	....	0	2	0	0	0	0
1940-41	Providence Reds	AHL	1	0	0	0	....	....	....	0	....	....	....	....	....
1941-42	Providence Reds	AHL	2	0	1	1	....	....	....	0	....	....	....	....	....
1942-43	Providence Reds	AHL	3	1	1	2	....	....	....	4	....	....	....	....	....
	NHL Totals		**473**	**158**	**144**	**302**	**292**	**418**	**710**	**444**	**46**	**15**	**3**	**18**	**50**
	Other Major League Totals		58	25	8	33	....	....	....	66	4	0	1	1	0

• Brother of Bill and Bud • NHL Second All-Star Team (1931)

Signed as a free agent by **Saskatoon** (WCHL), September 20, 1924. Traded to **NY Rangers** by **Saskatoon** (WHL) for cash, October 18, 1926. Traded to **Boston** by **NY Rangers** for cash, September 10, 1936. • Served as playing-coach for **Providence** (AHL), 1937-1943.

• COOK, Lloyd Lloyd Trambly "Farmer"

D – L. 6', 170 lbs. b: Lynden, Ont., 3/21/1890 d: 10/9/1964.

Season	Club	League	GP	G	A	Pts	AG	AA	APts	PIM	GP	G	A	Pts	PIM
1912-13	Fernie Ghostriders	BHL	STATISTICS NOT AVAILABLE												
	Taber Chiefs	ASHL	....	....	....	....	....	....	....	....	2	1	0	1	4
1913-14	Edmonton Dominions	ASHL	4	8	0	8	....	....	....	13	7	4	0	4	16
♦1914-15	Vancouver Millionaires	PCHA	17	11	6	17	....	....	....	15	3	3	0	3	9
	PCHA All-Stars	X-Games	2	0	1	1	....	....	....	0	....	....	....	....	....
1915-16	Vancouver Millionaires	PCHA	18	18	3	21	....	....	....	24	....	....	....	....	....
	PCHA All-Stars	X-Games	2	1	0	1	....	....	....	3	....	....	....	....	....
1916-17	Spokane Canaries	PCHA	23	13	9	22	....	....	....	32	....	....	....	....	....
1917-18	Vancouver Millionaires	PCHA	18	6	4	10	....	....	....	11	6	2	0	2	12
1918-19	Vancouver Millionaires	PCHA	20	8	6	14	....	....	....	22	2	1	0	1	0
1919-20	Vancouver Millionaires	PCHA	21	10	4	14	....	....	....	15	2	1	0	1	0
1920-21	Vancouver Millionaires	PCHA	24	12	9	21	....	....	....	18	2	1	1	2	0
	Vancouver Millionaires	St-Cup	5	2	0	2	....	....	....	1	....	....	....	....	....
1921-22	Vancouver Millionaires	PCHA	24	2	3	5	....	....	....	9	2	1	0	1	0
	Vancouver Millionaires	St-Cup	7	2	0	2	....	....	....	8	....	....	....	....	....
1922-23	Vancouver Maroons	PCHA	30	19	11	30	....	....	....	33	2	0	0	0	6
	Vancouver Maroons	St-Cup	4	0	1	1	....	....	....	4	....	....	....	....	....
1923-24	Vancouver Maroons	PCHA	28	7	5	12	....	....	....	18	2	0	2	2	0
	Vancouver Maroons	St-Cup	2	2	1	3	....	....	....	6	....	....	....	....	....
1924-25	**Boston Bruins**	**NHL**	**4**	**1**	**0**	**1**	**2**	**0**	**2**	**0**	....	....	....	....	....
1925-26	Culver City Pros	Cal-Pro	30	8	3	11	....	....	....	18	....	....	....	....	....
1926-27	LA Globe Ice Cream	Cal-Pro	STATISTICS NOT AVAILABLE												
1927-28	Los Angeles Richfields	Cal-Pro	22	13	2	15	....	....	....	18	....	....	....	....	....
1928-29	San Francisco Tigers	Cal-Pro	36	8	4	12	....	....	....	14	....	....	....	....	....
1929-30	San Francisco Tigers	Cal-Pro	36	4	3	7	....	....	....	....	....	....	....	....	....
1930-31	San Francisco Hawks	Cal-Pro	27	8	6	14	....	....	....	....	....	....	....	....	....
1931-32	San Francisco Rangers	Cal-Pro	DID NOT PLAY – COACHING												
	NHL Totals		**4**	**1**	**0**	**1**	**2**	**0**	**2**	**0**	....	....	....	....	....
	Other Major League Totals		223	106	60	166	....	....	....	197	21	9	3	12	27

ASHL First All-Star Team (1914) • PCHA Second All-Star Team (1916, 1918, 1919) • PCHA First All-Star Team (1920, 1921, 1923)

Signed as a free agent by **Vancouver** (PCHA), December 25, 1917. Traded to **Boston** by **Vancouver** (WCHL) for cash, November 18, 1924. • 1922 St-Cup totals include series vs. Regina.

• COOK, Tom Tom John
C – L. 5'7", 140 lbs. b: Fort William, Ont., 5/7/1907 d: 10/2/1961.

			REGULAR SEASON								PLAYOFFS				
Season	Club	League	GP	G	A	Pts	AG	AA	APts	PIM	GP	G	A	Pts	PIM
1923-24	Fort William Dominions	TBJHL	STATISTICS NOT AVAILABLE												
1924-25	University of Manitoba	WJrHL	STATISTICS NOT AVAILABLE												
	University of Manitoba	M-Cup	5	*8	0	*8	....	....	....	*15	....	....	....	....	....
1925-26	Fort William Forts	TBSHL	19	7	4	11	....	....	....	26	3	0	0	0	6
1926-27	Fort William Forts	TBSHL	19	25	*12	*37	....	....	....	38	2	1	0	1	2
1927-28	Fort William Forts	TBSHL	20	*34	7	*41	....	....	....	29	2	0	0	0	2
1928-29	Tulsa Oilers	AHA	39	*22	11	*33	....	....	....	26	4	3	0	3	4
1929-30	Chicago Black Hawks	NHL	41	14	16	30	20	38	58	16	2	0	1	1	4
1930-31	Chicago Black Hawks	NHL	44	15	14	29	30	43	73	34	9	1	3	4	11
1931-32	Chicago Black Hawks	NHL	48	12	13	25	20	29	49	36	2	0	0	0	2
1932-33	Chicago Black Hawks	NHL	48	12	14	26	22	29	51	30	....	....	....	....	....
♦1933-34	Chicago Black Hawks	NHL	37	5	9	14	9	19	28	15	8	1	0	1	0
1934-35	Chicago Black Hawks	NHL	48	13	18	31	21	31	52	33	2	0	0	0	2
1935-36	Chicago Black Hawks	NHL	47	4	8	12	8	15	23	20	1	0	0	0	0
1936-37	Chicago Black Hawks	NHL	15	0	2	2	0	4	4	0	....	....	....	....	....
	Cleveland Barons	IAHL	24	7	8	15	....	....	....	13	....	....	....	....	....
1937-38	Montreal Maroons	NHL	21	2	4	6	3	6	9	0	....	....	....	....	....
	New Haven Eagles	IAHL	2	0	0	0	....	....	....	4	....	....	....	....	....
	NHL Totals		**349**	**77**	**98**	**175**	**133**	**214**	**347**	**184**	**24**	**2**	**4**	**6**	**19**

Claimed by **Chicago** from **Tulsa** (AHA) in Inter-League Draft, May 13, 1929. Traded to **Cleveland** (AHL) by **Chicago** for cash, January 15, 1937. Claimed by **Montreal Maroons** from **Cleveland** (AHL) in Inter-League Draft, May 9, 1937.

• COOPER, Carson Carson Eric "Shovel-Shot"
RW – R. 5'7", 160 lbs. b: Cornwall, Ont., 7/17/1899 d: 7/4/1955.

Season	Club	League	GP	G	A	Pts	AG	AA	APts	PIM	GP	G	A	Pts	PIM
1916-17	Montreal Canada Cement	MCHL	STATISTICS NOT AVAILABLE												
1917-18	Hamilton Tigers	OHA-I	STATISTICS NOT AVAILABLE												
1918-19	Hamilton Tigers	OHA-Sr.	7	1	1	2	....	....	....	....	....	....	....	....	....
1919-20	Hamilton Tigers	OHA-Sr.	6	*18	2	20	....	....	....	....	2	2	0	2	0
1920-21	Hamilton Tigers	OHA-Sr.	10	*14	2	16	....	....	....	....	....	....	....	....	....
1921-22	Hamilton Tigers	OHA-Sr.	10	*22	1	*23	....	....	....	....	....	....	....	....	....
1922-23	Hamilton Tigers	OHA-Sr.	12	20	7	27	....	....	....	....	2	1	1	2	2
1923-24	Hamilton Tigers	OHA-Sr.	10	*33	7	*40	....	....	....	....	2	*5	1	*6	....
1924-25	Boston Bruins	NHL	12	5	3	8	9	12	21	4	....	....	....	....	....
1925-26	Boston Bruins	NHL	36	28	3	31	50	19	69	10	....	....	....	....	....
1926-27	Boston Bruins	NHL	10	0	0	0	0	0	0	0	....	....	....	....	....
	Montreal Canadiens	NHL	14	9	3	12	16	16	32	16	3	0	0	0	0
1927-28	Detroit Cougars	NHL	43	15	2	17	31	11	42	32	....	....	....	....	....
1928-29	Detroit Cougars	NHL	43	18	9	27	53	61	114	14	2	0	0	0	2
1929-30	Detroit Cougars	NHL	44	18	18	36	26	43	69	14	....	....	....	....	....
1930-31	Detroit Falcons	NHL	44	14	14	28	28	43	71	10	....	....	....	....	....
1931-32	Detroit Falcons	NHL	48	3	5	8	5	11	16	11	2	0	0	0	0
1932-33	Detroit Olympics	IHL	2	0	0	0	....	....	....	0	....	....	....	....	....
1933-34	Detroit Olympics	IHL	37	11	6	17	....	....	....	16	6	1	1	2	2
1934-35	Windsor Bulldogs	IHL	14	4	5	9	....	....	....	4	....	....	....	....	....
	Detroit Olympics	IHL	12	2	4	6	....	....	....	0	3	0	0	0	2
	NHL Totals		**294**	**110**	**57**	**167**	**218**	**216**	**434**	**111**	**7**	**0**	**0**	**0**	**2**

OHA-Sr. First All-Star Team (1921, 1922, 1923)

Signed as a free agent by **Boston**, November 2, 1924. • Missed majority of 1924-25 season recovering from knee injury suffered in game vs. Hamilton, December 10, 1924. Traded to **Montreal Canadiens** by **Boston** for Billy Boucher with both teams holding right of recall, January 17, 1927. • Players returned to original teams May 22, 1927. Traded to **Detroit Cougars** by **Boston** for cash, May 22, 1927.

• COOPER, Hal Hal Wallace
RW – R. 5'5", 155 lbs. b: New Liskeard, Ont., 8/29/1915 Deceased.

Season	Club	League	GP	G	A	Pts	AG	AA	APts	PIM	GP	G	A	Pts	PIM
1931-32	Hamilton Victorias	OHA-Jr.	3	1	2	3	....	....	....	4	3	2	0	2	2
1932-33	Hamilton Victorias	OHA-Jr.	STATISTICS NOT AVAILABLE												
1933-34	Sudbury Cub Wolves	NBHL	8	7	3	10	....	....	....	17	2	1	*4	5	*7
1934-35	Falconbridge Falcons	NBHL	8	8	2	10	....	....	....	10	2	0	1	1	0
1935-36	Falconbridge Falcons	NBHL	10	7	7	14	....	....	....	12	3	1	2	3	0
	Falconbridge Falcons	Al-Cup	13	5	3	8	....	....	....	4	....	....	....	....	....
1936-37	Falconbridge Falcons	NBHL	14	7	3	10	....	....	....	16	4	*2	*4	*6	2
1937-38	Falconbridge Falcons	NBHL	15	3	2	5	....	....	....	22	3	1	2	3	2
	Falconbridge Falcons	Al-Cup	9	4	5	9	....	....	....	4	....	....	....	....	....
1938-39	Kirkland Lake Blue Devils	GBHL	8	7	12	19	....	....	....	10	2	1	3	4	2
	Kirkland Lake Blue Devils	Al-Cup	7	3	4	7	....	....	....	4	....	....	....	....	....
1939-40	Kirkland Lake Blue Devils	X-Games	15	*20	5	25	....	....	....	16	....	....	....	....	....
	Kirkland Lake Blue Devils	Al-Cup	20	11	12	23	....	....	....	14	....	....	....	....	....
1940-41	Niagara Falls Cataracts	OHA-Sr.	32	21	20	41	....	....	....	22	3	0	2	2	2
	Toronto Telegram	TIHL	2	1	1	2	....	....	....	0	11	4	12	16	0
1941-42	Niagara Falls Cataracts	OHA-Sr.	25	12	13	25	....	....	....	13	7	7	0	7	6
1942-43	Niagara Falls Cataracts	OHA-Sr.	22	5	16	21	....	....	....	8	2	2	1	3	2
1943-44	Providence Reds	AHL	51	23	21	44	....	....	....	6	....	....	....	....	....
1944-45	New York Rangers	NHL	8	0	0	0	0	0	0	2	....	....	....	....	....
	Hershey Bears	AHL	46	24	17	41	....	....	....	9	11	6	6	12	6
1945-46	Hershey Bears	AHL	41	12	8	20	....	....	....	4	....	....	....	....	....
1946-47	Houston Huskies	USHL	9	0	6	6	....	....	....	2	....	....	....	....	....
1947-48			REINSTATED AS AN AMATEUR												
1948-49	Hamilton Tigers	OHA-Sr.	27	12	5	17	....	....	....	4	6	1	4	5	4
1949-50	Hamilton Tigers	OHA-Sr.	13	0	1	1	....	....	....	11	....	....	....	....	....
	NHL Totals		**8**	**0**	**0**	**0**	**0**	**0**	**0**	**2**	....	....	....	....	....

Claimed by **NY Rangers** from **Providence** (IAHL) in Inter-League Draft, May 12, 1939.

• COOPER, Joe
D – R. 6'2", 200 lbs. b: Winnipeg, Man., 12/14/1914 d: 4/3/1979.

Season	Club	League	GP	G	A	Pts	AG	AA	APts	PIM	GP	G	A	Pts	PIM
1931-32	Winnipeg K. of C.	MJHL	2	0	0	0	....	....	....	0	....	....	....	....	....
1932-33	Winnipeg K. of C.	MJHL	11	8	3	11	....	....	....	24	3	0	1	1	2
1933-34	Selkirk Fishermen	MJHL	13	12	3	15	....	....	....	28	5	3	*4	7	17
	Selkirk Fishermen	MHL-Sr.	1	0	0	0	....	....	....	6	....	....	....	....	....
1934-35	New York Crescents	EAHL	21	5	14	19	....	....	....	*70	7	5	0	5	*16
1935-36	New York Rangers	NHL	1	0	0	0	0	0	0	0	....	....	....	....	....
	Philadelphia Ramblers	Can-Am	48	5	10	15	....	....	....	86	4	1	0	1	6
1936-37	New York Rangers	NHL	48	0	3	3	0	5	5	42	9	1	1	2	12
1937-38	New York Rangers	NHL	46	3	2	5	5	3	8	56	3	0	0	0	4
1938-39	Philadelphia Ramblers	IAHL	35	8	15	23	....	....	....	50	....	....	....	....	....
	Chicago Black Hawks	NHL	17	3	3	6	5	5	10	10	....	....	....	....	....
1939-40	Chicago Black Hawks	NHL	44	4	7	11	7	11	18	59	2	0	0	0	0
1940-41	Chicago Black Hawks	NHL	45	5	5	10	8	7	15	66	5	1	0	1	8
1941-42	Chicago Black Hawks	NHL	47	6	14	20	8	17	25	58	3	0	2	2	2
1942-43	Ottawa Commandos	OCHL	12	4	4	8	....	....	....	*22	....	....	....	....	....
	Ottawa Commandos	Al-Cup	12	4	6	10	....	....	....	18	....	....	....	....	....
1943-44	Chicago Black Hawks	NHL	13	1	0	1	1	0	1	17	9	1	1	2	18
	Ottawa Commandos	QSHL	10	0	1	1	....	....	....	18	....	....	....	....	....
1944-45	Chicago Black Hawks	NHL	50	4	17	21	4	20	24	50	....	....	....	....	....
1945-46	Chicago Black Hawks	NHL	50	2	7	9	2	10	12	46	4	0	1	1	14
1946-47	New York Rangers	NHL	59	2	8	10	2	10	12	38	....	....	....	....	....
1947-48	Cleveland Barons	AHL	24	2	8	10	....	....	....	20	....	....	....	....	....
	Hershey Bears	AHL	29	5	6	11	....	....	....	36	2	0	0	0	2
	NHL Totals		**420**	**30**	**66**	**96**	**42**	**88**	**130**	**442**	**35**	**3**	**5**	**8**	**58**

EAHL First All-Star Team (1935) • Can-Am First All-Star Team (1936)

Signed as a free agent by **NY Rangers**, October 24, 1935. Traded to **Chicago** by **NY Rangers** for Alex Levinsky and $5,000, January 16, 1939. Claimed on waivers by **Boston** from **Chicago**, September 7, 1945. Traded to **Chicago** by **Boston** for cash, October, 1945. Traded to **NY Rangers** by **Chicago** for cash, November 1, 1946. Traded to **Cleveland** (AHL) by **NY Rangers** with Ab DeMarco for cash, May 5, 1947. Traded to **Hershey** (AHL) by **Cleveland** (AHL) with Babe Pratt for Hy Buller, December 24, 1947.

• COPP, Bob Robert Alonzo
D – L. 5'11", 180 lbs. b: Port Elgin, N.B., 11/15/1918.

Season	Club	League	GP	G	A	Pts	AG	AA	APts	PIM	GP	G	A	Pts	PIM
1934-35	Mount Allison University	MIAA	3	0	1	1	....	....	....	2	....	....	....	....	....
1935-36	Mount Allison University	MIAA	6	3	3	6	....	....	....	0	....	....	....	....	....
1936-37	Mount Allison University	MIAA	4	3	*4	7	....	....	....	6	1	0	0	0	0
	Amherst Pats	X-Games	5	1	3	4	....	....	....	2	....	....	....	....	....
	Amherst Pats	M-Cup	8	10	5	15	....	....	....	6	....	....	....	....	....
1937-38	Mount Allison University	MIAA	4	2	*7	*9	....	....	....	2	1	1	1	2	0
1938-39	University of Toronto	IIHL	9	2	2	4	....	....	....	0	....	....	....	....	....
1939-40	University of Toronto	IIHL	8	6	6	12	....	....	....	10	....	....	....	....	....
1940-41	Toronto Marlboros	OHA-Sr.	31	4	2	6	....	....	....	19	11	4	2	6	6
	Toronto RCAF	TMHL	1	0	1	1	....	....	....	0	....	....	....	....	....
	Toronto Marlboros	Al-Cup	6	0	2	2	....	....	....	2	....	....	....	....	....
1941-42	Toronto Marlboros	OHA-Sr.	28	7	11	18	....	....	....	21	6	0	0	0	4
1942-43	Toronto Maple Leafs	NHL	38	3	9	12	3	8	11	24	....	....	....	....	....
	Halifax RCAF	NSDHL	....	....	....	....	....	....	....	....	7	1	3	4	0
1943-44	Ottawa Commandos	OCHL	2	2	1	3	....	....	....	2	....	....	....	....	....
1944-45	Uplands RCAF	OCHL	12	3	7	10	....	....	....	4	4	1	2	3	2
1945-46	Ottawa Senators	QSHL	35	11	19	30	....	....	....	46	5	0	1	1	4
	Ottawa RCAF	OCHL	....	....	....	....	....	....	....	....	3	0	1	1	0
1946-47	Ottawa Senators	QSHL	28	2	8	10	....	....	....	32	11	1	1	2	8
1947-48	Ottawa Senators	QSHL	48	10	21	31	....	....	....	16	12	2	5	7	4
	Ottawa Senators	Al-Cup	14	5	7	12	....	....	....	20	....	....	....	....	....
1948-49	Ottawa Senators	QSHL	60	21	34	55	....	....	....	15	11	1	3	4	6
	Ottawa Senators	Al-Cup	12	0	6	6	....	....	....	4	....	....	....	....	....
1949-50	Ottawa Senators	QSHL	45	9	12	21	....	....	....	15	7	1	0	1	4
1950-51	Toronto Maple Leafs	NHL	2	0	0	0	0	0	0	2	....	....	....	....	....
	Ottawa Senators	QMHL	54	7	18	25	....	....	....	16	11	0	1	1	6
1951-52	Ottawa Senators	QMHL	4	0	0	0	....	....	....	0	....	....	....	....	....
1952-53	Ottawa Senators	QMHL	14	1	1	2	....	....	....	0	9	1	0	1	0
	Smiths Falls Rideaus	EOHL	32	1	14	15	....	....	....	6	....	....	....	....	....
1953-54	Ottawa Senators	QHL	42	0	5	5	....	....	....	8	21	0	1	1	6
1954-55	Ottawa Senators	QHL	27	0	4	4	....	....	....	6	....	....	....	....	....
	NHL Totals		**40**	**3**	**9**	**12**	**3**	**8**	**11**	**26**	....	....	....	....	....

QMHL First All-Star Team (1951)

• CORBEAU, Bert Bert Orian "Pig Iron"
D – R. 5'11", 200 lbs. b: Penetanguishene, Ont., 2/9/1894 d: 9/21/1942.

Season	Club	League	GP	G	A	Pts	AG	AA	APts	PIM	GP	G	A	Pts	PIM
1913-14	Halifax Crescents	MPHL	22	5	0	5	....	....	....	31	....	....	....	....	....
1914-15	Montreal Canadiens	NHA	18	1	1	2	....	....	....	35	....	....	....	....	....
♦1915-16	Montreal Canadiens	NHA	23	7	0	7	....	....	....	*134	5	0	0	0	35
1916-17	Montreal Canadiens	NHA	19	9	5	14	....	....	....	103	6	4	1	5	22
1917-18	Montreal Canadiens	NHL	21	8	8	16	10	34	44	41	2	1	1	2	11
1918-19	Montreal Canadiens	NHL	16	2	3	5	3	16	19	51	5	1	1	2	17
	Montreal Canadiens	St-Cup	5	0	1	1	....	....	....	3	....	....	....	....	....
1919-20	Montreal Canadiens	NHL	23	11	6	17	12	20	32	65	....	....	....	....	....
1920-21	Montreal Canadiens	NHL	24	11	2	13	14	8	22	86	....	....	....	....	....
1921-22	Montreal Canadiens	NHL	22	3	7	10	4	22	26	26	....	....	....	....	....
1922-23	Hamilton Tigers	NHL	21	10	4	14	17	15	32	22	....	....	....	....	....
1923-24	Toronto St. Pats	NHL	24	8	6	14	16	36	52	*55	....	....	....	....	....
1924-25	Toronto St. Pats	NHL	30	4	6	10	7	25	32	74	2	0	0	0	10
1925-26	Toronto St. Pats	NHL	36	5	5	10	9	32	41	*121	....	....	....	....	....
1926-27	Toronto Pats/Leafs	NHL	41	1	2	3	2	10	12	88	....	....	....	....	....
1927-28	Toronto Falcons	Can-Pro	41	5	2	7	....	....	....	*112	2	0	0	0	10
1928-29	London Panthers	Can-Pro	9	0	0	0	....	....	....	16	....	....	....	....	....
	NHL Totals		**258**	**63**	**49**	**112**	**94**	**218**	**312**	**629**	**9**	**2**	**2**	**4**	**38**
	Other Major League Totals		82	22	6	28	....	....	....	303	11	4	1	5	57

Rights retained by **Montreal Canadiens** after NHA folded, November 26, 1917. Traded to **Hamilton** by **Montreal Canadiens** for cash, October 1, 1922. Traded to **Toronto** by **Hamilton** with Amos Arbour and George Carey for Ken Randall, the NHL rights to Corb Denneny and cash, December 14, 1923. Signed as a free agent by **Toronto** (Can-Pro) after clearing NHL Waivers, October 20, 1927.

• CORCORAN, Norm Norman
C/RW – R. 5'10", 160 lbs. b: Toronto, Ont., 8/15/1931.

Season	Club	League	GP	G	A	Pts	AG	AA	APts	PIM	GP	G	A	Pts	PIM
1948-49	St. Michael's Majors	OHA-Jr.	28	2	2	4	....	....	....	32	....	....	....	....	....
1949-50	St. Catharines Teepees	OHA-Jr.	46	33	36	69	....	....	....	102	5	6	0	6	4
	Boston Bruins	NHL	1	0	0	0	0	0	0	0	....	....	....	....	....
	Boston Olympics	EAHL	2	3	2	5	....	....	....	4	5	1	1	2	12
1950-51	Hershey Bears	AHL	68	17	24	41	....	....	....	96	2	0	0	0	0
1951-52	Hershey Bears	AHL	54	22	21	43	....	....	....	71	5	1	0	1	6
1952-53	Boston Bruins	NHL	1	0	0	0	0	0	0	0	....	....	....	....	....
	Hershey Bears	AHL	60	15	22	37	....	....	....	92	3	1	0	1	0
1953-54	Hershey Bears	AHL	69	22	36	58	....	....	....	70	11	5	7	12	18
1954-55	Boston Bruins	NHL	2	0	0	0	0	0	0	2	4	0	0	0	6
	Hershey Bears	AHL	61	16	30	46	....	....	....	90	....	....	....	....	....

			REGULAR SEASON								PLAYOFFS				
Season	Club	League	GP	G	A	Pts	AG	AA	APts	PIM	GP	G	A	Pts	PIM
1955-56	Detroit Red Wings	NHL	2	0	0	0	0	0	0	0	....	....	....	....	....
	Edmonton Flyers	WHL	35	12	15	27	....	....	....	48	....	....	....	....	....
	Chicago Black Hawks	NHL	23	1	3	4	1	4	5	19	....	....	....	....	....
1956-57	Trois-Rivieres Lions	QHL	49	16	25	41	....	....	....	72	4	2	1	3	4
	Springfield Indians	AHL	12	0	1	1	....	....	....	2	....	....	....	....	....
1957-58	Buffalo Bisons	AHL	67	14	37	51	....	....	....	26	....	....	....	....	....
1958-59	Trois-Rivieres Lions	QHL	58	13	32	45	....	....	....	51	6	0	0	0	2
1959-60	Quebec Aces	AHL	56	18	27	45	....	....	....	52	....	....	....	....	....
1960-61	Quebec Aces	AHL	61	22	35	57	....	....	....	57	....	....	....	....	....
1961-62	Pittsburgh Hornets	AHL	67	17	34	51	....	....	....	41	....	....	....	....	....
1962-63	Pittsburgh Hornets	AHL	25	1	1	2	....	....	....	4	....	....	....	....	....
	Edmonton Flyers	WHL	30	9	10	19	....	....	....	4	3	0	0	0	0
1963-64	Providence Reds	AHL	52	11	14	25	....	....	....	19	2	3	0	3	0
1964-65	Providence Reds	AHL	36	7	11	18	....	....	....	12	....	....	....	....	....
1965-66	Buffalo Bisons	AHL	31	2	4	6	....	....	....	14	....	....	....	....	....
	NHL Totals		29	1	3	4	1	4	5	21	4	0	0	0	6

Played in NHL All-Star Game (1955)

Signed as a free agent by **Boston**, March 23, 1950. Traded to **Detroit** by **Boston** with Gilles Boisvert, Real Chevrefils, Warren Godfrey and Ed Sandford for Vic Stasiuk, Marcel Bonin, Lorne Davis and Terry Sawchuk, June 3, 1955. Traded to **Chicago** by **Detroit** for Wally Blaisdell, October 4, 1955. • Deal was voided when Blaisdell was unable to report. Traded to **Chicago** by **Detroit** (Edmonton-WHL) for cash and the loan of Gord Pennell, January 17, 1956. Traded to **Buffalo** (AHL) by **Springfield** (AHL) for Tony Schneider, August 17, 1957. Traded to **Toronto** (Rochester-AHL) by **Montreal** (Quebec-AHL) for Guy Rousseau, June 1, 1961. Traded to **Pittsburgh** (AHL) by **Toronto** for cash, June 2, 1961. Traded to **Providence** (AHL) by **Detroit** (Pittsburgh-AHL) for cash, August 8, 1963.

• CORMIER, Roger
Roger Albert
RW – R. 5'10", 167 lbs. b: Montreal, Que., 3/23/1905 d: 2/9/1971.

Season	Club	League	GP	G	A	Pts	AG	AA	APts	PIM	GP	G	A	Pts	PIM
1924-25	Montreal St. FX	MCHL	STATISTICS NOT AVAILABLE												
1925-26	Montreal St. FX	MCHL	STATISTICS NOT AVAILABLE												
	Montreal Canadiens	NHL	1	0	0	0	0	0	0	0	....	....	....	....	....
	Montreal Nationale	MBHL	9	4	3	7	....	....	....	6	....	....	....	....	....
1926-27	Providence Reds	Can-Am	32	6	2	8	....	....	....	47	....	....	....	....	....
1927-28	Providence Reds	Can-Am	38	7	2	9	....	....	....	36	....	....	....	....	....
1928-29	Providence Reds	Can-Am	29	1	1	2	....	....	....	23	....	....	....	....	....
	Kitchener Dutchmen	Can-Pro	11	4	0	4	....	....	....	14	3	0	0	0	0
1929-30	Providence Reds	Can-Am	39	9	4	13	....	....	....	54	3	1	1	2	4
1930-31	Providence Reds	Can-Am	39	11	14	25	....	....	....	51	2	1	1	2	0
1931-32	Providence Reds	Can-Am	39	6	8	14	....	....	....	50	5	0	0	0	4
1932-33	Windsor Bulldogs	IHL	44	8	12	20	....	....	....	79	5	2	2	4	12
1933-34	Cleveland Indians	IHL	44	10	9	19	....	....	....	28	....	....	....	....	....
1934-35	Cleveland Falcons	IHL	44	17	16	33	....	....	....	52	2	0	0	0	4
1935-36	Cleveland Falcons	IHL	8	1	2	3	....	....	....	4	....	....	....	....	....
	Pittsburgh Shamrocks	IHL	3	0	0	0	....	....	....	2	....	....	....	....	....
	Rochester Cardinals	IHL	30	7	3	10	....	....	....	17	....	....	....	....	....
1936-37			REINSTATED AS AN AMATEUR												
1937-38	Sherbrooke Red Raiders	QPHL	21	12	8	20	....	....	....	15	9	4	4	8	2
1938-39	Sherbrooke Red Raiders	QPHL	37	12	16	28	....	....	....	41	4	2	1	3	4
1939-40	Sherbrooke Red Raiders	QPHL	40	2	3	5	....	....	....	4	10	0	1	1	2
	Sherbrooke Red Raiders	Al-Cup	2	0	1	1	....	....	....	2	....	....	....	....	....
	NHL Totals		1	0	0	0	0	0	0	0	....	....	....	....	....

Signed as a free agent by **Montreal Canadiens**, January 15, 1926. Traded to **Windsor** (IHL) by **Providence** (Can-Am) for Roy Hinsperger, October, 1932. Signed to three-game try-out contract by **Pittsburgh** (IHL) after securing release from **Cleveland** (IHL), December 6, 1935. Signed as a free agent by **Rochester** (IHL), December 16, 1935.

• CORRIGAN, Chuck
Hubert Patrick
RW – R. 6'2", 192 lbs. b: Moosomin, Sask., 5/22/1916.

Season	Club	League	GP	G	A	Pts	AG	AA	APts	PIM	GP	G	A	Pts	PIM
1935-36	Toronto Goodyears	OHA-Sr.	8	1	3	4	....	....	....	8	8	3	1	4	4
1936-37	Toronto Goodyears	OHA-Sr.	9	4	1	5	....	....	....	8	5	1	1	2	6
1937-38	Toronto Maple Leafs	NHL	3	0	0	0	0	0	0	0	....	....	....	....	....
	Syracuse Stars	IAHL	20	3	2	5	....	....	....	11	....	....	....	....	....
	Springfield Indians	IAHL	22	5	2	7	....	....	....	10	....	....	....	....	....
1938-39	Springfield Indians	IAHL	21	1	2	3	....	....	....	0	....	....	....	....	....
	Hershey Bears	IAHL	21	1	4	5	....	....	....	11	5	0	1	1	0
1939-40	Springfield Indians	IAHL	54	12	31	43	....	....	....	14	3	0	1	1	0
1940-41	Springfield Indians	AHL	22	3	1	4	....	....	....	7	3	0	1	1	0
	New York Americans	NHL	16	2	2	4	3	3	6	2	....	....	....	....	....
1941-42	Springfield Indians	AHL	35	6	32	38	....	....	....	4	....	....	....	....	....
	Springfield Indians	AHL	12	1	1	2	....	....	....	8	....	....	....	....	....
1942-43	Pittsburgh Hornets	AHL	52	17	25	42	....	....	....	10	2	0	1	1	5
1943-44	Pittsburgh Hornets	AHL	3	0	2	2	....	....	....	2	....	....	....	....	....
	Kingston Army	OHA-Sr.	13	7	8	15	....	....	....	10	....	....	....	....	....
1944-45			MILITARY SERVICE												
1945-46	Toronto Peoples Credit	TIHL	2	1	0	1	....	....	....	4	....	....	....	....	....
	Fort Worth Rangers	USHL	6	2	2	4	....	....	....	6	....	....	....	....	....
	St. Paul Saints	USHL	23	6	5	11	....	....	....	8	3	0	0	0	0
1946-47	Toronto Peoples Credit	TIHL	21	4	13	17	....	....	....	8	5	2	0	2	0
1947-48	Fresno Falcons	PCHL	65	36	37	73	....	....	....	24	9	4	4	8	16
1948-49	Fresno Falcons	PCHL	16	5	12	17	....	....	....	2	2	0	0	0	2
	NHL Totals		19	2	2	4	3	3	6	2	....	....	....	....	....

Signed as a free agent by **Toronto**, October 17, 1937. Signed as a free agent by **NY Americans**, January 30, 1941. Traded to **Buffalo** (AHL) by **Springfield** (AHL) for cash, August, 1942. Traded to **Pittsburgh** (AHL) by **Buffalo** (AHL) for cash, October 13, 1942.

• CORRIVEAU, Andre
Fred Andre
RW – L. 5'8", 135 lbs. b: Grand'Mere, Que., 5/15/1928 d: 10/1/1993.

Season	Club	League	GP	G	A	Pts	AG	AA	APts	PIM	GP	G	A	Pts	PIM
1944-45	Montreal Nationale	QJHL	10	2	4	6	....	....	....	4	....	....	....	....	....
1945-46	Montreal Nationale	QJHL	20	12	*16	28	....	....	....	8	4	2	0	2	2
1946-47	Montreal Nationale	QJHL	26	33	*46	*79	....	....	....	26	11	12	14	26	12
1947-48	Valleyfield Braves	QSHL	43	22	31	53	....	....	....	20	6	1	3	4	2
1948-49	Valleyfield Braves	QSHL	62	32	43	75	....	....	....	40	3	2	1	3	0
1949-50	Valleyfield Braves	QSHL	60	33	*54	*87	....	....	....	25	5	3	0	3	0
1950-51	Valleyfield Braves	QMHL	58	38	*51	*89	....	....	....	15	16	10	*14	*24	0
	Valleyfield Braves	Alx-Cup	12	6	*13	*19	....	....	....	4	....	....	....	....	....
1951-52	Valleyfield Braves	QMHL	60	27	36	63	....	....	....	8	6	1	6	7	2
1952-53	Valleyfield Braves	QMHL	60	40	45	85	....	....	....	10	4	0	1	1	0
1953-54	Montreal Canadiens	NHL	3	0	1	1	0	1	1	0	....	....	....	....	....
	Valleyfield Braves	QHL	69	37	51	88	....	....	....	8	7	3	4	7	2
1954-55	Valleyfield Braves	QHL	56	31	32	63	....	....	....	28	....	....	....	....	....
1955-56	Montreal Royals	QHL	62	*37	40	77	....	....	....	2	11	1	7	8	2
	Montreal Royals	Ed-Cup	6	2	4	6	....	....	....	0	....	....	....	....	....
1956-57	Montreal Royals	QHL	63	22	34	56	....	....	....	8	3	1	1	2	2
	NHL Totals		3	0	1	1	0	1	1	0	....	....	....	....	....

QJHL Second All-Star Team (1947) • QSHL Second All-Star Team (1950) • QMHL Second All-Star Team (1951, 1952, 1953) • QHL Second All-Star Team (1954, 1955, 1957) • QHL First All-Star Team (1956) • Won Byng of Vimy Trophy (MVP - QHL) (1956)

• COSTELLO, Les
Leslie John Thomas
LW – L. 5'8", 158 lbs. b: South Porcupine, Ont., 2/16/1928.

Season	Club	League	GP	G	A	Pts	AG	AA	APts	PIM	GP	G	A	Pts	PIM
1943-44	South Porcupine Porkies	OHA-B	STATISTICS NOT AVAILABLE												
1944-45	St. Michael's Majors	OHA-Jr.	17	11	8	19	....	....	....	4	9	7	7	14	7
	St. Michael's Majors	M-Cup	14	8	8	16	....	....	....	14	....	....	....	....	....
1945-46	St. Michael's Majors	OHA-Jr.	24	17	23	40	....	....	....	17	11	8	10	18	12
1946-47	St. Michael's Majors	OHA-Jr.	29	29	33	62	....	....	....	78	9	9	7	16	13
	St. Michael's Majors	M-Cup	10	12	9	21	....	....	....	13	....	....	....	....	....
1947-48	Pittsburgh Hornets	AHL	68	32	22	54	....	....	....	40	2	0	0	0	2
♦	Toronto Maple Leafs	NHL	....	....	....	....	....	....	....	....	5	2	2	4	2
1948-49	Toronto Maple Leafs	NHL	15	2	3	5	3	4	7	11	....	....	....	....	....
	Pittsburgh Hornets	AHL	46	13	19	32	....	....	....	63	....	....	....	....	....
1949-50	Pittsburgh Hornets	AHL	70	18	31	49	....	....	....	69	....	....	....	....	....
	Toronto Maple Leafs	NHL	....	....	....	....	....	....	....	....	1	0	0	0	0
	NHL Totals		15	2	3	5	3	4	7	11	6	2	2	4	2

• Brother of Murray • Played in NHL All-Star Game (1948)

• Retired from NHL to begin Seminary studies, May, 1950.

• COSTELLO, Murray
C – R. 6'3", 190 lbs. b: South Porcupine, Ont., 2/24/1934.

Season	Club	League	GP	G	A	Pts	AG	AA	APts	PIM	GP	G	A	Pts	PIM
1950-51	St. Michael's Majors	OHA-Jr.	50	18	16	34	....	....	....	24	....	....	....	....	....
1951-52	St. Michael's Majors	OHA-Jr.	51	16	27	43	....	....	....	18	8	5	8	13	4
1952-53	St. Michael's Majors	OHA-Jr.	51	30	28	58	....	....	....	38	17	7	8	15	13
1953-54	Galt Black Hawks	OHA-Jr.	3	1	0	1	....	....	....	0	....	....	....	....	....
	Chicago Black Hawks	NHL	40	3	2	5	4	2	6	6	....	....	....	....	....
	Hershey Bears	AHL	26	7	13	20	....	....	....	10	11	4	4	8	9
1954-55	Boston Bruins	NHL	54	4	11	15	5	13	18	25	1	0	0	0	2
1955-56	Boston Bruins	NHL	41	6	6	12	8	7	15	19	....	....	....	....	....
	Detroit Red Wings	NHL	24	0	0	0	0	0	0	4	4	0	0	0	0
1956-57	Detroit Red Wings	NHL	3	0	0	0	0	0	0	0	....	....	....	....	....
	Edmonton Flyers	WHL	65	19	26	45	....	....	....	37	7	0	2	2	12
1957-58			REINSTATED AS AN AMATEUR												
1958-59	Windsor Bulldogs	OHA-Sr.	35	14	20	34	....	....	....	26	....	....	....	....	....
1959-60	Windsor Bulldogs	OHA-Sr.	43	18	20	38	....	....	....	23	17	5	7	12	12
	NHL Totals		162	13	19	32	17	22	39	54	5	0	0	0	2

• Brother of Les

Traded to **Boston** by **Chicago** for Frank Martin, October 4, 1954. Traded to **Detroit** by **Boston** with Lorne Ferguson for Real Chevrifils and Jerry Toppazzini, January 17, 1956.

• COTCH, Charlie
LW – L. 5'11", 175 lbs. b: Sarnia, Ont., 1902 Deceased.

Season	Club	League	GP	G	A	Pts	AG	AA	APts	PIM	GP	G	A	Pts	PIM
1921-22	London Tecumsehs	OHA-Sr.	STATISTICS NOT AVAILABLE												
1922-23	Vancouver Maroons	PCHA	15	0	0	0	....	....	....	0	2	0	0	0	0
	Vancouver Maroons	St-Cup	2	0	0	0	....	....	....	0	....	....	....	....	....
1923-24	Vancouver Maroons	PCHA	14	2	0	2	....	....	....	4	2	0	0	0	0
	Vancouver Maroons	St-Cup	1	0	0	0	....	....	....	0	....	....	....	....	....
1924-25	Hamilton Tigers	NHL	7	1	0	1	2	0	2	0	....	....	....	....	....
	Toronto St. Pats	NHL	5	0	0	0	0	0	0	0	....	....	....	....	....
	NHL Totals		12	1	0	1	2	0	2	0	....	....	....	....	....
	Other Major League Totals		29	2	0	2	....	....	....	4	4	0	0	0	0

Signed as a free agent by **Vancouver** (PCHA), November 7, 1922. Traded to **Montreal Canadiens** by **Vancouver** (PCHA) for Robert Boucher, March 26, 1924. Rights traded to **Hamilton** by **Montreal Canadiens** for cash, December 24, 1924. Signed as a free agent by **Toronto**, February 9, 1925.

• COTTON, Baldy
William Harold
LW – L. 5'10", 155 lbs. b: Nanticoke, Ont., 11/5/1902 d: 9/9/1984.

Season	Club	League	GP	G	A	Pts	AG	AA	APts	PIM	GP	G	A	Pts	PIM
1919-20	Parkdale Canoe Club	OHA-Jr.	6	3	0	3	....	....	....	0	....	....	....	....	....
1920-21	Toronto Maitlands	OHA-Jr.	STATISTICS NOT AVAILABLE												
1921-22	Toronto Aura Lee	OHA-Jr.	6	8	1	9	....	....	....	....	....	....	....	....	....
1922-23	Toronto Aura Lee	OHA-Jr.	11	5	3	8	....	....	....	....	....	....	....	....	....
1923-24	Pittsburgh Yellowjackets	USAHA	20	7	0	7	....	....	....	0	13	2	3	5	....
1924-25	Pittsburgh Yellowjackets	USAHA	40	7	0	7	....	....	....	0	8	2	0	2	....
1925-26	Pittsburgh Pirates	NHL	33	7	1	8	12	6	18	22	2	1	0	1	0
1926-27	Pittsburgh Pirates	NHL	37	5	0	5	9	0	9	17	....	....	....	....	....
1927-28	Pittsburgh Pirates	NHL	42	9	3	12	18	17	35	40	2	1	1	2	2
1928-29	Pittsburgh Pirates	NHL	32	3	2	5	9	13	22	38	....	....	....	....	....
	Toronto Maple Leafs	NHL	11	1	2	3	3	13	16	8	4	0	0	0	2
1929-30	Toronto Maple Leafs	NHL	41	21	17	38	30	40	70	47	....	....	....	....	....
1930-31	Toronto Maple Leafs	NHL	43	12	17	29	24	52	76	45	2	0	0	0	2
♦1931-32	Toronto Maple Leafs	NHL	48	5	13	18	8	29	37	41	7	2	2	4	8
1932-33	Toronto Maple Leafs	NHL	48	10	11	21	18	23	41	29	9	0	3	3	6
1933-34	Toronto Maple Leafs	NHL	47	8	14	22	14	29	43	46	5	0	2	2	0
1934-35	Toronto Maple Leafs	NHL	47	11	14	25	18	24	42	36	7	0	0	0	17
1935-36	New York Americans	NHL	45	7	9	16	13	17	30	27	5	0	1	1	9
1936-37	New York Americans	NHL	29	2	0	2	3	0	3	23	....	....	....	....	....
	New Haven Eagles	IAHL	18	4	8	12	....	....	....	48	....	....	....	....	....
	NHL Totals		503	101	103	204	179	263	442	419	43	4	9	13	46

Played in NHL All-Star Game (1934)

Signed as a free agent by **Pittsburgh**, September 26, 1925. Traded to **Toronto** by **Pittsburgh** for Gerry Lowrey and $9,500, February 12, 1929. Traded to **NY Americans** by **Toronto** for cash, October 9, 1935.

Season	Club	League	GP	G	A	Pts	AG	AA	APts	PIM	GP	G	A	Pts	PIM
			REGULAR SEASON								PLAYOFFS				

• COUGHLIN, Jack

Jack Joseph
RW – R. 5'10", 170 lbs. b: Douro, Ont., 6/6/1892 Deceased.

Season	Club	League	GP	G	A	Pts	AG	AA	APts	PIM	GP	G	A	Pts	PIM
1912-13	Peterborough Seniors	OHA-Sr.	6	4	0	4	....	....	....	4	....	....	....	....	....
1913-14	Ingersoll Seniors	OHA-Sr.	STATISTICS NOT AVAILABLE												
1914-15	NY Irish-Americans	AAHA	STATISTICS NOT AVAILABLE												
1915-16	Peterborough Electrics	OHA-Sr.	STATISTICS NOT AVAILABLE												
	Houghton Seniors	USHA	STATISTICS NOT AVAILABLE												
1916-17	Toronto Blueshirts	NHA	7	2	0	2	....	....	....	0	....	....	....	....	....
♦**1917-18**	**Toronto Arenas**	**NHL**	**5**	**2**	**0**	**2**	**2**	**0**	**2**	**3**	....	....	....	....	....
1918-19			DID NOT PLAY												
1919-20	**Quebec Bulldogs**	**NHL**	**9**	**0**	**0**	**0**	**0**	**0**	**0**	**0**	....	....	....	....	....
	Montreal Canadiens	**NHL**	**3**	**0**	**0**	**0**	**0**	**0**	**0**	**0**	....	....	....	....	....
1920-21	**Hamilton Tigers**	**NHL**	**2**	**0**	**0**	**0**	**0**	**0**	**0**	**0**	....	....	....	....	....
	NHL Totals		**19**	**2**	**0**	**2**	**2**	**0**	**2**	**3**	....	....	....	....	....
	Other Major League Totals		7	2	0	2	....	....	....	0	....	....	....	....	....

Signed as a free agent by **Toronto Arenas**, December 5, 1917. Signed as a free agent by **Quebec**, January 13, 1920. Signed as a free agent by **Montreal Canadiens**, February 18, 1920. Traded to **Hamilton** by **Montreal Canadiens** with Goldie Prodgers, Joe Matte and loan of Billy Coutu for 1920-21 season for Harry Mummery, Jack McDonald and Dave Ritchie, November 27, 1920.

• COULSON, D'arcy

D – R. 5'11", 175 lbs. b: Sudbury, Ont., 2/17/1908.

Season	Club	League	GP	G	A	Pts	AG	AA	APts	PIM	GP	G	A	Pts	PIM
1925-26	Loyola College	OHA-Jr.	STATISTICS NOT AVAILABLE												
1926-27	St. Michael's Majors	OHA-Jr.	6	5	2	7	....	....	....	....	6	0	3	3	....
1927-28	Ottawa Shamrocks	OCHL	15	5	2	7	....	....	....	....	1	0	0	0	0
1928-29	Ottawa Shamrocks	OCHL	5	2	0	2	....	....	....	....	5	1	3	*4	8
1929-30	Ottawa Shamrocks	OCHL	20	5	1	6	....	....	....	*89	6	2	1	3	26
	Chicago Shamrocks	USAHA	7	0	6	6	....	....	....	23	....	....	....	....	....
1930-31	**Philadelphia Quakers**	**NHL**	**28**	**0**	**0**	**0**	**0**	**0**	**0**	**103**	....	....	....	....	....
1931/34			OUT OF HOCKEY – RETIRED												
1934-35	Ottawa RCAF	OCHL	3	0	0	0	....	....	....	0	5	0	0	0	18
1935-36	Ottawa RCAF	OCHL	6	0	0	0	....	....	....	5	7	0	1	1	22
	NHL Totals		**28**	**0**	**0**	**0**	**0**	**0**	**0**	**103**	....	....	....	....	....

Signed as a free agent by **Philadelphia**, December 15, 1930. Claimed by **Montreal Canadiens** from **Philadelphia** in Dispersal Draft, November 26, 1931. Loaned to **Montreal Maroons** after **Philadelphia** franchise folded, September 12, 1931.

• COULTER, Art

Arthur Edmund **HHOF**
D – R. 5'11", 185 lbs. b: Winnipeg, Man., 5/31/1909.

Season	Club	League	GP	G	A	Pts	AG	AA	APts	PIM	GP	G	A	Pts	PIM
1924-25	Winnipeg Pilgrims	WJrHL	STATISTICS NOT AVAILABLE												
1925-26	Winnipeg Pilgrims	WJrHL	9	3	1	4	....	....	....	10	....	....	....	....	....
1926-27	Winnipeg Pilgrims	WJrHL	5	3	2	5	....	....	....	6	....	....	....	....	....
1927-28			STATISTICS NOT AVAILABLE												
1928-29			STATISTICS NOT AVAILABLE												
1929-30	Philadelphia Arrows	Can-Am	35	2	2	4	....	....	....	40	2	0	0	0	2
1930-31	Philadelphia Arrows	Can-Am	40	4	8	12	....	....	....	*109	....	....	....	....	....
1931-32	Philadelphia Arrows	Can-Am	26	9	4	13	....	....	....	42	....	....	....	....	....
	Chicago Black Hawks	**NHL**	**13**	**0**	**1**	**1**	**0**	**2**	**2**	**23**	**2**	**1**	**0**	**1**	**0**
1932-33	**Chicago Black Hawks**	**NHL**	**46**	**3**	**2**	**5**	**5**	**4**	**9**	**53**	....	....	....	....	....
♦**1933-34**	**Chicago Black Hawks**	**NHL**	**46**	**5**	**2**	**7**	**9**	**4**	**13**	**39**	**8**	**1**	**0**	**1**	**10**
1934-35	**Chicago Black Hawks**	**NHL**	**48**	**4**	**8**	**12**	**7**	**14**	**21**	**68**	**2**	**0**	**0**	**0**	**5**
1935-36	**Chicago Black Hawks**	**NHL**	**25**	**0**	**2**	**2**	**0**	**4**	**4**	**18**	....	....	....	....	....
	New York Rangers	**NHL**	**23**	**1**	**5**	**6**	**2**	**9**	**11**	**26**	....	....	....	....	....
1936-37	**New York Rangers**	**NHL**	**47**	**1**	**5**	**6**	**2**	**9**	**11**	**27**	**9**	**0**	**3**	**3**	**15**
1937-38	**New York Rangers**	**NHL**	**43**	**5**	**10**	**15**	**8**	**16**	**24**	**90**	....	....	....	....	....
1938-39	**New York Rangers**	**NHL**	**44**	**4**	**8**	**12**	**7**	**12**	**19**	**58**	**7**	**1**	**1**	**2**	**6**
♦**1939-40**	**New York Rangers**	**NHL**	**48**	**1**	**9**	**10**	**2**	**14**	**16**	**68**	**12**	**1**	**0**	**1**	**21**
1940-41	**New York Rangers**	**NHL**	**35**	**5**	**14**	**19**	**8**	**20**	**28**	**42**	**3**	**0**	**0**	**0**	**0**
1941-42	**New York Rangers**	**NHL**	**47**	**1**	**16**	**17**	**1**	**19**	**20**	**31**	**6**	**0**	**1**	**1**	**4**
1942-43	Coast Guard Cutters	EAHL	37	13	20	33	....	....	....	32	10	4	1	5	8
1943-44	Coast Guard Cutters	X-Games	26	10	13	23	....	....	....	10	12	6	8	14	8
	NHL Totals		**465**	**30**	**82**	**112**	**51**	**127**	**178**	**543**	**49**	**4**	**5**	**9**	**61**

NHL Second All-Star Team (1935, 1938, 1939, 1940) • EAHL First All-Star Team (1943)

Played in NHL All-Star Game (1939)

Traded to **NY Rangers** by **Chicago** for Earl Seibert, January 15, 1936.

• COULTER, Thomas

Thomas Henry
D – L. 6'2", 195 lbs. b: Winnipeg, Man., 4/21/1911.

Season	Club	League	GP	G	A	Pts	AG	AA	APts	PIM	GP	G	A	Pts	PIM
1930-31	Winnipeg Carnegie Tech	WSrHL	STATISTICS NOT AVAILABLE												
1931-32			DID NOT PLAY												
1932-33			DID NOT PLAY												
1933-34	**Chicago Black Hawks**	**NHL**	**2**	**0**	**0**	**0**	**0**	**0**	**0**	**0**	....	....	....	....	....
	Oklahoma City Warriors	AHA	47	2	1	3	....	....	....	30	....	....	....	....	....
1934-35	Cleveland Falcons	IHL	6	0	0	0	....	....	....	0	....	....	....	....	....
	NHL Totals		**2**	**0**	**0**	**0**	**0**	**0**	**0**	**0**	....	....	....	....	....

• Missed entire 1931-32 and 1932-33 seasons competing for Canada in the 1932 Olympics and 1933 World Championships in the 400-metre hurdles. • Missed majority of 1934-35 season recovering from leg injury suffered in training camp, October 21, 1934.

• COURNOYER, Yvan

— *see page 992*

• COUTU, Billy

Wilfred Arthur "Beaver"
D – L. 5'11", 190 lbs. b: North Bay, Ont., 3/1/1892 d: 2/25/1977.

Season	Club	League	GP	G	A	Pts	AG	AA	APts	PIM	GP	G	A	Pts	PIM
1915-16	Michigan Soo Indians	NMHL	STATISTICS NOT AVAILABLE												
1916-17	Montreal Canadiens	NHA	18	0	0	0	....	....	....	9	6	0	0	0	46
1917-18	**Montreal Canadiens**	**NHL**	**20**	**2**	**2**	**4**	**2**	**8**	**10**	**49**	**2**	**0**	**0**	**0**	**3**
1918-19	**Montreal Canadiens**	**NHL**	**15**	**1**	**2**	**3**	**2**	**11**	**13**	**18**	**5**	**0**	**1**	**1**	**6**
	Montreal Canadiens	St-Cup	5	0	1	1	....	....	....	0	....	....	....	....	....
1919-20	**Montreal Canadiens**	**NHL**	**20**	**4**	**0**	**4**	**4**	**0**	**4**	**67**	....	....	....	....	....
1920-21	**Hamilton Tigers**	**NHL**	**24**	**8**	**4**	**12**	**10**	**15**	**25**	***95**	....	....	....	....	....
1921-22	**Montreal Canadiens**	**NHL**	**24**	**4**	**3**	**7**	**5**	**9**	**14**	**8**	....	....	....	....	....
1922-23	**Montreal Canadiens**	**NHL**	**24**	**5**	**2**	**7**	**8**	**7**	**15**	**37**	**1**	**0**	**0**	**0**	***22**
1923-24	**Montreal Canadiens**	**NHL**	**16**	**3**	**1**	**4**	**6**	**6**	**12**	**18**	**2**	**0**	**0**	**0**	**0**
♦	Montreal Canadiens	St-Cup	4	0	0	0	....	....	....	0	....	....	....	....	....
1924-25	**Montreal Canadiens**	**NHL**	**28**	**3**	**2**	**5**	**5**	**8**	**13**	**56**	**2**	**0**	**0**	**0**	**0**
	Montreal Canadiens	St-Cup	4	1	0	1	....	....	....	10	....	....	....	....	....
1925-26	**Montreal Canadiens**	**NHL**	**33**	**2**	**4**	**6**	**3**	**26**	**29**	**95**	....	....	....	....	....
1926-27	**Boston Bruins**	**NHL**	**40**	**1**	**1**	**2**	**2**	**5**	**7**	**35**	**7**	**1**	**0**	**1**	**4**
1927-28	New Haven Eagles	Can-Am	37	11	1	12	....	....	....	*108	....	....	....	....	....
1928-29	Newark Bulldogs	Can-Am	40	0	1	1	....	....	....	42	....	....	....	....	....
1929-30	Minneapolis Millers	AHA	47	8	2	10	....	....	....	*105	....	....	....	....	....
1930-31	Minneapolis Millers	AHA	33	0	1	1	....	....	....	46	....	....	....	....	....
1931-32	Providence Reds	Can-Am	DID NOT PLAY – COACHING												
1932-33	Providence Reds	Can-Am	1	0	0	0	....	....	....	0	....	....	....	....	....
	NHL Totals		**244**	**33**	**21**	**54**	**47**	**95**	**142**	**478**	**19**	**1**	**1**	**2**	**35**
	Other Major League Totals		18	0	0	0	....	....	....	9	6	0	0	0	46

Rights retained by **Montreal Canadiens** after NHA folded, November 26, 1917. Loaned to **Hamilton** by **Montreal** for 1920-21 season with the trade of Jack McDonald, Dave Ritchie and Harry Mummery for Goldie Prodgers, Jack Coughlin and Joe Matte, November 27, 1920. Returned to **Montreal Canadiens** by **Hamilton**, November 15, 1921. • 1923-24 Stanley Cup totals includes series with Calgary (WCHL) and Vancouver (PCHA). Traded to **Boston** by **Montreal Canadiens** for Amby Moran, October 22, 1926. • Suspended for life by NHL for assault on referee Jerry LaFlamme, April 13, 1927. Traded to **New Haven** (Can-Am) by **Boston** with Nobby Clark for cash, January 5, 1928.

• COUTURE, Gerry

Gerald Joseph "Doc"
RW – R. 6'2", 185 lbs. b: Saskatoon, Sask., 8/6/1925 d: 7/13/1994.

Season	Club	League	GP	G	A	Pts	AG	AA	APts	PIM	GP	G	A	Pts	PIM
1940-41	St. Joseph's High School	H.S.	STATISTICS NOT AVAILABLE												
1941-42	Saskatoon Jr. Quakers	N-SJHL	8	*12	6	*18	....	....	....	0	6	*9	5	*14	0
	Saskatoon Jr. Quakers	M-Cup	3	1	0	1	....	....	....	0	....	....	....	....	....
1942-43	Saskatoon Jr. Quakers	N-SJHL	8	14	10	*24	....	....	....	26	3	4	1	5	2
	Saskatoon Jr. Quakers	M-Cup	8	14	7	21	....	....	....	2	....	....	....	....	....
1943-44	Saskatoon Jr. Quakers	N-SJHL	1	1	1	2	....	....	....	2	....	....	....	....	....
	U. of Saskatchewan	SCJHL	2	6	3	9	....	....	....	2	1	3	1	4	2
	Saskatoon HMCS Unicorn	N-SSHL	11	15	11	26	....	....	....	9	2	1	1	2	2
	U. of Saskatchewan	M-Cup	2	1	1	2	....	....	....	4	....	....	....	....	....
	Flin Flon Bombers	Al-Cup	4	1	3	4	....	....	....	10	....	....	....	....	....
1944-45	U. of Saskatchewan	N-SJHL	9	19	10	29	....	....	....	14	2	1	1	2	0
	Moose Jaw Canucks	N-SJHL	....	....	....	....	....	....	....	....	4	4	3	7	2
	Detroit Red Wings	**NHL**	....	....	....	....	....	....	....	....	**2**	**0**	**0**	**0**	**0**
1945-46	**Detroit Red Wings**	**NHL**	**43**	**3**	**7**	**10**	**4**	**10**	**14**	**18**	**5**	**0**	**2**	**2**	**0**
1946-47	**Detroit Red Wings**	**NHL**	**30**	**5**	**10**	**15**	**6**	**12**	**18**	**0**	**1**	**0**	**0**	**0**	**0**
	Indianapolis Capitols	AHL	34	24	18	42	....	....	....	21	....	....	....	....	....
1947-48	**Detroit Red Wings**	**NHL**	**19**	**3**	**6**	**9**	**4**	**8**	**12**	**2**	....	....	....	....	....
	Indianapolis Capitols	AHL	42	26	25	51	....	....	....	8	....	....	....	....	....
1948-49	**Detroit Red Wings**	**NHL**	**51**	**19**	**10**	**29**	**27**	**14**	**41**	**6**	**10**	**2**	**0**	**2**	**2**
♦**1949-50**	**Detroit Red Wings**	**NHL**	**69**	**24**	**7**	**31**	**31**	**8**	**39**	**21**	**14**	**5**	**4**	**9**	**2**
1950-51	**Detroit Red Wings**	**NHL**	**53**	**7**	**6**	**13**	**9**	**7**	**16**	**2**	**6**	**1**	**1**	**2**	**0**
1951-52	**Montreal Canadiens**	**NHL**	**10**	**0**	**1**	**1**	**0**	**1**	**1**	**4**	....	....	....	....	....
	Montreal Royals	QMHL	6	1	4	5	....	....	....	0	....	....	....	....	....
	Buffalo Bisons	AHL	9	2	3	5	....	....	....	2	....	....	....	....	....
	Cleveland Barons	AHL	38	21	19	40	....	....	....	2	5	1	0	1	0
1952-53	**Chicago Black Hawks**	**NHL**	**70**	**19**	**18**	**37**	**25**	**22**	**47**	**22**	**7**	**1**	**0**	**1**	**0**
1953-54	**Chicago Black Hawks**	**NHL**	**40**	**6**	**5**	**11**	**8**	**6**	**14**	**14**	....	....	....	....	....
	Providence Reds	AHL	19	10	7	17	....	....	....	2	....	....	....	....	....
1954-55	Calgary Stampeders	WHL	70	33	49	82	....	....	....	8	9	5	6	11	0
1955-56	Calgary Stampeders	WHL	66	32	50	82	....	....	....	10	8	3	7	10	8
1956-57	Calgary Stampeders	WHL	63	19	26	45	....	....	....	20	3	1	0	1	0
1957-58	Saskatoon–St. Paul	WHL	58	23	31	54	....	....	....	22	....	....	....	....	....
1958-59			REINSTATED AS AN AMATEUR												
1959-60	Saskatoon Quakers	SSHL	23	*26	*29	*55	....	....	....	26	7	7	*13	20	0
	Saskatoon Quakers	Al-Cup	5	2	1	3	....	....	....	0	....	....	....	....	....
	NHL Totals		**385**	**86**	**70**	**156**	**114**	**88**	**202**	**89**	**45**	**9**	**7**	**16**	**4**

WHL First All-Star Team (1955) • Played in NHL All-Star Game (1950)

Traded to **Montreal** by **Detroit** for Bert Hirschfeld, June 19, 1951. Traded to **Chicago** by **Montreal** for cash, September 22, 1952.

• COUTURE, Rosie

Rosario "Lolo"
RW – R. 5'11", 164 lbs. b: St. Bonfiace, Man., 7/24/1905 d: 3/1/1986.

Season	Club	League	GP	G	A	Pts	AG	AA	APts	PIM	GP	G	A	Pts	PIM
1922-23	St. Boniface Canadiens	MJHL	7	6	2	8	....	....	....	4	....	....	....	....	....
1923-24	Winnipeg Argonauts	MHL-Sr.	STATISTICS NOT AVAILABLE												
1924-25	Winnipeg Argonauts	MHL-Sr.	8	7	2	9	....	....	....	6	....	....	....	....	....
1925-26	Winnipeg Argonauts	MHL-Sr.	7	*9	*3	*12	....	....	....	4	2	3	0	3	2
1926-27	Winnipeg Winnipegs	MHL-Sr.	8	*16	1	*17	....	....	....	6	5	4	1	5	2
	Winnipeg Winnipegs	Al-Cup	2	2	0	2	....	....	....	0	....	....	....	....	....
1927-28	Winnipeg Maroons	AHA	39	14	6	20	....	....	....	20	....	....	....	....	....
1928-29	**Chicago Black Hawks**	**NHL**	**43**	**1**	**3**	**4**	**3**	**20**	**23**	**22**	....	....	....	....	....
1929-30	**Chicago Black Hawks**	**NHL**	**43**	**8**	**8**	**16**	**11**	**19**	**30**	**63**	**2**	**0**	**0**	**0**	**2**
1930-31	**Chicago Black Hawks**	**NHL**	**44**	**8**	**11**	**19**	**16**	**33**	**49**	**30**	**9**	**0**	**3**	**3**	**2**
1931-32	**Chicago Black Hawks**	**NHL**	**48**	**9**	**9**	**18**	**15**	**20**	**35**	**8**	**2**	**0**	**0**	**0**	**2**
1932-33	**Chicago Black Hawks**	**NHL**	**46**	**10**	**7**	**17**	**18**	**14**	**32**	**26**	....	....	....	....	....
♦**1933-34**	**Chicago Black Hawks**	**NHL**	**48**	**5**	**8**	**13**	**9**	**17**	**26**	**21**	**8**	**1**	**2**	**3**	**4**
1934-35	**Chicago Black Hawks**	**NHL**	**27**	**7**	**9**	**16**	**11**	**16**	**27**	**14**	**2**	**0**	**0**	**0**	**5**
1935-36	**Montreal Canadiens**	**NHL**	**10**	**0**	**1**	**1**	**0**	**2**	**2**	**0**	....	....	....	....	....
	Providence Reds	Can-Am	8	1	0	1	....	....	....	0	4	0	0	0	4
	London Tecumsehs	IHL	26	5	3	8	....	....	....	8	....	....	....	....	....
	NHL Totals		**309**	**48**	**56**	**104**	**83**	**141**	**224**	**184**	**23**	**1**	**5**	**6**	**15**

Traded to **Cleveland** (IHL) by **Chicago** for cash, June, 1935. Traded to **Montreal Canadiens** by **Cleveland** (IHL) for $2,500, October 21, 1935.

• COWLEY, Bill

William Mailes "Cowboy" **HHOF**
C – L. 5'10", 165 lbs. b: Bristol, Que., 6/12/1912 d: 12/31/1993.

Season	Club	League	GP	G	A	Pts	AG	AA	APts	PIM	GP	G	A	Pts	PIM
1929-30	Ottawa Glebe Collegiate	H.S.	STATISTICS NOT AVAILABLE												
1930-31	Ottawa Primrose	OCJHL	14	10	2	12	....	....	....	16	4	*4	1	5	8
	Ottawa Primrose	M-Cup	9	9	3	12	....	....	....	4	....	....	....	....	....
1931-32	Ottawa Jr. Shamrocks	OCJHL	2	2	1	3	....	....	....	2	3	4	*4	*8	2
	Ottawa Shamrocks	OCHL	....	....	....	....	....	....	....	....	1	0	0	0	0
1932-33	Ottawa Shamrocks	OCHL	14	7	6	13	....	....	....	24	4	1	0	1	4
1933-34	Halifax Wolverines	MSHL	38	*25	*25	*50	....	....	....	42	6	2	2	4	2
1934-35	**St. Louis Eagles**	**NHL**	**41**	**5**	**7**	**12**	**8**	**12**	**20**	**10**	....	....	....	....	....
	Tulsa Oilers	AHA	1	0	0	0	....	....	....	5	....	....	....	....	....
1935-36	**Boston Bruins**	**NHL**	**48**	**11**	**10**	**21**	**21**	**19**	**40**	**17**	**2**	**2**	**1**	**3**	**2**
1936-37	**Boston Bruins**	**NHL**	**46**	**13**	**22**	**35**	**22**	**41**	**63**	**4**	**3**	**0**	**3**	**3**	**0**

Season	Club	League	REGULAR SEASON GP	G	A	Pts	AG	AA	APts	PIM	PLAYOFFS GP	G	A	Pts	PIM
1937-38	**Boston Bruins**	**NHL**	**48**	**17**	**22**	**39**	**28**	**36**	**64**	**8**	**3**	**2**	**0**	**2**	**0**
♦1938-39	**Boston Bruins**	**NHL**	**34**	**8**	***34**	**42**	**14**	**54**	**68**	**2**	**12**	**3**	**11**	***14**	**2**
1939-40	**Boston Bruins**	**NHL**	**48**	**13**	**27**	**40**	**22**	**43**	**65**	**24**	**6**	**0**	**1**	**1**	**7**
♦1940-41	**Boston Bruins**	**NHL**	**46**	**17**	***45**	***62**	**26**	**66**	**92**	**16**	**2**	**0**	**0**	**0**	**0**
1941-42	**Boston Bruins**	**NHL**	**28**	**4**	**23**	**27**	**5**	**27**	**32**	**6**	**5**	**0**	**3**	**3**	**5**
1942-43	**Boston Bruins**	**NHL**	**48**	**27**	***45**	**72**	**28**	**43**	**71**	**10**	**9**	**1**	**7**	**8**	**4**
1943-44	**Boston Bruins**	**NHL**	**36**	**30**	**41**	**71**	**27**	**36**	**63**	**12**	....	....	....	....	....
1944-45	**Boston Bruins**	**NHL**	**49**	**25**	**40**	**65**	**25**	**47**	**72**	**12**	**7**	**3**	**3**	**6**	**0**
1945-46	**Boston Bruins**	**NHL**	**26**	**12**	**12**	**24**	**14**	**17**	**31**	**6**	**10**	**1**	**3**	**4**	**2**
1946-47	**Boston Bruins**	**NHL**	**51**	**13**	**25**	**38**	**15**	**30**	**45**	**16**	**5**	**0**	**2**	**2**	**0**
1947-48	Ottawa Army	OHA-Sr.	DID NOT PLAY – COACHING												
	NHL Totals		**549**	**195**	**353**	**548**	**255**	**471**	**726**	**143**	**64**	**12**	**34**	**46**	**22**

NHL First All-Star Team (1938, 1941, 1943, 1944) • NHL Scoring Leader (1941) • Won Hart Trophy (1941, 1943) • NHL Second All-Star Team (1945)

Signed as a free agent by **St. Louis**, October 22, 1934. Claimed by **Boston** from **St. Louis** in Dispersal Draft, October 15, 1935. • Missed majority of 1941-42 season recovering from jaw injury suffered in game vs. Detroit, January 22, 1942.

• COX, Danny

Daniel Smith "Silent Danny"
LW – L. 5'10", 180 lbs. b: Little Current, Ont., 10/12/1903 d: 8/8/1982.

Season	Club	League	GP	G	A	Pts	AG	AA	APts	PIM	GP	G	A	Pts	PIM
1922-23	Port Arthur Ports	TBSHL	16	*23	3	26	....	....	....	7	2	0	1	1	0
1923-24	Port Arthur Ports	TBSHL	16	12	*9	21	....	....	....	3	2	0	0	0	0
1924-25	Port Arthur Ports	TBSHL	20	12	4	16	....	....	....	7	10	8	3	11	0
1925-26	Port Arthur Ports	TBSHL	20	5	3	8	....	....	....	6	3	1	0	1	0
	Port Arthur Ports	Al-Cup	6	1	0	1	....	....	....	8	....	....	....	....	....
1926-27	**Toronto Pats/Leafs**	**NHL**	**14**	**0**	**1**	**1**	**0**	**5**	**5**	**4**	....	....	....	....	....
	Hamilton Tigers	Can-Pro	19	7	2	9	....	....	....	6	2	1	1	2	0
1927-28	**Toronto Maple Leafs**	**NHL**	**41**	**9**	**6**	**15**	**18**	**34**	**52**	**27**	....	....	....	....	....
1928-29	**Toronto Maple Leafs**	**NHL**	**42**	**12**	**7**	**19**	**35**	**47**	**82**	**14**	**4**	**0**	**1**	**1**	**4**
1929-30	**Toronto Maple Leafs**	**NHL**	**18**	**1**	**4**	**5**	**1**	**9**	**10**	**18**	....	....	....	....	....
	Ottawa Senators	**NHL**	**24**	**3**	**2**	**5**	**4**	**5**	**9**	**20**	**2**	**0**	**0**	**0**	**0**
1930-31	**Ottawa Senators**	**NHL**	**44**	**9**	**12**	**21**	**18**	**36**	**54**	**12**	....	....	....	....	....
1931-32	**Detroit Falcons**	**NHL**	**47**	**4**	**6**	**10**	**7**	**13**	**20**	**23**	**2**	**0**	**0**	**0**	**2**
1932-33	**Ottawa Senators**	**NHL**	**47**	**4**	**7**	**11**	**7**	**14**	**21**	**8**	....	....	....	....	....
1933-34	**Ottawa Senators**	**NHL**	**29**	**0**	**4**	**4**	**0**	**8**	**8**	**0**	....	....	....	....	....
	New York Rangers	**NHL**	**13**	**5**	**0**	**5**	**9**	**0**	**9**	**2**	**2**	**0**	**0**	**0**	**0**
1934-35	Minneapolis Millers	CHL	48	21	24	45	....	....	....	8	5	0	1	1	4
	Quebec Castors	Can-Am	....	....	....	....	....	....	....	....	3	0	0	0	0
1935-36	Philadelphia Ramblers	Can-Am	48	*24	23	47	....	....	....	36	4	1	1	2	0
1936-37	Philadelphia Ramblers	IAHL	46	12	15	27	....	....	....	18	6	0	1	1	14
1937-38	Seattle Seahawks	PCHL	38	7	7	14	....	....	....	6	4	0	0	0	4
1938-39	Seattle Seahawks	PCHL	39	11	13	24	....	....	....	18	7	3	1	4	9
1939-40	Wichita Skyhawks	AHA	31	10	19	29	....	....	....	4	....	....	....	....	....
1940-41	Seattle Olympics	PCHL	DID NOT PLAY – COACHING												
	NHL Totals		**319**	**47**	**49**	**96**	**99**	**171**	**270**	**128**	**10**	**0**	**1**	**1**	**6**

Can-Am Second All-Star Team (1936)

Signed as a free agent by **Toronto St. Pats**, October 13, 1926. Traded to **Ottawa** by **Toronto** with cash for Frank Nighbor, January 31, 1930. Claimed by **Detroit Falcons** from **Ottawa** for 1931-32 season in Dispersal Draft, September 26, 1931. Signed as a free agent by **NY Rangers** after securing release from **Ottawa** (January 30, 1934), February 3, 1934.

• CRASHLEY, Bart

— *see page 996*

• CRAWFORD, Jack

John Shea
D – R. 5'11", 200 lbs. b: Dublin, Ont., 10/26/1916 d: 1/19/1973.

Season	Club	League	GP	G	A	Pts	AG	AA	APts	PIM	GP	G	A	Pts	PIM
1933-34	St. Michael's Buzzers	OHA-B	STATISTICS NOT AVAILABLE												
	St. Michael's Buzzers	M-Cup	13	9	4	13	....	....	....	14	....	....	....	....	....
1934-35	St. Michael's Majors	OHA-Jr.	12	5	3	8	....	....	....	14	3	1	1	2	8
1935-36	West Toronto Nationals	OHA-Jr.	9	3	3	6	....	....	....	4	5	2	2	4	5
	McColl Frontenacs	TIHL	15	0	0	0	....	....	....	20	4	1	0	1	4
	West Toronto Nationals	M-Cup	11	7	4	11	....	....	....	12	....	....	....	....	....
1936-37	Kirkland Lake Blue Devils	GBHL	9	6	4	10	....	....	....	20	4	0	1	1	8
1937-38	**Boston Bruins**	**NHL**	**2**	**0**	**0**	**0**	**0**	**0**	**0**	**0**	....	....	....	....	....
	Providence Reds	AHL	46	6	7	13	....	....	....	33	7	5	8	13	4
♦1938-39	**Boston Bruins**	**NHL**	**48**	**4**	**8**	**12**	**7**	**12**	**19**	**12**	**12**	**1**	**1**	**2**	**9**
1939-40	**Boston Bruins**	**NHL**	**35**	**1**	**4**	**5**	**2**	**6**	**8**	**26**	**6**	**0**	**0**	**0**	**0**
♦1940-41	**Boston Bruins**	**NHL**	**45**	**2**	**8**	**10**	**3**	**11**	**14**	**27**	**11**	**0**	**2**	**2**	**7**
1941-42	**Boston Bruins**	**NHL**	**43**	**2**	**9**	**11**	**3**	**11**	**14**	**37**	**5**	**0**	**1**	**1**	**4**
1942-43	**Boston Bruins**	**NHL**	**49**	**5**	**18**	**23**	**5**	**17**	**22**	**24**	**6**	**1**	**1**	**2**	**10**
1943-44	**Boston Bruins**	**NHL**	**34**	**4**	**16**	**20**	**4**	**14**	**18**	**8**	....	....	....	....	....
1944-45	**Boston Bruins**	**NHL**	**40**	**5**	**19**	**24**	**5**	**22**	**27**	**10**	**7**	**0**	**5**	**5**	**0**
1945-46	**Boston Bruins**	**NHL**	**48**	**7**	**9**	**16**	**8**	**13**	**21**	**10**	**10**	**1**	**2**	**3**	**4**
1946-47	**Boston Bruins**	**NHL**	**58**	**1**	**17**	**18**	**1**	**20**	**21**	**16**	**2**	**0**	**0**	**0**	**0**
1947-48	**Boston Bruins**	**NHL**	**45**	**3**	**11**	**14**	**4**	**14**	**18**	**10**	**4**	**0**	**1**	**1**	**2**
1948-49	**Boston Bruins**	**NHL**	**55**	**2**	**13**	**15**	**3**	**18**	**21**	**14**	**3**	**0**	**0**	**0**	**0**
1949-50	**Boston Bruins**	**NHL**	**46**	**2**	**8**	**10**	**2**	**10**	**12**	**8**	....	....	....	....	....
1950-51	Hershey Bears	AHL	35	1	10	11	....	....	....	14	5	0	2	2	0
1951-52	Hershey Bears	AHL	23	0	2	2	....	....	....	8	3	0	0	0	0
1952-53	Hershey Bears	AHL	DID NOT PLAY – COACHING												
	NHL Totals		**548**	**38**	**140**	**178**	**47**	**168**	**215**	**202**	**66**	**3**	**13**	**16**	**36**

NHL Second All-Star Team (1943) • NHL First All-Star Team (1946)

Signed as a free agent by **Boston**, October 26, 1937.

• CRAWFORD, Rusty

Samuel Russell **HHOF**
LW – L. 5'11", 165 lbs. b: Cardinal, Ont., 11/7/1885 d: 12/19/1971.

Season	Club	League	GP	G	A	Pts	AG	AA	APts	PIM	GP	G	A	Pts	PIM
1907-08	Montreal Montegnards	MCHL	STATISTICS NOT AVAILABLE												
1908-09	Newington Ontarios	OHA-Sr.	STATISTICS NOT AVAILABLE												
1909-10	Prince Albert Mintos	N-SSHL	3	4	0	4	....	....	....	....	....	....	....	....	....
	Prince Albert Mintos	SPHL	....	....	....	....	....	....	....	....	4	1	0	1	14
1910-11	Prince Albert Mintos	SPHL	7	26	0	26	....	....	....	....	4	4	0	4	32
1911-12	Saskatoon Hoo-Hoos	SPHL	7	7	0	7	....	....	....	....	....	....	....	....	....
	Saskatoon Wholesalers	SPHL	1	2	0	2	....	....	....	....	2	2	0	2	*12
♦1912-13	Quebec Bulldogs	NHA	19	4	0	4	....	....	....	29	1	0	0	0	0
1913-14	Quebec Bulldogs	NHA	19	15	10	25	....	....	....	14	....	....	....	....	....
1914-15	Quebec Bulldogs	NHA	20	18	8	26	....	....	....	30	....	....	....	....	....
1915-16	Quebec Bulldogs	NHA	22	18	5	23	....	....	....	54	....	....	....	....	....
1916-17	Quebec Bulldogs	NHA	19	11	9	20	....	....	....	77	....	....	....	....	....
1917-18	**Ottawa Senators**	**NHL**	**12**	**2**	**2**	**4**	**2**	**8**	**10**	**15**	....	....	....	....	....
♦	**Toronto Arenas**	**NHL**	**8**	**1**	**2**	**3**	**1**	**8**	**9**	**51**	**2**	**2**	**1**	**3**	**9**
1918-19	**Toronto Arenas**	**NHL**	**18**	**7**	**4**	**11**	**12**	**22**	**34**	**51**	....	....	....	....	....
1919-20	Saskatoon Crescents	N-SSHL	12	3	3	6	....	....	....	14	....	....	....	....	....
1920-21	Saskatoon Crescents	N-SSHL	14	11	7	18	....	....	....	12	4	2	2	4	4
1921-22	Saskatoon-Moose Jaw	WCHL	24	8	8	16	....	....	....	29	....	....	....	....	....
1922-23	Saskatoon Sheiks	WCHL	19	7	6	13	....	....	....	10	....	....	....	....	....
	Calgary Tigers	WCHL	11	3	1	4	....	....	....	7	....	....	....	....	....
1923-24	Calgary Tigers	WCHL	26	4	4	8	....	....	....	21	2	1	0	1	2
	Calgary Tigers	St-Cup	2	0	1	1	....	....	....	4	....	....	....	....	....
1924-25	Calgary Tigers	WCHL	27	12	2	14	....	....	....	27	2	0	0	0	4
1925-26	Vancouver Maroons	WHL	14	0	0	0	....	....	....	8	....	....	....	....	....
1926-27	Minneapolis Millers	AHA	32	2	3	5	....	....	....	51	6	3	0	3	*13
1927-28	Minneapolis Millers	AHA	34	4	2	6	....	....	....	27	8	3	0	3	10
1928-29	Minneapolis Millers	AHA	40	9	3	12	....	....	....	33	4	0	0	0	0
1929-30	Minneapolis Millers	AHA	45	3	4	7	....	....	....	32	....	....	....	....	....
1930-31	Prince Albert Mintos	N-SSHL	DID NOT PLAY – COACHING												
	NHL Totals		**38**	**10**	**8**	**18**	**15**	**38**	**53**	**117**	**2**	**2**	**1**	**3**	**9**
	Other Major League Totals		220	100	53	153	....	....	....	306	5	1	0	1	6

Claimed by **Ottawa** from **Quebec** in Dispersal Draft, November 28, 1917. Signed as a free agent by **Toronto Arenas**, February 9, 1918. Signed as a free agent by **Ottawa**, December 2, 1918. Traded to **Toronto Arenas** by **Ottawa** for future considerations (loan of Harry Cameron, January 19, 1919), December 14, 1918. Rights transferred to **Quebec** by **Toronto Arenas** when Quebec franchise returned to NHL, November 25, 1919. Reinstated as a amateur to sign with the **Saskatoon Crescents** (SSHL), December 29, 1919. Signed as a free agent by **Saskatoon** (WCHL), November 12, 1921. Traded to **Calgary** (WCHL) by **Saskatoon** (WCHL) for cash, February 10, 1923. Traded to **Vancouver** (WHL) by **Calgary** (WHL) for Fern Headley, November 3, 1925.

• CREIGHTON, Dave

David Theodore
C – L. 6'1", 195 lbs. b: Port Arthur, Ont., 6/24/1930.

Season	Club	League	GP	G	A	Pts	AG	AA	APts	PIM	GP	G	A	Pts	PIM
1946-47	Port Arthur Bruins	TBJHL	6	8	7	15	....	....	....	2	4	5	3	8	0
	Fort William K of C	M-Cup	4	1	0	1	....	....	....	10	....	....	....	....	....
1947-48	Port Arthur Bruins	TBJHL	9	*19	*12	*31	....	....	....	4	5	5	4	9	4
	Port Arthur Bruins	M-Cup	17	21	15	36	....	....	....	16	....	....	....	....	....
1948-49	**Boston Bruins**	**NHL**	**12**	**1**	**3**	**4**	**1**	**4**	**5**	**0**	**3**	**0**	**0**	**0**	**0**
	Hershey Bears	AHL	49	19	18	37	....	....	....	12	....	....	....	....	....
1949-50	**Boston Bruins**	**NHL**	**64**	**18**	**13**	**31**	**23**	**16**	**39**	**13**	....	....	....	....	....
1950-51	**Boston Bruins**	**NHL**	**56**	**5**	**4**	**9**	**6**	**5**	**11**	**4**	**5**	**0**	**1**	**1**	**0**
	Hershey Bears	AHL	11	2	5	7	....	....	....	0	....	....	....	....	....
1951-52	**Boston Bruins**	**NHL**	**49**	**20**	**17**	**37**	**27**	**21**	**48**	**18**	**7**	**2**	**1**	**3**	**2**
	Hershey Bears	AHL	19	9	15	24	....	....	....	4	....	....	....	....	....
1952-53	**Boston Bruins**	**NHL**	**45**	**8**	**8**	**16**	**10**	**10**	**20**	**14**	**11**	**4**	**5**	**9**	**10**
1953-54	**Boston Bruins**	**NHL**	**69**	**20**	**20**	**40**	**27**	**24**	**51**	**27**	**4**	**0**	**0**	**0**	**0**
1954-55	**Toronto Maple Leafs**	**NHL**	**14**	**2**	**1**	**3**	**3**	**1**	**4**	**8**	....	....	....	....	....
	Chicago Black Hawks	**NHL**	**49**	**7**	**7**	**14**	**9**	**8**	**17**	**6**	....	....	....	....	....
1955-56	**New York Rangers**	**NHL**	**70**	**20**	**31**	**51**	**27**	**37**	**64**	**43**	**5**	**0**	**0**	**0**	**4**
1956-57	**New York Rangers**	**NHL**	**70**	**18**	**21**	**39**	**23**	**23**	**46**	**42**	**5**	**2**	**2**	**4**	**2**
1957-58	**New York Rangers**	**NHL**	**70**	**17**	**35**	**52**	**21**	**36**	**57**	**40**	**6**	**3**	**3**	**6**	**2**
1958-59	**Toronto Maple Leafs**	**NHL**	**34**	**3**	**9**	**12**	**4**	**9**	**13**	**4**	**5**	**0**	**1**	**1**	**0**
	Rochester Americans	AHL	33	14	17	31	....	....	....	46	5	1	3	4	4
1959-60	**Toronto Maple Leafs**	**NHL**	**14**	**1**	**5**	**6**	**1**	**5**	**6**	**4**	....	....	....	....	....
	Rochester Americans	AHL	58	25	34	59	....	....	....	30	12	3	3	6	10
1960-61	Rochester Americans	AHL	71	30	42	72	....	....	....	31	....	....	....	....	....
1961-62	Buffalo Bisons	AHL	68	21	48	69	....	....	....	54	11	2	6	8	4
1962-63	Baltimore Clippers	AHL	71	24	48	72	....	....	....	14	3	1	2	3	25
1963-64	Baltimore Clippers	AHL	72	17	25	42	....	....	....	20	....	....	....	....	....
1964-65	Baltimore Clippers	AHL	62	23	28	51	....	....	....	10	5	2	2	4	6
1965-66	Baltimore Clippers	AHL	14	3	2	5	....	....	....	2	....	....	....	....	....
	Providence Reds	AHL	56	16	37	53	....	....	....	14	....	....	....	....	....
1966-67	Providence Reds	AHL	72	22	42	64	....	....	....	63	....	....	....	....	....
1967-68	Providence Reds	AHL	72	22	53	75	....	....	....	54	8	6	2	8	0
1968-69	Providence Reds	AHL	72	11	20	31	....	....	....	36	1	0	0	0	0
	NHL Totals		**616**	**140**	**174**	**314**	**182**	**199**	**381**	**223**	**51**	**11**	**13**	**24**	**20**

• Father of Adam • AHL Second All-Star Team (1968) • Won Les Cunningham Award (MVP - AHL) (1968) • Played in NHL All-Star Game (1952, 1953, 1954, 1955, 1956)

Signed as a free agent by **Boston**, October 5, 1948. Traded to **Toronto** by **Boston** for Fern Flaman, July 20, 1954. Traded to **Chicago** by **Toronto** for cash, November 16, 1954. Traded to **Detroit** by **Chicago** with Jerry Toppazzini, John McCormack and Gord Hollingworth for Tony Leswick, John Wilson, Glen Skov and Benny Woit, May 27, 1955. Traded to **NY Rangers** by **Detroit** with Bronco Horvath for Billy Dea, Aggie Kukulowicz and cash, August 18, 1955. Claimed by **Montreal** from **NY Rangers** in Intra-League Draft, June 3, 1958. Claimed by **Toronto** from **Montreal** on waivers, September 25, 1958. Traded to **Buffalo** (AHL) by **Toronto** for Dick Gamble, June, 1961. Traded to **Baltimore** (AHL) by **Buffalo** (AHL) for cash, July, 1961. Traded to **Providence** (AHL) by **Baltimore** (AHL) for Ed MacQueen, November 26, 1965.

• CREIGHTON, Jimmy

F – L. 5'9", 150 lbs. b: Brandon, Man., 11/18/1905 d: 1993.

Season	Club	League	GP	G	A	Pts	AG	AA	APts	PIM	GP	G	A	Pts	PIM
1924-25	University of Manitoba	WJrHL	STATISTICS NOT AVAILABLE												
	University of Manitoba	M-Cup	2	1	1	2	....	....	....	10	....	....	....	....	....
1925-26	Melville Millionaires	S-SJHL	14	15	2	17	....	....	....	6	....	....	....	....	....
1926-27	Brandon Wheat Kings	MHL-Sr.	7	6	2	8	....	....	....	12	2	0	0	0	8
1927-28	Brandon Wheat Kings	MHL-Sr.	16	11	3	14	....	....	....	29	....	....	....	....	....
1928-29	Port Arthur Ports	TBSHL	19	13	9	22	....	....	....	40	2	1	0	1	2
	Port Arthur Ports	Al-Cup	7	9	3	12	....	....	....	9	....	....	....	....	....
1929-30	Detroit Olympics	IHL	23	10	8	18	....	....	....	24	....	....	....	....	....
1930-31	**Detroit Falcons**	**NHL**	**11**	**1**	**0**	**1**	**2**	**0**	**2**	**2**	....	....	....	....	....
	Detroit Olympics	IHL	5	0	0	0	....	....	....	8	....	....	....	....	....
1931-32	Detroit Olympics	IHL	3	0	0	0	....	....	....	0	....	....	....	....	....
	Philadelphia Arrows	Can-Am	5	2	0	2	....	....	....	15	....	....	....	....	....
	Boston Cubs	Can-Am	4	1	0	1	....	....	....	4	....	....	....	....	....
1932-33	Kansas City Pla-Mors	AHA	10	1	3	4	....	....	....	9	....	....	....	....	....
	Duluth-Wichita	AHA	1	0	0	0	....	....	....	2	....	....	....	....	....
	NHL Totals		**11**	**1**	**0**	**1**	**2**	**0**	**2**	**2**	....	....	....	....	....

• Missed remainder of 1929-30 and majority of 1930-31 seasons recovering from fractured pelvis suffered on January 24, 1930. Traded to **Detroit** by **Kansas City** (AHA) for cash, April 3, 1929. Signed as a free agent by **Philadelphia** (Can-Am) following release by Detroit (IHL), December 24, 1931.

• CRESSMAN, Glen

C – R. 5'9", 155 lbs. b: Petersburg, Ont., 8/29/1934.

Season	Club	League	GP	G	A	Pts	AG	AA	APts	PIM	GP	G	A	Pts	PIM
			REGULAR SEASON								PLAYOFFS				
1951-52	Kitchener Greenshirts	OHA-Jr.	3	0	3	3	....	....	....	0	4	0	2	2	0
1952-53	Kitchener Greenshirts	OHA-Jr.	56	6	11	17	....	....	....	2	....	....	....	....	....
1953-54	Kitchener Greenshirts	OHA-Jr.	59	20	28	48	....	....	....	10	4	0	1	1	0
1954-55	Toronto Marlboros	OHA-Jr.	51	23	19	42	....	....	....	16	13	2	7	9	17
	Toronto Marlboros	M-Cup	11	7	6	13	....	....	....	2	....	....	....	....	....
1955-56	Chicoutimi Sagueneens	QHL	64	12	18	30	....	....	....	7	5	0	1	1	0
1956-57	**Montreal Canadiens**	**NHL**	**4**	**0**	**0**	**0**	**0**	**0**	**0**	**2**	....	....	....	....	....
	Montreal Royals	QHL	34	11	13	24	....	....	....	4	4	0	0	0	2
	Rochester Americans	AHL	13	2	1	3	....	....	....	4	....	....	....	....	....
1957-58	Montreal Royals	QHL	64	14	21	35	....	....	....	8	7	0	2	2	0
1958-59	Chicoutimi Sagueneens	QHL	59	15	26	41	....	....	....	2	....	....	....	....	....
1959-60	Kingston Frontenacs	EPHL	62	13	22	35	....	....	....	6	....	....	....	....	....
1960-61	Montreal Royals	EPHL	47	5	9	14	....	....	....	6	....	....	....	....	....
1961-62	Knoxville Knights	EHL	46	13	17	30	....	....	....	8	8	2	2	4	0
1962-63	Knoxville Knights	EHL	68	34	36	70	....	....	....	6	5	0	0	0	2
1963-64	Knoxville Knights	EHL	72	27	47	74	....	....	....	23	8	3	2	5	4
1964-65	Knoxville Knights	EHL	71	43	40	83	....	....	....	24	10	6	4	10	0
1965-66	Knoxville Knights	EHL	72	26	43	69	....	....	....	4	3	0	0	0	0
	NHL Totals		**4**	**0**	**0**	**0**	**0**	**0**	**0**	**2**	....	....	....	....	....

• CRISP, Terry *— see page 998*

• CROGHAN, Maurice "Moe"

D – L. 5'11", 185 lbs. b: Montreal, Que., 11/19/1914 Deceased.

Season	Club	League	GP	G	A	Pts	AG	AA	APts	PIM	GP	G	A	Pts	PIM
1933-34	Montreal Jr. Royals	OJHL	6	2	1	3	....	....	....	14	4	3	0	3	*19
1934-35	Verdun Maple Leafs	QJHL	6	1	0	1	....	....	....	6	6	3	1	4	6
	Montreal Royals	MCHL	20	2	0	2	....	....	....	14	7	0	2	2	6
1935-36	Verdun Maple Leafs	QJHL	4	0	4	4	....	....	....	0	2	2	0	2	4
	Verdun Maple Leafs	MCHL	1	0	0	0	....	....	....	0	7	0	0	0	0
1936-37	Quebec Aces	QSHL	24	1	9	10	....	....	....	34	6	1	2	3	2
	Quebec Aces	Al-Cup	5	1	3	4	....	....	....	6	....	....	....	....	....
1937-38	**Montreal Maroons**	**NHL**	**16**	**0**	**0**	**0**	**0**	**0**	**0**	**4**	....	....	....	....	....
	Montreal Royals	MCHL	1	0	0	0	....	....	....	0	....	....	....	....	....
1938-39	Providence Reds	IAHL	13	0	1	1	....	....	....	6	....	....	....	....	....
	Springfield Indians	IAHL	16	0	1	1	....	....	....	10	3	0	0	0	0
1939-40	Montreal Victorias	MCHL	11	0	1	1	....	....	....	4	....	....	....	....	....
1940-41	Montreal Royals	QSHL	20	1	1	2	....	....	....	27	....	....	....	....	....
	NHL Totals		**16**	**0**	**0**	**0**	**0**	**0**	**0**	**4**	....	....	....	....	....

Signed as a free agent by **Mtl. Maroons**, October 27, 1937. Traded to **Springfield** (IAHL) by **Providence** (IAHL) with Norm Schultz for Hub Wilson and Joe McGoldrick, January 9, 1939.

• CROSSETT, Stan Stan Roy

D – R. 6', 200 lbs. b: Tillsonburg, Ont., 4/18/1900 Deceased.

Season	Club	League	GP	G	A	Pts	AG	AA	APts	PIM	GP	G	A	Pts	PIM
1929-30	Port Hope Eagles	OHA-Sr.	STATISTICS NOT AVAILABLE												
1930-31	**Philadelphia Quakers**	**NHL**	**21**	**0**	**0**	**0**	**0**	**0**	**0**	**10**	....	....	....	....	....
	NHL Totals		**21**	**0**	**0**	**0**	**0**	**0**	**0**	**10**	....	....	....	....	....

Signed as a free agent by **Philadelphia**, January 9, 1931.

• CROZIER, Joe Joseph Richard

D – R. 6', 185 lbs. b: Winnipeg, Man., 2/19/1929.

Season	Club	League	GP	G	A	Pts	AG	AA	APts	PIM	GP	G	A	Pts	PIM
1947-48	Brandon Wheat Kings	MJHL	23	1	10	11	....	....	....	18	5	0	1	1	0
1948-49	Brandon Wheat Kings	MJHL	30	4	23	27	....	....	....	14	7	1	5	6	6
	Brandon Wheat Kings	M-Cup	18	2	3	5	....	....	....	10	....	....	....	....	....
1949-50	San Francisco Shamrocks	PCHL	71	7	20	27	....	....	....	39	4	1	0	1	2
1950-51	Denver Falcons	USHL	9	1	2	3	....	....	....	6	....	....	....	....	....
	Vancouver Canucks	PCHL	46	2	15	17	....	....	....	24	....	....	....	....	....
1951-52	Quebec Aces	QMHL	60	2	24	26	....	....	....	60	15	1	4	5	16
	Quebec Aces	Alx-Cup	5	1	4	5	....	....	....	2	....	....	....	....	....
1952-53	Quebec Aces	QMHL	60	6	14	20	....	....	....	40	22	1	12	13	15
1953-54	Quebec Aces	QHL	71	6	21	27	....	....	....	63	16	0	5	5	2
	Quebec Aces	Ed-Cup	7	1	2	3	....	....	....	4	....	....	....	....	....
1954-55	Quebec Aces	QHL	59	5	21	26	....	....	....	34	8	3	1	4	8
1955-56	Quebec Aces	QHL	37	2	12	14	....	....	....	50	....	....	....	....	....
1956-57	Quebec Aces	QHL	67	7	30	37	....	....	....	61	10	1	2	3	6
	Quebec Aces	Ed-Cup	6	1	6	7	....	....	....	6	....	....	....	....	....
1957-58	Quebec Aces	QHL	51	3	11	14	....	....	....	59	13	0	2	2	*30
	Springfield Indians	AHL	2	0	1	1	....	....	....	0	....	....	....	....	....
1958-59	Quebec Aces	QHL	42	1	12	13	....	....	....	26	....	....	....	....	....
	Providence Reds	AHL	3	0	0	0	....	....	....	8	....	....	....	....	....
1959-60	**Toronto Maple Leafs**	**NHL**	**5**	**0**	**3**	**3**	**0**	**3**	**3**	**2**	....	....	....	....	....
	Spokane Comets	WHL	45	1	10	11	....	....	....	50	....	....	....	....	....
	Rochester Americans	AHL	25	1	11	12	....	....	....	12	12	0	2	2	11
1960-61	Rochester Americans	AHL	35	1	13	14	....	....	....	14	....	....	....	....	....
1961-62	Charlotte Checkers	EHL	DID NOT PLAY – COACHING												
	NHL Totals		**5**	**0**	**3**	**3**	**0**	**3**	**3**	**2**	....	....	....	....	....

MJHL Second All-Star Team (1948) • MJHL First All-Star Team (1949) • QHL Second All-Star Team (1954) • QHL First All-Star Team (1957)

• CRUTCHFIELD, Nels

C – L. 6'1", 175 lbs. b: Knowlton, Que., 7/12/1911 Deceased.

Season	Club	League	GP	G	A	Pts	AG	AA	APts	PIM	GP	G	A	Pts	PIM
1928-29	Shawinigan Cataracts	ECHA	24	8	1	9	....	....	....	39	....	....	....	....	....
1929-30	Shawinigan Cataracts	ECHA	24	5	4	9	....	....	....	38	....	....	....	....	....
1930-31	Shawinigan Cataracts	ECHA	12	6	4	10	....	....	....	6	....	....	....	....	....
	McGill Redmen	MCHL	12	2	2	4	....	....	....	21	4	2	0	2	8
	McGill Redmen	Al-Cup	6	2	0	2	....	....	....	14	....	....	....	....	....
1931-32	McGill Redmen	MCHL	12	7	6	13	....	....	....	*41	2	1	0	1	11
1932-33	McGill Redmen	MCHL	10	7	4	11	....	....	....	33	7	1	1	2	28
1933-34	McGill Redmen	MCHL	12	3	8	11	....	....	....	34	2	1	0	1	6
	McGill Redmen	Al-Cup	4	3	1	4	....	....	....	12	....	....	....	....	....
1934-35	**Montreal Canadiens**	**NHL**	**41**	**5**	**5**	**10**	**8**	**9**	**17**	**20**	**2**	**0**	**1**	**1**	**22**
	NHL Totals		**41**	**5**	**5**	**10**	**8**	**9**	**17**	**20**	**2**	**0**	**1**	**1**	**22**

Rights traded to **Montreal Canadiens** by **Montreal Maroons** for Lionel Conacher and the rights to Herb Cain, October 3, 1934. • Suffered career-ending injuries in automobile accident, September 28, 1935.

• CULLEN, Barry Charles Francis

RW – R. 6', 183 lbs. b: Ottawa, Ont., 6/16/1935.

Season	Club	League	GP	G	A	Pts	AG	AA	APts	PIM	GP	G	A	Pts	PIM
			REGULAR SEASON								PLAYOFFS				
1953-54	St. Catharines Teepees	OHA-Jr.	58	62	45	107	....	....	....	35	15	9	7	16	13
	St. Catharines Teepees	M-Cup	11	8	9	17	....	....	....	12	....	....	....	....	....
1954-55	St. Catharines Teepees	OHA-Jr.	49	45	42	87	....	....	....	87	11	9	5	14	34
1955-56	**Toronto Maple Leafs**	**NHL**	**3**	**0**	**0**	**0**	**0**	**0**	**0**	**4**	....	....	....	....	....
	Winnipeg Warriors	WHL	67	38	34	72	....	....	....	72	14	7	6	13	14
	Winnipeg Warriors	Ed-Cup	6	3	2	5	....	....	....	8	....	....	....	....	....
1956-57	**Toronto Maple Leafs**	**NHL**	**51**	**6**	**10**	**16**	**8**	**11**	**19**	**30**	....	....	....	....	....
	Rochester Americans	AHL	7	4	4	8	....	....	....	6	....	....	....	....	....
1957-58	**Toronto Maple Leafs**	**NHL**	**70**	**16**	**25**	**41**	**20**	**26**	**46**	**37**	....	....	....	....	....
1958-59	**Toronto Maple Leafs**	**NHL**	**40**	**6**	**8**	**14**	**7**	**8**	**15**	**17**	**2**	**0**	**0**	**0**	**0**
1959-60	**Detroit Red Wings**	**NHL**	**55**	**4**	**9**	**13**	**5**	**9**	**14**	**23**	**4**	**0**	**0**	**0**	**2**
	Hershey Bears	AHL	7	2	2	4	....	....	....	0	....	....	....	....	....
1960-61	Buffalo Bisons	AHL	71	16	37	53	....	....	....	59	4	1	0	1	10
1961-62	Buffalo Bisons	AHL	69	*41	53	94	....	....	....	61	11	2	4	6	10
1962-63	Buffalo Bisons	AHL	53	20	23	43	....	....	....	20	13	3	3	6	14
1963-64	Buffalo Bisons	AHL	72	23	38	61	....	....	....	32	....	....	....	....	....
	NHL Totals		**219**	**32**	**52**	**84**	**40**	**54**	**94**	**111**	**6**	**0**	**0**	**0**	**2**

• Father of John • Brother of Brian and Ray • Won WHL Rookie of the Year Award (1956) • AHL First All-Star Team (1962)

Signed as a free agent by **Toronto**, June, 1955. Traded to **Detroit** by **Toronto** for Frank Roggeveen and Johnny Wilson, June 9, 1959. Traded to **NY Rangers** (Buffalo-AHL) by **Detroit** for Pete Conacher, August, 1960.

• CULLEN, Brian Brian Joseph

C – L. 5'10", 160 lbs. b: Ottawa, Ont., 11/11/1933.

Season	Club	League	GP	G	A	Pts	AG	AA	APts	PIM	GP	G	A	Pts	PIM
1951-52	St. Catharines Teepees	OHA-Jr.	54	30	31	61	....	....	....	25	14	7	6	13	4
	Buffalo Bisons	AHL	1	0	0	0	....	....	....	0	....	....	....	....	....
1952-53	St. Catharines Teepees	OHA-Jr.	56	41	28	69	....	....	....	29	3	4	0	4	2
	Buffalo Bisons	AHL	3	1	5	6	....	....	....	0	....	....	....	....	....
1953-54	St. Catharines Teepees	OHA-Jr.	59	*68	*93	*161	....	....	....	40	15	*12	*17	*29	18
	St. Catharines Teepees	M-Cup	11	10	14	24	....	....	....	18	....	....	....	....	....
1954-55	**Toronto Maple Leafs**	**NHL**	**27**	**3**	**5**	**8**	**4**	**6**	**10**	**6**	**4**	**1**	**0**	**1**	**0**
	Pittsburgh Hornets	AHL	36	11	25	36	....	....	....	20	....	....	....	....	....
1955-56	**Toronto Maple Leafs**	**NHL**	**21**	**2**	**6**	**8**	**3**	**7**	**10**	**8**	**5**	**1**	**0**	**1**	**2**
	Winnipeg Warriors	WHL	50	16	35	51	....	....	....	10	....	....	....	....	....
1956-57	**Toronto Maple Leafs**	**NHL**	**46**	**8**	**12**	**20**	**10**	**13**	**23**	**27**	....	....	....	....	....
	Rochester Americans	AHL	9	2	10	12	....	....	....	2	....	....	....	....	....
1957-58	**Toronto Maple Leafs**	**NHL**	**67**	**20**	**23**	**43**	**25**	**24**	**49**	**29**	....	....	....	....	....
1958-59	**Toronto Maple Leafs**	**NHL**	**59**	**4**	**14**	**18**	**5**	**14**	**19**	**10**	**10**	**1**	**0**	**1**	**0**
1959-60	**New York Rangers**	**NHL**	**64**	**8**	**21**	**29**	**9**	**20**	**29**	**6**	....	....	....	....	....
1960-61	**New York Rangers**	**NHL**	**42**	**11**	**19**	**30**	**13**	**18**	**31**	**6**	....	....	....	....	....
	Buffalo Bisons	AHL	15	6	6	12	....	....	....	9	4	0	0	0	0
1961-62	Buffalo Bisons	AHL	67	22	59	81	....	....	....	18	11	5	3	8	11
1962-63	Buffalo Bisons	AHL	31	5	17	22	....	....	....	23	5	1	0	1	0
	NHL Totals		**326**	**56**	**100**	**156**	**69**	**102**	**171**	**92**	**19**	**3**	**0**	**3**	**2**

• Brother of Barry and Ray • Won Red Tilson Trophy (OHA-Jr. MVP) (1954) • OHA-Jr. First All-Star Team (1954)

Traded to **Toronto** by **Chicago** (Buffalo-AHL) for George Blair, Frank Sullivan and Jackie LeClair, May 4, 1954. Claimed by **NY Rangers** from **Toronto** in Intra-League Draft, June 10, 1959.

• CULLEN, Ray *— see page 1003*

• CUNNINGHAM, Bob Robert Gordon

C – L. 5'11", 168 lbs. b: Welland, Ont., 2/26/1941.

Season	Club	League	GP	G	A	Pts	AG	AA	APts	PIM	GP	G	A	Pts	PIM
1958-59	Guelph Biltmores	OHA-Jr.	54	19	27	46	....	....	....	25	10	1	6	7	8
1959-60	Guelph Biltmores	OHA-Jr.	48	14	23	37	....	....	....	26	3	1	2	3	0
	Trois-Rivieres Lions	EPHL	3	1	3	4	....	....	....	2	5	1	1	2	0
1960-61	Guelph Biltmores	OHA-Jr.	47	34	52	86	....	....	....	78	14	11	10	21	39
	New York Rangers	**NHL**	**3**	**0**	**1**	**1**	**0**	**1**	**1**	**0**	....	....	....	....	....
1961-62	**New York Rangers**	**NHL**	**1**	**0**	**0**	**0**	**0**	**0**	**0**	**0**	....	....	....	....	....
	Kitchener Beavers	EPHL	38	5	11	16	....	....	....	18	7	0	1	1	4
1962-63	Baltimore Clippers	AHL	57	9	17	26	....	....	....	21	3	0	1	1	0
1963-64	St. Paul Rangers	CPHL	69	25	47	72	....	....	....	32	8	1	5	6	7
1964-65	St. Louis Braves	CPHL	47	15	35	50	....	....	....	14	....	....	....	....	....
1965-66	Pittsburgh Hornets	AHL	65	10	21	31	....	....	....	14	3	0	0	0	0
1966-67	Baltimore Clippers	AHL	63	17	35	52	....	....	....	6	9	2	3	5	0
1967-68	Baltimore Clippers	AHL	71	13	30	43	....	....	....	8	....	....	....	....	....
1968-69	Baltimore Clippers	AHL	46	5	12	17	....	....	....	22	....	....	....	....	....
	Denver Spurs	WHL	17	8	5	13	....	....	....	0	....	....	....	....	....
1969-70	Denver Spurs	WHL	22	4	13	17	....	....	....	2	....	....	....	....	....
	Port Huron Flags	IHL	22	8	17	25	....	....	....	24	8	3	3	6	2
1970-71	Orillia Terriers	OHA-Sr.	40	15	29	44	....	....	....	32	....	....	....	....	....
1971-72	Barrie Flyers	OHA-Sr.	40	24	45	69	....	....	....	53	16	6	15	21	22
1972-73	Barrie Flyers	OHA-Sr.	35	23	43	66	....	....	....	10	....	....	....	....	....
1973-74	Brantford Forresters	OHA-Sr.	32	19	31	50	....	....	....	8	....	....	....	....	....
	NHL Totals		**4**	**0**	**1**	**1**	**0**	**1**	**1**	**0**	....	....	....	....	....

OHA-Jr. Second All-Star Team (1961) • OHA-Sr. First All-Star Team (1972)

Traded to **Detroit** (Pittsburgh-AHL) by **NY Rangers** for Dunc McCallum, June, 1965. Claimed by **NY Rangers** (Baltimore-AHL) from **Detroit** in Reverse Draft, June 15, 1966. Traded to **Phoenix** (WHL) by **Baltimore** (AHL) for Andre Pronovost, February, 1969.

• CUNNINGHAM, Les Leslie Roy

C – L. 5'8", 165 lbs. b: Calgary, Alta., 10/4/1913.

Season	Club	League	GP	G	A	Pts	AG	AA	APts	PIM	GP	G	A	Pts	PIM
1931-32	Calgary Jimmies	CCJHL	12	3	2	5	....	....	....	15	3	1	0	1	6
	Calgary Jimmies	M-Cup	8	4	0	4	....	....	....	4	....	....	....	....	....
1932-33	Regina Pats	S-SJHL	3	3	0	3	....	....	....	0	2	1	0	1	0
	Regina Pats	M-Cup	13	5	0	5	....	....	....	12	....	....	....	....	....
1933-34	Saskatoon Elites	N-SJHL	20	16	10	26	....	....	....	18	4	2	0	2	4
1934-35	Buffalo Bisons	IHL	42	12	12	24	....	....	....	34	....	....	....	....	....
1935-36	Buffalo Bisons	IHL	37	9	13	22	....	....	....	37	5	1	1	2	0
1936-37	Cleveland Falcons	IAHL	20	4	4	8	....	....	....	17	....	....	....	....	....
	New York Americans	**NHL**	**23**	**1**	**8**	**9**	**2**	**15**	**17**	**19**	....	....	....	....	....
1937-38	Cleveland Barons	IAHL	48	19	28	47	....	....	....	55	2	1	2	3	0
1938-39	Cleveland Barons	IAHL	52	26	20	46	....	....	....	49	9	6	4	*10	0

			REGULAR SEASON								PLAYOFFS				
Season	Club	League	GP	G	A	Pts	AG	AA	APts	PIM	GP	G	A	Pts	PIM
1939-40	**Chicago Black Hawks**	**NHL**	**37**	**6**	**11**	**17**	**10**	**17**	**27**	**2**	**1**	**0**	**0**	**0**	**0**
1940-41	Cleveland Barons	AHL	56	22	*42	*64	....	....	....	10	9	3	4	7	2
1941-42	Cleveland Barons	AHL	56	25	35	60	....	....	....	23	5	4	2	6	4
1942-43	Cleveland Barons	AHL	55	35	47	82	....	....	....	24	4	2	2	4	0
1943-44	Cleveland Barons	AHL	52	26	52	78	....	....	....	13	11	6	4	10	0
1944-45	Cleveland Barons	AHL	56	35	45	80	....	....	....	4	11	3	8	11	2
1945-46	Cleveland Barons	AHL	62	33	44	77	....	....	....	10	7	4	6	10	5
1946-47	Cleveland Barons	AHL	61	8	29	37	....	....	....	11	....	....	....	....	....
1947-48	San Francisco Shamrocks	PCHL	39	15	24	39	....	....	....	27	3	0	5	5	2
1948-49	San Francisco Shamrocks	PCHL	9	4	4	8	....	....	....	14	....	....	....	....	....
1949-50	Brandon Wheat Kings	MJHL	DID NOT PLAY – COACHING												
	NHL Totals		**60**	**7**	**19**	**26**	**12**	**32**	**44**	**21**	**1**	**0**	**0**	**0**	**0**

AHL Second All-Star Team (1941, 1943, 1944) • AHL First All-Star Team (1942)

Traded to **NY Americans** by **Cleveland** (IAHL) for Jim Klein, January 14, 1937. Traded to **Cleveland** (IAHL) by **NY Americans** for cash, October, 1937. Claimed by **Chicago** from **Cleveland** (IAHL) in Inter-League Draft, May 14, 1939. Traded to **Cleveland** (AHL) by **Chicago** for cash, May 12, 1940.

• CUPOLO, Bill William Donald

RW – R. 5′8″, 170 lbs. b: Niagara Falls, Ont., 1/8/1924.

Season	Club	League	GP	G	A	Pts	AG	AA	APts	PIM	GP	G	A	Pts	PIM
1941-42	Stratford Kist	OHA-B	12	14	24	38	....	....	....	13	....	....	....	....	....
1942-43	Stratford Kroehlers	OHA-Jr.	16	14	22	36	....	....	....	6	2	3	3	6	0
	Stratford Kroehlers	M-Cup	9	1	8	9	....	....	....	14	....	....	....	....	....
1943-44	Stratford Kroehlers	OHA-Jr.	STATISTICS NOT AVAILABLE												
1944-45	**Boston Bruins**	**NHL**	**47**	**11**	**13**	**24**	**11**	**15**	**26**	**10**	**7**	**1**	**2**	**3**	**0**
1945-46	Hershey Bears	AHL	25	4	9	13	....	....	....	21	....	....	....	....	....
	New Haven Ramblers	AHL	17	4	5	9	....	....	....	4	....	....	....	....	....
1946-47	Springfield Indians	AHL	50	8	12	20	....	....	....	38	2	0	0	0	2
1947-48	Springfield Indians	AHL	17	1	4	5	....	....	....	2	....	....	....	....	....
1948-49	Fort Worth Rangers	USHL	50	12	20	32	....	....	....	32	2	1	0	1	0
1949-50	San Diego–Seattle	PCHL	70	25	20	45	....	....	....	26	4	0	2	2	0
1950-51	Sydney Millionaires	CBMHL	49	20	28	48	....	....	....	54	....	....	....	....	....
	Sydney Millionaires	Alx-Cup	11	4	5	9	....	....	....	11	....	....	....	....	....
1951-52	Sydney Millionaires	MMHL	41	12	19	31	....	....	....	42	....	....	....	....	....
	New Haven Tomahawks	EAHL	29	19	10	29	....	....	....	25	9	3	2	5	2
1952-53	Washington Lions	EAHL	13	4	2	6	....	....	....	12	....	....	....	....	....
	Kitchener–Chatham	OHA-Sr.	41	12	16	28	....	....	....	36	....	....	....	....	....
1953-54	Chatham–Stratford	OHA-Sr.	54	9	27	36	....	....	....	47	7	1	4	5	4
	NHL Totals		**47**	**11**	**13**	**24**	**11**	**15**	**26**	**10**	**7**	**1**	**2**	**3**	**0**

• CURRIE, Hugh Hugh Roy

D – R. 6′, 190 lbs. b: Saskatoon, Sask., 10/22/1925.

Season	Club	League	GP	G	A	Pts	AG	AA	APts	PIM	GP	G	A	Pts	PIM
1943-44	Saskatoon Lions	SAHA	4	1	4	5	....	....	....	4	2	0	3	3	2
1944-45	Baltimore Orioles	EAHL	47	3	15	18	....	....	....	44	11	2	4	6	18
1945-46	Dallas Texans	USHL	18	3	1	4	....	....	....	14	....	....	....	....	....
	Washington Lions	EAHL	22	1	5	6	....	....	....	33	12	0	6	6	10
1946-47	Houston Huskies	USHL	36	4	8	12	....	....	....	30	....	....	....	....	....
	Tacoma Rockets	PCHL	18	5	8	13	....	....	....	44	....	....	....	....	....
1947-48	Buffalo Bisons	AHL	9	0	0	0	....	....	....	10	....	....	....	....	....
	Houston Huskies	USHL	52	5	7	12	....	....	....	67	12	1	0	1	2
1948-49	Houston Huskies	USHL	11	1	1	2	....	....	....	13	....	....	....	....	....
	San Diego Skyhawks	PCHL	51	4	11	15	....	....	....	52	14	2	6	8	30
1949-50	Louisville Blades	USHL	7	1	6	7	....	....	....	8	....	....	....	....	....
	Buffalo Bisons	AHL	54	3	25	28	....	....	....	64	5	0	0	0	13
1950-51	**Montreal Canadiens**	**NHL**	**1**	**0**	**0**	**0**	**0**	**0**	**0**	**0**	....	....	....	....	....
	Buffalo Bisons	AHL	57	9	56	65	....	....	....	54	4	0	1	1	2
1951-52	Buffalo Bisons	AHL	11	0	4	4	....	....	....	4	....	....	....	....	....
	Vancouver Canucks	PCHL	34	5	20	25	....	....	....	36	....	....	....	....	....
1952-53	Vancouver Canucks	WHL	68	3	25	28	....	....	....	77	9	2	5	7	10
1953-54	Springfield Indians	QHL	31	5	21	26	....	....	....	11	....	....	....	....	....
	Syracuse Warriors	AHL	41	2	13	15	....	....	....	26	....	....	....	....	....
1954-55	Springfield Indians	AHL	64	5	43	48	....	....	....	60	4	0	1	1	4
1955-56	Vancouver Canucks	WHL	69	6	30	36	....	....	....	36	15	0	3	3	6
1956-57	Vancouver Canucks	WHL	68	6	32	38	....	....	....	47	....	....	....	....	....
1957-58	Seattle Totems	WHL	70	3	40	43	....	....	....	72	11	1	1	2	10
1958-59	Vancouver Canucks	WHL	67	4	26	30	....	....	....	36	9	0	4	4	10
1959-60	Calgary Stampeders	WHL	66	1	25	26	....	....	....	30	....	....	....	....	....
1960-61	Victoria Cougars	WHL	70	1	16	17	....	....	....	39	5	0	1	1	0
1961-62	San Francisco Seals	WHL	7	0	1	1	....	....	....	2	....	....	....	....	....
	Vancouver Canucks	WHL	43	1	13	14	....	....	....	16	....	....	....	....	....
1962-63	Philadelphia Ramblers	EHL	65	2	50	52	....	....	....	31	3	1	0	1	2
1963-64	Edmonton Nuggets	ASHL	DID NOT PLAY – COACHING												
1964-65	Edmonton Nuggets	ASHL	DID NOT PLAY – COACHING												
1965-66	Edmonton Nuggets	WCSHL	7	0	6	6	....	....	....	5	....	....	....	....	....
	NHL Totals		**1**	**0**	**0**	**0**	**0**	**0**	**0**	**0**	....	....	....	....	....

AHL Second All-Star Team (1951) • WHL Coast Division Second All-Star Team (1957) • WHL Coast Division First All-Star Team (1958, 1959)

• Named coach of Vancouver Canucks (WHL), February 8, 1962. • Named playing coach of Philadelphia Ramblers (EHL), October 8, 1962

• CURRY, Floyd Floyd James "Busher"

RW – R. 5′11″, 174 lbs. b: Chapleau, Ont., 8/11/1925.

Season	Club	League	GP	G	A	Pts	AG	AA	APts	PIM	GP	G	A	Pts	PIM
1940-41	Kirkland Golden Gate	NOJHA	20	9	4	13	....	....	....	5	....	....	....	....	....
1941-42	Oshawa Generals	OHA-Jr.	24	11	15	26	....	....	....	20	12	9	10	19	15
	Oshawa Generals	M-Cup	11	11	6	17	....	....	....	4	....	....	....	....	....
1942-43	Oshawa Generals	OHA-Jr.	22	22	24	46	....	....	....	16	10	8	5	13	8
	Oshawa Generals	M-Cup	8	7	6	13	....	....	....	2	....	....	....	....	....
1943-44	Oshawa Generals	OHA-Jr.	26	22	26	48	....	....	....	13	10	4	7	11	6
	Oshawa Generals	M-Cup	10	11	8	19	....	....	....	14	....	....	....	....	....
1944-45	Toronto Navy Bulldogs	TNDHL	7	7	7	14	....	....	....	2	7	9	6	15	4
	Toronto Uptown Tires	TMHL	2	2	1	3	....	....	....	0	2	1	1	2	0
	Toronto Fuels	TMHL	7	2	2	4	....	....	....	0	....	....	....	....	....
1945-46	Montreal Royals	QSHL	32	22	23	45	....	....	....	8	11	3	6	9	4
1946-47	Montreal Royals	QSHL	40	23	20	43	....	....	....	26	11	3	4	7	4
	Montreal Royals	Al-Cup	14	6	2	8	....	....	....	14	....	....	....	....	....
1947-48	**Montreal Canadiens**	**NHL**	**31**	**1**	**5**	**6**	**1**	**6**	**7**	**0**	....	....	....	....	....
	Buffalo Bisons	AHL	14	6	8	14	....	....	....	10	....	....	....	....	....
1948-49	Buffalo Bisons	AHL	67	24	19	43	....	....	....	12	....	....	....	....	....
	Montreal Canadiens	**NHL**	....	....	....	....	....	....	....	....	**2**	**0**	**0**	**0**	**2**
1949-50	**Montreal Canadiens**	**NHL**	**49**	**8**	**8**	**16**	**10**	**10**	**20**	**8**	**5**	**1**	**0**	**1**	**2**
	Buffalo Bisons	AHL	24	4	6	10	....	....	....	6	....	....	....	....	....
1950-51	**Montreal Canadiens**	**NHL**	**69**	**13**	**14**	**27**	**17**	**17**	**34**	**23**	**11**	**0**	**2**	**2**	**2**
1951-52	**Montreal Canadiens**	**NHL**	**64**	**20**	**18**	**38**	**27**	**22**	**49**	**10**	**11**	**4**	**3**	***7**	**6**
♦1952-53	**Montreal Canadiens**	**NHL**	**68**	**16**	**6**	**22**	**21**	**7**	**28**	**10**	**12**	**2**	**1**	**3**	**2**
1953-54	**Montreal Canadiens**	**NHL**	**70**	**13**	**8**	**21**	**18**	**10**	**28**	**22**	**11**	**4**	**0**	**4**	**4**
1954-55	**Montreal Canadiens**	**NHL**	**68**	**11**	**10**	**21**	**14**	**11**	**25**	**36**	**12**	**8**	**4**	**12**	**4**
♦1955-56	**Montreal Canadiens**	**NHL**	**70**	**14**	**18**	**32**	**19**	**21**	**40**	**10**	**10**	**1**	**5**	**6**	**12**
♦1956-57	**Montreal Canadiens**	**NHL**	**70**	**7**	**9**	**16**	**9**	**10**	**19**	**20**	**10**	**3**	**2**	**5**	**2**
♦1957-58	**Montreal Canadiens**	**NHL**	**42**	**2**	**3**	**5**	**2**	**3**	**5**	**8**	**7**	**0**	**0**	**0**	**2**
1958-59	Montreal Royals	QHL	57	9	13	22	....	....	....	40	8	1	3	4	2
	Rochester Americans	AHL	2	0	0	0	....	....	....	4	....	....	....	....	....
1959-60	Montreal Royals	EPHL	DID NOT PLAY – COACHING												
	NHL Totals		**601**	**105**	**99**	**204**	**138**	**117**	**255**	**147**	**91**	**23**	**17**	**40**	**38**

Played in NHL All-Star Game (1951, 1952, 1953, 1956, 1957)

Signed as a free agent by **Montreal**, October 18, 1945.

• CUSHENAN, Ian Ian Robertson

D – L. 6′2″, 195 lbs. b: Hamilton, Ont., 11/29/1933.

Season	Club	League	GP	G	A	Pts	AG	AA	APts	PIM	GP	G	A	Pts	PIM
1952-53	St. Catharines Teepees	OHA-Jr.	49	3	9	12	....	....	....	60	3	0	1	1	8
1953-54	St. Catharines Teepees	OHA-Jr.	59	5	25	30	....	....	....	86	15	0	3	3	23
	St. Catharines Teepees	M-Cup	11	0	1	1	....	....	....	34	....	....	....	....	....
1954-55	Cleveland Barons	AHL	56	1	13	14	....	....	....	84	4	0	0	0	12
	Quebec Aces	QHL	6	0	2	2	....	....	....	4	....	....	....	....	....
1955-56	Cleveland Barons	AHL	63	2	16	18	....	....	....	113	8	0	3	3	*38
1956-57	**Chicago Black Hawks**	**NHL**	**11**	**0**	**0**	**0**	**0**	**0**	**0**	**13**	....	....	....	....	....
	Cleveland Barons	AHL	54	0	17	17	....	....	....	151	....	....	....	....	....
1957-58	**Chicago Black Hawks**	**NHL**	**61**	**2**	**8**	**10**	**2**	**8**	**10**	**67**	....	....	....	....	....
♦1958-59	**Montreal Canadiens**	**NHL**	**35**	**1**	**2**	**3**	**1**	**2**	**3**	**28**	....	....	....	....	....
1959-60	**New York Rangers**	**NHL**	**17**	**0**	**1**	**1**	**0**	**1**	**1**	**22**	....	....	....	....	....
	Springfield Indians	AHL	49	0	12	12	....	....	....	67	10	0	1	1	8
1960-61	Springfield Indians	AHL	71	5	41	46	....	....	....	81	8	2	3	5	18
1961-62	Buffalo Bisons	AHL	69	2	21	23	....	....	....	84	11	0	3	3	8
1962-63	Buffalo Bisons	AHL	72	3	29	32	....	....	....	97	13	1	6	7	34
1963-64	**Detroit Red Wings**	**NHL**	**5**	**0**	**0**	**0**	**0**	**0**	**0**	**4**	....	....	....	....	....
	Pittsburgh Hornets	AHL	56	4	16	20	....	....	....	77	5	0	3	3	9
1964-65	Buffalo Bisons	AHL	69	4	23	27	....	....	....	89	9	3	0	3	12
1965-66	Buffalo Bisons	AHL	69	0	13	13	....	....	....	66	....	....	....	....	....
	NHL Totals		**129**	**3**	**11**	**14**	**3**	**11**	**14**	**134**	....	....	....	....	....

AHL Second All-Star Team (1963) • Played in NHL All-Star Game (1958)

Traded to **Chicago** by **Cleveland** (AHL) for Ron Ingram, September 4, 1956. Traded to **Montreal** by **Chicago** for cash, September, 1958. Traded to **Chicago** by **Montreal** for cash, June, 1959. Claimed by **NY Rangers** from **Chicago** in Intra-League Draft, June 10, 1959. Claimed by **Detroit** from **Buffalo** (AHL) in Inter-League Draft, June 4, 1963. Traded to **Chicago** by **Detroit** with John Miszuk and Art Stratton for Aut Erickson and Ron Murphy, June 9, 1964.

• DAHLSTROM, Cully Carl S. USHOF

C – L. 5′11″, 175 lbs. b: Minneapolis, MN, 7/3/1913.

Season	Club	League	GP	G	A	Pts	AG	AA	APts	PIM	GP	G	A	Pts	PIM
1931-32	Minneapolis Millers	CHL	30	9	1	10	....	....	....	10	....	....	....	....	....
1932-33	Minneapolis Millers	CHL	27	3	9	12	....	....	....	27	7	1	0	1	0
1933-34	Minneapolis Millers	CHL	43	13	15	28	....	....	....	20	3	2	*4	*6	0
1934-35	St. Paul Saints	CHL	44	16	20	36	....	....	....	30	8	3	0	3	2
1935-36	St. Paul Saints	AHA	46	20	23	43	....	....	....	26	3	0	0	0	4
1936-37	St. Paul Saints	AHA	47	23	19	42	....	....	....	25	3	1	0	1	0
♦1937-38	**Chicago Black Hawks**	**NHL**	**48**	**10**	**9**	**19**	**16**	**14**	**30**	**11**	**10**	**3**	**1**	**4**	**2**
1938-39	**Chicago Black Hawks**	**NHL**	**48**	**6**	**14**	**20**	**10**	**22**	**32**	**2**	....	....	....	....	....
1939-40	**Chicago Black Hawks**	**NHL**	**45**	**11**	**19**	**30**	**18**	**30**	**48**	**15**	**2**	**0**	**0**	**0**	**0**
1940-41	**Chicago Black Hawks**	**NHL**	**40**	**11**	**14**	**25**	**17**	**20**	**37**	**6**	**5**	**3**	**3**	**6**	**2**
1941-42	**Chicago Black Hawks**	**NHL**	**33**	**13**	**14**	**27**	**17**	**17**	**34**	**6**	**3**	**0**	**0**	**0**	**0**
1942-43	**Chicago Black Hawks**	**NHL**	**38**	**11**	**13**	**24**	**11**	**12**	**23**	**10**	....	....	....	....	....
1943-44	**Chicago Black Hawks**	**NHL**	**50**	**20**	**22**	**42**	**18**	**19**	**37**	**8**	**9**	**0**	**4**	**4**	**0**
1944-45	**Chicago Black Hawks**	**NHL**	**40**	**6**	**13**	**19**	**6**	**15**	**21**	**0**	....	....	....	....	....
	NHL Totals		**342**	**88**	**118**	**206**	**113**	**149**	**262**	**58**	**29**	**6**	**8**	**14**	**4**

CHL Second All-Star Team (1935) • AHA First All-Star Team (1936) • Won Calder Trophy (1938)

Traded to **Boston** by **Minneapolis** (CHL) for cash with Minneapolis retaining right to repurchase if he did not make the Bruins, June 27, 1932. Traded to **Chicago** by **St. Paul** (CHL) for cash with St. Paul retaining right to repurchase if he did not make the Black Hawks, January 27, 1935. Claimed by **Chicago** from **St. Paul** (AHA) in Inter-League Draft, May 9, 1937. Traded to **Seattle** (PCHL) by **Chicago** for cash, November 26, 1945.

• DALEY, Frank Frank Patrick "Dapper Dan"

LW/C – L. 5′11″, 178 lbs. b: Port Arthur, Ont., 8/22/1909 d: 10/15/1968.

Season	Club	League	GP	G	A	Pts	AG	AA	APts	PIM	GP	G	A	Pts	PIM
1926-27	Fort William Forts	TBJHL	STATISTICS NOT AVAILABLE												
1927-28	Fort William Forts	TBSHL	1	0	0	0	....	....	....	2	....	....	....	....	....
1928-29	Houghton Cougars	NMHL	STATISTICS NOT AVAILABLE												
	Detroit Cougars	**NHL**	**5**	**0**	**0**	**0**	**0**	**0**	**0**	**0**	**2**	**0**	**0**	**0**	**0**
1929-30	Detroit Olympics	IHL	30	1	0	1	....	....	....	19	2	0	0	0	0
1930-31	Detroit Olympics	IHL	47	4	8	12	....	....	....	52	....	....	....	....	....
1931-32	Cleveland Indians	IHL	44	2	3	5	....	....	....	54	....	....	....	....	....
1932-33	Cleveland Indians	IHL	39	14	8	22	....	....	....	45	....	....	....	....	....
1933-34	Windsor–London	IHL	42	9	9	18	....	....	....	30	6	2	5	7	2
1934-35	Cleveland Falcons	IHL	43	16	*25	41	....	....	....	44	2	0	0	0	0
1935-36	Cleveland Falcons	IHL	48	17	*36	*53	....	....	....	45	2	0	0	0	2
1936-37	Cleveland Barons	IAHL	17	3	4	7	....	....	....	11	....	....	....	....	....
	Springfield Indians	IAHL	16	3	4	7	....	....	....	4	4	0	1	1	0
1937-38	St. Louis Flyers	AHA	25	6	6	12	....	....	....	10	....	....	....	....	....
	Seattle Seahawks	PCHL	18	5	7	12	....	....	....	10	4	0	0	0	0
1938-39	Seattle Seahawks	PCHL	47	15	25	40	....	....	....	32	7	2	2	4	12
1939-40	Seattle Seahawks	PCHL	40	26	14	40	....	....	....	20	....	....	....	....	....
1940-41	Seattle Olympics	PCHL	47	28	31	59	....	....	....	32	2	0	0	0	0
1941-42	Philadelphia Rockets	AHL	56	16	35	51	....	....	....	12	....	....	....	....	....
1942-43	Hershey Bears	AHL	56	15	33	48	....	....	....	31	6	0	2	2	2

Season	Club	League	REGULAR SEASON GP	G	A	Pts	AG	AA	APts	PIM	PLAYOFFS GP	G	A	Pts	PIM
1943-44	Seattle Ironmen	PCHL	5	11	6	17	....	....	....	18	....	....	....	....	....
	Hershey Bears	AHL	41	3	12	15	....	....	....	14	3	0	0	0	0
1944-45	Seattle Stars	PCHL	STATISTICS NOT AVAILABLE												
	NHL Totals		**5**	**0**	**0**	**0**	**0**	**0**	**0**	**0**	**2**	**0**	**0**	**0**	**0**

Traded to **Detroit** by **Houghton** (NMHL) for cash, February 23, 1929. Traded to **Cleveland** (IHL) by **Detroit** for cash, October 28, 1931. Traded to **London** (IHL) by **Windsor** (IHL) with Ellis Pringle for Farrand Gillie, October 31, 1934.

• DAME, Bunny
Aurelia Napoleon
LW – L. 5'9", 160 lbs. b: Edmonton, Alta., 12/6/1913.

Season	Club	League	GP	G	A	Pts	AG	AA	APts	PIM	GP	G	A	Pts	PIM
1930-31	Edmonton Canadians	EJrHL	3	1	0	1	....	....	....	0	....	....	....	....	....
1931-32	Edmonton Canadians	EJrHL	13	*14	2	*16	....	....	....	....	4	2	0	2	2
1932-33	Edmonton Canadians	EJrHL	11	....	....	....	....	....	....	16	3	1	0	1	0
	Edmonton Canadians	M-Cup	3	3	0	3	....	....	....	4	....	....	....	....	....
1933-34	Rossland Miners	WKHL	18	14	5	19	....	....	....	5	....	....	....	....	....
1934-35	Rossland Miners	WKHL	12	8	5	13	....	....	....	19	....	....	....	....	....
1935-36	Rossland Miners	WKHL	16	7	9	16	....	....	....	15	2	1	1	2	0
1936-37	Trail Smoke Eaters	WKHL	13	10	*12	22	....	....	....	6	3	0	0	0	0
1937-38	Trail Smoke Eaters	WKHL	18	9	10	19	....	....	....	4	4	0	1	1	0
	Trail Smoke Eaters	Al-Cup	12	7	10	17	....	....	....	8	....	....	....	....	....
1938-39	Trail Smoke Eaters	X-Games	STATISTICS NOT AVAILABLE												
	Canada	WEC	7	*8	4	*12	....	....	....	....	....	....	....	....	....
1939-40	Trail Smoke Eaters	WKHL	27	28	34	62	....	....	....	14	4	4	3	7	6
	Trail Smoke Eaters	Al-Cup	3	0	1	1	....	....	....	0	....	....	....	....	....
1940-41	Trail Smoke Eaters	WKHL	28	23	26	49	....	....	....	26	3	2	1	3	2
	Trail Smoke Eaters	Al-Cup	6	1	2	3	....	....	....	6	....	....	....	....	....
1941-42	**Montreal Canadiens**	**NHL**	**34**	**2**	**5**	**7**	**3**	**6**	**9**	**4**	....	....	....	....	....
1942-43			MILITARY SERVICE												
1943-44			MILITARY SERVICE												
1944-45	Calgary Currie Army	CNDHL	14	6	9	15	....	....	....	6	3	0	2	2	2
1945-46	Calgary Stampeders	WCSHL	36	23	31	54	....	....	....	14	4	3	3	6	0
	Calgary Stampeders	Al-Cup	11	6	5	11	....	....	....	5	....	....	....	....	....
1946-47	Calgary Stampeders	WCSHL	17	10	17	27	....	....	....	12	7	7	4	11	2
	Calgary Stampeders	Al-Cup	18	7	4	11	....	....	....	16	....	....	....	....	....
1947-48	Calgary Stampeders	WCSHL	46	14	22	36	....	....	....	22	11	4	4	8	8
1948-49	Calgary Stampeders	WCSHL	46	17	20	37	....	....	....	34	4	0	0	0	2
1949-50	Calgary Stampeders	WCSHL	44	14	15	29	....	....	....	23	11	1	2	3	4
	Calgary Stampeders	Al-Cup	14	2	2	4	....	....	....	4	....	....	....	....	....
	NHL Totals		**34**	**2**	**5**	**7**	**3**	**6**	**9**	**4**	....	....	....	....	....

• Only regular season games played and penalty minute totals available for Edmonton (EJrHL) in 1932-33. Signed as a free agent by **Montreal**, October 16, 1941.

• DAMORE, Hank
Henry John "Lou Costello"
C – L. 5'6", 200 lbs. b: Niagara Falls, Ont., 7/17/1919.

Season	Club	League	GP	G	A	Pts	AG	AA	APts	PIM	GP	G	A	Pts	PIM
1935-36	Niagara Falls Cataracts	OHA-Jr.	8	4	3	7	....	....	....	10	2	2	0	2	0
1936-37	Stratford Midgets	OHA-Jr.	13	*19	7	*26	....	....	....	30	2	3	*2	*5	*17
1937-38	Stratford Midgets	OHA-Jr.	14	13	17	30	....	....	....	*43	7	5	1	6	12
1938-39	Verdun Maple Leafs	QSHL	14	3	4	7	....	....	....	26	....	....	....	....	....
	Stratford Majors	OHA-Sr.	10	0	3	3	....	....	....	16	2	0	1	1	2
1939-40	Stratford Canadians	MOHL	38	18	16	34	....	....	....	40	4	3	3	6	10
1940-41	London Mohawks	OHA-Sr.	18	3	5	8	....	....	....	28	....	....	....	....	....
	Toronto Peoples Credit	TIHL	9	3	4	7	....	....	....	28	3	0	2	2	0
1941-42	Detroit Mansfields	MOHL	17	11	26	37	....	....	....	8	....	....	....	....	....
	Toledo Babcocks	MOHL	....	....	....	....	....	....	....	....	7	5	*6	*11	*28
	Toronto Peoples Credit	TIHL	3	0	0	0	....	....	....	4	....	....	....	....	....
1942-43	Windsor Colonial Tools	MOHL	15	17	*30	*47	....	....	....	*38	7	*16	10	*26	*14
1943-44	**New York Rangers**	**NHL**	**4**	**1**	**0**	**1**	**1**	**0**	**1**	**2**	....	....	....	....	....
	New Haven Eagles	EAHL	12	*6	*16	*22	....	....	....	12	....	....	....	....	....
	Brooklyn Crescents	EAHL	28	*34	*29	*63	....	....	....	26	11	8	12	20	6
1944-45	Washington Lions	EAHL	1	1	0	1	....	....	....	0	....	....	....	....	....
	Hershey Bears	AHL	1	0	0	0	....	....	....	0	....	....	....	....	....
	Baltimore Orioles	EAHL	....	....	....	....	....	....	....	....	1	0	0	0	0
	New York Rovers	EAHL	39	19	41	60	....	....	....	40	12	8	9	17	14
1945-46	Philadelphia Falcons	EAHL	50	13	38	51	....	....	....	28	12	4	7	11	4
1946-47	Fresno Falcons	PCHL	59	25	55	80	....	....	....	30	2	0	2	2	0
1947-48	Los Angeles Monarchs	PCHL	43	12	23	35	....	....	....	30	....	....	....	....	....
	NHL Totals		**4**	**1**	**0**	**1**	**1**	**0**	**1**	**2**	....	....	....	....	....

• Brother of Nick • EAHL First All-Star Team (1944) • Won John Carlin Trophy (Top Scorer - EAHL) (1944)

• DARRAGH, Harold
Harold Edward "Howl"
LW – R. 5'10", 145 lbs. b: Ottawa, Ont., 9/13/1902 d: 10/28/1993.

Season	Club	League	GP	G	A	Pts	AG	AA	APts	PIM	GP	G	A	Pts	PIM
1918-19	Ottawa CPR Bluebirds	OCHL	STATISTICS NOT AVAILABLE												
1919-20	Ottawa Gunners	OCHL	7	4	0	4	....	....	....	....	....	....	....	....	....
1920-21	Ottawa Gunners	OCHL	12	8	0	8	....	....	....	....	7	5	*6	11	3
1921-22	Ottawa Gunners	OCHL	14	12	*7	19	....	....	....	0	6	*12	*7	*19	0
1922-23	Ottawa Gunners	OCHL	1	0	0	0	....	....	....	0	....	....	....	....	....
	Pittsburgh Yellowjackets	USAHA	16	8	0	8	....	....	....	....	....	....	....	....	....
1923-24	Ottawa New Edinburghs	OCHL	12	6	*4	10	....	....	....	....	2	0	0	0	....
1924-25	Pittsburgh Yellowjackets	USAHA	40	14	0	14	....	....	....	....	8	3	0	3	....
1925-26	**Pittsburgh Pirates**	**NHL**	**35**	**10**	**7**	**17**	**17**	**46**	**63**	**6**	**2**	**1**	**0**	**1**	**0**
1926-27	**Pittsburgh Pirates**	**NHL**	**42**	**12**	**3**	**15**	**21**	**16**	**37**	**4**	....	....	....	....	....
1927-28	**Pittsburgh Pirates**	**NHL**	**44**	**13**	**2**	**15**	**26**	**11**	**37**	**16**	**2**	**0**	**1**	**1**	**0**
1928-29	**Pittsburgh Pirates**	**NHL**	**43**	**9**	**3**	**12**	**26**	**20**	**46**	**6**	....	....	....	....	....
1929-30	**Pittsburgh Pirates**	**NHL**	**42**	**15**	**17**	**32**	**21**	**40**	**61**	**6**	....	....	....	....	....
1930-31	**Philadelphia Quakers**	**NHL**	**10**	**1**	**1**	**2**	**2**	**3**	**5**	**2**	....	....	....	....	....
	Boston Bruins	**NHL**	**25**	**2**	**4**	**6**	**4**	**12**	**16**	**4**	**5**	**0**	**1**	**1**	**2**
♦1931-32	**Toronto Maple Leafs**	**NHL**	**48**	**5**	**10**	**15**	**8**	**22**	**30**	**6**	**7**	**0**	**1**	**1**	**2**
1932-33	**Toronto Maple Leafs**	**NHL**	**19**	**1**	**2**	**3**	**2**	**4**	**6**	**0**	....	....	....	....	....
	Syracuse Stars	IHL	24	7	13	20	....	....	....	4	6	2	0	2	0
1933-34	Syracuse Stars	IHL	44	9	10	19	....	....	....	12	6	0	1	1	0
1934-35			DID NOT PLAY												
1935-36	Pittsburgh Yellowjackets	IHL	41	7	14	21	....	....	....	4	....	....	....	....	....
	NHL Totals		**308**	**68**	**49**	**117**	**127**	**174**	**301**	**50**	**16**	**1**	**3**	**4**	**4**

• Brother of Jack • OCHL Second All-Star Team (1920, 1921) • OCHL First All-Star Team (1922)

Signed as a free agent by **Pittsburgh**, September 26, 1925. Transferred to **Philadelphia** after **Pittsburgh** franchise relocated, October 18, 1930. Traded to **Boston** by **Philadelphia** for Ron Lyons and Bill Hutton, December 8, 1930. Claimed on waivers by **Toronto** from **Boston**, June 8, 1931. Traded to **Syracuse** (IHL) by **Toronto** for Bill Thoms, January 3, 1933.

• DARRAGH, Jack
John Proctor **HHOF**
RW – R. 5'10", 168 lbs. b: Ottawa, Ont., 12/4/1890 d: 6/25/1924.

Season	Club	League	GP	G	A	Pts	AG	AA	APts	PIM	GP	G	A	Pts	PIM
1908-09	Ottawa Stewartons	OCHL	STATISTICS NOT AVAILABLE												
1909-10	Ottawa Stewartons	OCHL	5	11	0	11	....	....	....	11	1	0	0	0	3
	Ottawa Cliffsides	OCHL	....	....	....	....	....	....	....	....	3	4	0	4	0
1910-11	Ottawa Stewartons	OCHL	3	7	0	7	....	....	....	0	....	....	....	....	....
♦	Ottawa Senators	NHA	16	18	0	18	....	....	....	36	2	0	0	0	6
1911-12	Ottawa Senators	NHA	17	15	0	15	....	....	....	10	....	....	....	....	....
	East All-Stars	X-Games	3	4	0	4	....	....	....	8	....	....	....	....	....
1912-13	Ottawa Senators	NHA	20	15	0	15	....	....	....	16	....	....	....	....	....
1913-14	Ottawa Senators	NHA	20	23	5	28	....	....	....	69	....	....	....	....	....
1914-15	Ottawa Senators	NHA	18	11	2	13	....	....	....	32	5	4	0	4	9
1915-16	Ottawa Senators	NHA	21	16	5	21	....	....	....	41	....	....	....	....	....
1916-17	Ottawa Senators	NHA	20	24	4	28	....	....	....	17	2	2	0	2	3
1917-18	**Ottawa Senators**	**NHL**	**18**	**14**	**5**	**19**	**18**	**21**	**39**	**26**	....	....	....	....	....
1918-19	**Ottawa Senators**	**NHL**	**14**	**11**	**3**	**14**	**20**	**16**	**36**	**33**	**5**	**2**	**0**	**2**	**3**
1919-20	**Ottawa Senators**	**NHL**	**23**	**22**	**14**	**36**	**25**	**49**	**74**	**22**	....	....	....	....	....
♦	Ottawa Senators	St-Cup	5	5	2	7	....	....	....	3	....	....	....	....	....
1920-21	**Ottawa Senators**	**NHL**	**24**	**11**	***15**	**26**	**14**	**61**	**75**	**20**	**2**	**0**	**0**	**0**	**2**
♦	Ottawa Senators	St-Cup	5	5	0	5	....	....	....	12	....	....	....	....	....
1921-22			OUT OF HOCKEY – RETIRED												
♦1922-23	**Ottawa Senators**	**NHL**	**24**	**6**	**9**	**15**	**10**	**35**	**45**	**10**	**2**	**1**	**0**	**1**	**2**
1923-24	**Ottawa Senators**	**NHL**	**18**	**2**	**0**	**2**	**4**	**0**	**4**	**2**	**2**	**0**	**0**	**0**	**2**
	NHL Totals		**121**	**66**	**46**	**112**	**91**	**182**	**273**	**113**	**11**	**3**	**0**	**3**	**9**
	Other Major League Totals		132	122	16	138	....	....	....	221	9	6	0	6	18

• Brother of Harold

Signed as a free agent by **Ottawa** (NHA), December 27, 1910. Rights retained by **Ottawa** after NHA folded, November 26, 1917. Signed as a free agent by **Ottawa**, December 4, 1922.
• Died of peritonitis (ruptured appendix), June 25, 1924.

• DAVIDSON, Bob
Robert Earl
LW – L. 5'11", 185 lbs. b: Toronto, Ont., 2/10/1912 d: 9/26/1996.

Season	Club	League	GP	G	A	Pts	AG	AA	APts	PIM	GP	G	A	Pts	PIM
1928-29	Toronto Canoe Club	OHA-Jr.	STATISTICS NOT AVAILABLE												
1929-30	Toronto City Services	TMHL	STATISTICS NOT AVAILABLE												
	Toronto Canoe Club	OHA-Jr.	9	0	0	0	....	....	....	2	....	....	....	....	....
1930-31	Toronto Canoe Club	OHA-Jr.	9	6	4	10	....	....	....	10	2	1	0	1	2
1931-32	Toronto Canoe Club	OHA-Jr.	8	6	3	9	....	....	....	7	1	1	0	1	0
	Toronto City Services	TMHL	12	6	3	9	....	....	....	10	2	1	0	1	0
1932-33	Toronto Marlboros	OHA-Jr.	21	8	8	16	....	....	....	15	2	2	0	2	4
	Toronto City Services	TMHL	18	11	5	16	....	....	....	18	6	2	0	2	14
1933-34	Toronto Marlboros	OHA-Sr.	6	6	2	8	....	....	....	6	....	....	....	....	....
1934-35	**Toronto Maple Leafs**	**NHL**	**5**	**0**	**0**	**0**	**0**	**0**	**0**	**6**	....	....	....	....	....
	Syracuse Stars	IHL	28	4	12	16	....	....	....	17	2	0	0	0	2
1935-36	**Toronto Maple Leafs**	**NHL**	**35**	**4**	**4**	**8**	**8**	**8**	**16**	**32**	**9**	**1**	**3**	**4**	**2**
	Syracuse Stars	IHL	13	3	4	7	....	....	....	22	....	....	....	....	....
1936-37	**Toronto Maple Leafs**	**NHL**	**46**	**8**	**7**	**15**	**13**	**13**	**26**	**43**	**2**	**0**	**0**	**0**	**5**
1937-38	**Toronto Maple Leafs**	**NHL**	**48**	**3**	**17**	**20**	**5**	**27**	**32**	**52**	**4**	**0**	**2**	**2**	**7**
1938-39	**Toronto Maple Leafs**	**NHL**	**47**	**4**	**10**	**14**	**7**	**16**	**23**	**29**	**10**	**1**	**1**	**2**	**6**
1939-40	**Toronto Maple Leafs**	**NHL**	**48**	**8**	**18**	**26**	**13**	**28**	**41**	**56**	**10**	**0**	**3**	**3**	**16**
1940-41	**Toronto Maple Leafs**	**NHL**	**37**	**3**	**6**	**9**	**5**	**9**	**14**	**39**	**7**	**0**	**2**	**2**	**7**
♦1941-42	**Toronto Maple Leafs**	**NHL**	**37**	**6**	**20**	**26**	**8**	**24**	**32**	**39**	**13**	**1**	**2**	**3**	**20**
1942-43	**Toronto Maple Leafs**	**NHL**	**50**	**13**	**23**	**36**	**13**	**21**	**34**	**20**	**6**	**1**	**2**	**3**	**7**
1943-44	**Toronto Maple Leafs**	**NHL**	**47**	**19**	**28**	**47**	**17**	**25**	**42**	**21**	**5**	**0**	**0**	**0**	**4**
♦1944-45	**Toronto Maple Leafs**	**NHL**	**50**	**17**	**18**	**35**	**17**	**21**	**38**	**49**	**13**	**1**	**2**	**3**	**2**
1945-46	**Toronto Maple Leafs**	**NHL**	**41**	**9**	**9**	**18**	**11**	**13**	**24**	**12**	....	....	....	....	....
1946-47	St. Louis Flyers	AHL	DID NOT PLAY – COACHING												
	NHL Totals		**491**	**94**	**160**	**254**	**117**	**205**	**322**	**398**	**79**	**5**	**17**	**22**	**76**

• DAVIDSON, Gord
Gordon John
D – L. 5'11", 188 lbs. b: Stratford, Ont., 8/5/1918 Deceased.

Season	Club	League	GP	G	A	Pts	AG	AA	APts	PIM	GP	G	A	Pts	PIM
1935-36	Moose Jaw Canucks	S-SJHL	3	1	0	1	....	....	....	2	1	1	1	2	0
1936-37	Moose Jaw Canucks	S-SJHL	5	3	0	3	....	....	....	6	5	1	3	4	6
1937-38	Moose Jaw Canucks	S-SJHL	6	2	4	6	....	....	....	0	7	1	3	4	6
1938-39	Regina Aces	S-SSHL	27	1	3	4	....	....	....	22	....	....	....	....	....
1939-40	Regina Aces	S-SSHL	17	1	3	4	....	....	....	23	9	1	0	1	0
1940-41	Regina Rangers	S-SSHL	32	0	5	5	....	....	....	30	8	0	0	0	6
	Regina Rangers	Al-Cup	14	0	2	2	....	....	....	31	....	....	....	....	....
1941-42	New York Rovers	EAHL	58	9	31	40	....	....	....	55	7	1	6	7	6
1942-43	**New York Rangers**	**NHL**	**35**	**2**	**3**	**5**	**2**	**3**	**5**	**4**	....	....	....	....	....
1943-44	**New York Rangers**	**NHL**	**16**	**1**	**3**	**4**	**1**	**3**	**4**	**4**	....	....	....	....	....
	Buffalo Bisons	AHL	30	2	15	17	....	....	....	19	9	1	6	7	2
1944-45	Buffalo Bisons	AHL	59	10	20	30	....	....	....	20	6	1	0	1	4
1945-46	New Haven Eagles	AHL	17	1	3	4	....	....	....	16	....	....	....	....	....
	Cleveland Barons	AHL	43	5	20	25	....	....	....	16	12	1	5	6	4
1946-47	Cleveland Barons	AHL	58	5	10	15	....	....	....	14	4	0	0	0	0
1947-48	Cleveland Barons	AHL	58	2	15	17	....	....	....	16	9	2	2	4	2
1948-49	Cleveland Barons	AHL	62	5	20	25	....	....	....	10	5	0	0	0	0
1949-50	Buffalo Bisons	AHL	67	4	19	23	....	....	....	25	1	0	0	0	0
1950-51	Springfield Indians	AHL	54	5	24	29	....	....	....	10	3	0	1	1	4
	NHL Totals		**51**	**3**	**6**	**9**	**3**	**6**	**9**	**8**	....	....	....	....	....

EAHL First All-Star Team (1942) • AHL First All-Star Team (1945)

Loaned to **Montreal** (Buffalo-AHL) by **NY Rangers** with the trade of Roger Leger for Bob Dill, January 4, 1944. Traded to **Cleveland** (AHL) by **NY Rangers** for Harvey Fraser, November 25, 1945. Traded to **Buffalo** (AHL) by **Cleveland** (AHL) for Les Douglas, June 15, 1949. Traded to **Springfield** (AHL) by **Buffalo** (AHL) for cash, September 9, 1950.

• DAVIE, Bob
Robert Howard "Pinkie"
D – R. 6', 170 lbs. b: Beausejour, Man., 9/12/1912 d: 10/27/1990.

			REGULAR SEASON								PLAYOFFS				
Season	Club	League	GP	G	A	Pts	AG	AA	APts	PIM	GP	G	A	Pts	PIM
1930-31	Winnipeg Monarchs	WJrHL	1	0	0	0	....	....	....	2	4	1	0	1	0
1931-32	Winnipeg Monarchs	MJHL	12	1	2	3	....	....	....	36	4	1	0	1	4
	Winnipeg Monarchs	M-Cup	8	2	1	3	....	....	....	8	....	....	....	....	....
1932-33	Boston Cubs	Can-Am	46	4	7	11	....	....	....	70	7	1	3	4	4
1933-34	**Boston Bruins**	**NHL**	**9**	**0**	**0**	**0**	**0**	**0**	**0**	**6**	....	....	....	....	....
	Boston Cubs	Can-Am	33	6	8	14	....	....	....	47	5	0	1	1	11
1934-35	**Boston Bruins**	**NHL**	**30**	**0**	**1**	**1**	**0**	**2**	**2**	**17**	....	....	....	....	....
	Boston Cubs	Can-Am	19	3	5	8	....	....	....	16	....	....	....	....	....
1935-36	**Boston Bruins**	**NHL**	**2**	**0**	**0**	**0**	**0**	**0**	**0**	**2**	....	....	....	....	....
	Boston Cubs	Can-Am	23	2	8	10	....	....	....	29	....	....	....	....	....
	Springfield Indians	Can-Am	6	0	0	0	....	....	....	8	....	....	....	....	....
1936-37	Minneapolis Millers	AHA	44	9	8	17	....	....	....	51	6	2	3	5	6
1937-38	Minneapolis Millers	AHA	10	1	3	4	....	....	....	10	....	....	....	....	....
	Springfield Indians	IAHL	37	2	4	6	....	....	....	59	....	....	....	....	....
1938-39			DID NOT PLAY – INJURED												
1939-40			DID NOT PLAY – INJURED												
1940-41	Dauphin Dolphins	MIHA	....	....	....	....	....	....	....	....	7	2	2	4	6
	NHL Totals		**41**	**0**	**1**	**1**	**0**	**2**	**2**	**25**	....	....	....	....	....

Loaned to **Minneapolis** (AHA) by **Springfield** (IAHL) for cash, November 7, 1937 and recalled December, 1937. • Missed entire 1938-39 and 1939-40 seasons recovering from injuries suffered in industrial accident, June, 1938.

• DAVIES, Buck
Kenneth George
C – L. 5'6", 162 lbs. b: Bowmanville, Ont., 8/10/1922.

			REGULAR SEASON								PLAYOFFS				
Season	Club	League	GP	G	A	Pts	AG	AA	APts	PIM	GP	G	A	Pts	PIM
1941-42	Oshawa Generals	OHA-Jr.	24	17	21	38	....	....	....	2	12	9	6	15	4
	Oshawa Generals	M-Cup	11	6	6	12	....	....	....	6	....	....	....	....	....
1942-43	Toronto Army Daggers	OHA-Sr.	10	1	3	4	....	....	....	2	....	....	....	....	....
1943-44			MILITARY SERVICE												
1944-45	Toronto Army Shamrocks	TIHL	30	14	15	29	....	....	....	15	4	3	3	6	2
	Toronto Army Daggers	TNDHL	5	6	4	10	....	....	....	0	3	3	4	7	2
	Toronto Army Daggers	OHA-Sr.	4	3	0	3	....	....	....	2	....	....	....	....	....
1945-46	Toronto Mahers	TIHL	31	18	21	39	....	....	....	13	10	6	13	19	4
1946-47	St. Paul Saints	USHL	58	19	45	64	....	....	....	26	....	....	....	....	....
1947-48	New Haven Ramblers	AHL	67	29	43	72	....	....	....	35	4	0	1	1	9
	New York Rangers	**NHL**	....	....	....	....	....	....	....	....	**1**	**0**	**0**	**0**	**0**
1948-49	New Haven Ramblers	AHL	67	32	26	58	....	....	....	20	....	....	....	....	....
1949-50	Providence Reds	AHL	51	13	22	35	....	....	....	10	1	0	0	0	0
1950-51	Providence Reds	AHL	62	12	30	42	....	....	....	14	....	....	....	....	....
1951-52	Providence Reds	AHL	22	6	11	17	....	....	....	10	....	....	....	....	....
	Cleveland Barons	AHL	42	12	34	46	....	....	....	16	5	1	0	1	4
1952-53	Buffalo Bisons	AHL	59	9	20	29	....	....	....	25	....	....	....	....	....
1953-54	Providence Reds	AHL	56	22	27	49	....	....	....	26	....	....	....	....	....
1954-55	Providence Reds	AHL	56	17	32	49	....	....	....	42	....	....	....	....	....
1955-56	Providence Reds	AHL	34	12	14	26	....	....	....	40	9	2	1	3	0
1956-57	Providence Reds	AHL	60	18	25	43	....	....	....	76	5	0	0	0	4
1957-58	Providence Reds	AHL	58	7	15	22	....	....	....	33	1	0	0	0	0
1958-59	Washington Presidents	EHL	48	17	31	48	....	....	....	34	....	....	....	....	....
1959-60	Washington Presidents	EHL	64	27	36	63	....	....	....	40	....	....	....	....	....
1960-61	Philadelphia Ramblers	EHL	62	12	34	46	....	....	....	17	2	0	0	0	0
	NHL Totals		....	....	....	....	....	....	....	....	**1**	**0**	**0**	**0**	**0**

USHL Second All-Star Team (1947) • Won Outstanding Rookie Cup (Top Rookie - USHL) (1947)

Traded to **Providence** (AHL) by **NY Rangers** to complete transaction that sent Allan Stanley to NY Rangers (December, 1948), June, 1949. Traded to **Cleveland** (AHL) by **Boston** (Providence-AHL) with Vic Lynn for Joe Lund and Jean-Paul Gladu, December 10, 1951.

• DAVIS, Bob
Robert Amos "Friday"
RW – R. 6', 202 lbs. b: Lachine, Que., 2/2/1899 d: 7/5/1970.

			REGULAR SEASON								PLAYOFFS				
Season	Club	League	GP	G	A	Pts	AG	AA	APts	PIM	GP	G	A	Pts	PIM
1922-23	Eveleth Rangers	USAHA	19	3	0	3	....	....	....	....	....	....	....	....	....
1923-24	Fort William Forts	TBSHL	12	2	2	4	....	....	....	2	....	....	....	....	....
1924-25	Fort William Forts	TBSHL	19	2	2	4	....	....	....	....	....	....	....	....	....
1925-26	Fort William Forts	TBSHL	17	4	0	4	....	....	....	22	3	1	0	1	*12
1926-27	Fort William Forts	TBSHL	20	10	1	11	....	....	....	18	2	0	0	0	0
1927-28	Fort William Forts	TBSHL	21	10	3	13	....	....	....	12	2	0	0	0	2
1928-29	Duluth Hornets	AHA	40	6	3	9	....	....	....	79	....	....	....	....	....
1929-30	Duluth Hornets	AHA	48	7	4	11	....	....	....	61	4	0	0	0	2
1930-31	Duluth Hornets	AHA	48	7	8	15	....	....	....	68	4	0	1	1	4
1931-32	Duluth Hornets	AHA	48	10	6	16	....	....	....	64	8	1	0	1	8
1932-33	**Detroit Red Wings**	**NHL**	**3**	**0**	**0**	**0**	**0**	**0**	**0**	**0**	....	....	....	....	....
	Detroit Olympics	IHL	22	1	1	2	....	....	....	26	....	....	....	....	....
1933-34	Montreal LaFontaine	MCHL	16	5	7	12	....	....	....	2	....	....	....	....	....
1934-35	Montreal LaFontaine	MCHL	19	2	4	6	....	....	....	4	....	....	....	....	....
1935-36	Fort William Wanderers	TBSHL	DID NOT PLAY – COACHING												
	NHL Totals		**3**	**0**	**0**	**0**	**0**	**0**	**0**	**0**					

Signed as a free agent by **Duluth** (AHA), October 30, 1928. Signed as a free agent by **Detroit**, December 5, 1932. Traded to **Buffalo** (IAHL) by **Detroit** with Tip O'Neill and John Newman for Gamey Lederman, September 24, 1933.

• DAVIS, Lorne
Lorne Austin
RW – R. 5'11", 190 lbs. b: Regina, Sask., 7/20/1930.

			REGULAR SEASON								PLAYOFFS				
Season	Club	League	GP	G	A	Pts	AG	AA	APts	PIM	GP	G	A	Pts	PIM
1947-48	Regina Pats	S-SJHL	28	8	5	13	....	....	....	7	5	1	1	2	2
1948-49	Regina Pats	WCJHL	26	16	12	28	....	....	....	36	7	5	3	8	4
1949-50	Regina Pats	WCJHL	40	25	17	42	....	....	....	22	9	6	1	7	8
	Regina Pats	M-Cup	17	7	5	12	....	....	....	6	....	....	....	....	....
1950-51	Montreal Royals	QMHL	50	14	17	31	....	....	....	4	7	5	1	6	4
	Victoria Cougars	PCHL	3	1	1	2	....	....	....	0	....	....	....	....	....
1951-52	**Montreal Canadiens**	**NHL**	**3**	**1**	**1**	**2**	**1**	**1**	**2**	**2**	....	....	....	....	....
	Vancouver Canucks	PCHL	15	11	10	21	....	....	....	4	....	....	....	....	....
	Buffalo Bisons	AHL	48	19	19	38	....	....	....	18	3	1	0	1	0
1952-53	Buffalo Bisons	AHL	64	33	34	67	....	....	....	49	....	....	....	....	....
♦	**Montreal Canadiens**	**NHL**	....	....	....	....	....	....	....	....	**7**	**1**	**1**	**2**	**2**
1953-54	**Montreal Canadiens**	**NHL**	**37**	**6**	**4**	**10**	**8**	**5**	**13**	**2**	**11**	**2**	**0**	**2**	**8**
	Montreal Royals	QHL	37	13	22	35	....	....	....	25	....	....	....	....	....
1954-55	Montreal Royals	QHL	1	0	2	2	....	....	....	0	....	....	....	....	....
	Chicago Black Hawks	**NHL**	**8**	**0**	**0**	**0**	**0**	**0**	**0**	**4**	....	....	....	....	....
	Detroit Red Wings	**NHL**	**22**	**0**	**5**	**5**	**0**	**6**	**6**	**2**	....	....	....	....	....
	Edmonton Flyers	WHL	29	11	5	16	....	....	....	10	9	*7	4	*11	2
	Edmonton Flyers	Ed-Cup	7	3	2	5	....	....	....	6	....	....	....	....	....
1955-56	**Boston Bruins**	**NHL**	**15**	**0**	**1**	**1**	**0**	**1**	**1**	**0**	....	....	....	....	....
	Hershey Bears	AHL	45	19	21	40	....	....	....	42	....	....	....	....	....
1956-57	Hershey Bears	AHL	64	16	24	40	....	....	....	55	7	1	0	1	2
1957-58	Hershey Bears	AHL	68	18	16	34	....	....	....	36	11	0	0	0	12
1958-59	Providence Reds	AHL	70	22	24	46	....	....	....	65	....	....	....	....	....
1959-60	**Boston Bruins**	**NHL**	**10**	**1**	**1**	**2**	**1**	**1**	**2**	**10**	....	....	....	....	....
	Providence Reds	AHL	54	19	32	51	....	....	....	24	....	....	....	....	....
	Calgary Spurs	Al-Cup	3	1	0	1	....	....	....	0	....	....	....	....	....
1960-61	Winnipeg Warriors	WHL	70	22	22	44	....	....	....	18	....	....	....	....	....
1961-62			REINSTATED AS AN AMATEUR												
1962-63	Regina Capitals	SSHL	20	14	16	30	....	....	....	14	7	3	11	14	8
1963-64	Regina Capitals	SSHL	37	43	47	90	....	....	....	4	1	1	0	1	0
1964-65	Muskegon Zephyrs	IHL	67	20	39	59	....	....	....	30	....	....	....	....	....
1965-66	Regina Capitals	SSHL	11	8	19	27	....	....	....	0	....	....	....	....	....
	Canada	WEC-A	7	1	0	1	....	....	....	2	....	....	....	....	....
1966-67	Regina Capitals	SSHL	33	22	22	44	....	....	....	17	3	0	0	0	0
	NHL Totals		**95**	**8**	**12**	**20**	**10**	**14**	**24**	**20**	**18**	**3**	**1**	**4**	**10**

AHL Second All-Star Team (1953) • Played in NHL All-Star Game (1953)

Traded to **Chicago** by **Montreal** for Ike Hildebrand and future considerations, October 13, 1954. Traded to **Detroit** by **Chicago** for Metro Prystai, November 9, 1954. Traded to **Boston** by **Detroit** with Terry Sawchuk, Vic Stasiuk and Marcel Bonin for Ed Sandford, Real Chevrifils, Norm Corcoran, Gilles Boisvert and Warren Godfrey, June 3, 1955.

• DAVISON, Murray
Murray Dennis
D – R. 6'2", 190 lbs. b: Brantford, Ont., 6/10/1938 d: 1/13/2000.

			REGULAR SEASON								PLAYOFFS				
Season	Club	League	GP	G	A	Pts	AG	AA	APts	PIM	GP	G	A	Pts	PIM
1955-56	Barrie Flyers	OHA-Jr.	47	2	7	9	....	....	....	82	18	0	2	2	32
1956-57	Barrie Flyers	OHA-Jr.	52	6	7	13	....	....	....	53	3	0	0	0	8
1957-58	Barrie Flyers	OHA-Jr.	51	7	20	27	....	....	....	171	4	2	0	2	12
1958-59	Quebec Aces	QHL	3	0	0	0	....	....	....	0	....	....	....	....	....
	Kitchener Dutchmen	OHA-Sr.	54	3	13	16	....	....	....	*125	11	1	3	4	*36
1959-60	Kitchener Dutchmen	OHA-Sr.	48	0	11	11	....	....	....	63	8	2	4	6	4
1960-61	Cleveland Barons	AHL	1	0	0	0	....	....	....	0	4	0	0	0	0
	Greensboro Generals	EHL	64	4	37	41	....	....	....	106	9	0	4	4	10
1961-62	Cleveland Barons	AHL	65	1	6	7	....	....	....	53	6	0	0	0	0
1962-63	Cleveland Barons	AHL	3	0	0	0	....	....	....	6	....	....	....	....	....
	Springfield Indians	AHL	33	3	8	11	....	....	....	20	....	....	....	....	....
1963-64	Springfield Indians	AHL	DID NOT PLAY – SUSPENDED												
1964-65	Welland Wildcats	OHA-Sr.	25	5	10	15	....	....	....	33	....	....	....	....	....
1965-66	**Boston Bruins**	**NHL**	**1**	**0**	**0**	**0**	**0**	**0**	**0**	**0**	....	....	....	....	....
	Oklahoma City Blazers	CPHL	58	1	12	13	....	....	....	88	9	0	6	6	6
1966-67	Oklahoma City Blazers	CPHL	41	0	6	6	....	....	....	83	5	1	0	1	8
1967-68	Oklahoma City Blazers	CPHL	57	3	13	16	....	....	....	128	5	0	2	2	25
1968-69	Oklahoma City Blazers	CHL	28	1	3	4	....	....	....	63	7	0	1	1	21
1969-70	Oklahoma City Blazers	CHL	38	0	4	4	....	....	....	176	....	....	....	....	....
1970-71	Oklahoma City Blazers	CHL	1	0	0	0	....	....	....	0	....	....	....	....	....
1971/76			OUT OF HOCKEY – RETIRED												
1976-77	Oklahoma City Blazers	CHL	29	1	5	6	....	....	....	81	....	....	....	....	....
	NHL Totals		**1**	**0**	**0**	**0**	**0**	**0**	**0**	**0**					

Traded to **Springfield** (AHL) by **Cleveland** (AHL) with Wayne Larkin for Dick Mattiussi, October 17, 1962. • Suspended for entire 1963-64 season by Springfield (AHL) for refusing to report to team, September, 1963.

• DAWES, Bobby
Robert James
D/C – L. 6'1", 170 lbs. b: Saskatoon, Sask., 11/29/1924.

			REGULAR SEASON								PLAYOFFS				
Season	Club	League	GP	G	A	Pts	AG	AA	APts	PIM	GP	G	A	Pts	PIM
1942-43	Saskatoon Quakers	N-SJHL	7	7	6	13	....	....	....	20	3	3	1	4	0
	Saskatoon Quakers	M-Cup	8	4	8	12	....	....	....	4	....	....	....	....	....
1943-44	Oshawa Generals	OHA-Jr.	26	8	19	27	....	....	....	32	10	2	4	6	4
	Oshawa Generals	M-Cup	9	5	7	12	....	....	....	14	....	....	....	....	....
1944-45	Saskatoon Falcons	N-SJHL	2	2	3	5	....	....	....	0	....	....	....	....	....
1945-46	New Haven Eagles	AHL	57	9	18	27	....	....	....	33	....	....	....	....	....
1946-47	**Toronto Maple Leafs**	**NHL**	**1**	**0**	**0**	**0**	**0**	**0**	**0**	**0**	....	....	....	....	....
	Springfield Indians	AHL	42	4	17	21	....	....	....	27	2	0	2	2	0
1947-48	Pittsburgh Hornets	AHL	68	13	31	44	....	....	....	35	2	1	1	2	5
♦1948-49	**Toronto Maple Leafs**	**NHL**	**5**	**1**	**0**	**1**	**1**	**0**	**1**	**0**	**9**	**0**	**0**	**0**	**2**
	Pittsburgh Hornets	AHL	55	16	35	51	....	....	....	31	....	....	....	....	....
1949-50	**Toronto Maple Leafs**	**NHL**	**11**	**1**	**2**	**3**	**1**	**2**	**3**	**2**	....	....	....	....	....
	Cleveland Barons	AHL	47	3	19	22	....	....	....	41	9	1	3	4	10
1950-51	Buffalo Bisons	AHL	10	2	3	5	....	....	....	6	....	....	....	....	....
	Cincinnati Mohawks	AHL	15	4	3	7	....	....	....	4	....	....	....	....	....
	Seattle Ironmen	PCHL	20	2	11	13	....	....	....	10	....	....	....	....	....
	Montreal Canadiens	**NHL**	**15**	**0**	**5**	**5**	**0**	**6**	**6**	**4**	**1**	**0**	**0**	**0**	**0**
1951-52	Montreal Royals	QMHL	5	0	0	0	....	....	....	2	....	....	....	....	....
	Buffalo Bisons	AHL	2	0	3	3	....	....	....	0	....	....	....	....	....
1952-53	Montreal Royals	QMHL	DID NOT PLAY – INJURED												
1953-54	Galt Black Hawks	OHA-Jr.	DID NOT PLAY – COACHING												
	Sudbury Wolves	NOHA	19	2	10	12	....	....	....	4	10	0	5	5	4
1954-55	New Westminster Royals	WHL	12	3	3	6	....	....	....	2	....	....	....	....	....
	Kelowna Packers	OSHL	51	12	23	35	....	....	....	34	4	1	3	4	0
1955-56	New Westminster Royals	WHL	56	8	25	33	....	....	....	47	4	2	1	3	0
1956-57	Kamloops Chiefs	OSHL	54	4	42	46	....	....	....	52	12	5	6	11	15
1957-58	Kamloops Chiefs	OSHL	48	11	35	46	....	....	....	36	15	0	5	5	2
1958-59	Johnstown Jets	EHL	37	14	23	37	....	....	....	24	12	4	6	10	8
1959-60	Johnstown Jets	EHL	50	19	40	59	....	....	....	8	13	0	*12	12	9
1960-61	Johnstown Jets	EHL	56	12	26	38	....	....	....	12	11	4	7	11	2
1961-62	Johnstown Jets	EHL	68	16	30	46	....	....	....	24	13	6	8	14	2
1962-63	Saskatoon Quakers	SSHL	27	12	23	35	....	....	....	14	6	2	7	9	2
1963-64	Saskatoon Quakers	SSHL	8	8	12	20	....	....	....	0	11	4	4	8	4
	Saskatoon Quakers	Al-Cup	6	0	1	1	....	....	....	4	....	....	....	....	....

			REGULAR SEASON								PLAYOFFS				
Season	Club	League	GP	G	A	Pts	AG	AA	APts	PIM	GP	G	A	Pts	PIM
1964-65	Yorkton Terriers	SSHL	2	0	2	2	....	....	....	2	11	0	3	3	12
1965-66	Yorkton Terriers	SSHL	DID NOT PLAY – COACHING												
1966-67	Saskatoon Quakers	SSHL	16	2	11	13	....	....	....	4	14	1	9	10	2
	NHL Totals		**32**	**2**	**7**	**9**	**2**	**8**	**10**	**6**	**10**	**0**	**0**	**0**	**2**

OSHL First All-Star Team (1955) • OSHL Second All-Star Team (1957, 1958)

Played in NHL All-Star Game (1949)

Traded to **Cleveland** (AHL) by **Toronto** with $40,000 and future considerations (Phil Samis, Eric Pogue and rights to Bob Shropshire, April 6, 1950) for Al Rollins, November 29, 1949. Traded to **Buffalo** (AHL) by **Cleveland** (AHL) for Joe McArthur, September 6, 1950. Traded to **Cincinnati** (AHL) by **Buffalo** (AHL) for cash, January 12, 1951. Traded to **Montreal** by **Cincinnati** (AHL) for Paul Masnick, February 13, 1951. • Missed majority of 1951-52 season recovering from leg injury suffered in game vs. Toronto, April 21, 1951. • Sat out entire 1952-53 season to rehabilitate broken leg suffered in game vs. Toronto, April 21, 1951.

• DAY, Hap Clarence Henry **HHOF**

D – L. 5'11", 175 lbs. b: Owen Sound, Ont., 6/14/1901 d: 2/17/1990.

Season	Club	League	GP	G	A	Pts	AG	AA	APts	PIM	GP	G	A	Pts	PIM
1921-22	Collingwood Sailors	OHA-Jr.	STATISTICS NOT AVAILABLE												
1922-23	Hamilton Tigers	OHA-Sr.	11	4	11	15	....	....	....	4	2	0	0	0	0
1923-24	Hamilton Tigers	OHA-Sr.	10	6	11	17	....	....	....	....	2	1	1	2	....
1924-25	**Toronto St. Pats**	**NHL**	**26**	**10**	**12**	**22**	**17**	**51**	**68**	**33**	**2**	**0**	**0**	**0**	**0**
1925-26	**Toronto St. Pats**	**NHL**	**36**	**14**	**2**	**16**	**24**	**13**	**37**	**26**	....	....	....	....	....
1926-27	**Toronto Pats/Leafs**	**NHL**	**44**	**11**	**5**	**16**	**20**	**26**	**46**	**50**	....	....	....	....	....
1927-28	**Toronto Maple Leafs**	**NHL**	**22**	**9**	**8**	**17**	**18**	**45**	**63**	**48**	....	....	....	....	....
1928-29	**Toronto Maple Leafs**	**NHL**	**44**	**6**	**6**	**12**	**17**	**40**	**57**	**84**	**4**	**1**	**0**	**1**	**4**
1929-30	**Toronto Maple Leafs**	**NHL**	**43**	**7**	**14**	**21**	**10**	**33**	**43**	**77**	....	....	....	....	....
1930-31	**Toronto Maple Leafs**	**NHL**	**44**	**1**	**13**	**14**	**2**	**39**	**41**	**56**	**2**	**0**	**3**	**3**	**7**
♦**1931-32**	**Toronto Maple Leafs**	**NHL**	**47**	**7**	**8**	**15**	**12**	**18**	**30**	**33**	**7**	**3**	**3**	**6**	**6**
1932-33	**Toronto Maple Leafs**	**NHL**	**47**	**6**	**14**	**20**	**11**	**29**	**40**	**46**	**9**	**0**	**1**	**1**	***21**
1933-34	**Toronto Maple Leafs**	**NHL**	**48**	**9**	**10**	**19**	**15**	**21**	**36**	**35**	**5**	**0**	**0**	**0**	**6**
1934-35	**Toronto Maple Leafs**	**NHL**	**45**	**2**	**4**	**6**	**3**	**7**	**10**	**38**	**7**	**0**	**0**	**0**	**4**
1935-36	**Toronto Maple Leafs**	**NHL**	**44**	**1**	**13**	**14**	**2**	**25**	**27**	**41**	**9**	**0**	**0**	**0**	**8**
1936-37	**Toronto Maple Leafs**	**NHL**	**48**	**3**	**4**	**7**	**5**	**7**	**12**	**20**	**2**	**0**	**0**	**0**	**0**
1937-38	**New York Americans**	**NHL**	**43**	**0**	**3**	**3**	**0**	**5**	**5**	**14**	**6**	**0**	**0**	**0**	**0**
	NHL Totals		**581**	**86**	**116**	**202**	**156**	**359**	**515**	**601**	**53**	**4**	**7**	**11**	**56**

OHA-Sr. First All-Star Team (1923) • Played in NHL All-Star Game (1934, 1937)

Signed as a free agent by **Toronto St. Pats**, December 9, 1924. Traded to **NY Americans** by **Toronto** for cash, September 23, 1937.

• DEA, Billy — *see page 1015*

• DEACON, Don Donald John

LW – L. 5'9", 190 lbs. b: Regina, Sask., 6/2/1913 d: 12/25/1943.

Season	Club	League	GP	G	A	Pts	AG	AA	APts	PIM	GP	G	A	Pts	PIM
1929-30	Regina Olympics	RCJHL	1	0	0	0	....	....	....	0	....	....	....	....	....
1930-31	Regina Pats	S-SJHL	3	1	0	1	....	....	....	4	....	....	....	....	....
	Regina Pats	M-Cup	1	0	0	0	....	....	....	0	....	....	....	....	....
1931-32	Regina Pats	S-SJHL	4	1	0	1	....	....	....	0	2	3	0	3	0
	Regina Pats	M-Cup	4	1	0	1	....	....	....	9	....	....	....	....	....
1932-33	Prince Albert Mintos	N-SSHL	18	6	1	7	....	....	....	31	....	....	....	....	....
	Prince Albert Mintos	Al-Cup	3	1	0	1	....	....	....	6	....	....	....	....	....
1933-34	Prince Albert Mintos	N-SSHL	15	13	7	20	....	....	....	28	4	*3	0	*3	2
	Prince Albert Mintos	Al-Cup	2	1	0	1	....	....	....	0	....	....	....	....	....
1934-35	Prince Albert Mintos	N-SSHL	22	*26	10	36	....	....	....	44	4	*5	2	7	2
1935-36	Detroit Olympics	IHL	44	14	17	31	....	....	....	70	6	1	4	5	7
1936-37	**Detroit Red Wings**	**NHL**	**4**	**0**	**0**	**0**	**0**	**0**	**0**	**2**	....	....	....	....	....
	Pittsburgh Hornets	IAHL	43	14	15	29	....	....	....	18	5	2	2	4	14
1937-38	Pittsburgh Hornets	IAHL	42	18	19	37	....	....	....	28	2	0	3	3	0
1938-39	**Detroit Red Wings**	**NHL**	**8**	**1**	**3**	**4**	**2**	**5**	**7**	**2**	**2**	**2**	**1**	**3**	**0**
	Pittsburgh Hornets	IAHL	46	25	*41	*66	....	....	....	41	....	....	....	....	....
1939-40	**Detroit Red Wings**	**NHL**	**18**	**5**	**1**	**6**	**8**	**2**	**10**	**2**	....	....	....	....	....
	Indianapolis Capitols	IAHL	21	7	18	25	....	....	....	18	....	....	....	....	....
	Cleveland Barons	IAHL	18	6	7	13	....	....	....	8	....	....	....	....	....
1940-41	Cleveland Barons	AHL	53	15	15	30	....	....	....	46	9	1	5	6	10
1941-42	Cleveland Barons	AHL	49	13	14	27	....	....	....	15	1	1	0	1	0
1942-43	Calgary Currie Army	CNDHL	23	21	31	52	....	....	....	39	3	4	2	6	2
	Calgary Currie Army	Al-Cup	5	4	5	9	....	....	....	2	....	....	....	....	....
	NHL Totals		**30**	**6**	**4**	**10**	**10**	**7**	**17**	**6**	**2**	**2**	**1**	**3**	**0**

IAHL First All-Star Team (1939, 1940) • CNDHL First All-Star Team (1943)

Signed as a free agent by **Detroit**, October 11, 1934. Traded to **Cleveland** (IAHL) by **Detroit** (Indianapolis-IAHL) for Bob Gracie and $30,000, February 5, 1940.

• DELMONTE, Armand Armand Romeo "Dutch"

RW – R. 5'10", 170 lbs. b: Timmins, Ont., 6/3/1927 Deceased.

Season	Club	League	GP	G	A	Pts	AG	AA	APts	PIM	GP	G	A	Pts	PIM
1943-44	St. Catharines Falcons	OHA-Jr.	23	8	4	12	....	....	....	32	6	4	0	4	4
1944-45	St. Catharines Falcons	OHA-Jr.	21	17	14	31	....	....	....	36	5	2	2	4	4
1945-46	**Boston Bruins**	**NHL**	**1**	**0**	**0**	**0**	**0**	**0**	**0**	**0**	....	....	....	....	....
	Boston Olympics	EAHL	46	30	20	50	....	....	....	58	12	2	3	5	15
1946-47	Boston Olympics	EAHL	56	26	15	41	....	....	....	71	9	4	2	6	11
	Los Angeles Monarchs	PCHL	....	....	....	....	....	....	....	....	7	0	6	6	0
1947-48	St. Paul Saints	USHL	43	4	6	10	....	....	....	26	....	....	....	....	....
1948-49	St. Paul Saints	USHL	66	33	39	72	....	....	....	64	7	5	2	7	2
1949-50	St. Paul Saints	USHL	69	18	36	54	....	....	....	37	3	0	1	1	0
1950-51	St. Paul Saints	USHL	57	25	26	51	....	....	....	54	....	....	....	....	....
1951-52	Tacoma Rockets	PCHL	62	20	26	46	....	....	....	64	7	2	6	8	4
1952-53	Cleveland Barons	AHL	33	7	6	13	....	....	....	45	....	....	....	....	....
1953-54	Ottawa Senators	QHL	8	1	0	1	....	....	....	4	....	....	....	....	....
	Marion Barons	IHL	48	30	35	65	....	....	....	87	5	0	4	4	10
	NHL Totals		**1**	**0**	**0**	**0**	**0**	**0**	**0**	**0**	....	....	....	....	....

• DELORY, Val Val Arthur

LW – L. 5'10", 160 lbs. b: Toronto, Ont., 2/14/1927.

Season	Club	League	GP	G	A	Pts	AG	AA	APts	PIM	GP	G	A	Pts	PIM
1944-45	Toronto Victory Aircraft	OHA-B	9	7	4	11	....	....	....	4	2	1	0	1	*6
	Oshawa Generals	OHA-Jr.	1	0	0	0	....	....	....	0	....	....	....	....	....
1945-46	St. Catharines Falcons	OHA-Jr.	23	7	15	22	....	....	....	21	4	0	4	4	0
1946-47	Hamilton Szabos	OHA-Jr.	16	8	6	14	....	....	....	24	....	....	....	....	....
1947-48	New York Rovers	EAHL	15	8	5	13	....	....	....	6	....	....	....	....	....
	New York Rovers	QSHL	39	9	12	21	....	....	....	14	3	1	0	1	0

			REGULAR SEASON								PLAYOFFS				
Season	Club	League	GP	G	A	Pts	AG	AA	APts	PIM	GP	G	A	Pts	PIM
1948-49	**New York Rangers**	**NHL**	**1**	**0**	**0**	**0**	**0**	**0**	**0**	**0**	....	....	....	....	....
	New York Rovers	EAHL	57	19	34	53	....	....	....	12	....	....	....	....	....
1949-50	St. Paul Saints	USHL	2	0	0	0	....	....	....	0	....	....	....	....	....
	Tacoma Rockets	PCHL	1	0	0	0	....	....	....	0	....	....	....	....	....
	New York Rovers	EAHL	47	*36	37	*73	....	....	....	20	12	7	8	*15	18
1950-51	St. Paul–Kansas City	USHL	62	14	18	32	....	....	....	21	....	....	....	....	....
1951-52	Boston Olympics	EAHL	62	32	53	85	....	....	....	16	....	....	....	....	....
1952-53	Troy Uncle Sam Trojans	EAHL	40	24	37	61	....	....	....	2	....	....	....	....	....
	Owen Sound Mercurys	OHA-Sr.	7	1	3	4	....	....	....	2	....	....	....	....	....
	NHL Totals		**1**	**0**	**0**	**0**	**0**	**0**	**0**	**0**	....	....	....	....	....

EAHL First All-Star Team (1950) • Won John Carlin Trophy (Top Scorer - EAHL) (1950)

• DELVECCHIO, Alex — *see page 1020*

• DEMARCO, Ab Sr. Albert George

C – R. 6', 168 lbs. b: North Bay, Ont., 5/10/1916 d: 5/25/1989.

Season	Club	League	GP	G	A	Pts	AG	AA	APts	PIM	GP	G	A	Pts	PIM
1933-34	North Bay T & NO	NOHA	STATISTICS NOT AVAILABLE												
1934-35	North Bay Trappers	X-Games	STATISTICS NOT AVAILABLE												
1935-36	Barrie Colts	OHA-B	STATISTICS NOT AVAILABLE												
1936-37	Falconbridge Falcons	NOHA	13	4	5	9	....	....	....	6	4	0	0	0	0
1937-38	Baltimore Orioles	EAHL	56	25	27	52	....	....	....	12	....	....	....	....	....
1938-39	**Chicago Black Hawks**	**NHL**	**2**	**1**	**0**	**1**	**2**	**0**	**2**	**0**	....	....	....	....	....
	Providence Reds	IAHL	53	6	12	18	....	....	....	8	5	0	0	0	2
1939-40	**Chicago Black Hawks**	**NHL**	**17**	**0**	**5**	**5**	**0**	**8**	**8**	**17**	**2**	**0**	**0**	**0**	**0**
	Providence Reds	IAHL	20	5	9	14	....	....	....	16	....	....	....	....	....
1940-41	Providence Reds	AHL	55	20	34	54	....	....	....	13	4	0	3	3	5
1941-42	Providence Reds	AHL	52	23	38	61	....	....	....	17	....	....	....	....	....
1942-43	Providence Reds	AHL	39	27	39	66	....	....	....	9	....	....	....	....	....
	Toronto Maple Leafs	**NHL**	**4**	**0**	**1**	**1**	**0**	**1**	**1**	**0**	....	....	....	....	....
	Boston Bruins	**NHL**	**3**	**4**	**1**	**5**	**4**	**1**	**5**	**0**	**9**	**3**	**0**	**3**	**2**
1943-44	**Boston Bruins**	**NHL**	**3**	**0**	**0**	**0**	**0**	**0**	**0**	**0**	....	....	....	....	....
	New York Rangers	**NHL**	**36**	**14**	**19**	**33**	**13**	**17**	**30**	**2**	....	....	....	....	....
1944-45	**New York Rangers**	**NHL**	**50**	**24**	**30**	**54**	**24**	**35**	**59**	**10**	....	....	....	....	....
1945-46	**New York Rangers**	**NHL**	**50**	**20**	**27**	**47**	**24**	**40**	**64**	**20**	....	....	....	....	....
1946-47	**New York Rangers**	**NHL**	**44**	**9**	**10**	**19**	**10**	**12**	**22**	**4**	....	....	....	....	....
1947-48	Cleveland Barons	AHL	60	20	61	81	....	....	....	37	9	1	8	9	10
1948-49	Cleveland Barons	AHL	34	15	19	34	....	....	....	28	....	....	....	....	....
	Washington Lions	AHL	5	1	3	4	....	....	....	0	....	....	....	....	....
	Buffalo Bisons	AHL	25	7	15	22	....	....	....	12	....	....	....	....	....
1949-50	Buffalo Bisons	AHL	70	40	54	94	....	....	....	16	5	1	5	6	9
1950-51	Buffalo Bisons	AHL	64	37	*76	*113	....	....	....	35	4	0	3	3	0
1951-52	Buffalo Bisons	AHL	67	28	49	77	....	....	....	34	3	1	0	1	0
1952-53	North Bay Trappers	NOHA	40	20	37	57	....	....	....	38	7	0	5	5	2
1953-54	North Bay Trappers	NOHA	59	23	*69	*92	....	....	....	8	6	2	7	9	2
1954-55	North Bay Trappers	NOHA	50	19	34	53	....	....	....	4	13	4	*7	*11	24
1955-56	North Bay Trappers	NOHA	6	0	4	4	....	....	....	2	....	....	....	....	....
1956-57	North Bay Trappers	NOHA	4	1	1	2	....	....	....	0	....	....	....	....	....
1957-58	North Bay Trappers	NOHA	DID NOT PLAY – COACHING												
1958-59	North Bay Trappers	NOHA	4	1	1	2	....	....	....	0	....	....	....	....	....
	NHL Totals		**209**	**72**	**93**	**165**	**77**	**114**	**191**	**53**	**11**	**3**	**0**	**3**	**2**

• Father of Ab Jr. • EAHL Second All-Star Team (1938) • AHL Second All-Star Team (1950) • AHL First All-Star Team (1951) • Won John B. Sollenberger Trophy (Top Scorer - AHL) (1951) • Won Les Cunningham Award (MVP - AHL) (1951)

Signed as a free agent by **Chicago**, September 28, 1938. Traded to **Providence** (AHL) by **Chicago** for cash, May 14, 1940. Loaned to **Toronto** by **Providence** (AHL) with the trade of Buck Jones for the loan of Jack Forsey and George Boothman, February 3, 1943. Traded to **Boston** by **Providence** (AHL) with Oscar Aubuchon and Norm Calladine for cash, March 8, 1943. Traded to **NY Rangers** by **Boston** for cash, November, 1943. Traded to **Detroit** by **NY Rangers** with Hank Goldup for Flash Hollett, June 19, 1946. Transaction voided when Hollett decided to retire, June, 1946. Traded to **Cleveland** (AHL) by **NY Rangers** with Joe Cooper for cash, May 5, 1947. Traded to **Washington** (AHL) by **Cleveland** (AHL) with Bryan Hextall Sr. for Dan Porteous, Frank Porteous and Ken Schultz, January 20, 1949. Traded to **Montreal** (Buffalo-AHL) by **Washington** (AHL) for George Robertson with Montreal retaining right of recall, January 28, 1949.

• DEMERS, Tony Antonio

RW – R. 5'9", 180 lbs. b: Chambly Basin, Que., 7/22/1917 d: 1997.

Season	Club	League	GP	G	A	Pts	AG	AA	APts	PIM	GP	G	A	Pts	PIM
1935-36	Montreal Lafontaine	MCJHL	1	1	0	1	....	....	....	2	....	....	....	....	....
1936-37	Southampton Vikings	Britain	....	21	7	28	....	....	....	16	....	....	....	....	....
1937-38	**Montreal Canadiens**	**NHL**	**6**	**0**	**0**	**0**	**0**	**0**	**0**	**0**	....	....	....	....	....
	New Haven Eagles	IAHL	5	0	0	0	....	....	....	0	2	0	0	0	0
	Lachine Rapides	QPHL	STATISTICS NOT AVAILABLE												
1938-39	Lachine Rapides	QPHL	29	24	12	36	....	....	....	39	6	2	2	4	7
1939-40	**Montreal Canadiens**	**NHL**	**14**	**2**	**3**	**5**	**3**	**5**	**8**	**2**	....	....	....	....	....
	Valleyfield Braves	QPHL	35	30	23	53	....	....	....	37	....	....	....	....	....
1940-41	**Montreal Canadiens**	**NHL**	**46**	**13**	**10**	**23**	**20**	**14**	**34**	**17**	**2**	**0**	**0**	**0**	**0**
1941-42	**Montreal Canadiens**	**NHL**	**7**	**3**	**4**	**7**	**4**	**5**	**9**	**4**	....	....	....	....	....
	Valleyfield V's	MCHL	14	2	3	5	....	....	....	16	9	1	2	3	21
1942-43	**Montreal Canadiens**	**NHL**	**9**	**2**	**5**	**7**	**2**	**5**	**7**	**0**	....	....	....	....	....
	Montreal Army	MCHL	13	3	1	4	....	....	....	0	4	0	2	2	0
1943-44	**New York Rangers**	**NHL**	**1**	**0**	**0**	**0**	**0**	**0**	**0**	**0**	....	....	....	....	....
	Providence Reds	AHL	25	11	10	21	....	....	....	10	....	....	....	....	....
1944-45	Lachine Rapides	QPHL	11	2	3	5	....	....	....	12	....	....	....	....	....
1945-46	St-Hyacinthe Saints	QPHL	34	*50	29	*79	....	....	....	26	....	....	....	....	....
1946-47	Sherbrooke Saints	QPHL	43	32	36	68	....	....	....	8	10	8	*15	*23	2
	Sherbrooke Saints	Al-Cup	4	2	2	4	....	....	....	2	....	....	....	....	....
1947-48	Sherbrooke St. Xavier	QPHL	52	*62	46	108	....	....	....	24	10	6	6	12	9
1948-49	Sherbrooke Red Raiders	QSHL	60	53	58	111	....	....	....	29	10	*10	2	12	8
	NHL Totals		**83**	**20**	**22**	**42**	**29**	**29**	**58**	**23**	**2**	**0**	**0**	**0**	**0**

QSHL Second All-Star Team (1949) • Won Byng of Vimy Trophy (Sportsmanship - QSHL) (1949)

Signed as a free agent by **Montreal Canadiens**, October 30, 1937. Loaned to **NY Rangers** by **Montreal** for the remainder of the 1943-44 season to complete transaction that sent Phil Watson to Montreal (October 27, 1943), December, 1943. • Charged with manslaughter and sentenced to 15 years in prison, September 19, 1949.

• DENIS, Jean-Paul "Johnny"

RW – R. 5'8", 170 lbs. b: Montreal, Que., 2/28/1924.

Season	Club	League	GP	G	A	Pts	AG	AA	APts	PIM	GP	G	A	Pts	PIM
			REGULAR SEASON								PLAYOFFS				
1941-42	Montreal Concordias	MMJHL	12	11	6	17				2	2	2	2	4	0
1942-43	Montreal Concordias	MMJHL	20	13	9	22				13	4	1	0	1	2
1943-44	Montreal Concordias	MMJHL	10	4	4	8				14	5	3	1	4	6
	University of Montreal	QSHL	2	0	1	1				0					
	Montreal Royals	M-Cup	4	2	*4	*6				2					
1944-45	Hull Volants	QSHL	2	0	0	0				0					
	Montreal Army	QSHL	9	10	10	20				7					
1945-46	Montreal Royals	QSHL	1	0	0	0				0					
1946-47	**New York Rangers**	**NHL**	**6**	**0**	**1**	**1**	**0**	**1**	**1**	**0**					
	New Haven Ramblers	AHL	26	9	3	12				14					
	New York Rovers	EAHL	16	6	15	21				15					
	Montreal Royals	QSHL	1	0	0	0				0	1	0	0	0	0
1947-48	New Haven Ramblers	AHL	65	19	19	38				59	4	0	1	1	0
1948-49	New Haven Ramblers	AHL	63	24	23	47				108					
1949-50	**New York Rangers**	**NHL**	**4**	**0**	**1**	**1**	**0**	**1**	**1**	**2**					
	New Haven Ramblers	AHL	65	20	24	44				42					
1950-51	Cincinnati Mohawks	AHL	61	22	31	53				109					
1951-52	Cincinnati Mohawks	AHL	35	15	16	31				53					
	Providence Reds	AHL	4	2	3	5				4	6	2	0	2	11
1952-53	Providence Reds	AHL	57	21	17	38				74					
1953-54	Quebec Aces	QHL	6	1	0	1				2					
	Providence Reds	AHL	15	3	5	8				15					
1954-55	Shawinigan Cataracts	QHL	42	18	25	43				46	13	3	8	11	25
	Shawinigan Cataracts	Ed-Cup	7	3	3	6				12					
1955-56	Shawinigan Cataracts	QHL	59	24	42	66				63	11	2	3	5	7
1956-57	Shawinigan Cataracts	QHL	62	19	33	52				57					
1957-58	Shawinigan Cataracts	QHL	64	39	50	*89				68	8	1	7	8	2
1958-59	Montreal Royals	QHL	48	22	23	45				69	6	2	0	2	0
1959-60	Trois-Rivieres Lions	EPHL	69	30	40	70				51	7	4	1	5	6
1960-61	St. Paul Saints	IHL	67	41	52	93				52	13	8	6	14	9
1961-62	St. Paul Saints	IHL	64	32	56	88				49	11	*7	4	11	26
	NHL Totals		**10**	**0**	**2**	**2**	**0**	**2**	**2**	**2**					

QHL First All-Star Team (1958) • Won President's Cup (Scoring Champion - QHL) (1958)

Traded to **Providence** (AHL) by **NY Rangers** with Zellio Toppazzini and Pat Egan for Jack Stoddard, January 1, 1952.

• DENIS, Lulu Louis Gilbert

RW – R. 5'8", 140 lbs. b: Vonda, Sask., 6/7/1928.

Season	Club	League	GP	G	A	Pts	AG	AA	APts	PIM	GP	G	A	Pts	PIM
1945-46	Montreal Jr. Royals	QJHL	17	8	3	11				6					
1946-47	Montreal Jr. Royals	QJHL	28	11	19	30				28	8	3	4	7	0
1947-48	Montreal Jr. Royals	QJHL	31	22	21	43				10	12	3	12	15	0
1948-49	Montreal Royals	QSHL	53	12	17	29				21	9	1	0	1	10
1949-50	**Montreal Canadiens**	**NHL**	**2**	**0**	**1**	**1**	**0**	**1**	**1**	**0**					
	Montreal Royals	QSHL	57	24	23	47				51	6	1	1	2	2
1950-51	**Montreal Canadiens**	**NHL**	**1**	**0**	**0**	**0**	**0**	**0**	**0**	**0**					
	Montreal Royals	QMHL	57	22	32	54				27	7	2	3	5	4
1951-52	Montreal Royals	QMHL	59	21	21	42				8	7	2	1	3	4
1952-53	Buffalo Bisons	AHL	2	1	0	1				0					
	Montreal Royals	QMHL	51	23	16	39				14	14	3	4	7	4
1953-54	Montreal Royals	QHL	68	16	36	52				14	11	0	6	6	4
1954-55	Montreal Royals	QHL	62	20	*47	67				8	4	0	0	0	2
1955-56	Montreal Royals	QHL	61	14	25	39				17	13	8	*10	*18	0
	Montreal Royals	Ed-Cup	6	1	3	4				2					
1956-57	Montreal Royals	QHL	68	22	26	48				34	4	0	1	1	0
1957-58	Montreal Royals	QHL	61	21	31	52				11	7	4	4	8	4
1958-59	Montreal Royals	QHL	61	15	31	46				39	8	3	3	6	4
1959-60	Montreal Royals	EPHL	67	22	31	53				33	14	2	3	5	4
1960-61	Montreal Royals	EPHL	34	8	9	17				6					
	NHL Totals		**3**	**0**	**1**	**1**	**0**	**1**	**1**	**0**					

QHL First All-Star Team (1955)

• DENNENY, Corb Corbett Charles

C – R. 5'8", 160 lbs. b: Cornwall, Ont., 1/25/1894 d: 1/16/1963.

Season	Club	League	GP	G	A	Pts	AG	AA	APts	PIM	GP	G	A	Pts	PIM
1909-10	Cornwall Sons of England	LOVHL	STATISTICS NOT AVAILABLE												
1910-11	Cornwall Internationals	LOVHL	8	5	0	5									
1911-12	Cornwall Internationals	LOVHL	8	5	0	5				16					
1912-13	Cobalt McKinley Mines	CoMHL	9	7	0	7				9					
1913-14	Cobalt McKinley Mines	CoMHL	9	13	0	13				11					
1914-15	Toronto Shamrocks	NHA	19	13	3	16				18					
1915-16	Toronto Blueshirts	NHA	22	20	3	23				75					
1916-17	Toronto Blueshirts	NHA	14	14	2	16				23					
	Ottawa Senators	NHA	6	5	0	5				12	2	0	0	0	6
1917-18	**Toronto Arenas**	**NHL**	**21**	**20**	**9**	**29**	**26**	**39**	**65**	**14**	**2**	**0**	**0**	**0**	**0**
♦	Toronto Arenas	St-Cup	5	3	1	4				0					
1918-19	**Toronto Arenas**	**NHL**	**16**	**8**	**3**	**11**	**14**	**16**	**30**	**15**					
1919-20	**Toronto St. Pats**	**NHL**	**24**	**24**	**12**	**36**	**28**	**42**	**70**	**20**					
1920-21	**Toronto St. Pats**	**NHL**	**20**	**19**	**7**	**26**	**25**	**27**	**52**	**29**	**2**	**0**	**0**	**0**	**4**
1921-22	**Toronto St. Pats**	**NHL**	**24**	**19**	**9**	**28**	**26**	**29**	**55**	**28**	**2**	**1**	**0**	**1**	**0**
♦	Toronto St. Pats	St-Cup	5	3	2	5				2					
1922-23	**Toronto St. Pats**	**NHL**	**1**	**1**	**0**	**1**	**2**	**0**	**2**	**0**					
	Vancouver Maroons	PCHA	21	7	3	10				3	2	0	0	0	2
	Vancouver Maroons	St-Cup	3	0	0	0				0					
1923-24	**Hamilton Tigers**	**NHL**	**23**	**0**	**1**	**1**	**0**	**6**	**6**	**6**					
1924-25	Saskatoon Crescents	WCHL	28	15	3	18				24	2	2	0	2	2
1925-26	Saskatoon Crescents	WHL	30	18	*16	34				12	2	0	0	0	2
1926-27	**Toronto Pats/Leafs**	**NHL**	**29**	**7**	**1**	**8**	**12**	**5**	**17**	**24**					
	Saskatoon Shieks	PrHL	4	0	2	2				0	4	2	0	2	4
1927-28	**Chicago Black Hawks**	**NHL**	**18**	**5**	**0**	**5**	**10**	**0**	**10**	**12**					
	Saskatoon Shieks	PrHL	16	*15	6	21				10					
1928-29	Minneapolis Millers	AHA	7	0	1	1				0					
	Newark Bulldogs	Can-Am	27	11	7	18				36					
1929-30	Minneapolis Millers	AHA	48	26	8	34				22					
1930-31	Chicago Shamrocks	AHA	28	2	6	8				14					
	NHL Totals		**176**	**103**	**42**	**145**	**143**	**164**	**307**	**148**	**6**	**1**	**0**	**1**	**4**
	Other Major League Totals		140	92	30	122				167	8	2	0	2	12

• Brother of Cy • PCHA Second All-Star Team (1923) • WHL All-Star Team (1926)

Signed as a free agent by **Toronto** (NHA), November 12, 1915. Assigned to **Ottawa** (NHA) by NHA in dispersal of Toronto (NHA) players, February 11, 1917. Signed as a free agent by **Toronto**, December 5, 1917. PCHA rights traded to **Vancouver** (PCHA) by **Toronto** for Jack Adams, December 18, 1922. NHL rights traded to **Hamilton** by **Toronto** with Ken Randall and cash for Amos Arbour, Bert Corbeau and George Carey, December 14, 1923. Claimed on waivers by **Saskatoon** (WCHL) from **Hamilton**, November 21, 1924. Traded to **Toronto** by **Saskatoon** (PrHL) with Leo Bourgeault and Laurie Scott for cash, September 27, 1926. Rights returned to **Saskatoon** (PrHL) by **Toronto** when terms of transaction were voided, February, 1927. Traded to **Chicago** by **Saskatoon** (PrHL) for cash, June, 1927. Traded to **Saskatoon** (PrHL) by **Chicago** with Nick Wasnie for Cally McCalmon and Earl Miller, January 11, 1928. Signed as a free agent by **Minneapolis** (AHA), October 28, 1929.

• DENNENY, Cy Cyril Joseph HHOF

LW – L. 5'7", 168 lbs. b: Farrow's Point, Ont., 12/23/1891 d: 10/12/1970.

Season	Club	League	GP	G	A	Pts	AG	AA	APts	PIM	GP	G	A	Pts	PIM
1909-10	Cornwall Sons of England	LOVHL	STATISTICS NOT AVAILABLE												
1910-11	Cornwall Internationals	LOVHL	8	4	0	4									
1911-12	Cornwall Internationals	LOVHL	8	9	0	9				16					
1912-13	Russell Athletics	LOVHL	STATISTICS NOT AVAILABLE												
1913-14	Cobalt O'Brien Mines	CoMHL	9	12	0	12				8					
1914-15	Russel H.C.	LOVHL	3	3	0	3									
	Toronto Shamrocks	NHA	8	6	0	6				43					
1915-16	Toronto Blueshirts	NHA	24	24	4	28				57					
1916-17	Ottawa Senators	NHA	10	3	0	3				17	2	1	0	1	8
1917-18	**Ottawa Senators**	**NHL**	**20**	**36**	***10**	**46**	**49**	**43**	**92**	**80**					
1918-19	**Ottawa Senators**	**NHL**	**18**	**18**	**4**	**22**	**33**	**22**	**55**	**58**	**5**	**3**	**2**	**5**	**0**
1919-20	**Ottawa Senators**	**NHL**	**24**	**16**	**6**	**22**	**18**	**20**	**38**	**31**					
♦	Ottawa Senators	St-Cup	5	0	2	2				3					
1920-21	**Ottawa Senators**	**NHL**	**24**	**34**	**5**	**39**	**46**	**19**	**65**	**10**	**2**	**2**	**0**	**2**	**5**
♦	Ottawa Senators	St-Cup	5	2	2	4				10					
1921-22	**Ottawa Senators**	**NHL**	**22**	**27**	**12**	**39**	**38**	**39**	**77**	**20**	**2**	**2**	**0**	**2**	**4**
1922-23	**Ottawa Senators**	**NHL**	**24**	**23**	**11**	**34**	**40**	**43**	**83**	**28**	**2**	**2**	**0**	**2**	**2**
♦	Ottawa Senators	St-Cup	6	1	1	2				8					
1923-24	**Ottawa Senators**	**NHL**	**22**	***22**	**2**	***24**	**48**	**11**	**59**	**10**	**2**	**2**	**0**	**2**	**2**
1924-25	**Ottawa Senators**	**NHL**	**29**	**27**	***15**	**42**	**48**	**64**	**112**	**16**					
1925-26	**Ottawa Senators**	**NHL**	**36**	**24**	**12**	**36**	**42**	**80**	**122**	**18**	**2**	**0**	**0**	**0**	**4**
♦1926-27	**Ottawa Senators**	**NHL**	**42**	**17**	**6**	**23**	**30**	**31**	**61**	**16**	**6**	***5**	**0**	**5**	**0**
1927-28	**Ottawa Senators**	**NHL**	**44**	**3**	**0**	**3**	**6**	**0**	**6**	**12**	**2**	**0**	**0**	**0**	**0**
♦1928-29	**Boston Bruins**	**NHL**	**23**	**1**	**2**	**3**	**3**	**13**	**16**	**2**	**2**	**0**	**0**	**0**	**0**
	NHL Totals		**328**	**248**	**85**	**333**	**401**	**385**	**786**	**301**	**25**	**16**	**2**	**18**	**17**
	Other Major League Totals		42	33	4	37				117	2	1	0	1	8

• Brother of Corb • NHL Scoring Leader (1924)

Signed as a free agent by **Montreal Canadiens** (NHA), November 29, 1912 but released after training camp ended, December, 1912. Signed as a free agent by **Toronto** (NHA), November 12, 1915. • Suspended by Toronto (NHA) for failing to report to training camp, November 15, 1916. Traded to **Ottawa** (NHA) by **Toronto** (NHA) for cash, January, 1917. Rights retained by **Ottawa** after NHA folded, November 26, 1917. • 1922-23 Stanley Cup totals includes series with Regina (WCHL) and Edmonton (PCHA). Traded to **Boston** by **Ottawa** for cash, October 25, 1928.

• DENOIRD, Gerry

C – R. 5'10", 170 lbs. b: Toronto, Ont., 8/4/1902 Deceased.

Season	Club	League	GP	G	A	Pts	AG	AA	APts	PIM	GP	G	A	Pts	PIM
1920-21	Toronto Aura Lee	OHA-Jr.	3	1	0	1				0					
1921-22	Toronto Aura Lee	OHA-Jr.	6	10	0	10				0					
1922-23	**Toronto St. Pats**	**NHL**	**17**	**0**	**1**	**1**	**0**	**4**	**4**	**0**					
1923-24			REINSTATED AS AN AMATEUR												
1924-25	Toronto Aura Lee	OHA-Sr.	2	1	0	1				0					
	Toronto AA Clarke	TIHL	STATISTICS NOT AVAILABLE												
	NHL Totals		**17**	**0**	**1**	**1**	**0**	**4**	**4**	**0**					

Signed as a free agent by **Toronto**, October 25, 1922.

• DESAULNIERS, Gerard

C – L. 5'11", 152 lbs. b: Shawinigan Falls, Que., 12/31/1928 Deceased.

Season	Club	League	GP	G	A	Pts	AG	AA	APts	PIM	GP	G	A	Pts	PIM
1946-47	Laval Nationale	QJHL	STATISTICS NOT AVAILABLE												
1947-48	Laval Nationale	QJHL	32	21	27	48				26	12	*15	6	21	6
	Laval Nationale	M-Cup	8	5	5	10				6					
1948-49	Laval Nationale	QJHL	48	41	34	75				57	9	2	11	13	14
	Montreal Royals	QSHL	3	0	0	0				0	8	0	4	4	2
1949-50	Montreal Royals	QSHL	59	21	34	55				49	6	2	2	4	4
1950-51	**Montreal Canadiens**	**NHL**	**3**	**0**	**1**	**1**	**0**	**1**	**1**	**2**					
	Montreal Royals	QMHL	51	24	26	50				30	7	0	3	3	2
1951-52	Montreal Royals	QMHL	57	19	23	42				33	7	1	1	2	0
1952-53	**Montreal Canadiens**	**NHL**	**2**	**0**	**1**	**1**	**0**	**1**	**1**	**2**					
	Montreal Royals	QMHL	45	13	22	35				18	16	3	10	13	4
1953-54	**Montreal Canadiens**	**NHL**	**3**	**0**	**0**	**0**	**0**	**0**	**0**	**0**					
	Montreal Royals	QHL	66	11	26	37				31	11	4	4	8	0
1954-55	Shawinigan Cataracts	QHL	61	31	30	61				10	11	5	5	10	4
	Shawinigan Cataracts	Ed-Cup	6	0	2	2				0					
1955-56	Shawinigan Cataracts	QHL	62	14	23	37				35	11	7	3	10	0
1956-57	Shawinigan Cataracts	QHL	68	20	29	49				18					
1957-58	Shawinigan Cataracts	QHL	58	14	24	38				12	14	4	7	11	6
1958-59	Trois-Rivieres Lions	QHL	60	17	24	41				12	8	6	1	7	0
1959-60	Trois-Rivieres Lions	EPHL	56	13	28	41				4					
	NHL Totals		**8**	**0**	**2**	**2**	**0**	**2**	**2**	**4**					

QJHL First All-Star Team (1949) • Won Byng of Vimy Trophy (MVP - QHL) (1959)

• DESILETS, Joffre Joffre Wilfred

RW – R. 5'10", 170 lbs. b: Capreol, Ont., 4/16/1915 d: 11/30/1994.

Season	Club	League	GP	G	A	Pts	AG	AA	APts	PIM	GP	G	A	Pts	PIM
1929-30	Capreol Caps	OHA-Sr.	10	1	0	1				4					
1930-31	Capreol Caps	OHA-Sr.	12	4	0	4				4	1	0	0	0	0
1931-32	Stratford Midgets	OHA-Jr.	9	6	1	7				6	2	4	2	6	2

			REGULAR SEASON								PLAYOFFS				
Season	Club	League	GP	G	A	Pts	AG	AA	APts	PIM	GP	G	A	Pts	PIM
1932-33	Stratford Midgets	OHA-Jr.	14	*22	7	*29	....	....	....	30	3	4	0	4	0
	Stratford Midgets	M-Cup	8	11	2	13	....	....	....	16	....	....	....	....	....
1933-34	Stratford Midgets	OHA-Jr.	15	*34	13	*47	....	....	....	27	12	*14	7	*21	12
1934-35	Charlottetown Islanders	NBSHL	20	10	13	23	....	....	....	16	....	....	....	....	....
	Saint John Beavers	NBSHL	17	*35	*27	*62	....	....	....	2	12	*14	7	21	12
1935-36	**Montreal Canadiens**	**NHL**	**38**	**7**	**6**	**13**	**13**	**11**	**24**	**0**	....	....	....	....	....
	London Tecumsehs	IHL	9	1	2	3	....	....	....	4	2	0	0	0	0
1936-37	**Montreal Canadiens**	**NHL**	**48**	**7**	**12**	**19**	**12**	**22**	**34**	**17**	**5**	**1**	**0**	**1**	**0**
1937-38	**Montreal Canadiens**	**NHL**	**32**	**6**	**7**	**13**	**10**	**11**	**21**	**6**	**2**	**0**	**0**	**0**	**7**
1938-39	**Chicago Black Hawks**	**NHL**	**48**	**11**	**13**	**24**	**19**	**20**	**39**	**28**	....	....	....	....	....
1939-40	**Chicago Black Hawks**	**NHL**	**26**	**6**	**7**	**13**	**10**	**11**	**21**	**6**	....	....	....	....	....
	Providence Reds	IAHL	22	7	8	15	....	....	....	8	1	0	0	0	2
1940-41	Cleveland Barons	AHL	53	15	29	44	....	....	....	13	5	1	0	1	4
1941-42	Cleveland Barons	AHL	56	24	24	48	....	....	....	26	4	2	0	2	0
1942-43	Victoria Army	NNDHL	19	21	12	33	....	....	....	16	5	*7	3	10	2
	Victoria Army	Al-Cup	18	24	6	30	....	....	....	14	....	....	....	....	....
1943-44	Nanaimo Clippers	PCHL	14	7	3	10	....	....	....	10	....	....	....	....	....
	Vancouver Army	NNDHL	3	0	2	2	....	....	....	0	....	....	....	....	....
	Vernon Army	NNDHL	....	....	....	....	....	....	....	....	1	0	0	0	0
1944-45	Toronto Army Shamrocks	TIHL	31	14	31	45	....	....	....	18	4	2	4	6	2
	Toronto Army Daggers	TNDHL	4	4	10	14	....	....	....	0	2	4	4	8	0
	Toronto Army	OHA-Sr.	3	2	2	4	....	....	....	0	....	....	....	....	....
1945-46	New Haven Eagles	AHL	30	6	3	9	....	....	....	10	....	....	....	....	....
	Fort Worth Rangers	USHL	23	6	13	19	....	....	....	0	....	....	....	....	....
1946-47	Dallas Texans	USHL	49	16	23	39	....	....	....	8	....	....	....	....	....
1947-48	San Diego–Fresno	PCHL	53	5	21	26	....	....	....	16	9	4	2	6	0
1948-49			REINSTATED AS AN AMATEUR												
1949-50	Renfrew Lions	EOHL	12	0	1	1	....	....	....	2	....	....	....	....	....
1950-51	Renfrew Millionaires	EOHL	DID NOT PLAY – COACHING												
1951-52	Renfrew Millionaires	EOHL	16	3	4	7	....	....	....	2	....	....	....	....	....
	NHL Totals		**192**	**37**	**45**	**82**	**64**	**75**	**139**	**57**	**7**	**1**	**0**	**1**	**7**

AHL Second All-Star Team (1941, 1942)

Signed as a free agent by **Montreal Canadiens**, October 22, 1935. Traded to **Chicago** by **Montreal** for Louis Trudel, August 26, 1938. Traded to **Cleveland** (AHL) by **Chicago** for cash, May 12, 1940.

• DESJARDINS, Vic   Victor Arthur   USHOF

C – R. 5'9", 160 lbs.   b: S.S. Marie, MI, 7/4/1900   Deceased.

Season	Club	League	GP	G	A	Pts	AG	AA	APts	PIM	GP	G	A	Pts	PIM
1918-19	S.S. Marie Nationals	NOHA	STATISTICS NOT AVAILABLE												
1919-20	Michigan Soo Indians	USAHA	14	12	4	16	....	....	....	....	....	....	....	....	....
1920-21	S.S. Marie Greyhounds	NMHL	13	11	4	15	....	....	....	....	....	....	....	....	....
	S.S. Marie Greyhounds	NOHA	9	11	4	15	....	....	....	4	5	1	1	2	....
1921-22	Eveleth Rangers	USAHA	STATISTICS NOT AVAILABLE												
1922-23	Eveleth Rangers	USAHA	20	8	0	8	....	....	....	....	....	....	....	....	....
1923-24	Eveleth Rangers	USAHA	20	5	0	5	....	....	....	....	....	....	....	....	....
1924-25	Eveleth Arrowheads	USAHA	40	14	0	14	....	....	....	....	4	2	0	2	....
1925-26	Eveleth Rangers	CHL	38	18	4	22	....	....	....	40	....	....	....	....	....
1926-27	St. Paul Saints	AHA	34	13	4	17	....	....	....	30	....	....	....	....	....
1927-28	St. Paul Saints	AHA	40	20	*8	28	....	....	....	46	....	....	....	....	....
1928-29	St. Paul Saints	AHA	39	16	10	26	....	....	....	48	8	*4	1	*5	6
1929-30	St. Paul Saints	AHA	45	25	10	35	....	....	....	47	....	....	....	....	....
1930-31	**Chicago Black Hawks**	**NHL**	**39**	**3**	**12**	**15**	**6**	**36**	**42**	**11**	**9**	**0**	**0**	**0**	**0**
1931-32	**New York Rangers**	**NHL**	**48**	**3**	**3**	**6**	**5**	**7**	**12**	**16**	**7**	**0**	**0**	**0**	**0**
1932-33	St. Paul–Tulsa	AHA	31	16	12	28	....	....	....	10	4	*4	0	4	6
	Springfield Indians	Can-Am	13	5	9	14	....	....	....	4	....	....	....	....	....
1933-34	Tulsa Oilers	AHA	46	21	13	34	....	....	....	37	4	1	2	3	4
1934-35	Tulsa Oilers	AHA	46	16	18	34	....	....	....	37	5	2	*5	*7	4
1935-36	Tulsa Oilers	AHA	45	20	21	41	....	....	....	27	3	0	0	0	0
1936-37	Kansas City Greyhounds	AHA	48	13	16	29	....	....	....	37	3	1	0	1	0
1937-38	Kansas City Greyhounds	AHA	36	6	7	13	....	....	....	2	....	....	....	....	....
	NHL Totals		**87**	**6**	**15**	**21**	**11**	**43**	**54**	**27**	**16**	**0**	**0**	**0**	**0**

USAHA First All-Star Team (1920) • NOHA Second All-Star Team (1921) • AHA First All-Star Team (1927, 1935) • AHA Second All-Star Team (1936)

Signed as a free agent by **St. Paul** (AHA), October 21, 1926. Traded to **Chicago** by **St. Paul** (AHA) for cash, October 28, 1930. Traded to **NY Rangers** by **Chicago** with Art Somers for Paul Thompson, September 27, 1931.

• DESLAURIERS, Jacques

D – L. 6', 170 lbs.   b: Montreal, Que., 9/3/1928.

Season	Club	League	GP	G	A	Pts	AG	AA	APts	PIM	GP	G	A	Pts	PIM
1945-46	Montreal Nationale	QJHL	19	3	4	7	....	....	....	19	4	0	0	0	2
1946-47	Laval Nationale	QJHL	27	7	12	19	....	....	....	47	12	2	7	9	11
1947-48	Laval Nationale	QJHL	32	6	8	14	....	....	....	24	12	1	7	8	29
	Laval Nationale	M-Cup	8	1	4	5	....	....	....	10	....	....	....	....	....
1948-49	Dallas Texans	USHL	56	2	11	13	....	....	....	36	4	0	0	0	0
1949-50	Cincinnati Mohawks	AHL	52	0	4	4	....	....	....	18	....	....	....	....	....
1950-51	Valleyfield Braves	QMHL	53	2	13	15	....	....	....	32	15	2	4	6	8
	Valleyfield Braves	Alx-Cup	6	0	0	0	....	....	....	4	....	....	....	....	....
1951-52	Valleyfield Braves	QMHL	60	7	9	16	....	....	....	22	6	1	0	1	2
1952-53	Valleyfield Braves	QMHL	60	8	17	25	....	....	....	18	4	0	0	0	6
1953-54	Valleyfield Braves	QHL	57	6	14	20	....	....	....	14	7	1	1	2	0
1954-55	Valleyfield Braves	QHL	61	7	25	32	....	....	....	40	....	....	....	....	....
1955-56	**Montreal Canadiens**	**NHL**	**2**	**0**	**0**	**0**	**0**	**0**	**0**	**0**	....	....	....	....	....
	Montreal Royals	QHL	63	4	21	25	....	....	....	26	13	2	2	4	12
	Montreal Royals	Ed-Cup	5	0	2	2	....	....	....	0	....	....	....	....	....
1956-57	Montreal Royals	QHL	68	11	21	32	....	....	....	46	4	0	1	1	0
	Rochester Americans	AHL	2	0	1	1	....	....	....	0	....	....	....	....	....
1957-58	Chicoutimi Sagueneens	QHL	56	8	16	24	....	....	....	26	6	1	0	1	2
1958-59	Montreal Royals	QHL	51	5	15	20	....	....	....	32	8	0	2	2	4
1959-60	Montreal Royals	EPHL	52	3	9	12	....	....	....	44	14	0	5	5	4
1960-61	Granby Vics	ETSHL	STATISTICS NOT AVAILABLE												
1961-62	Granby Vics	ETSHL	STATISTICS NOT AVAILABLE												
	Granby Vics	Al-Cup	7	0	2	2	....	....	....	4	....	....	....	....	....
	NHL Totals		**2**	**0**	**0**	**0**	**0**	**0**	**0**	**0**	....	....	....	....	....

QJHL Second All-Star Team (1947) • QHL First All-Star Team (1956, 1957, 1959) • QHL Second All-Star Team (1958)

Traded to **Chicoutimi** (QHL) by **Montreal** with Jackie LeClair and Guy Rousseau for Stan Smrke, October 27, 1957.

• DEWAR, Tom

D – L. 5'9", 170 lbs.   b: Frobisher, Sask., 6/10/1913   Deceased.

			REGULAR SEASON								PLAYOFFS				
Season	Club	League	GP	G	A	Pts	AG	AA	APts	PIM	GP	G	A	Pts	PIM
1929-30	Moose Jaw Cubs	S-SJHL	STATISTICS NOT AVAILABLE												
	Moose Jaw Cubs	M-Cup	2	1	0	1	....	....	....	0	....	....	....	....	....
1930-31	Moose Jaw Cubs	S-SJHL	STATISTICS NOT AVAILABLE												
1931-32	Moose Jaw Cubs	S-SJHL	STATISTICS NOT AVAILABLE												
	Moose Jaw Cubs	M-Cup	4	4	2	6	....	....	....	8	....	....	....	....	....
1932-33	Moose Jaw Cubs	S-SJHL	STATISTICS NOT AVAILABLE												
	Moose Jaw Cubs	M-Cup	2	0	0	0	....	....	....	0	....	....	....	....	....
1933-34	Moose Jaw Cubs	S-SJHL	1	0	0	0	....	....	....	0	....	....	....	....	....
	BKE Budapest	Hungary	STATISTICS NOT AVAILABLE												
1934-35	Moose Jaw Millers	S-SSHL	13	2	0	2	....	....	....	12	....	....	....	....	....
	Saskatoon Standards	S-SSHL	24	4	6	10	....	....	....	20	2	0	0	0	4
1935-36	Prince Albert Mintos	S-SSHL	20	13	6	19	....	....	....	12	3	0	0	0	8
	Prince Albert Mintos	Al-Cup	7	2	0	2	....	....	....	....	....	....	....	....	....
1936-37	Earls Court Royals	Britain	....	8	8	16	....	....	....	60	....	....	....	....	....
1937-38	Moose Jaw Millers	S-SSHL	24	4	4	8	....	....	....	18	6	1	1	2	6
	Moose Jaw Canucks	Al-Cup	4	1	0	1	....	....	....	4	....	....	....	....	....
1938-39	Moose Jaw Millers	S-SSHL	30	8	5	13	....	....	....	18	8	0	0	0	0
1939-40	Calgary Stampeders	S-SSHL	32	6	11	17	....	....	....	6	8	2	1	3	2
1940-41	Calgary Stampeders	S-SSHL	30	8	4	12	....	....	....	10	8	2	0	2	2
1941-42	Calgary Stampeders	S-SSHL	29	2	6	8	....	....	....	4	6	0	2	2	8
1942-43	Calgary Buffalos	WCSHL	29	6	5	11	....	....	....	8	....	....	....	....	....
1943-44	**New York Rangers**	**NHL**	**9**	**0**	**2**	**2**	**0**	**2**	**2**	**4**	....	....	....	....	....
	Brooklyn Crescents	EAHL	2	1	0	1	....	....	....	0	....	....	....	....	....
	NHL Totals		**9**	**0**	**2**	**2**	**0**	**2**	**2**	**4**	....	....	....	....	....

• DEWSBURY, Al   Alan Percy "Dews"

D – L. 6'2", 202 lbs.   b: Goderich, Ont., 4/12/1926.

Season	Club	League	GP	G	A	Pts	AG	AA	APts	PIM	GP	G	A	Pts	PIM
1941-42	Toronto Young Rangers	OHA-B	STATISTICS NOT AVAILABLE												
	Toronto Native Sons	OHA-Jr.	1	0	0	0	....	....	....	0	....	....	....	....	....
1942-43	Toronto Young Rangers	OHA-B	STATISTICS NOT AVAILABLE												
1943-44	Toronto Young Rangers	OHA-Jr.	19	12	8	20	....	....	....	34	....	....	....	....	....
	Toronto C.I.L.	TIHL	11	10	6	16	....	....	....	12	7	2	3	5	2
	Hamilton Szabos	OHA-Jr.	....	....	....	....	....	....	....	....	3	1	0	1	0
1944-45	Toronto Young Rangers	OHA-Jr.	19	12	8	20	....	....	....	34	4	0	0	0	8
	Toronto Fuels	TMHL	9	1	3	4	....	....	....	24	....	....	....	....	....
	Toronto Maher Jewels	TIHL	3	0	0	0	....	....	....	0	....	....	....	....	....
	Porcupine Combines	M-Cup	3	0	0	0	....	....	....	2	....	....	....	....	....
1945-46	Omaha Knights	USHL	41	6	6	12	....	....	....	28	7	1	2	3	0
1946-47	**Detroit Red Wings**	**NHL**	**23**	**2**	**1**	**3**	**2**	**1**	**3**	**12**	**2**	**0**	**0**	**0**	**4**
	Indianapolis Capitols	AHL	34	6	4	10	....	....	....	80	....	....	....	....	....
1947-48	Indianapolis Capitols	AHL	10	0	4	4	....	....	....	34	....	....	....	....	....
	Omaha Knights	USHL	32	11	7	18	....	....	....	57	3	0	2	2	9
	Detroit Red Wings	**NHL**	....	....	....	....	....	....	....	....	**1**	**0**	**0**	**0**	**0**
1948-49	Indianapolis Capitols	AHL	65	8	24	32	....	....	....	103	2	0	2	2	0
♦**1949-50**	**Detroit Red Wings**	**NHL**	**11**	**2**	**2**	**4**	**2**	**2**	**4**	**2**	**4**	**0**	**3**	**3**	**8**
	Indianapolis Capitols	AHL	30	15	22	37	....	....	....	75	8	2	5	7	16
1950-51	**Chicago Black Hawks**	**NHL**	**67**	**5**	**14**	**19**	**6**	**17**	**23**	**79**	....	....	....	....	....
1951-52	**Chicago Black Hawks**	**NHL**	**69**	**7**	**17**	**24**	**9**	**21**	**30**	**99**	....	....	....	....	....
1952-53	**Chicago Black Hawks**	**NHL**	**69**	**5**	**16**	**21**	**7**	**19**	**26**	**97**	**7**	**1**	**2**	**3**	**4**
1953-54	**Chicago Black Hawks**	**NHL**	**69**	**6**	**15**	**21**	**8**	**18**	**26**	**44**	....	....	....	....	....
1954-55	**Chicago Black Hawks**	**NHL**	**2**	**0**	**1**	**1**	**0**	**1**	**1**	**10**	....	....	....	....	....
	Montreal Royals	QHL	41	7	9	16	....	....	....	80	14	3	2	5	*34
1955-56	**Chicago Black Hawks**	**NHL**	**37**	**3**	**12**	**15**	**4**	**14**	**18**	**22**	....	....	....	....	....
	Buffalo Bisons	AHL	31	8	18	26	....	....	....	48	5	0	3	3	4
1956-57	Buffalo–Hershey	AHL	59	6	31	37	....	....	....	101	5	0	0	0	2
1957-58	Hershey Bears	AHL	60	7	31	38	....	....	....	114	1	0	0	0	0
1958-59	Belleville McFarlands	EOHL	40	7	31	38	....	....	....	114	....	....	....	....	....
	Canada	WEC-A	8	3	2	5	....	....	....	*28	....	....	....	....	....
	NHL Totals		**347**	**30**	**78**	**108**	**38**	**93**	**131**	**365**	**14**	**1**	**5**	**6**	**16**

AHL Second All-Star Team (1950) • Played in NHL All-Star Game (1951)

Traded to **Chicago** by **Detroit** with Harry Lumley, Jack Stewart, Don Morrison and Pete Babando for Jim Henry, Bob Goldham, Gaye Stewart and Metro Prystai, July 13, 1950. Loaned to **Montreal** (Montreal-QHL) by **Chicago** with cash and the option on Paul Masnick, November 9, 1954. Returned to **Chicago** by **Montreal** for the return of Paul Masnick, December 10, 1954. Traded to **Hershey** (AHL) by **Chicago** (Buffalo-AHL) for Bob Hassard, February 14, 1957. Traded to **Windsor** (OHA-Sr.) by **Belleville** (OHA-Sr.) for Dennis Boucher, December, 1959.

• DHEERE, Marcel   Marcel Albert "Ching"

LW – L. 5'7", 175 lbs.   b: St. Boniface, Man., 12/19/1920.

Season	Club	League	GP	G	A	Pts	AG	AA	APts	PIM	GP	G	A	Pts	PIM
1939-40	Treherne Juniors	MJHL	STATISTICS NOT AVAILABLE												
1940-41	Portland Buckaroos	PCHL	48	18	6	24	....	....	....	58	....	....	....	....	....
1941-42	Montreal Sr. Canadiens	QSHL	37	7	3	10	....	....	....	67	6	0	0	0	2
1942-43	**Montreal Canadiens**	**NHL**	**11**	**1**	**2**	**3**	**1**	**2**	**3**	**2**	**5**	**0**	**0**	**0**	**6**
	Montreal Sr. Canadiens	QSHL	25	2	7	9	....	....	....	12	....	....	....	....	....
1943-44	Montreal Canada Car	MCHL	1	0	2	2	....	....	....	0	....	....	....	....	....
	Montreal RCAF	MCHL	4	0	0	0	....	....	....	0	....	....	....	....	....
1944-45			MILITARY SERVICE												
1945-46	Hull Volants	QSHL	28	10	9	19	....	....	....	15	....	....	....	....	....
1946-47	Houston Huskies	USHL	58	20	28	48	....	....	....	22	....	....	....	....	....
1947-48	Houston Huskies	USHL	18	8	9	17	....	....	....	4	....	....	....	....	....
	Tulsa Oilers	USHL	38	15	15	30	....	....	....	10	2	0	0	0	0
1948-49	Tulsa Oilers	USHL	66	20	35	55	....	....	....	18	7	1	2	3	2
1949-50	Tulsa Oilers	USHL	6	1	3	4	....	....	....	2	....	....	....	....	....
	St. Paul Saints	USHL	15	3	7	10	....	....	....	2	3	0	0	0	2
	Tacoma Rockets	PCHL	47	16	33	49	....	....	....	12	....	....	....	....	....
1950-51	Tacoma Rockets	PCHL	45	9	16	25	....	....	....	14	6	0	2	2	0
1951-52	Vernon Canadians	QMHL	43	14	24	38	....	....	....	33	....	....	....	....	....
1952-53	Melville Millionaires	SSHL	32	7	21	28	....	....	....	22	3	0	2	2	0
	NHL Totals		**11**	**1**	**2**	**3**	**1**	**2**	**3**	**2**	**5**	**0**	**0**	**0**	**6**

Traded to **Montreal** by **Portland** (PCHL) for cash, December 25, 1940.

• DIACHUK, Edward

Edward Henry
LW – L. 6'1", 185 lbs. b: Vegreville, Alta., 8/16/1936.

Season	Club	League	GP	G	A	Pts	AG	AA	APts	PIM	GP	G	A	Pts	PIM
			REGULAR SEASON								PLAYOFFS				
1953-54	Edmonton Oil Kings	WCJHL	27	4	5	9	....	....	....	17	20	3	2	5	12
	Edmonton Oil Kings	M-Cup	13	2	0	2	....	....	....	10	....	....	....	....	....
1954-55	Edmonton Oil Kings	WCJHL	35	15	12	27	....	....	....	70	5	0	0	0	0
1955-56	Edmonton Oil Kings	WCJHL	15	12	8	20	....	....	....	31	6	2	2	4	5
	Edmonton Flyers	WHL	1	0	0	0	....	....	....	0	....	....	....	....	....
1956-57	Edmonton Oil Kings	CAHL	STATISTICS NOT AVAILABLE												
	Edmonton Flyers	WHL	1	0	1	1	....	....	....	2	....	....	....	....	....
	Edmonton Oil Kings	M-Cup	6	1	3	4	....	....	....	20	....	....	....	....	....
1957-58	Penticton Vees	OSHL	39	11	9	20	....	....	....	84	5	0	0	0	6
	Edmonton Flyers	WHL	3	0	0	0	....	....	....	8	....	....	....	....	....
1958-59	Edmonton Flyers	WHL	37	8	13	21	....	....	....	60	1	0	0	0	2
1959-60	Edmonton Flyers	WHL	64	15	12	27	....	....	....	94	4	0	0	0	18
1960-61	**Detroit Red Wings**	**NHL**	**12**	**0**	**0**	**0**	**0**	**0**	**0**	**19**	....	....	....	....	....
	Edmonton Flyers	WHL	51	11	18	29	....	....	....	103	....	....	....	....	....
1961-62	Sudbury Wolves	EPHL	28	4	9	13	....	....	....	46	....	....	....	....	....
	Vancouver Canucks	WHL	19	2	3	5	....	....	....	20	....	....	....	....	....
1962-63	Los Angeles Blades	WHL	55	9	7	16	....	....	....	50	....	....	....	....	....
	NHL Totals		**12**	**0**	**0**	**0**	**0**	**0**	**0**	**19**	....	....	....	....	....

Traded to **LA Blades** (WHL) by **Detroit** for cash, July, 1962.

• DICK, Harry

D – L. 5'11", 210 lbs. b: Port Colborne, Ont., 11/22/1922.

Season	Club	League	GP	G	A	Pts	AG	AA	APts	PIM	GP	G	A	Pts	PIM
1938-39	Guelph Voyageurs	OHA-B	STATISTICS NOT AVAILABLE												
	Hershey Bears	EAHL	6	0	0	0	....	....	....	0	....	....	....	....	....
1939-40	Guelph Biltmores	OHA-Jr.	20	4	4	8	....	....	....	33	3	2	1	3	0
	Atlantic City Sea Gulls	EAHL	5	0	0	0	....	....	....	9	3	0	0	0	14
1940-41	Atlantic City Sea Gulls	EAHL	62	13	32	45	....	....	....	*202	6	0	2	2	6
1941-42	Minneapolis Millers	AHA	48	8	14	22	....	....	....	*91	....	....	....	....	....
	Philadelphia Rockets	AHL	2	0	0	0	....	....	....	4	....	....	....	....	....
	Cleveland Barons	AHL	3	0	0	0	....	....	....	12	....	....	....	....	....
	Atlantic City Sea Gulls	EAHL	....	....	....	....	....	....	....	....	2	2	1	3	2
1942-43	Cleveland Barons	AHL	2	0	0	0	....	....	....	0	....	....	....	....	....
	Toronto Army Daggers	OHA-Sr.	8	1	2	3	....	....	....	14	....	....	....	....	....
	Toronto Peoples Credit	TIHL	....	....	....	....	....	....	....	....	7	0	5	5	20
1943-44	Toronto Army Shamrocks	TIHL	31	12	23	35	....	....	....	109	4	0	3	3	6
1944-45	Toronto Army Shamrocks	TIHL	22	11	12	23	....	....	....	79	2	0	0	0	*10
	Toronto Army Daggers	TNDHL	2	1	3	4	....	....	....	2	....	....	....	....	....
	Toronto Army	OHA-Sr.	4	1	0	1	....	....	....	0	....	....	....	....	....
1945-46	Kansas City Pla-Mors	USHL	51	17	19	36	....	....	....	107	12	1	2	3	*34
1946-47	**Chicago Black Hawks**	**NHL**	**12**	**0**	**1**	**1**	**0**	**1**	**1**	**12**	....	....	....	....	....
	Kansas City Pla-Mors	USHL	40	6	14	20	....	....	....	80	11	4	3	7	12
1947-48	Tulsa Oilers	USHL	66	13	23	36	....	....	....	*191	2	0	0	0	19
1948-49	Washington Lions	AHL	64	8	17	25	....	....	....	118	....	....	....	....	....
1949-50	Louisville Blades	USHL	68	14	32	46	....	....	....	137	....	....	....	....	....
1950-51	Buffalo Bisons	AHL	67	6	35	41	....	....	....	*212	4	0	0	0	12
1951-52	Buffalo Bisons	AHL	54	3	22	25	....	....	....	119	2	0	0	0	5
1952-53	Vancouver Canucks	WHL	67	8	34	42	....	....	....	161	9	2	6	8	18
1953-54	Vancouver Canucks	WHL	54	4	15	19	....	....	....	116	12	3	2	5	*45
1954-55	Vancouver Canucks	WHL	69	10	23	33	....	....	....	*208	5	0	1	1	27
	NHL Totals		**12**	**0**	**1**	**1**	**0**	**1**	**1**	**12**	....	....	....	....	....

• DICKENS, Ernie

Ernest Leslie
D – L. 6', 175 lbs. b: Winnipeg, Man., 6/25/1921.

Season	Club	League	GP	G	A	Pts	AG	AA	APts	PIM	GP	G	A	Pts	PIM
1937-38	Winnipeg Rangers	MJHL	22	2	1	3	....	....	....	*63	2	1	0	1	*12
1938-39	St. James Canadians	MJHL	18	6	7	13	....	....	....	*66	2	2	0	2	4
1939-40	Winnipeg Monarchs	MJHL	19	3	6	9	....	....	....	24	7	2	0	2	10
1940-41	Toronto Marlboros	OHA-Jr.	15	2	7	9	....	....	....	50	12	3	8	11	10
	Toronto Marlboros	OHA-Sr.	1	0	0	0	....	....	....	2	....	....	....	....	....
♦1941-42	**Toronto Maple Leafs**	**NHL**	**10**	**2**	**2**	**4**	**3**	**2**	**5**	**6**	**13**	**0**	**0**	**0**	**4**
	Providence Reds	AHL	39	8	15	23	....	....	....	14	....	....	....	....	....
1942-43	Toronto RCAF	OHA-Sr.	10	4	7	11	....	....	....	10	9	3	1	4	11
	Toronto RCAF	Al-Cup	7	2	3	5	....	....	....	6	....	....	....	....	....
1943-44	Toronto RCAF	OHA-Sr.	10	1	2	3	....	....	....	6	....	....	....	....	....
1944-45			MILITARY SERVICE												
1945-46	**Toronto Maple Leafs**	**NHL**	**15**	**1**	**3**	**4**	**1**	**4**	**5**	**6**	....	....	....	....	....
	Pittsburgh Hornets	AHL	29	4	16	20	....	....	....	16	6	1	2	3	0
1946-47	Pittsburgh Hornets	AHL	64	11	40	51	....	....	....	21	12	1	1	2	6
1947-48	Pittsburgh Hornets	AHL	9	0	4	4	....	....	....	2	....	....	....	....	....
	Chicago Black Hawks	**NHL**	**54**	**5**	**15**	**20**	**6**	**20**	**26**	**30**	....	....	....	....	....
1948-49	**Chicago Black Hawks**	**NHL**	**59**	**2**	**3**	**5**	**3**	**4**	**7**	**14**	....	....	....	....	....
1949-50	**Chicago Black Hawks**	**NHL**	**70**	**0**	**13**	**13**	**0**	**16**	**16**	**22**	....	....	....	....	....
1950-51	**Chicago Black Hawks**	**NHL**	**70**	**2**	**8**	**10**	**3**	**10**	**13**	**20**	....	....	....	....	....
1951-52	Calgary Stampeders	PCHL	69	14	34	48	....	....	....	20	....	....	....	....	....
1952-53			OUT OF HOCKEY – RETIRED												
1953-54	Oshawa Truckmen	OIHA	DID NOT PLAY – COACHING												
	NHL Totals		**278**	**12**	**44**	**56**	**16**	**56**	**72**	**98**	**13**	**0**	**0**	**0**	**4**

AHL First All-Star Team (1947)

Traded to **Chicago** by **Toronto** with Gus Bodnar, Bud Poile, Gaye Stewart and Bob Goldham for Max Bentley and Cy Thomas, November 2, 1947. Traded to **Calgary** (PCHL) by **Chicago** for Sid Finney, October 1, 1951.

• DICKENSON, Herb

John Herbert
W – L. 5'11", 175 lbs. b: Hamilton, Ont., 6/11/1931.

Season	Club	League	GP	G	A	Pts	AG	AA	APts	PIM	GP	G	A	Pts	PIM
1949-50	Guelph Biltmores	OHA-Jr.	48	24	22	46	....	....	....	43	15	*15	3	18	6
	Guelph Biltmores	M-Cup	9	3	5	8	....	....	....	6	....	....	....	....	....
1950-51	Guelph Biltmores	OHA-Jr.	49	27	36	63	....	....	....	44	4	1	3	4	4
1951-52	**New York Rangers**	**NHL**	**37**	**14**	**13**	**27**	**19**	**16**	**35**	**8**	....	....	....	....	....
	Cincinnati Mohawks	AHL	36	15	8	23	....	....	....	30	....	....	....	....	....
1952-53	**New York Rangers**	**NHL**	**11**	**4**	**4**	**8**	**5**	**5**	**10**	**2**	....	....	....	....	....
	NHL Totals		**48**	**18**	**17**	**35**	**24**	**21**	**45**	**10**	....	....	....	....	....

• Suffered career-ending eye injury during warm-up prior to game vs.Toronto, November 5, 1952.

• DILL, Bob

Robert Edward — USHOF
D – L. 5'8", 185 lbs. b: St. Paul, MN, 4/25/1920 d: 4/16/1991.

Season	Club	League	GP	G	A	Pts	AG	AA	APts	PIM	GP	G	A	Pts	PIM
1938-39	Miami Clippers	TrHL	14	5	5	10	....	....	....	23	....	....	....	....	....
1939-40	S.S. Marie Indians	NMHL	STATISTICS NOT AVAILABLE												
1940-41	Baltimore Orioles	EAHL	56	12	11	23	....	....	....	130	....	....	....	....	....
1941-42	Springfield Indians	AHL	50	8	13	21	....	....	....	106	5	3	2	5	0
1942-43	Buffalo Bisons	AHL	19	2	7	9	....	....	....	46	....	....	....	....	....
	Coast Guard Clippers	EAHL	29	15	20	35	....	....	....	48	11	6	4	10	22
1943-44	Buffalo Bisons	AHL	23	5	9	14	....	....	....	75	....	....	....	....	....
	New York Rangers	**NHL**	**28**	**6**	**10**	**16**	**5**	**9**	**14**	**66**	....	....	....	....	....
1944-45	**New York Rangers**	**NHL**	**48**	**9**	**5**	**14**	**9**	**6**	**15**	**69**	....	....	....	....	....
1945-46	St. Paul Saints	USHL	30	11	11	22	....	....	....	62	....	....	....	....	....
1946-47	St. Paul Saints	USHL	58	12	18	30	....	....	....	*154	....	....	....	....	....
1947-48	St. Paul Saints	USHL	59	10	34	44	....	....	....	101	....	....	....	....	....
1948-49	St. Paul Saints	USHL	63	15	29	44	....	....	....	134	7	4	1	5	10
1949-50	St. Paul Saints	USHL	52	6	17	23	....	....	....	116	3	0	1	1	6
1950-51	St. Paul 7-Ups	AmAHL	DID NOT PLAY – COACHING												
1951-52	Springfield Indians	EAHL	37	3	16	19	....	....	....	58	....	....	....	....	....
	NHL Totals		**76**	**15**	**15**	**30**	**14**	**15**	**29**	**135**	....	....	....	....	....

EAHL Second All-Star Team (1943) • USHL First All-Star Team (1947, 1950)

• Suspended by AHL for assaulting referee George Parsons in game vs. Pittsburgh, January 1, 1944. Traded to **NY Rangers** by **Montreal** (Buffalo-AHL) for Roger Leger and the loan of Gord Davidson, January 4, 1944.

• DILLABOUGH, Bob

— *see page 1024*

• DILLON, Cecil

Cecil Graham "Ceece"
RW – L. 5'11", 173 lbs. b: Toledo, OH, 4/26/1908 d: 11/14/1969.

Season	Club	League	GP	G	A	Pts	AG	AA	APts	PIM	GP	G	A	Pts	PIM
1927-28	Owen Sound Greys	OHA-Sr.	STATISTICS NOT AVAILABLE												
1928-29	Springfield Indians	Can-Am	33	4	3	7	....	....	....	18	....	....	....	....	....
1929-30	Springfield Indians	Can-Am	39	19	13	32	....	....	....	38	....	....	....	....	....
1930-31	Springfield Indians	Can-Am	14	9	15	24	....	....	....	10	....	....	....	....	....
	New York Rangers	**NHL**	**25**	**7**	**3**	**10**	**14**	**9**	**23**	**8**	**4**	**0**	**1**	**1**	**2**
1931-32	**New York Rangers**	**NHL**	**48**	**23**	**15**	**38**	**39**	**33**	**72**	**22**	**7**	**2**	**1**	**3**	**4**
♦1932-33	**New York Rangers**	**NHL**	**48**	**21**	**10**	**31**	**39**	**21**	**60**	**12**	**8**	***8**	**2**	***10**	**6**
1933-34	**New York Rangers**	**NHL**	**48**	**13**	**26**	**39**	**22**	**55**	**77**	**10**	**2**	**0**	**1**	**1**	**2**
1934-35	**New York Rangers**	**NHL**	**48**	**25**	**9**	**34**	**42**	**16**	**58**	**4**	**4**	**2**	**1**	**3**	**0**
1935-36	**New York Rangers**	**NHL**	**48**	**18**	**14**	**32**	**35**	**27**	**62**	**12**	....	....	....	....	....
1936-37	**New York Rangers**	**NHL**	**48**	**20**	**11**	**31**	**34**	**20**	**54**	**13**	**9**	**0**	**3**	**3**	**0**
1937-38	**New York Rangers**	**NHL**	**48**	**21**	**18**	**39**	**35**	**29**	**64**	**6**	**3**	**1**	**0**	**1**	**0**
1938-39	**New York Rangers**	**NHL**	**48**	**12**	**15**	**27**	**21**	**23**	**44**	**6**	**1**	**0**	**0**	**0**	**0**
1939-40	**Detroit Red Wings**	**NHL**	**44**	**7**	**10**	**17**	**12**	**16**	**28**	**12**	**5**	**1**	**0**	**1**	**0**
1940-41	Indianapolis Capitols	AHL	15	1	6	7	....	....	....	2	....	....	....	....	....
	Providence Reds	AHL	34	8	14	22	....	....	....	2	4	0	0	0	2
1941-42	Pittsburgh Hornets	AHL	51	13	23	36	....	....	....	2	....	....	....	....	....
	NHL Totals		**453**	**167**	**131**	**298**	**293**	**249**	**542**	**105**	**43**	**14**	**9**	**23**	**14**

NHL Second All-Star Team (1936, 1937) • NHL First All-Star Team (1938) • Played in NHL All-Star Game (1937)

Traded to **NY Rangers** by **Springfield** (Can-Am) for cash, January 1, 1931. Traded to **Detroit** by **NY Rangers** for cash, May 17, 1939. Traded to **Providence** (AHL) by **Detroit** with Eddie Bush for Harold Jackson, December 15, 1940.

• DINEEN, Bill

William Patrick
RW – R. 5'11", 180 lbs. b: Arvida, Que., 9/18/1932.

Season	Club	League	GP	G	A	Pts	AG	AA	APts	PIM	GP	G	A	Pts	PIM
1948-49	Ottawa St. Pats	OCJHL	STATISTICS NOT AVAILABLE												
1949-50	St. Michael's Majors	OHA-Jr.	43	15	18	33	....	....	....	43	5	2	3	5	4
1950-51	St. Michael's Majors	OHA-Jr.	45	25	26	51	....	....	....	50	....	....	....	....	....
1951-52	St. Michael's Majors	OHA-Jr.	47	21	30	51	....	....	....	37	8	3	3	6	0
1952-53	St. Michael's Majors	OHA-Jr.	55	27	20	47	....	....	....	63	17	*13	7	20	18
♦1953-54	**Detroit Red Wings**	**NHL**	**70**	**17**	**8**	**25**	**23**	**10**	**33**	**34**	**12**	**0**	**0**	**0**	**2**
♦1954-55	**Detroit Red Wings**	**NHL**	**69**	**10**	**9**	**19**	**13**	**10**	**23**	**36**	**11**	**0**	**1**	**1**	**8**
1955-56	**Detroit Red Wings**	**NHL**	**70**	**12**	**7**	**19**	**16**	**8**	**24**	**30**	**10**	**1**	**0**	**1**	**8**
1956-57	**Detroit Red Wings**	**NHL**	**51**	**6**	**7**	**13**	**8**	**8**	**16**	**12**	**4**	**0**	**0**	**0**	**0**
1957-58	**Detroit Red Wings**	**NHL**	**22**	**2**	**4**	**6**	**2**	**4**	**6**	**2**	....	....	....	....	....
	Chicago Black Hawks	**NHL**	**41**	**4**	**9**	**13**	**5**	**9**	**14**	**8**	....	....	....	....	....
1958-59	Buffalo Bisons	AHL	49	8	19	27	....	....	....	17	11	3	5	8	10
1959-60	Buffalo Bisons	AHL	5	0	1	1	....	....	....	2	....	....	....	....	....
	Cleveland Barons	AHL	62	26	27	53	....	....	....	17	7	2	3	5	4
1960-61	Cleveland Barons	AHL	72	28	31	59	....	....	....	24	4	0	3	3	0
1961-62	Rochester Americans	AHL	70	19	19	38	....	....	....	20	2	0	0	0	2
1962-63	Quebec Aces	AHL	72	24	17	41	....	....	....	22	....	....	....	....	....
1963-64	Quebec Aces	AHL	61	27	25	52	....	....	....	26	9	3	3	6	0
1964-65	Seattle Totems	WHL	69	25	17	42	....	....	....	4	7	0	1	1	8
1965-66	Seattle Totems	WHL	71	23	16	39	....	....	....	10	....	....	....	....	....
1966-67	Seattle Totems	WHL	62	32	33	65	....	....	....	8	10	2	*7	9	4
1967-68	Seattle Totems	WHL	72	28	33	61	....	....	....	10	9	3	6	9	2
1968-69	Seattle Totems	WHL	74	9	16	25	....	....	....	8	4	0	0	0	0
1969-70	Denver Spurs	WHL	51	10	8	18	....	....	....	4	....	....	....	....	....
1970-71	Denver Spurs	WHL	16	5	6	11	....	....	....	4	....	....	....	....	....
	NHL Totals		**323**	**51**	**44**	**95**	**67**	**49**	**116**	**122**	**37**	**1**	**1**	**2**	**18**

• Father of Peter, Gord and Kevin • WHL Second All-Star Team (1967) • Played in NHL All-Star Game (1954, 1955)

Rights traded to **Detroit** by **Cleveland** (AHL) with the rights to Lou Jankowski for Bob Bailey and John Bailey, June, 1951. Traded to **Chicago** by **Detroit** with Billy Dea, Lorne Ferguson and Earl Reibel for Nick Mickoski, Bob Bailey, Hec Lalande and Jack McIntyre, December 17, 1957. Traded to **Cleveland** (AHL) by **Buffalo** (AHL) for Bob Bailey, October 20, 1959. Traded to **Toronto** (Rochester-AHL) by **Cleveland** (AHL) with cash for Hank Ciesla, August, 1961. Traded to **Quebec** (AHL) by **Toronto**(Rochester-AHL) for cash, July, 1962. Traded to **Seattle** (WHL) by **Quebec** (AHL) for cash, February 15, 1964.

• DINSMORE, Dinny

Charles Adrian
C – L. 5'6", 155 lbs. b: Toronto, Ont., 7/23/1903 Deceased.

Season	Club	League	GP	G	A	Pts	AG	AA	APts	PIM	GP	G	A	Pts	PIM
1919-20	Toronto Aura Lee	OHA-Jr.	6	0	0	0	....	....	....	....	....	....	....	....	....
1920-21	Toronto Aura Lee	OHA-Jr.	3	0	0	0	....	....	....	....	....	....	....	....	....
1921-22	Toronto Aura Lee	OHA-Jr.	6	1	0	1	....	....	....	....	....	....	....	....	....
1922-23	Toronto Aura Lee	OHA-Jr.	1	0	0	0	....	....	....	....	....	....	....	....	....
	Toronto Aura Lee	OHA-Jr.	8	2	1	3	....	....	....	....	....	....	....	....	....

			REGULAR SEASON								PLAYOFFS				
Season	Club	League	GP	G	A	Pts	AG	AA	APts	PIM	GP	G	A	Pts	PIM
1923-24	Toronto Aura Lee	OHA-Sr.	9	4	6	10									
1924-25	**Montreal Maroons**	**NHL**	**30**	**2**	**1**	**3**	**3**	**4**	**7**	**26**					
1925-26	**Montreal Maroons**	**NHL**	**33**	**3**	**1**	**4**	**5**	**6**	**11**	**18**	**4**	**1**	**0**	**1**	**2**
♦	Montreal Maroons	St-Cup	4	0	0	0				2					
1926-27	**Montreal Maroons**	**NHL**	**28**	**1**	**0**	**1**	**2**	**0**	**2**	**6**					
1927-28	Montreal CNR	MCHL	STATISTICS NOT AVAILABLE												
1928-29	Montreal CNR	MCHL	STATISTICS NOT AVAILABLE												
1929-30	**Montreal Maroons**	**NHL**	**9**	**0**	**0**	**0**	**0**	**0**	**0**	**0**	**4**	**0**	**0**	**0**	**0**
	NHL Totals		**100**	**6**	**2**	**8**	**10**	**10**	**20**	**50**	**8**	**1**	**0**	**1**	**2**

Signed as a free agent by **Montreal Maroons**, November 18, 1924. • 1925-26 Montreal Maroons playoff totals includes series against Ottawa and Pittsburgh.

• DOAK, Gary

— see page 1028

• DOHERTY, Fred "Doc"

RW – L. 5'8", 160 lbs. b: Norwood, Ont., Deceased.

			REGULAR SEASON								PLAYOFFS				
Season	Club	League	GP	G	A	Pts	AG	AA	APts	PIM	GP	G	A	Pts	PIM
1908-09	Guelph Professionals	OPHL	7	6	0	6				6					
	Galt Professionals	OPHL	10	10	0	10				24					
1909-10	Galt Professionals	X-Games	4	6	0	6				6					
	Galt Professionals	OPHL	16	19	0	19				35	2	1	0	1	*6
1910-11	Galt Professionals	OPHL	13	4	0	4					3	2	0	2	
	Belleville Professionals	EOPHL	3	1	0	1									
	Renfrew Creamery Kings	NHA	1	0	0	0				0					
1911-12	Moncton Victorias	MPHL	16	16	0	16				31	2	0	0	0	2
1912-13	Toronto Blueshirts	NHA	1	0	0	0				0					
	Moncton Victorias	MPHL	12	12	0	12				14					
	Halifax Crescents	MPHL	1	0	0	0				0					
1913-14	Toronto Ontarios	NHA	19	9	5	14				20					
1914-15	Quebec Bulldogs	NHA	1	0	0	0				0					
1915-16	Montreal Wanderers	NHA	1	0	0	0				0					
1916-17			MILITARY SERVICE												
1917-18			MILITARY SERVICE												
1918-19	**Montreal Canadiens**	**NHL**	**1**	**0**	**0**	**0**	**0**	**0**	**0**	**0**					
	NHL Totals		**1**	**0**	**0**	**0**	**0**	**0**	**0**	**0**					
	Other Major League Totals		98	76	5	81				130	7	3	0	3	8

Signed as a free agent by **Montreal Canadiens**, December 13, 1918.

• DONNELLY, Babe James Joseph

D – L. 5'7", 180 lbs. b: Sault Ste. Marie, Ont., 12/22/1895 Deceased.

			REGULAR SEASON								PLAYOFFS				
Season	Club	League	GP	G	A	Pts	AG	AA	APts	PIM	GP	G	A	Pts	PIM
1916-17	Hamilton 227th	OHA-Sr.	9	7	0	7									
	Toronto 204th	OHA-Sr.	STATISTICS NOT AVAILABLE												
1917-18			MILITARY SERVICE												
1918-19			MILITARY SERVICE												
1919-20	Edmonton Eskimos	Big-4	11	3	1	4				6	2	0	1	1	2
1920-21	S.S. Marie Greyhounds	NOHA	9	3	4	7				18	5	2	3	5	
	S.S. Marie Greyhounds	NMHL	14	8	4	12									
1921-22	S.S. Marie Greyhounds	NOHA	8	9	3	12				12	2	1	1	2	*6
	S.S. Marie Greyhounds	NMHL	11	9	4	13									
1922-23	S.S. Marie Greyhounds	NOHA	7	3	0	3				*25	2	1	0	1	4
	S.S. Marie Greyhounds	Al-Cup	5	2	2	4				4					
1923-24	S.S. Marie Greyhounds	NOHA	7	8	2	10				18					
	S.S. Marie Greyhounds	Al-Cup	7	6	1	7				21					
1924-25	S.S. Marie Greyhounds	NOHA	STATISTICS NOT AVAILABLE												
1925-26	S.S. Marie Greyhounds	CHL	32	8	2	10				40					
1926-27	**Montreal Maroons**	**NHL**	**34**	**0**	**1**	**1**	**0**	**5**	**5**	**14**	**2**	**0**	**0**	**0**	**0**
	Stratford Nationals	Can-Pro	1	0	0	0				2					
	Detroit Greyhounds	AHA	6	1	0	1				13					
1927-28	Minneapolis Millers	AHA	26	1	2	3				32					
1928-29	Philadelphia Arrows	Can-Am	22	1	1	2				20					
1929-30	London Panthers	IHL	12	4	1	5				16					
	Toronto Millionaires	IHL	3	0	0	0				2					
1930-31	Buffalo Majors	AHA	39	5	9	14				90					
1931-32	Buffalo Majors	AHA	16	4	2	6				21					
	Tulsa Oilers	AHA	21	1	0	1				30					
1932-33	Falconbridge Falcons	NOHA	STATISTICS NOT AVAILABLE												
1933-34	Falconbridge Falcons	NOHA	STATISTICS NOT AVAILABLE												
1934-35	Falconbridge Falcons	NOHA	5	0	1	1				8	2	1	0	1	0
1935-36	Streatham Hockey Club	Ln-Cup	....	1	2	3				2					
	Streatham Hockey Club	Britain	....	2	7	9				16					
1936-37	Streatham Hockey Club	Britain	DID NOT PLAY – COACHING												
	NHL Totals		**34**	**0**	**1**	**1**	**0**	**5**	**5**	**14**	**2**	**0**	**0**	**0**	**0**

NOHA 1st All-Star Team (1921, 1922)

Signed as a free agent by **Montreal Maroons** and loaned to **Detroit** (AHA), September 30, 1926. Rights traded to **London** (IHL) by **Minneapolis** (AHA) for George Redding, October 24, 1929. Traded to **Toronto Millionaires** (IHL) by **London** (IHL) for George Hiller, December 16, 1929.

• DORAN, John John Michael "Red"

D – L. 5'11", 195 lbs. b: Belleville, Ont., 5/24/1911 d: 2/11/1975.

			REGULAR SEASON								PLAYOFFS				
Season	Club	League	GP	G	A	Pts	AG	AA	APts	PIM	GP	G	A	Pts	PIM
1928-29	West Toronto Redmen	OHA-Jr.	STATISTICS NOT AVAILABLE												
1929-30	West Toronto Nationals	OHA-Jr.	4	2	0	2				2					
	Toronto Stockyards	TMHL	2	1	0	1				2					
	West Toronto Nationals	M-Cup	7	2	1	3				14					
1930-31	West Toronto Nationals	OHA-Jr.	STATISTICS NOT AVAILABLE												
1931-32	Toronto Marlboros	OHA-Sr.	7	0	0	0				8					
	Toronto Eaton's	TMHL	9	3	1	4				8	4	0	1	1	2
1932-33	New Haven Eagles	Can-Am	41	4	2	6				38					
1933-34	**New York Americans**	**NHL**	**39**	**1**	**4**	**5**	**2**	**8**	**10**	**40**					
	Quebec Castors	Can-Am	8	1	0	1				20					
1934-35	Quebec Castors	Can-Am	44	7	11	18				*105	3	1	0	1	4
1935-36	**New York Americans**	**NHL**	**25**	**4**	**2**	**6**	**8**	**4**	**12**	**44**	**3**	**0**	**0**	**0**	**0**
	New Haven Eagles	Can-Am	24	0	0	0				87					
1936-37	**New York Americans**	**NHL**	**21**	**0**	**1**	**1**	**0**	**2**	**2**	**10**					
	New Haven Eagles	IAHL	6	1	2	3				16					
	Pittsburgh Hornets	IAHL	21	2	8	10				34	5	1	1	2	11
1937-38	**Detroit Red Wings**	**NHL**	**7**	**0**	**0**	**0**	**0**	**0**	**0**	**10**					
	Pittsburgh Hornets	IAHL	25	4	6	10				24					
	New Haven Eagles	IAHL	11	0	6	6				14	2	0	0	0	2
1938-39	New Haven Eagles	IAHL	7	0	0	0				24					
	Providence Reds	IAHL	33	2	10	12				63	5	1	1	2	8
1939-40	Providence Reds	IAHL	46	14	19	33				82	8	4	2	6	16
	Montreal Canadiens	**NHL**	**6**	**0**	**3**	**3**	**0**	**5**	**5**	**6**					
1940-41	Hershey Bears	AHL	16	0	5	5				20					
	Buffalo Bisons	AHL	42	2	11	13				36					
1941-42	Truro Bearcats	NSAPC	1	0	0	0				0	5	2	1	3	0
	Truro Bearcats	Al-Cup	8	1	5	6				4					
1942-43	Montreal Army	MCHL	4	1	5	6				4	5	5	*7	*12	12
	NHL Totals		**98**	**5**	**10**	**15**	**10**	**19**	**29**	**110**	**3**	**0**	**0**	**0**	**0**

Traded to **Detroit** by **NY Americans** with $7,500 for Earl Robertson, May 9, 1937. Signed as a free agent by **Providence**, October 9, 1939. Loaned to **Montreal** by **Providence** (IAHL), January 15, 1940. Traded to **Buffalo** (AHL) by **Hershey** (AHL) for cash, December 11, 1940.

• DORAN, Lloyd Lloyd George "Red"

C – L. 6', 175 lbs. b: South Porcupine, Ont., 1/10/1921.

			REGULAR SEASON								PLAYOFFS				
Season	Club	League	GP	G	A	Pts	AG	AA	APts	PIM	GP	G	A	Pts	PIM
1940-41	Dome Porkies	NOJHA	23	9	12	21				28					
1941-42	Omaha Knights	AHA	39	6	18	24				25	8	4	3	7	*22
1942-43	Montreal Army	QSHL	30	9	16	25				46	7	2	1	3	10
1943-44	Kingston Army	OHA-Sr.	11	8	14	22				14					
1944-45			MILITARY SERVICE												
1945-46			MILITARY SERVICE												
1946-47	**Detroit Red Wings**	**NHL**	**24**	**3**	**2**	**5**	**3**	**2**	**5**	**10**					
	Indianapolis Capitols	AHL	35	9	24	33				77					
1947-48	Indianapolis Capitols	AHL	45	14	21	35				50					
1948-49	St. Louis Flyers	AHL	67	19	55	74				39	7	3	5	8	0
1949-50	St. Louis Flyers	AHL	70	14	42	56				60	2	0	1	1	0
1950-51	St. Louis Flyers	AHL	13	1	2	3				10					
	Denver Falcons	USHL	12	3	2	5				6					
	Cleveland Barons	AHL	22	2	9	11				16	8	3	4	7	6
	NHL Totals		**24**	**3**	**2**	**5**	**3**	**2**	**5**	**10**					

Signed as a free agent by **Detroit**, October 21, 1941. Traded to **Chicago** (St. Louis-AHL) by **Detroit** with Red Almas, Tony Licari, Barry Sullivan and Thain Simon for Joe Lund and Hec Highton, September 9, 1948. Traded to **Cleveland** (AHL) by **Chicago** (St. Louis-AHL) for Eric Pogue, November 17, 1950. • Diagnosed with leukemia, October, 1966.

• DORATY, Ken Kenneth Edward "Cagie"

F – R. 5'7", 133 lbs. b: Stittsville, Ont., 6/23/1906 d: 4/4/1981.

			REGULAR SEASON								PLAYOFFS				
Season	Club	League	GP	G	A	Pts	AG	AA	APts	PIM	GP	G	A	Pts	PIM
1921-22	Rouleau Athletic Club	SAHA	STATISTICS NOT AVAILABLE												
1922-23	Rouleau Athletic Club	RCSHL	STATISTICS NOT AVAILABLE												
1923-24	Regina Pats	RCJHL	6	5	2	7				0					
	Regina Pats	M-Cup	5	3	3	6				0					
1924-25	Regina Pats	RCJHL	4	5	4	9				2					
	Regina Pats	M-Cup	12	13	7	20				24					
1925-26	Portland Rosebuds	WHL	30	4	1	5				4					
1926-27	**Chicago Black Hawks**	**NHL**	**18**	**0**	**0**	**0**	**0**	**0**	**0**	**0**					
	Minneapolis Millers	AHA	7	0	0	0				0					
1927-28	Kitchener Millionaires	Can-Pro	39	19	6	25				35	5	2	0	2	6
1928-29	Toronto Millionaires	Can-Pro	39	*26	5	31				42	2	1	1	2	2
1929-30	Cleveland Indians	IHL	42	26	16	42				43	6	*5	0	5	*14
1930-31	Cleveland Indians	IHL	48	25	24	49				43	6	1	4	5	6
1931-32	Cleveland Indians	IHL	48	21	15	36				45					
1932-33	**Toronto Maple Leafs**	**NHL**	**38**	**5**	**11**	**16**	**9**	**23**	**32**	**16**	**9**	**5**	**0**	**5**	**2**
	Syracuse Stars	IHL	10	5	4	9				14					
1933-34	**Toronto Maple Leafs**	**NHL**	**34**	**9**	**10**	**19**	**15**	**21**	**36**	**6**	**5**	**2**	**2**	**4**	**0**
	Buffalo Bisons	IHL	4	0	0	0				2					
1934-35	**Toronto Maple Leafs**	**NHL**	**11**	**1**	**4**	**5**	**2**	**7**	**9**	**0**	**1**	**0**	**0**	**0**	**0**
	Syracuse Stars	IHL	30	12	17	29				37	2	0	1	1	0
	New Haven Eagles	Can-Am	1	0	0	0				0					
1935-36	Syracuse Stars	IHL	7	*1	2	3				4	2	0	2	2	0
	Cleveland Falcons	IHL	39	*27	18	45				38					
1936-37	Cleveland Barons	IAHL	6	1	2	3				0					
	Pittsburgh Hornets	IAHL	39	13	13	26				21	5	1	0	1	4
1937-38	**Detroit Red Wings**	**NHL**	**2**	**0**	**1**	**1**	**0**	**2**	**2**	**2**					
	Pittsburgh Hornets	IAHL	48	12	17	29				22	2	0	0	0	0
1938-39	Seattle Seahawks	PCHL	48	25	17	42				23	7	1	2	3	6
	NHL Totals		**103**	**15**	**26**	**41**	**26**	**53**	**79**	**24**	**15**	**7**	**2**	**9**	**2**
	Other Major League Totals		30	4	1	5				4					

IHL Second All-Star Team (1935, 1936) • Played in NHL All-Star Game (1934)

Rights transferred to **Chicago** after NHL club purchased **Portland** (WHL) franchise, May 15, 1926. Traded to **Kitchener** (Can-Pro) by **Minneapolis** (AHA) for cash, October, 1927. Traded to **Toronto** (Syracuse-IHL) by **Cleveland** (IHL) for cash, October 6, 1932. Traded to **Cleveland** (IHL) by **Toronto** for cash, December 2, 1935. Signed as a free agent by **Detroit**, December 3, 1936.

• DORNHOEFER, Gary

— see page 1034

• DOROHOY, Eddie "The Great Gabbo"

C/LW – L. 5'9", 155 lbs. b: Medicine Hat, Alta., 3/13/1929.

			REGULAR SEASON								PLAYOFFS				
Season	Club	League	GP	G	A	Pts	AG	AA	APts	PIM	GP	G	A	Pts	PIM
1946-47	Lethbridge Native Sons	AJHL	11	2	1	3				4	3	2	0	2	0
1947-48	Lethbridge Native Sons	AJHL	27	32	*49	81				22	6	6	*15	*21	9
	Lethbridge Native Sons	M-Cup	11	4	7	11				6					
1948-49	**Montreal Canadiens**	**NHL**	**16**	**0**	**0**	**0**	**0**	**0**	**0**	**6**					
	Dallas Texans	USHL	34	19	21	40				76	4	2	2	4	0
1949-50	Cincinnati Mohawks	AHL	6	0	0	0				2					
	Victoria Cougars	PCHL	31	15	16	31				25					
1950-51	Victoria Cougars	PCHL	68	29	*58	*87				64	12	*6	8	*14	8
1951-52	Victoria Cougars	PCHL	68	29	*56	85				66	13	3	4	7	12
1952-53	Victoria Cougars	WHL	70	24	54	78				97					
1953-54	Victoria Cougars	WHL	70	26	53	79				46	5	1	2	3	4
1954-55	Victoria Cougars	WHL	68	33	52	85				41	5	2	2	4	10
1955-56	Seattle Americans	WHL	69	18	41	59				131					
1956-57	Seattle Americans	WHL	70	31	55	86				70	6	2	6	8	4
1957-58	Victoria Cougars	WHL	58	34	41	75				51					
1958-59	Calgary Stampeders	WHL	64	35	*74	109				56	8	2	4	6	6
1959-60	Vancouver Canucks	WHL	33	17	21	38				30					
1960-61	Vancouver Canucks	WHL	2	0	0	0				0					
1961-62	Los Angeles–Vancouver	WHL	37	6	10	16				14					

Season	Club	League	GP	G	A	Pts	AG	AA	APts	PIM	GP	G	A	Pts	PIM
			REGULAR SEASON								PLAYOFFS				
1962-63	Vancouver Canucks	WHL	6	0	2	2	....	....	....	0	....	....	....	....	....
	Knoxville Knights	EHL	20	7	20	27	....	....	....	2	5	1	2	3	0
1963-64	New Haven Blades	EHL	18	11	18	29	....	....	....	6	5	2	3	5	2
1964-65	Spokane Jets	WIHL	47	20	50	70	....	....	....	118	3	0	2	2	12
	NHL Totals		**16**	**0**	**0**	**0**	**0**	**0**	**0**	**6**	....	....	....	....	....

PCHL Second All-Star Team (1952) • WHL Prairie Division First All-Star Team (1959) • Won Leader Cup (WHL Prairie Division - MVP) (1959)

Rights traded to **NY Rangers** by **Montreal** (Victoria-WHL) with Dick Gamble for Hy Buller with Montreal holding right of recall if Dorohoy failed to make NY Rangers roster, June 8, 1954. Transaction cancelled after Buller retired, September, 1954. Loaned to **Victoria** (WHL) by **Montreal** for cash, August, 1955. Loan transferred to **Seattle** (WHL) by **Montreal** for cash, September 12, 1955. Traded to **Victoria** (WHL) by **Montreal** (Seattle-WHL) for Bill Davidson and Don Chiupka, September, 1957. Traded to **Calgary** (WHL) by **Victoria** (WHL) for George Ford, Enio Sclisizzi and Murray Wilkie, July, 1958. • Missed majority of 1959-60 and 1960-61 seasons recovering from broken leg suffered in WHL game, December, 1959. Signed as a free agent by Knoxville (EHL), January 23, 1963.

• DOUGLAS, Kent

— see page 1035

• DOUGLAS, Les

Leslie Gordon
C – L. 5'9", 165 lbs. b: Perth, Ont., 12/5/1918.

Season	Club	League	GP	G	A	Pts	AG	AA	APts	PIM	GP	G	A	Pts	PIM
1934-35	Perth Crescents	OVJHL	STATISTICS NOT AVAILABLE												
	Perth Crescents	OVHL	2	0	0	0	....	....	....	2	....	....	....	....	....
1935-36	Perth Crescents	OVJHL	STATISTICS NOT AVAILABLE												
1936-37	Perth Crescents	OVJHL	12	*21	*19	*40	....	....	....	10	2	*3	*4	*7	0
1937-38	Perth Blue Devils	OVJHL	8	*18	16	*34	....	....	....	10	2	*8	*0	*8	0
	Perth Blue Devils	M-Cup	12	27	18	45	....	....	....	8	....	....	....	....	....
1938-39	Detroit Pontiacs	MOHL	27	*27	20	*47	....	....	....	25	7	5	4	9	13
1939-40	Indianapolis Capitols	IAHL	54	15	19	34	....	....	....	20	5	0	3	3	0
1940-41	**Detroit Red Wings**	**NHL**	**18**	**1**	**2**	**3**	**2**	**3**	**5**	**2**	....	....	....	....	....
	Indianapolis Capitols	AHL	31	3	5	8	....	....	....	4	....	....	....	....	....
1941-42	Indianapolis Capitols	AHL	56	15	33	48	....	....	....	9	10	8	9	*17	6
♦1942-43	**Detroit Red Wings**	**NHL**	**21**	**5**	**8**	**13**	**5**	**7**	**12**	**4**	**10**	**3**	**2**	**5**	**2**
	Indianapolis Capitols	AHL	33	13	26	39	....	....	....	7	1	1	0	1	0
1943-44	Toronto Maher Jewels	TIHL	8	4	6	10	....	....	....	2	....	....	....	....	....
	Toronto RCAF Manning	TNDHL	2	4	2	6	....	....	....	0	....	....	....	....	....
	Ottawa Commandos	QSHL	....	....	....	....	....	....	....	....	3	3	0	3	0
1944-45	Toronto Auto Workers	TMHL	13	9	25	34	....	....	....	4	3	0	0	0	0
	Toronto Orphans	TMHL	....	....	....	....	....	....	....	....	1	1	2	3	0
1945-46	**Detroit Red Wings**	**NHL**	**1**	**0**	**0**	**0**	**0**	**0**	**0**	**0**	....	....	....	....	....
	Indianapolis Capitols	AHL	62	44	46	*90	....	....	....	35	5	1	2	3	2
1946-47	**Detroit Red Wings**	**NHL**	**12**	**0**	**2**	**2**	**0**	**2**	**2**	**2**	....	....	....	....	....
	Indianapolis Capitols	AHL	51	26	57	83	....	....	....	26	....	....	....	....	....
1947-48	Buffalo Bisons	AHL	68	27	50	77	....	....	....	23	8	2	3	5	0
1948-49	Buffalo Bisons	AHL	68	20	52	72	....	....	....	20	....	....	....	....	....
1949-50	Cleveland Barons	AHL	67	32	*68	*100	....	....	....	27	9	2	2	4	11
1950-51	Cleveland Barons	AHL	70	31	39	70	....	....	....	20	11	3	4	7	0
1951-52	Montreal Royals	QMHL	60	30	*50	80	....	....	....	20	7	3	7	10	2
	Buffalo Bisons	AHL	....	....	....	....	....	....	....	....	1	0	1	1	0
1952-53	Montreal Royals	QMHL	55	19	29	48	....	....	....	8	14	5	3	8	4
1953-54	Sarnia Sailors	OHA-Sr.	22	8	15	23	....	....	....	6	....	....	....	....	....
1954-55	Kingston Goodyears	OHA-I	STATISTICS NOT AVAILABLE												
1955-56	Kingston Goodyears	OHA-I	27	8	12	20	....	....	....	52	1	0	0	0	0
	NHL Totals		**52**	**6**	**12**	**18**	**7**	**12**	**19**	**8**	**10**	**3**	**2**	**5**	**2**

AHL First All-Star Team (1946, 1950) • AHL Second All-Star Team (1947) • Won John B. Sollenberger Trophy (Top Scorer - AHL) (1950) • Won Les Cunningham Award (MVP - AHL) (1950) • Won Byng of Vimy Trophy (QMHL MVP) (1952)

Signed as a free agent by **Detroit**, October 9, 1939. Traded to **Buffalo** (AHL) by **Detroit** with Harold Jackson for Jim McFadden, June, 1947. Traded to **Cleveland** (AHL) by **Buffalo** (AHL) for Gord Davidson, June 15, 1949.

• DOWNIE, Dave

David Michael "Wildcat"
C/RW – R. 5'8", 168 lbs. b: Burke's Falls, Ont., 3/11/1909 d: 1962.

Season	Club	League	GP	G	A	Pts	AG	AA	APts	PIM	GP	G	A	Pts	PIM
1925-26	Regina Falcons	S-SJHL	8	7	3	10	....	....	....	4	....	....	....	....	....
	Regina Falcons	M-Cup	3	2	1	3	....	....	....	10	....	....	....	....	....
1926-27	Regina Falcons	S-SJHL	6	6	1	*7	....	....	....	0	1	0	0	0	0
1927-28	Vancouver Monarchs	VCAHL	8	10	1	11	....	....	....	10	2	2	1	3	0
	Vancouver Maroons	Al-Cup	2	4	1	5	....	....	....	4	....	....	....	....	....
1928-29	Victoria Cubs	PCHL	9	3	1	4	....	....	....	2	....	....	....	....	....
	Portland Buckaroos	PCHL	26	4	11	15	....	....	....	59	2	0	0	0	8
1929-30	Portland Buckaroos	PCHL	27	6	0	6	....	....	....	37	4	*3	0	*3	0
1930-31	Portland Buckaroos	PCHL	34	*13	4	*17	....	....	....	78	....	....	....	....	....
1931-32	Boston Cubs	Can-Am	8	1	0	1	....	....	....	12	....	....	....	....	....
	Syracuse Stars	IHL	37	12	7	19	....	....	....	46	....	....	....	....	....
1932-33	Syracuse Stars	IHL	34	15	12	27	....	....	....	52	6	1	2	3	*29
	Toronto Maple Leafs	**NHL**	**11**	**0**	**1**	**1**	**0**	**2**	**2**	**2**	....	....	....	....	....
1933-34	Syracuse Stars	IHL	26	12	10	22	....	....	....	31	6	0	0	0	0
1934-35	Syracuse Stars	IHL	43	14	14	28	....	....	....	71	2	0	0	0	0
1935-36	Windsor Bulldogs	IHL	43	15	15	30	....	....	....	*97	8	1	4	5	14
1936-37	Seattle Seahawks	PCHL	37	13	8	21	....	....	....	50	....	....	....	....	....
1937-38	Seattle Seahawks	PCHL	42	17	19	36	....	....	....	67	4	1	0	1	0
1938-39	Seattle Seahawks	PCHL	48	*35	29	64	....	....	....	32	7	3	2	5	9
1939-40	Seattle Seahawks	PCHL	40	22	*26	*48	....	....	....	26	....	....	....	....	....
1940-41	Seattle Olympics	PCHL	40	24	29	53	....	....	....	60	2	0	0	0	2
1941-42	Philadelphia Rockets	AHL	9	1	0	1	....	....	....	0	....	....	....	....	....
1942-43			DID NOT PLAY												
1943-44	Seattle Ironmen	PCSHL	9	*19	9	28	....	....	....	7	2	2	5	7	12
	Portland Oilers	PCSHL	....	....	....	....	....	....	....	....	4	7	1	8	2
1944-45	Seattle Stars	PCHL	STATISTICS NOT AVAILABLE												
	NHL Totals		**11**	**0**	**1**	**1**	**0**	**2**	**2**	**2**					

Traded to **Portland** (PCHL) by **Victoria** (PCHL) for Paul Runge, December 21, 1928. Signed as a free agent by **Boston**, November 4, 1931. Loaned to **Toronto** by **Syracuse** (IHL), February 12, 1933. Traded to **Windsor** (IHL) by **Syracuse** (IHL) for cash, October 17, 1935.

• DRAPER, Bruce

C – L. 5'10", 157 lbs. b: Toronto, Ont., 10/2/1940 d: 1/26/1968.

Season	Club	League	GP	G	A	Pts	AG	AA	APts	PIM	GP	G	A	Pts	PIM
			REGULAR SEASON								PLAYOFFS				
1957-58	St. Michael's Buzzers	OHA-B	STATISTICS NOT AVAILABLE												
	St. Michael's Majors	OHA-Jr.	2	0	0	0	....	....	....	2	....	....	....	....	....
1958-59	St. Michael's Majors	OHA-Jr.	48	24	25	49	....	....	....	58	15	5	7	12	24
1959-60	St. Michael's Majors	OHA-Jr.	38	16	22	38	....	....	....	23	10	6	6	12	10
1960-61	St. Michael's Majors	OHA-Jr.	46	44	33	77	....	....	....	77	19	10	*16	26	18
	St. Michael's Majors	M-Cup	9	5	7	12	....	....	....	2	....	....	....	....	....
1961-62	Rochester Americans	AHL	70	25	40	65	....	....	....	31	2	0	0	0	0
1962-63	**Toronto Maple Leafs**	**NHL**	**1**	**0**	**0**	**0**	**0**	**0**	**0**	**0**	....	....	....	....	....
	Sudbury Wolves	EPHL	11	3	10	13	....	....	....	10	....	....	....	....	....
	Rochester Americans	AHL	55	8	18	26	....	....	....	12	2	0	1	1	0
1963-64	Denver Invaders	WHL	68	15	30	45	....	....	....	30	6	0	3	3	0
1964-65	Hershey Bears	AHL	42	12	20	32	....	....	....	10	15	7	3	10	6
1965-66	Hershey Bears	AHL	41	14	21	35	....	....	....	49	....	....	....	....	....
1966-67	Hershey Bears	AHL	2	1	0	1	....	....	....	0	....	....	....	....	....
	NHL Totals		**1**	**0**	**0**	**0**	**0**	**0**	**0**	**0**	....	....	....	....	....

OHA-Jr. First All-Team (1961) • Won Max Kaminsky Trophy (OHA-Jr. MVP) (1961)

Traded to **Hershey** (AHL) by **Toronto** to complete transaction that sent Les Duff to Toronto (September, 1963), September, 1964.

• DRILLON, Gordie

Gordon Arthur **HHOF**
RW – R. 6'2", 178 lbs. b: Moncton, N.B., 10/23/1913 d: 9/23/1985.

Season	Club	League	GP	G	A	Pts	AG	AA	APts	PIM	GP	G	A	Pts	PIM
1926-27	Edith Cavell School	MSBL	5	4	0	4	....	....	....	....	....	....	....	....	....
1927-28	Victoria Street School	MSBL	5	1	1	2	....	....	....	....	....	....	....	....	....
1928-29	Moncton Aberdeens	H.S.	2	0	0	0	....	....	....	0	....	....	....	....	....
1929-30	Moncton Chalmers Club	SNBJL	6	8	4	12	....	....	....	2	....	....	....	....	....
1930-31	Moncton Athletics	MJHL	6	*15	4	*19	....	....	....	....	....	....	....	....	....
	Moncton Aberdeens	H.S.	3	1	0	1	....	....	....	0	1	1	0	*1	....
	Moncton Athletics	M-Cup	2	3	2	5	....	....	....	0	....	....	....	....	....
1931-32	Moncton Wheelers	MJHL	6	6	4	10	....	....	....	....	3	5	1	6	5
1932-33	Moncton Hawks	MJHL	4	13	3	16	....	....	....	0	2	*2	1	3	4
	Moncton Swift's	MCIHL	7	11	3	14	....	....	....	....	6	*13	4	*17	....
1933-34	Toronto Young Rangers	OHA-Jr.	11	*20	*13	*33	....	....	....	4	2	*5	*3	*8	4
	Toronto CCM	TMHL	2	0	1	1	....	....	....	0	....	....	....	....	....
	Toronto Young Rangers	M-Cup	2	0	0	0	....	....	....	16	....	....	....	....	....
1934-35	Toronto Lions	OHA-Jr.	11	17	9	26	....	....	....	2	5	2	1	3	6
	Toronto Dominions	OHA-Sr.	11	12	6	18	....	....	....	2	3	2	1	3	4
1935-36	Pittsburgh Yellowjackets	EAHL	40	22	12	34	....	....	....	4	8	3	2	5	0
1936-37	**Toronto Maple Leafs**	**NHL**	**41**	**16**	**17**	**33**	**27**	**31**	**58**	**2**	**2**	**0**	**0**	**0**	**0**
	Syracuse Stars	IAHL	7	2	3	5	....	....	....	2	....	....	....	....	....
1937-38	**Toronto Maple Leafs**	**NHL**	**48**	***26**	**26**	***52**	**43**	**42**	**85**	**4**	**7**	***7**	**1**	**8**	**2**
1938-39	**Toronto Maple Leafs**	**NHL**	**40**	**18**	**16**	**34**	**32**	**25**	**57**	**15**	**10**	***7**	**6**	**13**	**4**
1939-40	**Toronto Maple Leafs**	**NHL**	**43**	**21**	**19**	**40**	**35**	**30**	**65**	**13**	**10**	**3**	**1**	**4**	**0**
1940-41	**Toronto Maple Leafs**	**NHL**	**42**	**23**	**21**	**44**	**36**	**30**	**66**	**2**	**7**	**3**	**2**	**5**	**2**
♦1941-42	**Toronto Maple Leafs**	**NHL**	**48**	**23**	**18**	**41**	**31**	**21**	**52**	**6**	**9**	**2**	**3**	**5**	**2**
1942-43	**Montreal Canadiens**	**NHL**	**49**	**28**	**22**	**50**	**29**	**21**	**50**	**14**	**5**	**4**	**2**	**6**	**0**
1943-44	Toronto Army Daggers	OHA-Sr.	1	1	1	2	....	....	....	0	....	....	....	....	....
1944-45	Dartmouth RCAF	NSDHL	1	0	1	1	....	....	....	0	....	....	....	....	....
	Valleyfield Braves	QPHL	8	11	4	15	....	....	....	0	11	8	6	14	2
	Valleyfield Braves	Al-Cup	3	0	0	0	....	....	....	0	....	....	....	....	....
1945-46	Halifax RCAF	NSDHL	3	7	8	15	....	....	....	4	....	....	....	....	....
1946-47	Charlottetown Legion	NSSHL	4	10	8	18	....	....	....	16	11	*41	12	*53	4
1947-48	North Sydney Victorias	NSSHL	2	0	1	1	....	....	....	0	....	....	....	....	....
1948-49	Grand Falls All-Stars	Nfld-Sr.	DID NOT PLAY – COACHING												
	Maritime All-Stars	X-Games	2	11	7	18	....	....	....	2	....	....	....	....	....
1949-50	Saint John Beavers	NBSHL	49	48	24	72	....	....	....	40	11	1	4	5	12
1950-51	Moncton Hawks	MMHL	DID NOT PLAY – COACHING												
	NHL Totals		**311**	**155**	**139**	**294**	**233**	**200**	**433**	**56**	**50**	**26**	**15**	**41**	**10**

NHL First All-Star Team (1938, 1939) • Won Lady Byng Trophy (1938) • NHL Scoring Leader (1938) • NHL Second All-Star Team (1942) • Played in NHL All-Star Game (1939)

Traded to **Montreal** by **Toronto** for $30,000, October 4, 1942.

• DROUILLARD, Clarence

Clarence Joseph "Clare"
C – L. 5'7", 150 lbs. b: Windsor, Ont., 3/2/1914 Deceased.

Season	Club	League	GP	G	A	Pts	AG	AA	APts	PIM	GP	G	A	Pts	PIM
1932-33	Windsor Walkerton Tech	H.S.	3	3	*3	6	....	....	....	0	....	....	....	....	....
	Windsor Wanderers	MOHL	18	9	3	12	....	....	....	14	....	....	....	....	....
1933-34	St. Michael's Majors	OHA-Jr.	11	14	11	25	....	....	....	4	3	*4	2	6	4
	St. Michael's Majors	M-Cup	11	15	20	35	....	....	....	14	....	....	....	....	....
1934-35	Windsor Bulldogs	IHL	44	7	15	22	....	....	....	12	....	....	....	....	....
1935-36	Windsor Bulldogs	IHL	48	14	15	29	....	....	....	43	8	2	3	5	6
1936-37	Pittsburgh Hornets	IAHL	50	15	16	31	....	....	....	28	5	0	1	1	2
1937-38	**Detroit Red Wings**	**NHL**	**10**	**0**	**1**	**1**	**0**	**2**	**2**	**0**	....	....	....	....	....
	Pittsburgh Hornets	IAHL	5	0	4	4	....	....	....	4	....	....	....	....	....
	Providence Reds	IAHL	31	6	8	14	....	....	....	17	7	1	5	6	0
1938-39	Hershey Bears	IAHL	50	9	17	26	....	....	....	20	1	0	0	0	0
1939-40	Pittsburgh Hornets	IAHL	56	12	25	37	....	....	....	22	9	3	4	7	6
1940-41	Pittsburgh Hornets	AHL	31	6	13	19	....	....	....	6	....	....	....	....	....
	Springfield Indians	AHL	6	0	1	1	....	....	....	2	....	....	....	....	....
	Buffalo Bisons	AHL	9	0	2	2	....	....	....	6	....	....	....	....	....
1941-42	Buffalo Bisons	AHL	48	3	10	13	....	....	....	6	....	....	....	....	....
	Philadelphia Rockets	AHL	2	1	0	1	....	....	....	0	....	....	....	....	....
1942-43	Windsor Abars	WIHL	11	9	14	23	....	....	....	2	7	9	2	11	0
1943-44	Windsor Gotfredson	WIHL	9	14	11	25	....	....	....	2	3	2	3	5	2
1944-45	Windsor Gotfredson	WIHL	2	2	0	2	....	....	....	2	2	4	4	8	0
	NHL Totals		**10**	**0**	**1**	**1**	**0**	**2**	**2**	**0**					

Traded to **Detroit** by **Windsor** (IHL) for cash, February 26, 1936. Traded to **Boston** by **Detroit** with cash for Alex Motter, December 22, 1937. Signed as a free agent by **Toronto** (Pittsburgh-IAHL), September, 1939. Traded to **NY Americans** (Springfield-AHL) by **Toronto** (Pittsburgh-AHL) for Jack Howard and the loan of Peanuts O'Flaherty, January 17, 1941. Signed as a free agent by **Buffalo** (AHL), February 25, 1941. Loaned to **Philadelphia** (AHL) by **Buffalo** (AHL) for the loan of Alfie Moore, February 13, 1942.

			REGULAR SEASON								PLAYOFFS				
Season	Club	League	GP	G	A	Pts	AG	AA	APts	PIM	GP	G	A	Pts	PIM

• DROUIN, Polly Paul-Emile
LW – L. 5′7″, 160 lbs. b: Verdun, Que., 1/16/1916 d: 1/1/1968.

Season	Club	League	GP	G	A	Pts	AG	AA	APts	PIM	GP	G	A	Pts	PIM
1931-32	Ottawa Primrose	OCJHL	15	6	3	9	....	....	....	8	4	0	1	1	0
1932-33	Ottawa Primrose	OCJHL	13	5	3	8	....	....	....	6	4	2	1	3	6
1933-34	Hull Lasalle	OCJHL	16	20	*18	*38	....	....	....	47	4	4	3	7	4
	Hull Lasalle Seniors	OCHL	1	0	0	0	....	....	....	0	....	....	....	....	....
1934-35	**Montreal Canadiens**	**NHL**	**4**	**0**	**0**	**0**	**0**	**0**	**0**	**0**	....	....	....	....	....
	Ottawa Senators	OCHL	20	10	7	17	....	....	....	8	8	2	0	2	*20
1935-36	**Montreal Canadiens**	**NHL**	**30**	**1**	**8**	**9**	**2**	**15**	**17**	**19**	....	....	....	....	....
	Ottawa Senators	OCHL	12	7	7	14	....	....	....	12	....	....	....	....	....
1936-37	**Montreal Canadiens**	**NHL**	**4**	**0**	**0**	**0**	**0**	**0**	**0**	**0**	....	....	....	....	....
	New Haven Eagles	IAHL	27	10	13	23	....	....	....	33	....	....	....	....	....
1937-38	**Montreal Canadiens**	**NHL**	**31**	**7**	**13**	**20**	**11**	**21**	**32**	**8**	**1**	**0**	**0**	**0**	**0**
1938-39	**Montreal Canadiens**	**NHL**	**28**	**7**	**11**	**18**	**12**	**17**	**29**	**2**	**3**	**0**	**1**	**1**	**5**
1939-40	**Montreal Canadiens**	**NHL**	**42**	**4**	**11**	**15**	**7**	**17**	**24**	**51**	**1**	**0**	**0**	**0**	**0**
	New Haven Eagles	IAHL	7	1	6	7	....	....	....	0	....	....	....	....	....
1940-41	**Montreal Canadiens**	**NHL**	**21**	**4**	**7**	**11**	**6**	**10**	**16**	**0**	....	....	....	....	....
	New Haven Eagles	AHL	19	8	4	12	....	....	....	8	2	0	1	1	0
1941-42	Washington Lions	AHL	56	23	21	44	....	....	....	31	2	0	2	2	0
1942-43	Ottawa Commandos	QSHL	29	22	14	36	....	....	....	31	....	....	....	....	....
	Ottawa RCAF	QSHL	11	10	19	29	....	....	....	6	....	....	....	....	....
1943-44			MILITARY SERVICE												
1944-45			MILITARY SERVICE												
1945-46	Hull Volants	QSHL	13	8	13	21	....	....	....	10	....	....	....	....	....
	Ottawa QMG	OCHL	....	....	....	....	....	....	....	....	4	6	*14	*20	....
1946-47	St-Hyacinthe Gaulois	QPHL	40	24	30	54	....	....	....	20	4	1	0	1	0
	NHL Totals		**160**	**23**	**50**	**73**	**38**	**80**	**118**	**80**	**5**	**0**	**1**	**1**	**5**

Played in NHL All-Star Game (1939)

Claimed by **Montreal Canadiens** from **St. Louis** in Dispersal Draft, October 13, 1935. Traded to **Washington** (AHL) by **Montreal** for cash, October 9, 1941.

• DRUMMOND, Jim James Henry
D – L. 5′9″, 170 lbs. b: Toronto, Ont., 10/20/1918 d: 12/12/1950.

Season	Club	League	GP	G	A	Pts	AG	AA	APts	PIM	GP	G	A	Pts	PIM
1937-38	Toronto Marlboros	OHA-Jr.	12	3	5	8	....	....	....	8	6	0	4	4	6
1938-39	Oshawa Generals	OHA-Jr.	14	7	12	19	....	....	....	14	7	1	2	3	5
	Oshawa G-Men	OHA-Sr.	1	0	0	0	....	....	....	0	....	....	....	....	....
	Oshawa Generals	M-Cup	9	5	8	13	....	....	....	14	....	....	....	....	....
1939-40	Toronto Goodyears	OHA-Sr.	28	5	13	18	....	....	....	18	7	0	1	1	4
	Toronto Red Indians	TOHL	1	0	0	0	....	....	....	0	....	....	....	....	....
	Toronto RCAF	TMHL	6	3	3	6	....	....	....	4	3	1	2	3	2
	Toronto Goodyears	Al-Cup	4	0	0	0	....	....	....	2	....	....	....	....	....
1940-41	Toronto Marlboros	OHA-Sr.	30	8	8	16	....	....	....	18	10	0	0	0	11
	Toronto RCAF	TMHL	6	3	3	6	....	....	....	4	3	1	2	3	2
	Toronto Marlboros	Al-Cup	7	0	1	1	....	....	....	6	....	....	....	....	....
1941-42	Cornwall Flyers	QSHL	37	3	11	14	....	....	....	36	5	0	0	0	0
1942-43	Cornwall Flyers	QSHL	27	5	6	11	....	....	....	16	6	0	0	0	4
1943-44			MILITARY SERVICE												
1944-45	**New York Rangers**	**NHL**	**2**	**0**	**0**	**0**	**0**	**0**	**0**	**0**	....	....	....	....	....
	New York Rovers	EAHL	12	2	5	7	....	....	....	7	....	....	....	....	....
	Hershey Bears	AHL	24	1	4	5	....	....	....	4	11	3	2	5	2
	Toronto Orphans	TMHL	4	1	1	2	....	....	....	5	....	....	....	....	....
1945-46	Hershey Bears	AHL	55	4	11	15	....	....	....	16	3	0	1	1	0
1946-47	Cleveland Barons	AHL	53	5	17	22	....	....	....	26	4	0	0	0	2
1947-48	Philadelphia Rockets	AHL	23	4	7	11	....	....	....	10	....	....	....	....	....
1948-49	Philadelphia Rockets	AHL	24	0	6	6	....	....	....	15	....	....	....	....	....
	NHL Totals		**2**	**0**	**0**	**0**	**0**	**0**	**0**	**0**	....	....	....	....	....

Signed as a free agent by **NY Rangers**, December 5, 1944. Traded to **Hershey** (AHL) by **NY Rangers** for cash, January, 1945.

• DRURY, Herb Herbert Joseph
D/RW – R. 5′7″, 165 lbs. b: Midland, Ont., 3/2/1895 Deceased.

Season	Club	League	GP	G	A	Pts	AG	AA	APts	PIM	GP	G	A	Pts	PIM
1914-15	Midland Seniors	OHA-Sr.	1	2	0	2	....	....	....	....	....	....	....	....	....
1915-16	Port Colborne Seniors	OHA-Sr.	1	0	0	0	....	....	....	0	....	....	....	....	....
1916-17	St. Paul Saints	X-Games	STATISTICS NOT AVAILABLE												
	Pittsburgh AA	X-Games	6	0	1	1	....	....	....	6	....	....	....	....	....
1917-18	Pittsburgh AA	USAHA	12	10	0	10	....	....	....	....	....	....	....	....	....
1918-19			MILITARY SERVICE												
1919-20	United States	WEC-A	5	23	0	23	....	....	....	....	....	....	....	....	....
1920-21			DID NOT PLAY												
1921-22	Pittsburgh Stars	USAHA	STATISTICS NOT AVAILABLE												
1922-23	Pittsburgh Yellowjackets	USAHA	20	5	0	5	....	....	....	....	....	....	....	....	....
1923-24	Pittsburgh Yellowjackets	USAHA	2	2	0	2	....	....	....	....	13	5	0	5	....
	United States	Olympics	5	22	3	25	....	....	....	....	....	....	....	....	....
1924-25	Pittsburgh Yellowjackets	USAHA	33	7	0	7	....	....	....	....	8	4	0	4	....
1925-26	**Pittsburgh Pirates**	**NHL**	**33**	**6**	**2**	**8**	**10**	**13**	**23**	**40**	**2**	**1**	**0**	**1**	**0**
1926-27	**Pittsburgh Pirates**	**NHL**	**42**	**5**	**1**	**6**	**9**	**5**	**14**	**48**	....	....	....	....	....
1927-28	**Pittsburgh Pirates**	**NHL**	**44**	**6**	**4**	**10**	**12**	**23**	**35**	**44**	**2**	**0**	**1**	**1**	**0**
1928-29	**Pittsburgh Pirates**	**NHL**	**43**	**5**	**4**	**9**	**14**	**27**	**41**	**49**	....	....	....	....	....
1929-30	**Pittsburgh Pirates**	**NHL**	**27**	**2**	**0**	**2**	**3**	**0**	**3**	**12**	....	....	....	....	....
1930-31	**Philadelphia Quakers**	**NHL**	**24**	**0**	**2**	**2**	**0**	**6**	**6**	**10**	....	....	....	....	....
	NHL Totals		**213**	**24**	**13**	**37**	**48**	**74**	**122**	**203**	**4**	**1**	**1**	**2**	**0**

Signed as a free agent by **Pittsburgh**, September 26, 1925. Transferred to **Philadelphia** after **Pittsburgh** franchise relocated, October 18, 1930.

• DUBE, Gilles Joseph Gilles
LW – L. 5′10″, 165 lbs. b: Sherbrooke, Que., 6/2/1927.

Season	Club	League	GP	G	A	Pts	AG	AA	APts	PIM	GP	G	A	Pts	PIM
1945-46	Sherbrooke Randies	QPHL	7	1	3	4	....	....	....	0	....	....	....	....	....
1946-47	Montreal Jr. Canadiens	QJHL	12	16	16	32	....	....	....	8	2	1	2	3	2
1947-48	Sherbrooke St. Xavier	QPHL	43	31	41	72	....	....	....	44	8	6	10	16	13
1948-49	Sherbrooke Saints	QSHL	62	30	56	86	....	....	....	56	12	3	7	10	6
1949-50	**Montreal Canadiens**	**NHL**	**12**	**1**	**2**	**3**	**1**	**2**	**3**	**2**	....	....	....	....	....
	Cincinnati Mohawks	AHL	46	19	18	37	....	....	....	12	....	....	....	....	....
1950-51	Cincinnati Mohawks	AHL	62	16	26	42	....	....	....	29	....	....	....	....	....
1951-52	Sherbrooke Saints	QMHL	51	17	15	32	....	....	....	33	11	5	6	11	10
1952-53	Sherbrooke Saints	QMHL	60	21	32	53	....	....	....	55	7	3	2	5	14
1953-54	Sherbrooke Saints	QHL	72	17	45	62	....	....	....	68	5	1	5	6	4
♦	**Detroit Red Wings**	**NHL**	....	....	....	....	....	....	....	....	**2**	**0**	**0**	**0**	**0**
1954-55	Shawinigan Cataracts	QHL	56	18	41	59	....	....	....	30	13	1	7	8	7
	Shawinigan Cataracts	Ed-Cup	7	4	3	7	....	....	....	2	....	....	....	....	....
1955-56	Shawinigan Cataracts	QHL	64	*37	*54	*91	....	....	....	68	11	3	5	8	2
1956-57	Shawinigan Cataracts	QHL	58	12	31	43	....	....	....	38	....	....	....	....	....
1957/60			STATISTICS NOT AVAILABLE												
1960-61	Sherbrooke Cantons	QSHL	30	14	22	36	....	....	....	30	3	1	1	2	19
1961-62	Sherbrooke Cantons	ETSHL	18	6	17	23	....	....	....	18	7	0	8	8	8
	NHL Totals		**12**	**1**	**2**	**3**	**1**	**2**	**3**	**2**	**2**	**0**	**0**	**0**	**0**

QHL First All-Star Team (1956) • Won President's Cup (Scoring Champion - QHL) (1956)

Signed as a free agent by **Montreal**, September 27, 1949. Loaned to **Sherbrooke** (QMHL) by **Montreal** for cash, September, 1951. Signed as a free agent by **Detroit** to three game try-out contract, April 10, 1954.

• DUFF, Dick — *see page 1041*

• DUFOUR, Marc — *see page 1042*

• DUGGAN, John John Herbert "Jack"
LW – L. 5′8″, 185 lbs. b: Ottawa, Ont., 12/17/1898 Deceased.

Season	Club	League	GP	G	A	Pts	AG	AA	APts	PIM	GP	G	A	Pts	PIM
1917-18	Ottawa St. Brigids	OCHL	11	5	0	5	....	....	....	9	....	....	....	....	....
	Ottawa St. Brigids	OCHL	5	4	0	4	....	....	....	0	....	....	....	....	....
1918-19	Ottawa Munitions	OCHL	7	3	1	4	....	....	....	3	....	....	....	....	....
1919-20	Ottawa Munitions	OCHL	8	8	0	8	....	....	....	....	5	5	*5	10	....
1920-21	Ottawa Munitions	OCHL	8	8	0	8	....	....	....	....	1	0	1	1	0
1921-22	Ottawa Munitions	OCHL	13	8	6	14	....	....	....	6	....	....	....	....	....
1922-23	Ottawa St. Pats	OCHL	14	3	1	4	....	....	....	....	3	1	0	1	0
	Ottawa St. Pats	Al-Cup	7	4	0	4	....	....	....	2	....	....	....	....	....
1923-24	Ottawa Montagnards	OCHL	12	3	0	3	....	....	....	....	2	1	0	1	....
	Ottawa Montagnards	Al-Cup	4	2	1	3	....	....	....	....	....	....	....	....	....
1924-25	Ottawa Montagnards	OCHL	16	3	1	4	....	....	....	....	3	1	0	1	0
	Ottawa Montagnards	Al-Cup	4	0	1	1	....	....	....	8	....	....	....	....	....
1925-26	**Ottawa Senators**	**NHL**	**27**	**0**	**0**	**0**	**0**	**0**	**0**	**0**	**2**	**0**	**0**	**0**	**0**
	Ottawa Canadiens	OCHL	1	0	0	0	....	....	....	0	....	....	....	....	....
1926-27	London Panthers	Can-Pro	32	4	1	5	....	....	....	38	4	1	0	1	6
1927-28	London Panthers	Can-Pro	34	3	0	3	....	....	....	32	....	....	....	....	....
1928-29	Niagara Falls Cataracts	Can-Pro	42	2	1	3	....	....	....	53	....	....	....	....	....
	NHL Totals		**27**	**0**	**0**	**0**	**0**	**0**	**0**	**0**	**2**	**0**	**0**	**0**	**0**

OCHL Second All-Star Team (1919) • OCHL First All-Star Team (1920, 1921, 1922)

Signed as a free agent by **Ottawa**, December 14, 1925. Loaned to **London** (Can-Pro) by **Ottawa** for cash, November, 1926 and November 27, 1927. Traded to **Hamilton** (IHL) by **Ottawa** for cash, November 7, 1929.

• DUGUID, Lorne Lorne Wallace
LW – L. 5′11″, 185 lbs. b: Bolton, Ont., 4/4/1910 d: 5/21/1981.

Season	Club	League	GP	G	A	Pts	AG	AA	APts	PIM	GP	G	A	Pts	PIM
1927-28	Montreal Victorias	MCJHL	11	*10	0	*10	....	....	....	4	....	....	....	....	....
1928-29	Montreal Victorias	MCJHL	10	*8	0	*8	....	....	....	14	....	....	....	....	....
1929-30	Montreal Victorias	MRTHL	10	3	0	3	....	....	....	12	1	0	0	0	0
1930-31	Windsor Bulldogs	IHL	48	22	19	41	....	....	....	13	6	3	2	5	6
1931-32	**Montreal Maroons**	**NHL**	**13**	**0**	**0**	**0**	**0**	**0**	**0**	**6**	....	....	....	....	....
	Windsor Bulldogs	IHL	35	11	8	19	....	....	....	36	6	2	1	3	4
1932-33	**Montreal Maroons**	**NHL**	**48**	**4**	**7**	**11**	**7**	**14**	**21**	**38**	**2**	**0**	**0**	**0**	**4**
1933-34	**Montreal Maroons**	**NHL**	**5**	**0**	**1**	**1**	**0**	**2**	**2**	**0**	....	....	....	....	....
	Windsor Bulldogs	IHL	38	13	9	22	....	....	....	34	....	....	....	....	....
1934-35	**Detroit Red Wings**	**NHL**	**34**	**3**	**3**	**6**	**5**	**5**	**10**	**9**	....	....	....	....	....
	Detroit Olympics	IHL	17	12	5	17	....	....	....	0	....	....	....	....	....
1935-36	**Detroit Red Wings**	**NHL**	**5**	**0**	**0**	**0**	**0**	**0**	**0**	**0**	....	....	....	....	....
	Detroit Olympics	IHL	12	4	6	10	....	....	....	14	....	....	....	....	....
	Boston Bruins	**NHL**	**29**	**1**	**4**	**5**	**2**	**8**	**10**	**2**	**2**	**1**	**0**	**1**	**2**
1936-37	**Boston Bruins**	**NHL**	**1**	**1**	**0**	**1**	**2**	**0**	**2**	**2**	....	....	....	....	....
	Providence Reds	IAHL	49	20	21	41	....	....	....	16	3	2	0	2	2
1937-38	Cleveland Barons	IAHL	48	22	27	49	....	....	....	22	2	1	1	2	0
1938-39	Cleveland Barons	IAHL	54	19	32	51	....	....	....	23	9	2	*7	9	4
1939-40	Cleveland Barons	IAHL	24	5	6	11	....	....	....	18	....	....	....	....	....
	Pittsburgh Hornets	IAHL	20	4	6	10	....	....	....	8	9	1	0	1	2
1940-41	Pittsburgh Hornets	AHL	48	7	21	28	....	....	....	12	6	1	0	1	4
	NHL Totals		**135**	**9**	**15**	**24**	**16**	**29**	**45**	**57**	**4**	**1**	**0**	**1**	**6**

IAHL First All-Star Team (1938)

Signed as a free agent by **Windsor** (IHL), November 3, 1930. Signed as a free agent by **Montreal Maroons**, October 19, 1931. Traded to **Detroit** by **Montreal Maroons** for cash, October 28, 1934. Traded to **Boston** by **Detroit** for Gene Carrigan, December 29, 1935.

• DUKOWSKI, Duke Laudas Joseph
D – L. 5′10″, 185 lbs. b: Regina, Sask., 8/30/1902 Deceased.

Season	Club	League	GP	G	A	Pts	AG	AA	APts	PIM	GP	G	A	Pts	PIM
1916-17	Regina Vics	S-SSHL	3	0	1	1	....	....	....	0	....	....	....	....	....
1917-18	Regina Pats	RCJHL	6	12	2	14	....	....	....	6	1	0	0	0	2
	Regina Pats	Al-Cup	4	13	8	21	....	....	....	5	....	....	....	....	....
1918-19	Regina Pats	RCJHL	10	*40	8	*48	....	....	....	6	1	*2	0	2	*6
	Regina Pats	M-Cup	7	30	6	36	....	....	....	6	....	....	....	....	....
1919-20	Regina Pats	RCJHL	5	*14	1	*15	....	....	....	*16	....	....	....	....	....
	Regina Reginas	S-SSHL	1	0	0	0	....	....	....	0	....	....	....	....	....
	Regina Braves	S-SSHL	1	1	0	1	....	....	....	0	....	....	....	....	....
1920-21	Regina Vics	S-SSHL	14	4	1	5	....	....	....	42	4	1	0	1	6
1921-22	Saskatoon-Moose Jaw	WCHL	21	13	2	15	....	....	....	19	....	....	....	....	....
1922-23	Regina Capitals	WCHL	29	6	0	6	....	....	....	20	2	0	1	1	2
1923-24	Regina Capitals	WCHL	30	8	3	11	....	....	....	39	2	0	0	0	4
1924-25	Regina Capitals	WCHL	27	13	4	17	....	....	....	86	....	....	....	....	....
1925-26	Portland Rosebuds	WHL	29	5	7	12	....	....	....	46	....	....	....	....	....
1926-27	**Chicago Black Hawks**	**NHL**	**28**	**3**	**2**	**5**	**5**	**10**	**15**	**16**	**2**	**0**	**0**	**0**	**0**
1927-28	Kansas City Pla-Mors	AHA	37	9	3	12	....	....	....	87	3	0	0	0	2
1928-29	Kansas City Pla-Mors	AHA	40	10	5	15	....	....	....	101	....	....	....	....	....
1929-30	**Chicago Black Hawks**	**NHL**	**44**	**7**	**10**	**17**	**10**	**24**	**34**	**42**	**2**	**0**	**0**	**0**	**6**
1930-31	**Chicago Black Hawks**	**NHL**	**25**	**1**	**3**	**4**	**2**	**9**	**11**	**28**	....	....	....	....	....
	New York Americans	**NHL**	**12**	**1**	**1**	**2**	**2**	**3**	**5**	**12**	....	....	....	....	....
1931-32	New Haven Eagles	Can-Am	40	6	9	15	....	....	....	102	2	0	1	1	6
1932-33	**New York Americans**	**NHL**	**48**	**4**	**7**	**11**	**7**	**14**	**21**	**43**	....	....	....	....	....

			REGULAR SEASON								PLAYOFFS				
Season	**Club**	**League**	**GP**	**G**	**A**	**Pts**	**AG**	**AA**	**APts**	**PIM**	**GP**	**G**	**A**	**Pts**	**PIM**
1933-34	**New York Americans**	**NHL**	**9**	**0**	**1**	**1**	**0**	**2**	**2**	**11**	....	....	....	....	....
	Chicago Black Hawks	**NHL**	**5**	**0**	**0**	**0**	**0**	**0**	**0**	**2**	....	....	....	....	....
	New York Rangers	**NHL**	**29**	**0**	**6**	**6**	**0**	**13**	**13**	**18**	**2**	**0**	**0**	**0**	**0**
	Syracuse Stars	IHL	4	0	0	0	....	....	....	8	....	....	....	....	....
	NHL Totals		**200**	**16**	**30**	**46**	**26**	**75**	**101**	**172**	**6**	**0**	**0**	**0**	**6**
	Other Major League Totals		136	45	16	61	....	....	....	210	4	0	1	1	6

• Also known as Dutkowski. Prior to his death, Mr. Dukowski requested the "t" be dropped from his last name.

Signed as a free agent by **Saskatoon** (WCHL), November 17, 1921. Transferred to **Moose Jaw** (WCHL) after **Saskatoon** (WCHL) franchise relocated, February 1, 1922. Rights transferred to **Chicago** after NHL club purchased **Portland** (WHL) franchise, May 15, 1926. Claimed on waivers by **NY Americans** from **Chicago**, February 13, 1931. Loaned to **Chicago** by **NY Americans** for remainder of 1933-34 season, December 15, 1933. Recalled by **NY Americans** and traded to **NY Rangers** for cash, January 3, 1934.

• DUMART, Woody

Woodrow Wilson Clarence "Porky" **HHOF**

LW – L. 6', 190 lbs. b: Berlin, Ont., 12/23/1916.

Season	Club	League	GP	G	A	Pts	AG	AA	APts	PIM	GP	G	A	Pts	PIM
1933-34	Kitchener Empires	OHA-Jr.	12	8	3	11	....	....	....	12	3	1	*3	4	0
1934-35	Kitchener Greenshirts	OHA-Jr.	17	17	11	*28	....	....	....	10	3	3	1	4	2
1935-36	**Boston Bruins**	**NHL**	**1**	**0**	**0**	**0**	**0**	**0**	**0**	**0**	....	....	....	....	....
	Boston Cubs	Can-Am	46	11	10	21	....	....	....	15	....	....	....	....	....
1936-37	**Boston Bruins**	**NHL**	**17**	**4**	**4**	**8**	**7**	**7**	**14**	**2**	**3**	**0**	**0**	**0**	**0**
	Providence Reds	IAHL	34	4	7	11	....	....	....	10	....	....	....	....	....
1937-38	**Boston Bruins**	**NHL**	**48**	**13**	**14**	**27**	**21**	**23**	**44**	**6**	**3**	**0**	**0**	**0**	**0**
♦1938-39	**Boston Bruins**	**NHL**	**46**	**14**	**15**	**29**	**25**	**23**	**48**	**2**	**12**	**1**	**3**	**4**	**6**
1939-40	**Boston Bruins**	**NHL**	**48**	**22**	**21**	**43**	**37**	**33**	**70**	**16**	**6**	**1**	**0**	**1**	**0**
♦1940-41	**Boston Bruins**	**NHL**	**40**	**18**	**15**	**33**	**28**	**21**	**49**	**2**	**11**	**1**	**3**	**4**	**9**
1941-42	**Boston Bruins**	**NHL**	**35**	**14**	**15**	**29**	**19**	**18**	**37**	**8**	....	....	....	....	....
	Ottawa RCAF	OCHL	....	....	....	....	....	....	....	....	6	7	5	12	2
	Ottawa RCAF	Al-Cup	13	14	9	23	....	....	....	8	....	....	....	....	....
1942-43	Ottawa RCAF	OHA-Sr.	6	6	5	11	....	....	....	....	....	....	....	....	....
	Millward RCAF	Britain	STATISTICS NOT AVAILABLE												
1943-44			MILITARY SERVICE												
1944-45			MILITARY SERVICE												
1945-46	**Boston Bruins**	**NHL**	**50**	**22**	**12**	**34**	**26**	**17**	**43**	**2**	**10**	**4**	**3**	**7**	**0**
1946-47	**Boston Bruins**	**NHL**	**60**	**24**	**28**	**52**	**27**	**34**	**61**	**12**	**5**	**1**	**1**	**2**	**8**
1947-48	**Boston Bruins**	**NHL**	**59**	**21**	**16**	**37**	**27**	**21**	**48**	**14**	**5**	**0**	**0**	**0**	**0**
1948-49	**Boston Bruins**	**NHL**	**59**	**11**	**12**	**23**	**15**	**17**	**32**	**6**	**5**	**3**	**0**	**3**	**0**
1949-50	**Boston Bruins**	**NHL**	**69**	**14**	**25**	**39**	**18**	**30**	**48**	**14**	....	....	....	....	....
1950-51	**Boston Bruins**	**NHL**	**70**	**20**	**21**	**41**	**26**	**26**	**52**	**7**	**6**	**1**	**2**	**3**	**0**
1951-52	**Boston Bruins**	**NHL**	**39**	**5**	**8**	**13**	**7**	**10**	**17**	**0**	**7**	**0**	**1**	**1**	**0**
1952-53	**Boston Bruins**	**NHL**	**62**	**5**	**9**	**14**	**7**	**11**	**18**	**2**	**11**	**0**	**2**	**2**	**0**
1953-54	**Boston Bruins**	**NHL**	**69**	**4**	**3**	**7**	**5**	**4**	**9**	**6**	**4**	**0**	**0**	**0**	**0**
1954-55	Providence Reds	AHL	15	2	2	4	....	....	....	0	....	....	....	....	....
	NHL Totals		**772**	**211**	**218**	**429**	**295**	**295**	**590**	**99**	**88**	**12**	**15**	**27**	**23**

NHL Second All-Star Team (1940, 1941, 1947) • Played in NHL All-Star Game (1947, 1948)

Signed as a free agent by **Boston**, October 9, 1935.

• DUNCAN, Art

William John Arthur "Dunc"

D – R. 6'1", 190 lbs. b: Sault Ste. Marie, Ont., 7/4/1894 d: 4/13/1975.

Season	Club	League	GP	G	A	Pts	AG	AA	APts	PIM	GP	G	A	Pts	PIM
1912-13	Sudbury Wolves	NOHA	STATISTICS NOT AVAILABLE												
1913-14	Edmonton Eskimos	ASHL	5	2	0	2	....	....	....	16	3	1	0	1	3
1914-15	Edmonton Albertas	ASHL	3	1	0	1	....	....	....	11	....	....	....	....	....
1915-16	Vancouver Millionaires	PCHA	17	7	4	11	....	....	....	25	....	....	....	....	....
1916-17	Toronto 228th Battalion	NHA	6	3	1	4	....	....	....	6	....	....	....	....	....
1917-18			MILITARY SERVICE												
1918-19	Vancouver Millionaires	PCHA	17	2	1	3	....	....	....	0	2	0	0	0	0
1919-20	Vancouver Millionaires	PCHA	22	5	9	14	....	....	....	3	2	0	0	0	0
1920-21	Vancouver Millionaires	PCHA	24	3	5	8	....	....	....	6	2	0	3	3	0
	Vancouver Millionaires	St-Cup	5	2	1	3	....	....	....	3	....	....	....	....	....
1921-22	Vancouver Millionaires	PCHA	24	5	9	14	....	....	....	25	2	0	0	0	0
	Vancouver Millionaires	St-Cup	7	3	1	4	....	....	....	9	....	....	....	....	....
1922-23	Vancouver Maroons	PCHA	25	15	6	21	....	....	....	8	2	1	0	1	0
	Vancouver Maroons	St-Cup	4	2	2	4	....	....	....	0	....	....	....	....	....
1923-24	Vancouver Maroons	PCHA	30	*21	*10	*31	....	....	....	44	2	0	1	1	4
	Vancouver Maroons	St-Cup	2	1	1	2	....	....	....	8	....	....	....	....	....
1924-25	Vancouver Maroons	WCHL	26	5	5	10	....	....	....	28	....	....	....	....	....
1925-26	Calgary Tigers	WHL	29	9	4	13	....	....	....	30	....	....	....	....	....
1926-27	**Detroit Cougars**	**NHL**	**34**	**3**	**2**	**5**	**5**	**10**	**15**	**26**	....	....	....	....	....
1927-28	**Toronto Maple Leafs**	**NHL**	**43**	**7**	**5**	**12**	**14**	**28**	**42**	**97**	....	....	....	....	....
1928-29	**Toronto Maple Leafs**	**NHL**	**39**	**4**	**4**	**8**	**11**	**27**	**38**	**53**	**4**	**0**	**0**	**0**	**4**
1929-30	**Toronto Maple Leafs**	**NHL**	**38**	**4**	**5**	**9**	**6**	**12**	**18**	**49**	....	....	....	....	....
1930-31	**Toronto Maple Leafs**	**NHL**	**2**	**0**	**0**	**0**	**0**	**0**	**0**	**0**	**1**	**0**	**0**	**0**	**0**
1931-32	**Toronto Maple Leafs**	**NHL**	DID NOT PLAY – COACHING												
	NHL Totals		**156**	**18**	**16**	**34**	**36**	**77**	**113**	**225**	**5**	**0**	**0**	**0**	**4**
	Other Major League Totals		220	75	54	129	....	....	....	175	12	1	4	5	4

PCHA Second All-Star Team (1919, 1923) • PCHA First All-Star Team (1920, 1922, 1924)

Signed as a free agent by **Vancouver** (PCHA), November 26, 1915. Signed as a free agent by **Vancouver** (PCHA), December 27, 1918. Traded to **Calgary** (WHL) by **Vancouver** (WHL) for Reg Mackey, October 16, 1925. Traded to **Chicago** by **Calgary** (WHL) for cash, May 15, 1926. Rights traded to **Detroit** by **Chicago** for Art Gagne and Gord Fraser, October 18, 1926. Traded to **Toronto** by **Detroit** for Bill Brydge, May 16, 1927. • 1922 St-Cup totals include series vs. Regina.

• DUNLAP, Frank

"Judge / Biff"

W – L. 6', 185 lbs. b: Ottawa, Ont., 8/10/1924 d: 10/26/1993.

Season	Club	League	GP	G	A	Pts	AG	AA	APts	PIM	GP	G	A	Pts	PIM
1941-42	Ottawa St. Pats	OCJHL	....	....	....	....	....	....	....	....	7	9	8	17	4
1942-43	St. Michael's Majors	OHA-Jr.	11	8	6	14	....	....	....	10	6	4	2	6	2
1943-44	St. Michael's Majors	OHA-Jr.	15	11	14	25	....	....	....	20	12	6	8	14	10
	Toronto Maple Leafs	**NHL**	**15**	**0**	**1**	**1**	**0**	**1**	**1**	**2**	....	....	....	....	....
1944-45	Ottawa Commandos	QSHL	24	16	18	34	....	....	....	20	2	0	0	0	0
	Ottawa Navy	QSHL	7	4	8	12	....	....	....	9	....	....	....	....	....
1945-46	Hull Volants	QSHL	33	17	19	36	....	....	....	0	....	....	....	....	....
1946-47	Ottawa Senators	QSHL	17	7	5	12	....	....	....	4	1	0	0	0	0
	Ottawa Senators	OCHL	1	1	3	4	....	....	....	0	....	....	....	....	....

			REGULAR SEASON								PLAYOFFS				
Season	**Club**	**League**	**GP**	**G**	**A**	**Pts**	**AG**	**AA**	**APts**	**PIM**	**GP**	**G**	**A**	**Pts**	**PIM**
1947-48	Pembroke Lumber Kings	UOVHL	14	10	12	22	....	....	....	2	5	4	1	5	2
	Renfrew Lions	UOVHL	....	....	....	....	....	....	....	....	5	1	4	5	0
	Renfrew Lions	Al-Cup	5	1	4	5	....	....	....	0	....	....	....	....	....
	NHL Totals		**15**	**0**	**1**	**1**	**0**	**1**	**1**	**2**	....	....	....	....	....

• Played NHL home games only w/ St. Michael's (OHA-Jr.) and Toronto during 1943-44 season while attending law school

• DUSSAULT, Norm

Joseph Normand

C – L. 5'8", 165 lbs. b: Springfield, MA, 9/26/1925.

Season	Club	League	GP	G	A	Pts	AG	AA	APts	PIM	GP	G	A	Pts	PIM
1944-45	Petawawa Engineers	OVSHL	STATISTICS NOT AVAILABLE												
1945-46	Baltimore Clippers	EAHL	43	12	16	28	....	....	....	13	7	0	0	0	0
1946-47	Victoriaville Tigers	QPHL	42	35	36	71	....	....	....	39	5	2	1	3	6
1947-48	**Montreal Canadiens**	**NHL**	**28**	**5**	**10**	**15**	**6**	**13**	**19**	**4**	....	....	....	....	....
	Victoriaville Tigers	QPHL	31	24	24	48	....	....	....	9	....	....	....	....	....
1948-49	**Montreal Canadiens**	**NHL**	**47**	**9**	**8**	**17**	**12**	**11**	**23**	**6**	**2**	**0**	**0**	**0**	**0**
1949-50	**Montreal Canadiens**	**NHL**	**67**	**13**	**24**	**37**	**16**	**29**	**45**	**22**	**5**	**3**	**1**	**4**	**0**
1950-51	**Montreal Canadiens**	**NHL**	**64**	**4**	**20**	**24**	**5**	**24**	**29**	**15**	....	....	....	....	....
1951-52	Chicoutimi Sagueneens	QMHL	48	16	23	39	....	....	....	21	18	3	11	14	4
1952-53	Chicoutimi Sagueneens	QMHL	60	23	20	43	....	....	....	10	20	4	2	6	6
1953-54	Chicoutimi Sagueneens	QHL	68	25	34	59	....	....	....	14	5	0	2	2	0
1954-55	Chicoutimi Sagueneens	QHL	60	10	32	42	....	....	....	14	5	0	1	1	2
1955/60			STATISTICS NOT AVAILABLE												
1960-61	Sherbrooke Cantons	QSHL	21	7	9	16	....	....	....	10	7	2	1	3	8
1961-62	Sherbrooke Castors	ETSHL	....	....	....	....	....	....	....	....	7	1	3	4	6
	NHL Totals		**206**	**31**	**62**	**93**	**39**	**77**	**116**	**47**	**7**	**3**	**1**	**4**	**0**

Traded to **Chicoutimi** (QMHL) by **Montreal** for cash, November 21, 1951.

• DUTTON, Red

Mervyn Alexander **HHOF**

D – R. 6', 185 lbs. b: Russell, Man., 7/23/1898 d: 3/15/1987.

Season	Club	League	GP	G	A	Pts	AG	AA	APts	PIM	GP	G	A	Pts	PIM
1914-15	Winnipeg St. John's	WJrHL	STATISTICS NOT AVAILABLE												
1915/19			MILITARY SERVICE												
1919-20	Winnipeg Winnipegs	MHL-Sr.	8	6	7	13	....	....	....	10	....	....	....	....	....
	Winnipeg Winnipegs	Al-Cup	2	0	0	0	....	....	....	6	....	....	....	....	....
1920-21	Calgary Tigers	Big-4	15	5	3	8	....	....	....	*38	....	....	....	....	....
1921-22	Calgary Tigers	WCHL	22	16	5	21	....	....	....	*73	2	0	0	0	0
1922-23	Calgary Tigers	WCHL	18	2	4	6	....	....	....	24	....	....	....	....	....
1923-24	Calgary Tigers	WCHL	30	6	7	13	....	....	....	*54	2	0	1	1	2
	Calgary Tigers	St-Cup	2	1	0	1	....	....	....	8	....	....	....	....	....
1924-25	Calgary Tigers	WCHL	23	8	4	12	....	....	....	72	2	0	0	0	8
1925-26	Calgary Tigers	WHL	30	10	5	15	....	....	....	87	....	....	....	....	....
1926-27	**Montreal Maroons**	**NHL**	**44**	**4**	**4**	**8**	**7**	**21**	**28**	**108**	**2**	**0**	**0**	**0**	**4**
1927-28	**Montreal Maroons**	**NHL**	**42**	**7**	**6**	**13**	**14**	**34**	**48**	**94**	**9**	**1**	**0**	**1**	**27**
1928-29	**Montreal Maroons**	**NHL**	**44**	**1**	**3**	**4**	**3**	**20**	**23**	***139**	....	....	....	....	....
1929-30	**Montreal Maroons**	**NHL**	**43**	**3**	**13**	**16**	**4**	**31**	**35**	**98**	**4**	**0**	**0**	**0**	**2**
1930-31	**New York Americans**	**NHL**	**44**	**1**	**11**	**12**	**2**	**33**	**35**	**71**	....	....	....	....	....
1931-32	**New York Americans**	**NHL**	**47**	**3**	**5**	**8**	**5**	**11**	**16**	***107**	....	....	....	....	....
1932-33	**New York Americans**	**NHL**	**43**	**0**	**2**	**2**	**0**	**4**	**4**	**74**	....	....	....	....	....
1933-34	**New York Americans**	**NHL**	**48**	**2**	**8**	**10**	**3**	**17**	**20**	**65**	....	....	....	....	....
1934-35	**New York Americans**	**NHL**	**48**	**3**	**7**	**10**	**5**	**12**	**17**	**46**	....	....	....	....	....
1935-36	**New York Americans**	**NHL**	**46**	**5**	**8**	**13**	**10**	**15**	**25**	**69**	**3**	**0**	**0**	**0**	**0**
	NHL Totals		**449**	**29**	**67**	**96**	**53**	**198**	**251**	**871**	**18**	**1**	**0**	**1**	**33**
	Other Major League Totals		123	42	25	67	....	....	....	310	6	0	1	1	10

WCHL First All-Star Team (1922, 1924) • Won Lester Patrick Trophy (1993) • Played in NHL All-Star Game (1934)

Signed as a free agent by **Calgary** (WCHL), November 20, 1921. Traded to **Montreal Maroons** by **Calgary** (WHL) for cash, September 11, 1926. Traded to **NY Americans** by **Montreal Maroons** with Mike Neville, Hap Emms and Frank Carson for $35,000, May 14, 1930.

• DYCK, Henry

Henry Richard

C/LW – L. 5'8", 155 lbs. b: Herbert, Sask., 9/5/1912 Deceased.

Season	Club	League	GP	G	A	Pts	AG	AA	APts	PIM	GP	G	A	Pts	PIM
1928-29	Calgary Jimmies	CCJHL	4	4	0	4	....	....	....	0	....	....	....	....	....
1929-30	Calgary Canadians	CCJHL	STATISTICS NOT AVAILABLE												
	Calgary Canadians	M-Cup	7	9	2	11	....	....	....	4	....	....	....	....	....
1930-31	Seattle Eskimos	PCHL	34	1	1	2	....	....	....	18	4	0	0	0	2
1931-32	Syracuse Stars	IHL	2	0	0	0	....	....	....	0	....	....	....	....	....
	Hollywood Stars	Cal-Pro	....	13	12	25	....	....	....	....	....	....	....	....	....
1932-33	Saskatoon Crescents	WCHL	....	23	12	35	....	....	....	18	....	....	....	....	....
1933-34	Seattle Seahawks	NWHL	34	11	9	20	....	....	....	24	....	....	....	....	....
1934-35	Vancouver Lions	NWHL	32	11	8	19	....	....	....	20	8	0	1	1	6
	Vancouver Lions	L-W-S	5	*4	1	5	....	....	....	2	....	....	....	....	....
1935-36	Vancouver Lions	NWHL	25	10	4	14	....	....	....	6	....	....	....	....	....
	Edmonton Eskimos	NWHL	16	7	2	9	....	....	....	5	....	....	....	....	....
1936-37	Spokane–Seattle	PCHL	10	2	0	2	....	....	....	2	....	....	....	....	....
1937-38	Tulsa Oilers	AHA	43	10	20	30	....	....	....	22	4	1	2	3	5
1938-39	Tulsa Oilers	AHA	48	16	18	34	....	....	....	31	8	4	1	5	0
1939-40	Kansas City Greyhounds	AHA	39	14	16	30	....	....	....	19	....	....	....	....	....
1940-41	Kansas City Americans	AHA	5	0	1	1	....	....	....	0	....	....	....	....	....
1941-42	Johnstown Bluebirds	EAHL	58	46	40	86	....	....	....	32	7	11	5	16	2
1942-43	Washington Lions	AHL	27	4	9	13	....	....	....	6	....	....	....	....	....
	Buffalo Bisons	AHL	4	0	2	2	....	....	....	2	....	....	....	....	....
1943-44	**New York Rangers**	**NHL**	**1**	**0**	**0**	**0**	**0**	**0**	**0**	**0**	....	....	....	....	....
	Boston Olympics	EAHL	1	1	0	1	....	....	....	0	9	7	8	15	4
	Toronto Staffords	TMHL	24	23	18	41	....	....	....	14	11	15	12	*27	6
1944-45	Toronto Staffords	OHA-Sr.	1	0	0	0	....	....	....	0	....	....	....	....	....
	NHL Totals		**1**	**0**	**0**	**0**	**0**	**0**	**0**	**0**	....	....	....	....	....

EAHL First All-Star Team (1942)

Traded to **Vancouver** (NWHL) by **Seattle** (NWHL) for Sam McAdam, November, 1934. Loaned to **Edmonton** (NWHL) by **Vancouver** (NWHL) to complete deal that sent Bill Carse to Edmonton (January 22, 1936), January 26, 1936. Traded to **Buffalo** (AHL) by **Washington** (AHL) for cash, February 6, 1943.

• DYE, Babe

Cecil Henry **HHOF**

RW – R. 5'8", 150 lbs. b: Hamilton, Ont., 5/13/1898 d: 1/2/1962.

Season	Club	League	GP	G	A	Pts	AG	AA	APts	PIM	GP	G	A	Pts	PIM
1916-17	Toronto Aura Lee	OHA-Jr.	8	*31	0	*31	....	....	....	....	....	....	....	....	....
1917-18	Toronto De LaSalle	OHA-Jr.	STATISTICS NOT AVAILABLE												
1918-19	Toronto St. Pats	OHA-Sr.	9	13	1	14	....	....	....	....	2	3	0	3	0

Season	Club	League	GP	G	A	Pts	AG	AA	APts	PIM	GP	G	A	Pts	PIM
			REGULAR SEASON								PLAYOFFS				
1919-20	Toronto St. Pats	NHL	23	11	3	14	12	10	22	10	....	....	....	....	....
1920-21	Hamilton Tigers	NHL	1	*2	0	2	2	0	2	0	....	....	....	....	....
	Toronto St. Pats	NHL	23	*33	5	38	44	19	63	32	2	0	0	0	7
1921-22	Toronto St. Pats	NHL	24	31	7	38	45	22	67	39	2	2	0	2	2
♦	Toronto St. Pats	St-Cup	5	9	1	10	....	....	....	3	....	....	....	....	....
1922-23	Toronto St. Pats	NHL	22	*26	11	*37	46	43	89	19	....	....	....	....	....
1923-24	Toronto St. Pats	NHL	19	16	3	19	34	17	51	23	....	....	....	....	....
1924-25	Toronto St. Pats	NHL	29	*38	8	*46	70	33	103	41	2	0	0	0	0
1925-26	Toronto St. Pats	NHL	31	18	5	23	31	32	63	26	....	....	....	....	....
1926-27	Chicago Black Hawks	NHL	41	25	5	30	45	26	71	14	2	0	0	0	2
1927-28	Chicago Black Hawks	NHL	10	0	0	0	0	0	0	0	....	....	....	....	....
1928-29	New York Americans	NHL	42	1	0	1	3	0	3	17	2	0	0	0	0
1929-30	New Haven Eagles	Can-Am	34	11	4	15	....	....	....	16	....	....	....	....	....
1930-31	Toronto Maple Leafs	NHL	6	0	0	0	0	0	0	0	....	....	....	....	....
	St. Louis Flyers	AHA	DID NOT PLAY – COACHING												
1931-32	Chicago Shamrocks	AHA	DID NOT PLAY – COACHING												
	NHL Totals		271	201	47	248	332	202	534	221	10	2	0	2	11

OHA-Sr. Second All-Star Team (1919) • NHL Scoring Leader (1923, 1925)

Signed as a free agent by **Toronto**, December 15, 1919. Loaned to **Hamilton** by **Toronto**, December 4, 1920. Recalled by **Toronto** from **Hamilton**, December 24, 1920. • Retired from hockey to play professional baseball, September 6, 1923. Signed as a free agent by **Toronto**, January 2, 1924. Traded to **Chicago** by **Toronto** for $15,000, October 18, 1926. • Missed majority of 1927-28 season recovering from broken leg suffered in training camp, October 30, 1927. Traded to **NY Americans** by **Chicago** for $15,000, October 17, 1928. Traded to **New Haven** (Can-Am) by **NY Americans** for George Massecar, November 13, 1929. Signed as a free agent by **Toronto**, February 10, 1930. • Released by Toronto, December 8, 1930.

• DYTE, Jack

John Leonard
D – L. 6', 190 lbs. b: New Liskeard, Ont., 10/13/1918.

Season	Club	League	GP	G	A	Pts	AG	AA	APts	PIM	GP	G	A	Pts	PIM
1933/38	Barrie Colts	OHA-B	STATISTICS NOT AVAILABLE												
1938-39	Niagara Falls Cataracts	OHA-Sr.	20	3	3	6	....	....	....	31	....	....	....	....	....
1939-40	Baltimore Orioles	EAHL	57	8	18	26	....	....	....	57	9	0	2	2	6
1940-41	Baltimore Orioles	EAHL	64	15	16	31	....	....	....	68	....	....	....	....	....
1941-42	Johnstown Bluebirds	EAHL	60	15	21	36	....	....	....	88	7	4	4	8	8
1942-43	Montreal Royals	QSHL	13	1	1	2	....	....	....	20	....	....	....	....	....
1943-44	Chicago Black Hawks	NHL	27	1	0	1	1	0	1	31	....	....	....	....	....
	Providence Reds	AHL	7	0	0	0	....	....	....	6	....	....	....	....	....
	Buffalo Bisons	AHL	15	0	1	1	....	....	....	10	9	0	0	0	2
1944-45	Buffalo Bisons	AHL	52	2	8	10	....	....	....	56	6	0	0	0	2
1945-46	St. Louis Flyers	AHL	60	1	6	7	....	....	....	67	....	....	....	....	....
1946-47	New Liskeard Pioneers	OVHL	DID NOT PLAY – COACHING												
1947-48	New Liskeard Pioneers	OVHL	DID NOT PLAY – COACHING												
1948-49	North Sydney Victorias	CBSHL	58	6	18	24	....	....	....	65	6	3	1	4	4
	NHL Totals		27	1	0	1	1	0	1	31	....	....	....	....	....

EAHL Second All-Star Team (1940) • EAHL First All-Star Team (1941) • CBSHL Second All-Star Team (1949)

Signed as a free agent by **Chicago**, October 7, 1943. Traded to **Buffalo** (AHL) by **Chicago** for cash, June, 1944.

• EDDOLLS, Frank

Frank Herbert
D – L. 5'8", 180 lbs. b: Lachine, Que., 7/5/1921 d: 8/13/1961.

Season	Club	League	GP	G	A	Pts	AG	AA	APts	PIM	GP	G	A	Pts	PIM
1937-38	Verdun Jr. Maple Leafs	MMJHL	12	2	5	7	....	....	....	8	4	0	1	1	2
	Verdun Maple Leafs	QSHL	1	0	0	0	....	....	....	0	....	....	....	....	....
	Verdun Maple Leafs	M-Cup	5	4	5	9	....	....	....	12	....	....	....	....	....
1938-39	Verdun Jr. Maple Leafs	QJHL	10	9	5	14	....	....	....	24	3	1	1	2	8
	Verdun Maple Leafs	QSHL	1	0	0	0	....	....	....	0	....	....	....	....	....
	Verdun Jr. Maple Leafs	M-Cup	7	4	4	8	....	....	....	22	....	....	....	....	....
1939-40	Oshawa Generals	OHA-Jr.	15	13	8	21	....	....	....	8	7	3	5	8	8
	Oshawa Generals	M-Cup	8	1	2	3	....	....	....	24	....	....	....	....	....
1940-41	Oshawa Generals	OHA-Jr.	16	9	12	21	....	....	....	31	12	3	8	11	6
	Oshawa Generals	M-Cup	5	2	8	10	....	....	....	*14	....	....	....	....	....
1941-42	Hershey Bears	AHL	54	8	11	19	....	....	....	30	10	0	1	1	8
1942-43	Montreal RCAF	QSHL	35	8	10	18	....	....	....	42	12	2	6	8	8
1943-44	Montreal RCAF	MCHL	1	0	0	0	....	....	....	2	....	....	....	....	....
	Montreal Canada Car	MCHL	1	0	0	0	....	....	....	0	....	....	....	....	....
	Montreal Services	MCHL	3	0	0	0	....	....	....	0	....	....	....	....	....
1944-45	Montreal Canadiens	NHL	43	5	8	13	5	9	14	20	3	0	0	0	0
♦1945-46	Montreal Canadiens	NHL	8	0	1	1	0	1	1	6	8	0	1	1	2
	Buffalo Bisons	AHL	34	6	23	29	....	....	....	52	....	....	....	....	....
1946-47	Montreal Canadiens	NHL	6	0	0	0	0	0	0	0	7	0	0	0	4
	Buffalo Bisons	AHL	29	3	7	10	....	....	....	18	4	0	5	5	0
1947-48	New York Rangers	NHL	58	6	13	19	8	17	25	16	2	0	0	0	0
1948-49	New York Rangers	NHL	34	4	2	6	6	3	9	10	....	....	....	....	....
1949-50	New York Rangers	NHL	58	2	6	8	2	7	9	20	11	0	1	1	4
1950-51	New York Rangers	NHL	68	3	8	11	4	10	14	24	....	....	....	....	....
1951-52	New York Rangers	NHL	42	3	5	8	4	6	10	18	....	....	....	....	....
	Saskatoon Quakers	PCHL	12	3	6	9	....	....	....	6	....	....	....	....	....
	Cincinnati Mohawks	AHL	12	0	4	4	....	....	....	8	....	....	....	....	....
1952-53	Buffalo Bisons	AHL	50	5	25	30	....	....	....	24	....	....	....	....	....
1953-54	Buffalo Bisons	AHL	63	3	52	55	....	....	....	45	3	0	2	2	2
1954-55	Chicago Black Hawks	NHL	....	....	....	....	....	....	....	....	....	....	....	....	....
	NHL Totals		317	23	43	66	29	53	82	114	31	0	2	2	10

Won Byng of Vimy Trophy (Sportsmanship - QSHL) (1943) • AHL First All-Star Team (1954) • Played in NHL All-Star Game (1951)

Rights traded to **Toronto** by **Montreal** for the rights to Joe Benoit, June 7, 1940. Traded to **Montreal** by **Toronto** for the rights to Ted Kennedy, September 10, 1943. Loaned to **Buffalo** (AHL) by **Montreal** with Wilf Field, Kenny Mosdell and cash for Lorran Thibeault, October 24, 1945. Traded to **NY Rangers** by **Montreal** with Buddy O'Connor for Hal Laycoe, Joe Bell and George Robertson, August 19, 1947. • Missed majority of 1948-49 season recovering from knee injury suffered in automobile accident, October 8, 1948. Traded to **Montreal** by **NY Rangers** for cash, October 8, 1952. • Named player/coach of Buffalo Bisons (AHL), October 8, 1952.

• EDMUNDSON, Garry

Garry Frank "Duke"
LW – L. 6', 173 lbs. b: Sexsmith, Alta., 5/6/1932.

Season	Club	League	GP	G	A	Pts	AG	AA	APts	PIM	GP	G	A	Pts	PIM
1948-49	Edmonton Athletic Club	EJrHL	....	5	10	15	....	....	....	14	6	2	2	4	16
	Edmonton Athletic Club	M-Cup	7	1	1	2	....	....	....	4	....	....	....	....	....
1949-50	Edmonton Athletic Club	AAHA	....	19	13	32	....	....	....	11	....	....	....	....	....
1950-51	Regina Pats	WCJHL	23	12	6	18	....	....	....	38	12	11	8	19	13
	Regina Pats	M-Cup	15	7	6	13	....	....	....	18	....	....	....	....	....
1951-52	Kitchener Greenshirts	OHA-Jr.	51	35	53	88	....	....	....	80	4	1	1	2	6
	Montreal Canadiens	NHL	1	0	0	0	0	0	0	2	2	0	0	0	4
1952-53	Montreal Royals	QMHL	12	4	3	7	....	....	....	8	12	3	4	7	16
1953-54	Cincinnati Mohawks	IHL	64	25	53	78	....	....	....	105	11	2	4	6	9
1954-55	Cincinnati Mohawks	IHL	60	24	32	56	....	....	....	86	9	3	6	9	20
1955-56	Cincinnati Mohawks	IHL	56	35	52	87	....	....	....	95	8	3	3	6	10
	Winnipeg Warriors	WHL	2	0	0	0	....	....	....	2	....	....	....	....	....
1956-57	Shawinigan Cataracts	QHL	3	0	1	1	....	....	....	16	....	....	....	....	....
	Cincinnati Mohawks	IHL	52	23	25	48	....	....	....	74	7	3	5	8	*28
1957-58	New Westminster Royals	WHL	69	21	43	64	....	....	....	*188	4	1	3	4	2
1958-59	Springfield Indians	AHL	62	17	27	44	....	....	....	113	....	....	....	....	....
1959-60	Toronto Maple Leafs	NHL	39	4	6	10	5	6	11	47	9	0	1	1	4
1960-61	Toronto Maple Leafs	NHL	3	0	0	0	0	0	0	0	....	....	....	....	....
	Rochester Americans	AHL	68	25	44	69	....	....	....	62	....	....	....	....	....
1961-62	San Francisco Seals	WHL	51	15	21	36	....	....	....	53	2	0	0	0	0
1962-63	San Francisco Seals	WHL	70	34	42	76	....	....	....	96	17	5	3	8	12
1963-64	San Francisco Seals	WHL	46	13	21	34	....	....	....	55	....	....	....	....	....
	NHL Totals		43	4	6	10	5	6	11	49	11	0	1	1	8

IHL First All-Star Team (1956) • IHL Second All-Star Team (1957)

Claimed by **Springfield** (AHL) from **New Westminster** (WHL) in Inter-League Draft, June 3, 1958. Traded to **Toronto** by **Springfield** (AHL) for Frank Roggeveen, June 9, 1959. • Officially announced retirement, February 4, 1964.

• EGAN, Pat

Martin Joseph "Box-Car"
D – R. 5'10", 195 lbs. b: Blackie, Alta., 4/25/1918.

Season	Club	League	GP	G	A	Pts	AG	AA	APts	PIM	GP	G	A	Pts	PIM
1935-36	Calgary Radios	AAHA	6	1	2	3	....	....	....	*14	3	0	0	0	*11
1936-37	Nelson Maple Leafs	WKHL	14	2	2	4	....	....	....	14	....	....	....	....	....
1937-38	Sudbury Frood Tigers	NOHA	11	0	0	0	....	....	....	19	2	0	1	1	0
1938-39	Seattle Seahawks	PCHL	44	9	11	20	....	....	....	*185	7	1	2	3	*25
1939-40	New York Americans	NHL	10	4	3	7	7	5	12	6	2	0	0	0	4
	Springfield Indians	IAHL	47	12	11	23	....	....	....	74	3	0	0	0	10
1940-41	New York Americans	NHL	39	4	9	13	6	13	19	51	....	....	....	....	....
1941-42	Brooklyn Americans	NHL	48	8	20	28	11	24	35	*124	....	....	....	....	....
1942-43	Montreal Army	MCHL	19	6	8	14	....	....	....	56	7	0	0	0	*28
1943-44	Detroit Red Wings	NHL	23	4	15	19	4	13	17	40	....	....	....	....	....
	Boston Bruins	NHL	25	11	13	24	10	11	21	55	....	....	....	....	....
1944-45	Boston Bruins	NHL	48	7	15	22	7	17	24	*86	7	2	0	2	6
1945-46	Boston Bruins	NHL	41	8	10	18	9	14	23	32	10	3	0	3	8
1946-47	Boston Bruins	NHL	60	7	18	25	8	22	30	89	5	0	2	2	6
1947-48	Boston Bruins	NHL	60	8	11	19	10	14	24	81	5	1	1	2	2
1948-49	Boston Bruins	NHL	60	6	18	24	8	26	34	92	5	0	0	0	16
1949-50	New York Rangers	NHL	70	5	11	16	6	13	19	50	12	3	1	4	6
1950-51	New York Rangers	NHL	70	5	10	15	6	12	18	70	....	....	....	....	....
1951-52	Cincinnati Mohawks	AHL	36	6	8	14	....	....	....	85	....	....	....	....	....
	Providence Reds	AHL	32	3	22	25	....	....	....	64	15	2	7	9	49
1952-53	Providence Reds	AHL	26	6	9	15	....	....	....	48	....	....	....	....	....
1953-54	Providence Reds	AHL	70	10	19	29	....	....	....	127	....	....	....	....	....
1954-55	Providence Reds	AHL	59	6	28	34	....	....	....	*149	....	....	....	....	....
1955-56	Vancouver Canucks	WHL	70	4	22	26	....	....	....	*163	15	0	5	5	20
1956-57	Nelson Maple Leafs	WIHL	36	8	19	27	....	....	....	118	5	0	0	0	11
1957-58	Victoria Cougars	WHL	59	9	27	36	....	....	....	163	....	....	....	....	....
	Nelson Maple Leafs	WIHL	5	1	1	2	....	....	....	30	....	....	....	....	....
1958-59	Victoria Cougars	WHL	3	0	1	1	....	....	....	4	....	....	....	....	....
1959-60	Victoria Cougars	WHL	DID NOT PLAY – COACHING												
	NHL Totals		554	77	153	230	92	184	276	776	46	9	4	13	48

NHL Second All-Star Team (1942) • Played in NHL All-Star Game (1949)

Signed as a free agent by **NY Americans**, October 13, 1939. Rights transferred to **Detroit** from **Brooklyn** in Special Dispersal Draw, October 9, 1942. Traded to **Boston** by **Detroit** for Flash Hollett, January 5, 1944. Traded to **NY Rangers** by **Boston** for Billy Moe, the rights to Lorne Ferguson and future considerations, October 7, 1949. Traded to **Providence** (AHL) by **NY Rangers** with Zellio Toppazzini and Jean-Paul Denis for Jack Stoddard, January 1, 1952. • Suspended for life by AHL for assaulting linesman Patsy Callighen in game vs. St. Louis, November 5, 1952. Suspension lifted on December 14, 1952. • Missed remainder of 1952-53 season recovering from knee injury suffered in game vs. Pittsburgh (AHL), January 6, 1953.

• EHMAN, Gerry

— see page 1053

• ELIK, Bo

Boris
LW – L. 5'11", 190 lbs. b: Geralton, Ont., 10/17/1929.

Season	Club	League	GP	G	A	Pts	AG	AA	APts	PIM	GP	G	A	Pts	PIM
1949-50	Sunridge Beavers	OIHA	STATISTICS NOT AVAILABLE												
1950-51	North Bay Black Hawks	EOHL	37	18	18	36	....	....	....	32	....	....	....	....	....
1951-52	North Bay Black Hawks	EOHL	31	13	8	21	....	....	....	45	11	3	5	8	19
1952-53	North Bay Trappers	NOHA	48	18	17	35	....	....	....	67	7	2	1	3	17
1953-54	North Bay Trappers	NOHA	33	12	18	30	....	....	....	33	4	2	1	3	18
1954-55	North Bay Trappers	NOHA	55	18	25	43	....	....	....	52	12	7	6	13	6
1955-56	North Bay Trappers	NOHA	55	20	23	43	....	....	....	50	8	5	2	7	8
	Cleveland Barons	AHL	1	0	1	1	....	....	....	0	....	....	....	....	....
1956-57	Cleveland Barons	AHL	61	40	40	80	....	....	....	82	12	4	6	10	8
1957-58	Cleveland Barons	AHL	70	31	37	68	....	....	....	129	7	0	4	4	4
1958-59	Rochester Americans	AHL	14	1	7	8	....	....	....	28	....	....	....	....	....
	Providence Reds	AHL	50	19	27	46	....	....	....	44	....	....	....	....	....
1959-60	Providence Reds	AHL	69	26	27	53	....	....	....	75	5	0	1	1	2
1960-61	Providence Reds	AHL	51	10	20	30	....	....	....	46	....	....	....	....	....
1961-62	Pittsburgh Hornets	AHL	64	21	19	40	....	....	....	112	....	....	....	....	....
1962-63	Detroit Red Wings	NHL	3	0	0	0	0	0	0	0	....	....	....	....	....
	Pittsburgh Hornets	AHL	7	0	0	0	....	....	....	0	....	....	....	....	....
	Edmonton Flyers	WHL	58	22	25	47	....	....	....	79	3	5	0	5	0
	NHL Totals		3	0	0	0	0	0	0	0	....	....	....	....	....

AHL First All-Star Team (1957) • Won Dudley "Red" Garrett Memorial Award (Top Rookie - AHL) (1957) • AHL Second All-Star Team (1958)

Traded to **Rochester** (AHL) by **Cleveland** (AHL) for Eddie Mazur, September 23, 1958. Traded to **Providence** (AHL) by **Rochester** (AHL) for Gord Redahl, November 21, 1958.

• ELLIOT, Fred

RW – R. 5'8", 165 lbs. b: Clinton, Ont., 2/18/1903 Deceased.

Season	Club	League	REGULAR SEASON GP	G	A	Pts	AG	AA	APts	PIM	PLAYOFFS GP	G	A	Pts	PIM
1927-28	Toronto Falcons	Can-Pro	42	9	7	16	....	....	....	14	2	0	0	0	0
1928-29	**Ottawa Senators**	**NHL**	**43**	**2**	**0**	**2**	**6**	**0**	**6**	**6**	....	....	....	....	....
1929-30	Windsor Bulldogs	IHL	3	0	1	1	....	....	....	4	....	....	....	....	....
	London Panthers	IHL	5	1	0	1	....	....	....	16	....	....	....	....	....
	Niagara Falls Cataracts	IHL	33	2	5	7	....	....	....	10	....	....	....	....	....
1930-31	Philadelphia Arrows	Can-Am	13	1	2	3	....	....	....	11	....	....	....	....	....
	Stratford Nationals	OPHL	1	0	0	0	....	....	....	0	....	....	....	....	....
	London Panthers	IHL	19	0	1	1	....	....	....	0	....	....	....	....	....
	NHL Totals		**43**	**2**	**0**	**2**	**6**	**0**	**6**	**6**					

Traded to **Montreal Maroons** by **Toronto** for George Horne, October 1, 1928. Loaned to **Ottawa** by **Montreal Maroons** for 1928-29 season for cash, November 13, 1928. Signed as a free agent by **Windsor** (IHL), October 29, 1929. Traded to **London** (IHL) by **Windsor** (IHL) for Fred Brown and Ed Kuntz, November 21, 1929. Traded to **Toronto** (IHL) by **London** (IHL) for Steve Rice, December 7, 1929. Traded to **Niagara Falls** (IHL) by **Toronto** (IHL) with Lloyd Gross for Ike Morrison, Harry Lott and Jim Smith, December 15, 1929. Signed as a free agent by **London** (IHL), January 28, 1931.

• ELLIS, Ron

— see page 1056

• EMBERG, Eddie

C – L. 5'10", 160 lbs. b: Montreal, Que., 11/18/1921.

Season	Club	League	REGULAR SEASON GP	G	A	Pts	AG	AA	APts	PIM	PLAYOFFS GP	G	A	Pts	PIM
1939-40	Loyola Collegiate	H.S.	STATISTICS NOT AVAILABLE												
1940-41	Verdun Maple Leafs	QJHL	12	11	6	17	....	....	....	4	2	1	0	1	0
1941-42	Montreal Jr. Royals	QJHL	12	11	9	20	....	....	....	4	2	*5	2	7	2
	Montreal Royals	QSHL	1	1	0	1	....	....	....	0	....	....	....	....	....
	Montreal Jr. Royals	M-Cup	9	8	8	16	....	....	....	9	....	....	....	....	....
1942-43	Montreal RCAF	QSHL	26	7	10	17	....	....	....	0	12	1	2	3	0
	Montreal RCAF	MCHL	8	4	12	16	....	....	....	0	1	0	0	0	0
1943-44	Montreal RCAF	QSHL	1	0	0	0	....	....	....	0	3	*7	2	9	2
1944-45	Montreal RCAF	MCHL	3	3	2	5	....	....	....	0	....	....	....	....	....
	Quebec Aces	QSHL	12	5	3	8	....	....	....	7	7	6	4	*10	4
	Montreal Canadiens	**NHL**	....	....	....	....	....	....	....	....	**2**	**1**	**0**	**1**	**0**
	Quebec Aces	Al-Cup	3	1	0	1	....	....	....	0	....	....	....	....	....
1945-46	Quebec Aces	QSHL	31	19	7	26	....	....	....	18	6	2	2	4	0
1946-47	Valleyfield Braves	QSHL	40	23	*44	67	....	....	....	10	....	....	....	....	....
	Boston Olympics	EAHL	....	....	....	....	....	....	....	....	2	4	1	5	2
1947-48	Ottawa Senators	QSHL	36	29	24	53	....	....	....	13	12	4	4	8	2
	Ottawa Senators	Al-Cup	14	6	8	14	....	....	....	2	....	....	....	....	....
1948-49	Ottawa Senators	QSHL	62	31	53	84	....	....	....	27	11	2	5	7	8
	Ottawa Senators	Al-Cup	6	3	0	3	....	....	....	0	....	....	....	....	....
1949-50	Ottawa Senators	QSHL	59	22	47	69	....	....	....	16	7	3	5	8	2
1950-51	Ottawa Senators	QMHL	58	19	41	60	....	....	....	16	5	0	3	3	0
1951-52	Ottawa Senators	QMHL	60	11	26	37	....	....	....	28	....	....	....	....	....
	NHL Totals		....	....	....	....	....	....	....	....	**2**	**1**	**0**	**1**	**0**

QSHL Second All-Star Team (1948)

• EMMS, Hap

Leighton

LW/D – L. 6', 190 lbs. b: Barrie, Ont., 1/12/1905 d: 10/22/1988.

Season	Club	League	REGULAR SEASON GP	G	A	Pts	AG	AA	APts	PIM	PLAYOFFS GP	G	A	Pts	PIM
1921/24	Barris Colts	OHA-Jr.	STATISTICS NOT AVAILABLE												
1924-25	Midland HC	OHA-Jr.	STATISTICS NOT AVAILABLE												
1925-26	Brantford Seniors	OHA-Sr.	STATISTICS NOT AVAILABLE												
1926-27	**Montreal Maroons**	**NHL**	**8**	**0**	**0**	**0**	**0**	**0**	**0**	**0**	....	....	....	....	....
	Stratford Nationals	Can-Pro	25	11	5	16	....	....	....	59	2	0	0	0	2
1927-28	**Montreal Maroons**	**NHL**	**10**	**0**	**1**	**1**	**0**	**6**	**6**	**10**	....	....	....	....	....
	Stratford Nationals	Can-Pro	29	8	5	13	....	....	....	56	5	1	0	1	*20
1928-29	Windsor Bulldogs	Can-Pro	42	21	5	26	....	....	....	104	8	*6	3	*9	30
1929-30	Windsor Bulldogs	IHL	38	21	16	37	....	....	....	107	....	....	....	....	....
1930-31	**New York Americans**	**NHL**	**44**	**5**	**4**	**9**	**10**	**12**	**22**	**56**	....	....	....	....	....
1931-32	**New York Americans**	**NHL**	**13**	**1**	**0**	**1**	**2**	**0**	**2**	**11**	....	....	....	....	....
	New Haven Eagles	Can-Am	5	0	0	0	....	....	....	8	....	....	....	....	....
	Detroit Falcons	**NHL**	**20**	**5**	**9**	**14**	**8**	**20**	**28**	**27**	**2**	**0**	**0**	**0**	**2**
1932-33	**Detroit Red Wings**	**NHL**	**43**	**9**	**13**	**22**	**16**	**27**	**43**	**63**	**4**	**0**	**0**	**0**	**8**
1933-34	**Detroit Red Wings**	**NHL**	**45**	**7**	**7**	**14**	**12**	**15**	**27**	**51**	**8**	**0**	**0**	**0**	**2**
1934-35	**Boston Bruins**	**NHL**	**11**	**1**	**1**	**2**	**2**	**2**	**4**	**8**	....	....	....	....	....
	New York Americans	**NHL**	**28**	**2**	**2**	**4**	**3**	**3**	**6**	**19**	....	....	....	....	....
1935-36	**New York Americans**	**NHL**	**32**	**1**	**5**	**6**	**2**	**9**	**11**	**12**	....	....	....	....	....
1936-37	**New York Americans**	**NHL**	**46**	**4**	**8**	**12**	**7**	**15**	**22**	**48**	....	....	....	....	....
1937-38	**New York Americans**	**NHL**	**20**	**1**	**3**	**4**	**2**	**5**	**7**	**6**	....	....	....	....	....
	Pittsburgh Hornets	IAHL	26	5	13	18	....	....	....	39	2	1	1	2	0
1938-39	Pittsburgh Hornets	IAHL	55	9	26	35	....	....	....	62	....	....	....	....	....
1939-40	Omaha Knights	AHA	48	18	15	33	....	....	....	93	9	0	4	4	0
1940-41	Omaha Knights	AHA	27	7	11	18	....	....	....	31	....	....	....	....	....
1941-42	Omaha Knights	AHA	26	2	5	7	....	....	....	40	....	....	....	....	....
1942-43			MILITARY SERVICE												
1943-44			MILITARY SERVICE												
1944-45	St. Louis Flyers	AHL	2	0	0	0	....	....	....	0	....	....	....	....	....
	NHL Totals		**320**	**36**	**53**	**89**	**64**	**114**	**178**	**311**	**14**	**0**	**0**	**0**	**12**

Signed as a free agent by **Montreal Maroons**, November 10, 1926. Traded to **NY Americans** by **Montreal Maroons** (Windsor-IHL) with Frank Carson, Red Dutton and Mike Neville for $35,000, May 14, 1930. Traded to **Detroit** by **NY Americans** with Frank Carson for Tommy Filmore and Bert McInenly, December 29, 1931. Signed as a free agent by **Boston** after securing release from **Detroit**, October 28, 1934. Traded to **NY Americans** by **Boston** with Obs Heximer for Walter Jackson, December 13, 1934. Traded to **Detroit** by **NY Americans** for John Sorrell, February 13, 1938.

• ERICKSON, Aut

— see page 1059

• ESPOSITO, Phil

— see page 1062

• EVANS, Jack

William John Trevor "Tex"

D – L. 6', 185 lbs. b: Morriston, Wales, 4/21/1928 d: 11/10/1996.

Season	Club	League	REGULAR SEASON GP	G	A	Pts	AG	AA	APts	PIM	PLAYOFFS GP	G	A	Pts	PIM
1947-48	Lethbridge Native Sons	WCJHL	23	10	21	31	....	....	....	58	6	5	3	8	8
	Lethbridge Maple Leafs	WCSHL	1	0	0	0	....	....	....	0	....	....	....	....	....
	Lethbridge Native Sons	M-Cup	12	4	4	8	....	....	....	26	....	....	....	....	....
1948-49	**New York Rangers**	**NHL**	**3**	**0**	**0**	**0**	**0**	**0**	**0**	**4**	....	....	....	....	....
	Lethbridge Maple Leafs	WCSHL	48	7	10	17	....	....	....	124	3	0	0	0	8
1949-50	**New York Rangers**	**NHL**	**2**	**0**	**0**	**0**	**0**	**0**	**0**	**2**	....	....	....	....	....
	New Haven Ramblers	AHL	69	3	12	15	....	....	....	150	....	....	....	....	....
1950-51	**New York Rangers**	**NHL**	**49**	**1**	**0**	**1**	**1**	**0**	**1**	**95**	....	....	....	....	....
	Cincinnati Mohawks	AHL	16	3	3	6	....	....	....	56	....	....	....	....	....
1951-52	**New York Rangers**	**NHL**	**52**	**1**	**6**	**7**	**1**	**7**	**8**	**83**	....	....	....	....	....
1952-53	Saskatoon Quakers	WHL	68	9	22	31	....	....	....	179	13	0	3	3	16
1953-54	**New York Rangers**	**NHL**	**44**	**4**	**4**	**8**	**5**	**5**	**10**	**73**	....	....	....	....	....
	Saskatoon Quakers	WHL	27	2	3	5	....	....	....	49	....	....	....	....	....
1954-55	**New York Rangers**	**NHL**	**47**	**0**	**5**	**5**	**0**	**6**	**6**	**91**	....	....	....	....	....
	Saskatoon Quakers	WHL	22	2	4	6	....	....	....	16	....	....	....	....	....
	Victoria Cougars	WHL	....	....	....	....	....	....	....	....	1	0	0	0	2
1955-56	**New York Rangers**	**NHL**	**70**	**2**	**9**	**11**	**3**	**11**	**14**	**104**	**5**	**1**	**0**	**1**	**18**
1956-57	**New York Rangers**	**NHL**	**70**	**3**	**6**	**9**	**4**	**7**	**11**	**110**	**5**	**0**	**1**	**1**	**4**
1957-58	**New York Rangers**	**NHL**	**70**	**4**	**8**	**12**	**5**	**8**	**13**	**108**	**6**	**0**	**0**	**0**	**17**
1958-59	**Chicago Black Hawks**	**NHL**	**70**	**1**	**8**	**9**	**1**	**8**	**9**	**75**	**6**	**0**	**0**	**0**	**10**
1959-60	**Chicago Black Hawks**	**NHL**	**68**	**0**	**4**	**4**	**0**	**4**	**4**	**60**	**4**	**0**	**0**	**0**	**4**
♦1960-61	**Chicago Black Hawks**	**NHL**	**69**	**0**	**8**	**8**	**0**	**8**	**8**	**58**	**12**	**1**	**1**	**2**	**14**
1961-62	**Chicago Black Hawks**	**NHL**	**70**	**3**	**14**	**17**	**3**	**13**	**16**	**80**	**12**	**0**	**0**	**0**	**26**
1962-63	**Chicago Black Hawks**	**NHL**	**68**	**0**	**8**	**8**	**0**	**8**	**8**	**46**	**6**	**0**	**0**	**0**	**4**
1963-64	Buffalo Bisons	AHL	72	0	17	17	....	....	....	87	....	....	....	....	....
1964-65	Los Angeles Blades	WHL	69	2	13	15	....	....	....	91	....	....	....	....	....
1965-66	Vancouver Canucks	WHL	72	2	31	33	....	....	....	103	7	0	1	1	20
1966-67	California Seals	WHL	71	3	18	21	....	....	....	52	6	0	2	2	4
1967-68	San Diego Gulls	WHL	65	1	15	16	....	....	....	36	7	0	3	3	8
1968-69	San Diego Gulls	WHL	73	1	11	12	....	....	....	50	7	0	0	0	0
1969-70	San Diego Gulls	WHL	67	0	8	8	....	....	....	46	6	0	0	0	2
1970-71	San Diego Gulls	WHL	69	1	10	11	....	....	....	82	6	0	2	2	12
1971-72	San Diego Gulls	WHL	72	0	20	20	....	....	....	87	4	0	0	0	4
	NHL Totals		**752**	**19**	**80**	**99**	**23**	**85**	**108**	**989**	**56**	**2**	**2**	**4**	**97**

WHL First All-Star Team (1953) • Played in NHL All-Star Game (1961, 1962)

Claimed by **Chicago** from **NY Rangers** in Intra-League Draft, June 3, 1958. Claimed by **Boston** (Hershey-AHL) from **Chicago** in Reverse Draft, June 15, 1966. Traded to **San Diego** (WHL) by **Boston** for cash, October, 1967.

• EVANS, Stewart

"Stew"

D – L. 5'10", 170 lbs. b: Ottawa, Ont., 6/19/1908 d: 6/9/1996.

Season	Club	League	REGULAR SEASON GP	G	A	Pts	AG	AA	APts	PIM	PLAYOFFS GP	G	A	Pts	PIM
1926-27	McIntyre Mines	NOHA	STATISTICS NOT AVAILABLE												
1927-28	Iroquois Papermakers	NOHA	STATISTICS NOT AVAILABLE												
1928-29	Iroquois Papermakers	NOHA	STATISTICS NOT AVAILABLE												
1929-30	Detroit Olympics	IHL	38	8	11	19	....	....	....	113	3	1	0	1	7
1930-31	**Detroit Falcons**	**NHL**	**43**	**1**	**4**	**5**	**2**	**12**	**14**	**14**	....	....	....	....	....
1931-32	Detroit Olympics	IHL	45	3	9	12	....	....	....	72	6	0	0	0	18
1932-33	**Detroit Red Wings**	**NHL**	**48**	**2**	**6**	**8**	**4**	**12**	**16**	**74**	**4**	**0**	**0**	**0**	**6**
1933-34	**Detroit Red Wings**	**NHL**	**17**	**0**	**0**	**0**	**0**	**0**	**0**	**20**	....	....	....	....	....
	Montreal Maroons	**NHL**	**27**	**4**	**2**	**6**	**7**	**4**	**11**	**35**	**4**	**0**	**0**	**0**	**4**
♦1934-35	**Montreal Maroons**	**NHL**	**46**	**5**	**7**	**12**	**8**	**12**	**20**	**54**	**7**	**0**	**0**	**0**	**8**
1935-36	**Montreal Maroons**	**NHL**	**48**	**3**	**5**	**8**	**6**	**9**	**15**	**57**	**3**	**0**	**0**	**0**	**0**
1936-37	**Montreal Maroons**	**NHL**	**47**	**6**	**7**	**13**	**10**	**13**	**23**	**54**	**5**	**0**	**0**	**0**	**0**
1937-38	**Montreal Maroons**	**NHL**	**48**	**5**	**11**	**16**	**8**	**18**	**26**	**59**	....	....	....	....	....
1938-39	**Montreal Canadiens**	**NHL**	**43**	**2**	**7**	**9**	**3**	**11**	**14**	**58**	**3**	**0**	**0**	**0**	**2**
1939-40	Detroit Holzbaugh	MOHL	DID NOT PLAY – COACHING												
	NHL Totals		**367**	**28**	**49**	**77**	**48**	**91**	**139**	**425**	**26**	**0**	**0**	**0**	**20**

Signed as a free agent by **Detroit Cougars**, September 12, 1929. Traded to **Montreal Maroons** by **Detroit** for Ted Graham, January 2, 1934. Traded to **Montreal Canadiens** by **Montreal Maroons** for cash, September 14, 1938.

• EZINICKI, Bill

William "Wild Bill"

RW – R. 5'10", 170 lbs. b: Winnipeg, Man., 3/11/1924.

Season	Club	League	REGULAR SEASON GP	G	A	Pts	AG	AA	APts	PIM	PLAYOFFS GP	G	A	Pts	PIM
1941-42	Winnipeg Rangers	MJHL	2	3	0	3	....	....	....	0	....	....	....	....	....
1942-43	Oshawa Generals	OHA-Jr.	16	21	10	31	....	....	....	21	10	13	10	23	26
	Oshawa Generals	M-Cup	11	17	6	23	....	....	....	*33	....	....	....	....	....
1943-44	Oshawa Generals	OHA-Jr.	25	38	25	63	....	....	....	33	11	*13	3	16	*49
	Oshawa Generals	M-Cup	10	12	11	23	....	....	....	34	....	....	....	....	....
1944-45	**Toronto Maple Leafs**	**NHL**	**8**	**1**	**4**	**5**	**1**	**5**	**6**	**17**	....	....	....	....	....
	Toronto Army Sharocks	TIHL	1	1	2	3	....	....	....	10	....	....	....	....	....
1945-46	**Toronto Maple Leafs**	**NHL**	**24**	**4**	**8**	**12**	**5**	**12**	**17**	**29**	....	....	....	....	....
	Pittsburgh Hornets	AHL	27	9	12	21	....	....	....	23	....	....	....	....	....
♦1946-47	**Toronto Maple Leafs**	**NHL**	**60**	**17**	**20**	**37**	**19**	**24**	**43**	**93**	**11**	**0**	**2**	**2**	**30**
♦1947-48	**Toronto Maple Leafs**	**NHL**	**60**	**11**	**20**	**31**	**14**	**26**	**40**	**97**	**9**	**3**	**1**	**4**	**6**
♦1948-49	**Toronto Maple Leafs**	**NHL**	**52**	**13**	**15**	**28**	**18**	**21**	**39**	***145**	**9**	**1**	**4**	**5**	**20**
1949-50	**Toronto Maple Leafs**	**NHL**	**67**	**10**	**12**	**22**	**13**	**14**	**27**	***144**	**5**	**0**	**0**	**0**	**13**
1950-51	Pittsburgh Hornets	AHL	13	6	3	9	....	....	....	24	....	....	....	....	....
	Boston Bruins	**NHL**	**53**	**16**	**19**	**35**	**20**	**23**	**43**	**119**	**6**	**1**	**1**	**2**	**18**
1951-52	**Boston Bruins**	**NHL**	**28**	**5**	**5**	**10**	**7**	**6**	**13**	**47**	....	....	....	....	....
	Pittsburgh Hornets	AHL	16	4	9	13	....	....	....	53	11	3	1	4	*67
1952-53	Pittsburgh Hornets	AHL	41	15	13	28	....	....	....	*115	7	0	3	3	8
1953-54			PLAYED PRO GOLF												
1954-55	Ottawa Senators	QHL	18	5	6	11	....	....	....	39	....	....	....	....	....
	Vancouver Canucks	WHL	15	5	2	7	....	....	....	50	....	....	....	....	....
	New York Rangers	**NHL**	**16**	**2**	**2**	**4**	**3**	**2**	**5**	**22**	....	....	....	....	....
1955-56			PLAYED PRO GOLF												
1956-57	Sudbury Wolves	NOHA	19	5	4	9	....	....	....	32	12	1	9	10	29
	NHL Totals		**368**	**79**	**105**	**184**	**100**	**133**	**233**	**713**	**40**	**5**	**8**	**13**	**87**

Played in NHL All-Star Game (1947, 1948)

Rights traded to **Toronto** by **Buffalo** (AHL) for George Boothman and Don Webster, October 13, 1944. Signed as a free agent by **Pittsburgh** (AHL), October 10, 1950. Traded to **Boston** by **Toronto** with Vic Lynn for Fern Flaman, Ken Smith, Phil Maloney and Leo Boivin, November 16, 1950. Traded to **Toronto** by **Boston** for cash, January 28, 1952. Traded to **Vancouver** (WHL) by **Toronto** with Phil Maloney and Hugh Barlow for $10,000, December 21, 1954. Traded to **NY Rangers** by **Vancouver** (WHL) for Jackie McLeod and cash, February 12, 1955. Traded to **Providence** (AHL) by **NY Rangers** with cash for Jean-Guy Gendron, May 8, 1955.

• FAHEY, Trevor John Trevor

LW – L. 6'1", 175 lbs. b: New Waterford, N.S., 1/4/1944.

Season	Club	League	GP	G	A	Pts	AG	AA	APts	PIM	GP	G	A	Pts	PIM
			REGULAR SEASON								PLAYOFFS				
1960-61	Guelph Royals	OHA-Jr.	4	1	1	2	....	....	....	0	13	0	1	1	0
1961-62	Guelph Royals	OHA-Jr.	26	3	2	5	....	....	....	6	....	....	....	....	....
1962-63	Guelph Royals	OHA-Jr.	39	26	17	43	....	....	....	26	....	....	....	....	....
1963-64	Kitchener Rangers	OHA-Jr.	35	17	11	28	....	....	....	23	....	....	....	....	....
1964-65	**New York Rangers**	**NHL**	**1**	**0**	**0**	**0**	**0**	**0**	**0**	**0**	....	....	....	....	....
	New York Rovers	EHL	72	30	25	55	....	....	....	41	....	....	....	....	....
1965-66	Minnesota Rangers	CHL	67	13	9	22	....	....	....	4	6	1	2	3	0
1966-67	Omaha Knights	CHL	54	8	5	13	....	....	....	22	7	0	2	2	8
1967-68	Toledo Blades	IHL	4	0	0	0	....	....	....	0	....	....	....	....	....
	Des Moines Oak Leafs	IHL	53	37	39	76	....	....	....	22	....	....	....	....	....
1968-69	Des Moines Oak Leafs	IHL	66	27	43	70	....	....	....	56	....	....	....	....	....
	Denver Spurs	WHL	5	1	1	2	....	....	....	0	....	....	....	....	....
1969-70	Des Moines–Fort Wayne	IHL	67	25	33	58	....	....	....	74	3	1	1	2	5
1970-71	St. Francis Xavier X-Men	AUAA	20	19	23	42	....	....	....	44	....	....	....	....	....
1971-72	St. Francis Xavier X-Men	AUAA	20	15	13	28	....	....	....	87	....	....	....	....	....
1972-73	St. Francis Xavier X-Men	AUAA	20	19	22	41	....	....	....	28	....	....	....	....	....
1973-74	St. Francis Xavier X-Men	AUAA	19	17	16	33	....	....	....	34	....	....	....	....	....
1974-75	Brandon University	CWUAA	DID NOT PLAY – COACHING												
	NHL Totals		**1**	**0**	**0**	**0**	**0**	**0**	**0**	**0**	....	....	....	....	....

IHL First All-Star Team (1969)

Traded to **LA Kings** by **NY Rangers** with Jim Murray and Ken Turlick for Barclay Plager, June 16, 1967. Claimed on waivers by **Des Moines** (IHL) from **Omaha** (CHL), November, 1967. Traded to **Fort Wayne** (IHL) by **Des Moines** (IHL) for Ron Burman, November, 1969.

• FALKENBERG, Bob — *see page 1066*

• FARRANT, Walt Walter Leslie "Whitey"

RW – R. 5'10", 155 lbs. b: Toronto, Ont., 8/12/1912.

Season	Club	League	GP	G	A	Pts	AG	AA	APts	PIM	GP	G	A	Pts	PIM
1929-30	Parkdale Canoe Club	OHA-Jr.	2	0	0	0	....	....	....	0	....	....	....	....	....
1930-31	Parkdale Canoe Club	OHA-Jr.	9	*9	2	11	....	....	....	4	....	....	....	....	....
1931-32	Parkdale Canoe Club	OHA-Jr.	10	*13	2	15	....	....	....	10	....	....	....	....	....
	Toronto City Hall	TMHL	4	0	1	1	....	....	....	5	....	....	....	....	....
1932-33	Toronto Marlboros	OHA-Sr.	19	8	8	16	....	....	....	10	2	0	0	0	0
	Toronto City Services	TMHL	18	6	3	9	....	....	....	6	6	3	3	6	2
1933-34	Toronto Marlboros	OHA-Sr.	16	4	9	13	....	....	....	10	1	0	0	0	0
	Toronto City Services	TMHL	14	*15	9	*24	....	....	....	8	9	3	*7	10	8
1934-35	Toronto All-Stars	TIHL	2	1	0	1	....	....	....	2	2	0	1	1	0
	Toronto City Service	TIHL	13	*14	9	23	....	....	....	4	7	*7	4	*11	4
1935-36	Rochester Cardinals	IHL	46	26	19	45	....	....	....	12	....	....	....	....	....
	Springfield Indians	Can-Am	1	0	0	0	....	....	....	0	....	....	....	....	....
1936-37	New Haven Eagles	IAHL	25	6	6	12	....	....	....	4	....	....	....	....	....
	Providence Reds	IAHL	14	2	3	5	....	....	....	2	2	0	0	0	0
1937-38	Minneapolis Millers	AHA	47	18	20	38	....	....	....	25	5	2	3	5	5
1938-39	Minneapolis Millers	AHA	47	35	34	69	....	....	....	8	4	1	2	3	0
1939-40	Minneapolis Millers	AHA	48	29	35	64	....	....	....	9	3	1	1	2	0
1940-41	Minneapolis Millers	AHA	11	1	5	6	....	....	....	0	....	....	....	....	....
	Tulsa Oilers	AHA	36	15	12	27	....	....	....	0	....	....	....	....	....
1941-42	Toronto Marlboros	OHA-Sr.	21	22	15	37	....	....	....	0	6	5	3	8	2
	Toronto Peoples Credit	TIHL	8	3	10	13	....	....	....	0	5	1	2	3	0
1942-43	Toronto Peoples Credit	TIHL	29	*32	29	*61	....	....	....	21	9	12	7	19	0
1943-44	Toronto Peoples Credit	TIHL	29	*31	29	*60	....	....	....	6	10	*13	6	*19	2
	Chicago Black Hawks	**NHL**	**1**	**0**	**0**	**0**	**0**	**0**	**0**	**0**	....	....	....	....	....
1944-45	Toronto Peoples Credit	TIHL	33	*56	28	*84	....	....	....	7	9	8	8	16	0
1945-46	Toronto Peoples Credit	TIHL	32	30	20	50	....	....	....	4	5	2	3	5	6
	NHL Totals		**1**	**0**	**0**	**0**	**0**	**0**	**0**	**0**	....	....	....	....	....

AHA Second All-Star Team (1940)

Signed as a free agent by **NY Americans**, November, 1936. Traded to **Providence** (IAHL) by **New Haven** (IAHL) for Max Kaminsky, January 25, 1937. Loaned to **Chicago** by **Toronto** (TIHL.) as an emergency injury replacement, March, 1944.

• FASHOWAY, Gordie Gordon

LW – L. 5'11", 180 lbs. b: Portage la Prairie, Man., 6/16/1926.

Season	Club	League	GP	G	A	Pts	AG	AA	APts	PIM	GP	G	A	Pts	PIM
1944-45	Winnipeg Monarchs	MJHL	8	4	3	7	....	....	....	4	8	8	2	10	16
	Winnipeg Army	WNDHL	....	....	....	....	....	....	....	....	2	0	0	0	0
1945-46	Winnipeg Monarchs	MJHL	8	10	4	14	....	....	....	12	7	6	1	7	0
	Winnipeg Monarchs	M-Cup	17	4	3	7	....	....	....	10	....	....	....	....	....
1946-47	Harringay Racers	Britain	36	*63	22	85	....	....	....	44	....	....	....	....	....
	Harringay Racers	Nat-Tmt	3	6	0	6	....	....	....	2	....	....	....	....	....
1947-48	New Westminster Royals	PCHL	60	47	36	83	....	....	....	50	5	4	6	10	32
1948-49	Kansas City Pla-Mors	USHL	64	13	22	35	....	....	....	42	2	1	0	1	0
1949-50	Kansas City Pla-Mors	USHL	66	*52	32	84	....	....	....	71	3	0	0	0	0
1950-51	**Chicago Black Hawks**	**NHL**	**13**	**3**	**2**	**5**	**4**	**2**	**6**	**14**	....	....	....	....	....
	Milwaukee Seagulls	USHL	10	4	9	13	....	....	....	4	....	....	....	....	....
	New Westminster Royals	PCHL	32	12	13	25	....	....	....	26	11	4	2	6	4
1951-52	New Westminster Royals	PCHL	70	*51	34	85	....	....	....	46	7	5	0	5	2
1952-53	New Westminster Royals	WHL	68	35	28	63	....	....	....	31	7	3	2	5	0
1953-54	New Westminster Royals	WHL	70	43	26	69	....	....	....	35	7	2	3	5	4
1954-55	New Westminster Royals	WHL	70	45	32	77	....	....	....	20	....	....	....	....	....
1955-56	New Westminster Royals	WHL	69	*47	32	79	....	....	....	16	4	0	1	1	0
1956-57	New Westminster Royals	WHL	70	41	25	66	....	....	....	36	11	*6	5	11	6
1957-58	New Westminster Royals	WHL	69	33	33	66	....	....	....	43	4	1	0	1	0
1958-59	New Westminster Royals	WHL	67	37	24	61	....	....	....	16	....	....	....	....	....
1959-60	Victoria Cougars	WHL	70	34	33	67	....	....	....	12	11	4	3	7	2
1960-61	Portland Buckaroos	WHL	66	42	32	74	....	....	....	8	14	6	*10	16	2
1961-62	Portland Buckaroos	WHL	60	29	27	56	....	....	....	14	7	3	3	6	10
1962-63	Portland Buckaroos	WHL	61	36	20	56	....	....	....	8	7	3	0	3	0
1963-64	Portland Buckaroos	WHL	1	0	0	0	....	....	....	0	....	....	....	....	....
	NHL Totals		**13**	**3**	**2**	**5**	**4**	**2**	**6**	**14**	....	....	....	....	....

USHL First All-Star Team (1950) • PCHL First All-Star Team (1952) • WHL Coast Division Second All-Star Team (1957, 1958, 1961) • Won Fred J. Hume Cup (WHL Most Gentlemanly Player) (1961)

Traded to **Quebec** (AHL) by **New Westminster** (WHL) for Claude Robert, January 4, 1953. • Rights returned to **New Westminster** (WHL) by **Quebec** when Fashoway refused to report to Quebec. New Westminster paid cash to complete transaction, January 7, 1953.

• FAULKNER, Alex Selm Alexander

C – L. 5'8", 165 lbs. b: Bishop Falls, Nfld., 5/21/1936.

Season	Club	League	GP	G	A	Pts	AG	AA	APts	PIM	GP	G	A	Pts	PIM
			REGULAR SEASON								PLAYOFFS				
1951-52	Bishop's Falls Woodsmen	GFSHL	8	2	4	6	....	....	....	0	5	11	11	22	2
	Bishop's Falls Woodsmen	H.S.	6	9	6	15	....	....	....	0	5	11	*12	23	4
1952-53	Bishop's Falls Woodsmen	GFSHL	12	13	11	24	....	....	....	2	....	....	....	....	....
	Grand Falls All-Stars	Nfld-Sr.	1	3	1	4	....	....	....	0	....	....	....	....	....
	Bishop's Falls Woodsmen	Nfld-Sr.	3	3	4	7	....	....	....	0	2	0	4	4	0
1953-54	Bishop's Falls Woodsmen	GFSHL	14	13	17	30	....	....	....	5	2	1	2	3	0
	Grand Falls Bees	Nfld-Sr.	2	0	0	0	....	....	....	2	2	0	3	3	2
1954-55	Bishop's Falls Woodsmen	GFSHL	11	18	11	29	....	....	....	0	5	5	5	10	4
	Grand Falls All-Stars	Nfld-Sr.	9	10	12	22	....	....	....	0	4	*4	2	6	4
1955-56	Bishop's Falls Kinsemen	GFSHL	12	*20	*17	*37	....	....	....	8	....	....	....	....	....
	Grand Falls Andcos	Nfld-Sr.	5	6	3	9	....	....	....	0	3	4	*6	*10	4
1956-57	Bishop's Falls Kinsemen	GFSHL	12	*20	*17	*37	....	....	....	8	....	....	....	....	....
	Grand Falls Bees	Nfld-Sr.	....	....	....	....	....	....	....	....	4	*8	*8	*16	4
1957-58	Bishop's Falls Kinsemen	GFSHL	12	*38	22	*60	....	....	....	9	5	9	*9	*18	0
	Grand Falls Bees	Nfld-Sr.	....	....	....	....	....	....	....	....	12	14	11	25	4
1958-59	Conception Bay Cee Bees	Nfld-Sr.	25	103	49	152	....	....	....	32	8	23	13	36	6
1959-60	Conception Bay Cee Bees	Nfld-Sr.	19	*47	*36	*83	....	....	....	33	11	*41	*45	*86	18
1960-61	Conception Bay Cee Bees	Nfld-Sr.	STATISTICS NOT AVAILABLE												
	Rochester Americans	AHL	41	5	13	18	....	....	....	6	....	....	....	....	....
1961-62	**Toronto Maple Leafs**	**NHL**	**1**	**0**	**0**	**0**	**0**	**0**	**0**	**0**	....	....	....	....	....
	Rochester Americans	AHL	65	19	54	73	....	....	....	26	2	1	1	2	0
1962-63	**Detroit Red Wings**	**NHL**	**70**	**10**	**10**	**20**	**12**	**10**	**22**	**6**	**8**	**5**	**0**	**5**	**2**
1963-64	**Detroit Red Wings**	**NHL**	**30**	**5**	**7**	**12**	**6**	**7**	**13**	**9**	**4**	**0**	**0**	**0**	**0**
	Cincinnati Wings	CHL	11	4	8	12	....	....	....	6	....	....	....	....	....
	Pittsburgh Hornets	AHL	8	1	4	5	....	....	....	2	....	....	....	....	....
1964-65	Conception Bay Cee Bees	Nfld-Sr.	19	22	*57	*79	....	....	....	52	11	*23	*22	*45	12
1965-66	Conception Bay Cee Bees	Nfld-Sr.	5	5	16	21	....	....	....	4	6	4	13	17	10
1966-67	Memphis Wings	CHL	70	28	*60	88	....	....	....	32	7	2	5	7	14
1967-68	San Diego Gulls	WHL	71	26	41	67	....	....	....	32	7	2	2	4	2
1968-69	San Diego Gulls	WHL	73	17	51	68	....	....	....	16	7	2	4	6	4
1969-70	San Diego Gulls	WHL	60	17	48	65	....	....	....	14	6	0	6	6	4
1970-71	San Diego Gulls	WHL	4	1	1	2	....	....	....	0	....	....	....	....	....
	St. John's Capitals	Nfld-Sr.	36	26	47	73	....	....	....	18	11	9	*21	*30	....
	Grand Falls Cataracts	Al-Cup	5	3	4	7	....	....	....	2	....	....	....	....	....
1971-72	St. John's Capitals	Nfld-Sr.	24	18	42	60	....	....	....	52	4	2	3	5	2
	Grand Falls Cataracts	Al-Cup	4	0	3	3	....	....	....	0	....	....	....	....	....
1972-73			DID NOT PLAY												
1973-74	Gander Flyers	Nfld-Sr.	9	5	8	13	....	....	....	4	....	....	....	....	....
1974-75			DID NOT PLAY												
1975-76	Grand Falls Cataracts	Nfld-Sr.	8	6	10	16	....	....	....	4	7	10	8	18	14
	NHL Totals		**101**	**15**	**17**	**32**	**18**	**17**	**35**	**15**	**12**	**5**	**0**	**5**	**2**

CHL Second All-Star Team (1967)

• Led Nfld-Sr. league in regular season and playoff goals, assists and points in 1958-59. Signed as a free agent by **Toronto**, December, 1960. Claimed by **Detroit** from **Toronto** in Intra-League Draft, June 4, 1962. • Missed majority of 1965-66 season recovering from arm injury suffered in game vs. Gander (Nfld-Sr.), December 17, 1965 and knee injury suffered in game vs. Gander (Nfld-Sr.), March 21, 1965.

• FERGUSON, John — *see page 1073*

• FERGUSON, Lorne Lorne Robert "Fergie"

LW – L. 6', 175 lbs. b: Palmerston, Ont., 5/26/1930.

Season	Club	League	GP	G	A	Pts	AG	AA	APts	PIM	GP	G	A	Pts	PIM
1947-48	Guelph Biltmores	OHA-Jr.	35	28	11	39	....	....	....	87	....	....	....	....	....
1948-49	Guelph Biltmores	OHA-Jr.	46	38	24	62	....	....	....	52	....	....	....	....	....
1949-50	**Boston Bruins**	**NHL**	**3**	**1**	**1**	**2**	**1**	**1**	**2**	**0**	....	....	....	....	....
	Tulsa Oilers	USHL	70	35	35	70	....	....	....	21	....	....	....	....	....
1950-51	**Boston Bruins**	**NHL**	**70**	**16**	**17**	**33**	**20**	**21**	**41**	**31**	**6**	**1**	**0**	**1**	**2**
1951-52	**Boston Bruins**	**NHL**	**27**	**3**	**4**	**7**	**4**	**5**	**9**	**14**	....	....	....	....	....
	Hershey Bears	AHL	8	5	1	6	....	....	....	2	....	....	....	....	....
1952-53	Hershey Bears	AHL	64	25	40	65	....	....	....	56	3	0	2	2	6
1953-54	Hershey Bears	AHL	70	*45	42	87	....	....	....	34	11	2	3	5	11
1954-55	**Boston Bruins**	**NHL**	**69**	**20**	**14**	**34**	**26**	**16**	**42**	**24**	**4**	**1**	**0**	**1**	**2**
1955-56	**Boston Bruins**	**NHL**	**32**	**7**	**5**	**12**	**9**	**6**	**15**	**18**	....	....	....	....	....
	Detroit Red Wings	**NHL**	**31**	**8**	**7**	**15**	**11**	**8**	**19**	**12**	**10**	**1**	**2**	**3**	**12**
1956-57	**Detroit Red Wings**	**NHL**	**70**	**13**	**10**	**23**	**17**	**11**	**28**	**26**	**5**	**1**	**0**	**1**	**6**
1957-58	**Detroit Red Wings**	**NHL**	**15**	**1**	**3**	**4**	**1**	**3**	**4**	**0**	....	....	....	....	....
	Chicago Black Hawks	**NHL**	**38**	**6**	**9**	**15**	**7**	**9**	**16**	**24**	....	....	....	....	....
1958-59	**Chicago Black Hawks**	**NHL**	**67**	**7**	**10**	**17**	**8**	**10**	**18**	**44**	**6**	**2**	**1**	**3**	**2**
1959-60	Buffalo Bisons	AHL	70	13	35	48	....	....	....	54	....	....	....	....	....
1960-61	Quebec Aces	AHL	13	1	1	2	....	....	....	2	....	....	....	....	....
	Kingston Frontenacs	EPHL	26	5	17	22	....	....	....	2	4	0	0	0	2
1961-62	Kingston Frontenacs	EPHL	48	9	15	24	....	....	....	35	2	0	0	0	14
1962/65			OUT OF HOCKEY – RETIRED												
1965-66	Kingston Aces	OHA-Sr.	12	6	4	10	....	....	....	8	....	....	....	....	....
1966-67	Kingston Aces	OHA-Sr.	PLAYER/COACH – STATISTICS UNAVAILABLE												
1967-68	Kingston Aces	OHA-Sr.	10	8	4	12	....	....	....	2	....	....	....	....	....
1968-69			DID NOT PLAY												
1969-70	Belleville Mohawks	OHA-Sr.	9	2	2	4	....	....	....	2	....	....	....	....	....
	NHL Totals		**422**	**82**	**80**	**162**	**104**	**90**	**194**	**193**	**31**	**6**	**3**	**9**	**24**

AHL Second All-Star Team (1954)

Rights traded to **Boston** by **NY Rangers** with Billly Moe and future considerations for Pat Egan, October 7, 1949. Traded to **Detroit** by **Boston** with Murray Costello for Real Chevrefils and Jerry Toppazzini, January 17, 1956. Traded to **Chicago** by **Detroit** with Earl Reibel, Billy Dea and Bill Dineen for Bob Bailey, Nick Mickoski, Jack McIntyre and Hec Lalande, December 17, 1957. Traded to **Montreal** by **Chicago** with Glen Skov, the rights to Danny Lewicki, Terry Gray and Bob Bailey for Cec Hoekstra, Reggie Fleming, Ab McDonald and Bob Courcy, June 7, 1960.

• FIELD, Wilf Wilfred Spence

D – R. 5'11", 185 lbs. b: Winnipeg, Man., 4/29/1915 d: 3/17/1979.

Season	Club	League	GP	G	A	Pts	AG	AA	APts	PIM	GP	G	A	Pts	PIM
1933-34	Winnipeg Monarchs	MJHL	14	3	2	5	....	....	....	18	3	2	1	3	2
1934-35	Winnipeg Monarchs	MJHL	10	6	1	7	....	....	....	16	4	3	1	4	10
	Winnipeg Monarchs	M-Cup	9	5	2	7	....	....	....	14	....	....	....	....	....
1935-36	Winnipeg Monarchs	MJHL	2	0	1	1	....	....	....	0	....	....	....	....	....
	Providence Reds	IAHL	42	0	1	1	....	....	....	5	7	0	0	0	8

			REGULAR SEASON								PLAYOFFS				
Season	Club	League	GP	G	A	Pts	AG	AA	APts	PIM	GP	G	A	Pts	PIM
1936-37	New York Americans	NHL	2	0	0	0	0	0	0	0	....	....	....	....	....
	New Haven Eagles	IAHL	46	3	3	6	....	....	....	61	....	....	....	....	....
1937-38	Seattle Seahawks	PCHL	41	12	12	24	....	....	....	38	4	0	1	1	2
1938-39	New York Americans	NHL	47	1	3	4	2	5	7	37	2	0	0	0	2
1939-40	New York Americans	NHL	45	1	3	4	2	5	7	28	....	....	....	....	....
1940-41	New York Americans	NHL	36	5	6	11	8	9	17	31	....	....	....	....	....
1941-42	Brooklyn Americans	NHL	41	6	9	15	8	11	19	23	....	....	....	....	....
1942-43	Winnipeg RCAF	MHL-Sr.	2	0	1	1	....	....	....	5	....	....	....	....	....
	Calgary RCAF Mustangs	ASHL	16	1	4	5	....	....	....	32	8	2	4	6	8
1943-44	Ottawa Commandos	QSHL	8	0	4	4	....	....	....	22	....	....	....	....	....
1944-45	Montreal Canadiens	NHL	9	1	0	1	1	0	1	10	....	....	....	....	....
	Chicago Black Hawks	NHL	39	3	4	7	3	5	8	22	....	....	....	....	....
1945-46	Buffalo Bisons	AHL	36	1	10	11	....	....	....	22	12	0	2	2	8
1946-47	Buffalo Bisons	AHL	62	2	14	16	....	....	....	34	4	0	0	0	4
1947-48	Buffalo Bisons	AHL	51	0	17	17	....	....	....	28	6	0	2	2	2
1948-49	Houston Huskies	USHL	64	6	18	24	....	....	....	34	....	....	....	....	....
1949-50	Buffalo Bisons	AHL	66	3	7	10	....	....	....	31	5	0	0	0	0
1950-51	Kansas City Royals	USHL	52	4	13	17	....	....	....	16	....	....	....	....	....
1951-52	Halifax Saints	MMHL	5	0	1	1	....	....	....	12	....	....	....	....	....
1952-53	Troy Uncle Sam Trojans	EHL	DID NOT PLAY – COACHING												
	NHL Totals		219	17	25	42	24	35	59	151	2	0	0	0	2

Signed as a free agent by **NY Americans**, November, 1936. Rights transferred to **Montreal** from **Brooklyn** in Special Dispersal Draw, September 11, 1943. Loaned to **Chicago** by **Montreal** for the remainder of the 1944-45 season, December 7, 1944. Loaned to **Buffalo** (AHL) by **Montreal** with Frank Eddolls, Kenny Mosdell and cash for Lorran Thibeault, October 24, 1945.

• FIELDER, Guyle Guyle Abner

C – L. 5'9", 165 lbs. b: Potlatch, ID, 11/21/1930.

Season	Club	League	GP	G	A	Pts	AG	AA	APts	PIM	GP	G	A	Pts	PIM
1947-48	Prince Albert Mintos	SJHL	25	26	15	41	....	....	....	20	2	0	1	1	0
1948-49	Prince Albert Mintos	SJHL	20	17	*26	43	....	....	....	22	9	9	*14	23	4
	Lethbridge Native Sons	WCJHL	2	1	1	2	....	....	....	0	....	....	....	....	....
1949-50	Lethbridge Native Sons	WCJHL	39	47	*58	*105	....	....	....	19	10	2	7	9	14
1950-51	Lethbridge Native Sons	WCJHL	37	*44	*56	*100	....	....	....	6	7	3	5	8	8
	Chicago Black Hawks	NHL	3	0	0	0	0	0	0	0	....	....	....	....	....
1951-52	New Westminster Royals	PCHL	57	25	50	75	....	....	....	10	7	1	3	4	2
1952-53	St. Louis Flyers	AHL	62	22	*61	83	....	....	....	12	....	....	....	....	....
	Edmonton Flyers	WHL	3	0	1	1	....	....	....	0	....	....	....	....	....
	Detroit Red Wings	NHL	....	....	....	....	....	....	....	....	4	0	0	0	0
1953-54	Seattle Bombers	WHL	68	24	*64	*88	....	....	....	20	....	....	....	....	....
	Boston Bruins	NHL	....	....	....	....	....	....	....	....	2	0	0	0	2
1954-55	New Westminster Royals	WHL	70	20	*67	87	....	....	....	37	....	....	....	....	....
1955-56	Seattle Americans	WHL	70	18	61	79	....	....	....	42	....	....	....	....	....
1956-57	Seattle Americans	WHL	69	33	*89	*122	....	....	....	30	6	2	4	6	0
1957-58	Detroit Red Wings	NHL	6	0	0	0	0	0	0	2	....	....	....	....	....
	Seattle Totems	WHL	62	26	*85	*111	....	....	....	22	9	2	9	11	2
1958-59	Seattle Totems	WHL	69	24	*95	*119	....	....	....	18	12	4	9	13	4
1959-60	Seattle Totems	WHL	69	31	*64	*95	....	....	....	12	4	1	1	2	0
1960-61	Seattle Totems	WHL	69	24	*71	95	....	....	....	32	11	2	9	11	4
1961-62	Seattle Totems	WHL	69	21	52	73	....	....	....	46	2	0	0	0	0
1962-63	Seattle Totems	WHL	69	17	*80	*97	....	....	....	20	17	5	*17	*22	6
1963-64	Seattle Totems	WHL	66	17	*85	*102	....	....	....	34	....	....	....	....	....
	Quebec Aces	AHL	....	....	....	....	....	....	....	....	1	0	0	0	0
1964-65	Seattle Totems	WHL	70	14	*78	*92	....	....	....	38	7	0	7	7	2
1965-66	Seattle Totems	WHL	70	19	*75	94	....	....	....	10	....	....	....	....	....
1966-67	Seattle Totems	WHL	72	20	*71	*91	....	....	....	22	10	2	*7	9	12
1967-68	Seattle Totems	WHL	70	15	*55	70	....	....	....	26	9	6	5	11	2
1968-69	Seattle Totems	WHL	74	20	74	94	....	....	....	12	4	0	2	2	4
1969-70	Salt Lake Golden Eagles	WHL	55	8	58	66	....	....	....	20	....	....	....	....	....
1970-71	Salt Lake Golden Eagles	WHL	64	15	46	61	....	....	....	22	....	....	....	....	....
1971-72	Salt Lake Golden Eagles	WHL	30	5	22	27	....	....	....	4	....	....	....	....	....
	Portland Buckaroos	WHL	40	9	40	49	....	....	....	10	11	0	*10	10	2
1972-73	Portland Buckaroos	WHL	70	11	47	58	....	....	....	4	....	....	....	....	....
	NHL Totals		9	0	0	0	0	0	0	2	6	0	0	0	2

Rookie of the Year - PCHL (1952) • AHL First All-Star Team (1953) • Won Dudley "Red" Garrett Memorial Award (Top Rookie - AHL) (1953) • WHL First All-Star Team (1954, 1960, 1963, 1964, 1967) • WHL Coast Division First All-Star Team (1957, 1958, 1959) • Won Leader Cup (WHL Coast Division - MVP) (1957, 1958, 1959) • Won Leader Cup (WHL - MVP) (Tied with Hank Bassen) (1960) • WHL Second All-Star Team (1961, 1965, 1966, 1968) • Won Leader Cup (WHL - MVP) (1964, 1967) • Won Fred J. Hume Cup (WHL Most Gentlemanly Player) (1966, 1967, 1969)

Signed as a free agent by **Chicago**, March 9, 1951. Loaned to **New Westminster** (PCHL) by **Chicago** for cash, August, 1951. Traded to **Detroit** by **Chicago** with Steve Hrymnak and Red Almas for cash, September 23, 1952. Loaned to **Chicago** by **Detroit** (Edmonton-WHL) for 1952-53 season for the loan of Ray Hannigan for 1952-53 season, October 15, 1952. Claimed on waivers by **NY Rangers** from **Detroit**, September 29, 1953. Traded to **Seattle** (WHL) by **NY Rangers** for the rights to Lee Hyssop, October, 1953. NHL rights traded to **Boston** by **Seattle** (WHL) for cash, October, 1953. Claimed by **Boston** from **Seattle** (WHL) in Inter-League Draft, June 5, 1957. Traded to **Detroit** by **Boston** for cash, June 15, 1957. Claimed by **Toronto** from **Seattle** (WHL) in Inter-League Draft, June 3, 1958. • Fielder refused to sign with Toronto and remained the property of Seattle. Traded to **Salt Lake** (WHL) by **Seattle** (WHL) for Bobby Schmautz, November 15, 1969. Traded to **Portland** (WHL) by **California** (Salt Lake-WHL) with the loan of John Rathwell for Fred Hilts and Lyle Bradley, January, 1972. Selected by **Dayton-Houston** (WHA) in WHA General Player Draft, February 12, 1972.

• FILLION, Bob Robert Louis

LW – L. 5'10", 170 lbs. b: Thetford Mines, Que., 7/12/1921.

Season	Club	League	GP	G	A	Pts	AG	AA	APts	PIM	GP	G	A	Pts	PIM
1938-39	Verdun Maple Leafs	QJHL	11	4	12	16	....	....	....	8	3	1	1	2	2
	Verdun Maple Leafs	M-Cup	7	4	3	7	....	....	....	10	....	....	....	....	....
1939-40	Verdun Maple Leafs	QJHL	11	10	6	16	....	....	....	6	....	....	....	....	....
	Verdun Maple Leafs	QSHL	6	0	3	3	....	....	....	0	8	0	2	2	0
1940-41	Shawinigan Cataracts	QSHL	24	10	20	30	....	....	....	25	10	3	6	9	15
1941-42	Shawinigan Cataracts	QSHL	8	1	5	6	....	....	....	4	8	6	6	12	4
1942-43	Montreal Army	QSHL	33	4	13	17	....	....	....	8	7	1	3	4	2
♦1943-44	Montreal Canadiens	NHL	41	7	23	30	6	20	26	14	3	0	0	0	0
1944-45	Montreal Canadiens	NHL	31	6	8	14	6	9	15	12	1	3	0	3	0
♦1945-46	Montreal Canadiens	NHL	50	10	6	16	12	9	21	12	9	4	3	7	6
1946-47	Montreal Canadiens	NHL	57	6	3	9	7	4	11	16	8	0	0	0	0
1947-48	Montreal Canadiens	NHL	32	9	9	18	12	12	24	8	....	....	....	....	....
	Buffalo Bisons	AHL	18	9	9	18	....	....	....	4	....	....	....	....	....
1948-49	Montreal Canadiens	NHL	59	3	9	12	4	13	17	14	7	0	1	1	4
1949-50	Montreal Canadiens	NHL	57	1	3	4	1	4	5	8	5	0	0	0	0
1950-51	Sherbrooke Saints	QMHL	44	15	18	33	....	....	....	45	7	1	1	2	6
	NHL Totals		327	42	61	103	48	71	119	84	33	7	4	11	10

• Brother of Marcel

• FILLION, Marcel

LW – L. 5'7", 175 lbs. b: Thetford Mines, Que., 5/28/1923 d: 1998.

Season	Club	League	GP	G	A	Pts	AG	AA	APts	PIM	GP	G	A	Pts	PIM
1940-41	Shawinigan Cataracts	QSHL	27	11	13	24	....	....	....	2	10	4	2	6	8
1941-42	Shawinigan Cataracts	QSHL	33	15	17	32	....	....	....	16	10	2	1	3	2
1942-43	Quebec Sea Gulls	QCHL	....	....	....	....	....	....	....	....	10	*17	*23	*40	....
1943-44			DID NOT PLAY												
1944-45	Boston Bruins	NHL	1	0	0	0	0	0	0	0	....	....	....	....	....
	Boston Olympics	EAHL	46	38	40	78	....	....	....	84	12	10	8	18	2
1945-46	Shawinigan Cataracts	QSHL	20	8	6	14	....	....	....	14	4	1	0	1	4
1946-47	Providence Reds	AHL	21	2	6	8	....	....	....	6	....	....	....	....	....
	Boston Olympics	EAHL	27	19	6	25	....	....	....	18	9	7	*8	*15	14
1947-48	Boston Olympics	QSHL	48	25	32	57	....	....	....	22	....	....	....	....	....
	Boston Olympics	EAHL	19	14	17	31	....	....	....	15	....	....	....	....	....
1948-49	Boston–Sherbrooke	QSHL	63	39	34	73	....	....	....	41	12	7	2	9	4
1949-50	Sherbrooke Saints	QSHL	60	21	29	50	....	....	....	24	6	0	0	0	2
	Sherbrooke Saints	Al-Cup	9	2	1	3	....	....	....	11	....	....	....	....	....
1950-51	Sherbrooke Saints	QMHL	58	14	14	28	....	....	....	31	7	0	1	1	6
1951-52			OUT OF HOCKEY – RETIRED												
1952-53	Rimouski Renards	LSLHL	58	24	36	60	....	....	....	44	....	....	....	....	....
1953-54	Rimouski Renards	LSLHL	65	13	14	27	....	....	....	8	....	....	....	....	....
	NHL Totals		1	0	0	0	0	0	0	0	....	....	....	....	....

• Brother of Bob • EAHL Second All-Star Team (1945)

• FILMORE, Tommy

RW – R. 5'11", 189 lbs. b: Thamesford, Ont., Deceased.

Season	Club	League	GP	G	A	Pts	AG	AA	APts	PIM	GP	G	A	Pts	PIM
1926-27	London 12th Battery	OHA-Sr.	....	....	....	....	....	....	....	....	13	*19	7	*26	....
1927-28	London Panthers	Can-Pro	40	19	7	26	....	....	....	18	....	....	....	....	....
1928-29	London Panthers	Can-Pro	15	1	2	3	....	....	....	11	....	....	....	....	....
	Detroit Olympics	Can-Pro	25	10	6	16	....	....	....	12	7	2	1	3	9
1929-30	Detroit Olympics	IHL	42	18	16	34	....	....	....	34	3	1	0	1	0
1930-31	Detroit Falcons	NHL	39	6	2	8	12	6	18	10	....	....	....	....	....
1931-32	Detroit Falcons	NHL	9	0	0	0	0	0	0	2	....	....	....	....	....
	Detroit Olympics	IHL	11	2	1	3	....	....	....	4	....	....	....	....	....
	New York Americans	NHL	31	8	6	14	13	13	26	12	....	....	....	....	....
1932-33	New York Americans	NHL	34	1	4	5	2	8	10	9	....	....	....	....	....
	Boston Bruins	NHL	1	0	0	0	0	0	0	0	....	....	....	....	....
	Boston Cubs	Can-Am	10	3	4	7	....	....	....	0	7	0	*4	4	4
1933-34	Boston Bruins	NHL	3	0	0	0	0	0	0	0	....	....	....	....	....
	Boston Cubs	Can-Am	35	16	11	27	....	....	....	10	5	2	1	3	6
1934-35	Quebec Beavers	Can-Am	15	3	4	7	....	....	....	6	3	1	0	1	10
1935-36	Providence Reds	Can-Am	42	10	7	17	....	....	....	6	7	1	*5	*6	6
1936-37	Springfield Indians	IAHL	41	9	19	28	....	....	....	14	5	0	0	0	0
1937-38	Springfield Indians	IAHL	37	16	14	30	....	....	....	19	....	....	....	....	....
1938-39	Springfield Indians	IAHL	28	16	13	29	....	....	....	4	3	0	0	0	0
1939-40	Springfield Indians	IAHL	39	16	20	36	....	....	....	6	3	3	1	4	7
1940-41			DID NOT PLAY												
1941-42	Fort Worth Rangers	AHA	1	0	0	0	....	....	....	0	....	....	....	....	....
	NHL Totals		117	15	12	27	27	27	54	33	....	....	....	....	....

• Regular season totals for London (OHA-Sr.) in 1926-27 season unavailable. Signed as a free agent by **London** (Can-Pro), November 9, 1927. Traded to **NY Americans** by **Detroit** with Bert McInenly for Hap Emms and Frank Carson, December 29, 1931. Traded to **Boston** by **NY Americans** for Jim Klein, February 12, 1933. Traded to **Montreal Canadiens** by **Boston** with cash for Tony Savage, November 5, 1934. • Missed majority of 1934-35 season due to illness in the family. Re-assigned to **Quebec** (Can-Am) by **Montreal Canadiens**, February, 1935. Traded to **Springfield** (IAHL) by **Montreal Canadiens** for cash, April, 1936.

• FINKBEINER, Lloyd

LW/D – L. 5'10", 175 lbs. b: Guelph, Ont., 4/12/1920 d: 3/30/1999.

Season	Club	League	GP	G	A	Pts	AG	AA	APts	PIM	GP	G	A	Pts	PIM
1937-38	Guelph Indians	OHA-Jr.	14	3	2	5	....	....	....	14	9	3	2	5	10
	Guelph Indians	M-Cup	3	0	0	0	....	....	....	2	....	....	....	....	....
1938-39	Guelph Indians	OHA-Jr.	14	0	1	1	....	....	....	23	2	0	0	0	4
1939-40	Guelph Indians	OHA-Jr.	19	2	3	5	....	....	....	*63	3	0	0	0	6
1940-41	New York Americans	NHL	2	0	0	0	0	0	0	0	....	....	....	....	....
	Springfield Indians	AHL	34	3	5	8	....	....	....	8	....	....	....	....	....
	Atlantic City Seagulls	EAHL	6	0	0	0	....	....	....	0	....	....	....	....	....
1941-42	Camp Borden Army	NBSHL	4	8	5	13	....	....	....	4	....	....	....	....	....
1942-43	Toronto Army Daggers	OHA-Sr.	12	6	5	11	....	....	....	26	4	1	1	2	6
	Toronto CPR	TIHL	1	0	0	0	....	....	....	2	3	0	0	0	0
	Camp Borden Army	NSDHL	....	....	....	....	....	....	....	....	4	8	5	13	4
1943-44	Toronto Army Daggers	OHA-Sr.	1	0	0	0	....	....	....	0	....	....	....	....	....
	Toronto Army Shamrocks	TIHL	14	8	9	17	....	....	....	10	....	....	....	....	....
1944-45	Montreal Royals	QSHL	2	0	0	0	....	....	....	0	....	....	....	....	....
	Toronto Army Shamrocks	TIHL	1	0	0	0	....	....	....	0	....	....	....	....	....
1945-46	Buffalo Bisons	AHL	14	1	0	1	....	....	....	2	....	....	....	....	....
	Dallas Texans	USHL	42	13	8	21	....	....	....	28	....	....	....	....	....
1946-47	Dallas Texans	USHL	57	8	22	30	....	....	....	128	6	1	4	5	4
1947-48	Dallas Texans	USHL	66	9	18	27	....	....	....	78	....	....	....	....	....
1948-49	Houston Huskies	USHL	3	0	1	1	....	....	....	2	....	....	....	....	....
	Buffalo Bisons	AHL	63	7	14	21	....	....	....	95	....	....	....	....	....
1949-50	Buffalo Bisons	AHL	70	9	14	23	....	....	....	110	5	1	2	3	10
1950-51	Buffalo Bisons	AHL	64	6	20	26	....	....	....	85	4	1	1	2	10
1951-52	Buffalo Bisons	AHL	29	0	13	13	....	....	....	38	1	0	0	0	2
	Montreal Royals	QMHL	23	1	5	6	....	....	....	29	5	0	1	1	6
1952-53	Cincinnati Mohawks	IHL	48	5	26	31	....	....	....	87	9	2	5	7	32
1953-54	Stratford Indians	OHA-Sr.	52	9	21	30	....	....	....	100	3	1	0	1	12
1954-55	Stratford Indians	OHA-Sr.	50	2	16	18	....	....	....	103	7	1	6	7	8
1955-56	Stratford Indians	OHA-Sr.	48	6	21	27	....	....	....	60	6	2	1	3	6
1956-57	Strathroy Rockets	OIHA	....	6	13	19	....	....	....	....	....	....	....	....	....
	NHL Totals		2	0	0	0	0	0	0	0	....	....	....	....	....

USHL Second All-Star Team (1948)

Signed as a free agent by **NY Americans**, October 22, 1940.

• FINNEY, Sid Joseph Sidney

C – L. 5'11", 160 lbs. b: Banbridge, Ireland, 5/1/1929.

			REGULAR SEASON								PLAYOFFS				
Season	**Club**	**League**	**GP**	**G**	**A**	**Pts**	**AG**	**AA**	**APts**	**PIM**	**GP**	**G**	**A**	**Pts**	**PIM**
1947-48	Calgary Buffalos	AJHL	15	6	8	14	....	....	....	9	8	2	2	4	0
1948-49	Calgary Buffalos	WCJHL	32	27	16	43	....	....	....	14	8	*9	3	12	2
	Calgary Buffalos	M-Cup	16	12	7	19	....	....	....	4	....	....	....	....	....
1949-50	Calgary Stampeders	WCSHL	17	7	5	12	....	....	....	4	....	....	....	....	....
1950-51	Calgary Stampeders	WCMHL	57	*44	37	*81	....	....	....	12	8	4	1	5	0
1951-52	**Chicago Black Hawks**	**NHL**	**35**	**6**	**5**	**11**	**8**	**6**	**14**	**0**	....	....	....	....	....
	St. Louis Flyers	AHL	23	8	5	13	....	....	....	2	....	....	....	....	....
1952-53	**Chicago Black Hawks**	**NHL**	**18**	**4**	**2**	**6**	**5**	**2**	**7**	**4**	**7**	**0**	**2**	**2**	**0**
	Calgary Stampeders	WHL	39	25	19	44	....	....	....	12	....	....	....	....	....
1953-54	**Chicago Black Hawks**	**NHL**	**6**	**0**	**0**	**0**	**0**	**0**	**0**	**0**	....	....	....	....	....
	Calgary Stampeders	WHL	47	29	33	62	....	....	....	9	18	*15	5	*20	4
	Calgary Stampeders	Ed-Cup	7	*5	4	*9	....	....	....	0	....	....	....	....	....
1954-55	Calgary Stampeders	WHL	70	35	42	77	....	....	....	20	9	4	5	9	0
1955-56	Calgary Stampeders	WHL	69	43	36	79	....	....	....	24	8	7	4	11	0
1956-57	Calgary Stampeders	WHL	68	41	38	79	....	....	....	47	3	0	0	0	8
1957-58	Calgary Stampeders	WHL	58	*45	43	88	....	....	....	8	12	5	9	14	12
1958-59	Calgary Stampeders	WHL	60	29	30	59	....	....	....	24	8	1	5	6	2
1959-60	Calgary Stampeders	WHL	59	28	32	60	....	....	....	6	....	....	....	....	....
1960-61	Calgary Stampeders	WHL	59	26	42	68	....	....	....	12	5	2	4	6	0
1961-62	Calgary Stampeders	WHL	61	35	32	67	....	....	....	4	7	2	2	4	0
1962-63	Edmonton Flyers	WHL	65	23	42	65	....	....	....	16	3	1	3	4	0
1963-64	Cincinnati Wings	CHL	13	3	3	6	....	....	....	4	....	....	....	....	....
	Portland Buckaroos	WHL	39	9	10	19	....	....	....	2	....	....	....	....	....
1964-65			DID NOT PLAY												
1965-66	Drumheller Miners	ASHL	24	13	21	34	....	....	....	4	12	6	9	*15	0
	Drumheller Miners	Al-Cup	16	13	15	28	....	....	....	4	....	....	....	....	....
1966-67			OUT OF HOCKEY – RETIRED												
1967-68			OUT OF HOCKEY – RETIRED												
1968-69	Calgary Stampeders	ASHL	....	7	12	19	....	....	....	12	4	2	1	3	0
	NHL Totals		**59**	**10**	**7**	**17**	**13**	**8**	**21**	**4**	**7**	**0**	**2**	**2**	**0**

WHL Prairie Division First All-Star Team (1957, 1958) • Won Leader Cup (WHL Prairie Division - MVP) (1958)

Traded to **Chicago** by **Calgary** ((WCMHL) for Ernie Dickens, October 1, 1951. Claimed by **Chicago** from **Buffalo** (AHL) in Inter-League Draft, June 4, 1957. Claimed by **Hershey** (AHL) from **Chicago** (Calgary-WHL), June 3, 1958. Traded to **Edmonton** (WHL) by **Calgary** (WHL) for Gord Strate and future considerations (Jack Turner, October, 1962), September, 1962. Traded to **Portland** (WHL) by **Edmonton** (WHL) for Ken Laufman and Roger Leopold, November, 1963.

• FINNIGAN, Ed Edward David

LW – L. 5'8", 170 lbs. b: Shawville, Que., 5/23/1913 Deceased.

			REGULAR SEASON								PLAYOFFS				
Season	**Club**	**League**	**GP**	**G**	**A**	**Pts**	**AG**	**AA**	**APts**	**PIM**	**GP**	**G**	**A**	**Pts**	**PIM**
1927-28	North Bay Trappers	NOJHA	12	3	13	16	....	....	....	....	2	0	0	0	0
1928-29	Ottawa Shamrocks	OHA-Jr.	7	5	3	8	....	....	....	6	2	1	2	3	2
1929-30	Ottawa Rideaus	OHA-Jr.	12	5	1	6	....	....	....	19	2	1	*2	*3	4
	Ottawa Rideaus	M-Cup	2	2	0	2	....	....	....	8	....	....	....	....	....
1930-31	Ottawa Rideaus	OHA-Jr.	15	12	4	16	....	....	....	*49	2	0	1	1	10
	Ottawa Rideaus	OCHL	....	....	....	....	....	....	....	....	7	*3	1	4	14
	Ottawa Rideaus	Al-Cup	5	1	0	1	....	....	....	0	....	....	....	....	....
1931-32	Ottawa Rideaus	OCHL	23	12	5	17	....	....	....	46	4	1	0	1	2
1932-33	Ottawa Rideaus	OCHL	19	9	3	12	....	....	....	12	6	*4	1	*5	4
	Ottawa Rideaus	Al-Cup	4	2	2	4	....	....	....	4	....	....	....	....	....
1933-34	Ottawa New Edinburghs	OCHL	20	14	7	21	....	....	....	28	3	1	3	4	2
	Ottawa New Edinburghs	Al-Cup	7	6	3	9	....	....	....	14	....	....	....	....	....
1934-35	**St. Louis Eagles**	**NHL**	**12**	**1**	**1**	**2**	**2**	**2**	**4**	**2**	....	....	....	....	....
	Ottawa Senators	OCHL	20	15	*22	37	....	....	....	16	....	....	....	....	....
1935-36	Rochester Cardinals	IHL	11	2	0	2	....	....	....	10	....	....	....	....	....
	Boston Bruins	**NHL**	**3**	**0**	**0**	**0**	**0**	**0**	**0**	**0**	....	....	....	....	....
	Boston Cubs	Can-Am	29	9	4	13	....	....	....	4	....	....	....	....	....
1936-37	Providence Reds	IAHL	DID NOT PLAY – SUSPENDED												
1937-38	Ottawa Senators	OCHL	22	10	9	19	....	....	....	8	4	1	1	2	0
1938-39			REINSTATED AS AN AMATEUR												
1939-40	Ottawa RCAF	OCHL	2	2	0	2	....	....	....	2	....	....	....	....	....
1940-41	Hull Volants	OCHL	19	11	19	30	....	....	....	5	10	6	9	15	6
1941-42	Hull Volants	OCHL	12	7	13	20	....	....	....	0	7	5	3	8	2
1942-43	Hull–Ottawa Senators	QSHL	18	6	10	16	....	....	....	0	....	....	....	....	....
1943-44	Ottawa Montagnards	OCHL	13	*14	*16	*30	....	....	....	6	2	3	2	5	0
	Ottawa Canadiens	OCHL	....	....	....	....	....	....	....	....	5	8	1	9	0
1944-45	Ottawa Commandos	QSHL	15	6	4	10	....	....	....	7	2	0	0	0	0
1945-46	Spencerville Sagueenens	SLSHL	STATISTICS NOT AVAILABLE												
1946-47	Renfrew Lions	UOVHL	23	8	7	15	....	....	....	4	3	0	2	2	2
	NHL Totals		**15**	**1**	**1**	**2**	**2**	**2**	**4**	**2**	....	....	....	....	....

• Brother of Frank

Claimed by **NY Americans** from **St. Louis** in Dispersal Draft, October 14, 1935. Traded to **Boston** by **NY Americans** for cash, December 19, 1935. Traded to **Providence** (IAHL) by **Boston** for cash, October 7, 1936. • Suspended for entire 1936-37 season by **Providence** (IAHL) for refusing to report to team, October 12, 1936.

• FINNIGAN, Frank Frank Arthur "The Shawville Express"

RW – R. 5'9", 165 lbs. b: Shawville, Que., 7/9/1903 d: 12/25/1991.

			REGULAR SEASON								PLAYOFFS				
Season	**Club**	**League**	**GP**	**G**	**A**	**Pts**	**AG**	**AA**	**APts**	**PIM**	**GP**	**G**	**A**	**Pts**	**PIM**
1921-22	University of Ottawa	OCHL	5	1	3	4	....	....	....	0	....	....	....	....	....
1922-23	Ottawa Collegiate	OCHL	9	7	5	12	....	....	....	0	....	....	....	....	....
1923-24	Ottawa Montagnards	OCHL	10	4	1	5	....	....	....	....	3	0	0	0	....
	Ottawa Senators	**NHL**	**2**	**0**	**0**	**0**	**0**	**0**	**0**	**0**	**2**	**0**	**0**	**0**	**2**
1924-25	**Ottawa Senators**	**NHL**	**29**	**0**	**0**	**0**	**0**	**0**	**0**	**22**	....	....	....	....	....
1925-26	**Ottawa Senators**	**NHL**	**36**	**2**	**0**	**2**	**3**	**0**	**3**	**24**	**2**	**0**	**0**	**0**	**0**
♦1926-27	**Ottawa Senators**	**NHL**	**36**	**15**	**1**	**16**	**27**	**5**	**32**	**52**	**6**	**3**	**0**	**3**	**0**
1927-28	**Ottawa Senators**	**NHL**	**38**	**20**	**5**	**25**	**41**	**28**	**69**	**34**	**2**	**0**	**1**	**1**	**6**
1928-29	**Ottawa Senators**	**NHL**	**44**	**15**	**4**	**19**	**44**	**27**	**71**	**71**	....	....	....	....	....
1929-30	**Ottawa Senators**	**NHL**	**43**	**21**	**15**	**36**	**30**	**36**	**66**	**46**	**1**	**0**	**0**	**0**	**4**
1930-31	**Ottawa Senators**	**NHL**	**44**	**9**	**8**	**17**	**18**	**24**	**42**	**40**	....	....	....	....	....
♦1931-32	**Toronto Maple Leafs**	**NHL**	**47**	**8**	**13**	**21**	**13**	**29**	**42**	**45**	**7**	**2**	**3**	**5**	**8**
1932-33	**Ottawa Senators**	**NHL**	**45**	**4**	**14**	**18**	**7**	**29**	**36**	**37**	....	....	....	....	....
1933-34	**Ottawa Senators**	**NHL**	**48**	**10**	**10**	**20**	**17**	**21**	**38**	**10**	....	....	....	....	....
1934-35	**St. Louis Eagles**	**NHL**	**34**	**5**	**5**	**10**	**8**	**9**	**17**	**10**	....	....	....	....	....
	Toronto Maple Leafs	**NHL**	**11**	**2**	**0**	**2**	**3**	**0**	**3**	**2**	**7**	**1**	**2**	**3**	**2**
1935-36	**Toronto Maple Leafs**	**NHL**	**48**	**2**	**6**	**8**	**4**	**11**	**15**	**10**	**9**	**0**	**3**	**3**	**0**
1936-37	**Toronto Maple Leafs**	**NHL**	**48**	**2**	**7**	**9**	**3**	**13**	**16**	**4**	**2**	**0**	**0**	**0**	**0**
1937/39			OUT OF HOCKEY – RETIRED												
1939-40	Ottawa RCAF	OCHL	4	0	2	2	....	....	....	3	....	....	....	....	....
1940-41	Toronto RCAF	TMHL	13	1	2	3	....	....	....	8	3	1	0	1	0
1941-42			MILITARY SERVICE												
1942-43			MILITARY SERVICE												
1943-44			MILITARY SERVICE												
1944-45	Ottawa #17 Depot	OCHL	7	0	4	4	....	....	....	4	....	....	....	....	....
	NHL Totals		**553**	**115**	**88**	**203**	**218**	**232**	**450**	**407**	**38**	**6**	**9**	**15**	**22**

• Brother of Ed • Played in NHL All-Star Game (1934)

Signed as a free agent by **Ottawa**, February 21, 1924. Claimed by **Toronto** from **Ottawa** for 1931-32 season in Dispersal Draft, September 26, 1931. Transferred to **St. Louis** after **Ottawa** franchise relocated, September 30, 1934. Traded to **Toronto** by **St. Louis** for cash, February 13, 1935.

• FISHER, Alvin Alvin Thomas

RW – R. 6'1", 175 lbs. b: Sault Ste. Marie, Ont., Deceased.

			REGULAR SEASON								PLAYOFFS				
Season	**Club**	**League**	**GP**	**G**	**A**	**Pts**	**AG**	**AA**	**APts**	**PIM**	**GP**	**G**	**A**	**Pts**	**PIM**
1919-20	Hamilton Tigers	OHA-Sr.	4	0	1	1	....	....	....	....	2	0	0	0	0
1920-21	S.S. Marie Greyhounds	NMHL	14	6	3	9	....	....	....	....	....	....	....	....	....
	S.S. Marie Greyhounds	NOHA	9	7	1	8	....	....	....	12	5	1	0	1	0
1921-22	S.S. Marie Greyhounds	NMHL	12	2	5	7	....	....	....	....	....	....	....	....	....
	S.S. Marie Greyhounds	NOHA	8	2	1	3	....	....	....	15	2	0	1	1	2
1922-23	Calgary Tigers	WCHL	18	5	3	8	....	....	....	10	....	....	....	....	....
1923-24	Seattle Metropolitans	PCHA	15	1	1	2	....	....	....	2	2	0	0	0	0
1924-25	**Toronto St. Pats**	**NHL**	**9**	**1**	**0**	**1**	**2**	**0**	**2**	**4**	....	....	....	....	....
	NHL Totals		**9**	**1**	**0**	**1**	**2**	**0**	**2**	**4**	....	....	....	....	....
	Other Major League Totals		33	6	4	10	....	....	....	12	2	0	0	0	0

NOHA Second All-Star Team (1922)

Signed as a free agent by **Calgary** (WCHL), August 21, 1922. Traded to **Seattle** (PCHA) by **Calgary** (WCHL) with Jack Arbour for cash, August 21, 1923. Signed as a free agent by **Toronto**, November 24, 1925.

• FISHER, Dunc Duncan Robert

RW – R. 5'7", 170 lbs. b: Regina, Sask., 8/30/1927.

			REGULAR SEASON								PLAYOFFS				
Season	**Club**	**League**	**GP**	**G**	**A**	**Pts**	**AG**	**AA**	**APts**	**PIM**	**GP**	**G**	**A**	**Pts**	**PIM**
1944-45	Regina Abbotts	SJHL	15	5	6	11	....	....	....	30	....	....	....	....	....
1945-46	Regina Abbotts	SJHL	18	19	13	32	....	....	....	22	7	9	2	11	12
1946-47	Regina Pats	SJHL	26	28	16	44	....	....	....	12	6	5	7	12	8
1947-48	New Haven Ramblers	AHL	68	25	34	59	....	....	....	29	4	2	1	3	0
	New York Rangers	**NHL**	....	....	....	....	....	....	....	....	**1**	**0**	**1**	**1**	**0**
1948-49	**New York Rangers**	**NHL**	**60**	**9**	**16**	**25**	**12**	**23**	**35**	**40**	....	....	....	....	....
1949-50	**New York Rangers**	**NHL**	**70**	**12**	**21**	**33**	**15**	**25**	**40**	**42**	**12**	**3**	**3**	**6**	**14**
1950-51	**New York Rangers**	**NHL**	**12**	**0**	**0**	**0**	**0**	**0**	**0**	**0**	....	....	....	....	....
	St. Paul Saints	USHL	2	0	1	1	....	....	....	0	....	....	....	....	....
	Boston Bruins	**NHL**	**53**	**9**	**20**	**29**	**11**	**24**	**35**	**20**	**6**	**1**	**0**	**1**	**0**
1951-52	**Boston Bruins**	**NHL**	**65**	**15**	**12**	**27**	**20**	**15**	**35**	**2**	**2**	**0**	**0**	**0**	**0**
1952-53	**Boston Bruins**	**NHL**	**7**	**0**	**1**	**1**	**0**	**1**	**1**	**0**	....	....	....	....	....
	Hershey Bears	AHL	55	29	24	53	....	....	....	2	3	0	3	3	0
1953-54	Hershey Bears	AHL	69	41	39	80	....	....	....	24	11	4	1	5	2
1954-55	Hershey Bears	AHL	62	28	35	63	....	....	....	36	....	....	....	....	....
1955-56	Hershey Bears	AHL	60	40	43	83	....	....	....	73	....	....	....	....	....
1956-57	Hershey Bears	AHL	64	40	38	78	....	....	....	59	7	6	3	9	0
1957-58	Hershey Bears	AHL	70	*41	47	88	....	....	....	56	11	6	7	13	0
1958-59	**Detroit Red Wings**	**NHL**	**8**	**0**	**0**	**0**	**0**	**0**	**0**	**0**	....	....	....	....	....
	Hershey Bears	AHL	62	19	32	51	....	....	....	28	13	4	9	13	12
1959-60	Hershey Bears	AHL	69	22	43	65	....	....	....	58	....	....	....	....	....
	NHL Totals		**275**	**45**	**70**	**115**	**58**	**88**	**146**	**104**	**21**	**4**	**4**	**8**	**14**

AHL Second All-Star Team (1954, 1955, 1956, 1957) • AHL First All-Star Team (1958)

Traded to **Boston** by **NY Rangers** with future considerations (loan of Alex Kaleta to Hershey-AHL, November 20, 1950) for Ed Harrison and Zellio Toppazzini, November 16, 1950. Traded to **Hershey** (AHL) by **Boston** with Obie O'Brien for Ray Gariepy, June, 1953. Traded to **Detroit** by **Hershey** (AHL) for Don Poile, Hec Lalande and cash, April 23, 1958.

• FISHER, Joe

RW – R. 6', 175 lbs. b: Medicine Hat, Alta., 7/4/1916.

			REGULAR SEASON								PLAYOFFS				
Season	**Club**	**League**	**GP**	**G**	**A**	**Pts**	**AG**	**AA**	**APts**	**PIM**	**GP**	**G**	**A**	**Pts**	**PIM**
1934-35	Edmonton Athletic Club	AAHA	9	0	3	3	....	....	....	7	....	....	....	....	....
1935-36	Coleman Canadians	S-SSHL	5	1	2	3	....	....	....	2	....	....	....	....	....
1936-37	Coleman Canadians	S-SSHL	STATISTICS NOT AVAILABLE												
1937-38	Kirkland Lake Blue Devils	NOHA	9	3	*14	17	....	....	....	6	2	*4	0	*4	0
1938-39	Pittsburgh Hornets	AHL	48	9	22	31	....	....	....	17	....	....	....	....	....
1939-40	**Detroit Red Wings**	**NHL**	**34**	**2**	**4**	**6**	**3**	**6**	**9**	**2**	**5**	**1**	**1**	**2**	**0**
	Indianapolis Capitols	AHL	17	7	16	23	....	....	....	9	....	....	....	....	....
1940-41	**Detroit Red Wings**	**NHL**	**27**	**5**	**8**	**13**	**8**	**11**	**19**	**11**	**5**	**1**	**0**	**1**	**6**
	Indianapolis Capitols	AHL	24	8	12	20	....	....	....	7	....	....	....	....	....
1941-42	**Detroit Red Wings**	**NHL**	**3**	**0**	**0**	**0**	**0**	**0**	**0**	**0**	**1**	**0**	**0**	**0**	**0**
	Indianapolis Capitols	AHL	41	21	18	39	....	....	....	15	10	4	4	8	2
♦1942-43	**Detroit Red Wings**	**NHL**	**1**	**1**	**0**	**1**	**1**	**0**	**1**	**0**	**1**	**0**	**0**	**0**	**0**
	Indianapolis Capitols	AHL	56	24	37	61	....	....	....	9	7	2	5	7	0
1943-44			MILITARY SERVICE												
1944-45	Winnipeg RCAF	WNDHL	4	3	2	5	....	....	....	0	3	2	2	4	5
1945-46	Calgary Stampeders	WCSHL	12	12	4	16	....	....	....	0	5	2	3	5	2
	Calgary Stampeders	Al-Cup	13	9	13	22	....	....	....	6	....	....	....	....	....
1946-47	Lethbridge Maple Leafs	WCSHL	35	15	44	59	....	....	....	22	7	4	3	7	12
	Calgary Stampeders	Al-Cup	11	3	2	5	....	....	....	8	....	....	....	....	....
1947-48	Regina Caps	WCSHL	32	17	24	41	....	....	....	2	1	2	0	2	0
1948-49	Regina Caps	WCSHL	1	0	0	0	....	....	....	0	7	2	6	8	2
	Regina Caps	Al-Cup	5	2	1	3	....	....	....	12	....	....	....	....	....
1949-50	Medicine Hat Tigers	WCJHL	DID NOT PLAY – COACHING												
	NHL Totals		**65**	**8**	**12**	**20**	**12**	**17**	**29**	**13**	**12**	**2**	**1**	**3**	**6**

• Statistics for Coleman Canadians (1935-36) are for playoffs only.

• FITZPATRICK, Sandy — *see page 1079*

• FLAMAN, Fern Ferdinand Charles HHOF

D – R. 5'10", 190 lbs. b: Dysart, Sask., 1/25/1927.

			REGULAR SEASON								PLAYOFFS				
Season	**Club**	**League**	**GP**	**G**	**A**	**Pts**	**AG**	**AA**	**APts**	**PIM**	**GP**	**G**	**A**	**Pts**	**PIM**
1942-43	Regina Abbots	MJHL	1	0	0	0	....	....	....	0	....	....	....	....	....
1943-44	Boston Olympics	EAHL	32	12	7	19	....	....	....	31	12	2	6	8	14
	Brooklyn Crescents	EAHL	11	5	9	14	....	....	....	12	....	....	....	....	....

Season	Club	League	GP	G	A	Pts	AG	AA	APts	PIM	GP	G	A	Pts	PIM
			REGULAR SEASON								PLAYOFFS				
1944-45	Boston Bruins	NHL	1	0	0	0	0	0	0	0	....	....	....	....	....
	Boston Olympics	EAHL	46	16	27	43	....	....	....	75	10	3	5	8	13
1945-46	Boston Bruins	NHL	1	0	0	0	0	0	0	0	....	....	....	....	....
	Boston Olympics	EAHL	45	11	23	34	....	....	....	80	12	2	7	9	11
1946-47	Boston Bruins	NHL	23	1	4	5	1	5	6	41	5	0	0	0	8
	Hershey Bears	AHL	38	4	8	12	....	....	....	64	....	....	....	....	....
1947-48	Boston Bruins	NHL	56	4	6	10	5	8	13	69	5	0	0	0	12
1948-49	Boston Bruins	NHL	60	4	12	16	6	17	23	62	5	0	1	1	8
1949-50	Boston Bruins	NHL	69	2	5	7	2	6	8	122	....	....	....	....	....
1950-51	Boston Bruins	NHL	14	1	1	2	1	1	2	37	....	....	....	....	....
♦	Toronto Maple Leafs	NHL	39	2	6	8	3	7	10	64	9	1	0	1	8
	Pittsburgh Hornets	AHL	11	1	6	7	....	....	....	24	....	....	....	....	....
1951-52	Toronto Maple Leafs	NHL	61	0	7	7	0	9	9	110	4	0	2	2	18
1952-53	Toronto Maple Leafs	NHL	66	2	6	8	3	7	10	110	....	....	....	....	....
1953-54	Toronto Maple Leafs	NHL	62	0	8	8	0	10	10	84	2	0	0	0	0
1954-55	Boston Bruins	NHL	70	4	14	18	5	16	21	*150	4	1	0	1	2
1955-56	Boston Bruins	NHL	62	4	17	21	5	20	25	70	....	....	....	....	....
1956-57	Boston Bruins	NHL	68	6	25	31	8	28	36	108	10	0	3	3	19
1957-58	Boston Bruins	NHL	66	0	15	15	0	15	15	71	12	2	2	4	10
1958-59	Boston Bruins	NHL	70	0	21	21	0	21	21	101	7	0	0	0	8
1959-60	Boston Bruins	NHL	60	2	18	20	2	17	19	112	....	....	....	....	....
1960-61	Boston Bruins	NHL	62	2	9	11	2	9	11	59	....	....	....	....	....
1961-62	Providence Reds	AHL	65	3	33	36	....	....	....	95	3	0	1	1	6
1962-63	Providence Reds	AHL	68	4	17	21	....	....	....	65	6	0	2	2	0
1963-64	Providence Reds	AHL	22	1	5	6	....	....	....	21	3	0	1	1	4
1964-65	Providence Reds	AHL	DID NOT PLAY – COACHING												
	NHL Totals		910	34	174	208	43	196	239	1370	63	4	8	12	93

EAHL First All-Star Team (1945, 1946) • NHL Second All-Star Team (1955, 1957, 1958) • Played in NHL All-Star Game (1952, 1955, 1956, 1957, 1958, 1959)

Traded to **Toronto** by **Boston** with Ken Smith, Phil Maloney and Leo Boivin for Bill Ezinicki and Vic Lynn. November 16, 1950. Traded to **Boston** by **Toronto** for Dave Creighton, July 20, 1954.

• FLEMING, Reggie — *see page 1080*

• FOGOLIN, Lee Sr. Lidio John

D – L. 5'11", 195 lbs. b: Fort William, Ont., 2/27/1926.

Season	Club	League	GP	G	A	Pts	AG	AA	APts	PIM	GP	G	A	Pts	PIM
1942-43	Port Arthur Juniors	TBJHL	1	0	0	0	....	....	....	0	....	....	....	....	....
1943-44	Galt Kists	OHA-Jr.	22	0	2	2	....	....	....	25	3	0	1	1	2
1944-45	Galt Red Wings	OHA-Jr.	17	3	7	10	....	....	....	32	10	1	3	4	*25
1945-46	Galt Red Wings	OHA-Jr.	27	13	24	37	....	....	....	51	5	1	1	2	8
1946-47	Omaha Knights	USHL	59	2	9	11	....	....	....	117	11	1	3	4	27
1947-48	Indianapolis Capitols	AHL	65	2	9	11	....	....	....	113	....	....	....	....	....
	Detroit Red Wings	NHL	....	....	....	....	....	....	....	....	2	0	1	1	6
1948-49	Detroit Red Wings	NHL	43	1	2	3	1	3	4	59	9	0	0	0	4
	Indianapolis Capitols	AHL	20	2	6	8	....	....	....	30	....	....	....	....	....
♦1949-50	Detroit Red Wings	NHL	63	4	8	12	5	10	15	63	10	0	0	0	16
1950-51	Detroit Red Wings	NHL	19	0	1	1	0	1	1	16	....	....	....	....	....
	Chicago Black Hawks	NHL	35	3	10	13	4	12	16	63	....	....	....	....	....
1951-52	Chicago Black Hawks	NHL	69	0	9	9	0	11	11	96	....	....	....	....	....
1952-53	Chicago Black Hawks	NHL	70	2	8	10	3	10	13	79	7	0	1	1	4
1953-54	Chicago Black Hawks	NHL	68	0	1	1	0	1	1	95	....	....	....	....	....
1954-55	Chicago Black Hawks	NHL	9	0	1	1	0	1	1	16	....	....	....	....	....
1955-56	Chicago Black Hawks	NHL	51	0	8	8	0	9	9	88	....	....	....	....	....
1956-57	Calgary Stampeders	WHL	61	1	9	10	....	....	....	84	3	0	0	0	2
	NHL Totals		427	10	48	58	13	58	71	575	28	0	2	2	30

• Father of Lee Jr. • Played in NHL All-Star Game (1950, 1951)

Traded to **Chicago** by **Detroit** with Stephen Black for Bert Olmstead and Vic Stasiuk, December 2, 1950. • Missed majority of 1954-55 season recovering from elbow injury originally suffered in training camp, September 30, 1954.

• FOLEY, Gerry — *see page 1084*

• FOLK, Bill William Joseph

D – L. 5'11", 190 lbs. b: Regina, Sask., 7/11/1927.

Season	Club	League	GP	G	A	Pts	AG	AA	APts	PIM	GP	G	A	Pts	PIM
1944-45	Regina Abbotts	SJHL	16	1	2	3	....	....	....	54	....	....	....	....	....
1945-46	Regina Abbotts	SJHL	18	3	1	4	....	....	....	30	7	2	1	3	26
1946-47	Regina Caps	SJHL	29	7	5	12	....	....	....	40	6	2	0	2	10
1947-48	Boston Olympics	EAHL	19	2	4	6	....	....	....	39	....	....	....	....	....
	Boston Olympics	QSHL	38	5	5	10	....	....	....	64	....	....	....	....	....
1948-49	Omaha Knights	USHL	62	4	14	18	....	....	....	84	4	0	2	2	6
1949-50	Omaha Knights	USHL	65	14	33	47	....	....	....	78	....	....	....	....	....
1950-51	Indianapolis Capitols	AHL	64	4	26	30	....	....	....	58	3	0	1	1	4
	Omaha Knights	USHL	....	....	....	....	....	....	....	....	6	*7	3	10	16
1951-52	Detroit Red Wings	NHL	4	0	0	0	0	0	0	2	....	....	....	....	....
	Indianapolis Capitols	AHL	50	4	14	18	....	....	....	56	....	....	....	....	....
1952-53	Detroit Red Wings	NHL	8	0	0	0	0	0	0	2	....	....	....	....	....
	Edmonton Flyers	WHL	56	9	19	28	....	....	....	74	15	1	7	8	24
1953-54	Edmonton Flyers	WHL	49	4	14	18	....	....	....	66	....	....	....	....	....
1954-55	Providence Reds	AHL	45	5	21	26	....	....	....	52	....	....	....	....	....
1955-56	Providence Reds	AHL	15	1	8	9	....	....	....	18	9	2	3	5	15
	Saskatoon Quakers	WHL	51	6	14	20	....	....	....	66	....	....	....	....	....
1956-57	Providence Reds	AHL	60	1	15	16	....	....	....	56	4	0	1	1	6
1957-58	Vancouver Canucks	WHL	68	7	21	28	....	....	....	72	11	1	9	10	18
1958-59	Winnipeg Warriors	WHL	56	7	25	32	....	....	....	61	7	0	6	6	6
1959-60	Winnipeg Warriors	WHL	56	4	32	36	....	....	....	53	....	....	....	....	....
1960-61	Spokane Comets	WHL	65	8	23	31	....	....	....	68	2	0	0	0	2
1961-62	Spokane Comets	WHL	2	0	1	1	....	....	....	4	....	....	....	....	....
1962-63			DID NOT PLAY												
1963-64			DID NOT PLAY												
1964-65	Regina Capitals	SSHL	8	3	6	9	....	....	....	6	5	1	1	2	9
1965-66	Regina Capitals	SSHL	6	0	8	8	....	....	....	10	....	....	....	....	....
	NHL Totals		12	0	0	0	0	0	0	4	....	....	....	....	....

Missed remainder of 1961-62 and entire 1962-63 and 1963-64 seasons recovering from heart attack suffered following game vs. San Francisco (WHL), October 14, 1961.

• FONTEYNE, Val — *see page 1085*

• FONTINATO, Lou Louis "Leapin' Louie"

D – L. 6'1", 195 lbs. b: Guelph, Ont., 1/20/1932.

Season	Club	League	GP	G	A	Pts	AG	AA	APts	PIM	GP	G	A	Pts	PIM
			REGULAR SEASON								PLAYOFFS				
1949-50	Guelph Biltmores	OHA-B	STATISTICS NOT AVAILABLE												
1950-51	Guelph Biltmores	OHA-Jr.	45	3	11	14	....	....	....	93	5	0	0	0	0
1951-52	Guelph Biltmores	OHA-Jr.	48	6	15	21	....	....	....	152	11	0	1	1	37
	Guelph Biltmores	M-Cup	12	1	3	4	....	....	....	*50	....	....	....	....	....
1952-53	Vancouver Canucks	WHL	65	3	18	21	....	....	....	169	9	1	3	4	12
1953-54	Vancouver–Saskatoon	WHL	63	4	14	18	....	....	....	147	6	0	1	1	25
1954-55	New York Rangers	NHL	27	2	2	4	3	2	5	60	....	....	....	....	....
	Saskatoon Quakers	WHL	35	4	6	10	....	....	....	55	....	....	....	....	....
1955-56	New York Rangers	NHL	70	3	15	18	4	18	22	*202	4	0	0	0	6
1956-57	New York Rangers	NHL	70	3	12	15	4	13	17	139	5	0	0	0	7
1957-58	New York Rangers	NHL	70	3	8	11	4	8	12	*152	6	0	1	1	6
1958-59	New York Rangers	NHL	64	7	6	13	8	6	14	149	....	....	....	....	....
1959-60	New York Rangers	NHL	64	2	11	13	2	11	13	137	....	....	....	....	....
1960-61	New York Rangers	NHL	53	2	3	5	2	3	5	100	....	....	....	....	....
1961-62	Montreal Canadiens	NHL	54	2	13	15	2	12	14	*167	6	0	1	1	23
1962-63	Montreal Canadiens	NHL	63	2	8	10	2	8	10	141	....	....	....	....	....
	NHL Totals		535	26	78	104	31	81	112	1247	21	0	2	2	42

Traded to **Montreal** by **NY Rangers** for Doug Harvey, June 13, 1961. • Suffered career-ending neck injury in game vs. NY Rangers, March 9, 1963.

• FORSEY, Jack

RW – R. 5'11", 170 lbs. b: Swift Current, Sask., 11/7/1914 Deceased.

Season	Club	League	GP	G	A	Pts	AG	AA	APts	PIM	GP	G	A	Pts	PIM
1931-32	Calgary Jimmies	CCJHL	7	3	1	4	....	....	....	12	3	0	2	2	4
	Calgary Jimmies	M-Cup	8	2	1	3	....	....	....	0	....	....	....	....	....
1932-33	Calgary Jimmies	CCJHL	5	4	*6	*10	....	....	....	6	....	....	....	....	....
	Calgary Jimmies	M-Cup	7	6	4	10	....	....	....	11	....	....	....	....	....
1933-34	Nelson Red Wings	WKHL	7	2	4	6	....	....	....	5	1	1	0	1	0
1934-35	Kimberley Dynamiters	WKHL	7	3	5	8	....	....	....	7	9	*6	4	*10	8
	Kimberley Dynamiters	Al-Cup	6	3	2	5	....	....	....	4	....	....	....	....	....
1935-36	Kimberley Dynamiters	WKHL	7	4	5	9	....	....	....	9	4	4	0	4	0
1936-37	Earls Court Rangers	Britain	....	39	20	59	....	....	....	8	....	....	....	....	....
	Canada	WEC-A	8	8	0	8	....	....	....	....	....	....	....	....	....
1937-38	Earls Court Rangers	Ln-Cup	....	4	3	7	....	....	....	....	....	....	....	....	....
	Earls Court Rangers	Britain	....	6	4	10	....	....	....	....	....	....	....	....	....
	Earls Court Rangers	Nat-Tmt	....	5	7	12	....	....	....	....	....	....	....	....	....
1938-39	Earls Court Rangers	Ln-Cup	....	6	1	7	....	....	....	....	....	....	....	....	....
	Earls Court Rangers	Britain	....	20	11	31	....	....	....	....	....	....	....	....	....
	Earls Court Rangers	Nat-Tmt	....	8	6	14	....	....	....	....	....	....	....	....	....
1939-40	Sherbrooke Red Raiders	QPHL	41	29	54	83	....	....	....	45	7	5	*9	14	2
	Sherbrooke Red Raiders	Al-Cup	2	3	6	9	....	....	....	2	....	....	....	....	....
1940-41	Cornwall Flyers	QSHL	36	14	17	31	....	....	....	16	4	2	0	2	2
1941-42	Providence Reds	AHL	52	19	27	46	....	....	....	10	....	....	....	....	....
1942-43	Toronto Maple Leafs	NHL	19	7	9	16	7	8	15	10	3	0	1	1	0
	Providence Reds	AHL	33	18	20	38	....	....	....	2	....	....	....	....	....
1943-44	Red Deer Wranglers	WCSHL	16	8	9	17	....	....	....	0	5	0	2	2	0
1944-45			MILITARY SERVICE												
1945-46	Tulsa Oilers	USHL	11	1	3	4	....	....	....	0	....	....	....	....	....
	Regina Caps	WCSHL	16	6	8	14	....	....	....	4	....	....	....	....	....
1946-47	Kimberley Dynamiters	WIHL	36	18	24	42	....	....	....	8	4	3	3	6	0
	Kimberley Dynamiters	Al-Cup	5	1	2	3	....	....	....	0	....	....	....	....	....
1947-48	Saskatoon Quakers	WCSHL	7	2	1	3	....	....	....	0	....	....	....	....	....
	Swift Current Indians	SIHL	STATISTICS NOT AVAILABLE												
1948-49	Kimberley Dynamiters	WIHL	6	2	2	4	....	....	....	0	....	....	....	....	....
1949-50	Kamloops Elks	OSHL	33	20	21	41	....	....	....	4	7	1	3	4	0
	NHL Totals		19	7	9	16	7	8	15	10	3	0	1	1	0

Loaned to **Providence** (AHL) by **Toronto** with George Boothman for Buck Jones and the loan of Ab DeMarco, February 3, 1943.

• FORSLUND, Gus

RW – R. 5'10", 150 lbs. b: Umea, Sweden, 4/25/1908 Deceased.

Season	Club	League	GP	G	A	Pts	AG	AA	APts	PIM	GP	G	A	Pts	PIM
1926-27	Port Arthur Ports	TBSHL	16	1	1	2	....	....	....	2	....	....	....	....	....
1927-28	Fort William Forts	TBSHL	19	10	1	11	....	....	....	10	2	0	0	0	0
1928-29	Fort William Forts	TBSHL	DID NOT PLAY – INJURED												
1929-30	Duluth Hornets	AHA	48	9	5	14	....	....	....	32	4	0	*2	2	4
1930-31	Duluth Hornets	AHA	47	18	10	28	....	....	....	30	4	1	0	1	10
1931-32	Duluth Hornets	AHA	48	14	13	27	....	....	....	24	8	*5	1	*6	7
1932-33	Ottawa Senators	NHL	48	4	9	13	7	19	26	2	....	....	....	....	....
1933-34	Syracuse–Windsor	IHL	43	8	12	20	....	....	....	12	....	....	....	....	....
1934-35	Philadelphia Arrows	Can-Am	48	20	32	52	....	....	....	15	....	....	....	....	....
1935-36	New Haven Eagles	Can-Am	48	16	17	33	....	....	....	26	....	....	....	....	....
1936-37	Fort William Wanderers	TBSHL	DID NOT PLAY – COACHING												
1937-38	Fort William Wanderers	TBSHL	1	2	0	2	....	....	....	0	....	....	....	....	....
1938-39	Duluth Zephyrs	TBSHL	11	8	13	21	....	....	....	....	....	....	....	....	....
	Duluth Zephyrs	USHL	26	18	13	31	....	....	....	7	....	....	....	....	....
1939-40	Geraldton Gold Miners	TBSHL	24	18	*21	*39	....	....	....	8	3	1	0	1	2
1940-41	Geraldton Gold Miners	TBSHL	12	6	3	9	....	....	....	2	4	0	1	1	0
	NHL Totals		48	4	9	13	7	19	26	2	....	....	....	....	....

Traded to **Windsor** (IHL) by **Syracuse** (IHL) with Sparky Vail for Andy Bellemer, December, 1933.

• FOSTER, Herb Herbert Stanley

LW – L. 5'10", 168 lbs. b: Brockville, Ont., 8/9/1913.

Season	Club	League	GP	G	A	Pts	AG	AA	APts	PIM	GP	G	A	Pts	PIM
1932-33	Atlantic City Sea Gulls	EAHL	18	18	5	23	....	....	....	0	3	2	0	2	0
1933-34	Atlantic City Sea Gulls	EAHL	19	20	6	26	....	....	....	16	5	4	3	7	4
1934-35	Atlantic City Sea Gulls	EAHL	18	4	3	7	....	....	....	2	10	6	2	8	0
1935-36	Atlantic City Sea Gulls	EAHL	40	*25	3	28	....	....	....	24	8	5	2	7	2
1936-37	Atlantic City Sea Gulls	EAHL	48	*43	11	*54	....	....	....	12	3	*5	0	*5	0
1937-38	Atlantic City Sea Gulls	EAHL	57	*39	32	*71	....	....	....	13	....	....	....	....	....
1938-39	Atlantic City Sea Gulls	EAHL	52	*52	23	75	....	....	....	2	....	....	....	....	....
1939-40	Philadelphia Ramblers	IAHL	54	21	22	43	....	....	....	14	....	....	....	....	....
1940-41	New York Rangers	NHL	5	1	0	1	2	0	2	5	....	....	....	....	....
	Philadelphia Ramblers	AHL	53	24	22	46	....	....	....	18	....	....	....	....	....
1941-42	Cleveland Barons	AHL	57	23	15	38	....	....	....	10	5	1	1	2	0
1942-43	Cleveland Barons	AHL	37	6	16	22	....	....	....	0	....	....	....	....	....
	Pittsburgh Hornets	AHL	1	0	0	0	....	....	....	0	....	....	....	....	....
	Washington Lions	AHL	19	12	13	25	....	....	....	0	....	....	....	....	....
1943-44	Kingston Army	OHA-Sr.	14	12	15	27	....	....	....	2	....	....	....	....	....

Season	Club	League	GP	G	A	Pts	AG	AA	APts	PIM	GP	G	A	Pts	PIM
			REGULAR SEASON								PLAYOFFS				
1944-45			MILITARY SERVICE												
1945-46			MILITARY SERVICE												
1946-47	Shawinigan Cataracts	QSHL	37	13	11	24	....	....	....	29	3	0	1	1	4
1947-48	**New York Rangers**	**NHL**	**1**	**0**	**0**	**0**	**0**	**0**	**0**	**0**	....	....	....	....	....
	NY Rovers–Atlantic City	EAHL	34	37	24	61	....	....	....	8	....	....	....	....	....
	New York Rovers	QSHL	21	7	5	12	....	....	....	0	4	3	1	4	0
1948-49			DID NOT PLAY												
1949-50	Atlantic City Sea Gulls	EAHL	47	27	29	56	....	....	....	12	6	3	3	6	0
1950-51	Atlantic City Sea Gulls	EAHL	DID NOT PLAY – COACHING												
	NHL Totals		**6**	**1**	**0**	**1**	**2**	**0**	**2**	**5**	....	....	....	....	....

EAHL First All-Star Team (1933, 1934, 1937, 1938, 1939, 1948) • Won John Carlin Trophy (Top Scorer - EAHL) (1937, 1938, 1939) • EAHL Second All-Star Team (1950)

Signed as a free agent by **NY Rangers**, October 21, 1940. Traded to **Cleveland** (AHL) by **NY Rangers** for cash, September 9, 1941. Traded to **Washington** (AHL) by **Cleveland** (AHL) with future considerations for Lou Trudel, February 2, 1943.

• FOSTER, Yip
Harry Charles
D – L. 6'6", 198 lbs. b: Guelph, Ont., 11/25/1907 Deceased.

Season	Club	League	GP	G	A	Pts	AG	AA	APts	PIM	GP	G	A	Pts	PIM
1923-24	Toronto Canoe Club	OHA-Jr.	1	0	0	0	....	....	....	....	....	....	....	....	....
1924-25	Toronto Aura Lee	OHA-Jr.	8	7	4	11	....	....	....	....	10	4	4	8	....
1925-26	Toronto Aura Lee	OHA-Jr.	7	2	1	3	....	....	....	....	....	....	....	....	....
1926-27	Toronto City Hall	TIHL	STATISTICS NOT AVAILABLE												
1927-28	Springfield Indians	Can-Am	37	1	1	2	....	....	....	40	4	1	0	1	8
1928-29	Springfield Indians	Can-Am	38	5	1	6	....	....	....	83	....	....	....	....	....
1929-30	**New York Rangers**	**NHL**	**31**	**0**	**0**	**0**	**0**	**0**	**0**	**10**	....	....	....	....	....
	Boston Tigers	Can-Am	11	2	4	6	....	....	....	10	5	0	0	0	0
1930-31	Boston Tigers/Cubs	Can-Am	36	7	13	20	....	....	....	80	9	3	5	8	*28
1931-32	**Boston Bruins**	**NHL**	**34**	**1**	**2**	**3**	**2**	**4**	**6**	**12**	....	....	....	....	....
1932-33	Boston Cubs	Can-Am	12	2	3	5	....	....	....	34	....	....	....	....	....
	St. Paul-Tulsa	AHA	24	4	3	7	....	....	....	23	4	0	1	1	4
1933-34	**Detroit Red Wings**	**NHL**	**6**	**0**	**0**	**0**	**0**	**0**	**0**	**2**	....	....	....	....	....
	Detroit Olympics	IHL	37	4	8	12	....	....	....	35	6	0	1	1	4
1934-35	**Detroit Red Wings**	**NHL**	**12**	**2**	**0**	**2**	**3**	**0**	**3**	**8**	....	....	....	....	....
	Detroit Olympics	IHL	30	7	2	9	....	....	....	27	5	0	2	2	6
	Detroit Olympics	L-W-S	5	1	1	2	....	....	....	2	....	....	....	....	....
1935-36	Detroit Olympics	IHL	47	4	12	16	....	....	....	31	6	0	2	2	6
1936-37	Cleveland Barons	IAHL	44	3	15	18	....	....	....	27	....	....	....	....	....
1937-38	Cleveland Barons	IAHL	47	4	3	7	....	....	....	13	2	0	0	0	0
1938-39	Cleveland Barons	IAHL	52	2	12	14	....	....	....	34	9	0	1	1	0
1939-40	Syracuse Stars	IAHL	55	2	11	13	....	....	....	14	....	....	....	....	....
1940-41	Minneapolis Millers	AHA	47	4	5	9	....	....	....	10	3	0	0	0	0
1941-42	Minneapolis Millers	AHA	44	5	6	11	....	....	....	17	....	....	....	....	....
1942-43	Cleveland Barons	AHL	53	1	8	9	....	....	....	14	1	0	0	0	0
1943-44	Cleveland Barons	AHL	34	1	5	6	....	....	....	16	10	0	1	1	7
	NHL Totals		**83**	**3**	**2**	**5**	**5**	**4**	**9**	**32**	....	....	....	....	....

Signed as a free agent by **NY Rangers**, September, 1927. • Toronto also claimed to have his rights. NHL arranged for Eric Pettinger to be sent to Toronto as compensation, October, 1927. Traded to **Boston** by **NY Rangers** with $15,000 for Bill Regan, February 17, 1930. Traded to **Tulsa** (AHA) by **Boston** for cash, January 6, 1933. Signed as a free agent by **Detroit**, October 17, 1933. Traded to **Cleveland** (IAHL) by **Detroit** for cash, October 14, 1936.

• FOWLER, Jimmy
Jimmy William "The Blonde Bouncer"
D – L. 5'11", 168 lbs. b: Toronto, Ont., 4/6/1915 d: 10/17/1985.

Season	Club	League	GP	G	A	Pts	AG	AA	APts	PIM	GP	G	A	Pts	PIM
1932-33	West Toronto Nationals	OHA-Jr.	9	4	2	6	....	....	....	0	5	0	0	0	2
	West Toronto Nationals	M-Cup	6	1	0	1	....	....	....	0	....	....	....	....	....
1933-34	Toronto Young Rangers	OHA-Jr.	11	9	7	16	....	....	....	10	1	1	0	1	0
	Toronto City Services	TMHL	7	1	2	3	....	....	....	2	9	6	*7	13	12
	Toronto Young Rangers	M-Cup	2	0	1	1	....	....	....	4	....	....	....	....	....
1934-35	Toronto City Service	TIHL	11	3	3	6	....	....	....	4	7	2	6	8	8
	Toronto All-Stars	OHA-Sr.	10	4	0	4	....	....	....	4	6	2	2	4	4
1935-36	Syracuse Stars	IHL	45	10	15	25	....	....	....	23	3	1	0	1	0
1936-37	**Toronto Maple Leafs**	**NHL**	**48**	**7**	**11**	**18**	**12**	**20**	**32**	**22**	**2**	**0**	**0**	**0**	**0**
1937-38	**Toronto Maple Leafs**	**NHL**	**48**	**10**	**12**	**22**	**16**	**19**	**35**	**8**	**7**	**0**	**2**	**2**	**0**
1938-39	**Toronto Maple Leafs**	**NHL**	**39**	**1**	**6**	**7**	**2**	**9**	**11**	**9**	**9**	**0**	**1**	**1**	**2**
	Syracuse Stars	IAHL	7	3	1	4	....	....	....	0	....	....	....	....	....
	NHL Totals		**135**	**18**	**29**	**47**	**30**	**48**	**78**	**39**	**18**	**0**	**3**	**3**	**2**

Signed as a free agent by **Toronto**, October 22, 1935. Traded to **NY Americans** by **Toronto** with Busher Jackson, Murray Armstrong, Buzz Boll and Doc Romnes for Sweeney Schriner, May 18, 1939.

• FOWLER, Tom
C – L. 5'11", 165 lbs. b: Winnipeg, Man., 5/18/1924.

Season	Club	League	GP	G	A	Pts	AG	AA	APts	PIM	GP	G	A	Pts	PIM
1941-42	Winnipeg Monarchs	MJHL	5	0	0	0	....	....	....	0	2	0	0	0	2
1942-43	Winnipeg Monarchs	MJHL	13	4	12	16	....	....	....	0	2	0	0	0	0
	Winnipeg Rangers	M-Cup	8	3	3	6	....	....	....	2	....	....	....	....	....
1943-44	Winnipeg Monarchs	MJHL	10	9	*16	*25	....	....	....	12	3	5	1	6	2
	Winnipeg Esquires	WJrHL	....	....	....	....	....	....	....	....	3	3	1	4	0
1944-45	Winnipeg Navy	WNDHL	16	10	7	17	....	....	....	12	6	3	1	4	6
1945-46	Kansas City Pla-Mors	USHL	54	12	33	45	....	....	....	34	12	1	5	6	2
1946-47	**Chicago Black Hawks**	**NHL**	**24**	**0**	**1**	**1**	**0**	**1**	**1**	**18**	....	....	....	....	....
	Kansas City Pla-Mors	USHL	22	8	10	18	....	....	....	14	....	....	....	....	....
1947-48	Tulsa Oilers	USHL	14	1	4	5	....	....	....	8	....	....	....	....	....
	Fort Worth Rangers	USHL	49	9	28	37	....	....	....	33	4	1	2	3	0
1948-49	Oakland Oaks	PCHL	63	29	57	86	....	....	....	32	3	0	1	1	0
1949-50	Oakland–Los Angeles	PCHL	66	19	32	51	....	....	....	23	17	2	*18	20	15
1950-51	St. Michael's Monarchs	OMHL	32	9	19	28	....	....	....	32	9	2	2	4	4
	St. Michael's Monarchs	Alx-Cup	10	1	6	7	....	....	....	27	....	....	....	....	....
1951-52	Saskatoon Quakers	PCHL	57	8	18	26	....	....	....	22	13	3	3	6	4
1952-53	Saskatoon Quakers	WHL	1	0	1	1	....	....	....	0	....	....	....	....	....
	Moose Jaw Millers	SSHL	32	25	*58	*83	....	....	....	8	10	6	6	12	4
	NHL Totals		**24**	**0**	**1**	**1**	**0**	**1**	**1**	**18**	....	....	....	....	....

PCHL Southern First All-Star Team (1949) • MVP - PCHL Southern Division (1949) • SSHL First All-Star Team (1953)

Traded to **Toronto** (LA Monarchs-PCHL) by **Oakland** (PCHL) for cash, November 7, 1949.

• FOYSTON, Frank
Frank Corbett — HHOF
C/RW – L. 5'9", 158 lbs. b: Minesing, Ont., 2/2/1891 d: 1/19/1966.

Season	Club	League	GP	G	A	Pts	AG	AA	APts	PIM	GP	G	A	Pts	PIM
1908-09	Barrie Athletic Club	OHA-Jr.	6	17	0	17	....	....	....	9	....	....	....	....	....
1909-10	Barrie Athletic Club	OHA-Jr.	STATISTICS NOT AVAILABLE												
1910-11	Barrie Athletic Club	OHA-Sr.	6	14	0	14	....	....	....	....	....	....	....	....	....
1911-12	Toronto Eaton's	TMHL	6	15	0	15	....	....	....	....	4	*5	0	*5	9
1912-13	Toronto Blueshirts	NHA	16	8	0	8	....	....	....	8	....	....	....	....	....
♦1913-14	Toronto Blueshirts	NHA	19	16	2	18	....	....	....	8	5	4	0	4	0
1914-15	Toronto Blueshirts	NHA	20	13	9	22	....	....	....	11	....	....	....	....	....
1915-16	Toronto Blueshirts	NHA	1	0	0	0	....	....	....	0	....	....	....	....	....
	Seattle Metropolitans	PCHA	18	9	4	13	....	....	....	6	....	....	....	....	....
♦1916-17	Seattle Metropolitans	PCHA	24	36	12	48	....	....	....	51	4	7	3	10	3
1917-18	Seattle Metropolitans	PCHA	13	9	5	14	....	....	....	9	2	0	0	0	3
1918-19	Seattle Metropolitans	PCHA	18	15	4	19	....	....	....	0	2	*3	0	*3	0
	Seattle Metropolitans	St-Cup	5	9	1	10	....	....	....	0	....	....	....	....	....
1919-20	Seattle Metropolitans	PCHA	22	*26	3	29	....	....	....	3	2	3	0	3	0
	Seattle Metropolitans	St-Cup	5	6	1	7	....	....	....	7	....	....	....	....	....
1920-21	Seattle Metropolitans	PCHA	23	*26	4	30	....	....	....	10	2	1	0	1	0
1921-22	Seattle Metropolitans	PCHA	24	16	7	23	....	....	....	25	2	0	0	0	3
1922-23	Seattle Metropolitans	PCHA	30	20	8	28	....	....	....	21	....	....	....	....	....
1923-24	Seattle Metropolitans	PCHA	30	17	6	23	....	....	....	8	2	1	0	1	0
1924-25	Victoria Cougars	WCHL	27	6	5	11	....	....	....	6	4	1	1	2	2
♦	Victoria Cougars	St-Cup	4	1	0	1	....	....	....	0	....	....	....	....	....
1925-26	Victoria Cougars	WHL	12	6	3	9	....	....	....	8	3	2	0	2	4
	Victoria Cougars	St-Cup	4	0	0	0	....	....	....	2	....	....	....	....	....
1926-27	**Detroit Cougars**	**NHL**	**41**	**10**	**5**	**15**	**18**	**26**	**44**	**16**	....	....	....	....	....
1927-28	Detroit Olympics	Can-Am	19	3	2	5	....	....	....	14	....	....	....	....	....
	Detroit Cougars	**NHL**	**23**	**7**	**2**	**9**	**14**	**11**	**25**	**16**	....	....	....	....	....
1928-29	Detroit Olympics	Can-Am	42	18	6	24	....	....	....	20	7	0	0	0	9
1929-30	Detroit Olympics	IHL	31	2	1	3	....	....	....	6	3	0	0	0	0
1930-31			DID NOT PLAY – REFEREE												
1931-32	Bronx Tigers	Can-Am	DID NOT PLAY – COACHING												
	NHL Totals		**64**	**17**	**7**	**24**	**32**	**37**	**69**	**32**	....	....	....	....	....
	Other Major League Totals		297	223	72	295	....	....	....	174	28	22	4	26	15

OHA-Jr. First All-Star Team (1909) • PCHA First All-Star Team (1917, 1918, 1920, 1921, 1923, 1924) • PCHA MVP (1917) • PCHA Second All-Star Team (1919, 1922)

Signed as a free agent by **Seattle** (PCHA), December, 1915. Signed as a free agent by **Victoria** (WCHL) after **Seattle** (PCHA) franchise folded, November 10, 1924. • 1924-25 playoff totals includes WCHL series against Calgary and Saskatoon. • Missed majority of the 1925-26 season after announcing his retirement, October 25, 1925. • Resumed his playing career, January, 1926. • 1925-26 playoff totals includes WHL series against Edmonton and Saskatoon. NHL rights transferred to **Detroit** after NHL club purchased **Victoria** (WHL) franchise, May 15, 1926. • Named playing coach of **Detroit Olympics** (Can-Pro), October 11, 1927. Traded to **Detroit** by **Detroit Olympics** (Can-Pro) for cash, January 10, 1928.

• FRAMPTON, Bob
Percy James "Bob"
LW – L. 5'10", 175 lbs. b: Toronto, Ont., 1/20/1929.

Season	Club	League	GP	G	A	Pts	AG	AA	APts	PIM	GP	G	A	Pts	PIM
1946-47	Montreal Jr. Royals	QJHL	27	22	9	31	....	....	....	25	8	4	4	8	4
1947-48	Montreal Jr. Royals	QJHL	27	19	27	46	....	....	....	40	7	3	2	5	11
1948-49	Montreal Jr. Royals	QJHL	46	32	33	65	....	....	....	44	10	11	4	15	8
	Montreal Royals	QSHL	2	0	1	1	....	....	....	2	....	....	....	....	....
	Montreal Jr. Royals	M-Cup	15	13	4	17	....	....	....	12	....	....	....	....	....
1949-50	**Montreal Canadiens**	**NHL**	**2**	**0**	**0**	**0**	**0**	**0**	**0**	**0**	**3**	**0**	**0**	**0**	**0**
	Cincinnati Mohawks	AHL	60	9	19	28	....	....	....	29	....	....	....	....	....
1950-51	Victoria Cougars	PCHL	52	20	21	41	....	....	....	40	12	2	5	7	2
1951-52	Victoria Cougars	PCHL	69	34	26	60	....	....	....	50	13	8	3	11	4
1952-53	Montreal Royals	QMHL	59	19	18	37	....	....	....	32	16	4	8	12	10
1953-54	Montreal Royals	QHL	55	12	18	30	....	....	....	18	8	0	1	1	16
1954-55	Montreal Royals	QHL	6	1	1	2	....	....	....	0	....	....	....	....	....
	NHL Totals		**2**	**0**	**0**	**0**	**0**	**0**	**0**	**0**	**3**	**0**	**0**	**0**	**0**

QJHL First All-Star Team (1947)

Signed as a free agent by **Montreal**, June 28, 1949. Claimed by **Chicago** from **Montreal Royals** (QHL) in Reverse Draft, June 10, 1953.

• FRASER, Archie
Archibald McKay "Arch"
C – L. 5'11", 160 lbs. b: Souris, Man., 2/9/1914 Deceased.

Season	Club	League	GP	G	A	Pts	AG	AA	APts	PIM	GP	G	A	Pts	PIM
1932-33	Yorkton Terriers	S-SJHL	STATISTICS NOT AVAILABLE												
	Yorkton Terriers	M-Cup	2	0	0	0	....	....	....	0	....	....	....	....	....
1933/35	Yorkton Terriers	X-Games	STATISTICS NOT AVAILABLE												
1935-36	Yorkton Terriers	S-SSHL	17	5	7	12	....	....	....	4	3	0	1	1	4
1936-37	Yorkton Terriers	S-SSHL	24	14	11	25	....	....	....	20	7	1	*4	5	6
1937-38	Yorkton Terriers	S-SSHL	24	25	12	37	....	....	....	14	5	3	2	5	0
1938-39	Wembley Monarchs	Britain	....	29	13	42	....	....	....	....	....	....	....	....	....
1939-40	Yorkton Terriers	S-SSHL	27	20	20	40	....	....	....	6	5	3	0	3	8
1940-41	Yorkton Terriers	S-SSHL	31	18	19	37	....	....	....	8	8	3	5	8	2
1941-42	Yorkton Terriers	S-SSHL	32	17	17	34	....	....	....	10	....	....	....	....	....
1942-43	Yorkton Flyers	S-SSHL	24	11	9	20	....	....	....	10	....	....	....	....	....
1943-44	**New York Rangers**	**NHL**	**3**	**0**	**1**	**1**	**0**	**1**	**1**	**0**	....	....	....	....	....
	Moose Jaw Millers	S-SSHL	1	2	2	4	....	....	....	0	....	....	....	....	....
1944-45			MILITARY SERVICE												
1945-46			MILITARY SERVICE												
1946-47	Yorkton Terriers	SIHA	STATISTICS NOT AVAILABLE												
1947-48	Tacoma Rockets	PCHL	10	1	1	2	....	....	....	2	....	....	....	....	....
1948-49	Yorkton Terriers	SIHA	STATISTICS NOT AVAILABLE												
1949-50	Yorkton Terriers	SIHA	STATISTICS NOT AVAILABLE												
1950-51	Yorkton Legionnaires	S-SSHL	2	1	1	2	....	....	....	0	5	6	3	9	0
	Yorkton Legionnaires	Al-Cup	4	0	3	3	....	....	....	2	....	....	....	....	....
1951-52	Yorkton Legionnaires	S-SSHL	2	0	0	0	....	....	....	0	....	....	....	....	....
	NHL Totals		**3**	**0**	**1**	**1**	**0**	**1**	**1**	**0**	....	....	....	....	....

• Brother of Harvey

• FRASER, Charles
D – L. , b: Stellarton, N.S., Deceased.

Season	Club	League	GP	G	A	Pts	AG	AA	APts	PIM	GP	G	A	Pts	PIM
1919-20	Stellarton Seniors	NSSHL	11	4	0	4	....	....	....	....	....	....	....	....	....
1920-21	Stellarton Seniors	NSSHL	3	0	0	0	....	....	....	6	2	0	0	0	3
1921-22	New Glascow Black Foxes	NSSHL	STATISTICS NOT AVAILABLE												
	Stellerton Pros	MIL	....	....	....	....	....	....	....	....	6	4	0	4	....

Season	Club	League	GP	G	A	Pts	AG	AA	APts	PIM	GP	G	A	Pts	PIM
			REGULAR SEASON								PLAYOFFS				
1922-23	Stellerton Pros	MIL	5	0	0	0	....	....	....	6	....	....	....	....	....
	Amherst Ramblers	MIL	7	3	0	3	....	....	....	14	....	....	....	....	....
1923-24	**Hamilton Tigers**	**NHL**	**1**	**0**	**0**	**0**	**0**	**0**	**0**	**0**	....	....	....	....	....
	Amherst Ramblers	MIL	15	3	3	6	....	....	....	22	....	....	....	....	....
1924-25	Stellerton Pros	X-Games	2	4	0	4	....	....	....	2	1	0	0	0	5
	NHL Totals		**1**	**0**	**0**	**0**	**0**	**0**	**0**	**0**	....	....	....	....	....

Signed as a free agent by **Hamilton**, December 14, 1923.

• FRASER, Gord

Gordon Charles

D – L. 6', 180 lbs. b: Pembroke, Ont., 1/3/1902 d: 1966.

Season	Club	League	GP	G	A	Pts	AG	AA	APts	PIM	GP	G	A	Pts	PIM
1916-17	Pembroke Munitions	OVHL	5	2	0	2	....	....	....	....	....	....	....	....	....
1917-18	Pembroke Munitions	OVHL	3	1	0	1	....	....	....	....	....	....	....	....	....
1918-19	Port Arthur Ports	TBJHL	6	4	0	4	....	....	....	....	....	....	....	....	....
1919-20	Calgary Wanderers	Big-4	10	2	1	3	....	....	....	20	2	1	0	1	0
1920-21	Calgary Tigers	Big-4	15	11	6	17	....	....	....	33	....	....	....	....	....
1921-22	Seattle Metropolitans	PCHA	24	5	2	7	....	....	....	32	2	0	0	0	0
1922-23	Seattle Metropolitans	PCHA	29	4	4	8	....	....	....	46	....	....	....	....	....
1923-24	Seattle Metropolitans	PCHA	30	14	3	17	....	....	....	*64	2	0	0	0	4
1924-25	Victoria Cougars	WCHL	28	9	3	12	....	....	....	64	4	0	0	0	12
♦	Victoria Cougars	St-Cup	4	2	1	3	....	....	....	6	....	....	....	....	....
1925-26	Victoria Cougars	WHL	7	1	0	1	....	....	....	12	4	2	0	2	10
	Victoria Cougars	St-Cup	4	0	0	0	....	....	....	14	....	....	....	....	....
1926-27	**Chicago Black Hawks**	**NHL**	**44**	**14**	**6**	**20**	**25**	**31**	**56**	**89**	**2**	**1**	**0**	**1**	**6**
1927-28	**Chicago Black Hawks**	**NHL**	**11**	**1**	**1**	**2**	**2**	**6**	**8**	**10**	....	....	....	....	....
	Detroit Cougars	**NHL**	**30**	**3**	**1**	**4**	**6**	**6**	**12**	**50**	....	....	....	....	....
1928-29	**Detroit Cougars**	**NHL**	**14**	**0**	**0**	**0**	**0**	**0**	**0**	**12**	....	....	....	....	....
	Detroit Olympics	Can-Pro	28	0	0	0	....	....	....	27	7	1	1	2	23
1929-30	**Montreal Canadiens**	**NHL**	**10**	**0**	**0**	**0**	**0**	**0**	**0**	**4**	....	....	....	....	....
	Providence Reds	Can-Am	7	5	1	6	....	....	....	34	....	....	....	....	....
	Pittsburgh Pirates	**NHL**	**30**	**6**	**4**	**10**	**8**	**9**	**17**	**37**	....	....	....	....	....
1930-31	**Philadelphia Quakers**	**NHL**	**5**	**0**	**0**	**0**	**0**	**0**	**0**	**22**	....	....	....	....	....
	Pittsburgh Yellowjackets	IHL	38	7	3	10	....	....	....	75	....	....	....	....	....
1931-32	Pittsburgh Yellowjackets	IHL	45	10	15	25	....	....	....	90	....	....	....	....	....
1932-33	London Tecumsehs	IHL	44	3	8	11	....	....	....	60	6	0	0	0	16
1933-34	Seattle Sawhawks	NWHL	27	11	8	19	....	....	....	48	....	....	....	....	....
	London Tecumsehs	IHL	6	0	0	0	....	....	....	4	....	....	....	....	....
1934-35	Portland Buckaroos	NWHL	32	10	7	17	....	....	....	66	3	1	0	1	10
1935-36	Pittsburgh Shamrocks	IHL	15	4	2	6	....	....	....	14	....	....	....	....	....
1936-37	Baltimore Orioles	EAHL	DID NOT PLAY – COACHING												
	NHL Totals		**144**	**24**	**12**	**36**	**41**	**52**	**93**	**224**	**2**	**1**	**0**	**1**	**6**
	Other Major League Totals		118	33	12	45	....	....	....	218	12	2	0	2	26

PCHA Second All-Star Team (1923) • PCHA First All-Star Team (1924) • WCHL Second All-Star Team (1925)

Signed as a free agent by **Seattle** (PCHA), November, 1921. Signed as a free agent by **Victoria** (WCHL) after **Seattle** (PCHA) franchise folded, November 7, 1924. • 1924-25 playoff totals includes WCHL series against Calgary and Saskatoon. • 1925-26 playoff totals includes WHL series against Edmonton and Saskatoon. NHL rights transferred to **Detroit** after NHL club purchased **Victoria** (WHL) franchise, May 15, 1926. Traded to **Chicago** by **Detroit** with Art Gagne for the rights to Art Duncan, October 18, 1926. Traded to **Detroit** by **Chicago** with $5,000 for Duke Keats, December 16, 1927. Traded to **Montreal Canadiens** by **Detroit** for cash, October 10, 1929. Loaned to **Providence** (Can-Am) by **Montreal** for cash, December 12, 1929. Traded to **Pittsburgh** by **Montreal Canadiens** for Bert McCaffery, December 23, 1929. Transferred to **Philadelphia** after **Pittsburgh** franchise relocated, October 18, 1930. Traded to **Pittsburgh** (IHL) by **Philadelphia** for cash, November 28, 1930.

• FRASER, Harvey

Harvey James

C – R. 5'10", 168 lbs. b: Souris, Man., 10/14/1918.

Season	Club	League	GP	G	A	Pts	AG	AA	APts	PIM	GP	G	A	Pts	PIM
1935-36	Yorkton Terriers	S-SSHL	17	12	5	17	....	....	....	8	3	*5	1	6	0
1936-37	Yorkton Terriers	S-SSHL	24	13	8	21	....	....	....	16	7	*5	1	*6	6
1937-38	Yorkton Terriers	S-SSHL	24	27	*24	*51	....	....	....	29	5	3	2	5	4
1938-39	Wembley Monarchs	Ln-Cup	....	2	1	3	....	....	....	....	....	....	....	....	....
	Wembley Monarchs	Britain	....	11	15	26	....	....	....	....	....	....	....	....	....
	Wembley Monarchs	Nat-Tmt	....	7	3	10	....	....	....	....	....	....	....	....	....
1939-40	Yorkton Terriers	S-SSHL	31	32	17	49	....	....	....	14	5	3	1	4	10
1940-41	Yorkton Terriers	S-SSHL	30	26	18	44	....	....	....	16	9	*9	4	13	2
1941-42	Yorkton Terriers	S-SSHL	4	3	2	5	....	....	....	4	....	....	....	....	....
1942-43	Flin Flon Bombers	S-SSHL	22	8	11	19	....	....	....	10	8	7	5	12	6
1943-44	Moose Jaw Victorias	S-SSHL	5	12	4	16	....	....	....	0	....	....	....	....	....
	Seattle Ironmen	PCHL	2	2	3	5	....	....	....	0	....	....	....	....	....
	N-Westminster Lodes	PCHL	11	9	7	16	....	....	....	4	3	6	*5	*11	5
	N-Westminster Lodes	Al-Cup	15	5	12	17	....	....	....	6	....	....	....	....	....
1944-45	**Chicago Black Hawks**	**NHL**	**21**	**5**	**4**	**9**	**5**	**5**	**10**	**0**	....	....	....	....	....
	Providence Reds	AHL	8	7	6	13	....	....	....	4	....	....	....	....	....
	Cleveland Barons	AHL	13	6	11	17	....	....	....	4	12	1	3	4	4
1945-46	Cleveland Barons	AHL	11	2	5	7	....	....	....	6	....	....	....	....	....
	New Haven Eagles	AHL	22	4	12	16	....	....	....	4	....	....	....	....	....
	St. Louis Flyers	AHL	17	9	9	18	....	....	....	6	....	....	....	....	....
1946-47	St. Louis Flyers	AHL	49	21	16	37	....	....	....	17	....	....	....	....	....
	Providence Reds	AHL	15	7	9	16	....	....	....	4	....	....	....	....	....
1947-48	Providence Reds	AHL	64	45	52	97	....	....	....	12	5	1	2	3	4
1948-49	Providence Reds	AHL	68	34	55	89	....	....	....	16	14	4	7	11	14
1949-50	Providence Reds	AHL	52	20	30	50	....	....	....	4	3	0	2	2	4
1950-51	Hamilton Tigers	OMHL	28	15	16	31	....	....	....	12	8	2	4	6	4
	NHL Totals		**21**	**5**	**4**	**9**	**5**	**5**	**10**	**0**	....	....	....	....	....

• Brother of Archie • AHL Second All-Star Team (1949)

Signed as a free agent by **Chicago**, October 14, 1944. Traded to **Cleveland** (AHL) by **Chicago** for cash, February 6, 1945. Traded to **New Haven** (AHL) by **Cleveland** (AHL) for Gord Davidson, November 25, 1945. Traded to **St. Louis** (AHL) by **New Haven** (AHL) for cash, February 3, 1946. Traded to **Providence** (AHL) by **St. Louis** (AHL) for cash, February 10, 1947.

• FREDRICKSON, Frank

Frank Sigudor **HHOF**

C – L. 5'11", 180 lbs. b: Winnipeg, Man., 6/11/1895 d: 4/28/1979.

Season	Club	League	GP	G	A	Pts	AG	AA	APts	PIM	GP	G	A	Pts	PIM
1913-14	Winnipeg Falcons	MIHL	11	13	7	20	....	....	....	0	....	....	....	....	....
1914-15	Winnipeg Falcons	MIHL	8	10	5	15	....	....	....	0	1	1	0	1	0
1915-16	Winnipeg Falcons	MHL-Sr.	6	*13	3	*16	....	....	....	14	....	....	....	....	....
1916-17	Winnipeg 223rd Battalion	MHL-Sr.	8	*17	3	*20	....	....	....	*40	....	....	....	....	....
1917-18			MILITARY SERVICE												
1918-19			MILITARY SERVICE												
1919-20	Winnipeg Falcons	MHL-Sr.	10	*23	5	*28	....	....	....	12	....	....	....	....	....
	Canada	Olympics	3	*10	1	11	....	....	....		....	....	....	....	....
	Winnipeg Falcons	Al-Cup	6	22	5	27	....	....	....	2	....	....	....	....	....
1920-21	Victoria Aristocrats	PCHA	21	20	12	32	....	....	....	3	....	....	....	....	....
1921-22	Victoria Aristocrats	PCHA	24	15	10	25	....	....	....	26	....	....	....	....	....
1922-23	Victoria Cougars	PCHA	30	*39	*16	*55	....	....	....	26	2	2	0	2	4
1923-24	Victoria Cougars	PCHA	30	19	8	27	....	....	....	28	....	....	....	....	....
1924-25	Victoria Cougars	WCHL	28	22	8	30	....	....	....	43	4	3	1	4	2
♦	Victoria Cougars	St-Cup	4	3	3	6	....	....	....	6	....	....	....	....	....
1925-26	Victoria Cougars	WHL	30	16	8	24	....	....	....	89	4	2	0	2	6
	Victoria Cougars	St-Cup	4	1	1	2	....	....	....	10	....	....	....	....	....
1926-27	**Detroit Cougars**	**NHL**	**16**	**4**	**6**	**10**	**7**	**31**	**38**	**12**	....	....	....	....	....
	Boston Bruins	**NHL**	**28**	**14**	**7**	**21**	**25**	**37**	**62**	**33**	**8**	**2**	***2**	**4**	**20**
1927-28	**Boston Bruins**	**NHL**	**41**	**10**	**4**	**14**	**20**	**23**	**43**	**83**	**2**	**0**	**1**	**1**	**4**
1928-29	**Boston Bruins**	**NHL**	**12**	**3**	**1**	**4**	**9**	**7**	**16**	**24**	....	....	....	....	....
	Pittsburgh Pirates	**NHL**	**31**	**3**	**7**	**10**	**9**	**47**	**56**	**28**	....	....	....	....	....
1929-30	**Pittsburgh Pirates**	**NHL**	**9**	**4**	**7**	**11**	**6**	**16**	**22**	**20**	....	....	....	....	....
1930-31	**Detroit Falcons**	**NHL**	**24**	**1**	**2**	**3**	**2**	**6**	**8**	**6**	....	....	....	....	....
	Detroit Olympics	IHL	6	0	1	1	....	....	....	2	....	....	....	....	....
1931-32	Winnipeg Winnipegs	WJrHL	DID NOT PLAY – COACHING												
	NHL Totals		**161**	**39**	**34**	**73**	**78**	**167**	**245**	**206**	**10**	**2**	**3**	**5**	**24**
	Other Major League Totals		163	131	62	193	....	....	....	215	10	7	1	8	12

PCHA First All-Star Team (1921, 1922, 1923, 1924) • WHL First All-Star Team (1926)

Signed as a free agent by **Victoria** (PCHA), December 23, 1920. • 1924-25 playoff totals includes WCHL series against Calgary and Saskatoon. • 1925-26 playoff totals includes WHL series against Edmonton and Saskatoon. NHL rights transferred to **Detroit Cougars** after NHL club purchased **Victoria** (WHL) franchise, May 15, 1926. Traded to **Boston** by **Detroit Cougars** with Harry Meeking for Duke Keats and Archie Briden, January 7, 1927. Traded to **Pittsburgh** by **Boston** for Mickey MacKay and $12,000, December 21, 1928. • Missed majority of the 1929-30 season after undergoing knee surgery, December 21, 1929. Transferred to **Philadelphia** after **Pittsburgh** franchise relocated. • Released by **Philadelphia**, October 20, 1930. Signed as a free agent by **Detroit**, November 23, 1930. Signed as a free agent by **Detroit Olympics** (IAHL) after clearing NHL waivers, February 13, 1931.

• FREW, Irv

Irvine Bell "Ranger"

D – R. 5'10", 180 lbs. b: Kilsyth, Scotland, 8/16/1907 Deceased.

Season	Club	League	GP	G	A	Pts	AG	AA	APts	PIM	GP	G	A	Pts	PIM
1925-26	Calgary Canadians	CCJHL	STATISTICS NOT AVAILABLE												
	Calgary Canadians	M-Cup	9	1	2	3	....	....	....	20	....	....	....	....	....
1926-27	Calgary Tigers	PrHL	27	0	0	0	....	....	....	8	2	0	0	0	0
1927-28	Stratford Nationals	Can-Pro	41	6	1	7	....	....	....	72	5	1	0	1	12
1928-29	Buffalo Bisons	Can-Pro	24	1	1	2	....	....	....	43	....	....	....	....	....
	Toronto Millionaires	Can-Pro	20	2	0	2	....	....	....	34	2	0	0	0	12
1929-30	Cleveland Indians	IHL	41	3	3	6	....	....	....	61	6	0	0	0	8
1930-31	Cleveland Indians	IHL	45	3	5	8	....	....	....	59	6	0	0	0	6
1931-32	Cleveland Indians	IHL	9	1	0	1	....	....	....	31	....	....	....	....	....
1932-33	Cleveland Indians	IHL	19	2	0	2	....	....	....	56	....	....	....	....	....
	Quebec Beavers	Can-Am	26	1	2	3	....	....	....	57	....	....	....	....	....
1933-34	**Montreal Maroons**	**NHL**	**30**	**2**	**1**	**3**	**3**	**2**	**5**	**41**	**4**	**0**	**0**	**0**	**6**
	Quebec Beavers	Can-Am	14	3	1	4	....	....	....	16	....	....	....	....	....
1934-35	**St. Louis Eagles**	**NHL**	**48**	**0**	**2**	**2**	**0**	**3**	**3**	**89**	....	....	....	....	....
1935-36	**Montreal Canadiens**	**NHL**	**18**	**0**	**2**	**2**	**0**	**4**	**4**	**16**	....	....	....	....	....
	Springfield Indians	Can-Am	14	0	2	2	....	....	....	23	2	0	0	0	4
1936-37	Springfield Indians	IAHL	47	5	6	11	....	....	....	65	5	0	0	0	11
1937-38	Springfield Indians	IAHL	14	0	0	0	....	....	....	19	....	....	....	....	....
	Vancouver Lions	PCHL	10	0	1	1	....	....	....	25	6	0	0	0	*22
1938-39	Spokane Clippers	PCHL	45	1	7	8	....	....	....	106	....	....	....	....	....
1939-40	Springfield Indians	IAHL	50	2	4	6	....	....	....	69	3	0	1	1	2
1940-41	St. Louis Flyers	AHA	39	6	5	11	....	....	....	37	9	1	0	1	17
	NHL Totals		**96**	**2**	**5**	**7**	**3**	**9**	**12**	**146**	**4**	**0**	**0**	**0**	**6**

AHA Second All-Star Team (1941)

Signed as a free agent by **Stratford** (Can-Pro), November 20, 1927. Traded to **Ottawa** by **Montreal Maroons** with future considerations (Vern Ayres and Norman Smith, October 22, 1934) for Al Shields, September 20, 1934. Transferred to **St. Louis** after **Ottawa** franchise relocated, September 22, 1934. Claimed by **Montreal Canadiens** from **St. Louis** in Dispersal Draft, October 15, 1935.

• FROST, Harry

RW – R. 5'11", 165 lbs. b: Kerr Lake, Ont., 8/17/1914.

Season	Club	League	GP	G	A	Pts	AG	AA	APts	PIM	GP	G	A	Pts	PIM
1934-35	Sudbury Frood Tigers	NOHA	8	9	1	10	....	....	....	6	3	0	0	0	4
1935-36	Hershey B'ars	EAHL	38	7	2	9	....	....	....	8	5	1	2	3	0
1936-37	Hershey B'ars	EAHL	47	7	7	14	....	....	....	11	4	1	1	2	2
1937-38	Hershey B'ars	EAHL	57	37	25	62	....	....	....	6	....	....	....	....	....
♦1938-39	**Boston Bruins**	**NHL**	**4**	**0**	**0**	**0**	**0**	**0**	**0**	**0**	**1**	**0**	**0**	**0**	**0**
	Hershey Bears	IAHL	35	10	7	17	....	....	....	8	4	0	2	2	4
1939-40	Hershey Bears	IAHL	52	12	18	30	....	....	....	6	6	1	2	3	0
1940-41	Hershey Bears	AHL	55	25	15	40	....	....	....	2	10	*4	3	7	0
1941-42	Hershey Bears	AHL	52	18	22	40	....	....	....	6	5	1	1	2	2
	Philadelphia Rockets	AHL	3	1	3	4	....	....	....	0	....	....	....	....	....
1942-43	Hershey Bears	AHL	56	*43	40	83	....	....	....	6	6	2	0	2	0
1943-44			MILITARY SERVICE												
1944-45			MILITARY SERVICE												
1945-46	Hershey Bears	AHL	39	9	6	15	....	....	....	8	3	0	1	1	4
1946-47	Springfield Indians	AHL	62	28	21	49	....	....	....	10	2	1	0	1	0
1947-48	Springfield Indians	AHL	67	21	23	44	....	....	....	19	....	....	....	....	....
1948-49	Fort Worth Rangers	USHL	6	2	3	5	....	....	....	2	....	....	....	....	....
	Springfield Indians	AHL	1	0	0	0	....	....	....	0	....	....	....	....	....
	Washington Lions	AHL	54	25	14	39	....	....	....	2	....	....	....	....	....
1949-50	Louisville Blades	USHL	16	4	5	9	....	....	....	4	....	....	....	....	....
	Fresno Falcons	PCHL	42	9	7	16	....	....	....	2	....	....	....	....	....
	St. Louis Flyers	AHL	9	1	0	1	....	....	....	0	....	....	....	....	....
1950-51	Johnstown Jets	EAHL	54	16	38	54	....	....	....	10	6	0	1	1	0
1951-52	Washington Lions	EAHL	34	16	19	35	....	....	....	8	....	....	....	....	....
	NHL Totals		**4**	**0**	**0**	**0**	**0**	**0**	**0**	**0**	**1**	**0**	**0**	**0**	**0**

EAHL First All-Star Team (1938) • AHL First All-Star Team (1941, 1942, 1943)

Traded to **Washington** (AHL) by **Springfield** (AHL) for cash, November 10, 1948.

• FRYDAY, Bob   Bob George

RW – R. 5'10", 155 lbs.   b: Toronto, Ont., 12/5/1928.

			REGULAR SEASON								PLAYOFFS				
Season	Club	League	GP	G	A	Pts	AG	AA	APts	PIM	GP	G	A	Pts	PIM
1944-45	Etobicoke Indians	OHA-B	STATISTICS NOT AVAILABLE												
1945-46	Toronto Marlboros	OHA-Jr.	25	10	7	17	....	....	....	18	4	3	1	4	0
	Toronto Mahers	TIHL	20	11	13	24	....	....	....	8	10	9	4	13	0
1946-47	Montreal Royals	QJHL	27	26	26	52	....	....	....	11	8	8	7	15	6
	Montreal Royals	M-Cup	7	9	10	19	....	....	....	5	....	....	....	....	....
1947-48	Montreal Royals	QSHL	44	22	8	30	....	....	....	21	3	0	1	1	0
1948-49	Montreal Royals	QSHL	64	24	20	44	....	....	....	32	8	3	3	6	11
1949-50	**Montreal Canadiens**	**NHL**	**2**	**1**	**0**	**1**	**1**	**0**	**1**	**0**	....	....	....	....	....
	Montreal Royals	QSHL	55	15	32	47	....	....	....	28	5	0	0	0	0
1950-51	Montreal Royals	QMHL	43	17	26	43	....	....	....	35	7	2	2	4	2
1951-52	**Montreal Canadiens**	**NHL**	**3**	**0**	**0**	**0**	**0**	**0**	**0**	**0**	....	....	....	....	....
	Montreal Royals	QMHL	51	15	15	30	....	....	....	32	6	1	0	1	2
	Cincinnati Mohawks	AHL	....	....	....	....	....	....	....	....	5	1	4	5	2
1952-53	Buffalo Bisons	AHL	57	18	13	31	....	....	....	6	....	....	....	....	....
	NHL Totals		**5**	**1**	**0**	**1**	**1**	**0**	**1**	**0**	....	....	....	....	....

• GADSBY, Bill   William Alexander "Gads"   HHOF

D – L. 6', 180 lbs.   b: Calgary, Alta., 8/8/1927.

Season	Club	League	GP	G	A	Pts	AG	AA	APts	PIM	GP	G	A	Pts	PIM
1943-44	Calgary Grills	AHA-B	9	4	1	5	....	....	....	4	....	....	....	....	....
1944-45	Edmonton Canadians	AJHL	STATISTICS NOT AVAILABLE												
1945-46	Edmonton Canadians	AJHL	....	14	12	26	....	....	....	....	....	....	....	....	....
	Edmonton Canadians	M-Cup	14	12	5	17	....	....	....	22	....	....	....	....	....
1946-47	**Chicago Black Hawks**	**NHL**	**48**	**8**	**10**	**18**	**9**	**12**	**21**	**31**	....	....	....	....	....
	Kansas City Pla-Mors	USHL	12	2	3	5	....	....	....	8	....	....	....	....	....
1947-48	**Chicago Black Hawks**	**NHL**	**60**	**6**	**10**	**16**	**8**	**13**	**21**	**66**	....	....	....	....	....
1948-49	**Chicago Black Hawks**	**NHL**	**50**	**3**	**10**	**13**	**4**	**14**	**18**	**85**	....	....	....	....	....
1949-50	**Chicago Black Hawks**	**NHL**	**70**	**10**	**25**	**35**	**13**	**30**	**43**	**138**	....	....	....	....	....
1950-51	**Chicago Black Hawks**	**NHL**	**25**	**3**	**7**	**10**	**4**	**9**	**13**	**32**	....	....	....	....	....
1951-52	**Chicago Black Hawks**	**NHL**	**59**	**7**	**15**	**22**	**9**	**18**	**27**	**87**	....	....	....	....	....
1952-53	**Chicago Black Hawks**	**NHL**	**68**	**2**	**20**	**22**	**3**	**24**	**27**	**84**	**7**	**0**	**1**	**1**	**4**
1953-54	**Chicago Black Hawks**	**NHL**	**70**	**12**	**29**	**41**	**16**	**35**	**51**	**108**	....	....	....	....	....
1954-55	**Chicago Black Hawks**	**NHL**	**18**	**3**	**5**	**8**	**4**	**6**	**10**	**17**	....	....	....	....	....
	New York Rangers	**NHL**	**52**	**8**	**8**	**16**	**10**	**9**	**19**	**44**	....	....	....	....	....
1955-56	**New York Rangers**	**NHL**	**70**	**9**	**42**	**51**	**12**	**50**	**62**	**84**	**5**	**1**	**3**	**4**	**4**
1956-57	**New York Rangers**	**NHL**	**70**	**4**	**37**	**41**	**5**	**41**	**46**	**72**	**5**	**1**	**2**	**3**	**2**
1957-58	**New York Rangers**	**NHL**	**65**	**14**	**32**	**46**	**17**	**33**	**50**	**48**	**6**	**0**	**3**	**3**	**4**
1958-59	**New York Rangers**	**NHL**	**70**	**5**	**46**	**51**	**6**	**47**	**53**	**56**	....	....	....	....	....
1959-60	**New York Rangers**	**NHL**	**65**	**9**	**22**	**31**	**10**	**21**	**31**	**60**	....	....	....	....	....
1960-61	**New York Rangers**	**NHL**	**65**	**9**	**26**	**35**	**10**	**25**	**35**	**49**	....	....	....	....	....
1961-62	**Detroit Red Wings**	**NHL**	**70**	**7**	**30**	**37**	**8**	**29**	**37**	**88**	....	....	....	....	....
1962-63	**Detroit Red Wings**	**NHL**	**70**	**4**	**24**	**28**	**5**	**24**	**29**	**116**	**11**	**1**	**4**	**5**	***36**
1963-64	**Detroit Red Wings**	**NHL**	**64**	**2**	**16**	**18**	**2**	**17**	**19**	**80**	**14**	**0**	**4**	**4**	**22**
1964-65	**Detroit Red Wings**	**NHL**	**61**	**0**	**12**	**12**	**0**	**12**	**12**	**122**	**7**	**0**	**3**	**3**	**8**
1965-66	**Detroit Red Wings**	**NHL**	**58**	**5**	**12**	**17**	**6**	**11**	**17**	**72**	**12**	**1**	**3**	**4**	**12**
	NHL Totals		**1248**	**130**	**438**	**568**	**161**	**480**	**641**	**1539**	**67**	**4**	**23**	**27**	**92**

NHL Second All-Star Team (1953, 1954, 1957, 1965) • NHL First All-Star Team (1956, 1958, 1959) • Played in NHL All-Star Game (1953, 1954, 1956, 1957, 1958, 1959, 1960, 1965)

Signed as a free agent by **Chicago**, July 14, 1946. • Missed majority of 1950-51 season recovering from leg injury suffered in game vs. Toronto, November 22, 1950. Traded to **NY Rangers** by **Chicago** with Pete Conacher for Allan Stanley, Nick Mickoski and Rich Lamoureux, November 23, 1954. Traded to **Detroit** by **NY Rangers** with Eddie Shack for Billy McNeill and Red Kelly, February 5, 1960. • Kelly and McNeill refused to report and transaction was cancelled, February 7, 1960. Traded to **Detroit** by **NY Rangers** for Les Hunt, June 12, 1961.

• GAGNE, Art

RW – R. 5'7", 160 lbs.   b: Ottawa, Ont., 10/11/1897   Deceased.

Season	Club	League	GP	G	A	Pts	AG	AA	APts	PIM	GP	G	A	Pts	PIM
1914-15	Ottawa Aberdeens	OCHL	3	1	0	1	....	....	....	....	1	0	0	0	....
	Ottawa Royal Canadians	OCHL	5	2	0	2	....	....	....	....	2	0	0	0	....
1915-16	Ottawa Aberdeens	OCHL	5	4	0	4	....	....	....	....	....	....	....	....	....
1916-17	Ottawa Grand Trunks	OCHL	2	1	0	1	....	....	....	....	....	....	....	....	....
	Laval University	MCHL	7	11	5	16	....	....	....	....	....	....	....	....	....
1917-18	Quebec Sons of Ireland	QCHL	4	9	1	10	....	....	....	....	1	1	0	1	0
1918-19	Quebec Montagnais	QSHL	5	7	0	7	....	....	....	....	3	5	0	5	9
1919-20	Quebec Montagnais	QCHL	STATISTICS NOT AVAILABLE												
1920-21	Edmonton Eskimos	Big-4	15	9	4	13	....	....	....	22	....	....	....	....	....
1921-22	Edmonton Eskimos	WCHL	20	15	7	22	....	....	....	24	2	0	....	....	....
1922-23	Edmonton Eskimos	WCHL	29	22	*21	*43	....	....	....	63	2	1	0	1	0
	Edmonton Eskimos	St-Cup	2	0	0	0	....	....	....	2	....	....	....	....	....
1923-24	Regina Capitals	WCHL	25	7	7	14	....	....	....	39	2	0	0	0	0
1924-25	Regina Capitals	WCHL	28	8	7	15	....	....	....	32	....	....	....	....	....
1925-26	Edmonton Eskimos	WHL	24	35	10	45	....	....	....	24	2	1	2	3	6
1926-27	**Montreal Canadiens**	**NHL**	**44**	**14**	**3**	**17**	**25**	**16**	**41**	**42**	**4**	**0**	**0**	**0**	**0**
1927-28	**Montreal Canadiens**	**NHL**	**44**	**20**	**10**	**30**	**41**	**57**	**98**	**75**	**2**	**1**	**1**	**2**	**4**
1928-29	**Montreal Canadiens**	**NHL**	**44**	**7**	**3**	**10**	**20**	**20**	**40**	**52**	**3**	**0**	**0**	**0**	**12**
1929-30	**Boston Bruins**	**NHL**	**6**	**0**	**1**	**1**	**0**	**2**	**2**	**6**	....	....	....	....	....
	Ottawa Senators	**NHL**	**33**	**6**	**4**	**10**	**8**	**9**	**17**	**32**	**2**	**1**	**0**	**1**	**4**
1930-31	**Ottawa Senators**	**NHL**	**44**	**19**	**11**	**30**	**39**	**33**	**72**	**50**	....	....	....	....	....
1931-32	**Detroit Falcons**	**NHL**	**13**	**1**	**1**	**2**	**2**	**2**	**4**	**0**	....	....	....	....	....
	Detroit Olympics	IHL	29	6	7	13	....	....	....	18	6	0	1	1	2
1932-33	Edmonton Eskimos	WCHL	29	25	7	32	....	....	....	25	8	*6	1	*7	7
1933-34	Edmonton Eskimos	NWHL	33	18	*21	39	....	....	....	29	2	1	1	2	0
1934-35	Edmonton Eskimos	NWHL	28	20	12	32	....	....	....	18	....	....	....	....	....
1935-36	Seattle Seahawks	NWHL	10	1	4	5	....	....	....	6	....	....	....	....	....
	Edmonton Eskimos	NWHL	17	10	5	15	....	....	....	9	....	....	....	....	....
	NHL Totals		**228**	**67**	**33**	**100**	**135**	**139**	**274**	**257**	**11**	**2**	**1**	**3**	**20**
	Other Major League Totals		126	87	52	139	....	....	....	182	8	2	2	4	6

OCHL Second All-Star Team (1916) • WCHL Second All-Star Team (1922) • WCHL First All-Star Team (1923) • WHL First All-Star Team (1926)

Signed as a free agent by **Edmonton** (WCHL), November 4, 1921. Traded to **Regina** (WCHL) by **Edmonton** (WCHL) for Emory Sparrow and $1,500, October 3, 1923. Transferred to **Portland** (WHL) after **Regina** (WCHL) franchise relocated, September 28, 1925. Traded to **Edmonton** (WHL) by **Portland** (WHL) with Eddie Shore for Joe McCormack and Bob Trapp, October 7, 1925. Traded to **Detroit** by **Edmonton** (WHL) for cash, October 5, 1926. Traded to **Chicago** by **Detroit** with Gord Fraser for the rights to Art Duncan, October 18, 1926. Traded to **Montreal Canadiens** by **Chicago** for cash, October 18, 1926. Traded to **Boston** by **Montreal Canadiens** for cash, May 13, 1929. Traded to **Ottawa** by **Boston** for cash, December 21, 1929. Claimed by **Detroit** from **Ottawa** for 1931-32 season in Dispersal Draft, September 26, 1931. Traded to **Seattle** (NWHL) by **Edmonton** (NWHL) for Les Whittles, September, 1935. Signed as a free agent by **Edmonton** (NWHL) following release by **Seattle** (NWHL), December 20, 1935.

• GAGNE, Pierre   Pierre Reynald

LW – L. 6'1", 180 lbs.   b: North Bay, Ont., 6/5/1940.

Season	Club	League	GP	G	A	Pts	AG	AA	APts	PIM	GP	G	A	Pts	PIM
1958-59	Barrie Flyers	OHA-Jr.	54	20	18	38	....	....	....	10	6	1	4	5	14
1959-60	Barrie Flyers	OHA-Jr.	48	32	34	66	....	....	....	14	6	6	3	9	6
	Boston Bruins	**NHL**	**2**	**0**	**0**	**0**	**0**	**0**	**0**	**0**	....	....	....	....	....
1960-61	Clinton Comets	EHL	16	5	9	14	....	....	....	24	....	....	....	....	....
	New York Rovers	EHL	29	5	10	15	....	....	....	7	....	....	....	....	....
1961-62	North Bay Trappers	EPHL	1	0	0	0	....	....	....	0	....	....	....	....	....
	Fort Wayne Komets	IHL	59	19	32	51	....	....	....	39	....	....	....	....	....
1962-63	University of Ottawa	OQAA	STATISTICS NOT AVAILABLE												
1963-64	University of Ottawa	OQAA	STATISTICS NOT AVAILABLE												
1964-65	Hull Volants	QSHL	STATISTICS NOT AVAILABLE												
1965-66	Hull Volants	QSHL	STATISTICS NOT AVAILABLE												
	Shawinigan Bruins	M-Cup	3	0	0	0	....	....	....	2	....	....	....	....	....
1966-67	Providence Reds	AHL	70	20	21	41	....	....	....	18	....	....	....	....	....
1967-68	Providence Reds	AHL	28	5	13	18	....	....	....	6	5	0	0	0	2
1968-69	Providence Reds	AHL	67	17	22	39	....	....	....	18	9	3	5	8	4
1969-70	Nashville Dixie Flyers	EHL	67	41	44	85	....	....	....	35	....	....	....	....	....
1970-71	Dalhousie University	AUAA	18	27	35	*62	....	....	....	16	....	....	....	....	....
1971-72	Dalhousie University	AUAA	18	10	*24	34	....	....	....	70	....	....	....	....	....
	NHL Totals		**2**	**0**	**0**	**0**	**0**	**0**	**0**	**0**	....	....	....	....	....

OHA-Jr. First All-Star Team (1960) • AUAA First All-Star Team (1971)

• GAGNON, Johnny   "Black Cat"

RW – R. 5'5", 140 lbs.   b: Chicoutimi, Que., 6/8/1905   d: 3/22/1984.

Season	Club	League	GP	G	A	Pts	AG	AA	APts	PIM	GP	G	A	Pts	PIM
1922-23	Chicoutimi Bluets	QPHL	7	0	0	0	....	....	....	....	1	0	0	0	....
	Quebec Bulldogs	Big-4	3	0	0	0	....	....	....	....	....	....	....	....	....
1923-24	Trois-Rivieres Renards	ECHL	9	2	0	2	....	....	....	....	....	....	....	....	....
1924-25	Trois-Rivieres Renards	ECHL	16	18	0	18	....	....	....	....	2	5	0	5	....
1925-26	Quebec Sons of Ireland	QAHA	10	5	0	5	....	....	....	....	6	4	0	4	....
1926-27	Quebec Beavers	Can-Am	32	*27	6	*33	....	....	....	54	2	0	0	0	5
1927-28	Providence Reds	Can-Am	39	20	4	24	....	....	....	80	....	....	....	....	....
1928-29	Providence Reds	Can-Am	39	7	3	10	....	....	....	50	6	*4	0	*4	10
1929-30	Providence Reds	Can-Am	39	21	17	38	....	....	....	72	3	2	*4	*6	6
♦1930-31	**Montreal Canadiens**	**NHL**	**41**	**18**	**7**	**25**	**36**	**21**	**57**	**43**	**10**	***6**	**2**	**8**	**8**
1931-32	**Montreal Canadiens**	**NHL**	**48**	**19**	**18**	**37**	**32**	**40**	**72**	**40**	**4**	**1**	**1**	**2**	**4**
1932-33	**Montreal Canadiens**	**NHL**	**48**	**12**	**23**	**35**	**22**	**48**	**70**	**64**	**2**	**0**	**2**	**2**	**0**
1933-34	**Montreal Canadiens**	**NHL**	**48**	**9**	**15**	**24**	**15**	**32**	**47**	**25**	**2**	**1**	**0**	**1**	**2**
1934-35	**Boston Bruins**	**NHL**	**24**	**1**	**1**	**2**	**2**	**2**	**4**	**9**	....	....	....	....	....
	Montreal Canadiens	**NHL**	**23**	**1**	**5**	**6**	**2**	**9**	**11**	**2**	**2**	**0**	**1**	**1**	**2**
1935-36	**Montreal Canadiens**	**NHL**	**48**	**7**	**9**	**16**	**13**	**17**	**30**	**42**	....	....	....	....	....
1936-37	**Montreal Canadiens**	**NHL**	**48**	**20**	**16**	**36**	**34**	**29**	**63**	**38**	**5**	**2**	**1**	**3**	**9**
1937-38	**Montreal Canadiens**	**NHL**	**47**	**13**	**17**	**30**	**21**	**27**	**48**	**9**	**3**	**1**	**3**	**4**	**2**
1938-39	**Montreal Canadiens**	**NHL**	**45**	**12**	**22**	**34**	**21**	**35**	**56**	**23**	**3**	**0**	**2**	**2**	**10**
1939-40	**Montreal Canadiens**	**NHL**	**10**	**4**	**5**	**9**	**7**	**8**	**15**	**0**	....	....	....	....	....
	New York Americans	**NHL**	**24**	**4**	**3**	**7**	**7**	**5**	**12**	**0**	**1**	**1**	**0**	**1**	**0**
1940-41	Shawinigan Cataracts	QSHL	33	15	26	41	....	....	....	58	10	3	*8	11	12
1941-42	North Sydney Victorias	CBSHL	23	5	11	16	....	....	....	6	6	2	4	6	4
1942-43	Providence Reds	AHL	50	9	10	19	....	....	....	12	....	....	....	....	....
1943-44	Providence Reds	AHL	DID NOT PLAY – COACHING												
1944-45	Providence Reds	AHL	9	0	5	5	....	....	....	0	....	....	....	....	....
	NHL Totals		**454**	**120**	**141**	**261**	**212**	**273**	**485**	**295**	**32**	**12**	**12**	**24**	**37**

Played in NHL All-Star Game (1937, 1939)

Traded to **Montreal Canadiens** by **Providece** (Can-Am) for Gerry Carson, the loan of Jean Pusie and cash, October 21, 1930. Traded to **Boston** by **Montreal Canadiens** for Joe Lamb, October 2, 1934. Traded to **Montreal Canadiens** by **Boston** for cash, January 9, 1935. Traded to **NY Americans** by **Montreal** for cash, January 3, 1940. Signed as a free agent by **North Sydney** (CBSHL), December 18, 1941.

• GAINOR, Norm   "Dutch"

C – L. 6'1", 170 lbs.   b: Calgary, Alta., 4/10/1904   d: 1/16/1962.

Season	Club	League	GP	G	A	Pts	AG	AA	APts	PIM	GP	G	A	Pts	PIM
1923-24	Bellevue Bulldogs	ASHL	STATISTICS NOT AVAILABLE												
	Bellevue Bulldogs	Al-Cup	1	0	0	0	....	....	....	0	....	....	....	....	....
1924-25	Crows Nest Pass	ASHL	STATISTICS NOT AVAILABLE												
1925-26	Duluth Hornets	CHL	15	1	0	1	....	....	....	0	5	0	0	0	0
1926-27	Calgary Tigers	PrHL	23	16	11	27	....	....	....	38	2	0	0	0	0
1927-28	**Boston Bruins**	**NHL**	**42**	**8**	**4**	**12**	**16**	**23**	**39**	**35**	**2**	**0**	**0**	**0**	**6**
♦1928-29	**Boston Bruins**	**NHL**	**44**	**14**	**5**	**19**	**41**	**33**	**74**	**30**	**5**	**2**	**0**	**2**	**4**
1929-30	**Boston Bruins**	**NHL**	**42**	**18**	**31**	**49**	**26**	**75**	**101**	**39**	**3**	**0**	**0**	**0**	**0**
1930-31	**Boston Bruins**	**NHL**	**35**	**8**	**3**	**11**	**16**	**9**	**25**	**14**	**5**	**0**	**1**	**1**	**2**
1931-32	**New York Rangers**	**NHL**	**46**	**3**	**9**	**12**	**5**	**20**	**25**	**9**	**7**	**0**	**0**	**0**	**2**
1932-33	Springfield Indians	Can-Am	13	7	5	12	....	....	....	....	....	....	....	....	....
	Ottawa Senators	**NHL**	**2**	**0**	**0**	**0**	**0**	**0**	**0**	**0**	....	....	....	....	....
	Saskatoon Crescents	WCHL	21	10	11	21	....	....	....	4	....	....	....	....	....
1933-34	Calgary Tigers	NWHL	34	23	19	*42	....	....	....	24	5	2	0	2	2

Season	Club	League	GP	G	A	Pts	AG	AA	APts	PIM	GP	G	A	Pts	PIM
			REGULAR SEASON								PLAYOFFS				
♦1934-35	Montreal Maroons	NHL	35	0	4	4	0	7	7	2	....	....	....	....	....
1935-36	Calgary Tigers	NWHL	40	21	14	35	....	....	....	6	....	....	....	....	....
1936-37	Portland Buckaroos	PCHL	13	0	0	0	....	....	....	0	....	....	....	....	....
	NHL Totals		246	51	56	107	104	167	271	129	22	2	1	3	14

Signed as a free agent by **Calgary** (PrHL), November 8, 1926. Traded to **Boston** by **Minneapolis** (AHA) with Nobby Clark for Red Stuart, cash and future considerations, October 24, 1927. Traded to **NY Rangers** by **Boston** for Joe Jerwa, August 25, 1931. Traded to **Ottawa** by **NY Rangers** for cash after Springfield (Can-Am) franchise folded (December 18, 1932), December 23, 1932. Signed as a free agent by **Montreal Maroons**, October 22, 1934.

• GALBRAITH, Percy

Walter Percival "Perk"
LW/D – L. 5'10", 162 lbs. b: Toronto, Ont., 12/5/1898 d: 6/21/1961.

Season	Club	League	GP	G	A	Pts	AG	AA	APts	PIM	GP	G	A	Pts	PIM
1914-15	Winnipeg Winnipegs	MHL-Sr.	8	2	2	4	....	....	....	6	....	....	....	....	....
1915-16	Winnipeg Victorias	MHL-Sr.	2	3	1	4	....	....	....	2	....	....	....	....	....
1916-17	Winnipeg Victorias	WSrHL	STATISTICS NOT AVAILABLE												
1917-18			MILITARY SERVICE												
1918-19			MILITARY SERVICE												
1919-20	Winnipeg Monarchs	MHL-Sr.	7	6	1	7	....	....	....	6	....	....	....	....	....
1920-21	Eveleth Rangers	USAHA	STATISTICS NOT AVAILABLE												
1921-22	Eveleth Rangers	USAHA	STATISTICS NOT AVAILABLE												
1922-23	Eveleth Rangers	USAHA	20	4	0	4	....	....	....	....	....	....	....	....	....
1923-24	Eveleth Rangers	USAHA	21	9	2	11	....	....	....	....	....	....	....	....	....
1924-25	Eveleth Arrowheads	USAHA	38	10	0	10	....	....	....	....	4	0	0	0	0
1925-26	Eveleth-Hibbing Rangers	CHL	37	6	5	11	....	....	....	40	....	....	....	....	....
1926-27	Boston Bruins	NHL	42	9	8	17	16	42	58	26	8	3	3	*6	2
1927-28	Boston Bruins	NHL	42	6	5	11	12	28	40	26	2	0	1	1	6
♦1928-29	Boston Bruins	NHL	38	2	1	3	6	7	13	44	5	0	0	0	2
1929-30	Boston Bruins	NHL	44	7	9	16	10	21	31	38	6	1	3	4	8
1930-31	Boston Bruins	NHL	43	2	3	5	4	9	13	28	5	0	0	0	6
1931-32	Boston Bruins	NHL	47	2	1	3	3	2	5	28	....	....	....	....	....
1932-33	Boston Bruins	NHL	47	1	2	3	2	4	6	28	5	0	0	0	0
1933-34	Ottawa Senators	NHL	2	0	0	0	0	0	0	0	....	....	....	....	....
	Boston Bruins	NHL	42	0	2	2	0	4	4	6	....	....	....	....	....
1934-35	Eveleth Rangers	CHL	45	4	5	9	....	....	....	6	....	....	....	....	....
1935-36	Wichita Skyhawks	AHA	47	4	5	9	....	....	....	34	....	....	....	....	....
1936-37	Wichita Skyhawks	AHA	48	4	4	8	....	....	....	38	....	....	....	....	....
1937-38	St. Paul Saints	AHA	34	3	0	3	....	....	....	10	....	....	....	....	....
1938-39	St. Paul Saints	AHA	3	0	0	0	....	....	....	0	....	....	....	....	....
1939-40	St. Paul Saints	AHA	DID NOT PLAY – COACHING												
	NHL Totals		347	29	31	60	53	117	170	224	31	4	7	11	24

• CHL First All-Star Team (1926)

Rights traded to **Boston** by **St. Paul** (AHA) with the rights to Bill Hill for cash, January 3, 1926. Traded to **Ottawa** by **Boston** with Ted Saunders and Bud Cook for Bob Gracie, October 4, 1933. • Released by Ottawa, November 17, 1933. Signed as a free agent by **Boston**, November 21, 1933.

• GALLAGHER, John

John James
D – L. 5'11", 188 lbs. b: Kenora, Ont., 1/19/1909 d: 9/16/1981.

Season	Club	League	GP	G	A	Pts	AG	AA	APts	PIM	GP	G	A	Pts	PIM
1925-26	Kenora Thistles	TBSHL	16	4	3	7	....	....	....	12	....	....	....	....	....
1926-27	Kenora Thistles	TBJHL	12	5	4	9	....	....	....	18	....	....	....	....	....
1927-28	Kenora Thistles	TBJHL	STATISTICS NOT AVAILABLE												
1928-29	Kenora Thistles	TBJHL	16	4	3	7	....	....	....	12	....	....	....	....	....
1929-30	Montreal AAA	MCHL	10	3	0	3	....	....	....	25	2	0	0	0	0
	Montreal CPR	MCHL	STATISTICS NOT AVAILABLE												
1930-31	Montreal Maroons	NHL	35	4	2	6	8	6	14	35	2	0	0	0	0
1931-32	Montreal Maroons	NHL	19	1	0	1	2	0	2	18	....	....	....	....	....
	Windsor Bulldogs	IHL	29	6	4	10	....	....	....	48	6	2	1	3	13
1932-33	Montreal Maroons	NHL	6	1	0	1	2	0	2	0	....	....	....	....	....
	Detroit Red Wings	NHL	35	3	6	9	5	12	17	48	4	1	1	2	4
	Detroit Olympics	IHL	3	0	0	0	....	....	....	0	....	....	....	....	....
1933-34	Detroit Red Wings	NHL	1	0	0	0	0	0	0	0	....	....	....	....	....
1934-35	Windsor Bulldogs	IHL	26	3	5	8	....	....	....	8	....	....	....	....	....
1935-36	Detroit Olympics	IHL	44	4	3	7	....	....	....	40	6	3	0	3	2
1936-37	New York Americans	NHL	9	0	0	0	0	0	0	8	....	....	....	....	....
	Pittsburgh Hornets	IAHL	31	6	7	13	....	....	....	22	5	0	0	0	0
♦	Detroit Red Wings	NHL	11	1	0	1	2	0	2	4	10	1	0	1	17
1937-38	New York Americans	NHL	46	3	6	9	5	10	15	18	6	0	2	2	6
1938-39	New York Americans	NHL	43	1	5	6	2	8	10	22	2	0	0	0	0
	NHL Totals		205	14	19	33	26	36	62	153	24	2	3	5	27

Signed as a free agent by **Toronto**, July 30, 1930. • Montreal Maroons also claimed Gallagher's rights. NHL ruled he was property of Maroons, September 27, 1930. Traded to **Detroit** by **Montreal Maroons** for Reg Noble, December 9, 1932. • Missed majority of 1933-34 season recovering from injuries suffered in an automobile accident, November, 1933. Loaned to **Windsor** (IHL) by **Detroit** and played games in Canada only because he was denied entry into the U.S.A., November 30, 1934. Traded to **NY Americans** by **Detroit** for $6,000, October 7, 1936. Traded to **Detroit** by **NY Americans** for cash, November 29, 1936. Traded to **NY Americans** by **Detroit** for $6,000, October 7, 1937.

• GALLINGER, Don

Donald Calvin
C – L. 6', 170 lbs. b: Port Colborne, Ont., 4/16/1925 d: 2/7/2000.

Season	Club	League	GP	G	A	Pts	AG	AA	APts	PIM	GP	G	A	Pts	PIM
1939-40	Port Colbourne Incos	OIHA	....	....	....	....	....	....	....	....	3	0	0	0	4
1940-41	Port Colbourne Incos	OIHA	STATISTICS NOT AVAILABLE												
1941-42	St. Catharines Teepees	OHA-Jr.	STATISTICS NOT AVAILABLE												
1942-43	Boston Bruins	NHL	48	14	20	34	14	19	33	16	9	3	1	4	10
1943-44	Boston Bruins	NHL	23	13	5	18	12	4	16	6	....	....	....	....	....
	Toronto Bowsers	TIHL	3	3	4	7	....	....	....	11	9	5	7	12	10
1944-45	Winnipeg RCAF	WSrHL	9	10	5	15	....	....	....	18	4	1	6	7	8
1945-46	Boston Bruins	NHL	50	17	23	40	20	34	54	18	10	2	4	6	2
1946-47	Boston Bruins	NHL	47	11	19	30	12	23	35	12	4	0	0	0	7
1947-48	Boston Bruins	NHL	54	10	21	31	13	28	41	37	....	....	....	....	....
	NHL Totals		222	65	88	153	71	108	179	89	23	5	5	10	19

• Suspended for remainder of 1947-48 season by NHL for gambling violations, March 9, 1948. • Suspended for life by NHL for gambling violations, September 27, 1948. • Suspension lifted by NHL, August 28, 1970.

• GAMBLE, Dick

Richard Frank
LW – L. 6', 178 lbs. b: Moncton, N.B., 11/16/1928.

Season	Club	League	GP	G	A	Pts	AG	AA	APts	PIM	GP	G	A	Pts	PIM
1944-45	Moncton Bruins	NBJHL	3	*3	1	*4	....	....	....	2	10	*25	*9	*34	2
1945-46	Moncton Bruins	NBJHL	3	1	0	1	....	....	....	7	3	*6	3	*9	2
	Saint John Pontiacs	M-Cup	4	8	3	11	....	....	....	0	....	....	....	....	....
	Halifax St. Mary's	M-Cup	1	1	0	1	....	....	....	0	....	....	....	....	....
1946-47	Oshawa Generals	OHA-Jr.	24	15	20	35	....	....	....	26	5	3	0	3	0
1947-48	Oshawa Generals	OHA-Jr.	34	31	16	47	....	....	....	21	3	0	0	0	2
1948-49	Oshawa Generals	OHA-Jr.	46	39	23	62	....	....	....	10	2	2	0	2	0
1949-50	Quebec Aces	QSHL	56	20	25	45	....	....	....	18	12	9	3	12	4
1950-51	Quebec Aces	QMHL	58	*46	34	80	....	....	....	44	19	10	8	18	14
	Montreal Canadiens	NHL	1	0	0	0	0	0	0	0	....	....	....	....	....
1951-52	Montreal Canadiens	NHL	64	23	17	40	31	21	52	8	7	0	2	2	0
♦1952-53	Montreal Canadiens	NHL	69	11	13	24	14	16	30	26	5	1	0	1	2
1953-54	Montreal Canadiens	NHL	32	4	8	12	5	10	15	18	....	....	....	....	....
	Montreal Royals	QHL	32	20	25	45	....	....	....	49	10	5	1	6	4
1954-55	Chicago Black Hawks	NHL	14	2	0	2	3	0	3	6	....	....	....	....	....
	Buffalo Bisons	AHL	45	38	21	59	....	....	....	26	10	4	4	8	6
	Montreal Canadiens	NHL	....	....	....	....	....	....	....	....	2	0	0	0	2
1955-56	Montreal Canadiens	NHL	12	0	3	3	0	4	4	8	....	....	....	....	....
	Quebec Aces	QHL	52	23	24	47	....	....	....	45	7	4	5	9	14
1956-57	Quebec Aces	QHL	63	35	14	49	....	....	....	28	10	4	4	8	8
	Quebec Aces	Ed-Cup	6	3	2	5	....	....	....	8	....	....	....	....	....
1957-58	Buffalo Bisons	AHL	70	32	22	54	....	....	....	32	....	....	....	....	....
1958-59	Buffalo Bisons	AHL	70	31	30	61	....	....	....	24	11	2	2	4	14
1959-60	Buffalo Bisons	AHL	72	27	50	77	....	....	....	22	....	....	....	....	....
1960-61	Buffalo Bisons	AHL	72	40	36	76	....	....	....	18	4	2	0	2	6
1961-62	Rochester Americans	AHL	66	39	29	68	....	....	....	32	2	0	2	2	0
1962-63	Rochester Americans	AHL	70	35	22	57	....	....	....	16	2	0	1	1	0
1963-64	Rochester Americans	AHL	72	34	34	68	....	....	....	4	2	0	0	0	0
1964-65	Rochester Americans	AHL	70	48	29	77	....	....	....	16	10	5	8	13	6
1965-66	Toronto Maple Leafs	NHL	2	1	0	1	1	0	1	0	....	....	....	....	....
	Rochester Americans	AHL	71	*47	51	*98	....	....	....	22	12	2	*9	11	16
1966-67	Toronto Maple Leafs	NHL	1	0	0	0	0	0	0	0	....	....	....	....	....
	Rochester Americans	AHL	72	46	37	83	....	....	....	22	13	4	2	6	8
1967-68	Rochester Americans	AHL	67	20	22	42	....	....	....	77	4	0	1	1	8
1968-69	Rochester Americans	AHL	74	30	37	67	....	....	....	37	....	....	....	....	....
1969-70	Rochester Americans	AHL	8	1	4	5	....	....	....	6	....	....	....	....	....
	NHL Totals		195	41	41	82	54	51	105	66	14	1	2	3	4

QMHL First Team All-Star (1951) • AHL Second All-Star Team (1955, 1962, 1965, 1967) • AHL First All-Star Team (1961, 1966) • Won John B. Sollenberger Trophy (Top Scorer - AHL) (1966) • Won Les Cunningham Award (MVP - AHL) (1966) • Played in NHL All-Star Game (1953)

Signed as a free agent by **Montreal**, September 24, 1951. • Montreal loaned Murdo MacKay to Quebec (QMHL) as compensation. Traded to **NY Rangers** by **Montreal** with the rights to Ed Dorohoy for Hy Buller, June 8, 1954. • Transaction cancelled after Buller retired, September, 1954. Traded to **Chicago** by **Montreal** for Bill Shevtz and cash with Montreal holding right of recall, October 9, 1954. Rights returned to **Montreal by Chicago**, November 23, 1954. Traded to **Buffalo** (AHL) by **Montreal** for cash, July, 1957. Traded to **Toronto** by **Buffalo** (AHL) for Dave Creighton, July, 1961. Rights transferred to **Vancouver** (WHL) after WHL club purchased **Rochester** (AHL) franchise, August 13, 1968. • Named as playing coach of **Rochester** (AHL) by **Vancouver** (WHL), August 23, 1968.

• GARDINER, Herb

Herbert Martin **HHOF**
D – L. 5'10", 190 lbs. b: Winnipeg, Man., 5/8/1891 d: 1/11/1972.

Season	Club	League	GP	G	A	Pts	AG	AA	APts	PIM	GP	G	A	Pts	PIM
1908/10	Winnipeg Victorias	WSrHL	STATISTICS NOT AVAILABLE												
1910/14			OUT OF HOCKEY – RETIRED												
1914-15	Calgary Monarchs	AAHL	STATISTICS NOT AVAILABLE												
1915/18			MILITARY SERVICE												
1918-19	Calgary Wanderers	CSrHL	STATISTICS NOT AVAILABLE												
1919-20	Calgary Wanderers	Big-4	12	8	9	17	....	....	....	6	2	0	0	0	2
1920-21	Calgary Wanderers	Big-4	13	3	7	10	....	....	....	6	....	....	....	....	....
1921-22	Calgary Tigers	WCHL	24	4	1	5	....	....	....	6	2	0	0	0	0
1922-23	Calgary Tigers	WCHL	29	9	3	12	....	....	....	9	....	....	....	....	....
1923-24	Calgary Tigers	WCHL	22	5	5	10	....	....	....	4	2	1	0	1	0
	Calgary Tigers	St-Cup	2	2	1	3	....	....	....	0	....	....	....	....	....
1924-25	Calgary Tigers	WCHL	28	12	8	20	....	....	....	18	2	0	0	0	0
1925-26	Calgary Tigers	WHL	27	3	1	4	....	....	....	10	....	....	....	....	....
1926-27	Montreal Canadiens	NHL	44	6	6	12	11	31	42	26	4	0	0	0	10
1927-28	Montreal Canadiens	NHL	44	4	3	7	8	17	25	26	2	0	1	1	4
1928-29	Chicago Black Hawks	NHL	13	0	0	0	0	0	0	0	....	....	....	....	....
	Montreal Canadiens	NHL	7	0	0	0	0	0	0	0	3	0	0	0	2
1929-30	Philadelphia Arrows	Can-Am	1	0	0	0	....	....	....	0	....	....	....	....	....
1930-31	Philadelphia Arrows	Can-Am	DID NOT PLAY – COACHING												
1931-32	Philadelphia Arrows	Can-Am	1	0	0	0	....	....	....	0	....	....	....	....	....
1932-33	Philadelphia Arrows	Can-Am	DID NOT PLAY – COACHING												
1933-34	Philadelphia Arrows	Can-Am	DID NOT PLAY – COACHING												
1934-35	Philadelphia Arrows	Can-Am	12	0	0	0	....	....	....	0	....	....	....	....	....
1935-36	Philadelphia Ramblers	Can-Am	DID NOT PLAY – COACHING												
	NHL Totals		108	10	9	19	19	48	67	52	9	0	1	1	16
	Other Major League Totals		130	33	18	51	....	....	....	47	6	1	0	1	0

WCHL First All-Star Team (1923, 1925) • Won Hart Trophy (1927)

Signed as a free agent by **Calgary** (WCHL), November 4, 1921. Rights traded to **Montreal Canadiens** by **Calgary** (WHL) for cash, October 20, 1926. Loaned to **Chicago** by **Montreal Canadiens** and named playing coach of Black Hawks, August 27, 1928. • Recalled by Montreal Canadiens, February 12, 1929. Traded to **Boston** by **Montreal Canadiens** for cash, May 13, 1929. Traded to **Philadelphia** (Can-Am) by **Boston** for cash, October 4, 1929.

• GARDNER, Cal

Calvin Pearly "Ginger"
C – L. 6'1", 172 lbs. b: Transcona, Man., 10/30/1924.

Season	Club	League	GP	G	A	Pts	AG	AA	APts	PIM	GP	G	A	Pts	PIM
1940-41	St. Boniface Canadiens	WJrHL	STATISTICS NOT AVAILABLE												
1941-42	Winnipeg CUAC	WJrHL	9	6	3	9	....	....	....	11	....	....	....	....	....
1942-43	Winnipeg Esquires	WJrHL	15	18	9	27	....	....	....	37	6	8	5	13	2
	Winnipeg Rangers	M-Cup	10	11	3	14	....	....	....	30	....	....	....	....	....
1943-44	Port Arthur Navy	TBSHL	10	18	*24	42	....	....	....	15	2	5	3	8	4
	Port Arthur Navy	M-Cup	2	5	2	7	....	....	....	4	....	....	....	....	....
1944-45			MILITARY SERVICE												
1945-46	New York Rangers	NHL	16	8	2	10	9	3	12	2	....	....	....	....	....
	New York Rovers	EAHL	40	*41	32	*73	....	....	....	28	....	....	....	....	....

Season	Club	League	Regular Season GP	G	A	Pts	AG	AA	APts	PIM	Playoffs GP	G	A	Pts	PIM
1946-47	**New York Rangers**	**NHL**	**52**	**13**	**16**	**29**	**15**	**19**	**34**	**30**	....	....	....	....	....
1947-48	**New York Rangers**	**NHL**	**58**	**7**	**18**	**25**	**9**	**24**	**33**	**71**	**5**	**0**	**0**	**0**	**0**
♦**1948-49**	**Toronto Maple Leafs**	**NHL**	**53**	**13**	**22**	**35**	**18**	**31**	**49**	**35**	**9**	**2**	**5**	**7**	**0**
1949-50	**Toronto Maple Leafs**	**NHL**	**31**	**7**	**19**	**26**	**9**	**23**	**32**	**12**	**7**	**1**	**0**	**1**	**4**
♦**1950-51**	**Toronto Maple Leafs**	**NHL**	**66**	**23**	**28**	**51**	**29**	**34**	**63**	**42**	**11**	**1**	**1**	**2**	**4**
1951-52	**Toronto Maple Leafs**	**NHL**	**70**	**15**	**26**	**41**	**20**	**32**	**52**	**40**	**3**	**0**	**0**	**0**	**2**
1952-53	**Chicago Black Hawks**	**NHL**	**70**	**11**	**24**	**35**	**14**	**29**	**43**	**60**	**7**	**0**	**2**	**2**	**4**
1953-54	**Boston Bruins**	**NHL**	**70**	**14**	**20**	**34**	**19**	**24**	**43**	**62**	**4**	**1**	**1**	**2**	**0**
1954-55	**Boston Bruins**	**NHL**	**70**	**16**	**22**	**38**	**21**	**25**	**46**	**40**	**5**	**0**	**0**	**0**	**4**
1955-56	**Boston Bruins**	**NHL**	**70**	**15**	**21**	**36**	**20**	**25**	**45**	**57**	....	....	....	....	....
1956-57	**Boston Bruins**	**NHL**	**70**	**12**	**20**	**32**	**15**	**22**	**37**	**66**	**10**	**2**	**1**	**3**	**2**
1957-58	Springfield Indians	AHL	69	24	57	81	....	....	....	49	13	4	*12	16	4
1958-59	Providence Reds	AHL	68	24	39	63	....	....	....	73	....	....	....	....	....
1959-60	Kingston Frontenacs	EPHL	65	32	61	93	....	....	....	57	....	....	....	....	....
1960-61	Cleveland Barons	AHL	72	25	39	64	....	....	....	24	4	1	0	1	0
	NHL Totals		**696**	**154**	**238**	**392**	**198**	**291**	**489**	**517**	**61**	**7**	**10**	**17**	**20**

• Father of Dave and Paul • EAHL First All-Star Team (1946) • Won John Carlin Trophy (Top Scorer - EAHL) (1946) • AHL Second All-Star Team (1958) • Played in NHL All-Star Game (1948, 1949)

Traded to **Toronto** by **NY Rangers** with Bill Juzda, Rene Trudell and the rights to Frank Mathers for Wally Stanowski and Moe Morris, April 26, 1948. • Missed majority of 1949-50 season recovering from broken jaw suffered in game vs. Montreal, November 11, 1949. Traded to **Chicago** by **Toronto** with Ray Hannigan, Al Rollins and Gus Mortson for Harry Lumley, September 11, 1952. Traded to **Boston** by **Chicago** for cash, June 26, 1953. • Named playing coach of **Springfield** (AHL), July 27, 1957.

• GARIEPY, Ray "Rockabye Ray"

D – L. 5'9", 180 lbs. b: Toronto, Ont., 9/4/1928.

Season	Club	League	GP	G	A	Pts	AG	AA	APts	PIM	GP	G	A	Pts	PIM
1945-46	Barrie Flyers	OHA-Jr.	28	3	6	9	....	....	....	79	....	....	....	....	....
1946-47	Barrie Flyers	OHA-Jr.	31	8	16	24	....	....	....	*133	5	3	3	6	6
1947-48	Barrie Flyers	OHA-Jr.	35	7	21	28	....	....	....	72	13	7	9	16	32
	Barrie Flyers	M-Cup	10	0	3	3	....	....	....	31	....	....	....	....	....
1948-49	Buffalo Bisons	AHL	35	2	3	5	....	....	....	41	....	....	....	....	....
	Houston Huskies	USHL	36	3	10	13	....	....	....	45	....	....	....	....	....
1949-50	Buffalo Bisons	AHL	11	0	1	1	....	....	....	10	....	....	....	....	....
	Louisville Blades	USHL	54	3	14	17	....	....	....	87	....	....	....	....	....
1950-51	Hershey Bears	AHL	64	2	8	10	....	....	....	147	5	0	0	0	10
1951-52	Hershey Bears	AHL	57	2	7	9	....	....	....	111	5	1	0	1	2
1952-53	Hershey Bears	AHL	62	4	8	12	....	....	....	90	3	0	0	0	2
1953-54	**Boston Bruins**	**NHL**	**35**	**1**	**6**	**7**	**1**	**7**	**8**	**39**	....	....	....	....	....
	Hershey Bears	AHL	24	2	12	14	....	....	....	42	11	0	4	4	9
1954-55	Pittsburgh Hornets	AHL	56	2	20	22	....	....	....	96	10	0	2	2	8
1955-56	**Toronto Maple Leafs**	**NHL**	**1**	**0**	**0**	**0**	**0**	**0**	**0**	**4**	....	....	....	....	....
	Pittsburgh Hornets	AHL	54	1	13	14	....	....	....	95	4	0	3	3	11
1956-57	Owen Sound Mercury's	OHA-Sr.	26	6	11	17	....	....	....	39	....	....	....	....	....
1957-58	Chatham Maroons	OHA-Sr.	1	0	0	0	....	....	....	6	....	....	....	....	....
1958/66			OUT OF HOCKEY – RETIRED												
1966-67	Collingwood Georgians	OHA-Sr.	37	4	26	30	....	....	....	38	....	....	....	....	....
1967-68	Barrie Flyers	OHA-Sr.	40	1	23	24	....	....	....	45	....	....	....	....	....
1968-69	Barrie Flyers	OHA-Sr.	3	0	1	1	....	....	....	6	....	....	....	....	....
1969-70	Barrie Flyers	OHA-Sr.	DID NOT PLAY – COACHING												
	NHL Totals		**36**	**1**	**6**	**7**	**1**	**7**	**8**	**43**	....	....	....	....	....

Traded to **Hershey** (AHL) by **Buffalo** (AHL) for Rollie McLenahan, October 4, 1950. Signed as a free agent by **Boston**, October 8, 1953. Traded to **Toronto** by **Boston** for John Henderson, September 23, 1954. Traded to **Hershey** (AHL) by **Toronto** with Gil Mayer, Jack Price, Willie Marshall, Bob Hassard and Bob Solinger for cash, July 7, 1956.

• GARRETT, Red Dudley

D – L. 5'11", 190 lbs. b: Toronto, Ont., 7/24/1924 d: 11/25/1944.

Season	Club	League	GP	G	A	Pts	AG	AA	APts	PIM	GP	G	A	Pts	PIM
1940-41	Toronto Shamrocks	OMHA	STATISTICS NOT AVAILABLE												
1941-42	Toronto Marlboros	OHA-Jr.	18	2	5	7	....	....	....	*61	2	1	1	2	6
	Toronto Red Indian Chiefs	TIHL	12	1	4	5	....	....	....	22	....	....	....	....	....
1942-43	**New York Rangers**	**NHL**	**23**	**1**	**1**	**2**	**1**	**1**	**2**	**18**	....	....	....	....	....
	Providence Reds	AHL	6	0	0	0	....	....	....	2	....	....	....	....	....
	Sydney Navy	NSDHL	1	0	0	0	....	....	....	2	....	....	....	....	....
1943-44	Toronto Navy	OHA-Sr.	13	0	1	1	....	....	....	12	....	....	....	....	....
	Cornwallis Navy	NSDHL	4	4	5	9	....	....	....	18	3	1	0	1	15
	NHL Totals		**23**	**1**	**1**	**2**	**1**	**1**	**2**	**18**	....	....	....	....	....

Traded to **NY Rangers** by **Toronto** with Hank Goldup for Babe Pratt, November 27, 1942. • Killed in action during destroyer escort run off the coast of Port-aux-Basques, Newfoundland, November 25, 1944.

• GAUDREAULT, Armand Armand Gerard

LW – L. 5'9", 155 lbs. b: Lac St. Jean, Que., 7/14/1921.

Season	Club	League	GP	G	A	Pts	AG	AA	APts	PIM	GP	G	A	Pts	PIM
1940-41	Quebec Aces	QSHL	33	11	12	23	....	....	....	23	4	0	0	0	2
1941-42	Quebec Aces	QSHL	40	19	25	44	....	....	....	19	7	3	2	5	4
	Quebec Aces	Al-Cup	8	4	5	9	....	....	....	2	....	....	....	....	....
1942-43	Quebec Aces	QSHL	34	16	26	42	....	....	....	4	6	0	2	2	2
1943-44	Quebec Aces	QSHL	25	18	28	46	....	....	....	21	6	4	3	7	4
	Quebec Aces	Al-Cup	9	6	3	9	....	....	....	6	....	....	....	....	....
1944-45	**Boston Bruins**	**NHL**	**44**	**15**	**9**	**24**	**15**	**10**	**25**	**27**	**7**	**0**	**2**	**2**	**8**
1945-46	Hershey Bears	AHL	47	21	24	45	....	....	....	42	3	1	0	1	4
1946-47	Hershey Bears	AHL	61	23	31	54	....	....	....	34	11	3	3	6	10
	Quebec Aces	QSHL	1	0	0	0	....	....	....	0	....	....	....	....	....
1947-48	Hershey–Cleveland	AHL	17	10	11	21	....	....	....	6	2	1	0	1	15
	Sherbrooke Saints	QPHL	10	10	15	25	....	....	....	22	....	....	....	....	....
1948-49	Quebec Aces	QSHL	1	1	1	2	....	....	....	0	1	0	0	0	2
	Alma Eagles	LSJHL	STATISTICS NOT AVAILABLE												
1949-50	Quebec Aces	QSHL	60	31	32	63	....	....	....	48	12	9	6	15	6
1950-51	Quebec Aces	QMHL	56	24	27	51	....	....	....	16	19	7	10	17	9
1951-52	Quebec Aces	QMHL	60	29	28	57	....	....	....	52	6	3	4	7	4
	Quebec Aces	Alx-Cup	9	6	3	9	....	....	....	6	....	....	....	....	....
	NHL Totals		**44**	**15**	**9**	**24**	**15**	**10**	**25**	**27**	**7**	**0**	**2**	**2**	**8**

Signed as a free agent by **Boston**, November 2, 1944.

• GAUDREAULT, Leo Leopold

LW/C – L. 5'10", 152 lbs. b: Chicoutimi, Que., 10/19/1905 d: 1950.

Season	Club	League	GP	G	A	Pts	AG	AA	APts	PIM	GP	G	A	Pts	PIM
1921-22	Chicoutimi Bluets	QPHL	5	1	0	1	....	....	....	....	....	....	....	....	....
1922-23	Chicoutimi Bluets	QPHL	10	2	0	2	....	....	....	2	1	0	0	0	0
1923-24	Quebec Sons of Ireland	ECHA	12	3	0	3	....	....	....	....	9	0	0	0	0
1924-25	Montreal Nationale	MCHL	6	2	0	2	....	....	....	....	....	....	....	....	....
1925-26	Montreal Nationale	MBHL	9	6	2	8	....	....	....	6	....	....	....	....	....
1926-27	St. Francis Xavier	MCHL	12	6	3	9	....	....	....	20	5	1	4	5	2
	Montreal Nationale	MBHL	10	6	4	10	....	....	....	14	1	1	0	1	4
1927-28	**Montreal Canadiens**	**NHL**	**32**	**6**	**2**	**8**	**12**	**11**	**23**	**24**	....	....	....	....	....
1928-29	**Montreal Canadiens**	**NHL**	**11**	**0**	**0**	**0**	**0**	**0**	**0**	**4**	....	....	....	....	....
	Providence Reds	Can-Am	28	2	0	2	....	....	....	45	6	0	0	0	14
1929-30	Providence Reds	Can-Am	39	7	12	19	....	....	....	64	3	1	0	1	0
1930-31	Providence Reds	Can-Am	40	22	20	42	....	....	....	44	2	1	2	3	8
1931-32	Providence Reds	Can-Am	40	13	15	28	....	....	....	22	5	1	0	1	6
1932-33	**Montreal Canadiens**	**NHL**	**24**	**2**	**2**	**4**	**4**	**4**	**8**	**2**	....	....	....	....	....
	Providence Reds	Can-Am	26	12	15	27	....	....	....	26	2	0	1	1	0
1933-34	Providence Reds	Can-Am	40	9	23	32	....	....	....	14	3	1	3	4	2
1934-35	Providence Reds	Can-Am	48	23	26	49	....	....	....	12	4	0	1	1	0
1935-36	Providence Reds	Can-Am	46	7	17	24	....	....	....	8	7	0	0	0	2
1936-37	Minneapolis Millers	AHA	42	8	15	23	....	....	....	20	6	2	5	7	2
	NHL Totals		**67**	**8**	**4**	**12**	**16**	**15**	**31**	**30**	....	....	....	....	....

Signed as a free agent by **Montreal Canadiens**, October 7, 1927. Traded to **Providence** (Can-Am) by **Montreal Canadiens** for Armand Mondou, December 19, 1928. Signed as a free agent by **Montreal Canadiens**, September, 1932. Traded to **Providence** (Can-Am) by **Montreal** with Armand Mondou for Hago Harrington and Leo Murray with Montreal holding right of recall, January, 1933.

• GAUTHIER, Art "Nosey"

C – L. 5'8", 158 lbs. b: Espanola, Ont., 10/10/1904 Deceased.

Season	Club	League	GP	G	A	Pts	AG	AA	APts	PIM	GP	G	A	Pts	PIM
1921-22	Iroquois Falls Eskimos	NOJHA	....	....	....	....	....	....	....	....	7	5	5	10	....
1922-23	Iroquois Falls Eskimos	NOJHA	STATISTICS NOT AVAILABLE												
1923-24	North Bay Trappers	NOHA	6	2	0	2	....	....	....	....	5	9	0	9	....
1924-25	Galt Terriers	OHA-Sr.	20	7	10	17	....	....	....	34	....	....	....	....	....
1925-26	Galt Terriers	OHA-Sr.	20	13	7	20	....	....	....	31	2	2	*2	4	0
1926-27	Galt Terriers	OHA-Sr.	11	6	7	13	....	....	....	23	....	....	....	....	....
	Montreal Canadiens	**NHL**	**13**	**0**	**0**	**0**	**0**	**0**	**0**	**0**	**1**	**0**	**0**	**0**	**0**
1927-28	London Panthers	Can-Pro	23	8	3	11	....	....	....	22	....	....	....	....	....
	Providence Reds	Can-Am	16	2	0	2	....	....	....	6	....	....	....	....	....
1928-29	Toronto Ravinas	Can-Pro	38	10	5	15	....	....	....	24	2	0	1	1	2
1929-30	Hamilton Tigers	IHL	21	2	1	3	....	....	....	6	....	....	....	....	....
	Niagara Falls Cataracts	IHL	19	4	2	6	....	....	....	36	....	....	....	....	....
1930-31	Galt Terriers	OPHL	10	0	0	0	....	....	....	0	....	....	....	....	....
	London Tecumsehs	IHL	1	0	0	0	....	....	....	0	....	....	....	....	....
	Buffalo Bisons	IHL	22	3	0	3	....	....	....	8	6	0	0	0	0
1931-32	Buffalo Bisons	IHL	23	2	1	3	....	....	....	0	....	....	....	....	....
	NHL Totals		**13**	**0**	**0**	**0**	**0**	**0**	**0**	**0**	**1**	**0**	**0**	**0**	**0**

Signed as a free agent by **Montreal Canadiens**, February 9, 1927. Traded to **London** (Can-Pro) by **Montreal Canadiens** (Providence-Can-Am) for cash, January 10, 1928. Traded to **Hamilton** (IHL) by **Toronto** (IHL) for cash, November 4, 1929. Traded to **Niagara Falls** (IHL) by **Hamilton** (IHL) for Wilfred Desy, January 21, 1930. • Named playing-coach of **Galt** (OPHL), December 22, 1930. Signed as a free agent by **London** (IHL), January, 1931. Signed as a free agent by **Buffalo** (IHL) after release by **London** (IHL), January 23, 1931.

• GAUTHIER, Fern Rene Fernand

RW – R. 5'11", 175 lbs. b: Chicoutimi, Que., 8/31/1919 d: 11/7/1992.

Season	Club	League	GP	G	A	Pts	AG	AA	APts	PIM	GP	G	A	Pts	PIM
1938-39	Shawinigan Cataracts	QPHL	30	1	7	8	....	....	....	11	....	....	....	....	....
1939-40	Shawinigan Cataracts	QPHL	38	16	10	26	....	....	....	23	....	....	....	....	....
1940-41	Shawinigan Cataracts	QSHL	31	27	26	53	....	....	....	33	10	6	5	11	2
1941-42	Shawinigan Cataracts	QSHL	32	30	21	51	....	....	....	22	10	7	4	11	6
	Washington Lions	AHL	7	0	0	0	....	....	....	0	....	....	....	....	....
1942-43	Washington Lions	AHL	35	11	6	17	....	....	....	11	....	....	....	....	....
	Buffalo Bisons	AHL	14	1	7	8	....	....	....	11	6	0	0	0	2
1943-44	**New York Rangers**	**NHL**	**33**	**14**	**10**	**24**	**13**	**9**	**22**	**0**	....	....	....	....	....
	Montreal Royals	QSHL	1	0	0	0	....	....	....	0	....	....	....	....	....
1944-45	**Montreal Canadiens**	**NHL**	**50**	**18**	**13**	**31**	**18**	**15**	**33**	**23**	**4**	**0**	**0**	**0**	**0**
1945-46	**Detroit Red Wings**	**NHL**	**30**	**9**	**8**	**17**	**11**	**12**	**23**	**6**	**5**	**3**	**0**	**3**	**2**
	Indianapolis Capitols	AHL	14	4	8	12	....	....	....	0	....	....	....	....	....
1946-47	**Detroit Red Wings**	**NHL**	**40**	**1**	**12**	**13**	**1**	**14**	**15**	**2**	**3**	**1**	**0**	**1**	**0**
	Indianapolis Capitols	AHL	16	7	17	24	....	....	....	6	....	....	....	....	....
1947-48	**Detroit Red Wings**	**NHL**	**35**	**1**	**5**	**6**	**1**	**6**	**7**	**2**	**10**	**1**	**1**	**2**	**5**
	Indianapolis Capitols	AHL	32	16	17	33	....	....	....	4	....	....	....	....	....
1948-49	**Detroit Red Wings**	**NHL**	**41**	**3**	**2**	**5**	**4**	**3**	**7**	**2**	....	....	....	....	....
	Indianapolis Capitols	AHL	11	1	3	4	....	....	....	0	....	....	....	....	....
1949-50	St. Louis Flyers	AHL	41	16	15	31	....	....	....	6	....	....	....	....	....
1950-51	Sherbrooke Saints	QMHL	10	2	5	7	....	....	....	6	....	....	....	....	....
	Quebec Aces	QMHL	25	6	19	25	....	....	....	8	19	4	4	8	4
1951-52	St-Laurent Castors	QPHL	46	33	32	65	....	....	....	....	....	....	....	....	....
	NHL Totals		**229**	**46**	**50**	**96**	**48**	**59**	**107**	**35**	**22**	**5**	**1**	**6**	**7**

Traded to **Montreal** (Buffalo-AHL) by **Washington** (AHL) for cash, February 8, 1943. Loaned to **NY Rangers** by **Montreal** with Dutch Hiller, John Mahaffy, Charlie Sands and future considerations (Tony Demers, December, 1943) for the loan of Phil Watson, October 27, 1943. Traded to **Detroit** by **Montreal** to complete transaction that sent Billy Reay to Montreal (September 11, 1945), October 18, 1945. Traded to **St. Louis** (AHL) by **Detroit** with Cliff Simpson, Ed Nicholson and future considerations for Stephen Black and Bill Brennan, August 29, 1949.

• GAUTHIER, Jean — see page 1104

• GEE, George

C – L. 5'11", 180 lbs. b: Stratford, Ont., 6/28/1922 d: 1/14/1971.

Season	Club	League	GP	G	A	Pts	AG	AA	APts	PIM	GP	G	A	Pts	PIM
1939-40	Owen Sound Greys	OHA-B	11	8	2	10	....	....	....	10	....	....	....	....	....
1940-41	Falconbridge Falcons	GBHL	2	*6	0	6	....	....	....	2	....	....	....	....	....
1941-42	Kansas City Americans	AHA	37	16	15	31	....	....	....	16	6	3	1	4	8
1942-43	Sudbury Frood Tigers	NBHL	9	15	4	19	....	....	....	14	3	4	1	5	2
	Sudbury Frood Tigers	Al-Cup	3	3	1	4	....	....	....	0	....	....	....	....	....

Season	Club	League	GP	G	A	Pts	AG	AA	APts	PIM	GP	G	A	Pts	PIM
			REGULAR SEASON								PLAYOFFS				
1943-44	Toronto Navy	OHA-Sr.	11	2	1	3	....	....	....	0	....	....	....	....	....
	Cornwallis Navy	NSDHL	17	*18	9	27	....	....	....	....	....	....	....	....	....
	Cornwallis Navy	Al-Cup	12	14	10	24	....	....	....	11	....	....	....	....	....
1944-45	Cornwallis Navy	NSDHL	15	9	7	16	....	....	....	6	3	3	1	4	2
1945-46	**Chicago Black Hawks**	**NHL**	**35**	**14**	**15**	**29**	**17**	**22**	**39**	**12**	**4**	**1**	**1**	**2**	**4**
	Kansas City Pla-Mors	USHL	14	13	9	22	....	....	....	15	....	....	....	....	....
1946-47	**Chicago Black Hawks**	**NHL**	**60**	**20**	**20**	**40**	**23**	**24**	**47**	**26**	....	....	....	....	....
1947-48	**Chicago Black Hawks**	**NHL**	**60**	**14**	**25**	**39**	**18**	**33**	**51**	**18**	....	....	....	....	....
1948-49	**Chicago Black Hawks**	**NHL**	**4**	**0**	**2**	**2**	**0**	**3**	**3**	**4**	....	....	....	....	....
	Detroit Red Wings	**NHL**	**47**	**7**	**12**	**19**	**10**	**17**	**27**	**27**	**10**	**1**	**3**	**4**	**22**
♦1949-50	**Detroit Red Wings**	**NHL**	**69**	**17**	**21**	**38**	**21**	**25**	**46**	**42**	**14**	**3**	***6**	**9**	**0**
1950-51	**Detroit Red Wings**	**NHL**	**70**	**17**	**20**	**37**	**22**	**24**	**46**	**19**	**6**	**0**	**1**	**1**	**0**
1951-52	**Chicago Black Hawks**	**NHL**	**70**	**18**	**31**	**49**	**24**	**38**	**62**	**39**	....	....	....	....	....
1952-53	**Chicago Black Hawks**	**NHL**	**67**	**18**	**21**	**39**	**24**	**25**	**49**	**99**	**7**	**1**	**2**	**3**	**6**
1953-54	**Chicago Black Hawks**	**NHL**	**69**	**10**	**16**	**26**	**13**	**19**	**32**	**59**	....	....	....	....	....
1954-55	Windsor Bulldogs	OHA-Sr.	31	25	32	57	....	....	....	36	12	4	11	15	19
1955-56	Windsor Bulldogs	OHA-Sr.	44	24	18	42	....	....	....	36	....	....	....	....	....
1956-57	Windsor Bulldogs	OHA-Sr.	5	0	1	1	....	....	....	4	6	0	4	4	0
	NHL Totals		**551**	**135**	**183**	**318**	**172**	**230**	**402**	**345**	**41**	**6**	**13**	**19**	**32**

Played in NHL All-Star Game (1950)

Signed as a free agent by **Chicago**, November 10, 1941. Traded to **Detroit** by **Chicago** with Bud Poile for Jim Conacher, Bep Guidolin and Doug McCaig, October 25, 1948. Traded to **Chicago** by **Detroit** with Jim McFadden, Max McNab, Jimmy Peters Sr., Clare Martin and Rags Raglan for $75,000 and future considerations (Hugh Coflin, October, 1951), August 20, 1951. • Died while playing for Detroit Old-Timers in game vs. Wyandotte Juniors, January 14, 1971.

• GENDRON, Jean-Guy

— see page 1106

• GEOFFRION, Bernie

— see page 1106

• GERAN, Gerry

Gerald George Pierce "Duke"
C – R. 5'9", 180 lbs. b: Holyoke, MA, 8/3/1896 d: 1968.

Season	Club	League	GP	G	A	Pts	AG	AA	APts	PIM	GP	G	A	Pts	PIM
1915-16	Dartmouth College	Ivy	6	1	0	1	....	....	....	12	....	....	....	....	....
1916-17	Dartmouth College	Ivy	DID NOT PLAY												
1917-18	**Montreal Wanderers**	**NHL**	**4**	**0**	**0**	**0**	**0**	**0**	**0**	**0**	....	....	....	....	....
	Boston Navy	USNHL	11	7	0	7	....	....	....	....	....	....	....	....	....
1918-19			MILITARY SERVICE												
1919-20	Boston Shoe Trades	USAHA	STATISTICS NOT AVAILABLE												
	United States	Olympics	3	4	0	4	....	....	....	....	....	....	....	....	....
1920-21	Boston Shoe Trades	USAHA	6	3	0	3	....	....	....	....	....	....	....	....	....
1921-22	Paris Volants	France	8	*88	0	*88	....	....	....	....	....	....	....	....	....
1922-23	Boston A. A. Unicorn	USAHA	9	14	0	14	....	....	....	....	4	*4	0	*4	....
1923-24	Boston A. A. Unicorn	USAHA	10	9	0	9	....	....	....	....	3	3	1	*4	....
1924-25	Boston A. A. Unicorn	USAHA	19	13	0	13	....	....	....	....	4	0	0	0	0
1925-26	**Boston Bruins**	**NHL**	**33**	**5**	**1**	**6**	**9**	**6**	**15**	**6**	....	....	....	....	....
1926-27	St. Paul Saints	AHA	12	1	1	2	....	....	....	0	....	....	....	....	....
	NHL Totals		**37**	**5**	**1**	**6**	**9**	**6**	**15**	**6**	....	....	....	....	....

Signed as a free agent by **Montreal Wanderers**, December 3, 1917. Signed as a free agent by **Boston**, November 23, 1925. Traded to **St. Paul** (AHA) by **Boston** for cash, November 4, 1926.

• GERARD, Eddie

Edward George **HHOF**
LW/D – L. 5'9", 168 lbs. b: Ottawa, Ont., 2/22/1890 d: 12/7/1937.

Season	Club	League	GP	G	A	Pts	AG	AA	APts	PIM	GP	G	A	Pts	PIM
1907-08	Ottawa Seconds	OCHL	7	8	0	8	....	....	....	....	....	....	....	....	....
1908-09	Ottawa Seconds	OCHL	5	11	0	11	....	....	....	....	2	1	0	1	5
1909-10	Ottawa Seconds	OCHL	9	17	0	17	....	....	....	....	3	1	0	1	*14
1910-11	Ottawa New Edinburghs	OCHL	2	1	0	1	....	....	....	0	....	....	....	....	....
	Ottawa New Edinburghs	IPAHU	6	9	0	9	....	....	....	18	3	6	0	6	*6
1911-12	Ottawa New Edinburghs	IPAHU	10	12	0	12	....	....	....	8	4	8	0	8	*6
1912-13	Ottawa New Edinburghs	IPAHU	8	*16	0	*16	....	....	....	16	6	6	0	6	*6
1913-14	Ottawa Senators	NHA	11	6	7	13	....	....	....	34	....	....	....	....	....
1914-15	Ottawa Senators	NHA	20	9	10	19	....	....	....	39	5	1	0	1	6
	East All-Stars	X-Games	3	1	2	3	....	....	....	*14	....	....	....	....	....
1915-16	Ottawa Senators	NHA	24	13	5	18	....	....	....	57	....	....	....	....	....
1916-17	Ottawa Senators	NHA	19	18	*16	34	....	....	....	48	2	1	2	3	6
1917-18	**Ottawa Senators**	**NHL**	**20**	**13**	**7**	**20**	**16**	**30**	**46**	**26**	....	....	....	....	....
1918-19	**Ottawa Senators**	**NHL**	**18**	**4**	***6**	**10**	**7**	**33**	**40**	**17**	**5**	**3**	**0**	**3**	**3**
1919-20	**Ottawa Senators**	**NHL**	**22**	**9**	**7**	**16**	**10**	**24**	**34**	**19**	....	....	....	....	....
♦	Ottawa Senators	St-Cup	5	2	1	3	....	....	....	3	....	....	....	....	....
1920-21	**Ottawa Senators**	**NHL**	**24**	**11**	**4**	**15**	**14**	**15**	**29**	**18**	**7**	**1**	**0**	**1**	***50**
♦	Ottawa Senators	St-Cup	5	0	0	0	....	....	....	44	....	....	....	....	....
1921-22	**Ottawa Senators**	**NHL**	**21**	**7**	**11**	**18**	**9**	**35**	**44**	**16**	**2**	**0**	**0**	**0**	**8**
♦	Toronto St. Pats	St-Cup	....	....	....	....	....	....	....	....	1	0	0	0	0
1922-23	**Ottawa Senators**	**NHL**	**23**	**6**	**13**	**19**	**10**	**52**	**62**	**12**	**2**	**0**	**0**	**0**	**0**
♦	Ottawa Senators	St-Cup	6	1	0	1	....	....	....	4	....	....	....	....	....
	NHL Totals		**128**	**50**	**48**	**98**	**66**	**189**	**255**	**108**	**16**	**4**	**0**	**4**	**61**
	Other Major League Totals		74	46	38	84	....	....	....	178	7	2	2	4	12

Rights retained by **Ottawa** after NHA folded, November 26, 1917. Loaned to **Toronto** by **Ottawa** as an emergency injury replacement, March 25, 1922. • 1922-23 Stanley Cup totals includes series with Regina (WCHL) and Edmonton (PCHA).

• GETLIFFE, Ray

C/LW – L. 5'11", 175 lbs. b: Galt, Ont., 4/3/1914.

Season	Club	League	GP	G	A	Pts	AG	AA	APts	PIM	GP	G	A	Pts	PIM
1930-31	London Athletic Club	OIHA	9	9	0	9	....	....	....	0	2	0	0	0	4
1931-32	London Diamonds	OHA-B	6	8	4	12	....	....	....	....	....	....	....	....	....
1932-33	Stratford Midgets	OHA-B	6	4	7	11	....	....	....	12	11	6	0	6	20
1933-34	Stratford Midgets	OHA-Jr.	13	26	*17	43	....	....	....	18	2	*6	1	*7	2
1934-35	Charlottetown Abbies	MSHL	20	15	4	19	....	....	....	29	....	....	....	....	....
	Saint John St. Peters	SJCSL	17	*35	25	60	....	....	....	15	12	9	*14	*23	11
	Saint John Beavers	X-Games	2	1	1	2	....	....	....	6	....	....	....	....	....
1935-36	London Tecumsehs	IHL	17	6	3	9	....	....	....	17	....	....	....	....	....
	Boston Bruins	**NHL**	**1**	**0**	**0**	**0**	**0**	**0**	**0**	**2**	**2**	**0**	**0**	**0**	**0**
	Boston Cubs	Can-Am	29	16	14	30	....	....	....	14	....	....	....	....	....
1936-37	**Boston Bruins**	**NHL**	**48**	**16**	**15**	**31**	**27**	**28**	**55**	**28**	**3**	**2**	**1**	**3**	**2**
1937-38	**Boston Bruins**	**NHL**	**36**	**11**	**13**	**24**	**18**	**21**	**39**	**16**	**3**	**0**	**1**	**1**	**2**
♦1938-39	**Boston Bruins**	**NHL**	**43**	**10**	**12**	**22**	**17**	**19**	**36**	**11**	**11**	**1**	**1**	**2**	**2**
	Hershey Bears	IAHL	4	1	4	5	....	....	....	2	....	....	....	....	....
1939-40	**Montreal Canadiens**	**NHL**	**46**	**11**	**12**	**23**	**18**	**19**	**37**	**29**	....	....	....	....	....
1940-41	**Montreal Canadiens**	**NHL**	**39**	**15**	**10**	**25**	**23**	**14**	**37**	**25**	**3**	**1**	**1**	**2**	**0**
1941-42	**Montreal Canadiens**	**NHL**	**45**	**11**	**15**	**26**	**15**	**18**	**33**	**35**	**3**	**0**	**0**	**0**	**0**
1942-43	**Montreal Canadiens**	**NHL**	**50**	**18**	**28**	**46**	**18**	**26**	**44**	**26**	**5**	**0**	**1**	**1**	**8**
♦1943-44	**Montreal Canadiens**	**NHL**	**44**	**28**	**25**	**53**	**26**	**22**	**48**	**44**	**9**	**5**	**4**	**9**	**16**
1944-45	**Montreal Canadiens**	**NHL**	**41**	**16**	**7**	**23**	**16**	**8**	**24**	**34**	**6**	**0**	**1**	**1**	**0**
	NHL Totals		**393**	**136**	**137**	**273**	**178**	**175**	**353**	**250**	**45**	**9**	**10**	**19**	**30**

MSHL Second All-Star Team (1935) • Played in NHL All-Star Game (1939)

Signed as a free agent by **NY Rangers**, November 8, 1935. Loaned to **London** (IHL) for the 1935-36 season for cash, November, 1935. Traded to **Boston** by **NY Rangers** for cash, December 28, 1935. • Walter Jackson loaned to London (IHL) as compensation, December 31, 1935. Traded to **Montreal** by **Boston** with Charlie Sands for Herb Cain, October 10, 1939. Traded to **Detroit** by **Montreal** with Roly Rossignol for Billy Reay, September 11, 1945. Detroit received Fern Gauthier as compensation when Getliffe decided to retire, October 18, 1945.

• GIESEBRECHT, Gus

August Roy
C – L. 6', 177 lbs. b: Pembroke, Ont., 9/14/1917.

Season	Club	League	GP	G	A	Pts	AG	AA	APts	PIM	GP	G	A	Pts	PIM
1933-34	Ottawa St. Malachy's	OCJHL	15	6	11	17	....	....	....	4	....	....	....	....	....
1934-35	Ottawa Senators	OCJHL	5	7	7	14	....	....	....	0	....	....	....	....	....
	Pembroke Lumber Kings	OVJHL	5	7	3	10	....	....	....	....	....	....	....	....	....
	Pembroke Falcons	NOHA	4	4	4	8	....	....	....	....	....	....	....	....	....
1935-36	Pembroke Lumber Kings	OVJHL	8	*12	*12	*24	....	....	....	8	2	3	0	3	2
	Pembroke Lumber Kings	M-Cup	13	25	26	51	....	....	....	2	....	....	....	....	....
1936-37	Pittsburgh Yellowjackets	EAHL	47	12	18	30	....	....	....	11	....	....	....	....	....
1937-38	Detroit Pontiacs	MOHL	28	23	25	48	....	....	....	2	3	2	1	3	0
	Pittsburgh Hornets	IAHL	3	0	0	0	....	....	....	0	2	0	0	0	0
1938-39	**Detroit Red Wings**	**NHL**	**28**	**10**	**10**	**20**	**17**	**16**	**33**	**2**	**6**	**0**	**2**	**2**	**0**
	Pittsburgh Hornets	IAHL	24	6	6	12	....	....	....	4	....	....	....	....	....
1939-40	**Detroit Red Wings**	**NHL**	**30**	**4**	**7**	**11**	**7**	**11**	**18**	**2**	....	....	....	....	....
	Indianapolis Capitols	IAHL	21	10	9	19	....	....	....	0	....	4	1	5	0
1940-41	**Detroit Red Wings**	**NHL**	**43**	**7**	**18**	**25**	**11**	**26**	**37**	**7**	**9**	**2**	**1**	**3**	**0**
1941-42	**Detroit Red Wings**	**NHL**	**34**	**6**	**16**	**22**	**8**	**19**	**27**	**2**	**2**	**0**	**0**	**0**	**0**
	Indianapolis Capitols	AHL	15	6	7	13	....	....	....	4	....	1	3	4	0
1942-43	Kingston Frontenacs	OHA-Sr.	8	5	4	9	....	....	....	4	....	....	....	....	....
	Ottawa Canadians	Al-Cup	18	18	15	33	....	....	....	8	....	....	....	....	....
1943-44	Kingston Army	OHA-Sr.	11	8	20	28	....	....	....	12	....	....	....	....	....
	Truro Bearcats	NSNDL	4	8	6	14	....	....	....	2	....	....	....	....	....
1944-45	Kingston Army	LOVHL	3	2	5	7	....	....	....	0	....	....	....	....	....
1945-46	Pembroke Lumber Kings	UOVHL	17	*35	*14	*49	....	....	....	17	3	9	4	13	0
	Pembroke Lumber Kings	Al-Cup	8	13	9	22	....	....	....	2	....	....	....	....	....
1946-47	Pembroke Lumber Kings	UOVHL	24	*27	38	*65	....	....	....	6	4	*10	4	*14	0
	Ottawa Senators	QSHL	....	....	....	....	....	....	....	....	4	1	0	1	0
1947-48	Pembroke Lumber Kings	UOVHL	16	*21	*22	*43	....	....	....	12	5	2	*8	*10	2
1948-49	Pembroke Lumber Kings	UOVHL	9	8	*9	17	....	....	....	0	4	*10	4	*18	0
	Pembroke Lumber Kings	Al-Cup	9	4	3	7	....	....	....	4	....	....	....	....	....
1949-50	Pembroke Lumber Kings	ECSHL	32	20	23	43	....	....	....	8	4	2	0	2	0
1950-51	Pembroke Lumber Kings	ECSHL	17	11	16	27	....	....	....	2	8	3	3	6	2
1951-52	Pembroke Lumber Kings	ECSHL	44	27	44	71	....	....	....	12	7	0	1	1	0
	Pembroke Lumber Kings	Al-Cup	13	13	8	21	....	....	....	2	....	....	....	....	....
	NHL Totals		**135**	**27**	**51**	**78**	**43**	**72**	**115**	**13**	**17**	**2**	**3**	**5**	**0**

• GILBERT, Jeannot

Jeannot Elmourt "Gil"
C – L. 5'10", 170 lbs. b: Grande Baie, Que., 12/29/1940.

Season	Club	League	GP	G	A	Pts	AG	AA	APts	PIM	GP	G	A	Pts	PIM
1959-60	Barrie Flyers	OHA-Jr.	44	28	36	64	....	....	....	28	6	2	5	7	0
1960-61	Niagara Falls Flyers	OHA-Jr.	48	36	28	64	....	....	....	21	7	2	8	10	0
	Kingston Frontenacs	EPHL	1	0	1	1	....	....	....	0	....	....	....	....	....
1961-62	Clinton Comets	EHL	67	38	51	89	....	....	....	33	6	4	1	5	0
	Kingston Frontenacs	EPHL	5	1	2	3	....	....	....	0	3	2	0	2	0
1962-63	**Boston Bruins**	**NHL**	**5**	**0**	**0**	**0**	**0**	**0**	**0**	**4**	....	....	....	....	....
	Kingston Frontenacs	EPHL	64	34	53	87	....	....	....	25	5	1	6	7	2
1963-64	Minneapolis Bruins	CPHL	72	50	50	100	....	....	....	18	5	4	1	5	2
1964-65	**Boston Bruins**	**NHL**	**4**	**0**	**1**	**1**	**0**	**1**	**1**	**0**	....	....	....	....	....
	Providence Reds	AHL	64	25	30	55	....	....	....	16	....	....	....	....	....
1965-66	Hershey Bears	AHL	69	20	51	71	....	....	....	13	3	0	2	2	0
1966-67	Hershey Bears	AHL	72	26	57	83	....	....	....	48	5	0	2	2	0
1967-68	Hershey Bears	AHL	72	28	47	75	....	....	....	24	5	1	1	2	0
1968-69	Hershey Bears	AHL	71	35	65	100	....	....	....	13	11	3	3	6	10
1969-70	Hershey Bears	AHL	67	23	41	64	....	....	....	8	7	2	6	8	2
1970-71	Hershey Bears	AHL	56	14	28	42	....	....	....	8	4	0	2	2	4
1971-72	Hershey Bears	AHL	74	29	42	71	....	....	....	24	4	0	1	1	0
1972-73	Hershey Bears	AHL	71	31	58	89	....	....	....	8	7	3	8	11	2
1973-74	Quebec Nordiques	WHA	75	17	39	56	....	....	....	20	....	....	....	....	....
1974-75	Quebec Nordiques	WHA	58	7	21	28	....	....	....	12	11	3	6	9	2
	NHL Totals		**9**	**0**	**1**	**1**	**0**	**1**	**1**	**4**	....	....	....	....	....
	Other Major League Totals		133	24	60	84	....	....	....	32	11	3	6	9	2

EHL Rookie of the Year (1962) • Won Tommy Ivan Trophy (MVP - CPHL) (1964) • AHL First All-Star Team (1969) • Won John B. Sollenberger Trophy (Top Scorer - AHL) (1969)

Claimed by **Pittsburgh** from **Boston** in Expansion Draft, June 6, 1967. Traded to **Hershey** (AHL) by **Pittsburgh** for Gene Ubriaco, October, 1967. Signed as a free agent by **Quebec** (WHA), August, 1973.

• GILBERT, Rod

— see page 1109

• GILLIE, Farrand

Farrand Douglas "Bud"
LW/D – R. 5'10", 150 lbs. b: Cornwall, Ont., 5/11/1905 Deceased.

Season	Club	League	GP	G	A	Pts	AG	AA	APts	PIM	GP	G	A	Pts	PIM
1926-27	Cornwall Colts	LOVHL	STATISTICS NOT AVAILABLE												
1927-28	Detroit Olympics	Can-Pro	10	0	0	0	....	....	....	0	....	....	....	....	....
1928-29	**Detroit Cougars**	**NHL**	**1**	**0**	**0**	**0**	**0**	**0**	**0**	**0**	....	....	....	....	....
	Detroit Olympics	Can-Pro	41	5	4	9	....	....	....	31	7	0	0	0	8
1929-30	Detroit Olympics	IHL	42	9	7	16	....	....	....	38	3	0	0	0	0
1930-31	Detroit Olympics	IHL	46	19	6	25	....	....	....	36	....	....	....	....	....
1931-32	Detroit Olympics	IHL	48	16	10	26	....	....	....	31	6	0	0	0	8
1932-33	London Tecumsehs	IHL	44	13	9	22	....	....	....	36	6	3	1	4	6
1933-34	London Tecumsehs	IHL	44	11	5	16	....	....	....	26	6	2	2	4	2
1934-35	Windsor Bulldogs	IHL	43	4	7	11	....	....	....	22	....	....	....	....	....

Season	Club	League	GP	G	A	Pts	AG	AA	APts	PIM	GP	G	A	Pts	PIM
			REGULAR SEASON								PLAYOFFS				
1935-36	Windsor Bulldogs	IHL	11	0	0	0	....	....	....	4	....	....	....	....	....
	Rochester Cardinals	IHL	38	5	9	14	....	....	....	10	....	....	....	....	....
1936-37			REINSTATED AS AN AMATEUR												
1937-38	Cornwall Flyers	QSHL	24	8	9	17	....	....	....	18	6	3	1	4	8
	Cornwall Flyers	Al-Cup	11	4	5	9	....	....	....	22	....	....	....	....	....
1938-39	Brighton Tigers	Ln-Cup	....	2	0	2	....	....	....	....	....	....	....	....	....
	Brighton Tigers	Britain	....	11	6	17	....	....	....	....	....	....	....	....	....
	Brighton Tigers	Nat-Tmt	....	3	4	7	....	....	....	....	....	....	....	....	....
1939-40	Cornwall Flyers	QSHL	28	4	2	6	....	....	....	20	5	2	3	5	7
1940-41	Cornwall Flyers	QSHL	34	7	21	28	....	....	....	8	4	0	2	2	2
1941-42	Cornwall Flyers	QSHL	1	0	0	0	....	....	....	0	....	....	....	....	....
	NHL Totals		**1**	**0**	**0**	**0**	**0**	**0**	**0**	**0**	....	....	....	....	....

Signed as a free agent by **Detroit**, November 1, 1927. Transferred to **London** (IHL) by **Detroit** as compensation for Detroit's signing of free agent Gord Brydson, October 24, 1932. Traded to **Windsor** (IHL) by **London** (IHL) for Ellis Pringle, October 31, 1934. Loaned to **Rochester** (IHL) by **Windsor** (IHL), December 9, 1935.

• GIRARD, Kenny

RW – R. 6', 184 lbs. b: Toronto, Ont., 12/8/1936.

Season	Club	League	GP	G	A	Pts	AG	AA	APts	PIM	GP	G	A	Pts	PIM
1952-53	Toronto Midget Marlboros	OMHA	STATISTICS NOT AVAILABLE												
1953-54	Weston Dukes	OHA-B	STATISTICS NOT AVAILABLE												
1954-55	Toronto Marlboros	OHA-Jr.	47	15	14	29	....	....	....	4	12	8	5	13	17
	Toronto Marlboros	M-Cup	11	3	2	5	....	....	....	0	....	....	....	....	....
1955-56	Toronto Marlboros	OHA-Jr.	41	20	12	32	....	....	....	4	11	7	9	16	0
	Toronto Marlboros	M-Cup	13	9	7	16	....	....	....	8	....	....	....	....	....
1956-57	Toronto Marlboros	OHA-Jr.	35	23	11	34	....	....	....	4	1	0	0	0	0
	Toronto Maple Leafs	**NHL**	**3**	**0**	**1**	**1**	**0**	**1**	**1**	**2**	....	....	....	....	....
1957-58	**Toronto Maple Leafs**	**NHL**	**3**	**0**	**0**	**0**	**0**	**0**	**0**	**0**	....	....	....	....	....
	Rochester Americans	AHL	52	13	10	23	....	....	....	2	....	....	....	....	....
	Shawinigan Cataracts	QHL	9	0	5	5	....	....	....	6	14	2	5	7	2
1958-59			PLAYED PRO GOLF												
1959-60	**Toronto Maple Leafs**	**NHL**	**1**	**0**	**0**	**0**	**0**	**0**	**0**	**0**	....	....	....	....	....
	Sudbury Wolves	EPHL	15	5	2	7	....	....	....	0	9	0	1	1	4
1960-61	Sudbury Wolves	EPHL	65	23	18	41	....	....	....	6	....	....	....	....	....
	Rochester Americans	AHL	9	0	3	3	....	....	....	0	....	....	....	....	....
1961-62	Pittsburgh Hornets	AHL	21	4	2	6	....	....	....	2	....	....	....	....	....
	San Francisco Seals	WHL	31	9	11	20	....	....	....	2	2	0	0	0	0
	NHL Totals		**7**	**0**	**1**	**1**	**0**	**1**	**1**	**2**	....	....	....	....	....

• GIROUX, Art

Arthur Joseph

RW – R. 5'10", 165 lbs. b: Winnipeg, Man., 6/6/1908 d: 6/5/1982.

Season	Club	League	GP	G	A	Pts	AG	AA	APts	PIM	GP	G	A	Pts	PIM
1926-27	Saskatoon Sheiks	PrHL	27	1	0	1	....	....	....	4	2	0	0	0	0
1927-28	Saskatoon Sheiks	PrHL	19	6	1	7	....	....	....	2	....	....	....	....	....
1928-29	LA Richfields	Cal-Pro	....	7	1	8	....	....	....	....	....	....	....	....	....
1929-30	San Francisco Tigers	Cal-Pro	....	*34	10	44	....	....	....	59	....	....	....	....	....
1930-31	Providence Reds	Can-Am	39	16	7	23	....	....	....	41	2	0	0	0	4
1931-32	Providence Reds	Can-Am	36	11	10	21	....	....	....	25	5	3	1	4	2
1932-33	**Montreal Canadiens**	**NHL**	**40**	**5**	**2**	**7**	**9**	**4**	**13**	**14**	**2**	**0**	**0**	**0**	**0**
	Providence Reds	Can-Am	6	5	1	6	....	....	....	4	....	....	....	....	....
1933-34	Providence Reds	Can-Am	40	20	15	35	....	....	....	28	3	*7	1	*8	6
1934-35	**Boston Bruins**	**NHL**	**10**	**1**	**0**	**1**	**2**	**0**	**2**	**0**	....	....	....	....	....
	Boston Cubs	Can-Am	32	20	16	36	....	....	....	19	3	1	0	1	0
1935-36	**Detroit Red Wings**	**NHL**	**4**	**0**	**2**	**2**	**0**	**4**	**4**	**0**	....	....	....	....	....
	Detroit Olympics	IHL	35	17	12	29	....	....	....	28	6	4	4	8	4
1936-37	Pittsburgh Hornets	IAHL	47	21	7	28	....	....	....	30	5	3	0	3	2
1937-38	Providence Reds	IAHL	43	12	10	22	....	....	....	13	7	3	5	8	2
1938-39	Providence Reds	IAHL	51	23	24	47	....	....	....	4	5	1	1	2	0
1939-40	Providence Reds	IAHL	54	17	23	40	....	....	....	21	8	2	2	4	0
1940-41	Providence Reds	AHL	48	20	19	39	....	....	....	12	4	1	1	2	0
1941-42	Cleveland Barons	AHL	54	18	22	40	....	....	....	18	5	1	0	1	2
1942-43	Cleveland Barons	AHL	53	13	11	24	....	....	....	22	2	0	0	0	0
1943-44	Providence Reds	AHL	31	12	10	22	....	....	....	5	....	....	....	....	....
	Pittsburgh Hornets	AHL	11	11	5	16	....	....	....	0	....	....	....	....	....
1944-45	Pittsburgh Hornets	AHL	3	0	2	2	....	....	....	2	....	....	....	....	....
	St. Louis Flyers	AHL	40	18	15	33	....	....	....	6	....	....	....	....	....
	NHL Totals		**54**	**6**	**4**	**10**	**11**	**8**	**19**	**14**	**2**	**0**	**0**	**0**	**0**

IAHL Second All-Star Team (1940)

Traded to **Montreal Canadiens** by **San Francisco** (Cal-Pro) for $5,000, February 13, 1930. Traded to **Boston** by **Montreal Canadiens** for cash, October 18, 1934. Traded to **Detroit** by **Boston** with Marty Barry for Cooney Weiland and Walt Buswell, July 11, 1935.

• GLADU, Jean-Paul

Jean-Paul Joseph

LW – L. 5'11", 180 lbs. b: St. Hyacinthe, Que., 6/20/1921.

Season	Club	League	GP	G	A	Pts	AG	AA	APts	PIM	GP	G	A	Pts	PIM
1939-40	Verdun Jr. Maple Leafs	QJHL	11	5	3	8	....	....	....	4	4	5	0	5	0
	Verdun Maple Leafs	M-Cup	6	3	2	5	....	....	....	6	....	....	....	....	....
1940-41	Shawinigan Cataracts	QSHL	36	27	41	68	....	....	....	42	10	4	3	7	6
1941-42	Shawinigan Cataracts	QSHL	28	13	24	37	....	....	....	37	10	3	10	13	0
1942-43	Quebec Sea Gulls	QCHL	....	....	....	....	....	....	....	....	10	13	20	33	....
1943-44	Quebec Sea Gulls	QCHL	STATISTICS NOT AVAILABLE												
1944-45	**Boston Bruins**	**NHL**	**40**	**6**	**14**	**20**	**6**	**16**	**22**	**2**	**7**	**2**	**2**	**4**	**0**
1945-46	Hershey Bears	AHL	4	0	1	1	....	....	....	4	....	....	....	....	....
	St. Louis Flyers	AHL	40	19	23	42	....	....	....	14	....	....	....	....	....
1946-47	St. Louis Flyers	AHL	62	30	19	49	....	....	....	48	....	....	....	....	....
1947-48	St. Louis Flyers	AHL	67	34	47	81	....	....	....	24	....	....	....	....	....
1948-49	St. Louis Flyers	AHL	67	51	34	85	....	....	....	28	7	3	0	3	0
1949-50	St. Louis Flyers	AHL	38	19	19	38	....	....	....	4	2	0	1	1	0
1950-51	St. Louis Flyers	AHL	66	25	25	50	....	....	....	10	....	....	....	....	....
1951-52	Cleveland Barons	AHL	23	7	12	19	....	....	....	2	....	....	....	....	....
	Providence Reds	AHL	43	24	21	45	....	....	....	28	15	*8	7	15	16
1952-53	Providence Reds	AHL	63	21	25	46	....	....	....	46	....	....	....	....	....
1953-54	Providence Reds	AHL	49	8	20	28	....	....	....	22	....	....	....	....	....
1954-55			DID NOT PLAY												
1955-56	Trois-Rivieres Lions	QHL	5	0	3	3	....	....	....	8	....	....	....	....	....
	NHL Totals		**40**	**6**	**14**	**20**	**6**	**16**	**22**	**2**	**7**	**2**	**2**	**4**	**0**

AHL Second All-Star Team (1948)

Traded to **St. Louis** (AHL) by **Boston** (Hershey-AHL) for cash, December 6, 1945. Traded to **Cleveland** (AHL) by **Chicago** (St. Louis-AHL) for Harry Taylor, August 19, 1951. Traded to **Boston** (Providence-AHL) by **Cleveland** (AHL) with Joe Lund for Buck Davies and Vic Lynn, December 10, 1951. Traded to **Syracuse** (AHL) by **Providence** (AHL), February 5, 1954. Loaned to **Springfield** (QHL) by **Syracuse** (AHL) for cash, February 5, 1954. • Suspended for remainder of 1953-54 season by **Springfield** (AHL) for refusing to report to club, February 7, 1954.

• GLOVER, Fred

Frederick Austin

C – R. 5'9",,170 lbs. b: Toronto, Ont., 1/5/1928.

Season	Club	League	GP	G	A	Pts	AG	AA	APts	PIM	GP	G	A	Pts	PIM
1943-44	Toronto Young Leafs	OMHA	8	16	6	22	....	....	....	8	....	....	....	....	....
1944-45	Toronto Young Leafs	OMHA	11	*22	5	*27	....	....	....	12	....	....	....	....	....
1945-46	Galt Red Wings	OHA-Jr.	20	20	9	29	....	....	....	16	5	1	2	3	4
1946-47	Galt Red Wings	OHA-Jr.	32	34	26	60	....	....	....	67	9	6	2	8	21
1947-48	Omaha Knights	USHL	66	16	39	55	....	....	....	79	3	0	0	0	0
1948-49	Indianapolis Capitols	AHL	68	35	48	83	....	....	....	59	2	0	0	0	2
	Detroit Red Wings	**NHL**	....	....	....	....	....	....	....	....	**2**	**0**	**0**	**0**	**0**
1949-50	**Detroit Red Wings**	**NHL**	**7**	**0**	**0**	**0**	**0**	**0**	**0**	**0**	....	....	....	....	....
	Indianapolis Capitols	AHL	55	22	29	51	....	....	....	65	8	5	4	9	8
1950-51	Indianapolis Capitols	AHL	69	*48	36	84	....	....	....	106	3	0	1	1	8
	Detroit Red Wings	**NHL**	....	....	....	....	....	....	....	....	**6**	**0**	**0**	**0**	**0**
♦1951-52	**Detroit Red Wings**	**NHL**	**54**	**9**	**9**	**18**	**12**	**11**	**23**	**25**	....	....	....	....	....
	Indianapolis Capitols	AHL	10	5	6	11	....	....	....	8	....	....	....	....	....
1952-53	**Chicago Black Hawks**	**NHL**	**31**	**4**	**2**	**6**	**5**	**2**	**7**	**37**	....	....	....	....	....
	St. Louis Flyers	AHL	7	3	3	6	....	....	....	8	....	....	....	....	....
	Cleveland Barons	AHL	29	9	16	25	....	....	....	74	11	2	2	4	*36
1953-54	Cleveland Barons	AHL	55	23	42	65	....	....	....	117	9	*8	6	14	15
1954-55	Cleveland Barons	AHL	58	33	42	75	....	....	....	108	4	4	1	5	8
1955-56	Cleveland Barons	AHL	64	31	48	79	....	....	....	187	8	2	9	11	2
1956-57	Cleveland Barons	AHL	64	42	57	*99	....	....	....	111	12	6	8	*14	34
1957-58	Cleveland Barons	AHL	64	28	48	76	....	....	....	147	7	4	2	6	26
1958-59	Cleveland Barons	AHL	66	22	39	61	....	....	....	136	7	3	2	5	31
1959-60	Cleveland Barons	AHL	72	38	*69	*107	....	....	....	143	7	4	3	7	30
1960-61	Cleveland Barons	AHL	61	23	46	69	....	....	....	138	4	1	2	3	9
1961-62	Cleveland Barons	AHL	70	40	45	85	....	....	....	148	6	2	4	6	14
1962-63	Cleveland Barons	AHL	71	26	54	80	....	....	....	171	6	3	4	7	12
1963-64	Cleveland Barons	AHL	69	26	50	76	....	....	....	155	9	3	4	7	21
1964-65	Cleveland Barons	AHL	72	20	41	61	....	....	....	*208	....	....	....	....	....
1965-66	Cleveland Barons	AHL	47	8	28	36	....	....	....	74	12	0	3	3	41
1966-67	Cleveland Barons	AHL	60	25	35	60	....	....	....	107	5	1	1	2	10
1967-68	Cleveland Barons	AHL	70	13	32	45	....	....	....	132	....	....	....	....	....
	NHL Totals		**92**	**13**	**11**	**24**	**17**	**13**	**30**	**62**	**8**	**0**	**0**	**0**	**0**

• Brother of Howie • AHL First All-Star Team (1951, 1955, 1957, 1960, 1962) • Won John B. Sollenberger Trophy (Top Scorer - AHL) (1957, 1960) • AHL Second All-Star Team (1958, 1964) • Won Les Cunningham Award (MVP - AHL) (1960, 1962, 1964)

Traded to **Chicago** by **Detroit** with Enio Sclisizzi for cash, August 14, 1952. Traded to **Cleveland** (AHL) by **Chicago** to complete transaction that sent Vic Lynn to Chicago (January 4, 1953), January 16, 1953.

• GLOVER, Howie

— see page 1116

• GODFREY, Warren

— see page 1116

• GODIN, Sam

Hogomer Gabriel

RW – R. 5'10", 156 lbs. b: Rockland, Ont., 9/20/1909 Deceased.

Season	Club	League	GP	G	A	Pts	AG	AA	APts	PIM	GP	G	A	Pts	PIM
1926-27	Rockland Hockey Club	OVHL	STATISTICS NOT AVAILABLE												
1927-28	Rockland Hockey Club	OVHL	8	8	2	10	....	....	....	6	....	....	....	....	....
	Ottawa Senators	**NHL**	**24**	**0**	**0**	**0**	**0**	**0**	**0**	**0**	....	....	....	....	....
1928-29	**Ottawa Senators**	**NHL**	**23**	**2**	**1**	**3**	**6**	**7**	**13**	**21**	....	....	....	....	....
	Niagara Falls Cataracts	Can-Pro	18	8	1	9	....	....	....	33	....	....	....	....	....
1929-30	Buffalo Bisons	IHL	39	9	6	15	....	....	....	22	7	0	0	0	8
1930-31	Buffalo Bisons	IHL	26	3	5	8	....	....	....	16	6	0	0	0	2
1931-32	Buffalo Bisons	IHL	47	5	5	10	....	....	....	21	5	0	0	0	2
1932-33	Buffalo Bisons	IHL	42	15	12	27	....	....	....	45	6	*4	0	4	8
1933-34	**Montreal Canadiens**	**NHL**	**36**	**2**	**2**	**4**	**3**	**4**	**7**	**15**	....	....	....	....	....
	Windsor Bulldogs	IHL	9	0	0	0	....	....	....	2	....	....	....	....	....
1934-35	Buffalo Bisons	IHL	17	2	3	5	....	....	....	16	....	....	....	....	....
	London Tecumsehs	IHL	27	11	7	18	....	....	....	24	5	0	2	2	2
1935-36	Buffalo Bisons	IHL	48	19	18	37	....	....	....	14	5	2	1	3	0
1936-37	Buffalo Bisons	IAHL	11	1	2	3	....	....	....	4	....	....	....	....	....
	Vancouver Lions	PCHL	31	8	7	15	....	....	....	14	3	1	2	3	0
1937-38	Springfield Indians	IAHL	3	0	1	1	....	....	....	2	....	....	....	....	....
	Minneapolis Millers	AHA	44	24	17	41	....	....	....	19	7	*5	1	*6	0
1938-39	Minneapolis Millers	AHA	9	2	4	6	....	....	....	4	....	....	....	....	....
	Kansas City Greyhounds	AHA	29	6	12	18	....	....	....	10	....	....	....	....	....
1939-40	Wichita Skyhawks	AHA	15	1	4	5	....	....	....	10	....	....	....	....	....
1940-41	Ottawa Canadians	OCHL	8	1	1	2	....	....	....	2	....	....	....	....	....
	Hamilton Dofascos	OHA-Sr.	13	1	2	3	....	....	....	20	....	....	....	....	....
1941-42	Ottawa Canadians	OCHL	DID NOT PLAY – COACHING												
1942-43	Hamilton Majors	OHA-Sr.	1	0	0	0	....	....	....	0	....	....	....	....	....
	NHL Totals		**83**	**4**	**3**	**7**	**9**	**11**	**20**	**36**	....	....	....	....	....

Signed as a free agent by **Ottawa**, January 24, 1928. Traded to **Buffalo** (IHL) by **Ottawa** for cash, November, 1929. Traded to **Montreal Canadiens** by **Buffalo** (IHL) for cash, October, 1933. Signed as a free agent by **Vancouver** (PCHL) after **Buffalo** (IAHL) folded, December 9, 1936. Loaned to **London** (IHL) by **Montreal Canadiens**, December 30, 1934. Traded to **Springfield** (IAHL) by **Montreal Canadiens** for Hugh Conn, September 30, 1937. Traded to **Minneapolis** (AHA) by **Springfield** (IAHL) for cash, November 7, 1937.

• GOEGAN, Pete

— see page 1117

• GOLDHAM, Bob
Robert John "Golden Boy"
D – L. 6'2", 195 lbs. b: Georgetown, Ont., 5/12/1922 d: 11/6/1991.

			REGULAR SEASON								PLAYOFFS				
Season	Club	League	GP	G	A	Pts	AG	AA	APts	PIM	GP	G	A	Pts	PIM
1938-39	Toronto Ostranders	TMHL	1	0	0	0	....	....	....	0	....	....	....	....	....
1939-40	Northern Vocational	OHA-B	9	8	8	16	....	....	....	12	4	2	2	4	11
	Toronto Ostranders	TMHL	1	0	0	0	....	....	....	5	....	....	....	....	....
	Toronto Marlboros	OHA-Jr.	19	11	11	22	....	....	....	9	8	3	4	7	*30
1940-41	Toronto Marlboros	OHA-Jr.	14	13	9	22	....	....	....	*55	12	11	13	24	*22
1941-42	Washington Lions	AHL	1	0	0	0	....	....	....	0	....	....	....	....	....
	Hershey Bears	AHL	34	7	10	17	....	....	....	44	....	....	....	....	....
♦	**Toronto Maple Leafs**	**NHL**	**19**	**4**	**7**	**11**	**5**	**8**	**13**	**25**	**13**	**2**	**2**	**4**	**31**
1942-43	Toronto Navy	OHA-Sr.	12	1	6	7	....	....	....	29	....	....	....	....	....
	Victoria Navy	BCDHL	....	....	....	....	....	....	....	....	3	0	3	3	2
1943-44	Cornwallis Navy	NSDHL	8	6	*9	15	....	....	....	9	....	....	....	....	....
	Toronto Ostranders	TMHL	1	0	0	0	....	....	....	5	....	....	....	....	....
	Cornwallis Navy	Al-Cup	11	4	7	11	....	....	....	12	....	....	....	....	....
1944-45	Cornwallis Navy	NSSHL	12	2	9	11	....	....	....	4	2	0	1	1	4
1945-46	**Toronto Maple Leafs**	**NHL**	**49**	**7**	**14**	**21**	**8**	**20**	**28**	**44**	....	....	....	....	....
1946-47	**Toronto Maple Leafs**	**NHL**	**11**	**1**	**1**	**2**	**1**	**1**	**2**	**10**	....	....	....	....	....
1947-48	Pittsburgh Hornets	AHL	7	0	5	5	....	....	....	16	....	....	....	....	....
	Chicago Black Hawks	**NHL**	**38**	**2**	**9**	**11**	**3**	**12**	**15**	**38**	....	....	....	....	....
1948-49	**Chicago Black Hawks**	**NHL**	**60**	**1**	**10**	**11**	**1**	**14**	**15**	**43**	....	....	....	....	....
1949-50	**Chicago Black Hawks**	**NHL**	**67**	**2**	**10**	**12**	**2**	**12**	**14**	**57**	....	....	....	....	....
1950-51	**Detroit Red Wings**	**NHL**	**61**	**5**	**18**	**23**	**6**	**22**	**28**	**31**	**6**	**0**	**1**	**1**	**2**
♦1951-52	**Detroit Red Wings**	**NHL**	**69**	**0**	**14**	**14**	**0**	**17**	**17**	**24**	**8**	**0**	**1**	**1**	**8**
1952-53	**Detroit Red Wings**	**NHL**	**70**	**1**	**13**	**14**	**1**	**16**	**17**	**32**	**6**	**1**	**1**	**2**	**2**
♦1953-54	**Detroit Red Wings**	**NHL**	**69**	**1**	**15**	**16**	**1**	**18**	**19**	**50**	**12**	**0**	**2**	**2**	**2**
♦1954-55	**Detroit Red Wings**	**NHL**	**69**	**1**	**16**	**17**	**1**	**18**	**19**	**14**	**11**	**0**	**4**	**4**	**4**
1955-56	**Detroit Red Wings**	**NHL**	**68**	**3**	**16**	**19**	**4**	**19**	**23**	**32**	**10**	**0**	**3**	**3**	**4**
	NHL Totals		**650**	**28**	**143**	**171**	**33**	**177**	**210**	**400**	**66**	**3**	**14**	**17**	**53**

AHL Second All-Star Team (1942) • NHL Second All-Star Team (1955) • Played in NHL All-Star Game (1947, 1949, 1950, 1952, 1954, 1955)

Transferred to **Victoria Navy** (BCDHL) from **Toronto Navy** (OHA-Sr.), February 1, 1943. • Missed remainder of 1946-47 season recovering from arm injury suffered in game vs. Boston, December 4, 1946. Traded to **Chicago** by **Toronto** with Gus Bodnar, Bud Poile, Gaye Stewart and Ernie Dickens for Max Bentley and Cy Thomas, November 2, 1947. Traded to **Detroit** by **Chicago** with Jim Henry, Gaye Stewart and Metro Prystai for Al Dewsbury, Harry Lumley, Jack Stewart, Don Morrison and Pete Babando, July 13, 1950.

• GOLDSWORTHY, Bill
— *see page 1118*

• GOLDSWORTHY, Leroy
Leroy Delano
RW – R. 6', 165 lbs. b: Two Harbors, MN, 10/18/1906 d: 3/16/1980.

			REGULAR SEASON								PLAYOFFS				
Season	Club	League	GP	G	A	Pts	AG	AA	APts	PIM	GP	G	A	Pts	PIM
1924-25	Edmonton Victorias	EJrHL	1	0	0	0	....	....	....	0	3	0	0	0	2
1925-26	Edmonton Eskimos	WHL	11	0	0	0	....	....	....	0	....	....	....	....	....
1926-27	Springfield Indians	Can-Am	31	2	1	3	....	....	....	4	6	1	0	1	8
1927-28	Springfield Indians	Can-Am	38	8	5	13	....	....	....	32	4	2	0	2	2
1928-29	Springfield Indians	Can-Am	39	9	7	16	....	....	....	40	....	....	....	....	....
	New York Rangers	**NHL**	....	....	....	....	....	....	....	....	**1**	**0**	**0**	**0**	**0**
1929-30	**New York Rangers**	**NHL**	**44**	**4**	**1**	**5**	**6**	**2**	**8**	**16**	**4**	**0**	**0**	**0**	**2**
1930-31	London Tecumsehs	IHL	25	9	5	14	....	....	....	27	....	....	....	....	....
	Detroit Falcons	**NHL**	**12**	**1**	**0**	**1**	**2**	**0**	**2**	**2**	....	....	....	....	....
	Detroit Olympics	IHL	9	4	0	4	....	....	....	4	....	....	....	....	....
1931-32	Detroit Olympics	IHL	47	16	9	25	....	....	....	16	6	2	0	2	2
1932-33	**Detroit Red Wings**	**NHL**	**25**	**3**	**6**	**9**	**5**	**12**	**17**	**6**	**2**	**0**	**0**	**0**	**0**
	Detroit Olympics	IHL	17	12	2	14	....	....	....	22	....	....	....	....	....
♦1933-34	**Chicago Black Hawks**	**NHL**	**27**	**3**	**3**	**6**	**5**	**6**	**11**	**0**	**7**	**0**	**0**	**0**	**0**
	London Tecumsehs	IHL	18	11	4	15	....	....	....	10	....	....	....	....	....
1934-35	**Chicago Black Hawks**	**NHL**	**7**	**0**	**0**	**0**	**0**	**0**	**0**	**2**	....	....	....	....	....
	Montreal Canadiens	**NHL**	**33**	**20**	**9**	**29**	**33**	**16**	**49**	**13**	**2**	**1**	**0**	**1**	**0**
	London Tecumsehs	IHL	7	4	1	5	....	....	....	6	....	....	....	....	....
1935-36	**Montreal Canadiens**	**NHL**	**47**	**15**	**11**	**26**	**29**	**21**	**50**	**8**	....	....	....	....	....
1936-37	**Boston Bruins**	**NHL**	**47**	**8**	**6**	**14**	**13**	**11**	**24**	**8**	**3**	**0**	**0**	**0**	**0**
1937-38	**Boston Bruins**	**NHL**	**46**	**9**	**10**	**19**	**15**	**16**	**31**	**14**	**3**	**0**	**0**	**0**	**2**
1938-39	**New York Americans**	**NHL**	**48**	**3**	**11**	**14**	**5**	**17**	**22**	**10**	**2**	**0**	**0**	**0**	**0**
1939-40	Cleveland Barons	IAHL	56	9	22	31	....	....	....	10	....	....	....	....	....
1940-41	Buffalo Bisons	AHL	56	6	18	24	....	....	....	8	....	....	....	....	....
1941-42	Dallas Texans	AHA	50	15	24	39	....	....	....	31	....	....	....	....	....
1942-43			MILITARY SERVICE												
1943-44	Edmonton Vics	X-Games	STATISTICS NOT AVAILABLE												
	Edmonton Vics	Al-Cup	4	0	0	0	....	....	....	0	....	....	....	....	....
1944-45			MILITARY SERVICE												
1945-46	Dallas Texans	USHL	1	0	0	0	....	....	....	0	....	....	....	....	....
	NHL Totals		**336**	**66**	**57**	**123**	**113**	**101**	**214**	**79**	**24**	**1**	**0**	**1**	**4**
	Other Major League Totals		11	0	0	0				0					

Signed as a free agent by **Edmonton** (WHL), December 2, 1925. Traded to **NY Rangers** by **Edmonton** (WHL) for cash, October 19, 1926. Traded to **London** (IHL) by **NY Rangers** for cash, October 29, 1930. Traded to **Detroit** by **London** (IHL) for Harold Hicks, January 12, 1931. Traded to **Chicago** (London-IAHL) by **Detroit** with Frank Waite for Gene Carrigan, October 19, 1933. Traded to **London** (IHL) by **Chicago** for cash, November 22, 1933. Traded to **Chicago** by **London** (IHL) for $3,000 and the loan of Bill Kendall, January 4, 1934. Traded to **Montreal Canadiens** by **Chicago** with Roger Jenkins and Lionel Conacher for Howie Morenz, Marty Burke and Lorne Chabot, October 3, 1934. Traded to **Chicago** by **Montreal Canadiens** for cash, October 17, 1934. Traded to **Montreal Canadiens** by **Chicago** for cash, December 18, 1934. Traded to **Boston** by **Montreal Canadiens** with Sammy McManus and $10,000 for Babe Siebert and Roger Jenkins, September 10, 1936. Traded to **NY Americans** by **Boston** with the loan of Art Jackson for 1938-39 season for cash, October 24, 1938. Traded to **Cleveland** (IAHL) by **NY Americans** for cash, October 12, 1939.

• GOLDUP, Hank
Henry George
LW – L. 5'11", 175 lbs. b: Kingston, Ont., 10/29/1918.

			REGULAR SEASON								PLAYOFFS				
Season	Club	League	GP	G	A	Pts	AG	AA	APts	PIM	GP	G	A	Pts	PIM
1935-36	Kingston Dunlop Forts	KCHL	16	*29	14	43	....	....	....	....	....	....	....	....	....
1936-37	Northern Vocational	OHA-B	STATISTICS NOT AVAILABLE												
1937-38	Toronto Marlboros	OHA-Jr.	14	*25	*16	*41	....	....	....	12	6	6	4	10	4
1938-39	Toronto Goodyears	OHA-Sr.	16	18	11	29	....	....	....	18	3	1	0	1	0
	Toronto Goodyears	Al-Cup	10	5	9	14	....	....	....	12	....	....	....	....	....
1939-40	**Toronto Maple Leafs**	**NHL**	**21**	**6**	**4**	**10**	**10**	**6**	**16**	**2**	**10**	***5**	**1**	**6**	**4**
	Pittsburgh Hornets	IAHL	17	12	12	24	....	....	....	4	....	....	....	....	....
1940-41	**Toronto Maple Leafs**	**NHL**	**26**	**10**	**5**	**15**	**15**	**7**	**22**	**9**	**7**	**0**	**0**	**0**	**0**
♦1941-42	**Toronto Maple Leafs**	**NHL**	**44**	**12**	**18**	**30**	**16**	**21**	**37**	**13**	**9**	**0**	**0**	**0**	**2**
1942-43	**Toronto Maple Leafs**	**NHL**	**8**	**1**	**7**	**8**	**1**	**6**	**7**	**4**	....	....	....	....	....
	New York Rangers	**NHL**	**36**	**11**	**20**	**31**	**11**	**19**	**30**	**33**	....	....	....	....	....
1943-44	Toronto Army Daggers	OHA-Sr.	1	1	0	1	....	....	....	7	....	....	....	....	....
	Toronto Army Shamrocks	TIHL	13	7	9	16	....	....	....	36	4	6	4	10	6
1944-45	**New York Rangers**	**NHL**	**48**	**17**	**25**	**42**	**17**	**29**	**46**	**25**	....	....	....	....	....
1945-46	**New York Rangers**	**NHL**	**19**	**6**	**1**	**7**	**7**	**1**	**8**	**11**	....	....	....	....	....
	New Haven Eagles	AHL	25	13	11	24	....	....	....	7	....	....	....	....	....
1946-47	Cleveland Barons	AHL	61	30	19	49	....	....	....	22	4	0	1	1	0
1947-48			DID NOT PLAY												
1948-49	Washington Lions	AHL	7	0	0	0	....	....	....	2	....	....	....	....	....
	Shawinigan Cataracts	QSHL	3	0	3	3	....	....	....	0	....	....	....	....	....
	Fenelon Falls Generals	OIHA	DID NOT PLAY – COACHING												
	NHL Totals		**202**	**63**	**80**	**143**	**77**	**89**	**166**	**97**	**26**	**5**	**1**	**6**	**6**

• Father of Glenn

Traded to **NY Rangers** by **Toronto** with Red Garrett for Babe Pratt, November 27, 1942. Traded to **Detroit** by **NY Rangers** with Ab DeMarco for Flash Hollett, June 19, 1946. Transaction voided when Hollett decided to retire, June, 1946. Traded to **Cleveland** (AHL) by **NY Rangers** for cash, October 4, 1946.

• GOODEN, Bill
William Francis Charles
LW – L. 5'9", 175 lbs. b: Winnipeg, Man., 9/8/1923 d: 12/17/1998.

			REGULAR SEASON								PLAYOFFS				
Season	Club	League	GP	G	A	Pts	AG	AA	APts	PIM	GP	G	A	Pts	PIM
1940-41	Winnipeg Maroons	MJHL	7	8	2	10	....	....	....	6	3	4	0	4	2
1941-42	Portage Terriers	MJHL	18	15	22	37	....	....	....	25	5	7	4	11	15
	Portage Terriers	M-Cup	10	15	12	27	....	....	....	16	....	....	....	....	....
1942-43	**New York Rangers**	**NHL**	**12**	**0**	**3**	**3**	**0**	**3**	**3**	**0**	....	....	....	....	....
	Niagara Falls Cataracts	OHA-Sr.	22	11	12	23	....	....	....	21	2	0	0	0	4
1943-44	**New York Rangers**	**NHL**	**41**	**9**	**8**	**17**	**8**	**7**	**15**	**15**	....	....	....	....	....
1944-45	Hershey Bears	AHL	59	27	41	68	....	....	....	12	11	4	5	9	11
1945-46	Hershey Bears	AHL	37	13	9	22	....	....	....	18	....	....	....	....	....
	New Haven Eagles	AHL	19	6	7	13	....	....	....	6	....	....	....	....	....
1946-47	Springfield Indians	AHL	62	17	22	39	....	....	....	40	2	0	0	0	5
1947-48	Springfield Indians	AHL	68	32	36	68	....	....	....	14	....	....	....	....	....
1948-49	Fort Worth Rangers	USHL	5	4	0	4	....	....	....	2	....	....	....	....	....
	Springfield Indians	AHL	60	34	32	66	....	....	....	24	3	3	1	4	2
1949-50	Springfield Indians	AHL	67	29	37	66	....	....	....	23	2	1	0	1	0
1950-51	Springfield Indians	AHL	63	32	37	69	....	....	....	28	1	0	1	1	0
1951-52	Syracuse Warriors	AHL	65	21	25	46	....	....	....	33	....	....	....	....	....
1952-53	Syracuse Warriors	AHL	60	21	28	49	....	....	....	21	4	0	0	0	2
1953-54	Syracuse Warriors	AHL	41	15	20	35	....	....	....	6	....	....	....	....	....
1954-55	Vancouver Canucks	WHL	15	0	4	4	....	....	....	0	....	....	....	....	....
	Providence Reds	AHL	20	3	8	11	....	....	....	6	....	....	....	....	....
1955-56	Trois-Rivieres Lions	QHL	38	13	17	30	....	....	....	8	....	....	....	....	....
	Providence Reds	AHL	6	1	0	1	....	....	....	2	....	....	....	....	....
1956-57	Clinton Comets	EHL	25	7	10	17	....	....	....	4	....	....	....	....	....
	NHL Totals		**53**	**9**	**11**	**20**	**8**	**10**	**18**	**15**	....	....	....	....	....

AHL Second All-Star Team (1951)

Signed as a free agent by **NY Rangers**, October 30, 1942. Traded to **New Haven** (AHL) by **Hershey** (AHL) for Norm Larson, January 28, 1946. Loaned to **Springfield** (QHL) by **Syracuse** (AHL) for cash (February 11, 1954) but refused to report and was suspended by Springfield for remainder of 1953-54 season, February 13, 1954. Traded to **Vancouver** (WHL) by **Springfield** (AHL) for Dale Sweany and cash, December 2, 1954. Traded to **Providence** (AHL) by **Vancouver** (WHL) for cash, February 3, 1955.

• GOODFELLOW, Ebbie
Ebenezer Ralston **HHOF**
C/D – L. 6', 175 lbs. b: Ottawa, Ont., 4/9/1907 d: 9/10/1965.

			REGULAR SEASON								PLAYOFFS				
Season	Club	League	GP	G	A	Pts	AG	AA	APts	PIM	GP	G	A	Pts	PIM
1926-27	Ottawa Montagnards	OCHL	4	3	1	4	....	....	....	....	2	0	0	0	0
1927-28	Ottawa Montagnards	OCHL	15	7	2	9	....	....	....	....	6	*4	1	*5	....
1928-29	Detroit Olympics	Can-Pro	42	*26	8	*34	....	....	....	45	7	3	2	5	8
1929-30	**Detroit Cougars**	**NHL**	**44**	**17**	**17**	**34**	**24**	**40**	**64**	**54**	....	....	....	....	....
1930-31	**Detroit Falcons**	**NHL**	**44**	**25**	**23**	**48**	**51**	**71**	**122**	**32**	....	....	....	....	....
1931-32	**Detroit Falcons**	**NHL**	**48**	**14**	**16**	**30**	**23**	**35**	**58**	**56**	**2**	**0**	**0**	**0**	**0**
1932-33	**Detroit Red Wings**	**NHL**	**41**	**12**	**8**	**20**	**22**	**17**	**39**	**47**	**4**	**1**	**0**	**1**	**11**
1933-34	**Detroit Red Wings**	**NHL**	**48**	**13**	**13**	**26**	**22**	**27**	**49**	**45**	**9**	**4**	**3**	**7**	**12**
1934-35	**Detroit Red Wings**	**NHL**	**48**	**12**	**24**	**36**	**20**	**42**	**62**	**44**	....	....	....	....	....
♦1935-36	**Detroit Red Wings**	**NHL**	**48**	**5**	**18**	**23**	**10**	**34**	**44**	**69**	**7**	**1**	**0**	**1**	**4**
♦1936-37	**Detroit Red Wings**	**NHL**	**48**	**9**	**16**	**25**	**15**	**29**	**44**	**43**	**9**	**2**	**2**	**4**	**12**
1937-38	**Detroit Red Wings**	**NHL**	**30**	**0**	**7**	**7**	**0**	**11**	**11**	**13**	....	....	....	....	....
1938-39	**Detroit Red Wings**	**NHL**	**48**	**8**	**8**	**16**	**14**	**12**	**26**	**36**	**6**	**0**	**0**	**0**	**8**
1939-40	**Detroit Red Wings**	**NHL**	**43**	**11**	**17**	**28**	**18**	**27**	**45**	**31**	**5**	**0**	**2**	**2**	**9**
1940-41	**Detroit Red Wings**	**NHL**	**47**	**5**	**17**	**22**	**8**	**24**	**32**	**35**	**3**	**0**	**1**	**1**	**9**
1941-42	**Detroit Red Wings**	**NHL**	**9**	**2**	**2**	**4**	**3**	**2**	**5**	**2**	....	....	....	....	....
♦1942-43	**Detroit Red Wings**	**NHL**	**11**	**1**	**4**	**5**	**1**	**4**	**5**	**4**	....	....	....	....	....
	NHL Totals		**557**	**134**	**190**	**324**	**231**	**375**	**606**	**511**	**45**	**8**	**8**	**16**	**65**

NHL Second All-Star Team (1936) • NHL First All-Star Team (1937, 1940) • Won Hart Trophy (1940) • Played in NHL All-Star Game (1937, 1939)

Signed as a free agent by **Saskatoon** (WCHL), December 25, 1924. • Suspended by Saskatoon (PrHL) for refusing to report to team, December 22, 1926. • Barred from playing in the NHL after it was determined he had a valid contract with Saskatoon (PrHL), January 17, 1927. Traded to **Detroit** by **Saskatoon** (PrHL) for $4,000, February 2, 1927. • Missed majority of the 1941-42 and 1942-43 seasons recovering from knee surgery, December 1, 1941.

• GORDON, Fred
Frederick Kenneth
RW – R. 5'10", 185 lbs. b: Fleming, Sask., 5/6/1900.

			REGULAR SEASON								PLAYOFFS				
Season	Club	League	GP	G	A	Pts	AG	AA	APts	PIM	GP	G	A	Pts	PIM
1921-22	Indian Head Tigers	S-SSHL	8	*10	0	10	....	....	....	8	1	*2	0	2	0
1922-23	Indian Head Tigers	S-SSHL	STATISTICS NOT AVAILABLE												
1923-24	Brandon Regals	S-SSHL	12	4	5	9	....	....	....	5	2	0	0	0	2
1924-25	Saskatoon Crescents	WCHL	19	2	2	4	....	....	....	11	2	1	0	1	2
1925-26	Saskatoon Crescents	WHL	30	9	2	11	....	....	....	36	2	0	0	0	2
1926-27	**Detroit Cougars**	**NHL**	**38**	**5**	**5**	**10**	**9**	**26**	**35**	**28**	....	....	....	....	....
1927-28	**Boston Bruins**	**NHL**	**43**	**3**	**2**	**5**	**6**	**11**	**17**	**40**	**2**	**0**	**0**	**0**	**0**
1928-29	Minneapolis Millers	AHA	39	4	3	7	....	....	....	47	4	0	0	0	8
1929-30	Minneapolis Millers	AHA	40	4	7	11	....	....	....	102	....	....	....	....	....
1930-31	Minneapolis Millers	AHA	43	10	9	19	....	....	....	81	....	....	....	....	....
1931-32	Buffalo Majors	AHA	17	5	0	5	....	....	....	26	....	....	....	....	....
1932-33	Saskatoon Crescents	WCHL	3	0	0	0	....	....	....	0	....	....	....	....	....
1933-34	Kansas City Greyhounds	AHA	47	12	10	22	....	....	....	52	3	0	0	0	4

Season	Club	League	GP	G	A	Pts	AG	AA	APts	PIM	GP	G	A	Pts	PIM
1934-35	Kansas City Greyhounds	AHA	21	1	2	3	....	....	....	16	....	....	....	....	....
1935-36			DID NOT PLAY – REFEREE												
1936-37	Tulsa Oilers	AHA	DID NOT PLAY – COACHING												
	NHL Totals		**81**	**8**	**7**	**15**	**15**	**37**	**52**	**68**	**2**	**0**	**0**	**0**	**0**
	Other Major League Totals		49	11	4	15	....	....	....	47	4	1	0	1	4

Traded to **Detroit Cougars** by **Saskatoon** (WHL) for cash, October 27, 1926. Traded to **Boston** by **Detroit Cougars** for Harry Meeking, May 22, 1927. Signed as a free agent by **Saskatoon**, November 8, 1932.

• GORDON, Jackie John

C – R. 5'9", 154 lbs. b: Winnipeg, Man., 3/3/1928.

Season	Club	League	GP	G	A	Pts	AG	AA	APts	PIM	GP	G	A	Pts	PIM
1945-46	Winnipeg Rangers	MAHA	STATISTICS NOT AVAILABLE												
1946-47	New York Rovers	EAHL	54	37	40	77	....	....	....	6	7	4	5	9	0
1947-48	New Haven Ramblers	AHL	37	11	24	35	....	....	....	2	4	0	3	3	0
1948-49	**New York Rangers**	**NHL**	**31**	**3**	**9**	**12**	**4**	**13**	**17**	**0**	....	....	....	....	....
	New Haven Ramblers	AHL	36	10	28	38	....	....	....	14	....	....	....	....	....
1949-50	**New York Rangers**	**NHL**	**1**	**0**	**0**	**0**	**0**	**0**	**0**	**0**	**9**	**1**	**1**	**2**	**7**
	New Haven Ramblers	AHL	70	23	60	83	....	....	....	2	....	....	....	....	....
1950-51	**New York Rangers**	**NHL**	**4**	**0**	**1**	**1**	**0**	**1**	**1**	**0**	....	....	....	....	....
	Cincinnati Mohawks	AHL	59	23	42	65	....	....	....	10	....	....	....	....	....
1951-52	Cleveland Barons	AHL	20	7	20	27	....	....	....	0	2	0	2	2	0
1952-53	Cleveland Barons	AHL	64	20	58	78	....	....	....	6	11	4	7	*11	0
1953-54	Cleveland Barons	AHL	70	31	71	102	....	....	....	20	9	5	*13	*18	4
1954-55	Cleveland Barons	AHL	57	17	50	67	....	....	....	22	4	1	3	4	0
1955-56	Cleveland Barons	AHL	54	26	43	69	....	....	....	33	6	5	4	9	2
1956-57	Cleveland Barons	AHL	33	4	14	18	....	....	....	0	12	2	2	4	2
1957-58	Cleveland Barons	AHL	51	6	18	24	....	....	....	10	6	1	2	3	2
1958-59	Cleveland Barons	AHL	38	3	5	8	....	....	....	0	....	....	....	....	....
1959-60	Cleveland Barons	AHL	8	0	1	1	....	....	....	0	....	....	....	....	....
1960-61	Cleveland Barons	AHL	5	0	0	0	....	....	....	0	....	....	....	....	....
1961-62	Cleveland Barons	AHL	DID NOT PLAY – COACHING												
	NHL Totals		**36**	**3**	**10**	**13**	**4**	**14**	**18**	**0**	**9**	**1**	**1**	**2**	**7**

EAHL Second All-Star Team (1947)

Traded to **Cleveland** (AHL) by **NY Rangers** with Ed Reigle, Fred Shero, Fern Perreault and cash for Wally Hergesheimer and Hy Buller, May 14, 1951.

• GORMAN, Ed Edward Frederick

D – L. 6', 180 lbs. b: Buckingham, Quebec, 9/25/1892 d: 3/10/1963.

Season	Club	League	GP	G	A	Pts	AG	AA	APts	PIM	GP	G	A	Pts	PIM
1913-14	Buckingham Seniors	MCHL	4	1	0	1	....	....	....	....	1	1	0	1	....
1914-15	Buckingham Seniors	MCHL	8	3	0	3	....	....	....	....	4	1	0	1	....
1915-16	Pittsburgh Duquesne	USAHA	STATISTICS NOT AVAILABLE												
1916-17	Pittsburgh AA	USAHA	39	13	0	13	....	....	....		....	....	....	....	....
1917-18	Pembroke Munitions	OVHL	STATISTICS NOT AVAILABLE												
1918-19	Ottawa Royal Canadians	OCHL	8	1	3	4	....	....	....	13	....	....	....	....	....
1919-20	Ottawa Munitions	OCHL	7	1	0	1	....	....	....	19	5	3	5	8	....
1920-21	Ottawa St. Brigid's	OCHL	11	6	0	6	....	....	....	....	6	2	1	3	*15
1921-22	Ottawa Montagnards	OCHL	14	13	*9	*22	....	....	....	42	8	8	5	13	*15
1922-23	Ottawa Montagnards	OCHL	9	4	3	7	....	....	....	20	2	1	0	1	4
1923-24	Ottawa Montagnards	OCHL	12	4	0	4	....	....	....	....	2	*2	0	*2	....
	Ottawa Montagnards	Al-Cup	4	4	1	5	....	....	....	....	....	....	....	....	....
1924-25	**Ottawa Senators**	**NHL**	**28**	**11**	**4**	**15**	**19**	**16**	**35**	**49**	....	....	....	....	....
1925-26	**Ottawa Senators**	**NHL**	**23**	**2**	**1**	**3**	**3**	**6**	**9**	**12**	**2**	**0**	**0**	**0**	**2**
♦1926-27	**Ottawa Senators**	**NHL**	**41**	**1**	**0**	**1**	**2**	**0**	**2**	**17**	**6**	**0**	**0**	**0**	**0**
1927-28	**Toronto Maple Leafs**	**NHL**	**19**	**0**	**1**	**1**	**0**	**6**	**6**	**30**	....	....	....	....	....
	Kitchener Millionaires	Can-Pro	12	4	1	5	....	....	....	20	5	0	0	0	14
	NHL Totals		**111**	**14**	**6**	**20**	**24**	**28**	**52**	**108**	**8**	**0**	**0**	**0**	**2**

Signed as a free agent by **Ottawa**, November 6, 1924. Traded to **Toronto** by **Ottawa** for cash, October 26, 1927. • Suspended by Toronto for refusing assignment to Toronto Ravinas (Can-Pro), February 10, 1928. Traded to **Kitchener** (Can-Pro) by **Toronto** for cash, February 13, 1928.

• GOTTSELIG, Johnny

LW – L. 5'11", 158 lbs. b: Odessa, Russia, 6/24/1905 d: 5/15/1986.

Season	Club	League	GP	G	A	Pts	AG	AA	APts	PIM	GP	G	A	Pts	PIM
1923-24	Regina Pats	S-SJHL	6	6	0	6	....	....	....	6	....	....	....	....	....
	Regina Pats	M-Cup	5	8	1	9	....	....	....	8	....	....	....	....	....
1924-25	Regina Pats	S-SJHL	5	*18	2	*20	....	....	....	0	....	....	....	....	....
	Regina Victorias	S-SSHL	1	1	0	1	....	....	....	2	....	....	....	....	....
	Regina Pats	M-Cup	4	13	2	15	....	....	....	2	....	....	....	....	....
1925-26	Regina Victorias	S-SSHL	16	8	1	9	....	....	....	2	....	....	....	....	....
	Regina Victorias	Al-Cup	9	8	0	8	....	....	....	2	....	....	....	....	....
1926-27	Regina Capitals	PrHL	32	23	7	30	....	....	....	21	2	1	0	1	0
1927-28	Winnipeg Maroons	AHA	39	15	4	19	....	....	....	24	....	....	....	....	....
1928-29	**Chicago Black Hawks**	**NHL**	**44**	**5**	**3**	**8**	**14**	**20**	**34**	**26**	....	....	....	....	....
1929-30	**Chicago Black Hawks**	**NHL**	**39**	**21**	**4**	**25**	**30**	**9**	**39**	**28**	**2**	**0**	**0**	**0**	**4**
1930-31	**Chicago Black Hawks**	**NHL**	**42**	**20**	**12**	**32**	**41**	**36**	**77**	**14**	**9**	**3**	**3**	**6**	**2**
1931-32	**Chicago Black Hawks**	**NHL**	**44**	**13**	**15**	**28**	**22**	**33**	**55**	**28**	**2**	**0**	**0**	**0**	**2**
1932-33	**Chicago Black Hawks**	**NHL**	**41**	**11**	**11**	**22**	**20**	**23**	**43**	**6**	....	....	....	....	....
♦1933-34	**Chicago Black Hawks**	**NHL**	**48**	**16**	**14**	**30**	**28**	**29**	**57**	**4**	**8**	**4**	**3**	**7**	**4**
1934-35	**Chicago Black Hawks**	**NHL**	**48**	**19**	**18**	**37**	**31**	**31**	**62**	**16**	**2**	**0**	**0**	**0**	**0**
1935-36	**Chicago Black Hawks**	**NHL**	**40**	**14**	**15**	**29**	**27**	**28**	**55**	**4**	**2**	**0**	**2**	**2**	**0**
1936-37	**Chicago Black Hawks**	**NHL**	**47**	**9**	**21**	**30**	**15**	**39**	**54**	**10**	....	....	....	....	....
♦1937-38	**Chicago Black Hawks**	**NHL**	**48**	**13**	**19**	**32**	**21**	**31**	**52**	**22**	**10**	**5**	**3**	***8**	**4**
1938-39	**Chicago Black Hawks**	**NHL**	**48**	**16**	**23**	**39**	**28**	**36**	**64**	**15**	....	....	....	....	....
1939-40	**Chicago Black Hawks**	**NHL**	**39**	**8**	**15**	**23**	**13**	**24**	**37**	**7**	**2**	**0**	**1**	**1**	**0**
1940-41	**Chicago Black Hawks**	**NHL**	**5**	**1**	**4**	**5**	**2**	**6**	**8**	**5**	....	....	....	....	....
	Kansas City Americans	AHA	13	9	6	15	....	....	....	2	8	3	1	4	2
1941-42	Kansas City Americans	AHA	40	25	35	60	....	....	....	22	6	2	5	7	2
1942-43	**Chicago Black Hawks**	**NHL**	**10**	**2**	**6**	**8**	**2**	**6**	**8**	**12**	....	....	....	....	....
1943-44	**Chicago Black Hawks**	**NHL**	**45**	**8**	**15**	**23**	**7**	**13**	**20**	**6**	**6**	**1**	**1**	**2**	**2**
1944-45	**Chicago Black Hawks**	**NHL**	**1**	**0**	**0**	**0**	**0**	**0**	**0**	**0**	....	....	....	....	....
1945-46	**Chicago Black Hawks**	**NHL**	DID NOT PLAY – COACHING												
	NHL Totals		**589**	**176**	**195**	**371**	**301**	**364**	**665**	**203**	**43**	**13**	**13**	**26**	**18**

NHL Second All-Star Team (1939) • Played in NHL All-Star Game (1937, 1939)

Claimed by **Chicago** from **Winnipeg** (AHA) in Inter-League Draft, May 14, 1928.

• GOUPILLE, Red Clifford

D – L. 6', 190 lbs. b: Trois Rivieres, Que., 9/2/1915.

Season	Club	League	GP	G	A	Pts	AG	AA	APts	PIM	GP	G	A	Pts	PIM
1935-36	**Montreal Canadiens**	**NHL**	**4**	**0**	**0**	**0**	**0**	**0**	**0**	**0**	....	....	....	....	....
	Montreal Lafontaine	MCHL	22	7	11	18	....	....	....	54	....	....	....	....	....
1936-37	**Montreal Canadiens**	**NHL**	**4**	**0**	**0**	**0**	**0**	**0**	**0**	**0**	....	....	....	....	....
	New Haven Eagles	IAHL	34	6	4	10	....	....	....	78	....	....	....	....	....
1937-38	**Montreal Canadiens**	**NHL**	**47**	**4**	**5**	**9**	**6**	**8**	**14**	**44**	**3**	**2**	**0**	**2**	**4**
1938-39	**Montreal Canadiens**	**NHL**	**18**	**0**	**2**	**2**	**0**	**3**	**3**	**24**	....	....	....	....	....
	New Haven Eagles	IAHL	36	6	6	12	....	....	....	54	....	....	....	....	....
1939-40	**Montreal Canadiens**	**NHL**	**48**	**2**	**10**	**12**	**3**	**16**	**19**	**48**	....	....	....	....	....
1940-41	**Montreal Canadiens**	**NHL**	**48**	**3**	**6**	**9**	**5**	**9**	**14**	**81**	**2**	**0**	**0**	**0**	**0**
1941-42	**Montreal Canadiens**	**NHL**	**47**	**1**	**5**	**6**	**1**	**6**	**7**	**51**	**3**	**0**	**0**	**0**	**2**
1942-43	**Montreal Canadiens**	**NHL**	**6**	**2**	**0**	**2**	**2**	**0**	**2**	**8**	....	....	....	....	....
	Montreal Army	QSHL	22	3	5	8	....	....	....	37	7	0	3	3	20
1943-44			MILITARY SERVICE												
1944-45			MILITARY SERVICE												
1945-46	Hull Volants	QSHL	40	4	13	17	....	....	....	*95	....	....	....	....	....
1946-47	Sherbrooke Saints	QPHL	42	9	19	28	....	....	....	*112	10	4	7	11	10
	Sherbrooke Saints	Al-Cup	4	0	1	1	....	....	....	8	....	....	....	....	....
1947-48	Sherbrooke St. Francis	QPHL	61	12	31	43	....	....	....	101	9	1	3	4	20
1948-49	Sherbrooke Saints	QSHL	63	6	16	22	....	....	....	90	12	1	1	2	24
1949-50	Sherbrooke Saints	QSHL	57	4	19	23	....	....	....	51	12	0	2	2	2
	Sherbrooke Saints	Al-Cup	5	1	1	2	....	....	....	6	....	....	....	....	....
1950-51	Sherbrooke Saints	QMHL	59	1	15	16	....	....	....	54	7	0	0	0	6
	NHL Totals		**222**	**12**	**28**	**40**	**17**	**42**	**59**	**256**	**8**	**2**	**0**	**2**	**6**

Played in NHL All-Star Game (1939)

• GOYETTE, Phil — see page 1124

• GRABOSKI, Tony Anthony Rudel

LW/D – L. 5'10", 178 lbs. b: Timmins, Ont., 5/9/1916.

Season	Club	League	GP	G	A	Pts	AG	AA	APts	PIM	GP	G	A	Pts	PIM
1933-34	Oshawa Majors	OHA-Jr.	16	6	6	12	....	....	....	16	3	0	1	1	8
1934-35	Oshawa Majors	OHA-Jr.	13	3	7	10	....	....	....	6	2	1	2	3	2
1935-36	Sudbury Wolves	NOJHA	10	5	3	8	....	....	....	10	4	*8	2	10	4
	Falconbridge Falcons	Al-Cup	5	2	0	2	....	....	....	4	....	....	....	....	....
1936-37	Hershey B'ars	EAHL	48	17	9	26	....	....	....	36	4	2	1	3	2
1937-38	Hershey B'ars	EAHL	50	29	26	55	....	....	....	17	....	....	....	....	....
1938-39	Hershey Cubs	EAHL	52	27	13	40	....	....	....	12	....	....	....	....	....
1939-40	Sydney Millionaires	CBSHL	34	*29	*27	*56	....	....	....	50	4	4	4	*8	*14
1940-41	**Montreal Canadiens**	**NHL**	**34**	**4**	**3**	**7**	**6**	**4**	**10**	**12**	**3**	**0**	**0**	**0**	**6**
	New Haven Eagles	AHL	10	3	4	7	....	....	....	4	....	....	....	....	....
1941-42	**Montreal Canadiens**	**NHL**	**23**	**2**	**5**	**7**	**3**	**6**	**9**	**8**	....	....	....	....	....
	Washington Lions	AHL	24	3	2	5	....	....	....	12	2	0	0	0	0
1942-43	**Montreal Canadiens**	**NHL**	**9**	**0**	**2**	**2**	**0**	**2**	**2**	**4**	....	....	....	....	....
	Washington Lions	AHL	14	2	4	6	....	....	....	4	....	....	....	....	....
	Hershey Bears	AHL	38	8	26	34	....	....	....	10	6	0	0	0	2
1943/45			MILITARY SERVICE												
1945-46	Ottawa Senators	QSHL	19	5	5	10	....	....	....	32	9	1	3	4	10
	NHL Totals		**66**	**6**	**10**	**16**	**9**	**12**	**21**	**24**	**3**	**0**	**0**	**0**	**6**

Signed as a free agent by **Montreal**, October 25, 1940. Traded to **Hershey** (AHL) by **Montreal** (Washington-AHL) for cash, January 18, 1943.

• GRACIE, Bob Robert Joseph

C/LW – L. 5'9", 155 lbs. b: North Bay, Ont., 11/8/1910 d: 8/10/1963.

Season	Club	League	GP	G	A	Pts	AG	AA	APts	PIM	GP	G	A	Pts	PIM
1926-27	North Bay Collegiate	NOJHA	4	8	4	12	....	....	....	2	....	....	....	....	....
1927-28	North Bay Trappers	NOJHA	11	11	1	12	....	....	....	6	2	1	0	1	0
1928-29	Kirkland Lake Lakers	NOHA	6	*24	6	*30	....	....	....	4	4	3	3	6	2
1929-30	West Toronto Nationals	OHA-Jr.	7	*17	6	*23	....	....	....	12	2	*2	1	*3	0
	West Toronto Nationals	M-Cup	13	*15	6	21	....	....	....	2	....	....	....	....	....
1930-31	Toronto Eatons	TMHL	15	11	4	15	....	....	....	45	....	....	....	....	....
	Toronto Marlboros	OHA-Jr.	10	4	*6	10	....	....	....	6	3	2	0	2	6
	Toronto Maple Leafs	**NHL**	**8**	**4**	**2**	**6**	**8**	**6**	**14**	**4**	**2**	**0**	**0**	**0**	**0**
♦1931-32	**Toronto Maple Leafs**	**NHL**	**48**	**13**	**8**	**21**	**22**	**18**	**40**	**29**	**7**	**3**	**1**	**4**	**0**
1932-33	**Toronto Maple Leafs**	**NHL**	**48**	**9**	**13**	**22**	**16**	**27**	**43**	**27**	**9**	**0**	**1**	**1**	**0**
1933-34	**Boston Bruins**	**NHL**	**24**	**2**	**6**	**8**	**3**	**13**	**16**	**8**	....	....	....	....	....
	New York Americans	**NHL**	**24**	**4**	**6**	**10**	**7**	**13**	**20**	**10**	....	....	....	....	....
1934-35	**New York Americans**	**NHL**	**14**	**2**	**1**	**3**	**3**	**2**	**5**	**4**	....	....	....	....	....
	New Haven Eagles	Can-Am	1	1	2	3	....	....	....	0	....	....	....	....	....
♦	**Montreal Maroons**	**NHL**	**32**	**10**	**8**	**18**	**16**	**14**	**30**	**11**	**7**	**0**	**2**	**2**	**2**
1935-36	**Montreal Maroons**	**NHL**	**48**	**11**	**14**	**25**	**21**	**27**	**48**	**31**	**3**	**0**	**1**	**1**	**0**
1936-37	**Montreal Maroons**	**NHL**	**47**	**11**	**25**	**36**	**18**	**46**	**64**	**18**	**5**	**1**	**2**	**3**	**2**
1937-38	**Montreal Maroons**	**NHL**	**48**	**12**	**19**	**31**	**20**	**31**	**51**	**32**	....	....	....	....	....
1938-39	**Montreal Canadiens**	**NHL**	**7**	**0**	**1**	**1**	**0**	**2**	**2**	**4**	....	....	....	....	....
	Chicago Black Hawks	**NHL**	**31**	**4**	**6**	**10**	**7**	**9**	**16**	**27**	....	....	....	....	....
	Cleveland Barons	IAHL	11	1	5	6	....	....	....	0	9	4	2	6	0
1939-40	Cleveland Barons	IAHL	37	10	11	21	....	....	....	13	....	....	....	....	....
	Indianapolis Capitols	IAHL	19	5	9	14	....	....	....	19	5	1	0	1	0
1940-41	Buffalo Bisons	AHL	56	22	26	48	....	....	....	2	....	....	....	....	....
1941-42	Buffalo Bisons	AHL	35	10	10	20	....	....	....	8	....	....	....	....	....
	Pittsburgh Hornets	AHL	1	0	0	0	....	....	....	0	....	....	....	....	....
	Hershey Bears	AHL	17	8	6	14	....	....	....	0	7	2	3	5	0
1942-43	Hershey Bears	AHL	11	0	4	4	....	....	....	6	....	....	....	....	....
	Washington Lions	AHL	46	27	32	59	....	....	....	12	....	....	....	....	....
1943-44	Pittsburgh Hornets	AHL	41	13	24	37	....	....	....	13	....	....	....	....	....
1944-45	Pittsburgh Hornets	AHL	58	40	55	*95	....	....	....	4	....	....	....	....	....

Season	Club	League	GP	G	A	Pts	AG	AA	APts	PIM	GP	G	A	Pts	PIM
			REGULAR SEASON								PLAYOFFS				
1945-46	Pittsburgh Hornets	AHL	4	4	4	8	....	....	....	0	....	....	....	....	....
	Hollywood Wolves	PCHL	16	7	7	14	....	....	....	13	....	....	....	....	....
1946-47	Hollywood Wolves	PCHL	2	4	0	4	....	....	....	10	....	....	....	....	....
1947-48	Fresno Falcons	PCHL	8	3	2	5	....	....	....	2	....	....	....	....	....
	NHL Totals		**379**	**82**	**109**	**191**	**141**	**208**	**349**	**205**	**33**	**4**	**7**	**11**	**4**

Signed as a free agent by **Toronto**, February 27, 1931. Traded to **Ottawa** by **Toronto** with $10,000 for Hec Kilrea, October 4, 1933. Traded to **Boston** by **Ottawa** for Percy Galbraith, Bud Cook and Ted Saunders, October 4, 1933. Traded to **NY Americans** by **Boston** with Art Chapman for Lloyd Gross and George Patterson, January 11, 1934. Traded to **Montreal Maroons** by **NY Americans** for cash, December 25, 1934. Traded to **Montreal Canadiens** by **Montreal Maroons** for cash, September 14, 1938. Traded to **Chicago** by **Montreal** for cash, November 25, 1938. Traded to **Detroit** (Indianapolis-IAHL) by **Cleveland** (IAHL) with $30,000 for Don Deacon, February 5, 1940. Traded to **Buffalo** (AHL) by **Detroit** for cash, October 20, 1940. Traded to **Hershey** (AHL) by **Buffalo** (AHL) for Kilby MacDonald, February 2, 1942. Traded to **Washington** (AHL) by **Hershey** (AHL) for Jim O'Neill, November 21, 1942.

• GRAHAM, Leth

LW – L. 5'9", 150 lbs. b: Ottawa, Ont., 1894 d: 1/18/1944.

Season	Club	League	GP	G	A	Pts	AG	AA	APts	PIM	GP	G	A	Pts	PIM
1909-10	Hull Excelsiors	H-OHL	5	4	0	4	....	....	....	....	....	....	....	....	....
1910-11	Ottawa New Edinburghs	IPAHU	1	1	0	1	....	....	....	0	....	....	....	....	....
	Ottawa Stewartons	OCHL	5	2	0	2	....	....	....	3	....	....	....	....	....
1911-12	Ottawa Stewartons	IPAHU	8	8	0	8	....	....	....	6	....	....	....	....	....
1912-13	Ottawa Stewartons	IPAHU	7	7	0	7	....	....	....	18	....	....	....	....	....
1913-14	Ottawa Senators	NHA	17	1	1	2	....	....	....	2	....	....	....	....	....
1914-15	Ottawa Senators	NHA	17	9	3	12	....	....	....	34	5	1	0	1	0
1915/19			MILITARY SERVICE												
1919-20			DID NOT PLAY												
♦**1920-21**	**Ottawa Senators**	**NHL**	**14**	**0**	**0**	**0**	**0**	**0**	**0**	**0**	**1**	**0**	**0**	**0**	**0**
1921-22	**Ottawa Senators**	**NHL**	**1**	**2**	**0**	**2**	**3**	**0**	**3**	**0**	....	....	....	....	....
1922-23	**Hamilton Tigers**	**NHL**	**5**	**1**	**0**	**1**	**2**	**0**	**2**	**0**	....	....	....	....	....
1923-24	**Ottawa Senators**	**NHL**	**3**	**0**	**0**	**0**	**0**	**0**	**0**	**0**	....	....	....	....	....
1924-25	**Ottawa Senators**	**NHL**	**3**	**0**	**0**	**0**	**0**	**0**	**0**	**0**	....	....	....	....	....
1925-26	**Ottawa Senators**	**NHL**	**1**	**0**	**0**	**0**	**0**	**0**	**0**	**0**	....	....	....	....	....
	NHL Totals		**27**	**3**	**0**	**3**	**5**	**0**	**5**	**0**	**1**	**0**	**0**	**0**	**0**
	Other Major League Totals		34	10	4	14	....	....	....	36	5	1	0	1	0

Signed as a free agent by **Ottawa**, November 10, 1920. Traded to **Saskatoon** (WCHL) by **Ottawa** for cash, December 2, 1921. • Released by Saskatoon (WCHL), December 10, 1921. Signed as a free agent by **Ottawa**, December, 1921. Signed as a free agent by **Hamilton**, November 15, 1922. Traded to **Ottawa** by **Hamilton** for cash, December 18, 1923.

• GRAHAM, Teddy

Edward Dixon

D – L. 5'8", 170 lbs. b: Owen Sound, Ont., 1/30/1906 d: 1/11/1979.

Season	Club	League	GP	G	A	Pts	AG	AA	APts	PIM	GP	G	A	Pts	PIM
1923-24	Owen Sound Greys	X-Games	11	3	*7	10	....	....	....	....	....	....	....	....	....
	Owen Sound Greys	M-Cup	15	7	4	11	....	....	....	....	....	....	....	....	....
1924-25	Stratford Indians	OHA-Sr.	20	3	2	5	....	....	....	22	....	....	....	....	....
1925-26	London Ravens	OHA-Sr.	20	4	3	7	....	....	....	6	4	0	1	1	2
1926-27	Chicago Cardinals	AHA	32	1	1	2	....	....	....	23	....	....	....	....	....
1927-28	**Chicago Black Hawks**	**NHL**	**19**	**1**	**0**	**1**	**2**	**0**	**2**	**8**	....	....	....	....	....
	Saskatoon Shieks	PrHL	12	3	5	8	....	....	....	7	....	....	....	....	....
1928-29	Tulsa Oilers	AHA	34	10	*15	25	....	....	....	38	4	1	0	1	4
1929-30	Tulsa Oilers	AHA	15	4	0	4	....	....	....	12	....	....	....	....	....
	Chicago Black Hawks	**NHL**	**26**	**1**	**2**	**3**	**1**	**5**	**6**	**23**	**2**	**0**	**0**	**0**	**8**
1930-31	**Chicago Black Hawks**	**NHL**	**42**	**0**	**7**	**7**	**0**	**21**	**21**	**38**	**9**	**0**	**0**	**0**	**12**
1931-32	**Chicago Black Hawks**	**NHL**	**48**	**0**	**3**	**3**	**0**	**7**	**7**	**40**	**2**	**0**	**0**	**0**	**2**
1932-33	**Chicago Black Hawks**	**NHL**	**47**	**3**	**8**	**11**	**5**	**17**	**22**	**57**	....	....	....	....	....
1933-34	**Montreal Maroons**	**NHL**	**19**	**2**	**1**	**3**	**3**	**2**	**5**	**10**	....	....	....	....	....
	Detroit Red Wings	**NHL**	**28**	**1**	**0**	**1**	**2**	**0**	**2**	**29**	**9**	**3**	**1**	**4**	**8**
1934-35	**Detroit Red Wings**	**NHL**	**24**	**0**	**2**	**2**	**0**	**3**	**3**	**26**	....	....	....	....	....
	Detroit Olympics	IHL	7	0	0	0	....	....	....	10	....	....	....	....	....
	St. Louis Eagles	**NHL**	**13**	**0**	**0**	**0**	**0**	**0**	**0**	**2**	....	....	....	....	....
1935-36	**Boston Bruins**	**NHL**	**48**	**4**	**1**	**5**	**8**	**2**	**10**	**37**	**2**	**0**	**0**	**0**	**0**
1936-37	**Boston Bruins**	**NHL**	**1**	**0**	**0**	**0**	**0**	**0**	**0**	**0**	....	....	....	....	....
	New York Americans	**NHL**	**31**	**2**	**1**	**3**	**3**	**2**	**5**	**30**	....	....	....	....	....
	Providence Reds	IAHL	9	0	0	0	....	....	....	2	....	....	....	....	....
1937-38	New Haven Eagles	IAHL	29	0	2	2	....	....	....	14	2	0	0	0	0
1938-39			DID NOT PLAY – REFEREE												
	NHL Totals		**346**	**14**	**25**	**39**	**24**	**59**	**83**	**300**	**24**	**3**	**1**	**4**	**30**

Signed as a free agent by **Chicago** (Chicago-AHA), October 4, 1926. Traded to **Moose Jaw** (PrHL) by **Chicago** for Amby Moran and future considerations (Vic Hoffinger, January 23, 1928), January 11, 1928. Traded to **Saskatoon** (PrHL) by **Moose Jaw** (PrHL) for cash, January 11, 1928. Signed as a free agent by **Tulsa** (AHA), October 29, 1928. Traded to **Chicago** by **Tulsa** (AHA) for Ralph Taylor and cash, January 4, 1930. • Cash amount in January 4, 1930 transaction was increased after Taylor was returned to Chicago by NHL after they determined that Taylor was not offered on waivers to other NHL clubs. Traded to **Montreal Maroons** by **Chicago** for Lionel Conacher, October 1, 1933. Traded to **Detroit** by **Montreal Maroons** for Stewart Evans, January 2, 1934. Traded to **St. Louis** by **Detroit** with $50,000 for Syd Howe and Ralph Bowman, February 11, 1935. Claimed by **Boston** from **St. Louis** in Dispersal Draft, October 15, 1935. Traded to **NY Americans** by **Boston** for Walter Kalbfleish, December 19, 1936.

• GRANT, Danny

— *see page 1126*

• GRAVELLE, Leo

Leo Joseph Gerard "The Gazelle"

RW – R. 5'9", 160 lbs. b: Aylmer, Que., 6/10/1925.

Season	Club	League	GP	G	A	Pts	AG	AA	APts	PIM	GP	G	A	Pts	PIM
1942-43	Port Colborne Sailors	OHA-B	STATISTICS NOT AVAILABLE												
1943-44	Brantford Lions	OHA-B	STATISTICS NOT AVAILABLE												
1944-45	St. Michael's Majors	OHA-Jr.	17	*30	22	*52	....	....	....	6	9	*12	9	*21	0
	St. Michael's Majors	M-Cup	13	10	3	13	....	....	....	8	....	....	....	....	....
1945-46	Montreal Royals	QSHL	34	21	21	42	....	....	....	20	11	*10	4	*14	4
1946-47	**Montreal Canadiens**	**NHL**	**53**	**16**	**14**	**30**	**18**	**17**	**35**	**12**	**6**	**2**	**0**	**2**	**2**
	Montreal Royals	QSHL	2	2	2	4	....	....	....	0	....	....	....	....	....
1947-48	**Montreal Canadiens**	**NHL**	**15**	**0**	**0**	**0**	**0**	**0**	**0**	**0**	....	....	....	....	....
	Buffalo Bisons	AHL	29	11	13	24	....	....	....	7	....	....	....	....	....
	Houston Huskies	USHL	24	14	15	29	....	....	....	7	12	4	3	7	0
1948-49	**Montreal Canadiens**	**NHL**	**36**	**4**	**6**	**10**	**6**	**8**	**14**	**6**	**7**	**2**	**1**	**3**	**0**
	Buffalo Bisons	AHL	25	6	4	10	....	....	....	20	....	....	....	....	....
1949-50	**Montreal Canadiens**	**NHL**	**70**	**19**	**10**	**29**	**24**	**12**	**36**	**18**	**4**	**0**	**0**	**0**	**0**

Season	Club	League	GP	G	A	Pts	AG	AA	APts	PIM	GP	G	A	Pts	PIM
			REGULAR SEASON								PLAYOFFS				
1950-51	**Montreal Canadiens**	**NHL**	**31**	**4**	**2**	**6**	**5**	**2**	**7**	**0**	....	....	....	....	....
	Detroit Red Wings	**NHL**	**18**	**1**	**2**	**3**	**1**	**2**	**3**	**6**	....	....	....	....	....
	Indianapolis Capitols	AHL	15	4	6	10	....	....	....	0	....	....	....	....	....
1951-52	Ottawa Senators	QMHL	59	18	26	44	....	....	....	17	7	3	2	5	0
1952-53	Ottawa Senators	QMHL	60	28	28	56	....	....	....	4	11	2	5	7	0
1953-54	Ottawa Senators	QHL	68	*45	41	86	....	....	....	6	22	*9	7	16	8
1954-55	Ottawa–Chicoutimi	QHL	45	13	14	27	....	....	....	6	7	2	1	3	0
1955-56	Montreal Royals	QHL	42	13	12	25	....	....	....	11	....	....	....	....	....
	NHL Totals		**223**	**44**	**34**	**78**	**54**	**41**	**95**	**42**	**17**	**4**	**1**	**5**	**2**

QHL First All-Star Team (1954)

Traded to **Detroit** by **Montreal** for Bert Olmstead, December 19, 1950. Traded to **Ottawa** (QMHL) by **Detroit** for cash, September 5, 1951.

• GRAY, Alex

"Peanuts"

RW – R. 5'10", 170 lbs. b: Glasgow, Scotland, 6/21/1899 d: 4/10/1986.

Season	Club	League	GP	G	A	Pts	AG	AA	APts	PIM	GP	G	A	Pts	PIM
1920-21	Port Arthur Bruins	TBJHL	STATISTICS NOT AVAILABLE												
1921-22	Eveleth Rangers	USAHA	STATISTICS NOT AVAILABLE												
1922-23	Port Arthur Ports	TBSHL	14	18	8	26	....	....	....	10	2	0	1	1	0
1923-24	Port Arthur Ports	TBSHL	14	*20	5	*25	....	....	....	4	2	1	1	2	0
1924-25	Port Arthur Ports	TBSHL	20	*17	7	*24	....	....	....	9	10	11	4	15	4
1925-26	Port Arthur Ports	TBSHL	18	12	*9	21	....	....	....	14	3	0	0	0	0
	Port Arthur Ports	Al-Cup	6	4	1	5	....	....	....	0	....	....	....	....	....
1926-27	Port Arthur Ports	TBSHL	19	*27	6	33	....	....	....	31	9	1	0	1	0
♦**1927-28**	**New York Rangers**	**NHL**	**43**	**7**	**0**	**7**	**14**	**0**	**14**	**30**	**9**	**1**	**0**	**1**	**0**
1928-29	**Toronto Maple Leafs**	**NHL**	**7**	**0**	**0**	**0**	**0**	**0**	**0**	**2**	**4**	**0**	**0**	**0**	**0**
	Toronto Ravinas	Can-Pro	37	11	3	14	....	....	....	51	2	3	0	3	4
1929-30	Cleveland Indians	IHL	42	21	12	33	....	....	....	54	6	4	*3	*7	4
1930-31	Cleveland Indians	IHL	48	29	8	37	....	....	....	55	6	4	2	6	6
1931-32	Cleveland Indians	IHL	48	16	10	26	....	....	....	35	....	....	....	....	....
1932-33	Cleveland–Windsor	IHL	39	7	8	15	....	....	....	15	....	....	....	....	....
	NHL Totals		**50**	**7**	**0**	**7**	**14**	**0**	**14**	**32**	**13**	**1**	**0**	**1**	**0**

Signed as a free agent by **NY Rangers**, August 22, 1926. Traded to **Toronto** by **NY Rangers** for Butch Keeling, April 16, 1928. Traded to **Toronto Ravinas** (Can-Pro) by **Toronto** for cash, November 28, 1928.

• GRAY, Terry

— *see page 1128*

• GREEN, Red

Christopher Redvers

LW – L. 5'8", 148 lbs. b: Sudbury, Ont., 12/12/1899 Deceased.

Season	Club	League	GP	G	A	Pts	AG	AA	APts	PIM	GP	G	A	Pts	PIM
1917-18	Toronto De LaSalle	OHA-Jr.	STATISTICS NOT AVAILABLE												
1918-19	Parkdale Canoe Club	OHA-Jr.	STATISTICS NOT AVAILABLE												
1919-20	Sudbury Wolves	NOHA	5	15	4	19	....	....	....	2	2	*13	3	16	2
1920-21	Port Colborne Sailors	OHA-Sr.	STATISTICS NOT AVAILABLE												
1921-22	Sudbury Wolves	NOHA	9	*22	*9	*31	....	....	....	8	....	....	....	....	....
1922-23	Sudbury Wolves	NOHA	7	6	*5	*11	....	....	....	16	2	1	*2	*3	*4
1923-24	**Hamilton Tigers**	**NHL**	**23**	**11**	**2**	**13**	**23**	**11**	**34**	**31**	....	....	....	....	....
1924-25	**Hamilton Tigers**	**NHL**	**30**	**19**	***15**	**34**	**33**	**64**	**97**	**81**	....	....	....	....	....
1925-26	**New York Americans**	**NHL**	**35**	**13**	**4**	**17**	**22**	**26**	**48**	**42**	....	....	....	....	....
1926-27	**New York Americans**	**NHL**	**43**	**10**	**4**	**14**	**18**	**21**	**39**	**53**	....	....	....	....	....
1927-28	**New York Americans**	**NHL**	**40**	**6**	**1**	**7**	**12**	**6**	**18**	**67**	....	....	....	....	....
♦**1928-29**	**Boston Bruins**	**NHL**	**22**	**0**	**0**	**0**	**0**	**0**	**0**	**16**	**1**	**0**	**0**	**0**	**0**
	Detroit Cougars	**NHL**	**2**	**0**	**0**	**0**	**0**	**0**	**0**	**0**	....	....	....	....	....
	Providence Reds	Can-Am	7	2	1	3	....	....	....	4	....	....	....	....	....
1929-30	Duluth Hornets	AHA	48	14	3	17	....	....	....	81	3	0	0	0	10
1930-31	Duluth Hornets	AHA	42	8	2	10	....	....	....	60	3	0	0	0	0
1931-32	Tulsa Oilers	AHA	2	0	0	0	....	....	....	2	....	....	....	....	....
	NHL Totals		**195**	**59**	**26**	**85**	**108**	**128**	**236**	**290**	**1**	**0**	**0**	**0**	**0**

• Brother of Shorty • NOHA First All-Star Team (1922)

Signed as a free agent by **Hamilton**, November 13, 1923. Transferred to **NY Americans** after NHL club purchased **Hamilton** franchise, September 25, 1925. Traded to **Boston** by **NY Americans** for Harry Connor, May 18, 1928. Claimed on waivers by **Detroit** from **Boston**, February 16, 1929. Claimed on waivers by **Boston** from **Detroit**, March 4, 1929.

• GREEN, Shorty

Wilfred Thomas **HHOF**

RW – R. 5'10", 152 lbs. b: Sudbury, Ont., 7/17/1896 d: 4/19/1960.

Season	Club	League	GP	G	A	Pts	AG	AA	APts	PIM	GP	G	A	Pts	PIM
1914-15	Sudbury All-Stars	X-Games	12	*19	3	*22	....	....	....	....	....	....	....	....	....
	Sudbury All-Stars	Al-Cup	3	6	0	6	....	....	....	....	....	....	....	....	....
1915-16	Sudbury All-Stars	X-Games	STATISTICS NOT AVAILABLE												
1916-17	Hamilton 227th	OHA-Sr.	8	*17	0	*17	....	....	....	....	....	....	....	....	....
1917-18			MILITARY SERVICE												
1918-19	Hamilton Tigers	OHA-Sr.	8	12	3	15	....	....	....	....	4	*5	3	*8	....
	Hamilton Tigers	Al-Cup	2	3	0	3	....	....	....	....	....	....	....	....	....
1919-20	Sudbury Wolves	NOHA	6	*23	4	*27	....	....	....	*16	7	*13	4	*17	8
1920-21	Sudbury Wolves	NOHA	4	4	2	6	....	....	....	7	....	....	....	....	....
1921-22	Sudbury Wolves	NOHA	9	5	4	9	....	....	....	9	....	....	....	....	....
1922-23	Sudbury Wolves	NOHA	7	3	1	4	....	....	....	16	1	0	1	1	2
1923-24	**Hamilton Tigers**	**NHL**	**22**	**7**	**6**	**13**	**14**	**36**	**50**	**31**	....	....	....	....	....
1924-25	**Hamilton Tigers**	**NHL**	**28**	**18**	**9**	**27**	**32**	**38**	**70**	**63**	....	....	....	....	....
1925-26	**New York Americans**	**NHL**	**32**	**6**	**4**	**10**	**10**	**26**	**36**	**40**	....	....	....	....	....
1926-27	**New York Americans**	**NHL**	**21**	**2**	**1**	**3**	**4**	**5**	**9**	**17**	....	....	....	....	....
1927-28	**New York Americans**	**NHL**	DID NOT PLAY – COACHING												
1928-29	Duluth Hornets	AHA	DID NOT PLAY – COACHING												
1929-30	Duluth Hornets	AHA	2	0	0	0	....	....	....	2	....	....	....	....	....
1930-31	Duluth Hornets	AHA	1	0	0	0	....	....	....	8	....	....	....	....	....
	NHL Totals		**103**	**36**	**20**	**56**	**60**	**105**	**165**	**220**	....	....	....	....	....

• Brother of Red

Signed as a free agent by **Hamilton**, November 22, 1923. Transferred to **NY Americans** after NHL club purchased **Hamilton** franchise, September 25, 1925.

• GREEN, Ted

— *see page 1129*

• GRIGOR, George "Shorty"

C – R. 5'7", 150 lbs. b: Edinburgh, Scotland, 9/3/1916.

Season	Club	League	REGULAR SEASON GP	G	A	Pts	AG	AA	APts	PIM	PLAYOFFS GP	G	A	Pts	PIM
1934-35	Toronto Young Rangers	OHA-Jr.	9	3	2	5	....	....	....	11	2	1	0	1	0
1935-36	Toronto Young Rangers	OHA-Jr.	11	8	6	14	....	....	....	*25	2	0	0	0	0
	Toronto Dominions	TIHL	16	3	4	7	....	....	....	16	....	....	....	....	....
1936-37	Toronto Dominions	TIHL	9	1	3	4	....	....	....	12	3	0	1	1	4
1937-38			DID NOT PLAY												
1938-39	Niagara Falls Brights	OHA-Sr.	20	4	11	15	....	....	....	*48	....	....	....	....	....
	Niagara Falls Brights	Al-Cup	7	6	5	11	....	....	....	28	....	....	....	....	....
1939-40	Baltimore Orioles	EAHL	59	21	23	44	....	....	....	58	9	2	*7	*9	9
1940-41	Baltimore Orioles	EAHL	59	22	32	54	....	....	....	95	....	....	....	....	....
1941-42	Toronto Marlboros	OHA-Sr.	25	9	12	21	....	....	....	*71	6	0	3	3	10
	Toronto Kodaks	TMHL	11	8	13	21	....	....	....	4	7	1	4	5	8
1942-43	Research Colonels	OHA-Sr.	10	6	15	21	....	....	....	6	....	....	....	....	....
	Toronto Staffords	TIHL	18	11	17	28	....	....	....	42	6	2	5	7	6
1943-44	Toronto Staffords	TMHL	26	14	*36	50	....	....	....	20	7	3	4	7	*34
	Chicago Black Hawks	**NHL**	**2**	**1**	**0**	**1**	**1**	**0**	**1**	**0**	**1**	**0**	**0**	**0**	**0**
1944-45	Toronto Staffords	OHA-Sr.	8	1	4	5	....	....	....	8	....	....	....	....	....
	Toronto Peoples Credit	TIHL	29	18	26	44	....	....	....	20	6	5	10	15	4
1945-46	Toronto Peoples Credit	TIHL	29	13	20	33	....	....	....	23	5	1	4	5	14
1946-47	Toronto Peoples Credit	TIHL	27	12	27	39	....	....	....	51	3	0	0	0	10
1947-48	Toronto Peoples Credit	TIHL	26	7	25	32	....	....	....	22	5	0	2	2	12
	NHL Totals		**2**	**1**	**0**	**1**	**1**	**0**	**1**	**0**	**1**	**0**	**0**	**0**	**0**

Signed as a free agent by **Chicago**, October 7, 1943. • Military authorities allowed him to play only part-time with Chicago because of his essential wartime position in Toronto.

• GRONSDAHL, Lloyd Lloyd Gifford "Gabby"

RW – R. 5'9", 170 lbs. b: Norquay, Sask., 5/10/1921.

Season	Club	League	GP	G	A	Pts	AG	AA	APts	PIM	GP	G	A	Pts	PIM
1940-41	Regina Capitals	S-SJHL	16	7	11	18	....	....	....	6	4	*4	3	*7	2
1941-42	**Boston Bruins**	**NHL**	**10**	**1**	**2**	**3**	**1**	**2**	**3**	**0**	....	....	....	....	....
	Boston Olympics	EAHL	43	29	14	43	....	....	....	11	1	0	1	1	0
1942-43	Toronto RCAF	OHA-Sr.	5	6	0	6	....	....	....	10	9	*13	3	16	4
	Toronto RCAF	Al-Cup	7	6	1	7	....	....	....	6	....	....	....	....	....
1943-44	Toronto RCAF	OHA-Sr.	15	7	3	10	....	....	....	6	....	....	....	....	....
	Toronto Orphans	TMHL	8	5	6	11	....	....	....	4	13	13	13	26	4
1944-45	Toronto RCAF	TNDHL	2	1	3	4	....	....	....	0	....	....	....	....	....
	Toronto Orphans	TMHL	3	2	3	5	....	....	....	6	....	....	....	....	....
1945-46	Milward RCAF	Britain	STATISTICS NOT AVAILABLE												
1946-47	Hershey Bears	AHL	64	19	21	40	....	....	....	17	11	1	2	3	4
1947-48	Hershey Bears	AHL	66	11	11	22	....	....	....	7	2	1	0	1	2
1948-49	Tulsa Oilers	USHL	63	38	25	63	....	....	....	17	7	3	3	6	2
1949-50	Tulsa Oilers	USHL	60	20	23	43	....	....	....	21	....	....	....	....	....
1950-51	Tulsa Oilers	USHL	61	23	23	46	....	....	....	8	9	1	2	3	6
	NHL Totals		**10**	**1**	**2**	**3**	**1**	**2**	**3**	**0**	....	....	....	....	....

• GROSS, Lloyd Lloyd George "Bomber"

LW – L. 5'9", 175 lbs. b: Berlin, Ont., 9/5/1905.

Season	Club	League	GP	G	A	Pts	AG	AA	APts	PIM	GP	G	A	Pts	PIM
1924-25	Kitchener Greenshirts	OHA-Jr.	8	14	4	18	....	....	....	....	....	....	....	....	....
1925-26	Kitchener Greenshirts	OHA-Jr.	11	7	*11	18	....	....	....	....	....	....	....	....	....
1926-27	Kitchener Greenshirts	OHA-Sr.	11	7	4	11	....	....	....	4	4	0	2	2	2
	Toronto Maple Leafs	**NHL**	**16**	**1**	**1**	**2**	**2**	**5**	**7**	**0**	....	....	....	....	....
1927-28	Toronto Ravinas	Can-Pro	41	12	3	15	....	....	....	42	2	0	0	0	10
1928-29	Kitchener Dutchmen	Can-Pro	40	9	4	13	....	....	....	59	3	0	0	0	4
1929-30	Toronto Millionaires	IHL	11	3	0	3	....	....	....	8	....	....	....	....	....
	Niagara Falls Cataracts	IHL	12	6	3	9	....	....	....	7	....	....	....	....	....
	Buffalo Bisons	IHL	19	9	4	13	....	....	....	34	....	....	....	....	....
1930-31	Buffalo Bisons	IHL	47	13	15	28	....	....	....	57	6	2	1	3	2
1931-32	Buffalo Bisons	IHL	48	*24	16	40	....	....	....	65	6	*3	2	5	4
1932-33	Buffalo Bisons	IHL	42	*30	20	*50	....	....	....	83	6	*4	0	4	2
1933-34	**New York Americans**	**NHL**	**21**	**7**	**3**	**10**	**12**	**6**	**18**	**10**	....	....	....	....	....
	Boston Bruins	**NHL**	**6**	**1**	**0**	**1**	**2**	**0**	**2**	**6**	....	....	....	....	....
	Boston Cubs	Can-Am	3	1	1	2	....	....	....	0	....	....	....	....	....
	Detroit Red Wings	**NHL**	**13**	**1**	**1**	**2**	**2**	**2**	**4**	**2**	**1**	**0**	**0**	**0**	**0**
1934-35	**Detroit Red Wings**	**NHL**	**6**	**1**	**0**	**1**	**2**	**0**	**2**	**2**	....	....	....	....	....
	Detroit Olympics	IHL	18	4	6	10	....	....	....	19	....	....	....	....	....
	Buffalo Bisons	IHL	25	8	11	19	....	....	....	20	....	....	....	....	....
1935-36	Cleveland Falcons	IHL	48	17	10	27	....	....	....	30	2	1	0	1	2
1936-37	Buffalo Bisons	IAHL	3	0	1	1	....	....	....	0	....	....	....	....	....
	Cleveland Barons	IAHL	3	0	0	0	....	....	....	2	....	....	....	....	....
1937-38	Tulsa Oilers	AHA	48	24	20	44	....	....	....	36	3	0	0	0	0
1938-39	Tulsa Oilers	AHA	46	29	23	52	....	....	....	30	8	2	4	6	6
1939-40	Tulsa Oilers	AHA	45	13	24	37	....	....	....	24	....	....	....	....	....
1940-41	St. Paul Saints	AHA	48	12	20	32	....	....	....	22	4	0	0	0	5
1941-42	St. Paul Saints	AHA	50	8	9	17	....	....	....	33	2	0	0	0	0
	NHL Totals		**62**	**11**	**5**	**16**	**20**	**13**	**33**	**20**	**1**	**0**	**0**	**0**	**0**

IHL First All-Star Team (1935) • AHA Second All-Star Team (1938, 1939)

Signed as a free agent by **Toronto**, March 7, 1927. Traded to **Niagara Falls** (IHL) by **Toronto** (IHL) with Fred Elliot for Ike Morrison, Harry Lott and Jim Smith, December 16, 1929. Traded to **Buffalo** (IHL) by **Niagara Falls** (IHL) with Gamey Lederman for Wilf McDonald, January 9, 1930. Claimed by **NY Rangers** from **Buffalo** (IHL) in Inter-League Draft, May 13, 1933. Rights returned to **Buffalo** (IHL) by **NY Rangers** when NHL club failed to complete terms of purchase, May 25, 1933. Traded to **NY Americans** by **Buffalo** (IHL) for cash, October 11, 1933. Traded to **Boston** by **NY Americans** with George Patterson for Art Chapman and Bob Gracie, January 11, 1934. Traded to **Detroit** by **Boston** for cash, February 13, 1934. Traded to **Buffalo** (IHL) by **Detroit** with Garney Lederman for Bucko McDonald, January 9, 1935.

• GROSSO, Don Donald Joseph "Count"

LW/C – L. 5'11", 170 lbs. b: Sault Ste. Marie, Ont., 4/12/1915 d: 5/14/1985.

Season	Club	League	GP	G	A	Pts	AG	AA	APts	PIM	GP	G	A	Pts	PIM
1933-34	Detroit Mundus	MOHL	10	8	1	9	....	....	....	17	6	3	0	3	8
1934-35	Sudbury Cub Wolves	NBHL	7	3	0	3	....	....	....	4	5	1	2	3	2
1935-36	Falconbridge Falcons	NBHL	10	7	6	13	....	....	....	10	3	4	1	5	4
	Falconbridge Falcons	Al-Cup	13	8	3	11	....	....	....	18	....	....	....	....	....
1936-37	Sudbury Frood Miners	NBHL	14	11	5	16	....	....	....	6	2	0	1	1	2
	Sudbury Frood Miners	Al-Cup	14	13	5	18	....	....	....	4	....	....	....	....	....
1937-38	Falconbridge Falcons	NBHL	13	*13	8	*21	....	....	....	2	3	1	2	3	6
	Falconbridge Falcons	Al-Cup	9	5	9	14	....	....	....	15	....	....	....	....	....
1938-39	Kirkland Lake Blue Devils	NBHL	7	*17	12	*29	....	....	....	2	2	4	2	*6	0
	Detroit Red Wings	**NHL**	**1**	**1**	**1**	**2**	**2**	**2**	**4**	**0**	**3**	**1**	**2**	**3**	**7**
	Kirkland Lake Blue Devils	Al-Cup	7	14	3	17	....	....	....	2	....	....	....	....	....
1939-40	**Detroit Red Wings**	**NHL**	**29**	**2**	**3**	**5**	**3**	**5**	**8**	**11**	**5**	**0**	**0**	**0**	**0**
1940-41	**Detroit Red Wings**	**NHL**	**45**	**8**	**7**	**15**	**12**	**10**	**22**	**14**	**9**	**1**	**4**	**5**	**0**
1941-42	**Detroit Red Wings**	**NHL**	**48**	**23**	**30**	**53**	**31**	**36**	**67**	**13**	**12**	***8**	**6**	***14**	**29**
♦1942-43	**Detroit Red Wings**	**NHL**	**50**	**15**	**17**	**32**	**15**	**16**	**31**	**10**	**10**	**4**	**2**	**6**	**10**
1943-44	**Detroit Red Wings**	**NHL**	**42**	**16**	**31**	**47**	**14**	**27**	**41**	**13**	**5**	**1**	**0**	**1**	**0**
1944-45	**Detroit Red Wings**	**NHL**	**20**	**6**	**10**	**16**	**6**	**12**	**18**	**6**	....	....	....	....	....
	Chicago Black Hawks	**NHL**	**21**	**9**	**6**	**15**	**9**	**7**	**16**	**4**	....	....	....	....	....
1945-46	**Chicago Black Hawks**	**NHL**	**47**	**7**	**10**	**17**	**8**	**14**	**22**	**17**	**4**	**0**	**0**	**0**	**17**
1946-47	**Boston Bruins**	**NHL**	**33**	**0**	**2**	**2**	**0**	**2**	**2**	**2**	....	....	....	....	....
	Hershey Bears	AHL	25	8	14	22	....	....	....	34	11	4	6	10	2
1947-48	St. Louis Flyers	AHL	65	34	47	81	....	....	....	10	....	....	....	....	....
1948-49	St. Louis Flyers	AHL	63	10	45	55	....	....	....	17	7	0	2	2	4
1949-50	S.S. Marie Greyhounds	NOHA	....	....	....	....	....	....	....	....	11	5	6	11	....
1950-51	S.S. Marie Greyhounds	NOHA	DID NOT PLAY – COACHING												
1951-52	S.S. Marie Greyhounds	NOHA	4	0	1	1	....	....	....	0	8	2	2	4	12
	NHL Totals		**336**	**87**	**117**	**204**	**100**	**131**	**231**	**90**	**48**	**15**	**14**	**29**	**63**

Won Jack Fox Trophy (Sportsmanship-AHL) (1948)

Traded to **Chicago** by **Detroit** with Cully Simon and Byron McDonald for Earl Seibert and future considerations (Fido Purpur, January 4, 1945), January 2, 1945. Traded to **Boston** by **Chicago** for cash, June, 1946. Traded to **St. Louis** (AHL) by **Boston** for cash, June 14, 1947.

• GROSVENOR, Len Leonard Cecil

C/RW – R. 5'9", 172 lbs. b: Ottawa, Ont., 7/21/1905.

Season	Club	League	GP	G	A	Pts	AG	AA	APts	PIM	GP	G	A	Pts	PIM
1925-26	Ottawa Rideaus	OCHL	....	1	0	1	....	....	....	....	....	....	....	....	....
1926-27	Ottawa Rideaus	OCHL	14	9	4	13	....	....	....	....	....	....	....	....	....
1927-28	**Ottawa Senators**	**NHL**	**43**	**1**	**2**	**3**	**2**	**11**	**13**	**18**	**2**	**0**	**0**	**0**	**2**
1928-29	**Ottawa Senators**	**NHL**	**42**	**3**	**2**	**5**	**9**	**13**	**22**	**16**	....	....	....	....	....
1929-30	**Ottawa Senators**	**NHL**	**15**	**0**	**3**	**3**	**0**	**7**	**7**	**19**	....	....	....	....	....
	London Panthers	IHL	27	6	1	7	....	....	....	24	2	0	0	0	0
1930-31	London Tecumsehs	IHL	9	4	1	5	....	....	....	9	....	....	....	....	....
	Ottawa Senators	**NHL**	**33**	**5**	**4**	**9**	**10**	**12**	**22**	**25**	....	....	....	....	....
1931-32	**New York Americans**	**NHL**	**12**	**0**	**0**	**0**	**0**	**0**	**0**	**0**	....	....	....	....	....
	Bronx Tigers	Can-Am	30	6	5	11	....	....	....	28	2	0	0	0	0
1932-33	**Montreal Canadiens**	**NHL**	**4**	**0**	**0**	**0**	**0**	**0**	**0**	**0**	**2**	**0**	**0**	**0**	**0**
	NHL Totals		**149**	**9**	**11**	**20**	**21**	**43**	**64**	**78**	**4**	**0**	**0**	**0**	**2**

Signed as a free agent by **Ottawa**, October 24, 1927. Loaned to **London** (IHL) by **Ottawa** for cash, December 26, 1929. Traded to **London** (IHL) by **Ottawa** for cash, October 24, 1930. Traded to **Ottawa** by **London** (IHL) for Harry Connor, December 1, 1930. Claimed by **NY Americans** from **Ottawa** for 1931-32 season in Dispersal Draft, September 26, 1931. Signed as a free agent by **Montreal Canadiens**, January 7, 1933.

• GUIDOLIN, Aldo Aldo Reno

RW/D – R. 6', 180 lbs. b: Forks of Credit, Ont., 6/6/1932.

Season	Club	League	GP	G	A	Pts	AG	AA	APts	PIM	GP	G	A	Pts	PIM
1949-50	Guelph Biltmores	OHA-Jr.	38	8	8	16	....	....	....	21	15	2	0	2	18
	Guelph Biltmores	M-Cup	11	0	3	3	....	....	....	8	....	....	....	....	....
1950-51	Guelph Biltmores	OHA-Jr.	38	7	11	18	....	....	....	35	5	0	1	1	0
1951-52	Guelph Biltmores	OHA-Jr.	47	21	33	54	....	....	....	95	10	2	4	6	16
	Guelph Biltmores	M-Cup	4	2	1	3	....	....	....	2	....	....	....	....	....
1952-53	**New York Rangers**	**NHL**	**30**	**4**	**4**	**8**	**5**	**5**	**10**	**24**	....	....	....	....	....
	Vancouver Canucks	WHL	3	2	0	2	....	....	....	4	....	....	....	....	....
	Valleyfield Braves	QMHL	24	3	5	8	....	....	....	29	....	....	....	....	....
1953-54	**New York Rangers**	**NHL**	**68**	**2**	**6**	**8**	**3**	**7**	**10**	**51**	....	....	....	....	....
1954-55	**New York Rangers**	**NHL**	**70**	**2**	**5**	**7**	**3**	**6**	**9**	**34**	....	....	....	....	....
1955-56	**New York Rangers**	**NHL**	**14**	**1**	**0**	**1**	**1**	**0**	**1**	**8**	....	....	....	....	....
	Providence Reds	AHL	51	5	26	31	....	....	....	111	8	4	3	7	11
1956-57	Providence Reds	AHL	34	8	16	24	....	....	....	28	5	1	1	2	6
1957-58	Providence Reds	AHL	59	6	16	22	....	....	....	64	5	1	2	3	12
1958-59	Springfield Indians	AHL	55	3	18	21	....	....	....	90	....	....	....	....	....
1959-60	Cleveland Barons	AHL	66	10	22	32	....	....	....	168	7	0	2	2	16
1960-61	Cleveland Barons	AHL	72	10	37	47	....	....	....	152	4	0	1	1	8
1961-62	Cleveland Barons	AHL	68	7	34	41	....	....	....	*177	6	1	2	3	10
1962-63	Baltimore Clippers	AHL	59	8	28	36	....	....	....	144	....	....	....	....	....
1963-64	Baltimore Clippers	AHL	72	7	17	24	....	....	....	165	....	....	....	....	....
1964-65	Baltimore Clippers	AHL	67	1	28	29	....	....	....	143	....	....	....	....	....
1965-66	Providence Reds	AHL	71	4	21	25	....	....	....	157	....	....	....	....	....
1966-67	Baltimore Clippers	AHL	64	3	14	17	....	....	....	108	9	0	1	1	20
1967-68	Baltimore Clippers	AHL	69	6	12	18	....	....	....	95	....	....	....	....	....
1968-69	Baltimore Clippers	AHL	72	0	8	8	....	....	....	60	....	....	....	....	....
	NHL Totals		**182**	**9**	**15**	**24**	**12**	**18**	**30**	**117**	....	....	....	....	....

AHL First All-Star Team (1961, 1962)

Traded to **Cleveland** (AHL) by **NY Rangers** with Ed Hoekstra for Art Stratton with NY Rangers holding rights of recall, June, 1959. Traded to **Baltimore** (AHL) by **Cleveland** (AHL) for cash, August, 1962. Traded to **Providence** (AHL) by **NY Rangers** (Baltimore-AHL) with Marcel Paille, Jim Mikol and Sandy McGregor for Ed Giacomin, May 18, 1965. Traded to **Baltimore** (AHL) by **Providence** (AHL) with Willie Marshall, Jim Bartlett and Ian Anderson for Mike Corbett, Ed Lawson and Ken Stephanson, June, 1966.

• GUIDOLIN, Bep Armand

LW – L. 5'8", 175 lbs. b: Thorold, Ont., 12/9/1925.

Season	Club	League	GP	G	A	Pts	AG	AA	APts	PIM	GP	G	A	Pts	PIM
1941-42	Oshawa Generals	OHA-Jr.	21	4	13	17	....	....	....	38	11	0	3	3	22
	Oshawa Generals	M-Cup	11	5	5	10	....	....	....	56	....	....	....	....	....
1942-43	**Boston Bruins**	**NHL**	**42**	**7**	**15**	**22**	**7**	**14**	**21**	**43**	**9**	**0**	**4**	**4**	**12**
1943-44	**Boston Bruins**	**NHL**	**47**	**17**	**25**	**42**	**15**	**22**	**37**	**58**	....	....	....	....	....
1944-45	Newmarket Navy	TNDHL	7	11	12	23	....	....	....	*18	8	9	8	17	*23
	Toronto Army Shamrocks	TIHL	18	13	10	23	....	....	....	61	3	2	2	4	*10
	Toronto Army	OHA-Sr.	2	1	1	2	....	....	....	0	....	....	....	....	....
1945-46	**Boston Bruins**	**NHL**	**50**	**15**	**17**	**32**	**18**	**25**	**43**	**62**	**10**	**5**	**2**	**7**	**13**
1946-47	**Boston Bruins**	**NHL**	**56**	**10**	**13**	**23**	**11**	**16**	**27**	**73**	**3**	**0**	**1**	**1**	**6**
1947-48	**Detroit Red Wings**	**NHL**	**58**	**12**	**10**	**22**	**15**	**13**	**28**	**78**	**2**	**0**	**0**	**0**	**4**
1948-49	**Detroit Red Wings**	**NHL**	**4**	**0**	**0**	**0**	**0**	**0**	**0**	**0**	....	....	....	....	....
	Chicago Black Hawks	**NHL**	**56**	**4**	**17**	**21**	**6**	**24**	**30**	**116**	....	....	....	....	....
1949-50	**Chicago Black Hawks**	**NHL**	**70**	**17**	**34**	**51**	**21**	**41**	**62**	**42**	....	....	....	....	....
1950-51	**Chicago Black Hawks**	**NHL**	**69**	**12**	**22**	**34**	**15**	**27**	**42**	**56**	....	....	....	....	....
1951-52	**Chicago Black Hawks**	**NHL**	**67**	**13**	**18**	**31**	**17**	**22**	**39**	**78**	....	....	....	....	....
1952-53	Syracuse Warriors	AHL	23	1	8	9	....	....	....	24	3	0	0	0	8
	Ottawa Senators	QMHL	43	9	24	33	....	....	....	54	....	....	....	....	....

Season	Club	League	GP	G	A	Pts	AG	AA	APts	PIM	GP	G	A	Pts	PIM
			REGULAR SEASON								PLAYOFFS				
1953-54	Ottawa Senators	QHL	71	18	38	56	....	....	....	*148	22	2	11	13	39
1954-55	Ottawa Senators	QHL	19	5	12	17	....	....	....	77	....	....	....	....	....
	North Bay Trappers	NOHA	20	8	12	20	....	....	....	40	13	2	6	8	36
1955-56	Val d'Or Miners	QSHL	STATISTICS NOT AVAILABLE												
	North Bay Trappers	NOHA	1	1	2	3	....	....	....	2	....	....	....	....	....
1956-57	Belleville McFarlands	EOHL	48	16	29	45	....	....	....	*156	10	4	3	7	12
1957-58	Windsor Bulldogs	NOHA	7	2	6	8	....	....	....	24	....	....	....	....	....
	Belleville McFarlands	EOHL	35	12	18	30	....	....	....	60	13	3	10	13	*32
	Belleville McFarlands	Al-Cup	13	7	*14	*21	....	....	....	20	....	....	....	....	....
1958-59	Kingston Merchants	EOHL	43	11	26	37	....	....	....	62	12	0	4	4	24
1959-60			DID NOT PLAY												
1960-61	Omaha–Indianapolis	IHL	64	14	33	47	....	....	....	63	....	....	....	....	....
	NHL Totals		**519**	**107**	**171**	**278**	**125**	**204**	**329**	**606**	**24**	**5**	**7**	**12**	**35**

• Youngest player (16 years, 11 months) to play in a NHL game, November 12, 1942. (Toronto 3, Boston 1). Traded to **Detroit** by **Boston** for Billy Taylor, October 15, 1947. Traded to **Chicago** by **Detroit** with Jim Conacher and Doug McCaig for George Gee and Bud Poile, October 25, 1948. Traded to **North Bay** (NOHA) by **Ottawa** (QHL) for cash, December 17, 1954.

• HADDON, Lloyd Lloyd Ward

D – L. 6', 195 lbs. b: Sarnia, Ont., 8/10/1938.

Season	Club	League	GP	G	A	Pts	AG	AA	APts	PIM	GP	G	A	Pts	PIM
1954-55	Hamilton Tiger Cubs	OHA-Jr.	2	1	0	1	....	....	....	0	....	....	....	....	....
1955-56	Hamilton Tiger Cubs	OHA-Jr.	34	5	1	6	....	....	....	4	....	....	....	....	....
1956-57	Hamilton Tiger Cubs	OHA-Jr.	19	1	1	2	....	....	....	4	....	....	....	....	....
1957-58	Hamilton Tiger Cubs	OHA-Jr.	52	9	19	28	....	....	....	32	15	7	8	15	10
1958-59	Hamilton Tiger Cubs	OHA-Jr.	54	15	30	45	....	....	....	51	....	....	....	....	....
	Hershey Bears	AHL	1	0	0	0	....	....	....	0	....	....	....	....	....
	Edmonton Flyers	WHL	9	1	1	2	....	....	....	0	2	0	0	0	0
1959-60	**Detroit Red Wings**	**NHL**	**8**	**0**	**0**	**0**	**0**	**0**	**0**	**2**	**1**	**0**	**0**	**0**	**0**
	Edmonton Flyers	WHL	53	3	17	20	....	....	....	22	....	....	....	....	....
1960-61	Edmonton Flyers	WHL	68	15	20	35	....	....	....	25	....	....	....	....	....
1961-62	Edmonton Flyers	WHL	70	22	27	49	....	....	....	22	4	0	2	2	0
1962-63	Los Angeles Blades	WHL	70	19	32	51	....	....	....	4	3	1	3	4	0
1963-64	St. Louis Braves	CPHL	72	14	49	63	....	....	....	24	6	1	2	3	2
1964-65	Los Angeles Blades	WHL	65	7	28	35	....	....	....	12	....	....	....	....	....
	NHL Totals		**8**	**0**	**0**	**0**	**0**	**0**	**0**	**2**	**1**	**0**	**0**	**0**	**0**

OHA-Jr. First All-Star Team (1959) • WHL First Alll-Star Team (1962)

Traded to **LA Blades** (WHL) by **Detroit** for cash, July, 1962. Traded to **Chicago** (St. Louis - AHL) by **LA Blades** (WHL) for Norm Johnson, Ron Leopold and Gord Vejprava, August 12, 1963. Traded to **LA Blades** (WHL) by **St. Louis** (AHL) for cash, August 12, 1964.

• HADFIELD, Vic *— see page 1142*

• HAGGARTY, Jim

LW – L. 5'11", 167 lbs. b: Port Arthur, Ont., 4/14/1914 d: 3/8/1998.

Season	Club	League	GP	G	A	Pts	AG	AA	APts	PIM	GP	G	A	Pts	PIM
1932-33	Port Arthur Ports	TBJHL	12	*14	5	*19	....	....	....	4	2	0	0	0	0
	Port Arthur Ports	M-Cup	4	2	1	3	....	....	....	0	....	....	....	....	....
1933-34	Port Arthur Ports	TBJHL	10	6	4	10	....	....	....	9	2	3	0	3	0
	Port Arthur Ports	M-Cup	5	10	4	14	....	....	....	2	....	....	....	....	....
1934-35	Port Arthur Ports	TBSHL	16	11	2	13	....	....	....	21	3	*5	1	*6	5
	Port Arthur Ports	Al-Cup	7	8	1	9	....	....	....	4	....	....	....	....	....
1935-36	Wembley Canadians	Ln-Cup	....	8	2	10	....	....	....	....	....	....	....	....	....
	Wembley Canadians	Britain	....	15	2	17	....	....	....	....	....	....	....	....	....
	Canada	Olympics	2	2	3	5	....	....	....	0	....	....	....	....	....
1936-37	Wembley Monarchs	Britain	40	29	14	43	....	....	....	6	....	....	....	....	....
1937-38	Wembley Monarchs	Ln-Cup	....	0	1	1	....	....	....	....	....	....	....	....	....
	Wembley Monarchs	Britain	....	11	7	18	....	....	....	....	....	....	....	....	....
	Wembley Monarchs	Olympics	....	7	1	8	....	....	....	....	....	....	....	....	....
1938-39	Wembley Monarchs	Ln-Cup	....	0	1	1	....	....	....	....	....	....	....	....	....
	Wembley Monarchs	Britain	....	10	16	26	....	....	....	....	....	....	....	....	....
	Wembley Monarchs	Olympics	....	5	4	9	....	....	....	....	....	....	....	....	....
1939-40	Montreal Royals	QSHL	28	7	8	15	....	....	....	0	4	0	2	2	2
	Montreal Royals	Al-Cup	2	1	1	2	....	....	....	0	....	....	....	....	....
1940-41	Montreal Royals	QSHL	21	8	10	18	....	....	....	4	9	2	3	5	14
	Montreal Royals	Al-Cup	14	7	6	13	....	....	....	8	....	....	....	....	....
1941-42	Montreal Royals	QSHL	36	24	14	38	....	....	....	12	....	....	....	....	....
	Montreal Canadiens	**NHL**	**5**	**1**	**1**	**2**	**1**	**1**	**2**	**0**	**3**	**2**	**1**	**3**	**0**
1942-43	Montreal RCAF	QSHL	35	15	17	32	....	....	....	6	12	8	1	9	4
1943-44	Malton RCAF	TNDHL	4	5	2	7	....	....	....	2	2	*5	3	*8	0
1944-45	Montreal RCAF	QSHL	5	9	11	20	....	....	....	2	....	....	....	....	....
	Valleyfield Braves	QPHL	9	7	2	9	....	....	....	0	....	....	....	....	....
1945-46	Middleton RCAF	Britain	STATISTICS NOT AVAILABLE												
	Montreal Royals	QSHL	....	....	....	....	....	....	....	....	3	1	0	1	0
1946-47	Montreal Royals	QSHL	36	15	17	32	....	....	....	8	10	3	0	3	2
	Montreal Royals	Al-Cup	6	1	2	3	....	....	....	0	....	....	....	....	....
1947-48	Montreal Royals	QSHL	48	20	42	62	....	....	....	12	3	0	0	0	0
1948-49	Montreal Royals	QSHL	29	17	30	47	....	....	....	8	9	1	7	8	0
1949-50	Montreal Royals	QSHL	8	1	6	7	....	....	....	0	....	....	....	....	....
	Valleyfield Braves	QSHL	24	2	6	8	....	....	....	0	....	....	....	....	....
	NHL Totals		**5**	**1**	**1**	**2**	**1**	**1**	**2**	**0**	**3**	**2**	**1**	**3**	**0**

Signed as a free agent by **Montreal**, March 3, 1942.

• HAIDY, Gord Gordon Adam

RW – R. 5'11", 185 lbs. b: Winnipeg, Man., 4/11/1928.

Season	Club	League	GP	G	A	Pts	AG	AA	APts	PIM	GP	G	A	Pts	PIM
1944-45	Windsor Jr. Spitfires	OHA-B	10	6	8	14	....	....	....	6	2	1	2	3	4
1945-46	Windsor Spitfires	IHL	15	9	6	15	....	....	....	22	....	....	....	....	....
1946-47	Windsor Jr. Spitfires	OHA-Jr.	15	23	7	30	....	....	....	17	....	....	....	....	....
	Windsor Spitfires	IHL	26	31	25	56	....	....	....	35	6	*19	6	*25	8
1947-48	Windsor Jr. Spitfires	OHA-Jr.	28	38	19	57	....	....	....	43	12	10	5	15	34
	Windsor Spitfires	IHL	25	*32	11	43	....	....	....	48	....	....	....	....	....
1948-49	Omaha Knights	USHL	6	3	4	7	....	....	....	0	....	....	....	....	....
	Indianapolis Capitols	AHL	48	14	10	24	....	....	....	51	2	0	0	0	0
1949-50	Indianapolis Capitols	AHL	47	20	10	30	....	....	....	32	8	5	1	6	4
♦	**Detroit Red Wings**	**NHL**	....	....	....	....	....	....	....	....	**1**	**0**	**0**	**0**	**0**
1950-51	Indianapolis Capitols	AHL	59	26	18	44	....	....	....	40	3	0	0	0	0
1951-52			DID NOT PLAY – SUSPENDED												
1952-53	New Westminster Royals	WHL	18	6	4	10	....	....	....	14	....	....	....	....	....
	Buffalo Bisons	AHL	10	0	0	0	....	....	....	4	....	....	....	....	....

Season	Club	League	GP	G	A	Pts	AG	AA	APts	PIM	GP	G	A	Pts	PIM
			REGULAR SEASON								PLAYOFFS				
1953-54	Windsor Bulldogs	OHA-Sr.	54	*47	33	80	....	....	....	*191	4	2	1	3	8
1954-55	Windsor Bulldogs	OHA-Sr.	48	30	30	60	....	....	....	88	12	2	*13	15	*27
1955-56	Windsor Bulldogs	OHA-Sr.	48	23	27	50	....	....	....	114	....	....	....	....	....
1956-57	Windsor Bulldogs	OHA-Sr.	52	28	30	58	....	....	....	62	11	5	11	16	*48
1957-58	Chatham Maroons	NOHA	58	22	25	47	....	....	....	91	....	....	....	....	....
1958-59	Windsor Bulldogs	NOHA	27	9	15	24	....	....	....	45	....	....	....	....	....
1959-60	Windsor Bulldogs	OHA-Sr.	47	21	27	48	....	....	....	77	17	12	15	27	12
1960-61	Milwaukee–Indianapolis	IHL	14	5	6	11	....	....	....	8	....	....	....	....	....
	Windsor Bulldogs	WOHL	....	14	5	19	....	....	....	6	....	....	....	....	....
1961-62	Windsor Bulldogs	OHA-Sr.	17	13	12	25	....	....	....	16	13	9	9	18	12
1962-63	Sarnia Rams	OHA-Sr.	6	3	4	7	....	....	....	2	....	....	....	....	....
1963-64	Windsor Bulldogs	IHL	17	7	4	11	....	....	....	18	....	....	....	....	....
	NHL Totals		....	....	....	....	....	....	....	....	**1**	**0**	**0**	**0**	**0**

• Suspended for entire 1951-52 season by **Detroit** for refusing to report to **Indianapolis** (AHL), September 30, 1951.

• HALDERSON, Harold "Slim"

D – R. 6'3", 200 lbs. b: Winnipeg, Man., 1/6/1900 d: 8/1/1965.

Season	Club	League	GP	G	A	Pts	AG	AA	APts	PIM	GP	G	A	Pts	PIM
1917-18	Winnipeg Ypres	MHL-Sr.	7	5	6	11	....	....	....	4	....	....	....	....	....
	Winnipeg Ypres	Al-Cup	4	4	3	7	....	....	....	4	....	....	....	....	....
1918-19	Winnipeg Monarchs	MHL-Sr.	9	3	5	8	....	....	....	4	....	....	....	....	....
1919-20	Winnipeg Falcons	MHL-Sr.	9	10	*11	21	....	....	....	10	....	....	....	....	....
	Canada	Olympics	3	9	*2	11	....	....	....	....	....	....	....	....	....
	Winnipeg Falcons	Al-Cup	6	4	6	10	....	....	....	6	....	....	....	....	....
1920-21	Saskatoon Crescents	N-SSHL	16	12	3	15	....	....	....	38	4	*8	0	*8	9
1921-22	Victoria Aristocrats	PCHA	23	7	3	10	....	....	....	13	....	....	....	....	....
1922-23	Victoria Cougars	PCHA	29	10	5	15	....	....	....	26	2	0	0	0	0
1923-24	Victoria Cougars	PCHA	30	6	2	8	....	....	....	50	....	....	....	....	....
1924-25	Victoria Cougars	WCHL	28	3	6	9	....	....	....	71	4	1	0	1	12
♦	Victoria Cougars	St-Cup	4	1	2	3	....	....	....	8	....	....	....	....	....
1925-26	Victoria Cougars	WHL	23	3	1	4	....	....	....	51	3	1	0	1	6
	Victoria Cougars	St-Cup	4	1	0	1	....	....	....	8	....	....	....	....	....
1926-27	**Detroit Cougars**	**NHL**	**19**	**2**	**0**	**2**	**4**	**0**	**4**	**29**	....	....	....	....	....
	Toronto Pats/Leafs	**NHL**	**25**	**1**	**2**	**3**	**2**	**10**	**12**	**36**	....	....	....	....	....
1927-28	Quebec Castors	Can-Am	40	13	5	18	....	....	....	71	6	1	1	2	14
1928-29	Newark Bulldogs	Can-Am	40	6	3	9	....	....	....	107	....	....	....	....	....
1929-30	Kansas City Pla-Mors	AHA	48	8	7	15	....	....	....	76	5	0	0	0	8
1930-31	Kansas City Pla-Mors	AHA	47	5	7	12	....	....	....	77	8	1	1	2	10
1931-32	Kansas City Pla-Mors	AHA	46	9	3	12	....	....	....	69	4	2	0	2	0
1932-33	Kansas City Pla-Mors	AHA	26	1	4	5	....	....	....	30	....	....	....	....	....
	Duluth-Wichita	AHA	24	7	2	9	....	....	....	40	....	....	....	....	....
1933-34	Tulsa Oilers	AHA	48	9	12	21	....	....	....	66	4	0	2	2	4
	Wichita Vikings	AHA	2	0	0	0	....	....	....	0	....	....	....	....	....
1934-35	Tulsa Oilers	AHA	48	6	13	19	....	....	....	65	5	1	2	3	2
1935-36	Tulsa Oilers	AHA	48	6	14	20	....	....	....	25	3	0	0	0	4
1936-37	Wichita Skyhawks	AHA	48	5	4	9	....	....	....	30	....	....	....	....	....
	NHL Totals		**44**	**3**	**2**	**5**	**6**	**10**	**16**	**65**	....	....	....	....	....
	Other Major League Totals		133	29	17	46	....	....	....	211	9	2	0	2	18

PCHA Second All-Star Team (1922) • PCHA First All-Star Team (1923) • AHA First All-Star Team (1930, 1936, 1937)

Signed as a free agent by **Victoria** (PCHA), October 5, 1921. • 1924-25 playoff totals includes WCHL series against Calgary and Saskatoon. • 1925-26 playoff totals includes WHL series against Edmonton and Saskatoon. Transferred to **Detroit** after NHL club purchased **Victoria** (WHL) franchise, May 15, 1926. Traded to **Toronto** by **Detroit** for Pete Bellefeuille, January 10, 1927. Signed as a free agent by **Quebec** (Can-Am), November 1, 1927.

• HALEY, Len Leonard Frank "Comet"

RW – R. 5'6", 160 lbs. b: Edmonton, Alta., 9/15/1931.

Season	Club	League	GP	G	A	Pts	AG	AA	APts	PIM	GP	G	A	Pts	PIM
1947-48	Edmonton Canadians	EJrHL	1	0	0	0	....	....	....	0	....	....	....	....	....
1948-49	Westaskiwin Canadians	EJrHL	STATISTICS NOT AVAILABLE												
	Westaskiwin Canadians	M-Cup	3	1	0	1	....	....	....	6	....	....	....	....	....
1949-50	Medicine Hat Tigers	WCJHL	40	26	28	54	....	....	....	76	5	0	3	3	6
	Medicine Hat Tigers	M-Cup	12	7	11	18	....	....	....	52	....	....	....	....	....
1950-51	Medicine Hat Tigers	WCJHL	40	37	30	67	....	....	....	53	5	3	3	6	14
	Omaha Knights	USHL	3	1	3	4	....	....	....	0	....	....	....	....	....
1951-52	Glace Bay Miners	MMHL	86	44	58	*102	....	....	....	71	5	2	1	3	4
1952-53	Edmonton Flyers	WHL	69	18	17	35	....	....	....	23	15	4	6	10	6
1953-54	Edmonton Flyers	WHL	70	17	25	42	....	....	....	40	13	3	4	7	18
1954-55	Edmonton–Saskatoon	WHL	68	20	23	43	....	....	....	43	....	....	....	....	....
1955-56	Saskatoon Quakers	WHL	68	17	22	39	....	....	....	95	3	1	3	4	4
1956-57	Brandon Regals	WHL	69	21	33	54	....	....	....	77	9	5	2	7	4
	Brandon Regals	Ed-Cup	6	1	3	4	....	....	....	0	....	....	....	....	....
1957-58	Hershey Bears	AHL	70	30	19	49	....	....	....	34	11	4	4	8	4
1958-59	Hershey Bears	AHL	59	17	11	28	....	....	....	38	11	1	0	1	20
1959-60	**Detroit Red Wings**	**NHL**	**27**	**1**	**2**	**3**	**1**	**2**	**3**	**12**	**6**	**1**	**3**	**4**	**6**
	Edmonton Flyers	WHL	39	19	16	35	....	....	....	35	....	....	....	....	....
1960-61	**Detroit Red Wings**	**NHL**	**3**	**1**	**0**	**1**	**1**	**0**	**1**	**2**	....	....	....	....	....
	Edmonton Flyers	WHL	66	15	30	45	....	....	....	36	....	....	....	....	....
1961-62	San Francisco Seals	WHL	66	20	30	50	....	....	....	56	2	0	0	0	2
1962-63	San Francisco Seals	WHL	70	36	24	60	....	....	....	76	17	8	6	14	23
1963-64	San Francisco Seals	WHL	70	35	33	68	....	....	....	112	11	4	10	14	14
1964-65	San Francisco Seals	WHL	70	26	46	72	....	....	....	113	....	....	....	....	....
1965-66	Seattle Totems	WHL	69	27	39	66	....	....	....	89	....	....	....	....	....
1966-67	San Diego Gulls	WHL	69	13	33	46	....	....	....	71	....	....	....	....	....
1967-68	Tulsa Oilers	CPHL	70	*34	46	80	....	....	....	67	11	*6	9	15	15
1968-69	Omaha Knights	CHL	70	16	25	41	....	....	....	63	7	2	4	6	0
	Edmonton Monarchs	ASHL	2	0	2	2	....	....	....	0	....	....	....	....	....

Season	Club	League	GP	G	A	Pts	AG	AA	APts	PIM	GP	G	A	Pts	PIM
			REGULAR SEASON								PLAYOFFS				
1969-70	Grand Falls Cataracts	Nfld-Sr.	12	7	11	18	....	....	....	52	....	....	....	....	....
	New Haven Blades	EHL	39	12	31	43	....	....	....	16	11	5	3	8	16
1970-71	Edmonton Monarchs	PrSHL	40	23	26	49	....	....	....	76	....	....	....	....	....
1971-72	Edmonton Monarchs	PrSHL	40	18	23	41	....	....	....	63	....	....	....	....	....
	NHL Totals		**30**	**2**	**2**	**4**	**2**	**2**	**4**	**14**	**6**	**1**	**3**	**4**	**6**

WCJHL Second All-Star Team (1950) • CPHL First All-Star Team (1968)

• Assigned to Glace Bay (MMHL) by Detroit, October 16, 1951. Traded to **Saskatoon** (WHL) by **Detroit** (Edmonton-WHL) for cash, November, 1954. Claimed by **Hershey** (AHL) from **Brandon** (WHL) in Inter-League Draft, June 4, 1957. Traded to **Detroit** (Edmonton-WHL) by **Hershey** (AHL) for Ray Kinasewich, September, 1959. Traded to **Montreal** (Seattle-WHL) by **San Francisco** (WHL) for Gerry Brisson, October 22, 1965. Claimed by **Detroit** (Pittsburgh-AHL) from **Montreal** (Seattle-WHL) in Reverse Draft, June 15, 1966. Traded to **San Diego** (WHL) by **Detroit** (Pittsburgh-AHL) with Ed Ehrenverth and Al Nicholson for $20,000, June 20, 1966. Loaned to **Tulsa** (CPHL) by **San Diego** for 1967-68 season, September, 1967. Traded to **NY Rangers** by **San Diego** for Bruce Carmichael, September, 1968. Traded to **Des Moines** (IHL) by **NY Rangers** (New Haven-EHL) for Nelson Tremblay, September, 1970.

• HALL, Bob "Red"

F – L. 5'8", 165 lbs. b: Oak Park, IL, 10/13/1899 d: 12/3/1950.

Season	Club	League	GP	G	A	Pts	AG	AA	APts	PIM	GP	G	A	Pts	PIM
1917-18	Brooklyn Crescents	AAHL	4	3	0	3	....	....	....	....	....	....	....	....	....
1918-19	Brooklyn Crescents	AAHL	7	11	3	14	....	....	....	8	....	....	....	....	....
	Brooklyn Crescents	NYSHL	4	0	3	3	....	....	....	2	....	....	....	....	....
1919-20	Dartmouth College	Ivy	STATISTICS NOT AVAILABLE												
1920-21	Dartmouth College	Ivy	STATISTICS NOT AVAILABLE												
1921-22	Dartmouth College	Ivy	STATISTICS NOT AVAILABLE												
1922-23	New York St. Nicholas	USAHA	....	2	0	2	....	....	....	....	....	....	....	....	....
1923-24	Boston A.A. Unicorn	USAHA	1	0	0	0	....	....	....	....	1	0	0	0	....
	Dartmouth College	Ivy	STATISTICS NOT AVAILABLE												
1924-25	Boston A.A. Unicorn	USAHA	8	2	0	2	....	....	....	....	....	....	....	....	....
	Boston Maples	USAHA	4	0	0	0	....	....	....	....	....	....	....	....	....
	Minneapolis Rockets	USAHA	6	0	0	0	....	....	....	0	....	....	....	....	....
1925-26	New York Athletic Club	NYSHL	STATISTICS NOT AVAILABLE												
	New York Americans	NHL	8	0	0	0	0	0	0	0	....	....	....	....	....
	NHL Totals		**8**	**0**	**0**	**0**	**0**	**0**	**0**	**0**	....	....	....	....	....

Signed as a free agent **NY Americans**, February 8, 1926.

• HALL, Joe Joseph Henry "Bad Joe" HHOF

D – R. 5'10", 175 lbs. b: Staffordshire, England, 5/3/1882 d: 4/5/1919.

Season	Club	League	GP	G	A	Pts	AG	AA	APts	PIM	GP	G	A	Pts	PIM
1902-03	Brandon Regals	MHL-Sr.	6	8	0	8	....	....	....	....	....	....	....	....	....
1903-04	Winnipeg Rowing Club	MHL-Sr.	6	6	0	6	....	....	....	....	3	1	0	1	....
1904-05	Brandon Hockey Club	MHL-Sr.	8	11	0	11	....	....	....	....	....	....	....	....	....
1905-06	Portage Lakes Professionals	IHL	20	33	0	33	....	....	....	*98	....	....	....	....	....
	Quebec Bulldogs	ECAHA	3	2	0	2	....	....	....	3	....	....	....	....	....
1906-07	Brandon Regals	MHL-Sr.	9	14	0	14	....	....	....	....	2	5	0	5	5
1907-08	Montreal AAA	ECAHA	4	5	0	5	....	....	....	11	....	....	....	....	....
	Montreal Shamrocks	ECAHA	4	4	0	4	....	....	....	6	....	....	....	....	....
1908-09	Edmonton Pros	APHL	1	8	0	8	....	....	....	6	....	....	....	....	....
	Montreal Wanderers	ECHA	5	10	0	10	....	....	....	18	....	....	....	....	....
	Winnipeg Maple Leafs	MHL	2	2	1	3	....	....	....	0	2	2	1	3	9
1909-10	Montreal Shamrocks	NHA	10	8	0	8	....	....	....	47	....	....	....	....	....
	Montreal Shamrocks	CHA	1	7	0	7	....	....	....	6	....	....	....	....	....
1910-11	Quebec Bulldogs	NHA	10	0	0	0	....	....	....	20	....	....	....	....	....
♦1911-12	Quebec Bulldogs	NHA	18	15	0	15	....	....	....	30	2	2	0	2	2
♦1912-13	Quebec Bulldogs	NHA	17	8	0	8	....	....	....	78	2	3	0	3	0
1913-14	Quebec Bulldogs	NHA	19	13	4	17	....	....	....	61	....	....	....	....	....
1914-15	Quebec Bulldogs	NHA	20	3	2	5	....	....	....	52	....	....	....	....	....
1915-16	Quebec Bulldogs	NHA	23	1	2	3	....	....	....	89	....	....	....	....	....
1916-17	Quebec Bulldogs	NHA	19	6	5	11	....	....	....	95	....	....	....	....	....
1917-18	**Montreal Canadiens**	**NHL**	**21**	**8**	**7**	**15**	**10**	**30**	**40**	***100**	**2**	**0**	**1**	**1**	**12**
1918-19	**Montreal Canadiens**	**NHL**	**17**	**7**	**1**	**8**	**12**	**5**	**17**	***89**	**5**	**0**	**0**	**0**	***17**
	Montreal Canadiens	St-Cup	5	0	0	0	....	....	....	6	....	....	....	....	....
	NHL Totals		**38**	**15**	**8**	**23**	**22**	**35**	**57**	**189**	**7**	**0**	**1**	**1**	**29**
	Other Major League Totals		182	129	13	142	....	....	....	614	6	10	0	10	7

IHL First All-Star Team (1906)

Signed as a free agent by **Portage Lakes** (IHL), November 2, 1906. • Jumped contract with Portage Lakes (IHL) and signed with **Brandon** (MHL-Sr.), November 19, 1906. Signed as a free agent by **Winnipeg Maple Leafs** (MHL-Sr.), December 2, 1907. Signed as a free agent by **Montreal AAA** (ECAHA), January 18, 1908. Signed as a free agent by **Montreal Shamrocks** (ECAHA) after being released by Montreal AAA, February 11, 1908. Signed as a free agent by **Edmonton** (APHL), December 7, 1908. • Released by Edmonton (APHL), December 15, 1908. Claimed by **Montreal Canadiens** from **Quebec** in Dispersal Draft, November 26, 1917. • Died in a Seattle hospital from complications brought on by influenza, April 5, 1919.

• HALL, Murray — *see page 1145*

• HALL, Wayne Gary Wayne

LW – L. 5'9", 165 lbs. b: Melita, Man., 5/22/1939.

Season	Club	League	GP	G	A	Pts	AG	AA	APts	PIM	GP	G	A	Pts	PIM
1956-57	Flin Flon Midget Bombs	SAHA	STATISTICS NOT AVAILABLE												
	Flin Flon Bombers	M-Cup	1	0	0	0	....	....	....	0	....	....	....	....	....
1957-58	Flin Flon Bombers	SJHL	38	8	19	27	....	....	....	20	2	0	1	1	2
1958-59	Flin Flon Bombers	SJHL	45	36	48	84	....	....	....	24	11	5	10	15	16
	Flin Flon Bombers	M-Cup	8	7	7	14	....	....	....	2	....	....	....	....	....
1959-60	Trois-Rivieres Lions	EPHL	64	9	29	38	....	....	....	16	7	0	1	1	0
1960-61	**New York Rangers**	**NHL**	**4**	**0**	**0**	**0**	**0**	**0**	**0**	**0**	....	....	....	....	....
	Kitchener Dutchmen	EPHL	56	9	27	36	....	....	....	14	7	0	1	1	5
1961-62	Vancouver Canucks	WHL	61	12	30	42	....	....	....	4	....	....	....	....	....
1962-63	Seattle Totems	WHL	53	10	14	24	....	....	....	8	17	1	8	9	0
1963-64	St. Paul Rangers	CPHL	72	15	28	43	....	....	....	14	10	3	4	7	0
1964-65	Providence Reds	AHL	23	4	13	17	....	....	....	14	....	....	....	....	....
	St. Louis Braves	CPHL	24	3	9	12	....	....	....	4	....	....	....	....	....
	St. Paul Rangers	CPHL	....	....	....	....	....	....	....	....	1	1	0	1	0
1965-66	Minneosta Rangers	CPHL	60	17	35	52	....	....	....	10	7	1	2	3	2
1966-67	Omaha Knights	CPHL	58	12	29	41	....	....	....	20	....	....	....	....	....
1967-68	Omaha Knights	CPHL	65	18	23	41	....	....	....	0	....	....	....	....	....
1968-69	Omaha Knights	CHL	1	0	0	0	....	....	....	0	....	....	....	....	....
	Buffalo Bisons	AHL	54	5	18	23	....	....	....	16	6	0	0	0	2
1969/71			OUT OF HOCKEY – RETIRED												
1971-72	Waterloo Black Hawks	USHL	35	8	17	25	....	....	....	32	....	....	....	....	....
	NHL Totals		**4**	**0**	**0**	**0**	**0**	**0**	**0**	**0**	....	....	....	....	....

• HALLIDAY, Milt

LW – L. 5'10", 180 lbs. b: Ottawa, Ont., 9/21/1906 d: 8/16/1989.

Season	Club	League	GP	G	A	Pts	AG	AA	APts	PIM	GP	G	A	Pts	PIM
1923-24	Ottawa Stewartons	OCHL	STATISTICS NOT AVAILABLE												
1924-25	Ottawa Gunners	OCHL	16	7	1	8	....	....	....	....	....	....	....	....	....
1925-26	Ottawa Gunners	OCHL	....	10	2	12	....	....	....	....	6	*3	0	*3	....
♦1926-27	**Ottawa Senators**	**NHL**	**38**	**1**	**0**	**1**	**2**	**0**	**2**	**2**	**6**	**0**	**0**	**0**	**0**
1927-28	**Ottawa Senators**	**NHL**	**13**	**0**	**0**	**0**	**0**	**0**	**0**	**2**	....	....	....	....	....
	London Panthers	Can-Pro	29	8	1	9	....	....	....	6	....	....	....	....	....
1928-29	**Ottawa Senators**	**NHL**	**16**	**0**	**0**	**0**	**0**	**0**	**0**	**0**	....	....	....	....	....
	Niagara Falls Cataracts	Can-Pro	25	4	1	5	....	....	....	10	....	....	....	....	....
1929-30	Hamilton Tigers	IHL	41	12	3	15	....	....	....	10	....	....	....	....	....
1930-31	Pittsburgh Yellowjackets	IHL	44	11	2	13	....	....	....	14	6	0	0	0	2
1931-32	Pittsburgh Hornets	IHL	16	1	2	3	....	....	....	8	....	....	....	....	....
	Cleveland Indians	IHL	29	14	2	16	....	....	....	6	....	....	....	....	....
1932-33	Cleveland Falcons	IHL	42	14	8	22	....	....	....	10	....	....	....	....	....
1933-34	Boston Cubs	Can-Am	39	9	9	18	....	....	....	8	5	2	1	3	0
1934-35	Boston Cubs	Can-Am	13	2	4	6	....	....	....	2	3	0	0	0	0
	Cleveland Falcons	IHL	31	12	7	19	....	....	....	10	....	....	....	....	....
1935-36	Cleveland Falcons	IHL	10	1	1	2	....	....	....	2	....	....	....	....	....
	Buffalo Bisons	IHL	17	1	5	6	....	....	....	0	....	....	....	....	....
	Rochester Cardinals	IHL	18	3	2	5	....	....	....	4	....	....	....	....	....
1936-37			REINSTATED AS AN AMATEUR												
1937-38	Ottawa Montagnards	OCHL	18	12	2	14	....	....	....	0	....	....	....	....	....
1938-39	Ottawa Montagnards	OCHL	3	0	0	0	....	....	....	2	....	....	....	....	....
	NHL Totals		**67**	**1**	**0**	**1**	**2**	**0**	**2**	**4**	**6**	**0**	**0**	**0**	**0**

Signed as a free agent by **Ottawa**, October 24, 1926. Traded to **Hamilton** (IHL) by **Ottawa** for cash, November 7, 1929. Traded to **Cleveland** (IHL) by **Pittsburgh** (IHL) for Stew Dunning, January 5, 1932. Signed as a free agent by **Buffalo** (IHL) after securing release from **Cleveland** (IHL), December 18, 1935. Signed as a free agent by **Rochester** (IHL) after securing release from Buffalo, February 7, 1936.

• HAMEL, Herb "Hap"

RW – R. 5'11", 155 lbs. b: New Hamburg, Ont., 6/8/1904 Deceased.

Season	Club	League	GP	G	A	Pts	AG	AA	APts	PIM	GP	G	A	Pts	PIM
1925-26	New Hamburg Seniors	OHA-Sr.	STATISTICS NOT AVAILABLE												
1926-27	Stratford Nationals	Can-Pro	16	3	1	4	....	....	....	4	....	....	....	....	....
	Niagara Falls Cataracts	Can-Pro	15	3	1	4	....	....	....	2	....	....	....	....	....
1927-28	Hamilton Tigers	Can-Pro	1	0	0	0	....	....	....	0	....	....	....	....	....
1928-29	Hamilton Tigers	Can-Pro	38	10	2	12	....	....	....	27	....	....	....	....	....
1929-30	Brantford Indians	Can-Pro	28	13	7	20	....	....	....	37	....	....	....	....	....
1930-31	**Toronto Maple Leafs**	**NHL**	**2**	**0**	**0**	**0**	**0**	**0**	**0**	**4**	....	....	....	....	....
	Stratford Nationals	OPHL	10	4	2	6	....	....	....	12	....	....	....	....	....
	Oshawa Patricias	OPHL	17	10	9	19	....	....	....	2	7	3	3	6	0
	NHL Totals		**2**	**0**	**0**	**0**	**0**	**0**	**0**	**4**	....	....	....	....	....

Signed as a free agent by **Stratford** (Can-Pro), October 19, 1926. Traded to **Niagara Falls** (Can-Pro) by **Stratford** (Can-Pro) for Gene Chouinard, January 17, 1927. Signed as a free agent by **Toronto**, December 8, 1930. Traded to **Oshawa** (OPHL) by **Stratford** (OPHL) for Gene Chouinard, January 17, 1931.

• HAMILL, Red Robert George

LW – L. 5'11", 180 lbs. b: Toronto, Ont., 1/11/1917 d: 12/12/1985.

Season	Club	League	GP	G	A	Pts	AG	AA	APts	PIM	GP	G	A	Pts	PIM
1934-35	Toronto Young Rangers	OHA-B	STATISTICS NOT AVAILABLE												
1935-36	South Porcupine Porkies	NOJHA	STATISTICS NOT AVAILABLE												
1936-37	Copper Cliff Redmen	NOJHA	3	*10	2	12	....	....	....	10	12	*21	14	35	11
	Copper Cliff Redmen	NOHA	12	10	2	12	....	....	....	17	....	....	....	....	....
1937-38	**Boston Bruins**	**NHL**	**6**	**0**	**1**	**1**	**0**	**2**	**2**	**2**	....	....	....	....	....
	Providence Reds	IAHL	40	8	9	17	....	....	....	31	7	2	2	4	*12
♦1938-39	**Boston Bruins**	**NHL**	**6**	**0**	**1**	**1**	**0**	**2**	**2**	**0**	**12**	**0**	**0**	**0**	**8**
	Hershey Bears	IAHL	45	12	12	24	....	....	....	29	....	....	....	....	....
1939-40	**Boston Bruins**	**NHL**	**30**	**10**	**8**	**18**	**17**	**12**	**29**	**16**	**5**	**0**	**1**	**1**	**5**
	Hershey Bears	IAHL	22	9	10	19	....	....	....	20	....	....	....	....	....
1940-41	**Boston Bruins**	**NHL**	**8**	**0**	**1**	**1**	**0**	**1**	**1**	**0**	....	....	....	....	....
	Hershey Bears	AHL	36	13	17	30	....	....	....	20	9	3	3	6	11
1941-42	**Boston Bruins**	**NHL**	**9**	**6**	**3**	**9**	**8**	**4**	**12**	**2**	....	....	....	....	....
	Hershey Bears	AHL	10	6	8	14	....	....	....	2	....	....	....	....	....
	Chicago Black Hawks	**NHL**	**34**	**18**	**9**	**27**	**24**	**11**	**35**	**21**	**3**	**0**	**1**	**1**	**0**
1942-43	**Chicago Black Hawks**	**NHL**	**50**	**28**	**16**	**44**	**29**	**15**	**44**	**44**	....	....	....	....	....
1943-44	Kingston Army	OHA-Sr.	14	10	16	26	....	....	....	*28	....	....	....	....	....
1944-45			MILITARY SERVICE												
1945-46	**Chicago Black Hawks**	**NHL**	**38**	**20**	**17**	**37**	**24**	**25**	**49**	**23**	**4**	**1**	**0**	**1**	**7**
1946-47	**Chicago Black Hawks**	**NHL**	**60**	**21**	**19**	**40**	**24**	**23**	**47**	**12**	....	....	....	....	....
1947-48	**Chicago Black Hawks**	**NHL**	**60**	**11**	**13**	**24**	**14**	**17**	**31**	**18**	....	....	....	....	....
1948-49	**Chicago Black Hawks**	**NHL**	**57**	**8**	**4**	**12**	**11**	**6**	**17**	**16**	....	....	....	....	....
1949-50	**Chicago Black Hawks**	**NHL**	**59**	**6**	**2**	**8**	**8**	**2**	**10**	**6**	....	....	....	....	....
1950-51	**Chicago Black Hawks**	**NHL**	**2**	**0**	**0**	**0**	**0**	**0**	**0**	**0**	....	....	....	....	....
	Milwaukee Seagulls	USHL	52	7	27	34	....	....	....	47	....	....	....	....	....
1951-52	Galt Black Hawks	OHA-Jr.	DID NOT PLAY – COACHING												
	NHL Totals		**419**	**128**	**94**	**222**	**159**	**120**	**279**	**160**	**24**	**1**	**2**	**3**	**20**

Signed as a free agent by **Boston**, October 26, 1937. Traded to **Chicago** by **Boston** for cash, December 18, 1941.

• HAMILTON, Al — *see page 1148*

• HAMILTON, Chuck — *see page 1148*

• HAMILTON, Jack John McIvor

C – L. 5'7", 170 lbs. b: Trenton, Ont., 6/2/1925 Deceased.

Season	Club	League	GP	G	A	Pts	AG	AA	APts	PIM	GP	G	A	Pts	PIM
1939-40	Toronto Young Rangers	OHA-Jr.	13	0	0	0	....	....	....	0	2	0	0	0	0
1940-41	Toronto Young Rangers	OHA-Jr.	7	2	0	2	....	....	....	0	5	0	0	0	0
1941-42	Toronto Kodaks	TMHL	11	10	4	14	....	....	....	2	5	0	1	1	0
	Toronto Young Rangers	OHA-Jr.	17	9	8	17	....	....	....	9	6	2	5	7	0

Season	Club	League	GP	G	A	Pts	AG	AA	APts	PIM	GP	G	A	Pts	PIM
			REGULAR SEASON								PLAYOFFS				
1942-43	Toronto Staffords	TIHL	9	7	4	11	....	....	....	6	....	....	....	....	....
	Toronto Maple Leafs	**NHL**	**13**	**1**	**6**	**7**	**1**	**6**	**7**	**4**	**6**	**1**	**1**	**2**	**0**
1943-44	**Toronto Maple Leafs**	**NHL**	**49**	**20**	**17**	**37**	**18**	**15**	**33**	**4**	**5**	**1**	**0**	**1**	**0**
1944-45	Cornwallis Navy	NSDHL	13	10	8	18	....	....	....	6	3	2	3	5	0
1945-46	**Toronto Maple Leafs**	**NHL**	**40**	**7**	**9**	**16**	**8**	**13**	**21**	**12**	....	....	....	....	....
	Pittsburgh Hornets	AHL	8	5	3	8	....	....	....	12	....	....	....	....	....
1946-47	Pittsburgh Hornets	AHL	64	27	41	68	....	....	....	63	12	3	5	8	13
1947-48	Pittsburgh Hornets	AHL	67	21	29	50	....	....	....	52	2	0	0	0	5
1948-49	Providence Reds	AHL	59	26	54	80	....	....	....	32	14	3	6	9	6
1949-50	Providence Reds	AHL	55	19	35	54	....	....	....	20	4	2	2	4	0
1950-51	Providence Reds	AHL	45	21	26	47	....	....	....	29	....	....	....	....	....
	St. Louis Flyers	AHL	22	12	18	30	....	....	....	10	....	....	....	....	....
1951-52	St. Louis Flyers	AHL	67	27	50	77	....	....	....	34	....	....	....	....	....
1952-53	Shawinigan Cataracts	QMHL	17	3	7	10	....	....	....	31	....	....	....	....	....
	New Westminster Royals	WHL	45	12	19	31	....	....	....	52	7	1	2	3	2
1953-54	New Westminster Royals	WHL	63	15	31	46	....	....	....	54	7	2	3	5	8
1954-55	Kitchener Dutchmen	OHA-Sr.	40	7	30	37	....	....	....	22	10	5	9	14	6
	Kitchener Dutchmen	Al-Cup	17	4	10	14	....	....	....	4	....	....	....	....	....
1955-56	Owen Sound Mercurys	OHA-Sr.	48	18	35	53	....	....	....	27	6	0	3	3	0
1956-57	Owen Sound Mercurys	OHA-Sr.	8	0	5	5	....	....	....	16	....	....	....	....	....
	Troy Bruins	IHL	15	3	4	7	....	....	....	18	....	....	....	....	....
1957-58	North Bay Trappers	NOHA	10	0	4	4	....	....	....	14	....	....	....	....	....
	NHL Totals		**102**	**28**	**32**	**60**	**27**	**34**	**61**	**20**	**11**	**2**	**1**	**3**	**0**

AHL Second All-Star Team (1952)

Traded to **Providence** (AHL) by **Toronto** with cash to complete transaction that sent the rights to Danny Lewicki to Toronto (July 27, 1948), October 27, 1948. Traded to **Chicago** (St. Louis-AHL) by **Providence** (AHL) for Barry Sullivan, January 29, 1951. Traded to **New Westminster** (WHL) by **Shawinigan** (QMHL) for cash, December 7, 1952.

• HAMILTON, Reg

D – L. 5'11", 180 lbs. b: Toronto, Ont., 4/29/1914 d: 6/12/1991.

Season	Club	League	GP	G	A	Pts	AG	AA	APts	PIM	GP	G	A	Pts	PIM
1930-31	Toronto Marlboros	OHA-Jr.	8	2	1	3	....	....	....	8	2	0	0	0	4
1931-32	Toronto Marlboros	OHA-Jr.	10	5	3	8	....	....	....	10	4	0	0	0	*18
1932-33	Toronto Marlboros	OHA-Jr.	10	3	3	6	....	....	....	*45	3	0	0	0	*12
1933-34	St. Michael's Majors	OHA-Jr.	5	2	1	3	....	....	....	12	3	0	2	2	12
	Toronto CCM	TMHL	2	0	0	0	....	....	....	6	....	....	....	....	....
	St. Michael's Majors	M-Cup	13	4	12	16	....	....	....	46	....	....	....	....	....
1934-35	Syracuse Stars	IHL	40	4	4	8	....	....	....	38	2	0	0	0	2
1935-36	**Toronto Maple Leafs**	**NHL**	**7**	**0**	**0**	**0**	**0**	**0**	**0**	**0**	....	....	....	....	....
	Syracuse Stars	IHL	40	4	19	23	....	....	....	86	3	0	1	1	2
1936-37	**Toronto Maple Leafs**	**NHL**	**39**	**3**	**7**	**10**	**5**	**13**	**18**	**32**	**2**	**0**	**1**	**1**	**2**
	Syracuse Stars	AHL	9	0	3	3	....	....	....	12	....	....	....	....	....
1937-38	**Toronto Maple Leafs**	**NHL**	**45**	**1**	**4**	**5**	**2**	**6**	**8**	**43**	**7**	**0**	**1**	**1**	**2**
1938-39	**Toronto Maple Leafs**	**NHL**	**48**	**0**	**7**	**7**	**0**	**11**	**11**	**54**	**10**	**0**	**2**	**2**	**4**
1939-40	**Toronto Maple Leafs**	**NHL**	**23**	**2**	**2**	**4**	**3**	**3**	**6**	**23**	**10**	**0**	**0**	**0**	**0**
1940-41	**Toronto Maple Leafs**	**NHL**	**45**	**3**	**12**	**15**	**5**	**17**	**22**	**59**	**7**	**1**	**2**	**3**	**13**
1941-42	**Toronto Maple Leafs**	**NHL**	**22**	**0**	**4**	**4**	**0**	**5**	**5**	**27**	....	....	....	....	....
1942-43	**Toronto Maple Leafs**	**NHL**	**48**	**4**	**17**	**21**	**4**	**16**	**20**	**68**	**6**	**1**	**1**	**2**	**9**
1943-44	**Toronto Maple Leafs**	**NHL**	**39**	**4**	**12**	**16**	**4**	**10**	**14**	**32**	**5**	**1**	**0**	**1**	**8**
♦**1944-45**	**Toronto Maple Leafs**	**NHL**	**50**	**3**	**12**	**15**	**3**	**14**	**17**	**41**	**13**	**0**	**0**	**0**	**6**
1945-46	**Chicago Black Hawks**	**NHL**	**48**	**1**	**7**	**8**	**1**	**10**	**11**	**31**	**4**	**0**	**1**	**1**	**2**
1946-47	**Chicago Black Hawks**	**NHL**	**10**	**0**	**3**	**3**	**0**	**4**	**4**	**2**	....	....	....	....	....
	Kansas City Pla-Mors	USHL	26	0	10	10	....	....	....	30	10	0	3	3	0
1947-48	Kansas City Pla-Mors	USHL	14	0	2	2	....	....	....	6	....	....	....	....	....
1948-49	Kansas City Pla-Mors	USHL	DID NOT PLAY – COACHING												
	NHL Totals		**424**	**21**	**87**	**108**	**27**	**109**	**136**	**412**	**64**	**3**	**8**	**11**	**46**

Traded to **Chicago** by **Toronto** for cash and future considerations, July 9, 1945. • Named playing coach of **Kansas City** (USHL), December 1, 1946.

• HAMPSON, Ted *— see page 1149*

• HANNA, John *— see page 1152*

• HANNIGAN, Gord

John Gordon

C – L. 5'8", 155 lbs. b: Schumacher, Ont., 1/19/1929 d: 11/16/1966.

Season	Club	League	GP	G	A	Pts	AG	AA	APts	PIM	GP	G	A	Pts	PIM
1945/47	Schumacher Lions	NOHA	STATISTICS NOT AVAILABLE												
1947-48	St. Michael's Majors	OHA-Jr.	32	14	13	27	....	....	....	55	....	....	....	....	....
1948-49	St. Michael's Majors	OHA-Jr.	32	21	13	34	....	....	....	59	....	....	....	....	....
1949-50	Toronto Marlboros	OHA-Jr.	25	6	12	18	....	....	....	19	14	2	4	6	14
1950-51	St. Michael's Monarchs	OMHL	30	19	20	39	....	....	....	26	9	4	6	10	6
	St. Michael's Monarchs	Alx-Cup	10	9	6	15	....	....	....	4	....	....	....	....	....
1951-52	Pittsburgh Hornets	AHL	67	24	26	50	....	....	....	80	11	2	5	7	15
1952-53	**Toronto Maple Leafs**	**NHL**	**65**	**17**	**18**	**35**	**22**	**22**	**44**	**51**	....	....	....	....	....
1953-54	**Toronto Maple Leafs**	**NHL**	**35**	**4**	**4**	**8**	**5**	**5**	**10**	**18**	**5**	**2**	**0**	**2**	**4**
1954-55	**Toronto Maple Leafs**	**NHL**	**13**	**0**	**2**	**2**	**0**	**2**	**2**	**8**	....	....	....	....	....
	Pittsburgh Hornets	AHL	35	9	16	25	....	....	....	19	10	1	7	8	16
1955-56	**Toronto Maple Leafs**	**NHL**	**48**	**8**	**7**	**15**	**11**	**8**	**19**	**40**	**4**	**0**	**0**	**0**	**4**
	Pittsburgh Hornets	AHL	17	10	10	20	....	....	....	20	....	....	....	....	....
1956-57	Rochester Americans	AHL	64	21	40	61	....	....	....	111	10	2	4	6	*37
1957-58	Edmonton Flyers	WHL	25	6	8	14	....	....	....	15	....	....	....	....	....
	NHL Totals		**161**	**29**	**31**	**60**	**38**	**37**	**75**	**117**	**9**	**2**	**0**	**2**	**8**

• Brother of Pat and Ray

Traded to **Edmonton** (WHL) by **Toronto** for $5,000, February 25, 1958.

• HANNIGAN, Pat *— see page 1153*

• HANNIGAN, Ray

Raymond James

RW – R. 5'8", 155 lbs. b: Schumacher, Ont., 7/14/1927.

Season	Club	League	GP	G	A	Pts	AG	AA	APts	PIM	GP	G	A	Pts	PIM
1944-45	South Porcupine Porkies	NOJHA	....	15	3	18	....	....	....	2	....	....	....	....	....
	South Porcupine Porkies	M-Cup	2	2	2	4	....	....	....	0	....	....	....	....	....
1945-46	St. Michael's Buzzers	H.S.	8	*23	12	*35	....	....	....	29	2	3	1	4	0
	St. Michael's Majors	OHA-Jr.	2	1	0	1	....	....	....	0	....	....	....	....	....
1946-47	St. Michael's Majors	OHA-Jr.	22	13	8	21	....	....	....	21	9	11	2	13	6
	St. Michael's Majors	M-Cup	10	3	11	14	....	....	....	23	....	....	....	....	....

Season	Club	League	GP	G	A	Pts	AG	AA	APts	PIM	GP	G	A	Pts	PIM
			REGULAR SEASON								PLAYOFFS				
1947-48	Toronto Marlboros	OHA-Sr.	35	27	21	48	....	....	....	26	5	2	0	2	10
1948-49	**Toronto Maple Leafs**	**NHL**	**3**	**0**	**0**	**0**	**0**	**0**	**0**	**2**	....	....	....	....	....
	Toronto Marlboros	OHA-Sr.	38	24	21	45	....	....	....	24	9	7	5	12	18
	Toronto Marlboros	Al-Cup	13	9	6	15	....	....	....	8	....	....	....	....	....
1949-50	Pittsburgh Hornets	AHL	64	30	21	51	....	....	....	14	....	....	....	....	....
	Toronto Marlboros	Al-Cup	12	2	7	9	....	....	....	25	....	....	....	....	....
1950-51	Pittsburgh Hornets	AHL	65	24	17	41	....	....	....	31	13	9	6	15	20
1951-52	Pittsburgh Hornets	AHL	49	17	18	35	....	....	....	56	10	4	1	5	11
1952-53	Edmonton Flyers	WHL	64	22	19	41	....	....	....	53	15	7	6	13	6
1953-54	Edmonton Flyers	WHL	66	30	31	61	....	....	....	29	13	3	7	10	11
1954-55	Edmonton Flyers	WHL	56	21	16	37	....	....	....	27	....	....	....	....	....
	Edmonton Flyers	Ed-Cup	5	0	1	1	....	....	....	2	....	....	....	....	....
1955-56	Edmonton Oil Kings	WCJHL	DID NOT PLAY – COACHING												
	NHL Totals		**3**	**0**	**0**	**0**	**0**	**0**	**0**	**2**	....	....	....	....	....

• Brother of Pat and Gord

Traded to **Chicago** by **Toronto** with Cal Gardner, Gus Mortson and Al Rollins for Harry Lumley, September 11, 1952. Loaned to **Detroit** (Edmonton-WHL) by **Chicago** for 1952-53 season for loan of Guyle Fielder for 1952-53 season, October 15, 1952. Traded to **Detroit** (Edmonton-WHL) by **Chicago** for Bill Brennan, August 4, 1953.

• HANSON, Emil

Emil Clarence

RW/D – L. 5'8", 165 lbs. b: Camrose, Alta., 11/18/1907 d: 1955.

Season	Club	League	GP	G	A	Pts	AG	AA	APts	PIM	GP	G	A	Pts	PIM
1927-28	Augsburg Auggies	MIAC	STATISTICS NOT AVAILABLE												
1928-29	Tulsa Oilers	AHA	1	0	0	0	....	....	....	0	....	....	....	....	....
1929-30	Tulsa Oilers	AHA	34	6	1	7	....	....	....	23	9	0	0	0	6
1930-31	Tulsa Oilers	AHA	47	5	9	14	....	....	....	64	4	1	1	2	2
1931-32	Tulsa Oilers	AHA	48	9	12	21	....	....	....	39	....	....	....	....	....
1932-33	**Detroit Red Wings**	**NHL**	**7**	**0**	**0**	**0**	**0**	**0**	**0**	**6**	....	....	....	....	....
	Detroit Olympics	IHL	30	5	4	9	....	....	....	17	....	....	....	....	....
1933-34	Kansas City Greyhounds	AHA	48	6	11	17	....	....	....	25	3	1	1	2	4
1934-35	St. Paul Saints	CHL	46	17	14	31	....	....	....	50	8	3	1	4	8
1935-36	St. Paul Saints	AHA	46	7	16	23	....	....	....	36	5	1	0	1	2
1936-37	St. Paul Saints	AHA	46	6	5	11	....	....	....	23	3	1	0	1	4
1937-38	Wichita Skyhawks	AHA	47	6	9	15	....	....	....	20	4	1	0	1	2
1938-39	St. Paul Saints	AHA	43	11	14	25	....	....	....	14	3	0	0	0	0
1939-40	St. Paul Saints	AHA	46	4	9	13	....	....	....	20	7	1	2	3	0
1940-41	Minneapolis Millers	AHA	26	0	2	2	....	....	....	16	3	0	1	1	0
1941-42	Minneapolis Millers	AHA	46	4	4	8	....	....	....	10	....	....	....	....	....
1942-43			REINSTATED AS AN AMATEUR												
1943-44	Edmonton Vics	ESrHL	....	....	....	....	....	....	....	....	3	1	0	1	4
	NHL Totals		**7**	**0**	**0**	**0**	**0**	**0**	**0**	**6**	....	....	....	....	....

• Brother of Oscar • CHL First All-Star Team (1935) • AHA First All-Star Team (1936) • AHA Second All-Star Team (1937)

Signed as a free agent by **Chicago Shamrocks** (AHA), August 14, 1932. NHL rights transferred to **Detroit** from **Chicago Shamrocks** (AHA) after AHA club owners purchased Detroit (NHL and IHL) franchises, September 2, 1932. Traded to **Minneapolis** (AHA) by **St. Paul** (AHA) for cash, October 13, 1940.

• HANSON, Oscar

Oscar Edward "Ossie"

C – L. 5'10", 175 lbs. b: Camrose, Alta., 12/27/1909.

Season	Club	League	GP	G	A	Pts	AG	AA	APts	PIM	GP	G	A	Pts	PIM
1926/29	Augsburg Auggies	MIAC	STATISTICS NOT AVAILABLE												
1929-30			STATISTICS NOT AVAILABLE												
1930-31	St. Paul Saints	NWHL	STATISTICS NOT AVAILABLE												
1931-32	St. Paul Saints	CHL	35	*25	18	*43	....	....	....	29	....	....	....	....	....
1932-33	St. Paul Saints	CHL	37	*22	*17	*39	....	....	....	63	4	2	0	2	4
1933-34	Oklahoma City Warriors	AHA	42	16	6	22	....	....	....	50	....	....	....	....	....
1934-35	St. Paul Saints	CHL	47	*29	*30	*59	....	....	....	53	8	*7	5	*12	8
1935-36	St. Paul Saints	AHA	47	*30	*30	*60	....	....	....	....	5	2	1	3	11
1936-37	St. Louis Flyers	AHA	47	*33	*29	*62	....	....	....	25	6	4	3	7	14
1937-38	**Chicago Black Hawks**	**NHL**	**8**	**0**	**0**	**0**	**0**	**0**	**0**	**0**	....	....	....	....	....
	St. Louis Flyers	AHA	22	12	14	26	....	....	....	13	....	....	....	....	....
	Cleveland Barons	IAHL	21	3	3	6	....	....	....	0	2	0	0	0	0
1938-39	Minneapolis Millers	AHA	48	*37	*52	*89	....	....	....	38	4	4	0	4	6
1939-40	Minneapolis Millers	AHA	47	32	22	54	....	....	....	27	3	0	1	1	0
1940-41	Minneapolis Millers	AHA	37	12	12	24	....	....	....	20	3	0	0	0	0
1941-42	Minneapolis Millers	AHA	47	24	20	44	....	....	....	24	....	....	....	....	....
1942-43			REINSTATED AS AN AMATEUR												
1943-44	Flin Flon Bombers	MHL-Sr.	STATISTICS NOT AVAILABLE												
	Edmonton Vics	X-Games	STATISTICS NOT AVAILABLE												
	Edmonton Vics	Al-Cup	4	0	0	0	....	....	....	0	....	....	....	....	....
	NHL Totals		**8**	**0**	**0**	**0**	**0**	**0**	**0**	**0**	....	....	....	....	....

• Brother of Emil • AHA First All-Star Team (1936, 1937, 1939, 1940)

Traded to **Chicago** by **St. Louis** (AHA) for cash, January 27, 1937. Traded to **St. Louis** (AHA) by **Chicago** with Bill Kendall for cash, December 2, 1937. Traded to **Cleveland** (IAHL) by **St. Louis** (AHA) for Walt Brenneman, January 25, 1938.

• HARMON, Glen

David Glen

D – L. 5'9", 165 lbs. b: Holland, Man., 1/2/1921.

Season	Club	League	GP	G	A	Pts	AG	AA	APts	PIM	GP	G	A	Pts	PIM
1937-38	East Kildonen Bisons	MAHA	STATISTICS NOT AVAILABLE												
	Winnipeg Gordon Bell	H.S.	STATISTICS NOT AVAILABLE												
1938-39	Brandon Elks	MJHL	17	2	5	7	....	....	....	47	8	3	3	6	28
	Brandon Wheat Kings	MJHL	....	....	....	....	....	....	....	....	7	1	2	3	10
	Brandon Wheat Kings	M-Cup	6	2	1	3	....	....	....	18	....	....	....	....	....
1939-40	Brandon Elks	MJHL	23	4	10	14	....	....	....	67	2	1	0	1	0
1940-41	Winnipeg Rangers	MJHL	17	5	5	10	....	....	....	42	6	4	1	5	14
	Winnipeg Rangers	M-Cup	14	4	5	9	....	....	....	20	....	....	....	....	....
1941-42	Montreal Sr. Canadiens	QSHL	39	8	8	16	....	....	....	40	6	0	1	1	6
1942-43	**Montreal Canadiens**	**NHL**	**27**	**5**	**9**	**14**	**5**	**8**	**13**	**25**	**5**	**0**	**1**	**1**	**2**
	Montreal Sr. Canadiens	QSHL	20	5	8	13	....	....	....	35	....	....	....	....	....
♦**1943-44**	**Montreal Canadiens**	**NHL**	**43**	**5**	**16**	**21**	**4**	**14**	**18**	**36**	**9**	**1**	**2**	**3**	**4**
1944-45	**Montreal Canadiens**	**NHL**	**42**	**5**	**8**	**13**	**5**	**9**	**14**	**41**	**6**	**1**	**0**	**1**	**2**
♦**1945-46**	**Montreal Canadiens**	**NHL**	**49**	**7**	**10**	**17**	**8**	**14**	**22**	**28**	**9**	**1**	**4**	**5**	**0**
1946-47	**Montreal Canadiens**	**NHL**	**57**	**5**	**9**	**14**	**6**	**11**	**17**	**53**	**11**	**1**	**1**	**2**	**4**
1947-48	**Montreal Canadiens**	**NHL**	**56**	**10**	**4**	**14**	**13**	**5**	**18**	**52**	....	....	....	....	....
1948-49	**Montreal Canadiens**	**NHL**	**59**	**8**	**12**	**20**	**11**	**17**	**28**	**44**	**7**	**1**	**1**	**2**	**4**
1949-50	**Montreal Canadiens**	**NHL**	**62**	**3**	**16**	**19**	**4**	**19**	**23**	**28**	**5**	**0**	**1**	**1**	**21**
1950-51	**Montreal Canadiens**	**NHL**	**57**	**2**	**12**	**14**	**3**	**15**	**18**	**27**	**1**	**0**	**0**	**0**	**0**
1951-52	Montreal Royals	QMHL	55	5	20	25	....	....	....	33	5	3	4	7	2

Season	Club	League	GP	G	A	Pts	AG	AA	APts	PIM	GP	G	A	Pts	PIM
1952-53	Montreal Royals	QMHL	58	5	17	22	....	....	....	26	16	5	4	9	4
1953-54	Montreal Royals	QHL	65	8	22	30	....	....	....	31	8	0	2	2	2
1954-55	Montreal Royals	QHL	62	5	22	27	....	....	....	64	14	2	5	7	6
	NHL Totals		**452**	**50**	**96**	**146**	**59**	**112**	**171**	**334**	**53**	**5**	**10**	**15**	**37**

NHL Second All-Star Team (1945, 1949) • Played in NHL All-Star Game (1949, 1950)

Claimed by **Montreal** from **Tulsa** (AHA) in Inter-League Draft, June, 27. 1941.

• HARMS, John

RW – R. 5'8", 160 lbs. b: Saskatoon, Sask., 4/25/1925.

Season	Club	League	GP	G	A	Pts	AG	AA	APts	PIM	GP	G	A	Pts	PIM
1942-43	Saskatoon Quakers	N-SJHL	8	4	3	7	....	....	....	*28	3	2	*3	5	6
	Saskatoon Quakers	M-Cup	8	4	2	6	....	....	....	12	....	....	....	....	....
1943-44	**Chicago Black Hawks**	**NHL**	**1**	**0**	**0**	**0**	**0**	**0**	**0**	**0**	**4**	**3**	**0**	**3**	**2**
	Hershey Bears	AHL	52	10	21	31	....	....	....	35	7	2	1	3	6
1944-45	**Chicago Black Hawks**	**NHL**	**43**	**5**	**5**	**10**	**5**	**6**	**11**	**21**	....	....	....	....	....
	Providence Reds	AHL	3	0	4	4	....	....	....	0	....	....	....	....	....
1945-46	Kansas City Pla-Mors	USHL	45	26	25	51	....	....	....	73	12	2	2	4	14
1946-47	Kansas City Pla-Mors	USHL	60	21	34	55	....	....	....	80	12	3	9	12	9
1947-48	Kansas City Pla-Mors	USHL	66	29	40	69	....	....	....	56	7	2	6	8	0
1948-49	Kansas City Pla-Mors	USHL	57	19	48	67	....	....	....	64	2	0	0	0	0
1949-50	Kansas City Pla-Mors	USHL	64	15	27	42	....	....	....	38	3	2	0	2	2
1950-51	Regina Caps	WCMHL	21	0	7	7	....	....	....	12	....	....	....	....	....
	Nelson Maple Leafs	WIHL	25	8	12	20	....	....	....	99	4	1	2	3	12
1951-52	Nelson Maple Leafs	WIHL	37	14	30	44	....	....	....	80	3	2	2	4	5
	Vernon Canadians	OSHL	1	0	0	0	....	....	....	0	....	....	....	....	....
1952-53	Vernon Canadians	OSHL	52	30	37	67	....	....	....	110	5	2	2	4	20
1953-54	Vernon Canadians	OSHL	55	27	23	50	....	....	....	113	5	1	3	4	4
1954-55	Vernon Canadians	OSHL	53	17	23	40	....	....	....	52	5	2	4	6	2
	Vernon Canadians	Al-Cup	17	5	13	18	....	....	....	16	....	....	....	....	....
1955-56	Vernon Canadians	OSHL	39	16	25	41	....	....	....	58	8	4	3	7	32
	Vernon Canadians	Al-Cup	13	5	16	21	....	....	....	10	....	....	....	....	....
1956-57	Vernon Canadians	OSHL	49	20	38	58	....	....	....	87	12	3	6	9	*26
1957-58	Vernon Canadians	OSHL	37	9	11	20	....	....	....	62	8	0	4	4	16
1958-59	Vernon Canadians	OSHL	....	....	....	....	....	....	....	....	2	0	1	1	2
1959-60	Kelowna Packers	Al-Cup	6	1	3	4	....	....	....	2	....	....	....	....	....
1960-61	Vernon Canadians	OSHL	39	9	34	43	....	....	....	*131	5	1	6	7	6
	NHL Totals		**44**	**5**	**5**	**10**	**5**	**6**	**11**	**21**	**4**	**3**	**0**	**3**	**2**

USHL Second All-Star Team (1948) • OSHL First All-Star Team (1961)

• HARNOTT, Walter

Walter Herbert "Happy"

LW – L. 5'10", 175 lbs. b: Montreal, Que., 9/24/1909 Deceased.

Season	Club	League	GP	G	A	Pts	AG	AA	APts	PIM	GP	G	A	Pts	PIM
1928-29	Montreal Bell Telephone	MTRHL	2	1	1	2	....	....	....	2	....	....	....	....	....
1929-30	Montreal Columbus	MCHL	10	2	0	2	....	....	....	2	....	....	....	....	....
1930-31	Montreal Columbus	MCHL	9	3	0	3	....	....	....	6	2	0	0	0	6
1931-32	Boston Cubs	Can-Am	18	2	1	3	....	....	....	6	5	1	0	1	6
	Montreal AAA	MCHL	8	4	1	5	....	....	....	12	....	....	....	....	....
1932-33	Boston Cubs	Can-Am	23	4	1	5	....	....	....	10	....	....	....	....	....
1933-34	**Boston Bruins**	**NHL**	**6**	**0**	**0**	**0**	**0**	**0**	**0**	**2**	....	....	....	....	....
	Boston Cubs	Can-Am	38	10	5	15	....	....	....	16	3	0	1	1	0
1934-35	Syracuse Stars	IHL	5	0	1	1	....	....	....	0	....	....	....	....	....
	Boston Cubs	Can-Am	40	11	15	26	....	....	....	20	3	1	0	1	0
1935-36	Boston Cubs	Can-Am	22	3	4	7	....	....	....	14	....	....	....	....	....
	Calgary Tigers	NWHL	14	4	3	7	....	....	....	0	....	....	....	....	....
1936-37	St. Louis Flyers	AHA	7	1	0	1	....	....	....	2	....	....	....	....	....
1937-38	St. Paul Saints	AHA	34	12	15	27	....	....	....	4	....	....	....	....	....
	St. Louis Flyers	AHA	8	0	1	1	....	....	....	0	....	....	....	....	....
1938-39	St. Louis Flyers	AHA	47	16	25	41	....	....	....	31	7	3	4	7	2
1939-40	St. Louis Flyers	AHA	48	24	29	53	....	....	....	18	5	1	2	3	5
	Omaha Knights	AHA	....	....	....	....	....	....	....	....	3	1	1	2	0
1940-41	St. Louis Flyers	AHA	48	13	24	37	....	....	....	10	9	0	3	3	2
1941-42	St. Louis Flyers	AHA	42	7	10	17	....	....	....	8	3	0	0	0	2
1942-43	Montreal Royals	QSHL	9	0	2	2	....	....	....	2	....	....	....	....	....
	Montreal RCAF	MCHL	7	2	3	5	....	....	....	2	2	4	1	5	2
1943-44	Montreal RCAF	MCHL	4	0	0	0	....	....	....	0	2	0	0	0	0
1944-45	Montreal RCAF	MCHL	12	6	*18	24	....	....	....	0	6	1	3	4	6
	Valleyfield Braves	QPHL	....	....	....	....	....	....	....	....	1	0	0	0	0
	NHL Totals		**6**	**0**	**0**	**0**	**0**	**0**	**0**	**2**	....	....	....	....	....

AHA Second All-Star Team (1940)

Loaned to **Syracuse** (IHL) by **Boston** with Don Smillie for cash, November 27, 1934.

• HARPER, Terry

— see page 1157

• HARRINGTON, Hago

Leland Kitteridge

LW – L. 5'8", 163 lbs. b: Melrose, MA, 8/13/1904 d: 1959.

Season	Club	League	GP	G	A	Pts	AG	AA	APts	PIM	GP	G	A	Pts	PIM
1922-23	Melrose Monarchs	H.S.	STATISTICS NOT AVAILABLE												
1923-24	Boston A.A. Unicorns	USAHA	12	9	0	9	....	....	....	....	5	2	0	2	....
1924-25	Boston A.A. Unicorns	USAHA	18	14	0	14	....	....	....	....	4	1	0	1	....
1925-26	**Boston Bruins**	**NHL**	**26**	**7**	**2**	**9**	**12**	**13**	**25**	**6**	....	....	....	....	....
1926-27	New Haven Eagles	Can-Am	32	21	4	25	....	....	....	36	4	2	1	3	0
1927-28	**Boston Bruins**	**NHL**	**22**	**1**	**0**	**1**	**2**	**0**	**2**	**7**	**2**	**0**	**0**	**0**	**0**
	New Haven Eagles	Can-Am	16	13	5	18	....	....	....	22	....	....	....	....	....
1928-29	Providence Reds	Can-Am	31	5	3	8	....	....	....	44	6	3	0	3	14
1929-30	Providence Reds	Can-Am	37	11	6	17	....	....	....	51	3	1	1	2	2
1930-31	Providence Reds	Can-Am	39	8	16	24	....	....	....	41	2	1	0	1	2
1931-32	Providence Reds	Can-Am	39	15	*20	35	....	....	....	44	5	3	1	4	0
1932-33	Providence Reds	Can-Am	22	11	12	23	....	....	....	20	....	....	....	....	....
	Montreal Canadiens	**NHL**	**24**	**1**	**1**	**2**	**2**	**2**	**4**	**2**	**2**	**1**	**0**	**1**	**2**
1933-34	Providence Reds	Can-Am	40	13	19	32	....	....	....	26	3	0	2	2	0
1934-35	Providence Reds	Can-Am	46	17	32	49	....	....	....	32	6	0	1	1	8
1935-36	Providence Reds	Can-Am	45	12	3	15	....	....	....	22	7	0	0	0	8
	NHL Totals		**72**	**9**	**3**	**12**	**16**	**15**	**31**	**15**	**4**	**1**	**0**	**1**	**2**

Signed as a free agent by **Boston**, January 4, 1926. Traded to **Providence** (Can-Am) by **Boston** for cash, October, 1928. Traded to **Montreal Canadiens** by **Providence** (Can-Am) with Leo Murray for Leo Gaudreault and Armand Mondou with Montreal holding right of recall, January, 1933.

• HARRIS, Billy

— see page 1157

• HARRIS, Henry

RW – L. 5'11", 185 lbs. b: Kenora, Ont., 4/28/1906 Deceased.

Season	Club	League	GP	G	A	Pts	AG	AA	APts	PIM	GP	G	A	Pts	PIM
1927-28	Regina Capitals	PrHL	23	2	2	4	....	....	....	12	....	....	....	....	....
1928-29	Seattle Eskimos	PCHL	36	8	3	11	....	....	....	*138	5	1	0	1	10
1929-30	Seattle Eskimos	PCHL	34	11	3	14	....	....	....	128	....	....	....	....	....
1930-31	**Boston Bruins**	**NHL**	**32**	**2**	**4**	**6**	**4**	**12**	**16**	**20**	....	....	....	....	....
	Boston Cubs	Can-Am	12	2	3	5	....	....	....	32	9	1	2	3	30
1931-32	Buffalo Majors	AHA	15	0	4	4	....	....	....	32	....	....	....	....	....
1932-33	Calgary Tigers	WCHL	30	6	6	12	....	....	....	65	6	0	2	2	9
1933-34	Calgary Tigers	NWHL	34	9	10	19	....	....	....	46	5	3	0	3	2
1934-35	Calgary Tigers	NWHL	22	5	5	10	....	....	....	22	....	....	....	....	....
	NHL Totals		**32**	**2**	**4**	**6**	**4**	**12**	**16**	**20**	....	....	....	....	....

• Brother of Fred (Smokey)

Traded to **Boston** by **Seattle** (PCHL) for cash, February 4, 1930. Loaned to **Seattle** (PCHL) by **Boston** for the remainder of the 1929-30 season, February 4, 1930. Signed as a free agent by **Buffalo** (AHA), October 29, 1931.

• HARRIS, Ron

— see page 1158

• HARRIS, Smokey

Thomas Wilfred "Fred"

LW – L. 5'11", 165 lbs. b: Port Arthur, Ont., 10/11/1890 d: 6/4/1974.

Season	Club	League	GP	G	A	Pts	AG	AA	APts	PIM	GP	G	A	Pts	PIM
1909-10	Kenora Thistles	NOHA	STATISTICS NOT AVAILABLE												
1910-11	Kenora Thistles	Man-Pro	6	*13	0	*13	....	....	....	....	2	*3	0	*3	....
1911-12	Vancouver Millionaires	PCHA	15	4	0	4	....	....	....	55	....	....	....	....	....
	PCHA All-Stars	X-Games	1	0	0	0	....	....	....	0	....	....	....	....	....
1912-13	Vancouver Millionaires	PCHA	16	14	6	20	....	....	....	61	....	....	....	....	....
1913-14	Vancouver Millionaires	PCHA	15	14	3	17	....	....	....	33	....	....	....	....	....
1914-15	Portland Rosebuds	PCHA	18	14	3	17	....	....	....	39	....	....	....	....	....
1915-16	Portland Rosebuds	PCHA	18	10	6	16	....	....	....	*75	5	*4	0	*4	*21
	PCHA All-Stars	X-Games	3	3	2	5	....	....	....	3	....	....	....	....	....
1916-17	Portland Rosebuds	PCHA	23	18	13	31	....	....	....	39	....	....	....	....	....
1917-18	Portland Rosebuds	PCHA	8	6	5	11	....	....	....	19	....	....	....	....	....
1918-19	Vancouver Millionaires	PCHA	20	19	6	25	....	....	....	0	2	2	0	2	3
	Vancouver Millionaires	St-Cup	2	2	0	2	....	....	....	3	....	....	....	....	....
1919-20	Vancouver Millionaires	PCHA	22	14	11	25	....	....	....	12	2	0	1	1	0
1920-21	Vancouver Millionaires	PCHA	24	15	*17	*32	....	....	....	6	2	6	2	8	0
	Vancouver Millionaires	St-Cup	5	2	1	3	....	....	....	6	....	....	....	....	....
1921-22	Vancouver Millionaires	PCHA	23	10	4	14	....	....	....	21	....	....	....	....	....
1922-23	Vancouver Maroons	PCHA	20	10	6	16	....	....	....	26	2	0	0	0	0
	Vancouver Maroons	St-Cup	4	1	0	1	....	....	....	8	....	....	....	....	....
1923-24	Seattle Metropolitans	PCHA	30	8	*10	18	....	....	....	30	2	0	0	0	4
1924-25	**Boston Bruins**	**NHL**	**6**	**3**	**1**	**4**	**5**	**4**	**9**	**8**	....	....	....	....	....
	Vancouver Maroons	WCHL	14	0	1	1	....	....	....	16	....	....	....	....	....
1925-26	LA Richfield Oil	Cal-Pro	....	6	3	9	....	....	....	24	....	....	....	....	....
1926-27	Edmonton Eskimos	PrHL	32	12	12	24	....	....	....	68	....	....	....	....	....
1927-28	LA Richfield Oil	Cal-Pro	STATISTICS NOT AVAILABLE												
1928-29	San Francisco Tigers	Cal-Pro	36	13	13	26	....	....	....	43	....	....	....	....	....
1929-30	Hollywood Millionaires	Cal-Pro	42	7	12	19	....	....	....	28	....	....	....	....	....
1930-31	San Francisco Hawks	Cal-Pro	31	8	10	18	....	....	....	....	....	....	....	....	....
1931-32	San Francisco Rangers	Cal-Pro	30	3	8	11	....	....	....	....	....	....	....	....	....
	NHL Totals		**6**	**3**	**1**	**4**	**5**	**4**	**9**	**8**	....	....	....	....	....
	Other Major League Totals		266	156	91	247	....	....	....	432	15	12	3	15	28

• Brother of Henry • PCHA First All-Team (1913, 1916, 1919, 1920) • PCHA Second All-Star Team (1922)

Traded to **Portland** (PCHA) by **Vancouver** (PCHA) for Ken Mallen, 1914. Transferred to **Vancouver** (PCHA) after **Portland** (PCHA) franchise folded, November 29, 1918. Traded to **Seattle** (PCHA) by **Vancouver** (PCHA) for cash, October 30, 1923. Traded to **Boston** by **Seattle** (PCHA) for cash, November 2, 1924. Traded to **Vancouver** (WCHL) by **Boston** for cash, December 21, 1924. Signed as a free agent by **Edmonton** (PrHL), December 3, 1926. Signed as a free agent by **LA Richfield** (Cal-Pro), October 17, 1927.

• HARRIS, Ted

— see page 1159

• HARRISON, Ed

Edward Francis

C/LW – L. 6', 165 lbs. b: Mimico, Ont., 7/25/1927.

Season	Club	League	GP	G	A	Pts	AG	AA	APts	PIM	GP	G	A	Pts	PIM
1943-44	St. Michael's Midgets	OMHA	4	10	4	14	....	....	....	....	....	....	....	....	....
1944-45	St. Michael's Majors	OHA-Jr.	1	1	0	1	....	....	....	0	....	....	....	....	....
1945-46	St. Michael's Majors	OHA-Jr.	22	16	14	30	....	....	....	8	11	11	8	19	4
1946-47	St. Michael's Majors	OHA-Jr.	29	29	25	54	....	....	....	33	9	11	7	18	14
	St. Michael's Majors	M-Cup	10	*19	7	26	....	....	....	6	....	....	....	....	....
1947-48	**Boston Bruins**	**NHL**	**52**	**6**	**7**	**13**	**8**	**9**	**17**	**8**	**5**	**1**	**0**	**1**	**2**
1948-49	**Boston Bruins**	**NHL**	**59**	**5**	**5**	**10**	**7**	**7**	**14**	**20**	**4**	**0**	**0**	**0**	**0**
1949-50	**Boston Bruins**	**NHL**	**70**	**14**	**12**	**26**	**18**	**14**	**32**	**23**	....	....	....	....	....
1950-51	**Boston Bruins**	**NHL**	**9**	**1**	**0**	**1**	**1**	**0**	**1**	**0**	....	....	....	....	....
	New York Rangers	**NHL**	**4**	**1**	**0**	**1**	**1**	**0**	**1**	**2**	....	....	....	....	....
	Hershey Bears	AHL	48	24	14	38	....	....	....	23	6	1	6	7	0
1951-52	Cincinnati Mohawks	AHL	57	20	9	29	....	....	....	19	7	3	2	5	0
1952-53	Vancouver Canucks	WHL	5	0	1	1	....	....	....	0	....	....	....	....	....
	Syracuse Warriors	AHL	2	0	1	1	....	....	....	0	....	....	....	....	....
	St. Louis Flyers	AHL	10	2	1	3	....	....	....	2	....	....	....	....	....
	Washington Lions	EAHL	17	5	10	15	....	....	....	4	....	....	....	....	....
	Quebec Aces	QMHL	16	6	2	8	....	....	....	6	22	6	9	15	13
1953-54	Quebec Aces	QHL	33	3	2	5	....	....	....	4	....	....	....	....	....
	Sudbury Wolves	NOHA	13	8	3	11	....	....	....	0	11	5	3	8	2
1954/60	Woodstock Athletics	OSrBL	STATISTICS NOT AVAILABLE												
1960-61	Woodstock Athletics	OSrBL	28	12	11	23	....	....	....	2	....	....	....	....	....
1961-62	Woodstock Athletics	OSrBL	28	9	17	26	....	....	....	0	12	1	1	2	0
	NHL Totals		**194**	**27**	**24**	**51**	**35**	**30**	**65**	**53**	**9**	**1**	**0**	**1**	**2**

Traded to **NY Rangers** by **Boston** with Zellio Toppazzini for Dunc Fisher and future considerations (loan of Alex Kaleta to Hershey-AHL, November 20, 1950), November 16, 1950.

• HART, Gizzy

Wilfred Harold

LW – L. 5'9", 171 lbs. b: Weyburn, Sask., 6/1/1902 d: 6/22/1964.

Season	Club	League	GP	G	A	Pts	AG	AA	APts	PIM	GP	G	A	Pts	PIM
1919-20	Weyburn Wanderers	S-SSHL	10	16	0	16	....	....	....	0	2	2	0	2	0
1920-21	Weyburn Wanderers	S-SSHL	11	2	2	4	....	....	....	0	....	....	....	....	....
1921-22	Moose Jaw Maple Leafs	S-SSHL	7	3	0	3	....	....	....	2	....	....	....	....	....

			REGULAR SEASON								PLAYOFFS				
Season	Club	League	GP	G	A	Pts	AG	AA	APts	PIM	GP	G	A	Pts	PIM
1922-23	Weyburn Wanderers	S-SSHL	10	17	6	23	....	....	....	4	5	*6	*2	*8	2
1923-24	Victoria Cougars	PCHA	29	15	1	16	....	....	....	10	....	....	....	....	....
1924-25	Victoria Cougars	WCHL	26	8	6	14	....	....	....	8	4	0	0	0	0
♦	Victoria Cougars	St-Cup	4	2	1	3	....	....	....	0	....	....	....	....	....
1925-26	Victoria Cougars	WHL	27	6	4	10	....	....	....	2	2	1	0	1	2
	Victoria Cougars	St-Cup	4	0	0	0	....	....	....	2	....	....	....	....	....
1926-27	**Detroit Cougars**	**NHL**	**2**	**0**	**0**	**0**	**0**	**0**	**0**	**0**	....	....	....	....	....
	Windsor Hornets	Can-Pro	5	4	1	5	....	....	....	6	....	....	....	....	....
	Montreal Canadiens	**NHL**	**40**	**3**	**3**	**6**	**5**	**16**	**21**	**8**	**4**	**0**	**0**	**0**	**0**
1927-28	**Montreal Canadiens**	**NHL**	**44**	**3**	**2**	**5**	**6**	**11**	**17**	**4**	**2**	**0**	**0**	**0**	**0**
1928-29	Providence Reds	Can-Am	38	13	1	14	....	....	....	14	....	....	....	....	....
1929-30	Providence Reds	Can-Am	39	24	12	36	....	....	....	28	3	2	3	5	0
1930-31	Providence Reds	Can-Am	37	25	13	38	....	....	....	16	2	1	1	2	0
1931-32	Providence Reds	Can-Am	40	21	17	38	....	....	....	29	5	2	*2	4	6
1932-33	**Montreal Canadiens**	**NHL**	**18**	**0**	**3**	**3**	**0**	**6**	**6**	**0**	**2**	**0**	**1**	**1**	**0**
	Providence Reds	Can-Am	46	7	9	16	....	....	....	60	....	....	....	....	....
1933-34	Providence Reds	Can-Am	40	13	9	22	....	....	....	12	3	0	*4	4	7
1934-35	Weyburn Beavers	S-SSHL	1	0	0	0	....	....	....	0	....	....	....	....	....
1935-36	Weyburn Beavers	S-SSHL	DID NOT PLAY – COACHING												
1936-37	Weyburn Beavers	S-SSHL	DID NOT PLAY – COACHING												
1937-38	Weyburn Beavers	S-SSHL	1	0	0	0	....	....	....	0	....	....	....	....	....
	NHL Totals		**104**	**6**	**8**	**14**	**11**	**33**	**44**	**12**	**8**	**0**	**1**	**1**	**0**
	Other Major League Totals		82	29	11	40	....	....	....	20	6	1	0	1	2

PCHA All-Star Team (1924)

Signed as a free agent by **Victoria** (WCHL), October 24, 1923. • 1924-25 playoff totals includes WCHL series against Calgary and Saskatoon. • 1925-26 playoff totals includes WHL series against Edmonton and Saskatoon. Transferred to **Detroit** after NHL club purchased **Victoria** (WHL) franchise, May 15, 1926. Loaned to **Windsor** (Can-Pro) by **Detroit** for cash, November 24, 1926. Traded to **Montreal Canadiens** by **Detroit** for cash, December 12, 1926. Traded to **Providence** (Can-Am) by **Montreal** for cash, October 17, 1928.

• HARVEY, Doug — *see page 1161*

• HASSARD, Bob Robert Harry

C – R. 6′, 167 lbs. b: Lloydminster, Sask., 3/26/1929.

Season	Club	League	GP	G	A	Pts	AG	AA	APts	PIM	GP	G	A	Pts	PIM
1945-46	Toronto Marlboros	OHA-Jr.	23	4	8	12	....	....	....	6	4	2	3	5	0
1946-47	Toronto Marlboros	OHA-Jr.	17	9	16	25	....	....	....	7	2	1	1	2	0
	Toronto Dorsts	TMHL	12	14	16	30	....	....	....	2	12	*14	*15	*29	8
1947-48	Toronto Marlboros	OHA-Jr.	31	19	16	35	....	....	....	18	....	....	....	....	....
	Toronto Marlboros	OHA-Sr.	4	3	0	3	....	....	....	0	5	1	1	2	2
1948-49	Toronto Marlboros	OHA-Jr.	35	33	36	69	....	....	....	28	1	1	0	1	0
	Toronto Marlboros	OHA-Sr.	1	0	1	1	....	....	....	0	....	....	....	....	....
1949-50	**Toronto Maple Leafs**	**NHL**	**1**	**0**	**0**	**0**	**0**	**0**	**0**	**0**	....	....	....	....	....
	Toronto Marlboros	OHA-Sr.	41	12	21	33	....	....	....	22	14	3	*10	13	4
	Toronto Marlboros	Al-Cup	17	7	16	23	....	....	....	14	....	....	....	....	....
1950-51	**Toronto Maple Leafs**	**NHL**	**12**	**0**	**1**	**1**	**0**	**1**	**1**	**0**	....	....	....	....	....
	Toronto Marlboros	OMHL	28	19	17	36	....	....	....	12	....	....	....	....	....
1951-52	Pittsburgh Hornets	AHL	67	18	46	64	....	....	....	36	11	5	5	10	10
1952-53	**Toronto Maple Leafs**	**NHL**	**70**	**8**	**23**	**31**	**10**	**28**	**38**	**14**	....	....	....	....	....
1953-54	**Toronto Maple Leafs**	**NHL**	**26**	**1**	**4**	**5**	**1**	**5**	**6**	**4**	....	....	....	....	....
	Pittsburgh Hornets	AHL	46	15	24	39	....	....	....	44	5	3	1	4	8
1954-55	**Chicago Black Hawks**	**NHL**	**17**	**0**	**0**	**0**	**0**	**0**	**0**	**4**	....	....	....	....	....
	Pittsburgh Hornets	AHL	39	9	16	25	....	....	....	38	10	7	1	8	8
1955-56	Pittsburgh Hornets	AHL	64	22	48	70	....	....	....	47	4	1	3	4	4
1956-57	Hershey–Buffalo	AHL	61	12	19	31	....	....	....	20	....	....	....	....	....
1957-58	Buffalo Bisons	AHL	70	14	31	45	....	....	....	13	....	....	....	....	....
1958-59	Whitby Dunlops	EOHL	23	11	23	34	....	....	....	6	10	6	5	11	4
	Whitby Dunlops	Al-Cup	12	5	4	9	....	....	....	4	....	....	....	....	....
1959-60	Whitby Dunlops	OHA-Sr.	43	15	23	38	....	....	....	16	11	2	4	6	2
	NHL Totals		**126**	**9**	**28**	**37**	**11**	**34**	**45**	**22**	....	....	....	....	....

Traded to **Chicago** by **Toronto** for cash, August 10, 1954. Traded to **Toronto** (Pittsburgh-AHL) by **Chicago** for cash, November 16, 1954. Traded to **Detroit** (Hershey-AHL) by **Toronto** (Pittsburgh-AHL) with Gilles Mayer, Jack Price, Willie Marshall, Bob Solinger and Ray Gariepy for cash, July 7, 1956. Traded to **Chicago** (Buffalo-AHL) by **Hershey** (AHL) for Al Dewsbury, February 14, 1957.

• HAWORTH, Gord Gordon Joseph "Red"

C – L. 5′10″, 165 lbs. b: Drummondville, Que., 2/20/1932.

Season	Club	League	GP	G	A	Pts	AG	AA	APts	PIM	GP	G	A	Pts	PIM
1947-48	Drummondville College	H.S.	STATISTICS NOT AVAILABLE												
	Drummondville Diggers	QAAA	STATISTICS NOT AVAILABLE												
1948-49	Victoriaville Tigers	QJHL	46	9	13	22	....	....	....	36	4	0	1	1	6
1949-50	Atlantic City Seagulls	EAHL	7	0	1	1	....	....	....	2	....	....	....	....	....
	Quebec Citadelle	QJHL	STATISTICS NOT AVAILABLE												
1950-51	Quebec Citadelle	QJHL	46	27	30	57	....	....	....	43	13	5	3	8	8
	Quebec Citadelle	M-Cup	10	5	5	10	....	....	....	14	....	....	....	....	....
1951-52	Quebec Citadelle	QJHL	46	31	51	82	....	....	....	49	15	7	6	13	18
1952-53	**New York Rangers**	**NHL**	**2**	**0**	**1**	**1**	**0**	**1**	**1**	**0**	....	....	....	....	....
	Valleyfield Braves	QMHL	53	9	21	30	....	....	....	26	4	0	1	1	2
1953-54	Valleyfield Braves	QHL	69	24	28	52	....	....	....	64	6	1	0	1	0
1954-55	Valleyfield Braves	QHL	60	16	32	48	....	....	....	33	....	....	....	....	....
1955-56	Springfield Indians	AHL	30	3	13	16	....	....	....	30	....	....	....	....	....
	Trois-Rivieres Lions	QHL	16	4	6	10	....	....	....	8	....	....	....	....	....
1956-57	Victoria Cougars	WHL	64	17	35	52	....	....	....	26	3	0	0	0	0
1957-58	Victoria Cougars	WHL	67	23	37	60	....	....	....	18	....	....	....	....	....
1958-59	Victoria Cougars	WHL	65	21	52	73	....	....	....	32	3	2	0	2	0
1959-60	Victoria Cougars	WHL	70	27	33	60	....	....	....	24	11	3	7	10	4
1960-61	Portland Buckaroos	WHL	68	18	47	65	....	....	....	24	14	3	3	6	0
1961-62	Sudbury Wolves	EPHL	63	14	41	55	....	....	....	32	5	2	1	3	4
1962-63	Los Angeles Blades	WHL	69	11	40	51	....	....	....	16	3	2	3	5	2
1963-64	Los Angeles Blades	WHL	68	17	36	53	....	....	....	24	12	2	7	9	4
1964-65	Los Angeles Blades	WHL	47	7	18	25	....	....	....	15	....	....	....	....	....
1965-66	Drummondville Eagles	QSHL	41	14	30	44	....	....	....	26	5	0	2	2	6
1966-67	Drummondville Eagles	QSHL	40	13	28	41	....	....	....	26	9	2	*10	*12	4
	Drummondville Eagles	Al-Cup	11	4	*12	*16	....	....	....	2	....	....	....	....	....
1967-68	Drummondville Eagles	QSHL	48	15	31	46	....	....	....	21	10	3	*10	13	0
1968-69			DID NOT PLAY												
1969-70	Jacksonville Rockets	EHL	70	16	56	72	....	....	....	6	4	0	1	1	2
1970-71	Drummondville Rangers	QJHL	DID NOT PLAY – COACHING												
	NHL Totals		**2**	**0**	**1**	**1**	**0**	**1**	**1**	**0**	....	....	....	....	....

• Father of Alan

Traded to **Springfield** (AHL) by **Valleyfield** (QHL) for cash, September, 1955. Traded to **Boston** (Victoria-WHL) by **NY Rangers** for cash, September, 1956. Traded to **Detroit** by **Boston** for Gene Achtymichuk, August, 1961. Traded to **LA Blades** (WHL) by **Detroit** for cash, July, 1962.

• HAY, Bill William Charles "Red"

C – L. 6′3″, 190 lbs. b: Lumsden, Sask., 12/9/1935.

Season	Club	League	GP	G	A	Pts	AG	AA	APts	PIM	GP	G	A	Pts	PIM
1952-53	Regina Pats	WCJHL	29	14	17	31	....	....	....	22	7	0	2	2	0
1953-54	U. of Saskatchewan	WCIAA	5	4	1	5	....	....	....	4	....	....	....	....	....
1954-55	Regina Pats	WCJHL	33	16	31	47	....	....	....	68	14	8	2	10	6
	Regina Pats	M-Cup	15	12	11	23	....	....	....	12	....	....	....	....	....
1955-56	Colorado College	WIHA	DID NOT PLAY – FRESHMAN												
1956-57	Colorado College	WIHA	30	28	45	73	....	....	....	....	....	....	....	....	....
1957-58	Colorado College	WIHA	30	32	48	*80	....	....	....	23	....	....	....	....	....
1958-59	Calgary Stampeders	WHL	53	24	30	54	....	....	....	27	8	3	5	8	6
1959-60	**Chicago Black Hawks**	**NHL**	**70**	**18**	**37**	**55**	**21**	**36**	**57**	**31**	**4**	**1**	**2**	**3**	**2**
♦1960-61	**Chicago Black Hawks**	**NHL**	**69**	**11**	**48**	**59**	**13**	**47**	**60**	**45**	**12**	**2**	**5**	**7**	**20**
1961-62	**Chicago Black Hawks**	**NHL**	**60**	**11**	**52**	**63**	**13**	**51**	**64**	**34**	**12**	**3**	**7**	**10**	**18**
1962-63	**Chicago Black Hawks**	**NHL**	**64**	**12**	**33**	**45**	**14**	**33**	**47**	**36**	**6**	**3**	**2**	**5**	**6**
1963-64	**Chicago Black Hawks**	**NHL**	**70**	**23**	**33**	**56**	**29**	**35**	**64**	**30**	**7**	**3**	**1**	**4**	**4**
1964-65	**Chicago Black Hawks**	**NHL**	**69**	**11**	**26**	**37**	**13**	**27**	**40**	**36**	**14**	**3**	**1**	**4**	**4**
1965-66	**Chicago Black Hawks**	**NHL**	**68**	**20**	**31**	**51**	**23**	**30**	**53**	**20**	**6**	**0**	**2**	**2**	**4**
1966-67	**Chicago Black Hawks**	**NHL**	**36**	**7**	**13**	**20**	**8**	**13**	**21**	**12**	**6**	**0**	**1**	**1**	**4**
	NHL Totals		**506**	**113**	**273**	**386**	**134**	**272**	**406**	**244**	**67**	**15**	**21**	**36**	**62**

WCHA First All-Star Team (1957, 1958) • NCAA West First All-American Team (1957, 1958) • NCAA Championship All-Tournament Team (1957) • Won Calder Memorial Trophy (1960) • Played in NHL All-Star Game (1960, 1961)

Traded to **Chicago** by **Montreal** for cash, April, 1959. Claimed by **St. Louis** from **Chicago** in Expansion Draft, June 6, 1967. Claimed by **Chicago** (Providence-AHL) from **St. Louis** in Reverse Draft, June 13, 1968. Selected by **Calgary-Cleveland** (WHA) in WHA General Player Draft, February 12, 1972.

• HAY, George HHOF

LW – L. 5′10″, 155 lbs. b: Listowel, Ont., 1/10/1898 d: 7/13/1975.

Season	Club	League	GP	G	A	Pts	AG	AA	APts	PIM	GP	G	A	Pts	PIM
1914-15	Winnipeg Strathconas	MHL-Sr.	7	4	0	4	....	....	....	....	....	....	....	....	....
1915-16	Winnipeg Monarchs	MHL-Sr.	7	6	4	10	....	....	....	10	2	2	2	4	4
1916-17	Winnipeg Monarchs	WJrHL	STATISTICS NOT AVAILABLE												
1917-18			MILITARY SERVICE												
1918-19			MILITARY SERVICE												
1919-20	Regina Vics	S-SSHL	12	8	3	11	....	....	....	5	2	1	0	1	0
1920-21	Regina Vics	S-SSHL	16	9	4	13	....	....	....	7	4	5	2	7	2
1921-22	Regina Capitals	WCHL	25	21	11	32	....	....	....	9	6	1	0	1	5
1922-23	Regina Capitals	WCHL	30	28	8	36	....	....	....	12	2	1	0	1	0
1923-24	Regina Capitals	WCHL	25	20	11	31	....	....	....	8	2	1	1	2	0
1924-25	Regina Capitals	WCHL	20	16	6	22	....	....	....	6	....	....	....	....	....
1925-26	Portland Rosebuds	WHL	30	*19	12	31	....	....	....	4	....	....	....	....	....
1926-27	**Chicago Black Hawks**	**NHL**	**35**	**14**	**8**	**22**	**25**	**42**	**67**	**12**	**2**	**1**	**2**	**3**	**2**
1927-28	**Detroit Cougars**	**NHL**	**42**	**22**	**13**	**35**	**45**	**75**	**120**	**20**	....	....	....	....	....
1928-29	**Detroit Cougars**	**NHL**	**39**	**11**	**8**	**19**	**32**	**54**	**86**	**14**	**2**	**1**	**0**	**1**	**0**
1929-30	**Detroit Cougars**	**NHL**	**44**	**18**	**15**	**33**	**26**	**36**	**62**	**8**	....	....	....	....	....
1930-31	**Detroit Falcons**	**NHL**	**44**	**8**	**10**	**18**	**16**	**30**	**46**	**24**	....	....	....	....	....
1931-32	Detroit Olympics	IHL	48	10	9	19	....	....	....	26	6	0	0	0	2
1932-33	**Detroit Red Wings**	**NHL**	**34**	**1**	**6**	**7**	**2**	**12**	**14**	**6**	**4**	**0**	**1**	**1**	**0**
	Detroit Olympics	IHL	9	6	1	7	....	....	....	6	....	....	....	....	....
1933-34	**Detroit Red Wings**	**NHL**	**1**	**0**	**0**	**0**	**0**	**0**	**0**	**0**	....	....	....	....	....
	Detroit Olympics	IHL	4	0	0	0	....	....	....	5	....	....	....	....	....
	NHL Totals		**239**	**74**	**60**	**134**	**146**	**249**	**395**	**84**	**8**	**2**	**3**	**5**	**2**
	Other Major League Totals		130	104	48	152	....	....	....	39	10	3	1	4	5

WCHL First All-Star Team (1922, 1923, 1924) • WHL First All-Star Team (1926)

Signed as a free agent by **Regina** (WCHL), December 1, 1921. Transferred to **Portland** (WHL) after **Regina** (WCHL) franchise relocated, September 1, 1925. Transferred to **Chicago** after NHL club purchased **Portland** (WHL) franchise, May 15, 1926. Traded to **Detroit** by **Chicago** with Percy Traub for $15,000, April 11, 1927.

• HAY, Jim James Alexander "Red Eye"

D – R. 5′11″, 185 lbs. b: Saskatoon, Sask., 5/15/1931.

Season	Club	League	GP	G	A	Pts	AG	AA	APts	PIM	GP	G	A	Pts	PIM
1946-47	Saskatoon Legionaires	SJHL	3	2	0	2	....	....	....	0	....	....	....	....	....
1947-48	Windsor Spitfires	OHA-Jr.	29	10	15	25	....	....	....	40	10	2	0	2	10
	Detroit Auto Club	IHL	25	10	15	25	....	....	....	37	....	....	....	....	....
1948-49	Windsor Spitfires	OHA-Jr.	48	9	8	17	....	....	....	74	4	0	0	0	2
	Saskatoon Quakers	SJHL	2	1	0	1	....	....	....	0	2	2	1	3	4
	Detroit Auto Club	IHL	10	5	3	8	....	....	....	5	6	2	2	4	4
1949-50	Windsor Spitfires	OHA	48	5	15	20	....	....	....	98	11	2	1	3	6
1950-51	Omaha Knights	USHL	64	24	22	46	....	....	....	150	4	1	2	3	4
1951-52	Indianapolis Capitols	AHL	68	7	15	22	....	....	....	129	....	....	....	....	....
1952-53	**Detroit Red Wings**	**NHL**	**42**	**1**	**4**	**5**	**1**	**5**	**6**	**2**	**4**	**0**	**0**	**0**	**2**
	Edmonton Flyers	WHL	26	2	1	3	....	....	....	49	....	....	....	....	....
1953-54	**Detroit Red Wings**	**NHL**	**12**	**0**	**0**	**0**	**0**	**0**	**0**	**0**	....	....	....	....	....
	Sherbrooke Saints	QHL	54	4	6	10	....	....	....	98	5	0	0	0	10
♦1954-55	**Detroit Red Wings**	**NHL**	**21**	**0**	**1**	**1**	**0**	**1**	**1**	**20**	**5**	**1**	**0**	**1**	**0**
	Quebec Aces	QHL	38	5	13	18	....	....	....	107	....	....	....	....	....
1955-56	Brandon Regals	WHL	70	7	7	14	....	....	....	158	....	....	....	....	....
1956-57	Edmonton Flyers	WHL	52	3	13	16	....	....	....	120	....	....	....	....	....
1957-58	Troy Bruins	IHL	64	14	29	43	....	....	....	125	....	....	....	....	....
1958-59	Victoria Cougars	WHL	67	5	23	28	....	....	....	110	3	0	1	1	4
1959-60	Victoria Cougars	WHL	70	4	19	23	....	....	....	118	11	1	2	3	17
1960-61	Victoria Cougars	WHL	70	7	21	28	....	....	....	88	5	0	0	0	0
1961-62	San Francisco Seals	WHL	61	4	16	20	....	....	....	101	2	0	1	1	0
1962-63	Seattle Totems	WHL	70	9	21	30	....	....	....	109	17	2	5	7	10
1963-64	Seattle Totems	WHL	70	3	6	9	....	....	....	65	....	....	....	....	....
1964-65	Portland Buckaroos	WHL	64	2	15	17	....	....	....	115	10	0	4	4	14
1965-66	Portland Buckaroos	WHL	72	3	20	23	....	....	....	115	14	0	1	1	8
1966-67	Portland Buckaroos	WHL	51	1	9	10	....	....	....	49	....	....	....	....	....
1967-68	Portland Buckaroos	WHL	72	5	18	23	....	....	....	75	12	0	2	2	15

			REGULAR SEASON								PLAYOFFS				
Season	Club	League	GP	G	A	Pts	AG	AA	APts	PIM	GP	G	A	Pts	PIM
1968-69	Portland Buckaroos	WHL	74	0	23	23	....	....	....	71	10	0	2	2	17
1969-70	Salt Lake Golden Eagles	WHL	61	2	7	9	....	....	....	105	....	....	....	....	....
	Portland Buckaroos	WHL	....	....	....	....	....	....	....	....	3	1	1	2	6
1970-71	Salt Lake Golden Eagles	WHL	11	1	0	1	....	....	....	14	....	....	....	....	....
	Jersey Devils	EHL	18	1	6	7	....	....	....	37	....	....	....	....	....
1971-72	Jersey Devils	EHL	74	2	18	20	....	....	....	134	....	....	....	....	....
1972-73	Jersey Devils	EHL	DID NOT PLAY – COACHING												
	NHL Totals		**75**	**1**	**5**	**6**	**1**	**6**	**7**	**22**	**9**	**1**	**0**	**1**	**2**

USHL Second All-Star Team (1951)

Traded to **LA Blades** (WHL) by **San Francisco** (WHL) for cash, June, 1962. Traded to **Seattle** (WHL) by **LA Blades** (WHL) with Terry Slater and Jim Powers for Frank Arnett and Marc Boileau, July, 1962. Traded to **Portland** (WHL) by **Seattle** (WHL) for cash, October, 1964. Signed as a free agent by **Salt Lake** (WHL), November, 1969. Loaned to **Portland** (WHL) by **Salt Lake** (WHL) for the 1970 WHL playoffs, April, 1970.

• HAYNES, Paul

C – L. 5'10", 160 lbs. b: Montreal, Que., 3/1/1910 Deceased.

Season	Club	League	GP	G	A	Pts	AG	AA	APts	PIM	GP	G	A	Pts	PIM
1928-29	Montreal Champetre	MCJHL	....	2	0	2	....	....	....	....	....	....	....	....	....
	Loyola College	QCHL	STATISTICS NOT AVAILABLE												
1929-30	Montreal AAA	MCHL	10	2	1	3	....	....	....	4	2	0	0	0	0
1930-31	**Montreal Maroons**	**NHL**	**19**	**1**	**0**	**1**	**2**	**0**	**2**	**0**	....	....	....	....	....
	Windsor Bulldogs	IHL	27	11	16	27	....	....	....	16	6	4	*6	*10	2
1931-32	**Montreal Maroons**	**NHL**	**12**	**1**	**0**	**1**	**2**	**0**	**2**	**0**	**4**	**0**	**0**	**0**	**0**
	Windsor Bulldogs	IHL	33	10	14	24	....	....	....	6	....	....	....	....	....
1932-33	**Montreal Maroons**	**NHL**	**48**	**16**	**25**	**41**	**29**	**53**	**82**	**18**	**2**	**0**	**0**	**0**	**2**
1933-34	**Montreal Maroons**	**NHL**	**44**	**5**	**4**	**9**	**9**	**8**	**17**	**18**	**4**	**0**	**1**	**1**	**2**
	Windsor Bulldogs	IHL	4	0	0	0	....	....	....	0	....	....	....	....	....
1934-35	**Montreal Maroons**	**NHL**	**11**	**1**	**2**	**3**	**2**	**3**	**5**	**0**	....	....	....	....	....
	Boston Bruins	**NHL**	**37**	**4**	**3**	**7**	**7**	**5**	**12**	**8**	**3**	**0**	**0**	**0**	**0**
1935-36	**Montreal Canadiens**	**NHL**	**48**	**5**	**19**	**24**	**10**	**36**	**46**	**24**	....	....	....	....	....
1936-37	**Montreal Canadiens**	**NHL**	**47**	**8**	**18**	**26**	**13**	**33**	**46**	**24**	**5**	**2**	**3**	**5**	**0**
1937-38	**Montreal Canadiens**	**NHL**	**48**	**13**	**22**	**35**	**21**	**36**	**57**	**25**	**3**	**0**	**4**	**4**	**5**
1938-39	**Montreal Canadiens**	**NHL**	**47**	**5**	**33**	**38**	**9**	**52**	**61**	**27**	**3**	**0**	**0**	**0**	**4**
1939-40	**Montreal Canadiens**	**NHL**	**23**	**2**	**8**	**10**	**3**	**12**	**15**	**8**	....	....	....	....	....
1940-41	**Montreal Canadiens**	**NHL**	**7**	**0**	**0**	**0**	**0**	**0**	**0**	**12**	....	....	....	....	....
	New Haven Eagles	AHL	31	3	11	14	....	....	....	4	2	0	0	0	0
1941-42	Montreal Sr. Canadiens	QSHL	DID NOT PLAY – COACHING												
	NHL Totals		**391**	**61**	**134**	**195**	**107**	**238**	**345**	**164**	**24**	**2**	**8**	**10**	**13**

Played in NHL All-Star Game (1937, 1939)

Traded to **Boston** by **Montreal Maroons** for cash, December 28, 1934. Traded to **Montreal Canadiens** by **Boston** for Jack Riley, September 30, 1935.

• HEADLEY, Fern

Fern James "Curly"

D – L. 5'11", 175 lbs. b: Crystal, ND, 3/2/1901 d: 1950.

Season	Club	League	GP	G	A	Pts	AG	AA	APts	PIM	GP	G	A	Pts	PIM
1919-20	Saskatoon Quakers	S-SSHL	3	6	1	7	....	....	....	4	3	3	1	4	4
	Saskatoon Quakers	SJHL	....	....	....	....	....	....	....	....	3	6	1	7	4
1920-21	Saskatoon Collegiate	S-SSHL	4	6	2	8	....	....	....	....	5	4	0	4	6
1921-22	Saskatoon 5th Battalion	S-SSHL	9	7	2	9	....	....	....	2	....	....	....	....	....
1922-23	Saskatoon Sheiks	WCHL	10	2	0	2	....	....	....	4	....	....	....	....	....
1923-24	Saskatoon Crescents	WCHL	20	2	0	2	....	....	....	6	....	....	....	....	....
1924-25	**Boston Bruins**	**NHL**	**13**	**1**	**2**	**3**	**2**	**8**	**10**	**4**	....	....	....	....	....
	Montreal Canadiens	**NHL**	**17**	**0**	**1**	**1**	**0**	**4**	**4**	**6**	**1**	**0**	**0**	**0**	**0**
	Montreal Canadiens	St-Cup	4	0	0	0	....	....	....	0	....	....	....	....	....
1925-26	Calgary Tigers	WHL	29	2	1	3	....	....	....	47	....	....	....	....	....
1926-27	Calgary Tigers	PHL	30	16	10	26	....	....	....	30	2	0	0	0	4
1927-28	Minneapolis Millers	AHA	37	6	5	11	....	....	....	37	8	0	0	0	0
1928-29	St. Louis Flyers	AHA	40	14	11	25	....	....	....	54	....	....	....	....	....
1929-30	St. Louis Flyers	AHA	48	5	6	11	....	....	....	47	....	....	....	....	....
1930-31	Chicago Shamrocks	AHA	47	5	8	13	....	....	....	44	....	....	....	....	....
1931-32	Chicago Shamrocks	AHA	47	6	5	11	....	....	....	50	4	0	0	0	5
1932-33	Duluth-Wichita	AHA	41	10	9	19	....	....	....	37	....	....	....	....	....
1933-34	Tulsa Oilers	AHA	32	6	2	8	....	....	....	34	4	0	0	0	4
1934-35	Tulsa Oilers	AHA	48	5	11	16	....	....	....	31	5	0	0	0	2
1935-36	Tulsa Oilers	AHA	43	1	4	5	....	....	....	33	3	0	0	0	4
1936-37	Kansas City Greyhounds	AHA	7	1	1	2	....	....	....	13	....	....	....	....	....
	Tulsa Oilers	AHA	18	0	0	0	....	....	....	6	....	....	....	....	....
1937-38			DID NOT PLAY												
1938-39	Wichita Skyhawks	AHA	33	6	7	13	....	....	....	36	....	....	....	....	....
	NHL Totals		**30**	**1**	**3**	**4**	**2**	**12**	**14**	**10**	**1**	**0**	**0**	**0**	**0**
	Other Major League Totals		59	6	1	7	....	....	....	57	....	....	....	....	....

PrHL First All-Star Team (1927) • AHA Second All-Star Team (1935)

Signed as a free agent by **Saskatoon** (WCHL), October 30, 1922. Traded to **Boston** by **Saskatoon** (WCHL) for cash, November 2, 1924. Loaned to **Montreal Canadiens** by **Boston** for remainder of the 1924-25 season, January 14, 1925. Traded to **Vancouver** (WHL) by **Boston** for cash, October 29, 1925. Traded to **Calgary** (WHL) by **Vancouver** (WHL) for Rusty Crawford, November 3, 1925. Signed as a free agent by **Calgary** (PHL), November 19, 1926. Traded to **Minneapolis** (AHA) by **Calgary** (PHL) for cash, October 13, 1927. Rights transferred to **Detroit** from **Chicago Shamrocks** (AHA) after AHA club owners purchased Detroit (NHL and IHL) franchises, September 2, 1932.

• HEALEY, Rich

Richard Thomas

D – L. 5'10", 170 lbs. b: Vancouver, B.C., 3/12/1938.

Season	Club	League	GP	G	A	Pts	AG	AA	APts	PIM	GP	G	A	Pts	PIM
1955-56	Edmonton Oil Kings	WCJHL	35	3	9	12	....	....	....	69	6	0	0	0	6
1956-57	Edmonton Oil Kings	CAHL	STATISTICS NOT AVAILABLE												
	Edmonton Oil Kings	M-Cup	6	0	1	1	....	....	....	6	....	....	....	....	....
1957-58	Red Deer Rustlers	CAHL	STATISTICS NOT AVAILABLE												
	Edmonton Oil Kings	M-Cup	4	1	0	1	....	....	....	4	....	....	....	....	....
1958-59	Red Deer Rustlers	AIHA	STATISTICS NOT AVAILABLE												
1959-60	Sudbury Wolves	EPHL	66	1	10	11	....	....	....	75	12	0	3	3	8
1960-61	**Detroit Red Wings**	**NHL**	**1**	**0**	**0**	**0**	**0**	**0**	**0**	**2**	....	....	....	....	....
	Sudbury Wolves	EPHL	30	1	8	9	....	....	....	35	....	....	....	....	....
	Edmonton Flyers	WHL	10	0	0	0	....	....	....	11	....	....	....	....	....
	Hershey Bears	AHL	16	0	2	2	....	....	....	6	7	1	0	1	2
1961-62	S.S. Marie Thunderbirds	EPHL	61	2	22	24	....	....	....	68	....	....	....	....	....
1962-63	Edmonton Flyers	WHL	2	0	1	1	....	....	....	0	....	....	....	....	....
1963-64	Lacombe Rockets	CAHL	....	....	....	....	....	....	....	....	5	2	4	6	6
1964-65	Lacombe Rockets	CAHL	STATISTICS NOT AVAILABLE												
1965-66	Lacombe Rockets	ASHL	25	6	8	14	....	....	....	36	4	3	1	4	0
1966-67	Edmonton Nuggets	ASHL	17	1	2	3	....	....	....	24	....	....	....	....	....
1967-68	Vermilion Tigers	AIHA	STATISTICS NOT AVAILABLE												
1968-69	Edmonton Monarchs	ASHL	....	3	35	38	....	....	....	37	....	0	7	7	10
	NHL Totals		**1**	**0**	**0**	**0**	**0**	**0**	**0**	**2**	....	....	....	....	....

ASHL First All-Star Team (1969)

• Regular season totals for **Lacombe** (ASHL) in 1963-64 unavailable.

• HEBENTON, Andy

Andrew Alexander "Spuds"

RW – L. 5'9", 180 lbs. b: Winnipeg, Man., 10/3/1929.

Season	Club	League	GP	G	A	Pts	AG	AA	APts	PIM	GP	G	A	Pts	PIM
1946-47	St. Boniface Canadiens	MAHA	STATISTICS NOT AVAILABLE												
1947-48	Winnipeg Canadians	MJHL	24	21	13	34	....	....	....	15	6	5	3	8	6
1948-49	Winnipeg Canadians	MJHL	30	*30	13	43	....	....	....	34	10	*9	7	*16	10
1949-50	Cincinnati Mohawks	AHL	44	8	7	15	....	....	....	0	....	....	....	....	....
	Montreal Royals	QSHL	5	0	2	2	....	....	....	0	....	....	....	....	....
1950-51	Victoria Cougars	PCHL	56	16	16	32	....	....	....	12	12	*6	3	9	2
1951-52	Victoria Cougars	PCHL	67	31	25	56	....	....	....	81	13	6	6	12	5
1952-53	Victoria Cougars	WHL	70	27	24	51	....	....	....	46	....	....	....	....	....
1953-54	Victoria Cougars	WHL	70	21	24	45	....	....	....	29	5	3	1	4	0
1954-55	Victoria Cougars	WHL	70	46	34	80	....	....	....	20	5	1	1	2	2
1955-56	**New York Rangers**	**NHL**	**70**	**24**	**14**	**38**	**33**	**17**	**50**	**8**	**5**	**1**	**0**	**1**	**2**
1956-57	**New York Rangers**	**NHL**	**70**	**21**	**23**	**44**	**27**	**25**	**52**	**10**	**5**	**2**	**0**	**2**	**2**
1957-58	**New York Rangers**	**NHL**	**70**	**21**	**24**	**45**	**26**	**25**	**51**	**17**	**6**	**2**	**3**	**5**	**4**
1958-59	**New York Rangers**	**NHL**	**70**	**33**	**29**	**62**	**40**	**29**	**69**	**8**	....	....	....	....	....
1959-60	**New York Rangers**	**NHL**	**70**	**19**	**27**	**46**	**22**	**26**	**48**	**4**	....	....	....	....	....
1960-61	**New York Rangers**	**NHL**	**70**	**26**	**28**	**54**	**30**	**27**	**57**	**10**	....	....	....	....	....
1961-62	**New York Rangers**	**NHL**	**70**	**18**	**24**	**42**	**21**	**23**	**44**	**10**	**6**	**1**	**2**	**3**	**0**
1962-63	**New York Rangers**	**NHL**	**70**	**15**	**22**	**37**	**17**	**22**	**39**	**8**	....	....	....	....	....
1963-64	**Boston Bruins**	**NHL**	**70**	**12**	**11**	**23**	**15**	**11**	**26**	**8**	....	....	....	....	....
1964-65	Portland Buckaroos	WHL	70	34	40	74	....	....	....	16	10	*7	6	13	0
1965-66	Victoria Maple Leafs	WHL	72	31	45	76	....	....	....	12	14	6	11	17	14
1966-67	Victoria Maple Leafs	WHL	72	24	36	60	....	....	....	19	....	....	....	....	....
1967-68	Portland Buckaroos	WHL	70	16	29	45	....	....	....	10	12	3	4	7	0
1968-69	Portland Buckaroos	WHL	74	26	51	77	....	....	....	26	11	2	1	3	0
1969-70	Portland Buckaroos	WHL	72	36	42	78	....	....	....	9	11	2	7	9	0
1970-71	Portland Buckaroos	WHL	72	29	52	81	....	....	....	10	11	6	3	9	14
1971-72	Portland Buckaroos	WHL	72	30	34	64	....	....	....	12	11	3	4	7	2
1972-73	Portland Buckaroos	WHL	72	30	36	66	....	....	....	26	....	....	....	....	....
1973-74	Portland Buckaroos	WHL	78	28	44	72	....	....	....	16	10	2	4	6	2
1974-75	Seattle Totems	CHL	4	0	0	0	....	....	....	0	....	....	....	....	....
	Portland Buckaroos	WIHL	20	4	11	15	....	....	....	0	....	....	....	....	....
	NHL Totals		**630**	**189**	**202**	**391**	**231**	**205**	**436**	**83**	**22**	**6**	**5**	**11**	**8**

MJHL Second All-Star Team (1949) • WHL First All-Star Team (1971, 1973) • WHL Second All-Star Team • (1955, 1965, 1970) • Won Lady Byng Trophy (1957) • Won Fred J. Hume Cup (WHL Most Gentlemanly Player) (1965, 1970, 1971, 1972, 1973, 1974) • Played in NHL All-Star Game (1960)

Signed as a free agent by **Montreal**, April 30, 1947. Traded to **NY Rangers** by **Victoria** (WHL) for cash, April 28, 1955. Claimed by **Boston** from **NY Rangers** in Intra-League Draft, June 4, 1963. Traded to **Portland** (WHL) by **Boston** for cash, June 5, 1964. Traded to **Toronto** by **Boston** with Orland Kurtenbach and Pat Stapleton for Ron Stewart, June 8, 1965. Traded to **Phoenix** (WHL) by **Toronto** (Victoria-WHL) for cash, September, 1967. Traded to **Portland** (WHL) by **Phoenix** (WHL) for Rick Charron, Brian S. Smith and Tom McVie, September, 1967. Selected by **Miami-Philadelphia** (WHA) in WHA General Draft, February 12, 1972.

• HEFFERNAN, Frank

"Moose"

D – L. 6', 210 lbs. b: Peterborough, Ont., Deceased.

Season	Club	League	GP	G	A	Pts	AG	AA	APts	PIM	GP	G	A	Pts	PIM
1910-11	Peterborough Juniors	OHA-Jr.	STATISTICS NOT AVAILABLE												
1911-12	Ottawa College	OCHL	STATISTICS NOT AVAILABLE												
1912-13	Toronto R & AA	OHA-Sr.	6	2	0	2	....	....	....	0	4	2	0	2	....
1913-14	Toronto R & AA	OHA-Sr.	6	4	0	4	....	....	....	....	2	0	0	0	....
1914-15	Toronto Victorias	OHA-Sr.	6	5	0	5	....	....	....	....	4	0	0	0	....
1915-16	New York Crescents	USAHA	8	7	0	7	....	....	....	....	....	....	....	....	....
1916-17	Springhill Miners	NSAPC	2	6	0	6	....	....	....	....	....	....	....	....	....
	New York Crescents	USAHA	2	1	0	1	....	....	....	....	6	2	0	....	....
1917-18	New York Wanderers	USAHA	4	1	0	1	....	....	....	....	....	....	....	....	....
1918-19	Toronto St. Pats	OHA-Sr.	9	6	3	9	....	....	....	....	1	1	0	1	....
1919-20	**Toronto St. Pats**	**NHL**	**19**	**0**	**1**	**1**	**0**	**3**	**3**	**10**	....	....	....	....	....
	NHL Totals		**19**	**0**	**1**	**1**	**0**	**3**	**3**	**10**	....	....	....	....	....

OHA-Jr. First All-Star Team (1911)

Signed as a free agent by **Toronto St. Pats**, December 8, 1919.

• HEFFERNAN, Gerry

Gerald Joseph

RW – R. 5'9", 160 lbs. b: Montreal, Que., 7/24/1916.

Season	Club	League	GP	G	A	Pts	AG	AA	APts	PIM	GP	G	A	Pts	PIM
1934-35	Montreal Jr. Royals	QJHL	12	8	6	14	....	....	....	2	2	1	0	1	2
1935-36	Montreal Jr. Royals	QJHL	9	5	3	8	....	....	....	2	2	3	1	4	0
	Montreal Royals	QSHL	....	....	....	....	....	....	....	....	5	0	0	0	0
1936-37	Montreal Royals	QSHL	21	6	15	21	....	....	....	12	5	2	0	2	2
1937-38	Harringay Greyhounds	Britain	18	18	12	30	....	....	....	....	....	....	....	....	....
1938-39	Montreal Royals	QSHL	21	12	10	22	....	....	....	35	5	2	*8	*10	8
	Montreal Royals	Al-Cup	15	9	13	22	....	....	....	14	....	....	....	....	....
1939-40	Montreal Royals	QSHL	29	11	19	30	....	....	....	38	8	4	6	10	2
	Montreal Royals	Al-Cup	5	1	5	6	....	....	....	9	....	....	....	....	....
1940-41	Montreal Royals	QSHL	33	15	18	33	....	....	....	24	8	4	3	7	2
	Montreal Royals	Al-Cup	14	4	4	8	....	....	....	6	....	....	....	....	....
1941-42	**Montreal Canadiens**	**NHL**	**40**	**5**	**15**	**20**	**7**	**18**	**25**	**15**	**2**	**2**	**1**	**3**	**0**
	Montreal Royals	QSHL	9	2	4	6	....	....	....	6	....	....	....	....	....
1942-43	Montreal Royals	QSHL	22	19	15	34	....	....	....	28	4	0	1	1	2
	Montreal Canadiens	**NHL**	....	....	....	....	....	....	....	....	**2**	**0**	**0**	**0**	**0**
♦**1943-44**	**Montreal Canadiens**	**NHL**	**43**	**28**	**20**	**48**	**26**	**18**	**44**	**12**	**7**	**1**	**2**	**3**	**8**
1944-45	Montreal Royals	QSHL	23	23	28	51	....	....	....	14	7	4	4	8	2
1945-46	Montreal Royals	QSHL	38	20	24	44	....	....	....	41	11	7	6	13	4
	NHL Totals		**83**	**33**	**35**	**68**	**33**	**36**	**69**	**27**	**11**	**3**	**3**	**6**	**8**

Signed as a free agent by **Montreal**, November 28, 1941.

• HEINRICH, Lionel Lionel Grant

LW – L. 5'10", 180 lbs. b: Churchbridge, Sask., 4/20/1934.

Season	Club	League	GP	G	A	Pts	AG	AA	APts	PIM	GP	G	A	Pts	PIM
			REGULAR SEASON								PLAYOFFS				
1951-52	Humboldt Indians	SJHL	45	3	3	6	....	....	....	65	10	1	1	2	12
1952-53	Humboldt Indians	SJHL	27	10	11	21	....	....	....	92	10	3	2	5	12
1953-54	Humboldt Indians	SJHL	42	19	21	40	....	....	....	96	5	2	1	3	4
	Melville Millionaires	SSHL	2	1	0	1	....	....	....	4	9	3	4	7	17
1954-55	Hershey Bears	AHL	54	8	15	23	....	....	....	45	....	....	....	....	....
1955-56	**Boston Bruins**	**NHL**	**35**	**1**	**1**	**2**	**1**	**1**	**2**	**33**	....	....	....	....	....
	Hershey Bears	AHL	15	0	1	1	....	....	....	22	....	....	....	....	....
1956-57	Victoria Cougars	WHL	69	2	11	13	....	....	....	96	3	1	0	1	9
1957-58	Quebec Aces	QHL	4	0	1	1	....	....	....	10	....	....	....	....	....
	Windsor Bulldogs	OHA-Sr.	43	5	9	14	....	....	....	64	....	....	....	....	....
1958-59	Regina Capitals	SSHL	9	0	3	3	....	....	....	10	7	0	3	3	18
1959-60	Regina Capitals	SSHL	3	0	1	1	....	....	....	35	....	....	....	....	....
1960-61			DID NOT PLAY												
1961-62	Regina Capitals	SSHL	3	0	1	1	....	....	....	0	....	....	....	....	....
	NHL Totals		**35**	**1**	**1**	**2**	**1**	**1**	**2**	**33**	....	....	....	....	....

• HELLER, Ott Eberhardt Henry

D – R. 6', 190 lbs. b: Berlin, Ont., 6/2/1910 d: 6/15/1980.

Season	Club	League	GP	G	A	Pts	AG	AA	APts	PIM	GP	G	A	Pts	PIM
1928-29	Kitchener Greenshirts	OHA-Jr.	STATISTICS NOT AVAILABLE												
1929-30	Springfield Indians	Can-Am	26	6	2	8	....	....	....	32	....	....	....	....	....
1930-31	Springfield Indians	Can-Am	38	16	15	31	....	....	....	85	7	0	2	2	26
1931-32	Springfield Indians	Can-Am	21	7	7	14	....	....	....	30	....	....	....	....	....
	New York Rangers	**NHL**	**21**	**2**	**2**	**4**	**3**	**4**	**7**	**9**	**7**	**3**	**1**	**4**	**8**
♦1932-33	**New York Rangers**	**NHL**	**40**	**5**	**7**	**12**	**9**	**14**	**23**	**31**	**8**	**3**	**0**	**3**	**10**
1933-34	**New York Rangers**	**NHL**	**48**	**2**	**5**	**7**	**3**	**10**	**13**	**29**	**2**	**0**	**0**	**0**	**0**
1934-35	**New York Rangers**	**NHL**	**47**	**3**	**11**	**14**	**5**	**19**	**24**	**31**	**4**	**0**	**1**	**1**	**4**
1935-36	**New York Rangers**	**NHL**	**43**	**2**	**11**	**13**	**4**	**21**	**25**	**40**	....	....	....	....	....
1936-37	**New York Rangers**	**NHL**	**48**	**5**	**12**	**17**	**8**	**22**	**30**	**42**	**9**	**0**	**0**	**0**	**11**
1937-38	**New York Rangers**	**NHL**	**48**	**2**	**14**	**16**	**3**	**23**	**26**	**68**	**3**	**0**	**1**	**1**	**2**
1938-39	**New York Rangers**	**NHL**	**48**	**0**	**23**	**23**	**0**	**36**	**36**	**42**	**7**	**0**	**1**	**1**	**10**
♦1939-40	**New York Rangers**	**NHL**	**47**	**5**	**14**	**19**	**8**	**22**	**30**	**26**	**12**	**0**	**3**	**3**	**12**
1940-41	**New York Rangers**	**NHL**	**48**	**2**	**16**	**18**	**3**	**23**	**26**	**42**	**3**	**0**	**1**	**1**	**4**
1941-42	**New York Rangers**	**NHL**	**35**	**6**	**5**	**11**	**8**	**6**	**14**	**22**	**6**	**0**	**0**	**0**	**0**
1942-43	**New York Rangers**	**NHL**	**45**	**4**	**14**	**18**	**4**	**13**	**17**	**14**	....	....	....	....	....
1943-44	**New York Rangers**	**NHL**	**50**	**8**	**27**	**35**	**7**	**24**	**31**	**29**	....	....	....	....	....
1944-45	**New York Rangers**	**NHL**	**45**	**7**	**12**	**19**	**7**	**14**	**21**	**26**	....	....	....	....	....
1945-46	**New York Rangers**	**NHL**	**34**	**2**	**3**	**5**	**2**	**4**	**6**	**14**	....	....	....	....	....
	St. Paul Saints	USHL	16	2	5	7	....	....	....	4	6	0	1	1	4
1946-47	New Haven Ramblers	AHL	64	7	29	36	....	....	....	40	3	0	0	0	6
1947-48	New Haven Ramblers	AHL	67	6	25	31	....	....	....	40	4	1	0	1	6
1948-49	Indianapolis Capitols	AHL	55	6	21	27	....	....	....	24	2	0	0	0	4
1949-50	Indianapolis Capitols	AHL	30	0	1	1	....	....	....	6	4	0	0	0	2
1950-51	Indianapolis Capitols	AHL	48	4	12	16	....	....	....	34	2	0	1	1	2
1951-52	Indianapolis Capitols	AHL	48	4	15	19	....	....	....	40	....	....	....	....	....
1952-53	New Haven Nutmegs	EAHL	21	2	6	8	....	....	....	14	....	....	....	....	....
	Kitchener Dutchmen	OHA-Sr.	24	3	10	13	....	....	....	20	....	....	....	....	....
	Cleveland Barons	AHL	....	....	....	....	....	....	....	....	5	0	0	0	2
1953-54	Marion Barons	IHL	64	4	25	29	....	....	....	70	5	0	2	2	6
1954-55	Valleyfield Braves	QHL	18	0	3	3	....	....	....	4	....	....	....	....	....
	Cleveland Barons	AHL	6	0	1	1	....	....	....	2	3	0	1	1	4
1955-56	Chatham Maroons	OHA-Sr.	7	0	2	2	....	....	....	10	....	....	....	....	....
	NHL Totals		**647**	**55**	**176**	**231**	**74**	**255**	**329**	**465**	**61**	**6**	**8**	**14**	**61**

NHL Second All-Star Team (1941) • AHL Second All-Star Team (1947) • AHL First All-Star Team (1948) • IHL Second All-Star Team (1954)

Traded to **NY Rangers** by **Springfield** (Can-Am) for cash, May 9, 1931. Loaned to **Springfield** (Can-Am) by **NY Rangers** for cash, November 2, 1931.

• HELMAN, Harry Harry Herbert

RW – R. 5'6", 145 lbs. b: Ottawa, Ont., 8/28/1894.

Season	Club	League	GP	G	A	Pts	AG	AA	APts	PIM	GP	G	A	Pts	PIM
1916-17	Ottawa Munitions	OCHL	7	0	0	0	....	....	....	6	....	....	....	....	....
1917-18			MILITARY SERVICE												
1918-19			MILITARY SERVICE												
1919-20	Ottawa GWVA	OCHL	7	4	0	4	....	....	....	....	....	....	....	....	....
1920-21	Ottawa Munitions	OCHL	9	4	0	4	....	....	....	....	1	0	0	0	10
1921-22	Ottawa Munitions	OCHL	11	4	3	7	....	....	....	21	....	....	....	....	....
1922-23	**Ottawa Senators**	**NHL**	**24**	**0**	**0**	**0**	**0**	**0**	**0**	**5**	**2**	**0**	**0**	**0**	**0**
♦	Ottawa Senators	St-Cup	2	0	0	0	....	....	....	0	....	....	....	....	....
1923-24	**Ottawa Senators**	**NHL**	**19**	**1**	**0**	**1**	**2**	**0**	**2**	**2**	....	....	....	....	....
1924-25	**Ottawa Senators**	**NHL**	**1**	**0**	**0**	**0**	**0**	**0**	**0**	**0**	....	....	....	....	....
1925-26			REINSTATED AS AN AMATEUR												
1926-27	Saskatoon Shieks	PrHL	5	0	0	0	....	....	....	8	....	....	....	....	....
	NHL Totals		**44**	**1**	**0**	**1**	**2**	**0**	**2**	**7**	**2**	**0**	**0**	**0**	**0**

OCHL Second All-Star Team (1920, 1921)

Signed as a free agent by **Ottawa**, November 16, 1922. • 1922-23 Stanley Cup totals includes series with Regina (WCHL) and Edmonton (PCHA). Signed as a free agent by **Saskatoon** (PrHL), November 10, 1926.

• HEMMERLING, Tony Anthony Elmer Charles

LW – L. 5'11", 178 lbs. b: Landis, Sask., 5/15/1914 Deceased.

Season	Club	League	GP	G	A	Pts	AG	AA	APts	PIM	GP	G	A	Pts	PIM
1929-30	Biggar Nationals	S-SSHL	6	1	1	2	....	....	....	2	....	....	....	....	....
	Wilkie Outlaws	S-SJHL	....	....	....	....	....	....	....	....	2	1	0	1	6
1930-31	North Battleford Beavers	N-SSHL	15	3	8	11	....	....	....	20	4	0	0	0	8
	North Battleford Beavers	Al-Cup	4	0	0	0	....	....	....	6	....	....	....	....	....
1931-32	North Battleford Beavers	N-SSHL	20	11	5	16	....	....	....	24	....	....	....	....	....
1932-33	Saskatoon Quakers	N-SSHL	16	3	1	4	....	....	....	23	3	0	0	0	6
	Saskatoon Quakers	Al-Cup	13	1	0	1	....	....	....	21	....	....	....	....	....
1933-34	Seattle Seahawks	NWHL	34	13	4	17	....	....	....	46	....	....	....	....	....
1934-35	Seattle Seahawks	NWHL	36	21	12	33	....	....	....	46	5	1	2	3	0
1935-36	Seattle Seahawks	NWHL	6	0	1	1	....	....	....	2	....	....	....	....	....
	Calgary Tigers	NWHL	1	0	0	0	....	....	....	0	....	....	....	....	....
	New York Americans	**NHL**	**3**	**0**	**0**	**0**	**0**	**0**	**0**	**0**	....	....	....	....	....
	Rochester Cardinals	IHL	11	2	5	7	....	....	....	2	....	....	....	....	....
	New Haven Eagles	Can-Am	18	4	6	10	....	....	....	8	....	....	....	....	....
1936-37	**New York Americans**	**NHL**	**19**	**3**	**3**	**6**	**5**	**5**	**10**	**4**	....	....	....	....	....
	New Haven Eagles	IAHL	24	4	10	14	....	....	....	15	....	....	....	....	....
1937-38	New Haven Eagles	IAHL	42	11	11	22	....	....	....	14	2	1	1	2	2
1938-39	New Haven Eagles	IAHL	50	13	13	26	....	....	....	9	....	....	....	....	....
1939-40	New Haven Eagles	IAHL	51	26	31	57	....	....	....	4	3	2	2	4	0
1940-41	Buffalo Bisons	AHL	56	14	10	24	....	....	....	22	....	....	....	....	....
1941-42	Buffalo Bisons	AHL	55	20	19	39	....	....	....	7	....	....	....	....	....
1942-43	Pittsburgh Hornets	AHL	42	17	19	36	....	....	....	16	2	0	0	0	0
1943-44	Pittsburgh Hornets	AHL	51	19	24	43	....	....	....	23	....	....	....	....	....
1944-45	Pittsburgh Hornets	AHL	57	31	33	64	....	....	....	6	....	....	....	....	....
1945-46	Pittsburgh Hornets	AHL	1	0	0	0	....	....	....	0	....	....	....	....	....
	Buffalo Bisons	AHL	9	1	1	2	....	....	....	2	....	....	....	....	....
	Providence Reds	AHL	6	3	2	5	....	....	....	0	....	....	....	....	....
	Dallas Texans	USHL	7	1	1	2	....	....	....	2	....	....	....	....	....
1946-47	Fresno Falcons	PCHL	5	4	1	5	....	....	....	0	....	....	....	....	....
1947-48	Oakland Oaks	PCHL	DID NOT PLAY – COACHING												
	NHL Totals		**22**	**3**	**3**	**6**	**5**	**5**	**10**	**4**	....	....	....	....	....

IAHL Second All-Star Team (1940)

Traded to **Calgary** (NWHL) by **Seattle** (NWHL) for Jim Evans, November 28, 1935. Traded to **NY Americans** by **Calgary** (NWHL) for cash, December 2, 1935. Traded to **New Haven** (IAHL) by **NY Americans** for cash, January, 1937. Traded to **Buffalo** (AHL) by **New Haven** (AHL) for cash, September, 1940. Traded to **Pittsburgh** (AHL) by **Buffalo** (AHL) for cash, September, 1942.

• HENDERSON, Murray John Murray "Moe"

D – L. 6', 180 lbs. b: Toronto, Ont., 9/5/1921.

Season	Club	League	GP	G	A	Pts	AG	AA	APts	PIM	GP	G	A	Pts	PIM
1939-40	Toronto Young Rangers	OHA-Jr.	20	4	3	7	....	....	....	18	2	0	0	0	2
1940-41	Toronto Young Rangers	OHA-Jr.	15	5	0	5	....	....	....	8	5	2	0	2	8
1941-42	Toronto Marlboros	OHA-Jr.	28	2	4	6	....	....	....	10	6	2	1	3	8
	Toronto Kodaks	TMHL	5	4	0	4	....	....	....	0	6	1	3	4	15
1942-43	Toronto RCAF	OHA-Sr.	10	2	5	7	....	....	....	19	13	2	9	11	16
1943-44	Brantford RCAF	OHA-Sr.	STATISTICS NOT AVAILABLE												
	Toronto RCAF	OHA-Sr.	7	6	1	7	....	....	....	6	....	....	....	....	....
1944-45	**Boston Bruins**	**NHL**	**5**	**0**	**1**	**1**	**0**	**1**	**1**	**4**	**7**	**0**	**1**	**1**	**2**
	Boston Olympics	EAHL	3	1	2	3	....	....	....	4	3	2	2	4	2
	Toronto RCAF	TNDHL	2	2	1	3	....	....	....	0	....	....	....	....	....
1945-46	**Boston Bruins**	**NHL**	**48**	**4**	**11**	**15**	**5**	**16**	**21**	**30**	**10**	**1**	**1**	**2**	**4**
1946-47	**Boston Bruins**	**NHL**	**57**	**5**	**12**	**17**	**6**	**14**	**20**	**63**	**4**	**0**	**0**	**0**	**4**
1947-48	**Boston Bruins**	**NHL**	**49**	**6**	**8**	**14**	**8**	**10**	**18**	**50**	**3**	**1**	**0**	**1**	**5**
1948-49	**Boston Bruins**	**NHL**	**60**	**2**	**9**	**11**	**3**	**13**	**16**	**28**	**5**	**0**	**1**	**1**	**2**
1949-50	**Boston Bruins**	**NHL**	**64**	**3**	**8**	**11**	**4**	**10**	**14**	**42**	....	....	....	....	....
1950-51	**Boston Bruins**	**NHL**	**66**	**4**	**7**	**11**	**5**	**9**	**14**	**37**	**5**	**0**	**0**	**0**	**2**
1951-52	**Boston Bruins**	**NHL**	**56**	**0**	**6**	**6**	**0**	**7**	**7**	**51**	**7**	**0**	**0**	**0**	**4**
1952-53	Hershey Bears	AHL	61	4	19	23	....	....	....	49	3	0	0	0	0
1953-54	Hershey Bears	AHL	69	7	25	32	....	....	....	85	11	0	3	3	12
1954-55	Hershey Bears	AHL	59	4	14	18	....	....	....	61	....	....	....	....	....
1955-56	Hershey Bears	AHL	9	0	3	3	....	....	....	8	....	....	....	....	....
	NHL Totals		**405**	**24**	**62**	**86**	**31**	**80**	**111**	**305**	**41**	**2**	**3**	**5**	**23**

AHL Second All-Star Team (1955)

Signed as a free agent by **Boston**, February 28, 1945.

• HENDERSON, Paul — *see page 1171*

• HENDRICKSON, John John Gunnard "Jake"

D – R. 5'11", 175 lbs. b: Kingston, Ont., 12/5/1936.

Season	Club	League	GP	G	A	Pts	AG	AA	APts	PIM	GP	G	A	Pts	PIM
1953-54	Midland Greenshirts	OHA-B	STATISTICS NOT AVAILABLE												
1954-55	Hamilton Tiger Cubs	OHA-Jr.	38	1	7	8	....	....	....	15	3	0	0	0	0
1955-56	Hamilton Tiger Cubs	OHA-Jr.	44	10	14	24	....	....	....	98	....	....	....	....	....
1956-57	Hamilton Tiger Cubs	OHA-Jr.	46	6	9	15	....	....	....	120	4	0	0	0	2
	Springfield Indians	AHL	2	0	0	0	....	....	....	2	....	....	....	....	....
1957-58	**Detroit Red Wings**	**NHL**	**1**	**0**	**0**	**0**	**0**	**0**	**0**	**0**	....	....	....	....	....
	Edmonton Flyers	WHL	62	4	10	14	....	....	....	88	5	1	1	2	6
1958-59	**Detroit Red Wings**	**NHL**	**3**	**0**	**0**	**0**	**0**	**0**	**0**	**2**	....	....	....	....	....
	Hershey Bears	AHL	2	0	0	0	....	....	....	4	....	....	....	....	....
	Springfield Indians	AHL	13	0	0	0	....	....	....	4	....	....	....	....	....
	Edmonton Flyers	WHL	35	5	10	15	....	....	....	39	2	0	0	0	0
1959-60	Seattle Totems	WHL	1	0	0	0	....	....	....	0	....	....	....	....	....
	Sudbury Wolves	EPHL	64	8	27	35	....	....	....	71	3	1	1	2	4
1960-61	Sudbury Wolves	EPHL	48	9	14	23	....	....	....	67	....	....	....	....	....
1961-62	**Detroit Red Wings**	**NHL**	**1**	**0**	**0**	**0**	**0**	**0**	**0**	**2**	....	....	....	....	....
	Sudbury Wolves	EPHL	69	18	22	40	....	....	....	98	4	1	3	4	6
1962-63	Calgary Stampeders	WHL	61	14	35	49	....	....	....	64	....	....	....	....	....
1963-64	St. Louis Braves	CPHL	70	6	32	38	....	....	....	86	6	1	5	6	4
1964-65	St. Louis Braves	CPHL	25	2	12	14	....	....	....	30	....	....	....	....	....
	Los Angeles Blades	WHL	14	2	4	6	....	....	....	12	....	....	....	....	....
1965-66	Los Angeles Blades	WHL	67	10	44	54	....	....	....	61	....	....	....	....	....
1966-67	Los Angeles Blades	WHL	57	3	25	28	....	....	....	63	....	....	....	....	....
1967-68	Port Huron Flags	IHL	22	4	12	16	....	....	....	20	....	....	....	....	....
1968-69	Des Moines–Fort Wayne	IHL	66	5	25	30	....	....	....	52	6	1	3	4	0
1969-70	Long Island Ducks	EHL	46	5	40	45	....	....	....	38	....	....	....	....	....
1970-71	Port Huron Flags	IHL	21	5	3	8	....	....	....	16	....	....	....	....	....
	NHL Totals		**5**	**0**	**0**	**0**	**0**	**0**	**0**	**4**	....	....	....	....	....

Loaned to **Springfield** (AHL) by **Detroit** for cash, November 4, 1958. Traded to **Chicago** by **Detroit** for cash, July, 1962. Traded to **LA Blades** (WHL) by **Chicago** (St. Louis-AHL) for cash, March 1, 1965. Traded to **Des Moines** (IHL) by **Port Huron** (IHL) for cash, October, 1968. Traded to **Fort Wayne** (IHL) by **Des Moines** (IHL) with Ivan Robertson for Ron Hopkinson, January, 1969. Traded to **Long Island** (EHL) by **Fort Wayne** (IHL) for Ed Lawson, October, 1969. Traded to **Port Huron** (IHL) by **Long Island** (EHL) for cash, October, 1970.

• HENRY, Camille — *see page 1172*

• HERBERT, Jimmy James William "Sailor"

C/RW – R. 5'10", 185 lbs. b: Cayuga, Ont., 10/31/1897 d: 12/5/1968.

Season	Club	League	GP	G	A	Pts	AG	AA	APts	PIM	GP	G	A	Pts	PIM
1922-23	Hamilton Tigers	OHA-Sr.	12	3	2	5	....	....	....	....	2	1	0	1	8
1923-24	Eveleth Rangers	USAHA	19	3	0	3	....	....	....	....	....	....	....	....	....
1924-25	**Boston Bruins**	**NHL**	**30**	**17**	**7**	**24**	**30**	**29**	**59**	**55**	....	....	....	....	....
1925-26	**Boston Bruins**	**NHL**	**36**	**26**	**5**	**31**	**46**	**32**	**78**	**47**	....	....	....	....	....
1926-27	**Boston Bruins**	**NHL**	**34**	**15**	**7**	**22**	**27**	**37**	**64**	**51**	**8**	**3**	**0**	**3**	**8**
1927-28	**Boston Bruins**	**NHL**	**12**	**8**	**3**	**11**	**16**	**17**	**33**	**22**	....	....	....	....	....
	Toronto Maple Leafs	**NHL**	**31**	**7**	**1**	**8**	**14**	**6**	**20**	**40**	....	....	....	....	....

Season	Club	League	GP	G	A	Pts	AG	AA	APts	PIM	GP	G	A	Pts	PIM
			REGULAR SEASON								PLAYOFFS				
1928-29	**Detroit Cougars**	**NHL**	**40**	**9**	**5**	**14**	**26**	**33**	**59**	**34**	**1**	**0**	**0**	**0**	**2**
1929-30	**Detroit Cougars**	**NHL**	**23**	**1**	**3**	**4**	**1**	**7**	**8**	**4**	....	....	....	....	....
	London Panthers	IHL	1	0	0	0	....	....	....	0	....	....	....	....	....
1930-31	Detroit Olympics	IHL	44	14	11	25	....	....	....	34	....	....	....	....	....
1931-32	Detroit Olympics	IHL	43	5	5	10	....	....	....	34	6	0	0	0	2
1932-33	Syracuse Stars	IHL	2	0	0	0	....	....	....	0	....	....	....	....	....
	Windsor Bulldogs	IHL	7	2	0	2	....	....	....	0	....	....	....	....	....
	NHL Totals		**206**	**83**	**31**	**114**	**160**	**161**	**321**	**253**	**9**	**3**	**0**	**3**	**10**

Signed as a free agent by **Boston**, November 2, 1924. Traded to **Toronto** by **Boston** for the rights to Eric Pettinger and $15,000, December 21, 1927. Traded to **Detroit** by **Toronto** for the rights to Jack Arbour and $12,500, April 8, 1928.

• HERCHENRATTER, Art Arthur Jacob

LW – L. 6', 185 lbs. b: Berlin, Ont., 11/24/1917.

Season	Club	League	GP	G	A	Pts	AG	AA	APts	PIM	GP	G	A	Pts	PIM
1936-37	Kitchener Greenshirts	OHA-Jr.	13	7	1	8	....	....	....	6	2	0	0	0	5
1937-38	Kitchener Greenshirts	OHA-Jr.	11	4	6	10	....	....	....	0	....	....	....	....	....
1938-39	Detroit Holzbaugh	MOHL	26	9	5	14	....	....	....	4	7	1	2	3	2
1939-40	Windsor Bulldogs	MOHL	40	*31	16	47	....	....	....	14	4	2	1	3	0
1940-41	**Detroit Red Wings**	**NHL**	**10**	**1**	**2**	**3**	**2**	**3**	**5**	**2**	....	....	....	....	....
	Indianapolis Capitols	AHL	39	1	6	7	....	....	....	6	....	....	....	....	....
1941-42	New Haven Eagles	AHL	13	4	1	5	....	....	....	4	....	....	....	....	....
	Omaha Knights	AHA	22	7	5	12	....	....	....	8	....	....	....	....	....
	Kitchener Army	OHA-Sr.	....	....	....	....	....	....	....	....	1	1	1	2	2
1942-43	Kitchener Army	KNDHL	....	....	....	....	....	....	....	....	1	1	1	2	2
1943-44	Truro Bearcats	NSNDL	3	2	1	3	....	....	....	0	....	....	....	....	....
1944-45	MILITARY SERVICE														
1945-46	Stratford Indians	OHA-Sr.	2	0	0	0	....	....	....	0	5	0	5	5	0
1946-47	Springfield Indians	AHL	22	2	5	7	....	....	....	2	....	....	....	....	....
	Houston Huskies	USHL	15	6	7	13	....	....	....	4	....	....	....	....	....
1947-48	Kitchener Dutchmen	OHA-Sr.	19	5	16	21	....	....	....	10	10	2	5	7	8
1948-49	Kitchener Dutchmen	OHA-Sr.	32	7	10	17	....	....	....	14	4	0	0	0	0
1949-50	Kitchener Dutchmen	OHA-Sr.	14	2	1	3	....	....	....	4	....	....	....	....	....
	NHL Totals		**10**	**1**	**2**	**3**	**2**	**3**	**5**	**2**	....	....	....	....	....

Signed as a free agent by **Detroit**, October 16, 1940.

• HERGERTS, Fred

C – R. 6'1", 190 lbs. b: Calgary, Alta., 1/29/1913.

Season	Club	League	GP	G	A	Pts	AG	AA	APts	PIM	GP	G	A	Pts	PIM
1928-29	Calgary Shamrocks	CCJHL	3	0	0	0	....	....	....	0	....	....	....	....	....
1929-30	Calgary Shamrocks	CCJHL	STATISTICS NOT AVAILABLE												
1930-31	Calgary Canadians	CCJHL	2	1	*2	*3	....	....	....	0	2	0	0	0	0
	Calgary Canadians	M-Cup	8	3	2	5	....	....	....	4	....	....	....	....	....
1931-32	Calgary Bronks	ASHL	20	9	*12	21	....	....	....	*50	3	*2	1	*3	2
	Calgary Bronks	Al-Cup	11	*6	3	9	....	....	....	12	....	....	....	....	....
1932-33	Drumheller Miners	ASHL	15	11	*9	20	....	....	....	12	5	1	1	2	2
1933-34	Syracuse–Cleveland	IHL	40	1	3	4	....	....	....	11	6	1	0	1	2
1934-35	**New York Americans**	**NHL**	**19**	**2**	**4**	**6**	**3**	**7**	**10**	**2**	....	....	....	....	....
	Philadelphia Arrows	Can-Am	26	6	10	16	....	....	....	23	....	....	....	....	....
1935-36	**New York Americans**	**NHL**	**1**	**0**	**0**	**0**	**0**	**0**	**0**	**0**	....	....	....	....	....
	Rochester Cardinals	IHL	4	0	0	0	....	....	....	0	....	....	....	....	....
	Detroit Olympics	IHL	41	6	6	12	....	....	....	34	6	1	0	1	10
1936-37	Pittsburgh Hornets	AHL	24	1	6	7	....	....	....	20	....	....	....	....	....
	Cleveland Barons	AHL	26	3	9	12	....	....	....	27	5	0	0	0	0
1937-38	Kansas City Greyhounds	AHA	48	16	22	38	....	....	....	19	....	....	....	....	....
1938-39	St. Louis Flyers	AHA	39	16	36	52	....	....	....	40	2	0	1	1	0
1939-40	St. Louis Flyers	AHA	48	23	*48	*71	....	....	....	31	5	2	1	3	8
1940-41	St. Louis Flyers	AHA	48	11	*33	44	....	....	....	26	9	1	3	4	2
1941-42	St. Louis Flyers	AHA	44	15	13	28	....	....	....	22	3	1	1	2	0
1942-43	Hershey Bears	AHL	56	30	45	75	....	....	....	33	6	0	6	6	2
1943-44	Hershey Bears	AHL	53	19	31	50	....	....	....	43	7	2	4	6	2
1944-45	St. Louis Flyers	AHL	55	23	36	59	....	....	....	21	....	....	....	....	....
1945-46	St. Louis Flyers	AHL	58	9	32	41	....	....	....	34	....	....	....	....	....
1946-47	St. Louis Flyers	AHL	46	3	9	12	....	....	....	20	....	....	....	....	....
1947-48	Calgary Stampeders	WCSHL	45	2	12	14	....	....	....	78	11	3	4	7	6
1948-49	Nelson Maple Leafs	WIHL	36	14	27	41	....	....	....	56	5	1	4	5	6
1949-50	Nelson Maple Leafs	WIHL	PLAYER/COACH – STATISTICS UNAVAILABLE												
1950-51	Nelson Maple Leafs	WIHL	22	7	24	31	....	....	....	38	4	0	0	0	0
	NHL Totals		**20**	**2**	**4**	**6**	**3**	**7**	**10**	**2**	....	....	....	....	....

AHA First All-Star Team (1940)

Signed as a free agent by **Chicago**, October 15, 1933. Traded to **Detroit** by **NY Americans** with $7,500 for Eddie Wiseman, November 21, 1935. Loaned to **Rochester** (IHL) by **NY Americans**, November 10, 1935. Traded to **Cleveland** (AHL) by **Pittsburgh** (AHL) for cash, January 15, 1937. Traded to **St. Louis** (AHA) by **Cleveland** (AHL) for cash, October 13, 1938.

• HERGESHEIMER, Philip "Phantom"

RW – R. 5'10", 175 lbs. b: Winnipeg, Man., 7/9/1914.

Season	Club	League	GP	G	A	Pts	AG	AA	APts	PIM	GP	G	A	Pts	PIM
1932-33	Winnipeg Falcons	MJHL	8	8	2	10	....	....	....	6	....	....	....	....	....
1933-34	Winnipeg Falcons	MJHL	14	9	6	15	....	....	....	21	1	0	0	0	0
1934-35	Boston Cubs	Can-Am	46	10	6	16	....	....	....	16	3	1	0	1	2
1935-36	Boston Cubs	Can-Am	27	2	7	9	....	....	....	10	....	....	....	....	....
	Detroit Olympics	IHL	5	1	1	2	....	....	....	0	....	....	....	....	....
	London Tecumsehs	IHL	11	2	2	4	....	....	....	0	2	0	0	0	0
1936-37	Minneapolis Millers	AHA	48	23	26	49	....	....	....	22	6	1	4	5	4
1937-38	Cleveland Barons	IAHL	47	*25	20	45	....	....	....	13	2	2	1	3	0
1938-39	Cleveland Barons	IAHL	54	*34	19	53	....	....	....	23	9	*7	1	*8	14
1939-40	**Chicago Black Hawks**	**NHL**	**42**	**9**	**11**	**20**	**15**	**17**	**32**	**6**	**1**	**0**	**0**	**0**	**0**
1940-41	**Chicago Black Hawks**	**NHL**	**48**	**8**	**16**	**24**	**12**	**23**	**35**	**9**	**5**	**0**	**0**	**0**	**2**
1941-42	**Chicago Black Hawks**	**NHL**	**23**	**3**	**11**	**14**	**4**	**13**	**17**	**2**	....	....	....	....	....
	Boston Bruins	**NHL**	**3**	**0**	**0**	**0**	**0**	**0**	**0**	**2**	....	....	....	....	....
	Hershey Bears	AHL	12	8	7	15	....	....	....	2	10	6	5	11	4
1942-43	**Chicago Black Hawks**	**NHL**	**9**	**1**	**3**	**4**	**1**	**3**	**4**	**0**	....	....	....	....	....
	Cleveland Barons	AHL	36	14	27	41	....	....	....	4	4	1	1	2	2
1943-44	Cleveland Barons	AHL	33	21	19	40	....	....	....	6	....	....	....	....	....
	Ottawa Commandos	QSHL	1	0	2	2	....	....	....	0	1	0	0	0	2
1944-45	St. John's Navy	Nfld-Sr.	6	11	*15	*26	....	....	....	0	1	*3	*2	*5	0
1945-46	Cleveland Barons	AHL	54	21	27	48	....	....	....	4	12	6	10	*16	4
1946-47	Philadelphia Rockets	AHL	64	48	44	*92	....	....	....	20	....	....	....	....	....
1947-48	Philadelphia Rockets	AHL	57	42	31	73	....	....	....	6	....	....	....	....	....
1948-49	Philadelphia Rockets	AHL	67	38	28	66	....	....	....	14	....	....	....	....	....
1949-50	Cincinnati Mohawks	AHL	70	31	30	61	....	....	....	7	....	....	....	....	....
1950-51	Cincinnati Mohawks	AHL	54	6	13	19	....	....	....	8	....	....	....	....	....
1951-52	Kelowna Packers	OSHL	45	34	14	48	....	....	....	34	....	....	....	....	....
1952-53	Kelowna Packers	OSHL	54	20	26	46	....	....	....	10	4	2	2	4	2
1953-54	Kelowna Packers	OSHL	63	17	21	38	....	....	....	56	8	2	4	6	8
1954-55	Kamloops Elks	OSHL	40	10	8	18	....	....	....	18	9	2	0	2	2
	NHL Totals		**125**	**21**	**41**	**62**	**32**	**56**	**88**	**19**	**6**	**0**	**0**	**0**	**2**

• Brother of Wally • AHA Second All-Star Team (1937) • IAHL First All-Star Team (1939) • AHL First All-Star Team (1944, 1947) • AHL Second All-Star Team (1948, 1949) • OSHL First All-Star Team (1952) • OSHL Second All-Star Team (1953)

Loaned to **Detroit** (IHL) by **Boston** (Can-Am) for cash, January 1, 1936 and recalled, January 10, 1936. Loaned to **London** (IHL) by **Boston** (Can-Am) for cash, February 19, 1936. Traded to **Chicago** by **Cleveland** (IAHL) for Charley Mason, Harold Jackson and $15,000, May 17, 1939. • Suspended by **Chicago** for refusing assignment to **Kansas City** (AHA), January 16, 1942. Traded to **Boston** by **Chicago** for cash with Chicago holding right of recall, January 26, 1942. • Rights returned to **Chicago** by **Boston**, July 1, 1942.

• HERGESHEIMER, Wally Walter Edgar

RW – R. 5'8", 155 lbs. b: Winnipeg, Man., 1/8/1927.

Season	Club	League	GP	G	A	Pts	AG	AA	APts	PIM	GP	G	A	Pts	PIM
1943-44	Winnipeg Rangers	MJHL	2	2	1	3	....	....	....	2	....	....	....	....	....
1944-45	Winnipeg Rangers	MJHL	10	*20	10	*30	....	....	....	2	4	1	1	2	0
	Winnipeg Monarchs	M-Cup	10	9	5	14	....	....	....	2	....	....	....	....	....
1945-46	Brandon Elks	MJHL	10	15	11	26	....	....	....	4	7	3	1	4	0
1946-47	Brandon Elks	MJHL	16	*25	14	39	....	....	....	8	7	4	3	7	4
	Brandon Elks	M-Cup	12	18	6	24	....	....	....	4	....	....	....	....	....
1947-48	Minneapolis Millers	USHL	37	8	14	22	....	....	....	4	4	0	0	0	0
1948-49	San Francisco Shamrocks	PCHL	70	34	39	73	....	....	....	22	....	....	....	....	....
1949-50	Minneapolis Millers	USHL	69	43	37	80	....	....	....	22	7	5	5	10	0
1950-51	Cleveland Barons	AHL	71	42	41	83	....	....	....	8	11	*11	2	13	0
1951-52	**New York Rangers**	**NHL**	**68**	**26**	**12**	**38**	**35**	**15**	**50**	**6**	....	....	....	....	....
1952-53	**New York Rangers**	**NHL**	**70**	**30**	**29**	**59**	**40**	**35**	**75**	**10**	....	....	....	....	....
1953-54	**New York Rangers**	**NHL**	**66**	**27**	**16**	**43**	**37**	**19**	**56**	**42**	....	....	....	....	....
1954-55	**New York Rangers**	**NHL**	**14**	**4**	**2**	**6**	**5**	**2**	**7**	**4**	....	....	....	....	....
1955-56	**New York Rangers**	**NHL**	**70**	**22**	**18**	**40**	**30**	**21**	**51**	**26**	**5**	**1**	**0**	**1**	**0**
1956-57	**Chicago Black Hawks**	**NHL**	**41**	**2**	**8**	**10**	**3**	**9**	**12**	**12**	....	....	....	....	....
1957-58	Buffalo Bisons	AHL	70	26	21	47	....	....	....	18	....	....	....	....	....
1958-59	**New York Rangers**	**NHL**	**22**	**3**	**0**	**3**	**4**	**0**	**4**	**6**	....	....	....	....	....
	Buffalo Bisons	AHL	45	23	23	46	....	....	....	21	11	2	1	3	6
1959-60	Buffalo Bisons	AHL	72	25	29	54	....	....	....	13	....	....	....	....	....
1960-61	Calgary Stampeders	WHL	70	40	26	66	....	....	....	17	5	3	0	3	0
1961-62	Los Angeles Blades	WHL	66	21	44	65	....	....	....	6	....	....	....	....	....
	NHL Totals		**351**	**114**	**85**	**199**	**154**	**101**	**255**	**106**	**5**	**1**	**0**	**1**	**0**

• Brother of Philip • USHL First All-Star Team (1950) • AHL Second All-Star Team (1951) • Won Dudley "Red" Garrett Memorial Award (Top Rookie - AHL) (1951) • Played in NHL All-Star Game (1953, 1956)

Transferred to **Denver** (USHL) after **Minneapolis** (USHL) franchise relocated, August, 1950. Traded to **Cleveland** (AHL) by **NY Rangers** (Denver-USHL) for Bill Richardson, Neil Strain, Bob Jackson and Joe McArthur, September 5, 1950. Traded to **NY Rangers** by **Cleveland** (AHL) with Hy Buller for Ed Reigle, Jackie Gordon, Fred Shero, Fern Perreault and cash, May 14, 1951. • Missed remainder of 1954-55 season recovering from leg injury suffered in game vs. Toronto, December 18, 1954. Traded to **Chicago** by **NY Rangers** for Red Sullivan, June 19, 1956. Traded to **Buffalo** (AHL) by **Chicago** with Frank Martin for Ken Wharram, May 5, 1958. NHL rights transferred to **NY Rangers** from **Buffalo** after NHL club purchased AHL franchise, June, 1958. Claimed on waivers by **Montreal** from **NY Rangers**, December 10, 1958. Claimed on waivers by **NY Rangers** from **Montreal**, December 17, 1958.

• HERON, Red Robert Geatrex

C – L. 5'11", 170 lbs. b: Toronto, Ont., 12/31/1917.

Season	Club	League	GP	G	A	Pts	AG	AA	APts	PIM	GP	G	A	Pts	PIM
1932-33	Toronto Marlboros	OHA-Jr.	9	4	1	5	....	....	....	4	3	0	0	0	2
1933-34	Toronto Native Sons	OHA-Jr.	12	11	7	18	....	....	....	7	....	....	....	....	....
1934-35	West Toronto Nationals	OHA-Jr.	12	3	1	4	....	....	....	14	....	....	....	....	....
1935-36	West Toronto Nationals	OHA-Jr.	9	11	6	17	....	....	....	16	5	*6	*4	*10	2
	Toronto Goodyears	OHA-Sr.	13	*16	1	17	....	....	....	4	6	4	2	6	9
	West Toronto Nationals	M-Cup	12	*18	8	*26	....	....	....	20	....	....	....	....	....
1936-37	Toronto Goodyears	OHA-Sr.	8	5	3	8	....	....	....	16	5	3	0	3	8
1937-38	Toronto Goodyears	OHA-Sr.	16	*21	15	36	....	....	....	6	6	3	2	5	4
	Syracuse Stars	IAHL	1	0	0	0	....	....	....	0	6	1	2	3	0
1938-39	**Toronto Maple Leafs**	**NHL**	**6**	**0**	**0**	**0**	**0**	**0**	**0**	**0**	**2**	**0**	**0**	**0**	**4**
	Syracuse Stars	IAHL	46	12	14	26	....	....	....	26	3	0	1	1	10
1939-40	**Toronto Maple Leafs**	**NHL**	**42**	**11**	**12**	**23**	**18**	**19**	**37**	**12**	**9**	**2**	**0**	**2**	**2**
	Pittsburgh Hornets	IAHL	4	3	3	6	....	....	....	0	....	....	....	....	....
1940-41	**Toronto Maple Leafs**	**NHL**	**35**	**9**	**5**	**14**	**14**	**7**	**21**	**12**	**7**	**0**	**2**	**2**	**0**
	Pittsburgh Hornets	AHL	2	2	0	2	....	....	....	0	....	....	....	....	....
1941-42	**Brooklyn Americans**	**NHL**	**11**	**0**	**1**	**1**	**0**	**1**	**1**	**2**	....	....	....	....	....
	Springfield Indians	AHL	7	3	3	6	....	....	....	2	....	....	....	....	....
	Montreal Canadiens	**NHL**	**12**	**1**	**1**	**2**	**1**	**1**	**2**	**12**	**3**	**0**	**0**	**0**	**0**
	Pittsburgh Hornets	AHL	23	20	16	36	....	....	....	10	....	....	....	....	....
1942-43	Research Colonels	TMHL	12	*22	12	*34	....	....	....	4	....	....	....	....	....
	Toronto Peoples	TIHL	5	5	4	9	....	....	....	8	7	8	10	18	12
1943-44	Toronto RCAF	OHA-Sr.	15	6	10	16	....	....	....	12	....	....	....	....	....
	Toronto Staffords	TMHL	6	9	5	14	....	....	....	4	9	9	5	14	8
1944-45	Rockcliffe RCAF	ONDHL	....	....	....	....	....	....	....	....	2	0	2	2	0
1945-46	STATISTICS NOT AVAILABLE														
1946-47	Toronto Barkers	TIHL	26	37	25	62	....	....	....	6	6	*9	3	12	4
1947-48	Toronto Barkers	TIHL	27	20	14	34	....	....	....	8	9	6	5	11	4
	NHL Totals		**106**	**21**	**19**	**40**	**33**	**28**	**61**	**38**	**21**	**2**	**2**	**4**	**6**

Loaned to **Brooklyn** by **Toronto** with Nick Knott and Gus Marker and future considerations (cash, February 2, 1942) for Lorne Carr, October 30, 1941. Loaned to **Montreal** by **Brooklyn** for the loan of Murph Chamberlain, February 4, 1942.

• HEXIMER, Obs Orville Russell

LW/C – L. 5'7", 159 lbs. b: Niagara Falls, Ont., 2/16/1910.

Season	Club	League	GP	G	A	Pts	AG	AA	APts	PIM	GP	G	A	Pts	PIM
1926-27	Niagara Falls Cataracts	OHA-Jr.	....	....	....	....	....	....	....	....	4	*2	*3	*5	....
1927/29	Niagara Falls Cataracts	OHA-Jr.	STATISTICS NOT AVAILABLE												
1929-30	**New York Rangers**	**NHL**	**19**	**1**	**0**	**1**	**1**	**0**	**1**	**4**	....	....	....	....	....
	Springfield Indians	Can-Am	14	13	6	19	....	....	....	18	....	....	....	....	....
1930-31	Springfield Indians	Can-Am	40	*36	*25	*61	....	....	....	70	7	4	0	4	4
1931-32	Springfield Indians	Can-Am	40	11	17	28	....	....	....	51	....	....	....	....	....

			REGULAR SEASON								PLAYOFFS				
Season	Club	League	GP	G	A	Pts	AG	AA	APts	PIM	GP	G	A	Pts	PIM
1932-33	**Boston Bruins**	**NHL**	**48**	**7**	**5**	**12**	**13**	**10**	**23**	**12**	**5**	**0**	**0**	**0**	**2**
1933-34	Boston Cubs	Can-Am	39	12	15	27	....	....	....	53	5	1	2	3	2
1934-35	Boston Cubs	Can-Am	13	1	10	11	....	....	....	5	....	....	....	....	....
	New York Americans	**NHL**	**17**	**5**	**2**	**7**	**8**	**3**	**11**	**0**	....	....	....	....	....
	New Haven Eagles	Can-Am	12	11	5	16	....	....	....	7	....	....	....	....	....
1935-36	New Haven Eagles	Can-Am	39	15	10	25	....	....	....	35	....	....	....	....	....
1936-37	New Haven Eagles	IAHL	42	9	12	21	....	....	....	39	....	....	....	....	....
1937-38	New Haven Eagles	IAHL	36	13	11	24	....	....	....	21	....	....	....	....	....
	Springfield Indians	IAHL	6	2	1	3	....	....	....	0	....	....	....	....	....
1938-39	St. Paul Saints	AHA	41	22	25	47	....	....	....	43	3	0	2	2	0
1939-40			DID NOT PLAY												
1940-41	Niagara Falls Brights	OHA-Sr.	26	4	5	9	....	....	....	8	3	1	0	1	5
1941-42	Niagara Falls Weavers	OHA-Sr.	18	0	1	1	....	....	....	2	7	0	3	3	15
	NHL Totals		**84**	**13**	**7**	**20**	**22**	**13**	**35**	**16**	**5**	**0**	**0**	**0**	**2**

Signed as a free agent by **NY Rangers**, December 10, 1929. Traded to **Boston** by **NY Rangers** for $10,000, August 22, 1932. Traded to **NY Americans** by **Boston** with Hap Emms for Walter Jackson, December 13, 1934. Traded to **New Haven** (Can-Am) by **NY Americans** for cash, October 21, 1935. Traded to **Springfield** (IAHL) by **New Haven** (IAHL) for Bob McCulley, December 1, 1937.

• HEXTALL, Bryan Jr. *— see page 1175*

• HEXTALL, Bryan Sr. Bryan Aldwyn HHOF

RW – L. 5'10", 180 lbs. b: Grenfell, Sask., 7/31/1913 d: 7/25/1984.

			REGULAR SEASON								PLAYOFFS				
Season	Club	League	GP	G	A	Pts	AG	AA	APts	PIM	GP	G	A	Pts	PIM
1931-32	Winnipeg Monarchs	MJHL	4	0	0	0	....	....	....	0	1	2	0	2	0
1932-33	Portage Terriers	MJHL	12	10	*8	*18	....	....	....	6	2	0	0	0	4
1933-34	Portage Terriers	MJHL	7	6	4	10	....	....	....	8	....	....	....	....	....
	Vancouver Lions	NWHL	5	2	0	2	....	....	....	0	....	....	....	....	....
1934-35	Vancouver Lions	NWHL	32	14	10	24	....	....	....	27	8	0	0	0	*10
	Vancouver Lions	L-W-S	5	2	0	2	....	....	....	2	....	....	....	....	....
1935-36	Vancouver Lions	NWHL	40	*27	9	36	....	....	....	65	7	1	2	3	15
1936-37	Philadelphia Ramblers	IAHL	50	*27	25	52	....	....	....	40	6	2	4	6	6
	New York Rangers	**NHL**	**3**	**0**	**1**	**1**	**0**	**2**	**2**	**0**	....	....	....	....	....
1937-38	**New York Rangers**	**NHL**	**48**	**17**	**4**	**21**	**28**	**6**	**34**	**6**	**3**	**2**	**0**	**2**	**0**
1938-39	**New York Rangers**	**NHL**	**48**	**20**	**15**	**35**	**35**	**23**	**58**	**18**	**7**	**0**	**1**	**1**	**4**
♦1939-40	**New York Rangers**	**NHL**	**48**	***24**	**15**	**39**	**40**	**24**	**64**	**52**	**12**	**4**	**3**	**7**	**11**
1940-41	**New York Rangers**	**NHL**	**48**	***26**	**18**	**44**	**41**	**26**	**67**	**16**	**3**	**0**	**1**	**1**	**0**
1941-42	**New York Rangers**	**NHL**	**48**	**24**	**32**	***56**	**32**	**38**	**70**	**30**	**6**	**1**	**1**	**2**	**4**
1942-43	**New York Rangers**	**NHL**	**50**	**27**	**32**	**59**	**28**	**30**	**58**	**28**	....	....	....	....	....
1943-44	**New York Rangers**	**NHL**	**50**	**21**	**33**	**54**	**19**	**29**	**48**	**41**	....	....	....	....	....
1944-45	St. Catharines Saints	OHA-Sr.	1	0	1	1	....	....	....	0	....	....	....	....	....
1945-46	**New York Rangers**	**NHL**	**3**	**0**	**1**	**1**	**0**	**1**	**1**	**0**	....	....	....	....	....
1946-47	**New York Rangers**	**NHL**	**60**	**20**	**10**	**30**	**23**	**12**	**35**	**18**	....	....	....	....	....
1947-48	**New York Rangers**	**NHL**	**43**	**8**	**14**	**22**	**10**	**18**	**28**	**18**	**6**	**1**	**3**	**4**	**0**
1948-49	Cleveland Barons	AHL	32	12	17	29	....	....	....	14	....	....	....	....	....
	Washington Lions	AHL	25	6	6	12	....	....	....	2	....	....	....	....	....
	NHL Totals		**449**	**187**	**175**	**362**	**256**	**209**	**465**	**227**	**37**	**8**	**9**	**17**	**19**

• Father of Bryan Jr. and Dennis • NHL First All-Star Team (1940, 1941, 1942) • NHL Scoring Leader (1942) • NHL Second All-Star Team (1943)

• Missed entire 1944-45 and majority of 1945-46 seasons after being refused permission to enter USA by War Mobilization Command, November 22, 1944. Traded to **Cleveland** (AHL) by **NY Rangers** for cash, September 21, 1948. Traded to **Washington** (AHL) by **Cleveland** (AHL) with Ab DeMarco for Ken Schultz, Dan Porteous and Frank Porteous, January 20, 1949.

• HEYLIGER, Vic USHOF

C – L. 5'9", 175 lbs. b: Boston, MA, 9/26/1919.

Season	Club	League	GP	G	A	Pts	AG	AA	APts	PIM	GP	G	A	Pts	PIM
1934/37	University of Michigan	NCAA	STATISTICS NOT AVAILABLE												
1937-38	**Chicago Black Hawks**	**NHL**	**7**	**0**	**0**	**0**	**0**	**0**	**0**	**0**	....	....	....	....	....
	St. Paul Saints	AHA	3	0	0	0	....	....	....	0	....	....	....	....	....
1938-39	Detroit Holtzbaugh	MOHL	27	5	9	14	....	....	....	27	2	1	1	2	2
1939/43	University of Illinois	WIAA	DID NOT PLAY – COACHING												
1943-44	**Chicago Black Hawks**	**NHL**	**26**	**2**	**3**	**5**	**2**	**3**	**5**	**2**	....	....	....	....	....
1944-45	University of Michigan	NCAA	DID NOT PLAY – COACHING												
	NHL Totals		**33**	**2**	**3**	**5**	**2**	**3**	**5**	**2**	....	....	....	....	....

Signed as a free agent by **Chicago**, November 3, 1937. Signed as a free agent by **Chicago**, October 18, 1943.

• HICKE, Bill *— see page 1175*

• HICKS, Henry Henry Harold "Hal"

D – L. 5'7", 170 lbs. b: Sillery, Que., 12/10/1900 Deceased.

Season	Club	League	GP	G	A	Pts	AG	AA	APts	PIM	GP	G	A	Pts	PIM
1916-17	Ottawa Glebe Collegiate	OCJHL	STATISTICS NOT AVAILABLE												
1917-18	Ottawa Mallettes	OCHL	1	0	0	0	....	....	....	0	....	....	....	....	....
	Ottawa Glebe Collegiate	OCJHL	1	0	0	0	....	....	....	0	....	....	....	....	....
1918-19	Ottawa Grand Trunk	OCHL	STATISTICS NOT AVAILABLE												
1919-20	Ottawa Grand Trunk	OCHL	STATISTICS NOT AVAILABLE												
1920-21	Ottawa City Hall	OCHL	12	0	0	0	....	....	....						
1921-22	Ottawa St. Brigids	OCHL	6	0	0	0	....	....	....	6	....	....	....	....	....
1922-23	Ottawa ACC	OIHA	STATISTICS NOT AVAILABLE												
1923-24	Ottawa ACC	OIHA	STATISTICS NOT AVAILABLE												
1924-25	Ottawa Rideaus	OCHL	12	2	0	2	....	....	....	....	3	0	0	0	....
1925-26	Montreal CNR	MRTHL	7	3	1	4	....	....	....	10	1	0	0	0	0
	Ottawa Rideaus	OCHL	6	4	3	7	....	....	....	....	....	....	....	....	....
1926-27	Stratford Nationals	Can-Pro	31	5	4	9	....	....	....	76	2	0	0	0	0
1927-28	Stratford Nationals	Can-Pro	42	8	6	14	....	....	....	61	5	*4	1	5	8
1928-29	**Montreal Maroons**	**NHL**	**44**	**2**	**0**	**2**	**6**	**0**	**6**	**27**	....	....	....	....	....
1929-30	**Detroit Cougars**	**NHL**	**30**	**3**	**2**	**5**	**4**	**5**	**9**	**35**	....	....	....	....	....
	Detroit Olympics	IHL	15	0	1	1	....	....	....	21	3	0	0	0	0
1930-31	**Detroit Falcons**	**NHL**	**22**	**2**	**0**	**2**	**4**	**0**	**4**	**10**	....	....	....	....	....
	London Tecumsehs	IHL	27	4	3	7	....	....	....	10	....	....	....	....	....
1931-32	London Tecumsehs	IHL	47	3	9	12	....	....	....	53	6	0	1	1	2
1932-33	London Tecumsehs	IHL	44	9	15	24	....	....	....	51	6	0	0	0	5
1933-34	London Tecumsehs	IHL	15	1	1	2	....	....	....	8	....	....	....	....	....
	NHL Totals		**96**	**7**	**2**	**9**	**14**	**5**	**19**	**72**	....	....	....	....	....

Signed as a free agent by **Stratford** (Can-Pro), November 10, 1926. Traded to **Montreal Maroons** by **Stratford** (Can-Pro) for cash, April 23, 1928. Traded to **Detroit** by **Montreal Maroons** for $8,000, September 30, 1929. Traded to **London** (IHL) by **Detroit** for Leroy Goldsworthy, January 12, 1931.

• HICKS, Wayne *— see page 1177*

• HILDEBRAND, Ike Isaac Bruce

RW – R. 5'7", 147 lbs. b: Winnipeg, Man., 5/27/1927.

Season	Club	League	GP	G	A	Pts	AG	AA	APts	PIM	GP	G	A	Pts	PIM
1945-46	Oshawa Generals	OHA-Jr.	27	14	21	35	....	....	....	8	12	*21	11	*32	4
1946-47	Oshawa Generals	OHA-Jr.	29	28	25	53	....	....	....	23	5	3	1	4	16
1947-48	Toronto Marlboros	OHA-Jr.	35	29	37	66	....	....	....	29	5	2	0	2	6
1948-49	Los Angeles Monarchs	PCHL	45	17	19	36	....	....	....	32	7	1	5	6	17
1949-50	Los Angeles Monarchs	PCHL	63	24	36	60	....	....	....	28	17	6	8	14	20
1950-51	Kansas City Royals	USHL	63	*42	49	91	....	....	....	67	....	....	....	....	....
1951-52	Cleveland Barons	AHL	48	31	16	47	....	....	....	19	5	1	3	4	7
1952-53	Cleveland Barons	AHL	64	*38	34	72	....	....	....	40	11	1	1	2	11
1953-54	**New York Rangers**	**NHL**	**31**	**6**	**7**	**13**	**8**	**8**	**16**	**12**	....	....	....	....	....
	Vancouver Canucks	WHL	8	0	0	0	....	....	....	2	....	....	....	....	....
	Chicago Black Hawks	**NHL**	**7**	**1**	**4**	**5**	**1**	**5**	**6**	**4**	....	....	....	....	....
1954-55	**Chicago Black Hawks**	**NHL**	**3**	**0**	**0**	**0**	**0**	**0**	**0**	**0**	....	....	....	....	....
	Montreal Royals	QHL	53	17	25	42	....	....	....	27	14	1	6	7	14
1955-56	Cleveland Barons	AHL	54	9	19	28	....	....	....	43	8	1	1	2	10
1956-57	Pembroke Lumber Kings	EOHL	23	6	12	18	....	....	....	44	....	....	....	....	....
	Belleville McFarlands	EOHL	25	19	36	55	....	....	....	73	10	2	5	7	10
1957-58	Belleville McFarlands	EOHL	51	15	39	54	....	....	....	55	13	5	*19	24	2
	Belleville McFarlands	Al-Cup	14	6	12	18	....	....	....	12	....	....	....	....	....
1958-59	Belleville McFarlands	EOHL	46	30	36	66	....	....	....	31	....	....	....	....	....
	Canada	WEC-A	8	6	6	12	....	....	....	4	....	....	....	....	....
1959-60	Belleville McFarlands	OHA-Sr.	45	23	22	45	....	....	....	20	12	3	11	14	4
	NHL Totals		**41**	**7**	**11**	**18**	**9**	**13**	**22**	**16**	....	....	....	....	....

USHL First All-Star Team (1951) • AHL First All-Star Team (1953)

Traded to **Vancouver** (WHL) by **NY Rangers** for cash, January 7, 1954. Traded to **Chicago** by **Vancouver** (WHL) for cash, January 20, 1954. Traded to **Montreal** by **Chicago** with future considerations for Lorne Davis, October 13, 1954.

• HILL, Mel John Melvin "Sudden Death"

RW – R. 5'10", 175 lbs. b: Glenboro, Man., 2/15/1914 d: 4/11/1996.

Season	Club	League	GP	G	A	Pts	AG	AA	APts	PIM	GP	G	A	Pts	PIM
1932-33	Saskatoon Tigers	N-SJHL	3	*4	1	*5	....	....	....	0	....	....	....	....	....
	Saskatoon Tigers	M-Cup	3	4	0	4	....	....	....	0	....	....	....	....	....
1933-34	Saskatoon Wesleys	N-SJHL	4	3	2	5	....	....	....	0	9	12	7	19	2
1934-35	Sudbury Cub Wolves	NOJHA	10	9	4	13	....	....	....	8	5	2	1	3	0
1935-36	Sudbury Frood Miners	NBHL	10	7	6	13	....	....	....	15	....	....	....	....	....
1936-37	Sudbury Frood Miners	NBHL	15	*18	5	23	....	....	....	10	2	1	0	1	0
	Sudbury Frood Miners	Al-Cup	14	8	14	22	....	....	....	6	....	....	....	....	....
1937-38	**Boston Bruins**	**NHL**	**6**	**2**	**0**	**2**	**3**	**0**	**3**	**2**	**1**	**0**	**0**	**0**	**0**
	Providence Reds	IAHL	40	13	10	23	....	....	....	0	7	4	2	6	0
♦1938-39	**Boston Bruins**	**NHL**	**46**	**10**	**10**	**20**	**17**	**16**	**33**	**16**	**12**	**6**	**3**	**9**	**12**
1939-40	**Boston Bruins**	**NHL**	**38**	**9**	**11**	**20**	**15**	**17**	**32**	**19**	**3**	**0**	**0**	**0**	**0**
♦1940-41	**Boston Bruins**	**NHL**	**41**	**5**	**4**	**9**	**8**	**6**	**14**	**4**	**8**	**1**	**1**	**2**	**0**
	Hershey Bears	AHL	5	1	5	6	....	....	....	4	....	....	....	....	....
1941-42	Springfield Indians	AHL	1	0	0	0	....	....	....	0	....	....	....	....	....
	Brooklyn Americans	**NHL**	**47**	**14**	**23**	**37**	**19**	**27**	**46**	**10**	....	....	....	....	....
1942-43	**Toronto Maple Leafs**	**NHL**	**49**	**17**	**27**	**44**	**17**	**25**	**42**	**47**	**6**	**3**	**0**	**3**	**0**
1943-44	**Toronto Maple Leafs**	**NHL**	**17**	**9**	**10**	**19**	**8**	**9**	**17**	**6**	....	....	....	....	....
♦1944-45	**Toronto Maple Leafs**	**NHL**	**45**	**18**	**17**	**35**	**18**	**20**	**38**	**14**	**13**	**2**	**3**	**5**	**6**
1945-46	**Toronto Maple Leafs**	**NHL**	**35**	**5**	**7**	**12**	**6**	**10**	**16**	**10**	....	....	....	....	....
	Pittsburgh Hornets	AHL	13	7	8	15	....	....	....	0	6	1	2	3	0
1946-47	Pittsburgh Hornets	AHL	62	26	36	62	....	....	....	42	12	3	6	9	6
1947-48	Pittsburgh Hornets	AHL	63	10	22	32	....	....	....	14	2	0	0	0	2
1948-49	Regina Caps	WCSHL	43	23	30	53	....	....	....	11	8	4	6	10	4
	Regina Caps	Al-Cup	14	8	6	14	....	....	....	11	....	....	....	....	....
1949-50	Regina Caps	WCSHL	50	17	21	38	....	....	....	16	....	....	....	....	....
1950-51	Regina Caps	MCMHL	22	3	5	8	....	....	....	6	....	....	....	....	....
1951-52	Regina Caps	SSHL	17	7	11	18	....	....	....	16	3	1	0	1	9
	NHL Totals		**324**	**89**	**109**	**198**	**111**	**130**	**241**	**128**	**43**	**12**	**7**	**19**	**18**

Signed as a free agent by **Boston**, October 26, 1937. Traded to **Brooklyn** by **Boston** for cash, June 27, 1941. Rights transferred to **Toronto** from **Brooklyn** in Special Dispersal Draw, October 9, 1942. • Missed remainder of 1943-44 season recovering from broken ankle suffered in game vs. Detroit, December 16, 1943.

• HILLER, Dutch Wilbert Carl "Wib"

LW – L. 5'8", 170 lbs. b: Berlin, Ont., 5/11/1915.

Season	Club	League	GP	G	A	Pts	AG	AA	APts	PIM	GP	G	A	Pts	PIM
1932-33	Kitchener Empires	OHA-Jr.	11	7	3	10	....	....	....	19	5	*6	2	*8	4
1933-34	Sudbury Cub Wolves	NOJHA	8	7	0	7	....	....	....	15	2	*5	1	*6	2
1934-35	Sudbury Cub Wolves	NOJHA	4	5	0	5	....	....	....	8	3	2	0	2	*8
1935-36	Sudbury Frood Miners	NBHL	6	5	0	5	....	....	....	10	....	....	....	....	....
	Falconbridge Falcons	Al-Cup	13	6	1	7	....	....	....	4	....	....	....	....	....
1936-37	Harringay Greyhounds	Britain	42	22	11	33	....	....	....	16	....	....	....	....	....
1937-38	New York Rovers	EAHL	43	26	30	56	....	....	....	31	....	....	....	....	....
	New York Rangers	**NHL**	**8**	**0**	**1**	**1**	**0**	**2**	**2**	**2**	**1**	**0**	**0**	**0**	**0**
1938-39	**New York Rangers**	**NHL**	**48**	**10**	**19**	**29**	**17**	**30**	**47**	**22**	**7**	**1**	**0**	**1**	**9**
♦1939-40	**New York Rangers**	**NHL**	**48**	**13**	**18**	**31**	**22**	**28**	**50**	**57**	**12**	**2**	**4**	**6**	**2**
1940-41	**New York Rangers**	**NHL**	**44**	**8**	**10**	**18**	**12**	**14**	**26**	**20**	**3**	**0**	**0**	**0**	**0**
1941-42	**Detroit Red Wings**	**NHL**	**7**	**0**	**0**	**0**	**0**	**0**	**0**	**0**	....	....	....	....	....
	Boston Bruins	**NHL**	**43**	**7**	**10**	**17**	**9**	**12**	**21**	**19**	**5**	**0**	**1**	**1**	**0**
1942-43	**Boston Bruins**	**NHL**	**3**	**0**	**0**	**0**	**0**	**0**	**0**	**0**	....	....	....	....	....
	Montreal Canadiens	**NHL**	**39**	**8**	**6**	**14**	**8**	**6**	**14**	**4**	**5**	**1**	**0**	**1**	**4**
	Washington Lions	AHL	2	0	1	1	....	....	....	0	....	....	....	....	....
	San Diego Skyhawks	X-Games	STATISTICS NOT AVAILABLE												
1943-44	**New York Rangers**	**NHL**	**50**	**18**	**22**	**40**	**16**	**19**	**35**	**15**	....	....	....	....	....
1944-45	**Montreal Canadiens**	**NHL**	**48**	**20**	**16**	**36**	**20**	**19**	**39**	**20**	**6**	**1**	**1**	**2**	**4**
♦1945-46	**Montreal Canadiens**	**NHL**	**45**	**7**	**11**	**18**	**8**	**16**	**24**	**4**	**9**	**4**	**2**	**6**	**2**

Season	Club	League	GP	G	A	Pts	AG	AA	APts	PIM	GP	G	A	Pts	PIM
			REGULAR SEASON								PLAYOFFS				
1946-47	Pittsburgh Hornets	AHL	64	13	16	29	....	....	....	37	12	2	3	5	12
1947-48	Kitchener Dutchmen	OHA-Sr.	19	15	12	27	....	....	....	20	9	2	4	6	8
1948-49	Los Angeles Monarchs	PCHL	DID NOT PLAY – COACHING												
	NHL Totals		**383**	**91**	**113**	**204**	**112**	**146**	**258**	**163**	**48**	**9**	**8**	**17**	**21**

EAHL Second All-Star Team (1938)

Signed as a free agent by **NY Rangers**, February 24, 1938. Claimed on waivers by **Detroit** from **NY Rangers**, April 8, 1941. Traded to **Boston** by **Detroit** with $5,000 for Pat McReavy, November 24, 1941. Traded to **Montreal** by **Boston** for cash, August 15, 1942. Loaned to **NY Rangers** by **Montreal** with John Mahaffy, Fern Gauthier, Charlie Sands and future considerations (Tony Demers, December, 1943) for the loan of Phil Watson, October 27, 1943. Traded to **Toronto** (Pittsburgh-AHL) by **Montreal** (Buffalo-AHL) with Vic Lynn for John Mahaffy and Gerry Brown, September 21, 1946.

• HILLMAN, Floyd

Floyd Arthur
D – L. 5'11", 170 lbs. b: Ruthven, Ont., 11/19/1933.

Season	Club	League	GP	G	A	Pts	AG	AA	APts	PIM	GP	G	A	Pts	PIM
1950-51	Oshawa Chevies	OHA-B	STATISTICS NOT AVAILABLE												
	Oshawa Generals	OHA-Jr.	1	0	0	0	....	....	....	4	....	....	....	....	....
1951-52	Oshawa Chevies	OHA-B	STATISTICS NOT AVAILABLE												
1952-53	Oshawa Generals	OHA-Jr.	56	7	13	20	....	....	....	94	4	1	0	1	4
1953-54	Kitchener Greenshirts	OHA-Jr.	55	3	16	19	....	....	....	115	4	0	0	0	8
1954-55	Windsor Bulldogs	OHA-Sr.	46	2	10	12	....	....	....	*131	12	1	3	4	27
1955-56	Victoria Cougars	WHL	30	2	4	6	....	....	....	69	....	....	....	....	....
	Hershey Bears	AHL	41	1	6	7	....	....	....	70	....	....	....	....	....
1956-57	**Boston Bruins**	**NHL**	**6**	**0**	**0**	**0**	**0**	**0**	**0**	**10**	....	....	....	....	....
	Quebec Aces	QHL	62	4	8	12	....	....	....	140	10	0	2	2	14
	Quebec Aces	Ed-Cup	6	0	1	1	....	....	....	6	....	....	....	....	....
1957-58	Quebec Aces	QHL	23	0	5	5	....	....	....	49	13	0	2	2	15
	Springfield Indians	AHL	43	3	11	14	....	....	....	62	....	....	....	....	....
1958-59	Providence Reds	AHL	2	0	0	0	....	....	....	0	....	....	....	....	....
	Quebec Aces	QHL	59	1	18	19	....	....	....	149	....	....	....	....	....
1959-60	Providence Reds	AHL	72	4	27	31	....	....	....	132	5	0	1	1	10
1960-61	Providence Reds	AHL	39	0	8	8	....	....	....	53	....	....	....	....	....
	Kingston Frontenacs	EPHL	18	0	1	1	....	....	....	27	....	....	....	....	....
1961-62	San Francisco Seals	WHL	70	0	14	14	....	....	....	122	2	0	1	1	7
1962-63	Windsor Bulldogs	OHA-Sr.	33	3	20	23	....	....	....	72	11	0	2	2	27
	Windsor Bulldogs	Al-Cup	13	0	3	3	....	....	....	26	....	....	....	....	....
1963-64	Windsor Bulldogs	IHL	68	4	22	26	....	....	....	180	6	0	2	2	8
	NHL Totals		**6**	**0**	**0**	**0**	**0**	**0**	**0**	**10**	....	....	....	....	....

• Brother of Larry and Wayne

Traded to **Boston** by **Victoria** (WHL) for Arnott Whitney, December, 1955.

• HILLMAN, Larry

— see page 1180

• HILLMAN, Wayne

— see page 1181

• HIMES, Normie

Norman Lawrence
C – R. 5'9", 145 lbs. b: Galt, Ont., 4/13/1903 d: 9/14/1958.

Season	Club	League	GP	G	A	Pts	AG	AA	APts	PIM	GP	G	A	Pts	PIM
1918/20	Galt Terriers	OHA-Jr.	STATISTICS NOT AVAILABLE												
1920-21	Galt Terriers	OIHA	STATISTICS NOT AVAILABLE												
1921-22	Galt Terriers	OHA-Sr.	STATISTICS NOT AVAILABLE												
1922-23	Galt Terriers	OHA-Sr.	9	11	5	16	....	....	....	....	....	....	....	....	....
1923-24	Galt Terriers	OHA-Sr.	12	9	3	12	....	....	....	6	....	....	....	....	....
1924-25	Galt Terriers	OHA-Sr.	20	14	3	17	....	....	....	19	....	....	....	....	....
1925-26	Galt Terriers	OHA-Sr.	20	13	6	19	....	....	....	13	2	2	0	2	1
1926-27	**New York Americans**	**NHL**	**42**	**9**	**2**	**11**	**16**	**10**	**26**	**14**	....	....	....	....	....
1927-28	**New York Americans**	**NHL**	**44**	**14**	**5**	**19**	**29**	**28**	**57**	**22**	....	....	....	....	....
1928-29	**New York Americans**	**NHL**	**44**	**10**	**0**	**10**	**29**	**0**	**29**	**25**	**2**	**0**	**0**	**0**	**0**
1929-30	**New York Americans**	**NHL**	**44**	**28**	**22**	**50**	**40**	**52**	**92**	**15**	....	....	....	....	....
1930-31	**New York Americans**	**NHL**	**44**	**15**	**9**	**24**	**30**	**27**	**57**	**18**	....	....	....	....	....
1931-32	**New York Americans**	**NHL**	**48**	**7**	**21**	**28**	**12**	**47**	**59**	**9**	....	....	....	....	....
1932-33	**New York Americans**	**NHL**	**48**	**9**	**25**	**34**	**16**	**53**	**69**	**12**	....	....	....	....	....
1933-34	**New York Americans**	**NHL**	**48**	**9**	**16**	**25**	**15**	**34**	**49**	**10**	....	....	....	....	....
1934-35	**New York Americans**	**NHL**	**40**	**5**	**13**	**18**	**8**	**23**	**31**	**2**	....	....	....	....	....
1935-36	New Haven Eagles	Can-Am	46	4	14	18	....	....	....	26	....	....	....	....	....
1936-37	New Haven Eagles	IAHL	6	0	0	0	....	....	....	2	....	....	....	....	....
	NHL Totals		**402**	**106**	**113**	**219**	**195**	**274**	**469**	**127**	**2**	**0**	**0**	**0**	**0**

Played in NHL All-Star Game (1934)

Signed as a free agent by **NY Americans**, October 1, 1926.

• HIRSCHFELD, Bert

John Albert
LW – L. 5'10", 165 lbs. b: Halifax, N.S., 3/1/1929 d: 7/3/1996.

Season	Club	League	GP	G	A	Pts	AG	AA	APts	PIM	GP	G	A	Pts	PIM
1946-47	Halifax St. Mary's	X-Games	7	*13	*15	*28	....	....	....	0	....	....	....	....	....
	Halifax St. Mary's	M-Cup	7	8	12	20	....	....	....	2	....	....	....	....	....
1947-48	Halifax St. Mary's	X-Games	25	16	*39	55	....	....	....	11	....	....	....	....	....
	Halifax Crescents	HCSHL	2	1	3	4	....	....	....	2	....	....	....	....	....
	Halifax St. Mary's	M-Cup	8	19	8	27	....	....	....	0	....	....	....	....	....
1948-49	Montreal Jr. Royals	QJHL	40	32	26	58	....	....	....	17	10	11	4	15	5
	Montreal Royals	QSHL	1	0	0	0	....	....	....	0	....	....	....	....	....
	Montreal Royals	M-Cup	15	12	11	23	....	....	....	10	....	....	....	....	....
1949-50	**Montreal Canadiens**	**NHL**	**13**	**1**	**2**	**3**	**1**	**2**	**3**	**2**	**5**	**1**	**0**	**1**	**0**
	Cincinnati Mohawks	AHL	53	22	12	34	....	....	....	2	....	....	....	....	....
	Montreal Royals	QSHL	8	1	1	2	....	....	....	0	....	....	....	....	....
1950-51	**Montreal Canadiens**	**NHL**	**20**	**0**	**2**	**2**	**0**	**2**	**2**	**0**	....	....	....	....	....
	Cincinnati Mohawks	AHL	42	15	8	23	....	....	....	2	....	....	....	....	....
1951-52	Indianapolis Capitols	AHL	67	23	38	61	....	....	....	8	....	....	....	....	....
1952-53	St. Louis Flyers	AHL	58	12	27	39	....	....	....	4	....	....	....	....	....
1953-54	Providence Reds	AHL	60	10	26	36	....	....	....	10	....	....	....	....	....
1954-55	Moncton Hawks	ACSHL	66	29	27	56	....	....	....	10	13	7	8	15	0
	Moncton Hawks	Al-Cup	13	11	5	16	....	....	....	0	....	....	....	....	....
1955-56	Moncton Hawks	ACSHL	70	12	40	52	....	....	....	31	8	1	2	3	2
	New Haven Blades	EHL	1	0	2	2	....	....	....	0	....	....	....	....	....
1956-57	Campbellton Tigers	NNBHL	27	9	15	24	....	....	....	6	12	*10	4	14	4
1957-58			DID NOT PLAY												
1958-59	Halifax Wolves	NSSHL	28	3	9	12	....	....	....	0	....	....	....	....	....
1959-60	Halifax Wolves	NSSHL	28	11	6	17	....	....	....	9	....	....	....	....	....
1960-61	Halifax Wolves	NSSHL	28	25	17	42	....	....	....	2	5	3	2	5	2
1961-62	Halifax Wolves	NSSHL	25	11	20	31	....	....	....	2	5	6	6	12	2
1962-63	Halifax Tartans	NSSHL	DID NOT PLAY – COACHING												
	NHL Totals		**33**	**1**	**4**	**5**	**1**	**4**	**5**	**2**	**5**	**1**	**0**	**1**	**0**

Traded to **Detroit** by **Montreal** for Gerry Couture, June 19, 1951. Signed as a free agent by **Providence** (AHL), September 27, 1953. Traded to **Moncton** (ACSHL) by **Providence** (AHL) for cash, October 14, 1954.

• HITCHMAN, Lionel

Frederick Lionel
D – L. 6'1", 167 lbs. b: Toronto, Ont., 11/3/1901 d: 1/12/1969.

Season	Club	League	GP	G	A	Pts	AG	AA	APts	PIM	GP	G	A	Pts	PIM
1919-20	Toronto Aura Lee	OHA-Jr.	4	0	0	0	....	....	....	0	....	....	....	....	....
1920-21	Toronto Aura Lee	OHA-Jr.	3	1	0	1	....	....	....	4	....	....	....	....	....
1921-22	Ottawa New Edinburghs	OCHL	8	2	1	3	....	....	....	14	....	....	....	....	....
1922-23	Ottawa New Edinburghs	OCHL	16	5	1	6	....	....	....	30	3	0	0	0	*18
	Ottawa Senators	**NHL**	**3**	**0**	**1**	**1**	**0**	**4**	**4**	**12**	**2**	**0**	**0**	**0**	**0**
♦	Ottawa Senators	St-Cup	5	1	0	1	....	....	....	4	....	....	....	....	....
1923-24	**Ottawa Senators**	**NHL**	**24**	**2**	**6**	**8**	**4**	**36**	**40**	**24**	**2**	**0**	**0**	**0**	**4**
1924-25	**Ottawa Senators**	**NHL**	**12**	**0**	**0**	**0**	**0**	**0**	**0**	**2**	....	....	....	....	....
	Boston Bruins	**NHL**	**19**	**3**	**1**	**4**	**5**	**4**	**9**	**22**	....	....	....	....	....
1925-26	**Boston Bruins**	**NHL**	**36**	**7**	**4**	**11**	**12**	**26**	**38**	**70**	....	....	....	....	....
1926-27	**Boston Bruins**	**NHL**	**41**	**3**	**6**	**9**	**5**	**31**	**36**	**70**	**8**	**1**	**0**	**1**	**31**
1927-28	**Boston Bruins**	**NHL**	**44**	**5**	**3**	**8**	**10**	**17**	**27**	**87**	**2**	**0**	**0**	**0**	**2**
♦1928-29	**Boston Bruins**	**NHL**	**38**	**1**	**0**	**1**	**3**	**0**	**3**	**64**	**5**	**0**	**1**	**1**	**22**
1929-30	**Boston Bruins**	**NHL**	**39**	**2**	**7**	**9**	**3**	**16**	**19**	**58**	**6**	**1**	**0**	**1**	**14**
1930-31	**Boston Bruins**	**NHL**	**41**	**0**	**2**	**2**	**0**	**6**	**6**	**40**	**5**	**0**	**0**	**0**	**0**
1931-32	**Boston Bruins**	**NHL**	**48**	**4**	**3**	**7**	**7**	**7**	**14**	**36**	....	....	....	....	....
1932-33	**Boston Bruins**	**NHL**	**45**	**0**	**1**	**1**	**0**	**2**	**2**	**34**	**5**	**1**	**0**	**1**	**0**
1933-34	**Boston Bruins**	**NHL**	**27**	**1**	**0**	**1**	**2**	**0**	**2**	**4**	....	....	....	....	....
	Boston Cubs	Can-Am	4	0	0	0	....	....	....	2	....	....	....	....	....
	NHL Totals		**417**	**28**	**34**	**62**	**51**	**149**	**200**	**523**	**35**	**3**	**1**	**4**	**73**

OCHL Second All-Star Team (1922, 1923)

Signed as a free agent by **Ottawa**, February 28, 1923. • 1922-23 Stanley Cup totals includes series with Regina (WCHL) and Edmonton (PCHA). Traded to **Boston** by **Ottawa** for cash, January 10, 1925.

• HODGE, Ken

— see page 1184

• HODGSON, Ted

Edward James
RW – R. 5'11", 185 lbs. b: Hobbema, Alta., 6/30/1945.

Season	Club	League	GP	G	A	Pts	AG	AA	APts	PIM	GP	G	A	Pts	PIM
1963-64	Estevan Bruins	SJHL	60	19	17	36	....	....	....	123	11	4	4	8	32
1964-65	Estevan Bruins	SJHL	55	37	38	75	....	....	....	148	6	3	4	7	20
	Minneapolis Bruins	CPHL	2	0	0	0	....	....	....	2	5	0	0	0	0
1965-66	Estevan Bruins	SJHL	35	21	35	56	....	....	....	152	11	2	7	9	28
	Estevan Bruins	M-Cup	13	4	7	11	....	....	....	22	....	....	....	....	....
	Edmonton Oil Kings	M-Cup	6	2	3	5	....	....	....	9	....	....	....	....	....
1966-67	**Boston Bruins**	**NHL**	**4**	**0**	**0**	**0**	**0**	**0**	**0**	**0**	....	....	....	....	....
	Buffalo Bisons	AHL	7	2	2	4	....	....	....	16	....	....	....	....	....
	Oklahoma City Blazers	CPHL	53	5	7	12	....	....	....	101	9	2	1	3	10
1967-68	Oklahoma City Blazers	CPHL	62	11	10	21	....	....	....	136	7	0	1	1	15
1968-69	Oklahoma City Blazers	CHL	44	12	20	32	....	....	....	56	12	0	1	1	25
1969-70	Salt Lake Golden Eagles	WHL	57	18	22	40	....	....	....	54	....	....	....	....	....
1970-71	Salt Lake Golden Eagles	WHL	60	8	13	21	....	....	....	90	....	....	....	....	....
1971-72	Salt Lake Golden Eagles	WHL	72	22	17	39	....	....	....	86	....	....	....	....	....
1972-73	Cleveland Crusaders	WHA	74	15	23	38	....	....	....	93	9	1	3	4	13
1973-74	Cleveland Crusaders	WHA	10	0	2	2	....	....	....	6	....	....	....	....	....
	Jacksonville Barons	AHL	46	4	13	17	....	....	....	42	....	....	....	....	....
	Los Angeles Sharks	WHA	23	3	9	12	....	....	....	22	....	....	....	....	....
1974-75	Philadelphia Firebirds	NAHL	71	10	26	36	....	....	....	39	3	0	1	1	4
1975-76	Roanoke Valley Rebels	SHL	54	11	14	25	....	....	....	32	6	1	3	4	2
1976-77	Oklahoma City Blazers	CHL	46	5	23	28	....	....	....	83	....	....	....	....	....
	NHL Totals		**4**	**0**	**0**	**0**	**0**	**0**	**0**	**0**	....	....	....	....	....
	Other Major League Totals		107	18	34	52				121	9	1	3	4	13

Loaned to **Edmonton** by **Estevan** for Memorial Cup playoffs, April, 1964. Traded to **Salt Lake** (WHL) by **Boston** for cash, October 22, 1969. Traded to **NY Rangers** by **Salt Lake** (WHL) for cash, May 22, 1970. Traded to **Buffalo** by **NY Rangers** for cash, June, 1970. Selected by **Calgary-Cleveland** (WHA) in 1972 WHA General Player Draft, February 12, 1972. Traded to **LA Sharks** (WHA) by **Cleveland** (WHA) with Bill Young for Ron Ward, February, 1974. Rights transferred to **Michigan** (WHA) after **LA Sharks** (WHA) franchise relocated, April 11, 1974. Selected by **Phoenix** (WHA) from **Michigan** (WHA) in WHA Expansion Draft, May 30, 1974.

• HOEKSTRA, Cec

Cecil Thomas
C – L. 6', 175 lbs. b: Winnipeg, Man., 4/2/1935.

Season	Club	League	GP	G	A	Pts	AG	AA	APts	PIM	GP	G	A	Pts	PIM
1951-52	Weston Wildcats	OHA-B	25	15	15	30	....	....	....		....	....	....	....	....
1952-53	St. Boniface Canadiens	MJHL	31	11	17	28	....	....	....	10	8	5	6	11	2
	St. Boniface Canadiens	M-Cup	17	2	14	16	....	....	....	0	....	....	....	....	....
1953-54	St. Catharines Teepees	OHA-Jr.	59	24	35	59	....	....	....	8	14	4	8	12	0
	St. Catharines Teepees	M-Cup	11	2	5	7	....	....	....	2	....	....	....	....	....
1954-55	St. Catharines Teepees	OHA-Jr.	49	30	50	80	....	....	....	24	11	5	7	12	11
	Montreal Royals	QHL	....	....	....	....	....	....	....	....	3	1	0	1	0
1955-56	Montreal Royals	QHL	34	6	5	11	....	....	....	8	....	....	....	....	....
	Winnipeg Warriors	WHL	28	1	9	10	....	....	....	4	14	0	0	0	2
	Winnipeg Warriors	Ed-Cup	6	0	2	2	....	....	....	0	....	....	....	....	....
1956-57	Winnipeg Warriors	WHL	69	21	12	33	....	....	....	16	....	....	....	....	....
1957-58	Montreal Royals	QHL	31	13	24	37	....	....	....	11	7	3	4	7	0
	Rochester Americans	AHL	13	1	2	3	....	....	....	0	....	....	....	....	....
1958-59	Rochester Americans	AHL	70	26	24	50	....	....	....	4	5	1	1	2	0
1959-60	**Montreal Canadiens**	**NHL**	**4**	**0**	**0**	**0**	**0**	**0**	**0**	**0**	....	....	....	....	....
	Rochester Americans	AHL	69	17	32	49	....	....	....	2	5	1	1	2	0
1960-61	Buffalo Bisons	AHL	68	6	16	22	....	....	....	14	4	0	0	0	0
1961-62	Pittsburgh Hornets	AHL	68	16	31	47	....	....	....	16	....	....	....	....	....
1962-63	Calgary Stampeders	WHL	67	14	31	45	....	....	....	10	....	....	....	....	....
1963-64	Cleveland Barons	AHL	72	23	28	51	....	....	....	12	9	3	7	10	0
1964-65	Cleveland Barons	AHL	20	2	3	5	....	....	....	6	....	....	....	....	....
1965-66	Cleveland Barons	AHL	70	21	26	47	....	....	....	10	12	2	6	8	6
1966-67	Cleveland Barons	AHL	59	20	34	54	....	....	....	10	2	0	0	0	0
1967-68	Cleveland Barons	AHL	72	24	36	60	....	....	....	14	....	....	....	....	....
1968-69	Cleveland Barons	AHL	73	15	26	41	....	....	....	8	5	0	2	2	2

			REGULAR SEASON								PLAYOFFS				
Season	Club	League	GP	G	A	Pts	AG	AA	APts	PIM	GP	G	A	Pts	PIM
1969-70	Cleveland Barons	AHL	72	8	20	28	....	....	....	0	....	....	....	....	....
1970-71	Galt Hornets	OHA-Sr.	STATISTICS NOT AVAILABLE												
1971-72	Galt Hornets	OHA-Sr.	3	0	1	1	....	....	....	4	....	....	....	....	....
	NHL Totals		**4**	**0**	**0**	**0**	**0**	**0**	**0**	**0**	....	....	....	....	....

• Brother of Ed

Traded to **Chicago** by **Montreal** with Reggie Fleming, Ab McDonald and Bob Courcy for Terry Gray, Glen Skov, the rights to Danny Lewicki, Lorne Ferguson and Bob Bailey, June 7, 1960. Traded to **Pittsburgh** (AHL) by **Chicago** for cash, June, 1961. Traded to **Chicago** by **Pittsburgh** (AHL) for cash, September, 1962. Traded to **Boston** (San Francisco-WHL) by **Chicago** (Calgary-WHL) for Al Nicholson, January 22, 1963. • Transaction voided when Nicholson refused to report to club, January, 1963.

• HOFFINGER, Val — Val Edward "Doc"

D – L. 5′6″, 190 lbs. b: Seltz, Russia, 1/1/1901.

Season	Club	League	GP	G	A	Pts	AG	AA	APts	PIM	GP	G	A	Pts	PIM
1925-26	Saskatoon Empires	N-SSHL	4	6	1	7	....	....	....	*6	2	1	0	1	0
1926-27	Saskatoon Sheiks	PrHL	29	13	6	19	....	....	....	42	4	0	0	0	*8
1927-28	Saskatoon Sheiks	PrHL	16	5	1	6	....	....	....	14	....	....	....	....	....
	Chicago Black Hawks	**NHL**	**18**	**0**	**1**	**1**	**0**	**6**	**6**	**18**	....	....	....	....	....
1928-29	**Chicago Black Hawks**	**NHL**	**10**	**0**	**0**	**0**	**0**	**0**	**0**	**12**	....	....	....	....	....
	Duluth Hornets	AHA	6	0	1	1	....	....	....	4	....	....	....	....	....
	Kitchener Dutchmen	Can-Pro	4	0	0	0	....	....	....	0	....	....	....	....	....
	Hamilton Tigers	Can-Pro	21	3	3	6	....	....	....	28	....	....	....	....	....
1929-30	Hamilton–Kitchener	IHL	42	4	3	7	....	....	....	74	....	....	....	....	....
1930-31	Syracuse Stars	IHL	8	0	0	0	....	....	....	21	....	....	....	....	....
	Detroit Olympics	IHL	39	4	6	10	....	....	....	68	....	....	....	....	....
1931-32	London Tecumsehs	IHL	44	4	3	7	....	....	....	16	6	1	1	2	2
1932-33	London–Cleveland	IHL	33	6	6	12	....	....	....	18	....	....	....	....	....
1933-34	Edmonton Eskimos	PrHL	5	0	0	0	....	....	....	0	....	....	....	....	....
1934-35	Oklahoma City Warriors	AHA	46	4	4	8	....	....	....	46	....	....	....	....	....
	NHL Totals		**28**	**0**	**1**	**1**	**0**	**6**	**6**	**30**	....	....	....	....	....

Signed as a free agent by **Saskatoon** (PrHL), November 10, 1926. Traded to **Chicago** by **Saskatoon** (PrHL) to complete transaction that sent Teddy Graham to Saskatoon (January 11, 1928), January 23, 1928. Loaned to **Duluth** (AHA) by **Chicago** for cash, December, 1928. Loaned to **Kitchener** (Can-Pro) by **Chicago** for cash, January 7, 1929. Traded to **Hamilton** (Can-Pro) by **Kitchener** (Can-Pro) for cash with Chicago retaining NHL rights, January 24, 1929. Traded to **Detroit** by **Syracuse** (IHL) for Rusty Hughes, December 7, 1930. Traded to **Cleveland** (IHL) by **London** for cash, December, 1932.

• HOLLETT, Flash — Frank William

D – L. 6′, 180 lbs. b: North Sydney, N.S., 4/13/1912 d: 4/20/1999.

Season	Club	League	GP	G	A	Pts	AG	AA	APts	PIM	GP	G	A	Pts	PIM
1932-33	Syracuse Stars	IHL	19	0	2	2	....	....	....	16	6	3	0	3	9
1933-34	**Toronto Maple Leafs**	**NHL**	**4**	**0**	**0**	**0**	**0**	**0**	**0**	**4**	....	....	....	....	....
	Buffalo Bisons	IHL	13	5	4	9	....	....	....	8	....	....	....	....	....
	Ottawa Senators	**NHL**	**30**	**7**	**4**	**11**	**12**	**8**	**20**	**21**	....	....	....	....	....
1934-35	**Toronto Maple Leafs**	**NHL**	**48**	**10**	**16**	**26**	**16**	**28**	**44**	**38**	**7**	**0**	**0**	**0**	**6**
1935-36	**Toronto Maple Leafs**	**NHL**	**11**	**1**	**4**	**5**	**2**	**8**	**10**	**8**	....	....	....	....	....
	Syracuse Stars	IHL	4	2	1	3	....	....	....	8	....	....	....	....	....
	Boston Bruins	**NHL**	**6**	**1**	**2**	**3**	**2**	**4**	**6**	**2**	....	....	....	....	....
	Boston Cubs	Can-Am	18	6	15	21	....	....	....	24	....	....	....	....	....
1936-37	**Boston Bruins**	**NHL**	**48**	**3**	**7**	**10**	**5**	**13**	**18**	**22**	**3**	**0**	**0**	**0**	**2**
1937-38	**Boston Bruins**	**NHL**	**48**	**4**	**10**	**14**	**6**	**16**	**22**	**54**	**3**	**0**	**1**	**1**	**0**
♦1938-39	**Boston Bruins**	**NHL**	**44**	**10**	**17**	**27**	**17**	**27**	**44**	**35**	**12**	**1**	**3**	**4**	**2**
1939-40	**Boston Bruins**	**NHL**	**44**	**10**	**18**	**28**	**17**	**28**	**45**	**18**	**5**	**1**	**2**	**3**	**2**
♦1940-41	**Boston Bruins**	**NHL**	**41**	**9**	**15**	**24**	**14**	**21**	**35**	**23**	**11**	**3**	**4**	**7**	**8**
	Hershey Bears	AHL	5	4	2	6	....	....	....	2	....	....	....	....	....
1941-42	**Boston Bruins**	**NHL**	**48**	**19**	**14**	**33**	**25**	**17**	**42**	**21**	**5**	**0**	**1**	**1**	**2**
1942-43	**Boston Bruins**	**NHL**	**50**	**19**	**25**	**44**	**20**	**23**	**43**	**19**	**9**	**0**	**9**	**9**	**4**
1943-44	**Boston Bruins**	**NHL**	**25**	**9**	**7**	**16**	**8**	**6**	**14**	**4**	....	....	....	....	....
	Detroit Red Wings	**NHL**	**27**	**6**	**12**	**18**	**5**	**10**	**15**	**34**	**5**	**0**	**0**	**0**	**6**
1944-45	**Detroit Red Wings**	**NHL**	**50**	**20**	**21**	**41**	**20**	**24**	**44**	**39**	**14**	**3**	**4**	**7**	**6**
1945-46	**Detroit Red Wings**	**NHL**	**38**	**4**	**9**	**13**	**5**	**13**	**18**	**16**	**5**	**0**	**2**	**2**	**0**
1946-47	Toronto Staffords	TIHL	PLAYER/COACH – STATISTICS UNAVAILABLE												
1947-48	Kitchener Dutchmen	OHA-Sr.	15	6	11	17	....	....	....	24	....	....	....	....	....
1948-49	Toronto Marlboros	OHA-Sr.	31	6	15	21	....	....	....	20	7	2	3	5	4
	Toronto Marlboros	Al-Cup	13	3	10	13	....	....	....	11	....	....	....	....	....
1949-50	Toronto Marlboros	OHA-Sr.	42	7	27	34	....	....	....	29	14	1	8	9	14
	Toronto Marlboros	Al-Cup	17	5	12	17	....	....	....	8	....	....	....	....	....
	NHL Totals		**562**	**132**	**181**	**313**	**174**	**246**	**420**	**358**	**79**	**8**	**26**	**34**	**38**

NHL Second All-Star Team (1943) • NHL First All-Star Team (1945)

Loaned to **Ottawa** by **Toronto** for remainder of 1933-34 season, January 2, 1934. Traded to **Boston** by **Toronto** for $16,000, January 15 1936. Traded to **Detroit** by **Boston** for Pat Egan, January 5, 1944. Traded to **NY Rangers** by **Detroit** for Ab DeMarco and Hank Goldup, June 19, 1946. Transaction voided when Hollett decided to retire, June, 1946.

• HOLLINGWORTH, Gord — Gordon "Bucky"

D – L. 5′11″, 170 lbs. b: Montreal, Que., 7/24/1933 d: 2/2/1974.

Season	Club	League	GP	G	A	Pts	AG	AA	APts	PIM	GP	G	A	Pts	PIM
1949-50	Montreal Jr. Canadiens	QJHL	35	0	3	3	....	....	....	30	16	0	3	3	45
	Montreal Jr. Canadiens	M-Cup	12	0	1	1	....	....	....	24	....	....	....	....	....
1950-51	Montreal Jr. Canadiens	QJHL	45	2	16	18	....	....	....	122	9	2	1	3	*35
1951-52	Montreal Jr. Canadiens	QJHL	39	10	12	22	....	....	....	97	11	3	3	6	*16
	Montreal Jr. Canadiens	M-Cup	8	1	2	3	....	....	....	27	....	....	....	....	....
1952-53	Montreal Jr. Canadiens	QJHL	45	6	11	17	....	....	....	106	7	0	1	1	15
	Montreal Royals	QMHL	1	0	0	0	....	....	....	0	....	....	....	....	....
1953-54	Montreal Royals	QHL	63	2	16	18	....	....	....	78	11	1	4	5	14
1954-55	**Chicago Black Hawks**	**NHL**	**70**	**3**	**9**	**12**	**4**	**10**	**14**	**135**	....	....	....	....	....
1955-56	**Detroit Red Wings**	**NHL**	**41**	**0**	**2**	**2**	**0**	**2**	**2**	**28**	**3**	**0**	**0**	**0**	**2**
1956-57	**Detroit Red Wings**	**NHL**	**25**	**0**	**1**	**1**	**0**	**1**	**1**	**16**	....	....	....	....	....
	Springfield Indians	AHL	22	2	9	11	....	....	....	28	....	....	....	....	....
1957-58	**Detroit Red Wings**	**NHL**	**27**	**1**	**2**	**3**	**1**	**2**	**3**	**22**	....	....	....	....	....
	Hershey Bears	AHL	39	0	9	9	....	....	....	93	11	1	1	2	20
1958-59	Cleveland Barons	AHL	65	6	15	21	....	....	....	102	7	0	4	4	6

			REGULAR SEASON								PLAYOFFS				
Season	Club	League	GP	G	A	Pts	AG	AA	APts	PIM	GP	G	A	Pts	PIM
1959-60	Hershey Bears	AHL	63	5	15	20	....	....	....	131	....	....	....	....	....
1960-61	Hershey Bears	AHL	67	3	13	16	....	....	....	76	5	0	1	1	13
1961-62	Hershey Bears	AHL	45	0	11	11	....	....	....	63	....	....	....	....	....
	NHL Totals		**163**	**4**	**14**	**18**	**5**	**15**	**20**	**201**	**3**	**0**	**0**	**0**	**2**

QJHL Second All-Star Team (1952) • Played in NHL All-Star Game (1955)

Traded to **Chicago** by **Montreal** for $15,000, October 3, 1954. Traded to **Detroit** by **Chicago** with Jerry Toppazzini, John McCormack and Dave Creighton for Tony Leswick, Glen Skov, Johnny Wilson and Benny Woit, May 28, 1955. Traded to **Cleveland** (AHL) by **Detroit** with cash for Pete Goegan, February 20, 1958. Traded to **Hershey** (AHL) by **Cleveland** (AHL) with Claude Dufour for Gilles Mayer, June, 1959. • Officially announced retirement after being diagnosed with leukemia, February 23, 1962.

• HOLMES, Bill — William Orser

C – R. 6′, 200 lbs. b: Portage la Prairie, Man., 3/9/1899 d: 3/14/1961.

Season	Club	League	GP	G	A	Pts	AG	AA	APts	PIM	GP	G	A	Pts	PIM
1921-22	Brandon Elks	MHL-Sr.	12	8	1	9	....	....	....	4	2	0	0	0	6
	Brandon Elks	Al-Cup	4	4	1	5	....	....	....	0	....	....	....	....	....
1922-23	Brandon Elks	MHL-Sr.	16	16	2	18	....	....	....	19	....	....	....	....	....
1923-24	Brandon Elks	MHL-Sr.	11	1	2	3	....	....	....	5	3	0	1	1	6
1924-25	Edmonton Eskimos	WCHL	6	0	0	0	....	....	....	0	....	....	....	....	....
1925-26	**Montreal Canadiens**	**NHL**	**9**	**1**	**0**	**1**	**2**	**0**	**2**	**2**	....	....	....	....	....
1926-27	Niagara Falls Cataracts	Can-Pro	25	20	4	24	....	....	....	51	....	....	....	....	....
	New York Americans	**NHL**	**1**	**0**	**0**	**0**	**0**	**0**	**0**	**0**	....	....	....	....	....
1927-28	Niagara Falls Cataracts	Can-Pro	18	8	2	10	....	....	....	46	....	....	....	....	....
	London Panthers	Can-Pro	23	14	2	16	....	....	....	42	....	....	....	....	....
1928-29	New Haven Eagles	Can-Am	38	9	6	15	....	....	....	76	2	1	0	1	8
1929-30	**New York Americans**	**NHL**	**42**	**5**	**4**	**9**	**7**	**9**	**16**	**33**	....	....	....	....	....
1930-31	Syracuse Stars	IHL	48	19	*37	56	....	....	....	61	....	....	....	....	....
1931-32	Buffalo Majors	AHA	19	1	0	1	....	....	....	6	....	....	....	....	....
	Cleveland Indians	IHL	2	0	0	0	....	....	....	0	....	....	....	....	....
	Pittsburgh Yellowjackets	IHL	4	1	0	1	....	....	....	2	....	....	....	....	....
1932-33			DID NOT PLAY												
1933-34	Syracuse Stars	IHL	16	3	2	5	....	....	....	4	....	....	....	....	....
1934-35	London Tecumsehs	IHL	6	1	1	2	....	....	....	6	....	....	....	....	....
	New Haven Eagles	Can-Am	39	11	19	30	....	....	....	11	....	....	....	....	....
1935-36	Pittsburgh Yellowjackets	EAHL	21	1	4	5	....	....	....	8	....	....	....	....	....
	NHL Totals		**52**	**6**	**4**	**10**	**9**	**9**	**18**	**35**	....	....	....	....	....
	Other Major League Totals		6	0	0	0	....	....	....	0	....	....	....	....	....

Signed as a free agent by **Edmonton** (WCHL), November 13, 1924. Traded to **NY Americans** by **Edmonton** (WCHL) for cash, October 2, 1925. Signed as a free agent by **Montreal Canadiens** after being released by NY Americans, December 25, 1925. Signed as a free agent by **NY Americans** (Niagara Falls-Can-Pro), November 1, 1926. Traded to **Kitchener** (Can-Pro) by **Niagara Falls** (Can-Pro) for cash, January 13, 1928. Traded to **London** (Can-Pro) by **Kitchener** (Can-Pro) for $1,500 and future considerations (Albert Pudas, March, 1928), January 16, 1928. Traded to **NY Americans** by **London** for Mickey Roach, October 29, 1928. Signed as a free agent by **Buffalo** (AHA), November 6, 1931.

• HOLMES, Chuck — Charles Frank

RW – R. 6′, 185 lbs. b: Edmonton, Alta., 9/21/1934.

Season	Club	League	GP	G	A	Pts	AG	AA	APts	PIM	GP	G	A	Pts	PIM
1951-52	Edmonton Oil Kings	WCJHL	1	1	0	1	....	....	....	2	....	....	....	....	....
1952-53	Edmonton Oil Kings	WCJHL	14	12	8	20	....	....	....	17	11	5	4	9	6
1953-54	Edmonton Oil Kings	WCJHL	35	32	36	68	....	....	....	41	10	7	15	22	12
	Edmonton Oil Kings	M-Cup	13	5	11	16	....	....	....	30	....	....	....	....	....
1954-55	Edmonton Oil Kings	WCJHL	26	17	14	31	....	....	....	43	5	2	2	4	14
	Edmonton Flyers	WHL	8	1	2	3	....	....	....	0	9	2	1	3	2
	Edmonton Flyers	Ed-Cup	7	0	0	0	....	....	....	16	....	....	....	....	....
1955-56	Edmonton Flyers	WHL	69	16	22	38	....	....	....	54	3	1	0	1	0
1956-57	Edmonton Flyers	WHL	65	18	23	41	....	....	....	35	8	1	3	4	8
1957-58	Edmonton Flyers	WHL	57	23	34	57	....	....	....	58	5	0	0	0	2
1958-59	**Detroit Red Wings**	**NHL**	**15**	**0**	**3**	**3**	**0**	**3**	**3**	**6**	....	....	....	....	....
	Edmonton Flyers	WHL	43	13	22	35	....	....	....	44	3	0	0	0	0
1959-60	Edmonton Flyers	WHL	64	22	37	59	....	....	....	33	4	0	1	1	2
1960-61	Edmonton Flyers	WHL	68	19	32	51	....	....	....	19	....	....	....	....	....
1961-62	**Detroit Red Wings**	**NHL**	**8**	**1**	**0**	**1**	**1**	**0**	**1**	**4**	....	....	....	....	....
	Edmonton Flyers	WHL	60	27	47	74	....	....	....	43	12	3	8	11	6
1962-63	Edmonton Flyers	WHL	39	14	23	37	....	....	....	39	3	1	2	3	10
	Pittsburgh Hornets	AHL	30	1	15	16	....	....	....	8	....	....	....	....	....
1963-64	Pittsburgh Hornets	AHL	37	8	14	22	....	....	....	28	....	....	....	....	....
1964-65	Memphis Wings	CPHL	15	2	6	8	....	....	....	12	....	....	....	....	....
	Seattle Totems	WHL	42	11	13	24	....	....	....	41	7	3	1	4	12
1965-66	Portland Buckaroos	WHL	71	10	20	30	....	....	....	20	8	0	1	1	2
1966-67	Seattle Totems	WHL	71	14	13	27	....	....	....	44	10	5	2	7	13
1967-68	Seattle Totems	WHL	72	23	24	47	....	....	....	55	9	4	4	8	2
1968-69	Seattle Totems	WHL	74	25	38	63	....	....	....	40	4	0	1	1	0
1969-70	Seattle Totems	WHL	69	16	15	31	....	....	....	26	6	2	1	3	0
1970-71	Seattle Totems	WHL	44	11	18	29	....	....	....	31	....	....	....	....	....
	NHL Totals		**23**	**1**	**3**	**4**	**1**	**3**	**4**	**10**	....	....	....	....	....

• Son of Lou • WHL First All-Star Team (1968)

Traded to **Montreal** (Seattle-WHL) by **Detroit** (Pittsburgh-AHL) for Billy Carter with Detroit holding right of recall, December, 1964. Traded to **Portland** (WHL) by **Detroit** for cash, July, 1965. Traded to **Seattle** (WHL) by **Portland** (WHL) for Gordie Sinclair, July, 1966.

• HOLMES, Lou — Louis Charles Carter

C/LW – L. 5′10″, 150 lbs. b: Rushall, England, 1/29/1911.

Season	Club	League	GP	G	A	Pts	AG	AA	APts	PIM	GP	G	A	Pts	PIM
1929-30	Edmonton Bruins	EJrHL	2	2	1	3	....	....	....	2	2	2	1	3	2
1930-31	Edmonton Poolers	EJrHL	13	12	*7	*19	....	....	....	8	2	1	0	1	0
1931-32	**Chicago Black Hawks**	**NHL**	**41**	**1**	**4**	**5**	**2**	**9**	**11**	**6**	**2**	**0**	**0**	**0**	**2**
1932-33	**Chicago Black Hawks**	**NHL**	**18**	**0**	**0**	**0**	**0**	**0**	**0**	**0**	....	....	....	....	....
	St. Paul–Tulsa	AHA	26	11	9	20	....	....	....	11	4	0	0	0	0
1933-34	Edmonton Eskimos	NWHL	34	15	8	23	....	....	....	11	2	3	0	3	2
1934-35	Edmonton Eskimos	NWHL	13	13	4	17	....	....	....	2	....	....	....	....	....
	Oklahoma City Warriors	AHA	21	6	6	12	....	....	....	10	....	....	....	....	....
1935-36	Edmonton Eskimos	NWHL	39	13	14	27	....	....	....	42	....	....	....	....	....
1936-37	Spokane Clippers	PCHL	35	16	5	21	....	....	....	24	3	0	1	1	0
1937-38	Spokane Clippers	PCHL	43	14	21	35	....	....	....	30	....	....	....	....	....
	Portland Buckaroos	PCHL	....	....	....	....	....	....	....	....	1	0	2	2	2
1938-39	Portland Buckaroos	PCHL	48	34	40	*74	....	....	....	26	5	4	4	*8	8
1939-40	Portland Buckaroos	PCHL	38	13	13	26	....	....	....	23	5	1	1	2	4
1940-41	Portland Buckaroos	PCHL	47	24	26	50	....	....	....	28	....	....	....	....	....
1941-42	St. Paul Saints	AHA	48	15	16	31	....	....	....	18	2	0	1	1	6

Season	Club	League	GP	G	A	Pts	AG	AA	APts	PIM	GP	G	A	Pts	PIM
			REGULAR SEASON								PLAYOFFS				
1942-43			MILITARY SERVICE												
1943-44	Edmonton Vics	X-Games	STATISTICS NOT AVAILABLE												
	Edmonton Vics	Al-Cup	3	1	1	2	....	....	....	2	....	....	....	....	....
1944-45			MILITARY SERVICE												
1945-46	Edmonton All-Stars	AIHA	STATISTICS NOT AVAILABLE												
1946-47	Edmonton New Method	ESrHL	5	5	4	9	....	....	....	4	....	....	....	....	....
1947-48	Edmonton Flyers	WCSHL	36	8	17	25	....	....	....	0	....	....	....	....	....
1948-49	Edmonton Flyers	WCSHL	3	2	0	2	....	....	....	0	....	....	....	....	....
	NHL Totals		**59**	**1**	**4**	**5**	**2**	**9**	**11**	**6**	**2**	**0**	**0**	**0**	**2**

• Father of Chuck

Signed as a free agent by **Chicago**, October 14, 1931. Traded to **Tulsa** (AHA) by **Chicago** for cash, May, 1932. Traded to **Chicago** by **St. Paul** (AHA) for Gerry Lowrey, November 9, 1932. Traded to **Tulsa** (AHA) by **Chicago** for the rights to Norm Locking, March 7, 1933. • Loaned to **Portland** (PCHL) by **Spokane** (PCHL) as emergency injury replacement during 1937-38 PCHL playoffs. Later ruled ineligible to play by PCHL President Cyclone Taylor. Portland defaulted the series in protest.

• HOLOTA, John

John Paul
C – L. 5'6", 160 lbs. b: Hamilton, Ont., 2/25/1921 d: 3/10/1951.

Season	Club	League	GP	G	A	Pts	AG	AA	APts	PIM	GP	G	A	Pts	PIM
1939-40	Guelph Biltmores	OHA-Jr.	20	14	14	28	....	....	....	8	3	3	4	7	0
1940-41	Guelph Biltmores	OHA-Jr.	16	20	*21	41	....	....	....	7	5	3	9	12	4
1941-42	Omaha Knights	AHA	48	28	32	60	....	....	....	45	8	7	7	14	2
1942-43	**Detroit Red Wings**	**NHL**	**12**	**2**	**0**	**2**	**2**	**0**	**2**	**0**	....	....	....	....	....
	Indianapolis Capitols	AHL	13	8	15	23	....	....	....	5	....	....	....	....	....
	Toronto Army Shamrocks	TIHL	2	4	2	6	....	....	....	0	4	0	1	1	0
1943-44	Toronto Army Daggers	OHA-Sr.	1	0	0	0	....	....	....	0	....	....	....	....	....
	Toronto Army Shamrocks	TMHL	31	30	30	*60	....	....	....	25	4	2	6	8	0
1944-45	Toronto Army Shamrocks	TIHL	10	5	7	12	....	....	....	2	....	....	....	....	....
	Toronto Army Daggers	TNDHL	2	3	4	7	....	....	....	0	....	....	....	....	....
1945-46	**Detroit Red Wings**	**NHL**	**3**	**0**	**0**	**0**	**0**	**0**	**0**	**0**	....	....	....	....	....
	Indianapolis Capitols	AHL	34	20	17	37	....	....	....	8	....	....	....	....	....
	Omaha Knights	USHL	17	17	12	29	....	....	....	2	7	2	3	5	6
1946-47	Cleveland Barons	AHL	64	*52	35	87	....	....	....	28	4	1	0	1	0
1947-48	Cleveland Barons	AHL	68	48	38	86	....	....	....	11	9	4	4	8	8
1948-49	Cleveland Barons	AHL	62	34	44	78	....	....	....	12	5	4	1	5	0
1949-50	Cleveland Barons	AHL	44	14	28	42	....	....	....	16	5	3	2	5	5
1950-51	New Haven Ramblers	AHL	25	10	9	19	....	....	....	12	....	....	....	....	....
	Portland Eagles	PCHL	18	6	11	17	....	....	....	0	....	....	....	....	....
	Denver Falcons	USHL	11	3	4	7	....	....	....	0	....	....	....	....	....
	NHL Totals		**15**	**2**	**0**	**2**	**2**	**0**	**2**	**0**	....	....	....	....	....

AHA Second All-Star Team (1942) • TMHL MVP (1944) • AHL First All-Star Team (1947)

Signed as a free agent by **Detroit**, October 14, 1941. Traded to **Chicago** by **Detroit** for Bernie Strongman, September, 1946. • Died from injuries suffered in automobile accident (March 7, 1951), March 10, 1951.

• HOLWAY, Albert

Albert Robert "Toots"
D – L. 6'2", 190 lbs. b: Belleville, Ont., 9/24/1902 Deceased.

Season	Club	League	GP	G	A	Pts	AG	AA	APts	PIM	GP	G	A	Pts	PIM
1917/20	Belleville Juniors	OHA-Jr.	STATISTICS NOT AVAILABLE												
1920-21	S.S. Marie Greyhounds	NOHA	1	0	0	0	....	....	....	0	....	....	....	....	....
	Calumet Miners	NMHL	STATISTICS NOT AVAILABLE												
1921-22			STATISTICS NOT AVAILABLE												
1922-23			STATISTICS NOT AVAILABLE												
1923-24	Belleville Seniors	OHA-Sr.	STATISTICS NOT AVAILABLE												
	Toronto St. Pats	**NHL**	**5**	**1**	**0**	**1**	**2**	**0**	**2**	**0**	....	....	....	....	....
1924-25	**Toronto St. Pats**	**NHL**	**25**	**2**	**2**	**4**	**3**	**8**	**11**	**20**	**2**	**0**	**0**	**0**	**0**
1925-26	**Toronto St. Pats**	**NHL**	**12**	**0**	**0**	**0**	**0**	**0**	**0**	**0**	....	....	....	....	....
	Montreal Maroons	**NHL**	**17**	**0**	**0**	**0**	**0**	**0**	**0**	**6**	**4**	**0**	**0**	**0**	**0**
♦	Montreal Maroons	St-Cup	2	0	0	0	....	....	....	0	....	....	....	....	....
1926-27	**Montreal Maroons**	**NHL**	**13**	**0**	**0**	**0**	**0**	**0**	**0**	**2**	....	....	....	....	....
	Stratford Nationals	Can-Pro	20	3	3	6	....	....	....	16	2	1	0	1	9
1927-28	Stratford Nationals	Can-Pro	40	3	5	8	....	....	....	65	5	3	0	3	11
1928-29	**Pittsburgh Pirates**	**NHL**	**40**	**4**	**0**	**4**	**11**	**0**	**11**	**20**	....	....	....	....	....
1929-30	London Panthers	IHL	42	8	7	15	....	....	....	66	2	0	0	0	2
1930-31	London Tecumsehs	IHL	48	9	3	12	....	....	....	68	....	....	....	....	....
1931-32	London Tecumsehs	IHL	48	4	4	8	....	....	....	82	6	0	0	0	*26
1932-33	London Tecumsehs	IHL	43	2	10	12	....	....	....	101	6	0	1	1	6
1933-34	London Tecumsehs	IHL	44	3	3	6	....	....	....	39	6	0	0	0	2
1934-35	London Tecumsehs	IHL	32	2	4	6	....	....	....	23	5	0	0	0	6
1935-36	Cleveland Falcons	IHL	48	1	1	2	....	....	....	31	2	0	0	0	0
1936-37	Cleveland Barons	IAHL	3	0	0	0	....	....	....	0	....	....	....	....	....
	Seattle Seahawks	PCHL	26	0	0	0	....	....	....	6	....	....	....	....	....
	NHL Totals		**112**	**7**	**2**	**9**	**16**	**8**	**24**	**48**	**6**	**0**	**0**	**0**	**0**

Signed as a free agent by **Toronto**, February 15, 1924. Claimed on waivers by **Montreal Maroons** from **Toronto**, January 12, 1926. • 1925-26 Montreal Maroons playoff totals includes series against Ottawa and Pittsburgh. Traded to **Pittsburgh** by **Montreal Maroons** for Duke McCurry, September 30, 1928. Traded to **London** (IHL) by **Pittsburgh** for cash, October 22, 1929.

• HORECK, Pete

LW – L. 5'9", 158 lbs. b: Massey, Ont., 6/15/1923.

Season	Club	League	GP	G	A	Pts	AG	AA	APts	PIM	GP	G	A	Pts	PIM
1940-41	Parry Sound Pilots	OHA-B	STATISTICS NOT AVAILABLE												
1941-42	Atlantic City Sea Gulls	EAHL	59	24	30	54	....	....	....	66	14	2	5	7	6
1942-43	Washington Lions	AHL	1	1	1	2	....	....	....	2	....	....	....	....	....
	Providence Reds	AHL	16	8	8	16	....	....	....	18	....	....	....	....	....
	Cleveland Barons	AHL	43	16	11	27	....	....	....	38	4	1	1	2	2
1943-44	Cleveland Barons	AHL	54	*34	29	63	....	....	....	29	11	4	5	9	14
1944-45	**Chicago Black Hawks**	**NHL**	**50**	**20**	**16**	**36**	**20**	**19**	**39**	**44**	....	....	....	....	....
1945-46	**Chicago Black Hawks**	**NHL**	**50**	**20**	**21**	**41**	**24**	**31**	**55**	**34**	**4**	**0**	**0**	**0**	**2**
1946-47	**Chicago Black Hawks**	**NHL**	**18**	**4**	**6**	**10**	**4**	**7**	**11**	**12**	....	....	....	....	....
	Detroit Red Wings	**NHL**	**38**	**12**	**13**	**25**	**13**	**16**	**29**	**59**	**5**	**2**	**0**	**2**	**6**
1947-48	**Detroit Red Wings**	**NHL**	**50**	**12**	**17**	**29**	**15**	**22**	**37**	**44**	**10**	**3**	***7**	**10**	**12**
1948-49	**Detroit Red Wings**	**NHL**	**60**	**14**	**16**	**30**	**20**	**23**	**43**	**46**	**11**	**1**	**1**	**2**	**10**
1949-50	**Boston Bruins**	**NHL**	**34**	**5**	**5**	**10**	**6**	**6**	**12**	**22**	....	....	....	....	....
1950-51	**Boston Bruins**	**NHL**	**66**	**10**	**13**	**23**	**13**	**16**	**29**	**57**	**4**	**0**	**0**	**0**	**13**
1951-52	**Chicago Black Hawks**	**NHL**	**60**	**9**	**11**	**20**	**12**	**13**	**25**	**22**	....	....	....	....	....
1952-53	Sault Ste. Marie Indians	NOHA	19	4	8	12	....	....	....	18	3	0	1	1	7
1953-54	Sudbury Wolves	NOHA	12	3	5	8	....	....	....	25	11	2	4	6	18
1954-55	Sudbury Wolves	NOHA	38	18	18	36	....	....	....	42	....	....	....	....	....
1955-56	Sault Ste. Marie Indians	NOHA	36	12	24	36	....	....	....	30	7	2	1	3	22
1956-57	Sault Ste. Marie Indians	NOHA	47	22	20	42	....	....	....	91	10	3	2	5	18
1957-58	Louisville Rebels	IHL	15	6	7	13	....	....	....	69	....	....	....	....	....
	Chatham Maroons	OHA-Sr.	15	7	4	11	....	....	....	34	....	....	....	....	....
1958-59			DID NOT PLAY												
1959-60	Charlotte Clippers	EHL	15	1	1	2	....	....	....	22	....	....	....	....	....
	NHL Totals		**426**	**106**	**118**	**224**	**127**	**153**	**280**	**340**	**34**	**6**	**8**	**14**	**43**

Claimed by **Chicago** from **Cleveland** (AHL) in Inter-League Draft, May 12, 1944. Traded to **Detroit** by **Chicago** with Leo Reise for Adam Brown and Ray Powell, December 9, 1946. Traded to **Boston** by **Detroit** with Bill Quackenbush for Pete Babando, Clare Martin, Lloyd Durham and Jimmy Peters, August 16, 1949. Traded to **Chicago** by **Boston** for cash, November 1, 1951.

• HORNE, George

George Alexander "Shorty"
RW – R. 5'6", 165 lbs. b: Sudbury, Ont., 6/27/1904 d: 7/31/1929.

Season	Club	League	GP	G	A	Pts	AG	AA	APts	PIM	GP	G	A	Pts	PIM
1920-21	Sudbury Cub Wolves	NOJHA	4	2	1	3	....	....	....	....	4	2	0	2	....
1921-22	Sudbury Cub Wolves	NOJHA	4	2	3	5	....	....	....	6	2	1	1	2	2
	Sudbury Wolves	NOHA	....	....	....	....	....	....	....	....	4	2	3	5	6
1922-23	North Bay Trappers	NOHA	STATISTICS NOT AVAILABLE												
1923-24	North Bay Trappers	NOHA	6	6	0	6	....	....	....	....	5	*13	0	*13	....
1924-25	Grimsby Peach Kings	NOHA	STATISTICS NOT AVAILABLE												
♦1925-26	**Montreal Maroons**	**NHL**	**13**	**0**	**0**	**0**	**0**	**0**	**0**	**2**	....	....	....	....	....
1926-27	**Montreal Maroons**	**NHL**	**2**	**0**	**0**	**0**	**0**	**0**	**0**	**0**	....	....	....	....	....
	Stratford Nationals	Can-Pro	13	2	2	4	....	....	....	20	....	....	....	....	....
	London Panthers	Can-Pro	9	4	2	6	....	....	....	4	....	....	....	....	....
1927-28	Stratford Nationals	Can-Pro	40	*32	3	35	....	....	....	35	5	3	0	3	13
1928-29	**Toronto Maple Leafs**	**NHL**	**39**	**9**	**3**	**12**	**26**	**20**	**46**	**32**	**4**	**0**	**0**	**0**	**4**
	NHL Totals		**54**	**9**	**3**	**12**	**26**	**20**	**46**	**34**	**4**	**0**	**0**	**0**	**4**

Signed as a free agent by **Montreal Maroons**, October 8, 1925. Claimed on waivers by **Stratford** (Can-Pro) from **Montreal Maroons**, February 1, 1927. Traded to **Niagara Falls** (Can-Pro) by **Stratford** (Can-Pro) for George Herrington, February 2, 1927. Traded to **Toronto** by **Montreal Maroons** for Fred Elliot, October 1, 1928. • Drowned in Sagatoski Lake, Ontario, July 31, 1929.

• HORNER, Red

George Reginald **HHOF**
D – R. 6', 190 lbs. b: Lynden, Ont., 5/28/1909.

Season	Club	League	GP	G	A	Pts	AG	AA	APts	PIM	GP	G	A	Pts	PIM
1926-27	Toronto Marlboros	OHA-Jr.	9	5	1	6	....	....	....	....	2	0	0	0	....
1927-28	Toronto Marlboros	OHA-Jr.	9	4	5	9	....	....	....	2	2	0	0	0	....
	Toronto Marlboros	OHA-Sr.	1	0	0	0	....	....	....	0	....	....	....	....	....
	Toronto Marlboros	M-Cup	11	7	5	12	....	....	....		....	....	....	....	....
1928-29	Toronto Marlboros	OHA-Sr.	2	0	0	0	....	....	....		....	....	....	....	....
	Toronto Maple Leafs	**NHL**	**22**	**0**	**0**	**0**	**0**	**0**	**0**	**30**	**4**	**1**	**0**	**1**	**2**
1929-30	**Toronto Maple Leafs**	**NHL**	**33**	**2**	**7**	**9**	**3**	**16**	**19**	**96**	....	....	....	....	....
1930-31	**Toronto Maple Leafs**	**NHL**	**42**	**1**	**11**	**12**	**2**	**33**	**35**	**71**	**2**	**0**	**0**	**0**	**4**
♦1931-32	**Toronto Maple Leafs**	**NHL**	**42**	**7**	**9**	**16**	**12**	**20**	**32**	**97**	**7**	**2**	**2**	**4**	**20**
1932-33	**Toronto Maple Leafs**	**NHL**	**48**	**3**	**8**	**11**	**5**	**17**	**22**	***144**	**9**	**1**	**0**	**1**	**10**
1933-34	**Toronto Maple Leafs**	**NHL**	**40**	**11**	**10**	**21**	**19**	**21**	**40**	***146**	**5**	**1**	**0**	**1**	**6**
1934-35	**Toronto Maple Leafs**	**NHL**	**46**	**4**	**8**	**12**	**7**	**14**	**21**	***125**	**7**	**0**	**1**	**1**	**4**
1935-36	**Toronto Maple Leafs**	**NHL**	**43**	**2**	**9**	**11**	**4**	**17**	**21**	***167**	**9**	**1**	**2**	**3**	***22**
1936-37	**Toronto Maple Leafs**	**NHL**	**48**	**3**	**9**	**12**	**5**	**16**	**21**	***124**	**2**	**0**	**0**	**0**	**7**
1937-38	**Toronto Maple Leafs**	**NHL**	**47**	**4**	**20**	**24**	**6**	**32**	**38**	***82**	**7**	**0**	**1**	**1**	**14**
1938-39	**Toronto Maple Leafs**	**NHL**	**48**	**4**	**10**	**14**	**7**	**16**	**23**	***85**	**10**	**1**	**2**	**3**	***26**
1939-40	**Toronto Maple Leafs**	**NHL**	**31**	**1**	**9**	**10**	**2**	**14**	**16**	***87**	**9**	**0**	**2**	**2**	**55**
	NHL Totals		**490**	**42**	**110**	**152**	**72**	**216**	**288**	**1254**	**71**	**7**	**10**	**17**	**170**

Played in NHL All-Star Game (1934, 1937)

Signed as a free agent by **Toronto**, January 20, 1929.

• HORTON, Tim

— see page 1193

• HORVATH, Bronco

— see page 1194

• HOWARD, Jack

John Francis
D – L. 6', 190 lbs. b: London, Ont., 10/15/1911.

Season	Club	League	GP	G	A	Pts	AG	AA	APts	PIM	GP	G	A	Pts	PIM
1931-32	Hamilton Patricias	OSrB	STATISTICS NOT AVAILABLE												
1932-33	Hamilton Patricias	OSHA-B	STATISTICS NOT AVAILABLE												
	Hamilton Patricias	Al-Cup	6	3	0	3	....	....	....	6	....	....	....	....	....
1933-34	Hamilton Tigers	OHA-Sr.	23	5	1	6	....	....	....	28	4	0	1	1	2
	Hamilton Tigers	Al-Cup	8	2	0	2	....	....	....	16	....	....	....	....	....
1934-35	Hamilton Tigers	OHA-Sr.	20	6	6	12	....	....	....	41	6	2	1	3	6
1935-36	Syracuse Stars	IHL	48	5	6	11	....	....	....	48	3	0	0	0	0
1936-37	**Toronto Maple Leafs**	**NHL**	**2**	**0**	**0**	**0**	**0**	**0**	**0**	**0**	....	....	....	....	....
	Syracuse Stars	IAHL	48	6	9	15	....	....	....	46	9	2	0	2	2
1937-38	Syracuse Stars	IAHL	47	6	9	15	....	....	....	32	8	0	3	3	4
1938-39	Syracuse Stars	IAHL	23	1	0	1	....	....	....	10	....	....	....	....	....
1939-40	St. Louis Flyers	AHA	45	9	5	14	....	....	....	18	5	0	2	2	2
1940-41	St. Louis Flyers	AHA	8	0	1	1	....	....	....	10	....	....	....	....	....
	Springfield Indians	AHL	12	0	3	3	....	....	....	14	....	....	....	....	....
	Pittsburgh Hornets	AHL	24	0	5	5	....	....	....	10	6	0	0	0	8
1941-42	Pittsburgh Hornets	AHL	55	6	13	19	....	....	....	10	....	....	....	....	....
1942-43	Pittsburgh Hornets	AHL	54	1	16	17	....	....	....	12	2	0	2	2	4
1943-44	Pittsburgh Hornets	AHL	38	3	12	15	....	....	....	16	....	....	....	....	....
1944-45	Pittsburgh Hornets	AHL	26	1	6	7	....	....	....	16	....	....	....	....	....
	NHL Totals		**2**	**0**	**0**	**0**	**0**	**0**	**0**	**0**					

Signed as a free agent by **Toronto**, October 22, 1935. Traded to **St. Louis** (AHA) by **Toronto** for cash, October 13, 1939. Traded to **NY Americans** (Springfield-AHL) by **St. Louis** (AHA) for cash, November 29, 1940. Traded to **Toronto** (Pittsburgh-AHL) by **NY Americans** (Springfield-AHL) with the loan of Peanuts O'Flaherty for Clarence Drouillard, January 17, 1941.

• HOWE, Gordie

— see page 1198

• HOWE, Syd

Sydney Harris **HHOF**
C/LW – L. 5'9", 165 lbs. b: Ottawa, Ont., 9/28/1911 d: 5/20/1976.

Season	Club	League	GP	G	A	Pts	AG	AA	APts	PIM	GP	G	A	Pts	PIM
1927-28	Ottawa Gunners	OCHL	STATISTICS NOT AVAILABLE												
	Ottawa Gunners	M-Cup	8	9	4	13	....	....	....	8	....	....	....	....	....
1928-29	Ottawa Rideaus	OCHL	15	7	1	8	....	....	....		....	....	....	....	....

			REGULAR SEASON								PLAYOFFS				
Season	Club	League	GP	G	A	Pts	AG	AA	APts	PIM	GP	G	A	Pts	PIM
1929-30	Ottawa Rideaus	OCHL	11	8	1	9	....	....	....	9	....	....	....	....	....
	London Panthers	IHL	5	1	0	1	....	....	....	0	....	....	....	....	....
	Ottawa Senators	**NHL**	**12**	**1**	**1**	**2**	**1**	**2**	**3**	**0**	**2**	**0**	**0**	**0**	**0**
1930-31	**Philadelphia Quakers**	**NHL**	**44**	**9**	**11**	**20**	**18**	**33**	**51**	**20**	....	....	....	....	....
1931-32	**Toronto Maple Leafs**	**NHL**	**3**	**0**	**0**	**0**	**0**	**0**	**0**	**0**	....	....	....	....	....
	Syracuse Stars	IHL	45	9	12	21	....	....	....	44	....	....	....	....	....
1932-33	**Ottawa Senators**	**NHL**	**48**	**12**	**12**	**24**	**22**	**25**	**47**	**17**	....	....	....	....	....
1933-34	**Ottawa Senators**	**NHL**	**42**	**13**	**7**	**20**	**22**	**15**	**37**	**18**	....	....	....	....	....
1934-35	**St. Louis Eagles**	**NHL**	**36**	**14**	**13**	**27**	**23**	**23**	**46**	**23**	....	....	....	....	....
	Detroit Red Wings	**NHL**	**14**	**8**	**12**	**20**	**13**	**21**	**34**	**11**	....	....	....	....	....
♦1935-36	**Detroit Red Wings**	**NHL**	**48**	**16**	**14**	**30**	**31**	**27**	**58**	**26**	**7**	**3**	**3**	**6**	**2**
♦1936-37	**Detroit Red Wings**	**NHL**	**45**	**17**	**10**	**27**	**29**	**18**	**47**	**10**	**10**	**2**	**5**	**7**	**0**
1937-38	**Detroit Red Wings**	**NHL**	**48**	**8**	**19**	**27**	**13**	**31**	**44**	**14**	....	....	....	....	....
1938-39	**Detroit Red Wings**	**NHL**	**48**	**16**	**20**	**36**	**28**	**31**	**59**	**11**	**6**	**3**	**1**	**4**	**4**
1939-40	**Detroit Red Wings**	**NHL**	**46**	**14**	**23**	**37**	**23**	**36**	**59**	**17**	**5**	**2**	**2**	**4**	**2**
1940-41	**Detroit Red Wings**	**NHL**	**48**	**20**	**24**	**44**	**31**	**35**	**66**	**8**	**9**	**1**	***7**	**8**	**0**
1941-42	**Detroit Red Wings**	**NHL**	**48**	**16**	**19**	**35**	**21**	**23**	**44**	**6**	**12**	**3**	**5**	**8**	**0**
♦1942-43	**Detroit Red Wings**	**NHL**	**50**	**20**	**35**	**55**	**21**	**33**	**54**	**10**	**7**	**1**	**2**	**3**	**0**
1943-44	**Detroit Red Wings**	**NHL**	**46**	**32**	**28**	**60**	**29**	**25**	**54**	**6**	**5**	**2**	**2**	**4**	**0**
1944-45	**Detroit Red Wings**	**NHL**	**46**	**17**	**36**	**53**	**17**	**42**	**59**	**6**	**7**	**0**	**0**	**0**	**2**
1945-46	**Detroit Red Wings**	**NHL**	**26**	**4**	**7**	**11**	**5**	**10**	**15**	**9**	....	....	....	....	....
	Indianapolis Capitols	AHL	14	6	11	17	....	....	....	4	5	2	0	2	0
1946-47	Ottawa Senators	QSHL	24	19	21	40	....	....	....	4	11	2	1	3	0
	Ottawa Army	OCHL	1	2	1	3	....	....	....	0	....	....	....	....	....
1947-48	Ottawa Army	OCHL	PLAYER/COACH – STATISTICS UNAVAILABLE												
1948-49	Ottawa Army	OCHL	1	0	0	0	....	....	....	0	....	....	....	....	....
	NHL Totals		**698**	**237**	**291**	**528**	**347**	**430**	**777**	**212**	**70**	**17**	**27**	**44**	**10**

NHL Second All-Star Team (1945) • Played in NHL All-Star Game (1939)

Signed as a free agent by **Ottawa**, January 16, 1930. Loaned to **Philadelphia** by **Ottawa** for 1930-31 season, November, 1930. Claimed by **Toronto** from **Ottawa** for 1931-32 season in Dispersal Draft, September 26, 1931. Transferred to **St. Louis** after **Ottawa** franchise relocated, September 22, 1934. Traded to **Detroit** by **St. Louis** with Scotty Bowman for Ted Graham and $50,000, February 11, 1935. Traded to **St. Louis** (AHL) by **Detroit** (Indianapolis-AHL) for cash, August 17, 1946.

• HOWE, Vic Victor Stanley

RW – R. 6', 172 lbs. b: Saskatoon, Sask., 11/2/1929.

Season	Club	League	GP	G	A	Pts	AG	AA	APts	PIM	GP	G	A	Pts	PIM
1945/47	Saskatoon King George	H.S.	STATISTICS NOT AVAILABLE												
1947-48	Saskatoon Tech	SJrHL	STATISTICS NOT AVAILABLE												
1948-49	Windsor Hettche	IHL	31	16	14	30	....	....	....	17	13	8	5	13	2
1949-50	Windsor Spitfires	OHA-Jr.	41	9	11	20	....	....	....	15	11	2	6	8	6
1950-51	**New York Rangers**	**NHL**	**3**	**1**	**0**	**1**	**1**	**0**	**1**	**0**	....	....	....	....	....
	New York Rovers	EAHL	53	15	24	39	....	....	....	55	5	1	3	4	2
1951-52	Cincinnati Mohawks	AHL	2	0	1	1	....	....	....	0	....	....	....	....	....
	New York Rovers	EAHL	59	21	34	55	....	....	....	15	....	....	....	....	....
1952-53	Saskatoon Quakers	WHL	1	0	0	0	....	....	....	2	....	....	....	....	....
	Troy Uncle Sam Trojans	EAHL	59	27	52	79	....	....	....	23	....	....	....	....	....
1953-54	**New York Rangers**	**NHL**	**1**	**0**	**0**	**0**	**0**	**0**	**0**	**0**	....	....	....	....	....
	Saskatoon Quakers	WHL	65	15	23	38	....	....	....	35	6	0	2	2	0
1954-55	**New York Rangers**	**NHL**	**29**	**2**	**4**	**6**	**3**	**5**	**8**	**10**	....	....	....	....	....
	Saskatoon–Vancouver	WHL	22	3	6	9	....	....	....	2	....	....	....	....	....
	Valleyfield Braves	QHL	6	1	1	2	....	....	....	4	....	....	....	....	....
1955-56	Regina Regals	WHL	3	0	0	0	....	....	....	0	....	....	....	....	....
	Nelson Maple Leafs	WIHL	29	10	12	22	....	....	....	12	5	1	0	1	2
1956-57	Harringay Racers	Aut-Cup	30	15	16	31	....	....	....	14	....	....	....	....	....
	Harringay Racers	Britain	15	11	10	21	....	....	....	18	....	....	....	....	....
1957/61			OUT OF HOCKEY – RETIRED												
1961-62	Moncton Beavers	NSSHL	33	19	30	49	....	....	....	10	11	4	8	12	4
1962/65			OUT OF HOCKEY – RETIRED												
1965-66	Moncton Hawks	X-Games	....	....	....	....	....	....	....	....	7	3	4	7	2
	NHL Totals		**33**	**3**	**4**	**7**	**4**	**5**	**9**	**10**	....	....	....	....	....

• Brother of Gordie

Traded to **NY Rangers** by **Cleveland** (AHL) with Andy Bathgate for Glen Sonmor and Eric Pogue, November 15, 1954.

• HOWELL, Harry — see page 1199

• HOWELL, Ron

D/LW – L. 6', 185 lbs. b: Hamilton, Ont., 12/4/1935 d: 1992.

Season	Club	League	GP	G	A	Pts	AG	AA	APts	PIM	GP	G	A	Pts	PIM
1952-53	Kitchener–Guelph	OHA-Jr.	5	2	2	4	....	....	....	8	....	....	....	....	....
1953-54	Guelph Biltmores	OHA-Jr.	54	20	26	46	....	....	....	48	3	0	0	0	2
1954-55	Guelph Biltmores	OHA-Jr.	35	18	26	44	....	....	....	22	6	6	5	11	6
	New York Rangers	**NHL**	**3**	**0**	**0**	**0**	**0**	**0**	**0**	**0**	....	....	....	....	....
1955-56	Guelph Biltmores	OHA-Jr.	36	21	40	61	....	....	....	24	3	0	0	0	0
	New York Rangers	**NHL**	**1**	**0**	**0**	**0**	**0**	**0**	**0**	**0**	....	....	....	....	....
1956-57	Kitchener Dutchmen	OHA-Sr.	30	8	18	26	....	....	....	16	11	2	7	9	8
	Kitchener Dutchmen	Al-Cup	7	1	2	3	....	....	....	4	....	....	....	....	....
1957-58	Kitchener Dutchmen	OHA-Sr.	30	19	22	41	....	....	....	16	16	5	3	8	16
	Kitchener Dutchmen	Al-Cup	5	0	4	4	....	....	....	2	....	....	....	....	....
1958-59	Vancouver Canucks	WHL	37	9	9	18	....	....	....	12	9	2	3	5	4
1959-60			PLAYED PRO FOOTBALL												
1960-61	Rochester Americans	AHL	22	4	1	5	....	....	....	2	....	....	....	....	....
1961-62			PLAYED PRO FOOTBALL												
1962-63	Kitchener Tigers	OHA-Sr.	13	7	6	13	....	....	....	2	....	....	....	....	....
	Long Island Ducks	EHL	10	3	9	12	....	....	....	6	7	3	1	4	6
1963-64	Guelph Regals	OHA-Sr.	7	1	3	4	....	....	....	13	....	....	....	....	....
	Long Island Ducks	EHL	28	7	7	14	....	....	....	15	5	2	2	4	0
	NHL Totals		**4**	**0**	**0**	**0**	**0**	**0**	**0**	**0**					

• Brother of Harry

• Missed entire 1959-60 and 1961-62 seasons playing professional football in Canadian Football League w/ Hamilton Tiger-Cats. Claimed on waivers by **Toronto** from **NY Rangers**, December 4, 1960.

• HRYMNAK, Steve

D – L. 5'11", 178 lbs. b: Port Arthur, Ont., 3/3/1926.

			REGULAR SEASON								PLAYOFFS				
Season	Club	League	GP	G	A	Pts	AG	AA	APts	PIM	GP	G	A	Pts	PIM
1942-43	Port Arthur Flyers	TBJHL	9	8	3	11	....	....	....	8	5	0	0	0	10
1943-44	Port Arthur Flyers	TBJHL	10	0	5	5	....	....	....	19	6	3	4	7	4
	Port Arthur Flyers	M-Cup	8	0	1	1	....	....	....	12	....	....	....	....	....
1944-45			MILITARY SERVICE												
1945-46	Port Arthur Flyers	TBJHL	4	5	4	9	....	....	....	4	10	6	7	13	14
1946-47	New York Rovers	EAHL	53	0	7	7	....	....	....	52	7	0	0	0	7
1947-48	New Haven Ramblers	AHL	39	10	4	14	....	....	....	23	4	0	1	1	4
1948-49	New Haven Ramblers	AHL	55	10	11	21	....	....	....	28	....	....	....	....	....
1949-50	New Haven Ramblers	AHL	70	13	17	30	....	....	....	28	....	....	....	....	....
1950-51	St. Louis Flyers	AHL	57	11	11	22	....	....	....	32	....	....	....	....	....
1951-52	**Chicago Black Hawks**	**NHL**	**18**	**2**	**1**	**3**	**3**	**1**	**4**	**4**	....	....	....	....	....
	St. Louis Flyers	AHL	48	14	36	50	....	....	....	19	....	....	....	....	....
1952-53	St. Louis Flyers	AHL	64	14	27	41	....	....	....	31	....	....	....	....	....
	Detroit Red Wings	**NHL**	....	....	....	....	....	....	....	....	**2**	**0**	**0**	**0**	**0**
1953-54	Edmonton Flyers	WHL	69	13	17	30	....	....	....	41	13	3	4	7	5
1954-55	Edmonton Flyers	WHL	69	8	22	30	....	....	....	26	9	2	0	2	20
	Edmonton Flyers	Ed-Cup	7	0	2	2	....	....	....	14	....	....	....	....	....
1955-56	Edmonton Flyers	WHL	69	8	17	25	....	....	....	26	3	0	0	0	0
1956-57	New Westminster Royals	WHL	52	6	13	19	....	....	....	34	....	....	....	....	....
1957-58	New Westminster Royals	WHL	48	9	18	27	....	....	....	36	4	0	1	1	6
1958-59			REINSTATED AS AN AMATEUR												
1959-60	Port Arthur Bearcats	TBSHL	STATISTICS NOT AVAILABLE												
	Port Arthur Bearcats	Al-Cup	7	0	3	3	....	....	....	6	....	....	....	....	....
1960-61	Port Arthur Bearcats	TBSHL	....	....	....	....	....	....	....	....	5	2	2	4	2
	Port Arthur Bearcats	Al-Cup	4	1	2	3	....	....	....	4	....	....	....	....	....
1961/64	Port Arthur Bearcats	TBSHL	DID NOT PLAY – COACHING												
1964-65	Port Arthur Bearcats	TBSHL	10	0	1	1	....	....	....	22	....	....	....	....	....
	NHL Totals		**18**	**2**	**1**	**3**	**3**	**1**	**4**	**4**	**2**	**0**	**0**	**0**	**0**

Traded to **Chicago** (St. Louis-AHL) by **NY Rangers** for cash, September 19, 1950. Traded to **Detroit** by **Chicago** with Red Almas and Guyle Fielder for cash, September 23, 1952.

• HUARD, Rolly

C – L. 5'10", 170 lbs. b: Ottawa, Ont., 9/6/1902.

Season	Club	League	GP	G	A	Pts	AG	AA	APts	PIM	GP	G	A	Pts	PIM
1921-22	University of Ottawa	OCHL	12	10	7	17	....	....	....	12	....	....	....	....	....
1922-23	Ottawa Montagnards	OCHL	9	*8	4	12	....	....	....	2	2	0	0	0	0
1923-24	Ottawa Montagnards	OCHL	12	4	2	6	....	....	....	....	6	*5	1	6	6
1924-25	Ottawa Montagnards	OCHL	16	13	3	16	....	....	....	....	7	1	0	1	8
1925-26	Fort William Forts	TBSHL	20	13	4	17	....	....	....	18	3	0	0	0	2
1926-27	Windsor Hornets	Can-Pro	32	16	4	20	....	....	....	16	....	....	....	....	....
1927-28	Windsor Hornets	Can-Pro	42	21	7	28	....	....	....	8	....	....	....	....	....
1928-29	Windsor Bulldogs	Can-Pro	2	0	0	0	....	....	....	0	....	....	....	....	....
	Buffalo Bisons	Can-Pro	40	18	8	26	....	....	....	12	....	....	....	....	....
1929-30	Buffalo Bisons	IHL	40	8	6	14	....	....	....	16	7	1	1	2	10
1930-31	Buffalo Bisons	IHL	20	5	4	9	....	....	....	6	....	....	....	....	....
	Toronto Maple Leafs	**NHL**	**1**	**1**	**0**	**1**	**2**	**0**	**2**	**0**	....	....	....	....	....
	Syracuse Stars	IHL	10	1	2	3	....	....	....	0	....	....	....	....	....
	London Tecumsehs	IHL	17	2	1	3	....	....	....	6	....	....	....	....	....
1931-32	London Tecumsehs	IHL	45	3	11	14	....	....	....	12	6	1	2	3	0
1932-33	St. Louis Flyers	AHA	45	15	17	32	....	....	....	2	4	0	0	0	2
1933-34	St. Louis Flyers	AHA	42	5	5	10	....	....	....	14	7	0	1	1	2
1934-35			REINSTATED AS AN AMATEUR												
1935-36	Ottawa LaSalle	OCHL	DID NOT PLAY – COACHING												
	NHL Totals		**1**	**1**	**0**	**1**	**2**	**0**	**2**	**0**	....	....	....	....	....

OCHL First All-Star Team (1922) • OCHL Second All-Star Team (1923)

Signed as a free agent by **Windsor** (Can-Pro), October 14, 1926. Traded to **Buffalo** (Can-Pro) by **Windsor** (Can-Pro) for Mike Neville, November 18, 1928. Loaned to **Toronto** by **Buffalo** (IHL) as an emergency injury replacement, December 14, 1930. • One of only two players (Dean Morton) to score a goal in only NHL game. Traded to **Syracuse** (IHL) by **Buffalo** (IHL) for Martin Lauder, January 3, 1931. Traded to **Toronto** (London-IHL) by **Syracuse** (IHL) for Wallace Moore and Jimmy Smith, January 29, 1931.

• HUCUL, Fred — see page 1203

• HUDSON, Ron Ronald Justin

C – L. 5'8", 148 lbs. b: Calgary, Alta., 7/14/1911.

Season	Club	League	GP	G	A	Pts	AG	AA	APts	PIM	GP	G	A	Pts	PIM
1930-31	South Porcupine Porkies	NOJHA	STATISTICS NOT AVAILABLE												
1931-32	Truro Bearcats	NSSHL	16	6	3	9	....	....	....	25	5	0	1	1	0
1932-33	Charlottetown Abegweits	MSHL	25	5	1	6	....	....	....	27	2	0	0	0	2
1933-34	Charlottetown Abegweits	MSHL	23	6	8	14	....	....	....	16	3	1	0	1	0
1934-35	Halifax Wolverines	MSHL	20	6	3	9	....	....	....	14	....	....	....	....	....
	Halifax Wolverines	Big-3	4	1	0	1	....	....	....	0	6	*5	0	*5	6
	Halifax Wolverines	Al-Cup	8	12	2	14	....	....	....	4	....	....	....	....	....
1935-36	Detroit Olympics	IHL	47	7	19	26	....	....	....	10	6	1	1	2	0
1936-37	Pittsburgh Hornets	IAHL	47	9	7	16	....	....	....	27	5	1	1	2	2
1937-38	**Detroit Red Wings**	**NHL**	**32**	**5**	**2**	**7**	**8**	**3**	**11**	**2**	....	....	....	....	....
	Pittsburgh Hornets	IAHL	14	3	5	8	....	....	....	8	2	0	0	0	0
1938-39	Providence Reds	IAHL	51	16	22	38	....	....	....	7	5	1	3	4	0
1939-40	**Detroit Red Wings**	**NHL**	**1**	**0**	**0**	**0**	**0**	**0**	**0**	**0**	....	....	....	....	....
	Indianapolis Capitols	IAHL	54	27	27	54	....	....	....	19	5	0	1	1	0
1940-41	Omaha Knights	AHA	47	23	29	*52	....	....	....	19	....	....	....	....	....
1941-42	Omaha Knights	AHA	44	19	23	42	....	....	....	4	3	1	1	2	0
1942-43			MILITARY SERVICE												
1943-44			MILITARY SERVICE												
1944-45	St. Louis Flyers	AHL	21	0	2	2	....	....	....	8	....	....	....	....	....
	NHL Totals		**33**	**5**	**2**	**7**	**8**	**3**	**11**	**2**					

AHA First All-Star Team (1941)

Signed as a free agent by **Detroit**, October 15, 1935. Traded to **Providence** (IAHL) by **Detroit** (Pittsburgh-IAHL) for cash, November 1, 1938.

• HUGGINS, Al James Allan "Chink"

LW – L. 6', 160 lbs. b: Toronto, Ont., 12/21/1910.

Season	Club	League	GP	G	A	Pts	AG	AA	APts	PIM	GP	G	A	Pts	PIM
1926-27	Toronto Canoe Club	OHA-Jr.	9	0	0	0	....	....	....	0	....	....	....	....	....
1927-28	Montreal CPR	MCHL	STATISTICS NOT AVAILABLE												
1928-29	Iroquois Falls Paper	NOHA	STATISTICS NOT AVAILABLE												
1929-30	Montreal AAA	MCHL	7	3	0	3	....	....	....	16	2	*1	0	1	2
1930-31	**Montreal Maroons**	**NHL**	**20**	**1**	**1**	**2**	**2**	**3**	**5**	**2**	....	....	....	....	....
	Windsor Bulldogs	IHL	27	1	0	1	....	....	....	27	6	1	0	1	4
1931-32	Windsor Bulldogs	IHL	40	13	11	24	....	....	....	51	6	0	3	3	10
1932-33	Windsor–Detroit	IHL	41	9	9	18	....	....	....	47	6	0	2	2	4
1933-34	Syracuse Stars	IHL	43	14	23	37	....	....	....	24	6	0	3	3	4
1934-35	Syracuse Stars	IHL	42	10	19	29	....	....	....	41	....	....	....	....	....

			REGULAR SEASON								PLAYOFFS				
Season	Club	League	GP	G	A	Pts	AG	AA	APts	PIM	GP	G	A	Pts	PIM
1935-36	Syracuse Stars	IHL	DID NOT PLAY – COACHING												
1936-37	Syracuse Stars	IAHL	DID NOT PLAY – COACHING												
1937-38	South Porcupine Porkies	NOHA	8	3	5	8	....	....	....	8	....	....	....	....	....
1938-39	South Porcupine Porkies	NOHA	PLAYER/COACH – STATISTICS UNAVAILABLE												
1939-40	South Porcupine Porkies	NOHA	15	5	1	6	....	....	....	18	5	1	2	3	*8
	South Porcupine Porkies	Al-Cup	3	0	0	0	....	....	....	2	....	....	....	....	....
1940-41	South Porcupine Porkies	NOHA	22	8	8	16	....	....	....	18	....	....	....	....	....
1941-42	South Porcupine Porkies	NOHA	4	1	4	5	....	....	....	0	....	....	....	....	....
	NHL Totals		**20**	**1**	**1**	**2**	**2**	**3**	**5**	**2**	....	....	....	....	....

Signed as a free agent by **Montreal Maroons**, September 2, 1930. Traded to **Toronto** (Syracuse-IHL) by **Montreal Maroons** (Windsor-IHL) for Stew Adams, November 1, 1933.

• HUGHES, Albert

C/LW – R. 5'9", 165 lbs. b: Guelph, Ont., 5/13/1901.

Season	Club	League	GP	G	A	Pts	AG	AA	APts	PIM	GP	G	A	Pts	PIM
1921-22	Welland Sailors	OIHA	STATISTICS NOT AVAILABLE												
1922-23	Hamilton Tigers	OHA-Sr.	10	2	0	2	....	....	....	2	2	0	0	0	0
1923-24	Toronto AA Clarke	OHA-Sr.	STATISTICS NOT AVAILABLE												
1924-25	Toronto AA Clarke	OHA-Sr.	STATISTICS NOT AVAILABLE												
1925-26	New York Knickerbockers	USAHA	STATISTICS NOT AVAILABLE												
1926-27	New York Knickerbockers	USAHA	STATISTICS NOT AVAILABLE												
	Niagara Falls Cataracts	Can-Pro	14	2	0	2	....	....	....	8	....	....	....	....	....
1927-28	Niagara Falls Cataracts	Can-Pro	42	20	2	22	....	....	....	38	....	....	....	....	....
1928-29	New Haven Eagles	Can-Am	38	8	1	9	....	....	....	16	2	2	0	2	4
1929-30	New Haven Eagles	Can-Am	40	22	19	41	....	....	....	28	....	....	....	....	....
1930-31	**New York Americans**	**NHL**	**42**	**5**	**7**	**12**	**10**	**21**	**31**	**14**	....	....	....	....	....
1931-32	**New York Americans**	**NHL**	**18**	**1**	**1**	**2**	**2**	**2**	**4**	**8**	....	....	....	....	....
	New Haven Eagles	Can-Am	25	6	8	14	....	....	....	8	2	0	1	1	0
1932-33	St. Louis Flyers	AHA	44	14	15	29	....	....	....	20	4	1	1	2	0
1933-34	St. Louis Flyers	AHA	47	3	5	8	....	....	....	14	7	1	1	2	0
	NHL Totals		**60**	**6**	**8**	**14**	**12**	**23**	**35**	**22**	....	....	....	....	....

Signed as a free agent by **NY Americans**, January 18, 1927.

• HUGHES, James

James Romley "Rusty"

D – R. 5'9", 190 lbs. b: Webbwood, Ont., 5/12/1906.

Season	Club	League	GP	G	A	Pts	AG	AA	APts	PIM	GP	G	A	Pts	PIM
1923/25	Cobalt Jr. Miners	NOJHA	STATISTICS NOT AVAILABLE												
1925-26	Winnipeg Maroons	CHL	24	1	3	4	....	....	....	18	5	2	*2	*4	0
1926-27	Winnipeg Maroons	AHA	10	2	0	2	....	....	....	2	....	....	....	....	....
	Windsor Hornets	Can-Pro	1	1	0	1	....	....	....	0	....	....	....	....	....
1927-28	Windsor Bulldogs	Can-Pro	18	0	2	2	....	....	....	17	....	....	....	....	....
	Niagara Falls Cataracts	Can-Pro	16	0	0	0	....	....	....	34	....	....	....	....	....
1928-29	Buffalo Bisons	Can-Pro	40	4	1	5	....	....	....	79	....	....	....	....	....
1929-30	**Detroit Cougars**	**NHL**	**40**	**0**	**1**	**1**	**0**	**2**	**2**	**48**	....	....	....	....	....
1930-31	Detroit Olympics	IHL	7	0	0	0	....	....	....	4	....	....	....	....	....
	Syracuse Stars	IHL	39	1	2	3	....	....	....	75	....	....	....	....	....
1931-32	Syracuse Stars	IHL	48	1	2	3	....	....	....	80	....	....	....	....	....
1932-33	St. Louis Flyers	AHA	44	1	0	1	....	....	....	38	4	0	1	1	6
1933-34	Syracuse Stars	IHL	43	2	2	4	....	....	....	76	6	1	0	1	2
1934-35	Syracuse Stars	IHL	28	0	2	2	....	....	....	37	....	....	....	....	....
	Windsor Bulldogs	IHL	14	0	2	2	....	....	....	22	....	....	....	....	....
1935-36	Windsor Bulldogs	IHL	12	0	1	1	....	....	....	6	....	....	....	....	....
	Pittsburgh Shamrocks	IHL	32	1	4	5	....	....	....	48	....	....	....	....	....
	NHL Totals		**40**	**0**	**1**	**1**	**0**	**2**	**2**	**48**	....	....	....	....	....

Signed as a free agent by **Windsor** (Can-Pro), March 8, 1927. Claimed by **Detroit** from **Windsor** (Can-Pro) in Inter-League Draft, May 13, 1929. Traded to **Syracuse** (IHL) by **Detroit** for Val Hoffinger, December 7, 1930. Traded to **St. Louis** (AHA) by **Syracuse** (IHL) for cash, October 19, 1932. Signed as a free agent by **Syracuse** (IHL), October, 1933. Traded to **Windsor** (IHL) by **Syracuse** (IHL) for cash, October 17, 1935. • Signed as a free agent by **Pittsburgh** (IHL) after securing release from **Windsor** (IHL), December 18, 1935.

• HULL, Bobby

— see page 1207

• HULL, Dennis

— see page 1208

• HUNT, Fred

Frederick Tennyson "Fritz"

RW – R. 5'8", 160 lbs. b: Brantford, Ont., 1/17/1918 d: 10/4/1977.

Season	Club	League	GP	G	A	Pts	AG	AA	APts	PIM	GP	G	A	Pts	PIM
1933-34	Brantford Lions	OHA-Jr.	16	5	3	8	....	....	....	14	....	....	....	....	....
1934-35	Brantford Lions	OHA-Jr.	17	4	1	5	....	....	....	12	....	....	....	....	....
1935-36	St. Michael's Majors	OHA-Jr.	9	2	9	11	....	....	....	12	4	1	1	2	11
1936-37	St. Michael's Majors	OHA-Jr.	12	5	5	10	....	....	....	16	6	5	3	8	*19
	St. Michael's Majors	M-Cup	7	5	4	9	....	....	....	0	....	....	....	....	....
1937-38	Hershey B'ars	EAHL	57	10	14	24	....	....	....	45	....	....	....	....	....
1938-39	Hershey B'ars	EAHL	53	22	32	54	....	....	....	20	....	....	....	....	....
1939-40	Baltimore Orioles	EAHL	59	31	37	68	....	....	....	52	8	2	5	7	2
1940-41	**New York Americans**	**NHL**	**15**	**2**	**5**	**7**	**3**	**7**	**10**	**0**	....	....	....	....	....
	Springfield Indians	AHL	40	17	27	44	....	....	....	38	3	0	1	1	2
1941-42	Springfield Indians	AHL	51	19	21	40	....	....	....	45	2	0	0	0	0
1942-43	Buffalo Bisons	AHL	50	27	30	57	....	....	....	52	9	5	3	8	2
1943-44	Buffalo Bisons	AHL	52	27	*53	80	....	....	....	39	9	5	*11	16	0
1944-45	**New York Rangers**	**NHL**	**44**	**13**	**9**	**22**	**13**	**10**	**23**	**6**	....	....	....	....	....
1945-46	Buffalo Bisons	AHL	62	27	43	70	....	....	....	32	12	5	*11	*16	6
1946-47	Buffalo Bisons	AHL	63	26	21	47	....	....	....	29	2	0	1	1	0
1947-48	Buffalo Bisons	AHL	40	12	20	32	....	....	....	0	8	4	3	7	4
1948-49	Buffalo Bisons	AHL	48	12	26	38	....	....	....	6	....	....	....	....	....
	Hershey Bears	AHL	13	7	2	9	....	....	....	5	9	3	2	5	0
	NHL Totals		**59**	**15**	**14**	**29**	**16**	**17**	**33**	**6**	....	....	....	....	....

Signed as a free agent by **Hershey** (EAHL), October 25, 1937. Signed as a free agent by **NY Americans**, September 29, 1939. Rights transferred to **NY Rangers** from **Brooklyn** in Special Dispersal Draw, September 11, 1943. Traded to **Hershey** (AHL) by **Buffalo** (AHL) for cash, February 18, 1949.

• HURST, Ron

Ronald

RW – R. 5'9", 175 lbs. b: Toronto, Ont., 5/18/1931.

			REGULAR SEASON								PLAYOFFS				
Season	Club	League	GP	G	A	Pts	AG	AA	APts	PIM	GP	G	A	Pts	PIM
1946-47	Weston Dukes	OHA-B	STATISTICS NOT AVAILABLE												
	Toronto Young Rangers	OHA-Jr.	1	0	0	0	....	....	....	0	....	....	....	....	....
1947-48	Weston Dukes	OHA-B	STATISTICS NOT AVAILABLE												
1948-49	Weston Dukes	OHA-B	STATISTICS NOT AVAILABLE												
	Toronto Marlboros	OHA-Jr.	....	....	....	....	....	....	....	....	9	3	8	11	7
1949-50	Toronto Marlboros	OHA-Jr.	48	13	12	25	....	....	....	74	5	2	4	6	12
1950-51	Toronto Marlboros	OHA-Jr.	51	15	13	28	....	....	....	127	12	8	3	11	36
1951-52	Saint John Beavers	MMHL	63	17	25	42	....	....	....	51	10	2	1	3	24
	Saint John Beavers	Alx-Cup	5	2	2	4	....	....	....	6	....	....	....	....	....
1952-53	Ottawa Senators	QMHL	8	2	1	3	....	....	....	4	....	....	....	....	....
	Charlottetown Islanders	MMHL	70	23	21	44	....	....	....	104	18	3	9	12	35
1953-54	S.S. Marie Greyhounds	NOHA	53	11	30	41	....	....	....	63	9	4	5	9	8
1954-55	S.S. Marie Greyhounds	NOHA	57	24	29	53	....	....	....	60	14	5	4	9	29
1955-56	**Toronto Maple Leafs**	**NHL**	**50**	**7**	**5**	**12**	**9**	**6**	**15**	**62**	**3**	**0**	**2**	**2**	**4**
	Pittsburgh Hornets	AHL	13	7	8	15	....	....	....	44	....	....	....	....	....
1956-57	**Toronto Maple Leafs**	**NHL**	**14**	**2**	**2**	**4**	**3**	**2**	**5**	**8**	....	....	....	....	....
	Rochester Americans	AHL	26	7	16	23	....	....	....	58	10	1	4	5	20
1957-58	Rochester Americans	AHL	59	12	22	34	....	....	....	120	....	....	....	....	....
1958-59	Hershey Bears	AHL	19	2	8	10	....	....	....	47	....	....	....	....	....
1959-60	Hershey Bears	AHL	43	7	7	14	....	....	....	175	....	....	....	....	....
	NHL Totals		**64**	**9**	**7**	**16**	**12**	**8**	**20**	**70**	**3**	**0**	**2**	**2**	**4**

Signed as a free agent by **Saint John** (MMHL), September 17, 1951. Traded to **Hershey** (AHL) by **Toronto** with Mike Nykoluk and loan of Wally Boyer for 1958-59 and 1959-60 seasons for Willie Marshall, April 29, 1958.

• HUTCHINSON, Ron

Ronald Wayne

C – L. 5'10", 165 lbs. b: Flin Flon, Man., 10/24/1936.

Season	Club	League	GP	G	A	Pts	AG	AA	APts	PIM	GP	G	A	Pts	PIM
1954-55	Flin Flon Bombers	SJHL	16	1	6	7	....	....	....	0	....	....	....	....	....
1955-56	Flin Flon Bombers	SJHL	47	32	29	61	....	....	....	4	12	2	1	3	6
	Flin Flon Bombers	M-Cup	7	2	0	2	....	....	....	6	....	....	....	....	....
1956-57	Flin Flon Bombers	SJHL	55	28	54	82	....	....	....	10	10	7	12	19	2
	Flin Flon Bombers	M-Cup	17	4	13	17	....	....	....	11	....	....	....	....	....
1957-58	Vancouver Canucks	WHL	66	22	21	43	....	....	....	23	11	2	7	9	11
1958-59	Vancouver Canucks	WHL	70	15	33	48	....	....	....	21	9	2	4	6	9
1959-60	Vancouver Canucks	WHL	70	12	26	38	....	....	....	25	11	0	3	3	0
1960-61	**New York Rangers**	**NHL**	**9**	**0**	**0**	**0**	**0**	**0**	**0**	**0**	....	....	....	....	....
	Vancouver Canucks	WHL	53	11	5	16	....	....	....	10	9	0	1	1	0
1961-62	Vancouver–Seattle	WHL	70	18	16	34	....	....	....	14	2	0	0	0	0
1962-63	Vancouver Canucks	WHL	68	12	23	35	....	....	....	36	7	0	3	3	2
1963-64	Vancouver Canucks	WHL	70	10	19	29	....	....	....	8	....	....	....	....	....
1964-65	Vancouver Canucks	WHL	2	0	0	0	....	....	....	0	....	....	....	....	....
	Charlotte Checkers	EHL	59	20	30	50	....	....	....	33	3	1	1	2	0
1965-66	Vancouver Canucks	WHL	41	10	7	17	....	....	....	8	....	....	....	....	....
1966-67	Vancouver Canucks	WHL	13	0	1	1	....	....	....	4	....	....	....	....	....
1967-68			REINSTATED AS AN AMATEUR												
1968-69	Cranbrook Royals	WIHL	46	10	33	43	....	....	....	32	....	....	....	....	....
1969-70	Cranbrook Royals	WIHL	35	13	21	34	....	....	....	6	5	0	1	1	2
	NHL Totals		**9**	**0**	**0**	**0**	**0**	**0**	**0**	**0**	....	....	....	....	....

Traded to **Providence** (AHL) by **Vancouver** (WHL) with Wayne Muloin for Bob Blackburn, February 3, 1966. • Hutchinson failed to report to Providence (AHL).

• HUTTON, Bill

William David

D/RW – R. 5'11", 165 lbs. b: Calgary, Alta., 1/28/1910 d: 1977.

Season	Club	League	GP	G	A	Pts	AG	AA	APts	PIM	GP	G	A	Pts	PIM
1927-28	Calgary Canadians	X-Games	11	0	0	0	....	....	....	9	....	....	....	....	....
	Calgary Canadians	M-Cup	2	1	0	1	....	....	....	2	....	....	....	....	....
1928-29	Calgary Canadians	CCJHL	3	4	*3	*7	....	....	....	2	....	....	....	....	....
	Calgary Canadians	M-Cup	9	6	5	11	....	....	....	10	....	....	....	....	....
1929-30	**Boston Bruins**	**NHL**	**16**	**2**	**0**	**2**	**3**	**0**	**3**	**2**	....	....	....	....	....
	Ottawa Senators	**NHL**	**18**	**0**	**1**	**1**	**0**	**2**	**2**	**0**	**2**	**0**	**0**	**0**	**0**
	Philadelphia Arrows	Can-Am	6	1	1	2	....	....	....	0	....	....	....	....	....
1930-31	**Boston Bruins**	**NHL**	**9**	**0**	**0**	**0**	**0**	**0**	**0**	**2**	....	....	....	....	....
	Philadelphia Quakers	**NHL**	**21**	**1**	**1**	**2**	**2**	**3**	**5**	**4**	....	....	....	....	....
1931-32	Boston Cubs	Can-Am	6	0	0	0	....	....	....	2	....	....	....	....	....
	Detroit Olympics	IHL	4	0	0	0	....	....	....	0	....	....	....	....	....
	Duluth Hornets	AHA	2	0	0	0	....	....	....	0	....	....	....	....	....
	Syracuse Stars	IHL	4	0	0	0	....	....	....	0	....	....	....	....	....
1932-33	Calgary Tigers	WCHL	30	6	3	9	....	....	....	10	6	0	0	0	4
1933-34	Calgary Tigers	NWHL	32	11	1	12	....	....	....	25	5	2	0	2	2
1934-35	Vancouver Lions	NWHL	32	5	10	15	....	....	....	34	8	1	0	1	2
	Vancouver Lions	L-W-S	5	1	0	1	....	....	....	4	....	....	....	....	....
1935-36	Vancouver Lions	NWHL	40	4	7	11	....	....	....	10	7	0	0	0	2
1936-37	Spokane Clippers	PCHL	40	9	7	16	....	....	....	10	6	1	0	1	2
1937-38	Vancouver Lions	PCHL	42	4	5	9	....	....	....	24	6	1	1	2	4
1938-39	Vancouver Lions	PCHL	47	9	15	24	....	....	....	30	2	0	0	0	5
1939-40	Vancouver Lions	PCHL	39	7	3	10	....	....	....	28	5	1	3	4	4
1940-41	Vancouver Lions	PCHL	47	9	18	27	....	....	....	37	6	1	1	2	6
1941-42	Tulsa Oilers	AHA	50	5	8	13	....	....	....	12	2	1	0	1	0
1942-43	Vancouver St. Regis	PCHL	10	1	3	4	....	....	....	6	5	2	0	2	4
1943-44	Vancouver St. Regis	PCHL	23	5	7	12	....	....	....	6	3	0	0	0	2
	NHL Totals		**64**	**3**	**2**	**5**	**5**	**5**	**10**	**8**	**2**	**0**	**0**	**0**	**0**

Traded to **Ottawa** by **Boston** for Harry Connor, January 30, 1930. Traded to **Boston** by **Ottawa** for Harry Connor, October 16, 1930. Traded to **Philadelphia** by **Boston** with Ron Lyons for Harold Darragh, December 8, 1930. Traded to **Detroit** (IHL) by **Philadelphia** for cash, February 24, 1931.

• HYLAND, Harry

Harold Macarius **HHOF**

RW – R. 5'6", 156 lbs. b: Montreal, Que., 1/2/1889 d: 8/8/1969.

Season	Club	League	GP	G	A	Pts	AG	AA	APts	PIM	GP	G	A	Pts	PIM
1907-08	Montreal Shamrocks	CAIHL	STATISTICS NOT AVAILABLE												
1908-09	Montreal Shamrocks	ECHA	11	19	0	19	....	....	....	36	....	....	....	....	....
♦1909-10	Montreal Wanderers	NHA	11	24	0	24	....	....	....	23	1	3	0	3	3
1910-11	Montreal Wanderers	NHA	15	14	0	14	....	....	....	43	....	....	....	....	....
1911-12	New Westminster Royals	PCHA	15	26	0	26	....	....	....	44	....	....	....	....	....
	PCHA All-Stars	X-Games	3	*6	0	*6	....	....	....	8	....	....	....	....	....
1912-13	Montreal Wanderers	NHA	20	27	0	27	....	....	....	38	....	....	....	....	....
1913-14	Montreal Wanderers	NHA	18	30	12	42	....	....	....	18	....	....	....	....	....
1914-15	Montreal Wanderers	NHA	19	23	6	29	....	....	....	49	2	0	0	0	26
1915-16	Montreal Wanderers	NHA	20	14	0	14	....	....	....	69	....	....	....	....	....
1916-17	Montreal Wanderers	NHA	13	12	2	14	....	....	....	21	....	....	....	....	....
	Montreal St. Ann's	MCHL	....	3	1	4									

Season	Club	League	GP	G	A	Pts	AG	AA	APts	PIM	GP	G	A	Pts	PIM
			REGULAR SEASON								PLAYOFFS				
1917-18	**Montreal Wanderers**	**NHL**	**4**	**6**	**1**	**7**	**7**	**4**	**11**	**6**	....	....	....	....	....
	Ottawa Senators	**NHL**	**13**	**8**	**1**	**9**	**10**	**4**	**14**	**59**	....	....	....	....	....
1918-19	McGill University	MCHL	DID NOT PLAY – COACHING												
	NHL Totals		**17**	**14**	**2**	**16**	**17**	**8**	**25**	**65**	....	....	....	....	....
	Other Major League Totals		142	189	20	209	....	....	....	341	3	3	0	3	29

PCHA First All-Star Team (1912)

Signed as a free agent by **New Westminster** (PCHA), November 12, 1911. Rights retained by **Montreal Wanderers** after NHA folded, November 26, 1917. Claimed by **Ottawa** from **Montreal Wanderers** in Dispersal Draft, January 4, 1918. Traded to **Montreal Canadiens** by **Ottawa** for Skene Ronan, December 9, 1918.

• IMLACH, Brent

F – L. 5'8", 160 lbs. b: Quebec City, Que., 11/16/1946.

Season	Club	League	GP	G	A	Pts	AG	AA	APts	PIM	GP	G	A	Pts	PIM
1964-65	Toronto Marlboros	OHA-Jr.	4	0	0	0	....	....	....	0	....	....	....	....	....
1965-66	Toronto Marlboros	OHA-Jr.	45	23	18	41	....	....	....	15	14	0	5	5	4
	Toronto Maple Leafs	**NHL**	**2**	**0**	**0**	**0**	**0**	**0**	**0**	**0**	....	....	....	....	....
	Rochester Americans	AHL	1	0	0	0	....	....	....	2	....	....	....	....	....
1966-67	London Knights	OHA-Jr.	46	3	15	18	....	....	....	10	....	....	....	....	....
	Toronto Maple Leafs	**NHL**	**1**	**0**	**0**	**0**	**0**	**0**	**0**	**0**	....	....	....	....	....
1967-68	U. of Western Ontario	OQAA	15	11	15	26	....	....	....	9	....	....	....	....	....
1968-69	U. of Western Ontario	OQAA	15	14	20	34	....	....	....	8	....	....	....	....	....
1969-70	U. of Western Ontario	OQAA	15	3	10	13	....	....	....	8	....	....	....	....	....
1970-71	University of Toronto	OUAA	15	0	5	5	....	....	....	4	....	....	....	....	....
1971-72	York University	OUAA	20	16	22	38	....	....	....	28	....	....	....	....	....
	NHL Totals		**3**	**0**	**0**	**0**	**0**	**0**	**0**	**0**	....	....	....	....	....

Traded to **Buffalo** by **Toronto** for cash, August 31, 1970.

• INGARFIELD, Earl — *see page 1214*

• INGOLDSBY, Johnny John Gordon "Ding"

RW/D – R. 6'2", 210 lbs. b: Toronto, Ont., 6/21/1924 d: 8/10/1982.

Season	Club	League	GP	G	A	Pts	AG	AA	APts	PIM	GP	G	A	Pts	PIM
1941-42	Toronto De La Salle	OHA-B	8	*15	5	*20	....	....	....	16	3	0	2	2	0
	Toronto National Steel Car	TIHL	4	4	3	7	....	....	....	4	....	....	....	....	....
1942-43	**Toronto Maple Leafs**	**NHL**	**8**	**0**	**1**	**1**	**0**	**1**	**1**	**0**	....	....	....	....	....
	Providence Reds	AHL	24	10	12	22	....	....	....	2	2	0	0	0	0
1943-44	**Toronto Maple Leafs**	**NHL**	**21**	**5**	**0**	**5**	**4**	**0**	**4**	**15**	....	....	....	....	....
	Toronto C.I.L.	TIHL	4	4	3	7	....	....	....	0	....	....	....	....	....
	Toronto Army Daggers	TNDHL	....	....	....	....	....	....	....	....	2	3	2	5	0
1944-45	Toronto Uptown Tires	TMHL	16	5	11	16	....	....	....	9	....	....	....	....	....
1945-46	Toronto Staffords	OHA-Sr.	11	3	8	11	....	....	....	10	....	....	....	....	....
	Toronto Mahers	TIHL	13	11	5	16	....	....	....	24	10	*10	3	13	7
1946-47			PLAYER/COACH – STATISTICS UNAVAILABLE												
1947-48	Owen Sound Mercurys	OHA-Sr.	36	7	17	24	....	....	....	24	5	7	6	13	4
1948-49	Owen Sound Mercurys	OHA-Sr.	37	17	14	31	....	....	....	27	4	0	1	1	0
1949-50	Owen Sound Mercurys	OHA-Sr.	26	9	6	15	....	....	....	17	....	....	....	....	....
1950-51	Owen Sound Mercurys	OHA-Sr.	44	19	35	54	....	....	....	18	7	2	3	5	6
	Owen Sound Mercurys	Al-Cup	16	15	9	24	....	....	....	18	....	....	....	....	....
1951-52			DID NOT PLAY												
1952-53	New Haven Nutmegs	EAHL	60	29	52	81	....	....	....	20	....	....	....	....	....
1953-54	Marion Barons	IHL	61	19	18	37	....	....	....	30	5	0	1	1	10
1954-55	Grand Rapids Rockets	IHL	59	13	24	37	....	....	....	18	4	0	0	0	0
1955-56	Grand Rapids Rockets	IHL	58	16	30	46	....	....	....	18	....	....	....	....	....
1956-57	Huntington Hornets	IHL	60	18	10	28	....	....	....	6	4	3	1	4	0
1957-58	New Haven Blades	EHL	50	26	31	57	....	....	....	65	6	2	2	4	2
1958-59	New Haven Blades	EHL	64	15	23	38	....	....	....	8	....	....	....	....	....
1959-60	New Haven–Charlotte	EHL	40	8	15	23	....	....	....	18	....	....	....	....	....
	NHL Totals		**29**	**5**	**1**	**6**	**4**	**1**	**5**	**15**	....	....	....	....	....

Signed as a free agent by **Toronto**, November 18, 1942.

• INGRAM, Frank Frank Hamilton

RW – R. 5'8", 185 lbs. b: Craven, Sask., 9/17/1907.

Season	Club	League	GP	G	A	Pts	AG	AA	APts	PIM	GP	G	A	Pts	PIM
1922-23	Regina Boat Club	S-SJHL	2	1	1	2	....	....	....	0	....	....	....	....	....
1923-24	Regina Pats	S-SJHL	6	3	1	4	....	....	....	5	....	....	....	....	....
	Regina Pats	M-Cup	1	1	0	1	....	....	....	0	....	....	....	....	....
1924-25	Regina Pats	S-SJHL	5	11	1	12	....	....	....	5	....	....	....	....	....
	Regina Pats	M-Cup	12	10	5	15	....	....	....	*29	....	....	....	....	....
1925-26	Regina Victorias	S-SSHL	17	18	12	*30	....	....	....	13	....	....	....	....	....
	Regina Victorias	Al-Cup	9	12	*8	*20	....	....	....	4	....	....	....	....	....
1926-27	Fort William Forts	TBSHL	6	1	0	1	....	....	....	5	....	....	....	....	....
	Regina Capitals	PrHL	14	3	3	6	....	....	....	2	2	0	0	0	2
1927-28	St. Paul Saints	AHA	40	5	6	11	....	....	....	46	....	....	....	....	....
1928-29	St. Paul Saints	AHA	40	20	4	24	....	....	....	69	8	2	*2	4	4
1929-30	**Chicago Black Hawks**	**NHL**	**37**	**6**	**10**	**16**	**8**	**24**	**32**	**28**	**2**	**0**	**0**	**0**	**0**
1930-31	**Chicago Black Hawks**	**NHL**	**43**	**17**	**4**	**21**	**34**	**12**	**46**	**37**	**9**	**0**	**1**	**1**	**2**
1931-32	**Chicago Black Hawks**	**NHL**	**21**	**1**	**2**	**3**	**2**	**4**	**6**	**4**	....	....	....	....	....
	Philadelphia Arrows	Can-Am	8	1	3	4	....	....	....	13	....	....	....	....	....
	Pittsburgh Yellowjackets	IHL	15	6	3	9	....	....	....	21	....	....	....	....	....
1932-33	Boston Cubs	Can-Am	5	0	0	0	....	....	....	2	....	....	....	....	....
	Cleveland–Detroit	IHL	36	10	9	19	....	....	....	49	....	....	....	....	....
1933-34	Detroit Olympics	IHL	11	0	1	1	....	....	....	6	....	....	....	....	....
	Oklahoma City Warriors	AHA	42	6	7	13	....	....	....	40	....	....	....	....	....
1934-35	Oklahoma City Warriors	AHA	45	21	21	42	....	....	....	26	....	....	....	....	....
1935-36	Oklahoma–Minneapolis	AHA	48	20	18	38	....	....	....	8	....	....	....	....	....
1936-37	St. Louis Flyers	AHA	44	4	17	21	....	....	....	6	6	0	0	0	0
1937-38	Kansas City Greyhounds	AHA	48	12	24	36	....	....	....	11	....	....	....	....	....
1938-39	Kansas City Greyhounds	AHA	16	1	3	4	....	....	....	4	....	....	....	....	....
1939-40	Wichita Skyhawks	AHA	6	0	2	2	....	....	....	2	....	....	....	....	....
	Portage Lakes Lakers	NMHL	24	9	11	20	....	....	....	....	....	....	....	....	....
	NHL Totals		**101**	**24**	**16**	**40**	**44**	**40**	**84**	**69**	**11**	**0**	**1**	**1**	**2**

AHA Second All-Star Team (1935, 1936)

Signed as a free agent by **Regina** (PrHL), January 17, 1927. Signed as a free agent by **St. Paul** (AHA), October, 1927. Claimed by **Chicago** from **St. Paul** (AHA) in Inter-League Draft, May 13, 1929. Traded to **Boston** by **Chicago** for cash, October 17, 1932. Traded to **Cleveland** (IHL) by **Boston** (Boston-Can-Am) for cash, November, 1932. Signed as a free agent by **Detroit** (IHL) after being released by Cleveland (IHL) due to salary dispute, February 16, 1933.

• INGRAM, John J. "Jack"

C – L. 5'11", 170 lbs. b: Halifax, N.S., 1894 d: 12/14/1957.

Season	Club	League	GP	G	A	Pts	AG	AA	APts	PIM	GP	G	A	Pts	PIM
1912-13	Charlottetown Islanders	PEI-Sr.	STATISTICS NOT AVAILABLE												
1913-14	Moncton Machinists	MCHL	7	15	0	15	....	....	....	....	1	2	0	2	....
	Halifax Socials	MPHA	1	0	0	0	....	....	....	0	....	....	....	....	....
1914-15	Moncton Machinists	MCHL	4	4	0	4	....	....	....	....	....	....	....	....	....
1915-16	Moncton St. Bernards	X-Games	1	2	0	2	....	....	....	....	....	....	....	....	....
	Moncton Trojans	X-Games	STATISTICS NOT AVAILABLE												
1916-17	Moncton St. Bernards	X-Games	2	7	0	7	....	....	....	....	....	....	....	....	....
1917-18			DID NOT PLAY												
1918-19	Moncton Victorias	X-Games	1	3	0	3	....	....	....	....	....	....	....	....	....
1919-20	Moncton Victorias	ENBHL	6	8	3	11	....	....	....	4	9	*23	4	*27	4
1920-21	Moncton Victorias	MIAHL	9	*18	0	*18	....	....	....	6	2	4	0	4	2
1921-22	Moncton Victorias	MIAHL	13	*24	0	*24	....	....	....	36	....	....	....	....	....
1922-23	Moncton Victorias	MIAHL	12	18	0	18	....	....	....	39	....	....	....	....	....
1923-24	Moncton Victorias	MIAHL	16	12	0	12	....	....	....	19	....	....	....	....	....
1924-25	Moncton Victorias	MIAHL	3	*7	0	*7	....	....	....	2	....	....	....	....	....
	Boston Bruins	**NHL**	**1**	**0**	**0**	**0**	**0**	**0**	**0**	**0**	....	....	....	....	....
1925-26			DID NOT PLAY – REFEREE												
1926-27	Providence Reds	Can-Am	1	0	0	0	....	....	....	0	....	....	....	....	....
1927-28			DID NOT PLAY – REFEREE												
1928-29	Moncton Atlantics	SNBHL	12	7	3	10	....	....	....	16	2	1	0	1	2
1929-30	Moncton Atlantics	SNBHL	1	1	0	1	....	....	....	2	....	....	....	....	....
1930-31	Moncton Victorias	SNBHL	2	0	0	0	....	....	....	2	....	....	....	....	....
	NHL Totals		**1**	**0**	**0**	**0**	**0**	**0**	**0**	**0**	....	....	....	....	....

Signed as a free agent by **Boston**, January 5, 1925.

• INGRAM, Ron Ronald Walter

D – R. 5'11", 185 lbs. b: Toronto, Ont., 7/5/1933.

Season	Club	League	GP	G	A	Pts	AG	AA	APts	PIM	GP	G	A	Pts	PIM
1950-51	Toronto Marlboros	OHA-Jr.	3	0	1	1	....	....	....	2	....	....	....	....	....
1951-52	Toronto Marlboros	OHA-Jr.	40	8	15	23	....	....	....	27	5	1	0	1	6
1952-53	Toronto Marlboros	OHA-Jr.	47	3	12	15	....	....	....	98	7	1	1	2	30
1953-54	Stratford Indians	OHA-Sr.	54	10	13	23	....	....	....	113	12	3	6	9	34
1954-55	Stratford Indians	OHA-Sr.	50	6	20	26	....	....	....	96	7	2	4	6	12
1955-56	Montreal Royals	QHL	54	3	6	9	....	....	....	95	12	2	1	3	24
	Montreal Royals	Ed-Cup	6	0	3	3	....	....	....	14	....	....	....	....	....
1956-57	**Chicago Black Hawks**	**NHL**	**45**	**1**	**6**	**7**	**1**	**7**	**8**	**21**	....	....	....	....	....
	Cleveland Barons	AHL	18	0	4	4	....	....	....	18	12	3	5	8	31
1957-58	Buffalo Bisons	AHL	63	5	10	15	....	....	....	92	....	....	....	....	....
1958-59	Buffalo Bisons	AHL	58	3	14	17	....	....	....	57	11	0	6	6	38
1959-60	Buffalo Bisons	AHL	71	5	18	23	....	....	....	131	....	....	....	....	....
1960-61	Buffalo Bisons	AHL	72	5	18	23	....	....	....	108	4	1	0	1	16
1961-62	Buffalo Bisons	AHL	57	6	18	24	....	....	....	113	11	0	4	4	7
1962-63	Buffalo Bisons	AHL	65	3	29	32	....	....	....	113	12	1	5	6	32
	Chicago Black Hawks	**NHL**	....	....	....	....	....	....	....	....	**2**	**0**	**0**	**0**	**0**
1963-64	**Detroit Red Wings**	**NHL**	**50**	**3**	**6**	**9**	**4**	**6**	**10**	**50**	....	....	....	....	....
	New York Rangers	**NHL**	**16**	**1**	**3**	**4**	**1**	**3**	**4**	**8**	....	....	....	....	....
1964-65	**New York Rangers**	**NHL**	**3**	**0**	**0**	**0**	**0**	**0**	**0**	**2**	....	....	....	....	....
	Baltimore Clippers	AHL	63	12	31	43	....	....	....	92	5	0	0	0	10
1965-66	Baltimore Clippers	AHL	72	10	34	44	....	....	....	132	....	....	....	....	....
1966-67	Baltimore Clippers	AHL	59	4	31	35	....	....	....	65	8	1	3	4	12
1967-68	Buffalo Bisons	AHL	71	9	32	41	....	....	....	102	5	2	4	6	12
1968-69	Buffalo Bisons	AHL	62	4	33	37	....	....	....	97	6	0	3	3	8
1969-70	Seattle Totems	WHL	72	5	23	28	....	....	....	48	....	....	....	....	....
	NHL Totals		**114**	**5**	**15**	**20**	**6**	**16**	**22**	**81**	**2**	**0**	**0**	**0**	**0**

AHL First All-Star Team (1968) • AHL Second All-Star Team (1969)

Traded to **Cleveland** (AHL) by **Chicago** for Ian Cushenan, September, 1956. Traded to **Detroit** by **Chicago** with Roger Crozier for Howie Young, June 5, 1963. Traded to **NY Rangers** by **Detroit** for Albert Langlois, February 14, 1964. Traded to **Seattle** (WHL) by **NY Rangers** (Buffalo-AHL) for cash, October, 1969.

• IRVIN, Dick James Dickinson HHOF

C – L. 5'9", 162 lbs. b: Hamilton, Ont., 7/19/1892 d: 5/16/1957.

Season	Club	League	GP	G	A	Pts	AG	AA	APts	PIM	GP	G	A	Pts	PIM
1911-12	Winnipeg Monarchs	MIHA	5	16	0	16	....	....	....	0	1	5	0	5	0
1912-13	Winnipeg Strathconas	MIHA	7	*32	0	*32	....	....	....	12	1	0	0	0	0
	Winnipeg Monarchs	MIHA	2	5	0	5	....	....	....	....	....	....	....	....	....
1913-14	Winnipeg Strathconas	MIHA	3	11	0	11	....	....	....	....	....	....	....	....	....
	Winnipeg Monarchs	MHL-Sr.	7	*23	1	*24	....	....	....	....	....	....	....	....	....
1914-15	Winnipeg Monarchs	MHL-Sr.	6	*23	3	*26	....	....	....	30	2	10	0	10	2
	Winnipeg Monarchs	Al-Cup	6	*17	3	*20	....	....	....	20	....	....	....	....	....
1915-16	Winnipeg Monarchs	MHL-Sr.	8	*17	4	*21	....	....	....	38	2	7	1	8	2
1916-17	Portland Rosebuds	PCHA	23	35	10	45	....	....	....	24	....	....	....	....	....
1917-18	Winnipeg Ypres	MHL-Sr.	9	*29	8	*37	....	....	....	26	....	....	....	....	....
1918-19			MILITARY SERVICE												
1919-20	Regina Vics	S-SSHL	12	*32	4	*36	....	....	....	22	2	1	0	1	4
1920-21	Regina Vics	S-SSHL	11	19	5	24	....	....	....	12	4	*8	0	*8	4
1921-22	Regina Capitals	WCHL	20	21	7	28	....	....	....	17	4	*3	0	*3	2
1922-23	Regina Capitals	WCHL	25	9	4	13	....	....	....	12	2	1	0	1	0
1923-24	Regina Capitals	WCHL	29	15	8	23	....	....	....	33	2	0	0	0	4
1924-25	Regina Capitals	WCHL	28	13	5	18	....	....	....	38	....	....	....	....	....
1925-26	Portland Rosebuds	WHL	30	*31	5	36	....	....	....	29	....	....	....	....	....
1926-27	**Chicago Black Hawks**	**NHL**	**43**	**18**	***18**	**36**	**32**	**97**	**129**	**34**	**2**	**2**	**0**	**2**	**4**
1927-28	**Chicago Black Hawks**	**NHL**	**12**	**5**	**4**	**9**	**10**	**23**	**33**	**14**	....	....	....	....	....
1928-29	**Chicago Black Hawks**	**NHL**	**39**	**6**	**1**	**7**	**17**	**7**	**24**	**30**	....	....	....	....	....
	NHL Totals		**94**	**29**	**23**	**52**	**59**	**127**	**186**	**78**	**2**	**2**	**0**	**2**	**4**
	Other Major League Totals		155	124	39	163	....	....	....	153	8	4	0	4	6

PCHA Second All-Star Team (1917) • WCHL Second All-Star Team (1922) • WCHL First All-Star Team (1924)

Signed as a free agent by **Portland** (PCHA), November 9, 1916. • Re-instated as an amateur, November, 1917. Signed as a free agent by **Winnipeg** (MHL-Sr.), November 23, 1917. Signed as a free agent by **Regina** (WCHL), December 27, 1921. Transferred to **Portland** (WHL) after **Regina** (WCHL) franchise relocated, September 1, 1925. NHL rights transferred to **Chicago** after NHL club purchased **Portland** (WHL) franchise, May 15, 1926. • Missed remainder of 1927-28 season recovering from head injury suffered in game vs. Montreal Maroons, December 28, 1927.

• IRVINE, Ted — *see page 1215*

• IRWIN, Ivan
Ivan Duane "Ivan the Terrible"
D – L. 6'2", 185 lbs. b: Chicago, IL, 3/13/1927.

Season	Club	League	GP	G	A	Pts	AG	AA	APts	PIM	GP	G	A	Pts	PIM
			REGULAR SEASON								PLAYOFFS				
1943-44	Northern Vocational	H.S.	6	1	2	3	....	....	....	8	1	0	0	0	0
	Scarborough Colts	OHA-B	STATISTICS NOT AVAILABLE												
1944-45	Scarborough Colts	OHA-B	STATISTICS NOT AVAILABLE												
1945-46	Toronto Dorsts	TMHL	1	0	0	0	....	....	....	0	....	....	....	....	....
	Toronto Tip Tops	TIHL	5	2	0	2	....	....	....	0	....	....	....	....	....
	Scarborough Rangers	OHA-B	....	....	....	....	....	....	....	....	5	3	4	7	16
1946-47	Scarborough Rangers	OHA-B	STATISTICS NOT AVAILABLE												
1947-48	Boston Olympics	QSHL	40	1	3	4	....	....	....	30	....	....	....	....	....
	Boston Olympics	EAHL	16	2	1	3	....	....	....	36	....	....	....	....	....
1948-49	Sherbrooke Saints	QSHL	55	1	8	9	....	....	....	124	12	1	2	3	*36
1949-50	Sherbrooke Saints	QSHL	7	1	0	1	....	....	....	30	....	....	....	....	....
	Cincinnati Mohawks	AHL	52	2	7	9	....	....	....	114	....	....	....	....	....
1950-51	Cincinnati Mohawks	AHL	62	3	14	17	....	....	....	145	....	....	....	....	....
1951-52	Cincinnati Mohawks	AHL	67	4	10	14	....	....	....	111	7	0	1	1	18
1952-53	**Montreal Canadiens**	**NHL**	**4**	**0**	**1**	**1**	**0**	**1**	**1**	**0**	....	....	....	....	....
	Victoria Cougars	WHL	58	5	20	25	....	....	....	116	....	....	....	....	....
1953-54	**New York Rangers**	**NHL**	**56**	**2**	**12**	**14**	**3**	**15**	**18**	**109**	....	....	....	....	....
	Vancouver Canucks	WHL	13	1	0	1	....	....	....	20	....	....	....	....	....
1954-55	**New York Rangers**	**NHL**	**60**	**0**	**13**	**13**	**0**	**15**	**15**	**85**	....	....	....	....	....
1955-56	**New York Rangers**	**NHL**	**34**	**0**	**1**	**1**	**0**	**1**	**1**	**20**	**5**	**0**	**0**	**0**	**8**
	Providence Reds	AHL	19	0	5	5	....	....	....	43	....	....	....	....	....
1956-57	Providence Reds	AHL	62	4	14	18	....	....	....	149	5	0	1	1	8
1957-58	**New York Rangers**	**NHL**	**1**	**0**	**0**	**0**	**0**	**0**	**0**	**0**	....	....	....	....	....
	Providence Reds	AHL	63	2	16	18	....	....	....	146	5	1	2	3	6
1958-59	Buffalo Bisons	AHL	63	3	12	15	....	....	....	106	11	0	3	3	16
1959-60	Buffalo Bisons	AHL	40	1	8	9	....	....	....	53	....	....	....	....	....
1960/64	Toronto Westsides	OIHA	STATISTICS NOT AVAILABLE												
1964-65	New Glasgow Rangers	MSHL	12	1	2	3	....	....	....	4	....	....	....	....	....
1965-66	Providence Reds	AHL	DID NOT PLAY – COACHING												
1966-67	Orillia Pepsis	OHA-Sr.	23	4	10	14	....	....	....	30	....	....	....	....	....
	NHL Totals		**155**	**2**	**27**	**29**	**3**	**32**	**35**	**214**	**5**	**0**	**0**	**0**	**8**

AHL Second All-Star Team (1957) • AHL First All-Star Team (1958, 1959) • OHA-Sr. Second All-Star Team (1967)

Rights traded to **Montreal** by **Cincinnati** (AHL) for cash, October 3, 1951. Traded to **NY Rangers** by **Montreal** for Eddie Slowinski and Pete Babando, August 8, 1953.

• JACKSON, Art
Arthur Morris
C – L. 5'8", 165 lbs. b: Toronto, Ont., 12/15/1915 d: 5/15/1971.

Season	Club	League	GP	G	A	Pts	AG	AA	APts	PIM	GP	G	A	Pts	PIM
1931-32	Toronto Marlboros	OHA-Jr.	3	0	0	0	....	....	....	0	....	....	....	....	....
1932-33	Toronto Marlboros	OHA-Jr.	9	7	5	*12	....	....	....	10	3	2	0	2	6
1933-34	St. Michael's Majors	OHA-Jr.	12	23	13	36	....	....	....	6	3	*4	2	6	6
	Toronto CCM	TMHL	7	5	3	8	....	....	....	4	....	....	....	....	....
	St. Michael's Majors	M-Cup	13	21	15	36	....	....	....	26	....	....	....	....	....
1934-35	**Toronto Maple Leafs**	**NHL**	**20**	**1**	**3**	**4**	**2**	**5**	**7**	**4**	**1**	**0**	**0**	**0**	**2**
	Syracuse Stars	IHL	24	13	12	25	....	....	....	0	2	1	0	1	0
1935-36	**Toronto Maple Leafs**	**NHL**	**48**	**5**	**15**	**20**	**10**	**28**	**38**	**14**	**8**	**0**	**3**	**3**	**2**
	Syracuse Stars	IHL	1	0	0	0	....	....	....	0	....	....	....	....	....
1936-37	**Toronto Maple Leafs**	**NHL**	**14**	**2**	**0**	**2**	**3**	**0**	**3**	**2**	....	....	....	....	....
	Syracuse Stars	IAHL	30	17	21	38	....	....	....	37	9	1	3	4	0
1937-38	**Boston Bruins**	**NHL**	**48**	**9**	**3**	**12**	**15**	**5**	**20**	**24**	**3**	**0**	**0**	**0**	**0**
1938-39	**New York Americans**	**NHL**	**48**	**12**	**13**	**25**	**21**	**20**	**41**	**15**	**2**	**0**	**0**	**0**	**2**
1939-40	**Boston Bruins**	**NHL**	**46**	**7**	**18**	**25**	**12**	**28**	**40**	**6**	**5**	**1**	**2**	**3**	**0**
♦1940-41	**Boston Bruins**	**NHL**	**48**	**17**	**15**	**32**	**26**	**21**	**47**	**10**	**11**	**1**	**3**	**4**	**16**
1941-42	**Boston Bruins**	**NHL**	**47**	**6**	**18**	**24**	**8**	**21**	**29**	**25**	**5**	**0**	**1**	**1**	**0**
1942-43	**Boston Bruins**	**NHL**	**50**	**22**	**31**	**53**	**23**	**29**	**52**	**20**	**9**	**6**	**3**	**9**	**7**
1943-44	**Boston Bruins**	**NHL**	**49**	**28**	**41**	**69**	**26**	**36**	**62**	**8**	....	....	....	....	....
1944-45	**Boston Bruins**	**NHL**	**19**	**5**	**8**	**13**	**5**	**9**	**14**	**10**	....	....	....	....	....
♦	**Toronto Maple Leafs**	**NHL**	**31**	**9**	**13**	**22**	**9**	**15**	**24**	**6**	**8**	**0**	**0**	**0**	**0**
1945-46			STATISTICS NOT AVAILABLE												
1946-47	Toronto Barkers	TIHL	2	3	1	4	....	....	....	0	....	....	....	....	....
	NHL Totals		**468**	**123**	**178**	**301**	**160**	**217**	**377**	**144**	**52**	**8**	**12**	**20**	**29**

• Brother of Busher

Traded to **Boston** by **Toronto** for cash and future considerations, September 23, 1937. Loaned to **NY Americans** by **Boston** for the 1938-39 season with the trade of Leroy Goldsworthy for cash, October 24, 1938. Traded to **Toronto** by **Boston** for $7,500 and future considerations (Bingo Kampman, October 29, 1945), December 24, 1944.

• JACKSON, Busher
Harvey Ralph **HHOF**
LW – L. 5'11", 195 lbs. b: Toronto, Ont., 1/19/1911 d: 6/25/1966.

Season	Club	League	GP	G	A	Pts	AG	AA	APts	PIM	GP	G	A	Pts	PIM
1925/27	Humberside Collegiate	H.S.	STATISTICS NOT AVAILABLE												
1927-28	Toronto Marlboros	OHA-Jr.	4	4	0	4	....	....	....	2	2	0	0	0	0
1928-29	Toronto Marlboros	OHA-Jr.	9	10	4	14	....	....	....	0	3	*7	2	*9	....
	Toronto Marlboros	M-Cup	13	15	10	25	....	....	....	4	....	....	....	....	....
1929-30	**Toronto Maple Leafs**	**NHL**	**31**	**12**	**6**	**18**	**17**	**14**	**31**	**29**	....	....	....	....	....
1930-31	**Toronto Maple Leafs**	**NHL**	**43**	**18**	**13**	**31**	**36**	**39**	**75**	**81**	**2**	**0**	**0**	**0**	**0**
♦1931-32	**Toronto Maple Leafs**	**NHL**	**48**	**28**	**25**	***53**	**47**	**56**	**103**	**63**	**7**	**5**	**2**	**7**	**13**
1932-33	**Toronto Maple Leafs**	**NHL**	**48**	**27**	**17**	**44**	**50**	**35**	**85**	**43**	**9**	**3**	**1**	**4**	**2**
1933-34	**Toronto Maple Leafs**	**NHL**	**38**	**20**	**18**	**38**	**35**	**38**	**73**	**38**	**5**	**1**	**0**	**1**	**8**
1934-35	**Toronto Maple Leafs**	**NHL**	**42**	**22**	**22**	**44**	**36**	**39**	**75**	**27**	**7**	**3**	**2**	***5**	**2**
1935-36	**Toronto Maple Leafs**	**NHL**	**47**	**11**	**11**	**22**	**21**	**21**	**42**	**19**	**9**	**3**	**2**	**5**	**4**
1936-37	**Toronto Maple Leafs**	**NHL**	**46**	**21**	**19**	**40**	**36**	**35**	**71**	**12**	**2**	**1**	**0**	**1**	**2**
1937-38	**Toronto Maple Leafs**	**NHL**	**48**	**17**	**17**	**34**	**28**	**27**	**55**	**18**	**6**	**1**	**0**	**1**	**8**
1938-39	**Toronto Maple Leafs**	**NHL**	**41**	**10**	**17**	**27**	**17**	**27**	**44**	**12**	**7**	**0**	**1**	**1**	**2**
1939-40	**New York Americans**	**NHL**	**43**	**12**	**8**	**20**	**20**	**12**	**32**	**10**	**3**	**0**	**1**	**1**	**2**
1940-41	**New York Americans**	**NHL**	**46**	**8**	**18**	**26**	**12**	**26**	**38**	**4**	....	....	....	....	....
1941-42	**Boston Bruins**	**NHL**	**26**	**5**	**7**	**12**	**7**	**8**	**15**	**18**	**5**	**0**	**1**	**1**	**0**
1942-43	**Boston Bruins**	**NHL**	**44**	**19**	**15**	**34**	**20**	**14**	**34**	**38**	**9**	**1**	**2**	**3**	**10**
1943-44	**Boston Bruins**	**NHL**	**42**	**11**	**21**	**32**	**10**	**18**	**28**	**25**	....	....	....	....	....
	NHL Totals		**633**	**241**	**234**	**475**	**392**	**409**	**801**	**437**	**71**	**18**	**12**	**30**	**53**

• Brother of Art • NHL First All-Star Team (1932, 1934, 1935, 1937) • NHL Scoring Leader (1932) • NHL Second All-Star Team (1933) • Played in NHL All-Star Game (1934, 1937, 1939)

Signed as a free agent by **Toronto**, December 6, 1929. Traded to **NY Americans** by **Toronto** with Buzz Boll, Doc Romnes, Jimmy Fowler and Murray Armstrong for Sweeney Schriner, May 18, 1939. Traded to **Boston** by **NY Americans** for $7,500, January 4, 1942.

• JACKSON, Harold
Harold Russell "Hal"
D – R. 6'1", 195 lbs. b: Cedar Springs, Ont., 8/1/1918 Deceased.

Season	Club	League	GP	G	A	Pts	AG	AA	APts	PIM	GP	G	A	Pts	PIM
1933-34	Windsor Wanderers	MOHL	19	1	3	4	....	....	....	10	....	....	....	....	....
1934-35	Windsor Wanderers	MOHL	26	5	3	8	....	....	....	31	5	0	0	0	6
1935-36	St. Michael's Majors	OHA-Jr.	8	2	1	3	....	....	....	4	5	0	0	0	8
1936-37	**Chicago Black Hawks**	**NHL**	**38**	**1**	**3**	**4**	**2**	**5**	**7**	**6**	....	....	....	....	....
♦1937-38	**Chicago Black Hawks**	**NHL**	**3**	**0**	**0**	**0**	**0**	**0**	**0**	**0**	**1**	**0**	**0**	**0**	**2**
1938-39	Providence Reds	IAHL	51	5	6	11	....	....	....	57	5	0	3	3	6
1939-40	Cleveland Barons	IAHL	20	3	0	3	....	....	....	14	....	....	....	....	....
	Providence Reds	IAHL	27	2	7	9	....	....	....	24	8	1	1	2	4
1940-41	Providence Reds	AHL	19	1	2	3	....	....	....	20	....	....	....	....	....
	Detroit Red Wings	**NHL**	**1**	**0**	**0**	**0**	**0**	**0**	**0**	**0**	....	....	....	....	....
	Indianapolis Capitols	AHL	35	2	7	9	....	....	....	29	....	....	....	....	....
1941-42	Indianapolis Capitols	AHL	56	5	19	24	....	....	....	52	10	2	5	7	8
♦1942-43	**Detroit Red Wings**	**NHL**	**4**	**0**	**4**	**4**	**0**	**4**	**4**	**6**	**6**	**0**	**1**	**1**	**4**
	Indianapolis Capitols	AHL	53	9	16	25	....	....	....	30	4	0	3	3	14
1943-44	**Detroit Red Wings**	**NHL**	**50**	**7**	**12**	**19**	**6**	**10**	**16**	**76**	**5**	**0**	**0**	**0**	**11**
	Indianapolis Capitols	AHL	1	0	1	1	....	....	....	0	....	....	....	....	....
1944-45	**Detroit Red Wings**	**NHL**	**50**	**5**	**6**	**11**	**5**	**7**	**12**	**45**	**14**	**1**	**1**	**2**	**10**
1945-46	**Detroit Red Wings**	**NHL**	**36**	**3**	**4**	**7**	**4**	**6**	**10**	**36**	**5**	**0**	**0**	**0**	**6**
1946-47	**Detroit Red Wings**	**NHL**	**37**	**1**	**5**	**6**	**1**	**6**	**7**	**39**	....	....	....	....	....
1947-48	Buffalo Bisons	AHL	63	7	30	37	....	....	....	97	8	0	3	3	13
	NHL Totals		**219**	**17**	**34**	**51**	**18**	**38**	**56**	**208**	**31**	**1**	**2**	**3**	**33**

• Missed majority of 1937-38 season recovering from collarbone injury suffered in game vs. Boston, January 18, 1938. Traded to **Cleveland** (IAHL) by **Chicago** with Charley Mason and $15,000 for Phil Hergesheimer, May 17, 1939. Traded to **Detroit** by **Providence** (AHL) for Cecil Dillon and Eddie Bush, December 15, 1940. Traded to **Buffalo** (AHL) by **Detroit** with Les Douglas for Jim McFadden, June, 1947. Traded to **Boston** (Hershey-AHL) by **Montreal** (Buffalo-AHL) with Gerry Brown for Jack McGill, June 30, 1948.

• JACKSON, Jack
John Alexander
D – R. 5'10", 185 lbs. b: Windsor, Ont., 5/3/1925.

Season	Club	League	GP	G	A	Pts	AG	AA	APts	PIM	GP	G	A	Pts	PIM
1943-44	Stratford Kroehlers	OHA-Jr.	23	5	11	16	....	....	....	73	....	....	....	....	....
	Hamilton Whizzers	OHA-Jr.	....	....	....	....	....	....	....	....	2	0	1	1	7
1944-45	Montreal Jr. Royals	QJHL	5	1	2	3	....	....	....	0	3	2	1	3	0
1945-46	Kansas City Pla-Mors	USHL	39	11	11	22	....	....	....	28	12	0	1	1	12
1946-47	**Chicago Black Hawks**	**NHL**	**48**	**2**	**5**	**7**	**2**	**6**	**8**	**38**	....	....	....	....	....
	Kansas City Pla-Mors	USHL	15	1	3	4	....	....	....	24	....	....	....	....	....
1947-48	Kansas City Pla-Mors	USHL	66	6	19	25	....	....	....	72	7	0	1	1	0
1948-49	Kansas City Pla-Mors	USHL	66	11	17	28	....	....	....	82	2	1	0	1	0
1949-50	Kansas City Mohawks	USHL	70	9	30	39	....	....	....	34	3	0	0	0	0
1950-51	New Haven Ramblers	AHL	22	0	2	2	....	....	....	10	....	....	....	....	....
	Denver Falcons	USHL	28	3	9	12	....	....	....	28	5	1	5	6	20
1951-52	Seattle Ironmen	PCHL	54	6	13	19	....	....	....	72	....	....	....	....	....
	NHL Totals		**48**	**2**	**5**	**7**	**2**	**6**	**8**	**38**	....	....	....	....	....

• JACKSON, Lloyd
Lloyd Edgar
C – L. 5'9", 150 lbs. b: Ottawa, Ont., 1/7/1912 d: 2/15/1999.

Season	Club	League	GP	G	A	Pts	AG	AA	APts	PIM	GP	G	A	Pts	PIM
1929-30	Ottawa Montagnards	OCHL	12	8	*3	11	....	....	....	2	2	1	0	1	4
1930-31	Ottawa Montagnards	OCHL	4	0	2	2	....	....	....	0	....	....	....	....	....
	New Glasgow Tigers	NSEHL	24	15	5	20	....	....	....	14	2	0	0	0	2
1931-32	New Haven Eagles	Can-Am	40	9	11	20	....	....	....	3	2	1	0	1	0
1932-33	New Haven Eagles	Can-Am	36	4	14	18	....	....	....	16	....	....	....	....	....
1933-34	Cleveland–Syracuse	IHL	16	3	1	4	....	....	....	2	....	....	....	....	....
	Seattle Seahawks	NWHL	22	9	9	18	....	....	....	4	....	....	....	....	....
1934-35	New Haven Eagles	Can-Am	47	23	35	*58	....	....	....	10	....	....	....	....	....
1935-36	New Haven Eagles	Can-Am	47	17	28	45	....	....	....	3	....	....	....	....	....
1936-37	**New York Americans**	**NHL**	**14**	**1**	**1**	**2**	**2**	**2**	**4**	**0**	....	....	....	....	....
	New Haven Eagles	IAHL	44	6	19	25	....	....	....	2	....	....	....	....	....
1937-38	New Haven Eagles	IAHL	13	1	6	7	....	....	....	2	....	....	....	....	....
	Springfield Indians	IAHL	31	3	7	10	....	....	....	0	....	....	....	....	....
1938-39	Springfield Indians	IAHL	51	10	16	26	....	....	....	6	3	1	0	1	0
1939-40	Springfield Indians	IAHL	54	10	22	32	....	....	....	2	3	1	0	1	0
1940-41	Tulsa Oilers	AHA	15	5	5	10	....	....	....	0	....	....	....	....	....
	Kansas City Americans	AHA	24	5	8	13	....	....	....	12	....	....	....	....	....
1941-42	Fort Worth Rangers	AHA	50	15	37	52	....	....	....	2	5	2	3	5	2
	NHL Totals		**14**	**1**	**1**	**2**	**2**	**2**	**4**	**0**	....	....	....	....	....

Can-Am First All-Star Team (1936)

Traded to **New Haven** (AHL) by **NY Americans** with cash for Alfie Moore, November, 1936.

• JACKSON, Stan
Stanton James
LW – L. 6', 180 lbs. b: Parrsboro, N.S., 8/27/1898 d: 11/28/1955.

Season	Club	League	GP	G	A	Pts	AG	AA	APts	PIM	GP	G	A	Pts	PIM
1916-17	Amherst Academy	H.S.	STATISTICS NOT AVAILABLE												
1917-18	Toronto RFC	TNDHL	STATISTICS NOT AVAILABLE												
1918-19			MILITARY SERVICE												
1919-20	Amherst Ramblers	NSSHL	2	1	0	1	....	....	....	5	....	....	....	....	....
	Halifax Imperoyals	HCHL	STATISTICS NOT AVAILABLE												
1920-21	Amherst Ramblers	MIL	10	13	0	13	....	....	....	10	2	1	0	1	2
1921-22	Amherst Ramblers	MIL	8	9	0	9	....	....	....	10	....	....	....	....	....
	Toronto St. Pats	**NHL**	**1**	**0**	**0**	**0**	**0**	**0**	**0**	**0**	....	....	....	....	....
	Halifax Independents	X-Games	1	0	0	0	....	....	....	0	....	....	....	....	....
	Stellerton Millionaires	MIL	....	....	....	....	....	....	....	....	6	4	0	4	2
1922-23	Amherst Ramblers	MIL	12	14	0	14	....	....	....	24	....	....	....	....	....
1923-24	**Toronto St. Pats**	**NHL**	**22**	**1**	**1**	**2**	**2**	**6**	**8**	**6**	....	....	....	....	....
1924-25	**Toronto St. Pats**	**NHL**	**3**	**0**	**0**	**0**	**0**	**0**	**0**	**7**	....	....	....	....	....
	Boston Bruins	**NHL**	**24**	**5**	**2**	**7**	**9**	**8**	**17**	**30**	....	....	....	....	....
1925-26	**Boston Bruins**	**NHL**	**28**	**3**	**3**	**6**	**5**	**19**	**24**	**30**	....	....	....	....	....
1926-27	New Haven Eagles	Can-Am	7	5	0	5	....	....	....	8	....	....	....	....	....
	Ottawa Senators	**NHL**	**8**	**0**	**0**	**0**	**0**	**0**	**0**	**2**	....	....	....	....	....
	London Panthers	Can-Pro	16	3	0	3	....	....	....	36	4	2	1	3	8
1927-28	London Panthers	Can-Pro	42	16	9	25	....	....	....	91	....	....	....	....	....
1928-29	London Panthers	Can-Pro	14	4	1	5	....	....	....	30	....	....	....	....	....
	Philadelphia Arrows	Can-Am	18	2	1	3	....	....	....	24	....	....	....	....	....
1929-30	Philadelphia Arrows	Can-Am	38	8	13	21	....	....	....	60	2	0	1	1	4
1930-31	Buffalo Bisons	IHL	41	6	1	7	....	....	....	32	6	1	0	1	6

			REGULAR SEASON								PLAYOFFS				
Season	**Club**	**League**	**GP**	**G**	**A**	**Pts**	**AG**	**AA**	**APts**	**PIM**	**GP**	**G**	**A**	**Pts**	**PIM**
1931-32	Buffalo Bisons	IHL	38	1	3	4	....	....	....	8	....	....	....	....	....
1932-33			DID NOT PLAY												
1933-34	Charlottetown Abegweits	MSHL	DID NOT PLAY – COACHING												
	NHL Totals		**86**	**9**	**6**	**15**	**16**	**33**	**49**	**75**	....	....	....	....	....

Signed as a free agent by **Toronto St. Pats**, December 23, 1921. Signed as a free agent by **Boston**, December 17, 1924. Traded to **Ottawa** by **Boston** for cash, January 18, 1927. Traded to **London** (Can-Pro) by **Ottawa** for cash, February, 1927. Traded to **Philadelphia** (Can-Am) by **London** (Can-Pro) for Fred Lowrey, January 18, 1929.

• JACKSON, Walter "Red"

LW – L. 5'8", 164 lbs. b: Ibstock, England, 6/3/1908.

Season	Club	League	GP	G	A	Pts	AG	AA	APts	PIM	GP	G	A	Pts	PIM
1927-28	Winnipeg CPR	WSrHL	9	4	1	5	....	....	....	8	....	....	....	....	....
1928-29	Winnipeg CPR	WSrHL	8	3	3	6	....	....	....	10	3	1	0	1	0
	Winnipeg Maple Leafs	M-Cup	5	5	3	8	....	....	....	0	....	....	....	....	....
1929-30	Elmwood Maple Leafs	WSrHL	12	8	2	10	....	....	....	2	7	*5	3	*8	4
1930-31	Winnipeg Native Sons	WSrHL	4	2	2	4	....	....	....	2	....	....	....	....	....
	St. Louis Flyers	AHA	36	11	7	18	....	....	....	16	....	....	....	....	....
1931-32	St. Louis Flyers	AHA	48	8	5	13	....	....	....	24	....	....	....	....	....
1932-33	**New York Americans**	**NHL**	**34**	**10**	**2**	**12**	**18**	**4**	**22**	**6**	....	....	....	....	....
	New Haven Eagles	Can-Am	9	2	2	4	....	....	....	6	....	....	....	....	....
1933-34	**New York Americans**	**NHL**	**47**	**6**	**9**	**15**	**10**	**19**	**29**	**12**	....	....	....	....	....
1934-35	**New York Americans**	**NHL**	**1**	**0**	**0**	**0**	**0**	**0**	**0**	**0**	....	....	....	....	....
	Cleveland Falcons	IHL	4	0	0	0	....	....	....	0	....	....	....	....	....
	Boston Cubs	Can-Am	29	11	19	30	....	....	....	2	3	1	0	1	0
1935-36	**Boston Bruins**	**NHL**	**2**	**0**	**0**	**0**	**0**	**0**	**0**	**0**	....	....	....	....	....
	Boston Cubs	Can-Am	12	2	2	4	....	....	....	2	....	....	....	....	....
	London Tecumsehs	IHL	4	0	3	3	....	....	....	0	....	....	....	....	....
	New Haven Eagles	Can-Am	14	5	2	7	....	....	....	4	....	....	....	....	....
1936-37	New Haven Eagles	Can-Am	1	0	0	0	....	....	....	0	....	....	....	....	....
	Minneapolis Millers	AHA	30	8	9	17	....	....	....	8	6	4	1	5	2
1937-38	St. Louis Flyers	AHA	22	2	5	7	....	....	....	14	....	....	....	....	....
	NHL Totals		**84**	**16**	**11**	**27**	**28**	**23**	**51**	**18**	....	....	....	....	....

Traded to **NY Americans** by **St. Louis** (AHA) for George Massecar, October 30, 1932. Loaned to **Cleveland** by **NY Americans** to complete transaction that sent Lorne Carr to NY Americans, November 5, 1934. Traded to **Boston** by **NY Americans** for Obs Heximer and Hap Emms, December 13, 1934. Transferred to **London** (IHL) by **Boston** as compensation for Boston's trading for Ray Getliffe, December 31, 1935.

• JACOBS, Paul

D – L. 5'8", 160 lbs. b: Montreal, Quebec, Deceased.

Season	Club	League	GP	G	A	Pts	AG	AA	APts	PIM	GP	G	A	Pts	PIM
1912-13	Montreal Stars	MCHL	1	0	0	0	....	....	....	3	....	....	....	....	....
	Montreal Dominion Bridge	MTMHL	7	3	0	3	....	....	....		....	....	....	....	....
1913-14	Montreal Dominion Bridge	MTMHL	2	0	0	0	....	....	....	0	....	....	....	....	....
1914-15	Montreal Nationale	MCHL	1	0	0	0	....	....	....	3	....	....	....	....	....
	St. Lawrence Bridge	MTMHL	STATISTICS NOT AVAILABLE												
1915-16	New Haven Hockey Club	USAHA	STATISTICS NOT AVAILABLE												
1916-17			STATISTICS NOT AVAILABLE												
1917-18	Montreal Stars	MCHL	9	10	1	11	....	....	....	15	....	....	....	....	....
	Leeside Indians	X-Games	STATISTICS NOT AVAILABLE												
1918-19	**Toronto Arenas**	**NHL**	**1**	**0**	**0**	**0**	**0**	**0**	**0**	**0**	....	....	....	....	....
	Montreal Stars	MCHL	7	4	7	11	....	....	....	27	....	....	....	....	....
1919-20	Laval University	MCHL	10	6	0	6	....	....	....	24	....	....	....	....	....
1920-21			DID NOT PLAY												
1921-22	Quebec Voltigeurs	QPHL	6	2	1	3	....	....	....	....	....	....	....	....	....
1922-23	Cleveland Indians	USAHA	16	0	0	0	....	....	....	....	....	....	....	....	....
1923-24	Montreal Nationale	ECHA	8	0	0	0	....	....	....	....	....	....	....	....	....
1924-25	Cleveland Blues	USAHA	9	0	0	0	....	....	....	....	....	....	....	....	....
	NHL Totals		**1**	**0**	**0**	**0**	**0**	**0**	**0**	**0**	....	....	....	....	....

MTMHL First All-Star Team (1913) • MCHL First All-Star Team (1918) • MCHL Second All-Star Team (1919, 1920)

Signed as a free agent by **Toronto**, December 15, 1918.

• JAMES, Gerry Gerald Edwin

RW – R. 5'11", 185 lbs. b: Regina, Sask., 10/22/1934.

Season	Club	League	GP	G	A	Pts	AG	AA	APts	PIM	GP	G	A	Pts	PIM
1951-52	Toronto Marlboros	OHA-Jr.	3	0	0	0	....	....	....	4	6	2	5	7	14
1952-53	Toronto Marlboros	OHA-Jr.	49	19	15	34	....	....	....	131	7	0	1	1	20
1953-54	Toronto Marlboros	OHA-Jr.	41	23	17	40	....	....	....	123	15	8	2	10	26
1954-55	Toronto Marlboros	OHA-Jr.	38	8	13	21	....	....	....	60	13	4	4	8	28
	Toronto Maple Leafs	**NHL**	**1**	**0**	**0**	**0**	**0**	**0**	**0**	**0**	....	....	....	....	....
	Toronto Marlboros	M-Cup	11	1	3	4	....	....	....	54	....	....	....	....	....
1955-56	**Toronto Maple Leafs**	**NHL**	**46**	**3**	**3**	**6**	**4**	**4**	**8**	**50**	**5**	**1**	**0**	**1**	**8**
1956-57	**Toronto Maple Leafs**	**NHL**	**53**	**4**	**12**	**16**	**5**	**13**	**18**	**90**	....	....	....	....	....
1957-58	**Toronto Maple Leafs**	**NHL**	**15**	**3**	**2**	**5**	**4**	**2**	**6**	**61**	....	....	....	....	....
	Rochester Americans	AHL	15	2	4	6	....	....	....	46	....	....	....	....	....
1958-59	**Toronto Maple Leafs**	**NHL**	DID NOT PLAY – INJURED												
1959-60	**Toronto Maple Leafs**	**NHL**	**34**	**4**	**9**	**13**	**5**	**9**	**14**	**56**	**10**	**0**	**0**	**0**	**0**
1960-61	Winnipeg Warriors	WHL	26	2	7	9	....	....	....	50	....	....	....	....	....
1961-62			PLAYED PRO FOOTBALL												
1962-63	HC Davos	Switz.	DID NOT PLAY – COACHING												
1963-64	HC Davos	Switz.	DID NOT PLAY – COACHING												
1964-65	Yorkton Terriers	SSHL	36	11	31	42	....	....	....	89	11	0	4	4	33
1965-66	Yorkton Terriers	SSHL	29	11	22	33	....	....	....	*91	5	3	1	4	17
1966-67	Yorkton Terriers	SSHL	35	13	21	34	....	....	....	65	4	1	5	6	4
1967/71			DID NOT PLAY												
1971-72	Yorkton Terriers	PrSHL	40	8	30	38	....	....	....	143	....	....	....	....	....
	NHL Totals		**149**	**14**	**26**	**40**	**18**	**28**	**46**	**257**	**15**	**1**	**0**	**1**	**8**

• Missed the entire 1958-59 season recovering from leg injury suffered in football game between Winnipeg Blue Bombers (CFL) and Saskatchewan Roughriders (CFL), September 7, 1958. Loaned to **Winnipeg** (WHL) by **Toronto** (Victoria-WHL) for the remainder of the 1960-61 season for Barrie Ross, January, 1961.

• JAMIESON, Jim

D – L. 5'9", 170 lbs. b: Brantford, Ont., 3/21/1922.

Season	Club	League	GP	G	A	Pts	AG	AA	APts	PIM	GP	G	A	Pts	PIM
1940-41	Detroit Holtzbaugh	MOHL	27	14	6	20	....	....	....	47	7	*5	*7	*12	15
1941-42			STATISTICS NOT AVAILABLE												
1942-43	Windsor Ford	MOHL	15	10	6	16	....	....	....	8	3	0	2	2	4
	New York Rovers	EAHL	....	....	....	....	....	....	....	....	1	0	0	0	0
1943-44	**New York Rangers**	**NHL**	**1**	**0**	**1**	**1**	**0**	**1**	**1**	**0**	....	....	....	....	....
	New York Rovers	EAHL	40	6	10	16	....	....	....	73	11	3	2	5	22
1944-45	Pasadena Panthers	PCHL	STATISTICS NOT AVAILABLE												
1945-46			DID NOT PLAY												
1946-47	Baltimore Orioles	EAHL	50	9	23	32	....	....	....	29	9	2	2	4	8
1947-48	Powaasan Hawks	NBDHL	22	13	9	22	....	....	....	9	....	....	....	....	....
1948-49	Milwaukee–Akron	IHL	18	4	5	9	....	....	....	28	2	0	0	0	0
1949-50	Brantford Nationals	OSBHA	PLAYER/COACH – STATISTICS UNAVAILABLE												
1950-51	Brantford Nationals	OSBHA	DID NOT PLAY – COACHING												
1951-52	Brantford Redmen	OHA-Sr.	13	1	1	2	....	....	....	6	....	....	....	....	....
	NHL Totals		**1**	**0**	**1**	**1**	**0**	**1**	**1**	**0**	....	....	....	....	....

EAHL Second All-Star Team (1944) • EAHL First All-Star Team (1947)

• JANKOWSKI, Lou Louis Casimer

C/RW – R. 6', 180 lbs. b: Regina, Sask., 6/27/1931.

Season	Club	League	GP	G	A	Pts	AG	AA	APts	PIM	GP	G	A	Pts	PIM
1947-48	Hamilton Aerovox	OHA-B	STATISTICS NOT AVAILABLE												
1948-49	Oshawa Generals	OHA-Jr.	34	7	5	12	....	....	....	27	2	0	0	0	0
1949-50	Oshawa Generals	OHA-Jr.	45	20	32	52	....	....	....	31	....	....	....	....	....
1950-51	Oshawa Generals	OHA-Jr.	49	*61	54	115	....	....	....	14	5	6	4	10	2
	Detroit Red Wings	**NHL**	**1**	**0**	**1**	**1**	**0**	**1**	**1**	**0**	....	....	....	....	....
1951-52	Indianapolis Capitols	AHL	51	18	18	36	....	....	....	13	....	....	....	....	....
1952-53	**Detroit Red Wings**	**NHL**	**22**	**1**	**2**	**3**	**1**	**2**	**3**	**0**	**1**	**0**	**0**	**0**	**0**
	Edmonton Flyers	WHL	10	3	1	4	....	....	....	0	....	....	....	....	....
	St. Louis Flyers	AHL	37	14	19	33	....	....	....	4	....	....	....	....	....
1953-54	**Chicago Black Hawks**	**NHL**	**68**	**15**	**13**	**28**	**20**	**16**	**36**	**7**	....	....	....	....	....
1954-55	**Chicago Black Hawks**	**NHL**	**36**	**3**	**2**	**5**	**4**	**2**	**6**	**8**	....	....	....	....	....
	Buffalo Bisons	AHL	11	8	8	16	....	....	....	2	10	0	7	7	0
1955-56	Buffalo Bisons	AHL	62	14	20	34	....	....	....	8	4	1	2	3	0
1956-57	Buffalo Bisons	AHL	64	13	24	37	....	....	....	17	....	....	....	....	....
1957-58	Buffalo Bisons	AHL	59	21	25	46	....	....	....	0	....	....	....	....	....
1958-59	Calgary Stampeders	WHL	54	*45	47	92	....	....	....	13	4	1	1	2	0
1959-60	Calgary Stampeders	WHL	70	*42	42	84	....	....	....	9	....	....	....	....	....
1960-61	Calgary Stampeders	WHL	69	*57	42	99	....	....	....	7	5	3	2	5	2
1961-62	Calgary Stampeders	WHL	64	44	40	84	....	....	....	13	7	2	4	6	0
1962-63	Calgary Stampeders	WHL	67	24	26	50	....	....	....	4	....	....	....	....	....
1963-64	Denver Invaders	WHL	69	*41	44	85	....	....	....	10	6	5	2	7	2
1964-65	Victoria Maple Leafs	WHL	69	30	27	57	....	....	....	16	12	3	2	5	2
1965-66	Victoria Maple Leafs	WHL	68	32	32	64	....	....	....	10	14	4	2	6	8
1966-67	Victoria Maple Leafs	WHL	67	22	37	59	....	....	....	4	....	....	....	....	....
1967-68	Phoenix Roadrunners	WHL	72	25	23	48	....	....	....	6	4	0	0	0	0
1968-69	Denver Spurs	WHL	19	2	3	5	....	....	....	0	....	....	....	....	....
	Amarillo Wranglers	CHL	46	14	11	25	....	....	....	2	....	....	....	....	....
	NHL Totals		**127**	**19**	**18**	**37**	**25**	**21**	**46**	**15**	**1**	**0**	**0**	**0**	**0**

WHL Prairie Division First All-Star Team (1959) • WHL First All-Star Team (1960, 1961, 1964) • Won Leader Cup (WHL - MVP) (1961) • WHL Second All-Star Team (1962) • Won Fred J. Hume Cup (WHL Most Gentlemanly Player) (1964)

Rights traded to **Detroit** by **Cleveland** (AHL) with the rights to Bill Dineen for Bob Bailey and John Bailey, June, 1951. Traded to **Chicago** by **Detroit** with Larry Zeidel and Larry Wilson for cash, August 12, 1953. Signed as a free agent by **Denver** (WHL), September, 1963. Claimed by **Toronto** from **Toronto** (Denver-WHL) in Reverse Draft, June 8, 1964. Traded to **Phoenix** (WHL) by **Toronto** (Victoria-WHL) for cash, September, 1967. Traded to **Denver** (WHL) by **Phoenix** (WHL) for cash, July, 1968.

• JARRETT, Doug — *see page 1221*

• JARRETT, Gary — *see page 1221*

• JARVIS, Jim "Bud"

LW – L. 5'6", 165 lbs. b: Fort William, Ont., 12/7/1907.

Season	Club	League	GP	G	A	Pts	AG	AA	APts	PIM	GP	G	A	Pts	PIM
1927-28	Port Arthur Ports	TBSHL	20	13	7	20	....	....	....	14	....	....	....	....	....
1928-29	Port Arthur Ports	TBSHL	17	13	5	18	....	....	....	10	2	1	1	2	0
	Port Arthur Ports	Al-Cup	7	4	4	8	....	....	....	6	....	....	....	....	....
1929-30	**Pittsburgh Pirates**	**NHL**	**44**	**11**	**8**	**19**	**16**	**19**	**35**	**32**	....	....	....	....	....
1930-31	**Philadelphia Quakers**	**NHL**	**44**	**5**	**7**	**12**	**10**	**21**	**31**	**30**	....	....	....	....	....
1931-32	Springfield Indians	Can-Am	39	4	5	9	....	....	....	24	....	....	....	....	....
1932-33	Buffalo Bisons	IHL	37	11	6	17	....	....	....	14	6	0	3	3	0
1933-34	Buffalo Bisons	IHL	44	12	3	15	....	....	....	25	6	0	3	3	2
1934-35	Buffalo Bisons	IHL	44	8	11	19	....	....	....	16	....	....	....	....	....
1935-36	Buffalo Bisons	IHL	48	13	9	22	....	....	....	20	5	0	1	1	0
1936-37	Buffalo Bisons	IAHL	10	3	0	3	....	....	....	6	....	....	....	....	....
	Toronto Maple Leafs	**NHL**	**24**	**1**	**0**	**1**	**2**	**0**	**2**	**0**	....	....	....	....	....
	Syracuse Stars	IAHL	12	1	1	2	....	....	....	24	7	0	0	0	7
1937-38	Providence Reds	IAHL	47	6	6	12	....	....	....	4	7	1	1	2	0
1938-39	Providence Reds	IAHL	51	2	16	18	....	....	....	14	5	0	0	0	0
1939-40	Providence Reds	IAHL	27	9	15	24	....	....	....	6	....	....	....	....	....
	Hershey Bears	IAHL	23	9	12	21	....	....	....	4	6	1	0	1	2
1940-41	Geraldton Gold Miners	GBHL	19	4	4	8	....	....	....	4	4	1	0	1	0
1941-42			MILITARY SERVICE												
1942-43			MILITARY SERVICE												
1943-44	Hershey Bears	AHL	31	8	14	22	....	....	....	2	7	1	1	2	0
	NHL Totals		**112**	**17**	**15**	**32**	**28**	**40**	**68**	**62**	....	....	....	....	....

Signed as a free agent by **Pittsburgh**, October 31, 1929. Transferred to **Philadelphia** after **Pittsburgh** franchise relocated, October 18, 1930. Claimed by **NY Rangers** from **Philadelphia** in Dispersal Draft, September 26, 1931. Signed as a free agent by **Toronto** (Syracuse-IAHL) after **Buffalo** (IAHL) franchise folded, December 9, 1936. Traded to **Hershey** (AHL) by **Providence** (AHL) for Clarence Steele, January 17, 1940. • Re-instated as an amateur, December, 1940.

• JEFFREY, Larry — *see page 1223*

• JENKINS, Roger Joseph Roger "Broadway"

RW/D – R. 5'11", 173 lbs. b: Appleton, WI, 11/18/1911.

Season	Club	League	GP	G	A	Pts	AG	AA	APts	PIM	GP	G	A	Pts	PIM
1929-30	Edmonton Imperials	EJrHL	13	8	3	11	....	....	....	14	....	....	....	....	....
1930-31	**Chicago Black Hawks**	**NHL**	**10**	**0**	**1**	**1**	**0**	**3**	**3**	**2**	**3**	**0**	**0**	**0**	**0**
	London Tecumsehs	IHL	8	0	0	0	....	....	....	6	....	....	....	....	....
	Toronto Maple Leafs	**NHL**	**21**	**0**	**0**	**0**	**0**	**0**	**0**	**12**	....	....	....	....	....

Season	Club	League	GP	G	A	Pts	AG	AA	APts	PIM	GP	G	A	Pts	PIM
			REGULAR SEASON								PLAYOFFS				
1931-32	Bronx Tigers	Can-Am	39	9	7	16	....	....	....	66	2	0	0	0	6
1932-33	Chicago Black Hawks	NHL	46	3	10	13	5	21	26	42	....	....	....	....	....
♦1933-34	Chicago Black Hawks	NHL	48	2	2	4	3	4	7	37	8	0	0	0	0
1934-35	Montreal Canadiens	NHL	45	4	6	10	7	10	17	63	2	1	0	1	2
1935-36	Boston Bruins	NHL	40	2	6	8	4	11	15	51	2	0	1	1	2
	Boston Cubs	Can-Am	5	2	2	4	....	....	....	9	....	....	....	....	....
1936-37	Montreal Canadiens	NHL	10	0	0	0	0	0	0	8	....	....	....	....	....
	Montreal Maroons	NHL	1	0	0	0	0	0	0	0	....	....	....	....	....
	New York Americans	NHL	26	1	4	5	2	7	9	6	....	....	....	....	....
♦1937-38	Chicago Black Hawks	NHL	37	1	8	9	2	13	15	26	10	0	*6	6	8
1938-39	Chicago Black Hawks	NHL	14	1	1	2	2	2	4	2	....	....	....	....	....
	New York Americans	NHL	27	1	1	2	2	2	4	4	....	....	....	....	....
1939-40	Springfield Indians	AHL	50	8	18	26	....	....	....	29	2	0	0	0	0
1940-41	Hershey Bears	AHL	56	5	19	24	....	....	....	81	10	2	1	3	14
1941-42	Hershey Bears	AHL	55	9	28	37	....	....	....	110	10	3	5	8	12
1942-43	Hershey Bears	AHL	56	10	33	43	....	....	....	90	6	0	1	1	2
	Washington Lions	AHL	1	0	0	0	....	....	....	0	....	....	....	....	....
1943-44	Seattle Ironmen	PCHL	16	16	19	35	....	....	....	45	2	1	3	4	2
	Portland Oilers	PCHL	....	....	....	....	....	....	....	....	4	2	3	5	12
1944-45	Seattle Ironmen	PCHL	DID NOT PLAY – COACHING												
1945-46	Seattle Ironmen	PCHL	55	12	20	32	....	....	....	69	3	0	0	0	2
1946-47	Tacoma Rockets	PCHL	55	9	22	31	....	....	....	40	....	....	....	....	....
1947-48	Tacoma Rockets	PCHL	58	6	24	30	....	....	....	101	5	0	2	2	6
	NHL Totals		**325**	**15**	**39**	**54**	**27**	**73**	**100**	**253**	**25**	**1**	**7**	**8**	**12**

AHL First All-Star Team (1943)

Signed as a free agent by **Chicago**, October 28, 1930. Loaned to **Toronto** by **Chicago**, December 4, 1930. • Returned to **Chicago** by **Toronto**, February 3, 1931. Traded to **Montreal Canadiens** by **Chicago** with Leroy Goldsworthy and Lionel Conacher for Lorne Chabot, Howie Morenz and Marty Burke, October 3, 1934. Traded to **Boston** by **Montreal Canadiens** for Jean Pusie, Walt Buswell and cash, July 13, 1935. Traded to **Montreal Canadiens** by **Boston** with Babe Siebert for Leroy Goldsworthy, Sammy McManus and $10,000, September 10, 1936. Signed as a free agent by **Montreal Maroons** after securing release from **Montreal Canadiens**, December 17, 1936. Loaned to **NY Americans** by **Montreal Maroons** for cash, January 1, 1937. Signed as a free agent by **Chicago** after securing release from **Montreal Maroons**, November 20, 1937. Signed as a free agent by **NY Americans**, January 1, 1939. Traded to **Springfield** (IAHL) by **NY Americans** for cash, October 2, 1939.

• JENNINGS, Bill Joseph William

RW – R. 5'10", 165 lbs. b: Toronto, Ont., 6/28/1917.

Season	Club	League	GP	G	A	Pts	AG	AA	APts	PIM	GP	G	A	Pts	PIM
1934-35	West Toronto Nationals	TJrHL	12	6	0	6	....	....	....	22	....	....	....	....	....
1935-36	Toronto Dominions	TIHL	9	5	2	7	....	....	....	18	....	....	....	....	....
	West Toronto Nationals	OHA-Jr.	8	7	4	11	....	....	....	0	5	1	3	4	*17
	West Toronto Nationals	M-Cup	12	9	5	14	....	....	....	19	....	....	....	....	....
1936-37	Toronto Dominions	TIHL	8	3	*5	8	....	....	....	10	8	2	1	3	15
1937-38	Toronto Goodyears	TIHL	14	9	8	17	....	....	....	16	4	0	0	0	2
	Toronto Goodyears	Al-Cup	4	0	0	0	....	....	....	4	....	....	....	....	....
1938-39	Earls Court Rangers	Ln-Cup	....	1	1	2	....	....	....	....	....	....	....	....	....
	Earls Court Rangers	Britain	....	12	11	23	....	....	....	....	....	....	....	....	....
	Earls Court Rangers	Nat-Tmt	....	5	0	5	....	....	....	....	....	....	....	....	....
1939-40	Detroit Holtzbaugh	MOHL	35	24	20	44	....	....	....	38	11	6	1	7	29
1940-41	Detroit Red Wings	NHL	12	1	5	6	2	7	9	2	9	2	2	4	0
	Indianapolis Capitals	AHL	40	16	17	33	....	....	....	20	....	....	....	....	....
1941-42	Detroit Red Wings	NHL	16	2	1	3	3	1	4	6	....	....	....	....	....
	Indianapolis Capitals	AHL	34	9	25	34	....	....	....	10	10	4	2	6	4
1942-43	Detroit Red Wings	NHL	8	3	3	6	3	3	6	2	....	....	....	....	....
	Indianapolis Capitals	AHL	49	23	33	56	....	....	....	5	7	2	5	7	2
1943-44	Detroit Red Wings	NHL	33	6	11	17	5	10	15	10	4	0	0	0	0
1944-45	Boston Bruins	NHL	39	20	13	33	20	15	35	25	7	2	2	4	6
	Indianapolis Capitals	AHL	3	1	1	2	....	....	....	....	....	....	....	....	....
1945-46	Hershey Bears	AHL	37	17	14	31	....	....	....	12	....	....	....	....	....
	St. Louis Flyers	AHL	17	7	8	15	....	....	....	2	....	....	....	....	....
	NHL Totals		**108**	**32**	**33**	**65**	**33**	**36**	**69**	**45**	**20**	**4**	**4**	**8**	**6**

Signed as a free agent by **Detroit**, October 16, 1940. Traded to **Boston** by **Detroit** for Pete Leswick, October 30, 1944. Traded to **Chicago** (St. Louis-AHL) by **Boston** (Hershey-AHL) for Norm McAtee, February 5, 1946.

• JEREMIAH, Ed Edward John USHOF

RW/D – R. 5'9", 160 lbs. b: Worcester, MA, 11/4/1905 d: 8/15/1967.

Season	Club	League	GP	G	A	Pts	AG	AA	APts	PIM	GP	G	A	Pts	PIM
1925-26	Hebron Academy	H.S.	STATISTICS NOT AVAILABLE												
1926-27	Dartmouth University	Ivy	STATISTICS NOT AVAILABLE												
1927-28	Dartmouth College	Ivy	4	5	0	5	....	....	....	....	....	....	....	....	....
1928-29	Dartmouth College	Ivy	17	2	0	2	....	....	....	....	....	....	....	....	....
1929-30	Dartmouth College	Ivy	13	4	0	4	....	....	....	....	....	....	....	....	....
1930-31	New Haven Eagles	Can-Am	36	3	5	8	....	....	....	42	....	....	....	....	....
1931-32	New York Americans	NHL	9	0	1	1	0	2	2	0	....	....	....	....	....
	New Haven Eagles	Can-Am	13	0	8	8	....	....	....	15	....	....	....	....	....
	Boston Bruins	NHL	6	0	0	0	0	0	0	0	....	....	....	....	....
	Boston Cubs	Can-Am	15	2	0	2	....	....	....	6	....	....	....	....	....
1932-33	New Haven Eagles	Can-Am	17	2	1	3	....	....	....	6	....	....	....	....	....
1933-34	Philadelphia Arrows	Can-Am	37	2	2	4	....	....	....	55	2	0	0	0	2
1934-35	Cleveland Falcons	IHL	10	0	1	1	....	....	....	0	2	0	0	0	2
1935-36	Boston Olympics	USAHA	DID NOT PLAY – COACHING												
	NHL Totals		**15**	**0**	**1**	**1**	**0**	**2**	**2**	**0**	....	....	....	....	....

Won Lester Patrick Trophy (1969)

Traded to **Boston** by **NY Americans** for cash, February 1, 1932.

• JERWA, Frank Frank Ludwig

LW/D – L. 6'1", 179 lbs. b: Bankhead, Alta., 3/15/1909 Deceased.

Season	Club	League	GP	G	A	Pts	AG	AA	APts	PIM	GP	G	A	Pts	PIM
1926/28	Canmore Miners	ASHL	STATISTICS NOT AVAILABLE												
1928-29	Regina Pats	S-SSHL	5	4	*2	6	....	....	....	4	....	....	....	....	....
	Vancouver Lions	PCHL	5	3	0	3	....	....	....	4	1	0	0	0	0
1929-30	Vancouver Lions	PCHL	36	10	5	15	....	....	....	42	4	0	0	0	2
1930-31	Vancouver Lions	PCHL	32	11	5	16	....	....	....	54	4	1	1	2	12
1931-32	Boston Bruins	NHL	24	4	5	9	7	11	18	14	....	....	....	....	....
	Boston Cubs	Can-Am	22	6	14	20	....	....	....	50	....	....	....	....	....
1932-33	Boston Bruins	NHL	31	3	4	7	5	8	13	23	....	....	....	....	....
	Boston Cubs	Can-Am	19	5	11	16	....	....	....	34	7	4	1	5	12
1933-34	Boston Bruins	NHL	5	0	0	0	0	0	0	2	....	....	....	....	....
	Boston Cubs	Can-Am	34	12	19	31	....	....	....	75	5	1	2	3	22
1934-35	Boston Bruins	NHL	5	0	0	0	0	0	0	0	....	....	....	....	....
	Boston Cubs	Can-Am	25	24	12	36	....	....	....	14	....	....	....	....	....
	St. Louis Eagles	NHL	16	4	7	11	7	12	19	14	....	....	....	....	....
	Vancouver Lions	L-W-S	1	0	0	0	....	....	....	0	....	....	....	....	....
1935-36	New Haven Eagles	Can-Am	45	19	21	40	....	....	....	41	....	....	....	....	....
1936-37	Springfield Indians	IAHL	35	4	5	9	....	....	....	50	5	1	0	1	2
1937-38	Seattle Seahawks	PCHL	40	12	19	31	....	....	....	29	4	0	2	2	4
1938-39	Seattle Seahawks	PCHL	47	14	28	42	....	....	....	38	7	0	0	0	0
1939-40	Vancouver Lions	PCHL	22	5	8	13	....	....	....	36	5	2	0	2	*12
1940-41	Vancouver Lions	PCHL	44	27	20	47	....	....	....	33	6	1	1	2	*22
	NHL Totals		**81**	**11**	**16**	**27**	**19**	**31**	**50**	**53**	....	....	....	....	....

• Brother of Joe • Can-Am Second All-Star Team (1936)

Traded to **Boston** by **Vancouver** (PCHL) for cash, April 15, 1931. Traded to **St. Louis** by **Boston** for Gerry Shannon, January 10, 1935. Loaned to **Vancouver** by **St. Louis** for Little World Series, April, 1935. Traded to **Springfield** (AHL) by **New Haven** for cash, June 4, 1936.

• JERWA, Joe Joseph Charles

D – L. 6'2", 185 lbs. b: Bankhead, Alta., 1/20/1907 Deceased.

Season	Club	League	GP	G	A	Pts	AG	AA	APts	PIM	GP	G	A	Pts	PIM
1926/28	Canmore Miners	ASHL	STATISTICS NOT AVAILABLE												
1928-29	Vancouver Lions	NWHL	35	8	5	13	....	....	....	72	3	0	1	1	6
1929-30	Vancouver Lions	NWHL	35	12	6	18	....	....	....	76	4	1	0	1	6
1930-31	New York Rangers	NHL	33	4	7	11	8	21	29	72	4	0	0	0	4
	Springfield Indians	Can-Am	9	8	0	8	....	....	....	26	....	....	....	....	....
1931-32	Boston Bruins	NHL	11	0	0	0	0	0	0	8	....	....	....	....	....
	Boston Cubs	Can-Am	31	7	15	22	....	....	....	116	5	2	*2	4	*27
1932-33	Boston Cubs	Can-Am	39	10	18	28	....	....	....	108	7	4	2	6	*22
1933-34	Boston Bruins	NHL	2	0	0	0	0	0	0	2	....	....	....	....	....
	Boston Cubs	Can-Am	36	4	8	12	....	....	....	*101	5	2	0	2	*28
1934-35	Boston Cubs	Can-Am	44	21	17	38	....	....	....	95	3	1	*5	*6	*20
1935-36	New York Americans	NHL	47	9	12	21	17	23	40	65	5	2	3	5	2
1936-37	Boston Bruins	NHL	26	3	5	8	5	9	14	30	....	....	....	....	....
	New York Americans	NHL	20	6	8	14	10	15	25	27	....	....	....	....	....
1937-38	New York Americans	NHL	48	3	14	17	5	23	28	53	6	0	0	0	8
1938-39	New York Americans	NHL	47	4	12	16	7	19	26	52	2	0	0	0	2
1939-40	Cleveland Barons	IAHL	49	4	10	14	....	....	....	61	....	....	....	....	....
1940-41	Cleveland Barons	AHL	56	13	22	35	....	....	....	20	4	4	0	4	6
1941-42	Cleveland Barons	AHL	33	1	8	9	....	....	....	18	....	....	....	....	....
	NHL Totals		**234**	**29**	**58**	**87**	**52**	**110**	**162**	**309**	**17**	**2**	**3**	**5**	**16**

• Brother of Frank

Traded to **NY Rangers** by **Vancouver** (PCHL) with Red Beattie for $25,000, May 6, 1930. Traded to **Boston** by **NY Rangers** for Norm Gainor, August 25, 1931. Traded to **NY Americans** by **Boston** with Nels Stewart for cash, September 28, 1935. • Rights returned to **Boston** by **NY Americans** after NY Americans failed to complete purchase agreement, May 27, 1936. Traded to **NY Americans** by **Boston** for the loan of Al Shields and future considerations (the rights to Terry Reardon and Tom Cooper, October 17, 1937), January 25, 1937. Traded to **Cleveland** (IAHL) by **NY Americans** for cash, October 12, 1939.

• JOANETTE, Rosario "Kitouette"

C – R. 5'8", 165 lbs. b: Valleyfield, Que., 7/27/1919 d: 10/9/1998.

Season	Club	League	GP	G	A	Pts	AG	AA	APts	PIM	GP	G	A	Pts	PIM
1939-40	Valleyfield Braves	QPHL	26	3	8	11	....	....	....	2	4	2	1	3	6
1940-41	Valleyfield Braves	MCHL	37	28	37	65	....	....	....	18	3	0	0	0	2
1941-42	Valleyfield V's	MCHL	26	17	23	40	....	....	....	32	7	4	4	8	0
1942-43	Valleyfield Braves	MCHL	STATISTICS NOT AVAILABLE												
1943-44	Valleyfield Braves	MCHL	STATISTICS NOT AVAILABLE												
1944-45	Montreal Canadiens	NHL	2	0	1	1	0	1	1	4	....	....	....	....	....
	Valleyfield Braves	QPHL	37	*45	*56	*101	....	....	....	30	11	6	7	13	8
	Valleyfield Braves	Al-Cup	3	1	0	1	....	....	....	0	....	....	....	....	....
1945-46	Valleyfield Braves	QSHL	40	23	25	48	....	....	....	17	....	....	....	....	....
	Shawinigan Cataracts	QSHL	....	....	....	....	....	....	....	....	4	2	1	3	11
1946-47	Valleyfield Braves	QSHL	39	13	22	35	....	....	....	41	....	....	....	....	....
	Baltimore Clippers	EAHL	....	....	....	....	....	....	....	....	9	2	1	3	11
1947-48	Valleyfield Braves	QSHL	44	20	37	57	....	....	....	23	6	6	6	12	2
1948-49	Valleyfield Braves	QSHL	51	23	33	56	....	....	....	11	4	0	2	2	0
1949-50	Valleyfield Braves	QSHL	59	23	50	73	....	....	....	22	5	1	4	5	4
1950-51	Valleyfield Braves	QMHL	58	30	42	72	....	....	....	18	16	*13	6	19	8
	Valleyfield Braves	Alx-Cup	11	5	9	14	....	....	....	2	....	....	....	....	....
1951-52	Valleyfield Braves	QMHL	55	18	31	49	....	....	....	14	6	0	4	4	0
1952-53	Valleyfield Braves	QMHL	58	18	34	52	....	....	....	6	4	0	1	1	2
1953-54	Valleyfield Braves	QHL	60	13	16	29	....	....	....	10	7	2	4	6	0
1954-55	Valleyfield Braves	QHL	53	13	37	50	....	....	....	11	....	....	....	....	....
1955-56	Trois-Rivieres Lions	QHL	32	2	10	12	....	....	....	2	....	....	....	....	....
	Cornwall Colts	EOHL	16	21	20	41	....	....	....	18	7	2	8	10	18
1956-57	Cornwall Chevies	EOHL	49	22	31	53	....	....	....	20	6	0	2	2	4
	NHL Totals		**2**	**0**	**1**	**1**	**0**	**1**	**1**	**4**	....	....	....	....	....

• JOHANSEN, Bill William Odd

C/RW – R. 6', 163 lbs. b: Port Arthur, Ont., 7/27/1928.

Season	Club	League	GP	G	A	Pts	AG	AA	APts	PIM	GP	G	A	Pts	PIM
1945-46	Fort William Rangers	TBJHL	8	1	5	6	....	....	....	4	....	....	....	....	....
1946-47	Fort William Rangers	TBJHL	6	7	7	14	....	....	....	2	3	1	2	3	2
1947-48	Fort William Rangers	TBJHL	9	14	5	19	....	....	....	0	2	1	0	1	2
	Port Arthur Bruins	M-Cup	13	3	4	7	....	....	....	4	....	....	....	....	....
1948-49	Toronto Marlboros	OHA-Sr.	36	13	12	25	....	....	....	8	10	2	6	8	2
	Toronto Marlboros	Al-Cup	13	4	8	12	....	....	....	4	....	....	....	....	....
1949-50	Toronto Maple Leafs	NHL	1	0	0	0	0	0	0	0	....	....	....	....	....
	Toronto Marlboros	OHA-Sr.	41	22	33	55	....	....	....	9	14	6	6	12	4
	Toronto Marlboros	Al-Cup	17	8	17	25	....	....	....	2	....	....	....	....	....
1950-51	Toronto Marlboros	OMHL	32	14	24	38	....	....	....	8	3	1	2	3	0
1951-52	Ottawa Senators	QMHL	54	19	30	49	....	....	....	6	7	1	2	3	0
1952-53	Ottawa Senators	QMHL	60	16	24	40	....	....	....	19	7	0	1	1	2
1953-54	Ottawa Senators	QHL	67	16	35	51	....	....	....	23	22	6	9	15	8
1954-55	Ottawa Senators	QHL	27	5	12	17	....	....	....	6	....	....	....	....	....
	Providence Reds	AHL	23	5	8	13	....	....	....	10	....	....	....	....	....
1955-56	Providence Reds	AHL	53	8	27	35	....	....	....	14	9	3	4	7	4
1956-57	Providence Reds	AHL	49	7	18	25	....	....	....	14	5	0	1	1	2
1957-58	Vancouver Canucks	WHL	61	17	25	42	....	....	....	10	6	2	3	5	2
1958-59	Winnipeg Warriors	WHL	62	20	29	49	....	....	....	12	7	2	2	4	2
1959-60	Winnipeg Warriors	WHL	58	14	22	36	....	....	....	4	....	....	....	....	....

Season	Club	League	GP	G	A	Pts	AG	AA	APts	PIM	GP	G	A	Pts	PIM
			REGULAR SEASON								PLAYOFFS				
1960-61	Victoria Cougars	WHL	67	10	21	31	....	....	....	18	5	2	1	3	0
1961-62	Spokane Comets	WHL	67	14	23	37	....	....	....	8	8	2	1	3	0
1962-63	Spokane Comets	WHL	69	12	24	36	....	....	....	4	....	....	....	....	....
1963-64	Charlotte Checkers	EHL	27	16	10	26	....	....	....	6	....	....	....	....	....
1964-65	New York Rovers	EHL	62	20	33	53	....	....	....	4	....	....	....	....	....
1965/68			STATISTICS NOT AVAILABLE												
1968-69	Fort William Beavers	TBSHL	13	7	12	19	....	....	....	6	....	....	....	....	....
1969-70	Thunder Bay Beavers	TBSHL	STATISTICS NOT AVAILABLE												
	Thunder Bay Beavers	Al-Cup	4	1	1	2	....	....	....	0	....	....	....	....	....
	NHL Totals		**1**	**0**	**0**	**0**	**0**	**0**	**0**	**0**	....	....	....	....	....

• Known as "Johnson" during his playing career • Father of Trevor

Claimed by **Providence** (AHL) from **Toronto** (Ottawa-QHL) in Inter-League Draft, June 10, 1953. Traded to **Toronto** by **Providence** (AHL) for cash, October, 1953. Traded to **Providence** (AHL) by **Toronto** for cash, December 21, 1954. Rights transferred to **Toronto** after NHL club purchased **Spokane** (WHL) franchise, June 4, 1963.

• JOHNS, Don — see page 1228

• JOHNSON, Al Allan Edmund

RW/C – R. 5'11", 180 lbs. b: Winnipeg, Man., 3/30/1935.

Season	Club	League	GP	G	A	Pts	AG	AA	APts	PIM	GP	G	A	Pts	PIM
1951-52	St. Boniface Canadiens	MAHA	10	8	15	23	....	....	....	....	....	....	....	....	....
	St. Boniface Canadiens	MJHL	1	0	0	0	....	....	....	2	....	....	....	....	....
1952-53	St. Boniface Canadiens	MJHL	22	4	12	16	....	....	....	2	7	2	2	4	2
	St. Boniface Canadiens	M-Cup	17	4	7	11	....	....	....	8	....	....	....	....	....
1953-54	St. Boniface Canadiens	MJHL	36	13	*31	44	....	....	....	40	10	8	10	18	34
	St. Boniface Canadiens	M-Cup	8	3	2	5	....	....	....	8	....	....	....	....	....
1954-55	Trois-Rivieres Flambeaux	QJHL	44	14	17	31	....	....	....	23	10	5	5	10	2
	Montreal Royals	QHL	2	0	1	1	....	....	....	2	....	....	....	....	....
1955-56	Souris Elks	Big-6	28	33	30	63	....	....	....	18	....	....	....	....	....
	Winnipeg Warriors	WHL	2	0	0	0	....	....	....	0	....	....	....	....	....
	Winnipeg Maroons	Al-Cup	9	2	6	8	....	....	....	2	....	....	....	....	....
1956-57	**Montreal Canadiens**	**NHL**	**2**	**0**	**1**	**1**	**0**	**1**	**1**	**2**	....	....	....	....	....
	Cincinnati Mohawks	IHL	56	29	29	58	....	....	....	36	7	2	2	4	2
1957-58	Shawinigan Cataracts	QHL	57	15	28	43	....	....	....	18	14	8	10	18	2
1958-59	Spokane Spokes	WHL	68	30	33	63	....	....	....	28	4	0	0	0	7
1959-60	Spokane Spokes	WHL	69	29	27	56	....	....	....	28	....	....	....	....	....
1960-61	**Detroit Red Wings**	**NHL**	**70**	**16**	**21**	**37**	**18**	**20**	**38**	**14**	**11**	**2**	**2**	**4**	**6**
1961-62	**Detroit Red Wings**	**NHL**	**31**	**5**	**6**	**11**	**6**	**6**	**12**	**14**	....	....	....	....	....
	Hershey Bears	AHL	40	15	25	40	....	....	....	14	7	4	2	6	2
1962-63	**Detroit Red Wings**	**NHL**	**2**	**0**	**0**	**0**	**0**	**0**	**0**	**0**	....	....	....	....	....
	Pittsburgh Hornets	AHL	58	15	19	34	....	....	....	24	....	....	....	....	....
1963-64	Winnipeg Maroons	SSHL	6	6	4	10	....	....	....	2	....	....	....	....	....
	Winnipeg Maroons	Al-Cup	13	8	10	18	....	....	....	12	....	....	....	....	....
1964-65	Winnipeg Maroons	SSHL	6	6	8	14	....	....	....	6	....	....	....	....	....
	Canada	WEC-A	7	4	2	6	....	....	....	6	....	....	....	....	....
1965-66	Canada	Nat-Tm	STATISTICS NOT AVAILABLE												
1966-67			OUT OF HOCKEY – RETIRED												
1967-68	Fort Worth Wings	CPHL	46	23	27	50	....	....	....	27	....	....	....	....	....
1968-69	Denver Spurs	WHL	71	27	22	49	....	....	....	10	....	....	....	....	....
	NHL Totals		**105**	**21**	**28**	**49**	**24**	**27**	**51**	**30**	**11**	**2**	**2**	**4**	**6**

WHL Coast Division Second All-Star Team (1959) • WHL First All-Star Team (1960)

Claimed by **Detroit** from **Montreal** (Spokane-WHL) in Inter-League Draft, June, 1960.

• JOHNSON, Ching Ivan Wilfred HHOF

D – L. 5'11", 210 lbs. b: Winnipeg, Man., 12/7/1898 d: 6/17/1979.

Season	Club	League	GP	G	A	Pts	AG	AA	APts	PIM	GP	G	A	Pts	PIM
1919-20	Winnipeg Monarchs	WJrHL	7	6	3	9	....	....	....	10	....	....	....	....	....
1920-21	Eveleth Rangers	USAHA	STATISTICS NOT AVAILABLE												
1921-22	Eveleth Rangers	USAHA	STATISTICS NOT AVAILABLE												
1922-23	Eveleth Rangers	AHA	20	4	0	4	....	....	....	26	....	....	....	....	....
1923-24	Minneapolis Millers	USAHA	20	9	3	12	....	....	....	34	....	....	....	....	....
1924-25	Minneapolis Rockets	USAHA	40	8	0	8	....	....	....	43	....	....	....	....	....
1925-26	Minneapolis Millers	CHL	38	14	5	19	....	....	....	92	3	2	0	2	6
1926-27	**New York Rangers**	**NHL**	**27**	**3**	**2**	**5**	**5**	**10**	**15**	**66**	**2**	**0**	**0**	**0**	**8**
♦1927-28	**New York Rangers**	**NHL**	**42**	**10**	**6**	**16**	**20**	**34**	**54**	**146**	**9**	**1**	**1**	**2**	***46**
1928-29	**New York Rangers**	**NHL**	**8**	**0**	**0**	**0**	**0**	**0**	**0**	**14**	**6**	**0**	**0**	**0**	**26**
1929-30	**New York Rangers**	**NHL**	**30**	**3**	**3**	**6**	**4**	**7**	**11**	**82**	**4**	**0**	**0**	**0**	**14**
1930-31	**New York Rangers**	**NHL**	**44**	**2**	**6**	**8**	**4**	**18**	**22**	**77**	**4**	**1**	**0**	**1**	**17**
1931-32	**New York Rangers**	**NHL**	**47**	**3**	**10**	**13**	**5**	**22**	**27**	**106**	**7**	**2**	**0**	**2**	***24**
♦1932-33	**New York Rangers**	**NHL**	**48**	**8**	**9**	**17**	**14**	**19**	**33**	**127**	**8**	**1**	**0**	**1**	**14**
1933-34	**New York Rangers**	**NHL**	**48**	**2**	**6**	**8**	**3**	**13**	**16**	**86**	**2**	**0**	**0**	**0**	**4**
1934-35	**New York Rangers**	**NHL**	**29**	**2**	**3**	**5**	**3**	**5**	**8**	**34**	**4**	**0**	**0**	**0**	**2**
1935-36	**New York Rangers**	**NHL**	**47**	**5**	**3**	**8**	**10**	**6**	**16**	**58**	....	....	....	....	....
1936-37	**New York Rangers**	**NHL**	**35**	**0**	**0**	**0**	**0**	**0**	**0**	**2**	**9**	**0**	**1**	**1**	**4**
1937-38	**New York Americans**	**NHL**	**31**	**0**	**0**	**0**	**0**	**0**	**0**	**10**	**6**	**0**	**0**	**0**	**2**
1938-39	Minneapolis Millers	AHA	47	2	9	11	....	....	....	60	4	0	2	2	0
1939-40	Minneapolis Millers	AHA	48	0	4	4	....	....	....	26	3	0	0	0	2
1940-41	Marquette Ironmen	NMHL	PLAYER/COACH – STATISTICS UNAVAILABLE												
1941/43	Washington Lions	AHL	DID NOT PLAY – COACHING												
1943-44	Hollywood Wolves	PCHL	STATISTICS NOT AVAILABLE												
	NHL Totals		**436**	**38**	**48**	**86**	**68**	**134**	**202**	**808**	**61**	**5**	**2**	**7**	**161**

USAHA First All-Star Team (1924) • CHL First All-Star Team (1926) • NHL Second All-Star Team (1931, 1934) • NHL First All-Star Team (1932, 1933) • AHA Second All-Star Team (1939) • Played in NHL All-Star Game (1934)

Signed as a free agent by **NY Rangers**, September 2, 1926. • Missed majority of 1928-29 season recovering from ankle injury suffered in game vs. Montreal Maroons, December 1, 1928. Signed as a free agent by **NY Americans**, November 19, 1937.

• JOHNSON, Earl Earl Oswald "Ching"

LW – L. 6', 185 lbs. b: Fort Frances, Ont., 6/28/1931.

Season	Club	League	GP	G	A	Pts	AG	AA	APts	PIM	GP	G	A	Pts	PIM
1948-49	Windsor Spitfires	OHA-Jr.	54	39	29	68	....	....	....		....	....	....	....	....
1949-50	Windsor Spitfires	OHA-Jr.	42	18	18	36	....	....	....	6	2	1	0	1	0
	Detroit Hettche	IHL	39	18	16	34	....	....	....		....	....	....	....	....
1950-51	Windsor Spitfires	OHA-Jr.	54	39	28	67	....	....	....	19	8	2	3	5	0
1951-52	Edmonton Flyers	PCHL	69	37	34	71	....	....	....	19	4	0	1	1	2
1952-53	Edmonton Flyers	WHL	70	26	34	60	....	....	....	26	15	10	7	17	20
1953-54	**Detroit Red Wings**	**NHL**	**1**	**0**	**0**	**0**	**0**	**0**	**0**	**0**	....	....	....	....	....
	Edmonton Flyers	WHL	19	5	0	5	....	....	....	6	....	....	....	....	....
	Sherbrooke Saints	QHL	50	18	22	40	....	....	....	41	5	4	2	6	2
1954-55	Quebec Aces	QHL	21	12	6	18	....	....	....	18	....	....	....	....	....
	Vancouver Canucks	WHL	45	16	19	35	....	....	....	33	5	2	1	3	2
1955-56	Springfield Indians	AHL	7	4	2	6	....	....	....	6	....	....	....	....	....
	Vancouver–Edmonton	WHL	42	15	10	25	....	....	....	44	3	0	1	1	2
1956-57	Vancouver Canucks	WHL	54	17	14	31	....	....	....	49	....	....	....	....	....
	Providence Reds	AHL	9	2	4	6	....	....	....	6	....	....	....	....	....
1957-58	Trois-Rivieres Lions	QHL	50	14	8	22	....	....	....	6	....	....	....	....	....
1958-59	Spokane Comets	WHL	67	40	32	72	....	....	....	30	4	0	1	1	4
1959-60	Spokane Comets	WHL	69	31	31	62	....	....	....	20	....	....	....	....	....
1960-61	Spokane Comets	WHL	70	32	30	62	....	....	....	40	4	0	0	0	0
1961-62	Pittsburgh Hornets	AHL	18	3	3	6	....	....	....	2	....	....	....	....	....
	Los Angeles Blades	WHL	31	9	8	17	....	....	....	0	....	....	....	....	....
1962-63	New Haven Blades	EHL	53	20	25	45	....	....	....	11	....	....	....	....	....
1963-64	Spokane Jets	WIHL	38	41	30	71	....	....	....	4	12	*8	8	*16	0
	NHL Totals		**1**	**0**	**0**	**0**	**0**	**0**	**0**	**0**	....	....	....	....	....

WHL Coast Division Second All-Star Team (1959)

Loaned to **Quebec** (QHL) by **NY Rangers** for cash, October, 1954. Returned to **NY Rangers** from **Quebec** (QHL) with cash for the trade of Camille Henry to Providence (AHL), December 5, 1954.

• JOHNSON, Jim — see page 1230

• JOHNSON, Norm Norman Bruce

C – L. 5'10", 170 lbs. b: Moose Jaw, Sask., 11/27/1932.

Season	Club	League	GP	G	A	Pts	AG	AA	APts	PIM	GP	G	A	Pts	PIM
1949-50	Moose Jaw Canucks	WCJHL	3	0	0	0	....	....	....	0	....	....	....	....	....
1950-51	Moose Jaw Canucks	WCJHL	39	6	9	15	....	....	....	24	....	....	....	....	....
1951-52	Moose Jaw Canucks	WCJHL	44	16	13	29	....	....	....	96	....	....	....	....	....
1952-53	Moose Jaw Canucks	WCJHL	33	25	16	41	....	....	....	42	9	4	3	7	8
1953-54	Moose Jaw Millers	SSHL	37	22	35	57	....	....	....	40	8	2	3	5	6
	Moose Jaw Millers	Al-Cup	7	2	3	5	....	....	....	4	....	....	....	....	....
1954-55	Fort Wayne Komets	IHL	22	7	8	15	....	....	....	17	....	....	....	....	....
	Yorkton Terriers	WCSHL	....	....	....	....	....	....	....	....	6	1	1	2	4
1955-56	Brandon Regals	WHL	69	15	22	37	....	....	....	53	....	....	....	....	....
1956-57	Brandon Regals	WHL	70	32	46	78	....	....	....	75	9	2	7	9	2
	Brandon Regals	Ed-Cup	5	1	3	4	....	....	....	0	....	....	....	....	....
1957-58	**Boston Bruins**	**NHL**	**15**	**2**	**3**	**5**	**2**	**3**	**5**	**8**	**12**	**4**	**0**	**4**	**6**
	Springfield Indians	AHL	52	8	33	41	....	....	....	46	....	....	....	....	....
1958-59	**Boston Bruins**	**NHL**	**39**	**2**	**17**	**19**	**2**	**17**	**19**	**25**	....	....	....	....	....
	Chicago Black Hawks	**NHL**	**7**	**1**	**0**	**1**	**1**	**0**	**1**	**8**	....	....	....	....	....
	Rochester Americans	AHL	14	3	4	7	....	....	....	8	5	1	2	3	13
1959-60	Calgary Stampeders	WHL	45	20	40	60	....	....	....	32	....	....	....	....	....
	Buffalo Bisons	AHL	23	5	12	17	....	....	....	10	....	....	....	....	....
	Chicago Black Hawks	**NHL**	....	....	....	....	....	....	....	....	**2**	**0**	**0**	**0**	**0**
1960-61	Calgary Stampeders	WHL	58	23	64	87	....	....	....	19	5	1	3	4	2
1961-62	Calgary Stampeders	WHL	69	29	*64	93	....	....	....	25	7	0	5	5	2
1962-63	Calgary Stampeders	WHL	69	22	43	65	....	....	....	27	....	....	....	....	....
1963-64	Los Angeles Blades	WHL	70	33	53	86	....	....	....	38	12	5	14	19	18
	St. Paul Rangers	CPHL	1	0	1	1	....	....	....	2	....	....	....	....	....
1964-65	Los Angeles Blades	WHL	69	26	55	81	....	....	....	39	....	....	....	....	....
1965-66	Los Angeles Blades	WHL	71	23	54	77	....	....	....	34	....	....	....	....	....
1966-67	Los Angeles Blades	WHL	67	31	46	77	....	....	....	20	....	....	....	....	....
1967-68	Portland Buckaroos	WHL	72	23	40	63	....	....	....	24	12	1	9	10	14
1968-69	Portland Buckaroos	WHL	71	43	47	90	....	....	....	40	11	4	6	10	8
1969-70	Portland Buckaroos	WHL	71	34	62	96	....	....	....	34	11	7	10	17	24
1970-71	Portland Buckaroos	WHL	72	37	55	92	....	....	....	86	13	3	*11	14	29
1971-72	Spokane Jets	WIHL	DID NOT PLAY – COACHING												
	NHL Totals		**61**	**5**	**20**	**25**	**5**	**20**	**25**	**41**	**14**	**4**	**0**	**4**	**6**

WHL Prairie Division Second All-Star Team (1957) • WHL First All-Star Team (1961, 1962) • WHL Second All-Star Team (1969)

Claimed by **Boston** from **Brandon** (WHL) in Inter-League Draft, June 4, 1957. Claimed on waivers by **Chicago** from **Boston**, January 7, 1959. Loaned to **Montreal** (Rochester-AHL) by **Chicago** to complete transaction that sent Dollard St. Laurent to Chicago (June 3, 1958), February 20, 1959. Traded to **LA Blades** (WHL) by **Chicago** (St. Louis-AHL) with Ron Leopold and Gord Vejprava for Lloyd Haddon, August 12, 1963. Traded to **Portland** (WHL) by **LA Blades** (WHL) for cash, July, 1967.

• JOHNSON, Tom Thomas Christian HHOF

D – L. 6', 180 lbs. b: Baldur, Man., 2/18/1928.

Season	Club	League	GP	G	A	Pts	AG	AA	APts	PIM	GP	G	A	Pts	PIM
1946-47	Winnipeg Monarchs	MJHL	14	10	4	14	....	....	....	12	7	3	1	4	19
1947-48	**Montreal Canadiens**	**NHL**	**1**	**0**	**0**	**0**	**0**	**0**	**0**	**0**	....	....	....	....	....
	Montreal Royals	QSHL	16	0	4	4	....	....	....	10	....	....	....	....	....
1948-49	Buffalo Bisons	AHL	68	4	18	22	....	....	....	70	....	....	....	....	....
1949-50	Buffalo Bisons	AHL	58	7	19	26	....	....	....	52	5	0	0	0	20
	Montreal Canadiens	**NHL**	....	....	....	....	....	....	....	....	**1**	**0**	**0**	**0**	**0**
1950-51	**Montreal Canadiens**	**NHL**	**70**	**2**	**8**	**10**	**3**	**10**	**13**	**128**	**11**	**0**	**0**	**0**	**6**
1951-52	**Montreal Canadiens**	**NHL**	**67**	**0**	**7**	**7**	**0**	**9**	**9**	**76**	**11**	**1**	**0**	**1**	**2**
♦1952-53	**Montreal Canadiens**	**NHL**	**70**	**3**	**8**	**11**	**4**	**10**	**14**	**63**	**12**	**2**	**3**	**5**	**8**
1953-54	**Montreal Canadiens**	**NHL**	**70**	**7**	**11**	**18**	**9**	**13**	**22**	**85**	**11**	**1**	**2**	**3**	**30**
1954-55	**Montreal Canadiens**	**NHL**	**70**	**6**	**19**	**25**	**8**	**22**	**30**	**74**	**12**	**2**	**0**	**2**	**22**
♦1955-56	**Montreal Canadiens**	**NHL**	**64**	**3**	**10**	**13**	**4**	**12**	**16**	**75**	**10**	**0**	**2**	**2**	**8**
♦1956-57	**Montreal Canadiens**	**NHL**	**70**	**4**	**11**	**15**	**5**	**12**	**17**	**59**	**10**	**0**	**2**	**2**	**13**
♦1957-58	**Montreal Canadiens**	**NHL**	**66**	**3**	**18**	**21**	**4**	**19**	**23**	**75**	**2**	**0**	**0**	**0**	**0**
♦1958-59	**Montreal Canadiens**	**NHL**	**70**	**10**	**29**	**39**	**12**	**29**	**41**	**76**	**11**	**2**	**3**	**5**	**8**
♦1959-60	**Montreal Canadiens**	**NHL**	**64**	**4**	**25**	**29**	**5**	**24**	**29**	**59**	**8**	**0**	**1**	**1**	**4**
1960-61	**Montreal Canadiens**	**NHL**	**70**	**1**	**15**	**16**	**1**	**14**	**15**	**54**	**6**	**0**	**1**	**1**	**8**
1961-62	**Montreal Canadiens**	**NHL**	**62**	**1**	**17**	**18**	**1**	**16**	**17**	**45**	**6**	**0**	**1**	**1**	**0**
1962-63	**Montreal Canadiens**	**NHL**	**43**	**3**	**5**	**8**	**3**	**5**	**8**	**28**	....	....	....	....	....
1963-64	**Boston Bruins**	**NHL**	**70**	**4**	**21**	**25**	**5**	**22**	**27**	**33**	....	....	....	....	....
1964-65	**Boston Bruins**	**NHL**	**51**	**0**	**9**	**9**	**0**	**9**	**9**	**30**	....	....	....	....	....
	NHL Totals		**978**	**51**	**213**	**264**	**64**	**226**	**290**	**960**	**111**	**8**	**15**	**23**	**109**

NHL Second All-Star Team (1956) • NHL First All-Star Team (1959) • Won James Norris Trophy (1959) • Played in NHL All-Star Game (1952, 1953, 1956, 1957, 1958, 1959, 1960, 1963)

Signed as a free agent by **Montreal**, April 30, 1947. Claimed by **Boston** from **Montreal** in Waiver Draft, June 4, 1963. • Suffered career-ending leg injury in game vs. Chicago, February 28, 1965.

• JOHNSON, Virgil

USHOF

D – L. 5'9", 165 lbs. b: Minneapolis, MN, 3/4/1912 Deceased.

			REGULAR SEASON								PLAYOFFS				
Season	Club	League	GP	G	A	Pts	AG	AA	APts	PIM	GP	G	A	Pts	PIM
1930-31	Minneapolis Americans	NWHL	STATISTICS NOT AVAILABLE												
1931-32	Minneapolis Millers	CHL	34	9	4	13	....	....	....	24	....	....	....	....	....
1932-33	Minneapolis Millers	CHL	39	6	8	14	....	....	....	30	7	0	1	1	11
1933-34	Minneapolis Millers	CHL	36	9	13	22	....	....	....	21	3	0	2	2	2
1934-35	St. Paul Saints	CHL	45	6	13	19	....	....	....	38	8	2	*5	*7	8
1935-36	St. Paul Saints	AHA	47	9	20	29	....	....	....	14	5	0	1	1	4
1936-37	St. Paul Saints	AHA	48	4	15	19	....	....	....	35	3	0	2	2	4
♦1937-38	**Chicago Black Hawks**	**NHL**	**25**	**0**	**2**	**2**	**0**	**3**	**3**	**2**	**10**	**0**	**0**	**0**	**0**
	St. Paul Saints	AHA	24	2	6	8	....	....	....	14	....	....	....	....	....
1938-39	St. Paul Saints	AHA	48	5	12	17	....	....	....	22	3	1	0	1	0
1939-40	St. Paul Saints	AHA	45	6	16	22	....	....	....	15	7	0	1	1	6
1940-41	St. Paul Saints	AHA	48	6	15	21	....	....	....	14	4	0	0	0	4
1941-42	St. Paul Saints	AHA	49	8	17	25	....	....	....	18	2	1	0	1	0
1942-43	Hershey Bears	AHL	53	4	19	23	....	....	....	10	6	0	4	4	0
1943-44	**Chicago Black Hawks**	**NHL**	**48**	**1**	**8**	**9**	**1**	**7**	**8**	**23**	**9**	**0**	**3**	**3**	**4**
1944-45	**Chicago Black Hawks**	**NHL**	**2**	**0**	**1**	**1**	**0**	**1**	**1**	**2**	....	....	....	....	....
	Cleveland Barons	AHL	26	2	5	7	....	....	....	10	8	0	0	0	2
1945-46	Minneapolis Millers	USHL	53	9	17	26	....	....	....	12	....	....	....	....	....
1946-47	Minneapolis Millers	USHL	51	2	19	21	....	....	....	30	3	0	0	0	2
1947/50			DID NOT PLAY												
1950-51	Minneapolis Jerseys	AAHL	18	2	19	21	....	....	....	2	3	0	2	2	0
1951-52	St. Paul Saints	AAHL	34	10	19	29	....	....	....	12	3	0	5	5	0
	NHL Totals		**75**	**1**	**11**	**12**	**1**	**11**	**12**	**27**	**19**	**0**	**3**	**3**	**4**

AHA First All-Star Team (1942)

Traded to **Chicago** by **St. Paul** (AHA) for cash, January 8, 1938.

• JOHNSTON, George

George Joseph "Wingy"

RW – R. 5'8", 160 lbs. b: St. Charles, Man., 7/30/1920.

Season	Club	League	GP	G	A	Pts	AG	AA	APts	PIM	GP	G	A	Pts	PIM
1938-39	Duluth Zephyrs	TBSHL	11	5	2	7	....	....	....	14	....	....	....	....	....
1939-40	Saskatoon Quakers	N-SSHL	28	11	12	23	....	....	....	2	4	0	1	1	0
1940-41	Providence Reds	AHL	50	17	24	41	....	....	....	4	4	2	2	4	0
1941-42	**Chicago Black Hawks**	**NHL**	**2**	**2**	**0**	**2**	**3**	**0**	**3**	**0**	....	....	....	....	....
	Kansas City Americans	AHA	31	18	14	32	....	....	....	6	6	3	*9	12	0
1942-43	**Chicago Black Hawks**	**NHL**	**30**	**10**	**7**	**17**	**10**	**6**	**16**	**0**	....	....	....	....	....
1943-44	Vancouver RCAF	PCHL	10	12	5	17	....	....	....	2	....	....	....	....	....
1944-45	Saint John All-Stars	X-Games	STATISTICS NOT AVAILABLE												
1945-46	**Chicago Black Hawks**	**NHL**	**16**	**5**	**4**	**9**	**6**	**6**	**12**	**2**	....	....	....	....	....
	Kansas City Pla-Mors	USHL	38	38	34	72	....	....	....	6	12	4	8	12	2
1946-47	**Chicago Black Hawks**	**NHL**	**10**	**3**	**1**	**4**	**3**	**1**	**4**	**0**	....	....	....	....	....
	Kansas City Pla-Mors	USHL	47	29	29	58	....	....	....	6	12	5	4	9	4
1947-48	Cleveland Barons	AHL	15	4	4	8	....	....	....	4	....	....	....	....	....
	New Haven Ramblers	AHL	39	16	24	40	....	....	....	10	4	1	1	2	0
1948-49	New Haven Ramblers	AHL	39	14	23	37	....	....	....	2	....	....	....	....	....
	Tacoma Rockets	PCHL	28	17	14	31	....	....	....	4	6	0	5	5	0
1949-50	Tacoma Rockets	PCHL	70	46	44	90	....	....	....	64	5	0	2	2	0
1950-51	Tacoma Rockets	PCHL	70	27	31	58	....	....	....	17	6	1	2	3	0
1951-52	Tacoma Rockets	PCHL	70	32	45	77	....	....	....	8	7	2	4	6	0
1952-53	Tacoma Rockets	WHL	70	24	41	65	....	....	....	8	....	....	....	....	....
1953-54	Spokane Flyers	WIHL	66	35	39	74	....	....	....	45	5	2	4	6	0
1954-55	Spokane Flyers	WIHL	35	15	24	39	....	....	....	16	....	....	....	....	....
	NHL Totals		**58**	**20**	**12**	**32**	**22**	**13**	**35**	**2**	....	....	....	....	....

USHL First All-Star Team (1946, 1947) • PCHL Northern Second All-Star Team (1950) • PCHL Second All-Star Team (1952)

Traded to **NY Rangers** by **Cleveland** (AHL) for Church Russell, December 18, 1947.

• JOHNSTONE, Ross

Robert Ross

D – L. 6', 185 lbs. b: Montreal, Que., 4/7/1926.

Season	Club	League	GP	G	A	Pts	AG	AA	APts	PIM	GP	G	A	Pts	PIM
1942-43	Toronto Marlboros	OHA-Jr.	19	1	9	10	....	....	....	16	3	0	1	1	6
	Oshawa Generals	OHA-Jr.	....	....	....	....	....	....	....	....	13	3	3	6	27
	Oshawa Generals	M-Cup	11	2	3	5	....	....	....	23	....	....	....	....	....
1943-44	**Toronto Maple Leafs**	**NHL**	**18**	**2**	**0**	**2**	**2**	**0**	**2**	**6**	**3**	**0**	**0**	**0**	**0**
	Providence Reds	AHL	6	1	0	1	....	....	....	2	....	....	....	....	....
♦1944-45	**Toronto Maple Leafs**	**NHL**	**24**	**3**	**4**	**7**	**3**	**5**	**8**	**8**	....	....	....	....	....
1945-46	Pittsburgh Hornets	AHL	56	1	7	8	....	....	....	23	....	....	....	....	....
1946-47	Springfield Indians	AHL	33	1	7	8	....	....	....	2	2	1	0	1	0
1947-48	Springfield Indians	AHL	68	2	19	21	....	....	....	10	....	....	....	....	....
1948-49	New Haven Ramblers	AHL	10	1	3	4	....	....	....	2	....	....	....	....	....
1949-50	Detroit Hettche	IHL	18	7	3	10	....	....	....	6	3	1	0	1	0
1950-51	Toronto Marlboros	OMHL	31	7	6	13	....	....	....	36	3	1	1	2	0
1951-52	Atlantic City Seagulls	EAHL	38	7	10	17	....	....	....	8	....	....	....	....	....
1952-53			OUT OF HOCKEY – RETIRED												
1953/57	Sundridge Beavers	OIHA	STATISTICS NOT AVAILABLE												
	NHL Totals		**42**	**5**	**4**	**9**	**5**	**5**	**10**	**14**	**3**	**0**	**0**	**0**	**0**

Traded to **Toronto** by **Buffalo** (AHL) for cash, November 7, 1942. • Suspended by **Toronto** for refusing to report to **Tulsa** (USHL), October, 1946. Traded to **Springfield** (AHL) by **Toronto** for cash, December 31, 1946.

• JOLIAT, Aurel

Aurel Emile

HHOF

LW – L. 5'7", 136 lbs. b: Ottawa, Ont., 8/29/1901 d: 6/2/1986.

Season	Club	League	GP	G	A	Pts	AG	AA	APts	PIM	GP	G	A	Pts	PIM
1916-17	Ottawa New Edinburghs	OCHL	8	2	0	2	....	....	....	....	2	0	0	0	....
1917-18	Ottawa Aberdeens	OCJHL	3	2	0	2	....	....	....	3	....	....	....	....	....
1918-19	Ottawa New Edinburghs	OCHL	8	5	*3	8	....	....	....	9	....	....	....	....	....
1919-20	Ottawa New Edinburghs	OCHL	7	*12	0	*12	....	....	....	....	....	....	....	....	....
1920-21	Iroquois Falls Flyers	NOHA	STATISTICS NOT AVAILABLE												
1921-22	Iroquois Falls Flyers	NOHA	DID NOT PLAY – SUSPENDED												
1922-23	**Montreal Canadiens**	**NHL**	**24**	**12**	**9**	**21**	**20**	**35**	**55**	**37**	**2**	**1**	**0**	**1**	**11**
1923-24	**Montreal Canadiens**	**NHL**	**24**	**15**	**5**	**20**	**32**	**29**	**61**	**27**	**2**	**1**	**1**	**2**	**0**
♦	Montreal Canadiens	St-Cup	4	3	1	4	....	....	....	6	....	....	....	....	....
1924-25	**Montreal Canadiens**	**NHL**	**25**	**30**	**11**	**41**	**54**	**47**	**101**	**85**	**1**	**0**	**0**	**0**	**5**
	Montreal Canadiens	St-Cup	4	3	0	3	....	....	....	16	....	....	....	....	....
1925-26	**Montreal Canadiens**	**NHL**	**35**	**17**	**9**	**26**	**30**	**59**	**89**	**52**	....	....	....	....	....
1926-27	**Montreal Canadiens**	**NHL**	**43**	**14**	**4**	**18**	**25**	**21**	**46**	**79**	**4**	**1**	**0**	**1**	**10**
1927-28	**Montreal Canadiens**	**NHL**	**44**	**28**	**11**	**39**	**58**	**63**	**121**	**105**	**2**	**0**	**0**	**0**	**4**
1928-29	**Montreal Canadiens**	**NHL**	**44**	**12**	**5**	**17**	**35**	**33**	**68**	**59**	**3**	**1**	**1**	**2**	**10**
♦1929-30	**Montreal Canadiens**	**NHL**	**42**	**19**	**12**	**31**	**27**	**28**	**55**	**40**	**6**	**0**	**2**	**2**	**6**
♦1930-31	**Montreal Canadiens**	**NHL**	**43**	**13**	**22**	**35**	**26**	**67**	**93**	**73**	**10**	**0**	***4**	**4**	**12**
1931-32	**Montreal Canadiens**	**NHL**	**48**	**15**	**24**	**39**	**25**	**53**	**78**	**46**	**4**	**2**	**0**	**2**	**4**
1932-33	**Montreal Canadiens**	**NHL**	**48**	**18**	**21**	**39**	**33**	**44**	**77**	**53**	**2**	**2**	**1**	**3**	**2**
1933-34	**Montreal Canadiens**	**NHL**	**48**	**22**	**15**	**37**	**38**	**32**	**70**	**27**	**3**	**0**	**1**	**1**	**0**
1934-35	**Montreal Canadiens**	**NHL**	**48**	**17**	**12**	**29**	**28**	**21**	**49**	**18**	**2**	**1**	**0**	**1**	**0**
1935-36	**Montreal Canadiens**	**NHL**	**48**	**15**	**8**	**23**	**29**	**15**	**44**	**16**	....	....	....	....	....
1936-37	**Montreal Canadiens**	**NHL**	**47**	**17**	**15**	**32**	**29**	**28**	**57**	**30**	**5**	**0**	**3**	**3**	**2**
1937-38	**Montreal Canadiens**	**NHL**	**44**	**6**	**7**	**13**	**10**	**11**	**21**	**24**	....	....	....	....	....
	NHL Totals		**655**	**270**	**190**	**460**	**499**	**586**	**1085**	**771**	**46**	**9**	**13**	**22**	**66**

• Brother of Rene • NHL First All-Star Team (1931) • NHL Second All-Star Team (1932, 1934, 1935) • Won Hart Trophy (1934) • Played in NHL All-Star Game (1934, 1937)

• Suspended by NOHA from March, 1921 through November 21, 1922. Rights traded to **Montreal Canadiens** by **Saskatoon** (WCHL) with $3,500 for Newsy Lalonde, September 18, 1922. • 1923-24 Stanley Cup totals includes series with Calgary (WCHL) and Vancouver (PCHA).

• JOLIAT, Rene

Rene Robert

RW/D – L. 5'5", 140 lbs. b: Ottawa, Ont., 4/25/1898 d: 8/10/1953.

Season	Club	League	GP	G	A	Pts	AG	AA	APts	PIM	GP	G	A	Pts	PIM
1916-17	Ottawa Grand Trunks	OCHL	7	3	0	3	....	....	....	6	....	....	....	....	....
1917-18	Ottawa Aberdeens	OCHL	3	2	0	2	....	....	....	3	....	....	....	....	....
1918-19	Ottawa New Edinburghs	OCHL	8	4	1	5	....	....	....	9	....	....	....	....	....
1919-20	Ottawa New Edinburghs	OCHL	2	0	0	0	....	....	....	0	....	....	....	....	....
1920-21	Ottawa New Edinburghs	OCHL	7	2	0	2	....	....	....	9	....	....	....	....	....
	Iroquois Falls P-Makers	NOHA	STATISTICS NOT AVAILABLE												
1921-22	Ottawa New Edinburghs	OCHL	4	1	0	1	....	....	....	0	....	....	....	....	....
1922-23	Ottawa New Edinburghs	OCHL	16	1	1	2	....	....	....	0	3	0	0	0	0
1923-24	Hull Volants	OCHL	STATISTICS NOT AVAILABLE												
1924-25	**Montreal Canadiens**	**NHL**	**1**	**0**	**0**	**0**	**0**	**0**	**0**	**0**	....	....	....	....	....
	Boston Maples	USAHA	2	2	0	2	....	....	....	0	....	....	....	....	....
1925-26			REINSTATED AS AN AMATEUR												
1926/29			OUT OF HOCKEY – RETIRED												
1929-30	Ottawa Shamrocks	OCHL	15	0	0	0	....	....	....	20	6	0	0	0	4
	NHL Totals		**1**	**0**	**0**	**0**	**0**	**0**	**0**	**0**	....	....	....	....	....

• Brother of Aurel

Signed as a free agent by **Montreal Canadiens**, November 17, 1924.

• JONES, Buck

Alvin Bernard

D – R. 5'11", 200 lbs. b: Owen Sound, Ont., 8/17/1918.

Season	Club	League	GP	G	A	Pts	AG	AA	APts	PIM	GP	G	A	Pts	PIM
1936-37	Barrie Flyers	OHA-B	STATISTICS NOT AVAILABLE												
1937-38	Harringay Greyhounds	Britain	....	2	2	4	....	....	....	....	....	....	....	....	....
1938-39	Harringay Greyhounds	Britain	....	1	2	3	....	....	....	....	....	....	....	....	....
	Harringay Greyhounds	Nat-Tmt	....	1	0	1	....	....	....	....	....	....	....	....	....
	Detroit Red Wings	**NHL**	**11**	**0**	**1**	**1**	**0**	**2**	**2**	**6**	**6**	**0**	**1**	**1**	**10**
	Pittsburgh Hornets	IAHL	40	2	8	10	....	....	....	37	....	....	....	....	....
1939-40	**Detroit Red Wings**	**NHL**	**2**	**0**	**0**	**0**	**0**	**0**	**0**	**0**	....	....	....	....	....
	Indianapolis Capitols	IAHL	56	6	6	12	....	....	....	70	5	0	2	2	12
1940-41	Indianapolis Capitols	AHL	54	4	5	9	....	....	....	78	....	....	....	....	....
1941-42	**Detroit Red Wings**	**NHL**	**21**	**2**	**1**	**3**	**3**	**1**	**4**	**8**	....	....	....	....	....
	Indianapolis Capitols	AHL	13	4	1	5	....	....	....	27	....	....	....	....	....
	Providence Reds	AHL	19	5	8	13	....	....	....	22	....	....	....	....	....
1942-43	Providence Reds	AHL	39	4	11	15	....	....	....	79	....	....	....	....	....
	Toronto Maple Leafs	**NHL**	**16**	**0**	**0**	**0**	**0**	**0**	**0**	**22**	**6**	**0**	**0**	**0**	**8**
1943-44	Toronto Army Daggers	OHA-Sr.	1	0	0	0	....	....	....	0	....	....	....	....	....
	Kingston Army	OHA-Sr.	4	0	3	3	....	....	....	6	....	....	....	....	....
1944-45			MILITARY SERVICE												
1945-46			MILITARY SERVICE												
1946-47	Tulsa Oilers	USHL	58	7	4	11	....	....	....	127	5	0	1	1	12
1947-48	Tulsa Oilers	USHL	65	3	6	9	....	....	....	47	2	0	0	0	2
1948-49	Hershey Bears	AHL	65	1	5	6	....	....	....	76	11	0	2	2	*17
1949-50	Hershey Bears	AHL	66	0	6	6	....	....	....	60	....	....	....	....	....
1950-51	Tulsa Oilers	USHL	57	0	10	10	....	....	....	72	6	0	4	4	4
1951-52	Tacoma Rockets	PCHL	70	1	3	4	....	....	....	140	6	0	0	0	14
1952-53	Tacoma Rockets	WHL	69	7	14	21	....	....	....	105	....	....	....	....	....
1953-54	Seattle Bombers	WHL	26	1	1	2	....	....	....	34	....	....	....	....	....
	Nelson Maple Leafs	WIHL	7	0	0	0	....	....	....	10	8	1	0	1	12
	Nelson Maple Leafs	Al-Cup	8	0	1	1	....	....	....	4	....	....	....	....	....
	NHL Totals		**50**	**2**	**2**	**4**	**3**	**3**	**6**	**36**	**12**	**0**	**1**	**1**	**18**

Traded to **Providence** (AHL) by **Detroit** with Bob Whitelaw and for Eddie Bush and future considerations, February 3, 1942. Traded to **Toronto** by **Providence** (AHL) with the loan of Ab Demarco for the loan of Jack Forsey and George Boothman, February 3, 1943. Traded to **Tulsa** (USHL) by **Toronto** for cash, May 15, 1947. Signed as a free agent by **Seattle** (WHL), October 14, 1953.

• JOYAL, Eddie

— see page 1239

• JUCKES, Bing

Winston Bryan

LW – L. 5'10", 165 lbs. b: Hamiota, Man., 6/14/1926.

Season	Club	League	GP	G	A	Pts	AG	AA	APts	PIM	GP	G	A	Pts	PIM
1942-43	St. James Canadians	MJHL	1	1	0	1	....	....	....	0	1	0	0	0	0
1943-44	St. Catharines Falcons	OHA-Jr.	19	7	5	12	....	....	....	17	4	0	0	0	2
1944-45	Winnipeg Rangers	MJHL	3	5	0	5	....	....	....	12	3	5	1	6	8
	Winnipeg Navy	WNDHL	9	4	5	9	....	....	....	15	6	3	1	4	*14
1945-46	Brandon Elks	MJHL	10	23	16	39	....	....	....	*31	7	*16	4	*20	19
	Providence Reds	AHL	5	1	1	2	....	....	....	6	....	....	....	....	....
1946-47	Lethbridge Maple Leafs	WCSHL	34	31	9	40	....	....	....	47	4	3	1	4	0
1947-48	**New York Rangers**	**NHL**	**2**	**0**	**0**	**0**	**0**	**0**	**0**	**0**	....	....	....	....	....
	New Haven Ramblers	AHL	55	27	19	46	....	....	....	18	2	1	0	1	4
1948-49	St. Paul Saints	USHL	65	40	44	84	....	....	....	53	7	2	4	6	20
1949-50	**New York Rangers**	**NHL**	**14**	**2**	**1**	**3**	**2**	**1**	**3**	**6**	....	....	....	....	....
	New Haven Ramblers	AHL	46	5	12	17	....	....	....	16	....	....	....	....	....
1950-51	Denver Falcons	USHL	58	25	21	46	....	....	....	56	5	1	2	3	2
1951-52	Calgary Stampeders	PCHL	33	12	18	30	....	....	....	16	....	....	....	....	....
1952-53	Yorkton Legionnaires	SSHL	PLAYER/COACH – STATISTICS UNAVAILABLE												
1953-54	Vernon Canadians	OSHL	30	29	16	45	....	....	....	29	....	....	....	....	....
1954-55	Brandon Wheat Kings	MHL-Sr.	3	2	4	6	....	....	....	6	....	....	....	....	....
	NHL Totals		**16**	**2**	**1**	**3**	**2**	**1**	**3**	**6**	....	....	....	....	....

USHL First All-Star Team (1949)

Traded to **Denver** (USHL) by **NY Rangers** for cash, October 16, 1950.

• JUZDA, Bill

William "The Honest Brakeman"
D – R. 5'9", 190 lbs. b: Winnipeg, Man., 10/29/1920.

Season	Club	League	GP	G	A	Pts	AG	AA	APts	PIM	GP	G	A	Pts	PIM
			REGULAR SEASON								PLAYOFFS				
1937-38	Winnipeg St. John's	H.S.	STATISTICS NOT AVAILABLE												
1938-39	Elmwood Maple Leafs	WJrHL	16	1	0	1	....	....	....	36	5	1	1	2	0
1939-40	Kenora Thistles	WJrHL	24	3	6	9	....	....	....	29	9	2	3	5	20
	Kenora Thistles	M-Cup	11	1	4	5	....	....	....	42	....	....	....	....	....
1940-41	**New York Rangers**	**NHL**	**5**	**0**	**0**	**0**	**0**	**0**	**0**	**2**	....	....	....	....	....
	Philadelphia Rockets	AHL	52	7	14	21	....	....	....	47	....	....	....	....	....
1941-42	**New York Rangers**	**NHL**	**45**	**4**	**8**	**12**	**5**	**9**	**14**	**29**	**6**	**0**	**1**	**1**	**4**
1942-43	Buffalo Bisons	AHL	1	0	0	0	....	....	....	0	....	....	....	....	....
	Winnipeg RCAF	WNDHL	13	3	3	6	....	....	....	8	5	0	0	0	14
	Winnipeg RCAF	Al-Cup	12	1	3	4	....	....	....	14	....	....	....	....	....
1943-44	Winnipeg RCAF	WNDHL	3	0	0	0	....	....	....	4	....	....	....	....	....
1944-45	Dartmouth RCAF	NSDHL	4	0	0	0	....	....	....	12	3	0	4	4	4
1945-46	**New York Rangers**	**NHL**	**32**	**1**	**3**	**4**	**1**	**4**	**5**	**17**	....	....	....	....	....
	Providence Reds	AHL	18	4	3	7	....	....	....	20	2	0	0	0	9
1946-47	**New York Rangers**	**NHL**	**45**	**3**	**5**	**8**	**3**	**6**	**9**	**60**	....	....	....	....	....
	New Haven Ramblers	AHL	16	2	4	6	....	....	....	20	....	....	....	....	....
1947-48	**New York Rangers**	**NHL**	**60**	**3**	**9**	**12**	**4**	**12**	**16**	**70**	**6**	**0**	**0**	**0**	**9**
♦1948-49	**Toronto Maple Leafs**	**NHL**	**38**	**1**	**2**	**3**	**1**	**3**	**4**	**23**	**9**	**0**	**2**	**2**	**8**
	Pittsburgh Hornets	AHL	7	0	3	3	....	....	....	4	....	....	....	....	....
1949-50	**Toronto Maple Leafs**	**NHL**	**62**	**1**	**14**	**15**	**1**	**17**	**18**	**68**	**7**	**0**	**0**	**0**	**16**
♦1950-51	**Toronto Maple Leafs**	**NHL**	**65**	**0**	**9**	**9**	**0**	**11**	**11**	**64**	**11**	**0**	**0**	**0**	**7**
1951-52	**Toronto Maple Leafs**	**NHL**	**46**	**1**	**4**	**5**	**1**	**5**	**6**	**65**	**3**	**0**	**0**	**0**	**2**
1952-53	Pittsburgh Hornets	AHL	59	1	15	16	....	....	....	108	10	0	1	1	11
1953-54	Winnipeg Maroons	Al-Cup	23	4	8	12	....	....	....	*75	....	....	....	....	....
1954-55	Brandon Wheat Kings	MHL-Sr.	10	3	7	10	....	....	....	32	....	....	....	....	....
1955-56	Winnipeg Warriors	WHL	3	0	1	1	....	....	....	4	....	....	....	....	....
	Winnipeg Maroons	Al-Cup	9	1	5	6	....	....	....	32	....	....	....	....	....
1956-57	Pine Falls Falcons	X-Games	STATISTICS NOT AVAILABLE												
1957-58	Winnipeg Maroons	Al-Cup	13	0	4	4	....	....	....	21	....	....	....	....	....
1958-59	Winnipeg Maroons	Al-Cup	3	0	2	2	....	....	....	2	....	....	....	....	....
1959-60	Winnipeg Maroons	Al-Cup	3	1	0	1	....	....	....	2	....	....	....	....	....
1960-61	Winnipeg Maroons	Al-Cup	20	2	4	6	....	....	....	*43	....	....	....	....	....
1961-62	Winnipeg Maroons	SSHL	6	0	0	0	....	....	....	2	....	....	....	....	....
	Winnipeg Maroons	Al-Cup	9	0	0	0	....	....	....	*23	....	....	....	....	....
1962-63	Winnipeg Maroons	SSHL	6	0	0	0	....	....	....	2	....	....	....	....	....
	NHL Totals		**398**	**14**	**54**	**68**	**16**	**67**	**83**	**398**	**42**	**0**	**3**	**3**	**46**

AHL Second All-Star Team (1953) • Played in NHL All-Star Game (1948, 1949)

Signed as a free agent by **NY Rangers**, October 21, 1940. Traded to **Toronto** by **NY Rangers** with Cal Gardner, Rene Trudell and the rights to Frank Mathers for Wally Stanowski and Moe Morris, April 26, 1948.

• KABEL, Bob

Robert Gerald
C – R. 6', 183 lbs. b: Dauphin, Man., 11/11/1934.

Season	Club	League	GP	G	A	Pts	AG	AA	APts	PIM	GP	G	A	Pts	PIM
1952-53	Flin Flon Bombers	SJHL	47	26	12	38	....	....	....	54	11	5	2	7	4
	Flin Flon Bombers	M-Cup	2	1	0	1	....	....	....	2	....	....	....	....	....
1953-54	Flin Flon Bombers	SJHL	46	23	34	57	....	....	....	50	17	3	*14	17	37
	Flin Flon Bombers	M-Cup	4	0	3	3	....	....	....	4	....	....	....	....	....
1954-55	Saskatoon Wesleys	SJHL	46	19	21	40	....	....	....	62	5	1	1	2	17
	Saskatoon Quakers	WHL	1	0	0	0	....	....	....	2	....	....	....	....	....
1955-56	Vancouver Canucks	WHL	60	14	12	26	....	....	....	60	15	2	4	6	14
1956-57	Trois-Rivieres Lions	QHL	57	9	16	25	....	....	....	49	4	0	0	0	14
	Providence Reds	AHL	7	0	2	2	....	....	....	6	....	....	....	....	....
1957-58	Saskatoon–St. Paul	WHL	69	23	43	66	....	....	....	82	....	....	....	....	....
1958-59	Saskatoon Quakers	WHL	63	28	27	55	....	....	....	29	....	....	....	....	....
1959-60	**New York Rangers**	**NHL**	**44**	**5**	**11**	**16**	**6**	**11**	**17**	**32**	....	....	....	....	....
	Vancouver Canucks	WHL	25	9	4	13	....	....	....	22	....	....	....	....	....
1960-61	**New York Rangers**	**NHL**	**4**	**0**	**2**	**2**	**0**	**2**	**2**	**2**	....	....	....	....	....
	Springfield Indians	AHL	53	27	25	52	....	....	....	45	6	0	4	4	6
1961-62	Springfield Indians	AHL	50	8	28	36	....	....	....	26	11	1	5	6	12
1962-63	Vancouver Canucks	WHL	63	20	51	71	....	....	....	32	7	5	4	9	2
	Baltimore Clippers	AHL	3	0	0	0	....	....	....	0	....	....	....	....	....
1963-64	Vancouver Canucks	WHL	70	17	50	67	....	....	....	52	....	....	....	....	....
	St. Paul Rangers	CPHL	....	....	....	....	....	....	....	....	4	1	3	4	0
1964-65	Vancouver Canucks	WHL	70	20	40	60	....	....	....	62	5	0	1	1	4
1965-66	Providence Reds	AHL	27	8	6	14	....	....	....	6	....	....	....	....	....
	Vancouver Canucks	WHL	42	9	9	18	....	....	....	14	....	....	....	....	....
1966-67	California Seals	WHL	47	9	9	18	....	....	....	20	4	0	0	0	2
1967-68	Phoenix Roadrunners	WHL	70	16	32	48	....	....	....	12	4	0	3	3	2
1968-69	Phoenix Roadrunners	WHL	68	14	33	47	....	....	....	20	....	....	....	....	....
1969-70	Salt Lake Golden Eagles	WHL	3	0	2	2	....	....	....	7	....	....	....	....	....
	NHL Totals		**48**	**5**	**13**	**18**	**6**	**13**	**19**	**34**	....	....	....	....	....

Traded to **California** (WHL) by **NY Rangers** for Gerry Brisson with NY Rangers holding right of recall, October, 1966. Traded to **Phoenix** (WHL) by **NY Rangers** for cash, September, 1967. Traded to **Salt Lake** (WHL) by **Phoenix** (WHL) for cash, May, 1969.

• KACHUR, Ed

Edward Charles
RW – R. 5'8", 170 lbs. b: Fort William, Ont., 4/22/1934.

Season	Club	League	GP	G	A	Pts	AG	AA	APts	PIM	GP	G	A	Pts	PIM
1949-50	Fort William Canadiens	TBJHL	16	5	5	10	....	....	....	54	10	1	1	2	10
	Fort William Hurricanes	M-Cup	12	4	0	4	....	....	....	20	....	....	....	....	....
1950-51	Fort William Canadiens	TBJHL	14	5	3	8	....	....	....	32	6	3	3	6	12
1951-52	Fort William Canadiens	TBJHL	29	38	22	60	....	....	....	96	....	....	....	....	....
	Fort William Rangers	M-Cup	12	4	0	4	....	....	....	*28	....	....	....	....	....
1952-53	Fort William Canadiens	TBJHL	19	21	14	35	....	....	....	34	5	2	3	5	0
	Fort William Canadiens	M-Cup	5	2	4	6	....	....	....	5	....	....	....	....	....
1953-54	Cincinnati Mohawks	IHL	63	32	26	58	....	....	....	61	11	2	2	4	2
1954-55	Shawinigan Cataracts	QHL	59	25	14	39	....	....	....	46	13	5	3	8	18
	Shawinigan Cataracts	Ed-Cup	7	2	3	5	....	....	....	16	....	....	....	....	....
1955-56	Shawinigan Cataracts	QHL	64	31	34	65	....	....	....	91	11	6	5	11	16
1956-57	**Chicago Black Hawks**	**NHL**	**34**	**5**	**7**	**12**	**6**	**8**	**14**	**21**	....	....	....	....	....
	Shawinigan Cataracts	QHL	32	12	12	24	....	....	....	12	....	....	....	....	....
1957-58	**Chicago Black Hawks**	**NHL**	**62**	**5**	**7**	**12**	**6**	**7**	**13**	**14**	....	....	....	....	....
1958-59	Buffalo Bisons	AHL	68	15	17	32	....	....	....	26	11	*5	2	7	6
1959-60	Buffalo Bisons	AHL	57	19	19	38	....	....	....	10	....	....	....	....	....
1960-61	S.S. Marie Thunderbirds	EPHL	70	38	43	81	....	....	....	71	12	3	6	9	16
1961-62	S.S. Marie Thunderbirds	EPHL	70	22	32	54	....	....	....	65	....	....	....	....	....
1962-63	Buffalo Bisons	AHL	68	19	19	38	....	....	....	35	13	2	3	5	8
1963-64	Buffalo Bisons	AHL	64	13	14	27	....	....	....	10	....	....	....	....	....
1964-65	Los Angeles Blades	WHL	22	1	6	7	....	....	....	4	....	....	....	....	....
	Providence Reds	AHL	41	16	7	23	....	....	....	16	....	....	....	....	....
1965-66	Providence Reds	AHL	57	28	19	47	....	....	....	30	....	....	....	....	....
1966-67	Providence Reds	AHL	55	22	20	42	....	....	....	20	....	....	....	....	....
1967-68	Providence Reds	AHL	72	*47	29	76	....	....	....	30	8	3	2	5	8
1968-69	Providence Reds	AHL	71	26	26	52	....	....	....	24	9	1	4	5	6
1969-70	Providence Reds	AHL	21	9	4	13	....	....	....	2	....	....	....	....	....
1970-71	Thunder Bay Twins	USHL	15	12	7	19	....	....	....	35	....	....	....	....	....
1971-72	Johnstown Jets	EHL	25	18	11	29	....	....	....	6	....	....	....	....	....
	NHL Totals		**96**	**10**	**14**	**24**	**12**	**15**	**27**	**35**	....	....	....	....	....

QHL Second All-Star Team (1956) • EPHL Second All-Star Team (1961) • AHL First All-Star Team (1968)

Traded to **Chicago** by **Montreal** with Forbes Kennedy for $50,000, May 24, 1956. Traded to **LA Blades** (WHL) by **Chicago** (Buffalo-AHL) for cash, August 30, 1964. Traded to **Providence** (AHL) by **LA Blades** (WHL) for Harry Ottenbriet, January 2, 1965.

• KAISER, Vern

Vernon Charles
LW – L. 6', 180 lbs. b: Preston, Ont., 9/28/1926.

Season	Club	League	GP	G	A	Pts	AG	AA	APts	PIM	GP	G	A	Pts	PIM
1941/44	Preston Riversides	OMHA	STATISTICS NOT AVAILABLE												
1944-45	Winnipeg Navy	WSrHL	4	0	1	1	....	....	....	10	6	0	2	2	8
1945-46	Washington–NY Rovers	EAHL	46	5	6	11	....	....	....	83	12	0	0	0	*20
1946-47	Seattle Ironmen	PCHL	50	10	8	18	....	....	....	153	9	1	2	3	10
1947-48	Fort Worth Rangers	USHL	59	13	18	31	....	....	....	41	4	1	0	1	2
1948-49	Springfield Indians	AHL	61	25	17	42	....	....	....	32	3	1	1	2	4
1949-50	Springfield Indians	AHL	64	19	19	38	....	....	....	65	2	1	0	1	0
1950-51	**Montreal Canadiens**	**NHL**	**50**	**7**	**5**	**12**	**9**	**6**	**15**	**33**	**2**	**0**	**0**	**0**	**0**
	Buffalo Bisons	AHL	15	7	13	20	....	....	....	4	4	1	2	3	2
1951-52	Buffalo Bisons	AHL	58	24	26	50	....	....	....	67	2	0	1	1	2
1952-53	Buffalo Bisons	AHL	61	14	15	29	....	....	....	87	....	....	....	....	....
1953-54	Montreal Royals	QHL	43	14	22	36	....	....	....	27	....	....	....	....	....
	Syracuse Warriors	AHL	17	11	11	22	....	....	....	10	....	....	....	....	....
	NHL Totals		**50**	**7**	**5**	**12**	**9**	**6**	**15**	**33**	**2**	**0**	**0**	**0**	**0**

Traded to **Montreal** by **Springfield** (AHL) for Charles Gagnon and future considerations, April 18, 1950. Traded to **Syracuse** (AHL) by **Montreal** for cash, January 1, 1954.

• KALBFLEISH, Walter

Walter Morris "Jake"
D – R. 5'10", 175 lbs. b: New Hamburg, Ont., 12/18/1911 Deceased.

Season	Club	League	GP	G	A	Pts	AG	AA	APts	PIM	GP	G	A	Pts	PIM
1929-30	Niagara Falls Cataracts	OHA-Jr.	6	1	1	2	....	....	....	*16	2	1	0	1	2
1930-31	Niagara Falls Cataracts	OHA-Jr.	7	2	3	5	....	....	....	6	2	1	1	2	0
1931-32	Niagara Falls Cataracts	OHA-Jr.	20	0	1	1	....	....	....	54	2	0	0	0	2
1932-33	Niagara Falls Cataracts	OHA-Jr.	22	3	1	4	....	....	....	56	5	0	0	0	6
	Niagara Falls Cataracts	Al-Cup	6	1	1	2	....	....	....	18	....	....	....	....	....
1933-34	Niagara Falls Cataracts	OHA-Sr.	17	4	1	5	....	....	....	36	....	....	....	....	....
	Ottawa Senators	**NHL**	**22**	**0**	**4**	**4**	**0**	**8**	**8**	**20**	....	....	....	....	....
1934-35	**St. Louis Eagles**	**NHL**	**3**	**0**	**0**	**0**	**0**	**0**	**0**	**6**	....	....	....	....	....
	Buffalo Bisons	IHL	28	3	3	6	....	....	....	30	....	....	....	....	....
1935-36	**New York Americans**	**NHL**	**4**	**0**	**0**	**0**	**0**	**0**	**0**	**2**	**5**	**0**	**0**	**0**	**2**
	Rochester Cardinals	IHL	21	3	2	5	....	....	....	14	....	....	....	....	....
	Providence Reds	Can-Am	21	2	2	4	....	....	....	30	....	....	....	....	....
1936-37	**New York Americans**	**NHL**	**6**	**0**	**0**	**0**	**0**	**0**	**0**	**4**	....	....	....	....	....
	New Haven Eagles	IAHL	12	0	0	0	....	....	....	12	....	....	....	....	....
	Boston Bruins	**NHL**	**1**	**0**	**0**	**0**	**0**	**0**	**0**	**0**	....	....	....	....	....
	Providence Reds	IAHL	24	3	1	4	....	....	....	28	3	0	0	0	0
1937-38	Providence Reds	IAHL	48	1	9	10	....	....	....	46	7	0	0	0	2
1938-39	Hershey Bears	IAHL	45	4	4	8	....	....	....	42	....	....	....	....	....
1939-40	Hershey Bears	IAHL	53	3	4	7	....	....	....	72	6	0	1	1	4
1940-41	Niagara Falls Brights	OHA-Sr.	4	0	0	0	....	....	....	4	3	0	0	0	4
1941-42	Niagara Falls Weavers	OHA-Sr.	27	2	3	5	....	....	....	34	7	0	0	0	8
1942-43	Niagara Falls Cataracts	OHA-Sr.	5	0	2	2	....	....	....	6	1	0	0	0	0
	NHL Totals		**36**	**0**	**4**	**4**	**0**	**8**	**8**	**32**	**5**	**0**	**0**	**0**	**2**

Signed as a free agent by **Ottawa**, May 10, 1933. Transferred to **St. Louis** after **Ottawa** franchise relocated, September 22, 1934. Claimed by **NY Americans** from **St. Louis** in Dispersal Draft, October 15, 1935. Traded to **Boston** by **NY Americans** for Ted Graham, December 19, 1936.

• KALETA, Alex

Alexander "Killer"
LW – L. 6', 175 lbs. b: Canmore, Alta., 11/29/1919 d: 7/9/1987.

Season	Club	League	GP	G	A	Pts	AG	AA	APts	PIM	GP	G	A	Pts	PIM
1937-38	Canmore Briquettes	CCJHL	10	10	3	13	....	....	....	20	....	....	....	....	....
1938-39	Calgary Stampeders	ASHL	32	15	13	28	....	....	....	39	....	....	....	....	....
1939-40	Regina Aces	ASHL	32	19	20	39	....	....	....	33	9	4	6	10	10
1940-41	Lethbridge Maple Leafs	ASHL	24	20	*28	48	....	....	....	22	5	2	4	6	4
	Lethbridge Maple Leafs	Al-Cup	10	6	5	11	....	....	....	22	....	....	....	....	....
1941-42	**Chicago Black Hawks**	**NHL**	**48**	**7**	**21**	**28**	**9**	**25**	**34**	**12**	**3**	**1**	**2**	**3**	**0**
1942-43	Calgary Currie Army	CNDHL	24	23	*35	*58	....	....	....	23	5	4	3	7	6
	Calgary Currie Army	Al-Cup	5	2	4	6	....	....	....	0	....	....	....	....	....
1943-44	Calgary Currie Army	CNDHL	15	8	15	23	....	....	....	24	2	*5	1	6	4
1944-45	Calgary Currie Army	CNDHL	16	14	12	26	....	....	....	16	3	1	2	3	*12
1945-46	**Chicago Black Hawks**	**NHL**	**49**	**19**	**27**	**46**	**23**	**40**	**63**	**17**	**4**	**0**	**1**	**1**	**2**
1946-47	**Chicago Black Hawks**	**NHL**	**57**	**24**	**20**	**44**	**27**	**24**	**51**	**37**	....	....	....	....	....
1947-48	**Chicago Black Hawks**	**NHL**	**52**	**10**	**16**	**26**	**13**	**21**	**34**	**40**	....	....	....	....	....
1948-49	**New York Rangers**	**NHL**	**56**	**12**	**19**	**31**	**17**	**27**	**44**	**18**	....	....	....	....	....
1949-50	**New York Rangers**	**NHL**	**67**	**17**	**14**	**31**	**21**	**17**	**38**	**40**	**10**	**0**	**3**	**3**	**0**
1950-51	**New York Rangers**	**NHL**	**58**	**3**	**4**	**7**	**4**	**5**	**9**	**26**	....	....	....	....	....
	Hershey Bears	AHL	5	0	2	2	....	....	....	6	....	....	....	....	....
1951-52	Saskatoon Quakers	PCHL	62	38	44	82	....	....	....	23	13	6	*13	19	4
1952-53	Saskatoon Quakers	WHL	70	26	*57	83	....	....	....	6	13	9	*14	*23	2
1953-54	Saskatoon Quakers	WHL	70	19	53	72	....	....	....	52	6	0	5	5	4
1954-55	Saskatoon Quakers	WHL	13	2	9	11	....	....	....	10	....	....	....	....	....
	NHL Totals		**387**	**92**	**121**	**213**	**114**	**159**	**273**	**190**	**17**	**1**	**6**	**7**	**2**

CNDHL First All-Star Team (1943, 1944)

Traded to **NY Rangers** by **Chicago** with Emile Francis for Jim Henry, October 7, 1948. Loaned to **Boston** (Hershey-AHL) by **NY Rangers** to complete transaction that sent Zellio Toppazzini and Ed Harrison to NY Rangers (November 16, 1950), November 20, 1950.

• KAMINSKY, Max

C – L. 5'11", 160 lbs. b: Niagara Falls, Ont., 4/19/1913 d: 5/5/1961.

Season	Club	League	REGULAR SEASON GP	G	A	Pts	AG	AA	APts	PIM	PLAYOFFS GP	G	A	Pts	PIM
1929-30	Niagara Falls Cataracts	OHA-Jr.	6	9	*4	13				2	2	*5	1	*6	0
1930-31	Niagara Falls Cataracts	OHA-Jr.	7	14	*15	*29				0	2	*3	0	*3	4
	Niagara Falls Brights	OSHA-B	1	1	1	2				0					
1931-32	Niagara Falls Cataracts	OHA-Sr.	20	12	3	15				18	2	0	0	0	2
1932-33	Niagara Falls Cataracts	OHA-Sr.	21	11	7	18				36	5	2	1	3	13
	Niagara Falls Cataracts	Al-Cup	6	3	1	4				2					
1933-34	Niagara Falls Cataracts	OHA-Sr.	6	5	3	8				8					
	Ottawa Senators	**NHL**	**38**	**9**	**17**	**26**	**15**	**36**	**51**	**14**					
1934-35	**Boston Bruins**	**NHL**	**38**	**12**	**15**	**27**	**20**	**26**	**46**	**4**	**4**	**0**	**0**	**0**	**0**
	St. Louis Eagles	**NHL**	**12**	**0**	**0**	**0**	**0**	**0**	**0**	**0**					
1935-36	**Boston Bruins**	**NHL**	**36**	**1**	**2**	**3**	**2**	**4**	**6**	**20**					
1936-37	**Montreal Maroons**	**NHL**	**6**	**0**	**0**	**0**	**0**	**0**	**0**	**0**					
	Providence Reds	IAHL	2	0	0	0				0					
	New Haven Eagles	IAHL	20	3	5	8				6					
1937-38	New Haven Eagles	IAHL	15	2	4	6				4					
	Springfield Indians	IAHL	31	3	4	7				14					
1938-39	Springfield Indians	IAHL	46	7	14	21				8	3	0	1	1	2
1939-40	Springfield Indians	IAHL	53	11	29	40				20	3	0	2	2	0
1940-41	Springfield Indians	AHL	40	13	9	22				9	3	2	0	2	0
1941-42	Springfield Indians	AHL	53	18	23	41				9	5	0	2	2	0
1942-43	Buffalo Bisons	AHL	42	10	36	46				6	9	2	*12	14	4
1943-44	Buffalo Bisons	AHL	42	7	29	36				17	9	4	2	6	2
1944-45	Pittsburgh Hornets	AHL	54	5	28	33				17					
1945-46	Pittsburgh Hornets	AHL	DID NOT PLAY – COACHING												
	NHL Totals		**130**	**22**	**34**	**56**	**37**	**66**	**103**	**38**	**4**	**0**	**0**	**0**	**0**

IAHL Second All-Star Team (1940)

Signed as a free agent by **Ottawa**, December 4, 1933. Transferred to **St. Louis** after **Ottawa** franchise relocated, September 22, 1934. Traded to **Boston** by **St. Louis** with Des Roche for Joe Lamb, December 4, 1934. Traded to **Montreal Maroons** by **Boston** for cash, December 7, 1936. Traded to **New Haven** (IAHL) by **Providence** (IAHL) for Whitey Farrant, January 25, 1937. Traded to **Springfield** (IAHL) by **New Haven** (IAHL) for Paul Raymond, December 23, 1937.

• KAMPMAN, Rudolph "Bingo"

D – R. 5'10", 187 lbs. b: Berlin, Ont., 3/12/1914 d: 12/22/1987.

Season	Club	League	GP	G	A	Pts	AG	AA	APts	PIM	GP	G	A	Pts	PIM
1932-33	Kitchener Empires	OHA-B	1	1	1	2				0					
1933-34	Kitchener Greenshirts	OHA-Jr.	16	10	1	11				26	4	4	0	4	2
1934-35	Kitchener Greenshirts	OSBHL	13	4	2	6				10	3	1	0	1	4
	Kitchener Greenshirts	Al-Cup	2	0	0	0				2					
1935-36	Creighton Mines	NOHA	8	0	1	1				25	5	2	0	2	13
	Falconbridge Falcons	Al-Cup	17	3	4	7				31					
1936-37	Sudbury Frood Miners	NOHA	14	2	3	5				27	2	0	0	0	4
	Kitchener Greenshirts	OHA-Sr.	2	0	1	1				0					
	Sudbury Frood Miners	Al-Cup	11	2	4	6				10					
1937-38	**Toronto Maple Leafs**	**NHL**	**32**	**1**	**2**	**3**	**2**	**3**	**5**	**56**	**7**	**0**	**1**	**1**	**6**
	Syracuse Stars	IAHL	12	2	1	3				4					
1938-39	**Toronto Maple Leafs**	**NHL**	**41**	**2**	**8**	**10**	**3**	**12**	**15**	**52**	**10**	**1**	**1**	**2**	**20**
1939-40	**Toronto Maple Leafs**	**NHL**	**39**	**6**	**9**	**15**	**10**	**14**	**24**	**59**	**10**	**0**	**0**	**0**	**0**
1940-41	**Toronto Maple Leafs**	**NHL**	**39**	**1**	**4**	**5**	**2**	**6**	**8**	**53**	**7**	**0**	**0**	**0**	**0**
♦1941-42	**Toronto Maple Leafs**	**NHL**	**38**	**4**	**7**	**11**	**5**	**8**	**13**	**67**	**13**	**0**	**2**	**2**	**12**
1942-43	Halifax Army	NSDHL	8	4	3	7				18	4	0	1	1	14
	Ottawa Commandos	QSHL									1	0	0	0	0
	Ottawa Commandos	Al-Cup	12	3	4	7				14					
1943-44	Halifax Crescents	NSDHL	2	0	1	1				2					
	New Glasgow Bombers	NSAPC	2	0	0	0				4	2	0	0	0	0
1944-45	Dartmouth RCAF	NSDHL	5	0	0	0				8	3	0	0	0	4
1945-46	Providence Reds	AHL	27	4	8	12				12	2	0	0	0	0
1946-47	St. Louis Flyers	AHL	45	4	14	18				44					
1947-48	St. Louis Flyers	AHL	46	4	13	17				29					
1948-49	Fresno Falcons	PCHL	69	6	14	20				82	3	0	0	0	4
1949-50	Fresno Falcons	PCHL	37	3	6	9				27					
	Nanaimo Clippers	OSHL	9	2	2	4				14	8	1	0	1	8
1950-51	Kitchener Dutchmen	OMHL	23	2	3	5				20					
	NHL Totals		**189**	**14**	**30**	**44**	**22**	**43**	**65**	**287**	**47**	**1**	**4**	**5**	**38**

NSDHL First All-Star Team (1943) • PCHL Southern First All-Star Team (1949)

Traded to **Boston** by **Toronto** to complete transaction that sent Art Jackson to Toronto (December 24, 1944), October 29, 1945. Returned to **Toronto** by **Boston** and loaned to **Providence** (AHL), November 6, 1945.

• KANE, Francis Francis Joseph "Red"

D – L. 5'11", 186 lbs. b: Stratford, Ont., 1/19/1923.

Season	Club	League	GP	G	A	Pts	AG	AA	APts	PIM	GP	G	A	Pts	PIM
1941-42	Falconbridge Falcons	NOJHA	9	1	1	2				10	2	1	0	1	0
1942-43	Brantford Lions	OHA-Jr.	20	3	3	6				42	10	1	3	4	18
1943-44	**Detroit Red Wings**	**NHL**	**2**	**0**	**0**	**0**	**0**	**0**	**0**	**0**					
	Indianapolis Capitols	AHL	51	6	13	19				17	5	0	4	4	0
1944-45	Indianapolis Capitols	AHL	59	4	8	12				95	5	0	0	0	4
1945-46	St. Louis Flyers	AHL	5	0	0	0				10					
	Tulsa Oilers	USHL	47	8	7	15				*127	13	0	0	0	14
1946-47	Fort Worth Rangers	USHL	59	3	13	16				69	8	0	0	0	12
1947-48	Fort Worth Rangers	USHL	57	8	15	23				61	4	0	3	3	0
1948-49	Fort Worth Rangers	USHL	62	2	22	24				116	2	1	1	2	2
1949-50	Oakland–Los Angeles	PCHL	51	4	7	11				88	16	1	8	9	43
1950-51	New Haven Ramblers	AHL	28	1	7	8				45					
	Springfield Indians	AHL	11	0	1	1				4					
	Vancouver Canucks	PCHL	18	1	9	10				25					
	NHL Totals		**2**	**0**	**0**	**0**	**0**	**0**	**0**	**0**					

Traded to **Tulsa** (USHL) by **Detroit** for cash, November, 1945. Signed as a free agent by **Springfield** (AHL) and assigned to **Fort Worth** (USHL), October, 1946. Loaned to **LA Monarchs** (PCHL) by **Springfield** (AHL) after Oakland (PCHL) franchise folded, December 20, 1949. • Recalled by **Springfield** (AHL) when **New Haven** (AHL) franchise folded, December 10, 1950.

• KEATING, Jack John Thomas "Red"

LW – L. 6', 180 lbs. b: Kitchener, Ont., 10/9/1916 d: 12/29/1951.

Season	Club	League	GP	G	A	Pts	AG	AA	APts	PIM	GP	G	A	Pts	PIM
1934-35	Kitchener Greenshirts	OHA-Jr.	14	11	10	21				4	2	1	0	1	0
1935-36	Kitchener Greenshirts	OHA-Jr.	7	6	1	7				10	4	3	1	4	0
1936-37	Richmond Hawks	Britain	40	13	2	15				6					
1937-38	Harringay Racers	Ln-Cup		7	1	8									
	Harringay Racers	Britain		18	2	20									
	Harringay Racers	Nat-Tmt		4	0	4									
1938-39	**Detroit Red Wings**	**NHL**	**1**	**1**	**0**	**1**	**2**	**0**	**2**	**2**					
	Pittsburgh Hornets	AHL	50	19	12	31				18					
1939-40	**Detroit Red Wings**	**NHL**	**10**	**2**	**0**	**2**	**3**	**0**	**3**	**2**					
	Indianapolis Capitols	IAHL	32	8	12	20				4	5	1	2	3	0
1940-41	Indianapolis Capitols	AHL	53	21	18	39				6					
1941-42	Indianapolis Capitols	AHL	55	19	25	44				14	10	*9	9	*18	0
1942-43	Indianapolis Capitols	AHL	7	4	4	8				0					
1943-44			MILITARY SERVICE												
1944-45			MILITARY SERVICE												
1945-46	Indianapolis Capitols	AHL	14	8	3	11				0	5	1	1	2	0
	Hollywood Wolves	PCHL	8	5	2	7				6					
1946-47	Los Angeles Monarchs	PCHL	55	36	26	62				16	10	3	3	6	26
1947-48	Los Angeles Monarchs	PCHL	45	41	19	60				26					
	NHL Totals		**11**	**3**	**0**	**3**	**5**	**0**	**5**	**4**					

• KEATING, John John Richard

LW – L. 5'7", 145 lbs. b: St. John, N.B., 2/12/1908 d: 11/14/1984.

Season	Club	League	GP	G	A	Pts	AG	AA	APts	PIM	GP	G	A	Pts	PIM
1925-26	Chatham Ironmen	NNBHL	12	2	1	3				0	2	0	0	0	0
1926-27	Saint John Fusiliers	SNBHL	12	10	3	13				26	2	1	0	1	2
1927-28	Saint John Fusiliers	SNBHL	12	15	*8	*23				*42	2	1	0	1	8
	Saint John Fusiliers	Al-Cup	7	8	5	13				12					
1928-29	Saint John Fusiliers	SNBHL	12	12	*9	*21				16	2	1	0	1	4
1929-30	Saint John Beavers	SNBHL	11	9	6	15				35	2	0	0	0	4
	Saint John Beavers	Al-Cup	4	2	0	2				4					
1930-31	New Haven Eagles	Can-Am	39	9	2	11				49					
1931-32	**New York Americans**	**NHL**	**22**	**5**	**3**	**8**	**8**	**7**	**15**	**6**					
	New Haven Eagles	Can-Am	21	4	4	8				26					
1932-33	**New York Americans**	**NHL**	**13**	**0**	**2**	**2**	**0**	**4**	**4**	**11**					
	New Haven Eagles	Can-Am	39	12	8	20				71					
1933-34	Buffalo Bisons	IHL	43	8	4	12				21	6	0	0	0	2
1934-35	Providence Reds	Can-Am	46	16	19	35				27	6	*2	2	4	2
1935-36	Providence Reds	Can-Am	47	10	12	22				35	7	2	3	5	4
1936-37	Providence Reds	IAHL	51	12	31	43				22	3	1	2	3	2
1937-38	Providence Reds	IAHL	45	15	13	28				20	7	2	3	5	0
1938-39	Providence Reds	IAHL	51	5	18	23				16	5	0	1	1	0
1939-40	Syracuse Stars	IAHL	40	11	17	28				14					
1940-41	Buffalo Bisons	AHL	3	0	0	0				0					
	St. Paul Saints	AHA	34	5	3	8				6	4	0	1	1	6
1941-42	Saint John Beavers	X-Games	7	*9	5	14				0					
	Saint John Garrison	Al-Cup	2	2	1	3				2					
1942-43	Saint John Garrison	X-Games	3	1	3	4				2	2	0	*3	*3	0
	Saint John Garrison	Al-Cup	7	3	3	6				6					
1943-44	Saint John Garrison	X-Games	11	6	11	*17				2					
	Saint John Garrison	Al-Cup	5	9	4	13				0					
1944-45			MILITARY SERVICE												
1945-46	Saint John Beavers	X-Games	1	1	1	2				0					
1946-47	Saint John Beavers	MSHL	DID NOT PLAY – COACHING												
	NHL Totals		**35**	**5**	**5**	**10**	**8**	**11**	**19**	**17**					

Signed as a free agent by **NY Americans**, October 22, 1930. Loaned to **Buffalo** (IAHL) by **NY Americans** for cash, January 9, 1934. Traded to **Providence** (Can-Am) by **NY Americans** for cash, November 13, 1934. Signed as a free agent by **Syracuse** (AHL), October, 1940. Traded to **Buffalo** (AHL) by **Syracuse** (AHL) for cash, October, 1940. Loaned to **St. Paul** (AHA) by **Buffalo** (AHL), December 11, 1940.

• KEATS, Duke Gordon Blanchard HHOF

C – R. 5'11", 195 lbs. b: Montreal, Que., 3/1/1895 d: 1/16/1972.

Season	Club	League	GP	G	A	Pts	AG	AA	APts	PIM	GP	G	A	Pts	PIM
1912-13	Cobalt McKinley Mines	CoMHL	9	6	0	6				18					
1913-14	Cobalt O'Brien Mines	CoMHL	8	8	0	8				8					
	North Bay Trappers	NOHA	3	2	0	2				18	4	*6	0	*6	
1914-15	Haileybury Hawks	TBSHL	STATISTICS NOT AVAILABLE												
1915-16	Toronto Blueshirts	NHA	24	22	7	29				112					
1916-17	Toronto Blueshirts	NHA	13	15	3	18				54					
1917-18			MILITARY SERVICE												
1918-19			MILITARY SERVICE												
1919-20	Edmonton Eskimos	Big-4	12	*18	*14	*32				*41	2	*2	*2	*4	2
1920-21	Edmonton Dominions	Big-4	15	*23	6	*29				36					
1921-22	Edmonton Eskimos	WCHL	25	*31	*24	*55				47	2	0	1	1	6
1922-23	Edmonton Eskimos	WCHL	25	24	13	37				*72	2	2	2	4	0
	Edmonton Eskimos	St-Cup	2	0	0	0				4					
1923-24	Edmonton Eskimos	WCHL	29	19	12	31				41					
1924-25	Edmonton Eskimos	WCHL	28	23	9	32				63					
1925-26	Edmonton Eskimos	WHL	30	20	9	29				*134	2	0	1	1	28
1926-27	**Boston Bruins**	**NHL**	**17**	**4**	**7**	**11**	**7**	**37**	**44**	**20**					
	Detroit Cougars	**NHL**	**25**	**12**	**1**	**13**	**21**	**5**	**26**	**32**					
1927-28	**Detroit Cougars**	**NHL**	**5**	**0**	**2**	**2**	**0**	**11**	**11**	**6**					
	Chicago Black Hawks	**NHL**	**32**	**14**	**8**	**22**	**29**	**45**	**74**	**55**					
1928-29	**Chicago Black Hawks**	**NHL**	**3**	**0**	**1**	**1**	**0**	**7**	**7**	**0**					
	Tulsa Oilers	AHA	39	*22	11	*33				18	4	0	1	1	10
1929-30	Tulsa Oilers	AHA	3	2	2	4				2					
1930-31	Tulsa Oilers	AHA	43	14	10	24				44	4	0	1	1	6
1931-32			REINSTATED AS AN AMATEUR												

Season	Club	League	GP	G	A	Pts	AG	AA	APts	PIM	GP	G	A	Pts	PIM
			REGULAR SEASON								PLAYOFFS				
1932-33	Edmonton Eskimos	WCHL	25	8	7	15	....	....	....	*146	8	1	*4	5	0
1933-34	Edmonton Eskimos	NWHL	25	8	6	14	....	....	....	8	2	0	0	0	2
1934-35	Edmonton Eskimos	NWHL	DID NOT PLAY – COACHING												
	NHL Totals		**82**	**30**	**19**	**49**	**57**	**105**	**162**	**113**	....	....	....	....	....
	Other Major League Totals		174	154	77	231				523	6	2	4	6	34

WCHL First All-Star Team (1922, 1923, 1924, 1925) • WHL First All-Star Team (1926)

Signed as a free agent by **Toronto St. Pats**, December 9, 1919. Reinstated as an amateur and signed as a free agent by **Edmonton** (Big 4), December, 1919. Signed as a free agent by **Edmonton** (WCHL), November 4, 1921. Traded to **Boston** by **Edmonton** (WHL) for cash, September 4, 1926. Traded to **Detroit** by **Boston** with Archie Briden for Frank Fredrickson and Harry Meeking, January 7, 1927. Traded to **Chicago** by **Detroit** for Gord Fraser and $5,000, December 16, 1927. Traded to **Tulsa** (AHA) by **Chicago** for cash, November, 1928.

• KEELING, Butch Melville Sydney

LW – L. 5'11", 180 lbs. b: Owen Sound, Ont., 8/10/1905 d: 11/14/1984.

Season	Club	League	GP	G	A	Pts	AG	AA	APts	PIM	GP	G	A	Pts	PIM
1920/23	Owen Sound Greys	OHA-Jr.	STATISTICS NOT AVAILABLE												
1923-24	Owen Sound Greys	OHA-Jr.	11	24	4	28	....	....	....	....	....	....	....	....	....
	Owen Sound Greys	M-Cup	15	*37	*9	*46	....	....	....	....	....	....	....	....	....
1924-25	Owen Sound Greys	OHA-Jr.	16	22	8	30	....	....	....	....	....	....	....	....	....
	Owen Sound Greys	M-Cup	9	*15	5	*20	....	....	....	12	....	....	....	....	....
1925-26	London Ravens	OHA-Sr.	20	14	3	17	....	....	....	18	2	1	1	2	0
	London Ravens	Al-Cup	2	1	0	1	....	....	....	0	....	....	....	....	....
1926-27	London Panthers	Can-Pro	12	13	1	14	....	....	....	25	....	....	....	....	....
	Toronto Pats/Leafs	**NHL**	**30**	**11**	**2**	**13**	**20**	**10**	**30**	**29**	....	....	....	....	....
1927-28	**Toronto Maple Leafs**	**NHL**	**43**	**10**	**6**	**16**	**20**	**34**	**54**	**52**	....	....	....	....	....
1928-29	**New York Rangers**	**NHL**	**43**	**6**	**3**	**9**	**17**	**20**	**37**	**35**	**6**	***3**	**0**	***3**	**2**
1929-30	**New York Rangers**	**NHL**	**43**	**19**	**7**	**26**	**27**	**16**	**43**	**34**	**4**	**0**	**3**	**3**	**8**
1930-31	**New York Rangers**	**NHL**	**44**	**13**	**9**	**22**	**26**	**27**	**53**	**35**	**4**	**1**	**1**	**2**	**0**
1931-32	**New York Rangers**	**NHL**	**48**	**17**	**3**	**20**	**28**	**7**	**35**	**38**	**7**	**2**	**1**	**3**	**12**
♦1932-33	**New York Rangers**	**NHL**	**47**	**8**	**6**	**14**	**14**	**12**	**26**	**22**	**8**	**0**	**2**	**2**	**8**
1933-34	**New York Rangers**	**NHL**	**48**	**15**	**5**	**20**	**26**	**10**	**36**	**20**	**2**	**0**	**0**	**0**	**0**
1934-35	**New York Rangers**	**NHL**	**47**	**15**	**4**	**19**	**25**	**7**	**32**	**14**	**4**	**2**	**1**	**3**	**0**
1935-36	**New York Rangers**	**NHL**	**46**	**13**	**5**	**18**	**25**	**9**	**34**	**22**	....	....	....	....	....
1936-37	**New York Rangers**	**NHL**	**48**	**22**	**4**	**26**	**37**	**7**	**44**	**18**	**9**	**3**	**2**	**5**	**2**
1937-38	**New York Rangers**	**NHL**	**38**	**8**	**9**	**17**	**13**	**14**	**27**	**12**	**3**	**0**	**1**	**1**	**2**
1938-39	Philadelphia Ramblers	IAHL	48	6	13	19	....	....	....	16	9	2	1	3	5
1939-40	Kansas City Greyhounds	AHA	46	15	11	26	....	....	....	27	....	....	....	....	....
	NHL Totals		**525**	**157**	**63**	**220**	**278**	**173**	**451**	**331**	**47**	**11**	**11**	**22**	**34**

Signed as a free agent by **Toronto**, September 7, 1926. Traded to **NY Rangers** by **Toronto** for Alex Gray, April 16, 1928. • Named playing-coach of **Kansas City** (AHA), September 24, 1939.

• KEENAN, Larry *— see page 1251*

• KELLER, Ralph

D – R. 5'9", 174 lbs. b: Wilkie, Sask., 2/6/1936.

Season	Club	League	GP	G	A	Pts	AG	AA	APts	PIM	GP	G	A	Pts	PIM
1952-53	Prince Albert Mintos	SJHL	1	0	0	0	....	....	....	0	....	....	....	....	....
1953-54	Prince Albert Mintos	SJHL	48	7	21	28	....	....	....	83	15	1	1	2	34
1954-55	Prince Albert Mintos	SJHL	48	12	16	28	....	....	....	93	10	3	3	6	14
	Saskatoon Quakers	WHL	1	0	1	1	....	....	....	0	....	....	....	....	....
1955-56	Prince Albert Mintos	SJHL	50	20	35	55	....	....	....	56	12	6	7	13	12
	Saskatoon Quakers	WHL	4	0	0	0	....	....	....	2	3	0	0	0	2
1956-57	Vancouver Canucks	WHL	68	6	15	21	....	....	....	75	....	....	....	....	....
1957-58	Saskatoon–St. Paul	WHL	34	5	10	15	....	....	....	51	....	....	....	....	....
	Providence Reds	AHL	31	1	7	8	....	....	....	22	....	....	....	....	....
1958-59	Saskatoon Quakers	WHL	64	6	17	23	....	....	....	70	....	....	....	....	....
1959-60	Vancouver Canucks	WHL	70	12	19	31	....	....	....	102	11	2	4	6	16
1960-61	Vancouver Canucks	WHL	70	9	31	40	....	....	....	95	9	2	3	5	6
1961-62	Los Angeles Blades	WHL	70	17	38	55	....	....	....	136	....	....	....	....	....
1962-63	**New York Rangers**	**NHL**	**3**	**1**	**0**	**1**	**1**	**0**	**1**	**6**	....	....	....	....	....
	Baltimore Clippers	AHL	71	7	23	30	....	....	....	133	3	0	0	0	8
1963-64	Hershey Bears	AHL	61	5	20	25	....	....	....	102	6	1	2	3	10
1964-65	Hershey Bears	AHL	72	7	32	39	....	....	....	166	15	1	3	4	*38
1965-66	Hershey Bears	AHL	45	5	14	19	....	....	....	91	....	....	....	....	....
1966-67	Hershey Bears	AHL	69	11	33	44	....	....	....	109	5	0	4	4	6
1967-68	Hershey Bears	AHL	70	11	35	46	....	....	....	126	5	1	1	2	4
1968-69	Hershey Bears	AHL	74	9	46	55	....	....	....	104	11	3	4	7	*38
1969-70	Hershey Bears	AHL	62	13	21	34	....	....	....	94	7	1	3	4	21
1970-71	Hershey Bears	AHL	70	17	22	39	....	....	....	81	4	1	0	1	15
1971-72	Hershey Bears	AHL	67	8	26	34	....	....	....	100	4	0	1	1	2
1972-73	Hershey Bears	AHL	73	9	33	42	....	....	....	103	7	1	5	6	8
1973-74	Hershey Bears	AHL	74	8	23	31	....	....	....	99	10	2	1	3	6
	NHL Totals		**3**	**1**	**0**	**1**	**1**	**0**	**1**	**6**	....	....	....	....	....

WHL Second All-Star Team (1960) • WHL First All-Star Team (1961) • AHL First All-Star Team (1969) • AHL Second All-Star Team (1973)

Claimed by **Montreal** from **NY Rangers** (Baltimore-AHL) in Inter-League Draft, June 4, 1963. Traded to **Hershey** (AHL) by **Montreal** with the loan of Chuck Hamilton for Marc Reaume, June 11, 1963.

• KELLY, Pete Peter Cameron

RW – R. 5'11", 170 lbs. b: St. Vital, Man., 5/22/1913.

Season	Club	League	GP	G	A	Pts	AG	AA	APts	PIM	GP	G	A	Pts	PIM
1928-29	Montreal Camp Orelda	MCHL	....	....	....	....	....	....	....	....	....	....	....	....	....
1929-30	Montreal Victorias	MCJHL	10	3	0	3	....	....	....	4	....	....	....	....	....
1930-31	Montreal AAA	MCJHL	10	*7	0	*7	....	....	....	10	2	1	0	1	2
	Montreal AAA	MCHL	....	....	....	....	....	....	....	....	1	0	0	0	0
	Montreal AAA	M-Cup	4	4	3	7	....	....	....	4	....	....	....	....	....
1931-32	Montreal AAA	MCJHL	10	8	*9	*17	....	....	....	10	2	2	0	2	6
	Montreal AC	MCHL	....	....	....	....	....	....	....	....	1	0	0	0	0
	Montreal AAA	M-Cup	6	5	*5	*10	....	....	....	2	....	....	....	....	....
1932-33	Montreal Royals	MCHL	8	0	0	0	....	....	....	0	6	0	*2	2	11
1933-34	Charlottetown Abegweits	MSHL	39	14	11	25	....	....	....	67	3	1	0	1	2
1934-35	**St. Louis Eagles**	**NHL**	**25**	**3**	**10**	**13**	**5**	**17**	**22**	**14**	....	....	....	....	....
	Charlottetown Abegweits	MSHL	20	16	11	*27	....	....	....	27	....	....	....	....	....
♦1935-36	**Detroit Red Wings**	**NHL**	**46**	**6**	**8**	**14**	**11**	**15**	**26**	**30**	**7**	**1**	**1**	**2**	**2**
♦1936-37	**Detroit Red Wings**	**NHL**	**47**	**5**	**4**	**9**	**8**	**7**	**15**	**12**	**8**	**2**	**0**	**2**	**0**
1937-38	**Detroit Red Wings**	**NHL**	**9**	**0**	**1**	**1**	**0**	**2**	**2**	**2**	....	....	....	....	....
	Pittsburgh Hornets	IAHL	39	7	20	27	....	....	....	26	2	0	2	2	0
1938-39	**Detroit Red Wings**	**NHL**	**32**	**4**	**9**	**13**	**7**	**14**	**21**	**4**	**4**	**0**	**0**	**0**	**0**
	Pittsburgh Hornets	IAHL	6	2	6	8	....	....	....	0	....	....	....	....	....
1939-40	Pittsburgh Hornets	IAHL	54	20	20	40	....	....	....	22	9	2	5	7	9
1940-41	Pittsburgh Hornets	AHL	25	4	16	20	....	....	....	8	....	....	....	....	....
	New York Americans	**NHL**	**11**	**3**	**5**	**8**	**5**	**7**	**12**	**2**	....	....	....	....	....
	Springfield Indians	AHL	19	6	14	20	....	....	....	6	3	2	1	3	0
1941-42	**Brooklyn Americans**	**NHL**	**7**	**0**	**1**	**1**	**0**	**1**	**1**	**4**	....	....	....	....	....
	Springfield Indians	AHL	46	33	*44	*77	....	....	....	11	5	1	6	7	4
1942-43	Moncton RCAF	NBDHL	4	*9	6	*15	....	....	....	....	4	4	*8	*12	12
1943-44	Moncton Flyers	NBDHL	4	4	3	*7	....	....	....	0	....	....	....	....	....
	Charlottetown All-Stars	PEI-Sr.	4	3	6	9	....	....	....	2	....	....	....	....	....
	Saint John Beavers	X-Games	4	6	7	13	....	....	....	0	2	2	1	3	0
	Saint John Beavers	Al-Cup	3	6	3	9	....	....	....	0	....	....	....	....	....
1944-45	Charlottetown #2	PEI-Sr.	8	7	15	22	....	....	....	7	2	3	1	4	0
	New Glasgow Bombers	NSAPC	2	3	3	6	....	....	....	0	5	*11	4	*15	0
	New Glascow Bombers	Al-Cup	3	*5	5	*10	....	....	....	0	....	....	....	....	....
1945-46			MILITARY SERVICE												
1946-47	New Glasgow Bombers	NSAPC	16	14	14	28	....	....	....	....	3	2	1	3	0
	New Glascow Bombers	Al-Cup	2	0	0	0	....	....	....	0	....	....	....	....	....
1947-48	U. of New Brunswick	YCHL	1	0	3	3	....	....	....	0	4	4	6	10	2
1948-49	U. of New Brunswick	YCHL	3	2	1	3	....	....	....	0	5	*6	5	11	0
1949-50	U. of New Brunswick	SNBHL	5	7	5	12	....	....	....	4	1	0	0	0	0
1950-51	U. of New Brunswick	SNBHL	DID NOT PLAY – COACHING												
1951-52	U. of New Brunswick	X-Games	1	0	3	3	....	....	....	0	....	....	....	....	....
	NHL Totals		**177**	**21**	**38**	**59**	**36**	**63**	**99**	**68**	**19**	**3**	**1**	**4**	**2**

AHL First All-Star Team (1942)

Signed as a free agent by **St. Louis**, November, 1934. Claimed by **NY Americans** from **St. Louis** in Dispersal Draft, October 15, 1935. Traded to **Detroit** by **NY Americans** for Carl Voss, October 16, 1935. Traded to **Pittsburgh** (AHL) by **Detroit** for cash, December 2, 1937. Traded to **NY Americans** (Springfield-AHL) by **Pittsburgh** (AHL) for Norm Schultz, December 31, 1940.

• KELLY, Red Leonard Patrick HHOF

D/C – L. 5'11", 180 lbs. b: Simcoe, Ont., 7/9/1927.

Season	Club	League	GP	G	A	Pts	AG	AA	APts	PIM	GP	G	A	Pts	PIM
1943-44	St. Michael's Midgets	OMHA	8	10	5	15	....	....	....	....	....	....	....	....	....
1944-45	St. Michael's Buzzers	OHA-B	11	15	13	28	....	....	....	7	11	16	8	24	6
	St. Michael's Majors	OHA-Jr.	1	0	0	0	....	....	....	0	....	....	....	....	....
1945-46	St. Michael's Majors	OHA-Jr.	26	13	11	24	....	....	....	18	11	1	0	1	7
1946-47	St. Michael's Majors	OHA-Jr.	30	8	24	32	....	....	....	11	9	3	3	6	9
	St. Michael's Majors	M-Cup	9	5	5	10	....	....	....	2	....	....	....	....	....
1947-48	**Detroit Red Wings**	**NHL**	**60**	**6**	**14**	**20**	**8**	**18**	**26**	**13**	**10**	**3**	**2**	**5**	**2**
1948-49	**Detroit Red Wings**	**NHL**	**59**	**5**	**11**	**16**	**7**	**16**	**23**	**10**	**11**	**1**	**1**	**2**	**10**
♦1949-50	**Detroit Red Wings**	**NHL**	**70**	**15**	**25**	**40**	**19**	**30**	**49**	**9**	**14**	**1**	**3**	**4**	**2**
1950-51	**Detroit Red Wings**	**NHL**	**70**	**17**	**37**	**54**	**22**	**46**	**68**	**24**	**6**	**0**	**1**	**1**	**0**
♦1951-52	**Detroit Red Wings**	**NHL**	**67**	**16**	**31**	**47**	**21**	**38**	**59**	**16**	**5**	**1**	**0**	**1**	**0**
1952-53	**Detroit Red Wings**	**NHL**	**70**	**19**	**27**	**46**	**25**	**33**	**58**	**8**	**6**	**0**	**4**	**4**	**0**
♦1953-54	**Detroit Red Wings**	**NHL**	**62**	**16**	**33**	**49**	**22**	**40**	**62**	**18**	**12**	**5**	**1**	**6**	**0**
♦1954-55	**Detroit Red Wings**	**NHL**	**70**	**15**	**30**	**45**	**19**	**35**	**54**	**28**	**11**	**2**	**4**	**6**	**17**
1955-56	**Detroit Red Wings**	**NHL**	**70**	**16**	**34**	**50**	**22**	**41**	**63**	**39**	**10**	**2**	**4**	**6**	**2**
1956-57	**Detroit Red Wings**	**NHL**	**70**	**10**	**25**	**35**	**13**	**28**	**41**	**18**	**5**	**1**	**0**	**1**	**0**
1957-58	**Detroit Red Wings**	**NHL**	**61**	**13**	**18**	**31**	**16**	**19**	**35**	**26**	**4**	**0**	**1**	**1**	**2**
1958-59	**Detroit Red Wings**	**NHL**	**67**	**8**	**13**	**21**	**9**	**13**	**22**	**34**	....	....	....	....	....
1959-60	**Detroit Red Wings**	**NHL**	**50**	**6**	**12**	**18**	**7**	**12**	**19**	**10**	....	....	....	....	....
	Toronto Maple Leafs	**NHL**	**18**	**6**	**5**	**11**	**7**	**5**	**12**	**8**	**10**	**3**	**8**	**11**	**2**
1960-61	**Toronto Maple Leafs**	**NHL**	**64**	**20**	**50**	**70**	**23**	**49**	**72**	**12**	**2**	**1**	**0**	**1**	**0**
♦1961-62	**Toronto Maple Leafs**	**NHL**	**58**	**22**	**27**	**49**	**25**	**26**	**51**	**6**	**12**	**4**	**6**	**10**	**0**
♦1962-63	**Toronto Maple Leafs**	**NHL**	**66**	**20**	**40**	**60**	**23**	**40**	**63**	**8**	**10**	**2**	**6**	**8**	**6**
♦1963-64	**Toronto Maple Leafs**	**NHL**	**70**	**11**	**34**	**45**	**14**	**36**	**50**	**16**	**14**	**4**	**9**	**13**	**4**
1964-65	**Toronto Maple Leafs**	**NHL**	**70**	**18**	**28**	**46**	**22**	**29**	**51**	**8**	**6**	**3**	**2**	**5**	**2**
1965-66	**Toronto Maple Leafs**	**NHL**	**63**	**8**	**24**	**32**	**9**	**23**	**32**	**12**	**4**	**0**	**2**	**2**	**0**
♦1966-67	**Toronto Maple Leafs**	**NHL**	**61**	**14**	**24**	**38**	**16**	**23**	**39**	**4**	**12**	**0**	**5**	**5**	**2**
1967-68	**Los Angeles Kings**	**NHL**	DID NOT PLAY – COACHING												
	NHL Totals		**1316**	**281**	**542**	**823**	**349**	**600**	**949**	**327**	**164**	**33**	**59**	**92**	**51**

NHL Second All-Star Team (1950, 1956) • NHL First All-Star Team (1951, 1952, 1953, 1954, 1955, 1957) • Won Lady Byng Trophy (1951, 1953, 1954, 1961) • Won James Norris Trophy (1954) • Played in NHL All-Star Game (1950, 1951, 1952, 1953, 1954, 1955, 1956, 1957, 1958, 1960, 1961, 1962, 1963)

Traded to **NY Rangers** by **Detroit** with Billy McNeill for Bill Gadsby and Eddie Shack, February 5, 1960. Transaction voided when both Kelly and McNeill refused to report to NY Rangers, February 7, 1960. Traded to **Toronto** by **Detroit** for Marc Reaume, February 10, 1960. Rights traded to **LA Kings** by **Toronto** for Ken Block, June 8, 1967.

• KELLY, Regis Regis John "Pep"

RW – R. 5'7", 152 lbs. b: North Bay, Ont., 1/17/1914 d: 1990.

Season	Club	League	GP	G	A	Pts	AG	AA	APts	PIM	GP	G	A	Pts	PIM
1930/32	North Bay Trappers	NOJHA	STATISTICS NOT AVAILABLE												
1932-33	Newmarket Redmen	OHA-Jr.	17	14	5	19	....	....	....	....	....	....	....	....	....
	Newmarket Redmen	M-Cup	19	*13	3	*16	....	....	....	16	....	....	....	....	....
1933-34	St. Michael's Majors	OHA-Jr.	11	13	8	21	....	....	....	12	3	3	1	4	*15
	St. Michael's Majors	M-Cup	13	20	8	28	....	....	....	8	....	....	....	....	....
1934-35	**Toronto Maple Leafs**	**NHL**	**47**	**11**	**8**	**19**	**18**	**14**	**32**	**14**	**7**	**2**	**0**	**2**	**4**
	Syracuse Stars	IHL	1	0	0	0	....	....	....	0	....	....	....	....	....
1935-36	**Toronto Maple Leafs**	**NHL**	**42**	**11**	**8**	**19**	**21**	**15**	**36**	**24**	**9**	**2**	**3**	**5**	**4**
1936-37	**Toronto Maple Leafs**	**NHL**	**16**	**2**	**0**	**2**	**3**	**0**	**3**	**8**	....	....	....	....	....
	Chicago Black Hawks	**NHL**	**29**	**13**	**4**	**17**	**22**	**7**	**29**	**0**	....	....	....	....	....
1937-38	**Toronto Maple Leafs**	**NHL**	**43**	**9**	**10**	**19**	**15**	**16**	**31**	**25**	**7**	**2**	**2**	**4**	**2**
1938-39	**Toronto Maple Leafs**	**NHL**	**48**	**11**	**11**	**22**	**19**	**17**	**36**	**12**	**9**	**1**	**0**	**1**	**0**
1939-40	**Toronto Maple Leafs**	**NHL**	**34**	**11**	**9**	**20**	**18**	**14**	**32**	**15**	**6**	**0**	**1**	**1**	**0**
1940-41	**Chicago Black Hawks**	**NHL**	**21**	**5**	**3**	**8**	**8**	**4**	**12**	**7**	....	....	....	....	....
	Providence Reds	AHL	16	5	7	12	....	....	....	0	....	....	....	....	....
1941-42	**Brooklyn Americans**	**NHL**	**8**	**1**	**0**	**1**	**1**	**0**	**1**	**0**	....	....	....	....	....
	Springfield Indians	AHL	18	9	10	19	....	....	....	8	....	....	....	....	....
	Buffalo Bisons	AHL	34	8	14	22	....	....	....	12	....	....	....	....	....
1942-43	Pittsburgh Hornets	AHL	52	12	14	26	....	....	....	6	2	0	2	2	0
1943-44	Sudbury Open Pit	NBHL	6	3	1	4	....	....	....	2	....	....	....	....	....
	Sudbury Open Pit	Al-Cup	15	6	5	11	....	....	....	8	....	....	....	....	....
1944-45	Sudbury Open Pit	NBHL	4	5	2	7	....	....	....	0	4	1	1	2	2
	Powassen Hawks	NBHL	....	7	3	10	....	....	....	....	....	....	....	....	....
1945-46	North Bay Shamrocks	NBHL	STATISTICS NOT AVAILABLE												
1946-47	North Bay Holy Names	NBHL	STATISTICS NOT AVAILABLE												

			REGULAR SEASON								PLAYOFFS				
Season	Club	League	GP	G	A	Pts	AG	AA	APts	PIM	GP	G	A	Pts	PIM
1947-48	North Bay Hawks	NBHL	14	8	14	22	....	....	....	....	6	4	6	10	0
	North Bay Hawks	Al-Cup	3	0	1	1	....	....	....	2	....	....	....	....	....
1948-49	North Bay Hawks	NBHL	13	7	4	11	....	....	....	4	6	6	4	10	2
	North Bay Hawks	Al-Cup	11	3	5	8	....	....	....	0	....	....	....	....	....
	NHL Totals		**288**	**74**	**53**	**127**	**125**	**87**	**212**	**105**	**38**	**7**	**6**	**13**	**10**

Loaned to **Chicago** by **Toronto** for remainder of 1936-37 season for the loan of Bill Kendall, December 29, 1936. Traded to **Chicago** by **Toronto** for cash, May 10, 1940. Loaned to **Providence** (AHL) by **Chicago** for cash, February 5, 1941. Traded to **Buffalo** (AHL) by **Chicago** for cash, October, 1941. Traded to **Brooklyn** by **Buffalo** (AHL) for cash, October 19, 1941.

• KEMP, Stan "Bud"

D – R. 5'9", 165 lbs. b: Hamilton, Ont., 3/2/1924.

Season	Club	League	GP	G	A	Pts	AG	AA	APts	PIM	GP	G	A	Pts	PIM
1942-43	Hamilton Whizzers	OHA-Jr.	24	11	9	20	....	....	....	17	5	1	1	2	8
1943-44	Providence Reds	AHL	47	3	8	11	....	....	....	43	....	....	....	....	....
1944-45	Providence Reds	AHL	57	16	40	56	....	....	....	37	....	....	....	....	....
1945-46	Providence Reds	AHL	49	12	16	28	....	....	....	30	2	0	1	1	0
1946-47	Pittsburgh Hornets	AHL	64	3	11	14	....	....	....	64	12	1	0	1	13
1947-48	Pittsburgh Hornets	AHL	68	10	20	30	....	....	....	93	2	0	1	1	2
1948-49	**Toronto Maple Leafs**	**NHL**	**1**	**0**	**0**	**0**	**0**	**0**	**0**	**2**	....	....	....	....	....
	Pittsburgh Hornets	AHL	68	13	34	47	....	....	....	90	....	....	....	....	....
1949-50	Pittsburgh Hornets	AHL	70	11	17	28	....	....	....	82	....	....	....	....	....
1950-51	Hamilton Tigers	OMHL	2	0	0	0	....	....	....	0	....	....	....	....	....
	Toronto Marlboros	OMHL	22	3	8	11	....	....	....	46	3	0	0	0	6
1951-52	Hamilton–Brantford	OHA-Sr.	48	9	22	31	....	....	....	95	7	0	2	2	14
1952-53	Brantford Redmen	OHA-Sr.	48	6	20	26	....	....	....	73	5	1	3	4	10
1953-54	Hamilton Tigers	OHA-Sr.	44	8	28	36	....	....	....	74	2	0	0	0	0
1954-55	Kitchener Dutchmen	OHA-Sr.	49	15	17	32	....	....	....	74	10	1	3	4	18
	Kitchener Dutchmen	Al-Cup	17	1	3	4	....	....	....	*29	....	....	....	....	....
1955-56	Stratford Indians	OHA-Sr.	7	2	6	8	....	....	....	50	....	....	....	....	....
	Kitchener Dutchmen	OHA-Sr.	44	5	22	27	....	....	....	0	10	3	2	5	16
1956-57	Stratford Indians	OHA-Sr.	36	9	15	24	....	....	....	24	5	1	3	4	4
	NHL Totals		**1**	**0**	**0**	**0**	**0**	**0**	**0**	**2**	....	....	....	....	....

AHL Second All-Star Team (1949)

• KENDALL, Bill "Cowboy"

RW – R. 5'8", 168 lbs. b: Winnipeg, Man., 4/1/1910 Deceased.

Season	Club	League	GP	G	A	Pts	AG	AA	APts	PIM	GP	G	A	Pts	PIM
1928-29	Elmwood Millionaires	WJrHL	5	1	0	1	....	....	....	0	2	0	1	1	4
	Elmwood Millionaires	M-Cup	7	*6	2	*8	....	....	....	2	....	....	....	....	....
1929-30	Elmwood Millionaires	WJrHL	8	6	1	7	....	....	....	4	2	0	1	1	4
	Elmwood Millionaires	M-Cup	5	3	1	4	....	....	....	6	....	....	....	....	....
1930-31	Elmwood Maple Leafs	MHL-Sr.	3	1	0	1	....	....	....	0	....	....	....	....	....
	St. Louis Flyers	AHA	23	5	2	7	....	....	....	8	....	....	....	....	....
1931-32	St. Louis Flyers	AHA	47	4	4	8	....	....	....	41	....	....	....	....	....
1932-33	Duluth-Wichita	AHA	41	10	6	16	....	....	....	12	....	....	....	....	....
♦1933-34	**Chicago Black Hawks**	**NHL**	**21**	**3**	**0**	**3**	**5**	**0**	**5**	**0**	**2**	**0**	**0**	**0**	**0**
	London Tecumsehs	IHL	26	5	6	11	....	....	....	10	6	0	4	4	4
1934-35	**Chicago Black Hawks**	**NHL**	**47**	**6**	**4**	**10**	**10**	**7**	**17**	**16**	**2**	**0**	**0**	**0**	**0**
1935-36	London Tecumsehs	IHL	22	9	4	13	....	....	....	12	....	....	....	....	....
	Chicago Black Hawks	**NHL**	**22**	**2**	**1**	**3**	**4**	**2**	**6**	**0**	**2**	**0**	**0**	**0**	**0**
1936-37	**Chicago Black Hawks**	**NHL**	**17**	**3**	**0**	**3**	**5**	**0**	**5**	**6**	....	....	....	....	....
	Toronto Maple Leafs	**NHL**	**15**	**2**	**4**	**6**	**3**	**7**	**10**	**4**	....	....	....	....	....
1937-38	**Chicago Black Hawks**	**NHL**	**9**	**0**	**1**	**1**	**0**	**2**	**2**	**2**	....	....	....	....	....
	St. Louis Flyers	AHA	39	17	10	27	....	....	....	24	7	2	1	3	2
1938-39	St. Louis Flyers	AHA	48	27	27	54	....	....	....	47	7	3	4	7	5
1939-40	St. Louis Flyers	AHA	48	30	30	60	....	....	....	30	5	1	1	2	2
1940-41	St. Louis Flyers	AHA	30	23	12	35	....	....	....	11	9	1	2	3	4
1941-42	St. Louis Flyers	AHA	50	13	8	21	....	....	....	17	3	0	1	1	0
1942-43			MILITARY SERVICE												
1943-44			MILITARY SERVICE												
1944-45	St. Louis Flyers	AHL	60	15	31	46	....	....	....	4	....	....	....	....	....
1945-46	St. Louis Flyers	AHL	27	2	6	8	....	....	....	0	....	....	....	....	....
	NHL Totals		**131**	**16**	**10**	**26**	**27**	**18**	**45**	**28**	**6**	**0**	**0**	**0**	**0**

Signed as a free agent by **St. Louis** (AHA), December 26, 1930. Loaned to **London** (IHL) by **Chicago** with $3,000 for Leroy Goldsworthy, January 4, 1934. Loaned to **London** (IHL) by **Chicago**. for cash, October, 1935. Returned to **Chicago** by **London** (IHL) for the loan of Norm Locking, January 23, 1936. Loaned to **Toronto** by **Chicago** for the remainder of the 1936-37 season for the loan of Regis Kelly, December 29, 1936. Traded to **St. Louis** (AHA) by **Chicago** for cash, December 2, 1937.

• KENNEDY, Forbes — see page 1254

• KENNEDY, Ted Theodore Samuel "Teeder" HHOF

C – R. 5'11", 175 lbs. b: Humberstone, Ont., 12/12/1925.

Season	Club	League	GP	G	A	Pts	AG	AA	APts	PIM	GP	G	A	Pts	PIM
1942-43	Port Colborne Sailors	OHA-Sr.	23	23	*29	52	....	....	....	15	....	....	....	....	....
	Toronto Maple Leafs	**NHL**	**2**	**0**	**1**	**1**	**0**	**1**	**1**	**0**	....	....	....	....	....
1943-44	**Toronto Maple Leafs**	**NHL**	**49**	**26**	**23**	**49**	**24**	**20**	**44**	**2**	**5**	**1**	**1**	**2**	**4**
♦1944-45	**Toronto Maple Leafs**	**NHL**	**49**	**29**	**25**	**54**	**30**	**29**	**59**	**14**	**13**	***7**	**2**	**9**	**2**
1945-46	**Toronto Maple Leafs**	**NHL**	**21**	**3**	**2**	**5**	**4**	**3**	**7**	**4**	....	....	....	....	....
♦1946-47	**Toronto Maple Leafs**	**NHL**	**60**	**28**	**32**	**60**	**32**	**39**	**71**	**27**	**11**	**4**	**5**	**9**	**4**
♦1947-48	**Toronto Maple Leafs**	**NHL**	**60**	**25**	**21**	**46**	**33**	**28**	**61**	**32**	**9**	***8**	**6**	***14**	**0**
♦1948-49	**Toronto Maple Leafs**	**NHL**	**59**	**18**	**21**	**39**	**25**	**30**	**55**	**25**	**9**	**2**	***6**	**8**	**2**
1949-50	**Toronto Maple Leafs**	**NHL**	**53**	**20**	**24**	**44**	**25**	**29**	**54**	**34**	**7**	**1**	**2**	**3**	**8**
♦1950-51	**Toronto Maple Leafs**	**NHL**	**63**	**18**	***43**	**61**	**23**	**53**	**76**	**32**	**11**	**4**	**5**	**9**	**6**
1951-52	**Toronto Maple Leafs**	**NHL**	**70**	**19**	**33**	**52**	**25**	**41**	**66**	**33**	**4**	**0**	**0**	**0**	**4**
1952-53	**Toronto Maple Leafs**	**NHL**	**43**	**14**	**23**	**37**	**18**	**28**	**46**	**42**	....	....	....	....	....
1953-54	**Toronto Maple Leafs**	**NHL**	**67**	**15**	**23**	**38**	**20**	**28**	**48**	**78**	**5**	**1**	**1**	**2**	**2**
1954-55	**Toronto Maple Leafs**	**NHL**	**70**	**10**	**42**	**52**	**13**	**49**	**62**	**74**	**4**	**1**	**3**	**4**	**0**
1955-56			OUT OF HOCKEY – RETIRED												
1956-57	**Toronto Maple Leafs**	**NHL**	**30**	**6**	**16**	**22**	**8**	**18**	**26**	**35**	....	....	....	....	....
1957-58	Peterborough Petes	OHA-Jr.	DID NOT PLAY – COACHING												
	NHL Totals		**696**	**231**	**329**	**560**	**280**	**396**	**676**	**432**	**78**	**29**	**31**	**60**	**32**

NHL Second All-Star Team (1950, 1951, 1954) • Won Hart Trophy (1955) • Played in NHL All-Star Game (1947, 1948, 1949, 1950, 1951, 1954)

• Rights were held by Montreal at time of first appearance in NHL. Rights traded to **Toronto** by **Montreal** for the rights to Frank Eddolls, September 10, 1943. Missed majority of 1956-57 season while still in retirement but returned as an active player in game vs. Detroit, January 6, 1957.

• KENNY, Ernest Ernest William "Eddie"

D – L. 6'2", 195 lbs. b: Vermilion, Alta., 8/20/1907 d: 6/2/1970.

Season	Club	League	GP	G	A	Pts	AG	AA	APts	PIM	GP	G	A	Pts	PIM
1927-28	Edmonton Elks	ESrHL	STATISTICS NOT AVAILABLE												
1928-29	Victoria Cubs	PCHL	35	1	3	4	....	....	....	96	....	....	....	....	....
1929-30	Victoria Cubs	PCHL	36	5	0	5	....	....	....	116	....	....	....	....	....
1930-31	Tacoma Tigers	PCHL	10	0	0	0	....	....	....	48	....	....	....	....	....
	Detroit Olympics	IHL	17	0	0	0	....	....	....	54	....	....	....	....	....
	New York Rangers	**NHL**	**6**	**0**	**0**	**0**	**0**	**0**	**0**	**0**	....	....	....	....	....
1931-32	Portland Pirates	WKHL	STATISTICS NOT AVAILABLE												
1932-33	Edmonton Eskimos	WCHL	28	7	6	13	....	....	....	94	8	3	0	3	18
1933-34	Edmonton Eskimos	NWHL	34	13	10	23	....	....	....	91	2	0	0	0	*10
1934-35	**Chicago Black Hawks**	**NHL**	**4**	**0**	**0**	**0**	**0**	**0**	**0**	**18**	....	....	....	....	....
	London Tecumsehs	IHL	38	4	4	8	....	....	....	54	5	0	0	0	4
	Windsor Bulldogs	IHL	1	0	0	0	....	....	....	0	....	....	....	....	....
1935-36	London Tecumsehs	IHL	46	2	4	6	....	....	....	85	2	0	0	0	2
1936-37	Oakland–Spokane	PCHL	39	4	2	6	....	....	....	86	6	0	0	0	*17
1937-38	Spokane Clippers	PCHL	41	9	5	14	....	....	....	94	....	....	....	....	....
1938-39	Spokane Clippers	PCHL	48	9	13	22	....	....	....	70	....	....	....	....	....
1939-40	Seattle Seahawks	PCHL	39	3	9	12	....	....	....	57	....	....	....	....	....
	NHL Totals		**10**	**0**	**0**	**0**	**0**	**0**	**0**	**18**	....	....	....	....	....

Traded to **NY Rangers** by **Tacoma** (PCHL) for cash, January 3, 1931. Traded to **Chicago** by **Edmonton** (NWHL) for cash, October 22, 1934. Loaned to **Windsor** by **London** as an injury replacement, January 29, 1935.

• KEON, Dave — see page 1254

• KILREA, Brian — see page 1259

• KILREA, Hec Hector Joseph "Hurricane"

LW – L. 5'8", 175 lbs. b: Blackburn, Ont., 6/11/1907 d: 10/8/1969.

Season	Club	League	GP	G	A	Pts	AG	AA	APts	PIM	GP	G	A	Pts	PIM
1924-25	Ottawa Rideaus	OCHL	16	5	*4	9	....	....	....	....	3	0	0	0	0
1925-26	**Ottawa Senators**	**NHL**	**35**	**5**	**0**	**5**	**9**	**0**	**9**	**12**	**2**	**0**	**0**	**0**	**0**
♦1926-27	**Ottawa Senators**	**NHL**	**42**	**11**	**7**	**18**	**20**	**37**	**57**	**48**	**6**	**1**	**1**	**2**	**4**
1927-28	**Ottawa Senators**	**NHL**	**43**	**19**	**4**	**23**	**39**	**23**	**62**	**66**	**2**	**1**	**0**	**1**	**0**
1928-29	**Ottawa Senators**	**NHL**	**38**	**5**	**7**	**12**	**14**	**47**	**61**	**36**	....	....	....	....	....
1929-30	**Ottawa Senators**	**NHL**	**44**	**36**	**22**	**58**	**52**	**52**	**104**	**72**	**2**	**0**	**0**	**0**	**4**
1930-31	**Ottawa Senators**	**NHL**	**44**	**14**	**8**	**22**	**28**	**24**	**52**	**44**	....	....	....	....	....
1931-32	**Detroit Falcons**	**NHL**	**47**	**13**	**3**	**16**	**22**	**7**	**29**	**28**	**2**	**0**	**0**	**0**	**0**
1932-33	**Ottawa Senators**	**NHL**	**47**	**14**	**8**	**22**	**26**	**17**	**43**	**26**	....	....	....	....	....
1933-34	**Toronto Maple Leafs**	**NHL**	**43**	**10**	**13**	**23**	**17**	**27**	**44**	**15**	**5**	**2**	**0**	**2**	**2**
1934-35	**Toronto Maple Leafs**	**NHL**	**46**	**11**	**13**	**24**	**18**	**23**	**41**	**16**	**6**	**0**	**0**	**0**	**4**
♦1935-36	**Detroit Red Wings**	**NHL**	**48**	**6**	**17**	**23**	**11**	**32**	**43**	**37**	**7**	**0**	**3**	**3**	**2**
♦1936-37	**Detroit Red Wings**	**NHL**	**48**	**6**	**9**	**15**	**10**	**16**	**26**	**20**	**10**	**3**	**1**	**4**	**2**
1937-38	**Detroit Red Wings**	**NHL**	**48**	**9**	**9**	**18**	**15**	**14**	**29**	**10**	....	....	....	....	....
1938-39	**Detroit Red Wings**	**NHL**	**48**	**8**	**9**	**17**	**14**	**14**	**28**	**8**	**6**	**1**	**2**	**3**	**0**
1939-40	**Detroit Red Wings**	**NHL**	**12**	**0**	**0**	**0**	**0**	**0**	**0**	**0**	....	....	....	....	....
	Indianapolis Capitols	AHL	41	6	21	27	....	....	....	6	5	0	1	1	9
1940-41	Indianapolis Capitols	AHL	46	5	9	14	....	....	....	6	....	....	....	....	....
1941-42	Indianapolis Capitols	AHL	56	13	10	23	....	....	....	15	10	0	0	0	6
1942-43	Indianapolis Capitols	AHL	55	9	10	19	....	....	....	11	7	2	1	3	2
	NHL Totals		**633**	**167**	**129**	**296**	**295**	**333**	**628**	**438**	**48**	**8**	**7**	**15**	**18**

• Brother of Wally and Ken • Played in NHL All-Star Game (1934)

Signed as a free agent by **Ottawa**, November 12, 1925. Claimed by **Detroit** from **Ottawa** for 1931-32 season in Dispersal Draft, September 26, 1931. Traded to **Toronto** by **Ottawa** for Bob Gracie and $10,000, October 4, 1933. Traded to **Detroit** by **Toronto** for $7,000 and future considerations (Knucker Irvine, October, 1935), September 29, 1935.

• KILREA, Ken Kenneth Armstrong

LW – L. 6', 170 lbs. b: Ottawa, Ont., 1/16/1919 d: 1/14/1990.

Season	Club	League	GP	G	A	Pts	AG	AA	APts	PIM	GP	G	A	Pts	PIM
1935-36	University of Ottawa	OCJHL	9	*18	7	*25	....	....	....	9	4	*6	4	*10	*10
	University of Ottawa	M-Cup	3	2	1	3	....	....	....	4	....	....	....	....	....
1936-37	Detroit Pontiacs	MOHL	25	13	10	23	....	....	....	8	5	1	2	3	0
1937-38	Detroit Pontiacs	MOHL	28	*25	19	*44	....	....	....	4	3	0	2	2	2
1938-39	Pittsburgh Hornets	IAHL	51	14	28	42	....	....	....	21	....	....	....	....	....
	Detroit Red Wings	**NHL**	**1**	**0**	**0**	**0**	**0**	**0**	**0**	**0**	**3**	**1**	**1**	**2**	**4**
1939-40	**Detroit Red Wings**	**NHL**	**40**	**10**	**8**	**18**	**17**	**12**	**29**	**4**	**5**	**1**	**1**	**2**	**0**
	Indianapolis Capitols	AHL	11	4	15	19	....	....	....	2	....	....	....	....	....
1940-41	**Detroit Red Wings**	**NHL**	**15**	**2**	**0**	**2**	**3**	**0**	**3**	**0**	**5**	**0**	**0**	**0**	**0**
	Indianapolis Capitols	AHL	34	9	18	27	....	....	....	7	....	....	....	....	....
1941-42	**Detroit Red Wings**	**NHL**	**21**	**3**	**12**	**15**	**4**	**14**	**18**	**4**	....	....	....	....	....
	Indianapolis Capitols	AHL	27	15	29	44	....	....	....	8	10	1	8	9	2
1942-43	Ottawa Commandos	QSHL	20	12	18	30	....	....	....	6	11	6	5	11	12
	Ottawa Canadians	OCHL	2	1	3	4	....	....	....	0	....	....	....	....	....
	Ottawa Commandos	Al-Cup	9	4	6	10	....	....	....	6	....	....	....	....	....
	Ottawa Royal Canadians	ONDHL	11	23	*21	*44	....	....	....	0	....	....	....	....	....
1943-44	**Detroit Red Wings**	**NHL**	**14**	**1**	**3**	**4**	**1**	**3**	**4**	**0**	**2**	**0**	**0**	**0**	**0**
	Indianapolis Capitols	AHL	6	1	2	3	....	....	....	0	2	0	0	0	0
1944-45	Buffalo Bisons	AHL	51	19	46	65	....	....	....	14	6	3	*8	11	7
1945-46	New Haven Eagles	AHL	45	13	24	37	....	....	....	23	....	....	....	....	....
	Fort Worth Rangers	USHL	14	1	11	12	....	....	....	2	....	....	....	....	....
1946-47	Springfield Indians	AHL	14	3	1	4	....	....	....	2	....	....	....	....	....
	Fort Worth Rangers	USHL	33	18	21	39	....	....	....	16	9	2	6	8	2
1947-48	Philadelphia Rockets	AHL	63	15	35	50	....	....	....	20	....	....	....	....	....
1948-49	Philadelphia Rockets	AHL	64	15	28	43	....	....	....	32	....	....	....	....	....

Season	Club	League	GP	G	A	Pts	AG	AA	APts	PIM	GP	G	A	Pts	PIM
			REGULAR SEASON								PLAYOFFS				
1949-50	Ottawa Army	ECSHL	40	28	22	50	....	....	....	20	3	5	2	7	5
	Grand Rapids Rockets	IHL	4	2	1	3	....	....	....	0	8	3	8	11	4
1950-51	Ottawa Army	ECSHL	32	16	28	44	....	....	....	16	3	6	2	8	2
	Johnstown Jets	EAHL	1	0	0	0	....	....	....	10	6	3	4	7	2
	NHL Totals		**91**	**16**	**23**	**39**	**25**	**29**	**54**	**8**	**15**	**2**	**2**	**4**	**4**

• Brother of Wally and Hec

Signed as a free agent by **Detroit**, March 18, 1938.

• KILREA, Wally   Walter Charles

RW/C – R. 5'7", 150 lbs.   b: Ottawa, Ont., 2/18/1909.

Season	Club	League	GP	G	A	Pts	AG	AA	APts	PIM	GP	G	A	Pts	PIM
1927-28	Ottawa Montagnards	OCHL	15	5	3	8	....	....	....	....	4	0	1	1	0
	Ottawa Montagnards	Al-Cup	2	1	0	1	....	....	....	0	....	....	....	....	....
1928-29	Ottawa Montagnards	OCHL	12	5	*8	*13	....	....	....	....	....	....	....	....	....
1929-30	**Ottawa Senators**	**NHL**	**38**	**4**	**2**	**6**	**6**	**5**	**11**	**4**	**2**	**0**	**0**	**0**	**0**
	London Panthers	IHL	3	0	0	0	....	....	....	0	....	....	....	....	....
1930-31	**Philadelphia Quakers**	**NHL**	**44**	**8**	**12**	**20**	**16**	**36**	**52**	**22**	....	....	....	....	....
1931-32	**New York Americans**	**NHL**	**48**	**3**	**8**	**11**	**5**	**18**	**23**	**18**	....	....	....	....	....
1932-33	**Ottawa Senators**	**NHL**	**32**	**4**	**5**	**9**	**7**	**10**	**17**	**14**	....	....	....	....	....
	Montreal Maroons	**NHL**	**19**	**1**	**7**	**8**	**2**	**14**	**16**	**2**	**2**	**0**	**0**	**0**	**0**
1933-34	**Montreal Maroons**	**NHL**	**45**	**3**	**1**	**4**	**5**	**2**	**7**	**7**	**4**	**0**	**0**	**0**	**0**
	Windsor Bulldogs	IHL	3	0	0	0	....	....	....	2	....	....	....	....	....
1934-35	**Detroit Red Wings**	**NHL**	**3**	**0**	**0**	**0**	**0**	**0**	**0**	**0**	....	....	....	....	....
	Detroit Olympics	IHL	33	11	16	27	....	....	....	23	5	1	*4	5	0
	Detroit Olympics	L-W-S	5	1	*4	5	....	....	....	0	....	....	....	....	....
♦1935-36	**Detroit Red Wings**	**NHL**	**48**	**4**	**10**	**14**	**8**	**19**	**27**	**10**	**7**	**2**	**2**	**4**	**2**
	Detroit Olympics	IHL	3	4	2	6	....	....	....	0	....	....	....	....	....
♦1936-37	**Detroit Red Wings**	**NHL**	**47**	**8**	**13**	**21**	**13**	**24**	**37**	**6**	**10**	**0**	**2**	**2**	**4**
1937-38	**Detroit Red Wings**	**NHL**	**5**	**0**	**0**	**0**	**0**	**0**	**0**	**4**	....	....	....	....	....
	Pittsburgh Hornets	IAHL	44	6	11	17	....	....	....	28	2	0	0	0	0
1938-39	Hershey Bears	IAHL	42	17	31	48	....	....	....	35	5	5	2	7	5
1939-40	Hershey Bears	IAHL	56	12	29	41	....	....	....	18	10	2	5	7	4
1940-41	Hershey Bears	AHL	55	17	37	54	....	....	....	0	10	1	3	4	4
1941-42	Hershey Bears	AHL	56	12	35	47	....	....	....	14	10	4	2	6	2
1942-43	Hershey Bears	AHL	56	31	*68	*99	....	....	....	8	4	0	0	0	0
1943-44	Hershey Bears	AHL	33	15	30	45	....	....	....	8	....	....	....	....	....
	NHL Totals		**329**	**35**	**58**	**93**	**62**	**128**	**190**	**87**	**25**	**2**	**4**	**6**	**6**

• Brother of Hec and Ken • IHL First All-Star Team (1935) • AHL First All-Star Team (1943)

Loaned to **Philadelphia Quakers** by **Ottawa** for 1930-31 season, September, 1930. Claimed by **NY Americans** from **Ottawa** for 1931-32 season in Dispersal Draft, September 26, 1931. Traded to **Montreal Maroons** by **Ottawa** for Des Roche, February 3, 1933. Traded to **Detroit** by **Montreal Maroons** for Gus Marker, September 23, 1934. Traded to **Hershey** (IAHL) by **Detroit** for cash, June 23, 1938.

• KING, Frank   Frank Edward

C – L. 5'11", 185 lbs.   b: Toronto, Ont., 3/7/1929.

Season	Club	League	GP	G	A	Pts	AG	AA	APts	PIM	GP	G	A	Pts	PIM
1947-48	Brandon Wheat Kings	MJHL	22	13	8	21	....	....	....	31	5	4	0	4	10
1948-49	Brandon Wheat Kings	MJHL	30	27	14	41	....	....	....	*78	7	6	2	8	4
	Brandon Wheat Kings	M-Cup	18	*16	7	*23	....	....	....	7	....	....	....	....	....
1949-50	Minneapolis Millers	USHL	70	34	30	64	....	....	....	49	7	5	4	9	10
1950-51	**Montreal Canadiens**	**NHL**	**10**	**1**	**0**	**1**	**1**	**0**	**1**	**2**	....	....	....	....	....
	Cincinnati Mohawks	AHL	21	5	6	11	....	....	....	20	....	....	....	....	....
	Seattle Ironmen	PCHL	3	1	1	2	....	....	....	3	....	....	....	....	....
	Providence Reds	AHL	21	3	12	15	....	....	....	16	....	....	....	....	....
1951-52	Quebec Aces	QMHL	36	4	4	8	....	....	....	24	7	1	1	2	10
	Quebec Aces	Alx-Cup	1	0	0	0	....	....	....	0	....	....	....	....	....
1952-53	Halifax Atlantics	MMHL	72	38	40	78	....	....	....	92	15	7	8	15	31
1953-54	Sudbury Wolves	NOHA	45	14	11	25	....	....	....	26	1	0	0	0	0
1954-55	Vernon Canadians	OSHL	50	22	27	49	....	....	....	121	5	1	3	4	0
	Vernon Canadians	Al-Cup	17	*12	8	20	....	....	....	29	....	....	....	....	....
1955-56	Vernon Canadians	OSHL	56	40	34	74	....	....	....	115	8	4	6	10	14
	Vernon Canadians	Al-Cup	16	*18	3	21	....	....	....	*35	....	....	....	....	....
1956-57	Vernon Canadians	OSHL	50	17	33	50	....	....	....	90	12	7	*13	*20	18
1957-58	Vernon Canadians	OSHL	54	38	29	67	....	....	....	111	4	1	1	2	13
1958-59	Vernon Canadians	OSHL	52	23	28	51	....	....	....	....	16	3	9	12	*38
1959-60	Vernon Canadians	OSHL	12	11	8	19	....	....	....	2	13	11	9	20	24
	NHL Totals		**10**	**1**	**0**	**1**	**1**	**0**	**1**	**2**	....	....	....	....	....

Traded to **Montreal** by **Cleveland** (AHL) for cash, April 12, 1950. Loaned to **Seattle** (PCHL) by **Montreal** for cash, January 9, 1951. Traded to **Providence** (AHL) by **Montreal** (Cincinnati-AHL) for Roger Bedard, January 29, 1951. Signed as a free agent by **Halifax** (MMHL), October 6, 1952.

• KINSELLA, Ray   Thomas Raymond

LW – L. 5'10", 162 lbs.   b: Ottawa, Ont., 1/27/1911   d: 4/29/1996.

Season	Club	League	GP	G	A	Pts	AG	AA	APts	PIM	GP	G	A	Pts	PIM
1928-29	Ottawa Post Office	OCHL	STATISTICS NOT AVAILABLE												
	Ottawa CPR	OCHL	STATISTICS NOT AVAILABLE												
1929-30	Ottawa Shamrocks	OCHL	15	0	1	1	....	....	....	10	4	0	0	0	0
	Ottawa Shamrocks	Al-Cup	2	2	0	2	....	....	....	0	....	....	....	....	....
1930-31	Ottawa Rideaus	OCHL	18	3	4	7	....	....	....	34	....	....	....	....	....
	Ottawa Senators	**NHL**	**14**	**0**	**0**	**0**	**0**	**0**	**0**	**0**	....	....	....	....	....
1931-32	Philadelphia Arrows	Can-Am	31	8	3	11	....	....	....	12	....	....	....	....	....
1932-33	Quebec–New Haven	Can-Am	32	5	5	10	....	....	....	22	....	....	....	....	....
1933-34	New Haven Eagles	Can-Am	40	6	15	21	....	....	....	15	....	....	....	....	....
1934-35	London Tecumsehs	IHL	7	0	2	2	....	....	....	5	....	....	....	....	....
	Tulsa Oilers	AHA	43	11	16	27	....	....	....	27	5	0	0	0	0
1935-36			REINSTATED AS AN AMATEUR												
1936-37	Ottawa Senators	OCHL	19	7	7	14	....	....	....	7	....	....	....	....	....
1937-38	Ottawa Montagnards	OCHL	17	2	9	11	....	....	....	12	....	....	....	....	....
	NHL Totals		**14**	**0**	**0**	**0**	**0**	**0**	**0**	**0**	....	....	....	....	....

Signed as a free agent by **Ottawa**, February 3, 1931.

• KIRK, Bobby   "Cagey"

RW – R. 5'9", 180 lbs.   b: Dough Grange, Ireland, 8/8/1909   d: 7/11/1970.

Season	Club	League	GP	G	A	Pts	AG	AA	APts	PIM	GP	G	A	Pts	PIM
1927-28	Elmwood Millionaires	WJrHL	1	0	0	0	....	....	....	0	....	....	....	....	....
1928-29	Elmwood Millionaires	WJrHL	8	6	1	7	....	....	....		3	0	1	1	4
	Winnipeg CNR	WSrHL	5	0	1	1	....	....	....	4	....	....	....	....	....
	Elmwood Millionaires	M-Cup	7	5	2	7	....	....	....	11	....	....	....	....	....
1929-30	Elmwood Millionaires	WJrHL	5	*8	1	9	....	....	....	12	....	....	....	....	....
1930-31	Winnipeg Sr. Millionaires	WSrHL	3	0	0	0	....	....	....	0	....	....	....	....	....
	St. Louis Flyers	AHA	32	9	3	12	....	....	....	12	....	....	....	....	....
1931-32	St. Louis Flyers	AHA	39	1	4	5	....	....	....	16	....	....	....	....	....
1932-33	Regina–Vancouver	WCHL	29	10	2	12	....	....	....	14	2	0	0	0	0
1933-34	Vancouver Lions	NWHL	34	9	2	11	....	....	....	28	7	3	0	3	4
1934-35	Vancouver Lions	NWHL	32	*25	8	33	....	....	....	28	8	4	2	6	8
	Vancouver Lions	L-W-S	5	1	3	4	....	....	....	2	....	....	....	....	....
1935-36	Philadelphia Arrows	Can-Am	48	22	*29	*51	....	....	....	16	4	0	1	1	0
1936-37	Philadelphia Ramblers	IAHL	36	7	15	22	....	....	....	8	6	2	1	3	0
1937-38	**New York Rangers**	**NHL**	**39**	**4**	**8**	**12**	**6**	**13**	**19**	**14**	....	....	....	....	....
	Philadelphia Ramblers	IAHL	11	7	1	8	....	....	....	4	5	1	2	3	2
1938-39	Philadelphia Ramblers	IAHL	49	14	36	50	....	....	....	12	9	2	6	8	2
1939-40	Philadelphia Ramblers	AHL	11	0	4	4	....	....	....	0	....	....	....	....	....
	Hershey Bears	AHL	43	16	12	28	....	....	....	6	6	0	1	1	4
1940-41	Hershey Bears	AHL	52	19	26	45	....	....	....	6	10	*4	2	6	4
1941-42	Hershey Bears	AHL	53	14	27	41	....	....	....	18	10	1	4	5	0
	Philadelphia Ramblers	AHL	4	3	2	5	....	....	....	0	....	....	....	....	....
1942-43	Vancouver RCAF	NNDHL	11	9	11	20	....	....	....	4	....	....	....	....	....
	NHL Totals		**39**	**4**	**8**	**12**	**6**	**13**	**19**	**14**	....	....	....	....	....

Can-Am First All-Star Team (1936)

Claimed by **NY Rangers** from **Vancouver** (NWHL) in Inter-League Draft, May 11, 1935.

• KIRKPATRICK, Bob   Robert Dynan

C – L. 5'10", 165 lbs.   b: Regina, Sask., 12/1/1915.

Season	Club	League	GP	G	A	Pts	AG	AA	APts	PIM	GP	G	A	Pts	PIM
1933-34	Regina Pats	S-SJHL	STATISTICS NOT AVAILABLE												
	Regina Pats	M-Cup	4	1	0	1	....	....	....	4	....	....	....	....	....
1934-35	Regina Aces	S-SSHL	19	5	6	11	....	....	....	6	3	0	0	0	4
1935-36	Prince Albert Mintos	N-SSHL	16	13	3	16	....	....	....	23	3	0	*2	2	2
	Prince Albert Mintos	Al-Cup	6	4	0	4	....	....	....	2	....	....	....	....	....
1936-37	Earls Court Royals	Britain	....	30	21	51	....	....	....	26	....	....	....	....	....
1937-38	Lethbridge Maple Leafs	WKHL	23	23	17	40	....	....	....	16	2	1	2	3	2
1938-39	Lethbridge Maple Leafs	ASHL	31	21	*36	*57	....	....	....	36	7	*7	*7	*14	7
	Lethbridge Maple Leafs	Al-Cup	3	2	*3	*5	....	....	....	0	....	....	....	....	....
1939-40	Lethbridge Maple Leafs	ASHL	22	14	15	29	....	....	....	6	2	0	3	3	0
1940-41	Flin Flon Bombers	SSHL	32	14	10	24	....	....	....	6	3	4	2	6	0
1941-42	New York Rovers	EAHL	59	34	43	77	....	....	....	26	7	4	5	9	5
1942-43	**New York Rangers**	**NHL**	**49**	**12**	**12**	**24**	**12**	**11**	**23**	**6**	....	....	....	....	....
1943-44	Winnipeg Army	WNDHL	10	6	6	12	....	....	....	4	....	....	....	....	....
1944-45	Winnipeg Army	WNDHL	3	2	1	3	....	....	....	0	....	....	....	....	....
1945-46	St. Paul Saints	USHL	47	14	33	47	....	....	....	2	6	1	3	4	2
1946-47	St. Paul Saints	USHL	52	15	22	37	....	....	....	8	....	....	....	....	....
1947-48	Lethbridge Maple Leafs	ASHL	43	13	30	43	....	....	....	26	5	1	1	2	0
1948-49	Lethbridge Maple Leafs	ASHL	48	17	26	43	....	....	....	8	3	1	1	2	4
	NHL Totals		**49**	**12**	**12**	**24**	**12**	**11**	**23**	**6**	....	....	....	....	....

EAHL Second All-Star Team (1942)

• KITCHEN, Hobie   Chapman Hobart

D – L. 5'11", 187 lbs.   b: Toronto, Ont., 2/8/1904   Deceased.

Season	Club	League	GP	G	A	Pts	AG	AA	APts	PIM	GP	G	A	Pts	PIM
1920-21	Toronto Moose	OHA-Jr.	STATISTICS NOT AVAILABLE												
1921-22	Toronto Aura Lee	OHA-Jr.	2	0	0	0	....	....	....	0	....	....	....	....	....
1922-23	Toronto Aura Lee	OHA-Jr.	2	0	0	0	....	....	....	0	....	....	....	....	....
1923-24	Toronto St. Mary's	OHA-Jr.	8	5	0	5	....	....	....	15	....	....	....	....	....
1924-25	Niagara Falls Cataracts	OHA-Sr.	20	21	2	23	....	....	....	25	2	1	0	1	2
	Niagara Falls Cataracts	Al-Cup	8	4	2	6	....	....	....	2	....	....	....	....	....
♦1925-26	**Montreal Maroons**	**NHL**	**30**	**5**	**2**	**7**	**9**	**13**	**22**	**16**	....	....	....	....	....
1926-27	**Detroit Cougars**	**NHL**	**17**	**0**	**2**	**2**	**0**	**10**	**10**	**42**	....	....	....	....	....
	New Haven Eagles	Can-Am	6	0	0	0	....	....	....	10	....	....	....	....	....
1927-28	Kitchener Millionaires	Can-Pro	9	0	0	0	....	....	....	40	....	....	....	....	....
1928-29	Niagara Falls Cataracts	Can-Pro	6	0	0	0	....	....	....	6	....	....	....	....	....
	NHL Totals		**47**	**5**	**4**	**9**	**9**	**23**	**32**	**58**	....	....	....	....	....

Signed as a free agent by **Montreal Maroons**, April 13, 1925. Signed as a free agent by **Detroit**, October 27, 1926. Traded to **New Haven** (Can-Am) by **Detroit** for cash, January 28, 1927. Signed as a free agent by **Kitchener** (Can-Pro), October 27, 1927.

• KLEIN, Lloyd   James Lloyd "Deed"

LW – L. 6', 185 lbs.   b: Saskatoon, Sask., 1/13/1910   Deceased.

Season	Club	League	GP	G	A	Pts	AG	AA	APts	PIM	GP	G	A	Pts	PIM
1924-25	Saskatoon Wesleys	N-SJHL	7	5	*1	6	....	....	....	....	4	1	0	1	0
1925-26	Saskatoon Wesleys	N-SJHL	12	*19	0	*19	....	....	....	....	4	*7	0	*7	2
	Saskatoon Wesleys	M-Cup	6	*10	2	*12	....	....	....	2	....	....	....	....	....
1926-27	Saskatoon Wesleys	N-SJHL	6	*6	1	*7	....	....	....	17	2	*3	0	*3	2
	Saskatoon Wesleys	M-Cup	4	*8	1	*9	....	....	....	*11	....	....	....	....	....
1927-28	Saskatoon Sheiks	PrHL	27	*15	6	21	....	....	....	33	....	....	....	....	....
♦1928-29	**Boston Bruins**	**NHL**	**8**	**1**	**0**	**1**	**3**	**0**	**3**	**5**	....	....	....	....	....
	Minneapolis Millers	AHA	9	1	1	2	....	....	....	2	....	....	....	....	....
	Providence Reds	Can-Am	1	0	0	0	....	....	....	2	....	....	....	....	....
1929-30	Philadelphia Arrows	Can-Am	32	13	0	13	....	....	....	46	2	1	0	1	4
1930-31	Syracuse Stars	IHL	32	19	3	22	....	....	....	34	....	....	....	....	....
	Boston Cubs	Can-Am	10	7	3	10	....	....	....	12	8	*7	1	8	*32
1931-32	**Boston Bruins**	**NHL**	**5**	**1**	**0**	**1**	**2**	**0**	**2**	**0**	....	....	....	....	....
	Boston Cubs	Can-Am	37	*22	19	*41	....	....	....	19	5	*4	*2	*6	6
1932-33	Boston Cubs	Can-Am	28	15	15	30	....	....	....	30	....	....	....	....	....
	New York Americans	**NHL**	**15**	**2**	**2**	**4**	**4**	**4**	**8**	**4**	....	....	....	....	....
1933-34	**New York Americans**	**NHL**	**48**	**13**	**9**	**22**	**22**	**19**	**41**	**34**	....	....	....	....	....
1934-35	**New York Americans**	**NHL**	**29**	**7**	**3**	**10**	**11**	**5**	**16**	**9**	....	....	....	....	....
	New Haven Eagles	Can-Am	15	10	10	20	....	....	....	16	....	....	....	....	....
1935-36	**New York Americans**	**NHL**	**42**	**4**	**8**	**12**	**8**	**15**	**23**	**14**	**5**	**0**	**0**	**0**	**2**
	Rochester Cardinals	IHL	4	3	1	4	....	....	....	0	....	....	....	....	....
1936-37	**New York Americans**	**NHL**	**14**	**2**	**1**	**3**	**3**	**2**	**5**	**2**	....	....	....	....	....
	New Haven Eagles	IAHL	12	6	8	14	....	....	....	6	....	....	....	....	....
	Cleveland Barons	IAHL	25	6	7	13	....	....	....	8	....	....	....	....	....
1937-38	**New York Americans**	**NHL**	**3**	**0**	**1**	**1**	**0**	**2**	**2**	**0**	....	....	....	....	....
	Pittsburgh Hornets	IAHL	43	11	21	32	....	....	....	10	2	2	0	2	2
1938-39	Hershey Bears	IAHL	49	17	15	32	....	....	....	32	5	0	1	1	4
1939-40	Hershey Bears	IAHL	17	4	3	7	....	....	....	0	....	....	....	....	....
	Syracuse Stars	IAHL	35	12	18	30	....	....	....	8	....	....	....	....	....
1940-41	Buffalo Bisons	AHL	50	12	23	35	....	....	....	20	....	....	....	....	....
1941-42	Buffalo Bisons	AHL	55	20	22	42	....	....	....	20	....	....	....	....	....
1942-43	Buffalo Bisons	AHL	52	22	42	64	....	....	....	11	9	*5	10	*15	0
1943-44	Buffalo Bisons	AHL	47	23	22	45	....	....	....	22	9	1	4	5	0

Season	Club	League	GP	G	A	Pts	AG	AA	APts	PIM	GP	G	A	Pts	PIM
			REGULAR SEASON								PLAYOFFS				
1944-45	Pittsburgh Hornets	AHL	56	30	36	66	....	....	....	27	....	....	....	....	....
1945-46	Pittsburgh Hornets	AHL	8	1	5	6	....	....	....	2	....	....	....	....	....
	Hollywood Wolves	PCHL	33	24	12	36	....	....	....	14	12	10	6	16	8
1946-47	Saskatoon Quakers	WCSHL	35	12	17	29	....	....	....	30	3	1	1	2	2
1947-48	Tacoma Rockets	PCHL	46	28	27	55	....	....	....	32	5	0	1	1	0
	NHL Totals		**164**	**30**	**24**	**54**	**53**	**47**	**100**	**68**	**5**	**0**	**0**	**0**	**2**

Traded to **NY Americans** by **Boston** for Tommy Filmore, February 12, 1933. Traded to **Cleveland** (IAHL) by **NY Americans** for Les Cunningham, January 14, 1937.

• KLINGBEIL, Ike Ernest R.

D – L. 5'10", 180 lbs. b: Hancock, MI, 11/3/1908.

Season	Club	League	GP	G	A	Pts	AG	AA	APts	PIM	GP	G	A	Pts	PIM
1932-33	University of Michigan	MOHL	STATISTICS NOT AVAILABLE												
1933-34	Detroit Mundus	MOHL	11	5	1	6	....	....	....	27	6	2	2	4	*24
1934-35	Detroit Farm Crest	MOHL	16	3	1	4	....	....	....	26	1	1	0	1	0
1935-36	Detroit Tool Shop	MOHL	5	2	0	2	....	....	....	4	....	....	....	....	....
1936-37	**Chicago Black Hawks**	**NHL**	**5**	**1**	**2**	**3**	**2**	**4**	**6**	**2**	....	....	....	....	....
	Portage Lakes Lakers	NMHL	STATISTICS NOT AVAILABLE												
1937/40	Portage Lakes Lakers	NMHL	STATISTICS NOT AVAILABLE												
	NHL Totals		**5**	**1**	**2**	**3**	**2**	**4**	**6**	**2**	....	....	....	....	....

NMHL Second All-Star Team (1940)

• KLUKAY, Joe Joseph Francis "The Duke of Paducah"

LW – L. 6', 182 lbs. b: Sault Ste. Marie, Ont., 11/6/1922.

Season	Club	League	GP	G	A	Pts	AG	AA	APts	PIM	GP	G	A	Pts	PIM
1941-42	S.S. Marie Greyhounds	NOJHA	STATISTICS NOT AVAILABLE												
1942-43	Stratford Kroehlers	OHA-Jr.	14	11	18	29	....	....	....	11	2	4	4	8	0
	Toronto Maple Leafs	**NHL**	....	....	....	....	....	....	....	....	**1**	**0**	**0**	**0**	**0**
1943-44	Toronto Navy	OHA-Sr.	25	14	13	27	....	....	....	19	....	....	....	....	....
1944-45	Cornwallis Navy	NSDHL	13	8	4	12	....	....	....	8	3	3	3	6	6
1945-46	Pittsburgh Hornets	AHL	57	26	23	49	....	....	....	20	6	4	1	5	2
♦1946-47	**Toronto Maple Leafs**	**NHL**	**55**	**9**	**20**	**29**	**10**	**24**	**34**	**12**	**11**	**1**	**0**	**1**	**0**
♦1947-48	**Toronto Maple Leafs**	**NHL**	**59**	**15**	**15**	**30**	**19**	**20**	**39**	**28**	**9**	**1**	**1**	**2**	**2**
♦1948-49	**Toronto Maple Leafs**	**NHL**	**45**	**11**	**10**	**21**	**15**	**14**	**29**	**11**	**9**	**2**	**3**	**5**	**4**
1949-50	**Toronto Maple Leafs**	**NHL**	**70**	**15**	**16**	**31**	**19**	**19**	**38**	**19**	**7**	**3**	**0**	**3**	**4**
♦1950-51	**Toronto Maple Leafs**	**NHL**	**70**	**14**	**16**	**30**	**18**	**20**	**38**	**16**	**11**	**4**	**3**	**7**	**0**
1951-52	**Toronto Maple Leafs**	**NHL**	**43**	**4**	**8**	**12**	**5**	**10**	**15**	**6**	**4**	**1**	**1**	**2**	**0**
1952-53	**Boston Bruins**	**NHL**	**70**	**13**	**16**	**29**	**17**	**19**	**36**	**20**	**11**	**1**	**2**	**3**	**9**
1953-54	**Boston Bruins**	**NHL**	**70**	**20**	**17**	**37**	**27**	**21**	**48**	**27**	**4**	**0**	**0**	**0**	**0**
1954-55	**Boston Bruins**	**NHL**	**10**	**0**	**0**	**0**	**0**	**0**	**0**	**4**	....	....	....	....	....
	Toronto Maple Leafs	**NHL**	**56**	**8**	**8**	**16**	**10**	**9**	**19**	**44**	**4**	**0**	**0**	**0**	**4**
1955-56	**Toronto Maple Leafs**	**NHL**	**18**	**0**	**1**	**1**	**0**	**1**	**1**	**2**	....	....	....	....	....
	Pittsburgh Hornets	AHL	47	24	26	50	....	....	....	40	4	4	1	5	8
1956-57	Windsor Bulldogs	OHA-Sr.	52	23	30	53	....	....	....	80	12	6	4	10	9
1957-58	Windsor Bulldogs	NOHA	57	10	27	37	....	....	....	33	13	1	9	10	11
1958-59	Windsor Bulldogs	NOHA	49	21	21	42	....	....	....	25	....	....	....	....	....
1959-60			DID NOT PLAY												
1960-61	Windsor Bulldogs	OHA-Sr.	33	12	37	49	....	....	....	10	....	....	....	....	....
1961-62	Windsor Bulldogs	OHA-Sr.	33	12	20	32	....	....	....	32	13	1	7	8	6
1962-63	Windsor Bulldogs	OHA-Sr.	12	3	9	12	....	....	....	2	10	1	7	8	2
	Windsor Bulldogs	Al-Cup	10	3	8	11	....	....	....	13	....	....	....	....	....
1963-64	Windsor Bulldogs	IHL	1	0	1	1	....	....	....	0	....	....	....	....	....
	NHL Totals		**566**	**109**	**127**	**236**	**140**	**157**	**297**	**189**	**71**	**13**	**10**	**23**	**23**

Played in NHL All-Star Game (1947, 1948, 1949)

Signed as a free agent by **Toronto**, March 15, 1943. Traded to **Boston** by **Toronto** for cash, September 16, 1952. Traded to **Toronto** by **Boston** for Leo Boivin, November 9, 1954.

• KNIBBS, Bill William Arthur

C – L. 6'1", 180 lbs. b: Toronto, Ont., 1/24/1942.

Season	Club	League	GP	G	A	Pts	AG	AA	APts	PIM	GP	G	A	Pts	PIM
1959-60	Barrie Flyers	OHA-Jr.	48	14	25	39	....	....	....	29	6	2	1	3	19
1960-61	Niagara Falls Flyers	OHA-Jr.	48	22	35	57	....	....	....	31	7	4	1	5	2
1961-62	Niagara Falls Flyers	OHA-Jr.	50	28	34	62	....	....	....	19	10	2	4	6	5
	Kingston Frontenacs	EPHL	1	0	0	0	....	....	....	0	7	1	2	3	0
1962-63	Kingston Frontenacs	EPHL	69	22	25	47	....	....	....	8	5	0	1	1	5
1963-64	Minneapolis Bruins	CPHL	72	29	36	65	....	....	....	12	5	0	3	3	0
1964-65	**Boston Bruins**	**NHL**	**53**	**7**	**10**	**17**	**8**	**10**	**18**	**4**	....	....	....	....	....
	Minneapolis Bruins	CPHL	16	11	8	19	....	....	....	10	....	....	....	....	....
1965-66	Baltimore Clippers	AHL	71	21	17	38	....	....	....	12	....	....	....	....	....
1966-67	Baltimore Clippers	AHL	70	16	17	33	....	....	....	24	9	2	2	4	4
1967-68	Buffalo Bisons	AHL	49	13	27	40	....	....	....	21	5	3	0	3	2
1968-69	Buffalo Bisons	AHL	68	13	38	51	....	....	....	38	6	2	3	5	0
1969-70	Buffalo Bisons	AHL	69	17	43	60	....	....	....	18	8	1	4	5	10
1970-71	Seattle Totems	WHL	39	14	17	31	....	....	....	4	....	....	....	....	....
	Omaha Knights	CHL	19	10	22	32	....	....	....	70	11	2	9	11	2
1971-72	Providence Reds	AHL	76	13	33	46	....	....	....	34	5	0	2	2	2
1972-73	Providence Reds	AHL	67	17	39	56	....	....	....	32	4	0	1	1	0
1973-74	Rochester Americans	AHL	38	9	25	34	....	....	....	6	....	....	....	....	....
1974-75	HC Salzburg	Austria	STATISTICS NOT AVAILABLE												
	Rochester Americans	AHL	44	8	17	25	....	....	....	14	7	1	1	2	4
	NHL Totals		**53**	**7**	**10**	**17**	**8**	**10**	**18**	**4**	....	....	....	....	....

Claimed on waivers by **NY Rangers** from **Boston**, June 8, 1965. Selected by **LA Sharks** (WHA) in WHA General Player Draft, February 12, 1972. Traded to **Rochester** (AHL) by **NY Rangers** with $20,000 for Bob Kelly, June, 1973.

• KNOTT, Nick Nickolas Earl

D – L. 6'2", 200 lbs. b: Kingston, Ont., 7/23/1920 d: 4/12/1987.

Season	Club	League	GP	G	A	Pts	AG	AA	APts	PIM	GP	G	A	Pts	PIM
1938-39	Oshawa Generals	OHA-Jr.	14	15	7	22	....	....	....	17	7	5	5	10	4
	Oshawa Generals	M-Cup	9	*11	3	14	....	....	....	*22	....	....	....	....	....
1939-40	Oshawa Generals	OHA-Jr.	18	6	17	23	....	....	....	17	7	4	4	8	17
	Oshawa Generals	M-Cup	4	2	1	3	....	....	....	13	....	....	....	....	....
1940-41	Pittsburgh Hornets	AHL	30	7	11	18	....	....	....	20	6	2	3	5	6
1941-42	**Brooklyn Americans**	**NHL**	**14**	**3**	**1**	**4**	**4**	**1**	**5**	**9**	....	....	....	....	....
	Springfield Indians	AHL	38	13	28	41	....	....	....	74	5	0	3	3	2
1942-43	Cornwall Army	QSHL	32	17	26	43	....	....	....	51	6	1	1	2	22
1943-44			MILITARY SERVICE												
1944-45			MILITARY SERVICE												
1945-46	Tulsa Oilers	USHL	45	16	21	37	....	....	....	64	8	1	4	5	17
1946-47	Tulsa Oilers	USHL	57	10	29	39	....	....	....	120	5	1	1	2	14
1947-48	Tulsa Oilers	USHL	65	24	28	52	....	....	....	69	2	0	1	1	0
1948-49	Tulsa Oilers	USHL	56	31	24	55	....	....	....	79	6	2	3	5	4
1949-50	Tulsa Oilers	USHL	37	10	14	24	....	....	....	36	....	....	....	....	....
	NHL Totals		**14**	**3**	**1**	**4**	**4**	**1**	**5**	**9**	....	....	....	....	....

USHL Second All-Star Team (1946)

Signed as a free agent by **Toronto**, October 31, 1940. Loaned to **Brooklyn** by **Toronto** with Red Heron and Gus Marker and future considerations (cash, February 2, 1942) for Lorne Carr, October 30, 1941. Traded to **Tulsa** (USHL) by **Toronto** for cash, May 15, 1947. Traded to **Tacoma** (PCHL) by **Tulsa** (USHL) for cash, January 21, 1950. • Officially announced retirement, January 23, 1950.

• KNOX, Paul Paul Patrick

RW – R. 5'10", 160 lbs. b: Toronto, Ont., 11/23/1933.

Season	Club	League	GP	G	A	Pts	AG	AA	APts	PIM	GP	G	A	Pts	PIM
1950-51	St. Michael's Majors	OHA-Jr.	2	0	0	0	....	....	....	0	....	....	....	....	....
1951-52	St. Michael's Majors	OHA-Jr.	34	12	14	26	....	....	....	10	....	....	....	....	....
1952-53	St. Michael's Majors	OHA-Jr.	47	21	20	41	....	....	....	19	17	*13	7	20	2
1953-54	St. Michael's Majors	OHA-Jr.	58	40	28	68	....	....	....	20	8	9	10	19	4
1954-55	**Toronto Maple Leafs**	**NHL**	**1**	**0**	**0**	**0**	**0**	**0**	**0**	**0**	....	....	....	....	....
	University of Toronto	ICHL	STATISTICS NOT AVAILABLE												
1955-56	Kitchener Dutchmen	OHA-Sr.	48	19	24	43	....	....	....	6	10	6	4	10	2
	Canada	Olympics	8	7	7	*14	....	....	....	2	....	....	....	....	....
1956-57	Kitchener Dutchmen	OHA-Sr.	52	18	22	40	....	....	....	30	10	8	5	13	0
	Kitchener Dutchmen	Al-Cup	6	1	3	4	....	....	....	2	....	....	....	....	....
1957-58	Kitchener Dutchmen	NOHA	....	....	....	....	....	....	....	....	1	0	0	0	0
	Kitchener Dutchmen	Al-Cup	2	0	1	1	....	....	....	0	....	....	....	....	....
1958-59	Kitchener Dutchmen	NOHA	3	2	0	2	....	....	....	0	11	3	2	5	5
	NHL Totals		**1**	**0**	**0**	**0**	**0**	**0**	**0**	**0**	....	....	....	....	....

Signed as a free agent by **Kitcheer** (OHA-Sr.), October 3, 1955.

• KOPAK, Russ

C – L. 5'10", 158 lbs. b: Edmonton, Alta., 4/26/1924 d: 11/25/1998.

Season	Club	League	GP	G	A	Pts	AG	AA	APts	PIM	GP	G	A	Pts	PIM
1942-43	Regina Abbotts	S-SJHL	13	14	8	22	....	....	....	16	4	1	0	1	*13
1943-44	**Boston Bruins**	**NHL**	**24**	**7**	**9**	**16**	**6**	**8**	**14**	**0**	....	....	....	....	....
	Boston Olympics	EAHL	19	20	24	44	....	....	....	4	9	4	5	9	11
1944-45	Boston Olympics	EAHL	41	41	41	82	....	....	....	53	10	*15	10	25	6
1945-46	Fort Worth Rangers	USHL	56	21	31	52	....	....	....	23	....	....	....	....	....
1946-47	Fort Worth Rangers	USHL	59	22	25	47	....	....	....	30	9	0	2	2	2
1947-48	Fort Worth Rangers	USHL	44	15	28	43	....	....	....	23	....	....	....	....	....
1948-49	Fort Worth–Houston	USHL	66	17	33	50	....	....	....	14	2	0	0	0	0
1949-50	Seattle–Victoria	PCHL	72	13	20	33	....	....	....	21	....	....	....	....	....
	NHL Totals		**24**	**7**	**9**	**16**	**6**	**8**	**14**	**0**	....	....	....	....	....

EAHL Second All-Star Team (1944, 1945)

Signed as a free agent by **Victoria** (PCHL) after being released by **Seattle** (PCHL), November 16, 1949.

• KOTANEN, Dick

D – R. 5'11", 190 lbs. b: Port Arthur, Ont., 11/18/1925.

Season	Club	League	GP	G	A	Pts	AG	AA	APts	PIM	GP	G	A	Pts	PIM
1942-43	Port Arthur Bruins	TBJHL	8	3	2	5	....	....	....	2	3	0	1	1	2
1943-44	Port Arthur Bruins	TBJHL	11	3	4	7	....	....	....	6	4	0	3	3	4
	Port Arthur Shipbuilders	TBSHL	1	0	0	0	....	....	....	2	....	....	....	....	....
	Port Arthur Shipbuilders	Al-Cup	4	0	0	0	....	....	....	0	....	....	....	....	....
1944-45	Winnipeg Maroons	MJHL	4	1	1	2	....	....	....	0	2	0	1	1	2
	Winnipeg Army	WSrHL	9	0	2	2	....	....	....	2	2	0	0	0	2
1945-46	Brandon Elks	MJHL	8	2	3	5	....	....	....	2	7	1	2	3	16
1946-47	Port Arthur Bearcats	TBSHL	12	1	8	9	....	....	....	12	5	0	0	0	*8
	Port Arthur Bearcats	Al-Cup	8	0	1	1	....	....	....	0	....	....	....	....	....
1947-48	New York Rovers	EAHL	17	3	6	9	....	....	....	10	....	....	....	....	....
	New York Rovers	QSHL	45	3	8	11	....	....	....	34	4	1	2	3	4
1948-49	New York Rovers	EAHL	63	4	10	14	....	....	....	*52	....	....	....	....	....
1949-50	Regina Capitols	WCSHL	49	5	5	10	....	....	....	102	....	....	....	....	....
	New York Rovers	EAHL	1	0	0	0	....	....	....	0	12	0	0	0	22
1950-51	**New York Rangers**	**NHL**	**1**	**0**	**0**	**0**	**0**	**0**	**0**	**0**	....	....	....	....	....
	Sherbrooke Saints	QMHL	19	0	2	2	....	....	....	30	....	....	....	....	....
	New York Rovers	EAHL	32	2	4	6	....	....	....	79	6	0	1	1	*37
1951-52	Trail Smoke Eaters	WIHL	33	4	14	18	....	....	....	110	10	3	4	7	20
1952-53	Seattle Bombers	WHL	2	1	1	2	....	....	....	0	....	....	....	....	....
	Kamloops Elks	OSHL	51	3	16	19	....	....	....	107	12	3	4	7	24
1953-54	Windsor Bulldogs	OHA-Sr.	54	10	23	33	....	....	....	87	4	1	3	4	20
1954-55	Windsor–Chatham	OHA-Sr.	46	3	18	21	....	....	....	77	....	....	....	....	....
	Pembrooke Lumber Kings	NOHA	2	1	0	1	....	....	....	2	....	....	....	....	....
1955-56	Chatham Maroons	OHA-Sr.	48	1	8	9	....	....	....	109	10	0	4	4	22
	Chatham Maroons	Al-Cup	17	1	8	9	....	....	....	16	....	....	....	....	....
1956-57	Chatham Maroons	OHA-Sr.	17	0	4	4	....	....	....	22	....	....	....	....	....
	Kingston CKLC's	EOHL	29	1	9	10	....	....	....	40	5	1	0	1	8
1957-58	North Bay Trappers	NOHA	42	1	13	14	....	....	....	32	....	....	....	....	....
	NHL Totals		**1**	**0**	**0**	**0**	**0**	**0**	**0**	**0**	....	....	....	....	....

OSHL First All-Star Team (1953)

• KOZAK, Les Leslie Paul

LW – L. 6', 185 lbs. b: Dauphin, Man., 10/28/1940.

Season	Club	League	GP	G	A	Pts	AG	AA	APts	PIM	GP	G	A	Pts	PIM
1955-56	Melville Millionaires	SJHL	3	0	0	0	....	....	....	2	....	....	....	....	....
1956-57	Saskatoon Quakers	SJHL	1	0	0	0	....	....	....	0	....	....	....	....	....
	Toronto Marlboros	OHA-Jr.	1	0	1	1	....	....	....	0	8	0	1	1	0
1957-58	St. Michael's Majors	OHA-Jr.	38	9	15	24	....	....	....	10	3	0	0	0	0
1958-59	St. Michael's Majors	OHA-Jr.	43	10	8	18	....	....	....	18	15	4	1	5	10
1959-60	St. Michael's Majors	OHA-Jr.	42	18	17	35	....	....	....	34	10	2	2	4	10
1960-61			DID NOT PLAY												
1961-62	**Toronto Maple Leafs**	**NHL**	**12**	**1**	**0**	**1**	**1**	**0**	**1**	**2**	....	....	....	....	....
	Rochester Americans	AHL	45	14	9	23	....	....	....	31	....	....	....	....	....
	NHL Totals		**12**	**1**	**0**	**1**	**1**	**0**	**1**	**2**	....	....	....	....	....

• Missed the 1960-61 season while studying for the priesthood. • Suffered career-ending head injury in game vs. Providence (AHL), February 23, 1962.

• KRAFTCHECK, Stephen Stephen S.

D – R. 5'11", 190 lbs. b: Tinturn, Ont., 3/3/1929 d: 8/10/1997.

			REGULAR SEASON								PLAYOFFS				
Season	Club	League	GP	G	A	Pts	AG	AA	APts	PIM	GP	G	A	Pts	PIM
1945-46	Hamilton Lloyds	OHA-Jr.	2	0	0	0	....	....	....	2	....	....	....	....	....
	Hamilton Aerovox	OMHA	STATISTICS NOT AVAILABLE												
1946-47	Hamilton Aerovox	OHA-B	STATISTICS NOT AVAILABLE												
1947-48	Hamilton Aerovox	OHA-B	STATISTICS NOT AVAILABLE												
1948-49	San Francisco Shamrocks	PCHL	70	11	22	33	....	....	....	82	....	....	....	....	....
1949-50	Cleveland Barons	AHL	70	7	37	44	....	....	....	46	8	0	3	3	12
1950-51	**Boston Bruins**	**NHL**	**22**	**0**	**0**	**0**	**0**	**0**	**0**	**8**	**6**	**0**	**0**	**0**	**7**
	Indianapolis Capitols	AHL	47	6	27	33	....	....	....	39	3	0	0	0	2
1951-52	**New York Rangers**	**NHL**	**58**	**8**	**9**	**17**	**11**	**11**	**22**	**30**	....	....	....	....	....
1952-53	**New York Rangers**	**NHL**	**69**	**2**	**9**	**11**	**3**	**11**	**14**	**45**	....	....	....	....	....
1953-54	Cleveland Barons	AHL	70	5	20	25	....	....	....	62	7	2	1	3	10
1954-55	Cleveland Barons	AHL	60	9	26	35	....	....	....	38	4	0	2	2	0
1955-56	Cleveland Barons	AHL	57	5	29	34	....	....	....	40	8	1	4	5	10
1956-57	Cleveland Barons	AHL	63	7	33	40	....	....	....	42	12	2	*11	13	8
1957-58	Cleveland Barons	AHL	66	15	34	49	....	....	....	53	7	0	3	3	4
1958-59	**Toronto Maple Leafs**	**NHL**	**8**	**1**	**0**	**1**	**1**	**0**	**1**	**0**	....	....	....	....	....
	Rochester Americans	AHL	60	2	37	39	....	....	....	42	5	0	2	2	4
1959-60	Rochester Americans	AHL	68	1	41	42	....	....	....	47	12	1	3	4	12
1960-61	Rochester Americans	AHL	71	3	37	40	....	....	....	26	....	....	....	....	....
1961-62	Rochester Americans	AHL	69	4	41	45	....	....	....	45	2	0	0	0	2
1962-63	Providence Reds	AHL	69	2	19	21	....	....	....	22	6	0	2	2	2
1963-64	Providence Reds	AHL	69	1	5	6	....	....	....	22	....	....	....	....	....
	NHL Totals		**157**	**11**	**18**	**29**	**15**	**22**	**37**	**83**	**6**	**0**	**0**	**0**	**7**

PCHL Southern First All-Star Team (1949) • AHL Second All-Star Team (1956, 1961) • AHL First All-Star Team (1957, 1958, 1959, 1960) • Won Eddie Shore Award (Outstanding Defenseman - AHL) (1959)

Traded to **Boston** by **Cleveland** (AHL) for cash, April 17, 1950. Traded to **Detroit** (Indianapolis-AHL) by **Boston** for loan of Max Quackenbush for remainder of 1950-51 season, December 5, 1950. Traded to **NY Rangers** by **Detroit** with Ed Reigle for $30,000, May 14, 1951. Traded to **Cleveland** (AHL) by **NY Rangers** with cash for Bob Chrystal, June, 1953. Traded to **Toronto** by **Cleveland** (AHL) for Ian Anderson, April 30, 1958. Traded to **Providence** (AHL) by **Toronto** (Rochester-AHL) for cash, June, 1962.

• KRAKE, Skip — *see page 1274*

• KROL, Joe

LW – L. 5'11", 173 lbs. b: Winnipeg, Man., 8/13/1915 d: 10/26/1993.

Season	Club	League	GP	G	A	Pts	AG	AA	APts	PIM	GP	G	A	Pts	PIM
1932-33	Winnipeg K of C	WJrHL	11	6	3	9	....	....	....	18	3	1	1	2	2
1933-34	Selkirk Fishermen	WJrHL	14	3	3	6	....	....	....	43	5	0	2	2	13
1934-35	Winnipeg Monarchs	WJrHL	13	12	7	19	....	....	....	16	3	*6	2	*8	10
	Winnipeg Monarchs	M-Cup	9	11	7	18	....	....	....	21	....	....	....	....	....
1935-36	New York Rovers	EAHL	39	16	22	38	....	....	....	47	8	2	0	2	6
1936-37	**New York Rangers**	**NHL**	**1**	**0**	**0**	**0**	**0**	**0**	**0**	**0**	....	....	....	....	....
	Philadelphia Ramblers	IAHL	49	9	18	27	....	....	....	26	6	0	1	1	2
1937-38	Philadelphia Ramblers	IAHL	43	4	10	14	....	....	....	10	4	1	1	2	0
1938-39	**New York Rangers**	**NHL**	**1**	**1**	**1**	**2**	**2**	**2**	**4**	**0**	....	....	....	....	....
	Philadelphia Ramblers	IAHL	54	24	30	54	....	....	....	34	8	2	3	5	4
1939-40	Philadelphia Rockets	IAHL	52	7	11	18	....	....	....	23	....	....	....	....	....
1940-41	Hershey Bears	AHL	46	13	17	30	....	....	....	20	....	....	....	....	....
	Springfield Indians	AHL	6	2	3	5	....	....	....	12	3	0	2	2	2
1941-42	**Brooklyn Americans**	**NHL**	**24**	**9**	**3**	**12**	**12**	**4**	**16**	**8**	....	....	....	....	....
	Springfield Indians	AHL	18	3	12	15	....	....	....	5	....	....	....	....	....
1942-43	Vancouver RCAF	NNDHL	19	14	16	30	....	....	....	32	2	0	1	1	0
	Winnipeg RCAF	WNDHL	....	....	....	....	....	....	....	....	3	0	1	1	2
1943-44	Winnipeg RCAF	WNDHL	9	4	3	7	....	....	....	8	....	....	....	....	....
	NHL Totals		**26**	**10**	**4**	**14**	**14**	**6**	**20**	**8**	....	....	....	....	....

EAHL First All-Star Team (1936)

Signed as a free agent by **NY Rangers**, November, 1936. Traded to **Hershey** (IAHL) by **NY Rangers** for cash, April 4, 1940. Traded to **NY Americans** (Springfield-AHL) by **Hershey** for John Sorrell, February 14, 1941.

• KRYZANOWSKI, Ed Edward Lloyd

D – R. 5'11", 175 lbs. b: Fort Frances, Ont., 11/14/1925.

Season	Club	League	GP	G	A	Pts	AG	AA	APts	PIM	GP	G	A	Pts	PIM
1943-44	Fort Frances Maple Leafs	TBSHL	STATISTICS NOT AVAILABLE												
	Fort Frances Maple Leafs	Al-Cup	2	0	1	1	....	....	....	2	....	....	....	....	....
1944-45	HMCS Cornwallis	NNDHL	STATISTICS NOT AVAILABLE												
1945-46	University of Toronto	OUAA	6	1	3	4	....	....	....	4	1	0	0	0	2
1946-47	University of Toronto	CIAU	9	4	11	15	....	....	....	10	1	0	1	1	0
	Toronto Stoneys	TIHL	5	1	2	3	....	....	....	4	8	4	3	7	4
1947-48	University of Toronto	OUAA	12	10	12	22	....	....	....	12	1	2	0	2	0
	Fort Frances Canadians	TBSHL	STATISTICS NOT AVAILABLE												
1948-49	**Boston Bruins**	**NHL**	**36**	**1**	**3**	**4**	**1**	**4**	**5**	**10**	**5**	**0**	**1**	**1**	**2**
	Hershey Bears	AHL	18	0	8	8	....	....	....	6	....	....	....	....	....
1949-50	**Boston Bruins**	**NHL**	**57**	**6**	**10**	**16**	**8**	**12**	**20**	**12**	....	....	....	....	....
	Hershey Bears	AHL	10	1	1	2	....	....	....	4	....	....	....	....	....
1950-51	**Boston Bruins**	**NHL**	**69**	**3**	**6**	**9**	**4**	**7**	**11**	**10**	**6**	**0**	**0**	**0**	**2**
1951-52	**Boston Bruins**	**NHL**	**70**	**5**	**3**	**8**	**7**	**4**	**11**	**33**	**7**	**0**	**0**	**0**	**0**
1952-53	**Chicago Black Hawks**	**NHL**	**5**	**0**	**0**	**0**	**0**	**0**	**0**	**0**	....	....	....	....	....
	Providence Reds	AHL	51	5	26	31	....	....	....	19	....	....	....	....	....
1953-54	Providence Reds	AHL	70	2	14	16	....	....	....	37	....	....	....	....	....
1954-55	Hershey Bears	AHL	60	7	14	21	....	....	....	37	....	....	....	....	....
1955-56	Hershey Bears	AHL	64	9	26	35	....	....	....	53	....	....	....	....	....
1956/58			OUT OF HOCKEY – RETIRED												
1958/62	Warroad Lakers	AAHL	STATISTICS NOT AVAILABLE												
	NHL Totals		**237**	**15**	**22**	**37**	**20**	**27**	**47**	**65**	**18**	**0**	**1**	**1**	**4**

Signed as a free agent by **Boston**, October 8, 1948. Traded to **Chicago** by **Boston** for cash, August 14, 1952. Traded to **Boston** by **Chicago** for cash, October 31, 1952. Traded to **Providence** (AHL) by **Boston** for cash, November 8, 1952.

• KUHN, Gord Gordon Frederick "Doggie"

RW – R. 5'7", 145 lbs. b: Truro, N.S., 11/19/1905 d: 7/29/1978.

Season	Club	League	GP	G	A	Pts	AG	AA	APts	PIM	GP	G	A	Pts	PIM
1924-25	Truro Bearcats	NSSHL	8	15	0	15	....	....	....	....	1	0	0	0	2
	Truro Bearcats	Al-Cup	6	2	2	4	....	....	....	2	....	....	....	....	....
1925-26	Truro Bearcats	NSSHL	DID NOT PLAY – SUSPENDED												
1926-27	Windsor Maple Leafs	NSSHL	10	5	4	9	....	....	....	2	9	6	4	*10	2
1927-28	Truro Bearcats	NSSHL	11	10	*7	17	....	....	....	8	2	1	0	1	2
1928-29	Halifax Wolverines	HSrHL	12	13	3	16	....	....	....	25	2	3	1	4	2
	Halifax Wolverines	Al-Cup	8	*9	*5	*14	....	....	....	4	....	....	....	....	....
1929-30	Truro Bearcats	NSSHL	17	*14	5	*19	....	....	....	39	2	1	0	1	4
	Truro Bearcats	Al-Cup	8	*11	1	*12	....	....	....	2	....	....	....	....	....
1930-31	New Haven Eagles	Can-Am	36	5	5	10	....	....	....	48	....	....	....	....	....
1931-32	New Haven Eagles	Can-Am	40	16	6	22	....	....	....	52	....	....	....	....	....
1932-33	**New York Americans**	**NHL**	**12**	**1**	**1**	**2**	**2**	**2**	**4**	**4**	....	....	....	....	....
	New Haven Eagles	Can-Am	29	5	6	11	....	....	....	39	2	0	0	0	2
1933-34	Buffalo Bisons	IHL	36	4	5	9	....	....	....	20	6	1	0	1	20
1934-35	Providence Reds	Can-Am	46	13	22	35	....	....	....	26	6	0	1	1	6
1935-36	Providence Reds	Can-Am	46	8	9	17	....	....	....	47	7	2	2	4	*10
1936-37	Providence Reds	IAHL	48	17	13	30	....	....	....	34	3	1	1	2	7
1937-38	Providence Reds	IAHL	48	9	18	27	....	....	....	44	7	0	4	4	4
1938-39	Providence Reds	IAHL	52	13	9	22	....	....	....	13	5	0	2	2	0
1939-40	Syracuse Stars	IAHL	47	4	9	13	....	....	....	11	....	....	....	....	....
1940-41			DID NOT PLAY – REFEREE												
	NHL Totals		**12**	**1**	**1**	**2**	**2**	**2**	**4**	**4**	....	....	....	....	....

Signed as a free agent by **NY Americans**, October 27, 1930. Traded to **Buffalo** (IHL) by **NY Americans** for cash, January 9, 1934. Traded to **Providence** (Can-Am) by **Buffalo** (IHL) for cash, November 13, 1934.

• KUKULOWICZ, Aggie Adolph Frank

C – L. 6'3", 175 lbs. b: Winnipeg, Man., 4/2/1933.

Season	Club	League	GP	G	A	Pts	AG	AA	APts	PIM	GP	G	A	Pts	PIM
1950-51	Brandon Wheat Kings	MJHL	36	27	30	57	....	....	....	18	6	5	4	9	0
1951-52	Quebec Citadels	QJHL	50	24	35	59	....	....	....	54	15	2	*13	15	10
1952-53	**New York Rangers**	**NHL**	**3**	**1**	**0**	**1**	**1**	**0**	**1**	**0**	....	....	....	....	....
	Quebec Citadels	QJHL	46	13	24	37	....	....	....	109	9	6	2	8	4
	Quebec Citadels	M-Cup	8	3	5	8	....	....	....	0	....	....	....	....	....
1953-54	**New York Rangers**	**NHL**	**1**	**0**	**0**	**0**	**0**	**0**	**0**	**0**	....	....	....	....	....
	Saskatoon Quakers	WHL	70	14	27	41	....	....	....	38	6	0	1	1	2
1954-55	Saskatoon Quakers	WHL	57	12	25	37	....	....	....	31	....	....	....	....	....
1955-56	Brandon Regals	WHL	67	16	38	54	....	....	....	38	....	....	....	....	....
1956-57	New Westminster Royals	WHL	70	7	32	39	....	....	....	71	13	0	3	3	10
1957-58	Seattle Totems	WHL	67	5	23	28	....	....	....	61	9	2	2	4	15
1958-59	Saskatoon Quakers	WHL	9	1	6	7	....	....	....	0	....	....	....	....	....
	Quebec Aces	QHL	14	2	8	10	....	....	....	8	....	....	....	....	....
	Cornwall Chevies	EOHL	18	5	13	18	....	....	....	6	6	1	2	3	2
1959-60	St. Paul Saints	IHL	68	38	80	118	....	....	....	57	13	6	8	14	0
1960-61	St. Paul Saints	IHL	72	34	53	87	....	....	....	39	13	6	13	*19	19
1961-62	Minneapolis Millers	IHL	62	24	61	85	....	....	....	8	5	1	3	4	13
1962-63	Winnipeg Maroons	SSHL	10	3	12	15	....	....	....	0	....	....	....	....	....
	Winnipeg Maroons	Al-Cup	15	6	11	17	....	....	....	14	....	....	....	....	....
1963-64	Winnipeg Maroons	SSHL	16	12	15	27	....	....	....	14	....	....	....	....	....
	Winnipeg Maroons	Al-Cup	13	9	13	22	....	....	....	6	....	....	....	....	....
1964-65	Winnipeg Maroons	SSHL	6	2	3	5	....	....	....	0	....	....	....	....	....
1965-66	GKS Katowice	Poland	DID NOT PLAY – COACHING												
	NHL Totals		**4**	**1**	**0**	**1**	**1**	**0**	**1**	**0**	....	....	....	....	....

IHL Second All-Star Team (1960)

Traded to **Detroit** by **NY Rangers** with Billy Dea and cash for Dave Creighton and Bronco Horvath, August 18, 1955.

• KULLMAN, Arnie Arnold Edwin

C – L. 5'7", 170 lbs. b: Winnipeg, Man., 10/9/1927.

Season	Club	League	GP	G	A	Pts	AG	AA	APts	PIM	GP	G	A	Pts	PIM
1943-44	Winnipeg Rangers	MJHL	2	0	0	0	....	....	....	0	....	....	....	....	....
1944-45	Winnipeg Rangers	MJHL	10	11	6	17	....	....	....	12	4	4	1	5	0
1945-46	Brandon Elks	MJHL	4	4	3	7	....	....	....	4	7	4	3	7	8
1946-47	Stratford Kroehlers	OHA-Jr.	28	29	15	44	....	....	....	26	2	0	1	1	2
1947-48	**Boston Bruins**	**NHL**	**1**	**0**	**0**	**0**	**0**	**0**	**0**	**0**	....	....	....	....	....
	Boston Olympics	QSHL	45	25	18	43	....	....	....	45	....	....	....	....	....
	Boston Olympics	EAHL	17	4	5	9	....	....	....	24	....	....	....	....	....
1948-49	Hershey Bears	AHL	66	20	36	56	....	....	....	29	9	5	7	12	8
1949-50	**Boston Bruins**	**NHL**	**12**	**0**	**1**	**1**	**0**	**1**	**1**	**11**	....	....	....	....	....
	Hershey Bears	AHL	42	13	14	27	....	....	....	42	....	....	....	....	....
1950-51	Hershey Bears	AHL	69	32	33	65	....	....	....	52	4	3	2	5	4
1951-52	Hershey Bears	AHL	63	25	31	56	....	....	....	45	1	0	0	0	10
1952-53	Hershey Bears	AHL	64	25	39	64	....	....	....	22	3	0	1	1	4
1953-54	Hershey Bears	AHL	69	40	41	81	....	....	....	35	11	4	8	12	8
1954-55	Hershey Bears	AHL	62	23	48	71	....	....	....	67	....	....	....	....	....
1955-56	Hershey Bears	AHL	63	22	30	52	....	....	....	83	....	....	....	....	....
1956-57	Hershey Bears	AHL	57	18	24	42	....	....	....	53	7	0	1	1	29
1957-58	Hershey Bears	AHL	67	16	29	45	....	....	....	47	10	2	1	3	5
1958-59	Hershey Bears	AHL	59	10	17	27	....	....	....	70	13	2	4	6	16
1959-60	Hershey Bears	AHL	72	9	24	33	....	....	....	57	....	....	....	....	....
	NHL Totals		**13**	**0**	**1**	**1**	**0**	**1**	**1**	**11**	....	....	....	....	....

• Brother of Eddie

• KULLMAN, Eddie Edward George

RW – R. 5'7", 165 lbs. b: Winnipeg, Man., 12/12/1923 d: 1997.

Season	Club	League	GP	G	A	Pts	AG	AA	APts	PIM	GP	G	A	Pts	PIM
1941-42	Winnipeg Rangers	MJHL	18	14	5	19	....	....	....	9	....	....	....	....	....
1942-43	Winnipeg Rangers	MJHL	14	15	12	27	....	....	....	15	6	5	*8	13	8
	Winnipeg Rangers	M-Cup	13	*21	*12	*33	....	....	....	8	....	....	....	....	....
1943-44	Winnipeg Rangers	MJHL	2	0	0	0	....	....	....	0	....	....	....	....	....
	Toronto Maher Jewels	TIHL	2	1	1	2	....	....	....	0	....	....	....	....	....
	Stratford Kroehlers	OHA-Jr.	3	4	1	5	....	....	....	2	....	....	....	....	....
	St. Thomas RCAF	TNDHL	1	0	0	0	....	....	....	0	....	....	....	....	....
1944-45	Winnipeg Rangers	MJHL	1	0	0	0	....	....	....	0	....	....	....	....	....
	Vancouver RCAF	NNDHL	STATISTICS NOT AVAILABLE												
1945-46	Winnipeg Rangers	MJHL	10	6	4	10	....	....	....	4	....	....	....	....	....
1946-47	Portland Eagles	PCHL	60	*56	46	102	....	....	....	135	12	3	7	10	6
1947-48	**New York Rangers**	**NHL**	**51**	**15**	**17**	**32**	**19**	**22**	**41**	**32**	**6**	**1**	**0**	**1**	**2**
	New Haven Ramblers	AHL	12	5	4	9	....	....	....	8	....	....	....	....	....
1948-49	**New York Rangers**	**NHL**	**18**	**4**	**5**	**9**	**6**	**7**	**13**	**14**	....	....	....	....	....
	Providence Reds	AHL	41	16	24	40	....	....	....	22	10	5	4	9	6
1949-50	Providence Reds	AHL	69	32	34	66	....	....	....	62	4	2	2	4	2
1950-51	**New York Rangers**	**NHL**	**70**	**14**	**18**	**32**	**18**	**22**	**40**	**88**	....	....	....	....	....
1951-52	**New York Rangers**	**NHL**	**64**	**11**	**10**	**21**	**15**	**12**	**27**	**59**	....	....	....	....	....
	Cincinnati Mohawks	AHL	7	3	1	4	....	....	....	4	....	....	....	....	....
1952-53	**New York Rangers**	**NHL**	**70**	**8**	**10**	**18**	**10**	**12**	**22**	**61**	....	....	....	....	....

Season	Club	League	GP	G	A	Pts	AG	AA	APts	PIM	GP	G	A	Pts	PIM
			REGULAR SEASON								PLAYOFFS				
1953-54	**New York Rangers**	**NHL**	**70**	**4**	**10**	**14**	**5**	**12**	**17**	**44**	....	....	....	....	....
1954-55	Saskatoon–Vancouver	WHL	53	9	21	30	....	....	....	52	5	0	2	2	6
	Windsor Bulldogs	OHA-Sr.	3	0	1	1	....	....	....	6	....	....	....	....	....
	NHL Totals		**343**	**56**	**70**	**126**	**73**	**87**	**160**	**298**	**6**	**1**	**0**	**1**	**2**

• Brother of Arnie

Traded to **Providence** (AHL) by **NY Rangers** with Elwyn Morris, cash and future considerations (Buck Davies, June, 1949) for Allan Stanley, December 9, 1948. Traded to **NY Rangers** by **Providence** (AHL) for Orville LaValle and Sheldon Bloomer, August 16, 1950. Signed as a free agent by **Saskatoon** (WHL), October 19, 1954.

• KUNTZ, Alan
Alan Robert
LW – L. 5'11", 165 lbs. b: Toronto, Ont., 6/4/1919 d: 3/7/1987.

Season	Club	League	GP	G	A	Pts	AG	AA	APts	PIM	GP	G	A	Pts	PIM
1935-36	Ottawa Glebe Collegiate	H.S.				STATISTICS NOT AVAILABLE									
1936-37	Ottawa Jr. Senators	OCJHL	4	2	1	3	....	....	....	0	4	0	1	1	0
1937-38	Ottawa Glebe Collegiate	OCHL				STATISTICS NOT AVAILABLE									
1938-39	Guelph Indians	OHA-Jr.	14	9	10	19	....	....	....	9	2	0	2	2	2
1939-40	Washington Eagles	EAHL	41	22	27	49	....	....	....	2	4	1	0	1	2
1940-41	Philadelphia Rockets	AHL	48	11	14	25	....	....	....	23	....	....	....	....	....
1941-42	**New York Rangers**	**NHL**	**31**	**10**	**11**	**21**	**13**	**13**	**26**	**10**	**6**	**1**	**0**	**1**	**2**
	New Haven Eagles	AHL	21	5	9	14	....	....	....	2	....	....	....	....	....
1942-43	Montreal Army	QSHL	32	19	21	40	....	....	....	36	7	1	3	4	0
1944-45	Toronto Army Shamrocks	TIHL	5	3	4	7	....	....	....	0	....	....	....	....	....
	Toronto Army Daggers	OHA-Sr.	2	1	1	2	....	....	....	0	....	....	....	....	....
1945-46	**New York Rangers**	**NHL**	**14**	**0**	**1**	**1**	**0**	**1**	**1**	**2**	....	....	....	....	....
	St. Paul Saints	USHL	39	7	9	16	....	....	....	24	6	2	2	4	6
1946-47	New Haven Ramblers	AHL	55	17	27	44	....	....	....	27	....	....	....	....	....
1947-48	Springfield Indians	AHL	62	24	34	58	....	....	....	22	....	....	....	....	....
1948-49	Vancouver Canucks	PCHL	64	42	38	80	....	....	....	14	3	1	0	1	4
1949-50	Vancouver Canucks	PCHL	70	37	46	83	....	....	....	33	12	2	5	7	0
1950-51	Ottawa Senators	QMHL	53	10	17	27	....	....	....	22	11	4	2	6	0
1951-52	Ottawa Senators	QMHL	59	25	37	62	....	....	....	7	7	4	6	10	0
1952-53	Ottawa Senators	QMHL	49	14	19	33	....	....	....	6	10	2	2	4	0
1953-54	Ottawa Senators	QHL	62	13	19	32	....	....	....	9	22	2	7	9	2
1954-55	Ottawa Senators	QHL	27	8	8	16	....	....	....	11	....	....	....	....	....
	Pembroke Lumber Kings	NOHA	22	11	15	26	....	....	....	2	6	3	2	5	0
1955-56	Brockville Magedomas	EOHL	37	4	21	25	....	....	....	22	2	0	0	0	14
	NHL Totals		**45**	**10**	**12**	**22**	**13**	**14**	**27**	**12**	**6**	**1**	**0**	**1**	**2**

QMHL First All-Star Team (1952) • PCHL Northern Second All-Star Team (1949)

Traded to **Springfield** (AHL) by **NY Rangers** for $5,000, August, 1948. Traded to **Vancouver** (PCHL) by **Springfield** (AHL) for cash, October 20, 1948.

• KURTENBACH, Orland
— see page 1282

• KURYLUK, Merv
Mervin
LW – L. 5'11", 185 lbs. b: Yorkton, Sask., 8/10/1937.

Season	Club	League	GP	G	A	Pts	AG	AA	APts	PIM	GP	G	A	Pts	PIM
1954-55	Moose Jaw Canucks	WCJHL	39	10	21	31	....	....	....	78	....	....	....	....	....
1955-56	Yorkton Terriers	SJHL	48	26	34	60	....	....	....	113	5	2	1	3	11
1956-57	Melville Millionaires	SJHL	50	31	35	66	....	....	....	135	....	....	....	....	....
	Calgary Stampeders	WHL	4	1	0	1	....	....	....	0	3	0	1	1	2
1957-58	Calgary Stampeders	WHL	59	12	16	28	....	....	....	44	14	1	3	4	10
1958-59	Saskatoon Quakers	WHL	59	15	33	48	....	....	....	34	....	....	....	....	....
1959-60	S.S. Marie Thunderbirds	EPHL	45	15	26	41	....	....	....	40	....	....	....	....	....
	Calgary Stampeders	WHL	22	5	9	14	....	....	....	16	....	....	....	....	....
1960-61	S.S. Marie Thunderbirds	EPHL	69	22	20	42	....	....	....	84	12	4	7	11	13
1961-62	S.S. Marie Thunderbirds	EPHL	65	36	26	62	....	....	....	130	....	....	....	....	....
	Chicago Black Hawks	**NHL**	....	....	....	....	....	....	....	....	**2**	**0**	**0**	**0**	**0**
	Buffalo Bisons	AHL	....	....	....	....	....	....	....	....	2	0	0	0	0
1962-63	St. Louis Braves	EPHL	61	22	53	75	....	....	....	60	....	....	....	....	....
1963-64	Buffalo Bisons	AHL	72	14	25	39	....	....	....	45	....	....	....	....	....
1964-65	Buffalo Bisons	AHL	1	1	0	1	....	....	....	0	....	....	....	....	....
	St. Louis Braves	CPHL	58	9	31	40	....	....	....	66	....	....	....	....	....
	Los Angeles Blades	WHL	14	0	1	1	....	....	....	8	....	....	....	....	....
1965/71	Yorkton Terriers	SSHL				STATISTICS NOT AVAILABLE									
	NHL Totals		....	....	....	....	....	....	....	....	**2**	**0**	**0**	**0**	**0**

• KWONG, Larry
"King"
RW – R. 5'6", 150 lbs. b: Vernon, B.C., 6/17/1923.

Season	Club	League	GP	G	A	Pts	AG	AA	APts	PIM	GP	G	A	Pts	PIM
1939/41	Vernon Hydrophones	BCAHA				STATISTICS NOT AVAILABLE									
1941-42	Trail Smoke Eaters	ABCHL	29	9	13	22	....	....	....	10	3	0	0	0	0
1942-43	Nanaimo Clippers	WKHL	11	6	6	12	....	....	....	0	3	0	1	1	2
1943-44	Vancouver St. Regis	NNDHL	17	10	6	16	....	....	....	0	....	....	....	....	....
	Red Deer Wheelers	ASHL	2	0	0	0	....	....	....	0	5	1	2	3	0
1944-45						MILITARY SERVICE									
1945-46	Trail Smoke Eaters	WKHL	19	12	8	20	....	....	....	12	5	6	0	6	8
1946-47	New York Rovers	EAHL	47	19	18	37	....	....	....	15	9	7	3	10	0
1947-48	**New York Rangers**	**NHL**	**1**	**0**	**0**	**0**	**0**	**0**	**0**	**0**	....	....	....	....	....
	New York Rovers	EAHL	17	13	16	29	....	....	....	5	....	....	....	....	....
	New York Rovers	QSHL	48	20	37	57	....	....	....	23	4	1	0	1	0
1948-49	Valleyfield Braves	QSHL	63	37	47	84	....	....	....	8	3	1	0	1	7
1949-50	Valleyfield Braves	QSHL	60	25	35	60	....	....	....	16	5	2	1	3	2
1950-51	Valleyfield Braves	QMHL	60	34	*51	85	....	....	....	35	16	1	12	13	2
	Valleyfield Braves	Alx-Cup	12	6	9	15	....	....	....	4	....	....	....	....	....
1951-52	Valleyfield Braves	QMHL	60	38	28	66	....	....	....	16	6	1	5	6	0
1952-53	Valleyfield Braves	QMHL	56	10	22	32	....	....	....	6	3	0	2	2	0
1953-54	Valleyfield Braves	QHL	68	24	25	49	....	....	....	17	7	3	3	6	2
1954-55	Valleyfield Braves	QHL	50	24	30	54	....	....	....	8	....	....	....	....	....
1955-56	Trois-Rivieres Lions	QHL	29	3	6	9	....	....	....	10	....	....	....	....	....
	Troy Bruins	IHL	21	9	9	18	....	....	....	2	5	1	2	3	2
1956-57	Troy Bruins	IHL	9	1	0	1	....	....	....	0	....	....	....	....	....
	Cornwall Chevies	EOHL	33	14	15	29	....	....	....	22	6	5	1	6	0
1957-58	Nottingham Panthers	Aut-Cup	24	16	9	25	....	....	....	4	....	....	....	....	....
	Nottingham Panthers	Britain	31	39	15	54	....	....	....	6	....	....	....	....	....
	NHL Totals		**1**	**0**	**0**	**0**	**0**	**0**	**0**	**0**	....	....	....	....	....

QMHL First All-Star Team(1951) • Won Byng of Vimy Trophy (MVP - QSHL) (1951)

Signed as a free agent by **Valleyfield** (QSHL), October 5, 1948.

• KYLE, Bill
Bill Miller
C – R. 6'1", 210 lbs. b: Dysart, Sask., 12/23/1924 d: 4/17/1968.

Season	Club	League	GP	G	A	Pts	AG	AA	APts	PIM	GP	G	A	Pts	PIM
1939-40	Notre Dame Hounds	SAHA	5	1	0	1	....	....	....	2	....	....	....	....	....
1940-41	Dysart Devils	SIHA				STATISTICS NOT AVAILABLE									
1941-42	Notre Dame Hounds	SAHA	11	6	5	11	....	....	....	6	5	2	3	5	4
1942-43	Regina Commandos	RNDHL	12	10	10	20	....	....	....	14	6	*6	2	8	10
	Regina Commandos	M-Cup	2	0	1	1	....	....	....	0	....	....	....	....	....
1943-44						MILITARY SERVICE									
1944-45						MILITARY SERVICE									
1945-46	Portland Eagles	PCHL	58	38	33	71	....	....	....	60	8	7	2	9	6
1946-47	Portland Eagles	PCHL	54	40	59	99	....	....	....	60	14	7	*10	*17	4
1947-48	Regina Capitals	WCSHL	48	29	43	72	....	....	....	26	4	1	1	2	2
1948-49	Regina Capitals	WCSHL	48	21	41	62	....	....	....	56	4	1	1	2	2
	Regina Capitals	Al-Cup	14	5	*14	*19	....	....	....	14	....	....	....	....	....
1949-50	**New York Rangers**	**NHL**	**2**	**0**	**0**	**0**	**0**	**0**	**0**	**0**	....	....	....	....	....
	Regina Capitals	WCSHL	44	17	28	45	....	....	....	58	....	....	....	....	....
1950-51	**New York Rangers**	**NHL**	**1**	**0**	**3**	**3**	**0**	**4**	**4**	**0**	....	....	....	....	....
	Regina Capitals	WCMHL	44	17	28	45	....	....	....	55	....	....	....	....	....
	New York Rovers	EAHL	1	1	0	1	....	....	....	0	5	1	3	4	0
1951-52	Sherbrooke Saints	QMHL	60	20	31	51	....	....	....	36	11	1	2	3	2
1952-53	Regina Capitals	SSHL	31	23	38	61	....	....	....	23	7	7	*8	15	4
	Regina Capitals	Al-Cup	13	2	8	10	....	....	....	4	....	....	....	....	....
1953-54	Regina Capitals	SSHL	37	20	34	54	....	....	....	18	....	....	....	....	....
1954-55	Yorkton Terriers	X-Games	....	....	....	....	....	....	....	....	1	0	1	1	2
1955-56	Brandon Regals	WHL	66	13	45	58	....	....	....	44	....	....	....	....	....
1956-57						DID NOT PLAY									
1957-58						DID NOT PLAY									
1958-59	Regina Capitals	SSHL	9	6	10	16	....	....	....	2	....	....	....	....	....
1959-60	Regina Capitals	SSHL	13	6	16	22	....	....	....	22	9	6	7	13	2
1960-61	Regina Capitals	SSHL	14	12	5	17	....	....	....	10	9	1	4	5	0
	NHL Totals		**3**	**0**	**3**	**3**	**0**	**4**	**4**	**0**	....	....	....	....	....

• Brother of Gus • WCSHL First All-Star Team (1948) • SSHL Second All-Star Team (1953, 1954)

• KYLE, Gus
Gus Walter Lawrence
D – L. 6'1", 202 lbs. b: Dysart, Sask., 9/11/1923 d: 11/17/1996.

Season	Club	League	GP	G	A	Pts	AG	AA	APts	PIM	GP	G	A	Pts	PIM
1939-40	Notre Dame Hounds	H.S.	7	1	0	1	....	....	....	2	....	....	....	....	....
1940-41	Notre Dame Hounds	H.S.	17	7	8	15	....	....	....	29	2	0	0	0	2
1941-42	New York Rovers	EAHL	57	5	17	22	....	....	....	89	7	1	2	3	18
1942-43	Ottawa Postal Corps	OCHL	18	7	18	25	....	....	....	43	4	1	4	5	2
1943-44	Fredericton Army	NBDHL	5	*8	3	*11	....	....	....	....	....	....	....	....	....
	Saint John Beavers	NBDHL	1	1	0	1	....	....	....	0	1	2	0	2	0
1944-45	Saint John Beavers	Al-Cup	6	5	0	5	....	....	....	14	....	....	....	....	....
1945-46	Saint John Beavers	SJCHL	9	4	5	9	....	....	....	16	2	2	1	3	0
	Saint John Beavers	Al-Cup	8	4	4	*8	....	....	....	*32	....	....	....	....	....
1946-47	Saint John Beavers	MSHL	39	24	41	65	....	....	....	115	6	4	6	10	8
1947-48	Regina Caps	WCSHL	43	15	20	35	....	....	....	*76	4	1	0	1	4
1948-49	Regina Caps	WCSHL	40	5	10	15	....	....	....	100	7	0	0	0	8
	Regina Caps	Al-Cup	14	2	6	8	....	....	....	28	....	....	....	....	....
1949-50	**New York Rangers**	**NHL**	**70**	**3**	**5**	**8**	**4**	**6**	**10**	**143**	**12**	**1**	**2**	**3**	**30**
1950-51	**New York Rangers**	**NHL**	**64**	**2**	**3**	**5**	**3**	**4**	**7**	**92**	....	....	....	....	....
1951-52	**Boston Bruins**	**NHL**	**69**	**1**	**12**	**13**	**1**	**15**	**16**	***127**	**2**	**0**	**0**	**0**	**4**
1952-53	Calgary Stampeders	WHL	70	8	22	30	....	....	....	146	5	0	3	3	18
1953-54	Calgary Stampeders	WHL	69	10	17	27	....	....	....	94	12	0	5	5	23
	Calgary Stampeders	Ed-Cup	7	0	3	3	....	....	....	6	....	....	....	....	....
1954-55	Calgary Stampeders	WHL	66	5	16	21	....	....	....	88	9	0	3	3	8
1955-56	Calgary Stampeders	WHL	7	0	3	3	....	....	....	10	....	....	....	....	....
	NHL Totals		**203**	**6**	**20**	**26**	**8**	**25**	**33**	**362**	**14**	**1**	**2**	**3**	**34**

• Brother of Bill • MSHL First All-Star Team (1947) • WCSHL Second All-Star Team (1949)

Signed as a free agent by **NY Rangers**, October 7, 1949. Traded to **Boston** by **NY Rangers** with the rights to Penti Lund and cash for Paul Ronty, September 20, 1951.

• LABADIE, Mike
Michel Joseph Gilles
RW – R. 5'11", 170 lbs. b: St. Francis D'Assisi, Que., 8/17/1932.

Season	Club	League	GP	G	A	Pts	AG	AA	APts	PIM	GP	G	A	Pts	PIM
1950-51	Quebec Citadelle Bees	QJHL-B	10	6	8	14	....	....	....	11	....	....	....	....	....
	Quebec Citadelle	QJHL	2	0	1	1	....	....	....	0	....	....	....	....	....
1951-52	Quebec Citadelle	QJHL	50	34	43	77	....	....	....	31	15	6	7	13	6
1952-53	Quebec Citadelle	QJHL	47	35	43	78	....	....	....	60	9	3	*8	11	9
	New York Rangers	**NHL**	**3**	**0**	**0**	**0**	**0**	**0**	**0**	**0**	....	....	....	....	....
	Quebec Citadelle	M-Cup	8	4	6	10	....	....	....	28	....	....	....	....	....
1953-54	Quebec Aces	QHL	67	20	24	44	....	....	....	32	16	5	5	10	2
	Quebec Aces	Ed-Cup	7	0	2	2	....	....	....	0	....	....	....	....	....
1954-55	Quebec Aces	QHL	55	19	38	57	....	....	....	11	8	1	5	6	4
1955-56	Quebec Aces	QHL	61	18	21	39	....	....	....	35	7	4	3	7	0
1956-57	Quebec Aces	QHL	65	18	34	52	....	....	....	22	10	2	1	3	0
	Quebec Aces	Ed-Cup	7	0	3	3	....	....	....	6	....	....	....	....	....
1957-58	Quebec Aces	QHL	64	22	30	52	....	....	....	10	12	5	9	14	0
1958-59	Quebec Aces	QHL	10	4	3	7	....	....	....	2	....	....	....	....	....
	Cleveland Barons	AHL	59	23	35	58	....	....	....	16	7	0	2	2	2
1959-60	Cleveland Barons	AHL	72	24	22	46	....	....	....	20	7	1	5	6	2
1960-61	Quebec Aces	AHL	66	21	37	58	....	....	....	10	....	....	....	....	....
1961-62	Quebec Aces	AHL	56	17	22	39	....	....	....	8	....	....	....	....	....
1962-63	Quebec Aces	AHL	72	15	24	39	....	....	....	20	....	....	....	....	....
1963-64	Springfield Indians	AHL	70	31	34	65	....	....	....	12	....	....	....	....	....
1964-65	Springfield Indians	AHL	55	19	21	40	....	....	....	19	....	....	....	....	....
1965-66	Victoria Maple Leafs	WHL	72	8	21	29	....	....	....	14	14	4	3	7	4
1966-67	Victoria Maple Leafs	WHL	48	10	15	25	....	....	....	9	....	....	....	....	....
1967-68	Buffalo Bisons	AHL	70	23	30	53	....	....	....	16	5	1	3	4	2
1968-69	Buffalo Bisons	AHL	6	0	1	1	....	....	....	0	....	....	....	....	....
	NHL Totals		**3**	**0**	**0**	**0**	**0**	**0**	**0**	**0**	....	....	....	....	....

QJHL Second All-Star Team (1952) • QJHL First All-Star Team (1953) • Won William Northey Trophy (Top Rookie - QHL) (1954)

Traded to **Cleveland** (AHL) by **Quebec** (AHL) for Ian Anderson, November 7, 1958. Traded to **Quebec** (AHL) by **Cleveland** (AHL) for cash, May 6, 1960.

• LABINE, Leo
Leonard Gerald "The Lion"
RW – R. 5'10", 170 lbs. b: Haileybury, Ont., 7/22/1931.

Season	Club	League	GP	G	A	Pts	AG	AA	APts	PIM	GP	G	A	Pts	PIM
			REGULAR SEASON								PLAYOFFS				
1949-50	St. Michael's Majors	OHA-Jr.	47	20	22	42				77	5	1	2	3	13
1950-51	Barrie Flyers	OHA-Jr.	52	32	46	78				143	12	13	13	*26	*36
	Barrie Flyers	M-Cup	11	12	13	25				36					
1951-52	**Boston Bruins**	**NHL**	**15**	**2**	**4**	**6**	**3**	**5**	**8**	**9**	**5**	**0**	**1**	**1**	**4**
	Hershey Bears	AHL	53	23	23	46				88	5	0	1	1	20
1952-53	**Boston Bruins**	**NHL**	**51**	**8**	**15**	**23**	**10**	**18**	**28**	**69**	**7**	**2**	**1**	**3**	***19**
	Hershey Bears	AHL	16	7	3	10				33	3	1	2	3	8
1953-54	**Boston Bruins**	**NHL**	**68**	**16**	**19**	**35**	**22**	**23**	**45**	**57**	**4**	**0**	**1**	**1**	**8**
1954-55	**Boston Bruins**	**NHL**	**67**	**24**	**18**	**42**	**31**	**21**	**52**	**75**	**5**	**2**	**1**	**3**	**11**
1955-56	**Boston Bruins**	**NHL**	**68**	**16**	**18**	**34**	**22**	**21**	**43**	**104**					
1956-57	**Boston Bruins**	**NHL**	**67**	**18**	**29**	**47**	**23**	**32**	**55**	**128**	**10**	**3**	**2**	**5**	***14**
1957-58	**Boston Bruins**	**NHL**	**62**	**7**	**14**	**21**	**9**	**14**	**23**	**60**	**11**	**0**	**2**	**2**	**10**
1958-59	**Boston Bruins**	**NHL**	**70**	**9**	**23**	**32**	**11**	**23**	**34**	**74**	**7**	**2**	**1**	**3**	**12**
1959-60	**Boston Bruins**	**NHL**	**63**	**16**	**28**	**44**	**19**	**27**	**46**	**58**					
1960-61	**Boston Bruins**	**NHL**	**40**	**7**	**12**	**19**	**8**	**12**	**20**	**34**					
	Detroit Red Wings	**NHL**	**24**	**2**	**9**	**11**	**2**	**9**	**11**	**32**	**11**	**3**	**2**	**5**	**4**
1961-62	**Detroit Red Wings**	**NHL**	**48**	**3**	**4**	**7**	**3**	**4**	**7**	**30**					
	Sudbury Wolves	EPHL	9	10	10	20				18	5	0	4	4	4
1962-63	Los Angeles Blades	WHL	68	30	47	77				90	3	1	0	1	2
1963-64	Los Angeles Blades	WHL	70	31	46	77				56	12	*10	12	*22	10
1964-65	Los Angeles Blades	WHL	58	16	37	53				42					
1965-66	Los Angeles Blades	WHL	71	33	30	63				33					
1966-67	Los Angeles Blades	WHL	70	18	29	47				24					
	NHL Totals		**643**	**128**	**193**	**321**	**163**	**209**	**372**	**730**	**60**	**12**	**11**	**23**	**82**

WHL First All-Star Team (1964) • Played in NHL All-Star Game (1955, 1956)

Traded to **Detroit** by **Boston** with Vic Stasiuk for Gary Aldcorn, Murray Oliver and Tom McCarthy, January 23, 1961. Traded to **LA Blades** (WHL) by **Detroit** for cash, July, 1962.

• LABOSSIERE, Gord
— see page 1286

• LABOVITCH, Max
RW – R. 5'11", 165 lbs. b: Winnipeg, Man., 1/18/1924.

Season	Club	League	GP	G	A	Pts	AG	AA	APts	PIM	GP	G	A	Pts	PIM
1940-41	Winnipeg JV Rangers	MAHA	STATISTICS NOT AVAILABLE												
1941-42	Winnipeg Rangers	MJHL	17	13	8	21				14					
1942-43			MILITARY SERVICE												
1943-44	**New York Rangers**	**NHL**	**5**	**0**	**0**	**0**	**0**	**0**	**0**	**4**					
	New York Rovers	EAHL	24	11	13	24				20	11	6	10	16	0
1944-45			MILITARY SERVICE												
1945-46	Winnipeg Orioles	WSrHL	STATISTICS NOT AVAILABLE												
1946-47	Los Angeles Ramblers	WIHL	42	24	20	44				21					
1947-48	Toledo Mercurys	IHL	22	11	9	20				28	13	4	3	7	34
1948-49	Toledo-North Mercurys	IHL	18	6	6	12				4					
	Toledo-South Mercurys	IHL	14	2	3	5				6	12	4	5	9	20
1949-50	Toledo Buckeyes	IHL	49	12	30	42				73	8	1	3	4	12
	NHL Totals		**5**	**0**	**0**	**0**	**0**	**0**	**0**	**4**					

MAHA Second All-Star Team (1941)

• LABRIE, Guy
D – L. 6', 185 lbs. b: St. Charles Bellechasse, Que., 8/11/1920.

Season	Club	League	GP	G	A	Pts	AG	AA	APts	PIM	GP	G	A	Pts	PIM
1939-40	Quebec Beavers	QPHL	41	12	6	18				57					
1940-41	Valleyfield Braves	MCHL	41	14	12	26				48					
1941-42	Quebec Aces	QSHL	11	1	0	1				10					
1942-43			STATISTICS NOT AVAILABLE												
1943-44	**Boston Bruins**	**NHL**	**15**	**2**	**7**	**9**	**2**	**6**	**8**	**2**					
	Boston Olympics	QSHL	26	24	14	38				8	10	1	10	11	4
1944-45	Boston Olympics	QSHL	9	6	8	14				10					
	New York Rangers	**NHL**	**27**	**2**	**2**	**4**	**2**	**2**	**4**	**14**					
1945-46	Providence Reds	AHL	11	0	2	2				8					
	New Haven Ramblers	AHL	48	4	14	18				29					
1946-47	Quebec Aces	QSHL	17	1	2	3				18	2	1	1	2	0
1947-48	Quebec Aces	QSHL	45	6	18	24				42	10	2	4	6	21
1948-49	Quebec Aces	QSHL	48	6	8	14				64	3	0	0	0	0
1949-50	Sherbrooke Saints	QSHL	58	8	15	23				56	12	1	6	7	18
	Sherbrooke Saints	Al-Cup	10	0	4	4				13					
1950-51	Sherbrooke Saints	QMHL	47	3	18	21				56	7	1	3	4	2
1951-52	Sherbrooke Saints	QMHL	59	7	18	25				38	11	0	3	3	2
1952-53	Sherbrooke Saints	QMHL	56	11	15	26				38	4	1	1	2	2
1953-54	Riviere-du-Loup Raiders	SLVHL	60	6	11	17				30					
	NHL Totals		**42**	**4**	**9**	**13**	**4**	**8**	**12**	**16**					

QSHL Second All-Star Team (1948, 1950) • QMHL Second All-Star Team (1953)

Traded to **NY Rangers** by **Boston** for $12,000, November 27, 1944. Traded to **New Haven** (AHL) by **NY Rangers** (Providence-AHL) with Paul Courteau and Roland Forget for George Boothman and cash, November 19, 1945. Traded to **Sherbrooke** (QSHL) by **Quebec** (QSHL) with Jim Planche for Herb Carnegie, July 2, 1949.

• LACH, Elmer
Elmer James — HHOF
C – L. 5'10", 165 lbs. b: Nokomis, Sask., 1/22/1918.

Season	Club	League	GP	G	A	Pts	AG	AA	APts	PIM	GP	G	A	Pts	PIM
1935-36	Regina Abbotts	S-SJHL	2	0	1	1				2	4	3	0	3	6
1936-37	Weyburn Beavers	S-SSHL	23	16	6	22				27	3	0	1	1	4
1937-38	Weyburn Beavers	S-SSHL	22	12	12	24				44	3	2	1	3	0
1938-39	Moose Jaw Millers	S-SSHL	29	17	*20	37				23	10	6	*4	*10	8
1939-40	Moose Jaw Millers	S-SSHL	30	15	29	44				20	8	5	*9	*14	12
	Moose Jaw Millers	Al-Cup	3	1	1	2				4					
1940-41	**Montreal Canadiens**	**NHL**	**43**	**7**	**14**	**21**	**11**	**20**	**31**	**16**	**3**	**1**	**0**	**1**	**0**
1941-42	**Montreal Canadiens**	**NHL**	**1**	**0**	**1**	**1**	**0**	**1**	**1**	**0**					
1942-43	**Montreal Canadiens**	**NHL**	**45**	**18**	**40**	**58**	**18**	**38**	**56**	**14**	**5**	**2**	**4**	**6**	**6**
♦1943-44	**Montreal Canadiens**	**NHL**	**48**	**24**	**48**	**72**	**22**	**43**	**65**	**23**	**9**	**2**	***11**	**13**	**4**
1944-45	**Montreal Canadiens**	**NHL**	**50**	**26**	***54**	***80**	**26**	**65**	**91**	**37**	**6**	**4**	**4**	**8**	**2**
♦1945-46	**Montreal Canadiens**	**NHL**	**50**	**13**	***34**	**47**	**15**	**50**	**65**	**34**	**9**	**5**	***12**	***17**	**4**
1946-47	**Montreal Canadiens**	**NHL**	**31**	**14**	**16**	**30**	**16**	**19**	**35**	**22**					
1947-48	**Montreal Canadiens**	**NHL**	**60**	**30**	**31**	***61**	**39**	**41**	**80**	**72**					
1948-49	**Montreal Canadiens**	**NHL**	**36**	**11**	**18**	**29**	**15**	**26**	**41**	**59**	**1**	**0**	**0**	**0**	**4**
1949-50	**Montreal Canadiens**	**NHL**	**64**	**15**	**33**	**48**	**19**	**40**	**59**	**33**	**5**	**1**	**2**	**3**	**4**
1950-51	**Montreal Canadiens**	**NHL**	**65**	**21**	**24**	**45**	**27**	**29**	**56**	**48**	**11**	**2**	**2**	**4**	**2**
1951-52	**Montreal Canadiens**	**NHL**	**70**	**15**	***50**	**65**	**20**	**63**	**83**	**36**	**11**	**1**	**2**	**3**	**4**
♦1952-53	**Montreal Canadiens**	**NHL**	**53**	**16**	**25**	**41**	**21**	**30**	**51**	**56**	**12**	**1**	**6**	**7**	**6**
1953-54	**Montreal Canadiens**	**NHL**	**48**	**5**	**20**	**25**	**7**	**24**	**31**	**28**	**4**	**0**	**2**	**2**	**0**
	NHL Totals		**664**	**215**	**408**	**623**	**256**	**489**	**745**	**478**	**76**	**19**	**45**	**64**	**36**

S-SSHL First All-Star Team (1940) • NHL Second All-Star Team (1944, 1946) • NHL First All-Star Team (1945, 1948, 1952) • NHL Scoring Leader (1945) • Won Hart Trophy (1945) • Won Art Ross Trophy (1948) • Played in NHL All-Star Game (1948, 1952, 1953)

Signed as a free agent by **Montreal**, October 24, 1940. • Missed remainder of 1941-42 season after suffering elbow injury in game vs. Detroit, November 1, 1941.

• LAFLEUR, Roland
Roland Rene
LW – L. 5'6", 145 lbs. b: Ottawa, Ont., 1899 Deceased.

Season	Club	League	GP	G	A	Pts	AG	AA	APts	PIM	GP	G	A	Pts	PIM
1917-18	Ottawa St. Brigids	OCHL	5	3	0	3				3					
	Ottawa Royal Canadians	HOHL	1	0	0	0				0	1	1	0	1	3
1918-19	Ottawa Royal Canadians	OCHL	7	0	0	0				3	1	0	0	0	3
1919-20	Ottawa Mallettes	OCHL	7	3	0	3									
1920-21	Ottawa Lasalle	OCHL	11	4	0	4									
1921-22	Ottawa Montagnards	OCHL	14	*14	4	18				15	8	8	*6	14	10
1922-23	Ottawa Montagnards	OCHL	9	*8	*9	*17				14	2	0	0	0	*7
1923-24	Ottawa Royal Canadians	OCHL	12	3	0	3									
1924-25	**Montreal Canadiens**	**NHL**	**1**	**0**	**0**	**0**	**0**	**0**	**0**	**0**					
	Ottawa New Edinburghs	OCHL	16	8	1	9									
1925-26	Berlin Wanderers	OCHL	STATISTICS NOT AVAILABLE												
1926-27	Ottawa Gunners	OCHL	14	2	3	5									
1927-28	Ottawa Rideaus	OCHL	14	5	2	7									
1928-29	Ottawa Lasalle	OCHL	13	5	0	5					3	0	0	0	
1929-30	Ottawa Lasalle	OCHL	20	3	1	4				32					
1930-31	Ottawa Lasalle	OCHL	20	2	3	5				33	2	0	0	0	6
	NHL Totals		**1**	**0**	**0**	**0**	**0**	**0**	**0**	**0**					

OCHL Second All-Star Team (1922) • OCHL First All-Star Team (1923)

Signed as a free agent by **Montreal Canadiens**, November 17, 1924.

• LAFORCE, Ernie
D – L. 5'11", 175 lbs. b: Montreal, Que., 6/23/1916.

Season	Club	League	GP	G	A	Pts	AG	AA	APts	PIM	GP	G	A	Pts	PIM
1937-38	Montreal Lafontaine	QPHL	3	0	0	0				2					
1938-39	Verdun Maple Leafs	QSHL	18	4	4	8				14	2	0	0	0	4
1939-40	Verdun Bulldogs	QPHL	38	10	20	30				24	2	0	0	0	0
1940-41	Verdun Maple Leafs	QSHL	34	6	9	15				23					
1941-42	Montreal St. Pats	MCHL	37	5	15	20				12					
1942-43	**Montreal Canadiens**	**NHL**	**1**	**0**	**0**	**0**	**0**	**0**	**0**	**0**					
	Montreal Royals	QSHL	32	1	15	16				18	4	0	2	2	0
1943-44	Montreal Canada Car	MCHL	7	3	3	6				2					
	Montreal Royals	QSHL	19	1	15	16				6	7	0	1	1	8
1944-45	Montreal Royals	QSHL	22	7	13	20				19	7	0	3	3	2
1945-46	Montreal Royals	QSHL	24	9	7	16				4	6	0	1	1	6
1946-47	Montreal Royals	QSHL	21	3	6	9				18	11	1	7	8	10
	Montreal Royals	Al-Cup	14	2	3	5				4					
1947-48	Montreal Royals	QSHL	44	6	20	26				16	3	0	0	0	0
1948-49	Montreal Royals	QSHL	58	2	18	20				20	9	3	4	7	8
1949-50	Montreal Royals	QSHL	52	2	14	16				31	6	0	0	0	2
1950-51	Joliette Cyclones	QPHL	PLAYER/COACH – STATISTICS UNAVAILABLE												
	NHL Totals		**1**	**0**	**0**	**0**	**0**	**0**	**0**	**0**					

QPHL First All-Star Team (1940)

• LAFORGE, Claude
— see page 1291

• LAFRANCE, Adie
Adelard Henry
LW – L. 5'10", 165 lbs. b: Chapleau, Ont., 1/13/1912.

Season	Club	League	GP	G	A	Pts	AG	AA	APts	PIM	GP	G	A	Pts	PIM
1929-30	Sudbury St. Louis	NOJHA	8	4	1	5				0					
1930-31	Sudbury St. Louis	NOJHA	8	4	1	5				4	3	*4	0	*4	0
	Sudbury Wolf Cubs	NOJHA									1	0	0	0	0
	Sudbury St. Louis	Al-Cup	3	2	0	2				2					
	Sudbury Wolf Cubs	M-Cup	5	2	1	3				2					
1931-32	Falconbridge Falcons	NOHA	9	3	4	7				2	2	0	0	0	0
	Sudbury Wolves	NOHA	3	2	0	2				0					
1932-33	Sudbury Wolves	NOHA	7	4	2	6				10	2	1	0	1	2
1933-34	**Montreal Canadiens**	**NHL**	**3**	**0**	**0**	**0**	**0**	**0**	**0**	**2**	**2**	**0**	**0**	**0**	**0**
	Falconbridge Falcons	NOHA	8	5	1	6				12	2	1	0	1	2
1934-35	Quebec Beavers	Can-Am	46	4	4	8				10	3	0	0	0	2
1935-36	Springfield Indians	Can-Am	48	13	19	32				32	3	2	3	5	4
1936-37	Springfield Indians	IAHL	33	9	10	19				13					
1937-38	Springfield Indians	IAHL	41	8	13	21				17					
1938-39	Springfield Indians	IAHL	54	11	26	37				23	2	0	0	0	0
	NHL Totals		**3**	**0**	**0**	**0**	**0**	**0**	**0**	**2**	**2**	**0**	**0**	**0**	**0**

Signed as a free agent by **Montreal Canadiens**, March 9, 1934.

• LAFRANCE, Leo
Leonard Joseph
LW – L. 5'8", 160 lbs. b: Allomette, Que., 11/3/1902 d: 4/7/1993.

Season	Club	League	GP	G	A	Pts	AG	AA	APts	PIM	GP	G	A	Pts	PIM
1920-21	Sudbury Cub Wolves	NOJHA	2	2	2	4					5	*7	*4	*11	
1921-22	Iroquois Papermakers	NOHA									7	7	*5	*12	
1922-23	Iroquois Papermakers	NOHA	STATISTICS NOT AVAILABLE												
1923-24	Iroquois Papermakers	NOHA	8	2	1	3				15					
1924-25	Duluth Hornets	USAHA	31	6	0	6									
1925-26	Duluth Hornets	CHL	40	8	2	10				28	8	1	1	2	12
1926-27	**Montreal Canadiens**	**NHL**	**4**	**0**	**0**	**0**	**0**	**0**	**0**	**0**					
	Duluth Hornets	AHA	37	12	4	16				41	3	2	0	2	0
1927-28	**Montreal Canadiens**	**NHL**	**15**	**1**	**0**	**1**	**2**	**0**	**2**	**2**					
	Chicago Black Hawks	**NHL**	**14**	**1**	**0**	**1**	**2**	**0**	**2**	**4**					
	Kansas City Pla-Mors	AHA	13	1	0	1				8	3	0	0	0	2
1928-29	Tulsa Oilers	AHA	40	19	7	26				33	4	0	0	0	4
1929-30			DID NOT PLAY												
1930-31	Tulsa Oilers	AHA	48	27	15	42				41	4	*3	0	3	6
1931-32	Tulsa Oilers	AHA	48	11	5	16				51					
1932-33	Duluth-Wichita	AHA	39	16	8	24				32					
1933-34	Duluth Hornets	CHL	14	0	0	0				41					
	Tulsa Oilers	AHA	31	6	10	16				35	4	1	0	1	0

			REGULAR SEASON								PLAYOFFS				
Season	Club	League	GP	G	A	Pts	AG	AA	APts	PIM	GP	G	A	Pts	PIM
1934-35	Minneapolis Millers	CHL	46	16	11	27	....	....	....	26	5	2	3	5	2
1935-36	Rochester Cardinals	IHL	9	1	0	1	....	....	....	7	....	....	....	....	....
	Calgary Tigers	NWHL	3	0	0	0	....	....	....	2	....	....	....	....	....
	Seattle Seahawks	NWHL	26	8	4	12	....	....	....	25	4	3	2	5	2
	NHL Totals		**33**	**2**	**0**	**2**	**4**	**0**	**4**	**6**	....	....	....	....	....

CHL Second All-Star Team (1935)

Signed as a free agent by **Duluth** (AHA), November 2, 1926. Traded to **Montreal Canadiens** by **Duluth** (AHA) for cash, November 10, 1926. • Suspended by Montreal Canadiens for leaving the team, November, 24, 1926. Loaned to **Chicago** by **Montreal Canadiens** for cash, December 30, 1927. IHL rights transferred to **Rochester** (IHL) after IHL club purchased **Minneapolis** (CHL) franchise, October 16, 1935. Loaned to **Calgary** (NWHL) by **Montreal Canadiens**, December 19, 1935. Traded to **Seattle** (NWHL) by **Montreal Canadiens** for cash, January 1, 1936.

• LAFRENIERE, Roger *— see page 1292*

• LALANDE, Hec Hector J.

C – L. 5'9", 150 lbs. b: North Bay, Ont., 11/24/1934.

Season	Club	League	GP	G	A	Pts	AG	AA	APts	PIM	GP	G	A	Pts	PIM
1951-52	Belleville Bulls	OHA-B	STATISTICS NOT AVAILABLE												
1952-53	Galt Black Hawks	OHA-Jr.	56	9	24	33	....	....	....	65	11	6	6	12	27
1953-54	Galt Black Hawks	OHA-Jr.	59	17	22	39	....	....	....	118	....	....	....	....	....
	Chicago Black Hawks	**NHL**	**2**	**0**	**0**	**0**	**0**	**0**	**0**	**0**	....	....	....	....	....
1954-55	Galt Black Hawks	OHA-Jr.	49	31	48	79	....	....	....	93	4	5	0	5	8
	Buffalo Bisons	AHL	3	0	1	1	....	....	....	2	....	....	....	....	....
1955-56	**Chicago Black Hawks**	**NHL**	**65**	**8**	**18**	**26**	**11**	**21**	**32**	**70**	....	....	....	....	....
1956-57	**Chicago Black Hawks**	**NHL**	**50**	**11**	**17**	**28**	**14**	**19**	**33**	**38**	....	....	....	....	....
	Rochester Americans	AHL	13	5	2	7	....	....	....	17	....	....	....	....	....
1957-58	**Chicago Black Hawks**	**NHL**	**22**	**2**	**2**	**4**	**2**	**2**	**4**	**10**	....	....	....	....	....
	Detroit Red Wings	**NHL**	**12**	**0**	**2**	**2**	**0**	**2**	**2**	**2**	....	....	....	....	....
	Hershey Bears	AHL	11	7	7	14	....	....	....	12	11	3	4	7	10
1958-59	Hershey Bears	AHL	58	12	23	35	....	....	....	58	13	1	4	5	30
1959-60	Hershey Bears	AHL	61	14	28	42	....	....	....	71	....	....	....	....	....
1960-61	Hershey Bears	AHL	72	15	41	56	....	....	....	71	8	3	*7	*10	11
1961-62	Hershey Bears	AHL	64	21	36	57	....	....	....	19	7	0	2	2	0
1962-63	St. Louis Braves	EPHL	26	6	24	30	....	....	....	57	....	....	....	....	....
1963-64	Clinton Comets	EHL	62	27	75	102	....	....	....	33	15	11	10	21	11
1964-65	Clinton Comets	EHL	62	31	69	100	....	....	....	18	11	4	8	12	4
1965-66	Jersey Devils	EHL	36	8	25	33	....	....	....	2	....	....	....	....	....
1966-67	Jersey Devils	EHL	18	7	20	27	....	....	....	10	16	8	8	16	2
1967-68	Jersey Devils	EHL	2	1	0	1	....	....	....	0	....	....	....	....	....
	Belleville Monarchs	OHA-Sr.	28	5	12	17	....	....	....	2	....	....	....	....	....
	NHL Totals		**151**	**21**	**39**	**60**	**27**	**44**	**71**	**120**	....	....	....	....	....

Traded to **Detroit** by **Chicago** with Nick Mickoski, Bob Bailey and Jack McIntyre for Bill Dineen, Billy Dea, Lorne Ferguson and Earl Reibel, December 17, 1957. Traded to **Hershey** (AHL) by **Detroit** with Don Poile and cash for Dunc Fisher, April 23, 1958. Traded to **Jersey** (EHL) by **Clinton** (EHL) with Norm Defelice, Ted Sydlowski and Benny Woit for Ed Babiuk, Pat Kelly and Borden Smith, August, 1965.

• LALONDE, Newsy Edouard Charles HHOF

C – R. 5'9", 168 lbs. b: Cornwall, Ont., 10/31/1888 d: 11/21/1971.

Season	Club	League	GP	G	A	Pts	AG	AA	APts	PIM	GP	G	A	Pts	PIM
1904-05	Cornwall Athletics	OHA-Jr.	STATISTICS NOT AVAILABLE												
	Cornwall Victorias	FAHL	2	1	0	1	....	....	....	....	....	....	....	....	....
1905-06	Woodstock Seniors	OHA-Sr.	7	8	0	8	....	....	....	....	....	....	....	....	....
1906-07	Canadian Soo	IHL	18	29	4	33	....	....	....	27	....	....	....	....	....
1907-08	Portage-la-Prairie	MHL-Sr.	1	0	0	0	....	....	....	0	....	....	....	....	....
	Toronto Professionals	OPHL	9	*32	0	*32	....	....	....	37	1	2	0	2	0
	Haileybury Silver Kings	TPHL	....	....	....	....	....	....	....	....	1	3	0	3	0
1908-09	Toronto Professionals	OPHL	11	29	0	29	....	....	....	*79	....	....	....	....	....
1909-10	Montreal Canadiens	NHA	6	*16	0	*16	....	....	....	40	....	....	....	....	....
	Renfrew Creamery Kings	NHA	5	*22	0	*22	....	....	....	16	....	....	....	....	....
1910-11	Montreal Canadiens	NHA	16	19	0	19	....	....	....	63	....	....	....	....	....
1911-12	Vancouver Millionaires	PCHA	15	*27	0	*27	....	....	....	51	....	....	....	....	....
	PCHA All-Stars	X-Games	3	5	0	5	....	....	....	*11	....	....	....	....	....
1912-13	Montreal Canadiens	NHA	18	25	0	25	....	....	....	61	....	....	....	....	....
1913-14	Montreal Canadiens	NHA	14	22	5	27	....	....	....	23	2	0	0	0	2
1914-15	Montreal Canadiens	NHA	7	4	3	7	....	....	....	17	....	....	....	....	....
♦1915-16	Montreal Canadiens	NHA	24	*28	6	34	....	....	....	78	4	3	0	3	41
1916-17	Montreal Canadiens	NHA	18	28	7	35	....	....	....	61	5	2	0	2	*47
1917-18	**Montreal Canadiens**	**NHL**	**14**	**23**	**7**	**30**	**30**	**30**	**60**	**51**	**2**	**4**	**2**	**6**	**17**
1918-19	**Montreal Canadiens**	**NHL**	**17**	***22**	***10**	***32**	**42**	**58**	**100**	**40**	**5**	***11**	**22**	***13**	**6**
	Montreal Canadiens	St-Cup	5	6	0	6	....	....	....	3	....	....	....	....	....
1919-20	**Montreal Canadiens**	**NHL**	**23**	**37**	**9**	**46**	**44**	**31**	**75**	**34**	....	....	....	....	....
1920-21	**Montreal Canadiens**	**NHL**	**24**	**33**	**10**	***43**	**44**	**39**	**83**	**36**	....	....	....	....	....
1921-22	**Montreal Canadiens**	**NHL**	**20**	**9**	**5**	**14**	**12**	**16**	**28**	**20**	....	....	....	....	....
1922-23	Saskatoon Sheiks	WCHL	29	*30	4	34	....	....	....	44	....	....	....	....	....
1923-24	Saskatoon Crescents	WCHL	21	10	10	20	....	....	....	24	....	....	....	....	....
1924-25	Saskatoon Crescents	WCHL	22	8	6	14	....	....	....	42	2	0	0	0	4
1925-26	Saskatoon Crescents	WHL	3	0	0	0	....	....	....	2	2	0	0	0	2
1926-27	**New York Americans**	**NHL**	**1**	**0**	**0**	**0**	**0**	**0**	**0**	**2**	....	....	....	....	....
1927-28	Quebec Castors	Can-Am	1	0	0	0	....	....	....	0	....	....	....	....	....
1928-29	Niagara Falls Cataracts	Can-Pro	DID NOT PLAY – COACHING												
	NHL Totals		**99**	**124**	**41**	**165**	**172**	**174**	**346**	**183**	**7**	**15**	**24**	**19**	**23**
	Other Major League Totals		237	329	45	374	....	....	....	665	16	7	0	7	96

OPHL First All-Star Team (1908) • OPHL Second All-Star Team (1909) • IHL Second All-Star Team (1907) • PCHA First All-Star Team (1912) • NHL Scoring Leader (1919, 1921) • WCHL First All-Star Team (1924)

Signed as a free agent by **Canadian Soo** (IHL), January 2, 1907. Signed as a free agent by **American Soo** (IHL), November 3, 1907. Signed as a free agent by **Portage** (MHL-Sr.) after IHL folded, November 18, 1907. Signed as a free agent by **Toronto** (OPHL) after securing release from **Portage** (MHL-Sr.), January 15, 1908. Signed by **Haileybury** (TPHL) after leaving **Toronto** (OPHL), February 15, 1908. Signed as a free agent by **Vancouver** (PCHA), November 28, 1911. Rights traded to **Montreal Canadiens** (NHA) by **Vancouver** (PCHA) for $750, January, 1913. Rights retained by **Montreal Canadiens** after NHA folded, November 26, 1917. Traded to **Saskatoon** (WCHL) by **Montreal Canadiens** for $3,500 and the rights to Aurel Joliat, September 18, 1922. Traded to **NY Americans** by **Saskatoon** (WHL) for cash, September 27, 1926.

• LAMB, Joe

RW – R. 5'10", 170 lbs. b: Sussex, N.B., 6/18/1906 Deceased.

			REGULAR SEASON								PLAYOFFS				
Season	Club	League	GP	G	A	Pts	AG	AA	APts	PIM	GP	G	A	Pts	PIM
1922-23	Sussex Dairy Kings	SNBHL	8	1	0	1	....	....	....	4	4	2	0	2	2
1923-24	Sussex Dairy Kings	SNBHL	6	3	4	7	....	....	....	2	6	4	1	5	2
1924-25	Sussex Dairy Kings	SNBHL	12	14	4	18	....	....	....	8	6	2	3	5	6
1925-26	Montreal Royal Bank	MBHL	9	3	2	5	....	....	....	12	....	....	....	....	....
	Montreal Young Royals	MCJHL	6	6	4	10	....	....	....	6	....	....	....	....	....
	Montreal Young Royals	M-Cup	4	3	2	5	....	....	....	15	....	....	....	....	....
1926-27	Montreal Victorias	MCHL	7	5	3	8	....	....	....	26	....	....	....	....	....
	Montreal Victorias	X-Games	15	28	0	28	....	....	....	....	....	....	....	....	....
	Montreal Royal Bank	MBHL	4	3	4	7	....	....	....	14	1	0	0	0	0
1927-28	Montreal Victorias	MCHL	7	4	*4	8	....	....	....	6	....	....	....	....	....
	Montreal Royal Bank	MBHL	9	5	6	11	....	....	....	30	....	....	....	....	....
	Montreal Maroons	**NHL**	**21**	**8**	**5**	**13**	**16**	**28**	**44**	**39**	**8**	**1**	**0**	**1**	**32**
1928-29	**Montreal Maroons**	**NHL**	**30**	**4**	**1**	**5**	**11**	**7**	**18**	**44**	....	....	....	....	....
	Ottawa Senators	**NHL**	**6**	**0**	**0**	**0**	**0**	**0**	**0**	**8**	....	....	....	....	....
1929-30	**Ottawa Senators**	**NHL**	**44**	**29**	**20**	**49**	**42**	**48**	**90**	***119**	**2**	**0**	**0**	**0**	**11**
1930-31	**Ottawa Senators**	**NHL**	**44**	**11**	**14**	**25**	**22**	**43**	**65**	**91**	....	....	....	....	....
1931-32	**New York Americans**	**NHL**	**48**	**14**	**11**	**25**	**23**	**24**	**47**	**71**	....	....	....	....	....
1932-33	**Boston Bruins**	**NHL**	**42**	**11**	**8**	**19**	**20**	**17**	**37**	**68**	**5**	**0**	**1**	**1**	**6**
1933-34	**Boston Bruins**	**NHL**	**48**	**10**	**15**	**25**	**17**	**32**	**49**	**47**	....	....	....	....	....
1934-35	**Montreal Canadiens**	**NHL**	**7**	**3**	**2**	**5**	**5**	**3**	**8**	**4**	....	....	....	....	....
	St. Louis Eagles	**NHL**	**31**	**11**	**12**	**23**	**18**	**21**	**39**	**19**	....	....	....	....	....
1935-36	**Montreal Maroons**	**NHL**	**35**	**0**	**3**	**3**	**0**	**6**	**6**	**12**	**3**	**0**	**0**	**0**	**2**
1936-37	**New York Americans**	**NHL**	**48**	**3**	**9**	**12**	**5**	**16**	**21**	**53**	....	....	....	....	....
1937-38	**New York Americans**	**NHL**	**25**	**1**	**0**	**1**	**2**	**0**	**2**	**20**	....	....	....	....	....
	Detroit Red Wings	**NHL**	**14**	**3**	**1**	**4**	**5**	**2**	**7**	**6**	....	....	....	....	....
	Pittsburgh Hornets	IAHL	6	2	0	2	....	....	....	4	....	....	....	....	....
1938-39	Springfield Indians	IAHL	51	11	16	27	....	....	....	72	3	0	1	1	4
1939-40	Springfield Indians	IAHL	54	20	14	34	....	....	....	44	3	0	0	0	4
	NHL Totals		**443**	**108**	**101**	**209**	**186**	**247**	**433**	**601**	**18**	**1**	**1**	**2**	**51**

Signed as a free agent by **Montreal Maroons**, January 29, 1928. Traded to **Ottawa** by **Montreal Maroons** for George Boucher, February 14, 1929. Claimed by **NY Americans** from **Ottawa** for 1931-32 season in Dispersal Draft, September 26, 1931. Traded to **Boston** by **Ottawa** with $7,000 for Cooney Weiland, July 25, 1932. Traded to **Montreal Canadiens** by **Boston** for Johnny Gagnon, October 2, 1934. Traded to **Boston** by **Montreal Canadiens** for cash, December 4, 1934. Traded to **St. Louis** by **Boston** for Max Kaminsky and Des Roche, December 4, 1934. Claimed by **Montreal Maroons** from **St. Louis** in Dispersal Draft, October 15, 1935. Traded to **NY Americans** by **Montreal Maroons** with $10,000 for Carl Voss, September 6, 1936. Traded to **Detroit** by **NY Americans** for Red Beattie with NY Americans holding right of recall, January 24, 1938. • Recalled by NY Americans, October 9, 1938.

• LAMIRANDE, Jean-Paul

LW/D – R. 5'8", 170 lbs. b: Shawinigan Falls, Que., 8/21/1924 d: 1/30/1976.

Season	Club	League	GP	G	A	Pts	AG	AA	APts	PIM	GP	G	A	Pts	PIM
1943-44	Montreal Army	MCHl	2	0	0	0	....	....	....	0	2	0	0	0	2
1944-45	Montreal Army	MCHL	14	3	5	8	....	....	....	10	3	0	0	0	2
	Montreal Cyclones	MCHL	12	2	8	10	....	....	....	....	....	....	....	....	....
1945-46	Montreal Royals	QSHL	36	6	8	14	....	....	....	60	9	2	2	4	22
1946-47	**New York Rangers**	**NHL**	**14**	**1**	**1**	**2**	**1**	**1**	**2**	**14**	....	....	....	....	....
	New Haven Ramblers	AHL	4	0	1	1	....	....	....	6	....	....	....	....	....
	St. Paul Saints	USHL	26	0	4	4	....	....	....	18	....	....	....	....	....
1947-48	**New York Rangers**	**NHL**	**18**	**0**	**1**	**1**	**0**	**1**	**1**	**6**	**6**	**0**	**0**	**0**	**4**
	New Haven Ramblers	AHL	46	7	20	27	....	....	....	22	....	....	....	....	....
1948-49	New Haven Ramblers	AHL	30	3	7	10	....	....	....	18	....	....	....	....	....
1949-50	**New York Rangers**	**NHL**	**16**	**4**	**3**	**7**	**5**	**4**	**9**	**6**	**2**	**0**	**0**	**0**	**0**
	New Haven Ramblers	AHL	52	26	31	57	....	....	....	16	....	....	....	....	....
1950-51	St. Louis Flyers	AHL	64	13	36	49	....	....	....	6	....	....	....	....	....
1951-52	Chicoutimi Sagueneens	QMHL	58	11	28	39	....	....	....	32	18	2	7	9	4
1952-53	Chicoutimi Sagueneens	QMHL	56	4	19	23	....	....	....	36	20	2	6	8	17
1953-54	Chicoutimi Sagueneens	QHL	68	5	22	27	....	....	....	65	7	0	0	0	4
1954-55	**Montreal Canadiens**	**NHL**	**1**	**0**	**0**	**0**	**0**	**0**	**0**	**0**	....	....	....	....	....
	Shawinigan Cataracts	QHL	60	3	29	32	....	....	....	59	11	2	4	6	8
	Shawinigan Cataracts	Ed-Cup	7	2	2	4	....	....	....	4	....	....	....	....	....
1955-56	Trois-Rivieres–Shawinigan	QHL	58	6	16	22	....	....	....	44	11	1	2	3	10
1956-57	Quebec Aces	QHL	67	4	14	18	....	....	....	52	10	0	5	5	6
	Quebec Aces	Ed-Cup	6	1	0	1	....	....	....	6	....	....	....	....	....
1957-58	Quebec Aces	QHL	45	3	16	19	....	....	....	24	13	1	2	3	6
	Canada	WEC-A	7	1	4	5	....	....	....	0	....	....	....	....	....
1958-59	Belleville McFarlands	EOHL	20	5	8	13	....	....	....	10	....	....	....	....	....
	Canada	WEC-A	8	1	0	1	....	....	....	0	....	....	....	....	....
1959-60	Windsor Bulldogs	OHA-Sr.	49	6	16	22	....	....	....	50	14	0	4	4	2
1960-61	Kingston Frontenacs	EPHL	2	0	1	1	....	....	....	2	....	....	....	....	....
	Clinton Comets	EHL	52	6	27	33	....	....	....	22	4	0	1	1	7
	NHL Totals		**49**	**5**	**5**	**10**	**6**	**6**	**12**	**26**	**8**	**0**	**0**	**0**	**4**

QMHL First All-Star Team (1951, 1953) • QHL First All-Star Team (1955) • QHL Second All-Star Team (1956, 1957) • Named Best Defenseman at WEC-A (1959) • EHL Second All-Star Team (1961)

Traded to **Chicago** (St. Louis-AHL) by **NY Rangers** for cash, September 19, 1950. Traded to **Montreal** by **Chicago** for cash, October 25, 1954. Claimed on waivers by **Quebec** (QHL) from **Shawinigan** (QHL), October, 1956.

• LAMOUREUX, Leo Leonard Peter

C/D – L. 5'11", 175 lbs. b: Espanola, Ont., 10/1/1916 d: 1/11/1961.

Season	Club	League	GP	G	A	Pts	AG	AA	APts	PIM	GP	G	A	Pts	PIM
1932-33	Timmins Combines	NOHA	STATISTICS NOT AVAILABLE												
	Timmins Combines	Al-Cup	6	1	1	2	....	....	....	4	....	....	....	....	....
1933-34	Timmins Combines	NOHA	STATISTICS NOT AVAILABLE												
	Toronto CCM	TMHL	5	1	0	1	....	....	....	2	....	....	....	....	....
1934-35	Oshawa Generals	OHA-Jr.	14	6	14	20	....	....	....	8	2	4	0	4	4
1935-36	Timmins Black Shirts	NOHA	14	10	11	21	....	....	....	19	....	....	....	....	....
1936-37	Kirkland Lake Blue Devils	NOHA	6	4	5	9	....	....	....	0	4	1	0	1	2
1937-38	Windsor Chryslers	MOHL	31	13	15	28	....	....	....	36	8	4	5	9	6
1938-39	Earls Court Rangers	Britain	....	7	7	14	....	....	....	....	....	....	....	....	....
	Earls Court Rangers	Nat-Tmt	....	2	0	2	....	....	....	....	....	....	....	....	....
1939-40	Cornwall Royals	QSHL	29	7	9	16	....	....	....	29	5	1	2	3	6
1940-41	Hamilton Dofascos	OHA-Sr.	28	12	9	21	....	....	....	50	6	1	4	5	8
1941-42	**Montreal Canadiens**	**NHL**	**1**	**0**	**0**	**0**	**0**	**0**	**0**	**0**	....	....	....	....	....
	Washington Lions	AHL	55	5	19	24	....	....	....	40	2	0	2	2	0
1942-43	**Montreal Canadiens**	**NHL**	**46**	**2**	**16**	**18**	**2**	**15**	**17**	**53**	....	....	....	....	....
	Washington Lions	AHL	1	1	0	1	....	....	....	0	....	....	....	....	....

Season	Club	League	GP	G	A	Pts	AG	AA	APts	PIM	GP	G	A	Pts	PIM
			REGULAR SEASON								PLAYOFFS				
♦1943-44	Montreal Canadiens	NHL	44	8	23	31	7	20	27	32	9	0	3	3	8
1944-45	Montreal Canadiens	NHL	49	2	22	24	2	26	28	58	6	1	1	2	2
♦1945-46	Montreal Canadiens	NHL	45	5	7	12	6	10	16	18	9	0	2	2	2
1946-47	Montreal Canadiens	NHL	50	2	11	13	2	13	15	14	4	0	0	0	4
1947-48	Buffalo Bisons	AHL	15	1	3	4				2					
	Springfield Indians	AHL	40	1	14	15				16					
1948-49	Shawinigan Cataracts	QSHL	31	1	18	19				26					
1949-50	Shawinigan Cataracts	QSHL	22	1	15	16				8					
1950-51	Detroit Hettche	IHL	13	0	4	4				12					
	Charlottetown Islanders	MMHL	1	0	1	1				2					
1951-52	Charlottetown Islanders	MMHL	1	0	0	0				0					
1952-53	North Bay Trappers	NOHA	8	0	4	4				6					
1953-54			OUT OF HOCKEY – RETIRED												
1954-55			OUT OF HOCKEY – RETIRED												
1955-56	Indianapolis Chiefs	IHL	24	0	5	5				19					
	NHL Totals		**235**	**19**	**79**	**98**	**19**	**84**	**103**	**175**	**28**	**1**	**6**	**7**	**16**

QSHL First All-Star Team (1940)

Signed as a free agent by **Cornwall** (QSHL), October 2, 1939. Signed as a free agent by **Montreal**, October 16, 1941. Traded to **Springfield** (AHL) by **Montreal** for cash, December 17, 1947. • Named coach of Charlottetown (MMHL), November 15, 1950.

• LANCIEN, Jack John Gordon

D – L. 6', 188 lbs. b: Regina, Sask., 6/14/1923.

Season	Club	League	GP	G	A	Pts	AG	AA	APts	PIM	GP	G	A	Pts	PIM
1945-46	Swift Current Indians	SIHA	STATISTICS NOT AVAILABLE												
	Regina Capitals	WCSHL	12	1	2	3				12					
1946-47	New York Rangers	NHL	1	0	0	0	0	0	0	0					
	New York Rovers	EAHL	55	3	11	14				44	9	0	0	0	9
1947-48	New Haven Ramblers	AHL	68	7	20	27				64	4	0	1	1	4
	New York Rangers	NHL									2	0	0	0	2
1948-49	New Haven Ramblers	AHL	67	2	24	26				66					
1949-50	New York Rangers	NHL	43	1	4	5	1	5	6	27	4	0	1	1	0
	New Haven Ramblers	AHL	26	2	7	9				17					
	St. Paul Saints	USHL	4	0	2	2				4					
1950-51	New York Rangers	NHL	19	0	1	1	0	1	1	8					
	Cincinnati Mohawks	AHL	40	4	6	10				41					
1951-52	Cincinnati Mohawks	AHL	61	2	4	6				43	7	0	1	1	4
1952-53	Vancouver Canucks	WHL	64	10	12	22				39	9	0	1	1	4
1953-54	Vancouver Canucks	WHL	70	9	24	33				54	12	0	4	4	8
1954-55	Vancouver Canucks	WHL	70	5	30	35				17	5	0	1	1	4
1955-56	Spokane Flyers	WHL	44	7	32	39				13	10	1	9	10	2
	Spokane Flyers	Al-Cup	6	0	3	3				0					
1956-57	Spokane Flyers	WHL	48	9	23	32				23	9	0	*10	10	0
1957-58	Spokane Flyers	WHL	47	11	29	40				13	13	1	6	7	2
1958-59	Spokane Spokes	WHL	31	1	12	13				6	4	0	1	1	0
	Trail Smoke Eaters	WHL	5	1	3	4				0					
1959-60	Spokane Comets	WHL	1	0	0	0				0					
1960-61	Rossland Warriors	WHL	4	1	1	2									
	NHL Totals		**63**	**1**	**5**	**6**	**1**	**6**	**7**	**35**	**6**	**0**	**1**	**1**	**2**

• LANE, Myles USHOF

D – L. 6', 180 lbs. b: Melrose, MA, 10/2/1905 d: 1987.

Season	Club	League	GP	G	A	Pts	AG	AA	APts	PIM	GP	G	A	Pts	PIM
1923-24	Boston AAA	USAHA	4	0	0	0									
1924-25	Boston AAA	USAHA	1	1	0	1									
1925-26	Dartmouth College	Ivy	8	20	0	20									
1926-27	Dartmouth College	Ivy	4	10	0	10									
1927-28	Dartmouth College	Ivy	5	20	0	20									
1928-29	New York Rangers	NHL	24	1	0	1	3	0	3	22					
♦	Boston Bruins	NHL	19	1	0	1	3	0	3	2	5	0	0	0	0
1929-30	Boston Bruins	NHL	3	0	0	0	0	0	0	0	6	0	0	0	0
1930-31			DID NOT PLAY												
1931-32	Boston Cubs	Can-Am	40	3	4	7				48	5	0	1	1	2
1932-33	Boston Cubs	Can-Am	39	3	10	13				45	7	0	2	2	10
1933-34	Boston Bruins	NHL	25	2	1	3	3	2	5	17					
	Boston Cubs	Can-Am	16	3	2	5				8					
	NHL Totals		**71**	**4**	**1**	**5**	**9**	**2**	**11**	**41**	**11**	**0**	**0**	**0**	**0**

Signed as a free agent by **NY Rangers**, October 1, 1928. Traded to **Boston** by **NY Rangers** for $7,500, January 21, 1929.

• LANGELLE, Pete

C – L. 5'11", 170 lbs. b: Winnipeg, Man., 11/4/1917.

Season	Club	League	GP	G	A	Pts	AG	AA	APts	PIM	GP	G	A	Pts	PIM
1934-35	East Kildonan Stars	MAHA	STATISTICS NOT AVAILABLE												
1935-36	Winnipeg Monarchs	MJHL	15	5	4	9				6					
1936-37	Winnipeg Monarchs	MJHL	16	12	7	19				18	8	2	1	3	2
	Winnipeg Monarchs	M-Cup	9	1	9	10				2					
1937-38	Syracuse Stars	IAHL	48	4	14	18				8	8	*5	4	*9	2
1938-39	Toronto Maple Leafs	NHL	2	1	0	1	2	0	2	0	11	1	2	3	2
	Syracuse Stars	IAHL	51	10	13	23				8					
1939-40	Toronto Maple Leafs	NHL	39	7	14	21	12	22	34	2	10	0	3	3	0
1940-41	Toronto Maple Leafs	NHL	47	4	15	19	6	21	27	0	7	1	1	2	0
♦1941-42	Toronto Maple Leafs	NHL	48	10	22	32	13	26	39	9	13	3	3	6	2
1942-43	Winnipeg RCAF	WNDHL	13	11	*17	*28				12	5	*4	1	5	2
	Winnipeg RCAF	Al-Cup	12	7	6	13				2					
1943-44	Winnipeg RCAF	WNDHL	10	4	5	9				7					
1944-45	Winnipeg RCAF	WNDHL	10	4	6	10				2					
1945-46			MILITARY SERVICE												
1946-47	Pittsburgh Hornets	AHL	64	20	30	50				4	12	4	7	11	2
1947-48	Pittsburgh Hornets	AHL	67	21	37	58				8	2	0	0	0	0
1948-49	Pittsburgh Hornets	AHL	68	10	26	36				13					
1949-50	Pittsburgh Hornets	AHL	47	8	15	23				7					
1950-51	Pittsburgh Hornets	AHL	47	4	10	14				0	8	1	3	4	2
1951-52	Saint John Beavers	MMHL	72	16	18	34				35	10	3	1	4	4
	Saint John Beavers	Alx-Cup	5	0	2	2				0					
1952-53			REINSTATED AS AN AMATEUR												
1953-54	Pilot Mound Pioneers	MHL-Sr.	13	4	14	18				14					
	Winnipeg Maroons	Al-Cup	23	8	11	19				4					
	NHL Totals		**136**	**22**	**51**	**73**	**33**	**69**	**102**	**11**	**41**	**5**	**9**	**14**	**4**

Signed as a free agent by **Toronto**, October 27, 1937. Signed as a free agent by **Saint John** (MMHL), November 7, 1951.

• LANGLOIS, Albert "Junior"

D – L. 6', 205 lbs. b: Magog, Que., 11/6/1934.

Season	Club	League	GP	G	A	Pts	AG	AA	APts	PIM	GP	G	A	Pts	PIM
1952-53	Quebec Citadelle	QJHL	9	0	0	0				0					
1953-54	Quebec Frontenacs	QJHL	63	2	11	13				84	8	1	2	3	8
	Quebec Frontenacs	M-Cup	8	0	4	4				0					
1954-55	Quebec Citadelle	QJHL	43	2	18	20				73	9	1	3	4	12
	Quebec Citadelle	M-Cup	9	2	0	2				6					
1955-56	Shawinigan Cataracts	QHL	64	8	6	14				48	11	2	4	6	14
1956-57	Shawinigan Cataracts	QHL	16	0	2	2				12					
	Rochester Americans	AHL	47	5	24	29				64	10	0	4	4	18
♦1957-58	Montreal Canadiens	NHL	1	0	0	0	0	0	0	0	7	0	1	1	4
	Rochester Americans	AHL	68	0	11	11				88					
♦1958-59	Montreal Canadiens	NHL	48	0	3	3	0	3	3	26	7	0	0	0	4
♦1959-60	Montreal Canadiens	NHL	67	1	14	15	1	14	15	48	8	0	3	3	18
1960-61	Montreal Canadiens	NHL	61	1	12	13	1	12	13	56	5	0	0	0	6
1961-62	New York Rangers	NHL	69	7	18	25	8	17	25	90	6	0	1	1	2
1962-63	New York Rangers	NHL	60	2	14	16	2	14	16	62					
1963-64	New York Rangers	NHL	44	4	2	6	5	2	7	32					
	Baltimore Clippers	AHL	6	1	0	1				6					
	Detroit Red Wings	NHL	17	1	6	7	1	6	7	13	14	0	0	0	12
1964-65	Detroit Red Wings	NHL	65	1	12	13	1	12	13	107	6	1	0	1	4
1965-66	Boston Bruins	NHL	65	4	10	14	4	9	13	54					
1966-67	Los Angeles Blades	WHL	59	6	34	40				97					
	NHL Totals		**497**	**21**	**91**	**112**	**23**	**89**	**112**	**488**	**53**	**1**	**5**	**6**	**50**

QHL Second All-Star Team (1956) • Played in NHL All-Star Game (1959, 1960)

Traded to **NY Rangers** by **Montreal** for John Hanna, June 13, 1961. Traded to **Detroit** by **NY Rangers** for Ron Ingram, February 14, 1964. Traded to **Boston** by **Detroit** with Ron Harris, Parker MacDonald and Bob Dillabough for Ab McDonald, Bob McCord and Ken Stephanson, May 31, 1965.

• LANGLOIS, Charlie Louis Charles

RW/D – R. 6', 210 lbs. b: Lotbiniere, Que., 8/25/1894 d: 8/31/1965.

Season	Club	League	GP	G	A	Pts	AG	AA	APts	PIM	GP	G	A	Pts	PIM
1916-17	Montreal Stars	MCHL	10	2	*5	7				24	4	3	*2	*5	*15
	Montreal Lyalls	MCHL	11	8	0	8									
1917-18	Montreal Lyalls	MCHL	11	10	7	17				24	1	1	0	1	0
1918-19	Montreal Nationale	MCHL	3	5	3	8				3					
	Montreal Vickers	MCHL	6	4	0	4									
1919-20	Sudbury Wolves	NOHA	6	5	2	7				2	7	6	4	10	12
1920-21	Sudbury Wolves	NOHA	9	8	5	13				*61					
1921-22	Sudbury Wolves	NOHA	8	1	2	3				21					
1922-23	Sudbury Wolves	NOHA	7	1	1	2				6	2	0	0	0	0
1923-24	Sudbury Wolves	NOHA	STATISTICS NOT AVAILABLE												
1924-25	Hamilton Tigers	NHL	30	6	3	9	10	12	22	47					
1925-26	New York Americans	NHL	36	9	1	10	15	6	21	76					
1926-27	New York Americans	NHL	9	2	0	2	4	0	4	8					
	Pittsburgh Pirates	NHL	36	5	1	6	9	5	14	36					
1927-28	Pittsburgh Pirates	NHL	8	0	0	0	0	0	0	8					
	Montreal Canadiens	NHL	32	0	0	0	0	0	0	14	2	0	0	0	0
1928-29	Providence Reds	Can-Am	37	3	0	3				26	5	0	0	0	*24
1929-30	Duluth Hornets	AHA	46	7	1	8				87	4	0	0	0	0
1930-31	Duluth Hornets	AHA	47	2	6	8				64	4	0	0	0	6
1931-32	Tulsa Oilers	AHA	30	1	2	3				73					
	NHL Totals		**151**	**22**	**5**	**27**	**38**	**23**	**61**	**189**	**2**	**0**	**0**	**0**	**0**

MCHL Second All-Star Team (1917, 1918) • NOHA First All-Star Team (1921)

Signed as a free agent by **Hamilton**, October 16, 1924. Transferred to **NY Americans** after NHL club purchased **Hamilton** franchise, September 26, 1925. Traded to **Pittsburgh** by **NY Americans** with $2,000 for Lionel Conacher, December 16, 1926. Loaned to **Montreal Canadiens** by **Pittsburgh** for remainder of 1927-28 season for the loan of Marty Burke, December 16, 1927.

• LAPERRIERE, Jacques — see page 1301

• LAPRADE, Edgar Edgar Louis HHOF

C – R. 5'8", 160 lbs. b: Port Arthur, Ont., 10/10/1919.

Season	Club	League	GP	G	A	Pts	AG	AA	APts	PIM	GP	G	A	Pts	PIM
1935-36	Port Arthur Bruins	TBJHL	14	13	10	23				6	4	*4	*2	*6	2
1936-37	Port Arthur Bruins	TBJHL	18	*19	14	*33				2	3	*6	*3	*9	5
1937-38	Port Arthur Bruins	TBJHL	18	*23	11	*34				9	5	*6	0	*6	0
1938-39	Port Arthur Bruins	TBJHL	10	7	4	11									
	Port Arthur Bearcats	TBSHL	25	*31	9	*40				7	6	3	*3	*6	4
	Port Arthur Bearcats	Al-Cup	13	*22	4	*26				6					
1939-40	Port Arthur Bearcats	TBSHL	22	*20	15	35				8	3	*5	1	*6	2
	Port Arthur Bearcats	Al-Cup	12	13	10	23				6					
1940-41	Port Arthur Bearcats	TBSHL	20	*26	*21	*47				7	4	2	1	3	0
1941-42	Port Arthur Bearcats	TBSHL	15	18	*23	41				4					
	Port Arthur Bearcats	Al-Cup	17	12	*21	*33				6					
1942-43	Port Arthur Bearcats	TBSHL	8	7	10	17				0	3	7	4	11	4
	Port Arthur Bearcats	Al-Cup	8	6	10	16				2					
1943-44	Winnipeg Army	WNDHL	6	10	3	13				0					
1944-45	Barriefield Bears	OHA-Sr.	....	19	*28	*47				2	4	5	8	13	0
1945-46	New York Rangers	NHL	49	15	19	34	18	28	46	0					
1946-47	New York Rangers	NHL	58	15	25	40	17	30	47	9					
1947-48	New York Rangers	NHL	59	13	34	47	17	45	62	7	6	1	4	5	0
1948-49	New York Rangers	NHL	56	18	12	30	25	17	42	12					
1949-50	New York Rangers	NHL	60	22	22	44	28	27	55	2	12	3	5	8	4
1950-51	New York Rangers	NHL	42	10	13	23	13	16	29	0					
1951-52	New York Rangers	NHL	70	9	29	38	12	36	48	8					
1952-53	New York Rangers	NHL	11	2	1	3	3	1	4	2					
1953-54	New York Rangers	NHL	35	1	6	7	1	7	8	2					
1954-55	New York Rangers	NHL	60	3	11	14	4	13	17	0					
	NHL Totals		**500**	**108**	**172**	**280**	**138**	**220**	**358**	**42**	**18**	**4**	**9**	**13**	**4**

Won Calder Memorial Trophy (1946) • Won Lady Byng Trophy (1950) • Played in NHL All-Star Game (1947, 1948, 1949, 1950)

Signed as a free agent by **NY Rangers**, October 15, 1945.

• LAPRAIRIE, Benjamin "Bun"

D – R. 5'10", 160 lbs. b: Sault Ste. Marie, MI, .

			REGULAR SEASON								PLAYOFFS				
Season	Club	League	GP	G	A	Pts	AG	AA	APts	PIM	GP	G	A	Pts	PIM
1934-35	Chicago Baby Ruth	USAHA	2	1	0	1	....	....	....	....	2	1	0	1	0
1935-36	Kansas City Greyhounds	AHA	47	0	0	0	....	....	....	6	....	....	....	....	....
1936-37	**Chicago Black Hawks**	**NHL**	**7**	**0**	**0**	**0**	**0**	**0**	**0**	**0**	....	....	....	....	....
	Minneapolis Millers	AHA	5	0	0	0	....	....	....	6	....	....	....	....	....
	NHL Totals		**7**	**0**	**0**	**0**	**0**	**0**	**0**	**0**	....	....	....	....	....

• LAROCHELLE, Wildor

RW – R. 5'8", 158 lbs. b: Sorel, Que., 9/23/1906 d: 3/21/1964.

			REGULAR SEASON								PLAYOFFS				
Season	Club	League	GP	G	A	Pts	AG	AA	APts	PIM	GP	G	A	Pts	PIM
1925-26	**Montreal Canadiens**	**NHL**	**33**	**2**	**1**	**3**	**3**	**6**	**9**	**10**	....	....	....	....	....
1926-27	**Montreal Canadiens**	**NHL**	**41**	**0**	**1**	**1**	**0**	**5**	**5**	**6**	**4**	**0**	**0**	**0**	**0**
1927-28	**Montreal Canadiens**	**NHL**	**40**	**3**	**1**	**4**	**6**	**6**	**12**	**30**	**2**	**0**	**0**	**0**	**0**
1928-29	**Montreal Canadiens**	**NHL**	**2**	**0**	**0**	**0**	**0**	**0**	**0**	**0**	....	....	....	....	....
	Providence Reds	Can-Am	39	8	4	12	....	....	....	50	6	0	1	1	8
♦1929-30	**Montreal Canadiens**	**NHL**	**44**	**14**	**11**	**25**	**20**	**26**	**46**	**28**	**6**	**1**	**0**	**1**	**12**
♦1930-31	**Montreal Canadiens**	**NHL**	**40**	**8**	**5**	**13**	**16**	**15**	**31**	**35**	**10**	**1**	**2**	**3**	**8**
1931-32	**Montreal Canadiens**	**NHL**	**48**	**18**	**8**	**26**	**30**	**18**	**48**	**16**	**4**	**2**	**1**	**3**	**4**
1932-33	**Montreal Canadiens**	**NHL**	**47**	**11**	**4**	**15**	**20**	**8**	**28**	**27**	**2**	**1**	**0**	**1**	**0**
1933-34	**Montreal Canadiens**	**NHL**	**48**	**16**	**11**	**27**	**28**	**23**	**51**	**27**	**2**	**1**	**1**	**2**	**0**
1934-35	**Montreal Canadiens**	**NHL**	**48**	**9**	**19**	**28**	**15**	**33**	**48**	**12**	**2**	**0**	**0**	**0**	**0**
1935-36	**Montreal Canadiens**	**NHL**	**13**	**0**	**2**	**2**	**0**	**4**	**4**	**6**	....	....	....	....	....
	Chicago Black Hawks	**NHL**	**27**	**2**	**1**	**3**	**4**	**2**	**6**	**8**	**2**	**0**	**0**	**0**	**0**
	Philadelphia Arrows	Can-Am	6	2	3	5	....	....	....	0	....	....	....	....	....
1936-37	**Chicago Black Hawks**	**NHL**	**43**	**9**	**10**	**19**	**15**	**18**	**33**	**6**	....	....	....	....	....
1937-38			DID NOT PLAY												
1938-39	New Haven Eagles	IAHL	21	2	3	5	....	....	....	2	....	....	....	....	....
	NHL Totals		**474**	**92**	**74**	**166**	**157**	**164**	**321**	**211**	**34**	**6**	**4**	**10**	**24**

Signed as a free agent by **Montreal Canadiens**, November 23, 1925. Traded to **Chicago** by **Montreal Canadiens** for cash, December 21, 1935. Traded to **St. Louis** (AHA) by **Chicago** for cash, September 24, 1937. • Larochelle opted to retire rather than report to St. Louis.

• LAROSE, Bonner Charles

LW – R. 5'8", 170 lbs. b: Ottawa, Ont., 2/14/1901 d: 1/23/1961.

			REGULAR SEASON								PLAYOFFS				
Season	Club	League	GP	G	A	Pts	AG	AA	APts	PIM	GP	G	A	Pts	PIM
1917-18	Ottawa St. Brigids	OCHL	5	0	0	0	....	....	....	16	....	....	....	....	....
	Ottawa St. Brigids	HOHL	3	0	0	0	....	....	....	0	....	....	....	....	....
1918-19			MILITARY SERVICE												
1919-20	Ottawa St. Pats	OCHL	9	4	0	4	....	....	....	....	....	....	....	....	....
1920-21	Ottawa K of C	OCHL	6	1	0	1	....	....	....	....	....	....	....	....	....
1921-22	Ottawa K of C	OCHL	11	6	5	11	....	....	....	6	....	....	....	....	....
1922-23	Ottawa Royal Canadians	OCHL	14	10	4	14	....	....	....	23	....	....	....	....	....
1923-24	Ottawa Royal Canadians	OCHL	12	5	1	6	....	....	....	....	....	....	....	....	....
1924-25	Fort Pitt Hornets	USAHA	22	7	0	7	....	....	....	....	8	0	0	0	....
1925-26	St. Paul Saints	CHL	10	0	0	0	....	....	....	0	....	....	....	....	....
	Boston Bruins	**NHL**	**6**	**0**	**0**	**0**	**0**	**0**	**0**	**0**	....	....	....	....	....
1926-27	Boston Tigers	Can-Am	13	0	1	1	....	....	....	4	....	....	....	....	....
	New Haven Eagles	Can-Am	5	0	1	1	....	....	....	4	3	0	0	0	0
	NHL Totals		**6**	**0**	**0**	**0**	**0**	**0**	**0**	**0**	....	....	....	....	....

OCHL Second All-Star Team (1922) • OCHL First All-Star Team (1923)

Signed as a free agent by **Boston**, February 19, 1926. Traded to **New Haven** (Can-Am) by **Boston** (Boston-Can-Am) for Reg McLlwain, January 31, 1927.

• LAROSE, Claude — *see page 1305*

• LARSON, Norm Norm Lyle

RW – R. 6', 175 lbs. b: Moose Jaw, Sask., 10/13/1920.

			REGULAR SEASON								PLAYOFFS				
Season	Club	League	GP	G	A	Pts	AG	AA	APts	PIM	GP	G	A	Pts	PIM
1937-38	Moose Jaw Canucks	S-SJHL	8	*16	4	*20	....	....	....	4	7	*11	*5	*16	5
1938-39	Moose Jaw Millers	S-SSHL	24	16	6	22	....	....	....	2	10	*8	2	*10	2
1939-40	Moose Jaw Millers	S-SSHL	26	23	9	32	....	....	....	4	8	*10	2	12	4
	Moose Jaw Millers	Al-Cup	3	1	0	1	....	....	....	0	....	....	....	....	....
1940-41	**New York Americans**	**NHL**	**48**	**9**	**9**	**18**	**14**	**13**	**27**	**6**	....	....	....	....	....
1941-42	**Brooklyn Americans**	**NHL**	**40**	**16**	**9**	**25**	**21**	**11**	**32**	**6**	....	....	....	....	....
	Springfield Indians	AHL	5	3	3	6	....	....	....	0	4	1	2	3	0
1942-43	Port Arthur Shipbuilders	TBSHL	8	5	10	15	....	....	....	6	3	1	2	3	2
	Lakehead Army	TBDHL	1	2	3	5	....	....	....	0	....	....	....	....	....
	Port Arthur Shipbuilders	Al-Cup	13	16	11	27	....	....	....	9	....	....	....	....	....
	Port Arthur Bearcats	Al-Cup	8	6	8	14	....	....	....	13	....	....	....	....	....
1943-44	Port Arthur Shipbuilders	TBSHL	6	*20	3	*23	....	....	....	0	....	....	....	....	....
1944-45	Quebec Aces	QSHL	14	18	17	35	....	....	....	2	5	*7	3	*10	0
	Quebec Aces	Al-Cup	3	3	2	5	....	....	....	0	....	....	....	....	....
1945-46	New Haven Ramblers	AHL	40	19	26	45	....	....	....	18	....	....	....	....	....
	Hershey Bears	AHL	24	17	27	44	....	....	....	2	3	2	0	2	0
1946-47	**New York Rangers**	**NHL**	**1**	**0**	**0**	**0**	**0**	**0**	**0**	**0**	....	....	....	....	....
	New Haven Ramblers	AHL	11	1	5	6	....	....	....	0	....	....	....	....	....
1947-48	Hershey Bears	AHL	19	4	1	5	....	....	....	0	....	....	....	....	....
1948-49	Hershey Bears	AHL	55	13	24	37	....	....	....	13	8	0	2	2	0
1949-50	Hershey Bears	AHL	68	20	35	55	....	....	....	8	....	....	....	....	....
1950-51	Calgary Stampeders	WCMHL	47	28	35	63	....	....	....	20	8	1	3	4	2
1951-52	Calgary Stampeders	PCHL	65	30	25	55	....	....	....	18	....	....	....	....	....
1952-53	Calgary Stampeders	WHL	1	0	0	0	....	....	....	0	....	....	....	....	....
	Kamloops Elks	OSHL	45	26	21	47	....	....	....	22	12	4	8	12	0
1953-54	Kimberley Dynamiters	WIHL	39	23	29	52	....	....	....	12	9	1	4	5	8
	Kimberley Dynamiters	Al-Cup	5	1	0	1	....	....	....	4	....	....	....	....	....
1954-55	Kimberley Dynamiters	WIHL	26	10	16	26	....	....	....	17	8	2	3	5	2
1955-56	Kimberley Dynamiters	WIHL	43	35	37	72	....	....	....	6	5	1	1	2	2
	NHL Totals		**89**	**25**	**18**	**43**	**35**	**24**	**59**	**12**	....	....	....	....	....

WCMHL First All-Star Team (1951) • AHL Second All-Star Team (1946)

Signed as a free agent by **NY Americans**, October 23, 1940. Traded to **Hershey** (AHL) by **New Haven** (AHL) for Bill Gooden, January 28, 1946.

• LATREILLE, Phil

C/RW – R. 5'10", 185 lbs. b: Montreal, Que., 4/22/1938.

			REGULAR SEASON								PLAYOFFS				
Season	Club	League	GP	G	A	Pts	AG	AA	APts	PIM	GP	G	A	Pts	PIM
1956-57	Montreal D'arcy McGee	H.S.	10	*13	9	*22	....	....	....	....	....	....	....	....	....
1957-58	Middlebury College	ECAC-2	21	36	16	52	....	....	....	20	....	....	....	....	....
1958-59	Middlebury College	ECAC-2	22	*57	33	*90	....	....	....	....	....	....	....	....	....
1959-60	Middlebury College	ECAC-2	23	*77	19	*96	....	....	....	....	....	....	....	....	....
1960-61	Middlebury College	ECAC-2	25	*80	28	*108	....	....	....	....	....	....	....	....	....
	New York Rangers	**NHL**	**4**	**0**	**0**	**0**	**0**	**0**	**0**	**2**	....	....	....	....	....
1961-62	Long Island Ducks	EHL	6	0	2	2	....	....	....	0	....	....	....	....	....
	Montreal Olympiques	ETSHL	20	11	4	15	....	....	....	0	13	*11	4	15	8
	Montreal Olympiques	Al-Cup	16	6	3	9	....	....	....	0	....	....	....	....	....
1962-63	Montreal Olympiques	ETSHL	STATISTICS NOT AVAILABLE												
1963-64	Montreal Olympiques	QSHL	STATISTICS NOT AVAILABLE												
1964-65	Calgary Spurs	X-Games	STATISTICS NOT AVAILABLE												
	NHL Totals		**4**	**0**	**0**	**0**	**0**	**0**	**0**	**2**	....	....	....	....	....

ECAC-2 Second All-Star Team (1959) • ECAC-2 First All-Star Team (1960, 1961)

Signed as a free agent by **NY Rangers** to a five-game amateur tryout contract, March 10, 1961.

• LAUDER, Martin Martin Arthur "Harry"

D/C – L. 5'6", 165 lbs. b: Durham, Ont., 1/26/1907.

			REGULAR SEASON								PLAYOFFS				
Season	Club	League	GP	G	A	Pts	AG	AA	APts	PIM	GP	G	A	Pts	PIM
1925-26	Owen Sound Greys	OHA-Jr.	12	*18	*6	*24	....	....	....	....	8	*7	2	9	8
1926-27	Owen Sound Greys	OHA-Jr.	15	23	*13	36	....	....	....	....	....	....	....	....	....
1927-28	**Boston Bruins**	**NHL**	**3**	**0**	**0**	**0**	**0**	**0**	**0**	**2**	....	....	....	....	....
	Providence Reds	Can-Am	16	3	1	4	....	....	....	8	....	....	....	....	....
1928-29	Hamilton Tigers	Can-Pro	36	8	5	13	....	....	....	52	....	....	....	....	....
1929-30	Hamilton Tigers	IHL	40	19	11	30	....	....	....	39	....	....	....	....	....
1930-31	Syracuse Stars	IHL	20	6	2	8	....	....	....	26	....	....	....	....	....
	Buffalo Bisons	IHL	29	8	0	8	....	....	....	18	6	1	0	1	0
1931-32	Buffalo Bisons	IHL	46	7	3	10	....	....	....	24	6	0	0	0	0
1932-33	Buffalo Bisons	IHL	42	4	2	6	....	....	....	24	5	0	0	0	0
	NHL Totals		**3**	**0**	**0**	**0**	**0**	**0**	**0**	**2**	....	....	....	....	....

Signed as a free agent by **Boston**, October 2, 1927. Traded to **Buffalo** (IHL) by **Syracuse** (IHL) for Rolly Huard, January 3, 1931.

• LAVIOLETTE, Jack John Baptiste **HHOF**

D/RW – R. 5'11", 170 lbs. b: Belleville, Ont., 7/27/1879 d: 1/9/1960.

			REGULAR SEASON								PLAYOFFS				
Season	Club	League	GP	G	A	Pts	AG	AA	APts	PIM	GP	G	A	Pts	PIM
1902-03	Montreal Bell AAA	MCHL	STATISTICS NOT AVAILABLE												
1903-04	Montreal Nationals	FAHL	6	8	0	8	....	....	....	....	....	....	....	....	....
1904-05	Michigan Soo Indians	IHL	24	15	0	15	....	....	....	24	....	....	....	....	....
1905-06	Michigan Soo Indians	IHL	17	15	0	15	....	....	....	28	....	....	....	....	....
1906-07	Michigan Soo Indians	IHL	19	10	7	17	....	....	....	34	....	....	....	....	....
1907-08	Montreal Shamrocks	ECAHA	6	1	0	1	....	....	....	36	....	....	....	....	....
1908-09	Montreal Shamrocks	ECHA	9	1	0	1	....	....	....	36	....	....	....	....	....
1909-10	Montreal Canadiens	NHA	11	3	0	3	....	....	....	26	....	....	....	....	....
1910-11	Montreal Canadiens	NHA	16	0	0	0	....	....	....	24	....	....	....	....	....
1911-12	Montreal Canadiens	NHA	17	7	0	7	....	....	....	10	....	....	....	....	....
1912-13	Montreal Canadiens	NHA	20	8	0	8	....	....	....	77	....	....	....	....	....
1913-14	Montreal Canadiens	NHA	20	7	9	16	....	....	....	30	2	0	1	1	0
1914-15	Montreal Canadiens	NHA	18	6	3	9	....	....	....	35	....	....	....	....	....
♦1915-16	Montreal Canadiens	NHA	18	8	3	11	....	....	....	62	4	0	0	0	6
1916-17	Montreal Canadiens	NHA	17	7	3	10	....	....	....	24	6	1	2	3	9
1917-18	**Montreal Canadiens**	**NHL**	**18**	**2**	**1**	**3**	**2**	**4**	**6**	**6**	**2**	**0**	**0**	**0**	**0**
	NHL Totals		**18**	**2**	**1**	**3**	**2**	**4**	**6**	**6**	**2**	**0**	**0**	**0**	**0**
	Other Major League Totals		212	88	25	113	....	....	....	446	12	1	3	4	15

IHL First All-Star Team (1905, 1907) • IHL Second All-Star Team (1906)

Signed as a free agent by **Montreal Shamrocks** (ECAHA), December 15, 1907. Rights retained by **Montreal Canadiens** after NHA folded, November 26, 1917.

• LAYCOE, Hal Harold Richardson

D – L. 6'2", 185 lbs. b: Sutherland, Sask., 6/23/1922 d: 4/29/1997.

			REGULAR SEASON								PLAYOFFS				
Season	Club	League	GP	G	A	Pts	AG	AA	APts	PIM	GP	G	A	Pts	PIM
1938-39	Saskatoon Jr. Chiefs	N-SJHL	3	0	0	0	....	....	....	0	....	....	....	....	....
1939-40	Saskatoon Dodgers	N-SJHL	4	1	5	6	....	....	....	6	2	0	4	4	4
1940-41	Saskatoon Jr. Quakers	N-SJHL	11	12	11	23	....	....	....	13	2	3	4	*7	0
	Saskatoon Quakers	N-SSHL	1	0	0	0	....	....	....	0	....	....	....	....	....
	Saskatoon Jr. Quakers	M-Cup	10	4	8	12	....	....	....	22	....	....	....	....	....
1941-42	Saskatoon Quakers	N-SSHL	28	14	13	27	....	....	....	27	9	3	4	7	4
	Saskatoon Quakers	Al-Cup	4	0	1	1	....	....	....	0	....	....	....	....	....
1942-43	Ottawa CP Corps	OCHL	1	0	0	0	....	....	....	0	....	....	....	....	....
1943-44	Toronto Navy	OHA-Sr.	14	6	6	12	....	....	....	4	....	....	....	....	....
	Toronto Peoples Credit	TIHL	9	3	1	4	....	....	....	2	9	2	6	8	11
1944-45	Winnipeg Navy	WNDHL	15	10	15	25	....	....	....	8	5	5	*8	*13	0
1945-46	**New York Rangers**	**NHL**	**17**	**0**	**2**	**2**	**0**	**3**	**3**	**6**	....	....	....	....	....
	New York Rovers	EAHL	35	7	22	29	....	....	....	25	....	....	....	....	....
1946-47	**New York Rangers**	**NHL**	**58**	**1**	**12**	**13**	**1**	**14**	**15**	**25**	....	....	....	....	....
1947-48	**Montreal Canadiens**	**NHL**	**14**	**1**	**2**	**3**	**1**	**3**	**4**	**4**	....	....	....	....	....
	Buffalo Bisons	AHL	45	8	25	33	....	....	....	36	8	2	0	2	15
1948-49	**Montreal Canadiens**	**NHL**	**51**	**3**	**5**	**8**	**4**	**7**	**11**	**31**	**7**	**0**	**1**	**1**	**13**
	Buffalo Bisons	AHL	10	4	1	5	....	....	....	10	....	....	....	....	....
1949-50	**Montreal Canadiens**	**NHL**	**30**	**0**	**2**	**2**	**0**	**2**	**2**	**21**	**2**	**0**	**0**	**0**	**0**
1950-51	**Montreal Canadiens**	**NHL**	**38**	**0**	**2**	**2**	**0**	**2**	**2**	**25**	....	....	....	....	....
	Boston Bruins	**NHL**	**6**	**1**	**1**	**2**	**1**	**1**	**2**	**4**	**6**	**0**	**1**	**1**	**5**
1951-52	**Boston Bruins**	**NHL**	**70**	**5**	**7**	**12**	**7**	**9**	**16**	**61**	**7**	**1**	**1**	**2**	**11**
1952-53	**Boston Bruins**	**NHL**	**54**	**2**	**10**	**12**	**3**	**12**	**15**	**36**	**11**	**0**	**2**	**2**	**10**
1953-54	**Boston Bruins**	**NHL**	**58**	**3**	**16**	**19**	**4**	**19**	**23**	**29**	**2**	**0**	**0**	**0**	**0**
1954-55	**Boston Bruins**	**NHL**	**70**	**4**	**13**	**17**	**5**	**15**	**20**	**34**	**5**	**1**	**0**	**1**	**0**
1955-56	**Boston Bruins**	**NHL**	**65**	**5**	**5**	**10**	**7**	**6**	**13**	**16**	....	....	....	....	....
1956-57	New Westminster Royals	WHL	DID NOT PLAY – COACHING												
	NHL Totals		**531**	**25**	**77**	**102**	**33**	**93**	**126**	**292**	**40**	**2**	**5**	**7**	**39**

EAHL Second All-Star Team (1946)

Traded to **Montreal** by **NY Rangers** with Joe Bell and George Robertson for Buddy O'Connor and Frank Eddolls, August 19, 1947. Traded to **Boston** by **Montreal** for Ross Lowe, February 14, 1951.

• LEACH, Larry Lawrence Raymond

C – L. 6'2", 175 lbs. b: Lloydminster, Sask., 6/18/1936.

			REGULAR SEASON								PLAYOFFS				
Season	Club	League	GP	G	A	Pts	AG	AA	APts	PIM	GP	G	A	Pts	PIM
1953-54	Humboldt Indians	SJHL	46	8	6	14	....	....	....	20	5	1	0	1	2
1954-55	Humboldt Indians	SJHL	47	6	9	15	....	....	....	8	10	0	1	1	4
	Humboldt Indians	M-Cup	4	0	0	0	....	....	....	4	....	....	....	....	....
1955-56	Humboldt Indians	SJHL	45	22	35	57	....	....	....	27	5	2	3	5	8
	Victoria Cougars	WHL	3	1	0	1	....	....	....	6	4	0	0	0	0
1956-57	Victoria Cougars	WHL	66	6	10	16	....	....	....	72	3	0	0	0	2

			REGULAR SEASON								PLAYOFFS				
Season	Club	League	GP	G	A	Pts	AG	AA	APts	PIM	GP	G	A	Pts	PIM
1957-58	Victoria Cougars	WHL	33	7	9	16	....	....	....	23	....	....	....	....	....
	Springfield Indians	AHL	35	1	9	10	....	....	....	8	13	3	1	4	12
1958-59	**Boston Bruins**	**NHL**	**29**	**4**	**12**	**16**	**5**	**12**	**17**	**26**	**7**	**1**	**1**	**2**	**8**
	Providence Reds	AHL	37	12	17	29	....	....	....	24	....	....	....	....	....
1959-60	**Boston Bruins**	**NHL**	**69**	**7**	**12**	**19**	**8**	**12**	**20**	**47**	....	....	....	....	....
1960-61	Portland Buckaroos	WHL	54	13	16	29	....	....	....	80	14	6	7	13	22
1961-62	**Boston Bruins**	**NHL**	**28**	**2**	**5**	**7**	**2**	**5**	**7**	**18**	....	....	....	....	....
	Providence Reds	AHL	25	8	11	19	....	....	....	33	....	....	....	....	....
1962-63	Providence Reds	AHL	52	22	24	46	....	....	....	56	....	....	....	....	....
1963-64	Providence Reds	AHL	60	12	30	42	....	....	....	43	3	1	1	2	16
1964-65	Portland Buckaroos	WHL	52	7	10	17	....	....	....	48	10	2	1	3	6
1965-66	Portland Buckaroos	WHL	72	18	23	41	....	....	....	57	3	0	0	0	6
1966-67	Portland Buckaroos	WHL	60	18	17	35	....	....	....	43	4	0	0	0	0
1967-68	Portland Buckaroos	WHL	72	21	20	41	....	....	....	48	11	1	0	1	8
1968-69	Portland Buckaroos	WHL	72	8	18	26	....	....	....	50	9	0	0	0	2
1969-70	Portland Buckaroos	WHL	72	6	17	23	....	....	....	44	11	0	2	2	12
1970-71	Portland Buckaroos	WHL	60	6	15	21	....	....	....	28	11	3	3	6	6
1971-72	Portland Buckaroos	WHL	54	15	21	36	....	....	....	32	6	0	0	0	6
1972-73	Portland Buckaroos	WHL	71	5	14	19	....	....	....	42	....	....	....	....	....
1973-74	Lloydminster Blazers	AJHL	DID NOT PLAY – COACHING												
	NHL Totals		**126**	**13**	**29**	**42**	**15**	**29**	**44**	**91**	**7**	**1**	**1**	**2**	**8**

Traded to **Portland** (WHL) by **Boston** for cash, May 1964. Claimed by **Chicago** from **Portland** (WHL) in Inter-League Draft, June, 1968. Traded to **Portland** (WHL) by **Chicago** for cash, October, 1968.

• LeBRUN, Al Albert Ivan

D – R. 6', 185 lbs. b: Timmins, Ont., 12/1/1940.

Season	Club	League	GP	G	A	Pts	AG	AA	APts	PIM	GP	G	A	Pts	PIM
1957-58	Guelph Biltmores	OHA-Jr.	34	0	1	1	....	....	....	16	....	....	....	....	....
1958-59	Guelph Biltmores	OHA-Jr.	54	3	12	15	....	....	....	55	10	0	1	1	17
1959-60	Guelph Biltmores	OHA-Jr.	48	5	13	18	....	....	....	74	5	1	0	1	8
1960-61	Guelph Royals	OHA-Jr.	47	4	12	16	....	....	....	127	12	1	4	5	40
	New York Rangers	**NHL**	**4**	**0**	**2**	**2**	**0**	**2**	**2**	**4**	....	....	....	....	....
	Kitchener Beavers	EPHL	1	0	0	0	....	....	....	0	....	....	....	....	....
1961-62	Kitchener Beavers	EPHL	70	0	16	16	....	....	....	36	7	0	1	1	8
1962-63	Vancouver Canucks	WHL	55	5	8	13	....	....	....	31	....	....	....	....	....
1963-64	Vancouver Canucks	WHL	DID NOT PLAY – INJURED												
1964-65	St. Paul Rangers	CPHL	66	11	15	26	....	....	....	52	11	1	1	2	9
1965-66	**New York Rangers**	**NHL**	**2**	**0**	**0**	**0**	**0**	**0**	**0**	**0**	....	....	....	....	....
	St. Paul Rangers	CPHL	69	4	13	17	....	....	....	38	7	0	3	3	4
1966-67	Pittsburgh Hornets	AHL	26	1	8	9	....	....	....	24	....	....	....	....	....
	Los Angeles Blades	WHL	42	1	8	9	....	....	....	33	....	....	....	....	....
1967-68	Dallas Black Hawks	CPHL	61	6	17	23	....	....	....	53	4	0	0	0	4
1968-69	Memphis South Stars	CHL	34	1	4	5	....	....	....	20	....	....	....	....	....
	San Diego Gulls	WHL	29	1	4	5	....	....	....	8	3	0	0	0	2
1969-70	San Diego Gulls	WHL	72	7	18	25	....	....	....	37	6	0	1	1	2
1970-71	San Diego Gulls	WHL	66	3	13	16	....	....	....	50	....	....	....	....	....
1971-72	San Diego Gulls	WHL	72	2	17	19	....	....	....	67	4	0	0	0	2
1972-73	San Diego Gulls	WHL	72	2	16	18	....	....	....	101	6	0	0	0	2
1973-74	San Diego Gulls	WHL	37	0	4	4	....	....	....	10	4	0	1	1	0
	NHL Totals		**6**	**0**	**2**	**2**	**0**	**2**	**2**	**4**	....	....	....	....	....

OHA-Jr. First All-Star Team (1961) • CPHL First All-Star Team (1966) • Named Top Defenseman - CPHL (1966) • CPHL Second All-Star Team (1968) • WHL Second All-Star Team (1973)

• Missed entire 1963-64 season recovering from spinal surgery, July, 1963. Claimed by **Detroit** from **NY Rangers** in Intra-League Draft, June 15, 1966. Loaned to **Chicago** (LA Blades-WHL) by **Detroit** with Murray Hall for remainder of 1966-67 season and future considerations (Murray Hall, Al Lebrun and Rick Morris, June, 1967) for Howie Young, December 20, 1966. Traded to **Chicago** by **Detroit** with Murray Hall and Rick Morris to complete transaction that sent Howie Yound to Detroit (December 20, 1966), June, 1967. Claimed by **San Diego** (WHL) from **Chicago** in Reverse Draft, June 13, 1968. Selected by **Dayton-Houston** (WHA) in WHA General Player Draft, February 12, 1972.

• LECLAIR, Jackie John Louis

C – L. 5'10", 150 lbs. b: Quebec City, Que., 5/30/1929.

Season	Club	League	GP	G	A	Pts	AG	AA	APts	PIM	GP	G	A	Pts	PIM
1946-47	Ottawa St. Pats	OCJHL	22	16	19	35	....	....	....	14	7	*21	*11	*32	2
1947-48	Lethbridge Native Sons	AJHL	16	12	29	41	....	....	....	20	6	7	6	13	20
	Lethbridge Native Sons	M-Cup	11	6	4	10	....	....	....	4	....	....	....	....	....
1948-49	Quebec Citadelle	QJHL	36	21	27	48	....	....	....	30	13	4	9	13	4
1949-50	Ottawa Senators	QSHL	56	19	42	61	....	....	....	28	7	2	0	2	2
1950-51	Ottawa Senators	QMHL	56	20	22	42	....	....	....	43	7	0	1	1	0
1951-52	Quebec Aces	QMHL	57	25	29	54	....	....	....	22	12	7	4	11	9
	Quebec Aces	Alx-Cup	4	0	2	2	....	....	....	2	....	....	....	....	....
1952-53	Ottawa Senators	QMHL	54	22	37	59	....	....	....	27	11	8	2	10	0
1953-54	Ottawa Senators	QHL	4	3	7	10	....	....	....	7	....	....	....	....	....
	Pittsburgh Hornets	AHL	52	14	17	31	....	....	....	11	4	0	1	1	2
1954-55	**Montreal Canadiens**	**NHL**	**59**	**11**	**22**	**33**	**14**	**25**	**39**	**12**	**12**	**5**	**0**	**5**	**2**
♦1955-56	**Montreal Canadiens**	**NHL**	**54**	**6**	**8**	**14**	**8**	**9**	**17**	**30**	**8**	**1**	**1**	**2**	**4**
	Montreal Royals	QHL	12	5	10	15	....	....	....	8	....	....	....	....	....
♦1956-57	**Montreal Canadiens**	**NHL**	**47**	**3**	**10**	**13**	**4**	**11**	**15**	**14**	....	....	....	....	....
	Chicoutimi Sagueneens	QHL	14	8	9	17	....	....	....	4	10	1	*10	11	0
1957-58	Chicoutimi Sagueneens	QHL	48	20	40	60	....	....	....	32	6	0	1	1	4
1958-59	Quebec Aces	QHL	61	22	42	64	....	....	....	54	....	....	....	....	....
1959-60	Quebec Aces	AHL	72	22	39	61	....	....	....	22	....	....	....	....	....
1960-61	Quebec Aces	AHL	72	22	34	56	....	....	....	12	....	....	....	....	....
1961-62	Quebec Aces	AHL	50	3	11	14	....	....	....	18	....	....	....	....	....
1962-63	Charlotte Checkers	EHL	67	31	67	98	....	....	....	32	10	7	9	16	0
1963-64	Charlotte Checkers	EHL	57	27	56	83	....	....	....	34	3	1	2	3	0
1964-65	Charlotte–New Haven	EHL	44	23	35	58	....	....	....	78	....	....	....	....	....
	Knoxville Knights	EHL	....	....	....	....	....	....	....	....	10	4	3	7	6
1965-66	New Haven Blades	EHL	63	32	64	96	....	....	....	87	3	1	0	1	0
1966-67	New Haven Blades	EHL	68	20	55	75	....	....	....	49	....	....	....	....	....
1967-68	Florida Rockets	EHL	62	34	65	99	....	....	....	12	5	0	5	5	4
	NHL Totals		**160**	**20**	**40**	**60**	**26**	**45**	**71**	**56**	**20**	**6**	**1**	**7**	**6**

QJHL Second All-Star Team (1949) • QSHL Rookie of the Year (1950) • EHL North Second All-Star Team (1966) • Played in NHL All-Star Game (1956)

Traded to **Ottawa** (QHL) by **Toronto** for cash, October, 1952. Claimed by **Toronto** from **Ottawa** (QHL) in Inter-League Draft, June 10, 1953. Traded to **Chicago** (Buffalo-AHL) by **Toronto** with George Blair and Frank Sullivan for Brian Cullen, May 4, 1954. Traded to **Montreal** by **Buffalo** (AHL) with cash for Gaye Stewart, Eddie Slowinski and Pete Babando, August 17, 1954. Traded to **Chicoutimi** (QHL) by **Montreal** with Guy Rousseau and Jacques Deslauriers for Stan Smrke, October 27, 1957. Traded to **Florida** (EHL) by **New Haven** (EHL) for Russ McClenaghan, September, 1967.

• LEDUC, Albert "Battleship"

D – R. 5'9", 180 lbs. b: Valleyfield, Que., 11/22/1902 d: 7/31/1990.

Season	Club	League	GP	G	A	Pts	AG	AA	APts	PIM	GP	G	A	Pts	PIM
1920-21	Valleyfield Braves	MCHL	STATISTICS NOT AVAILABLE												
1921-22	University of Montreal	MCHL	STATISTICS NOT AVAILABLE												
1922-23	Quebec Aces	QCHL	STATISTICS NOT AVAILABLE												
1923-24	Montreal Hochelaga	MCHL	9	6	0	6	....	....	....	4	....	....	....	....	....
	Montreal Voltigeurs	MCHL	STATISTICS NOT AVAILABLE												
1924-25	Montreal Nationale	ECHL	11	9	0	9	....	....	....	....	....	....	....	....	....
1925-26	**Montreal Canadiens**	**NHL**	**32**	**10**	**3**	**13**	**17**	**19**	**36**	**62**	....	....	....	....	....
1926-27	**Montreal Canadiens**	**NHL**	**43**	**5**	**2**	**7**	**9**	**10**	**19**	**62**	**4**	**0**	**0**	**0**	**2**
1927-28	**Montreal Canadiens**	**NHL**	**42**	**8**	**5**	**13**	**16**	**28**	**44**	**73**	**2**	**1**	**0**	**1**	**5**
1928-29	**Montreal Canadiens**	**NHL**	**43**	**9**	**2**	**11**	**26**	**13**	**39**	**79**	**3**	**1**	**0**	**1**	**4**
♦1929-30	**Montreal Canadiens**	**NHL**	**44**	**6**	**8**	**14**	**8**	**19**	**27**	**90**	**6**	**1**	**3**	**4**	**8**
♦1930-31	**Montreal Canadiens**	**NHL**	**44**	**8**	**6**	**14**	**16**	**18**	**34**	**82**	**7**	**0**	**2**	**2**	**9**
1931-32	**Montreal Canadiens**	**NHL**	**41**	**5**	**3**	**8**	**8**	**7**	**15**	**60**	**4**	**1**	**1**	**2**	**2**
1932-33	**Montreal Canadiens**	**NHL**	**48**	**5**	**3**	**8**	**9**	**6**	**15**	**62**	**2**	**1**	**0**	**1**	**2**
1933-34	**Ottawa Senators**	**NHL**	**32**	**1**	**3**	**4**	**2**	**6**	**8**	**34**	....	....	....	....	....
	New York Rangers	**NHL**	**10**	**0**	**0**	**0**	**0**	**0**	**0**	**6**	....	....	....	....	....
1934-35	**Montreal Canadiens**	**NHL**	**4**	**0**	**0**	**0**	**0**	**0**	**0**	**4**	....	....	....	....	....
	Quebec Beavers	Can-Am	41	12	14	26	....	....	....	53	3	0	0	0	13
1935-36	Providence Reds	Can-Am	48	5	15	20	....	....	....	82	7	2	2	4	8
1936-37	Providence Reds	Can-Am	38	2	8	10	....	....	....	48	3	0	2	2	2
1937-38	Verdun Maple Leafs	QSHL	DID NOT PLAY – COACHING												
	NHL Totals		**383**	**57**	**35**	**92**	**111**	**126**	**237**	**614**	**28**	**5**	**6**	**11**	**32**

Can-Am Second All-Star Team (1936)

Signed as a free agent by **Montreal Canadiens**, April 16, 1925. Traded to **Ottawa** by **Montreal Canadiens** for cash with Montreal Canadiens retaining the rights of repurchase, October 22, 1933. Loaned to **NY Rangers** by **Ottawa** for remainder of 1933-34 season, February 15, 1934. Traded to **Montreal Canadiens** by **Ottawa** for cash, April 9, 1934. Signed as playing manager/coach of **Quebec Beavers** (Can-Am) with Montreal retaining right of recall, October 24, 1934. Traded to **Providence** (Can-Am) by **Springfield** (Can-Am) for Chris Speyer and Leo Murray and named playing-coach, October 12, 1935.

• LEE, Bobby

C – R. 5'10", 165 lbs. b: Verdun, Que., 12/28/1911 d: 12/31/1974.

Season	Club	League	GP	G	A	Pts	AG	AA	APts	PIM	GP	G	A	Pts	PIM
1929-30	Queens University	OHA-Sr.	9	3	0	3	....	....	....	0	....	....	....	....	....
1930-31	Montreal Columbus	MCJHL	9	4	0	4	....	....	....	8	....	....	....	....	....
1931-32	Queens University	OHA-Sr.	STATISTICS NOT AVAILABLE												
1932-33	Queens University	OHA-Sr.	STATISTICS NOT AVAILABLE												
1933-34	Montreal LaFontaine	MCJHL	15	6	2	8	....	....	....	10	....	....	....	....	....
1934-35	Montreal LaFontaine	MCJHL	18	9	6	15	....	....	....	24	....	....	....	....	....
	Baltimore Orioles	EAHL	4	0	1	1	....	....	....	4	9	5	2	7	4
1935-36	Baltimore Orioles	EAHL	40	19	20	39	....	....	....	45	8	4	6	10	15
1936-37	Brighton Tigers	Britain	36	32	21	53	....	....	....	22	....	....	....	....	....
1937-38	Earls Court Rangers	Ln-Cup	....	2	1	3	....	....	....	....	....	....	....	....	....
	Earls Court Rangers	Britain	....	14	8	22	....	....	....	17	....	....	....	....	....
	Earls Court Rangers	Nat-Tmt	....	6	4	10	....	....	....	....	....	....	....	....	....
1938-39	Earls Court Rangers	Ln-Cup	....	2	2	4	....	....	....	....	....	....	....	....	....
	Earls Court Rangers	Britain	....	13	19	32	....	....	....	....	....	....	....	....	....
	Earls Court Rangers	Nat-Tmt	....	4	4	8	....	....	....	....	....	....	....	....	....
1939-40	Quebec Aces	QSHL	30	8	13	21	....	....	....	27	....	....	....	....	....
1940-41	Quebec Aces	QSHL	36	14	24	38	....	....	....	15	4	3	1	4	2
1941-42	Quebec Aces	QSHL	40	20	30	50	....	....	....	10	7	0	7	7	2
	Quebec Aces	Al-Cup	8	5	*8	*13	....	....	....	4	....	....	....	....	....
1942-43	**Montreal Canadiens**	**NHL**	**1**	**0**	**0**	**0**	**0**	**0**	**0**	**0**	....	....	....	....	....
	Montreal Royals	QSHL	33	14	20	34	....	....	....	26	4	1	0	1	2
	Montreal RCAF	MCHL	....	....	....	....	....	....	....	....	5	2	2	4	4
1943-44	Montreal RCAF	MCHL	7	1	4	5	....	....	....	2	....	....	....	....	....
	Montreal Canada Car	MCHL	6	1	10	11	....	....	....	2	....	....	....	....	....
	Montreal RCAF	MCHL	8	8	12	20	....	....	....	4	4	4	7	11	6
1944-45	Toronto RCAF	Scotland	STATISTICS NOT AVAILABLE												
1945-46	Wembley Lions	Britain	STATISTICS NOT AVAILABLE												
1946-47	Brighton Tigers	Ln-Cup	2	3	2	5	....	....	....	0	....	....	....	....	....
	Brighton Tigers	A-Cup	12	19	9	28	....	....	....	4	....	....	....	....	....
	Brighton Tigers	Britain	36	57	*54	*111	....	....	....	22	2	3	2	5	8
	Brighton Tigers	Nat-Tmt	6	9	10	19	....	....	....	4	....	....	....	....	....
1947-48	Brighton Tigers	A-Cup	10	7	11	18	....	....	....	4	....	....	....	....	....
	Brighton Tigers	Britain	36	45	41	86	....	....	....	22	....	....	....	....	....
	Brighton Tigers	Nat-Tmt	12	11	7	18	....	....	....	7	....	....	....	....	....
1948-49	Brighton Tigers	A-Cup	11	17	4	21	....	....	....	8	....	....	....	....	....
	Brighton Tigers	Britain	28	20	31	51	....	....	....	12	....	....	....	....	....
	Brighton Tigers	Nat-Tmt	14	19	18	37	....	....	....	8	....	....	....	....	....
1949-50	Brighton Tigers	A-Cup	35	33	39	72	....	....	....	12	....	....	....	....	....
	Brighton Tigers	Britain	9	2	8	10	....	....	....	2	....	....	....	....	....
	Brighton Tigers	Nat-Tmt	8	3	4	7	....	....	....	6	....	....	....	....	....
1950-51	Brighton Tigers	A-Cup	30	29	24	53	....	....	....	16	....	....	....	....	....
	Brighton Tigers	Britain	30	12	13	25	....	....	....	2	....	....	....	....	....
1951-52	Brighton Tigers	A-Cup	30	14	12	26	....	....	....	16	....	....	....	....	....
	Brighton Tigers	Britain	30	22	15	37	....	....	....	10	....	....	....	....	....
1952-53	Brighton Tigers	A-Cup	30	12	10	22	....	....	....	30	....	....	....	....	....
	Brighton Tigers	Britain	30	8	7	15	....	....	....	6	....	....	....	....	....

Season	Club	League	GP	G	A	Pts	AG	AA	APts	PIM	GP	G	A	Pts	PIM
			REGULAR SEASON								PLAYOFFS				
1953-54	Brighton Tigers	A-Cup	21	20	15	35	....	....	....	10	....	....	....	....	....
	Brighton Tigers	Britain	24	23	25	48	....	....	....	14	....	....	....	....	....
	Brighton Tigers	Ln-Cup	12	13	17	30	....	....	....	10	....	....	....	....	....
	NHL Totals		**1**	**0**	**0**	**0**	**0**	**0**	**0**	**0**	....	....	....	....	....

Won John Carlin Trophy (Top Scorer - EHL) (1936)

• LEGER, Roger

D – R. 5'11", 200 lbs. b: L'Annonciation, Que., 3/26/1919 d: 4/7/1965.

Season	Club	League	GP	G	A	Pts	AG	AA	APts	PIM	GP	G	A	Pts	PIM
1940-41	Joliette Cyclones	MCHL	26	19	28	47	....	....	....	22	4	4	3	7	6
1941-42	Joliette Cyclones	MCHL	30	29	24	53	....	....	....	62	....	....	....	....	....
1942-43			MILITARY SERVICE												
1943-44	**New York Rangers**	**NHL**	**7**	**1**	**2**	**3**	**1**	**2**	**3**	**2**	....	....	....	....	....
	New York Rovers	EAHL	3	4	1	5	....	....	....	4	....	....	....	....	....
	Buffalo Bisons	AHL	29	7	17	24	....	....	....	10	9	6	7	13	4
1944-45	Buffalo Bisons	AHL	54	19	36	55	....	....	....	36	6	0	4	4	12
1945-46	Buffalo Bisons	AHL	57	22	35	57	....	....	....	41	12	1	8	9	4
1946-47	**Montreal Canadiens**	**NHL**	**49**	**4**	**18**	**22**	**4**	**22**	**26**	**12**	**11**	**0**	**6**	**6**	**10**
	Buffalo Bisons	AHL	10	2	3	5	....	....	....	8	....	....	....	....	....
1947-48	**Montreal Canadiens**	**NHL**	**48**	**4**	**14**	**18**	**5**	**18**	**23**	**26**	....	....	....	....	....
1948-49	**Montreal Canadiens**	**NHL**	**28**	**6**	**7**	**13**	**8**	**10**	**18**	**10**	**5**	**0**	**1**	**1**	**2**
	Buffalo Bisons	AHL	10	1	2	3	....	....	....	6	....	....	....	....	....
	Dallas Texans	USHL	12	3	5	8	....	....	....	12	....	....	....	....	....
1949-50	**Montreal Canadiens**	**NHL**	**55**	**3**	**12**	**15**	**4**	**14**	**18**	**21**	**4**	**0**	**0**	**0**	**2**
	Cincinnati Mohawks	AHL	11	4	4	8	....	....	....	2	....	....	....	....	....
1950-51	Victoria Cougars	PCHL	68	17	43	60	....	....	....	84	12	1	4	5	8
1951-52	Victoria Cougars	PCHL	70	16	47	63	....	....	....	68	13	2	9	11	14
1952-53	Montreal Royals	QMHL	60	5	30	35	....	....	....	22	16	2	7	9	15
1953-54	Montreal Royals	QHL	61	8	29	37	....	....	....	50	11	1	5	6	2
1954-55	Shawinigan Cataracts	QHL	59	2	29	31	....	....	....	83	11	1	9	10	6
	Shawinigan Cataracts	Ed-Cup	7	2	3	5	....	....	....	4	....	....	....	....	....
1955-56	Shawinigan Cataracts	QHL	45	4	17	21	....	....	....	29	10	0	0	0	0
	NHL Totals		**187**	**18**	**53**	**71**	**22**	**66**	**88**	**71**	**20**	**0**	**7**	**7**	**14**

AHL First All-Star Team (1945, 1946) • PCHL First All-Star Team (1951, 1952) • MVP - PCHL (1951) • QMHL First All-Star Team (1953) • QHL First All-Star Team (1954)

Signed as a free agent by **NY Rangers**, November 23, 1943. Traded to **Montreal** (Buffalo-AHL) by **NY Rangers** with the loan of Gord Davidson for Bob Dill, January 4, 1944. Traded to **Victoria** (WHL) by **Montreal** for cash and named playing-coach, September 16, 1950.

• LEIER, Edward

C – R. 5'11", 175 lbs. b: 11/3/1927.

Season	Club	League	GP	G	A	Pts	AG	AA	APts	PIM	GP	G	A	Pts	PIM
1945-46	Winnipeg Rangers	MAHA	STATISTICS NOT AVAILABLE												
1946-47	Winnipeg Rangers	MJHL	15	16	8	24	....	....	....	0	2	2	0	2	0
1947-48	Winnipeg Black Hawks	MJHL	19	12	10	22	....	....	....	2	....	....	....	....	....
	Winnipeg Nationals	WSrHL	2	3	2	5	....	....	....	0	....	....	....	....	....
1948-49	Saskatoon Quakers	WCSHL	25	3	17	20	....	....	....	4	....	....	....	....	....
1949-50	**Chicago Black Hawks**	**NHL**	**5**	**0**	**1**	**1**	**0**	**1**	**1**	**0**	....	....	....	....	....
	Kansas City Mohawks	USHL	59	19	21	40	....	....	....	2	3	1	1	2	0
1950-51	**Chicago Black Hawks**	**NHL**	**11**	**2**	**0**	**2**	**3**	**0**	**3**	**2**	....	....	....	....	....
	Milwaukee Seagulls	USHL	17	6	4	10	....	....	....	6	....	....	....	....	....
1951-52	Vancouver Canucks	PCHL	61	18	37	55	....	....	....	2	....	....	....	....	....
1952-53	Vancouver Canucks	WHL	59	10	27	37	....	....	....	9	9	1	1	2	0
1953-54	Springfield Indians	QHL	56	14	27	41	....	....	....	10	....	....	....	....	....
	Syracuse Warriors	AHL	17	5	6	11	....	....	....	2	....	....	....	....	....
1954-55	Springfield Indians	AHL	59	14	46	60	....	....	....	8	4	0	2	2	0
1955-56	Springfield Indians	AHL	62	9	48	57	....	....	....	14	....	....	....	....	....
	NHL Totals		**16**	**2**	**1**	**3**	**3**	**1**	**4**	**2**	....	....	....	....	....

MJHL Second All-Star Team (1948)

Signed as a free agent by **Saskatoon** (WCSHL), September 29, 1948.

• LEITER, Bobby

— *see page 1324*

• LEMIEUX, Real

— *see page 1328*

• LEPINE, Hec

Hector Theodule

C – R. 5'11", 185 lbs. b: St. Anne de Bellevue, Que., 12/7/1897 d: 3/29/1951.

Season	Club	League	GP	G	A	Pts	AG	AA	APts	PIM	GP	G	A	Pts	PIM
1917-18	Montreal La Casquette	MCHL	8	3	0	3	....	....	....	9	....	....	....	....	....
1918-19	Montreal Garnets	MCHL	6	0	0	0	....	....	....	0	....	....	....	....	....
1919/22	Ste-Anne de Bellevue	QIHA	STATISTICS NOT AVAILABLE												
1922-23	Montreal Sr. Royals	MCHL	4	14	0	14	....	....	....	....	....	....	....	....	....
1923-24	Montreal Hochelaga	MCHL	7	*15	0	*15	....	....	....	0	....	....	....	....	....
1924-25	Montreal Nationale	ECHL	3	2	0	2	....	....	....	0	....	....	....	....	....
	Fort Pitt Hornets	CHL	21	11	0	11	....	....	....	....	8	1	0	1	....
1925-26	**Montreal Canadiens**	**NHL**	**33**	**5**	**2**	**7**	**9**	**13**	**22**	**2**	....	....	....	....	....
1926-27	Providence Reds	Can-Am	28	6	1	7	....	....	....	28	....	....	....	....	....
1927-28			DID NOT PLAY – REFEREE												
	NHL Totals		**33**	**5**	**2**	**7**	**9**	**13**	**22**	**2**	....	....	....	....	....

• Brother of Alfred (Pit)

Signed as a free agent by **Montreal Canadiens**, December 29, 1925.

• LEPINE, Pit

Alfred Pierre

C – L. 5'11", 168 lbs. b: St. Anne de Bellevue, Que., 7/30/1901 d: 8/2/1955.

Season	Club	League	GP	G	A	Pts	AG	AA	APts	PIM	GP	G	A	Pts	PIM
1922-23	Montreal Royals	MCHL	4	2	0	2	....	....	....	....	....	....	....	....	....
	Montreal Shamrocks	MCHL	1	1	0	1	....	....	....	....	....	....	....	....	....
1923-24	Montreal Hochelaga	MCHL	9	3	0	3	....	....	....	2	....	....	....	....	....
1924-25	Montreal Nationale	ECHL	15	8	0	8	....	....	....	....	....	....	....	....	....
1925-26	**Montreal Canadiens**	**NHL**	**27**	**9**	**1**	**10**	**15**	**6**	**21**	**18**	....	....	....	....	....
	Montreal Nationale	ECHL	3	2	0	2	....	....	....	0	....	....	....	....	....
1926-27	**Montreal Canadiens**	**NHL**	**44**	**16**	**1**	**17**	**29**	**5**	**34**	**20**	**4**	**0**	**0**	**0**	**4**
1927-28	**Montreal Canadiens**	**NHL**	**20**	**4**	**1**	**5**	**8**	**6**	**14**	**6**	**1**	**0**	**0**	**0**	**0**
1928-29	**Montreal Canadiens**	**NHL**	**44**	**6**	**1**	**7**	**17**	**7**	**24**	**48**	**3**	**0**	**0**	**0**	**2**
♦1929-30	**Montreal Canadiens**	**NHL**	**44**	**24**	**9**	**33**	**34**	**21**	**55**	**47**	**6**	**2**	**2**	**4**	**6**
♦1930-31	**Montreal Canadiens**	**NHL**	**44**	**17**	**7**	**24**	**34**	**21**	**55**	**63**	**10**	**4**	**2**	**6**	**6**
1931-32	**Montreal Canadiens**	**NHL**	**48**	**19**	**11**	**30**	**32**	**24**	**56**	**42**	**3**	**1**	**0**	**1**	**4**
1932-33	**Montreal Canadiens**	**NHL**	**46**	**8**	**8**	**16**	**14**	**17**	**31**	**45**	**2**	**0**	**0**	**0**	**2**
1933-34	**Montreal Canadiens**	**NHL**	**48**	**10**	**8**	**18**	**17**	**17**	**34**	**44**	**2**	**0**	**0**	**0**	**0**
1934-35	**Montreal Canadiens**	**NHL**	**48**	**12**	**19**	**31**	**20**	**33**	**53**	**16**	**2**	**0**	**0**	**0**	**2**
1935-36	**Montreal Canadiens**	**NHL**	**32**	**6**	**10**	**16**	**11**	**19**	**30**	**4**	....	....	....	....	....
1936-37	**Montreal Canadiens**	**NHL**	**34**	**7**	**8**	**15**	**12**	**15**	**27**	**15**	**5**	**0**	**1**	**1**	**0**
1937-38	**Montreal Canadiens**	**NHL**	**47**	**5**	**14**	**19**	**8**	**23**	**31**	**24**	**3**	**0**	**0**	**0**	**0**
1938-39	New Haven Eagles	IAHL	52	8	23	31	....	....	....	16	....	....	....	....	....
1939-40	**Montreal Canadiens**	**NHL**	DID NOT PLAY – COACHING												
	NHL Totals		**526**	**143**	**98**	**241**	**251**	**214**	**465**	**392**	**41**	**7**	**5**	**12**	**26**

• Brother of Hec • Played in NHL All-Star Game (1937)

Signed as a free agent by **Montreal Canadiens**, November 13, 1925.

• LEROUX, Gaston

"Gus"

D – R. 6', 195 lbs. b: Montreal, Que., 1/9/1913.

Season	Club	League	GP	G	A	Pts	AG	AA	APts	PIM	GP	G	A	Pts	PIM
1930-31	Montreal Sr. Canadiens	MCHL	7	0	0	0	....	....	....	2	....	....	....	....	....
1931-32	St. Francois Xavier	MCHL	STATISTICS NOT AVAILABLE												
	Montreal Nationale	MBHL	STATISTICS NOT AVAILABLE												
1932-33	Montreal Nationale	MBHL	STATISTICS NOT AVAILABLE												
1933-34	Quebec Beavers	Can-Am	8	0	0	0	....	....	....	0	....	....	....	....	....
	Montreal LaFontaine	MCHL	14	4	2	6	....	....	....	11	....	....	....	....	....
1934-35	Cleveland Falcons	IHL	42	2	6	8	....	....	....	15	2	0	0	0	0
1935-36	**Montreal Canadiens**	**NHL**	**2**	**0**	**0**	**0**	**0**	**0**	**0**	**0**	....	....	....	....	....
	Windsor Bulldogs	IHL	12	1	1	2	....	....	....	2	7	0	0	0	0
	Springfield Indians	Can-Am	23	1	3	4	....	....	....	20	....	....	....	....	....
1936-37	Sherbrooke Red Raiders	QPHL	STATISTICS NOT AVAILABLE												
1937-38	Sherbrooke Red Raiders	QPHL	21	8	5	13	....	....	....	5	9	1	4	5	8
1938-39	Sherbrooke Red Raiders	QPHL	35	3	5	8	....	....	....	8	5	0	1	1	2
	NHL Totals		**2**	**0**	**0**	**0**	**0**	**0**	**0**	**0**	....	....	....	....	....

Signed as a free agent by **Montreal Canadiens**, October 24, 1935.

• LESIEUR, Art

D – R. 5'11", 191 lbs. b: Fall River, MA, 9/13/1907.

Season	Club	League	GP	G	A	Pts	AG	AA	APts	PIM	GP	G	A	Pts	PIM
1927-28	Nashua Nationals	NEHL	23	3	2	5	....	....	....	20	4	1	*2	*3	6
	Providence Reds	Can-Am	1	0	0	0	....	....	....	2	....	....	....	....	....
1928-29	**Montreal Canadiens**	**NHL**	**15**	**0**	**0**	**0**	**0**	**0**	**0**	**0**	....	....	....	....	....
	Chicago Black Hawks	**NHL**	**2**	**0**	**0**	**0**	**0**	**0**	**0**	**0**	....	....	....	....	....
	Providence Reds	Can-Am	16	1	0	1	....	....	....	16	4	0	0	0	2
1929-30	Providence Reds	Can-Am	40	3	0	3	....	....	....	57	3	0	0	0	4
♦1930-31	**Montreal Canadiens**	**NHL**	**21**	**2**	**0**	**2**	**4**	**0**	**4**	**14**	**10**	**0**	**0**	**0**	**4**
	Providence Reds	Can-Am	19	3	3	6	....	....	....	26	....	....	....	....	....
1931-32	**Montreal Canadiens**	**NHL**	**24**	**1**	**2**	**3**	**2**	**4**	**6**	**12**	**4**	**0**	**0**	**0**	**0**
	Providence Reds	Can-Am	18	4	3	7	....	....	....	35	....	....	....	....	....
1932-33	Providence Reds	Can-Am	25	1	3	4	....	....	....	34	....	....	....	....	....
1933-34	Providence Reds	Can-Am	40	2	1	3	....	....	....	68	3	0	1	1	8
1934-35	Providence Reds	Can-Am	47	5	9	14	....	....	....	80	6	1	0	1	10
1935-36	**Montreal Canadiens**	**NHL**	**38**	**1**	**0**	**1**	**2**	**0**	**2**	**24**	....	....	....	....	....
1936-37	Providence Reds	IAHL	51	3	7	10	....	....	....	54	3	0	0	0	2
1937-38	Providence Reds	IAHL	47	6	10	16	....	....	....	36	7	0	1	1	8
1938-39	Providence Reds	IAHL	54	5	7	12	....	....	....	53	5	0	0	0	4
1939-40	Providence Reds	IAHL	54	6	7	13	....	....	....	26	8	0	0	0	4
1940-41	Pittsburgh Hornets	AHL	32	2	0	2	....	....	....	22	....	....	....	....	....
	NHL Totals		**100**	**4**	**2**	**6**	**8**	**4**	**12**	**50**	**14**	**0**	**0**	**0**	**4**

NEHL First All-Star Team (1928) • IAHL Second All-Star Team (1938, 1939)

Signed as a free agent by **Montreal Canadiens**, October 30, 1928. Loaned to **Chicago** by **Montreal Canadiens** for the remainder of the 1928-29 season for the loan of Herb Gardiner, January 9, 1929. Traded to **Montreal Canadiens** by **Providence** (Can-Am) for cash and future considerations, September 30, 1935. Traded to **Pittsburgh** (AHL) by **Montreal** (Providence-AHL) for Babe Tapin, October 15, 1940.

• LESWICK, Jack

"Newsy"

C – R. 5'6", 155 lbs. b: Saskatoon, Sask., 1/1/1910 d: 8/7/1934.

Season	Club	League	GP	G	A	Pts	AG	AA	APts	PIM	GP	G	A	Pts	PIM
1929-30	Drumheller Miners	ASHL	11	14	5	19	....	....	....	15	....	....	....	....	....
	Duluth Hornets	AHA	13	1	1	2	....	....	....	6	3	0	0	0	4
1930-31	Duluth Hornets	AHA	41	22	9	31	....	....	....	27	4	0	1	1	4
1931-32	Duluth Hornets	AHA	34	9	7	16	....	....	....	36	8	0	*5	5	4
1932-33	Duluth-Wichita	AHA	41	*22	18	*40	....	....	....	76	....	....	....	....	....
1933-34	**Chicago Black Hawks**	**NHL**	**37**	**1**	**7**	**8**	**2**	**15**	**17**	**16**	....	....	....	....	....
	Kansas City Greyhounds	AHA	8	1	5	6	....	....	....	14	....	....	....	....	....
	NHL Totals		**37**	**1**	**7**	**8**	**2**	**15**	**17**	**16**	....	....	....	....	....

• Brother of Pete and Tony

Signed as a free agent by **Chicago** (Duluth-AHA), January, 1930.

• LESWICK, Pete

Peter John

W – R. 5'7", 163 lbs. b: Saskatoon, Sask., 7/12/1918.

Season	Club	League	GP	G	A	Pts	AG	AA	APts	PIM	GP	G	A	Pts	PIM
1933-34	Saskatoon Wesleys	S-SJHL	4	0	2	2	....	....	....	0	9	3	0	3	6
1934-35	Saskatoon Nutuna	S-SJHL	4	5	1	6	....	....	....	10	13	*20	*10	*30	2
1935-36	Saskatoon Wesleys	N-SSHL	5	4	1	5	....	....	....	0	....	....	....	....	....
	Saskatoon Wesleys	M-Cup	11	*17	*10	*27	....	....	....	2	....	....	....	....	....
1936-37	**New York Americans**	**NHL**	**1**	**1**	**0**	**1**	**2**	**0**	**2**	**0**	....	....	....	....	....
	New Haven Eagles	IAHL	19	4	3	7	....	....	....	0	....	....	....	....	....
1937-38	Seattle Seahawks	PCHL	42	20	10	30	....	....	....	22	3	0	0	0	2
1938-39	Kansas City Greyhounds	AHA	25	12	13	25	....	....	....	10	....	....	....	....	....
	Spokane Clippers	PCHL	20	7	3	10	....	....	....	9	....	....	....	....	....
1939-40	Kansas City Greyhounds	AHA	45	14	18	32	....	....	....	17	....	....	....	....	....
1940-41	Kansas City Americans	AHA	45	14	22	36	....	....	....	16	8	2	4	6	0
1941-42	Fort Worth Rangers	AHA	50	35	30	65	....	....	....	17	5	1	4	5	2
1942-43	Vancouver St. Regis	PCHL	3	6	1	7	....	....	....	2	5	3	2	5	4
1943-44	Portland Decleros	NWIHL	5	16	2	18	....	....	....	8	....	....	....	....	....
	New West-Lodestars	PCHL	19	25	11	36	....	....	....	10	2	0	*2	*2	0
	New West-Lodestars	Al-Cup	18	15	21	36	....	....	....	12	....	....	....	....	....
1944-45	**Boston Bruins**	**NHL**	**2**	**0**	**0**	**0**	**0**	**0**	**0**	**0**	....	....	....	....	....
	Indianapolis Capitols	AHL	53	29	39	68	....	....	....	12	3	1	0	1	0
1945-46	Indianapolis Capitols	AHL	61	29	52	81	....	....	....	10	5	1	1	2	0
1946-47	Cleveland Barons	AHL	64	32	41	73	....	....	....	35	4	1	1	2	0
1947-48	Cleveland Barons	AHL	59	36	40	76	....	....	....	8	6	2	4	6	2
1948-49	Cleveland Barons	AHL	68	44	35	79	....	....	....	10	5	0	2	2	0

Season	Club	League	GP	G	A	Pts	AG	AA	APts	PIM	GP	G	A	Pts	PIM
			REGULAR SEASON								PLAYOFFS				
1949-50	Cleveland Barons	AHL	64	36	50	86	....	....	....	18	9	2	2	4	0
1950-51	Buffalo Bisons	AHL	11	6	5	11	....	....	....	0	....	....	....	....	....
	Seattle Ironmen	PCHL	49	14	21	35	....	....	....	6	....	....	....	....	....
1951-52	Halifax St. Mary's	MMHL	70	32	36	68	....	....	....	6	9	3	4	7	4
	NHL Totals		**3**	**1**	**0**	**1**	**2**	**0**	**2**	**0**	....	....	....	....	....

• Brother of Jack and Tony • AHA First All-Star Team (1942) • AHL Second All-Star Team (1945, 1947) • AHL First All-Star Team (1946, 1948, 1949, 1950)

Signed as a free agent by **NY Americans**, October 15, 1935. Signed as a free agent by **Boston**, October 12, 1944. Traded to **Detroit** by **Boston** for Bill Jennings, October 30, 1944. Traded to **Cleveland** (AHL) by **Detroit** for cash, September 10, 1946. Traded to **Montreal** (Buffalo-AHL) by **Cleveland** (AHL) for Murdo MacKay, August 4, 1950.

• LESWICK, Tony

Anthony Joseph "Mighty Mouse"
W – R. 5'7", 160 lbs. b: Humboldt, Sask., 3/17/1923.

Season	Club	League	GP	G	A	Pts	AG	AA	APts	PIM	GP	G	A	Pts	PIM
1939-40	Saskatoon Dodgers	N-SJHL	4	5	2	7	....	....	....	13	2	4	1	5	0
1940-41	Saskatoon Jr. Quakers	N-SJHL	11	15	10	25	....	....	....	34	2	1	*6	*7	2
	Saskatoon Quakers	S-SSHL	1	0	0	0	....	....	....	2	....	....	....	....	....
	Saskatoon Jr. Quakers	M-Cup	12	7	4	11	....	....	....	14	....	....	....	....	....
1941-42	Saskatoon Quakers	S-SSHL	32	21	21	42	....	....	....	45	9	3	5	8	4
	Saskatoon Quakers	Al-Cup	5	2	3	5	....	....	....	4	....	....	....	....	....
1942-43	Cleveland Barons	AHL	52	14	26	40	....	....	....	43	4	3	3	6	4
	Victoria VMD	NNDHL	2	0	2	2	....	....	....	0	....	....	....	....	....
1943-44	Saskatoon Navy	S-SSHL	18	26	*26	52	....	....	....	*50	4	3	2	5	18
	New Westminster Royals	NWIHL	19	25	11	36	....	....	....	10	2	0	2	2	0
1944-45	Winnipeg Navy	WNDHL	12	9	8	17	....	....	....	*33	6	7	2	9	12
1945-46	**New York Rangers**	**NHL**	**50**	**15**	**9**	**24**	**18**	**13**	**31**	**26**	....	....	....	....	....
1946-47	**New York Rangers**	**NHL**	**59**	**27**	**14**	**41**	**31**	**17**	**48**	**51**	....	....	....	....	....
1947-48	**New York Rangers**	**NHL**	**60**	**24**	**16**	**40**	**31**	**21**	**52**	**76**	**6**	**3**	**2**	**5**	**8**
1948-49	**New York Rangers**	**NHL**	**60**	**13**	**14**	**27**	**18**	**20**	**38**	**70**	....	....	....	....	....
1949-50	**New York Rangers**	**NHL**	**69**	**19**	**25**	**44**	**24**	**30**	**54**	**85**	**12**	**2**	**4**	**6**	**12**
1950-51	**New York Rangers**	**NHL**	**70**	**15**	**11**	**26**	**19**	**13**	**32**	**112**	....	....	....	....	....
♦1951-52	**Detroit Red Wings**	**NHL**	**70**	**9**	**10**	**19**	**12**	**12**	**24**	**93**	**8**	**3**	**1**	**4**	**22**
1952-53	**Detroit Red Wings**	**NHL**	**70**	**15**	**12**	**27**	**20**	**14**	**34**	**87**	**6**	**1**	**0**	**1**	**11**
♦1953-54	**Detroit Red Wings**	**NHL**	**70**	**6**	**18**	**24**	**8**	**22**	**30**	**90**	**12**	**3**	**1**	**4**	**18**
♦1954-55	**Detroit Red Wings**	**NHL**	**70**	**10**	**17**	**27**	**13**	**19**	**32**	**137**	**11**	**1**	**2**	**3**	**20**
1955-56	**Chicago Black Hawks**	**NHL**	**70**	**11**	**11**	**22**	**15**	**13**	**28**	**71**	....	....	....	....	....
1956-57	Edmonton Flyers	WHL	60	22	31	53	....	....	....	107	8	2	1	3	6
1957-58	**Detroit Red Wings**	**NHL**	**22**	**1**	**2**	**3**	**1**	**2**	**3**	**2**	**4**	**0**	**0**	**0**	**0**
	Edmonton Flyers	WHL	42	10	15	25	....	....	....	46	....	....	....	....	....
1958-59	Edmonton Flyers	WHL	36	3	13	16	....	....	....	27	....	....	....	....	....
1959-60	Vancouver Canucks	WHL	9	3	6	9	....	....	....	0	11	0	1	1	0
	NHL Totals		**740**	**165**	**159**	**324**	**210**	**196**	**406**	**900**	**59**	**13**	**10**	**23**	**91**

• Brother of Jack and Pete • NHL Second All-Star Team (1950) • WHL Prairie Division Second All-Star Team (1957) • Played in NHL All-Star Game (1947, 1948, 1949, 1950, 1952, 1954)

Claimed by **NY Rangers** from **Buffalo** (AHL) in Inter-League Draft, June 14, 1945. Traded to **Detroit** by **NY Rangers** for Gaye Stewart, June 8, 1951. Traded to **Chicago** by **Detroit** with Glen Skov, John Wilson and Benny Woit for Jerry Toppazzini, John McCormack, Dave Creighton and Gord Hollingworth, May 28, 1955. Traded to **Detroit** by **Chicago** for cash, August 1, 1956.

• LEVANDOSKI, Joe

Joseph Thomas
RW – R. 5'11", 185 lbs. b: Cobalt, Ont., 3/17/1921.

Season	Club	League	GP	G	A	Pts	AG	AA	APts	PIM	GP	G	A	Pts	PIM
1939-40	Kirkland Lake Gales	GBHL	STATISTICS NOT AVAILABLE												
1940-41	Guelph Biltmores	OHA-Jr.	16	8	6	14	....	....	....	2	5	2	1	3	0
1941-42	Rivervale Skeeters	EAHL	55	26	27	53	....	....	....	51	7	9	4	13	0
1942-43	New Haven Eagles	AHL	28	8	9	17	....	....	....	10	....	....	....	....	....
	Hershey Bears	AHL	24	9	14	23	....	....	....	21	6	2	0	2	0
1943-44	Petawawa Grenades	UOVHL	6	0	3	3	....	....	....	4	....	....	....	....	....
1944-45	Petawawa Engineers	OVDHL	STATISTICS NOT AVAILABLE												
1945-46	St. Paul Saints	USHL	55	12	23	35	....	....	....	23	6	1	0	1	4
1946-47	**New York Rangers**	**NHL**	**8**	**1**	**1**	**2**	**1**	**1**	**2**	**0**	....	....	....	....	....
	New Haven Ramblers	AHL	47	10	12	22	....	....	....	47	3	2	0	2	2
1947-48	St. Paul Saints	USHL	56	20	24	44	....	....	....	41	....	....	....	....	....
1948-49	St. Paul Saints	USHL	36	9	13	22	....	....	....	40	....	....	....	....	....
	Buffalo Bisons	AHL	23	6	8	14	....	....	....	6	....	....	....	....	....
1949-50	St. Paul Saints	USHL	61	12	15	27	....	....	....	44	3	1	1	2	4
1950-51	Kansas City Royals	USHL	64	9	31	40	....	....	....	108	....	....	....	....	....
1951-52	Sydney Millionaires	MMHL	81	17	26	43	....	....	....	85	....	....	....	....	....
1952-53	Calgary Stampeders	WHL	70	7	21	28	....	....	....	79	5	1	4	5	0
1953-54	Providence Reds	AHL	61	2	5	7	....	....	....	62	....	....	....	....	....
	Sherbrooke Saints	QHL	....	....	....	....	....	....	....	....	2	1	0	1	0
1954-55	Providence Reds	AHL	16	1	3	4	....	....	....	18	....	....	....	....	....
	Quebec Aces	QHL	36	2	11	13	....	....	....	42	8	0	2	2	12
1955-56	Quebec Aces	QHL	8	0	3	3	....	....	....	23	....	....	....	....	....
	Kingston Goodyears	EOHL	27	8	23	31	....	....	....	80	14	1	11	12	29
1956-57	Kingston CKLC's	EOHL	37	3	8	11	....	....	....	50	5	0	1	1	18
1957-58	Kingston CKLC's	EOHL	49	7	23	30	....	....	....	60	7	0	2	2	20
1958-59	Kingston Merchants	EOHL	12	2	0	2	....	....	....	12	....	....	....	....	....
	NHL Totals		**8**	**1**	**1**	**2**	**1**	**1**	**2**	**0**	....	....	....	....	....

USHL Second All-Star Team (1951)

Traded to **Calgary** (WHL) by **NY Rangers** for cash, September 22, 1952. Traded to **Quebec** (QHL) by **Providence** (AHL) for Pierre Brilliant, December 5, 1954.

• LEVINSKY, Alex

"Mine Boy"
D – R. 5'10", 184 lbs. b: Syracuse, NY, 2/2/1910 d: 1990.

Season	Club	League	GP	G	A	Pts	AG	AA	APts	PIM	GP	G	A	Pts	PIM
1928-29	Toronto Marlboros	OHA-Jr.	8	4	1	5	....	....	....	....	3	0	*4	4	....
	Toronto Marlboros	M-Cup	12	2	5	7	....	....	....	20	....	....	....	....	....
1929-30	University of Toronto	OHA-Jr.	9	4	1	5	....	....	....	20	3	1	1	2	8
1930-31	Toronto Marlboros	OHA-Jr.	10	3	0	3	....	....	....	16	3	0	0	0	8
	Toronto Maple Leafs	**NHL**	**8**	**0**	**1**	**1**	**0**	**3**	**3**	**2**	**2**	**0**	**0**	**0**	**0**
♦1931-32	**Toronto Maple Leafs**	**NHL**	**47**	**5**	**5**	**10**	**8**	**11**	**19**	**29**	**7**	**0**	**0**	**0**	**6**
1932-33	**Toronto Maple Leafs**	**NHL**	**48**	**1**	**4**	**5**	**2**	**8**	**10**	**61**	**9**	**1**	**0**	**1**	**14**
1933-34	**Toronto Maple Leafs**	**NHL**	**47**	**5**	**11**	**16**	**9**	**23**	**32**	**38**	**5**	**0**	**0**	**0**	**6**
1934-35	**New York Rangers**	**NHL**	**20**	**0**	**4**	**4**	**0**	**7**	**7**	**6**	....	....	....	....	....
	Chicago Black Hawks	**NHL**	**23**	**3**	**4**	**7**	**5**	**7**	**12**	**16**	**2**	**0**	**0**	**0**	**0**
1935-36	**Chicago Black Hawks**	**NHL**	**48**	**1**	**7**	**8**	**2**	**13**	**15**	**69**	**2**	**0**	**1**	**1**	**0**
1936-37	**Chicago Black Hawks**	**NHL**	**48**	**0**	**8**	**8**	**0**	**15**	**15**	**32**	....	....	....	....	....
♦1937-38	**Chicago Black Hawks**	**NHL**	**48**	**3**	**2**	**5**	**5**	**3**	**8**	**18**	**10**	**1**	**0**	**1**	**0**
1938-39	**Chicago Black Hawks**	**NHL**	**30**	**1**	**3**	**4**	**2**	**5**	**7**	**36**	....	....	....	....	....
	Philadelphia Ramblers	IAHL	17	4	5	9	....	....	....	2	9	0	4	4	4
1939-40	Philadelphia Ramblers	IAHL	53	3	13	16	....	....	....	22	....	....	....	....	....
	NHL Totals		**367**	**19**	**49**	**68**	**33**	**95**	**128**	**307**	**37**	**2**	**1**	**3**	**26**

Played in NHL All-Star Game (1934)

Signed as a free agent by **Toronto**, March 2, 1931. Traded to **NY Rangers** by **Toronto** for cash, April 11, 1934. Traded to **Chicago** by **NY Rangers** for cash, January 16, 1935. Traded to **NY Rangers** by **Chicago** with $5,000 for Joe Cooper, January 16, 1939.

• LEWICKI, Danny

Daniel "Dashin' Danny"
LW – L. 5'8", 147 lbs. b: Fort William, Ont., 3/12/1931.

Season	Club	League	GP	G	A	Pts	AG	AA	APts	PIM	GP	G	A	Pts	PIM
1945-46	Fort William K of C	TBJHL	3	1	1	2	....	....	....	2	....	....	....	....	....
1946-47	Fort William K of C	TBJHL	16	*14	4	*18	....	....	....	4	4	*7	3	10	0
	Fort William K of C	M-Cup	4	1	3	4	....	....	....	4	....	....	....	....	....
1947-48	Fort William K of C	TBJHL	9	*19	7	26	....	....	....	14	7	*12	7	*19	8
	Port Arthur Bruins	M-Cup	17	*21	19	*40	....	....	....	15	....	....	....	....	....
1948-49	Stratford Kroehlers	OHA-Jr.	29	24	24	48	....	....	....	52	3	2	4	6	0
1949-50	Toronto Marlboros	OHA-Jr.	32	36	36	72	....	....	....	62	5	1	4	5	10
	Toronto Marlboros	OHA-Sr.	....	....	....	....	....	....	....	....	4	2	2	4	2
	Toronto Marlboros	Al-Cup	17	*22	*20	*42	....	....	....	32	....	....	....	....	....
♦1950-51	**Toronto Maple Leafs**	**NHL**	**61**	**16**	**18**	**34**	**20**	**22**	**42**	**26**	**9**	**0**	**0**	**0**	**0**
1951-52	**Toronto Maple Leafs**	**NHL**	**51**	**4**	**9**	**13**	**5**	**11**	**16**	**26**	....	....	....	....	....
	Pittsburgh Hornets	AHL	6	3	4	7	....	....	....	6	....	....	....	....	....
1952-53	**Toronto Maple Leafs**	**NHL**	**4**	**1**	**3**	**4**	**1**	**4**	**5**	**2**	....	....	....	....	....
	Pittsburgh Hornets	AHL	56	19	42	61	....	....	....	27	10	*6	4	10	12
1953-54	**Toronto Maple Leafs**	**NHL**	**7**	**0**	**1**	**1**	**0**	**1**	**1**	**12**	....	....	....	....	....
	Pittsburgh Hornets	AHL	60	36	45	81	....	....	....	19	5	0	2	2	16
1954-55	**New York Rangers**	**NHL**	**70**	**29**	**24**	**53**	**38**	**28**	**66**	**8**	....	....	....	....	....
1955-56	**New York Rangers**	**NHL**	**70**	**18**	**27**	**45**	**25**	**32**	**57**	**26**	**5**	**0**	**3**	**3**	**0**
1956-57	**New York Rangers**	**NHL**	**70**	**18**	**20**	**38**	**23**	**22**	**45**	**47**	**5**	**0**	**1**	**1**	**2**
1957-58	**New York Rangers**	**NHL**	**70**	**11**	**19**	**30**	**14**	**20**	**34**	**26**	**6**	**0**	**0**	**0**	**6**
1958-59	**Chicago Black Hawks**	**NHL**	**58**	**8**	**14**	**22**	**9**	**14**	**23**	**4**	**3**	**0**	**0**	**0**	**0**
1959-60	Buffalo Bisons	AHL	62	14	41	55	....	....	....	56	....	....	....	....	....
1960-61	Quebec Aces	AHL	67	18	25	43	....	....	....	42	....	....	....	....	....
1961-62	Quebec Aces	AHL	65	27	28	55	....	....	....	18	....	....	....	....	....
1962-63	Quebec Aces	AHL	64	23	25	48	....	....	....	30	....	....	....	....	....
	NHL Totals		**461**	**105**	**135**	**240**	**135**	**154**	**289**	**177**	**28**	**0**	**4**	**4**	**8**

AHL Second All-Star Team (1954) • NHL Second All-Star Team (1955) • Played in NHL All-Star Game (1955)

Rights traded to **Toronto** by **Providence** (AHL) for cash and future considerations (Jack Hamilton, October 27, 1948), July 27, 1948. Traded to **NY Rangers** by **Toronto** for cash, July 20, 1954. Claimed by **Montreal** from **NY Rangers** in Intra-League Draft, June 3, 1958. Claimed on waivers by **Chicago** from **Montreal**, September 23, 1958. Rights traded to **Montreal** by **Chicago** with Glen Skov, Bob Bailey, Terry Gray and Lorne Ferguson for Cec Hoekstra, Reggie Fleming, Ab McDonald and Bob Courcy, June 7, 1960.

• LEWIS, Doug

LW – L. 5'8", 155 lbs. b: Winnipeg, Man., 3/3/1921.

Season	Club	League	GP	G	A	Pts	AG	AA	APts	PIM	GP	G	A	Pts	PIM
1938-39	East Kildonan Bisons	MAHA	STATISTICS NOT AVAILABLE												
1939-40	Kenora Thistles	MJHL	23	8	6	14	....	....	....	6	18	2	0	2	14
	Kenora Thistles	M-Cup	10	1	0	1	....	....	....	12	....	....	....	....	....
1940-41	Edmonton Athletic Club	EJrHL	16	6	7	13	....	....	....	16	5	1	3	4	7
	Edmonton Athletic Club	M-Cup	5	3	0	3	....	....	....	4	....	....	....	....	....
1941-42	Springfield Indians	AHL	56	9	25	34	....	....	....	15	5	0	3	3	0
1942-43	Buffalo Bisons	AHL	55	9	27	36	....	....	....	21	7	0	4	4	7
1943-44	Winnipeg Navy	WNDHL	10	3	2	5	....	....	....	8	....	....	....	....	....
	Cornwallis Navy	NSDHL	2	2	4	6	....	....	....	2	1	1	1	2	0
1944-45	Buffalo Bisons	AHL	56	15	27	42	....	....	....	19	6	0	1	1	0
1945-46	Buffalo Bisons	AHL	62	20	32	52	....	....	....	8	2	0	0	0	0
1946-47	**Montreal Canadiens**	**NHL**	**3**	**0**	**0**	**0**	**0**	**0**	**0**	**0**	....	....	....	....	....
	Buffalo Bisons	AHL	55	10	25	35	....	....	....	16	4	0	1	1	0
1947-48	Buffalo Bisons	AHL	67	20	24	44	....	....	....	12	8	2	1	3	2
1948-49	Buffalo Bisons	AHL	64	22	16	38	....	....	....	23	....	....	....	....	....
1949-50	Buffalo Bisons	AHL	70	9	20	29	....	....	....	30	5	1	0	1	0
1950-51	Seattle Ironmen	PCHL	29	11	4	15	....	....	....	4	....	....	....	....	....
	Boston Olympics	EAHL	17	5	1	6	....	....	....	6	....	....	....	....	....
1951-52	Halifax St. Mary's	MMHL	46	10	8	18	....	....	....	0	....	....	....	....	....
1952-53	Winnipeg Maroons	X-Games	STATISTICS NOT AVAILABLE												
	Winnipeg Maroons	Al-Cup	5	1	1	2	....	....	....	12	....	....	....	....	....
1953-54	Winnipeg Maroons	X-Games	STATISTICS NOT AVAILABLE												
	Winnipeg Maroons	Al-Cup	2	2	0	2	....	....	....	0	....	....	....	....	....
	NHL Totals		**3**	**0**	**0**	**0**	**0**	**0**	**0**	**0**	....	....	....	....	....

Signed as a free agent by **Halifax** (MMHL), September 27, 1951.

• LEWIS, Herbie

Herbert A. "The Duke of Duluth" **HHOF**
LW – L. 5'9", 163 lbs. b: Calgary, Alta., 4/17/1906 d: 1/20/1991.

Season	Club	League	GP	G	A	Pts	AG	AA	APts	PIM	GP	G	A	Pts	PIM
1921-22	Calgary Hustlers	CCJHL	STATISTICS NOT AVAILABLE												
	Calgary Hustlers	M-Cup	6	5	1	6	....	....	....	2	....	....	....	....	....
1922-23	Calgary Canadians	CCJHL	12	*17	7	*24	....	....	....	24	....	....	....	....	....
	Calgary Canadians	M-Cup	4	5	4	9	....	....	....	8	....	....	....	....	....
1923-24	Calgary Canadians	CCJHL	STATISTICS NOT AVAILABLE												
	Calgary Canadians	M-Cup	7	12	8	20	....	....	....	13	....	....	....	....	....
1924-25	Duluth Hornets	USAHA	40	9	0	9	....	....	....	....	....	....	....	....	....
1925-26	Duluth Hornets	CHL	39	17	*11	*28	....	....	....	52	8	*3	1	*4	8
1926-27	Duluth Hornets	AHA	37	18	6	24	....	....	....	52	3	1	0	1	2
1927-28	Duluth Hornets	AHA	40	14	5	19	....	....	....	56	5	0	0	0	8
1928-29	**Detroit Cougars**	**NHL**	**36**	**9**	**5**	**14**	**26**	**33**	**59**	**33**	....	....	....	....	....
1929-30	**Detroit Cougars**	**NHL**	**44**	**20**	**11**	**31**	**29**	**26**	**55**	**36**	....	....	....	....	....
1930-31	**Detroit Falcons**	**NHL**	**43**	**15**	**6**	**21**	**30**	**18**	**48**	**38**	....	....	....	....	....
1931-32	**Detroit Falcons**	**NHL**	**48**	**5**	**14**	**19**	**8**	**31**	**39**	**21**	**2**	**0**	**0**	**0**	**0**
1932-33	**Detroit Red Wings**	**NHL**	**48**	**20**	**14**	**34**	**37**	**29**	**66**	**20**	**4**	**1**	**0**	**1**	**0**
1933-34	**Detroit Red Wings**	**NHL**	**43**	**16**	**15**	**31**	**28**	**32**	**60**	**15**	**9**	***5**	**2**	**7**	**2**
1934-35	**Detroit Red Wings**	**NHL**	**47**	**16**	**27**	**43**	**26**	**47**	**73**	**26**	....	....	....	....	....
♦1935-36	**Detroit Red Wings**	**NHL**	**45**	**14**	**23**	**37**	**27**	**44**	**71**	**25**	**7**	**2**	**3**	**5**	**0**
♦1936-37	**Detroit Red Wings**	**NHL**	**45**	**14**	**18**	**32**	**24**	**33**	**57**	**14**	**10**	***4**	**3**	**7**	**4**
1937-38	**Detroit Red Wings**	**NHL**	**42**	**13**	**18**	**31**	**21**	**29**	**50**	**12**	....	....	....	....	....
1938-39	**Detroit Red Wings**	**NHL**	**42**	**6**	**10**	**16**	**10**	**16**	**26**	**8**	**6**	**1**	**2**	**3**	**0**

Season	Club	League	GP	G	A	Pts	AG	AA	APts	PIM	GP	G	A	Pts	PIM
			REGULAR SEASON								PLAYOFFS				
1939-40	Indianapolis Capitols	IAHL	26	1	6	7				6	3	1	2	3	0
1940-41	Indianapolis Capitols	AHL	2	1	0	1				0					
1941-42	Indianapolis Capitols	AHL	DID NOT PLAY – COACHING												
	NHL Totals		483	148	161	309	266	338	604	248	38	13	10	23	6

CHL First All-Star Team (1926) • Played in NHL All-Star Game (1934)

Signed as a free agent by **Duluth** (CHL), November 4, 1926. Claimed by **Detroit** from **Duluth** (AHA) in Inter-League Draft, May 14, 1928.

• LICARI, Tony

RW – R. 5'7", 147 lbs. b: Ottawa, Ont., 4/9/1921.

Season	Club	League	GP	G	A	Pts	AG	AA	APts	PIM	GP	G	A	Pts	PIM
1938-39	Ottawa Glebe Collegiate	OCJHL	STATISTICS NOT AVAILABLE												
1939-40	Perth Blue Wings	OVHL	9	13	12	25				0	4	*6	6	*12	4
	Perth Blue Wings	M-Cup	8	9	6	15				2					
1940-41	Guelph Biltmores	OHA-Jr.	12	10	16	26				4	5	8	4	12	2
1941-42	Dallas Texans	AHA	49	15	18	33				10					
1942-43	Ottawa RCAF	OCHL	19	19	17	36				0	8	6	6	12	4
	Ottawa RCAF	Al-Cup	7	5	5	10				0					
1943-44	Vancouver RCAF	NNDHL	14	16	7	23				9	3	*4	1	5	0
1944-45	Ottawa #17 Depot	OCHL	7	13	*22	35				2					
1945-46			MILITARY SERVICE												
1946-47	**Detroit Red Wings**	**NHL**	**9**	**0**	**1**	**1**	**0**	**1**	**1**	**0**					
	Indianapolis Capitols	AHL	52	21	28	49				6					
1947-48	Indianapolis Capitols	AHL	65	20	39	59				10					
1948-49	St. Louis Flyers	AHL	68	22	52	74				8	7	1	4	5	2
1949-50	Ottawa RCAF	OCHL	40	28	29	57				22	5	4	3	7	4
1950-51	Ottawa Senators	QMHL	2	1	0	1				2					
	Ottawa RCAF	OCHL	40	23	28	51				14	7	*9	5	*14	6
1951-52	Harringay Racers	A-Cup	30	32	26	58				32					
	Harringay Racers	Britain	30	15	28	43				20					
1952-53	Harringay Racers	A-Cup	30	25	31	56				22					
	Harringay Racers	Britain	21	20	26	46				6					
1953-54	Harringay Racers	A-Cup	24	13	22	35				10					
	Harringay Racers	Britain	24	17	31	48				16					
	Harringay Racers	Ln-Cup	12	12	14	26				4					
1954-55	Pembroke Lumber Kings	NOHA	1	0	0	0				0					
	NHL Totals		**9**	**0**	**1**	**1**	**0**	**1**	**1**	**0**					

OCHL First All-Star Team (1951)

Traded to **Chicago** (St. Louis-AHL) by **Detroit** with Red Almas, Lloyd Doran, Barry Sullivan and Thain Simon for Joe Lund and Hec Highton, September 9, 1948.

• LINDSAY, Ted

Robert Blake Theodore "Terrible Teddie" HHOF

LW – L. 5'8", 163 lbs. b: Renfrew, Ont., 7/29/1925.

Season	Club	League	GP	G	A	Pts	AG	AA	APts	PIM	GP	G	A	Pts	PIM
1942-43	Kirkland Lake Lakers	GBHL	STATISTICS NOT AVAILABLE												
1943-44	St. Michael's Majors	OHA-Jr.	22	22	7	29				24	12	*13	6	*19	16
	Oshawa Generals	M-Cup	7	7	2	9				6					
1944-45	**Detroit Red Wings**	**NHL**	45	17	6	23	17	7	24	43	14	2	0	2	6
1945-46	**Detroit Red Wings**	**NHL**	47	7	10	17	8	14	22	14	5	0	1	1	0
1946-47	**Detroit Red Wings**	**NHL**	59	27	15	42	31	18	49	57	5	2	2	4	10
1947-48	**Detroit Red Wings**	**NHL**	60	*33	19	52	43	25	68	95	10	3	1	4	6
1948-49	**Detroit Red Wings**	**NHL**	50	26	28	54	37	40	77	97	11	2	*6	8	31
♦1949-50	**Detroit Red Wings**	**NHL**	69	23	*55	*78	29	68	97	141	13	4	4	8	16
1950-51	**Detroit Red Wings**	**NHL**	67	24	35	59	31	43	74	110	6	0	1	1	8
♦1951-52	**Detroit Red Wings**	**NHL**	70	30	39	69	40	49	89	123	8	*5	2	*7	8
1952-53	**Detroit Red Wings**	**NHL**	70	32	39	71	43	48	91	111	6	4	4	8	6
♦1953-54	**Detroit Red Wings**	**NHL**	70	26	36	62	36	44	80	110	12	4	4	8	14
♦1954-55	**Detroit Red Wings**	**NHL**	49	19	19	38	25	22	47	85	11	7	12	19	12
1955-56	**Detroit Red Wings**	**NHL**	67	27	23	50	37	27	64	161	10	6	3	9	22
1956-57	**Detroit Red Wings**	**NHL**	70	30	*55	85	39	62	101	103	5	2	4	6	8
1957-58	**Chicago Black Hawks**	**NHL**	68	15	24	39	18	25	43	110					
1958-59	**Chicago Black Hawks**	**NHL**	70	22	36	58	26	37	63	*184	6	2	4	6	13
1959-60	**Chicago Black Hawks**	**NHL**	68	7	19	26	8	18	26	91	4	1	1	2	0
1960/64			OUT OF HOCKEY – RETIRED												
1964-65	**Detroit Red Wings**	**NHL**	69	14	14	28	17	14	31	173	7	3	0	3	34
	NHL Totals		**1068**	**379**	**472**	**851**	**485**	**561**	**1046**	**1808**	**133**	**47**	**49**	**96**	**194**

• Son of Bert • NHL First All-Star Team (1948, 1950, 1951, 1952, 1953, 1954, 1956, 1957) • NHL Second All-Star Team (1949) • Won Art Ross Trophy (1950) • Played in NHL All-Star Game (1947, 1948, 1949, 1950, 1951, 1952, 1953, 1954, 1955, 1956, 1957)

• Loaned to **Oshawa** (OHA-Jr.) by **St. Michael's** (OHA-Jr.) for Memorial Cup Playoffs, March, 1943. Signed as a free agent by **Detroit**, October 18, 1944. Traded to **Chicago** by **Detroit** with Glenn Hall for Johnny Wilson, Forbes Kennedy, Hank Bassen and Bill Preston, July 23, 1957. Traded to **Detroit** by **Chicago** for cash, October 14, 1964.

• LISCOMBE, Carl

Harold Carlyle "Lefty"

LW – L. 5'7", 162 lbs. b: Perth, Ont., 5/17/1915.

Season	Club	League	GP	G	A	Pts	AG	AA	APts	PIM	GP	G	A	Pts	PIM
1933-34	Galt Terriers	OHA-B	13	6	1	7				20	2	1	0	1	8
1934-35	Hamilton Tigers	OHA-Sr.	19	*22	6	*28				20	6	1	0	1	2
1935-36	Detroit Olympics	IHL	47	12	8	20				37	6	1	1	2	4
1936-37	Pittsburgh Hornets	IAHL	50	8	13	21				23	5	0	1	1	2
1937-38	**Detroit Red Wings**	**NHL**	41	14	10	24	23	16	39	30					
	Pittsburgh Hornets	IAHL	5	3	1	4				17					
1938-39	**Detroit Red Wings**	**NHL**	41	8	18	26	14	28	42	13	6	0	0	0	2
1939-40	**Detroit Red Wings**	**NHL**	25	2	7	9	3	11	14	4					
	Indianapolis Capitols	IAHL	24	8	11	19				9	5	2	1	3	2
1940-41	**Detroit Red Wings**	**NHL**	33	10	10	20	15	14	29	0	8	4	3	7	12
	Indianapolis Capitols	AHL	19	4	5	9				7					
1941-42	**Detroit Red Wings**	**NHL**	47	13	17	30	17	20	37	14	12	6	6	12	2
♦1942-43	**Detroit Red Wings**	**NHL**	50	19	23	42	20	21	41	19	10	*6	8	*14	2
1943-44	**Detroit Red Wings**	**NHL**	50	36	37	73	33	33	66	17	5	1	0	1	2
1944-45	**Detroit Red Wings**	**NHL**	42	23	9	32	23	10	33	18	14	4	2	6	0
1945-46	**Detroit Red Wings**	**NHL**	44	12	9	21	14	13	27	2	4	1	0	1	0
1946-47	St. Louis Flyers	AHL	37	16	10	26				12					
	Providence Reds	AHL	26	19	22	41				4					
1947-48	Providence Reds	AHL	68	*50	68	*118				10	5	1	1	2	2
1948-49	Providence Reds	AHL	68	*55	47	102				2	14	3	2	5	2
1949-50	Providence Reds	AHL	57	13	29	42				16	3	0	0	0	0
1950-51	Sarnia–Detroit	IHL	45	29	23	52				9	3	1	0	1	0
	Hamilton Tigers	OMHL	4	0	0	0				0					
1951-52	Detroit Hettche	IHL	45	35	31	66				14					
1952-53	Chatham Maroons	OHA-Sr.	14	4	7	11				2					
1953-54	Chatham Maroons	OHA-Sr.	12	0	0	0				4					
	NHL Totals		**373**	**137**	**140**	**277**	**162**	**166**	**328**	**117**	**59**	**22**	**19**	**41**	**20**

AHL First All-Star Team (1948) • Won John B. Sollenberger Trophy (Top Scorer - AHL) (1948) • Won Les Cunningham Award (MVP - AHL) (1948, 1949) • AHL Second All-Star Team (1949) • IHL Second All-Star Team (1951)

Signed as a free agent by **Detroit**, September 24, 1935. Traded to **St. Louis** (AHL) by **Detroit** for cash, August 17, 1946. Traded to **Providence** (AHL) by **St. Louis** (AHL) with Eddie Bush, Roly Rossignol and cash for Bill McComb and Russell Brayshaw, January 9, 1947.

• LITZENBERGER, Ed

Edward C. "Litz"

C/RW – R. 6'1", 174 lbs. b: Neudorf, Sask., 7/15/1932.

Season	Club	League	GP	G	A	Pts	AG	AA	APts	PIM	GP	G	A	Pts	PIM
1949-50	Regina Pats	WCJHL	40	25	19	44				16	9	*11	4	15	4
	Regina Pats	M-Cup	14	12	10	22				2					
1950-51	Regina Pats	WCJHL	40	*44	35	79				23	12	*14	16	*30	6
	Regina Pats	M-Cup	17	12	10	22				14					
1951-52	Regina Pats	WCJHL	41	42	29	71				75	8	8	5	13	8
	Regina Pats	M-Cup	14	*14	12	*26				12					
1952-53	**Montreal Canadiens**	**NHL**	2	1	0	1	1	0	1	2					
	Montreal Royals	QMHL	59	26	24	50				42	16	8	4	12	15
1953-54	**Montreal Canadiens**	**NHL**	3	0	0	0	0	0	0	0					
	Montreal Royals	QHL	67	31	39	70				44	11	4	5	9	6
1954-55	**Montreal Canadiens**	**NHL**	29	7	4	11	9	5	14	12					
	Chicago Black Hawks	**NHL**	44	16	24	40	21	28	49	28					
1955-56	**Chicago Black Hawks**	**NHL**	70	10	29	39	14	35	49	36					
1956-57	**Chicago Black Hawks**	**NHL**	70	32	32	64	42	35	77	48					
1957-58	**Chicago Black Hawks**	**NHL**	70	32	30	62	40	31	71	63					
1958-59	**Chicago Black Hawks**	**NHL**	70	33	44	77	40	45	85	37	6	3	5	8	8
1959-60	**Chicago Black Hawks**	**NHL**	52	12	18	30	14	17	31	15	4	0	1	1	4
♦1960-61	**Chicago Black Hawks**	**NHL**	62	10	22	32	11	21	32	14	10	1	3	4	2
1961-62	**Detroit Red Wings**	**NHL**	32	8	12	20	9	11	20	4					
♦	**Toronto Maple Leafs**	**NHL**	37	10	10	20	11	10	21	14	10	0	2	2	4
♦1962-63	**Toronto Maple Leafs**	**NHL**	58	5	13	18	6	13	19	10	9	1	2	3	6
♦1963-64	**Toronto Maple Leafs**	**NHL**	19	2	0	2	2	0	2	0	1	0	0	0	10
	Rochester Americans	AHL	33	15	14	29				26	2	1	1	2	2
1964-65	Rochester Americans	AHL	72	25	61	86				34	10	1	3	4	6
1965-66	Victoria Maple Leafs	WHL	23	7	17	24				26					
	Rochester Americans	AHL	47	7	15	22				10	12	1	5	6	8
	NHL Totals		**618**	**178**	**238**	**416**	**220**	**251**	**471**	**283**	**40**	**5**	**13**	**18**	**34**

Won William Northey Trophy (Top Rookie - QMHL) (1953) • QMHL Second Team All-Star (!953) • QHL Second All-Star Team (1954) • Won Calder Memorial Trophy (1955) • NHL Second All-Star Team (1957) • Played in NHL All-Star Game (1955, 1957, 1958, 1959, 1962, 1963)

Traded to **Chicago** by **Montreal** for cash, December 10, 1954. Traded to **Detroit** by **Chicago** for Gerry Melnyk and Brian S. Smith, June 12, 1961. Claimed on waivers by **Toronto** from **Detroit**, December 29, 1961.

• LOCAS, Jacques

RW – R. 5'11", 175 lbs. b: Pointe aux Trembles, Que., 2/12/1926 Deceased.

Season	Club	League	GP	G	A	Pts	AG	AA	APts	PIM	GP	G	A	Pts	PIM
1943-44	Concordia Civics	QJHL	13	8	7	15				8	5	3	0	3	2
1944-45	Concordia Civics	QJHL	10	6	5	11				2	2	2	1	3	2
1945-46	Concordia Civics	QJHL	20	*25	8	*33				31	5	*7	3	10	4
1946-47	Montreal Royals	QSHL	38	23	12	35				69	10	*11	3	14	12
	Montreal Royals	Al-Cup	14	11	7	18				14					
1947-48	**Montreal Canadiens**	**NHL**	56	7	8	15	9	10	19	66					
1948-49	**Montreal Canadiens**	**NHL**	3	0	0	0	0	0	0	0					
	Dallas Texans	USHL	6	3	2	5				0					
1949-50	Cincinnati Mohawks	AHL	62	8	15	23				36					
1950-51	Montreal Royals	QMHL	22	15	7	22				63	7	2	2	4	10
1951-52	Montreal Royals	QMHL	41	11	15	26				44	7	0	1	1	0
1952-53	Sherbrooke Saints	QMHL	57	36	28	64				61	7	2	3	5	*24
1953-54	Chicoutimi Sagueneens	QHL	65	35	20	55				45	7	2	0	2	6
1954-55	Chicoutimi Sagueneens	QHL	46	24	14	38				36					
1955-56	Chicoutimi Sagueneens	QHL	62	27	23	50				80	5	2	0	2	2
1956-57	Chicoutimi Sagueneens	QHL	67	33	13	46				54	10	5	2	7	*24
1957-58	Chicoutimi Sagueneens	QHL	64	*40	16	56				54	5	2	0	2	6
1958-59	Chicoutimi Sagueneens	QHL	61	*49	24	73				46					
1959-60	Quebec Aces	AHL	39	9	8	17				20					
	NHL Totals		**59**	**7**	**8**	**15**	**9**	**10**	**19**	**66**					

QHL First All-Star Team (1958, 1959)

• LOCKING, Norm

Norman Wesley

LW/C – L. 6', 165 lbs. b: Owen Sound, Ont., 5/24/1911 d: 5/15/1995.

Season	Club	League	GP	G	A	Pts	AG	AA	APts	PIM	GP	G	A	Pts	PIM
1931-32	Pittsburgh Yellowjackets	IHL	29	2	0	2				12					
1932-33	St. Paul–Tulsa	AHA	39	11	11	22				32	4	1	0	1	*10
1933-34	Cleveland Indians	IHL	40	*24	10	34				21					
1934-35	**Chicago Black Hawks**	**NHL**	35	2	5	7	3	9	12	19					
1935-36	**Chicago Black Hawks**	**NHL**	13	0	1	1	0	2	2	7					
	London Tecumsehs	IHL	33	11	12	23				22	2	0	0	0	0
1936-37	Buffalo Bisons	IAHL	11	1	4	5				8					
	Syracuse Stars	IAHL	36	12	13	25				26	9	1	3	4	2
1937-38	Syracuse Stars	IAHL	48	19	17	36				13	8	4	3	7	0
1938-39	Syracuse Stars	IAHL	53	20	30	50				28	3	0	1	1	2
1939-40	Syracuse Stars	IAHL	55	*31	32	*63				12					
1940-41	Cleveland Barons	AHL	52	25	19	44				27	9	0	4	4	4
1941-42	Cleveland Barons	AHL	54	14	32	46				7	5	1	1	2	0
1942-43	Cleveland Barons	AHL	56	26	40	66				14	3	1	2	3	2
1943-44	Cleveland Barons	AHL	19	9	9	18				0	11	0	6	6	0
	NHL Totals		**48**	**2**	**6**	**8**	**3**	**11**	**14**	**26**					

IAHL First All-Star Team (1940) • AHL First All-Star Team (1941) • AHL Second All-Star Team (1943)

Rights traded to **Chicago** by **Tulsa** (AHA) for Lou Holmes, March 7, 1933. Traded to **Cleveland** (IHL) by **Chicago** for cash, November, 1933. Traded to **Chicago** by **Cleveland** (IHL) for cash, November 1, 1934. Loaned to **London** (IHL) by **Chicago** for the return from loan of Bill Kendall, January 23, 1936.

• LONG, Stanley
Stanley Gordon
D – L. 5'11", 190 lbs. b: Owen Sound, Ont., 11/6/1929 Deceased.

Season	Club	League	GP	G	A	Pts	AG	AA	APts	PIM	GP	G	A	Pts	PIM
			REGULAR SEASON								PLAYOFFS				
1946-47	Barrie Flyers	OHA-Jr.	14	1	1	2	....	....	....	29	5	0	1	1	4
1947-48	Barrie Flyers	OHA-Jr.	34	9	25	34	....	....	....	60	13	8	8	16	38
	Barrie Flyers	M-Cup	10	3	7	10	....	....	....	18	....	....	....	....	....
1948-49	Barrie Flyers	OHA-Jr.	42	11	39	50	....	....	....	89	8	2	9	11	11
	Barrie Flyers	M-Cup	8	2	3	5	....	....	....	6	....	....	....	....	....
1949-50	Barrie Flyers	OHA-Jr.	48	19	37	56	....	....	....	112	9	1	8	9	12
	Buffalo Bisons	AHL	1	0	0	0	....	....	....	0	....	....	....	....	....
1950-51	Victoria Cougars	PCHL	62	9	15	24	....	....	....	77	12	2	4	6	16
	Montreal Royals	QMHL	5	0	0	0	....	....	....	9	....	....	....	....	....
1951-52	Buffalo Bisons	AHL	61	11	20	31	....	....	....	96	3	2	1	3	2
	Montreal Canadiens	**NHL**	....	....	....	....	....	....	....	....	**3**	**0**	**0**	**0**	**0**
1952-53	Victoria Cougars	WHL	51	9	19	28	....	....	....	55	....	....	....	....	....
1953-54	Buffalo Bisons	AHL	6	0	4	4	....	....	....	10	....	....	....	....	....
1954-55	Kitchener Canucks	OHA-Jr.	DID NOT PLAY – COACHING												
	NHL Totals		....	....	....	....	....	....	....	....	**3**	**0**	**0**	**0**	**0**

Traded to **Buffalo** (AHL) by **Montreal** for cash, October 15, 1953.

• LONSBERRY, Ross
— see page 1342

• LORRAIN, Rod
Roderick Joseph
RW – R. 5'5", 156 lbs. b: Buckingham, Que., 7/26/1914 d: 10/22/1980.

Season	Club	League	GP	G	A	Pts	AG	AA	APts	PIM	GP	G	A	Pts	PIM
1932-33	Hull-Lasalle Juniors	HOHL	11	5	2	7	....	....	....	2	....	....	....	....	....
1933-34	Hull-Lasalle Juniors	HOHL	11	*21	14	35	....	....	....	2	4	3	6	9	2
1934-35	Ottawa Senators	OCHL	14	4	6	10	....	....	....	10	8	1	2	3	4
1935-36	**Montreal Canadiens**	**NHL**	**1**	**0**	**0**	**0**	**0**	**0**	**0**	**2**	....	....	....	....	....
	Ottawa Senators	OCHL	11	8	4	12	....	....	....	4	....	....	....	....	....
	Providence Reds	Can-Am	22	2	1	3	....	....	....	4	3	0	0	0	2
1936-37	**Montreal Canadiens**	**NHL**	**47**	**3**	**6**	**9**	**5**	**11**	**16**	**8**	**5**	**0**	**0**	**0**	**0**
1937-38	**Montreal Canadiens**	**NHL**	**48**	**13**	**19**	**32**	**21**	**31**	**52**	**14**	**3**	**0**	**0**	**0**	**0**
1938-39	**Montreal Canadiens**	**NHL**	**38**	**10**	**9**	**19**	**17**	**14**	**31**	**0**	**3**	**0**	**3**	**3**	**0**
	New Haven Eagles	IAHL	9	1	3	4	....	....	....	0	....	....	....	....	....
1939-40	**Montreal Canadiens**	**NHL**	**41**	**1**	**5**	**6**	**2**	**8**	**10**	**6**	....	....	....	....	....
1940-41	St-Jerome Papermakers	QPHL	34	34	24	58	....	....	....	12	13	*10	6	*16	11
1941-42	**Montreal Canadiens**	**NHL**	**4**	**1**	**0**	**1**	**1**	**0**	**1**	**0**	....	....	....	....	....
	Washington Lions	AHL	34	4	15	19	....	....	....	0	2	2	0	2	0
1942-43	Washington Lions	AHL	49	8	20	28	....	....	....	8	....	....	....	....	....
1943-44	University of Montreal	MCHL	3	1	2	3	....	....	....	0	....	....	....	....	....
	Montreal Vickers	MCHL	8	5	3	8	....	....	....	0	....	....	....	....	....
1944-45	Hull Volants	QSHL	11	2	9	11	....	....	....	0	....	....	....	....	....
	NHL Totals		**179**	**28**	**39**	**67**	**46**	**64**	**110**	**30**	**11**	**0**	**3**	**3**	**0**

Played in NHL All-Star Game (1939)

Signed as a free agent by **Montreal**, October 11, 1935.

• LOUGHLIN, Clem
Clem Joseph
D – L. 6', 180 lbs. b: Carroll, Man., 11/15/1894 d: 2/8/1977.

Season	Club	League	GP	G	A	Pts	AG	AA	APts	PIM	GP	G	A	Pts	PIM
1910-11	Winnipeg Monarchs	MHL-Sr.	1	0	0	0	....	....	....	....	....	....	....	....	....
1911-12	Winnipeg Monarchs	MHL-Sr.	STATISTICS NOT AVAILABLE												
1912-13	Winnipeg Strathconas	WSrHL	8	3	0	3	....	....	....	....	2	1	0	1	0
	Winnipeg Monarchs	MHL-Sr.	1	0	0	0	....	....	....	0	....	....	....	....	....
1913-14	Winnipeg Monarchs	MHL-Sr.	1	1	0	1	....	....	....	0	....	....	....	....	....
	Winnipeg Strathconas	MHL-Sr.	12	6	0	6	....	....	....	....	....	....	....	....	....
1914-15	Winnipeg Monarchs	MHL-Sr.	5	2	3	5	....	....	....	12	8	6	0	6	10
1915-16	Winnipeg Monarchs	WSrHL	8	1	1	2	....	....	....	6	2	0	0	0	0
1916-17	Portland Rosebuds	PCHA	24	3	1	4	....	....	....	43	....	....	....	....	....
1917-18	Portland Rosebuds	PCHA	16	2	0	2	....	....	....	6	....	....	....	....	....
1918-19	Victoria Aristocrats	PCHA	16	1	3	4	....	....	....	3	....	....	....	....	....
1919-20	Victoria Aristocrats	PCHA	22	2	2	4	....	....	....	18	....	....	....	....	....
1920-21	Victoria Aristocrats	PCHA	24	7	3	10	....	....	....	21	....	....	....	....	....
1921-22	Victoria Aristocrats	PCHA	24	6	3	9	....	....	....	6	....	....	....	....	....
1922-23	Victoria Cougars	PCHA	30	12	10	22	....	....	....	24	2	0	0	0	4
1923-24	Victoria Cougars	PCHA	30	10	7	17	....	....	....	26	....	....	....	....	....
1924-25	Victoria Cougars	WCHL	28	9	2	11	....	....	....	46	4	0	1	1	2
♦	Victoria Cougars	St-Cup	4	1	0	1	....	....	....	4	....	....	....	....	....
1925-26	Victoria Cougars	WHL	30	7	3	10	....	....	....	52	4	0	2	2	6
	Victoria Cougars	St-Cup	4	1	0	1	....	....	....	8	....	....	....	....	....
1926-27	**Detroit Cougars**	**NHL**	**34**	**7**	**3**	**10**	**12**	**16**	**28**	**40**	....	....	....	....	....
1927-28	**Detroit Cougars**	**NHL**	**43**	**1**	**2**	**3**	**2**	**11**	**13**	**21**	....	....	....	....	....
1928-29	**Chicago Black Hawks**	**NHL**	**24**	**0**	**1**	**1**	**0**	**7**	**7**	**16**	....	....	....	....	....
	Kitchener Millionaires	Can-Pro	18	3	1	4	....	....	....	21	3	0	0	0	8
1929-30	London Panthers	IHL	40	5	2	7	....	....	....	37	2	0	0	0	0
1930-31	London Tecumsehs	IHL	46	4	7	11	....	....	....	50	....	....	....	....	....
1931-32	London Tecumsehs	IHL	42	0	0	0	....	....	....	2	6	0	0	0	0
1932-33	London Tecumsehs	IHL	DID NOT PLAY – COACHING												
	NHL Totals		**101**	**8**	**6**	**14**	**14**	**34**	**48**	**77**	....	....	....	....	....
	Other Major League Totals		244	59	34	93	....	....	....	245	10	0	3	3	12

• Brother of Wilf • PCHA Second All-Star Team (1921, 1922, 1923) • PCHA First All-Star Team (1924)

Signed as a free agent by **Victoria** (PCHA) after **Portland** (PCHA) franchise folded, November 28, 1918. • 1924-25 playoff totals includes WCHL series against Calgary and Saskatoon. • 1925-26 playoff totals includes WHL series against Edmonton and Saskatoon. Transferred to **Detroit** after NHL club purchased **Victoria** (WHL) franchise, May 15, 1926. Traded to **Chicago** by **Detroit** for cash, October 18, 1928. Signed as a free agent by **Toronto**, November 12, 1929. Traded to **London** (IAHL) by **Toronto** for cash, November 12, 1929.

• LOUGHLIN, Wilf
D/LW – L. 6'2", 200 lbs. b: Carroll, Man., 2/28/1896 d: 6/25/1966.

Season	Club	League	GP	G	A	Pts	AG	AA	APts	PIM	GP	G	A	Pts	PIM
1915-16	Winnipeg Monarchs	WSrHL	1	0	0	0	....	....	....	6	....	....	....	....	....
1916-17	Winnipeg Monarchs	WSrHL	8	5	3	8	....	....	....	10	....	....	....	....	....
1917-18	Winnipeg Vimy	WSrHL	10	10	4	14	....	....	....	12	....	....	....	....	....
1918-19	Victoria Aristocrats	PCHA	7	1	3	4	....	....	....	0	....	....	....	....	....
	Winnipeg Monarchs	WSrHL	8	12	3	15	....	....	....	6	....	....	....	....	....
1919-20	Victoria Aristocrats	PCHA	20	4	1	5	....	....	....	19	....	....	....	....	....
1920-21	Victoria Aristocrats	PCHA	24	8	5	13	....	....	....	15	....	....	....	....	....
1921-22	Victoria Aristocrats	PCHA	24	8	3	11	....	....	....	27	....	....	....	....	....
1922-23	Victoria Cougars	PCHA	27	0	0	0	....	....	....	9	2	0	0	0	0
1923-24	**Toronto St. Pats**	**NHL**	**14**	**0**	**0**	**0**	**0**	**0**	**0**	**2**	....	....	....	....	....
1924-25	Regina Capitals	WCHL	18	0	0	0	....	....	....	6	....	....	....	....	....
1925-26	Edmonton Eskimos	WHL	5	1	0	1	....	....	....	0	....	....	....	....	....
	Winnipeg Maroons	AHA	3	0	0	0	....	....	....	0	....	....	....	....	....
1926-27	Moose Jaw Maroons	PrHL	5	0	0	0	....	....	....	0	....	....	....	....	....
	NHL Totals		**14**	**0**	**0**	**0**	**0**	**0**	**0**	**2**	....	....	....	....	....
	Other Major League Totals		125	22	12	34	....	....	....	76	2	0	0	0	0

• Brother of Clem • PCHA Second All-Star Team (1921)

Signed as a free agent by **Victoria** (PCHA), February 18, 1919. Traded to **Toronto St. Pats** by **Victoria** (PCHA) for cash, October 24, 1923. Signed as a free agent by **Regina** (WCHL), October 21, 1924. Transferred to **Portland** (WHL) after **Regina** (WCHL) franchise relocated, September 1, 1925. Traded to **Edmonton** (WHL) by **Portland** (WHL) for cash, November 16, 1925.

• LOWE, Odie
Norman Earl
C – R. 5'8", 140 lbs. b: Winnipeg, Man., 4/15/1928.

Season	Club	League	GP	G	A	Pts	AG	AA	APts	PIM	GP	G	A	Pts	PIM
1945-46	Winnipeg Rangers	MJHL	10	6	5	11	....	....	....	16	2	1	0	1	2
1946-47	Lethbridge Maple Leafs	AJHL	11	10	*22	*32	....	....	....	8	3	*5	*7	*12	4
	Lethbridge Maple Leafs	WCSHL	1	1	1	2	....	....	....	0	....	....	....	....	....
1947-48	Winnipeg Canadians	WJrHL	24	23	*28	*51	....	....	....	44	6	2	5	7	10
1948-49	New York Rovers	QSHL	62	27	39	66	....	....	....	29	....	....	....	....	....
1949-50	**New York Rangers**	**NHL**	**4**	**1**	**1**	**2**	**1**	**1**	**2**	**0**	....	....	....	....	....
	New York Rovers	EAHL	44	17	36	53	....	....	....	18	12	7	8	*15	6
1950-51	St. Paul Saints	USHL	63	12	24	36	....	....	....	16	4	0	0	0	2
1951-52	St. Paul Saints	AAHL	39	33	45	78	....	....	....	32	....	....	....	....	....
	Moncton Hawks	MMHL	2	0	0	0	....	....	....	0	....	....	....	....	....
1952-53	Nelson Maple Leafs	WIHL	45	24	34	58	....	....	....	22	....	....	....	....	....
	Winnipeg Maroons	Al-Cup	7	2	5	7	....	....	....	2	....	....	....	....	....
1953-54	Winnipeg Maroons	X-Games	STATISTICS NOT AVAILABLE												
	Winnipeg Maroons	Al-Cup	23	14	21	35	....	....	....	18	....	....	....	....	....
1954-55	Vernon Canadians	OSHL	54	17	28	45	....	....	....	28	5	2	4	6	0
	Vernon Canadians	Al-Cup	17	11	14	25	....	....	....	6	....	....	....	....	....
1955-56	Vernon Canadians	OSHL	56	43	48	91	....	....	....	21	8	5	7	12	0
	Vernon Canadians	Al-Cup	16	7	*18	*25	....	....	....	8	....	....	....	....	....
1956-57	Vernon Canadians	OSHL	54	*61	*53	*114	....	....	....	52	12	9	7	16	6
1957-58	Vernon Canadians	OSHL	54	25	28	53	....	....	....	54	8	6	2	8	6
1958-59	Vernon Canadians	OSHL	54	38	33	71	....	....	....	28	17	3	8	11	8
1959-60	Vernon Canadians	OSHL	45	35	44	79	....	....	....	16	13	*13	8	*21	2
1960-61	Vernon Canadians	OSHL	44	36	50	86	....	....	....	20	5	6	6	12	2
1961-62	Vernon Canadians	OSHL	DID NOT PLAY – COACHING												
	NHL Totals		**4**	**1**	**1**	**2**	**1**	**1**	**2**	**0**	....	....	....	....	....

OSHL First All-Star Team (1957) • OSHL Second All-Star Team (1961)

• LOWE, Ross
Ross Robert
D/LW – R. 6'2", 180 lbs. b: Oshawa, Ont., 9/21/1928 d: 8/8/1955.

Season	Club	League	GP	G	A	Pts	AG	AA	APts	PIM	GP	G	A	Pts	PIM
1944-45	Oshawa Generals	OHA-Jr.	17	3	0	3	....	....	....	20	3	1	1	2	0
1945-46	Oshawa Generals	OHA-Jr.	23	19	10	29	....	....	....	40	12	9	7	16	13
1946-47	Oshawa Generals	OHA-Jr.	13	5	4	9	....	....	....	11	5	2	0	2	2
1947-48	Oshawa Generals	OHA-Jr.	36	21	16	37	....	....	....	80	6	1	2	3	30
1948-49	Hershey Bears	AHL	43	4	7	11	....	....	....	55	11	0	0	0	2
1949-50	**Boston Bruins**	**NHL**	**3**	**0**	**0**	**0**	**0**	**0**	**0**	**0**	....	....	....	....	....
	Hershey Bears	AHL	57	7	15	22	....	....	....	76	....	....	....	....	....
1950-51	**Boston Bruins**	**NHL**	**43**	**5**	**3**	**8**	**6**	**4**	**10**	**40**	....	....	....	....	....
	Hershey Bears	AHL	10	1	3	4	....	....	....	28	....	....	....	....	....
	Buffalo Bisons	AHL	15	4	2	6	....	....	....	29	4	0	0	0	17
	Montreal Canadiens	**NHL**	....	....	....	....	....	....	....	....	**2**	**0**	**0**	**0**	**0**
1951-52	**Montreal Canadiens**	**NHL**	**31**	**1**	**5**	**6**	**1**	**6**	**7**	**42**	....	....	....	....	....
1952-53	Buffalo Bisons	AHL	43	5	15	20	....	....	....	53	....	....	....	....	....
1953-54	Victoria Cougars	WHL	66	15	23	38	....	....	....	101	5	0	1	1	10
1954-55	Springfield Indians	AHL	60	32	50	82	....	....	....	91	4	1	2	3	16
	NHL Totals		**77**	**6**	**8**	**14**	**7**	**10**	**17**	**82**	**2**	**0**	**0**	**0**	**0**

AHL First All-Star Team (1955) • Won Les Cunningham Award (MVP - AHL) (1955)

Traded to **Montreal** by **Boston** for Hal Laycoe, February 14, 1951. Claimed by **Syracuse** (AHL) from **Montreal** (Victoria-WHL) in Inter-League Draft, June 14, 1954. Transferred to **Springfield** (AHL) after **Syracuse** (AHL) franchise relocated, September, 1954. Claimed by **NY Rangers** from **Springfield** (AHL) in Inter-League Draft, May 31, 1955. • Drowned in Lake Haliburton, August 8, 1955.

• LOWREY, Ed
Edward James
C – R. 5'6", 160 lbs. b: Manotick, Ont., 8/13/1891 Deceased.

Season	Club	League	GP	G	A	Pts	AG	AA	APts	PIM	GP	G	A	Pts	PIM
1909-10	Ottawa Stewartons	OCHL	6	7	0	7	....	....	....	18	1	0	0	0	0
	Hull Volants	LOVHL	1	0	0	0	....	....	....	0	....	....	....	....	....
1910-11	Ottawa Buena Vistas	OCHL	10	4	0	4	....	....	....	23	....	....	....	....	....
1911-12	Ottawa Stewartons	IPAHU	10	9	0	9	....	....	....	20	....	....	....	....	....
1912-13	Ottawa Senators	NHA	13	4	0	4	....	....	....	14	....	....	....	....	....
	Ottawa New Edinburghs	IPAHU	2	2	0	2	....	....	....	15	....	....	....	....	....
1913-14	Toronto Ontarios	NHA	16	1	3	4	....	....	....	13	....	....	....	....	....
1914-15	Montreal Canadiens	NHA	1	0	0	0	....	....	....	0	....	....	....	....	....
	Ottawa Senators	NHA	4	2	1	3	....	....	....	3	2	0	0	0	0
1915-16	Toronto Blueshirts	NHA	2	0	0	0	....	....	....	0	....	....	....	....	....
1916-17	Ottawa Senators	NHA	19	3	1	4	....	....	....	3	2	0	0	0	0
1917-18	**Ottawa Senators**	**NHL**	**12**	**2**	**1**	**3**	**2**	**4**	**6**	**3**	....	....	....	....	....
1918-19	**Ottawa Senators**	**NHL**	**10**	**0**	**1**	**1**	**0**	**5**	**5**	**3**	....	....	....	....	....
1919-20	Ottawa Munitions	OCHL	DID NOT PLAY – COACHING												
1920-21	**Hamilton Tigers**	**NHL**	**5**	**0**	**0**	**0**	**0**	**0**	**0**	**0**	....	....	....	....	....
1921-22	Regina Capitals	WCHL	7	1	0	1	....	....	....	0	....	....	....	....	....
	University of Ottawa	OCHL	DID NOT PLAY – COACHING												
	NHL Totals		**27**	**2**	**2**	**4**	**2**	**9**	**11**	**6**	....	....	....	....	....
	Other Major League Totals		62	11	5	16	....	....	....	33	4	0	0	0	0

Traded to **Toronto Ontarios** (NHA) by **Ottawa** (NHA) for cash, January 1, 1914. Rights retained by **Ottawa** after NHA folded, November 26, 1917. Signed as a free agent by **Hamilton**, December 12, 1920. Signed as a free agent by **Regina** (WCHL), December 1, 1921.

• LOWREY, Fred

Frederick John "Frock"
RW – R. 5'9", 155 lbs. b: Ottawa, Ont., 8/12/1902 d: 1/24/1968.

Season	Club	League	GP	G	A	Pts	AG	AA	APts	PIM	GP	G	A	Pts	PIM
			REGULAR SEASON								PLAYOFFS				
1917-18	Ottawa Landsdownes	OCHL	1	0	0	0	....	....	....	0	....	....	....	....	....
1918-19	Ottawa Military HQ	OCHL	6	1	0	1	....	....	....	3	....	....	....	....	....
1919-20	Ottawa Munitions	OCHL	8	2	0	2	....	....	....	....	5	3	1	4	....
1920-21	Quebec Royal Rifles	OCHL	11	13	0	13	....	....	....	....	4	1	0	1	....
1921-22	Ottawa Munitions	OCHL	13	12	3	15	....	....	....	18	....	....	....	....	....
1922-23	New Haven Westminsters	USAHA	9	15	0	*15	....	....	....	....	....	....	....	....	....
1923-24	New Haven Bears	USAHA	12	7	0	7	....	....	....	....	....	....	....	....	....
1924-25	**Montreal Maroons**	**NHL**	**27**	**0**	**1**	**1**	**0**	**4**	**4**	**6**	....	....	....	....	....
1925-26	**Montreal Maroons**	**NHL**	**10**	**1**	**0**	**1**	**2**	**0**	**2**	**2**	....	....	....	....	....
	Pittsburgh Pirates	**NHL**	**16**	**0**	**0**	**0**	**0**	**0**	**0**	**2**	**2**	**0**	**0**	**0**	....
1926-27	Quebec Beavers	Can-Am	9	0	1	1	....	....	....	0	....	....	....	....	....
	New Haven Eagles	Can-Am	22	4	0	4	....	....	....	21	4	1	0	1	0
1927-28	Philadelphia Arrows	Can-Am	29	11	2	13	....	....	....	25	....	....	....	....	....
1928-29	Philadelphia Arrows	Can-Am	5	0	0	0	....	....	....	4	....	....	....	....	....
	London Panthers	Can-Pro	22	2	0	2	....	....	....	0	....	....	....	....	....
1929-30	Niagara Falls Cataracts	IHL	37	10	3	13	....	....	....	28	....	....	....	....	....
1930-31	Pittsburgh Yellowjackets	IHL	1	0	1	1	....	....	....	2	....	....	....	....	....
	Buffalo Majors	AHA	5	0	0	0	....	....	....	0	....	....	....	....	....
	Niagara Falls Cataracts	OPHL	26	11	2	13	....	....	....	6	5	2	3	5	0
1931-32	Philadelphia Arrows	Can-Am	13	1	1	2	....	....	....	4	....	....	....	....	....
1932-33			REINSTATED AS AN AMATEUR												
1933-34	Ottawa Rideaus	OCHL	10	4	0	4	....	....	....	10	....	....	....	....	....
1934-35	Ottawa RCAF	OCHL	8	10	0	10	....	....	....	8	5	1	0	1	4
1935-36	Ottawa RCAF	OCHL	17	1	0	1	....	....	....	4	....	....	....	....	....
1936-37	Trenton RCAF	OHA-Sr.	DID NOT PLAY – COACHING												
	NHL Totals		**53**	**1**	**1**	**2**	**2**	**4**	**6**	**10**	**2**	**0**	**0**	**0**	....

• Brother of Gerry

Signed as a free agent by **Montreal Maroons**, November 3, 1924. Claimed on waivers by **Pittsburgh** from **Montreal Maroons**, January 12, 1926. Traded to **London** (Can-Pro) by **Philadelphia** (Can-Am) for Stan Jackson, January 18, 1929.

• LOWREY, Gerry

Gerald Charles
LW – L. 5'8", 150 lbs. b: Ottawa, Ont., 2/14/1906 d: 10/20/1979.

Season	Club	League	GP	G	A	Pts	AG	AA	APts	PIM	GP	G	A	Pts	PIM
1921-22	University of Ottawa	OCHL	12	0	2	2	....	....	....	6	....	....	....	....	....
1922-23	Iroquois Falls Eskimos	NOHA	STATISTICS NOT AVAILABLE												
1923-24	North Bay Trappers	NOHA	6	4	0	4	....	....	....	0	5	9	0	9	0
1924-25	London AAA	OHA-Sr.	18	14	6	20	....	....	....	24	....	....	....	....	....
1925-26	London Ravens	OHA-Sr.	19	18	7	25	....	....	....	23	2	*4	1	*5	0
	London Ravens	Al-Cup	2	2	0	2	....	....	....	0	....	....	....	....	....
1926-27	London Panthers	Can-Pro	30	7	2	9	....	....	....	27	4	5	1	6	15
1927-28	**Toronto Maple Leafs**	**NHL**	**25**	**6**	**5**	**11**	**12**	**28**	**40**	**29**	....	....	....	....	....
	Toronto Falcons	Can-Pro	19	10	4	14	....	....	....	57	....	....	....	....	....
1928-29	**Toronto Maple Leafs**	**NHL**	**32**	**3**	**11**	**14**	**9**	**75**	**84**	**24**	....	....	....	....	....
	Pittsburgh Pirates	**NHL**	**12**	**2**	**1**	**3**	**6**	**7**	**13**	**6**	....	....	....	....	....
1929-30	**Pittsburgh Pirates**	**NHL**	**44**	**16**	**14**	**30**	**23**	**33**	**56**	**30**	....	....	....	....	....
1930-31	**Philadelphia Quakers**	**NHL**	**43**	**13**	**14**	**27**	**26**	**43**	**69**	**27**	....	....	....	....	....
1931-32	**Chicago Black Hawks**	**NHL**	**48**	**8**	**3**	**11**	**13**	**7**	**20**	**32**	**2**	**1**	**0**	**1**	**2**
1932-33	St. Paul-Tulsa	AHA	14	6	1	7	....	....	....	16	....	....	....	....	....
	Ottawa Senators	**NHL**	**7**	**0**	**0**	**0**	**0**	**0**	**0**	**0**	....	....	....	....	....
	Quebec Castors	Can-Am	26	12	14	26	....	....	....	43	....	....	....	....	....
1933-34	Quebec Castors	Can-Am	40	11	17	28	....	....	....	30	....	....	....	....	....
1934-35	Quebec Castors	Can-Am	31	13	10	23	....	....	....	30	....	....	....	....	....
	Providence Reds	Can-Am	19	7	13	20	....	....	....	19	6	*2	2	4	0
1935-36	Providence Reds	Can-Am	45	5	14	19	....	....	....	26	7	0	2	2	2
1936-37	Providence Reds	IAHL	40	3	16	19	....	....	....	17	3	1	0	1	0
1937-38			REINSTATED AS AN AMATEUR												
1938-39	Hull Volants	OCHL	5	2	6	8	....	....	....	2	9	*8	4	*12	8
	Hull Volants	Al-Cup	9	1	2	3	....	....	....	*7	....	....	....	....	....
1939-40	Ottawa Camerons	OCHL	15	13	8	21	....	....	....	12	....	....	....	....	....
1940-41	Ottawa Montagnards	OCHL	18	5	9	14	....	....	....	6	....	....	....	....	....
1941-42	Ottawa Montagnards	OCHL	1	0	0	0	....	....	....	0	....	....	....	....	....
	NHL Totals		**211**	**48**	**48**	**96**	**89**	**193**	**282**	**148**	**2**	**1**	**0**	**1**	**2**

• Brother of Fred

Signed as a free agent by **London** (Can-Pro), November 18, 1926. Traded to **Toronto** by **London** (Can-Pro) for Al Pudas, October 20, 1927. Traded to **Pittsburgh** by **Toronto** with $9,500 for Baldy Cotton, February 12, 1929. Transferred to **Philadelphia** after **Pittsburgh** franchise relocated, September 27, 1930. Claimed by **Chicago** from **Philadelphia** in Dispersal Draft, September 21, 1931. Traded to **St. Paul** (AHA) by **Chicago** for Lou Holmes, November 9, 1932. Signed as a free agent by **Ottawa** after securing release from **St. Paul** (AHA), January 4, 1933. Signed as a free agent by **Quebec** (Can-Am) after being released by **Ottawa**, January 19, 1933.

• LUCAS, Dave

David Charles
D – L. 6', 205 lbs. b: Downeyville, Ont., 3/22/1932.

Season	Club	League	GP	G	A	Pts	AG	AA	APts	PIM	GP	G	A	Pts	PIM
1951-52	Lindsay Braves	OHA-B	STATISTICS NOT AVAILABLE												
1952-53	Washington Lions	EAHL	62	2	14	16	....	....	....	43	....	....	....	....	....
1953-54	Troy Bruins	IHL	63	5	15	20	....	....	....	129	3	0	0	0	4
1954-55	Troy Bruins	IHL	3	0	1	1	....	....	....	4	....	....	....	....	....
	Washington Lions	EHL	48	7	27	34	....	....	....	95	8	3	5	8	9
1955-56	Washington Lions	EHL	64	10	14	24	....	....	....	132	4	1	1	2	0
1956-57	Johnstown Jets	EHL	62	12	28	40	....	....	....	100	6	1	2	3	4
1957-58	Johnstown Jets	EHL	64	11	36	47	....	....	....	55	6	0	3	3	4
1958-59	Johnstown Jets	EHL	61	10	24	34	....	....	....	50	....	....	....	....	....
1959-60	Johnstown Jets	EHL	63	13	19	32	....	....	....	91	13	3	6	9	17
1960-61	Johnstown Jets	EHL	61	9	34	43	....	....	....	70	12	1	4	5	8
1961-62	Johnstown Jets	EHL	68	14	30	44	....	....	....	70	15	2	5	7	8
1962-63	**Detroit Red Wings**	**NHL**	**1**	**0**	**0**	**0**	**0**	**0**	**0**	**0**	....	....	....	....	....
	Portland Buckaroos	WHL	1	0	0	0	....	....	....	0	....	....	....	....	....
	Pittsburgh Hornets	AHL	1	0	1	1	....	....	....	0	....	....	....	....	....
	Johnstown Jets	EHL	68	15	33	48	....	....	....	52	3	0	1	1	6
1963-64	Portland Buckaroos	WHL	2	0	0	0	....	....	....	0	....	....	....	....	....
	Johnstown Jets	EHL	70	17	36	53	....	....	....	86	10	0	6	6	34
1964-65	Johnstown Jets	EHL	72	12	48	60	....	....	....	126	5	2	4	6	16
1965-66	Johnstown Jets	EHL	72	13	35	48	....	....	....	84	2	0	0	0	2
	Pittsburgh Hornets	AHL	5	0	0	0	....	....	....	2	....	....	....	....	....
1966-67	Johnstown Jets	EHL	72	16	41	57	....	....	....	72	5	0	2	2	2
1967-68	Salem Rebels	EHL	PLAYER/COACH – STATISTICS UNAVAILABLE												
1968-69	Salem Rebels	EHL	63	7	28	35	....	....	....	112	....	....	....	....	....
	NHL Totals		**1**	**0**	**0**	**0**	**0**	**0**	**0**	**0**	....	....	....	....	....

EHL Second All-Star Team (1956, 1957, 1958, 1960, 1963) • EHL First All-Star Team (1962, 1964) • EHL North Second All-Star Team (1965, 1966)

Traded to **Salem** (EHL) by **Johnstown** (EHL) for cash, October, 1967. • Named playing-coach of Salem (EHL), October, 1967.

• LUND, Pentti

Pentti Alexander "Penny"
RW – R. 6', 185 lbs. b: Karijoki, Finland, 12/6/1925.

Season	Club	League	GP	G	A	Pts	AG	AA	APts	PIM	GP	G	A	Pts	PIM
1942-43	Port Arthur Bruins	TBJHL	9	5	11	16	....	....	....	4	3	3	3	6	5
	Fort William Forts	M-Cup	1	0	0	0	....	....	....	0	....	....	....	....	....
1943-44	Port Arthur Navy	TBJHL	10	21	*24	*45	....	....	....	10	2	3	2	5	0
	Port Arthur Navy	M-Cup	2	3	2	5	....	....	....	0	....	....	....	....	....
	Port Arthur Flyers	M-Cup	7	1	3	4	....	....	....	0	....	....	....	....	....
1944-45	Port Arthur Navy	TBJHL	9	*26	9	*35	....	....	....	9	....	....	....	....	....
	Port Arthur Bruins	M-Cup	5	5	2	7	....	....	....	0	....	....	....	....	....
1945-46	Boston Olympics	EAHL	34	14	19	33	....	....	....	10	12	*13	6	19	7
1946-47	Boston Olympics	EAHL	56	*49	43	*92	....	....	....	21	9	7	*8	*15	4
	Boston Bruins	**NHL**	....	....	....	....	....	....	....	....	**1**	**0**	**0**	**0**	**0**
1947-48	Hershey Bears	AHL	68	26	36	62	....	....	....	21	2	0	0	0	0
	Boston Bruins	**NHL**	....	....	....	....	....	....	....	....	**2**	**0**	**0**	**0**	**0**
1948-49	**New York Rangers**	**NHL**	**59**	**14**	**16**	**30**	**20**	**23**	**43**	**16**	....	....	....	....	....
1949-50	**New York Rangers**	**NHL**	**64**	**18**	**9**	**27**	**23**	**11**	**34**	**16**	**12**	***6**	**5**	***11**	**0**
1950-51	**New York Rangers**	**NHL**	**59**	**4**	**16**	**20**	**5**	**20**	**25**	**6**	....	....	....	....	....
1951-52	**Boston Bruins**	**NHL**	**23**	**0**	**5**	**5**	**0**	**6**	**6**	**0**	**2**	**1**	**0**	**1**	**0**
	Hershey Bears	AHL	7	1	1	2	....	....	....	5	....	....	....	....	....
1952-53	**Boston Bruins**	**NHL**	**54**	**8**	**9**	**17**	**10**	**11**	**21**	**2**	**2**	**0**	**0**	**0**	**0**
1953-54	S.S. Marie Greyhounds	NOHA	6	1	2	3	....	....	....	0	9	1	1	2	0
1954-55	S.S. Marie Greyhounds	NOHA	48	13	18	31	....	....	....	9	14	2	5	7	4
	NHL Totals		**259**	**44**	**55**	**99**	**58**	**71**	**129**	**40**	**19**	**7**	**5**	**12**	**0**

EAHL First All-Star Team (1947) • Won John Carlin Trophy (EAHL - Top Scorer) (1947) • Won Calder Memorial Trophy (1949)

Traded to **NY Rangers** by **Boston** with Ray Manson to complete transaction that sent Grant Warwick to Boston (February 6, 1948), June, 1948. Rights traded to **Boston** by **NY Rangers** with Gus Kyle and cash for Paul Ronty, September 20, 1951. Traded to **Victoria** (WHL) by **Boston** with Sam Bettio for cash, July 1, 1953.

• LUNDE, Len

— *see page 1348*

• LUNDY, Pat

Patrick Anthony
C – R. 5'11", 170 lbs. b: Saskatoon, Sask., 5/31/1925.

Season	Club	League	GP	G	A	Pts	AG	AA	APts	PIM	GP	G	A	Pts	PIM
1942-43	Saskatoon Jr. Quakers	N-SJHL	8	11	4	15	....	....	....	4	3	4	*3	*7	4
	Saskatoon Jr. Quakers	M-Cup	8	1	6	7	....	....	....	14	....	....	....	....	....
1943-44	Saskatoon Navy	N-SSHL	18	26	20	46	....	....	....	7	4	3	3	6	0
1944-45			MILITARY SERVICE												
1945-46	**Detroit Red Wings**	**NHL**	**4**	**3**	**2**	**5**	**4**	**3**	**7**	**2**	**2**	**1**	**0**	**1**	**0**
	Saskatoon Elks	WCSHL	34	19	22	41	....	....	....	24	3	0	0	0	0
1946-47	**Detroit Red Wings**	**NHL**	**59**	**17**	**17**	**34**	**19**	**20**	**39**	**10**	**5**	**0**	**1**	**1**	**2**
1947-48	**Detroit Red Wings**	**NHL**	**11**	**4**	**1**	**5**	**5**	**1**	**6**	**6**	**5**	**1**	**1**	**2**	**0**
	Indianapolis Capitols	AHL	39	17	28	45	....	....	....	20	....	....	....	....	....
1948-49	**Detroit Red Wings**	**NHL**	**15**	**4**	**3**	**7**	**6**	**4**	**10**	**4**	**4**	**0**	**0**	**0**	**0**
	Indianapolis Capitols	AHL	47	29	20	49	....	....	....	13	....	....	....	....	....
1949-50	Indianapolis Capitols	AHL	70	30	47	77	....	....	....	8	8	*7	7	*14	0
1950-51	**Chicago Black Hawks**	**NHL**	**61**	**9**	**9**	**18**	**11**	**11**	**22**	**9**	....	....	....	....	....
	Milwaukee Seagulls	USHL	9	7	6	13	....	....	....	0	....	....	....	....	....
1951-52	St. Louis Flyers	AHL	58	24	37	61	....	....	....	21	....	....	....	....	....
1952-53	Calgary Stampeders	WHL	68	25	24	49	....	....	....	20	5	1	5	6	0
1953-54	Calgary Stampeders	WHL	66	29	42	71	....	....	....	18	17	*15	10	*25	2
1954-55	Calgary Stampeders	WHL	65	28	33	61	....	....	....	10	9	3	3	6	2
1955-56	Brandon Regals	WHL	23	15	5	20	....	....	....	4	....	....	....	....	....
1956-57			DID NOT PLAY												
1957-58			DID NOT PLAY												
1958-59	Regina Capitals	SSHL	8	13	10	23	....	....	....	2	....	....	....	....	....
1959-60	Regina Capitals	SSHL	22	*26	21	47	....	....	....	4	9	8	6	14	4
1960-61	Regina Capitals	SSHL	26	27	32	59	....	....	....	2	8	7	5	12	0
1961-62	Regina Capitals	SSHL	17	15	12	27	....	....	....	9	....	....	....	....	....
	NHL Totals		**150**	**37**	**32**	**69**	**45**	**39**	**84**	**31**	**16**	**2**	**2**	**4**	**2**

Traded to **Chicago** by **Detroit** for cash, October 1, 1950.

• LYNN, Vic

Victor Ivan
LW/D – L. 5'10", 175 lbs. b: Saskatoon, Sask., 1/26/1925.

Season	Club	League	GP	G	A	Pts	AG	AA	APts	PIM	GP	G	A	Pts	PIM
1940-41	Saskatoon Embassys	SAHA	STATISTICS NOT AVAILABLE												
1941-42	Saskatoon Jr. Quakers	N-SJHL	7	6	8	14	....	....	....	12	6	0	2	2	10
	Saskatoon Jr. Quakers	M-Cup	3	1	0	1	....	....	....	12	....	....	....	....	....
1942-43	**New York Rangers**	**NHL**	**1**	**0**	**0**	**0**	**0**	**0**	**0**	**0**	....	....	....	....	....
	New York Rovers	EAHL	38	4	6	10	....	....	....	*122	10	3	3	6	30
1943-44	**Detroit Red Wings**	**NHL**	**3**	**0**	**0**	**0**	**0**	**0**	**0**	**4**	....	....	....	....	....
	Indianapolis Capitols	AHL	32	4	5	9	....	....	....	61	....	....	....	....	....
	Saskatoon Navy	N-SSHL	....	....	....	....	....	....	....	....	4	2	0	2	13
1944-45	St. Louis Flyers	AHL	60	15	23	38	....	....	....	92	....	....	....	....	....
1945-46	**Montreal Canadiens**	**NHL**	**2**	**0**	**0**	**0**	**0**	**0**	**0**	**0**	....	....	....	....	....
	Buffalo Bisons	AHL	53	26	25	51	....	....	....	60	12	5	5	10	10
♦1946-47	**Toronto Maple Leafs**	**NHL**	**31**	**6**	**14**	**20**	**7**	**17**	**24**	**44**	**11**	**4**	**1**	**5**	**16**
♦1947-48	**Toronto Maple Leafs**	**NHL**	**60**	**12**	**22**	**34**	**15**	**29**	**44**	**53**	**9**	**2**	**5**	**7**	***20**
♦1948-49	**Toronto Maple Leafs**	**NHL**	**52**	**7**	**9**	**16**	**10**	**13**	**23**	**36**	**8**	**0**	**1**	**1**	**2**
1949-50	**Toronto Maple Leafs**	**NHL**	**70**	**7**	**13**	**20**	**9**	**16**	**25**	**39**	**7**	**0**	**2**	**2**	**2**
1950-51	Pittsburgh Hornets	AHL	16	2	4	6	....	....	....	17	....	....	....	....	....
	Boston Bruins	**NHL**	**56**	**14**	**6**	**20**	**18**	**7**	**25**	**69**	**5**	**0**	**0**	**0**	**2**
1951-52	**Boston Bruins**	**NHL**	**12**	**2**	**2**	**4**	**3**	**2**	**5**	**4**	....	....	....	....	....
	Providence Reds	AHL	5	1	4	5	....	....	....	4	....	....	....	....	....
	Cleveland Barons	AHL	39	1	4	5	....	....	....	4	5	1	3	4	2
1952-53	Cleveland Barons	AHL	35	11	17	28	....	....	....	46	....	....	....	....	....
	Chicago Black Hawks	**NHL**	**29**	**0**	**10**	**10**	**0**	**12**	**12**	**23**	**7**	**1**	**1**	**2**	**4**
1953-54	**Chicago Black Hawks**	**NHL**	**11**	**1**	**0**	**1**	**1**	**0**	**1**	**2**	....	....	....	....	....
	Saskatoon Quakers	WHL	38	11	12	23	....	....	....	14	6	2	3	5	9
1954-55	Saskatoon Quakers	WHL	70	20	24	44	....	....	....	82	....	....	....	....	....

Season	Club	League	GP	G	A	Pts	AG	AA	APts	PIM	GP	G	A	Pts	PIM
			REGULAR SEASON								PLAYOFFS				
1955-56	Saskatoon Quakers	WHL	64	17	26	43				100	3	0	1	1	6
1956-57	Brandon Regals	WHL	61	10	21	31				137	9	2	7	9	8
	Brandon Regals	Ed-Cup	6	1	3	4				12					
1957-58	Saskatoon–St. Paul	WHL	38	13	19	32				49					
	Sudbury Wolves	NOHA	7	0	1	1				8					
1958-59	Prince Albert Mintos	SJHL	DID NOT PLAY – COACHING												
	Saskatoon Quakers	WHL	20	3	8	11				20					
1959-60	Saskatoon Quakers	SSHL	20	10	10	20				30	7	2	8	10	10
	Saskatoon Quakers	Al-Cup	2	0	0	0				2					
1960-61	Saskatoon Quakers	SSHL	PLAYER/COACH – STATISTICS UNAVAILABLE												
1961-62	Saskatoon Quakers	SSHL	12	5	5	10				16	8	1	3	4	6
	Saskatoon Quakers	Al-Cup	7	1	4	5				0					
1962-63	Saskatoon Quakers	SSHL	18	5	13	18				24					
1963-64	Saskatoon Quakers	SSHL	PLAYER/COACH – STATISTICS UNAVAILABLE												
	NHL Totals		**327**	**49**	**76**	**125**	**63**	**96**	**159**	**274**	**47**	**7**	**10**	**17**	**46**

Played in NHL All-Star Game (1947, 1948, 1949)

Traded to **Montreal** (Buffalo-AHL) by **Detroit** for cash, October 14,1945. Traded to **Toronto** (Pittsburgh-AHL) by **Montreal** (Buffalo-AHL) with Dutch Hiller for John Mahaffy and Gerry Brown, September 21, 1946. Traded to **Boston** by **Toronto** with Bill Ezinicki for Fern Flaman, Leo Boivin, Ken Smith and Phil Maloney, November 16, 1950. Traded to **Cleveland** (AHL) by **Boston** (Providence-AHL) with Ken Davies for Joe Lund and Jean-Paul Gladu, December 10, 1951. Traded to **Chicago** by **Cleveland** (AHL) for future considerations (Fred Glover, January 16, 1953), January 4, 1953.

• LYONS, Ron "Peaches"

LW – L. 5'11", 170 lbs. b: Portage la Prairie, Man., 2/15/1909.

Season	Club	League	GP	G	A	Pts	AG	AA	APts	PIM	GP	G	A	Pts	PIM
1926-27	International Falls AC	NMHL	STATISTICS NOT AVAILABLE												
1927-28	Medicine Hat Tigers	ASHL	STATISTICS NOT AVAILABLE												
1928-29	Trail Smoke Eaters	WKHL	STATISTICS NOT AVAILABLE												
1929-30	Portland Buckaroos	PCHL	35	4	1	5				4	4	1	0	1	4
1930-31	**Boston Bruins**	**NHL**	**14**	**0**	**0**	**0**	**0**	**0**	**0**	**19**	**5**	**0**	**0**	**0**	**0**
	Boston Tigers	Can-Am	7	2	3	5				33					
	Philadelphia Quakers	**NHL**	**22**	**2**	**4**	**6**	**4**	**12**	**16**	**8**					
1931-32	Boston Tigers	Can-Am	2	1	0	1				6					
	Springfield Indians	Can-Am	31	7	7	14				24					
1932-33	Windsor Bulldogs	IHL	5	1	2	3				4					
1933-34	Portland Buckaroos	NWHL	34	14	12	26				44					
1934-35	Portland Buckaroos	NWHL	32	13	10	23				45	3	1	0	1	2
1935-36	Portland Buckaroos	NWHL	9	0	1	1				4					
	Seattle Seahawks	NWHL	22	3	3	6				0					
1936-37	Seattle–Portland	PCHL	7	1	2	3				8					
1937-38	Portland Buckaroos	PCHL	6	0	0	0				0					
	Seattle Seahawks	PCHL	1	0	0	0				0					
	NHL Totals		**36**	**2**	**4**	**6**	**4**	**12**	**16**	**27**	**5**	**0**	**0**	**0**	**0**

Rights sold to **Boston** by **Portland** (PCHL) for $5,000, April 17, 1930. Traded to **Philadelphia** by **Boston** with Bill Hutton for Harold Darragh, December 8, 1930. Traded to **Boston** by **Philadelphia** for cash, February, 1931. Signed as a free agent by **Seattle** (NWHL) following release by Portland (NWHL), December 17, 1935.

• MacDONALD, Kilby James Allan Kilby

LW – L. 5'11", 178 lbs. b: Ottawa, Ont., 9/6/1914 d: 5/11/1986.

Season	Club	League	GP	G	A	Pts	AG	AA	APts	PIM	GP	G	A	Pts	PIM
1930-31	Ottawa Jr. Montagnards	OCJHL	15	2	0	2				14					
	Ottawa Montagnards	OCHL	4	0	0	0				2					
1931-32	Ottawa Jr. Montagnards	OCJHL	12	10	7	17				21	2	1	0	1	4
	Ottawa Montagnards	OCHL	1	0	0	0				0					
1932-33	Ottawa Jr. Montagnards	OCJHL	12	7	7	14				20	2	1	1	2	*12
	Ottawa Montagnards	OCHL	1	0	0	0				0					
1933-34	Lake Placid Seniors	NEHL	STATISTICS NOT AVAILABLE												
1934-35	Kirkland Lake Blue Devils	GBHL	13	7	8	15				20					
1935-36	Noranda Copper Kings	GBHL	16	14	10	24				48					
	Noranda Cooper Kings	Al-Cup	2	4	1	5				4					
1936-37	New York Rovers	EAHL	45	21	22	43				24	3	3	3	6	0
1937-38	Philadelphia Ramblers	IAHL	44	10	21	31				12	5	2	3	5	2
1938-39	Philadelphia Ramblers	IAHL	49	18	37	55				48	9	4	4	8	0
♦1939-40	**New York Rangers**	**NHL**	**44**	**15**	**13**	**28**	**25**	**20**	**45**	**19**	**12**	**0**	**2**	**2**	**4**
1940-41	**New York Rangers**	**NHL**	**47**	**5**	**6**	**11**	**8**	**9**	**17**	**12**	**3**	**1**	**0**	**1**	**0**
1941-42	Hershey Bears	AHL	37	14	16	30				16					
	Buffalo Bisons	AHL	21	14	14	28				12					
1942-43	Montreal Army	MCHL	29	11	20	31				10	7	3	6	9	16
	Montreal Army	MCHL	3	1	3	4				0	5	6	6	*12	12
1943-44	Montreal Army	MCHL	4	0	0	0				0					
	New York Rangers	**NHL**	**24**	**7**	**9**	**16**	**6**	**8**	**14**	**4**					
1944-45	**New York Rangers**	**NHL**	**36**	**9**	**6**	**15**	**9**	**7**	**16**	**12**					
1945-46	Hull Volants	QSHL	9	2	4	6				0					
	NHL Totals		**151**	**36**	**34**	**70**	**48**	**44**	**92**	**47**	**15**	**1**	**2**	**3**	**4**

EAHL First All-Star Team (1937) • IAHL First All-Star Team (1939) • Won Calder Trophy (1940)

Traded to **Hershey** (AHL) by **NY Rangers** for cash, September 11, 1941. Traded to **Buffalo** (AHL) by **Hershey** (AHL) for Bob Gracie, February 2, 1942. Traded to **NY Rangers** by **Buffalo** (AHL) for Hub Macey, Nestor Lubeck and Spencer Tatchell, January 12, 1944.

• MacDONALD, Lowell — see page 1353

• MacDONALD, Parker — see page 1354

• MACEY, Hub Hubert

LW – L. 5'8", 178 lbs. b: Big River, Sask., 4/13/1921.

Season	Club	League	GP	G	A	Pts	AG	AA	APts	PIM	GP	G	A	Pts	PIM
1938-39	Portage Terriers	MJHL	18	12	3	15				12	3	2	2	4	0
1939-40	Portage Terriers	MJHL	21	14	7	21				14	4	2	2	4	0
1940-41	Portage Terriers	MJHL	19	18	10	28				6	6	5	2	7	2
	Winnipeg Rangers	M-Cup									10	9	6	15	4
1941-42	**New York Rangers**	**NHL**	**9**	**3**	**5**	**8**	**4**	**6**	**10**	**0**	**1**	**0**	**0**	**0**	**0**
	New York Rovers	EAHL	47	39	33	72				8					
1942-43	**New York Rangers**	**NHL**	**9**	**3**	**3**	**6**	**3**	**3**	**6**	**0**					
	Kingston Frontenacs	OVHL	13	13	9	22				24	4	0	5	5	0
1943-44	Kingston Army	OHA-Sr.	2	2	1	3				2					
1944-45			MILITARY SERVICE												
1945-46	London Army	Britain	STATISTICS NOT AVAILABLE												
1946-47	**Montreal Canadiens**	**NHL**	**12**	**0**	**1**	**1**	**0**	**1**	**1**	**0**	**7**	**0**	**0**	**0**	**0**
	Buffalo Bisons	AHL	32	15	16	31				4					
	Houston Huskies	USHL	9	4	4	8				0					
1947-48	Houston Huskies	USHL	59	31	60	91				8	12	4	5	9	0
1948-49	Houston Huskies	USHL	14	6	9	15				0					
	Springfield Indians	AHL	43	20	29	49				2	3	0	1	1	0
1949-50	Springfield Indians	AHL	48	10	26	36				2	2	0	1	1	0
1950-51	Vancouver Canucks	PCHL	19	6	5	11				2					
	Tulsa Oilers	USHL	41	11	27	38				6	6	3	0	3	0
1951-52	Glace Bay Miners	MMHL	71	30	27	57				24	3	0	0	0	0
1952-53	Glace Bay Miners	MMHL	62	22	34	56				10	7	3	1	4	0
1953-54	Sault Ste. Marie Indians	NOHA	21	4	11	15				4					
1954-55			OUT OF HOCKEY – RETIRED												
1955-56	Kingston Goodyears	EOHL	30	20	22	42				4	14	7	*13	20	2
1956-57	Kingston CKLC's	EOHL	44	23	28	51				28	5	3	0	3	0
	NHL Totals		**30**	**6**	**9**	**15**	**7**	**10**	**17**	**0**	**8**	**0**	**0**	**0**	**0**

EAHL First All-Star Team (1942)

Traded to **Montreal** (Buffalo-AHL) by **NY Rangers** with Nestor Lubeck and Spencer Tatchell for Kilby MacDonald, January 12, 1944. Traded to **Springfield** (AHL) by **Montreal** for Gordie Bell and the rights to Sid McNabney, December 21, 1948. Signed as a free agent by **Vancouver** (PCHL), October, 1950. • Released by **Vancouver** (PCHL), November, 1950. Signed as a free agent by **Tulsa** (USHL), November, 23, 1950. Signed as a free agent by **Glace Bay** (MMHL), September 19, 1951.

• MacGREGOR, Bruce — see page 1354

• MacINTOSH, Ian Ian Ronald

RW – R. 5'11", 175 lbs. b: Selkirk, Man., 6/10/1927.

Season	Club	League	GP	G	A	Pts	AG	AA	APts	PIM	GP	G	A	Pts	PIM
1943-44	Winnipeg Rangers	WJrHL	10	15	10	25				20					
	Winnipeg St. James	WJrHL									6	7	5	12	6
1944-45	Winnipeg Rangers	WJrHL	7	8	5	13				5	4	0	5	5	0
	Winnipeg Navy	WNDHL	2	0	0	0				0					
1945-46	New York Rovers	EAHL	49	13	27	40				14	4	0	3	3	0
1946-47	New York Rovers	EAHL	53	22	23	45				17	9	5	5	10	4
	New Haven Ramblers	AHL	3	2	0	2				0					
1947-48	New Haven Ramblers	AHL	58	11	13	24				21	3	1	0	1	2
	New York Rovers	QSHL	3	0	0	0				0					
1948-49	St. Paul Saints	USHL	63	20	26	46				20	7	3	8	*11	0
1949-50	St. Paul Saints	USHL	70	35	42	77				33	3	1	2	3	0
1950-51	St. Paul Saints	USHL	64	39	38	77				82	4	1	1	2	2
1951-52	Cincinnati Mohawks	AHL	68	19	25	44				12	7	2	0	2	0
1952-53	**New York Rangers**	**NHL**	**4**	**0**	**0**	**0**	**0**	**0**	**0**	**4**					
	Vancouver Canucks	WHL	63	28	31	59				26	9	1	2	3	0
1953-54			REINSTATED AS AN AMATEUR												
1954-55	Winnipeg Maroons	X-Games	STATISTICS NOT AVAILABLE												
	Winnipeg Maroons	Al-Cup	5	4	3	7				2					
1955-56	Winnipeg Maroons	X-Games	STATISTICS NOT AVAILABLE												
	Winnipeg Maroons	Al-Cup	9	8	6	14				8					
1956-57	Winnipeg Maroons	X-Games	STATISTICS NOT AVAILABLE												
	Winnipeg Maroons	Al-Cup	8	1	2	3				2					
	NHL Totals		**4**	**0**	**0**	**0**	**0**	**0**	**0**	**4**					

• MacKAY, Calum "Baldy"

LW – L. 5'10", 178 lbs. b: Toronto, Ont., 1/1/1927.

Season	Club	League	GP	G	A	Pts	AG	AA	APts	PIM	GP	G	A	Pts	PIM
1943-44	Port Arthur Bruins	TBJHL	10	5	12	17				7	4	4	0	4	4
	Port Arthur Flyers	TBJHL									2	2	0	2	0
	Port Arthur Flyers	M-Cup	9	6	2	8				2					
1944-45	Port Arthur Bruins	TBJHL	10	12	15	27				24	8	3	*7	10	6
	Port Arthur Bruins	M-Cup	10	5	5	10				10					
1945-46	Port Arthur Bruins	TBJHL	3	3	4	7				9	6	*9	5	14	6
1946-47	Oshawa Generals	OHA-Jr.	27	16	22	38				54	5	1	0	1	25
	Detroit Red Wings	**NHL**	**5**	**0**	**0**	**0**	**0**	**0**	**0**	**0**					
1947-48	Omaha Knights	USHL	25	9	10	19				22					
	Indianapolis Capitols	AHL	36	18	16	34				18					
1948-49	**Detroit Red Wings**	**NHL**	**1**	**0**	**0**	**0**	**0**	**0**	**0**	**0**					
	Indianapolis Capitols	AHL	65	26	48	74				34	2	0	0	0	0
1949-50	Indianapolis Capitols	AHL	14	6	5	11				16					
	Montreal Canadiens	**NHL**	**52**	**8**	**10**	**18**	**10**	**12**	**22**	**44**	**5**	**0**	**1**	**1**	**2**
1950-51	**Montreal Canadiens**	**NHL**	**70**	**18**	**10**	**28**	**23**	**12**	**35**	**69**	**11**	**1**	**0**	**1**	**0**
1951-52	**Montreal Canadiens**	**NHL**	**12**	**0**	**1**	**1**	**0**	**1**	**1**	**8**					
	Buffalo Bisons	AHL	47	20	21	41				45	3	1	0	1	0
1952-53	Buffalo Bisons	AHL	64	28	42	70				65					
♦	**Montreal Canadiens**	**NHL**									**7**	**1**	**3**	**4**	**10**
1953-54	**Montreal Canadiens**	**NHL**	**47**	**10**	**13**	**23**	**13**	**16**	**29**	**54**	**3**	**0**	**1**	**1**	**0**
1954-55	**Montreal Canadiens**	**NHL**	**50**	**14**	**21**	**35**	**18**	**24**	**42**	**39**	**12**	**3**	**8**	**11**	**8**
1955-56	Montreal Royals	QHL	32	13	17	30				56	13	3	2	5	4
	Montreal Royals	Ed-Cup	1	1	0	1				0					
1956-57	Peterborough Petes	OHA-Jr.	DID NOT PLAY – COACHING												
	NHL Totals		**237**	**50**	**55**	**105**	**64**	**65**	**129**	**214**	**38**	**5**	**13**	**18**	**20**

Played in NHL All-Star Game (1953)

Traded to **Montreal** by **Detroit** for Joe Carveth, November 11, 1949. • Missed majority of 1955-56 season recovering from knee injury suffered in training camp, September 30, 1955.

• MacKAY, Dave

D – R. 6', 210 lbs. b: Edmonton, Alta., 1/14/1919.

Season	Club	League	GP	G	A	Pts	AG	AA	APts	PIM	GP	G	A	Pts	PIM
1936-37	Edmonton Athletic Club	EJrHL	6	3	1	4				12	3	0	1	1	0
1937-38	University of Alberta	ESrHL	22	17	9	26				59					
1938-39	University of Alberta	ESrHL	19	19	5	24				60					
1939-40	Edmonton Flyers	ESrHL	9	3	1	4				8					
1940-41	**Chicago Black Hawks**	**NHL**	**29**	**3**	**0**	**3**	**5**	**0**	**5**	**26**	**5**	**0**	**1**	**1**	**2**
	Providence Reds	AHL		2	5	7				6					
1941-42	Nanaimo Clippers	PCHL	27	3	0	3				26	5	0	1	1	2
1942-43	Nanaimo Clippers	PCHL	14	17	14	31				24	3	3	0	3	4
1943-44	Nanaimo Army	NNDHL	14	8	4	12				33					
	Vancouver Army	NNDHL									3	2	2	4	2
1944-45	Petawawa Engineers	OVHL	STATISTICS NOT AVAILABLE												
1945-46			MILITARY SERVICE												
1946-47			MILITARY SERVICE												

			REGULAR SEASON								PLAYOFFS				
Season	Club	League	GP	G	A	Pts	AG	AA	APts	PIM	GP	G	A	Pts	PIM
1947-48	New Westminster Royals	PCHL	13	3	11	14	....	....	....	47	5	1	1	2	14
1948-49	New Westminster Royals	PCHL	3	0	0	0	....	....	....	8	....	....	....	....	....
1949-50	Vernon Canadians	OSHL	43	13	9	22	....	....	....	86	4	2	1	3	8
1950-51	Vernon Canadians	OSHL	51	8	14	22	....	....	....	65	10	1	2	3	20
1951-52	Vernon Canadians	OSHL	5	0	1	1	....	....	....	4	....	....	....	....	....
1952-53	Vernon Canadians	OSHL	PLAYER/COACH – STATISTICS UNAVAILABLE												
1953-54	Vernon Canadians	OSHL	43	5	25	30	....	....	....	51	....	....	....	....	....
	NHL Totals		**29**	**3**	**0**	**3**	**5**	**0**	**5**	**26**	**5**	**0**	**1**	**1**	**2**

OSHL First All-Star Team (1951)

• Alberta Military Authority rejected his request to go to Chicago, October 10, 1941. Signed as a free agent by **Nanaimo** (PCHL), November 4, 1941.

• MacKAY, Mickey   Duncan McMillan   HHOF

C – L. 5'9", 162 lbs. b: Chelsey, Ont., 5/25/1894 d: 5/21/1940.

Season	Club	League	GP	G	A	Pts	AG	AA	APts	PIM	GP	G	A	Pts	PIM
1910-11	Chesley ACC	OHA-Jr.	STATISTICS NOT AVAILABLE												
1911-12	Chesley Intermediates	OIHA	STATISTICS NOT AVAILABLE												
1912-13	Edmonton Dominions	ASHL	7	14	0	14	....	....	....	3	2	*8	0	*8	0
1913-14	Grand Forks AC	BDHL	STATISTICS NOT AVAILABLE												
♦1914-15	Vancouver Millionaires	PCHA	17	*33	11	44	....	....	....	9	3	4	2	6	9
	PCHA All-Stars	X-Games	2	0	1	1	....	....	....	0	....	....	....	....	....
1915-16	Vancouver Millionaires	PCHA	14	12	7	19	....	....	....	32	....	....	....	....	....
	PCHA All-Stars	X-Games	2	3	0	3	....	....	....	0	....	....	....	....	....
1916-17	Vancouver Millionaires	PCHA	23	22	11	33	....	....	....	37	....	....	....	....	....
1917-18	Vancouver Millionaires	PCHA	18	10	8	18	....	....	....	31	2	2	1	3	0
	Vancouver Millionaires	St-Cup	5	5	5	10	....	....	....	12	....	....	....	....	....
1918-19	Vancouver Millionaires	PCHA	17	9	9	18	....	....	....	9	....	....	....	....	....
1919-20	Calgary Columbus Club	Big-4	11	4	6	10	....	....	....	14	....	....	....	....	....
1920-21	Vancouver Millionaires	PCHA	21	10	8	18	....	....	....	15	2	0	3	3	0
	Vancouver Millionaires	St-Cup	5	0	1	1	....	....	....	0	....	....	....	....	....
1921-22	Vancouver Millionaires	PCHA	24	14	*12	26	....	....	....	20	2	0	0	0	0
	Vancouver Millionaires	St-Cup	7	1	0	1	....	....	....	6	....	....	....	....	....
1922-23	Vancouver Maroons	PCHA	30	28	12	40	....	....	....	38	2	2	0	2	12
	Vancouver Maroons	St-Cup	4	1	0	1	....	....	....	4	....	....	....	....	....
1923-24	Vancouver Maroons	PCHA	28	*21	4	25	....	....	....	2	2	1	0	1	0
	Vancouver Maroons	St-Cup	2	2	0	2	....	....	....	2	....	....	....	....	....
1924-25	Vancouver Maroons	WCHL	28	*27	6	33	....	....	....	17	....	....	....	....	....
1925-26	Vancouver Maroons	WHL	27	12	4	16	....	....	....	24	....	....	....	....	....
1926-27	**Chicago Black Hawks**	**NHL**	**34**	**14**	**8**	**22**	**25**	**42**	**67**	**23**	**2**	**0**	**0**	**0**	**0**
1927-28	**Chicago Black Hawks**	**NHL**	**36**	**17**	**4**	**21**	**35**	**23**	**58**	**23**	....	....	....	....	....
1928-29	**Pittsburgh Pirates**	**NHL**	**10**	**1**	**0**	**1**	**3**	**0**	**3**	**2**	....	....	....	....	....
♦	**Boston Bruins**	**NHL**	**30**	**8**	**2**	**10**	**23**	**13**	**36**	**18**	**3**	**0**	**0**	**0**	**2**
1929-30	**Boston Bruins**	**NHL**	**37**	**4**	**5**	**9**	**6**	**12**	**18**	**13**	**6**	**0**	**0**	**0**	**4**
	NHL Totals		**147**	**44**	**19**	**63**	**92**	**90**	**182**	**79**	**11**	**0**	**0**	**0**	**6**
	Other Major League Totals		247	198	92	290	....	....	....	234	13	9	6	15	21

PCHA First All-Star Team (1915, 1917, 1919, 1922, 1923) • PCHA Second All-Star Team (1916, 1918, 1921) • WCHL First All-Star Team (1925) • WHL First All-Star Team (1926)

Signed as a free agent by **Grand Forks** (BDHL), November 24, 1913. Signed as a free agent by **Vancouver** (PCHA), November 3, 1914. • Re-instated as an amateur for 1919-20 season, November 23, 1919. Signed as a free agent by **Vancouver** (PCHA), November 29, 1920. Traded to **Chicago** by **Vancouver** (WHL) for cash, October 4, 1926. Traded to **Pittsburgh** by **Chicago** for cash, September, 1928. Traded to **Boston** by **Pittsburgh** with $12,000 for Frank Frederickson, December 21, 1928. • 1922 St-Cup totals include series vs. Regina.

• MacKAY, Murdo   John

RW/C – R. 5'11", 175 lbs. b: Fort William, Ont., 8/8/1917.

Season	Club	League	GP	G	A	Pts	AG	AA	APts	PIM	GP	G	A	Pts	PIM
1932-33	Fort William Forts	TBJHL	7	2	0	2	....	....	....	0	....	....	....	....	....
1933-34	Fort William Cubs	TBJHL	19	11	3	14	....	....	....	16	....	....	....	....	....
1934-35	Fort William Kams	TBJHL	16	8	3	11	....	....	....	6	....	....	....	....	....
1935-36	Fort William Kams	TBJHL	16	*23	9	*32	....	....	....	10	2	1	0	1	2
	Fort William Kams	M-Cup	4	*7	3	*10	....	....	....	0	....	....	....	....	....
1936-37	New York Rovers	EAHL	47	5	5	10	....	....	....	6	3	0	0	0	0
1937-38	New York Rovers	EAHL	39	7	6	13	....	....	....	4	....	....	....	....	....
1938-39	New York Rovers	EAHL	42	20	18	38	....	....	....	8	....	....	....	....	....
1939-40	New York Rovers	EAHL	58	44	44	88	....	....	....	29	....	....	....	....	....
1940-41	Philadelphia Rockets	AHL	56	20	15	35	....	....	....	12	....	....	....	....	....
1941-42	Buffalo Bisons	AHL	56	21	20	41	....	....	....	17	....	....	....	....	....
1942-43	Nanaimo Navy	NNDHL	20	22	7	29	....	....	....	8	6	5	3	8	6
1943-44	Nanaimo Navy	NNDHL	18	16	8	24	....	....	....	4	....	....	....	....	....
1944-45	Halifax Navy	NSDHL	12	8	6	14	....	....	....	0	6	3	1	4	0
1945-46	**Montreal Canadiens**	**NHL**	**5**	**0**	**1**	**1**	**0**	**1**	**1**	**0**	....	....	....	....	....
	Buffalo Bisons	AHL	58	32	31	63	....	....	....	18	12	5	8	13	2
1946-47	Buffalo Bisons	AHL	59	35	26	61	....	....	....	13	4	1	1	2	4
	Montreal Canadiens	**NHL**	....	....	....	....	....	....	....	....	**9**	**0**	**1**	**1**	**0**
1947-48	**Montreal Canadiens**	**NHL**	**14**	**0**	**2**	**2**	**0**	**3**	**3**	**0**	....	....	....	....	....
	Buffalo Bisons	AHL	55	37	39	76	....	....	....	15	8	4	4	8	0
1948-49	Buffalo Bisons	AHL	68	32	52	84	....	....	....	20	....	....	....	....	....
	Montreal Canadiens	**NHL**	....	....	....	....	....	....	....	....	**6**	**1**	**1**	**2**	**0**
1949-50	Buffalo Bisons	AHL	67	30	24	54	....	....	....	6	5	0	0	0	0
1950-51	Cleveland Barons	AHL	69	25	36	61	....	....	....	6	11	2	2	4	0
1951-52	Quebec Aces	QMHL	40	14	24	38	....	....	....	4	15	5	6	11	6
1952-53	Quebec Aces	QMHL	55	4	18	22	....	....	....	4	22	3	8	11	6
	NHL Totals		**19**	**0**	**3**	**3**	**0**	**4**	**4**	**0**	**15**	**1**	**2**	**3**	**0**

EAHL Second All-Star Team (1940) • AHL First All-Star Team (1949)

Signed as a free agent by **NY Rangers**, October 21, 1940. Traded to **Buffalo** (AHL) by **NY Rangers** for cash, September 11, 1941. Traded to **Montreal** by **Buffalo** (AHL) for John Adams and Moe White with Montreal holding right of recall, January 14, 1946. Traded to **Cleveland** (AHL) by **Montreal** (Buffalo-AHL) for Pete Leswick, August 4, 1950. Signed as a free agent by **Montreal**, September, 1951. Transferred to **Quebec** (QSHL) from **Montreal** as compensation for Montreal's signing of free agent Dick Gamble, September 24, 1951.

• MacKELL, Fleming   Fleming David "Mac"

C – L. 5'7", 156 lbs. b: Montreal, Que., 4/30/1929.

Season	Club	League	GP	G	A	Pts	AG	AA	APts	PIM	GP	G	A	Pts	PIM
1944-45	Montreal Jr. Royals	QJHL	9	3	4	7	....	....	....	0	6	2	3	5	2
1945-46	St. Michael's Majors	OHA-Jr.	24	25	25	50	....	....	....	29	11	13	9	22	*52
1946-47	St. Michael's Majors	OHA-Jr.	28	*49	33	*82	....	....	....	71	9	10	10	20	*33
	St. Michael's Majors	M-Cup	10	15	14	*29	....	....	....	*38	....	....	....	....	....
1947-48	**Toronto Maple Leafs**	**NHL**	**3**	**0**	**0**	**0**	**0**	**0**	**0**	**2**	....	....	....	....	....
	Pittsburgh Hornets	AHL	62	22	43	65	....	....	....	84	2	1	0	1	4
♦1948-49	**Toronto Maple Leafs**	**NHL**	**11**	**1**	**1**	**2**	**1**	**1**	**2**	**6**	**9**	**2**	**4**	**6**	**4**
	Pittsburgh Hornets	AHL	52	38	38	76	....	....	....	65	....	....	....	....	....
1949-50	**Toronto Maple Leafs**	**NHL**	**36**	**7**	**13**	**20**	**9**	**16**	**25**	**24**	**7**	**1**	**1**	**2**	**11**
	Pittsburgh Hornets	AHL	36	25	22	47	....	....	....	62	....	....	....	....	....
♦1950-51	**Toronto Maple Leafs**	**NHL**	**70**	**12**	**13**	**25**	**15**	**16**	**31**	**40**	**11**	**2**	**3**	**5**	**9**
1951-52	**Toronto Maple Leafs**	**NHL**	**32**	**2**	**8**	**10**	**3**	**10**	**13**	**16**	....	....	....	....	....
	Boston Bruins	**NHL**	**30**	**1**	**8**	**9**	**1**	**10**	**11**	**24**	**5**	**2**	**1**	**3**	**12**
1952-53	**Boston Bruins**	**NHL**	**65**	**27**	**17**	**44**	**36**	**21**	**57**	**63**	**11**	**2**	***7**	**9**	**7**
1953-54	**Boston Bruins**	**NHL**	**67**	**15**	**32**	**47**	**20**	**39**	**59**	**60**	**4**	**1**	**1**	**2**	**8**
1954-55	**Boston Bruins**	**NHL**	**60**	**11**	**24**	**35**	**14**	**28**	**42**	**76**	**4**	**0**	**1**	**1**	**0**
1955-56	**Boston Bruins**	**NHL**	**52**	**7**	**9**	**16**	**9**	**11**	**20**	**59**	....	....	....	....	....
1956-57	**Boston Bruins**	**NHL**	**65**	**22**	**17**	**39**	**28**	**19**	**47**	**73**	**10**	**5**	**3**	**8**	**4**
1957-58	**Boston Bruins**	**NHL**	**70**	**20**	**40**	**60**	**25**	**42**	**67**	**72**	**12**	**5**	**14**	***19**	**12**
1958-59	**Boston Bruins**	**NHL**	**57**	**17**	**23**	**40**	**20**	**23**	**43**	**28**	**7**	**2**	**6**	**8**	**8**
1959-60	**Boston Bruins**	**NHL**	**47**	**7**	**15**	**22**	**8**	**15**	**23**	**19**	....	....	....	....	....
1960-61	Quebec Aces	AHL	62	13	22	35	....	....	....	54	....	....	....	....	....
1961-62			DID NOT PLAY												
1962-63	Los Angeles Blades	WHL	29	10	21	31	....	....	....	26	3	1	1	2	2
1963-64	New Glasgow Rangers	NSSHL	7	5	14	19	....	....	....	4	4	2	2	4	4
1964-65	New Glasgow Rangers	NSSHL	57	49	*75	*124	....	....	....	85	....	....	....	....	....
1965-66	St-Hyacinthe Saints	QSHL	20	10	10	20	....	....	....	29	12	5	9	14	8
1966-67			STATISTICS NOT AVAILABLE												
1967-68	St. John's Capitals	Nfld-Sr.	33	11	19	30	....	....	....	53	....	....	....	....	....
	NHL Totals		**665**	**149**	**220**	**369**	**189**	**251**	**440**	**562**	**80**	**22**	**41**	**63**	**75**

• Son of Jack • NHL First All-Star Team (1953) • Played in NHL All-Star Game (1947, 1948, 1949, 1954)

Traded to **Boston** by **Toronto** for Jim Morrison, January 9, 1952. Traded to **LA Blades** (WHL) by **Quebec** (AHL) for cash, October 9, 1962. • Missed majority of 1962-63 and 1963-64 seasons recovering from knee injury suffered in game vs. San Francisco (WHL), November 29, 1962.

• MacKELL, Jack   John Ambrose

RW/D – R. 5'7", 150 lbs. b: Ottawa, Ont., 4/12/1896 Deceased.

Season	Club	League	GP	G	A	Pts	AG	AA	APts	PIM	GP	G	A	Pts	PIM
1914-15	Ottawa College	H.S.	STATISTICS NOT AVAILABLE												
1915-16	Ottawa New Edinburghs	OCHL	7	5	0	5	....	....	....	6	1	*2	0	*2	0
1916-17	Ottawa Munitions	OCHL	10	7	0	7	....	....	....	48	....	....	....	....	....
1917-18	Ottawa Munitions	OCHL	6	1	0	1	....	....	....	15	1	1	0	1	0
	Pembrooke Munitions	OCHL	STATISTICS NOT AVAILABLE												
1918-19	Ottawa Munitions	OCHL	7	*8	2	*10	....	....	....	39	....	....	....	....	....
1919-20	**Ottawa Senators**	**NHL**	**23**	**2**	**1**	**3**	**2**	**3**	**5**	**33**	....	....	....	....	....
♦	Ottawa Senators	St-Cup	5	0	0	0	....	....	....	0	....	....	....	....	....
♦1920-21	**Ottawa Senators**	**NHL**	**22**	**2**	**1**	**3**	**2**	**4**	**6**	**26**	**2**	**0**	**0**	**0**	**0**
1921-22			REINSTATED AS AN AMATEUR												
1922-23	Ottawa Munitions	OCHL	3	1	0	1	....	....	....	....	....	....	....	....	....
1923-24	Bank of Montreal	MBHL	8	1	0	1	....	....	....	3	....	....	....	....	....
	NHL Totals		**45**	**4**	**2**	**6**	**4**	**7**	**11**	**59**	**2**	**0**	**0**	**0**	**0**

• Father of Fleming

Signed as a free agent by **Ottawa**, December 19, 1919.

• MacKENZIE, Bill   William Kenneth

D – R. 5'11", 175 lbs. b: Winnipeg, Man., 12/12/1911 d: 5/29/1990.

Season	Club	League	GP	G	A	Pts	AG	AA	APts	PIM	GP	G	A	Pts	PIM
1929-30	Elmwood Maple Leafs	WJrHL	9	7	1	8	....	....	....	10	2	1	0	1	6
	Elmwood Maple Leafs	M-Cup	5	1	*2	3	....	....	....	0	....	....	....	....	....
1930-31	Elmwood Maple Leafs	WJrHL	11	8	6	14	....	....	....	6	12	6	3	9	2
	Elmwood Maple Leafs	M-Cup	9	*7	*4	*11	....	....	....	2	....	....	....	....	....
1931-32	Montreal AAA	MCHL	10	0	3	3	....	....	....	22	4	1	1	2	8
	Montreal AAA	Al-Cup	6	0	0	0	....	....	....	0	....	....	....	....	....
1932-33	**Chicago Black Hawks**	**NHL**	**36**	**4**	**4**	**8**	**7**	**8**	**15**	**13**	....	....	....	....	....
	Montreal Royals	MCHL	12	7	4	11	....	....	....	33	4	0	0	0	15
	Montreal Royals	Al-Cup	6	4	0	4	....	....	....	*23	....	....	....	....	....
1933-34	**Montreal Maroons**	**NHL**	**47**	**4**	**3**	**7**	**7**	**6**	**13**	**20**	**4**	**0**	**0**	**0**	**0**
1934-35	**Montreal Maroons**	**NHL**	**5**	**0**	**0**	**0**	**0**	**0**	**0**	**0**	....	....	....	....	....
	Windsor Bulldogs	IHL	21	3	1	4	....	....	....	19	....	....	....	....	....
	New York Rangers	**NHL**	**15**	**1**	**0**	**1**	**2**	**0**	**2**	**10**	**3**	**0**	**0**	**0**	**0**
1935-36	Windsor Bulldogs	IHL	42	10	8	18	....	....	....	52	8	0	1	1	6
1936-37	**Montreal Maroons**	**NHL**	**10**	**0**	**1**	**1**	**0**	**2**	**2**	**6**	....	....	....	....	....
	Montreal Canadiens	**NHL**	**39**	**4**	**3**	**7**	**7**	**5**	**12**	**22**	**5**	**1**	**0**	**1**	**0**
1937-38	**Montreal Canadiens**	**NHL**	**11**	**0**	**0**	**0**	**0**	**0**	**0**	**4**	....	....	....	....	....
♦	**Chicago Black Hawks**	**NHL**	**35**	**1**	**2**	**3**	**2**	**3**	**5**	**20**	**9**	**0**	**1**	**1**	**11**
1938-39	**Chicago Black Hawks**	**NHL**	**47**	**1**	**0**	**1**	**2**	**0**	**2**	**36**	....	....	....	....	....
1939-40	**Chicago Black Hawks**	**NHL**	**19**	**0**	**1**	**1**	**0**	**2**	**2**	**14**	....	....	....	....	....
	Providence Reds	IAHL	21	6	7	13	....	....	....	30	7	1	2	3	5
1940-41	Cleveland Barons	AHL	56	7	10	17	....	....	....	34	9	1	1	2	4
1941-42	Cleveland Barons	AHL	56	5	12	17	....	....	....	20	5	0	0	0	0
1942-43	Cleveland Barons	AHL	42	6	8	14	....	....	....	18	4	0	2	2	2
1943-44			MILITARY SERVICE												
1944-45	Cleveland Barons	AHL	13	0	2	2	....	....	....	6	....	....	....	....	....
	NHL Totals		**264**	**15**	**14**	**29**	**27**	**26**	**53**	**145**	**21**	**1**	**1**	**2**	**11**

AHL Second All-Star Team (1940, 1943) • AHL First All-Star Team (1941, 1942)

Signed as a free agent by **Montreal Maroons** after securing release from **Chicago**, June 25, 1933. Loaned to **NY Rangers** by **Montreal Maroons** for the remainder of the 1934-35 season, January 29, 1935. Traded to **Montreal Canadiens** by **Montreal Maroons** for Paul Runge, December 3, 1936. Traded to **Chicago** by **Montreal Canadiens** for Marty Burke, December 10, 1937. Traded to **Montreal** by **Chicago** for cash, May 11, 1940. Traded to **Cleveland** (AHL) by **Montreal** with Bill Summerhill for Jim O'Neill, May 17, 1940.

• MACKEY, Reg

D – L. 5'7", 155 lbs. b: Ottawa, Ont., 5/7/1900 Deceased.

Season	Club	League	GP	G	A	Pts	AG	AA	APts	PIM	GP	G	A	Pts	PIM
1919-20	Calgary Wanderers	Big-4	6	1	0	1	....	....	....	0	....	....	....	....	....
1920-21	Calgary City Seniors	CCSHL	....	....	....	....	....	....	....	....	....	....	....	....	....
1921-22	Calgary City Seniors	CCSHL	STATISTICS NOT AVAILABLE												
1922-23	Calgary City Seniors	CCSHL	STATISTICS NOT AVAILABLE												
	Calgary Tigers	WCHL	1	0	0	0	....	....	....	0	....	....	....	....	....
1923-24	Bellevue Bulldogs	ASHL	STATISTICS NOT AVAILABLE												
	Bellevue Bulldogs	Al-Cup	4	1	0	1	....	....	....	0	....	....	....	....	....
1924-25	Calgary Tigers	WCHL	16	3	0	3	....	....	....	15	2	0	0	0	2
1925-26	Vancouver Maroons	WHL	29	8	0	8	....	....	....	23	....	....	....	....	....
1926-27	**New York Rangers**	**NHL**	**34**	**0**	**0**	**0**	**0**	**0**	**0**	**16**	**1**	**0**	**0**	**0**	**0**
1927-28	Boston Tigers	Can-Am	36	18	2	20	....	....	....	78	2	0	0	0	2

			REGULAR SEASON								PLAYOFFS				
Season	Club	League	GP	G	A	Pts	AG	AA	APts	PIM	GP	G	A	Pts	PIM
1928-29	Boston Tigers	Can-Am	33	15	4	19	....	....	....	68	4	1	1	2	8
1929-30	Boston Tigers	Can-Am	37	19	7	26	....	....	....	104	4	3	1	4	16
1930-31	Boston Tigers	Can-Am	40	6	9	15	....	....	....	80	8	1	1	2	6
1931-32			REINSTATED AS AN AMATEUR												
1932-33	Calgary Tigers	WCHL	30	9	2	11	....	....	....	42	6	0	1	1	5
1933-34	Calgary Tigers	NWHL	3	0	0	0	....	....	....	0	....	....	....	....	....
	NHL Totals		**34**	**0**	**0**	**0**	**0**	**0**	**0**	**16**	**1**	**0**	**0**	**0**	**0**
	Other Major League Totals		46	11	0	11	....	....	....	38	2	0	0	0	2

Can-Am Second All-Star Team (1930)

Signed as a free agent by **Calgary** (WCHL), August 26, 1924. Traded to **Vancouver** (WHL) by **Calgary** (WHL) for Art Duncan, October 16, 1925. Traded to **NY Rangers** by **Vancouver** (WHL) for cash, October 9, 1926. Traded to **Boston** (Can-Am) by **NY Rangers** for cash, November 8, 1927.

• MACKIE, Howie

RW/D – L. 5'10", 190 lbs. b: Berlin, Ont., 8/30/1913 d: 3/9/1952.

Season	Club	League	GP	G	A	Pts	AG	AA	APts	PIM	GP	G	A	Pts	PIM
1930-31	Kitchener Redshirts	OHA-Jr.	8	2	0	2	....	....	....	8	2	1	0	1	6
1931-32	Kitchener Redshirts	OHA-Jr.	12	10	0	10	....	....	....	24	....	....	....	....	....
1932-33	Kitchener Emoires	OHA-B	12	12	4	16	....	....	....	24	5	2	3	5	4
1933-34	Kitchener Greenshirts	OHA-Jr.	15	4	4	8	....	....	....	8	....	....	....	....	....
1934-35	Kitchener Greenshirts	OSBHA	14	*19	8	*27	....	....	....	27	6	*9	3	*12	6
1935-36	Hamilton Tigers	OHA-Sr.	22	*24	11	35	....	....	....	21	9	*14	3	17	14
	Hamilton Tigers	Al-Cup	4	5	4	9	....	....	....	4	....	....	....	....	....
♦**1936-37**	**Detroit Red Wings**	**NHL**	**13**	**1**	**0**	**1**	**2**	**0**	**2**	**4**	**8**	**0**	**0**	**0**	**0**
	Pittsburgh Hornets	IAHL	33	8	5	13	....	....	....	12	1	0	0	0	0
1937-38	**Detroit Red Wings**	**NHL**	**7**	**0**	**0**	**0**	**0**	**0**	**0**	**0**	....	....	....	....	....
	Pittsburgh Hornets	IAHL	32	2	8	10	....	....	....	12	2	0	0	0	0
1938-39	Hershey Bears	IAHL	53	12	18	30	....	....	....	8	5	1	2	3	0
1939-40	Hershey Bears	IAHL	52	11	5	16	....	....	....	29	5	0	1	1	4
1940-41	Hershey Bears	AHL	43	15	19	34	....	....	....	19	10	0	2	2	4
1941-42	Hershey Bears	AHL	21	3	3	6	....	....	....	4	....	....	....	....	....
	Pittsburgh Hornets	AHL	1	0	0	0	....	....	....	0	....	....	....	....	....
	Philadelphia Rockets	AHL	21	12	12	24	....	....	....	8	....	....	....	....	....
1942-43	Pittsburgh Hornets	AHL	40	0	4	4	....	....	....	8	....	....	....	....	....
1943-44	Pittsburgh Hornets	AHL	29	2	11	13	....	....	....	21	....	....	....	....	....
1944-45	Pittsburgh Hornets	AHL	40	9	21	30	....	....	....	33	....	....	....	....	....
1945-46	Pittsburgh Hornets	AHL	31	5	9	14	....	....	....	31	4	0	0	0	0
	NHL Totals		**20**	**1**	**0**	**1**	**2**	**0**	**2**	**4**	**8**	**0**	**0**	**0**	**0**

Signed as a free agent by **Detroit**, September 20, 1936.

• MacMILLAN, John

John Stewart

RW – L. 5'10", 185 lbs. b: Lethbridge, Alta., 10/25/1935.

Season	Club	League	GP	G	A	Pts	AG	AA	APts	PIM	GP	G	A	Pts	PIM
1952-53	Crowsnest Pass Coalers	WCJHL	1	0	0	0	....	....	....	0	....	....	....	....	....
1953-54	Lethbridge Native Sons	WCJHL	28	5	9	14	....	....	....	12	4	0	0	0	2
1954-55	Lethbridge Native Sons	WCJHL	37	5	11	16	....	....	....	24	3	0	3	3	0
1955-56	Lethbridge Native Sons	WCJHL	45	27	27	54	....	....	....	34	9	4	6	10	6
1956-57	University of Denver	WCHA	DID NOT PLAY – FRESHMAN												
1957-58	University of Denver	WCHA	37	19	12	31	....	....	....	50	....	....	....	....	....
1958-59	University of Denver	WCHA	28	16	25	41	....	....	....	32	....	....	....	....	....
1959-60	University of Denver	WCHA	34	30	25	55	....	....	....	34	....	....	....	....	....
1960-61	**Toronto Maple Leafs**	**NHL**	**31**	**3**	**5**	**8**	**3**	**5**	**8**	**8**	**4**	**0**	**0**	**0**	**0**
	Rochester Americans	AHL	38	8	7	15	....	....	....	14	....	....	....	....	....
1961-62	Pittsburgh Hornets	AHL	33	6	10	16	....	....	....	25	....	....	....	....	....
♦	**Toronto Maple Leafs**	**NHL**	**31**	**1**	**0**	**1**	**1**	**0**	**1**	**8**	**3**	**0**	**0**	**0**	**0**
♦**1962-63**	**Toronto Maple Leafs**	**NHL**	**6**	**1**	**1**	**2**	**1**	**1**	**2**	**6**	**1**	**0**	**0**	**0**	**0**
	Rochester Americans	AHL	57	22	23	45	....	....	....	37	....	....	....	....	....
1963-64	**Toronto Maple Leafs**	**NHL**	**13**	**0**	**0**	**0**	**0**	**0**	**0**	**4**	....	....	....	....	....
	Detroit Red Wings	**NHL**	**20**	**0**	**3**	**3**	**0**	**3**	**3**	**6**	**4**	**0**	**1**	**1**	**2**
	Pittsburgh Hornets	AHL	31	4	8	12	....	....	....	8	5	1	1	2	0
1964-65	**Detroit Red Wings**	**NHL**	**3**	**0**	**1**	**1**	**0**	**1**	**1**	**0**	....	....	....	....	....
	Memphis Wings	CPHL	61	17	20	37	....	....	....	43	....	....	....	....	....
	St. Paul Rangers	CPHL	3	0	0	0	....	....	....	6	....	....	....	....	....
1965-66	Memphis Wings	CPHL	64	12	14	26	....	....	....	29	....	....	....	....	....
1966-67	San Diego Gulls	WHL	71	20	26	46	....	....	....	76	....	....	....	....	....
1967-68	San Diego Gulls	WHL	72	12	32	44	....	....	....	61	7	0	0	0	4
1968-69	San Diego Gulls	WHL	74	22	38	60	....	....	....	55	7	3	0	3	4
1969-70	San Diego Gulls	WHL	71	19	48	67	....	....	....	35	6	4	3	7	0
1970-71	San Diego Gulls	WHL	72	12	23	35	....	....	....	31	6	0	0	0	2
	NHL Totals		**104**	**5**	**10**	**15**	**5**	**10**	**15**	**32**	**12**	**0**	**1**	**1**	**2**

WCHA Second All-Star Team (1960) • Played in NHL All-Star Game (1962, 1963)

Claimed on waivers by **Detroit** from **Toronto**, December 3, 1963. Traded to **San Diego** (WHL) by **Detroit** for cash, June, 1966.

• MacNEIL, Al

— see page 1359

• MacPHERSON, Bud

James Albert

D – L. 6'4", 200 lbs. b: Edmonton, Alta., 3/31/1927 d: 1988.

Season	Club	League	GP	G	A	Pts	AG	AA	APts	PIM	GP	G	A	Pts	PIM
1943-44	Edmonton Maple Leafs	AJHL	STATISTICS NOT AVAILABLE												
1944-45	Edmonton Canadians	EJrHL	STATISTICS NOT AVAILABLE												
1945-46	Edmonton Canadians	EJrHL	STATISTICS NOT AVAILABLE												
1946-47	Oshawa Generals	OHA-Jr.	11	1	0	1	....	....	....	8	2	0	1	1	7
1947-48	Edmonton Flyers	ASHL	37	8	11	19	....	....	....	21	10	0	0	0	*41
	Edmonton Flyers	Al-Cup	14	3	3	6	....	....	....	26	....	....	....	....	....
1948-49	**Montreal Canadiens**	**NHL**	**3**	**0**	**0**	**0**	**0**	**0**	**0**	**2**	....	....	....	....	....
	Edmonton Flyers	WCSHL	44	5	17	22	....	....	....	65	9	0	3	3	10
1949-50	Cincinnati Mohawks	AHL	41	2	9	11	....	....	....	38	....	....	....	....	....
1950-51	**Montreal Canadiens**	**NHL**	**62**	**0**	**16**	**16**	**0**	**20**	**20**	**40**	**11**	**0**	**2**	**2**	**8**
	Cincinnati Mohawks	AHL	6	0	0	0	....	....	....	10	....	....	....	....	....
1951-52	**Montreal Canadiens**	**NHL**	**54**	**2**	**1**	**3**	**3**	**1**	**4**	**24**	**11**	**0**	**0**	**0**	**0**
♦**1952-53**	**Montreal Canadiens**	**NHL**	**59**	**2**	**3**	**5**	**3**	**4**	**7**	**67**	**4**	**0**	**1**	**1**	**9**
1953-54	**Montreal Canadiens**	**NHL**	**41**	**0**	**5**	**5**	**0**	**6**	**6**	**41**	**3**	**0**	**0**	**0**	**4**
	Montreal Royals	QHL	5	0	2	2	....	....	....	12	....	....	....	....	....
	Buffalo Bisons	AHL	8	0	1	1	....	....	....	6	....	....	....	....	....
1954-55	**Montreal Canadiens**	**NHL**	**30**	**1**	**8**	**9**	**1**	**9**	**10**	**55**	....	....	....	....	....
1955-56	Montreal Royals	QHL	31	2	9	11	....	....	....	63	13	2	1	3	30
	Montreal Royals	Ed-Cup	6	0	1	1	....	....	....	2	....	....	....	....	....
1956-57	**Montreal Canadiens**	**NHL**	**10**	**0**	**0**	**0**	**0**	**0**	**0**	**4**	....	....	....	....	....
	Montreal Royals	QHL	46	3	10	13	....	....	....	53	4	0	1	1	4
	Rochester Americans	AHL	7	0	3	3	....	....	....	12	....	....	....	....	....
1957-58	Edmonton Flyers	WHL	70	5	22	27	....	....	....	57	5	0	1	1	4
1958-59	Edmonton Flyers	WHL	63	3	13	16	....	....	....	54	3	1	1	2	12
	Hershey Bears	AHL	....	....	....	....	....	....	....	....	10	0	2	2	6
1959-60	Edmonton Flyers	WHL	62	7	12	19	....	....	....	20	4	0	1	1	4
1960-61	Edmonton Flyers	WHL	11	0	1	1	....	....	....	8	....	....	....	....	....
	NHL Totals		**259**	**5**	**33**	**38**	**7**	**40**	**47**	**233**	**29**	**0**	**3**	**3**	**21**

Played in NHL All-Star Game (1953)

Traded to **Chicago** by **Montreal** with Kenny Mosdell and Eddie Mazur for $55,000 with Montreal holding right of recall, May 17, 1956. • Returned to **Montreal** by **Chicago** after training camp, October 10, 1956. Traded to **Detroit** by **Montreal** with Gene Achtymichuk and Claude Laforge for cash, June 3, 1958.

• MAHAFFY, John

C – L. 5'7", 165 lbs. b: Montreal, Que., 7/18/1919.

Season	Club	League	GP	G	A	Pts	AG	AA	APts	PIM	GP	G	A	Pts	PIM
1934-35	Montreal Royals	QJHL	10	3	6	9	....	....	....	4	2	0	0	0	0
1935-36	Montreal Royals	QJHL	7	5	6	11	....	....	....	4	....	....	....	....	....
1936-37	Montreal Royals	MCHL	21	4	8	12	....	....	....	16	5	0	1	1	2
1937-38	Montreal Royals	MCHL	22	4	3	7	....	....	....	20	1	0	0	0	2
1938-39	Streatham Hockey Club	Ln-Cup	....	4	9	13	....	....	....	....	....	....	....	....	....
	Streatham Hockey Club	Britain	....	4	4	8	....	....	....	....	....	....	....	....	....
1939-40	Montreal Royals	MCHL	29	9	13	22	....	....	....	25	8	2	0	2	12
	Montreal Royals	Al-Cup	5	0	4	4	....	....	....	0	....	....	....	....	....
1940-41	Montreal Royals	MCHL	33	17	25	42	....	....	....	60	8	*6	5	*11	16
	Montreal Royals	Al-Cup	9	4	2	6	....	....	....	22	....	....	....	....	....
1941-42	Montreal Royals	QSHL	38	9	16	25	....	....	....	35	....	....	....	....	....
1942-43	**Montreal Canadiens**	**NHL**	**9**	**2**	**5**	**7**	**2**	**5**	**7**	**4**	....	....	....	....	....
	Montreal Royals	QSHL	28	21	16	37	....	....	....	14	7	4	2	6	4
1943-44	**New York Rangers**	**NHL**	**28**	**9**	**20**	**29**	**8**	**18**	**26**	**0**	....	....	....	....	....
	Montreal Army	MCHL	4	0	0	0	....	....	....	0	....	....	....	....	....
	Montreal Royals	QSHL	4	2	6	8	....	....	....	2	....	....	....	....	....
1944-45	Montreal Royals	QSHL	3	5	4	9	....	....	....	4	....	....	....	....	....
	Pittsburgh Hornets	AHL	37	17	23	40	....	....	....	10	....	....	....	....	....
	Montreal Canadiens	**NHL**	....	....	....	....	....	....	....	....	**1**	**0**	**1**	**1**	**0**
1945-46	Pittsburgh Hornets	AHL	58	28	36	64	....	....	....	35	6	4	2	6	10
1946-47	Buffalo Bisons	AHL	63	29	40	69	....	....	....	37	4	0	0	0	0
1947-48	Philadelphia Rockets	AHL	60	26	57	83	....	....	....	6	....	....	....	....	....
1948-49	Philadelphia Rockets	AHL	67	21	50	71	....	....	....	10	....	....	....	....	....
1949-50	Hershey Bears	AHL	69	23	36	59	....	....	....	13	....	....	....	....	....
1950-51	Hershey Bears	AHL	33	5	14	19	....	....	....	7	....	....	....	....	....
1951-52	Shawinigan Cataracts	QMHL	60	16	28	44	....	....	....	18	....	....	....	....	....
1952-53	St-Hyacinthe Saints	QPHL	61	28	58	86	....	....	....	....	....	....	....	....	....
	NHL Totals		**37**	**11**	**25**	**36**	**10**	**23**	**33**	**4**	**1**	**0**	**1**	**1**	**0**

Loaned to **NY Rangers** by **Montreal** with Dutch Hiller, Fern Gauthier, Charlie Sands and future considerations (Tony Demers, December, 1943) for the loan of Phil Watson, October 27, 1943. Traded to **Pittsburgh** (AHL) by **Montreal** for cash, November 24, 1944. • Played for Montreal in playoff game on March 24, 1945 though he was subsequently ruled ineligible to play in any further playoff games as his rights were still owned by Pittsburgh (AHL). Traded to **Montreal** (Buffalo-AHL) by **Toronto** (Pittsburgh-AHL) with Gerry Brown for Dutch Hiller and Vic Lynn, September 21, 1946.

• MAHOVLICH, Frank

— see page 1363

• MAHOVLICH, Pete

— see page 1364

• MAILLEY, Frank

D – L. 5'9", 182 lbs. b: Lachine, Que., 8/1/1916.

Season	Club	League	GP	G	A	Pts	AG	AA	APts	PIM	GP	G	A	Pts	PIM
1938-39	Miami Beach Pirates	TrHL	14	8	8	16	....	....	....	14	....	....	....	....	....
	Lachine Rapides	QSHL	1	0	0	0	....	....	....	0	....	....	....	....	....
1939-40	St-Hyacinthe Gaulois	QSHL	22	9	13	22	....	....	....	12	2	0	0	0	6
1940-41	Washington Eagles	EAHL	65	18	27	45	....	....	....	30	2	1	2	3	0
1941-42	Washington Lions	AHL	56	6	20	26	....	....	....	15	2	0	0	0	0
1942-43	**Montreal Canadiens**	**NHL**	**1**	**0**	**0**	**0**	**0**	**0**	**0**	**0**	....	....	....	....	....
	Washington Lions	AHL	51	4	14	18	....	....	....	30	....	....	....	....	....
1943-44			MILITARY SERVICE												
1944-45			MILITARY SERVICE												
1945-46	Quebec Aces	QSHL	6	0	0	0	....	....	....	4	6	0	0	0	0
	NHL Totals		**1**	**0**	**0**	**0**	**0**	**0**	**0**	**0**	....	....	....	....	....

• MAJEAU, Fern

C/LW – L. 5'9", 155 lbs. b: Verdun, Que., 5/3/1916 d: 6/21/1966.

Season	Club	League	GP	G	A	Pts	AG	AA	APts	PIM	GP	G	A	Pts	PIM
1934-35	Verdun Jr. Maple Leafs	MCJHL	10	9	12	21	....	....	....	12	5	*6	2	8	6
	Verdun Maple Leafs	MCHL	1	0	0	0	....	....	....	2	....	....	....	....	....
1935-36	Verdun Jr. Maple Leafs	MCJHL	9	8	*8	*16	....	....	....	10	....	....	....	....	....
	Verdun Maple Leafs	MCHL	5	0	3	3	....	....	....	0	7	2	2	4	2
1936-37	Verdun Maple Leafs	MCHL	21	3	6	9	....	....	....	40	....	....	....	....	....
1937-38	Montreal Royals	MCHL	12	4	5	9	....	....	....	8	1	0	1	1	0
1938-39	Lachine Rapides	QPHL	36	12	9	21	....	....	....	38	6	0	1	1	4
1939-40	Lachine Rapides	QPHL	41	17	25	42	....	....	....	54	9	8	6	14	4
1940-41	Verdun Maple Leafs	MCHL	34	16	18	34	....	....	....	31	....	....	....	....	....
1941-42	Montreal Pats	MCHL	28	11	8	19	....	....	....	22	....	....	....	....	....
1942-43	Montreal Sr. Canadiens	QSHL	24	8	5	13	....	....	....	17	4	4	2	6	2
♦**1943-44**	**Montreal Canadiens**	**NHL**	**44**	**20**	**18**	**38**	**18**	**16**	**34**	**39**	**1**	**0**	**0**	**0**	**0**
1944-45	**Montreal Canadiens**	**NHL**	**12**	**2**	**6**	**8**	**2**	**7**	**9**	**4**	....	....	....	....	....
	Montreal Royals	QSHL	9	6	7	13	....	....	....	10	7	4	0	4	10
1945-46	Valleyfield Braves	QSHL	39	17	27	44	....	....	....	46	....	....	....	....	....
1946-47	Valleyfield Braves	QSHL	33	10	25	35	....	....	....	32	....	....	....	....	....
1947-48	Lachine Rapides	QPHL	53	23	32	55	....	....	....	42	6	3	3	6	2
1948-49	Montreal Hydro Quebec	MCHL	11	6	10	16	....	....	....	....	....	....	....	....	....
	NHL Totals		**56**	**22**	**24**	**46**	**20**	**23**	**43**	**43**	**1**	**0**	**0**	**0**	**0**

Signed as a free agent by **Montreal Canadiens**, October 28, 1943.

• MAKI, Chico

— see page 1366

• MALONE, Cliff

RW – R. 5'10", 155 lbs. b: Quebec City, Que., 9/4/1925.

Season	Club	League	REGULAR SEASON								PLAYOFFS				
			GP	G	A	Pts	AG	AA	APts	PIM	GP	G	A	Pts	PIM
1943-44	Montreal Jr. Royals	QJHL	9	8	8	16	....	....	....	2	....	....	....	....	....
	Toronto Fuels	TMHL	3	3	5	8	....	....	....	0	....	....	....	....	....
1944-45	Montreal Jr. Royals	QJHL	13	14	9	23	....	....	....	2	7	7	3	10	4
	Montreal RCAF	MCHL	14	11	6	17	....	....	....	6	1	3	0	3	0
	Montreal Royals	QSHL	2	0	0	0	....	....	....	0	1	0	0	0	2
	Montreal Jr. Royals	M-Cup	8	5	6	11	....	....	....	0	....	....	....	....	....
1945-46	Montreal Royals	QSHL	....	....	....	....	....	....	....	....	2	1	0	1	0
1946-47	Montreal Royals	QSHL	31	16	19	35	....	....	....	6	11	4	4	8	12
	Montreal Royals	Al-Cup	14	8	13	21	....	....	....	4	....	....	....	....	....
1947-48	Montreal Royals	QSHL	46	18	49	67	....	....	....	21	3	1	0	1	2
1948-49	Montreal Royals	QSHL	64	35	60	95	....	....	....	40	9	3	4	7	10
1949-50	Montreal Royals	QSHL	60	21	36	57	....	....	....	55	6	2	1	3	4
1950-51	Montreal Royals	QMHL	60	25	24	49	....	....	....	54	7	0	4	4	2
1951-52	**Montreal Canadiens**	**NHL**	**3**	**0**	**0**	**0**	**0**	**0**	**0**	**0**	....	....	....	....	....
	Montreal Royals	QMHL	56	29	37	66	....	....	....	10	7	3	4	7	0
1952-53	Montreal Royals	QMHL	60	15	34	49	....	....	....	42	15	3	6	9	2
1953-54	Montreal Royals	QHL	13	0	3	3	....	....	....	8	....	....	....	....	....
	Ste-Therese Titans	QPHL	STATISTICS NOT AVAILABLE												
	NHL Totals		**3**	**0**	**0**	**0**	**0**	**0**	**0**	**0**	....	....	....	....	....

QMHL Second All-Star Team (1952)

• MALONE, Joe

Maurice Joseph "Phantom" **HHOF**

C/LW – L. 5'10", 150 lbs. b: Quebec City, Que., 2/28/1890 d: 5/15/1969.

Season	Club	League	REGULAR SEASON								PLAYOFFS				
			GP	G	A	Pts	AG	AA	APts	PIM	GP	G	A	Pts	PIM
1907-08	Quebec Crescents	QAAA	STATISTICS NOT AVAILABLE												
1908-09	Quebec Bulldogs	ECHA	12	8	0	8	....	....	....	17	....	....	....	....	....
1909-10	Quebec Bulldogs	CHA	2	5	0	5	....	....	....	3	....	....	....	....	....
	Waterloo Colts	OPHL	11	9	0	9	....	....	....	10	....	....	....	....	....
1910-11	Quebec Bulldogs	NHA	13	9	0	9	....	....	....	3	....	....	....	....	....
♦1911-12	Quebec Bulldogs	NHA	18	21	0	21	....	....	....	0	2	5	0	5	0
	East All-Stars	X-Games	2	0	0	0	....	....	....	0	....	....	....	....	....
♦1912-13	Quebec Bulldogs	NHA	20	*43	0	*43	....	....	....	34	4	*9	0	*9	0
1913-14	Quebec Bulldogs	NHA	17	24	4	28	....	....	....	20	....	....	....	....	....
1914-15	Quebec Bulldogs	NHA	12	16	5	21	....	....	....	21	....	....	....	....	....
1915-16	Quebec Bulldogs	NHA	24	25	10	35	....	....	....	21	....	....	....	....	....
1916-17	Quebec Bulldogs	NHA	19	*41	8	49	....	....	....	15	....	....	....	....	....
1917-18	**Montreal Canadiens**	**NHL**	**20**	***44**	**4**	***48**	**61**	**17**	**78**	**30**	**2**	**1**	**0**	**1**	**3**
1918-19	**Montreal Canadiens**	**NHL**	**8**	**7**	**2**	**9**	**12**	**11**	**23**	**3**	**5**	**5**	**0**	**5**	**0**
1919-20	**Quebec Bulldogs**	**NHL**	**24**	***39**	**10**	***49**	**47**	**35**	**82**	**12**	....	....	....	....	....
1920-21	**Hamilton Tigers**	**NHL**	**20**	**28**	**9**	**37**	**37**	**35**	**72**	**6**	....	....	....	....	....
1921-22	**Hamilton Tigers**	**NHL**	**24**	**24**	**7**	**31**	**34**	**22**	**56**	**4**	....	....	....	....	....
1922-23	**Montreal Canadiens**	**NHL**	**20**	**1**	**0**	**1**	**2**	**0**	**2**	**2**	**2**	**0**	**0**	**0**	**0**
♦1923-24	**Montreal Canadiens**	**NHL**	**10**	**0**	**0**	**0**	**0**	**0**	**0**	**0**	....	....	....	....	....
	NHL Totals		**126**	**143**	**32**	**175**	**193**	**120**	**313**	**57**	**9**	**6**	**0**	**6**	**3**
	Other Major League Totals		148	201	27	228	....	....	....	144	6	14	0	14	0

NHL Scoring Leader (1918, 1920)

Signed as a free agent by **Waterloo** (OPHL), January 20, 1910. Signed as a free agent by **Quebec** (NHA), November, 1910. Claimed by **Montreal Canadiens** from **Quebec** in Dispersal Draft, November 26, 1917. Transferred to **Quebec** by **Montreal Canadiens** when Quebec franchise returned to NHL, November 25, 1919. Transferred to **Hamilton** after **Quebec** franchise relocated, November 2, 1920. • Suspended by **Hamilton** for refusing to report to training camp, December 6, 1922. Traded to **Montreal Canadiens** by **Hamilton** for Edmond Bouchard, December 22, 1922.

• MALONEY, Phil

Philip Francis "The Fox"

C – L. 5'8", 165 lbs. b: Ottawa, Ont., 10/6/1927.

Season	Club	League	REGULAR SEASON								PLAYOFFS				
			GP	G	A	Pts	AG	AA	APts	PIM	GP	G	A	Pts	PIM
1944-45	Ottawa St. Pats	OCJHL	12	*14	6	20	....	....	....	5	5	5	4	9	0
	Ottawa St. Pats	M-Cup	5	0	2	2	....	....	....	5	....	....	....	....	....
1945-46	Ottawa St. Pats	OCJHL	12	*18	9	*27	....	....	....	9	5	0	8	8	0
1946-47	Shawinigan Cataracts	QSHL	34	10	15	25	....	....	....	4	4	3	3	6	0
1947-48	Shawinigan Cataracts	QSHL	48	18	46	64	....	....	....	24	7	2	6	8	0
1948-49	Hershey Bears	AHL	64	29	50	79	....	....	....	21	11	5	6	11	2
1949-50	**Boston Bruins**	**NHL**	**70**	**15**	**31**	**46**	**19**	**38**	**57**	**6**	....	....	....	....	....
1950-51	**Boston Bruins**	**NHL**	**13**	**2**	**0**	**2**	**3**	**0**	**3**	**2**	....	....	....	....	....
	Toronto Maple Leafs	**NHL**	**1**	**1**	**0**	**1**	**1**	**0**	**1**	**0**	....	....	....	....	....
	Pittsburgh Hornets	AHL	54	13	23	36	....	....	....	14	5	2	0	2	2
1951-52	Pittsburgh Hornets	AHL	66	19	37	56	....	....	....	25	5	0	1	1	0
1952-53	**Toronto Maple Leafs**	**NHL**	**29**	**2**	**6**	**8**	**3**	**7**	**10**	**2**	....	....	....	....	....
	Pittsburgh Hornets	AHL	28	8	22	30	....	....	....	22	....	....	....	....	....
1953-54	Pittsburgh Hornets	AHL	35	7	11	18	....	....	....	20	....	....	....	....	....
	Ottawa Senators	QHL	27	9	13	22	....	....	....	37	22	8	6	14	18
1954-55	Ottawa Senators	QHL	25	8	14	22	....	....	....	7	....	....	....	....	....
	Vancouver Canucks	WHL	37	16	27	43	....	....	....	9	5	2	2	4	0
1955-56	Vancouver Canucks	WHL	70	37	58	*95	....	....	....	14	15	8	7	15	4
1956-57	Vancouver Canucks	WHL	70	43	55	98	....	....	....	8	....	....	....	....	....
1957-58	Vancouver Canucks	WHL	70	35	59	94	....	....	....	0	11	8	*17	*25	4
1958-59	Vancouver Canucks	WHL	13	8	9	17	....	....	....	2	....	....	....	....	....
	Chicago Black Hawks	**NHL**	**24**	**2**	**2**	**4**	**2**	**2**	**4**	**6**	**6**	**0**	**0**	**0**	**0**
1959-60	**Chicago Black Hawks**	**NHL**	**21**	**6**	**4**	**10**	**7**	**4**	**11**	**0**	....	....	....	....	....
	Buffalo Bisons	AHL	46	21	41	62	....	....	....	14	....	....	....	....	....
1960-61	Buffalo Bisons	AHL	71	37	65	102	....	....	....	27	4	0	3	3	0
1961-62	Vancouver Canucks	WHL	70	34	52	86	....	....	....	2	....	....	....	....	....
1962-63	Vancouver Canucks	WHL	64	29	61	90	....	....	....	8	7	2	7	9	0
1963-64	Vancouver Canucks	WHL	65	28	53	81	....	....	....	38	....	....	....	....	....
1964-65	Vancouver Canucks	WHL	69	29	52	81	....	....	....	18	5	1	5	6	0
1965-66	Vancouver Canucks	WHL	65	22	51	73	....	....	....	16	7	5	8	13	0
1966-67	Vancouver Canucks	WHL	72	17	49	66	....	....	....	42	8	1	6	7	0
1967-68	Vancouver Canucks	WHL	72	22	46	68	....	....	....	6	....	....	....	....	....
1968-69	Vancouver Canucks	WHL	65	4	24	28	....	....	....	19	2	0	0	0	0
1969-70	Vancouver Canucks	WHL	16	2	1	3	....	....	....	0	....	....	....	....	....
	NHL Totals		**158**	**28**	**43**	**71**	**35**	**51**	**86**	**16**	**6**	**0**	**0**	**0**	**0**

WHL First All-Star Team (1956) • Won Leader Cup (WHL - MVP) (1956, 1962, 1963) • WHL Coast Division Second All-Star Team (1957, 1958) • AHL First All-Star Team (1961) • Won Les Cunningham Award (MVP - AHL) (1961) • WHL Second All-Star Team (1962, 1963) • Won Fred J. Hume Cup (WHL Most Gentlemanly Player) (1962, 1963, 1968)

Signed as a free agent by **Boston**, October 5, 1948. Traded to **Toronto** by **Boston** with Fern Flaman, Ken Smith and Leo Boivin for Bill Ezinicki and Vic Lynn, November 16, 1950. Traded to **Vancouver** (WHL) by **Toronto** with Bill Ezinicki and Hugh Barlow for $10,000, December 21, 1954. Claimed by **NY Rangers** from **Vancouver** (WHL) in Inter-League Draft, June 4, 1957. Traded to **Chicago** by **NY Rangers** (Vancouver-WHL) for $7,500, the loan of Ray Cyr and future considerations, December 21, 1958. Traded to **Vancouver** (WHL) by **Chicago** (Buffalo-AHL) for cash, September, 1961.

• MANASTERSKY, Tom

Thomas Timothy

D – R. 5'9", 185 lbs. b: Montreal, Que., 3/7/1929.

Season	Club	League	REGULAR SEASON								PLAYOFFS				
			GP	G	A	Pts	AG	AA	APts	PIM	GP	G	A	Pts	PIM
1944-45	Montreal Central High	H.S.	STATISTICS NOT AVAILABLE												
1945-46	Montreal Jr. Royals	QJHL	19	0	4	4	....	....	....	23	....	....	....	....	....
	Montreal Royals	QSHL	1	0	0	0	....	....	....	2	....	....	....	....	....
1946-47	Montreal Jr. Royals	QJHL	25	1	3	4	....	....	....	68	7	0	1	1	29
	Montreal Royals	QSHL	3	0	0	0	....	....	....	2	....	....	....	....	....
1947-48	Montreal Jr. Royals	QJHL	8	1	1	2	....	....	....	16	13	0	1	1	*38
1948-49	Montreal Jr. Royals	QJHL	30	2	5	7	....	....	....	63	10	2	4	6	16
	Montreal Royals	QSHL	2	0	0	0	....	....	....	0	....	....	....	....	....
	Montreal Jr. Royals	M-Cup	15	1	5	6	....	....	....	*67	....	....	....	....	....
1949-50	Montreal Royals	QSHL	27	2	7	9	....	....	....	87	3	0	0	0	25
1950-51	**Montreal Canadiens**	**NHL**	**6**	**0**	**0**	**0**	**0**	**0**	**0**	**11**	....	....	....	....	....
	Cincinnati Mohawks	AHL	5	0	0	0	....	....	....	18	....	....	....	....	....
	Victoria Cougars	PCHL	18	1	1	2	....	....	....	45	....	....	....	....	....
	Montreal Royals	QMHL	1	0	0	0	....	....	....	0	....	....	....	....	....
	NHL Totals		**6**	**0**	**0**	**0**	**0**	**0**	**0**	**11**	....	....	....	....	....

Signed as a free agent by **Montreal**, November 30, 1949.

• MANCUSO, Gus

Gus Felix

RW – L. 5'7", 160 lbs. b: Niagara Falls, Ont., 4/11/1914.

Season	Club	League	REGULAR SEASON								PLAYOFFS				
			GP	G	A	Pts	AG	AA	APts	PIM	GP	G	A	Pts	PIM
1930-31	Niagara Falls Cataracts	OHA-Jr.	3	1	2	3	....	....	....	0	....	....	....	....	....
1931-32	Niagara Falls Cataracts	OHA-Jr.	4	1	0	1	....	....	....	2	5	*3	0	3	2
1932-33	Niagara Falls Cataracts	OHA-Jr.	....	....	....	....	....	....	....	....	2	1	0	1	0
	Niagara Falls Cataracts	M-Cup	3	5	2	7	....	....	....	4	....	....	....	....	....
1933-34	Niagara Falls Cataracts	OHA-Sr.	24	9	1	10	....	....	....	20	2	0	0	0	0
1934-35	Hershey B'ars	EAHL	21	16	5	21	....	....	....	31	9	6	4	10	4
1935-36	Hershey B'ars	EAHL	40	24	12	36	....	....	....	37	8	3	0	3	18
1936-37	Hershey B'ars	EAHL	48	14	14	28	....	....	....	17	4	1	0	1	2
1937-38	**Montreal Canadiens**	**NHL**	**17**	**1**	**1**	**2**	**2**	**2**	**4**	**4**	....	....	....	....	....
	New Haven Eagles	IAHL	32	6	4	10	....	....	....	17	2	0	1	1	0
1938-39	**Montreal Canadiens**	**NHL**	**2**	**0**	**0**	**0**	**0**	**0**	**0**	**0**	....	....	....	....	....
	New Haven Eagles	IAHL	42	4	14	18	....	....	....	47	....	....	....	....	....
1939-40	**Montreal Canadiens**	**NHL**	**2**	**0**	**0**	**0**	**0**	**0**	**0**	**0**	....	....	....	....	....
	New Haven Eagles	IAHL	47	9	20	29	....	....	....	41	3	0	1	1	0
1940-41	New Haven Eagles	AHL	56	17	25	42	....	....	....	12	2	0	0	0	2
1941-42	New Haven Eagles	AHL	46	19	29	48	....	....	....	24	2	0	0	0	0
1942-43	**New York Rangers**	**NHL**	**21**	**6**	**8**	**14**	**6**	**7**	**13**	**13**	....	....	....	....	....
	New Haven Eagles	AHL	30	10	16	26	....	....	....	13	....	....	....	....	....
1943-44			MILITARY SERVICE												
1944-45			MILITARY SERVICE												
1945-46	Providence Reds	AHL	15	3	5	8	....	....	....	4	....	....	....	....	....
	Hollywood Wolves	PCHL	6	2	4	6	....	....	....	0	9	3	2	5	10
1946-47	Hollywood Wolves	PCHL	59	27	17	44	....	....	....	33	7	1	1	2	9
1947-48	Los Angeles Monarchs	PCHL	51	17	15	32	....	....	....	15	4	0	2	2	2
1948-49	Los Angeles Monarchs	PCHL	51	17	15	32	....	....	....	15	....	....	....	....	....
	NHL Totals		**42**	**7**	**9**	**16**	**8**	**9**	**17**	**17**	....	....	....	....	....

EAHL Second All-Star Team (1935) • EAHL First All-Star Team (1936)

Signed as a free agent by **Montreal Canadiens**, October 30, 1937. Traded to **NY Rangers** by **Montreal** for cash, November 4, 1942.

• MANN, Jack

John Edward Kingsley

C – L. 5'7", 160 lbs. b: Winnipeg, Man., 7/27/1919.

Season	Club	League	REGULAR SEASON								PLAYOFFS				
			GP	G	A	Pts	AG	AA	APts	PIM	GP	G	A	Pts	PIM
1937-38	Winnipeg Rangers	MJHL	9	0	1	1	....	....	....	6	2	0	0	0	0
1938-39	St. James Canadians	MJHL	17	7	7	14	....	....	....	10	2	0	3	3	2
1939-40	Nelson Maple Leafs	WKHL	27	20	9	29	....	....	....	21	7	*7	2	*9	6
1940-41	Nelson Maple Leafs	WKHL	27	*30	15	45	....	....	....	30	2	2	1	3	2
1941-42	Nanaimo Clippers	WKHL	26	*27	11	38	....	....	....	33	7	*7	2	*9	14
1942-43	Nanaimo Clippers	WKHL	19	16	12	28	....	....	....	8	3	1	0	1	0
1943-44	**New York Rangers**	**NHL**	**3**	**0**	**0**	**0**	**0**	**0**	**0**	**0**	....	....	....	....	....
	New York Rovers	EAHL	30	19	13	32	....	....	....	9	10	5	3	8	9
	Brooklyn Crescents	EAHL	2	0	0	0	....	....	....	5	....	....	....	....	....
1944-45	**New York Rangers**	**NHL**	**6**	**3**	**4**	**7**	**3**	**5**	**8**	**0**	....	....	....	....	....
	New York Rovers	EAHL	39	16	31	47	....	....	....	29	6	5	3	8	4
	Philadelphia Falcons	EAHL	2	1	0	1	....	....	....	0	....	....	....	....	....
1945-46	St. Paul Saints	USHL	36	12	11	23	....	....	....	6	6	0	4	4	0
1946-47	St. Paul Saints	USHL	6	1	2	3	....	....	....	0	....	....	....	....	....
	Fresno Falcons	PCHL	46	12	12	24	....	....	....	8	2	0	0	0	0
1947-48	New Westminster Royals	PCHL	56	18	34	52	....	....	....	16	....	....	....	....	....
	NHL Totals		**9**	**3**	**4**	**7**	**3**	**5**	**8**	**0**	....	....	....	....	....

• MANN, Norm

Norman Thomas

RW/C – R. 5'10", 155 lbs. b: Bradford, England, 3/3/1914.

Season	Club	League	REGULAR SEASON								PLAYOFFS				
			GP	G	A	Pts	AG	AA	APts	PIM	GP	G	A	Pts	PIM
1931-32	Newmarket Redmen	OHA-Jr.	7	1	1	2	....	....	....	*12	....	....	....	....	....
	Newmarket Redmen	M-Cup	5	1	2	3	....	....	....	2	....	....	....	....	....
1932-33	Newmarket Redmen	OHA-Jr.	17	11	8	19	....	....	....	....	....	....	....	....	....
	Newmarket Redmen	M-Cup	19	6	7	13	....	....	....	14	....	....	....	....	....
1933-34	Toronto Marlboros	OHA-Sr.	24	16	9	25	....	....	....	25	2	0	1	1	2
	Toronto British Consols	TMHL	11	8	4	12	....	....	....	14	5	1	1	2	16
1934-35	Toronto British Consols	TIHL	15	6	12	18	....	....	....	20	4	2	2	4	4
	Toronto All-Stars	TIHL	6	2	4	6	....	....	....	10	4	2	1	3	0

			REGULAR SEASON								PLAYOFFS				
Season	Club	League	GP	G	A	Pts	AG	AA	APts	PIM	GP	G	A	Pts	PIM
1935-36	Syracuse Stars	IHL	48	8	23	31				60	3	0	0	0	2
	Toronto Maple Leafs	**NHL**									**1**	**0**	**0**	**0**	**0**
1936-37	Syracuse Stars	IAHL	48	17	24	41				47	9	3	5	8	11
1937-38	Philadelphia Ramblers	IAHL	26	4	9	13				8	1	0	0	0	0
1938-39	Philadelphia Ramblers	IAHL	3	2	4	6				2					
	Toronto Maple Leafs	**NHL**	**16**	**0**	**0**	**0**	**0**	**0**	**0**	**2**					
	Syracuse Stars	IAHL	41	9	16	25				39	3	1	0	1	0
1939-40	Providence Reds	IAHL	36	11	16	27				25	8	3	5	8	6
1940-41	**Toronto Maple Leafs**	**NHL**	**15**	**0**	**3**	**3**	**0**	**4**	**4**	**2**	**1**	**0**	**0**	**0**	**0**
	Providence Reds	AHL	28	8	8	16				8	4	2	0	2	6
1941-42	Pittsburgh Hornets	AHL	41	16	36	52				11					
1942-43	Pittsburgh Hornets	AHL	54	31	45	76				83	2	0	1	1	0
	Cleveland Barons	AHL	1	0	0	0				0					
1943-44	Toronto Navy	OHA-Sr.	23	10	29	39				10					
1944-45	Toronto Navy	TNDHL	12	8	10	18				21	6	2	1	3	2
1945-46	Toronto Staffords	TIHL	13	4	11	15				10	13	2	3	5	4
1946-47	Cleveland Barons	AHL	27	5	6	11				17	4	0	0	0	2
1947-48			REINSTATED AS AN AMATEUR												
1948-49	Powassan Hawks	NBDHL	24	11	*34	45									
	NHL Totals		**31**	**0**	**3**	**3**	**0**	**4**	**4**	**4**	**2**	**0**	**0**	**0**	**0**

Signed as a free agent by **Toronto**, October 7, 1935. Claimed by **NY Rangers** from **Syracuse** (IAHL) in Inter-League Draft, May 9, 1937. Traded to **Toronto** by **NY Rangers** for $4,000, November 15, 1938. Traded to **Pittsburgh** (AHL) by **Toronto** for cash, October 30, 1941.

• MANNERS, Rennison Rennison Flint

C – L. 5'11", 160 lbs. b: Ottawa, Ont., 2/5/1904 d: 12/26/1944.

Season	Club	League	GP	G	A	Pts	AG	AA	APts	PIM	GP	G	A	Pts	PIM
1922-23	Pittsburgh Yellowjackets	USAHA	20	3	0	3									
1923-24	Pittsburgh Yellowjackets	USAHA	7	1	0	1					2	0	1	1	
1924-25	Fort Pitt Panthers	USAHA	19	7	0	7					8	4	0	4	
1925-26	Fort Pitt Panthers	USAHA	STATISTICS NOT AVAILABLE												
1926-27	Ottawa Montagnards	OCHL	15	3	2	5					2	0	0	0	0
1927-28	Ottawa Montagnards	OCHL	15	2	4	6					4	0	0	0	0
1928-29	Ottawa Montagnards	OCHL	12	*8	2	10									
1929-30	**Pittsburgh Pirates**	**NHL**	**33**	**3**	**2**	**5**	**4**	**5**	**9**	**14**					
	London Panthers	IHL	3	0	0	0				0					
1930-31	**Philadelphia Quakers**	**NHL**	**4**	**0**	**0**	**0**	**0**	**0**	**0**	**0**					
	Niagara Falls Cataracts	OPHL	27	9	8	17				23	2	0	0	0	2
1931-32			DID NOT PLAY												
1932-33			DID NOT PLAY												
1933-34	Ottawa Montagnards	OCHL	10	2	2	4				4	3	1	0	1	0
	NHL Totals		**37**	**3**	**2**	**5**	**4**	**5**	**9**	**14**					

Transferred to **Philadelphia** after **Pittsburgh** franchise relocated, September 26, 1930.

• MANSON, Ray Raymond Clifton

LW – L. 5'11", 180 lbs. b: St. Boniface, Man., 12/3/1926.

Season	Club	League	GP	G	A	Pts	AG	AA	APts	PIM	GP	G	A	Pts	PIM
1943-44	St. Boniface Canadiens	MJHL	10	8	3	11				2	9	3	3	6	0
1944-45	Winnipeg Esquires	MJHL	10	10	5	15				16	6	6	2	8	15
1945-46	Winnipeg Rangers	MJHL	10	10	5	15				13	2	1	0	1	2
1946-47	Brandon Elks	MJHL	16	22	*19	*41				10	7	*10	2	*12	5
1947-48	**Boston Bruins**	**NHL**	**1**	**0**	**0**	**0**	**0**	**0**	**0**	**0**					
	Boston Olympics	EAHL	20	20	17	37				6					
	Boston Olympics	QSHL	46	24	22	46				10					
1948-49	**New York Rangers**	**NHL**	**1**	**0**	**1**	**1**	**0**	**1**	**1**	**0**					
	New York Rovers	QSHL	41	17	13	30				8					
1949-50	New Haven Ramblers	AHL	70	11	15	26				26					
1950-51	New Haven Ramblers	AHL	26	9	7	16				2					
	St. Paul Saints	USHL	41	12	11	23				8	4	1	1	2	7
1951-52	Vancouver Canucks	PCHL	70	36	32	68				21					
1952-53	Vancouver–Saskatoon	WHL	69	20	25	45				8	13	6	*14	20	0
1953-54	Saskatoon Quakers	WHL	70	28	42	70				22	6	1	3	4	0
1954-55	Saskatoon Quakers	WHL	58	27	27	54				2					
1955-56	Brandon Regals	WHL	69	35	28	63				22					
1956-57	Brandon Regals	WHL	70	40	43	83				18	8	2	5	7	0
	Brandon Regals	Ed-Cup	6	3	5	8				2					
1957-58	Winnipeg Maroons	X-Games	STATISTICS NOT AVAILABLE												
	Winnipeg Maroons	Al-Cup	13	2	6	8				2					
	NHL Totals		**2**	**0**	**1**	**1**	**0**	**1**	**1**	**0**					

WHL Prairie Division First All-Star Team (1957)

Traded to **NY Rangers** by **Boston** with Pentti Lund to complete transaction that sent Grant Warwick to Boston (February 6, 1948), June, 1948.

• MANTHA, Georges Leon Georges

D/LW – L. 5'8", 165 lbs. b: Lachine, Que., 11/29/1908 d: 1/25/1990.

Season	Club	League	GP	G	A	Pts	AG	AA	APts	PIM	GP	G	A	Pts	PIM
1925-26	Montreal Bell Telephone	MTRHL	4	2	0	2				4					
1926-27	Montreal Bell Telephone	MTRHL	4	2	0	2				0					
1927-28	Montreal Bell Telephone	MTRHL	STATISTICS NOT AVAILABLE												
	Montreal Bell Telephone	MTRHL	3	1	1	2				4					
1928-29	University of Montreal	MCHL	3	0	1	1				2					
	Montreal Bell Telephone	MTRHL	4	1	1	2				14					
	Montreal Canadiens	**NHL**	**21**	**0**	**0**	**0**	**0**	**0**	**0**	**8**	**3**	**0**	**0**	**0**	**0**
♦1929-30	**Montreal Canadiens**	**NHL**	**44**	**5**	**2**	**7**	**7**	**5**	**12**	**16**	**6**	**0**	**0**	**0**	**8**
♦1930-31	**Montreal Canadiens**	**NHL**	**44**	**11**	**6**	**17**	**22**	**18**	**40**	**25**	**10**	**5**	**1**	**6**	**4**
1931-32	**Montreal Canadiens**	**NHL**	**48**	**1**	**7**	**8**	**2**	**15**	**17**	**8**	**4**	**0**	**1**	**1**	**8**
1932-33	**Montreal Canadiens**	**NHL**	**43**	**3**	**6**	**9**	**5**	**12**	**17**	**10**					
1933-34	**Montreal Canadiens**	**NHL**	**44**	**6**	**9**	**15**	**10**	**19**	**29**	**12**					
1934-35	**Montreal Canadiens**	**NHL**	**42**	**12**	**10**	**22**	**20**	**17**	**37**	**14**	**2**	**0**	**0**	**0**	**4**
1935-36	**Montreal Canadiens**	**NHL**	**35**	**1**	**12**	**13**	**2**	**23**	**25**	**14**					
1936-37	**Montreal Canadiens**	**NHL**	**47**	**13**	**14**	**27**	**22**	**26**	**48**	**17**	**5**	**0**	**0**	**0**	**0**
1937-38	**Montreal Canadiens**	**NHL**	**47**	**23**	**19**	**42**	**38**	**31**	**69**	**12**	**3**	**1**	**0**	**1**	**0**
1938-39	**Montreal Canadiens**	**NHL**	**25**	**5**	**5**	**10**	**9**	**8**	**17**	**6**	**3**	**0**	**0**	**0**	**0**
1939-40	**Montreal Canadiens**	**NHL**	**42**	**9**	**11**	**20**	**15**	**17**	**32**	**6**					
1940-41	**Montreal Canadiens**	**NHL**	**6**	**0**	**1**	**1**	**0**	**1**	**1**	**0**					
	New Haven Eagles	AHL	49	16	15	31				8					
1941-42	Washington Lions	AHL	50	18	25	43				4	1	0	0	0	0
1942-43	Washington Lions	AHL	19	2	2	4				4					
	NHL Totals		**488**	**89**	**102**	**191**	**152**	**192**	**344**	**148**	**36**	**6**	**2**	**8**	**24**

• Brother of Sylvio • AHL Second All-Star Team (1941) • Played in NHL All-Star Game (1937, 1939)

Traded to **Washington** (AHL) by **Montreal** for cash, October 9, 1941.

• MANTHA, Sylvio HHOF

D – R. 5'10", 178 lbs. b: Montreal, Que., 4/14/1902 d: 8/7/1974.

Season	Club	League	GP	G	A	Pts	AG	AA	APts	PIM	GP	G	A	Pts	PIM
1922-23	Montreal Nationale	MBHL	9	4	0	4									
1923-24	**Montreal Canadiens**	**NHL**	**24**	**1**	**3**	**4**	**2**	**17**	**19**	**11**	**2**	**0**	**0**	**0**	**0**
♦	Montreal Canadiens	St-Cup	4	0	0	0				0					
1924-25	**Montreal Canadiens**	**NHL**	**30**	**2**	**3**	**5**	**3**	**12**	**15**	**18**	**2**	**0**	**1**	**1**	**0**
	Montreal Canadiens	St-Cup	4	0	0	0									
1925-26	**Montreal Canadiens**	**NHL**	**34**	**2**	**1**	**3**	**3**	**6**	**9**	**66**					
1926-27	**Montreal Canadiens**	**NHL**	**43**	**10**	**5**	**15**	**18**	**26**	**44**	**77**	**4**	**1**	**0**	**1**	**0**
1927-28	**Montreal Canadiens**	**NHL**	**43**	**4**	**11**	**15**	**8**	**63**	**71**	**61**	**2**	**0**	**0**	**0**	**6**
1928-29	**Montreal Canadiens**	**NHL**	**44**	**9**	**4**	**13**	**26**	**27**	**53**	**56**	**3**	**0**	**0**	**0**	**0**
♦1929-30	**Montreal Canadiens**	**NHL**	**44**	**13**	**11**	**24**	**18**	**26**	**44**	**108**	**6**	**2**	**1**	**3**	**18**
♦1930-31	**Montreal Canadiens**	**NHL**	**44**	**4**	**7**	**11**	**8**	**21**	**29**	**75**	**10**	**2**	**1**	**3**	***26**
1931-32	**Montreal Canadiens**	**NHL**	**47**	**5**	**5**	**10**	**8**	**11**	**19**	**62**	**4**	**0**	**1**	**1**	**8**
1932-33	**Montreal Canadiens**	**NHL**	**48**	**4**	**7**	**11**	**7**	**14**	**21**	**50**	**2**	**0**	**1**	**1**	**2**
1933-34	**Montreal Canadiens**	**NHL**	**48**	**4**	**6**	**10**	**7**	**13**	**20**	**24**	**2**	**0**	**0**	**0**	**2**
1934-35	**Montreal Canadiens**	**NHL**	**47**	**3**	**11**	**14**	**5**	**19**	**24**	**36**	**2**	**0**	**0**	**0**	**2**
1935-36	**Montreal Canadiens**	**NHL**	**42**	**2**	**4**	**6**	**4**	**8**	**12**	**25**					
1936-37	**Boston Bruins**	**NHL**	**4**	**0**	**0**	**0**	**0**	**0**	**0**	**2**					
1937-38	Montreal Concordia	MCHL	DID NOT PLAY – COACHING												
	NHL Totals		**542**	**63**	**78**	**141**	**117**	**263**	**380**	**671**	**39**	**5**	**5**	**10**	**64**

• Brother of Georges • NHL Second All-Star Team (1931, 1932)

Signed as a free agent by **Montreal Canadiens**, December 3, 1923. • 1923-24 Stanley Cup totals includes series with Calgary (WCHL) and Vancouver (PCHA). Signed as a free agent by **Boston**, February 11, 1937.

• MARACLE, Bud Henry Elmer

LW – L. 5'11", 195 lbs. b: Ayr, Ont., 9/8/1904 Deceased.

Season	Club	League	GP	G	A	Pts	AG	AA	APts	PIM	GP	G	A	Pts	PIM
1921-22	Haileybury High School	H.S.									4	3	*5	*8	
1922-23	North Bay Trappers	NOHA	STATISTICS NOT AVAILABLE												
1923-24	North Bay Trappers	NOHA	6	*11	0	*11					5	11	0	11	
1924-25	North Bay Trappers	NOHA	STATISTICS NOT AVAILABLE												
1925-26	Toronto Industrial	TIHL	STATISTICS NOT AVAILABLE												
1926-27	Springfield Indians	Can-Am	32	5	1	6				44	6	2	1	3	4
1927-28	Springfield Indians	Can-Am	40	15	3	18				65	3	2	1	*3	0
1928-29	Springfield Indians	Can-Am	37	4	4	8				47					
1929-30	Springfield Indians	Can-Am	31	5	4	9				22					
1930-31	Springfield Indians	Can-Am	26	6	4	10				44					
	New York Rangers	**NHL**	**11**	**1**	**3**	**4**	**2**	**9**	**11**	**4**	**4**	**0**	**0**	**0**	**0**
1931-32	Bronx Tigers	Can-Am	1	0	0	0				0					
	Springfield Indians	Can-Am	27	3	9	12				14					
1932-33			DID NOT PLAY – INJURED												
1933-34	New Haven Eagles	Can-Am	40	11	6	17				31					
1934-35	New Haven Eagles	Can-Am	29	8	7	15				20					
	Philadelphia Arrows	Can-Am	14	6	3	9				4					
1935-36	Tulsa Oilers	AHA	48	12	8	20				17	3	0	0	0	0
1936-37	Tulsa Oilers	AHA	42	3	10	13				12					
1937-38			REINSTATED AS AN AMATEUR												
1938-39	Detroit Pontiacs	MOHL	22	3	5	8				2	7	1	0	1	6
	NHL Totals		**11**	**1**	**3**	**4**	**2**	**9**	**11**	**4**	**4**	**0**	**0**	**0**	**0**

Traded to **Bronx** (Can-Am) by **NY Rangers** for cash, November 1, 1931.

• MARCETTA, Milan

— see page 1374

• MARCH, Mush Harold

RW – R. 5'5", 154 lbs. b: Silton, Sask., 10/18/1908.

Season	Club	League	GP	G	A	Pts	AG	AA	APts	PIM	GP	G	A	Pts	PIM
1925-26	Regina Falcons	S-SJHL	8	*10	*7	*17				2					
	Regina Falcons	M-Cup	3	3	2	5				4					
1926-27	Regina Falcons	S-SJHL	5	*7	0	*7				4	1	0	0	0	0
1927-28	Regina Monarchs	S-SJHL	5	*13	*5	*18				*17	2	*4	0	*4	2
	Regina Monarchs	M-Cup	11	*36	4	*40				8					
1928-29	**Chicago Black Hawks**	**NHL**	**35**	**3**	**3**	**6**	**9**	**20**	**29**	**6**					
1929-30	**Chicago Black Hawks**	**NHL**	**43**	**8**	**7**	**15**	**11**	**16**	**27**	**48**					
1930-31	**Chicago Black Hawks**	**NHL**	**44**	**11**	**6**	**17**	**22**	**18**	**40**	**36**	**9**	**3**	**1**	**4**	**11**
1931-32	**Chicago Black Hawks**	**NHL**	**48**	**12**	**10**	**22**	**20**	**22**	**42**	**59**	**2**	**0**	**0**	**0**	**2**
1932-33	**Chicago Black Hawks**	**NHL**	**48**	**9**	**11**	**20**	**16**	**23**	**39**	**38**					
♦1933-34	**Chicago Black Hawks**	**NHL**	**48**	**4**	**13**	**17**	**7**	**27**	**34**	**26**	**8**	**2**	**2**	**4**	**6**
1934-35	**Chicago Black Hawks**	**NHL**	**48**	**13**	**17**	**30**	**21**	**30**	**51**	**48**	**2**	**0**	**0**	**0**	**0**
1935-36	**Chicago Black Hawks**	**NHL**	**48**	**16**	**19**	**35**	**31**	**36**	**67**	**42**	**2**	**2**	**3**	**5**	**0**
1936-37	**Chicago Black Hawks**	**NHL**	**37**	**11**	**6**	**17**	**18**	**11**	**29**	**31**					
♦1937-38	**Chicago Black Hawks**	**NHL**	**41**	**11**	**17**	**28**	**18**	**27**	**45**	**16**	**9**	**2**	**4**	**6**	**12**
1938-39	**Chicago Black Hawks**	**NHL**	**46**	**10**	**11**	**21**	**17**	**17**	**34**	**29**					
1939-40	**Chicago Black Hawks**	**NHL**	**45**	**9**	**14**	**23**	**15**	**22**	**37**	**49**	**2**	**1**	**0**	**1**	**2**
1940-41	**Chicago Black Hawks**	**NHL**	**44**	**8**	**9**	**17**	**12**	**13**	**25**	**16**	**4**	**2**	**3**	**5**	**0**
1941-42	**Chicago Black Hawks**	**NHL**	**48**	**6**	**26**	**32**	**8**	**31**	**39**	**22**	**3**	**0**	**2**	**2**	**4**
1942-43	**Chicago Black Hawks**	**NHL**	**50**	**7**	**29**	**36**	**7**	**27**	**34**	**46**					
1943-44	**Chicago Black Hawks**	**NHL**	**48**	**10**	**27**	**37**	**9**	**24**	**33**	**16**	**4**	**0**	**0**	**0**	**4**
1944-45	**Chicago Black Hawks**	**NHL**	**38**	**5**	**5**	**10**	**5**	**6**	**11**	**12**					
	NHL Totals		**759**	**153**	**230**	**383**	**246**	**370**	**616**	**540**	**45**	**12**	**15**	**27**	**41**

Played in NHL All-Star Game (1937)

Signed as a free agent by **Chicago**, November 29, 1928.

• MARCON, Lou Louis Angelo

D – R. 5'9", 168 lbs. b: Fort William, Ont., 5/28/1935.

Season	Club	League	GP	G	A	Pts	AG	AA	APts	PIM	GP	G	A	Pts	PIM
1951-52	Fort William Canadiens	TBJHL	28	1	0	1				10					
1952-53	Fort William Canadiens	TBJHL	30	1	2	3				20	6	0	2	2	4
	Fort William Canadiens	M-Cup	5	1	1	2				4					

Season	Club	League	GP	G	A	Pts	AG	AA	APts	PIM	GP	G	A	Pts	PIM
			REGULAR SEASON								PLAYOFFS				
1953-54	Fort William Canadiens	TBJHL	36	1	5	6	....	....	....	48	4	0	0	0	2
	Fort William Canadiens	M-Cup	13	1	3	4	....	....	....	6	....	....	....	....	....
1954-55	Fort William Canadiens	TBJHL	STATISTICS NOT AVAILABLE												
	Fort William Canadiens	M-Cup	7	2	1	3	....	....	....	9	....	....	....	....	....
1955-56	Cincinnati Mohawks	IHL	59	2	22	24	....	....	....	113	8	1	1	2	8
1956-57	Cincinnati Mohawks	IHL	55	0	17	17	....	....	....	49	7	0	1	1	4
	Rochester Americans	AHL	2	0	0	0	....	....	....	0	....	....	....	....	....
1957-58	Montreal Royals	QHL	3	0	0	0	....	....	....	2	....	....	....	....	....
	Cincinnati Mohawks	IHL	64	7	31	38	....	....	....	89	4	0	1	1	2
1958-59	**Detroit Red Wings**	**NHL**	**21**	**0**	**1**	**1**	**0**	**1**	**1**	**12**	....	....	....	....	....
	Edmonton Flyers	WHL	47	1	6	7	....	....	....	66	....	....	....	....	....
1959-60	**Detroit Red Wings**	**NHL**	**38**	**0**	**3**	**3**	**0**	**3**	**3**	**30**	....	....	....	....	....
	Edmonton Flyers	WHL	15	0	9	9	....	....	....	28	4	0	0	0	*22
1960-61	Edmonton Flyers	WHL	55	7	11	18	....	....	....	91	....	....	....	....	....
1961-62	Edmonton Flyers	WHL	62	2	15	17	....	....	....	68	12	1	2	3	23
1962-63	**Detroit Red Wings**	**NHL**	**1**	**0**	**0**	**0**	**0**	**0**	**0**	**0**	....	....	....	....	....
	Edmonton Flyers	WHL	28	5	8	13	....	....	....	61	....	....	....	....	....
	Pittsburgh Hornets	AHL	35	0	3	3	....	....	....	105	....	....	....	....	....
1963-64	Pittsburgh Hornets	AHL	49	3	15	18	....	....	....	108	5	0	0	0	15
1964-65	Pittsburgh Hornets	AHL	62	2	11	13	....	....	....	190	4	0	1	1	6
1965-66	Memphis Wings	CPHL	59	1	9	10	....	....	....	107	....	....	....	....	....
	Pittsburgh Hornets	AHL	11	0	2	2	....	....	....	25	3	0	0	0	12
1966-67	Memphis Wings	CPHL	67	4	10	14	....	....	....	206	7	1	2	3	25
1967-68	Fort Worth Wings	CPHL	66	0	7	7	....	....	....	157	13	0	0	0	32
1968-69	Thunder Bay Twins	TBSHL	10	0	6	6	....	....	....	6	8	1	1	2	8
1969-70	Thunder Bay Twins	TBSHL	STATISTICS NOT AVAILABLE												
1970-71	Thunder Bay Twins	TBSHL	STATISTICS NOT AVAILABLE												
1971-72	Thunder Bay Twins	USHL	27	2	12	14	....	....	....	83	....	....	....	....	....
1972-73	Thunder Bay Twins	USHL	22	1	5	6	....	....	....	20	....	....	....	....	....
	NHL Totals		**60**	**0**	**4**	**4**	**0**	**4**	**4**	**42**	....	....	....	....	....

IHL Second All-Star Team (1957) • IHL First All-Star Team (1958)

Claimed by **Detroit** from **Montreal** in Intra-League Draft, June 3, 1958.

• MARCOTTE, Don

— *see page 1376*

• MARIO, Frank

Frank George
C – L. 5'8", 170 lbs. b: Esterhazy, Sask., 2/25/1921 Deceased.

Season	Club	League	GP	G	A	Pts	AG	AA	APts	PIM	GP	G	A	Pts	PIM
1939-40	Regina Abbots	S-SJHL	12	8	9	17	....	....	....	6	2	0	1	1	0
	Regina Abbots	M-Cup	6	4	7	11	....	....	....	2	....	....	....	....	....
1940-41	Regina Rangers	S-SJHL	32	13	19	32	....	....	....	26	8	4	5	9	9
1941-42	**Boston Bruins**	**NHL**	**9**	**1**	**1**	**2**	**1**	**1**	**2**	**0**	....	....	....	....	....
	Hershey Bears	AHL	42	12	27	39	....	....	....	38	5	1	1	2	0
1942-43	Cornwall Army	QSHL	32	15	27	42	....	....	....	51	6	0	2	2	12
	Cornwall Army	Al-Cup	14	6	5	11	....	....	....	17	....	....	....	....	....
1943-44			MILITARY SERVICE												
1944-45	**Boston Bruins**	**NHL**	**44**	**8**	**18**	**26**	**8**	**21**	**29**	**24**	....	....	....	....	....
1945-46	Hershey Bears	AHL	37	6	24	30	....	....	....	29	3	1	0	1	2
1946-47	Hershey Bears	AHL	64	24	47	71	....	....	....	65	11	5	*13	*18	7
1947-48	Hershey Bears	AHL	68	30	36	66	....	....	....	32	2	1	0	1	0
1948-49	Hershey Bears	AHL	68	26	46	72	....	....	....	27	11	2	3	5	0
1949-50	Hershey Bears	AHL	48	9	25	34	....	....	....	25	....	....	....	....	....
1950-51	Hershey Bears	AHL	58	21	38	59	....	....	....	40	6	0	4	4	0
1951-52	Hershey Bears	AHL	68	15	38	53	....	....	....	26	5	0	4	4	0
1952-53	Quebec Aces	QMHL	55	8	22	30	....	....	....	30	22	3	9	12	2
1953-54	Cornwall Colts	EOHL	DID NOT PLAY – COACHING												
	Cornwall Colts	Al-Cup	5	0	1	1	....	....	....	2	....	....	....	....	....
	NHL Totals		**53**	**9**	**19**	**28**	**9**	**22**	**31**	**24**	....	....	....	....	....

Signed as a free agent by **Boston**, October 21, 1941.

• MARIUCCI, John

USHOF HHOF
D – L. 5'10", 200 lbs. b: Eveleth, MN, 5/8/1916 d: 3/23/1987.

Season	Club	League	GP	G	A	Pts	AG	AA	APts	PIM	GP	G	A	Pts	PIM
1939-40	University of Minnesota	AAU	STATISTICS NOT AVAILABLE												
1940-41	**Chicago Black Hawks**	**NHL**	**23**	**0**	**5**	**5**	**0**	**7**	**7**	**33**	**5**	**0**	**2**	**2**	**16**
	Providence Reds	AHL	17	3	3	6	....	....	....	15	....	....	....	....	....
1941-42	**Chicago Black Hawks**	**NHL**	**47**	**5**	**8**	**13**	**7**	**9**	**16**	**44**	**3**	**0**	**0**	**0**	**0**
1942-43	Coast Guard Clippers	EAHL	45	23	23	46	....	....	....	67	12	4	8	12	14
1943-44	Coast Guard Clippers	EAHL	34	11	16	27	....	....	....	*29	12	3	8	11	18
1944-45			MILITARY SERVICE												
1945-46	**Chicago Black Hawks**	**NHL**	**50**	**3**	**8**	**11**	**4**	**12**	**16**	**58**	**4**	**0**	**1**	**1**	**10**
1946-47	**Chicago Black Hawks**	**NHL**	**52**	**2**	**9**	**11**	**2**	**11**	**13**	**110**	....	....	....	....	....
1947-48	**Chicago Black Hawks**	**NHL**	**51**	**1**	**4**	**5**	**1**	**5**	**6**	**63**	....	....	....	....	....
1948-49	St. Louis Flyers	AHL	68	12	30	42	....	....	....	74	7	0	1	1	12
1949-50	Minneapolis Millers	USHL	67	8	24	32	....	....	....	87	7	0	2	2	23
1950-51	St. Paul Saints	USHL	59	2	28	30	....	....	....	85	4	0	0	0	0
1951-52	Minneapolis Millers	AAHL	39	18	31	49	....	....	....	45	....	....	....	....	....
1952/66	University of Minesota	WCHA	DID NOT PLAY – COACHING												
	NHL Totals		**223**	**11**	**34**	**45**	**14**	**44**	**58**	**308**	**12**	**0**	**3**	**3**	**26**

AAU First All-Star Team (1940) • NCAA All-American (1940) • EAHL First All-Star Team (1943) • Won Lester Patrick Trophy (1977)

Traded to **St. Louis** (AHL) by **Chicago** for cash, October 28, 1948. Traded to **Minneapolis** (USHL) by **St. Louis** (AHL) for cash, September 4, 1949.

• MARKER, Gus

August Solberg
RW – R. 5'9", 162 lbs. b: Wetaskiwin, Alta., 8/1/1907 Deceased.

Season	Club	League	GP	G	A	Pts	AG	AA	APts	PIM	GP	G	A	Pts	PIM
1927-28	Edmonton Elks	ESrHL	STATISTICS NOT AVAILABLE												
1928-29	Tulsa Oilers	AHA	36	10	5	15	....	....	....	39	4	1	0	1	2
1929-30	Tulsa Oilers	AHA	48	13	7	20	....	....	....	31	9	1	1	2	2
1930-31	Tulsa Oilers	AHA	48	21	11	32	....	....	....	42	4	1	1	2	8
1931-32	Tulsa Oilers	AHA	44	11	7	18	....	....	....	20	....	....	....	....	....
1932-33	**Detroit Red Wings**	**NHL**	**13**	**1**	**1**	**2**	**2**	**2**	**4**	**8**	....	....	....	....	....
	Detroit Olympics	IHL	27	6	7	13	....	....	....	31	....	....	....	....	....
1933-34	**Detroit Red Wings**	**NHL**	**7**	**1**	**0**	**1**	**2**	**0**	**2**	**2**	**4**	**0**	**0**	**0**	**2**
	Detroit Olympics	IHL	37	13	13	26	....	....	....	48	6	3	*6	*9	2
♦1934-35	**Montreal Maroons**	**NHL**	**44**	**11**	**4**	**15**	**18**	**7**	**25**	**18**	**7**	**1**	**1**	**2**	**4**
	Windsor Bulldogs	IHL	3	1	2	3	....	....	....	2	....	....	....	....	....
1935-36	**Montreal Maroons**	**NHL**	**48**	**7**	**12**	**19**	**13**	**23**	**36**	**10**	**3**	**1**	**0**	**1**	**2**
1936-37	**Montreal Maroons**	**NHL**	**47**	**10**	**12**	**22**	**17**	**22**	**39**	**22**	**5**	**0**	**1**	**1**	**0**
1937-38	**Montreal Maroons**	**NHL**	**48**	**9**	**15**	**24**	**15**	**24**	**39**	**35**	....	....	....	....	....
1938-39	**Toronto Maple Leafs**	**NHL**	**29**	**9**	**6**	**15**	**16**	**9**	**25**	**11**	**10**	**2**	**2**	**4**	**0**
1939-40	**Toronto Maple Leafs**	**NHL**	**42**	**10**	**9**	**19**	**17**	**14**	**31**	**15**	**10**	**1**	**3**	**4**	**23**
1940-41	**Toronto Maple Leafs**	**NHL**	**27**	**4**	**5**	**9**	**6**	**7**	**13**	**10**	**7**	**0**	**0**	**0**	**5**
1941-42	**Brooklyn Americans**	**NHL**	**17**	**2**	**5**	**7**	**3**	**6**	**9**	**2**	....	....	....	....	....
	Springfield Indians	AHL	16	10	6	16	....	....	....	6	....	....	....	....	....
1942-43	Kingston Frontenacs	OVHL	4	0	4	4	....	....	....	2	4	2	5	7	0
	NHL Totals		**322**	**64**	**69**	**133**	**109**	**114**	**223**	**133**	**46**	**5**	**7**	**12**	**36**

NHL rights transferred to **Detroit** from **Chicago Shamrocks** (AHA) after AHA club owners purchased Detroit (NHL and IAHL) franchises, September 2, 1932. Traded to **Montreal Maroons** by **Detroit** for Wally Kilrea, September 23, 1934. Traded to **Toronto** by **Montreal Maroons** for $4,000, November 3, 1938. Loaned to **Brooklyn** by **Toronto** with Red Heron and Nick Knott and future considerations (cash, February 2, 1942) for Lorne Carr, October 30, 1941.

• MARKLE, Jack

John Arthur
RW – R. 5'9", 155 lbs. b: Thessalon, Ont., 5/15/1907 d: 6/25/1956.

Season	Club	League	GP	G	A	Pts	AG	AA	APts	PIM	GP	G	A	Pts	PIM
1923-24	Owen Sound Greys	OHA-Jr.	2	0	0	0	....	....	....	0	....	....	....	....	....
1924-25	Owen Sound Collegiate	H.S.	STATISTICS NOT AVAILABLE												
1925-26	Owen Sound Greys	OHA-Jr.	12	4	1	5	....	....	....	....	8	5	0	5	7
1926-27	Owen Sound Greys	OHA-Jr.	16	*31	8	*39	....	....	....	....	....	....	....	....	....
1927-28	London Panthers	Can-Pro	29	3	1	4	....	....	....	60	....	....	....	....	....
1928-29	Hamilton Tigers	Can-Pro	36	12	4	16	....	....	....	10	....	....	....	....	....
1929-30	Hamilton Tigers	IHL	42	12	10	22	....	....	....	21	....	....	....	....	....
1930-31	Syracuse Stars	IHL	48	18	20	38	....	....	....	4	....	....	....	....	....
1931-32	Syracuse Stars	IHL	48	20	13	33	....	....	....	10	....	....	....	....	....
1932-33	Syracuse Stars	IHL	30	8	16	24	....	....	....	6	6	1	2	3	0
1933-34	Syracuse Stars	IHL	42	14	22	36	....	....	....	16	6	4	2	6	2
1934-35	Syracuse Stars	IHL	44	23	20	*43	....	....	....	4	2	0	0	0	5
1935-36	Syracuse Stars	IHL	43	27	24	51	....	....	....	4	3	0	1	1	0
	Toronto Maple Leafs	**NHL**	**8**	**0**	**1**	**1**	**0**	**2**	**2**	**0**	....	....	....	....	....
1936-37	Syracuse Stars	IAHL	50	21	*39	*60	....	....	....	4	9	2	4	6	0
1937-38	Syracuse Stars	IAHL	48	22	32	*54	....	....	....	8	8	*5	1	6	0
1938-39	Syracuse Stars	IAHL	53	16	32	48	....	....	....	4	3	2	1	3	0
1939-40	Syracuse Stars	IAHL	45	9	24	33	....	....	....	6	....	....	....	....	....
	NHL Totals		**8**	**0**	**1**	**1**	**0**	**2**	**2**	**0**	....	....	....	....	....

IHL First All-Star Team (1936) • IAHL Second All-Star Team (1938)

Loaned to **Toronto** by **Syracuse** (IHL), January 20, 1936.

• MARKS, Jack

LW/D – L. 6', 180 lbs. b: Brantford, Ont., 6/11/1885 d: 8/20/1945.

Season	Club	League	GP	G	A	Pts	AG	AA	APts	PIM	GP	G	A	Pts	PIM
1901-02	Belleville Intermediates	OIHA	STATISTICS NOT AVAILABLE												
1902-03			PLAYED PROFESSIONAL BASEBALL												
1903-04	Belleville Intermediates	OIHA	STATISTICS NOT AVAILABLE												
1904-05	Brockville Hockey Club	FAHL	8	6	0	6	....	....	....	....	....	....	....	....	....
1905-06	Brockville Hockey Club	FAHL	6	1	0	1	....	....	....	....	....	....	....	....	....
1906-07	New Glasgow Seniors	S-Cup	1	0	0	0	....	....	....	3	....	....	....	....	....
	S.S. Marie Pros	IHL	14	13	10	23	....	....	....	26	....	....	....	....	....
1907-08	Pittsburgh Lyceum	WPHL	STATISTICS NOT AVAILABLE												
	Brantford Professionals	OPHL	10	10	0	10	....	....	....	31	....	....	....	....	....
	Toronto Professionals	OPHL	....	....	....	....	....	....	....	....	1	0	0	0	0
1908-09	Brantford Hockey Club	OPHL	9	6	0	6	....	....	....	19	....	....	....	....	....
1909-10	Brantford Hockey Club	OPHL	1	5	0	5	....	....	....	....	....	....	....	....	....
	All-Montreal	CHA	4	7	0	7	....	....	....	3	....	....	....	....	....
1910-11	Chicago All-Americans	CCPHL	STATISTICS NOT AVAILABLE												
♦1911-12	Quebec Bulldogs	NHA	10	4	0	4	....	....	....	10	2	0	0	0	2
♦1912-13	Quebec Bulldogs	NHA	19	18	0	18	....	....	....	39	1	2	0	2	0
1913-14	Quebec Bulldogs	NHA	20	9	6	15	....	....	....	32	....	....	....	....	....
1914-15	Quebec Bulldogs	NHA	17	7	4	11	....	....	....	49	....	....	....	....	....
1915-16	Quebec Bulldogs	NHA	23	12	0	12	....	....	....	40	....	....	....	....	....
1916-17	Quebec Bulldogs	NHA	16	0	0	0	....	....	....	6	....	....	....	....	....
1917-18	**Montreal Wanderers**	**NHL**	**1**	**0**	**0**	**0**	**0**	**0**	**0**	**0**	....	....	....	....	....
♦	**Toronto Arenas**	**NHL**	**5**	**0**	**0**	**0**	**0**	**0**	**0**	**0**	....	....	....	....	....
1918-19			DID NOT PLAY												
1919-20	**Quebec Bulldogs**	**NHL**	**1**	**0**	**0**	**0**	**0**	**0**	**0**	**4**	....	....	....	....	....
	NHL Totals		**7**	**0**	**0**	**0**	**0**	**0**	**0**	**4**	....	....	....	....	....
	Other Major League Totals		139	84	20	104	....	....	....	252	4	2	0	2	2

IHL Second All-Star Team (1907)

Signed as a free agent by **S.S. Marie** (Cdn.) (IHL), January 14, 1907. Signed as a free agent by **S.S. Marie** (U.S.) (IHL), November 3, 1907. • Released by S.S. Marie (U.S.) after IHL folded, November, 1907. Signed as a free agent by **Pittsburgh** (WPHL), December 10, 1907. Signed by **Brantford** (OPHL) after leaving **Pittsburgh** (WPHL), January 7, 1908. • Named playing coach of Brantford (OPHL), November 22, 1909. • Resigned as playing-coach of Brantford (OPHL), December, 1909. Signed as a free agent by **All-Montreal** (CHA), December 13, 1909. Claimed by **Montreal Wanderers** from **Quebec** in Dispersal Draft, November 26, 1917. Claimed by **Montreal Canadiens** from **Montreal Wanderers** in Dispersal Draft, January 4, 1918. Loaned to **Toronto Arenas** by **Montreal Canadiens**, January 4, 1918. NHL rights transferred to **Quebec** from **Montreal Canadiens** when Quebec franchise returned to NHL, November 25, 1919.

• MAROTTE, Gilles

— *see page 1379*

• MARQUESS, Mark

Mark Clarence Emmett
RW – R. 5'8", 160 lbs. b: Bassano, Alta., 3/26/1924.

Season	Club	League	GP	G	A	Pts	AG	AA	APts	PIM	GP	G	A	Pts	PIM
1944-45	Moose Jaw Canucks	S-SJHL	15	19	*19	*38	....	....	....	4	4	*7	1	8	0
	Moose Jaw Canucks	M-Cup	16	*19	8	27	....	....	....	8	....	....	....	....	....
1945-46	Saskatoon Elks	WCSHL	4	0	2	2	....	....	....	4	....	....	....	....	....
	Boston Olympics	EAHL	36	18	22	40	....	....	....	10	12	7	6	13	2
1946-47	**Boston Bruins**	**NHL**	**27**	**5**	**4**	**9**	**6**	**5**	**11**	**6**	**4**	**0**	**0**	**0**	**0**
	Hershey Bears	AHL	27	10	13	23	....	....	....	14	....	....	....	....	....
1947-48	Hershey Bears	AHL	63	21	27	48	....	....	....	25	2	0	1	1	2
1948-49	Hershey Bears	AHL	58	25	23	48	....	....	....	33	11	3	8	11	4
1949-50	Hershey Bears	AHL	70	12	22	34	....	....	....	38	....	....	....	....	....
1950-51	Hershey Bears	AHL	57	9	27	36	....	....	....	32	5	1	2	3	2
1951-52	Tacoma Rockets	PCHL	70	17	38	55	....	....	....	67	7	6	2	8	8
1952-53	Tacoma Rockets	WHL	70	25	30	55	....	....	....	34	....	....	....	....	....
1953-54	Seattle Bombers	WHL	70	28	23	51	....	....	....	48	....	....	....	....	....
1954-55	Victoria Cougars	WHL	70	12	20	32	....	....	....	32	5	1	0	1	4

			REGULAR SEASON								PLAYOFFS				
Season	Club	League	GP	G	A	Pts	AG	AA	APts	PIM	GP	G	A	Pts	PIM
1955-56	Victoria–Vancouver	WHL	65	11	25	36	....	....	....	51	15	3	6	9	6
1956-57	Vernon–Kamloops	OSHL	39	15	28	43	....	....	....	23	5	0	3	3	2
1957-58	Kamloops Chiefs	OSHL	47	13	26	39	....	....	....	19	15	*8	4	12	6
	NHL Totals		**27**	**5**	**4**	**9**	**6**	**5**	**11**	**6**	**4**	**0**	**0**	**0**	**0**

• MARSHALL, Bert — *see page 1380*

• MARSHALL, Don — *see page 1380*

• MARSHALL, Willie
Willmott Charles "The Whip"

C – L. 5'10", 165 lbs. b: Kirkland Lake, Ont., 12/1/1931.

Season	Club	League	GP	G	A	Pts	AG	AA	APts	PIM	GP	G	A	Pts	PIM
1948-49	St. Michael's Majors	OHA-Jr.	32	13	18	31	....	....	....	14	....	....	....	....	....
1949-50	St. Michael's Majors	OHA-Jr.	48	39	27	66	....	....	....	32	5	6	1	7	10
1950-51	St. Michael's Majors	OHA-Jr.	43	29	30	59	....	....	....	20	....	....	....	....	....
	Guelph Biltmores	OHA-Jr.	4	4	3	7	....	....	....	2	....	....	....	....	....
	St. Michael's Monarchs	OMHL	2	1	1	2	....	....	....	0	6	1	1	2	2
1951-52	Charlottetown Islanders	MMHL	84	50	44	94	....	....	....	89	4	0	2	2	0
1952-53	**Toronto Maple Leafs**	**NHL**	**2**	**0**	**0**	**0**	**0**	**0**	**0**	**0**	....	....	....	....	....
	Pittsburgh Hornets	AHL	62	27	39	66	....	....	....	58	10	1	*8	9	13
1953-54	Pittsburgh Hornets	AHL	61	28	45	73	....	....	....	41	5	1	4	5	2
1954-55	**Toronto Maple Leafs**	**NHL**	**16**	**1**	**4**	**5**	**1**	**5**	**6**	**0**	....	....	....	....	....
	Pittsburgh Hornets	AHL	46	23	25	48	....	....	....	37	10	*9	7	*16	6
1955-56	**Toronto Maple Leafs**	**NHL**	**6**	**0**	**0**	**0**	**0**	**0**	**0**	**0**	....	....	....	....	....
	Pittsburgh Hornets	AHL	58	45	52	97	....	....	....	47	4	2	1	3	0
1956-57	Hershey Bears	AHL	64	35	59	94	....	....	....	18	7	3	7	10	4
1957-58	Hershey Bears	AHL	68	40	*64	*104	....	....	....	56	11	*10	9	*19	6
1958-59	**Toronto Maple Leafs**	**NHL**	**9**	**0**	**1**	**1**	**0**	**1**	**1**	**2**	....	....	....	....	....
	Rochester Americans	AHL	19	7	16	23	....	....	....	6	....	....	....	....	....
	Hershey Bears	AHL	37	22	16	38	....	....	....	4	9	*5	2	7	0
1959-60	Hershey Bears	AHL	72	38	40	78	....	....	....	99	....	....	....	....	....
1960-61	Hershey Bears	AHL	56	25	44	69	....	....	....	36	7	3	5	8	2
1961-62	Hershey Bears	AHL	70	30	65	95	....	....	....	24	7	0	6	6	0
1962-63	Hershey Bears	AHL	72	36	56	92	....	....	....	12	15	3	7	10	10
1963-64	Providence Reds	AHL	72	33	50	83	....	....	....	18	3	2	3	5	0
1964-65	Providence Reds	AHL	69	12	44	56	....	....	....	12	....	....	....	....	....
1965-66	Providence Reds	AHL	70	13	27	40	....	....	....	8	....	....	....	....	....
1966-67	Baltimore Clippers	AHL	68	33	56	89	....	....	....	22	9	6	7	13	0
1967-68	Baltimore Clippers	AHL	51	24	41	65	....	....	....	2	....	....	....	....	....
1968-69	Baltimore Clippers	AHL	74	26	52	78	....	....	....	18	4	1	2	3	0
1969-70	Baltimore Clippers	AHL	42	9	19	28	....	....	....	0	5	2	2	4	0
1970-71	Baltimore Clippers	AHL	64	15	40	55	....	....	....	0	6	0	1	1	0
1971-72	Toledo Hornets	IHL	46	15	32	47	....	....	....	89	....	....	....	....	....
	Rochester Americans	AHL	10	2	2	4	....	....	....	2	....	....	....	....	....
1972/75			DID NOT PLAY												
1975-76	Buffalo Norsemen	NAHL	DID NOT PLAY – GENERAL MANAGER												
	Buffalo Norsemen	NAHL	1	0	0	0	....	....	....	9	....	....	....	....	....
	NHL Totals		**33**	**1**	**5**	**6**	**1**	**6**	**7**	**2**	....	....	....	....	....

AHL First All-Star Team (1956, 1958) • Won John B. Sollenberger Trophy (Top Scorer - AHL) (1958) • AHL Second All-Star Team (1962)

Traded to **Detroit** (Hershey-AHL) by **Toronto** (Pittsburgh-AHL) with Gilles Mayer, Jack Price, Bob Hassard, Bob Solinger and Ray Gariepy for cash, July 7, 1956. Traded to **Toronto** by **Hershey** (AHL) for Mike Nykoluk, Ron Hurst and the loan of Wally Boyer for the 1958-59 and 1959-60 seasons, April 29, 1958. Loaned to **Detroit** (Hershey-AHL) by **Toronto** with cash for Gerry Ehman, December 23, 1958. Traded to **Boston** (Providence-AHL) by **Hershey** (AHL) for Dan Poliziani, June, 1963. Traded to **Baltimore** (AHL) by **Providence** (AHL) with Aldo Guidolin, Ian Anderson and Jim Bartlett for Ken Stephanson, Ed Lawson and Mike Corbett, June, 1966. Signed as a free agent by **Toledo** (IHL) following release by **Rochester** (AHL), October 15, 1971. Traded to **Rochester** (AHL) by **Toledo** (IHL) for cash, March 1, 1972. • Served as General Manager of **Buffalo Norsemen** (NAHL) and returned to active duty as an injury replacement, February, 1976.

• MARTIN, Clare
George Clarence

D – R. 5'11", 180 lbs. b: Waterloo, Ont., 2/25/1922 Deceased.

Season	Club	League	GP	G	A	Pts	AG	AA	APts	PIM	GP	G	A	Pts	PIM
1939-40	Waterloo Siskins	OHA-B	10	9	4	13	....	....	....	18	16	10	5	15	28
1940-41	Guelph Biltmores	OHA-Jr.	16	4	4	8	....	....	....	28	5	1	4	5	6
	Boston Olympics	EAHL	9	0	1	1	....	....	....	4	....	....	....	....	....
1941-42	**Boston Bruins**	**NHL**	**13**	**0**	**1**	**1**	**0**	**1**	**1**	**4**	**5**	**0**	**0**	**0**	**0**
	Boston Olympics	EAHL	43	11	18	29	....	....	....	31	1	0	1	1	0
1942-43	Ottawa Postal Corps	ONDHL	9	3	2	5	....	....	....	11	....	....	....	....	....
1943-44	Montreal Royals	QSHL	3	0	2	2	....	....	....	4	6	1	1	2	0
1944-45	Halifax Navy	NSDHL	....	....	....	....	....	....	....	....	5	0	3	3	2
1945-46	Boston Olympics	EAHL	51	19	22	41	....	....	....	26	12	4	10	14	2
1946-47	**Boston Bruins**	**NHL**	**6**	**3**	**0**	**3**	**3**	**0**	**3**	**0**	**5**	**0**	**1**	**1**	**0**
	Hershey Bears	AHL	42	4	11	15	....	....	....	38	....	....	....	....	....
1947-48	**Boston Bruins**	**NHL**	**59**	**5**	**13**	**18**	**6**	**17**	**23**	**34**	**5**	**0**	**0**	**0**	**6**
1948-49	Hershey Bears	AHL	26	3	13	16	....	....	....	18	11	1	7	8	10
♦1949-50	**Detroit Red Wings**	**NHL**	**64**	**2**	**5**	**7**	**2**	**6**	**8**	**14**	**10**	**0**	**1**	**1**	**0**
1950-51	**Detroit Red Wings**	**NHL**	**50**	**1**	**6**	**7**	**1**	**7**	**8**	**12**	**2**	**0**	**0**	**0**	**0**
1951-52	**Chicago Black Hawks**	**NHL**	**31**	**1**	**2**	**3**	**1**	**2**	**3**	**8**	....	....	....	....	....
	New York Rangers	**NHL**	**14**	**0**	**1**	**1**	**0**	**1**	**1**	**6**	....	....	....	....	....
	Cincinnati Mohawks	AHL	17	0	3	3	....	....	....	10	7	1	1	2	12
1952-53	Kitchener Dutchmen	OHA-Sr.	46	5	19	24	....	....	....	60	11	4	3	7	18
	Kitchener Dutchmen	Al-Cup	18	5	12	17	....	....	....	28	....	....	....	....	....
1953-54	Kitchener Dutchmen	OHA-Sr.	37	9	16	25	....	....	....	36	8	1	0	1	5
1954-55	Kitchener Dutchmen	OHA-Sr.	20	3	5	8	....	....	....	18	10	1	2	3	6
	Kitchener Dutchmen	Al-Cup	17	5	6	11	....	....	....	10	....	....	....	....	....
	NHL Totals		**237**	**12**	**28**	**40**	**13**	**34**	**47**	**78**	**27**	**0**	**2**	**2**	**6**

Traded to **Detroit** by **Boston** with Pete Babando, Lloyd Durham and Jimmy Peters for Bill Quackenbush and Pete Horeck, August 16, 1949. Traded to **Chicago** by **Detroit** with George Gee, Jimmy Peters Sr., Rags Raglan, Max McNab and Jim McFadden for $75,000 and future considerations (Hugh Coflin, October, 1951), August 20, 1951. Traded to **NY Rangers** by **Chicago** for cash, December 28, 1951.

• MARTIN, Frank
Francis William

D – L. 6'2", 190 lbs. b: Cayuga, Ont., 5/1/1933.

			REGULAR SEASON								PLAYOFFS				
Season	Club	League	GP	G	A	Pts	AG	AA	APts	PIM	GP	G	A	Pts	PIM
1949-50	St. Catharines Teepees	OHA-Jr.	44	5	13	18	....	....	....	44	5	1	3	4	10
1950-51	St. Catharines Teepees	OHA-Jr.	43	5	15	20	....	....	....	53	9	2	2	4	2
1951-52	St. Catharines Teepees	OHA-Jr.	54	25	30	55	....	....	....	40	12	1	2	3	6
1952-53	**Boston Bruins**	**NHL**	**14**	**0**	**2**	**2**	**0**	**2**	**2**	**6**	**6**	**0**	**1**	**1**	**2**
	Hershey Bears	AHL	41	5	4	9	....	....	....	14	3	0	1	1	0
1953-54	**Boston Bruins**	**NHL**	**68**	**3**	**17**	**20**	**4**	**21**	**25**	**38**	**4**	**0**	**1**	**1**	**0**
1954-55	**Chicago Black Hawks**	**NHL**	**66**	**4**	**8**	**12**	**5**	**9**	**14**	**35**	....	....	....	....	....
1955-56	**Chicago Black Hawks**	**NHL**	**61**	**3**	**11**	**14**	**4**	**13**	**17**	**21**	....	....	....	....	....
1956-57	**Chicago Black Hawks**	**NHL**	**70**	**1**	**8**	**9**	**1**	**9**	**10**	**12**	....	....	....	....	....
1957-58	**Chicago Black Hawks**	**NHL**	**3**	**0**	**0**	**0**	**0**	**0**	**0**	**10**	....	....	....	....	....
	Buffalo Bisons	AHL	52	2	20	22	....	....	....	14	....	....	....	....	....
1958-59	Buffalo Bisons	AHL	65	4	26	30	....	....	....	20	8	0	6	6	5
1959-60	Buffalo Bisons	AHL	72	4	21	25	....	....	....	15	....	....	....	....	....
1960-61	Quebec Aces	AHL	67	3	16	19	....	....	....	32	....	....	....	....	....
1961-62	Quebec Aces	AHL	58	4	14	18	....	....	....	18	....	....	....	....	....
1962-63	Quebec Aces	AHL	67	4	30	34	....	....	....	34	....	....	....	....	....
1963-64	Quebec Aces	AHL	71	5	18	23	....	....	....	36	9	0	1	1	2
1964-65	Cleveland Barons	AHL	67	7	23	30	....	....	....	22	....	....	....	....	....
	NHL Totals		**282**	**11**	**46**	**57**	**14**	**54**	**68**	**122**	**10**	**0**	**2**	**2**	**2**

AHL Second All-Star Team (1959) • Played in NHL All-Star Game (1955)

Traded to **Chicago** by **Boston** for Murray Costello, October 4, 1954. Traded to **Buffalo** (AHL) by **Chicago** with Wally Hergesheimer for Ken Wharram, May 5, 1958. Traded to **Quebec** (AHL) by **Buffalo** (AHL) for cash, July, 1960. Claimed by **Providence** (AHL) from **Montreal** in Reverse Draft, June 9, 1965.

• MARTIN, Jack
John Raymond

C – L. 5'11", 184 lbs. b: St. Catharines, Ont., 11/29/1940.

Season	Club	League	GP	G	A	Pts	AG	AA	APts	PIM	GP	G	A	Pts	PIM
1957-58	St. Michael's Majors	OHA-Jr.	50	11	15	26	....	....	....	32	9	2	4	6	10
1958-59	Toronto Marlboros	OHA-Jr.	51	15	14	29	....	....	....	62	5	3	0	3	13
1959-60	Toronto Marlboros	OHA-Jr.	42	30	30	60	....	....	....	63	4	1	3	4	10
	Sudbury Wolves	EPHL	....	....	....	....	....	....	....	....	4	1	0	1	2
1960-61	**Toronto Maple Leafs**	**NHL**	**1**	**0**	**0**	**0**	**0**	**0**	**0**	**0**	....	....	....	....	....
	Sudbury Wolves	EPHL	44	9	12	21	....	....	....	22	....	....	....	....	....
1961-62	S.S. Marie Thunderbirds	EPHL	10	1	1	2	....	....	....	8	....	....	....	....	....
	Pittsburgh Hornets	AHL	4	0	1	1	....	....	....	0	....	....	....	....	....
	San Francisco Seals	WHL	28	3	6	9	....	....	....	12	....	....	....	....	....
1962-63	Charlotte Checkers	EHL	67	32	33	65	....	....	....	57	10	2	6	8	4
1963-64	Nashville Dixie Flyers	EHL	71	47	60	107	....	....	....	10	2	1	0	1	2
1964-65	Knoxville Knights	EHL	67	39	69	108	....	....	....	8	10	5	5	10	4
	NHL Totals		**1**	**0**	**0**	**0**	**0**	**0**	**0**	**0**	....	....	....	....	....

• MARTIN, Pit — *see page 1382*

• MARTIN, Ron
Ronald Dennis Grant

RW – R. 5'6", 130 lbs. b: Calgary, Alta., 8/22/1909 d: 2/7/1971.

Season	Club	League	GP	G	A	Pts	AG	AA	APts	PIM	GP	G	A	Pts	PIM
1923-24	Calgary Canadians	CCJHL	STATISTICS NOT AVAILABLE												
	Calgary Canadiens	M-Cup	7	0	0	0	....	....	....	1	....	....	....	....	....
1924-25	Calgary Canadians	CCJHL	STATISTICS NOT AVAILABLE												
	Calgary Canadiens	M-Cup	2	0	0	0	....	....	....	2	....	....	....	....	....
1925-26	Calgary Canadians	CCJHL	STATISTICS NOT AVAILABLE												
	Calgary Canadiens	M-Cup	9	6	2	8	....	....	....	4	....	....	....	....	....
1926-27	Calgary Tigers	PrHL	32	13	5	18	....	....	....	20	2	1	0	1	0
1927-28	Kitchener Millionaires	Can-Pro	1	0	0	0	....	....	....	0	....	....	....	....	....
	Niagara Falls Cataracts	Can-Pro	34	13	5	18	....	....	....	20	....	....	....	....	....
1928-29	Toronto Millionaires	Can-Pro	16	4	1	5	....	....	....	14	....	....	....	....	....
	Buffalo Bisons	Can-Pro	27	7	1	8	....	....	....	12	....	....	....	....	....
1929-30	Buffalo Bisons	IHL	40	22	3	25	....	....	....	33	7	2	1	3	13
1930-31	Buffalo Bisons	IHL	48	28	13	41	....	....	....	24	6	1	3	4	0
1931-32	Buffalo Bisons	IHL	46	15	18	33	....	....	....	42	6	*3	2	5	2
1932-33	**New York Americans**	**NHL**	**47**	**5**	**7**	**12**	**9**	**14**	**23**	**6**	....	....	....	....	....
1933-34	**New York Americans**	**NHL**	**47**	**8**	**9**	**17**	**14**	**19**	**33**	**30**	....	....	....	....	....
1934-35	Syracuse Stars	IHL	43	6	12	18	....	....	....	18	2	0	1	1	2
1935-36	Edmonton Eskimos	NWHL	40	11	13	24	....	....	....	13	....	....	....	....	....
	Portland Buckaroos	NWHL	....	....	....	....	....	....	....	....	3	1	0	1	0
	Vancouver Lions	NWHL	....	....	....	....	....	....	....	....	2	3	1	4	0
1936-37	Portland Buckaroos	PCHL	39	9	9	18	....	....	....	10	3	*3	*3	*6	2
1937-38	Portland Buckaroos	PCHL	41	6	15	21	....	....	....	16	2	2	0	2	7
1938-39	Portland Buckaroos	PCHL	43	18	18	36	....	....	....	10	5	3	0	3	2
1939-40	Portland Buckaroos	PCHL	39	14	11	25	....	....	....	12	5	1	2	3	2
1940-41	Portland Buckaroos	PCHL	41	8	8	16	....	....	....	18	....	....	....	....	....
1941-42			MILITARY SERVICE												
1942-43			MILITARY SERVICE												
1943-44	Portland Decleros	NWIHL	16	12	13	25	....	....	....	2	....	....	....	....	....
	Portland Oilers	NWIHL	....	....	....	....	....	....	....	....	2	3	1	4	0
	NHL Totals		**94**	**13**	**16**	**29**	**23**	**33**	**56**	**36**	....	....	....	....	....

Signed as a free agent by **Calgary** (PrHL), November 8, 1926. Traded to **Buffalo** (Can-Pro) by **Toronto** (Can-Pro) for cash, January 13, 1929. Claimed by **Detroit** from **Buffalo** (IHL) in Inter-League Draft, May 9, 1931. Traded to **NY Americans** by **Detroit** for Doug Young, October 18, 1931. Traded to **Syracuse** (IHL) by **NY Americans** with the loan of Walter Jackson for the 1934-35 season for Lorne Carr, November 5, 1934. Loaned to **Portland** (NWHL) by **Edmonton** (NWHL) as emergency injury replacement (Jack Pratt) during NWHL playoffs, March 13, 1936. Loaned to **Vancouver** (NWHL) by **Edmonton** (NWHL) as emergency injury replacement (Bill Carse) during NWHL playoffs, March 23, 1936.

• MASNICK, Paul
Paul Andrew

C – R. 5'9", 165 lbs. b: Regina, Sask., 4/14/1931.

Season	Club	League	GP	G	A	Pts	AG	AA	APts	PIM	GP	G	A	Pts	PIM
1948-49	Regina Pats	WCJHL	26	7	10	17	....	....	....	4	7	1	1	2	0
1949-50	Regina Pats	WCJHL	40	44	43	87	....	....	....	62	9	9	14	23	4
	Regina Pats	M-Cup	14	13	14	27	....	....	....	12	....	....	....	....	....
1950-51	**Montreal Canadiens**	**NHL**	**43**	**4**	**1**	**5**	**5**	**1**	**6**	**14**	**11**	**2**	**1**	**3**	**4**
	Cincinnati Mohawks	AHL	19	5	7	12	....	....	....	15	....	....	....	....	....
1951-52	**Montreal Canadiens**	**NHL**	**15**	**1**	**2**	**3**	**1**	**2**	**3**	**2**	**6**	**1**	**0**	**1**	**12**
	Buffalo–Cincinnati	AHL	31	8	20	28	....	....	....	23	7	0	4	4	4
♦1952-53	**Montreal Canadiens**	**NHL**	**53**	**5**	**7**	**12**	**7**	**8**	**15**	**44**	**6**	**1**	**0**	**1**	**7**
	Montreal Royals	QMHL	10	6	6	12	....	....	....	10	....	....	....	....	....

Season	Club	League	GP	G	A	Pts	AG	AA	APts	PIM	GP	G	A	Pts	PIM
			REGULAR SEASON								PLAYOFFS				
1953-54	**Montreal Canadiens**	**NHL**	**50**	**5**	**21**	**26**	**7**	**26**	**33**	**57**	**10**	**0**	**4**	**4**	**4**
	Montreal Royals	QHL	14	3	14	17	....	....	....	9	....	....	....	....	....
1954-55	**Montreal Canadiens**	**NHL**	**11**	**0**	**0**	**0**	**0**	**0**	**0**	**0**	....	....	....	....	....
	Chicago Black Hawks	**NHL**	**11**	**1**	**0**	**1**	**1**	**0**	**1**	**8**	....	....	....	....	....
	Montreal Canadiens	**NHL**	**8**	**0**	**1**	**1**	**0**	**1**	**1**	**0**	....	....	....	....	....
	Montreal Royals	QHL	27	10	13	23	....	....	....	14	14	2	9	11	14
1955-56	Winnipeg Warriors	WHL	62	29	39	68	....	....	....	37	14	*11	9	20	14
	Winnipeg Warriors	Ed-Cup.	6	3	5	8	....	....	....	6	....	....	....	....	....
1956-57	Rochester Americans	AHL	64	24	38	62	....	....	....	46	10	5	5	10	17
1957-58	**Toronto Maple Leafs**	**NHL**	**41**	**2**	**9**	**11**	**2**	**9**	**11**	**14**	....	....	....	....	....
1958-59	Saskatoon Quakers	WHL	64	24	51	75	....	....	....	48	....	....	....	....	....
1959-60	Victoria–Winnipeg	WHL	68	16	29	45	....	....	....	16	11	2	5	7	2
1960-61	St. Paul Saints	IHL	60	31	59	90	....	....	....	34	11	2	6	8	12
1961-62	St. Paul Saints	IHL	31	11	21	33	....	....	....	4	....	....	....	....	....
	NHL Totals		**232**	**18**	**41**	**59**	**23**	**47**	**70**	**139**	**33**	**4**	**5**	**9**	**27**

Signed as a free agent by **Montreal**, October 10, 1950. Traded to **Cincinnati** (AHL) by **Montreal** for Bobby Dawes, February 13, 1951. Loaned to **Chicago** by **Montreal** for the loan of Al Dewsbury and cash, November 9, 1954. Returned to **Montreal** by **Chicago**, December 10, 1954. Traded to **Toronto** by **Montreal** for cash, September 30, 1957. Traded to **Winnipeg** (WHL) by **Victoria** (WHL) for cash, February 27, 1960.

• MASON, Charley

Charles Columbus "Dutch"

RW – R. 5'10", 160 lbs. b: Seaforth, Ont., 2/1/1912 d: 5/17/1971.

Season	Club	League	GP	G	A	Pts	AG	AA	APts	PIM	GP	G	A	Pts	PIM
1929-30	U. of Saskatchewan	S-SSHL	STATISTICS NOT AVAILABLE												
1930-31	U. of Saskatchewan	S-SSHL	7	4	1	5	....	....	....	4	....	....	....	....	....
	Saskatoon Wesleys	N-SJHL	3	0	1	1	....	....	....	0	2	0	0	0	0
1931-32	Saskatoon Wesleys	N-SJHL	4	4	1	5	....	....	....	2	8	2	0	2	0
	Saskatoon Crescents	N-SJHL	16	9	2	11	....	....	....	2	2	0	0	0	0
1932-33	Saskatoon Crescents	WCHL	29	13	7	20	....	....	....	6	....	....	....	....	....
1933-34	Vancouver Lions	NWHL	33	22	8	30	....	....	....	8	7	3	1	4	2
1934-35	**New York Rangers**	**NHL**	**46**	**5**	**9**	**14**	**8**	**16**	**24**	**14**	**4**	**0**	**1**	**1**	**0**
1935-36	**New York Rangers**	**NHL**	**28**	**1**	**5**	**6**	**2**	**9**	**11**	**30**	....	....	....	....	....
	Philadelphia Arrows	IHL	21	8	7	15	....	....	....	9	4	1	0	1	0
1936-37	Philadelphia Ramblers	IAHL	49	24	15	39	....	....	....	17	6	1	2	3	4
1937-38	**New York Americans**	**NHL**	**2**	**0**	**0**	**0**	**0**	**0**	**0**	**0**	....	....	....	....	....
	Philadelphia Ramblers	IAHL	45	24	20	44	....	....	....	11	5	1	1	2	2
1938-39	**Detroit Red Wings**	**NHL**	**6**	**0**	**1**	**1**	**0**	**2**	**2**	**0**	....	....	....	....	....
	Pittsburgh Hornets	IAHL	25	8	16	24	....	....	....	4	....	....	....	....	....
	Chicago Black Hawks	**NHL**	**13**	**1**	**3**	**4**	**2**	**5**	**7**	**0**	....	....	....	....	....
1939-40	Cleveland Barons	IAHL	40	12	12	24	....	....	....	15	....	....	....	....	....
1940-41	Buffalo Bisons	AHL	3	0	0	0	....	....	....	0	....	....	....	....	....
	Springfield Indians	AHL	41	17	18	35	....	....	....	14	2	0	0	0	0
1941-42	Providence Reds	AHL	15	0	8	8	....	....	....	7	....	....	....	....	....
	Philadelphia Ramblers	AHL	44	7	14	21	....	....	....	4	....	....	....	....	....
1942-43			DID NOT PLAY												
1943-44	U. of Saskatchewan	N-SSHL	DID NOT PLAY – COACHING												
	NHL Totals		**95**	**7**	**18**	**25**	**12**	**32**	**44**	**44**	**4**	**0**	**1**	**1**	**0**

IAHL First All-Star Team (1938)

Traded to **NY Rangers** by **Vancouver** (NWHL) for cash, September 27, 1934. Traded to **NY Americans** by **NY Rangers** (Philadelphia-AHL) for cash with NY Rangers holding rights of recall, October 7, 1937. Traded to **Detroit** by **NY Rangers** for cash, October 21, 1938. Traded to **Chicago** by **Detroit** for Phil Besler, January 27, 1939. Traded to **Cleveland** (IAHL) by **Chicago** with Harold Jackson and $15,000 for Phil Hergesheimer, May 17, 1939. Traded to **Buffalo** (AHL) by **Cleveland** (AHL) for cash, October 4, 1940. Traded to **Springfield** (AHL) by **Buffalo** (AHL) for Orville Waldriff, November 10, 1940. Signed as a free agent by **Providence** (AHL), October, 1941. Traded to **Philadelphia** (AHL) by **Providence** (AHL) for Art Shoquist, December 5, 1941.

• MASSECAR, George

George Sheldon

LW – L. 5'9", 165 lbs. b: Waterford, Ont., 7/10/1904 d: 7/14/1957.

Season	Club	League	GP	G	A	Pts	AG	AA	APts	PIM	GP	G	A	Pts	PIM
1925-26	Niagara Falls Cataracts	OHA-Sr.	19	4	3	7	....	....	....	10	....	....	....	....	....
1926-27	Niagara Falls Cataracts	Can-Pro	24	9	3	12	....	....	....	16	....	....	....	....	....
1927-28	Niagara Falls Cataracts	Can-Pro	40	6	3	9	....	....	....	25	....	....	....	....	....
1928-29	New Haven Eagles	Can-Am	40	8	1	9	....	....	....	39	2	0	0	0	4
1929-30	**New York Americans**	**NHL**	**43**	**7**	**3**	**10**	**10**	**7**	**17**	**18**	....	....	....	....	....
1930-31	**New York Americans**	**NHL**	**43**	**4**	**7**	**11**	**8**	**21**	**29**	**16**	....	....	....	....	....
1931-32	**New York Americans**	**NHL**	**14**	**1**	**1**	**2**	**2**	**2**	**4**	**12**	....	....	....	....	....
	Bronx Tigers	Can-Am	21	5	2	7	....	....	....	16	2	0	0	0	0
1932-33	St. Louis Flyers	AHA	45	14	*21	35	....	....	....	14	4	*4	0	4	8
1933-34	Detroit Olympics	IHL	44	10	12	22	....	....	....	13	6	1	1	2	0
1934-35	Buffalo Bisons	IHL	43	9	7	16	....	....	....	4	....	....	....	....	....
1935-36	Buffalo Bisons	IHL	48	10	11	21	....	....	....	12	5	1	0	1	0
1936-37	Buffalo Bisons	IAHL	11	1	0	1	....	....	....	0	....	....	....	....	....
	NHL Totals		**100**	**12**	**11**	**23**	**20**	**30**	**50**	**46**	....	....	....	....	....

Signed as a free agent by **Niagara Falls** (Can-Pro), November 1, 1926. Traded to **NY Americans** by **New Haven** (Can-Am) for Babe Dye, November 13, 1929. Traded to **St. Louis** (AHA) by **NY Americans** for Walter Jackson, October 30, 1932. Traded to **Detroit** by **St. Louis** (AHA) for cash, April 25, 1933. Traded to **Buffalo** (IHL) by **Detroit** (Detroit-IHL) for cash, October 31, 1934. Transferred to **Cleveland** (IAHL) after **Buffalo** (IAHL) franchise folded, December 10, 1936. • Officially announced retirement, December 13, 1936.

• MATHERS, Frank

Frank Sydney **HHOF**

D – L. 6'1", 182 lbs. b: Winnipeg, Man., 3/29/1924.

Season	Club	League	GP	G	A	Pts	AG	AA	APts	PIM	GP	G	A	Pts	PIM
1942-43	Winnipeg Rangers	WJrHL	10	7	8	15	....	....	....	0	....	....	....	....	....
1943-44	Regina Commandos	RNDHL	4	5	5	10	....	....	....	2	1	2	3	5	0
	Regina Pats	M-Cup	1	1	2	3	....	....	....	0	....	....	....	....	....
1944-45			MILITARY SERVICE												
1945-46	Ottawa Senators	QSHL	27	3	9	12	....	....	....	10	4	2	0	2	8
1946-47	Ottawa Senators	QSHL	36	5	7	12	....	....	....	27	10	5	1	6	12
1947-48	Ottawa Senators	QSHL	44	11	23	34	....	....	....	30	12	4	*5	*9	12
	Ottawa Senators	QSHL	14	5	9	14	....	....	....	18	....	....	....	....	....
1948-49	**Toronto Maple Leafs**	**NHL**	**15**	**1**	**2**	**3**	**1**	**3**	**4**	**2**	....	....	....	....	....
	Pittsburgh Hornets	AHL	46	7	23	30	....	....	....	50	....	....	....	....	....
1949-50	**Toronto Maple Leafs**	**NHL**	**6**	**0**	**1**	**1**	**0**	**1**	**1**	**2**	....	....	....	....	....
	Pittsburgh Hornets	AHL	58	3	20	23	....	....	....	28	....	....	....	....	....
1950-51	Pittsburgh Hornets	AHL	70	7	17	24	....	....	....	74	13	2	10	12	6
1951-52	**Toronto Maple Leafs**	**NHL**	**2**	**0**	**0**	**0**	**0**	**0**	**0**	**0**	....	....	....	....	....
	Pittsburgh Hornets	AHL	66	5	43	48	....	....	....	59	8	1	0	1	8
1952-53	Pittsburgh Hornets	AHL	55	8	26	34	....	....	....	46	10	1	4	5	18
1953-54	Pittsburgh Hornets	AHL	69	9	43	52	....	....	....	73	5	0	2	2	12
1954-55	Pittsburgh Hornets	AHL	62	10	30	40	....	....	....	38	10	2	3	5	0
1955-56	Pittsburgh Hornets	AHL	64	12	51	63	....	....	....	61	4	1	2	3	2
1956-57	Hershey Bears	AHL	49	1	15	16	....	....	....	51	7	1	2	3	6
1957-58	Hershey Bears	AHL	64	1	28	29	....	....	....	42	11	1	5	6	4
1958-59	Hershey Bears	AHL	64	1	22	23	....	....	....	62	3	0	1	1	0
1959-60	Hershey Bears	AHL	57	2	12	14	....	....	....	24	....	....	....	....	....
1960-61	Hershey Bears	AHL	62	1	7	8	....	....	....	22	8	0	5	5	2
1961-62	Hershey Bears	AHL	13	0	3	3	....	....	....	6	7	0	1	1	6
1962-63	Hershey Bears	AHL	DID NOT PLAY – COACHING												
	NHL Totals		**23**	**1**	**3**	**4**	**1**	**4**	**5**	**4**	....	....	....	....	....

AHL First All-Star Team (1952, 1953, 1954, 1955, 1956) • AHL Second All-Star Team (1958) • Won Lester Patrick Trophy (1987) • Played in NHL All-Star Game (1948)

Rights traded to **Toronto** by **NY Rangers** with Cal Gardner, Bill Juzda and Rene Trudell for Wally Stanowski and Moe Morris, April 26, 1948.

• MATTE, Joe

D – R. 5'11", 165 lbs. b: Bourget, Ont., 3/6/1893 d: 6/13/1961.

Season	Club	League	GP	G	A	Pts	AG	AA	APts	PIM	GP	G	A	Pts	PIM
1913-14	Montreal Gaiete Canadien	MCHL	5	3	0	3	....	....	....	....	....	....	....	....	....
1914-15	Van Cleek Hill	OVHL	STATISTICS NOT AVAILABLE												
1915-16	Montreal La Casquette	MCHL	12	4	0	4	....	....	....	6	....	....	....	....	....
1916-17	Montreal La Casquette	MCHL	10	*9	0	9	....	....	....	12	....	....	....	....	....
1917-18	Montreal Hochelaga	MCHL	11	*23	3	*26	....	....	....	9	3	*6	1	*7	....
1918-19	Hamilton Tigers	OHA-Sr.	8	12	5	17	....	....	....	3	4	2	1	3	....
	Hamilton Tigers	Al-Cup	2	2	0	2	....	....	....	0	....	....	....	....	....
1919-20	Hamilton Tigers	OHA-Sr.	1	0	1	1	....	....	....	0	....	....	....	....	....
	Toronto St. Pats	**NHL**	**17**	**8**	**3**	**11**	**9**	**10**	**19**	**19**	....	....	....	....	....
1920-21	**Hamilton Tigers**	**NHL**	**21**	**6**	**9**	**15**	**8**	**35**	**43**	**29**	....	....	....	....	....
1921-22	**Hamilton Tigers**	**NHL**	**21**	**3**	**3**	**6**	**4**	**9**	**13**	**6**	....	....	....	....	....
1922-23	Saskatoon Sheiks	WCHL	29	14	6	20	....	....	....	25	....	....	....	....	....
1923-24	Vancouver Maroons	PCHA	29	11	4	15	....	....	....	14	2	1	0	1	2
	Vancouver Maroons	St-Cup	2	0	1	1	....	....	....	6	....	....	....	....	....
1924-25	Vancouver Maroons	WCHL	24	8	1	9	....	....	....	20	....	....	....	....	....
1925-26	**Boston Bruins**	**NHL**	**3**	**0**	**0**	**0**	**0**	**0**	**0**	**0**	....	....	....	....	....
	Montreal Canadiens	**NHL**	**6**	**0**	**0**	**0**	**0**	**0**	**0**	**0**	....	....	....	....	....
	NHL Totals		**68**	**17**	**15**	**32**	**21**	**54**	**75**	**54**	....	....	....	....	....
	Other Major League Totals		82	33	11	44	....	....	....	59	2	1	0	1	2

OHA-Sr. First All-Star Team (1919)

Signed as a free agent by **Toronto**, January 16, 1920. Traded to **Montreal Canadiens** by **Toronto** with Goldie Prodgers for Harry Cameron, November 27, 1920. Traded to **Hamilton** by **Montreal** with Jack Coughlin, Goldie Prodgers and loan of Billy Coutu for 1920-21 season for Harry Mummery, Jack McDonald and Dave Ritchie, November 27, 1920. Traded to **Saskatoon** (WCHL) by **Hamilton** for cash, October 1, 1922. Traded to **Vancouver** (PCHA) by **Saskatoon** (WCHL) for cash, October 30, 1923. Signed as a free agent by **Boston**, December 5, 1925. Claimed on waivers by **Montreal Canadiens** from **Boston**, January 15, 1926.

• MATTE, Joe

Roland Joseph

D – R. 5'11", 178 lbs. b: Bourget, Ont., 3/15/1909 Deceased.

Season	Club	League	GP	G	A	Pts	AG	AA	APts	PIM	GP	G	A	Pts	PIM
1928-29	Ottawa Shamrocks	OCJHL	STATISTICS NOT AVAILABLE												
1929-30	**Detroit Cougars**	**NHL**	**12**	**0**	**1**	**1**	**0**	**2**	**2**	**0**	....	....	....	....	....
	Detroit Olympics	IHL	26	0	0	0	....	....	....	6	....	....	....	....	....
1930-31	Pittsburgh Yellowjackets	IHL	3	1	0	1	....	....	....	0	....	....	....	....	....
	Niagara Falls Cataracts	OPHL	25	9	1	10	....	....	....	45	5	2	0	2	10
	Detroit Olympics	IHL	2	0	0	0	....	....	....	0	....	....	....	....	....
1931-32	Pittsburgh Yellowjackets	IHL	48	4	4	8	....	....	....	82	....	....	....	....	....
1932-33	Cleveland Indians	IHL	34	3	4	7	....	....	....	34	....	....	....	....	....
1933-34	Cleveland Indians	IHL	1	0	0	0	....	....	....	0	....	....	....	....	....
	St. Louis Flyers	AHA	48	11	3	14	....	....	....	78	7	0	0	0	12
1934-35	St. Louis Flyers	AHA	48	14	10	24	....	....	....	50	6	1	1	2	10
1935-36	St. Louis Flyers	AHA	41	5	8	13	....	....	....	38	8	1	0	1	13
1936-37	St. Louis Flyers	AHA	41	5	8	13	....	....	....	36	6	1	0	1	4
1937-38	St. Louis Flyers	AHA	48	15	17	32	....	....	....	45	7	0	3	3	4
1938-39	St. Louis Flyers	AHA	40	13	15	28	....	....	....	28	7	2	1	3	4
1939-40	St. Louis Flyers	AHA	48	13	15	28	....	....	....	46	5	0	1	1	12
1940-41	Kansas City Americans	AHA	44	9	3	12	....	....	....	22	8	1	2	3	16
1941-42	Kansas City Americans	AHA	50	4	6	10	....	....	....	41	6	0	1	1	2
1942-43	**Chicago Black Hawks**	**NHL**	**12**	**0**	**2**	**2**	**0**	**2**	**2**	**8**	....	....	....	....	....
	Cleveland Barons	AHL	25	2	5	7	....	....	....	2	3	0	1	1	0
	NHL Totals		**24**	**0**	**3**	**3**	**0**	**4**	**4**	**8**	....	....	....	....	....

AHA First All-Star Team (1935, 1938, 1939, 1940) • AHA Second All-Star Team (1936, 1937)

• Father of NFL player Tom Matte (Baltimore Colts 1961-1972). Signed as a free agent by **Detroit**, September 12, 1929. Signed as a free agent by **Chicago**, September, 1942.

• MATZ, Johnny

John Reinhold

C – R. , b: Omaha, NB, 6/1/1891 d: 12/21/1969.

Season	Club	League	GP	G	A	Pts	AG	AA	APts	PIM	GP	G	A	Pts	PIM
1911-12	Edmonton YMCA	ESrHL	6	5	0	5	....	....	....	0	....	....	....	....	....
	Edmonton Maritimers	ESrHL	....	....	....	....	....	....	....	....	3	3	0	3	5
1912-13	Edmonton Dominions	ESrHL	7	7	0	7	....	....	....	4	....	....	....	....	....
1913-14	Grand Forks Clubs	BCBHL	STATISTICS NOT AVAILABLE												
1914-15	Grand Forks Clubs	BCBHL	STATISTICS NOT AVAILABLE												
	Vancouver Millionaires	PCHA	1	1	0	1	....	....	....	0	....	....	....	....	....
1915-16	Rossland Seniors	WKHL	STATISTICS NOT AVAILABLE												
1916/19			STATISTICS NOT AVAILABLE												
1919-20	Edmonton Hustlers	ESrHL	12	11	3	14	....	....	....	8	....	....	....	....	....
1920-21	Edmonton Dominos	Big-4	16	1	2	3	....	....	....	9	....	....	....	....	....
1921-22	Edmonton Eskimos	WCHL	24	4	1	5	....	....	....	2	2	0	0	0	0
1922-23	Edmonton Eskimos	WCHL	4	0	0	0	....	....	....	4	....	....	....	....	....
	Saskatoon Crescents	WCHL	24	4	3	7	....	....	....	6	....	....	....	....	....
1923-24	Saskatoon Crescents	WCHL	24	2	1	3	....	....	....	4	....	....	....	....	....
1924-25	**Montreal Canadiens**	**NHL**	**30**	**2**	**3**	**5**	**3**	**12**	**15**	**0**	**1**	**0**	**0**	**0**	**0**
	Montreal Canadiens	St-Cup	4	0	0	0	....	....	....	2	....	....	....	....	....

Season	Club	League	GP	G	A	Pts	AG	AA	APts	PIM	GP	G	A	Pts	PIM
			REGULAR SEASON								PLAYOFFS				
1925-26			DID NOT PLAY												
1926-27	Moose Jaw Maroons	PrHL	32	1	10	11	....	....	....	62	....	....	....	....	....
1927-28	Moose Jaw Maroons	PrHL	28	3	3	6	....	....	....	44	....	....	....	....	....
	NHL Totals		**30**	**2**	**3**	**5**	**3**	**12**	**15**	**0**	**1**	**0**	**0**	**0**	**0**
	Other Major League Totals		77	11	5	16	....	....	....	16	2	0	0	0	0

Signed as a free agent by **Grand Forks** (BCBHL), November 24, 1913. Signed as a free agent by **Vancouver** (PCHA), November 17, 1914. • Re-instated as an amateur, December, 1919. Signed as a free agent by **Edmonton** (WCHL), December 5, 1921. Traded to **Saskatoon** (WCHL) by **Edmonton** (WCHL) for Rube Brandow, January 1, 1923. Traded to **Montreal Canadiens** by **Saskatoon** (WCHL) for cash, November 25, 1924. Signed as a free agent by **Moose Jaw** (PrHL), November 19, 1926.

• MAXNER, Wayne Wayne Douglas

LW – L. 5'11", 180 lbs. b: Halifax, N.S., 9/27/1942.

Season	Club	League	GP	G	A	Pts	AG	AA	APts	PIM	GP	G	A	Pts	PIM
1959-60	Barrie Colts	OHA-B	STATISTICS NOT AVAILABLE												
	Barrie Flyers	OHA-Jr.	....	....	....	....	....	....	....	....	3	1	0	1	0
1960-61	Barrie Colts	OHA-B	STATISTICS NOT AVAILABLE												
1961-62	Niagara Falls Flyers	OHA-Jr.	28	14	15	29	....	....	....	38	10	7	4	11	4
1962-63	Niagara Falls Flyers	OHA-Jr.	50	32	*62	*94	....	....	....	48	7	*11	3	14	6
	Niagara Falls Flyers	M-Cup	16	*15	*20	*35	....	....	....	4	....	....	....	....	....
1963-64	Minneapolis Bruins	CPHL	70	27	29	56	....	....	....	44	5	2	1	3	0
1964-65	**Boston Bruins**	**NHL**	**54**	**7**	**6**	**13**	**8**	**6**	**14**	**42**	....	....	....	....	....
	Minneapolis Bruins	CPHL	16	8	11	19	....	....	....	20	....	....	....	....	....
1965-66	**Boston Bruins**	**NHL**	**8**	**1**	**3**	**4**	**1**	**3**	**4**	**6**	....	....	....	....	....
	San Francisco Seals	WHL	60	20	20	40	....	....	....	50	5	1	1	2	0
1966-67	California Seals	WHL	67	25	35	60	....	....	....	54	6	0	2	2	0
1967-68	Hershey Bears	AHL	54	13	20	33	....	....	....	16	2	0	0	0	2
1968-69	Hershey Bears	AHL	DID NOT PLAY – INJURED												
	Halifax Jr. Canadiens	MJrHL	DID NOT PLAY – COACHING												
1969-70	Long Island Ducks	EHL	64	41	41	82	....	....	....	30	....	....	....	....	....
1970-71	Montreal Voyageurs	AHL	4	0	0	0	....	....	....	0	....	....	....	....	....
	Long Island Ducks	EHL	64	44	43	87	....	....	....	12	....	....	....	....	....
1971-72	Gander Flyers	Nfld-Sr.	36	*52	*59	*111	....	....	....	10	8	7	10	17	2
1972-73	HYS-Intervam	Holland	10	*21	19	40	....	....	....	....	....	....	....	....	....
	Long Island Ducks	EHL	35	19	39	58	....	....	....	2	....	....	....	....	....
	Springfield Kings	AHL	4	0	1	1	....	....	....	2	....	....	....	....	....
1973-74	Windsor Spitfires	OJHL	DID NOT PLAY – COACHING												
	NHL Totals		**62**	**8**	**9**	**17**	**9**	**9**	**18**	**48**					

EHL North First All-Star Team (1971)

Traded to **Hershey** (AHL) by **Boston** for cash, June, 1968. • Missed entire 1968-69 season recovering from leg injury suffered while playing fastball in June, 1968. • Named coach of Halifax (MJrHL), January 3, 1969. Signed as a free agent by **Long Island** (EHL), November, 1970.

• MAXWELL, Wally

C – L. 5'10", 158 lbs. b: Ottawa, Ont., 8/24/1933.

Season	Club	League	GP	G	A	Pts	AG	AA	APts	PIM	GP	G	A	Pts	PIM
1950-51	Toronto Marlboros	OHA-Jr.	38	18	22	40	....	....	....	24	13	5	11	16	9
1951-52	Toronto Marlboros	OHA-Jr.	53	28	49	77	....	....	....	42	6	5	2	7	6
1952-53	Toronto Marlboros	OHA-Jr.	51	22	51	73	....	....	....	49	1	0	0	0	0
	Toronto Maple Leafs	**NHL**	**2**	**0**	**0**	**0**	**0**	**0**	**0**	**0**	....	....	....	....	....
1953-54	Toronto Marlboros	OHA-Jr.	59	42	32	74	....	....	....	82	15	11	5	16	20
1954-55	University of Michigan	WCHA	DID NOT PLAY – FRESHMAN												
1955-56	University of Michigan	WCHA	....	7	4	11	....	....	....	8	....	....	....	....	....
1956-57	University of Michigan	WCHA	....	10	6	16	....	....	....	14	....	....	....	....	....
1957-58	Whitby Dunlops	EOHL	14	1	6	7	....	....	....	2	....	....	....	....	....
	Windsor Bulldogs	OHA-Sr.	33	12	12	24	....	....	....	15	11	6	2	8	2
1958-59	Windsor Bulldogs	OHA-Sr.	31	8	15	23	....	....	....	17	....	....	....	....	....
1959-60	Toledo-St. Louis	IHL	3	0	0	0	....	....	....	2	....	....	....	....	....
1960-61	Oakville Oaks	OHA-Sr.	31	21	27	48	....	....	....	....	....	....	....	....	....
1961-62	Oakville Oaks	OHA-Sr.	10	7	3	10	....	....	....	....	....	....	....	....	....
	NHL Totals		**2**	**0**	**0**	**0**	**0**	**0**	**0**	**0**					

• MAYER, Shep Edwin

RW – R. 5'8", 180 lbs. b: Sturgeon Falls, Ont., 9/11/1923.

Season	Club	League	GP	G	A	Pts	AG	AA	APts	PIM	GP	G	A	Pts	PIM
1940-41	Sturgeon Falls Indians	NOJHA	STATISTICS NOT AVAILABLE												
1941-42	Guelph Biltmores	OHA-Jr.	23	9	8	17	....	....	....	34	11	8	7	15	20
1942-43	**Toronto Maple Leafs**	**NHL**	**12**	**1**	**2**	**3**	**1**	**2**	**3**	**4**	....	....	....	....	....
	Saskatoon RCAF	N-SSHL	16	6	3	9	....	....	....	27	3	2	0	2	4
1943-44	Camp Utopia Flyers	NBDHL	STATISTICS NOT AVAILABLE												
1944-45	North Bay RCAF	NOHA	....	14	3	17									
1945-46			MILITARY SERVICE												
1946-47	North Bay Rangers	NOHA	STATISTICS NOT AVAILABLE												
1947-48	S.S. Marie Indians	TBSHL	STATISTICS NOT AVAILABLE												
1948-49	S.S. Marie Indians	TBSHL	STATISTICS NOT AVAILABLE												
1949-50	Saskatoon Quakers	WCSHL	23	2	4	6	....	....	....	4	....	....	....	....	....
	Valleyfield Braves	QSHL	44	12	10	22	....	....	....	69	3	0	0	0	2
1950-51	Ottawa RCAF Flyers	ECSHL	34	12	9	21	....	....	....	20	7	5	8	13	14
	NHL Totals		**12**	**1**	**2**	**3**	**1**	**2**	**3**	**4**	....	....	....	....	....

• MAZUR, Eddie Edward Joseph "Spider"

D/LW – L. 6'2", 186 lbs. b: Winnipeg, Man., 7/25/1929 d: 7/3/1995.

Season	Club	League	GP	G	A	Pts	AG	AA	APts	PIM	GP	G	A	Pts	PIM
1947-48	Winnipeg Monarchs	MJHL	11	5	5	10	....	....	....	0	6	2	0	2	2
	Winnipeg Monarchs	M-Cup	4	2	3	5	....	....	....	2	....	....	....	....	....
1948-49	Dallas Texans	USHL	66	10	20	30	....	....	....	48	4	1	1	2	0
1949-50	Victoria Cougars	PCHL	65	33	26	59	....	....	....	17	....	....	....	....	....
1950-51	Victoria Cougars	PCHL	70	43	30	73	....	....	....	41	12	4	6	10	8
	Montreal Canadiens	**NHL**	....	....	....	....	....	....	....	....	**2**	**0**	**0**	**0**	**0**
1951-52	Buffalo Bisons	AHL	60	19	18	37	....	....	....	55	1	0	1	1	2
	Montreal Canadiens	**NHL**	....	....	....	....	....	....	....	....	**5**	**2**	**0**	**2**	**4**
1952-53	Victoria Cougars	WHL	51	20	18	38	....	....	....	54	....	....	....	....	....
♦	**Montreal Canadiens**	**NHL**	....	....	....	....	....	....	....	....	**7**	**2**	**2**	**4**	**11**
1953-54	**Montreal Canadiens**	**NHL**	**67**	**7**	**14**	**21**	**9**	**17**	**26**	**95**	**11**	**0**	**3**	**3**	**7**
1954-55	**Montreal Canadiens**	**NHL**	**25**	**1**	**5**	**6**	**1**	**6**	**7**	**21**	....	....	....	....	....
	Montreal Royals	QHL	19	4	8	12	....	....	....	16	14	*8	5	13	27
1955-56	Winnipeg Warriors	WHL	70	34	30	64	....	....	....	72	14	6	11	17	16
	Winnipeg Warriors	Ed-Cup	6	3	3	6	....	....	....	11	....	....	....	....	....
1956-57	**Chicago Black Hawks**	**NHL**	**15**	**0**	**1**	**1**	**0**	**1**	**1**	**4**	....	....	....	....	....
	Rochester Americans	AHL	47	24	40	64	....	....	....	90	10	3	9	12	18
1957-58	Rochester Americans	AHL	59	22	25	47	....	....	....	67	....	....	....	....	....
1958-59	Cleveland Barons	AHL	70	34	44	78	....	....	....	54	7	2	2	4	8
1959-60	Cleveland Barons	AHL	61	29	24	53	....	....	....	79	7	2	4	6	24
1960-61	Cleveland Barons	AHL	72	30	39	69	....	....	....	73	4	1	0	1	17
1961-62	Cleveland Barons	AHL	70	24	24	48	....	....	....	44	6	0	0	0	4
1962-63	Providence Reds	AHL	72	18	33	51	....	....	....	72	4	1	0	1	8
1963-64	Providence Reds	AHL	64	23	33	56	....	....	....	56	3	1	4	5	6
1964-65	Victoria Maple Leafs	WHL	62	16	30	46	....	....	....	97	11	1	0	1	6
1965-66	Grand Forks Flyers	MHL-Sr.	25	*22	*37	*59	....	....	....	23	....	....	....	....	....
	NHL Totals		**107**	**8**	**20**	**28**	**10**	**24**	**34**	**120**	**25**	**4**	**5**	**9**	**22**

PCHL Northern Second All-Star Team (1950) • PCHL Second All-Star Team (1951) • AHL Second All-Star Team (1957, 1959) • Played in NHL All-Star Game (1953)

Signed as a free agent by **Montreal**, September 27, 1948. Traded to **Chicago** by **Montreal** with Bud MacPherson and Kenny Mosdell for $55,000 with Montreal holding right of recall, May 24,1956. Traded to **Cleveland** (AHL) by **Rochester** (AHL) for Bo Elik, September 23, 1958. Traded to **Providence** (AHL) by **Cleveland** (AHL) for cash, September, 1962. Signed as a free agent by **Toronto** (Victoria-WHL), September, 1964. Traded to **Baltimore** (AHL) by **Toronto** for cash, September, 1965. • Did not report to Baltimore (AHL).

• McADAM, Sam

C/LW – L. 5'8", 175 lbs. b: Sterling, Scotland, 5/31/1908 Deceased.

Season	Club	League	GP	G	A	Pts	AG	AA	APts	PIM	GP	G	A	Pts	PIM
1924-25	Winnipeg Tigers	WJrHL	STATISTICS NOT AVAILABLE												
	Winnipeg Tigers	M-Cup	4	3	*2	5	....	....	....	4	....	....	....	....	....
1925-26	Tammany Tigers	MAHA	1	1	0	1	....	....	....	4	....	....	....	....	....
1926-27	Winnipeg Winnipegs	WSrHL	5	0	1	1	....	....	....	4	1	0	0	0	0
1927-28	Elmwood Millionaires	WJrHL	5	5	*3	8	....	....	....		2	1	1	2	6
	Winnipeg CPR	WSrHL	6	*6	*4	*10	....	....	....	12	....	....	....	....	....
	Elmwood Maple Leafs	M-Cup	3	10	0	10	....	....	....	0	....	....	....	....	....
1928-29	Vancouver Lions	PCHL	36	10	5	15	....	....	....	24	3	1	0	1	4
1929-30	Vancouver Lions	PCHL	35	11	7	18	....	....	....	38	4	1	1	2	0
1930-31	Vancouver Lions	PCHL	12	0	0	0	....	....	....	30	1	0	0	0	0
	New York Rangers	**NHL**	**5**	**0**	**0**	**0**	**0**	**0**	**0**	**0**	....	....	....	....	....
	Detroit Olympics	IHL	19	7	8	15	....	....	....	14	....	....	....	....	....
1931-32	Springfield Indians	IHL	39	10	6	16	....	....	....	33	....	....	....	....	....
1932-33	Vancouver Maroons	WCHL	29	15	13	28	....	....	....	113	2	4	1	5	0
1933-34	Vancouver Lions	WCHL	32	14	13	27	....	....	....	22	7	*6	2	8	2
1934-35	Seattle Seahawks	NWHL	36	11	17	28	....	....	....	32	5	2	1	3	4
1935-36	Seattle Seahawks	NWHL	39	23	14	37	....	....	....	14	4	3	*4	*7	0
1936-37	Seattle–Vancouver	PCHL	40	18	9	27	....	....	....	12	1	1	0	1	0
1937-38	Seattle Seahawks	PCHL	41	14	12	26	....	....	....	19	4	0	2	2	0
1938-39	Spokane Clippers	PCHL	48	18	21	39	....	....	....	6	....	....	....	....	....
1939-40	Portland Buckaroos	PCHL	36	2	8	10	....	....	....	12	5	0	1	1	2
1940-41	Spokane Bombers	PCHL	47	9	14	23	....	....	....	21	4	0	1	1	6
1941-42	N-Westminster Spitfires	PCHL	10	1	5	6	....	....	....	0	....	....	....	....	....
1942-43	Vancouver St. Regis	PCHL	2	0	1	1	....	....	....	0	....	....	....	....	....
1943-44	Vancouver St. Regis	PCHL	1	0	1	1	....	....	....	0	....	....	....	....	....
	NHL Totals		**5**	**0**	**0**	**0**	**0**	**0**	**0**	**0**					

NWHL Second All-Star Team (1935)

Traded to **NY Rangers** by **Vancouver** (PCHL) for $7,000, January 3, 1931. Traded to **Seattle** (NWHL) by **Vancouver** (NWHL) for Henry Dyck, November, 1934.

• McANDREW, Hazen Bernard Hazen

D – L. 5'10", 175 lbs. b: Mayo, Yukon, 8/7/1917 Deceased.

Season	Club	League	GP	G	A	Pts	AG	AA	APts	PIM	GP	G	A	Pts	PIM
1935-36	Niagara Falls Cataracts	OHA-Sr.	8	5	2	7	....	....	....	*24	2	0	0	0	4
	Niagara Falls Cataracts	Al-Cup	2	0	0	0	....	....	....	2	....	....	....	....	....
1936-37	Toronto British Consols	OHA-B	12	8	1	9	....	....	....	36	6	3	0	3	14
	Niagara Falls Cataracts	OHA-Sr.	....	....	....	....	....	....	....	....	4	0	0	0	2
1937-38	Harringay Greyhounds	Britain	....	1	1	2	....	....	....	....	....	....	....	....	....
	Harringay Greyhounds	Nat-Tmt	....	1	0	1	....	....	....	....	....	....	....	....	....
1938-39	Harringay Greyhounds	Ln-Cup	....	0	1	1	....	....	....	....	....	....	....	....	....
	Harringay Greyhounds	Britain	....	4	3	7	....	....	....	....	....	....	....	....	....
	Ottawa Senators	QSHL	9	0	0	0	....	....	....	10	....	....	....	....	....
	Harringay Greyhounds	Nat-Tmt	....	1	1	2	....	....	....	....	....	....	....	....	....
1939-40	Niagara Falls Cataracts	OHA-Sr.	3	1	1	2	....	....	....	4	....	....	....	....	....
	Atlantic City Seagulls	EAHL	34	10	9	19	....	....	....	26	3	2	0	2	6
1940-41	Niagara Falls Brights	OHA-Sr.	28	2	3	5	....	....	....	*78	3	0	1	1	0
	Springfield Indians	AHL	7	1	3	4	....	....	....	21	3	0	0	0	6
1941-42	**Brooklyn Americans**	**NHL**	**7**	**0**	**1**	**1**	**0**	**1**	**1**	**6**	....	....	....	....	....
	Hershey Bears	AHL	3	1	0	1	....	....	....	2	....	....	....	....	....
	Philadelphia Rockets	AHL	15	1	3	4	....	....	....	20	....	....	....	....	....
	Port Colborne Sailors	OHA-Sr.	2	0	0	0	....	....	....	0	....	....	....	....	....
	Springfield Indians	AHL	30	1	4	5	....	....	....	32	5	0	1	1	9
1942-43	Niagara Falls Cataracts	OHA-Sr.	24	9	10	19	....	....	....	*80	2	0	0	0	6
1943-44			MILITARY SERVICE												
1944-45			MILITARY SERVICE												
1945-46			MILITARY SERVICE												
1946-47	Springfield Indians	AHL	63	2	8	10	....	....	....	94	2	0	0	0	2
	Owen Sound Mercurys	OHA-Sr.	3	0	1	1	....	....	....	6	....	....	....	....	....
1947-48			DID NOT PLAY												
1948-49	Springfield Indians	AHL	63	3	8	11	....	....	....	70	3	0	0	0	0
1949-50	Vancouver Canucks	PCHL	63	1	14	15	....	....	....	67	3	0	0	0	16
	NHL Totals		**7**	**0**	**1**	**1**	**0**	**1**	**1**	**6**					

Signed as a free agent by **NY Americans** (Springfield-AHL), February 21, 1941. Traded to **Vancouver** (PCHL) by **Springfield** (AHL) for cash, September 14, 1949.

• McATEE, Jud Jerome F.

LW – L. 5'9", 170 lbs. b: Stratford, Ont., 2/5/1920.

Season	Club	League	GP	G	A	Pts	AG	AA	APts	PIM	GP	G	A	Pts	PIM
1936-37	Stratford Miners	OHA-B	9	7	7	14	....	....	....	2	....	....	....	....	....
1937-38	Stratford Midgets	OHA-Jr.	14	12	7	19	....	....	....	6	7	2	0	2	4
1938-39	Oshawa Generals	OHA-Jr.	14	2	3	5	....	....	....	6	7	3	1	4	2
	Oshawa Generals	M-Cup	7	3	1	4	....	....	....	2	....	....	....	....	....
1939-40	Oshawa Generals	OHA-Jr.	18	*25	*19	*44	....	....	....	12	15	*16	10	*26	28
	Oshawa Generals	M-Cup	8	7	6	13	....	....	....	20	....	....	....	....	....
1940-41	Indianapolis Capitols	AHL	54	11	13	24	....	....	....	6	....	....	....	....	....
1941-42	Indianapolis Capitols	AHL	54	16	23	39	....	....	....	4	10	3	3	6	0
1942-43	**Detroit Red Wings**	**NHL**	**1**	**0**	**0**	**0**	**0**	**0**	**0**	**0**	....	....	....	....	....
	Indianapolis Capitols	AHL	55	17	21	38	....	....	....	0	7	2	1	3	0
1943-44	**Detroit Red Wings**	**NHL**	**1**	**0**	**2**	**2**	**0**	**2**	**2**	**0**	....	....	....	....	....
	St. Catharines Saints	OHA-Sr.	20	14	9	23	....	....	....	14	5	1	2	3	0

			REGULAR SEASON								PLAYOFFS				
Season	Club	League	GP	G	A	Pts	AG	AA	APts	PIM	GP	G	A	Pts	PIM
1944-45	**Detroit Red Wings**	**NHL**	**44**	**15**	**11**	**26**	**15**	**13**	**28**	**6**	**14**	**2**	**1**	**3**	**0**
1945-46	Indianapolis Capitols	AHL	30	8	14	22	....	....	....	6	....	....	....	....	....
	St. Louis Flyers	AHL	32	7	10	17	....	....	....	8	....	....	....	....	....
1946-47	St. Louis Flyers	AHL	64	12	22	34	....	....	....	6	....	....	....	....	....
1947-48	St. Louis Flyers	AHL	14	1	4	5	....	....	....	0	....	....	....	....	....
	Hershey Bears	AHL	44	5	11	16	....	....	....	10	1	1	0	1	0
1948-49	Tulsa Oilers	USHL	49	22	34	56	....	....	....	4	....	....	....	....	....
	Hershey Bears	AHL	15	0	1	1	....	....	....	2	6	0	0	0	0
1949-50	Tulsa Oilers	USHL	42	9	13	22	....	....	....	12	....	....	....	....	....
	NHL Totals		**46**	**15**	**13**	**28**	**15**	**15**	**30**	**6**	**14**	**2**	**1**	**3**	**0**

• Brother of Norm

Signed as a free agent by **Detroit**, October 16, 1940. Traded to **Chicago** (St. Louis-AHL) by **Detroit** (Indianapolis-AHL) with Norm McAtee, George Ritchie and Roy Sawyer for Doug McCaig, George Blake and cash, December 26, 1945. Traded to **Hershey** (AHL) by **St. Louis** (AHL) for Norm Tustin, November 15, 1947.

• McATEE, Norm Norman Joseph

C – L. 5'8", 165 lbs. b: Stratford, Ont., 6/28/1921.

Season	Club	League	GP	G	A	Pts	AG	AA	APts	PIM	GP	G	A	Pts	PIM
1936-37	Stratford Miners	OHA-B	5	3	2	5	....	....	....	0	....	....	....	....	....
1937-38	Stratford Midgets	OHA-Jr.	14	9	8	17	....	....	....	6	7	2	1	3	0
1938-39	Oshawa Generals	OHA-Jr.	13	6	4	10	....	....	....	0	7	4	1	5	5
	Oshawa Generals	M-Cup	7	4	1	5	....	....	....	5	....	....	....	....	....
1939-40	Oshawa Generals	OHA-Jr.	18	17	18	35	....	....	....	9	15	2	*18	20	15
	Oshawa Generals	M-Cup	9	6	7	13	....	....	....	0	....	....	....	....	....
1940-41	Oshawa Generals	OHA-Jr.	14	15	12	27	....	....	....	2	10	10	9	19	2
	Oshawa Generals	M-Cup	5	4	2	6	....	....	....	2	....	....	....	....	....
1941-42	Philadelphia Capitals	AHL	18	1	6	7	....	....	....	4	....	....	....	....	....
	Philadelphia Rockets	AHL	12	8	9	17	....	....	....	2	....	....	....	....	....
	Omaha Knights	AHA	24	1	5	6	....	....	....	2	8	0	0	0	0
1942-43	Toronto RCAF	OHA-Sr.	2	0	1	1	....	....	....	5	9	7	5	12	10
	Toronto RCAF	Al-Cup	4	3	0	3	....	....	....	7	....	....	....	....	....
1943-44	Brantford RCAF	OHA-Sr.	STATISTICS NOT AVAILABLE												
1944-45			MILITARY SERVICE												
1945-46	Indianapolis Capitols	AHL	30	5	8	13	....	....	....	9	....	....	....	....	....
	St. Louis Flyers	AHL	17	3	6	9	....	....	....	4	....	....	....	....	....
	Hershey Bears	AHL	14	4	12	16	....	....	....	4	....	....	....	....	....
1946-47	**Boston Bruins**	**NHL**	**13**	**0**	**1**	**1**	**0**	**1**	**1**	**0**	....	....	....	....	....
	Hershey Bears	AHL	40	5	7	12	....	....	....	2	2	0	0	0	0
1947-48	Hershey Bears	AHL	9	0	2	2	....	....	....	0	....	....	....	....	....
	Tulsa Oilers	USHL	57	14	20	34	....	....	....	9	2	0	0	0	0
1948-49	Washington Lions	AHL	64	14	28	42	....	....	....	13	....	....	....	....	....
1949-50	Sherbrooke Saints	QSHL	36	15	16	31	....	....	....	10	12	*10	8	*18	2
	Sherbrooke Saints	Al-Cup	10	6	8	*14	....	....	....	6	....	....	....	....	....
1950-51	Sherbrooke Saints	QMHL	50	15	30	45	....	....	....	12	5	1	3	4	2
1951-52	Troy Bruins	IHL	33	11	17	28	....	....	....	29	7	0	4	4	4
1952-53	Troy Bruins	IHL	59	29	35	64	....	....	....	15	6	1	3	4	2
1953-54	Troy Bruins	IHL	62	20	48	68	....	....	....	22	3	0	2	2	0
	NHL Totals		**13**	**0**	**1**	**1**	**0**	**1**	**1**	**0**	....	....	....	....	....

• Brother of Jud

Traded to **Chicago** (St. Louis-AHL) by **Detroit** (Indianapolis-AHL) with Jud McAtee, George Ritchie and Roy Sawyer for Doug McCaig, George Blake and cash, December 26, 1945. Traded to **Boston** (Hershey-AHL) by **Chicago** (St. Louis-AHL) for Bill Jennings, February 5, 1946. Traded to **Washington** (AHL) by **Hershey** (AHL) for cash, October 9, 1949. Traded to **Seattle** (PCHL) by **Washington** (AHL) for cash, September, 1949. • Did not report to Seattle (PCHL).

• McAVOY, George

D – L. 6', 185 lbs. b: Edmonton, Alta., 6/21/1931 d: 5/15/1998.

Season	Club	League	GP	G	A	Pts	AG	AA	APts	PIM	GP	G	A	Pts	PIM
1947-48	Edmonton Athletic Club	EJrHL	17	2	3	5	....	....	....	6	4	0	0	0	4
1948-49	Edmonton Athletic Club	EJrHL	17	6	9	15	....	....	....	41	6	2	1	3	17
	Edmonton Athletic Club	M-Cup	8	1	5	6	....	....	....	10	....	....	....	....	....
1949-50	Laval Nationale	QJHL	36	2	6	8	....	....	....	73	7	1	1	2	15
1950-51	Montreal Jr. Canadiens	QJHL	41	7	12	19	....	....	....	54	9	1	1	2	18
1951-52	Halifax St. Mary's	MMHL	6	0	0	0	....	....	....	4	....	....	....	....	....
	Boston Olympics	EAHL	61	4	18	22	....	....	....	153	4	0	2	2	9
1952-53	Penticton Vees	OSHL	44	9	5	14	....	....	....	*162	10	1	1	2	16
	Penticton Vees	Al-Cup	18	4	6	10	....	....	....	70	....	....	....	....	....
1953-54	Penticton Vees	OSHL	61	11	24	35	....	....	....	*265	10	1	5	6	12
	Penticton Vees	Al-Cup	23	4	2	6	....	....	....	28	....	....	....	....	....
1954-55	Penticton Vees	OSHL	53	8	26	34	....	....	....	122	....	....	....	....	....
	Canada	WEC-A	8	2	2	4	....	....	....	14	....	....	....	....	....
	Montreal Canadiens	**NHL**	....	....	....	....	....	....	....	....	**4**	**0**	**0**	**0**	**0**
1955-56	Providence Reds	AHL	60	4	19	23	....	....	....	131	9	1	7	8	25
1956-57	Providence Reds	AHL	64	3	27	30	....	....	....	141	5	1	0	1	9
1957-58	Providence Reds	AHL	25	2	10	12	....	....	....	45	5	0	0	0	10
1958-59	New Westminster Royals	WHL	11	0	4	4	....	....	....	18	....	....	....	....	....
	Cleveland Barons	AHL	59	6	24	30	....	....	....	99	7	0	3	3	14
1959-60	Cleveland Barons	AHL	72	6	21	27	....	....	....	124	7	0	0	0	14
1960-61	Calgary Stampeders	WHL	70	5	28	33	....	....	....	111	5	0	2	2	10
1961-62	Calgary Stampeders	WHL	70	5	30	35	....	....	....	113	7	0	2	2	13
1962-63	Calgary Stampeders	WHL	70	9	16	25	....	....	....	141	....	....	....	....	....
1963-64			OUT OF HOCKEY – RETIRED												
1964-65	Edmonton Nuggets	X-Games	STATISTICS NOT AVAILABLE												
1965-66	Edmonton Nuggets	WCSHL	19	3	2	5	....	....	....	23	....	....	....	....	....
	NHL Totals		....	....	....	....	....	....	....	....	**4**	**0**	**0**	**0**	**0**

OSHL Second All-Star Team (1954) • OSHL First All-Star Team (1955)

Traded to **Cleveland** (AHL) by **Providence** (AHL) with Bob Robertson for Ed MacQueen, November 3, 1958.

• McBRIDE, Cliff

RW/D – R. 5'10", 180 lbs. b: Toronto, Ont., 1/10/1909.

Season	Club	League	GP	G	A	Pts	AG	AA	APts	PIM	GP	G	A	Pts	PIM
1926-27	Iroquois Falls Eskimos	NOJHA	STATISTICS NOT AVAILABLE												
	Iroquois Falls Eskimos	M-Cup	6	15	3	18	....	....	....	8	....	....	....	....	....
1927-28	Fort William Forts	TBSHL	20	12	5	17	....	....	....	*81	2	0	0	0	2
1928-29	**Montreal Maroons**	**NHL**	**1**	**0**	**0**	**0**	**0**	**0**	**0**	**0**	....	....	....	....	....
	Windsor Bulldogs	Can-Am	20	3	1	4	....	....	....	29	....	....	....	....	....

			REGULAR SEASON								PLAYOFFS				
Season	Club	League	GP	G	A	Pts	AG	AA	APts	PIM	GP	G	A	Pts	PIM
1929-30	**Toronto Maple Leafs**	**NHL**	**1**	**0**	**0**	**0**	**0**	**0**	**0**	**0**	....	....	....	....	....
	London Panthers	IHL	12	1	0	1	....	....	....	29	....	....	....	....	....
	Toronto Millionaires	IHL	25	2	7	9	....	....	....	5	....	....	....	....	....
	Galt Terriers	Can-Pro	1	0	0	0	....	....	....	0	....	....	....	....	....
	Brantford Indians	Can-Pro	8	0	1	1	....	....	....	2	....	....	....	....	....
1930-31	Pittsburgh Yellowjackets	IHL	4	0	0	0	....	....	....	8	....	....	....	....	....
	Cleveland Indians	IHL	38	2	3	5	....	....	....	34	6	0	1	1	0
1931-32	Syracuse Stars	IHL	46	4	5	9	....	....	....	54	....	....	....	....	....
1932-33			OUT OF HOCKEY – RETIRED												
1933-34	New Haven Eagles	Can-Am	39	7	8	15	....	....	....	51	....	....	....	....	....
1934-35	New Haven Eagles	Can-Am	44	13	11	24	....	....	....	32	....	....	....	....	....
1935-36	Springfield Indians	Can-Am	42	6	9	15	....	....	....	33	3	0	0	0	8
1936-37	Springfield Indians	IAHL	45	1	9	10	....	....	....	77	5	1	0	1	4
1937-38	Springfield Indians	IAHL	43	5	5	10	....	....	....	22	....	....	....	....	....
	NHL Totals		**2**	**0**	**0**	**0**	**0**	**0**	**0**	**0**	....	....	....	....	....

Traded to **Toronto** by **Montreal Maroons** for cash, October 23, 1929. Loaned to **London** (IHL) by **Toronto**, November 12, 1929. Traded to **Toronto Millionaires** (IHL) by **Toronto** for cash, February 6, 1930. Signed as a free agent by **Pittsburgh** (IHL) after **Toronto Millionaires** (IHL) franchise folded, October 30, 1930. Traded to **Cleveland** (IHL) by **Pittsburgh** (IHL) for Mickey McGuire, November 28, 1930.

• McBURNEY, Jim

LW – L. 5'7", 150 lbs. b: Sault Ste. Marie, Ont., 6/3/1933.

Season	Club	League	GP	G	A	Pts	AG	AA	APts	PIM	GP	G	A	Pts	PIM
1950-51	S.S. Marie Red Wings	NOJHA	5	7	3	10	....	....	....	4	2	1	3	4	0
1951-52	Galt Black Hawks	OHA-Jr.	47	35	31	66	....	....	....	27	3	2	1	3	0
1952-53	Galt Black Hawks	OHA-Jr.	55	*61	35	*96	....	....	....	18	11	4	5	9	6
	Chicago Black Hawks	**NHL**	**1**	**0**	**1**	**1**	**0**	**1**	**1**	**0**	....	....	....	....	....
1953-54	S.S. Marie Greyhounds	NOHA	58	30	21	51	....	....	....	6	1	0	0	0	0
1954-55	S.S. Marie Greyhounds	NOHA	51	*33	13	46	....	....	....	6	14	*8	2	10	8
1955-56	S.S. Marie Greyhounds	NOHA	50	26	12	38	....	....	....	2	5	0	1	1	0
1956-57			DID NOT PLAY												
1957-58	S.S. Marie Greyhounds	OHA-Sr.	47	17	11	28	....	....	....	10	4	1	0	1	0
1958-59	S.S. Marie Greyhounds	OHA-Sr.	54	*49	29	78	....	....	....	4	3	1	1	2	2
	NHL Totals		**1**	**0**	**1**	**1**	**0**	**1**	**1**	**0**	....	....	....	....	....

• McCABE, Stan

LW – L. 5'6", 165 lbs. b: Ottawa, Ont., 6/16/1908 d: 6/2/1958.

Season	Club	League	GP	G	A	Pts	AG	AA	APts	PIM	GP	G	A	Pts	PIM
1924-25	Ottawa Gunners	OCJHL	6	1	0	1	....	....	....	....	....	....	....	....	....
1925-26	Ottawa Rideaus	OCJHL	15	10	0	10	....	....	....	....	....	....	....	....	....
1926-27	North Bay Trappers	NOHA	11	18	8	26	....	....	....	42	4	2	4	6	10
1927-28	Detroit Olympics	Can-Pro	41	15	4	19	....	....	....	31	2	0	0	0	4
1928-29	Detroit Olympics	Can-Pro	39	17	2	19	....	....	....	70	7	2	0	2	11
1929-30	**Detroit Cougars**	**NHL**	**25**	**7**	**3**	**10**	**10**	**7**	**17**	**23**	....	....	....	....	....
	Detroit Olympics	IHL	17	7	3	10	....	....	....	39	....	....	....	....	....
1930-31	**Detroit Falcons**	**NHL**	**44**	**2**	**1**	**3**	**4**	**3**	**7**	**22**	....	....	....	....	....
1931-32	Detroit Olympics	IHL	47	10	8	18	....	....	....	61	6	0	0	0	14
1932-33	**Montreal Maroons**	**NHL**	**1**	**0**	**0**	**0**	**0**	**0**	**0**	**0**	....	....	....	....	....
	Quebec Beavers	Can-Am	47	11	19	30	....	....	....	46	....	....	....	....	....
1933-34	**Montreal Maroons**	**NHL**	**8**	**0**	**0**	**0**	**0**	**0**	**0**	**4**	....	....	....	....	....
	Quebec Castors	Can-Am	36	17	11	28	....	....	....	16	....	....	....	....	....
1934-35	Windsor Bulldogs	IHL	15	0	3	3	....	....	....	4	....	....	....	....	....
	Philadelphia Arrows	Can-Am	19	6	6	12	....	....	....	14	....	....	....	....	....
1935-36	Pittsburgh Yellowjackets	IHL	44	7	17	24	....	....	....	15	....	....	....	....	....
1936-37	Oakland–Spokane	PCHL	14	0	1	1	....	....	....	2	....	....	....	....	....
1937-38	Detroit Pontiacs	MOHL	23	10	7	17	....	....	....	4	3	0	0	0	0
1938-39	Detroit Pontiacs	MOHL	21	5	6	11	....	....	....	10	7	1	0	1	0
	NHL Totals		**78**	**9**	**4**	**13**	**14**	**10**	**24**	**49**	....	....	....	....	....

Signed as a free agent by **Detroit Cougars**, November 1, 1927. Claimed on waivers by **Montreal Maroons** from **Detroit**, November 14, 1932. Traded to **Quebec** (Can-Am) by **Montreal Maroons** for cash, November 27, 1932. Traded to **Montreal Maroons** by **Montreal Canadiens** (Quebec-Can-Am) for Paul Runge, December 6, 1933. • **Oakland** (PCHL) franchise transferred to **Spokane** (PCHL) during the 1936-37 season.

• McCAFFREY, Bert Albert John "Mac"

RW/D – R. 5'10", 180 lbs. b: Chesley, Ont., d: 4/15/1955.

Season	Club	League	GP	G	A	Pts	AG	AA	APts	PIM	GP	G	A	Pts	PIM
1915-16	Chesley ACC	OHA-I	STATISTICS NOT AVAILABLE												
1916-17	Toronto Riversides	OHA-Sr.	8	9	0	9	....	....	....	....	2	1	0	1	4
1917-18	Toronto Crescents	OHA-Sr.	9	*23	0	*23	....	....	....	....	....	....	....	....	....
1918-19	Toronto Dentals	OHA-Sr.	6	7	1	8	....	....	....	....	2	0	0	0	....
1919-20	Parkdale Canoe Club	OHA-Sr.	6	6	3	9	....	....	....	....	1	1	1	2	....
1920-21	Toronto Granites	OHA-Sr.	10	1	3	4	....	....	....	....	2	0	2	2	....
1921-22	Toronto Granites	OHA-Sr.	10	5	8	13	....	....	....	....	2	3	2	5	....
	Toronto Granites	Al-Cup	6	5	2	7	....	....	....	....	....	....	....	....	....
1922-23	Toronto Granites	OHA-Sr.	12	10	4	14	....	....	....	....	2	0	0	0	2
	Toronto Granites	Al-Cup	6	6	2	8	....	....	....	6	....	....	....	....	....
1923-24	Toronto Granites	X-Games	14	18	10	28	....	....	....	....	....	....	....	....	....
	Canada	Olympics	5	19	15	34	....	....	....	....	....	....	....	....	....
1924-25	**Toronto St. Pats**	**NHL**	**30**	**10**	**6**	**16**	**17**	**25**	**42**	**12**	**2**	**1**	**0**	**1**	**4**
1925-26	**Toronto St. Pats**	**NHL**	**36**	**14**	**7**	**21**	**24**	**46**	**70**	**42**	....	....	....	....	....
1926-27	**Toronto Pats/Leafs**	**NHL**	**43**	**5**	**5**	**10**	**9**	**26**	**35**	**43**	....	....	....	....	....
1927-28	**Toronto Maple Leafs**	**NHL**	**9**	**1**	**1**	**2**	**2**	**6**	**8**	**9**	....	....	....	....	....
	Pittsburgh Pirates	**NHL**	**35**	**6**	**3**	**9**	**12**	**17**	**29**	**14**	....	....	....	....	....
1928-29	**Pittsburgh Pirates**	**NHL**	**42**	**1**	**0**	**1**	**3**	**0**	**3**	**34**	....	....	....	....	....
1929-30	**Pittsburgh Pirates**	**NHL**	**15**	**3**	**4**	**7**	**4**	**9**	**13**	**12**	....	....	....	....	....
♦	**Montreal Canadiens**	**NHL**	**28**	**1**	**3**	**4**	**1**	**7**	**8**	**26**	**6**	**1**	**1**	**2**	**6**
1930-31	**Montreal Canadiens**	**NHL**	**22**	**2**	**1**	**3**	**4**	**3**	**7**	**10**	....	....	....	....	....
	Providence Reds	Can-Am	20	6	2	8	....	....	....	24	2	2	1	3	2
1931-32	Philadelphia Arrows	Can-Am	35	7	9	16	....	....	....	26	....	....	....	....	....
1932-33	Philadelphia Arrows	Can-Am	7	1	0	1	....	....	....	2	....	....	....	....	....
	NHL Totals		**260**	**43**	**30**	**73**	**76**	**139**	**215**	**202**	**8**	**2**	**1**	**3**	**10**

Signed as a free agent by **Toronto**, October 16, 1924. Traded to **Pittsburgh** by **Toronto** to complete three team transaction that sent Ty Arbour to Chicago and Ed Rodden to Toronto, December, 1927. Traded to **Montreal Canadiens** by **Pittsburgh** for Gord Fraser, December 23, 1929.

• McCAIG, Doug

D – R. 6', 190 lbs. b: Guelph, Ont., 2/24/1919.

Season	Club	League	GP	G	A	Pts	AG	AA	APts	PIM	GP	G	A	Pts	PIM
			REGULAR SEASON								PLAYOFFS				
1939-40	Detroit Holtzbaugh	MOHL	34	7	6	13	....	....	....	43	12	1	1	2	18
1940-41	Detroit Holtzbaugh	MOHL	11	1	4	5	....	....	....	12	....	....	....	....	....
	Indianapolis Capitols	AHL	27	1	1	2	....	....	....	14	....	....	....	....	....
1941-42	**Detroit Red Wings**	**NHL**	**9**	**0**	**1**	**1**	**0**	**1**	**1**	**6**	**2**	**0**	**0**	**0**	**6**
	Indianapolis Capitols	AHL	44	4	8	12	....	....	....	6	10	3	4	7	*13
1942-43	Toronto RCAF	TIHL	7	2	4	6	....	....	....	12	8	4	1	5	*23
	Toronto RCAF	Al-Cup	4	0	1	1	....	....	....	4	....	....	....	....	....
1943-44	Toronto RCAF	TIHL	7	1	1	2	....	....	....	16	....	....	....	....	....
	Brantford RCAF	OHA-Sr.	STATISTICS NOT AVAILABLE												
1944-45	Winnipeg RCAF	WNDHL	10	4	7	11	....	....	....	31	....	....	....	....	....
	Summerside RCAF	PEI-Sr.	....	....	....	....	....	....	....	....	3	1	0	1	0
1945-46	St. Louis Flyers	AHL	19	3	4	7	....	....	....	28	5	0	1	1	12
	Detroit Red Wings	**NHL**	**6**	**0**	**1**	**1**	**0**	**1**	**1**	**12**	....	....	....	....	....
	Indianapolis Capitols	AHL	24	1	8	9	....	....	....	27	5	0	1	1	12
1946-47	**Detroit Red Wings**	**NHL**	**47**	**2**	**4**	**6**	**2**	**5**	**7**	**62**	**5**	**0**	**1**	**1**	**4**
	Indianapolis Capitols	AHL	13	4	2	6	....	....	....	27	....	....	....	....	....
1947-48	**Detroit Red Wings**	**NHL**	**29**	**3**	**3**	**6**	**4**	**4**	**8**	**37**	....	....	....	....	....
1948-49	**Detroit Red Wings**	**NHL**	**1**	**0**	**0**	**0**	**0**	**0**	**0**	**0**	....	....	....	....	....
	Chicago Black Hawks	**NHL**	**55**	**1**	**3**	**4**	**1**	**4**	**5**	**60**	....	....	....	....	....
1949-50	**Chicago Black Hawks**	**NHL**	**63**	**0**	**4**	**4**	**0**	**5**	**5**	**49**	....	....	....	....	....
1950-51	**Chicago Black Hawks**	**NHL**	**53**	**2**	**5**	**7**	**3**	**6**	**9**	**29**	....	....	....	....	....
	Milwaukee Seagulls	USHL	6	1	1	2	....	....	....	4	....	....	....	....	....
1951-52	Edmonton Flyers	PCHL	70	4	7	11	....	....	....	*148	4	0	0	0	0
1952-53	Toledo Mercurys	IHL	59	7	12	19	....	....	....	73	5	0	0	0	4
1953-54	Toledo Mercurys	IHL	57	4	13	17	....	....	....	52	5	1	1	2	0
1954-55	Toledo Mercurys	IHL	34	1	8	9	....	....	....	25	....	....	....	....	....
1955-56	Fort Wayne Komets	IHL	38	11	15	26	....	....	....	39	....	....	....	....	....
1956-57	Fort Wayne Komets	IHL	DID NOT PLAY – COACHING												
	NHL Totals		**263**	**8**	**21**	**29**	**10**	**26**	**36**	**255**	**7**	**0**	**1**	**1**	**10**

AHL Second All-Star Team (1942) • IHL Second All-Star Team (1953, 1955)

Signed as a free agent by **Detroit**, December 31, 1940. Signed as a free agent by **St. Louis** (AHL), October, 1945. Traded to **Detroit** (Indianapolis-AHL) by **Chicago** (St. Louis-AHL) with George Blake and cash for Norm McAtee, Jud McAtee, George Ritchie and Roy Sawyer, December 26, 1945. Traded to **Chicago** by **Detroit** with Jim Conacher and Bep Guidolin for George Gee and Bud Poile, October 25, 1948. Traded to **Detroit** by **Chicago** for Max Quackenbush, September 18, 1951.

• McCALLUM, Dunc

— see page 1393

• McCALMON, Eddie

Edward Allison "Cally"

RW – R. 5'8", 170 lbs. b: Varney, Ont., 5/30/1902 Deceased.

Season	Club	League	GP	G	A	Pts	AG	AA	APts	PIM	GP	G	A	Pts	PIM
1917-18	Lumsden Athletic Club	SAHA	STATISTICS NOT AVAILABLE												
	Lumsden Athletic Club	M-Cup	3	6	0	6	....	....	....	0	....	....	....	....	....
1918-19	Lumsden Athletic Club	SAHA	10	21	0	21	....	....	....	3	....	....	....	....	....
1919-20			MILITARY SERVICE												
1920-21	Lumsden Athletic Club	SIHA	10	21	0	21	....	....	....	3	3	6	0	6	....
1921-22	Regina Victorias	SIHA	1	0	0	0	....	....	....	0	....	....	....	....	....
1922-23	Regina Victorias	SIHA	STATISTICS NOT AVAILABLE												
1923-24	U. of Saskatchewan	S-SSHL	STATISTICS NOT AVAILABLE												
1924-25	U. of Saskatchewan	S-SSHL	5	2	*4	6	....	....	....	4	....	....	....	....	....
1925-26	U. of Saskatchewan	S-SSHL	STATISTICS NOT AVAILABLE												
1926-27	U. of Saskatchewan	S-SSHL	STATISTICS NOT AVAILABLE												
1927-28	Saskatoon Shieks	PrHL	12	8	0	8	....	....	....	2	....	....	....	....	....
	Chicago Black Hawks	**NHL**	**23**	**2**	**0**	**2**	**4**	**0**	**4**	**8**	....	....	....	....	....
1928-29	Tulsa Oilers	AHA	2	0	0	0	....	....	....	5	....	....	....	....	....
1929-30	Toronto Millionaires	Can-Pro	34	6	4	10	....	....	....	10	....	....	....	....	....
1930-31	**Philadelphia Quakers**	**NHL**	**16**	**3**	**0**	**3**	**6**	**0**	**6**	**6**	....	....	....	....	....
	NHL Totals		**39**	**5**	**0**	**5**	**10**	**0**	**10**	**14**	....	....	....	....	....

Traded to **Chicago** by **Saskatoon** (PrHL) with Earl Miller for Nick Wasnie and Corb Denneny, January 11, 1928. Signed as a free agent by **Toronto Millionaires** (Can-Pro), December 3, 1929. Signed as a free agent by **Philadelphia** after **Toronto Millionaires** franchise folded, December 15, 1930.

• McCARTHY, Thomas

Thomas Joseph

RW – R. 5'11", 165 lbs. b: Hamilton, Ont., Deceased.

Season	Club	League	GP	G	A	Pts	AG	AA	APts	PIM	GP	G	A	Pts	PIM
1914-15	New York Irish-Americans	AAHL	8	5	0	5	....	....	....		....	....	....	....	....
1915-16	Brooklyn Crescents	AAHA	7	5	0	5	....	....	....		....	....	....	....	....
1916-17	Brooklyn Crescents	AAHA	12	14	0	14	....	....	....		....	....	....	....	....
1917-18	New York Wanderers	AAHA	10	4	0	4	....	....	....		....	....	....	....	....
1918-19	Hamilton Tigers	OHA-Sr.	8	*19	3	22	....	....	....		4	3	2	5	....
	Hamilton Tigers	Al-Cup	2	1	0	1	....	....	....	0	....	....	....	....	....
1919-20	**Quebec Bulldogs**	**NHL**	**12**	**12**	**6**	**18**	**14**	**20**	**34**	**0**	....	....	....	....	....
1920-21	**Hamilton Tigers**	**NHL**	**23**	**10**	**1**	**11**	**13**	**4**	**17**	**10**	....	....	....	....	....
1921-22	Saskatoon Sheiks	WCHL	7	1	0	1	....	....	....	0	....	....	....	....	....
1922-23	Seattle Metropolitans	PCHA	16	2	1	3	....	....	....	0	....	....	....	....	....
	NHL Totals		**35**	**22**	**7**	**29**	**27**	**24**	**51**	**10**	....	....	....	....	....
	Other Major League Totals		23	3	1	4	....	....	....	0	....	....	....	....	....

AAHA Second All-Star Team (1916) • AAHA First All-Star Team (1917, 1918)

• Refused amateur card by OHA, November 23, 1919. Signed as a free agent by **Quebec**, February 2, 1920. Transferred to **Hamilton** after **Quebec** franchise relocated, November 2, 1920. Signed as a free agent by **Saskatoon** (WCHL), December 17, 1921. Signed as a free agent by **Seattle** (PCHA), October 26, 1922.

• McCARTHY, Tom

Thomas Patrick Francis

LW – L. 6'1", 191 lbs. b: Toronto, Ont., 9/15/1934.

Season	Club	League	GP	G	A	Pts	AG	AA	APts	PIM	GP	G	A	Pts	PIM
1950-51	Weston Dukes	OHA-B	STATISTICS NOT AVAILABLE												
	Toronto Marlboros	OHA-Jr.	2	1	0	1	....	....	....	0	....	....	....	....	....
1951-52	Weston Dukes	OHA-B													
	Toronto Marlboros	OHA-Jr.	3	2	3	5	....	....	....	0	....	....	....	....	....
1952-53	Toronto Marlboros	OHA-Jr.	56	13	12	25	....	....	....	56	7	0	0	0	2
1953-54	Toronto Marlboros	OHA-Jr.	59	18	29	47	....	....	....	50	1	0	0	0	0
1954-55	Toronto–Guelph	OHA-Jr.	37	23	29	52	....	....	....	55	6	2	5	7	21
1955-56	Saskatoon–Vancouver	WHL	67	24	22	46	....	....	....	64	15	7	5	12	9
1956-57	**Detroit Red Wings**	**NHL**	**3**	**0**	**0**	**0**	**0**	**0**	**0**	**0**	....	....	....	....	....
	Edmonton Flyers	WHL	42	18	19	37	....	....	....	108	8	2	2	4	2
1957-58	**Detroit Red Wings**	**NHL**	**18**	**2**	**1**	**3**	**2**	**1**	**3**	**4**	....	....	....	....	....
	Victoria–Edmonton	WHL	45	22	31	53	....	....	....	36	....	....	....	....	....
	Providence Reds	AHL	1	0	0	0	....	....	....	2	5	0	1	1	4
1958-59	**Detroit Red Wings**	**NHL**	**15**	**2**	**3**	**5**	**2**	**3**	**5**	**4**	....	....	....	....	....
	Hershey Bears	AHL	40	4	6	10	....	....	....	14	5	1	0	1	0
1959-60	Sudbury Wolves	EPHL	70	46	62	*108	....	....	....	86	4	*8	*12	*20	6
1960-61	Sudbury Wolves	EPHL	45	30	24	54	....	....	....	60	....	....	....	....	....
	Boston Bruins	**NHL**	**24**	**4**	**5**	**9**	**5**	**5**	**10**	**0**	....	....	....	....	....
1961-62	Kingston Frontenacs	EPHL	70	53	45	98	....	....	....	68	11	7	3	10	35
1962-63	Portland Buckaroos	WHL	66	27	37	64	....	....	....	61	7	4	4	8	0
1963-64	Portland Buckaroos	WHL	55	11	23	34	....	....	....	31	5	2	3	5	0
1964-65	Tulsa Oilers	CPHL	68	*53	44	*97	....	....	....	110	12	3	7	10	29
1965-66	Cleveland Barons	AHL	72	33	34	67	....	....	....	27	12	7	5	*12	6
1966-67	Cleveland Barons	AHL	70	36	38	74	....	....	....	21	5	2	2	4	0
1967-68	Baltimore Clippers	AHL	70	34	49	83	....	....	....	52	....	....	....	....	....
1968-69	Rochester Americans	AHL	68	31	31	62	....	....	....	34	....	....	....	....	....
1969-70	Rochester Americans	AHL	24	5	8	13	....	....	....	24	....	....	....	....	....
1970-71	Orillia Terriers	OHA-Sr.	39	22	38	60	....	....	....	14	....	....	....	....	....
	Galt Hornets	Al-Cup	STATISTICS NOT AVAILABLE												
1971-72	Orillia Terriers	OHA-Sr.	5	0	3	3	....	....	....	0	....	....	....	....	....
1972-73	Orillia Terriers	OHA-Sr.	24	6	15	21	....	....	....	22	....	....	....	....	....
	Brantford Forresters	OHA-Sr.	12	9	12	21	....	....	....	5	....	....	....	....	....
	NHL Totals		**60**	**8**	**9**	**17**	**9**	**9**	**18**	**8**	....	....	....	....	....

EPHL First All-Star Team (1960) • EPHL Second All-Star Team (1962) • CPHL First All-Star Team (1965)

Traded to **NY Rangers** by **Toronto** for $2,000, August 29, 1955. Claimed by **Detroit** from **NY Rangers** in Intra-League Draft, September, 1956. Traded to **Boston** by **Detroit** with Murray Oliver and Gary Aldcorn for Vic Stasiuk and Leo Labine, January 23, 1961. Traded to **Toronto** by **Boston** for cash, August, 1964. Claimed by **Montreal** from **Toronto** (Tulsa-CPHL) in Inter-League Draft, June 8, 1965. Rights transferred to **Vancouver** (WHL) after WHL club purchased **Rochester** (AHL) franchise, August 13, 1968. NHL rights transferred to **Vancouver** after NHL club purchased **Vancouver** (WHL) franchise, December 19, 1969.

• McCARTNEY, Walt

Walter Herbert

LW – L. 5'10", 160 lbs. b: Regina, Sask., 4/26/1911 Deceased.

Season	Club	League	GP	G	A	Pts	AG	AA	APts	PIM	GP	G	A	Pts	PIM
1926-27	Indian Head Bengals	S-SJHL	6	2	0	2	....	....	....	0	....	....	....	....	....
1927-28	Weyburn Beavers	S-SSHL	9	4	2	6	....	....	....	2	....	....	....	....	....
1928-29	Weyburn Beavers	S-SSHL	20	15	4	19	....	....	....	0	2	0	0	0	2
1929-30	Weyburn Beavers	S-SSHL	20	5	5	10	....	....	....	8	4	0	0	0	0
	Weyburn Beavers	Al-Cup	2	1	0	1	....	....	....	0	....	....	....	....	....
1930-31	Weyburn Beavers	S-SSHL	20	11	0	11	....	....	....	10	....	....	....	....	....
1931-32	Weyburn Beavers	S-SSHL	17	*10	1	11	....	....	....	8	3	1	1	2	4
	Weyburn Beavers	Al-Cup	6	*6	1	*7	....	....	....	16	....	....	....	....	....
1932-33	**Montreal Canadiens**	**NHL**	**2**	**0**	**0**	**0**	**0**	**0**	**0**	**0**	....	....	....	....	....
	Quebec Beavers	Can-Am	12	0	0	0	....	....	....	4	....	....	....	....	....
1933-34	Vancouver Lions	NWHL	27	4	3	7	....	....	....	10	7	2	0	2	4
1934-35	Calgary Tigers	NWHL	14	12	2	14	....	....	....	2	....	....	....	....	....
1935-36	Calgary Tigers	NWHL	24	9	4	13	....	....	....	6	....	....	....	....	....
	Portland Buckaroos	NWHL	13	4	3	7	....	....	....	6	....	....	....	....	....
1936-37	Vancouver–Spokane	PCHL	32	6	10	16	....	....	....	16	6	*3	1	4	5
1937-38	Spokane Clippers	PCHL	42	6	7	13	....	....	....	19	....	....	....	....	....
1938-39	Portland Buckaroos	PCHL	45	21	19	40	....	....	....	49	5	2	1	3	6
1939-40	Portland Buckaroos	PCHL	37	14	9	23	....	....	....	26	5	2	0	2	6
1940-41	Portland–Seattle	PCHL	46	11	16	27	....	....	....	16	2	1	1	2	0
1941-42			DID NOT PLAY												
1942-43	Kingston Frontenacs	LOVHL	2	0	0	0	....	....	....	0	....	....	....	....	....
1943-44	Vancouver St. Regis	NWIHL	3	0	0	0	....	....	....	0	....	....	....	....	....
	Portland Oilers	NWIHL	15	15	10	25	....	....	....	2	6	*11	1	*12	6
	NHL Totals		**2**	**0**	**0**	**0**	**0**	**0**	**0**	**0**	....	....	....	....	....

• McCORD, Bob

— see page 1396

• McCORMACK, John

John Ronald "Goose"

C – L. 6', 185 lbs. b: Edmonton, Alta., 8/2/1925.

Season	Club	League	GP	G	A	Pts	AG	AA	APts	PIM	GP	G	A	Pts	PIM
1943-44	St. Michael's Majors	OHA-Jr.	24	18	30	48	....	....	....	6	25	15	24	39	14
1944-45	St. Michael's Majors	OHA-Jr.	15	18	23	41	....	....	....	6	9	10	*11	*21	8
	Toronto Tip Tops	TIHL	1	1	1	2	....	....	....	0	....	....	....	....	....
	St. Michael's Majors	M-Cup	14	8	16	24	....	....	....	8	....	....	....	....	....
1945-46	Tulsa Oilers	USHL	45	9	32	41	....	....	....	11	13	4	*12	*16	0
1946-47	Leaside Lions	OMHA	DID NOT PLAY – COACHING												
1947-48	**Toronto Maple Leafs**	**NHL**	**3**	**0**	**1**	**1**	**0**	**1**	**1**	**0**	....	....	....	....	....
	Toronto Marlboros	OHA-Sr.	33	28	*49	*77	....	....	....	10	5	0	4	4	2
1948-49	**Toronto Maple Leafs**	**NHL**	**1**	**0**	**0**	**0**	**0**	**0**	**0**	**0**	....	....	....	....	....
	Toronto Marlboros	OHA-Sr.	37	21	18	39	....	....	....	10	10	5	*11	16	2
	Toronto Marlboros	Al-Cup	13	7	8	15	....	....	....	0	....	....	....	....	....
1949-50	Toronto Marlboros	OHA-Sr.	29	17	33	50	....	....	....	14	....	....	....	....	....
	Toronto Maple Leafs	**NHL**	**34**	**6**	**5**	**11**	**8**	**6**	**14**	**0**	**6**	**1**	**0**	**1**	**0**
♦1950-51	**Toronto Maple Leafs**	**NHL**	**46**	**6**	**7**	**13**	**8**	**9**	**17**	**2**	....	....	....	....	....
	Pittsburgh Hornets	AHL	17	4	12	16	....	....	....	0	13	6	9	15	2
1951-52	**Montreal Canadiens**	**NHL**	**54**	**2**	**10**	**12**	**3**	**12**	**15**	**4**	....	....	....	....	....
	Buffalo Bisons	AHL	8	5	3	8	....	....	....	0	....	....	....	....	....
♦1952-53	**Montreal Canadiens**	**NHL**	**59**	**1**	**9**	**10**	**1**	**11**	**12**	**9**	**9**	**0**	**0**	**0**	**0**
1953-54	**Montreal Canadiens**	**NHL**	**51**	**5**	**10**	**15**	**7**	**12**	**19**	**12**	**7**	**0**	**1**	**1**	**0**
	Buffalo Bisons	AHL	16	7	15	22	....	....	....	0	....	....	....	....	....
1954-55	**Chicago Black Hawks**	**NHL**	**63**	**5**	**7**	**12**	**6**	**8**	**14**	**8**	....	....	....	....	....
1955-56	Edmonton Flyers	WHL	37	6	9	15	....	....	....	6	....	....	....	....	....
	NHL Totals		**311**	**25**	**49**	**74**	**33**	**59**	**92**	**35**	**22**	**1**	**1**	**2**	**0**

Played in NHL All-Star Game (1953)

• Missed entire 1946-47 season to commence seminary studies, October 9, 1946. Signed as a free agent by **Toronto**, January 11, 1950. Traded to **Montreal** by **Toronto** for cash, September 23, 1951. Claimed by **Chicago** from **Montreal** in Intra-League Draft, September 15, 1954. Traded to **Detroit** by **Chicago** with Dave Creighton, Gord Hollingworth and Jerry Toppazzini for Tony Leswick, Glen Skov, John Wilson and Benny Woit, May 27, 1955.

• McCREARY, Bill Sr.

— see page 1397

• McCREARY, Keith

— see page 1398

• McCREEDY, Johnny

RW – R. 5'9", 160 lbs. b: Winnipeg, Man., 3/23/1911 d: 12/7/1979.

Season	Club	League	GP	G	A	Pts	AG	AA	APts	PIM	GP	G	A	Pts	PIM
			REGULAR SEASON								PLAYOFFS				
1934-35	East Kildonan Northstars	MAHA	STATISTICS NOT AVAILABLE												
1935-36	Winnipeg Monarchs	MJHL	14	10	*11	21	....	....	....	6	....	....	....	....	....
1936-37	Winnipeg Monarchs	MJHL	9	7	9	16	....	....	....	2	8	*11	1	*12	4
	Winnipeg Monarchs	M-Cup	9	*13	5	18	....	....	....	4	....	....	....	....	....
1937-38	Trail Smoke Eaters	WKHL	20	19	17	36	....	....	....	46	5	2	*7	9	0
	Trail Smoke Eaters	Al-Cup	12	4	2	6	....	....	....	15	....	....	....	....	....
1938-39	Trail Smoke Eaters	X-Games	PLAYED EXHIBITION SEASON ONLY												
1939-40	Kirkland Lake Blue Devils	X-games	15	8	3	11	....	....	....	6	....	....	....	....	....
	Kirkland Lake Blue Devils	Al-Cup	20	*20	6	26	....	....	....	17	....	....	....	....	....
	Canada	WEC-A	7	4	3	7	....	....	....	....	....	....	....	....	....
1940-41	Sydney Millionaires	CBSHL	39	31	26	57	....	....	....	50	4	1	4	5	4
	Sydney Millionaires	Al-Cup	17	11	16	27	....	....	....	18	....	....	....	....	....
♦1941-42	**Toronto Maple Leafs**	**NHL**	**47**	**15**	**8**	**23**	**20**	**9**	**29**	**14**	**13**	**4**	**3**	**7**	**6**
1942-43	Toronto RCAF	TIHL	12	9	13	22	....	....	....	12	7	7	6	13	4
	Toronto RCAF	Al-Cup	4	1	2	3	....	....	....	5	....	....	....	....	....
1943-44	Brantford RCAF	OHA-Sr.	MILITARY SERVICE												
♦1944-45	**Toronto Maple Leafs**	**NHL**	**17**	**2**	**4**	**6**	**2**	**5**	**7**	**11**	**8**	**0**	**0**	**0**	**10**
	NHL Totals		**64**	**17**	**12**	**29**	**22**	**14**	**36**	**25**	**21**	**4**	**3**	**7**	**16**

• McCULLEY, Bob

Robert Keith

RW/D – R. 6'2", 210 lbs. b: Stratford, Ont., 2/8/1914.

Season	Club	League	GP	G	A	Pts	AG	AA	APts	PIM	GP	G	A	Pts	PIM
1929-30	Stratford Midgets	OHA-Jr.	6	6	1	7	....	....	....	12	2	1	0	1	8
1930-31	Stratford Midgets	OHA-Jr.	5	3	1	4	....	....	....	4	2	3	0	3	4
	Stratford Midgets	M-Cup	2	3	0	3	....	....	....	4	....	....	....	....	....
1931-32	Oshawa Generals	OHA-Jr.	STATISTICS NOT AVAILABLE												
1932-33	Providence Reds	Can-Am	41	7	2	9	....	....	....	38	2	0	0	0	0
1933-34	Providence Reds	Can-Am	2	0	0	0	....	....	....	0	....	....	....	....	....
	New Haven Eagles	Can-Am	38	13	3	16	....	....	....	24	....	....	....	....	....
1934-35	**Montreal Canadiens**	**NHL**	**1**	**0**	**0**	**0**	**0**	**0**	**0**	**0**	....	....	....	....	....
	New Haven Eagles	Can-Am	7	1	2	3	....	....	....	11	....	....	....	....	....
	Quebec Castors	Can-Am	8	1	2	3	....	....	....	4	....	....	....	....	....
	Boston Cubs	Can-Am	19	6	5	11	....	....	....	4	3	0	0	0	2
1935-36	Boston Cubs	Can-Am	42	14	7	21	....	....	....	20	....	....	....	....	....
	New Haven Eagles	Can-Am	5	4	1	5	....	....	....	2	....	....	....	....	....
1936-37	New Haven Eagles	IAHL	4	0	0	0	....	....	....	4	....	....	....	....	....
	Providence Reds	IAHL	4	1	2	3	....	....	....	6	....	....	....	....	....
	Springfield Indians	IAHL	33	7	7	14	....	....	....	10	5	1	2	3	2
1937-38	Springfield Indians	IAHL	8	0	0	0	....	....	....	4	....	....	....	....	....
	New Haven Eagles	IAHL	39	4	2	6	....	....	....	19	2	0	1	1	2
1938-39	New Haven Eagles	IAHL	53	13	12	25	....	....	....	10	....	....	....	....	....
1939-40	New Haven Eagles	IAHL	51	8	8	16	....	....	....	32	3	0	1	1	6
1940-41	Philadelphia Rockets	AHL	54	2	4	6	....	....	....	52	....	....	....	....	....
1941-42	Minneapolis Millers	AHA	17	2	2	4	....	....	....	10	....	....	....	....	....
	Providence Reds	AHL	20	1	3	4	....	....	....	9	....	....	....	....	....
	NHL Totals		**1**	**0**	**0**	**0**	**0**	**0**	**0**	**0**	....	....	....	....	....

Signed as a free agent by **Montreal Canadiens**, October 23, 1932. Traded to **Boston** (Can-Am) by **Montreal Canadiens** for Sheldon Buckles, December 2, 1934. Traded to **Providence** (AHL) by **Boston** for cash, October 7, 1936. Traded to **New Haven** (AHL) by **Springfield** (AHL) for Orville Heximer, December 1, 1937. Traded to **Cleveland** (AHL) by **NY Rangers** for cash, September 11, 1941. • Assigned to **Minneapolis** (AHA) by **Cleveland** (AHL), October, 1941. Signed as a free agent by **Providence** (AHL) after being released by **Minneapolis** (AHA), January 19, 1942.

• McCURRY, Duke

Francis Joseph

LW – L. 5'8", 160 lbs. b: Toronto, Ont., 6/13/1900 d: 11/8/1965.

Season	Club	League	GP	G	A	Pts	AG	AA	APts	PIM	GP	G	A	Pts	PIM
1917-18	Toronto De LaSalle	OHA-Jr.	STATISTICS NOT AVAILABLE												
1918-19	Parkdale Canoe Club	OHA-Jr.	STATISTICS NOT AVAILABLE												
1919-20	Toronto Canoe Club	OHA-Jr.	6	4	3	7	....	....	....	....	....	....	....	....	....
	Toronto Canoe Club	M-Cup	12	21	11	32	....	....	....	....	....	....	....	....	....
1920-21	Timmins AC	NOHA	STATISTICS NOT AVAILABLE												
1921-22	Timmins AC	NOHA	STATISTICS NOT AVAILABLE												
1922-23	Toronto Argonauts	OHA-Sr.	12	7	6	13	....	....	....	....	....	....	....	....	....
1923-24	Pittsburgh Yellowjackets	USAHA	20	6	0	6	....	....	....	....	13	4	0	4	....
1924-25	Pittsburgh Yellowjackets	USAHA	37	6	0	6	....	....	....	....	8	2	0	2	....
1925-26	**Pittsburgh Pirates**	**NHL**	**36**	**13**	**4**	**17**	**22**	**26**	**48**	**32**	**2**	**0**	**2**	**2**	**4**
1926-27	**Pittsburgh Pirates**	**NHL**	**33**	**3**	**3**	**6**	**5**	**16**	**21**	**23**	....	....	....	....	....
1927-28	**Pittsburgh Pirates**	**NHL**	**44**	**5**	**3**	**8**	**10**	**17**	**27**	**60**	**2**	**0**	**0**	**0**	**0**
1928-29	**Pittsburgh Pirates**	**NHL**	**35**	**0**	**1**	**1**	**0**	**7**	**7**	**4**	....	....	....	....	....
1929-30			DID NOT PLAY												
1930-31	Pittsburgh Yellowjackets	IHL	36	8	3	11	....	....	....	42	6	0	0	0	0
	NHL Totals		**148**	**21**	**11**	**32**	**37**	**66**	**103**	**119**	**4**	**0**	**2**	**2**	**4**

Signed as a free agent by **Pittsburgh**, September 26, 1925. Traded to **Montreal Maroons** by **Pittsburgh** for Albert Holway, September 30, 1929. Refused to report and sat out entire season. Signed as a free agent by **Pittsburgh** (IHL), November 20, 1930.

• McDONAGH, Bill

William James

LW – L. 5'9", 150 lbs. b: Rouyn, Que., 4/30/1928.

Season	Club	League	GP	G	A	Pts	AG	AA	APts	PIM	GP	G	A	Pts	PIM
1947-48	St. Michael's Buzzers	OHA-B	STATISTICS NOT AVAILABLE												
	St. Michael's Majors	OHA-Jr.	3	0	0	0	....	....	....	0	....	....	....	....	....
1948-49	Detroit Brights	IHL	29	19	20	39	....	....	....	25	2	1	0	1	0
1949-50	**New York Rangers**	**NHL**	**4**	**0**	**0**	**0**	**0**	**0**	**0**	**2**	....	....	....	....	....
	New Haven Ramblers	AHL	61	7	10	17	....	....	....	8	....	....	....	....	....
1950-51	St. Paul Saints	USHL	64	17	17	34	....	....	....	39	4	1	0	1	2
1951-52	Shawinigan Cataracts	QMHL	46	3	9	12	....	....	....	8	....	....	....	....	....
1952-53	Sydney Millionaires	MMHL	82	28	35	63	....	....	....	50	6	2	1	3	12
1953-54	Fredericton Capitals	NBSHL	49	19	26	45	....	....	....	61	15	7	7	14	21
	Fredericton Capitals	Al-Cup	8	3	7	10	....	....	....	6	....	....	....	....	....
1954-55	Fredericton Capitals	NBSHL	51	16	38	54	....	....	....	70	6	1	5	6	2
1955-56	Fredericton Capitals	NBSHL	60	21	49	70	....	....	....	46	9	2	5	7	2
1956-57	U. of New Brunswick	YCHL	6	11	9	20	....	....	....	0	2	0	1	1	2
	Fredericton Capitals	NBSHL	DID NOT PLAY – SUSPENDED												
	Fredericton Capitals	Al-Cup	4	6	6	12	....	....	....	5	....	....	....	....	....
1957-58	Sudbury Wolves	OHA-Sr.	16	3	5	8	....	....	....	6	....	....	....	....	....
	NHL Totals		**4**	**0**	**0**	**0**	**0**	**0**	**0**	**2**	....	....	....	....	....

IHL Northern Division Second All-Star Team (1949) • NBSHL First All-Star Team (1954)

Traded to **NY Rangers** by **Detroit** for cash, June, 1949. • Suspended for entire 1956-57 regular season by **Fredericton** (NBSHL) for refusing to play game vs. Saint John, March 7, 1956.

• McDONALD, Ab

— see page 1399

• McDONALD, Bucko

Wilfred Kennedy

D – L. 5'10", 205 lbs. b: Fergus, Ont., 10/31/1914 d: 7/21/1991.

Season	Club	League	GP	G	A	Pts	AG	AA	APts	PIM	GP	G	A	Pts	PIM
1933-34	Buffalo Bisons	IHL	41	3	1	4	....	....	....	14	6	1	0	1	0
1934-35	Buffalo Bisons	IHL	20	3	2	5	....	....	....	20	....	....	....	....	....
	Detroit Red Wings	**NHL**	**15**	**1**	**2**	**3**	**2**	**3**	**5**	**8**	....	....	....	....	....
	Detroit Olympics	IHL	12	3	1	4	....	....	....	8	....	....	....	....	....
♦1935-36	**Detroit Red Wings**	**NHL**	**47**	**4**	**6**	**10**	**8**	**11**	**19**	**32**	**7**	**3**	**0**	**3**	**10**
	Detroit Olympics	IHL	1	0	0	0	....	....	....	0	....	....	....	....	....
♦1936-37	**Detroit Red Wings**	**NHL**	**47**	**3**	**5**	**8**	**5**	**9**	**14**	**20**	**10**	**0**	**0**	**0**	**2**
1937-38	**Detroit Red Wings**	**NHL**	**47**	**3**	**7**	**10**	**5**	**11**	**16**	**14**	....	....	....	....	....
1938-39	**Detroit Red Wings**	**NHL**	**14**	**0**	**0**	**0**	**0**	**0**	**0**	**2**	....	....	....	....	....
	Toronto Maple Leafs	**NHL**	**33**	**3**	**3**	**6**	**5**	**5**	**10**	**20**	**10**	**0**	**0**	**0**	**4**
1939-40	**Toronto Maple Leafs**	**NHL**	**34**	**2**	**5**	**7**	**3**	**8**	**11**	**13**	**1**	**0**	**0**	**0**	**0**
1940-41	**Toronto Maple Leafs**	**NHL**	**31**	**6**	**11**	**17**	**9**	**16**	**25**	**12**	**7**	**2**	**0**	**2**	**2**
	Providence Reds	AHL	17	3	4	7	....	....	....	26	....	....	....	....	....
♦1941-42	**Toronto Maple Leafs**	**NHL**	**48**	**2**	**19**	**21**	**3**	**23**	**26**	**24**	**9**	**0**	**1**	**1**	**2**
1942-43	**Toronto Maple Leafs**	**NHL**	**40**	**2**	**11**	**13**	**2**	**10**	**12**	**39**	**6**	**1**	**0**	**1**	**4**
	Providence Reds	AHL	9	0	5	5	....	....	....	2	....	....	....	....	....
1943-44	**Toronto Maple Leafs**	**NHL**	**9**	**2**	**4**	**6**	**2**	**3**	**5**	**8**	....	....	....	....	....
	New York Rangers	**NHL**	**41**	**5**	**6**	**11**	**4**	**5**	**9**	**14**	....	....	....	....	....
1944-45	**New York Rangers**	**NHL**	**40**	**2**	**9**	**11**	**2**	**10**	**12**	**0**	....	....	....	....	....
1945-46	Hull Volants	QSHL	39	13	15	28	....	....	....	6	....	....	....	....	....
1946-47	Sundridge Beavers	NBHL	STATISTICS NOT AVAILABLE												
1947-48	Sundridge Beavers	NBHL	16	20	21	41	....	....	....	....	3	2	2	4	4
1948-49	Sundridge Beavers	NBHL	22	21	16	37	....	....	....	4	3	4	1	5	6
	NHL Totals		**446**	**35**	**88**	**123**	**50**	**114**	**164**	**206**	**50**	**6**	**1**	**7**	**24**

NHL Second All-Star Team (1942)

Traded to **Detroit** by **Buffalo** (IHL) for Gamey Lederman and Lloyd Gross, January 9, 1935. Traded to **Toronto** by **Detroit** for Bill Thomson and $10,000, December 19, 1938. Traded to **NY Rangers** by **Toronto** for cash, November, 1943.

• McDONALD, Butch

Byron Russell

LW/C – L. 6', 185 lbs. b: Moose Jaw, Sask., 11/21/1916.

Season	Club	League	GP	G	A	Pts	AG	AA	APts	PIM	GP	G	A	Pts	PIM
1934-35	Moose Jaw Canucks	S-SJHL	6	4	4	8	....	....	....	2	....	....	....	....	....
	Moose Jaw Canucks	M-Cup	6	4	4	8	....	....	....	12	....	....	....	....	....
1935-36			STATISTICS NOT AVAILABLE												
1936-37	Pittsburgh Yellowjackets	EAHL	47	16	20	36	....	....	....	30	....	....	....	....	....
1937-38	New Haven Eagles	IAHL	11	0	1	1	....	....	....	0	....	....	....	....	....
	Pittsburgh Hornets	IAHL	31	0	1	1	....	....	....	2	1	0	0	0	0
1938-39	Minneapolis Millers	AHA	48	31	42	73	....	....	....	21	4	0	1	1	0
	Pittsburgh Hornets	IAHL	1	1	0	1	....	....	....	0	....	....	....	....	....
1939-40	**Detroit Red Wings**	**NHL**	**37**	**1**	**6**	**7**	**2**	**9**	**11**	**2**	**5**	**0**	**2**	**2**	**10**
	Indianapolis Capitols	IAHL	15	4	13	17	....	....	....	4	....	....	....	....	....
1940-41	Indianapolis Capitols	AHL	51	13	30	43	....	....	....	2	....	....	....	....	....
1941-42	Moose Jaw Canucks	S-SSHL	30	13	17	30	....	....	....	8	9	2	7	9	2
1942-43	Regina Army Caps	S-SSHL	21	20	31	51	....	....	....	2	1	0	0	0	0
1943-44			MILITARY SERVICE												
1944-45	**Detroit Red Wings**	**NHL**	**3**	**1**	**1**	**2**	**1**	**1**	**2**	**0**	....	....	....	....	....
	Indianapolis Capitols	AHL	29	8	25	33	....	....	....	2	....	....	....	....	....
	Chicago Black Hawks	**NHL**	**26**	**6**	**13**	**19**	**6**	**15**	**21**	**0**	....	....	....	....	....
1945-46	Kansas City Pla-Mors	USHL	51	*39	*60	*99	....	....	....	5	12	2	8	10	0
1946-47	Kansas City Pla-Mors	USHL	51	16	*52	68	....	....	....	....	12	2	6	8	0
1947-48	Calgary Stampeders	WCSHL	47	21	*47	68	....	....	....	14	11	4	5	9	5
1948-49	Calgary Stampeders	WCSHL	47	17	*43	60	....	....	....	12	4	1	1	2	6
1949-50	Calgary Stampeders	WCSHL	10	4	7	11	....	....	....	0	....	....	....	....	....
1950-51	Calgary Stampeders	WCSHL	DID NOT PLAY – COACHING												
	NHL Totals		**66**	**8**	**20**	**28**	**9**	**25**	**34**	**2**	**5**	**0**	**2**	**2**	**10**

AHA First All-Star Team (1939) • USHL First All-Star Team (1946)

Signed as a free agent by **Detroit** (Pittsburgh-IAHL), October 30, 1937. Traded to **Chicago** by **Detroit** with Don Grosso and Cully Simon for Earl Seibert and future considerations (Fido Purpur, January 4, 1945), January 2, 1945.

• McDONALD, Jack

John Patrick

LW. , b: unknown d: 1/24/1958.

Season	Club	League	GP	G	A	Pts	AG	AA	APts	PIM	GP	G	A	Pts	PIM
1905-06	Quebec Crescents	QICHL	STATISTICS NOT AVAILABLE												
	Quebec Bulldogs	ECAHA	3	0	0	0	....	....	....	0	....	....	....	....	....
	New Glasgow Cubs	St-Cup	2	2	0	2	....	....	....	....	....	....	....	....	....
1906-07	Quebec Bulldogs	ECAHA	9	10	0	10	....	....	....	13	....	....	....	....	....
1907-08	Quebec Bulldogs	ECAHA	9	9	0	9	....	....	....	14	....	....	....	....	....
1908-09	Quebec Bulldogs	ECHA	9	8	0	8	....	....	....	17	....	....	....	....	....
1909-10	Quebec Bulldogs	CHA	3	9	0	9	....	....	....	3	....	....	....	....	....
	Waterloo Colts	OPHL	15	22	0	22	....	....	....	18	....	....	....	....	....
1910-11	Quebec Bulldogs	NHA	16	14	0	14	....	....	....	25	....	....	....	....	....
♦1911-12	Quebec Bulldogs	NHA	17	18	0	18	....	....	....	0	2	*9	0	*9	0
	NHA All-Stars	X-Games	2	1	0	1	....	....	....	0	....	....	....	....	....
1912-13	Vancouver Millionaires	PCHA	16	11	4	15	....	....	....	9	....	....	....	....	....
1913-14	Toronto Ontarios	NHA	20	27	8	35	....	....	....	12	....	....	....	....	....
1914-15	Quebec Bulldogs	NHA	19	9	8	17	....	....	....	17	....	....	....	....	....
1915-16	Quebec Bulldogs	NHA	20	9	5	14	....	....	....	10	....	....	....	....	....
1916-17	Quebec Bulldogs	NHA	19	13	8	21	....	....	....	0	....	....	....	....	....
1917-18	**Montreal Wanderers**	**NHL**	**4**	**3**	**1**	**4**	**4**	**4**	**8**	**3**	....	....	....	....	....
	Montreal Canadiens	**NHL**	**8**	**9**	**1**	**10**	**11**	**4**	**15**	**12**	**2**	**1**	**0**	**1**	**0**
1918-19	**Montreal Canadiens**	**NHL**	**18**	**8**	**4**	**12**	**14**	**22**	**36**	**9**	**5**	**0**	**1**	**1**	**3**
	Montreal Canadiens	St-Cup	5	1	1	2	....	....	....	3	....	....	....	....	....
1919-20	**Quebec Bulldogs**	**NHL**	**24**	**6**	**7**	**13**	**7**	**24**	**31**	**4**	....	....	....	....	....

Season	Club	League	REGULAR SEASON GP	G	A	Pts	AG	AA	APts	PIM	PLAYOFFS GP	G	A	Pts	PIM
1920-21	**Montreal Canadiens**	**NHL**	**6**	**0**	**1**	**1**	**0**	**4**	**4**	**0**					
	Toronto St. Pats	**NHL**	**6**	**0**	**0**	**0**	**0**	**0**	**0**	**2**					
1921-22	**Montreal Canadiens**	**NHL**	**3**	**0**	**0**	**0**	**0**	**0**	**0**	**0**					
	NHL Totals		**69**	**26**	**14**	**40**	**36**	**58**	**94**	**30**	**7**	**1**	**1**	**2**	**3**
	Other Major League Totals		172	150	33	183				135	2	9	0	9	0

Traded to **Quebec** (NHA) by **Toronto** (NHA) for Tommy Smith, December 21, 1914. Claimed by **Montreal Wanderers** from **Quebec** in Dispersal Draft, November 26, 1917. Claimed by **Montreal Canadiens** from **Montreal Wanderers** in Dispersal Draft, January 4, 1918. Transferred to **Quebec** by **Montreal Canadiens** when Quebec franchise returned to NHL, November 25, 1919. Transferred to **Hamilton** after **Quebec** franchise relocated, November 2, 1920. Traded to **Montreal Canadiens** by **Hamilton** with Harry Mummery and Dave Ritchie for Goldie Prodgers, Joe Matte, Jack Coughlin and loan of Billy Coutu for 1920-21 season, November 27, 1920. Loaned to **Toronto St. Pats** by **Montreal Canadiens** for the remainder of the 1920-21 season, February 11, 1921.

• McDONALD, Jack John Albert

RW – R. 5'11", 205 lbs. b: Swan River, Man., 11/24/1921 d: 1/24/1958.

Season	Club	League	GP	G	A	Pts	AG	AA	APts	PIM	GP	G	A	Pts	PIM
1938-39	Winnipeg St. John's	WJrHL	STATISTICS NOT AVAILABLE												
1939-40	Portage Terriers	MJHL	24	21	5	26				12	4	4	0	4	2
1940-41	Portage Terriers	MJHL	19	29	11	40				6	6	5	3	8	5
1941-42	Portage Terriers	MJHL	17	29	17	46				18	5	6	6	12	5
	Portage Terriers	M-Cup	10	*18	8	26				11					
1942-43	Flin Flon Bombers	N-SSHL	24	16	14	30				16	8	8	2	10	4
1943-44	**New York Rangers**	**NHL**	**43**	**10**	**9**	**19**	**9**	**8**	**17**	**6**					
1944-45			REINSTATED AS AN AMATEUR												
1945-46	Edmonton Flyers	WCSHL	26	24	18	42				2	6	3	1	4	2
1946-47	Portland Eagles	PCHL	60	34	26	60				40	14	7	5	12	6
1947-48	Winnipeg Eagles	X-Games	15	8	6	14				12					
1948-49	Winnipeg Eagles	X-Games	STATISTICS NOT AVAILABLE												
1949-50	New Westminster Royals	PCHL	6	0	0	0				0					
	NHL Totals		**43**	**10**	**9**	**19**	**9**	**8**	**17**	**6**					

• McDONALD, Robert

RW – L. 5'10", 170 lbs. b: Toronto, Ont., 1/4/1923.

Season	Club	League	GP	G	A	Pts	AG	AA	APts	PIM	GP	G	A	Pts	PIM
1940-41	St. James Canadians	MAHA	STATISTICS NOT AVAILABLE												
1941-42	St. James Canadians	MJHL	18	23	14	37				34	6	10	0	10	8
	Detroit Mansfields	MOHL	2	1	1	2				0					
1942-43	Windsor Army	WNDHL	11	8	10	18				10	3	1	0	1	2
1943-44	**New York Rangers**	**NHL**	**1**	**0**	**0**	**0**	**0**	**0**	**0**	**0**					
	New York Rovers	EAHL	41	15	36	51				12	11	5	8	13	0
1944-45	New York Rovers	EAHL	42	13	21	34				14	12	4	9	13	0
1945-46	Windsor Godfredson	IHL	15	10	*25	*35				10	2	0	1	1	0
1946-47	Detroit Auto Club	IHL	27	21	26	47				38					
1947-48	Detroit Brights	IHL	27	14	11	25				4	2	0	1	1	4
1948-49	Detroit Brights	IHL	18	0	4	4				0					
	NHL Totals		**1**	**0**	**0**	**0**	**0**	**0**	**0**	**0**					

EAHL Second All-Star Team (1944)

• McDONNELL, Moylan

D – R. 5'9", 145 lbs. b: Stony Mountain, Man., 8/27/1889 Deceased.

Season	Club	League	GP	G	A	Pts	AG	AA	APts	PIM	GP	G	A	Pts	PIM
1909-10	New York Crescents	AHAA	8	7	0	7									
1910-11	New York Crescents	AHAA	STATISTICS NOT AVAILABLE												
1911-12	Edmonton Maritimers	ASHL	6	5	0	5				6	4	1	0	1	10
1912-13	New York Irish Americans	AHAA	8	4	0	4				12					
1913-14	New York Irish Americans	AHAA	4	2	0	2									
1914-15	New York Hockey Club	AHAA	7	7	0	7									
1915-16	New York Hockey Club	AAHL	8	6	0	6									
1916/20			MILITARY SERVICE												
1920-21	**Hamilton Tigers**	**NHL**	**22**	**1**	**2**	**3**	**1**	**8**	**9**	**2**					
	NHL Totals		**22**	**1**	**2**	**3**	**1**	**8**	**9**	**2**					

AHAA First All-Star Team (1914, 1915) • AAHL Second All-Star Team (1916)

• Missed majority of 1913-14 season recovering from arm injury suffered in game vs. NY Crescents, February 6, 1914. Signed as a free agent by **Hamilton**, December 21, 1920.

• McFADDEN, Jim James Alexander

C – L. 5'7", 178 lbs. b: Belfast, Ireland, 4/15/1920.

Season	Club	League	GP	G	A	Pts	AG	AA	APts	PIM	GP	G	A	Pts	PIM
1939-40	Carman Beavers	AIHA	STATISTICS NOT AVAILABLE												
	Portland Buckaroos	PCHL	6	2	1	3				6	4	3	1	4	0
1940-41	Portland Buckaroos	PCHL	47	20	14	34				37					
1941-42	Montreal Sr. Canadiens	QSHL	27	8	6	14				12	5	0	1	1	4
1942-43	Winnipeg Army	WNDHL	12	14	10	24				6					
	Port Arthur Navy	Al-Cup	2	2	6	8				4					
1943-44	Winnipeg Army	WNDHL	8	7	2	9				2					
1944-45	Winnipeg Army	WNDHL	17	*20	*21	*41				16	2	0	1	1	2
	Winnipeg Army	Al-Cup	7	3	3	6				6					
1945-46	Ottawa Senators	QSHL	30	25	32	57				57	9	1	8	9	6
1946-47	Ottawa Senators	QSHL	16	17	17	34				2					
	Buffalo Bisons	AHL	31	19	15	34				37	4	2	0	2	2
	Detroit Red Wings	**NHL**									**4**	**0**	**2**	**2**	**0**
1947-48	**Detroit Red Wings**	**NHL**	**60**	**24**	**24**	**48**	**31**	**32**	**63**	**12**	**10**	**5**	**3**	**8**	**10**
1948-49	**Detroit Red Wings**	**NHL**	**55**	**12**	**20**	**32**	**17**	**28**	**45**	**10**	**8**	**0**	**1**	**1**	**6**
♦1949-50	**Detroit Red Wings**	**NHL**	**68**	**14**	**16**	**30**	**18**	**19**	**37**	**8**	**14**	**2**	**3**	**5**	**8**
1950-51	**Detroit Red Wings**	**NHL**	**70**	**14**	**18**	**32**	**18**	**22**	**40**	**10**	**6**	**0**	**0**	**0**	**2**
1951-52	**Chicago Black Hawks**	**NHL**	**70**	**10**	**24**	**34**	**13**	**30**	**43**	**14**					
1952-53	**Chicago Black Hawks**	**NHL**	**70**	**23**	**21**	**44**	**30**	**25**	**55**	**29**	**7**	**3**	**0**	**3**	**4**
1953-54	**Chicago Black Hawks**	**NHL**	**19**	**3**	**3**	**6**	**4**	**4**	**8**	**6**					
	Calgary Stampeders	WHL	37	27	28	55				16	18	10	12	22	4
	Calgary Stampeders	Ed-Cup	7	3	3	6				0					
1954-55	Calgary Stampeders	WHL	56	31	34	65				36	8	5	4	9	7
1955-56	Calgary Stampeders	WHL	64	23	37	60				26	8	4	4	8	4
1956-57	Calgary Stampeders	WHL	9	3	5	8				8					
1957/62	Miami Rockets	MSEHL	DID NOT PLAY – COACHING												
	NHL Totals		**412**	**100**	**126**	**226**	**131**	**160**	**291**	**89**	**49**	**10**	**9**	**19**	**30**

Won Calder Memorial Trophy (1948) • Played in NHL All-Star Game (1950)

Traded to **Montreal** by **Portland** (PCHL) for cash, December 25, 1940. Loaned to **Ottawa** (QSHL) by **Montreal** with Lude Check as compensation for Montreal's signing of Mike McMahon, October 24, 1945. Traded to **Buffalo** (AHL) by **Montreal** with Butch Stahan for Tom Rockey and cash, October 8, 1946. Traded to **Detroit** by **Buffalo** (AHL) for Les Douglas and Harold Jackson, June, 1947. Traded to **Chicago** by **Detroit** with George Gee, Max McNab, Jimmy Peters Sr., Clare Martin and Rags Raglan for $75,000 and future considerations (Hugh Coflin, October, 1951), August 20, 1951.

• McFADYEN, Don Donald Phillip

C/LW – L. 5'9", 163 lbs. b: Crossfield, Alta., 3/24/1907.

Season	Club	League	GP	G	A	Pts	AG	AA	APts	PIM	GP	G	A	Pts	PIM
1924-25	Calgary Canadians	CCJHL	STATISTICS NOT AVAILABLE												
	Calgary Canadians	M-Cup	2	0	0	0				0					
1925-26	Calgary Canadians	CCJHL	STATISTICS NOT AVAILABLE												
	Calgary Canadians	M-Cup	9	6	7	13				14					
1926/30	Marquette University	NIHA	STATISTICS NOT AVAILABLE												
1930-31	Chicago Shamrocks	AHA	47	21	11	32				60					
1931-32	Chicago Shamrocks	AHA	48	13	*17	30				40	4	0	1	1	4
1932-33	**Chicago Black Hawks**	**NHL**	**48**	**5**	**9**	**14**	**9**	**19**	**28**	**20**					
♦1933-34	**Chicago Black Hawks**	**NHL**	**46**	**1**	**3**	**4**	**2**	**6**	**8**	**20**	**8**	**2**	**2**	**4**	**5**
1934-35	**Chicago Black Hawks**	**NHL**	**37**	**2**	**5**	**7**	**3**	**9**	**12**	**4**	**2**	**0**	**0**	**0**	**0**
1935-36	**Chicago Black Hawks**	**NHL**	**48**	**4**	**16**	**20**	**8**	**30**	**38**	**33**	**1**	**0**	**0**	**0**	**0**
	NHL Totals		**179**	**12**	**33**	**45**	**22**	**64**	**86**	**77**	**11**	**2**	**2**	**4**	**5**

Signed as a free agent by **Chicago** (AHA), June 24, 1930. Traded to **Chicago** by **Chicago** (AHA) for cash, September 2, 1932.

• McFARLANE, Gord Gordon Lester "Red"

RW/D – R. 6'2", 180 lbs. b: Snowflake, Man., 7/18/1901 Deceased.

Season	Club	League	GP	G	A	Pts	AG	AA	APts	PIM	GP	G	A	Pts	PIM
1918-19	Edmonton Victorias	H.S.	STATISTICS NOT AVAILABLE												
1919-20	Calgary Columbus	Big-4	9	1	1	2				2					
1920-21	Calgary Fourex	CCSHL	STATISTICS NOT AVAILABLE												
1921-22	Calgary Fourex	CCSHL	STATISTICS NOT AVAILABLE												
1922-23	Calgary Fourex	CCSHL	STATISTICS NOT AVAILABLE												
1923-24	Seattle Metropolitans	PCHA	28	4	1	5				36	2	1	0	1	2
1924-25	Vancouver Maroons	WCHL	5	1	0	1				0					
	Calgary Tigers	WCHL	21	6	1	7				24	2	0	0	0	0
1925-26	Calgary Tigers	WHL	27	6	1	7				22					
1926-27	**Chicago Black Hawks**	**NHL**	**2**	**0**	**0**	**0**	**0**	**0**	**0**	**0**					
	Springfield Indians	Can-Am	23	5	0	5				26	3	0	0	0	2
1927-28	Kitchener Millionaires	Can-Pro	38	12	3	15				82	5	0	0	0	8
1928-29	Kitchener Dutchmen	Can-Pro	42	7	10	17				102	6	1	0	1	10
1929-30	Cleveland Indians	IHL	42	9	7	16				97	3	0	0	0	4
1930-31	Cleveland Indians	IHL	48	5	9	14				95	6	1	1	2	6
1931-32	Cleveland Indians	IHL	26	5	5	10				44					
1932-33	Cleveland Indians	IHL	40	5	7	12				53					
1933-34	Portland–Vancouver	NWHL	18	2	1	3				8					
1934-35	Vancouver–Calgary	NWHL	28	8	5	13				35	5	0	0	0	4
	Vancouver Lions	L-W-S	5	1	0	1				4					
1935-36	Calgary Tigers	NWHL	40	11	10	21				37					
1936-37			REINSTATED AS AN AMATEUR												
1937-38	Calgary Rangers	ASHL	26	9	16	25				37	6	2	1	3	10
	NHL Totals		**2**	**0**	**0**	**0**	**0**	**0**	**0**	**0**					
	Other Major League Totals		81	17	3	20				82	4	1	0	1	2

Rights traded to **Seattle** (PCHA) by **Calgary** (WCHL) with Bill Binney for Bernie Morris, October 7, 1923. Signed as a free agent by **Seattle**, October, 15, 1923. Signed as a free agent by **Vancouver** (WCHL) after **Seattle** (PCHA) franchise folded, November 10, 1924. Traded to **Calgary** (WCHL) by **Vancouver** (WCHL) for cash, December 21, 1924. Traded to **Chicago** by **Calgary** (WHL) for cash, November 16, 1926. Signed as a free agent by **Calgary** (PrHL), September, 1927. Traded to **Kitchener** (Can-Pro) by **Calgary** (PrHL), October 16, 1927. Traded to **Cleveland** (IHL) by **Kitchener** (IHL) for Bill Cameron and Clarence Wedgewood, October 18, 1929.

• McGIBBON, Irv Irvine John

RW – R. 6', 180 lbs. b: Antigonish, N.S., 10/11/1914 d: 2/1/1981.

Season	Club	League	GP	G	A	Pts	AG	AA	APts	PIM	GP	G	A	Pts	PIM
1934-35	Antigonish Bulldogs	NSAPC	....	21	12	*33				20					
1935-36	Antigonish Bulldogs	NSAPC	....	14	8	22				34					
1936-37	Antigonish Bulldogs	NSAPC	STATISTICS NOT AVAILABLE												
1937-38	Sydney Millionaires	CBSHL	STATISTICS NOT AVAILABLE												
1938-39	Sydney Millionaires	CBSHL	21	17	9	26				36	3	5	1	6	4
	Sydney Millionaires	Al-Cup	6	7	4	11				21					
1939-40	Glace Bay Miners	CBSHL	40	25	15	40				59	4	1	0	1	4
1940-41	Glace Bay Miners	CBSHL	42	16	7	23				75	4	0	0	0	4
1941-42	Montreal Sr. Canadiens	QSHL	24	5	4	9				18					
	Washington Lions	AHL	23	3	9	12				13	2	0	0	0	0
1942-43	**Montreal Canadiens**	**NHL**	**1**	**0**	**0**	**0**	**0**	**0**	**0**	**2**					
	New Glasgow Bombers	NSAPC									8	*4	5	9	9
1943-44			MILITARY SERVICE												
1944-45			MILITARY SERVICE												
1945-46	Pictou Royals	NSAPC	17	13	9	22				19	7	1	*10	*11	2
	Pictou Royals	Al-Cup	4	1	5	6				0					
1946-47	Antigonish Bulldogs	CBSHL	16	16	13	29									
1947-48	Antigonish Bulldogs	NSAPC	....	9	12	21				4					
1948-49	Antigonish Bulldogs	NSAPC	....	33	*43	76				10					
1949-50	Antigonish Bulldogs	NSAPC	DID NOT PLAY – COACHING												
	NHL Totals		**1**	**0**	**0**	**0**	**0**	**0**	**0**	**2**					

Signed as a free agent by **Montreal**, October 16, 1941.

• McGILL, Jack John George

C – L. 6'1", 180 lbs. b: Edmonton, Alta., 9/19/1921.

Season	Club	League	GP	G	A	Pts	AG	AA	APts	PIM	GP	G	A	Pts	PIM
1937-38	Edmonton Athletic Club	EJrHL	1	0	1	1				0					
1938-39	Edmonton Athletic Club	EJrHL	11	12	5	17				11					
	Edmonton Athletic Club	M-Cup	2	3	2	5				0					

			REGULAR SEASON								PLAYOFFS				
Season	Club	League	GP	G	A	Pts	AG	AA	APts	PIM	GP	G	A	Pts	PIM
1939-40	Edmonton Athletic Club	EJrHL	14	....	....	....	....	....	....	34	4	3	3	6	4
	Edmonton Athletic Club	M-Cup	14	14	14	28	....	....	....	16	....	....	....	....	....
1941-42	Boston Olympics	EAHL	36	34	34	68	....	....	....	50	1	1	0	1	2
	Boston Bruins	**NHL**	**13**	**8**	**11**	**19**	**11**	**13**	**24**	**2**	**5**	**4**	**1**	**5**	**6**
1942-43	Ottawa Army Medics	OCHL	11	9	6	15	....	....	....	10	....	....	....	....	....
	Ottawa Commandos	QSHL	10	4	6	10	....	....	....	18	2	0	0	0	15
	Ottawa Commandos	Al-Cup	2	0	2	2	....	....	....	2	....	....	....	....	....
1943-44	Winnipeg RCAF	WNDHL	1	0	0	0	....	....	....	0	....	....	....	....	....
1944-45	**Boston Bruins**	**NHL**	**14**	**4**	**2**	**6**	**4**	**2**	**6**	**0**	**7**	**3**	**3**	**6**	**0**
	Boston Olympics	EAHL	7	4	13	17	....	....	....	22	1	2	0	2	5
1945-46	**Boston Bruins**	**NHL**	**46**	**6**	**14**	**20**	**7**	**20**	**27**	**21**	**10**	**0**	**0**	**0**	**0**
1946-47	**Boston Bruins**	**NHL**	**24**	**5**	**9**	**14**	**6**	**11**	**17**	**19**	**5**	**0**	**0**	**0**	**11**
	Hershey Bears	AHL	36	21	28	49	....	....	....	57	....	....	....	....	....
1947-48	Hershey Bears	AHL	64	21	47	68	....	....	....	82	2	0	2	2	2
1948-49	Houston Huskies	USHL	3	0	3	3	....	....	....	6	....	....	....	....	....
	Buffalo Bisons	AHL	4	0	2	2	....	....	....	0	....	....	....	....	....
	Providence Reds	AHL	49	27	45	72	....	....	....	68	14	2	*12	14	15
1949-50	Providence Reds	AHL	66	24	58	82	....	....	....	67	4	1	2	3	4
1950-51	Providence Reds	AHL	69	29	69	98	....	....	....	58	....	....	....	....	....
1951-52	Providence Reds	AHL	50	19	42	61	....	....	....	36	15	1	4	5	27
1952-53	Edmonton Flyers	WHL	13	1	1	2	....	....	....	30	....	....	....	....	....
1953-54	New Westminster Royals	WHL	7	2	2	4	....	....	....	8	5	1	0	1	4
	NHL Totals		**97**	**23**	**36**	**59**	**28**	**46**	**74**	**42**	**27**	**7**	**4**	**11**	**17**

• Only games played and penalty minute totals available for Edmonton (EJrHL) in 1939-40 season. Traded to **Montreal** (Buffalo-AHL) by **Boston** (Hershey-AHL) for Gerry Brown and Hal Jackson, June 30, 1948. Traded to **Providence** (AHL) by **Buffalo** (AHL) for cash and the rights to Ferdinand Laliberte, October 25, 1948.

• McGILL, Jack

LW – L. 5'10", 150 lbs. b: Ottawa, Ont., 11/3/1910 Deceased.

Season	Club	League	GP	G	A	Pts	AG	AA	APts	PIM	GP	G	A	Pts	PIM
1928-29	Ottawa New Edinburghs	OCHL	15	3	0	3	....	....	....	....	2	0	0	0	0
1929-30	Ottawa New Edinburghs	OCHL	19	3	3	6	....	....	....	12	2	0	0	0	0
1930-31	McGill Redmen	MCHL	12	*6	0	6	....	....	....	29	4	6	0	6	*18
	McGill Redmen	Al-Cup	6	0	2	2	....	....	....	18	....	....	....	....	....
1931-32	McGill Redmen	MCHL	12	5	2	7	....	....	....	36	2	0	0	0	0
1932-33	McGill Redmen	MCHL	12	*12	6	*18	....	....	....	*45	3	0	2	2	8
1933-34	McGill Redmen	MCHL	12	9	8	17	....	....	....	24	4	2	4	6	6
	McGill Redmen	Al-Cup	4	3	1	4	....	....	....	8	....	....	....	....	....
1934-35	**Montreal Canadiens**	**NHL**	**44**	**9**	**1**	**10**	**15**	**2**	**17**	**34**	**2**	**2**	**0**	**2**	**0**
1935-36	**Montreal Canadiens**	**NHL**	**46**	**13**	**7**	**20**	**25**	**13**	**38**	**28**	....	....	....	....	....
1936-37	**Montreal Canadiens**	**NHL**	**44**	**5**	**2**	**7**	**8**	**4**	**12**	**9**	**1**	**0**	**0**	**0**	**0**
	NHL Totals		**134**	**27**	**10**	**37**	**48**	**19**	**67**	**71**	**3**	**2**	**0**	**2**	**0**

• McGREGOR, Sandy

Donald Alexander

RW – R. 5'11", 165 lbs. b: Toronto, Ont., 3/30/1939.

Season	Club	League	GP	G	A	Pts	AG	AA	APts	PIM	GP	G	A	Pts	PIM
1956-57	Toronto Marlboros	OHA-Jr.	1	0	0	0	....	....	....	0	....	....	....	....	....
1957-58	Guelph Biltmores	OHA-Jr.	32	7	10	17	....	....	....	2	....	....	....	....	....
1958-59	Guelph Biltmores	OHA-Jr.	54	34	36	70	....	....	....	26	6	0	4	4	2
1959-60	Trois-Rivieres Lions	EPHL	58	11	6	17	....	....	....	14	7	0	1	1	4
1960-61	Kitchener Beavers	EPHL	62	11	26	37	....	....	....	30	7	1	0	1	4
1961-62	Kitchener Beavers	EPHL	70	24	33	57	....	....	....	65	7	3	0	3	8
1962-63	Baltimore Clippers	AHL	69	21	28	49	....	....	....	22	3	0	0	0	0
1963-64	**New York Rangers**	**NHL**	**2**	**0**	**0**	**0**	**0**	**0**	**0**	**2**	....	....	....	....	....
	Baltimore Clippers	AHL	55	15	12	27	....	....	....	10	....	....	....	....	....
1964-65	Baltimore Clippers	AHL	66	23	16	39	....	....	....	14	5	1	0	1	2
1965-66	Baltimore Clippers	AHL	55	8	8	16	....	....	....	22	....	....	....	....	....
1966-67	Baltimore Clippers	AHL	54	12	16	28	....	....	....	25	7	1	3	4	0
1967-68	Baltimore Clippers	AHL	72	29	27	56	....	....	....	22	....	....	....	....	....
1968-69	Baltimore Clippers	AHL	73	44	19	63	....	....	....	34	4	0	2	2	2
	NHL Totals		**2**	**0**	**0**	**0**	**0**	**0**	**0**	**2**	....	....	....	....	....

Traded to **Providence** (AHL) by **NY Rangers** with Jim Mikol, Marcel Paille and Aldo Guidolin for Ed Giacomin, May 18, 1965. Traded to **Baltimore** (AHL) by **Providence** (AHL) for Buzz Dechamps, May 18, 1965.

• McGUIRE, Mickey

Francis Sheldon

LW – L. 5'10", 158 lbs. b: Gravenhurst, Ont., 7/7/1898 Deceased.

Season	Club	League	GP	G	A	Pts	AG	AA	APts	PIM	GP	G	A	Pts	PIM
1920-21	Timmins Gold Miners	GBHL	....	....	....	....	....	....	....	....	2	*3	0	*3	0
1921-22	Timmins Gold Miners	GBHL	STATISTICS NOT AVAILABLE												
1922-23	Porcupine Gold Miners	GBHL	STATISTICS NOT AVAILABLE												
1923-24	Cleveland Indians	USAHA	20	11	5	16	....	....	....	....	8	1	1	2	....
1924-25	Cleveland Blues	USAHA	38	9	0	9	....	....	....	....	....	....	....	....	....
1925-26	Minneapolis Millers	CHL	29	6	5	11	....	....	....	58	3	2	1	3	8
1926-27	**Pittsburgh Pirates**	**NHL**	**32**	**3**	**0**	**3**	**5**	**0**	**5**	**6**	....	....	....	....	....
1927-28	**Pittsburgh Pirates**	**NHL**	**4**	**0**	**0**	**0**	**0**	**0**	**0**	**0**	....	....	....	....	....
	Windsor Hornets	Can-Pro	33	16	3	19	....	....	....	31	....	....	....	....	....
1928-29	Windsor Bulldogs	Can-Pro	18	3	0	3	....	....	....	4	....	....	....	....	....
	London Panthers	Can-Pro	21	3	1	4	....	....	....	18	....	....	....	....	....
1929-30	Cleveland Indians	IHL	39	11	6	17	....	....	....	30	6	1	0	1	0
1930-31	Cleveland Indians	IHL	4	0	0	0	....	....	....	2	....	....	....	....	....
	Pittsburgh Yellowjackets	IHL	39	7	4	11	....	....	....	31	5	1	1	2	2
1931-32	Cleveland Indians	IHL	18	2	1	3	....	....	....	2	....	....	....	....	....
	NHL Totals		**36**	**3**	**0**	**3**	**5**	**0**	**5**	**6**	....	....	....	....	....

Signed as a free agent by **Pittsburgh**, October 7, 1926. Traded to **Windsor** (Can-Pro) by **Pittsburgh** for cash, December 1, 1927. Traded to **Toronto** (London-Can-Pro) by **Windsor** (Can-Pro) with cash for Jack Arbour, January 15, 1929. Traded to **Toronto** (IHL) by **London** (IHL) for cash, October 29, 1929. Transferred to **Cleveland** (IHL) after **Toronto** (IHL) franchise relocated for the 1929-30 season. Traded to **Pittsburgh** (IHL) by **Cleveland** (IHL) for Cliff McBride, November, 1930.

• McINENLY, Bert

Albert Harold

LW/D – L. 5'9", 160 lbs. b: Quebec City, Que., 5/6/1906 d: 10/15/1993.

Season	Club	League	GP	G	A	Pts	AG	AA	APts	PIM	GP	G	A	Pts	PIM
1924-25	Ottawa Rideaus	OCJHL	5	1	0	1	....	....	....	....	....	....	....	....	....
1925-26	Ottawa Shamrocks	OCHL	15	8	2	10	....	....	....	....	....	....	....	....	....
1926-27	Berlin Mountaineers	NEHL	30	24	9	33	....	....	....	19	....	....	....	....	....
	Ottawa Shamrocks	OCHL	2	2	1	3	....	....	....	....	....	....	....	....	....
1927-28	Ottawa Gunners	OCHL	14	3	3	6	....	....	....	....	....	....	....	....	....
1928-29	Detroit Olympics	Can-Pro	41	5	0	5	....	....	....	....	7	3	0	3	26
1929-30	Detroit Olympics	IHL	42	9	3	12	....	....	....	113	3	1	0	1	4
1930-31	**Detroit Falcons**	**NHL**	**44**	**3**	**5**	**8**	**6**	**15**	**21**	**48**	....	....	....	....	....
1931-32	**Detroit Falcons**	**NHL**	**17**	**0**	**1**	**1**	**0**	**2**	**2**	**16**	....	....	....	....	....
	New York Americans	**NHL**	**30**	**12**	**6**	**18**	**20**	**13**	**33**	**44**	....	....	....	....	....
1932-33	**Ottawa Senators**	**NHL**	**30**	**2**	**2**	**4**	**4**	**4**	**8**	**8**	....	....	....	....	....
1933-34	**Ottawa Senators**	**NHL**	**2**	**0**	**0**	**0**	**0**	**0**	**0**	**0**	....	....	....	....	....
	Boston Bruins	**NHL**	**7**	**0**	**0**	**0**	**0**	**0**	**0**	**4**	....	....	....	....	....
	Boston Cubs	Can-Am	26	4	9	13	....	....	....	36	5	0	1	1	25
1934-35	**Boston Bruins**	**NHL**	**33**	**2**	**1**	**3**	**3**	**2**	**5**	**24**	**4**	**0**	**0**	**0**	**2**
	Boston Cubs	Can-Am	15	2	3	5	....	....	....	29	....	....	....	....	....
1935-36	**Boston Bruins**	**NHL**	**3**	**0**	**0**	**0**	**0**	**0**	**0**	**0**	....	....	....	....	....
	Boston Cubs	Can-Am	40	4	10	14	....	....	....	24	....	....	....	....	....
1936-37	Providence Reds	IAHL	49	5	4	9	....	....	....	61	3	1	1	2	2
1937-38	Springfield Indians	IAHL	37	0	7	7	....	....	....	39	....	....	....	....	....
1938-39	Springfield Indians	IAHL	51	4	7	11	....	....	....	69	3	0	0	0	0
1939-40	Syracuse Stars	IAHL	56	2	13	15	....	....	....	26	....	....	....	....	....
1940-41	Buffalo Bisons	AHL	49	0	10	10	....	....	....	34	....	....	....	....	....
	NHL Totals		**166**	**19**	**15**	**34**	**33**	**36**	**69**	**144**	**4**	**0**	**0**	**0**	**2**

Signed as a free agent by **Detroit**, October 20, 1928. Traded to **NY Americans** by **Detroit** with Tommy Filmore for Hap Emms and Frank Carson, December 29, 1931. Traded to **Ottawa** by **NY Americans** for cash, October 19, 1932. Traded to **Boston** by **Ottawa** for cash, November, 1933. Traded to **Providence** (IAHL) by **Boston** for cash, October 7, 1936. Traded to **Springfield** (IAHL) by **Providence** (IAHL) for cash, November 12, 1937. Traded to **Syracuse** (IAHL) by **Springfield** (IAHL) for cash, September 28, 1939.

• McINTYRE, Jack

John Archibald

D – L. 5'11", 170 lbs. b: Brussels, Ont., 9/8/1930 d: 3/15/1998.

Season	Club	League	GP	G	A	Pts	AG	AA	APts	PIM	GP	G	A	Pts	PIM
1947-48	St. Catharines Teepees	OHA-Jr.	31	4	4	8	....	....	....	49	3	2	2	4	6
1948-49	St. Catharines Teepees	OHA-Jr.	46	14	16	30	....	....	....	64	5	0	3	3	10
1949-50	St. Catharines Teepees	OHA-Jr.	39	30	26	56	....	....	....	21	5	5	3	8	0
	Boston Bruins	**NHL**	**1**	**0**	**1**	**1**	**0**	**1**	**1**	**0**	....	....	....	....	....
	Boston Olympics	EAHL	15	4	5	9	....	....	....	6	5	2	1	3	2
1950-51	Hershey Bears	AHL	64	28	36	64	....	....	....	19	6	1	0	1	0
	Boston Bruins	**NHL**	....	....	....	....	....	....	....	....	**2**	**0**	**0**	**0**	**0**
1951-52	**Boston Bruins**	**NHL**	**52**	**12**	**19**	**31**	**16**	**23**	**39**	**18**	**7**	**1**	**2**	**3**	**2**
	Hershey Bears	AHL	5	1	2	3	....	....	....	2	....	....	....	....	....
1952-53	**Boston Bruins**	**NHL**	**70**	**7**	**15**	**22**	**9**	**18**	**27**	**31**	**10**	**4**	**2**	**6**	**2**
1953-54	Hershey Bears	AHL	44	15	17	32	....	....	....	99	....	....	....	....	....
	Chicago Black Hawks	**NHL**	**23**	**8**	**3**	**11**	**11**	**4**	**15**	**4**	....	....	....	....	....
1954-55	**Chicago Black Hawks**	**NHL**	**65**	**16**	**13**	**29**	**21**	**15**	**36**	**40**	....	....	....	....	....
1955-56	**Chicago Black Hawks**	**NHL**	**46**	**10**	**5**	**15**	**14**	**6**	**20**	**14**	....	....	....	....	....
	Buffalo Bisons	AHL	27	17	19	36	....	....	....	10	5	0	5	5	17
1956-57	**Chicago Black Hawks**	**NHL**	**70**	**18**	**14**	**32**	**23**	**15**	**38**	**32**	....	....	....	....	....
1957-58	**Chicago Black Hawks**	**NHL**	**27**	**0**	**4**	**4**	**0**	**4**	**4**	**10**	....	....	....	....	....
	Detroit Red Wings	**NHL**	**41**	**15**	**7**	**22**	**18**	**7**	**25**	**4**	**4**	**1**	**1**	**2**	**0**
1958-59	**Detroit Red Wings**	**NHL**	**55**	**15**	**14**	**29**	**18**	**14**	**32**	**14**	....	....	....	....	....
	Hershey Bears	AHL	10	7	3	10	....	....	....	2	....	....	....	....	....
1959-60	**Detroit Red Wings**	**NHL**	**49**	**8**	**7**	**15**	**9**	**7**	**16**	**6**	**6**	**1**	**1**	**2**	**0**
	Hershey Bears	AHL	17	7	9	16	....	....	....	4	....	....	....	....	....
1960-61	Hershey Bears	AHL	72	32	25	57	....	....	....	32	8	4	2	6	0
1961-62	Pittsburgh Hornets	AHL	67	25	23	48	....	....	....	32	....	....	....	....	....
1962-63	Edmonton Flyers	WHL	53	25	25	50	....	....	....	20	3	1	2	3	2
	Pittsburgh Hornets	AHL	8	0	1	1	....	....	....	6	....	....	....	....	....
1963-64	Cincinnati Wings	CPHL	12	0	4	4	....	....	....	12	....	....	....	....	....
	Guelph Regals	OHA-Sr.	20	10	27	37	....	....	....	2	5	3	1	4	6
1964-65	Guelph Regals	OHA-Sr.	29	22	20	42	....	....	....	10	7	5	4	9	4
1965-66	Guelph Regals	OHA-Sr.	1	0	0	0	....	....	....	0	....	....	....	....	....
1966-67	Johnstown Jets	EHL	5	0	1	1	....	....	....	4	....	....	....	....	....
1967-68			DID NOT PLAY												
1968-69	Woodstock Athletics	OHA-Sr.	33	11	15	26	....	....	....	22	....	....	....	....	....
	NHL Totals		**499**	**109**	**102**	**211**	**139**	**114**	**253**	**173**	**29**	**7**	**6**	**13**	**4**

Signed as a free agent by **Boston**, March 23, 1949. Traded to **Chicago** by **Boston** for cash, January 21, 1954. Traded to **Detroit** by **Chicago** with Bob Bailey, Nick Mickoski and Hec Lalonde for Earl Reibel, Billy Dea, Lorne Ferguson and Bill Dineen, December 17, 1957. Traded to **Hershey** (AHL) by **Detroit** with Pete Conacher and Marc Reaume for Howie Young, January, 1961.

• McKAY, Doug

Douglas Alvin

LW – L. 5'9", 165 lbs. b: Hamilton, Ont., 5/28/1929.

Season	Club	League	GP	G	A	Pts	AG	AA	APts	PIM	GP	G	A	Pts	PIM
1947-48	Windsor Spitfires	OHA-Jr.	33	18	32	50	....	....	....	25	12	1	4	5	21
	Detroit Brights	IHL	24	8	16	24	....	....	....	68	....	....	....	....	....
1948-49	Detroit Auto Club	IHL	6	2	4	6	....	....	....	26	6	1	3	4	36
	Windsor Spitfires	OHA-Jr.	42	19	29	48	....	....	....	98	4	0	1	1	2
1949-50	Indianapolis Capitols	AHL	65	16	31	47	....	....	....	37	8	2	6	8	*21
♦	**Detroit Red Wings**	**NHL**	....	....	....	....	....	....	....	....	**1**	**0**	**0**	**0**	**0**
1950-51	Indianapolis Capitols	AHL	35	7	8	15	....	....	....	31	....	....	....	....	....
	Omaha Knights	USHL	10	4	5	9	....	....	....	26	10	2	1	3	24
1951-52	Indianapolis Capitols	AHL	50	2	8	10	....	....	....	35	....	....	....	....	....
1952-53	Vernon Canadians	OSHL	16	2	2	4	....	....	....	16	....	....	....	....	....
	Brantford Redmen	OHA-Sr.	11	6	10	16	....	....	....	26	4	1	2	3	4
1953-54	Hamilton Tigers	OHA-Sr.	2	0	0	0	....	....	....	4	....	....	....	....	....
	Vernon Canadians	OSHL	43	5	25	30	....	....	....	51	....	....	....	....	....
1954-55			DID NOT PLAY												
1955-56	Stratford Indians	OHA-Sr.	27	8	14	22	....	....	....	59	7	2	3	5	22
1956-57	Stratford Indians	OHA-Sr.	25	3	12	15	....	....	....	44	3	0	1	1	2
	NHL Totals		....	....	....	....	....	....	....	....	**1**	**0**	**0**	**0**	**0**

• McKENNEY, Don — see page 1409

• McKENNY, Jim — see page 1409

• McKENZIE, John — see page 1410

• McKINNON, Alex
Robert Alexander
RW – R. 5'8", 175 lbs. b: Sault Ste. Marie, Ont., 4/17/1895 d: 10/8/1949.

			REGULAR SEASON								PLAYOFFS				
Season	Club	League	GP	G	A	Pts	AG	AA	APts	PIM	GP	G	A	Pts	PIM
1913-14	Sudbury Wolves	NOHA	4	1	0	1				0					
1914-15	Sudbury Wolves	X-Games	13	15	4	19									
	Sudbury Wolves	Al-Cup	3	1	0	1				0					
1915-16	Sudbury Wolves	X-Games	STATISTICS NOT AVAILABLE												
1916-17	Hamilton 227th Battalion	OHA-Sr.	6	5	0	5									
1917-18			MILITARY SERVICE												
1918-19	Sudbury Wolves	NOHA	STATISTICS NOT AVAILABLE												
1919-20	Sudbury Wolves	NOHA	6	5	*10	*15				10	7	3	*7	10	8
1920-21	Sudbury Wolves	NOHA	9	7	5	12				19					
1921-22	Sudbury Wolves	NOHA	9	10	8	18				18					
1922-23	Sudbury Wolves	NOHA	4	1	2	3				6	2	*2	0	2	2
1923-24	Pittsburgh Yellowjackets	USAHA	20	9	0	9					13	4	0	4	
1924-25	**Hamilton Tigers**	**NHL**	**29**	**8**	**3**	**11**	**14**	**12**	**26**	**47**					
1925-26	**New York Americans**	**NHL**	**35**	**5**	**3**	**8**	**9**	**19**	**28**	**34**					
1926-27	**New York Americans**	**NHL**	**42**	**2**	**1**	**3**	**4**	**5**	**9**	**29**					
1927-28	**New York Americans**	**NHL**	**43**	**3**	**3**	**6**	**6**	**17**	**23**	**71**					
1928-29	**Chicago Black Hawks**	**NHL**	**44**	**1**	**1**	**2**	**3**	**7**	**10**	**56**					
1929-30	Sudbury Wolves	NOHA	DID NOT PLAY – COACHING												
	NHL Totals		**193**	**19**	**11**	**30**	**36**	**60**	**96**	**237**					

NOHA Second All-Star Team (1921) • NOHA First All-Star Team (1922)

Signed as a free agent by **Hamilton**, October 16, 1924. Transferred to **NY Americans** after NHL club purchased **Hamilton** franchise, September 26, 1925. Traded to **Chicago** by **NY Americans** for Charley McVeigh, October 15, 1928.

• McKINNON, John
John Douglas
D – R. 5'8", 170 lbs. b: Guysborough, N.S., 7/15/1902 d: 2/8/1969.

Season	Club	League	GP	G	A	Pts	AG	AA	APts	PIM	GP	G	A	Pts	PIM
1923-24	Cleveland Indians	USAHA	10	0	0	0									
1924-25	Fort Pitt Hornets	USAHA	23	*24	0	*24					8	2	0	2	
1925-26	**Montreal Canadiens**	**NHL**	**2**	**0**	**0**	**0**	**0**	**0**	**0**	**0**					
	Minneapolis Millers	CHL	32	12	8	20				44	3	*3	1	*4	6
1926-27	**Pittsburgh Pirates**	**NHL**	**44**	**13**	**0**	**13**	**23**	**0**	**23**	**21**					
1927-28	**Pittsburgh Pirates**	**NHL**	**43**	**3**	**3**	**6**	**6**	**17**	**23**	**71**	**2**	**0**	**0**	**0**	**4**
1928-29	**Pittsburgh Pirates**	**NHL**	**39**	**1**	**0**	**1**	**3**	**0**	**3**	**44**					
1929-30	**Pittsburgh Pirates**	**NHL**	**41**	**10**	**7**	**17**	**14**	**16**	**30**	**42**					
1930-31	**Philadelphia Quakers**	**NHL**	**39**	**1**	**1**	**2**	**2**	**3**	**5**	**46**					
1931-32	Kansas City Pla-Mors	AHA	48	16	4	20				65	3	0	0	0	2
1932-33	Kansas City Pla-Mors	AHA	32	7	4	11				32	4	0	0	0	2
1933-34	Oklahoma City Warriors	AHA	46	10	4	14				16					
1934-35	Oklahoma City Warriors	AHA	43	3	4	7				15					
1935-36	St. Louis Flyers	AHA	39	1	9	10				12	8	2	2	4	*16
1936-37	St. Louis Flyers	AHA	47	5	9	14				16	6	1	0	1	2
1937-38	St. Louis Flyers	AHA	7	0	0	0				2					
1938-39	St. Louis Flyers	AHA	DID NOT PLAY – COACHING												
	NHL Totals		**208**	**28**	**11**	**39**	**48**	**36**	**84**	**224**	**2**	**0**	**0**	**0**	**4**

Signed as a free agent by **Montreal Canadiens**, November 23, 1925. Traded to **Pittsburgh** by **Montreal Canadiens** for cash, October 28, 1926. Transferred to **Philadelphia** after **Pittsburgh** franchise relocated, October 18, 1930.

• McLEAN, Fred
Frederick Ferguson
D – L. 6'2", 200 lbs. b: Lakeville Corner, N.B., 3/16/1893 Deceased.

Season	Club	League	GP	G	A	Pts	AG	AA	APts	PIM	GP	G	A	Pts	PIM
1908-09	Fredericton Capitals	YCHL	4	4	0	4				5	1	0	0	0	0
1909-10			DID NOT PLAY												
1910-11	Fredericton Capitals	NBSHL	6	3	0	3				13	3	1	0	1	3
1911-12	Fredericton Capitals	NBSHL	2	2	0	2				0	1	1	0	1	0
1912-13	Fredericton Capitals	YCHL	5	11	0	11				5	3	6	0	6	18
	Chatham Ironmen	X-Games	4	3	0	3				0					
1913-14	U. of New Brunswick	MIHL	3	5	0	5				12	1	5	0	5	0
	Fredericton Capitols	X-Games	2	4	0	4				5					
1914-15	Sydney Millionaires	EPHL	8	8	0	8				19					
1915-16	Maine Island Falls	NESHL	STATISTICS NOT AVAILABLE												
1916-17	Boston Arenas	X-Games	STATISTICS NOT AVAILABLE												
1917-18	Sydney Millionaires	CBHL	6	8	7	15				8	6	2	4	6	3
1918-19	Sydney Millionaires	CBHL	STATISTICS NOT AVAILABLE												
1919-20	Glace Bay Miners	CBHL	4	7	4	*11					2	2	2	4	2
	Quebec Bulldogs	**NHL**	**7**	**0**	**0**	**0**	**0**	**0**	**0**	**2**					
1920-21	**Hamilton Tigers**	**NHL**	**1**	**0**	**0**	**0**	**0**	**0**	**0**	**0**					
	Fredericton Capitols	SNBHL	3	2	0	2				10	2	2	0	2	6
1921/30	U. of New Brunswick	MIAU	DID NOT PLAY – COACHING												
1930/33			OUT OF HOCKEY – RETIRED												
1933/37	U. of New Brunswick	MIAU	DID NOT PLAY – COACHING												
	NHL Totals		**8**	**0**	**0**	**0**	**0**	**0**	**0**	**2**					

• Did not play in 1909-10 season as there was no rink available. Signed as a free agent by **Quebec**, February 16, 1920. Transferred to **Hamilton** after **Quebec** franchise relocated, November 2, 1920. • Named as coach of the University of New Brunswick, January 4, 1921.

• McLEAN, Jack
C/RW – R. 5'8", 165 lbs. b: Winnipeg, Man., 1/31/1923.

Season	Club	League	GP	G	A	Pts	AG	AA	APts	PIM	GP	G	A	Pts	PIM
1939-40	Toronto Young Rangers	OHA-Jr.	20	8	10	18				12	2	0	0	0	2
	Toronto People's Credit	TIHL	23	3	6	9				30	3	0	1	1	4
1940-41	Toronto Young Rangers	OHA-Jr.	14	8	7	15				27	5	4	3	7	8
	Toronto Peoples Credit	TIHL	23	3	6	9				30	3	0	1	1	4
1941-42	Toronto Young Rangers	OHA-Jr.	16	17	13	30				22	6	4	4	8	6
	Toronto Peoples Credit	TIHL	13	4	3	7				21	1	0	0	0	2
1942-43	**Toronto Maple Leafs**	**NHL**	**27**	**9**	**8**	**17**	**9**	**7**	**16**	**33**	**6**	**2**	**2**	**4**	**2**
1943-44	**Toronto Maple Leafs**	**NHL**	**32**	**3**	**15**	**18**	**3**	**13**	**16**	**30**	**3**	**0**	**0**	**0**	**6**
♦1944-45	**Toronto Maple Leafs**	**NHL**	**8**	**2**	**1**	**3**	**2**	**1**	**3**	**13**	**4**	**0**	**0**	**0**	**0**
1945-46	Toronto Staffords	OHA-Sr.	11	9	6	15				14	6	2	1	3	6
1946-47	Ottawa Senators	QSHL	24	11	17	28				35	7	0	2	2	8
1947-48	Ottawa Senators	QSHL	41	26	14	40				50	12	3	3	6	16
	Ottawa Senators	Al-Cup	12	4	3	7				20					
	NHL Totals		**67**	**14**	**24**	**38**	**14**	**21**	**35**	**76**	**13**	**2**	**2**	**4**	**8**

• Missed majority of 1944-45 season recovering from ankle injury suffered in game vs. Detroit, December 15, 1944.

• McLELLAN, John
Daniel John
C – L. 5'11", 150 lbs. b: South Porcupine, Ont., 8/6/1928 d: 10/27/1979.

Season	Club	League	GP	G	A	Pts	AG	AA	APts	PIM	GP	G	A	Pts	PIM
1945-46	St. Michael's Buzzers	H.S.	8	4	1	5				6	2	0	1	1	0
1946-47	St. Michael's Majors	OHA-Jr.	30	11	13	24				8	9	0	0	0	0
	St. Michael's Majors	M-Cup	8	1	3	4				2					
1947-48	Toronto Marlboros	OHA-Sr.	36	16	26	42				45	5	1	2	3	8
1948-49	Toronto Marlboros	OHA-Sr.	36	11	19	30				38	10	7	6	13	8
	Toronto Marlboros	Al-Cup	13	*9	9	*18				12					
1949-50	Toronto Marlboros	OHA-Sr.	36	12	20	32				41	14	3	7	10	14
	Toronto Marlboros	Al-Cup	17	7	8	15				15					
1950-51	Pittsburgh Hornets	AHL	37	8	6	14				23					
	Tulsa Oilers	USHL	14	9	5	14				16	9	4	1	5	9
1951-52	**Toronto Maple Leafs**	**NHL**	**2**	**0**	**0**	**0**	**0**	**0**	**0**	**0**					
	Pittsburgh Hornets	AHL	60	21	22	43				43	11	1	1	2	12
1952-53	Pittsburgh Hornets	AHL	51	13	24	37				59	10	2	2	4	20
1953-54	Pittsburgh Hornets	AHL	55	8	16	24				72	2	0	0	0	0
1954-55	Cleveland Barons	AHL	60	30	31	61				97	4	1	1	2	4
1955-56	Cleveland Barons	AHL	61	12	12	24				72	5	3	1	4	8
1956-57	Cleveland Barons	AHL	57	20	13	33				83	12	*7	2	9	12
1957-58	Cleveland Barons	AHL	46	11	15	26				53	4	0	0	0	2
1958-59	Belleville McFarlands	EOHL	45	17	27	44				74					
	Canada	WEC-A	7	4	*7	11				10					
1959-60	Milwaukee Falcons	IHL	23	7	18	25				29					
1960-61	Timmins Flyers	NOHA	STATISTICS NOT AVAILABLE												
	Rouyn-Noranda Alouettes	Al-Cup	3	2	1	3				4					
1961-62			DID NOT PLAY												
1962-63	Nashville Dixie Flyers	EHL	58	19	37	56				46	3	0	2	2	2
1963-64	Nashville Dixie Flyers	EHL	1	0	0	0				0					
1964-65	Nashville Dixie Flyers	EHL	DID NOT PLAY – COACHING												
	NHL Totals		**2**	**0**	**0**	**0**	**0**	**0**	**0**	**0**					

Traded to **Cleveland** (AHL) by **Toronto** with cash for Hugh Barlow, September 15, 1954. • Worked as surveyor for the Province of Ontario in 1961-62 season.

• McLENAHAN, Rollie
Roland Joseph "Mighty Mite"
D – L. 5'7", 169 lbs. b: Fredericton, N.B., 10/26/1921 d: 4/23/1984.

Season	Club	League	GP	G	A	Pts	AG	AA	APts	PIM	GP	G	A	Pts	PIM
1935-36	Marysville Royals	YCHL									2	0	0	0	4
1936-37	Devon Northsiders	YCHL									1	0	1	1	2
1937-38	Devon Northsiders	YCHL	4	6	2	8				8	6	6	1	7	*8
1938-39	Fredericton Merchants	YCHL	12	12	5	17									
1939-40	Windsor Mills	QAHA	STATISTICS NOT AVAILABLE												
	Windsor Mills	Al-Cup	2	0	0	0				2					
1940-41	Guelph Biltmores	OHA-Jr.	15	6	4	10				15	5	1	4	5	4
1941-42	Washington Eagles	EAHL	57	19	25	44				55	8	3	4	7	20
1942-43	Sudbury Tigers	NOHA	3	0	0	0				2	3	1	2	3	2
	Sudbury Wolves	Al-Cup	3	0	0	0				8					
1943-44	Sudbury Open Pit	NBHL	8	5	4	9				*20					
	Sudbury Open Pit	Al-Cup	16	4	4	8				*36					
1944-45	Sudbury Tigers	NOHA	6	7	6	13				10	7	0	4	4	12
1945-46	**Detroit Red Wings**	**NHL**	**9**	**2**	**1**	**3**	**2**	**1**	**3**	**10**	**2**	**0**	**0**	**0**	**0**
	Indianapolis Capitols	AHL	39	7	13	20				32					
1946-47	Cleveland Barons	AHL	64	6	17	23				55	4	0	0	0	2
1947-48	Hershey Bears	AHL	58	7	18	25				59	2	0	1	1	4
1948-49	Hershey Bears	AHL	64	15	33	48				86	11	4	6	10	8
1949-50	Hershey Bears	AHL	67	25	35	60				49					
1950-51	Buffalo Bisons	AHL	65	11	33	44				44	4	1	2	3	8
1951-52	Fredericton Capitals	X-Games	19	*23	17	40				*35					
1952-53	Fredericton Capitals	NBSHL	9	11	6	17				30	6	*5	*5	*10	8
	Sudbury Wolves	NOHA	36	27	34	61				31	7	3	5	8	0
	Sudbury Wolves	Al-Cup	7	4	6	10				6					
1953-54	Cincinnati Mohawks	IHL	47	24	29	53				96	11	3	3	6	*20
1954-55	Cincinnati Mohawks	IHL	57	27	47	74				80	10	1	8	9	25
1955-56	Cincinnati Mohawks	IHL	58	*34	32	66				62	8	2	*7	9	0
1956-57	Cincinnati Mohawks	IHL	50	7	10	17				31					
1957-58	Rochester Americans	AHL	DID NOT PLAY – COACHING												
	NHL Totals		**9**	**2**	**1**	**3**	**2**	**1**	**3**	**10**	**2**	**0**	**0**	**0**	**0**

AHL First All-Star Team (1950) • IHL First All-Star Team (1954, 1955, 1956)

• Regular season totals for Marysville (YCHL) and Devon (YCHL) in 1935-36 and 1936-37 unavailable. Traded to **Chicago** by **Detroit** for cash, April, 1946. Traded to **Buffalo** (AHL) by **Hershey** (AHL) for Ray Gariepy, October 4, 1950.

• McLEOD, Jackie
Robert John
RW – R. 5'9", 150 lbs. b: Regina, Sask., 4/30/1930.

Season	Club	League	GP	G	A	Pts	AG	AA	APts	PIM	GP	G	A	Pts	PIM
1945-46	Notre Dame Hounds	SAHA	1	0	0	0				0					
1946-47	Notre Dame Hounds	SAHA	24	8	9	17				10					
1947-48	Moose Jaw Canucks	SJHL	13	5	12	17				4	5	*11	5	*16	4
	Moose Jaw Canucks	M-Cup	6	4	3	7				4					
1948-49	Moose Jaw Canucks	WCJHL	26	19	20	39				25	7	4	2	6	10
1949-50	**New York Rangers**	**NHL**	**38**	**6**	**9**	**15**	**8**	**11**	**19**	**2**	**7**	**0**	**0**	**0**	**0**
1950-51	**New York Rangers**	**NHL**	**41**	**5**	**10**	**15**	**6**	**12**	**18**	**2**					
1951-52	**New York Rangers**	**NHL**	**13**	**2**	**3**	**5**	**3**	**4**	**7**	**2**					
	Cincinnati Mohawks	AHL	49	14	18	32				38	2	0	1	1	2
1952-53	**New York Rangers**	**NHL**	**3**	**0**	**0**	**0**	**0**	**0**	**0**	**2**					
	Saskatoon Quakers	WHL	55	30	47	77				28	13	8	11	19	19
1953-54	Saskatoon Quakers	WHL	69	33	38	71				46	6	4	1	5	4
1954-55	**New York Rangers**	**NHL**	**11**	**1**	**1**	**2**	**1**	**1**	**2**	**4**					
	Saskatoon–Vancouver	WHL	51	20	31	51				44	5	2	1	3	14
1955-56	Saskatoon Quakers	WHL	70	34	49	83				97	3	1	1	2	14
1956-57	Vancouver Canucks	WHL	41	30	19	49				30					
1957-58	Vancouver Canucks	WHL	68	44	27	71				45	9	*14	4	18	8
1958-59	Saskatoon Quakers	WHL	63	27	26	53				44					
1959-60	Calgary Stampeders	WHL	62	28	28	56				50					
1960-61	Moose Jaw Pla-Mors	SSHL	12	6	6	12				6					
	Trail Smoke Eaters	X-Games	STATISTICS NOT AVAILABLE												
	Canada	Nt-Team	19	14	*13	*27				21					
	Canada	WEC-A	7	*10	4	14				6					
	Moose Jaw Pla-Mors	Al-Cup	4	1	2	3				2					
1961-62	Moose Jaw Pla-Mors	SSHL	29	27	25	52				36					
	Canada	WEC-A	7	5	7	*12				6					
1962-63	Saskatoon Quakers	SSHL	31	37	*51	*88				22	1	0	0	0	2
	Canada	WEC-A	7	5	8	13				6					

Season	Club	League	GP	G	A	Pts	AG	AA	APts	PIM	GP	G	A	Pts	PIM
			REGULAR SEASON								PLAYOFFS				
1963-64	Saskatoon Quakers	SSHL	40	*52	52	104	....	....	....	22	11	7	8	15	6
	Saskatoon Quakers	Al-Cup	9	5	13	18	....	....	....	6	....	....	....	....	....
1964-65	Moose Jaw Canucks	SSHL	2	3	4	7	....	....	....	12	10	12	*12	24	10
1965-66	Canada	Nt-Team	PLAYER/COACH – STATISTICS UNAVAILABLE												
	Canada	WEC-A	7	4	2	6	....	....	....	4	....	....	....	....	....
	NHL Totals		**106**	**14**	**23**	**37**	**18**	**28**	**46**	**12**	**7**	**0**	**0**	**0**	**0**

WEC-A First All-Star Team (1962)

Signed as a free agent by **NY Rangers**, December 9, 1949. Traded to **Vancouver** (WHL) by **NY Rangers** with cash for Bill Ezinicki, February 12, 1955. Claimed by **NY Rangers** (Providence-AHL) from **NY Rangers** (Vancouver-WHL) in Inter-League Draft, June 4, 1957. Signed as a free agent by **Calgary** (WHL), October, 1959. Traded to **Victoria** (WHL) by **Calgary** (WHL) for cash, September, 1960.

• McMAHON, Mike Michael Clarence

D – L. 5'8", 215 lbs. b: Brockville, Ont., 2/1/1915 d: 12/3/1974.

Season	Club	League	GP	G	A	Pts	AG	AA	APts	PIM	GP	G	A	Pts	PIM
1935-36	Brockville Magedomas	LOVHL	17	11	8	19	....	....	....	27	7	6	3	9	8
	Brockville Magedomas	Al-Cup	6	3	3	6	....	....	....	13	....	....	....	....	....
1936-37	Cornwall Flyers	LOVHL	17	7	*13	20	....	....	....	48	6	2	2	4	6
1937-38	Cornwall Flyers	LOVHL	24	17	17	34	....	....	....	34	11	6	4	10	*33
	Cornwall Flyers	Al-Cup	11	6	4	10	....	....	....	33	....	....	....	....	....
1938-39	Cornwall Flyers	LOVHL	38	20	34	54	....	....	....	*144	9	3	5	8	*22
1939-40	Cornwall Royals	QSHL	30	2	7	9	....	....	....	81	5	2	3	5	14
1940-41	Quebec Aces	QSHL	33	5	11	16	....	....	....	57	4	1	1	2	4
1941-42	Quebec Aces	QSHL	40	16	11	27	....	....	....	76	7	4	2	6	14
	Quebec Aces	Al-Cup	6	1	3	4	....	....	....	*18	....	....	....	....	....
1942-43	Quebec Aces	QSHL	33	6	24	30	....	....	....	73	4	1	2	3	20
	Ottawa Commandos	QSHL	....	....	....	....	....	....	....	....	2	0	2	2	0
	Montreal Royals	QSHL	....	....	....	....	....	....	....	....	1	0	0	0	2
	Montreal Canadiens	**NHL**	....	....	....	....	....	....	....	....	**5**	**0**	**0**	**0**	**14**
♦**1943-44**	**Montreal Canadiens**	**NHL**	**42**	**7**	**17**	**24**	**6**	**15**	**21**	***98**	**8**	**1**	**2**	**3**	**16**
1944-45	Montreal Royals	QSHL	10	6	16	22	....	....	....	58	7	1	2	3	8
1945-46	**Montreal Canadiens**	**NHL**	**13**	**0**	**1**	**1**	**0**	**1**	**1**	**2**	....	....	....	....	....
	Boston Bruins	**NHL**	**2**	**0**	**0**	**0**	**0**	**0**	**0**	**2**	....	....	....	....	....
	Buffalo Bisons	AHL	26	2	14	16	....	....	....	50	12	5	1	6	14
1946-47	Dallas Texans	USHL	13	1	3	4	....	....	....	43	....	....	....	....	....
	Buffalo Bisons	AHL	50	12	28	40	....	....	....	68	4	1	0	1	4
1947-48	Houston Huskies	USHL	39	7	11	18	....	....	....	91	....	....	....	....	....
	Buffalo Bisons	AHL	17	2	9	11	....	....	....	15	8	0	2	2	16
1948-49	Springfield Indians	AHL	16	2	4	6	....	....	....	14	....	....	....	....	....
	NHL Totals		**57**	**7**	**18**	**25**	**6**	**16**	**22**	**102**	**13**	**1**	**2**	**3**	**30**

• Father of Mike Jr.

Signed as a free agent by **Ottawa** (QSHL), September, 1945. Signed as a free agent by **Montreal**, October 24, 1945. Loaned to **Boston** by **Montreal** as compensation for Montreal's recall of Paul Bibeault, January 8, 1946. Returned to **Montreal** by **Boston**, January 17, 1946.

• McMAHON, Mike

— *see page 1412*

• McMANUS, Sammy Andrew Samuel

LW – L. 5'9", 160 lbs. b: Belfast, Ireland, 10/22/1911 Deceased.

Season	Club	League	GP	G	A	Pts	AG	AA	APts	PIM	GP	G	A	Pts	PIM
1928-29	Toronto Canoe Club	OHA-Jr.	5	0	0	0	....	....	....	....	3	0	0	0	....
1929-30	Toronto Canoe Club	OHA-Jr.	9	2	3	5	....	....	....	8	....	....	....	....	....
	Toronto Overland	TMHL	13	5	7	12	....	....	....	10	....	....	....	....	....
1930-31	New Glasgow Tigers	NSEHL	24	7	10	17	....	....	....	28	2	0	0	0	0
1931-32	Fredericton Capitals	MSHL	24	11	10	21	....	....	....	18	2	0	0	0	0
1932-33	Moncton Hawks	MSHL	25	3	*5	8	....	....	....	43	5	1	2	3	4
	Moncton Hawks	Al-Cup	8	1	2	3	....	....	....	4	....	....	....	....	....
1933-34	Moncton Hawks	MSHL	38	*25	23	48	....	....	....	47	3	0	0	0	0
	Moncton Hawks	Al-Cup	12	8	9	17	....	....	....	12	....	....	....	....	....
♦**1934-35**	**Montreal Maroons**	**NHL**	**25**	**0**	**1**	**1**	**0**	**2**	**2**	**8**	**1**	**0**	**0**	**0**	**0**
	Windsor Bulldogs	IHL	10	2	4	6	....	....	....	6	....	....	....	....	....
	New Haven Eagles	Can-Am	8	6	1	7	....	....	....	7	....	....	....	....	....
1935-36	Philadelphia Ramblers	Can-Am	43	19	21	40	....	....	....	22	4	0	2	2	2
1936-37	**Boston Bruins**	**NHL**	**1**	**0**	**0**	**0**	**0**	**0**	**0**	**0**	....	....	....	....	....
	Providence Reds	IAHL	34	12	9	21	....	....	....	6	3	0	0	0	2
1937-38	Providence Reds	IAHL	45	8	19	27	....	....	....	18	7	3	1	4	2
1938-39	Hershey Bears	IAHL	36	12	19	31	....	....	....	10	5	1	2	3	2
1939-40	Pittsburgh Hornets	IAHL	46	4	20	24	....	....	....	10	9	2	5	7	4
	New Haven Eagles	IAHL	6	1	1	2	....	....	....	2	....	....	....	....	....
1940-41	Kansas City Americans	AHA	44	15	23	38	....	....	....	19	8	2	3	5	6
1941-42	St. Louis Flyers	AHA	50	18	39	57	....	....	....	12	3	0	0	0	0
1942-43	New Haven Eagles	AHL	28	13	13	26	....	....	....	4	....	....	....	....	....
	Washington Lions	AHL	23	6	22	28	....	....	....	2	....	....	....	....	....
1943-44	Saint John Beavers	X-Games	6	*7	8	*15	....	....	....	0	6	8	6	*14	10
	Saint John Beavers	Al-Cup	9	*28	15	*43	....	....	....	8	....	....	....	....	....
1944-45	Moncton RCAF Flyers	MNDHL	1	3	0	3	....	....	....	0	....	....	....	....	....
	Saint John Garrison	SJDHL	1	3	0	3	....	....	....	0	....	....	....	....	....
	Saint John Beavers	X-Games	1	0	1	1	....	....	....	0	....	....	....	....	....
	Saint John Beavers	Al-Cup	9	*20	13	*33	....	....	....	6	....	....	....	....	....
1945-46	Moncton Maroons	X-Games	13	*27	15	*42	....	....	....	11	....	....	....	....	....
	Moncton Maroons	Al-Cup	4	*15	3	*18	....	....	....	2	....	....	....	....	....
1946-47	Moncton Hawks	MSHL	32	37	34	71	....	....	....	13	9	*8	9	*17	2
	NHL Totals		**26**	**0**	**1**	**1**	**0**	**2**	**2**	**8**	**1**	**0**	**0**	**0**	**0**

Can-Am First All-Star Team (1936) • IAHL Second All-Star Team (1938) • AHA Second All-Star Team (1942)

Signed as a free agent by **Montreal Maroons**, October 31, 1934. Loaned to **New Haven** (Can-Am) by **Montreal Maroons** (Windsor-IHL) for cash, January 6, 1935. Traded to **NY Rangers** by **Montreal Maroons** for $10,000, October 26, 1935. Traded to **Montreal Maroons** by **NY Rangers** for cash, September, 1936. Traded to **Montreal Canadiens** by **Montreal Maroons** for the rights to Buddy O'Connor, September 10, 1936. Traded to **Boston** by **Montreal Canadiens** with Leroy Goldsworthy and $10,000 for Babe Siebert and Roger Jenkins, September 10, 1936. Loaned to **New Haven** (IAHL) by **Pittsburgh** (IAHL) for cash, February 12, 1940. Signed as a free agent by **Chicago**, October, 1940. Traded to **St. Louis** (AHA) by **Chicago** with cash for Fido Purpur, May 3, 1941.

• McNAB, Max Maxwell Douglas

C – L. 6'2", 179 lbs. b: Watson, Sask., 6/21/1924.

Season	Club	League	GP	G	A	Pts	AG	AA	APts	PIM	GP	G	A	Pts	PIM
			REGULAR SEASON								PLAYOFFS				
1942-43	Saskatoon Quakers	N-SJHL	4	7	8	15	....	....	....	6	2	1	2	3	0
1943-44			MILITARY SERVICE												
1944-45			MILITARY SERVICE												
1945-46	Saskatoon Elks	WCSHL	5	8	1	9	....	....	....	0	....	....	....	....	....
1946-47	Indianapolis Capitols	AHL	6	0	0	0	....	....	....	2	....	....	....	....	....
	Omaha Knights	USHL	37	20	19	39	....	....	....	15	11	6	6	12	0
	Detroit Metal Moldings	IHL	3	4	2	6	....	....	....	6	....	....	....	....	....
1947-48	**Detroit Red Wings**	**NHL**	**12**	**2**	**2**	**4**	**3**	**3**	**6**	**2**	**3**	**0**	**0**	**0**	**2**
	Omaha Knights	USHL	44	*44	32	76	....	....	....	10	3	3	2	5	0
1948-49	**Detroit Red Wings**	**NHL**	**51**	**10**	**13**	**23**	**14**	**18**	**32**	**14**	**10**	**1**	**0**	**1**	**2**
♦**1949-50**	**Detroit Red Wings**	**NHL**	**65**	**4**	**4**	**8**	**5**	**5**	**10**	**8**	**10**	**0**	**0**	**0**	**0**
1950-51	Indianapolis Capitols	AHL	70	36	48	84	....	....	....	36	3	1	2	3	2
	Detroit Red Wings	**NHL**	....	....	....	....	....	....	....	....	**2**	**0**	**0**	**0**	**0**
1951-52	New Westminster Royals	WHL	DID NOT PLAY – INJURED												
1952-53	New Westminster Royals	WHL	68	28	32	60	....	....	....	4	7	2	0	2	0
1953-54	New Westminster Royals	WHL	67	22	39	61	....	....	....	8	6	2	1	3	2
1954-55	New Westminster Royals	WHL	70	32	49	81	....	....	....	4	....	....	....	....	....
1955-56	New Westminster Royals	WHL	70	29	32	61	....	....	....	19	4	1	1	2	0
1956-57	New Westminster Royals	WHL	56	19	28	47	....	....	....	2	13	4	*8	*12	4
1957-58	New Westminster Royals	WHL	67	24	50	74	....	....	....	14	4	0	1	1	0
1958-59	New Westminster Royals	WHL	65	26	32	58	....	....	....	4	....	....	....	....	....
	NHL Totals		**128**	**16**	**19**	**35**	**22**	**26**	**48**	**24**	**25**	**1**	**0**	**1**	**4**

• Father of Peter • USHL Second All-Star Team (1948) • Won Leader Cup (WHL - MVP) (1955)

Traded to **Chicago** by **Detroit** with George Gee, Jimmy Peters, Clare Martin, Rags Raglan and Jim McFadden for $75,000 and future considerations (Hugh Coflin, October, 1951), August 20, 1951. • Missed entire 1951-52 season recovering from back surgery.

• McNABNEY, Sid

C – L. 5'7", 150 lbs. b: Toronto, Ont., 1/15/1929 d: 2/7/1957.

Season	Club	League	GP	G	A	Pts	AG	AA	APts	PIM	GP	G	A	Pts	PIM
1947-48	Barrie Flyers	OHA-Jr.	33	14	14	28	....	....	....	36	13	2	4	6	8
	Barrie Flyers	M-Cup	10	3	6	9	....	....	....	12	....	....	....	....	....
1948-49	Barrie Flyers	OHA-Jr.	45	27	37	64	....	....	....	91	8	5	7	12	16
	Barrie Flyers	M-Cup	8	5	4	9	....	....	....	22	....	....	....	....	....
1949-50	Buffalo Bisons	AHL	67	12	21	33	....	....	....	41	5	1	1	2	11
1950-51	Buffalo Bisons	AHL	70	28	42	70	....	....	....	35	4	2	3	5	8
	Montreal Canadiens	**NHL**	....	....	....	....	....	....	....	....	**5**	**0**	**1**	**1**	**2**
1951-52	Buffalo Bisons	AHL	57	19	23	42	....	....	....	51	3	0	0	0	2
	Edmonton Flyers	PCHL	4	5	1	6	....	....	....	2	....	....	....	....	....
1952-53	Syracuse Warriors	AHL	49	9	11	20	....	....	....	29	2	0	0	0	0
	NHL Totals		....	....	....	....	....	....	....	....	**5**	**0**	**1**	**1**	**2**

Rights traded to **Montreal** (Buffalo-AHL) by **Springfield** (AHL) with Gordie Bell for Hub Macey, December 21, 1948.

• McNAMARA, Howard Howard Dennis

D – L. 6', 240 lbs. b: Randolph, Ont., 8/3/1893 d: 9/4/1940.

Season	Club	League	GP	G	A	Pts	AG	AA	APts	PIM	GP	G	A	Pts	PIM
1908-09	Montreal Shamrocks	ECHA	10	4	0	4	....	....	....	61	....	....	....	....	....
	Canadian Soo Pros	X-Games	2	4	0	4	....	....	....	6	....	....	....	....	....
1909-10	Berlin Professionals	OPHL	3	0	0	0	....	....	....	8	....	....	....	....	....
	Cobalt Silver Kings	NHA	6	0	0	0	....	....	....	15	....	....	....	....	....
1910-11	Waterloo Colts	OPHL	15	2	0	2	....	....	....	....	....	....	....	....	....
1911-12	Halifax Crescents	MPHL	11	4	0	4	....	....	....	26	....	....	....	....	....
1912-13	Toronto Tecumsehs	X-Games	20	12	0	12	....	....	....	62	....	....	....	....	....
1913-14	Toronto Ontarios	NHA	20	7	6	13	....	....	....	36	....	....	....	....	....
1914-15	Toronto Shamrocks	NHA	18	4	1	5	....	....	....	67	....	....	....	....	....
♦1915-16	Montreal Canadiens	NHA	24	10	7	17	....	....	....	119	5	0	0	0	24
1916-17	Toronto 228th Battalion	NHA	12	11	3	14	....	....	....	36	....	....	....	....	....
1917-18			MILITARY SERVICE												
1918-19			MILITARY SERVICE												
1919-20	**Montreal Canadiens**	**NHL**	**10**	**1**	**0**	**1**	**1**	**0**	**1**	**4**	....	....	....	....	....
	NHL Totals		**10**	**1**	**0**	**1**	**1**	**0**	**1**	**4**	....	....	....	....	....
	Other Major League Totals		119	42	17	59	....	....	....	368	5	0	0	0	24

Signed with **Cobalt** (NHA) after jumping contract with **Berlin** (OPHL), February 1, 1910. Signed as a free agent by **Montreal Canadiens**, December 7, 1919.

• McNAUGHTON, George George Pabos

RW/C – R. 5'9", 150 lbs. b: Gaspe, Que., 4/4/1897 Deceased.

Season	Club	League	GP	G	A	Pts	AG	AA	APts	PIM	GP	G	A	Pts	PIM
1915-16	Quebec Sons of Ireland	QCHL	8	15	0	15	....	....	....	....	2	5	0	5	....
1916-17	Quebec Sons of Ireland	QCHL	10	15	2	17	....	....	....	....	3	2	1	3	3
1917-18	Quebec Sons of Ireland	QCHL	1	1	0	1	....	....	....	....	3	2	1	3	3
1918-19	Quebec Crescents	QCHL	STATISTICS NOT AVAILABLE												
1919-20	**Quebec Bulldogs**	**NHL**	**1**	**0**	**0**	**0**	**0**	**0**	**0**	**0**	....	....	....	....	....
	Winnipeg Virtlands	MHL-Sr.	1	2	0	2	....	....	....	0	....	....	....	....	....
1920-21	La Tuque Warriors	QPHL	STATISTICS NOT AVAILABLE												
1921-22	Grand Mere Seniors	QCHL	STATISTICS NOT AVAILABLE												
1922-23	Quebec Sons of Ireland	QCHL	15	14	0	14	....	....	....	....	5	*7	0	*7	....
1923-24	Quebec Sons of Ireland	QCHL	1	0	0	0	....	....	....	....	2	0	0	0	....
	Quebec Sons of Ireland	Al-Cup	6	3	0	3	....	....	....	....	....	....	....	....	....
	NHL Totals		**1**	**0**	**0**	**0**	**0**	**0**	**0**	**0**	....	....	....	....	....

Signed as a free agent by **Quebec**, December 21, 1919.

• McNEILL, Billy William Ronald

RW – R. 5'10", 175 lbs. b: Edmonton, Alta., 1/26/1936.

Season	Club	League	GP	G	A	Pts	AG	AA	APts	PIM	GP	G	A	Pts	PIM
1951-52	Edmonton Oil Kings	WCJHL	42	23	24	47	....	....	....	41	9	4	*10	14	2
1952-53	Edmonton Oil Kings	WCJHL	36	15	15	30	....	....	....	59	10	5	3	8	12
	Edmonton Flyers	WHL	1	0	0	0	....	....	....	0	....	....	....	....	....
1953-54	Edmonton Oil Kings	WCJHL	35	21	39	60	....	....	....	47	10	10	18	28	23
	Edmonton Oil Kings	M-Cup	14	4	13	17	....	....	....	27	....	....	....	....	....
1954-55	Hamilton Cubs	OHA-Jr.	49	22	28	50	....	....	....	66	3	3	2	5	2
	Edmonton Flyers	WHL	3	1	1	2	....	....	....	0	....	....	....	....	....
1955-56	Edmonton Flyers	WHL	68	19	31	50	....	....	....	69	1	0	0	0	0
1956-57	**Detroit Red Wings**	**NHL**	**64**	**5**	**10**	**15**	**6**	**11**	**17**	**34**	....	....	....	....	....
	Edmonton Flyers	WHL	4	1	0	1	....	....	....	26	....	....	....	....	....
1957-58	**Detroit Red Wings**	**NHL**	**35**	**5**	**10**	**15**	**6**	**10**	**16**	**29**	**4**	**1**	**1**	**2**	**4**
	Edmonton Flyers	WHL	31	17	14	31	....	....	....	42	....	....	....	....	....

Season	Club	League	GP	G	A	Pts	AG	AA	APts	PIM	GP	G	A	Pts	PIM
1958-59	**Detroit Red Wings**	**NHL**	**54**	**2**	**5**	**7**	**2**	**5**	**7**	**32**	....	....	....	....	....
	Edmonton Flyers	WHL	12	12	12	24	....	....	....	15	3	1	1	2	0
1959-60	**Detroit Red Wings**	**NHL**	**47**	**5**	**13**	**18**	**6**	**13**	**19**	**33**	....	....	....	....	....
1960-61	Edmonton Flyers	WHL	23	8	17	25	....	....	....	16	....	....	....	....	....
1961-62	Edmonton Flyers	WHL	26	13	28	41	....	....	....	68	12	7	4	11	19
1962-63	**Detroit Red Wings**	**NHL**	**42**	**3**	**7**	**10**	**3**	**7**	**10**	**12**	....	....	....	....	....
	Edmonton Flyers	WHL	22	5	19	24	....	....	....	8	3	0	3	3	0
1963-64	**Detroit Red Wings**	**NHL**	**15**	**1**	**1**	**2**	**1**	**1**	**2**	**2**	....	....	....	....	....
	Pittsburgh Hornets	AHL	20	1	6	7	....	....	....	23	....	....	....	....	....
	Vancouver Canucks	WHL	24	4	20	24	....	....	....	4	....	....	....	....	....
1964-65	Vancouver Canucks	WHL	68	29	59	88	....	....	....	86	5	2	4	6	0
1965-66	Vancouver Canucks	WHL	72	40	62	102	....	....	....	20	7	6	7	13	0
1966-67	Vancouver Canucks	WHL	6	3	5	8	....	....	....	4	....	....	....	....	....
1967-68	Vancouver Canucks	WHL	41	11	24	35	....	....	....	41	....	....	....	....	....
1968-69	Vancouver Canucks	WHL	22	3	2	5	....	....	....	10	....	....	....	....	....
	Rochester Americans	AHL	19	3	15	18	....	....	....	18	....	....	....	....	....
1969-70	Salt Lake Golden Eagles	WHL	24	6	16	22	....	....	....	4	....	....	....	....	....
1970-71	Salt Lake Golden Eagles	WHL	5	0	0	0	....	....	....	2	....	....	....	....	....
	San Diego Gulls	WHL	65	14	15	29	....	....	....	39	6	0	1	1	0
	NHL Totals		**257**	**21**	**46**	**67**	**24**	**47**	**71**	**142**	**4**	**1**	**1**	**2**	**4**

WHL First All-Star Team (1965, 1966) • Won Leader Cup (WHL - MVP) (1965, 1966)

Traded to **NY Rangers** by **Detroit** with Red Kelly for Eddie Shack and Bill Gadsby, February 5, 1960. • Kelly and McNeill refused to report and transaction was cancelled, February 7, 1960. • Suspended by Detroit for remainder of 1959-60 season for failing to report to NY Rangers, February 7, 1960. Claimed by **NY Rangers** from **Detroit** in Intra-League Draft, June 7, 1960. • Retired from hockey in order to pursue business interests in Edmonton, Summer, 1960. Rights traded to **Detroit** (Edmonton-WHL) by **NY Rangers** for cash, January, 1961. Traded to **Vancouver** (WHL) by **Detroit** for Barrie Ross and future considerations, January, 1964. Traded to **Salt Lake** (WHL) by **Vancouver** (WHL) for Germaine Gagnon and cash, August 19, 1969. • Missed majority of 1969-70 season recovering from ankle injury suffered in game vs. Phoenix (WHL), November 11, 1969.

• McNEILL, Stu

C – R. 5'10", 170 lbs. b: Port Arthur, Ont., 9/25/1938.

Season	Club	League	GP	G	A	Pts	AG	AA	APts	PIM	GP	G	A	Pts	PIM
1954-55	Port Arthur North Stars	TBJHL	32	11	3	14	....	....	....	10	....	....	....	....	....
1955-56	Port Arthur North Stars	TBJHL	30	16	23	39	....	....	....	2	9	3	4	7	2
	Port Arthur North Stars	M-Cup	13	8	7	15	....	....	....	6	....	....	....	....	....
	Regina Pats	M-Cup	3	0	0	0	....	....	....	0	....	....	....	....	....
1956-57	Port Arthur North Stars	TBJHL	30	27	28	55	....	....	....	0	8	3	4	7	0
	Fort William Canadiens	M-Cup	11	4	7	11	....	....	....	2	....	....	....	....	....
1957-58	Hamilton Tiger Cubs	OHA-Jr.	52	11	27	38	....	....	....	29	15	4	8	12	10
	Detroit Red Wings	**NHL**	**2**	**0**	**0**	**0**	**0**	**0**	**0**	**0**	....	....	....	....	....
1958-59	Hamilton Tiger Cubs	OHA	53	22	27	49	....	....	....	17	....	....	....	....	....
	Detroit Red Wings	**NHL**	**3**	**1**	**1**	**2**	**1**	**1**	**2**	**2**	....	....	....	....	....
1959-60	**Detroit Red Wings**	**NHL**	**5**	**0**	**0**	**0**	**0**	**0**	**0**	**0**	....	....	....	....	....
	Edmonton Flyers	WHL	59	10	17	27	....	....	....	4	4	0	1	1	0
	NHL Totals		**10**	**1**	**1**	**2**	**1**	**1**	**2**	**2**	....	....	....	....	....

• McREAVY, Pat

Patrick Joseph

C – R. 5'11", 165 lbs. b: Owen Sound, Ont., 1/16/1918.

Season	Club	League	GP	G	A	Pts	AG	AA	APts	PIM	GP	G	A	Pts	PIM
1935-36	St. Michael's Majors	OHA-Jr.	10	8	9	17	....	....	....	2	5	2	3	5	2
1936-37	Copper Cliff Jr. Redmen	NOJHA	4	5	4	9	....	....	....	4	....	....	....	....	....
	Copper Cliff Redmen	NOHA	14	7	7	14	....	....	....	12	....	....	....	....	....
	Copper Cliff Jr. Redmen	M-Cup	12	15	*21	*36	....	....	....	10	....	....	....	....	....
1937-38	Sudbury Wolves	NOHA	1	0	1	1	....	....	....	0	....	....	....	....	....
	Canada	WEC	7	2	1	3	....	....	....	2	....	....	....	....	....
1938-39	**Boston Bruins**	**NHL**	**6**	**0**	**0**	**0**	**0**	**0**	**0**	**0**	....	....	....	....	....
	Providence Reds	IAHL	47	11	16	27	....	....	....	23	5	0	1	1	0
1939-40	**Boston Bruins**	**NHL**	**2**	**0**	**0**	**0**	**0**	**0**	**0**	**2**	....	....	....	....	....
	Hershey Bears	IAHL	53	16	17	33	....	....	....	8	6	2	3	5	2
♦1940-41	**Boston Bruins**	**NHL**	**7**	**0**	**1**	**1**	**0**	**1**	**1**	**2**	**11**	**2**	**2**	**4**	**5**
	Hershey Bears	AHL	51	21	25	46	....	....	....	2	2	1	0	1	0
1941-42	**Boston Bruins**	**NHL**	**6**	**0**	**1**	**1**	**0**	**1**	**1**	**0**	....	....	....	....	....
	Detroit Red Wings	**NHL**	**34**	**5**	**8**	**13**	**7**	**9**	**16**	**0**	**11**	**1**	**1**	**2**	**4**
1942-43	Montreal RCAF	QSHL	14	2	4	6	....	....	....	8	....	....	....	....	....
	Toronto RCAF	OHA-Sr.	1	0	1	1	....	....	....	0	....	....	....	....	....
1943-44	Montreal RCAF	QSHL	7	2	2	4	....	....	....	2	....	....	....	....	....
1944-45	Valleyfield Braves	QPHL	3	2	2	4	....	....	....	0	....	....	....	....	....
1945-46	St. Louis Flyers	AHL	46	22	28	50	....	....	....	11	....	....	....	....	....
1946-47	St. Louis Flyers	AHL	64	18	29	47	....	....	....	21	....	....	....	....	....
1947-48	Owen Sound Mercurys	OHA-Sr.	27	20	28	48	....	....	....	2	5	3	7	10	0
1948-49	Owen Sound Mercurys	OHA-Sr.	39	17	22	39	....	....	....	4	4	1	4	5	0
1949-50	Owen Sound Mercurys	OHA-Sr.	42	26	25	51	....	....	....	6	....	....	....	....	....
1950-51	Owen Sound Mercurys	OHA-Sr.	DID NOT PLAY – COACHING												
	Owen Sound Mercurys	Al-Cup	16	7	*17	24	....	....	....	6	....	....	....	....	....
1951-52	Owen Sound Mercurys	OHA-Sr.	1	0	0	0	....	....	....	0	....	....	....	....	....
	NHL Totals		**55**	**5**	**10**	**15**	**7**	**11**	**18**	**4**	**22**	**3**	**3**	**6**	**9**

Traded to **Detroit** by **Boston** for Dutch Hiller and $5,000, November 24, 1941. Traded to **St. Louis** (AHL) by **Detroit** for cash, November 5, 1945.

• McVEIGH, Charley

Charley Henry "Rabbit"

C/LW – L. 5'6", 145 lbs. b: Kenora, Ont., 3/29/1898 d: 5/7/1984.

Season	Club	League	GP	G	A	Pts	AG	AA	APts	PIM	GP	G	A	Pts	PIM
1918-19	Winnipeg GTP	WJrHL	STATISTICS NOT AVAILABLE												
1919-20	Winnipeg Victorias	WSrHL	7	3	*12	15	....	....	....	12	....	....	....	....	....
1920-21	Moose Jaw Maple Leafs	S-SSHL	15	9	5	14	....	....	....	19	4	0	2	2	2
1921-22	Regina Capitals	WCHL	19	15	6	21	....	....	....	8	6	1	0	1	0
1922-23	Regina Capitals	WCHL	30	10	2	12	....	....	....	20	2	0	0	0	0
1923-24	Regina Capitals	WCHL	26	10	0	10	....	....	....	6	2	0	0	0	0
1924-25	Regina Capitals	WCHL	28	9	5	14	....	....	....	8	....	....	....	....	....
1925-26	Portland Rosebuds	WHL	27	8	3	11	....	....	....	14	....	....	....	....	....
1926-27	**Chicago Black Hawks**	**NHL**	**43**	**12**	**4**	**16**	**21**	**21**	**42**	**23**	**2**	**0**	**0**	**0**	**0**
1927-28	**Chicago Black Hawks**	**NHL**	**43**	**6**	**7**	**13**	**12**	**40**	**52**	**10**	....	....	....	....	....
1928-29	**New York Americans**	**NHL**	**44**	**6**	**2**	**8**	**17**	**13**	**30**	**16**	**2**	**0**	**0**	**0**	**2**
1929-30	**New York Americans**	**NHL**	**40**	**14**	**14**	**28**	**20**	**33**	**53**	**32**	....	....	....	....	....
1930-31	**New York Americans**	**NHL**	**44**	**5**	**11**	**16**	**10**	**33**	**43**	**23**	....	....	....	....	....
1931-32	**New York Americans**	**NHL**	**48**	**12**	**15**	**27**	**20**	**33**	**53**	**16**	....	....	....	....	....
1932-33	**New York Americans**	**NHL**	**40**	**7**	**12**	**19**	**13**	**25**	**38**	**10**	....	....	....	....	....
1933-34	**New York Americans**	**NHL**	**48**	**15**	**12**	**27**	**26**	**25**	**51**	**4**	....	....	....	....	....
1934-35	**New York Americans**	**NHL**	**47**	**7**	**11**	**18**	**11**	**19**	**30**	**4**	....	....	....	....	....
1935-36	London Tecumsehs	IHL	47	12	11	23	....	....	....	6	2	0	0	0	0
	NHL Totals		**397**	**84**	**88**	**172**	**150**	**242**	**392**	**138**	**4**	**0**	**0**	**0**	**2**
	Other Major League Totals		130	52	16	68	....	....	....	56	10	1	0	1	0

WCHL First All-Star Team (1923)

Signed as a free agent by **Regina** (WCHL), December 28, 1921. Transferred to **Portland** (WHL) after **Regina** (WHL) franchise relocated, September 1, 1925. Rights transferred to **Chicago** after NHL club purchased **Portland** (WHL) franchise, May 15, 1926. Traded to **NY Americans** by **Chicago** for Alex McKinnon, October 15, 1928. Signed as a free agent by **London** (IHL), October 23, 1935.

• McVICAR, Jack

John Richard "Slim"

D – R. 6', 160 lbs. b: Renfrew, Ont., 6/4/1904 Deceased.

Season	Club	League	GP	G	A	Pts	AG	AA	APts	PIM	GP	G	A	Pts	PIM
1920-21	Iroquois Papermakers	NOJHA	7	8	2	10	....	....	....	....	....	....	....	....	....
1921-22	Iroquois Papermakers	NOJHA	STATISTICS NOT AVAILABLE												
1922-23	North Bay Trappers	NOHA	STATISTICS NOT AVAILABLE												
1923-24	Grimsby Peach Kings	OHA-I	STATISTICS NOT AVAILABLE												
1924-25	Grimsby Peach Kings	OHA-I	STATISTICS NOT AVAILABLE												
1925-26	Grimsby Peach Kings	OHA-I	STATISTICS NOT AVAILABLE												
1926-27	Chicago Cardinals	AHA	6	0	0	0	....	....	....	2	....	....	....	....	....
	Quebec Castors	Can-Am	23	2	4	6	....	....	....	58	2	0	0	0	4
1927-28	Quebec Castors	Can-Am	39	5	4	9	....	....	....	42	6	1	1	2	8
1928-29	Newark Bulldogs	Can-Am	39	4	2	6	....	....	....	42	....	....	....	....	....
1929-30	Providence Reds	Can-Am	34	8	7	15	....	....	....	91	3	3	1	4	10
1930-31	**Montreal Maroons**	**NHL**	**40**	**2**	**4**	**6**	**4**	**12**	**16**	**35**	**2**	**0**	**0**	**0**	**2**
1931-32	**Montreal Maroons**	**NHL**	**48**	**0**	**0**	**0**	**0**	**0**	**0**	**28**	**4**	**0**	**0**	**0**	**0**
1932-33	Windsor Bulldogs	IHL	10	0	1	1	....	....	....	25	....	....	....	....	....
	Providence Reds	Can-Am	36	7	4	11	....	....	....	64	2	1	1	2	2
1933-34	Providence Reds	Can-Am	36	3	3	6	....	....	....	24	3	0	0	0	12
1934-35			OUT OF HOCKEY – RETIRED												
1935-36			OUT OF HOCKEY – RETIRED												
1936-37	Grimsby Peach Kings	OSBHL	13	0	2	2	....	....	....	14	2	0	0	0	0
	NHL Totals		**88**	**2**	**4**	**6**	**4**	**12**	**16**	**63**	**6**	**0**	**0**	**0**	**2**

Can-Am First All-Star Team (1930)

Signed as a free agent by **Chicago** (AHA), October 29, 1926. Signed as a free agent by **Quebec** (Can-Am) after release by Chicago (AHA), January 1, 1927. Transferred to **Newark** (Can-Am) after **Quebec** (Can-Am) franchise relocated, October, 1928. Traded to **Providence** (Can-Am) by **Newark** (Can-Am) for cash, October 8, 1929. Traded to **Montreal Maroons** by **Providence** (Can-Am) for cash, August, 1930. Traded to **Providence** (Can-Am) by **Montreal Maroons** (Windsor-IHL) for Harvey Rockburn, December 13, 1932.

• MEEKER, Howie

Howard William

RW – R. 5'9", 165 lbs. b: Kitchener, Ont., 11/4/1924.

Season	Club	League	GP	G	A	Pts	AG	AA	APts	PIM	GP	G	A	Pts	PIM
1939-40	New Hamburg Hahn's	OMHA	STATISTICS NOT AVAILABLE												
1940-41	Kitchener Greenshirts	OHA-B	9	13	10	23	....	....	....	2	4	4	2	6	0
1941-42	Stratford Kist	OHA-B	13	*29	16	45	....	....	....	20	4	8	*11	*19	4
	Stratford Kist	M-Cup	9	13	1	14	....	....	....	2	....	....	....	....	....
1942-43	Stratford Kroehlers	OHA-Jr.	6	6	4	10	....	....	....	4	2	0	1	1	0
	Brantford Lions	OHA-Jr.	....	....	....	....	....	....	....	....	2	0	1	1	4
1943-44			MILITARY SERVICE												
1944-45			MILITARY SERVICE												
1945-46	Stratford Indians	OHA-Sr.	7	8	5	13	....	....	....	4	5	6	5	11	0
♦1946-47	**Toronto Maple Leafs**	**NHL**	**55**	**27**	**18**	**45**	**31**	**22**	**53**	**76**	**11**	**3**	**3**	**6**	**6**
♦1947-48	**Toronto Maple Leafs**	**NHL**	**58**	**14**	**20**	**34**	**18**	**26**	**44**	**62**	**9**	**2**	**4**	**6**	**15**
♦1948-49	**Toronto Maple Leafs**	**NHL**	**30**	**7**	**7**	**14**	**10**	**10**	**20**	**56**	....	....	....	....	....
1949-50	**Toronto Maple Leafs**	**NHL**	**70**	**18**	**22**	**40**	**23**	**27**	**50**	**35**	**7**	**0**	**1**	**1**	**4**
♦1950-51	**Toronto Maple Leafs**	**NHL**	**49**	**6**	**14**	**20**	**8**	**17**	**25**	**24**	**11**	**1**	**1**	**2**	**14**
1951-52	**Toronto Maple Leafs**	**NHL**	**54**	**9**	**14**	**23**	**12**	**17**	**29**	**50**	**4**	**0**	**0**	**0**	**11**
1952-53	**Toronto Maple Leafs**	**NHL**	**25**	**1**	**7**	**8**	**1**	**8**	**9**	**26**	....	....	....	....	....
1953-54	**Toronto Maple Leafs**	**NHL**	**5**	**1**	**0**	**1**	**1**	**0**	**1**	**0**	....	....	....	....	....
1954-55	Pittsburgh Hornets	AHL	2	0	0	0	....	....	....	2	....	....	....	....	....
1955-56	Pittsburgh Hornets	AHL	DID NOT PLAY – COACHING												
1956-57	**Toronto Maple Leafs**	**NHL**	DID NOT PLAY – COACHING												
1957-58	St. John's City Council	SJCSL	12	7	*16	23	....	....	....		....	....	....	....	....
1958-59	St. John's City Council	SJCSL	DID NOT PLAY – COACHING												
1959-60	St. John's Capitals	X-Games	1	0	2	2	....	....	....	2	....	....	....	....	....
	Conception Bay Ceebees	X-Games	1	0	0	0	....	....	....	0	....	....	....	....	....
1960-61	St. John's Capitals	Nfld-Sr.	5	5	4	9	....	....	....	15	....	....	....	....	....
1961-62	St. John's Guards	SJJHL	DID NOT PLAY – COACHING												
	St. John's Guards	SJSHL	DID NOT PLAY – COACHING												
1962-63	St. John's Guards	SJSHL	....	....	....	....	....	....	....	....	4	2	2	4	0
1963-64	St. John's Guards	SJSHL	4	0	2	2	....	....	....	2	....	....	....	....	....
	St. John's Capitals	Nfld-Sr.	4	1	1	2	....	....	....	12	2	1	1	2	14
1964-65	St. John's Guards	SJSHL	1	0	2	2	....	....	....	2	....	....	....	....	....
1965-66	St. John's Guards	SJSHL	7	3	6	9	....	....	....	14	3	2	2	4	18
1966-67	St. John's Capitals	Nfld-Sr.	3	0	0	0	....	....	....	4	....	....	....	....	....
	St. John's Guards	SJSHL	....	....	....	....	....	....	....	....	7	3	6	9	18
1967-68	St. John's Feildians	SJSHL	7	3	14	17	....	....	....	6	1	1	1	2	0
1968-69	St. John's Feildians	SJSHL	14	4	12	16	....	....	....	....	16	7	12	19	8
	St. John's Capitals	Nfld-Sr.	3	0	2	2	....	....	....	2	1	0	0	0	0
	NHL Totals		**346**	**83**	**102**	**185**	**104**	**127**	**231**	**329**	**42**	**6**	**9**	**15**	**50**

Won Calder Memorial Trophy (1947) • Played in NHL All-Star Game (1947, 1948, 1949)

Signed as a free agent by **Toronto**, April 13, 1946. • Missed majority of 1948-49 season recovering from collarbone injury suffered in practice, December 27, 1948.

• MEEKING, Harry

"Hurricane Howie"

LW – L. 5'7", 160 lbs. b: Berlin, Ont., 11/4/1894 d: 2/12/1972.

Season	Club	League	GP	G	A	Pts	AG	AA	APts	PIM	GP	G	A	Pts	PIM
1912-13	Toronto Canoe Club	OHA-Jr.	STATISTICS NOT AVAILABLE												
	Toronto R & AA	OHA-Sr.	....	....	....	....	....	....	....	....	1	0	0	0	0
1913-14	Toronto R & AA	OHA-Sr.	4	5	0	5	....	....	....	....	2	2	0	2	4
1914-15	Toronto Victorias	OHA-Sr.	6	16	0	16	....	....	....	....	4	2	0	2	....
1915-16	Toronto Blueshirts	NHA	14	3	1	4	....	....	....	8	2	0	0	0	0
1916-17	Ottawa Signallers	OCHL	8	7	0	7	....	....	....	32	....	....	....	....	....
1917-18	**Toronto Arenas**	**NHL**	**21**	**10**	**9**	**19**	**12**	**39**	**51**	**28**	**2**	**3**	**0**	**3**	**6**
♦	Toronto Arenas	St-Cup	5	1	2	3	....	....	....	0	....	....	....	....	....
1918-19	**Toronto Arenas**	**NHL**	**14**	**7**	**3**	**10**	**12**	**16**	**28**	**32**	....	....	....	....	....
	Glace Bay Miners	CBHL	STATISTICS NOT AVAILABLE												
1919-20	Victoria Aristocrats	PCHA	21	4	4	8	....	....	....	*51					

Season	Club	League	GP	G	A	Pts	AG	AA	APts	PIM	GP	G	A	Pts	PIM
1920-21	Victoria Aristocrats	PCHA	24	13	2	15	....	....	....	15	....	....	....	....	....
1921-22	Victoria Aristocrats	PCHA	24	2	4	6	....	....	....	33	....	....	....	....	....
1922-23	Victoria Cougars	PCHA	28	17	9	26	....	....	....	43	2	0	0	0	2
1923-24	Victoria Cougars	PCHA	29	8	5	13	....	....	....	34	....	....	....	....	....
1924-25	Victoria Cougars	WCHL	28	12	2	14	....	....	....	24	4	0	0	0	2
♦	Victoria Cougars	St-Cup	4	0	1	1	....	....	....	2	....	....	....	....	....
1925-26	Victoria Cougars	WHL	19	1	1	2	....	....	....	20	4	0	0	0	0
	Victoria Cougars	St-Cup	4	0	0	0	....	....	....	6	....	....	....	....	....
1926-27	**Detroit Cougars**	**NHL**	**6**	**0**	**0**	**0**	**0**	**0**	**0**	**4**	....	....	....	....	....
	Windsor Hornets	Can-Pro	11	5	2	7	....	....	....	14	....	....	....	....	....
	Boston Bruins	**NHL**	**23**	**1**	**0**	**1**	**2**	**0**	**2**	**2**	**7**	**0**	**0**	**0**	**0**
1927-28	New Haven Eagles	Can-Am	39	9	6	15	....	....	....	61	....	....	....	....	....
1928-29	Philadelphia Arrows	Can-Am	38	5	1	6	....	....	....	60	....	....	....	....	....
1929-30	Toronto Millionaires	IHL	19	2	3	5	....	....	....	30	....	....	....	....	....
	London Tecumsehs	IHL	6	1	1	2	....	....	....	6	....	....	....	....	....
	Kitchener Dutchmen	Can-Pro	2	1	0	1	....	....	....	0	....	....	....	....	....
	NHL Totals		**64**	**18**	**12**	**30**	**26**	**55**	**81**	**66**	**9**	**3**	**0**	**3**	**6**
	Other Major League Totals		187	60	28	88	....	....	....	228	12	0	0	0	4

PCHA Second All-Star Team (1922, 1923)

Signed as a free agent by **Toronto Blueshirts** (NHA), December 21, 1915. Signed as a free agent by **Toronto Arenas**, December 5, 1917. • Suspended by Toronto for jumping contract to sign with Cape Breton (CBHL), February 19, 1919. Traded to **Victoria** (PCHA) by **Toronto St. Pats** for cash, December 7, 1919. • 1924-25 playoff totals includes WCHL series against Calgary and Saskatoon. • 1925-26 playoff totals includes WHL series against Edmonton and Saskatoon. Rights transferred to **Detroit** after NHL club purchased **Victoria** (WHL) franchise, May 15, 1926. Traded to **Boston** by **Detroit** with Frank Fredrickson for Duke Keats and Archie Briden, January 7, 1927. Traded to **Detroit** by **Boston** for Fred Gordon, May 22, 1927. Traded to **NY Rangers** by **Detroit** with Archie Briden for Stan Brown, October 10, 1927. Signed as a free agent by **Toronto Millionaires** (IHL), November 17, 1929. Traded to **London** (IHL) by **Toronto** (IHL) for cash, December 1, 1929.

• MEGER, Paul

Paul Carl
LW – L. 5'7", 160 lbs. b: Watrous, Sask., 2/17/1929.

Season	Club	League	GP	G	A	Pts	AG	AA	APts	PIM	GP	G	A	Pts	PIM
1945-46	Selkirk Fishermen	WSrHL	STATISTICS NOT AVAILABLE												
1946-47	Barrie Flyers	OHA-Jr.	31	13	14	27	....	....	....	20	5	3	2	5	9
1947-48	Barrie Flyers	OHA-Jr.	36	30	30	60	....	....	....	28	12	9	9	18	11
	Barrie Flyers	M-Cup	10	5	12	17	....	....	....	9	....	....	....	....	....
1948-49	Barrie Flyers	OHA-Jr.	40	33	42	75	....	....	....	79	8	5	4	9	2
	Barrie Flyers	M-Cup	8	3	4	7	....	....	....	6	....	....	....	....	....
1949-50	Buffalo Bisons	AHL	63	26	40	66	....	....	....	33	5	1	2	3	0
	Montreal Canadiens	**NHL**	....	....	....	....	....	....	....	....	**2**	**0**	**0**	**0**	**2**
1950-51	**Montreal Canadiens**	**NHL**	**17**	**2**	**4**	**6**	**3**	**5**	**8**	**6**	**11**	**1**	**3**	**4**	**4**
	Buffalo Bisons	AHL	46	34	35	69	....	....	....	16	....	....	....	....	....
1951-52	**Montreal Canadiens**	**NHL**	**69**	**24**	**18**	**42**	**32**	**22**	**54**	**44**	**11**	**0**	**3**	**3**	**2**
♦1952-53	**Montreal Canadiens**	**NHL**	**69**	**9**	**17**	**26**	**12**	**21**	**33**	**38**	**5**	**1**	**2**	**3**	**4**
1953-54	**Montreal Canadiens**	**NHL**	**44**	**4**	**9**	**13**	**5**	**11**	**16**	**24**	**6**	**1**	**0**	**1**	**4**
	Montreal Royals	QHL	23	13	17	30	....	....	....	28	....	....	....	....	....
1954-55	**Montreal Canadiens**	**NHL**	**13**	**0**	**4**	**4**	**0**	**5**	**5**	**6**	....	....	....	....	....
	NHL Totals		**212**	**39**	**52**	**91**	**52**	**64**	**116**	**118**	**35**	**3**	**8**	**11**	**16**

AHL Second All-Star Team (1950) • Won Dudley "Red" Garrett Memorial Award (Top Rookie - AHL) (1950) • AHL First All-Star Team (1951) • Played in NHL All-Star Game (1951, 1952, 1953) • Suffered career-ending head injury in game vs. Chicago, November 25, 1954.

• MEISSNER, Dick

Richard Donald
RW – R. 5'11", 200 lbs. b: Kindersley, Sask., 1/6/1940.

Season	Club	League	GP	G	A	Pts	AG	AA	APts	PIM	GP	G	A	Pts	PIM
1956-57	Humboldt Indians	SJHL	51	9	13	22	....	....	....	8	4	0	1	1	0
1957-58	Estevan Bruins	SJHL	51	49	24	73	....	....	....	9	6	2	5	7	0
1958-59	Estevan Bruins	SJHL	46	46	43	89	....	....	....	37	14	*18	*14	*32	9
	Flin Flon Bombers	M-Cup	6	2	2	4	....	....	....	2	....	....	....	....	....
1959-60	**Boston Bruins**	**NHL**	**60**	**5**	**6**	**11**	**6**	**6**	**12**	**22**	....	....	....	....	....
1960-61	**Boston Bruins**	**NHL**	**9**	**0**	**1**	**1**	**0**	**1**	**1**	**2**	....	....	....	....	....
	Kingston Frontenacs	EPHL	58	26	22	48	....	....	....	19	5	1	2	3	0
1961-62	**Boston Bruins**	**NHL**	**66**	**3**	**3**	**6**	**3**	**3**	**6**	**13**	....	....	....	....	....
1962-63	Hershey Bears	AHL	70	28	26	54	....	....	....	18	15	8	6	14	10
1963-64	**New York Rangers**	**NHL**	**35**	**3**	**5**	**8**	**4**	**5**	**9**	**0**	....	....	....	....	....
	Baltimore Clippers	AHL	12	5	5	10	....	....	....	4	....	....	....	....	....
1964-65	**New York Rangers**	**NHL**	**1**	**0**	**0**	**0**	**0**	**0**	**0**	**0**	....	....	....	....	....
	Baltimore Clippers	AHL	69	35	42	77	....	....	....	21	5	3	1	4	0
1965-66	St. Louis Braves	CPHL	62	27	12	39	....	....	....	23	5	2	1	3	0
1966-67	Los Angeles Blades	WHL	72	39	42	81	....	....	....	6	....	....	....	....	....
1967-68	Portland Buckaroos	WHL	6	1	1	2	....	....	....	2	....	....	....	....	....
	Baltimore Clippers	AHL	61	29	25	54	....	....	....	9	....	....	....	....	....
1968-69	Providence Reds	AHL	73	16	22	38	....	....	....	37	9	5	8	13	9
1969-70	Providence Reds	AHL	63	19	23	42	....	....	....	20	....	....	....	....	....
1970-71	Providence Reds	AHL	5	0	2	2	....	....	....	2	....	....	....	....	....
1971-72	Phoenix Roadrunners	WHL	14	4	4	8	....	....	....	11	....	....	....	....	....
	Seattle Totems	WHL	9	2	3	5	....	....	....	0	....	....	....	....	....
1972-73			DID NOT PLAY												
1973-74			DID NOT PLAY												
1974-75	Portland Buckaroos	WIHL	19	3	8	11	....	....	....	19	....	....	....	....	....
	NHL Totals		**171**	**11**	**15**	**26**	**13**	**15**	**28**	**37**	....	....	....	....	....

• Brother of Barrie • SJHL Second All-Star Team (1959) • WHL First All-Star Team (1967)

Traded to **NY Rangers** by **Boston** with Don McKenney for Dean Prentice, February 4, 1963. • Terms of transaction stipulated that Meissner would report to the NY Rangers following the 1962-63 season. Traded to **Chicago** by **NY Rangers** with Dave Richardson, Tracy Pratt and Mel Pearson for John McKenzie and Ray Cullen, June 4, 1965. Selected by **Providence** (AHL) from **Chicago** in Reverse Draft, June 13, 1968. Traded to **Phoenix** (WHL) by **Providence** (AHL) with Adam Keller for Jim Patterson, August, 1971.

• MELNYK, Gerry

— see page 1420

• MENARD, Hillary

Hillary Gilbert "Minnie"
LW – L. 5'8", 165 lbs. b: Timmins, Ont., 1/15/1934.

Season	Club	League	GP	G	A	Pts	AG	AA	APts	PIM	GP	G	A	Pts	PIM
1951-52	Barrie Flyers	OHA-Jr.	42	20	16	36	....	....	....	64	....	....	....	....	....
1952-53	Barrie–Galt Hawks	OHA-Jr.	55	23	19	42	....	....	....	143	10	11	7	18	9
1953-54	Galt Black Hawks	OHA-Jr.	19	6	15	21	....	....	....	30	....	....	....	....	....
	Hamilton Tiger Cubs	OHA-Jr.	4	0	0	0	....	....	....	0	....	....	....	....	....
	Chicago Black Hawks	**NHL**	**1**	**0**	**0**	**0**	**0**	**0**	**0**	**0**	....	....	....	....	....
	Guelph Biltmores	OHA-Jr.	34	17	23	40	....	....	....	42	3	3	0	3	21
1954-55	Pembroke Lumber Kings	NOHA	15	1	3	4	....	....	....	10	....	....	....	....	....
1955-56	Val D'Or Miners	QPHL	STATISTICS NOT AVAILABLE												
1956-57	Belleville McFarlands	EOHL	51	*50	28	78	....	....	....	134	10	5	4	9	10
1957-58	Belleville McFarlands	EOHL	51	22	24	46	....	....	....	46	13	7	4	11	18
	Belleville McFarlands	Al-Cup	14	*9	4	13	....	....	....	20	....	....	....	....	....
1958-59	Belleville McFarlands	EOHL	48	12	22	34	....	....	....	55	....	....	....	....	....
1959-60	New York Rovers	EHL	48	22	14	36	....	....	....	53	....	....	....	....	....
1960-61	Omaha Knights	IHL	55	18	30	48	....	....	....	88	....	....	....	....	....
	New York Rovers	EHL	2	0	0	0	....	....	....	0	....	....	....	....	....
1961-62	Omaha Knights	IHL	64	20	41	61	....	....	....	76	7	0	1	1	6
1962-63	Des Moines Oak Leafs	USHL	32	25	36	61	....	....	....	50	....	....	....	....	....
	Omaha Knights	IHL	7	4	2	6	....	....	....	16	7	6	2	8	8
1963-64	Des Moines Oak Leafs	IHL	39	11	22	33	....	....	....	49	....	....	....	....	....
1964-65	Des Moines Oak Leafs	IHL	1	0	0	0	....	....	....	0	....	....	....	....	....
1965-66	Des Moines Oak Leafs	IHL	3	1	0	1	....	....	....	2	....	....	....	....	....
1966-67	Belleville Mohawks	OHA-Sr.	40	13	26	39	....	....	....	18	....	....	....	....	....
1967-68	Belleville Mohawks	OHA-Sr.	34	22	11	33	....	....	....	23	....	....	....	....	....
	NHL Totals		**1**	**0**	**0**	**0**	**0**	**0**	**0**	**0**	....	....	....	....	....

• Brother of Howie

• MENARD, Howie

— see page 1420

• MERONEK, Bill

"Smiley"
C – L. 5'9", 155 lbs. b: Stony Mountain, Man., 4/15/1917 d: 5/25/1999.

Season	Club	League	GP	G	A	Pts	AG	AA	APts	PIM	GP	G	A	Pts	PIM
1934-35	St. Boniface Seals	MJHL	10	7	7	14	....	....	....	0	....	....	....	....	....
1935-36	Portage Terriers	MJHL	16	16	7	23	....	....	....	2	6	6	*6	12	6
1936-37	Portage Terriers	MJHL	16	*21	*20	*41	....	....	....	4	4	3	0	3	2
1937-38	Verdun Maple Leafs	QSHL	20	10	10	20	....	....	....	4	8	4	3	7	0
1938-39	Verdun Maple Leafs	QSHL	22	*17	17	34	....	....	....	9	2	0	1	1	0
1939-40	**Montreal Canadiens**	**NHL**	**7**	**2**	**2**	**4**	**3**	**3**	**6**	**0**	....	....	....	....	....
	Verdun Maple Leafs	QSHL	26	14	23	37	....	....	....	10	....	....	....	....	....
1940-41	Montreal Sr. Canadiens	QSHL	29	17	10	27	....	....	....	4	....	....	....	....	....
1941-42	Montreal Sr. Canadiens	QSHL	31	4	15	19	....	....	....	32	6	*8	6	*14	0
1942-43	Montreal Sr. Canadiens	QSHL	24	13	19	32	....	....	....	4	....	....	....	....	....
	Montreal Canadiens	**NHL**	**12**	**3**	**6**	**9**	**3**	**6**	**9**	**0**	**1**	**0**	**0**	**0**	**0**
1943-44	Montreal Noordyn	MCHL	10	*13	13	26	....	....	....	6	....	....	....	....	....
	Montreal Royals	QSHL	19	12	16	28	....	....	....	0	7	6	4	10	0
1944-45	Montreal Royals	QSHL	23	16	*32	48	....	....	....	8	6	3	4	7	0
1945-46	Montreal Royals	QSHL	35	15	36	51	....	....	....	18	8	0	4	4	2
1946-47	Lachine Rapides	QPHL	49	39	63	102	....	....	....	14	10	4	7	11	10
1947-48	Lachine Rapides	QPHL	1	0	0	0	....	....	....	0	....	....	....	....	....
1948-49	Hull Volants	ECSHL	15	11	*27	*38	....	....	....	4	7	8	3	11	2
1949-50	Cornwall Calumets	ECSHL	15	7	17	24	....	....	....	6	....	....	....	....	....
	Hull Volants	ECSHL	10	5	10	15	....	....	....	0	13	7	11	18	0
	NHL Totals		**19**	**5**	**8**	**13**	**6**	**9**	**15**	**0**	**1**	**0**	**0**	**0**	**0**

Signed as a free agent by **Montreal**, February 1, 1943. • Played home games only in 1942-43 because of work commitments.

• MERRILL, Horace

Horace Jefferson
D – L. 5'9", 176 lbs. b: Ottawa, Ont., 11/30/1885 d: 12/24/1958.

Season	Club	League	GP	G	A	Pts	AG	AA	APts	PIM	GP	G	A	Pts	PIM
1907-08	Ottawa Seconds	OCHL	7	5	0	5	....	....	....	....	....	....	....	....	....
1908-09	Ottawa Cliffsides	IPAHU	1	0	0	0	....	....	....	0	1	0	0	0	0
	Ottawa Seconds	OCHL	5	0	0	0	....	....	....	0	2	0	0	0	0
1909-10	Ottawa Seconds	OCHL	7	3	0	3	....	....	....	20	1	0	0	0	0
	Ottawa Seconds	Al-Cup	2	1	0	1	....	....	....	0	....	....	....	....	....
1910-11	Ottawa New Edinburghs	IPAHU	5	3	0	3	....	....	....	6	3	1	0	1	0
1911-12	Ottawa New Edinburghs	IPAHU	9	8	0	8	....	....	....	6	3	2	0	2	0
1912-13	Ottawa Senators	NHA	10	5	0	5	....	....	....	4	....	....	....	....	....
1913-14	Ottawa Senators	NHA	18	3	3	6	....	....	....	29	....	....	....	....	....
1914-15	Ottawa Senators	NHA	20	3	0	3	....	....	....	32	5	1	0	1	0
1915-16	Ottawa Senators	NHA	24	4	1	5	....	....	....	25	....	....	....	....	....
1916-17	Ottawa Senators	NHA	19	1	2	3	....	....	....	12	2	0	0	0	3
1917-18	**Ottawa Senators**	**NHL**	**3**	**0**	**0**	**0**	**0**	**0**	**0**	**3**	....	....	....	....	....
1918-19			DID NOT PLAY												
♦1919-20	**Ottawa Senators**	**NHL**	**5**	**0**	**0**	**0**	**0**	**0**	**0**	**0**	....	....	....	....	....
	NHL Totals		**8**	**0**	**0**	**0**	**0**	**0**	**0**	**3**	....	....	....	....	....
	Other Major League Totals		91	16	6	22	....	....	....	102	7	1	0	1	3

Signed as a free agent by **Ottawa** (NHA), January 13, 1913. Signed as a free agent by **Ottawa**, February 20, 1918. Signed as a free agent by **Ottawa**, November 28, 1919.

• METZ, Don

Donald Maurice
RW – R. 5'10", 165 lbs. b: Wilcox, Sask., 1/10/1916.

Season	Club	League	GP	G	A	Pts	AG	AA	APts	PIM	GP	G	A	Pts	PIM
1935-36	St. Michael's Majors	OHA-Jr.	10	9	4	13	....	....	....	5	5	3	0	3	8
	Toronto Goodyears	OHA-Sr.	13	6	3	9	....	....	....	4	9	3	4	7	10
1936-37	Toronto Goodyears	OHA-Sr.	9	3	2	5	....	....	....	6	5	0	2	2	6
1937-38	Toronto Goodyears	OHA-Sr.	16	20	*22	*42	....	....	....	4	6	6	2	*8	2
	Toronto Goodyears	Al-Cup	4	1	1	2	....	....	....	6	....	....	....	....	....
1938-39	Toronto Goodyears	OHA-Sr.	18	15	16	31	....	....	....	8	5	*4	5	*9	0
	Toronto Maple Leafs	**NHL**	....	....	....	....	....	....	....	....	**2**	**0**	**0**	**0**	**0**
	Toronto Goodyears	Al-Cup	10	*12	3	*15	....	....	....	17	....	....	....	....	....
1939-40	**Toronto Maple Leafs**	**NHL**	**10**	**1**	**1**	**2**	**2**	**2**	**4**	**4**	**2**	**0**	**0**	**0**	**0**
	Pittsburgh Hornets	IAHL	32	13	25	38	....	....	....	10	7	2	2	4	4
1940-41	**Toronto Maple Leafs**	**NHL**	**31**	**4**	**10**	**14**	**6**	**14**	**20**	**6**	**7**	**1**	**1**	**2**	**2**
♦1941-42	**Toronto Maple Leafs**	**NHL**	**25**	**2**	**3**	**5**	**3**	**4**	**7**	**8**	**4**	**4**	**3**	**7**	**0**
1942-43	Regina Army Caps	RNDHL	24	*43	26	*69	....	....	....	12	5	*10	4	14	6
1943-44	Toronto RCAF Seahawks	TIHL	....	....	....	....	....	....	....	....	2	1	1	2	4
♦1944-45	**Toronto Maple Leafs**	**NHL**	....	....	....	....	....	....	....	....	**11**	**0**	**1**	**1**	**4**
1945-46	**Toronto Maple Leafs**	**NHL**	**7**	**1**	**0**	**1**	**1**	**0**	**1**	**0**	....	....	....	....	....
	Pittsburgh Hornets	AHL	44	22	29	51	....	....	....	8	6	3	4	7	2

Season	Club	League	GP	G	A	Pts	AG	AA	APts	PIM	GP	G	A	Pts	PIM
			REGULAR SEASON								PLAYOFFS				
♦1946-47	Toronto Maple Leafs	NHL	40	4	9	13	4	11	15	10	11	2	3	5	4
	Pittsburgh Hornets	AHL	24	19	17	36	....	....	....	4	....	....	....	....	....
♦1947-48	Toronto Maple Leafs	NHL	26	4	6	10	5	8	13	2	2	0	0	0	2
	Pittsburgh Hornets	AHL	3	0	1	1	....	....	....	0	....	....	....	....	....
♦1948-49	Toronto Maple Leafs	NHL	33	4	6	10	6	8	14	12	3	0	0	0	0
	Pittsburgh Hornets	AHL	17	5	7	12	....	....	....	4	....	....	....	....	....
	NHL Totals		172	20	35	55	27	47	74	42	42	7	8	15	12

• Brother of Nick • Played in NHL All-Star Game (1947)

• METZ, Nick Nicholas John

LW – L. 5'11", 160 lbs. b: Wilcox, Sask., 2/16/1914 d: 8/24/1990.

Season	Club	League	GP	G	A	Pts	AG	AA	APts	PIM	GP	G	A	Pts	PIM
1930-31	Notre Dame Hounds	SAHA	STATISTICS NOT AVAILABLE												
1931-32	St. Michael's Buzzers	OHA-B	STATISTICS NOT AVAILABLE												
1932-33	St. Michael's Majors	OHA-Jr.	10	9	3	*12	....	....	....	14	2	0	*2	2	2
1933-34	St. Michael's Majors	OHA-Jr.	12	18	15	33	....	....	....	10	3	*4	0	4	6
	St. Michael's Majors	M-Cup	13	9	7	16	....	....	....	16	....	....	....	....	....
1934-35	Toronto Maple Leafs	NHL	18	2	2	4	3	3	6	4	6	1	1	2	0
	Syracuse Stars	IHL	26	13	13	26	....	....	....	6	....	....	....	....	....
1935-36	Toronto Maple Leafs	NHL	38	14	6	20	27	11	38	14	....	....	....	....	....
1936-37	Toronto Maple Leafs	NHL	48	9	11	20	15	20	35	19	2	0	0	0	0
1937-38	Toronto Maple Leafs	NHL	48	15	7	22	25	11	36	12	7	0	2	2	0
1938-39	Toronto Maple Leafs	NHL	47	11	10	21	19	16	35	15	10	3	3	6	6
1939-40	Toronto Maple Leafs	NHL	31	6	5	11	10	8	18	2	9	1	3	4	9
1940-41	Toronto Maple Leafs	NHL	47	14	21	35	22	30	52	10	7	3	4	7	0
♦1941-42	Toronto Maple Leafs	NHL	30	11	9	20	15	11	26	20	13	4	4	8	12
1942-43	Nanaimo Army	NNDHL	1	1	2	3	....	....	....	0	....	....	....	....	....
	Nanaimo Army	Al-Cup	13	3	3	6	....	....	....	10	....	....	....	....	....
1943-44	Nanaimo Army	PCHL	7	2	7	9	....	....	....	6	....	....	....	....	....
♦1944-45	Toronto Maple Leafs	NHL	50	22	13	35	22	15	37	26	7	1	1	2	2
1945-46	Toronto Maple Leafs	NHL	41	11	11	22	13	16	29	4	....	....	....	....	....
♦1946-47	Toronto Maple Leafs	NHL	60	12	16	28	13	19	32	15	6	4	2	6	0
♦1947-48	Toronto Maple Leafs	NHL	60	4	8	12	5	10	15	8	9	2	0	2	2
	NHL Totals		518	131	119	250	189	170	359	149	76	19	20	39	31

• Brother of Don

• MICHALUK, Art

D – R. 6', 180 lbs. b: Canmore, Alta., 5/4/1923.

Season	Club	League	GP	G	A	Pts	AG	AA	APts	PIM	GP	G	A	Pts	PIM
1939-40	Canmore Zephyrs	AJHL	9	1	1	2	....	....	....	0	2	0	2	2	2
1940-41			MILITARY SERVICE												
1941-42			MILITARY SERVICE												
1942-43	Calgary Mustangs	CNDHL	21	3	2	5	....	....	....	24	8	1	1	2	8
1943-44			MILITARY SERVICE												
1944-45	Calgary Mustangs	CNDHL	15	6	3	9	....	....	....	14	3	0	0	0	8
1945-46	Calgary Stampeders	WCSHL	35	5	9	14	....	....	....	24	5	0	1	1	6
	Calgary Stampeders	Al-Cup	13	0	2	2	....	....	....	12	....	....	....	....	....
1946-47	Calgary Stampeders	WCSHL	39	16	16	32	....	....	....	58	7	2	5	7	*15
	Calgary Stampeders	Al-Cup	18	1	4	5	....	....	....	16	....	....	....	....	....
1947-48	Chicago Black Hawks	NHL	5	0	0	0	0	0	0	0	....	....	....	....	....
	Pittsburgh Hornets	AHL	1	0	0	0	....	....	....	0	....	....	....	....	....
	Providence Reds	AHL	39	6	10	16	....	....	....	32	5	1	2	3	2
1948-49	Providence Reds	AHL	65	4	17	21	....	....	....	55	11	1	3	4	6
1949-50	Providence Reds	AHL	67	7	20	27	....	....	....	32	4	1	2	3	2
1950-51	Providence Reds	AHL	70	13	21	34	....	....	....	34	....	....	....	....	....
1951-52	Providence Reds	AHL	62	3	15	18	....	....	....	41	15	0	5	5	8
1952-53	Calgary Stampeders	WHL	70	10	26	36	....	....	....	22	5	0	2	2	8
1953-54	Calgary Stampeders	WHL	68	7	26	33	....	....	....	20	18	1	7	8	8
	Calgary Stampeders	Ed-Cup	7	1	3	4	....	....	....	0	....	....	....	....	....
1954-55	Calgary Stampeders	WHL	70	8	22	30	....	....	....	24	9	0	7	7	10
1955-56	Calgary Stampeders	WHL	54	3	14	17	....	....	....	28	8	0	2	2	6
1956-57	Calgary Stampeders	WHL	51	2	12	14	....	....	....	15	3	0	2	2	2
1957-58	Calgary Stampeders	WHL	17	3	15	18	....	....	....	2	14	0	3	3	6
	NHL Totals		5	0	0	0	0	0	0	0	....	....	....	....	....

• Brother of John • WHL First All-Star Team (1953, 1956) • WHL Prairie Division First All-Star Team (1957)

Signed as a free agent by **Chicago**, September 14, 1947.

• MICHALUK, John

LW – L. 5'10", 155 lbs. b: Canmore, Alta., 11/2/1928.

Season	Club	League	GP	G	A	Pts	AG	AA	APts	PIM	GP	G	A	Pts	PIM
1947-48	Westaskiwin Canadians	AJHL	STATISTICS NOT AVAILABLE												
	Westaskiwin Canadians	M-Cup	4	1	0	1	....	....	....	0	....	....	....	....	....
1948-49	Calgary Buffalos	WCJHL	30	26	17	43	....	....	....	24	8	6	5	11	8
	Calgary Stampeders	WCSHL	2	0	0	0	....	....	....	0	....	....	....	....	....
	Calgary Buffalos	M-Cup	16	3	7	10	....	....	....	22	....	....	....	....	....
1949-50	Spokane Flyers	WIHL	58	21	15	36	....	....	....	27	4	1	2	3	0
1950-51	Chicago Black Hawks	NHL	1	0	0	0	0	0	0	0	....	....	....	....	....
	Milwaukee Seagulls	USHL	56	13	11	24	....	....	....	41	....	....	....	....	....
1951-52	Providence Reds	AHL	46	13	12	25	....	....	....	16	3	0	1	1	0
1952-53	Providence Reds	AHL	18	1	3	4	....	....	....	6	....	....	....	....	....
	Quebec Aces	QMHL	22	3	3	6	....	....	....	17	21	0	2	2	5
1953-54	Calgary Stampeders	WHL	66	7	9	16	....	....	....	8	18	1	7	8	8
	Calgary Stampeders	Ed-Cup	2	1	0	1	....	....	....	0	....	....	....	....	....
1954-55	Calgary Stampeders	WHL	14	3	4	7	....	....	....	2	9	0	0	0	2
	NHL Totals		1	0	0	0	0	0	0	0	....	....	....	....	....

• Brother of Art

• MICKEY, Larry — *see page 1425*

• MICKOSKI, Nick Nicholas "Broadway Nick"

LW – L. 6'1", 183 lbs. b: Winnipeg, Man., 12/7/1927.

Season	Club	League	GP	G	A	Pts	AG	AA	APts	PIM	GP	G	A	Pts	PIM
1943-44	St. Catharines Falcons	OHA-Jr.	26	4	6	10	....	....	....	50	6	0	0	0	17
1944-45	Canadian Ukrainian A.C.	MJHL	12	11	4	15	....	....	....	2	4	5	4	9	0
1945-46	St. James Canadians	MJHL	10	10	6	16	....	....	....	8	2	0	0	0	0
	New York Rovers	EAHL	25	6	8	14	....	....	....	8	9	1	2	3	6
1946-47	New York Rovers	QSHL	30	25	16	41	....	....	....	16	....	....	....	....	....
	New York Rovers	EAHL	10	9	16	25	....	....	....	10	....	....	....	....	....
1947-48	New Haven Ramblers	AHL	22	11	16	27	....	....	....	4	4	2	1	3	2
	New York Rangers	NHL	....	....	....	....	....	....	....	....	2	0	1	1	0
1948-49	New York Rangers	NHL	54	13	9	22	18	13	31	20	....	....	....	....	....
1949-50	New York Rangers	NHL	45	10	10	20	13	12	25	10	12	1	5	6	2
	New Haven Ramblers	AHL	23	12	17	29	....	....	....	7	....	....	....	....	....
1950-51	New York Rangers	NHL	64	20	15	35	26	18	44	12	....	....	....	....	....
1951-52	New York Rangers	NHL	43	7	13	20	9	16	25	20	....	....	....	....	....
	Cincinnati Mohawks	AHL	22	11	10	21	....	....	....	15	5	2	3	5	4
1952-53	New York Rangers	NHL	70	19	16	35	25	19	44	39	....	....	....	....	....
1953-54	New York Rangers	NHL	68	19	16	35	26	19	45	22	....	....	....	....	....
1954-55	New York Rangers	NHL	18	0	14	14	0	16	16	6	....	....	....	....	....
	Chicago Black Hawks	NHL	52	10	19	29	13	22	35	42	....	....	....	....	....
1955-56	Chicago Black Hawks	NHL	70	19	20	39	26	24	50	52	....	....	....	....	....
1956-57	Chicago Black Hawks	NHL	70	16	20	36	21	22	43	24	....	....	....	....	....
1957-58	Chicago Black Hawks	NHL	28	5	6	11	6	6	12	20	....	....	....	....	....
	Detroit Red Wings	NHL	37	8	12	20	10	12	22	30	4	0	0	0	4
1958-59	Detroit Red Wings	NHL	66	11	15	26	13	15	28	20	....	....	....	....	....
1959-60	Boston Bruins	NHL	18	1	0	1	1	0	1	2	....	....	....	....	....
	Providence Reds	AHL	48	29	22	51	....	....	....	6	5	2	5	7	4
1960-61	Winnipeg Warriors	WHL	69	25	24	49	....	....	....	16	....	....	....	....	....
1961-62	San Francisco Seals	WHL	70	31	48	79	....	....	....	24	2	1	1	2	0
1962-63	San Francisco Seals	WHL	68	41	54	95	....	....	....	20	17	5	11	16	6
1963-64	San Francisco Seals	WHL	68	20	37	57	....	....	....	28	11	2	10	12	4
1964-65	San Francisco Seals	WHL	60	13	33	46	....	....	....	24	....	....	....	....	....
1965-66	San Francisco Seals	WHL	DID NOT PLAY – COACHING												
1966-67	Grand Falls Cataracts	Nfld-Sr.	37	27	49	76	....	....	....	12	....	....	....	....	....
1967-68	Grand Falls Cataracts	Nfld-Sr.	40	34	56	90	....	....	....	14	5	1	6	7	0
1968-69	Grand Falls Cataracts	Nfld-Sr.	40	24	28	52	....	....	....	26	6	2	4	6	4
	NHL Totals		703	158	185	343	207	214	421	319	18	1	6	7	6

WHL First All-Star Team (1963) • Played in NHL All-Star Game (1956)

Traded to **Chicago** by **NY Rangers** with Allan Stanley and Rich Lamoureux for Bill Gadsby and Pete Conacher, November 23, 1954. Traded to **Detroit** by **Chicago** with Hec Lalonde, Bob Bailey and Jack McIntyre for Bill Dineen, Billy Dea, Lorne Ferguson and Earl Reibel, December 17, 1957. Traded to **Boston** by **Detroit** for Jim Morrison, August 25, 1959.

• MIGAY, Rudy Rudolph Joseph

C – L. 5'6", 150 lbs. b: Fort William, Ont., 11/18/1928.

Season	Club	League	GP	G	A	Pts	AG	AA	APts	PIM	GP	G	A	Pts	PIM
1944-45	Port Arthur Flyers	TBJHL	11	22	10	32	....	....	....	22	3	2	2	4	6
1945-46	Port Arthur Flyers	TBJHL	6	11	*17	*28	....	....	....	0	10	7	10	17	6
1946-47	St. Michael's Majors	OHA-Jr.	28	25	18	43	....	....	....	15	9	2	11	13	0
	St. Michael's Majors	M-Cup	10	7	16	23	....	....	....	2	....	....	....	....	....
1947-48	Port Arthur Bruins	TBJHL	7	12	8	20	....	....	....	12	24	17	*30	47	18
	Port Arthur Bruins	M-Cup	17	13	24	37	....	....	....	16	....	....	....	....	....
1948-49	Pittsburgh Hornets	AHL	64	21	31	52	....	....	....	38	....	....	....	....	....
1949-50	Toronto Maple Leafs	NHL	18	1	5	6	1	6	7	8	....	....	....	....	....
	Pittsburgh Hornets	AHL	44	11	25	36	....	....	....	31	....	....	....	....	....
1950-51	Pittsburgh Hornets	AHL	58	20	38	58	....	....	....	45	13	1	*15	*16	11
1951-52	Toronto Maple Leafs	NHL	19	2	1	3	3	1	4	12	....	....	....	....	....
	Pittsburgh Hornets	AHL	32	20	26	46	....	....	....	10	11	7	4	11	8
1952-53	Toronto Maple Leafs	NHL	40	5	4	9	7	5	12	22	....	....	....	....	....
1953-54	Toronto Maple Leafs	NHL	70	8	15	23	11	18	29	60	5	1	0	1	4
1954-55	Toronto Maple Leafs	NHL	67	8	16	24	10	18	28	66	3	0	0	0	10
1955-56	Toronto Maple Leafs	NHL	70	12	16	28	16	19	35	52	5	0	0	0	6
1956-57	Toronto Maple Leafs	NHL	66	15	20	35	19	22	41	51	....	....	....	....	....
1957-58	Toronto Maple Leafs	NHL	48	7	14	21	9	14	23	18	....	....	....	....	....
	Rochester Americans	AHL	15	5	8	13	....	....	....	18	....	....	....	....	....
1958-59	Toronto Maple Leafs	NHL	19	1	1	2	1	1	2	4	2	0	0	0	0
	Rochester Americans	AHL	51	24	58	82	....	....	....	100	3	1	0	1	6
1959-60	Toronto Maple Leafs	NHL	1	0	0	0	0	0	0	0	....	....	....	....	....
	Rochester Americans	AHL	50	16	48	64	....	....	....	50	12	3	*10	13	19
1960-61	Port Arthur Bearcats	TBSHL	PLAYER/COACH – STATISTICS UNAVAILABLE												
1961-62	Port Arthur Bearcats	TBSHL	PLAYER/COACH – STATISTICS UNAVAILABLE												
1962-63	Rochester Americans	AHL	2	1	1	2	....	....	....	4	....	....	....	....	....
1963-64	Denver Invaders	WHL	56	20	31	51	....	....	....	30	6	0	3	3	32
1964-65	Tulsa Oilers	CPHL	50	5	26	31	....	....	....	53	....	....	....	....	....
1965-66	Tulsa Oilers	CPHL	DID NOT PLAY – COACHING												
	NHL Totals		418	59	92	151	77	104	181	293	15	1	0	1	20

AHL First All-Star Team (1959) • Shared Les Cunningham Award (MVP - AHL) with Bill Hicke (1959) • Played in NHL All-Star Game (1957)

• MIKITA, Stan — *see page 1426*

• MIKOL, Jim John Stanley

LW/D – R. 6', 175 lbs. b: Kitchener, Ont., 6/11/1938.

Season	Club	League	GP	G	A	Pts	AG	AA	APts	PIM	GP	G	A	Pts	PIM
1956-57	Peterborough Petes	OHA-Jr.	13	2	0	2	....	....	....	4	....	....	....	....	....
1957-58	Peterborough Petes	OHA-Jr.	35	6	12	18	....	....	....	37	5	0	2	2	13
1958-59	North Bay Trappers	NOHA	48	3	11	14	....	....	....	47	....	....	....	....	....
1959-60	Johnstown Jets	EHL	64	11	14	25	....	....	....	101	13	2	5	7	18
1960-61	Cleveland Barons	AHL	70	12	22	34	....	....	....	116	4	0	0	0	0
1961-62	Cleveland Barons	AHL	70	32	48	80	....	....	....	89	6	1	4	5	12
1962-63	Toronto Maple Leafs	NHL	4	0	1	1	0	1	1	2	....	....	....	....	....
	Cleveland Barons	AHL	49	20	30	50	....	....	....	58	5	0	5	5	4
1963-64	Cleveland Barons	AHL	72	24	44	68	....	....	....	52	9	3	4	7	6
1964-65	New York Rangers	NHL	30	1	3	4	1	3	4	6	....	....	....	....	....
	St. Paul Rangers	CPHL	33	14	33	47	....	....	....	30	11	1	7	8	12
1965-66	Providence Reds	AHL	72	24	26	50	....	....	....	35	....	....	....	....	....
1966-67	Providence Reds	AHL	31	8	9	17	....	....	....	8	....	....	....	....	....
1967-68	Providence Reds	AHL	63	19	30	49	....	....	....	30	8	1	3	4	12
1968-69	Cleveland Barons	AHL	72	20	35	55	....	....	....	27	5	0	0	0	0
1969-70	Cleveland Barons	AHL	68	8	19	27	....	....	....	18	....	....	....	....	....
	NHL Totals		34	1	4	5	1	4	5	8	....	....	....	....	....

Claimed by **Boston** from **Cleveland** (AHL) in Inter-League Draft, June 10, 1964. Claimed by **NY Rangers** from **Boston** in Intra-League Draft, June 10, 1964. Traded to **Providence** (AHL) by **NY Rangers** with Sandy McGregor, Marcel Paille and Aldo Guidolin for Ed Giacomin, May 17, 1965. Traded to **Montreal** by **Providence** (AHL) for Yves Locas, July 1, 1968. Traded to **Cleveland** (AHL) by **Montreal** with Bill Staub for Howie Glover, August 27, 1968.

• MILKS, Hib Hibbert

LW/C – L. 5'11", 165 lbs. b: Eardley, Ont., 4/1/1902 d: 1/21/1949.

			REGULAR SEASON								PLAYOFFS				
Season	Club	League	GP	G	A	Pts	AG	AA	APts	PIM	GP	G	A	Pts	PIM
1917-18	Ottawa Landsdownes	OCJHL	1	0	0	0	....	....	....	0	....	....	....	....	....
1918-19	Ottawa West-Enders	OCJHL	STATISTICS NOT AVAILABLE												
1919-20	Ottawa Gunners	OCHL	8	1	0	1	....	....	....	....	....	....	....	....	....
1920-21	Ottawa Gunners	OCHL	12	6	0	6	....	....	....	....	....	....	....	....	....
	Ottawa Gunners	Al-Cup	7	6	2	8	....	....	....	0	....	....	....	....	....
1921-22	Ottawa Gunners	OCHL	14	6	4	10	....	....	....	15	6	7	4	11	*18
1922-23	Pittsburgh Yellowjackets	USAHA	20	10	0	10	....	....	....	....	....	....	....	....	....
1923-24	Ottawa New Edinburghs	OCHL	12	*16	0	*16	....	....	....	....	2	0	0	0	....
1924-25	Pittsburgh Yellowjackets	USAHA	39	12	0	12	....	....	....	....	8	2	0	2	0
1925-26	**Pittsburgh Pirates**	**NHL**	**36**	**14**	**5**	**19**	**24**	**32**	**56**	**17**	**2**	**0**	**0**	**0**	**0**
1926-27	**Pittsburgh Pirates**	**NHL**	**44**	**16**	**6**	**22**	**29**	**31**	**60**	**18**	....	....	....	....	....
1927-28	**Pittsburgh Pirates**	**NHL**	**44**	**18**	**3**	**21**	**37**	**17**	**54**	**32**	**2**	**0**	**0**	**0**	**2**
1928-29	**Pittsburgh Pirates**	**NHL**	**44**	**9**	**3**	**12**	**26**	**20**	**46**	**22**	....	....	....	....	....
1929-30	**Pittsburgh Pirates**	**NHL**	**41**	**13**	**11**	**24**	**18**	**26**	**44**	**36**	....	....	....	....	....
1930-31	**Philadelphia Quakers**	**NHL**	**44**	**17**	**6**	**23**	**34**	**18**	**52**	**42**	....	....	....	....	....
1931-32	**New York Rangers**	**NHL**	**48**	**0**	**4**	**4**	**0**	**9**	**9**	**12**	**7**	**0**	**0**	**0**	**0**
1932-33	**Ottawa Senators**	**NHL**	**16**	**0**	**3**	**3**	**0**	**6**	**6**	**0**	....	....	....	....	....
	NHL Totals		**317**	**87**	**41**	**128**	**168**	**159**	**327**	**179**	**11**	**0**	**0**	**0**	**2**

OCHL Second All-Star Team (1922)

Signed as a free agent by **Pittsburgh**, September 26, 1925. Transferred to **Philadelphia** after **Pittsburgh** franchise relocated, October 18, 1930. Claimed by **NY Rangers** from **Philadelphia** in Dispersal Draft, September 26, 1931. Signed as a free agent by **Ottawa**, October 2, 1932. • Suffered career-ending knee injury in game vs. Detroit, January 4, 1933.

• MILLAR, Hugh Hugh Alexander

D – L. 5'9", 200 lbs. b: Edmonton, Alta., 4/3/1921.

Season	Club	League	GP	G	A	Pts	AG	AA	APts	PIM	GP	G	A	Pts	PIM
1937-38	Stoney Mountain Climbers	MIHA	STATISTICS NOT AVAILABLE												
1938-39	Winnipeg Rangers	MJHL	21	5	7	12	....	....	....	14	....	....	....	....	....
1939-40	Winnipeg Rangers	MJHL	22	9	1	10	....	....	....	27	....	....	....	....	....
1940-41	Winnipeg Rangers	MJHL	14	8	3	11	....	....	....	23	6	4	2	6	2
	Winnipeg Rangers	M-Cup	14	8	5	13	....	....	....	21	....	....	....	....	....
1941-42	Omaha Knights	AHA	50	3	8	11	....	....	....	34	8	5	1	6	4
1942-43	Winnipeg Navy	WNDHL	12	11	6	17	....	....	....	10	5	*4	2	*6	4
1943-44	Winnipeg Navy	WNDHL	9	3	2	5	....	....	....	15	....	....	....	....	....
	Calgary Combines	CNDHL	2	0	0	0	....	....	....	4	3	1	1	2	2
1944-45	Winnipeg Navy	WNDHL	2	0	0	0	....	....	....	2	....	....	....	....	....
	Cornwallis Navy	NSDHL	12	0	4	4	....	....	....	14	3	0	0	0	2
1945-46	Indianapolis Capitols	AHL	50	6	26	32	....	....	....	26	5	0	1	1	2
1946-47	**Detroit Red Wings**	**NHL**	**4**	**0**	**0**	**0**	**0**	**0**	**0**	**0**	**1**	**0**	**0**	**0**	**0**
	Indianapolis Capitols	AHL	57	18	12	30	....	....	....	43	....	....	....	....	....
1947-48	Indianapolis Capitols	AHL	68	8	36	44	....	....	....	39	....	....	....	....	....
1948-49	Indianapolis Capitols	AHL	DID NOT PLAY – SUSPENDED												
	NHL Totals		**4**	**0**	**0**	**0**	**0**	**0**	**0**	**0**	**1**	**0**	**0**	**0**	**0**

AHL Second All-Star Team (1946, 1948) • AHL First All-Star Team (1947)

• Suspended for entire 1948-49 season by **Detroit** for refusing to sign contract. CAHA recognized suspension and refused to permission to allow Millar to coach junior club in Winnipeg, October 26, 1948.

• MILLER, Bill Robert

C/D – R. 6', 160 lbs. b: Campbellton, N.B., 8/1/1908 d: 6/12/1986.

Season	Club	League	GP	G	A	Pts	AG	AA	APts	PIM	GP	G	A	Pts	PIM
1923-24	Campbellton Rink Rats	NNBHL	STATISTICS NOT AVAILABLE												
1924-25	Campbellton Tigers	NNBHL	6	5	2	7	....	....	....	2	....	....	....	....	....
1925-26	Campbellton Tigers	NNBHL	4	3	1	4	....	....	....	2	1	2	1	3	0
	Campbellton Tigers	Al-Cup	2	0	0	0	....	....	....	0	....	....	....	....	....
1926-27	Mount Allison University	MIHC	2	*4	0	*4	....	....	....	3	....	....	....	....	....
	Campbellton Tigers	NNBHL	2	2	0	2	....	....	....	0	....	....	....	....	....
1927-28	Mount Allison University	MIHC	2	*5	0	*5	....	....	....	0	....	....	....	....	....
	Campbellton Tigers	NNBHL	3	5	0	5	....	....	....	0	....	....	....	....	....
1928-29	Mount Allison University	MIHC	2	0	1	1	....	....	....	8	....	....	....	....	....
	Mount Allison University	MIHC	6	*13	1	*14	....	....	....	....	....	....	....	....	....
1929-30	Mount Allison University	MIHC	2	2	0	2	....	....	....	....	....	....	....	....	....
	Campbellton Tigers	X-Games	3	3	1	4	....	....	....	2	....	....	....	....	....
1930-31	Campbellton Tigers	NNBHL	11	*28	11	*39	....	....	....	6	....	....	....	....	....
	Campbellton Tigers	Al-Cup	5	8	3	11	....	....	....	2	....	....	....	....	....
1931-32	Campbellton Tigers	MSHL	23	*19	8	27	....	....	....	14	2	0	0	0	0
	Fredericton Capitals	X-Games	5	0	3	3	....	....	....	2	....	....	....	....	....
1932-33	Moncton Hawks	MSHL	23	5	0	5	....	....	....	0	5	1	1	2	0
	Moncton Hawks	Al-Cup	8	1	*6	*7	....	....	....	4	....	....	....	....	....
1933-34	Moncton Hawks	MSHL	41	8	19	27	....	....	....	30	3	1	*5	6	0
	Moncton Hawks	Al-Cup	12	9	7	16	....	....	....	4	....	....	....	....	....
♦1934-35	**Montreal Maroons**	**NHL**	**22**	**3**	**0**	**3**	**5**	**0**	**5**	**2**	**7**	**0**	**0**	**0**	**0**
	Moncton Hawks	MSHL	20	*17	5	22	....	....	....	4	3	*5	2	7	0
	Moncton Hawks	Big-3	4	2	1	3	....	....	....	2	....	....	....	....	....
1935-36	New Haven Eagles	Can-Am	11	0	0	0	....	....	....	0	....	....	....	....	....
	Montreal Maroons	**NHL**	**8**	**0**	**0**	**0**	**0**	**0**	**0**	**0**	....	....	....	....	....
	Montreal Canadiens	**NHL**	**17**	**1**	**2**	**3**	**2**	**4**	**6**	**2**	....	....	....	....	....
1936-37	**Montreal Canadiens**	**NHL**	**48**	**3**	**1**	**4**	**5**	**2**	**7**	**12**	**5**	**0**	**0**	**0**	**0**
	NHL Totals		**95**	**7**	**3**	**10**	**12**	**6**	**18**	**16**	**12**	**0**	**0**	**0**	**0**

• Recalled from **New Haven** (Can-Am) by **Montreal Maroons** to coach in Tommy Gorman's absence, January 3, 1936. Traded to **Montreal Canadiens** by **Montreal Maroons** with Toe Blake and Ken Gravell for Lorne Chabot, February, 1936.

• MILLER, Earl Ernest Earl

LW – L. 5'11", 180 lbs. b: Lumsden, Sask., 9/12/1905 Deceased.

Season	Club	League	GP	G	A	Pts	AG	AA	APts	PIM	GP	G	A	Pts	PIM
1923-24	Saskatoon Nutana	S-SJHL	STATISTICS NOT AVAILABLE												
1924-25	U. of Saskatchewan	N-SSHL	5	0	0	0	....	....	....	2	....	....	....	....	....
1925-26	U. of Saskatchewan	N-SSHL	1	0	1	1	....	....	....	0	....	....	....	....	....
1926-27	Saskatoon Sheiks	PrHL	20	4	2	6	....	....	....	14	4	*3	*1	*4	2
1927-28	Saskatoon Sheiks	PrHL	12	5	4	9	....	....	....	32	....	....	....	....	....
	Chicago Black Hawks	**NHL**	**21**	**1**	**1**	**2**	**2**	**6**	**8**	**32**	....	....	....	....	....
1928-29	**Chicago Black Hawks**	**NHL**	**17**	**1**	**1**	**2**	**3**	**7**	**10**	**24**	....	....	....	....	....
	Kitchener Dutchmen	Can-Pro	22	9	6	15	....	....	....	75	....	....	....	....	....
1929-30	**Chicago Black Hawks**	**NHL**	**28**	**11**	**5**	**16**	**16**	**12**	**28**	**50**	**2**	**1**	**0**	**1**	**6**
1930-31	**Chicago Black Hawks**	**NHL**	**19**	**3**	**4**	**7**	**6**	**12**	**18**	**8**	**1**	**0**	**0**	**0**	**0**
	London Panthers	IHL	4	0	3	3	....	....	....	4	....	....	....	....	....
1931-32	**Chicago Black Hawks**	**NHL**	**9**	**0**	**0**	**0**	**0**	**0**	**0**	**0**	....	....	....	....	....
	Pittsburgh Yellowjackets	IHL	22	3	2	5	....	....	....	14	....	....	....	....	....
♦	**Toronto Maple Leafs**	**NHL**	**15**	**3**	**3**	**6**	**5**	**7**	**12**	**10**	**7**	**0**	**0**	**0**	**0**
1932-33	Syracuse Stars	IHL	44	19	15	34	....	....	....	26	6	*4	0	4	6
1933-34	Syracuse Stars	IHL	43	21	19	*40	....	....	....	54	6	1	3	4	14
1934-35	Syracuse Stars	IHL	19	5	7	12	....	....	....	21	....	....	....	....	....
	Buffalo Bisons	IHL	20	2	2	4	....	....	....	18	....	....	....	....	....
1935-36	Buffalo Bisons	IHL	12	0	0	0	....	....	....	0	....	....	....	....	....
	Rochester Cardinals	IHL	5	0	3	3	....	....	....	4	....	....	....	....	....
	NHL Totals		**109**	**19**	**14**	**33**	**32**	**44**	**76**	**124**	**10**	**1**	**0**	**1**	**6**

Traded to **Chicago** by **Saskatoon** (PrHL) with Cally McCalmon for Corb Denneny and Nick Wasnie, January 11, 1928. Traded to **Toronto** by **Chicago** for cash, February 8, 1932. Signed as a free agent by **Buffalo** (IHL), January 8, 1935. Signed as a free agent by **Rochester** folowing release by **Buffalo** (IHL), December 18, 1935.

• MILLER, Jack John Leslie

C – L. 5'8", 155 lbs. b: Delisle, Sask., 9/16/1925.

Season	Club	League	GP	G	A	Pts	AG	AA	APts	PIM	GP	G	A	Pts	PIM
1941-42	Saskatoon Quakers	N-SJHL	8	2	1	3	....	....	....	2	2	0	0	0	0
1942-43	Prince Albert Blackhawks	N-SJHL	7	4	6	10	....	....	....	6	3	0	0	0	0
	Arnprior RCAF	UOVHL	8	6	7	13	....	....	....	2	2	1	1	2	0
1943-44	Arnprior RCAF	UOVHL	8	2	4	6	....	....	....	2	....	....	....	....	....
1944-45	Moose Jaw Canucks	S-SJHL	16	7	5	12	....	....	....	16	10	3	1	4	10
1945-46	Saskatoon Elks	WCSHL	30	12	11	23	....	....	....	6	....	....	....	....	....
1946-47	Los Angeles Ramblers	WKHL	48	8	20	28	....	....	....	38	....	....	....	....	....
1947-48	Kansas City Pla-Mors	USHL	66	23	28	51	....	....	....	59	7	2	1	3	2
1948-49	Kansas City Pla-Mors	USHL	66	18	36	54	....	....	....	46	2	0	2	2	2
1949-50	**Chicago Black Hawks**	**NHL**	**6**	**0**	**0**	**0**	**0**	**0**	**0**	**0**	....	....	....	....	....
	Kansas City Pla-Mors	USHL	62	19	31	50	....	....	....	38	3	0	2	2	2
1950-51	**Chicago Black Hawks**	**NHL**	**11**	**0**	**0**	**0**	**0**	**0**	**0**	**4**	....	....	....	....	....
	Milwaukee Seagulls	USHL	44	22	14	36	....	....	....	47	....	....	....	....	....
1951-52	Calgary Stampeders	PCHL	39	10	15	25	....	....	....	19	....	....	....	....	....
1952-53	Spokane Flyers	WIHL	59	*45	50	95	....	....	....	68	9	5	0	5	18
	Spokane Flyers	Al-Cup	4	4	2	6	....	....	....	2	....	....	....	....	....
1953-54	Vernon Canadians	OSHL	63	29	57	86	....	....	....	18	5	4	3	7	0
1954-55	Spokane Flyers	WIHL	32	21	30	51	....	....	....	40	4	2	2	4	2
1955-56	Spokane Flyers	WIHL	46	21	56	77	....	....	....	77	10	3	7	10	0
	Spokane Flyers	Al-Cup	6	4	1	5	....	....	....	0	....	....	....	....	....
	NHL Totals		**17**	**0**	**0**	**0**	**0**	**0**	**0**	**4**	....	....	....	....	....

OSHL Second All-Star Team (1954)

• MISZUK, John

— *see page 1433*

• MITCHELL, Bill William Richard

D – L. 5'11", 180 lbs. b: Port Dalhousie, Ont., 2/22/1930.

Season	Club	League	GP	G	A	Pts	AG	AA	APts	PIM	GP	G	A	Pts	PIM
1946-47	Stratford Kroehlers	OHA-Jr.	27	5	12	17	....	....	....	16	2	0	1	1	2
1947-48	Stratford Kroehlers	OHA-Jr.	34	4	10	14	....	....	....	41	2	0	1	1	0
	Kitchener Dutchmen	OHA-Sr.	2	1	0	1	....	....	....	0	....	....	....	....	....
1948-49	Stratford Kroehlers	OHA-Jr.	36	7	10	17	....	....	....	27	3	1	0	1	0
1949-50	Toronto Marlboros	OHA-Jr.	46	7	12	19	....	....	....	46	5	2	0	2	4
1950-51	Halifax St. Mary's	MMHL	3	0	0	0	....	....	....	0	....	....	....	....	....
	Moncton Hawks	MMHL	1	0	0	0	....	....	....	0	....	....	....	....	....
	Kitchener Dutchmen	OMHL	32	6	9	15	....	....	....	27	....	....	....	....	....
1951-52	Kitchener Dutchmen	OHA-Sr.	47	18	20	38	....	....	....	40	5	0	1	1	4
1952-53	Kitchener Dutchmen	OHA-Sr.	24	14	8	22	....	....	....	18	....	....	....	....	....
	Toledo Mercurys	IHL	15	3	9	12	....	....	....	4	5	1	1	2	10
1953-54	Toledo Mercurys	IHL	63	15	15	30	....	....	....	57	5	0	3	3	8
1954-55	Toledo Mercurys	IHL	60	18	30	48	....	....	....	55	3	1	1	2	4
1955-56	Toledo Mercurys	IHL	58	17	30	47	....	....	....	63	9	1	4	5	18
1956-57	Toledo Mercurys	IHL	60	12	31	43	....	....	....	36	5	3	3	6	6
1957-58	Toledo Mercurys	IHL	61	13	39	52	....	....	....	43	....	....	....	....	....
1958-59	Toledo Mercurys	IHL	60	12	33	45	....	....	....	50	....	....	....	....	....
	Fort Wayne Komets	IHL	....	....	....	....	....	....	....	....	11	0	7	7	6
1959-60	Toledo-St. Louis	IHL	55	11	26	37	....	....	....	34	....	....	....	....	....
1960-61	Chatham Maroons	OHA-Sr.	....	16	*40	56	....	....	....	26	....	....	....	....	....
1961-62	Galt–Windsor	OHA-Sr.	30	6	31	37	....	....	....	22	7	2	2	4	8
	Canada	WEC-A	6	0	1	1	....	....	....	19	....	....	....	....	....
	Toledo Mercurys	IHL	2	0	0	0	....	....	....	2	....	....	....	....	....
1962-63	Windsor Bulldogs	OHA-Sr.	43	1	23	24	....	....	....	14	8	1	2	3	8
	Windsor Bulldogs	Al-Cup	13	4	5	9	....	....	....	6	....	....	....	....	....
1963-64	Windsor Bulldogs	IHL	67	9	33	42	....	....	....	26	6	1	3	4	4
	Detroit Red Wings	**NHL**	**1**	**0**	**0**	**0**	**0**	**0**	**0**	**0**	....	....	....	....	....
	Cincinnati Wings	CHL	2	0	0	0	....	....	....	0	....	....	....	....	....
1964-65	Toledo Blades	IHL	48	5	21	26	....	....	....	42	4	0	1	1	2
1965-66	Fox Valley Astros	USHL	30	9	15	24	....	....	....	22	....	....	....	....	....
1966-67	University of Toledo	NCAA	DID NOT PLAY – COACHING												
	Toledo Blades	IHL	7	0	3	3	....	....	....	2	....	....	....	....	....
1967-68	Toledo Blades	IHL	39	4	12	16	....	....	....	26	....	....	....	....	....
1968-69			OUT OF HOCKEY – RETIRED												
1969-70	Toledo Blades	IHL	....	....	....	....	....	....	....	....	7	2	2	4	8
1970-71	Toledo Hornets	IHL	2	0	0	0	....	....	....	2	....	....	....	....	....
1971-72			OUT OF HOCKEY – RETIRED												
1972-73	Clinton Comets	EHL	3	0	1	1	....	....	....	6	....	....	....	....	....
	NHL Totals		**1**	**0**	**0**	**0**	**0**	**0**	**0**	**0**	....	....	....	....	....

IHL Second All-Star Team (1964)

Signed as a free agent by **Halifax** (MMHL), October 19, 1950. Signed as a free agent by **Moncton** (MMHL) following release by Halifax, October 25, 1950. Signed as a free agent by **Detroit**, February 22, 1964. • Served as playing/coach with **Toldeo** (IHL), 1969-70.

• MITCHELL, Herb "Hap"

LW – L. 5'10", 190 lbs. b: Meaford, Ont., 1/4/1896 d: 1/12/1969.

Season	Club	League	GP	G	A	Pts	AG	AA	APts	PIM	GP	G	A	Pts	PIM
1918-19	Hamilton Tigers	OHA-Sr.	STATISTICS NOT AVAILABLE												
	Hamilton Tiger Cats	OSrB	STATISTICS NOT AVAILABLE												
1919-20	Hamilton Tiger Cats	OSrB	STATISTICS NOT AVAILABLE												
1920-21	Hamilton Tigers	OSrB	STATISTICS NOT AVAILABLE												
1921-22	Hamilton Tigers	OHA-Sr.	10	5	1	6	....	....	....	....	....	....	....	....	....
1922-23	Hamilton Tigers	OHA-Sr.	12	8	8	16	....	....	....	....	2	1	0	1	8
1923-24	Hamilton Tigers	OHA-Sr.	9	10	0	10	....	....	....	....	2	1	0	1	....
1924-25	**Boston Bruins**	**NHL**	**18**	**3**	**0**	**3**	**5**	**0**	**5**	**22**					

			REGULAR SEASON								PLAYOFFS				
Season	Club	League	GP	G	A	Pts	AG	AA	APts	PIM	GP	G	A	Pts	PIM
1925-26	**Boston Bruins**	**NHL**	**26**	**3**	**0**	**3**	**5**	**0**	**5**	**14**	....	....	....	....	....
1926-27	New Haven Eagles	Can-Am	30	4	3	7	....	....	....	18	3	0	0	0	2
1927-28	Windsor Hornets	Can-Pro	10	0	1	1	....	....	....	2	....	....	....	....	....
1928-29	Windsor Bulldogs	OHA-Sr.	DID NOT PLAY – COACHING												
	NHL Totals		**44**	**6**	**0**	**6**	**10**	**0**	**10**	**36**	....	....	....	....	....

Signed as a free agent by **Boston**, November 2, 1924. • First player signed in Boston franchise history.

• MITCHELL, Red William Lawson

D – R. 5'10", 185 lbs. b: Toronto, Ont., 9/6/1912.

Season	Club	League	GP	G	A	Pts	AG	AA	APts	PIM	GP	G	A	Pts	PIM
1930-31	Toronto Marlboros	OHA-Jr.	2	0	0	0	....	....	....	2	1	0	0	0	0
1931-32	Toronto Marlboros	OHA-Jr.	8	1	1	2	....	....	....	6	4	0	0	0	6
1932-33	Kitchener Greenshirts	OHA-Sr.	10	3	1	4	....	....	....	34	....	....	....	....	....
	Detroit Olympics	IHL	19	0	0	0	....	....	....	54	....	....	....	....	....
1933-34	Detroit Olympics	IHL	43	2	2	4	....	....	....	26	6	1	1	2	0
1934-35	New Haven Eagles	Can-Am	46	1	4	5	....	....	....	75	....	....	....	....	....
1935-36	New Haven Eagles	Can-Am	37	2	4	6	....	....	....	49	....	....	....	....	....
1936-37	New Haven Eagles	Can-Am	3	0	0	0	....	....	....	0	....	....	....	....	....
	Minneapolis Millers	AHA	34	1	7	8	....	....	....	54	6	1	1	2	10
1937-38	Minneapolis Millers	AHA	46	3	9	12	....	....	....	70	7	0	1	1	8
1938-39	Minneapolis Millers	AHA	47	9	21	30	....	....	....	*87	4	0	2	2	0
1939-40	Minneapolis Millers	AHA	48	6	9	15	....	....	....	68	3	0	0	0	4
1940-41	Kansas City Americans	AHA	47	3	2	5	....	....	....	50	8	0	1	1	0
1941-42	**Chicago Black Hawks**	**NHL**	**1**	**0**	**0**	**0**	**0**	**0**	**0**	**4**	....	....	....	....	....
	Kansas City Americans	AHA	50	1	14	15	....	....	....	75	6	1	2	3	12
1942-43	**Chicago Black Hawks**	**NHL**	**42**	**1**	**1**	**2**	**1**	**1**	**2**	**47**	....	....	....	....	....
1943-44	Toronto Tip Tops	TIHL	8	1	4	5	....	....	....	8	....	....	....	....	....
	Toronto Peoples Credit	TIHL	20	1	7	8	....	....	....	11	10	2	1	3	18
1944-45	**Chicago Black Hawks**	**NHL**	**40**	**3**	**4**	**7**	**3**	**5**	**8**	**16**	....	....	....	....	....
1945-46	Kansas City Pla-Mors	USHL	49	2	27	29	....	....	....	47	12	0	4	4	6
1946-47	Kansas City Pla-Mors	USHL	60	8	31	39	....	....	....	72	12	1	6	7	6
1947-48	Providence Reds	AHL	10	1	1	2	....	....	....	6	....	....	....	....	....
	Kansas City Pla-Mors	USHL	54	6	12	18	....	....	....	47	7	1	1	2	5
	NHL Totals		**83**	**4**	**5**	**9**	**4**	**6**	**10**	**67**	....	....	....	....	....

Signed as a free agent by **Detroit**, December 29, 1932.

• MOE, Bill William Carl USHOF

D – L. 5'11", 170 lbs. b: Danvers, MA, 10/2/1916 d: 1998.

Season	Club	League	GP	G	A	Pts	AG	AA	APts	PIM	GP	G	A	Pts	PIM
1938-39	Cleveland Blues	X-Games	STATISTICS NOT AVAILABLE												
1939-40	Atlantic City Seagulls	EAHL	34	2	3	5	....	....	....	19	....	....	....	....	....
	Baltimore Orioles	EAHL	26	4	2	6	....	....	....	12	9	0	3	3	8
1940-41	Baltimore Orioles	EAHL	49	6	6	12	....	....	....	71	....	....	....	....	....
1941-42	Philadelphia Rockets	AHL	54	5	19	24	....	....	....	30	....	....	....	....	....
1942-43	Hershey Bears	AHL	55	8	12	20	....	....	....	69	6	0	1	1	9
1943-44	Hershey Bears	AHL	47	9	22	31	....	....	....	48	6	0	2	2	8
1944-45	**New York Rangers**	**NHL**	**35**	**2**	**4**	**6**	**2**	**5**	**7**	**14**	....	....	....	....	....
	Hershey Bears	AHL	12	1	5	6	....	....	....	12	....	....	....	....	....
1945-46	**New York Rangers**	**NHL**	**48**	**4**	**4**	**8**	**5**	**6**	**11**	**14**	....	....	....	....	....
1946-47	**New York Rangers**	**NHL**	**59**	**4**	**10**	**14**	**4**	**12**	**16**	**44**	....	....	....	....	....
1947-48	**New York Rangers**	**NHL**	**59**	**1**	**15**	**16**	**1**	**20**	**21**	**31**	**1**	**0**	**0**	**0**	**0**
1948-49	**New York Rangers**	**NHL**	**60**	**0**	**9**	**9**	**0**	**13**	**13**	**60**	....	....	....	....	....
1949-50	Hershey Bears	AHL	55	2	20	22	....	....	....	29	....	....	....	....	....
1950-51	Hershey Bears	AHL	59	3	12	15	....	....	....	41	6	0	4	4	0
1951-52	Calgary Stampeders	PCHL	57	5	15	20	....	....	....	48	....	....	....	....	....
1952-53	Troy Uncle Sam Trojans	EAHL	57	12	23	35	....	....	....	51	....	....	....	....	....
	NHL Totals		**261**	**11**	**42**	**53**	**12**	**56**	**68**	**163**	**1**	**0**	**0**	**0**	**0**

AHL First All-Star Team (1944)

Traded to **Baltimore** (EAHL) by **Atlantic City** (EAHL) for Ed Powers, January, 1940. Traded to **Boston** by **NY Rangers** with the rights to Lorne Ferguson for Pat Egan, October 7, 1949.

• MOFFAT, Ron Ronald Robert "Atlas"

LW – L. 5'11", 180 lbs. b: West Hope, N.D., 8/21/1905 d: 8/19/1960.

Season	Club	League	GP	G	A	Pts	AG	AA	APts	PIM	GP	G	A	Pts	PIM
1925-26	Saskatoon Crescents	WHL	8	0	0	0	....	....	....	2	....	....	....	....	....
1926-27	Saskatoon Sheiks	PrHL	29	12	5	17	....	....	....	6	4	0	0	0	2
1927-28	Saskatoon Sheiks	PrHL	28	12	*11	*23	....	....	....	18	....	....	....	....	....
1928-29	Tulsa Oilers	AHA	18	1	2	3	....	....	....	8	....	....	....	....	....
1929-30	Tulsa Oilers	AHA	48	14	5	19	....	....	....	45	9	2	0	2	4
1930-31	Tulsa Oilers	AHA	47	17	11	28	....	....	....	22	4	1	0	1	12
1931-32	Tulsa Oilers	AHA	41	11	1	12	....	....	....	34	....	....	....	....	....
1932-33	**Detroit Red Wings**	**NHL**	**24**	**1**	**1**	**2**	**2**	**2**	**4**	**6**	**4**	**0**	**0**	**0**	**0**
	Detroit Olympics	IHL	22	7	2	9	....	....	....	16	....	....	....	....	....
1933-34	**Detroit Red Wings**	**NHL**	**5**	**0**	**0**	**0**	**0**	**0**	**0**	**2**	**3**	**0**	**0**	**0**	**0**
	Detroit Olympics	IHL	38	17	10	27	....	....	....	25	6	*5	2	7	4
1934-35	**Detroit Red Wings**	**NHL**	**8**	**0**	**0**	**0**	**0**	**0**	**0**	**0**	....	....	....	....	....
	Detroit Olympics	IHL	36	11	15	26	....	....	....	37	5	3	1	4	5
	Windsor Bulldogs	IHL	1	0	0	0	....	....	....	4	....	....	....	....	....
	Detroit Olympics	L-W-S	5	2	1	3	....	....	....	4	....	....	....	....	....
1935-36	Windsor Bulldogs	IHL	47	18	12	30	....	....	....	34	8	2	3	5	4
1936-37	Spokane Clippers	PCHL	40	15	5	20	....	....	....	36	6	2	0	2	0
1937-38	Seattle Seahawks	PCHL	42	12	20	32	....	....	....	36	4	0	0	0	2
1938-39	Sea.–Port.–Spok.	PCHL	43	15	12	27	....	....	....	16	....	....	....	....	....
1939-40	Seattle Seahawks	PCHL	6	0	0	0	....	....	....	0	....	....	....	....	....
	NHL Totals		**37**	**1**	**1**	**2**	**2**	**2**	**4**	**8**	**7**	**0**	**0**	**0**	**0**
	Other Major League Totals		8	0	0	0	....	....	....	2	....	....	....	....	....

IHL Second All-Star Team (1936)

Signed as a free agent by **Saskatoon** (WHL), January 11, 1926. Transferred to **Saskatoon Sheiks** (PrHL) after WHL folded, May 22, 1926. Signed as a free agent by **Detroit**, August 1, 1932. Loaned to **Windsor** (IHL) by **Detroit** (IHL) as an injury replacement, January 4, 1935. Traded to **Windsor** (IHL) by **Detroit** for cash, October 18, 1935.

• MOHNS, Doug *— see page 1436*

• MOHNS, Lloyd Lloyd Warren "Dunc"

D – R. 5'9", 185 lbs. b: Petawawa, Ont., 7/31/1921.

Season	Club	League	GP	G	A	Pts	AG	AA	APts	PIM	GP	G	A	Pts	PIM
1938-39	Petawawa Cadets	OVJHL	STATISTICS NOT AVAILABLE												
1939-40	Pembroke Lumber Kings	OVJHL	8	3	4	7	....	....	....	2	2	0	0	0	0
1940-41	Pembroke Lumber Kings	OVJHL	10	4	3	7	....	....	....	10	4	0	0	0	7
1941-42	Pembroke Lumber Kings	OVHL	12	2	2	4	....	....	....	16	6	3	2	7	4
1942-43	New York Rovers	EAHL	3	1	0	1	....	....	....	0	10	2	0	2	14
	Petawawa Grenades	OVHL	8	9	1	10	....	....	....	4	7	3	0	3	0
	Vancouver Army	NNDHL	1	1	1	2	....	....	....	0	....	....	....	....	....
1943-44	**New York Rangers**	**NHL**	**1**	**0**	**0**	**0**	**0**	**0**	**0**	**0**	....	....	....	....	....
	New York Rovers	EAHL	15	2	2	4	....	....	....	25	....	....	....	....	....
	Brooklyn Crescents	EAHL	30	6	6	12	....	....	....	16	11	3	6	9	13
1944-45	Hershey Bears	AHL	26	3	1	4	....	....	....	27	....	....	....	....	....
	Philadelphia Falcons	EAHL	1	0	0	0	....	....	....	12	....	....	....	....	....
	New York Rovers	EAHL	22	4	8	12	....	....	....	31	5	1	1	2	6
1945-46	Pembroke Lumber Kings	OVSHL	16	4	2	6	....	....	....	14	3	1	2	3	2
	Pembroke Lumber Kings	Al-Cup	9	3	6	9	....	....	....	6	....	....	....	....	....
1946-47	Kirkland Lake Blue Devils	NOHA	STATISTICS NOT AVAILABLE												
1947-48	Oakland Oaks	PCHL	11	0	2	2	....	....	....	7	....	....	....	....	....
	Brantford Indians	OHA-Sr.	9	1	0	1	....	....	....	8	....	....	....	....	....
	NHL Totals		**1**	**0**	**0**	**0**	**0**	**0**	**0**	**0**	....	....	....	....	....

• Suspended for life by OHA-Sr. for assault on referee Frank Elliot in January 20, 1948 game vs. Owen Sound (OHA-Sr.), January 25, 1948.

• MOLYNEAUX, Larry

D – R. 5'11", 208 lbs. b: Sutton West, Ont., 7/9/1912.

Season	Club	League	GP	G	A	Pts	AG	AA	APts	PIM	GP	G	A	Pts	PIM
1931-32	Newmarket Redmen	OHA-Jr.	7	1	1	2	....	....	....	6	6	3	0	3	....
1932-33	Springfield Indians	Can-Am	13	0	1	1	....	....	....	17	....	....	....	....	....
	Quebec Castors	Can-Am	33	2	2	4	....	....	....	40	....	....	....	....	....
1933-34	Quebec Castors	Can-Am	40	2	5	7	....	....	....	60	....	....	....	....	....
1934-35	New Haven Eagles	Can-Am	48	6	11	17	....	....	....	60	....	....	....	....	....
1935-36	Philadelphia Ramblers	Can-Am	48	2	10	12	....	....	....	54	....	....	....	....	....
1936-37	Philadelphia Ramblers	IAHL	47	2	5	7	....	....	....	45	6	0	0	0	2
1937-38	**New York Rangers**	**NHL**	**2**	**0**	**0**	**0**	**0**	**0**	**0**	**2**	**3**	**0**	**0**	**0**	**8**
	Philadelphia Ramblers	IAHL	47	0	8	8	....	....	....	46	5	0	0	0	0
1938-39	**New York Rangers**	**NHL**	**43**	**0**	**1**	**1**	**0**	**2**	**2**	**18**	**7**	**0**	**0**	**0**	**0**
	Philadelphia Ramblers	IAHL	5	0	2	2	....	....	....	16	....	....	....	....	....
1939-40	Cleveland Barons	IAHL	54	2	6	8	....	....	....	46	....	....	....	....	....
1940-41	Cleveland Barons	AHL	19	1	2	3	....	....	....	17	....	....	....	....	....
	Pittsburgh Hornets	AHL	15	0	3	3	....	....	....	4	9	0	0	0	14
	NHL Totals		**45**	**0**	**1**	**1**	**0**	**2**	**2**	**20**	**10**	**0**	**0**	**0**	**8**

IAHL First All-Star Team (1938) • IAHL Second All-Star Team (1940)

• MONDOU, Armand

LW – L. 5'10", 175 lbs. b: Yamaska, Que., 6/27/1905 d: 9/13/1976.

Season	Club	League	GP	G	A	Pts	AG	AA	APts	PIM	GP	G	A	Pts	PIM
1925-26	Montreal St. Francis	MTRHL	STATISTICS NOT AVAILABLE												
	Montreal Nationale	MBHL	8	0	2	2	....	....	....	6	....	....	....	....	....
1926-27	Providence Reds	Can-Am	32	6	2	8	....	....	....	35	....	....	....	....	....
1927-28	Providence Reds	Can-Am	40	12	9	21	....	....	....	50	....	....	....	....	....
1928-29	Providence Reds	Can-Am	10	1	0	1	....	....	....	10	....	....	....	....	....
	Montreal Canadiens	**NHL**	**32**	**3**	**4**	**7**	**9**	**27**	**36**	**6**	**3**	**0**	**0**	**0**	**2**
♦1929-30	**Montreal Canadiens**	**NHL**	**44**	**3**	**5**	**8**	**4**	**12**	**16**	**24**	**6**	**1**	**1**	**2**	**6**
♦1930-31	**Montreal Canadiens**	**NHL**	**40**	**5**	**4**	**9**	**10**	**12**	**22**	**10**	**8**	**0**	**0**	**0**	**0**
1931-32	**Montreal Canadiens**	**NHL**	**47**	**6**	**12**	**18**	**10**	**26**	**36**	**22**	**4**	**1**	**2**	**3**	**2**
1932-33	**Montreal Canadiens**	**NHL**	**24**	**1**	**3**	**4**	**2**	**6**	**8**	**15**	....	....	....	....	....
	Providence Reds	Can-Am	23	9	8	17	....	....	....	14	....	....	....	....	....
1933-34	**Montreal Canadiens**	**NHL**	**48**	**5**	**3**	**8**	**9**	**6**	**15**	**4**	**1**	**0**	**1**	**1**	**0**
	Quebec Beavers	Can-Am	1	1	1	2	....	....	....	0	....	....	....	....	....
1934-35	**Montreal Canadiens**	**NHL**	**46**	**9**	**15**	**24**	**15**	**26**	**41**	**6**	**2**	**0**	**1**	**1**	**0**
1935-36	**Montreal Canadiens**	**NHL**	**36**	**7**	**11**	**18**	**13**	**21**	**34**	**10**	....	....	....	....	....
1936-37	**Montreal Canadiens**	**NHL**	**7**	**1**	**1**	**2**	**2**	**2**	**4**	**0**	**5**	**0**	**0**	**0**	**0**
	New Haven Eagles	IAHL	36	7	21	28	....	....	....	12	....	....	....	....	....
1937-38	**Montreal Canadiens**	**NHL**	**7**	**2**	**4**	**6**	**3**	**6**	**9**	**0**	....	....	....	....	....
1938-39	**Montreal Canadiens**	**NHL**	**34**	**3**	**7**	**10**	**5**	**11**	**16**	**2**	**3**	**1**	**0**	**1**	**2**
	New Haven Eagles	IAHL	14	8	5	13	....	....	....	26	....	....	....	....	....
1939-40	**Montreal Canadiens**	**NHL**	**21**	**2**	**2**	**4**	**3**	**3**	**6**	**0**	....	....	....	....	....
	New Haven Eagles	IAHL	21	6	15	21	....	....	....	4	3	0	0	0	2
	NHL Totals		**386**	**47**	**71**	**118**	**85**	**158**	**243**	**99**	**32**	**3**	**5**	**8**	**12**

Played in NHL All-Star Game (1939)

Traded to **Montreal Canadiens** by **Providence** (Can-Am) for Leo Gaudreault, December 19, 1928. Traded to **Providence** (Can-Am) by **Montreal Canadiens** with Leo Gaudreault for Hago Harrington and Leo Murray with Montreal holding rights of recall, January, 1933.

• MOORE, Dickie *— see page 1440*

• MORAN, Amby Ambrose Jason

D – L. 6', 200 lbs. b: Winnipeg, Man., 4/3/1895 d: 4/8/1958.

Season	Club	League	GP	G	A	Pts	AG	AA	APts	PIM	GP	G	A	Pts	PIM
1919-20	Winnipeg Winnipegs	MHL-Sr.	4	3	1	4	....	....	....	2	1	0	0	0	0
1920-21	Brandon Elks	MHL-Sr.	12	12	4	16	....	....	....	16	6	9	1	10	4
	Brandon Elks	Al-Cup	5	5	1	6	....	....	....	2	....	....	....	....	....
1921-22	Regina Capitals	WCHL	25	7	2	9	....	....	....	18	4	1	0	1	0
1922-23	Regina Capitals	WCHL	28	15	8	23	....	....	....	37	2	0	1	1	0
1923-24	Regina Capitals	WCHL	14	2	0	2	....	....	....	6	....	....	....	....	....
1924-25	Regina Capitals	WCHL	6	0	0	0	....	....	....	8	....	....	....	....	....
	Vancouver Maroons	WCHL	15	10	1	11	....	....	....	26	....	....	....	....	....
1925-26	Vancouver Maroons	WHL	30	5	0	5	....	....	....	30	....	....	....	....	....
1926-27	**Montreal Canadiens**	**NHL**	**12**	**0**	**0**	**0**	**0**	**0**	**0**	**10**	....	....	....	....	....
	New Haven Eagles	Can-Am	6	0	0	0	....	....	....	18	....	....	....	....	....
	Moose Jaw Canucks	PrHL	11	7	0	7	....	....	....	10	....	....	....	....	....
1927-28	Moose Jaw Canucks	PrHL	12	3	2	5	....	....	....	35	....	....	....	....	....
	Chicago Black Hawks	**NHL**	**23**	**1**	**1**	**2**	**2**	**6**	**8**	**14**	....	....	....	....	....
1928-29	Tulsa Oilers	AHA	34	3	1	4	....	....	....	26	4	0	0	0	0

			REGULAR SEASON								PLAYOFFS				
Season	Club	League	GP	G	A	Pts	AG	AA	APts	PIM	GP	G	A	Pts	PIM
1929-30	Tulsa Oilers	AHA	4	0	0	0				0					
	St. Louis Flyers	AHA	1	0	0	0				0					
1930-31	St. Louis Flyers	AHA	6	1	0	1				0					
	Buffalo Majors	AHA	1	0	1	1				0					
	NHL Totals		**35**	**1**	**1**	**2**	**2**	**6**	**8**	**24**					
	Other Major League Totals		118	39	11	50				125	6	1	1	2	0

Signed as a free agent by **Regina** (WCHL), November 30, 1921. • Missed majority of 1923-24 season after being arrested for assaulting police officer in Brandon, Manitoba, November 1, 1923. Traded to **Vancouver** (WCHL) by **Regina** (WCHL) for cash, December 10, 1925. Traded to **Boston** by **Vancouver** (WHL) for cash, September 4, 1926. Traded to **Montreal Canadiens** by **Boston** for Billy Coutu, October 22, 1926. Traded to **Boston** (Can-Am) by **Montreal** for cash, December 23, 1926. Signed as a free agent by **Moose Jaw** (PrHL) following release by Boston, January 29, 1927. Traded to **Chicago** by **Moose Jaw** (PrHL) for Ted Graham and future considerations (Vic Hoffinger), January 11, 1928. Signed as a free agent by **Buffalo** (AHA), December 15, 1930.

• MORENZ, Howie

Howarth William "The Stratford Streak" HHOF

C – L. 5'9", 165 lbs. b: Mitchell, Ont., 6/21/1902 d: 3/8/1937.

Season	Club	League	GP	G	A	Pts	AG	AA	APts	PIM	GP	G	A	Pts	PIM
1919-20	Stratford Midgets	OHA-Jr.	5	14	4	18					7	14	12	26	
1920-21	Stratford Midgets	OHA-Jr.	8	19	*12	*31					13	*38	*18	*56	
1921-22	Stratford Midgets	OHA-Jr.	4	17	6	23				10	5	*17	*4	*21	
	Stratford Indians	OHA-Sr.	4	10	3	13				2	8	*15	*8	*23	*21
1922-23	Stratford Indians	OHA-Sr.	10	15	*13	28				19	10	*28	7	*35	*36
1923-24	**Montreal Canadiens**	**NHL**	**24**	**13**	**3**	**16**	**27**	**17**	**44**	**20**	**2**	**3**	**1**	**4**	**6**
♦	Montreal Canadiens	St-Cup	4	4	2	6				4					
1924-25	**Montreal Canadiens**	**NHL**	**30**	**28**	**11**	**39**	**50**	**47**	**97**	**46**	**2**	**3**	**0**	**3**	**4**
	Montreal Canadiens	St-Cup	4	4	1	5				4					
1925-26	**Montreal Canadiens**	**NHL**	**31**	**23**	**3**	**26**	**40**	**19**	**59**	**39**					
1926-27	**Montreal Canadiens**	**NHL**	**44**	**25**	**7**	**32**	**45**	**37**	**82**	**49**	**4**	**1**	**0**	**1**	**4**
1927-28	**Montreal Canadiens**	**NHL**	**43**	***33**	***18**	***51**	**69**	**105**	**174**	**66**	**2**	**0**	**0**	**0**	**12**
1928-29	**Montreal Canadiens**	**NHL**	**42**	**17**	**10**	**27**	**50**	**68**	**118**	**47**	**3**	**0**	**0**	**0**	**6**
♦1929-30	**Montreal Canadiens**	**NHL**	**44**	**40**	**10**	**50**	**58**	**24**	**82**	**72**	**6**	**3**	**0**	**3**	**10**
♦1930-31	**Montreal Canadiens**	**NHL**	**39**	**28**	**23**	***51**	**57**	**71**	**128**	**49**	**10**	**1**	***4**	**5**	**10**
1931-32	**Montreal Canadiens**	**NHL**	**48**	**24**	**25**	**49**	**40**	**56**	**96**	**46**	**4**	**1**	**0**	**1**	**4**
1932-33	**Montreal Canadiens**	**NHL**	**46**	**14**	**21**	**35**	**26**	**44**	**70**	**32**	**2**	**0**	**3**	**3**	**2**
1933-34	**Montreal Canadiens**	**NHL**	**39**	**8**	**13**	**21**	**14**	**27**	**41**	**21**	**2**	**1**	**1**	**2**	**0**
1934-35	**Chicago Black Hawks**	**NHL**	**48**	**8**	**26**	**34**	**13**	**46**	**59**	**21**	**2**	**0**	**0**	**0**	**0**
1935-36	**Chicago Black Hawks**	**NHL**	**23**	**4**	**11**	**15**	**8**	**21**	**29**	**20**					
	New York Rangers	**NHL**	**19**	**2**	**4**	**6**	**4**	**8**	**12**	**6**					
1936-37	**Montreal Canadiens**	**NHL**	**30**	**4**	**16**	**20**	**7**	**29**	**36**	**12**					
	NHL Totals		**550**	**271**	**201**	**472**	**508**	**619**	**1127**	**546**	**39**	**13**	**9**	**22**	**58**

NHL Scoring Leader (1928, 1931) • Won Hart Trophy (1928, 1931, 1932) • NHL First All-Star Team (1931, 1932) • NHL Second All-Star Team (1933) • Played in NHL All-Star Game (1934)

Signed as a free agent by **Montreal Canadiens**, September 30, 1923. • 1923-24 Stanley Cup totals includes series with Calgary (WCHL) and Vancouver (PCHA). Traded to **Chicago** by **Montreal Canadiens** with Lorne Chabot and Marty Burke for Leroy Goldsworthy, Lionel Conacher and Roger Jenkins, October 3, 1934. Traded to **NY Rangers** by **Chicago** for Glenn Brydson, January 26, 1936. Traded to **Montreal Canadiens** by **NY Rangers** for cash, September 1, 1936. • Suffered career-ending leg injury in game vs. Chicago, January 28, 1937.

• MORIN, Pete

LW – L. 5'6", 150 lbs. b: Lachine, Que., 12/8/1915 d: 1/5/2000.

Season	Club	League	GP	G	A	Pts	AG	AA	APts	PIM	GP	G	A	Pts	PIM
1934-35	Paris Volants Francais	France	STATISTICS NOT AVAILABLE												
	Montreal Victorias	MMJHL	1	1	0	1				6					
1935-36	Montreal Victorias	MMJHL	STATISTICS NOT AVAILABLE												
1936-37	Montreal Royals	MCHL	21	17	5	22				15	5	3	1	4	4
1937-38	Montreal Royals	MCHL	22	4	4	8				14	1	0	0	0	0
1938-39	Montreal Royals	MCHL	17	7	12	19				16	5	*4	5	9	0
	Montreal Royals	Al-Cup	15	*17	8	*25				6					
1939-40	Montreal Royals	QSHL	29	14	20	34				4	8	3	7	10	5
	Montreal Royals	Al-Cup	5	2	3	5				2					
1940-41	Montreal Royals	QSHL	35	17	19	36				17	8	*6	2	8	4
	Montreal Royals	Al-Cup	14	11	5	16				29					
1941-42	**Montreal Canadiens**	**NHL**	**31**	**10**	**12**	**22**	**13**	**14**	**27**	**7**	**1**	**0**	**0**	**0**	**0**
	Montreal Royals	QSHL	11	3	1	4				4					
1942-43	Montreal RCAF	QSHL	35	15	21	36				4	12	3	6	9	4
1943-44	Montreal RCAF	QSHL	7	1	1	2				2					
1944-45	Lachine Rapides	QPHL	STATISTICS NOT AVAILABLE												
1945-46	Montreal Royals	QSHL	39	33	28	61				17	11	2	*12	*14	2
1946-47	Montreal Royals	QSHL	31	18	32	50				10	11	1	*15	*16	2
	Montreal Royals	Al-Cup	14	*3	15	18				2					
1947-48	Montreal Royals	QSHL	47	34	*57	*91				6	3	1	1	2	2
1948-49	Montreal Royals	QSHL	53	25	54	79				20	8	6	6	12	2
1949-50	Montreal Royals	QSHL	52	25	29	54				13	6	0	3	3	0
1950-51	Laval Nationale	QJHL	DID NOT PLAY – COACHING												
	NHL Totals		**31**	**10**	**12**	**22**	**13**	**14**	**27**	**7**	**1**	**0**	**0**	**0**	**0**

Won Byng of Vimy Trophy (MVP - QSHL) (1946) • QSHL First All-Star Team (1948) • QSHL Second All-Star Team (1949)

Signed as a free agent by **Montreal**, November 28, 1941.

• MORRIS, Bernie

Bernard Patrick

C/RW – R. 5'7", 145 lbs. b: Regina, Sask., Deceased.

Season	Club	League	GP	G	A	Pts	AG	AA	APts	PIM	GP	G	A	Pts	PIM
1910-11	Brandon Shamrocks	MIPHL	6	6	0	6									
1911-12	Moose Jaw Brewers	SPHL	8	*21	0	*21									
1912-13	Phoenix Hockey Club	BDHL	STATISTICS NOT AVAILABLE												
1913-14	Regina Victorias	S-SSHL	1	2	0	2				3					
1914-15	Victoria Aristocrats	PCHA	10	7	3	10				0					
♦1915-16	Seattle Metropolitans	PCHA	18	*23	9	32				27					
	PCHA All-Stars	X-Games	3	7	3	*10				0					
1916-17	Seattle Metropolitans	PCHA	24	37	17	*54				17	4	*14	2	*16	0
1917-18	Seattle Metropolitans	PCHA	18	20	*12	32				9	2	1	0	1	0
1918-19	Seattle Metropolitans	PCHA	20	22	7	29				15					
1919-20	Seattle Metropolitans	St-Cup									5	0	*2	2	0
1920-21	Seattle Metropolitans	PCHA	24	11	13	24				3	2	1	0	1	0
1921-22	Seattle Metropolitans	PCHA	24	14	10	24				36	2	0	0	0	0
1922-23	Seattle Metropolitans	PCHA	29	21	5	26				30					
1923-24	Calgary Tigers	WCHL	30	16	7	23				13	2	1	1	2	4
	Calgary Tigers	St-Cup	2	2	5	7				4					
1924-25	Calgary Tigers	WCHL	7	2	0	2				2					
	Boston Bruins	**NHL**	**6**	**1**	**0**	**1**	**2**	**0**	**2**	**0**					
	Regina Capitals	WCHL	7	1	2	3				2					
1925-26	Palais-de-Glace	Cal-Pro	10	10	*9	19				8					
1926-27	Edmonton Eskimos	PrHL	27	18	6	24				28					
1927-28	Detroit Olympics	Can-Pro	37	16	9	25				35	2	0	0	0	6
1928-29	Hamilton Tigers	Can-Pro	12	3	2	5				14					
1929-30	Hamilton Tigers	IHL	17	3	3	6				12					
	NHL Totals		**6**	**1**	**0**	**1**	**2**	**0**	**2**	**0**					
	Other Major League Totals		211	174	85	259				154	17	17	5	22	4

PCHA First All-Star Team (1916, 1917, 1918, 1919, 1922) • PCHA Second All-Star Team (1921, 1923)

• Missed remainder of 1918-19 and majority of 1919-20 seasons after being charged for Draft Evasion by U.S. authorities, March 16, 1918. All charges were dropped, March 19, 1920. Traded to **Calgary** (WCHL) by **Seattle** (PCHA) for Bill Binney and the rights to Gordon McFarlane, October 7, 1923. Traded to **Montreal Maroons** by **Calgary** (WCHL) for cash, January 3, 1925. Traded to **Boston** by **Montreal Maroons** with Bobby Benson for Alf Skinner, January 3, 1925. Signed as a free agent by **Regina** (WCHL) after release by **Boston**, February 10, 1925.

• MORRIS, Moe

Elwyn Gordon

D – L. 5'8", 187 lbs. b: Toronto, Ont., 1/3/1921 d: 2/6/2000.

Season	Club	League	GP	G	A	Pts	AG	AA	APts	PIM	GP	G	A	Pts	PIM
1937-38	Toronto Marlboros	OHA-Jr.	10	6	3	9				0	6	3	0	3	2
1938-39	Toronto Marlboros	OHA-Jr.	7	3	1	4				0	2	1	0	1	0
1939-40	Toronto Marlboros	OHA-Jr.	19	13	16	29				9	5	1	0	1	0
	Toronto Tip Tops	TIHL	22	5	6	11				6	3	0	0	0	2
	Toronto Ostranders	TMHL	6	9	3	12				4	4	3	2	5	0
1940-41	Toronto Marlboros	OHA-Jr.	16	7	17	24				12	12	1	4	5	2
	Toronto Tip Tops	TIHL	22	5	6	11				6	3	0	0	0	2
1941-42	Toronto Marlboros	OHA-Sr.	20	2	9	11				17	6	0	2	2	0
	Toronto Kodiacs	TMHL	13	1	0	1				0	2	0	1	1	0
1942-43	Toronto Navy	TNDHL	11	6	10	16				8	10	1	7	8	15
1943-44	**Toronto Maple Leafs**	**NHL**	**50**	**12**	**21**	**33**	**11**	**18**	**29**	**22**	**5**	**1**	**2**	**3**	**2**
	Toronto Ostranders	TIHL	6	9	3	12				4	4	3	2	5	0
♦1944-45	**Toronto Maple Leafs**	**NHL**	**29**	**0**	**2**	**2**	**0**	**2**	**2**	**18**	**13**	**3**	**0**	**3**	***14**
1945-46	**Toronto Maple Leafs**	**NHL**	**38**	**1**	**5**	**6**	**1**	**7**	**8**	**10**					
	Pittsburgh Hornets	AHL	10	0	7	7				0					
1946-47	Pittsburgh Hornets	AHL	64	2	15	17				45	12	0	2	2	6
1947-48	Pittsburgh Hornets	AHL	56	0	13	13				14	2	0	0	0	0
1948-49	**New York Rangers**	**NHL**	**18**	**0**	**1**	**1**	**0**	**1**	**1**	**8**					
	Providence Reds	AHL	45	1	18	19				13	14	1	0	1	4
1949-50	Providence Reds	AHL	58	1	12	13				11	4	0	2	2	0
1950-51	Providence Reds	AHL	69	8	13	21				18					
1951-52	Providence Reds	AHL	67	2	17	19				21	15	2	2	4	4
1952-53	Providence Reds	AHL	51	4	13	17				13					
1953-54	Owen Sound Mercurys	OHA-Sr.	52	9	28	37				12	10	0	7	7	2
	Owen Sound Mercurys	Al-Cup	7	0	2	2				2					
1954-55	Stratford Indians	OHA-Sr.	50	1	1	2				18					
	NHL Totals		**135**	**13**	**29**	**42**	**12**	**28**	**40**	**58**	**18**	**4**	**2**	**6**	**16**

AHL Second All-Star Team (1947)

Traded to **NY Rangers** by **Toronto** with Wally Stanowski for Cal Gardner, Bill Juzda, Rene Trudell and the rights to Frank Mathers, April 26, 1948. Traded to **Providence** (AHL) by **NY Rangers** with Eddie Kullman, cash and future considerations (Buck Davies, June, 1949) for Allan Stanley, December 9, 1948.

• MORRISON, Don

Donald MacRae

C – R. 5'10", 165 lbs. b: Saskatoon, Sask., 7/14/1923.

Season	Club	League	GP	G	A	Pts	AG	AA	APts	PIM	GP	G	A	Pts	PIM
1944-45	Winnipeg RCAF	WNDHL	STATISTICS NOT AVAILABLE												
1945-46	Omaha Knights	USHL	46	32	24	56				8	7	2	0	2	4
1946-47	Omaha Knights	USHL	59	32	44	*76				11	11	6	*12	*18	0
1947-48	**Detroit Red Wings**	**NHL**	**40**	**10**	**15**	**25**	**13**	**20**	**33**	**6**	**3**	**0**	**1**	**1**	**0**
	Indianapolis Capitols	AHL	27	12	16	28				9					
1948-49	**Detroit Red Wings**	**NHL**	**13**	**0**	**1**	**1**	**0**	**1**	**1**	**0**					
	Indianapolis Capitols	AHL	48	20	29	49				25	2	0	1	1	0
1949-50	Indianapolis Capitols	AHL	57	21	38	59				14	8	3	4	7	0
1950-51	**Chicago Black Hawks**	**NHL**	**59**	**8**	**12**	**20**	**10**	**15**	**25**	**6**					
1951-52	St. Louis Flyers	AHL	65	17	43	60				18					
	NHL Totals		**112**	**18**	**28**	**46**	**23**	**36**	**59**	**12**	**3**	**0**	**1**	**1**	**0**

• Brother of Rod • USHL First All-Star Team (1947)

Traded to **Chicago** by **Detroit** with Harry Lumley, Jack Stewart, Al Dewsbury and Pete Babando for Jim Henry, Bob Goldham, Gaye Stewart and Metro Prystai, July 13, 1950.

• MORRISON, Jim

— *see page 1444*

• MORRISON, John

John William "Crutchy"

LW – R. 5'8", 163 lbs. b: Selkirk, Man., 3/4/1895 Deceased.

Season	Club	League	GP	G	A	Pts	AG	AA	APts	PIM	GP	G	A	Pts	PIM
1913-14	Selkirk Fishermen	Man-Pro	10	5	0	5									
1914-15	Selkirk Fishermen	MSPHL	STATISTICS NOT AVAILABLE												
1915-16	Winnipeg 61st Battalion	WSrHL	8	7	2	9				8	3	1	0	1	6
	Winnipeg 61st Battalion	Al-Cup	2	1	0	1				0					
1916-17			MILITARY SERVICE												
1917-18			MILITARY SERVICE												
1918-19			MILITARY SERVICE												
1919-20	Selkirk Fishermen	MHL-Sr.	9	6	5	11				6					
1920-21	Winnipeg Falcons	MHL-Sr.	10	9	4	13				2					
1921-22	Selkirk Fishermen	MHL-Sr.	5	10	2	12				4					
	Edmonton Eskimos	WCHL	17	8	2	10				4	2	0	0	0	0
1922-23	Edmonton Eskimos	WCHL	26	10	2	12				5	2	0	0	0	0
	Edmonton Eskimos	St-Cup	2	1	0	1				0					
1923-24	Edmonton Eskimos	WCHL	23	1	2	3				2					
1924-25	Edmonton Eskimos	WCHL	27	5	2	7				11					
1925-26	**New York Americans**	**NHL**	**18**	**0**	**0**	**0**	**0**	**0**	**0**	**0**					
1926-27	Regina Capitals	PrHL	30	20	6	26				18	2	1	0	1	2
1927-28	Duluth Hornets	AHA	32	7	3	10				8	5	0	0	0	2
1928-29	Duluth Hornets	AHA	37	10	3	13				10					
1929-30	St. Paul Saints	AHA	45	9	4	13				10					

			REGULAR SEASON								PLAYOFFS				
Season	Club	League	GP	G	A	Pts	AG	AA	APts	PIM	GP	G	A	Pts	PIM
1930-31	Buffalo Majors	AHA	42	6	12	18	....	....	....	2	....	....	....	....	....
1931-32	Buffalo Majors	AHA	24	3	2	5	....	....	....	6	....	....	....	....	....
	Duluth Hornets	AHA	16	2	0	2	....	....	....	2	7	0	0	0	0
	NHL Totals		**18**	**0**	**0**	**0**	**0**	**0**	**0**	**0**	....	....	....	....	....
	Other Major League Totals		93	24	8	32	....	....	....	22	4	0	0	0	0

Signed as a free agent by **Edmonton** (WCHL), January 9, 1922. Traded to **NY Americans** by **Edmonton** (WHL) with Joe Simpson and Roy Rickey for $10,000, September 18, 1925. Signed as a free agent by **Regina** (PrHL), November 30, 1926. Transferred to **Buffalo**(AHA) after **St. Paul** (AHA) franchise relocated, October 5, 1930.

• MORRISON, Rod

RW – R. 5'9", 160 lbs. b: Saskatoon, Sask., 10/7/1925 d: 10/10/1998.

Season	Club	League	GP	G	A	Pts	AG	AA	APts	PIM	GP	G	A	Pts	PIM
1942-43	Saskatoon Quakers	N-SJHL	8	3	6	9	....	....	....	0	3	2	*3	5	0
	Saskatoon Quakers	M-Cup	8	9	2	11	....	....	....	12	....	....	....	....	....
1943-44	Indianapolis Capitols	AHL	54	13	10	23	....	....	....	4	5	0	0	0	0
1944-45	Saskatoon Falcons	S-SSHL	8	7	3	10	....	....	....	6	2	2	1	3	0
1945-46	Omaha Knights	USHL	36	8	7	15	....	....	....	8	7	1	1	2	2
1946-47	Indianapolis Capitols	AHL	37	7	17	24	....	....	....	6	....	....	....	....	....
1947-48	**Detroit Red Wings**	**NHL**	**34**	**8**	**7**	**15**	**10**	**9**	**19**	**4**	**3**	**0**	**0**	**0**	**0**
	Indianapolis Capitols	AHL	26	5	10	15	....	....	....	16	....	....	....	....	....
1948-49	Indianapolis Capitols	AHL	65	22	29	51	....	....	....	34	2	0	0	0	0
1949-50	Indianapolis Capitols	AHL	69	27	31	58	....	....	....	15	8	4	5	9	0
1950-51	Indianapolis Capitols	AHL	68	14	33	47	....	....	....	14	3	2	1	3	0
	NHL Totals		**34**	**8**	**7**	**15**	**10**	**9**	**19**	**4**	**3**	**0**	**0**	**0**	**0**

• Brother of Don

• MORTSON, Gus James Angus Gerald "Old Hardrock"

D – L. 5'11", 190 lbs. b: New Liskeard, Ont., 1/24/1925.

Season	Club	League	GP	G	A	Pts	AG	AA	APts	PIM	GP	G	A	Pts	PIM
1942-43	Kirkland Lake Lakers	GBHL	STATISTICS NOT AVAILABLE												
1943-44	St. Michael's Majors	OHA-Jr.	25	5	11	16	....	....	....	16	12	2	2	4	12
	Oshawa Generals	M-Cup	8	1	4	5	....	....	....	4	....	....	....	....	....
1944-45	St. Michael's Majors	OHA-Jr.	17	6	12	18	....	....	....	18	6	1	5	6	8
	St. Michael's Majors	M-Cup	14	6	4	10	....	....	....	12	....	....	....	....	....
1945-46	Tulsa Oilers	USHL	51	19	29	48	....	....	....	47	13	1	5	6	12
♦1946-47	**Toronto Maple Leafs**	**NHL**	**60**	**5**	**13**	**18**	**6**	**16**	**22**	***133**	**11**	**1**	**3**	**4**	**22**
♦1947-48	**Toronto Maple Leafs**	**NHL**	**58**	**7**	**11**	**18**	**9**	**14**	**23**	**118**	**5**	**1**	**2**	**3**	**2**
♦1948-49	**Toronto Maple Leafs**	**NHL**	**60**	**2**	**13**	**15**	**3**	**18**	**21**	**85**	**9**	**2**	**1**	**3**	**8**
1949-50	**Toronto Maple Leafs**	**NHL**	**68**	**3**	**14**	**17**	**4**	**17**	**21**	**125**	**7**	**0**	**0**	**0**	**18**
♦1950-51	**Toronto Maple Leafs**	**NHL**	**60**	**3**	**10**	**13**	**4**	**12**	**16**	***142**	**11**	**0**	**1**	**1**	**4**
1951-52	**Toronto Maple Leafs**	**NHL**	**65**	**1**	**10**	**11**	**1**	**12**	**13**	**106**	**4**	**0**	**0**	**0**	**8**
1952-53	**Chicago Black Hawks**	**NHL**	**68**	**5**	**18**	**23**	**7**	**22**	**29**	**88**	**7**	**1**	**1**	**2**	**6**
1953-54	**Chicago Black Hawks**	**NHL**	**68**	**5**	**13**	**18**	**7**	**16**	**23**	***132**	....	....	....	....	....
1954-55	**Chicago Black Hawks**	**NHL**	**65**	**2**	**11**	**13**	**3**	**13**	**16**	**133**	....	....	....	....	....
1955-56	**Chicago Black Hawks**	**NHL**	**52**	**5**	**10**	**15**	**7**	**12**	**19**	**87**	....	....	....	....	....
1956-57	**Chicago Black Hawks**	**NHL**	**70**	**5**	**18**	**23**	**6**	**20**	**26**	***147**	....	....	....	....	....
1957-58	**Chicago Black Hawks**	**NHL**	**67**	**3**	**10**	**13**	**4**	**10**	**14**	**62**	....	....	....	....	....
1958-59	**Detroit Red Wings**	**NHL**	**36**	**0**	**1**	**1**	**0**	**1**	**1**	**22**	....	....	....	....	....
	Buffalo Bisons	AHL	29	3	9	12	....	....	....	46	11	3	3	6	12
1959-60	Buffalo Bisons	AHL	72	10	32	42	....	....	....	37	....	....	....	....	....
1960-61			DID NOT PLAY												
1961-62	Dixie Beehives	OHA-B	DID NOT PLAY – COACHING												
1962-63	Chatham Maroons	OHA-Sr.	36	11	14	25	....	....	....	46	9	1	1	2	6
1963-64	Chatham Maroons	IHL	29	2	14	16	....	....	....	60	....	....	....	....	....
1964-65	Oakville Oaks	OHA-Sr.	31	7	18	25	....	....	....	78	11	1	5	6	18
	Buffalo Bisons	AHL	3	0	3	3	....	....	....	0	....	....	....	....	....
1965-66	Oakville Oaks	OHA-Sr.	27	7	15	22	....	....	....	48	....	....	....	....	....
1966-67	Oakville Oaks	OHA-Sr.	13	3	3	6	....	....	....	8	....	....	....	....	....
	NHL Totals		**797**	**46**	**152**	**198**	**61**	**183**	**244**	**1380**	**54**	**5**	**8**	**13**	**68**

NHL First All-Star Team (1950) • AHL Second All-Star Team (1960) • Played in NHL All-Star Game (1947, 1948, 1950, 1951, 1952, 1953, 1954, 1956)

Traded to **Chicago** by **Toronto** with Ray Hannigan, Al Rollins and Cal Gardner for Harry Lumley, September 11, 1952. Traded to **Detroit** by **Chicago** for future considerations, September 3, 1958. Claimed on waivers by **NY Rangers** (Buffalo-AHL) from **Detroit**, January 17, 1959.

• MOSDELL, Kenny Kenneth

C – L. 6'1", 170 lbs. b: Montreal, Que., 7/13/1922.

Season	Club	League	GP	G	A	Pts	AG	AA	APts	PIM	GP	G	A	Pts	PIM
1938-39	Montreal JV Royals	QAHA	STATISTICS NOT AVAILABLE												
1939-40	Montreal Jr. Royals	QJHL	12	7	9	16	....	....	....	4	2	0	0	0	0
	Montreal Royals	QSHL	1	0	0	0	....	....	....	2	....	....	....	....	....
1940-41	Montreal Jr. Royals	QJHL	12	7	10	17	....	....	....	18	2	0	*4	4	0
	Montreal Royals	QSHL	1	0	1	1	....	....	....	0	....	....	....	....	....
	Montreal Jr. Royals	M-Cup	10	10	16	26	....	....	....	15	....	....	....	....	....
1941-42	**Brooklyn Americans**	**NHL**	**41**	**7**	**9**	**16**	**9**	**11**	**20**	**16**	....	....	....	....	....
	Springfield Indians	AHL	1	0	0	0	....	....	....	0	....	....	....	....	....
1942-43	Lachine RCAF	QSHL	35	17	18	35	....	....	....	52	12	8	3	11	23
1943-44	Montreal RCAF	QSHL	7	3	7	10	....	....	....	13	....	....	....	....	....
	Montreal Fairchild	MCHL	6	7	6	13	....	....	....	5	....	....	....	....	....
1944-45	**Montreal Canadiens**	**NHL**	**31**	**12**	**6**	**18**	**12**	**7**	**19**	**16**	....	....	....	....	....
1945-46	Buffalo Bisons	AHL	43	21	23	44	....	....	....	46	....	....	....	....	....
♦	**Montreal Canadiens**	**NHL**	**13**	**2**	**1**	**3**	**2**	**1**	**3**	**8**	**9**	**4**	**1**	**5**	**6**
1946-47	**Montreal Canadiens**	**NHL**	**54**	**5**	**10**	**15**	**6**	**12**	**18**	**50**	**4**	**2**	**0**	**2**	**4**
1947-48	**Montreal Canadiens**	**NHL**	**23**	**1**	**0**	**1**	**1**	**0**	**1**	**19**	....	....	....	....	....
1948-49	**Montreal Canadiens**	**NHL**	**60**	**17**	**9**	**26**	**24**	**13**	**37**	**50**	**7**	**1**	**1**	**2**	**4**
1949-50	**Montreal Canadiens**	**NHL**	**67**	**15**	**12**	**27**	**19**	**14**	**33**	**42**	**5**	**0**	**0**	**0**	**12**
1950-51	**Montreal Canadiens**	**NHL**	**66**	**13**	**18**	**31**	**17**	**22**	**39**	**24**	**11**	**1**	**1**	**2**	**4**
1951-52	**Montreal Canadiens**	**NHL**	**44**	**5**	**11**	**16**	**7**	**13**	**20**	**19**	**2**	**1**	**0**	**1**	**0**
♦1952-53	**Montreal Canadiens**	**NHL**	**63**	**5**	**14**	**19**	**7**	**17**	**24**	**27**	**7**	**3**	**2**	**5**	**4**
1953-54	**Montreal Canadiens**	**NHL**	**67**	**22**	**24**	**46**	**30**	**29**	**59**	**64**	**11**	**1**	**0**	**1**	**4**
1954-55	**Montreal Canadiens**	**NHL**	**70**	**22**	**32**	**54**	**29**	**37**	**66**	**82**	**12**	**2**	**7**	**9**	**8**
♦1955-56	**Montreal Canadiens**	**NHL**	**67**	**13**	**17**	**30**	**18**	**20**	**38**	**48**	**9**	**1**	**1**	**2**	**2**
1956-57	**Chicago Black Hawks**	**NHL**	**25**	**2**	**4**	**6**	**3**	**4**	**7**	**10**	....	....	....	....	....
1957-58	**Montreal Canadiens**	**NHL**	**2**	**0**	**1**	**1**	**0**	**1**	**1**	**0**	....	....	....	....	....
	Montreal Royals	QHL	62	27	42	69	....	....	....	51	7	3	6	9	2
1958-59	Rochester Americans	AHL	2	0	0	0	....	....	....	0	....	....	....	....	....
	Montreal Royals	QHL	55	20	40	60	....	....	....	77	6	1	4	5	9
♦	**Montreal Canadiens**	**NHL**	....	....	....	....	....	....	....	....	**3**	**0**	**0**	**0**	**0**
1959-60	Montreal Royals	EPHL	61	26	36	62	....	....	....	50	14	3	3	6	12
	NHL Totals		**693**	**141**	**168**	**309**	**184**	**201**	**385**	**475**	**80**	**16**	**13**	**29**	**48**

NHL First All-Star Team (1954) • NHL Second All-Star Team (1955) • QHL Second All-Star Team (1959) • Played in NHL All-Star Game (1951, 1952, 1953, 1954, 1955)

Signed as a free agent by **Brooklyn**, October 28, 1941. Rights transferred to **Montreal** from **Brooklyn** in Special Dispersal Draw, September 11, 1943. Loaned to **Buffalo** (AHL) by **Montreal** with Frank Eddolls, Wilf Field and cash for Lorran Thibeault, October 24, 1945. • Missed majority of 1947-48 season recovering from knee injury suffered during softball game, August 15, 1947. Traded to **Chicago** by **Montreal** with Eddie Mazur and Bud MacPherson for $55,000 with Montreal holding right of recall, May 17, 1956. • Returned to **Montreal** by **Chicago**, September 20, 1957.

• MOSIENKO, Bill William "Mosie" HHOF

RW – R. 5'8", 160 lbs. b: Winnipeg, Man., 11/2/1921 d: 7/9/1994.

Season	Club	League	GP	G	A	Pts	AG	AA	APts	PIM	GP	G	A	Pts	PIM
1938-39	Winnipeg Sherburn AC	MAHA	STATISTICS NOT AVAILABLE												
1939-40	Winnipeg Monarchs	MJHL	24	21	8	29	....	....	....	14	7	8	3	11	2
1940-41	Providence Reds	AHL	36	14	19	33	....	....	....	8	....	....	....	....	....
	Kansas City Americans	AHA	7	2	2	4	....	....	....	0	8	4	1	5	2
1941-42	**Chicago Black Hawks**	**NHL**	**12**	**6**	**8**	**14**	**8**	**9**	**17**	**4**	**3**	**2**	**0**	**2**	**0**
	Kansas City Americans	AHA	33	12	19	31	....	....	....	9	....	....	....	....	....
1942-43	**Chicago Black Hawks**	**NHL**	**2**	**2**	**0**	**2**	**2**	**0**	**2**	**0**	....	....	....	....	....
	Quebec Aces	QSHL	8	5	3	8	....	....	....	2	4	2	2	4	2
1943-44	**Chicago Black Hawks**	**NHL**	**50**	**32**	**38**	**70**	**29**	**34**	**63**	**10**	**8**	**2**	**2**	**4**	**6**
1944-45	**Chicago Black Hawks**	**NHL**	**50**	**28**	**26**	**54**	**28**	**30**	**58**	**0**	....	....	....	....	....
1945-46	**Chicago Black Hawks**	**NHL**	**40**	**18**	**30**	**48**	**22**	**44**	**66**	**12**	**4**	**2**	**0**	**2**	**2**
1946-47	**Chicago Black Hawks**	**NHL**	**59**	**25**	**27**	**52**	**28**	**33**	**61**	**2**	....	....	....	....	....
1947-48	**Chicago Black Hawks**	**NHL**	**40**	**16**	**9**	**25**	**21**	**12**	**33**	**0**	....	....	....	....	....
1948-49	**Chicago Black Hawks**	**NHL**	**60**	**17**	**25**	**42**	**24**	**36**	**60**	**6**	....	....	....	....	....
1949-50	**Chicago Black Hawks**	**NHL**	**69**	**18**	**28**	**46**	**23**	**34**	**57**	**10**	....	....	....	....	....
1950-51	**Chicago Black Hawks**	**NHL**	**65**	**21**	**15**	**36**	**27**	**18**	**45**	**18**	....	....	....	....	....
1951-52	**Chicago Black Hawks**	**NHL**	**70**	**31**	**22**	**53**	**42**	**27**	**69**	**10**	....	....	....	....	....
1952-53	**Chicago Black Hawks**	**NHL**	**65**	**17**	**20**	**37**	**22**	**24**	**46**	**8**	**7**	**4**	**2**	**6**	**7**
1953-54	**Chicago Black Hawks**	**NHL**	**65**	**15**	**19**	**34**	**20**	**23**	**43**	**17**	....	....	....	....	....
1954-55	**Chicago Black Hawks**	**NHL**	**64**	**12**	**15**	**27**	**15**	**17**	**32**	**24**	....	....	....	....	....
1955-56	Winnipeg Warriors	WHL	64	22	23	45	....	....	....	37	14	6	*12	18	4
	Winnipeg Warriors	Ed-Cup	6	*6	3	9	....	....	....	6	....	....	....	....	....
1956-57	Winnipeg Warriors	WHL	61	27	26	53	....	....	....	25	....	....	....	....	....
1957-58	Winnipeg Warriors	WHL	65	38	36	74	....	....	....	43	7	1	0	1	6
1958-59	Winnipeg Warriors	WHL	63	42	46	88	....	....	....	55	7	1	3	4	10
1959-60	Winnipeg Warriors	WHL	DID NOT PLAY – COACHING												
	NHL Totals		**711**	**258**	**282**	**540**	**311**	**341**	**652**	**121**	**22**	**10**	**4**	**14**	**15**

NHL Second All-Star Team (1945, 1946) • Won Lady Byng Trophy (1945) • WHL Prairie Division First All-Star Team (1957, 1958, 1959) • Played in NHL All-Star Game (1947, 1949, 1950, 1952, 1953)

Signed as a free agent by **Chicago**, October 27, 1940.

• MOTTER, Alex Alexander Everett

C – L. 6', 175 lbs. b: Melville, Sask., 6/20/1913 d: 10/18/1996.

Season	Club	League	GP	G	A	Pts	AG	AA	APts	PIM	GP	G	A	Pts	PIM
1930-31	Melville Millionaires	S-SSHL	20	4	4	8	....	....	....	12	....	....	....	....	....
1931-32	Regina Pats	RJrHL	3	1	1	2	....	....	....	0	2	*1	0	*1	0
	Regina Pats	M-Cup	4	2	0	2	....	....	....	0	....	....	....	....	....
1932-33	Regina Pats	RJrHL	3	2	1	3	....	....	....	2	13	2	0	2	10
	Regina Pats	M-Cup	13	2	0	2	....	....	....	10	....	....	....	....	....
1933-34	Prince Albert Mintos	N-SSHL	22	17	*19	*36	....	....	....	22	4	0	1	1	2
1934-35	**Boston Bruins**	**NHL**	**3**	**0**	**0**	**0**	**0**	**0**	**0**	**0**	**4**	**0**	**0**	**0**	**0**
	Boston Cubs	Can-Am	42	14	11	25	....	....	....	34	3	1	2	3	0
1935-36	**Boston Bruins**	**NHL**	**23**	**1**	**4**	**5**	**2**	**8**	**10**	**4**	**2**	**0**	**0**	**0**	**0**
	Boston Cubs	Can-Am	15	2	8	10	....	....	....	13	....	....	....	....	....
1936-37	Providence Reds	IAHL	43	11	14	25	....	....	....	26	3	0	1	1	0
1937-38	Providence Reds	IAHL	17	6	6	12	....	....	....	4	....	....	....	....	....
	Detroit Red Wings	**NHL**	**32**	**5**	**17**	**22**	**8**	**27**	**35**	**6**	....	....	....	....	....
1938-39	**Detroit Red Wings**	**NHL**	**44**	**5**	**11**	**16**	**9**	**17**	**26**	**17**	**4**	**0**	**1**	**1**	**0**
1939-40	**Detroit Red Wings**	**NHL**	**37**	**7**	**12**	**19**	**12**	**19**	**31**	**28**	**5**	**1**	**1**	**2**	**15**
	Indianapolis Capitols	IAHL	16	5	4	9	....	....	....	16	....	....	....	....	....
1940-41	**Detroit Red Wings**	**NHL**	**47**	**13**	**12**	**25**	**20**	**17**	**37**	**18**	**9**	**1**	**3**	**4**	**4**
	Indianapolis Capitols	AHL	1	0	0	0	....	....	....	0	....	....	....	....	....
1941-42	**Detroit Red Wings**	**NHL**	**19**	**2**	**4**	**6**	**3**	**5**	**8**	**20**	**12**	**1**	**3**	**4**	**20**
♦1942-43	**Detroit Red Wings**	**NHL**	**50**	**6**	**4**	**10**	**6**	**4**	**10**	**42**	**5**	**0**	**1**	**1**	**2**
	Cleveland Barons	AHL	2	1	1	2	....	....	....	0	....	....	....	....	....
1943-44	Coast Guard Cutters	X-Games	33	12	21	33	....	....	....	12	12	4	10	14	9
1944-45			MILITARY SERVICE												
1945-46	Cleveland Barons	AHL	23	1	7	8	....	....	....	18	12	4	2	6	4
1946-47	Springfield Indians	AHL	61	6	14	20	....	....	....	50	2	1	0	1	0
1947-48	Philadelphia Rockets	AHL	63	6	22	28	....	....	....	55	....	....	....	....	....
	NHL Totals		**255**	**39**	**64**	**103**	**60**	**97**	**157**	**135**	**41**	**3**	**9**	**12**	**41**

Traded to **Detroit** by **Boston** for Clarence Drouillard and cash, December 22, 1937. Loaned to **Cleveland** (AHL) by **Detroit** as an injury replacement for Dick Adolph, October 23, 1942. Traded to **Cleveland** (AHL) by **Detroit** for cash, October 25, 1945.

• MULOIN, Wayne — *see page 1449*

• MUMMERY, Harry Harold "Mum"

D – L. 5'11", 220 lbs. b: Chicago, IL, 8/25/1889 d: 12/9/1945.

Season	Club	League	GP	G	A	Pts	AG	AA	APts	PIM	GP	G	A	Pts	PIM
1907-08	Brandon YMCA	MHL-Sr.	STATISTICS NOT AVAILABLE												
1908-09	Fort William Forts	NOHL	12	3	0	3	....	....	....	....	1	0	0	0	....
1909-10	Fort William Forts	NOHL	STATISTICS NOT AVAILABLE												
1910-11	Brandon Shamrocks	MIPHL	5	1	0	1	....	....	....	....	....	....	....	....	....
1911-12	Moose Jaw Brewers	SPHL	8	1	0	1	....	....	....	....	....	....	....	....	....
♦1912-13	Quebec Bulldogs	NHA	19	5	0	5	....	....	....	*87	2	1	0	1	0
1913-14	Quebec Bulldogs	NHA	20	8	5	13	....	....	....	29	....	....	....	....	....
1914-15	Quebec Bulldogs	NHA	20	7	4	11	....	....	....	88	....	....	....	....	....
1915-16	Quebec Bulldogs	NHA	23	2	1	3	....	....	....	84	....	....	....	....	....
1916-17	Montreal Canadiens	NHA	20	5	3	8	....	....	....	101	6	0	0	0	43
1917-18	**Toronto Arenas**	**NHL**	**18**	**3**	**3**	**6**	**4**	**12**	**16**	**41**	**2**	**1**	***1**	**2**	**17**
♦	Toronto Arenas	St-Cup	5	0	6	6	....	....	....	0	....	....	....	....	....

			REGULAR SEASON								PLAYOFFS				
Season	Club	League	GP	G	A	Pts	AG	AA	APts	PIM	GP	G	A	Pts	PIM
1918-19	Toronto Arenas	NHL	13	2	0	2	3	0	3	30	....	....	....	....	....
1919-20	Quebec Bulldogs	NHL	24	9	9	18	10	31	41	42	....	....	....	....	....
1920-21	Montreal Canadiens	NHL	24	15	5	20	19	19	38	69	....	....	....	....	....
1921-22	Hamilton Tigers	NHL	20	4	2	6	5	6	11	40	....	....	....	....	....
1922-23	Hamilton Tigers	NHL	7	0	0	0	0	0	0	4	....	....	....	....	....
	Saskatoon Sheiks	WCHL	4	0	0	0	....	....	....	2	....	....	....	....	....
	NHL Totals		106	33	19	52	41	68	109	226	2	1	1	2	17
	Other Major League Totals		118	30	13	43	....	....	....	391	9	1	0	1	43

NHL rights returned to **Quebec** (NHA) by **Montreal Canadiens** (NHA) prior to formation of NHL, November, 1917. Claimed by **Toronto Arenas** from **Quebec** in Dispersal Draft, November 26, 1917. Transferred to **Quebec** by **Toronto Arenas** when Quebec franchise returned to NHL, November 25, 1919. Transferred to **Hamilton** after **Quebec** franchise relocated, November 2, 1920. Traded to **Montreal Canadiens** by **Hamilton** with Jack McDonald and Dave Ritchie for Goldie Prodgers, Joe Matte, Jack Coughlin and the loan of Billy Coutu for the 1920-21 season, November 27, 1920. Traded to **Hamilton** by **Montreal Canadiens** with Amos Arbour for Sprague Cleghorn, November 26, 1921. Traded to **Saskatoon** (WCHL) by **Hamilton** for cash, February 8, 1923.

• MUNRO, Dunc — Duncan Brown

D – L. 5'8", 190 lbs. b: Moray, Scotland, 1/19/1901 d: 1/3/1958.

Season	Club	League	GP	G	A	Pts	AG	AA	APts	PIM	GP	G	A	Pts	PIM
1919-20	U. of Toronto Schools	OHA-Jr.	STATISTICS NOT AVAILABLE												
1920-21	Toronto Granites	OHA-Sr.	8	4	5	9	....	....	....	....	2	1	0	1	....
1921-22	Toronto Granites	OHA-Sr.	10	4	6	10	....	....	....	....	2	2	1	3	....
	Toronto Granites	Al-Cup	6	3	3	6	....	....	....	....	....	....	....	....	....
1922-23	Toronto Granites	OHA-Sr.	12	7	7	14	....	....	....	....	2	2	0	2	4
1923-24	Toronto Granites	X-Games	15	9	5	14	....	....	....	....	....	....	....	....	....
	Canada	Olympics	5	18	4	22	....	....	....	2	....	....	....	....	....
1924-25	Montreal Maroons	NHL	27	5	1	6	9	4	13	16	....	....	....	....	....
1925-26	Montreal Maroons	NHL	33	4	6	10	7	39	46	55	2	0	0	0	0
♦	Montreal Maroons	St-Cup	4	1	0	1	....	....	....	6	....	....	....	....	....
1926-27	Montreal Maroons	NHL	43	6	5	11	11	26	37	42	2	0	0	0	4
1927-28	Montreal Maroons	NHL	43	5	2	7	10	11	21	35	9	0	2	2	8
1928-29	Montreal Maroons	NHL	1	0	0	0	0	0	0	0	....	....	....	....	....
1929-30	Montreal Maroons	NHL	40	7	2	9	10	5	15	10	4	2	0	2	4
1930-31	Montreal Maroons	NHL	4	0	1	1	0	3	3	0	....	....	....	....	....
1931-32	Montreal Canadiens	NHL	48	1	1	2	2	2	4	14	4	0	0	0	2
	NHL Totals		239	28	18	46	49	90	139	172	21	2	2	4	18

Signed as a free agent by **Montreal Maroons**, October 30, 1924. • 1925-26 Montreal Maroons playoff totals includes series against Ottawa and Pittsburgh. • Missed remainder of 1928-29 season recovering from minor heart attack, November 15, 1928. • Named playing coach/manager by **Montreal Maroons**, September 23, 1929. Signed as a free agent by **Montreal Canadiens**, November 6, 1931.

• MUNRO, Gerry

D – L. 5'10", 175 lbs. b: Sault Ste. Marie, Ont., 11/28/1897 Deceased.

Season	Club	League	GP	G	A	Pts	AG	AA	APts	PIM	GP	G	A	Pts	PIM
1919-20	S.S. Marie Greyhounds	NMHL	2	2	0	2	....	....	....	2	....	....	....	....	....
	S.S. Marie Greyhounds	NOHA	3	5	1	6	....	....	....	2	....	....	....	....	....
1920-21	S.S. Marie Greyhounds	NMHL	10	5	2	7	....	....	....	....	....	....	....	....	....
	S.S. Marie Greyhounds	NOHA	4	2	0	2	....	....	....	4	5	*5	1	6	....
1921-22	S.S. Marie Greyhounds	NMHL	10	1	1	2	....	....	....	....	....	....	....	....	....
	S.S. Marie Greyhounds	NOHA	7	0	1	1	....	....	....	11	2	0	0	0	2
1922-23	Sudbury Wolves	NOHA	8	3	1	4	....	....	....	10	2	0	0	0	4
1923-24	Sudbury Mines	NOHA	STATISTICS NOT AVAILABLE												
1924-25	Montreal Maroons	NHL	30	1	0	1	2	0	2	37	....	....	....	....	....
1925-26	Toronto St. Pats	NHL	4	0	0	0	0	0	0	0	....	....	....	....	....
1926-27	Detroit Greyhounds	AHA	5	1	0	1	....	....	....	0	....	....	....	....	....
	Chicago Cardinals	AHA	10	0	2	2	....	....	....	8	....	....	....	....	....
	Winnipeg Maroons	AHA	20	2	2	4	....	....	....	20	3	0	0	0	0
1927-28	Kansas City Pla-Mors	AHA	22	3	1	4	....	....	....	37	....	....	....	....	....
1928-29	Kansas City Pla-Mors	AHA	30	1	0	1	....	....	....	12	....	....	....	....	....
1929-30	Kansas City Pla-Mors	AHA	48	2	1	3	....	....	....	34	4	2	0	2	7
1930-31	Minneapolis Millers	AHA	43	5	5	10	....	....	....	58	....	....	....	....	....
	NHL Totals		34	1	0	1	2	0	2	37	....	....	....	....	....

Signed as a free agent by **Montreal Maroons**, October 31, 1924. Traded to **Toronto St. Pats** by **Montreal Maroons** for cash, October 23, 1925. Signed as a free agent by **Detroit** (AHA), November 17, 1926. Signed as a free agent by **Minneapolis** (AHA), November 3, 1930.

• MURDOCH, Murray — John Murray

LW – L. 5'10", 180 lbs. b: Lucknow, Ont., 5/19/1904.

Season	Club	League	GP	G	A	Pts	AG	AA	APts	PIM	GP	G	A	Pts	PIM
1921-22	University of Manitoba	WJrHL	STATISTICS NOT AVAILABLE												
	University of Manitoba	M-Cup	2	*2	0	*2	....	....	....	0	....	....	....	....	....
1922-23	University of Manitoba	WJrHL	STATISTICS NOT AVAILABLE												
	University of Manitoba	M-Cup	8	*26	*4	*30	....	....	....	2	....	....	....	....	....
1923-24	University of Manitoba	MHL-Sr.	8	9	5	14	....	....	....	0	1	0	1	1	0
1924-25	Winnipeg Tiger Falcons	MHL-Sr.	18	12	2	14	....	....	....	2	....	....	....	....	....
1925-26	Winnipeg Maroons	CHL	34	9	2	11	....	....	....	12	5	0	1	1	0
1926-27	New York Rangers	NHL	44	6	4	10	11	21	32	12	2	0	0	0	0
♦1927-28	New York Rangers	NHL	44	7	3	10	14	17	31	14	9	2	1	3	12
1928-29	New York Rangers	NHL	44	8	6	14	23	40	63	18	6	0	0	0	2
1929-30	New York Rangers	NHL	44	13	13	26	18	31	49	22	4	3	0	3	6
1930-31	New York Rangers	NHL	44	7	7	14	14	21	35	8	4	0	2	2	0
1931-32	New York Rangers	NHL	48	5	16	21	8	35	43	32	7	0	2	2	2
♦1932-33	New York Rangers	NHL	48	5	11	16	9	23	32	23	8	3	*4	7	2
1933-34	New York Rangers	NHL	48	17	10	27	29	21	50	29	2	0	0	0	0
1934-35	New York Rangers	NHL	48	14	15	29	23	26	49	14	4	0	2	2	4
1935-36	New York Rangers	NHL	48	2	9	11	4	17	21	9	....	....	....	....	....
1936-37	New York Rangers	NHL	48	0	14	14	0	26	26	16	9	1	1	2	0
1937-38	Philadelphia Ramblers	IAHL	44	4	9	13	....	....	....	4	5	0	1	1	4
1938-39	Yale University	Ivy	DID NOT PLAY – COACHING												
	NHL Totals		508	84	108	192	153	278	431	197	55	9	12	21	28

Won Lester Patrick Trophy (1974)

Signed as a free agent by **NY Rangers**, September 2, 1926.

• MURPHY, Ron

— *see page 1454*

• MURRAY, Allan

D – L. 5'7", 165 lbs. b: Stratford, Ont., 11/10/1908.

Season	Club	League	GP	G	A	Pts	AG	AA	APts	PIM	GP	G	A	Pts	PIM
1926-27	Stratford Midgets	OHA-Jr.	STATISTICS NOT AVAILABLE												
1927-28	South Porcupine Porkies	NOHA	STATISTICS NOT AVAILABLE												
1928-29	Buffalo Bisons	Can-Pro	28	2	1	3	....	....	....	27	....	....	....	....	....
1929-30	Buffalo Bisons	IHL	37	1	0	1	....	....	....	54	....	....	....	....	....
1930-31	Buffalo Bisons	IHL	46	0	3	3	....	....	....	42	4	0	0	0	2
1931-32	Buffalo Bisons	IHL	46	2	7	9	....	....	....	39	6	0	0	0	2
1932-33	Buffalo Bisons	IHL	43	1	7	8	....	....	....	48	6	0	0	0	4
1933-34	New York Americans	NHL	39	1	1	2	2	2	4	20	....	....	....	....	....
	Syracuse Stars	IHL	9	1	0	1	....	....	....	28	....	....	....	....	....
1934-35	New York Americans	NHL	43	2	1	3	3	2	5	36	....	....	....	....	....
1935-36	New York Americans	NHL	48	1	0	1	2	0	2	33	5	0	0	0	2
1936-37	New York Americans	NHL	40	0	2	2	0	4	4	22	....	....	....	....	....
1937-38	New York Americans	NHL	47	0	1	1	0	2	2	34	6	0	0	0	6
1938-39	New York Americans	NHL	18	0	0	0	0	0	0	8	....	....	....	....	....
1939-40	New York Americans	NHL	36	1	4	5	2	6	8	10	3	0	0	0	2
	NHL Totals		271	5	9	14	9	16	25	163	14	0	0	0	10

Signed as a free agent by **NY Americans**, February 20, 1933. Traded to **Syracuse** (IHL) by **Buffalo** (IHL) for Graham Teasdale, September 24, 1933. • Missed majority of 1938-39 season recovering from shoulder injury suffered in game vs. Boston, December 29, 1938.

• MURRAY, Leo

C/LW – L. 5'9", 165 lbs. b: Portage la Prairie, Man., 2/15/1906 Deceased.

Season	Club	League	GP	G	A	Pts	AG	AA	APts	PIM	GP	G	A	Pts	PIM
1922-23	Montreal Ste-Anne's	MCHL	2	0	0	0	....	....	....	....	....	....	....	....	....
1923-24	Montreal Eurekas	MCHL	STATISTICS NOT AVAILABLE												
1924-25	Montreal Ste. Anne	ECHL	12	8	0	8	....	....	....	....	....	....	....	....	....
	Montreal Eurekas	MCHL	STATISTICS NOT AVAILABLE												
1925-26	Montreal Columbus Club	QAHA	8	5	0	5	....	....	....	15	....	....	....	....	....
	Montreal CNR	MRTHL	9	7	3	10	....	....	....	6	1	0	0	0	0
1926-27	Quebec Castors	Can-Am	32	13	4	17	....	....	....	36	2	0	0	0	2
1927-28	Quebec Castors	Can-Am	39	10	5	15	....	....	....	69	6	1	0	1	12
1928-29	Newark Bulldogs	Can-Am	40	6	3	9	....	....	....	78	....	....	....	....	....
1929-30	Providence Reds	Can-Am	22	3	3	6	....	....	....	47	....	....	....	....	....
1930-31	Detroit Olympics	IHL	27	3	5	8	....	....	....	18	....	....	....	....	....
	Philadelphia Arrows	Can-Am	15	5	1	6	....	....	....	27	....	....	....	....	....
1931-32	Providence Reds	Can-Am	39	17	11	28	....	....	....	65	5	2	*2	4	2
1932-33	Providence Reds	Can-Am	42	16	14	30	....	....	....	51	2	1	1	2	0
	Montreal Canadiens	NHL	6	0	0	0	0	0	0	2	....	....	....	....	....
1933-34	Providence Reds	Can-Am	40	9	12	21	....	....	....	60	3	0	0	0	9
1934-35	Providence Reds	Can-Am	39	2	10	12	....	....	....	32	6	1	0	1	6
1935-36	Springfield Indians	Can-Am	16	2	6	8	....	....	....	12	3	0	1	1	0
	NHL Totals		6	0	0	0	0	0	0	2	....	....	....	....	....

Signed as a free agent by **Quebec** (Can-Am), November 3, 1926. Transferred to **Newark** (Can-Am) after **Quebec** (Can-Am) franchise relocated, October, 1928. Rights traded to **Providence** (Can-Am) by **Newark** (Can-Am) for cash, October 8, 1929. Signed as a free agent by **NY Americans**, October 22, 1930. Signed as a free agent **Providence** (Can-Am), October, 1931. Traded to **Montreal Canadiens** by **Providence** (Can-Am) with Hago Harrington for Leo Gaudreault and Armand Mondou with both teams holding right of recall, January, 1933. Traded to **Springfield** (Can-Am) by **Providence** (Can-Am) with Chris Speyer for Albert Leduc, October 12, 1935.

• MYLES, Vic — Vic Robert William

D – R. 6'1", 208 lbs. b: Fairlight, Sask., 11/12/1915.

Season	Club	League	GP	G	A	Pts	AG	AA	APts	PIM	GP	G	A	Pts	PIM
1931-32	Moose Jaw Cubs	S-SJHL	....	....	....	....	....	....	....	....	4	0	0	0	4
	Moose Jaw Cubs	M-Cup	4	0	0	0	....	....	....	4	....	....	....	....	....
1932-33	Moose Jaw Cubs	S-SJHL	....	....	....	....	....	....	....	....	2	0	0	0	2
	Moose Jaw Cubs	M-Cup	2	0	0	0	....	....	....	2	....	....	....	....	....
1933-34	Moose Jaw Crescents	S-SSHL	20	9	2	11	....	....	....	38	3	0	1	1	*7
1934-35	North Battleford Beavers	N-SSHL	20	4	3	7	....	....	....	*45	6	4	*4	*8	16
1935-36	North Battleford Beavers	N-SSHL	16	10	9	19	....	....	....	38	3	2	0	2	2
1936-37	North Battleford Beavers	N-SSHL	25	2	10	12	....	....	....	*74	4	1	*4	5	6
1937-38	Moose Jaw Cresents	S-SSHL	23	9	17	26	....	....	....	*63	6	4	2	6	*8
1938-39	Moose Jaw Millers	S-SSHL	29	12	12	24	....	....	....	42	10	2	2	4	*14
1939-40	Philadelphia Rockets	IAHL	50	7	8	15	....	....	....	60	....	....	....	....	....
1940-41	New Haven Eagles	AHL	55	5	9	14	....	....	....	96	....	....	....	....	....
1941-42	New Haven Eagles	AHL	56	8	19	27	....	....	....	88	....	....	....	....	....
1942-43	New Haven Eagles	AHL	4	0	3	3	....	....	....	8	....	....	....	....	....
	New York Rangers	NHL	45	6	9	15	6	8	14	57	....	....	....	....	....
1943-44	Moose Jaw Victorias	S-SSHL	18	10	14	24	....	....	....	26	....	....	....	....	....
	Flin Flon Bombers	N-SSHL	4	5	2	7	....	....	....	13	....	....	....	....	....
	Flin Flon Bombers	Al-Cup	4	0	2	2	....	....	....	10	....	....	....	....	....
1944-45			MILITARY SERVICE												
1945-46	Tulsa Oilers	USHL	53	22	26	48	....	....	....	56	13	7	6	13	*27
1946-47	St. Paul Saints	USHL	58	14	27	41	....	....	....	73	....	....	....	....	....
1947-48	Regina Capitals	WCSHL	47	11	8	19	....	....	....	62	4	3	2	5	6
1948-49	Regina Capitals	WCSHL	45	12	10	22	....	....	....	87	8	1	7	8	6
	Regina Caps	Al-Cup	14	3	11	14	....	....	....	*32	....	....	....	....	....
1949-50	Saskatoon Quakers	WCSHL	50	7	15	22	....	....	....	99	5	0	0	0	10
1950-51	Regina Capitals	WCMHL	28	6	11	17	....	....	....	39	....	....	....	....	....
1951-52	Moose Jaw Canucks	WCSHL	DID NOT PLAY – COACHING												
	NHL Totals		45	6	9	15	6	8	14	57	....	....	....	....	....

WCSHL Second All-Star Team (1948) • WCSHL First All-Star Team (1949)

Signed as a free agent by **New Haven** (IAHL), October 12, 1939. Traded to **NY Rangers** by **New Haven** (AHL) for cash, November 17, 1942.

• NATTRASS, Ralph — Ralph William

D – R. 6', 185 lbs. b: Gainsboro, Sask., 5/26/1925.

Season	Club	League	GP	G	A	Pts	AG	AA	APts	PIM	GP	G	A	Pts	PIM
1943-44	Moose Jaw Canucks	SJHL	2	2	2	4	....	....	....	0	....	....	....	....	....
1944-45	Moose Jaw Canucks	SJHL	16	7	5	12	....	....	....	53	4	0	0	0	4
	Moose Jaw Canucks	M-Cup	17	9	5	14	....	....	....	*33	....	....	....	....	....
1945-46	Kansas City Pla-Mors	USHL	50	4	20	24	....	....	....	75	12	2	5	7	20
1946-47	Chicago Black Hawks	NHL	35	4	5	9	4	6	10	34	....	....	....	....	....
	Kansas City Pla-Mors	USHL	17	1	5	6	....	....	....	22	....	....	....	....	....
1947-48	Chicago Black Hawks	NHL	60	5	12	17	6	16	22	79	....	....	....	....	....

Season	Club	League	GP	G	A	Pts	AG	AA	APts	PIM	GP	G	A	Pts	PIM
			REGULAR SEASON								PLAYOFFS				
1948-49	**Chicago Black Hawks**	**NHL**	**60**	**4**	**10**	**14**	**6**	**14**	**20**	**99**	....	....	....	....	....
1949-50	**Chicago Black Hawks**	**NHL**	**68**	**5**	**11**	**16**	**6**	**13**	**19**	**96**	....	....	....	....	....
1950-51	Cincinnati Mohawks	AHL	55	0	30	30	....	....	....	84	....	....	....	....	....
	NHL Totals		**223**	**18**	**38**	**56**	**22**	**49**	**71**	**308**	....	....	....	....	....

Traded to **Montreal** by **Chicago** for cash, October 4, 1950.

• NEILSON, Jim

— see page 1465

• NESTERENKO, Eric

— see page 1467

• NEVILLE, Mike

Mike Joseph
C – R. 5'9", 168 lbs. b: Toronto, Ont., 10/11/1904 Deceased.

Season	Club	League	GP	G	A	Pts	AG	AA	APts	PIM	GP	G	A	Pts	PIM
1921-22	Grand'Mere Maroons	QPHL	8	7	0	7	....	....	....	....	....	....	....	....	....
1922-23	Quebec Sons Of Ireland	QPHL	8	2	0	2	....	....	....	....	5	1	0	1	....
1923-24	Trois-Rivieres Lions	QPHL	10	2	0	2	....	....	....	....	....	....	....	....	....
1924-25	London AAA	OHA-Sr.	8	5	4	9	....	....	....	2	....	....	....	....	....
	Toronto St. Pats	**NHL**	**13**	**1**	**2**	**3**	**2**	**8**	**10**	**4**	**2**	**0**	**0**	**0**	**0**
1925-26	**Toronto St. Pats**	**NHL**	**33**	**3**	**3**	**6**	**5**	**19**	**24**	**8**	....	....	....	....	....
1926-27	Hamilton Tigers	Can-Pro	32	15	4	19	....	....	....	38	2	0	0	0	0
1927-28	Hamilton Tigers	Can-Pro	11	8	3	11	....	....	....	15	....	....	....	....	....
	Stratford Nationals	Can-Pro	29	10	6	16	....	....	....	10	5	2	2	4	4
1928-29	Windsor Bulldogs	IHL	38	14	7	21	....	....	....	18	8	2	*5	7	6
1929-30	Windsor Bulldogs	IHL	39	11	17	28	....	....	....	20	....	....	....	....	....
1930-31	**New York Americans**	**NHL**	**19**	**1**	**0**	**1**	**2**	**0**	**2**	**2**	....	....	....	....	....
	New Haven Eagles	Can-Am	12	1	3	4	....	....	....	10	....	....	....	....	....
	London Panthers	IHL	19	2	5	7	....	....	....	15	....	....	....	....	....
1931-32	London Tecumsehs	IHL	48	10	11	21	....	....	....	25	5	0	0	0	2
1932-33	London Tecumsehs	IHL	42	9	8	17	....	....	....	15	6	1	2	3	0
1933-34	Cleveland–Syracuse	IHL	41	3	3	6	....	....	....	13	5	0	1	1	0
1934-35	Calgary–Portland	NWHL	24	6	6	12	....	....	....	6	....	....	....	....	....
1935-36	Rochester Cardinals	IHL	39	2	2	4	....	....	....	4	....	....	....	....	....
	NHL Totals		**65**	**5**	**5**	**10**	**9**	**27**	**36**	**14**	**2**	**0**	**0**	**0**	**0**

IHL First All-Star Team (1930)

Signed as a free agent by **Toronto**, January 14, 1925. Claimed on waivers by **Hamilton** (Can-Pro) from **Toronto**, October 16, 1926. Traded to **Stratford** (Can-Pro) by **Hamilton** (Can-Pro) with Fred Litzen for Butch Kelterborne, Shorty Quesnel and Roy Bogardis, December 19, 1927. Traded to **Montreal Maroons** (Windsor-Can-Pro) by **Buffalo** (Can-Pro) for Rollie Huard, November 18, 1928. Traded to **NY Americans** by **Montreal Maroons** (Windsor-IHL) with Frank Carson, Red Dutton and Hap Emms for $35,000, May 14, 1930. Traded to **London** (IHL) by **NY Americans** for cash, January 28, 1931.

• NEVIN, Bob

— see page 1468

• NEWMAN, John

C/LW – L. 5'8", 155 lbs. b: Ottawa, Ont., 4/24/1910 d: 4/17/1967.

Season	Club	League	GP	G	A	Pts	AG	AA	APts	PIM	GP	G	A	Pts	PIM
1928-29	Ottawa Shamrocks	OCHL	STATISTICS NOT AVAILABLE												
1929-30	Detroit Olympics	IHL	41	9	11	20	....	....	....	29	2	0	0	0	4
1930-31	**Detroit Falcons**	**NHL**	**8**	**1**	**1**	**2**	**2**	**3**	**5**	**0**	....	....	....	....	....
	Detroit Olympics	IHL	21	3	5	8	....	....	....	30	....	....	....	....	....
1931-32	Detroit Olympics	IHL	46	10	8	18	....	....	....	32	6	2	0	2	12
1932-33	Detroit Olympics	IHL	34	7	6	13	....	....	....	25	....	....	....	....	....
1933-34	Buffalo Bisons	IHL	43	5	2	7	....	....	....	16	6	0	2	2	2
1934-35	Cleveland Falcons	IHL	7	3	1	4	....	....	....	0	....	....	....	....	....
	Buffalo Bisons	IHL	32	4	10	14	....	....	....	4	....	....	....	....	....
1935-36	Buffalo Bisons	IHL	47	5	14	19	....	....	....	10	5	0	2	2	0
1936-37	Buffalo Bisons	IAHL	11	3	2	5	....	....	....	4	....	....	....	....	....
	Seattle Seahawks	PCHL	26	4	4	8	....	....	....	5	....	....	....	....	....
1937-38	Detroit Pontiacs	MOHL	28	10	12	22	....	....	....	23	3	2	1	3	4
1938-39	Detroit Pontiacs	MOHL	27	9	6	15	....	....	....	4	7	3	2	5	0
1939-40	Detroit Pontiacs	MOHL	23	9	2	11	....	....	....	11	....	....	....	....	....
	NHL Totals		**8**	**1**	**1**	**2**	**2**	**3**	**5**	**0**	....	....	....	....	....

Signed as a free agent by **Detroit**, September 12, 1929. Traded to **Buffalo** (IAHL) by **Detroit** with Bob Davis and Tip O'Neill for Gamey Lederman, September 24, 1933.

• NICHOLSON, Al

Allan Douglas
LW – L. 6'1", 180 lbs. b: Estevan, Sask., 4/26/1936.

Season	Club	League	GP	G	A	Pts	AG	AA	APts	PIM	GP	G	A	Pts	PIM
1951-52	Esteven Miners	SIHA	STATISTICS NOT AVAILABLE												
1952-53	Humboldt Indians	SJHL	40	6	9	15	....	....	....	24	12	3	1	4	2
1953-54	Humboldt Indians	SJHL	47	18	22	40	....	....	....	59	5	1	0	1	10
	Humboldt Indians	M-Cup	5	1	1	2	....	....	....	2	....	....	....	....	....
1954-55	Humboldt Indians	SJHL	38	37	34	71	....	....	....	52	10	6	7	13	8
	Humboldt Indians	M-Cup	5	1	1	2	....	....	....	2	....	....	....	....	....
1955-56	**Boston Bruins**	**NHL**	**14**	**0**	**0**	**0**	**0**	**0**	**0**	**4**	....	....	....	....	....
	Hershey Bears	AHL	38	9	15	24	....	....	....	32	....	....	....	....	....
1956-57	**Boston Bruins**	**NHL**	**5**	**0**	**1**	**1**	**0**	**1**	**1**	**0**	....	....	....	....	....
	Hershey Bears	AHL	55	22	27	49	....	....	....	51	3	0	0	0	2
1957-58	Springfield Indians	AHL	61	14	19	33	....	....	....	38	13	0	2	2	10
1958-59	Victoria Cougars	WHL	69	36	51	87	....	....	....	78	3	1	1	2	0
1959-60	Victoria–Winnipeg	WHL	71	21	34	55	....	....	....	22	....	....	....	....	....
1960-61	Winnipeg Warriors	WHL	70	15	33	48	....	....	....	51	....	....	....	....	....
1961-62	San Francisco Seals	WHL	70	25	35	60	....	....	....	8	2	1	1	2	0
1962-63	San Francisco Seals	WHL	70	27	35	62	....	....	....	4	17	5	9	14	6
1963-64	San Francisco Seals	WHL	69	24	30	54	....	....	....	31	11	6	8	14	4
1964-65	San Francisco Seals	WHL	70	28	30	58	....	....	....	37	....	....	....	....	....
1965-66	San Francisco Seals	WHL	70	23	28	51	....	....	....	23	7	1	0	1	0
1966-67	San Diego Gulls	WHL	72	25	27	52	....	....	....	24	....	....	....	....	....
1967-68	San Diego Gulls	WHL	72	28	33	61	....	....	....	23	7	3	2	5	4
1968-69	San Diego Gulls	WHL	74	22	33	55	....	....	....	49	7	3	5	8	4
1969-70	San Diego Gulls	WHL	72	28	25	53	....	....	....	14	6	1	5	6	10
1970-71	San Diego Gulls	WHL	72	28	44	72	....	....	....	27	6	2	1	3	8
1971-72	San Diego Gulls	WHL	72	26	36	62	....	....	....	26	4	0	0	0	2
	NHL Totals		**19**	**0**	**1**	**1**	**0**	**1**	**1**	**4**	....	....	....	....	....

Signed as a free agent by **Boston**, August 23, 1955. Traded to **Chicago** (Calgary-WHL) by **Boston** (San Francisco-WHL) for Cec Hoekstra, January 22, 1963. • Nicholson refused to report to Calgary (WHL) and transaction was cancelled, January, 1963. • Claimed by **Detroit** (Pittsburgh-AHL) from **Boston** in Reverse Draft, June 12, 1966. Traded to **San Diego** (WHL) by **Detroit** (Pittsburgh-AHL) with Len Haley and Ed Ehrenverth for $20,000, June 20, 1966.

• NICHOLSON, Ed

Edward George "Nicky"
D – L. 5'8", 180 lbs. b: Portsmouth, Ont., 9/9/1923 d: 1/15/1987.

Season	Club	League	GP	G	A	Pts	AG	AA	APts	PIM	GP	G	A	Pts	PIM
1943-44	Kingston Frontenacs	LOVHL	STATISTICS NOT AVAILABLE												
1944-45	Kingston Frontenacs	LOVHL	STATISTICS NOT AVAILABLE												
1945-46	Army Engineers	Scotland	STATISTICS NOT AVAILABLE												
1946-47	Indianapolis Capitols	AHL	57	4	10	14	....	....	....	79	....	....	....	....	....
1947-48	Indianapolis Capitols	AHL	65	5	16	21	....	....	....	63	....	....	....	....	....
	Detroit Red Wings	**NHL**	**1**	**0**	**0**	**0**	**0**	**0**	**0**	**0**	....	....	....	....	....
1948-49	Indianapolis Capitols	AHL	65	3	24	27	....	....	....	46	2	0	0	0	0
1949-50	St. Louis Flyers	AHL	70	12	19	31	....	....	....	20	2	0	0	0	2
1950-51	St. Louis Flyers	AHL	68	8	24	32	....	....	....	37	....	....	....	....	....
1951-52	St. Louis Flyers	AHL	50	2	11	13	....	....	....	23	....	....	....	....	....
1952-53	Kingston Goodyears	OSrBL	STATISTICS NOT AVAILABLE												
1953-54	Kingston Goodyears	OSBHL	STATISTICS NOT AVAILABLE												
1954-55	Kingston Goodyears	OSBHL	STATISTICS NOT AVAILABLE												
	NHL Totals		**1**	**0**	**0**	**0**	**0**	**0**	**0**	**0**	....	....	....	....	....

Signed as a free agent by **Detroit**, March 20, 1948. Traded to **St. Louis** (AHL) by **Detroit** with Fern Gauthier, Cliff Simpson and future considerations for Stephen Black and Bill Brennan, August 29, 1949.

• NICHOLSON, Hickey

John Ivan
LW – L. 5'10", 170 lbs. b: Charlottetown, P.E.I., 9/9/1911 d: 11/22/1956.

Season	Club	League	GP	G	A	Pts	AG	AA	APts	PIM	GP	G	A	Pts	PIM
1929-30	Charlottetown Abegweits	PEI-Sr.	8	6	1	7	....	....	....	28	2	*3	0	3	2
	Moncton Atlantics	NBSHL	1	1	1	2	....	....	....	0	....	....	....	....	....
	Charlottetown Islanders	Al-Cup	2	0	0	0	....	....	....	0	....	....	....	....	....
1930-31	Charlottetown Abegweits	PEI-Sr.	11	8	3	11	....	....	....	....	1	0	0	0	2
1931-32	Charlottetown Abegweits	MSHL	24	6	3	9	....	....	....	18	....	....	....	....	....
1932-33	Charlottetown Abegweits	MSHL	10	0	2	2	....	....	....	12	4	2	0	2	4
1933-34	Charlottetown Abegweits	MSHL	39	12	7	19	....	....	....	43	3	2	2	4	4
1934-35	Charlottetown Abegweits	MSHL	19	8	15	23	....	....	....	34	6	1	0	1	14
	Charlottetown Abegweits	Big-3	4	2	1	3	....	....	....	4	....	....	....	....	....
1935-36	Richmond Hawks	Ln-Cup	....	2	3	5	....	....	....	....	....	....	....	....	....
	Richmond Hawks	Britain	....	8	8	16	....	....	....	....	....	....	....	....	....
1936-37	Harringay Racers	Britain	34	9	8	17	....	....	....	30	....	....	....	....	....
1937-38	**Chicago Black Hawks**	**NHL**	**2**	**1**	**0**	**1**	**2**	**0**	**2**	**0**	....	....	....	....	....
	Kansas City Greyhounds	AHA	47	11	17	28	....	....	....	26	....	....	....	....	....
1938-39	Kansas City Greyhounds	AHA	48	16	35	51	....	....	....	33	....	....	....	....	....
1939-40	Kansas City Greyhounds	AHA	47	14	14	28	....	....	....	33	....	....	....	....	....
1940-41	Halifax Army	NSDHL	4	6	2	8	....	....	....	2	....	....	....	....	....
	NHL Totals		**2**	**1**	**0**	**1**	**2**	**0**	**2**	**0**	....	....	....	....	....

MSHL Second All-Star Team (1935)

• NIGHBOR, Frank

"The Pembroke Peach" HHOF
C – R. 5'9", 160 lbs. b: Pembroke, Ont., 1/26/1893 d: 4/13/1966.

Season	Club	League	GP	G	A	Pts	AG	AA	APts	PIM	GP	G	A	Pts	PIM
1910-11	Pembroke Debaters	UOVHL	6	6	*4	*10	....	....	....	3	2	*6	2	*8	0
1911-12	Port Arthur Bearcats	NOHL	4	0	0	0	....	....	....	9	....	....	....	....	....
1912-13	Toronto Blueshirts	NHA	19	25	0	25	....	....	....	9	....	....	....	....	....
1913-14	Vancouver Millionaires	PCHA	11	10	5	15	....	....	....	6	....	....	....	....	....
♦1914-15	Vancouver Millionaires	PCHA	17	23	7	30	....	....	....	12	3	4	*6	*10	6
1915-16	Ottawa Senators	NHA	23	19	5	24	....	....	....	26	....	....	....	....	....
1916-17	Ottawa Senators	NHA	19	*41	10	*51	....	....	....	24	2	1	1	2	6
1917-18	**Ottawa Senators**	**NHL**	**10**	**11**	**8**	**19**	**14**	**34**	**48**	**6**	....	....	....	....	....
1918-19	**Ottawa Senators**	**NHL**	**18**	**19**	**9**	**28**	**35**	**51**	**86**	**27**	**2**	**0**	**2**	**2**	**3**
1919-20	**Ottawa Senators**	**NHL**	**23**	**26**	***15**	**41**	**30**	**53**	**83**	**18**	....	....	....	....	....
♦	Ottawa Senators	St-Cup	5	6	1	7	....	....	....	2	....	....	....	....	....
1920-21	**Ottawa Senators**	**NHL**	**24**	**19**	**10**	**29**	**25**	**39**	**64**	**10**	**2**	**1**	**3**	**4**	**2**
♦	Ottawa Senators	St-Cup	5	0	1	1	....	....	....	0	....	....	....	....	....
1921-22	**Ottawa Senators**	**NHL**	**20**	**8**	**10**	**18**	**11**	**32**	**43**	**4**	**2**	**2**	**1**	**3**	**4**
1922-23	**Ottawa Senators**	**NHL**	**22**	**11**	**7**	**18**	**18**	**27**	**45**	**14**	**2**	**0**	**1**	**1**	**0**
♦	Ottawa Senators	St-Cup	6	1	1	2	....	....	....	10	....	....	....	....	....
1923-24	**Ottawa Senators**	**NHL**	**20**	**11**	**6**	**17**	**23**	**36**	**59**	**16**	**2**	**0**	**1**	**1**	**0**
1924-25	**Ottawa Senators**	**NHL**	**26**	**5**	**5**	**10**	**9**	**21**	**30**	**18**	....	....	....	....	....
1925-26	**Ottawa Senators**	**NHL**	**35**	**12**	***13**	**25**	**21**	**88**	**109**	**40**	**2**	**0**	**0**	**0**	**2**
♦1926-27	**Ottawa Senators**	**NHL**	**38**	**6**	**6**	**12**	**11**	**31**	**42**	**26**	**6**	**1**	**1**	**2**	**0**
1927-28	**Ottawa Senators**	**NHL**	**42**	**8**	**5**	**13**	**16**	**28**	**44**	**46**	**2**	**0**	**0**	**0**	**2**
1928-29	**Ottawa Senators**	**NHL**	**30**	**1**	**4**	**5**	**3**	**27**	**30**	**22**	....	....	....	....	....
1929-30	**Ottawa Senators**	**NHL**	**19**	**0**	**0**	**0**	**0**	**0**	**0**	**0**	....	....	....	....	....
	Toronto Maple Leafs	**NHL**	**22**	**2**	**0**	**2**	**3**	**0**	**3**	**2**	....	....	....	....	....
1930-31			OUT OF HOCKEY – RETIRED												
1931-32	Buffalo Bisons	IHL	1	0	0	0	....	....	....	0	....	....	....	....	....
	NHL Totals		**349**	**139**	**98**	**237**	**219**	**467**	**686**	**249**	**20**	**4**	**9**	**13**	**13**
	Other Major League Totals		93	118	27	145	....	....	....	86	5	5	7	12	12

PCHA First All-Star Team (1915) • Won Hart Trophy (1924) • Won Lady Byng Trophy (1925, 1926)

Signed as a free agent by **Vancouver** (PCHA), October 22, 1915. Signed by **Ottawa** (NHA) after jumping contract with **Vancouver** (PCHA), November 12, 1915. Signed as a free agent by **Ottawa**, December 22, 1917. • 1922-23 Stanley Cup totals includes series with Regina (WCHL) and Edmonton (PCHA). Traded to **Toronto** by **Ottawa** for Danny Cox and cash, January 31, 1930.

• NOBLE, Reg

Edward Reginald HHOF
C/D – L. 5'8", 180 lbs. b: Collingwood, Ont., 6/23/1896 d: 1/19/1962.

Season	Club	League	GP	G	A	Pts	AG	AA	APts	PIM	GP	G	A	Pts	PIM
1912-13	Collingwood Intermediates	OHA-I	STATISTICS NOT AVAILABLE												
	Collingwood Seniors	OHA-Sr.	1	0	0	0	....	....	....	0	....	....	....	....	....
1913-14	Collingwood ACC	OHA-Jr.	STATISTICS NOT AVAILABLE												
1914-15	Collingwood ACC	OHA-Jr.	STATISTICS NOT AVAILABLE												
1915-16	St. Michael's College	OHA-Jr.	....	....	....	....	....	....	....	....	6	*9	0	*9	....
	Toronto Riversides	OHA-Sr.	10	14	0	14	....	....	....	....	4	*6	0	*6	....

			REGULAR SEASON								PLAYOFFS				
Season	Club	League	GP	G	A	Pts	AG	AA	APts	PIM	GP	G	A	Pts	PIM
1916-17	Toronto Blueshirts	NHA	14	7	5	12	....	....	....	41	....	....	....	....	....
	Montreal Canadiens	NHA	6	4	0	4	....	....	....	15	2	0	1	1	3
1917-18	**Toronto Arenas**	**NHL**	**20**	**30**	***10**	**40**	**40**	**43**	**83**	**35**	**2**	**1**	**1**	**2**	**9**
♦	Toronto Arenas	St-Cup	5	2	1	3	....	....	....	0	....	....	....	....	....
1918-19	**Toronto Arenas**	**NHL**	**17**	**10**	**5**	**15**	**18**	**27**	**45**	**35**	....	....	....	....	....
1919-20	**Toronto St. Pats**	**NHL**	**24**	**24**	**9**	**33**	**28**	**31**	**59**	**52**	....	....	....	....	....
1920-21	**Toronto St. Pats**	**NHL**	**24**	**19**	**8**	**27**	**25**	**31**	**56**	**54**	**2**	**0**	**0**	**0**	**0**
1921-22	**Toronto St. Pats**	**NHL**	**24**	**17**	**11**	**28**	**24**	**35**	**59**	**19**	**2**	**0**	**0**	**0**	**12**
♦	Toronto St. Pats	St-Cup	5	0	1	1	....	....	....	9	....	....	....	....	....
1922-23	**Toronto St. Pats**	**NHL**	**24**	**12**	**11**	**23**	**20**	**43**	**63**	**47**	....	....	....	....	....
1923-24	**Toronto St. Pats**	**NHL**	**24**	**12**	**5**	**17**	**25**	**29**	**54**	**79**	....	....	....	....	....
1924-25	**Toronto St. Pats**	**NHL**	**3**	**1**	**0**	**1**	**2**	**0**	**2**	**8**	....	....	....	....	....
	Montreal Maroons	**NHL**	**27**	**8**	**11**	**19**	**14**	**47**	**61**	**56**	....	....	....	....	....
1925-26	**Montreal Maroons**	**NHL**	**33**	**9**	**9**	**18**	**15**	**59**	**74**	**96**	**4**	**1**	**1**	**2**	**6**
♦	Montreal Maroons	St-Cup	4	0	0	0	....	....	....	4	....	....	....	....	....
1926-27	**Montreal Maroons**	**NHL**	**43**	**3**	**3**	**6**	**5**	**16**	**21**	**112**	**2**	**0**	**0**	**0**	**2**
1927-28	**Detroit Cougars**	**NHL**	**44**	**6**	**8**	**14**	**12**	**45**	**57**	**63**	....	....	....	....	....
1928-29	**Detroit Cougars**	**NHL**	**43**	**6**	**4**	**10**	**17**	**27**	**44**	**52**	**2**	**0**	**0**	**0**	**2**
1929-30	**Detroit Cougars**	**NHL**	**43**	**6**	**4**	**10**	**8**	**9**	**17**	**72**	....	....	....	....	....
1930-31	**Detroit Falcons**	**NHL**	**44**	**2**	**5**	**7**	**4**	**15**	**19**	**42**	....	....	....	....	....
1931-32	**Detroit Falcons**	**NHL**	**48**	**3**	**3**	**6**	**5**	**7**	**12**	**72**	**2**	**0**	**0**	**0**	**0**
1932-33	**Detroit Red Wings**	**NHL**	**5**	**0**	**0**	**0**	**0**	**0**	**0**	**6**	....	....	....	....	....
	Montreal Maroons	**NHL**	**20**	**0**	**0**	**0**	**0**	**0**	**0**	**16**	**2**	**0**	**0**	**0**	**2**
1933-34	Cleveland Falcons	IHL	40	2	3	5	....	....	....	43	....	....	....	....	....
	NHL Totals		**510**	**168**	**106**	**274**	**262**	**464**	**726**	**916**	**18**	**2**	**2**	**4**	**33**
	Other Major League Totals		20	11	5	16	....	....	....	56	2	0	1	1	3

OHA-Jr. First All-Star Team (1915)

Signed as a free agent by **Toronto** (NHA), November 25, 1916. Assigned to **Montreal Canadiens** (NHA) by NHA in dispersal of **Toronto** (NHA) players, February 11, 1917. Signed as a free agent by **Toronto Arenas**, December 5, 1917. • Named player coach of Toronto, November 1, 1921. • Resigned as coach and captain of Toronto, November 1, 1922. Traded to **Montreal Maroons** by **Toronto** for $8,000, December 9, 1924. • 1925-26 Montreal Maroons playoff totals includes series against Ottawa and Pittsburgh. Traded to **Detroit** by **Montreal Maroons** for $7,500, October 4, 1927. Traded to **Montreal Maroons** by **Detroit** for John Gallagher, December 9, 1932.

• NOLAN, Paddy
James Patrick
LW/D – L. 5'8", 170 lbs. b: Charlottetown, PEI, 12/1/1897 d: 4/12/1957.

Season	Club	League	GP	G	A	Pts	AG	AA	APts	PIM	GP	G	A	Pts	PIM
1915-16	Glace Bay Miners	CBHL	8	16	4	20	....	....	....	....	4	9	0	9	....
1916-17	Glace Bay Miners	CBHL	1	1	1	2	....	....	....	....	1	*3	0	3	....
	New Glasgow Black Foxes	CBHL	2	2	0	2	....	....	....	12	....	....	....	....	....
1917-18	Glace Bay Miners	CBHL	8	10	2	12	....	....	....	5	6	4	2	6	2
1918-19	Glace Bay Miners	CBHL	STATISTICS NOT AVAILABLE												
1919-20	New Glasgow Black Foxes	NSPHL	6	6	0	6	....	....	....	....	....	....	....	....	....
1920-21	Stellerton Seniors	X-Games	4	7	3	10	....	....	....	....	2	0	1	1	3
1921-22	**Toronto St. Pats**	**NHL**	**2**	**0**	**0**	**0**	**0**	**0**	**0**	**0**	....	....	....	....	....
	New Glasgow Black Foxes	MIL	6	4	0	4	....	....	....	12	7	4	0	4	....
1922-23	Stellerton Professionals	MIL	12	15	0	15	....	....	....	30	3	6	0	6	5
1923-24	Stellerton Professionals	MIL	16	10	0	10	....	....	....	23	....	....	....	....	....
1924-25	New Glasgow Colts	X-Games	2	6	0	6	....	....	....	0	....	....	....	....	....
	Stellerton Professionals	X-Games	....	....	....	....	....	....	....	....	2	2	0	2	0
1925-26			REINSTATED AS AN AMATEUR												
1926-27	New Glasgow Colts	NSAPC	STATISTICS NOT AVAILABLE												
1927-28			DID NOT PLAY												
1928-29	New Glasgow Chevrolets	NSAPC	....	5	5	10	....	....	....	....	....	....	....	....	....
1929-30	New Glasgow Colts	NSEHL	15	12	0	12	....	....	....	11	3	2	0	2	....
1930-31	New Glasgow High	H.S.	DID NOT PLAY – COACHING												
	New Glasgow Tigers	NSEHL	2	2	0	2	....	....	....	0	....	....	....	....	....
	NHL Totals		**2**	**0**	**0**	**0**	**0**	**0**	**0**	**0**	....	....	....	....	....

Signed as a free agent by **Toronto St. Pats**, December 23, 1921.

• NORTHCOTT, Baldy
Lawrence McFarlane
D/LW – L. 6', 184 lbs. b: Calgary, Alta., 9/7/1908 d: 11/7/1986.

Season	Club	League	GP	G	A	Pts	AG	AA	APts	PIM	GP	G	A	Pts	PIM
1926-27	Brantford Redmen	OHA-Jr.	STATISTICS NOT AVAILABLE												
1927-28	Haileybury YMCA	NOHA	STATISTICS NOT AVAILABLE												
1928-29	North Bay Trappers	NOHA	STATISTICS NOT AVAILABLE												
	Montreal Maroons	**NHL**	**5**	**0**	**0**	**0**	**0**	**0**	**0**	**0**	....	....	....	....	....
1929-30	**Montreal Maroons**	**NHL**	**43**	**10**	**1**	**11**	**14**	**2**	**16**	**6**	**4**	**0**	**0**	**0**	**4**
1930-31	**Montreal Maroons**	**NHL**	**22**	**7**	**3**	**10**	**14**	**9**	**23**	**15**	**2**	**0**	**1**	**1**	**0**
	Windsor Bulldogs	IHL	21	12	6	18	....	....	....	18	....	....	....	....	....
1931-32	**Montreal Maroons**	**NHL**	**48**	**19**	**6**	**25**	**32**	**13**	**45**	**33**	**4**	**1**	**2**	**3**	**4**
1932-33	**Montreal Maroons**	**NHL**	**48**	**22**	**21**	**43**	**40**	**44**	**84**	**30**	**2**	**0**	**0**	**0**	**4**
1933-34	**Montreal Maroons**	**NHL**	**47**	**20**	**13**	**33**	**35**	**27**	**62**	**27**	**4**	**2**	**0**	**2**	**0**
♦1934-35	**Montreal Maroons**	**NHL**	**47**	**9**	**14**	**23**	**15**	**24**	**39**	**44**	**7**	***4**	**1**	***5**	**0**
1935-36	**Montreal Maroons**	**NHL**	**48**	**15**	**21**	**36**	**29**	**40**	**69**	**41**	**3**	**0**	**0**	**0**	**0**
1936-37	**Montreal Maroons**	**NHL**	**46**	**15**	**14**	**29**	**25**	**26**	**51**	**18**	**5**	**1**	**1**	**2**	**2**
1937-38	**Montreal Maroons**	**NHL**	**46**	**11**	**12**	**23**	**18**	**19**	**37**	**50**	....	....	....	....	....
1938-39	**Chicago Black Hawks**	**NHL**	**46**	**5**	**7**	**12**	**9**	**11**	**20**	**9**	....	....	....	....	....
1939-40	Winnipeg Rangers	MJHL	DID NOT PLAY – COACHING												
	NHL Totals		**446**	**133**	**112**	**245**	**231**	**215**	**446**	**273**	**31**	**8**	**5**	**13**	**14**

NHL First All-Star Team (1933) • Played in NHL All-Star Game (1937)

Traded to **Chicago** by **Montreal Maroons** with Earl Robinson and Russ Blinco for $30,000, September 15, 1938.

• NYKOLUK, Mike
RW – R. 5'11", 212 lbs. b: Toronto, Ont., 12/11/1934.

Season	Club	League	GP	G	A	Pts	AG	AA	APts	PIM	GP	G	A	Pts	PIM
1952-53	Weston Dukes	OHA-B	STATISTICS NOT AVAILABLE												
1953-54	Toronto Marlboros	OHA-Jr.	59	19	28	47	....	....	....	12	15	2	4	6	4
1954-55	Toronto Marlboros	OHA-Jr.	47	14	25	39	....	....	....	23	13	3	7	10	17
	Toronto Marlboros	M-Cup	10	4	9	13	....	....	....	4	....	....	....	....	....
1955-56	Winnipeg Warriors	WHL	70	10	25	35	....	....	....	18	14	10	*12	*22	7
	Winnipeg Warriors	Ed-Cup	6	3	3	6	....	....	....	0	....	....	....	....	....
1956-57	**Toronto Maple Leafs**	**NHL**	**32**	**3**	**1**	**4**	**4**	**1**	**5**	**20**	....	....	....	....	....
	Rochester Americans	AHL	28	9	13	22	....	....	....	30	9	3	2	5	4
1957-58	Rochester Americans	AHL	69	14	37	51	....	....	....	45	....	....	....	....	....
1958-59	Hershey Bears	AHL	66	15	38	53	....	....	....	60	13	*5	4	9	15
1959-60	Hershey Bears	AHL	71	13	32	45	....	....	....	55	....	....	....	....	....
1960-61	Hershey Bears	AHL	71	10	24	34	....	....	....	14	8	1	5	6	0
1961-62	Hershey Bears	AHL	59	4	20	24	....	....	....	13	7	1	2	3	12
1962-63	Hershey Bears	AHL	72	7	36	43	....	....	....	21	15	1	9	10	2
1963-64	Hershey Bears	AHL	72	9	63	72	....	....	....	39	6	1	3	4	0
1964-65	Hershey Bears	AHL	71	11	55	66	....	....	....	29	15	2	11	13	6
1965-66	Hershey Bears	AHL	67	10	53	63	....	....	....	14	3	0	1	1	0
1966-67	Hershey Bears	AHL	72	16	*68	84	....	....	....	26	5	0	4	4	4
1967-68	Hershey Bears	AHL	72	19	*66	85	....	....	....	30	5	2	6	8	0
1968-69	Hershey Bears	AHL	74	15	55	70	....	....	....	14	11	0	8	8	0
1969-70	Hershey Bears	AHL	72	16	57	73	....	....	....	12	7	0	2	2	2
1970-71	Hershey Bears	AHL	71	14	39	53	....	....	....	33	4	0	3	3	0
1971-72	Hershey Bears	AHL	62	13	30	43	....	....	....	20	4	0	2	2	4
	NHL Totals		**32**	**3**	**1**	**4**	**4**	**1**	**5**	**20**	....	....	....	....	....

AHL Second All-Star Team (1967) • Won Les Cunningham Award (MVP - AHL) (1967) • AHL First All-Star Team (1968)

Traded to **Hershey** (AHL) by **Toronto** with Ron Hurst and the loan of Wally Boyer for the 1958-59 and 1959-60 seasons for Willie Marshall, April 29, 1958

• OATMAN, Russell
Warren Russell
LW – L. 5'10", 195 lbs. b: Tillsonburg, Ont., 2/19/1905 d: 10/25/1964.

Season	Club	League	GP	G	A	Pts	AG	AA	APts	PIM	GP	G	A	Pts	PIM
1924-25	Minneapolis Rockets	CHL	27	4	0	4	....	....	....	....	....	....	....	....	....
1925-26	Victoria Cougars	WHL	30	8	4	12	....	....	....	38	4	1	0	1	22
	Victoria Cougars	St-Cup	4	0	0	0	....	....	....	10	....	....	....	....	....
1926-27	**Detroit Cougars**	**NHL**	**14**	**3**	**0**	**3**	**5**	**0**	**5**	**12**	....	....	....	....	....
	Montreal Maroons	**NHL**	**25**	**8**	**4**	**12**	**14**	**21**	**35**	**30**	**2**	**0**	**0**	**0**	**0**
	Windsor Hornets	Can-Pro	1	0	0	0	....	....	....	0	....	....	....	....	....
1927-28	**Montreal Maroons**	**NHL**	**43**	**7**	**4**	**11**	**14**	**23**	**37**	**36**	**9**	**1**	**0**	**1**	**18**
1928-29	**Montreal Maroons**	**NHL**	**11**	**1**	**0**	**1**	**3**	**0**	**3**	**12**	....	....	....	....	....
	New York Rangers	**NHL**	**27**	**1**	**1**	**2**	**3**	**7**	**10**	**10**	**4**	**0**	**0**	**0**	**0**
1929-30	Hamilton Tigers	IHL	7	2	0	2	....	....	....	8	....	....	....	....	....
	Niagara Falls Cataracts	IHL	20	6	2	8	....	....	....	2	....	....	....	....	....
	NHL Totals		**120**	**20**	**9**	**29**	**39**	**51**	**90**	**100**	**15**	**1**	**0**	**1**	**18**
	Other Major League Totals		30	8	4	12	....	....	....	38	4	1	0	1	22

Signed as a free agent by **Victoria** (WHL), October 25, 1925. • 1925-26 playoff totals includes WHL series against Edmonton and Saskatoon. Rights transferred to **Detroit** after NHL club purchased **Victoria** (WHL) franchise, May 15, 1926. • Suspended by Detroit for insubordination, January 4, 1927. Traded to **Montreal Maroons** by **Detroit** for cash, January 6, 1927. Traded to **NY Rangers** by **Montreal Maroons** for cash, December 12, 1928. Traded to **Hamilton** (IHL) by **NY Rangers** for cash, October 30, 1929. Traded to **Niagara Falls** (IHL) by **Hamilton** (IHL) for future considerations (Lloyd McIntyre), January 30, 1930. • Suffered career-ending leg injury in automobile accident, March 13, 1930.

• O'BRIEN, Ellard
Ellard John "Obie"
D – L. 6'3", 183 lbs. b: St. Catharines, Ont., 5/27/1930.

Season	Club	League	GP	G	A	Pts	AG	AA	APts	PIM	GP	G	A	Pts	PIM
1948-49	St. Catharines Teepees	OHA-Jr.	25	9	8	17	....	....	....	20	5	3	3	6	2
1949-50	St. Catharines Teepees	OHA-Jr.	48	58	43	101	....	....	....	79	5	1	2	3	13
	Boston Olympics	EAHL	3	1	2	3	....	....	....	0	5	0	1	1	0
1950-51	Tulsa Oilers	USHL	57	33	28	61	....	....	....	38	2	0	1	1	11
1951-52	Hershey Bears	AHL	54	13	28	41	....	....	....	22	5	0	1	1	2
1952-53	Hershey Bears	AHL	61	16	32	48	....	....	....	38	3	0	1	1	2
1953-54	Hershey Bears	AHL	63	20	31	51	....	....	....	23	11	5	9	14	6
1954-55	Hershey Bears	AHL	62	31	38	69	....	....	....	28	....	....	....	....	....
1955-56	**Boston Bruins**	**NHL**	**2**	**0**	**0**	**0**	**0**	**0**	**0**	**0**	....	....	....	....	....
	Hershey Bears	AHL	49	12	14	26	....	....	....	71	....	....	....	....	....
1956-57	Hershey Bears	AHL	64	20	35	55	....	....	....	78	7	1	3	4	4
1957-58	Hershey Bears	AHL	65	23	48	71	....	....	....	46	11	4	11	15	6
1958-59	Hershey Bears	AHL	63	16	26	42	....	....	....	48	13	4	3	7	18
1959-60	Quebec Aces	AHL	67	9	19	28	....	....	....	36	....	....	....	....	....
1960-61	Quebec Aces	AHL	68	8	7	15	....	....	....	25	....	....	....	....	....
1961-62	Philadelphia Ramblers	EHL	60	23	32	55	....	....	....	12	3	0	0	0	4
	NHL Totals		**2**	**0**	**0**	**0**	**0**	**0**	**0**	**0**	....	....	....	....	....

Signed as a free agent by **Boston**, October 3, 1950. Traded to **Hershey** (AHL) by **Boston** with Dunc Fisher for Ray Gariepy, June, 1953. Traded to **Quebec** (AHL) by **Hershey** (AHL) for cash, October 17, 1959.

• O'CONNOR, Buddy
Herbert William **HHOF**
C – R. 5'8", 142 lbs. b: Montreal, Que., 6/21/1916 d: 8/24/1977.

Season	Club	League	GP	G	A	Pts	AG	AA	APts	PIM	GP	G	A	Pts	PIM
1934-35	Montreal Jr. Royals	QJHL	10	*15	7	*22	....	....	....	4	2	1	1	2	0
	Montreal Royals	QSHL	....	....	....	....	....	....	....	....	4	1	0	1	2
	Montreal Royals	Al-Cup	1	1	0	1	....	....	....	0	....	....	....	....	....
1935-36	Montreal Royals	QSHL	22	14	10	24	....	....	....	6	8	6	5	*11	6
	Montreal Royals	Al-Cup	4	1	0	1	....	....	....	4	....	....	....	....	....
1936-37	Montreal Royals	QSHL	19	10	*17	27	....	....	....	27	5	0	4	*4	2
1937-38	Montreal Royals	QSHL	22	9	14	23	....	....	....	10	1	0	0	0	0
1938-39	Montreal Royals	QSHL	22	13	*23	*36	....	....	....	28	5	5	4	9	2
	Montreal Royals	Al-Cup	13	10	10	20	....	....	....	15	....	....	....	....	....
1939-40	Montreal Royals	QSHL	29	16	25	41	....	....	....	6	8	*8	6	*14	2
	Montreal Royals	Al-Cup	5	*5	5	*10	....	....	....	6	....	....	....	....	....
1940-41	Montreal Royals	QSHL	35	15	*38	53	....	....	....	12	8	2	*7	*9	4
	Montreal Royals	Al-Cup	14	6	*14	*20	....	....	....	4	....	....	....	....	....
1941-42	**Montreal Canadiens**	**NHL**	**36**	**9**	**16**	**25**	**12**	**19**	**31**	**4**	**3**	**0**	**1**	**1**	**0**
	Montreal Royals	QSHL	9	1	5	6	....	....	....	4	....	....	....	....	....
1942-43	**Montreal Canadiens**	**NHL**	**50**	**15**	**43**	**58**	**15**	**41**	**56**	**2**	**5**	**4**	**5**	**9**	**0**
♦1943-44	**Montreal Canadiens**	**NHL**	**44**	**12**	**42**	**54**	**11**	**37**	**48**	**6**	**8**	**1**	**2**	**3**	**2**
1944-45	**Montreal Canadiens**	**NHL**	**50**	**21**	**23**	**44**	**21**	**27**	**48**	**2**	**2**	**0**	**0**	**0**	**0**
♦1945-46	**Montreal Canadiens**	**NHL**	**45**	**11**	**11**	**22**	**13**	**16**	**29**	**2**	**9**	**2**	**3**	**5**	**0**
	Montreal Royals	QSHL	2	0	1	1	....	....	....	0	2	0	2	2	0
1946-47	**Montreal Canadiens**	**NHL**	**46**	**10**	**20**	**30**	**11**	**24**	**35**	**6**	**8**	**3**	**4**	**7**	**0**
1947-48	**New York Rangers**	**NHL**	**60**	**24**	**36**	**60**	**31**	**48**	**79**	**8**	**6**	**1**	**4**	**5**	**0**
1948-49	**New York Rangers**	**NHL**	**46**	**11**	**24**	**35**	**15**	**34**	**49**	**0**	....	....	....	....	....
1949-50	**New York Rangers**	**NHL**	**66**	**11**	**22**	**33**	**14**	**27**	**41**	**4**	**12**	**4**	**2**	**6**	**4**

Season	Club	League	GP	G	A	Pts	AG	AA	APts	PIM	GP	G	A	Pts	PIM
			REGULAR SEASON								PLAYOFFS				
1950-51	**New York Rangers**	**NHL**	**66**	**16**	**20**	**36**	**20**	**24**	**44**	**0**	....	....	....	....	....
1951-52	Cincinnati Mohawks	AHL	65	11	43	54	....	....	....	4	4	2	3	5	2
1952-53	Cincinnati Mohawks	IHL	1	0	0	0	....	....	....	0	....	....	....	....	....
	NHL Totals		**509**	**140**	**257**	**397**	**163**	**297**	**460**	**34**	**53**	**15**	**21**	**36**	**6**

NHL Second All-Star Team (1948) • Won Lady Byng Trophy (1948) • Won Hart Trophy (1948) • AHL Second All-Star Team (1952) • Played in NHL All-Star Game (1949)

Rights traded to **Montreal Maroons** by **Montreal Canadiens** for Sammy McManus, September 10, 1936. Traded to **Montreal Canadiens** by **Montreal Maroons** for cash, September 24, 1938. Traded to **NY Rangers** by **Montreal** with Frank Eddolls for Hal Laycoe, Joe Bell and George Robertson, August 19, 1947. • Named Player/Coach of **Cincinnati** (AHL), September 24, 1952.

• ODROWSKI, Gerry — *see page 1486*

• O'FLAHERTY, Peanuts John Benedict

RW – R. 5'7", 154 lbs. b: Toronto, Ont., 4/10/1918.

Season	Club	League	GP	G	A	Pts	AG	AA	APts	PIM	GP	G	A	Pts	PIM
1933-34	St. Michael's Buzzers	OHA-B	....	....	....	....	....	....	....	....	....	....	....	....	....
	St. Michael's Buzzers	M-Cup	13	11	8	19	....	....	....	12	....	....	....	....	....
1934-35	St. Michael's Majors	OHA-Jr.	12	10	6	16	....	....	....	10	3	1	0	1	0
1935-36	West Toronto Nationals	TJrHL	10	6	*14	*20	....	....	....	4	5	4	*4	8	9
	West Toronto Nationals	M-Cup	12	10	*9	19	....	....	....	10	....	....	....	....	....
1936-37	Toronto Dominions	OHA-Sr.	9	*7	*5	*12	....	....	....	4	8	2	*4	6	4
	Toronto Dominions	Al-Cup	3	2	0	2	....	....	....	2	....	....	....	....	....
1937-38	Toronto Marlboros	OHA-Jr.	12	20	10	30	....	....	....	16	6	5	4	9	6
	Toronto Goodyears	OHA-Sr.	....	....	....	....	....	....	....	....	2	2	1	3	0
	Toronto Goodyears	Al-Cup	4	0	0	0	....	....	....	0	....	....	....	....	....
1938-39	Toronto Goodyears	OHA-Sr.	20	*23	12	35	....	....	....	12	5	6	4	*10	0
	Toronto Goodyears	Al-Cup	10	7	5	12	....	....	....	6	....	....	....	....	....
1939-40	Toronto Goodyears	OHA-Sr.	29	*41	35	*76	....	....	....	18	7	*8	5	*13	6
	Toronto Goodyears	Al-Cup	4	*3	3	*6	....	....	....	2	....	....	....	....	....
1940-41	**New York Americans**	**NHL**	**10**	**4**	**0**	**4**	**6**	**0**	**6**	**0**	....	....	....	....	....
	Springfield Indians	AHL	11	2	8	10	....	....	....	0	....	....	....	....	....
	Pittsburgh Hornets	AHL	24	10	12	22	....	....	....	4	6	1	2	3	2
1941-42	**Brooklyn Americans**	**NHL**	**11**	**1**	**1**	**2**	**1**	**1**	**2**	**0**	....	....	....	....	....
	Springfield Indians	AHL	42	18	*44	62	....	....	....	14	5	5	1	6	0
1942-43	Pittsburgh Hornets	AHL	36	10	27	37	....	....	....	6	2	1	0	1	0
1943-44	Pittsburgh Hornets	AHL	2	1	2	3	....	....	....	0	....	....	....	....	....
	Toronto RCAF	OHA-Sr.	8	7	7	14	....	....	....	2	....	....	....	....	....
	Toronto Peoples Credit	TIHL	20	9	15	24	....	....	....	10	6	7	7	14	4
1944-45			MILITARY SERVICE												
1945-46	Pittsburgh Hornets	AHL	61	24	45	69	....	....	....	24	6	4	3	7	2
1946-47	Pittsburgh Hornets	AHL	64	33	35	68	....	....	....	24	12	0	5	5	4
1947-48	Pittsburgh Hornets	AHL	50	16	20	36	....	....	....	12	....	....	....	....	....
1948-49	Pittsburgh Hornets	AHL	67	24	25	49	....	....	....	22	....	....	....	....	....
1949-50	Pittsburgh Hornets	AHL	69	10	15	25	....	....	....	2	....	....	....	....	....
1950-51	St. Michael's Monarchs	OHA-Sr.	28	7	12	19	....	....	....	40	9	1	2	3	8
	St. Michael's Monarchs	Alx-Cup	7	0	4	4	....	....	....	2	....	....	....	....	....
1951-52	Saint John Beavers	MMHL	45	5	9	14	....	....	....	50	7	1	3	4	2
	Saint John Beavers	Alx-Cup	3	0	0	0	....	....	....	0	....	....	....	....	....
1952-53	Ottawa Senators	QSHL	DID NOT PLAY – COACHING												
1953-54	S.S. Marie Greyhounds	NOHA	4	0	0	0	....	....	....	2	....	....	....	....	....
1954-55	S.S. Marie Greyhounds	NOHA	3	0	0	0	....	....	....	0	....	....	....	....	....
1955-56	Sudbury Wolves	NOHA	8	0	1	1	....	....	....	4	....	....	....	....	....
1956-57			DID NOT PLAY – COACHING												
1957-58	Sudbury Wolves	NOHA	PLAYER/COACH – STATISTICS UNAVAILABLE												
1958-59	Sudbury Wolves	NOHA	1	0	0	0	....	....	....	0	....	....	....	....	....
	NHL Totals		**21**	**5**	**1**	**6**	**7**	**1**	**8**	**0**	....	....	....	....	....

• Father of Gerry

Signed as a free agent by **NY Americans**, October 17, 1940. Loaned to **Toronto** (Pittsburgh-AHL) by **NY Americans** (Springfield-AHL) with the trade of Jack Howard for Clarence Drouillard, January 17, 1941. Returned to **NY Americans** by **Toronto** (Pittsburgh-AHL) with the trade of Phil McAtee for Viv Allen and Glenn Brydson, October 8, 1941. Signed as a free agent by **Pittsburgh** (AHL), September 24, 1942.

• O'GRADY, George

D – L. 5'8", 175 lbs. b: Montreal, Que., Deceased.

Season	Club	League	GP	G	A	Pts	AG	AA	APts	PIM	GP	G	A	Pts	PIM
1911-12	Montreal Garnets	MCHL	6	5	0	5	....	....	....	2	2	0	0	0	0
1912-13	Montreal Garnets	MCHL	11	4	0	4	....	....	....	*33	....	....	....	....	....
1913-14	Montreal Wanderers	NHA	12	1	2	3	....	....	....	8	....	....	....	....	....
1914-15	Montreal Wanderers	NHA	2	1	0	1	....	....	....	0	1	0	0	0	0
1915-16	Montreal Wanderers	NHA	2	0	1	1	....	....	....	4	....	....	....	....	....
1916-17	Montreal Stars	MCHL	STATISTICS NOT AVAILABLE												
1917-18	**Montreal Wanderers**	**NHL**	**4**	**0**	**0**	**0**	**0**	**0**	**0**	**0**	....	....	....	....	....
	NHL Totals		**4**	**0**	**0**	**0**	**0**	**0**	**0**	**0**	....	....	....	....	....
	Other Major League Totals		16	2	3	5	....	....	....	12	1	0	0	0	0

Rights retained by **Montreal Wanderers** after NHA folded, November 26, 1917.

• OLIVER, Harry Harold "Pee Wee" HHOF

RW – R. 5'8", 155 lbs. b: Selkirk, Man., 10/26/1898 d: 6/16/1985.

Season	Club	League	GP	G	A	Pts	AG	AA	APts	PIM	GP	G	A	Pts	PIM
1917-18	Selkirk Fishermen	MHL-Jr.	STATISTICS NOT AVAILABLE												
	Selkirk Fishermen	M-Cup	2	*7	*4	*11	....	....	....	0	....	....	....	....	....
1918-19	Selkirk Fishermen	MHL-Sr.	9	15	9	24	....	....	....	6	4	5	1	6	0
	Selkirk Fishermen	Al-Cup	2	7	4	11	....	....	....	0	....	....	....	....	....
1919-20	Selkirk Fishermen	MHL-Sr.	10	7	7	14	....	....	....	4	....	....	....	....	....
1920-21	Calgary Canadians	Big-4	16	14	6	20	....	....	....	11	....	....	....	....	....
1921-22	Calgary Tigers	WCHL	20	10	4	14	....	....	....	7	2	1	0	1	0
1922-23	Calgary Tigers	WCHL	29	25	7	32	....	....	....	10	....	....	....	....	....
1923-24	Calgary Tigers	WCHL	27	22	12	34	....	....	....	14	2	0	1	1	2
	Calgary Tigers	St-Cup	2	2	1	3	....	....	....	4	....	....	....	....	....
1924-25	Calgary Tigers	WCHL	24	20	*13	*33	....	....	....	23	2	0	0	0	2
1925-26	Calgary Tigers	WHL	30	13	12	25	....	....	....	14	....	....	....	....	....
1926-27	**Boston Bruins**	**NHL**	**42**	**18**	**6**	**24**	**32**	**31**	**63**	**17**	**8**	**4**	**2**	***6**	**4**
1927-28	**Boston Bruins**	**NHL**	**43**	**13**	**5**	**18**	**26**	**28**	**54**	**20**	**2**	**2**	**0**	**2**	**4**
♦1928-29	**Boston Bruins**	**NHL**	**43**	**17**	**6**	**23**	**50**	**40**	**90**	**24**	**5**	**1**	**1**	**2**	**8**
1929-30	**Boston Bruins**	**NHL**	**40**	**16**	**5**	**21**	**23**	**12**	**35**	**12**	**6**	**2**	**1**	**3**	**6**
1930-31	**Boston Bruins**	**NHL**	**44**	**16**	**14**	**30**	**32**	**43**	**75**	**18**	**4**	**0**	**0**	**0**	**2**
1931-32	**Boston Bruins**	**NHL**	**44**	**13**	**7**	**20**	**22**	**15**	**37**	**22**	....	....	....	....	....
1932-33	**Boston Bruins**	**NHL**	**47**	**11**	**7**	**18**	**20**	**14**	**34**	**10**	**5**	**0**	**0**	**0**	**0**
1933-34	**Boston Bruins**	**NHL**	**48**	**5**	**9**	**14**	**9**	**19**	**28**	**6**	....	....	....	....	....
1934-35	**New York Americans**	**NHL**	**47**	**7**	**9**	**16**	**11**	**16**	**27**	**4**	....	....	....	....	....
1935-36	**New York Americans**	**NHL**	**45**	**9**	**16**	**25**	**17**	**30**	**47**	**12**	**5**	**1**	**2**	**3**	**0**
1936-37	**New York Americans**	**NHL**	**20**	**2**	**1**	**3**	**3**	**2**	**5**	**2**	....	....	....	....	....
	NHL Totals		**463**	**127**	**85**	**212**	**245**	**250**	**495**	**147**	**35**	**10**	**6**	**16**	**24**
	Other Major League Totals		130	90	48	138	....	....	....	68	6	1	1	2	4

WCHL First All-Star Team (1924, 1925)

Signed as a free agent by **Calgary** (WCHL), December 22, 1921. Traded to **Boston** by **Calgary** (WHL) for cash, September 4, 1926. Traded to **NY Americans** by **Boston** for cash, November 2, 1934.

• OLIVER, Murray — *see page 1490*

• OLMSTEAD, Bert Murray Albert HHOF

LW – L. 6'1", 180 lbs. b: Sceptre, Sask., 9/4/1926.

Season	Club	League	GP	G	A	Pts	AG	AA	APts	PIM	GP	G	A	Pts	PIM
1944-45	Moose Jaw Canucks	S-SJHL	16	0	3	3	....	....	....	8	4	2	0	2	8
	Moose Jaw Canucks	M-Cup	17	10	8	18	....	....	....	18	....	....	....	....	....
1945-46	Moose Jaw Canucks	S-SJHL	18	24	19	43	....	....	....	32	4	0	1	1	6
	Moose Jaw Canucks	M-Cup	8	2	8	10	....	....	....	6	....	....	....	....	....
1946-47	Kansas City Pla-Mors	USHL	60	27	15	42	....	....	....	34	12	2	3	5	4
1947-48	Kansas City Pla-Mors	USHL	66	26	26	52	....	....	....	42	7	1	4	5	0
1948-49	**Chicago Black Hawks**	**NHL**	**9**	**0**	**2**	**2**	**0**	**3**	**3**	**4**	....	....	....	....	....
	Kansas City Pla-Mors	USHL	52	33	44	77	....	....	....	54	2	0	1	1	0
1949-50	**Chicago Black Hawks**	**NHL**	**70**	**20**	**29**	**49**	**25**	**35**	**60**	**40**	....	....	....	....	....
1950-51	**Chicago Black Hawks**	**NHL**	**15**	**2**	**1**	**3**	**3**	**1**	**4**	**0**	....	....	....	....	....
	Milwaukee Seagulls	USHL	12	8	7	15	....	....	....	11	....	....	....	....	....
	Montreal Canadiens	**NHL**	**39**	**16**	**22**	**38**	**20**	**27**	**47**	**50**	**11**	**2**	**4**	**6**	**9**
1951-52	**Montreal Canadiens**	**NHL**	**69**	**7**	**28**	**35**	**9**	**35**	**44**	**49**	**11**	**0**	**1**	**1**	**4**
♦1952-53	**Montreal Canadiens**	**NHL**	**69**	**17**	**28**	**45**	**22**	**34**	**56**	**83**	**12**	**2**	**2**	**4**	**4**
1953-54	**Montreal Canadiens**	**NHL**	**70**	**15**	**37**	**52**	**20**	**45**	**65**	**85**	**11**	**0**	**1**	**1**	**19**
1954-55	**Montreal Canadiens**	**NHL**	**70**	**10**	***48**	**58**	**13**	**56**	**69**	**103**	**12**	**0**	**4**	**4**	**21**
♦1955-56	**Montreal Canadiens**	**NHL**	**70**	**14**	***56**	**70**	**19**	**68**	**87**	**94**	**10**	**4**	***10**	**14**	**8**
♦1956-57	**Montreal Canadiens**	**NHL**	**64**	**15**	**33**	**48**	**19**	**37**	**56**	**74**	**10**	**0**	***9**	**9**	**13**
♦1957-58	**Montreal Canadiens**	**NHL**	**57**	**9**	**28**	**37**	**11**	**29**	**40**	**71**	**9**	**0**	**3**	**3**	**0**
1958-59	**Toronto Maple Leafs**	**NHL**	**70**	**10**	**31**	**41**	**12**	**31**	**43**	**74**	**12**	**4**	**2**	**6**	**13**
1959-60	**Toronto Maple Leafs**	**NHL**	**53**	**15**	**21**	**36**	**18**	**20**	**38**	**63**	**10**	**3**	**4**	**7**	**0**
1960-61	**Toronto Maple Leafs**	**NHL**	**67**	**18**	**34**	**52**	**21**	**33**	**54**	**84**	**3**	**1**	**2**	**3**	**10**
♦1961-62	**Toronto Maple Leafs**	**NHL**	**56**	**13**	**23**	**36**	**15**	**22**	**37**	**10**	**4**	**0**	**1**	**1**	**0**
	NHL Totals		**848**	**181**	**421**	**602**	**227**	**476**	**703**	**884**	**115**	**16**	**43**	**59**	**101**

NHL Second All-Star Team (1953, 1956) • Played in NHL All-Star Game (1953, 1956, 1957, 1959)

Traded to **Detroit** by **Chicago** with Vic Stasiuk for Lee Fogolin Sr. and Stephen Black, December 2, 1950. Traded to **Montreal** by **Detroit** for Leo Gravelle, December 19, 1950. Claimed by **Toronto** from **Montreal** in Intra-League Draft, June 3, 1958. Claimed by **NY Rangers** from **Toronto** in Intra-League Draft, June 4, 1962.

• OLSON, Dennis

C – R. 6', 182 lbs. b: Kenora, Ont., 11/9/1934.

Season	Club	League	GP	G	A	Pts	AG	AA	APts	PIM	GP	G	A	Pts	PIM
1951-52	Port Arthur Flyers	TBJHL	30	16	15	31	....	....	....	18	3	0	1	1	0
1952-53	Port Arthur Flyers	TBJHL	30	24	23	47	....	....	....	39	8	3	4	7	2
1953-54	Port Arthur North Stars	TBJHL	36	31	22	53	....	....	....	43	5	4	2	6	12
	Fort William Canadiens	M-Cup	13	2	6	8	....	....	....	11	....	....	....	....	....
1954-55	Troy Bruins	IHL	57	9	24	33	....	....	....	36	11	1	6	7	7
1955-56	Troy Bruins	IHL	60	31	39	70	....	....	....	76	5	0	2	2	9
1956-57	New Westminster Royals	WHL	70	25	14	39	....	....	....	23	13	5	2	7	6
1957-58	**Detroit Red Wings**	**NHL**	**4**	**0**	**0**	**0**	**0**	**0**	**0**	**0**	....	....	....	....	....
	Seattle–Victoria	WHL	61	30	27	57	....	....	....	16	....	....	....	....	....
	Edmonton Flyers	WHL	1	0	0	0	....	....	....	0	....	....	....	....	....
1958-59	Springfield Indians	AHL	68	21	23	44	....	....	....	20	....	....	....	....	....
1959-60	Trois-Rivieres Lions	EPHL	6	1	1	2	....	....	....	2	....	....	....	....	....
	Springfield Indians	AHL	61	14	29	43	....	....	....	13	10	1	5	6	4
1960-61	Kitchener Beavers	EPHL	54	31	31	62	....	....	....	57	....	....	....	....	....
	Springfield Indians	AHL	17	1	7	8	....	....	....	2	8	4	6	*10	0
1961-62	Springfield Indians	AHL	70	24	22	46	....	....	....	30	11	4	3	7	4
1962-63	Springfield Indians	AHL	72	25	33	58	....	....	....	20	....	....	....	....	....
1963-64	Springfield Indians	AHL	72	20	33	53	....	....	....	16	....	....	....	....	....
1964-65	Springfield Indians	AHL	72	21	34	55	....	....	....	30	....	....	....	....	....
	NHL Totals		**4**	**0**	**0**	**0**	**0**	**0**	**0**	**0**	....	....	....	....	....

Won WHL Coast Division Rookie of the Year Award (1957)

Traded to **Springfield** (AHL) by **Detroit** with Bill McCreary and Hank Bassen for Gerry Ehman, May 1, 1958. Claimed by **NY Rangers** from **Springfield** (AHL) in Inter-League Draft, June, 1961.

• O'NEIL, Jim James Beaton "Peggy"

C/RW – R. 5'8", 160 lbs. b: Semans, Sask., 4/3/1913 d: 2/13/1973.

Season	Club	League	GP	G	A	Pts	AG	AA	APts	PIM	GP	G	A	Pts	PIM
1930-31	Saskatoon Wesleys	N-SJHL	4	*6	2	*8	....	....	....	2	2	0	0	0	2
1931-32	Saskatoon Wesleys	N-SJHL	4	3	0	3	....	....	....	5	8	3	0	3	10
	Saskatoon Crescents	N-SSHL	18	6	3	9	....	....	....	22	4	0	1	1	12
	Saskatoon Wesleys	M-Cup	2	0	0	0	....	....	....	2	....	....	....	....	....
1932-33	Boston Cubs	Can-Am	46	13	17	30	....	....	....	63	7	1	3	4	8
1933-34	**Boston Bruins**	**NHL**	**23**	**2**	**2**	**4**	**3**	**4**	**7**	**15**	....	....	....	....	....
	Boston Cubs	Can-Am	12	6	5	11	....	....	....	19	....	....	....	....	....
1934-35	**Boston Bruins**	**NHL**	**48**	**2**	**11**	**13**	**3**	**19**	**22**	**35**	**4**	**0**	**0**	**0**	**9**
1935-36	**Boston Bruins**	**NHL**	**48**	**2**	**11**	**13**	**4**	**21**	**25**	**49**	**2**	**1**	**1**	**2**	**4**
1936-37	**Boston Bruins**	**NHL**	**21**	**0**	**2**	**2**	**0**	**4**	**4**	**6**	....	....	....	....	....
	Providence Reds	IAHL	15	2	8	10	....	....	....	14	3	0	1	1	2
1937-38	Cleveland Barons	IAHL	38	5	24	29	....	....	....	66	2	0	0	0	0
1938-39	Cleveland Barons	IAHL	41	4	18	22	....	....	....	29	9	2	6	8	0
1939-40	Cleveland Barons	IAHL	56	7	20	27	....	....	....	35	....	....	....	....	....
1940-41	**Montreal Canadiens**	**NHL**	**12**	**0**	**3**	**3**	**0**	**4**	**4**	**0**	**3**	**0**	**0**	**0**	**0**
	New Haven Eagles	AHL	40	7	17	24	....	....	....	40	....	....	....	....	....
1941-42	**Montreal Canadiens**	**NHL**	**4**	**0**	**1**	**1**	**0**	**1**	**1**	**4**	....	....	....	....	....
	Washington Lions	AHL	41	7	33	40	....	....	....	22	2	0	0	0	6
1942-43	Washington Lions	AHL	10	2	7	9	....	....	....	4	....	....	....	....	....
	Hershey Bears	AHL	45	17	43	60	....	....	....	48	6	3	1	4	2

Season	Club	League	GP	G	A	Pts	AG	AA	APts	PIM	GP	G	A	Pts	PIM
			REGULAR SEASON								PLAYOFFS				
1943-44	Hershey Bears	AHL	54	20	33	53	....	....	....	18	7	0	6	6	2
1944-45	Hershey Bears	AHL	55	14	32	46	....	....	....	16	11	2	7	9	4
1945-46	Hershey Bears	AHL	52	5	26	31	....	....	....	33	3	0	0	0	2
	NHL Totals		**156**	**6**	**30**	**36**	**10**	**53**	**63**	**109**	**9**	**1**	**1**	**2**	**13**

Traded to **Montreal** by **Cleveland** (IAHL) for Bill Summerhill and Bill MacKenzie, May 17, 1940. Traded to **Hershey** (AHL) by **Washington** (AHL) for Bob Gracie, November 21, 1942.

• O'NEILL, Tom "Windy"

RW – R. 5'10", 155 lbs. b: Deseronto, Ont., 9/28/1923 Deceased.

Season	Club	League	GP	G	A	Pts	AG	AA	APts	PIM	GP	G	A	Pts	PIM
1940-41	St. Michael's Buzzers	OHA-B	6	1	3	4	....	....	....	0	2	0	*3	3	0
1941-42	St. Michael's Majors	OHA-Jr.	18	6	6	12	....	....	....	28	2	0	0	0	0
1942-43	St. Michael's Majors	OHA-Jr.	16	5	9	14	....	....	....	34	5	3	3	6	4
	Toronto Tip Tops	TIHL	6	1	6	7	....	....	....	2	....	....	....	....	....
1943-44	**Toronto Maple Leafs**	**NHL**	**33**	**8**	**7**	**15**	**7**	**6**	**13**	**29**	**4**	**0**	**0**	**0**	**6**
♦1944-45	**Toronto Maple Leafs**	**NHL**	**33**	**2**	**5**	**7**	**2**	**6**	**8**	**24**	....	....	....	....	....
1945-46	Quebec Aces	QSHL	39	6	14	20	....	....	....	33	5	0	1	1	0
1946-47	Halifax Crescents	MSHL	32	25	21	46	....	....	....	49	4	0	0	0	0
1947-48	Halifax Crescents	MSHL	26	14	16	30	....	....	....	36	4	0	4	4	0
1948-49	Halifax St. Mary's	MSHL	22	4	2	6	....	....	....	18	5	0	0	0	6
	Halifax St. Mary's	Al-Cup	2	0	0	0	....	....	....	4	....	....	....	....	....
	NHL Totals		**66**	**10**	**12**	**22**	**9**	**12**	**21**	**53**	**4**	**0**	**0**	**0**	**6**

• O'REE, Willie William Eldon

W – L. 5'10", 175 lbs. b: Fredericton, N.B., 10/15/1935.

Season	Club	League	GP	G	A	Pts	AG	AA	APts	PIM	GP	G	A	Pts	PIM
1950-51	Fredericton Falcons	NBAHA	....	....	....	....	....	....	....	....	2	0	0	0	4
1951-52	Fredericton Merchants	YCHL	6	10	4	14	....	....	....	2	8	10	5	15	18
	Fredericton Jr. Capitals	NBJHL	3	2	0	2	....	....	....	0	....	....	....	....	....
1952-53	Fredericton Jr. Capitals	NBJHL	12	15	3	18	....	....	....	6	4	5	0	5	2
	Fredericton Capitals	NBSHL	2	2	0	2	....	....	....	0	....	....	....	....	....
1953-54	Fredericton Capitals	NBSHL	23	7	11	18	....	....	....	15	18	*8	5	13	6
	Fredericton Capitals	Al-Cup	7	*7	5	12	....	....	....	4	....	....	....	....	....
1954-55	Quebec Frontenacs	QJHL	43	27	17	44	....	....	....	41	9	4	3	7	8
	Quebec Frontenacs	M-Cup	8	3	3	6	....	....	....	2	....	....	....	....	....
1955-56	Kitchener Canucks	OHA-Jr.	41	30	28	58	....	....	....	38	8	4	3	7	6
1956-57	Quebec Aces	QHL	68	22	12	34	....	....	....	80	10	3	3	6	10
	Quebec Aces	Ed-Cup	6	1	1	2	....	....	....	2	....	....	....	....	....
1957-58	**Boston Bruins**	**NHL**	**2**	**0**	**0**	**0**	**0**	**0**	**0**	**0**	....	....	....	....	....
	Springfield Indians	AHL	6	0	0	0	....	....	....	0	....	....	....	....	....
	Quebec Aces	QHL	57	13	19	32	....	....	....	43	9	4	2	6	8
1958-59	Quebec Aces	QHL	56	9	21	30	....	....	....	74	....	....	....	....	....
1959-60	Kingston Frontenacs	EPHL	50	21	25	46	....	....	....	41	....	....	....	....	....
1960-61	**Boston Bruins**	**NHL**	**43**	**4**	**10**	**14**	**5**	**10**	**15**	**26**	....	....	....	....	....
	Hull-Ottawa Canadiens	EPHL	16	10	9	19	....	....	....	21	....	....	....	....	....
1961-62	Hull-Ottawa Canadiens	EPHL	12	1	2	3	....	....	....	18	....	....	....	....	....
	Los Angeles Blades	WHL	54	28	26	54	....	....	....	57	....	....	....	....	....
1962-63	Los Angeles Blades	WHL	64	25	26	51	....	....	....	41	3	2	3	5	2
1963-64	Los Angeles Blades	WHL	60	17	18	35	....	....	....	45	12	4	8	12	10
1964-65	Los Angeles Blades	WHL	70	*38	21	59	....	....	....	75	....	....	....	....	....
1965-66	Los Angeles Blades	WHL	62	33	33	66	....	....	....	30	....	....	....	....	....
1966-67	Los Angeles Blades	WHL	68	34	26	60	....	....	....	58	....	....	....	....	....
1967-68	San Diego Gulls	WHL	66	21	33	54	....	....	....	54	7	2	2	4	6
1968-69	San Diego Gulls	WHL	70	38	41	79	....	....	....	63	7	3	3	6	12
1969-70	San Diego Gulls	WHL	66	24	22	46	....	....	....	50	6	6	3	9	4
1970-71	San Diego Gulls	WHL	66	18	15	33	....	....	....	47	6	4	1	5	14
1971-72	San Diego Gulls	WHL	48	16	17	33	....	....	....	42	4	0	1	1	2
1972-73	New Haven Nighthawks	AHL	50	21	24	45	....	....	....	41	....	....	....	....	....
	San Diego Gulls	WHL	18	6	5	11	....	....	....	18	6	1	4	5	2
1973-74	San Diego Gulls	WHL	73	30	28	58	....	....	....	89	4	3	3	6	0
1974-75	San Diego Charms	SCSHL	STATISTICS NOT AVAILABLE												
1975-76	San Diego Charms	SCSHL	STATISTICS NOT AVAILABLE												
1976-77			OUT OF HOCKEY – RETIRED												
1977-78			OUT OF HOCKEY – RETIRED												
1978-79	San Diego Hawks	PCL	53	21	25	46	....	....	....	37	....	....	....	....	....
	NHL Totals		**45**	**4**	**10**	**14**	**5**	**10**	**15**	**26**	....	....	....	....	....

WHL Second All-Star Team (1969)

Traded to **Montreal** by **Boston** with Stan Maxwell for Cliff Pennington and Terry Gray, June, 1961. Traded to **LA Blades** (WHL) by **Montreal** for cash, November 10, 1961. Traded to **San Diego** (WHL) by **LA Blades** (WHL) for cash, July, 1967. Selected by **LA Sharks** (WHA) in WHA General Player Draft, February 12, 1972.

• ORLANDO, Jimmy

D – L. 5'11", 185 lbs. b: Montreal, Que., 2/27/1916.

Season	Club	League	GP	G	A	Pts	AG	AA	APts	PIM	GP	G	A	Pts	PIM
1932-33	Montreal Victorias	MMJHL	11	2	0	2	....	....	....	33	....	....	....	....	....
1933-34	Montreal Victorias	MMJHL	8	0	4	4	....	....	....	44	2	0	0	0	8
	Montreal Victorias	MCHL	1	0	0	0	....	....	....	0	....	....	....	....	....
1934-35	Montreal Victorias	MMJHL	2	3	2	5	....	....	....	8	....	....	....	....	....
	Montreal Victorias	MCHL	7	0	0	0	....	....	....	18	....	....	....	....	....
1935-36	Rochester Cardinals	IHL	12	0	0	0	....	....	....	18	....	....	....	....	....
	Montreal Sr. Canadiens	MCHL	19	1	6	7	....	....	....	49	....	....	....	....	....
1936-37	**Detroit Red Wings**	**NHL**	**9**	**0**	**1**	**1**	**0**	**2**	**2**	**8**	....	....	....	....	....
	Pittsburgh Hornets	IAHL	38	0	5	5	....	....	....	61	5	0	0	0	5
1937-38	**Detroit Red Wings**	**NHL**	**6**	**0**	**0**	**0**	**0**	**0**	**0**	**4**	....	....	....	....	....
	Pittsburgh Hornets	IAHL	45	0	7	7	....	....	....	*82	2	0	0	0	0
1938-39	Springfield Indians	IAHL	54	7	9	16	....	....	....	106	3	0	0	0	8
1939-40	**Detroit Red Wings**	**NHL**	**48**	**1**	**3**	**4**	**2**	**5**	**7**	**54**	**5**	**0**	**0**	**0**	**15**
1940-41	**Detroit Red Wings**	**NHL**	**48**	**1**	**10**	**11**	**2**	**14**	**16**	**99**	**9**	**0**	**2**	**2**	**31**
1941-42	**Detroit Red Wings**	**NHL**	**48**	**1**	**7**	**8**	**1**	**8**	**9**	**111**	**12**	**0**	**4**	**4**	**45**
♦1942-43	**Detroit Red Wings**	**NHL**	**40**	**3**	**4**	**7**	**3**	**4**	**7**	**99**	**10**	**0**	**3**	**3**	**14**
1943-44			MILITARY SERVICE												
1944-45			MILITARY SERVICE												
1945-46	Valleyfield Braves	QSHL	40	3	19	22	....	....	....	52	....	....	....	....	....
	Ottawa Senators	QSHL	....	....	....	....	....	....	....	....	9	1	3	4	22
1946-47	Valleyfield Braves	QSHL	35	5	8	13	....	....	....	69	....	....	....	....	....
1947-48	Montreal Royals	QSHL	39	3	14	17	....	....	....	*124	3	0	0	0	4
1948-49	Montreal Royals	QSHL	45	3	20	23	....	....	....	*164	8	2	1	3	18
1949-50	Montreal Royals	QSHL	1	0	0	0	....	....	....	0	....	....	....	....	....
	Valleyfield Braves	QSHL	30	2	11	13	....	....	....	52	5	0	1	1	24
1950-51	Valleyfield Braves	QMHL	53	1	11	12	....	....	....	107	16	0	6	6	24
	Valleyfield Braves	Alx-Cup	12	0	1	1	....	....	....	28	....	....	....	....	....
	NHL Totals		**199**	**6**	**25**	**31**	**8**	**33**	**41**	**375**	**36**	**0**	**9**	**9**	**105**

AHL Second All-Star Team (1939) • QSHL First All-Star Team (1948, 1949)

Traded to **Springfield** (IAHL) by **Detroit** for cash, September 27, 1938. Traded to **Detroit** by **Springfield** (IAHL) for cash, October, 1939. Signed as a free agent by **Valleyfield** (QMHL), October 9, 1950.

• ORR, Bobby — *see page 1493*

• OUELLETTE, Eddie Adelard Edward

C – L. 5'9", 181 lbs. b: Ottawa, Ont., 3/9/1911.

Season	Club	League	GP	G	A	Pts	AG	AA	APts	PIM	GP	G	A	Pts	PIM
1928-29	Windsor-Walkerton Tech	MOHL	STATISTICS NOT AVAILABLE												
1929-30	Toronto Millionaires	IHL	18	3	5	8	....	....	....	15	....	....	....	....	....
1930-31	Pittsburgh Yellowjackets	IHL	44	2	5	7	....	....	....	26	6	0	0	0	2
1931-32	Pittsburgh Hornets	IHL	2	0	0	0	....	....	....	0	....	....	....	....	....
	Windsor Bulldogs	IHL	37	9	4	13	....	....	....	26	6	0	0	0	2
1932-33	Windsor Bulldogs	IHL	43	7	10	17	....	....	....	63	6	2	0	2	4
1933-34	Cleveland–London	IHL	42	9	19	28	....	....	....	15	6	2	0	2	6
1934-35	London Tecumsehs	IHL	44	15	*25	40	....	....	....	50	5	1	2	3	4
1935-36	**Chicago Black Hawks**	**NHL**	**43**	**3**	**2**	**5**	**6**	**4**	**10**	**11**	**1**	**0**	**0**	**0**	**0**
1936-37	Portland Buckaroos	PCHL	39	18	8	26	....	....	....	50	3	0	1	1	8
1937-38	Portland Buckaroos	PCHL	42	12	20	32	....	....	....	63	2	2	0	2	4
1938-39	Portland Buckaroos	PCHL	48	32	30	62	....	....	....	64	5	3	4	7	10
1939-40	Portland Buckaroos	PCHL	37	13	10	23	....	....	....	53	4	2	2	4	0
1940-41	Portland Buckaroos	PCHL	47	21	22	43	....	....	....	59	....	....	....	....	....
1941-42	Lachine Flyers	QPHL	18	4	5	9	....	....	....	12	2	0	0	0	2
	NHL Totals		**43**	**3**	**2**	**5**	**6**	**4**	**10**	**11**	**1**	**0**	**0**	**0**	**0**

Signed as a free agent by **Toronto Millionaires** (IHL), January 20, 1930. Signed as a free agent by **Pittsburgh** (IHL) after **Toronto** (IHL) franchise folded, October 30, 1930. Traded to **Montreal Canadiens** by **London** (IHL) for cash, April 1, 1935. Signed as a free agent by **Chicago**, October 27, 1935.

• OUELLETTE, Gerry Gerald Adrian "Red"

RW – R. 5'9", 170 lbs. b: Grand Falls, N.B., 11/1/1938.

Season	Club	League	GP	G	A	Pts	AG	AA	APts	PIM	GP	G	A	Pts	PIM
1958-59	Waterloo Siskins	OHA-B	STATISTICS NOT AVAILABLE												
1959-60	Kingston Frontenacs	EPHL	64	35	42	77	....	....	....	23	....	....	....	....	....
1960-61	**Boston Bruins**	**NHL**	**34**	**5**	**4**	**9**	**6**	**4**	**10**	**0**	....	....	....	....	....
	Kingston Frontenacs	EPHL	21	13	5	18	....	....	....	4	3	1	2	3	0
1961-62	Kingston Frontenacs	EPHL	32	15	10	25	....	....	....	11	....	....	....	....	....
	Providence Reds	AHL	34	8	14	22	....	....	....	4	....	....	....	....	....
1962-63	Kingston Frontenacs	EPHL	61	31	42	73	....	....	....	10	....	....	....	....	....
1963-64	Minneapolis Bruins	CPHL	69	32	47	79	....	....	....	4	5	0	2	2	2
1964-65	Minneapolis Bruins	CPHL	57	24	36	60	....	....	....	8	5	1	3	4	0
	San Francisco Seals	WHL	7	1	0	1	....	....	....	0	....	....	....	....	....
1965-66	Buffalo Bisons	AHL	72	11	21	32	....	....	....	6	....	....	....	....	....
1966-67	Buffalo Bisons	AHL	66	17	20	37	....	....	....	8	....	....	....	....	....
1967-68	Buffalo Bisons	AHL	66	18	32	50	....	....	....	6	5	0	6	6	2
1968-69	Buffalo Bisons	AHL	74	25	37	62	....	....	....	12	6	4	1	5	4
1969-70	Buffalo Bisons	AHL	67	26	46	72	....	....	....	10	11	2	7	9	2
1970-71	Omaha Knights	CHL	71	23	*58	81	....	....	....	14	11	5	*13	*18	0
1971-72	Campbellton Tigers	NNBHL	PLAYER/COACH – STATISTICS UNAVAILABLE												
1972-73	Campbellton Tigers	NNBHL	PLAYER/COACH – STATISTICS UNAVAILABLE												
1973-74	Campbellton Tigers	NNBHL	PLAYER/COACH – STATISTICS UNAVAILABLE												
1974-75	Campbellton Tigers	NNBHL	....	5	9	14	....	....	....	0	....	....	....	....	....
1975-76	Campbellton Tigers	NNBHL	....	10	16	26	....	....	....	4	....	....	....	....	....
	NHL Totals		**34**	**5**	**4**	**9**	**6**	**4**	**10**	**0**	....	....	....	....	....

• Shared Tommy Ivan Trophy (MVP - CHL) with Andre Dupont, Peter McDuffe and Joe Zanussi (1971)

Traded to **San Francisco** (WHL) by **Boston** to complete transaction that sent Orland Kurtenbach and Ed Panagabko to San Francisco (July 26, 1962), July 7, 1963. Loaned to **Minneapolis** (CPHL) by **San Francisco** (WHL) for cash, September, 1963. Claimed by **Buffalo** (AHL) from **Boston** in Reverse Draft, June 9, 1965.

• OWEN, George USHOF

D – L. 5'11", 190 lbs. b: Hamilton, Ont., 2/12/1901 d: 3/4/1986.

Season	Club	League	GP	G	A	Pts	AG	AA	APts	PIM	GP	G	A	Pts	PIM
1918-19	Newton High School	H.S.	STATISTICS NOT AVAILABLE												
1919-20	Harvard University	Ivy	DID NOT PLAY – FRESHMAN												
1920-21	Harvard University	Ivy	11	10	0	10	....	....	....	....	....	....	....	....	....
1921-22	Harvard University	Ivy	DID NOT PLAY												
1922-23	Harvard University	Ivy	STATISTICS NOT AVAILABLE												
1923-24	Boston AAA	USAHA	12	*10	0	*10	....	....	....	....	....	....	....	....	....
1924-25	Harvard University	Ivy	DID NOT PLAY – COACHING												
1925-26	Boston A. A. Unicorn	USAHA	....	....	....	....	....	....	....	....	2	0	2	2	....
1926-27	Boston University Club	MBHL	STATISTICS NOT AVAILABLE												
1927-28	Boston University Club	MBHL	STATISTICS NOT AVAILABLE												
♦1928-29	**Boston Bruins**	**NHL**	**27**	**5**	**4**	**9**	**14**	**27**	**41**	**48**	**5**	**0**	**0**	**0**	**0**
1929-30	**Boston Bruins**	**NHL**	**42**	**9**	**4**	**13**	**13**	**9**	**22**	**31**	**6**	**0**	**2**	**2**	**6**
1930-31	**Boston Bruins**	**NHL**	**38**	**12**	**13**	**25**	**24**	**39**	**63**	**33**	**5**	**2**	**3**	**5**	**13**
1931-32	**Boston Bruins**	**NHL**	**42**	**12**	**10**	**22**	**20**	**22**	**42**	**29**	....	....	....	....	....
1932-33	**Boston Bruins**	**NHL**	**34**	**6**	**2**	**8**	**11**	**4**	**15**	**10**	**5**	**0**	**0**	**0**	**6**
1933-34	Michigan Tech Huskies	WCHA	DID NOT PLAY – COACHING												
	NHL Totals		**183**	**44**	**33**	**77**	**82**	**101**	**183**	**151**	**21**	**2**	**5**	**7**	**25**

Rights traded to **Boston** by **Toronto** for Eric Pettinger and the rights to Hugh Plaxton, January 8, 1929.

• PALANGIO, Pete Peter Albert

LW – L. 5'11", 175 lbs. b: North Bay, Ont., 9/10/1908.

Season	Club	League	GP	G	A	Pts	AG	AA	APts	PIM	GP	G	A	Pts	PIM
1926-27	North Bay Trappers	NOHA	11	*25	10	*35	....	....	....	24	4	*9	3	*12	4
	Montreal Canadiens	**NHL**	**6**	**0**	**0**	**0**	**0**	**0**	**0**	**0**	**4**	**0**	**0**	**0**	**0**
1927-28	Windsor Hornets	Can-Pro	28	16	1	17	....	....	....	18	....	....	....	....	....
	Detroit Cougars	**NHL**	**14**	**3**	**0**	**3**	**6**	**0**	**6**	**8**	....	....	....	....	....
1928-29	**Montreal Canadiens**	**NHL**	**2**	**0**	**0**	**0**	**0**	**0**	**0**	**0**	....	....	....	....	....
	Kitchener Dutchmen	Can-Pro	37	17	7	24	....	....	....	26	3	1	0	1	4

Season	Club	League	REGULAR SEASON								PLAYOFFS				
			GP	G	A	Pts	AG	AA	APts	PIM	GP	G	A	Pts	PIM
1929-30	London Panthers	IHL	44	11	6	17	....	....	....	36	2	0	0	0	0
1930-31	London Tecumsehs	IHL	3	2	0	2	....	....	....	0	....	....	....	....	....
	Syracuse Stars	IHL	41	18	12	30	....	....	....	12	....	....	....	....	....
1931-32	Syracuse Stars	IHL	43	12	5	17	....	....	....	18	....	....	....	....	....
1932-33	St. Louis Flyers	AHA	43	21	14	35	....	....	....	38	4	0	1	1	2
1933-34	St. Louis Flyers	AHA	48	21	9	30	....	....	....	22	7	*3	1	*4	6
1934-35	St. Louis Flyers	AHA	47	34	19	53	....	....	....	8	6	*4	3	*7	11
1935-36	St. Louis Flyers	AHA	48	22	20	42	....	....	....	38	8	*5	1	*6	8
1936-37	St. Louis Flyers	AHA	16	12	12	24	....	....	....	4	....	....	....	....	....
	Chicago Black Hawks	**NHL**	**30**	**8**	**9**	**17**	**13**	**16**	**29**	**16**	....	....	....	....	....
♦**1937-38**	**Chicago Black Hawks**	**NHL**	**19**	**2**	**1**	**3**	**3**	**2**	**5**	**4**	**3**	**0**	**0**	**0**	**0**
	St. Louis Flyers	AHA	25	8	13	21	....	....	....	9	7	3	0	3	2
1938-39	Tulsa Oilers	AHA	34	12	18	30	....	....	....	16	8	1	3	4	2
1939-40	Tulsa Oilers	AHA	46	21	27	48	....	....	....	14	....	....	....	....	....
1940-41	Tulsa Oilers	AHA	48	12	21	33	....	....	....	17	....	....	....	....	....
1941-42	Dallas Texans	AHA	49	22	29	51	....	....	....	6	....	....	....	....	....
1942-43	Hershey Bears	AHL	5	0	1	1	....	....	....	0	....	....	....	....	....
	Pittsburgh Hornets	AHL	29	6	18	24	....	....	....	4	2	1	0	1	2
1943-44	Sudbury Open Pit Miners	NBHL	1	0	1	1	....	....	....	0	....	....	....	....	....
1944-45	North Bay Merchants	NBHL	....	*23	*12	*35	....	....	....	....	....	....	....	....	....
1945-46	North Bay Rangers	NBHL	STATISTICS NOT AVAILABLE												
1946-47	North Bay Rangers	NBHL	STATISTICS NOT AVAILABLE												
1947-48	North Bay Black Hawks	NBHL	14	19	22	41	....	....	....	....	6	8	7	15	2
	North Bay Black Hawks	Al-Cup	5	3	5	8	....	....	....	....	....	....	....	....	....
1948-49	North Bay Black Hawks	NBHL	8	4	2	6	....	....	....	0	....	....	....	....	....
	NHL Totals		**71**	**13**	**10**	**23**	**22**	**18**	**40**	**28**	**7**	**0**	**0**	**0**	**0**

AHA First All-Star Team (1935, 1936)

Signed as a free agent by **Montreal Canadiens**, February, 1927. Loaned to **Detroit** by **Montreal Canadiens** (Windsor-Can-Pro) with cash for Stan Brown, February 13, 1928. Loaned to **Kitchener** (Can-Pro) by **Montreal Canadiens** for cash, November 26, 1928. Traded to **London** (IHL) by **Montreal Canadiens** for cash, November 11, 1929. Traded to **Syracuse** (IHL) by **London** (IHL) for cash, November 28, 1930. Traded to **St. Louis** (AHA) by **Syracuse** (IHL) for cash, October 19, 1932. Traded to **Chicago** by **St. Louis** (AHA) for $25,000, December 19, 1936. Traded to **Tulsa** (AHA) by **Chicago** for cash, October 24, 1938.

• PALAZZARI, Aldo

RW – L. 5′7″, 168 lbs. b: Eveleth, MN, 7/25/1918.

Season	Club	League	GP	G	A	Pts	AG	AA	APts	PIM	GP	G	A	Pts	PIM
1938-39	Eveleth Rangers	USHL	30	25	13	38	....	....	....	24	5	2	2	4	2
1939-40	University of Illinois	MIAU	STATISTICS NOT AVAILABLE												
1940-41	University of Illinois	MIAU	STATISTICS NOT AVAILABLE												
1941-42	University of Illinois	MIAU	STATISTICS NOT AVAILABLE												
	Akron Clippers	USHL	12	2	5	7	....	....	....	10	2	1	2	3	6
1942-43	Akron Clippers	USHL	STATISTICS NOT AVAILABLE												
1943-44	**Boston Bruins**	**NHL**	**24**	**6**	**3**	**9**	**5**	**3**	**8**	**4**	....	....	....	....	....
	Boston Olympics	EAHL	17	15	17	32	....	....	....	14	....	....	....	....	....
	New York Rangers	**NHL**	**11**	**2**	**0**	**2**	**2**	**0**	**2**	**0**	....	....	....	....	....
1944-45	**New York Rangers**	**NHL**	DID NOT PLAY – INJURED												
	NHL Totals		**35**	**8**	**3**	**11**	**7**	**3**	**10**	**4**	....	....	....	....	....

• Father of Doug

Traded to **NY Rangers** by **Boston** for $3,000, February 22, 1944. • Suffered eventual career-ending eye injury in NY Rangers training camp, October 18, 1944.

• PANAGABKO, Ed

Edwin Arnold

C – L. 5′8″, 170 lbs. b: Norquay, Sask., 5/17/1934 d: 1/18/1979.

Season	Club	League	GP	G	A	Pts	AG	AA	APts	PIM	GP	G	A	Pts	PIM
1951-52	Humboldt Indians	SJHL	43	31	19	50	....	....	....	20	9	11	3	14	6
1952-53	Humboldt Indians	SJHL	33	24	27	51	....	....	....	2	12	5	7	12	4
1953-54	Humboldt Indians	SJHL	32	10	20	30	....	....	....	27	5	2	2	4	10
	Seattle Bombers	WHL	1	0	0	0	....	....	....	0	....	....	....	....	....
	Melville Millionaires	SSHL	....	....	....	....	....	....	....	....	4	1	1	2	2
1954-55	Grand Rapids Rockets	IHL	60	25	35	60	....	....	....	53	4	2	2	4	2
1955-56	**Boston Bruins**	**NHL**	**28**	**0**	**3**	**3**	**0**	**4**	**4**	**38**	....	....	....	....	....
	Hershey Bears	AHL	41	16	25	41	....	....	....	52	....	....	....	....	....
1956-57	**Boston Bruins**	**NHL**	**1**	**0**	**0**	**0**	**0**	**0**	**0**	**0**	....	....	....	....	....
	Hershey Bears	AHL	58	13	19	32	....	....	....	44	7	0	2	2	8
1957-58	Hershey Bears	AHL	61	12	14	26	....	....	....	24	10	0	0	0	6
1958-59	Providence Reds	AHL	69	13	36	49	....	....	....	50	....	....	....	....	....
1959-60	Providence Reds	AHL	49	7	21	28	....	....	....	25	5	5	2	7	2
1960-61	Providence Reds	AHL	68	20	32	52	....	....	....	45	....	....	....	....	....
1961-62	Portland–Los Angeles	WHL	69	24	52	76	....	....	....	37	....	....	....	....	....
1962-63	San Francisco Seals	WHL	70	31	47	78	....	....	....	42	17	3	11	14	2
1963-64	San Francisco Seals	WHL	67	15	29	44	....	....	....	35	11	8	9	17	6
1964-65	San Francisco Seals	WHL	70	21	43	64	....	....	....	59	....	....	....	....	....
1965-66			DID NOT PLAY												
1966-67	San Diego Gulls	WHL	57	9	22	31	....	....	....	14	....	....	....	....	....
1967-68	San Diego Gulls	WHL	44	2	2	4	....	....	....	29	7	0	1	1	0
	NHL Totals		**29**	**0**	**3**	**3**	**0**	**4**	**4**	**38**	....	....	....	....	....

Traded to **San Francisco** (WHL) by **Boston** with Orland Kurtenbach and future considerations (Gerry Ouelette, July 7, 1963) for Larry McNabb and cash, July 26, 1962.

• PAPIKE, Joe

Joseph John

RW – R. 6′, 175 lbs. b: Eveleth, MN, 3/28/1915 d: 5/28/1967.

Season	Club	League	GP	G	A	Pts	AG	AA	APts	PIM	GP	G	A	Pts	PIM
1931-32	Virginia Rockets	CHL	31	15	4	19	....	....	....	17	....	....	....	....	....
1932-33	Eveleth Rangers	CHL	37	13	7	20	....	....	....	6	3	1	1	2	4
1933-34	Eveleth Rangers	CHL	43	13	6	19	....	....	....	17	3	0	1	1	2
1934-35	Baltimore Orioles	EAHL	20	7	3	10	....	....	....	10	9	2	5	7	0
1935-36	Wichita Skyhawks	AHA	47	11	9	20	....	....	....	19	....	....	....	....	....
1936-37	Wichita Skyhawks	AHA	48	22	15	37	....	....	....	6	....	....	....	....	....
1937-38	Wichita Skyhawks	AHA	47	22	22	44	....	....	....	12	4	0	0	0	0
1938-39	Wichita Skyhawks	AHA	44	12	12	24	....	....	....	2	....	....	....	....	....
1939-40	Kansas City Greyhounds	AHA	38	12	19	31	....	....	....	12	....	....	....	....	....
1940-41	**Chicago Black Hawks**	**NHL**	**9**	**2**	**2**	**4**	**3**	**3**	**6**	**2**	**5**	**0**	**2**	**2**	**0**
	Kansas City Americans	AHA	39	20	23	43	....	....	....	15	....	....	....	....	....
1941-42	**Chicago Black Hawks**	**NHL**	**9**	**1**	**0**	**1**	**1**	**0**	**1**	**0**	....	....	....	....	....
	Kansas City Americans	AHA	34	22	24	46	....	....	....	6	6	2	5	7	4
1942-43			MILITARY SERVICE												
1943-44			MILITARY SERVICE												
1944-45	**Chicago Black Hawks**	**NHL**	**2**	**0**	**1**	**1**	**0**	**1**	**1**	**2**	....	....	....	....	....
1945-46			DID NOT PLAY												
1946-47	Duluth Coolerators	TBSHL	8	11	7	18	....	....	....	0	....	....	....	....	....
	NHL Totals		**20**	**3**	**3**	**6**	**4**	**4**	**8**	**4**	**5**	**0**	**2**	**2**	**0**

AHA Second All-Star Team (1938, 1941)

• PAPPIN, Jim

— see page 1499

• PARGETER, George

George William

LW – L. 5′7″, 168 lbs. b: Calgary, Alta., 2/24/1923.

Season	Club	League	GP	G	A	Pts	AG	AA	APts	PIM	GP	G	A	Pts	PIM
1941-42	Calgary Royals	CCJHL	STATISTICS NOT AVAILABLE												
	Calgary Royals	M-Cup	2	2	0	2	....	....	....	0	....	....	....	....	....
1942-43	Red Deer Wheelers	ASHL	24	18	9	27	....	....	....	8	....	....	....	....	....
1943-44	Red Deer Wheelers	ASHL	16	5	6	11	....	....	....	8	5	2	*6	*8	7
1944-45	Buffalo Bisons	AHL	53	25	14	39	....	....	....	12	6	3	5	8	0
1945-46	New Haven Eagles	AHL	48	21	15	36	....	....	....	6	....	....	....	....	....
	Fort Worth Rangers	USHL	14	8	4	12	....	....	....	0	....	....	....	....	....
1946-47	**Montreal Canadiens**	**NHL**	**4**	**0**	**0**	**0**	**0**	**0**	**0**	**0**	....	....	....	....	....
	Buffalo Bisons	AHL	45	6	15	21	....	....	....	14	4	0	1	1	0
1947-48	Houston Huskies	USHL	26	11	16	27	....	....	....	2	....	....	....	....	....
	Buffalo Bisons	AHL	33	3	4	7	....	....	....	2	8	1	1	2	0
1948-49	Buffalo Bisons	AHL	66	31	34	65	....	....	....	18	....	....	....	....	....
1949-50	Buffalo Bisons	AHL	68	21	23	44	....	....	....	9	5	1	0	1	2
1950-51	Buffalo Bisons	AHL	63	20	24	44	....	....	....	6	4	0	1	1	0
1951-52	Buffalo Bisons	AHL	51	7	15	22	....	....	....	8	3	0	0	0	0
1952-53	Seattle Bombers	WHL	69	16	33	49	....	....	....	4	5	2	0	2	0
1953-54	Calgary Stampeders	WHL	67	20	15	35	....	....	....	4	18	5	8	13	2
	Calgary Stampeders	Ed-Cup	7	2	2	4	....	....	....	....	....	....	....	....	....
1954-55	Calgary Stampeders	WHL	70	17	19	36	....	....	....	10	9	2	2	4	0
	NHL Totals		**4**	**0**	**0**	**0**	**0**	**0**	**0**	**0**	....	....	....	....	....

Traded to **Montreal** (Buffalo-AHL) by **Springfield** (AHL) for John Quilty, November 19, 1946.

• PARISE, Jean-Paul

— see page 1500

• PARKES, Ernie

George Ernest

RW – R. 5′10″, 150 lbs. b: Dunnville, Ont., 11/4/1898 d: 7/7/1948.

Season	Club	League	GP	G	A	Pts	AG	AA	APts	PIM	GP	G	A	Pts	PIM
1914-15	Toronto Argonauts	OHA-Sr.	2	3	0	3	....	....	....	....	....	....	....	....	....
1915-16	Toronto Argonauts	OHA-Sr.	10	13	0	13	....	....	....	....	2	0	0	0	0
1916-17	Toronto Riversides	OHA-Sr.	7	6	0	6	....	....	....	....	2	0	0	0	3
1917-18	Kitchener Greenshirts	OHA-Sr.	9	29	0	29	....	....	....	....	5	8	0	8	....
1918-19	Kitchener Greenshirts	OHA-Sr.	9	7	*8	15	....	....	....	....	....	....	....	....	....
1919-20	Kitchener Greenshirts	OHA-Sr.	8	*22	*6	*28	....	....	....	....	2	1	1	2	....
1920-21	Kitchener Greenshirts	OHA-Sr.	7	6	2	8	....	....	....	....	1	1	0	1	....
1921-22	Vancouver Millionaires	PCHA	24	8	3	11	....	....	....	0	2	0	0	0	0
	Vancouver Millionaires	St-Cup	7	0	3	3	....	....	....	0	....	....	....	....	....
1922-23	Vancouver Maroons	PCHA	30	11	4	15	....	....	....	2	2	2	0	2	0
	Vancouver Maroons	St-Cup	4	0	2	2	....	....	....	2	....	....	....	....	....
1923-24	Vancouver Maroons	PCHA	30	3	1	4	....	....	....	2	2	1	0	1	0
	Vancouver Maroons	St-Cup	2	0	0	0	....	....	....	0	....	....	....	....	....
1924-25	**Montreal Maroons**	**NHL**	**17**	**0**	**0**	**0**	**0**	**0**	**0**	**2**	....	....	....	....	....
	NHL Totals		**17**	**0**	**0**	**0**	**0**	**0**	**0**	**2**	....	....	....	....	....
	Other Major League Totals		84	22	8	30	....	....	....	4	6	3	0	3	0

OHA-Sr. Second All-Star Team (1918, 1921) • OHA-Sr. First All-Star Team (1919, 1920) • PCHA Second All-Star Team (1923)

Signed as a free agent by **Vancouver** (PCHA) November 16, 1921. Signed as a free agent by **Toronto St. Pats**, December 8, 1924. Traded to **Boston** by **Toronto St. Pats** for cash, December 8, 1924. Rights traded to **Montreal Maroons** by **Boston** for George Carroll, December 19, 1924. • 1922 St-Cup totals include series vs. Regina.

• PARSONS, George

George Henry

LW – L. 5′11″, 174 lbs. b: Toronto, Ont., 6/28/1914 d: 6/30/1998.

Season	Club	League	GP	G	A	Pts	AG	AA	APts	PIM	GP	G	A	Pts	PIM
1930-31	Toronto Native Sons	TJrHL	9	4	2	6	....	....	....	4	2	0	0	0	0
1931-32	Toronto Nationals	OHA-Jr.	10	11	2	13	....	....	....	11	3	0	1	1	2
	Toronto City Services	TMHL	9	6	1	7	....	....	....	4	2	0	0	0	0
1932-33	West Toronto Nationals	OHA-Jr.	9	8	2	10	....	....	....	10	5	*3	1	*4	8
	Toronto City Services	TMHL	14	3	2	5	....	....	....	6	5	*6	1	*7	10
	West Toronto Nationals	M-Cup	6	7	2	9	....	....	....	10	....	....	....	....	....
1933-34	Toronto Young Rangers	OHA-Jr.	6	13	9	22	....	....	....	8	1	0	1	1	0
	Toronto City Service	TMHL	14	11	1	12	....	....	....	6	9	*11	4	*15	*26
	Toronto Young Rangers	M-Cup	2	2	0	2	....	....	....	4	....	....	....	....	....
1934-35	Toronto City Service	TIHL	13	*14	4	*18	....	....	....	15	7	4	4	8	*17
	Toronto All-Stars	OHA-Sr.	13	13	1	14	....	....	....	10	6	3	1	4	2
	Toronto All-Stars	Al-Cup	6	*11	3	14	....	....	....	6	....	....	....	....	....
1935-36	Syracuse Stars	IHL	48	20	17	37	....	....	....	18	3	0	0	0	0
1936-37	**Toronto Maple Leafs**	**NHL**	**5**	**0**	**0**	**0**	**0**	**0**	**0**	**0**	....	....	....	....	....
	Syracuse Stars	IAHL	43	26	11	37	....	....	....	32	9	3	3	6	0
1937-38	**Toronto Maple Leafs**	**NHL**	**30**	**5**	**6**	**11**	**8**	**10**	**18**	**6**	**7**	**3**	**2**	**5**	**11**
	Syracuse Stars	IAHL	17	6	8	14	....	....	....	17	....	....	....	....	....
1938-39	**Toronto Maple Leafs**	**NHL**	**43**	**7**	**7**	**14**	**12**	**11**	**23**	**14**	....	....	....	....	....
	NHL Totals		**78**	**12**	**13**	**25**	**20**	**21**	**41**	**20**	**7**	**3**	**2**	**5**	**11**

Signed as a free agent by **Toronto**, October 22, 1935. • Suffered career-ending eye injury in game vs. Chicago, March 4, 1939.

• PATRICK, Lester

Curtis Lester "The Silver Fox" **HHOF**

D – L. 6′1″, 180 lbs. b: Drummondville, Que., 12/30/1883 d: 6/1/1960.

Season	Club	League	GP	G	A	Pts	AG	AA	APts	PIM	GP	G	A	Pts	PIM
1903-04	Brandon Hockey Club	NWHL	....	....	....	....	....	....	....	....	2	0	0	0	....
1904-05	Westmount Academy	CAHL	8	4	0	4	....	....	....	....	....	....	....	....	....
♦1905-06	Montreal Wanderers	ECAHA	9	17	0	17	....	....	....	26	2	3	0	3	3
♦1906-07	Montreal Wanderers	ECAHA	9	11	0	11	....	....	....	11	6	10	0	10	32
1907-08	Nelson Seniors	BCHL	....	....	....	....	....	....	....	....	2	1	0	1	....
1908-09	Edmonton Pros	X-Games	1	1	0	1	....	....	....	3	....	....	....	....	....
	Edmonton Pros	St-Cup	2	1	1	2	....	....	....	3	....	....	....	....	....
	Nelson Pros	X-Games	2	4	0	4	....	....	....	3	....	....	....	....	....
1909-10	Renfrew Creamery Kings	NHA	12	23	0	23	....	....	....	25	....	....	....	....	....
1910-11	Nelson Seniors	BCHL	STATISTICS NOT AVAILABLE												

			REGULAR SEASON								PLAYOFFS				
Season	Club	League	GP	G	A	Pts	AG	AA	APts	PIM	GP	G	A	Pts	PIM
1911-12	Victoria Aristocrats	PCHA	16	10	0	10	....	....	....	9	....	....	....	....	....
	PCHA All-Stars	X-Games	2	0	0	0	....	....	....	0	....	....	....	....	....
1912-13	Victoria Aristocrats	PCHA	15	14	5	19	....	....	....	12	3	4	0	4	....
1913-14	Victoria Aristocrats	PCHA	9	5	5	10	....	....	....	0	3	2	0	2	....
1914-15	Victoria Aristocrats	PCHA	17	12	5	17	....	....	....	15	....	....	....	....	....
	PCHA All-Stars	X-Games	2	1	0	1	....	....	....	0	....	....	....	....	....
1915-16	Victoria Aristocrats	PCHA	18	13	11	24	....	....	....	27	....	....	....	....	....
1916-17	Spokane Canaries	PCHA	23	10	11	21	....	....	....	15	....	....	....	....	....
1917-18	Seattle Metropolitans	PCHA	17	2	8	10	....	....	....	15	2	0	1	1	0
1918-19	Victoria Aristocrats	PCHA	9	2	5	7	....	....	....	0	....	....	....	....	....
1919-20	Victoria Aristocrats	PCHA	11	2	2	4	....	....	....	3	....	....	....	....	....
1920-21	Victoria Aristocrats	PCHA	5	2	3	5	....	....	....	13	....	....	....	....	....
1921-22	Victoria Aristocrats	PCHA	2	0	0	0	....	....	....	0	....	....	....	....	....
1922-23	Victoria Cougars	PCHA	DID NOT PLAY – COACHING												
1923-24	Victoria Cougars	PCHA	DID NOT PLAY – COACHING												
1924-25	Victoria Cougars	WCHL	DID NOT PLAY – COACHING												
1925-26	Victoria Cougars	WHL	23	5	8	13	....	....	....	20	2	0	0	0	2
1926-27	**New York Rangers**	**NHL**	**1**	**0**	**0**	**0**	**0**	**0**	**0**	**2**	....	....	....	....	....
1927/39	**New York Rangers**	**NHL**	DID NOT PLAY – COACHING												
1939/46	**New York Rangers**	**NHL**	DID NOT PLAY – GENERAL MANAGER												
	NHL Totals		**1**	**0**	**0**	**0**	**0**	**0**	**0**	**2**	....	....	....	....	....
	Other Major League Totals		195	128	63	191	....	....	....	191	18	19	1	20	37

• Father of Muzz and Lynn • PCHA First All-Star Team (1913, 1915, 1916, 1917) • PCHA Second All-Star Team (1918, 1920)

Signed as a free agent by **Edmonton Pros**, December 13, 1908. Signed as a free agent by **Renfrew** (NHA), December 13, 1909. • 1925-26 playoff totals includes WHL series against Edmonton and Saskatoon. • Named coach and general manager of **NY Rangers** replacing Conn Smythe and Frank Carroll, October 27, 1926.

• PATRICK, Lynn — Joseph Lynn — HHOF

C/LW – L. 6'1", 192 lbs. b: Victoria, B.C., 2/3/1912 d: 1/26/1980.

Season	Club	League	GP	G	A	Pts	AG	AA	APts	PIM	GP	G	A	Pts	PIM
1933-34	Montreal Royals	MCHL	15	5	3	8	....	....	....	4	2	0	0	0	0
1934-35	**New York Rangers**	**NHL**	**48**	**9**	**13**	**22**	**15**	**23**	**38**	**17**	**4**	**2**	**2**	**4**	**0**
1935-36	**New York Rangers**	**NHL**	**48**	**11**	**14**	**25**	**21**	**27**	**48**	**29**	....	....	....	....	....
1936-37	**New York Rangers**	**NHL**	**45**	**8**	**16**	**24**	**13**	**29**	**42**	**23**	**9**	**3**	**0**	**3**	**2**
1937-38	**New York Rangers**	**NHL**	**48**	**15**	**19**	**34**	**25**	**31**	**56**	**24**	**3**	**0**	**1**	**1**	**2**
1938-39	**New York Rangers**	**NHL**	**35**	**8**	**21**	**29**	**14**	**33**	**47**	**25**	**7**	**1**	**1**	**2**	**0**
♦1939-40	**New York Rangers**	**NHL**	**48**	**12**	**16**	**28**	**20**	**25**	**45**	**34**	**12**	**2**	**2**	**4**	**4**
1940-41	**New York Rangers**	**NHL**	**48**	**20**	**24**	**44**	**31**	**35**	**66**	**12**	**3**	**1**	**0**	**1**	**14**
1941-42	**New York Rangers**	**NHL**	**47**	***32**	**22**	**54**	**43**	**26**	**69**	**18**	**6**	**1**	**0**	**1**	**0**
1942-43	**New York Rangers**	**NHL**	**50**	**22**	**39**	**61**	**23**	**37**	**60**	**28**	....	....	....	....	....
1943-44			MILITARY SERVICE												
1944-45			MILITARY SERVICE												
1945-46	**New York Rangers**	**NHL**	**38**	**8**	**6**	**14**	**9**	**9**	**18**	**30**	....	....	....	....	....
1946-47	New Haven Ramblers	AHL	16	2	6	8	....	....	....	16	3	1	0	1	2
1947-48	New Haven Ramblers	AHL	DID NOT PLAY – COACHING												
	NHL Totals		**455**	**145**	**190**	**335**	**214**	**275**	**489**	**240**	**44**	**10**	**6**	**16**	**22**

• Son of Lester • Brother of Muzz • Father of Craig and Glenn • NHL First All-Star Team (1942) • NHL Second All-Star Team (1943) • Won Lester Patrick Trophy (1989)

• PATRICK, Muzz — Frederick Murray

D – L. 6'2", 200 lbs. b: Victoria, B.C., 6/28/1915 d: 7/27/1998.

Season	Club	League	GP	G	A	Pts	AG	AA	APts	PIM	GP	G	A	Pts	PIM
1933-34	Montreal Westmount High	H.S.	STATISTICS NOT AVAILABLE												
1934-35	New York Crescents	EAHL	21	3	3	6	....	....	....	16	6	2	3	5	9
1935-36	New York Rovers	EAHL	40	3	8	11	....	....	....	31	8	2	2	4	15
1936-37	Philadelphia Ramblers	IAHL	50	2	11	13	....	....	....	75	6	0	1	1	2
1937-38	Philadelphia Ramblers	IAHL	48	3	6	9	....	....	....	37	5	2	0	2	6
	New York Rangers	**NHL**	**1**	**0**	**2**	**2**	**0**	**3**	**3**	**0**	**3**	**0**	**0**	**0**	**2**
1938-39	**New York Rangers**	**NHL**	**48**	**1**	**10**	**11**	**2**	**16**	**18**	**64**	**7**	**1**	**0**	**1**	**17**
♦1939-40	**New York Rangers**	**NHL**	**46**	**2**	**4**	**6**	**3**	**6**	**9**	**44**	**12**	**3**	**0**	**3**	**13**
1940-41	**New York Rangers**	**NHL**	**47**	**2**	**8**	**10**	**3**	**11**	**14**	**21**	**3**	**0**	**0**	**0**	**2**
1941-42			MILITARY SERVICE												
1942-43			MILITARY SERVICE												
1943-44			MILITARY SERVICE												
1944-45			MILITARY SERVICE												
1945-46	**New York Rangers**	**NHL**	**24**	**0**	**2**	**2**	**0**	**3**	**3**	**4**	....	....	....	....	....
	Providence Reds	AHL	2	0	1	1	....	....	....	0	....	....	....	....	....
1946-47	St. Paul Saints	USHL	7	0	0	0				0					
1947-48	St. Paul Saints	USHL	DID NOT PLAY – COACHING												
1948-49	Tacoma Rockets	PCHL	DID NOT PLAY – COACHING												
1949-50	Tacoma Rockets	PCHL	8	0	0	0				12					
	NHL Totals		**166**	**5**	**26**	**31**	**8**	**39**	**47**	**133**	**25**	**4**	**0**	**4**	**34**

• Son of Lester • Brother of Lynn

Named playing-coach of **St. Paul** (USHL), October 7, 1946.

• PATTERSON, George — George Franklin "Paddy"

W – R. 6'1", 176 lbs. b: Kingston, Ont., 5/22/1906 d: 1/20/1977.

Season	Club	League	GP	G	A	Pts	AG	AA	APts	PIM	GP	G	A	Pts	PIM
1925-26	Kingston Frontenacs	OHA-Jr.	STATISTICS NOT AVAILABLE												
1926-27	Hamilton Tigers	Can-Pro	23	14	3	17	....	....	....	30	....	....	....	....	....
	Toronto Pats/Leafs	**NHL**	**17**	**4**	**2**	**6**	**7**	**10**	**17**	**17**	....	....	....	....	....
1927-28	**Toronto Maple Leafs**	**NHL**	**12**	**1**	**0**	**1**	**2**	**0**	**2**	**14**	....	....	....	....	....
	Toronto Ravinas	Can-Pro	16	7	0	7	....	....	....	37	....	....	....	....	....
	Montreal Canadiens	**NHL**	**16**	**0**	**1**	**1**	**0**	**6**	**6**	**0**	....	....	....	....	....
1928-29	**Montreal Canadiens**	**NHL**	**44**	**4**	**5**	**9**	**11**	**33**	**44**	**34**	**3**	**0**	**0**	**0**	**2**
1929-30	**New York Americans**	**NHL**	**39**	**13**	**4**	**17**	**18**	**9**	**27**	**24**	....	....	....	....	....
1930-31	**New York Americans**	**NHL**	**44**	**8**	**6**	**14**	**16**	**18**	**34**	**67**	....	....	....	....	....
1931-32	**New York Americans**	**NHL**	**20**	**6**	**0**	**6**	**10**	**0**	**10**	**26**	....	....	....	....	....
	New Haven Eagles	Can-Am	25	17	10	27	....	....	....	33	2	2	0	2	12
1932-33	**New York Americans**	**NHL**	**41**	**12**	**7**	**19**	**22**	**14**	**36**	**26**	....	....	....	....	....
1933-34	**New York Americans**	**NHL**	**13**	**3**	**0**	**3**	**5**	**0**	**5**	**6**	....	....	....	....	....
	Boston Bruins	**NHL**	**10**	**0**	**1**	**1**	**0**	**2**	**2**	**2**	....	....	....	....	....
	Boston Cubs	Can-Am	17	7	3	10	....	....	....	15	5	0	2	2	2
1934-35	**Detroit Red Wings**	**NHL**	**7**	**0**	**0**	**0**	**0**	**0**	**0**	**0**	....	....	....	....	....
	Detroit Olympics	IHL	3	0	0	0	....	....	....	2	....	....	....	....	....
	St. Louis Eagles	**NHL**	**21**	**0**	**1**	**1**	**0**	**2**	**2**	**2**	....	....	....	....	....
	Buffalo Bisons	IHL	25	10	9	19	....	....	....	56	....	....	....	....	....
1935-36	Buffalo Bisons	IHL	48	7	11	18	....	....	....	31	1	0	0	0	2
1936-37	Buffalo Bisons	IAHL	11	2	1	3	....	....	....	16	....	....	....	....	....
	Minneapolis Millers	AHA	35	19	17	36	....	....	....	35	6	*8	2	*10	6
1937-38	Minneapolis Millers	AHA	48	25	34	*59	....	....	....	46	7	1	*4	5	0
1938-39	Cleveland Barons	IAHL	53	11	5	16	....	....	....	20	9	1	1	2	0
1939-40	New Haven Eagles	IAHL	54	25	27	52	....	....	....	42	3	2	2	4	2
1940-41	New Haven Eagles	AHL	45	19	33	52	....	....	....	33	2	0	0	0	0
1941-42	New Haven Eagles	AHL	28	9	16	25	....	....	....	18	2	0	1	1	2
1942-43	New Haven Eagles	AHL	26	10	12	22	....	....	....	2	....	....	....	....	....
	Indianapolis Capitols	AHL	23	9	19	28	....	....	....	6	7	1	4	5	0
1943-44	Hershey Bears	AHL	48	15	31	46	....	....	....	16	7	1	1	2	4
1944-45	Hershey Bears	AHL	24	9	13	22	....	....	....	5	....	....	....	....	....
	Providence Reds	AHL	30	17	20	37	....	....	....	4	....	....	....	....	....
	NHL Totals		**284**	**51**	**27**	**78**	**91**	**94**	**185**	**218**	**3**	**0**	**0**	**0**	**2**

AHA Second All-Star Team (1937) • AHA First All-Star Team (1938)

Signed as a free agent by **Hamilton** (Can-Pro), September 21, 1926. Traded to **Toronto** by **Hamilton** (Can-Pro) for $5,000 and the loan of Al Pudas, February 1, 1927. Traded to **Montreal Canadiens** by **Toronto** for cash, February 8, 1928. Traded to **Boston** by **Montreal Canadiens** for cash, May 13, 1929. Claimed on waivers by **NY Americans** from **Boston**, October 23, 1929. Traded to **Boston** by **NY Americans** with Lloyd Gross for Art Chapman and Bob Gracie, January 11, 1934. Traded to **Detroit** by **Boston** for Gene Carrigan, October 10, 1934. Traded to **St. Louis** by **Detroit** for Mickey Blake and $3,500 with Detroit holding right of recall, November 28, 1934. Returned to **Detroit**, December 24, 1934. Traded to **Buffalo** (IHL) by **Detroit** for cash, January 4, 1935. Signed as a free agent by **Minneapolis** (AHA) after **Buffalo** (IAHL) franchise folded, December 9, 1936.

• PAUL, Butch — Arthur Stewart

C – R. 5'11", 160 lbs. b: Rocky Mountain House, Alta., 9/11/1943 d: 3/25/1966.

Season	Club	League	GP	G	A	Pts	AG	AA	APts	PIM	GP	G	A	Pts	PIM
1961-62	Edmonton Oil Kings	CAHL	STATISTICS NOT AVAILABLE												
	Edmonton Oil Kings	M-Cup	21	8	11	19	....	....	....	8	....	....	....	....	....
1962-63	Edmonton Oil Kings	CAHL	STATISTICS NOT AVAILABLE												
	Edmonton Oil Kings	M-Cup	20	17	13	30	....	....	....	14	....	....	....	....	....
1963-64	Edmonton Oil Kings	CAHL	37	27	*53	*80	....	....	....	19	5	4	1	5	0
	Cincinnati Wings	CPHL	1	0	1	1	....	....	....	5	....	....	....	....	....
	Edmonton Oil Kings	M-Cup	19	18	*25	*43	....	....	....	18	....	....	....	....	....
1964-65	**Detroit Red Wings**	**NHL**	**3**	**0**	**0**	**0**	**0**	**0**	**0**	**0**	....	....	....	....	....
	Charlotte Checkers	EHL	30	27	14	41	....	....	....	50	....	....	....	....	....
	Pittsburgh Hornets	AHL	30	7	16	23	....	....	....	16	4	1	0	1	2
1965-66	Memphis Wings	CPHL	68	13	47	60	....	....	....	44	....	....	....	....	....
	NHL Totals		**3**	**0**	**0**	**0**	**0**	**0**	**0**	**0**	....	....	....	....	....

CAHL First All-Star Team (1964) • Died of injuries suffered in an automobile accident, March 25, 1966.

• PAULHUS, Rollie — Roland Edmond "Tubby"

D – L. 5'8", 185 lbs. b: Montreal, Que., 9/1/1902 Deceased.

Season	Club	League	GP	G	A	Pts	AG	AA	APts	PIM	GP	G	A	Pts	PIM
1924-25	Verdun Maple Leafs	MCHL	STATISTICS NOT AVAILABLE												
1925-26	**Montreal Canadiens**	**NHL**	**33**	**0**	**0**	**0**	**0**	**0**	**0**	**0**	....	....	....	....	....
1926-27	Providence Reds	Can-Am	29	5	3	8	....	....	....	74	....	....	....	....	....
1927-28	Providence Reds	Can-Am	39	15	3	18	....	....	....	76	....	....	....	....	....
1928-29	Providence Reds	Can-Am	38	5	2	7	....	....	....	108	2	0	0	0	2
1929-30	Providence Reds	Can-Am	8	0	0	0	....	....	....	6	....	....	....	....	....
	London Panthers	IHL	2	0	0	0	....	....	....	0	....	....	....	....	....
	New Haven Eagles	Can-Am	10	0	1	1	....	....	....	20	....	....	....	....	....
	Windsor Bulldogs	IHL	1	0	0	0	....	....	....	0	....	....	....	....	....
1930-31	Philadelphia Arrows	Can-Am	29	0	3	3	....	....	....	63	....	....	....	....	....
1931-32	Philadelphia Arrows	Can-Am	22	1	1	2	....	....	....	26	....	....	....	....	....
	Cleveland Indians	IHL	8	0	0	0	....	....	....	2	....	....	....	....	....
	NHL Totals		**33**	**0**	**0**	**0**	**0**	**0**	**0**	**0**	....	....	....	....	....

Signed as a free agent by **Montreal Canadiens**, November 16, 1925. Traded to **London** (Can-Am) by **Providence** (Can-Am) for cash, January 27, 1930. Traded to **Providence** (Can-Am) by **London** (Can-Am) for cash, February 5, 1930. Traded to **New Haven** (Can-Am) by **Providence** (Can-Am) for cash, February 10, 1930.

• PAVELICH, Marty — Martin Nicholas

LW – L. 5'11", 168 lbs. b: Sault Ste. Marie, Ont., 11/6/1927.

Season	Club	League	GP	G	A	Pts	AG	AA	APts	PIM	GP	G	A	Pts	PIM
1944-45	Galt Red Wings	OHA-Jr.	21	8	12	20	....	....	....	10	9	7	5	12	6
1945-46	Galt Red Wings	OHA-Jr.	25	22	26	48	....	....	....	18	5	2	1	3	5
1946-47	Galt Red Wings	OHA-Jr.	28	22	28	50	....	....	....	32	9	4	5	9	6
1947-48	**Detroit Red Wings**	**NHL**	**41**	**4**	**8**	**12**	**5**	**10**	**15**	**10**	**10**	**2**	**2**	**4**	**6**
	Indianapolis Capitols	AHL	26	3	14	17	....	....	....	21	....	....	....	....	....
1948-49	**Detroit Red Wings**	**NHL**	**60**	**10**	**16**	**26**	**14**	**23**	**37**	**40**	**9**	**0**	**1**	**1**	**8**
♦1949-50	**Detroit Red Wings**	**NHL**	**65**	**8**	**15**	**23**	**10**	**18**	**28**	**58**	**14**	**4**	**2**	**6**	**13**
	Indianapolis Capitols	AHL	6	2	3	5	....	....	....	2	....	....	....	....	....
1950-51	**Detroit Red Wings**	**NHL**	**67**	**9**	**20**	**29**	**11**	**24**	**35**	**41**	**6**	**0**	**1**	**1**	**2**
♦1951-52	**Detroit Red Wings**	**NHL**	**68**	**17**	**19**	**36**	**23**	**23**	**46**	**54**	**8**	**2**	**2**	**4**	**2**
1952-53	**Detroit Red Wings**	**NHL**	**64**	**13**	**20**	**33**	**17**	**24**	**41**	**49**	**6**	**2**	**1**	**3**	**7**
♦1953-54	**Detroit Red Wings**	**NHL**	**65**	**9**	**20**	**29**	**12**	**24**	**36**	**57**	**12**	**2**	**2**	**4**	**4**
♦1954-55	**Detroit Red Wings**	**NHL**	**70**	**15**	**15**	**30**	**19**	**17**	**36**	**59**	**11**	**1**	**3**	**4**	**12**
1955-56	**Detroit Red Wings**	**NHL**	**70**	**5**	**13**	**18**	**7**	**15**	**22**	**38**	**10**	**0**	**1**	**1**	**14**
1956-57	**Detroit Red Wings**	**NHL**	**64**	**3**	**13**	**16**	**4**	**14**	**18**	**48**	**5**	**0**	**0**	**0**	**6**
	NHL Totals		**634**	**93**	**159**	**252**	**122**	**192**	**314**	**454**	**91**	**13**	**15**	**28**	**74**

Played in NHL All-Star Game (1950, 1952, 1954, 1955)

• PAYER, Evariste

C/LW – L. 5'6", 150 lbs. b: Rockland, Ont., 12/12/1887 d: 1963.

Season	Club	League	GP	G	A	Pts	AG	AA	APts	PIM	GP	G	A	Pts	PIM
1909-10	Rockland Seniors	LOHA	STATISTICS NOT AVAILABLE												
1910-11	Montreal Canadiens	NHA	5	0	0	0	....	....	....	3	....	....	....	....	....
1911-12	Montreal Canadiens	NHA	4	1	0	1	....	....	....	0	....	....	....	....	....
	Montreal Hochelaga	MCHL	7	6	0	6	....	....	....	6	....	....	....	....	....
1912-13	Montreal Champetre	MCHL	12	13	0	13	....	....	....	15	1	1	0	1	0
1913-14	Montreal Champetre	MCHL	10	10	0	10	....	....	....	20	....	....	....	....	....
1914-15	Rockland Seniors	LOHA	STATISTICS NOT AVAILABLE												
1915-16			MILITARY SERVICE												

			REGULAR SEASON								PLAYOFFS				
Season	Club	League	GP	G	A	Pts	AG	AA	APts	PIM	GP	G	A	Pts	PIM
1916-17			MILITARY SERVICE												
1917-18	Rockland Seniors	OCHL	STATISTICS NOT AVAILABLE												
	Montreal Canadiens	**NHL**	**1**	**0**	**0**	**0**	**0**	**0**	**0**	**0**	....	....	....	....	....
	NHL Totals		**1**	**0**	**0**	**0**	**0**	**0**	**0**	**0**	....	....	....	....	....
	Other Major League Totals		9	1	0	1	....	....	....	3	....	....	....	....	....

MCHL First All-Star Team (1912, 1913) • MCHL Second All-Star Team (1914)

Signed as a free agent by **Montreal Canadiens** (NHA), January 30, 1912. Signed as a free agent by **Montreal Canadiens**, January 29, 1918.

• PEARSON, Mel — *see page 1508*

• PEER, Bert

RW – R. 5′11″, 175 lbs. b: Port Credit, Ont., 11/12/1910.

Season	Club	League	GP	G	A	Pts	AG	AA	APts	PIM	GP	G	A	Pts	PIM
1932-33	Toronto Bell Telephone	TMHL	11	4	1	5	....	....	....	10	4	1	1	2	4
1933-34	Toronto Bell Telephone	TMHL	STATISTICS NOT AVAILABLE												
1934-35	British Consols	TIHL	12	7	3	10	....	....	....	2	4	2	0	2	6
	Oakville Villans	OHA-Sr.	14	9	3	12	....	....	....	20	2	0	2	2	0
1935-36	Oakville Villans	OHA-Sr.	15	10	4	14	....	....	....	15	2	1	0	1	2
	British Consols	TMHL	14	11	3	14	....	....	....	19	5	0	1	1	26
1936-37	Harringay Racers	Britain	....	38	22	60	....	....	....	26	....	....	....	....	....
1937-38	Harringay Racers	Ln-Cup	....	5	1	6	....	....	....	....	....	....	....	....	....
	Harringay Racers	Britain	....	8	5	13	....	....	....	....	....	....	....	....	....
	Harringay Racers	Nat-Tmt	....	6	2	8	....	....	....	....	....	....	....	....	....
1938-39	Valleyfield Braves	QPHL	36	25	24	49	....	....	....	61	11	5	6	11	8
1939-40	**Detroit Red Wings**	**NHL**	**1**	**0**	**0**	**0**	**0**	**0**	**0**	**0**	....	....	....	....	....
	Omaha Knights	AHA	34	14	17	31	....	....	....	14	9	1	*7	8	19
	Ottawa Senators	QCHL	8	0	2	2	....	....	....	0	....	....	....	....	....
1940-41	Omaha Knights	AHA	32	8	14	22	....	....	....	13	....	....	....	....	....
1941-42	Fort Worth Rangers	AHA	50	*38	40	*78	....	....	....	31	5	3	4	7	7
1942-43	Toronto Navy	OHA-Sr.	10	3	15	18	....	....	....	4	10	7	9	16	8
1943-44			MILITARY SERVICE												
1944-45			MILITARY SERVICE												
1945-46	Tulsa Oilers	USHL	11	7	8	15	....	....	....	4	13	5	4	9	2
	Valleyfield Braves	QSHL	16	6	9	15	....	....	....	4	....	....	....	....	....
1946-47	Hamilton Tigers	OHA-Sr.	24	16	17	33	....	....	....	2	7	3	3	6	0
	Hamilton Tigers	Al-Cup	9	5	3	8	....	....	....	6	....	....	....	....	....
1947-48	Hamilton Tigers	OHA-Sr.	35	6	13	19	....	....	....	10	10	0	2	2	6
	Hamilton Tigers	Al-Cup	6	0	1	1	....	....	....	0	....	....	....	....	....
	NHL Totals		**1**	**0**	**0**	**0**	**0**	**0**	**0**	**0**	....	....	....	....	....

AHA Second All-Star Team (1942)

• PEIRSON, Johnny John Frederick

RW – R. 5′11″, 170 lbs. b: Winnipeg, Man., 7/21/1925.

Season	Club	League	GP	G	A	Pts	AG	AA	APts	PIM	GP	G	A	Pts	PIM
1943-44	Montreal Jr. Canadiens	QJHL	15	1	2	3	....	....	....	4	3	2	0	2	8
1944-45			MILITARY SERVICE												
1945-46	McGill University	MCHL	6	13	5	18	....	....	....	....	....	....	....	....	....
1946-47	**Boston Bruins**	**NHL**	**5**	**0**	**0**	**0**	**0**	**0**	**0**	**0**	....	....	....	....	....
	Boston Olympics	EAHL	10	5	10	15	....	....	....	24	....	....	....	....	....
	Hershey Bears	AHL	26	11	11	22	....	....	....	32	11	3	2	5	10
1947-48	**Boston Bruins**	**NHL**	**15**	**4**	**2**	**6**	**5**	**3**	**8**	**0**	**5**	**3**	**2**	**5**	**0**
	Hershey Bears	AHL	36	14	26	40	....	....	....	39	....	....	....	....	....
1948-49	**Boston Bruins**	**NHL**	**59**	**22**	**21**	**43**	**31**	**30**	**61**	**45**	**5**	**3**	**1**	**4**	**4**
1949-50	**Boston Bruins**	**NHL**	**57**	**27**	**25**	**52**	**34**	**30**	**64**	**49**	....	....	....	....	....
1950-51	**Boston Bruins**	**NHL**	**70**	**19**	**19**	**38**	**24**	**23**	**47**	**43**	**2**	**1**	**1**	**2**	**2**
1951-52	**Boston Bruins**	**NHL**	**68**	**20**	**30**	**50**	**27**	**37**	**64**	**30**	**7**	**0**	**2**	**2**	**4**
1952-53	**Boston Bruins**	**NHL**	**49**	**14**	**15**	**29**	**18**	**18**	**36**	**32**	**11**	**3**	**6**	**9**	**2**
1953-54	**Boston Bruins**	**NHL**	**68**	**21**	**19**	**40**	**29**	**23**	**52**	**55**	**4**	**0**	**0**	**0**	**2**
1954-55			OUT OF HOCKEY – RETIRED												
1955-56	**Boston Bruins**	**NHL**	**33**	**11**	**14**	**25**	**15**	**17**	**32**	**10**	....	....	....	....	....
1956-57	**Boston Bruins**	**NHL**	**68**	**13**	**26**	**39**	**17**	**29**	**46**	**41**	**10**	**0**	**3**	**3**	**12**
1957-58	**Boston Bruins**	**NHL**	**53**	**2**	**2**	**4**	**2**	**2**	**4**	**10**	**5**	**0**	**1**	**1**	**0**
	NHL Totals		**545**	**153**	**173**	**326**	**202**	**212**	**414**	**315**	**49**	**10**	**16**	**26**	**26**

Played in NHL All-Star Game (1950, 1951)

• Missed majority of 1955-56 season while still in retirement but returned as an active player in game vs. Chicago, December 15, 1955.

• PENNINGTON, Cliff Clifford

C – R. 6′, 170 lbs. b: Winnipeg, Man., 4/18/1940.

Season	Club	League	GP	G	A	Pts	AG	AA	APts	PIM	GP	G	A	Pts	PIM
1955-56	St. Boniface Canadiens	MJHL	1	1	1	2	....	....	....	0	1	1	1	2	0
	St. Boniface Canadiens	M-Cup	4	1	0	1	....	....	....	2	....	....	....	....	....
1956-57	St. Boniface Canadiens	MJHL	30	28	27	55	....	....	....	2	7	3	1	4	0
1957-58	Flin Flon Bombers	MJHL	47	32	39	71	....	....	....	8	12	*12	5	17	0
1958-59	Flin Flon Bombers	MJHL	48	*62	50	*112	....	....	....	4	11	14	9	23	4
	Winnipeg Warriors	WHL	5	4	1	5	....	....	....	0	....	....	....	....	....
	Flin Flon Bombers	M-Cup	10	10	10	20	....	....	....	4	....	....	....	....	....
1959-60	Kitchener Dutchmen	OHA-Sr.	47	23	28	51	....	....	....	5	6	4	6	10	0
	Canada	Olympics	5	0	2	2	....	....	....	4	....	....	....	....	....
	Winnipeg Warriors	WHL	2	1	1	2	....	....	....	2	....	....	....	....	....
	Flin Flon Bombers	MJHL	....	....	....	....	....	....	....	....	1	0	0	0	0
	Flin Flon Bombers	M-Cup	5	9	4	13	....	....	....	6	....	....	....	....	....
	Edmonton Oil Kings	M-Cup	6	6	2	8	....	....	....	0	....	....	....	....	....
1960-61	**Montreal Canadiens**	**NHL**	**4**	**1**	**0**	**1**	**1**	**0**	**1**	**0**	....	....	....	....	....
	Hull-Ottawa Canadiens	EPHL	65	33	*69	*102	....	....	....	10	14	4	*11	15	0
1961-62	**Boston Bruins**	**NHL**	**70**	**9**	**32**	**41**	**10**	**31**	**41**	**2**	....	....	....	....	....
1962-63	**Boston Bruins**	**NHL**	**27**	**7**	**10**	**17**	**8**	**10**	**18**	**4**	....	....	....	....	....
	Kingston Frontenacs	EPHL	39	21	41	62	....	....	....	6	5	2	*9	*11	0
1963-64	San Francisco Seals	WHL	26	6	15	21	....	....	....	4	....	....	....	....	....
	Quebec Aces	AHL	43	11	19	30	....	....	....	2	7	1	1	2	0
1964-65	Verdun Pirates	QSHL	STATISTICS NOT AVAILABLE												
1965-66	Los Angeles Blades	WHL	36	6	8	14	....	....	....	6	....	....	....	....	....
1966-67	Florida Rockets	EHL	64	37	49	86	....	....	....	2	....	....	....	....	....
1967-68	Nashville Dixie Flyers	EHL	68	49	66	115	....	....	....	18	4	3	3	6	0
1968-69	Nashville Dixie Flyers	EHL	72	59	58	117	....	....	....	26	14	6	11	17	4
1969-70	Des Moines Oak Leafs	IHL	72	43	57	100	....	....	....	6	3	1	2	3	0
1970-71	Des Moines–Flint	IHL	54	22	42	64	....	....	....	8	....	....	....	....	....
1971-72	St. Petersburg Suns	EHL	66	25	56	81	....	....	....	61	2	1	2	3	2
1972-73	Sun Coast Suns	EHL	48	25	47	72	....	....	....	10	....	....	....	....	....
1973-74	Sun Coast Suns	SHL	5	0	5	5	....	....	....	0	....	....	....	....	....
	NHL Totals		**101**	**17**	**42**	**59**	**19**	**41**	**60**	**6**	....	....	....	....	....

EPHL First All-Star Team (1962) • EHL South First All-Star Team (1969) • IHL First All-Star Team (1970) • Won James Gatschene Memorial Trophy (MVP - IHL) (1970)

Traded to **Boston** by **Montreal** with Terry Gray for Willie O'Ree and Stan Maxwell, June, 1961. Traded to **San Francisco** (WHL) by **Boston** for cash, June, 1963. Traded to **Boston** by **San Francisco** (WHL) for Gerry Odrowski and future considerations (loan of Dallas Smith for 1964-65 season, July 8, 1964), December 17, 1963. Signed as a free agent by **LA Blades** (WHL), August 22, 1965. Claimed on waivers by **Nashville** (EHL) from **Jacksonville** (EHL), October, 1967. Traded to **Des Moines** (IHL) by **Nashville** (EHL) for cash, October, 1969. Traded to **Flint** (IHL) by **Des Moines** (IHL) for Peter Mara, December, 1970. Traded to **Jacksonville** (EHL) by **Flint** (IHL) for Pierre Farmer, September, 1971. Traded to **St. Petersburg** (EHL) by **Jacksonville** for cash, December, 1971.

• PERREAULT, Fern

LW – L. 5′11″, 174 lbs. b: Chambly Bassin, Que., 3/31/1927.

Season	Club	League	GP	G	A	Pts	AG	AA	APts	PIM	GP	G	A	Pts	PIM
1944-45	Montreal Nationale	QJHL	11	3	2	5	....	....	....	8	....	....	....	....	....
1945-46	Montreal Nationale	QJHL	20	8	10	18	....	....	....	18	4	3	0	3	4
1946-47	New York Rovers	EAHL	44	11	13	24	....	....	....	15	8	0	0	0	2
1947-48	**New York Rangers**	**NHL**	**2**	**0**	**0**	**0**	**0**	**0**	**0**	**0**	....	....	....	....	....
	New York Rovers	EAHL	21	12	13	25	....	....	....	26	....	....	....	....	....
	New York Rovers	QSHL	35	6	17	23	....	....	....	18	4	1	1	2	4
1948-49	Tacoma Rockets	PCHL	70	37	40	77	....	....	....	67	6	5	2	7	9
1949-50	**New York Rangers**	**NHL**	**1**	**0**	**0**	**0**	**0**	**0**	**0**	**0**	....	....	....	....	....
	New Haven Ramblers	AHL	65	25	24	49	....	....	....	23	....	....	....	....	....
1950-51	Cincinnati Mohawks	AHL	70	26	30	56	....	....	....	16	....	....	....	....	....
1951-52	Cleveland Barons	AHL	27	9	14	23	....	....	....	18	....	....	....	....	....
	Montreal Royals	QMHL	28	7	12	19	....	....	....	14	7	1	2	3	8
1952-53	Chicoutimi Sagueneens	QMHL	45	5	18	23	....	....	....	26	20	9	10	19	18
1953-54	Chicoutimi Sagueneens	QHL	68	18	41	59	....	....	....	18	7	0	3	3	2
1954-55	Shawinigan Cataracts	QHL	57	17	37	54	....	....	....	42	12	3	4	7	10
	Shawinigan Cataracts	Ed-Cup	7	3	2	5	....	....	....	12	....	....	....	....	....
1955-56	Chicoutimi Sagueneens	QHL	64	17	33	50	....	....	....	46	5	2	1	3	4
1956-57	Chicoutimi Sagueneens	QHL	67	22	39	61	....	....	....	48	10	*8	5	13	8
1957-58	Chicoutimi Sagueneens	QHL	50	30	23	53	....	....	....	42	6	1	0	1	6
1958-59	Montreal Royals	QHL	61	25	30	55	....	....	....	34	8	1	*5	6	4
1959-60	Montreal Royals	EPHL	30	6	3	9	....	....	....	14	....	....	....	....	....
	NHL Totals		**3**	**0**	**0**	**0**	**0**	**0**	**0**	**0**	....	....	....	....	....

PCHL Northern First All-Star Team (1949)

Traded to **Cleveland** (AHL) by **NY Rangers** with Ed Reigle, Jackie Gordon, Fred Shero and cash for Hy Buller and Wally Hergesheimer, May 14, 1951. Traded to **Chicoutimi** (QMHL) by **Montreal** (QMHL) for Jimmy Moore, September 25, 1952.

• PETERS, Frank "Frosty"

D – R. 5′11″, 160 lbs. b: Rouses Point, NY, 6/5/1905 Deceased.

Season	Club	League	GP	G	A	Pts	AG	AA	APts	PIM	GP	G	A	Pts	PIM
1922-23	Edmonton Yeomen	EJrHL	STATISTICS NOT AVAILABLE												
1923-24	Crowsnest Monarchs	ASHL	STATISTICS NOT AVAILABLE												
1924-25	Boston Maples	USAHA	7	2	0	2	....	....	....	....	....	....	....	....	....
1925-26	Eveleth-Hibbing Rangers	CHL	30	0	1	1	....	....	....	7	....	....	....	....	....
1926-27	Eveluth-Hibbing Rangers	CHL	STATISTICS NOT AVAILABLE												
1927-28	Philadelphia Arrows	Can-Am	18	3	0	3	....	....	....	22	....	....	....	....	....
	Windsor Hornets	Can-Pro	8	0	0	0	....	....	....	10	....	....	....	....	....
1928-29	Philadelphia Arrows	Can-Am	38	4	3	7	....	....	....	93	....	....	....	....	....
1929-30	Philadelphia Arrows	Can-Am	39	10	5	15	....	....	....	*135	2	0	0	0	0
1930-31	**New York Rangers**	**NHL**	**43**	**0**	**0**	**0**	**0**	**0**	**0**	**59**	**4**	**0**	**0**	**0**	**2**
1931-32	Detroit Olympics	IHL	48	1	11	12	....	....	....	75	6	0	0	0	4
1932-33	Philadelphia Arrows	Can-Am	46	3	1	4	....	....	....	103	3	0	0	0	2
1933-34	Philadelphia Arrows	Can-Am	40	2	2	4	....	....	....	61	2	0	0	0	2
	NHL Totals		**43**	**0**	**0**	**0**	**0**	**0**	**0**	**59**	**4**	**0**	**0**	**0**	**2**

Traded to **NY Rangers** by **Philadelphia** (Can-Am) for cash, February 18, 1930. Traded to **Detroit** by **NY Rangers** for cash, October 19, 1931. Traded to **NY Rangers** by **Detroit** for Sparky Vail, September, 1932. Traded to **Philadelphia** (Can-Am) by **NY Rangers** for George Nichols, September, 1932.

• PETERS, Garry — *see page 1515*

• PETERS, Jimmy Jr. — *see page 1515*

• PETERS, Jimmy Sr. James Meldrum

RW – R. 5′11″, 165 lbs. b: Montreal, Que., 10/2/1922.

Season	Club	League	GP	G	A	Pts	AG	AA	APts	PIM	GP	G	A	Pts	PIM
1939-40	Verdun Jr. Maple Leafs	QJHL	11	0	3	3	....	....	....	10	4	0	0	0	0
	Verdun Jr. Maple Leafs	M-Cup	7	1	3	4	....	....	....	0	....	....	....	....	....
1940-41	Montreal Jr. Canadiens	QJHL	11	7	8	15	....	....	....	6	4	1	*4	5	4
	Montreal Jr. Royals	M-Cup	16	8	11	19	....	....	....	22	....	....	....	....	....
	Montreal Sr. Canadiens	QSHL	1	0	0	0	....	....	....	0	....	....	....	....	....
1941-42	Springfield Indians	AHL	24	1	9	10	....	....	....	4	4	1	1	2	0
1942-43	Montreal Army	MCHL	5	3	5	8	....	....	....	4	....	....	....	....	....
	Montreal Army	MCHL	27	16	18	34	....	....	....	15	3	0	1	1	4
1943-44	Montreal Army	MCHL	2	0	0	0	....	....	....	0	....	....	....	....	....
	Kingston Army	OHA-Sr.	13	13	15	28	....	....	....	10	....	....	....	....	....
1944-45	Canadian Army Recovery	Belgium	STATISTICS NOT AVAILABLE												
♦1945-46	**Montreal Canadiens**	**NHL**	**47**	**11**	**19**	**30**	**13**	**28**	**41**	**10**	**9**	**3**	**1**	**4**	**6**
	Montreal Royals	QSHL	1	1	0	1	....	....	....	0	....	....	....	....	....
1946-47	**Montreal Canadiens**	**NHL**	**60**	**11**	**13**	**24**	**12**	**16**	**28**	**27**	**11**	**1**	**2**	**3**	**10**
1947-48	**Montreal Canadiens**	**NHL**	**22**	**1**	**3**	**4**	**1**	**4**	**5**	**6**	....	....	....	....	....
	Boston Bruins	**NHL**	**37**	**12**	**15**	**27**	**15**	**20**	**35**	**38**	**5**	**1**	**2**	**3**	**2**
1948-49	**Boston Bruins**	**NHL**	**60**	**16**	**15**	**31**	**22**	**21**	**43**	**8**	**4**	**0**	**1**	**1**	**0**
♦1949-50	**Detroit Red Wings**	**NHL**	**70**	**14**	**16**	**30**	**18**	**19**	**37**	**20**	**8**	**0**	**2**	**2**	**0**
1950-51	**Detroit Red Wings**	**NHL**	**68**	**17**	**21**	**38**	**22**	**26**	**48**	**14**	**6**	**0**	**0**	**0**	**0**
1951-52	**Chicago Black Hawks**	**NHL**	**70**	**15**	**21**	**36**	**20**	**26**	**46**	**16**	....	....	....	....	....
1952-53	**Chicago Black Hawks**	**NHL**	**69**	**22**	**19**	**41**	**29**	**23**	**52**	**16**	**7**	**0**	**1**	**1**	**4**

Season	Club	League	GP	G	A	Pts	AG	AA	APts	PIM	GP	G	A	Pts	PIM
			REGULAR SEASON								PLAYOFFS				
1953-54	**Chicago Black Hawks**	**NHL**	**46**	**6**	**4**	**10**	**8**	**5**	**13**	**21**	....	....	....	....	....
♦	**Detroit Red Wings**	**NHL**	**25**	**0**	**4**	**4**	**0**	**5**	**5**	**10**	**10**	**0**	**0**	**0**	**0**
1954-55	Windsor Bulldogs	OHA-Sr.	46	25	31	56	....	....	....	62	12	10	7	17	2
1955-56	Windsor Bulldogs	OHA-Sr.	48	12	37	49	....	....	....	72	....	....	....	....	....
	NHL Totals		**574**	**125**	**150**	**275**	**160**	**193**	**353**	**186**	**60**	**5**	**9**	**14**	**22**

• Father of Jimmy Jr. • Played in NHL All-Star Game (1950)

Signed as a free agent by **Brooklyn**, October 28, 1941. Rights transferred to **Buffalo** from **Brooklyn** in Special Dispersal Draft, October 9, 1942. Claimed by **Montreal** from **Buffalo** (AHL) in Inter-League Draft, June 14, 1945. Traded to **Boston** by **Montreal** with John Quilty for Joe Carveth, December 17, 1947. Traded to **Detroit** by **Boston** with Pete Babando, Clare Martin and Lloyd Durham for Bill Quakenbush and Pete Horeck, August 16, 1949. Traded to **Chicago** by **Detroit** with George Gee, Clare Martin, Rags Raglan, Max McNab and Jim McFadden for $75,000 and future considerations (Hugh Coflin, October, 1951), August 20, 1951. Traded to **Detroit** by **Chicago** for future considerations, January 25, 1954.

• PETTINGER, Eric

Eric Robinson "Cowboy"
LW/C – L. 6', 175 lbs. b: North Bierley, England, 12/14/1904 d: 12/24/1968.

Season	Club	League	GP	G	A	Pts	AG	AA	APts	PIM	GP	G	A	Pts	PIM
1921-22	Regina Pats	S-SJHL	5	4	1	5	....	....	....	2	....	....	....	....	....
	Regina Pats	M-Cup	8	1	0	1	....	....	....	*12	....	....	....	....	....
1922-23	Regina Pats	RJrHL	4	5	1	6	....	....	....	0	....	....	....	....	....
	Regina Victorias	S-SSHL	1	0	0	0	....	....	....	0	....	....	....	....	....
	Regina Pats	M-Cup	6	2	1	3	....	....	....	*8	....	....	....	....	....
1923-24	Regina Pats	RJrHL	6	8	3	11	....	....	....	*14	5	6	2	8	6
	Regina Victorias	S-SSHL	3	0	0	0	....	....	....	0	....	....	....	....	....
	Regina Pats	M-Cup	5	6	2	8	....	....	....	6	....	....	....	....	....
1924-25	Regina Victorias	S-SSHL	9	*9	*4	*13	....	....	....	4	....	....	....	....	....
	Regina Victorias	Al-Cup	5	4	2	6	....	....	....	4	....	....	....	....	....
1925-26	Regina Victorias	S-SSHL	17	17	10	27	....	....	....	24	9	7	4	11	6
	Regina Victorias	Al-Cup	9	7	4	11	....	....	....	6	....	....	....	....	....
1926-27	Fort William Forts	MTBHL	20	7	5	12	....	....	....	37	2	*2	*1	*3	0
1927-28	Fort William Forts	MTBHL	17	22	10	32	....	....	....	12	2	0	0	0	0
1928-29	**Boston Bruins**	**NHL**	**17**	**0**	**0**	**0**	**0**	**0**	**0**	**17**	....	....	....	....	....
	Toronto Maple Leafs	**NHL**	**25**	**3**	**3**	**6**	**9**	**20**	**29**	**24**	**4**	**1**	**0**	**1**	**8**
1929-30	**Toronto Maple Leafs**	**NHL**	**43**	**4**	**9**	**13**	**6**	**21**	**27**	**40**	....	....	....	....	....
1930-31	**Ottawa Senators**	**NHL**	**13**	**0**	**0**	**0**	**0**	**0**	**0**	**2**	....	....	....	....	....
	London Panthers	IHL	36	9	5	14	....	....	....	44	....	....	....	....	....
1931-32	London Tecumsehs	IHL	48	21	12	33	....	....	....	46	6	0	1	1	8
1932-33	London Tecumsehs	IHL	43	20	21	41	....	....	....	54	6	0	0	0	9
1933-34	London Tecumsehs	IHL	43	11	12	23	....	....	....	41	6	4	3	7	0
1934-35	London Tecumsehs	IHL	44	10	15	25	....	....	....	45	5	4	0	4	5
1935-36	London Tecumsehs	IHL	47	23	19	42	....	....	....	43	2	0	2	2	2
1936-37	Cleveland Barons	IAHL	10	1	0	1	....	....	....	0	....	....	....	....	....
	Portland Buckaroos	PCHL	1	0	0	0	....	....	....	0	....	....	....	....	....
	Pittsburgh Hornets	IAHL	2	0	0	0	....	....	....	0	....	....	....	....	....
	NHL Totals		**98**	**7**	**12**	**19**	**15**	**41**	**56**	**83**	**4**	**1**	**0**	**1**	**8**

• Brother of Gord • IHL First All-Star Team (1936)

Signed as a free agent by **NY Rangers**, September, 1927. Rights traded to **Toronto** by **NY Rangers** for the rights to Yip Foster, October, 1927. Rights traded to **Boston** by **Toronto** with $15,000 for Jimmy Herbert, December 21, 1927. Traded to **Toronto** by **Boston** with the rights to Hugh Plaxton for the rights to George Owen, January 10, 1929. Traded to **Ottawa** by **Toronto** with Art Smith and $35,000 for King Clancy, October 11, 1930. Traded to **London** (IHL) by **Ottawa** for cash, October 31, 1932.

• PETTINGER, Gord

Gordon Robert "Gosh"
C – L. 6', 175 lbs. b: Harrogate, England, 11/11/1911 d: 4/12/1986.

Season	Club	League	GP	G	A	Pts	AG	AA	APts	PIM	GP	G	A	Pts	PIM
1928-29	Regina Pats	S-SJHL	6	*5	1	6	....	....	....	2	....	....	....	....	....
	Regina Pats	M-Cup	6	6	0	6	....	....	....	4	....	....	....	....	....
1929-30	Regina Pats	S-SJHL	3	*2	*2	*4	....	....	....	4	....	....	....	....	....
	Regina Pats	M-Cup	8	*5	1	6	....	....	....	*12	....	....	....	....	....
1930-31	Vancouver Lions	NWHL	33	5	5	10	....	....	....	10	4	0	1	1	0
1931-32	Bronx Tigers	Can-Am	39	14	18	32	....	....	....	34	2	0	*2	2	6
♦1932-33	**New York Rangers**	**NHL**	**34**	**1**	**2**	**3**	**2**	**4**	**6**	**18**	**8**	**0**	**0**	**0**	**0**
	Springfield Indians	Can-Am	13	7	5	12	....	....	....	12	....	....	....	....	....
1933-34	**Detroit Red Wings**	**NHL**	**48**	**3**	**14**	**17**	**5**	**29**	**34**	**14**	**7**	**1**	**0**	**1**	**2**
	Detroit Olympics	IHL	1	0	0	0	....	....	....	0	....	....	....	....	....
1934-35	**Detroit Red Wings**	**NHL**	**13**	**2**	**3**	**5**	**3**	**5**	**8**	**2**	....	....	....	....	....
	London Tecumsehs	IHL	44	10	15	25	....	....	....	45	5	4	0	4	5
♦1935-36	**Detroit Red Wings**	**NHL**	**30**	**8**	**7**	**15**	**15**	**13**	**28**	**6**	**7**	**2**	**2**	**4**	**0**
	Detroit Olympics	IHL	18	9	16	25	....	....	....	10	....	....	....	....	....
♦1936-37	**Detroit Red Wings**	**NHL**	**48**	**7**	**15**	**22**	**12**	**28**	**40**	**13**	**10**	**0**	**2**	**2**	**2**
1937-38	**Detroit Red Wings**	**NHL**	**12**	**1**	**3**	**4**	**2**	**5**	**7**	**4**	....	....	....	....	....
	Boston Bruins	**NHL**	**35**	**7**	**10**	**17**	**11**	**16**	**27**	**10**	**3**	**0**	**0**	**0**	**0**
♦1938-39	**Boston Bruins**	**NHL**	**48**	**11**	**14**	**25**	**19**	**22**	**41**	**8**	**12**	**1**	**1**	**2**	**7**
1939-40	**Boston Bruins**	**NHL**	**24**	**2**	**6**	**8**	**3**	**9**	**12**	**2**	....	....	....	....	....
	Hershey Bears	IAHL	29	9	12	21	....	....	....	0	5	1	1	2	4
1940-41	Hershey Bears	AHL	52	13	28	41	....	....	....	4	6	2	*6	8	2
1941-42	Hershey Bears	AHL	56	12	38	50	....	....	....	8	10	2	8	10	2
1942-43			MILITARY SERVICE												
1943-44			MILITARY SERVICE												
1944-45	Hershey Bears	AHL	32	5	12	17	....	....	....	0	....	....	....	....	....
	Cleveland Barons	AHL	12	1	3	4	....	....	....	4	....	....	....	....	....
1945-46	Regina Capitals	WCSHL	8	2	6	8	....	....	....	0	....	....	....	....	....
	NHL Totals		**292**	**42**	**74**	**116**	**72**	**131**	**203**	**77**	**47**	**4**	**5**	**9**	**11**

• Brother of Eric

Signed as a free agent by **NY Rangers**, October 29, 1930. Traded to **Detroit** by **NY Rangers** for cash, October 23, 1933. Traded to **Boston** by **Detroit** for Red Beattie, December 19, 1937.

• PHILLIPS, Batt

William John Orville
C – L. 5'10", 163 lbs. b: Carleton Place, Ont., 9/23/1902 d: 1/10/1978.

Season	Club	League	GP	G	A	Pts	AG	AA	APts	PIM	GP	G	A	Pts	PIM
1922-23	Carelton Place Seniors	UOVHL	12	17	5	22	....	....	....	....	....	....	....	....	....
1923-24			STATISTICS NOT AVAILABLE												
1924-25	New York Athletics	USAHA	STATISTICS NOT AVAILABLE												
1925-26	Brandon Regals	S-SSHL	15	12	3	15	....	....	....	14	....	....	....	....	....
1926-27	Kenora Thistles	TBSHL	19	15	5	20	....	....	....	15	....	....	....	....	....
1927-28	Winnipeg Maroons	AHA	10	1	0	1	....	....	....	8	....	....	....	....	....
1928-29	Vancouver Lions	PCHL	32	10	9	19	....	....	....	81	3	1	1	2	4
1929-30	Vancouver Lions	PCHL	11	5	1	6	....	....	....	10	....	....	....	....	....
	Montreal Maroons	**NHL**	**27**	**1**	**1**	**2**	**1**	**2**	**3**	**6**	**4**	**0**	**0**	**0**	**2**
	Windsor Bulldogs	IHL	1	1	0	1	....	....	....	0	....	....	....	....	....
1930-31	Windsor Bulldogs	IHL	35	6	17	23	....	....	....	20	6	2	1	3	2
1931-32	Windsor Bulldogs	IHL	47	7	14	21	....	....	....	37	6	0	0	0	7
1932-33	Philadelphia Arrows	Can-Am	47	10	24	34	....	....	....	47	5	0	0	0	0
1933-34	Windsor Bulldogs	IHL	13	3	1	4	....	....	....	6	....	....	....	....	....
	Quebec Castors	Can-Am	31	4	4	8	....	....	....	6	....	....	....	....	....
1934-35	Quebec Castors	Can-Am	39	4	16	20	....	....	....	4	3	0	0	0	0
	Cleveland Falcons	IHL	2	0	0	0	....	....	....	2	....	....	....	....	....
1935-36			DID NOT PLAY – REFEREE												
1937-38	Carleton Place Red Wings	UOVHL	6	1	7	8	....	....	....	2	5	4	5	*9	4
1938-39	Carleton Place Red Wings	UOVHL	14	7	10	17	....	....	....	4	4	2	4	6	0
1939-40	Carleton Place Red Wings	UOVHL	11	3	9	12	....	....	....	4	3	0	0	0	0
1940-41	Nanaimo Clippers	PCSHL	STATISTICS NOT AVAILABLE												
1941-42	Nanaimo Clippers	PCSHL	15	2	4	6	....	....	....	9	....	....	....	....	....
	NHL Totals		**27**	**1**	**1**	**2**	**1**	**2**	**3**	**6**	**4**	**0**	**0**	**0**	**2**

Traded to **Montreal Maroons** by **Vancouver** (PCHL) for $10,000, December 17, 1929. Traded to **Philadelphia** (Can-Am) by **Montreal Maroons** for cash, October 22, 1932.

• PHILLIPS, Charlie

D – L. 5'11", 200 lbs. b: Toronto, Ont., 5/10/1917.

Season	Club	League	GP	G	A	Pts	AG	AA	APts	PIM	GP	G	A	Pts	PIM
1935-36	Toronto Young Rangers	OHA-Jr.	STATISTICS NOT AVAILABLE												
1936-37	Toronto Lions	OHA-B	12	8	2	10	....	....	....	14	....	....	....	....	....
1937-38	Moncton Maroons	SNBHL	29	24	9	33	....	....	....	*90	3	1	0	1	8
	Moncton Maroons	Al-Cup	8	8	3	11	....	....	....	*29	....	....	....	....	....
1938-39	Saint John Beavers	X-Games	34	16	16	32	....	....	....	*60	....	....	....	....	....
	Saint John Beavers	Al-Cup	13	7	9	16	....	....	....	20	....	....	....	....	....
1939-40	Glace Bay Miners	CBSHL	40	8	7	15	....	....	....	33	4	1	0	1	2
1940-41	Glace Bay Miners	CBSHL	43	6	14	20	....	....	....	51	4	1	0	1	10
1941-42	Glace Bay Miners	CBSHL	40	29	33	62	....	....	....	*97	7	*6	5	*11	*18
1942-43	**Montreal Canadiens**	**NHL**	**17**	**0**	**0**	**0**	**0**	**0**	**0**	**6**	....	....	....	....	....
	Washington Lions	AHL	10	5	3	8	....	....	....	14	....	....	....	....	....
1943-44	Kingston Army	OHA-Sr.	14	1	5	6	....	....	....	17	....	....	....	....	....
1944-45	Providence Reds	AHL	4	0	0	0	....	....	....	0	....	....	....	....	....
1945-46	Lachine Rapides	QPHL	3	0	0	0	....	....	....	0	4	2	2	4	2
1946-47	Montreal Royals	QSHL	1	0	0	0	....	....	....	0	....	....	....	....	....
	Lachine Rapides	QPHL	14	4	4	8	....	....	....	4	....	....	....	....	....
	Washington Lions	EAHL	14	9	7	16	....	....	....	21	9	4	3	7	9
1947-48	Glace Bay Miners	CBSHL	47	17	17	34	....	....	....	105	4	2	1	3	4
	Moncton Hawks	MSHL	....	....	....	....	....	....	....	....	1	1	0	1	0
1948-49	Saint John Beavers	MSHL	48	20	20	40	....	....	....	57	7	2	0	2	4
1949-50	Glace Bay Miners	CBSHL	66	11	29	40	....	....	....	31	10	1	3	4	6
1950-51	Moncton Hawks	MMHL	19	5	2	7	....	....	....	4	....	....	....	....	....
	Kentville Wildcats	NSAPC	DID NOT PLAY – COACHING												
1951-52	Dieppe Goats	MCIHL	STATISTICS NOT AVAILABLE												
	NHL Totals		**17**	**0**	**0**	**0**	**0**	**0**	**0**	**6**	....	....	....	....	....

• PHILLIPS, Merlyn

Merlyn John "Bill"
C – R. 5'7", 160 lbs. b: Richmond Hill, Ont., 5/24/1899 Deceased.

Season	Club	League	GP	G	A	Pts	AG	AA	APts	PIM	GP	G	A	Pts	PIM
1914-15	U. of Western Ontario	OHA-Jr.	STATISTICS NOT AVAILABLE												
1915-16	London Ontarios	OHA-Jr.	STATISTICS NOT AVAILABLE												
1916-17	London AAB	OHA-Jr.	STATISTICS NOT AVAILABLE												
	London 149th	OHA-Sr.	STATISTICS NOT AVAILABLE												
1917-18	Campbellton Army	NNBHL	STATISTICS NOT AVAILABLE												
1919-20	S. S. Marie Greyhounds	NOHA	2	1	1	2	....	....	....	2	....	....	....	....	....
	S. S. Marie Greyhounds	NMHL	5	5	3	8	....	....	....	....	....	....	....	....	....
1920-21	S. S. Marie Greyhounds	NOHA	9	8	*9	17	....	....	....	38	5	4	*3	*7	....
	S. S. Marie Greyhounds	NMHL	13	11	11	22	....	....	....	....	....	....	....	....	....
1921-22	S. S. Marie Greyhounds	NOHA	8	9	6	15	....	....	....	22	2	....	1	....	2
	S. S. Marie Greyhounds	NMHL	12	10	*14	24	....	....	....	....	....	....	....	....	....
1922-23	S. S. Marie Greyhounds	NOHA	8	*8	3	*11	....	....	....	12	2	1	0	1	*4
	S. S. Marie Greyhounds	Al-Cup	5	*9	1	*10	....	....	....	4	....	....	....	....	....
1923-24	S. S. Marie Greyhounds	NOHA	8	6	*8	*14	....	....	....	10	7	5	*6	11	8
1924-25	S. S. Marie Greyhounds	NOHA	STATISTICS NOT AVAILABLE												
1925-26	S. S. Marie Greyhounds	CHL	20	9	4	13	....	....	....	32	....	....	....	....	....
	Montreal Maroons	**NHL**	**12**	**3**	**1**	**4**	**5**	**6**	**11**	**6**	**4**	**3**	**0**	**3**	**4**
♦	Montreal Maroons	St-Cup	4	1	1	2	....	....	....	0	....	....	....	....	....
1926-27	**Montreal Maroons**	**NHL**	**43**	**15**	**1**	**16**	**27**	**5**	**32**	**45**	**2**	**0**	**0**	**0**	**0**
1927-28	**Montreal Maroons**	**NHL**	**40**	**7**	**5**	**12**	**14**	**28**	**42**	**33**	**9**	**2**	**1**	**3**	**9**
1928-29	**Montreal Maroons**	**NHL**	**42**	**6**	**5**	**11**	**17**	**33**	**50**	**41**	....	....	....	....	....
1929-30	**Montreal Maroons**	**NHL**	**44**	**13**	**10**	**23**	**18**	**24**	**42**	**48**	**4**	**0**	**0**	**0**	**2**
1930-31	**Montreal Maroons**	**NHL**	**43**	**6**	**1**	**7**	**12**	**3**	**15**	**38**	**1**	**0**	**0**	**0**	**2**
	Windsor Bulldogs	IHL	3	3	1	4	....	....	....	0	....	....	....	....	....
1931-32	**Montreal Maroons**	**NHL**	**46**	**1**	**1**	**2**	**2**	**2**	**4**	**11**	**4**	**0**	**0**	**0**	**2**
1932-33	**Montreal Maroons**	**NHL**	**2**	**0**	**0**	**0**	**0**	**0**	**0**	**0**	....	....	....	....	....
	New York Americans	**NHL**	**30**	**1**	**7**	**8**	**2**	**14**	**16**	**10**	....	....	....	....	....
	NHL Totals		**302**	**52**	**31**	**83**	**97**	**115**	**212**	**232**	**24**	**5**	**1**	**6**	**19**

Signed as a free agent by **Montreal Maroons**, February 17, 1926. • 1925-26 Montreal Maroons playoff totals includes series against Ottawa and Pittsburgh. Signed as a free agent by **NY Americans**, November 21, 1932.

• PICARD, Noel

— *see page 1519*

• PICKETTS, Hal

Frederick Harold
RW – R. 6', 183 lbs. b: Asquith, Sask., 4/22/1909.

Season	Club	League	GP	G	A	Pts	AG	AA	APts	PIM	GP	G	A	Pts	PIM
1927-28	Saskatoon Hilltops	N-SJHL	1	0	1	1	....	....	....	0	5	1	1	2	13
	Saskatoon Tigers	S-SSHL	2	0	0	0	....	....	....	0	....	....	....	....	....
1928-29	Saskatoon Hilltops	N-SJHL	STATISTICS NOT AVAILABLE												
1929-30	Biggar Nationals	W-SSHL	10	4	0	4	....	....	....	8	....	....	....	....	....
1930-31	North Battleford Beavers	N-SSHL	19	7	3	10	....	....	....	18	4	2	1	*3	6
1931-32	Bronx Tigers	Can-Am	37	2	0	2	....	....	....	30	2	0	0	0	0
1932-33	New Haven Eagles	Can-Am	46	8	3	11	....	....	....	90	....	....	....	....	....
1933-34	**New York Americans**	**NHL**	**48**	**3**	**1**	**4**	**5**	**2**	**7**	**32**	....	....	....	....	....
1934-35	Buffalo Bisons	IHL	30	8	2	10	....	....	....	30	....	....	....	....	....
1935-36	Rochester Cardinals	IHL	16	3	1	4	....	....	....	13	....	....	....	....	....
	London Tecumsehs	IHL	27	1	2	3	....	....	....	19	2	0	0	0	4
1936-37	Spokane Clippers	PCHL	32	7	1	8	....	....	....	53	6	1	0	1	6

Season	Club	League	REGULAR SEASON GP	G	A	Pts	AG	AA	APts	PIM	PLAYOFFS GP	G	A	Pts	PIM
1937-38	Spokane Clippers	PCHL	34	3	2	5	....	....	....	42	....	....	....	....	....
1938-39			REINSTATED AS AN AMATEUR												
1939-40	Saskatoon Quakers	N-SSHL	8	0	0	0	....	....	....	11	....	....	....	....	....
	Yorkton Terriers	S-SSHL	14	4	4	8	....	....	....	21	5	0	0	0	6
1940-41	Yorkton Terriers	S-SSHL	31	4	9	13	....	....	....	30	9	2	2	4	18
	NHL Totals		**48**	**3**	**1**	**4**	**5**	**2**	**7**	**32**	....	....	....	....	....

Loaned to **Rochester** (IHL) by **NY Americans** for cash, November 8, 1935. Traded to **London** (IHL) by **NY Americans** for cash, January 3, 1936.

• PIDHIRNY, Harry

C – L. 5′11″, 155 lbs. b: Toronto, Ont., 3/5/1928.

Season	Club	League	GP	G	A	Pts	AG	AA	APts	PIM	GP	G	A	Pts	PIM
1944-45	Toronto Young Rangers	OHA-Jr.	20	11	3	14	....	....	....	4	5	3	3	6	0
1945-46	Toronto Young Rangers	OHA-Jr.	25	9	13	22	....	....	....	0	2	2	0	2	0
	Toronto Mahers	TIHL	12	4	4	8	....	....	....	2	10	2	2	4	0
1946-47	Toronto Young Rangers	OHA-Jr.	14	11	8	19	....	....	....	5	....	....	....	....	....
1947-48	Galt Rockets	OHA-Jr.	36	22	26	48	....	....	....	23	8	*11	8	19	5
	Toronto Mahers	TIHL	....	....	....	....	....	....	....	....	4	2	2	4	4
1948-49	Philadelphia Rockets	AHL	68	19	20	39	....	....	....	13	....	....	....	....	....
1949-50	Springfield Indians	AHL	70	21	28	49	....	....	....	6	2	0	0	0	0
1950-51	Springfield Indians	AHL	64	30	28	58	....	....	....	8	1	0	0	0	0
1951-52	Syracuse Warriors	AHL	56	25	23	48	....	....	....	4	....	....	....	....	....
1952-53	Syracuse Warriors	AHL	63	34	30	64	....	....	....	2	4	2	1	3	0
1953-54	Syracuse Warriors	AHL	51	31	12	43	....	....	....	4	....	....	....	....	....
1954-55	Springfield Indians	AHL	64	23	27	50	....	....	....	14	4	2	0	2	0
1955-56	Springfield Indians	AHL	63	32	39	71	....	....	....	16	....	....	....	....	....
1956-57	Springfield Indians	AHL	60	23	28	51	....	....	....	8	....	....	....	....	....
1957-58	**Boston Bruins**	**NHL**	**2**	**0**	**0**	**0**	**0**	**0**	**0**	**0**	....	....	....	....	....
	Springfield Indians	AHL	68	20	28	48	....	....	....	6	13	0	4	4	0
1958-59	Springfield Indians	AHL	70	21	*60	81	....	....	....	26	....	....	....	....	....
1959-60	Springfield Indians	AHL	69	31	36	67	....	....	....	10	10	5	6	11	0
1960-61	Springfield Indians	AHL	71	34	37	71	....	....	....	19	8	*5	5	*10	0
1961-62	San Francisco Seals	WHL	66	24	34	58	....	....	....	12	2	1	2	3	0
1962-63	Providence Reds	AHL	53	13	22	35	....	....	....	4	4	0	1	1	2
1963-64	Baltimore Clippers	AHL	62	10	20	30	....	....	....	4	....	....	....	....	....
1964-65	Baltimore Clippers	AHL	72	8	11	19	....	....	....	12	5	0	0	0	2
1965-66	Baltimore Clippers	AHL	47	1	4	5	....	....	....	6	....	....	....	....	....
1966-67	Springfield Indians	AHL	DID NOT PLAY – COACHING												
1967-68	Muskegon Mohawks	IHL	36	15	23	38	....	....	....	4	9	5	2	7	0
1968-69	Syracuse Blazers	EHL	DID NOT PLAY – COACHING												
1969-70	Barrie Flyers	OHA-Sr.	4	1	1	2	....	....	....	0	....	....	....	....	....
	NHL Totals		**2**	**0**	**0**	**0**	**0**	**0**	**0**	**0**	....	....	....	....	....

AHL Second All-Star Team (1959)

Traded to **Springfield** (AHL) by **Philadelphia** (AHL) for cash, September, 1949. Transferred to **Syracuse** (AHL) after **Springfield** (AHL) franchise relocated, October, 1951. Transferred to **Springfield** (AHL) after **Syracuse** (AHL) franchise relocated, October, 1954. Traded to **San Francisco** (WHL) by **Boston** (Springfield-AHL) for cash, September, 1961. Traded to **Montreal** by **San Francisco** (WHL) for Moe Mantha and the loan of Camille Bedard, Gary Mork and Norm Waslowski, September 12, 1962. Traded to **Providence** (AHL) by **Montreal** for cash, October, 1962.

• PIKE, Alf

Alfred George "The Embalmer"

LW/C – L. 6′, 187 lbs. b: Winnipeg, Man., 9/15/1917.

Season	Club	League	GP	G	A	Pts	AG	AA	APts	PIM	GP	G	A	Pts	PIM
1934-35	East Kildonen Bisons	MAHA	STATISTICS NOT AVAILABLE												
1935-36	Winnipeg Monarchs	MJHL	14	10	11	21	....	....	....	20	....	....	....	....	....
1936-37	Winnipeg Monarchs	MJHL	14	10	10	20	....	....	....	21	8	2	*10	*12	*21
	Winnipeg Monarchs	M-Cup	9	7	6	13	....	....	....	4	....	....	....	....	....
1937-38	New York Rovers	EAHL	45	16	23	39	....	....	....	58	....	....	....	....	....
1938-39	New York Rovers	EAHL	25	9	4	13	....	....	....	12	....	....	....	....	....
	Philadelphia Ramblers	IAHL	3	1	1	2	....	....	....	0	9	4	2	6	4
♦1939-40	**New York Rangers**	**NHL**	**47**	**8**	**9**	**17**	**13**	**14**	**27**	**38**	**12**	**3**	**1**	**4**	**6**
1940-41	**New York Rangers**	**NHL**	**48**	**6**	**13**	**19**	**9**	**19**	**28**	**23**	**3**	**0**	**1**	**1**	**2**
1941-42	**New York Rangers**	**NHL**	**34**	**8**	**19**	**27**	**11**	**23**	**34**	**16**	**6**	**1**	**0**	**1**	**4**
1942-43	**New York Rangers**	**NHL**	**41**	**6**	**16**	**22**	**6**	**15**	**21**	**48**	....	....	....	....	....
1943-44	Winnipeg RCAF	WNDHL	9	3	4	7	....	....	....	10	....	....	....	....	....
1944-45	Winnipeg RCAF	WNDHL	9	5	2	7	....	....	....	20	....	....	....	....	....
1945-46	**New York Rangers**	**NHL**	**33**	**7**	**9**	**16**	**8**	**13**	**21**	**18**	....	....	....	....	....
1946-47	**New York Rangers**	**NHL**	**31**	**7**	**11**	**18**	**8**	**13**	**21**	**2**	....	....	....	....	....
1947-48	Winnipeg Nationals	MTBHL	11	5	1	6	....	....	....	17	....	....	....	....	....
1948-49	Winnipeg Nationals	MTBHL	2	2	4	6	....	....	....	4	....	....	....	....	....
1949-50	Guelph Biltmores	OHA-Jr.	DID NOT PLAY – COACHING												
	NHL Totals		**234**	**42**	**77**	**119**	**55**	**97**	**152**	**145**	**21**	**4**	**2**	**6**	**12**

• PILOTE, Pierre

— see page 1521

• PITRE, Didier

"Cannonball" **HHOF**

RW/D – R. 5′11″, 185 lbs. b: Valleyfield, Que., 9/1/1883 d: 7/29/1934.

Season	Club	League	GP	G	A	Pts	AG	AA	APts	PIM	GP	G	A	Pts	PIM
1903-04	Montreal Nationals	FAHL	2	1	0	1	....	....	....	0	....	....	....	....	....
1904-05	Montreal Nationals	CAHL	2	0	0	0	....	....	....	0	....	....	....	....	....
	American Soo Indians	IHL	13	11	0	11	....	....	....	6	....	....	....	....	....
1905-06	American Soo Indians	IHL	22	*41	0	*41	....	....	....	29	....	....	....	....	....
1906-07	American Soo Indians	IHL	23	25	11	36	....	....	....	28	....	....	....	....	....
1907-08	Montreal Shamrocks	ECAHA	10	3	0	3	....	....	....	15	....	....	....	....	....
1908-09	Edmonton Eskimos	ESrHL	3	0	0	0	....	....	....	0	2	0	2	2	11
	Renfrew Creamery Kings	FAHL	STATISTICS NOT AVAILABLE												
1909-10	Montreal Canadiens	NHA	12	10	0	10	....	....	....	5	....	....	....	....	....
1910-11	Montreal Canadiens	NHA	16	19	0	19	....	....	....	22	....	....	....	....	....
1911-12	Montreal Canadiens	NHA	18	27	0	27	....	....	....	40	....	....	....	....	....
1912-13	Montreal Canadiens	NHA	17	24	0	24	....	....	....	80	....	....	....	....	....
1913-14	Vancouver Millionaires	PCHA	15	14	2	16	....	....	....	12	....	....	....	....	....
1914-15	Montreal Canadiens	NHA	20	30	4	34	....	....	....	15	....	....	....	....	....
♦1915-16	Montreal Canadiens	NHA	24	24	*15	*39	....	....	....	42	5	*4	0	4	18
1916-17	Montreal Canadiens	NHA	21	21	6	27	....	....	....	50	6	7	0	7	32
1917-18	**Montreal Canadiens**	**NHL**	**20**	**17**	**6**	**23**	**22**	**25**	**47**	**29**	**2**	**0**	**1**	**1**	**13**
1918-19	**Montreal Canadiens**	**NHL**	**17**	**14**	**5**	**19**	**25**	**27**	**52**	**12**	**5**	**2**	***3**	**5**	**3**
	Montreal Canadiens	St-Cup	5	0	3	3	....	....	....	0	....	....	....	....	....
1919-20	**Montreal Canadiens**	**NHL**	**22**	**14**	**12**	**26**	**16**	**42**	**58**	**6**	....	....	....	....	....
1920-21	**Montreal Canadiens**	**NHL**	**23**	**16**	**5**	**21**	**21**	**19**	**40**	**25**	....	....	....	....	....
1921-22	**Montreal Canadiens**	**NHL**	**23**	**2**	**4**	**6**	**3**	**12**	**15**	**12**	....	....	....	....	....
1922-23	**Montreal Canadiens**	**NHL**	**22**	**1**	**2**	**3**	**2**	**7**	**9**	**0**	**2**	**0**	**0**	**0**	**0**
	NHL Totals		**127**	**64**	**34**	**98**	**89**	**132**	**221**	**84**	**9**	**2**	**4**	**6**	**16**
	Other Major League Totals		211	249	38	287	....	....	....	344	11	11	0	11	50

IHL First All-Star Team (1906, 1907)

Signed as a free agent by **American Soo** (IHL), January 5, 1905. Signed as a free agent by **Montreal Shamrocks** (ECAHA), December 15, 1907. Signed as a free agent by **Edmonton** (ESrHL), December 3, 1908. Signed by **Renfrew** (FAHL) after jumping contract with **Edmonton** (ESrHL), January 3, 1909. Signed as a free agent by **Montreal Nationals** (CHA), December 12, 1909. Signed as a free agent by **Montreal Canadiens** (NHA) after jumping contract with **Montreal Nationals** (CHA), December 19, 1909. Signed as a free agent by **New Westminster** (PCHA), November 22, 1912. Signed with **Quebec** (NHA) after jumping contract with **New Westminster** (PCHA), November 25, 1912. Traded to **Montreal Canadiens** (NHA) by **Quebec** (NHA) for cash, December, 1912. Rights retained by **Montreal Canadiens** after NHA folded, November 26, 1917.

• PLAGER, Bob

— see page 1523

• PLAMONDON, Gerry

Gerald Roger

LW – L. 5′8″, 170 lbs. b: Sherbrooke, Que., 1/5/1925.

Season	Club	League	GP	G	A	Pts	AG	AA	APts	PIM	GP	G	A	Pts	PIM
1943-44	Montreal Jr. Canadiens	QJHL	15	*21	7	28	....	....	....	2	3	*6	1	7	0
	Montreal Canada Car	MCHL	11	6	6	12	....	....	....	0	....	....	....	....	....
	Montreal Jr. Royals	M-Cup	4	1	3	4	....	....	....	4	....	....	....	....	....
1944-45	Pittsburgh Hornets	AHL	4	2	2	4	....	....	....	10	....	....	....	....	....
	Valleyfield Braves	QSHL	23	14	20	34	....	....	....	8	11	*13	7	*21	2
	Valleyfield Braves	Al-Cup	3	1	0	1	....	....	....	0	....	....	....	....	....
♦1945-46	**Montreal Canadiens**	**NHL**	**6**	**0**	**2**	**2**	**0**	**3**	**3**	**2**	**1**	**0**	**0**	**0**	**0**
	Valleyfield Braves	QSHL	39	*40	28	68	....	....	....	12	....	....	....	....	....
1946-47	Montreal Royals	QSHL	26	15	15	30	....	....	....	21	11	5	4	9	4
	Montreal Royals	Al-Cup	14	7	12	19	....	....	....	2	....	....	....	....	....
1947-48	**Montreal Canadiens**	**NHL**	**3**	**1**	**1**	**2**	**1**	**1**	**2**	**0**	....	....	....	....	....
	Montreal Royals	QSHL	46	*51	22	73	....	....	....	16	3	0	1	1	0
1948-49	**Montreal Canadiens**	**NHL**	**27**	**5**	**5**	**10**	**7**	**7**	**14**	**8**	**7**	**5**	**1**	**6**	**0**
	Montreal Royals	QSHL	36	34	25	59	....	....	....	24	....	....	....	....	....
1949-50	**Montreal Canadiens**	**NHL**	**37**	**1**	**5**	**6**	**1**	**6**	**7**	**0**	**3**	**0**	**1**	**1**	**2**
	Cincinnati Mohawks	AHL	20	8	9	17	....	....	....	6	....	....	....	....	....
1950-51	**Montreal Canadiens**	**NHL**	**1**	**0**	**0**	**0**	**0**	**0**	**0**	**0**	....	....	....	....	....
	Cincinnati Mohawks	AHL	70	21	29	50	....	....	....	43	....	....	....	....	....
1951-52	Montreal Royals	QMHL	60	23	29	52	....	....	....	21	7	3	1	4	0
1952-53	Montreal Royals	QMHL	57	18	22	40	....	....	....	6	16	2	4	6	2
1953-54	Matane Red Rockets	SLVHL	68	18	43	61	....	....	....	16	....	....	....	....	....
	Matane Red Rockets	Al-Cup	16	6	6	12	....	....	....	10	....	....	....	....	....
1954-55	Trois-Rivieres Flambeaux	QJHL	DID NOT PLAY – COACHING												
1955-56	Chicoutimi Sagueneens	QHL	7	1	1	2	....	....	....	12	....	....	....	....	....
1956-57	Cornwall Chevies	EOHL	50	7	24	31	....	....	....	20	6	0	0	0	10
1957-58	Pembroke Lumber Kings	EOHL	50	12	21	33	....	....	....	18	12	1	4	5	6
	NHL Totals		**74**	**7**	**13**	**20**	**9**	**17**	**26**	**10**	**11**	**5**	**2**	**7**	**2**

QSHL First All-Star Team (1948)

Traded to **Pittsburgh** (AHL) by **Montreal** for cash, November 24, 1944. Signed as a free agent by **Valleyfield** (QSHL), September 19, 1945.

• PLAXTON, Hugh

Hugh John

LW – L. 5′10″, 184 lbs. b: Barrie, Ont., 5/16/1904 Deceased.

Season	Club	League	GP	G	A	Pts	AG	AA	APts	PIM	GP	G	A	Pts	PIM
1921-22	University of Toronto	OHA-Jr.	3	0	0	0	....	....	....	....	....	....	....	....	....
	University of Toronto	OHA-B	STATISTICS NOT AVAILABLE												
1922-23	University of Toronto	OHA-Jr.	6	11	3	14	....	....	....	....	1	0	0	0	0
1923-24	University of Toronto	OHA-Jr.	8	*18	3	*21	....	....	....	10	3	1	1	2	*6
	University of Toronto	M-Cup	2	0	1	1	....	....	....	2	....	....	....	....	....
1924-25	University of Toronto	OHA-Sr.	8	4	2	6	....	....	....	....	....	....	....	....	....
	University of Toronto	Al-Cup	6	5	2	7	....	....	....	....	....	....	....	....	....
1925-26	Toronto Grads	OHA-Sr.	9	*31	7	*38	....	....	....	11	2	0	0	0	4
1926-27	Toronto Varsity Grads	OHA-Sr.	9	*31	7	*38	....	....	....	11	2	0	0	0	0
	Toronto Varsity Grads	Al-Cup	11	*21	5	*26	....	....	....	22	....	....	....	....	....
1927-28	Toronto Varsity Grads	X-Games	12	20	*10	30	....	....	....	....	....	....	....	....	....
	Canada	Olympics	3	*12	2	14	....	....	....	....	....	....	....	....	....
1928/32			OUT OF HOCKEY – RETIRED												
1932-33	**Montreal Maroons**	**NHL**	**15**	**1**	**2**	**3**	**2**	**4**	**6**	**4**	....	....	....	....	....
	Windsor Bulldogs	IHL	10	1	1	2	....	....	....	4	....	....	....	....	....
	Vancouver Maroons	WCHL	8	0	0	0	....	....	....	0	....	....	....	....	....
	NHL Totals		**15**	**1**	**2**	**3**	**2**	**4**	**6**	**4**	....	....	....	....	....

• Did not play from 1928 to 1932 while practicing law in Ontario. Rights traded to **Toronto** by **Boston** with Eric Pettinger for the rights to George Owen, January 10, 1929. Signed as a free agent by **Montreal Maroons**, October, 1932.

• PLETSCH, Charles

D. , b: Chesley, Ont., 1893.

Season	Club	League	GP	G	A	Pts	AG	AA	APts	PIM	GP	G	A	Pts	PIM
1911-12	Chesley ACC	OHA-Sr.	STATISTICS NOT AVAILABLE												
1912-13	Sudbury Wolves	NOHA	7	4	0	4	....	....	....	29	....	....	....	....	....
1913/16	Stratford Indians	OHA-I	STATISTICS NOT AVAILABLE												
1916/19	Detroit Michigans	X-Games	STATISTICS NOT AVAILABLE												
1919-20	Markdale Seniors	OIHA	STATISTICS NOT AVAILABLE												
1920-21	Markdale Seniors	OIHA	STATISTICS NOT AVAILABLE												
	Hamilton Tigers	**NHL**	**1**	**0**	**0**	**0**	**0**	**0**	**0**	**0**	....	....	....	....	....
	NHL Totals		**1**	**0**	**0**	**0**	**0**	**0**	**0**	**0**	....	....	....	....	....

Signed as a free agent by **Detroit Michigans**, December, 1916. Signed as a free agent by **Hamilton**, December 31, 1920.

• PODOLSKY, Nels

LW – L. 5′10″, 170 lbs. b: Winnipeg, Man., 12/19/1925.

Season	Club	League	GP	G	A	Pts	AG	AA	APts	PIM	GP	G	A	Pts	PIM
1942-43	Montreal Jr. Royals	QJHL	4	2	2	4	....	....	....	6	8	2	1	3	6
	Montreal Royals	QSHL	1	0	0	0	....	....	....	0	....	....	....	....	....
1943-44	Galt Kists	OHA-Jr.	26	25	16	41	....	....	....	54	3	1	0	1	4
1944-45	Halifax Navy	NSDHL	3	0	0	0	....	....	....	6	....	....	....	....	....
	Cornwallis Navy	NSDHL	MILITARY SERVICE												
1945-46	Omaha Knights	USHL	44	9	13	22	....	....	....	64	7	2	3	5	4

Season	Club	League	GP	G	A	Pts	AG	AA	APts	PIM	GP	G	A	Pts	PIM
			REGULAR SEASON								PLAYOFFS				
1946-47	Indianapolis Capitols	AHL	61	8	7	15	....	....	....	96	....	....	....	....	....
1947-48	Indianapolis Capitols	AHL	68	25	30	55	....	....	....	57	....	....	....	....	....
1948-49	**Detroit Red Wings**	**NHL**	**1**	**0**	**0**	**0**	**0**	**0**	**0**	**0**	**7**	**0**	**0**	**0**	**4**
	Indianapolis Capitols	AHL	64	26	30	56	....	....	....	92	2	1	0	1	0
1949-50	Indianapolis Capitols	AHL	52	18	24	42	....	....	....	67	8	1	4	5	8
1950-51	Indianapolis Capitols	AHL	19	3	4	7	....	....	....	13	1	0	0	0	0
1951-52	Edmonton Flyers	PCHL	59	14	16	30	....	....	....	112	2	0	1	1	0
1952-53	St. Louis Flyers	AHL	18	2	6	8	....	....	....	39	....	....	....	....	....
	Shawinigan Cataracts	QMHL	47	15	19	34	....	....	....	93	....	....	....	....	....
1953-54	Sherbrooke Saints	QHL	64	15	25	40	....	....	....	67	5	0	1	1	4
1954-55	Troy Bruins	IHL	60	16	18	34	....	....	....	156	11	1	4	5	9
1955-56	Troy Bruins	IHL	60	17	17	34	....	....	....	147	5	0	0	0	4
1956-57	Troy Bruins	IHL	52	9	14	23	....	....	....	105	....	....	....	....	....
1957-58	S.S. Marie Greyhounds	NOHA	35	4	9	13	....	....	....	54	4	0	0	0	10
	NHL Totals		**1**	**0**	**0**	**0**	**0**	**0**	**0**	**0**	**7**	**0**	**0**	**0**	**4**

• POETA, Tony Anthony Joseph

RW – L. 5'5", 168 lbs. b: North Bay, Ont., 3/4/1933.

Season	Club	League	GP	G	A	Pts	AG	AA	APts	PIM	GP	G	A	Pts	PIM
1950-51	Galt Black Hawks	OHA-Jr.	51	17	13	30	....	....	....	35	3	0	0	0	0
1951-52	Galt Black Hawks	OHA-Jr.	51	27	28	55	....	....	....	31	3	4	0	4	2
	Chicago Black Hawks	**NHL**	**1**	**0**	**0**	**0**	**0**	**0**	**0**	**0**	....	....	....	....	....
1952-53	Galt–Barrie Flyers	OHA-Jr.	54	29	34	63	....	....	....	49	15	10	9	19	27
1953-54	Cleveland Barons	AHL	2	0	0	0	....	....	....	2	5	1	0	1	2
	Marion Barons	IHL	55	29	35	64	....	....	....	37	5	3	3	6	6
1954-55	Valleyfield Braves	QHL	11	1	1	2	....	....	....	0	....	....	....	....	....
	North Bay Trappers	NOHA	42	8	11	19	....	....	....	10	13	0	1	1	17
1955-56	North Bay Trappers	NOHA	25	5	4	9	....	....	....	8	....	....	....	....	....
	Stratford Indians	OHA-Sr.	24	3	8	11	....	....	....	4	7	0	0	0	0
1956-57			REINSTATED AS AN AMATEUR												
1957-58	North Bay Trappers	NOHA	26	1	4	5	....	....	....	9	....	....	....	....	....
	Belleville McFarlands	EOHL	7	1	1	2	....	....	....	2	....	....	....	....	....
1958-59	North Bay Trappers	NOHA	54	15	22	37	....	....	....	31	....	....	....	....	....
1959-60	Greensboro–Johnstown	EHL	13	0	6	6	....	....	....	5	....	....	....	....	....
	Milwaukee Falcons	IHL	29	6	9	15	....	....	....	35	....	....	....	....	....
	NHL Totals		**1**	**0**	**0**	**0**	**0**	**0**	**0**	**0**	....	....	....	....	....

Loaned to **Valleyfield** (QHL) by **Cleveland** (AHL) for cash, September 29, 1954.

• POILE, Bud Norman Robert HHOF

RW – R. 6', 189 lbs. b: Fort William, Ont., 2/10/1924.

Season	Club	League	GP	G	A	Pts	AG	AA	APts	PIM	GP	G	A	Pts	PIM
1940-41	Fort William Rangers	TBJHL	17	25	10	35	....	....	....	14	2	3	2	5	4
1941-42	Fort William Rangers	TBJHL	18	*36	29	*65	....	....	....	*55	3	*5	*7	*12	11
	Fort William Forts	TBSHL	1	0	2	2	....	....	....	0	....	....	....	....	....
	Port Arthur Bearcats	M-Cup	....	....	....	....	....	....	....	....	6	1	2	3	2
1942-43	**Toronto Maple Leafs**	**NHL**	**48**	**16**	**19**	**35**	**16**	**18**	**34**	**24**	**6**	**2**	**4**	**6**	**4**
1943-44	**Toronto Maple Leafs**	**NHL**	**11**	**6**	**8**	**14**	**5**	**7**	**12**	**9**	....	....	....	....	....
	Toronto RCAF	OHA-Sr.	8	5	9	14	....	....	....	8	....	....	....	....	....
	Toronto Bowsers	TMHL	3	5	2	7	....	....	....	0	4	*16	5	21	2
1944-45			MILITARY SERVICE												
1945-46	**Toronto Maple Leafs**	**NHL**	**9**	**1**	**8**	**9**	**1**	**12**	**13**	**0**	....	....	....	....	....
♦1946-47	**Toronto Maple Leafs**	**NHL**	**59**	**19**	**17**	**36**	**21**	**20**	**41**	**19**	**7**	**2**	**0**	**2**	**2**
1947-48	**Toronto Maple Leafs**	**NHL**	**4**	**2**	**0**	**2**	**3**	**0**	**3**	**0**	....	....	....	....	....
	Chicago Black Hawks	**NHL**	**54**	**23**	**29**	**52**	**30**	**38**	**68**	**17**	....	....	....	....	....
1948-49	**Chicago Black Hawks**	**NHL**	**4**	**0**	**0**	**0**	**0**	**0**	**0**	**2**	....	....	....	....	....
	Detroit Red Wings	**NHL**	**56**	**21**	**21**	**42**	**30**	**30**	**60**	**6**	**10**	**0**	**1**	**1**	**2**
1949-50	**New York Rangers**	**NHL**	**27**	**3**	**6**	**9**	**4**	**7**	**11**	**8**	....	....	....	....	....
	Boston Bruins	**NHL**	**39**	**16**	**14**	**30**	**20**	**17**	**37**	**6**	....	....	....	....	....
1950-51	Tulsa Oilers	USHL	60	15	38	53	....	....	....	48	9	5	6	11	4
1951-52	Glace Bay Miners	MMHL	84	33	60	93	....	....	....	69	2	0	0	0	0
1952-53	Edmonton Flyers	WHL	70	20	29	49	....	....	....	62	15	0	7	7	12
1953-54	Edmonton Flyers	WHL	49	12	39	51	....	....	....	34	13	3	9	12	0
1954-55	Edmonton Flyers	WHL	3	1	2	3	....	....	....	0	....	....	....	....	....
	Edmonton Flyers	Ed-Cup	1	0	0	0	....	....	....	0	....	....	....	....	....
1955-56	Edmonton Flyers	WHL	DID NOT PLAY – COACHING												
	NHL Totals		**311**	**107**	**122**	**229**	**130**	**149**	**279**	**91**	**23**	**4**	**5**	**9**	**8**

• Brother of Don • MMHL First All-Star Team (1952) • NHL Second All-Star Team (1948) • Played in NHL All-Star Game (1947, 1948) • Won Lester Patrick Trophy (1989)

Traded to **Chicago** by **Toronto** with Gus Bodnar, Gaye Stewart, Ernie Dickens and Bob Goldham for Max Bentley and Cy Thomas, November 2, 1947. Traded to **Detroit** by **Chicago** with George Gee for Jim Conacher, Bep Guidolin and Doug McCaig, October 25, 1948. Traded to **NY Rangers** by **Detroit** for cash, August 16, 1949. Traded to **Boston** by **NY Rangers** for cash, December 22, 1949. Signed by **Tulsa** (USHL) as playing-coach, October 3, 1950.

• POILE, Don Donald B.

C – L. 5'11", 160 lbs. b: Fort William, Ont., 6/1/1932.

Season	Club	League	GP	G	A	Pts	AG	AA	APts	PIM	GP	G	A	Pts	PIM
1949-50	Fort William Hurricanes	TBJHL	12	8	2	10	....	....	....	8	5	1	0	1	4
1950-51	Fort William Hurricanes	TBJHL	21	2	7	9	....	....	....	14	12	7	7	14	12
1951-52	Fort William Hurricanes	TBJHL	30	30	36	66	....	....	....	46	9	*9	*10	*19	12
	Fort William Hurricanes	M-Cup	12	4	8	12	....	....	....	17	....	....	....	....	....
1952-53	Milwaukee Chiefs	IHL	56	42	34	76	....	....	....	14	....	....	....	....	....
	Edmonton Flyers	WHL	....	....	....	....	....	....	....	....	2	0	0	0	0
1953-54	Edmonton Flyers	WHL	70	26	33	59	....	....	....	16	13	2	2	4	8
1954-55	**Detroit Red Wings**	**NHL**	**4**	**0**	**0**	**0**	**0**	**0**	**0**	**0**	....	....	....	....	....
	Edmonton Flyers	WHL	52	16	29	45	....	....	....	21	9	5	1	6	0
	Edmonton Flyers	Ed-Cup	7	1	1	2	....	....	....	10	....	....	....	....	....
1955-56	Edmonton Flyers	WHL	70	22	29	51	....	....	....	63	3	2	0	2	2
1956-57	Edmonton Flyers	WHL	69	31	25	56	....	....	....	54	8	3	2	5	14
1957-58	**Detroit Red Wings**	**NHL**	**62**	**7**	**9**	**16**	**9**	**9**	**18**	**12**	**4**	**0**	**0**	**0**	**0**
	Edmonton Flyers	WHL	2	1	3	4	....	....	....	0	....	....	....	....	....
1958-59	Hershey Bears	AHL	4	0	0	0	....	....	....	0	....	....	....	....	....
	Edmonton Flyers	WHL	51	18	29	47	....	....	....	19	3	1	0	1	4
1959-60	Edmonton Flyers	WHL	70	20	34	54	....	....	....	28	4	0	1	1	12
1960-61	Edmonton Flyers	WHL	60	22	21	43	....	....	....	21	....	....	....	....	....
1961-62	Edmonton Flyers	WHL	63	23	27	50	....	....	....	20	12	7	7	14	2
	NHL Totals		**66**	**7**	**9**	**16**	**9**	**9**	**18**	**12**	**4**	**0**	**0**	**0**	**0**

• Brother of Bud • Won WHL Rookie of the Year Award (1954) • Played in NHL All-Star Game (1954)

Traded to **Hershey** (AHL) by **Detroit** with Hec Lalande and cash for Dunc Fisher, April 23, 1958.

• POIRER, Gordie Gordon Arthur

C – L. 5'6", 150 lbs. b: Maple Creek, Sask., 10/27/1914.

Season	Club	League	GP	G	A	Pts	AG	AA	APts	PIM	GP	G	A	Pts	PIM
1931-32	Montreal Columbus	QAHA	10	6	2	8	....	....	....	14	....	....	....	....	....
1932-33	St. Francis Xavier	QJHL	11	4	0	4	....	....	....	15	2	1	0	1	6
1933-34	Montreal Sr. Canadiens	MCHL	15	1	1	2	....	....	....	8	4	1	2	3	0
1934-35	Montreal Sr. Canadiens	MCHL	20	7	11	18	....	....	....	20	2	1	1	2	0
1935-36			DID NOT PLAY												
1936-37	Brighton Tigers	Britain	40	25	9	34	....	....	....	36	....	....	....	....	....
1937-38	Brighton Tigers	Ln-Cup	....	5	2	7	....	....	....	....	....	....	....	....	....
	Brighton Tigers	Britain	....	9	12	21	....	....	....	....	....	....	....	....	....
	Brighton Tigers	Nat-Tmt	....	6	2	8	....	....	....	....	....	....	....	....	....
1938-39	Brighton Tigers	Ln-Cup	....	3	2	5	....	....	....	....	....	....	....	....	....
	Brighton Tigers	Britain	....	14	15	29	....	....	....	....	....	....	....	....	....
	Brighton Tigers	Nat-Tmt	....	8	4	12	....	....	....	....	....	....	....	....	....
1939-40	St-Hyacinthe Gaulois	QPHL	36	37	43	80	....	....	....	22	....	....	....	....	....
	Montreal Canadiens	**NHL**	**10**	**0**	**0**	**0**	**0**	**0**	**0**	**0**	....	....	....	....	....
1940-41	Ottawa–Montreal	QSHL	29	8	23	31	....	....	....	16	8	0	5	5	10
1941-42	Ottawa Senators	QSHL	40	21	19	40	....	....	....	12	8	1	4	5	13
1942-43	Ottawa Commandos	QSHL	32	17	14	31	....	....	....	19	22	13	5	18	10
	Ottawa Army	OHA-Sr.	10	15	16	31	....	....	....	5	....	....	....	....	....
1943-44	Ottawa Commandos	QSHL	8	2	6	8	....	....	....	6	....	....	....	....	....
1944-45			MILITARY SERVICE												
1945-46	Ottawa GMC's	OCHL	....	9	13	22	....	....	....	....	4	6	10	16	....
	Ottawa Senators	QSHL	29	12	16	28	....	....	....	9	5	1	2	3	0
1946-47	Brighton Tigers	A-Cup	6	8	3	11	....	....	....	8	....	....	....	....	....
	Brighton Tigers	Britain	36	28	32	60	....	....	....	35	....	....	....	....	....
	Brighton Tigers	Ln-Cup	2	3	1	4	....	....	....	0	....	....	....	....	....
1947-48	Brighton Tigers	A-Cup	9	13	5	18	....	....	....	8	....	....	....	....	....
	Brighton Tigers	Britain	34	18	25	43	....	....	....	30	....	....	....	....	....
	Brighton Tigers	Nat-Tmt	4	0	1	1	....	....	....	6	....	....	....	....	....
1948-49	Brighton Tigers	A-Cup	10	8	6	14	....	....	....	14	....	....	....	....	....
	Brighton Tigers	Britain	25	9	12	21	....	....	....	22	....	....	....	....	....
	Brighton Tigers	Nat-Tmt	14	13	23	36	....	....	....	23	....	....	....	....	....
1949-50			DID NOT PLAY												
1950-51	Harringay Greyhounds	A-Cup	27	1	12	13	....	....	....	18	....	....	....	....	....
	Harringay Greyhounds	Britain	13	1	0	1	....	....	....	2	....	....	....	....	....
	NHL Totals		**10**	**0**	**0**	**0**	**0**	**0**	**0**	**0**	....	....	....	....	....

QPHL First All-Star Team (1940)

Signed as a free agent by **Montreal**, February 14, 1940.

• POLICH, John

RW – R. 6'2", 200 lbs. b: Hibbing, MN, 7/8/1916.

Season	Club	League	GP	G	A	Pts	AG	AA	APts	PIM	GP	G	A	Pts	PIM
1934-35	Hibbing Bluejackets	H.S.	STATISTICS NOT AVAILABLE												
1935/38	Loyola College Lions	SCSHL	STATISTICS NOT AVAILABLE												
1939-40	**New York Rangers**	**NHL**	**1**	**0**	**0**	**0**	**0**	**0**	**0**	**0**	....	....	....	....	....
	Philadelphia Rockets	IAHL	53	11	22	33	....	....	....	56	....	....	....	....	....
1940-41	**New York Rangers**	**NHL**	**2**	**0**	**1**	**1**	**0**	**1**	**1**	**0**	....	....	....	....	....
	Philadelphia Rockets	AHL	50	10	31	41	....	....	....	53	....	....	....	....	....
1941-42			REINSTATED AS AN AMATEUR												
1942-43	Los Angeles Monarchs	SCSHL	STATISTICS NOT AVAILABLE												
1943-44	Los Angeles Monarchs	SCSHL	STATISTICS NOT AVAILABLE												
1944-45	Los Angeles Monarchs	PCHL	18	10	18	28	....	....	....	0	....	....	....	....	....
1945-46	Los Angeles Monarchs	PCHL	34	11	14	25	....	....	....	86	7	2	1	3	14
1946-47	Los Angeles Monarchs	PCHL	50	25	37	62	....	....	....	37	10	6	5	11	9
1947-48	Los Angeles Monarchs	PCHL	53	17	30	47	....	....	....	59	4	3	0	3	6
	NHL Totals		**3**	**0**	**1**	**1**	**0**	**1**	**1**	**0**	....	....	....	....	....

Signed as a free agent by **NY Rangers**, October 13, 1939. Traded to **Pittsburgh** (AHL) by **NY Rangers** for cash, September 11, 1941. • Refused to report and retired from professional play, October 10, 1941.

• POLIZIANI, Dan Daniel

RW – R. 5'11", 158 lbs. b: Sydney, N.S., 1/8/1935.

Season	Club	League	GP	G	A	Pts	AG	AA	APts	PIM	GP	G	A	Pts	PIM
1952-53	St. Catharines Teepees	OHA-Jr.	54	9	13	22	....	....	....	18	3	0	2	2	2
1953-54	St. Catharines Teepees	OHA-Jr.	20	3	6	9	....	....	....	10	....	....	....	....	....
	Barrie Flyers	OHA-Jr.	35	24	27	51	....	....	....	29	....	....	....	....	....
1954-55	Barrie Flyers	OHA-Jr.	34	18	38	56	....	....	....	105	....	....	....	....	....
	Cleveland Barons	AHL	2	1	0	1	....	....	....	0	....	....	....	....	....
1955-56	Cleveland Barons	AHL	5	2	1	3	....	....	....	0	....	....	....	....	....
	Quebec Aces	QHL	42	14	16	30	....	....	....	62	5	0	2	2	4
1956-57	Cleveland Barons	AHL	58	21	25	46	....	....	....	74	7	2	1	3	0
1957-58	Cleveland Barons	AHL	65	23	19	42	....	....	....	60	6	5	2	7	6
1958-59	**Boston Bruins**	**NHL**	**1**	**0**	**0**	**0**	**0**	**0**	**0**	**0**	**3**	**0**	**0**	**0**	**0**
	Providence Reds	AHL	59	18	21	39	....	....	....	54	....	....	....	....	....
1959-60	Providence Reds	AHL	60	30	31	61	....	....	....	52	5	1	4	5	16
1960-61	Providence Reds	AHL	63	20	43	63	....	....	....	65	....	....	....	....	....
1961-62	Providence Reds	AHL	57	14	37	51	....	....	....	57	3	1	1	2	2
1962-63	Providence Reds	AHL	50	13	17	30	....	....	....	27	6	1	6	7	16
1963-64	Hershey Bears	AHL	66	14	20	34	....	....	....	36	5	2	1	3	4
1964-65	Hershey Bears	AHL	45	14	12	26	....	....	....	44	1	0	0	0	2
	NHL Totals		**1**	**0**	**0**	**0**	**0**	**0**	**0**	**0**	**3**	**0**	**0**	**0**	**0**

Claimed by **Boston** from **Cleveland** (AHL) in Inter-League Draft, June 3, 1958. Traded to **Hershey** by **Boston** (Providence-AHL) for Willie Marshall, June, 1963.

• POPEIN, Larry *— see page 1530*

• POPIEL, Poul *— see page 1530*

• PORTLAND, Jack
John Frederick
D – L. 6'2", 185 lbs. b: Waubaushene, Ont., 7/30/1912 Deceased.

			REGULAR SEASON								PLAYOFFS				
Season	Club	League	GP	G	A	Pts	AG	AA	APts	PIM	GP	G	A	Pts	PIM
1932-33	Collingwood Combines	OHA-Sr.	STATISTICS NOT AVAILABLE												
1933-34	Montreal Canadiens	NHL	31	0	2	2	0	4	4	10	2	0	0	0	0
1934-35	Montreal Canadiens	NHL	5	0	0	0	0	0	0	2	....	....	....	....	....
	Boston Bruins	NHL	15	1	1	2	2	2	4	2	....	....	....	....	....
	Boston Cubs	Can-Am	28	7	5	12	....	....	....	34	3	0	0	0	4
1935-36	Boston Bruins	NHL	2	0	0	0	0	0	0	0	....	....	....	....	....
	Boston Cubs	Can-Am	47	4	6	10	....	....	....	95	....	....	....	....	....
1936-37	Boston Bruins	NHL	46	2	4	6	3	7	10	58	3	0	0	0	4
1937-38	Boston Bruins	NHL	48	0	5	5	0	8	8	26	3	0	0	0	4
♦1938-39	Boston Bruins	NHL	48	4	5	9	7	8	15	46	12	0	0	0	11
1939-40	Boston Bruins	NHL	28	0	5	5	0	8	8	16	....	....	....	....	....
	Chicago Black Hawks	NHL	16	1	4	5	2	6	8	20	2	0	0	0	2
1940-41	Chicago Black Hawks	NHL	5	0	0	0	0	0	0	4	....	....	....	....	....
	Montreal Canadiens	NHL	42	2	7	9	3	10	13	34	3	0	1	1	2
1941-42	Montreal Canadiens	NHL	46	2	9	11	3	11	14	53	3	0	0	0	0
1942-43	Montreal Canadiens	NHL	49	3	14	17	3	13	16	52	5	1	2	3	2
1943-44			MILITARY SERVICE												
1944-45			MILITARY SERVICE												
1945-46			MILITARY SERVICE												
1946-47	Buffalo Bisons	AHL	50	2	14	16	....	....	....	25	2	0	0	0	0
1947-48	Philadelphia Rockets	AHL	1	0	1	1	....	....	....	0	....	....	....	....	....
	Washington Lions	AHL	56	5	14	19	....	....	....	19	....	....	....	....	....
	NHL Totals		381	15	56	71	23	77	100	323	33	1	3	4	25

Can-Am First All-Star Team (1936)

Traded to **Boston** by **Montreal Canadiens** for Tony Savage and $7,500, December 3, 1934. Traded to **Chicago** by **Boston** for Des Smith, January 27, 1940. Traded to **Montreal** by **Chicago** for $12,500, November 19, 1940.

• POWELL, Ray
Raymond Henry
C – L. 6', 170 lbs. b: Timmins, Ont., 11/16/1925.

Season	Club	League	GP	G	A	Pts	AG	AA	APts	PIM	GP	G	A	Pts	PIM
1942-43	Sudbury Open Pit	X-Games	STATISTICS NOT AVAILABLE												
1943-44	Brantford Lions	OHA-Jr.	21	10	21	31	....	....	....	17	3	1	2	3	2
	Pittsburgh Hornets	AHL	2	0	0	0	....	....	....	0	....	....	....	....	....
1944-45	Baltimore Blades	EAHL	43	33	*62	95	....	....	....	19	9	9	9	18	2
	New York Rovers	EAHL	1	0	0	0	....	....	....	0	....	....	....	....	....
	Buffalo Bisons	AHL	2	0	1	1	....	....	....	0	4	2	3	5	0
1945-46	New Haven Eagles	AHL	14	2	10	12	....	....	....	2	....	....	....	....	....
	Fort Worth Rangers	USHL	33	19	29	48	....	....	....	6	....	....	....	....	....
1946-47	Omaha–Kansas City	USHL	55	28	42	70	....	....	....	6	....	....	....	....	....
1947-48	Kansas City Pla-Mors	USHL	62	37	47	84	....	....	....	16	12	5	8	13	0
1948-49	Kansas City Pla-Mors	USHL	61	*48	58	*106	....	....	....	22	2	0	2	2	0
1949-50	Kansas City Pla-Mors	USHL	64	27	*84	*111	....	....	....	11	3	0	1	1	0
1950-51	Chicago Black Hawks	NHL	31	7	15	22	9	18	27	2	....	....	....	....	....
	Milwaukee Seagulls	USHL	35	18	19	37	....	....	....	16	....	....	....	....	....
1951-52	Providence Reds	AHL	67	35	*62	*97	....	....	....	6	15	*8	7	15	6
1952-53	Providence Reds	AHL	59	17	41	58	....	....	....	6	....	....	....	....	....
1953-54	Quebec Aces	QHL	68	22	55	77	....	....	....	10	16	3	8	11	6
	Quebec Aces	Ed-Cup	6	3	1	4	....	....	....	0	....	....	....	....	....
1954-55	Quebec Aces	QHL	53	22	43	65	....	....	....	22	8	1	3	4	0
1955-56	Quebec Aces	QHL	59	15	33	48	....	....	....	30	6	1	0	1	8
1956-57	Victoria Cougars	WHL	34	10	9	19	....	....	....	4	3	1	2	3	0
1957-58	Kelowna Packers	OSHL	48	27	42	69	....	....	....	21	10	3	1	4	0
1958-59	Kelowna Packers	OSHL	DID NOT PLAY – INJURED												
1959-60			OUT OF HOCKEY – RETIRED												
1960-61	Kelowna Packers	OSHL	2	2	1	3	....	....	....	2	....	....	....	....	....
	NHL Totals		31	7	15	22	9	18	27	2	....	....	....	....	....

EAHL First All-Star Team (1945) • USHL First All-Star Team (1949, 1950) • Won Herman W. Paterson Cup (USHL - MVP) (1950) • AHL First All-Star Team (1952) • Won John B. Sollenberger Trophy (Top Scorer - AHL) (1952) • Won Les Cunningham Award (MVP - AHL) (1952) • QHL Second All-Star Team (1955) • OSHL Second All-Star Team (1958)

Claimed by **Toronto** from **Fort Worth** (USHL) in Inter-League Draft, June, 1946. Traded to **Detroit** by **Toronto** with Doug Baldwin for Gerry Brown, September 21, 1946. Traded to **Chicago** by **Detroit** with Adam Brown for Leo Reise and Pete Horeck, December 9, 1946. Traded to **Providence** (AHL) by **Chicago** for cash, August 30, 1951. Traded to **Quebec** (QHL) by **Providence** (AHL) for cash, July 14, 1953.

• PRATT, Babe
Walter — HHOF
D – L. 6'3", 212 lbs. b: Stony Mountain, Man., 1/7/1916 d: 12/16/1988.

Season	Club	League	GP	G	A	Pts	AG	AA	APts	PIM	GP	G	A	Pts	PIM
1932-33	Elmwood Millionaires	MAHA	STATISTICS NOT AVAILABLE												
1933-34	Kenora Thistles	NOJHA	16	14	7	21	....	....	....	33	9	6	2	8	18
	Kenora Thistles	M-Cup	4	4	4	8	....	....	....	14	....	....	....	....	....
1934-35	Kenora Thistles	NOJHA	18	19	*23	*42	....	....	....	18	2	0	4	4	2
	Brandon Wheat Kings	MHL-Sr.	1	0	0	0	....	....	....	0	....	....	....	....	....
1935-36	New York Rangers	NHL	17	1	1	2	2	2	4	16	....	....	....	....	....
	Philadelphia Ramblers	Can-Am	28	7	8	15	....	....	....	48	4	0	0	0	2
1936-37	New York Rangers	NHL	47	8	7	15	13	13	26	23	9	3	1	4	11
1937-38	New York Rangers	NHL	47	5	14	19	8	23	31	56	2	0	0	0	2
1938-39	New York Rangers	NHL	48	2	19	21	3	30	33	20	7	1	2	3	9
♦1939-40	New York Rangers	NHL	48	4	13	17	7	20	27	61	12	3	1	4	18
1940-41	New York Rangers	NHL	47	3	17	20	5	24	29	52	3	1	1	2	6
1941-42	New York Rangers	NHL	47	4	24	28	5	29	34	55	6	1	3	4	24
1942-43	New York Rangers	NHL	4	0	2	2	0	2	2	6	....	....	....	....	....
	Toronto Maple Leafs	NHL	40	12	25	37	12	23	35	44	6	1	2	3	8
1943-44	Toronto Maple Leafs	NHL	50	17	40	57	15	36	51	30	5	0	3	3	4
♦1944-45	Toronto Maple Leafs	NHL	50	18	23	41	18	27	45	39	13	2	4	6	8
1945-46	Toronto Maple Leafs	NHL	41	5	20	25	6	29	35	36	....	....	....	....	....
1946-47	Boston Bruins	NHL	31	4	4	8	4	5	9	25	....	....	....	....	....
	Hershey Bears	AHL	21	5	10	15	....	....	....	23	11	3	5	8	*19
1947-48	Cleveland Barons	AHL	17	1	4	5	....	....	....	8	....	....	....	....	....
	Hershey Bears	AHL	36	2	14	16	....	....	....	39	2	0	0	0	0
1948-49	New Westminster Royals	PCHL	63	18	48	66	....	....	....	64	12	1	8	9	10
1949-50	New Westminster Royals	PCHL	59	8	29	37	....	....	....	56	18	2	6	8	22
1950-51	New Westminster Royals	PCHL	65	8	15	23	....	....	....	54	7	0	0	0	4
1951-52	Tacoma Rockets	PCHL	63	7	31	38	....	....	....	20	5	0	1	1	0
1952-53	New Westminster Royals	PCHL	DID NOT PLAY – COACHING												
	NHL Totals		517	83	209	292	98	263	361	463	63	12	17	29	90

• Father of Tracy • NHL First All-Star Team (1944) • Won Hart Trophy (1944) • NHL Second All-Star Team (1945) • PCHL Northern First All-Star Team (1949, 1950) • MVP - PCHL Northern Division (1949, 1950) • PCHL First All-Star Team (1951)

Signed as a free agent by **NY Rangers**, October 18, 1935. Traded to **Toronto** by **NY Rangers** for Hank Goldup and Red Garrett, November 27, 1942. • Suspended by NHL President Red Dutton for gambling violations, January 29, 1946. • Suspension lifted by NHL President Red Dutton, February 15, 1946. Traded to **Boston** by **Toronto** for the rights to Eric Pogue and cash, June 19, 1946. Traded to **Cleveland** (AHL) by **Boston** for cash, May 15, 1947. Traded to **Hershey** (AHL) by **Cleveland** (AHL) with Joe Cooper for Hy Buller, December 24, 1947. Traded to **New Westminster** (PCHL) by **Hershey** (AHL) for cash, October 5, 1948.

• PRATT, Jack
C/D – R. 6', 190 lbs. b: Edinburgh, Scotland, 4/13/1906.

Season	Club	League	GP	G	A	Pts	AG	AA	APts	PIM	GP	G	A	Pts	PIM
1927-28	Rossland Ramblers	WKHL	STATISTICS NOT AVAILABLE												
1928-29	Portland Buckaroos	PCHL	36	5	3	8	....	....	....	98	2	0	0	0	6
1929-30	Portland Buckaroos	PCHL	34	5	3	8	....	....	....	*162	4	0	*3	*3	*10
1930-31	Boston Bruins	NHL	32	2	0	2	4	0	4	36	4	0	0	0	0
	Boston Cubs	Can-Am	5	1	1	2	....	....	....	8	9	1	2	3	30
1931-32	Boston Bruins	NHL	5	0	0	0	0	0	0	6	....	....	....	....	....
	Boston Cubs	Can-Am	37	12	8	20	....	....	....	*137	5	0	1	1	6
1932-33	Philadelphia Arrows	Can-Am	43	16	14	30	....	....	....	75	5	2	0	2	8
1933-34	Kimberley Dynamiters	WKHL	PLAYER/COACH – STATISTICS UNAVAILABLE												
1934-35	Kimberley Dynamiters	WKHL	PLAYER/COACH – STATISTICS UNAVAILABLE												
1935-36	Portland Buckaroos	NWHL	27	19	15	34	....	....	....	43	....	....	....	....	....
1936-37	Kimberley Dynamiters	WKHL	PLAYER/COACH – STATISTICS UNAVAILABLE												
1937-38	Kimberley Dynamiters	WKHL	12	6	7	13	....	....	....	27	....	....	....	....	....
1938-39	Kimberley Dynamiters	WKHL	PLAYER/COACH – STATISTICS UNAVAILABLE												
1939-40	Kimberley Dynamiters	WKHL	5	0	1	1	....	....	....	8	....	....	....	....	....
	NHL Totals		37	2	0	2	4	0	4	42	4	0	0	0	0

Signed as a free agent by **Boston**, November 5, 1930.

• PRENTICE, Dean
— see page 1536

• PRENTICE, Eric
Eric Dayton "Doc"
LW – L. 5'11", 150 lbs. b: Schumacher, Ont., 8/22/1926.

Season	Club	League	GP	G	A	Pts	AG	AA	APts	PIM	GP	G	A	Pts	PIM
1942-43	Timmins Buffalo Ankerites	TBSHL	STATISTICS NOT AVAILABLE												
1943-44	Toronto Maple Leafs	NHL	5	0	0	0	0	0	0	4	....	....	....	....	....
	Providence Reds	AHL	7	0	1	1	....	....	....	2	....	....	....	....	....
	Hershey Bears	AHL	6	3	2	5	....	....	....	12	7	2	0	2	0
1944-45	Pittsburgh Hornets	AHL	33	9	7	16	....	....	....	10	....	....	....	....	....
1945-46	Omaha Knights	USHL	3	0	2	2	....	....	....	2	....	....	....	....	....
	Hollywood Wolves	PCHL	21	6	6	12	....	....	....	19	12	4	9	13	12
1946-47	Hollywood Wolves	PCHL	60	18	22	40	....	....	....	12	7	2	3	5	6
1947-48	Fresno Falcons	PCHL	62	18	12	30	....	....	....	58	6	1	2	3	9
1948-49	Philadelphia Rockets	AHL	63	22	24	46	....	....	....	10	....	....	....	....	....
1949-50	Oakland–L.A.–Fresno	PCHL	65	20	16	36	....	....	....	22	....	....	....	....	....
	NHL Totals		5	0	0	0	0	0	0	4	....	....	....	....	....

• Brother of Dean

Loaned to **Los Angeles** (PCHL) by **Springfield** (AHL) after **Oakland** (PCHL) folded, December 20, 1949.

• PRICE, Jack
John Rees
D – L. 5'9", 180 lbs. b: Goderich, Ont., 5/8/1932.

Season	Club	League	GP	G	A	Pts	AG	AA	APts	PIM	GP	G	A	Pts	PIM
1949-50	Galt Red Wings	OHA-Jr.	45	7	6	13	....	....	....	102	....	....	....	....	....
1950-51	Galt Black Hawks	OHA-Jr.	54	5	15	20	....	....	....	74	3	1	0	1	8
1951-52	Galt Black Hawks	OHA-Jr.	53	7	28	35	....	....	....	102	3	0	1	1	0
	Chicago Black Hawks	NHL	1	0	0	0	0	0	0	0	....	....	....	....	....
1952-53	Chicago Black Hawks	NHL	10	0	0	0	0	0	0	2	4	0	0	0	0
	Chatham Maroons	OHA-Sr.	46	15	19	34	....	....	....	98	....	....	....	....	....
1953-54	Chicago Black Hawks	NHL	46	4	6	10	5	7	12	22	....	....	....	....	....
	Ottawa Senators	QHL	17	1	3	4	....	....	....	26	....	....	....	....	....
1954-55	Pittsburgh Hornets	AHL	57	3	8	11	....	....	....	78	10	0	0	0	6
1955-56	Winnipeg Warriors	WHL	3	0	0	0	....	....	....	6	....	....	....	....	....
	Pittsburgh Hornets	AHL	61	6	12	18	....	....	....	65	4	0	0	0	10
1956-57	Hershey Bears	AHL	64	4	21	25	....	....	....	56	7	0	2	2	14
1957-58	Hershey Bears	AHL	70	2	14	16	....	....	....	46	11	1	1	2	8
1958-59	Hershey Bears	AHL	65	2	7	9	....	....	....	44	13	0	1	1	10
1959-60	Hershey Bears	AHL	71	1	11	12	....	....	....	63	....	....	....	....	....
1960-61	Sudbury Wolves	EPHL	30	4	14	18	....	....	....	20	....	....	....	....	....
	Edmonton Flyers	WHL	37	1	6	7	....	....	....	14	....	....	....	....	....
1961-62	Pittsburgh Hornets	AHL	69	1	14	15	....	....	....	64	....	....	....	....	....
1962-63	Pittsburgh Hornets	AHL	22	1	5	6	....	....	....	14	....	....	....	....	....
	Edmonton Flyers	WHL	38	1	9	10	....	....	....	20	3	0	0	0	7
	Sarnia Rams	OHA-Sr.	8	1	2	3	....	....	....	30	....	....	....	....	....
1963-64	Windsor Bulldogs	IHL	7	1	1	2	....	....	....	5	....	....	....	....	....
	NHL Totals		57	4	6	10	5	7	12	24	4	0	0	0	0

Traded to **Toronto** by **Chicago** for Ray Timgren, October 4, 1954. Traded to **Detroit** (Hershey - AHL) by **Toronto** (Pittsburgh - AHL) with Gilles Mayer, Willie Marshall, Bob Hassard, Bob Solinger and Ray Gariepy for cash, July 7, 1956.

• PRICE, Noel
— see page 1537

• PRIMEAU, Joe
Alfred Joseph "Gentleman Joe" — HHOF
C – L. 5'11", 153 lbs. b: Lindsay, Ont., 1/29/1906 d: 5/14/1989.

Season	Club	League	GP	G	A	Pts	AG	AA	APts	PIM	GP	G	A	Pts	PIM
1923-24	St. Michael's Majors	OHA-Jr.	6	1	1	2	....	....	....	....	....	....	....	....	....
1924-25	Toronto St. Mary's	OHA-Jr.	8	7	3	10	....	....	....	....	....	....	....	....	....
1925-26	Toronto St. Mary's	OHA-Jr.	7	*15	2	*17	....	....	....	2	2	2	*1	3	....
1926-27	Toronto Marlboros	OHA-Jr.	10	11	3	14	....	....	....	4	....	....	....	....	....
1927-28	Toronto Maple Leafs	NHL	2	0	0	0	0	0	0	0	....	....	....	....	....
	Toronto Ravinas	Can-Pro	41	26	13	39	....	....	....	36	2	1	0	1	0

Season	Club	League	GP	G	A	Pts	AG	AA	APts	PIM	GP	G	A	Pts	PIM
			REGULAR SEASON								PLAYOFFS				
1928-29	**Toronto Maple Leafs**	**NHL**	**6**	**0**	**1**	**1**	**0**	**7**	**7**	**2**	....	....	....	....	....
	London Panthers	Can-Pro	35	12	10	22	....	....	....	16	....	....	....	....	....
1929-30	**Toronto Maple Leafs**	**NHL**	**43**	**5**	**21**	**26**	**7**	**50**	**57**	**22**	....	....	....	....	....
1930-31	**Toronto Maple Leafs**	**NHL**	**38**	**9**	***32**	**41**	**18**	**99**	**117**	**18**	**2**	**0**	**0**	**0**	**0**
♦1931-32	**Toronto Maple Leafs**	**NHL**	**46**	**13**	***37**	**50**	**22**	**84**	**106**	**25**	**7**	**0**	***6**	**6**	**2**
1932-33	**Toronto Maple Leafs**	**NHL**	**48**	**11**	**21**	**32**	**20**	**44**	**64**	**4**	**8**	**0**	**1**	**1**	**4**
1933-34	**Toronto Maple Leafs**	**NHL**	**45**	**14**	***32**	**46**	**24**	**68**	**92**	**8**	**5**	**2**	**4**	**6**	**6**
1934-35	**Toronto Maple Leafs**	**NHL**	**37**	**10**	**20**	**30**	**16**	**35**	**51**	**16**	**7**	**0**	**3**	**3**	**0**
1935-36	**Toronto Maple Leafs**	**NHL**	**45**	**4**	**13**	**17**	**8**	**25**	**33**	**10**	**9**	**3**	**4**	**7**	**0**
	NHL Totals		**310**	**66**	**177**	**243**	**115**	**412**	**527**	**105**	**38**	**5**	**18**	**23**	**12**

Won Lady Byng Trophy (1932) • NHL Second All-Star Team (1934) • Played in NHL All-Star Game (1934)

Signed as a free agent by **Toronto**, July 17, 1928.

• PRINGLE, Ellie
William Ellis "Moose"
D – L. 6'2", 205 lbs. b: Toronto, Ont., 8/31/1911 Deceased.

Season	Club	League	GP	G	A	Pts	AG	AA	APts	PIM	GP	G	A	Pts	PIM
1928-29	Newmarket Royals	OHA-Jr.	STATISTICS NOT AVAILABLE												
	Toronto Marlboros	OHA-Jr.	9	6	0	6	....	....	....	....	2	1	0	1	....
1929-30	Toronto Marlboros	OHA-Jr.	8	0	0	0	....	....	....	22	....	....	....	....	....
	Toronto Willys-Overland	TIHL	STATISTICS NOT AVAILABLE												
1930-31	**New York Americans**	**NHL**	**6**	**0**	**0**	**0**	**0**	**0**	**0**	**0**	....	....	....	....	....
	New Haven Eagles	Can-Am	30	3	1	4	....	....	....	66	....	....	....	....	....
1931-32	Bronx Tigers	Can-Am	38	2	3	5	....	....	....	83	2	0	0	0	0
1932-33	New Haven Eagles	Can-Am	42	5	3	8	....	....	....	103	....	....	....	....	....
1933-34	Windsor Bulldogs	IHL	44	0	0	0	....	....	....	82	....	....	....	....	....
1934-35	London Tecumsehs	IHL	25	3	1	4	....	....	....	58	....	....	....	....	....
	St. Paul Saints	CHL	15	2	3	5	....	....	....	36	....	....	....	....	....
1935-36	London Tecumsehs	IHL	20	1	1	2	....	....	....	29	....	....	....	....	....
	Rochester Cardinals	IHL	16	1	3	4	....	....	....	30	....	....	....	....	....
1936-37	Tulsa Oilers	AHA	48	4	7	11	....	....	....	72	....	....	....	....	....
1937-38	Vancouver Lions	PCHL	38	2	5	7	....	....	....	56	6	2	0	2	6
1938-39	Vancouver Lions	PCHL	43	6	9	15	....	....	....	37	2	0	0	0	4
1939-40	Toronto Red Indians	TOHL	5	0	2	2	....	....	....	6	3	0	1	1	0
1940-41	Toronto Red Indians	TIHL	5	0	2	2	....	....	....	6	3	0	1	1	0
1941-42	Sutton Greenshirts	OIHA	STATISTICS NOT AVAILABLE												
1942-43	Toronto Dehavillands	TMHL	20	1	1	2	....	....	....	8	7	1	1	2	20
	NHL Totals		**6**	**0**	**0**	**0**	**0**	**0**	**0**	**0**	....	....	....	....	....

Signed as a free agent by **NY Americans**, October 22, 1930. Traded to **London** (IHL) by **Windsor** (IHL) for Farrand Gillie, October 31, 1934. Loaned to **Rochester** (IHL) by **London** (IHL) for cash, January 3, 1936.

• PRODGERS, Goldie
Samuel George
F/D – R. 5'10", 180 lbs. b: London, Ont., 10/18/1891 d: 10/25/1935.

Season	Club	League	GP	G	A	Pts	AG	AA	APts	PIM	GP	G	A	Pts	PIM
1908-09	London Athletics	OHA-Jr.	STATISTICS NOT AVAILABLE												
1909-10	London Wingers	OIHA	STATISTICS NOT AVAILABLE												
1910-11	Waterloo Colts	OPHL	16	9	0	9	....	....	....	....	....	....	....	....	....
♦1911-12	Quebec Bulldogs	NHA	18	3	0	3	....	....	....	15	2	0	0	0	0
1912-13	Victoria Aristocrats	PCHA	15	6	0	6	....	....	....	21	3	1	0	1	0
1913-14	Quebec Bulldogs	NHA	20	2	3	5	....	....	....	11	....	....	....	....	....
1914-15	Montreal Wanderers	NHA	18	8	5	13	....	....	....	54	2	0	0	0	15
♦1915-16	Montreal Canadiens	NHA	24	8	3	11	....	....	....	86	4	3	0	3	13
1916-17	Toronto 228th Battalion	NHA	12	16	3	19	....	....	....	30	....	....	....	....	....
1917-18			MILITARY SERVICE												
1918-19			MILITARY SERVICE												
1919-20	**Toronto St. Pats**	**NHL**	**16**	**8**	**6**	**14**	**9**	**20**	**29**	**4**	....	....	....	....	....
1920-21	**Hamilton Tigers**	**NHL**	**24**	**18**	**9**	**27**	**23**	**35**	**58**	**8**	....	....	....	....	....
1921-22	**Hamilton Tigers**	**NHL**	**24**	**15**	**6**	**21**	**21**	**19**	**40**	**4**	....	....	....	....	....
1922-23	**Hamilton Tigers**	**NHL**	**23**	**13**	**4**	**17**	**22**	**15**	**37**	**17**	....	....	....	....	....
1923-24	**Hamilton Tigers**	**NHL**	**23**	**9**	**4**	**13**	**18**	**23**	**41**	**6**	....	....	....	....	....
1924-25	**Hamilton Tigers**	**NHL**	**1**	**0**	**0**	**0**	**0**	**0**	**0**	**0**	....	....	....	....	....
1925-26			OUT OF HOCKEY – RETIRED												
1926-27	London Panthers	Can-Pro	16	1	0	1	....	....	....	10	....	....	....	....	....
1927-28	London Panthers	Can-Pro	DID NOT PLAY – COACHING												
	NHL Totals		**111**	**63**	**29**	**92**	**93**	**112**	**205**	**39**	....	....	....	....	....
	Other Major League Totals		123	52	14	66	....	....	....	217	11	4	0	4	28

OHA-Jr. First All-Star Team (1909)

Signed as a free agent by **Waterloo** (OPHL), January 5, 1911. Signed by **Victoria** (PCHA) after jumping contract with **Quebec** (NHA), November 18, 1912. Traded to **Montreal Wanderers** (NHA) by **Quebec** (NHA) for cash, December 4, 1914. NHL rights transferred to **Quebec** by **NHL** when Quebec franchise returned to NHL, November 25, 1919. • Suspended by **Quebec** after refusing to report to training camp, November 27, 1919. Traded to **Montreal Canadiens** by **Quebec** for Eddie Carpenter, December 21, 1919. Traded to **Toronto** by **Montreal Canadiens** for Harry Cameron, January 14, 1920. Traded to **Montreal Canadiens** by **Toronto** with Joe Matte for Harry Cameron, November 27, 1920. Traded to **Hamilton** by **Toronto** with Jack Coughlin, Joe Matte and loan of Billy Coutu for 1920-21 season for Harry Mummery, Jack McDonald and Dave Ritchie, November 27, 1920.

• PRONOVOST, Andre
— see page 1541

• PRONOVOST, Marcel
— see page 1542

• PROVOST, Claude
— see page 1543

• PRYSTAI, Metro
C – L. 5'8", 155 lbs. b: Yorkton, Sask., 11/7/1927.

Season	Club	League	GP	G	A	Pts	AG	AA	APts	PIM	GP	G	A	Pts	PIM
1943-44	Moose Jaw Canucks	S-SJHL	2	1	0	1	....	....	....	0	1	0	0	0	0
	Moose Jaw Victorias	S-SSHL					....	....	....	....	2	0	0	0	0
1944-45	Moose Jaw Canucks	S-SJHL	15	13	8	21	....	....	....	6	4	7	5	12	0
	Moose Jaw Canucks	M-Cup	17	8	10	18	....	....	....	19	....	....	....	....	....
1945-46	Moose Jaw Canucks	SJHL	16	25	25	*50	....	....	....	8	4	5	8	13	0
	Moose Jaw Canucks	M-Cup	8	11	7	18	....	....	....	6	....	....	....	....	....
1946-47	Moose Jaw Canucks	SJHL	22	32	39	*71	....	....	....	8	6	5	*9	*14	0
	Moose Jaw Canucks	M-Cup	15	9	*17	*26	....	....	....	6	....	....	....	....	....
1947-48	**Chicago Black Hawks**	**NHL**	**54**	**7**	**11**	**18**	**9**	**14**	**23**	**25**	....	....	....	....	....
1948-49	**Chicago Black Hawks**	**NHL**	**59**	**12**	**7**	**19**	**17**	**10**	**27**	**19**	....	....	....	....	....
1949-50	**Chicago Black Hawks**	**NHL**	**65**	**29**	**22**	**51**	**37**	**27**	**64**	**31**	....	....	....	....	....
1950-51	**Detroit Red Wings**	**NHL**	**62**	**20**	**17**	**37**	**26**	**21**	**47**	**27**	**3**	**1**	**0**	**1**	**0**
♦1951-52	**Detroit Red Wings**	**NHL**	**69**	**21**	**22**	**43**	**28**	**27**	**55**	**16**	**8**	**2**	***5**	***7**	**0**
1952-53	**Detroit Red Wings**	**NHL**	**70**	**16**	**34**	**50**	**21**	**42**	**63**	**12**	**6**	**4**	**4**	**8**	**2**
♦1953-54	**Detroit Red Wings**	**NHL**	**70**	**12**	**15**	**27**	**16**	**18**	**34**	**26**	**12**	**2**	**3**	**5**	**0**
1954-55	**Detroit Red Wings**	**NHL**	**12**	**2**	**3**	**5**	**3**	**3**	**6**	**9**	....	....	....	....	....
	Chicago Black Hawks	**NHL**	**57**	**11**	**13**	**24**	**14**	**15**	**29**	**28**	....	....	....	....	....
1955-56	**Chicago Black Hawks**	**NHL**	**8**	**1**	**3**	**4**	**1**	**4**	**5**	**8**	....	....	....	....	....
	Detroit Red Wings	**NHL**	**63**	**12**	**16**	**28**	**16**	**19**	**35**	**10**	**9**	**1**	**2**	**3**	**6**
1956-57	**Detroit Red Wings**	**NHL**	**70**	**7**	**15**	**22**	**9**	**16**	**25**	**16**	**5**	**2**	**0**	**2**	**0**
1957-58	Edmonton Flyers	WHL	21	13	14	27	....	....	....	6	....	....	....	....	....
	Detroit Red Wings	**NHL**	**15**	**1**	**1**	**2**	**1**	**1**	**2**	**4**	....	....	....	....	....
1958-59	Edmonton Flyers	WHL	4	1	0	1	....	....	....	4	....	....	....	....	....
1959-60	Omaha Knights	IHL	DID NOT PLAY – COACHING												
	NHL Totals		**674**	**151**	**179**	**330**	**198**	**217**	**415**	**231**	**43**	**12**	**14**	**26**	**8**

Played in NHL All-Star Game (1950, 1953, 1954)

Traded to **Detroit** by **Chicago** with Jim Henry, Gaye Stewart and Bob Goldham for Al Dewsbury, Harry Lumley, Jack Stewart, Don Morrison and Pete Babando, July 13, 1950. Traded to **Chicago** by **Detroit** for Lorne Davis, November 9, 1954. Traded to **Detroit** by **Chicago** for Ed Sandford, October 24, 1955.

• PUDAS, Al
John Albert
W – R. 5'10", 160 lbs. b: Siikajoki, Finland, 2/17/1899 d: 10/28/1976.

Season	Club	League	GP	G	A	Pts	AG	AA	APts	PIM	GP	G	A	Pts	PIM
1918/22	Port Arthur Pascoes	TBSHL	STATISTICS NOT AVAILABLE												
1922-23	Port Arthur Ports	MHL-Sr.	16	17	8	25	....	....	....	5	2	1	0	1	0
1923-24	Port Arthur Bearcats	MHL-Sr.	16	11	2	13	....	....	....	2	2	1	0	1	2
1924-25	Port Arthur Bearcats	MHL-Sr.	20	3	3	6	....	....	....	....	10	11	10	21	13
1925-26	Port Arthur Bearcats	MHL-Sr.	20	11	2	13	....	....	....	20	9	*7	*6	*13	18
1926-27	Windsor Bulldogs	Can-Pro	18	10	2	12	....	....	....	8	....	....	....	....	....
	Toronto St. Pats	**NHL**	**4**	**0**	**0**	**0**	**0**	**0**	**0**	**0**	....	....	....	....	....
	Hamilton Tigers	Can-Pro	9	8	0	8	....	....	....	2	2	3	0	3	0
1927-28	London Panthers	Can-Pro	10	2	2	4	....	....	....	4	....	....	....	....	....
	Stratford Nationals	Can-Pro	1	0	0	0	....	....	....	0	....	....	....	....	....
	Detroit Olympics	Can-Pro	19	4	1	5	....	....	....	0	2	0	0	0	0
	NHL Totals		**4**	**0**	**0**	**0**	**0**	**0**	**0**	**0**	....	....	....	....	....

Signed as a free agent by **Toronto**, October 28, 1926. Loaned to **Windsor** by **Toronto** for cash, November 10, 1926. Loaned to **Hamilton** (Can-Pro) by **Toronto** with $5,000 for George Patterson, February 1, 1927. Traded to **London** (Can-Pro) by **Toronto** for Gerry Lowrey, October 20, 1927. Traded to **Kitchener** (Can-Pro) by **London** (Can-Pro) to complete transaction that sent Bill Holmes to London (Can-Pro) (January 16, 1928), March, 1928. Traded to **Stratford** (Can-Pro) by **Kitchener** (Can-Pro) for Jack Kentner, January 19, 1928. Traded to **Detroit** (Can-Pro) by **Stratford** (Can-Pro) for Harry Lott, January 22, 1928.

• PULFORD, Bob
— see page 1544

• PURPUR, Fido
Clifford Joseph **USHOF**
RW – R. 5'6", 155 lbs. b: Grand Forks, ND, 9/26/1914.

Season	Club	League	GP	G	A	Pts	AG	AA	APts	PIM	GP	G	A	Pts	PIM
1931-32	Grand Forks Falcons	H.S.	STATISTICS NOT AVAILABLE												
1932-33	Minneapolis Millers	CHL	37	13	3	16	....	....	....	13	7	1	1	2	6
1933-34	Minneapolis Millers	CHL	44	15	10	25	....	....	....	79	3	2	1	3	2
1934-35	Minneapolis Millers	CHL	14	4	2	6	....	....	....	29	....	....	....	....	....
	St. Louis Eagles	**NHL**	**25**	**1**	**2**	**3**	**2**	**3**	**5**	**8**	....	....	....	....	....
1935-36	St. Louis Flyers	AHA	47	13	5	18	....	....	....	34	7	1	*3	4	2
1936-37	St. Louis Flyers	AHA	32	7	15	22	....	....	....	29	6	2	3	5	2
1937-38	St. Louis Flyers	AHA	48	23	15	38	....	....	....	15	7	0	3	3	4
1938-39	St. Louis Flyers	AHA	48	35	43	78	....	....	....	34	7	3	3	6	4
1939-40	St. Louis Flyers	AHA	46	32	38	70	....	....	....	44	5	1	3	4	4
1940-41	St. Louis Flyers	AHA	46	25	16	41	....	....	....	32	9	*5	0	5	4
1941-42	**Chicago Black Hawks**	**NHL**	**8**	**0**	**0**	**0**	**0**	**0**	**0**	**0**	....	....	....	....	....
	Kansas City Americans	AHA	39	18	30	48	....	....	....	19	6	*10	5	*15	10
1942-43	**Chicago Black Hawks**	**NHL**	**50**	**13**	**16**	**29**	**13**	**15**	**28**	**14**	....	....	....	....	....
1943-44	**Chicago Black Hawks**	**NHL**	**40**	**9**	**10**	**19**	**8**	**9**	**17**	**13**	**9**	**1**	**1**	**2**	**0**
1944-45	**Chicago Black Hawks**	**NHL**	**21**	**2**	**7**	**9**	**2**	**8**	**10**	**11**	....	....	....	....	....
	Indianapolis Capitols	AHL	26	8	14	22	....	....	....	10	5	1	2	3	2
	Detroit Red Wings	**NHL**	....	....	....	....	....	....	....	2	**7**	**0**	**1**	**1**	**4**
1945-46	St. Louis Flyers	AHL	56	18	15	33	....	....	....	21	....	....	....	....	....
1946-47	St. Paul Saints	USHL	56	15	23	38	....	....	....	16	....	....	....	....	....
	NHL Totals		**144**	**25**	**35**	**60**	**25**	**35**	**60**	**46**	**16**	**1**	**2**	**3**	**4**

AHA First All-Star Team (1939, 1940)

Traded to **St. Louis** by **Minneapolis** (CHL) for Nick Wasnie and $1,600, December 28, 1934. Claimed by **Toronto** from **St. Louis** in Dispersal Draft, October 15, 1935. Traded to **St. Louis** (AHA) by **Toronto** for cash, November 6, 1935. Traded to **Chicago** by **St. Louis** (AHA) for Sammy McManus and cash, May 3, 1941. Traded to **Detroit** by **Chicago** to complete transaction that sent Earl Seibert to Detroit (January 2, 1945), January 4, 1945. Traded to **St. Louis** (AHL) by **Detroit** for cash, August 24, 1945.

• PUSIE, Jean
Jean Baptiste
D – L. 6', 205 lbs. b: Montreal, Que., 10/15/1910 d: 4/21/1956.

Season	Club	League	GP	G	A	Pts	AG	AA	APts	PIM	GP	G	A	Pts	PIM
1927-28	Montreal-Rousseau	H.S.	STATISTICS NOT AVAILABLE												
1928-29	Montreal Nationale	MCBHL	STATISTICS NOT AVAILABLE												
1929-30	Verdun CPR	MMRHL	STATISTICS NOT AVAILABLE												
	Montreal Northern Electric	MTRHL	STATISTICS NOT AVAILABLE												
	London Panthers	IHL	11	1	0	1	....	....	....	2	2	0	0	0	2
1930-31	Galt Terriers	OPHL	22	16	8	24	....	....	....	29	2	0	1	1	0
♦	**Montreal Canadiens**	**NHL**	**6**	**0**	**0**	**0**	**0**	**0**	**0**	**0**	**3**	**0**	**0**	**0**	**0**
	Detroit Olympics	IHL	4	0	0	0	....	....	....	0	....	....	....	....	....
1931-32	**Montreal Canadiens**	**NHL**	**1**	**0**	**0**	**0**	**0**	**0**	**0**	**0**	....	....	....	....	....
	Philadelphia Arrows	Can-Am	14	0	4	4	....	....	....	8	....	....	....	....	....
	Trois-Rivieres Renards	ECHL	14	5	2	7	....	....	....	24	....	....	....	....	....
1932-33	Quebec Castors	Can-Am	1	0	1	1	....	....	....	0	....	....	....	....	....
	Regina–Vancouver	WCHL	30	*30	*22	*52	....	....	....	31	2	0	1	1	0
1933-34	**New York Rangers**	**NHL**	**19**	**0**	**2**	**2**	**0**	**4**	**4**	**17**	....	....	....	....	....
	London Tecumsehs	IHL	26	6	6	12	....	....	....	47	6	3	2	5	2
1934-35	**Boston Bruins**	**NHL**	**4**	**1**	**0**	**1**	**2**	**0**	**2**	**0**	**4**	**0**	**0**	**0**	**0**
	Boston Cubs	Can-Am	34	14	13	27	....	....	....	59	....	....	....	....	....
1935-36	**Montreal Canadiens**	**NHL**	**31**	**0**	**2**	**2**	**0**	**4**	**4**	**11**	....	....	....	....	....
	Boston Cubs	Can-Am	16	4	5	9	....	....	....	18	....	....	....	....	....
1936-37	Providence Reds	IAHL	29	5	8	13	....	....	....	39	2	0	0	0	0
1937-38	Cleveland Barons	IAHL	39	0	6	6	....	....	....	13	2	1	1	2	0

Season	Club	League	GP	G	A	Pts	AG	AA	APts	PIM	GP	G	A	Pts	PIM
			REGULAR SEASON								PLAYOFFS				
1938-39	St. Louis Flyers	AHA	35	18	12	30	....	....	....	60	5	2	2	4	16
1939-40	Vancouver Lions	PCHL	30	13	12	25	....	....	....	*85	....	....	....	....	....
1940-41	Seattle Olympics	PCHL	28	10	13	23	....	....	....	48	....	....	....	....	....
1941-42	St. Louis Flyers	AHA	35	9	12	21	....	....	....	19	....	....	....	....	....
1942-43	Montreal Locomotive	MCHL	STATISTICS NOT AVAILABLE												
1943-44	Montreal Army	MCHL	6	0	2	2	....	....	....	12	2	0	1	1	2
1944-45	Montreal NDG Monarchs	MCHL	STATISTICS NOT AVAILABLE												
1945-46			DID NOT PLAY												
1946-47	Verdun Eagles	QPHL	6	3	4	7	....	....	....	0	....	....	....	....	....
	NHL Totals		**61**	**1**	**4**	**5**	**2**	**8**	**10**	**28**	**7**	**0**	**0**	**0**	**0**

Signed as a free agent by **Montreal Canadiens**, February 4, 1930. Loaned to **Providence** (Can-Am) by **Montreal Canadiens** with cash and Gerry Carson for Johnny Gagnon, October 21, 1930. Loan transferred to **Galt** (OPHL) by **Montreal Canadiens** for cash, October 30, 1930. Signed as a free agent by **Regina** (WCHL) after being released by **Quebec** (Can-Am), November 16, 1932. Traded to **NY Rangers** by **Vancouver** (WCHL) for cash, March 11, 1933. Traded to **Boston** by **NY Rangers** for Percy Jackson, November 1, 1934. Traded to **Montreal Canadiens** by **Boston** with Walt Buswell and cash for Roger Jenkins, July 13, 1935. Traded to **Boston** (Can-Am) by **Montreal Canadiens** for cash, February 9, 1936. Signed as a free agent by **St. Louis** (AHA), September 24, 1938. Traded to **Vancouver** (PCHL) by **St. Louis** (AHA) for cash, October 11, 1939. Traded to **St. Louis** (AHA) by **St. Paul** (AHA) for cash, November 3, 1941. Traded to **Fort Worth** (AHA) by **St. Louis** (AHA) for Andre Maloney, February 12, 1942.

• QUACKENBUSH, Bill — Hubert George — HHOF

D – L. 5'11", 190 lbs. b: Toronto, Ont., 3/2/1922 d: 9/12/1999.

Season	Club	League	GP	G	A	Pts	AG	AA	APts	PIM	GP	G	A	Pts	PIM
1939-40	Toronto Western High	H.S.	STATISTICS NOT AVAILABLE												
1940-41	Toronto Native Sons	OHA-Jr.	13	4	9	13	....	....	....	0	....	....	....	....	....
	Toronto Campbell's	TMHL	20	7	9	16	....	....	....	4	....	....	....	....	....
1941-42	Brantford Lions	OHA-Jr.	23	5	29	34	....	....	....	16	7	2	4	6	8
	Toronto Tip Tops	TIHL	....	....	....	....	....	....	....	....	14	2	7	9	6
1942-43	**Detroit Red Wings**	**NHL**	**10**	**1**	**1**	**2**	**1**	**1**	**2**	**4**	....	....	....	....	....
	Indianapolis Capitols	AHL	37	6	13	19	....	....	....	0	7	0	1	1	6
1943-44	**Detroit Red Wings**	**NHL**	**43**	**4**	**14**	**18**	**4**	**12**	**16**	**6**	**2**	**1**	**0**	**1**	**0**
	Indianapolis Capitols	AHL	1	1	0	1	....	....	....	0	....	....	....	....	....
1944-45	**Detroit Red Wings**	**NHL**	**50**	**7**	**14**	**21**	**7**	**16**	**23**	**10**	**14**	**0**	**2**	**2**	**2**
1945-46	**Detroit Red Wings**	**NHL**	**48**	**11**	**10**	**21**	**13**	**14**	**27**	**6**	**5**	**0**	**1**	**1**	**0**
1946-47	**Detroit Red Wings**	**NHL**	**44**	**5**	**17**	**22**	**6**	**20**	**26**	**6**	**5**	**0**	**0**	**0**	**2**
1947-48	**Detroit Red Wings**	**NHL**	**58**	**6**	**16**	**22**	**8**	**21**	**29**	**17**	**10**	**0**	**2**	**2**	**0**
1948-49	**Detroit Red Wings**	**NHL**	**60**	**6**	**17**	**23**	**8**	**24**	**32**	**0**	**11**	**1**	**1**	**2**	**0**
1949-50	**Boston Bruins**	**NHL**	**70**	**8**	**17**	**25**	**10**	**20**	**30**	**4**	....	....	....	....	....
1950-51	**Boston Bruins**	**NHL**	**70**	**5**	**24**	**29**	**6**	**29**	**35**	**12**	**6**	**0**	**1**	**1**	**0**
1951-52	**Boston Bruins**	**NHL**	**69**	**2**	**17**	**19**	**3**	**21**	**24**	**6**	**7**	**0**	**3**	**3**	**0**
1952-53	**Boston Bruins**	**NHL**	**69**	**2**	**16**	**18**	**3**	**19**	**22**	**6**	**11**	**0**	**4**	**4**	**4**
1953-54	**Boston Bruins**	**NHL**	**45**	**0**	**17**	**17**	**0**	**21**	**21**	**6**	**4**	**0**	**0**	**0**	**0**
1954-55	**Boston Bruins**	**NHL**	**68**	**2**	**20**	**22**	**3**	**23**	**26**	**8**	**5**	**0**	**5**	**5**	**0**
1955-56	**Boston Bruins**	**NHL**	**70**	**3**	**22**	**25**	**4**	**26**	**30**	**4**	....	....	....	....	....
	NHL Totals		**774**	**62**	**222**	**284**	**76**	**267**	**343**	**95**	**80**	**2**	**19**	**21**	**8**

• Brother of Max • NHL Second All-Star Team (1947, 1953) • NHL First All-Star Team (1948, 1949, 1951) • Won Lady Byng Trophy (1949) • Played in NHL All-Star Game (1947, 1948, 1949, 1950, 1951, 1952, 1953, 1954)

Signed as a free agent by **Detroit**, October 19, 1942. Traded to **Boston** by **Detroit** with Pete Horeck for Pete Babando, Lloyd Durham, Clare Martin and Jimmy Peters, August 16, 1949.

• QUACKENBUSH, Max — Maxwell Joseph

D – L. 6'2", 180 lbs. b: Toronto, Ont., 8/29/1928.

Season	Club	League	GP	G	A	Pts	AG	AA	APts	PIM	GP	G	A	Pts	PIM
1944-45	DeLasalle Oaklands	H.S.	11	14	13	27	....	....	....	18	2	2	1	3	2
1945-46	DeLasalle Oaklands	H.S.	8	18	13	31	....	....	....	12	12	9	7	16	6
1946-47	DeLasalle Oaklands	H.S.	8	*16	10	*26	....	....	....	18	11	11	5	16	39
1947-48	Windsor Spitfires	OHA-Jr.	35	8	22	30	....	....	....	82	12	1	0	1	23
	Windsor Hettche	IHL	23	5	9	14	....	....	....	71	....	....	....	....	....
1948-49	Omaha Knights	USHL	66	3	14	17	....	....	....	61	4	0	1	1	0
1949-50	Indianapolis Capitols	AHL	68	6	22	28	....	....	....	34	4	0	1	1	0
1950-51	Indianapolis Capitols	AHL	23	2	4	6	....	....	....	24	....	....	....	....	....
	Boston Bruins	**NHL**	**47**	**4**	**6**	**10**	**5**	**7**	**12**	**26**	**6**	**0**	**0**	**0**	**4**
1951-52	St. Louis Flyers	AHL	50	5	15	20	....	....	....	54	....	....	....	....	....
	Chicago Black Hawks	**NHL**	**14**	**0**	**1**	**1**	**0**	**1**	**1**	**4**	....	....	....	....	....
1952-53	Calgary Stampeders	WHL	65	2	21	23	....	....	....	31	3	0	1	1	0
1953-54	Calgary Stampeders	WHL	70	11	28	39	....	....	....	48	18	3	4	7	2
	Calgary Stampeders	Ed-Cup	7	2	*6	8	....	....	....	2	....	....	....	....	....
1954-55	Calgary Stampeders	WHL	63	8	24	32	....	....	....	56	9	1	3	4	4
	NHL Totals		**61**	**4**	**7**	**11**	**5**	**8**	**13**	**30**	**6**	**0**	**0**	**0**	**4**

• Brother of Bill

Loaned to **Boston** by **Detroit** (Indianapolis-AHL) for remainder of 1950-51 season for Steve Kraftcheck, December 5, 1950. Traded to **Chicago** by **Detroit** for Doug McCaig, September 18, 1951. Claimed by **Chicago** from **Calgary-WHL** (Chicago) in Inter-League Draft, June 14, 1954. Traded to **Montreal** by **Chicago** for Fred Burchell, July 3, 1955.
• Transaction voided when Quackenbush officially announced retirement, July 15, 1955.

• QUENNEVILLE, Leo

LW/C – L. 5'10", 170 lbs. b: St. Anicet, Que., 6/15/1900 Deceased.

Season	Club	League	GP	G	A	Pts	AG	AA	APts	PIM	GP	G	A	Pts	PIM
1921-22	Chicoutimi Bluets	QPHL	9	13	0	13	....	....	....	....	1	0	0	0	....
1922-23	Chicoutimi Bluets	QPHL	10	6	0	6	....	....	....	....	1	0	0	0	....
1923-24	Trois-Rivieres Renards	ECHL	11	5	0	5	....	....	....	....	....	....	....	....	....
1924-25	Trois-Rivieres Renards	ECHL	16	14	0	14	....	....	....	....	2	0	0	0	0
1925-26	Chicoutimi Sagueneens	QPHL	STATISTICS NOT AVAILABLE												
1926-27	Quebec Beavers	Can-Am	31	4	2	6	....	....	....	56	2	0	0	0	4
1927-28	Quebec Beavers	Can-Am	40	10	9	19	....	....	....	58	6	2	0	2	*18
1928-29	Hamilton Tigers	IHL	7	1	0	1	....	....	....	16	....	....	....	....	....
	Newark Bulldogs	Can-Am	40	11	6	17	....	....	....	68	....	....	....	....	....
1929-30	**New York Rangers**	**NHL**	**25**	**0**	**3**	**3**	**0**	**7**	**7**	**10**	**3**	**0**	**0**	**0**	**0**
	Springfield Indians	Can-Am	12	2	1	3	....	....	....	19	....	....	....	....	....
1930-31	London Panthers	IHL	48	14	6	20	....	....	....	50	....	....	....	....	....
1931-32	London Tecumsehs	IHL	45	11	17	28	....	....	....	41	6	0	0	0	4
1932-33	London Tecumsehs	IHL	40	11	8	19	....	....	....	55	6	2	1	3	4
1933-34	Quebec Beavers	Can-Am	36	6	17	23	....	....	....	23	....	....	....	....	....
1934-35	Quebec Beavers	Can-Am	41	9	12	21	....	....	....	19	3	0	0	0	0
	NHL Totals		**25**	**0**	**3**	**3**	**0**	**7**	**7**	**10**	**3**	**0**	**0**	**0**	**0**

Claimed by **NY Rangers** from **Newark** (Can-Am) in Inter-League Draft, May 13, 1929. Traded to **London** (IHL) by **NY Rangers** for cash, October 14, 1930.

• QUILTY, John — John Francis

C – L. 5'10", 175 lbs. b: Ottawa, Ont., 1/21/1921 d: 9/12/1969.

Season	Club	League	GP	G	A	Pts	AG	AA	APts	PIM	GP	G	A	Pts	PIM
1936-37	Ottawa Glebe Collegiate	H.S.	STATISTICS NOT AVAILABLE												
1937-38	Ottawa St. Pats	OCJHL	STATISTICS NOT AVAILABLE												
1938-39	Ottawa St. Pats	OCJHL	STATISTICS NOT AVAILABLE												
	Ottawa St. Pats	M-Cup	5	*11	5	*16	....	....	....	0	....	....	....	....	....
1939-40	Ottawa St. Pats	OCJHL	STATISTICS NOT AVAILABLE												
1940-41	**Montreal Canadiens**	**NHL**	**48**	**18**	**16**	**34**	**28**	**23**	**51**	**31**	**3**	**0**	**2**	**2**	**0**
1941-42	**Montreal Canadiens**	**NHL**	**48**	**12**	**12**	**24**	**16**	**14**	**30**	**44**	**3**	**0**	**1**	**1**	**0**
1942-43	Toronto RCAF	OHA-Sr.	9	6	9	15	....	....	....	12	....	....	....	....	....
1943-44	Vancouver RCAF	NNDHL	14	12	14	26	....	....	....	8	3	1	2	3	2
1944-45			MILITARY SERVICE												
1945-46	Ottawa Senators	QSHL	2	0	0	0	....	....	....	0	3	1	0	1	0
1946-47	**Montreal Canadiens**	**NHL**	**3**	**1**	**1**	**2**	**1**	**1**	**2**	**0**	**7**	**3**	**2**	**5**	**9**
	Buffalo Bisons	AHL	5	0	2	2	....	....	....	2	....	....	....	....	....
	Springfield Indians	AHL	46	17	15	32	....	....	....	36	2	0	0	0	0
1947-48	**Montreal Canadiens**	**NHL**	**20**	**2**	**3**	**5**	**3**	**4**	**7**	**4**	....	....	....	....	....
	Boston Bruins	**NHL**	**6**	**3**	**2**	**5**	**4**	**3**	**7**	**2**	....	....	....	....	....
1948-49	North Sydney Victorias	CBSHL	31	5	15	20	....	....	....	18	6	2	3	5	0
1949-50	Ottawa RCAF Flyers	ECSHL	27	10	12	22	....	....	....	6	5	2	4	6	2
1950-51	Ottawa RCAF Flyers	ECSHL	38	0	12	12	....	....	....	54	7	1	3	4	14
	Ottawa Senators	QMHL	....	....	....	....	....	....	....	....	3	0	0	0	4
1951-52	Ottawa Senators	QMHL	3	0	0	0	....	....	....	0	....	....	....	....	....
	Renfrew Millionaires	ECSHL	40	9	27	36	....	....	....	52	3	1	1	2	10
	NHL Totals		**125**	**36**	**34**	**70**	**52**	**45**	**97**	**81**	**13**	**3**	**5**	**8**	**9**

Won Calder Trophy (1941) • ECSHL MVP (1952)

Signed as a free agent by **Montreal**, October 29, 1940. Traded to **Springfield** (AHL) by **Montreal** (Buffalo-AHL) for George Pargeter, November 19, 1946. Traded to **Montreal** by **Springfield** (AHL) for cash, March 3, 1947. Traded to **Boston** by **Montreal** with Jimmy Peters for Joe Carveth December 16, 1947.

• RADLEY, Yip — Harold Henry John

D – L. 6'00", 198 lbs. b: Ottawa, Ont., 6/27/1908 d: 8/19/1963.

Season	Club	League	GP	G	A	Pts	AG	AA	APts	PIM	GP	G	A	Pts	PIM
1926-27	Ottawa Rideaus	OCHL	14	1	2	3	....	....	....	....	....	....	....	....	....
1927-28	Ottawa Rideaus	OCHL	4	0	0	0	....	....	....	....	....	....	....	....	....
1928-29	Ottawa Montagnards	OCHL	15	2	1	3	....	....	....	....	....	....	....	....	....
1929-30	Ottawa Montagnards	OCHL	20	3	1	4	....	....	....	57	6	3	1	4	*20
1930-31	**New York Americans**	**NHL**	**1**	**0**	**0**	**0**	**0**	**0**	**0**	**0**	....	....	....	....	....
	New Haven Eagles	Can-Am	34	1	2	3	....	....	....	77	....	....	....	....	....
1931-32	New Haven Eagles	Can-Am	39	4	0	4	....	....	....	26	2	0	0	0	0
1932-33	New Haven Eagles	Can-Am	27	1	0	1	....	....	....	34	....	....	....	....	....
1933-34	Cleveland Indians	IHL	43	4	6	10	....	....	....	92	....	....	....	....	....
1934-35	Cleveland Indians	IHL	5	0	0	0	....	....	....	4	....	....	....	....	....
	St. Louis Flyers	AHA	40	6	6	12	....	....	....	63	6	1	1	2	*26
1935-36	Tulsa Oilers	AHA	47	5	6	11	....	....	....	*72	2	1	1	2	2
1936-37	**Montreal Maroons**	**NHL**	**17**	**0**	**1**	**1**	**0**	**2**	**2**	**13**	....	....	....	....	....
	Providence Reds	IAHL	4	1	0	1	....	....	....	0	....	....	....	....	....
	New Haven Eagles	IAHL	2	0	0	0	....	....	....	0	....	....	....	....	....
1937-38	Tulsa Oilers	AHA	47	0	10	10	....	....	....	68	4	0	1	1	5
1938-39	Kansas City Greyhounds	AHA	10	0	1	1	....	....	....	12	....	....	....	....	....
	Wichita Skyhawks	AHA	19	4	5	9	....	....	....	8	....	....	....	....	....
1939-40	Wichita Skyhawks	AHA	6	0	1	1	....	....	....	6	....	....	....	....	....
1940-41	Kingston Combines	OHA-Sr.	PLAYER/COACH – STATISTICS UNAVAILABLE												
1941-42	Kingston Combines	OHA-Sr.	16	0	2	2	....	....	....	13	....	....	....	....	....
	NHL Totals		**18**	**0**	**1**	**1**	**0**	**2**	**2**	**13**	....	....	....	....	....

AHA Second All-Star Team (1936)

Signed as a free agent by **NY Americans**, October 22, 1930. Signed as a free agent by **Montreal Maroons**, October 16, 1936 .

• RAGLAN, Rags — Clarence Eldon

D – L. 6'1", 193 lbs. b: Pembroke, Ont., 9/4/1927.

Season	Club	League	GP	G	A	Pts	AG	AA	APts	PIM	GP	G	A	Pts	PIM
1943-44	Toronto Sammy Tafts	OMHA	STATISTICS NOT AVAILABLE												
1944-45	Toronto Marlboros	OHA-Jr.	6	0	1	1	....	....	....	16	....	....	....	....	....
	Toronto Uptown Tires	TMHL	5	0	0	0	....	....	....	4	....	....	....	....	....
1945-46	Toronto Marlboros	OHA-Jr.	25	2	10	12	....	....	....	41	4	0	2	2	6
	Toronto Dorsts	TMHL	1	0	0	0	....	....	....	0	....	....	....	....	....
	Toronto People's Credit	TIHL	3	0	1	1	....	....	....	0	....	....	....	....	....
1946-47	Toronto Marlboros	OHA-Jr.	20	5	4	9	....	....	....	50	2	0	2	2	0
	Toronto Dorsts	TMHL	2	0	2	2	....	....	....	0	11	9	8	17	26
1947-48	Quebec Aces	QSHL	45	9	11	20	....	....	....	106	10	0	1	1	16
1948-49	Quebec Aces	QSHL	63	11	24	35	....	....	....	121	3	0	2	2	4
1949-50	Indianapolis Capitols	AHL	68	4	17	21	....	....	....	61	8	0	2	2	11
1950-51	**Detroit Red Wings**	**NHL**	**33**	**3**	**1**	**4**	**4**	**1**	**5**	**14**	....	....	....	....	....
	Indianapolis Capitols	AHL	30	2	10	12	....	....	....	35	3	0	1	1	4
1951-52	**Chicago Black Hawks**	**NHL**	**35**	**0**	**5**	**5**	**0**	**6**	**6**	**28**	....	....	....	....	....
	St. Louis Flyers	AHL	30	2	12	14	....	....	....	42	....	....	....	....	....
1952-53	**Chicago Black Hawks**	**NHL**	**32**	**1**	**3**	**4**	**1**	**4**	**5**	**10**	**3**	**0**	**0**	**0**	**0**
	Edmonton Flyers	WHL	18	3	2	5	....	....	....	38	....	....	....	....	....
1953-54	Quebec Aces	QHL	63	10	12	22	....	....	....	86	14	0	1	1	4
	Quebec Aces	Ed-Cup	7	0	2	2	....	....	....	*9	....	....	....	....	....
1954-55	Buffalo Bisons	AHL	57	5	8	13	....	....	....	92	10	0	4	4	14
1955-56	Buffalo Bisons	AHL	43	2	18	20	....	....	....	48	3	0	1	1	6
1956-57	Vancouver Canucks	WHL	18	2	3	5	....	....	....	16	....	....	....	....	....
1957-58	Saskatoon–Victoria	WHL	50	4	13	17	....	....	....	50	....	....	....	....	....

Season	Club	League	GP	G	A	Pts	AG	AA	APts	PIM	GP	G	A	Pts	PIM
			REGULAR SEASON								PLAYOFFS				
1958-59	Belleville Merchants	EOHL	22	0	9	9	....	....	....	26	....	....	....	....	....
	Kingston CKLC's	EOHL	30	4	24	28	....	....	....	44	12	0	5	5	6
1959-60	Washington Presidents	EHL	49	3	12	15	....	....	....	41	....	....	....	....	....
1960-61	Windsor Bulldogs	OHA-Sr.	8	1	4	5	....	....	....	20	....	....	....	....	....
	NHL Totals		**100**	**4**	**9**	**13**	**5**	**11**	**16**	**52**	**3**	**0**	**0**	**0**	**0**

• Father of Herb •QSHL First All-Star Team (1949)

Traded to **Chicago** by **Detroit** with George Gee, Jimmy Peters Sr., Clare Martin, Max McNab and Jim McFadden for $75,000 and future considerations (Hugh Coflin, October, 1951), August 20, 1951.

• RALEIGH, Don James Donald "Bones"

C – L. 5′11″, 150 lbs. b: Kenora, Ont., 6/27/1926.

Season	Club	League	GP	G	A	Pts	AG	AA	APts	PIM	GP	G	A	Pts	PIM
1941-42	East Kildonan High	H.S.	STATISTICS NOT AVAILABLE												
	Winnipeg Excelsiors	MAHA	STATISTICS NOT AVAILABLE												
1942-43	Winnipeg Monarchs	MJHL	12	8	1	9	....	....	....	0	2	1	1	2	0
1943-44	**New York Rangers**	**NHL**	**15**	**2**	**2**	**4**	**2**	**2**	**4**	**2**	....	....	....	....	....
	Brooklyn Crescents	EAHL	26	23	20	43	....	....	....	6	11	*16	9	25	4
1944-45	Winnipeg Monarchs	MJHL	5	14	9	23	....	....	....	2	7	5	7	12	19
	Winnipeg Army	WNDHL	4	3	1	4	....	....	....	0	2	1	2	3	0
1945-46	Brandon Elks	MJHL	10	*24	*24	*48	....	....	....	2	7	7	11	18	18
1946-47	University of Manitoba	WSrHL	3	8	6	14	....	....	....	2	....	....	....	....	....
	Winnipeg Flyers	WSrHL	3	4	1	5	....	....	....	0	4	3	*15	*18	0
	Winnipeg Flyers	Al-Cup	8	*8	7	*15	....	....	....	0	....	....	....	....	....
1947-48	**New York Rangers**	**NHL**	**52**	**15**	**18**	**33**	**19**	**24**	**43**	**2**	**6**	**2**	**0**	**2**	**2**
1948-49	**New York Rangers**	**NHL**	**41**	**10**	**16**	**26**	**14**	**23**	**37**	**8**	....	....	....	....	....
1949-50	**New York Rangers**	**NHL**	**70**	**12**	**25**	**37**	**15**	**30**	**45**	**11**	**12**	**4**	**5**	**9**	**4**
1950-51	**New York Rangers**	**NHL**	**64**	**15**	**24**	**39**	**19**	**29**	**48**	**18**	....	....	....	....	....
	New York Rovers	EAHL	2	0	0	0	....	....	....	0	....	....	....	....	....
1951-52	**New York Rangers**	**NHL**	**70**	**19**	**42**	**61**	**25**	**52**	**77**	**14**	....	....	....	....	....
1952-53	**New York Rangers**	**NHL**	**55**	**4**	**18**	**22**	**5**	**22**	**27**	**2**	....	....	....	....	....
1953-54	**New York Rangers**	**NHL**	**70**	**15**	**30**	**45**	**20**	**37**	**57**	**16**	....	....	....	....	....
1954-55	**New York Rangers**	**NHL**	**69**	**8**	**32**	**40**	**10**	**37**	**47**	**19**	....	....	....	....	....
1955-56	**New York Rangers**	**NHL**	**29**	**1**	**12**	**13**	**1**	**14**	**15**	**4**	....	....	....	....	....
	Providence Reds	AHL	13	4	20	24	....	....	....	0	....	....	....	....	....
	Saskatoon Quakers	WHL	25	17	19	36	....	....	....	2	3	1	1	2	2
1956-57	Brandon Regals	WHL	68	13	47	60	....	....	....	14	9	0	3	3	0
	Brandon Regals	Ed-Cup	6	2	6	8	....	....	....	2	....	....	....	....	....
1957-58	Saskatoon Quakers	WHL	40	10	23	33	....	....	....	8	....	....	....	....	....
	NHL Totals		**535**	**101**	**219**	**320**	**130**	**270**	**400**	**96**	**18**	**6**	**5**	**11**	**6**

Played in NHL All-Star Game (1951, 1954)

• RAMSAY, Beattie William Beattie

D – L. 5′7″, 143 lbs. b: Lumsden, Sask., 12/12/1895 d: 9/30/1952.

Season	Club	League	GP	G	A	Pts	AG	AA	APts	PIM	GP	G	A	Pts	PIM
1919-20	University of Toronto	OHA-Sr.	6	3	2	5	....	....	....	....	6	4	*4	8	....
1920-21	University of Toronto	OHA-Sr.	10	5	4	9	....	....	....	....	3	0	1	1	....
	University of Toronto	Al-Cup	5	6	2	8	....	....	....	....	....	....	....	....	....
1921-22	University of Toronto	OHA-Sr.	10	11	4	15	....	....	....	....	....	....	....	....	....
1922-23	Toronto Granites	OHA-Sr.	....	....	....	....	....	....	....	....	2	0	0	0	0
	University of Toronto	Al-Cup	6	3	3	6	....	....	....	0	....	....	....	....	....
1923-24	Toronto Granites	X-Games	12	7	7	14	....	....	....	....	....	....	....	....	....
	Canada	Olympics	5	9	6	15	....	....	....	....	....	....	....	....	....
1924-25	Princeton University	Ivy	DID NOT PLAY – COACHING												
1925-26	Princeton University	Ivy	DID NOT PLAY – COACHING												
1926-27	Princeton University	Ivy	DID NOT PLAY – COACHING												
1927-28	**Toronto Maple Leafs**	**NHL**	**43**	**0**	**2**	**2**	**0**	**11**	**11**	**10**	....	....	....	....	....
1928-29	Yorkton Terriers	S-SSHL	DID NOT PLAY – COACHING												
	NHL Totals		**43**	**0**	**2**	**2**	**0**	**11**	**11**	**10**	....	....	....	....	....

OHA-Sr. First All-Star Team (1921, 1922)

Signed as a free agent by **Toronto**, March 17, 1927.

• RAMSAY, Les

LW – L. 5′9″, 155 lbs. b: Verdun, Que., 7/1/1920.

Season	Club	League	GP	G	A	Pts	AG	AA	APts	PIM	GP	G	A	Pts	PIM
1936-37	Verdun Jr. Maple Leafs	QJHL	11	1	5	6	....	....	....	6	....	....	....	....	....
	Verdun Maple Leafs	QSHL	4	1	0	1	....	....	....	0	....	....	....	....	....
1937-38	Verdun Jr. Maple Leafs	QJHL	9	2	5	7	....	....	....	12	....	....	....	....	....
	Verdun Maple Leafs	QSHL	7	3	1	4	....	....	....	2	5	0	1	1	10
1938-39	Verdun Jr. Maple Leafs	QJHL	11	2	10	12	....	....	....	31	3	0	3	3	4
	Verdun Maple Leafs	QSHL	1	0	0	0	....	....	....	0	....	....	....	....	....
	Verdun Jr. Maple Leafs	M-Cup	7	*6	2	*8	....	....	....	6	....	....	....	....	....
1939-40	Washington Eagles	EAHL	61	25	52	77	....	....	....	24	3	2	1	3	0
1940-41	Verdun Maple Leafs	QSHL	34	16	23	39	....	....	....	39	....	....	....	....	....
1941-42	Verdun Maple Leafs	QSHL	28	8	12	20	....	....	....	16	6	1	2	3	12
	Glace Bay Miners	CBSHL	10	7	2	9	....	....	....	38	....	....	....	....	....
1942-43	Ottawa Flyers	OCHL	18	11	16	27	....	....	....	33	8	8	5	13	2
1943-44	Ottawa Commandos	QSHL	7	2	1	3	....	....	....	8	....	....	....	....	....
1944-45	**Chicago Black Hawks**	**NHL**	**11**	**2**	**2**	**4**	**2**	**2**	**4**	**2**	....	....	....	....	....
	Ottawa Commandos	QSHL	9	5	5	10	....	....	....	6	....	....	....	....	....
1945-46	Hull Volants	QSHL	13	2	6	8	....	....	....	8	....	....	....	....	....
	Lachine Rapides	QPHL	29	4	21	25	....	....	....	20	4	1	2	3	6
1946-47	Lachine Rapides	QPHL	50	22	41	63	....	....	....	44	11	3	4	7	6
1947-48	Moncton Hawks	MMHL	46	20	32	52	....	....	....	21	11	5	3	8	2
1948-49	Moncton Hawks	MMHL	5	2	1	3	....	....	....	2	....	....	....	....	....
	Glace Bay Miners	CBSHL	3	2	2	4	....	....	....	2	....	....	....	....	....
	Antigonish Bulldogs	NSAPC	STATISTICS NOT AVAILABLE												
1949-50	Plouefe Raftsmen	QPHL	STATISTICS NOT AVAILABLE												
1950-51	Saint John Beavers	MMHL	7	5	2	7	....	....	....	0	7	1	2	3	0
	NHL Totals		**11**	**2**	**2**	**4**	**2**	**2**	**4**	**2**	....	....	....	....	....

• RANDALL, Ken Kenneth Fenwick

RW/D – R. 5′10″, 180 lbs. b: Kingston, Ont., Deceased.

Season	Club	League	GP	G	A	Pts	AG	AA	APts	PIM	GP	G	A	Pts	PIM
1906-07	Lindsay Midgets	OHA-Jr.	4	2	0	2	....	....	....	....	6	9	0	9	....
1907-08	Lindsay Midgets	OIHA	6	10	0	10	....	....	....	....	....	....	....	....	....
1908-09	Lindsay Midgets	OIHA	STATISTICS NOT AVAILABLE												
1909-10	Brantford Professionals	OPHL	10	10	0	10	....	....	....	....	....	....	....	....	....
1910-11	Port Hope Professionals	EOPHL	6	*19	0	*19	....	....	....	....	2	*4	0	*4	....
1911-12	Montreal Wanderers	NHA	1	0	0	0	....	....	....	0	....	....	....	....	....
	Saskatoon Hoo Hoos	SPHL	1	0	0	0	....	....	....	0	....	....	....	....	....
	Saskatoon Real Estates	SPHL	2	2	0	2	....	....	....	....	....	....	....	....	....
1912-13	Toronto Blueshirts	NHA	2	0	0	0	....	....	....	0	....	....	....	....	....
	Sydney Millionaires	MPHL	12	17	0	17	....	....	....	18	2	1	0	1	0
1913-14	Sydney Millionaires	MPHL	24	28	0	28	....	....	....	68	2	*5	0	*5	8
1914-15	Sydney Millionaires	MPHL	8	*11	0	*11	....	....	....	17	....	....	....	....	....
1915-16	Toronto Blueshirts	NHA	24	7	5	12	....	....	....	111	....	....	....	....	....
1916-17	Toronto Blueshirts	NHA	13	8	2	10	....	....	....	*64	....	....	....	....	....
	Montreal Wanderers	NHA	5	3	2	5	....	....	....	*40	....	....	....	....	....
1917-18	**Toronto Arenas**	**NHL**	**21**	**12**	**2**	**14**	**15**	**8**	**23**	**96**	**2**	**1**	**1**	**2**	***12**
♦	Toronto Arenas	St-Cup	5	1	0	1	....	....	....	0	....	....	....	....	....
1918-19	**Toronto Arenas**	**NHL**	**14**	**8**	**6**	**14**	**14**	**33**	**47**	**27**	....	....	....	....	....
1919-20	**Toronto St. Pats**	**NHL**	**22**	**10**	**8**	**18**	**11**	**27**	**38**	**42**	....	....	....	....	....
1920-21	**Toronto St. Pats**	**NHL**	**22**	**6**	**5**	**11**	**8**	**19**	**27**	**74**	**2**	**0**	**0**	**0**	**11**
1921-22	**Toronto St. Pats**	**NHL**	**24**	**10**	**6**	**16**	**14**	**19**	**33**	**32**	**2**	**1**	**0**	**1**	**4**
♦	Toronto St. Pats	St-Cup	4	1	0	1	....	....	....	19	....	....	....	....	....
1922-23	**Toronto St. Pats**	**NHL**	**24**	**3**	**5**	**8**	**5**	**19**	**24**	**58**	....	....	....	....	....
1923-24	**Hamilton Tigers**	**NHL**	**24**	**7**	**6**	**13**	**14**	**36**	**50**	**58**	....	....	....	....	....
1924-25	**Hamilton Tigers**	**NHL**	**30**	**8**	**10**	**18**	**14**	**42**	**56**	**52**	....	....	....	....	....
1925-26	**New York Americans**	**NHL**	**34**	**4**	**2**	**6**	**7**	**13**	**20**	**94**	....	....	....	....	....
1926-27	**New York Americans**	**NHL**	**3**	**0**	**0**	**0**	**0**	**0**	**0**	**0**	....	....	....	....	....
	Niagara Falls Cataracts	Can-Pro	15	4	0	4	....	....	....	25	....	....	....	....	....
	Hamilton Tigers	Can-Pro	13	3	2	5	....	....	....	21	2	0	0	0	7
1927-28	Providence Reds	Can-Am	19	0	0	0	....	....	....	6	....	....	....	....	....
1928-29	New Haven Eagles	Can-Am	DID NOT PLAY – COACHING												
1929-30	Kitchener Dutchmen	Can-Pro	DID NOT PLAY – COACHING												
1930-31	Oshawa Patricians	OPHL	2	0	0	0	....	....	....	0	7	0	0	0	4
1931-32	Amherst Ramblers	NSAPC	DID NOT PLAY – COACHING												
	NHL Totals		**218**	**68**	**50**	**118**	**102**	**216**	**318**	**533**	**6**	**2**	**1**	**3**	**27**
	Other Major League Totals		99	84	9	93	....	....	....	318	4	6	0	6	8

OPHL Second All-Star Team (1910) • EOPHL First All-Star Team (1911)

Signed as a free agent by **Brantford** (OPHL), January 5, 1910. Signed as a free agent by **Sydney** (MPHL) after release by **Toronto** (NHA), December 29, 1912. Assigned to **Montreal Wanderers** (NHA) by NHA in dispersal of **Toronto Blueshirts** (NHA) players, February 11, 1917. Signed as a free agent by **Toronto**, December 9, 1917. Traded to **Hamilton** by **Toronto** with the NHL rights to Corb Denneny and cash for Amos Arbour, George Carey and Bert Corbeau, December 14, 1923. Transferred to **NY Americans** after NHL club purchased **Hamilton** franchise, September 26, 1925. Loaned to **Niagara Falls** (Can-Pro) by **NY Americans** for cash, November 22, 1926. Loaned to **Niagara Falls** (Can-Pro) by **NY Americans** for cash, January 26, 1927. Loaned to **Providence** (Can-Am) by **NY Americans** for cash, December 7, 1927.

• RANIERI, George George Dominic

LW – L. 5′8″, 190 lbs. b: Toronto, Ont., 1/14/1936.

Season	Club	League	GP	G	A	Pts	AG	AA	APts	PIM	GP	G	A	Pts	PIM
1953-54	Hamilton Tiger Cubs	OHA-Jr.	6	0	1	1	....	....	....	4	....	....	....	....	....
	Barrie Flyers	OHA-Jr.	48	20	18	38	....	....	....	92	....	....	....	....	....
1954-55	Barrie Flyers	OHA-Jr.	49	14	28	42	....	....	....	101	....	....	....	....	....
	Edmonton Flyers	WHL	2	0	0	0	....	....	....	0	....	....	....	....	....
1955-56	Barrie Flyers	OHA-Jr.	48	29	28	57	....	....	....	74	18	6	*14	20	28
	Edmonton Flyers	WHL	2	0	1	1	....	....	....	8	....	....	....	....	....
1956-57	**Boston Bruins**	**NHL**	**2**	**0**	**0**	**0**	**0**	**0**	**0**	**0**	....	....	....	....	....
	Victoria Cougars	WHL	50	7	12	19	....	....	....	64	....	....	....	....	....
	Hershey Bears	AHL	4	1	0	1	....	....	....	0	....	....	....	....	....
1957-58	Quebec Aces	QHL	5	0	1	1	....	....	....	4	....	....	....	....	....
	Hershey Bears	AHL	8	0	2	2	....	....	....	4	....	....	....	....	....
	Louisville Rebels	IHL	52	25	19	44	....	....	....	54	11	3	8	11	22
1958-59	Louisville Rebels	IHL	59	*60	64	*124	....	....	....	64	11	*11	13	*24	6
1959-60	Louisville Rebels	IHL	8	8	4	12	....	....	....	18	....	....	....	....	....
	New York Rovers	EHL	64	35	45	80	....	....	....	45	....	....	....	....	....
1960-61	Providence Reds	AHL	72	30	41	71	....	....	....	30	....	....	....	....	....
1961-62	Providence Reds	AHL	49	21	22	43	....	....	....	38	....	....	....	....	....
1962-63	Providence Reds	AHL	58	21	23	44	....	....	....	52	6	1	1	2	2
1963-64	Providence Reds	AHL	54	20	26	46	....	....	....	38	....	....	....	....	....
1964-65	Providence Reds	AHL	61	18	22	40	....	....	....	38	....	....	....	....	....
	NHL Totals		**2**	**0**	**0**	**0**	**0**	**0**	**0**	**0**	....	....	....	....	....

IHL First All-Star Team (1959) • Won George H. Wilkinson Trophy (Top Scorer - IHL) (1959)

• RATELLE, Jean — *see page 1550*

• RAVLICH, Matt — *see page 1552*

• RAYMOND, Armand

D – L. 5′9″, 185 lbs. b: Mechanicsville, NY, 1/12/1913 Deceased.

Season	Club	League	GP	G	A	Pts	AG	AA	APts	PIM	GP	G	A	Pts	PIM
1931-32	Montreal Jr. Xavier	MCJHL	10	0	0	0	....	....	....	8	2	0	0	0	8
1932-33	Montreal Jr. Xavier	MCJHL	10	1	0	1	....	....	....	15	2	0	0	0	2
1933-34	Montreal Jr. Xavier	MCJHL	7	1	1	2	....	....	....	20	....	....	....	....	....
	Montreal Sr. Xavier	MCHL	13	2	0	2	....	....	....	*36	....	....	....	....	....
1934-35			DID NOT PLAY												
1935-36	Atlantic City Seagulls	EAHL	21	0	4	4	....	....	....	14	8	1	1	2	6
1936-37	Montreal Sr. Canadiens	QSHL	21	3	3	6	....	....	....	30	2	0	0	0	4
1937-38	**Montreal Canadiens**	**NHL**	**11**	**0**	**1**	**1**	**0**	**2**	**2**	**10**	....	....	....	....	....
	Montreal Concordia	MCHL	21	6	7	13	....	....	....	32	1	0	0	0	2
1938-39	Montreal Concordia	MCHL	STATISTICS NOT AVAILABLE												
1939-40	**Montreal Canadiens**	**NHL**	**11**	**0**	**1**	**1**	**0**	**2**	**2**	**0**	....	....	....	....	....
	Providence Reds	IAHL	22	0	4	4	....	....	....	14	....	....	....	....	....
1940-41	St-Jerome Papermakers	QPHL	33	18	20	38	....	....	....	86	8	2	5	7	6
	St-Jerome Papermakers	Al-Cup	4	0	0	0	....	....	....	0	....	....	....	....	....
1941-42	Shawinigan Cataracts	QPHL	28	1	21	22	....	....	....	40	10	1	1	2	12
	NHL Totals		**22**	**0**	**2**	**2**	**0**	**4**	**4**	**10**	....	....	....	....	....

• RAYMOND, Paul Paul Marcel

RW – R. 5′8″, 150 lbs. b: Montreal, Que., 2/27/1913 d: 4/4/1995.

Season	Club	League	GP	G	A	Pts	AG	AA	APts	PIM	GP	G	A	Pts	PIM
1930-31	Montreal Jr. Canadiens	MCJHL	4	2	1	3	....	....	....	2	....	....	....	....	....
1931-32	Montreal Sr. Canadiens	MCHL	11	5	4	9	....	....	....	8	2	2	0	2	0
1932-33	**Montreal Canadiens**	**NHL**	**16**	**0**	**0**	**0**	**0**	**0**	**0**	**0**	....	....	....	....	....
	Providence Reds	IHL	20	1	5	6	....	....	....	0	2	0	0	0	0

			REGULAR SEASON								PLAYOFFS				
Season	Club	League	GP	G	A	Pts	AG	AA	APts	PIM	GP	G	A	Pts	PIM
1933-34	Montreal Canadiens	NHL	29	1	0	1	2	0	2	2	2	0	0	0	0
	Windsor Bulldogs	IHL	20	1	1	2	....	....	....	6	....	....	....	....	....
1934-35	Montreal Canadiens	NHL	20	1	1	2	2	2	4	0	....	....	....	....	....
	Quebec Beavers	Can-Am	30	9	12	21	....	....	....	24	3	0	0	0	4
1935-36	Springfield Indians	Can-Am	48	6	27	33	....	....	....	55	3	2	1	3	0
1936-37	Springfield Indians	IAHL	43	11	17	28	....	....	....	49	5	0	2	2	0
1937-38	Springfield Indians	IAHL	14	0	4	4	....	....	....	0	....	....	....	....	....
	New Haven Eagles	IAHL	33	10	14	24	....	....	....	14	2	0	0	0	0
1938-39	Montreal Canadiens	NHL	11	0	2	2	0	3	3	4	3	0	0	0	2
	New Haven Eagles	IAHL	51	2	5	7	....	....	....	22	....	....	....	....	....
1939-40	Montreal Royals	QSHL	26	6	27	33	....	....	....	12	6	3	*5	8	0
	Montreal Royals	Al-Cup	5	2	*7	9	....	....	....	0	....	....	....	....	....
1940-41	Montreal Royals	QSHL	33	13	19	32	....	....	....	31	4	0	0	0	0
	Montreal Royals	Al-Cup	10	1	4	5	....	....	....	6	....	....	....	....	....
1941-42	Montreal Royals	QSHL	38	17	18	35	....	....	....	24	....	....	....	....	....
1942-43	Montreal Royals	QSHL	5	0	0	0	....	....	....	8	....	....	....	....	....
1943-44			MILITARY SERVICE												
1944-45			MILITARY SERVICE												
1945-46	Montreal Royals	QSHL	26	8	14	22	....	....	....	6	9	2	6	8	6
1946-47	Montreal Royals	QSHL	2	0	1	1	....	....	....	0	....	....	....	....	....
	Lachine Rapides	QPHL	26	9	15	24	....	....	....	13	9	1	1	2	2
	NHL Totals		76	2	3	5	4	5	9	6	5	0	0	0	2

QSHL Second Team All-Star (1940)

Signed as a free agent by **Montreal Canadiens**, October 28, 1932. Traded to **New Haven** (IAHL) by **Springfield** (IAHL) for Max Kaminsky, December 23, 1937. Signed as a free agent by **Montreal Canadiens**, February 21, 1938.

• READ, Mel

Melvin Dean "Pee Wee"
C – L. 5'8", 165 lbs. b: Montreal, Que., 4/10/1924.

Season	Club	League	GP	G	A	Pts	AG	AA	APts	PIM	GP	G	A	Pts	PIM
1940-41	Verdun Jr. Maple Leafs	QJHL	12	7	8	15	....	....	....	2	2	0	0	0	0
	Verdun Maple Leafs	QSHL	1	0	0	0	....	....	....	0	....	....	....	....	....
1941-42	Cornwall Flyers	QSHL	40	11	10	21	....	....	....	14	5	0	0	0	4
1942-43	Montreal Sr. Canadiens	QSHL	22	7	7	14	....	....	....	4	....	....	....	....	....
1943-44	Montreal Navy	MCHL	11	12	*13	*25	....	....	....	4	6	*7	3	10	4
1944-45	Montreal Royals	QSHL	12	4	3	7	....	....	....	9	3	0	1	1	0
1945-46	Dallas Texans	USHL	56	*39	53	92	....	....	....	28	....	....	....	....	....
1946-47	New York Rangers	NHL	1	0	0	0	0	0	0	0	....	....	....	....	....
	New Haven Ramblers	AHL	59	13	27	40	....	....	....	42	3	1	2	3	2
1947-48	St. Paul Saints	USHL	62	19	30	49	....	....	....	36	....	....	....	....	....
1948-49	Tacoma Rockets	PCHL	70	27	43	70	....	....	....	41	6	2	5	7	0
	Shawinigan Cataracts	QSHL	1	0	1	1	....	....	....	0	....	....	....	....	....
1949-50	Tacoma Rockets	PCHL	70	20	*67	87	....	....	....	23	5	3	3	6	0
1950-51	Tacoma Rockets	PCHL	70	22	42	64	....	....	....	18	6	1	2	3	2
1951-52	Shawinigan Cataracts	QMHL	58	7	23	30	....	....	....	8	....	....	....	....	....
	NHL Totals		1	0	0	0	0	0	0	0	....	....	....	....	....

USHL Second All-Star Team (1946) • PCHL Northern First All-Star Team (1950)

Loaned to **Tacoma** (PCHL) by **NY Rangers** for cash, September 30, 1948.

• REARDON, Ken

Kenneth Joseph **HHOF**
D – L. 5'10", 180 lbs. b: Winnipeg, Man., 4/1/1921.

Season	Club	League	GP	G	A	Pts	AG	AA	APts	PIM	GP	G	A	Pts	PIM
1937-38	Blue River Rebels	BCJHL	STATISTICS NOT AVAILABLE												
1938-39	Edmonton Athletic Club	EJrHL	9	0	1	1	....	....	....	15	2	0	2	2	....
	Edmonton Athletic Club	M-Cup	2	0	1	1	....	....	....	0	....	....	....	....	....
1939-40	Edmonton Athletic Club	EJrHL	10	....	....	....	....	....	....	*42	4	0	2	2	*8
	Edmonton Athletic Club	M-Cup	14	18	13	31	....	....	....	46	....	....	....	....	....
1940-41	Montreal Canadiens	NHL	34	2	8	10	3	11	14	41	3	0	0	0	4
1941-42	Montreal Canadiens	NHL	41	3	12	15	4	14	18	93	3	0	0	0	4
1942-43	Ottawa Commandos	OCHL	26	7	16	23	....	....	....	77	23	3	9	12	*47
	Ottawa Army	OCHL	10	10	7	17	....	....	....	15	....	....	....	....	....
1943-44	Ottawa Commandos	OCHL	1	1	0	1	....	....	....	0	....	....	....	....	....
1944-45			MILITARY SERVICE												
♦1945-46	Montreal Canadiens	NHL	43	5	4	9	6	6	12	45	9	1	1	2	4
	Montreal Royals	QSHL	2	0	0	0	....	....	....	4	....	....	....	....	....
1946-47	Montreal Canadiens	NHL	52	5	17	22	6	20	26	84	7	1	2	3	20
1947-48	Montreal Canadiens	NHL	58	7	15	22	9	20	29	129	....	....	....	....	....
1948-49	Montreal Canadiens	NHL	46	3	13	16	4	18	22	103	7	0	0	0	18
1949-50	Montreal Canadiens	NHL	67	1	27	28	1	33	34	109	2	0	2	2	12
	NHL Totals		341	26	96	122	33	122	155	604	31	2	5	7	62

• Brother of Terry • NHL Second All-Star Team (1946, 1948, 1949) • NHL First All-Star Team (1947, 1950) • Played in NHL All-Star Game (1947, 1948, 1949)

• Only games played and penalty minute totals available for Edmonton (EJrHL) in 1939-40 season. Signed as a free agent by **Montreal**, October 26, 1940.

• REARDON, Terry

Terry George
C/RW – R. 5'10", 170 lbs. b: Winnipeg, Man., 4/6/1919 d: 2/14/1993.

Season	Club	League	GP	G	A	Pts	AG	AA	APts	PIM	GP	G	A	Pts	PIM
1934-35	East Kildonan North Stars	MAHA	STATISTICS NOT AVAILABLE												
1935-36	St. Boniface Seals	MJHL	13	9	3	12	....	....	....	4	....	....	....	....	....
1936-37	St. Boniface Seals	MJHL	16	*22	10	32	....	....	....	27	7	*8	2	*10	*17
1937-38	Brandon Wheat Kings	MJHL	16	*29	*16	*45	....	....	....	20	5	5	1	6	6
1938-39	Boston Bruins	NHL	4	0	0	0	0	0	0	0	....	....	....	....	....
	Hershey Bears	IAHL	50	7	20	27	....	....	....	31	5	1	0	1	2
1939-40	Hershey Bears	IAHL	55	13	24	37	....	....	....	26	4	4	0	4	2
	Boston Bruins	NHL	....	....	....	....	....	....	....	....	1	0	1	1	0
♦1940-41	Boston Bruins	NHL	34	6	5	11	9	7	16	19	11	2	4	6	6
	Hershey Bears	AHL	19	3	8	11	....	....	....	10	....	....	....	....	....
1941-42	Montreal Canadiens	NHL	33	17	17	34	23	20	43	14	3	2	2	4	2
1942-43	Montreal Canadiens	NHL	13	6	6	12	6	6	12	2	....	....	....	....	....
	Montreal Army	MCHL	19	7	17	24	....	....	....	6	7	4	2	6	2
1943-44	Nanaimo Army	NNDHL	11	6	7	13	....	....	....	12	....	....	....	....	....
1944-45			MILITARY SERVICE												
1945-46	Boston Bruins	NHL	49	12	11	23	14	16	30	21	10	4	0	4	2
1946-47	Boston Bruins	NHL	60	6	14	20	7	17	24	17	5	0	3	3	2
1947-48	Providence Reds	AHL	49	4	10	14	....	....	....	28	5	2	1	3	10
1948-49	Providence Reds	AHL	68	2	10	12	....	....	....	16	14	4	1	5	2
1949-50	Providence Reds	AHL	61	2	9	11	....	....	....	9	1	0	0	0	12
1950-51	Providence Reds	AHL	46	5	16	21	....	....	....	12	....	....	....	....	....
1951-52	Providence Reds	AHL	19	2	6	8	....	....	....	16	11	0	7	7	12
1952-53	Providence Reds	AHL	15	0	2	2	....	....	....	6	....	....	....	....	....
1953-54	Sydney Millionaires	MMHL	58	6	25	31	....	....	....	32	13	0	4	4	2
1954-55	Providence Reds	AHL	15	1	8	9	....	....	....	2	....	....	....	....	....
	NHL Totals		193	47	53	100	59	66	125	73	30	8	10	18	12

• Brother of Ken

Rights traded to **Boston** by **NY Americans** with the rights to Tom Cooper to complete transaction that sent Joe Jerwa to Boston (January 25, 1937), October 17, 1937. Loaned to **Montreal** by **Boston** for the loan of Paul Gauthier's NHL rights, November 5, 1941. Named playing-coach of **Providence** (AHL), September 24, 1947. Named playing-coach of **Sydney** (MMHL), September 3, 1953.

• REAUME, Marc

— *see page 1552*

• REAY, Billy

William T.
C – L. 5'7", 155 lbs. b: Winnipeg, Man., 8/21/1918.

Season	Club	League	GP	G	A	Pts	AG	AA	APts	PIM	GP	G	A	Pts	PIM
1936-37	St. Boniface Seals	MJHL	15	4	4	8	....	....	....	6	7	1	0	1	2
1937-38	St. Boniface Seals	MJHL	15	15	7	22	....	....	....	14	10	5	5	10	12
	Winnipeg Hudson's Bay	WSrHL	8	5	3	8	....	....	....	4	....	....	....	....	....
1938-39	Calgary Stampeders	CCSHL	32	11	8	19	....	....	....	44	....	....	....	....	....
1939-40	Omaha Knights	AHA	48	18	20	38	....	....	....	23	9	*6	1	7	4
1940-41	Omaha Knights	AHA	46	18	22	40	....	....	....	32	....	....	....	....	....
1941-42	Quebec Aces	QSHL	1	1	0	1	....	....	....	0	7	1	3	4	4
	Sydney Millionaires	CBSHL	DID NOT PLAY – COACHING												
	Quebec Aces	Al-Cup	11	6	3	9	....	....	....	8	....	....	....	....	....
1942-43	Quebec Aces	QSHL	29	16	26	42	....	....	....	22	4	2	0	2	2
1943-44	Detroit Red Wings	NHL	2	2	0	2	2	0	2	0	....	....	....	....	....
	Quebec Aces	QSHL	25	15	*31	46	....	....	....	19	5	2	7	9	2
	Quebec Aces	Al-Cup	9	3	9	12	....	....	....	0	....	....	....	....	....
1944-45	Detroit Red Wings	NHL	2	0	0	0	0	0	0	0	....	....	....	....	....
	Quebec Aces	QSHL	20	17	29	46	....	....	....	6	7	3	1	4	4
	Quebec Aces	Al-Cup	3	0	0	0	....	....	....	0	....	....	....	....	....
♦1945-46	Montreal Canadiens	NHL	44	17	12	29	20	17	37	10	9	1	2	3	4
1946-47	Montreal Canadiens	NHL	59	22	20	42	25	24	49	17	11	6	1	7	14
1947-48	Montreal Canadiens	NHL	60	6	14	20	8	18	26	24	....	....	....	....	....
1948-49	Montreal Canadiens	NHL	60	22	23	45	31	33	64	33	7	1	5	6	4
1949-50	Montreal Canadiens	NHL	68	19	26	45	24	31	55	48	4	0	1	1	0
1950-51	Montreal Canadiens	NHL	60	6	18	24	8	22	30	24	11	3	3	6	10
1951-52	Montreal Canadiens	NHL	68	7	34	41	9	42	51	20	10	2	2	4	7
♦1952-53	Montreal Canadiens	NHL	56	4	15	19	5	18	23	26	11	0	2	2	4
1953-54	Victoria Cougars	WHL	69	10	14	24	....	....	....	30	5	0	0	0	2
1954-55	Victoria Cougars	WHL	70	3	28	31	....	....	....	43	5	1	1	2	4
	NHL Totals		479	105	162	267	132	205	337	202	63	13	16	29	43

Won Byng of Vimy Trophy (Sportsmanship - QSHL) (1945) • Played in NHL All-Star Game (1952)

Signed as a free agent by **Detroit**, October 2, 1939. • Served as coach of Sydney (CBSHL) from November 18 through December 28, 1941. Awarded to **Quebec** (QSHL) by QSHL, February 23, 1942. Traded to **Montreal** by **Detroit** for Ray Getliffe and Rolly Rossignol, September 11, 1945. • Detroit received Fern Gauthier (October 18, 1945) as compensation after Getliffe decided to retire. Named playing-coach of **Victoria** (WHL), June 25, 1953.

• REDAHL, Gord

Gordon Charles
RW – L. 5'11", 170 lbs. b: Kinistino, Sask., 8/28/1935.

Season	Club	League	GP	G	A	Pts	AG	AA	APts	PIM	GP	G	A	Pts	PIM
1952-53	Flin Flon Bombers	SJHL	1	0	0	0	....	....	....	0	....	....	....	....	....
1953-54	Flin Flon Bombers	SJHL	39	27	19	46	....	....	....	10	17	8	8	16	8
	Saskatoon Quakers	WHL	1	1	0	1	....	....	....	0	....	....	....	....	....
	Flin Flon Bombers	M-Cup	4	0	0	0	....	....	....	2	....	....	....	....	....
1954-55	Flin Flon Bombers	SJHL	45	33	23	56	....	....	....	49	5	2	1	3	4
1955-56	Flin Flon Bombers	SJHL	48	39	39	78	....	....	....	62	12	9	5	14	8
	Saskatoon Quakers	WHL	1	0	0	0	....	....	....	2	....	....	....	....	....
	Flin Flon Bombers	M-Cup	7	2	1	3	....	....	....	12	....	....	....	....	....
1956-57	Winnipeg Warriors	WHL	65	14	12	26	....	....	....	19	....	....	....	....	....
1957-58	Winnipeg Warriors	WHL	57	20	27	47	....	....	....	30	7	5	3	8	4
1958-59	Boston Bruins	NHL	18	0	1	1	0	1	1	2	....	....	....	....	....
	Providence Reds	AHL	16	0	0	0	....	....	....	11	....	....	....	....	....
	Rochester Americans	AHL	15	4	2	6	....	....	....	2	....	....	....	....	....
1959-60	Winnipeg Warriors	WHL	70	24	22	46	....	....	....	20	....	....	....	....	....
1960-61	Winnipeg Warriors	WHL	67	19	24	43	....	....	....	19	....	....	....	....	....
1961-62	San Francisco Seals	WHL	51	16	17	33	....	....	....	10	....	....	....	....	....
	Pittsburgh Hornets	AHL	10	3	3	6	....	....	....	6	....	....	....	....	....
1962-63	Pittsburgh Hornets	AHL	5	1	0	1	....	....	....	2	....	....	....	....	....
	Calgary Stampeders	WHL	55	14	25	39	....	....	....	10	....	....	....	....	....
1963-64	Denver Invaders	WHL	69	25	33	58	....	....	....	24	6	2	4	6	4
1964-65	Victoria Maple Leafs	WHL	70	32	29	61	....	....	....	22	12	3	4	7	6
1965-66	Victoria Maple Leafs	WHL	66	23	26	49	....	....	....	12	14	3	3	6	2
1966-67	Rochester Americans	AHL	6	0	3	3	....	....	....	0	....	....	....	....	....
	Victoria Maple Leafs	WHL	41	9	10	19	....	....	....	12	5	0	1	1	0
1967-68	Phoenix Roadrunners	WHL	52	16	16	32	....	....	....	10	4	0	0	0	0
1968-69	Denver Spurs	WHL	65	18	17	35	....	....	....	18	....	....	....	....	....
1969-70	Denver Spurs	WHL	14	0	3	3	....	....	....	0	....	....	....	....	....
1970-71	The Pass Huskies	AIHA	STATISTICS NOT AVAILABLE												
	NHL Totals		18	0	1	1	0	1	1	2	....	....	....	....	....

Claimed by **Boston** from **NY Rangers** in Intra-League Draft, June 3, 1958. Traded to **Toronto** (Rochester-AHL) by **Boston** (Providence-AHL) for Bo Elik, November 21, 1958. Traded to **Pittsburgh** (AHL) by **San Francisco** (WHL) for Bob Bailey, February 27, 1962. Traded to **Calgary** (WHL) by **Pittsburgh** (AHL) for cash, October 24, 1962. Claimed by **Toronto** from **Denver** (WHL) in Inter-League Draft, June 8, 1964. Traded to **Denver** (WHL) by **Toronto** for cash, July, 1968.

• REDDING, George

"Shorty"
LW/D – L. 5'7", 145 lbs. b: Peterborough, Ont., 3/6/1903 Deceased.

Season	Club	League	GP	G	A	Pts	AG	AA	APts	PIM	GP	G	A	Pts	PIM
1920-21	Hamilton Beavers	OHA-Jr.	STATISTICS NOT AVAILABLE												
1921-22	Hamilton Tigers	OHA-Sr.	10	1	4	5	....	....	....	....	....	....	....	....	....
1922-23	Hamilton Tigers	OHA-Sr.	11	0	1	1	....	....	....	....	2	0	0	0	2
1923-24	Hamilton Tigers	OHA-Sr.	10	4	4	8	....	....	....	....	2	0	0	0	....
1924-25	Boston Bruins	NHL	27	3	2	5	5	8	13	10	....	....	....	....	....
1925-26	Boston Bruins	NHL	28	0	0	0	0	0	0	13	....	....	....	....	....
1926-27	Boston Tigers	Can-Am	31	7	0	7	....	....	....	39	....	....	....	....	....
1927-28	Boston Tigers	Can-Am	39	7	3	10	....	....	....	48	2	1	0	1	2

Season	Club	League	GP	G	A	Pts	AG	AA	APts	PIM	GP	G	A	Pts	PIM
			REGULAR SEASON								PLAYOFFS				
1928-29	London Panthers	Can-Pro	33	0	0	0	....	....	....	60	....	....	....	....	....
1929-30	Minneapolis Millers	AHA	47	4	3	7	....	....	....	64	....	....	....	....	....
1930-31	Minneapolis Millers	AHA	43	9	3	12	....	....	....	73	....	....	....	....	....
1931-32	Buffalo Majors	AHA	13	0	2	2	....	....	....	8	....	....	....	....	....
1932-33	Hamilton Pats	OHA-Sr.	DID NOT PLAY – COACHING												
	NHL Totals		**55**	**3**	**2**	**5**	**5**	**8**	**13**	**23**	....	....	....	....	....

Signed as a free agent by **Boston**, October 16, 1924. Traded to **Minneapolis** (AHA) by **London** (IHL) for the rights to Babe Donnelly, October 24, 1929.

• REGAN, Bill — William Ronald

D – L. 6'1", 190 lbs. b: Creighton Mines, Ont., 12/11/1908 Deceased.

Season	Club	League	GP	G	A	Pts	AG	AA	APts	PIM	GP	G	A	Pts	PIM
1925-26	St. Michael's Majors	OHA-Jr.	5	2	1	3	....	....	....	....	....	....	....	....	....
1926-27	St. Michael's Majors	OHA-Jr.	1	0	0	0	....	....	....	....	6	4	1	5	....
1927-28	St. Michael's Majors	OHA-Jr.	6	12	3	15	....	....	....	....	6	2	2	4	....
1928-29	St. Michael's Majors	OHA-Jr.	6	3	4	7	....	....	....	....	....	....	....	....	....
1929-30	Boston Tigers	Can-Am	28	6	5	11	....	....	....	45	....	....	....	....	....
	New York Rangers	**NHL**	**10**	**0**	**0**	**0**	**0**	**0**	**0**	**4**	**4**	**0**	**0**	**0**	**0**
1930-31	**New York Rangers**	**NHL**	**42**	**2**	**1**	**3**	**4**	**3**	**7**	**49**	**4**	**0**	**0**	**0**	**2**
1931-32	Bronx Tigers	Can-Am	40	5	10	15	....	....	....	106	2	0	0	0	6
1932-33	Springfield Indians	Can-Am	13	1	2	3	....	....	....	30	....	....	....	....	....
	New York Americans	**NHL**	**15**	**1**	**1**	**2**	**2**	**2**	**4**	**14**	....	....	....	....	....
	New Haven Eagles	Can-Am	15	7	3	10	....	....	....	32	....	....	....	....	....
1933-34	Buffalo–Cleveland	IHL	45	9	13	22	....	....	....	85	....	....	....	....	....
1934-35			DID NOT PLAY												
1935-36			DID NOT PLAY												
1936-37	Creighton Mines	GBHL	13	2	0	2	....	....	....	34	2	0	0	0	*8
	Sudbury Frood Miners	NBHL	....	....	....	....	....	....	....	....	6	1	1	2	4
	NHL Totals		**67**	**3**	**2**	**5**	**6**	**5**	**11**	**67**	**8**	**0**	**0**	**0**	**2**

• Missed majority of 1926-27 season recovering from arm injury suffered in exhibition game vs. North Bay, December 26, 1926. Traded to **NY Rangers** by **Boston** for Yip Foster and $15,000, February 17, 1930. Loaned to **Bronx** (Can-Am) by **NY Rangers** for cash, November 1, 1931. Loaned to **NY Americans** by **NY Rangers** for the remainder of 1932-33 season for cash, December 27, 1932.

• REGAN, Larry — Lawrence Emmett

RW – R. 5'9", 162 lbs. b: North Bay, Ont., 8/9/1930.

Season	Club	League	GP	G	A	Pts	AG	AA	APts	PIM	GP	G	A	Pts	PIM
1946-47	Ottawa Jr. Senators	OCJHL	24	22	18	40	....	....	....	2	2	0	2	2	0
	Ottawa Senators	QSHL	3	1	0	1	....	....	....	0	3	0	0	0	0
1947-48	Ottawa Senators	QSHL	41	17	14	31	....	....	....	35	5	0	2	2	0
1948-49	Toronto Marlboros	OHA-Jr.	40	19	15	34	....	....	....	25	10	4	2	6	0
1949-50	Toronto Marlboros	OHA-Jr.	48	38	36	74	....	....	....	22	5	1	3	4	0
1950-51	Ottawa Senators	QMHL	52	14	31	45	....	....	....	28	9	0	3	3	0
1951-52	Ottawa Senators	QMHL	50	11	10	21	....	....	....	27	7	0	0	0	8
1952-53	Shawinigan Cataracts	QMHL	52	15	27	42	....	....	....	21	....	....	....	....	....
1953-54	Quebec Aces	QHL	70	19	32	51	....	....	....	14	16	5	5	10	4
	Quebec Aces	Ed-Cup	7	2	1	3	....	....	....	0	....	....	....	....	....
1954-55	Quebec Aces	QHL	51	11	30	41	....	....	....	39	8	1	2	3	6
1955-56	Quebec Aces	QHL	3	3	1	4	....	....	....	2	7	4	4	8	4
	Pembroke Lumber Kings	NOHA	22	5	14	19	....	....	....	10	....	....	....	....	....
1956-57	**Boston Bruins**	**NHL**	**69**	**14**	**19**	**33**	**18**	**21**	**39**	**29**	**8**	**0**	**2**	**2**	**10**
1957-58	**Boston Bruins**	**NHL**	**59**	**11**	**28**	**39**	**14**	**29**	**43**	**22**	**12**	**3**	**8**	**11**	**6**
1958-59	**Boston Bruins**	**NHL**	**36**	**5**	**6**	**11**	**6**	**6**	**12**	**10**	....	....	....	....	....
	Toronto Maple Leafs	**NHL**	**32**	**4**	**21**	**25**	**5**	**21**	**26**	**2**	**8**	**1**	**1**	**2**	**2**
1959-60	**Toronto Maple Leafs**	**NHL**	**47**	**4**	**16**	**20**	**5**	**16**	**21**	**6**	**10**	**3**	**3**	**6**	**0**
1960-61	**Toronto Maple Leafs**	**NHL**	**37**	**3**	**5**	**8**	**3**	**5**	**8**	**2**	**4**	**0**	**0**	**0**	**0**
1961-62	Pittsburgh Hornets	AHL	49	10	19	29	....	....	....	12	....	....	....	....	....
1962-63	IEV Innsbruck	Austria	DID NOT PLAY – COACHING												
1963-64	IEV Innsbruck	Austria	DID NOT PLAY – COACHING												
1964-65	Etobicoke Indians	OHA-B	DID NOT PLAY – COACHING												
1965-66	Baltimore Clippers	AHL	64	16	34	50	....	....	....	41	....	....	....	....	....
	NHL Totals		**280**	**41**	**95**	**136**	**51**	**98**	**149**	**71**	**42**	**7**	**14**	**21**	**18**

Won Calder Memorial Trophy (1957)

Claimed by **Boston** from **Quebec** (QHL) in Inter-League Draft, June 5, 1956. Claimed on waivers by **Toronto** from **Boston**, January 7, 1959. Named playing-coach of **Pittsburgh** (AHL), June 12, 1961.

• REIBEL, Earl — "Dutch"

C – R. 5'8", 160 lbs. b: Kitchener, Ont., 7/21/1930.

Season	Club	League	GP	G	A	Pts	AG	AA	APts	PIM	GP	G	A	Pts	PIM
1948-49	Kitchener Greenshirts	OHA-B	STATISTICS NOT AVAILABLE												
1949-50	Windsor Spitfires	OHA-Jr.	48	53	*76	*129	....	....	....	14	11	7	*14	*21	2
1950-51	Omaha Knights	USHL	32	13	25	38	....	....	....	6	10	0	6	6	2
1951-52	Indianapolis Capitols	AHL	68	33	34	67	....	....	....	8	....	....	....	....	....
1952-53	Edmonton Flyers	WHL	70	34	56	*90	....	....	....	14	12	6	6	12	4
♦1953-54	**Detroit Red Wings**	**NHL**	**69**	**15**	**33**	**48**	**20**	**40**	**60**	**18**	**9**	**1**	**3**	**4**	**0**
♦1954-55	**Detroit Red Wings**	**NHL**	**70**	**25**	**41**	**66**	**33**	**48**	**81**	**15**	**11**	**5**	**7**	**12**	**2**
1955-56	**Detroit Red Wings**	**NHL**	**68**	**17**	**39**	**56**	**23**	**47**	**70**	**10**	**10**	**0**	**2**	**2**	**2**
1956-57	**Detroit Red Wings**	**NHL**	**70**	**13**	**23**	**36**	**17**	**25**	**42**	**6**	**5**	**0**	**2**	**2**	**0**
1957-58	**Detroit Red Wings**	**NHL**	**29**	**4**	**5**	**9**	**5**	**5**	**10**	**4**	....	....	....	....	....
	Chicago Black Hawks	**NHL**	**40**	**4**	**12**	**16**	**5**	**12**	**17**	**6**	....	....	....	....	....
1958-59	**Boston Bruins**	**NHL**	**63**	**6**	**8**	**14**	**7**	**8**	**15**	**16**	**4**	**0**	**0**	**0**	**0**
1959-60	Providence Reds	AHL	69	20	46	66	....	....	....	6	5	0	1	1	0
1960-61	Providence Reds	AHL	43	7	18	25	....	....	....	2	....	....	....	....	....
	NHL Totals		**409**	**84**	**161**	**245**	**110**	**185**	**295**	**75**	**39**	**6**	**14**	**20**	**4**

Won Dudley "Red" Garrett Memorial Award (Top Rookie - AHL) (1952) • WHL First All-Star Team (1953) • Won Lady Byng Trophy (1956) • Played in NHL All-Star Game (1954, 1955)

Traded to **Chicago** by **Detroit** with Billy Dea, Bill Dineen and Lorne Ferguson for Hec Lalande, Nick Mickoski, Bob Bailey and Jack McIntyre, December 17, 1957. Claimed by **Boston** from **Chicago** in Intra-League Draft, June 3, 1958.

• REID, Dave

C – L. 6'2", 180 lbs. b: Toronto, Ont., 1/11/1934 d: 1978.

Season	Club	League	GP	G	A	Pts	AG	AA	APts	PIM	GP	G	A	Pts	PIM
1951-52	Weston Dukes	OHA-B	STATISTICS NOT AVAILABLE												
	Toronto Marlboros	OHA-Jr.	3	2	2	4	....	....	....	0	....	....	....	....	....
1952-53	Toronto Marlboros	OHA-Jr.	52	12	19	31	....	....	....	29	7	0	1	1	4
	Toronto Maple Leafs	**NHL**	**2**	**0**	**0**	**0**	**0**	**0**	**0**	**0**	....	....	....	....	....
1953-54	Toronto Marlboros	OHA-Jr.	59	22	31	53	....	....	....	38	15	8	11	19	4
1954-55	**Toronto Maple Leafs**	**NHL**	**1**	**0**	**0**	**0**	**0**	**0**	**0**	**0**	....	....	....	....	....
	University of Toronto	OQAA	STATISTICS NOT AVAILABLE												
1955-56	**Toronto Maple Leafs**	**NHL**	**4**	**0**	**0**	**0**	**0**	**0**	**0**	**0**	....	....	....	....	....
	University of Toronto	OQAA	STATISTICS NOT AVAILABLE												
1956-57	Hull-Ottawa Canadiens	QHL	15	4	1	5	....	....	....	2	....	....	....	....	....
	Hull-Ottawa Canadiens	EOHL	12	8	5	13	....	....	....	6	....	....	....	....	....
	NHL Totals		**7**	**0**	**0**	**0**	**0**	**0**	**0**	**0**	....	....	....	....	....

• REID, Gerry — Gerald Roland

C – R. 6'1", 180 lbs. b: Owen Sound, Ont., 10/13/1928.

Season	Club	League	GP	G	A	Pts	AG	AA	APts	PIM	GP	G	A	Pts	PIM
1946-47	Owen Sound Mercuries	OHA-Sr.	12	6	8	14	....	....	....	0	6	4	4	8	0
1947-48	Barrie Flyers	OHA-Jr.	36	28	34	62	....	....	....	10	13	10	9	*19	10
	Barrie Flyers	M-Cup	8	11	5	16	....	....	....	4	....	....	....	....	....
1948-49	Indianapolis Capitols	AHL	68	31	47	78	....	....	....	18	2	0	0	0	2
	Detroit Red Wings	**NHL**	....	....	....	....	....	....	....	....	**2**	**0**	**0**	**0**	**2**
1949-50	Indianapolis Capitols	AHL	62	28	31	59	....	....	....	10	8	3	6	9	2
1950-51	Indianapolis Capitols	AHL	69	17	51	68	....	....	....	4	3	1	0	1	2
1951-52	Cleveland Barons	AHL	52	15	22	37	....	....	....	9	5	0	0	0	0
1952-53	Owen Sound Mercury's	OHA-Sr.	21	15	20	35	....	....	....	4	11	7	3	10	0
1953-54	Owen Sound Mercury's	OHA-Sr.	48	37	34	71	....	....	....	8	7	6	9	15	2
	Owen Sound Mercury's	Al-Cup	7	1	2	3	....	....	....	2	....	....	....	....	....
1954-55	Owen Sound Mercury's	OHA-Sr.	50	24	33	57	....	....	....	10	5	2	3	5	0
1955-56	Owen Sound Mercury's	OHA-Sr.	48	23	20	43	....	....	....	10	6	0	1	1	2
1956-57	Owen Sound Mercury's	OHA-Sr.	52	20	29	49	....	....	....	10	....	....	....	....	....
	NHL Totals		....	....	....	....	....	....	....	....	**2**	**0**	**0**	**0**	**2**

• REID, Gord — Gordon John

D – L. 5'10", 195 lbs. b: Mount Albert, Ont., 2/19/1912.

Season	Club	League	GP	G	A	Pts	AG	AA	APts	PIM	GP	G	A	Pts	PIM
1929-30	Port Colborne Ports	OHA-Sr.	2	0	0	0	....	....	....	0	2	0	0	0	0
1930/34	Port Colborne Ports	OHA-Sr.	STATISTICS NOT AVAILABLE												
1934-35	New Haven Eagles	Can-Am	47	9	5	14	....	....	....	76	....	....	....	....	....
1935-36	New Haven Eagles	Can-Am	48	3	9	12	....	....	....	*102	....	....	....	....	....
1936-37	**New York Americans**	**NHL**	**1**	**0**	**0**	**0**	**0**	**0**	**0**	**2**	....	....	....	....	....
	New Haven Eagles	IAHL	40	0	4	4	....	....	....	54	....	....	....	....	....
1937-38	New Haven Eagles	IAHL	12	0	1	1	....	....	....	10	....	....	....	....	....
	Kansas City Greyhounds	AHA	36	3	1	4	....	....	....	51	....	....	....	....	....
1938-39	St. Paul Saints	AHA	46	3	4	7	....	....	....	50	3	0	0	0	2
1939-40	St. Paul Saints	AHA	47	4	19	23	....	....	....	56	7	1	0	1	12
1940-41	St. Paul Saints	AHA	40	3	4	7	....	....	....	30	4	0	0	0	0
1941-42	St. Paul Saints	AHA	50	4	7	11	....	....	....	51	2	1	0	1	5
1942-43	New Haven Eagles	AHL	18	1	2	3	....	....	....	10	....	....	....	....	....
1943-44	Providence Reds	AHL	40	2	8	10	....	....	....	30	....	....	....	....	....
	NHL Totals		**1**	**0**	**0**	**0**	**0**	**0**	**0**	**2**	....	....	....	....	....

• REID, Reg — Reginald Sutherland "Rusty"

LW – L. 5'8", 138 lbs. b: Seaforth, Ont., 2/17/1899 Deceased.

Season	Club	League	GP	G	A	Pts	AG	AA	APts	PIM	GP	G	A	Pts	PIM
1916-17	Seaforth Hockey Club	OIHA	STATISTICS NOT AVAILABLE												
1917-18	Seaforth Juniors	OHA-Jr.	6	18	0	18	....	....	....	2	....	....	....	....	....
1918-19	Seaforth Juniors	OHA-Jr.	STATISTICS NOT AVAILABLE												
	Seaforth Hockey Club	OIHA	STATISTICS NOT AVAILABLE												
1919-20	Seaforth Hockey Club	OIHA	4	12	0	12									
1921-22	Seaforth Hockey Club	OIHA	6	16	0	16	....	....	....	4	....	....	....	....	....
1922-23	Seaforth Hockey Club	OIHA	STATISTICS NOT AVAILABLE												
1923-24	Seaforth Hockey Club	OIHA	STATISTICS NOT AVAILABLE												
1924-25	**Toronto St. Pats**	**NHL**	**27**	**1**	**0**	**1**	**2**	**0**	**2**	**2**	**2**	**0**	**0**	**0**	**0**
1925-26	**Toronto St. Pats**	**NHL**	**12**	**0**	**0**	**0**	**0**	**0**	**0**	**2**	....	....	....	....	....
1926-27	Stratford Nationals	Can-Pro	25	8	3	11	....	....	....	4	1	0	0	0	0
	Windsor Bulldogs	Can-Pro	1	0	0	0	....	....	....	0	....	....	....	....	....
1927-28	Stratford Nationals	Can-Pro	14	0	0	0	....	....	....	0	....	....	....	....	....
1928-29			OUT OF HOCKEY – RETIRED												
1929-30	Seaforth Hockey Club	OIHA	STATISTICS NOT AVAILABLE												
1930-31	Stratford Nationals	OPHL	5	0	0	0	....	....	....	0	....	....	....	....	....
	NHL Totals		**39**	**1**	**0**	**1**	**2**	**0**	**2**	**4**	**2**	**0**	**0**	**0**	**0**

Signed as a free agent by **Toronto St. Pats**, November 12, 1924. Signed as a free agent by **Stratford** (Can-Pro), October 15, 1926. Loaned to **Windsor** (Can-Pro) by **Stratford** (Can-Pro) for cash, January 30, 1927.

• REIGLE, Ed — "Rags"

D – L. 5'9", 180 lbs. b: Winnipeg, Man., 6/19/1924.

Season	Club	League	GP	G	A	Pts	AG	AA	APts	PIM	GP	G	A	Pts	PIM
1940-41	East Kildonan Northstars	MJHL	1	0	0	0	....	....	....	2	....	....	....	....	....
1941-42	East Kildonan Northstars	MJHL	18	4	7	11	....	....	....	29	2	1	0	1	4
1942-43	Oshawa Generals	OHA-Jr.	22	4	6	10	....	....	....	28	20	5	5	10	31
	Oshawa Generals	M-Cup	10	1	2	3	....	....	....	10	....	....	....	....	....
1943-44			MILITARY SERVICE												
1944-45	Toronto Army Shamrocks	TIHL	1	0	0	0	....	....	....	2	....	....	....	....	....
	Indianapolis Capitols	AHL	28	1	5	6	....	....	....	24	5	1	3	4	2
1945-46	Omaha Knights	USHL	46	12	11	23	....	....	....	100	7	0	4	4	7
	Indianapolis Capitols	AHL	7	0	3	3	....	....	....	7	....	....	....	....	....
1946-47	Omaha Knights	USHL	19	0	0	0	....	....	....	22	11	1	1	2	2
	Detroit Metal Mouldings	IHL	4	1	0	1	....	....	....	2	....	....	....	....	....
1947-48	Omaha Knights	USHL	53	16	17	33	....	....	....	58	3	0	0	0	*20
1948-49	Omaha Knights	USHL	62	9	25	34	....	....	....	109	4	0	0	0	2
1949-50	Cleveland Barons	AHL	62	5	20	25	....	....	....	62	9	0	4	4	16
1950-51	**Boston Bruins**	**NHL**	**17**	**0**	**2**	**2**	**0**	**2**	**2**	**25**	....	....	....	....	....
	Hershey Bears	AHL	50	6	31	37	....	....	....	76	3	0	0	0	6
1951-52	Cleveland Barons	AHL	64	10	35	45	....	....	....	119	5	0	3	3	6
1952-53	Cleveland Barons	AHL	49	3	35	38	....	....	....	47	....	....	....	....	....
1953-54	Cleveland Barons	AHL	68	10	26	36	....	....	....	95	7	1	4	5	8
1954-55	Cleveland Barons	AHL	62	7	30	37	....	....	....	90	4	0	1	1	2
1955-56	North Bay Trappers	NOHA	51	7	18	25	....	....	....	66	10	0	6	6	8
1956-57	North Bay Trappers	NOHA	54	8	22	30	....	....	....	62	13	3	5	8	16
	NHL Totals		**17**	**0**	**2**	**2**	**0**	**2**	**2**	**25**	....	....	....	....	....

AHL Second All-Star Team (1952, 1953) • NOHA First All-Star Team (1956)

Traded to **Boston** by **Cleveland** (AHL) for cash, April 17, 1950. Traded to **Detroit** by **Boston** for cash, May, 1951.Traded to **NY Rangers** by **Detroit** with Steve Kraftcheck for $30,000, May 14, 1951. Traded to **Cleveland** (AHL) by **NY Rangers** with Jackie Gordon, Fred Shero, Fern Perreault and cash for Wally Hergesheimer and Hy Buller, May 14, 1951.

• REINIKKA, Ollie   Oliver Mathias "Rocco"

C/RW – R. 5'10", 160 lbs. b: Shuswap, B.C., 8/2/1901 d: 1962.

			REGULAR SEASON								PLAYOFFS				
Season	Club	League	GP	G	A	Pts	AG	AA	APts	PIM	GP	G	A	Pts	PIM
1920-21	Canmore Roses	ASHL	6	1	0	1	....	....	....	0	....	....	....	....	....
1921-22	Canmore Roses	ASHL	STATISTICS NOT AVAILABLE												
1922-23	Canmore Roses	ASHL	6	2	0	2	....	....	....	....	....	....	....	....	....
1923-24	Canmore Roses	ASHL	STATISTICS NOT AVAILABLE												
1924-25	Vancouver Maroons	WCHL	19	1	0	1	....	....	....	4	....	....	....	....	....
1925-26	Vancouver Maroons	WHL	27	10	2	12	....	....	....	8	....	....	....	....	....
1926-27	**New York Rangers**	**NHL**	**16**	**0**	**0**	**0**	**0**	**0**	**0**	**0**	....	....	....	....	....
	Springfield Indians	Can-Am	16	0	0	0	....	....	....	10	4	1	0	1	4
1927-28	Stratford Nationals	Can-Pro	42	8	3	11	....	....	....	12	5	1	0	1	2
1928-29	Hamilton Tigers	Can-Pro	19	0	3	3	....	....	....	6	....	....	....	....	....
	Seattle Seahawks	PCHL	15	2	1	3	....	....	....	2	5	1	1	2	0
1929-30	Seattle Eskimos	PCHL	35	12	3	15	....	....	....	12	....	....	....	....	....
1930-31	London Tecumsehs	IHL	44	7	5	12	....	....	....	19	....	....	....	....	....
1931-32	London Tecumsehs	IHL	26	2	0	2	....	....	....	2	....	....	....	....	....
1932-33			OUT OF HOCKEY – RETIRED												
1933-34			OUT OF HOCKEY – RETIRED												
1934-35	Rossland Miners	WKHL	16	6	8	14	....	....	....	3	2	0	1	1	2
1935-36	Rossland Miners	WKHL	4	1	2	3	....	....	....	1	2	1	3	4	0
1936-37	Rossland Miners	WKHL	14	1	7	8	....	....	....	6	....	....	....	....	....
	NHL Totals		**16**	**0**	**0**	**0**	**0**	**0**	**0**	**0**	....	....	....	....	....
	Other Major League Totals		46	11	2	13	....	....	....	12	....	....	....	....	....

Signed as a free agent by **Vancouver** (WCHL), November 17, 1924. Traded to **NY Rangers** by **Vancouver** (WHL) for cash, October 25, 1926. Traded to **Stratford** (Can-Pro) by **NY Rangers** for cash, November 11, 1927. Signed as a free agent by **Hamilton** (Can-Pro), November 6, 1928. Traded to **Seattle** (PCHL) by **Hamilton** (Can-Pro) for cash, January 30, 1929. Traded to **London** (IHL) by **Seattle** (PCHL) for cash, September 11, 1930.

• REISE, Leo   Leonard Charles

D – R. 5'11", 175 lbs. b: Pembroke, Ont., 6/1/1892 d: 7/8/1975.

			REGULAR SEASON								PLAYOFFS				
Season	Club	League	GP	G	A	Pts	AG	AA	APts	PIM	GP	G	A	Pts	PIM
1913-14	Hamilton Tiger Cubs	OIHA	STATISTICS NOT AVAILABLE												
	New Liskeard Seniors	NOHA	4	1	0	1	....	....	....	....	....	....	....	....	....
1914-15	Hamilton Tigers-2	OHA-I	STATISTICS NOT AVAILABLE												
1915-16	Hamilton Tigers-2	OHA-I	2	0	0	0	....	....	....	0	....	....	....	....	....
1916-17	Hamilton Tigers-2	OHA-I	6	8	0	8	....	....	....	....	....	....	....	....	....
1917-18	Hamilton Sr. Tigers	OHA-Sr.	8	8	0	8	....	....	....	....	....	....	....	....	....
1918-19	Hamilton Sr. Tigers	OHA-Sr.	8	5	1	6	....	....	....	....	6	2	0	2	....
1919-20	Hamilton Sr. Tigers	OHA-Sr.	5	8	3	11	....	....	....	....	2	0	0	0	....
1920-21	Hamilton Sr. Tigers	OHA-Sr.	9	4	4	8	....	....	....	....	....	....	....	....	....
	Hamilton Tigers	**NHL**	**24**	**9**	**14**	**23**	**11**	**56**	**67**	**11**	....	....	....	....	....
1921-22	**Hamilton Tigers**	**NHL**	**24**	**9**	**14**	**23**	**12**	**46**	**58**	**11**	....	....	....	....	....
1922-23	**Hamilton Tigers**	**NHL**	**24**	**6**	**6**	**12**	**10**	**23**	**33**	**35**	....	....	....	....	....
1923-24	**Hamilton Tigers**	**NHL**	**4**	**0**	**0**	**0**	**0**	**0**	**0**	**4**	....	....	....	....	....
	Saskatoon Crescents	WCHL	18	4	2	6	....	....	....	6	....	....	....	....	....
1924-25	Saskatoon Crescents	WCHL	28	8	3	11	....	....	....	46	2	0	0	0	0
1925-26	Saskatoon Crescents	WHL	30	2	10	12	....	....	....	32	2	0	0	0	4
1926-27	Niagara Falls Cataracts	Can-Pro	3	3	1	4	....	....	....	0	....	....	....	....	....
	New York Americans	**NHL**	**40**	**7**	**6**	**13**	**12**	**31**	**43**	**24**	....	....	....	....	....
1927-28	**New York Americans**	**NHL**	**43**	**8**	**1**	**9**	**16**	**6**	**22**	**62**	....	....	....	....	....
1928-29	**New York Americans**	**NHL**	**44**	**4**	**1**	**5**	**11**	**7**	**18**	**32**	**2**	**0**	**0**	**0**	**0**
1929-30	**New York Americans**	**NHL**	**24**	**0**	**0**	**0**	**0**	**0**	**0**	**0**	....	....	....	....	....
	New York Rangers	**NHL**	**14**	**0**	**1**	**1**	**0**	**2**	**2**	**8**	**4**	**0**	**0**	**0**	**16**
1930-31	London Tecumsehs	IHL	8	0	0	0	....	....	....	6	....	....	....	....	....
	Pittsburgh Yellowjackets	IHL	37	5	5	10	....	....	....	18	6	1	2	3	2
1931-32	Pittsburgh Yellowjackets	IHL	21	0	0	0	....	....	....	19	....	....	....	....	....
	NHL Totals		**241**	**43**	**43**	**86**	**72**	**171**	**243**	**187**	**6**	**0**	**0**	**0**	**16**
	Other Major League Totals		76	14	15	29	....	....	....	84	4	0	0	0	4

• Father of Leo Jr. • OHA-Sr. Second All-Star Team (1918, 1921) • OHA-Sr. First All-Star Team (1920)

Signed as a free agent by **Hamilton**, February 23, 1921. Traded to **Saskatoon** (WCHL) by **Hamilton** for cash, December 29, 1923. Signed as a free agent by **Niagara Falls** (Can-Pro), November 1, 1926. Traded to **NY Americans** by **Niagara Falls** (Can-Pro) for cash, November 22, 1926. Traded to **NY Rangers** by **NY Americans** for cash, February 6, 1930. Traded to **London** (IHL) by **NY Rangers** for cash, October 22, 1930. Traded to **Pittsburgh** (IHL) by **London** (IHL) for Steve Yankoski and $500, December 8, 1930.

• REISE, Leo   Leonard Charles

D – L. 6', 205 lbs. b: Stoney Creek, Ont., 6/7/1922.

			REGULAR SEASON								PLAYOFFS				
Season	Club	League	GP	G	A	Pts	AG	AA	APts	PIM	GP	G	A	Pts	PIM
1939-40	Brantford Lions	OHA-B	12	12	4	16	....	....	....	36	11	9	8	17	10
	Brantford Lions	M-Cup	2	1	5	6	....	....	....	5	....	....	....	....	....
1940-41	Brantford Lions	OHA-B	10	8	7	15	....	....	....	32	16	12	11	23	22
	Brantford Lions	M-Cup	11	10	11	21	....	....	....	20	....	....	....	....	....
1941-42	Guelph Biltmores	OHA-Jr.	14	5	7	12	....	....	....	28	10	1	3	4	22
1942-43			MILITARY SERVICE												
1943-44	Victoria Navy	NNDHL	17	1	2	3	....	....	....	24	....	....	....	....	....
	Halifax Navy	NSDHL	....	....	....	....	....	....	....	....	4	0	0	0	2
1944-45	Winnipeg Navy	WNDHL	17	9	2	11	....	....	....	26	6	1	2	3	11
1945-46	**Chicago Black Hawks**	**NHL**	**6**	**0**	**0**	**0**	**0**	**0**	**0**	**6**	....	....	....	....	....
	Kansas City Pla-Mors	USHL	50	7	18	25	....	....	....	30	....	....	....	....	....
1946-47	**Chicago Black Hawks**	**NHL**	**17**	**0**	**0**	**0**	**0**	**0**	**0**	**18**	....	....	....	....	....
	Kansas City Pla-Mors	USHL	2	0	1	1	....	....	....	0	....	....	....	....	....
	Indianapolis Capitols	AHL	5	0	4	4	....	....	....	8	....	....	....	....	....
	Detroit Red Wings	**NHL**	**31**	**4**	**6**	**10**	**4**	**7**	**11**	**14**	**5**	**0**	**1**	**1**	**4**
1947-48	**Detroit Red Wings**	**NHL**	**58**	**5**	**4**	**9**	**6**	**5**	**11**	**30**	**10**	**2**	**1**	**3**	**12**
1948-49	**Detroit Red Wings**	**NHL**	**59**	**3**	**7**	**10**	**4**	**10**	**14**	**60**	**11**	**1**	**0**	**1**	**4**
♦1949-50	**Detroit Red Wings**	**NHL**	**70**	**4**	**17**	**21**	**5**	**20**	**25**	**46**	**14**	**2**	**0**	**2**	**19**
1950-51	**Detroit Red Wings**	**NHL**	**68**	**5**	**16**	**21**	**6**	**20**	**26**	**67**	**6**	**2**	**3**	**5**	**2**
♦1951-52	**Detroit Red Wings**	**NHL**	**54**	**0**	**11**	**11**	**0**	**13**	**13**	**34**	**6**	**1**	**0**	**1**	***27**
1952-53	**New York Rangers**	**NHL**	**61**	**4**	**15**	**19**	**5**	**18**	**23**	**53**	....	....	....	....	....
1953-54	**New York Rangers**	**NHL**	**70**	**3**	**5**	**8**	**4**	**6**	**10**	**71**	....	....	....	....	....
1954-55	Owen Sound Mercuries	OHA-Sr.	8	1	1	2	....	....	....	4	5	1	1	2	6
	NHL Totals		**494**	**28**	**81**	**109**	**34**	**99**	**133**	**399**	**52**	**8**	**5**	**13**	**68**

• Son of Leo Sr. • USHL First All-Star Team (1946) • NHL Second All-Star Team (1950, 1951) • Played in NHL All-Star Game (1950, 1951, 1952, 1953)

Traded to **Detroit** by **Chicago** with Pete Horeck for Adam Brown and Ray Powell, December 9, 1946. Traded to **NY Rangers** by **Detroit** for Reg Sinclair and John Morrison, August 18, 1952.

• RICHARD, Henri   — see page 1560

• RICHARD, Maurice   Joseph Henri Maurice "The Rocket"   HHOF

RW – L. 5'10", 170 lbs. b: Montreal, Que., 8/4/1921 d: 5/27/2000.

			REGULAR SEASON								PLAYOFFS				
Season	Club	League	GP	G	A	Pts	AG	AA	APts	PIM	GP	G	A	Pts	PIM
1937-38	St-Francois-de-Laval	H.S.	STATISTICS NOT AVAILABLE												
1938-39	St-Georges Norchet	QAHA	46	90	46	136	....	....	....	....	....	....	....	....	....
1939-40	Verdun Jr. Maple Leafs	QJHL	10	4	1	5	....	....	....	2	4	*6	*3	*9	2
	Verdun Maple Leafs	QSHL	1	0	0	0	....	....	....	0	....	....	....	....	....
	Verdun Jr. Maple Leafs	M-Cup	7	7	9	16	....	....	....	16	....	....	....	....	....
1940-41	Montreal Sr. Canadiens	QSHL	1	0	1	1	....	....	....	0	....	....	....	....	....
1941-42	Montreal Sr. Canadiens	QSHL	31	8	9	17	....	....	....	27	6	2	1	3	6
1942-43	**Montreal Canadiens**	**NHL**	**16**	**5**	**6**	**11**	**5**	**6**	**11**	**4**	....	....	....	....	....
♦1943-44	**Montreal Canadiens**	**NHL**	**46**	**32**	**22**	**54**	**29**	**19**	**48**	**45**	**9**	***12**	**5**	**17**	**10**
1944-45	**Montreal Canadiens**	**NHL**	**50**	***50**	**23**	**73**	**52**	**27**	**79**	**46**	**6**	**6**	**2**	**8**	**10**
♦1945-46	**Montreal Canadiens**	**NHL**	**50**	**27**	**21**	**48**	**33**	**31**	**64**	**50**	**9**	***7**	**4**	**11**	**15**
1946-47	**Montreal Canadiens**	**NHL**	**60**	***45**	**26**	**71**	**52**	**31**	**83**	**69**	**10**	***6**	**5**	***11**	***44**
1947-48	**Montreal Canadiens**	**NHL**	**53**	**28**	**25**	**53**	**37**	**33**	**70**	**89**	....	....	....	....	....
1948-49	**Montreal Canadiens**	**NHL**	**59**	**20**	**18**	**38**	**28**	**26**	**54**	**110**	**7**	**2**	**1**	**3**	**14**
1949-50	**Montreal Canadiens**	**NHL**	**70**	***43**	**22**	**65**	**56**	**27**	**83**	**114**	**5**	**1**	**1**	**2**	**6**
1950-51	**Montreal Canadiens**	**NHL**	**65**	**42**	**24**	**66**	**55**	**29**	**84**	**97**	**11**	***9**	**4**	***13**	**13**
1951-52	**Montreal Canadiens**	**NHL**	**48**	**27**	**17**	**44**	**36**	**21**	**57**	**44**	**11**	**4**	**2**	**6**	**6**
♦1952-53	**Montreal Canadiens**	**NHL**	**70**	**28**	**33**	**61**	**37**	**40**	**77**	***112**	**12**	**7**	**1**	**8**	**2**
1953-54	**Montreal Canadiens**	**NHL**	**70**	***37**	**30**	**67**	**51**	**37**	**88**	**112**	**11**	**3**	**0**	**3**	**22**
1954-55	**Montreal Canadiens**	**NHL**	**67**	***38**	**36**	**74**	**50**	**42**	**92**	**125**	....	....	....	....	....
♦1955-56	**Montreal Canadiens**	**NHL**	**70**	**38**	**33**	**71**	**53**	**39**	**92**	**89**	**10**	**5**	**9**	**14**	***24**
♦1956-57	**Montreal Canadiens**	**NHL**	**63**	**33**	**29**	**62**	**43**	**32**	**75**	**74**	**10**	**8**	**3**	**11**	**8**
♦1957-58	**Montreal Canadiens**	**NHL**	**28**	**15**	**19**	**34**	**18**	**20**	**38**	**28**	**10**	***11**	**4**	**15**	**10**
♦1958-59	**Montreal Canadiens**	**NHL**	**42**	**17**	**21**	**38**	**20**	**21**	**41**	**27**	**4**	**0**	**0**	**0**	**2**
♦1959-60	**Montreal Canadiens**	**NHL**	**51**	**19**	**16**	**35**	**22**	**16**	**38**	**50**	**8**	**1**	**3**	**4**	**2**
	NHL Totals		**978**	**544**	**421**	**965**	**677**	**497**	**1174**	**1285**	**133**	**82**	**44**	**126**	**188**

• Brother of Henri • NHL Second All-Star Team (1944, 1951, 1952, 1953, 1954, 1957) • NHL First All-Star Team (1945, 1946, 1947, 1948, 1949, 1950, 1955, 1956) • Won Hart Trophy (1947) • Played in NHL All-Star Game (1947, 1948, 1949, 1950, 1951, 1952, 1953, 1954, 1955, 1956, 1957, 1958, 1959)

• Missed majority of 1940-41 season recovering from ankle injury suffered in game vs. Boston, November 3, 1940. Signed as a free agent by **Montreal**, October 29, 1942. • Missed majority of 1957-58 season recovering from achilles tendon injury suffered in game vs. Toronto, November 13, 1957. Missed remainder of 1958-59 regular season recovering from ankle injury suffered in game vs. Chicago, January 18, 1959.

• RICHARDSON, Dave   — see page 1561

• RILEY, Jack

C – L. 5'11", 160 lbs. b: Berckenla, Ireland, 12/29/1910.

			REGULAR SEASON								PLAYOFFS				
Season	Club	League	GP	G	A	Pts	AG	AA	APts	PIM	GP	G	A	Pts	PIM
1926-27	Calgary Canadians	CCJHL	6	11	3	14	....	....	....	....	....	....	....	....	....
	Calgary Canadians	M-Cup	2	0	0	0	....	....	....	0	....	....	....	....	....
1927-28	Vancouver King George	VCAHL	8	5	0	5	....	....	....	2	3	3	0	3	0
1928-29	Calgary Canadians	CCJHL	STATISTICS NOT AVAILABLE												
1929-30	Seattle Eskimos	PCHL	5	0	0	0	....	....	....	0	....	....	....	....	....
1930-31	Chicago Shamrocks	AHA	26	6	8	14	....	....	....	16	....	....	....	....	....
	Minneapolis Millers	AHA	16	4	2	6	....	....	....	8	....	....	....	....	....
1931-32	Chicago Shamrocks	AHA	46	17	16	33	....	....	....	28	4	3	0	3	2
1932-33	**Detroit Red Wings**	**NHL**	**1**	**0**	**0**	**0**	**0**	**0**	**0**	**0**	....	....	....	....	....
	Detroit–Cleveland	IHL	42	10	15	25	....	....	....	20	....	....	....	....	....
1933-34	**Montreal Canadiens**	**NHL**	**48**	**6**	**11**	**17**	**10**	**23**	**33**	**4**	**2**	**0**	**1**	**1**	**0**
1934-35	**Montreal Canadiens**	**NHL**	**47**	**4**	**11**	**15**	**7**	**19**	**26**	**4**	**2**	**0**	**2**	**2**	**0**
1935-36	**Boston Bruins**	**NHL**	**8**	**0**	**0**	**0**	**0**	**0**	**0**	**0**	....	....	....	....	....
	Boston Cubs	Can-Am	30	3	10	13	....	....	....	8	....	....	....	....	....
1936-37	Tulsa Oilers	AHA	48	14	17	31	....	....	....	16	....	....	....	....	....
1937-38	Tulsa Oilers	AHA	47	13	23	36	....	....	....	19	4	1	0	1	2
1938-39	Tulsa Oilers	AHA	43	16	25	41	....	....	....	14	8	2	2	4	9
1939-40	Wichita Skyhawks	AHA	44	19	18	37	....	....	....	19	....	....	....	....	....
1940-41	Vancouver Lions	PCHL	47	16	*40	56	....	....	....	14	6	2	1	3	0
1941-42	Philadelphia Rockets	AHL	2	1	0	1	....	....	....	0	....	....	....	....	....
	Hershey Bears	AHL	6	3	0	3	....	....	....	0	10	0	0	0	0
	Montreal Pats	MCHL	31	15	11	26	....	....	....	8	....	....	....	....	....
1942-43	Cornwall Army	MCHL	20	7	13	20	....	....	....	11	6	0	1	1	0
	Vancouver Norvans	PCHL	6	5	9	14	....	....	....	0	3	0	1	1	0
1943-44	Vancouver St. Regis	PCHL	2	0	0	0	....	....	....	0	....	....	....	....	....
1944-45	Hershey Bears	AHL	35	5	7	12	....	....	....	7	6	0	0	0	0
	NHL Totals		**104**	**10**	**22**	**32**	**17**	**42**	**59**	**8**	**4**	**0**	**3**	**3**	**0**

Traded to **Chicago** (AHA) by **Minneapolis** (AHA) for George Burland and Stan Fuller, January 8, 1931. NHL rights transferred to **Detroit** from **Chicago** (AHA) after AHA club owners purchased Detroit (NHL and IHL) franchises, September 2, 1932. Traded to **Cleveland** (IHL) by **Detroit** with Tony Prelesnik for Frank Waite, December 2, 1932. Traded to **Montreal Canadiens** by **Cleveland** (IHL) for cash, June, 1933. Traded to **Boston** by **Montreal Canadiens** for Paul Haynes, September 30, 1935.

• RILEY, Jim   James Norman

LW – L. 5'11", 180 lbs. b: Bayfield, NB, 5/25/1897 d: 5/25/1969.

			REGULAR SEASON								PLAYOFFS				
Season	Club	League	GP	G	A	Pts	AG	AA	APts	PIM	GP	G	A	Pts	PIM
1914-15	Calgary Victorias	ASHL	STATISTICS NOT AVAILABLE												
1915-16	Victoria Aristocrats	PCHA	12	4	1	5	....	....	....	14	....	....	....	....	....
♦1916-17	Seattle Metropolitans	PCHA	24	11	5	16	....	....	....	34	4	0	0	0	3
1917-18	Seattle Metropolitans	PCHA	18	4	3	7	....	....	....	15	2	1	0	1	3
1918-19			MILITARY SERVICE												
1919-20	Seattle Metropolitans	PCHA	22	11	4	15	....	....	....	49	2	1	2	3	0
	Seattle Metropolitans	St-Cup	5	0	1	1	....	....	....	0	....	....	....	....	....
1920-21	Seattle Metropolitans	PCHA	24	23	5	28	....	....	....	20	2	0	0	0	0
1921-22	Seattle Metropolitans	PCHA	24	16	2	18	....	....	....	27	2	0	0	0	3
1922-23	Seattle Metropolitans	PCHA	30	23	4	27	....	....	....	70	....	....	....	....	....
1923-24	Seattle Metropolitans	PCHA	13	2	2	4	....	....	....	11	2	0	1	1	2
1924-25			PLAYED PROFESSIONAL BASEBALL												
1925-26			PLAYED PROFESSIONAL BASEBALL												

			REGULAR SEASON								PLAYOFFS				
Season	Club	League	GP	G	A	Pts	AG	AA	APts	PIM	GP	G	A	Pts	PIM
1926-27	Dallas Texans	X-Games	STATISTICS NOT AVAILABLE												
	Chicago Black Hawks	**NHL**	**3**	**0**	**0**	**0**	**0**	**0**	**0**	**0**	....	....	....	....	....
	Detroit Cougars	**NHL**	**6**	**0**	**2**	**2**	**0**	**10**	**10**	**14**	....	....	....	....	....
1927-28			PLAYED PROFESSIONAL BASEBALL												
1928-29	Los Angeles Richfields	Cal-Pro	....	2	2	4	....	....	....	....	....	....	....	....	....
	NHL Totals		**9**	**0**	**2**	**2**	**0**	**10**	**10**	**14**	....	....	....	....	....
	Other Major League Totals		167	94	26	120	....	....	....	240	14	2	3	5	11

PCHA Second All-Star Team (1920, 1921, 1922) • PCHA First All-Star Team (1923)

• Only athlete to play both major league baseball (St. Louis - AL, Washington) and NHL hockey. Signed as a free agent by **Chicago**, January 19, 1927. Traded to **Detroit** by **Chicago** for cash, January 31, 1927. Traded to **Detroit Olympics** (Can-Pro) by **Detroit** for cash, October 11, 1927.

• RIOPELLE, Rip   Howard Joseph

LW – L. 5′11″, 165 lbs.   b: Ottawa, Ont., 1/30/1922.

Season	Club	League	GP	G	A	Pts	AG	AA	APts	PIM	GP	G	A	Pts	PIM
1936-37	St. Malachi's Collegiate	H.S.	STATISTICS NOT AVAILABLE												
1937-38	Ottawa Lasalle	OCJHL	13	7	2	9	....	....	....	4	....	....	....	....	....
	Ottawa Lasalle	OCHL	1	0	0	0	....	....	....	0	....	....	....	....	....
1938-39	Ottawa St. Pats	OCJHL	STATISTICS NOT AVAILABLE												
1939-40	Ottawa St. Pats	OCJHL	STATISTICS NOT AVAILABLE												
1940-41	Ottawa St. Pats	OCHL	STATISTICS NOT AVAILABLE												
	Ottawa Car Bombers	UOVHL	1	0	1	1	....	....	....	2	....	....	....	....	....
1941-42	Ottawa St. Pats	OCJHL	....	....	....	....	....	....	....	....	5	2	5	7	2
1942-43	Toronto RCAF	OHA-Sr.	10	14	6	20	....	....	....	2	9	5	4	9	2
1943-44	Arnprior RCAF	UOVHL	5	6	6	12	....	....	....	2	....	....	....	....	....
1944-45			MILITARY SERVICE												
1945-46	Montreal Royals	QSHL	36	20	21	41	....	....	....	16	11	7	6	13	4
1946-47	Montreal Royals	QSHL	34	10	19	29	....	....	....	26	11	3	6	9	4
	Montreal Royals	Al-Cup	14	0	6	6	....	....	....	8	....	....	....	....	....
1947-48	**Montreal Canadiens**	**NHL**	**55**	**5**	**2**	**7**	**6**	**3**	**9**	**12**	....	....	....	....	....
1948-49	**Montreal Canadiens**	**NHL**	**48**	**10**	**6**	**16**	**14**	**8**	**22**	**34**	**7**	**1**	**1**	**2**	**2**
1949-50	**Montreal Canadiens**	**NHL**	**66**	**12**	**8**	**20**	**15**	**10**	**25**	**27**	**1**	**0**	**0**	**0**	**0**
1950-51			DID NOT PLAY – INJURED												
1951-52	Ottawa Senators	QMHL	54	18	28	46	....	....	....	18	7	1	4	5	0
1952-53	Ottawa Senators	QMHL	60	20	31	51	....	....	....	20	11	3	7	10	4
1953-54	Ottawa Senators	QHL	72	31	*60	*91	....	....	....	46	22	3	9	12	4
1954-55	Ottawa Senators	QHL	20	4	4	8	....	....	....	12	....	....	....	....	....
	NHL Totals		**169**	**27**	**16**	**43**	**35**	**21**	**56**	**73**	**8**	**1**	**1**	**2**	**2**

QMHL Second All-Star Team (1953) • QHL First All-Star Team (1954) • Won President's Cup (Scoring Champion - QHL) (1954)

• Missed entire 1950-51 season recovering from back injury, June, 1950. Traded to **Ottawa** (QMHL) by **Montreal** for cash, October 4, 1951.

• RIPLEY, Vic   Victor Merrick

LW – L. 5′8″, 170 lbs.   b: Elgin, Ont., 5/30/1906   Deceased.

Season	Club	League	GP	G	A	Pts	AG	AA	APts	PIM	GP	G	A	Pts	PIM
1922-23	Calgary Canadians	CCJHL	13	15	8	23	....	....	....	....	....	....	....	....	....
	Calgary Canadians	M-Cup	4	3	0	3	....	....	....	4	....	....	....	....	....
1923-24	Calgary Canadians	CCJHL	STATISTICS NOT AVAILABLE												
	Calgary Canadians	M-Cup	7	10	9	19	....	....	....	6	....	....	....	....	....
1924-25	Calgary Canadians	CCJHL	STATISTICS NOT AVAILABLE												
	Calgary Canadians	M-Cup	2	4	0	4	....	....	....	2	....	....	....	....	....
1925-26	Minneapolis Millers	CHL	35	6	2	8	....	....	....	16	3	1	0	1	2
1926-27	Minneapolis Millers	AHA	34	7	1	8	....	....	....	30	6	0	0	0	2
1927-28	Kitchener Millionaires	Can-Pro	39	26	*14	*40	....	....	....	69	5	1	1	2	12
1928-29	**Chicago Black Hawks**	**NHL**	**34**	**11**	**2**	**13**	**32**	**13**	**45**	**31**	....	....	....	....	....
1929-30	**Chicago Black Hawks**	**NHL**	**40**	**8**	**8**	**16**	**11**	**19**	**30**	**33**	**2**	**0**	**0**	**0**	**2**
1930-31	**Chicago Black Hawks**	**NHL**	**37**	**8**	**4**	**12**	**16**	**12**	**28**	**9**	**9**	**2**	**1**	**3**	**4**
1931-32	**Chicago Black Hawks**	**NHL**	**46**	**12**	**6**	**18**	**20**	**13**	**33**	**47**	**2**	**0**	**0**	**0**	**0**
1932-33	**Chicago Black Hawks**	**NHL**	**15**	**2**	**4**	**6**	**4**	**8**	**12**	**6**	....	....	....	....	....
	Boston Bruins	**NHL**	**23**	**2**	**5**	**7**	**4**	**10**	**14**	**21**	**5**	**1**	**0**	**1**	**0**
1933-34	**Boston Bruins**	**NHL**	**14**	**2**	**1**	**3**	**3**	**2**	**5**	**6**	....	....	....	....	....
	New York Rangers	**NHL**	**34**	**5**	**12**	**17**	**9**	**25**	**34**	**10**	**2**	**1**	**0**	**1**	**4**
1934-35	**New York Rangers**	**NHL**	**4**	**0**	**2**	**2**	**0**	**3**	**3**	**0**	....	....	....	....	....
	St. Louis Eagles	**NHL**	**31**	**1**	**5**	**6**	**2**	**9**	**11**	**10**	....	....	....	....	....
1935-36	Cleveland Falcons	IHL	48	14	32	46	....	....	....	51	2	0	0	0	0
1936-37	Cleveland Barons	IAHL	13	0	2	2	....	....	....	6	....	....	....	....	....
	New Haven Eagles	IAHL	13	0	1	1	....	....	....	4	....	....	....	....	....
1937-38	Spokane Clippers	PCHL	42	19	16	35	....	....	....	19	....	....	....	....	....
1938-39	Spokane Clippers	PCHL	44	20	22	42	....	....	....	22	....	....	....	....	....
1939-40	Seattle Seahawks	PCHL	36	11	15	26	....	....	....	24	....	....	....	....	....
1940-41	Portland Buckaroos	PCHL	47	11	20	31	....	....	....	37	....	....	....	....	....
1941-42			MILITARY SERVICE												
1942-43			MILITARY SERVICE												
1943-44	Portland Declercs	NNDHL	15	13	8	21	....	....	....	10	....	....	....	....	....
	Portland Oilers	NNDHL	1	1	1	2	....	....	....	4	4	1	1	2	4
	NHL Totals		**278**	**51**	**49**	**100**	**101**	**114**	**215**	**173**	**20**	**4**	**1**	**5**	**10**

Signed as a free agent by **Minneapolis** (CHL), November 15, 1925. Signed as a free agent by **Minneapolis** (AHA), November 1, 1926. Traded to **Calgary** (PrHL) by **Minneapolis** (AHA) for cash, June, 1927. Traded to **Kitchener** (Can-Pro) by **Calgary** (PrHL) for cash, October 16, 1927. Claimed by **Chicago** from **Kitchener** (Can-Pro) in Inter-League Draft, May 14, 1928. Traded to **Boston** by **Chicago** for Billy Burch, January 17, 1933. Traded to **NY Rangers** by **Boston** with Roy Burmeister for Babe Siebert, December 18, 1933. Traded to **St. Louis** by **NY Rangers** for cash, November 29, 1934. Signed as a free agent by **New Haven** (IAHL) after release by **Cleveland** (IAHL), January 19, 1937.

• RITCHIE, Dave

D – R. 5′7″, 180 lbs.   b: Montreal, Que., 1/12/1892   Deceased.

Season	Club	League	GP	G	A	Pts	AG	AA	APts	PIM	GP	G	A	Pts	PIM
1909-10	Montreal Westmount	SLVHL	STATISTICS NOT AVAILABLE												
1910-11	Grand'Mere HC	IPAHU	STATISTICS NOT AVAILABLE												
1911-12	Grand'Mere HC	IPAHU	8	13	0	13	....	....	....	....	2	*5	0	*5	....
1912-13	Grand'Mere HC	IPAHU	5	3	0	3	....	....	....	....	4	4	0	4	0
	Grand'Mere HC	Al-Cup	2	1	0	1	....	....	....	0	....	....	....	....	....
1913-14	Grand'Mere HC	IPAHU	STATISTICS NOT AVAILABLE												
1914-15	Quebec Bulldogs	NHA	14	2	1	3	....	....	....	0	....	....	....	....	....
1915-16	Quebec Bulldogs	NHA	23	9	4	13	....	....	....	38	....	....	....	....	....
1916-17	Quebec Bulldogs	NHA	19	17	10	27	....	....	....	20	....	....	....	....	....
1917-18	**Montreal Wanderers**	**NHL**	**4**	**5**	**2**	**7**	**6**	**8**	**14**	**3**	....	....	....	....	....
	Ottawa Senators	**NHL**	**14**	**4**	**1**	**5**	**5**	**4**	**9**	**18**	....	....	....	....	....
1918-19	**Toronto Arenas**	**NHL**	**4**	**0**	**0**	**0**	**0**	**0**	**0**	**9**	....	....	....	....	....
1919-20	**Quebec Bulldogs**	**NHL**	**23**	**6**	**3**	**9**	**7**	**10**	**17**	**18**	....	....	....	....	....
1920-21	**Montreal Canadiens**	**NHL**	**6**	**0**	**0**	**0**	**0**	**0**	**0**	**2**	....	....	....	....	....
1921-22			DID NOT PLAY – REFEREE												
1922-23			DID NOT PLAY – REFEREE												
1923-24			DID NOT PLAY – REFEREE												
1924-25	**Montreal Canadiens**	**NHL**	**5**	**0**	**0**	**0**	**0**	**0**	**0**	**0**	**1**	**0**	**0**	**0**	**0**
1925-26	**Montreal Canadiens**	**NHL**	**2**	**0**	**0**	**0**	**0**	**0**	**0**	**0**	....	....	....	....	....
	NHL Totals		**58**	**15**	**6**	**21**	**18**	**22**	**40**	**50**	**1**	**0**	**0**	**0**	**0**
	Other Major League Totals		56	28	15	43	....	....	....	58	....	....	....	....	....

Signed as a free agent by **Quebec** (NHA), December 1, 1914. Claimed by **Montreal Wanderers** from **Quebec** in Dispersal Draft, November 26, 1917. Claimed by **Ottawa** from **Montreal Wanderers** in Dispersal Draft, January 4, 1918. Signed as a free agent by **Toronto Arenas**, January 17, 1919. Transferred to **Quebec** by **Toronto Arenas** when Quebec franchise returned to NHL, November 25, 1919. Transferred to **Hamilton** after **Quebec** franchise relocated, November 2, 1920. Traded to **Montreal Canadiens** by **Hamilton** with Harry Mummery and Jack McDonald for Goldie Prodgers, Joe Matte, Jack Coughlin and the loan of Bill Coutu for the 1920-21 season, November 27, 1920. Signed as a free agent by **Montreal Canadiens**, January 28, 1925. Signed as a free agent by **Montreal Canadiens**, January 13, 1926.

• RITSON, Alex   Alexander Clive

C – L. 5′11″, 172 lbs.   b: Peace River, Alta., 3/7/1922.

Season	Club	League	GP	G	A	Pts	AG	AA	APts	PIM	GP	G	A	Pts	PIM
1940-41	Regina Generals	S-SJHL	19	9	12	21	....	....	....	14	4	1	5	6	2
1941-42	Tulsa Oilers	AHA	50	14	13	27	....	....	....	12	2	0	0	0	0
1942-43	Washington Lions	AHL	12	5	7	12	....	....	....	0	....	....	....	....	....
	Providence Reds	AHL	40	9	23	32	....	....	....	19	2	0	0	0	0
1943-44	Indianapolis Capitols	AHL	53	22	21	43	....	....	....	13	5	0	1	1	0
1944-45	**New York Rangers**	**NHL**	**1**	**0**	**0**	**0**	**0**	**0**	**0**	**0**	....	....	....	....	....
	Hershey Bears	AHL	42	13	29	42	....	....	....	13	11	5	3	8	4
1945-46	Hershey Bears	AHL	11	0	2	2	....	....	....	4	....	....	....	....	....
	New Haven Eagles	AHL	14	4	2	6	....	....	....	0	....	....	....	....	....
	Omaha Knights	USHL	3	0	0	0	....	....	....	5	....	....	....	....	....
	Fort Worth Rangers	USHL	7	0	4	4	....	....	....	0	....	....	....	....	....
1946-47	Fort Worth Rangers	USHL	60	21	26	47	....	....	....	37	9	1	1	2	0
1947-48	Fort Worth Rangers	USHL	66	22	40	62	....	....	....	42	4	0	1	1	0
1948-49	Tulsa Oilers	USHL	66	16	43	59	....	....	....	73	7	1	1	2	12
1949-50	Cincinnati Mohawks	AHL	6	0	0	0	....	....	....	7	....	....	....	....	....
	Louisville Blades	USHL	45	10	18	28	....	....	....	18	....	....	....	....	....
	Seattle Ironmen	PCHL	16	1	4	5	....	....	....	11	4	2	0	2	0
1950-51	Seattle Ironmen	PCHL	3	0	0	0	....	....	....	0	....	....	....	....	....
	Vernon Canadians	OSHL	47	33	36	69	....	....	....	44	10	4	2	6	4
1951-52	Vernon Canadians	OSHL	48	24	25	49	....	....	....	47	....	....	....	....	....
	NHL Totals		**1**	**0**	**0**	**0**	**0**	**0**	**0**	**0**	....	....	....	....	....

Claimed by **NY Rangers** from **Indianapolis** (AHL) in Inter-League Draft, May 12, 1944. Traded to **Tulsa** (USHL) by **Fort Worth** (USHL) for Doug McMurdy, October 9, 1948. Traded to **Buffalo** (AHL) by **Tulsa** (USHL) for Len Haldorsen, September 8, 1949.

• RITTINGER, Alan   Alan Wilbur

W – R. 5′9″, 155 lbs.   b: Regina, Sask., 1/28/1925.

Season	Club	League	GP	G	A	Pts	AG	AA	APts	PIM	GP	G	A	Pts	PIM
1941-42	Regina Abbotts	SAHA	STATISTICS NOT AVAILABLE												
1942-43	Regina Abbotts	S-SJHL	10	1	4	5	....	....	....	17	4	1	1	2	0
1943-44	**Boston Bruins**	**NHL**	**19**	**3**	**7**	**10**	**3**	**6**	**9**	**0**	....	....	....	....	....
	Boston Olympics	EAHL	31	18	25	43	....	....	....	16	8	3	4	7	10
1944-45	Boston Olympics	EAHL	48	29	39	68	....	....	....	100	12	7	12	19	19
1945-46	New Haven Eagles	AHL	14	0	7	7	....	....	....	12	....	....	....	....	....
	Fort Worth Rangers	USHL	41	12	25	37	....	....	....	32	....	....	....	....	....
1946-47	Seattle Ironmen	PCHL	60	24	26	50	....	....	....	73	10	2	4	6	17
1947-48	Oakland Oaks	PCHL	53	17	29	46	....	....	....	72	....	....	....	....	....
1948-49	Vancouver Canucks	PCHL	16	4	0	4	....	....	....	8	....	....	....	....	....
1949-50	Kerrisdale Monarchs	WKHL	34	23	19	42	....	....	....	68	4	1	1	2	4
1950-51	Kerrisdale Monarchs	WKHL	42	13	17	30	....	....	....	58	5	1	2	3	4
1951-52	Vancouver Wheelers	WKHL	21	20	14	34	....	....	....	38	6	4	3	7	8
	NHL Totals		**19**	**3**	**7**	**10**	**3**	**6**	**9**	**0**	....	....	....	....	....

• RIVERS, Gus   Gus George

RW – R. 5′11″, 180 lbs.   b: Winnipeg, Man., 11/19/1909   d: 10/15/1985.

Season	Club	League	GP	G	A	Pts	AG	AA	APts	PIM	GP	G	A	Pts	PIM
1925-26	Winnipeg Vics	WJrHL	STATISTICS NOT AVAILABLE												
1926-27	Elmwood Millionaires	WJrHL	STATISTICS NOT AVAILABLE												
1927-28	Elmwood Millionaires	WJrHL	5	2	1	3	....	....	....	6	2	2	1	3	0
	Winnipeg Eaton's	WSrHL	6	1	2	3	....	....	....	8	2	1	1	2	4
	Elmwood Millionaires	M-Cup	3	2	0	2	....	....	....	0	....	....	....	....	....
1928-29	University of Manitoba	MTBHL	5	6	2	8	....	....	....	4	1	0	0	0	0
	Winnipeg CPR	WSrHL	9	7	5	12	....	....	....	8	3	0	*2	2	2
1929-30	Winnipeg Winnipegs	MHL-Sr.	6	1	4	5	....	....	....	12	....	....	....	....	....
♦	**Montreal Canadiens**	**NHL**	**19**	**1**	**0**	**1**	**1**	**0**	**1**	**2**	**6**	**1**	**0**	**1**	**2**
♦**1930-31**	**Montreal Canadiens**	**NHL**	**44**	**2**	**5**	**7**	**4**	**15**	**19**	**6**	**10**	**1**	**0**	**1**	**0**
1931-32	**Montreal Canadiens**	**NHL**	**25**	**1**	**0**	**1**	**2**	**0**	**2**	**4**	....	....	....	....	....
	Providence Reds	Can-Am	19	11	12	23	....	....	....	10	5	1	*2	3	2
1932-33	Providence Reds	Can-Am	43	11	18	29	....	....	....	25	2	1	1	2	0
1933-34	Providence Reds	Can-Am	35	11	8	19	....	....	....	17	3	0	0	0	0
1934-35	Providence Reds	Can-Am	45	18	23	41	....	....	....	8	6	1	1	2	7
1935-36	Providence Reds	Can-Am	45	13	17	30	....	....	....	25	7	*3	3	*6	2
1936-37	Providence Reds	IAHL	46	8	14	22	....	....	....	17	3	2	1	3	0
	NHL Totals		**88**	**4**	**5**	**9**	**7**	**15**	**22**	**12**	**16**	**2**	**0**	**2**	**2**

Signed as a free agent by **Montreal Canadiens**, January 22, 1930.

• RIVERS, Wayne   *— see page 1567*

• ROACH, Mickey   Michael Richard

C – L. 5′6″, 158 lbs.   b: Boston, MA, 5/1/1895   d: 4/1/1977.

Season	Club	League	GP	G	A	Pts	AG	AA	APts	PIM	GP	G	A	Pts	PIM
1913-14	Boston Pilgrims	X-Games	8	4	0	4	....	....	....	....	2	0	0	0	3
	Boston English High	H.S.	STATISTICS NOT AVAILABLE												
1914-15	Boston Arenas	AAHL	10	*14	0	*14	....	....	....	....	7	4	0	4	....
1915-16	Boston Arenas	AAHL	6	11	0	11	....	....	....	....	....	....	....	....	....
1916-17	New York Crescents	AAHL	6	5	0	5	....	....	....	....	6	4	0	4	....
1917-18	New York Wanderers	USNHL	10	12	0	12	....	....	....	....	....	....	....	....	....

Season	Club	League	GP	G	A	Pts	AG	AA	APts	PIM	GP	G	A	Pts	PIM
			REGULAR SEASON								PLAYOFFS				
1918-19	Hamilton Tigers	OHA-Sr.	8	17	*12	*29	....	....	....	....	4	4	*3	7	....
	Hamilton Tigers	Al-Cup	2	1	1	2	....	....	....	0	....	....	....	....	....
1919-20	**Toronto St. Pats**	**NHL**	**21**	**11**	**2**	**13**	**12**	**7**	**19**	**4**	....	....	....	....	....
1920-21	**Toronto St. Pats**	**NHL**	**9**	**1**	**1**	**2**	**1**	**4**	**5**	**2**	....	....	....	....	....
	Hamilton Tigers	**NHL**	**14**	**9**	**8**	**17**	**11**	**31**	**42**	**0**	....	....	....	....	....
1921-22	**Hamilton Tigers**	**NHL**	**24**	**14**	**6**	**20**	**19**	**19**	**38**	**7**	....	....	....	....	....
1922-23	**Hamilton Tigers**	**NHL**	**24**	**17**	**10**	**27**	**29**	**39**	**68**	**8**	....	....	....	....	....
1923-24	**Hamilton Tigers**	**NHL**	**20**	**5**	**3**	**8**	**10**	**17**	**27**	**7**	....	....	....	....	....
1924-25	**Hamilton Tigers**	**NHL**	**30**	**6**	**4**	**10**	**10**	**16**	**26**	**8**	....	....	....	....	....
1925-26	**New York Americans**	**NHL**	**25**	**3**	**0**	**3**	**5**	**0**	**5**	**4**	....	....	....	....	....
1926-27	**New York Americans**	**NHL**	**44**	**11**	**0**	**11**	**20**	**0**	**20**	**14**	....	....	....	....	....
1927-28	Niagara Falls Cataracts	Can-Pro	41	12	6	18	....	....	....	23	....	....	....	....	....
1928-29	Windsor Bulldogs	Can-Pro	42	8	9	17	....	....	....	0	7	1	0	1	2
1929-30	Buffalo Bisons	IHL	10	0	0	0	....	....	....	0	....	....	....	....	....
1930-31	Buffalo Bisons	IHL	DID NOT PLAY – COACHING												
	NHL Totals		**211**	**77**	**34**	**111**	**117**	**133**	**250**	**54**	....	....	....	....	....

AAHL First All-Star Team (1916, 1917) • USNHL First All-Star Team (1918) • OHA-Sr. First All-Star Team (1919)

Signed as a free agent by **Toronto**, December 16, 1919. Traded to **Hamilton** by **Toronto** for cash, January 21, 1921. Transferred to **NY Americans** after NHL club purchased **Hamilton** franchise, September 26, 1925. Traded to **Niagara Falls** (Can-Pro) by **NY Americans** and named playing coach for future considerations (Bill Holmes, October 29, 1928), October 5, 1927. Traded to **Windsor** (Can-Pro) by **London** (Can-Pro) for cash, October 30, 1928. Traded to **Buffalo** (IHL) by **Windsor** (IHL) for cash and named playing coach, July 8, 1929.

• ROBERT, Claude

LW – L. 5'11", 175 lbs. b: Montreal, Que., 8/10/1928.

Season	Club	League	GP	G	A	Pts	AG	AA	APts	PIM	GP	G	A	Pts	PIM
1947-48	Montreal Nationale	QJHL	32	21	22	43	....	....	....	41	12	4	11	15	8
	Montreal Nationale	M-Cup	8	4	6	10	....	....	....	10	....	....	....	....	....
1948-49	Montreal Royals	QSHL	44	14	7	21	....	....	....	28	....	....	....	....	....
1949-50	Chicoutimi Sagueneens	QSHL	60	31	25	56	....	....	....	79	5	1	6	7	2
1950-51	**Montreal Canadiens**	**NHL**	**23**	**1**	**0**	**1**	**1**	**0**	**1**	**9**	....	....	....	....	....
	Cincinnati Mohawks	AHL	26	5	5	10	....	....	....	28	....	....	....	....	....
1951-52	Quebec Aces	QMHL	60	22	27	49	....	....	....	53	15	6	7	13	20
	Quebec Aces	Alx-Cup	5	2	0	2	....	....	....	14	....	....	....	....	....
1952-53	Quebec Aces	QMHL	29	3	12	15	....	....	....	35	....	....	....	....	....
	New Westminster Royals	WHL	29	8	11	19	....	....	....	37	7	0	4	4	0
1953-54	Ottawa Senators	QHL	19	3	6	9	....	....	....	20	....	....	....	....	....
	Charlottetown Islanders	MMHL	38	23	32	55	....	....	....	34	7	2	0	2	4
1954-55	North Bay Trappers	NOHA	16	4	9	13	....	....	....	7	....	....	....	....	....
	Fort Wayne–Toledo	IHL	19	3	5	8	....	....	....	12	....	....	....	....	....
	NHL Totals		**23**	**1**	**0**	**1**	**1**	**0**	**1**	**9**	....	....	....	....	....

Traded to **New Westminster** (WHL) by **Quebec** (AHL) for Gordie Fashoway, January 4, 1953. • Fashoway refused to report to Quebec so New Westminster paid cash to complete transaction, January 7, 1953.

• ROBERTS, Doug — see page 1569

• ROBERTS, Jimmy — see page 1570

• ROBERTSON, Fred

D – L. 5'10", 198 lbs. b: Carlisle, England, 10/22/1911 d: 9/20/1997.

Season	Club	League	GP	G	A	Pts	AG	AA	APts	PIM	GP	G	A	Pts	PIM
1928-29	Toronto Canoe Club	OHA-Jr.	9	3	2	5	....	....	....	....	3	3	1	4	....
1929-30	Sudbury K of C	NOJHA	5	3	0	3	....	....	....	0	....	....	....	....	....
	Toronto Canoe Club	OHA-Jr.	4	2	0	2	....	....	....	20	....	....	....	....	....
	Toronto Eaton's	TMHL	15	7	4	11	....	....	....	28	2	0	1	1	8
1930-31	Toronto Marlboros	OHA-Sr.	8	0	0	0	....	....	....	14	3	0	0	0	4
	Toronto Eaton's	TMHL	14	6	2	8	....	....	....	29	6	0	2	2	12
1931-32	Toronto Eaton's	TMHL	9	4	2	6	....	....	....	16	....	....	....	....	....
	Toronto Marlboros	OHA-Sr.	20	7	6	13	....	....	....	*58	1	0	1	1	2
♦	**Toronto Maple Leafs**	**NHL**	**8**	**0**	**0**	**0**	**0**	**0**	**0**	**23**	**7**	**0**	**0**	**0**	**0**
1932-33	Syracuse Stars	IHL	42	3	4	7	....	....	....	*109	5	1	1	2	6
1933-34	**Toronto Maple Leafs**	**NHL**	**2**	**0**	**0**	**0**	**0**	**0**	**0**	**0**	....	....	....	....	....
	Detroit Red Wings	**NHL**	**24**	**1**	**0**	**1**	**2**	**0**	**2**	**12**	....	....	....	....	....
	Detroit Olympics	IHL	19	0	0	0	....	....	....	34	6	1	4	5	18
1934-35	Syracuse Stars	IHL	25	0	3	3	....	....	....	22	....	....	....	....	....
	Cleveland Falcons	IHL	20	3	1	4	....	....	....	20	2	0	0	0	2
1935-36	Cleveland Falcons	IHL	48	5	5	10	....	....	....	82	2	0	0	0	8
1936-37	Cleveland Falcons	IAHL	32	0	7	7	....	....	....	28	....	....	....	....	....
1937-38	Cleveland Barons	IAHL	48	3	4	7	....	....	....	74	2	0	0	0	8
1938-39	Cleveland Barons	IAHL	51	0	1	1	....	....	....	45	9	0	2	2	8
1939-40	Cleveland Barons	IAHL	45	5	3	8	....	....	....	38	....	....	....	....	....
1940-41	Cleveland Barons	AHL	56	7	8	15	....	....	....	45	7	1	0	1	6
1941-42	Cleveland Barons	AHL	48	5	8	13	....	....	....	22	5	0	1	1	2
1942-43	Cleveland Barons	AHL	56	2	9	11	....	....	....	33	4	0	1	1	22
1943-44	Cleveland Barons	AHL	3	1	1	2	....	....	....	2	....	....	....	....	....
	Pittsburgh Hornets	AHL	33	3	5	8	....	....	....	12	....	....	....	....	....
1944-45	Pittsburgh Hornets	AHL	35	1	17	18	....	....	....	22	....	....	....	....	....
	Hershey Bears	AHL	15	2	3	5	....	....	....	4	11	0	3	3	4
1945-46	Hershey Bears	AHL	24	2	3	5	....	....	....	4	....	....	....	....	....
	St. Louis Flyers	AHL	16	0	4	4	....	....	....	6	....	....	....	....	....
1946-47	Toronto Stoneys	TIHL	20	1	2	3	....	....	....	9	6	0	1	1	2
	NHL Totals		**34**	**1**	**0**	**1**	**2**	**0**	**2**	**35**	**7**	**0**	**0**	**0**	**0**

IAHL First All-Star Team (1940) • AHL Second All-Star Team (1941, 1942)

Signed as a free agent by **Toronto**, February 14, 1932. Traded to **Detroit** by **Toronto** for $6,500, November 13, 1933. Traded to **Pittsburgh** (AHL) by **Cleveland** (AHL) for Pete Bessone, November 1, 1943.

• ROBERTSON, George

George Thomas "Robbie"

LW/C – L. 6'1", 172 lbs. b: Winnipeg, Man., 5/11/1928.

Season	Club	League	GP	G	A	Pts	AG	AA	APts	PIM	GP	G	A	Pts	PIM
1944-45	Winnipeg Monarchs	MJHL	7	7	6	13	....	....	....	6	6	0	3	3	8
	Winnipeg Monarchs	M-Cup	10	4	7	11	....	....	....	12	....	....	....	....	....
1945-46	Winnipeg Monarchs	MJHL	9	8	2	10	....	....	....	2	23	17	12	29	24
	Winnipeg Monarchs	M-Cup	16	12	7	19	....	....	....	12	....	....	....	....	....
1946-47	Stratford Kroehlers	OHA-Jr.	30	20	27	47	....	....	....	20	2	1	3	4	0
1947-48	**Montreal Canadiens**	**NHL**	**1**	**0**	**0**	**0**	**0**	**0**	**0**	**0**	....	....	....	....	....
	Montreal Royals	QSHL	47	11	27	38	....	....	....	18	3	0	0	0	0
1948-49	**Montreal Canadiens**	**NHL**	**30**	**2**	**5**	**7**	**3**	**7**	**10**	**6**	....	....	....	....	....
	Buffalo Bisons	AHL	4	0	0	0	....	....	....	0	....	....	....	....	....
	Washington Lions	AHL	20	4	16	20	....	....	....	2	....	....	....	....	....
1949-50	Cincinnati Mohawks	AHL	26	3	5	8	....	....	....	0	....	....	....	....	....
	Victoria Cougars	PCHL	24	1	11	12	....	....	....	6	....	....	....	....	....
1950-51	Springfield Indians	AHL	5	1	3	4	....	....	....	0	....	....	....	....	....
	Sydney Millionaires	CBMHL	26	12	20	32	....	....	....	25	5	2	2	4	4
	Sydney Millionaires	Alx-Cup	12	2	7	9	....	....	....	9	....	....	....	....	....
1951-52	Sydney Millionaires	MMHL	86	26	44	70	....	....	....	56	....	....	....	....	....
1952-53	Sydney Millionaires	MMHL	74	18	48	66	....	....	....	24	6	1	2	3	0
1953-54	Sydney Millionaires	MMHL	70	32	48	80	....	....	....	30	14	4	2	6	2
1954-55	Saskatoon Quakers	WHL	35	4	15	19	....	....	....	8	....	....	....	....	....
	Grand Rapids Rockets	IHL	23	7	8	15	....	....	....	4	4	0	0	0	2
1955-56	S.S. Marie Greyhounds	NOHA	60	12	34	46	....	....	....	14	5	1	4	5	0
	NHL Totals		**31**	**2**	**5**	**7**	**3**	**7**	**10**	**6**	....	....	....	....	....

MMHL Second All-Star Team (1954)

Traded to **Montreal** by **NY Rangers** with Hal Laycoe and Joe Bell for Buddy O'Connor and Frank Eddolls, August 19, 1947. Traded to **Washington** (AHL) by **Montreal** (Buffalo-AHL) for Ab DeMarco with Montreal retaining right of recall, January 28, 1949. Traded to **Victoria** (PCHL) by **Montreal** for cash, December 11, 1949. Signed as a free agent by **Sydney** (CBMHL), January 7, 1951.

• ROBINSON, Doug — see page 1572

• ROBINSON, Earl

Henry Earle

RW/C – R. 5'10", 160 lbs. b: Montreal, Que., 3/11/1907 Deceased.

Season	Club	League	GP	G	A	Pts	AG	AA	APts	PIM	GP	G	A	Pts	PIM
1925-26	Montreal Royal Bank	MCBHL	9	5	2	7	....	....	....	4	....	....	....	....	....
	Montreal Royals	MCJHL	9	*9	*6	*15	....	....	....	4	4	*17	2	*19	7
1926-27	Montreal Royal Bank	MCBHL	4	7	4	*11	....	....	....	2	....	....	....	....	....
	Montreal Victorias	X-Games	15	*48	....	*48	....	....	....	....	....	....	....	....	....
	Montreal Victorias	MCHL	5	4	1	5	....	....	....	4	....	....	....	....	....
1927-28	Philadelphia Arrows	Can-Am	34	18	7	25	....	....	....	21	....	....	....	....	....
1928-29	**Montreal Maroons**	**NHL**	**38**	**2**	**1**	**3**	**6**	**7**	**13**	**2**	....	....	....	....	....
1929-30	**Montreal Maroons**	**NHL**	**31**	**1**	**2**	**3**	**1**	**5**	**6**	**10**	**4**	**0**	**0**	**0**	**0**
	Windsor Bulldogs	IHL	5	3	2	5	....	....	....	0	....	....	....	....	....
1930-31	Windsor Bulldogs	IHL	48	*44	19	*63	....	....	....	18	6	*6	4	*10	0
1931-32	**Montreal Maroons**	**NHL**	**26**	**0**	**3**	**3**	**0**	**7**	**7**	**2**	....	....	....	....	....
	Windsor Bulldogs	IHL	21	10	4	14	....	....	....	8	6	2	3	5	4
1932-33	**Montreal Maroons**	**NHL**	**44**	**15**	**9**	**24**	**27**	**19**	**46**	**6**	**2**	**0**	**0**	**0**	**0**
1933-34	**Montreal Maroons**	**NHL**	**47**	**12**	**16**	**28**	**21**	**34**	**55**	**14**	**4**	**2**	**0**	**2**	**0**
♦1934-35	**Montreal Maroons**	**NHL**	**48**	**17**	**18**	**35**	**28**	**31**	**59**	**23**	**7**	**2**	**2**	**4**	**0**
1935-36	**Montreal Maroons**	**NHL**	**39**	**6**	**14**	**20**	**11**	**27**	**38**	**27**	**3**	**0**	**0**	**0**	**0**
1936-37	**Montreal Maroons**	**NHL**	**47**	**16**	**18**	**34**	**27**	**33**	**60**	**19**	**5**	**1**	**2**	**3**	**0**
1937-38	**Montreal Maroons**	**NHL**	**39**	**4**	**7**	**11**	**6**	**11**	**17**	**13**	....	....	....	....	....
1938-39	**Chicago Black Hawks**	**NHL**	**47**	**9**	**6**	**15**	**16**	**9**	**25**	**13**	....	....	....	....	....
1939-40	**Montreal Canadiens**	**NHL**	**11**	**1**	**4**	**5**	**2**	**6**	**8**	**4**	....	....	....	....	....
	New Haven Eagles	IAHL	25	11	14	25	....	....	....	2	3	2	2	4	0
1940-41	New Haven Eagles	AHL	56	16	19	35	....	....	....	19	2	0	0	0	0
1941-42	Providence Reds	AHL	1	0	0	0	....	....	....	0	....	....	....	....	....
	New Haven Eagles	AHL	48	13	20	33	....	....	....	2	2	0	0	0	2
1942-43	Toronto Colonels	OHA-Sr.	10	13	*16	29	....	....	....	6	....	....	....	....	....
	Toronto Staffords	TIHL	16	13	5	18	....	....	....	8	2	2	0	2	2
1943-44	Toronto Army Daggers	OHA-Sr.	1	0	0	0	....	....	....	0	....	....	....	....	....
	Toronto Army Shamrocks	TIHL	25	13	11	24	....	....	....	20	4	3	1	4	2
	NHL Totals		**417**	**83**	**98**	**181**	**145**	**189**	**334**	**133**	**25**	**5**	**4**	**9**	**0**

MCBHL First All-Star Team (1927) • Played in NHL All-Star Game (1937, 1939)

Traded to **Chicago** by **Montreal Maroons** with Russ Blinco and Baldy Northcott for $30,000, September 15, 1938. Traded to **Montreal Canadiens** by **Chicago** for cash, October 11, 1939.

• ROCHE, Des

Michael Patrick

RW – R. 5'7", 165 lbs. b: Kemptville, Ont., 2/1/1909 Deceased.

Season	Club	League	GP	G	A	Pts	AG	AA	APts	PIM	GP	G	A	Pts	PIM
1925-26	Montreal Victorias	MCJHL	6	4	1	5	....	....	....	2	4	3	1	4	2
1926-27	Montreal Victorias	MCHL	1	0	0	0	....	....	....	0	....	....	....	....	....
1927-28	Montreal Bell Telephone	MRTHL	STATISTICS NOT AVAILABLE												
	Montreal St. Anthony	MRTHL	13	7	0	7	....	....	....	....	....	....	....	....	....
1928-29	Montreal Bell Telephone	MRTHL	....	5	4	9	....	....	....	20	....	....	....	....	....
	Montreal Martin	MRTHL	....	7	0	7	....	....	....	....	....	....	....	....	....
1929-30	Montreal Bell Telephone	MRTHL	10	6	0	6	....	....	....	8	2	1	0	1	2
1930-31	**Montreal Maroons**	**NHL**	**19**	**0**	**1**	**1**	**0**	**3**	**3**	**6**	....	....	....	....	....
	Windsor Bulldogs	IHL	26	10	2	12	....	....	....	16	6	1	0	1	2
1931-32	Windsor Bulldogs	IHL	42	11	12	23	....	....	....	42	6	2	0	2	6
1932-33	**Montreal Maroons**	**NHL**	**5**	**0**	**0**	**0**	**0**	**0**	**0**	**0**	....	....	....	....	....
	Windsor Bulldogs	IHL	20	7	4	11	....	....	....	32	....	....	....	....	....
	Ottawa Senators	**NHL**	**16**	**3**	**6**	**9**	**5**	**12**	**17**	**6**	....	....	....	....	....
1933-34	**Ottawa Senators**	**NHL**	**46**	**14**	**10**	**24**	**24**	**21**	**45**	**22**	....	....	....	....	....
1934-35	**St. Louis Eagles**	**NHL**	**7**	**0**	**0**	**0**	**0**	**0**	**0**	**0**	....	....	....	....	....
	Montreal Canadiens	**NHL**	**5**	**0**	**1**	**1**	**0**	**2**	**2**	**0**	....	....	....	....	....
	Buffalo Bisons	IHL	1	1	1	2	....	....	....	2	....	....	....	....	....
	Detroit Red Wings	**NHL**	**15**	**3**	**0**	**3**	**5**	**0**	**5**	**10**	....	....	....	....	....
	Detroit Olympics	IHL	7	0	3	3	....	....	....	6	5	*6	2	*8	4
	Detroit Olympics	L-W-S	5	2	2	4	....	....	....	4	....	....	....	....	....
1935-36	Pittsburgh Shamrocks	IHL	25	7	7	14	....	....	....	26	....	....	....	....	....
	Cleveland Falcons	IHL	19	3	5	8	....	....	....	10	2	0	0	0	0
1936-37	St. Louis Flyers	AHA	4	3	0	3	....	....	....	2	....	....	....	....	....
1937-38	Tulsa Oilers	AHA	32	12	9	21	....	....	....	27	....	....	....	....	....
1938-39	Spokane Clippers	PCHL	45	14	11	25	....	....	....	33	....	....	....	....	....
	NHL Totals		**113**	**20**	**18**	**38**	**34**	**38**	**72**	**44**	....	....	....	....	....

• Brother of Earl

Signed as a free agent by **Montreal Maroons**, September 2, 1930. Traded to **Ottawa** by **Montreal Maroons** for Wally Kilrea, February 3, 1933. Transferred to **St. Louis** after **Ottawa** franchise relocated, September 22, 1934. Traded to **Boston** by **St. Louis** with Max Kaminsky for Joe Lamb, December 4, 1934. Traded to **Montreal Canadiens** by **Boston** for cash, December 8, 1934. Traded to **Buffalo** (IHL) by **Montreal Canadiens** for cash, December 26, 1934. Traded to **Detroit** by **Buffalo** (IHL) for cash, January 1, 1935. Traded to **Pittsburgh** (IHL) by **Detroit** for cash, October 17, 1935. Traded to **Cleveland** (IHL) by **Pittsburgh** (IHL) for cash, February 3, 1936.

• ROCHE, Earl Earl Joseph
LW – L. 5'11", 175 lbs. b: Prescott, Ont., 2/22/1910 d: 1966.

Season	Club	League	GP	G	A	Pts	AG	AA	APts	PIM	GP	G	A	Pts	PIM
			REGULAR SEASON								PLAYOFFS				
1925-26	Montreal Victorias	MCJHL	5	1	1	2	....	....	....	2	....	....	....	....	....
1926-27	Montreal Bell Telephone	MRTHL	STATISTICS NOT AVAILABLE												
1927-28	Montreal Bell Telephone	MRTHL	STATISTICS NOT AVAILABLE												
	Montreal St. Anthony's	MMRHL	STATISTICS NOT AVAILABLE												
1928-29	Montreal Victorias	MCJHL	STATISTICS NOT AVAILABLE												
	Montreal Bell Telephone	MRTHL	15	*10	4	*14	....	....	....	24	....	....	....	....	....
	Montreal Martins	MMRHL	....	2	0	2	....	....	....	2	....	....	....	....	....
1929-30	Montreal Bell Telephone	MRTHL	10	6	0	6	....	....	....	18	2	*1	*1	*2	6
1930-31	**Montreal Maroons**	**NHL**	**42**	**2**	**0**	**2**	**4**	**0**	**4**	**18**	**2**	**0**	**0**	**0**	**0**
1931-32	Windsor Bulldogs	IHL	48	22	18	40	....	....	....	51	6	0	1	1	2
1932-33	**Montreal Maroons**	**NHL**	**5**	**0**	**0**	**0**	**0**	**0**	**0**	**0**	....	....	....	....	....
	Windsor Bulldogs	IHL	17	6	8	14	....	....	....	23	....	....	....	....	....
	Boston Bruins	**NHL**	**3**	**0**	**0**	**0**	**0**	**0**	**0**	**0**	....	....	....	....	....
	Ottawa Senators	**NHL**	**20**	**4**	**5**	**9**	**7**	**10**	**17**	**6**	....	....	....	....	....
1933-34	**Ottawa Senators**	**NHL**	**45**	**13**	**16**	**29**	**22**	**34**	**56**	**22**	....	....	....	....	....
	Detroit Olympics	IHL	5	0	0	0	....	....	....	2	....	....	....	....	....
1934-35	**St. Louis Eagles**	**NHL**	**19**	**3**	**3**	**6**	**5**	**5**	**10**	**2**	....	....	....	....	....
	Buffalo Bisons	IHL	1	1	1	2	....	....	....	0	....	....	....	....	....
	Detroit Red Wings	**NHL**	**13**	**3**	**3**	**6**	**5**	**5**	**10**	**0**	....	....	....	....	....
	Detroit Olympics	IHL	7	2	1	3	....	....	....	12	5	1	*4	5	0
	Detroit Olympics	L-W-S	4	3	0	3	....	....	....	*26	....	....	....	....	....
1935-36	Pittsburgh Shamrocks	IHL	28	12	11	23	....	....	....	30	....	....	....	....	....
	Cleveland Falcons	IHL	19	9	8	17	....	....	....	26	2	0	0	0	0
1936-37	Cleveland Barons	IAHL	39	11	17	28	....	....	....	49	....	....	....	....	....
1937-38	Cleveland Barons	IAHL	46	4	9	13	....	....	....	12	1	0	2	2	2
1938-39	Providence Reds	IAHL	1	0	0	0	....	....	....	0	....	....	....	....	....
	Cleveland Barons	IAHL	9	0	4	4	....	....	....	0	....	....	....	....	....
	Hershey Bears	IAHL	42	4	9	13	....	....	....	14	5	0	3	3	0
1939-40	New Haven Eagles	IAHL	54	13	28	41	....	....	....	14	3	0	3	3	0
1940-41	New Haven Eagles	AHL	51	18	17	35	....	....	....	22	2	0	0	0	2
1941-42	New Haven Eagles	AHL	56	9	20	29	....	....	....	19	2	0	0	0	2
1942-43			REINSTATED AS AN AMATEUR												
1943-44	Montreal Noordyn	MCHL	10	5	5	10	....	....	....	6	....	....	....	....	....
	NHL Totals		**147**	**25**	**27**	**52**	**43**	**54**	**97**	**48**	**2**	**0**	**0**	**0**	**0**

• Brother of Des

Signed as a free agent by **Montreal Maroons**, September 2, 1930. Signed as a free agent by **Boston**, January 14, 1933. Traded to **Ottawa** by **Boston** to complete transaction that sent Alex Smith to Boston, January 25, 1933. Transferred to **St. Louis** after **Ottawa** franchise relocated, September 22, 1934. Traded to **Buffalo** (IHL) by **St. Louis** for cash, December 20, 1934. Traded to **Detroit** by **Buffalo** (IHL) for cash, January 1, 1935. Traded to **Cleveland** (IHL) by **Pittsburgh** (IHL) for cash, February 3, 1936.

• ROCHE, Ernie Ernest Charles
D – L. 6'1", 170 lbs. b: Montreal, Que., 2/4/1930.

Season	Club	League	GP	G	A	Pts	AG	AA	APts	PIM	GP	G	A	Pts	PIM
1946-47	Montreal Jr. Canadiens	QJHL	27	3	9	12	....	....	....	52	8	2	9	11	14
	Montreal Jr. Canadiens	M-Cup	8	1	6	7	....	....	....	16	....	....	....	....	....
1947-48	Montreal Jr. Canadiens	QJHL	32	9	10	19	....	....	....	68	5	0	0	0	6
1948-49	Montreal Jr. Canadiens	QJHL	48	11	12	23	....	....	....	73	4	1	1	2	2
1949-50	Montreal Jr. Canadiens	QJHL	36	12	12	24	....	....	....	81	15	5	13	18	26
	Montreal Jr. Canadiens	M-Cup	13	1	10	11	....	....	....	30	....	....	....	....	....
1950-51	**Montreal Canadiens**	**NHL**	**4**	**0**	**0**	**0**	**0**	**0**	**0**	**2**	....	....	....	....	....
	Cincinnati Mohawks	AHL	60	3	10	13	....	....	....	21	....	....	....	....	....
1951-52	Buffalo Bisons	AHL	4	0	1	1	....	....	....	2	....	....	....	....	....
	Victoria Cougars	PCHL	64	6	17	23	....	....	....	60	10	0	1	1	4
1952-53	Victoria Cougars	WHL	65	10	25	35	....	....	....	69	....	....	....	....	....
1953-54	Montreal Royals	QHL	51	1	15	16	....	....	....	48	9	2	1	3	4
	Victoria Cougars	WHL	5	0	0	0	....	....	....	4	....	....	....	....	....
1954-55	Montreal Royals	QHL	56	11	11	22	....	....	....	52	14	1	4	5	14
1955-56	Springfield Indians	AHL	22	3	5	8	....	....	....	10	....	....	....	....	....
	Shawinigan Cataracts	QHL	24	2	8	10	....	....	....	10	11	0	1	1	4
1956-57	Montreal Royals	QHL	64	4	21	25	....	....	....	66	4	0	0	0	0
	Hull-Ottawa Canadiens	EOHL	1	0	0	0	....	....	....	0	....	....	....	....	....
1957-58	Montreal Royals	QHL	53	5	15	20	....	....	....	40	7	1	1	2	2
1958-59	Montreal Royals	QHL	51	1	8	9	....	....	....	16	3	0	0	0	0
1959-60	Sudbury Wolves	EPHL	62	4	29	33	....	....	....	38	14	2	3	5	22
1960-61	Sudbury Wolves	EPHL	5	0	2	2	....	....	....	2	....	....	....	....	....
	Milwaukee Falcons	IHL	10	2	0	2	....	....	....	4	....	....	....	....	....
	Windsor Maple Leafs	NSSHL	22	4	6	10	....	....	....	6	10	0	0	0	4
	NHL Totals		**4**	**0**	**0**	**0**	**0**	**0**	**0**	**2**	....	....	....	....	....

Claimed by **Springfield** (AHL) from **Montreal** (Montreal Royals-QHL) in Inter-League Draft, June 1, 1955.

• ROCHEFORT, Dave David Joseph
C – L. 6', 180 lbs. b: Red Deer, Alta., 7/22/1946.

Season	Club	League	GP	G	A	Pts	AG	AA	APts	PIM	GP	G	A	Pts	PIM
1962-63	Edmonton Oil Kings	CAHL	STATISTICS NOT AVAILABLE												
	Edmonton Oil Kings	M-Cup	11	0	1	1	....	....	....	4	....	....	....	....	....
1963-64	Edmonton Oil Kings	CAHL	6	3	5	8	....	....	....	21	....	....	....	....	....
1964-65	Edmonton Oil Kings	CAHL	....	....	....	....	....	....	....	....	5	2	2	4	0
	Edmonton Oil Kings	M-Cup	18	6	2	8	....	....	....	26	....	....	....	....	....
1965-66	Edmonton Oil Kings	ASHL	24	6	10	16	....	....	....	34	11	3	7	10	18
	Edmonton Oil Kings	M-Cup	19	7	9	16	....	....	....	39	....	....	....	....	....
1966-67	**Detroit Red Wings**	**NHL**	**1**	**0**	**0**	**0**	**0**	**0**	**0**	**0**	....	....	....	....	....
	Memphis Wings	CPHL	32	5	8	13	....	....	....	10	....	....	....	....	....
	Pittsburgh Hornets	AHL	1	0	0	0	....	....	....	0	....	....	....	....	....
1967-68	Fort Worth Wings	CPHL	65	15	18	33	....	....	....	55	12	2	0	2	16
1968-69	Baltimore Clippers	AHL	46	2	7	9	....	....	....	22	....	....	....	....	....
1969-70	Oklahoma City Blazers	CHL	3	0	1	1	....	....	....	2	....	....	....	....	....
	Salt Lake Golden Eagles	WHL	59	7	16	23	....	....	....	40	....	....	....	....	....
1970-71	Edmonton Monarchs	ASHL	STATISTICS NOT AVAILABLE												
1971-72	Edmonton Monarchs	PrSHL	30	29	23	42	....	....	....	43	....	....	....	....	....
	NHL Totals		**1**	**0**	**0**	**0**	**0**	**0**	**0**	**0**	....	....	....	....	....

• ROCHEFORT, Leon — see page 1574

• ROCKBURN, Harvey "Hard Rock"
D – L. 5'10", 180 lbs. b: Ottawa, Ont., 8/20/1908 d: 6/9/1977.

Season	Club	League	GP	G	A	Pts	AG	AA	APts	PIM	GP	G	A	Pts	PIM
1924-25	Ottawa Tigers	OCJHL	STATISTICS NOT AVAILABLE												
1925-26	Ottawa Gunners	OCHL	15	3	1	4	....	....	....	....	6	0	0	0	0
	Montreal CNR	MRTHL	1	0	0	0	....	....	....	0	....	....	....	....	....
1926-27	Ottawa Shamrocks	OCHL	2	1	1	2	....	....	....	....	....	....	....	....	....
	Berlin Mountaineers	NEHL	27	6	4	10	....	....	....	24	....	....	....	....	....
1927-28	Detroit Olympics	Can-Pro	36	2	1	3	....	....	....	82	2	0	0	0	8
1928-29	Detroit Olympics	Can-Pro	37	2	1	3	....	....	....	*176	7	1	0	1	*42
1929-30	**Detroit Cougars**	**NHL**	**36**	**4**	**0**	**4**	**6**	**0**	**6**	**97**	....	....	....	....	....
1930-31	**Detroit Falcons**	**NHL**	**42**	**0**	**1**	**1**	**0**	**3**	**3**	***118**	....	....	....	....	....
1931-32	Detroit Olympics	IHL	46	6	3	9	....	....	....	*149	6	1	0	1	20
1932-33	Providence Reds	Can-Am	4	0	0	0	....	....	....	20	....	....	....	....	....
	Windsor Bulldogs	IHL	18	1	0	1	....	....	....	36	....	....	....	....	....
	Ottawa Senators	**NHL**	**16**	**0**	**1**	**1**	**0**	**2**	**2**	**39**	....	....	....	....	....
1933-34	London Panthers	IHL	41	6	11	17	....	....	....	*113	4	0	0	0	12
1934-35	Windsor Bulldogs	IHL	40	4	2	6	....	....	....	*114	....	....	....	....	....
1935-36	Cleveland Falcons	IHL	32	0	1	1	....	....	....	83	....	....	....	....	....
	Rochester Cardinals	IHL	1	0	0	0	....	....	....	0	....	....	....	....	....
1936-37	Kansas City Greyhounds	AHA	48	5	3	8	....	....	....	73	2	0	0	0	4
1937-38	St. Paul Saints	AHA	32	2	5	7	....	....	....	46	....	....	....	....	....
	Portland Buckaroos	PCHL	6	0	0	0	....	....	....	16	....	....	....	....	....
1938-39			REINSTATED AS AN AMATEUR												
1939-40	Ottawa Lasalle	OCHL	15	0	5	5	....	....	....	36	4	2	1	3	9
	NHL Totals		**94**	**4**	**2**	**6**	**6**	**5**	**11**	**254**	....	....	....	....	....

NEHL First All-Star Team (1927) • IHL First All-Star Team (1935) • AHA Second All-Star Team (1937)

Signed as a free agent by **Stratford** (Can-Pro), October 24, 1927. Traded to **Detroit** by **Stratford** (Can-Pro) for cash, October 31, 1927. Traded to **Providence** (Can-Am) by **Detroit** for cash, September, 1932. Traded to **Montreal Maroons** (Windsor-IHL) by **Providence** (Can-Am) for Jack McVicar, December 13, 1932. Traded to **Ottawa** by **Montreal Maroons** (Windsor-IHL) for cash, February 2, 1933. Loaned to **Rochester** (IHL) by **Cleveland** (IHL) for the return of Bill Anderson, February 16, 1936.

• RODDEN, Eddie Edward Anthony
C – R. 5'7", 150 lbs. b: Mattawa, Ont., 3/22/1901 Deceased.

Season	Club	League	GP	G	A	Pts	AG	AA	APts	PIM	GP	G	A	Pts	PIM
1914-15	Haileybury Rexalls	NOHA	STATISTICS NOT AVAILABLE												
1915/18	New Liskeard Pioneers	NOHA	STATISTICS NOT AVAILABLE												
1918-19	Toronto Aura Lee	OHA-Jr.	STATISTICS NOT AVAILABLE												
1919-20	Woodstock Juniors	OHA-Jr.	4	6	0	6	....	....	....	....	....	....	....	....	....
	Woodstock Athletics	OIHA	STATISTICS NOT AVAILABLE												
1920-21	Toronto DeLasalle	OHA-Jr.	STATISTICS NOT AVAILABLE												
	Toronto Granites	X-Games	STATISTICS NOT AVAILABLE												
1921-22	Toronto Aura Lee	OHA-Sr.	10	9	6	15	....	....	....	....	2	0	1	1	....
1922-23	Toronto Granites	OHA-Sr.	7	3	1	4	....	....	....	....	....	....	....	....	....
	Toronto Granites	Al-Cup	4	4	1	5	....	....	....	4	....	....	....	....	....
1923-24	Eveleth Rangers	USAHA	21	9	0	9	....	....	....	....	....	....	....	....	....
1924-25	Eveleth Arrowheads	USAHA	39	1	0	1	....	....	....	....	3	0	0	0	....
1925-26	Eveleth Rangers	CHL	36	7	9	16	....	....	....	42	....	....	....	....	....
1926-27	Minneapolis Millers	AHA	19	6	3	9	....	....	....	8	....	....	....	....	....
	Chicago Black Hawks	**NHL**	**19**	**3**	**3**	**6**	**5**	**16**	**21**	**0**	**2**	**0**	**1**	**1**	**0**
1927-28	**Chicago Black Hawks**	**NHL**	**9**	**0**	**2**	**2**	**0**	**11**	**11**	**6**	....	....	....	....	....
	Toronto Maple Leafs	**NHL**	**25**	**3**	**6**	**9**	**6**	**34**	**40**	**36**	....	....	....	....	....
1928-29	**Boston Bruins**	**NHL**	**20**	**0**	**0**	**0**	**0**	**0**	**0**	**10**	....	....	....	....	....
	Windsor Bulldogs	Can-Pro	19	6	5	11	....	....	....	14	3	1	0	1	20
1929-30	London Panthers	IHL	42	13	*30	43	....	....	....	50	2	1	0	1	2
1930-31	**New York Rangers**	**NHL**	**24**	**0**	**3**	**3**	**0**	**9**	**9**	**8**	....	....	....	....	....
	Pittsburgh Yellowjackets	IHL	29	7	7	14	....	....	....	21	6	0	1	1	6
1931-32	Pittsburgh Yellowjackets	IHL	42	5	13	18	....	....	....	43	....	....	....	....	....
1932-33	Quebec Beavers	Can-Am	11	3	3	6	....	....	....	12	....	....	....	....	....
	Windsor Bulldogs	IHL	21	2	4	6	....	....	....	6	6	0	0	0	2
1933-34	Tulsa Oilers	AHA	13	2	6	8	....	....	....	10	4	1	1	2	0
	NHL Totals		**97**	**6**	**14**	**20**	**11**	**70**	**81**	**60**	**2**	**0**	**1**	**1**	**0**

OHA-Sr. Second All-Star Team (1922)

Signed as a free agent by **Minneapolis** (AHA), October 21, 1926. Traded to **Chicago** by **Minneapolis** (AHA) for cash, January, 1927. Traded to **Toronto** by **Chicago** to complete three team transaction that sent Bert McCaffrey to Pittsburgh and Ty Arbour to Chicago, December, 1927. Traded to **Boston** by **Toronto** for cash, June 20, 1928. Loaned to **Windsor** (Can-Pro) by **Boston** for cash, January 30, 1929. Traded to **London** (IHL) by **Boston** for cash, October 16, 1929. Traded to **NY Rangers** by **London** (IHL) for $8,500, September 11, 1930. Traded to **Pittsburgh** (IHL) by **NY Rangers** for cash, January 3, 1931. Traded to **Windsor** (IHL) by **Quebec** (Can-Am) for cash, January 19, 1933.

• ROLFE, Dale — see page 1577

• ROMNES, Doc Elwyn Nelson USHOF
LW/C – L. 5'11", 156 lbs. b: White Bear, MN, 1/1/1909 Deceased.

Season	Club	League	GP	G	A	Pts	AG	AA	APts	PIM	GP	G	A	Pts	PIM
1926-27	St. Paul Vocational	H.S.	STATISTICS NOT AVAILABLE												
1927-28	St. Paul Saints	AHA	40	2	3	5	....	....	....	16	....	....	....	....	....
1928-29	St. Paul Saints	AHA	39	7	3	10	....	....	....	22	8	2	0	2	6
1929-30	St. Paul Saints	AHA	36	15	4	19	....	....	....	26	....	....	....	....	....
1930-31	**Chicago Black Hawks**	**NHL**	**30**	**5**	**7**	**12**	**10**	**21**	**31**	**8**	**9**	**1**	**1**	**2**	**2**
	London Tecumsehs	IHL	13	5	5	10	....	....	....	14	....	....	....	....	....
1931-32	**Chicago Black Hawks**	**NHL**	**18**	**1**	**0**	**1**	**2**	**0**	**2**	**6**	**2**	**0**	**0**	**0**	**0**
	Pittsburgh Yellowjackets	IHL	31	11	2	13	....	....	....	6	....	....	....	....	....
1932-33	**Chicago Black Hawks**	**NHL**	**47**	**10**	**12**	**22**	**18**	**25**	**43**	**2**	....	....	....	....	....
♦1933-34	**Chicago Black Hawks**	**NHL**	**47**	**8**	**21**	**29**	**14**	**44**	**58**	**6**	**8**	**2**	***7**	**9**	**0**
1934-35	**Chicago Black Hawks**	**NHL**	**35**	**10**	**14**	**24**	**16**	**24**	**40**	**8**	**2**	**0**	**0**	**0**	**0**
1935-36	**Chicago Black Hawks**	**NHL**	**48**	**13**	**25**	**38**	**25**	**48**	**73**	**6**	**2**	**1**	**2**	**3**	**0**
1936-37	**Chicago Black Hawks**	**NHL**	**28**	**4**	**14**	**18**	**7**	**26**	**33**	**2**	....	....	....	....	....
♦1937-38	**Chicago Black Hawks**	**NHL**	**44**	**10**	**22**	**32**	**16**	**36**	**52**	**4**	**12**	**2**	**4**	**6**	**2**

			REGULAR SEASON								PLAYOFFS				
Season	Club	League	GP	G	A	Pts	AG	AA	APts	PIM	GP	G	A	Pts	PIM
1938-39	Chicago Black Hawks	NHL	12	0	4	4	0	6	6	0	....	....	....	....	....
	Toronto Maple Leafs	NHL	36	7	16	23	12	25	37	0	10	1	4	5	0
1939-40	New York Americans	NHL	15	0	1	1	0	2	2	0	....	....	....	....	....
	Omaha Knights	AHA	14	12	19	31	....	....	....	6	9	3	4	7	0
	NHL Totals		360	68	136	204	120	257	377	42	45	7	18	25	4

Won Lady Byng Trophy (1936)

Signed as a free agent by **St. Paul** (AHA), November 2, 1927. Traded to **Chicago** by **St. Paul** (AHA) for cash, October 28, 1930. Traded to **Toronto** by **Chicago** for Bill Thoms, December 8, 1938. Traded to **NY Americans** by **Toronto** with Buzz Boll, Busher Jackson, Murray Armstrong and Jimmy Fowler for Sweeny Schriner, May 18, 1939. Traded to **Omaha** (AHA) by **NY Americans** for cash, February 7, 1940.

• RONAN, Skene Erskine

D/C – L. 5'6", 150 lbs. b: Ottawa, Ont., Deceased.

Season	Club	League	GP	G	A	Pts	AG	AA	APts	PIM	GP	G	A	Pts	PIM
1906-07	Pembroke Lumber Kings	UOVHL	1	1	0	1	....	....	....	0	....	....	....	....	....
1907-08	Ottawa Primrose	OCHL	8	*15	0	*15	....	....	....	....	....	....	....	....	....
1908-09	Pittsburgh Bankers	WPHL	8	5	0	5	....	....	....	....	....	....	....	....	....
	Toronto Professionals	OPHL	7	4	0	4	....	....	....	4	....	....	....	....	....
	Haileybury Silver Kings	TPHL	5	6	0	6	....	....	....	7	2	1	0	1	6
1909-10	Haileybury Silver Kings	NHA	11	3	0	3	....	....	....	21	....	....	....	....	....
1910-11	Renfrew Creamery Kings	NHA	5	3	0	3	....	....	....	9	....	....	....	....	....
1911-12	Ottawa Senators	NHA	18	*35	0	*35	....	....	....	5	....	....	....	....	....
	NHA All-Stars	X-Games	3	2	0	2	....	....	....	0	....	....	....	....	....
1912-13	Ottawa Senators	NHA	20	18	0	18	....	....	....	39	....	....	....	....	....
1913-14	Ottawa Senators	NHA	19	18	5	23	....	....	....	65	....	....	....	....	....
1914-15	Toronto Shamrocks	NHA	18	21	4	25	....	....	....	55	....	....	....	....	....
1915-16	Toronto Blueshirts	NHA	9	0	3	3	....	....	....	8	....	....	....	....	....
♦	Montreal Canadiens	NHA	8	6	4	10	....	....	....	14	2	1	0	1	0
1916-17	Ottawa Munitions	OCHL	PLAYER/COACH – STATISTICS UNAVAILABLE												
1917-18	Ottawa Munitions	OCHL	PLAYER/COACH – STATISTICS UNAVAILABLE												
1918-19	Ottawa Senators	NHL	11	0	0	0	0	0	0	6	....	....	....	....	....
	NHL Totals		11	0	0	0	0	0	0	6	....	....	....	....	....
	Other Major League Totals		115	108	16	124	....	....	....	220	2	1	0	1	0

• Suspended for remainder of 1906-07 season for playing with Pembroke (UOVHL) under an assumed name (Johnston), December, 1906. Signed by **Toronto** (OPHL) after jumping contract with **Pittsburgh** (WPHL), December 22, 1908. Signed by **Haileybury** (TPHL) after jumping contract with **Toronto** (OPHL), January 27, 1909. Claimed by **Ottawa** (NHA) from **Renfrew** (NHA) in Dispersal Draft, November 12, 1911. Traded to **Toronto Shamrocks** (NHA) by **Ottawa** (NHA) for Sammy Hebert and cash, December 25, 1914. Traded to **Ottawa** by **Montreal Canadiens** for rights to Harry Hyland, December 9, 1918. Released by **Ottawa**, January 26, 1919. Re-signed as a free agent by **Ottawa**, February 17, 1919.

• RONSON, Len — *see page 1579*

• RONTY, Paul

C – L. 6', 160 lbs. b: Toronto, Ont., 6/12/1928.

Season	Club	League	GP	G	A	Pts	AG	AA	APts	PIM	GP	G	A	Pts	PIM
1944-45	Toronto Chevies Aces	OHA-B	9	7	6	13	....	....	....	7	5	*6	*6	*12	0
	Toronto Uptown Tires	TMHL	1	1	0	1	....	....	....	0	....	....	....	....	....
1945-46	Boston Olympics	EAHL	49	19	25	44	....	....	....	14	12	6	11	17	2
1946-47	Hershey Bears	AHL	64	19	40	59	....	....	....	12	11	0	2	2	2
1947-48	Boston Bruins	NHL	24	3	11	14	4	14	18	0	5	0	4	4	0
	Hershey Bears	AHL	31	15	24	39	....	....	....	2	....	....	....	....	....
1948-49	Boston Bruins	NHL	60	20	29	49	28	42	70	11	5	1	2	3	2
1949-50	Boston Bruins	NHL	70	23	36	59	29	44	73	8	....	....	....	....	....
1950-51	Boston Bruins	NHL	70	10	22	32	13	27	40	20	6	0	1	1	2
1951-52	New York Rangers	NHL	65	12	31	43	16	38	54	16	....	....	....	....	....
1952-53	New York Rangers	NHL	70	16	38	54	21	47	68	20	....	....	....	....	....
1953-54	New York Rangers	NHL	70	13	33	46	18	40	58	18	....	....	....	....	....
1954-55	New York Rangers	NHL	55	4	11	15	5	13	18	8	....	....	....	....	....
	Montreal Canadiens	NHL	4	0	0	0	0	0	0	2	5	0	0	0	2
	NHL Totals		488	101	211	312	134	265	399	103	21	1	7	8	6

Played in NHL All-Star Game (1949, 1950, 1953, 1954)

Traded to **NY Rangers** by **Boston** for Gus Kyle, cash and the rights to Pentti Lund, September 20, 1951. Claimed on waivers by **Montreal** from **NY Rangers**, February 20, 1955.

• ROSS, Art Arthur Howie HHOF

D – L. 5'11", 190 lbs. b: Naughton, Ont., 1/13/1886 d: 8/5/1964.

Season	Club	League	GP	G	A	Pts	AG	AA	APts	PIM	GP	G	A	Pts	PIM
1902-03	Westmount Academy	H.S.	STATISTICS NOT AVAILABLE												
	Montreal Westmount	CAHL	STATISTICS NOT AVAILABLE												
1903-04	Montreal Westmount	CAHL	STATISTICS NOT AVAILABLE												
1904-05	Montreal Merchants	CAHL	8	10	0	10	....	....	....	....	....	....	....	....	....
1905-06	Brandon Kings	MHL-Sr.	7	6	0	6	....	....	....	....	....	....	....	....	....
♦1906-07	Kenora Thistles	St-Cup	2	0	0	0	....	....	....	10	....	....	....	....	....
	Brandon Kings	MHL-Sr.	9	5	0	5	....	....	....	....	2	1	0	1	0
♦1907-08	Montreal Wanderers	ECAHA	10	8	0	8	....	....	....	27	5	3	0	3	23
	Pembroke Lumber Kings	UOVHL	1	5	0	5	....	....	....	....	....	....	....	....	....
1908-09	Montreal Wanderers	ECHA	9	2	0	2	....	....	....	30	2	0	0	0	*13
	Montreal Wanderers	NYSHL	2	2	0	2	....	....	....	3	....	....	....	....	....
	Cobalt Silver Kings	TPHL	....	....	....	....	....	....	....	....	2	1	0	1	0
1909-10	All-Montreal	CHA	4	4	0	4	....	....	....	3	....	....	....	....	....
	Haileybury Silver Kings	NHA	12	6	0	6	....	....	....	25	....	....	....	....	....
1910-11	Montreal Wanderers	NHA	11	4	0	4	....	....	....	24	....	....	....	....	....
1911-12	Montreal Wanderers	NHA	18	16	0	16	....	....	....	35	....	....	....	....	....
	NHA All-Stars	X-Games	3	4	0	4	....	....	....	0	....	....	....	....	....
1912-13	Montreal Wanderers	NHA	19	11	0	11	....	....	....	58	....	....	....	....	....
1913-14	Montreal Wanderers	NHA	18	4	5	9	....	....	....	74	....	....	....	....	....
1914-15	Ottawa Senators	NHA	16	3	1	4	....	....	....	55	5	2	0	2	0
1915-16	Ottawa Senators	NHA	21	8	8	16	....	....	....	69	....	....	....	....	....
1916-17	Montreal Wanderers	NHA	16	6	2	8	....	....	....	66	....	....	....	....	....
1917-18	Montreal Wanderers	NHL	3	1	0	1	1	0	1	12	....	....	....	....	....
	NHL Totals		3	1	0	1	1	0	1	12	....	....	....	....	....
	Other Major League Totals		165	77	16	93	....	....	....	476	14	6	0	6	36

Won Lester Patrick Trophy (1984)

Signed as a free agent by **Haileybury** (NHA) after CHA folded, January 16, 1910. Rights retained by **Montreal Wanderers** after NHA folded, November 26, 1917.

• ROSS, Jim

D – R. 6'3", 185 lbs. b: Edinburgh, Scotland, 5/20/1926.

Season	Club	League	GP	G	A	Pts	AG	AA	APts	PIM	GP	G	A	Pts	PIM
1942-43	Unionville Ushers	OMHA	STATISTICS NOT AVAILABLE												
1943-44	Toronto Sammy Tafts	OMHA	STATISTICS NOT AVAILABLE												
1944-45	DeLasalle Oaklands	OHA-B	11	0	4	4	....	....	....	12	2	0	0	0	0
1945-46	DeLasalle Oaklands	H.S.	8	5	9	14	....	....	....	6	14	2	6	8	8
1946-47	Perth Panthers	A-Cup	....	3	3	6	....	....	....	4	....	....	....	....	....
	Perth Panthers	S-land	....	9	12	21	....	....	....	25	8	8	3	11	19
	Perth Panthers	C-Cup	....	6	4	10	....	....	....	16	....	....	....	....	....
1947-48	Detroit Metal Moldings	IHL	30	7	13	20	....	....	....	35	3	0	1	1	6
1948-49	Detroit Jerry Lynch	IHL	31	9	20	29	....	....	....	38	2	0	1	1	0
1949-50	Sydney Millionaires	CBSHL	72	14	31	45	....	....	....	81	5	1	2	3	6
	Sydney Millionaires	Al-Cup	9	6	2	8	....	....	....	8	....	....	....	....	....
1950-51	Quebec Aces	QMHL	50	6	21	27	....	....	....	62	19	1	4	5	16
1951-52	New York Rangers	NHL	51	2	9	11	3	11	14	25	....	....	....	....	....
	Cincinnati Mohawks	AHL	7	0	3	3	....	....	....	4	....	....	....	....	....
1952-53	New York Rangers	NHL	11	0	2	2	0	2	2	4	....	....	....	....	....
	Saskatoon Quakers	WHL	42	3	10	13	....	....	....	40	13	1	7	8	12
1953-54	Saskatoon Quakers	WHL	57	5	17	22	....	....	....	38	6	2	1	3	2
1954-55	Saskatoon Quakers	WHL	65	6	11	17	....	....	....	31	....	....	....	....	....
	NHL Totals		62	2	11	13	3	13	16	29	....	....	....	....	....

IHL Northern Division First All-Star Team (1949) • CBSHL First All-Star Team (1950) • QMHL Second All-Star Team (1951) • WHL First All-Star Team (1954)

• ROSSIGNOL, Roly

RW – R. 5'9", 168 lbs. b: Edmundston, N.B., 10/18/1921.

Season	Club	League	GP	G	A	Pts	AG	AA	APts	PIM	GP	G	A	Pts	PIM
1936-37	Edmundston High School	H.S.	1	0	0	0	....	....	....	0	3	1	0	1	2
1937-38	Edmundston Fraser Pulp	NNBHL	8	7	2	9	....	....	....	6	2	1	0	1	6
1938-39	Edmundston Fraser Pulp	NNBHL	5	5	8	13	....	....	....	2	2	2	0	2	....
	Edmunston Eskimos	NNBHL	3	1	1	2	....	....	....	....	4	1	2	3	2
	Edmundston High Scool	H.S.	....	....	....	....	....	....	....	....	1	1	1	2	0
1939-40	Verdun Maple Leafs	QJHL	12	2	5	7	....	....	....	10	4	1	2	3	11
	Verdun Maple Leafs	M-Cup	7	7	4	11	....	....	....	8	....	....	....	....	....
1940-41	Verdun Maple Leafs	QJHL	1	0	0	0	....	....	....	0	....	....	....	....	....
	Washington Eagles	EAHL	65	23	23	46	....	....	....	44	2	0	0	0	0
1941-42	Quebec Aces	QSHL	32	12	10	22	....	....	....	30	7	1	1	2	2
	Quebec Aces	Al-Cup	6	0	1	1	....	....	....	0	....	....	....	....	....
1942-43	Quebec Aces	QSHL	34	16	16	32	....	....	....	18	4	1	1	2	4
1943-44	Quebec Aces	QSHL	25	22	18	40	....	....	....	20	6	3	7	10	0
	Detroit Red Wings	NHL	1	0	1	1	0	1	1	0	....	....	....	....	....
	Quebec Aces	Al-Cup	9	10	8	18	....	....	....	6	....	....	....	....	....
1944-45	Montreal Canadiens	NHL	5	2	2	4	2	2	4	2	1	0	0	0	2
	Pittsburgh Hornets	AHL	38	19	24	43	....	....	....	29	....	....	....	....	....
1945-46	Detroit Red Wings	NHL	8	1	2	3	1	3	4	4	....	....	....	....	....
	Indianapolis Capitols	AHL	48	26	21	47	....	....	....	25	5	1	1	2	4
1946-47	St. Louis Flyers	AHL	31	6	9	15	....	....	....	15	....	....	....	....	....
	Providence Reds	AHL	27	11	10	21	....	....	....	10	....	....	....	....	....
1947-48	Providence Reds	AHL	6	2	2	4	....	....	....	2	....	....	....	....	....
1948-49	Providence Reds	AHL	DID NOT PLAY – INJURED												
1949-50	Quebec Aces	QSHL	42	12	23	35	....	....	....	17	9	1	1	2	....
1950-51	Jonquiere Aces	QPHL	STATISTICS NOT AVAILABLE												
1951-52	Jonquiere Aces	SLSHL	STATISTICS NOT AVAILABLE												
1952-53	Mont Joli Castors	SLSHL	58	42	59	101	....	....	....	75	....	....	....	....	....
1953-54	Riviere-du-Loup 3 L's	SLSHL	8	2	5	7	....	....	....	4	....	....	....	....	....
	Dalhousie Rangers	NNBHL	32	25	24	49	....	....	....	41	....	....	....	....	....
1954-55	Dalhousie Rangers	NNBHL	32	*43	*62	*105	....	....	....	28	....	....	....	....	....
1955-56	Bathurst Papermakers	NNBHL	36	40	42	82	....	....	....	24	....	....	....	....	....
1956-57	Bathurst Papermakers	NNBHL	48	21	42	63	....	....	....	34	6	4	4	8	2
1957-58	Bathurst Papermakers	NNBHL	36	12	53	65	....	....	....	37	....	....	....	....	....
1958-59	Bathurst Papermakers	NNBHL	36	13	23	36	....	....	....	30	....	....	....	....	....
1959-60	Bathurst Papermakers	NNBHL	STATISTICS NOT AVAILABLE												
1960-61	Bathurst Papermakers	NNBHL	STATISTICS NOT AVAILABLE												
1961-62	Bathurst Papermakers	NNBHL	36	17	27	44	....	....	....	16	....	....	....	....	....
1962-63	Bathurst Papermakers	NNBHL	36	6	12	18	....	....	....	14	....	....	....	....	....
	NHL Totals		14	3	5	8	3	6	9	6	1	0	0	0	2

Loaned to **Detroit** by **Montreal** (Quebec-QSHL) as an emergency injury replacement, March 11, 1944. Traded to **Detroit** (Pittsburgh-AHL) by **Montreal** for cash, November 24, 1944. Traded to **Montreal** by **Detroit** (Pittsburgh-AHL) for cash, February, 1945. Traded to **Detroit** by **Montreal** with Ray Getliffe for Billy Reay, September 11, 1945. Getliffe decided to retire and Detroit was awarded the rights to Fern Gauthier as compensation, October 18, 1945. Signed as a free agent by **St. Louis** (AHL), October, 1946. Traded to **Providence** (AHL) by **St. Louis** (AHL) with Carl Liscombe, Eddie Bush and cash for Bill McComb and Russ Brayshaw, January 9, 1947. • Missed remainder of 1947-48 season and entire 1948-49 season recovering from leg injury suffered in game vs. Pittsburgh, October 26, 1947.

• ROTHSCHILD, Sam

LW – L. 5'6", 145 lbs. b: Sudbury, Ont., 10/16/1899 d: 4/15/1987.

Season	Club	League	GP	G	A	Pts	AG	AA	APts	PIM	GP	G	A	Pts	PIM
1915-16	Sudbury Midgets	NOHA	STATISTICS NOT AVAILABLE												
1916-17	Montreal Harmonia	QAAA	9	*16	0	*16	....	....	....	....	....	....	....	....	....
1917-18	Montreal 65th Regiment	MCHL	STATISTICS NOT AVAILABLE												
	Montreal Viciciers	MCHL	STATISTICS NOT AVAILABLE												
1918-19	Montreal Stars	MCHL	5	2	3	5	....	....	....	6	....	....	....	....	....
	Montreal Vickers	MCHL	1	5	0	5	....	....	....	....	....	....	....	....	....
1919-20	Sudbury Jr. Wolves	NOJHA	1	0	0	0	....	....	....	0	....	....	....	....	....
1920-21	Sudbury Wolves	NOHA	9	10	2	12	....	....	....	0	....	....	....	....	....
1921-22	Sudbury Wolves	NOHA	6	5	5	10	....	....	....	3	....	....	....	....	....
1922-23	Sudbury Wolves	NOHA	7	6	4	10	....	....	....	22	2	1	0	1	2
1923-24	Sudbury Wolves	NOHA	STATISTICS NOT AVAILABLE												
1924-25	Montreal Maroons	NHL	28	5	4	9	9	16	25	5	....	....	....	....	....
1925-26	Montreal Maroons	NHL	33	2	1	3	3	6	9	8	4	0	0	0	0
♦	Montreal Maroons	St-Cup	4	0	0	0	....	....	....	0	....	....	....	....	....
1926-27	Montreal Maroons	NHL	22	1	1	2	2	5	7	8	2	0	0	0	0
1927-28	Pittsburgh Pirates	NHL	12	0	0	0	0	0	0	0	....	....	....	....	....
	New York Americans	NHL	5	0	0	0	0	0	0	4	....	....	....	....	....
	NHL Totals		100	8	6	14	14	27	41	25	6	0	0	0	0

Signed as a free agent by **Montreal Maroons**, October 20, 1924. • 1925-26 Montreal Maroons playoff totals includes series against Ottawa and Pittsburgh. Signed as a free agent by **Pittsburgh**, November, 1927. • Suspended by Pittsburgh for breaking training rules, December 26, 1927. Signed as a free agent by **NY Americans**, January 5, 1928.

• ROULSTON, Rolly William Orville

LW/D – L. 6'1", 195 lbs. b: Toronto, Ont., 4/12/1911 d: 4/24/1983.

Season	Club	League	REGULAR SEASON GP	G	A	Pts	AG	AA	APts	PIM	PLAYOFFS GP	G	A	Pts	PIM
1928-29	Toronto Canoe Club	OHA-Jr.	1	0	0	0									
1929-30	Toronto Canoe Club	OHA-Jr.	9	3	0	3				10					
1930-31	Portland Buckaroos	PCHL	34	3	0	3				68					
1931-32	Cleveland Indians	IHL	36	0	3	3				34					
1932-33	Cleveland Indians	IHL	10	0	0	0				2					
	Hershey B'ars	TriHL	10	10	1	11				4	2	1	0	1	0
1933-34	Tulsa Oilers	AHA	47	20	12	32				36	4	0	0	0	2
	Wichita Vikings	AHA	1	0	0	0				6	4	0	0	0	2
1934-35	Detroit Olympics	IHL	40	3	2	5				23	5	0	1	1	2
	Windsor Bulldogs	IHL	2	0	0	0				0					
	Detroit Olympics	L-W-S	5	2	1	3				2					
1935-36	**Detroit Red Wings**	**NHL**	**1**	**0**	**0**	**0**	**0**	**0**	**0**	**0**					
	Detroit Olympics	IHL	44	9	8	17				40	6	2	1	3	6
1936-37	**Detroit Red Wings**	**NHL**	**21**	**0**	**5**	**5**	**0**	**9**	**9**	**10**					
	Pittsburgh Hornets	IAHL	10	3	1	4				10					
1937-38	**Detroit Red Wings**	**NHL**	**2**	**0**	**1**	**1**	**0**	**2**	**2**	**0**					
	Pittsburgh Hornets	IAHL	48	4	5	9				31	2	0	1	1	0
1938-39	Hershey Bears	IAHL	52	3	14	17				75	5	2	0	2	4
1939-40	Hershey Bears	IAHL	45	7	12	19				22	6	1	0	1	4
1940-41	Hershey Bears	AHL	50	4	9	13				20	10	0	0	0	4
1941-42	Philadelphia Rockets	AHL	39	6	9	15				16					
	Pittsburgh Hornets	AHL	1	0	0	0				0					
	NHL Totals		**24**	**0**	**6**	**6**	**0**	**11**	**11**	**10**					

TriHL First All-Star Team (1933)

Traded to **Detroit** by **Tulsa** (AHA) for cash, September, 1934. Traded to **Hershey** (IAHL) by **Detroit** for cash, June 23, 1938. Traded to **Philadelphia** (AHL) by **Hershey** (AHL) for cash, October 30, 1941.

• ROUSSEAU, Bobby — *see page 1581*

• ROUSSEAU, Guy Guy Lucien

LW – L. 5'6", 140 lbs. b: Montreal, Que., 12/21/1934.

Season	Club	League	REGULAR SEASON GP	G	A	Pts	AG	AA	APts	PIM	PLAYOFFS GP	G	A	Pts	PIM
1950-51	Verdun LaSalle	QJHL	41	6	21	27				21	3	0	1	1	0
1951-52	St-Jerome Eagles	QJHL	50	33	*66	99				28					
1952-53	Quebec Citadelle	QJHL	46	43	*52	*95				12	7	4	5	9	8
1953-54	Quebec Frontenacs	QJHL	51	42	47	89				21	8	*11	10	*21	4
	Quebec Frontenacs	M-Cup	8	5	13	18				8					
1954-55	Quebec Citadelle	QJHL	40	22	33	55				42	9	*8	7	*15	6
	Montreal Canadiens	**NHL**	**2**	**0**	**1**	**1**	**0**	**1**	**1**	**0**					
	Quebec Frontenacs	M-Cup	9	3	*11	14				6					
1955-56	Montreal Royals	QHL	61	11	27	38				36	13	1	6	7	4
	Montreal Royals	Ed-Cup	6	1	1	2				2					
1956-57	**Montreal Canadiens**	**NHL**	**2**	**0**	**0**	**0**	**0**	**0**	**0**	**0**					
	Montreal Royals	QHL	66	15	27	42				46	4	0	1	1	4
1957-58	Chicoutimi Sagueneens	QHL	63	29	41	70				30	6	0	2	2	0
1958-59	Rochester Americans	AHL	65	20	20	40				22	3	2	1	3	4
1959-60	Rochester Americans	AHL	42	15	16	31				16	11	7	4	11	2
1960-61	Rochester Americans	AHL	71	26	41	67				30					
1961-62	Quebec Aces	AHL	63	19	21	40				26					
1962-63	Quebec Aces	AHL	47	7	21	28				0					
1963-64	Cleveland Barons	AHL	70	18	16	34				11	9	6	3	9	4
1964-65	Quebec Aces	AHL	41	10	18	28				10	5	1	0	1	0
1965-66	Sherbrooke Saints	QSHL	40	8	10	18				10					
1966-67	St-Hyacinthe Gaulois	QSHL	STATISTICS NOT AVAILABLE												
1967-68	St-Hyacinthe Gaulois	QSHL	STATISTICS NOT AVAILABLE												
1968-69	St-Hyacinthe Gaulois	QSHL	STATISTICS NOT AVAILABLE												
	NHL Totals		**4**	**0**	**1**	**1**	**0**	**1**	**1**	**0**					

• Brother of Bobby and Roland • QJHL Second All-Star Team (1952) • QJHL First All-Star Team (1953) • QHL First All-Star Team (1958)

Traded to **Chicoutimi** (QHL) by **Montreal** with Jackie LeClair and Jacques Deslauriers for Stan Smrke, October 27, 1957. Traded to **Toronto** by **Montreal** for cash, June 7, 1960. Traded to **Montreal** (Quebec-AHL) by **Toronto** (Rochester-AHL) for Norm Corcoran, June 1, 1961. • Suspended for life by QAHA for assault on referee Jim Kierans during game vs. **Ottawa Nationals** (QSHL), February 23, 1969.

• ROUSSEAU, Roland

D – L. 5'8", 160 lbs. b: Montreal, Que., 12/1/1929.

Season	Club	League	REGULAR SEASON GP	G	A	Pts	AG	AA	APts	PIM	PLAYOFFS GP	G	A	Pts	PIM
1947-48	Verdun Jr. Maple Leafs	QJHL	32	3	7	10				20	4	0	0	0	2
1948-49	Montreal Jr. Royals	QJHL	47	5	8	13				73	10	2	3	5	6
	Montreal Royals	QSHL									2	0	0	0	0
	Montreal Jr. Royals	M-Cup	15	1	2	3				42					
1949-50	Montreal Jr. Royals	QJHL	1	1	1	2				8					
	Laval Nationale	MCHL	34	9	16	25				81	7	2	3	5	10
	Montreal Royals	QSHL	2	0	0	0				6	5	0	0	0	0
1950-51	Montreal Royals	QMHL	56	4	13	17				53	7	2	0	2	6
1951-52	Montreal Royals	QMHL	54	2	22	24				86	7	0	2	2	2
	Cincinnati Mohawks	AHL									3	0	0	0	2
1952-53	**Montreal Canadiens**	**NHL**	**2**	**0**	**0**	**0**	**0**	**0**	**0**	**0**					
	Montreal Royals	QMHL	49	4	15	19				48	16	1	2	3	14
1953-54	Buffalo Bisons	AHL	66	5	10	15				64	3	2	0	2	2
1954-55	Montreal Royals	QHL	59	3	11	14				78	10	0	1	1	4
1955-56	Montreal Royals	QHL	63	5	9	14				58	13	1	2	3	8
	Montreal Royals	Ed-Cup	6	0	1	1				2					
1956-57	Chicoutimi Sagueneens	QHL	65	1	16	17				74	10	2	1	3	2
1957-58	Chicoutimi Sagueneens	QHL	60	1	11	12				87	6	0	0	0	0
1958/60			DID NOT PLAY												
1960-61	Granby Vics	QSHL	30	3	15	18				15	9	1	2	3	2
	Granby Vics	Al-Cup	7	0	5	5				14					
1961-62	Granby Vics	ETSHL	20	0	5	5				14	7	2	2	4	12
	Montreal Olympics	Al-Cup	16	0	3	3				12					
1962/67			OUT OF HOCKEY – RETIRED												
1967-68	Granby Vics	QSHL	46	17	31	48				8					
	NHL Totals		**2**	**0**	**0**	**0**	**0**	**0**	**0**	**0**					

• Brother of Bobby and Guy

Claimed by **Montreal** from **Montreal** (Montreal-QHL) in Inter-League Draft, June 10, 1953.

• ROWE, Bobby Robert Price "Stubby"

RW/D – L. 5'6", 160 lbs. b: Heathcote, Ont., Deceased.

Season	Club	League	REGULAR SEASON GP	G	A	Pts	AG	AA	APts	PIM	PLAYOFFS GP	G	A	Pts	PIM
1902-03	Portage Lake Pros	X-Games	12	25	0	25					4	2	0	2	
1903-04	Meaford Juniors	OHA-Jr.	STATISTICS NOT AVAILABLE												
1904-05	Meaford Juniors	OHA-Jr.	STATISTICS NOT AVAILABLE												
1905-06	Barrie Hockey Club	OHA-Sr.	4	13	0	13				15					
1906-07	Barrie Pros	X-Games	1	4	0	4									
	Renfrew Riversides	UOVHL	STATISTICS NOT AVAILABLE												
	Latchford Pros	TPHL	1	1	0	1				0					
1907-08	Renfrew Creamery Kings	UOVHL									2	*9	0	*9	
1908-09	Haileybury Silver Kings	TPHL	1	0	0	0				0					
	Renfrew Creamery Kings	FAHL	STATISTICS NOT AVAILABLE												
1909-10	Renfrew Millionaires	NHA	8	11	0	11				38					
1910-11	Renfrew Millionaires	NHA	16	11	0	11				*82					
1911-12	Victoria Aristocrats	PCHA	16	10	0	10				*62					
	PCHA All-Stars	X-Games	1	0	0	0				0					
1912-13	Victoria Aristocrats	PCHA	15	8	7	15				34	2	1	0	1	0
1913-14	Victoria Aristocrats	PCHA	12	8	7	15				11	3	0	0	0	0
1914-15	Victoria Aristocrats	PCHA	12	6	1	7				13					
1915-16	Seattle Metropolitans	PCHA	17	3	5	8				25					
	PCHA All-Stars	X-Games	1	0	1	1				0					
♦1916-17	Seattle Metropolitans	PCHA	25	9	12	21				45	4	0	2	2	0
1917-18	Seattle Metropolitans	PCHA	17	3	2	5				28					
1918-19	Seattle Metropolitans	PCHA	20	5	6	11				19	2	0	1	1	0
	Seattle Metropolitans	St-Cup	5	1	0	1				6					
1919-20	Seattle Metropolitans	PCHA	22	2	4	6				16	2	0	1	1	0
	Seattle Metropolitans	St-Cup	5	2	0	2				13					
1920-21	Seattle Metropolitans	PCHA	24	0	2	2				29	2	0	1	1	0
1921-22	Seattle Metropolitans	PCHA	23	2	1	3				34	2	0	0	0	*6
1922-23	Seattle Metropolitans	PCHA	30	7	2	9				*71					
1923-24	Seattle Metropolitans	PCHA	24	10	2	12				30	2	0	0	0	*8
1924-25	**Boston Bruins**	**NHL**	**4**	**1**	**0**	**1**	**2**	**0**	**2**	**0**					
1925-26	Portland Rosebuds	WHL	2	0	0	0				0					
	NHL Totals		**4**	**1**	**0**	**1**	**2**	**0**	**2**	**0**					
	Other Major League Totals		283	95	51	146				537	19	1	5	6	14

PCHA Second All-Star Team (1917, 1920) • PCHA First All-Star Team (1918, 1919, 1923)

Signed as a free agent by **Renfrew** (UOVHL), January 10, 1907. Signed as a free agent by **Renfrew** (NHA), December 1, 1909. Claimed by **Toronto** (NHA) from **Renfrew** (NHA) in Dispersal Draft, November 12, 1911. Signed by **Victoria** (PCHA) after jumping contract with **Toronto** (NHA), November 28, 1911. Traded to **Seattle** (PCHA) by **Victoria** (PCHA) for cash, October 3, 1915. Traded to **Boston** by **Seattle** (WCHL) for cash, November 2, 1924. Signed as a free agent by **Portland** (WHL), January 26, 1926.

• ROWE, Ron Ronald Nickolas

C/LW – L. 5'8", 170 lbs. b: Toronto, Ont., 11/30/1923.

Season	Club	League	REGULAR SEASON GP	G	A	Pts	AG	AA	APts	PIM	PLAYOFFS GP	G	A	Pts	PIM
1940-41	Markham Waxers	OHA-B	STATISTICS NOT AVAILABLE												
1941-42	Markham Waxers	OHA-B	STATISTICS NOT AVAILABLE												
1942-43	Toronto Marlboros	OHA-Jr.	20	26	21	47				40	3	4	4	8	16
	Toronto CPR	TIHL	17	16	15	31				17	5	3	8	11	6
1943-44	Montreal Navy	MCHL	8	7	6	13				26	4	3	2	5	*19
	Montreal Canada Car	MCHL	2	1	2	3				0					
	Montreal Jr. Royals	QJHL	8	6	4	10				19	4	3	4	7	0
	Montreal Jr. Royals	M-Cup	4	1	0	1				0					
1944-45	St. John's Navy	Nfld-Sr.	6	13	4	17				7	1	1	1	2	0
1945-46	Toronto Tip Tops	TIHL	3	1	2	3				0					
	Halifax Navy	NSDHL	9	*15	7	22				25	3	6	4	10	6
	Halifax Navy	Al-Cup	9	*16	7	*23				*36					
1946-47	Boston Olympics	EAHL	56	41	40	81				78	7	4	2	6	*26
1947-48	**New York Rangers**	**NHL**	**5**	**1**	**0**	**1**	**1**	**0**	**1**	**0**					
	St. Paul Saints	USHL	3	0	1	1				0					
	New York Rovers	EAHL	14	9	6	15				28					
	New York Rovers	QSHL	28	17	17	34				49	2	2	0	2	4
1948-49	Tacoma Rockets	PCHL	70	30	37	67				105	1	1	0	1	0
1949-50	Tacoma Rockets	PCHL	68	47	44	*91				64	5	4	1	5	14
1950-51	Tacoma Rockets	PCHL	70	33	34	67				105	6	2	1	3	12
1951-52	Vancouver Canucks	PCHL	12	1	3	4				22					
	Sydney Millionaires	MMHL	5	0	0	0				0					
	Moncton Hawks	MMHL	58	31	31	62				12					
1952-53	Sydney Millionaires	MMHL	70	33	39	72				71	6	2	3	5	10
1953-54	North Bay Trappers	NOHA	15	7	6	13				0					
	S.S. Marie Greyhounds	NOHA	4	0	1	1				0					
	Pembroke Lumber Kings	NOHA	27	11	9	20				0	4	1	0	1	0
1954-55	Pembroke Lumber Kings	NOHA	15	6	2	8				10	2	0	0	0	0
1955-56	Pembroke Lumber Kings	NOHA	51	16	26	42				6					
1956-57	Pembroke Lumber Kings	EOHL	40	7	11	18				18					
	NHL Totals		**5**	**1**	**0**	**1**	**1**	**0**	**1**	**0**					

Loaned to **Tacoma** (PCHL) by **NY Rangers** for cash, September 30, 1948. Traded to **Sydney** (MMHL) by **NY Rangers** for cash, November 6, 1951. Traded to **Moncton** (MMHL) by **Sydney** (MMHL with Tom Rockey and Sam Kennedy for Ron Matthews, November 19, 1951.

• ROZZINI, Gino Gino William "Rosy"

C – L. 5'8", 150 lbs. b: Shawinigan Falls, Que., 10/24/1918.

Season	Club	League	REGULAR SEASON GP	G	A	Pts	AG	AA	APts	PIM	PLAYOFFS GP	G	A	Pts	PIM
1936-37	Creighton Mines	GBHL	17	5	7	12				18	2	0	2	2	4
1937-38	Creighton Eagles	GBHL	15	8	5	13				22	4	0	0	0	8
1938-39	Creighton Eagles	GBHL	12	5	1	6				6	6	2	*3	5	6
1939-40	Sudbury Open Pit Miners	NBHL	16	10	2	12				24					
1940-41	St. Catharines Saints	OHA-Sr.	31	15	13	28				67	12	7	5	12	8
1941-42	Quebec Aces	QSHL	40	14	28	42				34	7	5	4	9	4
	Quebec Aces	Al-Cup	7	0	4	4				0					
1942-43	Quebec Aces	QSHL	34	12	21	33				41	4	1	2	3	0
1943-44	Quebec Aces	QSHL	13	6	5	11				10	6	5	0	5	10
	Quebec Aces	Al-Cup	9	7	9	16				6					
1944-45	**Boston Bruins**	**NHL**	**31**	**5**	**10**	**15**	**5**	**12**	**17**	**20**	**6**	**1**	**2**	**3**	**6**
	Boston Olympics	EAHL	10	19	11	30				14					
1945-46	Hershey Bears	AHL	56	31	40	71				63	3	0	2	2	4
1946-47	Tulsa Oilers	USHL	13	3	5	8				6					
	Hershey Bears	AHL	37	5	10	15				14	11	3	2	5	0
1947-48	St. Paul Saints	USHL	65	22	60	82				79					
1948-49	New Haven Ramblers	AHL	58	16	33	49				45					

Season	Club	League	GP	G	A	Pts	AG	AA	APts	PIM	GP	G	A	Pts	PIM
			REGULAR SEASON								PLAYOFFS				
1949-50	St. Paul Saints	USHL	68	27	40	67	....	....	....	59	3	0	2	2	0
1950-51	Tacoma Rockets	PCHL	70	10	27	37	....	....	....	67	4	1	1	2	0
1951-52	Vancouver Canucks	PCHL	8	0	1	1	....	....	....	6	....	....	....	....	....
	Spokane Flyers	WIHL	52	23	41	64	....	....	....	100	4	1	2	3	5
1952-53	Spokane Flyers	WIHL	57	34	54	88	....	....	....	77	9	1	3	4	0
	Spokane Flyers	Al-Cup	7	1	4	5	....	....	....	6	....	....	....	....	....
1953-54	Spokane Flyers	WIHL	58	22	45	67	....	....	....	73	5	3	5	8	16
1954-55	Spokane Flyers	WIHL	24	9	12	21	....	....	....	31	....	....	....	....	....
1955-56	Spokane Flyers	WIHL	45	25	46	71	....	....	....	32	9	2	8	10	15
	Spokane Flyers	Al-Cup	6	0	3	3	....	....	....	4	....	....	....	....	....
1956-57			DID NOT PLAY												
1957-58	Rossland Warriors	WIHL	DID NOT PLAY – COACHING												
1958-59	Rossland Warriors	WIHL	2	0	2	2	....	....	....	6	....	....	....	....	....
	NHL Totals		**31**	**5**	**10**	**15**	**5**	**12**	**17**	**20**	**6**	**1**	**2**	**3**	**6**

Signed as a free agent by **Boston**, November 2, 1944.

• RUELLE, Bernie   Bernard Edward

LW – L. 5'9", 165 lbs.   b: Houghton, MI, 11/23/1920.

Season	Club	League	GP	G	A	Pts	AG	AA	APts	PIM	GP	G	A	Pts	PIM
1939-40	Detroit Pontiacs	MOHL	34	5	8	13	....	....	....	14	....	....	....	....	....
	Detroit Holzbaugh	MOHL	....	....	....	....	....	....	....	....	4	1	0	1	0
1940-41	Detroit Holtzbaugh	MOHL	25	6	6	12	....	....	....	11	5	4	2	6	8
1941-42	Toledo–Detroit	MOHL	28	16	14	30	....	....	....	6	7	3	2	5	4
1942-43			DID NOT PLAY												
1943-44	**Detroit Red Wings**	**NHL**	**2**	**1**	**0**	**1**	**1**	**0**	**1**	**0**	....	....	....	....	....
	Indianapolis Capitols	AHL	48	8	15	23	....	....	....	9	5	1	0	1	2
1944-45			MILITARY SERVICE												
1945-46			MILITARY SERVICE												
1946-47	Tacoma–Fresno	PCHL	44	14	9	23	....	....	....	20	2	0	0	0	0
	NHL Totals		**2**	**1**	**0**	**1**	**1**	**0**	**1**	**0**	....	....	....	....	....

• RUNGE, Paul

C/LW – L. 5'11", 167 lbs.   b: Edmonton, Alta., 9/10/1908   d: 4/27/1972.

Season	Club	League	GP	G	A	Pts	AG	AA	APts	PIM	GP	G	A	Pts	PIM
1927-28	Edmonton Superiors	EJrHL	STATISTICS NOT AVAILABLE												
1928-29	Portland Buckaroos	PCHL	6	1	0	1	....	....	....	0	....	....	....	....	....
	Victoria Cubs	PCHL	26	3	0	3	....	....	....	0	....	....	....	....	....
1929-30	Victoria Cubs	PCHL	36	5	5	10	....	....	....	35	....	....	....	....	....
1930-31	**Boston Bruins**	**NHL**	**1**	**0**	**0**	**0**	**0**	**0**	**0**	**0**	....	....	....	....	....
	Boston Cubs	Can-Am	39	9	11	20	....	....	....	35	9	*7	2	*9	17
1931-32	**Boston Bruins**	**NHL**	**14**	**0**	**1**	**1**	**0**	**2**	**2**	**8**	....	....	....	....	....
	Boston Cubs	Can-Am	29	11	11	22	....	....	....	29	....	....	....	....	....
1932-33	Philadelphia Arrows	Can-Am	44	21	*27	*48	....	....	....	38	5	2	1	3	2
1933-34	**Montreal Maroons**	**NHL**	**4**	**0**	**0**	**0**	**0**	**0**	**0**	**0**	....	....	....	....	....
	Windsor Bulldogs	IHL	25	7	12	19	....	....	....	10	....	....	....	....	....
	Quebec Beavers	Can-Am	8	1	3	4	....	....	....	2	....	....	....	....	....
1934-35	**Montreal Canadiens**	**NHL**	**3**	**0**	**0**	**0**	**0**	**0**	**0**	**2**	....	....	....	....	....
	Quebec Beavers	Can-Am	48	25	33	*58	....	....	....	28	3	0	1	1	0
1935-36	**Montreal Canadiens**	**NHL**	**12**	**0**	**2**	**2**	**0**	**4**	**4**	**4**	....	....	....	....	....
	Boston Bruins	**NHL**	**33**	**8**	**2**	**10**	**15**	**4**	**19**	**14**	**2**	**0**	**0**	**0**	**2**
1936-37	**Montreal Canadiens**	**NHL**	**4**	**1**	**0**	**1**	**2**	**0**	**2**	**2**	....	....	....	....	....
	Montreal Maroons	**NHL**	**30**	**4**	**10**	**14**	**7**	**18**	**25**	**6**	**5**	**0**	**0**	**0**	**4**
	New Haven Eagles	IAHL	8	1	3	4	....	....	....	5	....	....	....	....	....
1937-38	**Montreal Maroons**	**NHL**	**39**	**5**	**7**	**12**	**8**	**11**	**19**	**21**	....	....	....	....	....
1938-39	Cleveland Barons	IAHL	54	7	28	35	....	....	....	26	8	1	4	5	4
1939-40	Cleveland Barons	IAHL	48	7	15	22	....	....	....	7	....	....	....	....	....
1940-41	Buffalo Bisons	AHL	20	3	6	9	....	....	....	9	....	....	....	....	....
	Minneapolis Millers	AHA	29	12	14	26	....	....	....	4	3	0	2	2	0
1941-42	Dallas Texans	AHA	46	16	41	57	....	....	....	29	....	....	....	....	....
1942-43			DID NOT PLAY												
1943-44	Edmonton Vics	X-Games	STATISTICS NOT AVAILABLE												
	Edmonton Vics	Al-Cup	3	0	2	2	....	....	....	0	....	....	....	....	....
	NHL Totals		**140**	**18**	**22**	**40**	**32**	**39**	**71**	**57**	**7**	**0**	**0**	**0**	**6**

Traded to **Victoria** (PCHL) by **Portland** (PCHL) for Dave Downie, December 21, 1928. Signed as a free agent by **Boston**, November 5, 1930. Traded to **Philadelphia** (Can-Am) by **Boston** for cash, September, 1932. Traded to **Montreal Maroons** by **Philadelphia** (Can-Am) for cash, November 25, 1933. Traded to **Montreal Canadiens** (Quebec-Can-Am) by **Montreal Maroons** for Stan McCabe, December 6, 1933. Traded to **Boston** by **Montreal Canadiens** for cash, December 24, 1935. Traded to **Montreal Canadiens** by **Boston** for cash, April, 1936. Traded to **Montreal Maroons** by **Montreal Canadiens** for Bill MacKenzie, December 3, 1936. Traded to **Cleveland** (AHL) by **Montreal Maroons** for cash, October 3, 1938. Loaned to **Minneapolis** (AHA) by **Buffalo** (AHL) with cash for Bob Blake, December 27, 1940.

• RUPP, Duane   *— see page 1586*

• RUSSELL, Church   Church Davidson

LW/C – L. 5'11", 175 lbs.   b: Winnipeg, Man., 3/16/1923   d: 3/31/1999.

Season	Club	League	GP	G	A	Pts	AG	AA	APts	PIM	GP	G	A	Pts	PIM
1939-40	St. James Canadians	MAHA	STATISTICS NOT AVAILABLE												
1940-41	Winnipeg Rangers	WJrHL	STATISTICS NOT AVAILABLE												
1941-42	Winnipeg Rangers	WJrHL	18	6	11	17	....	....	....	0	....	....	....	....	....
1942-43	Winnipeg Rangers	WJrHL	12	*23	*13	*36	....	....	....	0	6	*16	4	*20	2
1943-44	Victoria Navy	PCHL	15	4	6	10	....	....	....	4	....	....	....	....	....
1944-45			MILITARY SERVICE												
1945-46	**New York Rangers**	**NHL**	**17**	**0**	**5**	**5**	**0**	**7**	**7**	**2**	....	....	....	....	....
	New York Rovers	EAHL	38	27	*43	70	....	....	....	4	....	....	....	....	....
1946-47	**New York Rangers**	**NHL**	**54**	**20**	**8**	**28**	**23**	**10**	**33**	**8**	....	....	....	....	....
1947-48	**New York Rangers**	**NHL**	**19**	**0**	**3**	**3**	**0**	**4**	**4**	**2**	....	....	....	....	....
	New York Rovers	QSHL	2	0	0	0	....	....	....	0	....	....	....	....	....
	Cleveland Barons	AHL	40	13	18	31	....	....	....	8	9	3	5	8	0
1948-49	Cleveland Barons	AHL	56	17	22	39	....	....	....	10	5	1	1	2	2
1949-50	Pittsburgh Hornets	AHL	67	7	22	29	....	....	....	15	....	....	....	....	....
1950-51	Vancouver Canucks	PCHL	58	12	21	33	....	....	....	8	....	....	....	....	....
1951-52	Winnipeg Maroons	Al-Cup	6	5	4	9	....	....	....	2	....	....	....	....	....
1952-53	Winnipeg Maroons	Al-Cup	4	1	1	2	....	....	....	5	....	....	....	....	....
1953-54	Brandon Regals	MHL-Sr.	STATISTICS NOT AVAILABLE												
1954-55	Brandon Regals	MHL-Sr.	8	5	4	9	....	....	....	2	....	....	....	....	....
	NHL Totals		**90**	**20**	**16**	**36**	**23**	**21**	**44**	**12**	....	....	....	....	....

EAHL First All-Star Team (1946)

Traded to **Cleveland** (AHL) by **NY Rangers** for George Johnston, December 18, 1947. Traded to **Pittsburgh** (AHL) by **Cleveland** (AHL) for cash, September 13, 1949.

• SABOURIN, Bob   Robert

LW – L. 5'9", 177 lbs.   b: Sudbury, Ont., 3/17/1933.

Season	Club	League	GP	G	A	Pts	AG	AA	APts	PIM	GP	G	A	Pts	PIM
1948-49	St. Michael's Majors	OHA-Jr.	10	2	2	4	....	....	....	0	....	....	....	....	....
1949-50	St. Michael's Majors	OHA-Jr.	47	21	11	32	....	....	....	38	5	3	0	3	2
1950-51	St. Michael's Majors	OHA-Jr.	54	25	18	43	....	....	....	54	....	....	....	....	....
1951-52	St. Michael's Majors	OHA-Jr.	51	31	23	54	....	....	....	26	8	2	4	6	4
	Toronto Maple Leafs	**NHL**	**1**	**0**	**0**	**0**	**0**	**0**	**0**	**2**	....	....	....	....	....
1952-53	Pittsburgh Hornets	AHL	51	22	20	42	....	....	....	19	10	*6	0	6	14
1953-54	Ottawa Senators	QHL	4	2	5	7	....	....	....	2	....	....	....	....	....
	Pittsburgh Hornets	AHL	64	16	30	46	....	....	....	29	5	3	1	4	6
1954-55	Pittsburgh Hornets	AHL	49	8	19	27	....	....	....	14	3	0	0	0	2
1955-56	Pittsburgh Hornets	AHL	47	6	16	22	....	....	....	39	3	0	0	0	0
1956-57	Springfield Indians	AHL	59	11	29	40	....	....	....	21	....	....	....	....	....
1957-58	Quebec Aces	QHL	64	28	32	60	....	....	....	8	13	5	1	6	12
1958-59	Trois-Rivieres Lions	QHL	59	25	25	50	....	....	....	12	8	1	2	3	5
1959-60	Trois-Rivieres Lions	EPHL	66	22	31	53	....	....	....	24	4	1	0	1	14
1960-61	Kitchener Dutchemen	EPHL	70	20	36	56	....	....	....	24	7	1	1	2	2
1961-62	North Bay Trappers	EPHL	67	12	24	36	....	....	....	16	....	....	....	....	....
1962-63	Sudbury Wolves	EPHL	1	0	0	0	....	....	....	0	....	....	....	....	....
	Calgary–Seattle	WHL	61	17	23	40	....	....	....	14	17	8	8	16	6
1963-64	Seattle Totems	WHL	68	13	19	32	....	....	....	15	....	....	....	....	....
1964-65	Seattle Totems	WHL	57	11	10	21	....	....	....	12	7	1	0	1	4
1965-66	Long Island Ducks	EHL	72	31	43	74	....	....	....	40	12	3	7	10	22
1966-67	Jacksonville Rockets	EHL	71	16	30	46	....	....	....	38	....	....	....	....	....
1967-68	Jacksonville Rockets	EHL	55	13	22	35	....	....	....	10	....	....	....	....	....
	NHL Totals		**1**	**0**	**0**	**0**	**0**	**0**	**0**	**2**	....	....	....	....	....

• Brother of Gary • EHL North Second All-Star Team (1966)

Loaned to **Toronto** by **St. Michael's** (OHA-Jr.) as an emergency injury replacement, March 13, 1952. Traded to **Springfield** (AHL) by **Toronto** (Pittsburgh-AHL) with Bob Bailey for $15,000, May, 1956.

• ST. LAURENT, Dollard   Dollard Herve Joseph

D – L. 5'11", 175 lbs.   b: Verdun, Que., 5/12/1929.

Season	Club	League	GP	G	A	Pts	AG	AA	APts	PIM	GP	G	A	Pts	PIM
1947-48	Montreal Jr. Canadiens	QJHL	15	3	10	13	....	....	....	12	....	....	....	....	....
1948-49	Montreal Jr. Canadiens	QJHL	44	15	27	42	....	....	....	77	4	0	4	4	8
1949-50	Montreal Royals	QSHL	45	7	15	22	....	....	....	66	....	....	....	....	....
1950-51	**Montreal Canadiens**	**NHL**	**3**	**0**	**0**	**0**	**0**	**0**	**0**	**0**	....	....	....	....	....
	Montreal Royals	QMHL	57	12	30	42	....	....	....	69	7	3	2	5	14
1951-52	**Montreal Canadiens**	**NHL**	**40**	**3**	**10**	**13**	**4**	**12**	**16**	**30**	**9**	**0**	**3**	**3**	**6**
	Montreal Royals	QMHL	27	10	16	26	....	....	....	22	....	....	....	....	....
♦1952-53	**Montreal Canadiens**	**NHL**	**54**	**2**	**6**	**8**	**3**	**7**	**10**	**34**	**12**	**0**	**3**	**3**	**4**
1953-54	**Montreal Canadiens**	**NHL**	**53**	**3**	**12**	**15**	**4**	**15**	**19**	**43**	**10**	**1**	**2**	**3**	**8**
1954-55	**Montreal Canadiens**	**NHL**	**58**	**3**	**14**	**17**	**4**	**16**	**20**	**24**	**12**	**0**	**5**	**5**	**12**
♦1955-56	**Montreal Canadiens**	**NHL**	**46**	**4**	**9**	**13**	**5**	**11**	**16**	**58**	**4**	**0**	**0**	**0**	**2**
♦1956-57	**Montreal Canadiens**	**NHL**	**64**	**1**	**11**	**12**	**1**	**12**	**13**	**49**	**7**	**0**	**1**	**1**	**13**
♦1957-58	**Montreal Canadiens**	**NHL**	**65**	**3**	**20**	**23**	**4**	**21**	**25**	**68**	**5**	**0**	**0**	**0**	**10**
1958-59	**Chicago Black Hawks**	**NHL**	**70**	**4**	**8**	**12**	**5**	**8**	**13**	**28**	**6**	**0**	**1**	**1**	**2**
1959-60	**Chicago Black Hawks**	**NHL**	**68**	**4**	**13**	**17**	**5**	**13**	**18**	**60**	**4**	**0**	**1**	**1**	**0**
♦1960-61	**Chicago Black Hawks**	**NHL**	**67**	**2**	**17**	**19**	**2**	**16**	**18**	**58**	**11**	**1**	**2**	**3**	**12**
1961-62	**Chicago Black Hawks**	**NHL**	**64**	**0**	**13**	**13**	**0**	**12**	**12**	**44**	**12**	**0**	**4**	**4**	**18**
1962-63	Quebec Aces	AHL	54	3	14	17	....	....	....	34	....	....	....	....	....
	NHL Totals		**652**	**29**	**133**	**162**	**37**	**143**	**180**	**496**	**92**	**2**	**22**	**24**	**87**

QJHL First All-Star Team (1949) • QMHL Second All-Star Team (1951) • Played in NHL All-Star Game (1953, 1956, 1957, 1958, 1961)

• Missed majority of 1947-48 season recovering from collarbone injury suffered in game vs. Verdun (QJHL), December 2, 1947. Traded to **Chicago** by **Montreal** for cash and future considerations (the loan of Norm Johnson, February 20, 1959), June 3, 1958. Traded to **Quebec** (AHL) by **Chicago** for cash, September 6, 1962.

• SAMIS, Phil   Phillip Lawrence

D – R. 5'9", 180 lbs.   b: Edmonton, Alta., 12/28/1927.

Season	Club	League	GP	G	A	Pts	AG	AA	APts	PIM	GP	G	A	Pts	PIM
1943-44	Edmonton Maple Leafs	EJrHL	STATISTICS NOT AVAILABLE												
1944-45	St. Michael's Majors	OHA-Jr.	9	7	10	17	....	....	....	8	9	3	6	9	*36
	St. Michael's Majors	OHA-Jr.	3	0	1	1	....	....	....	2	....	....	....	....	....
	St. Michael's Majors	M-Cup	2	0	0	0	....	....	....	2	....	....	....	....	....
1945-46	Oshawa Generals	OHA-Jr.	27	11	9	20	....	....	....	*83	12	1	3	4	18
1946-47	Oshawa Generals	OHA-Jr.	27	5	20	25	....	....	....	120	5	0	0	0	20
1947-48	Pittsburgh Hornets	AHL	68	4	10	14	....	....	....	*181	2	0	2	2	2
♦	**Toronto Maple Leafs**	**NHL**	....	....	....	....	....	....	....	....	**5**	**0**	**1**	**1**	**2**
1948-49	Pittsburgh Hornets	AHL	60	3	7	10	....	....	....	91	....	....	....	....	....
1949-50	**Toronto Maple Leafs**	**NHL**	**2**	**0**	**0**	**0**	**0**	**0**	**0**	**0**	....	....	....	....	....
	Pittsburgh Hornets	AHL	66	2	11	13	....	....	....	139	....	....	....	....	....
1950-51	Cleveland Barons	AHL	64	3	14	17	....	....	....	105	11	2	3	5	*21
1951-52	Cleveland Barons	AHL	60	11	14	25	....	....	....	117	5	1	1	2	13
1952-53	Cleveland Barons	AHL	1	0	0	0	....	....	....	0	....	....	....	....	....
	Montreal Royals	QMHL	56	4	11	15	....	....	....	76	15	0	1	1	15
	NHL Totals		**2**	**0**	**0**	**0**	**0**	**0**	**0**	**0**	**5**	**0**	**1**	**1**	**2**

Traded to **Cleveland** (AHL) by **Toronto** to complete transaction that sent Bobby Dawes, $40,000 and future considerations (Eric Pogue and rights to Bob Shropshire) to Toronto for Al Rollins (November 29, 1949), April 6, 1950

• SANDERSON, Derek   *— see page 1597*

• SANDFORD, Ed   Edward Michael "Sandy"

LW – R. 6'1", 180 lbs.   b: New Toronto, Ont., 8/20/1928.

Season	Club	League	GP	G	A	Pts	AG	AA	APts	PIM	GP	G	A	Pts	PIM
1943-44	St. Michael's Buzzers	OHA-B	3	1	0	1	....	....	....	0	....	....	....	....	....
1944-45	St. Michael's Buzzers	OHA-B	11	12	11	23	....	....	....	9	11	10	14	24	8
1945-46	St. Michael's Majors	OHA-Jr.	26	10	9	19	....	....	....	28	11	5	5	10	12

			REGULAR SEASON								PLAYOFFS				
Season	Club	League	GP	G	A	Pts	AG	AA	APts	PIM	GP	G	A	Pts	PIM
1946-47	St. Michael's Majors	OHA-Jr.	27	30	*37	67	....	....	....	38	9	*12	12	*24	31
	St. Michael's Majors	M-Cup	10	11	*17	28	....	....	....	26	....	....	....	....	....
1947-48	**Boston Bruins**	**NHL**	**59**	**10**	**15**	**25**	**13**	**20**	**33**	**25**	**5**	**1**	**0**	**1**	**0**
1948-49	**Boston Bruins**	**NHL**	**56**	**16**	**20**	**36**	**22**	**28**	**50**	**57**	**5**	**1**	**3**	**4**	**2**
1949-50	**Boston Bruins**	**NHL**	**19**	**1**	**4**	**5**	**1**	**5**	**6**	**6**	....	....	....	....	....
1950-51	**Boston Bruins**	**NHL**	**51**	**10**	**13**	**23**	**13**	**16**	**29**	**33**	**6**	**0**	**1**	**1**	**4**
1951-52	**Boston Bruins**	**NHL**	**65**	**13**	**12**	**25**	**17**	**15**	**32**	**54**	**7**	**2**	**2**	**4**	**0**
	Boston Olympics	EAHL	2	1	0	1	....	....	....	0	....	....	....	....	....
1952-53	**Boston Bruins**	**NHL**	**61**	**14**	**21**	**35**	**18**	**25**	**43**	**44**	**11**	***8**	**3**	***11**	**11**
1953-54	**Boston Bruins**	**NHL**	**70**	**16**	**31**	**47**	**22**	**38**	**60**	**42**	**3**	**0**	**1**	**1**	**4**
1954-55	**Boston Bruins**	**NHL**	**60**	**14**	**20**	**34**	**18**	**23**	**41**	**38**	**5**	**1**	**1**	**2**	**6**
1955-56	**Detroit Red Wings**	**NHL**	**4**	**0**	**0**	**0**	**0**	**0**	**0**	**0**	....	....	....	....	....
	Chicago Black Hawks	**NHL**	**57**	**12**	**9**	**21**	**16**	**11**	**27**	**56**	....	....	....	....	....
	NHL Totals		**502**	**106**	**145**	**251**	**140**	**181**	**321**	**355**	**42**	**13**	**11**	**24**	**27**

NHL Second All-Star Team (1954) • Played in NHL All-Star Game (1951, 1952, 1953, 1954, 1955)

• Missed remainder of 1949-50 season recovering from ankle injury suffered in game vs. Toronto, November 13, 1949. Traded to **Detroit** by **Boston** with Gilles Boisvert, Real Chevrefils, Warren Godfrey and Norm Corcoran for Marcel Bonin, Vic Stasiuk, Terry Sawchuk and Lorne Davis, June 3, 1955. Traded to **Chicago** by **Detroit** for Metro Prystai, October 24, 1955.

• SANDS, Charlie

C/RW – R. 5'9", 160 lbs. b: Fort William, Ont., 3/23/1911 Deceased.

Season	Club	League	GP	G	A	Pts	AG	AA	APts	PIM	GP	G	A	Pts	PIM
1929-30	Fort William Forts	TBSHL	14	1	1	2	....	....	....	0	....	....	....	....	....
1930-31	Port Arthur Ports	TBSHL	22	10	1	11	....	....	....	25	2	0	0	0	0
1931-32	Port Arthur Ports	TBSHL	17	6	3	9	....	....	....	10	2	1	0	1	9
1932-33	**Toronto Maple Leafs**	**NHL**	**3**	**0**	**3**	**3**	**0**	**6**	**6**	**0**	**9**	**2**	**2**	**4**	**2**
	Syracuse Stars	IHL	37	10	5	15	....	....	....	10	1	0	0	0	4
1933-34	**Toronto Maple Leafs**	**NHL**	**45**	**8**	**8**	**16**	**14**	**17**	**31**	**2**	**5**	**1**	**0**	**1**	**0**
1934-35	**Boston Bruins**	**NHL**	**41**	**15**	**12**	**27**	**25**	**21**	**46**	**0**	**4**	**0**	**0**	**0**	**0**
1935-36	**Boston Bruins**	**NHL**	**40**	**6**	**4**	**10**	**11**	**8**	**19**	**8**	**2**	**0**	**0**	**0**	**0**
	Boston Cubs	Can-Am	5	1	3	4	....	....	....	0	....	....	....	....	....
1936-37	**Boston Bruins**	**NHL**	**47**	**18**	**5**	**23**	**30**	**9**	**39**	**6**	**3**	**1**	**2**	**3**	**0**
1937-38	**Boston Bruins**	**NHL**	**46**	**17**	**12**	**29**	**28**	**19**	**47**	**12**	**3**	**1**	**1**	**2**	**0**
♦**1938-39**	**Boston Bruins**	**NHL**	**37**	**7**	**5**	**12**	**12**	**8**	**20**	**10**	**1**	**0**	**0**	**0**	**0**
	Hershey Bears	IAHL	4	3	1	4	....	....	....	0	....	....	....	....	....
1939-40	**Montreal Canadiens**	**NHL**	**47**	**9**	**20**	**29**	**15**	**32**	**47**	**10**	....	....	....	....	....
1940-41	**Montreal Canadiens**	**NHL**	**43**	**5**	**13**	**18**	**8**	**19**	**27**	**4**	**2**	**1**	**0**	**1**	**0**
1941-42	**Montreal Canadiens**	**NHL**	**38**	**11**	**16**	**27**	**15**	**19**	**34**	**6**	**3**	**0**	**1**	**1**	**2**
1942-43	**Montreal Canadiens**	**NHL**	**31**	**3**	**9**	**12**	**3**	**8**	**11**	**0**	**2**	**0**	**0**	**0**	**0**
	Washington Lions	AHL	1	0	1	1	....	....	....	0	....	....	....	....	....
	San Diego Skyhawks	X-Games	STATISTICS NOT AVAILABLE												
1943-44	**New York Rangers**	**NHL**	**9**	**0**	**2**	**2**	**0**	**2**	**2**	**0**	....	....	....	....	....
	Pasadena Panthers	CalHL	STATISTICS NOT AVAILABLE												
1944-45	Pasadena Panthers	PCHL	15	14	24	38	....	....	....	0	....	....	....	....	....
1945-46	Los Angeles Monarchs	PCHL	11	3	3	6	....	....	....	0	....	....	....	....	....
1946-47	Fresno Falcons	PCHL	3	1	6	7	....	....	....	0	....	....	....	....	....
	NHL Totals		**427**	**99**	**109**	**208**	**161**	**168**	**329**	**58**	**34**	**6**	**6**	**12**	**4**

Played in NHL All-Star Game (1934)

Traded to **Boston** by **Toronto** for cash, May 12, 1934. Traded to **Montreal** by **Boston** with Ray Getliffe for Herb Cain, October 10, 1939. Loaned to **NY Rangers** by **Montreal** with John Mahaffy, Dutch Hiller, Fern Gauthier and future considerations (Tony Demers, December, 1943) for the loan of Phil Watson, October 27, 1943.

• SASKAMOOSE, Fred "Chief Running Deer"

C – R. 5'8", 165 lbs. b: Sandy Lake Reserve, Sask., 12/25/1933.

Season	Club	League	GP	G	A	Pts	AG	AA	APts	PIM	GP	G	A	Pts	PIM
1948/50	Duck Lake Ducks	SAHA	STATISTICS NOT AVAILABLE												
1950-51	Moose Jaw Canucks	WCJHL	18	7	7	14	....	....	....	9	....	....	....	....	....
1951-52	Moose Jaw Canucks	WCJHL	42	19	22	41	....	....	....	59	....	....	....	....	....
1952-53	Moose Jaw Canucks	WCJHL	36	18	17	35	....	....	....	40	9	7	5	12	4
1953-54	Moose Jaw Canucks	WCJHL	34	31	26	57	....	....	....	56	5	4	2	6	8
	Chicago Black Hawks	**NHL**	**11**	**0**	**0**	**0**	**0**	**0**	**0**	**6**	....	....	....	....	....
1954-55	New Westminster Royals	WHL	21	3	8	11	....	....	....	6	....	....	....	....	....
	Chicoutimi Sagueneens	QHL	22	4	4	8	....	....	....	2	6	2	1	3	2
1955-56	Calgary Stampeders	WHL	2	0	0	0	....	....	....	2	....	....	....	....	....
1956-57	Kamloops Chiefs	OSHL	23	7	10	17	....	....	....	36	....	....	....	....	....
1957-58	Kamloops Chiefs	OSHL	51	26	27	53	....	....	....	63	15	7	6	13	34
1958-59			DID NOT PLAY												
1959-60	Kamloops Chiefs	OSHL	20	10	20	30	....	....	....	42	5	0	0	0	0
1960-61	North Battleford Beavers	SIHA	STATISTICS NOT AVAILABLE												
	NHL Totals		**11**	**0**	**0**	**0**	**0**	**0**	**0**	**6**	....	....	....	....	....

• SATHER, Glen — *see page 1600*

• SAUNDERS, Ted Theodore Clarence "Bud"

RW – R. 5'8", 165 lbs. b: Ottawa, Ont., 8/29/1911.

Season	Club	League	GP	G	A	Pts	AG	AA	APts	PIM	GP	G	A	Pts	PIM
1928-29	Ottawa New Edinburghs	OCHL	15	3	1	4	....	....	....	....	2	1	0	1	0
1929-30	Iroquois Falls Eskimos	NOHA	STATISTICS NOT AVAILABLE												
1930-31	Springfield Indians	Can-Am	38	19	4	23	....	....	....	28	7	3	2	5	6
1931-32	Springfield Indians	Can-Am	30	5	3	8	....	....	....	20	....	....	....	....	....
	Cleveland Indians	IHL	6	0	0	0	....	....	....	2	....	....	....	....	....
1932-33	Boston Cubs	Can-Am	47	*29	10	39	....	....	....	82	7	*5	2	*7	18
1933-34	**Ottawa Senators**	**NHL**	**18**	**1**	**3**	**4**	**2**	**6**	**8**	**4**	....	....	....	....	....
	Detroit Olympics	IHL	21	1	4	5	....	....	....	14	6	0	0	0	4
1934-35	Philadelphia Arrows	Can-Am	48	*28	20	48	....	....	....	35	....	....	....	....	....
1935-36	Springfield Indians	Can-Am	48	19	22	41	....	....	....	36	3	0	0	0	0
1936-37	Springfield Indians	IAHL	45	17	13	30	....	....	....	44	5	1	0	1	2
1937-38	Springfield Indians	IAHL	45	8	21	29	....	....	....	41	....	....	....	....	....
1938-39	Springfield Indians	IAHL	53	10	19	29	....	....	....	33	3	0	1	1	2
1939-40	St. Paul Saints	AHA	46	23	25	48	....	....	....	51	7	*6	4	*10	4
1940-41	St. Paul Saints	AHA	46	18	15	33	....	....	....	14	4	2	1	3	0
1941-42	Cornwall–Ottawa	QSHL	40	*31	25	*56	....	....	....	20	8	2	2	4	4
1942-43	Ottawa Commandos	QSHL	28	10	13	23	....	....	....	15	....	....	....	....	....
	Ottawa Army Medics	OCHL	9	10	8	18	....	....	....	2	....	....	....	....	....
1943-44	Truro Bearcats	NSAPC	10	*17	6	23	....	....	....	0	....	....	....	....	....
	NHL Totals		**18**	**1**	**3**	**4**	**2**	**6**	**8**	**4**	....	....	....	....	....

Can-Am Second All-Star Team (1936)

Traded to **Ottawa** by **Boston** with Percy Galbraith and Bud Cook for Bob Gracie, October 4, 1933. Traded to **Detroit** (IHL) by **Ottawa** for cash, December, 1933. Traded to **Springfield** (Can-Am) by **Philadelphia** (Can-Am) for cash, October 18, 1935. Traded to **St. Paul** (AHA) by **Springfield** (IAHL) for cash, September 28, 1939.

• SAVAGE, Tony Anthony Gordon Donald

D – L. 6', 175 lbs. b: Calgary, Alta., 7/18/1906 d: 2/28/1974.

Season	Club	League	GP	G	A	Pts	AG	AA	APts	PIM	GP	G	A	Pts	PIM
1925-26	Calgary Canadiens	CCJHL	STATISTICS NOT AVAILABLE												
	Calgary Canadiens	M-Cup	9	3	3	6	....	....	....	18	....	....	....	....	....
1926-27	Calgary Tigers	PrHL	29	1	2	3	....	....	....	27	2	0	0	0	0
1927-28	Kitchener / London	Can-Pro	32	1	4	5	....	....	....	59	....	....	....	....	....
1928-29	Kitchener Dutchmen	Can-Pro	37	8	1	9	....	....	....	33	3	0	0	0	4
1929-30	Seattle Eskimos	PCHL	35	7	1	8	....	....	....	28	....	....	....	....	....
1930-31	Seattle Eskimos	PCHL	33	11	5	16	....	....	....	83	4	*2	0	2	10
1931-32	Syracuse Stars	IHL	48	8	13	21	....	....	....	58	....	....	....	....	....
1932-33	Syracuse Stars	IHL	35	9	6	15	....	....	....	75	6	1	2	3	8
1933-34	Calgary Tigers	NWHL	29	9	12	21	....	....	....	48	5	3	1	4	4
1934-35	**Boston Bruins**	**NHL**	**8**	**0**	**0**	**0**	**0**	**0**	**0**	**2**	....	....	....	....	....
	Montreal Canadiens	**NHL**	**41**	**1**	**5**	**6**	**2**	**9**	**11**	**4**	**2**	**0**	**0**	**0**	**0**
1935-36	Calgary Tigers	NWHL	34	22	17	39	....	....	....	45	....	....	....	....	....
1936-37			REINSTATED AS AN AMATEUR												
1937-38	Olds Elks	ASHL	25	13	9	22	....	....	....	25	3	0	1	1	6
1938-39	Saskatoon Quakers	N-SSHL	7	1	2	3	....	....	....	2	....	....	....	....	....
1939-40	Lethbridge Maple Leafs	ASHL	5	0	2	2	....	....	....	2	....	....	....	....	....
	NHL Totals		**49**	**1**	**5**	**6**	**2**	**9**	**11**	**6**	**2**	**0**	**0**	**0**	**0**

Traded to **Kitchener** (Can-Pro) by **Calgary** (PrHL) for cash, October 16, 1927. Traded to **Seattle** (PCHL) by **Kitchener** (Can-Pro) for cash, October 31, 1929. Traded to **Montreal Canadiens** by **Calgary** (NWHL) for cash, October, 1934. Traded to **Boston** by **Montreal Canadiens** for Tommy Filmore and cash, November 5, 1934. Traded to **Montreal Canadiens** by **Boston** with $7,500 for Jack Portland, December 3, 1934.

• SAVARD, Serge — *see page 1603*

• SCHAEFFER, Butch Paul

D – R. 5'10", 190 lbs. b: Hinkley, MN, 11/7/1911.

Season	Club	League	GP	G	A	Pts	AG	AA	APts	PIM	GP	G	A	Pts	PIM
1934-35	Chicago Baby Ruth	AUAA	2	0	0	0	....	....	....	0	....	....	....	....	....
1935-36	Chicago Baby Ruth	AUAA	STATISTICS NOT AVAILABLE												
1936-37	**Chicago Black Hawks**	**NHL**	**5**	**0**	**0**	**0**	**0**	**0**	**0**	**6**	....	....	....	....	....
1937-38	Eveleth Rangers	USHL	STATISTICS NOT AVAILABLE												
1938-39	Eveleth Rangers	USHL	27	0	6	6	....	....	....	25	5	0	0	0	8
	NHL Totals		**5**	**0**	**0**	**0**	**0**	**0**	**0**	**6**	....	....	....	....	....

• SCHERZA, Chuck Charles

LW/C – L. 5'10", 190 lbs. b: Brandon, Man., 2/15/1923.

Season	Club	League	GP	G	A	Pts	AG	AA	APts	PIM	GP	G	A	Pts	PIM
1941-42	Regina Abbotts	S-SJHL	12	7	*7	14	....	....	....	8	5	1	2	3	6
	Regina Abbotts	M-Cup	9	8	5	13	....	....	....	16	....	....	....	....	....
1942-43	Oshawa Generals	OHA-Jr.	21	8	5	13	....	....	....	26	21	14	6	20	12
1943-44	**Boston Bruins**	**NHL**	**9**	**1**	**1**	**2**	**1**	**1**	**2**	**6**	....	....	....	....	....
	New York Rangers	**NHL**	**5**	**3**	**2**	**5**	**3**	**2**	**5**	**11**	....	....	....	....	....
1944-45	**New York Rangers**	**NHL**	**22**	**2**	**3**	**5**	**2**	**3**	**5**	**18**	....	....	....	....	....
	Hershey Bears	AHL	27	6	3	9	....	....	....	29	11	1	6	7	8
1945-46	Providence Reds	AHL	61	15	27	42	....	....	....	81	2	0	0	0	0
1946-47	Providence Reds	AHL	64	21	36	57	....	....	....	78	....	....	....	....	....
1947-48	Providence Reds	AHL	68	18	65	83	....	....	....	72	5	1	0	1	2
1948-49	Providence Reds	AHL	68	14	13	27	....	....	....	54	14	0	4	4	7
1949-50	Providence Reds	AHL	63	6	10	16	....	....	....	41	4	0	0	0	0
1950-51	Providence Reds	AHL	69	13	26	39	....	....	....	33	....	....	....	....	....
1951-52	Providence Reds	AHL	68	11	9	20	....	....	....	32	15	1	2	3	2
1952-53	Providence Reds	AHL	59	9	37	46	....	....	....	40	....	....	....	....	....
1953-54	Providence Reds	AHL	67	18	47	65	....	....	....	50	....	....	....	....	....
1954-55	Providence Reds	AHL	62	14	27	41	....	....	....	58	....	....	....	....	....
1955-56	Trois-Rivieres Lions	QHL	49	14	23	37	....	....	....	42	....	....	....	....	....
1956-57	North Bay Trappers	NOHA	47	13	33	46	....	....	....	64	13	1	*12	13	14
1957-58	North Bay Trappers	NOHA	6	1	4	5	....	....	....	6	....	....	....	....	....
1958-59	North Bay Trappers	NOHA	12	1	4	5	....	....	....	8	....	....	....	....	....
	NHL Totals		**36**	**6**	**6**	**12**	**6**	**6**	**12**	**35**	....	....	....	....	....

Traded to **NY Rangers** by **Boston** for cash, November, 1943.

• SCHINKEL, Ken — *see page 1606*

• SCHMIDT, Clarence Clarence Elmer

RW – R. 5'11", 165 lbs. b: Williams, MN, 9/17/1925 d: 11/2/1997.

Season	Club	League	GP	G	A	Pts	AG	AA	APts	PIM	GP	G	A	Pts	PIM
1942-43	Boston Olympics	EAHL	36	25	12	37	....	....	....	22	9	4	1	5	5
1943-44	**Boston Bruins**	**NHL**	**7**	**1**	**0**	**1**	**1**	**0**	**1**	**2**	....	....	....	....	....
	Boston Olympics	EAHL	13	7	6	13	....	....	....	14	8	6	3	9	5
1944-45	Warroad Lakers	MHL-Sr.	STATISTICS NOT AVAILABLE												
	NHL Totals		**7**	**1**	**0**	**1**	**1**	**0**	**1**	**2**	....	....	....	....	....

• SCHMIDT, Jackie John Robert

LW – L. 5'10", 155 lbs. b: Odessa, Sask., 11/11/1924.

Season	Club	League	GP	G	A	Pts	AG	AA	APts	PIM	GP	G	A	Pts	PIM
1941-42	Regina Abbotts	S-SJHL	11	10	3	13	....	....	....	4	5	2	0	2	6
	Regina Abbotts	M-Cup	9	5	5	10	....	....	....	6	....	....	....	....	....
1942-43	**Boston Bruins**	**NHL**	**45**	**6**	**7**	**13**	**6**	**6**	**12**	**6**	**5**	**0**	**0**	**0**	**0**
	Providence Reds	AHL	4	1	3	4	....	....	....	6	....	....	....	....	....
1943-44	Toronto RCAF	TIHL	4	0	0	0	....	....	....	0	....	....	....	....	....
	Toronto C.I.L.	TMHL	....	9	16	25	....	....	....	4	7	7	5	12	4
	Halifax Navy	NSDHL	....	....	....	....	....	....	....	....	4	0	0	0	2
1944-45	Dartmouth RCAF	NSDHL	7	5	4	9	....	....	....	4	....	....	....	....	....
1945-46			MILITARY SERVICE												

Season	Club	League	GP	G	A	Pts	AG	AA	APts	PIM	GP	G	A	Pts	PIM
			REGULAR SEASON								PLAYOFFS				
1946-47	N. Westminster-Portland	PCHL	61	13	20	33	....	....	....	23	14	0	0	0	4
1947-48	Valleyfield Braves	QSHL	40	23	14	37	....	....	....	15	6	2	3	5	2
1948-49	Valleyfield Braves	QSHL	63	28	41	69	....	....	....	32	4	0	0	0	0
1949-50	Valleyfield Braves	QSHL	57	33	22	55	....	....	....	28	5	1	3	4	....
1950-51	Valleyfield Braves	QMHL	56	27	40	67	....	....	....	37	16	11	6	17	0
	Valleyfield Braves	Alx-Cup	12	6	8	14	....	....	....	6	....	....	....	....	....
1951-52	Valleyfield Braves	QMHL	37	12	17	29	....	....	....	8	5	1	0	1	4
1952-53	Valleyfield Braves	QMHL	51	9	17	26	....	....	....	27	4	1	0	1	0
	NHL Totals		**45**	**6**	**7**	**13**	**6**	**6**	**12**	**6**	**5**	**0**	**0**	**0**	**0**

• Brother of Otto

• SCHMIDT, Milt

Milton Conrad HHOF

C/D – L. 6', 185 lbs. b: Kitchener, Ont., 3/5/1918.

Season	Club	League	GP	G	A	Pts	AG	AA	APts	PIM	GP	G	A	Pts	PIM
1933-34	Kitchener Empires	OHA-Jr.	7	2	4	6	....	....	....	2	4	2	*3	5	0
1934-35	Kitchener Greenshirts	OHA-Jr.	17	*20	6	26	....	....	....	14	3	2	2	4	0
1935-36	Kitchener Greenshirts	OHA-Jr.	5	4	3	7	....	....	....	2	4	4	1	*5	11
1936-37	**Boston Bruins**	**NHL**	**26**	**2**	**8**	**10**	**3**	**15**	**18**	**15**	**3**	**0**	**0**	**0**	**0**
	Providence Reds	IAHL	23	8	1	9	....	....	....	12	....	....	....	....	....
1937-38	**Boston Bruins**	**NHL**	**44**	**13**	**14**	**27**	**21**	**23**	**44**	**15**	**3**	**0**	**0**	**0**	**0**
♦1938-39	**Boston Bruins**	**NHL**	**41**	**15**	**17**	**32**	**26**	**27**	**53**	**13**	**12**	**3**	**3**	**6**	**2**
1939-40	**Boston Bruins**	**NHL**	**48**	**22**	***30**	***52**	**37**	**48**	**85**	**37**	**6**	**0**	**0**	**0**	**0**
♦1940-41	**Boston Bruins**	**NHL**	**45**	**13**	**25**	**38**	**20**	**36**	**56**	**23**	**11**	**5**	**6**	***11**	**9**
1941-42	**Boston Bruins**	**NHL**	**36**	**14**	**21**	**35**	**19**	**25**	**44**	**34**	....	....	....	....	....
	Ottawa RCAF	OCHL	....	....	....	....	....	....	....	....	6	4	7	11	*10
1941-43	Ottawa RCAF	Al-Cup	13	6	17	23	....	....	....	*19	....	....	....	....	....
1942-43			MILITARY SERVICE												
1943-44			MILITARY SERVICE												
1944-45	Middleton RCAF	X-Games	STATISTICS NOT AVAILABLE												
1945-46	**Boston Bruins**	**NHL**	**48**	**13**	**18**	**31**	**15**	**26**	**41**	**21**	**10**	**3**	**5**	**8**	**2**
1946-47	**Boston Bruins**	**NHL**	**59**	**27**	**35**	**62**	**31**	**42**	**73**	**40**	**5**	**3**	**1**	**4**	**4**
1947-48	**Boston Bruins**	**NHL**	**33**	**9**	**17**	**26**	**12**	**22**	**34**	**28**	**5**	**2**	**5**	**7**	**2**
1948-49	**Boston Bruins**	**NHL**	**44**	**10**	**22**	**32**	**14**	**31**	**45**	**25**	**4**	**0**	**2**	**2**	**8**
1949-50	**Boston Bruins**	**NHL**	**68**	**19**	**22**	**41**	**24**	**27**	**51**	**41**	....	....	....	....	....
1950-51	**Boston Bruins**	**NHL**	**62**	**22**	**39**	**61**	**28**	**48**	**76**	**33**	**6**	**0**	**1**	**1**	**7**
1951-52	**Boston Bruins**	**NHL**	**69**	**21**	**29**	**50**	**28**	**36**	**64**	**57**	**7**	**2**	**1**	**3**	**0**
1952-53	**Boston Bruins**	**NHL**	**68**	**11**	**23**	**34**	**14**	**28**	**42**	**30**	**10**	**5**	**1**	**6**	**6**
1953-54	**Boston Bruins**	**NHL**	**62**	**14**	**18**	**32**	**19**	**22**	**41**	**28**	**4**	**1**	**0**	**1**	**20**
1954-55	**Boston Bruins**	**NHL**	**23**	**4**	**8**	**12**	**5**	**9**	**14**	**26**	....	....	....	....	....
1955/61	**Boston Bruins**	**NHL**	DID NOT PLAY – COACHING												
	NHL Totals		**776**	**229**	**346**	**575**	**316**	**465**	**781**	**466**	**86**	**24**	**25**	**49**	**60**

NHL First All-Star Team (1940, 1947, 1951) • NHL Scoring Leader (1940) • Won Hart Trophy (1951) • NHL Second All-Star Team (1952) • Won Lester Patrick Trophy (1996) • Played in NHL All-Star Game (1947, 1948, 1951, 1952)

Signed as a free agent by **Boston**, October 9, 1935.

• SCHMIDT, Otto

Otto Joseph

D – R. 5'10", 157 lbs. b: Odessa, Sask., 11/5/1926.

Season	Club	League	GP	G	A	Pts	AG	AA	APts	PIM	GP	G	A	Pts	PIM
1942-43	Regina Abbotts	S-SJHL	1	0	0	0	....	....	....	2	....	....	....	....	....
1943-44	Regina Abbotts	S-SJHL	2	0	0	0	....	....	....	0	....	....	....	....	....
	Boston Bruins	**NHL**	**2**	**0**	**0**	**0**	**0**	**0**	**0**	**0**	....	....	....	....	....
	Boston Olympics	EAHL	32	12	22	34	....	....	....	8	9	1	2	3	2
	Toronto C.I.L.	TMHL	9	9	16	25	....	....	....	4	7	7	5	12	4
1944-45	Saskatoon Falcons	S-SJHL	7	0	0	0	....	....	....	10	2	0	0	0	9
	Boston Olympics	EAHL	48	31	36	67	....	....	....	16	12	14	4	18	7
1945-46	Boston Olympics	EAHL	11	1	2	3	....	....	....	2	....	....	....	....	....
	Seattle Ironmen	PCHL	17	0	0	0	....	....	....	20	....	....	....	....	....
	Fort Worth Rangers	USHL	26	1	1	2	....	....	....	26	....	....	....	....	....
1946-47	Houston–Fort Worth	USHL	35	1	3	4	....	....	....	28	....	....	....	....	....
1947-48	Fort Worth Rangers	USHL	55	17	11	28	....	....	....	55	5	0	2	2	0
1948-49	Fort Worth Rangers	USHL	8	4	2	6	....	....	....	17	....	....	....	....	....
	Springfield Indians	AHL	50	7	18	25	....	....	....	61	3	1	1	2	0
1949-50	Kerrisdale Monarchs	WKHL	STATISTICS NOT AVAILABLE												
1950-51	Vancouver Canucks	PCHL	11	1	2	3	....	....	....	12	....	....	....	....	....
	Kerrisdale Monarchs	WKHL	34	11	26	37	....	....	....	69	5	5	3	8	2
1951-52	Vancouver Wheelers	VCIHL	32	18	14	32	....	....	....	26	....	....	....	....	....
	NHL Totals		**2**	**0**	**0**	**0**	**0**	**0**	**0**	**0**	....	....	....	....	....

• Brother of Jackie

Signed as a free agent by **Boston**, December 7, 1943.

• SCHNARR, Werner

Werner Henry

C – L. 5'7", 145 lbs. b: Berlin, Ont., 3/23/1903 Deceased.

Season	Club	League	GP	G	A	Pts	AG	AA	APts	PIM	GP	G	A	Pts	PIM
1920-21	Kitchnener Union Jacks	OHA-Jr.	STATISTICS NOT AVAILABLE												
1921-22	Quaker City Seniors	USAHA	STATISTICS NOT AVAILABLE												
1922-23	Kitchener Union Jacks	OHA-Jr.	....	....	....	....	....	....	....	....	8	*14	*5	*19	....
1923-24	Kitchener Greenshirts	OHA-Sr.	1	0	0	0	....	....	....	0	....	....	....	....	....
	Kitchener Twin City	OHA-Sr.	10	10	5	15	....	....	....	....	....	....	....	....	....
1924-25	**Boston Bruins**	**NHL**	**25**	**0**	**0**	**0**	**0**	**0**	**0**	**0**	....	....	....	....	....
1925-26	**Boston Bruins**	**NHL**	**1**	**0**	**0**	**0**	**0**	**0**	**0**	**0**	....	....	....	....	....
1926-27	Stratford Nationals	Can-Pro	2	0	0	0	....	....	....	0	....	....	....	....	....
1927-28			REINSTATED AS AN AMATEUR												
1928-29	Kitchener Dutchmen	Can-Pro	2	0	0	0	....	....	....	0	....	....	....	....	....
1929-30	Guelph Maple Leafs	Can-Pro	27	17	*19	36	....	....	....	16	4	3	*5	8	8
1930-31	Kitchener Silverwoods	OPHL	30	13	7	20	....	....	....	29	4	2	2	4	0
	NHL Totals		**26**	**0**	**0**	**0**	**0**	**0**	**0**	**0**	....	....	....	....	....

Signed as a free agent by **Boston**, October 29, 1924. Signed as a free agent by **Stratford** (Can-Pro), November 28, 1926. Signed as a free agent by **Guelph** (Can-Pro), November 25, 1929.

• SCHOCK, Ron

— see page 1608

• SCHRINER, Sweeney

David HHOF

LW – L. 6', 185 lbs. b: Saratov, Russia, 11/30/1911 d: 7/4/1990.

Season	Club	League	GP	G	A	Pts	AG	AA	APts	PIM	GP	G	A	Pts	PIM
1925-26	Calgary North Hill	AAHA	STATISTICS NOT AVAILABLE												
1926-27	Calgary North Hill	AAHA	STATISTICS NOT AVAILABLE												
1927-28	Calgary North Hill	AAHA	STATISTICS NOT AVAILABLE												
1928-29	Calgary Canadians	CCJHL	STATISTICS NOT AVAILABLE												
1929-30	Calgary Canadians	CCJHL	STATISTICS NOT AVAILABLE												
	Calgary Canadians	M-Cup	5	0	2	2	....	....	....	8	....	....	....	....	....
1930-31	Calgary Canadians	CCJHL	2	*2	0	2	....	....	....	0	....	....	....	....	....
	Calgary Canadians	M-Cup	8	10	4	14	....	....	....	19	....	....	....	....	....
1931-32	Calgary Bronks	ASHL	18	*19	3	*22	....	....	....	32	3	1	*2	*3	0
	Calgary Bronks	Al-Cup	11	8	5	13	....	....	....	12	....	....	....	....	....
1932-33	Calgary Bronks	ASHL	15	*22	4	*26	....	....	....	8	5	*3	1	*4	6
	Calgary Bronks	Al-Cup	2	2	2	4	....	....	....	2	....	....	....	....	....
1933-34	Syracuse Stars	IHL	44	17	11	28	....	....	....	28	4	0	0	0	0
1934-35	**New York Americans**	**NHL**	**48**	**18**	**22**	**40**	**30**	**39**	**69**	**6**	....	....	....	....	....
1935-36	**New York Americans**	**NHL**	**48**	**19**	**26**	***45**	**37**	**50**	**87**	**8**	**5**	**3**	**1**	**4**	**2**
1936-37	**New York Americans**	**NHL**	**48**	**21**	**25**	***46**	**36**	**46**	**82**	**17**	....	....	....	....	....
1937-38	**New York Americans**	**NHL**	**48**	**21**	**17**	**38**	**35**	**27**	**62**	**22**	**6**	**1**	**0**	**1**	**0**
1938-39	**New York Americans**	**NHL**	**48**	**13**	**31**	**44**	**23**	**49**	**72**	**20**	**2**	**0**	**0**	**0**	**30**
1939-40	**Toronto Maple Leafs**	**NHL**	**39**	**11**	**15**	**26**	**18**	**24**	**42**	**10**	**9**	**1**	**3**	**4**	**4**
1940-41	**Toronto Maple Leafs**	**NHL**	**48**	**24**	**14**	**38**	**38**	**20**	**58**	**6**	**7**	**2**	**1**	**3**	**4**
♦1941-42	**Toronto Maple Leafs**	**NHL**	**47**	**20**	**16**	**36**	**27**	**19**	**46**	**21**	**13**	**6**	**3**	**9**	**10**
1942-43	**Toronto Maple Leafs**	**NHL**	**37**	**19**	**17**	**36**	**20**	**16**	**36**	**13**	**4**	**2**	**2**	**4**	**0**
1943-44	Calgary Combines	WCSHL	10	9	9	18	....	....	....	14	3	3	2	5	4
	Vancouver St. Regis	PCHL	....	....	....	....	....	....	....	....	3	6	3	9	0
♦1944-45	**Toronto Maple Leafs**	**NHL**	**26**	**22**	**15**	**37**	**22**	**17**	**39**	**10**	**13**	**3**	**1**	**4**	**4**
1945-46	**Toronto Maple Leafs**	**NHL**	**47**	**13**	**6**	**19**	**15**	**9**	**24**	**15**	....	....	....	....	....
1946-47	Lethbridge Maple Leafs	WCSHL	DID NOT PLAY – COACHING												
1947-48	Lethbridge Maple Leafs	WCSHL	DID NOT PLAY – COACHING												
1948-49	Regina Capitals	WCSHL	36	26	27	53	....	....	....	30	8	*10	2	12	0
	Regina Capitals	Al-Cup	14	3	8	11	....	....	....	18	....	....	....	....	....
	NHL Totals		**484**	**201**	**204**	**405**	**301**	**316**	**617**	**148**	**59**	**18**	**11**	**29**	**54**

NHL Rookie of the Year (1935) • NHL First All-Star Team (1936, 1941) • NHL Scoring Leader (1936, 1937) • NHL Second All-Star Team (1937) • Played in NHL All-Star Game (1937)

Traded to **Toronto** by **NY Americans** for Busher Jackson, Buzz Boll, Doc Romnes, Jimmy Fowler and Murray Armstrong, May 18, 1939.

• SCLISIZZI, Enio

James Enio

LW – L. 5'10", 170 lbs. b: Milton, Ont., 8/1/1925.

Season	Club	League	GP	G	A	Pts	AG	AA	APts	PIM	GP	G	A	Pts	PIM
1941-42	Milton Baby Bombers	OMHA	STATISTICS NOT AVAILABLE												
1942-43	Toronto Red Indians	TIHL	14	7	10	17	....	....	....	2	....	....	....	....	....
	Toronto Marlboros	OHA-Jr.	1	0	0	0	....	....	....	0	....	....	....	....	....
	Milton Bombers	OHA-B	....	....	....	....	....	....	....	....	10	10	10	20	15
1943-44	Stratford Kroehlers	OHA-Jr.	23	17	14	31	....	....	....	40	....	....	....	....	....
	Hamilton Whizzers	OHA-Jr.	....	....	....	....	....	....	....	....	2	2	2	4	0
1944-45	Cornwallis Navy	OHA-Sr.	STATISTICS NOT AVAILABLE												
1945-46	Stratford Indians	OHA-Sr.	14	6	5	11	....	....	....	2	5	5	4	9	4
	Toronto Bowser Orphans	TMHL	2	1	1	2	....	....	....	5	10	9	13	22	8
1946-47	Indianapolis Capitols	AHL	60	20	14	34	....	....	....	45	....	....	....	....	....
	Detroit Red Wings	**NHL**	....	....	....	....	....	....	....	....	**1**	**0**	**0**	**0**	**0**
1947-48	**Detroit Red Wings**	**NHL**	**4**	**1**	**0**	**1**	**1**	**0**	**1**	**0**	**6**	**0**	**0**	**0**	**4**
	Indianapolis Capitols	AHL	61	29	38	67	....	....	....	58	....	....	....	....	....
1948-49	**Detroit Red Wings**	**NHL**	**50**	**9**	**8**	**17**	**12**	**11**	**23**	**24**	**6**	**0**	**0**	**0**	**2**
	Indianapolis Capitols	AHL	12	3	7	10	....	....	....	6	....	....	....	....	....
1949-50	**Detroit Red Wings**	**NHL**	**4**	**0**	**0**	**0**	**0**	**0**	**0**	**2**	....	....	....	....	....
	Indianapolis Capitols	AHL	62	19	26	45	....	....	....	47	8	1	4	5	7
1950-51	Indianapolis Capitols	AHL	64	30	36	66	....	....	....	43	3	2	0	2	0
1951-52	**Detroit Red Wings**	**NHL**	**9**	**2**	**1**	**3**	**3**	**1**	**4**	**0**	....	....	....	....	....
	Indianapolis Capitols	AHL	55	24	34	58	....	....	....	35	....	....	....	....	....
1952-53	**Chicago Black Hawks**	**NHL**	**14**	**0**	**2**	**2**	**0**	**2**	**2**	**0**	....	....	....	....	....
	St. Louis Flyers	AHL	10	4	4	8	....	....	....	2	....	....	....	....	....
	Calgary Stampeders	WHL	16	12	11	23	....	....	....	12	5	5	2	7	4
1953-54	Edmonton Flyers	WHL	70	28	36	64	....	....	....	46	13	6	4	10	8
1954-55	Edmonton Flyers	WHL	59	29	24	53	....	....	....	50	9	0	5	5	12
	Edmonton Flyers	Ed-Cup	7	0	2	2	....	....	....	4	....	....	....	....	....
1955-56	Buffalo Bisons	AHL	60	18	28	46	....	....	....	56	5	1	3	4	2
1956-57	Calgary Stampeders	WHL	67	26	24	50	....	....	....	42	3	2	0	2	2
1957-58	Calgary Stampeders	WHL	68	22	15	37	....	....	....	19	14	5	3	8	16
1958-59	Victoria Cougars	WHL	60	12	29	41	....	....	....	22	3	1	1	2	2
	NHL Totals		**81**	**12**	**11**	**23**	**16**	**14**	**30**	**26**	**13**	**0**	**0**	**0**	**6**

AHL First All-Star Team (1952) • WHL First All-Star Team (1954)

Traded to **Chicago** by **Detroit** with Fred Glover for cash, August 14, 1952. Traded to **Victoria** (WHL) by **Calgary** (WHL) with George Ford and Murray Wilkie for Ed Dorohoy, July, 1958.

• SCOTT, Ganton

RW – R. 5'9", 165 lbs. b: Preston, Ont., 3/23/1903 Deceased.

Season	Club	League	GP	G	A	Pts	AG	AA	APts	PIM	GP	G	A	Pts	PIM
1921-22	Toronto Aura Lee	OHA-Jr.	6	*11	1	*12	....	....	....	....	....	....	....	....	....
1922-23	**Toronto St. Pats**	**NHL**	**17**	**0**	**0**	**0**	**0**	**0**	**0**	**0**	....	....	....	....	....
1923-24	**Toronto St. Pats**	**NHL**	**4**	**0**	**0**	**0**	**0**	**0**	**0**	**0**	....	....	....	....	....
	Hamilton Tigers	**NHL**	**8**	**0**	**0**	**0**	**0**	**0**	**0**	**0**	....	....	....	....	....
1924-25	**Montreal Maroons**	**NHL**	**28**	**1**	**1**	**2**	**2**	**4**	**6**	**0**	....	....	....	....	....
1925-26	Edmonton Eskimos	WHL	7	0	1	1	....	....	....	0	....	....	....	....	....
	Saskatoon Crescents	WHL	6	0	1	1	....	....	....	2	....	....	....	....	....
	Palais-de-Glace	Cal-Pro	STATISTICS NOT AVAILABLE												
1926-27	Los Angeles Richfields	Cal-Pro	STATISTICS NOT AVAILABLE												
1927-28	Los Angeles Richfields	Cal-Pro	STATISTICS NOT AVAILABLE												
1928-29	San Francisco Tigers	Cal-Pro	....	*31	6	*37	....	....	....	32	....	....	....	....	....
1929-30	San Francisco Tigers	Cal-Pro	....	12	6	18	....	....	....	....	....	....	....	....	....
1930-31	San Francisco Hawks	Cal-Pro	....	11	10	21	....	....	....	29	....	....	....	....	....
1931-32	Oakland Sheiks	Cal-Pro	....	15	5	20	....	....	....	....	....	....	....	....	....
	NHL Totals		**57**	**1**	**1**	**2**	**2**	**4**	**6**	**0**	....	....	....	....	....
	Other Major League Totals		13	0	2	2	....	....	....	2	....	....	....	....	....

Signed as a free agent by **Toronto St. Pats**, October 9, 1922. Traded to **Hamilton** by **Toronto St. Pats** for cash, January 16, 1924. Signed as a free agent by **Montreal Maroons**, October 31, 1924. Signed as a free agent by **Edmonton** (WHL), December 29, 1925. Traded to **Saskatoon** (WHL) by **Edmonton** (WHL) for cash, January 25, 1926.

• SCOTT, Laurie

LW/C – L. 5'6", 155 lbs. b: South River, Ont., 6/19/1900 d: 2/15/1977.

Season	Club	League	GP	G	A	Pts	AG	AA	APts	PIM	GP	G	A	Pts	PIM
1921-22	Melville Millionaires	S-SJHL	STATISTICS NOT AVAILABLE												
1922-23	Saskatoon Sheiks	WCHL	21	7	6	13	....	....	....	6	....	....	....	....	....
1923-24	Saskatoon Crescents	WCHL	30	20	5	25	....	....	....	8	....	....	....	....	....

Season	Club	League	GP	G	A	Pts	AG	AA	APts	PIM	GP	G	A	Pts	PIM
			REGULAR SEASON								PLAYOFFS				
1924-25	Saskatoon Crescents	WCHL	26	12	6	18	....	....	....	41	2	0	0	0	2
1925-26	Saskatoon Crescents	WHL	29	11	4	15	....	....	....	32	2	1	0	1	2
1926-27	**New York Americans**	**NHL**	**39**	**6**	**2**	**8**	**11**	**10**	**21**	**22**	....	....	....	....	....
♦1927-28	**New York Rangers**	**NHL**	**23**	**0**	**1**	**1**	**0**	**6**	**6**	**6**	....	....	....	....	....
	Springfield Indians	Can-Am	17	3	3	6	....	....	....	8	4	0	0	0	2
1928-29	Springfield Indians	Can-Am	40	9	1	10	....	....	....	42	....	....	....	....	....
1929-30	Duluth Hornets	AHA	48	19	13	32	....	....	....	46	4	3	1	4	4
1930-31	Duluth Hornets	AHA	48	29	11	40	....	....	....	51	4	1	1	2	4
1931-32	Duluth Hornets	AHA	48	12	9	21	....	....	....	47	8	3	0	3	7
1932-33	Eveleth Rangers	CHL	38	10	9	19	....	....	....	23	3	0	0	0	5
1933-34	Oklahoma City Warriors	AHA	37	9	10	19	....	....	....	7	....	....	....	....	....
1934-35	St. Louis Flyers	AHA	41	17	22	39	....	....	....	8	3	2	*4	6	0
	NHL Totals		**62**	**6**	**3**	**9**	**11**	**16**	**27**	**28**	....	....	....	....	....
	Other Major League Totals		106	50	21	71	....	....	....	87	4	1	0	1	4

Signed as a free agent by **Saskatoon** (WCHL), December 21, 1922. Traded to **Toronto** by **Saskatoon** (PrHL) with Corb Denneny and Leo Bourgeault for cash, September 27, 1926. • Ruled to be property of **Toronto** by NHL President Frank Calder after **NY Americans** claimed his rights, November 4, 1926. Traded to **NY Americans** by **Toronto** for Jesse Spring, November 15, 1926. Traded to **NY Rangers** by **NY Americans** for cash, October 14, 1927. Traded to **Duluth** (AHA) by **NY Rangers** for cash, October 18, 1929.

• SEIBERT, Earl

Earl Walter HHOF

D – R. 6'2", 198 lbs. b: Berlin, Ont., 12/7/1911 d: 5/12/1990.

Season	Club	League	GP	G	A	Pts	AG	AA	APts	PIM	GP	G	A	Pts	PIM
1927-28	Kitchener Jr. Greenshirts	OHA-Jr.	STATISTICS NOT AVAILABLE												
	Kitchener Greenshirts	OHA-Sr.	1	0	0	0	....	....	....	2	....	....	....	....	....
1928-29	Kitchener Jr. Greenshirts	OHA-Jr.	STATISTICS NOT AVAILABLE												
1929-30	Springfield Indians	Can-Am	40	4	1	5	....	....	....	84	....	....	....	....	....
1930-31	Springfield Indians	Can-Am	38	16	11	27	....	....	....	96	4	2	0	2	16
1931-32	**New York Rangers**	**NHL**	**46**	**4**	**6**	**10**	**7**	**13**	**20**	**88**	**7**	**1**	**2**	**3**	**14**
♦1932-33	**New York Rangers**	**NHL**	**45**	**2**	**3**	**5**	**4**	**6**	**10**	**92**	**8**	**1**	**0**	**1**	**14**
1933-34	**New York Rangers**	**NHL**	**48**	**13**	**10**	**23**	**22**	**21**	**43**	**66**	**2**	**0**	**0**	**0**	**4**
1934-35	**New York Rangers**	**NHL**	**48**	**6**	**19**	**25**	**10**	**33**	**43**	**86**	**4**	**0**	**0**	**0**	**6**
1935-36	**New York Rangers**	**NHL**	**17**	**2**	**3**	**5**	**4**	**6**	**10**	**6**	....	....	....	....	....
	Chicago Black Hawks	**NHL**	**15**	**3**	**6**	**9**	**6**	**11**	**17**	**19**	**2**	**2**	**0**	**2**	**0**
1936-37	**Chicago Black Hawks**	**NHL**	**43**	**9**	**6**	**15**	**15**	**11**	**26**	**46**	....	....	....	....	....
♦1937-38	**Chicago Black Hawks**	**NHL**	**48**	**8**	**13**	**21**	**13**	**21**	**34**	**38**	**10**	**5**	**2**	**7**	**12**
1938-39	**Chicago Black Hawks**	**NHL**	**48**	**4**	**11**	**15**	**7**	**17**	**24**	**57**	....	....	....	....	....
1939-40	**Chicago Black Hawks**	**NHL**	**36**	**3**	**7**	**10**	**5**	**11**	**16**	**35**	**2**	**0**	**1**	**1**	**8**
1940-41	**Chicago Black Hawks**	**NHL**	**46**	**3**	**17**	**20**	**5**	**24**	**29**	**52**	**5**	**0**	**0**	**0**	**12**
1941-42	**Chicago Black Hawks**	**NHL**	**46**	**7**	**14**	**21**	**9**	**17**	**26**	**52**	**3**	**0**	**0**	**0**	**0**
1942-43	**Chicago Black Hawks**	**NHL**	**44**	**5**	**27**	**32**	**5**	**25**	**30**	**48**	....	....	....	....	....
1943-44	**Chicago Black Hawks**	**NHL**	**50**	**8**	**25**	**33**	**7**	**22**	**29**	**20**	**9**	**0**	**2**	**2**	**2**
1944-45	**Chicago Black Hawks**	**NHL**	**22**	**7**	**8**	**15**	**7**	**9**	**16**	**13**	....	....	....	....	....
	Detroit Red Wings	**NHL**	**25**	**5**	**9**	**14**	**5**	**10**	**15**	**10**	**14**	**2**	**1**	**3**	**4**
1945-46	**Detroit Red Wings**	**NHL**	**18**	**0**	**3**	**3**	**0**	**4**	**4**	**18**	....	....	....	....	....
	Indianapolis Capitols	AHL	24	2	9	11	....	....	....	19	5	0	0	0	0
1946-47	Springfield Indians	AHL	DID NOT PLAY – COACHING												
	NHL Totals		**645**	**89**	**187**	**276**	**131**	**261**	**392**	**746**	**66**	**11**	**8**	**19**	**76**

Can-Am First All-Star Team (1931) • NHL First All-Star Team (1935, 1942, 1943, 1944) • NHL Second All-Star Team (1936, 1937, 1938, 1939, 1940, 1941) • Played in NHL All-Star Game (1939)

Traded to **NY Rangers** by **Springfield** (Can-Am) for cash, May 9, 1931. Traded to **Chicago** by **NY Rangers** for Art Coulter, January 15, 1936. Traded to **Detroit** by **Chicago** with future considerations (Fido Purpur, January 4, 1945) for Cully Simon, Don Grosso and Byron McDonald, January 2, 1945.

• SEILING, Rod

— see page 1613

• SELBY, Brit

— see page 1614

• SENICK, George

LW – L. 5'11", 195 lbs. b: Saskatoon, Sask., 9/16/1929.

Season	Club	League	GP	G	A	Pts	AG	AA	APts	PIM	GP	G	A	Pts	PIM
1946-47	Saskatoon Jr. Quakers	N-SJHL	23	21	28	49	....	....	....	66	2	0	0	0	0
1947-48	Omaha Knights	USHL	62	20	23	43	....	....	....	81	3	0	0	0	0
1948-49	Seattle Ironmen	PCHL	55	26	16	42	....	....	....	*166	....	....	....	....	....
	Houston Huskies	USHL	5	0	0	0	....	....	....	0	....	....	....	....	....
1949-50	Seattle Ironmen	PCHL	70	31	31	62	....	....	....	145	4	2	1	3	6
1950-51	Seattle Ironmen	PCHL	16	6	4	10	....	....	....	28	....	....	....	....	....
	Saskatoon Quakers	WCMHL	15	13	13	26	....	....	....	45	8	*10	8	*18	4
	Saskatoon Quakers	Alx-Cup	3	1	1	2	....	....	....	6	....	....	....	....	....
1951-52	Saskatoon Quakers	PCHL	67	26	23	49	....	....	....	98	13	*11	10	*21	*24
1952-53	**New York Rangers**	**NHL**	**13**	**2**	**3**	**5**	**3**	**4**	**7**	**8**	....	....	....	....	....
	Saskatoon Quakers	WHL	48	27	46	73	....	....	....	61	13	5	9	14	14
1953-54	Saskatoon Quakers	WHL	43	21	21	42	....	....	....	51	6	3	2	5	19
1954-55	Saskatoon–Vancouver	WHL	34	10	11	21	....	....	....	20	....	....	....	....	....
	Spokane Flyers	WIHL	11	7	10	17	....	....	....	19	4	3	2	5	4
1955-56	Brandon Regals	WHL	66	34	37	71	....	....	....	71	....	....	....	....	....
1956-57	Seattle Americans	WHL	50	26	26	52	....	....	....	40	....	....	....	....	....
1957-58	Sudbury Wolves	NOHA	50	26	32	58	....	....	....	59	7	2	4	6	18
1958-59	Sudbury Wolves	NOHA	30	11	15	26	....	....	....	74	1	0	0	0	0
1959-60	Saskatoon Quakers	SSHL	20	*26	22	48	....	....	....	54	7	*14	*13	*27	12
	Saskatoon Quakers	Al-Cup	6	1	3	4	....	....	....	10	....	....	....	....	....
1960-61	Yorkton Terriers	SSHL	1	1	0	1	....	....	....	0	....	....	....	....	....
	Saskatoon Quakers	SSHL	13	12	16	28	....	....	....	33	1	0	0	0	2
	Saskatoon Quakers	Al-Cup	13	13	8	21	....	....	....	25	....	....	....	....	....
1961-62	Saskatoon Quakers	SSHL	29	30	*54	*84	....	....	....	60	8	6	*17	*23	20
1962-63	Saskatoon Quakers	SSHL	28	*44	38	82	....	....	....	47	11	5	*21	*26	*23
1963-64			OUT OF HOCKEY – RETIRED												
1964-65	Saskatoon Quakers	SSHL	5	3	10	13	....	....	....	4	....	....	....	....	....
1965-66	Saskatoon Quakers	SSHL	30	27	32	59	....	....	....	40	12	8	*15	*23	13
	NHL Totals		**13**	**2**	**3**	**5**	**3**	**4**	**7**	**8**	....	....	....	....	....

WHL First All-Star Team (1953)

• SHACK, Eddie

— see page 1618

• SHACK, Joe

LW – L. 5'10", 170 lbs. b: Winnipeg, Man., 12/8/1915 d: 5/5/1987.

Season	Club	League	GP	G	A	Pts	AG	AA	APts	PIM	GP	G	A	Pts	PIM
1933-34	Elmwood Maple Leafs	MJHL	11	14	2	16	....	....	....	0	2	0	1	1	2
1934-35	Elmwood Maple Leafs	MJHL	10	6	7	13	....	....	....	16	4	2	1	3	6
1935-36	Elmwood Millionaires	MHL-Sr.	10	6	3	9	....	....	....	15	3	0	1	1	2
1936-37	Harringay Greyhounds	Britain	24	18	9	27	....	....	....	12	....	....	....	....	....
1937-38	Harringay Greyhounds	Ln-Cup	....	3	2	5	....	....	....	....	....	....	....	....	....
	Harringay Greyhounds	Britain	....	8	7	15	....	....	....	....	....	....	....	....	....
	Harringay Greyhounds	Nat-Tmt	....	3	10	13	....	....	....	....	....	....	....	....	....
1938-39	Harringay Greyhounds	Ln-Cup	....	6	1	7	....	....	....	....	....	....	....	....	....
	Harringay Greyhounds	Britain	....	24	19	43	....	....	....	....	....	....	....	....	....
	Harringay Greyhounds	Nat-Tmt	....	3	7	10	....	....	....	....	....	....	....	....	....
1939-40	Ottawa Senators	QSHL	28	10	17	27	....	....	....	16	....	....	....	....	....
1940-41	Ottawa Senators	QSHL	35	21	21	42	....	....	....	22	8	3	1	4	8
1941-42	New Haven Eagles	AHL	56	16	29	45	....	....	....	12	2	0	0	0	0
1942-43	**New York Rangers**	**NHL**	**20**	**5**	**9**	**14**	**5**	**8**	**13**	**6**	....	....	....	....	....
1943-44	Ottawa Commandos	QSHL	19	7	16	23	....	....	....	11	3	0	4	4	0
	Montreal Vics	MCHL	12	10	10	20	....	....	....	14	....	....	....	....	....
1944-45	**New York Rangers**	**NHL**	**50**	**4**	**18**	**22**	**4**	**21**	**25**	**14**	....	....	....	....	....
1945-46	St. Paul Saints	USHL	51	28	31	59	....	....	....	37	6	0	1	1	4
1946-47	St. Paul Saints	USHL	55	25	30	55	....	....	....	29	....	....	....	....	....
1947-48	St. Paul Saints	USHL	62	12	31	43	....	....	....	19	....	....	....	....	....
1948-49	Harringay Racers	A-Cup	14	9	14	23	....	....	....	8	....	....	....	....	....
	Harringay Racers	Britain	28	28	*41	*69	....	....	....	34	....	....	....	....	....
1949-50	Harringay Racers	A-Cup	36	20	37	57	....	....	....	44	....	....	....	....	....
	Harringay Racers	Britain	21	10	15	25	....	....	....	18	....	....	....	....	....
1950-51	Harringay Racers	A-Cup	28	24	24	48	....	....	....	48	....	....	....	....	....
	Harringay Racers	Britain	16	12	16	28	....	....	....	14	....	....	....	....	....
1951-52	Harringay Racers	A-Cup	29	18	22	40	....	....	....	30	....	....	....	....	....
	Harringay Racers	Britain	30	23	29	52	....	....	....	32	....	....	....	....	....
1952-53	Harringay Racers	A-Cup	30	31	27	58	....	....	....	56	....	....	....	....	....
	Harringay Racers	Britain	30	26	29	55	....	....	....	30	....	....	....	....	....
1953-54	Harringay Racers	Ln-Cup	4	0	5	5	....	....	....	0	....	....	....	....	....
	Harringay Racers	Britain	20	16	9	25	....	....	....	47	....	....	....	....	....
1954-55	Dunfermline Vikings	Britain	5	4	0	4	....	....	....	0	....	....	....	....	....
1955-56	Sweden	Nt-Team	DID NOT PLAY – COACHING												
	NHL Totals		**70**	**9**	**27**	**36**	**9**	**29**	**38**	**20**	....	....	....	....	....

Traded to **NY Rangers** by **New Haven** (AHL) for cash after New Haven (AHL) franchise folded, January 18, 1943.

• SHANNON, Chuck

Charles Kitchener "Specs"

D – L. 5'11", 192 lbs. b: Campbellford, Ont., 3/22/1916.

Season	Club	League	GP	G	A	Pts	AG	AA	APts	PIM	GP	G	A	Pts	PIM
1931-32	Niagara Falls Cataracts	OHA-Jr.	6	6	2	8	....	....	....	6	5	1	*2	3	0
1932-33	Niagara Falls Cataracts	OHA-Jr.	6	6	2	8	....	....	....	6	2	2	*2	4	4
	Niagara Falls Cataracts	M-Cup	3	1	1	2	....	....	....	4	....	....	....	....	....
1933-34	Sudbury Jr. Wolves	NOHA	8	*9	*6	*15	....	....	....	12	2	3	1	4	0
1934-35	Sudbury Jr. Wolves	NOHA	10	*19	5	*24	....	....	....	10	5	*5	*4	*9	4
1935-36	Syracuse Stars	IHL	46	10	14	24	....	....	....	16	3	0	0	0	0
1936-37	Syracuse Stars	IAHL	50	6	19	25	....	....	....	40	9	2	2	4	0
1937-38	Syracuse Stars	IAHL	43	6	20	26	....	....	....	33	8	0	4	4	4
1938-39	Springfield Indians	IAHL	1	0	0	0	....	....	....	0	....	....	....	....	....
	Syracuse Stars	IAHL	19	0	9	9	....	....	....	12	3	0	1	1	0
1939-40	**New York Americans**	**NHL**	**4**	**0**	**0**	**0**	**0**	**0**	**0**	**2**	....	....	....	....	....
	Kansas City Greyhounds	AHA	24	5	7	12	....	....	....	8	....	....	....	....	....
	Springfield Indians	IAHL	19	2	4	6	....	....	....	17	....	....	....	....	....
1940-41	Buffalo Bisons	AHL	53	10	24	34	....	....	....	42	....	....	....	....	....
1941-42	Buffalo Bisons	AHL	55	6	13	19	....	....	....	32	....	....	....	....	....
1942-43	Pittsburgh Hornets	AHL	50	8	12	20	....	....	....	36	2	0	2	2	4
1943-44	Pittsburgh Hornets	AHL	42	3	12	15	....	....	....	4	....	....	....	....	....
	Providence Reds	AHL	1	0	0	0	....	....	....	0	....	....	....	....	....
1944-45	Pittsburgh Hornets	AHL	23	1	4	5	....	....	....	10	....	....	....	....	....
	Toronto Army Shamrocks	TIHL	11	2	6	8	....	....	....	4	2	0	1	1	0
	Newmarket Army	TNDHL	....	....	....	....	....	....	....	....	5	3	5	8	12
	Toronto Army Daggers	TNDHL	....	....	....	....	....	....	....	....	1	2	0	2	4
1945-46	Toronto Staffords	OHA-Sr.	16	4	9	13	....	....	....	20	10	0	2	2	8
1946-47	Owen Sound Mohawks	OHA-Sr.	22	3	10	13	....	....	....	12	9	2	1	3	14
1947-48	Hamilton Pats	OHA-Sr.	13	1	5	6	....	....	....	2	2	0	1	1	2
	NHL Totals		**4**	**0**	**0**	**0**	**0**	**0**	**0**	**2**	....	....	....	....	....

• Brother of Gerry • AHL First All-Star Team (1938)

Traded to **NY Americans** by **Toronto** for cash, October 13, 1939. • Rights returned to **Toronto** when **NY Americans** failed to complete the transaction, July 1, 1940. Traded to **Buffalo** (IAHL) by **Toronto** for cash, October 20, 1940. Traded to **Pittsburgh** (AHL) by **Buffalo** (AHL) for cash, October 13, 1942.

• SHANNON, Gerry

Gerald Edmond "River"

LW – L. 5'11", 170 lbs. b: Campbellford, Ont., 10/25/1910 d: 5/6/1983.

Season	Club	League	GP	G	A	Pts	AG	AA	APts	PIM	GP	G	A	Pts	PIM
1926-27	Niagara Falls Cataracts	OHA-Jr.	....	....	....	....	....	....	....	....	4	*2	0	*2	0
1927-28	Niagara Falls Cataracts	OHA-Jr.	STATISTICS NOT AVAILABLE												
1928-29	Oakville Lions	OHA-Jr.	12	2	0	2	....	....	....	....	....	....	....	....	....
1929-30	Niagara Falls Cataracts	OHA-Sr.	4	7	*4	11	....	....	....	0	2	2	1	3	0
1930-31	Port Colborne Sailors	OHA-Sr.	10	3	3	6	....	....	....	15	5	1	2	3	8
1931-32	Port Colborne Sailors	OHA-Sr.	20	6	3	9	....	....	....	38	4	0	0	0	4
1932-33	Niagara Falls Cataracts	OHA-Sr.	22	16	12	*28	....	....	....	16	5	1	*3	4	10
	Niagara Falls Cataracts	Al-Cup	6	3	0	3	....	....	....	0	....	....	....	....	....
1933-34	**Ottawa Senators**	**NHL**	**48**	**11**	**15**	**26**	**19**	**32**	**51**	**26**	....	....	....	....	....
1934-35	**St. Louis Eagles**	**NHL**	**25**	**2**	**2**	**4**	**3**	**3**	**6**	**11**	....	....	....	....	....
	Boston Bruins	**NHL**	**17**	**1**	**1**	**2**	**2**	**2**	**4**	**4**	**4**	**0**	**0**	**0**	**2**
	Boston Cubs	Can-Am	7	4	2	6	....	....	....	2	....	....	....	....	....
1935-36	**Boston Bruins**	**NHL**	**23**	**0**	**1**	**1**	**0**	**2**	**2**	**6**	....	....	....	....	....
	Boston Cubs	Can-Am	22	11	6	17	....	....	....	24	....	....	....	....	....
1936-37	Providence Reds	IAHL	8	1	3	4	....	....	....	7	....	....	....	....	....
	Montreal Maroons	**NHL**	**31**	**9**	**7**	**16**	**15**	**13**	**28**	**13**	**5**	**0**	**1**	**1**	**0**

			REGULAR SEASON								PLAYOFFS				
Season	Club	League	GP	G	A	Pts	AG	AA	APts	PIM	GP	G	A	Pts	PIM
1937-38	**Montreal Maroons**	**NHL**	**36**	**0**	**3**	**3**	**0**	**5**	**5**	**20**	....	....	....	....	....
	Springfield Indians	IAHL	8	2	1	3	....	....	....	0	....	....	....	....	....
1938-39	Hershey Bears	IAHL	31	9	2	11	....	....	....	4	5	1	1	2	8
1939-40	Hershey Bears	IAHL	52	13	18	31	....	....	....	8	6	1	2	3	2
	NHL Totals		**180**	**23**	**29**	**52**	**39**	**57**	**96**	**80**	**9**	**0**	**1**	**1**	**2**

• Brother of Chuck

Signed as a free agent by **Ottawa**, May 10, 1933. Transferred to **St. Louis** after **Ottawa** franchise relocated, September 22, 1934. Traded to **Boston** by **St. Louis** for Frank Jerwa, January 10, 1935. Traded to **Montreal Maroons** by **Boston** to complete transaction that sent Hooley Smith to Boston (October 26, 1936), December 4, 1936. Traded to **Cleveland** (IAHL) by **Montreal Maroons** for cash, October 6, 1938. Traded to **Hershey** (IAHL) by **Cleveland** (IAHL) for cash, October 11, 1938.

• SHAY, Norm

D/RW – L. 5'9", 158 lbs. b: Huntsville, Ont., 2/3/1899 Deceased.

Season	Club	League	GP	G	A	Pts	AG	AA	APts	PIM	GP	G	A	Pts	PIM
1920-21	Port Colborne Sailors	OIHA	STATISTICS NOT AVAILABLE												
1921-22	Boston Westminsters	USAHA	....	....	....	....	....	....	....	....	4	1	0	1	....
1922-23	New Haven Westminsters	USAHA	....	7	0	7	....	....	....	....	....	....	....	....	....
1923-24	New Haven Bears	USAHA	12	6	0	6	....	....	....	....	....	....	....	....	....
1924-25	**Boston Bruins**	**NHL**	**18**	**1**	**2**	**3**	**2**	**8**	**10**	**14**	....	....	....	....	....
1925-26	**Boston Bruins**	**NHL**	**13**	**1**	**0**	**1**	**2**	**0**	**2**	**2**	....	....	....	....	....
	Toronto St. Pats	**NHL**	**22**	**3**	**1**	**4**	**5**	**6**	**11**	**18**	....	....	....	....	....
1926-27	New Haven Eagles	Can-Am	22	4	2	6	....	....	....	48	4	0	0	0	2
1927-28	Philadelphia Arrows	Can-Am	7	1	0	1	....	....	....	14	....	....	....	....	....
1928-29	Philadelphia Arrows	Can-Am	3	0	0	0	....	....	....	0	....	....	....	....	....
1929-30	New Haven Eagles	Can-Am	40	6	3	9	....	....	....	59	....	....	....	....	....
	NHL Totals		**53**	**5**	**3**	**8**	**9**	**14**	**23**	**34**	....	....	....	....	....

Signed as a free agent by **Boston**, January 9, 1925. Traded to **Toronto** by **Boston** for cash, January 14, 1926. Claimed on waivers by **New Haven** (Can-Am) from **Toronto**, October 18, 1926.

• SHEA, Pat Francis Patrick

D – L. 5'10", 190 lbs. b: Potlatch, ID, 10/29/1912 Deceased.

Season	Club	League	GP	G	A	Pts	AG	AA	APts	PIM	GP	G	A	Pts	PIM
1930-31	White Bear Lake	H.S.	STATISTICS NOT AVAILABLE												
1931-32	**Chicago Black Hawks**	**NHL**	**10**	**1**	**0**	**1**	**2**	**0**	**2**	**0**	....	....	....	....	....
	Pittsburgh Yellowjackets	IHL	3	0	0	0	....	....	....	0	....	....	....	....	....
1932-33	St. Paul-Tulsa	AHA	39	8	8	16	....	....	....	37	4	0	1	1	*10
1933-34	Minneapolis Millers	CHL	40	5	7	12	....	....	....	88	3	*3	0	3	4
1934-35	Minneapolis Millers	CHL	46	6	13	19	....	....	....	38	5	0	0	0	4
1935-36	Kansas City Greyhounds	AHA	41	10	9	19	....	....	....	33	....	....	....	....	....
	Rochester Cardinals	IHL	8	0	2	2	....	....	....	6	....	....	....	....	....
1936-37	Kansas City Greyhounds	AHA	40	2	6	8	....	....	....	26	3	0	0	0	11
1937-38	Kansas City Greyhounds	AHA	46	11	12	23	....	....	....	*73	....	....	....	....	....
1938-39	Kansas City Greyhounds	AHA	48	13	14	27	....	....	....	58	....	....	....	....	....
1939-40	Minneapolis Millers	AHA	48	12	13	25	....	....	....	57	3	2	0	2	5
1940-41	Minneapolis Millers	AHA	45	7	8	15	....	....	....	25	3	0	0	0	0
1941-42	Minneapolis Millers	AHA	46	2	11	13	....	....	....	38	....	....	....	....	....
	NHL Totals		**10**	**1**	**0**	**1**	**2**	**0**	**2**	**0**	....	....	....	....	....

CHL First All-Star Team (1935) • AHA Second All-Star Team (1940)

Signed as a free agent by **Chicago**, October 14, 1931. Traded to **St. Paul** (AHA) by **Chicago** for cash, October 26, 1932.

• SHEPPARD, Frank Francis Joseph Xavier

C/LW – L. 5'6", 157 lbs. b: Montreal, Que., 10/19/1907 Deceased.

Season	Club	League	GP	G	A	Pts	AG	AA	APts	PIM	GP	G	A	Pts	PIM
1925-26	Winnipeg Maroons	CHL	29	3	3	6	....	....	....	16	....	....	....	....	....
1926-27	Detroit Millionaires	MOHL	STATISTICS NOT AVAILABLE												
	Detroit Greyhounds	AHA	2	0	0	0	....	....	....	0	....	....	....	....	....
1927-28	**Detroit Cougars**	**NHL**	**8**	**1**	**1**	**2**	**2**	**6**	**8**	**0**	....	....	....	....	....
	St. Paul Saints	AHA	33	12	4	16	....	....	....	32	....	....	....	....	....
1928-29	St. Paul Saints	AHA	2	0	0	0	....	....	....	0	....	....	....	....	....
	Tulsa Oilers	AHA	40	21	10	31	....	....	....	31	4	2	0	2	2
1929-30	Tulsa Oilers	AHA	43	11	6	17	....	....	....	41	7	1	1	2	2
1930-31	Tulsa Oilers	AHA	48	21	11	32	....	....	....	54	4	1	1	2	8
1931-32	Tulsa Oilers	AHA	41	8	4	12	....	....	....	50	....	....	....	....	....
1932-33	Regina—Vancouver	WCHL	27	19	13	32	....	....	....	23	2	1	0	1	2
1933-34	Edmonton Eskimos	NWHL	7	1	2	3	....	....	....	2	....	....	....	....	....
1934-35	Calgary–Edmonton	NWHL	14	1	4	5	....	....	....	14	....	....	....	....	....
1935-36	Vancouver Lions	NWHL	39	10	7	17	....	....	....	50	7	3	3	6	5
1936-37	Vancouver Lions	PCHL	7	2	1	3	....	....	....	4	....	....	....	....	....
	NHL Totals		**8**	**1**	**1**	**2**	**2**	**6**	**8**	**0**	....	....	....	....	....

• Brother of Johnny

Signed as a free agent by **Detroit**, September 9, 1927. Traded to **St. Paul** (AHA) by **Detroit** for cash, December 19, 1927. Traded to **Tulsa** (AHA) by **St. Paul** (AHA) for cash, November 22, 1928.

• SHEPPARD, Johnny "Jake"

LW – L. 5'7", 165 lbs. b: Montreal, Que., 7/23/1903 d: 1968.

Season	Club	League	GP	G	A	Pts	AG	AA	APts	PIM	GP	G	A	Pts	PIM
1919-20	Selkirk Jr. Fishermen	MJHL	STATISTICS NOT AVAILABLE												
	Selkirk Jr. Fishermen	M-Cup	4	3	3	6	....	....	....	0	....	....	....	....	....
1921-22	Selkirk Fishermen	MHL-Sr.	11	10	2	12	....	....	....	19	....	....	....	....	....
1922-23	Edmonton Eskimos	WCHL	21	1	1	2	....	....	....	6	2	0	0	0	0
	Edmonton Eskimos	St-Cup	1	0	0	0	....	....	....	0	....	....	....	....	....
1923-24	Edmonton Eskimos	WCHL	25	6	2	8	....	....	....	14	....	....	....	....	....
1924-25	Edmonton Eskimos	WCHL	28	14	4	18	....	....	....	26	....	....	....	....	....
1925-26	Edmonton Eskimos	WHL	23	7	7	14	....	....	....	16	2	1	0	1	2
1926-27	**Detroit Cougars**	**NHL**	**43**	**13**	**8**	**21**	**23**	**42**	**65**	**60**	....	....	....	....	....
1927-28	**Detroit Cougars**	**NHL**	**44**	**10**	**10**	**20**	**20**	**57**	**77**	**40**	....	....	....	....	....
1928-29	**New York Americans**	**NHL**	**43**	**5**	**4**	**9**	**14**	**27**	**41**	**38**	**2**	**0**	**0**	**0**	**0**
1929-30	**New York Americans**	**NHL**	**43**	**14**	**15**	**29**	**20**	**36**	**56**	**32**	....	....	....	....	....
1930-31	**New York Americans**	**NHL**	**42**	**5**	**8**	**13**	**10**	**24**	**34**	**16**	....	....	....	....	....
1931-32	**New York Americans**	**NHL**	**5**	**1**	**0**	**1**	**2**	**0**	**2**	**2**	....	....	....	....	....
	Bronx Tigers	Can-Am	33	17	11	28	....	....	....	27	2	1	0	1	2
1932-33	**New York Americans**	**NHL**	**46**	**17**	**9**	**26**	**31**	**19**	**50**	**32**	....	....	....	....	....
1933-34	**Boston Bruins**	**NHL**	**4**	**0**	**0**	**0**	**0**	**0**	**0**	**0**	....	....	....	....	....
♦	**Chicago Black Hawks**	**NHL**	**38**	**3**	**4**	**7**	**5**	**8**	**13**	**4**	**8**	**0**	**0**	**0**	**0**
1934-35	Seattle Seahawks	NWHL	36	6	17	23	....	....	....	38	5	2	2	4	0
1935-36	Seattle Seahawks	NWHL	39	13	10	23	....	....	....	29	4	2	*4	6	2
	NHL Totals		**308**	**68**	**58**	**126**	**125**	**213**	**338**	**224**	**10**	**0**	**0**	**0**	**0**
	Other Major League Totals		97	28	14	42	....	....	....	62	4	1	0	1	2

• Brother of Frank

Signed as a free agent by **Edmonton** (WCHL), November 23, 1922. Traded to **Detroit** by **Edmonton** (PrHL) for cash, October 5, 1926. Traded to **NY Americans** by **Detroit** for cash, October 14, 1928. Traded to **Boston** by **NY Americans** with Lloyd Gross and George Patterson for Bob Gracie and Art Chapman, September 8, 1933. Signed as a free agent by **Chicago** after securing release from **Boston**, November 24, 1933.

• SHERF, John John Harold

LW – L. 5'11", 178 lbs. b: Calumet, MI, 4/8/1913 Deceased.

Season	Club	League	GP	G	A	Pts	AG	AA	APts	PIM	GP	G	A	Pts	PIM
1933-34	University of Michigan	MOHL	STATISTICS NOT AVAILABLE												
1934-35	University of Michigan	MOHL	STATISTICS NOT AVAILABLE												
1935-36	**Detroit Red Wings**	**NHL**	**1**	**0**	**0**	**0**	**0**	**0**	**0**	**0**	....	....	....	....	....
	Detroit Olympics	IHL	39	10	7	17	....	....	....	38	6	1	2	3	7
♦1936-37	**Detroit Red Wings**	**NHL**	**1**	**0**	**0**	**0**	**0**	**0**	**0**	**0**	**5**	**0**	**1**	**1**	**2**
	Pittsburgh Hornets	IAHL	48	7	11	18	....	....	....	36	4	1	0	1	2
1937-38	**Detroit Red Wings**	**NHL**	**6**	**0**	**0**	**0**	**0**	**0**	**0**	**2**	....	....	....	....	....
	Pittsburgh Hornets	IAHL	18	2	8	10	....	....	....	6	....	....	....	....	....
	Philadelphia Ramblers	IAHL	20	5	7	12	....	....	....	2	5	1	1	2	6
1938-39	**Detroit Red Wings**	**NHL**	**3**	**0**	**0**	**0**	**0**	**0**	**0**	**0**	**3**	**0**	**0**	**0**	**0**
	Pittsburgh Hornets	IAHL	54	18	22	40	....	....	....	26	....	....	....	....	....
1939-40	Pittsburgh Hornets	IAHL	55	20	15	35	....	....	....	38	9	1	4	5	2
1940-41	Pittsburgh Hornets	AHL	54	21	14	35	....	....	....	31	6	1	3	4	2
1941-42	Pittsburgh Hornets	AHL	56	19	37	56	....	....	....	10	....	....	....	....	....
1942-43			MILITARY SERVICE												
1943-44	**Detroit Red Wings**	**NHL**	**8**	**0**	**0**	**0**	**0**	**0**	**0**	**6**	....	....	....	....	....
	NHL Totals		**19**	**0**	**0**	**0**	**0**	**0**	**0**	**8**	**8**	**0**	**1**	**1**	**2**

Signed as a free agent by **Detroit**, October 15, 1935. Loaned to **NY Rangers** (Philadelphia-IAHL) by **Detroit** for remainder of 1937-38 season with cash for Ed Wares, January 17, 1938. Traded to **Pittsburgh** (IAHL) by **Detroit** for cash, October 18, 1939.

• SHERO, Fred Frederick Alexander "The Fog"

D – L. 5'10", 175 lbs. b: Winnipeg, Man., 10/23/1925 d: 11/24/1990.

Season	Club	League	GP	G	A	Pts	AG	AA	APts	PIM	GP	G	A	Pts	PIM
1941-42	St. James Canadians	MAHA	STATISTICS NOT AVAILABLE												
1942-43	St. James Monarchs	MJHL	16	3	3	6	....	....	....	2	4	1	1	2	2
1943-44	New York Rovers	EAHL	15	5	7	12	....	....	....	6	....	....	....	....	....
	Brooklyn Crescents	EAHL	29	11	14	25	....	....	....	7	10	2	5	7	8
1944-45	Port Arthur Navy	TBJHL	1	0	0	0	....	....	....	2	....	....	....	....	....
	Winnipeg Rangers	MJHL	2	0	5	5	....	....	....	0	3	1	1	2	8
	Winnipeg Navy	WNDHL	15	5	8	13	....	....	....	16	6	2	2	4	4
1945-46	New York Rovers	EAHL	30	10	15	25	....	....	....	20	12	2	5	7	8
1946-47	New Haven Ramblers	AHL	3	0	0	0	....	....	....	6	....	....	....	....	....
	New York Rovers	EAHL	46	9	22	31	....	....	....	44	9	1	3	4	25
1947-48	St. Paul Saints	USHL	40	9	14	23	....	....	....	20	....	....	....	....	....
	New York Rangers	**NHL**	**19**	**1**	**0**	**1**	**1**	**0**	**1**	**2**	**6**	**0**	**1**	**1**	**6**
1948-49	**New York Rangers**	**NHL**	**59**	**3**	**6**	**9**	**4**	**8**	**12**	**64**	....	....	....	....	....
1949-50	**New York Rangers**	**NHL**	**67**	**2**	**8**	**10**	**2**	**10**	**12**	**71**	**7**	**0**	**1**	**1**	**2**
	New Haven Ramblers	AHL	2	1	0	1	....	....	....	0	....	....	....	....	....
1950-51	Cincinnati Mohawks	AHL	65	5	17	22	....	....	....	94	....	....	....	....	....
1951-52	Cleveland Barons	AHL	15	2	2	4	....	....	....	10	3	0	1	1	2
	Seattle Ironmen	PCHL	43	1	16	17	....	....	....	46	....	....	....	....	....
1952-53	Cleveland Barons	AHL	64	4	14	18	....	....	....	54	9	2	1	3	16
1953-54	Cleveland Barons	AHL	69	21	32	53	....	....	....	95	9	2	3	5	16
1954-55	Cleveland Barons	AHL	37	8	14	22	....	....	....	54	....	....	....	....	....
1955-56	Winnipeg Warriors	WHL	59	8	24	32	....	....	....	99	6	0	2	2	8
	Winnipeg Warriors	Ed-Cup	6	0	2	2	....	....	....	12	....	....	....	....	....
1956-57	Winnipeg Warriors	WHL	66	8	24	32	....	....	....	52	....	....	....	....	....
1957-58	Shawinigan Cataracts	QHL	48	1	5	6	....	....	....	50	4	0	1	1	10
1958-59	Moose Jaw Canucks	SJHL	DID NOT PLAY – COACHING												
	NHL Totals		**145**	**6**	**14**	**20**	**7**	**18**	**25**	**137**	**13**	**0**	**2**	**2**	**8**

EAHL First All-Star Team (1947) • AHL Second All-Star Team (1954) • Won Jack Adams Award (1974) • Won Lester Patrick Trophy (1980)

Traded to **Cleveland** (AHL) by **NY Rangers** with Ed Reigle, Jackie Gordon, Fern Perreault and cash for Hy Buller and Wally Hergesheimer, May 14, 1951.

• SHERRITT, Gordon Gordon Ephraim "Moose"

D – L. 6'1", 195 lbs. b: Oakville, Man., 4/8/1922.

Season	Club	League	GP	G	A	Pts	AG	AA	APts	PIM	GP	G	A	Pts	PIM
1937-38	Portage Terriers	MJHL	10	1	0	1	....	....	....	12	....	....	....	....	....
1938-39	Portage Terriers	MJHL	16	1	0	1	....	....	....	16	2	0	0	0	0
1939-40	Harringay Greyhounds	Ln-Cup	....	2	1	3	....	....	....	....	....	....	....	....	....
	Harringay Greyhounds	Britain	....	6	2	8	....	....	....	....	....	....	....	....	....
	Harringay Greyhounds	Nat-Tmt	....	22	1	23	....	....	....	....	....	....	....	....	....
1940-41	Edmonton Flyers	ASHL	21	0	0	0	....	....	....	29	....	....	....	....	....
1941-42	Moose Jaw Millers	S-SSHL	32	0	8	8	....	....	....	46	9	0	2	2	18
1942-43	Indianapolis Capitols	AHL	53	2	13	15	....	....	....	63	7	0	1	1	8
	New Haven Eagles	AHL	4	0	5	5	....	....	....	4	....	....	....	....	....
1943-44	**Detroit Red Wings**	**NHL**	**8**	**0**	**0**	**0**	**0**	**0**	**0**	**12**	....	....	....	....	....
	Indianapolis Capitols	AHL	43	2	12	14	....	....	....	*165	5	1	2	3	*18
1944-45	Indianapolis Capitols	AHL	51	3	11	14	....	....	....	86	5	0	1	1	2
1945-46	Cleveland Barons	AHL	18	0	9	9	....	....	....	50	....	....	....	....	....
	Minneapolis Millers	USHL	18	1	5	6	....	....	....	24	....	....	....	....	....
1946-47	Minneapolis Millers	USHL	48	2	13	15	....	....	....	96	3	0	0	0	0
1947-48	Minneapolis Millers	USHL	61	1	12	13	....	....	....	76	10	1	3	4	10
1948-49	Minneapolis Millers	USHL	64	3	35	38	....	....	....	63	....	....	....	....	....
	NHL Totals		**8**	**0**	**0**	**0**	**0**	**0**	**0**	**12**	....	....	....	....	....

Signed as a free agent by **Detroit**, October 26, 1942. Loaned to **New Haven** (AHL) by **Detroit** (Indianapolis-AHL) for cash, December 11, 1942. Traded to **Cleveland** (AHL) by **Detroit** for cash, October 4, 1945. Traded to **Buffalo** (AHL) by **Minneapolis** (USHL) for cash, September, 1949. • Sherritt did not report to Buffalo (AHL) and later retired.

• SHEWCHUCK, Jack
John Michael
D – L. 6'1", 190 lbs. b: Brantford, Ont., 6/19/1917 d: 5/15/1989.

Season	Club	League	GP	G	A	Pts	AG	AA	APts	PIM	GP	G	A	Pts	PIM
			REGULAR SEASON								PLAYOFFS				
1935-36	Sudbury Cub Wolves	NOJHA	10	2	0	2	....	....	....	22	....	....	....	....	....
	Copper Cliff Jr. Redmen	NOJHA	4	6	4	10	....	....	....	6	....	....	....	....	....
	Sudbury Wolves	M-Cup	4	1	0	1	....	....	....	*10	....	....	....	....	....
1936-37	Copper Cliff Jr. Redmen	NOJHA	14	1	3	4	....	....	....	22	....	....	....	....	....
	Copper Cliff Jr. Redmen	M-Cup	12	4	3	7	....	....	....	*31	....	....	....	....	....
1937-38	Providence Reds	IAHL	42	4	3	7	....	....	....	69	7	0	0	0	6
1938-39	**Boston Bruins**	**NHL**	**3**	**0**	**0**	**0**	**0**	**0**	**0**	**2**	....	....	....	....	....
	Providence Reds	IAHL	46	8	17	25	....	....	....	72	5	1	1	2	8
1939-40	**Boston Bruins**	**NHL**	**47**	**2**	**4**	**6**	**3**	**6**	**9**	**55**	**6**	**0**	**0**	**0**	**0**
1940-41	**Boston Bruins**	**NHL**	**20**	**2**	**2**	**4**	**3**	**3**	**6**	**8**	....	....	....	....	....
	Hershey Bears	AHL	31	1	5	6	....	....	....	22	9	0	0	0	2
1941-42	**Boston Bruins**	**NHL**	**22**	**2**	**0**	**2**	**3**	**0**	**3**	**14**	**5**	**0**	**1**	**1**	**7**
	Hershey Bears	AHL	34	1	9	10	....	....	....	28	....	....	....	....	....
1942-43	**Boston Bruins**	**NHL**	**48**	**2**	**6**	**8**	**2**	**6**	**8**	**50**	**9**	**0**	**0**	**0**	**12**
1943-44			MILITARY SERVICE												
1944-45	**Boston Bruins**	**NHL**	**47**	**1**	**7**	**8**	**1**	**8**	**9**	**31**	....	....	....	....	....
1945-46	Hershey Bears	AHL	55	3	15	18	....	....	....	89	3	0	1	1	2
1946-47	St. Louis Flyers	AHL	51	1	9	10	....	....	....	34	....	....	....	....	....
1947-48	St. Louis Flyers	AHL	65	1	12	13	....	....	....	58	....	....	....	....	....
1948-49	Kitchener Dutchmen	OHA-Sr.	35	3	11	14	....	....	....	43	12	0	0	0	20
1949-50	Kitchener Dutchmen	OHA-Sr.	41	7	7	14	....	....	....	69	13	1	2	3	26
1950-51	Kitchener Dutchmen	OHA-Sr.	3	0	0	0	....	....	....	8	....	....	....	....	....
1951-52	Brantford Redmen	OHA-Sr.	10	0	1	1	....	....	....	0	....	....	....	....	....
	NHL Totals		**187**	**9**	**19**	**28**	**12**	**23**	**35**	**160**	**20**	**0**	**1**	**1**	**19**

Signed as a free agent by **Boston**, October 26, 1937.

• SHIBICKY, Alex
Alexandre Dimitri
RW – R. 6', 180 lbs. b: Winnipeg, Man., 5/19/1914.

Season	Club	League	GP	G	A	Pts	AG	AA	APts	PIM	GP	G	A	Pts	PIM
1931-32	Winnipeg Columbus Club	MAHA	STATISTICS NOT AVAILABLE												
1932-33	Winnipeg Columbus Club	MJHL	11	3	0	3	....	....	....	18	3	1	0	1	0
1933-34	Selkirk Jr. Fishermen	MJHL	12	11	4	15	....	....	....	19	5	6	3	9	0
	Selkirk Fishermen	MHL-Sr.	1	0	0	0	....	....	....	0	....	....	....	....	....
1934-35	Brooklyn Crescents	EAHL	21	16	9	25	....	....	....	31	8	*8	1	9	4
1935-36	**New York Rangers**	**NHL**	**18**	**4**	**2**	**6**	**8**	**4**	**12**	**6**	....	....	....	....	....
	Philadelphia Ramblers	Can-Am	28	16	6	22	....	....	....	13	....	....	....	....	....
1936-37	**New York Rangers**	**NHL**	**47**	**14**	**8**	**22**	**24**	**15**	**39**	**30**	**9**	**1**	**4**	**5**	**0**
1937-38	**New York Rangers**	**NHL**	**48**	**17**	**18**	**35**	**28**	**29**	**57**	**26**	**3**	**2**	**0**	**2**	**2**
1938-39	**New York Rangers**	**NHL**	**48**	**24**	**9**	**33**	**43**	**14**	**57**	**24**	**7**	**3**	**1**	**4**	**2**
♦1939-40	**New York Rangers**	**NHL**	**44**	**11**	**21**	**32**	**18**	**33**	**51**	**33**	**11**	**2**	**5**	**7**	**4**
1940-41	**New York Rangers**	**NHL**	**41**	**10**	**14**	**24**	**15**	**20**	**35**	**14**	**3**	**1**	**0**	**1**	**2**
1941-42	**New York Rangers**	**NHL**	**45**	**20**	**14**	**34**	**27**	**17**	**44**	**16**	**6**	**3**	**2**	**5**	**2**
1942-43	Ottawa Engineers	OCHL	9	9	13	22	....	....	....	6	....	....	....	....	....
	Ottawa Commandos	QSHL	18	15	7	22	....	....	....	25	11	7	5	12	12
	Ottawa Commandos	Al-Cup	11	11	13	24	....	....	....	2	....	....	....	....	....
1943-44	Ottawa Commandos	QSHL	10	6	6	12	....	....	....	6	....	....	....	....	....
1944-45	Ottawa Engineers	OCHL	4	3	5	8	....	....	....	0	5	8	3	11	4
1945-46	**New York Rangers**	**NHL**	**33**	**10**	**5**	**15**	**12**	**7**	**19**	**12**	....	....	....	....	....
	Providence Reds	AHL	18	7	12	19	....	....	....	4	1	0	0	0	0
1946-47	New Haven Ramblers	AHL	53	20	12	32	....	....	....	28	3	0	2	2	0
1947-48	New Westminster Royals	PCHL	DID NOT PLAY – COACHING												
	NHL Totals		**324**	**110**	**91**	**201**	**175**	**139**	**314**	**161**	**39**	**12**	**12**	**24**	**12**

EAHL First All-Star Team (1935)

Signed as a free agent by **NY Rangers**, October 18, 1934.

• SHIELDS, Al
D – R. 6', 188 lbs. b: Ottawa, Ont., 5/10/1907 d: 9/24/1975.

Season	Club	League	GP	G	A	Pts	AG	AA	APts	PIM	GP	G	A	Pts	PIM
1927-28	Ottawa Montagnards	OCHL	15	6	0	6	....	....	....	....	4	0	0	0	0
	New Haven Eagles	Can-Am	5	0	0	0	....	....	....	0	....	....	....	....	....
	Ottawa Senators	**NHL**	**7**	**0**	**1**	**1**	**0**	**6**	**6**	**2**	**2**	**0**	**0**	**0**	**0**
	Ottawa Montagnards	Al-Cup	2	0	0	0	....	....	....	0	....	....	....	....	....
1928-29	**Ottawa Senators**	**NHL**	**42**	**0**	**1**	**1**	**0**	**7**	**7**	**10**	....	....	....	....	....
	St. Louis Flyers	AHA	6	1	1	2	....	....	....	2	....	....	....	....	....
1929-30	**Ottawa Senators**	**NHL**	**44**	**6**	**3**	**9**	**8**	**7**	**15**	**32**	**2**	**0**	**0**	**0**	**0**
1930-31	**Philadelphia Quakers**	**NHL**	**43**	**7**	**3**	**10**	**14**	**9**	**23**	**98**	....	....	....	....	....
1931-32	**New York Americans**	**NHL**	**48**	**4**	**1**	**5**	**7**	**2**	**9**	**45**	....	....	....	....	....
1932-33	**Ottawa Senators**	**NHL**	**48**	**7**	**4**	**11**	**13**	**8**	**21**	**119**	....	....	....	....	....
1933-34	**Ottawa Senators**	**NHL**	**47**	**4**	**7**	**11**	**7**	**15**	**22**	**44**	....	....	....	....	....
♦1934-35	**Montreal Maroons**	**NHL**	**42**	**4**	**8**	**12**	**7**	**14**	**21**	**45**	**7**	**0**	**1**	**1**	**6**
1935-36	**Montreal Maroons**	**NHL**	**45**	**2**	**7**	**9**	**4**	**13**	**17**	**81**	**3**	**0**	**0**	**0**	**6**
1936-37	**New York Americans**	**NHL**	**27**	**3**	**0**	**3**	**5**	**0**	**5**	**79**	....	....	....	....	....
	Boston Bruins	**NHL**	**18**	**0**	**4**	**4**	**0**	**7**	**7**	**15**	**3**	**0**	**0**	**0**	**2**
1937-38	**Montreal Maroons**	**NHL**	**48**	**5**	**7**	**12**	**8**	**11**	**19**	**67**	....	....	....	....	....
1938-39	New Haven Eagles	IAHL	25	2	2	4	....	....	....	17	....	....	....	....	....
1939-40	New Haven Eagles	IAHL	45	5	9	14	....	....	....	26	3	0	2	2	2
1940-41	New Haven Eagles	AHL	48	9	16	25	....	....	....	59	2	0	0	0	2
	Buffalo Bisons	AHL	3	0	0	0	....	....	....	0	....	....	....	....	....
1941-42	Washington Lions	AHL	51	3	10	13	....	....	....	24	2	0	0	0	0
1942-43	Arnprior RCAF	OVHL	8	4	6	10	....	....	....	16	2	0	1	1	4
1943-44	Arnprior RCAF	OVHL	5	1	3	4	....	....	....	6	....	....	....	....	....
	NHL Totals		**459**	**42**	**46**	**88**	**73**	**99**	**172**	**637**	**17**	**0**	**1**	**1**	**14**

Played in NHL All-Star Game (1934)

Signed as a free agent by **Ottawa**, March 3, 1928. Traded to **Philadelphia** by **Ottawa** with Syd Howe and Wally Kilrea for $35,000, November 6, 1930. Claimed by **NY Americans** from **Ottawa** for 1931-32 season in Dispersal Draft, September 26, 1931. Traded to **Montreal Maroons** by **Ottawa** for Irv Frew and future considerations (Normie Smith and Vern Ayres, October 22, 1934), September 20, 1934. Loaned to **NY Americans** by **Montreal Maroons** for cash, September 15, 1936. Loaned to **Boston** by **NY Americans** with future considerations (the rights to Terry Reardon and Tom Cooper, October 17, 1937) for Joe Jerwa, January 25, 1937. Returned to **Montreal Maroons** July 1,1937. Signed as a free agent by **Montreal** (New Haven-IAHL), October 4, 1939. Loaned to **Buffalo** (AHL) by **Montreal** (New Haven-AHL) for cash, December 1, 1940 and recalled December 10, 1940. Traded to **Washington** (AHL) by **Montreal** for cash, October 9, 1941.

• SHILL, Bill
William Roy
RW – R. 6'1", 175 lbs. b: Toronto, Ont., 3/6/1923.

Season	Club	League	GP	G	A	Pts	AG	AA	APts	PIM	GP	G	A	Pts	PIM
1939-40	Toronto Red Indians	TIHL	19	12	7	19	....	....	....	16	4	0	2	2	4
1940-41	Toronto Young Rangers	OHA-Jr.	12	7	5	12	....	....	....	10	5	3	0	3	4
	Toronto Red Indians	TIHL	19	14	7	21	....	....	....	16	4	0	2	2	4
1941-42	Toronto Young Rangers	OHA-Jr.	16	23	11	34	....	....	....	36	6	8	2	10	8
	Toronto Small Arms	TNDHL	7	9	5	14	....	....	....	8	....	....	....	....	....
	Toronto Red Indians	TIHL	18	15	10	25	....	....	....	14	....	....	....	....	....
1942-43	**Boston Bruins**	**NHL**	**7**	**4**	**1**	**5**	**4**	**1**	**5**	**4**	....	....	....	....	....
	Toronto Tip Tops	TIHL	2	5	0	5	....	....	....	4	3	3	4	7	6
	Toronto Navy	OHA-Sr.	6	6	6	12	....	....	....	11	7	3	3	6	2
1943-44	St. John's Navy	Nfld-Sr.	2	3	4	7	....	....	....	0	....	....	....	....	....
1944-45	Cornwallis Navy	NSNDL	13	7	6	13	....	....	....	2	3	4	1	5	0
1945-46	**Boston Bruins**	**NHL**	**45**	**15**	**12**	**27**	**18**	**17**	**35**	**12**	**7**	**1**	**2**	**3**	**2**
1946-47	**Boston Bruins**	**NHL**	**27**	**2**	**0**	**2**	**2**	**0**	**2**	**2**	....	....	....	....	....
	Hershey Bears	AHL	13	1	3	4	....	....	....	2	....	....	....	....	....
1947-48	Dallas Texans	USHL	66	16	21	37	....	....	....	30	....	....	....	....	....
1948-49	Seattle–Vancouver	PCHL	63	43	26	69	....	....	....	38	3	0	2	2	0
1949-50	Vancouver Canucks	PCHL	69	34	42	76	....	....	....	20	12	7	6	13	2
1950-51	Vancouver Canucks	PCHL	70	36	21	57	....	....	....	33	....	....	....	....	....
1951-52	Vancouver Canucks	PCHL	17	5	3	8	....	....	....	9	....	....	....	....	....
	Ottawa Senators	QMHL	3	0	1	1	....	....	....	0	....	....	....	....	....
	Brantford Redmen	OHA-Sr.	31	25	25	50	....	....	....	16	7	2	5	7	6
1952-53	Brantford Redmen	OHA-Sr.	46	36	27	63	....	....	....	44	5	2	3	5	4
1953-54	Toronto Lyndhursts	TIHL	DID NOT PLAY – COACHING												
	Canada	WEC-A	7	6	3	9	....	....	....	2	....	....	....	....	....
	NHL Totals		**79**	**21**	**13**	**34**	**24**	**18**	**42**	**18**	**7**	**1**	**2**	**3**	**2**

• Brother of Jack • PCHL First All-Star Team (1951) • WEC-A First All-Star Team (1954)

Signed as a free agent by **Toronto**, March 1, 1934. Traded to **Montreal** by **Boston** for cash, February 15, 1947. Traded to **Vancouver** (PCHL) by **Seattle** (PCHL) with Ab Collings for Paul Waldner, Russ Brayshaw and cash, November 8, 1948.

• SHILL, Jack
John Walker
C – L. 5'9", 175 lbs. b: Toronto, Ont., 1/12/1913 d: 10/25/1976.

Season	Club	League	GP	G	A	Pts	AG	AA	APts	PIM	GP	G	A	Pts	PIM
1929-30	Toronto Marlboros	OHA-Jr.	1	0	0	0	....	....	....	0	....	....	....	....	....
1930-31	Toronto Marlboros	OHA-Jr.	8	5	3	8	....	....	....	19	2	1	1	2	6
1931-32	Toronto Marlboros	OHA-Jr.	10	12	4	*16	....	....	....	*31	4	1	0	1	2
	Toronto Marlboros	OHA-Sr.	....	....	....	....	....	....	....	....	1	0	0	0	0
1932-33	Toronto Marlboros	OHA-Jr.	3	3	1	4	....	....	....	6	....	....	....	....	....
	Toronto Marlboros	OHA-Sr.	11	5	1	6	....	....	....	18	2	0	0	0	8
1933-34	**Toronto Maple Leafs**	**NHL**	**7**	**0**	**1**	**1**	**0**	**2**	**2**	**0**	**2**	**0**	**0**	**0**	**0**
	Toronto Marlboros	OHA-Sr.	22	15	10	25	....	....	....	34	2	1	0	1	2
	Toronto British Consols	TMHL	8	3	3	6	....	....	....	36	....	....	....	....	....
1934-35	**Boston Bruins**	**NHL**	**45**	**4**	**4**	**8**	**7**	**7**	**14**	**22**	**2**	**0**	**0**	**0**	**0**
	Boston Cubs	Can-Am	6	2	2	4	....	....	....	4	....	....	....	....	....
1935-36	**Toronto Maple Leafs**	**NHL**	**3**	**0**	**1**	**1**	**0**	**2**	**2**	**0**	**9**	**0**	**3**	**3**	**8**
	Syracuse Stars	IHL	46	20	20	40	....	....	....	82	1	0	0	0	0
1936-37	**Toronto Maple Leafs**	**NHL**	**32**	**4**	**4**	**8**	**7**	**7**	**14**	**26**	**2**	**0**	**0**	**0**	**0**
1937-38	**New York Americans**	**NHL**	**22**	**1**	**3**	**4**	**2**	**5**	**7**	**10**	....	....	....	....	....
♦	**Chicago Black Hawks**	**NHL**	**23**	**4**	**3**	**7**	**6**	**5**	**11**	**8**	**10**	**1**	**3**	**4**	**15**
1938-39	**Chicago Black Hawks**	**NHL**	**28**	**2**	**4**	**6**	**3**	**6**	**9**	**4**	....	....	....	....	....
1939-40	Providence Reds	IAHL	50	14	26	40	....	....	....	51	8	3	7	10	2
1940-41	Providence Reds	AHL	41	16	22	38	....	....	....	20	3	1	0	1	9
1941-42	Providence Reds	AHL	55	18	28	46	....	....	....	17	....	....	....	....	....
1942-43	Toronto Colonels	TIHL	2	0	0	0	....	....	....	0	....	....	....	....	....
	Toronto Dehavillands	TNDHL	9	7	4	11	....	....	....	15	13	11	*18	29	18
1943-44	Toronto Tip Tops	TIHL	21	20	15	35	....	....	....	5	....	....	....	....	....
1944-45			STATISTICS NOT AVAILABLE												
1945-46	Toronto Mahers	TIHL	33	30	33	63	....	....	....	26	10	5	*15	*20	8
1946-47	Toronto Mahers	TIHL	28	9	19	28	....	....	....	6	....	....	....	....	....
1947-48	Toronto Mahers	TIHL	6	4	2	6	....	....	....	2	....	....	....	....	....
	NHL Totals		**160**	**15**	**20**	**35**	**25**	**34**	**59**	**70**	**25**	**1**	**6**	**7**	**23**

• Brother of Bill • IHL First All-Star Team (1936)

Loaned to **Boston** by **Toronto** for 1934-35 season for cash, May 12, 1934. Traded to **NY Americans** by **Toronto** for rights to Wally Stanowski, October 17, 1937. Traded to **Chicago** by **NY Americans** for cash, January 26, 1938. Traded to **Providence** (IAHL) by **Chicago** for cash, October 24, 1939. Rights traded to **Buffalo** (AHL) by **Providence** (AHL) for Jacques Toupin, October 29, 1942. • Suffered career-ending back injury in game vs. Toronto Barkers (TIHL), December 8, 1948.

• SHORE, Eddie
Edward William "The Edmonton Express" **HHOF**
D – R. 5'11", 190 lbs. b: Fort Qu'Appelle, Sask., 11/25/1902 d: 3/16/1985.

Season	Club	League	GP	G	A	Pts	AG	AA	APts	PIM	GP	G	A	Pts	PIM
1923-24	Melville Millionaires	S-SSHL	STATISTICS NOT AVAILABLE												
	Melville Millionaires	Al-Cup	9	*8	6	*14	....	....	....	0	....	....	....	....	....
1924-25	Regina Caps	WCHL	24	6	0	6	....	....	....	75	....	....	....	....	....
1925-26	Edmonton Eskimos	WHL	30	12	2	14	....	....	....	86	2	0	0	0	8
1926-27	**Boston Bruins**	**NHL**	**40**	**12**	**6**	**18**	**21**	**31**	**52**	**130**	**8**	**1**	**1**	**2**	***40**
1927-28	**Boston Bruins**	**NHL**	**43**	**11**	**6**	**17**	**22**	**34**	**56**	***165**	**2**	**0**	**0**	**0**	**8**
♦1928-29	**Boston Bruins**	**NHL**	**39**	**12**	**7**	**19**	**35**	**47**	**82**	**96**	**5**	**1**	**1**	**2**	***28**
1929-30	**Boston Bruins**	**NHL**	**42**	**12**	**19**	**31**	**17**	**45**	**62**	**105**	**6**	**1**	**0**	**1**	***26**
1930-31	**Boston Bruins**	**NHL**	**44**	**15**	**16**	**31**	**30**	**49**	**79**	**105**	**5**	**2**	**1**	**3**	**24**
1931-32	**Boston Bruins**	**NHL**	**45**	**9**	**13**	**22**	**15**	**29**	**44**	**80**	....	....	....	....	....
1932-33	**Boston Bruins**	**NHL**	**48**	**8**	**27**	**35**	**14**	**57**	**71**	**102**	**5**	**0**	**1**	**1**	**14**
1933-34	**Boston Bruins**	**NHL**	**30**	**2**	**10**	**12**	**3**	**21**	**24**	**57**	....	....	....	....	....
1934-35	**Boston Bruins**	**NHL**	**48**	**7**	**26**	**33**	**11**	**46**	**57**	**32**	**4**	**0**	**1**	**1**	**2**
1935-36	**Boston Bruins**	**NHL**	**45**	**3**	**16**	**19**	**6**	**30**	**36**	**61**	**2**	**1**	**1**	**2**	**12**
1936-37	**Boston Bruins**	**NHL**	**20**	**3**	**1**	**4**	**5**	**2**	**7**	**12**	....	....	....	....	....
1937-38	**Boston Bruins**	**NHL**	**48**	**3**	**14**	**17**	**5**	**23**	**28**	**42**	**3**	**0**	**1**	**1**	**6**
♦1938-39	**Boston Bruins**	**NHL**	**44**	**4**	**14**	**18**	**7**	**22**	**29**	**47**	**12**	**0**	**4**	**4**	**19**
1939-40	**Boston Bruins**	**NHL**	**4**	**2**	**1**	**3**	**3**	**2**	**5**	**4**	....	....	....	....	....
	New York Americans	**NHL**	**10**	**2**	**3**	**5**	**3**	**5**	**8**	**9**	**3**	**0**	**2**	**2**	**2**
	Springfield Indians	IAHL	15	1	14	15	....	....	....	18	2	0	1	1	0
1940-41	Springfield Indians	AHL	56	4	13	17	....	....	....	66	3	0	0	0	2

Season	Club	League	GP	G	A	Pts	AG	AA	APts	PIM	GP	G	A	Pts	PIM
			REGULAR SEASON								PLAYOFFS				
1941-42	Springfield Indians	AHL	35	5	12	17				61	5	0	3	3	6
1942-43			DID NOT PLAY												
1943-44	Buffalo Bisons	AHL	1	0	0	0				0					
	NHL Totals		550	105	179	284	197	443	640	1047	55	6	13	19	181
	Other Major League Totals		54	18	2	20				161	2	0	0	0	8

WHL First All-Star Team (1926) • NHL First All-Star Team (1931, 1932, 1933, 1935, 1936, 1938, 1939) • Won Hart Trophy (1933, 1935, 1936, 1938) • NHL Second All-Star Team (1934) • Won Lester Patrick Trophy (1970) • Played in NHL All-Star Game (1934, 1937, 1939)

Signed as a free agent by **Regina** (WCHL), December 2, 1924. Transferred to **Portland** (WHL) after **Regina** (WHL) franchise relocated, September 1, 1925. Traded to **Edmonton** (WHL) by **Portland** (WHL) with Art Gagne for Joe McCormick and Bob Trapp, October 7, 1925. Traded to **Boston** by **Edmonton** (WHL) for cash, August 20, 1926. • Suspended indefinitely by NHL following on-ice assault against Ace Bailey of Toronto, December 12, 1933. Shore assessed a sixteen-game suspension by NHL, January, 1934. • Missed remainder of 1936-37 season after suffering a back injury vs. NY Rangers, January 28, 1937. Traded to **NY Americans** by **Boston** for Ed Wiseman and $5,000, January 25, 1940.

• SHORE, Hamby — Samuel Hamilton

D/LW – L. 6', 175 lbs. b: Ottawa, Ont., 2/12/1886 d: 10/14/1918.

Season	Club	League	GP	G	A	Pts	AG	AA	APts	PIM	GP	G	A	Pts	PIM
♦1904-05	Ottawa Silver Seven	OCHL	3	6	0	6					1	2	0	2	
1905-06	Winnipeg Seniors	MHL-Sr.	STATISTICS NOT AVAILABLE												
1906-07	Pembroke Lumber Kings	OVHL	1	0	0	0				0					
	Ottawa Silver Seven	ECAHA	10	15	0	15									
1907-08	Winnipeg Strathconas	Man-Pro	14	23	0	23									
	Winnipeg Maple Leafs	Man-Pro	1	4	0	4					2	2	0	2	0
1908-09			DID NOT PLAY												
1909-10	Ottawa Senators	CHA	2	2	0	2									
	Ottawa Senators	NHA	12	6	0	6				44	4	3	0	3	6
♦1910-11	Ottawa Senators	NHA	16	7	0	7				53	2	0	0	0	6
1911-12	Ottawa Senators	NHA	18	8	0	8				35					
	NHA All-Stars	X-Games	3	0	0	0				10					
1912-13	Ottawa Senators	NHA	19	15	0	15				66					
1913-14	Ottawa Senators	NHA	13	6	3	9				46					
1914-15	Ottawa Senators	NHA	20	5	1	6				53	5	0	0	0	0
1915-16	Ottawa Senators	NHA	19	2	1	3				83					
1916-17	Ottawa Senators	NHA	19	11	6	17				88	2	0	0	0	6
1917-18	Ottawa Senators	NHL	18	3	8	11	4	34	38	51					
	NHL Totals		18	3	8	11	4	34	38	51					
	Other Major League Totals		148	77	11	88				468	13	3	0	3	18

• Missed entire 1908-09 season due to illness. Signed as a free agent by **Ottawa** (NHA), November, 1909. Rights retained by **Ottawa** after NHA folded, November 26, 1917.

• SIEBERT, Babe — Albert — HHOF

LW/D – L. 5'10", 182 lbs. b: Plattsville, Ont., 1/14/1904 d: 8/25/1939.

Season	Club	League	GP	G	A	Pts	AG	AA	APts	PIM	GP	G	A	Pts	PIM
1920-21	Zurich Intermediates	OIHA	STATISTICS NOT AVAILABLE												
1921-22	Exeter Hawks	OIHA	STATISTICS NOT AVAILABLE												
1922-23	Kitchener Greenshirts	OHA-Jr.									8	6	4	10	
1923-24	Kitchener Twin City	OHA-Sr.	10	9	4	13									
1924-25	Niagara Falls Cataracts	OHA-Sr.	20	9	2	11				26	2	*2	0	*2	3
	Niagara Falls Cataracts	Al-Cup	8	*5	0	5									
1925-26	Montreal Maroons	NHL	35	16	8	24	28	53	81	108	4	1	0	1	4
♦	Montreal Maroons	St-Cup	4	1	2	3				4					
1926-27	Montreal Maroons	NHL	42	5	3	8	9	16	25	116	2	1	0	1	2
1927-28	Montreal Maroons	NHL	39	8	9	17	16	51	67	109	9	2	0	2	26
1928-29	Montreal Maroons	NHL	40	3	5	8	9	33	42	52					
1929-30	Montreal Maroons	NHL	39	14	19	33	20	45	65	94	3	0	0	0	0
1930-31	Montreal Maroons	NHL	43	16	12	28	32	36	68	76	2	0	0	0	6
1931-32	Montreal Maroons	NHL	48	21	18	39	35	40	75	64	4	0	1	1	4
♦1932-33	New York Rangers	NHL	43	9	10	19	16	21	37	38	8	1	0	1	12
1933-34	New York Rangers	NHL	13	0	1	1	0	2	2	18					
	Boston Bruins	NHL	32	5	6	11	9	13	22	31					
1934-35	Boston Bruins	NHL	48	6	18	24	10	31	41	80	4	0	0	0	6
1935-36	Boston Bruins	NHL	45	12	9	21	23	17	40	66	2	0	1	1	0
1936-37	Montreal Canadiens	NHL	44	8	20	28	13	37	50	38	5	1	2	3	2
1937-38	Montreal Canadiens	NHL	37	8	11	19	13	18	31	56	3	1	1	2	0
1938-39	Montreal Canadiens	NHL	44	9	7	16	16	11	27	36	3	0	0	0	0
	NHL Totals		592	140	156	296	249	424	673	982	49	7	5	12	62

NHL First All-Star Team (1936, 1937, 1938) • Won Hart Trophy (1937) • Played in NHL All-Star Game (1937)

Signed as a free agent by **Montreal Maroons**, March 16, 1925. • 1925-26 Montreal Maroons playoff totals includes series against Ottawa and Pittsburgh. Traded to **NY Rangers** by **Montreal Maroons** for cash, July 2, 1932. Traded to **Boston** by **NY Rangers** for Vic Ripley and Roy Burmeister, December 18, 1933. Traded to **Montreal Canadiens** by **Boston** with Roger Jenkins for Leroy Goldsworthy, Sammy McManus and $10,000, September 10, 1936.

• SIMON, Cully — John Cullen

D – L. 5'10", 190 lbs. b: Brockville, Ont., 5/8/1918 d: 8/2/1980.

Season	Club	League	GP	G	A	Pts	AG	AA	APts	PIM	GP	G	A	Pts	PIM
1937-38	Pembroke Lumber Kings	OCJHL	7	5	5	10				14	2	2	2	4	*8
1938-39	Valleyfield Braves	QPHL	3	0	0	0				2					
1939-40	Verdun Bulldogs	QPHL	41	3	7	10				44	2	0	0	0	2
1940-41	Cornwall Flyers	QSHL	36	2	10	12				53	4	0	0	0	9
1941-42	Omaha Knights	AHA	38	0	5	5				49	8	0	1	1	20
	Kitchener Army	TIHL									1	0	0	0	2
1942-43	Indianapolis Capitols	AHL	17	1	4	5				8					
	Washington Lions	AHL	1	0	0	0				0					
♦	Detroit Red Wings	NHL	34	1	1	2	1	1	2	34	9	1	0	1	4
1943-44	Detroit Red Wings	NHL	46	3	7	10	3	6	9	52	5	0	0	0	2
1944-45	Detroit Red Wings	NHL	21	0	2	2	0	2	2	26					
	Chicago Black Hawks	NHL	29	0	1	1	0	1	1	9					
1945-46	Pembroke Lumber Kings	UOVHL	STATISTICS NOT AVAILABLE												
1946-47	Pembroke Lumber Kings	UOVHL	24	4	8	12				18	8	0	4	4	20
1947-48	Pembroke Lumber Kings	UOVHL	14	4	3	7				28	5	1	1	2	9
1948-49	Pembroke Lumber Kings	UOVHL	9	1	2	3				8	9	1	1	2	8
	Pembroke Lumber Kings	Al-Cup	9	4	3	7				*22					
1949-50	Pembroke Lumber Kings	ECSHL	34	5	16	21				47	4	0	1	1	9
1950-51	Pembroke Lumber Kings	ECSHL	31	1	12	13				40	8	0	4	4	10
1951-52	Pembroke Lumber Kings	ECSHL	36	2	16	18				46	9	3	3	6	19
	Pembroke Lumber Kings	Al-Cup	13	0	5	5				*28					
	NHL Totals		130	4	11	15	4	10	14	121	14	1	0	1	6

• Brother of Thain

Signed as a free agent by **Detroit**, October 14, 1941. Loaned to **Washington** (AHL) by **Detroit** (Indianapolis-AHL) as an emergency injury replacement for cash, December 2, 1942. Traded to **Chicago** by **Detroit** with Don Grosso and Byron McDonald for Earl Seibert and future considerations (Fido Purpur, January 4, 1945), January 2, 1945.

• SIMON, Thain — Thain Andrew

D – L. 6', 200 lbs. b: Brockville, Ont., 4/24/1922.

Season	Club	League	GP	G	A	Pts	AG	AA	APts	PIM	GP	G	A	Pts	PIM
1941-42	Brantford Lions	OHA-Jr.	23	15	8	23				21	7	1	6	7	10
1942-43	Ottawa RCAF	OCHL	16	1	4	5				4	8	0	2	2	16
1943-44			MILITARY SERVICE												
1944-45			MILITARY SERVICE												
1945-46	Pembroke Lumber Kings	UOVHL	7	1	1	2				4	3	0	0	0	7
	Pembroke Lumber Kings	Al-Cup	9	0	5	5				10					
	Ottawa RCAF	Al-Cup	9	0	0	0				6					
1946-47	Detroit Red Wings	NHL	3	0	0	0	0	0	0	0					
	Indianapolis Capitols	AHL	46	2	4	6				14					
1947-48	Omaha Knights	USHL	33	1	3	4				21					
	Indianapolis Capitols	AHL	9	1	0	1				4					
1948-49	St. Louis Flyers	AHL	65	4	6	10				14	7	0	1	1	4
1949-50	Pembroke Lumber Kings	ECSHL	34	3	11	14				28	3	0	1	1	4
1950-51	Pembroke Lumber Kings	ECSHL	32	3	8	11				26	8	2	4	6	2
1951-52	Pembroke Lumber Kings	ECSHL	40	4	15	19				24	11	0	1	1	6
	Pembroke Lumber Kings	Al-Cup	13	0	5	5				12					
1952-53	Pembroke Lumber Kings	UOVHL	DID NOT PLAY – COACHING												
	NHL Totals		3	0	0	0	0	0	0	0					

• Brother of Cully

Traded to **Chicago** (St. Louis-AHL) by **Detroit** with Red Almas, Lloyd Doran, Barry Sullivan and Tony Licari for Joe Lund and Hec Highton, September 9, 1948.

• SIMPSON, Cliff — Clifford Vernon

C – R. 5'11", 175 lbs. b: Toronto, Ont., 4/4/1923 d: 5/30/1987.

Season	Club	League	GP	G	A	Pts	AG	AA	APts	PIM	GP	G	A	Pts	PIM
1939-40	Toronto Young Rangers	OHA-Jr.	20	12	5	17				8	2	0	0	0	0
1940-41	Toronto Young Rangers	OHA-Jr.	13	11	8	19				17	5	2	3	5	2
1941-42	Brantford Lions	OHA-Jr.	23	39	26	65				26	7	5	14	19	22
1942-43	Indianapolis Capitols	AHL	18	1	12	13				13					
	Toronto Army Daggers	OHA-Sr.	7	12	4	16				12	4	6	3	9	14
	Toronto Tip Tops	TIHL	1	3	2	5				0	11	*16	14	*25	10
1943-44	Toronto Tip Tops	TIHL	1	1	0	1				0					
	Toronto Army Daggers	OHA-Sr.	1	0	1	1				2					
1944-45	Barriefield Bears	OHA-Sr.	15	*28	8	36				4					
	Toronto Bowsers	TMHL	1	2	0	2				0	1	3	1	4	0
	Toronto Uptown Tires	TMHL	11	20	16	36				32	1	1	3	4	6
1945-46	Indianapolis Capitols	AHL	52	21	15	36				10	5	2	4	6	0
1946-47	Detroit Red Wings	NHL	6	0	1	1	0	1	1	0	1	0	0	0	0
	Indianapolis Capitols	AHL	54	42	36	78				28					
1947-48	Indianapolis Capitols	AHL	68	48	62	110				31					
	Detroit Red Wings	NHL									1	0	0	0	2
1948-49	Indianapolis Capitols	AHL	52	25	21	46				12	2	2	0	2	0
1949-50	St. Louis Flyers	AHL	56	31	52	83				8	2	0	0	0	0
1950-51	St. Louis Flyers	AHL	65	40	34	74				8					
1951-52	St. Louis Flyers	AHL	47	26	26	52				6					
	NHL Totals		6	0	1	1	0	1	1	0	2	0	0	0	2

AHL Second All-Star Team (1947) • AHL First All-Star Team (1948)

Signed as a free agent by **Detroit**, October 19, 1942. Traded to **St. Louis** (AHL) by **Detroit** with Fern Gauthier, Ed Nicholson and future considerations for Stephen Black and Bill Brennan, August 29, 1949.

• SIMPSON, Joe — Harold Joseph Edward "Bullet" — HHOF

D – R. 5'10", 175 lbs. b: Selkirk, Man., 8/13/1893 d: 12/25/1973.

Season	Club	League	GP	G	A	Pts	AG	AA	APts	PIM	GP	G	A	Pts	PIM
1912-13	Winnipeg Strathconas	MHL-Sr.									2	0	0	0	0
1913-14	Selkirk Fishermen	WJrHL	11	12	0	12									
1914-15	Winnipeg Victorias	MHL-Sr.	8	8	2	10				16					
1915-16	Winnipeg 61st Battalion	MHL-Sr.	8	9	2	11				24	2	1	0	1	4
	Winnipeg 61st Battalion	Al-Cup	5	4	2	6				2					
1916-17			MILITARY SERVICE												
1917-18			MILITARY SERVICE												
1918-19	Selkirk Fishermen	MHL-Sr.	4	0	0	0				0	4	3	2	5	2
1919-20	Selkirk Fishermen	MHL-Sr.	10	19	4	23				6					
1920-21	Edmonton Eskimos	Big-4	15	2	6	8				21					
1921-22	Edmonton Eskimos	WCHL	25	21	12	33				15	2	1	0	1	2
1922-23	Edmonton Eskimos	WCHL	30	15	14	29				6	2	0	0	0	0
	Edmonton Eskimos	St-Cup	2	0	1	1				0					
1923-24	Edmonton Eskimos	WCHL	30	10	4	14				6					
1924-25	Edmonton Eskimos	WCHL	28	11	12	23				16					
1925-26	New York Americans	NHL	32	2	2	4	3	13	16	2					
1926-27	New York Americans	NHL	43	4	2	6	7	10	17	39					
1927-28	New York Americans	NHL	24	2	0	2	4	0	4	32					
1928-29	New York Americans	NHL	43	3	2	5	9	13	22	29	2	0	0	0	0
1929-30	New York Americans	NHL	44	8	13	21	11	31	42	41					
1930-31	New York Americans	NHL	42	2	0	2	4	0	4	13					
1931-32	New Haven Eagles	Can-Am	DID NOT PLAY – COACHING												
	NHL Totals		228	21	19	40	38	67	105	156	2	0	0	0	0
	Other Major League Totals		113	57	42	99				43	4	1	0	1	2

Big-4 First All-Star Team (1921) • WCHL First All-Star Team (1922, 1923, 1925) • WCHL Second All-Star Team (1924)

Signed as a free agent by **Edmonton** (WCHL), November 4, 1921. Traded to **NY Americans** by **Edmonton** (WHL) with John Morrison and Roy Rickey for $10,000, September 18, 1925.

• SINCLAIR, Reg
Reginald Alexander
RW/C – R. 6', 165 lbs. b: Lachine, Que., 3/6/1925.

Season	Club	League	GP	G	A	Pts	AG	AA	APts	PIM	GP	G	A	Pts	PIM
			REGULAR SEASON								PLAYOFFS				
1943-44	Notre Dame Monarchs	QAHA	STATISTICS NOT AVAILABLE												
1944-45	McGill University	MCHL	12	12	5	17	....	....	....	14	....	....	....	....	....
1945-46	McGill University	MCHL	9	9	3	12	....	....	....	10	3	3	2	5	4
1946-47	McGill University	MCHL	6	0	1	1	....	....	....	....	....	....	....	....	....
1947-48	McGill University	MCHL	12	11	6	17	....	....	....	28	....	....	....	....	....
1948-49	McGill University	MCHL	12	*21	14	*35	....	....	....	17	....	....	....	....	....
1949-50	Sherbrooke Saints	QSHL	56	15	31	46	....	....	....	94	12	*7	9	*16	24
	Sherbrooke Saints	Al-Cup	10	*8	6	*14	....	....	....	10	....	....	....	....	....
1950-51	**New York Rangers**	**NHL**	**70**	**18**	**21**	**39**	**23**	**26**	**49**	**70**	....	....	....	....	....
1951-52	**New York Rangers**	**NHL**	**69**	**20**	**10**	**30**	**27**	**12**	**39**	**33**	....	....	....	....	....
1952-53	**Detroit Red Wings**	**NHL**	**69**	**11**	**12**	**23**	**14**	**14**	**28**	**36**	**3**	**1**	**0**	**1**	**0**
	NHL Totals		**208**	**49**	**43**	**92**	**64**	**52**	**116**	**139**	**3**	**1**	**0**	**1**	**0**

Played in NHL All-Star Game (1951, 1952)

Signed as a free agent by **NY Rangers**, October 3, 1950. Traded to **Detroit** by **NY Rangers** with John Morrison for Leo Reise Jr., August 18, 1952.

• SINGBUSH, Alex
Alexander Edward
D – L. 5'11", 180 lbs. b: 1/31/1914 d: 3/8/1969.

Season	Club	League	GP	G	A	Pts	AG	AA	APts	PIM	GP	G	A	Pts	PIM
1932-33	Winnipeg K of C	MJHL	6	0	0	0	....	....	....	2	2	0	0	0	0
1933-34	Portage Terriers	MJHL	14	5	7	12	....	....	....	*48	2	0	0	0	4
1934-35	Sudbury Refinery ORC	NBHL	6	1	1	2	....	....	....	18	....	....	....	....	....
1935-36	Sudbury Refinery ORC	NBHL	9	3	4	7	....	....	....	26	....	....	....	....	....
1936-37	Sudbury Refinery ORC	NBHL	17	4	6	10	....	....	....	*64	....	....	....	....	....
1937-38	New Haven Eagles	IAHL	43	4	3	7	....	....	....	44	....	....	....	....	....
1938-39	New Haven Eagles	IAHL	18	0	0	0	....	....	....	25	....	....	....	....	....
	Philadelphia Rams	IAHL	38	2	1	3	....	....	....	52	9	0	1	1	6
1939-40	New Haven Eagles	IAHL	54	12	14	26	....	....	....	76	3	0	0	0	2
1940-41	**Montreal Canadiens**	**NHL**	**32**	**0**	**5**	**5**	**0**	**7**	**7**	**15**	**3**	**0**	**0**	**0**	**4**
	New Haven Eagles	AHL	8	0	2	2	....	....	....	2	....	....	....	....	....
1941-42	Washington Lions	AHL	55	6	7	13	....	....	....	50	2	0	0	0	4
1942-43	Washington Lions	AHL	11	1	5	6	....	....	....	31	....	....	....	....	....
	Providence Reds	AHL	35	6	6	12	....	....	....	32	2	0	0	0	0
1943-44	Sudbury Open Pit	NBHL	8	1	0	1	....	....	....	6	....	....	....	....	....
	Sudbury Open Pit	Al-Cup	16	4	5	9	....	....	....	30	....	....	....	....	....
1944-45	Sudbury Open Pit	NBHL	8	0	4	4	....	....	....	2	7	0	0	0	10
1945-46	Providence Reds	AHL	1	0	0	0	....	....	....	0	....	....	....	....	....
	Hull Volants	QSHL	5	0	0	0	....	....	....	4	....	....	....	....	....
	North Bay CPR	NOHA	STATISTICS NOT AVAILABLE												
	NHL Totals		**32**	**0**	**5**	**5**	**0**	**7**	**7**	**15**	**3**	**0**	**0**	**0**	**4**

Traded to **Washington** (AHL) by **Montreal** for cash, October 9, 1941.

• SKILTON, Raymie
Raymond Nelson
D – R. 5'10", 190 lbs. b: Cambridge, MA, 9/26/1889 d: 7/1/1961.

Season	Club	League	GP	G	A	Pts	AG	AA	APts	PIM	GP	G	A	Pts	PIM
1911-12	Boston AA	BSrHA	STATISTICS NOT AVAILABLE												
1912-13	Sherbrooke Saints	IPAHU	STATISTICS NOT AVAILABLE												
1913-14	Boston Irish Americans	X-Games	7	8	0	8	....	....	....	....	....	....	....	....	....
1914-15	Boston Arenas	X-Games	5	9	0	9	....	....	....	....	6	7	0	7	....
1915-16	Boston A.A. Unicorn	AAHL	7	2	0	2	....	....	....	....	3	2	0	2	....
1916-17	Boston Arenas	AAHL	8	4	0	4	....	....	....	....	....	....	....	....	....
1917-18	**Montreal Wanderers**	**NHL**	**1**	**0**	**0**	**0**	**0**	**0**	**0**	**0**	....	....	....	....	....
	Boston Navy Yard	USNHL	11	11	0	11	....	....	....	....	....	....	....	....	....
1918-19			REINSTATED AS AN AMATEUR												
1919-20			REINSTATED AS AN AMATEUR												
1920-21	Boston Shoe Trades	USAHA	3	2	0	2	....	....	....	....	....	....	....	....	....
1921-22	Boston Shoe Trades	USAHA	STATISTICS NOT AVAILABLE												
1922-23	Boston Vics	USAHA	3	1	0	1	....	....	....	....	....	....	....	....	....
	NHL Totals		**1**	**0**	**0**	**0**	**0**	**0**	**0**	**0**	....	....	....	....	....

AAHL First All-Star Team (1916, 1917) • USNHL First All-Star Team (1918)

Signed as a free agent by **Montreal Wanderers**, December 21, 1917.

• SKINNER, Alf
"Dutch"
RW – R. 5'10", 180 lbs. b: Toronto, Ont., 1/26/1896 d: 4/11/1961.

Season	Club	League	GP	G	A	Pts	AG	AA	APts	PIM	GP	G	A	Pts	PIM
1911-12	Toronto Argonauts	OHA-Jr.	STATISTICS NOT AVAILABLE												
1912-13	Parkdale Canoe Club	OHA-Jr.	STATISTICS NOT AVAILABLE												
1913-14	Toronto Rowing Club	OHA-Sr.	6	4	0	4	....	....	....	0	....	....	....	....	....
1914-15	Toronto Shamrocks	NHA	16	5	2	7	....	....	....	68	....	....	....	....	....
1915-16	Toronto Blueshirts	NHA	23	7	4	11	....	....	....	66	....	....	....	....	....
1916-17	Toronto Blueshirts	NHA	14	6	7	13	....	....	....	52	....	....	....	....	....
	Montreal Wanderers	NHA	6	5	0	5	....	....	....	23	....	....	....	....	....
1917-18	**Toronto Arenas**	**NHL**	**20**	**13**	**5**	**18**	**16**	**21**	**37**	**28**	**2**	**0**	**1**	***1**	**9**
♦	Toronto Arenas	St-Cup	5	8	2	10	....	....	....	0	....	....	....	....	....
1918-19	**Toronto Arenas**	**NHL**	**17**	**12**	**4**	**16**	**22**	**22**	**44**	**26**	....	....	....	....	....
1919-20	Vancouver Millionaires	PCHA	22	15	2	17	....	....	....	28	2	1	0	1	0
1920-21	Vancouver Millionaires	PCHA	24	20	4	24	....	....	....	22	2	3	1	4	6
	Vancouver Millionaires	St-Cup	3	4	0	4	....	....	....	14	....	....	....	....	....
1921-22	Vancouver Millionaires	PCHA	24	11	2	13	....	....	....	21	2	0	0	0	6
	Vancouver Millionaires	St-Cup	7	1	1	2	....	....	....	12	....	....	....	....	....
1922-23	Vancouver Maroons	PCHA	23	13	2	15	....	....	....	28	2	0	0	0	2
	Vancouver Maroons	St-Cup	3	1	1	2	....	....	....	4	....	....	....	....	....
1923-24	Vancouver Maroons	PCHA	29	5	2	7	....	....	....	38	2	0	0	0	2
	Vancouver Maroons	St-Cup	2	0	0	0	....	....	....	0	....	....	....	....	....
1924-25	**Boston Bruins**	**NHL**	**10**	**0**	**0**	**0**	**0**	**0**	**0**	**15**	....	....	....	....	....
	Montreal Maroons	**NHL**	**17**	**1**	**1**	**2**	**2**	**4**	**6**	**16**	....	....	....	....	....
1925-26	**Pittsburgh Pirates**	**NHL**	**7**	**0**	**0**	**0**	**0**	**0**	**0**	**2**	....	....	....	....	....
1926-27	Duluth Hornets	AHA	23	2	3	5	....	....	....	40	....	....	....	....	....
1927-28	Kitchener Millionaires	Can-Pro	18	4	0	4	....	....	....	42	....	....	....	....	....
1928-29	Kitchener Dutchmen	Can-Pro	39	14	5	19	....	....	....	63	3	0	0	0	10
1929-30	Guelph Maple Leafs	Can-Pro	DID NOT PLAY – COACHING												
	NHL Totals		**71**	**26**	**10**	**36**	**40**	**47**	**87**	**87**	**2**	**0**	**1**	**1**	**9**
	Other Major League Totals		181	87	25	112	....	....	....	346	10	4	1	5	16

PCHA Second All-Star Team (1920, 1921, 1922, 1923)

Signed as a free agent by **Toronto Shamrocks**, November, 1914. Signed as a free agent by **Toronto Blueshirts**, November, 1915. Claimed by **Montreal Wanderers** (NHA) in Dispersal Draft of Toronto (NHA) players, February 11, 1917. Signed as a free agent by **Toronto**, November 5, 1917. Traded to **Vancouver** (PCHA) by **Toronto** for cash, December 7, 1919. Traded to **Boston** by **Vancouver** (PCHA) for cash, November 2, 1924. Traded to **Montreal Maroons** by **Boston** for Bernie Morris and Bobby Benson, January 3, 1925. Signed as a free agent by **Pittsburgh**, November 10, 1925. Signed as a free agent by **Duluth** (AHA), November 10, 1926. Signed as a free agent by **Kitchener** (Can-Pro) and named playing coach, October 5, 1927. • 1922 St-Cup totals include series vs. Regina.

• SKOV, Glen
Glen Frederick
C/LW – L. 6'2", 180 lbs. b: Wheatley, Ont., 1/26/1931.

Season	Club	League	GP	G	A	Pts	AG	AA	APts	PIM	GP	G	A	Pts	PIM
1946-47	Windsor Spitfires	OHA-Jr.	2	0	0	0	....	....	....	0	....	....	....	....	....
1947-48	Detroit Hettche	IHL	18	4	4	8	....	....	....	8	8	5	3	8	6
1948-49	Windsor Spitfires	OHA-Jr.	35	16	12	28	....	....	....	42	4	0	0	0	2
	Windsor Ryancretes	IHL	11	2	7	9	....	....	....	4	3	0	6	6	0
1949-50	Windsor Spitfires	OHA-Jr.	47	51	51	102	....	....	....	23	8	7	2	9	0
	Detroit Red Wings	**NHL**	**2**	**0**	**0**	**0**	**0**	**0**	**0**	**0**	....	....	....	....	....
1950-51	**Detroit Red Wings**	**NHL**	**19**	**7**	**6**	**13**	**9**	**7**	**16**	**13**	**6**	**0**	**0**	**0**	**0**
	Omaha Knights	USHL	45	26	33	59	....	....	....	55	....	....	....	....	....
♦1951-52	**Detroit Red Wings**	**NHL**	**70**	**12**	**14**	**26**	**16**	**17**	**33**	**48**	**8**	**1**	**4**	**5**	**16**
1952-53	**Detroit Red Wings**	**NHL**	**70**	**12**	**15**	**27**	**16**	**18**	**34**	**54**	**6**	**1**	**0**	**1**	**2**
♦1953-54	**Detroit Red Wings**	**NHL**	**70**	**17**	**10**	**27**	**23**	**12**	**35**	**95**	**12**	**1**	**2**	**3**	**16**
♦1954-55	**Detroit Red Wings**	**NHL**	**70**	**14**	**16**	**30**	**18**	**18**	**36**	**53**	**11**	**2**	**0**	**2**	**8**
1955-56	**Chicago Black Hawks**	**NHL**	**70**	**7**	**20**	**27**	**9**	**24**	**33**	**26**	....	....	....	....	....
1956-57	**Chicago Black Hawks**	**NHL**	**67**	**14**	**28**	**42**	**18**	**31**	**49**	**69**	....	....	....	....	....
1957-58	**Chicago Black Hawks**	**NHL**	**70**	**17**	**18**	**35**	**21**	**19**	**40**	**35**	....	....	....	....	....
1958-59	**Chicago Black Hawks**	**NHL**	**70**	**3**	**5**	**8**	**4**	**5**	**9**	**4**	**6**	**2**	**1**	**3**	**4**
1959-60	**Chicago Black Hawks**	**NHL**	**69**	**3**	**4**	**7**	**3**	**4**	**7**	**16**	**4**	**0**	**0**	**0**	**2**
1960-61	**Montreal Canadiens**	**NHL**	**3**	**0**	**0**	**0**	**0**	**0**	**0**	**0**	....	....	....	....	....
	Hull-Ottawa Canadians	EPHL	67	16	26	42	....	....	....	24	14	2	6	8	2
	NHL Totals		**650**	**106**	**136**	**242**	**137**	**155**	**292**	**413**	**53**	**7**	**7**	**14**	**48**

Played in NHL All-Star Game (1954)

Traded to **Chicago** by **Detroit** with Tony Leswick, John Wilson and Ben Woit for Dave Creighton, Gord Hollingworth, John McCormack and Jerry Toppazzini, May 27, 1955. Traded to **Montreal** by **Chicago** with Terry Gray, the rights to Danny Lewicki, Bob Bailey and Lorne Ferguson for Ab McDonald, Reggie Fleming, Bob Courcy and Cec Hoekstra, June 7, 1960.

• SLEAVER, John
C – R. 6'1", 180 lbs. b: Copper Cliff, Ont., 8/18/1934.

Season	Club	League	GP	G	A	Pts	AG	AA	APts	PIM	GP	G	A	Pts	PIM
1950-51	Galt Black Hawks	OHA-Jr.	46	9	14	23	....	....	....	23	3	0	1	1	4
1951-52	Galt Black Hawks	OHA-Jr.	54	22	35	57	....	....	....	53	3	0	3	3	4
1952-53	Galt Black Hawks	OHA-Jr.	56	20	36	56	....	....	....	96	10	3	7	10	6
1953-54	Galt Black Hawks	OHA-Jr.	58	23	37	60	....	....	....	67	....	....	....	....	....
	Chicago Black Hawks	**NHL**	**1**	**0**	**0**	**0**	**0**	**0**	**0**	**2**	....	....	....	....	....
1954-55	Galt Black Hawks	OHA-Jr.	49	14	20	34	....	....	....	36	4	3	0	3	4
1955-56	Windsor Bulldogs	OHA-Sr.	48	13	17	30	....	....	....	27	....	....	....	....	....
	Buffalo Bisons	AHL	2	1	1	2	....	....	....	2	....	....	....	....	....
1956-57	**Chicago Black Hawks**	**NHL**	**12**	**1**	**0**	**1**	**1**	**0**	**1**	**4**	....	....	....	....	....
	Buffalo Bisons	AHL	29	7	9	16	....	....	....	2	....	....	....	....	....
	Windsor Bulldogs	OHA-Sr.	21	7	15	22	....	....	....	43	....	....	....	....	....
1957-58	Quebec Aces	QHL	59	17	19	36	....	....	....	56	13	3	5	8	23
	Buffalo Bisons	AHL	1	0	0	0	....	....	....	0	....	....	....	....	....
1958-59	Trois-Rivieres Lions	QHL	61	10	14	24	....	....	....	42	8	0	4	4	12
1959-60	Sudbury Wolves	EPHL	70	20	35	55	....	....	....	42	14	2	6	8	12
1960-61	Sudbury Wolves	EPHL	60	17	34	51	....	....	....	34	....	....	....	....	....
	Vancouver Canucks	WHL	3	0	0	0	....	....	....	2	....	....	....	....	....
1961-62	North Bay Trappers	EPHL	70	24	34	58	....	....	....	59	....	....	....	....	....
1962-63	Springfield Indians	AHL	38	6	16	22	....	....	....	8	....	....	....	....	....
1963-64	Denver Invaders	WHL	69	23	46	69	....	....	....	59	5	1	5	6	4
1964-65	Victoria Maple Leafs	WHL	70	14	49	63	....	....	....	39	12	3	6	9	16
1965-66	Victoria Maple Leafs	WHL	72	19	49	68	....	....	....	47	14	1	6	7	10
1966-67	Providence Reds	AHL	72	13	42	55	....	....	....	24	....	....	....	....	....
1967-68	Providence Reds	AHL	72	15	35	50	....	....	....	42	8	0	3	3	6
1968-69	Providence Reds	AHL	73	7	18	25	....	....	....	29	9	2	5	7	0
1969-70	Columbus Checkers	IHL	72	12	49	61	....	....	....	71	....	....	....	....	....
	NHL Totals		**13**	**1**	**0**	**1**	**1**	**0**	**1**	**6**	....	....	....	....	....

Signed as a free agent by **Detroit** (Sudbury-EPHL), October, 1959. Signed as a free agent by **Montreal** (North Bay-EPHL), October, 1961. NHL rights transferred to **Toronto** after NHL club purchased **Denver** (WHL) franchise and relocated team to Victoria, June, 1964. Claimed by **Providence** (AHL) from **Toronto** in Reverse Draft, June 15, 1966.

• SLOAN, Tod
Tod Aloysius Martin "Slinker"
C/RW – R. 5'10", 152 lbs. b: Pontiac, Que., 11/30/1927.

Season	Club	League	GP	G	A	Pts	AG	AA	APts	PIM	GP	G	A	Pts	PIM
1943-44	Copper Cliff Reps	NOJHA	STATISTICS NOT AVAILABLE												
1944-45	St. Michael's Majors	OHA-Jr.	19	21	16	37	....	....	....	14	9	10	10	20	0
	St. Michael's Majors	M-Cup	14	17	4	21	....	....	....	32	....	....	....	....	....
1945-46	St. Michael's Majors	OHA-Jr.	25	*43	*32	*75	....	....	....	49	11	16	6	22	16
1946-47	Pittsburgh Hornets	AHL	64	15	24	39	....	....	....	31	12	2	2	4	0
1947-48	**Toronto Maple Leafs**	**NHL**	**1**	**0**	**0**	**0**	**0**	**0**	**0**	**0**	....	....	....	....	....
	Pittsburgh Hornets	AHL	61	20	24	44	....	....	....	18	2	1	0	1	2
1948-49	**Toronto Maple Leafs**	**NHL**	**29**	**3**	**4**	**7**	**4**	**6**	**10**	**0**	....	....	....	....	....
	Pittsburgh Hornets	AHL	35	18	16	34	....	....	....	23	....	....	....	....	....
1949-50	Cleveland Barons	AHL	62	37	29	66	....	....	....	28	9	*10	4	*14	7
♦1950-51	**Toronto Maple Leafs**	**NHL**	**70**	**31**	**25**	**56**	**40**	**31**	**71**	**105**	**11**	**4**	**5**	**9**	**18**
1951-52	**Toronto Maple Leafs**	**NHL**	**68**	**25**	**23**	**48**	**34**	**28**	**62**	**89**	**4**	**0**	**0**	**0**	**10**
1952-53	**Toronto Maple Leafs**	**NHL**	**70**	**15**	**10**	**25**	**20**	**12**	**32**	**76**	....	....	....	....	....
1953-54	**Toronto Maple Leafs**	**NHL**	**67**	**11**	**32**	**43**	**15**	**39**	**54**	**100**	**5**	**1**	**1**	**2**	**4**
1954-55	**Toronto Maple Leafs**	**NHL**	**63**	**13**	**15**	**28**	**17**	**17**	**34**	**89**	**4**	**0**	**0**	**0**	**2**
1955-56	**Toronto Maple Leafs**	**NHL**	**70**	**37**	**29**	**66**	**52**	**35**	**87**	**100**	**2**	**0**	**0**	**0**	**5**
1956-57	**Toronto Maple Leafs**	**NHL**	**52**	**14**	**21**	**35**	**18**	**23**	**41**	**33**	....	....	....	....	....
1957-58	**Toronto Maple Leafs**	**NHL**	**59**	**13**	**25**	**38**	**16**	**26**	**42**	**58**	....	....	....	....	....
1958-59	**Chicago Black Hawks**	**NHL**	**59**	**27**	**35**	**62**	**32**	**36**	**68**	**79**	**6**	**3**	**5**	**8**	**0**

			REGULAR SEASON								PLAYOFFS				
Season	Club	League	GP	G	A	Pts	AG	AA	APts	PIM	GP	G	A	Pts	PIM
1959-60	Chicago Black Hawks	NHL	70	20	20	40	23	19	42	54	3	0	0	0	0
♦1960-61	Chicago Black Hawks	NHL	67	11	23	34	13	22	35	48	12	1	1	2	8
1961-62	Galt Terriers	OHA-Sr.	9	11	4	15	....	....	....	8	....	....	....	....	....
	Canada	WEC-A	6	6	4	10	....	....	....	4	....	....	....	....	....
	NHL Totals		**745**	**220**	**262**	**482**	**284**	**294**	**578**	**831**	**47**	**9**	**12**	**21**	**47**

NHL Second All-Star Team (1956) • Played in NHL All-Star Game (1951, 1952, 1956)

Signed as a free agent by **Toronto**, April 30, 1946. Loaned to **Cleveland** (AHL) by **Toronto** for the 1949-50 season with the trade of Ray Ceresino and Harry Taylor for Bob Solinger, September 6, 1949. Traded to **Chicago** by **Toronto** for cash, June 6, 1958.

• SLOBODIAN, Peter Peter Paul

D – L. 6'1", 185 lbs. b: Dauphin, Man., 4/24/1918 d: 11/17/1986.

Season	Club	League	GP	G	A	Pts	AG	AA	APts	PIM	GP	G	A	Pts	PIM
1936-37	Brandon Wheat Kings	MJHL	14	0	0	0	....	....	....	20	4	2	0	2	10
1937-38	Brandon Wheat Kings	MJHL	14	3	6	9	....	....	....	22	5	0	3	3	14
1938-39	Regina Aces	S-SSHL	30	5	5	10	....	....	....	*74	....	....	....	....	....
1939-40	Regina Aces	S-SSHL	18	4	10	14	....	....	....	48	9	3	1	4	26
1940-41	**New York Americans**	**NHL**	**41**	**3**	**2**	**5**	**5**	**3**	**8**	**54**	....	....	....	....	....
1941-42	Lethbridge Maple Leafs	ABCHL	30	4	14	18	....	....	....	*149	9	4	0	4	*32
	Lethbridge Maple Leafs	Al-Cup	4	0	0	0	....	....	....	18	....	....	....	....	....
1942-43	Lethbridge Bombers	ABCHL	20	8	6	14	....	....	....	*83	2	0	1	1	6
1943-44	Calgary Combines	CNDHL	9	2	0	2	....	....	....	15	....	....	....	....	....
1944-45	Calgary RCAF	CNDHL	11	2	2	4	....	....	....	*48	....	....	....	....	....
1945-46	Calgary Stampeders	WCSHL	....	....	....	....	....	....	....	....	5	0	1	1	16
	Calgary Stampeders	Al-Cup	13	0	0	0	....	....	....	14	....	....	....	....	....
1946-47	Hershey Bears	AHL	52	4	15	19	....	....	....	99	11	1	2	3	16
1947-48	Hershey Bears	AHL	54	2	8	10	....	....	....	105	2	0	1	1	6
1948-49	Lethbridge Maple Leafs	WCSHL	35	1	16	17	....	....	....	74	3	0	2	2	4
1949-50	Lethbridge Native Sons	AJHL	DID NOT PLAY – COACHING												
	NHL Totals		**41**	**3**	**2**	**5**	**5**	**3**	**8**	**54**	....	....	....	....	....

S-SSHL First All-Star Team (1940) • ABCHL First All-Star Team (1942, 1943) • CNDHL First All-Star Team (1944)

Signed as a free agent by **NY Americans**, October 11, 1940.

• SLOWINSKI, Eddie Edward Stanley

RW – R. 5'11", 195 lbs. b: Winnipeg, Man., 11/18/1922 d: 8/21/1999.

Season	Club	League	GP	G	A	Pts	AG	AA	APts	PIM	GP	G	A	Pts	PIM
1940-41	Winnipeg Monarchs	WJrHL	....	....	....	....	....	....	....	....	3	2	0	2	2
	Winnipeg St. Paul's	MAHA	STATISTICS NOT AVAILABLE												
1941-42	Winnipeg Monarchs	WJrHL	18	18	20	38	....	....	....	40	1	0	1	1	4
1942-43	Ottawa Army	OCHL	4	6	5	11	....	....	....	2	....	....	....	....	....
	Ottawa Commandos	OCHL	27	17	12	29	....	....	....	8	11	3	1	4	10
	Ottawa Commandos	Al-Cup	4	1	1	2	....	....	....	6	....	....	....	....	....
1943-44	Red Deer Rangers	ASHL	16	6	9	15	....	....	....	0	5	3	0	3	9
1944-45	Calgary Navy	ASHL	16	16	11	27	....	....	....	10	....	....	....	....	....
	Winnipeg Navy	WSrHL	....	....	....	....	....	....	....	....	4	0	0	0	0
1945-46	Ottawa Senators	QSHL	30	26	29	55	....	....	....	10	9	3	6	9	4
1946-47	Ottawa Senators	QSHL	40	*26	18	44	....	....	....	18	10	3	1	4	4
1947-48	**New York Rangers**	**NHL**	**38**	**6**	**5**	**11**	**8**	**6**	**14**	**2**	**4**	**0**	**0**	**0**	**0**
	New Haven Ramblers	AHL	18	9	9	18	....	....	....	2	....	....	....	....	....
1948-49	**New York Rangers**	**NHL**	**20**	**1**	**1**	**2**	**1**	**1**	**2**	**2**	....	....	....	....	....
	New Haven Ramblers	AHL	5	2	2	4	....	....	....	0	....	....	....	....	....
	St. Paul Saints	USHL	16	5	12	17	....	....	....	0	7	5	6	11	2
1949-50	**New York Rangers**	**NHL**	**63**	**14**	**23**	**37**	**18**	**28**	**46**	**12**	**12**	**2**	***6**	**8**	**6**
1950-51	**New York Rangers**	**NHL**	**69**	**14**	**18**	**32**	**18**	**22**	**40**	**15**	....	....	....	....	....
1951-52	**New York Rangers**	**NHL**	**64**	**21**	**22**	**43**	**28**	**27**	**55**	**18**	....	....	....	....	....
1952-53	**New York Rangers**	**NHL**	**37**	**2**	**5**	**7**	**3**	**6**	**9**	**14**	....	....	....	....	....
1953-54	Buffalo Bisons	AHL	67	38	41	79	....	....	....	16	3	1	0	1	2
1954-55	Buffalo Bisons	AHL	59	22	35	57	....	....	....	37	10	5	5	10	4
1955-56	Buffalo Bisons	AHL	63	23	26	49	....	....	....	24	5	1	0	1	2
1956-57	Springfield Indians	AHL	59	18	24	42	....	....	....	10	....	....	....	....	....
1957-58	Providence Reds	AHL	3	0	0	0	....	....	....	2	....	....	....	....	....
	NHL Totals		**291**	**58**	**74**	**132**	**76**	**90**	**166**	**63**	**16**	**2**	**6**	**8**	**6**

WJrHL First All-Star Team (1942) • AHL First All-Star Team (1954)

Signed as a free agent by **NY Rangers**, October 7, 1947. Traded to **Montreal** by **NY Rangers** with Pete Babando for Ivan Irwin, August 8, 1953. Traded to **Buffalo** (AHL) by **Montreal** with Gaye Stewart and Pete Babando for Jackie LeClair and cash, August 17, 1954.

• SLY, Darryl

— see page 1638

• SMART, Alex

LW – L. 5'10", 150 lbs. b: Brandon, Man., 5/29/1918.

Season	Club	League	GP	G	A	Pts	AG	AA	APts	PIM	GP	G	A	Pts	PIM
1935-36	Portage Terriers	MJHL	16	10	4	14	....	....	....	4	6	*9	*6	*15	2
1936-37	Portage Terriers	MJHL	16	15	4	19	....	....	....	10	4	0	2	2	6
1937-38	Toronto Marlboros	OHA-Sr.	12	12	11	23	....	....	....	10	6	4	8	12	9
1938-39	Verdun Maple Leafs	MCHL	22	6	9	15	....	....	....	18	2	1	1	2	4
1939-40	Verdun Maple Leafs	MCHL	21	8	9	17	....	....	....	13	8	7	1	8	9
1940-41	Montreal Sr. Canadiens	MCHL	33	7	15	22	....	....	....	21	....	....	....	....	....
1941-42	Montreal Sr. Canadiens	QSHL	36	15	6	21	....	....	....	40	6	4	4	8	4
1942-43	Montreal Sr. Canadiens	QSHL	23	12	11	23	....	....	....	8	....	....	....	....	....
	Montreal Canadiens	**NHL**	**8**	**5**	**2**	**7**	**5**	**2**	**7**	**0**	....	....	....	....	....
1943-44	Montreal Royals	QSHL	20	9	14	23	....	....	....	9	5	4	3	7	2
	Montreal Vickers	MCHL	10	8	13	21	....	....	....	12	....	....	....	....	....
1944-45	Montreal Royals	QSHL	24	19	19	38	....	....	....	12	7	2	3	5	2
1945-46	Montreal Royals	QSHL	37	16	24	40	....	....	....	33	11	5	5	10	6
1946-47	Ottawa Senators	QSHL	38	14	21	35	....	....	....	26	9	1	6	7	4
1947-48	Ottawa Senators	QSHL	47	28	38	66	....	....	....	11	12	2	8	10	6
	Ottawa Senators	Al-Cup	10	4	7	11	....	....	....	2	....	....	....	....	....
1948-49	Ottawa Senators	QSHL	40	14	27	41	....	....	....	29	11	3	4	5	6
	Ottawa Senators	Al-Cup	14	1	4	5	....	....	....	2	....	....	....	....	....
1949-50	Ottawa Senators	QSHL	28	8	12	20	....	....	....	28	7	0	3	3	12
1950-51	Eastview St. Charles	OVHL	DID NOT PLAY – COACHING												
	NHL Totals		**8**	**5**	**2**	**7**	**5**	**2**	**7**	**0**	....	....	....	....	....

Signed as a free agent by **Montreal**, February 1, 1943.

• SMILLIE, Don Donald William Winter

LW – L. 6', 185 lbs. b: Toronto, Ont., 9/13/1910.

Season	Club	League	GP	G	A	Pts	AG	AA	APts	PIM	GP	G	A	Pts	PIM
1928-29	Toronto Young Rangers	OHA-Jr.	12	10	0	10	....	....	....	....	4	1	0	1	....
	Toronto Young Rangers	M-Cup	5	5	1	6	....	....	....	....	....	....	....	....	....
1929-30	University of Toronto	OHA-Sr.	9	6	0	6	....	....	....	10	3	1	0	1	0
1930-31	University of Toronto	OHA-Sr.	10	1	2	3	....	....	....	16	....	....	....	....	....
1931-32	University of Toronto	OHA-Sr.	12	4	3	7	....	....	....	18	....	....	....	....	....
1932-33	University of Toronto	OHA-Sr.	11	5	3	8	....	....	....	16	....	....	....	....	....
	Toronto City Services	TMHL	1	0	0	0	....	....	....	0	....	....	....	....	....
1933-34	**Boston Bruins**	**NHL**	**12**	**2**	**2**	**4**	**3**	**4**	**7**	**4**	....	....	....	....	....
	Boston Cubs	Can-Am	15	1	2	3	....	....	....	11	....	....	....	....	....
	Toronto Nationals	OHA-Sr.	11	3	1	4	....	....	....	14	....	....	....	....	....
	Toronto Red Indians	TMHL	4	3	1	4	....	....	....	0	....	....	....	....	....
1934-35	Boston Cubs	Can-Am	6	0	1	1	....	....	....	4	....	....	....	....	....
	Syracuse Stars	IHL	9	0	2	2	....	....	....	4	....	....	....	....	....
	Windsor Bulldogs	IHL	25	8	2	10	....	....	....	12	....	....	....	....	....
1935-36	Windsor Bulldogs	IHL	26	6	9	15	....	....	....	19	8	1	0	1	7
	St. Louis Flyers	AHA	3	0	0	0	....	....	....	0	....	....	....	....	....
	London Tecumsehs	IHL	20	3	3	6	....	....	....	14	....	....	....	....	....
	NHL Totals		**12**	**2**	**2**	**4**	**3**	**4**	**7**	**4**	....	....	....	....	....

Loaned to **Syracuse** (IHL) by **Boston** with Walter Harnott for cash, November 27, 1934. Traded to **Windsor** (IHL) by **Boston** for cash, December 27, 1934. Traded to **London** (IHL) by **Windsor** (IHL) for Jim Arnott and cash, January 2, 1936. Traded to **Windsor** (IHL) by **London** (IHL) for cash, February 16, 1936.

• SMITH, Alex "Boots"

D – L. 5'11", 176 lbs. b: Liverpool, England, 4/2/1902 d: 11/29/1963.

Season	Club	League	GP	G	A	Pts	AG	AA	APts	PIM	GP	G	A	Pts	PIM
1922-23	Ottawa Gunners	OCHL	3	1	0	1	....	....	....	0	....	....	....	....	....
1923-24	Ottawa Collegiate	H.S.	STATISTICS NOT AVAILABLE												
1924-25	Ottawa Rideaus	OCHL	11	7	1	8	....	....	....	....	3	0	0	0	0
	Ottawa Senators	**NHL**	**7**	**0**	**0**	**0**	**0**	**0**	**0**	**4**	....	....	....	....	....
1925-26	**Ottawa Senators**	**NHL**	**36**	**0**	**0**	**0**	**0**	**0**	**0**	**36**	**2**	**0**	**0**	**0**	**2**
♦1926-27	**Ottawa Senators**	**NHL**	**42**	**4**	**1**	**5**	**7**	**5**	**12**	**58**	**6**	**0**	**0**	**0**	**8**
1927-28	**Ottawa Senators**	**NHL**	**44**	**9**	**4**	**13**	**18**	**23**	**41**	**90**	**2**	**0**	**0**	**0**	**4**
1928-29	**Ottawa Senators**	**NHL**	**44**	**1**	**7**	**8**	**3**	**47**	**50**	**96**	....	....	....	....	....
1929-30	**Ottawa Senators**	**NHL**	**43**	**2**	**6**	**8**	**3**	**14**	**17**	**91**	**2**	**0**	**0**	**0**	**4**
1930-31	**Ottawa Senators**	**NHL**	**37**	**5**	**6**	**11**	**10**	**18**	**28**	**73**	....	....	....	....	....
1931-32	**Detroit Falcons**	**NHL**	**48**	**6**	**8**	**14**	**10**	**18**	**28**	**47**	**2**	**0**	**0**	**0**	**4**
1932-33	**Ottawa Senators**	**NHL**	**34**	**2**	**0**	**2**	**4**	**0**	**4**	**42**	....	....	....	....	....
	Boston Bruins	**NHL**	**15**	**5**	**4**	**9**	**9**	**8**	**17**	**30**	**5**	**0**	**2**	**2**	**6**
1933-34	**Boston Bruins**	**NHL**	**45**	**4**	**6**	**10**	**7**	**13**	**20**	**32**	....	....	....	....	....
1934-35	**New York Americans**	**NHL**	**48**	**3**	**8**	**11**	**5**	**14**	**19**	**46**	....	....	....	....	....
1935-36	Ottawa RCAF	OCHL	DID NOT PLAY – COACHING												
	NHL Totals		**443**	**41**	**50**	**91**	**76**	**160**	**236**	**645**	**19**	**0**	**2**	**2**	**28**

Signed as a free agent by **Ottawa**, February 10, 1925. Claimed by **Detroit Falcons** from **Ottawa** for 1931-32 season in Dispersal Draft, September 26, 1931. Traded to **Boston** by **Ottawa** for future considerations (Earl Roche), January 25, 1933. Traded to **NY Americans** by **Boston** for cash, October 18, 1934.

• SMITH, Art

D – L. 5'10", 200 lbs. b: Toronto, Ont., 11/29/1906 d: 5/16/1962.

Season	Club	League	GP	G	A	Pts	AG	AA	APts	PIM	GP	G	A	Pts	PIM
1923-24	Oakwood Collegiate	OHA-Jr.	STATISTICS NOT AVAILABLE												
1924-25	Toronto Canoe Club	OHA-Jr.	8	5	4	9	....	....	....	....	2	*2	0	2	....
	Toronto Canoe Club	OHA-Sr.	2	1	0	1	....	....	....	....	....	....	....	....	....
1925-26	Toronto Canoe Club	OHA-Jr.	8	5	1	6	....	....	....	....	....	....	....	....	....
1926-27	Toronto Canoe Club	OHA-Sr.	10	8	3	11	....	....	....	4	....	....	....	....	....
1927-28	**Toronto Maple Leafs**	**NHL**	**15**	**5**	**3**	**8**	**10**	**17**	**27**	**22**	....	....	....	....	....
	Toronto Falcons	Can-Pro	29	11	1	12	....	....	....	46	....	....	....	....	....
1928-29	**Toronto Maple Leafs**	**NHL**	**43**	**5**	**0**	**5**	**14**	**0**	**14**	**91**	**4**	**1**	**1**	**2**	**8**
1929-30	**Toronto Maple Leafs**	**NHL**	**43**	**3**	**3**	**6**	**4**	**7**	**11**	**75**	....	....	....	....	....
1930-31	**Ottawa Senators**	**NHL**	**43**	**2**	**4**	**6**	**4**	**12**	**16**	**61**	....	....	....	....	....
1931-32	Boston Cubs	Can-Am	1	0	0	0	....	....	....	0	....	....	....	....	....
	Chicago Shamrocks	AHA	14	0	1	1	....	....	....	20	....	....	....	....	....
	NHL Totals		**144**	**15**	**10**	**25**	**32**	**36**	**68**	**249**	**4**	**1**	**1**	**2**	**8**

Signed as a free agent by **Toronto**, October 27, 1927. Traded to **Ottawa** by **Toronto** with Eric Pettinger and $35,000 for King Clancy, October 11, 1930.

• SMITH, Brian Brian Stuart

LW – L. 6', 180 lbs. b: Creighton Mine, Ont., 12/6/1937.

Season	Club	League	GP	G	A	Pts	AG	AA	APts	PIM	GP	G	A	Pts	PIM
1954-55	Hamilton Tiger Cubs	OHA-Jr.	33	7	3	10	....	....	....	14	3	0	1	1	7
1955-56	Hamilton Tiger Cubs	OHA-Jr.	41	20	17	37	....	....	....	24	....	....	....	....	....
1956-57	Hamilton Tiger Cubs	OHA-Jr.	52	27	23	50	....	....	....	32	4	1	0	1	0
1957-58	Hamilton Tiger Cubs	OHA-Jr.	50	24	17	41	....	....	....	65	13	6	2	8	29
	Detroit Red Wings	**NHL**	**4**	**0**	**1**	**1**	**0**	**1**	**1**	**0**	....	....	....	....	....
1958-59	Edmonton Flyers	WHL	20	4	4	8	....	....	....	12	....	....	....	....	....
1959-60	**Detroit Red Wings**	**NHL**	**31**	**2**	**5**	**7**	**2**	**5**	**7**	**2**	**5**	**0**	**0**	**0**	**0**
	Hershey Bears	AHL	34	13	9	22	....	....	....	29	....	....	....	....	....
1960-61	**Detroit Red Wings**	**NHL**	**26**	**0**	**2**	**2**	**0**	**2**	**2**	**10**	....	....	....	....	....
	Edmonton Flyers	WHL	11	5	3	8	....	....	....	2	....	....	....	....	....
	Hershey Bears	AHL	31	6	14	20	....	....	....	17	8	1	0	1	2
1961-62	Buffalo Bisons	AHL	58	10	18	28	....	....	....	14	11	1	0	1	0
1962-63	Buffalo Bisons	AHL	65	15	21	36	....	....	....	16	13	2	3	5	9
1963-64	Buffalo Bisons	AHL	58	6	3	9	....	....	....	13	....	....	....	....	....
1964-65	Los Angeles Blades	WHL	69	35	28	63	....	....	....	38	....	....	....	....	....
1965-66	Los Angeles Blades	WHL	71	19	20	39	....	....	....	16	....	....	....	....	....
1966-67	Buffalo Bisons	AHL	60	15	17	32	....	....	....	30	....	....	....	....	....
1967-68	Phoenix Roadrunners	WHL	52	11	12	23	....	....	....	5	....	....	....	....	....
1968-69	Jacksonville Rockets	EHL	21	7	8	15	....	....	....	0	....	....	....	....	....
	NHL Totals		**61**	**2**	**8**	**10**	**2**	**8**	**10**	**12**	**5**	**0**	**0**	**0**	**0**

• Son of Stu • WHL Second All-Star Team (1965)

Traded to **Chicago** by **Detroit** with Gerry Melnyk for Ed Litzenberger, June 12, 1961. Traded to **Phoenix** (WHL) by **Portland** (WHL) with Rick Charron and Tom McVie for Andy Hebenton, September, 1967.

• SMITH, Carl
Carl David "Winky"
RW – L. 5'5", 150 lbs. b: Cache Bay, Ont., 9/18/1917 d: 1/9/1967.

Season	Club	League	GP	G	A	Pts	AG	AA	APts	PIM	GP	G	A	Pts	PIM
			REGULAR SEASON								PLAYOFFS				
1933-34	St. Michael's Buzzers	OHA-B	STATISTICS NOT AVAILABLE												
	St. Michael's Buzzers	M-Cup	13	16	13	29	....	....	....	4	....	....	....	....	....
1934-35	St. Michael's Majors	OHA-Jr.	12	9	2	11	....	....	....	8	3	3	1	4	4
1935-36	Oshawa Chevies	TIHL	13	4	4	8	....	....	....	12	....	....	....	....	....
1936-37	Oshawa G-Men	TIHL	9	3	1	4	....	....	....	12	....	....	....	....	....
1937-38	Oshawa G-Men	OHA-Sr.	16	14	10	24	....	....	....	16	2	0	0	0	4
1938-39	Oshawa G-Men	OHA-Sr.	18	12	18	30	....	....	....	37	7	1	4	5	6
1939-40	Detroit Holzbaugh	MOHL	31	16	16	32	....	....	....	14	12	3	4	7	28
1940-41	St. Louis Flyers	AHA	48	21	19	40	....	....	....	18	9	2	3	5	6
1941-42	St. Louis Flyers	AHA	50	11	17	28	....	....	....	43	2	1	1	2	0
1942-43	New Haven Eagles	AHL	31	4	12	16	....	....	....	13	....	....	....	....	....
	Buffalo Bisons	AHL	22	10	12	22	....	....	....	8	9	2	7	9	0
1943-44	**Detroit Red Wings**	**NHL**	**7**	**1**	**1**	**2**	**1**	**1**	**2**	**2**	....	....	....	....	....
	Indianapolis Capitols	AHL	45	20	26	46	....	....	....	20	5	1	4	5	2
1944-45	St. Louis Flyers	AHL	58	10	26	36	....	....	....	23	....	....	....	....	....
1945-46	Indianapolis Capitols	AHL	5	0	2	2	....	....	....	2	....	....	....	....	....
	Omaha Knights	USHL	54	29	38	67	....	....	....	33	7	3	1	4	7
1946-47	Omaha Knights	USHL	56	15	21	36	....	....	....	20	11	8	7	15	0
1947-48	Omaha Knights	USHL	38	19	34	53	....	....	....	2	3	1	0	1	0
1948-49	Omaha Knights	USHL	61	11	33	44	....	....	....	36	4	0	0	0	0
	NHL Totals		**7**	**1**	**1**	**2**	**1**	**1**	**2**	**2**	....	....	....	....	....

• Brother of Nakina • USHL First All-Star Team (1946)

Signed as a free agent by **Detroit**, September 28, 1939. Loaned to **New Haven** (AHL) by **Detroit** for cash, November, 1942. Loaned transferred to **Buffalo** (AHL) by **Detroit** for cash, January 21, 1943.

• SMITH, Clint
Clint James "Snuffy" HHOF
C – L. 5'8", 165 lbs. b: Assiniboia, Sask., 12/12/1913.

Season	Club	League	GP	G	A	Pts	AG	AA	APts	PIM	GP	G	A	Pts	PIM
1930-31	Saskatoon Wesleys	N-SJHL	1	0	0	0	....	....	....	0	2	0	0	0	0
1931-32	Saskatoon Wesleys	N-SJHL	4	*5	1	*6	....	....	....	0	9	*6	1	*7	2
	Saskatoon Crescents	N-SSHL	18	*19	3	22	....	....	....	0	4	*6	0	*6	4
1932-33	Springfield Indians	Can-Am	12	0	0	0	....	....	....	0	....	....	....	....	....
	Saskatoon Crescents	WCPHL	27	7	6	13	....	....	....	8	....	....	....	....	....
1933-34	Vancouver Lions	NWHL	34	*25	14	39	....	....	....	8	7	5	*4	*9	2
1934-35	Vancouver Lions	NWHL	32	22	*22	*44	....	....	....	2	8	3	*5	8	4
	Vancouver Lions	L-W-S	5	3	2	5	....	....	....	0	....	....	....	....	....
1935-36	Vancouver Lions	NWHL	40	21	*32	*53	....	....	....	10	7	2	*4	6	2
1936-37	**New York Rangers**	**NHL**	**2**	**1**	**0**	**1**	**2**	**0**	**2**	**0**	....	....	....	....	....
	Philadelphia Ramblers	IAHL	49	25	29	54	....	....	....	15	6	*4	3	7	0
1937-38	**New York Rangers**	**NHL**	**48**	**14**	**23**	**37**	**23**	**37**	**60**	**0**	**3**	**2**	**0**	**2**	**0**
1938-39	**New York Rangers**	**NHL**	**48**	**21**	**20**	**41**	**37**	**31**	**68**	**2**	**7**	**1**	**2**	**3**	**0**
♦1939-40	**New York Rangers**	**NHL**	**41**	**8**	**16**	**24**	**13**	**25**	**38**	**2**	**11**	**1**	**3**	**4**	**2**
1940-41	**New York Rangers**	**NHL**	**48**	**14**	**11**	**25**	**22**	**16**	**38**	**0**	**3**	**0**	**0**	**0**	**0**
1941-42	**New York Rangers**	**NHL**	**47**	**10**	**24**	**34**	**13**	**29**	**42**	**4**	**5**	**0**	**0**	**0**	**0**
1942-43	**New York Rangers**	**NHL**	**47**	**12**	**21**	**33**	**12**	**20**	**32**	**4**	....	....	....	....	....
1943-44	**Chicago Black Hawks**	**NHL**	**50**	**23**	***49**	**72**	**21**	**44**	**65**	**4**	**9**	**4**	**8**	**12**	**0**
1944-45	**Chicago Black Hawks**	**NHL**	**50**	**23**	**31**	**54**	**23**	**36**	**59**	**0**	....	....	....	....	....
1945-46	**Chicago Black Hawks**	**NHL**	**50**	**26**	**24**	**50**	**31**	**35**	**66**	**2**	**4**	**2**	**1**	**3**	**0**
1946-47	**Chicago Black Hawks**	**NHL**	**52**	**9**	**17**	**26**	**10**	**20**	**30**	**6**	....	....	....	....	....
1947-48	Tulsa Oilers	USHL	64	38	33	71	....	....	....	10	2	0	1	1	0
1948-49	St. Paul Saints	USHL	2	2	0	2	....	....	....	2	....	....	....	....	....
1949-50	St. Paul Saints	USHL	21	7	15	22	....	....	....	2	2	0	0	0	2
1950-51	St. Paul Saints	USHL	23	3	9	12	....	....	....	0	....	....	....	....	....
1951-52	Cincinnati Mohawks	AHL	2	0	0	0	....	....	....	2	....	....	....	....	....
	NHL Totals		**483**	**161**	**236**	**397**	**207**	**293**	**500**	**24**	**42**	**10**	**14**	**24**	**2**

Won Lady Byng Trophy (1939, 1944) • Won Herman W. Paterson Cup (USHL - MVP) (1948)

Signed as a free agent by **NY Rangers**, October 13, 1932. Signed as a free agent by **Chicago**, September, 1943. • Named coach of Cincinnati (AHL), June 18, 1951.

• SMITH, Dallas
— see page 1641

• SMITH, Des
Desmond Patrick
D – L. 6', 185 lbs. b: Ottawa, Ont., 2/22/1914 Deceased.

Season	Club	League	GP	G	A	Pts	AG	AA	APts	PIM	GP	G	A	Pts	PIM
1930-31	Ottawa St. Malachys	OCHL	13	1	0	1	....	....	....	32	....	....	....	....	....
1931-32	Ottawa Jr. Montagnards	OCJHL	12	2	4	6	....	....	....	18	2	0	0	0	11
	Ottawa Montagnards	OCHL	1	0	0	0	....	....	....	0	....	....	....	....	....
1932-33	Ottawa Jr. Montagnards	OCJHL	15	3	5	8	....	....	....	25	2	0	0	0	4
	Ottawa Montagnards	OCHL	1	0	0	0	....	....	....	0	1	0	0	0	0
1933-34	Ottawa Montagnards	OCHL	21	6	5	11	....	....	....	37	3	0	1	1	4
1934-35	Charlottetown Abegweits	MSHL	19	0	2	2	....	....	....	54	....	....	....	....	....
	Saint John St. Peters	SJCHL	14	6	15	21	....	....	....	*19	12	4	1	5	*21
1935-36	Wembley Lions	Ln-Cup	....	4	1	5	....	....	....	....	....	....	....	....	....
	Wembley Lions	Britain	....	7	4	11	....	....	....	....	....	....	....	....	....
1936-37	Wembley Monarchs	Britain	34	8	8	16	....	....	....	40	....	....	....	....	....
1937-38	**Montreal Maroons**	**NHL**	**40**	**3**	**1**	**4**	**5**	**2**	**7**	**47**	....	....	....	....	....
1938-39	**Montreal Canadiens**	**NHL**	**16**	**3**	**3**	**6**	**5**	**5**	**10**	**8**	**3**	**0**	**0**	**0**	**4**
	New Haven Eagles	IAHL	34	4	9	13	....	....	....	34	....	....	....	....	....
1939-40	**Chicago Black Hawks**	**NHL**	**24**	**1**	**4**	**5**	**2**	**6**	**8**	**27**	....	....	....	....	....
	Boston Bruins	**NHL**	**20**	**2**	**2**	**4**	**3**	**3**	**6**	**23**	**6**	**0**	**0**	**0**	**0**
♦1940-41	**Boston Bruins**	**NHL**	**48**	**6**	**8**	**14**	**9**	**11**	**20**	**61**	**11**	**0**	**2**	**2**	**12**
1941-42	**Boston Bruins**	**NHL**	**48**	**7**	**7**	**14**	**9**	**8**	**17**	**70**	**5**	**1**	**2**	**3**	**2**
1942-43	Ottawa Army	OCHL	DID NOT PLAY – COACHING												
1943-44	Ottawa Army	OCHL	DID NOT PLAY – COACHING												
1944-45	Montreal Army	MCHL	10	6	2	8	....	....	....	10	3	0	1	1	4
1945-46	Shawinigan Cataracts	QSHL	14	0	3	3	....	....	....	12	....	....	....	....	....
1946-47	Springfield Indians	AHL	2	1	0	1	....	....	....	0	....	....	....	....	....
	NHL Totals		**196**	**22**	**25**	**47**	**33**	**35**	**68**	**236**	**25**	**1**	**4**	**5**	**18**

• Brother of Rodger • Father of Brian and Gary

Signed as a free agent by **Montreal Maroons**, October 7, 1937. Traded to **Montreal Canadiens** by **Montreal Maroons** for cash, September 14, 1938. Traded to **Chicago** by **Montreal Canadiens** for cash, May 15, 1939. Traded to **Boston** by **Chicago** for Jack Portland, January 27, 1940.

• SMITH, Don
LW/C – L. 5'7", 160 lbs. b: Cornwall, Ont., Deceased.

Season	Club	League	GP	G	A	Pts	AG	AA	APts	PIM	GP	G	A	Pts	PIM
1904-05	Cornwall Seniors	FAHL	7	4	0	4	....	....	....	....	....	....	....	....	....
1905-06	Cornwall Hockey Club	FAHL	5	2	0	2	....	....	....	....	....	....	....	....	....
1906-07	Cornwall Hockey Club	FAHL	9	*16	0	*16	....	....	....	....	....	....	....	....	....
1907-08	Portage la Prairie	MPHL	14	19	0	19	....	....	....	....	....	....	....	....	....
1908-09	St. Catharines Pros	OPHL	6	10	0	10	....	....	....	12	....	....	....	....	....
	Toronto Torontos	OPHL	8	11	0	11	....	....	....	15	....	....	....	....	....
1909-10	Montreal Shamrocks	CHA	3	7	0	7	....	....	....	3	....	....	....	....	....
	Montreal Shamrocks	NHA	12	14	0	14	....	....	....	*58	....	....	....	....	....
	Montreal ACB	MCHL	7	6	0	6	....	....	....	....	....	....	....	....	....
1910-11	Renfrew Creamery Kings	NHA	16	26	0	26	....	....	....	49	....	....	....	....	....
1911-12	Victoria Aristocrats	PCHA	16	19	0	19	....	....	....	22	....	....	....	....	....
1912-13	Montreal Canadiens	NHA	20	19	0	19	....	....	....	52	....	....	....	....	....
1913-14	Montreal Canadiens	NHA	20	18	10	28	....	....	....	18	2	1	0	1	7
1914-15	Montreal Canadiens	NHA	11	2	5	7	....	....	....	18	....	....	....	....	....
	Montreal Wanderers	NHA	8	4	3	7	....	....	....	21	2	1	0	1	12
1915-16	Montreal Wanderers	NHA	23	14	2	16	....	....	....	56	....	....	....	....	....
1916-17			MILITARY SERVICE												
1917-18			MILITARY SERVICE												
1918-19			MILITARY SERVICE												
1919-20	**Montreal Canadiens**	**NHL**	**12**	**1**	**0**	**1**	**1**	**0**	**1**	**6**	....	....	....	....	....
	NHL Totals		**12**	**1**	**0**	**1**	**1**	**0**	**1**	**6**	....	....	....	....	....
	Other Major League Totals		157	163	20	183	....	....	....	324	4	2	0	2	19

Signed as a free agent by **St. Catharines** (OPHL), December 8, 1908. Signed as a free agent by **Toronto** (OPHL) after **St. Catharines** (OPHL) folded, January 22, 1909. Signed as a free agent by **Trenton** (EOPHL), December 22, 1910. Signed by **Renfrew** (NHA) after jumping contract with **Trenton** (EOPHL), December 27, 1910. Claimed by **Montreal Wanderers** (NHA) in Dispersal Draft of **Renfrew** (NHA) players, November 12, 1911. Signed by **Victoria** (PCHA) after jumping contract with **Montreal Wanderers** (NHA), December, 1911. Signed as a free agent by **Montreal Canadiens** (NHA), November 26, 1912. Traded to **Montreal Wanderers** by **Montreal Canadiens** for cash, February 2, 1915. Rights not retained by **Montreal Wanderers** after NHA folded, November 26, 1917. Signed as a free agent by **Montreal Canadiens**, December 11, 1919.

• SMITH, Don
Donald Arthur
LW/C – L. 5'10", 165 lbs. b: Regina, Sask., 5/4/1929.

Season	Club	League	GP	G	A	Pts	AG	AA	APts	PIM	GP	G	A	Pts	PIM
1946-47	Humboldt Indians	SJHL	22	7	15	22	....	....	....	4	....	....	....	....	....
1946-48	Humboldt Indians	SJHL	17	0	1	1	....	....	....	2	....	....	....	....	....
1947-48	Medicine Hat Tigers	AJHL	12	4	3	7	....	....	....	2	....	....	....	....	....
1948-49	Medicine Hat Tigers	AJHL	17	5	8	13	....	....	....	8	....	....	....	....	....
1949-50	**New York Rangers**	**NHL**	**11**	**1**	**1**	**2**	**1**	**1**	**2**	**0**	**1**	**0**	**0**	**0**	**0**
	New York Rovers	EAHL	32	15	9	24	....	....	....	2	....	....	....	....	....
1950-51	St. Paul Saints	USHL	59	18	19	37	....	....	....	34	4	1	1	2	2
1951-52	Cincinnati Mohawks	AHL	7	2	1	3	....	....	....	0	....	....	....	....	....
	Vancouver Canucks	PCHL	35	11	16	27	....	....	....	47	....	....	....	....	....
1952-53	Vancouver Canucks	WHL	66	13	15	28	....	....	....	29	9	2	2	4	18
	Fort Wayne Komets	IHL	7	1	0	1	....	....	....	2	....	....	....	....	....
1953-54	Vancouver Canucks	WHL	19	1	1	2	....	....	....	6	....	....	....	....	....
	Cincinnati Mohawks	IHL	53	27	31	58	....	....	....	110	11	3	1	4	20
1954-55	Cincinnati Mohawks	IHL	60	14	13	27	....	....	....	99	10	3	5	8	8
1955-56	Cincinnati Mohawks	IHL	59	37	44	81	....	....	....	45	8	*7	3	*10	2
1956-57	Cincinnati Mohawks	IHL	60	32	32	64	....	....	....	64	7	*5	3	8	6
1957-58	Cincinnati Mohawks	IHL	59	28	49	77	....	....	....	76	4	1	1	2	2
1958-59	Indianapolis Chiefs	IHL	30	21	19	40	....	....	....	26	....	....	....	....	....
1959-60	Regina Caps	SSHL	21	18	18	36	....	....	....	38	9	7	7	14	8
1960-61	Regina Caps	SSHL	27	31	35	66	....	....	....	20	5	6	3	9	6
	Moose Jaw Pla-Mors	Al-Cup	3	1	3	4	....	....	....	0	....	....	....	....	....
1961-62	Saskatoon Quakers	SSHL	29	23	33	56	....	....	....	4	8	*9	5	14	2
	Regina Capitals	Al-Cup	13	6	8	14	....	....	....	10	....	....	....	....	....
1962-63	Saskatoon Quakers	SSHL	25	19	30	49	....	....	....	8	11	7	10	17	4
1963-64	Saskatoon Quakers	SSHL	40	20	31	51	....	....	....	51	11	7	10	17	16
	Saskatoon Quakers	Al-Cup	9	6	6	12	....	....	....	6	....	....	....	....	....
1964-65			DID NOT PLAY												
1965-66	Yorkton Terriers	WCSHL	30	7	12	19	....	....	....	25	5	1	1	2	2
1966-67	Yorkton Terriers	WCSHL	13	3	1	4	....	....	....	0	....	....	....	....	....
	Saskatoon Quakers	WCSHL	34	6	13	19	....	....	....	59	4	0	1	1	4
1967-68	Saskatoon Quakers	WCSHL	20	2	10	12	....	....	....	40	4	0	0	0	10
	NHL Totals		**11**	**1**	**1**	**2**	**1**	**1**	**2**	**0**	**1**	**0**	**0**	**0**	**0**

• Brother of Ken • IHL Second All-Star Team (1956) • IHL First All-Star Team (1957, 1958) • SSHL First All-Star Team (1961, 1962)

• SMITH, Floyd
— see page 1643

• SMITH, Glen
Raymond Glen
RW – R. 5'8", 155 lbs. b: Lucky Lake, Sask., 3/19/1931.

Season	Club	League	GP	G	A	Pts	AG	AA	APts	PIM	GP	G	A	Pts	PIM
1948-49	Moose Jaw Canucks	WCJHL	26	7	1	8	....	....	....	10	9	4	2	6	11
	Moose Jaw Canucks	M-Cup	6	0	1	1	....	....	....	11	....	....	....	....	....
1949-50	Moose Jaw Canucks	WCJHL	33	20	22	42	....	....	....	28	4	1	0	1	0
1950-51	**Chicago Black Hawks**	**NHL**	**2**	**0**	**0**	**0**	**0**	**0**	**0**	**0**	....	....	....	....	....
	Milwaukee Seagulls	USHL	64	10	14	24	....	....	....	31	....	....	....	....	....
1951-52	Nelson Maple Leafs	WIHL	42	16	15	31	....	....	....	19	9	4	3	7	2
1952-53	Nelson Maple Leafs	WIHL	39	13	8	21	....	....	....	10	5	2	0	2	2
1953-54	Moose Jaw Millers	SSHL	39	25	37	62	....	....	....	15	7	1	4	5	2
	Moose Jaw Millers	Al-Cup	8	1	0	1	....	....	....	0	....	....	....	....	....
1954-55	Fort Wayne Komets	IHL	24	4	6	10	....	....	....	4	....	....	....	....	....
1955-56			DID NOT PLAY												
1956-57	Gravelbourg Hornets	SIHA	STATISTICS NOT AVAILABLE												
1957-58	Gravelbourg Hornets	SIHA	STATISTICS NOT AVAILABLE												
1958-59	Moose Jaw Canucks	SSHL	10	5	6	11	....	....	....	2	....	....	....	....	....
1959-60	Moose Jaw Canucks	SSHL	25	18	9	27	....	....	....	35	5	4	8	12	2
1960-61	Moose Jaw Canucks	SSHL	32	12	22	34	....	....	....	10	8	4	0	4	2
1961-62	Moose Jaw Canucks	SSHL	30	9	24	33	....	....	....	8	6	2	0	2	2
1962-63	Moose Jaw Canucks	SSHL	31	13	18	31	....	....	....	17	....	....	....	....	....
1963-64	Moose Jaw Canucks	SSHL	31	21	18	39	....	....	....	10	....	....	....	....	....
1964-65	Moose Jaw Canucks	SSHL	9	0	2	2	....	....	....	2	....	....	....	....	....
1965-66	Moose Jaw Canucks	SSHL	5	0	2	2	....	....	....	2	....	....	....	....	....
	NHL Totals		**2**	**0**	**0**	**0**	**0**	**0**	**0**	**0**	....	....	....	....	....

• SMITH, Glenn

Glenn Grafton "George"
D – L. 5'8", 180 lbs. b: Meaford, Ont., 1895 Deceased.

Season	Club	League	GP	G	A	Pts	AG	AA	APts	PIM	GP	G	A	Pts	PIM
			REGULAR SEASON								PLAYOFFS				
1910-11	Woodstock Athletics	OHA-Jr.	6	4	0	4	....	....	....	....	....	....	....	....	....
1911-12	Woodstock Athletics	OHA-Jr.	STATISTICS NOT AVAILABLE												
1912-13	Woodstock Athletics	OHA-Jr.	STATISTICS NOT AVAILABLE												
1913-14	Woodstock Athletics	OHA-Jr.	STATISTICS NOT AVAILABLE												
1914-15			MILITARY SERVICE												
1915-16	Toronto Riversides	OHA-Sr.	7	5	0	5	....	....	....	....	2	1	0	1	0
	Toronto Riversides	Al-Cup	4	4	0	4	....	....	....	0	....	....	....	....	....
1916-17	Toronto Riversides	OHA-Sr.	8	4	0	4	....	....	....	....	2	0	0	0	4
1917-18	Toronto Crescents	OHA-Sr.	9	10	0	10	....	....	....	....	....	....	....	....	....
1918-19	Toronto Dentals	OHA-Sr.	7	8	1	9	....	....	....	....	1	0	0	0	....
1919-20	Toronto Dentals	OHA-Sr.	5	8	3	11	....	....	....	....	....	....	....	....	....
1920-21	Toronto St. Francis	OHA-Sr.	1	0	0	0	....	....	....	0	....	....	....	....	....
1921-22	**Toronto St. Pats**	**NHL**	**9**	**0**	**0**	**0**	**0**	**0**	**0**	**0**	....	....	....	....	....
	NHL Totals		**9**	**0**	**0**	**0**	**0**	**0**	**0**	**0**	....	....	....	....	....

OHA-Sr. First All-Star Team (1918)

Signed as a free agent by **Toronto**, December 16, 1921.

• SMITH, Hooley

Reginald Joseph HHOF
C/RW – R. 5'10", 155 lbs. b: Toronto, Ont., 1/7/1903 d: 8/24/1963.

Season	Club	League	GP	G	A	Pts	AG	AA	APts	PIM	GP	G	A	Pts	PIM
1919-20	Toronto Beaches	OHA-Jr.	STATISTICS NOT AVAILABLE												
1920-21	Parkdale Canoe Club	OHA-Jr.	3	3	0	3	....	....	....	....	....	....	....	....	....
1921-22	Toronto Granites	OHA-Jr.	5	1	0	1	....	....	....	....	1	0	0	0	....
1922-23	Toronto Granites	OHA-Sr.	8	3	3	6	....	....	....	....	2	1	0	1	2
	Toronto Granites	Al-Cup	6	1	*6	7	....	....	....	12	....	....	....	....	....
1923-24	Toronto Granites	X-Games	15	10	*14	24	....	....	....	....	5	17	*16	33	....
	Canada	Olympics	5	17	16	33	....	....	....	4	....	....	....	....	....
1924-25	**Ottawa Senators**	**NHL**	**30**	**10**	**13**	**23**	**17**	**55**	**72**	**81**	....	....	....	....	....
1925-26	**Ottawa Senators**	**NHL**	**28**	**16**	**9**	**25**	**28**	**59**	**87**	**53**	**2**	**0**	**0**	**0**	**14**
♦1926-27	**Ottawa Senators**	**NHL**	**43**	**9**	**6**	**15**	**16**	**31**	**47**	**125**	**6**	**1**	**0**	**1**	**16**
1927-28	**Montreal Maroons**	**NHL**	**34**	**14**	**5**	**19**	**29**	**28**	**57**	**72**	**9**	**2**	**1**	**3**	**23**
1928-29	**Montreal Maroons**	**NHL**	**41**	**10**	**9**	**19**	**29**	**61**	**90**	**120**	....	....	....	....	....
1929-30	**Montreal Maroons**	**NHL**	**42**	**21**	**9**	**30**	**30**	**21**	**51**	**83**	**4**	**1**	**1**	**2**	**14**
1930-31	**Montreal Maroons**	**NHL**	**39**	**12**	**14**	**26**	**24**	**43**	**67**	**68**	....	....	....	....	....
1931-32	**Montreal Maroons**	**NHL**	**43**	**11**	**33**	**44**	**18**	**74**	**92**	**49**	**4**	**2**	**1**	**3**	**2**
1932-33	**Montreal Maroons**	**NHL**	**48**	**20**	**21**	**41**	**37**	**44**	**81**	**66**	**2**	**2**	**0**	**2**	**2**
1933-34	**Montreal Maroons**	**NHL**	**47**	**18**	**19**	**37**	**31**	**40**	**71**	**58**	**4**	**0**	**1**	**1**	**6**
♦1934-35	**Montreal Maroons**	**NHL**	**46**	**5**	**22**	**27**	**8**	**39**	**47**	**41**	**6**	**0**	**0**	**0**	**14**
1935-36	**Montreal Maroons**	**NHL**	**47**	**19**	**19**	**38**	**37**	**36**	**73**	**75**	**3**	**0**	**0**	**0**	**2**
1936-37	**Boston Bruins**	**NHL**	**44**	**8**	**10**	**18**	**13**	**18**	**31**	**36**	**3**	**0**	**0**	**0**	**0**
1937-38	**New York Americans**	**NHL**	**47**	**10**	**10**	**20**	**16**	**16**	**32**	**23**	**6**	**0**	**3**	**3**	**0**
1938-39	**New York Americans**	**NHL**	**48**	**8**	**11**	**19**	**14**	**17**	**31**	**18**	**2**	**0**	**0**	**0**	**14**
1939-40	**New York Americans**	**NHL**	**47**	**7**	**8**	**15**	**12**	**12**	**24**	**41**	**3**	**3**	**1**	**4**	**2**
1940-41	**New York Americans**	**NHL**	**41**	**2**	**7**	**9**	**3**	**10**	**13**	**4**	....	....	....	....	....
	NHL Totals		**715**	**200**	**225**	**425**	**362**	**604**	**966**	**1013**	**54**	**11**	**8**	**19**	**109**

NHL Second All-Star Team (1932) • NHL First All-Star Team (1936) • Played in NHL All-Star Game (1934)

Signed as a free agent by **Ottawa**, October 31, 1924. Traded to **Montreal Maroons** by **Ottawa** for Harry Broadbent and $22,500, October 7, 1927. Traded to **Boston** by **Montreal Maroons** for cash and future considerations (Gerry Shannon, December 4, 1936), October 26, 1936. Traded to **NY Americans** by **Boston** for cash, November, 5, 1937.

• SMITH, Ken

Kenneth Alvin
LW – L. 5'7", 150 lbs. b: Moose Jaw, Sask., 5/8/1924.

Season	Club	League	GP	G	A	Pts	AG	AA	APts	PIM	GP	G	A	Pts	PIM
1940-41	Regina Pats	S-SJHL	15	13	7	20	....	....	....	2	4	*4	1	5	0
1941-42	Oshawa Generals	OHA-Jr.	24	17	14	31	....	....	....	0	23	19	11	30	12
	Oshawa Generals	M-Cup	11	7	5	12	....	....	....	2	....	....	....	....	....
1942-43	Oshawa Generals	OHA-Jr.	22	33	21	54	....	....	....	2	21	*31	23	*54	16
	Oshawa Generals	M-Cup	11	*16	8	*24	....	....	....	4	....	....	....	....	....
1943-44	Oshawa Generals	OHA-Jr.	26	*53	26	*79	....	....	....	2	10	6	7	13	0
	Oshawa Generals	M-Cup	10	14	*13	*27	....	....	....	0	....	....	....	....	....
1944-45	**Boston Bruins**	**NHL**	**49**	**20**	**14**	**34**	**20**	**16**	**36**	**2**	**7**	**3**	**4**	**7**	**0**
1945-46	**Boston Bruins**	**NHL**	**23**	**2**	**6**	**8**	**2**	**9**	**11**	**0**	**8**	**0**	**4**	**4**	**0**
	Hershey Bears	AHL	27	10	13	23	....	....	....	8	....	....	....	....	....
1946-47	**Boston Bruins**	**NHL**	**60**	**14**	**7**	**21**	**16**	**8**	**24**	**4**	**5**	**3**	**0**	**3**	**2**
1947-48	**Boston Bruins**	**NHL**	**60**	**11**	**12**	**23**	**14**	**16**	**30**	**14**	**5**	**2**	**3**	**5**	**0**
1948-49	**Boston Bruins**	**NHL**	**59**	**20**	**20**	**40**	**28**	**28**	**56**	**6**	**5**	**0**	**2**	**2**	**4**
1949-50	**Boston Bruins**	**NHL**	**66**	**10**	**31**	**41**	**13**	**38**	**51**	**12**	....	....	....	....	....
1950-51	**Boston Bruins**	**NHL**	**14**	**1**	**3**	**4**	**1**	**4**	**5**	**11**	....	....	....	....	....
	Pittsburgh Hornets	AHL	55	8	23	31	....	....	....	33	13	2	7	9	4
1951-52	Pittsburgh Hornets	AHL	3	0	0	0	....	....	....	6	....	....	....	....	....
	Pittsburgh Hornets	AHL	56	20	36	56	....	....	....	20	15	3	1	4	8
1952-53	Providence Reds	AHL	25	4	7	11	....	....	....	13	....	....	....	....	....
1953-54	Providence Reds	AHL	23	3	9	12	....	....	....	12	....	....	....	....	....
	Sydney Millionaires	MMHL	6	0	0	0	....	....	....	0	....	....	....	....	....
1954-55	Hershey Bears	AHL	50	12	16	28	....	....	....	16	....	....	....	....	....
1955-56	Hershey Bears	AHL	64	16	35	51	....	....	....	22	....	....	....	....	....
1956-57	Hershey Bears	AHL	17	0	2	2	....	....	....	4	....	....	....	....	....
	NHL Totals		**331**	**78**	**93**	**171**	**94**	**119**	**213**	**49**	**30**	**8**	**13**	**21**	**6**

• Brother of Don A.

Traded to **Toronto** by **Boston** with Fern Flaman, Phil Maloney and Leo Boivin for Bill Ezinicki and Vic Lynn, November 16, 1950. Traded to **Providence** (AHL) by **Toronto** for cash, November 10, 1951.

• SMITH, Nakina

Dalton Joseph
C – L. 5'10", 150 lbs. b: Cache Bay, Ont., 7/26/1915.

Season	Club	League	GP	G	A	Pts	AG	AA	APts	PIM	GP	G	A	Pts	PIM
1931-32	Sudbury Jr. Wolves	NOJHA	3	*5	2	*7	....	....	....	4	....	....	....	....	....
	Sudbury Wolves	NOHA	9	7	2	9	....	....	....	6	....	....	....	....	....
1932-33	Sudbury Jr. Wolves	NOJHA	7	4	1	5	....	....	....	16	2	0	1	1	2
1933-34	Toronto Torontos	OHA-Sr.	5	4	3	7	....	....	....	7	2	0	0	0	0
	Toronto British Consols	TMHL	15	9	10	19	....	....	....	2	5	3	2	5	2
1934-35	Oshawa Chevies	TIHL	15	8	*19	*27	....	....	....	2	....	....	....	....	....
1935-36	Rochester Cardinals	IHL	34	5	8	13	....	....	....	4	....	....	....	....	....
	London Tecumsehs	IHL	12	0	3	3	....	....	....	4	....	....	....	....	....
1936-37	New Haven Eagles	IAHL	46	4	17	21	....	....	....	10	....	....	....	....	....
1937-38	Minneapolis Millers	AHA	48	15	25	40	....	....	....	30	7	1	2	3	0
1938-39	Minneapolis Millers	AHA	48	30	*52	82	....	....	....	10	4	1	0	1	0
1939-40	Minneapolis Millers	AHA	45	32	36	68	....	....	....	12	3	0	2	2	2
1940-41	St. Louis Flyers	AHA	46	6	21	27	....	....	....	8	9	3	5	*8	10
1941-42	St. Louis Flyers	AHA	50	19	39	58	....	....	....	27	3	0	1	1	0
1942-43	New Haven Eagles	AHL	32	11	21	32	....	....	....	14	....	....	....	....	....
	Washington Lions	AHL	23	3	8	11	....	....	....	14	....	....	....	....	....
	Philadelphia Falcons	EAHL	....	....	....	....	....	....	....	....	9	8	9	17	2
1943-44	**Detroit Red Wings**	**NHL**	**10**	**1**	**2**	**3**	**1**	**2**	**3**	**0**	....	....	....	....	....
	Indianapolis Capitols	AHL	34	11	23	34	....	....	....	11	5	0	1	1	0
1944-45	St. Louis Flyers	AHL	60	11	31	42	....	....	....	22	....	....	....	....	....
1945-46	Dallas Texans	USHL	25	5	13	18	....	....	....	2	....	....	....	....	....
	Minneapolis Millers	USHL	27	11	13	24	....	....	....	4	....	....	....	....	....
	Buffalo Bisons	AHL	3	0	3	3	....	....	....	0	....	....	....	....	....
1946-47	St. Paul Saints	USHL	60	14	32	46	....	....	....	6	....	....	....	....	....
1947-48	St. Paul Saints	USHL	53	9	13	22	....	....	....	2	....	....	....	....	....
1948-49	Los Angeles Monarchs	PCHL	63	34	28	62	....	....	....	34	7	0	4	4	10
1949-50	Los Angeles Monarchs	PCHL	1	0	1	1	....	....	....	0	....	....	....	....	....
	NHL Totals		**10**	**1**	**2**	**3**	**1**	**2**	**3**	**0**	....	....	....	....	....

• Brother of Carl • AHA First All-Star Team (1939) • AHA Second All-Star Team (1940) • PCHL Southern Second All-Star Team (1949)

Signed as a free agent by **Rochester** (IHL), October, 1935. Loaned to **London** (IHL) by **Rochester** (IHL) for cash, November 20, 1935 and recalled January 1, 1936. Signed as a free agent by **Detroit**, October 19, 1943.

• SMITH, Rodger

Rodger Dennis
D – L. 6', 175 lbs. b: Ottawa, Ont., 7/26/1896 d: 1/31/1935.

Season	Club	League	GP	G	A	Pts	AG	AA	APts	PIM	GP	G	A	Pts	PIM
1918-19	Hamilton Tigers	OHA	STATISTICS NOT AVAILABLE												
1919-20	Ottawa War Vets	OCHL	7	3	0	3	....	....	....	22	....	....	....	....	....
1920-21	Ottawa Gunners	OCHL	13	6	0	6	....	....	....	....	6	1	3	4	*9
1921-22	Ottawa Gunners	OCHL	10	6	3	9	....	....	....	9	6	6	5	11	15
1922-23	Ottawa Gunners	OCHL	17	*19	*10	*29	....	....	....	21	....	....	....	....	....
1923-24	Pittsburgh Yellow Jackets	USAHA	20	9	2	11	....	....	....	....	12	4	1	5	12
1924-25	Pittsburgh Yellow Jackets	USAHA	34	8	0	8	....	....	....	....	8	1	0	1	....
1925-26	**Pittsburgh Pirates**	**NHL**	**36**	**9**	**1**	**10**	**15**	**6**	**21**	**22**	**2**	**1**	**0**	**1**	**0**
1926-27	**Pittsburgh Pirates**	**NHL**	**36**	**4**	**0**	**4**	**7**	**0**	**7**	**6**	....	....	....	....	....
1927-28	**Pittsburgh Pirates**	**NHL**	**43**	**1**	**0**	**1**	**2**	**0**	**2**	**30**	**2**	**2**	**0**	**2**	**0**
1928-29	**Pittsburgh Pirates**	**NHL**	**44**	**4**	**2**	**6**	**11**	**13**	**24**	**49**	....	....	....	....	....
1929-30	**Pittsburgh Pirates**	**NHL**	**42**	**2**	**1**	**3**	**3**	**2**	**5**	**65**	....	....	....	....	....
1930-31	**Philadelphia Quakers**	**NHL**	**9**	**0**	**0**	**0**	**0**	**0**	**0**	**0**	....	....	....	....	....
	Pittsburgh Yellow Jackets	IHL	26	1	0	1	....	....	....	2	6	0	0	0	4
	Niagara Falls Cataracts	Can-Pro	12	0	0	0	....	....	....	0	....	....	....	....	....
1931-32	Chicoutimi Carabins	ECHL	23	6	10	16	....	....	....	36	3	0	0	0	2
	NHL Totals		**210**	**20**	**4**	**24**	**38**	**21**	**59**	**172**	**4**	**3**	**0**	**3**	**0**

• Brother of Des • OCHL First All-Star Team (1920, 1921, 1922, 1923) • ECHL First All-Star Team (1932)

Signed as a free agent by **Pittsburgh**, September 26, 1925. Transferred to **Philadelphia** after **Pittsburgh** franchise relocated, October 18, 1930. Traded to **Pittsburgh** (IHL) by **Philadelphia**, December 16, 1930.

• SMITH, Sid

Sidney James
LW – L. 5'10", 173 lbs. b: Toronto, Ont., 7/11/1925.

Season	Club	League	GP	G	A	Pts	AG	AA	APts	PIM	GP	G	A	Pts	PIM
1943-44	Toronto DeLasalle	OHA-B	9	1	1	2	....	....	....	2	9	4	2	6	8
1944-45	Oshawa Generals	OHA-Jr.	20	10	7	17	....	....	....	18	3	0	1	1	0
	Porcupine Combines	M-Cup	2	2	0	2	....	....	....	0	....	....	....	....	....
1945-46	Toronto Staffords	OHA-Sr.	13	9	12	21	....	....	....	2	10	6	7	13	0
1946-47	Quebec Aces	QSHL	15	12	5	17	....	....	....	6	....	....	....	....	....
	Toronto Maple Leafs	**NHL**	**14**	**2**	**1**	**3**	**2**	**1**	**3**	**0**	....	....	....	....	....
	Pittsburgh Hornets	AHL	23	12	5	17	....	....	....	4	....	....	....	....	....
♦1947-48	**Toronto Maple Leafs**	**NHL**	**31**	**7**	**10**	**17**	**9**	**13**	**22**	**10**	**2**	**0**	**0**	**0**	**0**
	Pittsburgh Hornets	AHL	30	23	17	40	....	....	....	11	....	....	....	....	....
♦1948-49	**Toronto Maple Leafs**	**NHL**	**1**	**0**	**0**	**0**	**0**	**0**	**0**	**0**	**6**	**5**	**2**	**7**	**0**
	Pittsburgh Hornets	AHL	68	*55	57	*112	....	....	....	4	....	....	....	....	....
1949-50	**Toronto Maple Leafs**	**NHL**	**68**	**22**	**23**	**45**	**28**	**28**	**56**	**6**	**7**	**0**	**3**	**3**	**2**
♦1950-51	**Toronto Maple Leafs**	**NHL**	**70**	**30**	**21**	**51**	**39**	**26**	**65**	**10**	**11**	**7**	**3**	**10**	**0**
1951-52	**Toronto Maple Leafs**	**NHL**	**70**	**27**	**30**	**57**	**36**	**37**	**73**	**6**	**4**	**0**	**0**	**0**	**0**
1952-53	**Toronto Maple Leafs**	**NHL**	**70**	**20**	**19**	**39**	**26**	**23**	**49**	**6**	....	....	....	....	....
1953-54	**Toronto Maple Leafs**	**NHL**	**70**	**22**	**16**	**38**	**30**	**19**	**49**	**28**	**5**	**1**	**1**	**2**	**0**
1954-55	**Toronto Maple Leafs**	**NHL**	**70**	**33**	**21**	**54**	**43**	**24**	**67**	**14**	**4**	**3**	**1**	**4**	**0**
1955-56	**Toronto Maple Leafs**	**NHL**	**55**	**4**	**17**	**21**	**5**	**20**	**25**	**8**	**5**	**1**	**0**	**1**	**0**
1956-57	**Toronto Maple Leafs**	**NHL**	**70**	**17**	**24**	**41**	**22**	**26**	**48**	**4**	....	....	....	....	....
1957-58	**Toronto Maple Leafs**	**NHL**	**12**	**2**	**1**	**3**	**2**	**1**	**3**	**2**	....	....	....	....	....
	Whitby Dunlops	OHA-Sr.	28	24	19	43	....	....	....	4	....	....	....	....	....
	Canada	WEC-A	7	9	5	14	....	....	....	2	....	....	....	....	....
1958-59	Whitby Dunlops	OHA-Sr.	51	*35	35	70	....	....	....	20	10	*7	4	11	2
	Whitby Dunlops	Al-Cup	12	*12	8	*20	....	....	....	8	....	....	....	....	....
	NHL Totals		**601**	**186**	**183**	**369**	**242**	**218**	**460**	**94**	**44**	**17**	**10**	**27**	**2**

AHL First All-Star Team (1949) • Won John B. Sollenberger Trophy (Top Scorer - AHL) (1949) • NHL Second All-Star Team (1951, 1952) • Won Lady Byng Trophy (1952, 1955) • NHL First All-Star Team (1955) • Played in NHL All-Star Game (1949, 1950, 1951, 1952, 1953, 1954, 1955)

Signed as a free agent by **Quebec** (QSHL), October 15, 1946. Signed as a free agent by **Toronto**, December 8, 1946.

• SMITH, Stan

Stanley George
C – L. 5'10", 165 lbs. b: Coal Creek, B.C., 8/13/1917.

Season	Club	League	GP	G	A	Pts	AG	AA	APts	PIM	GP	G	A	Pts	PIM
1936-37	Trail Smoke Eaters	WKJHL	STATISTICS NOT AVAILABLE												
1937-38	Rossland Miners	WKHL	23	19	17	36	....	....	....	14	....	....	....	....	....
1938-39	New York Rovers	EAHL	53	23	27	50	....	....	....	12	....	....	....	....	....
♦1939-40	**New York Rangers**	**NHL**	**1**	**0**	**0**	**0**	**0**	**0**	**0**	**0**	**1**	**0**	**0**	**0**	**0**
	Philadelphia Rockets	IAHL	53	11	22	33	....	....	....	9	....	....	....	....	....
1940-41	**New York Rangers**	**NHL**	**8**	**2**	**1**	**3**	**3**	**1**	**4**	**0**	....	....	....	....	....
	Philadelphia Rockets	AHL	49	18	22	40	....	....	....	2	....	....	....	....	....
1941-42	Cleveland Barons	AHL	21	9	6	15	....	....	....	0	5	1	2	3	0
1942-43	Calgary Army	ASHL	8	1	3	4	....	....	....	0	2	0	3	3	0
1943-44	Nanaimo Clippers	WKHL					....	....	....	....	2	0	2	2	0
1944-45			MILITARY SERVICE												
1945-46			MILITARY SERVICE												
1946-47	Minneapolis Millers	USHL	42	15	27	42	....	....	....	0	2	0	0	0	0
1947-48	Minneapolis Millers	USHL	51	17	25	42	....	....	....	2	10	3	5	8	0

			REGULAR SEASON								PLAYOFFS				
Season	Club	League	GP	G	A	Pts	AG	AA	APts	PIM	GP	G	A	Pts	PIM
1948-49	Minneapolis Millers	USHL	64	18	32	50	....	....	....	0	....	....	....	....	....
1949-50	Minneapolis Millers	USHL	32	1	10	11	....	....	....	2	....	....	....	....	....
	San Francisco Shamrocks	PCHL	31	2	14	16	....	....	....	2	4	0	0	0	0
	NHL Totals		**9**	**2**	**1**	**3**	**3**	**1**	**4**	**0**	**1**	**0**	**0**	**0**	**0**

Signed as a free agent by **NY Rangers**, October 23, 1939. Traded to **Cleveland** (AHL) by **NY Rangers** for cash, September 9, 1941.

• SMITH, Stu Stuart Ernest

LW – L. 5'8", 165 lbs. b: Basswood, Man., 9/25/1918.

Season	Club	League	GP	G	A	Pts	AG	AA	APts	PIM	GP	G	A	Pts	PIM
1932-33	Kenora Thistles	NOJHA	10	*12	1	*13	....	....	....	4	7	3	1	4	6
1933-34	Kenora Thistles	NOJHA	16	*22	6	*28	....	....	....	10	9	*11	1	*12	12
	Kenora Thistles	M-Cup	4	1	1	2	....	....	....	4	....	....	....	....	....
1934-35	Kenora Canadians	TBSHL	11	9	4	13	....	....	....	5	....	....	....	....	....
1935-36	Kenora Thistles	MTBHL	12	*11	2	13	....	....	....	5	....	....	....	....	....
1936-37	Sudbury Creighton Mines	NBHL	14	*13	5	18	....	....	....	20	2	*2	0	2	0
1937-38	Sudbury Creighton Mines	NBHL	9	5	2	7	....	....	....	2	5	*3	0	3	8
1938-39	Kirkland Lake Blue Devils	GBHL	7	13	8	21	....	....	....	2	2	*6	0	6	2
	Kirkland Lake Blue Devils	Al-Cup	6	4	2	6	....	....	....	2	....	....	....	....	....
1939-40	Kirkland Lake Blue Devils	X-Games	15	9	8	17	....	....	....	8	....	....	....	....	....
	Kirkland Lake Blue Devils	Al-Cup	20	8	9	17	....	....	....	12	....	....	....	....	....
1940-41	**Montreal Canadiens**	**NHL**	**3**	**2**	**1**	**3**	**3**	**1**	**4**	**2**	**1**	**0**	**0**	**0**	**0**
	Quebec Royal Rifles	QCHL	35	*33	26	*59	....	....	....	37	4	0	0	0	4
1941-42	**Montreal Canadiens**	**NHL**	**1**	**0**	**1**	**1**	**0**	**1**	**1**	**0**	....	....	....	....	....
	Washington Lions	AHL	55	22	28	50	....	....	....	2	2	0	0	0	0
1942-43	Ottawa Canadiens	OCHL	10	11	14	25	....	....	....	6	8	6	7	13	2
	Washington Lions	AHL	42	14	26	40	....	....	....	28	....	....	....	....	....
1943-44	Ottawa Commandos	OCHL	25	10	17	27	....	....	....	2	3	1	1	2	2
	Hull Volants	Al-Cup	4	3	3	6	....	....	....	0	....	....	....	....	....
1944-45	Ottawa Commandos	OCHL	24	20	25	45	....	....	....	11	2	2	0	2	2
1945-46	Ottawa Senators	QSHL	36	29	35	64	....	....	....	10	7	7	2	9	9
1946-47	Ottawa Senators	QSHL	34	20	27	47	....	....	....	14	8	2	1	3	2
1947-48	Ottawa Senators	QSHL	45	21	42	63	....	....	....	6	12	5	7	12	8
	Ottawa Senators	Al-Cup	14	3	7	10	....	....	....	11	....	....	....	....	....
1948-49	Ottawa Senators	QSHL	40	12	18	30	....	....	....	2	....	....	....	....	....
	Ottawa Senators	Al-Cup	11	5	5	10	....	....	....	0	....	....	....	....	....
1949-50	Ottawa Senators	QSHL	53	27	22	49	....	....	....	6	5	2	2	4	0
1950-51	Smiths Falls Rideaus	ECSHL	17	25	11	36	....	....	....	....	5	10	4	14	....
	Smiths Falls Rideaus	Al-Cup	16	12	12	24	....	....	....	14	....	....	....	....	....
1951-52	Smiths Falls Rideaus	ECSHL	43	38	46	84	....	....	....	6	8	2	3	5	0
1952-53	Smiths Falls Rideaus	ECSHL	47	38	38	*76	....	....	....	12	13	8	7	*15	2
	Smiths Falls Rideaus	Al-Cup	11	5	*9	14	....	....	....	4	....	....	....	....	....
1953-54	Smiths Falls Rideaus	ECSHL	19	19	23	42	....	....	....	6	13	0	5	5	12
	NHL Totals		**4**	**2**	**2**	**4**	**3**	**2**	**5**	**2**	**1**	**0**	**0**	**0**	**0**

Father of Brian

Signed as a free agent by **Montreal**, October 16, 1941.

• SMITH, Tommy Thomas James HHOF

C – L. 5'6", 150 lbs. b: Ottawa, Ont., 9/27/1886 d: 8/1/1966.

Season	Club	League	GP	G	A	Pts	AG	AA	APts	PIM	GP	G	A	Pts	PIM
1904-05	Ottawa Emmetts	OCHL	STATISTICS NOT AVAILABLE												
1905-06	Ottawa Vics	FAHL	8	*12	0	*12	....	....	....	....	....	....	....	....	....
	Ottawa Senators	ECAHA	3	6	0	6	....	....	....	12	1	0	0	0	9
1906-07	Pittsburgh Hockey Club	IHL	23	31	13	44	....	....	....	47	....	....	....	....	....
1907-08	Pittsburgh Lyceum	WPHL	16	*33	0	*33	....	....	....	....	1	2	0	2	....
1908-09	Pittsburgh Lyceum	WPHL	6	15	0	15	....	....	....	....	....	....	....	....	....
	Brantford Redmen	OPHL	13	*40	0	*40	....	....	....	30	....	....	....	....	....
	Pittsburgh Bankers	WPHL	....	....	....	....	....	....	....	....	3	3	0	3	3
	Haileybury Silver Kings	TPHL	1	3	0	3	....	....	....	2	2	*3	0	*3	0
1909-10	Brantford Redmen	OPHL	2	1	0	1	....	....	....	3	....	....	....	....	....
1910-11	Galt Professionals	OPHL	18	22	0	22	....	....	....	....	3	*7	0	*7	0
1911-12	Moncton Victorias	MPHL	18	53	0	53	....	....	....	*48	2	2	0	2	3
1912-13	Quebec Bulldogs	NHA	18	39	0	39	....	....	....	30	2	4	0	4	0
1913-14	Quebec Bulldogs	NHA	20	*39	6	*45	....	....	....	35	....	....	....	....	....
1914-15	Toronto Shamrocks	NHA	10	*17	2	*19	....	....	....	14	....	....	....	....	....
	Quebec Bulldogs	NHA	9	*23	2	*25	....	....	....	29	....	....	....	....	....
1915-16	Quebec Bulldogs	NHA	22	16	3	19	....	....	....	30	....	....	....	....	....
1916-17	Montreal Canadiens	NHA	14	7	4	11	....	....	....	32	6	4	0	4	14
1917-18	Ottawa Transport	OCHL	DID NOT PLAY – COACHING												
1918-19	Glace Bay Miners	CBSHL	DID NOT PLAY – COACHING												
1919-20	**Quebec Bulldogs**	**NHL**	**10**	**0**	**1**	**1**	**0**	**3**	**3**	**11**	....	....	....	....	....
	NHL Totals		**10**	**0**	**1**	**1**	**0**	**3**	**3**	**11**					
	Other Major League Totals		170	294	30	324				310	14	17	0	17	26

Signed as a free agent by **Pittsburgh Lyceum** (WPHL), December 10, 1907. Signed by **Brantford** (OPHL) after jumping contract with **Pittsburgh Lyceum** (WPHL), December 18, 1908. Signed by **Haileybury** (TPHL) after jumping contract with **Brantford** (OPHL), February 14, 1909. Signed as a free agent by **Brantford** (OPHL), January 25, 1910. • Missed majority of 1909-10 season while suffering from typhoid fever. Signed as a free agent by **Quebec** (NHA), December 1, 1912. Traded to **Toronto** (NHA) by **Quebec** (NHA) for Jack McDonald, December 21, 1914. Traded to **Quebec** (NHA) by **Toronto** (NHA) for cash, January 29, 1915. Traded to **Montreal Canadiens** (NHA) by **Quebec** (NHA) for Sammy Hebert, January 16, 1917. Rights retained by **Montreal Canadiens** after NHA folded, November 26, 1917. Traded to **Ottawa** by **Montreal Canadiens** for cash, November 28, 1918. Transferred to **Quebec** by **Ottawa** when Quebec franchise returned to NHL, November 25, 1919.

• SMITH, Wayne Wayne Clifford

D – L. 6', 195 lbs. b: Kamsack, Sask., 2/12/1943.

Season	Club	League	GP	G	A	Pts	AG	AA	APts	PIM	GP	G	A	Pts	PIM
1959-60	Saskatoon Quakers	SJHL	2	0	1	1	....	....	....	0	....	....	....	....	....
1960-61	Saskatoon Quakers	SJHL	60	12	19	31	....	....	....	79	....	....	....	....	....
1961-62	Saskatoon Quakers	SJHL	48	12	19	31	....	....	....	99	7	3	5	8	16
1962-63	University of Denver	WCHA	6	8	3	11	....	....	....	24	....	....	....	....	....
1963-64	University of Denver	WCHA	31	6	5	11	....	....	....	85	....	....	....	....	....
1964-65	University of Denver	WCHA	STATISTICS NOT AVAILABLE												
1965-66	University of Denver	WCHA	32	8	17	25	....	....	....	72					
1966-67	**Chicago Black Hawks**	**NHL**	**2**	**1**	**1**	**2**	**1**	**1**	**2**	**2**	**1**	**0**	**0**	**0**	**0**
	St. Louis Braves	CPHL	70	4	9	13	....	....	....	50	....	....	....	....	....
1967-68	Portland Buckaroos	WHL	68	2	14	16	....	....	....	52	12	0	0	0	0
1968-69	San Diego Gulls	WHL	1	0	0	0	....	....	....	0	....	....	....	....	....
	NHL Totals		**2**	**1**	**1**	**2**	**1**	**1**	**2**	**2**	**1**	**0**	**0**	**0**	**0**

SJHL First All-Star Team (1962) • WCHA Second All-Star Team (1964) • NCAA Championship All-Tournament Team (1964, 1966) • WCHA First All-Star Team (1965, 1966) • NCAA West First All-American Team (1965, 1966)

Rights traded to **Chicago** by **LA Blades** (WHL) to complete transaction that sent Howie Young to LA Blades (WHL) (February 11, 1964), July, 1964.

• SMRKE, Stan Stanley

LW – L. 5'11", 180 lbs. b: Belgrade, Yugoslavia, 9/2/1928 d: 4/14/1977.

Season	Club	League	GP	G	A	Pts	AG	AA	APts	PIM	GP	G	A	Pts	PIM
1945-46	Copper Cliff Jr. Redmen	NOJHA	3	4	0	4	....	....	....	0	....	....	....	....	....
1946-47	Toronto Young Rangers	OHA-Jr.	5	0	0	0	....	....	....	0	....	....	....	....	....
1947-48	Atlantic City–Baltimore	EAHL	28	9	16	25	....	....	....	14	....	....	....	....	....
1948-49	Chicoutimi Volants	LSLHL	36	27	18	45	....	....	....	....	....	....	....	....	....
1949-50	Chicoutimi Sagueneens	LSLHL	58	24	26	50	....	....	....	64	5	5	0	5	5
1950-51	Chicoutimi Sagueneens	QMHL	54	16	36	52	....	....	....	48	6	0	2	2	2
1951-52	Chicoutimi Sagueneens	QMHL	40	10	13	23	....	....	....	25	18	5	6	11	15
1952-53	Chicoutimi Sagueneens	QMHL	59	35	46	81	....	....	....	28	20	5	8	13	13
1953-54	Chicoutimi Sagueneens	QHL	62	11	32	43	....	....	....	24	7	0	2	2	0
1954-55	Chicoutimi Sagueneens	QHL	60	25	36	61	....	....	....	34	7	2	2	4	2
1955-56	Chicoutimi Sagueneens	QHL	45	26	32	58	....	....	....	20	5	1	3	4	7
1956-57	**Montreal Canadiens**	**NHL**	**4**	**0**	**0**	**0**	**0**	**0**	**0**	**0**	....	....	....	....	....
	Chicoutimi Sagueneens	QHL	33	20	18	38	....	....	....	22	....	....	....	....	....
1957-58	**Montreal Canadiens**	**NHL**	**5**	**0**	**3**	**3**	**0**	**3**	**3**	**0**	....	....	....	....	....
	Rochester Americans	AHL	63	20	19	39	....	....	....	32	....	....	....	....	....
1958-59	Chicoutimi Sagueneens	QHL	57	36	32	68	....	....	....	40	....	....	....	....	....
1959-60	Rochester Americans	AHL	67	*40	36	76	....	....	....	18	11	*7	6	13	2
1960-61	Rochester Americans	AHL	21	10	12	22	....	....	....	6	....	....	....	....	....
1961-62	Rochester Americans	AHL	40	7	19	26	....	....	....	14	2	0	0	0	0
1962-63	Rochester Americans	AHL	71	22	25	47	....	....	....	16	2	1	0	1	0
1963-64	Rochester Americans	AHL	59	23	19	42	....	....	....	26	2	0	0	0	0
1964-65	Rochester Americans	AHL	71	33	59	92	....	....	....	28	10	5	4	9	4
1965-66	Rochester Americans	AHL	50	11	20	31	....	....	....	8	8	0	1	1	0
1966-67	Rochester Americans	AHL	71	31	30	61	....	....	....	24	13	2	7	9	2
	NHL Totals		**9**	**0**	**3**	**3**	**0**	**3**	**3**	**0**	....	....	....	....	....

• Father of John • QMHL Second All-Star Team (1951) • QMHL First All-Star Team (1953) • QHL Second All-Star Team (1956, 1959) • AHL First All-Star Team (1960) • Played in NHL All-Star Game (1957)

• Scored a goal in 1957 All-Star Game, October 5, 1957. Traded to **Montreal** by **Chicoutimi** (QHL) for Jackie LeClair, Jacques DesLauriers and Guy Rousseau, October 27, 1957. Traded to **Toronto** by **Montreal** for Al MacNeil, June 7, 1960.

• SMYLIE, Rod Roderick Thomas "Doctor"

W – R. 5'10", 170 lbs. b: Toronto, Ont., 9/28/1895 Deceased.

Season	Club	League	GP	G	A	Pts	AG	AA	APts	PIM	GP	G	A	Pts	PIM
1915-16	Toronto R & AA	OHA-Jr.	STATISTICS NOT AVAILABLE												
1916-17	Toronto Dentals	OHA-Sr.	7	7	0	7	....	....	....	....	3	3	0	3	0
	Toronto Dentals	Al-Cup	4	2	2	4	....	....	....	4	....	....	....	....	....
1917-18	Toronto Dentals	OHA-Sr.	8	13	0	13	....	....	....	....	2	0	0	0	0
1918-19	Toronto Dentals	OHA-Sr.	7	8	5	13	....	....	....	....	2	1	1	2	0
1919-20	Toronto Dentals	OHA-Sr.	5	8	3	11	....	....	....	0	....	....	....	....	....
1920-21	**Toronto St. Pats**	**NHL**	**23**	**2**	**1**	**3**	**2**	**4**	**6**	**2**	**2**	**0**	**0**	**0**	**0**
1921-22	**Toronto St. Pats**	**NHL**	**20**	**0**	**0**	**0**	**0**	**0**	**0**	**2**	**1**	**0**	***0**	**0**	**2**
♦	Toronto St. Pats	St-Cup	5	1	3	4	....	....	....	0	....	....	....	....	....
1922-23	**Toronto St. Pats**	**NHL**	**2**	**0**	**0**	**0**	**0**	**0**	**0**	**0**	....	....	....	....	....
1923-24	**Ottawa Senators**	**NHL**	**13**	**1**	**1**	**2**	**2**	**6**	**8**	**8**	....	....	....	....	....
1924-25	**Toronto St. Pats**	**NHL**	**11**	**1**	**0**	**1**	**2**	**0**	**2**	**0**	**1**	**0**	**0**	**0**	**0**
1925-26	**Toronto St. Pats**	**NHL**	**5**	**0**	**0**	**0**	**0**	**0**	**0**	**0**	....	....	....	....	....
	NHL Totals		**74**	**4**	**2**	**6**	**6**	**10**	**16**	**12**	**4**	**0**	**0**	**0**	**2**

OHA-Sr. Second All-Star Team (1918, 1919)

Signed as a free agent by **Toronto**, December 15, 1920. Signed as a free agent by **Ottawa**, January 2, 1924. Signed as a free agent by **Toronto**, January 27, 1925.

• SOLINGER, Bob Robert Edward "Solly"

W – L. 5'9", 170 lbs. b: Star City, Sask., 12/23/1925.

Season	Club	League	GP	G	A	Pts	AG	AA	APts	PIM	GP	G	A	Pts	PIM
1944-45	Prince Albert Hawks	SJHL	12	14	3	17	....	....	....	6	5	7	5	*12	6
	Prince Albert Hawks	M-Cup	3	0	1	1	....	....	....	*12	....	....	....	....	....
1945-46	Cleveland Barons	AHL	1	0	0	0	....	....	....	0	....	....	....	....	....
	Philadelphia Falcons	EAHL	44	10	9	19	....	....	....	50	12	5	3	8	11
1946-47	Minneapolis Millers	USHL	2	0	0	0	....	....	....	0	....	....	....	....	....
	Edmonton Flyers	WCSHL	38	11	16	27	....	....	....	*72	4	4	3	7	10
1947-48	Cleveland Barons	AHL	67	40	29	69	....	....	....	41	9	*7	6	*13	0
1948-49	Cleveland Barons	AHL	68	16	31	47	....	....	....	29	5	3	3	6	4
1949-50	Pittsburgh Hornets	AHL	44	10	17	27	....	....	....	34	....	....	....	....	....
1950-51	Pittsburgh Hornets	AHL	69	22	32	54	....	....	....	34	13	10	6	*16	4
1951-52	**Toronto Maple Leafs**	**NHL**	**24**	**5**	**3**	**8**	**7**	**4**	**11**	**4**	....	....	....	....	....
	Pittsburgh Hornets	AHL	44	23	20	43	....	....	....	24	11	3	6	9	4
1952-53	**Toronto Maple Leafs**	**NHL**	**18**	**1**	**1**	**2**	**1**	**1**	**2**	**2**	....	....	....	....	....
	Pittsburgh Hornets	AHL	42	26	30	56	....	....	....	51	10	4	5	9	24
1953-54	**Toronto Maple Leafs**	**NHL**	**39**	**3**	**2**	**5**	**4**	**2**	**6**	**2**	....	....	....	....	....
	Pittsburgh Hornets	AHL	22	10	19	29	....	....	....	4	5	1	1	2	12
1954-55	**Toronto Maple Leafs**	**NHL**	**17**	**1**	**5**	**6**	**1**	**6**	**7**	**11**	....	....	....	....	....
	Pittsburgh Hornets	AHL	46	12	24	36	....	....	....	36	10	6	7	13	6
1955-56	Pittsburgh Hornets	AHL	63	27	46	73	....	....	....	74	4	0	3	3	0
1956-57	Hershey Bears	AHL	61	19	30	49	....	....	....	16	7	1	1	2	11
1957-58	Hershey Bears	AHL	66	16	32	48	....	....	....	28	11	1	8	9	4
1958-59	Hershey Bears	AHL	69	12	24	36	....	....	....	46	12	3	7	10	23
1959-60	**Detroit Red Wings**	**NHL**	**1**	**0**	**0**	**0**	**0**	**0**	**0**	**0**	....	....	....	....	....
	Hershey Bears	AHL	45	8	15	23	....	....	....	18	....	....	....	....	....
	Edmonton Flyers	WHL	21	10	9	19	....	....	....	14	4	0	1	1	0
1960-61	Edmonton Flyers	WHL	67	23	19	42	....	....	....	10	....	....	....	....	....
1961-62	San Francisco Seals	WHL	70	30	55	85	....	....	....	4	2	1	0	1	0
1962-63	Los Angeles Blades	WHL	67	33	43	76	....	....	....	28	3	2	1	3	2
1963-64	Los Angeles Blades	WHL	59	13	20	33	....	....	....	25	6	2	2	4	0
1964-65	Red Deer Rustlers	AIHA	STATISTICS NOT AVAILABLE												
	Lacombe Rockets	CAHL	STATISTICS NOT AVAILABLE												

			REGULAR SEASON								PLAYOFFS				
Season	Club	League	GP	G	A	Pts	AG	AA	APts	PIM	GP	G	A	Pts	PIM
1965-66	Lacombe Rockets	ASHL	30	12	10	22	....	....	....	59	4	2	2	4	0
	Drumheller Rockets	Al-Cup	16	4	4	8	....	....	....	2	....	....	....	....	....
1966-67	Edmonton Nuggets	ASHL	25	7	17	24	....	....	....	26	8	4	3	7	10
1967-68	Edmonton Nuggets	ASHL	....	2	4	6	....	....	....	6	....	3	6	9	6
1968-69	Edmonton Monarchs	ASHL	30	8	25	33	....	....	....	36	6	0	7	7	2
	NHL Totals		**99**	**10**	**11**	**21**	**13**	**13**	**26**	**19**	....	....	....	....	....

Won Dudley "Red" Garrett Memorial Award (Top Rookie - AHL) (1948) • AHL Second All-Star Team (1953) • WHL Second All-Star Team (1962, 1963)

Traded to **Toronto** by **Cleveland** (AHL) for Ray Ceresino, Harry Taylor and the loan of Tod Sloan for the 1949-50 season, September 6, 1949. Traded to **Detroit** (Hershey-AHL) by **Toronto** (Pittsburgh-AHL) with Gilles Mayer, Jack Price, Willie Marshall, Bob Hassard and Ray Gariepy for cash, July 7, 1956. Traded to **San Francisco** (WHL) by **Detroit** for cash, July, 1962. Traded to **NY Rangers** (LA Blades-WHL) by **San Francisco** (WHL) for Danny Belisle with NY Rangers holding right of recall, July, 1962.

• SOMERS, Art

Arthur Ernest
C – L. 5'5", 167 lbs. b: Winnipeg, Man., 1/19/1902 d: 1/29/1992.

Season	Club	League	GP	G	A	Pts	AG	AA	APts	PIM	GP	G	A	Pts	PIM
1920-21	Winnipeg Falcons	WJrHL	....	....	....	....	....	....	....	....	....	....	....	....	....
1921-22	Winnipeg Victorias	TBSHL	STATISTICS NOT AVAILABLE												
1922-23	Winnipeg Falcons	MTBHL	16	10	6	16	....	....	....	33	2	0	0	0	2
	Winnipeg Falcons	Al-Cup	3	2	0	2	....	....	....	*14	....	....	....	....	....
1923-24	Winnipeg Falcons	MTBHL	12	10	6	16	....	....	....	14	....	....	....	....	....
1924-25	Fort William Forts	MTBHL	20	5	2	7	....	....	....	41	....	....	....	....	....
1925-26	Winnipeg Maroons	CHL	36	*21	5	26	....	....	....	61	5	1	1	2	12
1926-27	Winnipeg Maroons	AHA	32	11	10	21	....	....	....	73	3	0	1	1	7
1927-28	Winnipeg Maroons	AHA	40	8	6	14	....	....	....	71	....	....	....	....	....
1928-29	Vancouver Lions	PCHL	35	*23	7	*30	....	....	....	66	3	*3	0	3	2
1929-30	**Chicago Black Hawks**	**NHL**	**44**	**11**	**13**	**24**	**16**	**31**	**47**	**74**	**2**	**0**	**0**	**0**	**2**
1930-31	**Chicago Black Hawks**	**NHL**	**33**	**3**	**6**	**9**	**6**	**18**	**24**	**33**	**9**	**0**	**0**	**0**	**0**
1931-32	**New York Rangers**	**NHL**	**48**	**11**	**15**	**26**	**18**	**33**	**51**	**45**	**7**	**0**	**1**	**1**	**8**
♦1932-33	**New York Rangers**	**NHL**	**48**	**7**	**15**	**22**	**13**	**31**	**44**	**28**	**8**	**1**	***4**	**5**	**8**
1933-34	**New York Rangers**	**NHL**	**8**	**1**	**2**	**3**	**2**	**4**	**6**	**5**	**2**	**0**	**0**	**0**	**0**
	Windsor Bulldogs	IHL	7	2	2	4	....	....	....	5	....	....	....	....	....
1934-35	**New York Rangers**	**NHL**	**41**	**0**	**5**	**5**	**0**	**9**	**9**	**4**	**2**	**0**	**0**	**0**	**2**
1935-36	Prince Albert Mintos	AJHL	DID NOT PLAY – COACHING												
	NHL Totals		**222**	**33**	**56**	**89**	**55**	**126**	**181**	**189**	**30**	**1**	**5**	**6**	**20**

Signed as a free agent by **Winnipeg** (AHA), November 3, 1926. Traded to **NY Rangers** by **Chicago** with Vic Desjardins for Paul Thompson, September 27, 1931.

• SONMOR, Glen

Glen Robert
LW – L. 5'11", 165 lbs. b: Moose Jaw, Sask., 4/22/1929.

Season	Club	League	GP	G	A	Pts	AG	AA	APts	PIM	GP	G	A	Pts	PIM
1945-46	Hamilton Lloyds	OHA-B	1	0	1	1	....	....	....	0	....	....	....	....	....
1946-47	Hamilton Lloyds	OHA-B	STATISTICS NOT AVAILABLE												
1947-48	Guelph Biltmores	OHA-Jr.	36	21	15	36	....	....	....	20	....	....	....	....	....
1948-49	Brandon Wheat Kings	WCJHL	30	18	*30	48	....	....	....	40	7	2	*5	7	11
	Brandon Wheat Kings	M-Cup	18	8	9	17	....	....	....	33	....	....	....	....	....
1949-50	Minneapolis Millers	USHL	55	17	43	60	....	....	....	25	7	2	4	6	7
1950-51	Cleveland Barons	AHL	65	14	35	49	....	....	....	47	11	3	4	7	14
1951-52	St. Louis Flyers	AHL	67	24	30	54	....	....	....	42	....	....	....	....	....
1952-53	Cleveland Barons	AHL	64	25	26	51	....	....	....	62	11	0	2	2	18
1953-54	**New York Rangers**	**NHL**	**15**	**2**	**0**	**2**	**3**	**0**	**3**	**17**	....	....	....	....	....
	Cleveland Barons	AHL	31	13	12	25	....	....	....	45	....	....	....	....	....
1954-55	**New York Rangers**	**NHL**	**13**	**0**	**0**	**0**	**0**	**0**	**0**	**4**	....	....	....	....	....
	Cleveland Barons	AHL	36	11	21	32	....	....	....	34	....	....	....	....	....
1955-56	Cleveland Barons	AHL	DID NOT PLAY – INJURED												
1956-57	Ohio State University	CCHA	DID NOT PLAY – COACHING												
	NHL Totals		**28**	**2**	**0**	**2**	**3**	**0**	**3**	**21**	....	....	....	....	....

WCJHL Second All-Star Team (1949)

Traded to **Cleveland** (AHL) by **NY Rangers** with Eric Pogue for Andy Bathgate and Vic Howe, November 15, 1954. • Suffered career-ending eye injury in game vs. Pittsburgh (AHL) February 27, 1955.

• SORRELL, John

John Arthur "Long John"
LW – L. 5'11", 155 lbs. b: Chesterville, Ont., 1/16/1906 d: 11/30/1984.

Season	Club	League	GP	G	A	Pts	AG	AA	APts	PIM	GP	G	A	Pts	PIM
1926-27	Chesterville Colts	OIHA	STATISTICS NOT AVAILABLE												
1927-28	Quebec Beavers	Can-Am	40	7	3	10	....	....	....	27	6	1	0	1	2
1928-29	Windsor Bulldogs	Can-Pro	42	16	7	23	....	....	....	36	8	1	1	2	6
1929-30	London Panthers	IHL	42	*31	13	44	....	....	....	26	2	0	0	0	0
1930-31	**Detroit Falcons**	**NHL**	**39**	**9**	**7**	**16**	**18**	**21**	**39**	**10**	....	....	....	....	....
1931-32	**Detroit Falcons**	**NHL**	**48**	**8**	**5**	**13**	**13**	**11**	**24**	**22**	**2**	**1**	**0**	**1**	**0**
1932-33	**Detroit Red Wings**	**NHL**	**47**	**14**	**10**	**24**	**26**	**21**	**47**	**11**	**4**	**2**	**2**	**4**	**4**
1933-34	**Detroit Red Wings**	**NHL**	**47**	**21**	**10**	**31**	**36**	**21**	**57**	**8**	**8**	**0**	**2**	**2**	**0**
1934-35	**Detroit Red Wings**	**NHL**	**47**	**20**	**16**	**36**	**33**	**28**	**61**	**12**	....	....	....	....	....
	Detroit Olympics	IHL	1	1	2	3	....	....	....	0	....	....	....	....	....
♦1935-36	**Detroit Red Wings**	**NHL**	**48**	**13**	**15**	**28**	**25**	**28**	**53**	**8**	**7**	**3**	**4**	**7**	**0**
♦1936-37	**Detroit Red Wings**	**NHL**	**48**	**8**	**16**	**24**	**13**	**29**	**42**	**4**	**10**	**2**	**4**	**6**	**2**
1937-38	**Detroit Red Wings**	**NHL**	**23**	**3**	**7**	**10**	**5**	**11**	**16**	**0**	....	....	....	....	....
	New York Americans	**NHL**	**17**	**8**	**2**	**10**	**13**	**3**	**16**	**9**	**6**	**4**	**0**	**4**	**2**
1938-39	**New York Americans**	**NHL**	**48**	**13**	**9**	**22**	**23**	**14**	**37**	**10**	**2**	**0**	**0**	**0**	**0**
1939-40	**New York Americans**	**NHL**	**48**	**8**	**16**	**24**	**13**	**25**	**38**	**4**	**3**	**0**	**3**	**3**	**2**
1940-41	**New York Americans**	**NHL**	**30**	**2**	**6**	**8**	**3**	**9**	**12**	**2**	....	....	....	....	....
	Springfield Indians	AHL	10	0	1	1	....	....	....	2	....	....	....	....	....
	Hershey Bears	AHL	10	1	6	7	....	....	....	14	10	1	2	3	10
1941-42	Hershey Bears	AHL	53	23	14	37	....	....	....	2	10	0	4	4	0
1942-43	Hershey Bears	AHL	49	24	28	52	....	....	....	8	6	4	2	6	0
1943-44	Indianapolis Capitols	AHL	51	16	22	38	....	....	....	6	5	4	4	8	2
1944-45	Indianapolis Capitols	AHL	56	21	21	42	....	....	....	8	5	2	0	2	2
1945-46	Indianapolis Capitols	AHL	DID NOT PLAY – COACHING												
	NHL Totals		**490**	**127**	**119**	**246**	**221**	**221**	**442**	**100**	**42**	**12**	**15**	**27**	**10**

IHL First All-Star Team (1930)

Traded to **London** (IHL) by **Montreal Canadiens** for cash, November 5, 1929. Traded to **Detroit** by **London** (IHL) for cash and future considerations (Herb Stuart, November 10, 1930), April 8, 1930. Traded to **NY Americans** by **Detroit** for Hap Emms, February 13, 1938. Traded to **Hershey** by **NY Americans** (Springfield-AHL) for Joe Krol, February 14, 1941.

• SPARROW, Emory

Emory William "Spunk"
RW/C – L. 5'11", 180 lbs. b: Hartney, Man., 9/15/1898 d: 2/2/1965.

			REGULAR SEASON								PLAYOFFS				
Season	Club	League	GP	G	A	Pts	AG	AA	APts	PIM	GP	G	A	Pts	PIM
1913-14	St. John's College	WJrHL	STATISTICS NOT AVAILABLE												
1914-15	Winnipeg Winnipeg's	WSrHL	STATISTICS NOT AVAILABLE												
1915-16	Winnipeg 61st Battalion	MHL-Sr.	7	4	4	8	....	....	....	20	....	....	....	....	....
1916-17			MILITARY SERVICE												
1917-18	Winnipeg Somme	MHL-Sr.	8	14	7	21	....	....	....	22	....	....	....	....	....
1918-19	Winnipeg Argonauts	MHL-Sr.	9	22	*10	*32	....	....	....	6	....	....	....	....	....
1919-20	Moose Jaw Maple Leafs	S-SSHL	10	11	1	12	....	....	....	30	2	1	0	1	3
	Moose Jaw Maple Leafs	Al-Cup	5	2	1	3	....	....	....	0	....	....	....	....	....
1920-21	Moose Jaw Maple Leafs	S-SSHL	13	15	6	21	....	....	....	*56	4	3	0	3	6
1921-22	Regina Capitals	WCHL	14	10	2	12	....	....	....	6	4	0	0	0	7
1922-23	Regina Capitals	WCHL	23	6	4	10	....	....	....	33	....	....	....	....	....
1923-24	Edmonton Eskimos	WCHL	23	11	6	17	....	....	....	34	....	....	....	....	....
1924-25	Calgary Tigers	WCHL	16	7	8	15	....	....	....	48	2	0	0	0	2
	Boston Bruins	**NHL**	**8**	**0**	**0**	**0**	**0**	**0**	**0**	**4**	....	....	....	....	....
1925-26	Calgary Tigers	WHL	11	3	2	5	....	....	....	34	....	....	....	....	....
	Edmonton Eskimos	WHL	17	11	2	13	....	....	....	32	2	0	0	0	6
1926-27	Calgary Tigers	PHL	32	26	*25	51	....	....	....	58	2	2	0	2	2
1927-28	Minneapolis Millers	AHA	5	1	1	2	....	....	....	8	....	....	....	....	....
	Regina Capitals	PHL	16	9	7	16	....	....	....	14	....	....	....	....	....
1928-29	Philadelphia Arrows	Can-Am	23	2	2	4	....	....	....	22	....	....	....	....	....
	NHL Totals		**8**	**0**	**0**	**0**	**0**	**0**	**0**	**4**	....	....	....	....	....
	Other Major League Totals		104	48	24	72	....	....	....	187	8	0	0	0	15

PHL First All-Star Team (1927)

Signed as a free agent by **Regina** (WCHL), December 27, 1921. Traded to **Edmonton** (WCHL) by **Regina** (WCHL) with $1,500 for Art Gagne, October 3, 1923. Traded to **Calgary** (WCHL) by **Edmonton** (WCHL) with Hal Winkler for cash, August 28, 1924. Loaned to **Boston** by **Calgary** (WCHL) for cash, December 8, 1924. Returned to **Calgary** (WCHL) from **Boston** after breaking training rules, January 5, 1925. Traded to **Edmonton** (WHL) by **Calgary** (WHL) for cash, January 19, 1926. Traded to **Detroit** by **Edmonton** (WHL) for cash, October 5, 1926. Signed as a free agent by **Calgary** (PHL), November 17, 1926. Traded to **Minneapolis** (AHA) by **Calgary** (PHL) for cash, October 13, 1927. • Suspended for life by AHA for assaulting referee Moose Goheen with his stick, December 28, 1927.

• SPENCE, Gordon

Gordon Edmund
LW – L. 5'7", 150 lbs. b: Haileybury, Ont., 7/25/1897 Deceased.

Season	Club	League	GP	G	A	Pts	AG	AA	APts	PIM	GP	G	A	Pts	PIM
1915-16	Haileybury Rexalls	NOJHA	STATISTICS NOT AVAILABLE												
1916-17	Toronto 228th Battalion	OHA-Jr.	STATISTICS NOT AVAILABLE												
	Toronto 228th Battalion	NHA	1	0	0	0	....	....	....	....					
1917-18			MILITARY SERVICE												
1918-19	New Liskeard Seniors	NOHA	STATISTICS NOT AVAILABLE												
1919-20	Haileybury Rexalls	NOHA	STATISTICS NOT AVAILABLE												
1920-21	New Liskeard Seniors	NOHA	STATISTICS NOT AVAILABLE												
1921-22	New Liskeard Seniors	NOHA	STATISTICS NOT AVAILABLE												
1922-23			DID NOT PLAY												
1923-24			DID NOT PLAY												
1924-25	New Liskeard Seniors	NOHA	STATISTICS NOT AVAILABLE												
1925-26	**Toronto St. Pats**	**NHL**	**3**	**0**	**0**	**0**	**0**	**0**	**0**	**0**					
1926/29	South Porcupine Porkies	NOHA	STATISTICS NOT AVAILABLE												
1929-30	Cornwall Colts	LOVHL	3	0	0	0	....	....	....	0	2	0	0	0	0
	Cornwall Colts	Al-Cup	4	2	1	3	....	....	....	....	....	....	....	....	....
	NHL Totals		**3**	**0**	**0**	**0**	**0**	**0**	**0**	**0**					
	Other Major League Totals		1	0	0	0									

Signed as a free agent by **Toronto St. Pats**, December 31, 1925.

• SPENCER, Irv

— *see page 1653*

• SPEYER, Chris

"Duke"
D – L. 5'10", 170 lbs. b: Toronto, Ont., 2/6/1907 Deceased.

Season	Club	League	GP	G	A	Pts	AG	AA	APts	PIM	GP	G	A	Pts	PIM
1921-22	Toronto Granites	OHA-Jr.	5	0	1	1	....	....	....	....	....	....	....	....	....
1922-23	Toronto Aura Lee	OHA-Sr.	12	1	0	1	....	....	....	....	....	....	....	....	....
1923-24	**Toronto St. Pats**	**NHL**	**3**	**0**	**0**	**0**	**0**	**0**	**0**	**0**	....	....	....	....	....
	Toronto Aura Lee	OHA-Sr.	6	3	1	4	....	....	....	....	....	....	....	....	....
1924-25	**Toronto St. Pats**	**NHL**	**2**	**0**	**0**	**0**	**0**	**0**	**0**	**0**	....	....	....	....	....
1925-26			DID NOT PLAY												
1926-27	Niagara Falls Cataracts	Can-Pro	20	3	0	3	....	....	....	22	....	....	....	....	....
	London Panthers	Can-Pro	4	0	0	0	....	....	....	2	4	0	0	0	0
1927-28	Niagara Falls Cataracts	Can-Pro	38	3	5	8	....	....	....	46	....	....	....	....	....
1928-29	New Haven Eagles	Can-Am	39	3	2	5	....	....	....	38	2	0	0	0	6
1929-30	New Haven Eagles	Can-Am	40	8	8	16	....	....	....	87	....	....	....	....	....
1930-31	New Haven Eagles	Can-Am	40	8	10	18	....	....	....	83	....	....	....	....	....
1931-32	New Haven Eagles	Can-Am	38	6	13	19	....	....	....	53	2	1	1	2	2
1932-33	New Haven Eagles	Can-Am	48	13	13	26	....	....	....	50	....	....	....	....	....
1933-34	**New York Americans**	**NHL**	**9**	**0**	**0**	**0**	**0**	**0**	**0**	**0**	....	....	....	....	....
	Syracuse Stars	IHL	4	0	0	0	....	....	....	0	....	....	....	....	....
	New Haven Eagles	Can-Am	20	2	3	5	....	....	....	10	....	....	....	....	....
1934-35	Providence Reds	Can-Am	47	7	3	10	....	....	....	21	6	0	1	1	0
1935-36	Springfield Indians	Can-Am	48	8	12	20	....	....	....	18	2	0	1	1	2
	NHL Totals		**14**	**0**	**0**	**0**	**0**	**0**	**0**	**0**	....	....	....	....	....

Can-Am Second All-Star Team (1936)

Signed as a free agent by **Toronto**, February 23, 1924. Signed as a free agent by **Niagara Falls** (Can-Pro), November 1, 1926. Loaned to **London** (Can-Pro) by **Niagara Falls** (Can-Pro) for cash, February 1, 1927. Signed as a free agent by **NY Americans**, November 1, 1933. Signed as a free agent by **Providence** (Can-Am), November 5, 1934. Traded to **Springfield** (Can-Am) by **Providence** (Can-Am) with Leo Murray for Albert Leduc, October 12, 1935.

• SPRING, Jesse

D – L. 6', 185 lbs. b: Alba, PA, 1/18/1901 d: 3/25/1942.

Season	Club	League	GP	G	A	Pts	AG	AA	APts	PIM	GP	G	A	Pts	PIM
1917-18	Toronto DeLasalle	OHA-Jr.	STATISTICS NOT AVAILABLE												
1918-19	Toronto Parkdales	OHA-Jr.	STATISTICS NOT AVAILABLE												
1919-20	Toronto A.R. Clarke	TMHL	STATISTICS NOT AVAILABLE												
1920-21	Timmins Open Mine	GBHL	STATISTICS NOT AVAILABLE												
1921-22	Toronto A.R. Clarke	TMHL	STATISTICS NOT AVAILABLE												
1922-23	Toronto A.R. Clarke	TIHL	STATISTICS NOT AVAILABLE												
1923-24	**Hamilton Tigers**	**NHL**	**20**	**3**	**3**	**6**	**6**	**17**	**23**	**20**	....	....	....	....	....

Season	Club	League	GP	G	A	Pts	AG	AA	APts	PIM	GP	G	A	Pts	PIM
			REGULAR SEASON								PLAYOFFS				
1924-25	**Hamilton Tigers**	**NHL**	**29**	**2**	**1**	**3**	**3**	**4**	**7**	**11**	....	....	....	....	....
1925-26	**Pittsburgh Pirates**	**NHL**	**32**	**5**	**0**	**5**	**9**	**0**	**9**	**23**	**2**	**0**	**2**	**2**	**2**
1926-27	**Toronto Maple Leafs**	**NHL**	**2**	**0**	**0**	**0**	**0**	**0**	**0**	**0**	....	....	....	....	....
	Niagara Falls Cataracts	Can-Pro	10	0	0	0	....	....	....	14	....	....	....	....	....
1927-28	Niagara Falls Cataracts	Can-Pro	39	1	3	4	....	....	....	57	....	....	....	....	....
1928-29	**New York Americans**	**NHL**	**23**	**0**	**0**	**0**	**0**	**0**	**0**	**0**	....	....	....	....	....
	New Haven Eagles	Can-Am	1	0	0	0	....	....	....	0	....	....	....	....	....
	Pittsburgh Pirates	**NHL**	**5**	**0**	**0**	**0**	**0**	**0**	**0**	**2**	....	....	....	....	....
1929-30	**Pittsburgh Pirates**	**NHL**	**22**	**1**	**0**	**1**	**1**	**0**	**1**	**18**	....	....	....	....	....
1930-31	Detroit Olympics	IHL	28	2	3	5	....	....	....	22	....	....	....	....	....
1931-32	Cleveland Indians	IHL	30	3	1	4	....	....	....	22	....	....	....	....	....
1932-33	Oshawa Blue Imps	OHA-Sr.	DID NOT PLAY – COACHING												
	NHL Totals		**133**	**11**	**4**	**15**	**19**	**21**	**40**	**74**	**2**	**0**	**2**	**2**	**2**

Signed as a free agent by **Hamilton**, December 18, 1923. Transferred to **NY Americans** after NHL club purchased **Hamilton** franchise, September 26, 1925. Loaned to **Pittsburgh** by **NY Americans** for 1925-26 season for future considerations (Joe Miller, February 23, 1926), November 25, 1925. Traded to **Toronto** by **NY Americans** for Laurie Scott, November 15, 1926. Traded to **NY Americans** by **Toronto** for cash, January, 1927. Traded to **Pittsburgh** by **NY Americans** with loan of Edmond Bouchard for remainder of 1928-29 season for loan of Tex White for remainder of 1928-29 season, February 15, 1929. Signed as a free agent by **Detroit**, November 6, 1930.

• STACKHOUSE, Ted

D – R. 6'1", 200 lbs. b: Wolfville, N.S., d: 11/24/1975.

Season	Club	League	GP	G	A	Pts	AG	AA	APts	PIM	GP	G	A	Pts	PIM
1913-14	Wolfville YMCA	WNSHL	STATISTICS NOT AVAILABLE												
	Acadia University	WNSHL	STATISTICS NOT AVAILABLE												
1914-15	Wolfville YMCA	WNSHL	STATISTICS NOT AVAILABLE												
	Acadia University	WNSHL	STATISTICS NOT AVAILABLE												
1915-16			DID NOT PLAY												
1916-17	New Glasgow Tigers	NSEHL	STATISTICS NOT AVAILABLE												
1917-18	New Glasgow Tigers	X-Games	STATISTICS NOT AVAILABLE												
1918-19	New Glasgow Tigers	X-Games	STATISTICS NOT AVAILABLE												
1919-20	Acadia University	WNSHL	DID NOT PLAY – COACHING												
1920-21	Wolfville AAA	NSVHL	1	0	1	1	....	....	....	0	....	....	....	....	....
1921-22	**Toronto St. Pats**	**NHL**	**13**	**0**	**0**	**0**	**0**	**0**	**0**	**2**	**1**	**0**	**0**	**0**	**0**
♦	Toronto St. Pats	St-Cup	4	0	0	0	....	....	....	0	....	....	....	....	....
1922-23	Amherst Ramblers	MIL	1	0	0	0	....	....	....	0	....	....	....	....	....
	Sydney Millionaires	X-Games	2	0	2	2	....	....	....	2	....	....	....	....	....
1923-24			REINSTATED AS AN AMATEUR												
1924-25			DID NOT PLAY – REFEREE												
1925-26	Manchester New England	NEHL	STATISTICS NOT AVAILABLE												
1926-27	Nashua Nationals	NEHL	26	9	3	12	....	....	....	9	4	1	1	2	2
	Providence Reds	Can-Am	5	0	0	0	....	....	....	2	....	....	....	....	....
1927-28	Nashua Nationals	NEHL	20	4	3	7	....	....	....	10	4	1	1	2	2
	NHL Totals		**13**	**0**	**0**	**0**	**0**	**0**	**0**	**2**	**1**	**0**	**0**	**0**	**0**

NEHL First All-Star Team (1927) • NEHL Second All-Star Team (1928)

Signed as a free agent by **Toronto St. Pats**, December 23, 1921. Signed as a free agent by **Toronto St. Pats**, January 25, 1922.

• STAHAN, Butch

Francis Ralph

D – L. 6'1", 195 lbs. b: Minnedosa, Man., 10/29/1918 d: 5/25/1995.

Season	Club	League	GP	G	A	Pts	AG	AA	APts	PIM	GP	G	A	Pts	PIM
1934-35	Portage Terriers	MJHL	16	2	3	5	....	....	....	18	....	....	....	....	....
1935-36	Portage Terriers	MJHL	16	6	5	11	....	....	....	17	6	1	1	2	4
1936-37	Portage Terriers	MJHL	6	0	0	0	....	....	....	2	....	....	....	....	....
	Flin Flon Bombers	N-SSHL	18	6	4	10	....	....	....	43	6	0	0	0	*8
1937-38	Brandon Wheat Kings	MJHL	16	1	6	7	....	....	....	16	5	0	0	0	0
	Flin Flon Bombers	N-SSHL	24	0	1	1	....	....	....	6	8	2	0	2	10
1938-39	Creighton Eagles	GBHL	7	3	0	3	....	....	....	*27	1	0	0	0	2
1939-40	Kirkland Lake Blue Devils	X-Games	13	2	2	4	....	....	....	32	....	....	....	....	....
	Kirkland Lake Blue Devils	Al-Cup	5	1	1	2	....	....	....	4	....	....	....	....	....
1940-41	Quebec Aces	QSHL	36	6	12	18	....	....	....	60	4	0	1	1	22
1941-42	Quebec Aces	Al-Cup	8	1	4	5	....	....	....	*18	....	....	....	....	....
1942-43	Quebec Aces	QSHL	34	12	23	35	....	....	....	83	4	3	1	4	8
	Port Arthur Bearcats	Al-Cup	3	0	0	0	....	....	....	6	....	....	....	....	....
1943-44	Quebec Aces	QSHL	25	7	21	28	....	....	....	74	6	1	2	3	20
	Quebec Aces	Al-Cup	9	6	5	11	....	....	....	*24	....	....	....	....	....
1944-45	Montreal Royals	QSHL	19	7	11	18	....	....	....	72	4	0	1	1	14
	Montreal Canadiens	**NHL**	....	....	....	....	....	....	....	....	**3**	**0**	**1**	**1**	**2**
	Sudbury Open Pit	Al-Cup	1	0	0	0	....	....	....	0	....	....	....	....	....
1945-46	Montreal Royals	QSHL	39	9	15	24	....	....	....	76	11	3	2	5	34
1946-47	Ottawa Senators	QSHL	40	10	26	36	....	....	....	116	9	2	8	10	30
1947-48	Ottawa Senators	QSHL	41	12	21	33	....	....	....	44	12	1	7	8	*23
	Ottawa Senators	Al-Cup	13	1	4	5	....	....	....	*44	....	....	....	....	....
1948-49	Ottawa Senators	QSHL	62	9	34	43	....	....	....	92	11	0	3	3	14
	Ottawa Senators	Al-Cup	3	0	0	0	....	....	....	0	....	....	....	....	....
1949-50	Ottawa Senators	QSHL	60	9	18	27	....	....	....	116	7	0	4	4	16
1950-51	Ottawa Senators	QMHL	56	2	22	24	....	....	....	106	11	2	3	5	18
1951-52	Ottawa Senators	QMHL	59	10	16	26	....	....	....	76	7	2	0	2	4
1952-53	Ottawa Senators	QMHL	56	3	13	16	....	....	....	118	9	0	2	2	14
1953-54	Ottawa Senators	QHL	34	0	5	5	....	....	....	56	2	0	0	0	4
	Pembroke Lumber Kings	NOHA	11	1	1	2	....	....	....	24	....	....	....	....	....
1954-55	Ottawa Senators	QHL	8	0	1	1	....	....	....	23	....	....	....	....	....
	Toledo Mercurys	IHL	30	0	13	13	....	....	....	63	2	0	1	1	4
1955-56	Toledo-Marion Mercurys	IHL	59	4	29	33	....	....	....	198	9	2	3	5	12
1956-57	Toledo Mercurys	IHL	60	7	22	29	....	....	....	96	5	1	2	3	4
	NHL Totals		....	....	....	....	....	....	....	....	**3**	**0**	**1**	**1**	**2**

QSHL Second All-Star Team (1941, 1948)

Traded to **Buffalo** (AHL) by **Montreal** with Jim McFadden for Tom Rockey and cash, October 8, 1946.

• STALEY, Al

Allan Ramon "Red"

C – R. 6'1", 175 lbs. b: Regina, Sask., 9/21/1928.

Season	Club	League	GP	G	A	Pts	AG	AA	APts	PIM	GP	G	A	Pts	PIM
1944-45	Regina Commandos	S-SJHL	17	3	3	6	....	....	....	4	9	4	0	4	6
1945-46	Regina Commandos	S-SJHL	17	12	12	24	....	....	....	10	9	2	4	6	10
1946-47	Regina Pats	S-SJHL	23	22	27	49	....	....	....	21	6	*9	4	13	6
1947-48	Regina Pats	S-SJHL	28	37	30	67	....	....	....	43	5	3	*7	10	14
1948-49	**New York Rangers**	**NHL**	**1**	**0**	**1**	**1**	**0**	**1**	**1**	**0**	....	....	....	....	....
	New Haven Ramblers	AHL	2	0	0	0	....	....	....	0	....	....	....	....	....
	New York Rovers	QSHL	51	17	21	38	....	....	....	15	....	....	....	....	....
1949-50	Regina Capitals	WCSHL	10	1	2	3	....	....	....	4	....	....	....	....	....
	Saskatoon Quakers	WCSHL	16	7	2	9	....	....	....	2	5	2	1	3	8
1950-51	Saskatoon Quakers	WCMHL	59	28	29	57	....	....	....	46	4	0	3	3	0
1951-52	Trail Smoke Eaters	WIHL	43	20	24	44	....	....	....	61	3	1	3	4	0
1952-53	Moose Jaw Millers	SSHL	30	23	27	50	....	....	....	57	10	6	4	10	4
	NHL Totals		**1**	**0**	**1**	**1**	**0**	**1**	**1**	**0**	....	....	....	....	....

SSHL First All-Star Team (1953)

• STANFIELD, Fred

— see page 1656

• STANFIELD, Jack

John Gordon

LW – L. 5'11", 176 lbs. b: Toronto, Ont., 5/30/1942.

Season	Club	League	GP	G	A	Pts	AG	AA	APts	PIM	GP	G	A	Pts	PIM
1960-61	Dixie Beehives	OHA-B	STATISTICS NOT AVAILABLE												
1961-62	St. Catharines Teepees	OHA-Jr.	42	8	11	19	....	....	....	12	6	1	0	1	0
1962-63	Philadelphia Ramblers	EHL	68	33	34	67	....	....	....	38	3	0	0	0	4
1963-64	St. Louis Braves	CPHL	63	23	33	56	....	....	....	39	6	1	1	2	0
1964-65	Buffalo Bisons	AHL	72	19	20	39	....	....	....	34	9	2	5	7	4
1965-66	Buffalo Bisons	AHL	59	13	11	24	....	....	....	42	....	....	....	....	....
	Chicago Black Hawks	**NHL**	....	....	....	....	....	....	....	....	**1**	**0**	**0**	**0**	**0**
1966-67	Los Angeles Blades	WHL	47	12	10	22	....	....	....	29	....	....	....	....	....
1967-68	Dallas Black Hawks	CPHL	67	20	21	41	....	....	....	31	2	0	0	0	0
1968-69	San Diego Gulls	WHL	68	14	13	27	....	....	....	18	7	1	1	2	0
1969-70	Rochester Americans	AHL	66	21	21	42	....	....	....	19	....	....	....	....	....
1970-71	Rochester Americans	AHL	48	11	9	20	....	....	....	35	....	....	....	....	....
1971-72	Rochester Americans	AHL	62	11	16	27	....	....	....	74	....	....	....	....	....
1972-73	Houston Aeros	WHA	71	8	12	20	....	....	....	8	9	1	0	1	0
1973-74	Houston Aeros	WHA	41	1	3	4	....	....	....	2	7	0	0	0	2
	Macon Whoopees	SHL	3	6	1	7	....	....	....	4	....	....	....	....	....
	NHL Totals		....	....	....	....	....	....	....	....	**1**	**0**	**0**	**0**	**0**
	Other Major League Totals		112	9	15	24	....	....	....	10	16	1	0	1	2

• Brother of Fred and Jim

Claimed by **Vancouver** (WHL) from **Chicago** in Reverse Draft, June, 1969. NHL rights transferred to **Vancouver** after NHL club purchased **Vancouver** (WHL) franchise, December 19, 1969. Selected by **Dayton-Houston** (WHA) in WHA General Player Draft, February 12, 1972.

• STANKIEWICZ, Ed

Edward

C – R. 5'9", 165 lbs. b: Kitchener, Ont., 12/1/1929.

Season	Club	League	GP	G	A	Pts	AG	AA	APts	PIM	GP	G	A	Pts	PIM
1949-50	Windsor Spitfires	OHA-Jr.	47	54	48	102	....	....	....	48	11	6	11	17	23
1950-51	Toronto Marlboros	OMHL	32	7	17	24	....	....	....	42	3	0	0	0	6
1951-52	St. Louis Flyers	AHL	2	2	2	4	....	....	....	0	....	....	....	....	....
	Kitchener Dutchmen	OHA-Sr.	48	41	46	87	....	....	....	34	5	1	3	4	11
1952-53	St. Louis Flyers	AHL	61	13	25	38	....	....	....	48	....	....	....	....	....
1953-54	**Detroit Red Wings**	**NHL**	**1**	**0**	**0**	**0**	**0**	**0**	**0**	**2**	....	....	....	....	....
	Sherbrooke Saints	QHL	71	31	30	61	....	....	....	67	5	1	1	2	2
1954-55	Edmonton Flyers	WHL	59	27	45	72	....	....	....	96	9	1	5	6	*28
	Edmonton Flyers	Ed-Cup	7	1	5	6	....	....	....	25	....	....	....	....	....
1955-56	**Detroit Red Wings**	**NHL**	**5**	**0**	**0**	**0**	**0**	**0**	**0**	**0**	....	....	....	....	....
	Edmonton Flyers	WHL	54	33	30	63	....	....	....	54	3	2	0	2	4
1956-57	Edmonton Flyers	WHL	16	2	8	10	....	....	....	26	....	....	....	....	....
1957-58	Hershey Bears	AHL	65	13	19	32	....	....	....	56	11	3	1	4	18
1958-59	Hershey Bears	AHL	59	16	17	33	....	....	....	88	13	*5	2	7	34
1959-60	Seattle–Spokane	WHL	69	19	27	46	....	....	....	56	....	....	....	....	....
1960-61	Spokane–Seattle	WHL	66	19	20	39	....	....	....	73	11	1	2	3	21
1961-62	Sudbury Wolves	EPHL	69	31	24	55	....	....	....	86	5	3	0	3	8
1962-63	Los Angeles Blades	WHL	56	9	15	24	....	....	....	82	....	....	....	....	....
1963-64	Long Island Ducks	EHL	67	34	34	68	....	....	....	94	5	1	1	2	23
1964-65	Long Island Ducks	EHL	71	48	47	95	....	....	....	84	15	2	4	6	18
	NHL Totals		**6**	**0**	**0**	**0**	**0**	**0**	**0**	**2**	....	....	....	....	....

• Brother of Myron • EHL Second All-Star Team (1964) • EHL North Second All-Star Team (1965)

Traded to **Spokane** (WHL) by **Seattle** (WHL) for Jim Powers, November 7, 1959. Traded to **Seattle** (WHL) by **Spokane** (WHL) for Jim Powers, November 6, 1960. Traded to **LA Blades** (WHL) by **Detroit** for cash, July, 1962.

• STANLEY, Allan

— see page 1657

• STANLEY, Barney

Russell **HHOF**

RW – L. 6', 175 lbs. b: Paisley, Ont., 1/1/1893 d: 5/16/1971.

Season	Club	League	GP	G	A	Pts	AG	AA	APts	PIM	GP	G	A	Pts	PIM
1911-12	Edmonton Maritimers	ASHL	5	4	0	4	....	....	....	4	4	*8	0	*8	10
1912-13	Edmonton Dominions	ASHL	7	7	0	7	....	....	....	4	2	6	0	6	2
1913-14	Edmonton Dominions	ASHL	5	6	0	6	....	....	....	25	6	3	0	3	7
1914-15	Edmonton Albertas	ASHL	3	2	0	2	....	....	....	6	....	....	....	....	....
♦	Vancouver Millionaires	PCHA	5	7	1	8	....	....	....	0	3	5	1	6	0
	PCHA All-Stars	X-Games	2	2	1	3	....	....	....	0	....	....	....	....	....
1915-16	Vancouver Millionaires	PCHA	14	6	6	12	....	....	....	9	....	....	....	....	....
1916-17	Edmonton Dominions	X-Games	1	2	0	2	....	....	....	0	....	....	....	....	....
	Vancouver Millionaires	PCHA	23	28	*18	46	....	....	....	9	....	....	....	....	....
1917-18	Vancouver Millionaires	PCHA	18	11	6	17	....	....	....	9	2	1	0	1	9
	Vancouver Millionaires	St-Cup	5	2	0	2	....	....	....	6	....	....	....	....	....
1918-19	Vancouver Millionaires	PCHA	20	10	6	16	....	....	....	19	2	0	0	0	0
1919-20	Edmonton Eskimos	Big-4	12	10	12	22	....	....	....	20	2	0	1	1	*5
1920-21	Calgary Canadians	Big-4	15	11	*10	21	....	....	....	5	....	....	....	....	....
1921-22	Calgary Tigers	WCHL	24	26	5	31	....	....	....	17	....	....	....	....	....
1922-23	Regina Capitals	WCHL	29	14	7	21	....	....	....	10	2	1	0	1	2
1923-24	Regina Capitals	WCHL	30	15	11	26	....	....	....	27	2	1	0	1	2
1924-25	Edmonton Eskimos	WCHL	25	12	5	17	....	....	....	36	....	....	....	....	....
1925-26	Edmonton Eskimos	WHL	29	14	8	22	....	....	....	47	2	1	0	1	0
1926-27	Winnipeg Maroons	AHA	35	8	8	16	....	....	....	78	3	0	0	0	2

Season	Club	League	GP	G	A	Pts	AG	AA	APts	PIM	GP	G	A	Pts	PIM
			REGULAR SEASON								PLAYOFFS				
1927-28	Chicago Black Hawks	NHL	1	0	0	0	0	0	0	0	....	....	....	....	....
1928-29	Minneapolis Millers	AHA	40	8	5	13	....	....	....	34	4	1	0	1	2
1929-30	Edmonton Poolers	EJrHL	DID NOT PLAY – COACHING												
	NHL Totals		1	0	0	0	0	0	0	0	....	....	....	....	....
	Other Major League Totals		217	143	73	216	....	....	....	183	13	9	1	10	13

PCHA Second All-Star Team (1918) • WCHL First All-Star Team (1922, 1923)

Signed as a free agent by **Vancouver** (PCHA), February, 1915. Reinstated as an amateur, November 23, 1919. Signed as a free agent by **Calgary** (WCHL), November 30, 1921. Traded to **Regina** (WCHL) by **Calgary** (WCHL) for cash, November 13, 1922. Signed as a free agent by **Edmonton** (WCHL), November 7, 1924. Named playing coach of **Edmonton** (PrHL), October 28, 1926. Named playing coach of **Winnipeg** (AHA) after resigning position with **Edmonton** (AHA), October 28, 1926. Signed as a free agent by **Chicago** as manager/coach, September, 1927.

• STANOWSKI, Wally

Walter Peter "The Whirling Dervish"
D – L. 5'11", 180 lbs. b: Winnipeg, Man., 4/28/1919.

Season	Club	League	GP	G	A	Pts	AG	AA	APts	PIM	GP	G	A	Pts	PIM
1935-36	East Kildonan Bisons	MAHA	STATISTICS NOT AVAILABLE												
1936-37	St. Boniface Seals	MJHL	15	7	6	13	....	....	....	4	7	3	1	4	4
1937-38	St. Boniface Seals	MJHL	15	8	13	21	....	....	....	7	10	4	*7	11	6
	Winnipeg CP Air	WSrHL	6	4	3	7	....	....	....	0	....	....	....	....	....
	St. Boniface Seals	M-Cup	11	6	4	10	....	....	....	2	....	....	....	....	....
1938-39	Syracuse Stars	IAHL	54	1	16	17	....	....	....	8	3	0	2	2	0
1939-40	Toronto Maple Leafs	NHL	27	2	7	9	3	11	14	11	10	1	0	1	2
	Providence Reds	IAHL	8	0	3	3	....	....	....	6	....	....	....	....	....
1940-41	Toronto Maple Leafs	NHL	47	7	14	21	11	20	31	35	7	0	3	3	2
♦1941-42	Toronto Maple Leafs	NHL	24	1	7	8	1	8	9	10	13	2	8	10	2
1942-43	Winnipeg RCAF	WNDHL	13	5	12	17	....	....	....	20	5	2	1	3	16
	Winnipeg RCAF	Al-Cup	12	6	5	11	....	....	....	4	....	....	....	....	....
1943-44	Winnipeg RCAF	WNDHL	9	1	3	4	....	....	....	12	....	....	....	....	....
1944-45	Winnipeg RCAF	WNDHL	3	1	1	2	....	....	....	8	....	....	....	....	....
♦	Toronto Maple Leafs	NHL	34	2	9	11	2	10	12	16	13	0	1	1	5
1945-46	Toronto Maple Leafs	NHL	45	3	10	13	4	14	18	10	....	....	....	....	....
♦1946-47	Toronto Maple Leafs	NHL	51	3	16	19	3	19	22	12	8	0	0	0	0
♦1947-48	Toronto Maple Leafs	NHL	54	2	11	13	3	14	17	12	9	0	2	2	2
1948-49	New York Rangers	NHL	60	1	8	9	1	11	12	16	....	....	....	....	....
1949-50	New York Rangers	NHL	37	1	1	2	1	1	2	10	....	....	....	....	....
1950-51	New York Rangers	NHL	49	1	5	6	1	6	7	28	....	....	....	....	....
	Cincinnati Mohawks	AHL	7	0	0	0	....	....	....	2	....	....	....	....	....
1951-52	Cincinnati Mohawks	AHL	33	0	11	11	....	....	....	42	....	....	....	....	....
	NHL Totals		428	23	88	111	30	114	144	160	60	3	14	17	13

NHL First All-Star Team (1941) • Played in NHL All-Star Game (1947)

Rights traded to **Toronto** by **NY Americans** for Jack Shill, October 17, 1937. Traded to **NY Rangers** by **Toronto** with Moe Morris for Cal Gardner, Bill Juzda, Rene Trudell and the rights to Frank Mathers, April 26, 1948.

• STAPLETON, Pat

— *see page 1658*

• STARR, Harold

Harold William "Twinkle"
D – L. 5'11", 176 lbs. b: Ottawa, Ont., 7/6/1906 Deceased.

Season	Club	League	GP	G	A	Pts	AG	AA	APts	PIM	GP	G	A	Pts	PIM
1921-22	Ottawa Gunners	OCHL	1	0	0	0	....	....	....	0	....	....	....	....	....
1922-23	Ottawa St. Brigids	OCHL	2	0	0	0	....	....	....	0	....	....	....	....	....
1923-24	Ottawa Gunners	OCHL	STATISTICS NOT AVAILABLE												
1924-25	Ottawa Gunners	OCHL	STATISTICS NOT AVAILABLE												
1925-26	Ottawa Shamrocks	OCHL	2	1	0	1	....	....	....	0	....	....	....	....	....
1926-27	Ottawa Shamrocks	OCHL	15	3	2	5	....	....	....	....	....	....	....	....	....
1927-28	Ottawa Shamrocks	OCHL	STATISTICS NOT AVAILABLE												
1928-29	Ottawa Shamrocks	OCHL	11	1	1	2	....	....	....	....	5	*4	0	*4	10
1929-30	Ottawa Senators	NHL	28	2	1	3	3	2	5	12	2	1	0	1	0
	London Panthers	IHL	13	2	2	4	....	....	....	22	....	....	....	....	....
1930-31	Ottawa Senators	NHL	35	2	1	3	4	3	7	48	....	....	....	....	....
1931-32	Montreal Maroons	NHL	47	1	2	3	2	4	6	47	4	0	0	0	0
1932-33	Ottawa Senators	NHL	31	0	0	0	0	0	0	30	....	....	....	....	....
	Montreal Canadiens	NHL	15	0	0	0	0	0	0	6	2	0	0	0	2
1933-34	Montreal Maroons	NHL	....	....	....	....	....	....	....	....	3	0	0	0	0
	Windsor Bulldogs	IHL	41	5	2	7	....	....	....	40	....	....	....	....	....
1934-35	New York Rangers	NHL	33	1	1	2	2	2	4	31	4	0	0	0	2
	Windsor Bulldogs	IHL	15	0	0	0	....	....	....	12	....	....	....	....	....
1935-36	New York Rangers	NHL	16	0	0	0	0	0	0	12	....	....	....	....	....
	Cleveland Falcons	IHL	16	1	1	2	....	....	....	19	2	0	0	0	0
1936-37			REINSTATED AS AN AMATEUR												
1937-38	Ottawa Senators	OCHL	22	1	2	3	....	....	....	12	5	0	0	0	0
1938-39	Ottawa LaSalle	OCHL	16	3	0	3	....	....	....	12	5	1	2	3	10
	NHL Totals		205	6	5	11	11	11	22	186	15	1	0	1	4

Claimed by **Montreal Maroons** from **Ottawa** for 1931-32 season in Dispersal Draft, September 26, 1931. Traded to **Montreal Canadiens** by **Ottawa** with Leo Bourgeault for Marty Burke and future considerations (Nick Wasnie, March 23, 1933), February 14, 1933. Claimed on waivers by **Montreal Maroons** from **Montreal Canadiens**, December 5, 1933. Traded to **NY Rangers** by **Montreal Maroons** for cash, December 23, 1934. Traded to **Cleveland** (IHL) by **NY Rangers** for cash, January 30, 1936.

• STARR, Wilf

"Twinkie"
C – L. 5'11", 190 lbs. b: St. Boniface, Man., 7/22/1909.

Season	Club	League	GP	G	A	Pts	AG	AA	APts	PIM	GP	G	A	Pts	PIM
1927-28	Winnipeg Columbus Club	WJrHL	3	2	2	4	....	....	....	....	2	2	0	2	2
	Winnipeg CPR	WSrHL	3	2	0	2	....	....	....	8	....	....	....	....	....
1928-29	Winnipeg CPR	WSrHL	7	6	1	7	....	....	....	14	3	0	0	0	0
	University of Manitoba	WSrHL	6	6	4	10	....	....	....	12	2	0	0	0	2
1929-30	Winnipeg Winnipegs	WSrHL	12	7	*5	*12	....	....	....	10	2	0	0	0	0
1930-31	Springfield Indians	Can-Am	25	8	4	12	....	....	....	35	7	0	0	0	16
1931-32	Springfield Indians	Can-Am	38	19	11	30	....	....	....	38	....	....	....	....	....
1932-33	Springfield Indians	Can-Am	8	1	0	1	....	....	....	4	....	....	....	....	....
	New York Americans	NHL	26	4	3	7	7	6	13	8	....	....	....	....	....
1933-34	Detroit Red Wings	NHL	28	2	2	4	3	4	7	17	7	0	2	2	2
	Detroit Olympics	IHL	19	8	2	10	....	....	....	22	....	....	....	....	....
1934-35	Detroit Red Wings	NHL	24	1	1	2	2	2	4	0	....	....	....	....	....
	Detroit Olympics	IHL	18	8	9	17	....	....	....	21	....	....	....	....	....
	Windsor Bulldogs	IHL	1	0	0	0	....	....	....	0	....	....	....	....	....
1935-36	Detroit Red Wings	NHL	9	1	0	1	2	0	2	0	....	....	....	....	....
	Detroit Olympics	IHL	24	5	13	18	....	....	....	38	6	*6	*6	*12	*22
1936-37	Pittsburgh Hornets	IAHL	48	5	21	26	....	....	....	87	5	0	2	2	10
1937-38	Providence Reds	IAHL	31	5	13	18	....	....	....	28	7	3	4	7	4
1938-39	Providence Reds	IAHL	50	16	33	49	....	....	....	61	5	0	3	3	*15
1939-40	Providence Reds	IAHL	53	15	26	41	....	....	....	71	8	2	5	7	2
	NHL Totals		87	8	6	14	14	12	26	25	7	0	2	2	2

Signed as a free agent by **NY Rangers**, October 29, 1930. Traded to **NY Americans** by **NY Rangers** for cash after Springfield (Can-Am) franchise folded, December 22, 1932. Traded to **Detroit** by **NY Americans** for cash, September, 1933. Loaned to **Windsor** (IHL) by **Detroit**, January 30, 1935.

• STASIUK, Vic

Victor John "Yogi"
LW – L. 6', 185 lbs. b: Lethbridge, Alta., 5/23/1929.

Season	Club	League	GP	G	A	Pts	AG	AA	APts	PIM	GP	G	A	Pts	PIM
1946-47	Lethbridge Maple Leafs	AJHL	9	0	6	6	....	....	....	11	1	1	1	2	0
1947-48	Wetaskiwin Canadians	EJrHL	STATISTICS NOT AVAILABLE												
1948-49	Kansas City Pla-Mors	USHL	66	7	13	20	....	....	....	52	2	0	0	0	0
1949-50	Chicago Black Hawks	NHL	17	1	1	2	1	1	2	2	....	....	....	....	....
	Kansas City Pla-Mors	USHL	39	10	13	23	....	....	....	27	....	....	....	....	....
1950-51	Chicago Black Hawks	NHL	20	5	3	8	6	4	10	6	....	....	....	....	....
	Detroit Red Wings	NHL	50	3	10	13	4	12	16	12	....	....	....	....	....
♦1951-52	Detroit Red Wings	NHL	58	5	9	14	7	11	18	19	7	0	2	2	0
	Indianapolis Capitols	AHL	8	7	1	8	....	....	....	6	....	....	....	....	....
1952-53	Detroit Red Wings	NHL	3	0	0	0	0	0	0	0	....	....	....	....	....
	Edmonton Flyers	WHL	48	37	43	80	....	....	....	71	....	....	....	....	....
♦1953-54	Detroit Red Wings	NHL	42	5	2	7	7	2	9	4	....	....	....	....	....
	Edmonton Flyers	WHL	21	6	12	18	....	....	....	37	13	2	6	8	23
♦1954-55	Detroit Red Wings	NHL	59	8	11	19	10	13	23	67	11	5	3	8	6
	Edmonton Flyers	WHL	11	7	6	13	....	....	....	32	....	....	....	....	....
1955-56	Boston Bruins	NHL	59	19	18	37	26	21	47	118	....	....	....	....	....
1956-57	Boston Bruins	NHL	64	24	16	40	31	18	49	69	10	2	1	3	2
1957-58	Boston Bruins	NHL	70	21	35	56	26	36	62	55	12	0	5	5	13
1958-59	Boston Bruins	NHL	70	27	33	60	32	33	65	63	7	4	2	6	11
1959-60	Boston Bruins	NHL	69	29	39	68	34	38	72	121	....	....	....	....	....
1960-61	Boston Bruins	NHL	46	5	25	30	6	24	30	35	....	....	....	....	....
	Detroit Red Wings	NHL	23	10	13	23	11	12	23	16	11	2	5	7	4
1961-62	Detroit Red Wings	NHL	59	15	28	43	17	27	44	45	....	....	....	....	....
1962-63	Detroit Red Wings	NHL	36	6	11	17	7	11	18	37	11	3	0	3	4
	Pittsburgh Hornets	AHL	22	9	20	29	....	....	....	24	....	....	....	....	....
1963-64	Pittsburgh Hornets	AHL	42	10	10	20	....	....	....	32	5	0	0	0	4
1964-65	Pittsburgh Hornets	AHL	63	14	21	35	....	....	....	58	3	0	0	0	0
1965-66	Memphis Wings	CPHL	25	9	3	12	....	....	....	14	....	....	....	....	....
	NHL Totals		745	183	254	437	225	263	488	669	69	16	18	34	40

WHL First All-Star Team (1953) • Played in NHL All-Star Game (1960)

Traded to **Detroit** by **Chicago** with Bert Olmstead for Stephen Black and Lee Fogolin, December 2, 1950. Traded to **Boston** by **Detroit** with Marcel Bonin, Lorne Davis and Terry Sawchuk for Gilles Boisvert, Real Chevrefils, Norm Corcoran, Warren Godfrey and Ed Sandford, June 3, 1955. Traded to **Detroit** by **Boston** with Leo Labine for Gary Aldcorn, Murray Oliver and Tom McCarthy, January 23, 1961.

• STEELE, Frank

Harold Franklin
RW/D – R. 5'11", 170 lbs. b: Niagara Falls, Ont., 3/19/1905 Deceased.

Season	Club	League	GP	G	A	Pts	AG	AA	APts	PIM	GP	G	A	Pts	PIM
1923-24	Niagara Falls Cataracts	OHA-Jr.	6	4	0	4	....	....	....	....	....	....	....	....	....
1924-25	Niagara Falls Cataracts	OHA-Jr.	STATISTICS NOT AVAILABLE												
1925-26	Niagara Falls Falcons	OIHA	STATISTICS NOT AVAILABLE												
1926-27	Niagara Falls Falcons	OIHA	STATISTICS NOT AVAILABLE												
	Hamilton Tigers	Can-Pro	5	0	0	0	....	....	....	0	....	....	....	....	....
1927-28	Calumet Miners	NMHL	....	....	....	....	....	....	....	....	....	....	....	....	....
1928-29	Niagara Falls Cataracts	Can-Pro	40	7	2	9	....	....	....	47	....	....	....	....	....
1929-30	Detroit Olympics	IHL	42	15	3	18	....	....	....	47	3	0	0	0	2
1930-31	Detroit Falcons	NHL	1	0	0	0	0	0	0	0	....	....	....	....	....
	Detroit Olympics	IHL	40	10	6	16	....	....	....	34	....	....	....	....	....
1931-32	Detroit Olympics	IHL	48	7	6	13	....	....	....	44	6	0	0	0	4
1932-33	Detroit Olympics	IHL	16	3	0	3	....	....	....	12	....	....	....	....	....
	Kansas City Pla-Mors	AHA	7	0	0	0	....	....	....	4	....	....	....	....	....
	Duluth-Wichita	AHA	24	0	8	8	....	....	....	17	....	....	....	....	....
1933-34	Windsor Bulldogs	IHL	44	10	13	23	....	....	....	39	....	....	....	....	....
1934-35	Windsor Bulldogs	IHL	43	11	9	20	....	....	....	12	....	....	....	....	....
1935-36	Windsor Bulldogs	IHL	45	9	4	13	....	....	....	30	7	0	1	1	12
1936-37			REINSTATED AS AN AMATEUR												
1937-38	Detroit Holzbaugh	MOHL	4	1	0	1	....	....	....	4	....	....	....	....	....
	Detroit Pontiacs	MOHL	20	3	4	7	....	....	....	21	2	0	0	0	5
1938-39	Detroit Pontiacs	MOHL	27	2	5	7	....	....	....	18	7	1	1	2	8
1939-40	Detroit Pontiacs	MOHL	29	1	2	3	....	....	....	13	....	....	....	....	....
	NHL Totals		1	0	0	0	0	0	0	0					

Signed as a free agent by **Hamilton** (Can-Pro), November 2, 1926. Signed as a free agent by **Detroit Cougars**, August 30, 1929.

• STEMKOWSKI, Pete

— *see page 1661*

• STERNER, Ulf

LW – L. 6'2", 187 lbs. b: Deje, Sweden, 2/11/1941.

Season	Club	League	GP	G	A	Pts	AG	AA	APts	PIM	GP	G	A	Pts	PIM
1956-57	Forshaga IF	Sweden	7	3	0	3	....	....	....	....	....	....	....	....	....
1957-58	Forshaga IF	Sweden	14	2	0	2	....	....	....	....	....	....	....	....	....
1958-59	Forshaga IF	Sweden	11	7	8	15	....	....	....	....	....	....	....	....	....
1959-60	Forshaga IF	Sweden	14	17	6	23	....	....	....	14	....	....	....	....	....
	Sweden	Olympics	5	0	1	1	....	....	....	0	....	....	....	....	....
1960-61	Forshaga IF	Sweden	13	14	8	22	....	....	....	2	....	....	....	....	....
	Sweden	WEC-A	7	5	0	5	....	....	....	2	....	....	....	....	....
1961-62	Vastra Frolunda	Sweden	13	12	9	21	....	....	....	26	7	6	4	10	5
	Sweden	WEC-A	7	9	7	16	....	....	....	2	....	....	....	....	....
1962-63	Vastra Frolunda	Sweden	14	14	6	20	....	....	....	6	7	7	4	11	0
	Sweden	WEC-A	7	7	2	9	....	....	....	2	....	....	....	....	....
1963-64	Vastra Frolunda	Sweden	12	10	2	12	....	....	....	6	7	1	4	5	10
	Sweden	Olympics	7	6	5	*11	....	....	....	0	....	....	....	....	....
1964-65	New York Rangers	NHL	4	0	0	0	0	0	0	0	....	....	....	....	....
	St. Paul Rangers	CPHL	16	12	9	21	....	....	....	2	....	....	....	....	....
	Baltimore Clippers	AHL	52	18	26	44	....	....	....	12	5	1	0	1	2
1965-66	Rogle BK Angelholm	Swede-2	15	32	11	43	....	....	....	....	6	12	3	15	....
	Sweden	WEC-A	7	4	1	5	....	....	....	0	....	....	....	....	....

Season	Club	League	GP	G	A	Pts	AG	AA	APts	PIM	GP	G	A	Pts	PIM
			REGULAR SEASON								PLAYOFFS				
1966-67	Rogle BK Angelholm	Swede-2	19	4	11	15	....	....	....	11	....	....	....	....	....
	Sweden	WEC-A	7	2	3	5	....	....	....	7	....	....	....	....	....
1967-68	Farjestads BK Karlstad	Sweden	21	16	8	24	....	....	....	19	....	....	....	....	....
1968-69	Vastra Frolunda	Sweden	19	19	20	39	....	....	....	10	7	5	7	12	2
	Sweden	WEC-A	10	5	9	14	....	....	....	8	....	....	....	....	....
1969-70	Farjestads BK Karlstad	Swede-2	17	14	22	36	....	....	....	....	5	3	4	7	2
	Sweden	WEC-A	10	1	7	8	....	....	....	7	....	....	....	....	....
1970-71	Farjestads BK Karlstad	Sweden	6	4	7	11	....	....	....	13	14	10	3	13	14
	Sweden	WEC-A	10	2	2	4	....	....	....	2	....	....	....	....	....
1971-72	Farjestads BK Karlstad	Sweden	14	10	15	*25	....	....	....	28	14	5	6	11	24
1972-73	Farjestads BK Karlstad	Sweden	14	7	*15	22	....	....	....	23	14	10	2	12	29
	Sweden	WEC-A	9	5	2	7	....	....	....	6	....	....	....	....	....
1973-74	London Lions	Britain	64	27	88	115	....	....	....	71	2	0	2	2	0
1974-75	BK Backen	Swede-2	22	14	*30	44	....	....	....	*63	....	....	....	....	....
1975-76	BK Backen	Swede-2	22	17	*23	40	....	....	....	31	....	....	....	....	....
1976-77	BK Backen	Swede-2	24	14	24	38	....	....	....	....	....	....	....	....	....
1977-78	Vanesborgs HC	Swede-3	15	17	16	33	....	....	....	....	....	....	....	....	....
1978/89	Hammaro HC	Swede-3	DID NOT PLAY – COACHING												
1989-90	Hammaro HC	Swede-3	1	0	0	0	....	....	....	0	....	....	....	....	....
	NHL Totals		**4**	**0**	**0**	**0**	**0**	**0**	**0**	**0**	....	....	....	....	....

WEC-A All-Star Team (1962, 1969) • Swedish Player of the Year (1963) • Named Best Forward at WEC-A (1969)

Signed as a free agent by **NY Rangers**, October 1, 1964. Selected by **New York** (WHA) in WHA General Player Draft, February 12, 1972.

• STEVENS, Phil
Phillip Collins
C/D – R. 5'11", 165 lbs. b: St. Lambert, Ont., 2/15/1893 d: 4/8/1968.

Season	Club	League	GP	G	A	Pts	AG	AA	APts	PIM	GP	G	A	Pts	PIM
1911-12	Montreal AAA	IPAHU	5	3	0	3	....	....	....	15	....	....	....	....	....
	Montreal St-Jacques	MCHL	STATISTICS NOT AVAILABLE												
1912-13	Grand'Mere AAA	IPAHU	5	0	0	0	....	....	....	12	....	....	....	....	....
	Grand'Mere AAA	Al-Cup	2	0	0	0	....	....	....	0	....	....	....	....	....
1913-14	Grand'Mere AAA	IPAHU	STATISTICS NOT AVAILABLE												
1914-15	Montreal Wanderers	NHA	15	0	1	1	....	....	....	6	2	0	0	0	....
1915-16	Montreal Wanderers	NHA	22	2	2	4	....	....	....	33	....	....	....	....	....
1916-17	Montreal Wanderers	NHA	15	4	2	6	....	....	....	38	....	....	....	....	....
1917-18	**Montreal Wanderers**	**NHL**	**4**	**1**	**0**	**1**	**1**	**0**	**1**	**3**	....	....	....	....	....
1918-19			MILITARY SERVICE												
1919-20			DID NOT PLAY												
1920-21			DID NOT PLAY												
1921-22	**Montreal Canadiens**	**NHL**	**4**	**0**	**0**	**0**	**0**	**0**	**0**	**0**	....	....	....	....	....
1922-23	Saskatoon Sheiks	WCHL	15	0	0	0	....	....	....	3	....	....	....	....	....
1923-24	Saskatoon Crescents	WCHL	26	6	2	8	....	....	....	14	....	....	....	....	....
1924-25	Saskatoon Crescents	WCHL	25	2	0	2	....	....	....	30	2	0	0	0	0
1925-26	**Boston Bruins**	**NHL**	**17**	**0**	**0**	**0**	**0**	**0**	**0**	**0**	....	....	....	....	....
1926-27	Springfield Indians	Can-Am	6	0	1	1	....	....	....	0	....	....	....	....	....
	Saskatoon Sheiks	PHL	23	8	2	10	....	....	....	11	4	1	1	2	6
1927-28	Saskatoon Sheiks	PHL	28	3	1	4	....	....	....	8	....	....	....	....	....
1928-29	Oakland Shieks	Cal-Pro	....	6	2	8	....	....	....	....	....	....	....	....	....
1929-30	Oakland Sheiks	Cal-Pro	STATISTICS NOT AVAILABLE												
1930-31	Oakland Sheiks	Cal-Pro	....	12	4	16	....	....	....	....	4	0	1	1	....
1931-32	Oakland Sheiks	Cal-Pro	....	1	0	1	....	....	....	....	....	....	....	....	....
	NHL Totals		**25**	**1**	**0**	**1**	**1**	**0**	**1**	**3**	....	....	....	....	....
	Other Major League Totals		118	14	7	21	....	....	....	124	4	0	0	0	0

PHL First All-Star Team (1927)

Signed as a free agent by **Montreal Wanderers** (NHA), December 4, 1914. Rights retained by **Montreal Wanderers** after NHA folded, November 26, 1917. Signed as a free agent by **Montreal Canadiens**, December 6, 1921. Claimed on waivers by **Saskatoon** (WCHL) from **Montreal Canadiens**, November 13, 1922. Signed as a free agent by **Boston**, November 14, 1925. Signed as a free agent by **NY Rangers**, October, 1926. Loaned to **Springfield** (Can-Am) by **NY Rangers** for cash, November 15, 1926. Signed as a free agent by **Saskatoon** (PHL), December 29, 1926.

• STEWART, Gaye
James Gaye "Box Car"
LW – L. 5'11", 175 lbs. b: Fort William, Ont., 6/28/1923.

Season	Club	League	GP	G	A	Pts	AG	AA	APts	PIM	GP	G	A	Pts	PIM
1939-40	Port Arthur Bruins	TBJHL	16	*17	6	23	....	....	....	18	5	*8	2	*10	4
1940-41	Toronto Marlboros	OHA-Jr.	16	*31	13	*44	....	....	....	16	12	13	7	20	10
1941-42	Toronto Marlboros	OHA-Jr.	13	13	8	21	....	....	....	2	6	3	4	7	4
	Hershey Bears	AHL	5	4	2	6	....	....	....	0	10	4	5	9	0
♦	**Toronto Maple Leafs**	**NHL**	....	....	....	....	....	....	....	....	**1**	**0**	**0**	**0**	**0**
1942-43	**Toronto Maple Leafs**	**NHL**	**48**	**24**	**23**	**47**	**25**	**21**	**46**	**20**	**4**	**0**	**2**	**2**	**4**
1943-44	Montreal Royals	QSHL	10	4	7	11	....	....	....	8	4	6	2	8	0
	Montreal Navy	MCHL	6	5	7	12	....	....	....	2	5	*7	4	11	4
1944-45	Cornwallis Navy	NSDHL	11	9	7	16	....	....	....	12	3	3	4	*7	2
1945-46	**Toronto Maple Leafs**	**NHL**	**50**	***37**	**15**	**52**	**45**	**22**	**67**	**8**	....	....	....	....	....
♦**1946-47**	**Toronto Maple Leafs**	**NHL**	**60**	**19**	**14**	**33**	**21**	**17**	**38**	**15**	**11**	**2**	**5**	**7**	**8**
	Valleyfield Braves	QSHL	1	1	0	1	....	....	....	0	....	....	....	....	....
1947-48	**Toronto Maple Leafs**	**NHL**	**7**	**1**	**0**	**1**	**1**	**0**	**1**	**0**	....	....	....	....	....
	Chicago Black Hawks	**NHL**	**54**	**26**	**29**	**55**	**34**	**38**	**72**	**83**	....	....	....	....	....
1948-49	**Chicago Black Hawks**	**NHL**	**54**	**20**	**18**	**38**	**28**	**26**	**54**	**57**	....	....	....	....	....
1949-50	**Chicago Black Hawks**	**NHL**	**70**	**24**	**19**	**43**	**31**	**23**	**54**	**43**	....	....	....	....	....
1950-51	**Detroit Red Wings**	**NHL**	**67**	**18**	**13**	**31**	**23**	**16**	**39**	**18**	**6**	**0**	**2**	**2**	**4**
1951-52	**New York Rangers**	**NHL**	**69**	**15**	**25**	**40**	**20**	**31**	**51**	**22**	....	....	....	....	....
1952-53	**New York Rangers**	**NHL**	**18**	**1**	**1**	**2**	**1**	**1**	**2**	**8**	....	....	....	....	....
	Montreal Canadiens	**NHL**	**5**	**0**	**2**	**2**	**0**	**2**	**2**	**0**	....	....	....	....	....
	Quebec Aces	QMHL	29	13	20	33	....	....	....	28	22	*16	12	28	8
1953-54	Buffalo Bisons	AHL	70	42	53	95	....	....	....	38	3	0	2	2	4
	Montreal Canadiens	**NHL**	....	....	....	....	....	....	....	....	**3**	**0**	**0**	**0**	**0**
1954-55	Buffalo Bisons	AHL	60	17	19	36	....	....	....	36	....	....	....	....	....
	NHL Totals		**502**	**185**	**159**	**344**	**229**	**197**	**426**	**274**	**25**	**2**	**9**	**11**	**16**

Won Calder Trophy (1943) • NHL First All-Star Team (1946) • NHL Second All-Star Team (1948) • AHL First All-Star Team (1954) • Played in NHL All-Star Game (1947, 1948, 1950, 1951)

Signed as a free agent by **Toronto**, March 6, 1942. Traded to **Chicago** by **Toronto** with Bud Poile, Bob Goldham, Gus Bodnar and Ernie Dickens for Max Bentley and Cy Thomas, November 2, 1947. Traded to **Detroit** by **Chicago** with Metro Prystai, Bob Goldham and Jim Henry for Harry Lumley, Jack Stewart, Al Dewsbury, Pete Babando and Don Morrison, July 13, 1950. Traded to **NY Rangers** by **Detroit** for Tony Leswick, June 8, 1951. Claimed on waivers by **Montreal** from **NY Rangers**, December 1, 1952. Traded to **Buffalo** (AHL) by **Montreal** with Eddie Slowinski and Pete Babando for Jackie LeClair and cash, August 17, 1954. Named playing coach of **Buffalo**, September 1, 1954.

• STEWART, Jack
John Sherratt "Black Jack" HHOF
D – L. 5'10", 190 lbs. b: Pilot Mound, Man., 5/6/1917 d: 5/25/1983.

Season	Club	League	GP	G	A	Pts	AG	AA	APts	PIM	GP	G	A	Pts	PIM
1935-36	Portage Terriers	MJHL	16	0	0	0	....	....	....	6	6	0	1	1	4
1936-37	Portage Terriers	MJHL	16	4	1	5	....	....	....	20	4	1	1	2	2
1937-38	Pittsburgh Hornets	IAHL	48	0	1	1	....	....	....	16	2	0	0	0	0
1938-39	Pittsburgh Hornets	IAHL	21	0	0	0	....	....	....	20	....	....	....	....	....
	Detroit Red Wings	**NHL**	**32**	**0**	**1**	**1**	**0**	**2**	**2**	**18**	....	....	....	....	....
1939-40	**Detroit Red Wings**	**NHL**	**48**	**1**	**0**	**1**	**2**	**0**	**2**	**40**	**5**	**0**	**0**	**0**	**4**
1940-41	**Detroit Red Wings**	**NHL**	**47**	**2**	**6**	**8**	**3**	**9**	**12**	**56**	**9**	**1**	**2**	**3**	**8**
1941-42	**Detroit Red Wings**	**NHL**	**44**	**4**	**7**	**11**	**5**	**8**	**13**	**93**	**12**	**0**	**1**	**1**	**12**
♦**1942-43**	**Detroit Red Wings**	**NHL**	**44**	**2**	**9**	**11**	**2**	**8**	**10**	**68**	**10**	**1**	**2**	**3**	***35**
1943-44	Montreal RCAF	MDSHL	7	3	5	8	....	....	....	18	....	....	....	....	....
1944-45	Winnipeg RCAF	WNDHL	2	0	1	1	....	....	....	2	....	....	....	....	....
1945-46	**Detroit Red Wings**	**NHL**	**47**	**4**	**11**	**15**	**5**	**16**	**21**	***73**	**5**	**0**	**0**	**0**	**14**
1946-47	**Detroit Red Wings**	**NHL**	**55**	**5**	**9**	**14**	**6**	**11**	**17**	**83**	**5**	**0**	**1**	**1**	**12**
1947-48	**Detroit Red Wings**	**NHL**	**60**	**5**	**14**	**19**	**6**	**18**	**24**	**91**	**9**	**1**	**3**	**4**	**6**
1948-49	**Detroit Red Wings**	**NHL**	**60**	**4**	**11**	**15**	**6**	**16**	**22**	**96**	**11**	**1**	**1**	**2**	***32**
♦**1949-50**	**Detroit Red Wings**	**NHL**	**65**	**3**	**11**	**14**	**4**	**13**	**17**	**86**	**14**	**1**	**4**	**5**	**20**
1950-51	**Chicago Black Hawks**	**NHL**	**26**	**0**	**2**	**2**	**0**	**2**	**2**	**49**	....	....	....	....	....
1951-52	**Chicago Black Hawks**	**NHL**	**37**	**1**	**3**	**4**	**1**	**4**	**5**	**12**	....	....	....	....	....
1952-53	Chatham Maroons	OHA-Sr.	45	2	27	29	....	....	....	*134	....	....	....	....	....
1953-54	Chatham Maroons	OHA-Sr.	21	0	8	8	....	....	....	35	6	0	0	0	8
	NHL Totals		**565**	**31**	**84**	**115**	**40**	**107**	**147**	**765**	**80**	**5**	**14**	**19**	**143**

NHL First All-Star Team (1943, 1948, 1949) • NHL Second All-Star Team (1946, 1947) • Played in NHL All-Star Game (1947, 1948, 1949, 1950)

Signed as a free agent by **Detroit**, October 27, 1937. Traded to **Chicago** by **Detroit** with Harry Lumley, Al Dewsbury, Pete Babando and Don Morrison for Metro Prystai, Bob Goldham, Gaye Stewart and Jim Henry, July 13, 1950. • Missed remainder of 1950-51 season recovering from back injury suffered in game vs. Toronto, December 14, 1950.

• STEWART, Ken
D – L. 6', 175 lbs. b: Port Arthur, Ont., 3/29/1913 Deceased.

Season	Club	League	GP	G	A	Pts	AG	AA	APts	PIM	GP	G	A	Pts	PIM
1930-31	Edmonton Strathconas	EJrHL	13	3	2	5	....	....	....	7	2	0	1	1	0
	Edmonton Strathconas	M-Cup	2	1	0	1	....	....	....	0	....	....	....	....	....
1931-32	Edmonton Strathconas	EJrHL	13	7	1	8	....	....	....	....	....	....	....	....	....
	Edmonton Superiors	ESrHL	1	0	0	0	....	....	....	0	....	....	....	....	....
1932-33	Luscar Indians	ASHL	STATISTICS NOT AVAILABLE												
1933-34	Luscar Indians	ASHL	STATISTICS NOT AVAILABLE												
1934-35	Cadomin Colts	AIHA	STATISTICS NOT AVAILABLE												
1935-36	Luscar Indians	ASHL	....	....	....	....				....	8	3	2	5	4
1936-37	Lethbridge Maple Leafs	ASHL	STATISTICS NOT AVAILABLE												
1937-38	Lethbridge Maple Leafs	ASHL	24	13	*26	39	....	....	....	2	2	2	2	4	2
1938-39	Lethbridge Maple Leafs	ASHL	31	17	18	35	....	....	....	20	9	7	2	9	4
1939-40	Lethbridge Maple Leafs	ASHL	30	16	12	28	....	....	....	4	2	2	0	2	2
1940-41	Lethbridge Maple Leafs	ASHL	30	28	16	44	....	....	....	2	5	0	1	1	0
	Lethbridge Maple Leafs	Al-Cup	10	2	7	9	....	....	....	8	....	....	....	....	....
1941-42	**Chicago Black Hawks**	**NHL**	**6**	**1**	**1**	**2**	**1**	**1**	**2**	**2**	....	....	....	....	....
	Kansas City Americans	AHA	41	17	25	42	....	....	....	6	5	6	2	8	0
1942-43	Calgary Army	CNDHL	23	13	15	28	....	....	....	16	5	0	2	2	4
	Calgary Army	Al-Cup	5	1	2	3	....	....	....	4	....	....	....	....	....
1943-44	Calgary Army	CNDHL	15	5	2	7	....	....	....	6	2	1	1	2	0
1944-45	Calgary Army	CNDHL	15	8	7	15	....	....	....	0	....	....	....	....	....
1945-46	Regina Caps	WCSHL	23	15	16	31	....	....	....	16	....	....	....	....	....
1946-47	Los Angeles Ramblers	WKHL	48	26	35	61	....	....	....	14	....	....	....	....	....
1947-48	Calgary Stampeders	WCSHL	47	14	22	36	....	....	....	20	11	1	2	3	4
1948-49			DID NOT PLAY												
1949-50	Kelowna Packers	OSHL	19	10	10	20	....	....	....	14	....	....	....	....	....
1950-51	Kamloops Elks	OSHL	52	24	31	55	....	....	....	11	5	3	1	4	4
	NHL Totals		**6**	**1**	**1**	**2**	**1**	**1**	**2**	**2**	....	....	....	....	....

• STEWART, Nels
Nelson Robert "Old Poison" HHOF
C – L. 6'1", 195 lbs. b: Montreal, Que., 12/29/1902 d: 8/21/1957.

Season	Club	League	GP	G	A	Pts	AG	AA	APts	PIM	GP	G	A	Pts	PIM
1917/19	Toronto Beaches	OHA-Jr.	STATISTICS NOT AVAILABLE												
1919-20	Parkdale Canoe Club	OHA-Sr.	8	18	2	20	....	....	....	....	1	1	0	1	....
1920-21	Cleveland Indians	USAHA	10	*23	0	*23	....	....	....	....	8	*6	0	*6	....
1921-22	Cleveland Indians	USAHA	12	13	0	13	....	....	....	....	....	....	....	....	....
1922-23	Cleveland Indians	USAHA	20	*22	0	*22	....	....	....	....	....	....	....	....	....
1923-24	Cleveland Indians	USAHA	20	*21	*8	*29	....	....	....	....	8	*5	2	*7	....
1924-25	Cleveland Blues	USAHA	40	*21	0	*21	....	....	....	....	8	*6	3	*9	24
1925-26	**Montreal Maroons**	**NHL**	**36**	***34**	**8**	***42**	**61**	**53**	**114**	**119**	**4**	**0**	**2**	**2**	**10**
♦	Montreal Maroons	St-Cup	4	6	1	7	....	....	....	14	....	....	....	....	....
1926-27	**Montreal Maroons**	**NHL**	**43**	**17**	**4**	**21**	**30**	**21**	**51**	***133**	**2**	**0**	**0**	**0**	**4**
1927-28	**Montreal Maroons**	**NHL**	**41**	**27**	**7**	**34**	**56**	**40**	**96**	**104**	**9**	**2**	**2**	**4**	**13**
1928-29	**Montreal Maroons**	**NHL**	**44**	**21**	**8**	**29**	**62**	**54**	**116**	**74**	....	....	....	....	....
1929-30	**Montreal Maroons**	**NHL**	**44**	**39**	**16**	**55**	**56**	**38**	**94**	**81**	**4**	**1**	**1**	**2**	**2**
1930-31	**Montreal Maroons**	**NHL**	**42**	**25**	**14**	**39**	**51**	**43**	**94**	**75**	**2**	**1**	**0**	**1**	**6**
1931-32	**Montreal Maroons**	**NHL**	**38**	**22**	**11**	**33**	**37**	**24**	**61**	**61**	**4**	**0**	**1**	**1**	**2**
1932-33	**Boston Bruins**	**NHL**	**47**	**18**	**18**	**36**	**33**	**38**	**71**	**62**	**5**	**2**	**0**	**2**	**4**
1933-34	**Boston Bruins**	**NHL**	**48**	**22**	**17**	**39**	**38**	**36**	**74**	**68**	....	....	....	....	....
1934-35	**Boston Bruins**	**NHL**	**47**	**21**	**18**	**39**	**35**	**31**	**66**	**45**	**4**	**0**	**1**	**1**	**0**
1935-36	**New York Americans**	**NHL**	**48**	**14**	**15**	**29**	**27**	**28**	**55**	**16**	**5**	**1**	**2**	**3**	**4**

			REGULAR SEASON								PLAYOFFS				
Season	Club	League	GP	G	A	Pts	AG	AA	APts	PIM	GP	G	A	Pts	PIM
1936-37	**Boston Bruins**	**NHL**	**11**	***3**	**2**	**5**	**5**	**4**	**9**	**6**	....	....	....	....	....
	New York Americans	**NHL**	**32**	***20**	**10**	**30**	**34**	**18**	**52**	**31**	....	....	....	....	....
1937-38	**New York Americans**	**NHL**	**48**	**19**	**17**	**36**	**31**	**27**	**58**	**29**	**6**	**2**	**3**	**5**	**2**
1938-39	**New York Americans**	**NHL**	**46**	**16**	**19**	**35**	**28**	**30**	**58**	**43**	**2**	**0**	**0**	**0**	**0**
1939-40	**New York Americans**	**NHL**	**35**	**6**	**7**	**13**	**10**	**11**	**21**	**6**	**3**	**0**	**0**	**0**	**0**
	NHL Totals		**650**	**324**	**191**	**515**	**594**	**496**	**1090**	**953**	**50**	**9**	**12**	**21**	**47**

NHL Scoring Leader (1926) • Won Hart Trophy (1926, 1930) • Played in NHL All-Star Game (1934)

Signed as a free agent by **Montreal Maroons**, June 25, 1925. • 1925-26 Montreal Maroons playoff totals includes series against Ottawa and Pittsburgh. Traded to **Boston** by **Montreal Maroons** for cash, October 17, 1932. Traded to **NY Americans** by **Boston** with Joe Jerwa for cash, September 28, 1935. Rights returned to **Boston** by **NY Americans** after NY Americans were unable to complete purchase agreement, May 27, 1936. Traded to **NY Americans** by **Boston** for cash, December 19, 1936.

• STEWART, Ron

— see page 1667

• STODDARD, Jack John Edward

RW – R. 6'3", 185 lbs. b: Stoney Creek, Ont., 9/26/1926.

Season	Club	League	GP	G	A	Pts	AG	AA	APts	PIM	GP	G	A	Pts	PIM
1943-44	Stratford Kroehlers	OHA-Jr.	13	7	6	13	....	....	....	0	....	....	....	....	....
	Hamilton Whizzies	OHA-Jr.	5	4	4	8	....	....	....	2	....	....	....	....	....
1944-45	Hamilton Pats	OHA-Sr.	4	4	1	5	....	....	....	0	....	....	....	....	....
1945-46	Hamilton Lloyds	OHA-Jr.	16	4	7	11	....	....	....	17	....	....	....	....	....
1946-47	Baltimore Clippers	EAHL	53	22	19	41	....	....	....	22	9	*8	3	11	2
1947-48	Providence Reds	AHL	45	6	7	13	....	....	....	4	5	1	1	2	0
	Quebec Aces	QSHL	10	5	1	6	....	....	....	16	....	....	....	....	....
1948-49	Providence Reds	AHL	61	25	28	53	....	....	....	36	14	4	4	8	6
1949-50	Providence Reds	AHL	69	32	29	61	....	....	....	31	4	1	2	3	2
1950-51	Providence Reds	AHL	70	37	27	64	....	....	....	24	....	....	....	....	....
1951-52	Providence Reds	AHL	35	20	28	48	....	....	....	16	....	....	....	....	....
	New York Rangers	**NHL**	**20**	**4**	**2**	**6**	**5**	**2**	**7**	**2**	....	....	....	....	....
1952-53	**New York Rangers**	**NHL**	**60**	**12**	**13**	**25**	**16**	**16**	**32**	**29**	....	....	....	....	....
1953-54	Cleveland Barons	AHL	66	23	34	57	....	....	....	43	5	0	0	0	0
1954-55	Providence Reds	AHL	58	13	16	29	....	....	....	15	....	....	....	....	....
1955-56	Trois-Rivieres Lions	QHL	27	5	13	18	....	....	....	19	....	....	....	....	....
	Owen Sound Mercurys	OHA-Sr.	6	4	3	7	....	....	....	4	6	2	2	4	6
1956-57	Owen Sound Mercurys	OHA-Sr.	52	15	28	43	....	....	....	56	....	....	....	....	....
1957-58	Kitchener Dutchmen	NOHA	32	10	16	26	....	....	....	22	....	....	....	....	....
1958-59			OUT OF HOCKEY – RETIRED												
1959-60	Chatham Maroons	OHA-Sr.	1	0	0	0	....	....	....	0	8	4	1	5	2
	Chatham Maroons	Al-Cup	12	3	5	8	....	....	....	2	....	....	....	....	....
1960-61	Woodstock Athletics	OHA-Sr.	....	14	17	31	....	....	....	22	....	....	....	....	....
1961-62	Woodstock Athletics	OHA-Sr.	1	0	2	2	....	....	....	0	....	....	....	....	....
	NHL Totals		**80**	**16**	**15**	**31**	**21**	**18**	**39**	**31**	....	....	....	....	....

Traded to **NY Rangers** by **Providence** (AHL) for Pat Egan, Zellio Toppazzini and Jean-Paul Denis, January 1, 1952. Traded to **Providence** (AHL) by **Cleveland** (AHL) for cash, June 19, 1954.

• STRAIN, Neil Neil Gilbert

LW/C – L. 5'9", 165 lbs. b: Kenora, Ont., 2/24/1926 d: 1975.

Season	Club	League	GP	G	A	Pts	AG	AA	APts	PIM	GP	G	A	Pts	PIM
1945-46	Portage Terriers	MJHL	10	12	10	22	....	....	....	0	....	....	....	....	....
1946-47	Valleyfield Braves	QSHL	38	13	21	34	....	....	....	18	....	....	....	....	....
1947-48	San Francisco Shamrocks	PCHL	66	21	22	43	....	....	....	36	4	6	1	7	6
1948-49	San Francisco Shamrocks	PCHL	67	29	24	53	....	....	....	42	....	....	....	....	....
1949-50	Cleveland Barons	AHL	4	2	3	5	....	....	....	0	....	....	....	....	....
	Minneapolis Millers	USHL	37	12	13	25	....	....	....	6	7	2	2	4	2
1950-51	Denver Falcons	USHL	39	10	21	31	....	....	....	10	....	....	....	....	....
1951-52	Saskatoon Quakers	PCHL	69	33	40	73	....	....	....	26	13	5	7	12	0
1952-53	**New York Rangers**	**NHL**	**52**	**11**	**13**	**24**	**14**	**16**	**30**	**12**	....	....	....	....	....
	Saskatoon Quakers	WHL	19	9	9	18	....	....	....	0	....	....	....	....	....
1953-54	Edmonton Flyers	WHL	8	1	1	2	....	....	....	0	....	....	....	....	....
	NHL Totals		**52**	**11**	**13**	**24**	**14**	**16**	**30**	**12**	....	....	....	....	....

Signed as a free agent by **Valleyfield** (QSHL), October 10, 1946. Traded to **NY Rangers** (Denver-USHL) by **Cleveland** (AHL) with Bill Richardson, Bob Jackson and Joe McArthur for Wally Hergesheimer, September 5, 1950. Traded to **Cleveland** (AHL) by **NY Rangers** with Emile Francis and cash for Johnny Bower and Eldred Kobussen, July 20, 1953. Traded to **Edmonton** (WHL) by **Cleveland** (AHL) for cash, November 16, 1953.

• STRATE, Gord Gordon Lynn

D – L. 6'1", 190 lbs. b: Edmonton, Alta., 5/28/1935.

Season	Club	League	GP	G	A	Pts	AG	AA	APts	PIM	GP	G	A	Pts	PIM
1952-53	Edmonton Oil Kings	WCJHL	31	3	3	6	....	....	....	32	13	0	1	1	6
1953-54	Edmonton Oil Kings	WCJHL	33	1	7	8	....	....	....	41	10	3	3	6	12
	Edmonton Oil Kings	M-Cup	14	0	2	2	....	....	....	28	....	....	....	....	....
1954-55	Edmonton Oil Kings	WCJHL	40	6	12	18	....	....	....	55	3	0	0	0	2
	Edmonton Flyers	WHL	2	1	0	1	....	....	....	0	....	....	....	....	....
1955-56	Brandon Regals	WHL	60	0	6	6	....	....	....	64	....	....	....	....	....
1956-57	**Detroit Red Wings**	**NHL**	**5**	**0**	**0**	**0**	**0**	**0**	**0**	**4**	....	....	....	....	....
	Edmonton Flyers	WHL	64	0	15	15	....	....	....	33	8	0	0	0	0
1957-58	**Detroit Red Wings**	**NHL**	**45**	**0**	**0**	**0**	**0**	**0**	**0**	**24**	....	....	....	....	....
	Cleveland Barons	AHL	15	0	1	1	....	....	....	4	7	0	1	1	2
1958-59	**Detroit Red Wings**	**NHL**	**11**	**0**	**0**	**0**	**0**	**0**	**0**	**6**	....	....	....	....	....
	Hershey Bears	AHL	53	0	2	2	....	....	....	40	13	0	0	0	5
1959-60	Edmonton Flyers	WHL	69	1	8	9	....	....	....	47	4	1	0	1	0
1960-61	Sudbury Wolves	EPHL	14	0	3	3	....	....	....	10	....	....	....	....	....
	Edmonton Flyers	WHL	57	1	7	8	....	....	....	40	....	....	....	....	....
1961-62	Sudbury Wolves	EPHL	70	2	17	19	....	....	....	83	5	0	0	0	4
	NHL Totals		**61**	**0**	**0**	**0**	**0**	**0**	**0**	**34**	....	....	....	....	....

WHL Prairie Division Second All-Star Team (1957)

Traded to **Calgary** (WHL) by **Edmonton** (WHL) with future considerations (Jack Turner, October, 1962) for Sid Finney, September, 1962.

• STRATTON, Art

— see page 1670

• STROBEL, Art Art George

LW – L. 5'6", 160 lbs. b: Regina, Sask., 11/28/1922.

Season	Club	League	GP	G	A	Pts	AG	AA	APts	PIM	GP	G	A	Pts	PIM
1941-42	Regina Abbotts	S-SJHL	7	0	0	0	....	....	....	0	....	....	....	....	....
1942-43	Regina Commandos	S-SJHL	13	4	5	9	....	....	....	2	6	2	*3	5	4
	Yorkton Wings	N-SSHL	1	0	0	0	....	....	....	0	....	....	....	....	....
	Regina Pats	M-Cup	2	0	0	0	....	....	....	0	....	....	....	....	....
1943-44	**New York Rangers**	**NHL**	**7**	**0**	**0**	**0**	**0**	**0**	**0**	**0**	....	....	....	....	....
	New York Rovers	EAHL	30	12	18	30	....	....	....	2	9	6	7	13	10
1944-45	Hershey Bears	AHL	56	11	15	26	....	....	....	8	11	5	0	5	4
1945-46	Hershey Bears	AHL	4	0	3	3	....	....	....	0	....	....	....	....	....
	Minneapolis Millers	USHL	43	6	8	14	....	....	....	6	....	....	....	....	....
1946-47	Minneapolis Millers	USHL	59	17	17	34	....	....	....	27	3	0	0	0	4
1947-48	Minneapolis Millers	USHL	59	19	23	42	....	....	....	15	10	0	2	2	2
1948-49	Minneapolis Millers	USHL	61	14	29	43	....	....	....	13	....	....	....	....	....
1949-50	Portland Buckaroos	PCHL	71	20	23	43	....	....	....	28	....	....	....	....	....
1950-51			OUT OF HOCKEY – RETIRED												
1951-52			OUT OF HOCKEY – RETIRED												
1952-53	Rochester Mustangs	USHL	32	32	30	62	....	....	....	6	....	....	....	....	....
1953-57	Rochester Mustangs	X-Games	STATISTICS NOT AVAILABLE												
1957-58	Rochester Mustangs	CHL	30	16	18	34	....	....	....	....	....	....	....	....	....
1958-59	Rochester Mustangs	CHL	30	22	17	39	....	....	....	....	....	....	....	....	....
	NHL Totals		**7**	**0**	**0**	**0**	**0**	**0**	**0**	**0**	....	....	....	....	....

Signed as a free agent by **NY Rangers**, October 21, 1943. Traded to **Portland** (PCHL) by **Minneapolis** (USHL) for cash, September, 1949.

• STUART, Billy William Roxborough "Red"

D – L. 5'11", 190 lbs. b: Sackville, N.B., 2/1/1900 d: 3/7/1978.

Season	Club	League	GP	G	A	Pts	AG	AA	APts	PIM	GP	G	A	Pts	PIM
1916-17	Amherst Ramblers	NSCHL	4	6	0	6	....	....	....	....	4	*7	0	*7	....
1917-18	Amherst Victorias	X-Games	7	8	2	10	....	....	....	....	5	4	*3	7	....
1918-19	Springhill Miners	X-Games	STATISTICS NOT AVAILABLE												
1919-20	Amherst Ramblers	X-Games	6	*21	3	*24	....	....	....	18	13	*30	8	*38	*35
1920-21	Amherst Ramblers	MIL	1	0	0	0	....	....	....	0	....	....	....	....	....
	Toronto St. Pats	**NHL**	**19**	**2**	**1**	**3**	**2**	**4**	**6**	**4**	**2**	**0**	**0**	**0**	**0**
1921-22	**Toronto St. Pats**	**NHL**	**24**	**3**	**7**	**10**	**4**	**22**	**26**	**16**	**2**	**1**	**1**	**2**	**0**
♦	Toronto St. Pats	St-Cup	5	0	2	2	....	....	....	6	....	....	....	....	....
1922-23	**Toronto St. Pats**	**NHL**	**23**	**7**	**3**	**10**	**12**	**11**	**23**	**16**	....	....	....	....	....
1923-24	**Toronto St. Pats**	**NHL**	**24**	**4**	**3**	**7**	**8**	**17**	**25**	**22**	....	....	....	....	....
1924-25	**Toronto St. Pats**	**NHL**	**4**	**0**	**1**	**1**	**0**	**4**	**4**	**2**	....	....	....	....	....
	Boston Bruins	**NHL**	**25**	**5**	**3**	**8**	**9**	**12**	**21**	**30**	....	....	....	....	....
1925-26	**Boston Bruins**	**NHL**	**33**	**6**	**1**	**7**	**10**	**6**	**16**	**41**	....	....	....	....	....
1926-27	**Boston Bruins**	**NHL**	**43**	**3**	**1**	**4**	**5**	**5**	**10**	**20**	**8**	**0**	**0**	**0**	**6**
1927-28	Minneapolis Millers	AHA	39	5	2	7	....	....	....	80	7	1	0	1	12
1928-29	Minneapolis Millers	AHA	39	17	6	23	....	....	....	87	4	0	*2	2	6
1929-30	Minneapolis Millers	AHA	48	12	8	20	....	....	....	70	....	....	....	....	....
1930-31	Seattle Eskimos	PCHL	34	5	8	13	....	....	....	20	4	0	1	1	*14
1931-32	Duluth Hornets	AHA	48	15	2	17	....	....	....	56	8	0	1	1	10
1932-33	Minneapolis Millers	CHL	39	3	1	4	....	....	....	37	7	1	1	2	6
1933-34	Halifax Wolverines	NSSHL	DID NOT PLAY – COACHING												
	NHL Totals		**195**	**30**	**20**	**50**	**50**	**81**	**131**	**151**	**12**	**1**	**1**	**2**	**6**

AHA MVP (1929)

Signed as a free agent by **Toronto**, January 5, 1920. Traded to **Boston** by **Toronto** for cash, December 14, 1924. Traded to **Minneapolis** (AHA) by **Boston** with cash and future considerations for Nobby Clark and Dutch Gainor, October 24, 1927. Traded to **Seattle** (PCHL) by **Minneapolis** (AHA) for cash, July 25, 1930.

• SULLIVAN, Barry Barry Carter "Big Ben"

RW – R. 6', 185 lbs. b: Preston, Ont., 9/21/1927.

Season	Club	League	GP	G	A	Pts	AG	AA	APts	PIM	GP	G	A	Pts	PIM
1943-44	Stratford Koehlers	OHA-Jr.	8	9	3	12	....	....	....	4	....	....	....	....	....
	Galt Red Wings	OHA-Jr.	13	10	9	19	....	....	....	0	2	0	1	1	2
1944-45	Oshawa Generals	OHA-Jr.	20	21	14	35	....	....	....	19	3	2	4	6	0
	Porcupine Combines	M-Cup	3	1	1	2	....	....	....	2	....	....	....	....	....
1945-46	Omaha Knights	USHL	40	11	14	25	....	....	....	15	....	....	....	....	....
1946-47	Omaha Knights	USHL	38	21	21	42	....	....	....	12	11	7	9	16	8
	Indianapolis Capitols	AHL	19	0	1	1	....	....	....	2	....	....	....	....	....
1947-48	**Detroit Red Wings**	**NHL**	**1**	**0**	**0**	**0**	**0**	**0**	**0**	**0**	....	....	....	....	....
	Indianapolis Capitols	AHL	68	22	26	48	....	....	....	14	....	....	....	....	....
1948-49	St. Louis Flyers	AHL	63	32	38	70	....	....	....	21	7	3	3	6	0
1949-50	St. Louis Flyers	AHL	69	19	38	57	....	....	....	20	2	0	0	0	0
1950-51	St. Louis Flyers	AHL	28	3	13	16	....	....	....	6	....	....	....	....	....
	New Haven Ramblers	AHL	14	7	10	17	....	....	....	2	....	....	....	....	....
	Providence Reds	AHL	11	6	6	12	....	....	....	0	....	....	....	....	....
1951-52	Providence Reds	AHL	61	25	47	72	....	....	....	12	14	6	*12	*18	8
1952-53	Providence Reds	AHL	61	23	37	60	....	....	....	31	....	....	....	....	....
	NHL Totals		**1**	**0**	**0**	**0**	**0**	**0**	**0**	**0**	....	....	....	....	....

AHL Second All-Star Team (1952)

• Loaned to **Porcupine** (NOHA) by **Oshawa** (OHA-Jr.) for Memorial Cup playoffs, March, 1945. Traded to **Chicago** (St. Louis-AHL) by **Detroit** with Red Almas, Lloyd Doran, Tony Licari and Thain Simon for Joe Lund and Hec Highton, September 9, 1948. Loaned to **New Haven** (AHL) by **Chicago** (St. Louis-AHL) for cash, November 7, 1950 and recalled when New Haven franchise folded, December 11, 1950. Traded to **Providence** (AHL) by **Chicago** (St. Louis-AHL) for Jack Hamilton, January 29, 1951.

• SULLIVAN, Frank Frank Taylor "Sully"

D – R. 5'11", 178 lbs. b: Toronto, Ont., 6/16/1929.

Season	Club	League	GP	G	A	Pts	AG	AA	APts	PIM	GP	G	A	Pts	PIM
1945-46	DeLasalle Oaklands	H.S.	6	2	1	3	....	....	....	0	9	6	1	7	0
1946-47	Toronto Marlboros	OHA-Jr.	2	2	0	2	....	....	....	0	....	....	....	....	....
1947-48	Oshawa Generals	OHA-Jr.	33	8	18	26	....	....	....	60	6	1	4	5	16
1948-49	Oshawa Generals	OHA-Jr.	44	14	22	36	....	....	....	112	2	1	3	4	2
1949-50	**Toronto Maple Leafs**	**NHL**	**1**	**0**	**0**	**0**	**0**	**0**	**0**	**0**	....	....	....	....	....
	Toronto Marlboros	OHA-Sr.	41	4	6	10	....	....	....	38	14	6	*10	*16	14
	Toronto Marlboros	Al-Cup	16	6	18	24	....	....	....	22	....	....	....	....	....
1950-51	St. Michael's Monarchs	OMHL	33	4	9	13	....	....	....	54	8	0	7	7	24
	St. Michael's Monarchs	Alx-Cup	10	1	*8	9	....	....	....	16	....	....	....	....	....
1951-52	Pittsburgh Hornets	AHL	61	10	16	26	....	....	....	76	11	0	9	9	4
1952-53	**Toronto Maple Leafs**	**NHL**	**5**	**0**	**0**	**0**	**0**	**0**	**0**	**2**	....	....	....	....	....
	Pittsburgh Hornets	AHL	51	11	16	27	....	....	....	88	10	0	2	2	4
1953-54	Pittsburgh Hornets	AHL	62	6	36	42	....	....	....	56	5	1	1	2	10

Season	Club	League	GP	G	A	Pts	AG	AA	APts	PIM	GP	G	A	Pts	PIM
1954-55	**Chicago Black Hawks**	**NHL**	**1**	**0**	**0**	**0**	**0**	**0**	**0**	**0**	....	....	....	....	....
	Buffalo Bisons	AHL	64	11	33	44	....	....	....	34	10	2	6	8	6
1955-56	**Chicago Black Hawks**	**NHL**	**1**	**0**	**0**	**0**	**0**	**0**	**0**	**0**	....	....	....	....	....
	Buffalo Bisons	AHL	55	6	40	46	....	....	....	40	5	1	1	2	4
1956-57	Buffalo Bisons	AHL	56	4	41	45	....	....	....	46	....	....	....	....	....
1957-58	Buffalo Bisons	AHL	65	2	36	38	....	....	....	34	....	....	....	....	....
1958-59	Springfield Indians	AHL	69	9	28	37	....	....	....	48	....	....	....	....	....
	NHL Totals		**8**	**0**	**0**	**0**	**0**	**0**	**0**	**2**	....	....	....	....	....

• Brother of Peter • AHL Second All-Star Team (1955, 1957) • AHL First All-Star Team (1956)

Traded to **Chicago** (Buffalo-AHL) by **Toronto** with George Blair and Jackie LeClair for Brian Cullen, May 4, 1954.

• SULLIVAN, Red George James

C – L. 5'11", 155 lbs. b: Peterborough, Ont., 12/24/1929.

Season	Club	League	GP	G	A	Pts	AG	AA	APts	PIM	GP	G	A	Pts	PIM
1947-48	St. Catharines Teepees	OHA-Jr.	26	10	12	22	....	....	....	34	3	2	3	5	0
1948-49	St. Catharines Teepees	OHA-Jr.	46	32	*48	80	....	....	....	53	5	6	4	10	6
1949-50	St. Catharines Teepees	OHA-Jr.	13	14	15	29	....	....	....	19	....	....	....	....	....
	Boston Bruins	**NHL**	**3**	**0**	**1**	**1**	**0**	**1**	**1**	**0**	....	....	....	....	....
	Hershey Bears	AHL	51	10	30	40	....	....	....	36	....	....	....	....	....
1950-51	Hershey Bears	AHL	70	28	56	84	....	....	....	36	6	1	2	3	0
	Boston Bruins	**NHL**	....	....	....	....	....	....	....	....	**2**	**0**	**0**	**0**	**2**
1951-52	**Boston Bruins**	**NHL**	**67**	**12**	**12**	**24**	**16**	**15**	**31**	**24**	**7**	**0**	**0**	**0**	**0**
1952-53	**Boston Bruins**	**NHL**	**32**	**3**	**8**	**11**	**4**	**10**	**14**	**8**	**3**	**0**	**0**	**0**	**0**
	Hershey Bears	AHL	36	10	40	50	....	....	....	18	....	....	....	....	....
1953-54	Hershey Bears	AHL	69	30	*89	*119	....	....	....	54	11	2	7	9	4
1954-55	**Chicago Black Hawks**	**NHL**	**70**	**19**	**42**	**61**	**25**	**49**	**74**	**51**	....	....	....	....	....
1955-56	**Chicago Black Hawks**	**NHL**	**63**	**14**	**26**	**40**	**19**	**31**	**50**	**58**	....	....	....	....	....
1956-57	**New York Rangers**	**NHL**	**42**	**6**	**17**	**23**	**8**	**19**	**27**	**36**	**5**	**1**	**2**	**3**	**4**
1957-58	**New York Rangers**	**NHL**	**70**	**11**	**35**	**46**	**14**	**36**	**50**	**61**	**1**	**0**	**0**	**0**	**0**
1958-59	**New York Rangers**	**NHL**	**70**	**21**	**42**	**63**	**25**	**43**	**68**	**56**	....	....	....	....	....
1959-60	**New York Rangers**	**NHL**	**70**	**12**	**25**	**37**	**14**	**24**	**38**	**81**	....	....	....	....	....
1960-61	**New York Rangers**	**NHL**	**70**	**9**	**31**	**40**	**10**	**30**	**40**	**66**	....	....	....	....	....
1961-62	Kitchener Beavers	EPHL	61	16	46	62	....	....	....	81	7	1	6	7	4
1962-63	Baltimore Clippers	AHL	31	14	22	36	....	....	....	25	....	....	....	....	....
1963/65	**New York Rangers**	**NHL**	DID NOT PLAY – COACHING												
	NHL Totals		**557**	**107**	**239**	**346**	**135**	**258**	**393**	**441**	**18**	**1**	**2**	**3**	**6**

AHL First All-Star Team (1954) • Won John B. Sollenberger Trophy (Top Scorer - AHL) (1954) • Won Les Cunningham Award (MVP - AHL) (1954) • Played in NHL All-Star Game (1955, 1956, 1958, 1959, 1960)

Traded to **Chicago** by **Boston** for cash, September 10, 1954. Traded to **NY Rangers** by **Chicago** for Wally Hergesheimer, June 19, 1956.

• SUMMERHILL, Bill William Arthur

RW – R. 5'9", 170 lbs. b: Toronto, Ont., 7/9/1915 d: 10/29/1978.

Season	Club	League	GP	G	A	Pts	AG	AA	APts	PIM	GP	G	A	Pts	PIM
1937-38	Verdun Maple Leafs	MCHL	22	16	*20	*36	....	....	....	20	8	*8	1	9	18
	Montreal Canadiens	**NHL**	....	....	....	....	....	....	....	....	**1**	**0**	**0**	**0**	**0**
1938-39	**Montreal Canadiens**	**NHL**	**43**	**6**	**10**	**16**	**10**	**16**	**26**	**28**	**2**	**0**	**0**	**0**	**2**
	New Haven Eagles	IAHL	6	1	2	3	....	....	....	0	....	....	....	....	....
1939-40	**Montreal Canadiens**	**NHL**	**13**	**3**	**2**	**5**	**5**	**3**	**8**	**24**	....	....	....	....	....
	New Haven Eagles	IAHL	27	14	27	41	....	....	....	16	3	1	1	2	2
1940-41	Cleveland Barons	AHL	49	14	13	27	....	....	....	48	8	2	2	4	8
1941-42	**Brooklyn Americans**	**NHL**	**16**	**5**	**5**	**10**	**7**	**6**	**13**	**18**	....	....	....	....	....
	Springfield Indians	AHL	36	21	28	49	....	....	....	42	5	5	1	6	2
1942-43	Buffalo Bisons	AHL	56	41	27	68	....	....	....	64	9	*5	9	*14	2
1943-44	Toronto Army Daggers	OHA-Sr.	1	0	0	0	....	....	....	0	....	....	....	....	....
1944-45	Toronto Shamrocks	TIHL	14	13	11	24	....	....	....	16	4	7	2	9	4
	Toronto Army	TNDHL	....	....	....	....	....	....	....	....	3	5	5	10	0
1945-46	New Haven Eagles	AHL	21	5	7	12	....	....	....	16	....	....	....	....	....
	Fort Worth Rangers	USHL	13	4	3	7	....	....	....	8	....	....	....	....	....
1946-47	Springfield Indians	AHL	61	26	30	56	....	....	....	37	2	1	1	2	0
1947-48	Springfield Indians	AHL	67	27	47	74	....	....	....	22	....	....	....	....	....
1948-49	Springfield Indians	AHL	65	30	36	66	....	....	....	36	3	3	4	7	2
1949-50	Springfield Indians	AHL	25	10	15	25	....	....	....	18	....	....	....	....	....
1950-51	New Haven Ramblers	AHL	27	12	11	23	....	....	....	16	....	....	....	....	....
	Portland Eagles	PCHL	40	15	16	31	....	....	....	10	6	1	0	1	4
	NHL Totals		**72**	**14**	**17**	**31**	**22**	**25**	**47**	**70**	**3**	**0**	**0**	**0**	**2**

MCHL First All-Star Team (1938) • AHL Second All-Star Team (1943)

Traded to **Cleveland** (AHL) by **Montreal Canadiens** with Bill MacKenzie for Jim O'Neill, May 17, 1940. Traded to **Brooklyn** by **Cleveland** (AHL) for cash, October 6, 1941.

• SUOMI, Al Al William

LW – L. 5'10", 170 lbs. b: Eveleth, MN, 10/29/1913 Deceased.

Season	Club	League	GP	G	A	Pts	AG	AA	APts	PIM	GP	G	A	Pts	PIM
1934-35	Chicago Baby Ruth	USAHA	....	....	....	....	....	....	....	....	2	2	0	2	....
1935-36	Detroit Tool Shop	MOHL	17	8	5	13	....	....	....	6	4	0	1	1	0
1936-37	**Chicago Black Hawks**	**NHL**	**5**	**0**	**0**	**0**	**0**	**0**	**0**	**0**	....	....	....	....	....
	Virginia Americans	TBSHL	20	8	4	12	....	....	....	12	....	....	....	....	....
	Detroit Pontiacs	MOHL	20	2	0	2	....	....	....	14	....	....	....	....	....
	NHL Totals		**5**	**0**	**0**	**0**	**0**	**0**	**0**	**0**	....	....	....	....	....

• SUTHERLAND, Bill — see page 1677

• SUTHERLAND, Max Ronald Maxwell

LW – L. 5'10", 165 lbs. b: Grenfell, Sask., 2/8/1907 Deceased.

Season	Club	League	GP	G	A	Pts	AG	AA	APts	PIM	GP	G	A	Pts	PIM
1921-22	Moose Jaw Monarchs	S-SJHL	1	0	0	0	....	....	....	0	....	....	....	....	....
1922-23	Moose Jaw Maple Leafs	S-SSHL	10	5	0	5	....	....	....	4	....	....	....	....	....
1923-24	Moose Jaw Canucks	S-SJHL	6	2	4	6	....	....	....	3	....	....	....	....	....
	Pense Wanderers	S-SSHL	2	1	2	3	....	....	....	0	....	....	....	....	....
1924-25	Moose Jaw Millers	S-SSHL	8	6	0	6	....	....	....	14	....	....	....	....	....
1925-26	Moose Jaw Millers	S-SSHL	18	13	5	18	....	....	....	12	....	....	....	....	....
1926-27	Moose Jaw Maroons	PrHL	32	17	7	24	....	....	....	38	....	....	....	....	....
1927-28	Moose Jaw Maroons	PrHL	28	13	5	18	....	....	....	*53	....	....	....	....	....
1928-29	Seattle Eskimos	PCHL	30	5	1	6	....	....	....	80	5	0	0	0	*12
1929-30	Seattle Eskimos	PCHL	36	10	3	13	....	....	....	102	....	....	....	....	....
1930-31	Seattle Eskimos	PCHL	34	9	2	11	....	....	....	96	4	1	0	1	2
1931-32	**Boston Bruins**	**NHL**	**2**	**0**	**0**	**0**	**0**	**0**	**0**	**0**	....	....	....	....	....
	Boston Cubs	Can-Am	35	7	7	14	....	....	....	51	5	0	1	1	8
1932-33	Calgary Tigers	WCHL	30	10	4	14	....	....	....	51	6	2	0	2	11
1933-34	Calgary Tigers	NWHL	28	14	4	18	....	....	....	50	5	2	0	2	4
1934-35	Calgary Tigers	NWHL	18	5	3	8	....	....	....	4	....	....	....	....	....
1935-36			DID NOT PLAY												
1936-37	Olds Elks	ASHL	DID NOT PLAY – COACHING												
1937-38	Olds Elks	ASHL	25	12	10	22	....	....	....	31	3	1	0	1	6
1938-39	Olds Elks	ASHL	13	7	6	13	....	....	....	30	....	....	....	....	....
	NHL Totals		**2**	**0**	**0**	**0**	**0**	**0**	**0**	**0**	....	....	....	....	....

Traded to **Boston** by **Seattle** (PCHL) for cash, October 21, 1931.

• SWEENEY, Bill William

C – L. 5'10", 165 lbs. b: Guelph, Ont., 1/30/1937 d: 1991.

Season	Club	League	GP	G	A	Pts	AG	AA	APts	PIM	GP	G	A	Pts	PIM
1953-54	Guelph Biltmores	OHA-Jr.	14	4	3	7	....	....	....	0	3	0	1	1	2
1954-55	Guelph Biltmores	OHA-Jr.	47	18	37	55	....	....	....	25	6	5	5	10	7
1955-56	Guelph Biltmores	OHA-Jr.	48	29	38	67	....	....	....	16	3	0	1	1	2
1956-57	Guelph Biltmores	OHA-Jr.	52	49	*57	*106	....	....	....	20	10	*19	7	*26	11
	Guelph Biltmores	M-Cup	6	2	3	5	....	....	....	0	....	....	....	....	....
1957-58	Providence Reds	AHL	70	31	46	77	....	....	....	24	5	1	1	2	2
1958-59	Buffalo Bisons	AHL	70	31	44	75	....	....	....	12	11	4	5	9	4
1959-60	**New York Rangers**	**NHL**	**4**	**1**	**0**	**1**	**1**	**0**	**1**	**0**	....	....	....	....	....
	Springfield Indians	AHL	67	37	59	96	....	....	....	14	10	*7	7	*14	0
1960-61	Springfield Indians	AHL	70	40	*68	*108	....	....	....	26	8	4	5	9	2
1961-62	Springfield Indians	AHL	70	40	61	*101	....	....	....	14	11	5	5	*10	0
1962-63	Springfield Indians	AHL	69	38	65	*103	....	....	....	16	....	....	....	....	....
1963-64	Springfield Indians	AHL	72	25	48	73	....	....	....	18	....	....	....	....	....
1964-65	Springfield Indians	AHL	51	13	31	44	....	....	....	26	....	....	....	....	....
1965-66	Springfield Indians	AHL	72	22	37	59	....	....	....	10	6	2	3	5	0
1966-67	Springfield Indians	AHL	65	16	50	66	....	....	....	12	....	....	....	....	....
1967-68	Springfield Kings	AHL	9	1	1	2	....	....	....	0	....	....	....	....	....
	Vancouver Canucks	WHL	15	3	5	8	....	....	....	2	....	....	....	....	....
	Memphis South Stars	CPHL	1	0	0	0	....	....	....	0	....	....	....	....	....
1968-69	Rochester Americans	AHL	10	0	0	0	....	....	....	2	....	....	....	....	....
1969-70	Oakville Oaks	OHA-Sr.	11	2	10	12	....	....	....	0	....	....	....	....	....
	NHL Totals		**4**	**1**	**0**	**1**	**1**	**0**	**1**	**0**	....	....	....	....	....

Won Dudley "Red" Garrett Memorial Award (Top Rookie - AHL) (1958) • AHL First All-Star Team (1960, 1962) • AHL Second All-Star Team (1961) • Won John B. Sollenberger Trophy (Top Scorer - AHL) (1961, 1962, 1963)

NHL rights transferred to **LA Kings** after NHL club purchased **Springfield** (AHL) franchise, May, 1967. Traded to **Vancouver** (WHL) by **LA Kings** with the loan of Mike Corbett and Larry Mavety for cash, October, 1967.

• TALBOT, Jean-Guy — see page 1686

• TATCHELL, Spence Spence Henry

D – L. 5'11", 175 lbs. b: Lloydminster, Sask., 7/16/1924.

Season	Club	League	GP	G	A	Pts	AG	AA	APts	PIM	GP	G	A	Pts	PIM
1940-41	Winnipeg Rangers	MAHA	STATISTICS NOT AVAILABLE												
1941-42	Winnipeg Rangers	MJHL	1	0	0	0	....	....	....	2	....	....	....	....	....
1942-43	Winnipeg Monarchs	MJHL	7	9	2	11	....	....	....	8	....	....	....	....	....
	New York Rangers	**NHL**	**1**	**0**	**0**	**0**	**0**	**0**	**0**	**0**	....	....	....	....	....
	New York Rovers	EAHL	43	3	10	13	....	....	....	27	9	0	2	2	4
1943-44	Cornwallis Navy	NSDHL	5	4	6	10	....	....	....	....	....	....	....	....	....
	Cornwallis Navy	Al-Cup	10	1	8	9	....	....	....	9	....	....	....	....	....
1944-45			MILITARY SERVICE												
1945-46	Nelson Maple Leafs	WKHL	20	7	3	10	....	....	....	10	8	2	2	4	9
1946-47	Nelson Maple Leafs	WIHL	34	16	14	30	....	....	....	8	7	2	1	3	0
1947-48	Nelson Maple Leafs	WIHL	35	7	13	20	....	....	....	6	3	0	1	1	2
1948-49	Nelson Maple Leafs	WIHL	42	9	13	22	....	....	....	6	5	2	3	5	0
1949-50	Nelson Maple Leafs	WIHL	1	0	0	0	....	....	....	0	....	....	....	....	....
	Kimberley Dynamiters	WIHL	33	15	18	33	....	....	....	9	5	2	4	6	2
1950-51	Kimberley Dynamiters	WIHL	32	10	20	30	....	....	....	8	7	1	2	3	....
1951-52	Kimberley Dynamiters	WIHL	35	15	18	33	....	....	....	8	2	1	1	2	0
1952-53	Kimberley Dynamiters	WIHL	30	6	12	18	....	....	....	6	4	0	2	2	0
1953-54	Kimberley Dynamiters	WIHL	18	1	9	10	....	....	....	8	....	....	....	....	....
	NHL Totals		**1**	**0**	**0**	**0**	**0**	**0**	**0**	**0**	....	....	....	....	....

Traded to **Montreal** (Buffalo-AHL) by **NY Rangers** with Hub Macey and Nestor Lubeck for Kilby MacDonald, January 12, 1944.

• TAYLOR, Billy William James "Billy the Kid"

C – R. 5'9", 150 lbs. b: Winnipeg, Man., 5/3/1919 d: 6/12/1990.

Season	Club	League	GP	G	A	Pts	AG	AA	APts	PIM	GP	G	A	Pts	PIM
1935-36	St. Michael's Buzzers	OHA-B	7	*9	*9	18	....	....	....	2	11	*27	7	*34	7
1936-37	Toronto British Consols	TMHL	12	12	14	*26	....	....	....	20	6	7	3	*10	0
1937-38	Oshawa Generals	OHA-Jr.	12	19	7	26	....	....	....	27	7	*8	*9	*17	10
	Oshawa Generals	M-Cup	13	*17	*19	*36	....	....	....	12	....	....	....	....	....
1938-39	Oshawa Generals	OHA-Jr.	14	*22	*31	*53	....	....	....	37	7	*7	*7	*14	8
	Oshawa Sr. Generals	OHA-Sr.	....	....	....	....	....	....	....	....	1	0	0	0	0
	Oshawa Generals	M-Cup	9	*11	*17	*28	....	....	....	14	....	....	....	....	....
1939-40	**Toronto Maple Leafs**	**NHL**	**29**	**4**	**6**	**10**	**7**	**9**	**16**	**9**	**2**	**1**	**0**	**1**	**0**
	Pittsburgh Hornets	AHL	17	14	14	28	....	....	....	11	9	*7	5	*12	4
1940-41	**Toronto Maple Leafs**	**NHL**	**47**	**9**	**26**	**35**	**14**	**37**	**51**	**15**	**7**	**0**	**3**	**3**	**5**
♦1941-42	**Toronto Maple Leafs**	**NHL**	**48**	**12**	**26**	**38**	**16**	**31**	**47**	**20**	**13**	**2**	***8**	**10**	**4**
1942-43	**Toronto Maple Leafs**	**NHL**	**50**	**18**	**42**	**60**	**18**	**40**	**58**	**2**	**6**	**2**	**2**	**4**	**0**
1943-44	Toronto Army Daggers	OHA-Sr.	1	0	0	0	....	....	....	5	....	....	....	....	....
1944-45	Newmarket Army	TNDHL	8	12	17	29	....	....	....	4	8	17	15	32	4
	Toronto Army Shamrocks	TIHL	14	9	11	20	....	....	....	12	1	1	2	3	0
1945-46	**Toronto Maple Leafs**	**NHL**	**48**	**23**	**18**	**41**	**28**	**26**	**54**	**14**	....	....	....	....	....
1946-47	**Detroit Red Wings**	**NHL**	**60**	**17**	***46**	**63**	**19**	**56**	**75**	**35**	**5**	**1**	**5**	**6**	**4**
1947-48	**Boston Bruins**	**NHL**	**39**	**4**	**16**	**20**	**5**	**21**	**26**	**25**	....	....	....	....	....
	New York Rangers	**NHL**	**2**	**0**	**0**	**0**	**0**	**0**	**0**	**0**	....	....	....	....	....
	NHL Totals		**323**	**87**	**180**	**267**	**107**	**220**	**327**	**120**	**33**	**6**	**18**	**24**	**13**

• Father of Billy

Traded to **Detroit** by **Toronto** for Harry Watson, September 21, 1946. Traded to **Boston** by **Detroit** for Bep Guidolin, October 15, 1947. Traded to **NY Rangers** by **Boston** with future considerations (Pentti Lund and Ray Manson, June, 1948) for Grant Warwick, February 6, 1948. • Suspended for life by NHL for gambling infractions, March 9, 1948. • Suspension lifted by NHL, August 25, 1970.

• TAYLOR, Billy William Gordon

C – L. 6'1", 175 lbs. b: Winnipeg, Man., 10/14/1942.

Season	Club	League	GP	G	A	Pts	AG	AA	APts	PIM	GP	G	A	Pts	PIM
			REGULAR SEASON								PLAYOFFS				
1958-59	St. John's PWC	H.S.	6	*10	*5	*15	....	....	....	....	....	....	....	....	....
	St. John's Jr. Guards	SJSHL	....	....	....	....	....	....	....	....	4	4	2	6	2
1959-60	St. John's PWC	H.S.	5	4	*4	8	....	....	....	23	....	....	....	....	....
	St. John's Jr. Guards	SJJHL	12	21	8	29	....	....	....	38	7	5	2	7	13
	St. John's Guards	SJSHL	6	2	3	5	....	....	....	2	....	....	....	....	....
	St. John's Caps	Nfld-Jr.	....	....	....	....	....	....	....	....	6	2	5	7	6
	St. John's All-Stars	Nfld-Sr.	....	....	....	....	....	....	....	....	2	1	2	3	0
1960-61	Guelph Royals	OHA-Jr.	48	12	19	31	....	....	....	89	14	7	5	12	*77
1961-62	Guelph Royals	OHA-Jr.	38	20	26	46	....	....	....	81	....	....	....	....	....
	Kitchener Beavers	EPHL	2	0	0	0	....	....	....	0	....	....	....	....	....
1962-63	Guelph Royals	OHA-Jr.	49	32	31	63	....	....	....	61	....	....	....	....	....
	Sudbury Wolves	EPHL	4	0	1	1	....	....	....	4	4	0	0	0	0
1963-64	St. Paul Rangers	CPHL	69	30	29	59	....	....	....	87	11	4	4	8	10
1964-65	**New York Rangers**	**NHL**	**2**	**0**	**0**	**0**	**0**	**0**	**0**	**0**	....	....	....	....	....
	Baltimore Clippers	AHL	5	1	1	2	....	....	....	4	....	....	....	....	....
	St. Paul–St. Louis	CPHL	43	17	24	41	....	....	....	65	....	....	....	....	....
1965-66	St. Louis Braves	CPHL	68	13	21	34	....	....	....	72	5	1	1	2	2
1966-67	Buffalo Bisons	AHL	63	9	26	35	....	....	....	38	....	....	....	....	....
1967-68	Memphis South Stars	CPHL	30	2	7	9	....	....	....	34	1	0	0	0	2
	NHL Totals		**2**	**0**	**0**	**0**	**0**	**0**	**0**	**0**	....	....	....	....	....

• Son of Billy. Traded to **Chicago** by **NY Rangers** with Camille Henry, Don Johns and Wally Chevrier for Doug Robinson, Wayne Hillman and John Brenneman, February 4, 1965. Claimed by **Minnesota** from **Chicago** in Intra-League Draft, June, 1967.

• TAYLOR, Bob

RW – R. 6'1", 190 lbs. b: Newton, MA, 8/12/1904 d: 12/12/1993.

Season	Club	League	GP	G	A	Pts	AG	AA	APts	PIM	GP	G	A	Pts	PIM
1924-25	Boston AA Unicorn	USAHA	5	2	0	2	....	....	....	4	....	....	....	....	....
1925-26	Boston AA Unicorn	USAHA	4	2	0	2	....	....	....	....	2	0	0	0	0
1926-27	Boston Tigers	Can-Am	32	11	1	12	....	....	....	24	....	....	....	....	....
1927-28	Boston Tigers	Can-Am	40	8	2	10	....	....	....	30	2	0	0	0	2
1928-29	Boston Tigers	Can-Am	37	12	4	16	....	....	....	56	4	2	0	2	6
1929-30	**Boston Bruins**	**NHL**	**8**	**0**	**0**	**0**	**0**	**0**	**0**	**6**	....	....	....	....	....
	Philadelphia Arrows	Can-Am	34	11	3	14	....	....	....	46	2	0	0	0	8
1930-31	Boston Cubs	Can-Am	40	8	3	11	....	....	....	40	9	1	2	3	10
1931-32	Boston Cubs	Can-Am	1	0	0	0	....	....	....	2	....	....	....	....	....
	Providence Reds	Can-Am	37	6	5	11	....	....	....	20	5	1	*2	3	0
1932-33	Providence Reds	Can-Am	45	10	4	14	....	....	....	12	2	0	0	0	0
1933-34	Providence Reds	Can-Am	39	3	7	10	....	....	....	0	3	2	1	3	0
1934-35	Providence Reds	Can-Am	38	2	5	7	....	....	....	0	2	0	0	0	0
1935-36	Providence Reds	Can-Am	2	0	0	0	....	....	....	4	....	....	....	....	....
	NHL Totals		**8**	**0**	**0**	**0**	**0**	**0**	**0**	**6**	....	....	....	....	....

Claimed by **Boston** from **Boston Tigers** (Can-Am) in Inter-League Draft, May 13, 1929.

• TAYLOR, Harry

C – R. 5'8", 165 lbs. b: St. James, Man., 3/28/1926.

Season	Club	League	GP	G	A	Pts	AG	AA	APts	PIM	GP	G	A	Pts	PIM
1939-40	Linwood St. James	H.S.	2	0	0	0	....	....	....	0	....	....	....	....	....
	St. James Deer Lodge	MAHA	....	....	....	....	....	....	....	....	4	8	1	9	0
1940-41	St. James Deer Lodge	MAHA	4	10	0	10	....	....	....	....	....	....	....	....	....
1941-42	St. James Collegiate	H.S.	5	3	1	4	....	....	....	....	1	2	0	2	....
	St. James Canadians	MAHA	6	5	1	6	....	....	....	....	5	1	0	1	....
1942-43	St. James Collegiate	H.S.	6	6	1	7	....	....	....	....	4	4	2	6	....
	St. James Canadians	MAHA	11	7	0	7	....	....	....	....	7	4	6	10	4
1943-44	St. James Canadians	MJHL	10	9	7	16	....	....	....	4	10	*14	5	*19	2
1944-45	St. James Canadians	MJHL	DID NOT PLAY – SUSPENDED												
	Winnipeg CPR Railway	WNDHL	8	5	2	7	....	....	....	....	3	2	3	5	....
	Winnipeg Monarchs	M-Cup	1	1	2	3	....	....	....	0	....	....	....	....	....
1945-46	Winnipeg Monarchs	MJHL	8	5	10	15	....	....	....	4	17	3	6	9	4
	Winnipeg CPR Railway	WNDHL	5	18	15	33	....	....	....	....	2	0	0	0	....
	Winnipeg Monarchs	M-Cup	17	16	18	34	....	....	....	8	....	....	....	....	....
1946-47	**Toronto Maple Leafs**	**NHL**	**9**	**0**	**2**	**2**	**0**	**2**	**2**	**0**	....	....	....	....	....
	Tulsa Oilers	USHL	5	2	6	8	....	....	....	2	....	....	....	....	....
	Pittsburgh Hornets	AHL	38	4	10	14	....	....	....	18	12	1	0	1	8
1947-48	Providence Reds	AHL	54	24	39	63	....	....	....	44	5	1	0	1	4
♦1948-49	**Toronto Maple Leafs**	**NHL**	**42**	**4**	**7**	**11**	**6**	**10**	**16**	**30**	**1**	**0**	**0**	**0**	**0**
	Pittsburgh Hornets	AHL	16	2	8	10	....	....	....	15	....	....	....	....	....
1949-50	Cleveland Barons	AHL	57	27	27	54	....	....	....	39	9	1	3	4	10
1950-51	Cleveland Barons	AHL	61	9	31	40	....	....	....	15	10	4	5	9	4
1951-52	**Chicago Black Hawks**	**NHL**	**15**	**1**	**1**	**2**	**1**	**1**	**2**	**0**	....	....	....	....	....
	St. Louis Flyers	AHL	46	19	22	41	....	....	....	30	....	....	....	....	....
1952-53	St. Louis Flyers	AHL	39	14	14	28	....	....	....	16	....	....	....	....	....
1953-54	Buffalo Bisons	AHL	70	10	31	41	....	....	....	24	2	0	1	1	0
1954-55	Buffalo Bisons	AHL	1	0	0	0	....	....	....	0	....	....	....	....	....
	Ottawa Senators	QHL	12	0	4	4	....	....	....	4	....	....	....	....	....
	S.S. Marie Greyhounds	NOHA	24	5	9	14	....	....	....	18	14	3	3	6	4
1955-56	S.S. Marie Greyhounds	NOHA	48	12	21	33	....	....	....	28	5	3	1	4	0
1956-57	Dauphin Kings	MHA-I	10	12	0	12	....	....	....	....	10	5	8	13	....
1957-58	St. Boniface Saints	MHA-I	5	5	0	5	....	....	....	....	10	10	2	12	....
	NHL Totals		**66**	**5**	**10**	**15**	**7**	**13**	**20**	**30**	**1**	**0**	**0**	**0**	**0**

• Statistics for 1939-40 and 1940-41 seasons are for playoffs only. • Suspended for the entire 1944-45 regular season by MJHL when transfer request to join Winnipeg Monarchs was denied, September, 1944. Signed as a free agent by **Toronto**, May 1, 1946. Traded to **Cleveland,** (AHL) by **Toronto** with Ray Ceresino and the loan of Tod Sloan for the 1949-50 season for Bob Solinger, September 6, 1949. Traded to **Chicago** (St. Louis-AHL) by **Cleveland** (AHL) for Jean-Paul Gladu, August 19, 1951. Traded to **Sault Ste. Marie** (NOHA) by **Buffalo** (AHL) for cash, December, 1954.

• TAYLOR, Ralph "Bouncer"

D – R. 5'9", 180 lbs. b: Toronto, Ont., 10/2/1905 d: 7/3/1976.

Season	Club	League	GP	G	A	Pts	AG	AA	APts	PIM	GP	G	A	Pts	PIM
1923-24	Toronto Canoe Club	OHA-Jr.	5	3	2	5	....	....	....	8	....	....	....	....	....
1924-25	Toronto Canoe Club	OHA-Jr.	8	9	2	11	....	....	....	0	2	0	2	2	....
1925-26	Toronto Canoe Club	OHA-Jr.	8	2	2	4	....	....	....	....	....	....	....	....	....
1926-27	Chicago Cardinals	AHA	29	4	1	5	....	....	....	57	....	....	....	....	....
1927-28	**Chicago Black Hawks**	**NHL**	**22**	**1**	**1**	**2**	**2**	**6**	**8**	**39**	....	....	....	....	....
	Moose Jaw Maroons	PrHL	16	7	2	9	....	....	....	20	....	....	....	....	....
1928-29	**Chicago Black Hawks**	**NHL**	**38**	**0**	**0**	**0**	**0**	**0**	**0**	**56**	....	....	....	....	....
	St. Louis Flyers	AHA	8	2	0	2	....	....	....	14	....	....	....	....	....
1929-30	**Chicago Black Hawks**	**NHL**	**17**	**1**	**0**	**1**	**1**	**0**	**1**	**42**	....	....	....	....	....
	New York Rangers	**NHL**	**22**	**2**	**0**	**2**	**3**	**0**	**3**	**32**	**4**	**0**	**0**	**0**	**10**
1930-31	Chicago Shamrocks	AHA	34	6	6	12	....	....	....	68	....	....	....	....	....
1931-32	Chicago Shamrocks	AHA	48	4	2	6	....	....	....	81	4	0	0	0	8
1932-33	Detroit Olympics	IHL	35	3	4	7	....	....	....	62	....	....	....	....	....
1933-34	Tulsa Oilers	AHA	2	2	1	3	....	....	....	2	....	....	....	....	....
	Kansas City Greyhounds	AHA	46	4	6	10	....	....	....	47	3	2	1	3	10
1934-35	Kansas City Greyhounds	AHA	44	6	1	7	....	....	....	59	2	0	0	0	2
1935-36	Kansas City Greyhounds	AHA	48	6	8	14	....	....	....	44	....	....	....	....	....
1936-37	Kansas City Greyhounds	AHA	42	5	3	8	....	....	....	30	3	0	0	0	7
	Tulsa Oilers	AHA	1	0	0	0	....	....	....	0	....	....	....	....	....
1937-38	Kansas City Greyhounds	AHA	6	1	0	1	....	....	....	6	....	....	....	....	....
	St. Louis Flyers	AHA	21	0	1	1	....	....	....	14	7	0	0	0	6
1938-39	St. Louis Flyers	AHA	38	0	1	1	....	....	....	27	7	1	2	3	10
	NHL Totals		**99**	**4**	**1**	**5**	**6**	**6**	**12**	**169**	**4**	**0**	**0**	**0**	**10**

Signed as a free agent by **Chicago** (AHA), October 29, 1926. Loaned to **St. Louis** (AHA) by **Chicago** for cash, November 23, 1928. Traded to **Tulsa** (AHA) by **Chicago** with cash for Teddy Graham, January 4, 1930. Transaction voided when NHL determined Taylor had not passed through waivers. Claimed on waivers by **NY Rangers** from **Chicago**, January 8, 1930. Traded to **Chicago Shamrocks** (AHA) by **NY Rangers** for $7,500, October 27, 1930. NHL rights transferred to **Detroit** from **Chicago Shamrocks** (AHA) after AHA club owners purchased Detroit (NHL and IHL) franchises, September 2, 1932.

• TAYLOR, Ted — see page 1690

• TEAL, Skip Allan Leslie

C – L. 5'8", 155 lbs. b: Ridgeway, Ont., 7/17/1933.

Season	Club	League	GP	G	A	Pts	AG	AA	APts	PIM	GP	G	A	Pts	PIM
1949-50	St. Catharines Lions	OHA-B	STATISTICS NOT AVAILABLE												
	St. Catharines Teepees	OHA-Jr.	....	....	....	....	....	....	....	....	3	1	2	3	0
1950-51	St. Catharines Teepees	OHA-Jr.	51	37	28	65	....	....	....	87	8	1	3	4	4
1951-52	Barrie Flyers	OHA-Jr.	14	4	9	13	....	....	....	56	....	....	....	....	....
1952-53	Barrie Flyers	OHA-Jr.	36	26	24	50	....	....	....	48	14	12	6	18	15
	Barrie Flyers	M-Cup	10	12	15	27	....	....	....	31	....	....	....	....	....
1953-54	Hershey Bears	AHL	66	16	21	37	....	....	....	38	11	3	4	7	16
1954-55	**Boston Bruins**	**NHL**	**1**	**0**	**0**	**0**	**0**	**0**	**0**	**0**	....	....	....	....	....
	Hershey Bears	AHL	58	14	29	43	....	....	....	87	....	....	....	....	....
1955-56	Victoria Cougars	WHL	67	22	21	43	....	....	....	34	8	1	1	2	2
1956-57	Quebec Aces	QHL	66	23	41	64	....	....	....	48	10	2	6	8	0
	Quebec Aces	Ed-Cup	6	2	7	9	....	....	....	0	....	....	....	....	....
1957-58	Quebec Aces	QHL	60	16	56	72	....	....	....	19	13	6	*14	20	4
	Springfield Indians	AHL	4	0	1	1	....	....	....	0	....	....	....	....	....
1958-59	Quebec Aces	QHL	62	24	38	62	....	....	....	42	....	....	....	....	....
1959-60	Kingston Frontenacs	EPHL	70	27	43	70	....	....	....	30	....	....	....	....	....
1960-61	Clinton Comets	EHL	63	46	66	112	....	....	....	32	4	1	1	2	0
1961-62	Clinton Comets	EHL	59	34	66	100	....	....	....	26	6	2	3	5	2
1962-63	Clinton Comets	EHL	51	35	58	93	....	....	....	12	13	10	8	18	10
	NHL Totals		**1**	**0**	**0**	**0**	**0**	**0**	**0**	**0**	....	....	....	....	....

• Brother of Vic • EHL Second All-Star Team (1961, 1962, 1963)

• TESSIER, Orval Orval Roy

C – L. 5'8", 160 lbs. b: Cornwall, Ont., 6/30/1933.

Season	Club	League	GP	G	A	Pts	AG	AA	APts	PIM	GP	G	A	Pts	PIM
1951-52	Kitchener Greenshirts	OHA-Jr.	52	*62	25	87	....	....	....	18	4	3	1	4	8
1952-53	Kitchener–Barrie	OHA-Jr.	55	54	40	94	....	....	....	19	15	7	13	20	12
	Barrie Flyers	M-Cup	10	10	18	28	....	....	....	14	....	....	....	....	....
1953-54	Montreal Royals	QHL	60	21	18	39	....	....	....	13	9	2	1	3	6
1954-55	**Montreal Canadiens**	**NHL**	**4**	**0**	**0**	**0**	**0**	**0**	**0**	**0**	....	....	....	....	....
	Montreal Royals	QHL	60	*36	30	66	....	....	....	8	12	4	7	11	0
1955-56	**Boston Bruins**	**NHL**	**23**	**2**	**3**	**5**	**3**	**4**	**7**	**6**	....	....	....	....	....
	Hershey Bears	AHL	2	0	1	1	....	....	....	0	....	....	....	....	....
	Quebec Aces	QHL	28	5	10	15	....	....	....	4	7	1	2	3	2
1956-57	Quebec Aces	QHL	68	*43	38	*81	....	....	....	24	10	7	5	12	0
	Quebec Aces	Ed-Cup	6	*9	3	*12	....	....	....	0	....	....	....	....	....
1957-58	Springfield Indians	AHL	12	5	3	8	....	....	....	2	....	....	....	....	....
1958-59	Trois-Rivieres Lions	QHL	62	27	39	66	....	....	....	4	8	2	3	5	9
1959-60	Kingston Frontenacs	EPHL	70	*59	*67	*126	....	....	....	10	....	....	....	....	....
1960-61	**Boston Bruins**	**NHL**	**32**	**3**	**4**	**7**	**3**	**4**	**7**	**0**	....	....	....	....	....
	Kingston Frontenacs	EPHL	34	22	21	43	....	....	....	6	5	4	2	6	0
1961-62	Kingston Frontenacs	EPHL	66	54	60	*114	....	....	....	12	11	5	9	14	0
1962-63	Portland Buckaroos	WHL	36	15	21	36	....	....	....	9	7	0	0	0	0
1963-64	Portland Buckaroos	WHL	66	14	34	48	....	....	....	4	5	1	2	3	0
1964-65	Clinton Comets	EHL	66	60	58	118	....	....	....	8	11	2	7	9	0
	NHL Totals		**59**	**5**	**7**	**12**	**6**	**8**	**14**	**6**	....	....	....	....	....

QHL First All-Star Team (1955, 1957) • Won President's Cup (Scoring Champion - QHL) (1957) • QHL Second All-Star Team (1959) • EHL North Second All-Star Team (1965) • Won Jack Adams Award (1983)

Claimed by **Boston** from **Montreal** in Intra-League Draft, June 1, 1955. Traded to **Montreal** by **Boston** (Portland-WHL) for cash, August, 1964.

• THIBEAULT, Lorrain Lorrain Laurence "Larry Half-n-Half"

LW – L. 5'7", 180 lbs. b: Charletone, Ont., 10/2/1918.

Season	Club	League	GP	G	A	Pts	AG	AA	APts	PIM	GP	G	A	Pts	PIM
1936-37	Cornwall Flyers	OCHL	23	3	4	7	....	....	....	10	6	0	0	0	0
1937-38	Hull Volants	OCHL	20	10	4	14	....	....	....	6	9	2	2	4	5
1938-39	Hull Volants	OCHL	9	15	2	17	....	....	....	14	....	....	....	....	....
	Springfield Indians	IAHL	8	0	1	1	....	....	....	7	3	0	0	0	0
1939-40	Springfield Indians	IAHL	29	11	14	25	....	....	....	6	3	0	0	0	2
1940-41	Springfield Indians	AHL	54	14	18	32	....	....	....	32	3	1	0	1	2
1941-42	Cornwall Flyers	QSHL	36	17	18	35	....	....	....	45	5	1	4	5	6
1942-43	Cornwall Flyers	QSHL	33	21	27	*48	....	....	....	22	6	1	2	3	2
1943-44	Buffalo Bisons	AHL	51	18	45	63	....	....	....	46	9	7	10	17	14
1944-45	**Detroit Red Wings**	**NHL**	**4**	**0**	**2**	**2**	**0**	**2**	**2**	**2**	....	....	....	....	....
	Indianapolis Capitols	AHL	31	2	12	14	....	....	....	20	2	0	0	0	2
1945-46	Buffalo Bisons	AHL	6	2	3	5	....	....	....	4	....	....	....	....	....
	Montreal Canadiens	**NHL**	**1**	**0**	**0**	**0**	**0**	**0**	**0**	**0**	....	....	....	....	....
	Hull Volants	QSHL	25	9	18	27	....	....	....	48	....	....	....	....	....
1946-47	Victoriaville Tigers	QPHL	35	21	41	62	....	....	....	40	5	2	3	5	2
1947-48	Houston Huskies	USHL	46	12	17	29	....	....	....	28	4	0	0	0	0
1948-49	Houston Huskies	USHL	22	7	6	13	....	....	....	14	....	....	....	....	....
	San Diego Skyhawks	PCHL	15	6	4	10	....	....	....	18	....	....	....	....	....

Season	Club	League	GP	G	A	Pts	AG	AA	APts	PIM	GP	G	A	Pts	PIM
			REGULAR SEASON								PLAYOFFS				
1949-50	Victoria Cougars	AHL	66	20	28	48	....	....	....	46	....	....	....	....	....
1950-51	Buckingham Beavers	ECSHL	DID NOT PLAY – COACHING												
1951-52	Buckingham Beavers	ECSHL	24	10	16	26	....	....	....	24	....	....	....	....	....
	Thurso Lumber Kings	ECSHL	10	3	3	6	....	....	....	15	6	1	1	2	4
1952-53	Thurso Lumber Kings	ECSHL	STATISTICS NOT AVAILABLE												
1953-54	Edmonton Flyers	WHL	61	4	8	12	....	....	....	16	13	2	1	3	2
1954-55	Quebec Aces	QHL	39	1	8	9	....	....	....	27	1	0	0	0	0
1955-56	Quebec Aces	QHL	28	1	5	6	....	....	....	6	....	....	....	....	....
	NHL Totals		**5**	**0**	**2**	**2**	**0**	**2**	**2**	**2**	....	....	....	....	....

Signed as a free agent by **Detroit**, October 21, 1944. Traded to **Buffalo** (AHL) by **Detroit** for cash, October 17, 1945. Loaned to **Montreal** by **Buffalo** (AHL) for the loan of Wilf Field, Kenny Mosdell and Frank Eddolls, October 29, 1945. Returned to **Buffalo** (AHL) from **Montreal** and requested that his amateur status be reinstated, November 6, 1945. Signed with **Hull** (QSHL), November, 1945.

• THOMAS, Cy
Cyril James

W – L. 5'11", 185 lbs. b: Dowlais, Wales, 8/5/1926.

Season	Club	League	GP	G	A	Pts	AG	AA	APts	PIM	GP	G	A	Pts	PIM
1945-46	Edmonton Canadians	EJrHL	STATISTICS NOT AVAILABLE												
	Edmonton Canadians	M-Cup	14	10	*9	19	....	....	....	18	....	....	....	....	....
1946-47	Edmonton Flyers	WCSHL	30	12	7	19	....	....	....	18	4	0	3	3	7
1947-48	Chicago Black Hawks	NHL	6	1	0	1	1	0	1	8	....	....	....	....	....
	Toronto Maple Leafs	NHL	8	1	2	3	1	3	4	4	....	....	....	....	....
	Pittsburgh Hornets	AHL	29	2	4	6	....	....	....	14	2	0	0	0	0
	Spokane Spartans	WIHL	18	9	19	28	....	....	....	28	....	....	....	....	....
1948-49	University of Alberta	ESrHL	8	8	8	16	....	....	....	16	....	....	....	....	....
1949-50	Saskatoon Quakers	WCSHL	50	30	24	54	....	....	....	90	5	1	1	2	6
1950-51	Halifax St. Mary's	MMHL	60	29	29	58	....	....	....	103	12	6	5	11	25
1951-52	Calgary Stampeders	PCHL	69	24	43	67	....	....	....	83	....	....	....	....	....
	NHL Totals		**14**	**2**	**2**	**4**	**2**	**3**	**5**	**12**	....	....	....	....	....

Traded to **Toronto** by **Chicago** with Max Bentley for Bob Goldham, Ernie Dickens, Bud Poile, Gus Bodnar and Gaye Stewart, November 2, 1947. Signed as a free agent by **Halifax** (MMHL), September 28, 1950.

• THOMPSON, Cliff

D – L. 5'11", 185 lbs. b: Winchester, MA, 12/9/1918.

Season	Club	League	GP	G	A	Pts	AG	AA	APts	PIM	GP	G	A	Pts	PIM
1938-39	Hebron Academy	H.S.	STATISTICS NOT AVAILABLE												
	Boston Olympics	QPHL	4	3	1	4	....	....	....	2	....	....	....	....	....
1939-40	Boston Olympics	EAHL	35	16	14	30	....	....	....	33	5	0	2	2	4
1940-41	Boston Olympics	EAHL	65	12	18	30	....	....	....	80	4	0	4	4	4
1941-42	Boston Bruins	NHL	3	0	0	0	0	0	0	2	....	....	....	....	....
	Hershey Bears	AHL	20	3	5	8	....	....	....	2	....	....	....	....	....
	St. Paul Saints	AHA	28	5	6	11	....	....	....	22	2	1	0	1	0
	Boston Olympics	EAHL	....	....	....	....	....	....	....	....	1	0	1	1	0
1942-43			MILITARY SERVICE												
1943-44			MILITARY SERVICE												
1944-45			MILITARY SERVICE												
1945-46	Boston Olympics	EAHL	43	7	13	20	....	....	....	18	12	2	4	6	0
1946-47	Boston Olympics	EAHL	53	11	19	30	....	....	....	51	9	2	6	8	6
1947-48	Boston Olympics	EAHL	19	5	16	21	....	....	....	22	....	....	....	....	....
	Boston Olympics	QSHL	48	10	20	30	....	....	....	57	....	....	....	....	....
1948-49	Boston Bruins	NHL	10	0	1	1	0	1	1	0	....	....	....	....	....
	Hershey Bears	AHL	9	0	0	0	....	....	....	2	....	....	....	....	....
	Boston Olympics	QSHL	26	4	18	22	....	....	....	35	....	....	....	....	....
1949-50	Boston Olympics	EAHL	26	7	14	21	....	....	....	57	3	2	1	3	0
	NHL Totals		**13**	**0**	**1**	**1**	**0**	**1**	**1**	**2**	....	....	....	....	....

EAHL Second All-Star Team (1947, 1948)

Signed as a free agent by **Boston**, October 22, 1941.

• THOMPSON, Ken
Kenworthy

LW/C – L. 5'10", 160 lbs. b: Oakengates, England, 5/29/1881 Deceased.

Season	Club	League	GP	G	A	Pts	AG	AA	APts	PIM	GP	G	A	Pts	PIM
1913-14	Montreal HLP	MTMHL	10	7	0	7	....	....	....	15	....	....	....	....	....
	Montreal Shamrocks	MCHL	1	0	0	0	....	....	....	0	....	....	....	....	....
	Laval University	MTMHL	3	0	3	3	....	....	....	....	1	0	0	0	0
1914-15	Montreal All-Montreal	MCHL	11	14	0	14	....	....	....	9	....	....	....	....	....
1915-16	Laval University	MCHL	10	8	0	8	....	....	....	6	1	0	0	0	0
1916-17	Montreal Wanderers	NHA	14	1	0	1	....	....	....	8	....	....	....	....	....
1917-18	Montreal Wanderers	NHL	1	0	0	0	0	0	0	0	....	....	....	....	....
	NHL Totals		**1**	**0**	**0**	**0**	**0**	**0**	**0**	**0**	....	....	....	....	....
	Other Major League Totals		14	1	0	1	....	....	....	8	....	....	....	....	....

Rights retained by **Montreal Wanderers** after NHA folded, November 26, 1917.

• THOMPSON, Paul
Paul Ivan

LW – L. 5'11", 180 lbs. b: Calgary, Alta., 11/2/1906 Deceased.

Season	Club	League	GP	G	A	Pts	AG	AA	APts	PIM	GP	G	A	Pts	PIM
1924-25	Calgary Canadians	CCJHL	STATISTICS NOT AVAILABLE												
	Calgary Canadians	M-Cup	2	0	0	0	....	....	....	0	....	....	....	....	....
1925-26	Calgary Canadians	CCJHL	STATISTICS NOT AVAILABLE												
	Calgary Canadians	M-Cup	9	12	2	14	....	....	....	10	....	....	....	....	....
1926-27	New York Rangers	NHL	43	7	3	10	12	16	28	12	2	0	0	0	0
♦1927-28	New York Rangers	NHL	42	4	4	8	8	23	31	22	8	0	0	0	30
1928-29	New York Rangers	NHL	44	10	7	17	29	47	76	38	6	0	*2	2	6
1929-30	New York Rangers	NHL	44	7	12	19	10	28	38	36	4	0	0	0	2
1930-31	New York Rangers	NHL	44	7	7	14	14	21	35	36	4	3	0	3	2
1931-32	Chicago Black Hawks	NHL	48	8	14	22	13	31	44	34	2	0	0	0	2
1932-33	Chicago Black Hawks	NHL	48	13	20	33	24	42	66	27	....	....	....	....	....
♦1933-34	Chicago Black Hawks	NHL	48	20	16	36	35	34	69	17	8	4	3	7	6
1934-35	Chicago Black Hawks	NHL	48	16	23	39	26	40	66	20	2	0	0	0	0
1935-36	Chicago Black Hawks	NHL	45	17	23	40	33	44	77	19	2	0	3	3	0
1936-37	Chicago Black Hawks	NHL	47	17	18	35	29	33	62	28	....	....	....	....	....
♦1937-38	Chicago Black Hawks	NHL	48	22	22	44	36	36	72	14	10	4	3	7	6
1938-39	Chicago Black Hawks	NHL	33	5	10	15	9	16	25	33	....	....	....	....	....
1939-40	Chicago Black Hawks	NHL	DID NOT PLAY – COACHING												
	NHL Totals		**582**	**153**	**179**	**332**	**278**	**411**	**689**	**336**	**48**	**11**	**11**	**22**	**54**

• Brother of Tiny • NHL Second All-Star Team (1936)

Signed as a free agent by **NY Rangers**, October 12, 1926. Traded to **Chicago** by **NY Rangers** for Art Somers and Vic Desjardins, September 27, 1931.

• THOMS, Bill

C – L. 5'9", 170 lbs. b: Newmarket, Ont., 3/5/1910 d: 12/26/1964.

Season	Club	League	GP	G	A	Pts	AG	AA	APts	PIM	GP	G	A	Pts	PIM
1928-29	Newmarket Redmen	OHA-Jr.	STATISTICS NOT AVAILABLE												
1929-30	West Toronto Nationals	OHA-Jr.	7	7	*13	20	....	....	....	6	2	0	0	0	0
	West Toronto Nationals	M-Cup	9	*9	*5	*14	....	....	....	10	....	....	....	....	....
1930-31	Toronto Marlboros	OHA-Jr.	10	*11	2	*13	....	....	....	4	3	0	0	0	2
	Toronto Eaton's	TMHL	15	11	*7	*18	....	....	....	0	6	0	*4	4	0
1931-32	Toronto Marlboros	OHA-Jr.	20	*16	6	*22	....	....	....	26	2	1	0	1	0
	Syracuse Stars	IHL	12	2	4	6	....	....	....	2	....	....	....	....	....
	Toronto Eaton's	TMHL	6	4	4	8	....	....	....	0	2	*4	1	*5	0
1932-33	Syracuse Stars	IHL	20	7	7	14	....	....	....	18	....	....	....	....	....
	Toronto Marlboros	OHA-Sr.	1	0	0	0	....	....	....	0	....	....	....	....	....
	Toronto Maple Leafs	NHL	29	3	9	12	5	19	24	15	9	1	1	2	4
1933-34	Toronto Maple Leafs	NHL	47	8	18	26	14	38	52	24	5	0	2	2	0
1934-35	Toronto Maple Leafs	NHL	47	9	13	22	15	23	38	15	7	2	0	2	0
1935-36	Toronto Maple Leafs	NHL	48	*23	15	38	45	28	73	29	9	3	*5	8	0
1936-37	Toronto Maple Leafs	NHL	48	10	9	19	17	16	33	14	2	0	0	0	0
1937-38	Toronto Maple Leafs	NHL	48	14	24	38	23	39	62	14	7	0	1	1	0
1938-39	Toronto Maple Leafs	NHL	12	1	4	5	2	6	8	4	....	....	....	....	....
	Chicago Black Hawks	NHL	36	6	11	17	10	17	27	16	....	....	....	....	....
1939-40	Chicago Black Hawks	NHL	47	9	13	22	15	20	35	2	1	0	0	0	0
1940-41	Chicago Black Hawks	NHL	47	13	19	32	20	27	47	4	....	....	....	....	....
1941-42	Chicago Black Hawks	NHL	47	15	30	45	20	36	56	4	3	0	1	1	0
1942-43	Chicago Black Hawks	NHL	47	15	28	43	15	26	41	3	....	....	....	....	....
1943-44	Chicago Black Hawks	NHL	7	3	5	8	3	4	7	2	....	....	....	....	....
1944-45	Chicago Black Hawks	NHL	21	2	6	8	2	7	9	8	....	....	....	....	....
	Boston Bruins	NHL	17	4	2	6	4	2	6	0	1	0	0	0	2
1945/47			OUT OF HOCKEY – RETIRED												
1947-48	Toronto Mahers	TIHL	26	4	16	20	....	....	....	10	3	2	0	2	7
	NHL Totals		**548**	**135**	**206**	**341**	**210**	**308**	**518**	**154**	**44**	**6**	**10**	**16**	**6**

NHL Second All-Star Team (1936) • Played in NHL All-Star Game (1934)

Traded to **Toronto** by **Syracuse** (IHL) for Harold Darraugh, January 3, 1933. Traded to **Chicago** by **Toronto** for Doc Romnes, December 8, 1938. Traded to **Boston** by **Chicago** for cash, January 14, 1945.

• THOMSON, Bill
William Ferguson

C/RW – R. 5'9", 162 lbs. b: Troon, Scotland, 3/23/1914 d: 8/6/1993.

Season	Club	League	GP	G	A	Pts	AG	AA	APts	PIM	GP	G	A	Pts	PIM
1930-31	Kenora Thistles	MJHL	12	7	8	*15	....	....	....	2	3	0	0	0	0
1931-32	Port Arthur Ports	TBSHL	17	4	*7	11	....	....	....	6	2	1	0	1	0
1932-33	Port Arthur Ports	TBSHL	19	7	3	10	....	....	....	4	5	1	0	1	6
1933-34	Port Arthur Ports	TBSHL	13	8	4	12	....	....	....	20	4	1	0	1	0
1934-35	Port Arthur Ports	TBSHL	14	5	2	7	....	....	....	8	4	2	1	3	0
	Port Arthur Bearcats	Al-Cup	7	7	1	8	....	....	....	0	....	....	....	....	....
1935-36	Port Arthur Indians	TBSHL	8	7	0	7	....	....	....	2	....	....	....	....	....
	Canada	Nt-Team	11	*7	3	*10	....	....	....	4	....	....	....	....	....
	Canada	Olympics	8	7	0	7	....	....	....	2	....	....	....	....	....
1936-37	Port Arthur Bearcats	TBSHL	31	34	15	49	....	....	....	31	3	2	0	2	2
1937-38	Syracuse Stars	IAHL	47	7	9	16	....	....	....	17	8	0	0	0	0
1938-39	Pittsburgh Hornets	IAHL	35	8	14	22	....	....	....	10	....	....	....	....	....
	Detroit Red Wings	NHL	4	0	0	0	0	0	0	0	....	....	....	....	....
	Syracuse Stars	IAHL	14	1	3	4	....	....	....	2	....	....	....	....	....
1939-40	Indianapolis Capitols	IAHL	38	10	26	36	....	....	....	12	5	0	4	4	2
	Syracuse Stars	AHL	2	0	0	0	....	....	....	0	....	....	....	....	....
1940-41	Indianapolis Capitols	AHL	44	5	15	20	....	....	....	23	....	....	....	....	....
	Pittsburgh Hornets	AHL	1	0	0	0	....	....	....	0	....	....	....	....	....
1941-42	Omaha Knights	AHA	50	26	27	53	....	....	....	11	8	6	*7	13	0
1942-43	Indianapolis Capitols	AHL	55	23	22	45	....	....	....	4	7	4	2	6	10
1943-44	Detroit Red Wings	NHL	5	2	2	4	2	2	4	0	2	0	0	0	0
	Indianapolis Capitols	AHL	45	20	38	58	....	....	....	6	5	2	4	6	0
1944-45	Indianapolis Capitols	AHL	32	9	19	28	....	....	....	17	5	1	3	4	0
1945-46	St. Louis Flyers	AHL	23	2	10	12	....	....	....	0	....	....	....	....	....
	Hershey Bears	AHL	28	5	13	18	....	....	....	6	3	0	3	3	2
1946-47	Hershey Bears	AHL	13	2	5	7	....	....	....	0	....	....	....	....	....
	Minneapolis Millers	USHL	26	8	13	21	....	....	....	12	3	0	1	1	0
1947-48	Tulsa Oilers	USHL	56	10	24	34	....	....	....	0	1	1	0	1	0
1948-49	Dallas Texans	USHL	11	4	3	7	....	....	....	0	....	....	....	....	....
	Seattle Ironmen	PCHL	9	0	7	7	....	....	....	0	....	....	....	....	....
	NHL Totals		**9**	**2**	**2**	**4**	**2**	**2**	**4**	**0**	**2**	**0**	**0**	**0**	**0**

Signed as a free agent by **Toronto**, October 13, 1937. Traded to **Detroit** by **Toronto** with $10,000 for Bucko McDonald, December 19, 1938. Traded to **St. Louis** (AHL) by **Indianapolis** (AHL) for cash with Detroit holding right of recall, January, 1946. Traded to **Tulsa** (USHL) by **Cleveland** (AHL) for cash, October 6, 1947.

• THOMSON, Jimmy
James Richard "Jeems"

D – R. 5'11", 175 lbs. b: Winnipeg, Man., 2/23/1927 d: 5/18/1991.

Season	Club	League	GP	G	A	Pts	AG	AA	APts	PIM	GP	G	A	Pts	PIM
1943-44	St. Michael's Majors	OHA-Jr.	21	2	2	4	....	....	....	40	12	2	2	4	20
1944-45	St. Michael's Majors	OHA-Jr.	18	13	12	25	....	....	....	*52	9	5	2	7	14
	St. Michael's Majors	M-Cup	14	6	4	10	....	....	....	30	....	....	....	....	....
1945-46	Toronto Maple Leafs	NHL	5	0	1	1	0	1	1	4	....	....	....	....	....
	Pittsburgh Hornets	AHL	28	2	5	7	....	....	....	16	6	0	2	2	2
♦1946-47	Toronto Maple Leafs	NHL	60	2	14	16	2	17	19	97	11	0	1	1	22
♦1947-48	Toronto Maple Leafs	NHL	59	0	29	29	0	38	38	82	9	1	1	2	9
♦1948-49	Toronto Maple Leafs	NHL	60	4	16	20	6	23	29	56	9	1	5	6	10
1949-50	Toronto Maple Leafs	NHL	70	0	13	13	0	16	16	76	7	0	2	2	7
♦1950-51	Toronto Maple Leafs	NHL	69	3	33	36	4	41	45	76	11	0	1	1	*34
1951-52	Toronto Maple Leafs	NHL	70	0	25	25	0	31	31	86	4	0	0	0	25
1952-53	Toronto Maple Leafs	NHL	69	0	22	22	0	27	27	73	....	....	....	....	....
1953-54	Toronto Maple Leafs	NHL	61	2	24	26	3	29	32	86	3	0	0	0	2
1954-55	Toronto Maple Leafs	NHL	70	4	12	16	5	14	19	63	4	0	0	0	16
1955-56	Toronto Maple Leafs	NHL	62	0	7	7	0	8	8	96	5	0	3	3	10
1956-57	Toronto Maple Leafs	NHL	62	0	12	12	0	13	13	50	....	....	....	....	....
1957-58	Chicago Black Hawks	NHL	70	4	7	11	5	7	12	75	....	....	....	....	....
	NHL Totals		**787**	**19**	**215**	**234**	**25**	**265**	**290**	**920**	**63**	**2**	**13**	**15**	**135**

NHL Second All-Star Team (1951, 1952) • Played in NHL All-Star Game (1947, 1948, 1949, 1950, 1951, 1952, 1953)

Signed as a free agent by **Toronto**, October 16, 1945. Traded to **Chicago** by **Toronto** for cash, August, 1957. Traded to **Toronto** by **Chicago** for cash, July, 1958.

• THOMSON, Rhys "Tommy"

D – L. 6'1", 195 lbs. b: Toronto, Ont., 8/9/1918 Deceased.

			REGULAR SEASON								PLAYOFFS				
Season	Club	League	GP	G	A	Pts	AG	AA	APts	PIM	GP	G	A	Pts	PIM
1935-36	Toronto Young Rangers	OHA-B	9	3	2	5				20	2	0	0	0	2
1936-37	Toronto Young Rangers	OHA-B	11	1	2	3				13	3	0	0	0	2
1937-38	Toronto Young Rangers	OHA-Jr.	9	5	2	7				13	3	2	1	3	8
1938-39	New Haven Eagles	IAHL	19	1	3	4				6					
1939-40	**Montreal Canadiens**	**NHL**	**7**	**0**	**0**	**0**	**0**	**0**	**0**	**16**					
	New Haven Eagles	IAHL	18	0	1	1				10					
1940-41	Springfield Indians	AHL	51	3	7	10				30					
1941-42	Springfield Indians	AHL	50	1	15	16				39					
1942-43	**Toronto Maple Leafs**	**NHL**	**18**	**0**	**2**	**2**	**0**	**2**	**2**	**22**					
	Providence Reds	AHL	23	2	12	14				48	2	0	0	0	0
1943-44	Kingston Army	OHA-Sr.	2	0	0	0				4					
	Petawawa Grenades	UOVHL	5	1	6	7				17					
1944-45	Toronto Army Daggers	OHA-Sr.	2	0	0	0				0					
	Toronto Army Daggers	TNDHL									2	2	1	3	2
	Toronto Army Shamrocks	TIHL	18	2	5	7				26	1	0	2	2	2
1945-46	Toronto Staffords	TIHL	14	2	2	4				19	10	2	0	2	8
	NHL Totals		**25**	**0**	**2**	**2**	**0**	**2**	**2**	**38**					

Signed as a free agent by **Montreal** (New Haven-IAHL), January 18, 1939. Traded to **NY Americans** (Springfield-AHL) by **Montreal** for cash, October, 1940. Rights transferred to **Toronto** from **Brooklyn** in Special Dispersal Draw, September 11, 1942.

• THORSTEINSON, Joe Johan Magnus "Stony"

RW – R. 5'9", 157 lbs. b: Winnipeg, Man., 3/19/1905 d: 8/24/1948.

Season	Club	League	GP	G	A	Pts	AG	AA	APts	PIM	GP	G	A	Pts	PIM
1919-20	Selkirk Jr. Fishermen	MJHL	STATISTICS NOT AVAILABLE												
	Selkirk Jr. Fishermen	M-Cup	4	6	3	9				0					
1920-21	Selkirk Jr. Fishermen	MJHL	STATISTICS NOT AVAILABLE												
1921-22	Selkirk Jr. Fishermen	MJHL	STATISTICS NOT AVAILABLE												
1922-23	Selkirk Fishermen	MHL-Sr.	14	3	7	10				10					
1923-24	Selkirk Fishermen	MHL-Sr.	2	0	1	1				0					
1924-25	Coleman Tigers	ASHL	STATISTICS NOT AVAILABLE												
1925-26	Winnipeg Maroons	CHL	21	4	1	5				22	5	1	1	2	0
1926-27	Winnipeg Maroons	AHA	26	4	1	5				53	3	1	0	1	2
	Moose Jaw Maroons	PrHL	16	3	0	3				4					
1927-28	Regina Capitals	PrHL	26	7	3	10				26					
1928-29	Duluth Hornets	AHA	39	8	4	12				32					
1929-30	St. Paul Saints	AHA	48	9	6	15				44					
1930-31	Buffalo Majors	AHA	42	20	14	34				38					
1931-32	Bufalo Majors	AHA	9	1	0	1				6					
	Duluth Hornets	AHA	37	5	4	9				26	4	0	0	0	2
1932-33	**New York Americans**	**NHL**	**4**	**0**	**0**	**0**	**0**	**0**	**0**	**0**					
	Edmonton Eskimos	WCHL	5	2	0	2				4					
	New Haven Eagles	Can-Am	3	0	0	0				2					
1933-34	Wichita Vikings	AHA	2	2	1	3				4					
	St. Louis Flyers	AHA	14	0	0	0				2					
	Tulsa Oilers	AHA	9	1	3	4				23					
1934-35	Minneapolis Millers	CHL	28	2	5	7				21	5	1	2	3	2
	NHL Totals		**4**	**0**	**0**	**0**	**0**	**0**	**0**	**0**					

Signed as a free agent by **Winnipeg** (AHA), November 5, 1926.

• THURIER, Fred Alfred Michael

C – R. 5'11", 160 lbs. b: Granby, Que., 1/11/1916 d: 11/20/1999.

Season	Club	League	GP	G	A	Pts	AG	AA	APts	PIM	GP	G	A	Pts	PIM
1936-37	Montreal Sr. Canadiens	QSHL	22	12	6	18				20	2	0	0	0	4
1937-38	Springfield Indians	IAHL	46	10	9	19				18					
1938-39	Springfield Indians	IAHL	36	11	8	19				21	3	0	0	0	0
1939-40	Springfield Indians	IAHL	54	28	32	60				27	3	2	1	3	12
1940-41	**New York Americans**	**NHL**	**3**	**2**	**1**	**3**	**3**	**1**	**4**	**0**					
	Springfield Indians	AHL	41	*29	31	60				36	3	0	1	1	0
1941-42	**Brooklyn Americans**	**NHL**	**27**	**7**	**7**	**14**	**9**	**8**	**17**	**4**					
	Springfield Indians	AHL	22	20	24	44				6	5	2	5	7	2
1942-43	Buffalo Bisons	AHL	7	6	9	15				2					
	Montreal Army	QSHL	13	8	5	13				6	7	3	2	5	6
	Montreal Army	MCHL	2	4	1	5				0					
1943-44	Montreal Army	MCHL	1	0	0	0				0					
	Buffalo Bisons	AHL	39	33	40	73				43	9	*8	10	*18	14
1944-45	**New York Rangers**	**NHL**	**50**	**16**	**19**	**35**	**16**	**22**	**38**	**14**					
1945-46	Cleveland Barons	AHL	47	21	32	53				18	12	*9	7	*16	6
1946-47	Cleveland Barons	AHL	63	18	33	51				58	4	0	0	0	0
1947-48	Cleveland Barons	AHL	68	36	38	74				38	9	5	8	*13	4
1948-49	Cleveland Barons	AHL	51	26	31	57				47	5	2	7	9	2
1949-50	Cleveland Barons	AHL	57	30	52	82				22	4	2	0	2	0
1950-51	Cleveland Barons	AHL	64	32	63	95				19	10	1	12	12	0
1951-52	Cleveland Barons	AHL	47	19	23	42				12	4	1	2	3	4
	NHL Totals		**80**	**25**	**27**	**52**	**28**	**31**	**59**	**18**					

AHL First All-Star Team (1941) • AHL Second All-Star Team (1942, 1951)

Traded to **NY Americans** by **Springfield** (AHL) for cash, October 10, 1940. Claimed by **NY Rangers** from **Brooklyn** in Special Dispersal Draw, September 11, 1943.

• TIMGREN, Ray Raymond Charles "Golden Boy"

LW – L. 5'9", 150 lbs. b: Windsor, Ont., 9/29/1928 d: 11/25/1999.

Season	Club	League	GP	G	A	Pts	AG	AA	APts	PIM	GP	G	A	Pts	PIM
1943-44	Toronto Young Leafs	OMHA	STATISTICS NOT AVAILABLE												
1944-45	Toronto Young Leafs	OHA									10	10	8	18	
1946-47	Toronto Marlboros	OHA-Jr.	20	20	7	27				6	2	2	3	5	0
	Toronto Dorsts	TMHL	13	17	15	32				5	12	11	*15	26	4
1947-48	Toronto Marlboros	OHA-Jr.	30	20	20	40				33					
	Toronto Marlboros	OHA-Jr.	3	1	0	1				0	5	1	1	2	2
♦1948-49	**Toronto Maple Leafs**	**NHL**	**36**	**3**	**12**	**15**	**4**	**17**	**21**	**9**	**9**	**3**	**3**	**6**	**2**
	Toronto Marlboros	OHA-Sr.	26	6	22	28				27					
1949-50	**Toronto Maple Leafs**	**NHL**	**68**	**7**	**18**	**25**	**9**	**22**	**31**	**22**	**6**	**0**	**4**	**4**	**2**
♦1950-51	**Toronto Maple Leafs**	**NHL**	**70**	**1**	**9**	**10**	**1**	**11**	**12**	**20**	**11**	**0**	**1**	**1**	**2**
1951-52	**Toronto Maple Leafs**	**NHL**	**50**	**2**	**4**	**6**	**3**	**5**	**8**	**11**	**4**	**0**	**1**	**1**	**0**
	Pittsburgh Hornets	AHL	19	13	5	18				11					
1952-53	**Toronto Maple Leafs**	**NHL**	**12**	**0**	**0**	**0**	**0**	**0**	**0**	**4**					
	Pittsburgh Hornets	AHL	50	16	12	28				23	10	2	0	2	0
1953-54	Pittsburgh Hornets	AHL	70	22	30	52				27	5	1	1	2	2
1954-55	**Chicago Black Hawks**	**NHL**	**14**	**1**	**1**	**2**	**1**	**1**	**2**	**2**					
	Pittsburgh Hornets	AHL	45	12	13	25				24	10	3	4	7	2
	Toronto Maple Leafs	**NHL**	**1**	**0**	**0**	**0**	**0**	**0**	**0**	**2**					
1955-56	Pittsburgh Hornets	AHL	8	0	4	4				13					
	NHL Totals		**251**	**14**	**44**	**58**	**18**	**56**	**74**	**70**	**30**	**3**	**9**	**12**	**6**

Played in NHL All-Star Game (1949)

• Regular season totals for Toronto (OHA) in 1944-45 season are unavailable. Traded to **Chicago** by **Toronto** for Jack Price, October 4, 1954. Loaned to **Toronto** (Pittsburgh-AHL) by **Chicago**, November 16, 1954.

• TOMSON, Jack John Fraser

D – R. 6'1", 175 lbs. b: Uxbridge, England, 1/31/1918.

Season	Club	League	GP	G	A	Pts	AG	AA	APts	PIM	GP	G	A	Pts	PIM
1934-35	Regina Wares	RJrHL	6	3	2	5				0					
1935-36	Regina Christies	RJrHL	3	4	0	4				4					
	Regina Jr. Aces	S-SJHL	3	1	1	2				6	4	0	1	1	2
	Regina Aces	M-Cup	2	1	1	2				0					
1936-37	Regina Jr. Aces	S-SJHL	5	6	0	6				0	2	0	0	0	0
1937-38	Regina Aces	S-SSHL	24	15	8	23				23	3	1	0	1	0
1938-39	Seattle Seahawks	PCHL	7	0	0	0				0					
	Philadelphia Ramblers	IAHL	45	2	9	11				36	7	0	0	0	6
	New York Americans	**NHL**									**2**	**0**	**0**	**0**	**0**
1939-40	**New York Americans**	**NHL**	**12**	**1**	**1**	**2**	**2**	**2**	**4**	**0**					
	Kansas City Greyhounds	AHA	11	0	2	2				6					
	Springfield Indians	IAHL	22	2	3	5				2	2	0	0	0	2
1940-41	**New York Americans**	**NHL**	**3**	**0**	**0**	**0**	**0**	**0**	**0**	**0**					
	Seattle Olympics	PCHL	40	16	15	31				55	2	0	0	0	2
1941-42	Regina Rangers	S-SSHL	27	6	12	18				41	3	0	0	0	2
1942-43	Victoria Navy	VNDHL	18	8	10	18				41	6	6	5	*11	11
1943-44	Victoria Navy	PCHL	16	5	4	9				22					
1944-45			MILITARY SERVICE												
1945-46	New Westminster Royals	PCHL	53	16	22	38				65					
1946-47	New Westminster Royals	PCHL	57	28	21	49				98	4	0	1	1	0
1947-48	New Westminster Royals	PCHL	54	14	23	37				84	4	1	1	2	0
1948-49	Seattle Ironmen	PCHL	69	12	20	32				31					
1949-50	Kerrisdale Monarchs	OkMHL	24	5	8	13				25	3	0	0	0	2
1950-51	Kerrisdale Monarchs	OkMHL	STATISTICS NOT AVAILABLE												
	NHL Totals		**15**	**1**	**1**	**2**	**2**	**2**	**4**	**0**	**2**	**0**	**0**	**0**	**0**

Signed as a free agent by **NY Americans**, October 24, 1938. Loaned to **Seattle** (PCHL) by **NY Americans** for cash, November, 1938. Loaned to **Philadelphia** (IAHL) by **NY Americans** for cash, November 25, 1938.

• TOPPAZZINI, Jerry Gerald J. "Topper"

RW – R. 6', 180 lbs. b: Copper Cliff, Ont., 7/29/1931.

Season	Club	League	GP	G	A	Pts	AG	AA	APts	PIM	GP	G	A	Pts	PIM
1947-48	Copper Cliff Jr. Redmen	NOJHA	9	4	1	5				0	3	2	1	3	0
	Copper Cliff Jr. Redmen	M-Cup	7	2	3	5				2					
1948-49	St. Catharines Teepees	OHA-Jr.	45	24	20	44				37	5	2	2	4	4
1949-50	Barrie Flyers	OHA-Jr.	36	15	17	32				60	9	1	4	5	4
1950-51	Barrie Flyers	OHA-Jr.	54	40	50	90				116	12	7	9	16	15
	Barrie Flyers	M-Cup	11	7	11	18				28					
1951-52	Hershey Bears	AHL	54	20	25	45				26	5	0	1	1	4
1952-53	**Boston Bruins**	**NHL**	**69**	**10**	**13**	**23**	**13**	**16**	**29**	**36**	**11**	**0**	**3**	**3**	**9**
1953-54	**Boston Bruins**	**NHL**	**37**	**0**	**5**	**5**	**0**	**6**	**6**	**24**					
	Hershey Bears	AHL	16	5	10	15				23					
	Chicago Black Hawks	**NHL**	**14**	**5**	**3**	**8**	**7**	**4**	**11**	**18**					
1954-55	**Chicago Black Hawks**	**NHL**	**70**	**9**	**18**	**27**	**12**	**21**	**33**	**59**					
1955-56	**Detroit Red Wings**	**NHL**	**40**	**1**	**7**	**8**	**1**	**8**	**9**	**31**					
	Boston Bruins	**NHL**	**28**	**7**	**7**	**14**	**9**	**8**	**17**	**22**					
1956-57	**Boston Bruins**	**NHL**	**55**	**15**	**23**	**38**	**19**	**25**	**44**	**26**	**10**	**0**	**1**	**1**	**2**
1957-58	**Boston Bruins**	**NHL**	**64**	**25**	**24**	**49**	**31**	**25**	**56**	**51**	**12**	**9**	**3**	**12**	**2**
1958-59	**Boston Bruins**	**NHL**	**70**	**21**	**23**	**44**	**25**	**23**	**48**	**61**	**7**	**4**	**2**	**6**	**0**
1959-60	**Boston Bruins**	**NHL**	**69**	**12**	**33**	**45**	**14**	**32**	**46**	**26**					
1960-61	**Boston Bruins**	**NHL**	**67**	**15**	**35**	**50**	**17**	**34**	**51**	**35**					
1961-62	**Boston Bruins**	**NHL**	**70**	**19**	**31**	**50**	**22**	**30**	**52**	**26**					
1962-63	**Boston Bruins**	**NHL**	**65**	**17**	**18**	**35**	**20**	**18**	**38**	**6**					
1963-64	**Boston Bruins**	**NHL**	**65**	**7**	**4**	**11**	**9**	**4**	**13**	**15**					
1964-65	Pittsburgh Hornets	AHL	65	16	31	47				32	4	2	6	8	0
1965-66	Los Angeles Blades	WHL	47	6	17	23				8					
1966-67	Los Angeles Blades	WHL	59	19	37	56				22					
1967-68	Port Huron Flags	IHL	37	11	26	37				25					
	NHL Totals		**783**	**163**	**244**	**407**	**199**	**254**	**453**	**436**	**40**	**13**	**9**	**22**	**13**

• Brother of Zellio • Played in NHL All-Star Game (1955, 1958, 1959)

Traded to **Chicago** by **Boston** for Gus Bodnar, February 16, 1954. Traded to **Detroit** by **Chicago** with Dave Creighton, Gord Hollingworth and John McCormack for Tony Leswick, Glen Skov, John Wilson and Benny Woit, May 27, 1955. Traded to **Boston** by **Detroit** with Real Chevrefils for Murray Costello and Lorne Ferguson, January 17, 1956. Traded to **Chicago** by **Boston** with Matt Ravlich for Murray Balfour and Mike Draper, June 9, 1964. Traded to **Detroit** (Pittsburgh-AHL) by **Chicago** (Buffalo-AHL) for Hank Ciesla, October 10, 1964. Claimed by **LA Blades** (WHL) from **Detroit** in Reverse Draft, June 9, 1965.

• TOPPAZZINI, Zellio Zellio Louis Peter

RW – R. 5'11", 180 lbs. b: Copper Cliff, Ont., 1/5/1930.

Season	Club	League	GP	G	A	Pts	AG	AA	APts	PIM	GP	G	A	Pts	PIM
1946-47	Copper Cliff Jr. Redmen	NOJHA	9	10	3	13				6	5	4	4	8	5
1947-48	St. Catharines Teepees	OHA-Jr.	33	27	18	45				53	3	4	4	8	2
1948-49	**Boston Bruins**	**NHL**	**5**	**1**	**1**	**2**	**1**	**1**	**2**	**0**	**2**	**0**	**0**	**0**	**0**
	Hershey Bears	AHL	49	9	14	23				15					
1949-50	**Boston Bruins**	**NHL**	**36**	**5**	**5**	**10**	**6**	**6**	**12**	**18**					
	Hershey Bears	AHL	34	16	9	25				6					
1950-51	**Boston Bruins**	**NHL**	**4**	**0**	**1**	**1**	**0**	**1**	**1**	**0**					
	Hershey Bears	AHL	12	6	5	11				2					
	New York Rangers	**NHL**	**55**	**14**	**14**	**28**	**18**	**17**	**35**	**27**					
1951-52	**New York Rangers**	**NHL**	**16**	**1**	**1**	**2**	**1**	**1**	**2**	**4**					
	Cincinnati Mohawks	AHL	7	2	4	6				0					
	Providence Reds	AHL	33	20	25	45				6	11	3	7	10	2
1952-53	Providence Reds	AHL	64	35	32	67				23					
1953-54	Providence Reds	AHL	70	33	43	76				18					
1954-55	Providence Reds	AHL	62	21	*53	74				12					
1955-56	Providence Reds	AHL	64	42	*71	*113				44	9	7	*13	*20	2
1956-57	**Chicago Black Hawks**	**NHL**	**7**	**0**	**0**	**0**	**0**	**0**	**0**	**0**					
	Providence Reds	AHL	44	13	40	53				16	5	0	1	1	4

Season	Club	League	GP	G	A	Pts	AG	AA	APts	PIM	GP	G	A	Pts	PIM
			REGULAR SEASON								PLAYOFFS				
1957-58	Providence Reds	AHL	70	27	42	69	....	....	....	14	5	1	1	2	0
1958-59	Providence Reds	AHL	67	17	38	55	....	....	....	14	....	....	....	....	....
1959-60			OUT OF HOCKEY – RETIRED												
1960-61	Providence Reds	AHL	68	31	34	65	....	....	....	2	....	....	....	....	....
1961-62	Providence Reds	AHL	66	21	36	57	....	....	....	2	3	1	2	3	0
1962-63	Providence Reds	AHL	61	16	24	40	....	....	....	10	6	4	4	8	0
1963-64	Providence Reds	AHL	14	1	6	7	....	....	....	0	1	0	0	0	0
1964-65	Providence College	Ivy	DID NOT PLAY – COACHING												
	NHL Totals		**123**	**21**	**22**	**43**	**26**	**26**	**52**	**49**	**2**	**0**	**0**	**0**	**0**

• Brother of Jerry • AHL Second All-Star Team (1955) • AHL First All-Star Team (1956) • Won John B. Sollenberger Trophy (Top Scorer - AHL) (1956)

Traded to **NY Rangers** by **Boston** with Ed Harrison for Dunc Fisher and future considerations (loan of Alex Kaleta to Hershey-AHL, November 20, 1950), November 16, 1950. Traded to **Providence** (AHL) by **NY Rangers** with Pat Egan and Jean-Paul Denis for Jack Stoddard, January 1, 1952. Claimed by **Chicago** from **Providence** (AHL) in Inter-League Draft, June 5, 1956.

• TOUHEY, Bill William James

LW – L. 5'9", 155 lbs. b: Ottawa, Ont., 3/23/1906 d: 3/28/1999.

Season	Club	League	GP	G	A	Pts	AG	AA	APts	PIM	GP	G	A	Pts	PIM
1920-21	Ottawa St. Brigids	OCHL	STATISTICS NOT AVAILABLE												
1921-22	Ottawa St. Brigids	OCHL	2	0	0	0	....	....	....	0	....	....	....	....	....
1922-23	Ottawa St. Pats	OCHL	STATISTICS NOT AVAILABLE												
1923-24	Ottawa College	OCHL	STATISTICS NOT AVAILABLE												
1924-25	Ottawa Gunners	OCHL	16	*15	3	*18	....	....	....	....	....	....	....	....	....
1925-26	Montreal CNR	MRTHL	3	0	0	0	....	....	....	2	1	0	0	0	0
	Ottawa Montagnards	OCHL	15	7	*5	12	....	....	....	....	5	1	0	1	....
1926-27	Stratford Nationals	Can-Pro	30	19	*10	*29	....	....	....	18	2	0	0	0	6
1927-28	**Montreal Maroons**	**NHL**	**29**	**2**	**0**	**2**	**4**	**0**	**4**	**2**	....	....	....	....	....
	Stratford Nationals	Can-Pro	11	2	3	5	....	....	....	15	5	*4	1	5	4
1928-29	**Ottawa Senators**	**NHL**	**44**	**9**	**3**	**12**	**26**	**20**	**46**	**28**	....	....	....	....	....
1929-30	**Ottawa Senators**	**NHL**	**44**	**10**	**3**	**13**	**14**	**7**	**21**	**24**	**2**	**1**	**0**	**1**	**0**
1930-31	**Ottawa Senators**	**NHL**	**44**	**15**	**15**	**30**	**30**	**46**	**76**	**8**	....	....	....	....	....
1931-32	**Boston Bruins**	**NHL**	**26**	**5**	**4**	**9**	**8**	**9**	**17**	**12**	....	....	....	....	....
	Boston Cubs	Can-Am	5	1	0	1	....	....	....	2	....	....	....	....	....
	Philadelphia Arrows	Can-Am	11	1	5	6	....	....	....	4	....	....	....	....	....
1932-33	**Ottawa Senators**	**NHL**	**47**	**12**	**7**	**19**	**22**	**14**	**36**	**12**	....	....	....	....	....
1933-34	**Ottawa Senators**	**NHL**	**46**	**12**	**8**	**20**	**21**	**17**	**38**	**21**	....	....	....	....	....
1934-35	Windsor Bulldogs	IHL	25	4	14	18	....	....	....	0	....	....	....	....	....
	Syracuse Stars	IHL	12	1	2	3	....	....	....	2	....	....	....	....	....
1935-36	Buffalo Bisons	IHL	40	15	15	30	....	....	....	8	5	0	0	0	0
1936-37	Buffalo Bisons	AHL	10	0	0	0	....	....	....	0	....	....	....	....	....
1937-38	Ottawa Senators	OCHL	21	8	12	20	....	....	....	2	2	1	1	2	0
1938-39	Ottawa Senators	OCHL	22	11	11	22	....	....	....	6	6	2	4	6	2
1939-40	Ottawa Senators	OCHL	30	9	18	27	....	....	....	4	....	....	....	....	....
	NHL Totals		**280**	**65**	**40**	**105**	**125**	**113**	**238**	**107**	**2**	**1**	**0**	**1**	**0**

Signed as a free agent by **Montreal Maroons**, November 2, 1927. Traded to **Stratford** (Can-Pro) by **Montreal Maroons** for Fred Brown with Montreal holding right of recall, February 14, 1928. Traded to **Ottawa** by **Montreal Maroons** for cash, October 25, 1928. Claimed by **Boston** from **Ottawa** for 1931-32 season in Dispersal Draft, September 26, 1931. Transferred to **St. Louis** after **Ottawa** franchise relocated, May 14, 1934. Loaned to **Syracuse** (IHL) by **St. Louis**, December 28, 1934.

• TOUPIN, Jacques Jean Jacques

RW – R. 5'7", 155 lbs. b: Trois Rivieres, Que., 11/10/1910 d: 2/17/1987.

Season	Club	League	GP	G	A	Pts	AG	AA	APts	PIM	GP	G	A	Pts	PIM
1928-29	Trois-Rivieres Renards	ECHA	21	9	1	10	....	....	....	12	....	....	....	....	....
1929-30	Trois-Rivieres Renards	ECHA	9	4	3	7	....	....	....	12	....	....	....	....	....
1930-31	Trois-Rivieres Renards	ECHA	18	9	*13	*22	....	....	....	15	2	0	0	0	2
1931-32	Quebec Castors	ECHA	24	13	8	21	....	....	....	12	3	3	*6	*9	0
1932-33	Quebec Castors	Can-Am	48	13	23	36	....	....	....	24	....	....	....	....	....
1933-34	Quebec Castors	Can-Am	40	12	14	26	....	....	....	14	....	....	....	....	....
1934-35	London Tecumsehs	IHL	15	2	8	10	....	....	....	0	5	2	2	4	2
	Quebec Beavers	Can-Am	27	5	10	15	....	....	....	0	....	....	....	....	....
1935-36	Springfield Indians	Can-Am	47	18	15	33	....	....	....	20	3	1	2	3	2
1936-37	Springfield Indians	IAHL	45	13	24	37	....	....	....	6	5	0	1	1	4
1937-38	Springfield Indians	IAHL	48	11	19	30	....	....	....	24	....	....	....	....	....
1938-39	Springfield Indians	IAHL	53	8	31	39	....	....	....	16	3	0	0	0	0
1939-40	Springfield Indians	IAHL	49	16	*34	50	....	....	....	12	....	....	....	....	....
1940-41	Buffalo Bisons	AHL	48	21	22	43	....	....	....	15	....	....	....	....	....
1941-42	Buffalo Bisons	AHL	56	15	36	51	....	....	....	34	....	....	....	....	....
1942-43	Providence Reds	AHL	53	22	39	61	....	....	....	8	2	0	2	2	0
1943-44	Providence Reds	AHL	25	16	26	42	....	....	....	14	....	....	....	....	....
	Chicago Black Hawks	**NHL**	**8**	**1**	**2**	**3**	**1**	**2**	**3**	**0**	**4**	**0**	**0**	**0**	**0**
1944-45	Shawinigan Cataracts	QPHL	22	23	25	48	....	....	....	6	6	5	4	9	0
	Valleyfield Braves	QPHL	....	....	....	....	....	....	....	....	5	2	1	3	2
	Valleyfield Braves	Al-Cup	3	2	2	4	....	....	....	0	....	....	....	....	....
1945-46	Shawinigan Cataracts	QSHL	24	13	12	25	....	....	....	22	4	0	0	0	10
	NHL Totals		**8**	**1**	**2**	**3**	**1**	**2**	**3**	**0**	**4**	**0**	**0**	**0**	**0**

Signed as a free agent by **Buffalo** (AHL), November 13, 1940. Traded to **Providence** (AHL) by **Buffalo** (AHL) for the rights to Jack Shill, October 29, 1942. Traded to **Chicago** by **Providence** (AHL) for cash, February 28, 1944.

• TOWNSEND, Art Elmer Albert "Bull"

D – L. 5'10", 185 lbs. b: Souris, Man., 10/9/1905 d: 5/7/1971.

Season	Club	League	GP	G	A	Pts	AG	AA	APts	PIM	GP	G	A	Pts	PIM
1923-24	Souris Eagles	MHL-Sr.	STATISTICS NOT AVAILABLE												
1924-25	Brandon Wheat Kings	MHL-Sr.	20	7	2	9	....	....	....		....	....	....	....	....
1925-26	Portland Rosebuds	WHL	29	4	2	6	....	....	....	48	....	....	....	....	....
1926-27	**Chicago Black Hawks**	**NHL**	**5**	**0**	**0**	**0**	**0**	**0**	**0**	**0**	....	....	....	....	....
	Springfield Indians	Can-Am	24	7	1	8	....	....	....	40	6	0	0	0	6
1927-28	Winnipeg Maroons	AHA	38	5	4	9	....	....	....	93	....	....	....	....	....
1928-29	Tulsa Oilers	AHA	20	1	1	2	....	....	....	39	....	....	....	....	....
1929-30	Seattle Eskimos	PCHL	28	3	1	4	....	....	....	118	....	....	....	....	....
1930-31	San Francisco Tigers	Cal-Pro	....	1	5	6	....	....	....	....	....	....	....	....	....
1931-32	London Tecumsehs	IHL	6	0	0	0	....	....	....	4	....	....	....	....	....
	Trois-Rivieres Renards	ECHA	23	5	3	8	....	....	....	38	....	....	....	....	....
1932-33	Regina—Edmonton	WCHL	25	4	4	8	....	....	....	37	8	1	2	3	8
1933-34	Edmonton Eskimos	NWHL	34	10	9	19	....	....	....	*102	2	0	1	1	4
1934-35	Edmonton–Portland	NWHL	29	4	8	12	....	....	....	53	....	....	....	....	....
1935-36	Edmonton Eskimos	NWHL	40	5	6	11	....	....	....	*84	....	....	....	....	....
1936-37	University of Alberta	ASHL	DID NOT PLAY – COACHING												
1937-38	Edmonton Superiors	ASHL	20	7	5	12	....	....	....	49	....	....	....	....	....
1938-39	Edmonton Superiors	ASHL	10	1	1	2	....	....	....	10	....	....	....	....	....
	NHL Totals		**5**	**0**	**0**	**0**	**0**	**0**	**0**	**0**	....	....	....	....	....
	Other Major League Totals		29	4	2	6	....	....	....	48	....	....	....	....	....

ECHA Second All-Star Team (1932)

Signed as a free agent by **Regina** (WCHL), March 9, 1925. Transferred to **Portland** (WHL) after **Regina** (WHL) franchise relocated, September 1, 1925. NHL rights transferred to **Chicago** after NHL club purchased **Portland** (WHL) franchise, May 16, 1926. Loaned to **Springfield** (Can-Am) by **Chicago** for cash, December 16, 1926. Signed as a free agent by **London** (IHL), October 30, 1931.

• TRAINOR, Wes Wes Thomas "Bucko"

C/LW – R. 5'8", 180 lbs. b: Charlottetown, P.E.I., 9/11/1922 Deceased.

Season	Club	League	GP	G	A	Pts	AG	AA	APts	PIM	GP	G	A	Pts	PIM
1937-38	Charlottetown Royals	PEI-Jr.	3	2	3	5	....	....	....	0	2	2	2	4	2
1938-39	Charlottetown Royals	PEI-Jr.	9	6	*18	24	....	....	....	2	4	4	3	7	0
1939-40	Charlottetown Army	PEI-Sr.	5	7	6	13	....	....	....	8	....	....	....	....	....
	Charlottetown Royals	PEI-Jr.	....	....	....	....	....	....	....	....	10	8	5	13	6
	Charlottetown Royals	M-Cup	6	4	2	6	....	....	....	6	....	....	....	....	....
1940-41	Petawawa Grenades	UOVHL	18	18	17	35	....	....	....	15	5	5	3	8	*5
	Petawawa Grenades	Al-Cup	4	3	*9	*12	....	....	....	*9	....	....	....	....	....
1941-42			MILITARY SERVICE												
1942-43			MILITARY SERVICE												
1943-44			MILITARY SERVICE												
1944-45			MILITARY SERVICE												
1945-46	Drummondville Intrepids	QPHL	31	18	24	42	....	....	....	27	....	....	....	....	....
1946-47	Moncton Hawks	MMHL	37	20	*45	65	....	....	....	42	9	4	*11	15	8
1947-48	St. Paul Saints	USHL	35	7	8	15	....	....	....	22	....	....	....	....	....
1948-49	**New York Rangers**	**NHL**	**17**	**1**	**2**	**3**	**1**	**3**	**4**	**6**	....	....	....	....	....
	St. Paul Saints	USHL	49	19	49	68	....	....	....	43	....	....	....	....	....
1949-50	New Haven Ramblers	AHL	44	6	16	22	....	....	....	21	....	....	....	....	....
	St. Paul Saints	USHL	14	3	6	9	....	....	....	11	3	1	0	1	0
1950-51	Charlottetown Islanders	MMHL	72	25	*73	98	....	....	....	81	11	4	7	11	8
	Charlottetown Islanders	Alx-Cup	7	2	5	7	....	....	....	0	....	....	....	....	....
1951-52	Charlottetown Islanders	MMHL	76	13	43	56	....	....	....	47	4	0	1	1	2
1952-53	Grand Falls Cataracts	Nfld-Jr.	DID NOT PLAY – COACHING												
	Grand Falls All-Stars	Nfld-Sr.	10	3	9	12	....	....	....	*33	4	0	3	3	8
1953-54	Charlottetown Islanders	MMHL	65	18	47	65	....	....	....	36	7	0	3	3	9
1954-55	Grand Falls All-Stars	Nfld-Sr.	7	1	3	4	....	....	....	2	4	1	2	3	2
1955-56	Grand Falls Cataracts	Nfld-Jr.	DID NOT PLAY – COACHING												
	Grand Falls Andcos	Nfld-Sr.	....	....	....	....	....	....	....	....	1	0	0	0	0
	NHL Totals		**17**	**1**	**2**	**3**	**1**	**3**	**4**	**6**	....	....	....	....	....

MMHL First All-Star Team (1947)

Signed as a free agent by **NY Rangers**, September, 1947.

• TRAPP, Bob Robert Albert

D – L. 5'10", 170 lbs. b: Pembroke, Ont., 12/16/1899 d: 11/20/1979.

Season	Club	League	GP	G	A	Pts	AG	AA	APts	PIM	GP	G	A	Pts	PIM
1914-15	Toronto R & AA	OHA-Sr.	STATISTICS NOT AVAILABLE												
1915-16	Toronto R & AA	OHA-Sr.	8	4	0	4	....	....	....		....	....	....	....	....
1916-17			MILITARY SERVICE												
1917-18			MILITARY SERVICE												
1918-19	Toronto Veterans	OHA-Sr.	3	2	1	3	....	....	....	0	....	....	....	....	....
1919-20	Edmonton Eskimos	Big-4	12	2	2	4	....	....	....	6	2	0	0	0	0
1920-21	Edmonton Dominions	Big-4	16	6	1	7	....	....	....	2	....	....	....	....	....
1921-22	Edmonton Eskimos	WCHL	24	5	4	9	....	....	....	5	2	1	0	1	0
1922-23	Edmonton Eskimos	WCHL	26	5	5	10	....	....	....	14	2	0	1	1	2
	Edmonton Eskimos	St-Cup	2	0	0	0	....	....	....	2	....	....	....	....	....
1923-24	Edmonton Eskimos	WCHL	30	5	4	9	....	....	....	20	....	....	....	....	....
1924-25	Edmonton Eskimos	WCHL	27	8	11	19	....	....	....	33	....	....	....	....	....
1925-26	Portland Rosebuds	WHL	30	4	12	16	....	....	....	55	....	....	....	....	....
1926-27	**Chicago Black Hawks**	**NHL**	**44**	**4**	**2**	**6**	**7**	**10**	**17**	**92**	**2**	**0**	**0**	**0**	**4**
1927-28	**Chicago Black Hawks**	**NHL**	**38**	**0**	**2**	**2**	**0**	**11**	**11**	**37**	....	....	....	....	....
1928-29	Tulsa Oilers	AHA	40	8	6	14	....	....	....	30	4	1	0	1	14
1929-30	Tulsa Oilers	AHA	23	1	3	4	....	....	....	10	....	....	....	....	....
1930-31	Tulsa Oilers	AHA	45	8	13	21	....	....	....	54	4	0	0	0	2
1931-32	Tulsa Oilers	AHA	25	4	3	7	....	....	....	30	....	....	....	....	....
	Providence Reds	Can-Am	14	2	2	4	....	....	....	12	5	0	*2	2	6
1932-33	Providence Reds	Can-Am	44	3	11	14	....	....	....	50	2	1	0	1	0
1933-34	Providence Reds	Can-Am	17	0	1	1	....	....	....	2	....	....	....	....	....
	NHL Totals		**82**	**4**	**4**	**8**	**7**	**21**	**28**	**129**	**2**	**0**	**0**	**0**	**4**
	Other Major League Totals		137	27	36	63	....	....	....	127	4	1	1	2	2

WCHL Second All-Star Team (1922) • WCHL First All-Star Team (1923) • WHL First All-Star Team (1926)

Signed as a free agent by **Edmonton** (WCHL), December 5, 1921. Traded to **Portland** (WHL) by **Edmonton** (WHL) with Joe McCormick for Eddie Shore and Art Gagne, October 7, 1925. NHL rights transferred to **Chicago** after NHL club purchased **Portland** (WHL) franchise, May 16, 1926.

• TRAUB, Percy "Puss"

D – L. 5'9", 175 lbs. b: Elmwood, Ont., 8/23/1896 d: 12/5/1948.

Season	Club	League	GP	G	A	Pts	AG	AA	APts	PIM	GP	G	A	Pts	PIM
1915-16	Regina Victorias	S-SSHL	9	1	0	1	....	....	....	11	....	....	....	....	....
1916-17	Regina 217 Battalion	S-SSHL	7	2	3	5	....	....	....	19	....	....	....	....	....
1917-18	Regina Depot	S-SSHL	6	0	1	1	....	....	....	23	....	....	....	....	....
1918-19			MILITARY SERVICE												
1919-20	Regina Victorias	S-SSHL	12	2	2	4	....	....	....	20	2	1	0	1	0
1920-21	Regina Victorias	S-SSHL	15	4	4	8	....	....	....	22	4	0	2	2	2
1921-22	Regina Capitals	WCHL	25	8	2	10	....	....	....	32	4	0	1	1	0
1922-23	Regina Capitals	WCHL	26	3	5	8	....	....	....	27	2	0	0	0	*4
1923-24	Regina Capitals	WCHL	27	2	4	6	....	....	....	48	2	0	0	0	4
1924-25	Regina Capitals	WCHL	26	4	5	9	....	....	....	61	....	....	....	....	....
1925-26	Portland Rosebuds	WHL	28	1	3	4	....	....	....	66	....	....	....	....	....
1926-27	**Chicago Black Hawks**	**NHL**	**42**	**0**	**2**	**2**	**0**	**10**	**10**	**93**	**2**	**0**	**0**	**0**	**6**
1927-28	**Detroit Cougars**	**NHL**	**44**	**3**	**1**	**4**	**6**	**6**	**12**	**78**	....	....	....	....	....

Season	Club	League	GP	G	A	Pts	AG	AA	APts	PIM	GP	G	A	Pts	PIM
			REGULAR SEASON								PLAYOFFS				
1928-29	**Detroit Cougars**	**NHL**	**44**	**0**	**0**	**0**	**0**	**0**	**0**	**46**	**2**	**0**	**0**	**0**	**0**
1929-30			DID NOT PLAY – REFEREE												
1930-31	Regina Vics	S-SSHL	DID NOT PLAY – COACHING												
	NHL Totals		**130**	**3**	**3**	**6**	**6**	**16**	**22**	**217**	**4**	**0**	**0**	**0**	**6**
	Other Major League Totals		132	18	19	37	....	....	....	234	8	0	1	1	8

WCHL Second All-Star Team (1922, 1923) • WCHL First All-Star Team (1924)

Signed as a free agent by **Regina** (WCHL), November 23, 1921. Transferred to **Portland** (WHL) after **Regina** (WHL) franchise relocated, September 1, 1925. NHL rights transferred to **Chicago** after NHL club purchased **Portland** (WHL) franchise, May 16, 1926. Traded to **Detroit** by **Chicago** with George Hay for $15,000, April 11, 1927.

• TREMBLAY, Gilles

— *see page 1707*

• TREMBLAY, J.C.

— *see page 1708*

• TREMBLAY, Marcel

Marcel Bernard

RW – R. 5'11", 165 lbs. b: St. Boniface, Man., 7/4/1915.

Season	Club	League	GP	G	A	Pts	AG	AA	APts	PIM	GP	G	A	Pts	PIM
1932-33	Winnipeg Monarchs	WJrHL	10	8	1	9	....	....	....	2	....	....	....	....	....
1933-34	Winnipeg Monarchs	WJrHL	14	6	4	10	....	....	....	2	3	1	1	2	4
1934-35			DID NOT PLAY												
1935-36			DID NOT PLAY												
1936-37	Flin Flon Bombers	N-SSHL	16	11	5	16	....	....	....	14	6	*5	2	7	2
1937-38	Flin Flon Bombers	N-SSHL	19	*19	10	29	....	....	....	22	....	....	....	....	....
1938-39	**Montreal Canadiens**	**NHL**	**10**	**0**	**2**	**2**	**0**	**3**	**3**	**0**	....	....	....	....	....
	New Haven Eagles	AHL	26	5	13	18	....	....	....	6	....	....	....	....	....
1939-40	New Haven Eagles	IAHL	51	23	24	47	....	....	....	23	3	2	0	2	0
1940-41	New Haven Eagles	AHL	48	11	18	29	....	....	....	24	2	0	0	0	0
1941-42	New Haven Eagles	AHL	20	7	5	12	....	....	....	18	....	....	....	....	....
1942-43			MILITARY SERVICE												
1943-44			MILITARY SERVICE												
1944-45	Montreal Army	MCHL	2	0	0	0	....	....	....	0	....	....	....	....	....
	NHL Totals		**10**	**0**	**2**	**2**	**0**	**3**	**3**	**0**	....	....	....	....	....

• TREMBLAY, Nil

Louis Nil

C – R. 5'9", 170 lbs. b: Matane, Que., 7/26/1923 Deceased.

Season	Club	League	GP	G	A	Pts	AG	AA	APts	PIM	GP	G	A	Pts	PIM
1941-42	Quebec Aces	QSHL	1	0	0	0	....	....	....	0	....	....	....	....	....
1942-43	Quebec Aces	QJHL	17	8	6	14	....	....	....	8	....	....	....	....	....
1943-44	Quebec Aces	QSHL	25	19	28	*47	....	....	....	15	6	5	4	9	2
	Quebec Aces	Al-Cup	9	10	11	21	....	....	....	12	....	....	....	....	....
1944-45	**Montreal Canadiens**	**NHL**	**1**	**0**	**1**	**1**	**0**	**1**	**1**	**0**	**2**	**0**	**0**	**0**	**0**
	Hull–Quebec	QSHL	21	23	31	*54	....	....	....	37	7	4	5	9	2
	Quebec Aces	Al-Cup	3	2	*4	*6	....	....	....	2	....	....	....	....	....
1945-46	**Montreal Canadiens**	**NHL**	**2**	**0**	**0**	**0**	**0**	**0**	**0**	**0**	....	....	....	....	....
	Quebec Aces	QSHL	32	19	20	39	....	....	....	51	6	3	5	8	18
1946-47	Quebec Aces	QSHL	37	25	35	60	....	....	....	43	4	3	5	8	10
1947-48	Quebec Aces	QSHL	2	0	2	2	....	....	....	2	....	....	....	....	....
	Seattle Ironmen	PCHL	3	0	2	2	....	....	....	10	....	....	....	....	....
1948-49	Ottawa Senators	QSHL	60	35	*71	106	....	....	....	51	11	3	7	10	8
	Ottawa Senators	Al-Cup	12	*11	*9	*20	....	....	....	2	....	....	....	....	....
1949-50	Ottawa Senators	QSHL	59	15	38	53	....	....	....	69	7	4	4	8	4
1950-51	Ottawa Senators	QMHL	52	21	29	50	....	....	....	22	11	2	2	4	4
1951-52	Sherbrooke Saints	QMHL	47	9	28	37	....	....	....	21	9	2	3	5	0
1952-53	Sherbrooke Saints	QMHL	46	13	18	31	....	....	....	21	7	0	5	5	2
1953-54	Riviere-du-Loup Raiders	SLSHL	57	15	33	48	....	....	....	8	....	....	....	....	....
	NHL Totals		**3**	**0**	**1**	**1**	**0**	**1**	**1**	**0**	**2**	**0**	**0**	**0**	**0**

QSHL Second All-Star Team (1949)

Signed as a free agent by **Montreal**, November 14, 1944.

• TROTTIER, Dave

David Thomas

LW – L. 5'10", 170 lbs. b: Pembroke, Ont., 6/25/1906 d: 12/13/1956.

Season	Club	League	GP	G	A	Pts	AG	AA	APts	PIM	GP	G	A	Pts	PIM
1923-24	St. Michael's Majors	OHA-Jr.	6	*13	2	15	....	....	....	....	....	....	....	....	....
1924-25	St. Michael's Majors	OHA-Jr.	6	7	*7	14	....	....	....	....	1	1	1	2	0
1925-26	Toronto Varsity Grads	OHA-Sr.	STATISTICS NOT AVAILABLE												
1926-27	Toronto Varsity Grads	OHA-Sr.	11	23	*8	31	....	....	....	7	2	1	0	1	2
	Toronto Varsity Grads	Al-Cup	12	9	*7	16	....	....	....	*32	....	....	....	....	....
1927-28	Toronto Varsity Grads	X-Games	12	*33	*10	*43	....	....	....	....	....	....	....	....	....
	Canada	Olympics	3	*12	*3	*15	....	....	....	....	....	....	....	....	....
1928-29	**Montreal Maroons**	**NHL**	**37**	**2**	**4**	**6**	**6**	**27**	**33**	**69**	....	....	....	....	....
	Montreal Victorias	MCHL	2	0	0	0	....	....	....	0	....	....	....	....	....
1929-30	**Montreal Maroons**	**NHL**	**41**	**17**	**10**	**27**	**24**	**24**	**48**	**73**	**4**	**0**	**2**	**2**	**8**
1930-31	**Montreal Maroons**	**NHL**	**43**	**9**	**8**	**17**	**18**	**24**	**42**	**58**	**2**	**0**	**0**	**0**	**6**
1931-32	**Montreal Maroons**	**NHL**	**48**	**26**	**18**	**44**	**44**	**40**	**84**	**94**	**4**	**1**	**0**	**1**	**0**
1932-33	**Montreal Maroons**	**NHL**	**48**	**16**	**15**	**31**	**29**	**31**	**60**	**38**	**2**	**0**	**0**	**0**	**6**
1933-34	**Montreal Maroons**	**NHL**	**48**	**9**	**17**	**26**	**15**	**36**	**51**	**47**	**4**	**0**	**0**	**0**	**6**
♦**1934-35**	**Montreal Maroons**	**NHL**	**34**	**10**	**9**	**19**	**16**	**16**	**32**	**22**	**7**	**2**	**1**	**3**	**4**
1935-36	**Montreal Maroons**	**NHL**	**46**	**10**	**10**	**20**	**19**	**19**	**38**	**25**	**3**	**0**	**0**	**0**	**4**
1936-37	**Montreal Maroons**	**NHL**	**43**	**12**	**11**	**23**	**20**	**20**	**40**	**33**	**5**	**1**	**0**	**1**	**5**
1937-38	**Montreal Maroons**	**NHL**	**47**	**9**	**10**	**19**	**15**	**16**	**31**	**42**	....	....	....	....	....
1938-39	**Detroit Red Wings**	**NHL**	**11**	**1**	**1**	**2**	**2**	**2**	**4**	**16**	....	....	....	....	....
	Pittsburgh Hornets	IAHL	10	5	3	8	....	....	....	6	....	....	....	....	....
	NHL Totals		**446**	**121**	**113**	**234**	**208**	**255**	**463**	**517**	**31**	**4**	**3**	**7**	**39**

Played in NHL All-Star Game (1937)

Signed as a free agent by **Montreal Maroons**, April 8, 1928. Rights later awarded to **Toronto**. Traded to **Montreal Maroons** by **Toronto** for $15,000, November 28, 1928. Traded to **Detroit** by **Montreal Maroons** for cash, December 13, 1938.

• TRUDEL, Lou

Louis Napoleon

LW – L. 5'11", 167 lbs. b: Salem, MA, 7/21/1912 d: 3/19/1972.

Season	Club	League	GP	G	A	Pts	AG	AA	APts	PIM	GP	G	A	Pts	PIM
1929-30	Edmonton Poolers	EJrHL	2	*4	0	*4	....	....	....	0	....	....	....	....	....
	Edmonton Poolers	M-Cup	2	1	0	1	....	....	....	4	....	....	....	....	....
1930-31	Edmonton Poolers	EJrHL	13	7	3	10	....	....	....	8	....	....	....	....	....
1931-32	Edmonton Poolers	EJrHL	10	10	1	11	....	....	....	....	4	*3	0	*3	4
	Edmonton Poolers	M-Cup	5	4	0	4	....	....	....	12	....	....	....	....	....
1932-33	St. Paul Greyhounds	AHA	16	5	4	9	....	....	....	11	....	....	....	....	....
	St. Paul-Tulsa	AHA	15	5	2	7	....	....	....	8	4	1	0	1	4
♦**1933-34**	**Chicago Black Hawks**	**NHL**	**31**	**1**	**3**	**4**	**2**	**6**	**8**	**13**	**7**	**0**	**0**	**0**	**0**
	Syracuse Stars	IHL	5	0	0	0	....	....	....	2	....	....	....	....	....
1934-35	**Chicago Black Hawks**	**NHL**	**47**	**11**	**11**	**22**	**18**	**19**	**37**	**28**	**2**	**0**	**0**	**0**	**0**
1935-36	**Chicago Black Hawks**	**NHL**	**47**	**3**	**4**	**7**	**6**	**8**	**14**	**27**	**2**	**0**	**0**	**0**	**2**
1936-37	**Chicago Black Hawks**	**NHL**	**45**	**6**	**12**	**18**	**10**	**22**	**32**	**11**	....	....	....	....	....
♦**1937-38**	**Chicago Black Hawks**	**NHL**	**42**	**6**	**16**	**22**	**10**	**26**	**36**	**15**	**10**	**0**	**3**	**3**	**2**
1938-39	**Montreal Canadiens**	**NHL**	**31**	**8**	**13**	**21**	**14**	**20**	**34**	**2**	**3**	**1**	**0**	**1**	**0**
	New Haven Eagles	IAHL	18	6	9	15	....	....	....	7	....	....	....	....	....
1939-40	**Montreal Canadiens**	**NHL**	**47**	**12**	**7**	**19**	**20**	**11**	**31**	**24**	....	....	....	....	....
1940-41	**Montreal Canadiens**	**NHL**	**16**	**2**	**3**	**5**	**3**	**4**	**7**	**2**	....	....	....	....	....
	New Haven Eagles	AHL	20	22	13	35	....	....	....	11	2	0	0	0	0
1941-42	Washington Lions	AHL	54	*37	29	66	....	....	....	11	2	1	0	1	0
1942-43	Cleveland Barons	AHL	18	8	5	13	....	....	....	0	4	0	1	1	2
1943-44	Cleveland Barons	AHL	52	29	47	76	....	....	....	13	11	4	2	6	2
1944-45	Cleveland Barons	AHL	60	*45	48	93	....	....	....	25	12	8	5	13	6
1945-46	Cleveland Barons	AHL	61	33	46	79	....	....	....	24	12	7	4	11	8
1946-47	Cleveland Barons	AHL	50	20	29	49	....	....	....	12	....	....	....	....	....
1947-48	Cleveland Barons	AHL	13	1	6	7	....	....	....	6	....	....	....	....	....
1948-49	Montreal Royals	QSHL	2	0	0	0	....	....	....	0	3	0	0	0	0
1949-50	Cleveland Knights	EAHL	STATISTICS NOT AVAILABLE												
1950-51	Grand Rapids Rockets	IHL	19	10	25	35	....	....	....	10	3	0	0	0	0
1951-52	Grand Rapids Rockets	IHL	17	2	10	12	....	....	....	20	13	2	3	5	12
1952-53	St-Jerome Alouettes	QPHL	62	18	25	43	....	....	....	....	....	....	....	....	....
1953-54	Milwaukee Chiefs	IHL	11	1	6	7	....	....	....	4	....	....	....	....	....
	NHL Totals		**306**	**49**	**69**	**118**	**83**	**116**	**199**	**122**	**24**	**1**	**3**	**4**	**4**

AHL Second All-Star Team (1942, 1945, 1946) • AHL First All-Star Team (1944) • Played in NHL All-Star Game (1939)

Traded to **Montreal Canadiens** by **Chicago** for Joffre Desilets, August 26, 1938. Traded to **Washington** (AHL) by **Montreal** for cash, October 9, 1941. Traded to **Cleveland** (AHL) by **Washington** (AHL) for Herb Foster and future considerations, February 2, 1943.

• TRUDELL, Rene

Rene Joseph

RW – R. 5'9", 165 lbs. b: Mariapolis, Man., 1/31/1919 d: 3/19/1972.

Season	Club	League	GP	G	A	Pts	AG	AA	APts	PIM	GP	G	A	Pts	PIM
1935-36	Kildonan North Stars	MJHL	2	0	0	0	....	....	....	3	....	....	....	....	....
1936-37	Winnipeg Canadians	MJHL	15	17	7	24	....	....	....	20	....	....	....	....	....
1937-38	Portage Terriers	MJHL	21	14	14	28	....	....	....	20	....	....	....	....	....
	Hudson's Bay Seniors	WPSHL	5	0	1	1	....	....	....	0	4	0	0	0	4
1938-39	Portage Terriers	MJHL	18	12	11	23	....	....	....	40	3	1	0	1	6
1939-40	Harringay Racers	Ln-Cup	....	10	4	14	....	....	....	....	....	....	....	....	....
	Harringay Racers	Britain	....	20	15	35	....	....	....	....	....	....	....	....	....
	Harringay Racers	Nat-Tmt	....	4	3	7	....	....	....	....	....	....	....	....	....
1940-41	Toledo Babcocks	USHL	22	8	21	29	....	....	....	46	2	2	0	2	4
1941-42	Yorkton Terriers	S-SSHL	30	11	28	39	....	....	....	62	....	....	....	....	....
1942-43	Winnipeg RCAF	WNDHL	13	6	12	18	....	....	....	26	5	1	1	2	6
	Winnipeg RCAF	Al-Cup	12	4	*13	*17	....	....	....	*30	....	....	....	....	....
1943-44	Winnipeg RCAF	WNDHL	9	5	0	5	....	....	....	20	....	....	....	....	....
1944-45	Winnipeg RCAF	WNDHL	10	12	3	15	....	....	....	6	2	0	0	0	6
1945-46	**New York Rangers**	**NHL**	**16**	**3**	**5**	**8**	**4**	**7**	**11**	**4**	....	....	....	....	....
	New York Rovers	EAHL	40	29	32	61	....	....	....	44	....	....	....	....	....
1946-47	**New York Rangers**	**NHL**	**59**	**8**	**16**	**24**	**9**	**19**	**28**	**38**	....	....	....	....	....
1947-48	**New York Rangers**	**NHL**	**54**	**13**	**7**	**20**	**17**	**9**	**26**	**30**	**5**	**0**	**0**	**0**	**2**
1948-49	Springfield Indians	AHL	48	18	28	46	....	....	....	34	3	3	3	6	0
	NHL Totals		**129**	**24**	**28**	**52**	**30**	**35**	**65**	**72**	**5**	**0**	**0**	**0**	**2**

EAHL First All-Star Team (1946)

Traded to **Toronto** by **NY Rangers** with Cal Gardner, Bill Juzda and the rights to Frank Mathers for Wally Stanowski and Moe Morris, April 26, 1948. Traded to **Springfield** (AHL) by **Toronto** (Pittsburgh-AHL) for $5,000 and future considerations, November 17, 1948.

• TUDIN, Connie

Cornell

C – L. 5'11", 170 lbs. b: Ottawa, Ont., 9/21/1917 Deceased.

Season	Club	League	GP	G	A	Pts	AG	AA	APts	PIM	GP	G	A	Pts	PIM
1936-37	Ottawa Rideaus	OCJHL	15	*31	*15	*46	....	....	....	4	4	*8	*4	*12	4
	Ottawa Rideaus	M-Cup	4	8	*8	16	....	....	....	8	....	....	....	....	....
1937-38	Arnprior Greenshirts	UOVHL	16	18	*17	*35	....	....	....	12	3	0	2	2	0
	Arnprior Greenshirts	Al-Cup	4	2	*8	10	....	....	....	2	....	....	....	....	....
1938-39	Wembley Lions	Ln-Cup	....	1	1	2	....	....	....	2	....	....	....	....	....
	Harringay Greyhounds	Britain	....	6	7	13	....	....	....	14	....	....	....	....	....
	Wembley Lions	Nat-Tmt	....	4	3	7	....	....	....	6	....	....	....	....	....
1939-40	Lachine Rapides	QPHL	41	27	12	39	....	....	....	76	9	5	4	9	10
1940-41	Montreal Sr. Canadiens	QSHL	31	11	9	20	....	....	....	52	....	....	....	....	....
	New Haven Eagles	AHL	10	2	7	9	....	....	....	2	2	1	0	1	0
1941-42	**Montreal Canadiens**	**NHL**	**4**	**0**	**1**	**1**	**0**	**1**	**1**	**4**	....	....	....	....	....
	Washington Lions	AHL	42	9	12	21	....	....	....	20	2	0	0	0	0
1942-43	Ottawa RCAF	OHA-Sr.	17	15	14	29	....	....	....	19	8	4	3	7	13
	Ottawa RCAF	Al-Cup	7	1	2	3	....	....	....	6	....	....	....	....	....
1943-44	Arnprior RCAF	OHA-Sr.	7	9	12	21	....	....	....	10	....	....	....	....	....
1944-45	Rockcliffe RCAF	ONDHL	12	16	21	37	....	....	....	7	3	7	2	9	4
	Ottawa Commandos	QSHL	1	1	0	1	....	....	....	0	....	....	....	....	....
1945-46	Ottawa–Hull	QSHL	25	9	22	31	....	....	....	2	....	....	....	....	....
	Arnprior Rams	UOVHL	4	0	2	2	....	....	....	4	....	....	....	....	....
	Ottawa RCAF	OCHL	10	9	8	17	....	....	....	....	4	2	2	4	....
1946-47	Ottawa Senators	QSHL	4	0	0	0	....	....	....	0	....	....	....	....	....
	Ottawa Senators	UOVHL	18	19	15	34	....	....	....	22	9	7	7	14	12
1947-48	Ottawa Senators	QSHL	43	24	30	54	....	....	....	18	12	*12	11	*23	6
	Ottawa Senators	Al-Cup	14	4	6	10	....	....	....	10	....	....	....	....	....
1948-49	Ottawa Senators	QSHL	57	22	36	58	....	....	....	19	11	2	4	6	4
	Ottawa Senators	Al-Cup	1	0	0	0	....	....	....	0	....	....	....	....	....
1949-50	Ottawa Senators	QSHL	41	10	14	24	....	....	....	52	7	0	1	1	4
1950-51	Ottawa Senators	QMHL	55	4	18	22	....	....	....	59	11	2	3	5	10
1951-52	Smiths Falls Rideaus	ECSHL	43	11	33	44	....	....	....	63	5	2	2	4	0
1952-53	Smiths Falls Rideaus	ECSHL	45	16	27	43	....	....	....	22	13	*4	4	8	7
	Smiths Falls Rideaus	Al-Cup	11	*6	4	10	....	....	....	8	....	....	....	....	....
1953-54	Brockville Magadonas	NYOHL	30	18	39	57	....	....	....	18	....	....	....	....	....
	NHL Totals		**4**	**0**	**1**	**1**	**0**	**1**	**1**	**4**	....	....	....	....	....

Signed as a free agent by **Montreal**, October 16, 1941.

• TURLICK, Gord

LW/C – L. 6'1", 170 lbs. b: Miskel, B.C., 9/17/1939.

			REGULAR SEASON								PLAYOFFS				
Season	Club	League	GP	G	A	Pts	AG	AA	APts	PIM	GP	G	A	Pts	PIM
1957-58	Melville Millionaires	SJHL	16	1	2	3	....	....	....	6	....	....	....	....	....
1958-59	Melville Millionaires	SJHL	3	0	0	0	....	....	....	0	....	....	....	....	....
	Prince Albert Mintos	SJHL	32	7	9	16	....	....	....	33	5	0	1	1	4
1959-60	Prince Albert Mintos	SJHL	58	*65	36	101	....	....	....	50	7	4	2	6	2
	Boston Bruins	**NHL**	**2**	**0**	**0**	**0**	**0**	**0**	**0**	**2**	....	....	....	....	....
1960-61	Sudbury Wolves	EPHL	5	0	0	0	....	....	....	4	....	....	....	....	....
	Clinton Comets	EHL	8	2	1	3	....	....	....	10	....	....	....	....	....
	New York Rovers	EHL	44	8	13	21	....	....	....	5	....	....	....	....	....
1961-62	Indianapolis Chiefs	IHL	4	0	0	0	....	....	....	0	....	....	....	....	....
	Kimberley Dynamiters	WIHL	24	12	7	19	....	....	....	4	....	....	....	....	....
1962-63			DID NOT PLAY												
1963-64	Spokane Jets	WIHL	50	25	35	60	....	....	....	18	4	4	1	5	6
1964-65	Spokane Jets	WIHL	43	20	16	36	....	....	....	27	3	1	0	1	0
1965-66	Spokane Jets	WIHL	50	27	37	64	....	....	....	36	10	8	5	13	4
1966-67	Spokane Jets	WIHL	48	19	34	53	....	....	....	29	....	....	....	....	....
1967-68	Spokane Jets	WIHL	43	18	27	45	....	....	....	24	10	2	4	6	6
1968-69	Spokane Jets	WIHL	38	11	13	24	....	....	....	27	9	2	4	6	6
	Spokane Jets	Al-Cup	5	1	0	1	....	....	....	4	....	....	....	....	....
1969-70	Spokane Jets	WIHL	50	22	26	48	....	....	....	38	9	5	4	9	2
	Spokane Jets	Al-Cup	13	2	1	3	....	....	....	2	....	....	....	....	....
1970-71	Spokane Jets	WIHL	50	19	25	44	....	....	....	20	....	....	....	....	....
1971-72	Spokane Jets	WIHL	36	8	17	25	....	....	....	9	19	1	0	1	....
	NHL Totals		**2**	**0**	**0**	**0**	**0**	**0**	**0**	**2**	....	....	....	....	....

• TURNER, Bob

Robert George

D – L. 6', 170 lbs. b: Regina, Sask., 1/31/1934.

Season	Club	League	GP	G	A	Pts	AG	AA	APts	PIM	GP	G	A	Pts	PIM
1951-52	Regina Pats	WCJHL	31	2	10	12	....	....	....	40	6	0	1	1	4
1952-53	Regina Pats	WCJHL	33	10	4	14	....	....	....	90	7	0	2	2	16
	Regina Capitals	SSHL	....	....	....	....	....	....	....	....	2	0	1	1	0
	Regina Capitals	Al-Cup	12	1	0	1	....	....	....	19	....	....	....	....	....
1953-54	Regina Pats	WCJHL	36	15	14	29	....	....	....	55	16	1	5	6	48
1954-55	Shawinigan Cataracts	QHL	61	4	14	18	....	....	....	98	13	0	2	2	4
	Shawinigan Cataracts	Ed-Cup	7	0	1	1	....	....	....	24	....	....	....	....	....
♦**1955-56**	**Montreal Canadiens**	**NHL**	**33**	**1**	**4**	**5**	**1**	**5**	**6**	**35**	**10**	**0**	**1**	**1**	**10**
	Shawinigan Cataracts	QHL	37	6	12	18	....	....	....	55	....	....	....	....	....
♦**1956-57**	**Montreal Canadiens**	**NHL**	**58**	**1**	**4**	**5**	**1**	**4**	**5**	**48**	**6**	**0**	**1**	**1**	**0**
	Rochester Americans	AHL	8	0	2	2	....	....	....	4	....	....	....	....	....
♦**1957-58**	**Montreal Canadiens**	**NHL**	**66**	**0**	**3**	**3**	**0**	**3**	**3**	**30**	**10**	**0**	**0**	**0**	**2**
♦**1958-59**	**Montreal Canadiens**	**NHL**	**68**	**4**	**24**	**28**	**5**	**24**	**29**	**66**	**11**	**0**	**2**	**2**	**20**
♦**1959-60**	**Montreal Canadiens**	**NHL**	**54**	**0**	**9**	**9**	**0**	**9**	**9**	**40**	**8**	**0**	**0**	**0**	**0**
1960-61	**Montreal Canadiens**	**NHL**	**60**	**2**	**2**	**4**	**2**	**2**	**4**	**16**	**5**	**0**	**0**	**0**	**0**
1961-62	**Chicago Black Hawks**	**NHL**	**69**	**8**	**2**	**10**	**9**	**2**	**11**	**52**	**12**	**1**	**0**	**1**	**6**
1962-63	**Chicago Black Hawks**	**NHL**	**70**	**3**	**3**	**6**	**3**	**3**	**6**	**20**	**6**	**0**	**0**	**0**	**6**
1963-64	Buffalo Bisons	AHL	68	6	15	21	....	....	....	84	....	....	....	....	....
	NHL Totals		**478**	**19**	**51**	**70**	**21**	**52**	**73**	**307**	**68**	**1**	**4**	**5**	**44**

WCJHL First All-Star Team (1954) • Played in NHL All-Star Game (1956, 1957, 1958, 1959, 1960, 1961)

Traded to **Chicago** by **Montreal** for Fred Hilts, June, 1961. Traded to **LA Sharks** (WHL) by **Chicago** for cash, August 6, 1964.

• TUSTIN, Norm

Norman Robert

LW – L. 5'11", 175 lbs. b: Regina, Sask., 1/3/1919 d: 8/16/1998.

Season	Club	League	GP	G	A	Pts	AG	AA	APts	PIM	GP	G	A	Pts	PIM
1938-39	Owen Sound Greys	OHA-Jr.	STATISTICS NOT AVAILABLE												
1939-40	Atlantic City Seagulls	EAHL	61	31	16	47	....	....	....	23	3	*6	1	*7	2
1940-41	Minneapolis Millers	AHA	48	*29	21	50	....	....	....	12	3	1	2	3	0
1941-42	**New York Rangers**	**NHL**	**18**	**2**	**4**	**6**	**3**	**5**	**8**	**0**	....	....	....	....	....
	New Haven Eagles	AHL	31	19	11	30	....	....	....	2	2	0	0	0	0
1942-43	Toronto RCAF	OHA-Sr.	6	4	5	9	....	....	....	5	3	2	0	2	2
	Toronto RCAF	Al-Cup	3	2	0	2	....	....	....	2	....	....	....	....	....
1943-44	Toronto RCAF	OHA-Sr.	15	7	9	16	....	....	....	12	....	....	....	....	....
1944-45			MILITARY SERVICE												
1945-46			MILITARY SERVICE												
1946-47	New Haven Ramblers	AHL	64	18	18	36	....	....	....	8	3	0	1	1	0
1947-48	Hershey Bears	AHL	13	1	6	7	....	....	....	4	....	....	....	....	....
	St. Louis Flyers	AHL	50	17	21	38	....	....	....	0	....	....	....	....	....
1948-49	St. Louis Flyers	AHL	28	5	13	18	....	....	....	2	....	....	....	....	....
1949-50	St. Louis Flyers	AHL	30	7	5	12	....	....	....	6	....	....	....	....	....
	Kansas City Mohawks	USHL	21	10	11	21	....	....	....	9	3	0	0	0	0
1950-51			REINSTATED AS AN AMATEUR												
1951-52	Sarnia Sailors	OHA-Sr.	5	3	2	5	....	....	....	2	....	....	....	....	....
	NHL Totals		**18**	**2**	**4**	**6**	**3**	**5**	**8**	**0**	....	....	....	....	....

AHA First All-Star Team (1941)

Traded to **St. Louis** (AHL) by **Hershey** (AHL) for Jud McAtee, November 15, 1947.

• TUTEN, Aut

Audley Kendrick

D – L. 5'10", 180 lbs. b: Enterprize, AL, 1/14/1915.

Season	Club	League	GP	G	A	Pts	AG	AA	APts	PIM	GP	G	A	Pts	PIM
1932-33	Melville Millionaires	S-SJHL	STATISTICS NOT AVAILABLE												
	Saskatoon Tigers	N-SJHL	4	1	1	2	....	....	....	0	2	0	0	0	7
	Saskatoon Tigers	M-Cup	3	1	0	1	....	....	....	7	....	....	....	....	....
1933-34	Regina Pats	S-SJHL	2	0	2	2	....	....	....	2	4	0	1	1	*8
	Regina Pats	M-Cup	4	0	1	1	....	....	....	*8	....	....	....	....	....
1934-35	Hershey B'ars	EAHL	21	3	6	9	....	....	....	35	9	3	1	4	*16
1935-36	Hershey B'ars	EAHL	40	9	5	14	....	....	....	64	8	3	2	5	*20
1936-37	Hershey B'ars	EAHL	46	7	8	15	....	....	....	*82	4	0	1	1	6
1937-38	Hershey B'ars	EAHL	43	6	9	15	....	....	....	62	....	....	....	....	....
1938-39	Baltimore Orioles	EAHL	53	13	9	22	....	....	....	*109	....	....	....	....	....
1939-40	Kansas City Greyhounds	AHA	48	10	15	25	....	....	....	104	....	....	....	....	....
1940-41	Kansas City Americans	AHA	47	11	16	27	....	....	....	75	8	1	1	2	12
1941-42	**Chicago Black Hawks**	**NHL**	**5**	**1**	**1**	**2**	**1**	**1**	**2**	**10**	....	....	....	....	....
	Kansas City Americans	AHA	45	13	17	30	....	....	....	72	6	2	4	6	19
1942-43	**Chicago Black Hawks**	**NHL**	**34**	**3**	**7**	**10**	**3**	**6**	**9**	**38**	....	....	....	....	....
1943-44			MILITARY SERVICE												
1944-45			MILITARY SERVICE												
1945-46			MILITARY SERVICE												
1946-47	Kansas City Pla-Mors	AHA	10	2	3	5	....	....	....	4	....	....	....	....	....
	Oakland Oaks	PCHL	45	23	22	45	....	....	....	41	....	....	....	....	....
1947-48			DID NOT PLAY – REFEREE												
1948-49	Los Angeles–San Diego	PCHL	24	2	5	7	....	....	....	33	....	....	....	....	....
	NHL Totals		**39**	**4**	**8**	**12**	**4**	**7**	**11**	**48**	....	....	....	....	....

EAHL Second All-Star Team (1937, 1938) • EAHL First All-Star Team (1939) • AHA Second All-Star Team (1940, 1942) • AHA First All-Star Team (1941)

• ULLMAN, Norm

— *see page 1717*

• VADNAIS, Carol

— *see page 1718*

• VAIL, Sparky

Melville Arthur

D/LW – L. 6', 185 lbs. b: Meaford, Ont., 7/5/1906 Deceased.

Season	Club	League	GP	G	A	Pts	AG	AA	APts	PIM	GP	G	A	Pts	PIM
1925-26	North Bay Trappers	NOJHA	STATISTICS NOT AVAILABLE												
1926-27	Springfield Indians	Can-Am	31	17	6	23	....	....	....	73	6	1	0	1	16
1927-28	Springfield Indians	Can-Am	39	18	4	22	....	....	....	92	4	1	1	2	14
1928-29	**New York Rangers**	**NHL**	**18**	**3**	**0**	**3**	**9**	**0**	**9**	**16**	**6**	**0**	**0**	**0**	**2**
	Springfield Indians	Can-Am	22	7	3	10	....	....	....	42	....	....	....	....	....
1929-30	**New York Rangers**	**NHL**	**32**	**1**	**1**	**2**	**1**	**2**	**3**	**2**	**4**	**0**	**0**	**0**	**0**
	Springfield Indians	Can-Am	9	1	2	3	....	....	....	30	....	....	....	....	....
1930-31	Providence Reds	Can-Am	38	12	21	33	....	....	....	44	....	....	....	....	....
1931-32	Providence Reds	Can-Am	36	7	18	25	....	....	....	40	1	0	0	0	2
1932-33	Providence Reds	Can-Am	41	6	12	18	....	....	....	20	2	0	0	0	0
1933-34	Syracuse–Windsor	IHL	42	4	8	12	....	....	....	53	....	....	....	....	....
1934-35	Cleveland Falcons	IHL	43	8	24	32	....	....	....	47	2	0	0	0	0
1935-36	Pittsburgh Yellowjackets	IHL	45	5	12	17	....	....	....	52	....	....	....	....	....
1936/38			DID NOT PLAY												
1938-39	Toronto Red Indians	TIHL	30	3	*15	18	....	....	....	*57	13	4	*14	*18	28
1939-40	Toronto Red Indians	TIHL	33	3	*25	28	....	....	....	30	3	0	5	5	0
1940-41	Toronto Red Indians	TIHL	27	6	12	18	....	....	....	18	4	0	1	1	0
1941-42	Toronto Red Indians	TIHL	16	1	9	10	....	....	....	4	....	....	....	....	....
1942-43	Toronto Red Indians	TIHL	9	0	8	8	....	....	....	2	....	....	....	....	....
	NHL Totals		**50**	**4**	**1**	**5**	**10**	**2**	**12**	**18**	**10**	**0**	**0**	**0**	**2**

Signed as a free agent by **NY Rangers**, September 2, 1926. Traded to **Providence** (Can-Am) by **NY Rangers** for cash, October 27, 1930. Traded to **Detroit** (IHL) by **Providence** (Can-Am) for Frank Peters, October 30, 1933. Traded to **Windsor** (IHL) by **Syracuse** (IHL) with Gus Forslund for Andy Bellemer, December, 1933.

• VAN IMPE, Ed

— *see page 1722*

• VASKO, Moose

— *see page 1724*

• VOKES, Ed

LW – L. 5'9", 160 lbs. b: Quill Lake, Sask., 1904 Deceased.

Season	Club	League	GP	G	A	Pts	AG	AA	APts	PIM	GP	G	A	Pts	PIM
1928-29	Oakland Shieks	Cal-Pro	10	0	0	0	....	....	....	....	....	....	....	....	....
1929-30	Oakland Shieks	Cal-Pro	....	25	8	33	....	....	....	29	....	....	....	....	....
1930-31	**Chicago Black Hawks**	**NHL**	**5**	**0**	**0**	**0**	**0**	**0**	**0**	**0**	....	....	....	....	....
	London Tecumsehs	IHL	12	0	0	0	....	....	....	0	....	....	....	....	....
	Niagara Falls Cataracts	Can-Pro	2	0	0	0	....	....	....	4	....	....	....	....	....
1931-32	San Francisco Rangers	Can-Pro	....	29	9	38	....	....	....	....	....	....	....	....	....
1932-33	San Francisco Rangers	Can-Pro	STATISTICS NOT AVAILABLE												
	NHL Totals		**5**	**0**	**0**	**0**	**0**	**0**	**0**	**0**	....	....	....	....	....

Traded to **Chicago** by **Oakland** (Cal-Pro) for cash, December 15, 1930. Traded to **Pittsburgh** (IHL) by **Chicago** for cash, February 12, 1931. Loaned to **Niagara Falls** (Can-Pro) by **Pittsburgh** (IHL), February 13, 1931.

• VOSS, Carl

Carl Potter **HHOF**

C – L. 5'9", 168 lbs. b: Chelsea, MA, 1/6/1907 d: 9/13/1993.

Season	Club	League	GP	G	A	Pts	AG	AA	APts	PIM	GP	G	A	Pts	PIM
1924-25	Queen's University	LOVHL	STATISTICS NOT AVAILABLE												
1925-26	Kingston Frontenacs	OHA-Sr.	STATISTICS NOT AVAILABLE												
1926-27	Toronto Marlboros	OHA-Jr.	4	0	0	0	....	....	....	....	2	0	1	1	....
	Toronto Marlboros	OHA-Jr.	2	0	0	0	....	....	....	0	....	....	....	....	....
	Toronto Maple Leafs	**NHL**	**12**	**0**	**0**	**0**	**0**	**0**	**0**	**0**	....	....	....	....	....
1927-28	Toronto Falcons	Can-Pro	23	3	4	7	....	....	....	15	2	0	0	0	2
1928-29	**Toronto Maple Leafs**	**NHL**	**2**	**0**	**0**	**0**	**0**	**0**	**0**	**0**	....	....	....	....	....
	London Panthers	Can-Pro	42	11	9	20	....	....	....	44	....	....	....	....	....
1929-30	Buffalo Bisons	IHL	42	14	8	22	....	....	....	22	7	3	0	3	6
1930-31	Buffalo Bisons	IHL	47	16	10	26	....	....	....	46	6	3	3	6	8
1931-32	Buffalo Bisons	IHL	46	18	23	*41	....	....	....	53	6	1	*5	*6	7
1932-33	**New York Rangers**	**NHL**	**10**	**2**	**1**	**3**	**4**	**2**	**6**	**4**	....	....	....	....	....
	Detroit Red Wings	**NHL**	**38**	**6**	**14**	**20**	**11**	**29**	**40**	**6**	**4**	**1**	**1**	**2**	**0**
1933-34	**Detroit Red Wings**	**NHL**	**8**	**0**	**2**	**2**	**0**	**4**	**4**	**2**	....	....	....	....	....
	Ottawa Senators	**NHL**	**40**	**7**	**16**	**23**	**12**	**34**	**46**	**10**	....	....	....	....	....
1934-35	**St. Louis Eagles**	**NHL**	**48**	**13**	**18**	**31**	**21**	**31**	**52**	**14**	....	....	....	....	....
1935-36	**New York Americans**	**NHL**	**46**	**3**	**9**	**12**	**6**	**17**	**23**	**10**	**5**	**0**	**0**	**0**	**0**
1936-37	**Montreal Maroons**	**NHL**	**20**	**0**	**2**	**2**	**0**	**4**	**4**	**4**	**5**	**1**	**0**	**1**	**0**
1937-38	**Montreal Maroons**	**NHL**	**3**	**0**	**0**	**0**	**0**	**0**	**0**	**0**	....	....	....	....	....
♦	**Chicago Black Hawks**	**NHL**	**34**	**3**	**8**	**11**	**5**	**13**	**18**	**0**	**10**	**3**	**2**	**5**	**0**
1938-39	**Chicago Black Hawks**	**NHL**	DID NOT PLAY – INJURED												
	NHL Totals		**261**	**34**	**70**	**104**	**59**	**134**	**193**	**50**	**24**	**5**	**3**	**8**	**0**

NHL Rookie of the Year (1933)

Signed as a free agent by **Toronto**, February 16, 1927. Traded to **Buffalo** (IHL) by **Toronto** with Wes King for Gord Brydson, October 10, 1929. Traded to **NY Rangers** by **Buffalo** (IHL) for Lorne Carr and $15,000, October 4, 1932. Traded to **Detroit** by **NY Rangers** for cash, December 11, 1932. Traded to **Ottawa** by **Detroit** with cash for Cooney Weiland, November 26, 1933. Transferred to **St. Louis** after **Ottawa** franchise relocated, September 22, 1934. Claimed by **Detroit** from **St. Louis** in Dispersal Draft, October 15, 1935. Traded to **NY Americans** by **Detroit** for Pete Kelly, October 16, 1935. Traded to **Montreal Maroons** by **NY Americans** for Joe Lamb and $10,000, September 6, 1936. Signed as a free agent by **Chicago**, December 6, 1937. • Suffered career-ending knee injury in training camp, September 30, 1938.

• WAITE, Frank "Deacon"

C – L. 5'11", 150 lbs. b: Fort Qu'Appelle, Sask., 4/9/1905 d: 7/18/1989.

Season	Club	League	GP	G	A	Pts	AG	AA	APts	PIM	GP	G	A	Pts	PIM
1918-19	Wolseley Wanderers	S-SJHL									2	1	0	1	0
1919-20	Wolseley Wanderers	S-SJHL	STATISTICS NOT AVAILABLE												
1920-21	Wolseley Wanderers	S-SJHL	STATISTICS NOT AVAILABLE												
1921-22	Indian Head Tigers	S-SSHL	5	0	2	2				0	1	0	0	0	0
1922-23	Weyburn Wanderers	S-SSHL	10	5	2	7				9	5	5	1	6	6
1923-24	Brandon Wheat Kings	MHL-Sr.	11	3	2	5				3	4	0	1	1	6
1924-25	Trail Smoke Eaters	WKHL	STATISTICS NOT AVAILABLE												
1925-26	Vancouver Maroons	WHL	28	0	1	1				4					
1926-27	Springfield Indians	Can-Am	25	7	4	11				24	6	1	1	2	4
1927-28	Springfield Indians	Can-Am	39	7	*15	22				36	4	1	1	2	6
1928-29	Boston Tigers	Can-Am	39	12	10	22				42	4	2	0	2	12
1929-30	Boston Tigers	Can-Am	40	23	*34	*57				57	5	2	3	5	6
1930-31	Springfield Indians	Can-Am	25	5	*25	30				28	6	0	1	1	0
	New York Rangers	**NHL**	**17**	**1**	**3**	**4**	**2**	**9**	**11**	**4**					
1931-32	Syracuse Stars	IHL	43	7	*26	33				33					
1932-33	Cleveland–Detroit	IHL	42	6	12	18				12					
1933-34	London Panthers	IHL	11	1	3	4				6					
	Philadelphia Arrows	Can-Am	31	11	19	30				15	2	0	1	1	10
	NHL Totals		**17**	**1**	**3**	**4**	**2**	**9**	**11**	**4**					
	Other Major League Totals		28	0	1	1				4					

Can-Am First All_Star Team (1930)

Signed as a free agent by **Vancouver** (WHL), September, 1925. Signed as a free agent by **NY Rangers**, September 2, 1926. Traded to **Boston** by **NY Rangers** for cash, September, 1928. Traded to **Springfield** (Can-Am) by **Boston** for cash, September, 1930. Traded to **NY Rangers** by **Springfield** (Can-Am) for cash, November 4, 1930. Traded to **Syracuse** (IAHL) by **NY Rangers** for cash, October 21, 1931. Signed as a free agent by **Cleveland** (IHL), November 5, 1932. Traded to **Detroit** by **Cleveland** (IHL) for Jack Riley and Tony Prelesnik, December 2, 1932. Traded to **Chicago** (London-IHL) by **Detroit** with Leroy Goldsworthy for Gene Carrigan, October 19, 1933.

• WALKER, Jack John Phillip HHOF

F – L. 5'8", 153 lbs. b: Silver Mountain, Ont., 11/29/1888 d: 2/16/1950.

Season	Club	League	GP	G	A	Pts	AG	AA	APts	PIM	GP	G	A	Pts	PIM
1905-06	Port Arthur East Greys	NOHL	STATISTICS NOT AVAILABLE												
1906-07	Port Arthur East Greys	NOHL	STATISTICS NOT AVAILABLE												
1907-08	Port Arthur Lake City	NOHL	6	3	0	3				0					
1908-09	Port Arthur Lake City	NOHL	12	8	0	8									
1909-10	Port Arthur Lake City	NOHL	12	20	0	20				21					
1910-11	Port Arthur Lake City	NOHL	14	30	0	30					3	3	0	3	0
1911-12	Port Arthur Lake City	NOHL	13	17	0	17				0	2	3	0	3	0
1912-13	Toronto Blueshirts	NHA	1	0	0	0				0					
	Moncton Victorias	MPHL	15	21	0	21				9					
♦1913-14	Toronto Blueshirts	NHA	20	20	*16	36				17	5	4	0	4	2
1914-15	Toronto Blueshirts	NHA	19	12	7	19				11					
1915-16	Seattle Metropolitans	PCHA	18	13	6	19				6					
	PCHA All-Stars	X-Games	3	0	4	*4				0					
♦1916-17	Seattle Metropolitans	PCHA	24	11	15	26				3	4	1	2	3	0
1917-18	Seattle Metropolitans	PCHA	1	0	0	0				0					
1918-19	Seattle Metropolitans	PCHA	20	9	6	15				9	2	0	2	2	*0
	Seattle Metropolitans	St-Cup	5	3	0	3				9					
1919-20	Seattle Metropolitans	PCHA	22	4	8	12				3	2	1	1	2	0
	Seattle Metropolitans	St-Cup	5	1	3	4				0					
1920-21	Seattle Metropolitans	PCHA	23	6	4	10				6	2	0	0	0	0
1921-22	Seattle Metropolitans	PCHA	20	8	4	12				0	2	0	0	0	0
1922-23	Seattle Metropolitans	PCHA	29	13	10	23				4					
1923-24	Seattle Metropolitans	PCHA	29	18	5	23				0	2	0	1	1	0
1924-25	Victoria Cougars	WCHL	28	7	7	*14				6	4	4	0	4	0
♦	Victoria Cougars	St-Cup	4	4	2	6				0					
1925-26	Victoria Cougars	WHL	30	9	8	17				16	4	0	0	0	0
	Victoria Cougars	St-Cup	4	4	2	6				0					
1926-27	**Detroit Cougars**	**NHL**	**37**	**3**	**4**	**7**	**5**	**21**	**26**	**6**					
1927-28	**Detroit Cougars**	**NHL**	**43**	**2**	**4**	**6**	**4**	**23**	**27**	**12**					
1928-29	Seattle Eskimos	PCHL	34	5	8	13				4	5	0	*2	2	2
1929-30	Seattle Eskimos	PCHL	26	6	*11	17				2					
1930-31	Seattle Eskimos	PCHL	34	2	*13	15				8	4	0	*3	*3	0
1931-32	Hollywood Stars	Cal-Pro		5	13	18									
1932-33	Oakland Sheiks	Cal-Pro	DID NOT PLAY – COACHING												
	NHL Totals		**80**	**5**	**8**	**13**	**9**	**44**	**53**	**18**					
	Other Major League Totals		356	229	96	325				111	32	16	6	22	2

PCHA Second All-Star Team (1917, 1919, 1920) • PCHA First All-Star Team (1921, 1922, 1924)

Jumped contract with Toronto (NHA) to sign with **Moncton** (MPHL), December 26, 1912. Jumped contract with Toronto (NHA) to sign with **Seattle** (PCHA), November 12, 1915. Signed as a free agent by **Victoria** (WCHL), November 10, 1924. • 1924-25 playoff totals includes WCHL series against Calgary and Saskatoon. • 1925-26 playoff totals includes WHL series against Edmonton and Saskatoon. Traded to **Detroit** by **Victoria** (WHL) for cash, May 15, 1926. • Obtained release from Detroit to become coach of Seattle (PCHL).

• WALL, Bob *— see page 1736*

• WALTON, Bobby

C/RW – R. 5'9", 165 lbs. b: Ottawa, Ont., 8/5/1912 d: 9/3/1992.

Season	Club	League	GP	G	A	Pts	AG	AA	APts	PIM	GP	G	A	Pts	PIM
1929-30	Ottawa Canoe Club	OCJHL	11	7	3	10				6					
1930-31	Ottawa Rideaus	OCJHL	16	*14	5	19				20	2	0	1	1	4
	Ottawa Rideaus	OCHL									2	0	0	0	2
	Ottawa Rideaus	M-Cup	3	0	0	0				2					
1931-32	Ottawa New Edinburghs	OCHL	26	6	4	10				77	2	0	0	0	0
1932-33	Ottawa New Edinburghs	OCHL	14	6	5	11				12					
1933-34	Ottawa Montagnards	OCHL	21	*17	*13	*30				12	3	0	0	0	2
1934-35	Wembley Lions	Britain	STATISTICS NOT AVAILABLE												
1935-36	Wembley Lions	Ln-Cup		6	9	15									
	Wembley Lions	Britain		14	9	23				15					
1936-37	Wembley Lions	Britain		27	17	44				22					
1937-38	Kirkland Lake Blue Devils	GBHL	10	8	8	16				10	2	0	1	1	*6
1938-39	Kirkland Lake Blue Devils	GBHL	10	7	9	16				22	3	0	1	1	0
1939-40	Kirkland Lake Blue Devils	GBHL	15	6	10	16				8	20	9	13	22	0
1940-41	Niagara Falls Brights	OHA-Sr.	24	15	11	26				10	3	0	1	1	0
	Sydney Millionaires	CBSHL	1	2	5	7				2	4	2	*4	6	0
	Sydney Millionaires	Al-Cup	17	16	17	33				8					
1941-42	Montreal Royals	QSHL	29	6	17	23				22	2	0	0	0	0
1942-43	Sudbury Open Pit Miners	NBHL	5	6	4	10				4					
1943-44	**Montreal Canadiens**	**NHL**	**4**	**0**	**0**	**0**	**0**	**0**	**0**	**0**					
	Buffalo Bisons	AHL	32	7	14	21				6	9	0	0	0	0
1944-45	Pittsburgh Hornets	AHL	58	37	58	*95				27					
1945-46	Pittsburgh Hornets	AHL	47	25	26	51				22	6	1	5	6	4
1946-47	Cleveland Barons	AHL	62	20	28	48				22	4	0	1	1	0
1947-48	Washington Lions	AHL	66	20	23	43				8					
	NHL Totals		**4**	**0**	**0**	**0**	**0**	**0**	**0**	**0**					

• Father of Mike • AHL First All-Star Team (1945)

Signed as a free agent by **Montreal Royals** (QSHL), November 5, 1941. Signed as a free agent by **Montreal** following release by Royals, February 2, 1942.

• WALTON, Mike *— see page 1738*

• WARD, Don Donald Joseph

D – L. 6'2", 200 lbs. b: Sarnia, Ont., 10/19/1935.

Season	Club	League	GP	G	A	Pts	AG	AA	APts	PIM	GP	G	A	Pts	PIM
1955-56	Sarnia Legionnaires	OHA-B	36	17	24	41									
1956-57	Windsor Bulldogs	OHA-Sr.	21	3	6	9				24					
	Buffalo Bisons	AHL	31	3	6	9				48					
1957-58	**Chicago Black Hawks**	**NHL**	**3**	**0**	**0**	**0**	**0**	**0**	**0**	**0**					
	Buffalo Bisons	AHL	54	1	11	12				65					
1958-59	Calgary Stampeders	WHL	64	4	18	22				131	8	1	4	5	8
1959-60	**Boston Bruins**	**NHL**	**31**	**0**	**1**	**1**	**0**	**1**	**1**	**16**					
	Providence Reds	AHL	27	2	3	5				54	5	0	0	0	0
1960-61	Winnipeg Warriors	WHL	70	5	12	17				95					
1961-62	Seattle Totems	WHL	70	7	23	30				91	2	0	0	0	4
1962-63	Seattle Totems	WHL	69	3	18	21				131	17	1	2	3	10
1963-64	Seattle Totems	WHL	70	5	25	30				122					
1964-65	Seattle Totems	WHL	70	3	8	11				140	7	1	1	2	10
1965-66	Seattle Totems	WHL	56	5	8	13				84					
1966-67	Seattle Totems	WHL	44	0	5	5				48	6	0	1	1	2
1967-68	Seattle Totems	WHL	70	2	12	14				107	9	1	2	3	14
1968-69	Seattle Totems	WHL	73	3	15	18				129	4	0	1	1	4
1969-70	Seattle Totems	WHL	72	3	17	20				96	6	0	2	2	20
1970-71	Seattle Totems	WHL	56	0	11	11				80					
1971-72	Seattle Totems	WHL	41	1	8	9				82					
1972-73	Greensboro Generals	EHL	13	0	1	1				30	7	1	2	3	24
	NHL Totals		**34**	**0**	**1**	**1**	**0**	**1**	**1**	**16**					

• Father of Joe

Claimed by **Boston** from **Calgary** (WHL) in Inter-League Draft, June 9, 1959. Traded to **Portland** (WHL) by **Boston** with Gene Achtymichuk as part of transaction that sent Don Head to Boston (May, 1961), August, 1961. Traded to **Seattle** (WHL) by **Portland** (WHL) for Tom McVie, August, 1961. Selected by **LA Sharks** (WHA) in WHA General Player Draft, February 12, 1972.

• WARD, Jimmy James William

RW – R. 5'11", 167 lbs. b: Fort William, Ont., 9/1/1906 d: 11/15/1990.

Season	Club	League	GP	G	A	Pts	AG	AA	APts	PIM	GP	G	A	Pts	PIM
1922/24	Kenora Thistles	TBJHL	STATISTICS NOT AVAILABLE												
1924-25	Kenora Thistles	TBIHA	STATISTICS NOT AVAILABLE												
1925-26	Kenora Thistles	TBSHL	16	10	3	13				16					
1926-27	Fort William Forts	TBSHL	20	18	5	23				20	2	0	0	0	0
1927-28	**Montreal Maroons**	**NHL**	**42**	**10**	**2**	**12**	**20**	**11**	**31**	**44**	**9**	**1**	**1**	**2**	**6**
1928-29	**Montreal Maroons**	**NHL**	**43**	**14**	**8**	**22**	**41**	**54**	**95**	**46**					
1929-30	**Montreal Maroons**	**NHL**	**44**	**10**	**7**	**17**	**14**	**16**	**30**	**54**	**4**	**0**	**1**	**1**	**12**
1930-31	**Montreal Maroons**	**NHL**	**41**	**14**	**8**	**22**	**28**	**24**	**52**	**52**	**2**	**0**	**0**	**0**	**2**
1931-32	**Montreal Maroons**	**NHL**	**48**	**19**	**19**	**38**	**32**	**42**	**74**	**39**	**4**	**2**	**1**	**3**	**0**
1932-33	**Montreal Maroons**	**NHL**	**48**	**16**	**17**	**33**	**29**	**35**	**64**	**52**	**2**	**0**	**0**	**0**	**0**
1933-34	**Montreal Maroons**	**NHL**	**48**	**14**	**9**	**23**	**24**	**19**	**43**	**46**	**4**	**0**	**0**	**0**	**0**
♦**1934-35**	**Montreal Maroons**	**NHL**	**41**	**9**	**6**	**15**	**15**	**10**	**25**	**24**	**7**	**1**	**1**	**2**	**0**
1935-36	**Montreal Maroons**	**NHL**	**48**	**12**	**19**	**31**	**23**	**36**	**59**	**30**	**3**	**0**	**0**	**0**	**6**
1936-37	**Montreal Maroons**	**NHL**	**40**	**14**	**14**	**28**	**24**	**26**	**50**	**34**					
1937-38	**Montreal Maroons**	**NHL**	**48**	**11**	**15**	**26**	**18**	**24**	**42**	**34**					
1938-39	**Montreal Canadiens**	**NHL**	**36**	**4**	**3**	**7**	**7**	**5**	**12**	**0**	**1**	**0**	**0**	**0**	**0**
1939-40	New Haven Eagles	AHL	49	5	14	19				28					
	NHL Totals		**527**	**147**	**127**	**274**	**275**	**302**	**577**	**455**	**36**	**4**	**4**	**8**	**26**

Played in NHL All-Star Game (1934, 1937)

Signed as a free agent by **Montreal Maroons**, August 26, 1927. Traded to **Montreal Canadiens** by **Montreal Maroons** for cash, September 14, 1938. • Named player coach of **New Haven** (IAHL), October 16, 1939.

• WARES, Eddie Edward George

D/RW – R. 5'11", 182 lbs. b: Calgary, Alta., 3/19/1915.

Season	Club	League	GP	G	A	Pts	AG	AA	APts	PIM	GP	G	A	Pts	PIM
1931-32	Calgary Shamrocks	CCJHL	1	0	0	0				0					
1932-33	Calgary Jimmies	CCJHL	STATISTICS NOT AVAILABLE												
	Calgary Jimmies	M-Cup	7	0	1	1				4					
1933-34	Calgary Jimmies	CCJHL	3	5	2	7				4					
	Calgary Jimmies	M-Cup	3	1	2	3				4					
1934-35	Calgary Bronks	ASHL	12	13	4	17				6	2	1	0	1	0
1935-36	Philadelphia Arrows	Can-Am	48	7	6	13				29	3	1	0	1	2
1936-37	**New York Rangers**	**NHL**	**2**	**2**	**0**	**2**	**3**	**0**	**3**	**0**					
	Philadelphia Ramblers	IAHL	50	10	23	33				30	6	1	1	2	8
1937-38	Philadelphia Ramblers	IAHL	25	12	14	26				4					
	Detroit Red Wings	**NHL**	**21**	**9**	**7**	**16**	**15**	**11**	**26**	**2**					
1938-39	**Detroit Red Wings**	**NHL**	**28**	**8**	**8**	**16**	**14**	**12**	**26**	**10**	**6**	**1**	**0**	**1**	**8**
1939-40	**Detroit Red Wings**	**NHL**	**33**	**2**	**6**	**8**	**3**	**9**	**12**	**19**	**5**	**0**	**0**	**0**	**0**
	Indianapolis Capitols	IAHL	1	0	0	0				0					
1940-41	**Detroit Red Wings**	**NHL**	**42**	**10**	**16**	**26**	**15**	**23**	**38**	**34**	**9**	**0**	**0**	**0**	**0**
	Indianapolis Capitols	AHL	1	0	0	0				0					
1941-42	**Detroit Red Wings**	**NHL**	**43**	**9**	**29**	**38**	**12**	**35**	**47**	**31**	**12**	**1**	**3**	**4**	**22**
♦**1942-43**	**Detroit Red Wings**	**NHL**	**47**	**12**	**18**	**30**	**12**	**17**	**29**	**10**	**10**	**3**	**3**	**6**	**4**
1943-44	Calgary Combines	CSrHL	16	4	4	8				18	2	2	2	4	6
1944-45	Calgary Navy	CNDHL	2	0	0	0				4					
	Halifax Navy	NSDHL									3	2	0	2	4
1945-46	**Chicago Black Hawks**	**NHL**	**45**	**4**	**11**	**15**	**5**	**16**	**21**	**34**	**3**	**0**	**1**	**1**	**0**

Season	Club	League	GP	G	A	Pts	AG	AA	APts	PIM	GP	G	A	Pts	PIM
			REGULAR SEASON								PLAYOFFS				
1946-47	**Chicago Black Hawks**	**NHL**	**60**	**4**	**7**	**11**	**4**	**8**	**12**	**21**					
1947-48	Cleveland Barons	AHL	66	6	22	28				20	9	0	1	1	2
1948-49	Cleveland Barons	AHL	44	1	17	18				10					
	Kansas City Pla-Mors	USHL	20	4	6	10				0	2	0	0	0	0
1949-50	Victoria Cougars	PCHL	42	5	11	16				6					
1950-51	Nelson Maple Leafs	WIHL	34	6	12	18				66	4	0	0	0	6
1951-52	Nelson Maple Leafs	WIHL	26	6	7	13				12	8	0	3	3	0
1952-53	Nelson Maple Leafs	WIHL	6	1	6	7				20					
	NHL Totals		**321**	**60**	**102**	**162**	**83**	**131**	**214**	**161**	**45**	**5**	**7**	**12**	**34**

ASHL First All-Star Team (1944)

Signed as a free agent by **Montreal Maroons**, September 30, 1935. Traded to **NY Rangers** by **Montreal Maroons** for the rights to George Brown, October 30, 1935. Traded to **Detroit** by **NY Rangers** (Philadelphia-IAHL) for the loan of John Sherf for the remainder of the 1937-38 season and cash, January 17, 1938. Traded to **Chicago** by **Detroit** for cash, October 11, 1945. Traded to **Cleveland** (AHL) by **Chicago** for cash, September, 1947. Traded to **Chicago** (Kansas City-USHL) by **Cleveland** for Doug Baldwin, January 28, 1949. • Named player coach of Victoria (PCHL), September 14, 1949.

• WARWICK, Bill

William Harvey

LW – L. 5'7", 155 lbs. b: Regina, Sask., 11/17/1924.

Season	Club	League	GP	G	A	Pts	AG	AA	APts	PIM	GP	G	A	Pts	PIM
1941-42	Regina Abbotts	S-SJHL	10	1	3	4				8	5	4	1	5	2
	Regina Abbotts	M-Cup	9	5	4	9				13					
1942-43	**New York Rangers**	**NHL**	**1**	**0**	**1**	**1**	**0**	**1**	**1**	**4**					
	New York Rovers	EAHL	43	26	29	55				47	10	9	4	13	6
1943-44	**New York Rangers**	**NHL**	**13**	**3**	**2**	**5**	**3**	**2**	**5**	**12**					
	Brooklyn Crescents	EAHL	2	0	1	1				0					
	New York Rovers	EAHL	27	14	14	28				34	11	7	9	16	12
1944-45	Hershey Bears	AHL	40	10	7	17				26	6	0	0	0	0
	New York Rovers	EAHL	1	2	1	3				2					
1945-46	Pittsburgh Hornets	AHL	8	0	4	4				14					
	Providence Reds	AHL	34	14	9	23				20	2	0	0	0	2
1946-47	Providence Reds	AHL	18	4	8	12				22					
	Philadelphia Rockets	AHL	46	21	19	40				20					
1947-48	Springfield Indians	AHL	3	0	0	0				2					
	Fort Worth Rangers	USHL	46	23	15	38				41	4	1	1	2	2
1948-49	Springfield Indians	AHL	14	3	4	7				10					
	Fort Worth Rangers	USHL	52	32	27	59				30	2	1	0	1	15
1949-50	Minneapolis Millers	USHL	70	35	46	81				47	7	3	0	3	4
	Cleveland Barons	AHL									2	0	3	3	2
1950-51	Denver Falcons	USHL	40	13	23	36				20					
1951-52	Ottawa Senators	QMHL	28	0	3	3				30					
	Halifax St. Mary's	MMHL	39	17	24	41				18	9	3	2	5	20
1952-53	Penticton Vees	OSHL	38	21	34	55				82	11	3	*11	14	*35
	Penticton Vees	Al-Cup	18	9	11	20				*73					
1953-54	Penticton Vees	OSHL	58	*50	45	*95				127	10	8	6	14	28
	Penticton Vees	Al-Cup	24	8	16	24				*60					
1954-55	Penticton Vees	OSHL	54	*36	37	*73				*168					
	Canada	WEC-A	8	14	8	*22				12					
1955-56	Penticton Vees	OSHL	49	32	44	76				210					
1956-57	Trail Smoke Eaters	WIHL	45	27	34	61				*166	9	2	5	7	*44
1957-58	Kamloops Chiefs	OSHL	47	17	28	45				*148	8	2	5	7	10
	NHL Totals		**14**	**3**	**3**	**6**	**3**	**3**	**6**	**16**					

• Brother of Grant • EAHL Second All-Star Team (1943) • OSHL First All-Star Team (1954, 1955) • WEC-A All-Star Team (1955) • Named Best Forward at WEC-A (1955)

Traded to **Philadelphia** (AHL) by **Providence** (AHL) for Ed Prokop, November 25, 1946. Traded to **Cleveland** (AHL) by **Springfield** (AHL) for John Black, September 11, 1949.

• WARWICK, Grant

Grant David "Nobby"

RW – R. 5'6", 155 lbs. b: Regina, Sask., 10/11/1921.

Season	Club	League	GP	G	A	Pts	AG	AA	APts	PIM	GP	G	A	Pts	PIM
1938-39	Regina Abbotts	S-SJHL	4	0	0	0				2					
1939-40	Regina Abbotts	S-SJHL	11	0	0	0				0	2	2	*4	*6	11
	Regina Abbotts	M-Cup	6	2	4	6				12					
1940-41	Regina Rangers	S-SSHL	31	14	18	32				16	8	5	1	6	2
	Regina Rangers	Al-Cup	14	6	9	15				8					
1941-42	**New York Rangers**	**NHL**	**44**	**16**	**17**	**33**	**21**	**20**	**41**	**36**	**6**	**0**	**1**	**1**	**2**
1942-43	**New York Rangers**	**NHL**	**50**	**17**	**18**	**35**	**17**	**17**	**34**	**31**					
1943-44	**New York Rangers**	**NHL**	**18**	**8**	**9**	**17**	**7**	**8**	**15**	**14**					
1944-45	**New York Rangers**	**NHL**	**42**	**20**	**22**	**42**	**20**	**26**	**46**	**25**					
1945-46	**New York Rangers**	**NHL**	**45**	**19**	**18**	**37**	**23**	**26**	**49**	**19**					
1946-47	**New York Rangers**	**NHL**	**54**	**20**	**20**	**40**	**23**	**24**	**47**	**24**					
1947-48	**New York Rangers**	**NHL**	**40**	**17**	**12**	**29**	**22**	**16**	**38**	**30**					
	Boston Bruins	**NHL**	**18**	**6**	**5**	**11**	**8**	**6**	**14**	**8**	**5**	**0**	**3**	**3**	**4**
1948-49	**Boston Bruins**	**NHL**	**58**	**22**	**15**	**37**	**31**	**21**	**52**	**14**	**5**	**2**	**0**	**2**	**0**
1949-50	**Montreal Canadiens**	**NHL**	**26**	**2**	**6**	**8**	**2**	**7**	**9**	**19**					
	Buffalo Bisons	AHL	37	19	28	47				33	3	2	0	2	0
1950-51	Buffalo Bisons	AHL	65	34	65	99				43	4	2	1	3	2
1951-52	Buffalo Bisons	AHL	55	24	41	65				35	3	0	0	0	2
	Halifax St. Mary's	MMHL									5	1	0	1	2
1952-53	Penticton Vees	OSHL	31	19	27	46				49	11	7	8	15	15
	Penticton Vees	Al-Cup	18	8	*13	*21				16					
1953-54	Penticton Vees	OSHL	54	36	43	79				79	10	*11	7	*18	8
	Penticton Vees	Al-Cup	23	*16	*30	*46				28					
1954-55	Penticton Vees	OSHL	38	22	34	56				62					
	Canada	WEC-A	8	6	*11	17				5					
1955-56	Penticton Vees	OSHL	54	*54	59	*113				44	7	5	3	8	16
1956-57	Trail Smoke Eaters	WIHL	43	18	30	48				70	8	5	5	10	8
1957-58	Kamloops Chiefs	OSHL	49	9	31	40				45	15	1	*13	14	14
	NHL Totals		**395**	**147**	**142**	**289**	**174**	**171**	**345**	**220**	**16**	**2**	**4**	**6**	**6**

• Brother of Bill • OSHL First All-Star Team (1953, 1954, 1955, 1956) • Won Calder Trophy (1942) • Played in NHL All-Star Game (1947)

Claimed by **NY Rangers** from **Cleveland** (AHL) in Inter-League Draft, June 27, 1941. • Missed majority of 1943-44 season recovering from head injury suffered in game vs. Detroit, December 23, 1943. Traded to **Boston** by **NY Rangers** for Billy Taylor and future considerations (Pentti Lund and Ray Manson, June, 1948), February 6, 1948. Traded to **Montreal** by **Boston** for cash, October 10, 1949.

• WASNIE, Nick

RW – R. 5'11", 174 lbs. b: Winnipeg, Man., 1/1/1904 d: 5/26/1991.

Season	Club	League	GP	G	A	Pts	AG	AA	APts	PIM	GP	G	A	Pts	PIM
1921/23	Selkirk Fishermen	MJHL	STATISTICS NOT AVAILABLE												
1923/25	Coleman Tigers	ASHL	STATISTICS NOT AVAILABLE												
1925-26	Winnipeg Maroons	CHL	31	7	1	8				35	5	1	0	1	0
1926-27	Winnipeg Maroons	AHA	21	7	3	10				33					
1927-28	**Chicago Black Hawks**	**NHL**	**14**	**1**	**0**	**1**	**2**	**0**	**2**	**22**					
	Quebec Beavers	Can-Am	22	8	3	11				32	6	*3	0	*3	*18
1928-29	Newark Bulldogs	Can-Am	40	14	6	20				76					
♦1929-30	**Montreal Canadiens**	**NHL**	**44**	**12**	**11**	**23**	**17**	**26**	**43**	**64**	**6**	**2**	**2**	**4**	**12**
♦1930-31	**Montreal Canadiens**	**NHL**	**44**	**9**	**2**	**11**	**18**	**6**	**24**	**26**	**10**	**4**	**1**	**5**	**8**
1931-32	**Montreal Canadiens**	**NHL**	**48**	**10**	**2**	**12**	**17**	**4**	**21**	**16**	**4**	**0**	**0**	**0**	**0**
1932-33	**New York Americans**	**NHL**	**48**	**11**	**12**	**23**	**20**	**25**	**45**	**36**					
1933-34	**Ottawa Senators**	**NHL**	**37**	**11**	**6**	**17**	**19**	**13**	**32**	**10**					
1934-35	**St. Louis Eagles**	**NHL**	**13**	**3**	**1**	**4**	**5**	**2**	**7**	**2**					
	Minneapolis Millers	CHL	33	16	19	35				32	5	2	3	5	4
1935-36	Rochester Cardinals	IHL	7	3	4	7				7					
	Pittsburgh Shamrocks	IHL	35	14	21	35				53					
1936-37	Kansas City Greyhounds	AHA	46	18	19	37				52	3	0	1	1	0
1937-38	Kansas City Greyhounds	AHA	45	9	12	21				14					
1938-39	Kansas City Greyhounds	AHA	48	34	27	61				19					
1939-40	Kansas City Greyhounds	AHA	48	18	21	39				36					
	NHL Totals		**248**	**57**	**34**	**91**	**98**	**76**	**174**	**176**	**20**	**6**	**3**	**9**	**20**

CHL First All-Star Team (1935) • AHA First All-Star Team (1937)

Signed as a free agent by **Chicago**, October 12, 1927. Traded to **Saskatoon** (PrHL) by **Chicago** with Corb Denneny for Cally McCalmon and Earl Miller, January 11, 1928. Signed as a free agent by **Montreal Canadiens**, November 10, 1929. Loaned to **NY Americans** by **Montreal Canadiens** for the 1932-33 season, October, 1932. Traded to **Ottawa** by **Montreal Canadiens** for cash to complete the transaction that sent Harold Starr and Leo Bourgeault to the Montreal Canadiens (February 14, 1933), March 23, 1933. Transferred to **St. Louis** after **Ottawa** franchise relocated, 1934. Traded to **Minneapolis** (CHL) by **St. Louis** with $1,600 for Fido Purpur, December 28, 1934. • Transferred to **Rochester** (IHL) after **Minneapolis** (CHL) franchise relocated, October 16, 1935. Traded to **Pittsburgh** (IHL) by **Rochester** (IHL) for Roger Cormier, December 12, 1935.

• WATSON, Bryan

— see page 1742

• WATSON, Harry

"Whipper" HHOF

LW – L. 6'1", 207 lbs. b: Saskatoon, Sask., 5/6/1923.

Season	Club	League	GP	G	A	Pts	AG	AA	APts	PIM	GP	G	A	Pts	PIM
1938-39	Saskatoon Jr. Chiefs	N-SJHL	3	0	1	1				0					
1939-40	Saskatoon Chiefs	SAHA									4	7	4	11	2
	Saskatoon Dodgers	SJHL									2	*6	2	8	2
	Saskatoon Dodgers	M-Cup	4	*7	4	11				2					
1940-41	Saskatoon Jr. Quakers	N-SJHL	6	10	8	18				4	2	3	1	4	0
	Saskatoon Jr. Quakers	M-Cup	14	14	5	19				4					
1941-42	**Brooklyn Americans**	**NHL**	**47**	**10**	**8**	**18**	**13**	**9**	**22**	**6**					
♦1942-43	**Detroit Red Wings**	**NHL**	**50**	**13**	**18**	**31**	**13**	**17**	**30**	**10**	**7**	**0**	**0**	**0**	**0**
1943-44	Montreal RCAF	QSHL	7	7	4	11				4					
	Saskatoon Navy	SNDHL	2	6	2	8				2					
1944-45	Winnipeg RCAF	WNDHL	1	2	0	2				0	4	7	0	7	2
1945-46	**Detroit Red Wings**	**NHL**	**44**	**14**	**10**	**24**	**17**	**14**	**31**	**4**	**5**	**2**	**0**	**2**	**0**
♦1946-47	**Toronto Maple Leafs**	**NHL**	**44**	**19**	**15**	**34**	**21**	**18**	**39**	**10**	**11**	**3**	**2**	**5**	**6**
♦1947-48	**Toronto Maple Leafs**	**NHL**	**57**	**21**	**20**	**41**	**27**	**26**	**53**	**16**	**9**	**5**	**2**	**7**	**9**
♦1948-49	**Toronto Maple Leafs**	**NHL**	**60**	**26**	**19**	**45**	**37**	**27**	**64**	**0**	**9**	**4**	**2**	**6**	**2**
1949-50	**Toronto Maple Leafs**	**NHL**	**60**	**19**	**16**	**35**	**24**	**19**	**43**	**11**	**7**	**0**	**0**	**0**	**2**
♦1950-51	**Toronto Maple Leafs**	**NHL**	**68**	**18**	**19**	**37**	**23**	**23**	**46**	**18**	**5**	**1**	**2**	**3**	**4**
1951-52	**Toronto Maple Leafs**	**NHL**	**70**	**22**	**17**	**39**	**29**	**21**	**50**	**18**	**4**	**1**	**0**	**1**	**2**
1952-53	**Toronto Maple Leafs**	**NHL**	**63**	**16**	**8**	**24**	**21**	**10**	**31**	**8**					
1953-54	**Toronto Maple Leafs**	**NHL**	**70**	**21**	**7**	**28**	**29**	**8**	**37**	**30**	**5**	**0**	**1**	**1**	**2**
1954-55	**Toronto Maple Leafs**	**NHL**	**8**	**1**	**1**	**2**	**1**	**1**	**2**	**0**					
	Chicago Black Hawks	**NHL**	**43**	**14**	**16**	**30**	**18**	**18**	**36**	**4**					
1955-56	**Chicago Black Hawks**	**NHL**	**55**	**11**	**14**	**25**	**15**	**17**	**32**	**6**					
1956-57	**Chicago Black Hawks**	**NHL**	**70**	**11**	**19**	**30**	**14**	**21**	**35**	**9**					
1957-58	Buffalo Bisons	AHL	52	8	15	23				10					
1958-59	St. Catharines Teepees	OHA-Jr.	DID NOT PLAY – COACHING												
	NHL Totals		**809**	**236**	**207**	**443**	**302**	**249**	**551**	**150**	**62**	**16**	**9**	**25**	**27**

Played in NHL All-Star Game (1947, 1948, 1949, 1951, 1952, 1953, 1955)

Signed as a free agent by **Brooklyn**, October 10, 1941. Rights transferred to **Detroit** from **Brooklyn** in Special Dispersal Draft October 9, 1942. Traded to **Toronto** by **Detroit** for Billy Taylor, September 21, 1946. Traded to **Chicago** by **Toronto** for cash, December 10, 1954.

• WATSON, Jim

— see page 1743

• WATSON, Joe

— see page 1743

• WATSON, Phil

Henry Philip

RW/C – R. 5'11", 165 lbs. b: Montreal, Que., 4/24/1914 Deceased.

Season	Club	League	GP	G	A	Pts	AG	AA	APts	PIM	GP	G	A	Pts	PIM
1932-33	Montreal St. Francis	MCJHL	11	10	5	15				16	2	0	0	0	0
1933-34	Montreal St. Francis	MCJHL	16	7	6	13				14					
1934-35	Montreal Jr. Royals	QJHL	19	7	7	14				24	7	1	2	3	4
1935-36	**New York Rangers**	**NHL**	**24**	**0**	**2**	**2**	**0**	**4**	**4**	**24**					
	Philadelphia Arrows	Can-Am	22	9	5	14				32					
1936-37	**New York Rangers**	**NHL**	**48**	**11**	**17**	**28**	**18**	**31**	**49**	**22**	**9**	**0**	**2**	**2**	**9**
1937-38	**New York Rangers**	**NHL**	**48**	**7**	**25**	**32**	**11**	**41**	**52**	**52**	**3**	**0**	**2**	**2**	**0**
1938-39	**New York Rangers**	**NHL**	**48**	**15**	**22**	**37**	**26**	**35**	**61**	**42**	**7**	**1**	**1**	**2**	**7**
♦1939-40	**New York Rangers**	**NHL**	**48**	**7**	**28**	**35**	**12**	**44**	**56**	**42**	**12**	**3**	**6**	***9**	**16**
1940-41	**New York Rangers**	**NHL**	**40**	**11**	**25**	**36**	**17**	**36**	**53**	**49**	**3**	**0**	**2**	**2**	**9**
1941-42	**New York Rangers**	**NHL**	**48**	**15**	***37**	**52**	**20**	**44**	**64**	**58**	**6**	**1**	**4**	**5**	**8**
1942-43	**New York Rangers**	**NHL**	**46**	**14**	**28**	**42**	**14**	**26**	**40**	**44**					
♦1943-44	**Montreal Canadiens**	**NHL**	**44**	**17**	**32**	**49**	**15**	**28**	**43**	**61**	**9**	**3**	**5**	**8**	**16**
1944-45	**New York Rangers**	**NHL**	**45**	**11**	**8**	**19**	**11**	**9**	**20**	**24**					
1945-46	**New York Rangers**	**NHL**	**49**	**12**	**14**	**26**	**14**	**20**	**34**	**43**					

			REGULAR SEASON								PLAYOFFS				
Season	Club	League	GP	G	A	Pts	AG	AA	APts	PIM	GP	G	A	Pts	PIM
1946-47	**New York Rangers**	**NHL**	**48**	**6**	**12**	**18**	**7**	**14**	**21**	**17**	....	....	....	....	....
1947-48	**New York Rangers**	**NHL**	**54**	**18**	**15**	**33**	**23**	**20**	**43**	**54**	**5**	**2**	**3**	**5**	**2**
1948-49	New York Rovers	QSHL	DID NOT PLAY – COACHING												
	NHL Totals		**590**	**144**	**265**	**409**	**188**	**352**	**540**	**532**	**54**	**10**	**25**	**35**	**67**

NHL Second All-Star Team (1942)

Signed as a free agent by **NY Rangers** for $4,500, October 27, 1935. Loaned to **Montreal** by **NY Rangers** for the 1943-44 season for the loan of Charlie Sands, Fern Gauthier, Dutch Hiller, John Mahaffy and future considerations (Tony Demers, December, 1943), October 27, 1943.

• WEBSTER, Aubrey

RW – R. 5'9", 168 lbs. b: Kenora, Ont., 9/25/1912 Deceased.

Season	Club	League	GP	G	A	Pts	AG	AA	APts	PIM	GP	G	A	Pts	PIM
1927/30	Kenora Thistles	TBJHL	STATISTICS NOT AVAILABLE												
1930-31	Weyburn Beavers	SSHL	12	9	2	11	....	....	....	8	....	....	....	....	....
	Philadelphia Quakers	**NHL**	**1**	**0**	**0**	**0**	**0**	**0**	**0**	**0**	....	....	....	....	....
1931-32	Fredericton Capitals	NBSHL	23	15	6	21	....	....	....	6	7	*7	1	8	2
1932-33	Moncton Hawks	NBSHL	18	2	2	4	....	....	....	7	3	0	0	0	6
	Moncton Hawks	Al-Cup	6	2	1	3	....	....	....	2	....	....	....	....	....
1933-34	Moncton Hawks	NBSHL	36	22	9	31	....	....	....	22	3	0	0	0	2
	Moncton Hawks	Al-Cup	11	*10	1	11	....	....	....	2	....	....	....	....	....
1934-35	**Montreal Maroons**	**NHL**	**4**	**0**	**0**	**0**	**0**	**0**	**0**	**0**	....	....	....	....	....
	Windsor Bulldogs	IHL	37	11	16	27	....	....	....	6	....	....	....	....	....
1935-36	Windsor Bulldogs	IHL	48	13	14	27	....	....	....	15	8	1	1	2	2
1936-37	Spokane Clippers	PCHL	40	9	7	16	....	....	....	32	6	0	2	2	2
1937-38	Spokane Clippers	PCHL	42	11	22	33	....	....	....	49	....	....	....	....	....
1938-39	Portland Buckaroos	PCHL	40	19	16	35	....	....	....	25	5	1	3	4	14
1939-40	Portland Buckaroos	PCHL	22	9	5	14	....	....	....	10	....	....	....	....	....
	Wichita Skyhawks	AHA	20	3	7	10	....	....	....	2	....	....	....	....	....
1940-41	Spokane Bombers	PCHL	32	9	19	28	....	....	....	14	....	....	....	....	....
1941-42			MILITARY SERVICE												
1942-43			MILITARY SERVICE												
1943-44	Portland Oilers	NNDHL	14	15	14	29	....	....	....	4	6	3	6	9	0
1944-45			MILITARY SERVICE												
1945-46	Portland Eagles	PCHL	57	9	21	30	....	....	....	44	8	2	3	5	2
	NHL Totals		**5**	**0**	**0**	**0**	**0**	**0**	**0**	**0**	....	....	....	....	....

Signed as a free agent by **Montreal Maroons**, August, 1934. Traded to **Windsor** (IHL) by **Montreal Maroons** for cash, December 26, 1934.

• WEBSTER, Don

LW – L. 5'8", 180 lbs. b: Toronto, Ont., 7/3/1924 d: 1978.

Season	Club	League	GP	G	A	Pts	AG	AA	APts	PIM	GP	G	A	Pts	PIM
1940-41	Etobicoke Indians	OHA-B	10	10	6	16	....	....	....	21	6	4	1	5	*27
	Toronto Stockyards	TIHL	10	2	2	4	....	....	....	*42	6	2	1	3	2
1941-42	Toronto Marlboros	OHA-Jr.	18	6	6	12	....	....	....	47	2	0	2	2	6
	Toronto Peoples Credit	TIHL	6	1	0	1	....	....	....	12	1	0	0	0	0
1942-43	Providence Reds	AHL	48	11	19	30	....	....	....	67	2	0	0	0	2
1943-44	**Toronto Maple Leafs**	**NHL**	**27**	**7**	**6**	**13**	**6**	**5**	**11**	**28**	**5**	**0**	**0**	**0**	**12**
1944-45	Buffalo Bisons	AHL	39	4	13	17	....	....	....	57	....	....	....	....	....
	Hershey Bears	AHL	9	1	1	2	....	....	....	4	....	....	....	....	....
1945-46	Hershey Bears	AHL	5	1	3	4	....	....	....	4	....	....	....	....	....
	Fort Worth Rangers	USHL	4	0	0	0	....	....	....	2	....	....	....	....	....
	Shawinigan Cataracts	QSHL	9	2	2	4	....	....	....	8	....	....	....	....	....
	Washington Lions	EAHL	27	5	7	12	....	....	....	49	11	4	2	6	4
1946-47	San Diego Skyhawks	PCHL	60	9	19	28	....	....	....	114	2	0	0	0	2
1947-48	Springfield Indians	AHL	17	1	2	3	....	....	....	24	....	....	....	....	....
	Tulsa Oilers	USHL	46	9	19	28	....	....	....	80	2	1	0	1	4
1948-49	Tulsa Oilers	USHL	52	7	11	18	....	....	....	*137	7	0	3	3	4
1949-50	Los Angeles Monarchs	PCHL	57	1	13	14	....	....	....	*187	17	3	2	5	52
1950-51	Victoria Cougars	PCHL	64	2	18	20	....	....	....	145	12	0	0	0	*41
1951-52			DID NOT PLAY												
1952-53	Victoria Cougars	WHL	66	0	15	15	....	....	....	123	....	....	....	....	....
	NHL Totals		**27**	**7**	**6**	**13**	**6**	**5**	**11**	**28**	**5**	**0**	**0**	**0**	**12**

• Brother of John

Traded to **Buffalo** (AHL) by **Toronto** with George Boothman for the rights to Bill Ezinicki, October 13, 1944. Traded to **Hershey** (AHL) by **Buffalo** (AHL) for Hec Pozzo and the rights to George Parsons, February 8, 1945.

• WEBSTER, John

John Robert "Chick"

C – L. 5'11", 160 lbs. b: Toronto, Ont., 11/3/1920.

Season	Club	League	GP	G	A	Pts	AG	AA	APts	PIM	GP	G	A	Pts	PIM
1937-38	Toronto Native Sons	OHA-Jr.	12	3	6	9	....	....	....	0	....	....	....	....	....
1938-39	Toronto Native Sons	OHA-Jr.	14	6	4	10	....	....	....	8	8	4	3	7	8
1939-40	Toronto Native Sons	OHA-Jr.	11	3	6	9	....	....	....	21	....	....	....	....	....
	Toronto Stockyards	TMHL	13	9	8	17	....	....	....	14	....	....	....	....	....
1940-41	Baltimore Orioles	EAHL	62	24	37	61	....	....	....	21	....	....	....	....	....
1941-42	St. Catharines Saints	OHA-Sr.	12	1	7	8	....	....	....	26	....	....	....	....	....
	Toronto Stockyards	TMHL	3	1	3	4	....	....	....	0	1	3	0	3	0
	Camp Borden Army	NDHL	....	....	....	....	....	....	....	....	1	0	1	1	0
1942-43	Petawawa Grenades	UOVHL	3	5	1	6	....	....	....	6	2	3	1	4	0
	Petawawa Grenades	Al-Cup	8	7	6	13	....	....	....	21	....	....	....	....	....
1943-44			MILITARY SERVICE												
1944-45			MILITARY SERVICE												
1945-46	Toronto Uptown Tires	TMHL	3	1	4	5	....	....	....	2	....	....	....	....	....
	Baltimore Orioles	EAHL	15	7	9	16	....	....	....	5	12	11	9	*20	2
1946-47	New York Rovers	EAHL	13	7	11	18	....	....	....	36	....	....	....	....	....
	New Haven Ramblers	AHL	47	9	15	24	....	....	....	26	....	....	....	....	....
1947-48	New Haven Ramblers	AHL	65	22	37	59	....	....	....	12	4	1	1	2	0
1948-49	New Haven Ramblers	AHL	65	16	33	49	....	....	....	24	....	....	....	....	....
1949-50	**New York Rangers**	**NHL**	**14**	**0**	**0**	**0**	**0**	**0**	**0**	**4**	....	....	....	....	....
	New Haven Ramblers	AHL	38	9	17	26	....	....	....	16	....	....	....	....	....
1950-51	Tacoma Rockets	PCHL	63	20	28	48	....	....	....	36	6	1	1	2	2
1951-52	Cincinnati Mohawks	AHL	49	6	12	18	....	....	....	15	7	3	2	5	0
1952-53	Syracuse Warriors	AHL	13	2	2	4	....	....	....	0	....	....	....	....	....
	Vancouver Canucks	WHL	5	0	0	0	....	....	....	0	....	....	....	....	....
	S.S. Marie Greyhounds	NOHA	12	1	7	8	....	....	....	4	2	0	1	1	0
	NHL Totals		**14**	**0**	**0**	**0**	**0**	**0**	**0**	**4**	....	....	....	....	....

• Brother of Don

• WEILAND, Cooney

Ralph — HHOF

C – L. 5'7", 150 lbs. b: Seaforth (Edmondville), Ont., 11/5/1904 d: 7/3/1985.

Season	Club	League	GP	G	A	Pts	AG	AA	APts	PIM	GP	G	A	Pts	PIM
1918/22	Seaforth Highlanders	OHA-Jr.	STATISTICS NOT AVAILABLE												
1922-23	Owen Sound Greys	OHA-Jr.	STATISTICS NOT AVAILABLE												
1923-24	Owen Sound Greys	X-Games	9	*33	5	*38	....	....	....	....	....	....	....	....	....
	Owen Sound Greys	M-Cup	....	....	....	....	....	....	....	....	....	....	....	....	....
1924-25	Minneapolis Rockets	USAHA	35	8	0	8	....	....	....	....	....	....	....	....	....
1925-26	Minneapolis Millers	CHL	26	10	4	14	....	....	....	20	3	1	1	2	0
1926-27	Minneapolis Millers	AHA	36	21	2	23	....	....	....	30	6	*4	1	*5	0
1927-28	Minneapolis Millers	AHA	40	*21	5	26	....	....	....	34	8	2	*2	*4	0
♦1928-29	**Boston Bruins**	**NHL**	**42**	**11**	**7**	**18**	**32**	**47**	**79**	**16**	**5**	**2**	**0**	**2**	**2**
1929-30	**Boston Bruins**	**NHL**	**44**	***43**	**30**	***73**	**62**	**72**	**134**	**27**	**6**	**1**	***5**	***6**	**2**
1930-31	**Boston Bruins**	**NHL**	**44**	**25**	**13**	**38**	**51**	**39**	**90**	**14**	**5**	***6**	**3**	***9**	**2**
1931-32	**Boston Bruins**	**NHL**	**46**	**14**	**12**	**26**	**23**	**26**	**49**	**20**	....	....	....	....	....
1932-33	**Ottawa Senators**	**NHL**	**48**	**16**	**11**	**27**	**29**	**23**	**52**	**4**	....	....	....	....	....
1933-34	**Ottawa Senators**	**NHL**	**9**	**2**	**0**	**2**	**3**	**0**	**3**	**4**	....	....	....	....	....
	Detroit Red Wings	**NHL**	**39**	**11**	**19**	**30**	**19**	**40**	**59**	**6**	**9**	**2**	**2**	**4**	**4**
1934-35	**Detroit Red Wings**	**NHL**	**48**	**13**	**25**	**38**	**21**	**44**	**65**	**10**	....	....	....	....	....
1935-36	**Boston Bruins**	**NHL**	**48**	**14**	**13**	**27**	**27**	**25**	**52**	**15**	**2**	**1**	**0**	**1**	**2**
1936-37	**Boston Bruins**	**NHL**	**48**	**6**	**9**	**15**	**10**	**16**	**26**	**6**	**3**	**0**	**0**	**0**	**0**
1937-38	**Boston Bruins**	**NHL**	**48**	**11**	**12**	**23**	**18**	**19**	**37**	**16**	**3**	**0**	**0**	**0**	**0**
♦1938-39	**Boston Bruins**	**NHL**	**45**	**7**	**9**	**16**	**12**	**14**	**26**	**9**	**12**	**0**	**0**	**0**	**0**
1939-40	**Boston Bruins**	**NHL**	DID NOT PLAY – COACHING												
	NHL Totals		**509**	**173**	**160**	**333**	**307**	**365**	**672**	**147**	**45**	**12**	**10**	**22**	**12**

NHL Scoring Leader (1930) • NHL Second All-Star Team (1935) • Won Lester Patrick Trophy (1972)

Signed as a free agent by **Minneapolis** (AHA), November 1, 1926. Traded to **Boston** by **Minneapolis** (AHA) for cash, December 23, 1927. • Weiland remained with Minneapolis (AHA) for the remainder of the 1927-28 season. Traded to **Ottawa** by **Boston** for Joe Lamb and $7,000, July 25, 1932. Traded to **Detroit** by **Ottawa** for Carl Voss and cash, November 26, 1933. Traded to **Boston** by **Detroit** with Walt Buswell for Marty Barry and Art Giroux, June 30, 1935.

• WELLINGTON, Alex

"Duke"

RW – R. , b: Port Arthur, Ont., Deceased.

Season	Club	League	GP	G	A	Pts	AG	AA	APts	PIM	GP	G	A	Pts	PIM
1910-11	Port Arthur Lake Cities	NOHL	5	9	0	9	....	....	....	6	3	7	0	7	3
1911-12	Port Arthur Lake Cities	NOHL	STATISTICS NOT AVAILABLE												
1912-13	Halifax Cresents	MPHL	6	0	0	0	....	....	....	0	....	....	....	....	....
1913-14	Cleveland Indians	X-Games	STATISTICS NOT AVAILABLE												
1914-15	Cleveland Indians	X-Games	STATISTICS NOT AVAILABLE												
1915-16	Pittsburgh Duquesne	X-Games	STATISTICS NOT AVAILABLE												
1916-17	New York Irish Americans	NYHL	STATISTICS NOT AVAILABLE												
1917-18	New York Wanderers	NYHL	8	1	0	1	....	....	....	....	....	....	....	....	....
1918-19			DID NOT PLAY – SUSPENDED												
1919-20	New York New Rochelle	USAHA	STATISTICS NOT AVAILABLE												
	Quebec Bulldogs	**NHL**	**1**	**0**	**0**	**0**	**0**	**0**	**0**	**0**	....	....	....	....	....
	NHL Totals		**1**	**0**	**0**	**0**	**0**	**0**	**0**	**0**	....	....	....	....	....
	Other Major League Totals		11	9	0	9	....	....	....	6	3	7	0	7	3

Signed as a free agent by **Quebec**, January 9, 1920.

• WENTWORTH, Cy

Marvin

D – R. 5'10", 170 lbs. b: Grimsby, Ont., 1/24/1905 Deceased.

Season	Club	League	GP	G	A	Pts	AG	AA	APts	PIM	GP	G	A	Pts	PIM
1921/23	Grimsby Lions	OHA-Jr.	STATISTICS NOT AVAILABLE												
1923-24	Hamilton Jr. Tigers	OHA-Jr.	STATISTICS NOT AVAILABLE												
1924-25	Brantford Lions	OIHA	STATISTICS NOT AVAILABLE												
1925-26	Windsor Hornets	OHA-Sr.	20	6	5	11	....	....	....	9	....	....	....	....	....
1926-27	Chicago Cardinals	AHA	34	8	4	12	....	....	....	40	....	....	....	....	....
1927-28	**Chicago Black Hawks**	**NHL**	**43**	**5**	**5**	**10**	**10**	**28**	**38**	**31**	....	....	....	....	....
1928-29	**Chicago Black Hawks**	**NHL**	**44**	**2**	**1**	**3**	**6**	**7**	**13**	**44**	....	....	....	....	....
1929-30	**Chicago Black Hawks**	**NHL**	**37**	**3**	**4**	**7**	**4**	**9**	**13**	**28**	....	....	....	....	....
1930-31	**Chicago Black Hawks**	**NHL**	**44**	**4**	**4**	**8**	**8**	**12**	**20**	**12**	**9**	**1**	**1**	**2**	**14**
1931-32	**Chicago Black Hawks**	**NHL**	**48**	**3**	**10**	**13**	**5**	**22**	**27**	**30**	**2**	**0**	**0**	**0**	**0**
1932-33	**Montreal Maroons**	**NHL**	**47**	**4**	**10**	**14**	**7**	**21**	**28**	**48**	**2**	**0**	**1**	**1**	**0**
1933-34	**Montreal Maroons**	**NHL**	**48**	**2**	**5**	**7**	**3**	**10**	**13**	**31**	**4**	**0**	**2**	**2**	**2**
♦1934-35	**Montreal Maroons**	**NHL**	**48**	**4**	**9**	**13**	**7**	**16**	**23**	**28**	**7**	**3**	**2**	***5**	**0**
1935-36	**Montreal Maroons**	**NHL**	**48**	**4**	**5**	**9**	**8**	**9**	**17**	**24**	**3**	**0**	**0**	**0**	**0**
1936-37	**Montreal Maroons**	**NHL**	**43**	**3**	**4**	**7**	**5**	**7**	**12**	**29**	**5**	**1**	**0**	**1**	**0**
1937-38	**Montreal Maroons**	**NHL**	**48**	**4**	**5**	**9**	**6**	**8**	**14**	**32**	....	....	....	....	....
1938-39	**Montreal Canadiens**	**NHL**	**45**	**0**	**3**	**3**	**0**	**5**	**5**	**12**	**3**	**0**	**0**	**0**	**4**
1939-40	**Montreal Canadiens**	**NHL**	**32**	**1**	**3**	**4**	**2**	**5**	**7**	**6**	....	....	....	....	....
	NHL Totals		**575**	**39**	**68**	**107**	**71**	**159**	**230**	**355**	**35**	**5**	**6**	**11**	**20**

NHL Second All-Star Team (1935) • Played in NHL All-Star Game (1937, 1939)

Traded to **Chicago** by **Windsor** (Can-Pro) for cash, December, 20, 1926. Traded to **Montreal Maroons** by **Chicago** for $10,000, October 24, 1932. Traded to **Montreal Canadiens** by **Montreal Maroons** for cash, September 14, 1938.

• WESTFALL, Ed

— see page 1748

• WHARRAM, Kenny

— see page 1748

• WHARTON, Len

D – L. 6', 170 lbs. b: Winnipeg, Man., 12/13/1927.

Season	Club	League	GP	G	A	Pts	AG	AA	APts	PIM	GP	G	A	Pts	PIM
1944-45	New York Rovers	EAHL	39	9	12	21	....	....	....	8	12	0	2	2	18
	New York Rangers	**NHL**	**1**	**0**	**0**	**0**	**0**	**0**	**0**	**0**	....	....	....	....	....
1945-46	New York Rovers	EAHL	36	3	9	12	....	....	....	26	9	0	0	0	2
1946-47	Stratford Kroehlers	OHA-Jr.	18	7	5	12	....	....	....	38	....	....	....	....	....
1947-48	San Diego Skyhawks	PCHL	47	11	15	26	....	....	....	18	....	....	....	....	....
1948-49	Louisville Blades	IHL	28	4	14	18	....	....	....	102	6	0	0	0	*23
1949-50	Toledo Buckeyes	EAHL	45	2	11	13	....	....	....	*151	7	1	1	2	20
1950-51	Toledo Mercurys	IHL	53	6	19	25	....	....	....	*186	21	1	8	9	28
1951-52	Toledo Mercurys	IHL	44	2	15	17	....	....	....	*148	10	1	3	4	10
1952-53	Fort Wayne Komets	IHL	59	5	24	29	....	....	....	77	....	....	....	....	....
1953-54	Fort Wayne Komets	IHL	52	1	10	11	....	....	....	84	2	0	1	1	16
	NHL Totals		**1**	**0**	**0**	**0**	**0**	**0**	**0**	**0**	....	....	....	....	....

Signed as a free agent by **NY Rangers** , October 10, 1944.

• WHITE, Moe Maurice Leonard

LW/C – L. 5'11", 178 lbs. b: Verdun, Que., 7/28/1919.

Season	Club	League	GP	G	A	Pts	AG	AA	APts	PIM	GP	G	A	Pts	PIM
			REGULAR SEASON								PLAYOFFS				
1935-36	Verdun Maple Leafs	QJHL	9	1	3	4				0	2	0	2	2	0
1936-37	Montreal Victorias	MCJHL	11	2	5	7				19	2	2	1	3	2
	Montreal Victorias	M-Cup	4	2	2	4				2					
1937-38	Montreal Victorias	MCJHL	19	7	5	12				19	6	6	2	8	16
	Montreal Victorias	M-Cup	4	2	2	4				2					
1938-39	Montreal Victorias	MCHL	22	9	10	19				19					
1939-40	Verdun Maple Leafs	QSHL	30	14	14	28				20	8	3	3	6	10
1940-41	Glace Bay Miners	CBSHL	11	4	5	9				14					
1941-42	Glace Bay Miners	CBSHL	40	31	31	62				44	7	5	4	9	6
1942-43	Montreal Army	MCHL	33	13	20	33				16	7	1	2	3	16
	Montreal Army	MCHL	6	6	7	13				2	5	6	4	10	0
1943-44	Kingston Army	OHA-Sr.	13	7	8	15				6					
	Montreal Army	MCHL	1	0	0	0				0					
1944-45			MILITARY SERVICE												
1945-46	**Montreal Canadiens**	**NHL**	**4**	**0**	**1**	**1**	**0**	**1**	**1**	**2**					
	Montreal Royals	QSHL	1	1	0	1				2					
	Buffalo Bisons	AHL	11	2	2	4				2					
1946-47	Houston Huskies	USHL	60	28	34	62				27					
1947-48	Valleyfield Braves	QSHL	46	23	29	52				37	6	0	2	2	10
1948-49	Glace Bay Miners	CBSHL	57	6	*44	50				111	12	1	3	4	*33
1949-50	Glace Bay Miners	CBSHL	70	18	27	45				33	10	0	9	9	2
1950-51	Joliette Cyclones	QPHL	STATISTICS NOT AVAILABLE												
1951-52	St-Laurent Castors	QPHL	STATISTICS NOT AVAILABLE												
	NHL Totals		**4**	**0**	**1**	**1**	**0**	**1**	**1**	**2**					

• Missed majority of 1940-41 recovering from ankle injury, November, 1940. Traded to **Buffalo** (AHL) by **Montreal** with John Adams for Murdo MacKay with Montreal holding right of recall, January 14, 1946. Traded to **Buffalo** (AHL) by **Montreal** for cash, October 8, 1946.

• WHITE, Sherman Sherman Beverley "Shermie"

C – L. 5'10", 165 lbs. b: Cape Tormentine, N.B., 5/12/1923 Deceased.

Season	Club	League	GP	G	A	Pts	AG	AA	APts	PIM	GP	G	A	Pts	PIM
1938-39	Amherst St. Pats	X-Games	9	*11	*5	*16				18					
	Amherst St. Pats	M-Cup	7	17	6	23				8					
1939-40	Amherst Ramblers	SNBHL	7	*17	5	*22				4	5	*8	1	9	0
1940-41	Amherst Ramblers	NBCHL	4	12	2	14				0					
1941-42	Amherst Ramblers	X-Games	7	*14	5	19				0					
1942-43	Amherst All-Stars	X-Games	5	*14	*7	*21				0					
	Amherst Busymen	NSDHL	5	*9	*8	*17				6	1	*4	1	*5	0
	Amherst All-Stars	Al-Cup	2	3	4	7				0					
1943-44	Amherst Victoria Bombers	X-Games	1	2	0	2				5	1	1	1	2	2
	Saint John Beavers	Al-Cup	1	0	1	1				0					
	Moncton #5 Providers	NBDHL	1	1	0	1				0	3	3	3	6	0
1944-45	Moncton #5 Providers	NBDHL	8	10	5	15				0	2	4	1	5	0
	Dartmouth RCAF	NSDHL	3	0	1	1				0	3	0	0	0	4
1945-46	Dartmouth RCAF	NSDHL	8	8	8	16				0	5	4	5	9	0
	Amherst Ramblers	NBCHL	3	6	3	9				0					
	Moncton Maroons	SNBHL	3	4	7	11				0	3	0	3	3	0
1946-47	**New York Rangers**	**NHL**	**1**	**0**	**0**	**0**	**0**	**0**	**0**	**0**					
	New York Rovers	EAHL	19	13	9	22				2					
	New Haven Ramblers	AHL	36	8	8	16				8	3	2	0	2	0
1947-48	New Haven Ramblers	AHL	58	9	30	39				10	4	0	2	2	2
1948-49	New Haven Ramblers	AHL	68	26	32	58				13					
1949-50	**New York Rangers**	**NHL**	**3**	**0**	**2**	**2**	**0**	**2**	**2**	**0**					
	New Haven Ramblers	AHL	70	17	35	52				6					
1950-51	St. Louis Flyers	AHL	66	11	42	53				6					
1951-52	Chicoutimi Sagueneens	QMHL	59	23	32	55				8	18	2	9	11	0
1952-53	Chicoutimi Sagueneens	QMHL	58	26	*57	83				6	20	3	*16	19	4
1953-54	Chicoutimi Sagueneens	QHL	51	10	36	46				4	3	1	1	2	0
1954-55	Amherst Ramblers	ACSHL	41	20	46	66				2	8	2	4	6	2
1955-56	Amherst Ramblers	ACSHL	63	42	*78	*120				2	14	10	9	*19	2
	Saint John Beavers	Al-Cup	2	0	2	2				0					
1956-57	Bathurst Papermakers	NNBSL	42	20	38	58				7					
1957-58	Bishop's Falls Flyers	Nfld-Sr.	11	20	15	35				0					
	Bishop's Falls Kinsmen	BFCHL	5	6	7	13				0					
	Grand Falls Andcos	Nfld-Sr.	1	1	2	3				0					
1958-59	Glace Bay Miners	CBSHL	34	23	*54	*77				8	3	1	3	4	0
	Glace Bay Miners	Al-Cup	6	7	12	19				0					
1959-60	Glace Bay Miners	CBSHL	32	24	29	53				2	9	5	8	13	2
1960-61	Amherst Ramblers	NSAPC	31	18	*55	*73				0	7	1	6	7	0
	Amherst Ramblers	Al-Cup	15	5	16	21				0					
1961-62	Amherst Ramblers	NSAPC	28	14	27	41				0	9	6	9	15	0
	Amherst Ramblers	Al-Cup	8	2	5	7									
1962-63	Amherst Ramblers	NSSHL	28	21	50	71				6	11	3	3	6	0
	Moncton Hawks	Al-Cup	14	4	7	11				6					
1963-64	Moncton Hawks	NSSHL	28	9	15	24				2	4	0	1	1	0
	NHL Totals		**4**	**0**	**2**	**2**	**0**	**2**	**2**	**0**					

QMHL Second All-Star Team (1953) • Won Byng of Vimy Trophy (MVP - QMHL) (1953)

Traded to **St. Louis** (AHL) by **NY Rangers** for cash, September 19, 1950. Traded to **Amherst** (ACSHL) by **Chicoutimi** (QHL) for cash, November 17, 1954. • Cash for Chicoutimi (QHL) purchase provided by fans who wanted White to finish his career in the Maritimes.

• WHITE, Tex Wilfred

RW – R. 5'11", 155 lbs. b: Hillbrough, Ont., 6/26/1900 d: 12/2/1949.

Season	Club	League	GP	G	A	Pts	AG	AA	APts	PIM	GP	G	A	Pts	PIM
1917/19	Barrie Canoe Club	OHA-Jr.	STATISTICS NOT AVAILABLE												
1919-20	Toronto Canoe Club	OHA-Jr.	STATISTICS NOT AVAILABLE												
	Toronto Canoe Club	M-Cup	12	35	3	38									
1920/23	Dunville Dunnies	OIHA	STATISTICS NOT AVAILABLE												
1923-24	Pittsburgh Yellowjackets	USAHA	20	11	0	11					13	1	1	2	
1924-25	Pittsburgh Yellowjackets	USAHA	39	7	0	7					8	1	0	1	
1925-26	**Pittsburgh Pirates**	**NHL**	**35**	**7**	**1**	**8**	**12**	**6**	**18**	**22**					
1926-27	**Pittsburgh Pirates**	**NHL**	**43**	**5**	**4**	**9**	**9**	**21**	**30**	**21**					
1927-28	**Pittsburgh Pirates**	**NHL**	**44**	**5**	**1**	**6**	**10**	**6**	**16**	**54**	**2**	**0**	**0**	**0**	**2**
1928-29	**Pittsburgh Pirates**	**NHL**	**30**	**3**	**4**	**7**	**9**	**27**	**36**	**18**					
	New York Americans	**NHL**	**13**	**2**	**1**	**3**	**6**	**7**	**13**	**8**	**2**	**0**	**0**	**0**	**2**
1929-30	**Pittsburgh Pirates**	**NHL**	**29**	**8**	**1**	**9**	**11**	**2**	**13**	**16**					
	New Haven Eagles	Can-Am	12	2	0	2				6					
1930-31	**Philadelphia Quakers**	**NHL**	**9**	**3**	**0**	**3**	**6**	**0**	**6**	**2**					
	Pittsburgh Yellowjackets	IHL	35	9	7	16				12	6	1	0	1	6
1931-32	Pittsburgh Yellowjackets	IHL	24	1	1	2				22					
	NHL Totals		**203**	**33**	**12**	**45**	**63**	**69**	**132**	**141**	**4**	**0**	**0**	**0**	**4**

Signed as a free agent by **Pittsburgh**, September 26, 1925. Loaned to **NY Americans** by **Pittsburgh** for remainder of 1928-29 season for Jesse Spring and loan of Edmond Bouchard for remainder of 1928-29 season, February 15, 1929. Transferred to **Philadelphia** after **Pittsburgh** franchise relocated, September 27, 1930. Traded to **Pittsburgh** (IHL) by **Philadelphia** for cash, December 16, 1930.

• WHITELAW, Bob

D – L. 5'11", 185 lbs. b: Motherwell, Scotland, 10/5/1916.

Season	Club	League	GP	G	A	Pts	AG	AA	APts	PIM	GP	G	A	Pts	PIM
1935-36	Winnipeg Rangers	MJHL	12	4	4	8				10	2	3	0	3	6
1936-37	Harringay Racers	Britain	....	5	3	8				10					
1937-38	Harringay Racers	Ln-Cup	....	0	1	1				....					
	Harringay Racers	Britain	....	8	4	12				15					
	Harringay Racers	Nat-Tmt	....	3	0	3									
1938-39	Pittsburgh Hornets	IAHL	50	1	7	8				23					
1939-40	Indianapolis Capitols	IAHL	56	6	7	13				22	5	0	0	0	0
1940-41	**Detroit Red Wings**	**NHL**	**23**	**0**	**2**	**2**	**0**	**3**	**3**	**2**	**8**	**0**	**0**	**0**	**0**
	Indianapolis Capitols	AHL	24	1	4	5				8					
1941-42	**Detroit Red Wings**	**NHL**	**9**	**0**	**0**	**0**	**0**	**0**	**0**	**0**					
	Indianapolis Capitols	AHL	9	1	2	3				5					
	Providence Reds	AHL	19	0	1	....				8					
1942-43	Providence Reds	AHL	55	7	15	22				27	2	0	0	0	0
1943-44			MILITARY SERVICE												
1944-45	Winnipeg RCAF	WNDHL	11	1	2	3				6					
1945-46	Wembley Lions	Britain	STATISTICS NOT AVAILABLE												
1946-47	Providence Reds	AHL	60	2	6	8				7					
1947-48	Winnipeg Nationals	WSrHL	7	1	1	2				0					
	NHL Totals		**32**	**0**	**2**	**2**	**0**	**3**	**3**	**2**	**8**	**0**	**0**	**0**	**0**

Signed as a free agent by **Detroit**, October 13, 1939. Traded to **Providence** (AHL) by **Detroit** with Buck Jones for Eddie Bush and future considerations, February 3, 1942.

• WIEBE, Art Walter Arthur Ronald

D – L. 5'10", 180 lbs. b: Rosthern, Sask., 9/28/1912 d: 6/6/1971.

Season	Club	League	GP	G	A	Pts	AG	AA	APts	PIM	GP	G	A	Pts	PIM
1930-31	Edmonton Poolers	EJrHL	10	0	1	1				6					
1931-32	Edmonton Poolers	AAHA	10	2	2	4				....	2	1	0	1	0
	Edmonton Poolers	M-Cup	5	0	0	0				6					
1932-33	Edmonton Superiors	ESrHL	STATISTICS NOT AVAILABLE												
	St. Paul Greyhounds	AHA	16	0	0	0				10					
	Chicago Black Hawks	**NHL**	**4**	**0**	**0**	**0**	**0**	**0**	**0**	**0**					
1933-34	Kansas City Greyhounds	AHA	15	1	1	2				9	4	0	0	0	0
1934-35	**Chicago Black Hawks**	**NHL**	**42**	**2**	**1**	**3**	**3**	**2**	**5**	**27**	**2**	**0**	**0**	**0**	**2**
1935-36	**Chicago Black Hawks**	**NHL**	**46**	**1**	**0**	**1**	**2**	**0**	**2**	**25**	**2**	**0**	**0**	**0**	**0**
1936-37	**Chicago Black Hawks**	**NHL**	**43**	**0**	**2**	**2**	**0**	**4**	**4**	**6**					
♦1937-38	**Chicago Black Hawks**	**NHL**	**43**	**0**	**3**	**3**	**0**	**5**	**5**	**24**	**10**	**0**	**1**	**1**	**2**
1938-39	**Chicago Black Hawks**	**NHL**	**47**	**1**	**2**	**3**	**2**	**3**	**5**	**24**					
1939-40	**Chicago Black Hawks**	**NHL**	**47**	**2**	**2**	**4**	**3**	**3**	**6**	**20**	**2**	**1**	**0**	**1**	**2**
1940-41	**Chicago Black Hawks**	**NHL**	**45**	**3**	**2**	**5**	**5**	**3**	**8**	**28**	**4**	**0**	**0**	**0**	**0**
1941-42	**Chicago Black Hawks**	**NHL**	**43**	**2**	**4**	**6**	**3**	**5**	**8**	**20**	**3**	**0**	**0**	**0**	**0**
1942-43	**Chicago Black Hawks**	**NHL**	**33**	**1**	**7**	**8**	**1**	**6**	**7**	**25**					
1943-44	**Chicago Black Hawks**	**NHL**	**21**	**2**	**4**	**6**	**2**	**3**	**5**	**2**	**8**	**0**	**2**	**2**	**4**
	NHL Totals		**414**	**14**	**27**	**41**	**21**	**34**	**55**	**201**	**31**	**1**	**3**	**4**	**10**

Traded to **Chicago** by **St. Paul** (AHA) for Helge Bostrom, December 29, 1932.

• WILCOX, Archie

RW/D – L. 5'11", 195 lbs. b: Montreal, Que., 5/9/1904 d: 1993.

Season	Club	League	GP	G	A	Pts	AG	AA	APts	PIM	GP	G	A	Pts	PIM
1924-25	Montreal Ste-Anne	ECHL	STATISTICS NOT AVAILABLE												
1925-26	Montreal CNR	MRTHL	9	3	3	6				12	1	0	0	0	0
	Montreal Victorias	MCHL	10	0	0	0				14	3	0	0	0	2
1926-27	Stratford Nationals	Can-Pro	6	0	0	0				6					
	Providence Reds	Can-Am	21	4	3	7				22					
1927-28	Providence Reds	Can-Am	38	12	2	14				50					
1928-29	Providence Reds	Can-Am	40	2	1	3				52	6	0	*2	2	14
1929-30	**Montreal Maroons**	**NHL**	**42**	**3**	**5**	**8**	**4**	**12**	**16**	**38**	**4**	**1**	**0**	**1**	**2**
1930-31	**Montreal Maroons**	**NHL**	**39**	**2**	**2**	**4**	**4**	**6**	**10**	**42**	**2**	**0**	**0**	**0**	**2**
1931-32	**Montreal Maroons**	**NHL**	**48**	**3**	**3**	**6**	**5**	**7**	**12**	**37**	**4**	**0**	**0**	**0**	**4**
1932-33	**Montreal Maroons**	**NHL**	**47**	**0**	**3**	**3**	**0**	**6**	**6**	**37**	**2**	**0**	**0**	**0**	**0**
1933-34	**Montreal Maroons**	**NHL**	**10**	**0**	**0**	**0**	**0**	**0**	**0**	**2**					
	Quebec Beavers	Can-Am	15	1	2	3				13					
	Boston Bruins	**NHL**	**14**	**0**	**1**	**1**	**0**	**2**	**2**	**2**					
1934-35	Boston Cubs	Can-Am	4	0	2	2				6					
	St. Louis Eagles	**NHL**	**8**	**0**	**0**	**0**	**0**	**0**	**0**	**2**					
	Syracuse Stars	IHL	15	0	5	5				8	2	0	0	0	0
	NHL Totals		**208**	**8**	**14**	**22**	**13**	**33**	**46**	**158**	**12**	**1**	**0**	**1**	**8**

Signed as a free agent by **Stratford** (Can-Pro), April 21, 1926. Signed as a free agent by **Providence** (Can-Am) following release by Stratford (Can-Pro), January 3, 1927. Traded to **Montreal Maroons** by **Providence** (Can-Am) for cash, September 23, 1929. Claimed on waivers by **Boston** from **Montreal Maroons**, January 29, 1934. Traded to **St. Louis** by **Boston** for Burr Williams, December 2, 1934. Traded to **Syracuse** (IHL) by **St. Louis** for cash, January 4, 1934.

• WILDER, Arch Archibald

LW – L. 5'9", 155 lbs. b: Melville, Sask., 4/30/1917.

Season	Club	League	GP	G	A	Pts	AG	AA	APts	PIM	GP	G	A	Pts	PIM
1935-36	Weyburn Beavers	N-SSHL	2	1	1	2				0					
1936-37	Saskatoon Wesleys	N-SJHL									3	5	1	6	2
	Saskatoon Wesleys	M-Cup	8	7	3	10				2					
1937-38	Detroit Pontiacs	MOHL	28	5	11	16				9	3	0	1	1	0
1938-39	Detroit Pontiac McLeans	MOHL	27	14	17	31				6	7	3	*6	9	6
1939-40	Indianapolis Capitols	IAHL	56	12	12	24				16	5	2	0	2	2
1940-41	**Detroit Red Wings**	**NHL**	**18**	**0**	**2**	**2**	**0**	**3**	**3**	**2**					
	Indianapolis Capitols	AHL	9	1	3	4				0					
	Omaha Knights	AHA	24	1	4	5				4					
1941-42	Saskatoon Quakers	N-SSHL	31	8	16	24				4	9	4	1	5	2
	Saskatoon Quakers	Al-Cup	3	1	3	4				0					
1942-43			MILITARY SERVICE												
1943-44			MILITARY SERVICE												

			REGULAR SEASON								PLAYOFFS				
Season	Club	League	GP	G	A	Pts	AG	AA	APts	PIM	GP	G	A	Pts	PIM
1944-45	Calgary RCAF	ASHL	16	13	8	21	....	....	....	2	3	0	*3	3	0
1945-46	Calgary Stampeders	WCSHL	34	17	21	38	....	....	....	20	4	2	1	3	10
	Calgary Stampeders	Al-Cup	12	4	1	5	....	....	....	4	....	....	....	....	....
1946-47	Calgary Stampeders	WCSHL	40	13	12	25	....	....	....	14	7	3	4	7	0
	Calgary Stampeders	Al-Cup	17	2	7	9	....	....	....	0	....	....	....	....	....
1947-48	Calgary Stampeders	WCSHL	46	10	16	26	....	....	....	10	11	2	5	7	4
1948-49	Calgary Stampeders	WCSHL	45	6	14	20	....	....	....	10	4	0	0	0	2
1949-50	Calgary Stampeders	WCSHL	42	4	10	14	....	....	....	12	10	1	2	3	2
	Calgary Stampeders	Al-Cup	15	0	9	9	....	....	....	10	....	....	....	....	....
1950-51	Calgary Stampeders	WCMHL	30	6	13	19	....	....	....	21	6	0	2	2	0
	NHL Totals		**18**	**0**	**2**	**2**	**0**	**3**	**3**	**2**	....	....	....	....	....

• Regular season totals for Saskatoon Wesleys (1936-37) unavailable. Signed as a free agent by **Detroit**, October 26, 1937.

• WILKINS, Barry — *see page 1754*

• WILKINSON, John

D – L. 5'11", 195 lbs. b: Ottawa, Ont., 7/9/1911 Deceased.

Season	Club	League	GP	G	A	Pts	AG	AA	APts	PIM	GP	G	A	Pts	PIM
1929-30	Ottawa Rideaus	OCJHL	12	2	0	2	....	....	....	21	2	0	0	0	*4
	Ottawa Rideaus	M-Cup	6	2	0	2	....	....	....	18	....	....	....	....	....
1930-31	Ottawa Rideaus	OCJHL	16	3	3	6	....	....	....	28	2	0	0	0	4
1931-32	Ottawa New Edinburghs	OCHL	26	2	3	5	....	....	....	61	2	0	0	0	8
1932-33	Ottawa New Edinburghs	OCHL	20	4	2	6	....	....	....	33	3	0	0	0	4
1933-34	Ottawa New Edinburghs	OCHL	13	2	2	4	....	....	....	15	3	1	0	1	*0
	Ottawa New Edinburghs	Al-Cup	7	2	1	3	....	....	....	20	....	....	....	....	....
1934-35	Ottawa Senators	OCHL	19	5	0	5	....	....	....	42	8	0	0	0	14
1935-36	Wembley Canadians	Ln-Cup	....	2	2	4	....	....	....	....	....	....	....	....	....
	Wembley Canadians	Britain	....	6	4	10	....	....	....	18	....	....	....	....	....
1936-37	Wembley Monarchs	Britain	40	17	9	26	....	....	....	60	....	....	....	....	....
1937-38	Ottawa Senators	QSHL	17	5	5	10	....	....	....	39	3	0	0	0	5
1938-39	Ottawa Senators	QSHL	21	6	7	13	....	....	....	*56	6	0	0	0	10
1939-40	Ottawa Senators	QSHL	21	1	4	5	....	....	....	38	....	....	....	....	....
1940-41	Ottawa Senators	QSHL	33	8	13	21	....	....	....	45	8	2	2	4	2
	Winnipeg Navy	WNDHL	3	1	1	2	....	....	....	10	....	....	....	....	....
1941-42	Montreal Pats	QSHL	21	2	2	4	....	....	....	18	....	....	....	....	....
	Halifax Navy	NSDHL	2	0	1	1	....	....	....	2	5	1	1	2	0
1942-43	Hull Volants	OHA-Sr.	14	2	4	6	....	....	....	11	4	0	1	1	4
	Halifax Navy	NSDHL	1	0	0	0	....	....	....	0	....	....	....	....	....
1943-44	**Boston Bruins**	**NHL**	**9**	**0**	**0**	**0**	**0**	**0**	**0**	**6**	....	....	....	....	....
	Ottawa Commandos	QSHL	7	1	1	2	....	....	....	6	3	0	0	0	0
	NHL Totals		**9**	**0**	**0**	**0**	**0**	**0**	**0**	**6**	....	....	....	....	....

QSHL First All-Star Team (1938, 1941)

• WILLIAMS, Burr Burton

D – R. 5'10", 183 lbs. b: Okemah, OK, 8/30/1909 d: 2/12/1981.

Season	Club	League	GP	G	A	Pts	AG	AA	APts	PIM	GP	G	A	Pts	PIM
1927-28	Duluth Hornets	AHA	36	7	3	10	....	....	....	61	5	1	0	1	12
1928-29	Duluth Hornets	AHA	26	5	2	7	....	....	....	44	....	....	....	....	....
1929-30	Tulsa Oilers	AHA	48	9	7	16	....	....	....	77	9	2	*2	*4	*21
1930-31	Tulsa Oilers	AHA	48	16	*16	32	....	....	....	107	4	0	0	0	13
1931-32	Tulsa Oilers	AHA	8	1	2	3	....	....	....	14	....	....	....	....	....
	St. Louis Flyers	AHA	42	10	3	13	....	....	....	72	....	....	....	....	....
1932-33	Duluth-Wichita	AHA	18	8	6	14	....	....	....	30	....	....	....	....	....
	Detroit Olympics	IAHL	14	3	1	4	....	....	....	20	....	....	....	....	....
1933-34	**Detroit Red Wings**	**NHL**	**1**	**0**	**1**	**1**	**0**	**2**	**2**	**12**	**7**	**0**	**0**	**0**	**8**
	Detroit Olympics	IHL	35	5	4	9	....	....	....	50	....	....	....	....	....
1934-35	**St. Louis Eagles**	**NHL**	**9**	**0**	**0**	**0**	**0**	**0**	**0**	**6**	....	....	....	....	....
	Boston Bruins	**NHL**	**7**	**0**	**0**	**0**	**0**	**0**	**0**	**6**	....	....	....	....	....
	Detroit Olympics	IHL	26	5	8	13	....	....	....	36	5	0	0	0	*8
	Detroit Olympics	L-W-S	5	2	0	2	....	....	....	16	....	....	....	....	....
1935-36	Detroit Olympics	IHL	47	7	9	16	....	....	....	53	6	1	1	2	14
1936-37	**Detroit Red Wings**	**NHL**	**2**	**0**	**0**	**0**	**0**	**0**	**0**	**4**	....	....	....	....	....
	Pittsburgh Hornets	IAHL	49	3	10	13	....	....	....	78	5	1	1	2	6
1937-38	New Haven Eagles	IAHL	2	0	0	0	....	....	....	0	....	....	....	....	....
	Pittsburgh Hornets	IAHL	3	0	0	0	....	....	....	2	....	....	....	....	....
	Tulsa Oilers	AHA	33	6	4	10	....	....	....	42	4	0	0	0	8
1938-39	Tulsa Oilers	AHA	48	5	8	13	....	....	....	71	8	0	2	2	*20
1939-40	Tulsa Oilers	AHA	46	8	13	21	....	....	....	39	....	....	....	....	....
1940-41	St. Louis Flyers	AHA	7	0	0	0	....	....	....	12	....	....	....	....	....
	Kansas City Americans	AHA	4	0	0	0	....	....	....	0	....	....	....	....	....
	Omaha Knights	AHA	19	0	1	1	....	....	....	4	....	....	....	....	....
	Minneapolis Millers	AHA	10	4	2	6	....	....	....	4	....	....	....	....	....
	NHL Totals		**19**	**0**	**1**	**1**	**0**	**2**	**2**	**28**	**7**	**0**	**0**	**0**	**8**

IHL Second All-Star Team (1936)

Claimed by **Toronto** from **Tulsa** (AHA) in Inter-League Draft, April 15, 1930. • Rights returned to **Tulsa** (AHA) when American Hockey Association severed working relationship with NHL. Traded to **St. Louis** (AHA) by **Tulsa** (AHA) for cash, December, 1931. Claimed by **Chicago** from **St. Louis** (AHA) in Inter-League Draft, September 2, 1932. Traded to **Duluth** (AHA) by **Chicago** for cash, October, 1932. Traded to **Detroit** by **Duluth** (AHA) for cash, January 29, 1933. Traded to **St. Louis** by **Detroit** for Normie Smith, October 22, 1934. Traded to **Boston** by **St. Louis** for Archie Wilcox, December 2, 1934. Traded to **Detroit** by **Boston** for cash, December 31, 1934. Signed as a free agent by **St. Louis** (AHA), November 14, 1940. Traded to **Kansas City** (AHA) by **St. Louis** (AHA) for cash, December 4, 1940.

• WILLIAMS, Tommy — *see page 1757*

• WILLSON, Don

C – L. 5'8", 157 lbs. b: Chatham, Ont., 1/1/1914.

			REGULAR SEASON								PLAYOFFS				
Season	Club	League	GP	G	A	Pts	AG	AA	APts	PIM	GP	G	A	Pts	PIM
1931-32	Newmarket Redmen	X-Games	7	6	0	6	....	....	....	2	....	....	....	....	....
	Newmarket Redmen	M-Cup	6	11	1	12	....	....	....	....	....	....	....	....	....
1932-33	Newmarket Redmen	X-Games	17	*15	5	*20	....	....	....	....	....	....	....	....	....
	Newmarket Redmen	M-Cup	19	7	2	9	....	....	....	10	....	....	....	....	....
1933-34	St. Michael's Majors	OHA-Jr.	8	9	9	18	....	....	....	0	3	1	1	2	0
	St. Michael's Majors	M-Cup	11	7	12	19	....	....	....	8	....	....	....	....	....
1934-35	Oshawa Chevies	OHA-Jr.	15	10	6	16	....	....	....	8	....	....	....	....	....
1935-36	Earls Court Rangers	Ln-Cup	....	15	7	22	....	....	....	....	....	....	....	....	....
	Earls Court Rangers	Britain	....	22	*16	38	....	....	....	....	....	....	....	....	....
1936-37	Earls Court Rangers	Britain	38	37	*28	65	....	....	....	16	....	....	....	....	....
1937-38	**Montreal Canadiens**	**NHL**	**18**	**2**	**7**	**9**	**3**	**11**	**14**	**0**	**3**	**0**	**0**	**0**	**0**
	Verdun Maple Leafs	QSHL	14	9	13	22	....	....	....	2	....	....	....	....	....
1938-39	**Montreal Canadiens**	**NHL**	**4**	**0**	**0**	**0**	**0**	**0**	**0**	**0**	....	....	....	....	....
	New Haven Eagles	AHL	42	10	10	20	....	....	....	2	....	....	....	....	....
1939-40	New Haven Eagles	IAHL	54	12	32	44	....	....	....	6	3	0	3	3	....
1940-41	New Haven Eagles	AHL	49	11	19	30	....	....	....	6	....	....	....	....	....
1941-42	New Haven Eagles	AHL	53	16	24	40	....	....	....	10	2	0	1	1	0
1942-43	Toronto RCAF	OHA-Sr.	9	7	9	16	....	....	....	2	2	1	0	1	2
1943-44			MILITARY SERVICE												
1944-45			MILITARY SERVICE												
1945-46	Toronto Staffords	OHA-Sr.	16	18	9	27	....	....	....	4	10	6	10	16	0
1946-47	Toronto Staffords	OHA-Sr.	24	2	5	7	....	....	....	20	5	1	2	3	2
1947-48	Toronto Marlboros	OHA-Sr.	11	0	2	2	....	....	....	5	....	....	....	....	....
	NHL Totals		**22**	**2**	**7**	**9**	**3**	**11**	**14**	**0**	**3**	**0**	**0**	**0**	**0**

QSHL First All-Star Team (1938)

• WILSON, Bob Robert Wayne

D – L. 5'9", 165 lbs. b: Sudbury, Ont., 2/18/1934.

Season	Club	League	GP	G	A	Pts	AG	AA	APts	PIM	GP	G	A	Pts	PIM
1952-53	Galt Black Hawks	OHA-Jr.	49	2	10	12	....	....	....	*165	11	1	2	3	24
1953-54	Galt Black Hawks	OHA-Jr.	55	5	17	22	....	....	....	127	....	....	....	....	....
	Chicago Black Hawks	**NHL**	**1**	**0**	**0**	**0**	**0**	**0**	**0**	**0**	....	....	....	....	....
1954-55	Belleville TPT's	EOHL	STATISTICS NOT AVAILABLE												
1955-56	Belleville TPT's	EOHL	34	4	15	19	....	....	....	88	....	....	....	....	....
1956-57	Buffalo Bisons	AHL	1	0	0	0	....	....	....	0	....	....	....	....	....
	Huntington Hornets	IHL	44	3	10	13	....	....	....	72	....	....	....	....	....
	Windsor Bulldogs	OHA-Sr.	9	0	3	3	....	....	....	16	12	0	4	4	45
1957-58	Buffalo Bisons	AHL	4	0	0	0	....	....	....	26	....	....	....	....	....
	Windsor Bulldogs	OHA-Sr.	31	2	4	6	....	....	....	53	....	....	....	....	....
1958-59	Buffalo Bisons	AHL	6	0	2	2	....	....	....	10	....	....	....	....	....
	Trois-Rivieres Lions	QHL	54	1	7	8	....	....	....	170	8	0	3	3	*21
1959-60	Soo Thunderbirds	EPHL	40	3	14	17	....	....	....	60	....	....	....	....	....
	Calgary Stampeders	WHL	21	0	4	4	....	....	....	41	....	....	....	....	....
	Buffalo Bisons	AHL	4	0	1	1	....	....	....	6	....	....	....	....	....
1960-61	S.S. Marie Thunderbirds	EPHL	33	3	9	12	....	....	....	131	....	....	....	....	....
	Buffalo Bisons	AHL	40	0	5	5	....	....	....	53	4	0	1	1	33
1961-62	S.S. Marie Thunderbirds	EPHL	55	3	15	18	....	....	....	120	....	....	....	....	....
	Buffalo Bisons	AHL	....	....	....	....	....	....	....	....	2	0	0	0	0
1962-63	Buffalo Bisons	AHL	60	0	6	6	....	....	....	95	9	0	2	2	15
1963-64	Buffalo Bisons	AHL	63	1	9	10	....	....	....	123	....	....	....	....	....
1964-65	St. Louis Braves	CPHL	13	1	3	4	....	....	....	27	....	....	....	....	....
	Buffalo Bisons	AHL	46	0	10	10	....	....	....	86	9	0	0	0	0
1965-66	Los Angeles Blades	WHL	68	0	7	7	....	....	....	102	....	....	....	....	....
1966-67	Baltimore Clippers	AHL	34	0	1	1	....	....	....	36	1	0	0	0	0
1967-68	Baltimore Clippers	AHL	39	1	5	6	....	....	....	59	....	....	....	....	....
1968-69			REINSTATED AS AN AMATEUR												
1969-70	Belleville Mohawks	OHA-Sr.	7	0	2	2	....	....	....	16	....	....	....	....	....
	NHL Totals		**1**	**0**	**0**	**0**	**0**	**0**	**0**	**0**	....	....	....	....	....

Claimed by **Baltimore** (AHL) from **Chicago** in Reverse Draft, June 15, 1966.

• WILSON, Cully Carol

RW – R. 5'8", 180 lbs. b: Winnipeg, Man., Deceased.

Season	Club	League	GP	G	A	Pts	AG	AA	APts	PIM	GP	G	A	Pts	PIM
1910-11	Winnipeg Falcons	MIPHL	4	4	0	4	....	....	....	....	....	....	....	....	....
	Kenora Thistles	MIPHL	2	0	0	0	....	....	....	....	....	....	....	....	....
	Winnipeg Monarchs	MHL-Sr.	1	2	0	2	....	....	....	....	....	....	....	....	....
1911-12	Winnipeg Falcons	MHL-Sr.	8	11	0	11	....	....	....	....	....	....	....	....	....
1912-13	Toronto Blueshirts	NHA	19	12	0	12	....	....	....	45	....	....	....	....	....
♦1913-14	Toronto Blueshirts	NHA	20	9	4	13	....	....	....	33	2	0	0	0	2
1914-15	Toronto Blueshirts	NHA	20	22	5	27	....	....	....	*138	....	....	....	....	....
1915-16	Toronto Blueshirts	NHA	3	0	0	0	....	....	....	0	....	....	....	....	....
	Seattle Metropolitans	PCHA	18	12	5	17	....	....	....	57	....	....	....	....	....
	PCHA All-Stars	X-Games	1	8	0	8	....	....	....	0	....	....	....	....	....
♦1916-17	Seattle Metropolitans	PCHA	15	13	7	20	....	....	....	58	4	1	4	5	6
1917-18	Seattle Metropolitans	PCHA	17	8	6	14	....	....	....	46	2	0	0	0	3
1918-19	Seattle Metropolitans	PCHA	18	11	5	16	....	....	....	*37	2	1	1	2	0
	Seattle Metropolitans	St-Cup	5	3	1	4	....	....	....	6	....	....	....	....	....
1919-20	**Toronto St. Pats**	**NHL**	**23**	**20**	**6**	**26**	**23**	**20**	**43**	***86**	....	....	....	....	....
1920-21	**Toronto St. Pats**	**NHL**	**8**	**2**	**3**	**5**	**2**	**11**	**13**	**22**	....	....	....	....	....
	Montreal Canadiens	**NHL**	**11**	**6**	**1**	**7**	**8**	**4**	**12**	**29**	....	....	....	....	....
1921-22	**Hamilton Tigers**	**NHL**	**23**	**7**	**9**	**16**	**9**	**29**	**38**	**20**	....	....	....	....	....
1922-23	**Hamilton Tigers**	**NHL**	**23**	**16**	**5**	**21**	**27**	**19**	**46**	**46**	....	....	....	....	....
1923-24	Calgary Tigers	WCHL	30	16	7	23	....	....	....	37	2	1	0	1	4
	Calgary Tigers	St-Cup	2	3	0	3	....	....	....	2	....	....	....	....	....
1924-25	Calgary Tigers	WCHL	28	14	6	20	....	....	....	20	2	1	0	1	6
1925-26	Calgary Tigers	WHL	30	11	4	15	....	....	....	63	....	....	....	....	....
1926-27	**Chicago Black Hawks**	**NHL**	**39**	**8**	**4**	**12**	**14**	**21**	**35**	**40**	**2**	**1**	**0**	**1**	**6**
1927-28	St. Paul Saints	AHA	38	10	2	12	....	....	....	64	....	....	....	....	....
1928-29	St. Paul Saints	AHA	40	10	5	15	....	....	....	40	8	2	*2	4	14
1929-30	St. Paul Saints	AHA	48	7	6	13	....	....	....	57	....	....	....	....	....
1930-31	San Francisco Tigers	Cal-Pro	....	10	2	12	....	....	....	....	....	....	....	....	....
	Duluth Hornets	AHA	24	10	6	16	....	....	....	24	4	0	0	0	2
1931-32	Kansas City Pla-Mors	AHA	34	1	2	3	....	....	....	28	4	0	0	0	2
	NHL Totals		**127**	**59**	**28**	**87**	**83**	**104**	**187**	**243**	**2**	**1**	**0**	**1**	**6**
	Other Major League Totals		218	128	49	177	....	....	....	534	14	4	5	9	21

PCHA First All-Star Team (1919) • WCHL Second All-Star Team (1925)

Signed as a free agent by **Seattle** (PCHA), December, 1915. Signed as a free agent by **Toronto**, November 27, 1919. Loaned to **Montreal Canadiens** by **Toronto**, January 21, 1921. • Suspended for remainder of the 1920-21 season by **Toronto** for refusing to report to NHL club after being recalled from Montreal Canadiens, February 11, 1921. Traded to **Hamilton** by **Toronto** for Eddie Carpenter, November 9, 1921. Traded to **Calgary** (WCHL) by **Hamilton** for cash, November 22, 1923. Traded to **Chicago** by **Calgary** (WHL) for cash, October 25, 1926. Traded to **St. Paul** (AHA) by **Chicago**, September, 1927. Transferred to **Buffalo** (AHA) after **St. Paul** (AHA) franchise relocated, October 5, 1930. Signed as a free agent by **San Francisco** (Cal-Pro), October, 1930. Traded to **Duluth** (AHA) by **San Francisco** (Cal-Pro) for cash, February 7, 1931.

• WILSON, Gord Gordon Allan

LW – L. 6', 175 lbs. b: Port Arthur, Ont., 8/13/1932.

Season	Club	League	GP	G	A	Pts	AG	AA	APts	PIM	GP	G	A	Pts	PIM
			REGULAR SEASON								PLAYOFFS				
1948/51	Port Arthur Bruins	TBJHL	STATISTICS NOT AVAILABLE												
1951-52	Fort William Hurricanes	M-Cup	12	6	4	10	....	....	....	2	....	....	....	....	....
1952-53	Port Arthur Bearcats	TBSHL	STATISTICS NOT AVAILABLE												
	Hershey Bears	AHL	7	3	2	5	....	....	....	0	....	....	....	....	....
1953-54	Hershey Bears	AHL	4	1	0	1	....	....	....	0	....	....	....	....	....
1954-55	Hershey Bears	AHL	63	27	25	52	....	....	....	12	....	....	....	....	....
	Boston Bruins	**NHL**	....	....	....	....	....	....	....	....	**2**	**0**	**0**	**0**	**0**
1955-56	Hershey Bears	AHL	55	27	38	65	....	....	....	8	....	....	....	....	....
1956-57	Quebec Aces	QHL	5	1	1	2	....	....	....	2	....	....	....	....	....
	Victoria Cougars	WHL	14	0	1	1	....	....	....	0	....	....	....	....	....
1957-58	Victoria Cougars	WHL	65	26	38	64	....	....	....	4	....	....	....	....	....
1958-59	Victoria Cougars	WHL	40	12	15	27	....	....	....	0	3	0	1	1	2
1959-60	Victoria Cougars	WHL	43	5	7	12	....	....	....	0	....	....	....	....	....
	Quebec Aces	AHL	15	1	0	1	....	....	....	2	....	....	....	....	....
	NHL Totals		....	....	....	....	....	....	....	....	**2**	**0**	**0**	**0**	**0**

• Missed majority of 1953-54 season recovering from knee inury that originally occurred in training camp and eventually required surgery, January 14, 1954. • Missed majority of 1956-57 season recovering from knee injury suffered in training camp, September 28, 1956.

• WILSON, Hub James

LW – L. 5'10", 180 lbs. b: Ottawa, Ont., 5/13/1909.

Season	Club	League	GP	G	A	Pts	AG	AA	APts	PIM	GP	G	A	Pts	PIM
1930-31	Montreal CPR	MRTHL	STATISTICS NOT AVAILABLE												
	Montreal AAA	MCHL	11	3	1	4	....	....	....	10	2	2	0	2	2
1931-32	**New York Americans**	**NHL**	**2**	**0**	**0**	**0**	**0**	**0**	**0**	**0**	....	....	....	....	....
	New Haven Eagles	Can-Am	37	6	2	8	....	....	....	20	2	0	0	0	0
1932-33	New Haven–Philadelphia	Can-Am	43	13	12	25	....	....	....	44	5	0	0	0	0
1933-34	Quebec Beavers	Can-Am	40	13	10	23	....	....	....	15	....	....	....	....	....
1934-35	Quebec Beavers	Can-Am	47	13	16	29	....	....	....	23	3	0	0	0	0
1935-36	Springfield Indians	Can-Am	38	17	17	34	....	....	....	30	3	1	1	2	0
1936-37	Springfield Indians	IAHL	49	10	11	21	....	....	....	23	5	1	0	1	2
1937-38	Springfield Indians	IAHL	42	12	8	20	....	....	....	24	....	....	....	....	....
1938-39	Springfield Indians	IAHL	25	2	3	5	....	....	....	6	....	....	....	....	....
	Providence Reds	IAHL	28	8	13	21	....	....	....	10	5	0	3	3	0
1939-40	Providence Reds	IAHL	53	15	14	29	....	....	....	20	8	3	3	6	8
1940-41	Providence Reds	AHL	45	14	10	24	....	....	....	14	4	2	0	2	2
1941-42	Philadelphia Rockets	AHL	1	0	0	0	....	....	....	0	....	....	....	....	....
	Pittsburgh Hornets	AHL	48	7	10	17	....	....	....	2	....	....	....	....	....
	NHL Totals		**2**	**0**	**0**	**0**	**0**	**0**	**0**	**0**	....	....	....	....	....

Traded to **Philadelphia** (Can-Am) by **NY Americans** with Norm Clooings for Eddie Burke, February 11, 1933. Traded to **Providence** (IAHL) by **Springfield** (IAHL) with Joe McGoldrick for Norm Schultz and Maurice Croghan, January 9, 1939. Traded to **Pittsburgh** (AHL) by **Providence** (AHL) for cash, October 10, 1941.

• WILSON, Jerry Jerold

C – L. 6'2", 200 lbs. b: Edmonton, Alta., 4/10/1937.

Season	Club	League	GP	G	A	Pts	AG	AA	APts	PIM	GP	G	A	Pts	PIM
1951-52	Winnipeg Canadians	MAHA	20	12	7	19	....	....	....	19	....	....	....	....	....
1952-53	Winnipeg Canadians	WJrHL	STATISTICS NOT AVAILABLE												
1953-54	St. Boniface Canadiens	MJHL	31	12	16	28	....	....	....	50	10	6	8	14	19
	St. Boniface Canadiens	M-Cup	8	2	3	5	....	....	....	4	....	....	....	....	....
1954-55	St. Boniface Canadiens	MJHL	31	35	32	67	....	....	....	59	....	....	....	....	....
1955-56	Montreal Jr. Canadiens	QJHL	DID NOT PLAY – INJURED												
	Montreal Jr. Canadiens	M-Cup	10	3	4	7	....	....	....	10	....	....	....	....	....
1956-57	Hull-Ottawa Canadiens	OHA-Jr.	24	9	19	28	....	....	....	47	....	....	....	....	....
	Montreal Canadiens	**NHL**	**3**	**0**	**0**	**0**	**0**	**0**	**0**	**2**	....	....	....	....	....
	Hull-Ottawa Canadiens	EOHL	14	10	8	18	....	....	....	13	....	....	....	....	....
	Hull-Ottawa Canadiens	QHL	12	5	5	10	....	....	....	8	....	....	....	....	....
	Hull-Ottawa Canadiens	M-Cup	3	0	0	0	....	....	....	0	....	....	....	....	....
1957-58	Hull-Ottawa Canadiens	QHL	DID NOT PLAY – INJURED												
1958-59	Hull-Ottawa Canadiens	QHL	DID NOT PLAY – INJURED												
1959-60	Minneapolis Millers	IHL	2	0	3	3	....	....	....	2	....	....	....	....	....
	NHL Totals		**3**	**0**	**0**	**0**	**0**	**0**	**0**	**2**	....	....	....	....	....

• Father of Carey

• Suffered eventual career-ending knee injury in training camp in September of 1955 that forced him to miss entire 1955-56 regular season and entire 1957-58 and 1958-59 seasons. • Hull-Ottawa played partial schedule against OHA-Jr. teams in 1956-57 that counted for the opposition only.

• WILSON, Johnny John Edward "Iron Man"

LW – L. 5'11", 168 lbs. b: Kincardine, Ont., 6/14/1929.

Season	Club	League	GP	G	A	Pts	AG	AA	APts	PIM	GP	G	A	Pts	PIM
1947-48	Windsor Spitfires	OHA-Jr.	34	23	28	51	....	....	....	15	12	4	6	10	11
	Detroit Hettche	IHL	25	21	13	34	....	....	....	19	....	....	....	....	....
1948-49	Windsor Spitfires	OHA-Jr.	25	30	20	50	....	....	....	24	4	1	0	1	2
	Detroit Hettche	IHL	4	5	4	9	....	....	....	0	13	*16	7	*23	16
1949-50	Omaha Knights	USHL	70	41	39	80	....	....	....	46	7	2	5	7	4
♦	**Detroit Red Wings**	**NHL**	**1**	**0**	**0**	**0**	**0**	**0**	**0**	**0**	**8**	**0**	**1**	**1**	**0**
1950-51	Indianapolis Capitols	AHL	70	34	21	55	....	....	....	48	3	1	0	1	4
	Detroit Red Wings	**NHL**	....	....	....	....	....	....	....	....	**1**	**0**	**0**	**0**	**0**
♦1951-52	**Detroit Red Wings**	**NHL**	**28**	**4**	**5**	**9**	**5**	**6**	**11**	**18**	**8**	**4**	**1**	**5**	**5**
	Indianapolis Capitols	AHL	42	25	14	39	....	....	....	16	....	....	....	....	....
1952-53	**Detroit Red Wings**	**NHL**	**70**	**23**	**19**	**42**	**30**	**23**	**53**	**22**	**6**	**2**	**5**	**7**	**0**
♦1953-54	**Detroit Red Wings**	**NHL**	**70**	**17**	**17**	**34**	**23**	**21**	**44**	**22**	**12**	**3**	**0**	**3**	**0**
♦1954-55	**Detroit Red Wings**	**NHL**	**70**	**12**	**15**	**27**	**15**	**17**	**32**	**14**	**11**	**0**	**1**	**1**	**0**
1955-56	**Chicago Black Hawks**	**NHL**	**70**	**24**	**9**	**33**	**33**	**11**	**44**	**12**	....	....	....	....	....
1956-57	**Chicago Black Hawks**	**NHL**	**70**	**18**	**30**	**48**	**23**	**33**	**56**	**24**	....	....	....	....	....
1957-58	**Detroit Red Wings**	**NHL**	**70**	**12**	**27**	**39**	**15**	**28**	**43**	**14**	**4**	**2**	**1**	**3**	**0**
1958-59	**Detroit Red Wings**	**NHL**	**70**	**11**	**17**	**28**	**13**	**17**	**30**	**18**	....	....	....	....	....
1959-60	**Toronto Maple Leafs**	**NHL**	**70**	**15**	**16**	**31**	**18**	**16**	**34**	**8**	**10**	**1**	**2**	**3**	**2**
1960-61	**Toronto Maple Leafs**	**NHL**	**3**	**0**	**1**	**1**	**0**	**1**	**1**	**0**	....	....	....	....	....
	Rochester Americans	AHL	2	2	2	4	....	....	....	0	....	....	....	....	....
	New York Rangers	**NHL**	**56**	**14**	**12**	**26**	**16**	**12**	**28**	**24**	....	....	....	....	....
1961-62	**New York Rangers**	**NHL**	**40**	**11**	**3**	**14**	**13**	**3**	**16**	**14**	**6**	**2**	**2**	**4**	**4**
	NHL Totals		**688**	**161**	**171**	**332**	**204**	**188**	**392**	**190**	**66**	**14**	**13**	**27**	**11**

• Brother of Larry • USHL Second All-Star Team (1950) • Played in NHL All-Star Game (1954, 1956)

Traded to **Chicago** by **Detroit** with Tony Leswick, Glen Skov and Benny Woit for Dave Creighton, Gord Hollingworth, John McCormack and Jerry Toppazzini, May 27, 1955. Traded to **Detroit** by **Chicago** with Forbes Kennedy, Bill Preston and Hank Bassen for Ted Lindsay and Glenn Hall, July 23, 1957. Traded to **Toronto** by **Detroit** with Frank Roggeveen for Barry Cullen, June 9, 1959. Traded to **NY Rangers** by **Toronto** with Pat Hannigan for Eddie Shack, November 7, 1960.

• WILSON, Larry Lawrence

C – L. 5'11", 160 lbs. b: Kincardine, Ont., 10/23/1930 d: 8/16/1979.

Season	Club	League	GP	G	A	Pts	AG	AA	APts	PIM	GP	G	A	Pts	PIM
1947-48	Windsor Spitfires	OHA-Jr.	12	4	13	17	....	....	....	2	12	3	3	6	9
	Windsor Hettche	IHL	25	13	29	42	....	....	....	6	....	....	....	....	....
1948-49	Windsor Spitfires	OHA-Jr.	45	23	37	60	....	....	....	22	4	1	1	2	2
	Detroit Hettche	IHL	9	10	7	17	....	....	....	6	13	4	*17	21	20
1949-50	Omaha Knights	USHL	70	22	57	79	....	....	....	51	7	2	6	8	10
♦	**Detroit Red Wings**	**NHL**	**1**	**0**	**0**	**0**	**0**	**0**	**0**	**2**	**4**	**0**	**0**	**0**	**0**
1950-51	Indianapolis Capitols	AHL	53	12	23	35	....	....	....	14	3	0	1	1	0
1951-52	**Detroit Red Wings**	**NHL**	**5**	**0**	**0**	**0**	**0**	**0**	**0**	**4**	....	....	....	....	....
	Indianapolis Capitols	AHL	62	19	40	59	....	....	....	30	....	....	....	....	....
1952-53	**Detroit Red Wings**	**NHL**	**15**	**0**	**4**	**4**	**0**	**5**	**5**	**6**	....	....	....	....	....
	Edmonton Flyers	WHL	49	17	29	46	....	....	....	24	14	6	7	13	4
1953-54	**Chicago Black Hawks**	**NHL**	**66**	**9**	**33**	**42**	**12**	**40**	**52**	**22**	....	....	....	....	....
1954-55	**Chicago Black Hawks**	**NHL**	**63**	**12**	**11**	**23**	**15**	**13**	**28**	**39**	....	....	....	....	....
1955-56	**Chicago Black Hawks**	**NHL**	**2**	**0**	**0**	**0**	**0**	**0**	**0**	**2**	....	....	....	....	....
	Buffalo Bisons	AHL	62	39	39	78	....	....	....	74	5	0	2	2	4
1956-57	Buffalo Bisons	AHL	64	22	45	67	....	....	....	71	....	....	....	....	....
1957-58	Buffalo Bisons	AHL	70	26	53	79	....	....	....	48	....	....	....	....	....
1958-59	Buffalo Bisons	AHL	66	24	39	63	....	....	....	26	11	0	5	5	7
1959-60	Buffalo Bisons	AHL	64	33	45	78	....	....	....	18	....	....	....	....	....
1960-61	Buffalo Bisons	AHL	72	30	54	84	....	....	....	62	4	0	2	2	0
1961-62	Buffalo Bisons	AHL	68	9	25	34	....	....	....	28	10	3	0	3	4
1962-63	Buffalo Bisons	AHL	72	16	29	45	....	....	....	30	13	1	3	4	0
1963-64	Buffalo Bisons	AHL	71	17	26	43	....	....	....	38	....	....	....	....	....
1964-65	Buffalo Bisons	AHL	31	0	7	7	....	....	....	12	....	....	....	....	....
1965-66	Buffalo Bisons	AHL	38	13	12	25	....	....	....	8	....	....	....	....	....
1966-67	Buffalo Bisons	AHL	65	28	37	65	....	....	....	60	....	....	....	....	....
1967-68	Buffalo Bisons	AHL	41	10	18	28	....	....	....	24	....	....	....	....	....
1968-69	Dayton Gems	IHL	50	19	42	61	....	....	....	36	....	....	....	....	....
1969-70	Dayton Gems	IHL	68	20	43	63	....	....	....	54	13	2	4	6	0
	NHL Totals		**152**	**21**	**48**	**69**	**27**	**58**	**85**	**75**	**4**	**0**	**0**	**0**	**0**

• Brother of Johnny • Father of Ron • AHL Second All-Star Team (1956, 1960)

Traded to **Chicago** by **Detroit** with Larry Zeidel and Lou Jankowski for cash, August 12, 1953. Traded to **Buffalo** (AHL) by **Chicago** for cash, August 12, 1957.

• WILSON, Wally Walter Lloyd

C – R. 5'11", 165 lbs. b: Berwick, N.S., 5/25/1921.

Season	Club	League	GP	G	A	Pts	AG	AA	APts	PIM	GP	G	A	Pts	PIM
1938-39	Oshawa Bees	OHA-B	STATISTICS NOT AVAILABLE												
1939-40	Oshawa Generals	OHA-Jr.	11	10	9	19	....	....	....	0	15	2	4	6	4
	Oshawa Generals	M-Cup	6	8	8	16	....	....	....	2	....	....	....	....	....
1940-41	Oshawa Generals	OHA-Jr.	16	15	7	22	....	....	....	27	12	14	*14	*28	7
	Oshawa Generals	M-Cup	5	0	8	8	....	....	....	6	....	....	....	....	....
1941-42	Hershey Bears	AHL	48	16	20	36	....	....	....	8	10	4	1	5	2
1942-43	Toronto RCAF	OHA-Sr.	10	13	12	25	....	....	....	10	9	3	*16	*19	18
	Toronto RCAF	Al-Cup	4	2	4	6	....	....	....	2	....	....	....	....	....
1943-44	Toronto RCAF	OHA-Sr.	11	6	5	11	....	....	....	2	....	....	....	....	....
	Camp Borden RCAF	NDHL	STATISTICS NOT AVAILABLE												
	Brantford RCAF	NDHL	STATISTICS NOT AVAILABLE												
1944-45	Quebec Aces	QSHL	3	5	0	5	....	....	....	4	3	1	5	6	0
	Quebec Aces	Al-Cup	3	3	1	4	....	....	....	2	....	....	....	....	....
1945-46	Pittsburgh Hornets	AHL	57	34	41	75	....	....	....	32	5	4	6	10	2
1946-47	Pittsburgh Hornets	AHL	51	21	30	51	....	....	....	38	12	5	5	10	8
1947-48	**Boston Bruins**	**NHL**	**53**	**11**	**8**	**19**	**14**	**10**	**24**	**18**	**1**	**0**	**0**	**0**	**0**
	NHL Totals		**53**	**11**	**8**	**19**	**14**	**10**	**24**	**18**	**1**	**0**	**0**	**0**	**0**

Claimed by **Toronto** from **Hershey** (AHL) in Inter-League Draft, June 14, 1945. Traded to **Boston** by **Toronto** for cash, August 17, 1947.

• WISEMAN, Eddie Edward Randall

RW – R. 5'7", 160 lbs. b: Newcastle, N.B., 12/28/1912 d: 5/6/1977.

Season	Club	League	GP	G	A	Pts	AG	AA	APts	PIM	GP	G	A	Pts	PIM
1924/28	Regina Crescents	RJrHL	STATISTICS NOT AVAILABLE												
1928-29	Regina Argos	S-SJHL	5	1	1	2	....	....	....	2	....	....	....	....	....
1929-30	Regina Pats	S-SJHL	3	1	0	1	....	....	....	4	....	....	....	....	....
1930-31	Chicago Shamrocks	AHA	44	8	11	19	....	....	....	16	....	....	....	....	....
1931-32	Chicago Shamrocks	AHA	44	17	17	*34	....	....	....	26	4	2	2	4	0
1932-33	**Detroit Red Wings**	**NHL**	**43**	**8**	**8**	**16**	**14**	**17**	**31**	**16**	**2**	**0**	**0**	**0**	**0**
1933-34	**Detroit Red Wings**	**NHL**	**48**	**5**	**9**	**14**	**9**	**19**	**28**	**13**	**7**	**0**	**1**	**1**	**4**
	Detroit Olympics	IHL	1	1	0	1	....	....	....	0	....	....	....	....	....
1934-35	**Detroit Red Wings**	**NHL**	**39**	**11**	**13**	**24**	**18**	**23**	**41**	**14**	....	....	....	....	....
	Detroit Olympics	IHL	12	3	3	6	....	....	....	8	....	....	....	....	....
	Detroit Olympics	L-W-S	5	1	2	3	....	....	....	12	....	....	....	....	....
1935-36	**Detroit Red Wings**	**NHL**	**1**	**0**	**0**	**0**	**0**	**0**	**0**	**0**	....	....	....	....	....
	Detroit Olympics	IHL	3	2	1	3	....	....	....	10	....	....	....	....	....
	New York Americans	**NHL**	**44**	**12**	**16**	**28**	**23**	**30**	**53**	**15**	**4**	**2**	**1**	**3**	**0**
1936-37	**New York Americans**	**NHL**	**44**	**14**	**19**	**33**	**24**	**35**	**59**	**12**	....	....	....	....	....
1937-38	**New York Americans**	**NHL**	**48**	**18**	**14**	**32**	**30**	**23**	**53**	**32**	**6**	**0**	**4**	**4**	**10**
1938-39	**New York Americans**	**NHL**	**47**	**12**	**21**	**33**	**21**	**33**	**54**	**8**	**2**	**0**	**0**	**0**	**0**
1939-40	**New York Americans**	**NHL**	**31**	**5**	**13**	**18**	**8**	**20**	**28**	**8**	....	....	....	....	....
	Boston Bruins	**NHL**	**18**	**2**	**6**	**8**	**3**	**9**	**12**	**0**	**6**	**2**	**1**	**3**	**2**
♦1940-41	**Boston Bruins**	**NHL**	**48**	**16**	**24**	**40**	**25**	**35**	**60**	**10**	**11**	***6**	**2**	**8**	**0**
1941-42	**Boston Bruins**	**NHL**	**45**	**12**	**22**	**34**	**16**	**26**	**42**	**8**	**5**	**0**	**1**	**1**	**0**
1942-43	Saskatoon RCAF	SSHL	15	8	10	18	....	....	....	11	1	1	1	2	0

Season	Club	League	GP	G	A	Pts	AG	AA	APts	PIM	GP	G	A	Pts	PIM
			REGULAR SEASON								PLAYOFFS				
1943-44			MILITARY SERVICE												
1944-45	Montreal Royals	QSHL	1	1	0	1	....	....	....	0	1	0	0	0	0
1945-46	Moose Jaw Canucks	SJHL	DID NOT PLAY – COACHING												
	NHL Totals		**456**	**115**	**165**	**280**	**191**	**270**	**461**	**136**	**43**	**10**	**10**	**20**	**16**

Signed as a free agent by **Chicago** (AHA), October 29, 1930. NHL rights transferred to **Detroit** from **Chicago Shamrocks** (AHA) after AHA club owners purchased Detroit (NHL and IHL) franchises, September 2, 1932. Traded to **NY Americans** by **Detroit** for Fred Hergert and $7,500, November 21, 1935. Traded to **Boston** by **NY Americans** with $5,000 for Eddie Shore, January 25, 1940.

• WITIUK, Steve

RW – R. 5'7", 165 lbs. b: Winnipeg, Man., 1/8/1929.

Season	Club	League	GP	G	A	Pts	AG	AA	APts	PIM	GP	G	A	Pts	PIM
1946-47	Winnipeg Rangers	MJHL	16	5	6	11	....	....	....	4	2	0	1	1	2
1947-48	Winnipeg Black Hawks	MJHL	22	12	5	17	....	....	....	10	....	....	....	....	....
1948-49	Winnipeg Black Hawks	MJHL	28	16	20	36	....	....	....	49	....	....	....	....	....
1949-50	Regina Caps	WCSHL	8	0	1	1	....	....	....	0	....	....	....	....	....
	Kamloops Elks	OSHL	33	20	7	27	....	....	....	45	7	6	6	12	6
1950-51	Edmonton Flyers	WCMHL	48	22	23	45	....	....	....	71	8	2	2	4	10
1951-52	**Chicago Black Hawks**	**NHL**	**33**	**3**	**8**	**11**	**4**	**10**	**14**	**14**	....	....	....	....	....
	St. Louis Flyers	AHL	14	5	2	7	....	....	....	11	....	....	....	....	....
1952-53	Calgary Stampeders	WHL	60	21	20	41	....	....	....	66	1	0	0	0	0
1953-54	Calgary Stampeders	WHL	69	19	36	55	....	....	....	52	18	3	6	9	20
	Calgary Stampeders	Ed-Cup	7	3	1	4	....	....	....	2	....	....	....	....	....
1954-55	Calgary Stampeders	WHL	60	26	37	63	....	....	....	61	9	5	2	7	14
1955-56	Calgary Stampeders	WHL	66	30	34	64	....	....	....	76	8	5	6	11	12
1956-57	Calgary Stampeders	WHL	47	17	18	35	....	....	....	55	....	....	....	....	....
1957-58	Calgary–Winnipeg	WHL	65	27	46	73	....	....	....	43	7	0	2	2	2
1958-59	Winnipeg Warriors	WHL	62	12	33	45	....	....	....	43	6	1	4	5	2
1959-60	Winnipeg Warriors	WHL	62	20	27	47	....	....	....	40	....	....	....	....	....
1960-61	Spokane Spokes	WHL	67	28	24	52	....	....	....	79	4	0	1	1	4
1961-62	Spokane Comets	WHL	64	26	40	66	....	....	....	49	16	4	9	13	34
1962-63	Spokane Comets	WHL	66	21	33	54	....	....	....	96	....	....	....	....	....
1963-64	Denver Invaders	WHL	70	25	28	53	....	....	....	62	4	0	0	0	10
1964-65	Victoria Maple Leafs	WHL	56	11	21	32	....	....	....	37	11	2	2	4	16
1965-66	Victoria Maple Leafs	WHL	72	6	16	22	....	....	....	47	3	0	0	0	0
1966-67	Victoria Maple Leafs	WHL	59	5	10	15	....	....	....	34	....	....	....	....	....
1967-68	Spokane Jets	WIHL	41	20	34	54	....	....	....	57	8	7	*9	16	13
	Spokane Jets	Al-Cup	4	0	1	1	....	....	....	9	....	....	....	....	....
1968-69	Spokane Jets	WIHL	40	6	18	24	....	....	....	30	6	2	1	3	2
	NHL Totals		**33**	**3**	**8**	**11**	**4**	**10**	**14**	**14**	....	....	....	....	....

Signed as a free agent by **Chicago**, October 1, 1951. Traded to **Toronto** (Winnipeg-WHL) by **Chicago** (Calgary-WHL) for George Ford and Murray Wilkie, January, 1958. Rights transferred to **Toronto** after NHL club purchased **Spokane** (WHL) franchise, June 4, 1963. Transferred to **Phoenix** (WHL) after **Victoria** (WHL) franchise relocated, August, 1967. Traded to **Toronto** by **Phoenix** for Walt McKechnie, October 15, 1967.

• WOIT, Benny

Benedict Francis

RW/D – R. 5'11", 195 lbs. b: Fort William, Ont., 1/7/1928.

Season	Club	League	GP	G	A	Pts	AG	AA	APts	PIM	GP	G	A	Pts	PIM
1944-45	Port Arthur Flyers	TBJHL	11	3	6	9	....	....	....	6	3	0	0	0	4
1945-46	Port Arthur Flyers	TBJHL	4	1	1	2	....	....	....	8	10	0	6	6	10
1946-47	St. Michael's Majors	OHA-Jr.	27	5	16	21	....	....	....	42	9	0	1	1	16
	St. Michael's Majors	M-Cup	10	1	6	7	....	....	....	10	....	....	....	....	....
1947-48	Port Arthur Bruins	TBJHL	8	3	11	14	....	....	....	21	5	4	0	4	*26
	Port Arthur Bruins	M-Cup	17	5	7	12	....	....	....	41	....	....	....	....	....
1948-49	Indianapolis Capitols	AHL	68	3	12	15	....	....	....	30	2	0	1	1	0
1949-50	Indianapolis Capitols	AHL	70	7	17	24	....	....	....	29	8	2	0	2	4
1950-51	Indianapolis Capitols	AHL	69	8	22	30	....	....	....	40	3	0	0	0	0
	Detroit Red Wings	**NHL**	**2**	**0**	**0**	**0**	**0**	**0**	**0**	**2**	**4**	**0**	**0**	**0**	**2**
♦1951-52	**Detroit Red Wings**	**NHL**	**58**	**3**	**8**	**11**	**4**	**10**	**14**	**20**	**8**	**1**	**1**	**2**	**2**
1952-53	**Detroit Red Wings**	**NHL**	**70**	**1**	**5**	**6**	**1**	**6**	**7**	**40**	**6**	**1**	**3**	**4**	**0**
♦1953-54	**Detroit Red Wings**	**NHL**	**70**	**0**	**2**	**2**	**0**	**2**	**2**	**38**	**12**	**0**	**1**	**1**	**8**
♦1954-55	**Detroit Red Wings**	**NHL**	**62**	**2**	**3**	**5**	**3**	**3**	**6**	**22**	**11**	**0**	**1**	**1**	**6**
1955-56	**Chicago Black Hawks**	**NHL**	**63**	**1**	**8**	**9**	**1**	**9**	**10**	**46**	....	....	....	....	....
1956-57	**Chicago Black Hawks**	**NHL**	**9**	**0**	**0**	**0**	**0**	**0**	**0**	**2**	....	....	....	....	....
	Rochester Americans	AHL	47	4	12	16	....	....	....	54	8	1	1	2	6
1957-58	Rochester Americans	AHL	52	2	7	9	....	....	....	40	....	....	....	....	....
1958-59	Spokane Comets	WHL	61	5	9	14	....	....	....	54	4	0	3	3	4
1959-60	Providence Reds	AHL	30	1	2	3	....	....	....	16	5	1	1	2	0
1960-61	Providence Reds	AHL	58	2	10	12	....	....	....	26	....	....	....	....	....
1961-62	Kingston Frontenacs	EPHL	5	0	1	1	....	....	....	6	1	0	0	0	6
	Clinton Comets	EHL	51	8	23	31	....	....	....	51	6	1	2	3	4
1962-63	Clinton Comets	EHL	63	8	15	23	....	....	....	57	13	3	6	9	12
1963-64	Clinton Comets	EHL	69	12	35	47	....	....	....	78	15	5	7	12	31
1964-65	Clinton Comets	EHL	71	4	36	40	....	....	....	68	11	0	4	4	4
1965-66	Jersey Devils	EHL	38	3	19	22	....	....	....	60	....	....	....	....	....
1966-67	Westfort Hurricanes	TBJHL	DID NOT PLAY – COACHING												
1967-68	Port Arthur Bearcats	TBSHL	12	3	7	10	....	....	....	0	....	....	....	....	....
	Port Arthur Bearcats	M-Cup	3	0	1	1	....	....	....	2	....	....	....	....	....
1968-69	Fort William Beavers	TBSHL	10	0	6	6	....	....	....	2	....	....	....	....	....
	NHL Totals		**334**	**7**	**26**	**33**	**9**	**30**	**39**	**170**	**41**	**2**	**6**	**8**	**18**

EHL First All-Star Team (1962, 1963) • EHL Second All-Star Team (1964) • EHL North First All-Star Team (1965) • Played in NHL All-Star Game (1954)

Traded to **Chicago** by **Detroit** with Tony Leswick, Glen Skov and John Wilson for Dave Creighton, Gord Hollingworth, John McCormack and Jerry Toppazzini, May 27, 1955. Claimed on waivers by **Montreal** from **Chicago**, November, 1956. Traded to **Jersey** (EHL) by **Clinton** (EHL) with Norm Defelice, Hec Lalande and Ted Sydlowski for Ed Babiuk, Pat Kelly and Borden Smith, August, 1965.

• WOJCIECHOWSKI, Steve

Steven

RW – R. 5'8", 158 lbs. b: Fort William, Ont., 12/25/1922.

Season	Club	League	GP	G	A	Pts	AG	AA	APts	PIM	GP	G	A	Pts	PIM
1938-39	Fort William Maroons	TBJHL	18	14	*11	*25	....	....	....	20	5	4	0	4	7
1939-40	Port Arthur Bruins	TBJHL	16	16	9	*25	....	....	....	2	....	....	....	....	....
	Port Arthur Bearcats	TBSHL	1	0	0	0	....	....	....	0	....	....	....	....	....
1940-41	Port Arthur Bruins	TBJHL	16	16	*21	37	....	....	....	29	6	*8	4	12	4
1941-42	Port Arthur Bruins	TBJHL	18	22	*41	63	....	....	....	55	3	4	5	9	13
	Port Arthur Bearcats	TBSHL	1	1	1	2	....	....	....	0	....	....	....	....	....
	Port Arthur Bearcats	Al-Cup	17	10	7	17	....	....	....	17	....	....	....	....	....
1942-43	St. Catharines Saints	OHA-Sr.	17	21	15	36	....	....	....	7	3	1	1	2	0
1943-44	Winnipeg Army	WNDHL	10	8	8	16	....	....	....	2	....	....	....	....	....

Season	Club	League	GP	G	A	Pts	AG	AA	APts	PIM	GP	G	A	Pts	PIM
			REGULAR SEASON								PLAYOFFS				
1944-45	**Detroit Red Wings**	**NHL**	**49**	**19**	**20**	**39**	**19**	**23**	**42**	**17**	**6**	**0**	**1**	**1**	**0**
1945-46	Indianapolis Capitols	AHL	30	14	20	34	....	....	....	14	....	....	....	....	....
	Omaha Knights	USHL	17	4	10	14	....	....	....	4	7	1	2	3	2
1946-47	**Detroit Red Wings**	**NHL**	**5**	**0**	**0**	**0**	**0**	**0**	**0**	**0**	....	....	....	....	....
	Indianapolis Capitols	AHL	56	21	24	45	....	....	....	4	....	....	....	....	....
1947-48	Philadelphia Rockets	AHL	68	37	29	66	....	....	....	27	....	....	....	....	....
1948-49	Philadelphia Rockets	AHL	68	29	28	57	....	....	....	37	....	....	....	....	....
1949-50	Cleveland Barons	AHL	47	21	23	44	....	....	....	12	6	3	3	6	4
1950-51	Cleveland Barons	AHL	58	26	30	56	....	....	....	24	....	....	....	....	....
1951-52	Cleveland Barons	AHL	68	*37	41	78	....	....	....	42	5	2	0	2	2
1952-53	Cleveland Barons	AHL	64	37	31	68	....	....	....	16	10	1	4	5	2
1953-54	Buffalo Bisons	AHL	70	26	32	58	....	....	....	18	3	0	1	1	2
1954-55	Buffalo Bisons	AHL	17	5	4	9	....	....	....	2	....	....	....	....	....
	S.S. Marie Greyhounds	NOHA	23	10	7	17	....	....	....	13	....	....	....	....	....
	NHL Totals		**54**	**19**	**20**	**39**	**19**	**23**	**42**	**17**	**6**	**0**	**1**	**1**	**0**

• Also known as Steve Wochy • AHL First All-Star Team (1952)

Traded to **Cleveland** (AHL) by **Detroit** for cash, June 15, 1947. Traded to **Philadelphia** (AHL) by **Cleveland** (AHL) for cash, August, 1947. Traded to **Cleveland** (AHL) by **Philadelphia** (AHL) for cash, August, 1949. Traded to **Buffalo** (AHL) by **Cleveland** (AHL) for Don Ashbee, July, 1953. Traded to **Sault Ste. Marie** (NOHA) by **Buffalo** (AHL) for cash, December, 1954.

• WOOD, Robert

Robert Owen

D – L. 6'1", 185 lbs. b: Lethbridge, Alta., 7/9/1930.

Season	Club	League	GP	G	A	Pts	AG	AA	APts	PIM	GP	G	A	Pts	PIM
1946-47	Lethbridge Native Sons	AJHL	1	0	1	1	....	....	....	8	....	....	....	....	....
1947-48	Lethbridge Native Sons	AJHL	22	5	9	14	....	....	....	26	6	0	0	0	2
1948-49	Lethbridge Native Sons	WCJHL	25	1	7	8	....	....	....	48	6	0	3	3	14
1949-50	Lethbridge Native Sons	WCJHL	37	3	24	27	....	....	....	56	....	....	....	....	....
1950-51	**New York Rangers**	**NHL**	**1**	**0**	**0**	**0**	**0**	**0**	**0**	**0**	....	....	....	....	....
	New York Rovers	EAHL	53	3	4	7	....	....	....	77	5	0	0	0	14
	NHL Totals		**1**	**0**	**0**	**0**	**0**	**0**	**0**	**0**	....	....	....	....	....

• WOYTOWICH, Bob

— see page 1765

• WYCHERLEY, Ralph

Ralph Harold "Bus"

LW – L. 6', 185 lbs. b: Saskatoon, Sask., 2/26/1920.

Season	Club	League	GP	G	A	Pts	AG	AA	APts	PIM	GP	G	A	Pts	PIM
1937-38	Saskatoon Wesleys	SCJHL	2	0	1	1	....	....	....	5	....	....	....	....	....
1938-39	Brandon Elks	MJHL	15	*25	11	*36	....	....	....	15	7	*7	2	9	6
	Brandon Elks	M-Cup	6	*7	3	*10	....	....	....	4	....	....	....	....	....
1939-40	Brandon Elks	MJHL	24	24	12	36	....	....	....	14	3	0	1	1	2
1940-41	**New York Americans**	**NHL**	**26**	**4**	**5**	**9**	**6**	**7**	**13**	**4**	....	....	....	....	....
	Springfield Indians	AHL	13	5	4	9	....	....	....	7	....	....	....	....	....
1941-42	**Brooklyn Americans**	**NHL**	**2**	**0**	**2**	**2**	**0**	**2**	**2**	**2**	....	....	....	....	....
	Springfield Indians	AHL	12	3	5	8	....	....	....	6	....	....	....	....	....
	Philadelphia Rockets	AHL	21	10	8	18	....	....	....	6	....	....	....	....	....
	Hershey Bears	AHL	5	1	4	5	....	....	....	0	3	0	1	1	0
1942-43	Toronto RCAF	OHA-Sr.	7	4	2	6	....	....	....	2	9	12	7	*19	10
	Toronto RCAF	Al-Cup	4	5	5	10	....	....	....	4	....	....	....	....	....
1943-44	Toronto RCAF	OHA-Sr.	6	6	1	7	....	....	....	2	....	....	....	....	....
	Toronto Fuels	TMHL	8	13	7	20	....	....	....	7	6	8	8	16	4
1944-45	Toronto RCAF	TNDHL	2	2	2	4	....	....	....	0	....	....	....	....	....
	Toronto Orphans	TMHL	8	16	10	26	....	....	....	4	....	....	....	....	....
1945-46			MILITARY SERVICE												
1946-47	Hershey Bears	AHL	4	0	0	0	....	....	....	0	....	....	....	....	....
	Tulsa Oilers	USHL	51	32	22	54	....	....	....	6	5	2	1	3	0
1947-48	Minneapolis Millers	USHL	61	40	38	78	....	....	....	4	10	3	7	10	0
1948-49	Cleveland Barons	AHL	39	16	18	34	....	....	....	8	4	0	0	0	0
1949-50	Kansas City Mohawks	USHL	63	30	32	62	....	....	....	5	3	0	0	0	0
1950-51	Toronto Marlboros	OMHL	30	14	18	32	....	....	....	8	3	1	0	1	2
	NHL Totals		**28**	**4**	**7**	**11**	**6**	**9**	**15**	**6**	....	....	....	....	....

USHL First All-Star Team (1947, 1948)

• Statistics for Saskatoon Wesleys (1937-38) are for playoffs only. Signed as a free agent by **NY Americans**, October 11, 1940. Traded to **Chicago** (Kansas City-USHL) by **Cleveland** (AHL) with Doug Baldwin for Al Rollins, September 13, 1949.

• WYLIE, Bill

William Vance "Wiggie"

C – L. 5'7", 145 lbs. b: Galt, Ont., 7/15/1928 d: 11/24/1983.

Season	Club	League	GP	G	A	Pts	AG	AA	APts	PIM	GP	G	A	Pts	PIM
1944-45	Brantford Lions	OHA-B	12	10	20	30	....	....	....	4	4	2	1	3	2
1945-46	Brantford Lions	OHA-B	STATISTICS NOT AVAILABLE												
1946-47	Galt Red Wings	OHA-Jr.	24	11	23	34	....	....	....	16	8	3	6	9	0
1947-48	Galt Rockets	OHA-Jr.	28	26	27	53	....	....	....	10	8	6	10	16	6
1948-49	Quebec Aces	QSHL	55	18	33	51	....	....	....	22	1	0	0	0	2
1949-50	Quebec Aces	QSHL	55	15	24	39	....	....	....	14	12	3	*12	15	6
1950-51	**New York Rangers**	**NHL**	**1**	**0**	**0**	**0**	**0**	**0**	**0**	**0**	....	....	....	....	....
	New York Rovers	EAHL	48	23	35	58	....	....	....	10	6	1	5	6	0
	St. Paul Saints	USHL	2	1	1	2	....	....	....	0	....	....	....	....	....
1951-52	Cincinnati Mohawks	AHL	68	21	32	53	....	....	....	10	7	2	3	5	0
1952-53	Vancouver Canucks	WHL	48	9	19	28	....	....	....	4	....	....	....	....	....
1953-54	Vancouver Canucks	WHL	54	13	26	39	....	....	....	6	13	1	6	7	0
1954-55	Vancouver Canucks	WHL	56	9	35	44	....	....	....	4	5	1	2	3	2
1955-56	Vancouver Canucks	WHL	49	13	31	44	....	....	....	14	....	....	....	....	....
1956-57	Vancouver Canucks	WHL	68	18	52	70	....	....	....	16	....	....	....	....	....
1957-58	Kitchener Dutchmen	NOHA	50	18	45	63	....	....	....	8	14	6	*14	*20	0
	Kitchener Dutchmen	Al-Cup	5	0	1	1	....	....	....	0	....	....	....	....	....
1958-59	Kitchener Dutchmen	NOHA	54	20	55	75	....	....	....	4	11	5	*9	14	0
1959-60	Kitchener Dutchmen	OHA-Sr.	20	5	13	18	....	....	....	0	8	0	6	6	0
1960-61	Galt Terriers	X-Games	4	4	8	12	....	....	....	2	....	....	....	....	....
	Galt Terriers	Al-Cup	12	4	12	16	....	....	....	0	....	....	....	....	....
1961-62	Galt Terriers	OHA-Sr.	19	13	18	31	....	....	....	2	....	....	....	....	....
1962-63	Galt Terriers	OHA-Sr.	9	3	4	7	....	....	....	0	....	....	....	....	....
	NHL Totals		**1**	**0**	**0**	**0**	**0**	**0**	**0**	**0**	....	....	....	....	....

EAHL Second All-Star Team (1951)

• YACKEL, Ken   Kenneth James   USHOF

RW – R. 5'11", 195 lbs.   b: St. Paul, MN, 3/5/1932   d: 7/12/1998.

			REGULAR SEASON								PLAYOFFS				
Season	Club	League	GP	G	A	Pts	AG	AA	APts	PIM	GP	G	A	Pts	PIM
1950-51	St. Paul 7-Up-Kopps	AAHL	24	15	14	29	....	....	....	55	....	....	....	....	....
1951-52	United Staes	Nt-Team	STATISTICS NOT AVAILABLE												
	United States	Olympics	8	6	0	6	....	....	....	2	....	....	....	....	....
1952-53	University of Minnesota	WCHA	27	10	16	26	....	....	....	40	....	....	....	....	....
1953-54	University of Minnesota	WCHA	27	11	17	28	....	....	....	62	....	....	....	....	....
1954-55	University of Minnesota	WCHA	28	18	18	36	....	....	....	51	....	....	....	....	....
1955-56	University of Minnesota	WCHA	30	31	27	58	....	....	....	102	....	....	....	....	....
	Cleveland Barons	AHL	3	0	1	1	....	....	....	6	....	....	....	....	....
1956-57	Edina Hornets	H.S.	DID NOT PLAY – COACHING												
1957-58	Saskatoon–St. Paul	WHL	21	12	8	20	....	....	....	30	....	....	....	....	....
1958-59	**Boston Bruins**	**NHL**	**6**	**0**	**0**	**0**	**0**	**0**	**0**	**2**	**2**	**0**	**0**	**0**	**2**
	Providence Reds	AHL	66	16	33	49	....	....	....	83	....	....	....	....	....
1959-60	Providence Reds	AHL	57	14	21	35	....	....	....	68	5	2	1	3	16
1960-61	Minneapolis Millers	IHL	72	40	74	*114	....	....	....	102	8	5	2	7	8
1961-62	Minneapolis Millers	IHL	66	50	48	98	....	....	....	103	5	1	3	4	13
1962-63	Minneapolis Millers	IHL	70	40	60	100	....	....	....	70	12	7	11	18	12
1963-64	Muskegon Zephyrs	IHL	1	0	0	0	....	....	....	0	....	....	....	....	....
	NHL Totals		**6**	**0**	**0**	**0**	**0**	**0**	**0**	**2**	**2**	**0**	**0**	**0**	**2**

WCHA First All-Star Team (1954, 1955, 1956) • NCAA West First All-American Team (1954) • NCAA Championship All-Tournament Team (1954) • IHL First All-Star Team (1961, 1962) • Won Leo P. Lamoureux Memorial Trophy (Top Scorer - IHL) (1961) • IHL Second All-Star Team (1963)

Traded to **Boston** by **NY Rangers** (Saskatoon-WHL) for cash, September 30, 1958.

• YOUNG, Doug   Douglas Gordon "The Gleichen Cowboy"

D – R. 5'10", 190 lbs.   b: Medicine Hat, Alta., 10/1/1908   d: 5/15/1990.

			REGULAR SEASON								PLAYOFFS				
Season	Club	League	GP	G	A	Pts	AG	AA	APts	PIM	GP	G	A	Pts	PIM
1926-27	Calgary Canadians	CCJHL	STATISTICS NOT AVAILABLE												
	Calgary Canadians	M-Cup	2	0	1	1	....	....	....	2	....	....	....	....	....
1927-28	Kitchener Millionaires	Can-Pro	8	1	1	2	....	....	....	10	5	0	1	1	12
1928-29	Toronto Millionaires	Can-Pro	41	7	3	10	....	....	....	75	2	0	0	0	8
1929-30	Cleveland Indians	IHL	41	13	5	18	....	....	....	68	6	2	0	2	2
1930-31	Cleveland Indians	IHL	47	16	6	22	....	....	....	46	6	3	1	4	8
1931-32	**Detroit Falcons**	**NHL**	**47**	**10**	**2**	**12**	**17**	**4**	**21**	**45**	**2**	**0**	**0**	**0**	**2**
1932-33	**Detroit Red Wings**	**NHL**	**48**	**5**	**6**	**11**	**9**	**12**	**21**	**59**	**4**	**1**	**1**	**2**	**0**
1933-34	**Detroit Red Wings**	**NHL**	**47**	**4**	**0**	**4**	**7**	**0**	**7**	**36**	**9**	**0**	**0**	**0**	**10**
1934-35	**Detroit Red Wings**	**NHL**	**48**	**4**	**6**	**10**	**7**	**10**	**17**	**37**	....	....	....	....	....
	Detroit Olympics	IHL	1	0	0	0	....	....	....	0	....	....	....	....	....
♦**1935-36**	**Detroit Red Wings**	**NHL**	**47**	**5**	**12**	**17**	**10**	**23**	**33**	**54**	**7**	**0**	**2**	**2**	**0**
1936-37	**Detroit Red Wings**	**NHL**	**11**	**0**	**0**	**0**	**0**	**0**	**0**	**6**	....	....	....	....	....
1937-38	**Detroit Red Wings**	**NHL**	**48**	**3**	**5**	**8**	**5**	**8**	**13**	**24**	....	....	....	....	....
1938-39	**Detroit Red Wings**	**NHL**	**42**	**1**	**5**	**6**	**2**	**8**	**10**	**16**	**6**	**0**	**2**	**2**	**4**
1939-40	**Montreal Canadiens**	**NHL**	**47**	**3**	**9**	**12**	**5**	**14**	**19**	**22**	....	....	....	....	....
1940-41	**Montreal Canadiens**	**NHL**	**3**	**0**	**0**	**0**	**0**	**0**	**0**	**4**	....	....	....	....	....
	Providence Reds	AHL	42	9	13	22	....	....	....	22	4	0	1	1	7
	NHL Totals		**388**	**35**	**45**	**80**	**62**	**79**	**141**	**303**	**28**	**1**	**5**	**6**	**16**

IHL First All-Star Team (1930) • AHL First All-Star Team (1941) • Played in NHL All-Star Game (1939)

Signed as a free agent by **Kitchener** (Can-Pro), February 5, 1928. Claimed by **Philadelphia** from **Cleveland** (IHL) in Inter-League Draft, May 9, 1931. Claimed by **NY Americans** from **Philadelphia** in Dispersal Draft, September 17, 1931. Traded to **Detroit** by **NY Americans** for Ron Martin, October 18, 1931. • Missed majority of 1936-37 season recovering from ankle injury, December, 1936. Signed as a free agent by **Montreal**, October 30, 1939. Traded to **Buffalo** (AHL) by **Montreal** for cash pending waiver claim, November 27, 1940. Claimed on waivers by **Toronto** from **Montreal** and assigned to **Providence** (AHL), November 29, 1940.

• YOUNG, Howie   — *see page 1772*

• ZEIDEL, Larry   — *see page 1777*

• ZENIUK, Ed   Edward William

D – L. 5'11", 180 lbs.   b: Landis, Sask., 3/8/1933.

			REGULAR SEASON								PLAYOFFS				
Season	Club	League	GP	G	A	Pts	AG	AA	APts	PIM	GP	G	A	Pts	PIM
1950-51	Edmonton Poolers	EJrHL	STATISTICS NOT AVAILABLE												
	Edmonton Oil Kings	M-Cup	6	0	2	2	....	....	....	4	....	....	....	....	....
1951-52	Edmonton Oil Kings	WCJHL	43	5	16	21	....	....	....	110	9	1	4	5	*32
1952-53	Edmonton Oil Kings	WCJHL	30	3	8	11	....	....	....	104	11	0	1	1	22
1953-54	Edmonton–Seattle	WHL	58	4	11	15	....	....	....	69	4	0	0	0	2
1954-55	**Detroit Red Wings**	**NHL**	**2**	**0**	**0**	**0**	**0**	**0**	**0**	**0**	....	....	....	....	....
	Edmonton Flyers	WHL	57	2	7	9	....	....	....	88	9	0	0	0	6
	Edmonton Flyers	Ed-Cup	6	0	0	0	....	....	....	24	....	....	....	....	....
1955-56	New Westminster Royals	WHL	14	1	3	4	....	....	....	31	....	....	....	....	....
	Quebec Aces	QHL	26	0	4	4	....	....	....	54	6	0	0	0	10
	NHL Totals		**2**	**0**	**0**	**0**	**0**	**0**	**0**	**0**	....	....	....	....	....

• ZOBOROSKY, Marty   "Buster"

D – R. 5'10", 180 lbs.   b: Moose Jaw, Sask., .

			REGULAR SEASON								PLAYOFFS				
Season	Club	League	GP	G	A	Pts	AG	AA	APts	PIM	GP	G	A	Pts	PIM
1934-35	Moose Jaw Canucks	S-SJHL	6	4	0	4	....	....	....	9	....	....	....	....	....
	Moose Jaw Canucks	M-Cup	1	0	0	0	....	....	....	2	....	....	....	....	....
1935-36	Moose Jaw Canucks	S-SJHL	3	0	0	0	....	....	....	8	....	....	....	....	....
	Moose Jaw Hardware	S-SSHL	6	1	0	1	....	....	....	*12	4	0	1	1	8
1936-37	Prince Albert Mintos	N-SSHL	20	0	1	1	....	....	....	28	2	0	0	0	4
1937/41	Swift Current Indians	SIHA	STATISTICS NOT AVAILABLE												
1941-42	Kimberley Dynamiters	ABCHL	27	1	1	2	....	....	....	24	1	0	0	0	2
	Kimberley Dynamiters	Al-Cup	1	0	0	0	....	....	....	0	....	....	....	....	....
1942-43	Vancouver RCAF	PCHL	11	2	1	3	....	....	....	*32	4	0	0	0	*20
	Vancouver RCAF	Al-Cup	5	1	2	3	....	....	....	*20	....	....	....	....	....
1943-44	Vancouver St. Regis	NNDHL	7	1	0	1	....	....	....	6	....	....	....	....	....
1944-45	**Chicago Black Hawks**	**NHL**	**1**	**0**	**0**	**0**	**0**	**0**	**0**	**2**	....	....	....	....	....
	Providence Reds	AHL	1	0	0	0	....	....	....	0	....	....	....	....	....
	NHL Totals		**1**	**0**	**0**	**0**	**0**	**0**	**0**	**2**	....	....	....	....	....

• Probably played under the name Marty Edwards from 1937 to 1941. No statistics are available.

• ZUNICH, Rudy   Rudolph Ralph

D – L. 5'9", 170 lbs.   b: Calumet, MI, 11/24/1910.

			REGULAR SEASON								PLAYOFFS				
Season	Club	League	GP	G	A	Pts	AG	AA	APts	PIM	GP	G	A	Pts	PIM
1934-35	Detroit Holzbaugh	MOHL	27	18	8	26	....	....	....	*49	6	1	0	1	10
1935-36	Detroit Holzbaugh	MOHL	19	4	6	10	....	....	....	16	4	0	1	1	0
1936-37	Detroit Holzbaugh	MOHL	24	13	11	24	....	....	....	30	7	1	2	3	6
1937-38	Detroit Holzbaugh	MOHL	27	8	8	16	....	....	....	43	6	4	1	5	0
1938-39	Detroit Holzbaugh	MOHL	20	4	4	8	....	....	....	6	2	1	1	2	0
1939-40	Detroit Holzbaugh	MOHL	33	14	16	30	....	....	....	32	12	4	4	8	12
1940-41	Detroit Holzbaugh	MOHL	25	9	13	22	....	....	....	29	7	4	1	5	2
1941-42	Detroit Parisclean	MOHL	24	11	26	37	....	....	....	16	7	3	3	6	0
1942-43			MILITARY SERVICE												
1943-44	**Detroit Red Wings**	**NHL**	**2**	**0**	**0**	**0**	**0**	**0**	**0**	**2**	....	....	....	....	....
	NHL Totals		**2**	**0**	**0**	**0**	**0**	**0**	**0**	**2**	....	....	....	....	....

Signed as a free agent by **Detroit** to a three-game tryout contract, October 31, 1943.

CHAPTER 77

Using the Modern Player Register

James Duplacey

THE MODERN PLAYER REGISTER begins on the facing page. It contains the complete statistical history of every player whose NHL career began in 1967–68 or later plus the complete statistical history of every player who played in the NHL both before and after the start of the 1967–68 season. The 1967–68 season marks the beginning of the modern era in the tabulation of NHL statistics because additional categories such as power-play goals and shots on goal first began to be tracked.

Here are notes on the various statistical categories used in the Modern Player Register:

Biographical – This field contains the player's last name and popular name in **bold** type. It is followed by the player's proper name, middle name and nickname. If a player's proper name is the one he is commonly known by (**William**), both it and his middle name follow (**William Joseph**). If the player goes by his common name (**Bill**), then both his proper name (**William**) and his middle name (**William Joseph**) are included. The player's "nickname" follows his proper and middle names (William Joseph "**Soupy**"). The name field is followed by position (**C** – center, **RW** – right wing, **LW** – left wing, **W** – wing, **F** – forward, **D** – defense), shooting side (**R** – right, **L**– left), height in feet and inches, weight in pounds, date of birth (month/day/year), place of birth and date of death. If the death date is not known, the date is represented by "Deceased." If any other biographical information is not known, the appropriate field is left blank.

If a player was selected in the NHL's Amateur or Entry Draft (1963 to 2000), that information is noted here as *NY Islanders 3rd, 45th overall in 1998*. If a player was selected in the Supplemental Draft, that information is included as well. For those players who re-entered the Draft, the second team that selected the player is noted here, while details of his first selection are found in the trade notes field. Draft information for those players selected in the WHA Amateur and Professional Drafts and who played in both the NHL and WHA can be found in his notes section. If the player is a member of the Hockey Hall of Fame (**HHOF**) and/or the United States Hockey Hall of Fame (**USHOF**), it is noted here.

Season – The hockey season starts in the fall and ends the following spring. It is represented as one four digit date, a hyphen and a two-digit date (1997–98). For players who did not play for three or more seasons but later returned to play or coach, those years are represented as 1994–1999.

Club – This field gives information as to which team or teams the player performed with during the season. If statistics for a particular team or season could not be located, the club name has been included with a Statistics not Available footnote.

League – This field contains the league or abbreviated league name for each team line. Several new categories have been introduced for this field in the second edition of *Total Hockey*, including Allan Cup and Memorial Cup statistics and other Championship Cup competitions. Complete details on these new innovations and can be found on pages 610 and 1973.

GP – Games Played – Games in which a player appears on the ice during a game. Players who are dressed but do not step on the ice during play are not credited with a game played.

G – Goals scored – A goal is credited to the last player from the scoring team to touch the puck before it completely crosses the goal line. A player may not deliberately direct the puck into the net with a skate or deflect a puck into the net with his stick above the height of the crossbar of the goal frame.

A – Assists – An assist is awarded to any player, or players, taking part in the play immediately preceding the goal. No more than two assists are awarded for each goal.

Pts – Points – Any player credited with a goal or an assist receives one point.

AG – Adjusted goals – **AA** - Adjusted assists -**APts** - Adjusted points *(See page 613)*

PIM – Penalties in minutes – Number of minutes a player is penalized during the season. A player is penalized two minutes for each minor penalty, five minutes for each major penalty and 10 minutes for each misconduct, game misconduct and gross misconduct penalty.

PP – Power-play goals – Goals scored while the opposition has fewer players on the ice than the scoring team due to players being penalized.

SH – Shorthand goals – goals scored while the opposition has more players on the ice than the scoring team due to players being penalized.

GW – Game-winning goals – Goal scored that gives the winning team one more goal than the total number of goals the losing team eventually scores. For example, the fourth goal scored in a 6–3 victory is considered the winning goal, regardless of when it was scored.

S – Shots on goal – Shots taken on net by an individual player that either enter the net or would do so if not for intervention by an opposing player, usually the goaltender. A long clearing shot taken from behind center ice is not considered a shot on goal, unless it is directed at an empty net. Shots off the posts or crossbar are not counted as shots on goals.

% – Shooting percentage – Percentage of shots taken by an individual player that result in goals. The percentage is calculated by dividing the number of goals by shots. The resulting figure is expressed as a percentage to one decimal place.

TGF – Total Goals For – Total number of goals scored by a player's team while he is on the ice.

PGF – Power-play Goals For – Total number of power-play goals scored by a player's team while he is on the ice.

TGA – Total Goals Against – Total number of goals scored against a player's team while he is on the ice.

PGA – Total number of power play goals scored against a player's team while he is on the ice.

+/– – Plus/minus rating – Total number of goals scored by a player's team while he is on the ice (at even strength or short hand) less the total number of goals allowed by a player's team while he is on the ice (at even strength or on the power-play). Calculated as follows: (TGF – PGF) – (TGA – PGA)

NHL Totals – NHL statistics with the exception of +/– are totaled here.

Other Major League Totals – This field includes WHA totals for those players who played in both the WHA and the NHL. The WHA is the only "major" professional league to operate since 1926. A list of other major leagues is found on page 611. See page 1973 for a complete list of league and tournaments in *Total Hockey*.

Award and All-Star Notes – This field contains details of all-star selections, and major trophies and awards. Also included are IIHF awards and NHL All-Star Game appearances.

Trade Notes – This field contains notes on NHL trades, Drafts, and free agent signings. WHA transaction notes are included for those who played in both the WHA and the NHL.

Special notes concerning injuries and other oddities and curiosities are indicated by a bullet (•). An asterisk (*) is used to indicate league- or tournament-leading statistics.

CHAPTER 78

Modern Player Register

Career Records for Players Appearing in the NHL in 1967–68 or Later

• AALTO, Antti

C – L. 6'2", 210 lbs. b: Lappeenranta, Finland, 3/4/1975. Anaheim's 6th, 134th overall, in 1993.

Season	Club	League	GP	G	A	Pts	AG	AA	APts	PIM	PP	SH	GW	S	%	TGF	PGF	TGA	PGA	+/–	GP	G	A	Pts	PIM	PP	SH	GW
			REGULAR SEASON																		PLAYOFFS							
1991-92	SaiPa Lappeenranta	Finland-Jr.	13	7	9	16				38											6	3	1	4	6			
	SaiPa Lappeenranta	Finland-2	20	6	6	12				20																		
1992-93	SaiPa Lappeenranta-B	Finland-Jr.	3	0	1	1				2																		
	SaiPa Lappeenranta-2	Finland-Jr.	3	4	2	6				2																		
	TPS Turku	Finland-Jr.	14	6	8	14				18											6	2	2	4	8			
	TPS Turku	Finland	1	0	0	0				0																		
	SaiPa Lappeenranta	Finland-2	23	6	8	14				14																		
1993-94	TPS Turku	Finland-Jr.	10	3	8	11				14											5	1	4	5	12			
	Kiekko-67 Turku	Finland-2	4	2	2	4				27																		
	Finland	WJC-A	7	0	2	2				8																		
	TPS Turku	Finland	33	5	9	14				16											10	1	1	2	4			
1994-95	Kiekko-67 Turku	Finland-Jr.	2	1	2	3				2																		
	Kiekko-67 Turku	Finland-2	1	1	0	1				29																		
	Finland	WJC-A	7	2	3	5				18																		
	TPS Turku	Finland	44	11	7	18				18											5	0	1	1	2			
1995-96	Kiekko-67 Turku	Finland-2	2	0	2	2				2																		
	TPS Turku	Finland	40	15	16	31				22											11	3	5	8	14			
1996-97	TPS Turku	Finland	44	15	19	34				60											11	5	6	11	31			
	TPS Turku	EuroHL	5	3	3	6				2											2	1	1	2	0			
	Finland	WC-A	5	2	0	2				0																		
	Finland	Nat-Team	14	2	4	6				26																		
1997-98	**Mighty Ducks of Anaheim**	**NHL**	**3**	**0**	**0**	**0**	**0**	**0**	**0**	**0**	**0**	**0**	**0**	**1**	**0.0**	**0**	**0**	**1**	**0**	**–1**								
	Cincinnati Mighty Ducks	AHL	29	4	9	13				30																		
1998-99	**Mighty Ducks of Anaheim**	**NHL**	**73**	**3**	**5**	**8**	**4**	**5**	**9**	**24**	**2**	**0**	**0**	**61**	**4.9**	**13**	**7**	**18**	**0**	**–12**	**4**	**0**	**0**	**0**	**2**	**0**	**0**	**0**
99-2000	**Mighty Ducks of Anaheim**	**NHL**	**63**	**7**	**11**	**18**	**8**	**10**	**18**	**26**	**1**	**0**	**1**	**102**	**6.9**	**22**	**1**	**44**	**10**	**–13**								
	Finland	WC-A	8	0	0	0				6																		
	NHL Totals		**139**	**10**	**16**	**26**	**12**	**15**	**27**	**50**	**3**	**0**	**1**	**164**	**6.1**	**35**	**8**	**63**	**10**		**4**	**0**	**0**	**0**	**2**	**0**	**0**	**0**

• ABGRALL, Dennis

Dennis Harvey RW – R. 6'1", 180 lbs. b: Moosomin, Sask., 4/24/1953. Los Angeles' 3rd, 70th overall, in 1973.

Season	Club	League	GP	G	A	Pts	AG	AA	APts	PIM	PP	SH	GW	S	%	TGF	PGF	TGA	PGA	+/–	GP	G	A	Pts	PIM	PP	SH	GW
1969-70	Moose Jaw Canucks	SJHL	STATISTICS NOT AVAILABLE																									
1970-71	Saskatoon Blades	WCJHL	64	31	43	74				28											5	4	2	6	8			
1971-72	Saskatoon Blades	WCJHL	64	29	38	67				58											2	2	0	2	0			
1972-73	Saskatoon Blades	WCJHL	68	30	39	69				36											16	7	6	13	12			
1973-74	Portland Buckaroos	WHL	78	27	41	68				37											10	2	*7	9	8			
1974-75	Springfield Indians	AHL	75	25	40	65				17											17	9	11	20	8			
1975-76	**Los Angeles Kings**	**NHL**	**13**	**0**	**2**	**2**	**0**	**1**	**1**	**4**	**0**	**0**	**0**	**9**	**0.0**	**3**	**2**	**8**	**0**	**–7**								
	Fort Worth Texans	CHL	64	21	36	57				34																		
1976-77	Cincinnati Stingers	WHA	80	23	39	62				22											4	2	0	2	5			
1977-78	Cincinnati Stingers	WHA	65	13	11	24				13																		
1978-79	Binghamton Dusters	AHL	6	0	0	0				0																		
	Erie Blades	NEHL	56	30	49	79				8																		
1979-80	EC Bad Tolz	Germany-2	30	23	25	48																						
1980-81	EC Bad Tolz	Germany-2	STATISTICS NOT AVAILABLE																									
1981-82	CPS Liege	Belgium	23	46	32	78				16																		
	NHL Totals		**13**	**0**	**2**	**2**	**0**	**1**	**1**	**4**	**0**	**0**	**0**	**9**	**0.0**	**3**	**2**	**8**	**0**									
	Other Major League Totals		145	36	50	86				35											4	2	0	2	5			

Selected by **LA Sharks** (WHA) in 1973 WHA Amateur Draft, June, 1973. WHA rights transferred to **Cincinnati** (WHA) after **Michigan-Baltimore** (WHA) franchise folded, June, 1975. Claimed by **Winnipeg** from **LA Kings** in 1979 Expansion Draft, June 13, 1979.

• ABRAHAMSSON, Thommy

Thommy Ulf D – L. 6'2", 185 lbs. b: Umea, Sweden, 4/12/1947.

Season	Club	League	GP	G	A	Pts	AG	AA	APts	PIM	PP	SH	GW	S	%	TGF	PGF	TGA	PGA	+/–	GP	G	A	Pts	PIM	PP	SH	GW
1964-65	Leksands IF	Sweden	11	1	1	2				8											14	0	2	2	4			
1965-66	Leksands IF	Sweden	20	3	5	8				12											7	2	0	2	6			
1966-67	Leksands IF	Sweden	20	4	5	9				15											2	1	0	1	2			
1967-68	Leksands IF	Sweden	26	12	6	18																						
1968-69	Leksands IF	Sweden	26	11	9	20				19																		
1969-70	Leksands IF	Sweden	14	3	4	7				18											14	5	4	9	15			
	Sweden	WEC-A	10	3	1	4				8																		
1970-71	Leksands IF	Sweden	14	7	4	11				4											14	5	1	6	25			
	Sweden	WEC-A	9	2	1	3				10																		
1971-72	Leksands IF	Sweden	25	5	14	19				28																		
	Sweden	Olympics	6	1	1	2				2																		
	Sweden	WEC-A	10	0	1	1				14																		
1972-73	Leksands IF	Sweden	14	7	3	10				20											14	7	3	10	8			
	Sweden	WEC-A	2	1	1	2				0																		
1973-74	Leksands IF	Sweden	14	7	4	11				13											21	8	7	15	31			
	Sweden	WEC-A	10	0	3	3				6																		
1974-75	New England Whalers	WHA	76	8	22	30				46											6	0	0	0	0			
1975-76	New England Whalers	WHA	63	14	21	35				47											17	2	4	6	15			
1976-77	New England Whalers	WHA	64	6	24	30				33											5	0	3	3	0			
1977-78	Leksands IF	Sweden	28	17	5	22				56																		
1978-79	Leksands IF	Sweden	24	6	3	9				55											4	0	1	1	8			
1979-80	Leksands IF	Sweden	26	9	6	15				35																		
1980-81	**Hartford Whalers**	**NHL**	**32**	**6**	**11**	**17**	**5**	**7**	**12**	**16**	**4**	**0**	**1**	**66**	**9.1**	**46**	**17**	**34**	**1**	**–4**								
	Binghamton Whalers	AHL	2	0	0	0				2																		
1981-82	Timra IF	Sweden	28	10	4	14				44																		
1982-83	Timra IF	Sweden	36	18	18	36				49																		
	NHL Totals		**32**	**6**	**11**	**17**	**5**	**7**	**12**	**16**	**4**	**0**	**1**	**66**	**9.1**	**46**	**17**	**34**	**1**									
	Other Major League Totals		203	28	67	95				126											28	2	7	9	15			

Swedish Player of the Year (1973)

Signed as a free agent by **New England** (WHA), August, 1974. Signed as a free agent by **Hartford**, May 23, 1980.

● **ACOMB, Doug** Douglas Raymond C – L. 5'11", 165 lbs. b: Toronto, Ont., 5/15/1949.

Season	Club	League	REGULAR SEASON GP	G	A	Pts	AG	AA	APts	PIM	PP	SH	GW	S	%	TGF	PGF	TGA	PGA	+/–	PLAYOFFS GP	G	A	Pts	PIM	PP	SH	GW
1965-66	York Steel	OHA-B	40	26	32	58																						
	Toronto Marlboros	OHA-Jr.																			4	0	0	0	4			
1966-67	Toronto Marlboros	OHA-Jr.	43	20	18	38				41											17	11	10	21	22			
	Toronto Marlboros	Mem-Cup	9	10	8	18				23																		
1967-68	Toronto Marlboros	OHA-Jr.	52	22	44	66				51											5	2	3	5	4			
	Toronto Marlboros	OHA-Sr.	1	2	1	3				0																		
1968-69	Toronto Marlboros	OHA-Jr.	54	*55	38	93				71											6	2	1	3	6			
1969-70	**Toronto Maple Leafs**	**NHL**	**2**	**0**	**1**	**1**	**0**	**1**	**1**	**0**	**0**	**0**	**0**	**0**	**0.0**	**1**	**0**	**0**	**0**	**1**								
	Tulsa Oilers	CHL	52	17	22	39				34											5	0	2	2	4			
	Buffalo Bisons	AHL																			2	0	0	0	0			
1970-71	Phoenix Roadrunners	WHL	69	9	16	25				15											10	1	3	4	4			
1971-72	Barrie Flyers	OHA-Sr.	39	*37	41	*78				53											18	*15	7	22	6			
1972-73	Barrie Flyers	OHA-Sr.	40	34	39	73				34																		
1973-74	Barrie Flyers	OHA-Sr.	35	22	33	55				22																		
1974-75	WEV Wien	Austria	25	27	16	43				75																		
1975-76	Barrie Flyers	OHA-Sr.	44	33	42	75				34																		
	NHL Totals		**2**	**0**	**1**	**1**	**0**	**1**	**1**	**0**	**0**	**0**	**0**	**0**	**0.0**	**1**	**0**	**0**	**0**									

OHA-Sr. First All-Star Team (1973, 1976)

● **ACTON, Keith** Keith Edward C – L. 5'8", 170 lbs. b: Stouffville, Ont., 4/15/1958. Montreal's 8th, 103rd overall, in 1978.

Season	Club	League	GP	G	A	Pts	AG	AA	APts	PIM	PP	SH	GW	S	%	TGF	PGF	TGA	PGA	+/–	GP	G	A	Pts	PIM	PP	SH	GW
1974-75	Wexford Raiders	OHA-B	43	23	29	52				46																		
1975-76	Peterborough Petes	OMJHL	35	9	17	26				30																		
1976-77	Peterborough Petes	OMJHL	65	52	69	121				93											4	1	4	5	6			
1977-78	Peterborough Petes	OMJHL	68	42	86	128				52											21	10	8	18	16			
	Peterborough Petes	Mem-Cup	3	0	1	1				0																		
1978-79	Nova Scotia Voyageurs	AHL	79	15	26	41				22											10	4	2	6	4			
1979-80	**Montreal Canadiens**	**NHL**	**2**	**0**	**1**	**1**	**0**	**1**	**1**	**0**	**0**	**0**	**0**	**1**	**0.0**	**1**	**0**	**1**	**0**	**0**								
	Nova Scotia Voyageurs	AHL	75	45	53	98				38											6	1	2	3	8			
1980-81	**Montreal Canadiens**	**NHL**	**61**	**15**	**24**	**39**	**12**	**16**	**28**	**74**	**3**	**0**	**2**	**101**	**14.9**	**50**	**8**	**38**	**1**	**5**	**2**	**0**	**0**	**0**	**6**	**0**	**0**	**0**
1981-82	**Montreal Canadiens**	**NHL**	**78**	**36**	**52**	**88**	**28**	**35**	**63**	**88**	**10**	**0**	**5**	**218**	**16.5**	**128**	**35**	**51**	**6**	**48**	**5**	**0**	**4**	**4**	**16**	**0**	**0**	**0**
1982-83	**Montreal Canadiens**	**NHL**	**78**	**24**	**26**	**50**	**20**	**18**	**38**	**63**	**1**	**0**	**3**	**154**	**15.6**	**64**	**4**	**74**	**8**	**–6**	**3**	**0**	**0**	**0**	**0**	**0**	**0**	**0**
1983-84	**Montreal Canadiens**	**NHL**	**9**	**3**	**7**	**10**	**2**	**5**	**7**	**4**	**2**	**0**	**0**	**14**	**21.4**	**13**	**7**	**12**	**1**	**–5**								
	Minnesota North Stars	**NHL**	**62**	**17**	**38**	**55**	**14**	**26**	**40**	**60**	**4**	**2**	**5**	**151**	**11.3**	**73**	**18**	**72**	**19**	**2**	**15**	**4**	**7**	**11**	**12**	**1**	**0**	**1**
1984-85	**Minnesota North Stars**	**NHL**	**78**	**20**	**38**	**58**	**16**	**26**	**42**	**90**	**4**	**0**	**3**	**167**	**12.0**	**81**	**23**	**86**	**25**	**–3**	**9**	**4**	**4**	**8**	**6**	**1**	**0**	**2**
1985-86	**Minnesota North Stars**	**NHL**	**79**	**26**	**32**	**58**	**21**	**22**	**43**	**100**	**5**	**2**	**2**	**169**	**15.4**	**76**	**16**	**112**	**41**	**–11**	**5**	**0**	**3**	**3**	**6**	**0**	**0**	**0**
	Canada	WEC-A	10	3	0	3				2																		
1986-87	**Minnesota North Stars**	**NHL**	**78**	**16**	**29**	**45**	**14**	**21**	**35**	**56**	**1**	**1**	**3**	**126**	**12.7**	**61**	**8**	**107**	**39**	**–15**								
1987-88	**Minnesota North Stars**	**NHL**	**46**	**8**	**11**	**19**	**7**	**8**	**15**	**74**	**0**	**1**	**0**	**49**	**16.3**	**28**	**2**	**73**	**38**	**–9**								
	♦ **Edmonton Oilers**	**NHL**	**26**	**3**	**6**	**9**	**3**	**4**	**7**	**21**	**1**	**0**	**1**	**26**	**11.5**	**10**	**2**	**24**	**6**	**–10**	**7**	**2**	**0**	**2**	**16**	**0**	**0**	**2**
1988-89	**Edmonton Oilers**	**NHL**	**46**	**11**	**15**	**26**	**9**	**11**	**20**	**47**	**0**	**1**	**1**	**74**	**14.9**	**35**	**1**	**40**	**15**	**9**								
	Philadelphia Flyers	**NHL**	**25**	**3**	**10**	**13**	**3**	**7**	**10**	**64**	**0**	**1**	**0**	**38**	**7.9**	**21**	**0**	**27**	**7**	**1**	**16**	**2**	**3**	**5**	**18**	**0**	**0**	**0**
1989-90	**Philadelphia Flyers**	**NHL**	**69**	**13**	**14**	**27**	**11**	**10**	**21**	**80**	**0**	**2**	**0**	**94**	**13.8**	**41**	**0**	**65**	**22**	**–2**								
	Canada	WEC-A	10	2	0	2				0																		
1990-91	**Philadelphia Flyers**	**NHL**	**76**	**14**	**23**	**37**	**13**	**17**	**30**	**131**	**2**	**1**	**1**	**120**	**11.7**	**52**	**8**	**75**	**22**	**–9**								
1991-92	**Philadelphia Flyers**	**NHL**	**50**	**7**	**10**	**17**	**6**	**8**	**14**	**98**	**0**	**0**	**3**	**79**	**8.9**	**28**	**2**	**42**	**12**	**–4**								
	Canada	WC-A	6	1	0	1				2																		
1992-93	**Philadelphia Flyers**	**NHL**	**83**	**8**	**15**	**23**	**7**	**10**	**17**	**51**	**0**	**0**	**0**	**74**	**10.8**	**29**	**0**	**91**	**52**	**–10**								
1993-94	**Washington Capitals**	**NHL**	**6**	**0**	**0**	**0**	**0**	**0**	**0**	**21**	**0**	**0**	**0**	**2**	**0.0**	**0**	**0**	**4**	**0**	**–4**								
	New York Islanders	**NHL**	**71**	**2**	**7**	**9**	**2**	**5**	**7**	**50**	**0**	**0**	**0**	**33**	**6.1**	**10**	**0**	**35**	**24**	**–1**	**4**	**0**	**0**	**0**	**8**	**0**	**0**	**0**
1994-95	Hershey Bears	AHL	12	5	7	12				58																		
1995-1998	**Philadelphia Flyers**	**NHL**	DID NOT PLAY – ASSISTANT COACH																									
1998-2000	**New York Rangers**	**NHL**	DID NOT PLAY – ASSISTANT COACH																									
	NHL Totals		**1023**	**226**	**358**	**584**	**188**	**250**	**438**	**1172**	**33**	**11**	**29**	**1690**	**13.4**	**801**	**134**	**1029**	**338**		**66**	**12**	**21**	**33**	**88**	**2**	**0**	**5**

AHL Second All-Star Team (1980) • Played in NHL All-Star Game (1982)

Traded to **Minnesota** by **Montreal** with Mark Napier and Toronto's 3rd round choice (previously acquired, Minnesota selected Ken Hodge Jr.) in 1984 Entry Draft for Bobby Smith, October 28, 1983. Traded to **Edmonton** by **Minnesota** for Moe Mantha, January 22, 1988. Traded to **Philadelphia** by **Edmonton** with Edmonton's 6th round choice (Dimitri Yushkevich) in 1991 Entry Draft for Dave Brown, February 7, 1989. Traded to **Winnipeg** by **Philadelphia** with Pete Peeters for future considerations, September 28, 1989. Traded to **Philadelphia** by **Winnipeg** with Pete Peeters for Toronto's 5th round choice (previously acquired, Winnipeg selected Juha Ylonen) in 1991 Entry Draft and the cancellation of future considerations owed Philadelphia from the Shawn Cronin trade, October 3, 1989. Signed as a free agent by **Washington**, July 27, 1993. Claimed on waivers by **NY Islanders** from **Washington**, October 22, 1993.

● **ADAM, Russ** Russell Norman C – L. 5'10", 185 lbs. b: Windsor, Ont., 5/5/1961. Toronto's 7th, 137th overall, in 1980.

Season	Club	League	GP	G	A	Pts	AG	AA	APts	PIM	PP	SH	GW	S	%	TGF	PGF	TGA	PGA	+/–	GP	G	A	Pts	PIM	PP	SH	GW
1977-78	Windsor Royals	OHA-B	35	26	44	70																						
	Windsor Spitfires	OMJHL	3	1	2	3				0																		
1978-79	Kitchener Rangers	OMJHL	62	20	17	37				39											9	4	3	7	31			
1979-80	Kitchener Rangers	OMJHL	54	37	34	71				143																		
1980-81	Kitchener Rangers	OMJHL	64	37	50	87				215											10	0	2	2	17			
	Kitchener Rangers	Mem-Cup	5	0	4	4				6																		
1981-82	New Brunswick Hawks	AHL	52	11	21	32				50											12	3	5	8	32			
1982-83	**Toronto Maple Leafs**	**NHL**	**8**	**1**	**2**	**3**	**1**	**1**	**2**	**11**	**0**	**0**	**0**	**4**	**25.0**	**3**	**0**	**7**	**1**	**–3**								
	St. Catharines Saints	AHL	64	19	17	36				119																		
1983-84	St. Catharines Saints	AHL	70	32	24	56				76											7	0	1	1	10			
1984-85	Fort Wayne Komets	IHL	60	28	46	74				56																		
1985-86	Fort Wayne Komets	IHL	48	24	37	61				36											14	7	*13	20	9			
1986-87	St. John's Capitals	Nfld-Sr.	PLAYER/COACH – STATISTICS UNAVAILABLE																									
1987-88	St. John's Capitals	Nfld-Sr.	47	47	55	102				90																		
1988-89	ESV Kaufbeuren	Germany	36	8	6	14				8																		
1989-90	Augsburger EV	Germany-2	48	14	23	37				30																		
1990-91	Augsburger EV	Germany-2	52	20	44	64				32																		
1991-92	Augsburger EV	Germany-2	33	8	15	23				28																		
	Augsburger EV	Germany-Q	13	2	2	4				4																		
	NHL Totals		**8**	**1**	**2**	**3**	**1**	**1**	**2**	**11**	**0**	**0**	**0**	**4**	**25.0**	**3**	**0**	**7**	**1**									

● **ADAMS, Bryan** LW – L. 6', 185 lbs. b: Fort St. James, B.C., 3/20/1977.

Season	Club	League	GP	G	A	Pts	AG	AA	APts	PIM	PP	SH	GW	S	%	TGF	PGF	TGA	PGA	+/–	GP	G	A	Pts	PIM	PP	SH	GW
1994-95	Prince George Spruce Kings	BCJHL	48	37	53	90																						
1995-96	Michigan State Spartans	CCHA	42	3	8	11				12																		
1996-97	Michigan State Spartans	CCHA	29	7	7	14				51																		
1997-98	Michigan State Spartans	CCHA	31	9	21	30				39																		
1998-99	Michigan State Spartans	CCHA	42	21	16	37				56																		
99-2000	**Atlanta Thrashers**	**NHL**	**2**	**0**	**0**	**0**	**0**	**0**	**0**	**0**	**0**	**0**	**0**	**1**	**0.0**	**0**	**0**	**1**	**0**	**–1**								
	Orlando Solar Bears	IHL	64	16	18	34				27											4	0	1	1	6			
	NHL Totals		**2**	**0**	**0**	**0**	**0**	**0**	**0**	**0**	**0**	**0**	**0**	**1**	**0.0**	**0**	**0**	**1**	**0**									

Signed as a free agent by **Atlanta**, July 6, 1999.

● **ADAMS, Greg** Gregory Daren LW – L. 6'3", 195 lbs. b: Nelson, B.C., 8/15/1963.

Season	Club	League	GP	G	A	Pts	AG	AA	APts	PIM	PP	SH	GW	S	%	TGF	PGF	TGA	PGA	+/–	GP	G	A	Pts	PIM	PP	SH	GW
1980-81	Kelowna Buckaroos	BCJHL	48	40	50	90				16																		
1981-82	Kelowna Buckaroos	BCJHL	45	31	42	73				24																		
1982-83	Northern Arizona University	ACHA	29	14	21	35				46																		

Season	Club	League	GP	G	A	Pts	AG	AA	APts	PIM	PP	SH	GW	S	%	TGF	PGF	TGA	PGA	+/–	GP	G	A	Pts	PIM	PP	SH	GW
			REGULAR SEASON																		PLAYOFFS							
1983-84	Northern Arizona University	ACHA	26	44	29	73				24																		
1984-85	**New Jersey Devils**	**NHL**	**36**	**12**	**9**	**21**	**10**	**6**	**16**	**14**	**5**	**0**	**0**	**63**	**19.0**	**27**	**7**	**34**	**0**	**–14**								
	Maine Mariners	AHL	41	15	20	35				12											11	3	4	7	0			
1985-86	**New Jersey Devils**	**NHL**	**78**	**35**	**42**	**77**	**28**	**28**	**56**	**30**	**10**	**0**	**2**	**202**	**17.3**	**98**	**28**	**78**	**1**	**–7**								
	Canada	WEC-A	1	1	0	1				0																		
1986-87	**New Jersey Devils**	**NHL**	**72**	**20**	**27**	**47**	**17**	**20**	**37**	**19**	**6**	**0**	**1**	**143**	**14.0**	**75**	**25**	**66**	**0**	**–16**								
1987-88	**Vancouver Canucks**	**NHL**	**80**	**36**	**40**	**76**	**31**	**29**	**60**	**30**	**12**	**0**	**3**	**227**	**15.9**	**110**	**43**	**100**	**9**	**–24**								
1988-89	**Vancouver Canucks**	**NHL**	**61**	**19**	**14**	**33**	**16**	**10**	**26**	**24**	**9**	**0**	**2**	**144**	**13.2**	**58**	**29**	**51**	**1**	**–21**	**7**	**2**	**3**	**5**	**2**	**0**	**0**	**0**
1989-90	**Vancouver Canucks**	**NHL**	**65**	**30**	**20**	**50**	**26**	**14**	**40**	**18**	**13**	**0**	**1**	**181**	**16.6**	**64**	**23**	**50**	**1**	**–8**								
	Canada	WEC-A	10	8	1	9				10																		
1990-91	**Vancouver Canucks**	**NHL**	**55**	**21**	**24**	**45**	**19**	**18**	**37**	**10**	**5**	**1**	**2**	**148**	**14.2**	**65**	**21**	**53**	**4**	**–5**	**5**	**0**	**0**	**0**	**2**	**0**	**0**	**0**
1991-92	**Vancouver Canucks**	**NHL**	**76**	**30**	**27**	**57**	**27**	**20**	**47**	**26**	**13**	**1**	**5**	**184**	**16.3**	**92**	**37**	**61**	**14**	**8**	**6**	**0**	**2**	**2**	**4**	**0**	**0**	**0**
1992-93	**Vancouver Canucks**	**NHL**	**53**	**25**	**31**	**56**	**21**	**21**	**42**	**14**	**6**	**1**	**3**	**124**	**20.2**	**79**	**22**	**44**	**18**	**31**	**12**	**7**	**6**	**13**	**6**	**5**	**0**	**1**
1993-94	**Vancouver Canucks**	**NHL**	**68**	**13**	**24**	**37**	**12**	**19**	**31**	**20**	**5**	**1**	**2**	**139**	**9.4**	**60**	**18**	**51**	**8**	**–1**	**23**	**6**	**8**	**14**	**2**	**2**	**0**	**2**
1994-95	**Vancouver Canucks**	**NHL**	**31**	**5**	**10**	**15**	**9**	**15**	**24**	**12**	**2**	**2**	**0**	**56**	**8.9**	**27**	**5**	**30**	**9**	**1**								
	Dallas Stars	**NHL**	**12**	**3**	**3**	**6**	**5**	**4**	**9**	**4**	**1**	**0**	**0**	**16**	**18.8**	**11**	**5**	**10**	**0**	**–4**	**5**	**2**	**0**	**2**	**0**	**0**	**0**	**0**
1995-96	**Dallas Stars**	**NHL**	**66**	**22**	**21**	**43**	**22**	**17**	**39**	**33**	**11**	**1**	**1**	**140**	**15.7**	**62**	**31**	**70**	**18**	**–21**								
1996-97	**Dallas Stars**	**NHL**	**50**	**21**	**15**	**36**	**22**	**13**	**35**	**2**	**5**	**0**	**4**	**113**	**18.6**	**58**	**16**	**16**	**1**	**27**	**3**	**0**	**1**	**1**	**0**	**0**	**0**	**0**
1997-98	**Dallas Stars**	**NHL**	**49**	**14**	**18**	**32**	**16**	**18**	**34**	**20**	**7**	**0**	**1**	**75**	**18.7**	**55**	**21**	**23**	**0**	**11**	**12**	**2**	**2**	**4**	**0**	**0**	**0**	**2**
1998-99	**Phoenix Coyotes**	**NHL**	**75**	**19**	**24**	**43**	**22**	**23**	**45**	**26**	**5**	**0**	**3**	**176**	**10.8**	**68**	**20**	**53**	**4**	**–1**	**3**	**0**	**1**	**1**	**0**	**0**	**0**	**0**
99-2000	**Phoenix Coyotes**	**NHL**	**69**	**19**	**27**	**46**	**21**	**25**	**46**	**14**	**5**	**0**	**0**	**129**	**14.7**	**70**	**23**	**48**	**0**	**–1**	**5**	**0**	**0**	**0**	**0**	**0**	**0**	**0**
	NHL Totals	•	**996**	**344**	**376**	**720**	**324**	**300**	**624**	**316**	**120**	**7**	**30**	**2260**	**15.2**	**1079**	**374**	**838**	**88**		**81**	**19**	**23**	**42**	**16**	**7**	**0**	**5**

Played in NHL All-Star Game (1988) • Family name originally Adamakos

Signed as a free agent by **New Jersey**, June 25, 1984. Traded to **Vancouver** by **New Jersey** with Kirk McLean and New Jersey's 2nd round choice (Leif Rohlin) in 1988 Entry Draft for Patrik Sundstrom and Vancouver's 2nd (Jeff Christian) and 4th (Matt Ruchty) round choices in 1988 Entry Draft, September 15, 1987. Traded to **Dallas** by **Vancouver** with Dan Kesa and Vancouver's 5th round choice (later traded to LA Kings — LA Kings selected Jason Morgan) in 1995 Entry Draft for Russ Courtnall, April 7, 1995. Signed as a free agent by **Phoenix**, September 1, 1998.

• ADAMS, Greg

Gregory Charles LW – L. 6'1", 190 lbs. b: Duncan, B.C., 5/31/1960.

Season	Club	League	GP	G	A	Pts	AG	AA	APts	PIM	PP	SH	GW	S	%	TGF	PGF	TGA	PGA	+/–	GP	G	A	Pts	PIM	PP	SH	GW
1977-78	Nanaimo Clippers	BCJHL	62	53	60	113				150																		
1978-79	Victoria Cougars	WHL	71	23	31	54				151											14	5	0	5	59			
1979-80	Victoria Cougars	WHL	71	62	48	110				212											16	9	11	20	71			
1980-81	**Philadelphia Flyers**	**NHL**	**6**	**3**	**0**	**3**	**2**	**0**	**2**	**8**	**0**	**0**	**0**	**6**	**50.0**	**4**	**0**	**4**	**0**	**0**								
	Maine Mariners	AHL	71	19	20	39				158											20	2	3	5	89			
1981-82	**Philadelphia Flyers**	**NHL**	**33**	**4**	**15**	**19**	**3**	**10**	**13**	**105**	**0**	**0**	**0**	**29**	**13.8**	**25**	**3**	**15**	**0**	**7**								
	Maine Mariners	AHL	45	16	21	37				241											4	0	3	3	28			
1982-83	**Hartford Whalers**	**NHL**	**79**	**10**	**13**	**23**	**8**	**9**	**17**	**216**	**1**	**0**	**1**	**114**	**8.8**	**42**	**6**	**82**	**0**	**–46**								
1983-84	**Washington Capitals**	**NHL**	**57**	**2**	**6**	**8**	**2**	**4**	**6**	**133**	**0**	**0**	**0**	**37**	**5.4**	**21**	**1**	**19**	**0**	**1**	**1**	**0**	**0**	**0**	**0**	**0**	**0**	**0**
1984-85	**Washington Capitals**	**NHL**	**51**	**6**	**12**	**18**	**5**	**8**	**13**	**72**	**0**	**0**	**1**	**62**	**9.7**	**29**	**1**	**20**	**0**	**8**	**5**	**0**	**0**	**0**	**9**	**0**	**0**	**0**
	Binghamton Whalers	AHL	28	9	16	25				58																		
1985-86	**Washington Capitals**	**NHL**	**78**	**18**	**38**	**56**	**14**	**26**	**40**	**152**	**3**	**0**	**2**	**149**	**12.1**	**98**	**21**	**55**	**2**	**24**	**9**	**1**	**3**	**4**	**27**	**0**	**0**	**0**
1986-87	**Washington Capitals**	**NHL**	**67**	**14**	**30**	**44**	**12**	**22**	**34**	**184**	**2**	**0**	**0**	**92**	**15.2**	**70**	**17**	**45**	**1**	**9**	**7**	**1**	**3**	**4**	**38**	**1**	**0**	**0**
1987-88	**Washington Capitals**	**NHL**	**78**	**15**	**12**	**27**	**13**	**9**	**22**	**153**	**3**	**0**	**0**	**109**	**13.8**	**50**	**17**	**36**	**0**	**–3**	**14**	**0**	**5**	**5**	**58**	**0**	**0**	**0**
1988-89	**Edmonton Oilers**	**NHL**	**49**	**4**	**5**	**9**	**3**	**4**	**7**	**82**	**0**	**0**	**1**	**49**	**8.2**	**26**	**0**	**25**	**0**	**1**								
	Vancouver Canucks	**NHL**	**12**	**4**	**2**	**6**	**3**	**1**	**4**	**35**	**2**	**0**	**0**	**22**	**18.2**	**9**	**3**	**4**	**0**	**2**	**7**	**0**	**0**	**0**	**21**	**0**	**0**	**0**
1989-90	**Quebec Nordiques**	**NHL**	**7**	**1**	**3**	**4**	**1**	**2**	**3**	**17**	**0**	**0**	**0**	**8**	**12.5**	**9**	**5**	**6**	**0**	**–2**								
	Detroit Red Wings	**NHL**	**28**	**3**	**7**	**10**	**3**	**5**	**8**	**16**	**0**	**0**	**0**	**19**	**15.8**	**15**	**0**	**15**	**0**	**0**								
	NHL Totals		**545**	**84**	**143**	**227**	**69**	**100**	**169**	**1173**	**11**	**0**	**5**	**696**	**12.1**	**398**	**74**	**326**	**3**		**43**	**2**	**11**	**13**	**153**	**1**	**0**	**0**

WHL All-Star Team (1980)

Signed as a free agent by **Philadelphia**, September 28, 1979. Traded to **Hartford** by **Philadelphia** with Ken Linseman and Philadelphia's 1st (David Jensen) and 3rd (Leif Karlsson) round choices in 1982 Entry Draft for Mark Howe and Hartford's 3rd round choice (Derrick Smith) in 1983 Entry Draft, August 19, 1982. Traded to **Washington** by **Hartford** for Torrie Robertson, October 3, 1983. Traded to **Edmonton** by **Washington** for the rights to Geoff Courtnall, July 22, 1988. Traded to **Vancouver** by **Edmonton** with Doug Smith for John Leblanc and Vancouver's 5th round choice (Peter White) in 1989 Entry Draft, March 7, 1989. Claimed by **Quebec** from **Vancouver** in Waiver Draft, October 2, 1989. Traded to **Detroit** by **Quebec** with Robert Picard for Tony McKegney, December 4, 1989.

• ADAMS, Kevyn

Kevyn W. C – R. 6'1", 195 lbs. b: Washington, D.C., 10/8/1974. Boston's 1st, 25th overall, in 1993.

Season	Club	League	GP	G	A	Pts	AG	AA	APts	PIM	PP	SH	GW	S	%	TGF	PGF	TGA	PGA	+/–	GP	G	A	Pts	PIM	PP	SH	GW
1990-91	Niagara Scenics	NAJHL	55	17	20	37				24																		
1991-92	Niagara Scenics	NAJHL	40	25	33	58				51																		
1992-93	University of Miami-Ohio	CCHA	40	17	15	32				18																		
1993-94	University of Miami-Ohio	CCHA	36	15	28	43				24																		
	United States	WJC-A	7	3	4	7				2																		
1994-95	University of Miami-Ohio	CCHA	38	20	29	49				30																		
1995-96	University of Miami-Ohio	CCHA	36	17	30	47				30																		
1996-97	Grand Rapids Griffins	IHL	82	22	25	47				47											5	1	1	2	4			
1997-98	**Toronto Maple Leafs**	**NHL**	**5**	**0**	**0**	**0**	**0**	**0**	**0**	**7**	**0**	**0**	**0**	**3**	**0.0**	**0**	**0**	**1**	**1**	**0**								
	St. John's Maple Leafs	AHL	59	17	20	37				99											4	0	0	0	4			
1998-99	**Toronto Maple Leafs**	**NHL**	**1**	**0**	**0**	**0**	**0**	**0**	**0**	**0**	**0**	**0**	**0**	**1**	**0.0**	**0**	**0**	**0**	**0**	**0**	**7**	**0**	**2**	**2**	**14**	**0**	**0**	**0**
	St. John's Maple Leafs	AHL	80	15	35	50				85											5	2	0	2	4			
99-2000	**Toronto Maple Leafs**	**NHL**	**52**	**5**	**8**	**13**	**6**	**7**	**13**	**39**	**0**	**0**	**0**	**70**	**7.1**	**19**	**0**	**38**	**12**	**–7**	**12**	**1**	**0**	**1**	**7**	**0**	**1**	**0**
	St. John's Maple Leafs	AHL	23	6	11	17				24																		
	NHL Totals		**58**	**5**	**8**	**13**	**6**	**7**	**13**	**46**	**0**	**0**	**0**	**74**	**6.8**	**19**	**0**	**39**	**13**		**19**	**1**	**2**	**3**	**21**	**0**	**1**	**0**

CCHA Second All-Star Team (1995)

Signed as a free agent by **Toronto**, August 7, 1997. Selected by **Columbus** from **Toronto** in Expansion Draft, June 23, 2000.

• ADDUONO, Rick

Rick Norman C – . 5'11", 182 lbs. b: Fort William, Ont., 1/25/1955. Boston's 3rd, 60th overall, in 1975.

Season	Club	League	GP	G	A	Pts	AG	AA	APts	PIM	PP	SH	GW	S	%	TGF	PGF	TGA	PGA	+/–	GP	G	A	Pts	PIM	PP	SH	GW
1972-73	St. Catharines Black Hawks	OMJHL	55	45	64	109				58																		
1973-74	St. Catharines Black Hawks	OMJHL	70	51	*84	*135				24																		
	St. Catharines Black Hawks	Mem-Cup	3	1	0	1				2																		
1974-75	St. Catharines Black Hawks	OMJHL	55	27	39	66				31											4	0	1	1	6			
1975-76	**Boston Bruins**	**NHL**	**1**	**0**	**0**	**0**	**0**	**0**	**0**	**0**	**0**	**0**	**0**	**0**	**0.0**	**0**	**0**	**1**	**0**	**–1**								
	Rochester Americans	AHL	68	11	23	34				24											7	2	1	3	7			
	Binghamton Dusters	NAHL	2	2	0	2				0																		
1976-77	Rochester Americans	AHL	77	29	45	74				38											8	3	1	4	2			
1977-78	Rochester Americans	AHL	76	38	60	*98				34											6	1	2	3	6			
1978-79	Birmingham Bulls	WHA	80	20	33	53				67																		
1979-80	**Atlanta Flames**	**NHL**	**3**	**0**	**0**	**0**	**0**	**0**	**0**	**2**	**0**	**0**	**0**	**1**	**0.0**	**0**	**0**	**1**	**0**	**–1**								
	Birmingham Bulls	CHL	78	35	39	74				76											4	1	0	1	0			
1980-81	KAC Klagenfurt	Austria	7	4	5	9				4																		
	New Haven Nighthawks	AHL	51	6	12	18				57											4	0	1	1	6			
1981-82	Fredericton Express	AHL	5	1	1	2				2																		
1982-1990	Thunder Bay Twins	CASH	PLAYER/COACH – STATISTICS UNAVAILABLE																									

Season	Club	League	GP	G	A	Pts	AG	AA	APts	PIM	PP	SH	GW	S	%	TGF	PGF	TGA	PGA	+/–	GP	G	A	Pts	PIM	PP	SH	GW
			REGULAR SEASON																		PLAYOFFS							
1990-1994	Thunder Bay Flyers	USHL	DID NOT PLAY – COACHING																									
1994-1998	South Carolina Stingrays	ECHL	DID NOT PLAY – ASSISTANT COACH																									
1998-2000	South Carolina Stingrays	ECHL	DID NOT PLAY – COACHING																									
	NHL Totals		**4**	**0**	**0**	**0**	**0**	**0**	**0**	**2**	**0**	**0**	**0**	**1**	**0.0**	**0**	**0**	**2**	**0**		....	....	....	....	....	....	....	....
	Other Major League Totals		80	20	33	53	....	....	....	67	....	....	....	....	....	....	....	....	....	....	....	....	....	....	....	....	....	....

AHL Second All-Star Team (1978) • Won John B. Sollenberger Trophy (Top Scorer - AHL) (1978)

Selected by **San Diego** (WHA) in 1975 WHA Amateur Draft, May, 1975. Signed as a free agent by **Birmingham** (WHA) after **San Diego** franchise folded, July, 1978. Signed as a free agent by **Atlanta**, October 9, 1979. Signed as a free agent by **New Haven** (AHL), November, 1980.

• AFFLECK, Bruce

Robert Bruce D – L. 6', 205 lbs. b: Salmon Arm, B.C., 5/5/1954. California's 3rd, 21st overall, in 1974.

Season	Club	League	GP	G	A	Pts	AG	AA	APts	PIM	PP	SH	GW	S	%	TGF	PGF	TGA	PGA	+/–	GP	G	A	Pts	PIM	PP	SH	GW
1970-71	Penticton Broncos	BCJHL	60	23	46	69	....	....	....	49	....	....	....	....	....	....	....	....	....	....	....	....	....	....	....	....	....	....
1971-72	Penticton Broncos	BCJHL	57	31	69	100	....	....	....	91	....	....	....	....	....	....	....	....	....	....	....	....	....	....	....	....	....	....
1972-73	University of Denver	WCHA	39	6	19	25	....	....	....	30	....	....	....	....	....	....	....	....	....	....	....	....	....	....	....	....	....	....
1973-74	University of Denver	WCHA	38	8	23	31	....	....	....	42	....	....	....	....	....	....	....	....	....	....	....	....	....	....	....	....	....	....
1974-75	Salt Lake Golden Eagles	CHL	35	0	14	14	....	....	....	28	....	....	....	....	....	....	....	....	....	....	....	....	....	....	....	....	....	....
	St. Louis Blues	**NHL**	**13**	**0**	**2**	**2**	**0**	**1**	**1**	**4**	**0**	**0**	**0**	**3**	**0.0**	**13**	**0**	**6**	**0**	**7**	**1**	**0**	**0**	**0**	**0**	**0**	**0**	**0**
	Springfield Indians	AHL	8	1	3	4	....	....	....	12	....	....	....	....	....	....	....	....	....	....	....	....	....	....	....	....	....	....
1975-76	**St. Louis Blues**	**NHL**	**80**	**4**	**26**	**30**	**3**	**19**	**22**	**20**	**3**	**0**	**1**	**100**	**4.0**	**92**	**17**	**112**	**40**	**3**	**3**	**0**	**0**	**0**	**0**	**0**	**0**	**0**
1976-77	**St. Louis Blues**	**NHL**	**80**	**5**	**20**	**25**	**4**	**15**	**19**	**24**	**1**	**0**	**0**	**133**	**3.8**	**86**	**8**	**110**	**10**	**–22**	**4**	**0**	**0**	**0**	**0**	**0**	**0**	**0**
1977-78	**St. Louis Blues**	**NHL**	**75**	**4**	**14**	**18**	**4**	**11**	**15**	**26**	**0**	**0**	**1**	**95**	**4.2**	**54**	**6**	**122**	**18**	**–56**	....	....	....	....	....	....	....	....
1978-79	**St. Louis Blues**	**NHL**	**26**	**1**	**3**	**4**	**1**	**2**	**3**	**12**	**0**	**0**	**0**	**34**	**2.9**	**15**	**2**	**28**	**2**	**–13**	....	....	....	....	....	....	....	....
	Salt Lake Golden Eagles	CHL	48	8	31	39	....	....	....	30	....	....	....	....	....	....	....	....	....	....	10	0	4	4	2	....	....	....
1979-80	**Vancouver Canucks**	**NHL**	**5**	**0**	**1**	**1**	**0**	**1**	**1**	**0**	**0**	**0**	**0**	**3**	**0.0**	**2**	**0**	**3**	**1**	**0**	....	....	....	....	....	....	....	....
	Dallas Black Hawks	CHL	72	10	53	63	....	....	....	39	....	....	....	....	....	....	....	....	....	....	....	....	....	....	....	....	....	....
1980-81	Indianapolis Checkers	CHL	77	8	50	58	....	....	....	41	....	....	....	....	....	....	....	....	....	....	5	2	6	8	2	....	....	....
1981-82	EHC Kloten	Switz.	38	15	14	29	....	....	....	....	....	....	....	....	....	....	....	....	....	....	....	....	....	....	....	....	....	....
	Indianapolis Checkers	CHL	16	5	17	22	....	....	....	4	....	....	....	....	....	....	....	....	....	....	13	1	17	18	16	....	....	....
1982-83	EHC Kloten	Switz.	30	6	12	18	....	....	....	....	....	....	....	....	....	....	....	....	....	....	....	....	....	....	....	....	....	....
	Indianapolis Checkers	CHL	8	2	12	14	....	....	....	0	....	....	....	....	....	....	....	....	....	....	13	0	18	18	2	....	....	....
1983-84	**New York Islanders**	**NHL**	**1**	**0**	**0**	**0**	**0**	**0**	**0**	**0**	**0**	**0**	**0**	**2**	**0.0**	**0**	**0**	**1**	**0**	**–1**	....	....	....	....	....	....	....	....
	Indianapolis Checkers	CHL	54	13	40	53	....	....	....	18	....	....	....	....	....	....	....	....	....	....	2	0	0	0	0	....	....	....
	NHL Totals		**280**	**14**	**66**	**80**	**12**	**49**	**61**	**86**	**4**	**0**	**2**	**370**	**3.8**	**262**	**33**	**382**	**71**		**8**	**0**	**0**	**0**	**0**	**0**	**0**	**0**

BCJHL First All-Star Team (1971, 1972) • WCHA First All-Star Team (1973) • NCAA Championship All-Tournament Team (1973) • WCHA Second All-Star Team (1974) • CHL First All-Star Team (1980, 1981, 1984) • Won Bobby Orr Trophy (Top Defenseman - CHL) (1980, 1981, 1984) • Shared Tommy Ivan Trophy (MVP - CHL) with John Vanbiesbrouck (1984)

Traded to **St. Louis** by **California** for Frank Spring, January 9, 1975. Traded to **Vancouver** by **St. Louis** with Gord Buynak for cash, November 6, 1979. Traded to **St. Louis** by **Vancouver** with Gord Buynak for cash, February 28, 1980. Signed as a free agent by **NY Islanders**, September 22, 1980.

• AFINOGENOV, Maxim

Maxim Sergeyevich RW – L. 5'11", 176 lbs. b: Moscow, USSR, 9/4/1979. Buffalo's 3rd, 69th overall, in 1997.

Season	Club	League	GP	G	A	Pts	AG	AA	APts	PIM	PP	SH	GW	S	%	TGF	PGF	TGA	PGA	+/–	GP	G	A	Pts	PIM	PP	SH	GW
1995-96	Dynamo Moscow-2	Russia-2	STATISTICS NOT AVAILABLE																									
	Dynamo Moscow	CIS	1	0	0	0	....	....	....	0	....	....	....	....	....	....	....	....	....	....	....	....	....	....	....	....	....	....
	Russia	EJC-A	5	1	1	2	....	....	....	0	....	....	....	....	....	....	....	....	....	....	....	....	....	....	....	....	....	....
1996-97	Dynamo Moscow	Russia	29	6	5	11	....	....	....	10	....	....	....	....	....	....	....	....	....	....	4	0	2	2	0	....	....	....
	Dynamo Moscow	EuroHL	3	0	0	0	....	....	....	0	....	....	....	....	....	....	....	....	....	....	3	1	0	1	4	....	....	....
	Russia	EJC-A	6	4	3	7	....	....	....	18	....	....	....	....	....	....	....	....	....	....	....	....	....	....	....	....	....	....
1997-98	Dynamo Moscow	Russia	35	10	5	15	....	....	....	53	....	....	....	....	....	....	....	....	....	....	....	....	....	....	....	....	....	....
	Dynamo Moscow	EuroHL	6	3	1	4	....	....	....	27	....	....	....	....	....	....	....	....	....	....	....	....	....	....	....	....	....	....
	Russia	WJC-A	7	3	2	5	....	....	....	4	....	....	....	....	....	....	....	....	....	....	....	....	....	....	....	....	....	....
1998-99	Dynamo Moscow	Russia	38	8	13	21	....	....	....	24	....	....	....	....	....	....	....	....	....	....	16	*10	6	*16	14	....	....	....
	Dynamo Moscow	EuroHL	5	3	5	8	....	....	....	29	....	....	....	....	....	....	....	....	....	....	4	2	1	3	27	....	....	....
	Russia	WJC-A	7	3	5	8	....	....	....	0	....	....	....	....	....	....	....	....	....	....	....	....	....	....	....	....	....	....
	Russia	WC-A	6	2	1	3	....	....	....	2	....	....	....	....	....	....	....	....	....	....	....	....	....	....	....	....	....	....
99-2000	**Buffalo Sabres**	**NHL**	**65**	**16**	**18**	**34**	**18**	**17**	**35**	**41**	**2**	**0**	**2**	**128**	**12.5**	**38**	**8**	**34**	**0**	**–4**	**5**	**0**	**1**	**1**	**2**	**0**	**0**	**0**
	Rochester Americans	AHL	15	6	12	18	....	....	....	8	....	....	....	....	....	....	....	....	....	....	8	3	1	4	4	....	....	....
	Russia	WC-A	6	1	0	1	....	....	....	4	....	....	....	....	....	....	....	....	....	....	....	....	....	....	....	....	....	....
	NHL Totals		**65**	**16**	**18**	**34**	**18**	**17**	**35**	**41**	**2**	**0**	**2**	**128**	**12.5**	**38**	**8**	**34**	**0**		**5**	**0**	**1**	**1**	**2**	**0**	**0**	**0**

Named Best Forward at WJC-A (1999)

• AGNEW, Jim

D – L. 6'1", 190 lbs. b: Hartney, Man., 3/21/1966. Vancouver's 10th, 157th overall, in 1984.

Season	Club	League	GP	G	A	Pts	AG	AA	APts	PIM	PP	SH	GW	S	%	TGF	PGF	TGA	PGA	+/–	GP	G	A	Pts	PIM	PP	SH	GW
1982-83	Estevan Bruins	SJHL	STATISTICS NOT AVAILABLE																									
	Brandon Wheat Kings	WHL	14	1	1	2	....	....	....	9	....	....	....	....	....	....	....	....	....	....	....	....	....	....	....	....	....	....
1983-84	Brandon Wheat Kings	WHL	71	6	17	23	....	....	....	107	....	....	....	....	....	....	....	....	....	....	12	0	1	1	39	....	....	....
1984-85	Brandon Wheat Kings	WHL	19	3	15	18	....	....	....	82	....	....	....	....	....	....	....	....	....	....	....	....	....	....	....	....	....	....
	Portland Winter Hawks	WHL	44	5	24	29	....	....	....	223	....	....	....	....	....	....	....	....	....	....	6	0	2	2	44	....	....	....
1985-86	Portland Winter Hawks	WHL	70	6	30	36	....	....	....	286	....	....	....	....	....	....	....	....	....	....	9	0	1	1	48	....	....	....
1986-87	**Vancouver Canucks**	**NHL**	**4**	**0**	**0**	**0**	**0**	**0**	**0**	**0**	**0**	**0**	**0**	**1**	**0.0**	**0**	**0**	**0**	**0**	**0**	....	....	....	....	....	....	....	....
	Fredericton Express	AHL	67	0	5	5	....	....	....	261	....	....	....	....	....	....	....	....	....	....	....	....	....	....	....	....	....	....
1987-88	**Vancouver Canucks**	**NHL**	**10**	**0**	**1**	**1**	**0**	**1**	**1**	**16**	**0**	**0**	**0**	**4**	**0.0**	**6**	**0**	**7**	**2**	**1**	....	....	....	....	....	....	....	....
	Fredericton Express	AHL	63	2	8	10	....	....	....	188	....	....	....	....	....	....	....	....	....	....	14	0	2	2	43	....	....	....
1988-89	Milwaukee Admirals	IHL	47	2	10	12	....	....	....	181	....	....	....	....	....	....	....	....	....	....	11	0	2	2	34	....	....	....
1989-90	**Vancouver Canucks**	**NHL**	**7**	**0**	**0**	**0**	**0**	**0**	**0**	**36**	**0**	**0**	**0**	**3**	**0.0**	**3**	**0**	**4**	**0**	**–1**	....	....	....	....	....	....	....	....
	Milwaukee Admirals	IHL	51	4	10	14	....	....	....	238	....	....	....	....	....	....	....	....	....	....	....	....	....	....	....	....	....	....
1990-91	**Vancouver Canucks**	**NHL**	**20**	**0**	**0**	**0**	**0**	**0**	**0**	**81**	**0**	**0**	**0**	**12**	**0.0**	**5**	**0**	**16**	**0**	**–11**	....	....	....	....	....	....	....	....
	Milwaukee Admirals	IHL	3	0	0	0	....	....	....	33	....	....	....	....	....	....	....	....	....	....	....	....	....	....	....	....	....	....
1991-92	**Vancouver Canucks**	**NHL**	**24**	**0**	**0**	**0**	**0**	**0**	**0**	**56**	**0**	**0**	**0**	**9**	**0.0**	**3**	**0**	**8**	**4**	**–1**	**4**	**0**	**0**	**0**	**6**	**0**	**0**	**0**
1992-93	**Hartford Whalers**	**NHL**	**16**	**0**	**0**	**0**	**0**	**0**	**0**	**68**	**0**	**0**	**0**	**3**	**0.0**	**14**	**0**	**13**	**2**	**3**	....	....	....	....	....	....	....	....
	Springfield Indians	AHL	1	0	1	1	....	....	....	2	....	....	....	....	....	....	....	....	....	....	....	....	....	....	....	....	....	....
1993-94	**Hartford Whalers**	**NHL**	DID NOT PLAY – INJURED																									
	NHL Totals		**81**	**0**	**1**	**1**	**0**	**1**	**1**	**257**	**0**	**0**	**0**	**32**	**0.0**	**31**	**0**	**48**	**8**		**4**	**0**	**0**	**0**	**6**	**0**	**0**	**0**

WHL West First All-Star Team (1986) • IHL Second All-Star Team (1990)

• Missed majority of 1990-1993 and entire 1993-94 seasons recovering from knee injury originally suffered in game vs. Muskegon (IHL), January 6, 1990. Signed as a free agent by **Hartford**, July 8, 1992. • Suffered career-ending knee injury in exhibition game vs. Ottawa, September 14, 1994. • Officially announced retirement, September 22, 1994.

• AHERN, Fred

Frederick Vincent RW – R. 6', 180 lbs. b: Boston, MA, 2/12/1952.

Season	Club	League	GP	G	A	Pts	AG	AA	APts	PIM	PP	SH	GW	S	%	TGF	PGF	TGA	PGA	+/–	GP	G	A	Pts	PIM	PP	SH	GW
1970-71	Bowdoin College	ECAC-2	21	14	12	26	....	....	....	....	....	....	....	....	....	....	....	....	....	....	....	....	....	....	....	....	....	....
1971-72	Bowdoin College	ECAC-2	15	7	14	21	....	....	....	....	....	....	....	....	....	....	....	....	....	....	....	....	....	....	....	....	....	....
1972-73	Bowdoin College	ECAC-2	21	13	21	34	....	....	....	....	....	....	....	....	....	....	....	....	....	....	....	....	....	....	....	....	....	....
1973-74	Bowdoin College	ECAC-2	21	18	20	38	....	....	....	....	....	....	....	....	....	....	....	....	....	....	....	....	....	....	....	....	....	....
1974-75	**California Golden Seals**	**NHL**	**3**	**2**	**1**	**3**	**2**	**1**	**3**	**0**	**1**	**0**	**1**	**10**	**20.0**	**3**	**2**	**2**	**0**	**–1**	....	....	....	....	....	....	....	....
	Salt Lake Golden Eagles	CHL	64	26	26	52	....	....	....	101	....	....	....	....	....	....	....	....	....	....	9	5	3	8	11	....	....	....
1975-76	**California Golden Seals**	**NHL**	**44**	**17**	**8**	**25**	**15**	**6**	**21**	**43**	**3**	**0**	**4**	**88**	**19.3**	**38**	**9**	**32**	**1**	**–2**	....	....	....	....	....	....	....	....
	Salt Lake Golden Eagles	CHL	30	12	14	26	....	....	....	57	....	....	....	....	....	....	....	....	....	....	....	....	....	....	....	....	....	....
1976-77	United States	Can-Cup	5	2	0	2	....	....	....	0	....	....	....	....	....	....	....	....	....	....	....	....	....	....	....	....	....	....
	Cleveland Barons	**NHL**	**25**	**4**	**4**	**8**	**4**	**3**	**7**	**20**	**2**	**0**	**0**	**45**	**8.9**	**9**	**4**	**17**	**0**	**–12**	....	....	....	....	....	....	....	....
1977-78	**Cleveland Barons**	**NHL**	**36**	**3**	**4**	**7**	**3**	**3**	**6**	**48**	**0**	**0**	**1**	**37**	**8.1**	**10**	**1**	**26**	**1**	**–16**	....	....	....	....	....	....	....	....
	Colorado Rockies	**NHL**	**38**	**5**	**13**	**18**	**5**	**10**	**15**	**19**	**1**	**0**	**0**	**66**	**7.6**	**24**	**4**	**36**	**0**	**–16**	**2**	**0**	**1**	**1**	**2**	**0**	**0**	**0**
1978-79	Binghamton Dusters	AHL	75	25	32	57	....	....	....	56	....	....	....	....	....	....	....	....	....	....	5	1	4	5	4	....	....	....
1979-80	Adirondack Red Wings	AHL	38	4	6	10	....	....	....	34	....	....	....	....	....	....	....	....	....	....	5	0	1	1	2	....	....	....
	Oklahoma City Stars	CHL	25	4	9	13	....	....	....	45	....	....	....	....	....	....	....	....	....	....	....	....	....	....	....	....	....	....

			REGULAR SEASON																		PLAYOFFS							
Season	Club	League	GP	G	A	Pts	AG	AA	APts	PIM	PP	SH	GW	S	%	TGF	PGF	TGA	PGA	+/-	GP	G	A	Pts	PIM	PP	SH	GW
1980-81	HC Neuchatel	Switz-2	STATISTICS NOT AVAILABLE																									
	Baltimore Clippers	EHL	7	3	1	4	....	....	....	0	....	....	....	....	....	....	....	....	....	....	....	....	....	....	....	....	....	....
1981-82	Cape Cod Buccaneers	ACHL	38	9	27	36	....	....	....	38	....	....	....	....	....	....	....	....	....	....	....	....	....	....	....	....	....	....
	NHL Totals		**146**	**31**	**30**	**61**	**29**	**23**	**52**	**130**	**7**	**0**	**6**	**246**	**12.6**	**84**	**20**	**113**	**2**		**2**	**0**	**1**	**1**	**2**	**0**	**0**	**0**

Signed as a free agent by **California**, September, 1974. Transferred to **Cleveland** after **California** franchise relocated, August 26, 1976. Traded to **Colorado** by **Cleveland** with Ralph Klassen for Rick Jodzio and Chuck Arnason, January 9, 1978. Traded to **Cleveland** by **Colorado** for cash, May 11, 1978. Placed on **Minnesota** reserve list after **Cleveland-Minnesota** Dispersal Draft, June 15, 1979.

• AHOLA, Peter

Peter Kristian D – L. 6'3", 205 lbs. b: Espoo, Finland, 5/14/1968.

Season	Club	League	GP	G	A	Pts	AG	AA	APts	PIM	PP	SH	GW	S	%	TGF	PGF	TGA	PGA	+/-	GP	G	A	Pts	PIM	PP	SH	GW
1985-86	Kiekko-Espoo	Finland-Jr.	5	0	0	0	....	....	....	0	....	....	....	....	....	....	....	....	....	....	....	....	....	....	....	....	....	....
1986-87	Kiekko-Espoo	Finland-Jr.	33	6	12	18	....	....	....	97	....	....	....	....	....	....	....	....	....	....	....	....	....	....	....	....	....	....
1987-88	Kiekko-Espoo	Finland-3	28	6	10	16	....	....	....	44	....	....	....	....	....	....	....	....	....	....	....	....	....	....	....	....	....	....
1988-89	Kiekko-Espoo	Finland-Jr.	7	3	0	3	....	....	....	18	....	....	....	....	....	....	....	....	....	....	....	....	....	....	....	....	....	....
	Sports Academy	Finland-Jr.	5	2	6	8	....	....	....	6	....	....	....	....	....	....	....	....	....	....	....	....	....	....	....	....	....	....
	Kiekko-Espoo	Finland-Jr.	7	2	1	3	....	....	....	8	....	....	....	....	....	....	....	....	....	....	3	0	6	6	2	....	....	....
	Kiekko-Espoo	Finland-2	44	5	10	15	....	....	....	62	....	....	....	....	....	....	....	....	....	....	....	....	....	....	....	....	....	....
1989-90	Boston University	H-East	43	3	20	23	....	....	....	65	....	....	....	....	....	....	....	....	....	....	....	....	....	....	....	....	....	....
1990-91	Boston University	H-East	39	12	24	36	....	....	....	88	....	....	....	....	....	....	....	....	....	....	....	....	....	....	....	....	....	....
1991-92	**Los Angeles Kings**	**NHL**	**71**	**7**	**12**	**19**	**6**	**9**	**15**	**101**	**0**	**0**	**0**	**74**	**9.5**	**66**	**3**	**76**	**25**	**12**	**6**	**0**	**0**	**0**	**2**	**0**	**0**	**0**
	Phoenix Roadrunners	IHL	7	3	3	6	....	....	....	34	....	....	....	....	....	....	....	....	....	....	....	....	....	....	....	....	....	....
1992-93	**Los Angeles Kings**	**NHL**	**8**	**1**	**1**	**2**	**1**	**1**	**2**	**6**	**0**	**0**	**0**	**3**	**33.3**	**5**	**0**	**7**	**0**	**–2**	....	....	....	....	....	....	....	....
	Pittsburgh Penguins	**NHL**	**22**	**0**	**1**	**1**	**0**	**1**	**1**	**14**	**0**	**0**	**0**	**5**	**0.0**	**8**	**0**	**13**	**3**	**–2**	....	....	....	....	....	....	....	....
	Cleveland Lumberjacks	IHL	9	1	0	1	....	....	....	4	....	....	....	....	....	....	....	....	....	....	....	....	....	....	....	....	....	....
	San Jose Sharks	**NHL**	**20**	**2**	**3**	**5**	**2**	**2**	**4**	**16**	**0**	**0**	**0**	**32**	**6.3**	**19**	**6**	**26**	**7**	**–6**	....	....	....	....	....	....	....	....
1993-94	**Calgary Flames**	**NHL**	**2**	**0**	**0**	**0**	**0**	**0**	**0**	**0**	**0**	**0**	**0**	**1**	**0.0**	**0**	**0**	**0**	**0**	**0**	....	....	....	....	....	....	....	....
	Saint John Flames	AHL	66	9	19	28	....	....	....	59	....	....	....	....	....	....	....	....	....	....	6	1	2	3	12	....	....	....
1994-95	Kiekko-Espoo	Finland	50	12	21	33	....	....	....	96	....	....	....	....	....	....	....	....	....	....	4	5	1	6	10	....	....	....
	Finland	Nat-Team	15	0	4	4	....	....	....	12	....	....	....	....	....	....	....	....	....	....	....	....	....	....	....	....	....	....
1995-96	HIFK Helsinki	Finland	34	7	7	14	....	....	....	58	....	....	....	....	....	....	....	....	....	....	3	1	0	1	2	....	....	....
	Finland	Nat-Team	2	0	0	0	....	....	....	4	....	....	....	....	....	....	....	....	....	....	....	....	....	....	....	....	....	....
1996-97	HIFK Helsinki	Finland	34	7	7	14	....	....	....	58	....	....	....	....	....	....	....	....	....	....	3	1	0	1	2	....	....	....
	Finland	Nat-Team	6	1	0	1	....	....	....	4	....	....	....	....	....	....	....	....	....	....	....	....	....	....	....	....	....	....
1997-98	TPS Turku	Finland	46	6	17	23	....	....	....	36	....	....	....	....	....	....	....	....	....	....	4	0	0	0	6	....	....	....
	TPS Turku	EuroHL	6	0	0	0	....	....	....	8	....	....	....	....	....	....	....	....	....	....	....	....	....	....	....	....	....	....
	Finland	Nat-Team	6	2	3	5	....	....	....	4	....	....	....	....	....	....	....	....	....	....	....	....	....	....	....	....	....	....
1998-99	TPS Turku	Finland	47	12	21	33	....	....	....	93	....	....	....	....	....	....	....	....	....	....	10	3	7	10	12	....	....	....
99-2000	Blues Espoo	Finland	50	12	24	36	....	....	....	110	....	....	....	....	....	....	....	....	....	....	4	1	2	3	*38	....	....	....
	NHL Totals		**123**	**10**	**17**	**27**	**9**	**13**	**22**	**137**	**0**	**0**	**0**	**115**	**8.7**	**98**	**9**	**122**	**35**		**6**	**0**	**0**	**0**	**2**	**0**	**0**	**0**

Signed as a free agent by **LA Kings**, April 5, 1991. Traded to **Pittsburgh** by **LA Kings** for Jeff Chychrun, November 6, 1992. Traded to **San Jose** by **Pittsburgh** for future considerations, February 26, 1993. Traded to **Tampa Bay** by **San Jose** for Dave Capuano, June 19, 1993. Traded to **Calgary** by **Tampa Bay** for cash, October 5, 1993.

• AHRENS, Chris

Christopher Alfred D – R. 6', 185 lbs. b: San Bernadino, CA, 7/31/1952. Minnesota's 4th, 76th overall, in 1972.

Season	Club	League	GP	G	A	Pts	AG	AA	APts	PIM	PP	SH	GW	S	%	TGF	PGF	TGA	PGA	+/-	GP	G	A	Pts	PIM	PP	SH	GW
1969-70	Kitchener Greenshirts	OHA-B	38	10	19	29	....	....	....	134	....	....	....	....	....	....	....	....	....	....	....	....	....	....	....	....	....	....
	Kitchener Rangers	OHA-Jr.	4	1	0	1	....	....	....	0	....	....	....	....	....	....	....	....	....	....	....	....	....	....	....	....	....	....
1970-71	Kitchener Rangers	OHA-Jr.	54	7	14	21	....	....	....	203	....	....	....	....	....	....	....	....	....	....	4	0	2	2	11	....	....	....
1971-72	Kitchener Rangers	OMJHL	40	3	22	25	....	....	....	64	....	....	....	....	....	....	....	....	....	....	....	....	....	....	....	....	....	....
1972-73	Cleveland-Jacksonville Barons	AHL	76	2	17	19	....	....	....	*248	....	....	....	....	....	....	....	....	....	....	....	....	....	....	....	....	....	....
	Minnesota North Stars	**NHL**	....	....	....	....	....	....	....	....	....	....	....	....	....	....	....	....	....	....	**1**	**0**	**0**	**0**	**0**	**0**	**0**	**0**
1973-74	**Minnesota North Stars**	**NHL**	**3**	**0**	**1**	**1**	**0**	**1**	**1**	**0**	**0**	**0**	**0**	**4**	**0.0**	**1**	**0**	**0**	**0**	**1**	....	....	....	....	....	....	....	....
	New Haven Nighthawks	AHL	73	4	20	24	....	....	....	177	....	....	....	....	....	....	....	....	....	....	10	1	0	1	*45	....	....	....
1974-75	**Minnesota North Stars**	**NHL**	**44**	**0**	**2**	**2**	**0**	**1**	**1**	**77**	**0**	**0**	**0**	**20**	**0.0**	**8**	**1**	**41**	**7**	**–27**	....	....	....	....	....	....	....	....
	New Haven Nighthawks	AHL	23	1	10	11	....	....	....	132	....	....	....	....	....	....	....	....	....	....	16	2	5	7	*106	....	....	....
1975-76	**Minnesota North Stars**	**NHL**	**2**	**0**	**0**	**0**	**0**	**0**	**0**	**2**	**0**	**0**	**0**	**1**	**0.0**	**0**	**0**	**1**	**0**	**–1**	....	....	....	....	....	....	....	....
	New Haven Nighthawks	AHL	70	2	8	10	....	....	....	121	....	....	....	....	....	....	....	....	....	....	3	0	0	0	12	....	....	....
1976-77	**Minnesota North Stars**	**NHL**	**2**	**0**	**0**	**0**	**0**	**0**	**0**	**5**	**0**	**0**	**0**	**1**	**0.0**	**1**	**0**	**0**	**0**	**1**	....	....	....	....	....	....	....	....
	Rhode Island Reds	AHL	42	1	7	8	....	....	....	82	....	....	....	....	....	....	....	....	....	....	....	....	....	....	....	....	....	....
	New Haven Nighthawks	AHL	29	1	6	7	....	....	....	82	....	....	....	....	....	....	....	....	....	....	....	....	....	....	....	....	....	....
1977-78	**Minnesota North Stars**	**NHL**	**1**	**0**	**0**	**0**	**0**	**0**	**0**	**0**	**0**	**0**	**0**	**0**	**0.0**	**1**	**0**	**1**	**0**	**0**	....	....	....	....	....	....	....	....
	Fort Worth Texans	CHL	50	1	10	11	....	....	....	137	....	....	....	....	....	....	....	....	....	....	....	....	....	....	....	....	....	....
	Edmonton Oilers	WHA	4	0	0	0	....	....	....	15	....	....	....	....	....	....	....	....	....	....	....	....	....	....	....	....	....	....
	NHL Totals		**52**	**0**	**3**	**3**	**0**	**2**	**2**	**84**	**0**	**0**	**0**	**26**	**0.0**	**11**	**1**	**43**	**7**		**1**	**0**	**0**	**0**	**0**	**0**	**0**	**0**
	Other Major League Totals		4	0	0	0	....	....	....	15	....	....	....	....	....	....	....	....	....	....	....	....	....	....	....	....	....	....

Selected by **NY Raiders** (WHA) in 1972 WHA General Player Draft, February 12, 1972. Traded to **Edmonton** (WHA) by **Minnesota** with Pierre Jarry for future considerations, March, 1978.

• AITKEN, Brad

Bradley E. LW – L. 6'2", 200 lbs. b: Scarborough, Ont., 10/30/1967. Pittsburgh's 3rd, 46th overall, in 1986.

Season	Club	League	GP	G	A	Pts	AG	AA	APts	PIM	PP	SH	GW	S	%	TGF	PGF	TGA	PGA	+/-	GP	G	A	Pts	PIM	PP	SH	GW
1983-84	Chatham Maroons	OJHL-B	48	18	30	48	....	....	....	113	....	....	....	....	....	....	....	....	....	....	....	....	....	....	....	....	....	....
1984-85	Peterborough Petes	OHL	63	18	26	44	....	....	....	36	....	....	....	....	....	....	....	....	....	....	13	1	2	3	2	....	....	....
1985-86	Peterborough Petes	OHL	48	9	28	37	....	....	....	77	....	....	....	....	....	....	....	....	....	....	....	....	....	....	....	....	....	....
	Sault Ste. Marie Greyhounds	OHL	20	8	19	27	....	....	....	11	....	....	....	....	....	....	....	....	....	....	....	....	....	....	....	....	....	....
1986-87	Sault Ste. Marie Greyhounds	OHL	52	27	38	65	....	....	....	86	....	....	....	....	....	....	....	....	....	....	4	1	2	3	5	....	....	....
1987-88	**Pittsburgh Penguins**	**NHL**	**5**	**1**	**1**	**2**	**1**	**1**	**2**	**0**	**0**	**0**	**0**	**4**	**25.0**	**2**	**0**	**1**	**0**	**1**	....	....	....	....	....	....	....	....
	Muskegon Lumberjacks	IHL	74	32	31	63	....	....	....	128	....	....	....	....	....	....	....	....	....	....	1	0	0	0	0	....	....	....
1988-89	Muskegon Lumberjacks	IHL	74	35	30	65	....	....	....	139	....	....	....	....	....	....	....	....	....	....	13	5	5	10	75	....	....	....
1989-90	Muskegon Lumberjacks	IHL	46	10	23	33	....	....	....	172	....	....	....	....	....	....	....	....	....	....	....	....	....	....	....	....	....	....
	Phoenix Roadrunners	IHL	8	2	1	3	....	....	....	18	....	....	....	....	....	....	....	....	....	....	....	....	....	....	....	....	....	....
	Fort Wayne Komets	IHL	13	5	2	7	....	....	....	0	....	....	....	....	....	....	....	....	....	....	5	2	1	3	12	....	....	....
1990-91	**Pittsburgh Penguins**	**NHL**	**6**	**0**	**1**	**1**	**0**	**1**	**1**	**25**	**0**	**0**	**0**	**3**	**0.0**	**1**	**0**	**3**	**0**	**–2**	....	....	....	....	....	....	....	....
	Muskegon Lumberjacks	IHL	44	14	17	31	....	....	....	143	....	....	....	....	....	....	....	....	....	....	....	....	....	....	....	....	....	....
	Kansas City Blades	IHL	6	4	6	10	....	....	....	2	....	....	....	....	....	....	....	....	....	....	....	....	....	....	....	....	....	....
	Edmonton Oilers	**NHL**	**3**	**0**	**1**	**1**	**0**	**1**	**1**	**0**	**0**	**0**	**0**	**0**	**0.0**	**1**	**0**	**2**	**0**	**–1**	....	....	....	....	....	....	....	....
	Cape Breton Oilers	AHL	6	2	3	5	....	....	....	17	....	....	....	....	....	....	....	....	....	....	3	0	2	2	6	....	....	....
1991-92	St. John's Maple Leafs	AHL	59	12	27	39	....	....	....	169	....	....	....	....	....	....	....	....	....	....	....	....	....	....	....	....	....	....
1992-93	St. John's Maple Leafs	AHL	4	0	1	1	....	....	....	2	....	....	....	....	....	....	....	....	....	....	....	....	....	....	....	....	....	....
	EV Landshut	Germany	1	0	0	0	....	....	....	0	....	....	....	....	....	....	....	....	....	....	....	....	....	....	....	....	....	....
	Raleigh IceCaps	ECHL	25	11	12	23	....	....	....	129	....	....	....	....	....	....	....	....	....	....	10	1	9	10	12	....	....	....
	NHL Totals		**14**	**1**	**3**	**4**	**1**	**3**	**4**	**25**	**0**	**0**	**0**	**7**	**14.3**	**4**	**0**	**6**	**0**		....	....	....	....	....	....	....	....

Traded to **Edmonton** by **Pittsburgh** for Kim Issel, March 5, 1991. Signed as a free agent by **Toronto**, July 30, 1991.

• AITKEN, Johnathan

Johnathan James D – L. 6'4", 215 lbs. b: Edmonton, Alta., 5/24/1978. Boston's 1st, 8th overall, in 1996.

Season	Club	League	GP	G	A	Pts	AG	AA	APts	PIM	PP	SH	GW	S	%	TGF	PGF	TGA	PGA	+/-	GP	G	A	Pts	PIM	PP	SH	GW
1993-94	Sherwood Park Kings	AAHA	31	4	9	13	....	....	....	54	....	....	....	....	....	....	....	....	....	....	....	....	....	....	....	....	....	....
1994-95	Medicine Hat Tigers	WHL	53	0	5	5	....	....	....	71	....	....	....	....	....	....	....	....	....	....	5	0	0	0	0	....	....	....
1995-96	Medicine Hat Tigers	WHL	71	6	14	20	....	....	....	131	....	....	....	....	....	....	....	....	....	....	5	1	0	1	6	....	....	....
1996-97	Brandon Wheat Kings	WHL	65	4	18	22	....	....	....	211	....	....	....	....	....	....	....	....	....	....	6	0	0	0	4	....	....	....
1997-98	Brandon Wheat Kings	WHL	69	9	25	34	....	....	....	183	....	....	....	....	....	....	....	....	....	....	18	0	8	8	67	....	....	....

			REGULAR SEASON																		PLAYOFFS							
Season	Club	League	GP	G	A	Pts	AG	AA	APts	PIM	PP	SH	GW	S	%	TGF	PGF	TGA	PGA	+/–	GP	G	A	Pts	PIM	PP	SH	GW
1998-99	Providence Bruins	AHL	65	2	9	11	....	....	....	92	....	....	....	....	....	....	....	....	....	....	13	0	0	0	17	....	....	....
99-2000	**Boston Bruins**	**NHL**	**3**	**0**	**0**	**0**	**0**	**0**	**0**	**0**	**0**	**0**	**0**	**2**	**0.0**	**0**	**0**	**3**	**0**	**–3**	....	....	....	....	....	....	....	....
	Providence Bruins	AHL	70	2	12	14	....	....	....	121	....	....	....	....	....	....	....	....	....	....	11	1	0	1	26	....	....	....
	NHL Totals		**3**	**0**	**0**	**0**	**0**	**0**	**0**	**0**	**0**	**0**	**0**	**2**	**0.0**	**0**	**0**	**3**	**0**		....	....	....	....	....	....	....	....

WHL East Second All-Star Team (1998)

• AIVAZOFF, Micah

C – L. 6′, 195 lbs. b: Powell River, B.C., 5/4/1969. Los Angeles' 6th, 109th overall, in 1988.

Season	Club	League	GP	G	A	Pts	AG	AA	APts	PIM	PP	SH	GW	S	%	TGF	PGF	TGA	PGA	+/–	GP	G	A	Pts	PIM	PP	SH	GW
1985-86	Powell River A's	BCAHA	STATISTICS NOT AVAILABLE																									
	Victoria Cougars	WHL	25	3	4	7	....	....	....	25	....	....	....	....	....	....	....	....	....	....	....	....	....	....	....	....	....	....
1986-87	Victoria Cougars	WHL	72	18	39	57	....	....	....	112	....	....	....	....	....	....	....	....	....	....	5	1	0	1	2	....	....	....
1987-88	Victoria Cougars	WHL	69	26	57	83	....	....	....	79	....	....	....	....	....	....	....	....	....	....	8	3	4	7	14	....	....	....
1988-89	Victoria Cougars	WHL	70	35	65	100	....	....	....	136	....	....	....	....	....	....	....	....	....	....	8	5	7	12	2	....	....	....
1989-90	New Haven Nighthawks	AHL	77	20	39	59	....	....	....	71	....	....	....	....	....	....	....	....	....	....	....	....	....	....	....	....	....	....
1990-91	New Haven Nighthawks	AHL	79	11	29	40	....	....	....	84	....	....	....	....	....	....	....	....	....	....	....	....	....	....	....	....	....	....
1991-92	Adirondack Red Wings	AHL	61	9	20	29	....	....	....	50	....	....	....	....	....	....	....	....	....	....	19	2	8	10	25	....	....	....
1992-93	Adirondack Red Wings	AHL	79	32	53	85	....	....	....	100	....	....	....	....	....	....	....	....	....	....	11	8	6	14	10	....	....	....
1993-94	**Detroit Red Wings**	**NHL**	**59**	**4**	**4**	**8**	**4**	**3**	**7**	**38**	**0**	**0**	**0**	**52**	**7.7**	**16**	**1**	**20**	**4**	**–1**	....	....	....	....	....	....	....	....
1994-95	**Edmonton Oilers**	**NHL**	**21**	**0**	**1**	**1**	**0**	**1**	**1**	**2**	**0**	**0**	**0**	**6**	**0.0**	**2**	**0**	**4**	**0**	**–2**	....	....	....	....	....	....	....	....
1995-96	**New York Islanders**	**NHL**	**12**	**0**	**1**	**1**	**0**	**1**	**1**	**6**	**0**	**0**	**0**	**8**	**0.0**	**2**	**1**	**8**	**1**	**–6**	....	....	....	....	....	....	....	....
	Utah Grizzlies	IHL	59	14	21	35	....	....	....	58	....	....	....	....	....	....	....	....	....	....	22	3	5	8	33	....	....	....
1996-97	Binghamton Rangers	AHL	75	12	36	48	....	....	....	70	....	....	....	....	....	....	....	....	....	....	4	1	1	2	0	....	....	....
1997-98	ERC Ingolstadt	Germany-2	19	9	19	28	....	....	....	59	....	....	....	....	....	....	....	....	....	....	....	....	....	....	....	....	....	....
	San Antonio Dragons	IHL	54	13	33	46	....	....	....	33	....	....	....	....	....	....	....	....	....	....	....	....	....	....	....	....	....	....
1998-99	Utah Grizzlies	IHL	79	25	22	47	....	....	....	67	....	....	....	....	....	....	....	....	....	....	....	....	....	....	....	....	....	....
99-2000	Utah Grizzlies	IHL	80	15	31	46	....	....	....	81	....	....	....	....	....	....	....	....	....	....	5	0	0	0	4	....	....	....
	NHL Totals		**92**	**4**	**6**	**10**	**4**	**5**	**9**	**46**	**0**	**0**	**0**	**66**	**6.1**	**20**	**2**	**32**	**5**		....	....	....	....	....	....	....	....

Signed as a free agent by **Detroit**, March 18, 1993. Claimed by **Pittsburgh** from **Detroit** in Waiver Draft, January 18, 1995. Claimed by **Edmonton** from **Pittsburgh** in Waiver Draft, January 18, 1995. Signed as a free agent by **NY Islanders**, August 23, 1995. Signed as a free agent by **NY Rangers**, August 23, 1996.

• ALATALO, Mika

Mika Antero LW – L. 6′, 190 lbs. b: Oulu, Finland, 5/11/1971. Winnipeg's 11th, 203rd overall, in 1990.

Season	Club	League	GP	G	A	Pts	AG	AA	APts	PIM	PP	SH	GW	S	%	TGF	PGF	TGA	PGA	+/–	GP	G	A	Pts	PIM	PP	SH	GW
1988-89	KooKoo Kouvola	Finland	34	8	6	14	....	....	....	10	....	....	....	....	....	....	....	....	....	....	....	....	....	....	....	....	....	....
	Finland	EJC-A	6	3	3	6	....	....	....	10	....	....	....	....	....	....	....	....	....	....	....	....	....	....	....	....	....	....
1989-90	KooKoo Kouvola	Finland	41	3	5	8	....	....	....	22	....	....	....	....	....	....	....	....	....	....	....	....	....	....	....	....	....	....
1990-91	Lukko Rauma	Finland	39	10	1	11	....	....	....	10	....	....	....	....	....	....	....	....	....	....	....	....	....	....	....	....	....	....
1991-92	Lukko Rauma	Finland	43	20	17	37	....	....	....	32	....	....	....	....	....	....	....	....	....	....	2	0	0	0	0	....	....	....
1992-93	Lukko Rauma	Finland	48	16	19	35	....	....	....	38	....	....	....	....	....	....	....	....	....	....	3	0	0	0	0	....	....	....
1993-94	Lukko Rauma	Finland	45	19	15	34	....	....	....	77	....	....	....	....	....	....	....	....	....	....	9	2	2	4	4	....	....	....
	Finland	Olympics	7	2	1	3	....	....	....	2	....	....	....	....	....	....	....	....	....	....	....	....	....	....	....	....	....	....
1994-95	TPS Turku	Finland	44	23	13	36	....	....	....	79	....	....	....	....	....	....	....	....	....	....	13	2	5	7	8	....	....	....
1995-96	TPS Turku	Finland	49	19	18	37	....	....	....	44	....	....	....	....	....	....	....	....	....	....	11	3	4	7	8	....	....	....
1996-97	Lulea HF	Sweden	50	19	18	37	....	....	....	54	....	....	....	....	....	....	....	....	....	....	10	2	3	5	22	....	....	....
1997-98	Lulea HF	Sweden	45	14	10	24	....	....	....	22	....	....	....	....	....	....	....	....	....	....	2	0	0	0	0	....	....	....
1998-99	TPS Turku	Finland	53	14	23	37	....	....	....	44	....	....	....	....	....	....	....	....	....	....	10	6	3	9	6	....	....	....
99-2000	**Phoenix Coyotes**	**NHL**	**82**	**10**	**17**	**27**	**11**	**16**	**27**	**36**	**1**	**0**	**1**	**107**	**9.3**	**42**	**2**	**43**	**0**	**–3**	**5**	**0**	**0**	**0**	**2**	**0**	**0**	**0**
	NHL Totals		**82**	**10**	**17**	**27**	**11**	**16**	**27**	**36**	**1**	**0**	**1**	**107**	**9.3**	**42**	**2**	**43**	**0**		**5**	**0**	**0**	**0**	**2**	**0**	**0**	**0**

Transferred to **Phoenix** after **Winnipeg** franchise relocated, July 1, 1996.

• ALBELIN, Tommy

D – L. 6′1″, 194 lbs. b: Stockholm, Sweden, 5/21/1964. Quebec's 7th, 158th overall, in 1983.

Season	Club	League	GP	G	A	Pts	AG	AA	APts	PIM	PP	SH	GW	S	%	TGF	PGF	TGA	PGA	+/–	GP	G	A	Pts	PIM	PP	SH	GW
1980-81	Stocksunds IF	Sweden-3	18	6	1	7	....	....	....	....	....	....	....	....	....	....	....	....	....	....	....	....	....	....	....	....	....	....
1981-82	Stocksunds IF	Sweden-3	22	6	2	8	....	....	....	....	....	....	....	....	....	....	....	....	....	....	....	....	....	....	....	....	....	....
1982-83	Djurgardens IF Stockholm	Sweden	19	2	5	7	....	....	....	4	....	....	....	....	....	....	....	....	....	....	6	1	0	1	2	....	....	....
	Sweden	WJC-A	7	0	3	3	....	....	....	....	....	....	....	....	....	....	....	....	....	....	....	....	....	....	....	....	....	....
1983-84	Djurgardens IF Stockholm	Sweden	30	9	5	14	....	....	....	26	....	....	....	....	....	....	....	....	....	....	4	0	1	1	2	....	....	....
	Sweden	WJC-A	7	1	3	4	....	....	....	10	....	....	....	....	....	....	....	....	....	....	....	....	....	....	....	....	....	....
1984-85	Djurgardens IF Stockholm	Sweden	32	9	8	17	....	....	....	22	....	....	....	....	....	....	....	....	....	....	8	2	1	3	4	....	....	....
	Sweden	WEC-A	10	1	0	1	....	....	....	10	....	....	....	....	....	....	....	....	....	....	....	....	....	....	....	....	....	....
1985-86	Djurgardens IF Stockholm	Sweden	35	4	8	12	....	....	....	26	....	....	....	....	....	....	....	....	....	....	....	....	....	....	....	....	....	....
	Sweden	WEC-A	10	3	0	3	....	....	....	12	....	....	....	....	....	....	....	....	....	....	....	....	....	....	....	....	....	....
1986-87	Djurgardens IF Stockholm	Sweden	33	7	5	12	....	....	....	49	....	....	....	....	....	....	....	....	....	....	2	0	0	0	0	....	....	....
	Sweden	WEC-A	10	1	5	6	....	....	....	12	....	....	....	....	....	....	....	....	....	....	....	....	....	....	....	....	....	....
1987-88	Sweden	Can-Cup	6	2	2	4	....	....	....	2	....	....	....	....	....	....	....	....	....	....	....	....	....	....	....	....	....	....
	Quebec Nordiques	**NHL**	**60**	**3**	**23**	**26**	**3**	**16**	**19**	**47**	**0**	**0**	**0**	**98**	**3.1**	**66**	**26**	**59**	**12**	**–7**	....	....	....	....	....	....	....	....
1988-89	**Quebec Nordiques**	**NHL**	**14**	**2**	**4**	**6**	**2**	**3**	**5**	**27**	**1**	**0**	**1**	**16**	**12.5**	**16**	**5**	**17**	**0**	**–6**	....	....	....	....	....	....	....	....
	Halifax Citadels	AHL	8	2	5	7	....	....	....	4	....	....	....	....	....	....	....	....	....	....	....	....	....	....	....	....	....	....
	New Jersey Devils	**NHL**	**46**	**7**	**24**	**31**	**6**	**17**	**23**	**40**	**1**	**1**	**1**	**82**	**8.5**	**83**	**23**	**50**	**8**	**18**	....	....	....	....	....	....	....	....
	Sweden	WEC-A	7	0	2	2	....	....	....	8	....	....	....	....	....	....	....	....	....	....	....	....	....	....	....	....	....	....
1989-90	**New Jersey Devils**	**NHL**	**68**	**6**	**23**	**29**	**5**	**16**	**21**	**63**	**4**	**0**	**0**	**125**	**4.8**	**86**	**23**	**74**	**10**	**–1**	....	....	....	....	....	....	....	....
1990-91	**New Jersey Devils**	**NHL**	**47**	**2**	**12**	**14**	**2**	**9**	**11**	**44**	**1**	**0**	**0**	**66**	**3.0**	**47**	**14**	**36**	**4**	**1**	**3**	**0**	**1**	**1**	**2**	**0**	**0**	**0**
	Utica Devils	AHL	14	4	2	6	....	....	....	10	....	....	....	....	....	....	....	....	....	....	....	....	....	....	....	....	....	....
1991-92	Sweden	Can-Cup	6	0	0	0	....	....	....	6	....	....	....	....	....	....	....	....	....	....	....	....	....	....	....	....	....	....
	New Jersey Devils	**NHL**	**19**	**0**	**4**	**4**	**0**	**3**	**3**	**4**	**0**	**0**	**0**	**18**	**0.0**	**19**	**0**	**15**	**3**	**7**	**1**	**1**	**1**	**2**	**0**	**0**	**0**	**0**
	Utica Devils	AHL	11	4	6	10	....	....	....	4	....	....	....	....	....	....	....	....	....	....	....	....	....	....	....	....	....	....
1992-93	**New Jersey Devils**	**NHL**	**36**	**1**	**5**	**6**	**1**	**3**	**4**	**14**	**1**	**0**	**1**	**33**	**3.0**	**33**	**7**	**35**	**9**	**0**	**5**	**2**	**0**	**2**	**0**	**1**	**0**	**1**
1993-94	**New Jersey Devils**	**NHL**	**62**	**2**	**17**	**19**	**2**	**13**	**15**	**36**	**1**	**0**	**1**	**62**	**3.2**	**61**	**13**	**50**	**22**	**20**	**20**	**2**	**5**	**7**	**14**	**1**	**0**	**1**
	Albany River Rats	AHL	4	0	2	2	....	....	....	17	....	....	....	....	....	....	....	....	....	....	....	....	....	....	....	....	....	....
1994-95♦	**New Jersey Devils**	**NHL**	**48**	**5**	**10**	**15**	**9**	**15**	**24**	**20**	**2**	**0**	**0**	**60**	**8.3**	**43**	**4**	**39**	**9**	**9**	**20**	**1**	**7**	**8**	**2**	**0**	**0**	**0**
1995-96	**New Jersey Devils**	**NHL**	**53**	**1**	**12**	**13**	**1**	**10**	**11**	**14**	**0**	**0**	**0**	**90**	**1.1**	**37**	**12**	**31**	**6**	**0**	....	....	....	....	....	....	....	....
	Calgary Flames	**NHL**	**20**	**0**	**1**	**1**	**0**	**1**	**1**	**4**	**0**	**0**	**0**	**31**	**0.0**	**13**	**2**	**17**	**7**	**1**	**4**	**0**	**0**	**0**	**0**	**0**	**0**	**0**
1996-97	Sweden	W-Cup	4	1	0	1	....	....	....	2	....	....	....	....	....	....	....	....	....	....	....	....	....	....	....	....	....	....
	Calgary Flames	**NHL**	**72**	**4**	**11**	**15**	**4**	**10**	**14**	**14**	**2**	**0**	**0**	**103**	**3.9**	**69**	**21**	**75**	**19**	**–8**	....	....	....	....	....	....	....	....
	Sweden	WC-A	11	1	3	4	....	....	....	2	....	....	....	....	....	....	....	....	....	....	....	....	....	....	....	....	....	....
1997-98	**Calgary Flames**	**NHL**	**69**	**2**	**17**	**19**	**2**	**17**	**19**	**32**	**1**	**0**	**2**	**88**	**2.3**	**67**	**11**	**82**	**35**	**9**	....	....	....	....	....	....	....	....
	Sweden	Olympics	3	0	0	0	....	....	....	4	....	....	....	....	....	....	....	....	....	....	....	....	....	....	....	....	....	....
1998-99	**Calgary Flames**	**NHL**	**60**	**1**	**5**	**6**	**1**	**5**	**6**	**8**	**0**	**0**	**0**	**54**	**1.9**	**27**	**0**	**67**	**29**	**–11**	....	....	....	....	....	....	....	....
99-2000	**Calgary Flames**	**NHL**	**41**	**4**	**6**	**10**	**4**	**6**	**10**	**12**	**1**	**1**	**1**	**37**	**10.8**	**28**	**5**	**39**	**13**	**–3**	....	....	....	....	....	....	....	....
	NHL Totals		**715**	**40**	**174**	**214**	**42**	**144**	**186**	**379**	**15**	**2**	**7**	**963**	**4.2**	**695**	**166**	**686**	**186**		**53**	**6**	**14**	**20**	**18**	**2**	**0**	**2**

Swedish World All-Star Team (1987, 1997)

Traded to **New Jersey** by **Quebec** for New Jersey's 4th round choice (Niclas Andersson) in 1989 Entry Draft, December 12, 1988. Traded to **Calgary** by **New Jersey** with Cale Hulse and Jocelyn Lemieux for Phil Housley and Dan Keczmer, February 26, 1996.

• ALDRIDGE, Keith

D – R. 5′11″, 185 lbs. b: Detroit, MI, 7/20/1973.

Season	Club	League	GP	G	A	Pts	AG	AA	APts	PIM	PP	SH	GW	S	%	TGF	PGF	TGA	PGA	+/–	GP	G	A	Pts	PIM	PP	SH	GW
1989-90	Detroit Central Parts	MNHL	STATISTICS NOT AVAILABLE																									
1990-91	Detroit Little Ceasars	MNHL	STATISTICS NOT AVAILABLE																									
1991-92	Rochester Mustangs	USHL	STATISTICS NOT AVAILABLE																									
1992-93	Lake Superior State	CCHA	37	3	11	14	....	....	....	30	....	....	....	....	....	....	....	....	....	....	....	....	....	....	....	....	....	....
1993-94	Lake Superior State	CCHA	45	10	24	34	....	....	....	86	....	....	....	....	....	....	....	....	....	....	....	....	....	....	....	....	....	....
1994-95	Lake Superior State	CCHA	40	10	31	41	....	....	....	89	....	....	....	....	....	....	....	....	....	....	....	....	....	....	....	....	....	....

Season	Club	League	GP	G	A	Pts	AG	AA	APts	PIM	PP	SH	GW	S	%	TGF	PGF	TGA	PGA	+/-	GP	G	A	Pts	PIM	PP	SH	GW
			REGULAR SEASON																		PLAYOFFS							
1995-96	Lake Superior State	CCHA	38	14	36	50	....	....	....	88	....	....	....	....	....	....	....	....	....	....	....	....	....	....	....	....	....	....
	Baltimore Bandits	AHL	7	0	2	2	....	....	....	2	....	....	....	....	....	....	....	....	....	....	....	....	....	....	....	....	....	....
1996-97	Baltimore Bandits	AHL	51	4	9	13	....	....	....	92	....	....	....	....	....	....	....	....	....	....	3	0	0	0	4	....	....	....
1997-98	Detroit Vipers	IHL	79	13	21	34	....	....	....	89	....	....	....	....	....	....	....	....	....	....	23	1	9	10	67	....	....	....
1998-99	Detroit Vipers	IHL	66	15	28	43	....	....	....	130	....	....	....	....	....	....	....	....	....	....	11	2	7	9	49	....	....	....
99-2000	**Dallas Stars**	**NHL**	**4**	**0**	**0**	**0**	**0**	**0**	**0**	**0**	**0**	**0**	**0**	**6**	**0.0**	**1**	**0**	**0**	**0**	**1**	....	....	....	....	....	....	....	....
	Michigan K-Wings	IHL	55	2	10	12	....	....	....	55	....	....	....	....	....	....	....	....	....	....	....	....	....	....	....	....	....	....
	NHL Totals		**4**	**0**	**0**	**0**	**0**	**0**	**0**	**0**	**0**	**0**	**0**	**6**	**0.0**	**1**	**0**	**0**	**0**		....	....	....	....	....	....	....	....

Signed as a free agent by **Dallas**, September 1, 1999.

• ALEXANDER, Claire

Claire Arthur "The Milkman" D – R. 6'1", 175 lbs. b: Collingwood, Ont., 6/16/1945.

Season	Club	League	GP	G	A	Pts	AG	AA	APts	PIM	PP	SH	GW	S	%	TGF	PGF	TGA	PGA	+/-	GP	G	A	Pts	PIM	PP	SH	GW
1965-66	Kitchener Rangers	OHA-Jr.	45	2	15	17	....	....	....	26	....	....	....	....	....	....	....	....	....	....	15	0	0	0	0	....	....	....
1966-67	Johnstown–Knoxville	EHL	67	17	20	37	....	....	....	39	....	....	....	....	....	....	....	....	....	....	....	....	....	....	....	....	....	....
1967-68	Collingwood Kings	OHA-Sr.	40	17	32	49	....	....	....	36	....	....	....	....	....	....	....	....	....	....	....	....	....	....	....	....	....	....
1968-69	Collingwood Kings	OHA-Sr.	39	30	32	62	....	....	....	16	....	....	....	....	....	....	....	....	....	....	....	....	....	....	....	....	....	....
1969-70	Orillia Terriers	OHA-Sr.	27	23	5	28	....	....	....	24	....	....	....	....	....	....	....	....	....	....	....	....	....	....	....	....	....	....
1970-71	Orillia Terriers	OHA-Sr.	37	26	25	51	....	....	....	48	....	....	....	....	....	....	....	....	....	....	....	....	....	....	....	....	....	....
1971-72	Orillia Terriers	OHA-Sr.	41	13	28	41	....	....	....	42	....	....	....	....	....	....	....	....	....	....	....	....	....	....	....	....	....	....
1972-73	Orillia Terriers	OHA-Sr.	38	17	29	46	....	....	....	40	....	....	....	....	....	....	....	....	....	....	....	....	....	....	....	....	....	....
	Tulsa Oilers	CHL	5	5	1	6	....	....	....	9	....	....	....	....	....	....	....	....	....	....	....	....	....	....	....	....	....	....
1973-74	Oklahoma City Blazers	CHL	72	23	37	60	....	....	....	34	....	....	....	....	....	....	....	....	....	....	9	3	4	7	2	....	....	....
1974-75	**Toronto Maple Leafs**	**NHL**	**42**	**7**	**11**	**18**	**6**	**8**	**14**	**12**	**4**	**0**	**1**	**90**	**7.8**	**54**	**13**	**32**	**2**	**11**	**7**	**0**	**0**	**0**	**0**	**0**	**0**	**0**
	Oklahoma City Blazers	CHL	33	8	17	25	....	....	....	14	....	....	....	....	....	....	....	....	....	....	....	....	....	....	....	....	....	....
1975-76	**Toronto Maple Leafs**	**NHL**	**33**	**2**	**6**	**8**	**2**	**4**	**6**	**6**	**0**	**0**	**0**	**46**	**4.3**	**23**	**7**	**18**	**2**	**0**	**9**	**2**	**4**	**6**	**4**	**1**	**0**	**0**
	Oklahoma City Blazers	CHL	43	25	31	56	....	....	....	22	....	....	....	....	....	....	....	....	....	....	....	....	....	....	....	....	....	....
1976-77	**Toronto Maple Leafs**	**NHL**	**48**	**1**	**12**	**13**	**1**	**9**	**10**	**12**	**0**	**0**	**0**	**61**	**1.6**	**31**	**5**	**32**	**2**	**–4**	....	....	....	....	....	....	....	....
1977-78	Tulsa Oilers	CHL	46	14	42	56	....	....	....	22	....	....	....	....	....	....	....	....	....	....	....	....	....	....	....	....	....	....
	Vancouver Canucks	**NHL**	**32**	**8**	**18**	**26**	**7**	**14**	**21**	**6**	**4**	**0**	**0**	**105**	**7.6**	**53**	**21**	**47**	**8**	**–7**	....	....	....	....	....	....	....	....
1978-79	Edmonton Oilers	WHA	54	8	23	31	....	....	....	16	....	....	....	....	....	....	....	....	....	....	....	....	....	....	....	....	....	....
	Dallas Black Hawks	CHL	7	1	2	3	....	....	....	0	....	....	....	....	....	....	....	....	....	....	6	1	2	3	4	....	....	....
1979-80	VfL Bad Nauheim	Germany	44	32	18	50	....	....	....	96	....	....	....	....	....	....	....	....	....	....	....	....	....	....	....	....	....	....
1980-81	VfL Bad Nauheim	Germany	38	16	18	34	....	....	....	48	....	....	....	....	....	....	....	....	....	....	5	4	1	5	27	....	....	....
1981-82	ZSC Zurich	Switz-2	STATISTICS NOT AVAILABLE																									
	NHL Totals		**155**	**18**	**47**	**65**	**16**	**35**	**51**	**36**	**8**	**0**	**1**	**302**	**6.0**	**161**	**46**	**129**	**14**		**16**	**2**	**4**	**6**	**4**	**1**	**0**	**0**
	Other Major League Totals		54	8	23	31	....	....	....	16	....	....	....	....	....	....	....	....	....	....	....	....	....	....	....	....	....	....

CHL First All-Star Team (1974) • Won Ken McKenzie Trophy (CHL's Rookie of the Year) (1974) • Named CHL's Top Defenseman (1974) • CHL Second All-Star Team (1978)

Signed to a five-game tryout by **Tulsa** (CHL), January, 1973. Signed as a free agent by **Toronto**, September, 1974. Traded to **Vancouver** by **Toronto** for cash, January 29, 1978. Signed as a free agent by **Edmonton** (WHA), June, 1978.

• ALFREDSSON, Daniel

RW – R. 5'11", 195 lbs. b: Goteborg, Sweden, 12/11/1972. Ottawa's 5th, 133rd overall, in 1994.

Season	Club	League	GP	G	A	Pts	AG	AA	APts	PIM	PP	SH	GW	S	%	TGF	PGF	TGA	PGA	+/-	GP	G	A	Pts	PIM	PP	SH	GW
1990-91	IF Molndal	Sweden-2	3	0	0	0	....	....	....	2	....	....	....	....	....	....	....	....	....	....	8	4	4	8	4	....	....	....
1991-92	IF Molndal	Sweden-2	32	12	8	20	....	....	....	43	....	....	....	....	....	....	....	....	....	....	....	....	....	....	....	....	....	....
1992-93	Vastra Frolunda	Sweden	20	1	5	6	....	....	....	8	....	....	....	....	....	....	....	....	....	....	....	....	....	....	....	....	....	....
1993-94	Vastra Frolunda	Sweden	39	20	10	30	....	....	....	18	....	....	....	....	....	....	....	....	....	....	4	1	1	2	....	....	....	....
1994-95	Vastra Frolunda	Sweden	22	7	11	18	....	....	....	22	....	....	....	....	....	....	....	....	....	....	....	....	....	....	....	....	....	....
	Sweden	WC-A	8	3	1	4	....	....	....	4	....	....	....	....	....	....	....	....	....	....	....	....	....	....	....	....	....	....
1995-96	**Ottawa Senators**	**NHL**	**82**	**26**	**35**	**61**	**26**	**29**	**55**	**28**	**8**	**2**	**3**	**212**	**12.3**	**89**	**38**	**82**	**13**	**–18**	....	....	....	....	....	....	....	....
	Sweden	WC-A	6	1	2	3	....	....	....	4	....	....	....	....	....	....	....	....	....	....	....	....	....	....	....	....	....	....
1996-97	Sweden	W-Cup	4	0	0	0	....	....	....	2	....	....	....	....	....	....	....	....	....	....	....	....	....	....	....	....	....	....
	Ottawa Senators	**NHL**	**76**	**24**	**47**	**71**	**25**	**42**	**67**	**30**	**11**	**1**	**1**	**247**	**9.7**	**97**	**37**	**67**	**12**	**5**	**7**	**5**	**2**	**7**	**6**	**3**	**0**	**2**
1997-98	**Ottawa Senators**	**NHL**	**55**	**17**	**28**	**45**	**20**	**27**	**47**	**18**	**7**	**0**	**7**	**149**	**11.4**	**59**	**24**	**33**	**5**	**7**	**11**	**7**	**2**	**9**	**20**	**2**	**1**	**1**
	Sweden	Olympics	4	2	3	5	....	....	....	2	....	....	....	....	....	....	....	....	....	....	....	....	....	....	....	....	....	....
1998-99	**Ottawa Senators**	**NHL**	**58**	**11**	**22**	**33**	**13**	**21**	**34**	**14**	**3**	**0**	**5**	**163**	**6.7**	**54**	**19**	**28**	**1**	**8**	**4**	**1**	**2**	**3**	**4**	**1**	**0**	**0**
	Sweden	WC-A	10	4	5	9	....	....	....	8	....	....	....	....	....	....	....	....	....	....	....	....	....	....	....	....	....	....
99-2000	**Ottawa Senators**	**NHL**	**57**	**21**	**38**	**59**	**24**	**35**	**59**	**28**	**4**	**2**	**0**	**164**	**12.8**	**77**	**23**	**49**	**6**	**11**	**6**	**1**	**3**	**4**	**2**	**1**	**0**	**0**
	NHL Totals		**328**	**99**	**170**	**269**	**108**	**154**	**262**	**118**	**33**	**5**	**16**	**935**	**10.6**	**376**	**141**	**259**	**37**		**28**	**14**	**9**	**23**	**32**	**7**	**1**	**3**

NHL All-Rookie Team (1996) • Won Calder Memorial Trophy (1996) • Played in NHL All-Star Game (1996, 1997, 1998)

• ALLAN, Jeff

D – L. 6' 1", 194 lbs. b: Hull, Que., 5/17/1957. Cleveland's 7th, 95th overall, in 1977.

Season	Club	League	GP	G	A	Pts	AG	AA	APts	PIM	PP	SH	GW	S	%	TGF	PGF	TGA	PGA	+/-	GP	G	A	Pts	PIM	PP	SH	GW
1974-75	Cornwall Royals	QMJHL	71	10	30	40	....	....	....	86	....	....	....	....	....	....	....	....	....	....	....	....	....	....	....	....	....	....
1975-76	Cornwall Royals	QMJHL	17	5	8	13	....	....	....	40	....	....	....	....	....	....	....	....	....	....	....	....	....	....	....	....	....	....
	Peterborough Petes	OMJHL	43	1	8	9	....	....	....	47	....	....	....	....	....	....	....	....	....	....	....	....	....	....	....	....	....	....
1976-77	Hull Festivals	QMJHL	68	15	33	48	....	....	....	76	....	....	....	....	....	....	....	....	....	....	....	....	....	....	....	....	....	....
1977-78	**Cleveland Barons**	**NHL**	**4**	**0**	**0**	**0**	**0**	**0**	**0**	**2**	**0**	**0**	**0**	**5**	**0.0**	**3**	**0**	**3**	**0**	**0**	....	....	....	....	....	....	....	....
	Cincinnati Stingers	WHA	2	0	0	0	....	....	....	0	....	....	....	....	....	....	....	....	....	....	....	....	....	....	....	....	....	....
	Hampton Gulls	AHL	8	0	0	0	....	....	....	4	....	....	....	....	....	....	....	....	....	....	....	....	....	....	....	....	....	....
	Phoenix Roadrunners	CHL	6	0	0	0	....	....	....	2	....	....	....	....	....	....	....	....	....	....	....	....	....	....	....	....	....	....
	Toledo Goaldiggers	IHL	44	7	20	27	....	....	....	89	....	....	....	....	....	....	....	....	....	....	17	2	2	4	20	....	....	....
1978-79	Toledo Goaldiggers	IHL	3	0	0	0	....	....	....	11	....	....	....	....	....	....	....	....	....	....	....	....	....	....	....	....	....	....
	Los Angeles Blades	PHL	19	6	5	11	....	....	....	100	....	....	....	....	....	....	....	....	....	....	....	....	....	....	....	....	....	....
	NHL Totals		**4**	**0**	**0**	**0**	**0**	**0**	**0**	**2**	**0**	**0**	**0**	**5**	**0.0**	**3**	**0**	**3**	**0**		....	....	....	....	....	....	....	....
	Other Major League Totals		2	0	0	0	....	....	....	0	....	....	....	....	....	....	....	....	....	....	....	....	....	....	....	....	....	....

Selected by **Cincinnati** (WHA) in 1977 WHA Amateur Draft, May, 1977.

• ALLEN, Chris

D – R. 6'2", 197 lbs. b: Chatham, Ont., 5/8/1978. Florida's 2nd, 60th overall, in 1996.

Season	Club	League	GP	G	A	Pts	AG	AA	APts	PIM	PP	SH	GW	S	%	TGF	PGF	TGA	PGA	+/-	GP	G	A	Pts	PIM	PP	SH	GW
1992-93	Blenheim Blades	OJHL-C	3	0	0	0	....	....	....	0	....	....	....	....	....	....	....	....	....	....	....	....	....	....	....	....	....	....
1993-94	Leamington Flyers	OJHL-B	52	6	20	26	....	....	....	38	....	....	....	....	....	....	....	....	....	....	....	....	....	....	....	....	....	....
1994-95	Kingston Frontenacs	OHL	43	3	5	8	....	....	....	15	....	....	....	....	....	....	....	....	....	....	2	0	0	0	0	....	....	....
1995-96	Kingston Frontenacs	OHL	55	21	18	39	....	....	....	58	....	....	....	....	....	....	....	....	....	....	6	0	2	2	8	....	....	....
1996-97	Kingston Frontenacs	OHL	61	14	29	43	....	....	....	81	....	....	....	....	....	....	....	....	....	....	5	1	2	3	4	....	....	....
	Carolina Monarchs	AHL	9	0	0	0	....	....	....	2	....	....	....	....	....	....	....	....	....	....	....	....	....	....	....	....	....	....
1997-98	Kingston Frontenacs	OHL	66	38	57	95	....	....	....	91	....	....	....	....	....	....	....	....	....	....	10	4	2	6	6	....	....	....
	Florida Panthers	**NHL**	**1**	**0**	**0**	**0**	**0**	**0**	**0**	**2**	**0**	**0**	**0**	**1**	**0.0**	**1**	**0**	**1**	**0**	**0**	....	....	....	....	....	....	....	....
1998-99	**Florida Panthers**	**NHL**	**1**	**0**	**0**	**0**	**0**	**0**	**0**	**0**	**0**	**0**	**0**	**0**	**0.0**	**1**	**0**	**0**	**0**	**1**	....	....	....	....	....	....	....	....
	Beast of New Haven	AHL	58	8	27	35	....	....	....	43	....	....	....	....	....	....	....	....	....	....	....	....	....	....	....	....	....	....
99-2000	Louisville Panthers	AHL	36	5	6	11	....	....	....	12	....	....	....	....	....	....	....	....	....	....	....	....	....	....	....	....	....	....
	Port Huron Border Cats	UHL	6	2	1	3	....	....	....	4	....	....	....	....	....	....	....	....	....	....	....	....	....	....	....	....	....	....
	NHL Totals		**2**	**0**	**0**	**0**	**0**	**0**	**0**	**2**	**0**	**0**	**0**	**1**	**0.0**	**2**	**0**	**1**	**0**		....	....	....	....	....	....	....	....

OHL First All-Star Team (1998) • Canadian Major Junior First All-Star Team (1998)

• ALLEN, Peter

D – R. 6'2", 200 lbs. b: Calgary, Alta., 3/6/1970. Boston's 1st, 24th overall, in 1991 Supplemental Draft.

Season	Club	League	GP	G	A	Pts	AG	AA	APts	PIM	PP	SH	GW	S	%	TGF	PGF	TGA	PGA	+/-	GP	G	A	Pts	PIM	PP	SH	GW
1988-89	Calgary Western College	ACAC	24	7	30	37	....	....	....	....	....	....	....	....	....	....	....	....	....	....	....	....	....	....	....	....	....	....
1989-90	Yale University	ECAC	26	2	4	6	....	....	....	16	....	....	....	....	....	....	....	....	....	....	....	....	....	....	....	....	....	....
1990-91	Yale University	ECAC	17	0	6	6	....	....	....	14	....	....	....	....	....	....	....	....	....	....	....	....	....	....	....	....	....	....
1991-92	Yale University	ECAC	26	5	13	18	....	....	....	26	....	....	....	....	....	....	....	....	....	....	....	....	....	....	....	....	....	....
1992-93	Yale University	ECAC	30	3	15	18	....	....	....	32	....	....	....	....	....	....	....	....	....	....	....	....	....	....	....	....	....	....

			REGULAR SEASON																		PLAYOFFS							
Season	**Club**	**League**	**GP**	**G**	**A**	**Pts**	**AG**	**AA**	**APts**	**PIM**	**PP**	**SH**	**GW**	**S**	**%**	**TGF**	**PGF**	**TGA**	**PGA**	**+/–**	**GP**	**G**	**A**	**Pts**	**PIM**	**PP**	**SH**	**GW**
1993-94	Richmond Renegades	ECHL	52	2	16	18	....	....	....	62	....	....	....	....	....	....	....	....	....	....	....	....	....	....	....	....	....	....
	P.E.I. Senators	AHL	6	0	1	1	....	....	....	6	....	....	....	....	....	....	....	....	....	....	....	....	....	....	....	....	....	....
1994-95	Canada	Nat-Team	52	5	15	20	....	....	....	36	....	....	....	....	....	....	....	....	....	....	....	....	....	....	....	....	....	....
	Canada	WC-A	7	0	0	0	....	....	....	4	....	....	....	....	....	....	....	....	....	....	....	....	....	....	....	....	....	....
1995-96	**Pittsburgh Penguins**	**NHL**	**8**	**0**	**0**	**0**	**0**	**0**	**0**	**8**	**0**	**0**	**0**	**2**	**0.0**	**4**	**0**	**2**	**0**	**2**	....	....	....	....	....	....	....	....
	Cleveland Lumberjacks	IHL	65	3	45	48	....	....	....	55	....	....	....	....	....	....	....	....	....	....	3	0	0	0	2	....	....	....
1996-97	Cleveland Lumberjacks	IHL	81	14	31	45	....	....	....	75	....	....	....	....	....	....	....	....	....	....	14	0	6	6	24	....	....	....
1997-98	Kentucky Thoroughblades	AHL	72	0	18	18	....	....	....	73	....	....	....	....	....	....	....	....	....	....	3	0	1	1	4	....	....	....
1998-99	Kentucky Thoroughblades	AHL	72	3	17	20	....	....	....	48	....	....	....	....	....	....	....	....	....	....	12	1	1	2	8	....	....	....
99-2000	Canada	Nat-Team	49	5	20	25	....	....	....	30	....	....	....	....	....	....	....	....	....	....	....	....	....	....	....	....	....	....
	Canada	WC-A	1	0	0	0	....	....	....	0	....	....	....	....	....	....	....	....	....	....	....	....	....	....	....	....	....	....
	NHL Totals		**8**	**0**	**0**	**0**	**0**	**0**	**0**	**8**	**0**	**0**	**0**	**2**	**0.0**	**4**	**0**	**2**	**0**		....	....	....	....	....	....	....	....

Signed as a free agent by **Pittsburgh**, August 10, 1995. Signed as a free agent by **San Jose**, August 19, 1997.

• ALLEY, Steve LW – L. 6', 185 lbs. b: Anoka, MN, 12/29/1953. Chicago's 10th, 141st overall, in 1973.

Season	Club	League	GP	G	A	Pts	AG	AA	APts	PIM	PP	SH	GW	S	%	TGF	PGF	TGA	PGA	+/–	GP	G	A	Pts	PIM	PP	SH	GW
1971-72	Anoka High School	Hi-School	28	25	49	74	....	....	....	....	....	....	....	....	....	....	....	....	....	....	....	....	....	....	....	....	....	....
1972-73	University of Wisconsin	WCHA	40	8	15	23	....	....	....	12	....	....	....	....	....	....	....	....	....	....	....	....	....	....	....	....	....	....
1973-74	University of Wisconsin	WCHA	36	12	19	31	....	....	....	16	....	....	....	....	....	....	....	....	....	....	....	....	....	....	....	....	....	....
1974-75	University of Wisconsin	WCHA	38	23	25	48	....	....	....	84	....	....	....	....	....	....	....	....	....	....	....	....	....	....	....	....	....	....
	United States	WEC-A	9	1	1	2	....	....	....	2	....	....	....	....	....	....	....	....	....	....	....	....	....	....	....	....	....	....
1975-76	United States	Nat-Team	64	29	33	62	....	....	....	67	....	....	....	....	....	....	....	....	....	....	....	....	....	....	....	....	....	....
	United States	Olympics	6	1	1	2	....	....	....	4	....	....	....	....	....	....	....	....	....	....	....	....	....	....	....	....	....	....
1976-77	University of Wisconsin	WCHA	45	32	31	63	....	....	....	50	....	....	....	....	....	....	....	....	....	....	....	....	....	....	....	....	....	....
1977-78	Birmingham Bulls	WHA	27	8	12	20	....	....	....	11	....	....	....	....	....	....	....	....	....	....	5	1	0	1	5	....	....	....
	Hampton Gulls	AHL	30	6	3	9	....	....	....	27	....	....	....	....	....	....	....	....	....	....	....	....	....	....	....	....	....	....
	Springfield Indians	AHL	1	0	0	0	....	....	....	0	....	....	....	....	....	....	....	....	....	....	....	....	....	....	....	....	....	....
	United States	WEC-A	3	0	0	0	....	....	....	0	....	....	....	....	....	....	....	....	....	....	....	....	....	....	....	....	....	....
1978-79	Birmingham Bulls	WHA	78	17	24	41	....	....	....	36	....	....	....	....	....	....	....	....	....	....	....	....	....	....	....	....	....	....
1979-80	**Hartford Whalers**	**NHL**	**7**	**1**	**1**	**2**	**1**	**1**	**2**	**0**	**0**	**0**	**0**	**5**	**20.0**	**2**	**0**	**6**	**0**	**–4**	**3**	**0**	**1**	**1**	**0**	**0**	**0**	**0**
	Springfield Indians	AHL	59	25	28	53	....	....	....	46	....	....	....	....	....	....	....	....	....	....	....	....	....	....	....	....	....	....
	Cincinnati Stingers	CHL	10	3	6	9	....	....	....	12	....	....	....	....	....	....	....	....	....	....	....	....	....	....	....	....	....	....
1980-81	**Hartford Whalers**	**NHL**	**8**	**2**	**2**	**4**	**2**	**1**	**3**	**11**	**0**	**0**	**0**	**10**	**20.0**	**8**	**0**	**7**	**0**	**1**	....	....	....	....	....	....	....	....
	Binghamton Whalers	AHL	69	26	32	58	....	....	....	34	....	....	....	....	....	....	....	....	....	....	6	3	1	4	9	....	....	....
	NHL Totals		**15**	**3**	**3**	**6**	**3**	**2**	**5**	**11**	**0**	**0**	**0**	**15**	**20.0**	**10**	**0**	**13**	**0**		**3**	**0**	**1**	**1**	**0**	**0**	**0**	**0**
	Other Major League Totals		105	25	36	61	....	....	....	47	....	....	....	....	....	....	....	....	....	....	5	1	0	1	5	....	....	....

Selected by **New England** (WHA) in 1973 WHA Amateur Draft, June, 1973. WHA rights traded to **Birmingham** (WHA) by **New England** (WHA) for future considerations, July, 1977. Claimed by **Hartford** from **Birmingham** (WHA) in 1979 WHA Dispersal Draft, June 9, 1979.

• ALLISON, Dave David Bryan D – R. 6'1", 200 lbs. b: Fort Frances, Ont., 4/14/1959.

Season	Club	League	GP	G	A	Pts	AG	AA	APts	PIM	PP	SH	GW	S	%	TGF	PGF	TGA	PGA	+/–	GP	G	A	Pts	PIM	PP	SH	GW
1976-77	Cornwall Royals	QMJHL	63	2	11	13	....	....	....	180	....	....	....	....	....	....	....	....	....	....	12	0	4	4	60	....	....	....
1977-78	Cornwall Royals	QMJHL	60	9	29	38	....	....	....	302	....	....	....	....	....	....	....	....	....	....	5	2	3	5	32	....	....	....
1978-79	Cornwall Royals	QMJHL	66	7	31	38	....	....	....	*407	....	....	....	....	....	....	....	....	....	....	7	1	6	7	34	....	....	....
1979-80	Nova Scotia Voyageurs	AHL	49	1	12	13	....	....	....	119	....	....	....	....	....	....	....	....	....	....	4	0	0	0	46	....	....	....
1980-81	Nova Scotia Voyageurs	AHL	70	5	12	17	....	....	....	298	....	....	....	....	....	....	....	....	....	....	6	0	0	0	15	....	....	....
1981-82	Nova Scotia Voyageurs	AHL	78	8	25	33	....	....	....	*332	....	....	....	....	....	....	....	....	....	....	9	0	3	3	*84	....	....	....
1982-83	Nova Scotia Voyageurs	AHL	70	3	22	25	....	....	....	180	....	....	....	....	....	....	....	....	....	....	7	0	2	2	24	....	....	....
1983-84	**Montreal Canadiens**	**NHL**	**3**	**0**	**0**	**0**	**0**	**0**	**0**	**12**	**0**	**0**	**0**	**2**	**0.0**	**1**	**0**	**3**	**0**	**–2**	....	....	....	....	....	....	....	....
	Nova Scotia Voyageurs	AHL	53	2	18	20	....	....	....	155	....	....	....	....	....	....	....	....	....	....	6	0	3	3	25	....	....	....
1984-85	Sherbrooke Canadiens	AHL	4	0	1	1	....	....	....	19	....	....	....	....	....	....	....	....	....	....	....	....	....	....	....	....	....	....
	Nova Scotia Voyageurs	AHL	68	4	18	22	....	....	....	175	....	....	....	....	....	....	....	....	....	....	6	0	2	2	15	....	....	....
1985-86	Muskegon Lumberjacks	IHL	66	7	30	37	....	....	....	247	....	....	....	....	....	....	....	....	....	....	14	2	9	11	46	....	....	....
1986-87	Muskegon Lumberjacks	IHL	67	11	35	46	....	....	....	337	....	....	....	....	....	....	....	....	....	....	15	4	3	7	20	....	....	....
1987-88	Newmarket Saints	AHL	48	1	9	10	....	....	....	166	....	....	....	....	....	....	....	....	....	....	....	....	....	....	....	....	....	....
1988-89	Halifax Citadels	AHL	12	1	2	3	....	....	....	29	....	....	....	....	....	....	....	....	....	....	....	....	....	....	....	....	....	....
	Indianapolis Ice	IHL	34	0	7	7	....	....	....	105	....	....	....	....	....	....	....	....	....	....	....	....	....	....	....	....	....	....
1989-1992	Virginia Lancers	ECHL	DID NOT PLAY – COACHING																									
1992-1994	Kingston Frontenacs	OHL	DID NOT PLAY – COACHING																									
1994-1995	P.E.I. Senators	AHL	DID NOT PLAY – COACHING																									
	Ottawa Senators	**NHL**	DID NOT PLAY – COACHING																									
1995-1996			OUT OF HOCKEY – RETIRED																									
1996-1998	Grand Rapids Griffins	IHL	DID NOT PLAY – COACHING																									
1998-1999			OUT OF HOCKEY – RETIRED																									
1999-2000	Fort Wayne Komets	UHL	DID NOT PLAY – COACHING																									
	NHL Totals		**3**	**0**	**0**	**0**	**0**	**0**	**0**	**12**	**0**	**0**	**0**	**2**	**0.0**	**1**	**0**	**3**	**0**		....	....	....	....	....	....	....	....

• Brother of Mike

Signed as a free agent by **Montreal**, October 4, 1979. Named Head Coach of **Milwaukee** (IHL), June 1, 2000.

• ALLISON, Jamie D – L. 6'1", 200 lbs. b: Lindsay, Ont., 5/13/1975. Calgary's 2nd, 44th overall, in 1993.

Season	Club	League	GP	G	A	Pts	AG	AA	APts	PIM	PP	SH	GW	S	%	TGF	PGF	TGA	PGA	+/–	GP	G	A	Pts	PIM	PP	SH	GW
1990-91	Waterloo Siskins	OJHL-B	38	3	8	11	....	....	....	91	....	....	....	....	....	....	....	....	....	....	....	....	....	....	....	....	....	....
1991-92	Windsor Spitfires	OHL	59	4	8	12	....	....	....	70	....	....	....	....	....	....	....	....	....	....	4	1	1	2	2	....	....	....
1992-93	Detroit Jr. Red Wings	OHL	61	0	13	13	....	....	....	64	....	....	....	....	....	....	....	....	....	....	15	2	5	7	23	....	....	....
1993-94	Detroit Jr. Red Wings	OHL	40	2	22	24	....	....	....	69	....	....	....	....	....	....	....	....	....	....	17	2	9	11	35	....	....	....
1994-95	Detroit Jr. Red Wings	OHL	50	1	14	15	....	....	....	119	....	....	....	....	....	....	....	....	....	....	18	2	7	9	35	....	....	....
	Calgary Flames	**NHL**	**1**	**0**	**0**	**0**	**0**	**0**	**0**	**0**	**0**	**0**	**0**	**0**	**0.0**	**0**	**0**	**0**	**0**	**0**	....	....	....	....	....	....	....	....
	Detroit Jr. Red Wings	Mem-Cup	5	0	0	0	....	....	....	4	....	....	....	....	....	....	....	....	....	....	....	....	....	....	....	....	....	....
1995-96	Saint John Flames	AHL	71	3	16	19	....	....	....	223	....	....	....	....	....	....	....	....	....	....	14	0	2	2	16	....	....	....
1996-97	**Calgary Flames**	**NHL**	**20**	**0**	**0**	**0**	**0**	**0**	**0**	**35**	**0**	**0**	**0**	**8**	**0.0**	**6**	**0**	**16**	**6**	**–4**	....	....	....	....	....	....	....	....
	Saint John Flames	AHL	46	3	6	9	....	....	....	139	....	....	....	....	....	....	....	....	....	....	5	0	1	1	4	....	....	....
1997-98	**Calgary Flames**	**NHL**	**43**	**3**	**8**	**11**	**4**	**8**	**12**	**104**	**0**	**0**	**1**	**27**	**11.1**	**28**	**0**	**29**	**4**	**3**	....	....	....	....	....	....	....	....
	Saint John Flames	AHL	16	0	5	5	....	....	....	49	....	....	....	....	....	....	....	....	....	....	....	....	....	....	....	....	....	....
1998-99	Saint John Flames	AHL	5	0	0	0	....	....	....	23	....	....	....	....	....	....	....	....	....	....	....	....	....	....	....	....	....	....
	Chicago Blackhawks	**NHL**	**39**	**2**	**2**	**4**	**2**	**2**	**4**	**62**	**0**	**0**	**0**	**24**	**8.3**	**22**	**1**	**28**	**7**	**0**	....	....	....	....	....	....	....	....
	Indianapolis Ice	IHL	3	1	0	1	....	....	....	10	....	....	....	....	....	....	....	....	....	....	....	....	....	....	....	....	....	....
99-2000	**Chicago Blackhawks**	**NHL**	**59**	**1**	**3**	**4**	**1**	**3**	**4**	**102**	**0**	**0**	**0**	**24**	**4.2**	**30**	**0**	**45**	**10**	**–5**	....	....	....	....	....	....	....	....
	NHL Totals		**162**	**6**	**13**	**19**	**7**	**13**	**20**	**303**	**0**	**0**	**1**	**83**	**7.2**	**86**	**1**	**118**	**27**		....	....	....	....	....	....	....	....

Traded to **Chicago** by **Calgary** with Marty McInnis and Eric Andersson for Jeff Shantz and Steve Dubinsky, October 27, 1998.

• ALLISON, Jason Jason Paul C – R. 6'3", 205 lbs. b: North York, Ont., 5/29/1975. Washington's 2nd, 17th overall, in 1993.

Season	Club	League	GP	G	A	Pts	AG	AA	APts	PIM	PP	SH	GW	S	%	TGF	PGF	TGA	PGA	+/–	GP	G	A	Pts	PIM	PP	SH	GW
1990-91	North York Rangers	MTHL	63	53	41	94	....	....	....	....	....	....	....	....	....	....	....	....	....	....	....	....	....	....	....	....	....	....
1991-92	London Knights	OHL	65	11	19	30	....	....	....	15	....	....	....	....	....	....	....	....	....	....	7	0	0	0	0	....	....	....
1992-93	London Knights	OHL	66	42	76	118	....	....	....	50	....	....	....	....	....	....	....	....	....	....	12	7	13	20	8	....	....	....
1993-94	London Knights	OHL	56	55	87	*142	....	....	....	68	....	....	....	....	....	....	....	....	....	....	5	2	13	15	13	....	....	....
	Canada	WJC-A	7	3	6	9	....	....	....	2	....	....	....	....	....	....	....	....	....	....	....	....	....	....	....	....	....	....
	Washington Capitals	**NHL**	**2**	**0**	**1**	**1**	**0**	**1**	**1**	**0**	**0**	**0**	**0**	**5**	**0.0**	**3**	**1**	**1**	**0**	**1**	....	....	....	....	....	....	....	....
	Portland Pirates	AHL	....	....	....	....	....	....	....	....	....	....	....	....	....	....	....	....	....	....	6	2	1	3	0	....	....	....

Season	Club	League	GP	G	A	Pts	AG	AA	APts	PIM	PP	SH	GW	S	%	TGF	PGF	TGA	PGA	+/-	GP	G	A	Pts	PIM	PP	SH	GW
			REGULAR SEASON																		PLAYOFFS							
1994-95	London Knights	OHL	15	15	21	36	....	....	....	43	....	....	....	....	....	....	....	....	....	....	....	....	....	....	....	....	....	....
	Canada	WJC-A	7	3	*12	*15	....	....	....	6	....	....	....	....	....	....	....	....	....	....	....	....	....	....	....	....	....	....
	Washington Capitals	**NHL**	**12**	**2**	**1**	**3**	**4**	**1**	**5**	**6**	**2**	**0**	**0**	**9**	**22.2**	**5**	**4**	**4**	**0**	**–3**	....	....	....	....	....	....	....	....
	Portland Pirates	AHL	8	5	4	9	....	....	....	2	....	....	....	....	....	....	....	....	....	....	7	3	8	11	2	....	....	....
1995-96	**Washington Capitals**	**NHL**	**19**	**0**	**3**	**3**	**0**	**2**	**2**	**2**	**0**	**0**	**0**	**18**	**0.0**	**7**	**2**	**8**	**0**	**–3**	....	....	....	....	....	....	....	....
	Portland Pirates	AHL	57	28	41	69	....	....	....	42	....	....	....	....	....	....	....	....	....	....	6	1	6	7	9	....	....	....
1996-97	**Washington Capitals**	**NHL**	**53**	**5**	**17**	**22**	**5**	**15**	**20**	**25**	**1**	**0**	**1**	**71**	**7.0**	**32**	**10**	**25**	**0**	**–3**	....	....	....	....	....	....	....	....
	Boston Bruins	**NHL**	**19**	**3**	**9**	**12**	**3**	**8**	**11**	**9**	**1**	**0**	**0**	**28**	**10.7**	**17**	**6**	**14**	**0**	**–3**	....	....	....	....	....	....	....	....
1997-98	**Boston Bruins**	**NHL**	**81**	**33**	**50**	**83**	**39**	**49**	**88**	**60**	**5**	**0**	**8**	**158**	**20.9**	**113**	**40**	**44**	**4**	**33**	**6**	**2**	**6**	**8**	**4**	**1**	**0**	**0**
1998-99	**Boston Bruins**	**NHL**	**82**	**23**	**53**	**76**	**27**	**51**	**78**	**68**	**5**	**1**	**3**	**158**	**14.6**	**108**	**42**	**71**	**10**	**5**	**12**	**2**	**9**	**11**	**6**	**1**	**0**	**0**
99-2000	**Boston Bruins**	**NHL**	**37**	**10**	**18**	**28**	**11**	**17**	**28**	**20**	**3**	**0**	**1**	**66**	**15.2**	**44**	**20**	**25**	**6**	**5**	....	....	....	....	....	....	....	....
	NHL Totals		**305**	**76**	**152**	**228**	**89**	**144**	**233**	**190**	**17**	**1**	**13**	**513**	**14.8**	**329**	**125**	**192**	**20**		**18**	**4**	**15**	**19**	**10**	**2**	**0**	**0**

OHL First All-Star Team (1994) • Canadian Major Junior First All-Star Team (1994) • Canadian Major Junior Player of the Year (1994) • WJC-A All-Star Team (1995)

Traded to **Boston** by **Washington** with Jim Carey, Anson Carter and Washington's 3rd round choice (Lee Goren) in 1997 Entry Draft for Bill Ranford, Adam Oates and Rick Tocchet, March 1, 1997. • Missed majority of 1999-2000 season recovering from thumb injury suffered in game vs. NY Islanders, January 8, 2000.

• ALLISON, Mike

Michael Earnest "Red Dog" LW – R. 6', 200 lbs. b: Fort Frances, Ont., 3/28/1961. NY Rangers' 2nd, 35th overall, in 1980.

Season	Club	League	GP	G	A	Pts	AG	AA	APts	PIM	PP	SH	GW	S	%	TGF	PGF	TGA	PGA	+/-	GP	G	A	Pts	PIM	PP	SH	GW
1977-78	Kenora Thistles	NOJHA	47	30	36	66	....	....	....	70	....	....	....	....	....	....	....	....	....	....	....	....	....	....	....	....	....	....
	New Westminster Bruins	WCJHL	5	0	1	1	....	....	....	2	....	....	....	....	....	....	....	....	....	....	....	....	....	....	....	....	....	....
1978-79	Sudbury Wolves	OMJHL	59	24	32	56	....	....	....	41	....	....	....	....	....	....	....	....	....	....	10	4	2	6	18	....	....	....
1979-80	Sudbury Wolves	OMJHL	67	24	71	95	....	....	....	74	....	....	....	....	....	....	....	....	....	....	9	8	6	14	6	....	....	....
1980-81	**New York Rangers**	**NHL**	**75**	**26**	**38**	**64**	**20**	**25**	**45**	**83**	**4**	**0**	**2**	**122**	**21.3**	**96**	**23**	**67**	**6**	**12**	**14**	**3**	**1**	**4**	**20**	**1**	**0**	**2**
1981-82	New York Rangers	DN-Cup	4	3	2	....	....	....	....	....	....	....	....	....	....	....	....	....	....	....	....	....	....	....	....	....	....	....
	New York Rangers	**NHL**	**48**	**7**	**15**	**22**	**6**	**10**	**16**	**74**	**0**	**0**	**0**	**62**	**11.3**	**32**	**2**	**34**	**1**	**–3**	**10**	**1**	**3**	**4**	**18**	**0**	**0**	**0**
	Springfield Indians	AHL	2	0	0	0	....	....	....	0	....	....	....	....	....	....	....	....	....	....	....	....	....	....	....	....	....	....
1982-83	**New York Rangers**	**NHL**	**39**	**11**	**9**	**20**	**9**	**6**	**15**	**37**	**1**	**0**	**0**	**45**	**24.4**	**30**	**5**	**18**	**1**	**8**	**8**	**0**	**5**	**5**	**10**	**0**	**0**	**0**
	Tulsa Oilers	CHL	6	2	2	4	....	....	....	2	....	....	....	....	....	....	....	....	....	....	....	....	....	....	....	....	....	....
1983-84	**New York Rangers**	**NHL**	**45**	**8**	**12**	**20**	**6**	**8**	**14**	**64**	**0**	**0**	**2**	**52**	**15.4**	**31**	**0**	**34**	**8**	**5**	**5**	**0**	**1**	**1**	**6**	**0**	**0**	**0**
1984-85	**New York Rangers**	**NHL**	**31**	**9**	**15**	**24**	**7**	**10**	**17**	**17**	**2**	**0**	**1**	**46**	**19.6**	**33**	**7**	**32**	**6**	**0**	....	....	....	....	....	....	....	....
1985-86	**New York Rangers**	**NHL**	**28**	**2**	**13**	**15**	**2**	**9**	**11**	**22**	**0**	**0**	**0**	**26**	**7.7**	**18**	**0**	**15**	**1**	**4**	**16**	**0**	**2**	**2**	**38**	**0**	**0**	**0**
	New Haven Nighthawks	AHL	9	6	6	12	....	....	....	4	....	....	....	....	....	....	....	....	....	....	....	....	....	....	....	....	....	....
1986-87	**Toronto Maple Leafs**	**NHL**	**71**	**7**	**16**	**23**	**6**	**12**	**18**	**66**	**1**	**3**	**2**	**48**	**14.6**	**41**	**3**	**70**	**33**	**1**	**13**	**3**	**5**	**8**	**15**	**1**	**0**	**2**
1987-88	**Toronto Maple Leafs**	**NHL**	**15**	**0**	**3**	**3**	**0**	**2**	**2**	**10**	**0**	**0**	**0**	**7**	**0.0**	**4**	**0**	**4**	**0**	**0**	....	....	....	....	....	....	....	....
	Los Angeles Kings	**NHL**	**37**	**16**	**12**	**28**	**14**	**9**	**23**	**57**	**5**	**1**	**2**	**54**	**29.6**	**45**	**15**	**38**	**11**	**3**	**5**	**0**	**0**	**0**	**16**	**0**	**0**	**0**
1988-89	**Los Angeles Kings**	**NHL**	**55**	**14**	**22**	**36**	**12**	**16**	**28**	**122**	**6**	**0**	**2**	**71**	**19.7**	**58**	**15**	**40**	**4**	**7**	**7**	**1**	**0**	**1**	**10**	**0**	**0**	**0**
1989-90	**Los Angeles Kings**	**NHL**	**55**	**2**	**11**	**13**	**2**	**8**	**10**	**78**	**0**	**0**	**1**	**25**	**8.0**	**29**	**2**	**44**	**11**	**–6**	**4**	**1**	**0**	**1**	**2**	**0**	**1**	**0**
	New Haven Nighthawks	AHL	5	2	2	4	....	....	....	14	....	....	....	....	....	....	....	....	....	....	....	....	....	....	....	....	....	....
	NHL Totals		**499**	**102**	**166**	**268**	**84**	**115**	**199**	**630**	**19**	**4**	**12**	**558**	**18.3**	**417**	**72**	**396**	**82**		**82**	**9**	**17**	**26**	**135**	**2**	**1**	**4**

• Brother of Dave

Traded to **Toronto** by **NY Rangers** for Walt Poddubny, August 18, 1986. Traded to **LA Kings** by **Toronto** for Sean McKenna, December 14, 1987.

• ALLISON, Ray

Raymond Peter RW – R. 5'10", 195 lbs. b: Cranbrook, B.C., 3/4/1959. Hartford's 1st, 18th overall, in 1979.

Season	Club	League	GP	G	A	Pts	AG	AA	APts	PIM	PP	SH	GW	S	%	TGF	PGF	TGA	PGA	+/-	GP	G	A	Pts	PIM	PP	SH	GW
1974-75	Brandon Travellers	MJHL	STATISTICS NOT AVAILABLE																									
	Brandon Wheat Kings	WCJHL	2	0	0	0	....	....	....	0	....	....	....	....	....	....	....	....	....	....	....	....	....	....	....	....	....	....
1975-76	Brandon Travellers	MJHL	31	22	21	43	....	....	....	158	....	....	....	....	....	....	....	....	....	....	....	....	....	....	....	....	....	....
	Brandon Wheat Kings	WCJHL	36	9	17	26	....	....	....	50	....	....	....	....	....	....	....	....	....	....	5	2	1	3	0	....	....	....
1976-77	Brandon Wheat Kings	WCJHL	71	45	92	137	....	....	....	198	....	....	....	....	....	....	....	....	....	....	14	9	11	20	37	....	....	....
1977-78	Brandon Wheat Kings	WCJHL	71	74	86	160	....	....	....	254	....	....	....	....	....	....	....	....	....	....	8	7	8	15	35	....	....	....
1978-79	Brandon Wheat Kings	WHL	62	60	93	153	....	....	....	191	....	....	....	....	....	....	....	....	....	....	22	18	19	37	28	....	....	....
	Canada	WJC-A	5	0	5	5	....	....	....	4	....	....	....	....	....	....	....	....	....	....	....	....	....	....	....	....	....	....
	Brandon Wheat Kings	Mem-Cup	5	*5	3	8	....	....	....	8	....	....	....	....	....	....	....	....	....	....	....	....	....	....	....	....	....	....
1979-80	**Hartford Whalers**	**NHL**	**64**	**16**	**12**	**28**	**14**	**9**	**23**	**13**	**0**	**0**	**2**	**79**	**20.3**	**40**	**0**	**43**	**0**	**–3**	**2**	**0**	**1**	**1**	**0**	**0**	**0**	**0**
	Springfield Indians	AHL	13	6	9	15	....	....	....	18	....	....	....	....	....	....	....	....	....	....	....	....	....	....	....	....	....	....
1980-81	**Hartford Whalers**	**NHL**	**6**	**1**	**0**	**1**	**1**	**0**	**1**	**0**	**0**	**0**	**0**	**6**	**16.7**	**2**	**0**	**3**	**0**	**–1**	....	....	....	....	....	....	....	....
	Binghamton Whalers	AHL	74	31	39	70	....	....	....	81	....	....	....	....	....	....	....	....	....	....	2	0	1	1	0	....	....	....
1981-82	**Philadelphia Flyers**	**NHL**	**51**	**17**	**37**	**54**	**13**	**25**	**38**	**104**	**5**	**0**	**2**	**131**	**13.0**	**78**	**25**	**41**	**1**	**13**	**3**	**2**	**0**	**2**	**2**	**2**	**0**	**0**
	Maine Mariners	AHL	26	15	13	28	....	....	....	75	....	....	....	....	....	....	....	....	....	....	....	....	....	....	....	....	....	....
1982-83	**Philadelphia Flyers**	**NHL**	**67**	**21**	**30**	**51**	**17**	**21**	**38**	**57**	**4**	**0**	**1**	**148**	**14.2**	**87**	**18**	**45**	**6**	**30**	**3**	**0**	**1**	**1**	**12**	**0**	**0**	**0**
1983-84	**Philadelphia Flyers**	**NHL**	**37**	**8**	**13**	**21**	**6**	**9**	**15**	**47**	**0**	**0**	**0**	**73**	**11.0**	**37**	**7**	**20**	**1**	**11**	**3**	**0**	**1**	**1**	**4**	**0**	**0**	**0**
1984-85	**Philadelphia Flyers**	**NHL**	**11**	**1**	**1**	**2**	**1**	**1**	**2**	**2**	**0**	**0**	**0**	**16**	**6.3**	**4**	**0**	**1**	**0**	**3**	**1**	**0**	**0**	**0**	**2**	**0**	**0**	**0**
	Hershey Bears	AHL	49	17	22	39	....	....	....	61	....	....	....	....	....	....	....	....	....	....	....	....	....	....	....	....	....	....
1985-86	Hershey Bears	AHL	77	32	46	78	....	....	....	131	....	....	....	....	....	....	....	....	....	....	18	4	6	10	28	....	....	....
1986-87	**Philadelphia Flyers**	**NHL**	**2**	**0**	**0**	**0**	**0**	**0**	**0**	**0**	**0**	**0**	**0**	**1**	**0.0**	**0**	**0**	**3**	**1**	**–2**	....	....	....	....	....	....	....	....
	Hershey Bears	AHL	78	29	55	84	....	....	....	57	....	....	....	....	....	....	....	....	....	....	5	3	1	4	12	....	....	....
1987-88	EHC Olten	Switz-2	38	33	18	51	....	....	....	....	....	....	....	....	....	....	....	....	....	....	5	*6	3	*9	....	....	....	....
	Hershey Bears	AHL	....	....	....	....	....	....	....	....	....	....	....	....	....	....	....	....	....	....	9	2	9	11	17	....	....	....
1988-89	EHC Olten	Switz.	36	23	16	39	....	....	....	....	....	....	....	....	....	....	....	....	....	....	2	2	0	2	2	....	....	....
	Hershey Bears	AHL	15	6	11	17	....	....	....	18	....	....	....	....	....	....	....	....	....	....	12	4	7	11	6	....	....	....
1989-90	Hershey Bears	AHL	70	25	30	55	....	....	....	66	....	....	....	....	....	....	....	....	....	....	....	....	....	....	....	....	....	....
1990-1993			OUT OF HOCKEY – RETIRED																									
1993-94	HC Rapperswil-Jona	Switz-2	30	17	19	36	....	....	....	....	....	....	....	....	....	....	....	....	....	....	....	....	....	....	....	....	....	....
	NHL Totals		**238**	**64**	**93**	**157**	**52**	**65**	**117**	**223**	**9**	**0**	**5**	**454**	**14.1**	**248**	**50**	**156**	**9**		**12**	**2**	**3**	**5**	**20**	**2**	**0**	**0**

WHL All-Star Team (1979) • Memorial Cup All-Star Team (1979)

Traded to **Philadelphia** by **Hartford** with Fred Arthur and Hartford's 1st (Ron Sutter) and 3rd (Miroslav Dvorak) round choices in 1982 Entry Draft for Rick MacLeish, Blake Wesley, Don Gillen and Philadelphia's 1st (Paul Lawless), 2nd (Mark Patterson) and 3rd (Kevin Dineen) round choices in 1982 Entry Draft, July 3, 1981.

• AMADIO, Dave

David A. D – R. 6'1", 207 lbs. b: Glace Bay, N.S., 4/23/1939 d: 4/1/1981.

Season	Club	League	GP	G	A	Pts	AG	AA	APts	PIM	PP	SH	GW	S	%	TGF	PGF	TGA	PGA	+/-	GP	G	A	Pts	PIM	PP	SH	GW
1954-55	Glace Bay Miners	CBJHL	30	7	18	25	....	....	....	50	....	....	....	....	....	....	....	....	....	....	....	....	....	....	....	....	....	....
1955-56	Burlington Cougars	OHA-B	STATISTICS NOT AVAILABLE																									
1956-57	Hamilton Tiger Cubs	OHA-Jr.	44	10	9	19	....	....	....	117	....	....	....	....	....	....	....	....	....	....	4	0	1	1	2	....	....	....
1957-58	Hamilton Tiger Cubs	OHA-Jr.	52	13	21	34	....	....	....	122	....	....	....	....	....	....	....	....	....	....	15	2	5	7	56	....	....	....
	Detroit Red Wings	**NHL**	**2**	**0**	**0**	**0**	**0**	**0**	**0**	**2**	....	....	....	....	....	....	....	....	....	....	....	....	....	....	....	....	....	....
	Hershey Bears	AHL	....	....	....	....	....	....	....	....	....	....	....	....	....	....	....	....	....	....	1	0	0	0	0	....	....	....
1958-59	Edmonton Flyers	WHL	58	7	7	14	....	....	....	110	....	....	....	....	....	....	....	....	....	....	3	0	1	1	2	....	....	....
1959-60	Edmonton Flyers	WHL	13	1	4	5	....	....	....	35	....	....	....	....	....	....	....	....	....	....	....	....	....	....	....	....	....	....
	Sudbury Wolves	EPHL	50	13	17	30	....	....	....	139	....	....	....	....	....	....	....	....	....	....	14	3	7	10	14	....	....	....
1960-61	Sudbury Wolves	EPHL	25	2	14	16	....	....	....	50	....	....	....	....	....	....	....	....	....	....	....	....	....	....	....	....	....	....
1961-62	Sudbury Wolves	EPHL	9	0	5	5	....	....	....	15	....	....	....	....	....	....	....	....	....	....	....	....	....	....	....	....	....	....
	Springfield Indians	AHL	58	4	11	15	....	....	....	56	....	....	....	....	....	....	....	....	....	....	11	0	1	1	19	....	....	....
1962-63	Springfield Indians	AHL	71	8	19	27	....	....	....	95	....	....	....	....	....	....	....	....	....	....	....	....	....	....	....	....	....	....
1963-64	Springfield Indians	AHL	72	11	24	35	....	....	....	120	....	....	....	....	....	....	....	....	....	....	....	....	....	....	....	....	....	....
1964-65	Springfield Indians	AHL	72	10	24	34	....	....	....	100	....	....	....	....	....	....	....	....	....	....	....	....	....	....	....	....	....	....
1965-66	Springfield Indians	AHL	72	9	11	20	....	....	....	124	....	....	....	....	....	....	....	....	....	....	6	0	3	3	6	....	....	....
1966-67	Springfield Indians	AHL	66	11	29	40	....	....	....	89	....	....	....	....	....	....	....	....	....	....	....	....	....	....	....	....	....	....
1967-68	**Los Angeles Kings**	**NHL**	**58**	**4**	**6**	**10**	**5**	**6**	**11**	**101**	**0**	**0**	**0**	**92**	**4.3**	**59**	**10**	**77**	**18**	**–10**	**7**	**0**	**2**	**2**	**8**	**0**	**0**	**0**
	Springfield Kings	AHL	17	2	6	8	....	....	....	25	....	....	....	....	....	....	....	....	....	....	....	....	....	....	....	....	....	....
1968-69	**Los Angeles Kings**	**NHL**	**65**	**1**	**5**	**6**	**1**	**4**	**5**	**60**	**1**	**0**	**1**	**72**	**1.4**	**43**	**6**	**67**	**9**	**–21**	**9**	**1**	**0**	**1**	**10**	**0**	**0**	**0**
1969-70	Springfield Kings	AHL	40	4	15	19	....	....	....	78	....	....	....	....	....	....	....	....	....	....	13	1	1	2	10	....	....	....

			REGULAR SEASON																		PLAYOFFS							
Season	Club	League	GP	G	A	Pts	AG	AA	APts	PIM	PP	SH	GW	S	%	TGF	PGF	TGA	PGA	+/–	GP	G	A	Pts	PIM	PP	SH	GW
1970-71	Kansas City Blues	CHL	30	2	13	15	....	....	....	45	....	....	....	....	....	....	....	....	....	....	....	....	....	....	....	....	....	....
	Denver Spurs	WHL	35	0	6	6	....	....	....	42	....	....	....	....	....	....	....	....	....	....	....	....	....	....	....	....	....	....
1971-72	Salt Lake Golden Eagles	WHL	68	6	22	28	....	....	....	93	....	....	....	....	....	....	....	....	....	....	....	....	....	....	....	....	....	....
1972-73	Salt Lake Golden Eagles	WHL	72	6	33	39	....	....	....	129	....	....	....	....	....	....	....	....	....	....	9	3	2	5	16	....	....	....
1973-74	Seattle Totems	WHL	70	6	13	19	....	....	....	60	....	....	....	....	....	....	....	....	....	....	....	....	....	....	....	....	....	....
	NHL Totals		**125**	**5**	**11**	**16**	**6**	**10**	**16**	**163**	....	....	....	....	....	....	....	....	....	....	**16**	**1**	**2**	**3**	**18**	....	....	....

Traded to **Springfield** (AHL) by **Detroit** for cash, June, 1961. NHL rights transferred to **LA Kings** after NHL club purchased **Springfield** (AHL) franchise, May, 1967.

• AMBROZIAK, Peter

Peter A. LW – L. 6', 206 lbs. b: Toronto, Ont., 9/15/1971. Buffalo's 4th, 72nd overall, in 1991.

Season	Club	League	GP	G	A	Pts	AG	AA	APts	PIM	PP	SH	GW	S	%	TGF	PGF	TGA	PGA	+/–	GP	G	A	Pts	PIM	PP	SH	GW
1987-88	South Ottawa Canadians	OMHA	STATISTICS NOT AVAILABLE																									
	Ottawa Jr. Senators	OJHL	1	0	0	0	....	....	....	0	....	....	....	....	....	....	....	....	....	....	....	....	....	....	....	....	....	....
1988-89	Ottawa 67's	OHL	50	8	15	23	....	....	....	11	....	....	....	....	....	....	....	....	....	....	12	1	2	3	2	....	....	....
1989-90	Ottawa 67's	OHL	60	13	19	32	....	....	....	37	....	....	....	....	....	....	....	....	....	....	4	0	0	0	2	....	....	....
1990-91	Ottawa 67's	OHL	62	30	32	62	....	....	....	56	....	....	....	....	....	....	....	....	....	....	17	15	9	24	24	....	....	....
1991-92	Ottawa 67's	OHL	49	32	49	81	....	....	....	50	....	....	....	....	....	....	....	....	....	....	11	3	7	10	33	....	....	....
	Rochester Americans	AHL	2	0	1	1	....	....	....	0	....	....	....	....	....	....	....	....	....	....	....	....	....	....	....	....	....	....
1992-93	Rochester Americans	AHL	50	8	10	18	....	....	....	37	....	....	....	....	....	....	....	....	....	....	12	4	3	7	16	....	....	....
1993-94	Rochester Americans	AHL	22	3	4	7	....	....	....	53	....	....	....	....	....	....	....	....	....	....	....	....	....	....	....	....	....	....
1994-95	**Buffalo Sabres**	**NHL**	**12**	**0**	**1**	**1**	**0**	**1**	**1**	**0**	**0**	**0**	**0**	**3**	**0.0**	**1**	**0**	**3**	**1**	**–1**	....	....	....	....	....	....	....	....
	Rochester Americans	AHL	46	14	11	25	....	....	....	35	....	....	....	....	....	....	....	....	....	....	4	0	0	0	6	....	....	....
1995-96	Albany River Rats	AHL	8	2	1	3	....	....	....	25	....	....	....	....	....	....	....	....	....	....	....	....	....	....	....	....	....	....
	Cornwall Aces	AHL	50	9	15	24	....	....	....	42	....	....	....	....	....	....	....	....	....	....	8	1	1	2	4	....	....	....
1996-97	Fort Wayne Komets	IHL	57	15	5	20	....	....	....	28	....	....	....	....	....	....	....	....	....	....	....	....	....	....	....	....	....	....
1997-98	Hershey Bears	AHL	63	7	11	18	....	....	....	61	....	....	....	....	....	....	....	....	....	....	5	0	1	1	6	....	....	....
1998-99	Flint Generals	UHL	40	19	27	46	....	....	....	90	....	....	....	....	....	....	....	....	....	....	5	0	2	2	12	....	....	....
	Detroit Vipers	IHL	33	5	8	13	....	....	....	30	....	....	....	....	....	....	....	....	....	....	2	0	0	0	0	....	....	....
99-2000	New Mexico Scorpions	WPHL	57	43	44	87	....	....	....	86	....	....	....	....	....	....	....	....	....	....	9	3	4	7	30	....	....	....
	NHL Totals		**12**	**0**	**1**	**1**	**0**	**1**	**1**	**0**	**0**	**0**	**0**	**3**	**0.0**	**1**	**0**	**3**	**1**		....	....	....	....	....	....	....	....

Signed as a free agent by **New Mexico** (WPHL) and named as player/assistant coach, July 7, 1999.

• AMODEO, Mike

Michael Anthony D – L. 5'10", 190 lbs. b: Toronto, Ont., 6/22/1952. California's 7th, 102nd overall, in 1972.

Season	Club	League	GP	G	A	Pts	AG	AA	APts	PIM	PP	SH	GW	S	%	TGF	PGF	TGA	PGA	+/–	GP	G	A	Pts	PIM	PP	SH	GW
1968-69	Toronto Midget Marlboros	MTHL	STATISTICS NOT AVAILABLE																									
	Toronto Marlboros	OHA-Jr.	....	....	....	....	....	....	....	....	....	....	....	....	....	....	....	....	....	....	1	0	0	0	0	....	....	....
1969-70	Toronto Marlboros	OHA-Jr.	54	5	11	16	....	....	....	161	....	....	....	....	....	....	....	....	....	....	....	....	....	....	....	....	....	....
1970-71	Toronto Marlboros	OHA-Jr.	11	0	3	3	....	....	....	31	....	....	....	....	....	....	....	....	....	....	....	....	....	....	....	....	....	....
	Niagara Falls Flyers	OMJHL	3	0	0	0	....	....	....	2	....	....	....	....	....	....	....	....	....	....	....	....	....	....	....	....	....	....
	Oshawa Generals	OMJHL	24	0	12	12	....	....	....	65	....	....	....	....	....	....	....	....	....	....	....	....	....	....	....	....	....	....
1971-72	Oshawa Generals	OMJHL	63	6	34	40	....	....	....	130	....	....	....	....	....	....	....	....	....	....	....	....	....	....	....	....	....	....
1972-73	Ottawa Nationals	WHA	61	1	14	15	....	....	....	77	....	....	....	....	....	....	....	....	....	....	5	0	1	1	10	....	....	....
1973-74	Toronto Toros	WHA	77	0	11	11	....	....	....	82	....	....	....	....	....	....	....	....	....	....	12	0	2	2	26	....	....	....
1974-75	Toronto Toros	WHA	64	1	13	14	....	....	....	50	....	....	....	....	....	....	....	....	....	....	3	0	1	1	4	....	....	....
1975-76	Toronto Toros	WHA	31	4	8	12	....	....	....	35	....	....	....	....	....	....	....	....	....	....	....	....	....	....	....	....	....	....
	Rochester Americans	AHL	10	0	2	2	....	....	....	4	....	....	....	....	....	....	....	....	....	....	4	0	1	1	0	....	....	....
1976-77	Orebro IK	Sweden	34	5	3	8	....	....	....	38	....	....	....	....	....	....	....	....	....	....	....	....	....	....	....	....	....	....
1977-78	Orebro IK	Sweden	34	2	6	8	....	....	....	44	....	....	....	....	....	....	....	....	....	....	....	....	....	....	....	....	....	....
	Winnipeg Jets	WHA	3	1	1	2	....	....	....	0	....	....	....	....	....	....	....	....	....	....	7	1	3	4	19	....	....	....
1978-79	Orebro IK	Sweden	1	0	1	1	....	....	....	0	....	....	....	....	....	....	....	....	....	....	....	....	....	....	....	....	....	....
	Winnipeg Jets	WHA	64	4	18	22	....	....	....	29	....	....	....	....	....	....	....	....	....	....	....	....	....	....	....	....	....	....
1979-80	**Winnipeg Jets**	**NHL**	**19**	**0**	**0**	**0**	**0**	**0**	**0**	**2**	**0**	**0**	**0**	**14**	**0.0**	**6**	**0**	**21**	**0**	**–15**	....	....	....	....	....	....	....	....
	Tulsa Oilers	CHL	20	3	6	9	....	....	....	32	....	....	....	....	....	....	....	....	....	....	....	....	....	....	....	....	....	....
1980-81	Orebro IK	Sweden-2	31	7	6	13	....	....	....	43	....	....	....	....	....	....	....	....	....	....	....	....	....	....	....	....	....	....
1981-82	HC Merano	Italy	31	20	21	41	....	....	....	14	....	....	....	....	....	....	....	....	....	....	....	....	....	....	....	....	....	....
	Italy	WEC-A	7	0	0	0	....	....	....	2	....	....	....	....	....	....	....	....	....	....	....	....	....	....	....	....	....	....
1982-83	HC Merano	Italy	32	12	21	33	....	....	....	20	....	....	....	....	....	....	....	....	....	....	....	....	....	....	....	....	....	....
	NHL Totals		**19**	**0**	**0**	**0**	**0**	**0**	**0**	**2**	**0**	**0**	**0**	**14**	**0.0**	**6**	**0**	**21**	**0**		....	....	....	....	....	....	....	....
	Other Major League Totals		300	11	65	76	....	....	....	273	....	....	....	....	....	....	....	....	....	....	27	1	7	8	59	....	....	....

Selected by **Ontario-Ottawa** (WHA) in 1972 WHA General Player Draft, February 12, 1972. Transferred to **Toronto** (WHA) after **Ottawa** (WHA) franchise relocated, May, 1973. Signed as a free agent by **Winnipeg** (WHA), March, 1978. Rights retained by **Winnipeg** prior to Expansion Draft, June 9, 1979.

• AMONTE, Tony

Anthony RW – L. 6', 200 lbs. b: Hingham, MA, 8/2/1970. NY Rangers' 3rd, 68th overall, in 1988.

Season	Club	League	GP	G	A	Pts	AG	AA	APts	PIM	PP	SH	GW	S	%	TGF	PGF	TGA	PGA	+/–	GP	G	A	Pts	PIM	PP	SH	GW
1985-86	Thayer Academy	Hi-School	2	0	0	0	....	....	....	0	....	....	....	....	....	....	....	....	....	....	....	....	....	....	....	....	....	....
1986-87	Thayer Academy	Hi-School	25	25	32	57	....	....	....	....	....	....	....	....	....	....	....	....	....	....	....	....	....	....	....	....	....	....
1987-88	Thayer Academy	Hi-School	28	30	38	68	....	....	....	....	....	....	....	....	....	....	....	....	....	....	....	....	....	....	....	....	....	....
1988-89	Thayer Academy	Hi-School	25	35	38	73	....	....	....	....	....	....	....	....	....	....	....	....	....	....	....	....	....	....	....	....	....	....
	United States	WJC-A	7	1	3	4	....	....	....	2	....	....	....	....	....	....	....	....	....	....	....	....	....	....	....	....	....	....
1989-90	Boston University	H-East	41	25	33	58	....	....	....	52	....	....	....	....	....	....	....	....	....	....	....	....	....	....	....	....	....	....
	United States	WJC-A	7	5	2	7	....	....	....	4	....	....	....	....	....	....	....	....	....	....	....	....	....	....	....	....	....	....
1990-91	Boston University	H-East	38	31	37	68	....	....	....	82	....	....	....	....	....	....	....	....	....	....	....	....	....	....	....	....	....	....
	United States	WEC-A	10	2	5	7	....	....	....	4	....	....	....	....	....	....	....	....	....	....	....	....	....	....	....	....	....	....
	New York Rangers	**NHL**	....	....	....	....	....	....	....	....	....	....	....	....	....	....	....	....	....	....	**2**	**0**	**2**	**2**	**2**	**0**	**0**	**0**
1991-92	**New York Rangers**	**NHL**	**79**	**35**	**34**	**69**	**32**	**26**	**58**	**55**	**9**	**0**	**4**	**234**	**15.0**	**100**	**28**	**60**	**0**	**12**	**13**	**3**	**6**	**9**	**2**	**2**	**0**	**0**
1992-93	**New York Rangers**	**NHL**	**83**	**33**	**43**	**76**	**27**	**30**	**57**	**49**	**13**	**0**	**4**	**270**	**12.2**	**112**	**43**	**71**	**2**	**0**	....	....	....	....	....	....	....	....
	United States	WC-A	6	1	2	3	....	....	....	8	....	....	....	....	....	....	....	....	....	....	....	....	....	....	....	....	....	....
1993-94	**New York Rangers**	**NHL**	**72**	**16**	**22**	**38**	**15**	**17**	**32**	**31**	**3**	**0**	**4**	**179**	**8.9**	**67**	**22**	**46**	**6**	**5**	....	....	....	....	....	....	....	....
	Chicago Blackhawks	**NHL**	**7**	**1**	**3**	**4**	**1**	**2**	**3**	**6**	**1**	**0**	**0**	**16**	**6.3**	**7**	**4**	**8**	**0**	**–5**	**6**	**4**	**2**	**6**	**4**	**1**	**0**	**1**
1994-95	HC Fassa	Alpenliga	14	22	16	38	....	....	....	10	....	....	....	....	....	....	....	....	....	....	....	....	....	....	....	....	....	....
	HC Fassa	EuroHL	2	5	1	6	....	....	....	0	....	....	....	....	....	....	....	....	....	....	....	....	....	....	....	....	....	....
	Chicago Blackhawks	**NHL**	**48**	**15**	**20**	**35**	**27**	**30**	**57**	**41**	**6**	**1**	**3**	**105**	**14.3**	**50**	**17**	**34**	**8**	**7**	**16**	**3**	**3**	**6**	**10**	**0**	**0**	**0**
1995-96	**Chicago Blackhawks**	**NHL**	**81**	**31**	**32**	**63**	**30**	**26**	**56**	**62**	**5**	**4**	**5**	**216**	**14.4**	**91**	**31**	**70**	**20**	**10**	**7**	**2**	**4**	**6**	**6**	**1**	**0**	**0**
1996-97	United States	W-Cup	7	2	4	6	....	....	....	6	....	....	....	....	....	....	....	....	....	....	....	....	....	....	....	....	....	....
	Chicago Blackhawks	**NHL**	**81**	**41**	**36**	**77**	**44**	**32**	**76**	**64**	**9**	**2**	**4**	**266**	**15.4**	**96**	**23**	**56**	**18**	**35**	**6**	**4**	**2**	**6**	**8**	**0**	**0**	**0**
1997-98	**Chicago Blackhawks**	**NHL**	**82**	**31**	**42**	**73**	**36**	**41**	**77**	**66**	**7**	**3**	**5**	**296**	**10.5**	**102**	**30**	**75**	**24**	**21**	....	....	....	....	....	....	....	....
	United States	Olympics	4	0	1	1	....	....	....	4	....	....	....	....	....	....	....	....	....	....	....	....	....	....	....	....	....	....
1998-99	**Chicago Blackhawks**	**NHL**	**82**	**44**	**31**	**75**	**52**	**30**	**82**	**60**	**14**	**3**	**8**	**256**	**17.2**	**104**	**40**	**90**	**26**	**0**	....	....	....	....	....	....	....	....
99-2000	**Chicago Blackhawks**	**NHL**	**82**	**43**	**41**	**84**	**49**	**38**	**87**	**48**	**11**	**5**	**2**	**260**	**16.5**	**113**	**29**	**86**	**12**	**10**	....	....	....	....	....	....	....	....
	NHL Totals		**697**	**290**	**304**	**594**	**313**	**272**	**585**	**482**	**78**	**18**	**39**	**2098**	**13.8**	**842**	**267**	**596**	**116**		**50**	**16**	**19**	**35**	**32**	**4**	**0**	**1**

Hockey East Second All-Star Team (1991) • NCAA Championship All-Tournament Team (1991) • NHL All-Rookie Team (1992) • Played in NHL All-Star Game (1997, 1998, 1999, 2000)

• Missed remainder of 1985-86 season recovering from knee injury, October, 1985. Traded to **Chicago** by **NY Rangers** with the rights to Matt Oates for Stephane Matteau and Brian Noonan, March 21, 1994.

• ANDERSON, Earl

Earl Orlin RW – R. 6'1", 185 lbs. b: Roseau, MN, 2/24/1951. Detroit's 5th, 58th overall, in 1971.

Season	Club	League	GP	G	A	Pts	AG	AA	APts	PIM	PP	SH	GW	S	%	TGF	PGF	TGA	PGA	+/–	GP	G	A	Pts	PIM	PP	SH	GW
1967-1970	Roseau Rams	Hi-School	STATISTICS NOT AVAILABLE																									
1970-71	University of North Dakota	WCHA	32	12	17	29	....	....	....	22	....	....	....	....	....	....	....	....	....	....	....	....	....	....	....	....	....	....
1971-72	University of North Dakota	WCHA	36	23	22	45	....	....	....	24	....	....	....	....	....	....	....	....	....	....	....	....	....	....	....	....	....	....
1972-73	University of North Dakota	WCHA	36	17	30	47	....	....	....	12	....	....	....	....	....	....	....	....	....	....	....	....	....	....	....	....	....	....
	United States	WEC-B	7	8	4	12	....	....	....	....	....	....	....	....	....	....	....	....	....	....	....	....	....	....	....	....	....	....
1973-74	London Lions	Britain	70	62	48	110	....	....	....	41	....	....	....	....	....	....	....	....	....	....								

			REGULAR SEASON																		PLAYOFFS							
Season	Club	League	GP	G	A	Pts	AG	AA	APts	PIM	PP	SH	GW	S	%	TGF	PGF	TGA	PGA	+/–	GP	G	A	Pts	PIM	PP	SH	GW
1974-75	**Detroit Red Wings**	**NHL**	**45**	**7**	**3**	**10**	**6**	**2**	**8**	**12**	**1**	**0**	**1**	**61**	**11.5**	**19**	**1**	**29**	**0**	**–11**	....	....	....	....	....	....	....	....
	Virginia Wings	AHL	4	0	3	3	....	....	....	2	....	....	....	....	....	....	....	....	....	....	....	....	....	....	....	....	....	....
	Boston Bruins	**NHL**	**19**	**2**	**4**	**6**	**2**	**3**	**5**	**4**	**0**	**0**	**1**	**24**	**8.3**	**7**	**0**	**2**	**0**	**5**	**3**	**0**	**1**	**1**	**0**	**0**	**0**	**0**
1975-76	**Boston Bruins**	**NHL**	**5**	**0**	**1**	**1**	**0**	**1**	**1**	**2**	**0**	**0**	**0**	**5**	**0.0**	**1**	**1**	**5**	**3**	**–2**	....	....	....	....	....	....	....	....
1976-77	**Boston Bruins**	**NHL**	**40**	**10**	**11**	**21**	**9**	**8**	**17**	**4**	**1**	**0**	**3**	**65**	**15.4**	**35**	**3**	**30**	**2**	**4**	**2**	**0**	**0**	**0**	**0**	**0**	**0**	**0**
	Rochester Americans	AHL	32	19	14	33	....	....	....	16	....	....	....	....	....	....	....	....	....	....	....	....	....	....	....	....	....	....
1977-78	Rochester Americans	AHL	72	26	40	66	....	....	....	22	....	....	....	....	....	....	....	....	....	....	6	1	2	3	2	....	....	....
	NHL Totals		**109**	**19**	**19**	**38**	**17**	**14**	**31**	**22**	**2**	**0**	**5**	**155**	**12.3**	**62**	**5**	**66**	**5**		**5**	**0**	**1**	**1**	**0**	**0**	**0**	**0**

Traded to **Boston** by **Detroit** with Hank Nowak for Walt McKechnie and Boston's 3rd round choice (Clarke Hamilton) in 1975 Amateur Draft, February 18, 1975

• ANDERSON, Glenn

Glenn Christopher RW – L. 6'1", 190 lbs. b: Vancouver, B.C., 10/2/1960. Edmonton's 3rd, 69th overall, in 1979.

Season	Club	League	GP	G	A	Pts	AG	AA	APts	PIM	PP	SH	GW	S	%	TGF	PGF	TGA	PGA	+/–	GP	G	A	Pts	PIM	PP	SH	GW
1977-78	Bellingham Blazers	BCJHL	64	62	69	131	....	....	....	46	....	....	....	....	....	....	....	....	....	....	....	....	....	....	....	....	....	....
	New Westminster Bruins	WCJHL	1	0	1	1	....	....	....	2	....	....	....	....	....	....	....	....	....	....	....	....	....	....	....	....	....	....
1978-79	Seattle Breakers	WHL	2	0	1	1	....	....	....	0	....	....	....	....	....	....	....	....	....	....	....	....	....	....	....	....	....	....
	University of Denver	WCHA	40	26	29	55	....	....	....	58	....	....	....	....	....	....	....	....	....	....	....	....	....	....	....	....	....	....
1979-80	Seattle Breakers	WHL	7	5	5	10	....	....	....	4	....	....	....	....	....	....	....	....	....	....	2	0	1	1	0	....	....	....
	Canada	Nat-Team	49	21	21	42	....	....	....	46	....	....	....	....	....	....	....	....	....	....	....	....	....	....	....	....	....	....
	Canada	Olympics	6	2	2	4	....	....	....	4	....	....	....	....	....	....	....	....	....	....	....	....	....	....	....	....	....	....
1980-81	**Edmonton Oilers**	**NHL**	**58**	**30**	**23**	**53**	**23**	**15**	**38**	**24**	**10**	**3**	**5**	**160**	**18.8**	**77**	**16**	**70**	**13**	**4**	**9**	**5**	**7**	**12**	**12**	**3**	**0**	**0**
1981-82	**Edmonton Oilers**	**NHL**	**80**	**38**	**67**	**105**	**30**	**45**	**75**	**71**	**9**	**0**	**8**	**252**	**15.1**	**177**	**52**	**88**	**9**	**46**	**5**	**2**	**5**	**7**	**8**	**0**	**0**	**1**
1982-83	**Edmonton Oilers**	**NHL**	**72**	**48**	**56**	**104**	**39**	**39**	**78**	**70**	**11**	**0**	**10**	**243**	**19.8**	**153**	**51**	**61**	**0**	**41**	**16**	**10**	**10**	**20**	**32**	**1**	**0**	**2**
1983-84♦	**Edmonton Oilers**	**NHL**	**80**	**54**	**45**	**99**	**44**	**31**	**75**	**65**	**11**	**4**	**11**	**277**	**19.5**	**153**	**46**	**73**	**7**	**41**	**19**	**6**	**11**	**17**	**33**	**1**	**0**	**1**
1984-85	Canada	Can-Cup	8	1	4	5	....	....	....	16	....	....	....	....	....	....	....	....	....	....	....	....	....	....	....	....	....	....
♦	**Edmonton Oilers**	**NHL**	**80**	**42**	**39**	**81**	**34**	**27**	**61**	**69**	**12**	**1**	**6**	**258**	**16.3**	**125**	**41**	**67**	**7**	**24**	**18**	**10**	**16**	**26**	**38**	**2**	**0**	**1**
1985-86	**Edmonton Oilers**	**NHL**	**72**	**54**	**48**	**102**	**43**	**32**	**75**	**90**	**18**	**2**	**9**	**243**	**22.2**	**147**	**43**	**79**	**13**	**38**	**10**	**8**	**3**	**11**	**14**	**1**	**0**	**2**
1986-87♦	**Edmonton Oilers**	**NHL**	**80**	**35**	**38**	**73**	**30**	**28**	**58**	**65**	**7**	**1**	**5**	**188**	**18.6**	**127**	**37**	**67**	**4**	**27**	**21**	**14**	**13**	**27**	**59**	**4**	**0**	**2**
	NHL All-Stars	RV-87	2	1	0	1	....	....	....	2	....	....	....	....	....	....	....	....	....	....	....	....	....	....	....	....	....	....
1987-88	Canada	Can-Cup	7	2	1	3	....	....	....	4	....	....	....	....	....	....	....	....	....	....	....	....	....	....	....	....	....	....
♦	**Edmonton Oilers**	**NHL**	**80**	**38**	**50**	**88**	**32**	**36**	**68**	**58**	**16**	**1**	**3**	**255**	**14.9**	**137**	**55**	**95**	**18**	**5**	**19**	**9**	**16**	**25**	**49**	**4**	**0**	**1**
1988-89	**Edmonton Oilers**	**NHL**	**79**	**16**	**48**	**64**	**14**	**34**	**48**	**93**	**7**	**0**	**3**	**212**	**7.5**	**99**	**38**	**82**	**5**	**–16**	**7**	**1**	**2**	**3**	**8**	**1**	**0**	**0**
	Canada	WEC-A	6	2	2	4	....	....	....	4	....	....	....	....	....	....	....	....	....	....	....	....	....	....	....	....	....	....
1989-90♦	**Edmonton Oilers**	**NHL**	**73**	**34**	**38**	**72**	**29**	**27**	**56**	**107**	**17**	**1**	**7**	**204**	**16.7**	**105**	**42**	**75**	**11**	**–1**	**22**	**10**	**12**	**22**	**20**	**2**	**0**	**2**
1990-91	**Edmonton Oilers**	**NHL**	**74**	**24**	**31**	**55**	**22**	**24**	**46**	**59**	**8**	**0**	**4**	**193**	**12.4**	**84**	**31**	**73**	**13**	**–7**	**18**	**6**	**7**	**13**	**41**	**3**	**0**	**0**
1991-92	**Toronto Maple Leafs**	**NHL**	**72**	**24**	**33**	**57**	**22**	**25**	**47**	**100**	**5**	**0**	**4**	**188**	**12.8**	**76**	**23**	**88**	**22**	**–13**	....	....	....	....	....	....	....	....
	Canada	WC-A	6	2	1	3	....	....	....	16	....	....	....	....	....	....	....	....	....	....	....	....	....	....	....	....	....	....
1992-93	**Toronto Maple Leafs**	**NHL**	**76**	**22**	**43**	**65**	**18**	**30**	**48**	**117**	**11**	**0**	**3**	**161**	**13.7**	**101**	**46**	**37**	**1**	**19**	**21**	**7**	**11**	**18**	**31**	**0**	**0**	**2**
1993-94	**Toronto Maple Leafs**	**NHL**	**73**	**17**	**18**	**35**	**16**	**14**	**30**	**50**	**5**	**0**	**3**	**127**	**13.4**	**60**	**22**	**44**	**0**	**–6**	....	....	....	....	....	....	....	....
♦	**New York Rangers**	**NHL**	**12**	**4**	**2**	**6**	**4**	**2**	**6**	**12**	**2**	**0**	**0**	**22**	**18.2**	**11**	**4**	**6**	**0**	**1**	**23**	**3**	**3**	**6**	**42**	**0**	**1**	**2**
1994-95	Augsburger EV Panther	Germany	5	6	2	8	....	....	....	10	....	....	....	....	....	....	....	....	....	....	....	....	....	....	....	....	....	....
	Lukko Rauma	Finland	4	1	1	2	....	....	....	0	....	....	....	....	....	....	....	....	....	....	....	....	....	....	....	....	....	....
	Canada	Nat-Team	26	11	8	19	....	....	....	40	....	....	....	....	....	....	....	....	....	....	....	....	....	....	....	....	....	....
	St. Louis Blues	**NHL**	**36**	**12**	**14**	**26**	**21**	**21**	**42**	**37**	**0**	**0**	**3**	**54**	**22.2**	**34**	**4**	**25**	**4**	**9**	**6**	**1**	**1**	**2**	***49**	**0**	**0**	**0**
1995-96	Canada	Nat-Team	11	4	4	8	....	....	....	39	....	....	....	....	....	....	....	....	....	....	....	....	....	....	....	....	....	....
	Augsburger EV Panther	Germany	9	5	3	8	....	....	....	48	....	....	....	....	....	....	....	....	....	....	....	....	....	....	....	....	....	....
	Edmonton Oilers	**NHL**	**17**	**4**	**6**	**10**	**4**	**5**	**9**	**27**	**0**	**0**	**1**	**36**	**11.1**	**14**	**1**	**13**	**0**	**0**	....	....	....	....	....	....	....	....
	St. Louis Blues	**NHL**	**15**	**2**	**2**	**4**	**2**	**2**	**4**	**6**	**2**	**0**	**0**	**35**	**5.7**	**7**	**4**	**18**	**4**	**–11**	**11**	**1**	**4**	**5**	**6**	**0**	**0**	**1**
1996-97	HC Bolzano	Alpenliga	2	0	1	1	....	....	....	0	....	....	....	....	....	....	....	....	....	....	....	....	....	....	....	....	....	....
	HC La Chaux-de-Fonds	Switz.	23	14	15	29	....	....	....	103	....	....	....	....	....	....	....	....	....	....	....	....	....	....	....	....	....	....
	NHL Totals		**1129**	**498**	**601**	**1099**	**427**	**437**	**864**	**1120**	**151**	**13**	**85**	**3108**	**16.0**	**1687**	**556**	**1061**	**131**		**225**	**93**	**121**	**214**	**442**	**22**	**1**	**17**

Played in NHL All-Star Game (1984, 1985, 1986, 1988)

Traded to **Toronto** by **Edmonton** with Grant Fuhr and Craig Berube for Vincent Damphousse, Peter Ing, Scott Thornton, Luke Richardson, future considerations and cash, September 19, 1991. Traded to **NY Rangers** by **Toronto** with the rights to Scott Malone and Toronto's 4th round choice (Alexander Korobolin) in 1994 Entry Draft for Mike Gartner, March 21, 1994. Signed as a free agent by **St. Louis**, February 13, 1995. Signed as a free agent by **Vancouver**, January 22, 1996. Claimed on waivers by **Edmonton** from **Vancouver**, January 25, 1996. Claimed on waivers by **St. Louis** from **Edmonton**, March 12, 1996.

• ANDERSON, Jim

James William LW – L. 5'10", 165 lbs. b: Pembroke, Ont., 12/1/1930.

Season	Club	League	GP	G	A	Pts	AG	AA	APts	PIM	PP	SH	GW	S	%	TGF	PGF	TGA	PGA	+/–	GP	G	A	Pts	PIM	PP	SH	GW
1949-50	Windsor Spitfires	OHA-Jr.	3	0	0	0	....	....	....	2	....	....	....	....	....	....	....	....	....	....	9	1	4	5	0	....	....	....
	Detroit Hettche	IHL	31	18	14	32	....	....	....	12	....	....	....	....	....	....	....	....	....	....	....	....	....	....	....	....	....	....
1950-51	Windsor Spitfires	OHA-Jr.	53	21	22	43	....	....	....	35	....	....	....	....	....	....	....	....	....	....	7	2	2	4	6	....	....	....
1951-52	Glace Bay Miners	MMHL	88	*51	33	84	....	....	....	14	....	....	....	....	....	....	....	....	....	....	4	3	0	3	2	....	....	....
1952-53	Edmonton Flyers	WHL	44	11	11	22	....	....	....	8	....	....	....	....	....	....	....	....	....	....	15	*12	3	15	0	....	....	....
	Shawinigan Cataracts	QMHL	22	7	4	11	....	....	....	8	....	....	....	....	....	....	....	....	....	....	....	....	....	....	....	....	....	....
1953-54	Edmonton Flyers	WHL	66	23	21	44	....	....	....	22	....	....	....	....	....	....	....	....	....	....	13	6	2	8	2	....	....	....
1954-55	Springfield Indians	AHL	63	39	32	71	....	....	....	40	....	....	....	....	....	....	....	....	....	....	4	0	0	0	0	....	....	....
1955-56	Springfield Indians	AHL	61	28	23	51	....	....	....	44	....	....	....	....	....	....	....	....	....	....	....	....	....	....	....	....	....	....
1956-57	Springfield Indians	AHL	64	30	25	55	....	....	....	32	....	....	....	....	....	....	....	....	....	....	....	....	....	....	....	....	....	....
1957-58	Trois-Rivieres Lions	QHL	34	14	18	32	....	....	....	2	....	....	....	....	....	....	....	....	....	....	....	....	....	....	....	....	....	....
	Springfield Indians	AHL	11	3	0	3	....	....	....	12	....	....	....	....	....	....	....	....	....	....	....	....	....	....	....	....	....	....
	Buffalo Bisons	AHL	14	1	4	5	....	....	....	4	....	....	....	....	....	....	....	....	....	....	....	....	....	....	....	....	....	....
1958-59	Springfield Indians	AHL	69	27	36	63	....	....	....	16	....	....	....	....	....	....	....	....	....	....	....	....	....	....	....	....	....	....
1959-60	Springfield Indians	AHL	56	16	21	37	....	....	....	10	....	....	....	....	....	....	....	....	....	....	4	1	0	1	0	....	....	....
1960-61	Springfield Indians	AHL	72	*43	38	81	....	....	....	18	....	....	....	....	....	....	....	....	....	....	8	*5	0	5	0	....	....	....
1961-62	Springfield Indians	AHL	70	38	41	79	....	....	....	24	....	....	....	....	....	....	....	....	....	....	11	*7	1	8	2	....	....	....
1962-63	Springfield Indians	AHL	70	35	26	61	....	....	....	6	....	....	....	....	....	....	....	....	....	....	....	....	....	....	....	....	....	....
1963-64	Springfield Indians	AHL	72	*40	32	72	....	....	....	14	....	....	....	....	....	....	....	....	....	....	....	....	....	....	....	....	....	....
1964-65	Springfield Indians	AHL	72	40	29	69	....	....	....	14	....	....	....	....	....	....	....	....	....	....	....	....	....	....	....	....	....	....
1965-66	Springfield Indians	AHL	69	27	20	47	....	....	....	12	....	....	....	....	....	....	....	....	....	....	6	1	1	2	0	....	....	....
1966-67	Springfield Indians	AHL	63	25	29	54	....	....	....	4	....	....	....	....	....	....	....	....	....	....	....	....	....	....	....	....	....	....
1967-68	**Los Angeles Kings**	**NHL**	**7**	**1**	**2**	**3**	**1**	**2**	**3**	**2**	**0**	**0**	**0**	**20**	**5.0**	**4**	**0**	**6**	**0**	**–2**	....	....	....	....	....	....	....	....
	Springfield Kings	AHL	62	22	24	46	....	....	....	26	....	....	....	....	....	....	....	....	....	....	4	0	1	1	2	....	....	....
1968-69	Springfield Kings	AHL	54	12	15	27	....	....	....	10	....	....	....	....	....	....	....	....	....	....	....	....	....	....	....	....	....	....
1969-70	Springfield Kings	AHL	1	0	0	0	....	....	....	0	....	....	....	....	....	....	....	....	....	....	....	....	....	....	....	....	....	....
	NHL Totals		**7**	**1**	**2**	**3**	**1**	**2**	**3**	**2**	**0**	**0**	**0**	**20**	**5.0**	**4**	**0**	**6**	**0**		....	....	....	....	....	....	....	....

Won Dudley "Red" Garrett Memorial Award (Top Rookie - AHL) (1955) • AHL Second All-Star Team (1961, 1964)

Loaned to **Glace Bay** (MMHL) by **Detroit**, September 20, 1951. Loaned to **Shawinigan**, (QMHL) by **Detroit**, December 5, 1952. Loaned to **Buffalo** (AHL) by **Springfield** (AHL), February 23, 1958. NHL rights transferred to **LA Kings** after NHL club purchased **Springfield** (AHL) franchise, May, 1967.

• ANDERSON, John

John Murray RW – L. 5'11", 200 lbs. b: Toronto, Ont., 3/28/1957. Toronto's 1st, 11th overall, in 1977.

Season	Club	League	GP	G	A	Pts	AG	AA	APts	PIM	PP	SH	GW	S	%	TGF	PGF	TGA	PGA	+/–	GP	G	A	Pts	PIM	PP	SH	GW
1972-73	Markham Waxers	OHA-B	STATISTICS NOT AVAILABLE																									
1973-74	Toronto Marlboros	OMJHL	38	22	22	44	....	....	....	6	....	....	....	....	....	....	....	....	....	....	....	....	....	....	....	....	....	....
1974-75	Toronto Marlboros	OMJHL	70	49	64	113	....	....	....	31	....	....	....	....	....	....	....	....	....	....	22	16	14	30	14	....	....	....
	Toronto Marlboros	Mem-Cup	4	4	*6	*10	....	....	....	2	....	....	....	....	....	....	....	....	....	....	....	....	....	....	....	....	....	....
1975-76	Toronto Marlboros	OMJHL	39	26	25	51	....	....	....	19	....	....	....	....	....	....	....	....	....	....	10	7	4	11	7	....	....	....
1976-77	Toronto Marlboros	OMJHL	64	57	62	119	....	....	....	42	....	....	....	....	....	....	....	....	....	....	6	3	5	8	0	....	....	....
	Canada	WJC-A	7	10	5	15	....	....	....	6	....	....	....	....	....	....	....	....	....	....	....	....	....	....	....	....	....	....
1977-78	**Toronto Maple Leafs**	**NHL**	**17**	**1**	**2**	**3**	**1**	**2**	**3**	**2**	**0**	**0**	**0**	**14**	**7.1**	**6**	**0**	**5**	**0**	**1**	**2**	**0**	**0**	**0**	**0**	**0**	**0**	**0**
	Dallas Black Hawks	CHL	55	22	23	45	....	....	....	6	....	....	....	....	....	....	....	....	....	....	13	*11	8	*19	2	....	....	....
1978-79	**Toronto Maple Leafs**	**NHL**	**71**	**15**	**11**	**26**	**13**	**8**	**21**	**10**	**0**	**0**	**2**	**123**	**12.2**	**48**	**4**	**43**	**1**	**2**	**6**	**0**	**2**	**2**	**0**	**0**	**0**	**0**
1979-80	**Toronto Maple Leafs**	**NHL**	**74**	**25**	**28**	**53**	**21**	**20**	**41**	**22**	**3**	**0**	**5**	**207**	**12.1**	**76**	**12**	**59**	**0**	**5**	**3**	**1**	**1**	**2**	**0**	**0**	**0**	**0**

			REGULAR SEASON																		PLAYOFFS							
Season	Club	League	GP	G	A	Pts	AG	AA	APts	PIM	PP	SH	GW	S	%	TGF	PGF	TGA	PGA	+/–	GP	G	A	Pts	PIM	PP	SH	GW
1980-81	**Toronto Maple Leafs**	**NHL**	75	17	26	43	13	17	30	31	2	0	1	142	12.0	64	10	65	0	–11	2	0	0	0	0	0	0	0
1981-82	**Toronto Maple Leafs**	**NHL**	69	31	26	57	24	17	41	30	7	0	3	191	16.2	94	16	82	12	8	....	....	....	....	....	....	....	....
1982-83	**Toronto Maple Leafs**	**NHL**	80	31	49	80	25	34	59	24	9	0	6	199	15.6	127	46	93	6	–6	4	2	4	6	0	1	0	0
	Canada	WEC-A	6	2	2	4	....	....	....	6	....	....	....	....	....	....	....	....	....	....	....	....	....	....	....	....	....	....
1983-84	**Toronto Maple Leafs**	**NHL**	73	37	31	68	30	21	51	22	14	0	5	192	19.3	108	48	72	0	–12	....	....	....	....	....	....	....	....
1984-85	**Toronto Maple Leafs**	**NHL**	75	32	31	63	26	21	47	27	14	1	5	194	16.5	99	38	88	7	–20	....	....	....	....	....	....	....	....
	Canada	WEC-A	9	5	2	7	....	....	....	18	....	....	....	....	....	....	....	....	....	....	....	....	....	....	....	....	....	....
1985-86	**Quebec Nordiques**	**NHL**	65	21	28	49	17	19	36	26	8	3	5	190	11.1	97	52	59	13	–1	....	....	....	....	....	....	....	....
	Hartford Whalers	**NHL**	14	8	17	25	6	11	17	2	1	0	1	50	16.0	33	7	9	1	18	10	5	8	13	0	3	0	0
1986-87	**Hartford Whalers**	**NHL**	76	31	44	75	27	32	59	19	7	0	5	223	13.9	111	45	57	2	11	6	1	2	3	0	1	0	0
1987-88	**Hartford Whalers**	**NHL**	63	17	32	49	14	23	37	20	9	0	3	149	11.4	75	46	40	6	–5	....	....	....	....	....	....	....	....
1988-89	**Hartford Whalers**	**NHL**	62	16	24	40	14	17	31	28	1	0	0	132	12.1	71	19	41	4	15	4	0	1	1	2	0	0	0
1989-90	Binghamton Whalers	AHL	3	1	1	2	....	....	....	0	....	....	....	....	....	....	....	....	....	....	....	....	....	....	....	....	....	....
	HC Milano Saima	Italy	9	7	9	16	....	....	....	18	....	....	....	....	....	....	....	....	....	....	....	....	....	....	....	....	....	....
1990-91	Fort Wayne Komets	IHL	63	40	43	83	....	....	....	24	....	....	....	....	....	....	....	....	....	....	1	3	0	3	0	....	....	....
1991-92	New Haven Nighthawks	AHL	68	41	54	95	....	....	....	24	....	....	....	....	....	....	....	....	....	....	4	0	4	4	0	....	....	....
1992-93	San Diego Gulls	IHL	65	34	46	80	....	....	....	18	....	....	....	....	....	....	....	....	....	....	11	5	6	11	4	....	....	....
1993-94	San Diego Gulls	IHL	72	24	24	48	....	....	....	32	....	....	....	....	....	....	....	....	....	....	4	1	1	2	8	....	....	....
1994-1995	San Diego Gulls	IHL	DID NOT PLAY – ASSISTANT COACH																									
1995-1996	Winston-Salem Mammoths	SHL	DID NOT PLAY – COACHING																									
1996-1997	Quad City Mallards	ColHL	DID NOT PLAY – COACHING																									
1997-2000	Chicago Wolves	IHL	DID NOT PLAY – COACHING																									
	NHL Totals		814	282	349	631	231	242	473	263	75	4	41	2006	14.1	1009	343	713	52		37	9	18	27	2	5	0	0

Memorial Cup All-Star Team (1975) • OMJHL First All-Star Team (1977) • CHL Second All-Star Team (1978) • AHL First All-Star Team (1992) • Won Fred T. Hunt Memorial Trophy (Sportsmanship - AHL) (1992) • Won Les Cunningham Award (MVP - AHL) (1992)

Traded to **Quebec** by **Toronto** for Brad Maxwell, August 21, 1985. Traded to **Hartford** by **Quebec** for Risto Siltanen, March 8, 1986.

• ANDERSON, Murray

Murray Craig D – L. 5'10", 175 lbs. b: The Pas, Man., 8/28/1949. Montreal's 4th, 44th overall, in 1969.

Season	Club	League	GP	G	A	Pts	AG	AA	APts	PIM	PP	SH	GW	S	%	TGF	PGF	TGA	PGA	+/–	GP	G	A	Pts	PIM	PP	SH	GW
1966-67	Selkirk Steelers	MJHL	47	3	13	16	....	....	....	82	....	....	....	....	....	....	....	....	....	....	....	....	....	....	....	....	....	....
1967-68	Flin Flon Bombers	WCJHL	55	5	14	19	....	....	....	87	....	....	....	....	....	....	....	....	....	....	15	1	2	3	19	....	....	....
1968-69	Flin Flon Bombers	WCJHL	53	17	30	47	....	....	....	120	....	....	....	....	....	....	....	....	....	....	18	0	6	6	0	....	....	....
1969-70	Flin Flon Bombers	WCJHL	50	5	23	28	....	....	....	150	....	....	....	....	....	....	....	....	....	....	17	2	11	13	20	....	....	....
1970-71	Rochester–Montreal	AHL	52	0	5	5	....	....	....	48	....	....	....	....	....	....	....	....	....	....	....	....	....	....	....	....	....	....
1971-72	Nova Scotia Voyageurs	AHL	64	11	6	17	....	....	....	35	....	....	....	....	....	....	....	....	....	....	15	2	3	5	2	....	....	....
1972-73	Nova Scotia Voyageurs	AHL	71	1	24	25	....	....	....	52	....	....	....	....	....	....	....	....	....	....	13	1	2	3	22	....	....	....
1973-74	New Haven Nighthawks	AHL	76	9	34	43	....	....	....	79	....	....	....	....	....	....	....	....	....	....	10	0	3	3	6	....	....	....
1974-75	**Washington Capitals**	**NHL**	40	0	1	1	0	1	1	68	0	0	0	24	0.0	13	2	70	19	–40	....	....	....	....	....	....	....	....
	Richmond Robins	AHL	35	3	9	12	....	....	....	56	....	....	....	....	....	....	....	....	....	....	7	1	2	3	4	....	....	....
1975-76	Springfield Indians	AHL	75	3	21	24	....	....	....	62	....	....	....	....	....	....	....	....	....	....	....	....	....	....	....	....	....	....
1976-77	Tulsa Oilers	CHL	3	0	0	0	....	....	....	4	....	....	....	....	....	....	....	....	....	....	....	....	....	....	....	....	....	....
	NHL Totals		40	0	1	1	0	1	1	68	0	0	0	24	0.0	13	2	70	19		....	....	....	....	....	....	....	....

WCJHL All-Star Team (1970)

Traded to **Minnesota** by **Montreal** with Tony Featherstone for cash, May 29, 1973. Claimed by **Washington** from **Minnesota** in Expansion Draft, June 12, 1974

• ANDERSON, Perry

Perry Lynn LW – L. 6'1", 225 lbs. b: Barrie, Ont., 10/14/1961. St. Louis' 5th, 117th overall, in 1980.

Season	Club	League	GP	G	A	Pts	AG	AA	APts	PIM	PP	SH	GW	S	%	TGF	PGF	TGA	PGA	+/–	GP	G	A	Pts	PIM	PP	SH	GW
1977-78	Alliston Hornets	OHA-C	45	26	34	60	....	....	....	90	....	....	....	....	....	....	....	....	....	....	....	....	....	....	....	....	....	....
1978-79	Kingston Canadians	OMJHL	61	6	13	19	....	....	....	85	....	....	....	....	....	....	....	....	....	....	5	2	1	3	6	....	....	....
1979-80	Kingston Canadians	OMJHL	63	17	16	33	....	....	....	52	....	....	....	....	....	....	....	....	....	....	3	0	0	0	6	....	....	....
1980-81	Kingston Canadians	OMJHL	38	9	13	22	....	....	....	118	....	....	....	....	....	....	....	....	....	....	....	....	....	....	....	....	....	....
	Brantford Alexanders	OMJHL	31	8	27	35	....	....	....	43	....	....	....	....	....	....	....	....	....	....	6	4	2	6	15	....	....	....
1981-82	**St. Louis Blues**	**NHL**	5	1	2	3	1	1	2	0	0	0	0	9	11.1	4	0	3	0	1	10	2	0	2	4	1	0	0
	Salt Lake Golden Eagles	CHL	71	32	32	64	....	....	....	117	....	....	....	....	....	....	....	....	....	....	2	1	0	1	2	....	....	....
1982-83	**St. Louis Blues**	**NHL**	18	5	2	7	4	1	5	14	0	0	0	27	18.5	9	1	15	1	–6	....	....	....	....	....	....	....	....
	Salt Lake Golden Eagles	CHL	57	23	19	42	....	....	....	140	....	....	....	....	....	....	....	....	....	....	....	....	....	....	....	....	....	....
1983-84	**St. Louis Blues**	**NHL**	50	7	5	12	6	3	9	195	0	0	1	49	14.3	22	0	36	1	–13	9	0	0	0	27	0	0	0
	Montana Magic	CHL	8	7	3	10	....	....	....	34	....	....	....	....	....	....	....	....	....	....	....	....	....	....	....	....	....	....
1984-85	**St. Louis Blues**	**NHL**	71	9	9	18	7	6	13	146	0	0	1	86	10.5	30	0	28	0	2	3	0	0	0	7	0	0	0
1985-86	**New Jersey Devils**	**NHL**	51	7	12	19	6	8	14	91	1	0	1	61	11.5	25	2	31	1	–7	....	....	....	....	....	....	....	....
1986-87	**New Jersey Devils**	**NHL**	57	10	9	19	9	7	16	107	2	0	1	46	21.7	33	8	38	0	–13	....	....	....	....	....	....	....	....
	Maine Mariners	AHL	9	5	4	9	....	....	....	42	....	....	....	....	....	....	....	....	....	....	....	....	....	....	....	....	....	....
1987-88	**New Jersey Devils**	**NHL**	60	4	6	10	3	4	7	222	1	0	0	40	10.0	22	5	26	1	–8	10	0	0	0	113	0	0	0
1988-89	**New Jersey Devils**	**NHL**	39	3	6	9	3	4	7	128	0	0	0	36	8.3	15	0	10	0	5	....	....	....	....	....	....	....	....
1989-90	Utica Devils	AHL	71	13	17	30	....	....	....	128	....	....	....	....	....	....	....	....	....	....	5	0	0	0	24	....	....	....
1990-91	**New Jersey Devils**	**NHL**	1	0	0	0	0	0	0	5	0	0	0	1	0.0	0	0	0	0	0	4	0	1	1	10	0	0	0
	Utica Devils	AHL	68	19	14	33	....	....	....	245	....	....	....	....	....	....	....	....	....	....	....	....	....	....	....	....	....	....
1991-92	**San Jose Sharks**	**NHL**	48	4	8	12	4	6	10	143	0	0	0	57	7.0	16	0	33	0	–17	....	....	....	....	....	....	....	....
1992-93	San Diego Gulls	IHL	51	8	13	21	....	....	....	217	....	....	....	....	....	....	....	....	....	....	5	0	0	0	14	....	....	....
1993-94	Salt Lake Golden Eagles	IHL	2	0	0	0	....	....	....	21	....	....	....	....	....	....	....	....	....	....	....	....	....	....	....	....	....	....
	NHL Totals		400	50	59	109	43	40	83	1051	4	0	4	412	12.1	176	16	220	4		36	2	1	3	161	1	0	0

CHL Second All-Star Team (1982)

Traded to **New Jersey** by **St. Louis** for Rick Meagher and New Jersey's 12th round choice (Bill Butler) in 1986 Entry Draft, August 29, 1985. Signed as a free agent by **San Jose**, July 8, 1991.

• ANDERSON, Ron

Ronald Henry RW – R. 5'10", 165 lbs. b: Moncton, N.B., 1/21/1950.

Season	Club	League	GP	G	A	Pts	AG	AA	APts	PIM	PP	SH	GW	S	%	TGF	PGF	TGA	PGA	+/–	GP	G	A	Pts	PIM	PP	SH	GW
1963-64	Moncton Rovers	NBAHA	....	*17	10	*27	....	....	....	7	....	....	....	....	....	....	....	....	....	....	....	....	....	....	....	....	....	....
1964-65	Moncton Aces	NBAHA	....	15	7	22	....	....	....	4	....	....	....	....	....	....	....	....	....	....	....	....	....	....	....	....	....	....
1965-66	Moncton Beavers	NBAHA	....	*20	21	*41	....	....	....	10	....	....	....	....	....	....	....	....	....	....	....	....	....	....	....	....	....	....
1966-67	Moncton Seals	NBJHL	....	26	*34	*60	....	....	....	....	....	....	....	....	....	....	....	....	....	....	....	*17	21	*38	0	....	....	....
	Moncton Seals	SNBHL	....	15	20	35	....	....	....	34	....	....	....	....	....	....	....	....	....	....	....	....	....	....	....	....	....	....
1967-68	Moncton Hawks	SNBHL	30	17	23	40	....	....	....	2	....	....	....	....	....	....	....	....	....	....	....	....	....	....	....	....	....	....
	Moncton Seals	NBJHL	....	....	....	....	....	....	....	....	....	....	....	....	....	....	....	....	....	....	6	2	3	5	12	....	....	....
	Fredericton Jr. Red Wings	NBJHL	....	....	....	....	....	....	....	....	....	....	....	....	....	....	....	....	....	....	5	*6	4	10	2	....	....	....
	Halifax Jr. Canadians	Mem-Cup	4	0	2	2	....	....	....	6	....	....	....	....	....	....	....	....	....	....	....	....	....	....	....	....	....	....
	Fredericton Red Wings	Mem-Cup	6	3	5	8	....	....	....	2	....	....	....	....	....	....	....	....	....	....	....	....	....	....	....	....	....	....
1968-69	Moncton Alpines	SNBHL	20	*30	36	*66	....	....	....	34	....	....	....	....	....	....	....	....	....	....	....	....	....	....	....	....	....	....
1969-70	Boston University	ECAC	DID NOT PLAY – FRESHMAN																									
1970-71	Boston University	ECAC	31	20	21	41	....	....	....	17	....	....	....	....	....	....	....	....	....	....	....	....	....	....	....	....	....	....
1971-72	Boston University	ECAC	31	19	27	46	....	....	....	26	....	....	....	....	....	....	....	....	....	....	....	....	....	....	....	....	....	....
1972-73	Boston Braves	AHL	73	41	29	70	....	....	....	53	....	....	....	....	....	....	....	....	....	....	....	....	....	....	....	....	....	....
1973-74	Boston Braves	AHL	75	24	31	55	....	....	....	28	....	....	....	....	....	....	....	....	....	....	....	....	....	....	....	....	....	....
1974-75	**Washington Capitals**	**NHL**	28	9	7	16	8	5	13	8	4	0	0	43	20.9	23	9	34	0	–20	....	....	....	....	....	....	....	....
	Richmond Robins	AHL	38	20	19	39	....	....	....	19	....	....	....	....	....	....	....	....	....	....	....	....	....	....	....	....	....	....

			REGULAR SEASON																		PLAYOFFS							
Season	Club	League	GP	G	A	Pts	AG	AA	APts	PIM	PP	SH	GW	S	%	TGF	PGF	TGA	PGA	+/–	GP	G	A	Pts	PIM	PP	SH	GW
1975-76	Richmond Robins	AHL	20	2	3	5	....	....	....	6	....	....	....	....	....	....	....	....	....	....	....	....	....	....	....	....	....	....
	New Haven Nighthawks	AHL	17	1	3	4	....	....	....	8	....	....	....	....	....	....	....	....	....	....	3	0	0	0	0	....	....	....
1976-77	VSV Veicherung	Austria-2	24	26	14	40	....	....	....	....	....	....	....	....	....	....	....	....	....	....	....	....	....	....	....	....	....	....
1977-78	WEV Wein	Germany	26	28	8	36	....	....	....	14	....	....	....	....	....	....	....	....	....	....	....	....	....	....	....	....	....	....
	NHL Totals		**28**	**9**	**7**	**16**	**8**	**5**	**13**	**8**	**4**	**0**	**0**	**43**	**20.9**	**23**	**9**	**34**	**0**		....	....	....	....	....	....	....	....

AHL Second All-Star Team (1973) • Won Dudley "Red" Garrett Memorial Award (Top Rookie - AHL) (1973)

Signed as a free agent by **Boston**, June, 1972. Claimed by **Washington** from **Boston** in Expansion Draft, June 12, 1974. • Missed majority of 1975-76 season after suffering a knee injury during training camp, September, 1975. Traded to **New Haven** (AHL) by **Washington** with Bob Gryp for Rich Nantais and Alain Langlais, February 23, 1976

• ANDERSON, Ron

Ronald Chester "Goings" RW – R. 6', 170 lbs. b: Red Deer, Alta., 7/29/1945.

Season	Club	League	GP	G	A	Pts	AG	AA	APts	PIM	PP	SH	GW	S	%	TGF	PGF	TGA	PGA	+/–	GP	G	A	Pts	PIM	PP	SH	GW
1962-63	Edmonton Oil Kings	CAHL	STATISTICS NOT AVAILABLE																									
	Edmonton Oil Kings	Mem-Cup	20	1	3	4	....	....	....	8	....	....	....	....	....	....	....	....	....	....	....	....	....	....	....	....	....	....
1963-64	Edmonton Oil Kings	CAHL	14	6	5	11	....	....	....	4	....	....	....	....	....	....	....	....	....	....	3	0	0	0	2	....	....	....
	Edmonton Oil Kings	Mem-Cup	17	8	5	13	....	....	....	17	....	....	....	....	....	....	....	....	....	....	....	....	....	....	....	....	....	....
1964-65	Edmonton Oil Kings	CAHL	....	....	....	....	....	....	....	....	....	....	....	....	....	....	....	....	....	....	5	5	2	7	6	....	....	....
	Edmonton Oil Kings	Mem-Cup	19	11	17	28	....	....	....	42	....	....	....	....	....	....	....	....	....	....	....	....	....	....	....	....	....	....
1965-66	Edmonton Oil Kings	ASHL	30	15	19	34	....	....	....	51	....	....	....	....	....	....	....	....	....	....	11	7	3	10	31	....	....	....
	Hamilton Red Wings	OHA-Jr.	6	1	0	1	....	....	....	2	....	....	....	....	....	....	....	....	....	....	....	....	....	....	....	....	....	....
	Memphis Wings	CPHL	3	1	3	4	....	....	....	4	....	....	....	....	....	....	....	....	....	....	....	....	....	....	....	....	....	....
	Edmonton Oil Kings	Mem-Cup	17	11	10	21	....	....	....	21	....	....	....	....	....	....	....	....	....	....	....	....	....	....	....	....	....	....
1966-67	Memphis Wings	CPHL	67	12	22	34	....	....	....	51	....	....	....	....	....	....	....	....	....	....	7	2	2	4	2	....	....	....
1967-68	**Detroit Red Wings**	**NHL**	**18**	**2**	**0**	**2**	**2**	**0**	**2**	**13**	**0**	**0**	**0**	**21**	**9.5**	**6**	**0**	**10**	**0**	**–4**	....	....	....	....	....	....	....	....
	Fort Worth Wings	CPHL	39	21	19	40	....	....	....	46	....	....	....	....	....	....	....	....	....	....	....	....	....	....	....	....	....	....
1968-69	**Detroit Red Wings**	**NHL**	**7**	**0**	**0**	**0**	**0**	**0**	**0**	**8**	**0**	**0**	**0**	**4**	**0.0**	**1**	**0**	**4**	**0**	**–3**	....	....	....	....	....	....	....	....
	Los Angeles Kings	**NHL**	**56**	**3**	**5**	**8**	**3**	**4**	**7**	**26**	**0**	**0**	**0**	**68**	**4.4**	**14**	**1**	**38**	**16**	**–9**	**4**	**0**	**0**	**0**	**2**	**0**	**0**	**0**
1969-70	**St. Louis Blues**	**NHL**	**59**	**9**	**9**	**18**	**10**	**8**	**18**	**36**	**0**	**0**	**0**	**197**	**4.6**	**33**	**3**	**19**	**0**	**11**	**1**	**0**	**0**	**0**	**2**	**0**	**0**	**0**
	Buffalo Bisons	AHL	9	8	3	11	....	....	....	16	....	....	....	....	....	....	....	....	....	....	....	....	....	....	....	....	....	....
1970-71	**Buffalo Sabres**	**NHL**	**74**	**14**	**12**	**26**	**14**	**10**	**24**	**44**	**0**	**1**	**3**	**139**	**10.1**	**38**	**1**	**70**	**22**	**–11**	....	....	....	....	....	....	....	....
1971-72	**Buffalo Sabres**	**NHL**	**37**	**0**	**4**	**4**	**0**	**3**	**3**	**19**	**0**	**0**	**0**	**35**	**0.0**	**10**	**0**	**22**	**2**	**–10**	....	....	....	....	....	....	....	....
	Salt Lake Golden Eagles	WHL	26	7	10	17	....	....	....	8	....	....	....	....	....	....	....	....	....	....	....	....	....	....	....	....	....	....
1972-73	Alberta Oilers	WHA	73	14	15	29	....	....	....	43	....	....	....	....	....	....	....	....	....	....	....	....	....	....	....	....	....	....
1973-74	Edmonton Oilers	WHA	19	5	2	7	....	....	....	6	....	....	....	....	....	....	....	....	....	....	1	0	0	0	0	....	....	....
	Winston-Salem Polar Bears	SHL	49	28	31	59	....	....	....	33	....	....	....	....	....	....	....	....	....	....	....	....	....	....	....	....	....	....
1974-75	Mohawk Valley Comets	NAHL	64	18	34	52	....	....	....	21	....	....	....	....	....	....	....	....	....	....	....	....	....	....	....	....	....	....
1975-76	Winston-Salem Polar Bears	SHL	27	0	7	7	....	....	....	14	....	....	....	....	....	....	....	....	....	....	....	....	....	....	....	....	....	....
	Tidewater Sharks	SHL	41	1	14	15	....	....	....	49	....	....	....	....	....	....	....	....	....	....	....	....	....	....	....	....	....	....
1976-77	Winston-Salem Polar Twins	SHL	24	1	6	7	....	....	....	10	....	....	....	....	....	....	....	....	....	....	....	....	....	....	....	....	....	....
	NHL Totals		**251**	**28**	**30**	**58**	**29**	**25**	**54**	**146**	**0**	**1**	**3**	**464**	**6.0**	**102**	**5**	**163**	**40**		**5**	**0**	**0**	**0**	**4**	**0**	**0**	**0**
	Other Major League Totals		92	19	17	36	....	....	....	49	....	....	....	....	....	....	....	....	....	....	1	0	0	0	0	....	....	....

SHL Second All-Star Team (1974) • SHL First All-Star Team (1976)

Traded to **LA Kings** by **Detroit** for Poul Popiel, November 12, 1968. Claimed by **St. Louis** from **LA Kings** in Intra-League Draft, June 11, 1969. Traded to **Buffalo** by **St. Louis** for Craig Cameron, October 2, 1970. Selected by **Alberta** (WHA) in 1972 WHA General Player Draft, February 12, 1972. Claimed by **San Diego** (WHL) from **Buffalo** (Salt Lake-WHL) in Reverse Draft, June, 1972.

• ANDERSON, Russ

Russ Vincent D – L. 6'3", 210 lbs. b: Minneapolis, MN, 2/12/1955. Pittsburgh's 2nd, 31st overall, in 1975.

Season	Club	League	GP	G	A	Pts	AG	AA	APts	PIM	PP	SH	GW	S	%	TGF	PGF	TGA	PGA	+/–	GP	G	A	Pts	PIM	PP	SH	GW
1974-75	University of Minnesota	WCHA	30	2	7	9	....	....	....	56	....	....	....	....	....	....	....	....	....	....	....	....	....	....	....	....	....	....
1975-76	University of Minnesota	WCHA	28	0	5	5	....	....	....	81	....	....	....	....	....	....	....	....	....	....	....	....	....	....	....	....	....	....
1976-77	**Pittsburgh Penguins**	**NHL**	**66**	**2**	**11**	**13**	**2**	**8**	**10**	**81**	**0**	**0**	**1**	**45**	**4.4**	**63**	**6**	**62**	**10**	**5**	**3**	**0**	**1**	**1**	**14**	**0**	**0**	**0**
	Hershey Bears	AHL	11	0	4	4	....	....	....	35	....	....	....	....	....	....	....	....	....	....	....	....	....	....	....	....	....	....
	United States	WEC-A	10	0	0	0	....	....	....	16	....	....	....	....	....	....	....	....	....	....	....	....	....	....	....	....	....	....
1977-78	**Pittsburgh Penguins**	**NHL**	**74**	**2**	**16**	**18**	**2**	**12**	**14**	**150**	**0**	**0**	**1**	**51**	**3.9**	**67**	**2**	**81**	**11**	**–5**	....	....	....	....	....	....	....	....
1978-79	**Pittsburgh Penguins**	**NHL**	**72**	**3**	**13**	**16**	**3**	**9**	**12**	**93**	**0**	**0**	**0**	**48**	**6.3**	**52**	**0**	**64**	**13**	**1**	**2**	**0**	**0**	**0**	**0**	**0**	**0**	**0**
1979-80	**Pittsburgh Penguins**	**NHL**	**76**	**5**	**22**	**27**	**4**	**16**	**20**	**150**	**0**	**0**	**0**	**78**	**6.4**	**93**	**3**	**107**	**28**	**11**	**5**	**0**	**2**	**2**	**14**	**0**	**0**	**0**
1980-81	**Pittsburgh Penguins**	**NHL**	**34**	**3**	**14**	**17**	**2**	**9**	**11**	**112**	**1**	**0**	**1**	**38**	**7.9**	**46**	**7**	**44**	**17**	**12**	....	....	....	....	....	....	....	....
1981-82	**Pittsburgh Penguins**	**NHL**	**31**	**0**	**1**	**1**	**0**	**1**	**1**	**98**	**0**	**0**	**0**	**13**	**0.0**	**11**	**0**	**18**	**3**	**–4**	....	....	....	....	....	....	....	....
	Hartford Whalers	**NHL**	**25**	**1**	**3**	**4**	**1**	**2**	**3**	**85**	**0**	**0**	**1**	**24**	**4.2**	**20**	**0**	**46**	**9**	**–17**	....	....	....	....	....	....	....	....
1982-83	**Hartford Whalers**	**NHL**	**57**	**0**	**6**	**6**	**0**	**4**	**4**	**171**	**0**	**0**	**0**	**18**	**0.0**	**35**	**0**	**77**	**9**	**–33**	....	....	....	....	....	....	....	....
1983-84	**Los Angeles Kings**	**NHL**	**70**	**5**	**12**	**17**	**4**	**8**	**12**	**126**	**0**	**0**	**1**	**47**	**10.6**	**60**	**2**	**110**	**22**	**–30**	....	....	....	....	....	....	....	....
1984-85	**Los Angeles Kings**	**NHL**	**14**	**1**	**1**	**2**	**1**	**1**	**2**	**20**	**0**	**0**	**0**	**11**	**9.1**	**9**	**0**	**12**	**1**	**–2**	....	....	....	....	....	....	....	....
	New Haven Nighthawks	AHL	6	0	2	2	....	....	....	2	....	....	....	....	....	....	....	....	....	....	....	....	....	....	....	....	....	....
	NHL Totals		**519**	**22**	**99**	**121**	**19**	**70**	**89**	**1086**	**1**	**0**	**5**	**373**	**5.9**	**456**	**20**	**621**	**123**		**10**	**0**	**3**	**3**	**28**	**0**	**0**	**0**

Traded to **Hartford** by **Pittsburgh** with Pittsburgh 8th round choice (Chris Duperron) in 1983 Entry Draft for Rick MacLeish, December 29, 1981. Signed as a free agent by **LA Kings**, September 2, 1983.

• ANDERSON, Shawn

Shawn Stephen D – L. 6'1", 200 lbs. b: Montreal, Que., 2/7/1968. Buffalo's 1st, 5th overall, in 1986.

Season	Club	League	GP	G	A	Pts	AG	AA	APts	PIM	PP	SH	GW	S	%	TGF	PGF	TGA	PGA	+/–	GP	G	A	Pts	PIM	PP	SH	GW
1983-84	Lac St-Louis Lions	QAAA	42	25	23	48	....	....	....	....	....	....	....	....	....	....	....	....	....	....	....	....	....	....	....	....	....	....
1984-85	Lac St-Louis Lions	QAAA	42	23	42	65	....	....	....	10	....	....	....	....	....	....	....	....	....	....	....	....	....	....	....	....	....	....
1985-86	University of Maine	H-East	16	5	8	13	....	....	....	22	....	....	....	....	....	....	....	....	....	....	....	....	....	....	....	....	....	....
	Canada	Nat-Team	33	2	6	8	....	....	....	16	....	....	....	....	....	....	....	....	....	....	....	....	....	....	....	....	....	....
1986-87	**Buffalo Sabres**	**NHL**	**41**	**2**	**11**	**13**	**2**	**8**	**10**	**23**	**0**	**0**	**0**	**26**	**7.7**	**30**	**5**	**29**	**4**	**0**	....	....	....	....	....	....	....	....
	Rochester Americans	AHL	15	2	5	7	....	....	....	11	....	....	....	....	....	....	....	....	....	....	....	....	....	....	....	....	....	....
1987-88	**Buffalo Sabres**	**NHL**	**23**	**1**	**2**	**3**	**1**	**1**	**2**	**17**	**1**	**0**	**0**	**29**	**3.4**	**25**	**8**	**25**	**5**	**–3**	....	....	....	....	....	....	....	....
	Rochester Americans	AHL	22	5	16	21	....	....	....	19	....	....	....	....	....	....	....	....	....	....	6	0	0	0	0	....	....	....
1988-89	**Buffalo Sabres**	**NHL**	**33**	**2**	**10**	**12**	**2**	**7**	**9**	**18**	**2**	**0**	**0**	**26**	**7.7**	**31**	**5**	**31**	**8**	**3**	**5**	**0**	**1**	**1**	**4**	**0**	**0**	**0**
	Rochester Americans	AHL	31	5	14	19	....	....	....	24	....	....	....	....	....	....	....	....	....	....	....	....	....	....	....	....	....	....
1989-90	**Buffalo Sabres**	**NHL**	**16**	**1**	**3**	**4**	**1**	**2**	**3**	**8**	**0**	**0**	**0**	**16**	**6.3**	**17**	**4**	**11**	**0**	**2**	....	....	....	....	....	....	....	....
	Rochester Americans	AHL	39	2	16	18	....	....	....	41	....	....	....	....	....	....	....	....	....	....	9	1	0	1	4	....	....	....
1990-91	**Quebec Nordiques**	**NHL**	**31**	**3**	**10**	**13**	**3**	**8**	**11**	**21**	**2**	**0**	**0**	**44**	**6.8**	**31**	**7**	**22**	**0**	**2**	....	....	....	....	....	....	....	....
	Halifax Citadels	AHL	4	0	1	1	....	....	....	2	....	....	....	....	....	....	....	....	....	....	....	....	....	....	....	....	....	....
1991-92	EC Weiswasser	Germany	38	7	15	22	....	....	....	83	....	....	....	....	....	....	....	....	....	....	6	5	4	9	8	....	....	....
1992-93	**Washington Capitals**	**NHL**	**60**	**2**	**6**	**8**	**2**	**4**	**6**	**18**	**1**	**0**	**0**	**42**	**4.8**	**22**	**5**	**19**	**0**	**–2**	**6**	**0**	**0**	**0**	**0**	**0**	**0**	**0**
	Baltimore Skipjacks	AHL	10	1	5	6	....	....	....	8	....	....	....	....	....	....	....	....	....	....	....	....	....	....	....	....	....	....
1993-94	**Washington Capitals**	**NHL**	**50**	**0**	**9**	**9**	**0**	**7**	**7**	**12**	**0**	**0**	**0**	**31**	**0.0**	**21**	**2**	**23**	**3**	**–1**	**8**	**1**	**0**	**1**	**12**	**0**	**0**	**0**
1994-95	**Philadelphia Flyers**	**NHL**	**1**	**0**	**0**	**0**	**0**	**0**	**0**	**0**	**0**	**0**	**0**	**0**	**0.0**	**1**	**0**	**1**	**0**	**0**	....	....	....	....	....	....	....	....
	Hershey Bears	AHL	31	9	21	30	....	....	....	18	....	....	....	....	....	....	....	....	....	....	6	2	3	5	19	....	....	....
1995-96	Milwaukee Admirals	IHL	79	22	39	61	....	....	....	68	....	....	....	....	....	....	....	....	....	....	5	0	7	7	0	....	....	....
1996-97	Wedemark Scorpions	Germany	8	1	0	1	....	....	....	4	....	....	....	....	....	....	....	....	....	....	....	....	....	....	....	....	....	....
	Utah Grizzlies	IHL	31	2	12	14	....	....	....	21	....	....	....	....	....	....	....	....	....	....	....	....	....	....	....	....	....	....
	Manitoba Moose	IHL	17	2	7	9	....	....	....	5	....	....	....	....	....	....	....	....	....	....	....	....	....	....	....	....	....	....
1997-98	Revier Lowen	Germany	32	5	14	19	....	....	....	45	....	....	....	....	....	....	....	....	....	....	....	....	....	....	....	....	....	....
1998-99	KAC Klagenfurt	Alpenliga	33	8	11	19	....	....	....	34	....	....	....	....	....	....	....	....	....	....	....	....	....	....	....	....	....	....
	KAC Klagenfurt	Austria	21	9	6	15	....	....	....	10	....	....	....	....	....	....	....	....	....	....	....	....	....	....	....	....	....	....
99-2000	Augsburger Panther	Germany	34	3	11	14	....	....	....	14	....	....	....	....	....	....	....	....	....	....	2	1	0	1	2	....	....	....
	Michigan K-Wings	IHL	6	0	2	2	....	....	....	2	....	....	....	....	....	....	....	....	....	....	....	....	....	....	....	....	....	....
	NHL Totals		**255**	**11**	**51**	**62**	**11**	**37**	**48**	**117**	**6**	**0**	**0**	**214**	**5.1**	**178**	**36**	**161**	**20**		**19**	**1**	**1**	**2**	**16**	**0**	**0**	**0**

Traded to **Washington** by **Buffalo** for Bill Houlder, September 30, 1990. Claimed by **Quebec** from **Washington** in NHL Waiver Draft, October 1, 1990. Traded to **Winnipeg** by **Quebec** for Sergei Kharin, October 22, 1991. • 1991-92 playoff totals for **EC Weiswasser** are Qualifcation Round statistics. Traded to **Washington** by **Winnipeg** for future considerations, October 23, 1991. Signed as a free agent by **Philadelphia**, August 16, 1994.

• ANDERSSON, Erik

C – L. 6'3", 210 lbs. b: Stockholm, Sweden, 8/19/1971. Calgary's 6th, 70th overall, in 1997.

Season	Club	League	GP	G	A	Pts	AG	AA	APts	PIM	PP	SH	GW	S	%	TGF	PGF	TGA	PGA	+/–	GP	G	A	Pts	PIM	PP	SH	GW
			REGULAR SEASON																		PLAYOFFS							
1988-89	Vallentuna BK	Sweden-2	24	2	6	8	....	....	....	4	....	....	....	....	....	....	....	....	....	....	....	....	....	....	....	....	....	....
1989-90	Danderyd IK	Sweden-2	30	14	5	19	....	....	....	16	....	....	....	....	....	....	....	....	....	....	....	....	....	....	....	....	....	....
1990-91	AIK Solna Stockholm	Sweden	32	1	1	2	....	....	....	10	....	....	....	....	....	....	....	....	....	....	....	....	....	....	....	....	....	....
	Sweden	WJC-A	7	2	1	3	....	....	....	4	....	....	....	....	....	....	....	....	....	....	....	....	....	....	....	....	....	....
1991-92	AIK Solna Stockholm	Sweden	3	0	0	0	....	....	....	0	....	....	....	....	....	....	....	....	....	....	....	....	....	....	....	....	....	....
1992-93	University of Denver	WCHA	DID NOT PLAY – ACADEMICALLY INELIGIBLE								....	....	....	....	....	....	....	....	....	....	....	....	....	....	....	....	....	....
1993-94	University of Denver	WCHA	38	10	20	30	....	....	....	26	....	....	....	....	....	....	....	....	....	....	....	....	....	....	....	....	....	....
1994-95	University of Denver	WCHA	42	12	19	31	....	....	....	42	....	....	....	....	....	....	....	....	....	....	....	....	....	....	....	....	....	....
1995-96	University of Denver	WCHA	39	12	35	47	....	....	....	40	....	....	....	....	....	....	....	....	....	....	....	....	....	....	....	....	....	....
1996-97	University of Denver	WCHA	39	17	17	34	....	....	....	42	....	....	....	....	....	....	....	....	....	....	....	....	....	....	....	....	....	....
1997-98	**Calgary Flames**	**NHL**	**12**	**2**	**1**	**3**	**2**	**1**	**3**	**8**	**0**	**0**	**0**	**11**	**18.2**	**4**	**0**	**9**	**1**	**–4**	....	....	....	....	....	....	....	....
	Saint John Flames	AHL	29	5	9	14	....	....	....	29	....	....	....	....	....	....	....	....	....	....	....	....	....	....	....	....	....	....
1998-99	Saint John Flames	AHL	5	0	0	0	....	....	....	4	....	....	....	....	....	....	....	....	....	....	....	....	....	....	....	....	....	....
	Indianapolis Ice	IHL	48	5	7	12	....	....	....	24	....	....	....	....	....	....	....	....	....	....	4	0	0	0	44	....	....	....
99-2000	AIK Solna Stockholm	Sweden	50	7	8	15	....	....	....	62	....	....	....	....	....	....	....	....	....	....	....	....	....	....	....	....	....	....
	NHL Totals		**12**	**2**	**1**	**3**	**2**	**1**	**3**	**8**	**0**	**0**	**0**	**11**	**18.2**	**4**	**0**	**9**	**1**		....	....	....	....	....	....	....	....

• Re-entered NHL draft. Originally LA Kings' 5th choice, 112th overall, in 1990 Entry Draft. Traded to **Chicago** by **Calgary** with Marty McInnis and Jamie Allison for Jeff Shantz and Steve Dubinsky, October 27, 1998.

• ANDERSSON, Kent-Erik

Kent-Erik H. RW – . 6'2", 185 lbs. b: Orebro, Sweden, 5/24/1951.

Season	Club	League	GP	G	A	Pts	AG	AA	APts	PIM	PP	SH	GW	S	%	TGF	PGF	TGA	PGA	+/–	GP	G	A	Pts	PIM	PP	SH	GW
1971-72	Farjestads BK Karlstad	Sweden	22	9	6	15	....	....	....	2	....	....	....	....	....	....	....	....	....	....	....	....	....	....	....	....	....	....
1972-73	Farjestads BK Karlstad	Sweden	14	10	7	17	....	....	....	6	....	....	....	....	....	....	....	....	....	....	....	....	....	....	....	....	....	....
1973-74	Farjestads BK Karlstad	Sweden	12	10	6	16	....	....	....	12	....	....	....	....	....	....	....	....	....	....	20	15	6	21	4	....	....	....
1974-75	Farjestads BK Karlstad	Sweden	27	18	11	29	....	....	....	2	....	....	....	....	....	....	....	....	....	....	....	....	....	....	....	....	....	....
1975-76	Farjestads BK Karlstad	Sweden	26	8	5	13	....	....	....	6	....	....	....	....	....	....	....	....	....	....	4	1	1	2	2	....	....	....
1976-77	Farjestads BK Karlstad	Sweden	33	17	17	34	....	....	....	30	....	....	....	....	....	....	....	....	....	....	5	2	1	3	4	....	....	....
	Sweden	WEC-A	10	4	1	5	....	....	....	0	....	....	....	....	....	....	....	....	....	....	....	....	....	....	....	....	....	....
1977-78	**Minnesota North Stars**	**NHL**	**73**	**15**	**18**	**33**	**14**	**14**	**28**	**4**	**3**	**0**	**1**	**121**	**12.4**	**48**	**12**	**71**	**18**	**–17**	....	....	....	....	....	....	....	....
	Sweden	WEC-A	10	5	1	6	....	....	....	12	....	....	....	....	....	....	....	....	....	....	....	....	....	....	....	....	....	....
1978-79	**Minnesota North Stars**	**NHL**	**41**	**9**	**4**	**13**	**8**	**3**	**11**	**4**	**2**	**2**	**4**	**59**	**15.3**	**20**	**4**	**30**	**8**	**–6**	....	....	....	....	....	....	....	....
1979-80	**Minnesota North Stars**	**NHL**	**61**	**9**	**10**	**19**	**8**	**7**	**15**	**8**	**1**	**0**	**3**	**87**	**10.3**	**37**	**2**	**45**	**7**	**–3**	**13**	**2**	**4**	**6**	**2**	**0**	**0**	**1**
	Oklahoma City Stars	CHL	3	0	2	2	....	....	....	2	....	....	....	....	....	....	....	....	....	....	....	....	....	....	....	....	....	....
1980-81	Minnesota North Stars	DN-Cup	3	1	1	2	....	....	....	0	....	....	....	....	....	....	....	....	....	....	....	....	....	....	....	....	....	....
	Minnesota North Stars	**NHL**	**77**	**17**	**24**	**41**	**13**	**16**	**29**	**22**	**1**	**4**	**2**	**127**	**13.4**	**56**	**3**	**63**	**18**	**8**	**19**	**2**	**4**	**6**	**2**	**0**	**0**	**0**
1981-82	Sweden	Can-Cup	5	0	1	1	....	....	....	0	....	....	....	....	....	....	....	....	....	....	....	....	....	....	....	....	....	....
	Minnesota North Stars	**NHL**	**70**	**9**	**12**	**21**	**7**	**8**	**15**	**18**	**0**	**0**	**2**	**78**	**11.5**	**35**	**1**	**57**	**18**	**–5**	**4**	**0**	**2**	**2**	**0**	**0**	**0**	**0**
1982-83	**New York Rangers**	**NHL**	**71**	**8**	**20**	**28**	**7**	**14**	**21**	**14**	**0**	**0**	**1**	**91**	**8.8**	**46**	**5**	**53**	**18**	**6**	**9**	**0**	**0**	**0**	**0**	**0**	**0**	**0**
1983-84	**New York Rangers**	**NHL**	**63**	**5**	**15**	**20**	**4**	**10**	**14**	**8**	**0**	**0**	**1**	**70**	**7.1**	**36**	**1**	**43**	**13**	**5**	**5**	**0**	**1**	**1**	**0**	**0**	**0**	**0**
1984-85	Farjestads BK Karlstad	Sweden	32	8	12	20	....	....	....	10	....	....	....	....	....	....	....	....	....	....	3	2	0	2	2	....	....	....
1985-86	Farjestads BK Karlstad	Sweden	25	6	7	13	....	....	....	12	....	....	....	....	....	....	....	....	....	....	8	*5	6	*11	2	....	....	....
	NHL Totals		**456**	**72**	**103**	**175**	**61**	**72**	**133**	**78**	**7**	**6**	**14**	**633**	**11.4**	**278**	**28**	**362**	**100**		**50**	**4**	**11**	**15**	**4**	**0**	**0**	**1**

Won Golden Puck Award as Swedish Player of the Year (1977)

Signed as a free agent by **Minnesota**, June 15, 1977. Traded to **Hartford** by **Minnesota** with Mark Johnson for Jordy Douglas and Hartford's 5th round choice (Jiri Poner) in 1984 Entry Draft, October 1, 1982. Traded to **NY Rangers** by **Hartford** for Ed Hospodar, October 1, 1982.

• ANDERSSON, Mikael

LW – L. 5'11", 181 lbs. b: Malmo, Sweden, 5/10/1966. Buffalo's 1st, 18th overall, in 1984.

Season	Club	League	GP	G	A	Pts	AG	AA	APts	PIM	PP	SH	GW	S	%	TGF	PGF	TGA	PGA	+/–	GP	G	A	Pts	PIM	PP	SH	GW
1980-81	Kungalv-Ytterby HK	Sweden-3	16	9	2	11	....	....	....	....	....	....	....	....	....	....	....	....	....	....	....	....	....	....	....	....	....	....
1981-82	Vastra Frolunda	Sweden-Jr.	STATISTICS NOT AVAILABLE																									
1982-83	Vastra Frolunda	Sweden-Jr.	STATISTICS NOT AVAILABLE																									
	Vastra Frolunda	Sweden	1	1	0	1	....	....	....	0	....	....	....	....	....	....	....	....	....	....	....	....	....	....	....	....	....	....
1983-84	Vastra Frolunda	Sweden	18	0	3	3	....	....	....	6	....	....	....	....	....	....	....	....	....	....	....	....	....	....	....	....	....	....
	Sweden	WJC-A	7	1	2	3	....	....	....	8	....	....	....	....	....	....	....	....	....	....	....	....	....	....	....	....	....	....
1984-85	Vastra Frolunda	Sweden	30	16	11	27	....	....	....	18	....	....	....	....	....	....	....	....	....	....	6	3	2	5	2	....	....	....
	Sweden	WJC-A	6	2	3	5	....	....	....	0	....	....	....	....	....	....	....	....	....	....	....	....	....	....	....	....	....	....
1985-86	**Buffalo Sabres**	**NHL**	**32**	**1**	**9**	**10**	**1**	**6**	**7**	**4**	**0**	**0**	**0**	**13**	**7.7**	**20**	**4**	**16**	**0**	**0**	....	....	....	....	....	....	....	....
	Sweden	WJC-A	7	4	3	7	....	....	....	10	....	....	....	....	....	....	....	....	....	....	....	....	....	....	....	....	....	....
	Rochester Americans	AHL	20	10	4	14	....	....	....	6	....	....	....	....	....	....	....	....	....	....	....	....	....	....	....	....	....	....
1986-87	**Buffalo Sabres**	**NHL**	**16**	**0**	**3**	**3**	**0**	**2**	**2**	**0**	**0**	**0**	**0**	**6**	**0.0**	**8**	**1**	**15**	**6**	**–2**	....	....	....	....	....	....	....	....
	Rochester Americans	AHL	42	6	20	26	....	....	....	14	....	....	....	....	....	....	....	....	....	....	9	1	2	3	2	....	....	....
1987-88	**Buffalo Sabres**	**NHL**	**37**	**3**	**20**	**23**	**3**	**14**	**17**	**10**	**0**	**1**	**1**	**34**	**8.8**	**33**	**3**	**35**	**12**	**7**	**1**	**1**	**0**	**1**	**0**	**0**	**0**	**0**
	Rochester Americans	AHL	35	12	24	36	....	....	....	16	....	....	....	....	....	....	....	....	....	....	....	....	....	....	....	....	....	....
1988-89	**Buffalo Sabres**	**NHL**	**14**	**0**	**1**	**1**	**0**	**1**	**1**	**4**	**0**	**0**	**0**	**12**	**0.0**	**6**	**0**	**9**	**2**	**–1**	....	....	....	....	....	....	....	....
	Rochester Americans	AHL	56	18	33	51	....	....	....	12	....	....	....	....	....	....	....	....	....	....	....	....	....	....	....	....	....	....
1989-90	**Hartford Whalers**	**NHL**	**50**	**13**	**24**	**37**	**11**	**17**	**28**	**6**	**1**	**2**	**2**	**86**	**15.1**	**45**	**11**	**48**	**14**	**0**	**5**	**0**	**3**	**3**	**2**	**0**	**0**	**0**
1990-91	**Hartford Whalers**	**NHL**	**41**	**4**	**7**	**11**	**4**	**5**	**9**	**8**	**0**	**0**	**0**	**57**	**7.0**	**19**	**2**	**28**	**11**	**0**	....	....	....	....	....	....	....	....
	Springfield Indians	AHL	26	7	22	29	....	....	....	10	....	....	....	....	....	....	....	....	....	....	18	*10	8	18	12	....	....	....
1991-92	Sweden	Can-Cup	6	0	1	1	....	....	....	2	....	....	....	....	....	....	....	....	....	....	....	....	....	....	....	....	....	....
	Hartford Whalers	**NHL**	**74**	**18**	**29**	**47**	**16**	**22**	**38**	**14**	**1**	**3**	**1**	**149**	**12.1**	**65**	**8**	**69**	**30**	**18**	**7**	**0**	**2**	**2**	**6**	**0**	**0**	**0**
	Sweden	WC-A	5	1	1	2	....	....	....	0	....	....	....	....	....	....	....	....	....	....	....	....	....	....	....	....	....	....
1992-93	**Tampa Bay Lightning**	**NHL**	**77**	**16**	**11**	**27**	**13**	**8**	**21**	**14**	**3**	**2**	**4**	**169**	**9.5**	**43**	**6**	**76**	**25**	**–14**	....	....	....	....	....	....	....	....
	Sweden	WC-A	8	2	2	4	....	....	....	2	....	....	....	....	....	....	....	....	....	....	....	....	....	....	....	....	....	....
1993-94	**Tampa Bay Lightning**	**NHL**	**76**	**13**	**12**	**25**	**12**	**9**	**21**	**23**	**1**	**1**	**2**	**136**	**9.6**	**43**	**2**	**45**	**12**	**8**	....	....	....	....	....	....	....	....
	Sweden	WC-A	8	2	0	2	....	....	....	0	....	....	....	....	....	....	....	....	....	....	....	....	....	....	....	....	....	....
1994-95	Vastra Frolunda	Sweden	7	1	0	1	....	....	....	31	....	....	....	....	....	....	....	....	....	....	....	....	....	....	....	....	....	....
	Tampa Bay Lightning	**NHL**	**36**	**4**	**7**	**11**	**7**	**10**	**17**	**4**	**0**	**0**	**0**	**36**	**11.1**	**18**	**1**	**27**	**7**	**–3**	....	....	....	....	....	....	....	....
1995-96	**Tampa Bay Lightning**	**NHL**	**64**	**8**	**11**	**19**	**8**	**9**	**17**	**2**	**0**	**0**	**1**	**104**	**7.7**	**27**	**0**	**51**	**24**	**0**	**6**	**1**	**1**	**2**	**0**	**0**	**0**	**0**
1996-97	Sweden	W-Cup	4	0	1	1	....	....	....	2	....	....	....	....	....	....	....	....	....	....	....	....	....	....	....	....	....	....
	Tampa Bay Lightning	**NHL**	**70**	**5**	**14**	**19**	**5**	**12**	**17**	**8**	**0**	**3**	**1**	**102**	**4.9**	**28**	**0**	**51**	**24**	**1**	....	....	....	....	....	....	....	....
1997-98	**Tampa Bay Lightning**	**NHL**	**72**	**6**	**11**	**17**	**7**	**11**	**18**	**29**	**0**	**1**	**1**	**105**	**5.7**	**22**	**0**	**49**	**23**	**–4**	....	....	....	....	....	....	....	....
	Sweden	Olympics	4	1	1	2	....	....	....	0	....	....	....	....	....	....	....	....	....	....	....	....	....	....	....	....	....	....
1998-99	**Tampa Bay Lightning**	**NHL**	**40**	**2**	**3**	**5**	**2**	**3**	**5**	**4**	**0**	**0**	**0**	**40**	**5.0**	**12**	**0**	**33**	**13**	**–8**	....	....	....	....	....	....	....	....
	Philadelphia Flyers	**NHL**	**7**	**0**	**1**	**1**	**0**	**1**	**1**	**0**	**0**	**0**	**0**	**11**	**0.0**	**2**	**0**	**2**	**1**	**1**	**6**	**0**	**1**	**1**	**2**	**0**	**0**	**0**
99-2000	**Philadelphia Flyers**	**NHL**	**36**	**2**	**3**	**5**	**2**	**3**	**5**	**0**	**0**	**1**	**0**	**38**	**5.3**	**8**	**0**	**16**	**6**	**–2**	....	....	....	....	....	....	....	....
	New York Islanders	**NHL**	**19**	**0**	**3**	**3**	**0**	**3**	**3**	**4**	**0**	**0**	**0**	**19**	**0.0**	**3**	**0**	**8**	**4**	**–1**	....	....	....	....	....	....	....	....
	NHL Totals		**761**	**95**	**169**	**264**	**91**	**136**	**227**	**134**	**6**	**14**	**13**	**1117**	**8.5**	**402**	**38**	**578**	**214**		**25**	**2**	**7**	**9**	**10**	**0**	**0**	**0**

• Brother of Niklas

Claimed by **Hartford** from **Buffalo** in NHL Waiver Draft, October 2, 1989. Signed as a free agent by **Tampa Bay**, June 29, 1992. Traded to **Philadelphia** by **Tampa Bay** with Sandy McCarthy for Colin Forbes and Philadelphia's 4th round choice (Michal Lanisak) in 1999 Entry Draft, March 20, 1999. Traded to **NY Islanders** by **Philadelphia** with Carolina's 5th round choice (previously acquired, NY Islanders selected Kristofer Ottoson) in 2000 Entry Draft for Gino Odjick, February 15, 2000.

• ANDERSSON, Niklas

Niklas P. LW – L. 5'9", 175 lbs. b: Kungalv, Sweden, 5/20/1971. Quebec's 5th, 68th overall, in 1989.

Season	Club	League	GP	G	A	Pts	AG	AA	APts	PIM	PP	SH	GW	S	%	TGF	PGF	TGA	PGA	+/–	GP	G	A	Pts	PIM	PP	SH	GW
1987-88	Vastra Frolunda	Sweden-2	15	5	5	10	....	....	....	6	....	....	....	....	....	....	....	....	....	....	8	6	4	10	4	....	....	....
	Sweden	EJC-A	6	4	9	13	....	....	....	2	....	....	....	....	....	....	....	....	....	....	....	....	....	....	....	....	....	....
1988-89	Vastra Frolunda	Sweden-2	30	12	24	36	....	....	....	24	....	....	....	....	....	....	....	....	....	....	10	4	6	10	4	....	....	....
	Sweden	WJC-A	7	2	0	2	....	....	....	0	....	....	....	....	....	....	....	....	....	....	....	....	....	....	....	....	....	....
1989-90	Vastra Frolunda	Sweden	38	10	21	31	....	....	....	14	....	....	....	....	....	....	....	....	....	....	....	....	....	....	....	....	....	....
	Sweden	WJC-A	7	3	3	6	....	....	....	6	....	....	....	....	....	....	....	....	....	....	....	....	....	....	....	....	....	....

Season	Club	League	REGULAR SEASON GP	G	A	Pts	AG	AA	APts	PIM	PP	SH	GW	S	%	TGF	PGF	TGA	PGA	+/-	PLAYOFFS GP	G	A	Pts	PIM	PP	SH	GW
1990-91	Vastra Frolunda	Sweden	22	6	10	16				16																		
	Sweden	WJC-A	7	5	3	8				8																		
1991-92	Sweden	Can-Cup	6	0	1	1				0																		
	Halifax Citadels	AHL	57	8	26	34				41																		
1992-93	**Quebec Nordiques**	**NHL**	**3**	**0**	**1**	**1**	**0**	**1**	**1**	**2**	**0**	**0**	**0**	**4**	**0.0**	**3**	**0**	**3**	**0**	**0**								
	Halifax Citadels	AHL	76	32	50	82				42																		
1993-94	Cornwall Aces	AHL	42	18	34	52				8																		
1994-95	Denver Grizzlies	IHL	66	22	39	61				28											15	8	13	21	10			
1995-96	**New York Islanders**	**NHL**	**47**	**14**	**12**	**26**	**14**	**10**	**24**	**12**	**3**	**2**	**1**	**89**	**15.7**	**35**	**7**	**40**	**9**	**–3**								
	Utah Grizzlies	IHL	30	13	22	35				25																		
	Sweden	WC-A	6	1	1	2				8																		
1996-97	Sweden	W-Cup	1	0	0	0				0																		
	New York Islanders	**NHL**	**74**	**12**	**31**	**43**	**13**	**28**	**41**	**57**	**1**	**1**	**1**	**122**	**9.8**	**61**	**15**	**52**	**10**	**4**								
	Sweden	WC-A	11	0	2	2				8																		
1997-98	**San Jose Sharks**	**NHL**	**5**	**0**	**0**	**0**	**0**	**0**	**0**	**2**	**0**	**0**	**0**	**6**	**0.0**	**0**	**0**	**1**	**0**	**–1**								
	Kentucky Thoroughblades	AHL	37	10	28	38				54																		
	Utah Grizzlies	IHL	21	6	20	26				24											4	3	1	4	4			
1998-99	Chicago Wolves	IHL	65	17	47	64				49											10	2	2	4	10			
99-2000	**New York Islanders**	**NHL**	**17**	**3**	**7**	**10**	**3**	**6**	**9**	**8**	**1**	**0**	**0**	**24**	**12.5**	**13**	**5**	**15**	**4**	**–3**								
	Chicago Wolves	IHL	52	20	21	41				59											9	6	1	7	4			
	Nashville Predators	**NHL**	**7**	**0**	**1**	**1**	**0**	**1**	**1**	**0**	**0**	**0**	**0**	**7**	**0.0**	**2**	**1**	**1**	**0**	**0**								
	NHL Totals		**153**	**29**	**52**	**81**	**30**	**46**	**76**	**81**	**5**	**3**	**2**	**252**	**11.5**	**114**	**28**	**112**	**23**									

• Brother of Mikael • IHL Second All-Star Team (2000)

Signed as a free agent by **NY Islanders**, July 15, 1994. Signed as a free agent by **San Jose**, September 17, 1997. Signed as a free agent by **Toronto**, September 4, 1998. Traded to **NY Islanders** by **Toronto** for Craig Charron, August 17, 1999. Claimed on waivers by **Nashville** from **NY Islanders**, January 20, 2000.

• ANDERSSON, Peter

D – R. 6'2", 200 lbs. b: Sodertalje, Sweden, 3/2/1962. Washington's 8th, 173rd overall, in 1980.

Season	Club	League	GP	G	A	Pts	AG	AA	APts	PIM	PP	SH	GW	S	%	TGF	PGF	TGA	PGA	+/-	GP	G	A	Pts	PIM	PP	SH	GW
1980-81	Timra IF	Sweden-Jr.	STATISTICS NOT AVAILABLE																									
	Sweden	WJC-A	5	1	1	2				22																		
	IF Bjorkloven Umea	Sweden	31	1	2	3				16																		
1981-82	IF Bjorkloven Umea	Sweden	33	7	7	14				36											7	1	1	2	8			
	Sweden	WJC-A	7	3	6	9				12																		
	Sweden	WEC-A	10	2	1	3				2																		
1982-83	Sweden	Nat-Team	25	3	1	4				18																		
	IF Bjorkloven Umea	Sweden	34	8	16	24				30											3	0	0	0	4			
	Sweden	WEC-A	10	1	1	2				8																		
1983-84	**Washington Capitals**	**NHL**	**42**	**3**	**7**	**10**	**2**	**5**	**7**	**20**	**2**	**0**	**0**	**49**	**6.1**	**43**	**15**	**17**	**1**	**12**	**3**	**0**	**1**	**1**	**2**	**0**	**0**	**0**
1984-85	Sweden	Can-Cup	8	1	1	2				4																		
	Washington Capitals	**NHL**	**57**	**0**	**10**	**10**	**0**	**7**	**7**	**21**	**0**	**0**	**0**	**58**	**0.0**	**51**	**14**	**36**	**4**	**5**	**2**	**0**	**0**	**0**	**0**	**0**	**0**	**0**
	Binghamton Whalers	AHL	13	2	3	5				6																		
1985-86	**Washington Capitals**	**NHL**	**61**	**6**	**16**	**22**	**5**	**11**	**16**	**36**	**3**	**0**	**3**	**83**	**7.2**	**66**	**31**	**48**	**5**	**–8**								
	Quebec Nordiques	**NHL**	**12**	**1**	**8**	**9**	**1**	**5**	**6**	**4**	**1**	**0**	**0**	**16**	**6.3**	**26**	**8**	**10**	**0**	**8**	**2**	**0**	**1**	**1**	**0**	**0**	**0**	**0**
1986-87	IF Bjorkloven Umea	Sweden	36	6	10	16				30											6	2	1	3	4			
	Sweden	WEC-A	10	0	5	5				8																		
1987-88	Sweden	Can-Cup	5	1	1	2				2																		
	IF Bjorkloven Umea	Sweden	40	6	12	18				40											8	1	5	6	2			
	Sweden	Olympics	8	2	2	4				4																		
1988-89	IF Bjorkloven Umea	Sweden	16	0	12	12				16											7	4	3	7	2			
	Sweden	WEC-A	8	0	1	1				4																		
1989-90	EV Zug	Switz.	26	5	9	14																						
	EHC Kloten	Switz.	8	3	0	3				0											5	1	2	3	4			
	Sweden	WEC-A	10	0	2	2				6																		
1990-91	IF Bjorkloven Umea	Sweden-2	36	11	18	29				18											2	1	0	1	0			
	Sweden	WEC-A	10	1	0	1				4																		
1991-92	Sweden	Can-Cup	6	0	0	0				2																		
	IF Bjorkloven Umea	Sweden	35	9	20	29				30											3	0	0	0	4			
	Sweden	Olympics	8	1	2	3				4																		
1992-93	IF Bjorkloven Umea	Sweden-2	35	10	23	33				32											9	1	1	2	12			
1993-94	IF Bjorkloven Umea	Sweden-2	22	1	5	6				14																		
	IF Bjorkloven Umea	Sweden-Q	16	0	4	4				18											2	0	0	0	0			
1994-95	IF Bjorkloven Umea	Sweden-2	28	6	7	13				18											4	1	3	4	0			
	NHL Totals		**172**	**10**	**41**	**51**	**8**	**28**	**36**	**81**	**6**	**0**	**3**	**206**	**4.9**	**186**	**68**	**111**	**10**		**7**	**0**	**2**	**2**	**2**	**0**	**0**	**0**

EJC-A All-Star Team (1980) • Swedish World All-Star Team (1982, 1983, 1992)

Traded to **Quebec** by **Washington** for Quebec's 3rd round choice (Shawn Simpson) in 1986 Entry Draft, March 10, 1986. • Totals for Bjorkloven IF in 1988-89 and 1993-94 are Relegation Round statistics.

• ANDERSSON, Peter

D – L. 6', 196 lbs. b: Orebro, Sweden, 8/29/1965. NY Rangers' 5th, 75th overall, in 1983.

Season	Club	League	GP	G	A	Pts	AG	AA	APts	PIM	PP	SH	GW	S	%	TGF	PGF	TGA	PGA	+/-	GP	G	A	Pts	PIM	PP	SH	GW
1981-82	Orebro IK	Sweden-2	31	8	5	13				30											2	0	0	0	0			
	Sweden	EJC-A	5	0	0	0				2																		
1982-83	Orebro IK	Sweden-2	25	10	10	20				16											2	1	2	3	2			
	Sweden	WJC-A	7	3	0	3																						
1983-84	Farjestads BK Stockholm	Sweden	36	4	7	11				22																		
	Sweden	WJC-A	7	0	1	1				4																		
1984-85	Farjestads BK Stockholm	Sweden	35	5	12	17				24																		
	Sweden	WJC-A	7	4	10	14				20																		
1985-86	Farjestads BK Stockholm	Sweden	34	6	10	16				18																		
1986-87	Farjestads BK Stockholm	Sweden	32	9	8	17				32																		
1987-88	Farjestads BK Stockholm	Sweden	38	14	20	34				44											8	2	2	4	4			
1988-89	Farjestads BK Stockholm	Sweden	33	6	17	23				44																		
1989-90	Malmo IF	Sweden	33	15	25	40				32																		
1990-91	Malmo IF	Sweden	34	9	17	26				26																		
1991-92	Malmo IF	Sweden	40	12	20	32				80																		
	Sweden	Olympics	8	0	1	1				4																		
1992-93	**New York Rangers**	**NHL**	**31**	**4**	**11**	**15**	**3**	**8**	**11**	**18**	**3**	**0**	**1**	**68**	**5.9**	**35**	**15**	**18**	**2**	**4**								
	Binghamton Rangers	AHL	27	11	22	33				16																		
	Sweden	WC-A	7	1	6	7				8																		
1993-94	**New York Rangers**	**NHL**	**8**	**1**	**1**	**2**	**1**	**1**	**2**	**2**	**0**	**1**	**1**	**10**	**10.0**	**2**	**1**	**4**	**0**	**–3**								
	Florida Panthers	**NHL**	**8**	**1**	**1**	**2**	**1**	**1**	**2**	**0**	**0**	**0**	**0**	**11**	**9.1**	**7**	**2**	**10**	**0**	**–5**								
	Sweden	WC-A	8	0	1	1				6																		
1994-95	Malmo IF	Sweden	27	1	9	10				18											9	5	0	5	16			
1995-96	Malmo IF	Sweden	27	7	15	22				14																		
	Dusseldorfer EG	Germany	5	1	4	5				6											13	4	6	10	8			
1996-97	HC Bolzano	Italy	6	0	5	5				8																		
	Dusseldorfer EG	Germany	45	11	20	31				54											4	1	1	2	0			
1997-98	HC Lugano	Switz.	36	11	16	27				26											7	1	5	6	0			
1998-99	HC Lugano	Switz.	43	11	29	40				38											16	4	*15	19	20			

Season	Club	League	GP	G	A	Pts	AG	AA	APts	PIM	PP	SH	GW	S	%	TGF	PGF	TGA	PGA	+/–	GP	G	A	Pts	PIM	PP	SH	GW
			REGULAR SEASON																		PLAYOFFS							
99-2000	HC Lugano	Switz.	42	7	33	40	....	....	....	46	....	....	....	....	....	....	....	....	....	....	12	3	*15	18	12	....	....	....
	HC Lugano	EuroHL	4	0	2	2	....	....	....	6	....	....	....	....	....	....	....	....	....	....	....	....	....	....	....	....	....	....
	Sweden	WC-A	7	1	3	4	....	....	....	12	....	....	....	....	....	....	....	....	....	....	....	....	....	....	....	....	....	....
	NHL Totals		**47**	**6**	**13**	**19**	**5**	**10**	**15**	**20**	**3**	**1**	**2**	**89**	**6.7**	**44**	**18**	**32**	**2**		....	....	....	....	....	....	....	....

Swedish Junior Player-of-the-Year (1983)

Traded to **Florida** by **NY Rangers** for Florida's 9th round choice (Vitali Yeremeyev) in 1994 Entry Draft, March 21, 1994.

• ANDRASCIK, Steve

Steven George RW – R. 5'11", 200 lbs. b: Sherridon, Man., 11/6/1948. Detroit's 1st, 11th overall, in 1968.

Season	Club	League	GP	G	A	Pts	AG	AA	APts	PIM	PP	SH	GW	S	%	TGF	PGF	TGA	PGA	+/–	GP	G	A	Pts	PIM	PP	SH	GW
1967-68	Flin Flon Bombers	WCJHL	60	30	26	56	....	....	....	88	....	....	....	....	....	....	....	....	....	....	15	4	3	7	11	....	....	....
1968-69	Flin Flon Bombers	WCJHL	50	32	36	68	....	....	....	142	....	....	....	....	....	....	....	....	....	....	18	7	8	15	....	....	....	....
1969-70	Fort Worth Wings	CHL	69	8	7	15	....	....	....	80	....	....	....	....	....	....	....	....	....	....	7	0	1	1	5	....	....	....
1970-71	Fort Worth Wings	CHL	8	2	1	3	....	....	....	23	....	....	....	....	....	....	....	....	....	....	....	....	....	....	....	....	....	....
	Omaha Knights	CHL	65	23	14	37	....	....	....	81	....	....	....	....	....	....	....	....	....	....	11	2	0	2	24	....	....	....
1971-72	Providence Reds	AHL	74	14	10	24	....	....	....	104	....	....	....	....	....	....	....	....	....	....	5	2	0	2	8	....	....	....
	New York Rangers	**NHL**	....	....	....	....	....	....	....	....	....	....	....	....	....	....	....	....	....	....	**1**	**0**	**0**	**0**	**0**	**0**	**0**	**0**
1972-73	Providence Reds	AHL	41	8	9	17	....	....	....	44	....	....	....	....	....	....	....	....	....	....	4	0	3	3	9	....	....	....
1973-74	Hershey Bears	AHL	70	23	43	66	....	....	....	36	....	....	....	....	....	....	....	....	....	....	14	3	7	10	44	....	....	....
1974-75	Indianapolis Racers	WHA	20	2	4	6	....	....	....	16	....	....	....	....	....	....	....	....	....	....	....	....	....	....	....	....	....	....
	Greensboro Generals	SHL	3	1	0	1	....	....	....	0	....	....	....	....	....	....	....	....	....	....	....	....	....	....	....	....	....	....
	Michigan–Baltimore Blades	WHA	57	4	7	11	....	....	....	42	....	....	....	....	....	....	....	....	....	....	....	....	....	....	....	....	....	....
1975-76	Cincinnati Stingers	WHA	20	3	2	5	....	....	....	21	....	....	....	....	....	....	....	....	....	....	....	....	....	....	....	....	....	....
	Hampton Gulls	SHL	32	16	15	31	....	....	....	26	....	....	....	....	....	....	....	....	....	....	9	*6	5	11	24	....	....	....
1976-77	Hershey Bears	AHL	79	16	23	39	....	....	....	59	....	....	....	....	....	....	....	....	....	....	6	1	1	2	11	....	....	....
1977-78	Hershey Bears	AHL	79	4	9	13	....	....	....	21	....	....	....	....	....	....	....	....	....	....	....	....	....	....	....	....	....	....
	NHL Totals		....	....	....	....	....	....	....	....	....	....	....	....	....	....	....	....	....		**1**	**0**	**0**	**0**	**0**	**0**	**0**	**0**
	Other Major League Totals		97	9	13	22	....	....	....	79	....	....	....	....	....	....	....	....	....	....	....	....	....	....	....	....	....	....

Traded to **NY Rangers** by **Detroit** for Don Luce, November 2, 1970. Selected by **Alberta** (WHA) in 1972 WHA General Player Draft, February 12, 1972. Traded to **Pittsburgh** by **NY Rangers** to complete transaction that sent Sheldon Kannegiesser to NY Rangers (March 2, 1973), May 16, 1973. WHA rights traded to **Cincinnati** (WHA) by **Edmonton** (WHA) for future considerations, July, 1974. Loaned to **Indianapolis** (WHA) by **Cincinnati** (WHA) for 1974-75 season, July, 1974. Traded to **Michigan** (WHA) by **Indianapolis** (WHA) with Steve Richardson for Jacques Lucas and Brian McDonald, November, 1974.

• ANDREA, Paul

Paul Lawrence RW – L. 5'10", 174 lbs. b: North Sydney, N.S., 7/31/1941.

Season	Club	League	GP	G	A	Pts	AG	AA	APts	PIM	PP	SH	GW	S	%	TGF	PGF	TGA	PGA	+/–	GP	G	A	Pts	PIM	PP	SH	GW
1958-59	Guelph Biltmores	OHA-Jr.	23	5	0	5	....	....	....	2	....	....	....	....	....	....	....	....	....	....	9	1	2	3	5	....	....	....
1959-60	Guelph Biltmores	OHA-Jr.	48	11	20	31	....	....	....	21	....	....	....	....	....	....	....	....	....	....	5	0	2	2	0	....	....	....
1960-61	Guelph Royals	OHA-Jr.	48	29	33	62	....	....	....	30	....	....	....	....	....	....	....	....	....	....	14	3	11	14	20	....	....	....
	Kitchener-Waterloo Beavers	EPHL	2	0	0	0	....	....	....	0	....	....	....	....	....	....	....	....	....	....	....	....	....	....	....	....	....	....
1961-62	Kitchener-Waterloo Beavers	EPHL	16	4	0	4	....	....	....	8	....	....	....	....	....	....	....	....	....	....	7	2	2	4	2	....	....	....
	Vancouver Canucks	WHL	24	4	1	5	....	....	....	0	....	....	....	....	....	....	....	....	....	....	....	....	....	....	....	....	....	....
1962-63	Sudbury Wolves	EPHL	28	9	10	19	....	....	....	8	....	....	....	....	....	....	....	....	....	....	8	2	1	3	4	....	....	....
1963-64	St. Paul Rangers	CPHL	71	27	30	57	....	....	....	12	....	....	....	....	....	....	....	....	....	....	11	2	2	4	2	....	....	....
1964-65	St. Paul Rangers	CPHL	65	25	39	64	....	....	....	8	....	....	....	....	....	....	....	....	....	....	11	3	4	7	0	....	....	....
1965-66	**New York Rangers**	**NHL**	**4**	**1**	**1**	**2**	**1**	**1**	**2**	**0**	....	....	....	....	....	....	....	....	....	....	....	....	....	....	....	....	....	....
	Minnesota Rangers	CPHL	64	37	43	80	....	....	....	12	....	....	....	....	....	....	....	....	....	....	7	1	3	4	2	....	....	....
1966-67	Omaha Knights	CPHL	69	*37	46	83	....	....	....	22	....	....	....	....	....	....	....	....	....	....	12	6	7	13	2	....	....	....
1967-68	**Pittsburgh Penguins**	**NHL**	**65**	**11**	**21**	**32**	**13**	**21**	**34**	**2**	**5**	**0**	**1**	**92**	**12.0**	**45**	**19**	**29**	**1**	**–2**	....	....	....	....	....	....	....	....
1968-69	**Pittsburgh Penguins**	**NHL**	**25**	**7**	**6**	**13**	**7**	**5**	**12**	**2**	**5**	**0**	**1**	**45**	**15.6**	**16**	**12**	**14**	**0**	**–10**	....	....	....	....	....	....	....	....
	Amarillo Wranglers	CHL	47	23	29	52	....	....	....	22	....	....	....	....	....	....	....	....	....	....	....	....	....	....	....	....	....	....
1969-70	Vancouver Canucks	WHL	72	44	47	91	....	....	....	13	....	....	....	....	....	....	....	....	....	....	11	5	7	12	6	....	....	....
1970-71	**California Golden Seals**	**NHL**	**9**	**1**	**0**	**1**	**1**	**0**	**1**	**2**	**1**	**0**	**0**	**14**	**7.1**	**1**	**1**	**6**	**0**	**–6**	....	....	....	....	....	....	....	....
	Buffalo Sabres	**NHL**	**47**	**11**	**21**	**32**	**11**	**18**	**29**	**4**	**2**	**0**	**3**	**99**	**11.1**	**55**	**31**	**40**	**0**	**–16**	....	....	....	....	....	....	....	....
1971-72	Cincinnati Swords	AHL	69	14	58	72	....	....	....	18	....	....	....	....	....	....	....	....	....	....	10	5	6	11	6	....	....	....
1972-73	Cleveland Crusaders	WHA	66	21	30	51	....	....	....	12	....	....	....	....	....	....	....	....	....	....	9	2	8	10	2	....	....	....
1973-74	Cleveland Crusaders	WHA	69	15	18	33	....	....	....	14	....	....	....	....	....	....	....	....	....	....	5	1	0	1	0	....	....	....
	Jacksonville Barons	AHL	8	1	3	4	....	....	....	2	....	....	....	....	....	....	....	....	....	....	....	....	....	....	....	....	....	....
1974-75	Tulsa Oilers	CHL	9	5	1	6	....	....	....	0	....	....	....	....	....	....	....	....	....	....	....	....	....	....	....	....	....	....
	Cape Cod Codders	NAHL	33	8	32	40	....	....	....	26	....	....	....	....	....	....	....	....	....	....	....	....	....	....	....	....	....	....
	NHL Totals		**150**	**31**	**49**	**80**	**33**	**45**	**78**	**10**	....	....	....	....	....	....	....	....			....	....	....	....	....	....	....	....
	Other Major League Totals		135	36	48	84	....	....	....	26	....	....	....	....	....	....	....	....	....	....	14	3	8	11	2	....	....	....

CPHL First All-Star Team (1966) • WHL Second All-Star Team (1970)

Traded to **Pittsburgh** by **NY Rangers** with George Konik, Dunc McCallum and Frank Francis for Larry Jeffrey, June 6, 1967. Traded to **Vancouver** (WHL) by **Pittsburgh** with John Arbour and the loan of Andy Bathgate for the 1969-70 season for Bryan Hextall Jr., May 20, 1969. Claimed by **Oakland** from **Vancouver** (WHL) in Intra-League Draft, June 9, 1970. Claimed on waivers by **Buffalo** from **California**, November 4, 1970. Selected by **Dayton-Houston** (WHA) in 1972 WHA General Player Draft, February 12, 1972. WHA rights traded to **Cleveland** (WHA) by **Houston** (WHA) for future considerations, June, 1972.

• ANDREYCHUK, Dave

David John LW – R. 6'4", 220 lbs. b: Hamilton, Ont., 9/29/1963. Buffalo's 3rd, 16th overall, in 1982.

Season	Club	League	GP	G	A	Pts	AG	AA	APts	PIM	PP	SH	GW	S	%	TGF	PGF	TGA	PGA	+/–	GP	G	A	Pts	PIM	PP	SH	GW
1979-80	Hamilton Hawks	OMHA	21	25	24	49	....	....	....	....	....	....	....	....	....	....	....	....	....	....	....	....	....	....	....	....	....	....
1980-81	Oshawa Generals	OMJHL	67	22	22	44	....	....	....	80	....	....	....	....	....	....	....	....	....	....	10	3	2	5	20	....	....	....
1981-82	Oshawa Generals	OHL	67	57	43	100	....	....	....	71	....	....	....	....	....	....	....	....	....	....	3	1	4	5	16	....	....	....
1982-83	Oshawa Generals	OHL	14	8	24	32	....	....	....	6	....	....	....	....	....	....	....	....	....	....	....	....	....	....	....	....	....	....
	Canada	WJC-A	7	6	5	11	....	....	....	14	....	....	....	....	....	....	....	....	....	....	....	....	....	....	....	....	....	....
	Buffalo Sabres	**NHL**	**43**	**14**	**23**	**37**	**11**	**16**	**27**	**16**	**3**	**0**	**1**	**66**	**21.2**	**55**	**24**	**25**	**0**	**6**	**4**	**1**	**0**	**1**	**4**	**0**	**0**	**0**
1983-84	**Buffalo Sabres**	**NHL**	**78**	**38**	**42**	**80**	**31**	**29**	**60**	**42**	**10**	**0**	**7**	**178**	**21.3**	**110**	**36**	**55**	**1**	**20**	**2**	**0**	**1**	**1**	**2**	**0**	**0**	**0**
1984-85	**Buffalo Sabres**	**NHL**	**64**	**31**	**30**	**61**	**25**	**20**	**45**	**54**	**14**	**0**	**2**	**153**	**20.3**	**89**	**43**	**50**	**0**	**–4**	**5**	**4**	**2**	**6**	**4**	**0**	**0**	**2**
1985-86	**Buffalo Sabres**	**NHL**	**80**	**36**	**51**	**87**	**29**	**34**	**63**	**61**	**12**	**0**	**3**	**225**	**16.0**	**126**	**45**	**80**	**2**	**3**	....	....	....	....	....	....	....	....
	Canada	WEC-A	10	3	2	5	....	....	....	18	....	....	....	....	....	....	....	....	....	....	....	....	....	....	....	....	....	....
1986-87	**Buffalo Sabres**	**NHL**	**77**	**25**	**48**	**73**	**22**	**35**	**57**	**46**	**13**	**0**	**2**	**255**	**9.8**	**111**	**41**	**69**	**1**	**2**	....	....	....	....	....	....	....	....
1987-88	**Buffalo Sabres**	**NHL**	**80**	**30**	**48**	**78**	**26**	**34**	**60**	**112**	**15**	**0**	**5**	**253**	**11.9**	**112**	**47**	**66**	**2**	**1**	**6**	**2**	**4**	**6**	**0**	**1**	**0**	**0**
1988-89	**Buffalo Sabres**	**NHL**	**56**	**28**	**24**	**52**	**24**	**17**	**41**	**40**	**7**	**0**	**3**	**145**	**19.3**	**76**	**28**	**48**	**0**	**0**	**5**	**0**	**3**	**3**	**0**	**0**	**0**	**0**
1989-90	**Buffalo Sabres**	**NHL**	**73**	**40**	**42**	**82**	**34**	**30**	**64**	**42**	**18**	**0**	**3**	**206**	**19.4**	**131**	**62**	**63**	**0**	**6**	**6**	**2**	**5**	**7**	**2**	**1**	**0**	**0**
1990-91	**Buffalo Sabres**	**NHL**	**80**	**36**	**33**	**69**	**33**	**25**	**58**	**32**	**13**	**0**	**4**	**234**	**15.4**	**122**	**50**	**61**	**0**	**11**	**6**	**2**	**2**	**4**	**8**	**1**	**0**	**0**
1991-92	**Buffalo Sabres**	**NHL**	**80**	**41**	**50**	**91**	**37**	**38**	**75**	**71**	**28**	**0**	**2**	**337**	**12.2**	**155**	**86**	**79**	**1**	**–9**	**7**	**1**	**3**	**4**	**12**	**0**	**0**	**0**
1992-93	**Buffalo Sabres**	**NHL**	**52**	**29**	**32**	**61**	**24**	**22**	**46**	**48**	**20**	**0**	**2**	**171**	**17.0**	**92**	**54**	**46**	**0**	**–8**	....	....	....	....	....	....	....	....
	Toronto Maple Leafs	**NHL**	**31**	**25**	**13**	**38**	**21**	**9**	**30**	**8**	**12**	**0**	**2**	**139**	**18.0**	**54**	**28**	**14**	**0**	**12**	**21**	**12**	**7**	**19**	**35**	**4**	**0**	**3**
1993-94	**Toronto Maple Leafs**	**NHL**	**83**	**53**	**46**	**99**	**49**	**36**	**85**	**98**	**21**	**5**	**8**	**333**	**15.9**	**148**	**69**	**77**	**20**	**22**	**18**	**5**	**5**	**10**	**16**	**3**	**1**	**0**
1994-95	**Toronto Maple Leafs**	**NHL**	**48**	**22**	**16**	**38**	**39**	**24**	**63**	**34**	**8**	**0**	**2**	**168**	**13.1**	**61**	**25**	**44**	**1**	**–7**	**7**	**3**	**2**	**5**	**25**	**2**	**0**	**0**
1995-96	**Toronto Maple Leafs**	**NHL**	**61**	**20**	**24**	**44**	**20**	**20**	**40**	**54**	**12**	**2**	**3**	**200**	**10.0**	**71**	**40**	**46**	**4**	**–11**	....	....	....	....	....	....	....	....
	New Jersey Devils	**NHL**	**15**	**8**	**5**	**13**	**8**	**4**	**12**	**10**	**2**	**0**	**0**	**41**	**19.5**	**13**	**2**	**9**	**0**	**2**	....	....	....	....	....	....	....	....
1996-97	**New Jersey Devils**	**NHL**	**82**	**27**	**34**	**61**	**29**	**30**	**59**	**48**	**4**	**1**	**2**	**233**	**11.6**	**83**	**16**	**30**	**1**	**38**	**1**	**0**	**0**	**0**	**0**	**0**	**0**	**0**
1997-98	**New Jersey Devils**	**NHL**	**75**	**14**	**34**	**48**	**16**	**33**	**49**	**26**	**4**	**0**	**2**	**180**	**7.8**	**78**	**27**	**46**	**14**	**19**	**6**	**1**	**0**	**1**	**4**	**1**	**0**	**0**

			REGULAR SEASON																		PLAYOFFS							
Season	Club	League	GP	G	A	Pts	AG	AA	APts	PIM	PP	SH	GW	S	%	TGF	PGF	TGA	PGA	+/–	GP	G	A	Pts	PIM	PP	SH	GW
1998-99	**New Jersey Devils**	**NHL**	**52**	**15**	**13**	**28**	**18**	**13**	**31**	**20**	**4**	**0**	**3**	**110**	**13.6**	**46**	**16**	**29**	**0**	**1**	**4**	**2**	**0**	**2**	**4**	**0**	**0**	**0**
99-2000	**Boston Bruins**	**NHL**	**63**	**19**	**14**	**33**	**21**	**13**	**34**	**28**	**7**	**0**	**2**	**192**	**9.9**	**53**	**23**	**60**	**19**	**–11**								
	Colorado Avalanche	**NHL**	**14**	**1**	**2**	**3**	**1**	**2**	**3**	**2**	**1**	**0**	**1**	**41**	**2.4**	**7**	**4**	**15**	**3**	**–9**	**17**	**3**	**2**	**5**	**18**	**2**	**0**	**0**
	NHL Totals		**1287**	**552**	**624**	**1176**	**518**	**484**	**1002**	**892**	**228**	**8**	**59**	**3860**	**14.3**	**1793**	**766**	**1012**	**69**		**115**	**38**	**36**	**74**	**134**	**15**	**1**	**5**

Played in NHL All-Star Game (1990, 1994)

Traded to **Toronto** by **Buffalo** with Daren Puppa and Buffalo's 1st round choice (Kenny Jonsson) in 1993 Entry Draft for Grant Fuhr and Toronto's 5th round choice (Kevin Popp) in 1995 Entry Draft, February 2, 1993. Traded to **New Jersey** by **Toronto** for New Jersey's 2nd round choice (Marek Posmyk) in 1996 Entry Draft and New Jersey's 3rd round choice (later traded back to New Jersey - New Jersey selected Andre Lakos) in 1999 Entry Draft, March 13, 1996. Signed as a free agent by Boston, July 29, 1999. Traded to **Colorado** by **Boston** with Ray Bourque for Brian Rolston, Martin Grenier, Sami Pahlsson and New Jersey's 1st round choice (previously acquired, Boston selected Martin Samuelsson) in 200 Entry Draft, March 6, 2000. Signed as a free agent by **Buffalo**, July 13, 2000.

• ANDRIEVSKI, Alexander

RW – R. 6'5", 211 lbs. b: Moscow, USSR, 8/10/1968. Chicago's 13th, 220th overall, in 1991.

Season	Club	League	GP	G	A	Pts	AG	AA	APts	PIM	PP	SH	GW	S	%	TGF	PGF	TGA	PGA	+/–	GP	G	A	Pts	PIM	PP	SH	GW
1988-89	Dynamo Minsk	USSR	7	1	1	2				2																		
1989-90	Dynamo Minsk	USSR	47	16	12	28				32																		
1990-91	Dynamo Moscow	USSR	44	9	8	17				28																		
1991-92	HC Fribourg	Switz.	1	0	0	0				0																		
	Dynamo Moscow	CIS	31	9	8	17				14																		
1992-93	**Chicago Blackhawks**	**NHL**	**1**	**0**	**0**	**0**	**0**	**0**	**0**	**0**	**0**	**0**	**0**	**0**	**0.0**	**0**	**0**	**0**	**0**	**0**								
	Indianapolis Ice	IHL	66	26	25	51				59											4	2	3	5	10			
1993-94	Indianapolis Ice	IHL	4	0	1	1				2																		
	Kalamazoo Wings	IHL	57	6	22	28				58											1	0	0	0	2			
1994-95	HPK Hameenlinna	Finland	17	8	9	17				18																		
	Tivali Minsk	CIS	4	1	1	2				4																		
	Belarus	WC-C	4	1	1	2				6																		
1995-96	HPK Hameenlinna	Finland	43	18	15	33				75											9	7	1	8	4			
	Belarus	WC-B	7	5	*7	*12				8																		
1996-97	HPK Hameenlinna	Finland	42	17	28	45				26											10	2	4	6	2			
	Belarus	WC-B	7	5	*7	*12				8																		
1997-98	HPK Hameenlinna	Finland	25	7	9	16				22																		
	HPK Hameenlinna	EuroHL	3	0	1	1				4											2	1	1	2	2			
	Belarus	Olympics	6	1	2	3				8																		
	Belarus	WC-A	6	1	3	4				12																		
1998-99	HC Bolzano	Alpenliga	35	23	14	37				16																		
	HC Bolzano	Italy	2	0	0	0				4																		
	HC Bolzano	EuroHL	6	0	1	1				4																		
	Krefeld Pinguine	Germany	13	5	4	9				8											4	0	1	1	6			
99-2000	EHC Neuwied	Germany-2	17	11	11	22																						
	Revier Lowen	Germany	43	16	28	44				44																		
	Belarus	WC-A	3	1	2	3				2																		
	NHL Totals		**1**	**0**	**0**	**0**	**0**	**0**	**0**	**0**	**0**	**0**	**0**	**0**	**0.0**	**0**	**0**	**0**	**0**									

WC-B All-Star Team (1996, 1997)

• ANDRUFF, Ron

Ronald Nicholas C – R. 6', 185 lbs. b: Port Alberni, B.C., 7/10/1953. Montreal's 4th, 32nd overall, in 1973.

Season	Club	League	GP	G	A	Pts	AG	AA	APts	PIM	PP	SH	GW	S	%	TGF	PGF	TGA	PGA	+/–	GP	G	A	Pts	PIM	PP	SH	GW
1971-72	Flin Flon Bombers	WCJHL	63	20	32	52				44											7	0	3	3	17			
1972-73	Flin Flon Bombers	WCJHL	66	43	48	91				114											8	2	4	6	15			
1973-74	Nova Scotia Voyageurs	AHL	72	11	27	38				93											6	4	0	4	0			
1974-75	**Montreal Canadiens**	**NHL**	**5**	**0**	**0**	**0**	**0**	**0**	**0**	**2**	**0**	**0**	**0**	**1**	**0.0**	**1**	**1**	**1**	**0**	**–1**								
	Nova Scotia Voyageurs	AHL	65	30	31	61				50											6	4	1	5	18			
1975-76	**Montreal Canadiens**	**NHL**	**1**	**0**	**0**	**0**	**0**	**0**	**0**	**0**	**0**	**0**	**0**	**0**	**0.0**	**0**	**0**	**0**	**0**	**0**								
	Nova Scotia Voyageurs	AHL	74	*42	46	88				58											9	5	8	13	9			
1976-77	**Colorado Rockies**	**NHL**	**66**	**4**	**18**	**22**	**4**	**14**	**18**	**21**	**0**	**0**	**0**	**106**	**3.8**	**34**	**5**	**52**	**5**	**–18**								
1977-78	**Colorado Rockies**	**NHL**	**78**	**15**	**18**	**33**	**14**	**14**	**28**	**31**	**0**	**0**	**1**	**133**	**11.3**	**43**	**6**	**55**	**2**	**–16**	**2**	**0**	**0**	**0**	**0**	**0**	**0**	**0**
1978-79	**Colorado Rockies**	**NHL**	**3**	**0**	**0**	**0**	**0**	**0**	**0**	**0**	**0**	**0**	**0**	**4**	**0.0**	**0**	**0**	**4**	**0**	**–4**								
	Philadelphia Firebirds	AHL	35	16	16	32				8																		
	New Haven Nighthawks	AHL	33	9	23	32				10											10	6	11	*17	0			
1979-80	Mannheimer ERC	Germany	47	44	40	84				117																		
1980-81	Mannheimer ERC	Germany	44	35	43	78				110											10	8	7	15	16			
1981-82	Dusseldorfer EG	Germany	4	1	3	4				6																		
	NHL Totals		**153**	**19**	**36**	**55**	**18**	**28**	**46**	**54**	**0**	**0**	**1**	**244**	**7.8**	**78**	**12**	**112**	**7**		**2**	**0**	**0**	**0**	**0**	**0**	**0**	**0**

AHL First All-Star Team (1976) • Won Les Cunningham Award (MVP - AHL) (1976)

Traded to **Colorado** by **Montreal** with Sean Shanahan for cash, September 13, 1976.

• ANDRUSAK, Greg

D – R. 6'1", 190 lbs. b: Cranbrook, B.C., 11/14/1969. Pittsburgh's 5th, 88th overall, in 1988.

Season	Club	League	GP	G	A	Pts	AG	AA	APts	PIM	PP	SH	GW	S	%	TGF	PGF	TGA	PGA	+/–	GP	G	A	Pts	PIM	PP	SH	GW
1985-86	Nelson North Stars	BCAHA	STATISTICS NOT AVAILABLE																									
1986-87	Kelowna Packers	BCJHL	45	10	24	34				95																		
1987-88	University of Minnesota-Duluth.	WCHA	37	4	5	9				42																		
1988-89	University of Minnesota-Duluth.	WCHA	35	4	8	12				74																		
	Canada	Nat-Team	2	0	0	0				0																		
1989-90	University of Minnesota-Duluth.	WCHA	35	5	29	34				74																		
1990-91	Canada	Nat-Team	53	4	11	15				34																		
1991-92	University of Minnesota-Duluth.	WCHA	36	7	27	34				125																		
1992-93	Cleveland Lumberjacks	IHL	55	3	22	25				78											2	0	0	0	2			
	Muskegon Fury	ColHL	2	0	3	3				7																		
1993-94	**Pittsburgh Penguins**	**NHL**	**3**	**0**	**0**	**0**	**0**	**0**	**0**	**2**	**0**	**0**	**0**	**4**	**0.0**	**1**	**0**	**2**	**0**	**–1**								
	Cleveland Lumberjacks	IHL	69	13	26	39				109																		
1994-95	**Pittsburgh Penguins**	**NHL**	**7**	**0**	**4**	**4**	**0**	**6**	**6**	**6**	**0**	**0**	**0**	**7**	**0.0**	**5**	**3**	**4**	**1**	**–1**								
	Cleveland Lumberjacks	IHL	8	0	8	8				14																		
	Detroit Vipers	IHL	37	5	26	31				50																		
	Canada	WC-A	7	0	0	0				12																		
1995-96	**Pittsburgh Penguins**	**NHL**	**2**	**0**	**0**	**0**	**0**	**0**	**0**	**0**	**0**	**0**	**0**	**1**	**0.0**	**1**	**0**	**2**	**0**	**–1**								
	Detroit Vipers	IHL	58	6	30	36				128																		
	Minnesota Moose	IHL	5	0	4	4				8																		
1996-97	Eisbaren Berlin	Germany	45	5	17	22				170											8	1	1	2	20			
1997-98	Eisbaren Berlin	Germany	34	3	7	10				65											9	0	1	1	8			
1998-99	Eisbaren Berlin	Germany	19	2	5	7				12																		
	Eisbaren Berlin	EuroHL	5	0	1	1				18																		
	HC Geneve-Servette	Switz-2	10	3	13	16																						
	Houston Aeros	IHL	3	0	1	1				2											6	1	4	5	16			
	Pittsburgh Penguins	**NHL**	**7**	**0**	**1**	**1**	**0**	**1**	**1**	**4**	**0**	**0**	**0**	**2**	**0.0**	**6**	**1**	**1**	**0**	**4**	**12**	**1**	**0**	**1**	**6**	**0**	**0**	**1**
99-2000	**Toronto Maple Leafs**	**NHL**	**9**	**0**	**1**	**1**	**0**	**1**	**1**	**4**	**0**	**0**	**0**	**5**	**0.0**	**9**	**1**	**7**	**0**	**1**	**3**	**0**	**0**	**0**	**2**	**0**	**0**	**0**
	Chicago Wolves	IHL	54	2	23	25				50											11	1	5	6	20			
	NHL Totals		**28**	**0**	**6**	**6**	**0**	**8**	**8**	**16**	**0**	**0**	**0**	**19**	**0.0**	**22**	**5**	**16**	**1**		**15**	**1**	**0**	**1**	**8**	**0**	**0**	**1**

WCHA First All-Star Team (1992)

Signed as a free agent by **Pittsburgh**, March 19, 1999. Signed as a free agent by **Toronto**, July 19, 1999.

• ANGOTTI, Lou

Louis Frederick C/RW – R. 5'9", 170 lbs. b: Toronto, Ont., 1/16/1938.

Season	Club	League	GP	G	A	Pts	AG	AA	APts	PIM	PP	SH	GW	S	%	TGF	PGF	TGA	PGA	+/–	GP	G	A	Pts	PIM	PP	SH	GW
1955-56	St. Michael's Majors	OHA-Jr.	48	6	6	12				29											8	4	0	4	20			
1956-57	St. Michael's Majors	OHA-Jr.	52	12	19	31				28											4	1	2	3	4			

			REGULAR SEASON																		PLAYOFFS							
Season	Club	League	GP	G	A	Pts	AG	AA	APts	PIM	PP	SH	GW	S	%	TGF	PGF	TGA	PGA	+/–	GP	G	A	Pts	PIM	PP	SH	GW
1957-58	St. Michael's Majors	OHA-Jr.	52	23	19	42	....	....	....	72	....	....	....	....	....	....	....	....	....	....	9	7	8	15	10	....	....	....
	Kitchener Dutchman	Al-Cup	1	0	0	0	....	....	....	2	....	....	....	....	....	....	....	....	....	....	....	....	....	....	....	....	....	....
1958-59	Michigan Tech JV Huskies	WCHA	5	10	9	19	....	....	....	....	....	....	....	....	....	....	....	....	....	....	....	....	....	....	....	....	....	....
1959-60	Michigan Tech Huskies	WCHA	30	18	21	39	....	....	....	30	....	....	....	....	....	....	....	....	....	....	....	....	....	....	....	....	....	....
1960-61	Michigan Tech Huskies	WCHA	28	25	17	42	....	....	....	52	....	....	....	....	....	....	....	....	....	....	....	....	....	....	....	....	....	....
1961-62	Michigan Tech Huskies	WCHA	31	28	23	51	....	....	....	50	....	....	....	....	....	....	....	....	....	....	....	....	....	....	....	....	....	....
1962-63	Kitchener-Waterloo Tigers	OHA-Sr.	16	19	7	26	....	....	....	26	....	....	....	....	....	....	....	....	....	....	....	....	....	....	....	....	....	....
	Rochester Americans	AHL	39	16	15	31	....	....	....	19	....	....	....	....	....	....	....	....	....	....	1	0	0	0	0	....	....	....
1963-64	Rochester Americans	AHL	60	15	30	45	....	....	....	28	....	....	....	....	....	....	....	....	....	....	2	1	1	2	0	....	....	....
1964-65	**New York Rangers**	**NHL**	**70**	**9**	**8**	**17**	**11**	**8**	**19**	**20**	....	....	....	....	....	....	....	....	....	....	....	....	....	....	....	....	....	....
1965-66	**New York Rangers**	**NHL**	**21**	**2**	**2**	**4**	**2**	**2**	**4**	**2**	....	....	....	....	....	....	....	....	....	....	....	....	....	....	....	....	....	....
	St. Louis Braves	CPHL	8	10	8	18	....	....	....	4	....	....	....	....	....	....	....	....	....	....	....	....	....	....	....	....	....	....
	Chicago Black Hawks	**NHL**	**30**	**4**	**10**	**14**	**4**	**9**	**13**	**12**	....	....	....	....	....	....	....	....	....	....	**6**	**0**	**0**	**0**	**2**	**0**	**0**	**0**
1966-67	**Chicago Black Hawks**	**NHL**	**63**	**6**	**12**	**18**	**7**	**12**	**19**	**21**	....	....	....	....	....	....	....	....	....	....	**6**	**2**	**1**	**3**	**2**	**0**	**0**	**0**
1967-68	**Philadelphia Flyers**	**NHL**	**70**	**12**	**37**	**49**	**14**	**37**	**51**	**35**	**2**	**0**	**1**	**146**	**8.2**	**57**	**12**	**47**	**6**	**4**	**7**	**0**	**0**	**0**	**2**	**0**	**0**	**0**
1968-69	**Pittsburgh Penguins**	**NHL**	**71**	**17**	**20**	**37**	**18**	**18**	**36**	**36**	**3**	**0**	**2**	**123**	**13.8**	**43**	**8**	**57**	**1**	**–21**	....	....	....	....	....	....	....	....
1969-70	**Chicago Black Hawks**	**NHL**	**70**	**12**	**26**	**38**	**13**	**24**	**37**	**25**	**5**	**0**	**2**	**97**	**12.4**	**53**	**16**	**37**	**2**	**2**	**8**	**0**	**0**	**0**	**0**	**0**	**0**	**0**
1970-71	**Chicago Black Hawks**	**NHL**	**65**	**9**	**16**	**25**	**9**	**13**	**22**	**19**	**1**	**1**	**2**	**83**	**10.8**	**32**	**2**	**35**	**22**	**17**	**16**	**3**	**3**	**6**	**9**	**0**	**0**	**1**
1971-72	**Chicago Black Hawks**	**NHL**	**65**	**5**	**10**	**15**	**5**	**9**	**14**	**23**	**0**	**0**	**0**	**58**	**8.6**	**20**	**2**	**31**	**13**	**0**	**6**	**0**	**0**	**0**	**0**	**0**	**0**	**0**
1972-73	**Chicago Black Hawks**	**NHL**	**77**	**15**	**22**	**37**	**14**	**17**	**31**	**26**	**4**	**1**	**4**	**91**	**16.5**	**41**	**8**	**59**	**23**	**–3**	**16**	**3**	**4**	**7**	**2**	**0**	**0**	**2**
1973-74	**St. Louis Blues**	**NHL**	**51**	**12**	**23**	**35**	**12**	**19**	**31**	**9**	**1**	**0**	**5**	**84**	**14.3**	**42**	**6**	**40**	**1**	**–3**	....	....	....	....	....	....	....	....
1974-75	Chicago Cougars	WHA	26	2	5	7	....	....	....	9	....	....	....	....	....	....	....	....	....	....	....	....	....	....	....	....	....	....
	NHL Totals		**653**	**103**	**186**	**289**	**109**	**168**	**277**	**228**	....	....	....	....	....	....	....	....	....	....	**65**	**8**	**8**	**16**	**17**	....	....	....
	Other Major League Totals		26	2	5	7	....	....	....	9	....	....	....	....	....	....	....	....	....	....	....	....	....	....	....	....	....	....

NCAA Championship All-Tournament Team (1960, 1962) • NCAA Championship Tournament MVP (1960, 1962) • WCHA Second All-Star Team (1961) • WCHA First All-Star Team (1962) • NCAA West First All-American Team (1962)

Traded to **NY Rangers** by **Toronto** (Rochester-AHL) with Ed Lawson for Duane Rupp and Ed Ehrenverth, June 25, 1964. Traded to **Chicago** by **NY Rangers** for cash, January 7, 1966. Claimed by **Philadelphia** from **Chicago** in Expansion Draft, June 6, 1967. Traded to **St. Louis** by **Philadelphia** with Ian Campbell for Darryl Edestrand and Gerry Melynk, June 11, 1968. Traded to **Pittsburgh** by **St. Louis** for Ab McDonald, June 11, 1968. Traded to **St. Louis** by **Pittsburgh** with Pittsburgh's 1st round choice (Gene Carr) in 1971 Amateur Draft for Ron Schock, Craig Cameron and St. Louis' 2nd round choice (Brian MacKenzie) in 1971 Amateur Draft, June 6, 1969. Claimed by **Chicago** from **St. Louis** in Intra-League Draft, June 11, 1969. Selected by **NY Raiders** (WHA) in 1972 WHA General Player Draft, February 12, 1972. Claimed by **St. Louis** from **Chicago** in Intra-League Draft, June 12, 1973. WHA rights traded to **Indianapolis** (WHA) by **San Diego** (WHA) for cash, July, 1974. WHA rights traded to **Chicago** (WHA) by **Indianapolis** (WHA) for future considerations, January, 1975.

• ANHOLT, Darrel

D – L. 6'2", 230 lbs. b: Hardisty, Alta., 11/23/1962. Chicago's 3rd, 54th overall, in 1981.

Season	Club	League	GP	G	A	Pts	AG	AA	APts	PIM	PP	SH	GW	S	%	TGF	PGF	TGA	PGA	+/–	GP	G	A	Pts	PIM	PP	SH	GW
1979-80	Red Deer Rustlers	AJHL	50	2	14	16	....	....	....	147	....	....	....	....	....	....	....	....	....	....	....	....	....	....	....	....	....	....
	Red Deer Rustlers	Cen-Cup	STATISTICS NOT AVAILABLE																									
1980-81	Calgary Wranglers	WHL	72	5	23	28	....	....	....	286	....	....	....	....	....	....	....	....	....	....	22	1	7	8	55	....	....	....
1981-82	Calgary Wranglers	WHL	64	10	29	39	....	....	....	294	....	....	....	....	....	....	....	....	....	....	9	1	4	5	16	....	....	....
1982-83	Springfield Indians	AHL	80	2	18	20	....	....	....	109	....	....	....	....	....	....	....	....	....	....	....	....	....	....	....	....	....	....
1983-84	**Chicago Black Hawks**	**NHL**	**1**	**0**	**0**	**0**	**0**	**0**	**0**	**0**	**0**	**0**	**0**	**0**	**0.0**	**2**	**0**	**0**	**0**	**2**	....	....	....	....	....	....	....	....
	Springfield Indians	AHL	80	13	21	34	....	....	....	142	....	....	....	....	....	....	....	....	....	....	4	0	1	1	2	....	....	....
1984-85	Milwaukee Admirals	IHL	82	5	22	27	....	....	....	125	....	....	....	....	....	....	....	....	....	....	....	....	....	....	....	....	....	....
	NHL Totals		**1**	**0**	**0**	**0**	**0**	**0**	**0**	**0**	**0**	**0**	**0**	**0**	**0.0**	**2**	**0**	**0**	**0**		....	....	....	....	....	....	....	....

• ANTONOVICH, Mike

Michael John C – L. 5'8", 165 lbs. b: Calumet, MN, 10/18/1951. Minnesota's 8th, 113th overall, in 1971.

Season	Club	League	GP	G	A	Pts	AG	AA	APts	PIM	PP	SH	GW	S	%	TGF	PGF	TGA	PGA	+/–	GP	G	A	Pts	PIM	PP	SH	GW
1969-70	University of Minnesota	WCHA	32	23	20	43	....	....	....	60	....	....	....	....	....	....	....	....	....	....	2	1	0	1	0	....	....	....
1970-71	University of Minnesota	WCHA	32	14	16	30	....	....	....	20	....	....	....	....	....	....	....	....	....	....	....	....	....	....	....	....	....	....
1971-72	University of Minnesota	WCHA	13	8	2	10	....	....	....	19	....	....	....	....	....	....	....	....	....	....	....	....	....	....	....	....	....	....
1972-73	Minnesota Fighting Saints	WHA	75	20	19	39	....	....	....	44	....	....	....	....	....	....	....	....	....	....	5	2	0	2	0	....	....	....
1973-74	Minnesota Fighting Saints	WHA	68	21	29	50	....	....	....	4	....	....	....	....	....	....	....	....	....	....	11	1	4	5	4	....	....	....
1974-75	Minnesota Fighting Saints	WHA	66	24	26	50	....	....	....	6	....	....	....	....	....	....	....	....	....	....	12	1	4	5	2	....	....	....
1975-76	Minnesota Fighting Saints	WHA	57	25	21	46	....	....	....	18	....	....	....	....	....	....	....	....	....	....	....	....	....	....	....	....	....	....
	Minnesota North Stars	**NHL**	**12**	**0**	**2**	**2**	**0**	**1**	**1**	**8**	**0**	**0**	**0**	**22**	**0.0**	**4**	**1**	**7**	**0**	**–4**	....	....	....	....	....	....	....	....
	United States	WEC-A	10	1	3	4	....	....	....	14	....	....	....	....	....	....	....	....	....	....	....	....	....	....	....	....	....	....
1976-77	Minnesota Fighting Saints	WHA	42	27	21	48	....	....	....	28	....	....	....	....	....	....	....	....	....	....	....	....	....	....	....	....	....	....
	Edmonton Oilers	WHA	7	1	1	2	....	....	....	0	....	....	....	....	....	....	....	....	....	....	....	....	....	....	....	....	....	....
	New England Whalers	WHA	26	12	9	21	....	....	....	10	....	....	....	....	....	....	....	....	....	....	5	2	2	4	4	....	....	....
	United States	WEC-A	DID NOT PLAY																									
1977-78	New England Whalers	WHA	75	32	35	67	....	....	....	32	....	....	....	....	....	....	....	....	....	....	14	*10	7	*17	4	....	....	....
1978-79	Springfield Indians	AHL	7	2	3	5	....	....	....	2	....	....	....	....	....	....	....	....	....	....	....	....	....	....	....	....	....	....
	New England Whalers	WHA	69	20	27	47	....	....	....	35	....	....	....	....	....	....	....	....	....	....	10	5	3	8	14	....	....	....
1979-80	**Hartford Whalers**	**NHL**	**5**	**0**	**1**	**1**	**0**	**1**	**1**	**2**	**0**	**0**	**0**	**4**	**0.0**	**1**	**0**	**1**	**0**	**0**	....	....	....	....	....	....	....	....
	Springfield Indians	AHL	24	14	6	20	....	....	....	35	....	....	....	....	....	....	....	....	....	....	....	....	....	....	....	....	....	....
1980-81	Tulsa Oilers	CHL	60	28	32	60	....	....	....	36	....	....	....	....	....	....	....	....	....	....	8	1	2	3	2	....	....	....
1981-82	**Minnesota North Stars**	**NHL**	**2**	**0**	**0**	**0**	**0**	**0**	**0**	**0**	**0**	**0**	**0**	**0**	**0.0**	**0**	**0**	**1**	**0**	**–1**	....	....	....	....	....	....	....	....
	Nashville South Stars	CHL	80	29	77	106	....	....	....	76	....	....	....	....	....	....	....	....	....	....	3	0	1	1	2	....	....	....
	United States	WEC-A	7	0	0	0	....	....	....	6	....	....	....	....	....	....	....	....	....	....	....	....	....	....	....	....	....	....
1982-83	**New Jersey Devils**	**NHL**	**30**	**7**	**7**	**14**	**6**	**5**	**11**	**11**	**2**	**0**	**0**	**47**	**14.9**	**19**	**5**	**21**	**0**	**–7**	....	....	....	....	....	....	....	....
	Wichita Wind	CHL	10	8	12	20	....	....	....	0	....	....	....	....	....	....	....	....	....	....	....	....	....	....	....	....	....	....
1983-84	**New Jersey Devils**	**NHL**	**38**	**3**	**5**	**8**	**2**	**3**	**5**	**16**	**0**	**0**	**0**	**47**	**6.4**	**20**	**6**	**29**	**0**	**–15**	....	....	....	....	....	....	....	....
	Maine Mariners	AHL	25	17	13	30	....	....	....	8	....	....	....	....	....	....	....	....	....	....	17	4	8	12	8	....	....	....
1984-1992			OUT OF HOCKEY – RETIRED																									
1992-93	Minnesota Iron Rangers	AmHA	2	0	2	2	....	....	....	2	....	....	....	....	....	....	....	....	....	....	....	....	....	....	....	....	....	....
1993-1994			OUT OF HOCKEY – RETIRED																									
1994-1996	Minnesota Moose	IHL	DID NOT PLAY – ASSISTANT COACH																									
1995-1996	Quad City Mallards	ColHL	2	0	1	1	....	....	....	4	....	....	....	....	....	....	....	....	....	....	....	....	....	....	....	....	....	....
1996-1997	Phoenix Roadrunners	IHL	DID NOT PLAY – ASSISTANT COACH																									
1997-2000	**St. Louis Blues**	**NHL**	DID NOT PLAY – SCOUTING																									
	NHL Totals		**87**	**10**	**15**	**25**	**8**	**10**	**18**	**37**	**2**	**0**	**0**	**120**	**8.3**	**44**	**12**	**59**	**0**		....	....	....	....	....	....	....	....
	Other Major League Totals		485	182	188	370	....	....	....	177	....	....	....	....	....	....	....	....	....	....	57	21	20	41	28	....	....	....

CHL Second All-Star Team (1982)

Selected by **Minnesota** (WHA) in 1972 WHA General Player Draft, February 12, 1972. Signed as a free agent by **Minnesota** (NHL) after **Minnesota** (WHA) franchise folded, March 10, 1976. Signed as a free agent by **Minnesota** (WHA), after being released by **Minnesota** (NHL), September, 1976. Traded to **Edmonton** (WHA) by **Minnesota** (WHA) with Jean-Louis Levasseur, Bill Butters, Dave Keon, Jack Carlson, Steve Carlson and John McKenzie for cash, January, 1977. Traded to **New England** (WHA) by **Edmonton** (WHA) with Bill Butters for Brett Callighen and Ron Busniuk, February, 1977. Signed as a free agent by **Hartford**, October 17,1979. Signed as a free agent by **Minnesota**, November 25, 1981. Signed as a free agent by **New Jersey**, October 1, 1982.

• ANTOSKI, Shawn

"Moose" LW – L. 6'4", 235 lbs. b: Brantford, Ont., 3/25/1970. Vancouver's 2nd, 18th overall, in 1990.

Season	Club	League	GP	G	A	Pts	AG	AA	APts	PIM	PP	SH	GW	S	%	TGF	PGF	TGA	PGA	+/–	GP	G	A	Pts	PIM	PP	SH	GW
1985-86	Don Mills Flyers	MTHL	27	10	15	25	....	....	....	50	....	....	....	....	....	....	....	....	....	....	....	....	....	....	....	....	....	....
1986-87	Don Mills Flyers	MTHL	33	12	13	25	....	....	....	75	....	....	....	....	....	....	....	....	....	....	....	....	....	....	....	....	....	....
1987-88	North Bay Centennials	OHL	52	3	4	7	....	....	....	163	....	....	....	....	....	....	....	....	....	....	....	....	....	....	....	....	....	....
1988-89	North Bay Centennials	OHL	57	6	21	27	....	....	....	201	....	....	....	....	....	....	....	....	....	....	9	5	3	8	24	....	....	....
1989-90	North Bay Centennials	OHL	59	25	31	56	....	....	....	201	....	....	....	....	....	....	....	....	....	....	5	1	2	3	17	....	....	....
1990-91	**Vancouver Canucks**	**NHL**	**2**	**0**	**0**	**0**	**0**	**0**	**0**	**0**	**0**	**0**	**0**	**2**	**0.0**	**0**	**0**	**2**	**0**	**–2**	....	....	....	....	....	....	....	....
	Milwaukee Admirals	IHL	62	17	7	24	....	....	....	330	....	....	....	....	....	....	....	....	....	....	5	1	2	3	10	....	....	....
1991-92	**Vancouver Canucks**	**NHL**	**4**	**0**	**0**	**0**	**0**	**0**	**0**	**29**	**0**	**0**	**0**	**6**	**0.0**	**0**	**0**	**1**	**0**	**–1**	....	....	....	....	....	....	....	....
	Milwaukee Admirals	IHL	52	17	16	33	....	....	....	346	....	....	....	....	....	....	....	....	....	....	5	2	0	2	20	....	....	....
1992-93	**Vancouver Canucks**	**NHL**	**2**	**0**	**0**	**0**	**0**	**0**	**0**	**0**	**0**	**0**	**0**	**0**	**0.0**	**0**	**0**	**0**	**0**	**0**	....	....	....	....	....	....	....	....
	Hamilton Canucks	AHL	41	3	4	7	....	....	....	172	....	....	....	....	....	....	....	....	....	....	....	....	....	....	....	....	....	....
1993-94	**Vancouver Canucks**	**NHL**	**55**	**1**	**2**	**3**	**1**	**2**	**3**	**190**	**0**	**0**	**1**	**25**	**4.0**	**9**	**1**	**19**	**0**	**–11**	**16**	**0**	**1**	**1**	**36**	**0**	**0**	**0**

			REGULAR SEASON																		PLAYOFFS							
Season	Club	League	GP	G	A	Pts	AG	AA	APts	PIM	PP	SH	GW	S	%	TGF	PGF	TGA	PGA	+/-	GP	G	A	Pts	PIM	PP	SH	GW
1994-95	Vancouver Canucks	NHL	7	0	0	0	0	0	0	46	0	0	0	4	0.0	0	0	4	0	–4	....	....	....	....	....	....	....	....
	Philadelphia Flyers	NHL	25	0	0	0	0	0	0	61	0	0	0	12	0.0	4	0	4	0	0	13	0	1	1	10	0	0	0
1995-96	Philadelphia Flyers	NHL	64	1	3	4	1	2	3	204	0	0	0	34	2.9	10	1	13	0	–4	7	1	1	2	28	0	0	1
1996-97	Pittsburgh Penguins	NHL	13	0	0	0	0	0	0	49	0	0	0	3	0.0	3	0	3	0	0	....	....	....	....	....	....	....	....
	Mighty Ducks of Anaheim	NHL	2	0	0	0	0	0	0	2	0	0	0	0	0.0	1	0	0	0	1	....	....	....	....	....	....	....	....
1997-98	Mighty Ducks of Anaheim	NHL	9	1	0	1	1	0	1	18	0	0	0	6	16.7	2	0	1	0	1	....	....	....	....	....	....	....	....
	NHL Totals		183	3	5	8	3	4	7	599	0	0	1	92	3.3	29	2	47	0		36	1	3	4	74	0	0	1

Traded to **Philadelphia** by **Vancouver** for Josef Beranek, February 15, 1995. Signed as a free agent by **Pittsburgh**, July 31, 1996. Traded to **Anaheim** by **Pittsburgh** with Dmitri Mironov for Alex Hicks and Fredrik Olausson, November 19, 1996. • Missed majority of 1996-97 season recovering from hernia surgery, February 4, 1997. • Suffered career-ending injuries in automobile accident, November 24, 1997.

• ANTROPOV, Nikolai

C – L. 6'5", 203 lbs. b: Vost, USSR, 2/18/1980. Toronto's 1st, 10th overall, in 1998.

Season	Club	League	GP	G	A	Pts	AG	AA	APts	PIM	PP	SH	GW	S	%	TGF	PGF	TGA	PGA	+/-	GP	G	A	Pts	PIM	PP	SH	GW
1995-96	Torpedo Ust-Kamenogorsk	Russia-Jr.	20	18	20	38	....	....	....	30	....	....	....	....	....	....	....	....	....	....	....	....	....	....	....	....	....	....
1996-97	Torpedo Ust-Kamenogorsk	Russia-2	8	2	1	3	....	....	....	6	....	....	....	....	....	....	....	....	....	....	....	....	....	....	....	....	....	....
1997-98	Torpedo Ust-Kamenogorsk	Russia-2	42	15	24	39	....	....	....	62	....	....	....	....	....	....	....	....	....	....	....	....	....	....	....	....	....	....
1998-99	Dynamo Moscow	Russia	30	5	9	14	....	....	....	30	....	....	....	....	....	....	....	....	....	....	11	0	1	1	4	....	....	....
	Dynamo Moscow	EuroHL	5	3	1	4	....	....	....	10	....	....	....	....	....	....	....	....	....	....	3	0	0	0	0	....	....	....
	Kazakhstan	WJC-A	6	3	5	8	....	....	....	14	....	....	....	....	....	....	....	....	....	....	....	....	....	....	....	....	....	....
99-2000	Toronto Maple Leafs	NHL	66	12	18	30	13	17	30	41	0	0	2	89	13.5	46	6	26	0	14	3	0	0	0	4	0	0	0
	St. John's Maple Leafs	AHL	2	0	0	0	....	....	....	4	....	....	....	....	....	....	....	....	....	....	....	....	....	....	....	....	....	....
	NHL Totals		66	12	18	30	13	17	30	41	0	0	2	89	13.5	46	6	26	0		3	0	0	0	4	0	0	0

• APPS, Syl Jr.

Sylvanus Marshall C – R. 6', 185 lbs. b: Toronto, Ont., 8/1/1947. NY Rangers' 4th, 21st overall, in 1964.

Season	Club	League	GP	G	A	Pts	AG	AA	APts	PIM	PP	SH	GW	S	%	TGF	PGF	TGA	PGA	+/-	GP	G	A	Pts	PIM	PP	SH	GW
1965-66	Kingston Frontenacs	OHA-B	STATISTICS NOT AVAILABLE																									
1966-67	Princeton University	ECAC-2	DID NOT PLAY – FRESHMAN																									
1967-68	Kingston Aces	OHA-Sr.	35	16	22	38	....	....	....	28	....	....	....	....	....	....	....	....	....	....	....	....	....	....	....	....	....	....
1968-69	Kingston Aces	OHA-Sr.	27	14	22	36	....	....	....	17	....	....	....	....	....	....	....	....	....	....	....	....	....	....	....	....	....	....
	Buffalo Bisons	AHL	2	1	2	3	....	....	....	4	....	....	....	....	....	....	....	....	....	....	....	....	....	....	....	....	....	....
1969-70	Omaha Rangers	CHL	68	16	38	54	....	....	....	43	....	....	....	....	....	....	....	....	....	....	12	*10	9	*19	4	....	....	....
	Buffalo Bisons	AHL	....	....	....	....	....	....	....	....	....	....	....	....	....	....	....	....	....	....	7	2	3	5	6	....	....	....
1970-71	New York Rangers	NHL	31	1	2	3	1	2	3	11	0	0	0	25	4.0	7	2	5	0	0	....	....	....	....	....	....	....	....
	Omaha Rangers	CHL	11	0	5	5	....	....	....	4	....	....	....	....	....	....	....	....	....	....	....	....	....	....	....	....	....	....
	Pittsburgh Penguins	NHL	31	9	16	25	9	13	22	21	4	0	1	75	12.0	34	12	21	2	3	....	....	....	....	....	....	....	....
1971-72	Pittsburgh Penguins	NHL	72	15	44	59	15	38	53	78	3	1	1	164	9.1	80	19	55	12	18	4	1	0	1	2	0	0	0
1972-73	Pittsburgh Penguins	NHL	77	29	56	85	27	45	72	18	6	2	4	186	15.6	106	23	77	19	25	....	....	....	....	....	....	....	....
1973-74	Pittsburgh Penguins	NHL	75	24	61	85	23	51	74	37	7	4	2	177	13.6	123	38	77	13	21	....	....	....	....	....	....	....	....
1974-75	Pittsburgh Penguins	NHL	79	24	55	79	21	41	62	43	4	1	6	181	13.3	110	29	92	19	8	9	2	3	5	9	1	0	1
1975-76	Pittsburgh Penguins	NHL	80	32	67	99	28	50	78	24	7	1	4	210	15.2	150	55	94	16	17	3	0	1	1	0	0	0	0
1976-77	Pittsburgh Penguins	NHL	72	18	43	61	16	33	49	20	3	2	2	164	11.0	80	22	70	14	2	3	1	0	1	12	1	0	0
1977-78	Pittsburgh Penguins	NHL	9	0	7	7	0	5	5	0	0	0	0	11	0.0	8	2	9	3	0	....	....	....	....	....	....	....	....
	Los Angeles Kings	NHL	70	19	26	45	17	20	37	18	4	0	1	131	14.5	58	13	56	0	–11	2	0	1	1	0	0	0	0
1978-79	Los Angeles Kings	NHL	80	7	30	37	6	22	28	29	0	0	1	128	5.5	49	10	65	1	–25	2	1	0	1	0	1	0	0
1979-80	Los Angeles Kings	NHL	51	5	16	21	4	12	16	12	1	0	0	53	9.4	26	4	39	0	–17	....	....	....	....	....	....	....	....
	NHL Totals		727	183	423	606	167	332	499	311	39	11	22	1505	12.2	831	229	660	99		23	5	5	10	23	3	0	1

• Son of Syl Sr. • Played in NHL All-Star Game (1975)

• Attended Queens University while playing with Kingston (OHA-Sr.) Traded to **Pittsburgh** by **NY Rangers** with Sheldon Kannegiesser for Glen Sather, January 26, 1971. Traded to **LA Kings** by **Pittsburgh** with Hartland Monahan for Dave Schultz, Gene Carr and L.A. Kings' 4th round choice (Shane Pearsall) in 1978 Amateur Draft, November 2, 1977.

• ARBOUR, Al

Alger Joseph "Radar" D – L. 6', 180 lbs. b: Sudbury, Ont., 11/1/1932. HHOF

Season	Club	League	GP	G	A	Pts	AG	AA	APts	PIM	PP	SH	GW	S	%	TGF	PGF	TGA	PGA	+/-	GP	G	A	Pts	PIM	PP	SH	GW
1949-50	Windsor Spitfires	OHA-Jr.	3	0	0	0	....	....	....	0	....	....	....	....	....	....	....	....	....	....	1	0	0	0	0	....	....	....
	Detroit Hettche	IHL	33	14	8	22	....	....	....	10	....	....	....	....	....	....	....	....	....	....	3	0	0	0	4	....	....	....
1950-51	Windsor Spitfires	OHA-Jr.	31	5	4	9	....	....	....	27	....	....	....	....	....	....	....	....	....	....	....	....	....	....	....	....	....	....
1951-52	Windsor Spitfires	OHA-Jr.	55	7	12	19	....	....	....	86	....	....	....	....	....	....	....	....	....	....	....	....	....	....	....	....	....	....
1952-53	Windsor Spitfires	OHA-Jr.	56	5	7	12	....	....	....	92	....	....	....	....	....	....	....	....	....	....	....	....	....	....	....	....	....	....
	Washington Lions	EAHL	4	0	2	2	....	....	....	0	....	....	....	....	....	....	....	....	....	....	....	....	....	....	....	....	....	....
	Edmonton Flyers	WHL	8	0	1	1	....	....	....	2	....	....	....	....	....	....	....	....	....	....	15	0	5	5	10	....	....	....
1953-54♦	Detroit Red Wings	NHL	36	0	1	1	0	1	1	18	....	....	....	....	....	....	....	....	....	....	....	....	....	....	....	....	....	....
	Sherbrooke Saints	QHL	19	1	3	4	....	....	....	24	....	....	....	....	....	....	....	....	....	....	2	0	0	0	2	....	....	....
1954-55	Edmonton Flyers	WHL	41	3	9	12	....	....	....	39	....	....	....	....	....	....	....	....	....	....	....	....	....	....	....	....	....	....
	Quebec Aces	QHL	20	4	5	9	....	....	....	55	....	....	....	....	....	....	....	....	....	....	4	0	0	0	2	....	....	....
1955-56	Edmonton Flyers	WHL	70	5	14	19	....	....	....	109	....	....	....	....	....	....	....	....	....	....	3	0	0	0	4	....	....	....
	Detroit Red Wings	NHL	....	....	....	....	....	....	....	....	....	....	....	....	....	....	....	....	....	....	4	0	1	1	0	0	0	0
1956-57	Detroit Red Wings	NHL	44	1	6	7	1	7	8	38	....	....	....	....	....	....	....	....	....	....	5	0	0	0	6	0	0	0
	Edmonton Flyers	WHL	24	2	3	5	....	....	....	24	....	....	....	....	....	....	....	....	....	....	....	....	....	....	....	....	....	....
1957-58	Detroit Red Wings	NHL	69	1	6	7	1	6	7	104	....	....	....	....	....	....	....	....	....	....	4	0	1	1	4	0	0	0
1958-59	Chicago Black Hawks	NHL	70	2	10	12	2	10	12	86	....	....	....	....	....	....	....	....	....	....	6	1	2	3	26	0	0	0
1959-60	Chicago Black Hawks	NHL	57	1	5	6	1	5	6	66	....	....	....	....	....	....	....	....	....	....	4	0	0	0	4	0	0	0
1960-61♦	Chicago Black Hawks	NHL	53	3	2	5	3	2	5	40	....	....	....	....	....	....	....	....	....	....	7	0	0	0	2	0	0	0
1961-62♦	Toronto Maple Leafs	NHL	52	1	5	6	1	5	6	68	....	....	....	....	....	....	....	....	....	....	8	0	0	0	6	0	0	0
1962-63	Toronto Maple Leafs	NHL	4	1	0	1	1	0	1	4	....	....	....	....	....	....	....	....	....	....	....	....	....	....	....	....	....	....
	Rochester Americans	AHL	63	6	21	27	....	....	....	97	....	....	....	....	....	....	....	....	....	....	2	0	2	2	2	....	....	....
1963-64♦	Toronto Maple Leafs	NHL	6	0	1	1	0	1	1	0	....	....	....	....	....	....	....	....	....	....	1	0	0	0	0	0	0	0
	Rochester Americans	AHL	60	3	19	22	....	....	....	62	....	....	....	....	....	....	....	....	....	....	2	1	0	1	0	....	....	....
1964-65	Rochester Americans	AHL	71	1	16	17	....	....	....	88	....	....	....	....	....	....	....	....	....	....	10	0	1	1	16	....	....	....
	Toronto Maple Leafs	NHL	....	....	....	....	....	....	....	....	....	....	....	....	....	....	....	....	....	....	1	0	0	0	2	0	0	0
1965-66	Toronto Maple Leafs	NHL	4	0	1	1	0	1	1	2	....	....	....	....	....	....	....	....	....	....	....	....	....	....	....	....	....	....
	Rochester Americans	AHL	59	2	11	13	....	....	....	86	....	....	....	....	....	....	....	....	....	....	12	0	2	2	8	....	....	....
1966-67	Rochester Americans	AHL	71	3	19	22	....	....	....	48	....	....	....	....	....	....	....	....	....	....	13	0	1	1	16	....	....	....
1967-68	St. Louis Blues	NHL	74	1	10	11	1	10	11	50	1	0	0	39	2.6	58	1	90	27	–6	14	0	3	3	10	0	0	0
1968-69	St. Louis Blues	NHL	67	1	6	7	1	5	6	50	0	0	1	25	4.0	54	0	62	28	20	12	0	0	0	10	0	0	0
1969-70	St. Louis Blues	NHL	68	0	3	3	0	3	3	85	0	0	0	30	0.0	54	1	73	27	7	14	0	1	1	16	0	0	0
1970-71	St. Louis Blues	NHL	22	0	2	2	0	2	2	6	0	0	0	3	0.0	14	0	13	5	6	6	0	0	0	6	0	0	0
	NHL Totals		626	12	58	70	12	58	70	617	....	....	....	....	....	....	....	....	....		86	1	8	9	92	....	....	....

WHL Second All-Star Team (1955) • AHL First All-Star Team (1963, 1964, 1965, 1966) • Won Eddie Shore Award (Outstanding Defenseman - AHL) (1965) • Won Jack Adams Award (1979) • Won Lester Patrick Trophy (1992) • Played in NHL All-Star Game (1969)

Claimed by **Chicago** from **Detroit** in Intra-League Draft, June 3, 1958. Claimed by **Toronto** from **Chicago** in Intra-League Draft, June 13, 1961. Claimed by **St. Louis** from **Toronto** in Expansion Draft, June 6, 1967. • Served as Head Coach of **St. Louis** from October 10, 1970 to February 5, 1971.

• ARBOUR, John

John Gilbert D – L. 5'11", 195 lbs. b: Niagara Falls, Ont., 9/28/1945.

Season	Club	League	GP	G	A	Pts	AG	AA	APts	PIM	PP	SH	GW	S	%	TGF	PGF	TGA	PGA	+/-	GP	G	A	Pts	PIM	PP	SH	GW
1962-63	Niagara Falls Flyers	OHA-Jr.	47	1	5	6	....	....	....	27	....	....	....	....	....	....	....	....	....	....	8	1	0	1	0	....	....	....
	Niagara Falls Flyers	Mem-Cup	16	0	1	1	....	....	....	12	....	....	....	....	....	....	....	....	....	....	....	....	....	....	....	....	....	....
1963-64	Niagara Falls Flyers	OHA-Jr.	56	12	6	18	....	....	....	94	....	....	....	....	....	....	....	....	....	....	4	0	1	1	12	....	....	....
1964-65	Niagara Falls Flyers	OHA-Jr.	....	....	....	....	....	....	....	....	....	....	....	....	....	....	....	....	....	....	11	0	6	6	40	....	....	....
	Niagara Falls Flyers	Mem-Cup	13	2	7	9	....	....	....	33	....	....	....	....	....	....	....	....	....	....	....	....	....	....	....	....	....	....
1965-66	Niagara Falls Flyers	OHA-Jr.	47	13	31	44	....	....	....	196	....	....	....	....	....	....	....	....	....	....	6	2	4	6	14	....	....	....
	Boston Bruins	NHL	2	0	0	0	0	0	0	0	....	....	....	....	....	....	....	....	....	....	....	....	....	....	....	....	....	....
	Oklahoma City Blazers	CPHL	3	0	0	0	....	....	....	0	....	....	....	....	....	....	....	....	....	....	3	0	0	0	0	....	....	....
1966-67	Oklahoma City Blazers	CPHL	67	3	21	24	....	....	....	140	....	....	....	....	....	....	....	....	....	....	9	0	1	1	11	....	....	....

			REGULAR SEASON																		PLAYOFFS							
Season	**Club**	**League**	**GP**	**G**	**A**	**Pts**	**AG**	**AA**	**APts**	**PIM**	**PP**	**SH**	**GW**	**S**	**%**	**TGF**	**PGF**	**TGA**	**PGA**	**+/–**	**GP**	**G**	**A**	**Pts**	**PIM**	**PP**	**SH**	**GW**
1967-68	**Boston Bruins**	**NHL**	**4**	**0**	**1**	**1**	**0**	**1**	**1**	**11**	**0**	**0**	**0**	**3**	**0.0**	**1**	**0**	**0**	**0**	**1**	....	....	....	....	....	....	....	....
	Oklahoma City Blazers	CPHL	62	2	15	17	....	....	....	224	....	....	....	....	....	....	....	....	....	....	7	1	0	1	42	....	....	....
1968-69	**Pittsburgh Penguins**	**NHL**	**17**	**0**	**2**	**2**	**0**	**2**	**2**	**35**	**0**	**0**	**0**	**19**	**0.0**	**6**	**0**	**21**	**1**	**–14**	....	....	....	....	....	....	....	....
	Baltimore Clippers	AHL	59	4	17	21	....	....	....	157	....	....	....	....	....	....	....	....	....	....	4	0	0	0	15	....	....	....
1969-70	Vancouver Canucks	WHL	72	7	28	35	....	....	....	*251	....	....	....	....	....	....	....	....	....	....	11	2	3	5	*42	....	....	....
1970-71	**Vancouver Canucks**	**NHL**	**13**	**0**	**0**	**0**	**0**	**0**	**0**	**12**	**0**	**0**	**0**	**9**	**0.0**	**3**	**0**	**10**	**3**	**–4**	....	....	....	....	....	....	....	....
	St. Louis Blues	**NHL**	**53**	**1**	**6**	**7**	**1**	**5**	**6**	**81**	**0**	**0**	**0**	**57**	**1.8**	**31**	**0**	**35**	**5**	**1**	**5**	**0**	**0**	**0**	**0**	**0**	**0**	**0**
1971-72	**St. Louis Blues**	**NHL**	**17**	**0**	**0**	**0**	**0**	**0**	**0**	**10**	**0**	**0**	**0**	**14**	**0.0**	**6**	**1**	**10**	**1**	**–4**	....	....	....	....	....	....	....	....
	Denver Spurs	WHL	20	4	12	16	....	....	....	73	....	....	....	....	....	....	....	....	....	....	....	....	....	....	....	....	....	....
1972-73	Minnesota Fighting Saints	WHA	76	6	27	33	....	....	....	188	....	....	....	....	....	....	....	....	....	....	5	0	1	1	12	....	....	....
1973-74	Minnesota Fighting Saints	WHA	77	6	43	49	....	....	....	192	....	....	....	....	....	....	....	....	....	....	11	3	6	9	27	....	....	....
1974-75	Minnesota Fighting Saints	WHA	71	11	43	54	....	....	....	67	....	....	....	....	....	....	....	....	....	....	12	0	6	6	23	....	....	....
1975-76	Denver-Ottawa Civics	WHA	34	2	13	15	....	....	....	49	....	....	....	....	....	....	....	....	....	....	....	....	....	....	....	....	....	....
	Minnesota Fighting Saints	WHA	7	0	4	4	....	....	....	14	....	....	....	....	....	....	....	....	....	....	....	....	....	....	....	....	....	....
1976-77	Minnesota Fighting Saints	WHA	33	3	19	22	....	....	....	22	....	....	....	....	....	....	....	....	....	....	....	....	....	....	....	....	....	....
	Calgary Cowboys	WHA	37	1	15	16	....	....	....	38	....	....	....	....	....	....	....	....	....	....	....	....	....	....	....	....	....	....
	NHL Totals		**106**	**1**	**9**	**10**	**1**	**8**	**9**	**149**	....	....	....	....	....	....	....	....	....		**5**	**0**	**0**	**0**	**0**	....	....	....
	Other Major League Totals		335	29	164	193	....	....	....	570	....	....	....	....	....	....	....	....	....	....	28	3	13	16	62	....	....	....

CPHL Second All-Star Team (1968)

• Regular season totals for **Niagara Falls** (OHA-Jr.) in 1964-65 unavailable. Traded to **Pittsburgh** by **Boston** with Jean Pronovost for cash, May 21, 1968. Traded to **Vancouver** (WHL) by **Pittsburgh** with Paul Andrea and the loan of Andy Bathgate for the 1969-70 season for Bryan Hextall Jr., May 20, 1969. Rights transferred to **Vancouver** after NHL franchise purchased WHL club, December 19, 1969. Traded to **St. Louis** by **Vancouver** for cash, December 3, 1970. Selected by **Minnesota** (WHA) in 1972 WHA General Player Draft, February 12, 1972. Traded to **Denver** (WHA) by **Minnesota** (WHA) for future considerations, October, 1975. Signed as a free agent by **Minnesota** (WHA) after **Denver-Ottawa** (WHA) franchise folded, January 17, 1976. Traded to **Calgary** (WHA) by **Minnesota** (WHA) with Butch Deadmarsh and Danny Gruen for cash, January, 1977.

• ARCHAMBAULT, Michel

Michel Joseph LW – L. 5'8", 160 lbs. b: St. Myacenthe, Que., 9/27/1950. Chicago's 2nd, 28th overall, in 1970.

Season	Club	League	GP	G	A	Pts	AG	AA	APts	PIM	PP	SH	GW	S	%	TGF	PGF	TGA	PGA	+/–	GP	G	A	Pts	PIM	PP	SH	GW
1966-67	Drummondville Rangers	QJHL	....	....	....	....	....	....	....	....	....	....	....	....	....	....	....	....	....	....	3	1	1	2	12	....	....	....
1967-68	Drummondville Rangers	QJHL	50	23	41	64	....	....	....	66	....	....	....	....	....	....	....	....	....	....	10	7	8	15	14	....	....	....
1968-69	Drummondville Rangers	QJHL	STATISTICS NOT AVAILABLE																									
1969-70	Drummondville Rangers	QJHL	55	69	82	151	....	....	....	167	....	....	....	....	....	....	....	....	....	....	6	6	8	14	17	....	....	....
	Quebec Remparts	Mem-Cup	3	1	3	4	....	....	....	6	....	....	....	....	....	....	....	....	....	....	....	....	....	....	....	....	....	....
1970-71	Dallas Black Hawks	CHL	61	17	17	34	....	....	....	56	....	....	....	....	....	....	....	....	....	....	10	5	2	7	10	....	....	....
1971-72	Dallas Black Hawks	CHL	65	31	26	57	....	....	....	115	....	....	....	....	....	....	....	....	....	....	12	6	6	12	14	....	....	....
1972-73	Quebec Nordiques	WHA	57	12	25	37	....	....	....	36	....	....	....	....	....	....	....	....	....	....	....	....	....	....	....	....	....	....
1973-74	Maine Nordiques	NAHL	72	43	65	108	....	....	....	83	....	....	....	....	....	....	....	....	....	....	8	1	7	8	0	....	....	....
1974-75	Dallas Black Hawks	CHL	70	26	40	66	....	....	....	49	....	....	....	....	....	....	....	....	....	....	8	4	2	6	8	....	....	....
1975-76	Dallas Black Hawks	CHL	76	26	47	73	....	....	....	41	....	....	....	....	....	....	....	....	....	....	10	2	2	4	2	....	....	....
1976-77	**Chicago Black Hawks**	**NHL**	**3**	**0**	**0**	**0**	**0**	**0**	**0**	**0**	**0**	**0**	**0**	**1**	**0.0**	**0**	**0**	**3**	**0**	**–3**	....	....	....	....	....	....	....	....
	Dallas Black Hawks	CHL	72	28	45	73	....	....	....	60	....	....	....	....	....	....	....	....	....	....	5	0	3	3	0	....	....	....
1977-78	VEU Feldkirch	Austria	19	18	9	27	....	....	....	70	....	....	....	....	....	....	....	....	....	....	....	....	....	....	....	....	....	....
	NHL Totals		**3**	**0**	**0**	**0**	**0**	**0**	**0**	**0**	**0**	**0**	**0**	**1**	**0.0**	**0**	**0**	**3**	**0**		....	....	....	....	....	....	....	....
	Other Major League Totals		57	12	25	37	....	....	....	36	....	....	....	....	....	....	....	....	....	....	....	....	....	....	....	....	....	....

QJHL Second All-Star Team (1970) • CHL First All-Star Team (1976, 1977)

Selected by **Quebec** (WHA) in 1972 WHA General Player Draft, February 12, 1972. Selected by **Indianapolis** (WHA) from **Quebec** (WHA) in WHA Expansion Draft, May 30, 1974.

• ARCHIBALD, Dave

David J. C/LW – L. 6'1", 210 lbs. b: Chilliwack, B.C., 4/14/1969. Minnesota's 1st, 6th overall, in 1987.

Season	Club	League	GP	G	A	Pts	AG	AA	APts	PIM	PP	SH	GW	S	%	TGF	PGF	TGA	PGA	+/–	GP	G	A	Pts	PIM	PP	SH	GW
1983-84	Chilliwack Auctioneers	BCAHA	STATISTICS NOT AVAILABLE																									
	Portland Winter Hawks	WHL	7	0	1	1	....	....	....	2	....	....	....	....	....	....	....	....	....	....	....	....	....	....	....	....	....	....
1984-85	Portland Winter Hawks	WHL	47	7	11	18	....	....	....	10	....	....	....	....	....	....	....	....	....	....	3	0	2	2	0	....	....	....
1985-86	Portland Winter Hawks	WHL	70	29	35	64	....	....	....	56	....	....	....	....	....	....	....	....	....	....	15	6	7	13	11	....	....	....
	Portland Winter Hawks	Mem-Cup	4	1	0	1	....	....	....	2	....	....	....	....	....	....	....	....	....	....	....	....	....	....	....	....	....	....
1986-87	Portland Winter Hawks	WHL	65	50	57	107	....	....	....	40	....	....	....	....	....	....	....	....	....	....	20	10	18	28	11	....	....	....
1987-88	**Minnesota North Stars**	**NHL**	**78**	**13**	**20**	**33**	**11**	**14**	**25**	**26**	**3**	**0**	**2**	**96**	**13.5**	**47**	**17**	**47**	**0**	**–17**	....	....	....	....	....	....	....	....
1988-89	**Minnesota North Stars**	**NHL**	**72**	**14**	**19**	**33**	**12**	**13**	**25**	**14**	**7**	**0**	**2**	**105**	**13.3**	**60**	**30**	**43**	**2**	**–11**	**5**	**0**	**1**	**1**	**0**	**0**	**0**	**0**
1989-90	**Minnesota North Stars**	**NHL**	**12**	**1**	**5**	**6**	**1**	**4**	**5**	**6**	**1**	**0**	**1**	**26**	**3.8**	**13**	**6**	**6**	**0**	**1**	....	....	....	....	....	....	....	....
	New York Rangers	**NHL**	**19**	**2**	**3**	**5**	**2**	**2**	**4**	**6**	**1**	**0**	**0**	**30**	**6.7**	**10**	**4**	**6**	**0**	**0**	....	....	....	....	....	....	....	....
	Flint Spirits	IHL	41	14	38	52	....	....	....	16	....	....	....	....	....	....	....	....	....	....	4	3	2	5	0	....	....	....
1990-91	Canada	Nat-Team	29	19	12	31	....	....	....	20	....	....	....	....	....	....	....	....	....	....	....	....	....	....	....	....	....	....
	Canada	WEC-A	10	0	1	1	....	....	....	8	....	....	....	....	....	....	....	....	....	....	....	....	....	....	....	....	....	....
1991-92	Canada	Nat-Team	58	20	43	63	....	....	....	64	....	....	....	....	....	....	....	....	....	....	....	....	....	....	....	....	....	....
	HC Bolzano	Italy	5	4	3	7	....	....	....	16	....	....	....	....	....	....	....	....	....	....	7	8	5	13	7	....	....	....
	Canada	Olympics	8	7	1	8	....	....	....	18	....	....	....	....	....	....	....	....	....	....	....	....	....	....	....	....	....	....
1992-93	Binghamton Rangers	AHL	8	6	3	9	....	....	....	10	....	....	....	....	....	....	....	....	....	....	....	....	....	....	....	....	....	....
	Ottawa Senators	**NHL**	**44**	**9**	**6**	**15**	**7**	**4**	**11**	**32**	**6**	**0**	**0**	**93**	**9.7**	**26**	**12**	**52**	**22**	**–16**	....	....	....	....	....	....	....	....
1993-94	**Ottawa Senators**	**NHL**	**33**	**10**	**8**	**18**	**9**	**6**	**15**	**14**	**2**	**0**	**1**	**65**	**15.4**	**34**	**12**	**54**	**25**	**–7**	....	....	....	....	....	....	....	....
1994-95	**Ottawa Senators**	**NHL**	**14**	**2**	**2**	**4**	**4**	**3**	**7**	**19**	**0**	**0**	**1**	**27**	**7.4**	**8**	**1**	**17**	**3**	**–7**	....	....	....	....	....	....	....	....
1995-96	**Ottawa Senators**	**NHL**	**44**	**6**	**4**	**10**	**6**	**3**	**9**	**18**	**0**	**0**	**1**	**56**	**10.7**	**12**	**3**	**41**	**18**	**–14**	....	....	....	....	....	....	....	....
	Utah Grizzlies	IHL	19	1	4	5	....	....	....	10	....	....	....	....	....	....	....	....	....	....	....	....	....	....	....	....	....	....
1996-97	**New York Islanders**	**NHL**	**7**	**0**	**0**	**0**	**0**	**0**	**0**	**4**	**0**	**0**	**0**	**4**	**0.0**	**0**	**0**	**7**	**3**	**–4**	....	....	....	....	....	....	....	....
	Frankfurt Lions	Germany	34	10	19	29	....	....	....	48	....	....	....	....	....	....	....	....	....	....	9	4	2	6	16	....	....	....
1997-98	San Antonio Dragons	IHL	55	11	21	32	....	....	....	10	....	....	....	....	....	....	....	....	....	....	....	....	....	....	....	....	....	....
1998-99	Utah Grizzlies	IHL	76	23	25	48	....	....	....	32	....	....	....	....	....	....	....	....	....	....	....	....	....	....	....	....	....	....
99-2000	Linkopings HC	Sweden	21	5	4	9	....	....	....	18	....	....	....	....	....	....	....	....	....	....	....	....	....	....	....	....	....	....
	Utah Grizzlies	IHL	27	7	4	11	....	....	....	10	....	....	....	....	....	....	....	....	....	....	5	0	0	0	0	....	....	....
	NHL Totals		**323**	**57**	**67**	**124**	**52**	**49**	**101**	**139**	**20**	**0**	**8**	**502**	**11.4**	**210**	**85**	**273**	**73**		**5**	**0**	**1**	**1**	**0**	**0**	**0**	**0**

Traded to **NY Rangers** by **Minnesota** for Jayson More, November 1, 1989. Traded to **Ottawa** by **NY Rangers** for Ottawa's 5th round choice (later traded to LA Kings — LA Kings selected Frederick Beaubien) in 1993 Entry Draft, November 6, 1992. Signed as a free agent by **NY Islanders**, October 10, 1996

• ARCHIBALD, Jim

James RW – R. 5'11", 175 lbs. b: Craik, Sask., 6/6/1961. Minnesota's 11th, 139th overall, in 1981.

Season	Club	League	GP	G	A	Pts	AG	AA	APts	PIM	PP	SH	GW	S	%	TGF	PGF	TGA	PGA	+/–	GP	G	A	Pts	PIM	PP	SH	GW
1979-80	Craik Warriors	SIHA	STATISTICS NOT AVAILABLE																									
1980-81	Moose Jaw Canucks	SJHL	52	46	42	88	....	....	....	308	....	....	....	....	....	....	....	....	....	....	....	....	....	....	....	....	....	....
1981-82	University of North Dakota	WCHA	41	10	16	26	....	....	....	96	....	....	....	....	....	....	....	....	....	....	....	....	....	....	....	....	....	....
1982-83	University of North Dakota	WCHA	33	7	14	21	....	....	....	91	....	....	....	....	....	....	....	....	....	....	....	....	....	....	....	....	....	....
1983-84	University of North Dakota	WCHA	44	21	15	36	....	....	....	156	....	....	....	....	....	....	....	....	....	....	....	....	....	....	....	....	....	....
1984-85	University of North Dakota	WCHA	41	37	24	61	....	....	....	197	....	....	....	....	....	....	....	....	....	....	....	....	....	....	....	....	....	....
	Springfield Indians	AHL	8	1	0	1	....	....	....	5	....	....	....	....	....	....	....	....	....	....	....	....	....	....	....	....	....	....
	Minnesota North Stars	**NHL**	**4**	**1**	**2**	**3**	**1**	**1**	**2**	**11**	**0**	**0**	**0**	**12**	**8.3**	**6**	**0**	**6**	**0**	**0**	....	....	....	....	....	....	....	....
1985-86	**Minnesota North Stars**	**NHL**	**11**	**0**	**0**	**0**	**0**	**0**	**0**	**32**	**0**	**0**	**0**	**7**	**0.0**	**1**	**1**	**3**	**0**	**–3**	....	....	....	....	....	....	....	....
	Springfield Indians	AHL	12	1	7	8	....	....	....	34	....	....	....	....	....	....	....	....	....	....	....	....	....	....	....	....	....	....
1986-87	**Minnesota North Stars**	**NHL**	**1**	**0**	**0**	**0**	**0**	**0**	**0**	**2**	**0**	**0**	**0**	**1**	**0.0**	**0**	**0**	**1**	**0**	**–1**	....	....	....	....	....	....	....	....
	Springfield Indians	AHL	66	10	17	27	....	....	....	303	....	....	....	....	....	....	....	....	....	....	....	....	....	....	....	....	....	....
1987-88	Kalamazoo Wings	IHL	12	0	1	1	....	....	....	73	....	....	....	....	....	....	....	....	....	....	....	....	....	....	....	....	....	....
	NHL Totals		**16**	**1**	**2**	**3**	**1**	**1**	**2**	**45**	**0**	**0**	**0**	**20**	**5.0**	**7**	**1**	**10**	**0**		....	....	....	....	....	....	....	....

WCHA First All-Star Team (1985)

• ARESHENKOFF, Ron

C – L. 6', 175 lbs. b: Grand Forks, B.C., 6/13/1957. Buffalo's 2nd, 32nd overall, in 1977.

Season	Club	League	GP	G	A	Pts	AG	AA	APts	PIM	PP	SH	GW	S	%	TGF	PGF	TGA	PGA	+/–	GP	G	A	Pts	PIM	PP	SH	GW
1974-75	Vernon Vikings	BCJHL	65	36	50	86	....	....	....	40	....	....	....	....	....	....	....	....	....	....	....	....	....	....	....	....	....	....
1975-76	Medicine Hat Tigers	WCJHL	71	25	35	60	....	....	....	77	....	....	....	....	....	....	....	....	....	....	3	1	2	3	0	....	....	....

Season	Club	League	GP	G	A	Pts	AG	AA	APts	PIM	PP	SH	GW	S	%	TGF	PGF	TGA	PGA	+/-	GP	G	A	Pts	PIM	PP	SH	GW
			REGULAR SEASON																		PLAYOFFS							
1976-77	Medicine Hat Tigers	WCJHL	60	51	42	93	....	....	....	57	....	....	....	....	....	....	....	....	....	....	4	1	0	1	0	....	....	....
1977-78	Hershey Bears	AHL	38	9	14	23	....	....	....	38	....	....	....	....	....	....	....	....	....	....	....	....	....	....	....	....	....	....
1978-79	Hershey Bears	AHL	DID NOT PLAY – INJURED																									
1979-80	**Edmonton Oilers**	**NHL**	**4**	**0**	**0**	**0**	**0**	**0**	**0**	**0**	**0**	**0**	**0**	**3**	**0.0**	**0**	**0**	**4**	**0**	**–4**	....	....	....	....	....	....	....	....
	Houston Apollos	CHL	55	14	24	38	....	....	....	72	....	....	....	....	....	....	....	....	....	....	2	0	0	0	0	....	....	....
1980-1983	Trail Smoke Eaters	WIHL	STATISTICS NOT AVAILABLE																									
1983-84	Trail Smoke Eaters	WIHL	45	12	20	32	....	....	....	....	....	....	....	....	....	....	....	....	....	....	....	....	....	....	....	....	....	....
	NHL Totals		**4**	**0**	**0**	**0**	**0**	**0**	**0**	**0**	**0**	**0**	**0**	**3**	**0.0**	**0**	**0**	**4**	**0**		....	....	....	....	....	....	....	....

• Missed majority of 1977-78 and all of 1978-79 seasons recovering from shoulder surgery, January, 1978. Claimed by **Edmonton** from **Buffalo** in Expansion Draft, June 13, 1979. Traded to **Philadelphia** by **Edmonton** with Edmonton's 10th round choice (Bob O'Brien) in 1980 Entry Draft for Barry Dean, June 11, 1980.

• ARMSTRONG, Bill

William Harold C – L. 6'2", 195 lbs. b: London, Ont., 6/25/1966.

Season	Club	League	GP	G	A	Pts	AG	AA	APts	PIM	PP	SH	GW	S	%	TGF	PGF	TGA	PGA	+/-	GP	G	A	Pts	PIM	PP	SH	GW
1983-84	Wexford Raiders	OJHL-B	25	6	20	26	....	....	....	8	....	....	....	....	....	....	....	....	....	....	....	....	....	....	....	....	....	....
1984-85	London Diamonds	OJHL-B	43	17	21	38	....	....	....	102	....	....	....	....	....	....	....	....	....	....	....	....	....	....	....	....	....	....
1985-86	London Diamonds	OJHL-B	41	26	23	49	....	....	....	81	....	....	....	....	....	....	....	....	....	....	....	....	....	....	....	....	....	....
1986-87	University of Western Michigan	CCHA	43	13	20	33	....	....	....	86	....	....	....	....	....	....	....	....	....	....	....	....	....	....	....	....	....	....
1987-88	University of Western Michigan	CCHA	41	22	17	39	....	....	....	88	....	....	....	....	....	....	....	....	....	....	....	....	....	....	....	....	....	....
1988-89	University of Western Michigan	CCHA	40	23	19	42	....	....	....	97	....	....	....	....	....	....	....	....	....	....	....	....	....	....	....	....	....	....
1989-90	Hershey Bears	AHL	58	10	6	16	....	....	....	99	....	....	....	....	....	....	....	....	....	....	....	....	....	....	....	....	....	....
1990-91	**Philadelphia Flyers**	**NHL**	**1**	**0**	**1**	**1**	**0**	**1**	**1**	**0**	**0**	**0**	**0**	**1**	**0.0**	**1**	**0**	**0**	**0**	**1**	....	....	....	....	....	....	....	....
	Hershey Bears	AHL	70	36	27	63	....	....	....	150	....	....	....	....	....	....	....	....	....	....	6	2	8	10	19	....	....	....
1991-92	Hershey Bears	AHL	64	26	22	48	....	....	....	186	....	....	....	....	....	....	....	....	....	....	6	2	2	4	6	....	....	....
1992-93	Cincinnati Cyclones	IHL	42	14	11	25	....	....	....	99	....	....	....	....	....	....	....	....	....	....	....	....	....	....	....	....	....	....
	Utica Devils	AHL	32	18	21	39	....	....	....	60	....	....	....	....	....	....	....	....	....	....	....	....	....	....	....	....	....	....
1993-94	Albany River Rats	AHL	74	32	50	82	....	....	....	188	....	....	....	....	....	....	....	....	....	....	....	....	....	....	....	....	....	....
1994-95	Albany River Rats	AHL	76	32	47	79	....	....	....	115	....	....	....	....	....	....	....	....	....	....	13	6	5	11	20	....	....	....
1995-96	Albany River Rats	AHL	10	3	4	7	....	....	....	22	....	....	....	....	....	....	....	....	....	....	....	....	....	....	....	....	....	....
	Indianapolis Ice	IHL	12	4	5	9	....	....	....	13	....	....	....	....	....	....	....	....	....	....	....	....	....	....	....	....	....	....
	Detroit Vipers	IHL	54	34	25	59	....	....	....	66	....	....	....	....	....	....	....	....	....	....	12	6	2	8	15	....	....	....
1996-97	Grand Rapids Griffins	IHL	35	1	8	9	....	....	....	39	....	....	....	....	....	....	....	....	....	....	....	....	....	....	....	....	....	....
	Orlando Solar Bears	IHL	34	4	25	29	....	....	....	55	....	....	....	....	....	....	....	....	....	....	10	3	6	9	29	....	....	....
1997-98	Orlando Solar Bears	IHL	62	19	18	37	....	....	....	106	....	....	....	....	....	....	....	....	....	....	....	....	....	....	....	....	....	....
	Kansas City Blades	IHL	9	1	4	5	....	....	....	24	....	....	....	....	....	....	....	....	....	....	5	0	2	2	11	....	....	....
1998-2000	Providence Bruins	AHL	DID NOT PLAY – ASSISTANT COACH																									
	NHL Totals		**1**	**0**	**1**	**1**	**0**	**1**	**1**	**0**	**0**	**0**	**0**	**1**	**0.0**	**1**	**0**	**0**	**0**		....	....	....	....	....	....	....	....

Signed as a free agent by **Philadelphia**, May 16, 1989. Signed as a free agent by **New Jersey**, March 21, 1993. • Diagnosed with career-ending brain tumour that required surgery, May 6, 1998.

• ARMSTRONG, Derek

C – R. 5'11", 188 lbs. b: Ottawa, Ont., 4/23/1973. NY Islanders' 5th, 128th overall, in 1992.

Season	Club	League	GP	G	A	Pts	AG	AA	APts	PIM	PP	SH	GW	S	%	TGF	PGF	TGA	PGA	+/-	GP	G	A	Pts	PIM	PP	SH	GW
1989-90	Hawkesbury Hawks	OJHL	48	8	10	18	....	....	....	30	....	....	....	....	....	....	....	....	....	....	....	....	....	....	....	....	....	....
1990-91	Hawkesbury Hawks	OJHL	54	27	45	72	....	....	....	49	....	....	....	....	....	....	....	....	....	....	....	....	....	....	....	....	....	....
	Sudbury Wolves	OHL	2	0	2	2	....	....	....	0	....	....	....	....	....	....	....	....	....	....	....	....	....	....	....	....	....	....
1991-92	Sudbury Wolves	OHL	66	31	54	85	....	....	....	22	....	....	....	....	....	....	....	....	....	....	9	2	2	4	2	....	....	....
1992-93	Sudbury Wolves	OHL	66	44	62	106	....	....	....	56	....	....	....	....	....	....	....	....	....	....	14	9	10	19	26	....	....	....
1993-94	**New York Islanders**	**NHL**	**1**	**0**	**0**	**0**	**0**	**0**	**0**	**0**	**0**	**0**	**0**	**2**	**0.0**	**0**	**0**	**0**	**0**	**0**	....	....	....	....	....	....	....	....
	Salt Lake Golden Eagles	IHL	76	23	35	58	....	....	....	61	....	....	....	....	....	....	....	....	....	....	....	....	....	....	....	....	....	....
1994-95	Denver Grizzlies	IHL	59	13	18	31	....	....	....	65	....	....	....	....	....	....	....	....	....	....	6	0	2	2	0	....	....	....
1995-96	**New York Islanders**	**NHL**	**19**	**1**	**3**	**4**	**1**	**2**	**3**	**14**	**0**	**0**	**0**	**23**	**4.3**	**5**	**1**	**12**	**2**	**–6**	....	....	....	....	....	....	....	....
	Worcester IceCats	AHL	51	11	15	26	....	....	....	33	....	....	....	....	....	....	....	....	....	....	4	2	1	3	0	....	....	....
1996-97	**New York Islanders**	**NHL**	**50**	**6**	**7**	**13**	**6**	**6**	**12**	**33**	**0**	**0**	**2**	**36**	**16.7**	**16**	**1**	**25**	**2**	**–8**	....	....	....	....	....	....	....	....
	Utah Grizzlies	IHL	17	4	8	12	....	....	....	10	....	....	....	....	....	....	....	....	....	....	6	0	4	4	4	....	....	....
1997-98	**Ottawa Senators**	**NHL**	**9**	**2**	**0**	**2**	**2**	**0**	**2**	**9**	**0**	**0**	**1**	**8**	**25.0**	**4**	**0**	**3**	**0**	**1**	....	....	....	....	....	....	....	....
	Detroit Vipers	IHL	10	0	1	1	....	....	....	2	....	....	....	....	....	....	....	....	....	....	....	....	....	....	....	....	....	....
	Hartford Wolf Pack	AHL	54	16	30	46	....	....	....	40	....	....	....	....	....	....	....	....	....	....	15	2	6	8	22	....	....	....
1998-99	**New York Rangers**	**NHL**	**3**	**0**	**0**	**0**	**0**	**0**	**0**	**0**	**0**	**0**	**0**	**1**	**0.0**	**0**	**0**	**0**	**0**	**0**	....	....	....	....	....	....	....	....
	Hartford Wolf Pack	AHL	59	29	51	80	....	....	....	73	....	....	....	....	....	....	....	....	....	....	7	5	4	9	10	....	....	....
99-2000	**New York Rangers**	**NHL**	**1**	**0**	**0**	**0**	**0**	**0**	**0**	**0**	**0**	**0**	**0**	**1**	**0.0**	**0**	**0**	**0**	**0**	**0**	....	....	....	....	....	....	....	....
	Hartford Wolf Pack	AHL	77	28	54	82	....	....	....	101	....	....	....	....	....	....	....	....	....	....	23	7	16	23	24	....	....	....
	NHL Totals		**83**	**9**	**10**	**19**	**9**	**8**	**17**	**56**	**0**	**0**	**3**	**71**	**12.7**	**25**	**2**	**40**	**4**		....	....	....	....	....	....	....	....

• AHL Second All-Star Team (2000)

Signed as a free agent by **Ottawa**, July 28, 1997. Signed as a free agent by **NY Rangers**, August 10, 1998.

• ARMSTRONG, George

George Edward "Chief" C/RW – R. 6'1", 184 lbs. b: Skead, Ont., 7/6/1930. **HHOF**

Season	Club	League	GP	G	A	Pts	AG	AA	APts	PIM	PP	SH	GW	S	%	TGF	PGF	TGA	PGA	+/-	GP	G	A	Pts	PIM	PP	SH	GW
1946-47	Copper Cliff Jr. Redmen	NOJHA	9	6	5	11	....	....	....	4	....	....	....	....	....	....	....	....	....	....	5	0	1	1	*10	....	....	....
1947-48	Stratford Kroehlers	OHA-Jr.	36	33	*40	*73	....	....	....	33	....	....	....	....	....	....	....	....	....	....	2	1	0	1	6	....	....	....
1948-49	Toronto Marlboros	OHA-Jr.	39	29	33	62	....	....	....	89	....	....	....	....	....	....	....	....	....	....	10	*7	*10	*17	2	....	....	....
	Toronto Marlboros	OHA-Sr.	3	0	0	0	....	....	....	2	....	....	....	....	....	....	....	....	....	....	....	....	....	....	....	....	....	....
	Toronto Marlboros	Al-Cup	10	2	5	7	....	....	....	6	....	....	....	....	....	....	....	....	....	....	....	....	....	....	....	....	....	....
1949-50	Toronto Marlboros	OHA-Sr.	45	64	51	115	....	....	....	74	....	....	....	....	....	....	....	....	....	....	3	0	0	0	0	....	....	....
	Toronto Maple Leafs	**NHL**	**2**	**0**	**0**	**0**	**0**	**0**	**0**	**0**	....	....	....	....	....	....	....	....	....	....	....	....	....	....	....	....	....	....
	Toronto Marlboros	Al-Cup	17	19	19	38	....	....	....	18	....	....	....	....	....	....	....	....	....	....	....	....	....	....	....	....	....	....
1950-51	Pittsburgh Hornets	AHL	71	15	33	48	....	....	....	49	....	....	....	....	....	....	....	....	....	....	13	4	9	13	6	....	....	....
1951-52	**Toronto Maple Leafs**	**NHL**	**20**	**3**	**3**	**6**	**4**	**4**	**8**	**30**	....	....	....	....	....	....	....	....	....	....	**4**	**0**	**0**	**0**	**2**	....	....	....
	Pittsburgh Hornets	AHL	50	30	29	59	....	....	....	62	....	....	....	....	....	....	....	....	....	....	....	....	....	....	....	....	....	....
1952-53	**Toronto Maple Leafs**	**NHL**	**52**	**14**	**11**	**25**	**18**	**13**	**31**	**54**	....	....	....	....	....	....	....	....	....	....	....	....	....	....	....	....	....	....
1953-54	**Toronto Maple Leafs**	**NHL**	**63**	**17**	**15**	**32**	**23**	**18**	**41**	**60**	....	....	....	....	....	....	....	....	....	....	**5**	**1**	**0**	**1**	**2**	....	....	....
1954-55	**Toronto Maple Leafs**	**NHL**	**66**	**10**	**18**	**28**	**13**	**21**	**34**	**80**	....	....	....	....	....	....	....	....	....	....	**4**	**1**	**0**	**1**	**4**	....	....	....
1955-56	**Toronto Maple Leafs**	**NHL**	**67**	**16**	**32**	**48**	**22**	**38**	**60**	**97**	....	....	....	....	....	....	....	....	....	....	**5**	**4**	**2**	**6**	**0**	....	....	....
1956-57	**Toronto Maple Leafs**	**NHL**	**54**	**18**	**26**	**44**	**23**	**29**	**52**	**37**	....	....	....	....	....	....	....	....	....	....	....	....	....	....	....	....	....	....
1957-58	**Toronto Maple Leafs**	**NHL**	**59**	**17**	**25**	**42**	**21**	**26**	**47**	**93**	....	....	....	....	....	....	....	....	....	....	....	....	....	....	....	....	....	....
1958-59	**Toronto Maple Leafs**	**NHL**	**59**	**20**	**16**	**36**	**24**	**16**	**40**	**37**	....	....	....	....	....	....	....	....	....	....	**12**	**0**	**4**	**4**	**10**	....	....	....
1959-60	**Toronto Maple Leafs**	**NHL**	**70**	**23**	**28**	**51**	**27**	**27**	**54**	**60**	....	....	....	....	....	....	....	....	....	....	**10**	**1**	**4**	**5**	**4**	....	....	....
1960-61	**Toronto Maple Leafs**	**NHL**	**47**	**14**	**19**	**33**	**16**	**18**	**34**	**21**	....	....	....	....	....	....	....	....	....	....	**5**	**1**	**1**	**2**	**0**	....	....	....
1961-62◆	**Toronto Maple Leafs**	**NHL**	**70**	**21**	**32**	**53**	**24**	**31**	**55**	**27**	....	....	....	....	....	....	....	....	....	....	**12**	**7**	**5**	**12**	**2**	....	....	....
1962-63◆	**Toronto Maple Leafs**	**NHL**	**70**	**19**	**24**	**43**	**22**	**24**	**46**	**27**	....	....	....	....	....	....	....	....	....	....	**10**	**3**	**6**	**9**	**4**	....	....	....
1963-64◆	**Toronto Maple Leafs**	**NHL**	**66**	**20**	**17**	**37**	**25**	**18**	**43**	**14**	....	....	....	....	....	....	....	....	....	....	**14**	**5**	**8**	**13**	**10**	....	....	....
1964-65	**Toronto Maple Leafs**	**NHL**	**59**	**15**	**22**	**37**	**18**	**23**	**41**	**14**	....	....	....	....	....	....	....	....	....	....	**6**	**1**	**0**	**1**	**4**	....	....	....
1965-66	**Toronto Maple Leafs**	**NHL**	**70**	**16**	**35**	**51**	**18**	**33**	**51**	**12**	....	....	....	....	....	....	....	....	....	....	**4**	**0**	**1**	**1**	**4**	....	....	....
1966-67◆	**Toronto Maple Leafs**	**NHL**	**70**	**9**	**24**	**33**	**10**	**23**	**33**	**26**	....	....	....	....	....	....	....	....	....	....	**9**	**2**	**1**	**3**	**6**	....	....	....
1967-68	**Toronto Maple Leafs**	**NHL**	**62**	**13**	**21**	**34**	**15**	**21**	**36**	**4**	**2**	**0**	**2**	**125**	**10.4**	**56**	**10**	**49**	**11**	**8**	....	....	....	....	....	....	....	....
1968-69	**Toronto Maple Leafs**	**NHL**	**53**	**11**	**16**	**27**	**12**	**14**	**26**	**10**	**1**	**1**	**1**	**103**	**10.7**	**36**	**10**	**56**	**21**	**–9**	**4**	**0**	**0**	**0**	**0**	**0**	**0**	**0**
1969-70	**Toronto Maple Leafs**	**NHL**	**49**	**13**	**15**	**28**	**14**	**14**	**28**	**12**	**2**	**0**	**3**	**93**	**14.0**	**37**	**4**	**39**	**15**	**9**	....	....	....	....	....	....	....	....
1970-71	**Toronto Maple Leafs**	**NHL**	**59**	**7**	**18**	**25**	**7**	**15**	**22**	**6**	**0**	**0**	**1**	**93**	**7.5**	**41**	**9**	**42**	**17**	**7**	**6**	**0**	**2**	**2**	**0**	**0**	**0**	**0**
	NHL Totals		**1187**	**296**	**417**	**713**	**356**	**426**	**782**	**721**	....	....	....	....	....	....	....	....	....	....	**110**	**26**	**34**	**60**	**52**	....	....	....

Played in NHL All-Star Game (1956, 1957, 1959, 1962, 1963, 1964, 1968)

• ARMSTRONG, Tim

Timothy S. C – R. 5'11", 170 lbs. b: Toronto, Ont., 5/12/1967. Toronto's 11th, 211th overall, in 1985.

Season	Club	League	GP	G	A	Pts	AG	AA	APts	PIM	PP	SH	GW	S	%	TGF	PGF	TGA	PGA	+/-	GP	G	A	Pts	PIM	PP	SH	GW
1983-84	Markham Waxers	OJHL	42	24	41	65	....	....	....	41	....	....	....	....	....	....	....	....	....	....	....	....	....	....	....	....	....	....
1984-85	Toronto Marlboros	OHL	63	17	45	62	....	....	....	28	....	....	....	....	....	....	....	....	....	....	5	5	2	7	0	....	....	....

Season	Club	League	GP	G	A	Pts	AG	AA	APts	PIM	PP	SH	GW	S	%	TGF	PGF	TGA	PGA	+/–	GP	G	A	Pts	PIM	PP	SH	GW
			REGULAR SEASON																		PLAYOFFS							
1985-86	Toronto Marlboros	OHL	64	35	69	104				36											4	1	3	4	9			
1986-87	Toronto Marlboros	OHL	66	29	55	84				61																		
	Newmarket Saints	AHL	5	3	0	3				2																		
1987-88	Newmarket Saints	AHL	78	19	40	59				26																		
1988-89	**Toronto Maple Leafs**	**NHL**	11	1	0	1	1	0	1	6	0	0	0	5	20.0	2	0	6	2	–2								
	Newmarket Saints	AHL	37	16	24	40				38																		
1989-90	Newmarket Saints	AHL	63	25	37	62				24																		
1990-91	VEU Feldkirch	Austria	5	0	2	2				8																		
	Binghamton Rangers	AHL	56	24	32	56				37											10	1	6	7	6			
	NHL Totals		11	1	0	1	1	0	1	6	0	0	0	5	20.0	2	0	6	2									

• ARNASON, Chuck

Ernest Charles RW – R. 5'10", 183 lbs. b: Ashburn, Man., 7/15/1951. Montreal's 2nd, 7th overall, in 1971.

Season	Club	League	GP	G	A	Pts	AG	AA	APts	PIM	PP	SH	GW	S	%	TGF	PGF	TGA	PGA	+/–	GP	G	A	Pts	PIM	PP	SH	GW
1968-69	Selkirk Fishermen	CMJHL	STATISTICS NOT AVAILABLE																									
1969-70	Flin Flon Bombers	WCJHL	60	34	27	61				91											17	14	18	*32	38			
1970-71	Flin Flon Bombers	WCJHL	66	*79	84	*163				153											17	15	*22	*37	30			
1971-72	**Montreal Canadiens**	**NHL**	17	3	0	3	3	0	3	4	0	0	0	12	25.0	7	1	7	0	–1								
	Nova Scotia Voyageurs	AHL	58	30	24	54				33											15	7	6	13	6			
1972-73	**Montreal Canadiens**	**NHL**	19	1	1	2	1	1	2	2	1	0	0	18	5.6	6	2	5	0	–1								
	Nova Scotia Voyageurs	AHL	38	18	20	38				4											13	5	10	15	16			
1973-74	**Atlanta Flames**	**NHL**	33	7	6	13	7	5	12	13	0	0	1	62	11.3	21	3	17	0	1								
	Pittsburgh Penguins	**NHL**	41	13	5	18	12	4	16	4	0	0	2	121	10.7	27	4	27	2	–2								
1974-75	**Pittsburgh Penguins**	**NHL**	78	26	32	58	23	24	47	32	7	0	3	214	12.1	85	17	68	0	0	9	2	4	6	4	1	0	0
1975-76	**Pittsburgh Penguins**	**NHL**	30	7	3	10	6	2	8	14	0	0	2	69	10.1	18	1	21	0	–4								
	Kansas City Scouts	**NHL**	39	14	10	24	12	7	19	21	5	0	0	122	11.5	32	14	55	2	–35								
1976-77	**Colorado Rockies**	**NHL**	61	13	10	23	12	8	20	10	3	0	1	152	8.6	35	9	49	0	–23								
1977-78	**Colorado Rockies**	**NHL**	29	4	8	12	4	6	10	10	2	0	0	50	8.0	22	7	18	0	–3								
	Phoenix Roadrunners	CHL	6	3	3	6				4																		
	Cleveland Barons	**NHL**	40	21	13	34	19	10	29	8	5	0	2	110	19.1	41	5	38	0	–2								
1978-79	**Minnesota North Stars**	**NHL**	1	0	0	0	0	0	0	0	0	0	0	0	0.0	0	0	1	1	0								
	Oklahoma City Stars	CHL	60	24	22	46				42																		
	Washington Capitals	**NHL**	13	0	2	2	0	1	1	4	0	0	0	17	0.0	5	2	4	0	–1								
1979-80	Dallas Black Hawks	CHL	68	15	17	32				28																		
1980-81	Kolner EC	Germany	DID NOT PLAY – INJURED																									
	NHL Totals		401	109	90	199	99	68	167	122	23	0	11	947	11.5	299	65	310	5		9	2	4	6	4	1	0	0

WCJHL All-Star Team (1971)

Traded to **Atlanta** by **Montreal** for Atlanta's 1st round choice (Rick Chartraw) in 1974 Amateur Draft, May 29, 1973. Traded to **Pittsburgh** by **Atlanta** with Bob Paradise for Al McDonough, January 4, 1974. Traded to **Kansas City** by **Pittsburgh** with Steve Durbano and Pittsburgh's 1st round choice (Paul Gardner) in 1976 Amateur Draft for Simon Nolet, Ed Gilbert and Kansas City's 1st round choice (Blair Chapman) in 1976 Amateur Draft, January 9, 1976. Transferred to **Colorado** after **Kansas City** franchise relocated, July 15, 1976. Traded to **Cleveland** by **Colorado** with Rick Jodzio for Ralph Klassen and Fred Ahern, January 9, 1978. Placed on **Minnesota** Reserve List after **Minnesota-Cleveland** Dispersal Draft, June 15, 1978. Traded to **Washington** by **Minnesota** for future considerations, March 12, 1979. Traded to **Minnesota** by **Washington** for cash, April 24, 1979. Traded to **Vancouver** by **Minnesota** for cash, July 19, 1979. • Suffered eventual career-ending knee injury in training camp, September, 1980.

• ARNIEL, Scott

Scott William LW – L. 6'1", 188 lbs. b: Kingston, Ont., 9/17/1962. Winnipeg's 2nd, 22nd overall, in 1981.

Season	Club	League	GP	G	A	Pts	AG	AA	APts	PIM	PP	SH	GW	S	%	TGF	PGF	TGA	PGA	+/–	GP	G	A	Pts	PIM	PP	SH	GW
1978-79	Kingston Voyageurs	OJHL	STATISTICS NOT AVAILABLE																									
	Kingston Canadians	OHL																			3	0	1	1	0			
1979-80	Cornwall Royals	QMJHL	61	22	28	50				51																		
	Cornwall Royals	Mem-Cup	5	0	2	2				2																		
1980-81	Cornwall Royals	QMJHL	68	52	71	123				102											19	14	19	33	24			
	Canada	WJC-A	5	3	1	4				4																		
	Cornwall Royals	Mem-Cup	5	6	2	8				4																		
1981-82	Cornwall Royals	OHL	24	18	26	44				43																		
	Canada	WJC-A	7	5	6	11				4																		
	Winnipeg Jets	**NHL**	17	1	8	9	1	5	6	14	1	0	0	18	5.6	11	2	7	0	2	3	0	0	0	0	0	0	0
1982-83	**Winnipeg Jets**	**NHL**	75	13	5	18	11	3	14	46	1	2	0	92	14.1	28	2	55	13	–16	2	0	0	0	0	0	0	0
1983-84	**Winnipeg Jets**	**NHL**	80	21	35	56	17	24	41	68	6	0	2	140	15.0	89	27	73	1	–10	2	0	0	0	5	0	0	0
1984-85	**Winnipeg Jets**	**NHL**	79	22	22	44	18	15	33	81	3	0	3	142	15.5	74	8	59	0	7	8	1	2	3	9	0	0	1
1985-86	**Winnipeg Jets**	**NHL**	80	18	25	43	14	17	31	40	3	0	0	125	14.4	72	9	73	2	–8	3	0	0	0	12	0	0	0
1986-87	**Buffalo Sabres**	**NHL**	63	11	14	25	9	10	19	59	0	0	3	90	12.2	40	2	65	26	–1								
1987-88	**Buffalo Sabres**	**NHL**	73	17	23	40	14	16	30	61	0	3	2	111	15.3	51	1	82	40	8	6	0	1	1	5	0	0	0
1988-89	**Buffalo Sabres**	**NHL**	80	18	23	41	15	16	31	46	0	2	3	122	14.8	67	4	91	38	10	5	1	0	1	4	0	1	0
1989-90	**Buffalo Sabres**	**NHL**	79	18	14	32	15	10	25	77	1	1	4	123	14.6	55	1	73	23	4	5	1	0	1	4	0	0	0
1990-91	**Winnipeg Jets**	**NHL**	75	5	17	22	5	13	18	87	0	0	1	91	5.5	40	1	67	16	–12								
1991-92	**Boston Bruins**	**NHL**	29	5	3	8	5	2	7	20	0	0	1	34	14.7	14	0	16	7	5								
	Maine Mariners	AHL	14	4	4	8				8																		
	New Haven Nighthawks	AHL	11	3	3	6				10																		
1992-93	San Diego Gulls	IHL	79	35	48	83				116											14	6	5	11	16			
1993-94	San Diego Gulls	IHL	79	34	43	77				121											7	6	3	9	24			
1994-95	Houston Aeros	IHL	72	37	40	77				102											4	1	0	1	10			
1995-96	Houston Aeros	IHL	64	18	28	46				94																		
	Utah Grizzlies	IHL	14	3	3	6				29											22	10	7	17	28			
1996-97	Manitoba Moose	IHL	73	23	27	50				67																		
1997-98	Manitoba Moose	IHL	79	28	42	70				84											3	1	0	1	10			
1998-99	Manitoba Moose	IHL	70	16	35	51				82											5	1	2	3	0			
	NHL Totals		730	149	189	338	124	131	255	599	15	8	19	1088	13.7	541	57	661	166		34	3	3	6	39	0	1	1

Traded to **Buffalo** by **Winnipeg** for Gilles Hamel, June 21, 1986. Traded to **Winnipeg** by **Buffalo** with Phil Housley, Jeff Parker and Buffalo's 1st round choice (Keith Tkachuk) in 1990 Entry Draft for Dale Hawerchuk, Winnipeg's 1st round choice (Brad May) in 1990 Entry Draft and future considerations, June 16, 1990. Traded to **Boston** by **Winnipeg** for future considerations, November 22, 1991. • Officially announced retirement, July 15, 1999.

• ARNOTT, Jason

Jason William C – R. 6'4", 225 lbs. b: Collingwood, Ont., 10/11/1974. Edmonton's 1st, 7th overall, in 1993.

Season	Club	League	GP	G	A	Pts	AG	AA	APts	PIM	PP	SH	GW	S	%	TGF	PGF	TGA	PGA	+/–	GP	G	A	Pts	PIM	PP	SH	GW
1989-90	Stayner Siskins	OJHL-C	34	21	31	52				12																		
1990-91	Lindsay Bears	OJHL-B	42	17	44	61				10											8	9	8	17	6			
1991-92	Oshawa Generals	OHL	57	9	15	24				12																		
1992-93	Oshawa Generals	OHL	56	41	57	98				74											13	9	9	18	20			
1993-94	**Edmonton Oilers**	**NHL**	78	33	35	68	31	27	58	104	10	0	4	194	17.0	93	36	61	5	1								
	Canada	WC-A	8	0	6	6				10																		
1994-95	**Edmonton Oilers**	**NHL**	42	15	22	37	27	33	60	128	7	0	1	156	9.6	55	27	44	2	–14								
1995-96	**Edmonton Oilers**	**NHL**	64	28	31	59	28	25	53	87	8	0	5	244	11.5	89	39	60	4	–6								
1996-97	**Edmonton Oilers**	**NHL**	67	19	38	57	20	34	54	92	10	1	2	248	7.7	91	47	76	11	–21	12	3	6	9	18	1	0	0
1997-98	**Edmonton Oilers**	**NHL**	35	5	13	18	6	13	19	78	1	0	0	100	5.0	26	13	32	3	–16								
	New Jersey Devils	**NHL**	35	5	10	15	6	10	16	21	3	0	2	99	5.1	28	16	20	0	–8	5	0	2	2	0	0	0	0
1998-99	**New Jersey Devils**	**NHL**	74	27	27	54	32	26	58	79	8	0	3	200	13.5	81	31	40	0	10	7	2	2	4	4	1	0	0
99-2000♦	**New Jersey Devils**	**NHL**	76	22	34	56	25	32	57	51	7	0	4	244	9.0	94	32	41	1	22	23	8	12	20	18	3	0	1
	NHL Totals		471	154	210	364	175	200	375	640	54	1	21	1485	10.4	557	241	374	26		47	13	22	35	40	5	0	1

NHL All-Rookie Team (1994) • Played in NHL All-Star Game (1997)

Traded to **New Jersey** by **Edmonton** with Bryan Muir for Valeri Zelepukin and Bill Guerin, January 4, 1998.

• ARTHUR, Fred
Frederick Edward D – L. 6'5", 210 lbs. b: Toronto, Ont., 3/6/1961. Hartford's 1st, 8th overall, in 1980.

Season	Club	League	GP	G	A	Pts	AG	AA	APts	PIM	PP	SH	GW	S	%	TGF	PGF	TGA	PGA	+/–	PO GP	PO G	PO A	PO Pts	PO PIM	PO PP	PO SH	PO GW
			REGULAR SEASON																		PLAYOFFS							
1977-78	Cornwall Royals	QMJHL	68	2	20	22				86																		
1978-79	Cornwall Royals	QMJHL	72	6	64	70				227																		
1979-80	Cornwall Royals	QMJHL	67	5	70	75				105											18	2	12	14	44			
	Cornwall Royals	Mem-Cup	5	0	5	5				13																		
1980-81	Cornwall Royals	QMJHL	36	3	22	25				134											19	1	11	12	45			
	Canada	WJC-A	5	0	2	2				10																		
	Hartford Whalers	**NHL**	**3**	**0**	**0**	**0**	**0**	**0**	**0**	**0**	**0**	**0**	**0**	**3**	**0.0**	**1**	**0**	**6**	**0**	**–5**								
	Cornwall Royals	Mem-Cup	5	0	3	3				10																		
1981-82	**Philadelphia Flyers**	**NHL**	**74**	**1**	**7**	**8**	**1**	**5**	**6**	**47**	**0**	**0**	**0**	**33**	**3.0**	**62**	**1**	**112**	**43**	**–8**	**4**	**0**	**0**	**0**	**2**	**0**	**0**	**0**
1982-83	**Philadelphia Flyers**	**NHL**	**3**	**0**	**1**	**1**	**0**	**1**	**1**	**2**	**0**	**0**	**0**	**1**	**0.0**	**2**	**0**	**3**	**0**	**–1**								
	NHL Totals		**80**	**1**	**8**	**9**	**1**	**6**	**7**	**49**	**0**	**0**	**0**	**37**	**2.7**	**65**	**1**	**121**	**43**		**4**	**0**	**0**	**0**	**2**	**0**	**0**	**0**

QMJHL First All-Star Team (1980) • Memorial Cup All-Star Team (1981)

Traded to **Philadelphia** by **Hartford** with Ray Allison and Hartford's 1st (Ron Sutter) and 3rd (Miroslav Dvorak) round choices in 1982 Entry Draft for Rick MacLeish, Blake Wesley, Don Gillen and Philadelphia's 1st (Paul Lawless), 2nd (Mark Patterson) and 3rd (Kevin Dineen) round choices in 1982 Entry Draft, July 3, 1981. • Officially announced retirement to attend medical school, October 20, 1982.

• ARVEDSSON, Magnus
C – L. 6'2", 198 lbs. b: Karlstad, Swe., 11/25/1971. Ottawa's 4th, 119th overall, in 1997.

Season	Club	League	GP	G	A	Pts	AG	AA	APts	PIM	PP	SH	GW	S	%	TGF	PGF	TGA	PGA	+/–	PO GP	PO G	PO A	PO Pts	PO PIM	PO PP	PO SH	PO GW
1990-91	Orebro IK	Sweden-2	29	7	11	18				12											2	0	1	1	2			
1991-92	Orebro IK	Sweden-2	32	12	21	33				30											7	4	4	8	4			
1992-93	Orebro IK	Sweden-2	36	11	18	29				34											6	2	1	3	0			
1993-94	Farjestads BK Karlstad	Sweden	16	1	7	8				10																		
1994-95	Farjestads BK Karlstad	Sweden-Jr.	1	0	0	0				0																		
	Farjestads BK Karlstad	Sweden	36	1	6	7				45											4	0	0	0	6			
1995-96	Farjestads BK Karlstad	Sweden	40	10	14	24				40											8	0	3	3	10			
1996-97	Farjestads BK Karlstad	Sweden	48	13	11	24				36											14	4	7	11	8			
	Farjestads BK Karlstad	EuroHL	5	1	0	1				2											2	0	1	1	2			
	Sweden	WC-A	10	2	1	3				6																		
1997-98	**Ottawa Senators**	**NHL**	**61**	**11**	**15**	**26**	**13**	**15**	**28**	**36**	**0**	**1**	**0**	**90**	**12.2**	**36**	**2**	**38**	**6**	**2**	**11**	**0**	**1**	**1**	**6**	**0**	**0**	**0**
1998-99	**Ottawa Senators**	**NHL**	**80**	**21**	**26**	**47**	**25**	**25**	**50**	**50**	**0**	**4**	**6**	**136**	**15.4**	**66**	**1**	**54**	**22**	**33**	**3**	**0**	**1**	**1**	**2**	**0**	**0**	**0**
99-2000	**Ottawa Senators**	**NHL**	**47**	**15**	**13**	**28**	**17**	**12**	**29**	**36**	**1**	**1**	**4**	**91**	**16.5**	**37**	**2**	**36**	**5**	**4**	**6**	**0**	**0**	**0**	**6**	**0**	**0**	**0**
	NHL Totals		**188**	**47**	**54**	**101**	**55**	**52**	**107**	**122**	**1**	**6**	**10**	**317**	**14.8**	**139**	**5**	**128**	**33**		**20**	**0**	**2**	**2**	**14**	**0**	**0**	**0**

• ASHAM, Arron
RW – R. 5'11", 194 lbs. b: Portage La Prairie, Man., 4/13/1978. Montreal's 3rd, 71st overall, in 1996.

Season	Club	League	GP	G	A	Pts	AG	AA	APts	PIM	PP	SH	GW	S	%	TGF	PGF	TGA	PGA	+/–	PO GP	PO G	PO A	PO Pts	PO PIM	PO PP	PO SH	PO GW
1993-94	Portage Bantam Terriers	MAHA	21	18	19	37				82																		
1994-95	Red Deer Rebels	WHL	62	11	16	27				126																		
1995-96	Red Deer Rebels	WHL	70	32	45	77				174											10	6	3	9	20			
1996-97	Red Deer Rebels	WHL	67	45	51	96				149											16	12	14	26	36			
1997-98	Red Deer Rebels	WHL	67	43	49	92				153											5	0	2	2	8			
	Fredericton Canadians	AHL	2	1	1	2				0											2	0	1	1	0			
1998-99	**Montreal Canadiens**	**NHL**	**7**	**0**	**0**	**0**	**0**	**0**	**0**	**0**	**0**	**0**	**0**	**5**	**0.0**	**0**	**0**	**4**	**0**	**–4**								
	Fredericton Canadiens	AHL	60	16	18	34				118											13	8	6	14	11			
99-2000	**Montreal Canadiens**	**NHL**	**33**	**4**	**2**	**6**	**4**	**2**	**6**	**24**	**0**	**1**	**1**	**29**	**13.8**	**8**	**1**	**14**	**0**	**–7**								
	Quebec Citadelles	AHL	13	4	5	9				32											2	0	0	0	2			
	NHL Totals		**40**	**4**	**2**	**6**	**4**	**2**	**6**	**24**	**0**	**1**	**1**	**34**	**11.8**	**8**	**1**	**18**	**0**									

• ASHBEE, Barry
William Barry D – R. 5'10", 180 lbs. b: Weston, Ont., 7/28/1939 d: 5/12/1977.

Season	Club	League	GP	G	A	Pts	AG	AA	APts	PIM	PP	SH	GW	S	%	TGF	PGF	TGA	PGA	+/–	PO GP	PO G	PO A	PO Pts	PO PIM	PO PP	PO SH	PO GW
1956-57	Barrie Flyers	OHA-Jr.	34	0	4	4				23											3	0	0	0	0			
1957-58	Lakeshore Bruins	OHA-B	STATISTICS NOT AVAILABLE																									
1958-59	Barrie Flyers	OHA-Jr.	53	8	22	30				108											6	0	3	3	12			
1959-60	Kingston Frontenacs	EPHL	62	2	11	13				72																		
1960-61	Kingston Frontenacs	EPHL	64	4	11	15				75											5	0	0	0	14			
1961-62	North Bay–Kingston	EPHL	35	2	7	9				87																		
1962-63	Hershey Bears	AHL	72	0	17	17				94											15	0	2	2	34			
1963-64	Hershey Bears	AHL	72	3	6	9				142											6	0	0	0	12			
1964-65	Hershey Bears	AHL	66	3	13	16				114											14	0	0	0	22			
1965-66	**Boston Bruins**	**NHL**	**14**	**0**	**3**	**3**	**0**	**3**	**3**	**14**																		
	Hershey Bears	AHL	36	1	10	11				100											3	0	0	0	6			
1966-67	Hershey Bears	AHL	DID NOT PLAY – INJURED																									
1967-68	Hershey Bears	AHL	65	5	15	20				86											5	0	1	1	4			
1968-69	Hershey Bears	AHL	71	5	29	34				130											11	2	5	7	14			
1969-70	Hershey Bears	AHL	72	5	25	30				80											7	0	1	1	24			
1970-71	**Philadelphia Flyers**	**NHL**	**64**	**4**	**23**	**27**	**4**	**19**	**23**	**44**	**2**	**0**	**1**	**99**	**4.0**	**84**	**26**	**70**	**15**	**3**								
1971-72	**Philadelphia Flyers**	**NHL**	**73**	**6**	**14**	**20**	**6**	**12**	**18**	**75**	**2**	**0**	**1**	**104**	**5.8**	**80**	**12**	**87**	**21**	**2**								
1972-73	**Philadelphia Flyers**	**NHL**	**64**	**1**	**17**	**18**	**1**	**13**	**14**	**106**	**0**	**1**	**0**	**61**	**1.6**	**69**	**3**	**92**	**24**	**–2**	**11**	**0**	**4**	**4**	**20**	**0**	**0**	**0**
1973-74♦	**Philadelphia Flyers**	**NHL**	**69**	**4**	**13**	**17**	**4**	**11**	**15**	**52**	**0**	**0**	**0**	**70**	**5.7**	**87**	**8**	**51**	**24**	**52**	**6**	**0**	**0**	**0**	**2**	**0**	**0**	**0**
1974-75	**Philadelphia Flyers**	**NHL**	DID NOT PLAY – ASSISTANT COACH																									
	NHL Totals		**284**	**15**	**70**	**85**	**15**	**58**	**73**	**291**											**17**	**0**	**4**	**4**	**22**			

NHL Second All-Star Team (1974)

Traded to **Detroit** (Hershey-AHL) by **Boston** with Ed Chadwick for Bob Perreault, June, 1962. • Missed entire 1966-67 season recovering from back surgery, September, 1966. Traded to **Philadelphia** by **Pittsburgh** (Hershey-AHL) for Darryl Edestrand and Larry McKillop, May 22, 1970. • Suffered career-ending eye injury in playoff game vs. NY Rangers, April 28, 1974.

• ASHBY, Don
Donald Allan "Ants" C – L. 6'1", 185 lbs. b: Kamloops, B.C., 3/8/1955 d: 5/30/1981. Toronto's 1st, 6th overall, in 1975.

Season	Club	League	GP	G	A	Pts	AG	AA	APts	PIM	PP	SH	GW	S	%	TGF	PGF	TGA	PGA	+/–	PO GP	PO G	PO A	PO Pts	PO PIM	PO PP	PO SH	PO GW
1972-73	Kamloops Rockets	BCJHL	28	22	22	44																						
	Calgary Centennials	WCJHL	36	10	12	22				0											6	0	1	1	0			
1973-74	Calgary Centennials	WCJHL	68	30	38	68				52											14	6	7	13	0			
1974-75	Calgary Centennials	WCJHL	70	52	68	120				71																		
1975-76	**Toronto Maple Leafs**	**NHL**	**50**	**6**	**15**	**21**	**5**	**11**	**16**	**10**	**1**	**0**	**0**	**63**	**9.5**	**31**	**1**	**29**	**4**	**5**								
	Oklahoma City Blazers	CHL	26	9	14	23				36											4	0	1	1	2			
1976-77	**Toronto Maple Leafs**	**NHL**	**76**	**19**	**23**	**42**	**17**	**18**	**35**	**24**	**3**	**0**	**4**	**118**	**16.1**	**58**	**10**	**69**	**7**	**–14**	**9**	**1**	**0**	**1**	**4**	**0**	**0**	**0**
	Dallas Black Hawks	CHL	3	1	0	1				0																		
1977-78	**Toronto Maple Leafs**	**NHL**	**12**	**1**	**2**	**3**	**1**	**2**	**3**	**0**	**0**	**0**	**0**	**8**	**12.5**	**4**	**1**	**7**	**0**	**–4**								
	Dallas Black Hawks	CHL	48	14	28	42				15											13	9	9	18	5			
1978-79	**Toronto Maple Leafs**	**NHL**	**3**	**0**	**0**	**0**	**0**	**0**	**0**	**0**	**0**	**0**	**0**	**2**	**0.0**	**0**	**0**	**3**	**0**	**–3**								
	New Brunswick Hawks	AHL	13	2	5	7				9																		
	Colorado Rockies	**NHL**	**12**	**2**	**3**	**5**	**2**	**2**	**4**	**0**	**2**	**0**	**0**	**24**	**8.3**	**9**	**5**	**7**	**0**	**–3**								
1979-80	**Colorado Rockies**	**NHL**	**11**	**0**	**1**	**1**	**0**	**1**	**1**	**4**	**0**	**0**	**0**	**10**	**0.0**	**4**	**0**	**9**	**3**	**–2**								
	Fort Worth Texans	CHL	45	27	27	54				18																		
	Edmonton Oilers	**NHL**	**18**	**10**	**9**	**19**	**8**	**7**	**15**	**0**	**3**	**0**	**1**	**31**	**32.3**	**28**	**6**	**22**	**1**	**1**	**3**	**0**	**0**	**0**	**0**	**0**	**0**	**0**
1980-81	**Edmonton Oilers**	**NHL**	**6**	**2**	**3**	**5**	**2**	**2**	**4**	**2**	**1**	**0**	**1**	**13**	**15.4**	**6**	**2**	**5**	**0**	**–1**								
	Wichita Wind	CHL	70	36	60	96				46											18	9	16	25	6			
	NHL Totals		**188**	**40**	**56**	**96**	**35**	**43**	**78**	**40**	**10**	**0**	**6**	**269**	**14.9**	**140**	**25**	**151**	**15**		**12**	**1**	**0**	**1**	**4**	**0**	**0**	**0**

CHL First All-Star Team (1981)

• Missed majority of 1978-79 season in retirement. Traded to **Colorado** by **Toronto** with Trevor Johansen for Paul Gardner, March 13, 1979. Traded to **Edmonton** by **Colorado** for Bobby Schmautz, February 25, 1980. • Died of injuries suffered in automobile accident following CHL finals, May 30, 1981.

• ASHTON, Brent

Brent Kenneth LW – L. 6'1", 210 lbs. b: Saskatoon, Sask., 5/18/1960. Vancouver's 2nd, 26th overall, in 1979.

			REGULAR SEASON																		PLAYOFFS							
Season	Club	League	GP	G	A	Pts	AG	AA	APts	PIM	PP	SH	GW	S	%	TGF	PGF	TGA	PGA	+/-	GP	G	A	Pts	PIM	PP	SH	GW
1975-76	Saskatoon Olympics	SJHL	47	40	50	90	....	....	....	....	....	....	....	....	....	....	....	....	....	....	....	....	....	....	....	....	....	....
	Saskatoon Blades	WCJHL	11	3	4	7	....	....	....	11	....	....	....	....	....	....	....	....	....	....	18	1	1	2	5	....	....	....
1976-77	Saskatoon Blades	WCJHL	54	26	25	51	....	....	....	84	....	....	....	....	....	....	....	....	....	....	6	1	2	3	15	....	....	....
1977-78	Saskatoon Blades	WCJHL	46	38	26	64	....	....	....	47	....	....	....	....	....	....	....	....	....	....	....	....	....	....	....	....	....	....
1978-79	Saskatoon Blades	WHL	62	64	55	119	....	....	....	80	....	....	....	....	....	....	....	....	....	....	11	14	4	18	5	....	....	....
1979-80	**Vancouver Canucks**	**NHL**	**47**	**5**	**14**	**19**	**4**	**10**	**14**	**11**	**0**	**0**	**0**	**69**	**7.2**	**36**	**5**	**27**	**0**	**4**	**4**	**1**	**0**	**1**	**6**	**0**	**0**	**0**
1980-81	**Vancouver Canucks**	**NHL**	**77**	**18**	**11**	**29**	**14**	**7**	**21**	**57**	**0**	**0**	**0**	**111**	**16.2**	**46**	**2**	**56**	**2**	**–10**	**3**	**0**	**0**	**0**	**0**	**0**	**0**	**0**
1981-82	**Colorado Rockies**	**NHL**	**80**	**24**	**36**	**60**	**19**	**24**	**43**	**26**	**3**	**0**	**4**	**182**	**13.2**	**89**	**25**	**106**	**11**	**–31**	....	....	....	....	....	....	....	....
1982-83	**New Jersey Devils**	**NHL**	**76**	**14**	**19**	**33**	**11**	**13**	**24**	**47**	**4**	**0**	**1**	**113**	**12.4**	**52**	**10**	**68**	**3**	**–23**	....	....	....	....	....	....	....	....
1983-84	**Minnesota North Stars**	**NHL**	**68**	**7**	**10**	**17**	**6**	**7**	**13**	**54**	**0**	**0**	**0**	**82**	**8.5**	**27**	**0**	**44**	**4**	**–13**	**12**	**1**	**2**	**3**	**22**	**0**	**0**	**0**
1984-85	**Minnesota North Stars**	**NHL**	**29**	**4**	**7**	**11**	**3**	**5**	**8**	**15**	**0**	**0**	**0**	**30**	**13.3**	**15**	**0**	**27**	**13**	**1**	....	....	....	....	....	....	....	....
	Quebec Nordiques	**NHL**	**49**	**27**	**24**	**51**	**22**	**16**	**38**	**38**	**6**	**1**	**2**	**122**	**22.1**	**61**	**14**	**39**	**10**	**18**	**18**	**6**	**4**	**10**	**13**	**1**	**1**	**1**
1985-86	**Quebec Nordiques**	**NHL**	**77**	**26**	**32**	**58**	**21**	**22**	**43**	**64**	**5**	**2**	**5**	**207**	**12.6**	**80**	**14**	**69**	**10**	**7**	**3**	**2**	**1**	**3**	**9**	**0**	**1**	**0**
1986-87	**Quebec Nordiques**	**NHL**	**46**	**25**	**19**	**44**	**22**	**14**	**36**	**17**	**12**	**2**	**1**	**98**	**25.5**	**55**	**26**	**46**	**5**	**–12**	....	....	....	....	....	....	....	....
	Detroit Red Wings	**NHL**	**35**	**15**	**16**	**31**	**13**	**12**	**25**	**22**	**3**	**1**	**3**	**86**	**17.4**	**41**	**16**	**35**	**7**	**–3**	**16**	**4**	**9**	**13**	**6**	**2**	**0**	**0**
1987-88	**Detroit Red Wings**	**NHL**	**73**	**26**	**27**	**53**	**22**	**19**	**41**	**50**	**7**	**2**	**3**	**161**	**16.1**	**81**	**23**	**57**	**9**	**10**	**16**	**7**	**5**	**12**	**10**	**2**	**1**	**0**
1988-89	**Winnipeg Jets**	**NHL**	**75**	**31**	**37**	**68**	**26**	**26**	**52**	**36**	**7**	**1**	**1**	**180**	**17.2**	**109**	**29**	**102**	**17**	**–5**	....	....	....	....	....	....	....	....
	Canada	WEC-A	10	3	3	6	....	....	....	2	....	....	....	....	....	....	....	....	....	....	....	....	....	....	....	....	....	....
1989-90	**Winnipeg Jets**	**NHL**	**79**	**22**	**34**	**56**	**19**	**24**	**43**	**37**	**3**	**0**	**5**	**167**	**13.2**	**80**	**12**	**77**	**13**	**4**	**7**	**3**	**1**	**4**	**2**	**2**	**0**	**1**
1990-91	**Winnipeg Jets**	**NHL**	**61**	**12**	**24**	**36**	**11**	**18**	**29**	**58**	**1**	**0**	**2**	**107**	**11.2**	**50**	**11**	**59**	**10**	**–10**	....	....	....	....	....	....	....	....
1991-92	**Winnipeg Jets**	**NHL**	**7**	**1**	**0**	**1**	**1**	**0**	**1**	**4**	**0**	**0**	**0**	**6**	**16.7**	**4**	**1**	**9**	**3**	**–3**	....	....	....	....	....	....	....	....
	Boston Bruins	**NHL**	**61**	**17**	**22**	**39**	**15**	**17**	**32**	**47**	**6**	**1**	**1**	**124**	**13.7**	**66**	**19**	**58**	**7**	**–4**	....	....	....	....	....	....	....	....
1992-93	**Boston Bruins**	**NHL**	**26**	**2**	**2**	**4**	**2**	**1**	**3**	**11**	**0**	**0**	**0**	**26**	**7.7**	**8**	**0**	**13**	**5**	**0**	....	....	....	....	....	....	....	....
	Providence Bruins	AHL	11	4	8	12	....	....	....	10	....	....	....	....	....	....	....	....	....	....	....	....	....	....	....	....	....	....
	Calgary Flames	**NHL**	**32**	**8**	**11**	**19**	**7**	**8**	**15**	**41**	**0**	**2**	**1**	**58**	**13.8**	**32**	**4**	**23**	**6**	**11**	**6**	**0**	**3**	**3**	**2**	**0**	**0**	**0**
1993-94	Las Vegas Thunder	IHL	16	4	10	14	....	....	....	29	....	....	....	....	....	....	....	....	....	....	....	....	....	....	....	....	....	....
	NHL Totals		**998**	**284**	**345**	**629**	**238**	**243**	**481**	**635**	**57**	**12**	**29**	**1929**	**14.7**	**932**	**211**	**915**	**135**		**85**	**24**	**25**	**49**	**70**	**7**	**3**	**2**

Rights traded to **Winnipeg** by **Vancouver** with Vancouver's 4th round choice (Tom Martin) in 1982 Entry Draft as compensation for Vancouver's signing of free agent Ivan Hlinka, July 15, 1981. Traded to **Colorado** by **Winnipeg** with Winnipeg's 3rd round choice (Dave Kasper) in 1982 Entry Draft for Lucien DeBlois, July 15, 1981. Transferred to **New Jersey** after **Colorado** franchise relocated, June 30, 1982. Traded to **Minnesota** by **New Jersey** for Dave Lewis, October 3, 1983. Traded to **Quebec** by **Minnesota** with Brad Maxwell for Tony McKegney and Bo Berglund, December 14, 1984. Traded to **Detroit** by **Quebec** with Gilbert Delorme and Mark Kumpel for Basil McRae, John Ogrodnick and Doug Shedden, January 17, 1987. Traded to **Winnipeg** by **Detroit** for Paul MacLean, June 13, 1988. Traded to **Boston** by **Winnipeg** for Petri Skriko, October 29, 1991. Traded to **Calgary** by **Boston** for C.J. Young, February 1, 1993. • Suffered career-ending knee injury, November, 1993.

• ASTASHENKO, Kaspars

D – L. 6'2", 183 lbs. b: Riga, Latvia, 2/17/1975. Tampa Bay's 5th, 127th overall, in 1999.

Season	Club	League	GP	G	A	Pts	AG	AA	APts	PIM	PP	SH	GW	S	%	TGF	PGF	TGA	PGA	+/-	GP	G	A	Pts	PIM	PP	SH	GW
1993-94	Pardaugava Riga	CIS	4	0	0	0	....	....	....	10	....	....	....	....	....	....	....	....	....	....	....	....	....	....	....	....	....	....
1994-95	Pardaugava Riga	CIS	25	0	0	0	....	....	....	24	....	....	....	....	....	....	....	....	....	....	....	....	....	....	....	....	....	....
1995-96	CSKA Moscow	CIS	26	0	1	1	....	....	....	10	....	....	....	....	....	....	....	....	....	....	....	....	....	....	....	....	....	....
1996-97	CSKA Moscow	Russia	41	0	0	0	....	....	....	48	....	....	....	....	....	....	....	....	....	....	2	0	1	1	4	....	....	....
1997-98	CSKA Moscow	Russia	25	1	3	4	....	....	....	6	....	....	....	....	....	....	....	....	....	....	....	....	....	....	....	....	....	....
1998-99	Cincinnati Cyclones	IHL	74	3	11	14	....	....	....	166	....	....	....	....	....	....	....	....	....	....	3	0	2	2	6	....	....	....
	Dayton Bombers	ECHL	2	0	1	1	....	....	....	4	....	....	....	....	....	....	....	....	....	....	....	....	....	....	....	....	....	....
99-2000	**Tampa Bay Lightning**	**NHL**	**8**	**0**	**1**	**1**	**0**	**1**	**1**	**4**	**0**	**0**	**0**	**3**	**0.0**	**7**	**0**	**10**	**1**	**–2**	....	....	....	....	....	....	....	....
	Detroit Vipers	IHL	51	1	10	11	....	....	....	86	....	....	....	....	....	....	....	....	....	....	....	....	....	....	....	....	....	....
	Long Beach Ice Dogs	IHL	14	0	3	3	....	....	....	10	....	....	....	....	....	....	....	....	....	....	....	....	....	....	....	....	....	....
	NHL Totals		**8**	**0**	**1**	**1**	**0**	**1**	**1**	**4**	**0**	**0**	**0**	**3**	**0.0**	**7**	**0**	**10**	**1**		....	....	....	....	....	....	....	....

• ASTLEY, Mark

D – L. 5'11", 185 lbs. b: Calgary, Alta., 3/30/1969. Buffalo's 9th, 194th overall, in 1989.

Season	Club	League	GP	G	A	Pts	AG	AA	APts	PIM	PP	SH	GW	S	%	TGF	PGF	TGA	PGA	+/-	GP	G	A	Pts	PIM	PP	SH	GW
1986-87	Calgary Royals	AAHA	STATISTICS NOT AVAILABLE																									
1987-88	Calgary Canucks	AJHL	52	25	39	64	....	....	....	106	....	....	....	....	....	....	....	....	....	....	25	9	12	21	....	....	....	....
1988-89	Lake Superior State	CCHA	42	3	12	15	....	....	....	26	....	....	....	....	....	....	....	....	....	....	....	....	....	....	....	....	....	....
1989-90	Lake Superior State	CCHA	43	7	25	32	....	....	....	29	....	....	....	....	....	....	....	....	....	....	....	....	....	....	....	....	....	....
1990-91	Lake Superior State	CCHA	45	19	27	46	....	....	....	50	....	....	....	....	....	....	....	....	....	....	....	....	....	....	....	....	....	....
1991-92	Lake Superior State	CCHA	39	11	36	47	....	....	....	65	....	....	....	....	....	....	....	....	....	....	....	....	....	....	....	....	....	....
	Canada	Nat-Team	11	2	2	4	....	....	....	6	....	....	....	....	....	....	....	....	....	....	....	....	....	....	....	....	....	....
1992-93	HC Lugano	Switz.	30	10	12	22	....	....	....	57	....	....	....	....	....	....	....	....	....	....	....	....	....	....	....	....	....	....
	Canada	Nat-Team	22	4	14	18	....	....	....	14	....	....	....	....	....	....	....	....	....	....	....	....	....	....	....	....	....	....
1993-94	HC Ambri-Piotta	Switz.	23	5	9	14	....	....	....	17	....	....	....	....	....	....	....	....	....	....	....	....	....	....	....	....	....	....
	Canada	Nat-Team	13	4	8	12	....	....	....	6	....	....	....	....	....	....	....	....	....	....	....	....	....	....	....	....	....	....
	Canada	Olympics	8	0	1	1	....	....	....	4	....	....	....	....	....	....	....	....	....	....	....	....	....	....	....	....	....	....
	Buffalo Sabres	**NHL**	**1**	**0**	**0**	**0**	**0**	**0**	**0**	**0**	**0**	**0**	**0**	**2**	**0.0**	**0**	**0**	**1**	**0**	**–1**	....	....	....	....	....	....	....	....
1994-95	**Buffalo Sabres**	**NHL**	**14**	**2**	**1**	**3**	**4**	**1**	**5**	**12**	**0**	**0**	**0**	**21**	**9.5**	**7**	**2**	**8**	**1**	**–2**	**2**	**0**	**0**	**0**	**0**	**0**	**0**	**0**
	Rochester Americans	AHL	46	5	24	29	....	....	....	49	....	....	....	....	....	....	....	....	....	....	3	0	2	2	2	....	....	....
1995-96	**Buffalo Sabres**	**NHL**	**60**	**2**	**18**	**20**	**2**	**15**	**17**	**80**	**0**	**0**	**0**	**80**	**2.5**	**58**	**17**	**57**	**4**	**–12**	....	....	....	....	....	....	....	....
1996-97	Phoenix Roadrunners	IHL	52	6	11	17	....	....	....	43	....	....	....	....	....	....	....	....	....	....	....	....	....	....	....	....	....	....
1997-98	HC Lugano	Switz.	19	1	5	6	....	....	....	19	....	....	....	....	....	....	....	....	....	....	4	0	1	1	0	....	....	....
1998-99	HC Lugano	Switz.	41	3	2	5	....	....	....	30	....	....	....	....	....	....	....	....	....	....	16	1	3	4	33	....	....	....
99-2000	HC Lugano	Switz.	40	1	13	14	....	....	....	46	....	....	....	....	....	....	....	....	....	....	13	0	5	5	14	....	....	....
	HC Lugano	EuroHL	6	0	1	1	....	....	....	8	....	....	....	....	....	....	....	....	....	....	4	0	0	0	4	....	....	....
	NHL Totals		**75**	**4**	**19**	**23**	**6**	**16**	**22**	**92**	**0**	**0**	**0**	**103**	**3.9**	**65**	**19**	**66**	**5**		**2**	**0**	**0**	**0**	**0**	**0**	**0**	**0**

CCHA Second All-Star Team (1991) • CCHA First All-Star Team (1992) • NCAA West First All-American Team (1992) • NCAA All-Tournament Team (1992)

Signed as a free agent by **LA Kings**, September 6, 1996.

• ATCHEYNUM, Blair

RW – R. 6'2", 198 lbs. b: Estevan, Sask., 4/20/1969. Hartford's 2nd, 52nd overall, in 1989.

Season	Club	League	GP	G	A	Pts	AG	AA	APts	PIM	PP	SH	GW	S	%	TGF	PGF	TGA	PGA	+/-	GP	G	A	Pts	PIM	PP	SH	GW
1984-85	North Battleford Bantam Stars	SAHA	26	25	21	46	....	....	....	106	....	....	....	....	....	....	....	....	....	....	....	....	....	....	....	....	....	....
1985-86	North Battleford North Stars	SJHL	33	16	14	30	....	....	....	41	....	....	....	....	....	....	....	....	....	....	6	2	0	2	6	....	....	....
	Saskatoon Blades	WHL	19	1	4	5	....	....	....	22	....	....	....	....	....	....	....	....	....	....	....	....	....	....	....	....	....	....
1986-87	Saskatoon Blades	WHL	21	0	4	4	....	....	....	4	....	....	....	....	....	....	....	....	....	....	....	....	....	....	....	....	....	....
	Swift Current Broncos	WHL	5	2	1	3	....	....	....	0	....	....	....	....	....	....	....	....	....	....	....	....	....	....	....	....	....	....
	Moose Jaw Warriors	WHL	12	3	0	3	....	....	....	2	....	....	....	....	....	....	....	....	....	....	....	....	....	....	....	....	....	....
1987-88	Moose Jaw Warriors	WHL	60	32	16	48	....	....	....	52	....	....	....	....	....	....	....	....	....	....	....	....	....	....	....	....	....	....
1988-89	Moose Jaw Warriors	WHL	71	70	68	138	....	....	....	70	....	....	....	....	....	....	....	....	....	....	....	....	....	....	....	....	....	....
1989-90	Binghamton Whalers	AHL	78	20	21	41	....	....	....	45	....	....	....	....	....	....	....	....	....	....	7	2	5	7	13	....	....	....
1990-91	Springfield Indians	AHL	72	25	27	52	....	....	....	42	....	....	....	....	....	....	....	....	....	....	13	0	6	6	6	....	....	....
1991-92	Springfield Indians	AHL	62	16	21	37	....	....	....	64	....	....	....	....	....	....	....	....	....	....	6	1	1	2	2	....	....	....
1992-93	**Ottawa Senators**	**NHL**	**4**	**0**	**1**	**1**	**0**	**1**	**1**	**0**	**0**	**0**	**0**	**2**	**0.0**	**1**	**0**	**4**	**0**	**–3**	....	....	....	....	....	....	....	....
	New Haven Senators	AHL	51	16	18	34	....	....	....	47	....	....	....	....	....	....	....	....	....	....	....	....	....	....	....	....	....	....
1993-94	Columbus Chill	ECHL	16	15	12	27	....	....	....	10	....	....	....	....	....	....	....	....	....	....	....	....	....	....	....	....	....	....
	Portland Pirates	AHL	2	0	0	0	....	....	....	0	....	....	....	....	....	....	....	....	....	....	....	....	....	....	....	....	....	....
	Springfield Indians	AHL	40	18	22	40	....	....	....	13	....	....	....	....	....	....	....	....	....	....	6	0	2	2	0	....	....	....
1994-95	Minnesota Moose	IHL	17	4	6	10	....	....	....	7	....	....	....	....	....	....	....	....	....	....	....	....	....	....	....	....	....	....
	Worcester IceCats	AHL	55	17	29	46	....	....	....	26	....	....	....	....	....	....	....	....	....	....	....	....	....	....	....	....	....	....
1995-96	Cape Breton Oilers	AHL	79	30	42	72	....	....	....	65	....	....	....	....	....	....	....	....	....	....	....	....	....	....	....	....	....	....
1996-97	Hershey Bears	AHL	77	42	45	87	....	....	....	57	....	....	....	....	....	....	....	....	....	....	13	6	11	17	6	....	....	....
1997-98	**St. Louis Blues**	**NHL**	**61**	**11**	**15**	**26**	**13**	**15**	**28**	**10**	**0**	**1**	**3**	**103**	**10.7**	**36**	**0**	**46**	**15**	**5**	**10**	**0**	**0**	**0**	**2**	**0**	**0**	**0**

Season	Club	League	GP	G	A	Pts	AG	AA	APts	PIM	PP	SH	GW	S	%	TGF	PGF	TGA	PGA	+/-	GP	G	A	Pts	PIM	PP	SH	GW
			REGULAR SEASON																		PLAYOFFS							
1998-99	**Nashville Predators**	**NHL**	**53**	**8**	**6**	**14**	**9**	**6**	**15**	**16**	**2**	**0**	**1**	**70**	**11.4**	**23**	**8**	**44**	**19**	**-10**	....	....	....	....	....	....	....	....
	St. Louis Blues	**NHL**	**12**	**2**	**2**	**4**	**2**	**2**	**4**	**2**	**0**	**0**	**1**	**23**	**8.7**	**4**	**0**	**4**	**2**	**2**	**13**	**1**	**3**	**4**	**6**	**0**	**0**	**0**
99-2000	**Chicago Blackhawks**	**NHL**	**47**	**5**	**7**	**12**	**6**	**6**	**12**	**6**	**0**	**0**	**0**	**48**	**10.4**	**13**	**0**	**28**	**7**	**-8**	....	....	....	....	....	....	....	....
	NHL Totals		**177**	**26**	**31**	**57**	**30**	**30**	**60**	**34**	**2**	**1**	**5**	**246**	**10.6**	**77**	**8**	**126**	**43**		**23**	**1**	**3**	**4**	**8**	**0**	**0**	**0**

WHL First All-Star Team (1989) • AHL First All-Star Team (1997)

Claimed by **Ottawa** from **Hartford** in Expansion Draft, June 18, 1992. Signed as a free agent by **St. Louis**, September 15, 1997. Claimed by **Nashville** from **St. Louis** in Expansion Draft, June 26, 1998. Traded to **St. Louis** by **Nashville** for St. Louis' 6th round choice (Zbynek Irgl) in 2000 Entry Draft, March 23, 1999. Signed as a free agent by **Chicago**, September 30, 1999.

• ATKINSON, Steve

Steven John RW – R. 5'11", 170 lbs. b: Toronto, Ont., 10/16/1948. Detroit's 1st, 6th overall, in 1966.

Season	Club	League	GP	G	A	Pts	AG	AA	APts	PIM	PP	SH	GW	S	%	TGF	PGF	TGA	PGA	+/-	GP	G	A	Pts	PIM	PP	SH	GW
1964-65	Niagara Falls Flyers	OHA-Jr.	15	1	0	1	....	....	....	0	....	....	....	....	....	....	....	....	....	....	....	....	....	....	....	....	....	....
	Niagara Falls Flyers	Mem-Cup	3	3	2	5	....	....	....	4	....	....	....	....	....	....	....	....	....	....	....	....	....	....	....	....	....	....
1965-66	Niagara Falls Flyers	OHA-Jr.	39	8	7	15	....	....	....	12	....	....	....	....	....	....	....	....	....	....	6	5	2	7	2	....	....	....
1966-67	Niagara Falls Flyers	OHA-Jr.	44	31	35	66	....	....	....	42	....	....	....	....	....	....	....	....	....	....	10	6	5	11	4	....	....	....
1967-68	Niagara Falls Flyers	OHA-Jr.	50	37	36	73	....	....	....	61	....	....	....	....	....	....	....	....	....	....	19	14	10	24	15	....	....	....
	Niagara Falls Flyers	Mem-Cup	10	7	9	16	....	....	....	2	....	....	....	....	....	....	....	....	....	....	....	....	....	....	....	....	....	....
1968-69	**Boston Bruins**	**NHL**	**1**	**0**	**0**	**0**	**0**	**0**	**0**	**0**	**0**	**0**	**0**	**0**	**0.0**	**0**	**0**	**1**	**0**	**-1**	....	....	....	....	....	....	....	....
	Oklahoma City Blazers	CHL	65	40	40	80	....	....	....	62	....	....	....	....	....	....	....	....	....	....	12	4	0	4	13	....	....	....
1969-70	Oklahoma City Blazers	CHL	63	29	23	52	....	....	....	63	....	....	....	....	....	....	....	....	....	....	....	....	....	....	....	....	....	....
1970-71	**Buffalo Sabres**	**NHL**	**57**	**20**	**18**	**38**	**20**	**15**	**35**	**12**	**0**	**1**	**2**	**126**	**15.9**	**55**	**8**	**48**	**2**	**1**	....	....	....	....	....	....	....	....
1971-72	**Buffalo Sabres**	**NHL**	**67**	**14**	**10**	**24**	**14**	**9**	**23**	**26**	**3**	**0**	**0**	**122**	**11.5**	**41**	**9**	**54**	**0**	**-22**	....	....	....	....	....	....	....	....
1972-73	**Buffalo Sabres**	**NHL**	**61**	**9**	**9**	**18**	**8**	**7**	**15**	**36**	**2**	**0**	**1**	**96**	**9.4**	**34**	**6**	**33**	**0**	**-5**	**1**	**0**	**0**	**0**	**0**	**0**	**0**	**0**
1973-74	**Buffalo Sabres**	**NHL**	**70**	**6**	**10**	**16**	**6**	**8**	**14**	**22**	**0**	**0**	**1**	**109**	**5.5**	**31**	**1**	**29**	**0**	**1**	....	....	....	....	....	....	....	....
1974-75	**Washington Capitals**	**NHL**	**46**	**11**	**4**	**15**	**10**	**3**	**13**	**8**	**3**	**2**	**0**	**92**	**12.0**	**26**	**8**	**60**	**16**	**-26**	....	....	....	....	....	....	....	....
	Richmond Robins	AHL	22	11	18	29	....	....	....	6	....	....	....	....	....	....	....	....	....	....	7	1	4	5	15	....	....	....
1975-76	Toronto Toros	WHA	52	2	6	8	....	....	....	22	....	....	....	....	....	....	....	....	....	....	....	....	....	....	....	....	....	....
	Buffalo Norsemen	NAHL	37	30	31	61	....	....	....	38	....	....	....	....	....	....	....	....	....	....	....	....	....	....	....	....	....	....
1976-77	Brantford Alexanders	OHA-Sr.	11	9	13	22	....	....	....	8	....	....	....	....	....	....	....	....	....	....	....	....	....	....	....	....	....	....
	Erie Blades	NAHL	28	18	20	38	....	....	....	19	....	....	....	....	....	....	....	....	....	....	....	....	....	....	....	....	....	....
1977-78	Brantford Alexanders	OHA-Sr.	33	15	28	43	....	....	....	4	....	....	....	....	....	....	....	....	....	....	....	....	....	....	....	....	....	....
	NHL Totals		**302**	**60**	**51**	**111**	**58**	**42**	**100**	**104**	**8**	**3**	**4**	**545**	**11.0**	**187**	**32**	**225**	**18**		**1**	**0**	**0**	**0**	**0**	**0**	**0**	**0**
	Other Major League Totals		52	2	6	8	....	....	....	22	....	....	....	....	....	....	....	....	....	....	....	....	....	....	....	....	....	....

CHL First All-Star Team (1969) • Won Ken McKenzie Trophy (Rookie of the Year - CHL) (1969)

Traded to **Boston** by **Detroit** to complete transaction that sent Leo Boivin and Dean Prentice to Detroit (February 16, 1966), June 6, 1966. Sold to **Hershey** (AHL) by **Boston** for cash, June, 1970. Claimed by **St. Louis** from **Hershey** (AHL) in Intra-League Draft, June 9, 1970. Claimed on waivers by **Buffalo** from **St. Louis**, November 1, 1970. Selected by **Dayton-Houston** (WHA) in 1972 WHA General Player Draft, February 12, 1972. Claimed by **Washington** from **Buffalo** in Expansion Draft, June 12, 1974. WHA rights traded to **Toronto** (WHA) by **Houston** (WHA) for cash, September, 1975.

• ATTWELL, Bob

Robert Allan RW – R. 6', 192 lbs. b: Spokane, WA, 12/26/1959. Colorado's 4th, 106th overall, in 1979.

Season	Club	League	GP	G	A	Pts	AG	AA	APts	PIM	PP	SH	GW	S	%	TGF	PGF	TGA	PGA	+/-	GP	G	A	Pts	PIM	PP	SH	GW
1975-76	Bramalae Blues	OHA-B	50	32	28	60	....	....	....	12	....	....	....	....	....	....	....	....	....	....	....	....	....	....	....	....	....	....
1976-77	Peterborough Petes	OMJHL	64	18	25	43	....	....	....	10	....	....	....	....	....	....	....	....	....	....	4	1	2	3	2	....	....	....
1977-78	Peterborough Petes	OMJHL	68	23	43	66	....	....	....	32	....	....	....	....	....	....	....	....	....	....	21	6	12	18	4	....	....	....
	Peterborough Petes	Mem-Cup	5	1	1	2	....	....	....	0	....	....	....	....	....	....	....	....	....	....	....	....	....	....	....	....	....	....
1978-79	Peterborough Petes	OMJHL	68	32	61	93	....	....	....	39	....	....	....	....	....	....	....	....	....	....	19	8	8	16	8	....	....	....
	Peterborough Petes	Mem-Cup	5	3	0	3	....	....	....	2	....	....	....	....	....	....	....	....	....	....	....	....	....	....	....	....	....	....
1979-80	**Colorado Rockies**	**NHL**	**7**	**1**	**1**	**2**	**1**	**1**	**2**	**0**	**0**	**0**	**0**	**2**	**50.0**	**3**	**0**	**8**	**0**	**-5**	....	....	....	....	....	....	....	....
	Fort Worth Texans	CHL	74	26	35	61	....	....	....	18	....	....	....	....	....	....	....	....	....	....	15	4	5	9	4	....	....	....
1980-81	**Colorado Rockies**	**NHL**	**15**	**0**	**4**	**4**	**0**	**3**	**3**	**0**	**0**	**0**	**0**	**11**	**0.0**	**9**	**0**	**10**	**2**	**1**	....	....	....	....	....	....	....	....
	Fort Worth Texans	CHL	60	13	18	31	....	....	....	30	....	....	....	....	....	....	....	....	....	....	5	1	2	3	0	....	....	....
1981-82	Fort Worth Texans	CHL	79	31	36	67	....	....	....	66	....	....	....	....	....	....	....	....	....	....	....	....	....	....	....	....	....	....
1982-83	Moncton Alpines	AHL	74	14	19	33	....	....	....	31	....	....	....	....	....	....	....	....	....	....	....	....	....	....	....	....	....	....
1983-84	Fort Wayne Komets	IHL	70	25	35	60	....	....	....	22	....	....	....	....	....	....	....	....	....	....	6	1	1	2	0	....	....	....
1984-85	EC Bad Tolz	Germany-2	36	42	18	60	....	....	....	54	....	....	....	....	....	....	....	....	....	....	18	12	11	23	20	....	....	....
1985-86	BSC Preussen Berlin	Germany-2	18	16	12	28	....	....	....	20	....	....	....	....	....	....	....	....	....	....	....	....	....	....	....	....	....	....
1986-87	BSC Preussen Berlin	Germany-2	13	10	8	18	....	....	....	19	....	....	....	....	....	....	....	....	....	....	....	....	....	....	....	....	....	....
1987-88	BSC Preussen Berlin	Germany	23	8	5	13	....	....	....	6	....	....	....	....	....	....	....	....	....	....	....	....	....	....	....	....	....	....
	BSC Preussen Berlin	Germany-Q	12	14	8	22	....	....	....	0	....	....	....	....	....	....	....	....	....	....	....	....	....	....	....	....	....	....
1988-89	Heilbronner EC	Germany-2	36	40	37	77	....	....	....	36	....	....	....	....	....	....	....	....	....	....	13	9	7	16	....	....	....	....
1989-90	Augsberger EV	Germany-2	30	20	21	41	....	....	....	14	....	....	....	....	....	....	....	....	....	....	....	....	....	....	....	....	....	....
	NHL Totals		**22**	**1**	**5**	**6**	**1**	**4**	**5**	**0**	**0**	**0**	**0**	**13**	**7.7**	**12**	**0**	**18**	**2**		....	....	....	....	....	....	....	....

• Son of Ron

Signed as a free agent by **Edmonton**, October 25, 1982.

• ATTWELL, Ron

Ronald Allan RW – R. 6', 185 lbs. b: Humber Summit, Ont., 2/9/1935.

Season	Club	League	GP	G	A	Pts	AG	AA	APts	PIM	PP	SH	GW	S	%	TGF	PGF	TGA	PGA	+/-	GP	G	A	Pts	PIM	PP	SH	GW
1952-53	Montreal Jr. Canadiens	QJHL	9	3	2	5	....	....	....	6	....	....	....	....	....	....	....	....	....	....	3	0	1	1	4	....	....	....
1953-54	Montreal Jr. Canadiens	QJHL	50	15	27	42	....	....	....	17	....	....	....	....	....	....	....	....	....	....	8	1	0	1	4	....	....	....
	Montreal Royals	QHL	1	0	0	0	....	....	....	0	....	....	....	....	....	....	....	....	....	....	....	....	....	....	....	....	....	....
1954-55	Montreal Jr. Canadiens	QJHL	42	14	27	41	....	....	....	35	....	....	....	....	....	....	....	....	....	....	5	2	5	7	8	....	....	....
	Providence Reds	AHL	2	0	1	1	....	....	....	2	....	....	....	....	....	....	....	....	....	....	....	....	....	....	....	....	....	....
1955-56	Providence Reds	AHL	44	7	14	21	....	....	....	23	....	....	....	....	....	....	....	....	....	....	1	0	0	0	2	....	....	....
1956-57	Trois-Rivieres Lions	QHL	67	15	21	36	....	....	....	27	....	....	....	....	....	....	....	....	....	....	4	0	1	1	2	....	....	....
1957-58	Shawinigan Cataracts	QHL	54	12	27	39	....	....	....	29	....	....	....	....	....	....	....	....	....	....	14	*9	8	17	6	....	....	....
	Rochester Americans	AHL	6	1	0	1	....	....	....	2	....	....	....	....	....	....	....	....	....	....	....	....	....	....	....	....	....	....
1958-59	Spokane Comets	WHL	34	7	10	17	....	....	....	4	....	....	....	....	....	....	....	....	....	....	4	1	1	2	4	....	....	....
	Chicoutimi Sagueneens	QHL	25	5	16	21	....	....	....	4	....	....	....	....	....	....	....	....	....	....	....	....	....	....	....	....	....	....
1959-60	Spokane Comets	WHL	70	20	34	54	....	....	....	41	....	....	....	....	....	....	....	....	....	....	....	....	....	....	....	....	....	....
1960-61	Cleveland Barons	AHL	66	23	35	58	....	....	....	37	....	....	....	....	....	....	....	....	....	....	4	2	1	3	0	....	....	....
1961-62	Cleveland Barons	AHL	70	28	55	83	....	....	....	43	....	....	....	....	....	....	....	....	....	....	6	2	2	4	4	....	....	....
1962-63	Quebec Aces	AHL	69	14	28	42	....	....	....	26	....	....	....	....	....	....	....	....	....	....	....	....	....	....	....	....	....	....
1963-64	Cleveland Barons	AHL	72	*30	38	68	....	....	....	32	....	....	....	....	....	....	....	....	....	....	9	1	5	6	2	....	....	....
1964-65	Cleveland Barons	AHL	72	14	49	63	....	....	....	43	....	....	....	....	....	....	....	....	....	....	....	....	....	....	....	....	....	....
1965-66	Cleveland Barons	AHL	68	23	25	48	....	....	....	64	....	....	....	....	....	....	....	....	....	....	4	1	0	1	2	....	....	....
1966-67	Cleveland Barons	AHL	70	24	37	61	....	....	....	46	....	....	....	....	....	....	....	....	....	....	5	1	4	5	10	....	....	....
1967-68	**St. Louis Blues**	**NHL**	**18**	**1**	**7**	**8**	**1**	**7**	**8**	**6**	**1**	**0**	**0**	**31**	**3.2**	**9**	**4**	**14**	**0**	**-9**	....	....	....	....	....	....	....	....
	New York Rangers	**NHL**	**4**	**0**	**0**	**0**	**0**	**0**	**0**	**2**	**0**	**0**	**0**	**0**	**0.0**	**0**	**0**	**0**	**0**	**0**	....	....	....	....	....	....	....	....
	Buffalo Bisons	AHL	35	7	11	18	....	....	....	4	....	....	....	....	....	....	....	....	....	....	5	1	2	3	4	....	....	....
1968-69	Buffalo Bisons	AHL	74	19	41	60	....	....	....	59	....	....	....	....	....	....	....	....	....	....	4	1	1	2	2	....	....	....
1969-70	Buffalo Bisons	AHL	71	9	39	48	....	....	....	28	....	....	....	....	....	....	....	....	....	....	7	2	0	2	2	....	....	....
	Omaha Knights	CHL	....	....	....	....	....	....	....	....	....	....	....	....	....	....	....	....	....	....	1	0	0	0	0	....	....	....
	NHL Totals		**22**	**1**	**7**	**8**	**1**	**7**	**8**	**8**	**1**	**0**	**0**	**31**	**3.2**	**9**	**4**	**14**	**0**		....	....	....	....	....	....	....	....

• Father of Bob

• Suspended for majority of 1952-53 season after CAHA refused to allow Attwell's transfer from **London** (OHA-B) to **Montreal Jr. Canadiens** (QJHL), September 2, 1952. Decision overturned by OHA, February 4, 1953. Traded to **Montreal** by **Cleveland** (AHL) for cash, June 14, 1967. Traded to **St. Louis** by **Montreal** with Pat Quinn for cash, June 14, 1967. Traded to **NY Rangers** by **St. Louis** with Ron Stewart for Red Berenson and Barclay Plager, November 29, 1967.

• AUBIN, Norm

Normand C – L. 6', 185 lbs. b: St. Leonard, Que., 7/26/1960. Toronto's 2nd, 51st overall, in 1979.

Season	Club	League	GP	G	A	Pts	AG	AA	APts	PIM	PP	SH	GW	S	%	TGF	PGF	TGA	PGA	+/-	Playoffs GP	G	A	Pts	PIM	PP	SH	GW
							REGULAR SEASON														PLAYOFFS							
1976-77	Sorel Eperviers	QMJHL	50	25	26	51	....	....	....	32	....	....	....	....	....	....	....	....	....	....	....	....	....	....	....	....	....	....
1977-78	Verdun Eperviers	QMJHL	71	62	73	135	....	....	....	107	....	....	....	....	....	....	....	....	....	....	....	....	....	....	....	....	....	....
1978-79	Verdun Eperviers	QMJHL	70	*80	69	149	....	....	....	84	....	....	....	....	....	....	....	....	....	....	11	14	11	25	8	....	....	....
1979-80	Sorel Eperviers	QMJHL	21	*41	29	70	....	....	....	28	....	....	....	....	....	....	....	....	....	....	....	....	....	....	....	....	....	....
	Sherbrooke Castors	QMJHL	42	*50	60	110	....	....	....	38	....	....	....	....	....	....	....	....	....	....	14	15	16	31	24	....	....	....
1980-81	New Brunswick Hawks	AHL	79	43	46	89	....	....	....	99	....	....	....	....	....	....	....	....	....	....	13	5	6	11	34	....	....	....
1981-82	**Toronto Maple Leafs**	**NHL**	**43**	**14**	**12**	**26**	**11**	**8**	**19**	**22**	**3**	**0**	**1**	**62**	**22.6**	**41**	**9**	**49**	**1**	**–16**	....	....	....	....	....	....	....	....
	Cincinnati Tigers	CHL	31	15	17	32	....	....	....	36	....	....	....	....	....	....	....	....	....	....	....	....	....	....	....	....	....	....
1982-83	**Toronto Maple Leafs**	**NHL**	**26**	**4**	**1**	**5**	**3**	**1**	**4**	**8**	**2**	**0**	**1**	**18**	**22.2**	**8**	**3**	**15**	**1**	**–9**	**1**	**0**	**0**	**0**	**0**	**0**	**0**	**0**
	St. Catharines Saints	AHL	49	31	26	57	....	....	....	40	....	....	....	....	....	....	....	....	....	....	....	....	....	....	....	....	....	....
1983-84	St. Catharines Saints	AHL	80	47	47	94	....	....	....	63	....	....	....	....	....	....	....	....	....	....	7	5	3	8	8	....	....	....
1984-85	Nova Scotia Voyageurs	AHL	48	23	26	49	....	....	....	26	....	....	....	....	....	....	....	....	....	....	6	2	5	7	8	....	....	....
	NHL Totals		**69**	**18**	**13**	**31**	**14**	**9**	**23**	**30**	**5**	**0**	**2**	**80**	**22.5**	**49**	**12**	**64**	**2**		**1**	**0**	**0**	**0**	**0**	**0**	**0**	**0**

QMJHL First All-Star Team (1979)

Signed as a free agent by **Edmonton**, December, 1984.

• AUBIN, Serge

C – L. 6'1", 194 lbs. b: Val d'Or, Que., 2/15/1975. Pittsburgh's 9th, 161st overall, in 1994.

Season	Club	League	GP	G	A	Pts	AG	AA	APts	PIM	PP	SH	GW	S	%	TGF	PGF	TGA	PGA	+/-	Playoffs GP	G	A	Pts	PIM	PP	SH	GW
1990-91	Temiscamingue Forestiers	QAAA	27	2	4	6	....	....	....	10	....	....	....	....	....	....	....	....	....	....	....	....	....	....	....	....	....	....
1991-92	Temiscamingue Forestiers	QAAA	42	28	32	60	....	....	....	36	....	....	....	....	....	....	....	....	....	....	....	....	....	....	....	....	....	....
1992-93	Drummondville Voltigeurs	QMJHL	65	16	34	50	....	....	....	30	....	....	....	....	....	....	....	....	....	....	8	0	1	1	16	....	....	....
1993-94	Granby Bisons	QMJHL	63	42	32	74	....	....	....	80	....	....	....	....	....	....	....	....	....	....	7	2	3	5	8	....	....	....
1994-95	Granby Bisons	QMJHL	60	37	73	110	....	....	....	55	....	....	....	....	....	....	....	....	....	....	11	8	15	23	4	....	....	....
1995-96	Hampton Roads Admirals	ECHL	62	24	62	86	....	....	....	74	....	....	....	....	....	....	....	....	....	....	3	1	4	5	10	....	....	....
	Cleveland Lumberjacks	IHL	2	0	0	0	....	....	....	0	....	....	....	....	....	....	....	....	....	....	2	0	0	0	0	....	....	....
1996-97	Cleveland Lumberjacks	IHL	57	9	16	25	....	....	....	38	....	....	....	....	....	....	....	....	....	....	2	0	0	0	0	....	....	....
1997-98	Syracuse Crunch	AHL	55	6	14	20	....	....	....	57	....	....	....	....	....	....	....	....	....	....	....	....	....	....	....	....	....	....
	Hershey Bears	AHL	5	2	1	3	....	....	....	0	....	....	....	....	....	....	....	....	....	....	7	1	3	4	6	....	....	....
1998-99	Hershey Bears	AHL	64	30	39	69	....	....	....	58	....	....	....	....	....	....	....	....	....	....	3	0	1	1	2	....	....	....
	Colorado Avalanche	**NHL**	**1**	**0**	**0**	**0**	**0**	**0**	**0**	**0**	**0**	**0**	**0**	**1**	**0.0**	**0**	**0**	**0**	**0**	**0**	....	....	....	....	....	....	....	....
99-2000	**Colorado Avalanche**	**NHL**	**15**	**2**	**1**	**3**	**2**	**1**	**3**	**6**	**0**	**0**	**1**	**14**	**14.3**	**3**	**0**	**2**	**0**	**1**	**17**	**0**	**1**	**1**	**6**	**0**	**0**	**0**
	Hershey Bears	AHL	58	42	38	80	....	....	....	56	....	....	....	....	....	....	....	....	....	....	....	....	....	....	....	....	....	....
	NHL Totals		**16**	**2**	**1**	**3**	**2**	**1**	**3**	**6**	**0**	**0**	**1**	**15**	**13.3**	**3**	**0**	**2**	**0**		**17**	**0**	**1**	**1**	**6**	**0**	**0**	**0**

• AHL First All-Star Team (2000)

Signed as a free agent by **Hershey** (AHL), July 24, 1998. Signed as a free agent by **Colorado**, December 22, 1998. Signed as a free agent by **Columbus**, July 11, 2000.

• AUBRY, Pierre

LW – L. 5'10", 170 lbs. b: Cap-de-la-Madeleine, Que., 4/15/1960.

Season	Club	League	GP	G	A	Pts	AG	AA	APts	PIM	PP	SH	GW	S	%	TGF	PGF	TGA	PGA	+/-	Playoffs GP	G	A	Pts	PIM	PP	SH	GW
1977-78	Quebec Remparts	QMJHL	32	18	19	37	....	....	....	19	....	....	....	....	....	....	....	....	....	....	....	....	....	....	....	....	....	....
	Trois-Rivieres Draveurs	QMJHL	41	20	25	45	....	....	....	34	....	....	....	....	....	....	....	....	....	....	....	....	....	....	....	....	....	....
1978-79	Quebec Remparts	QMJHL	7	2	3	5	....	....	....	5	....	....	....	....	....	....	....	....	....	....	....	....	....	....	....	....	....	....
	Trois-Rivieres Draveurs	QMJHL	67	53	45	98	....	....	....	97	....	....	....	....	....	....	....	....	....	....	13	2	5	7	10	....	....	....
	Trois-Rivieres Draveurs	Mem-Cup	4	0	1	1	....	....	....	0	....	....	....	....	....	....	....	....	....	....	....	....	....	....	....	....	....	....
1979-80	Trois-Rivieres Draveurs	QMJHL	72	85	62	147	....	....	....	118	....	....	....	....	....	....	....	....	....	....	7	5	3	8	14	....	....	....
1980-81	**Quebec Nordiques**	**NHL**	**1**	**0**	**0**	**0**	**0**	**0**	**0**	**0**	**0**	**0**	**0**	**0**	**0.0**	**0**	**0**	**0**	**0**	**0**	....	....	....	....	....	....	....	....
	Rochester Americans	AHL	1	0	0	0	....	....	....	0	....	....	....	....	....	....	....	....	....	....	....	....	....	....	....	....	....	....
	Erie Blades	EHL	71	*66	*68	*134	....	....	....	99	....	....	....	....	....	....	....	....	....	....	8	7	8	15	4	....	....	....
1981-82	**Quebec Nordiques**	**NHL**	**62**	**10**	**13**	**23**	**8**	**9**	**17**	**27**	**0**	**1**	**1**	**62**	**16.1**	**34**	**2**	**57**	**16**	**–9**	**15**	**1**	**1**	**2**	**30**	**0**	**0**	**1**
	Fredericton Express	AHL	11	6	5	11	....	....	....	10	....	....	....	....	....	....	....	....	....	....	....	....	....	....	....	....	....	....
1982-83	**Quebec Nordiques**	**NHL**	**77**	**7**	**9**	**16**	**6**	**6**	**12**	**48**	**0**	**0**	**1**	**63**	**11.1**	**26**	**0**	**65**	**33**	**–6**	**2**	**0**	**0**	**0**	**0**	**0**	**0**	**0**
1983-84	**Quebec Nordiques**	**NHL**	**23**	**1**	**1**	**2**	**1**	**1**	**2**	**17**	**0**	**0**	**0**	**9**	**11.1**	**2**	**0**	**7**	**2**	**–3**	....	....	....	....	....	....	....	....
	Fredericton Express	AHL	12	4	5	9	....	....	....	4	....	....	....	....	....	....	....	....	....	....	....	....	....	....	....	....	....	....
	Detroit Red Wings	**NHL**	**14**	**4**	**1**	**5**	**3**	**1**	**4**	**8**	**0**	**0**	**0**	**13**	**30.8**	**6**	**0**	**7**	**0**	**–1**	**3**	**0**	**0**	**0**	**2**	**0**	**0**	**0**
1984-85	**Detroit Red Wings**	**NHL**	**25**	**2**	**2**	**4**	**2**	**1**	**3**	**33**	**0**	**0**	**0**	**21**	**9.5**	**5**	**0**	**6**	**0**	**–1**	....	....	....	....	....	....	....	....
	Adirondack Red Wings	AHL	29	13	10	23	....	....	....	74	....	....	....	....	....	....	....	....	....	....	....	....	....	....	....	....	....	....
1985-86	Adirondack Red Wings	AHL	66	28	31	59	....	....	....	124	....	....	....	....	....	....	....	....	....	....	16	*11	4	15	20	....	....	....
1986-87	HC Chamonix	France	STATISTICS NOT AVAILABLE																									
	Adirondack Red Wings	AHL	17	3	7	10	....	....	....	23	....	....	....	....	....	....	....	....	....	....	9	1	3	4	32	....	....	....
1987-88	HC Chamonix	France	19	10	21	31	....	....	....	38	....	....	....	....	....	....	....	....	....	....	....	....	....	....	....	....	....	....
	HC Fassa	Italy	17	28	18	46	....	....	....	18	....	....	....	....	....	....	....	....	....	....	....	....	....	....	....	....	....	....
1988-89	HC Geneve-Servette	Switz-2	STATISTICS NOT AVAILABLE																									
1989-90	ASG Tours	France	32	31	35	66	....	....	....	100	....	....	....	....	....	....	....	....	....	....	....	....	....	....	....	....	....	....
1990-91	ASG Tours	France	14	5	12	17	....	....	....	62	....	....	....	....	....	....	....	....	....	....	3	2	2	4	18	....	....	....
1991-1993	Victoriaville Tigres	QMJHL	DID NOT PLAY – COACHING																									
1993-1995	Val-d'Or Foreurs	QMJHL	DID NOT PLAY – COACHING																									
1995-1997			OUT OF HOCKEY – RETIRED																									
1997-98	Asbestos Azteques	QSPHL	5	0	5	5				10																		
	NHL Totals		**202**	**24**	**26**	**50**	**20**	**18**	**38**	**133**	**0**	**1**	**2**	**168**	**14.3**	**73**	**2**	**142**	**51**		**20**	**1**	**1**	**2**	**32**	**0**	**0**	**1**

QMJHL Second All-Star Team (1980)

Signed as a free agent by **Quebec**, October 10, 1980. Traded to **Detroit** by **Quebec** for cash, February 29, 1984.

• AUCOIN, Adrian

D – R. 6'2", 210 lbs. b: Ottawa, Ont., 7/3/1973. Vancouver's 7th, 117th overall, in 1992.

Season	Club	League	GP	G	A	Pts	AG	AA	APts	PIM	PP	SH	GW	S	%	TGF	PGF	TGA	PGA	+/-	Playoffs GP	G	A	Pts	PIM	PP	SH	GW
1989-90	Nepean Raiders	OJHL	54	2	14	16	....	....	....	95	....	....	....	....	....	....	....	....	....	....	4	0	1	1	....	....	....	....
1990-91	Nepean Raiders	OJHL	56	17	33	50	....	....	....	125	....	....	....	....	....	....	....	....	....	....	....	....	....	....	....	....	....	....
1991-92	Boston University	H-East	32	2	10	12	....	....	....	60	....	....	....	....	....	....	....	....	....	....	....	....	....	....	....	....	....	....
1992-93	Canada	Nat-Team	42	8	10	18	....	....	....	71	....	....	....	....	....	....	....	....	....	....	....	....	....	....	....	....	....	....
	Canada	WJC-A	7	0	1	1	....	....	....	8	....	....	....	....	....	....	....	....	....	....	....	....	....	....	....	....	....	....
1993-94	Canada	Nat-Team	59	5	12	17	....	....	....	80	....	....	....	....	....	....	....	....	....	....	....	....	....	....	....	....	....	....
	Canada	Olympics	4	0	0	0	....	....	....	2	....	....	....	....	....	....	....	....	....	....	....	....	....	....	....	....	....	....
	Hamilton Canucks	AHL	13	1	2	3	....	....	....	19	....	....	....	....	....	....	....	....	....	....	4	0	2	2	6	....	....	....
1994-95	**Vancouver Canucks**	**NHL**	**1**	**1**	**0**	**1**	**2**	**0**	**2**	**0**	**0**	**0**	**0**	**2**	**50.0**	**1**	**0**	**0**	**0**	**1**	**4**	**1**	**0**	**1**	**0**	**1**	**0**	**0**
	Syracuse Crunch	AHL	71	13	18	31	....	....	....	52	....	....	....	....	....	....	....	....	....	....	....	....	....	....	....	....	....	....
1995-96	**Vancouver Canucks**	**NHL**	**49**	**4**	**14**	**18**	**4**	**11**	**15**	**34**	**2**	**0**	**0**	**85**	**4.7**	**56**	**15**	**37**	**4**	**8**	**6**	**0**	**0**	**0**	**2**	**0**	**0**	**0**
	Syracuse Crunch	AHL	29	5	13	18	....	....	....	47	....	....	....	....	....	....	....	....	....	....	....	....	....	....	....	....	....	....
1996-97	**Vancouver Canucks**	**NHL**	**70**	**5**	**16**	**21**	**5**	**14**	**19**	**63**	**1**	**0**	**0**	**116**	**4.3**	**72**	**9**	**74**	**11**	**0**	....	....	....	....	....	....	....	....
1997-98	**Vancouver Canucks**	**NHL**	**35**	**3**	**3**	**6**	**4**	**3**	**7**	**21**	**1**	**0**	**1**	**44**	**6.8**	**17**	**6**	**21**	**6**	**–4**	....	....	....	....	....	....	....	....
1998-99	**Vancouver Canucks**	**NHL**	**82**	**23**	**11**	**34**	**27**	**11**	**38**	**77**	**18**	**2**	**3**	**174**	**13.2**	**100**	**46**	**93**	**25**	**–14**	....	....	....	....	....	....	....	....
99-2000	Canada	Nat-Team	2	0	0	0	....	....	....	2	....	....	....	....	....	....	....	....	....	....	....	....	....	....	....	....	....	....
	Vancouver Canucks	**NHL**	**57**	**10**	**14**	**24**	**11**	**13**	**24**	**30**	**4**	**0**	**1**	**126**	**7.9**	**59**	**19**	**46**	**13**	**7**	....	....	....	....	....	....	....	....
	Canada	WC-A	9	3	3	6	....	....	....	14	....	....	....	....	....	....	....	....	....	....	....	....	....	....	....	....	....	....
	NHL Totals		**294**	**46**	**58**	**104**	**53**	**52**	**105**	**225**	**26**	**2**	**5**	**547**	**8.4**	**305**	**95**	**271**	**59**		**10**	**1**	**0**	**1**	**2**	**1**	**0**	**0**

• Missed majority of 1997-98 season recovering from ankle injury suffered in game vs. Anaheim (October 4, 1997) and groin injury suffered in game vs. Pittsburgh, November 1, 1997.

• AUDET, Philippe

LW – L. 6'2", 175 lbs. b: Ottawa, Ont., 6/4/1977. Detroit's 2nd, 52nd overall, in 1995.

			REGULAR SEASON																		PLAYOFFS							
Season	Club	League	GP	G	A	Pts	AG	AA	APts	PIM	PP	SH	GW	S	%	TGF	PGF	TGA	PGA	+/-	GP	G	A	Pts	PIM	PP	SH	GW
1992-93	Beauce-Amiante	QAAA	28	21	24	45	....	....	....	75	....	....	....	....	....	....	....	....	....	....	....	....	....	....	....	....	....	....
1993-94	Trois-Rivieres Estacades	QAAA	34	22	21	43	....	....	....	90	....	....	....	....	....	....	....	....	....	....	....	....	....	....	....	....	....	....
1994-95	Granby Bisons	QMJHL	62	19	17	36	....	....	....	93	....	....	....	....	....	....	....	....	....	....	13	2	5	7	10	....	....	....
1995-96	Granby Bisons	QMJHL	67	40	43	83	....	....	....	162	....	....	....	....	....	....	....	....	....	....	21	12	18	30	32	....	....	....
	Granby Bisons	Mem-Cup	4	*4	4	*8	....	....	....	10	....	....	....	....	....	....	....	....	....	....	....	....	....	....	....	....	....	....
1996-97	Granby Bisons	QMJHL	67	52	56	108	....	....	....	138	....	....	....	....	....	....	....	....	....	....	4	4	1	5	35	....	....	....
	Adirondack Red Wings	AHL	3	1	1	2	....	....	....	0	....	....	....	....	....	....	....	....	....	....	1	1	0	1	0	....	....	....
1997-98	Adirondack Red Wings	AHL	50	7	8	15	....	....	....	43	....	....	....	....	....	....	....	....	....	....	1	0	0	0	0	....	....	....
1998-99	**Detroit Red Wings**	**NHL**	**4**	**0**	**0**	**0**	**0**	**0**	**0**	**0**	**0**	**0**	**0**	**3**	**0.0**	**0**	**0**	**2**	**0**	**–2**	....	....	....	....	....	....	....	....
	Adirondack Red Wings	AHL	70	20	20	40	....	....	....	77	....	....	....	....	....	....	....	....	....	....	2	1	0	1	4	....	....	....
99-2000	Cincinnati Mighty Ducks	AHL	62	19	22	41	....	....	....	115	....	....	....	....	....	....	....	....	....	....	....	....	....	....	....	....	....	....
	Springfield Falcons	AHL	14	3	7	10	....	....	....	6	....	....	....	....	....	....	....	....	....	....	5	3	1	4	14	....	....	....
	NHL Totals		**4**	**0**	**0**	**0**	**0**	**0**	**0**	**0**	**0**	**0**	**0**	**3**	**0.0**	**0**	**0**	**2**	**0**		....	....	....	....	....	....	....	....

Memorial Cup All-Star Team (1996) • QMJHL First All-Star Team (1997)

Traded to **Phoenix** by **Detroit** for Todd Gill, March 13, 2000.

• AUDETTE, Donald

RW – R. 5'8", 190 lbs. b: Laval, Que., 9/23/1969. Buffalo's 8th, 183rd overall, in 1989.

Season	Club	League	GP	G	A	Pts	AG	AA	APts	PIM	PP	SH	GW	S	%	TGF	PGF	TGA	PGA	+/-	GP	G	A	Pts	PIM	PP	SH	GW
1985-86	Laval Laurentides	QAAA	41	32	38	70	....	....	....	....	....	....	....	....	....	....	....	....	....	....	....	....	....	....	....	....	....	....
1986-87	Laval Titan	QMJHL	66	17	22	39	....	....	....	36	....	....	....	....	....	....	....	....	....	....	14	2	6	8	10	....	....	....
1987-88	Laval Titan	QMJHL	63	48	61	109	....	....	....	56	....	....	....	....	....	....	....	....	....	....	14	7	12	19	20	....	....	....
1988-89	Laval Titan	QMJHL	70	76	85	161	....	....	....	123	....	....	....	....	....	....	....	....	....	....	17	17	12	29	43	....	....	....
	Laval Titan	Mem-Cup	4	3	6	9	....	....	....	6	....	....	....	....	....	....	....	....	....	....	....	....	....	....	....	....	....	....
1989-90	Rochester Americans	AHL	70	42	46	88	....	....	....	78	....	....	....	....	....	....	....	....	....	....	15	9	8	17	29	....	....	....
	Buffalo Sabres	**NHL**	....	....	....	....	....	....	....	....	....	....	....	....	....	....	....	....	....	....	**2**	**0**	**0**	**0**	**0**	**0**	**0**	**0**
1990-91	**Buffalo Sabres**	**NHL**	**8**	**4**	**3**	**7**	**4**	**2**	**6**	**4**	**2**	**0**	**1**	**17**	**23.5**	**8**	**2**	**7**	**0**	**–1**	....	....	....	....	....	....	....	....
	Rochester Americans	AHL	5	4	0	4	....	....	....	2	....	....	....	....	....	....	....	....	....	....	....	....	....	....	....	....	....	....
1991-92	**Buffalo Sabres**	**NHL**	**63**	**31**	**17**	**48**	**28**	**13**	**41**	**75**	**5**	**0**	**6**	**153**	**20.3**	**69**	**20**	**50**	**0**	**–1**	....	....	....	....	....	....	....	....
1992-93	**Buffalo Sabres**	**NHL**	**44**	**12**	**7**	**19**	**10**	**5**	**15**	**51**	**2**	**0**	**0**	**92**	**13.0**	**30**	**4**	**34**	**0**	**–8**	**8**	**2**	**2**	**4**	**6**	**0**	**0**	**0**
	Rochester Americans	AHL	6	8	4	12	....	....	....	10	....	....	....	....	....	....	....	....	....	....	....	....	....	....	....	....	....	....
1993-94	**Buffalo Sabres**	**NHL**	**77**	**29**	**30**	**59**	**27**	**23**	**50**	**41**	**16**	**1**	**4**	**207**	**14.0**	**78**	**35**	**41**	**0**	**2**	**7**	**0**	**1**	**1**	**6**	**0**	**0**	**0**
1994-95	**Buffalo Sabres**	**NHL**	**46**	**24**	**13**	**37**	**43**	**19**	**62**	**27**	**13**	**0**	**7**	**124**	**19.4**	**52**	**30**	**25**	**0**	**–3**	**5**	**1**	**1**	**2**	**4**	**1**	**0**	**0**
1995-96	**Buffalo Sabres**	**NHL**	**23**	**12**	**13**	**25**	**12**	**11**	**23**	**18**	**8**	**0**	**1**	**92**	**13.0**	**33**	**20**	**13**	**0**	**0**	....	....	....	....	....	....	....	....
1996-97	**Buffalo Sabres**	**NHL**	**73**	**28**	**22**	**50**	**30**	**20**	**50**	**48**	**8**	**0**	**5**	**182**	**15.4**	**65**	**20**	**51**	**0**	**–6**	**11**	**4**	**5**	**9**	**6**	**3**	**0**	**0**
1997-98	**Buffalo Sabres**	**NHL**	**75**	**24**	**20**	**44**	**28**	**20**	**48**	**59**	**10**	**0**	**5**	**198**	**12.1**	**68**	**26**	**33**	**1**	**10**	**15**	**5**	**8**	**13**	**10**	**3**	**0**	**2**
1998-99	**Los Angeles Kings**	**NHL**	**49**	**18**	**18**	**36**	**21**	**17**	**38**	**51**	**6**	**0**	**2**	**152**	**11.8**	**57**	**20**	**31**	**1**	**7**	....	....	....	....	....	....	....	....
99-2000	**Los Angeles Kings**	**NHL**	**49**	**12**	**20**	**32**	**13**	**19**	**32**	**45**	**1**	**0**	**3**	**112**	**10.7**	**50**	**15**	**30**	**1**	**6**	....	....	....	....	....	....	....	....
	Atlanta Thrashers	**NHL**	**14**	**7**	**4**	**11**	**8**	**4**	**12**	**12**	**0**	**1**	**1**	**50**	**14.0**	**15**	**6**	**19**	**6**	**–4**	....	....	....	....	....	....	....	....
	NHL Totals		**521**	**201**	**167**	**368**	**224**	**153**	**377**	**431**	**71**	**2**	**35**	**1379**	**14.6**	**525**	**198**	**334**	**9**		**48**	**12**	**17**	**29**	**32**	**7**	**0**	**2**

QMJHL First All-Star Team (1989) • AHL First All-Star Team (1990) • Won Dudley "Red" Garret Memorial Trophy (Top Rookie - AHL) (1990)

Traded to **Los Angeles** by **Buffalo** for Los Angeles' 2nd round choice (Milan Bartovic) in 1999 Entry Draft, December 18, 1998. Traded to **Atlanta** by **Los Angeles** with Frantisek Kaberle for Kelly Buchberger and Nelson Emerson, March 13, 2000.

• AUGE, Les

D – L. 6'1", 190 lbs. b: St. Paul, MN, 5/16/1953.

Season	Club	League	GP	G	A	Pts	AG	AA	APts	PIM	PP	SH	GW	S	%	TGF	PGF	TGA	PGA	+/-	GP	G	A	Pts	PIM	PP	SH	GW
1971-72	University of Minnesota	WCHA	22	2	14	16	....	....	....	8	....	....	....	....	....	....	....	....	....	....	....	....	....	....	....	....	....	....
1972-73	University of Minnesota	WCHA	28	3	20	23	....	....	....	28	....	....	....	....	....	....	....	....	....	....	....	....	....	....	....	....	....	....
1973-74	University of Minnesota	WCHA	28	7	25	32	....	....	....	36	....	....	....	....	....	....	....	....	....	....	....	....	....	....	....	....	....	....
1974-75	University of Minnesota	WCHA	38	6	20	26	....	....	....	52	....	....	....	....	....	....	....	....	....	....	....	....	....	....	....	....	....	....
1975-76	Rochester Americans	AHL	10	0	3	3	....	....	....	6	....	....	....	....	....	....	....	....	....	....	....	....	....	....	....	....	....	....
	Dayton Gems	IHL	65	11	29	40	....	....	....	59	....	....	....	....	....	....	....	....	....	....	15	1	6	7	10	....	....	....
1976-77	Dayton Gems	IHL	29	3	8	11	....	....	....	34	....	....	....	....	....	....	....	....	....	....	....	....	....	....	....	....	....	....
	Rochester Americans	AHL	10	0	3	3	....	....	....	6	....	....	....	....	....	....	....	....	....	....	....	....	....	....	....	....	....	....
1977-78	Hershey Bears	AHL	2	0	0	0	....	....	....	0	....	....	....	....	....	....	....	....	....	....	....	....	....	....	....	....	....	....
	Port Huron Flags	IHL	78	3	37	40	....	....	....	104	....	....	....	....	....	....	....	....	....	....	17	2	13	15	20	....	....	....
1978-79	Oklahoma City Stars	CHL	70	4	14	18	....	....	....	42	....	....	....	....	....	....	....	....	....	....	....	....	....	....	....	....	....	....
	United States	WEC-A	8	1	0	1	....	....	....	4	....	....	....	....	....	....	....	....	....	....	....	....	....	....	....	....	....	....
1979-80	United States	Nat-Team	29	0	14	14	....	....	....	14	....	....	....	....	....	....	....	....	....	....	....	....	....	....	....	....	....	....
	Hershey Bears	AHL	4	0	0	0	....	....	....	0	....	....	....	....	....	....	....	....	....	....	....	....	....	....	....	....	....	....
	Fort Worth Texans	CHL	50	6	24	30	....	....	....	26	....	....	....	....	....	....	....	....	....	....	15	1	3	4	2	....	....	....
1980-81	**Colorado Rockies**	**NHL**	**6**	**0**	**3**	**3**	**0**	**2**	**2**	**4**	**0**	**0**	**0**	**3**	**0.0**	**7**	**1**	**9**	**0**	**–3**	....	....	....	....	....	....	....	....
	Fort Worth Texans	CHL	70	6	17	23	....	....	....	56	....	....	....	....	....	....	....	....	....	....	5	0	3	3	4	....	....	....
1981-82	Fort Worth Texans	CHL	20	0	8	8	....	....	....	26	....	....	....	....	....	....	....	....	....	....	....	....	....	....	....	....	....	....
	NHL Totals		**6**	**0**	**3**	**3**	**0**	**2**	**2**	**4**	**0**	**0**	**0**	**3**	**0.0**	**7**	**1**	**9**	**0**		....	....	....	....	....	....	....	....

NCAA Championship All-Tournament Team (1974) • WCHA Second All-Star Team (1975) • NCAA West First All-American Team (1975)

Signed as a free agent by **Colorado**, July 15, 1979.

• AUGUSTA, Patrik

RW – L. 5'10", 170 lbs. b: Jihlava, Czech., 11/13/1969. Toronto's 8th, 149th overall, in 1992.

Season	Club	League	GP	G	A	Pts	AG	AA	APts	PIM	PP	SH	GW	S	%	TGF	PGF	TGA	PGA	+/-	GP	G	A	Pts	PIM	PP	SH	GW
1988-89	Dukla Jihlava	Czech.	15	3	1	4	....	....	....	4	....	....	....	....	....	....	....	....	....	....	....	....	....	....	....	....	....	....
1989-90	Dukla Jihlava	Czech.	39	9	11	20	....	....	....	....	....	....	....	....	....	....	....	....	....	....	7	3	1	4	....	....	....	....
1990-91	Dukla Jihlava	Czech.	51	20	23	43	....	....	....	....	....	....	....	....	....	....	....	....	....	....	....	....	....	....	....	....	....	....
1991-92	Dukla Jihlava	Czech.	42	16	16	32	....	....	....	26	....	....	....	....	....	....	....	....	....	....	....	....	....	....	....	....	....	....
	Czechoslovakia	Olympics	8	3	2	5	....	....	....	0	....	....	....	....	....	....	....	....	....	....	....	....	....	....	....	....	....	....
	Czechoslovakia	WC-A	5	2	2	4	....	....	....	4	....	....	....	....	....	....	....	....	....	....	....	....	....	....	....	....	....	....
1992-93	St. John's Maple Leafs	AHL	75	32	45	77	....	....	....	74	....	....	....	....	....	....	....	....	....	....	8	3	3	6	23	....	....	....
1993-94	**Toronto Maple Leafs**	**NHL**	**2**	**0**	**0**	**0**	**0**	**0**	**0**	**0**	**0**	**0**	**0**	**3**	**0.0**	**0**	**0**	**0**	**0**	**0**	....	....	....	....	....	....	....	....
	St. John's Maple Leafs	AHL	77	*53	43	96	....	....	....	105	....	....	....	....	....	....	....	....	....	....	11	4	8	12	4	....	....	....
1994-95	St. John's Maple Leafs	AHL	71	37	32	69	....	....	....	98	....	....	....	....	....	....	....	....	....	....	4	2	0	2	7	....	....	....
1995-96	Los Angeles Ice Dogs	IHL	79	34	51	85	....	....	....	83	....	....	....	....	....	....	....	....	....	....	....	....	....	....	....	....	....	....
1996-97	Long Beach Ice Dogs	IHL	82	45	42	87	....	....	....	96	....	....	....	....	....	....	....	....	....	....	18	4	4	8	33	....	....	....
1997-98	Long Beach Ice Dogs	IHL	82	41	40	81	....	....	....	84	....	....	....	....	....	....	....	....	....	....	17	11	7	18	20	....	....	....
1998-99	Long Beach Ice Dogs	IHL	68	24	35	59	....	....	....	125	....	....	....	....	....	....	....	....	....	....	8	4	6	10	4	....	....	....
	Washington Capitals	**NHL**	**2**	**0**	**0**	**0**	**0**	**0**	**0**	**0**	**0**	**0**	**0**	**4**	**0.0**	**0**	**0**	**0**	**0**	**0**	....	....	....	....	....	....	....	....
99-2000	Schwenningen Wild Wings	Germany	34	14	15	29	....	....	....	52	....	....	....	....	....	....	....	....	....	....	....	....	....	....	....	....	....	....
	NHL Totals		**4**	**0**	**0**	**0**	**0**	**0**	**0**	**0**	**0**	**0**	**0**	**7**	**0.0**	**0**	**0**	**0**	**0**		....	....	....	....	....	....	....	....

AHL Second All-Star Team (1994) • IHL Second All-Star Team (1997)

Signed as a free agent by **Washington**, December 11, 1998.

• AWREY, Don

Donald William D – L. 6', 175 lbs. b: Kitchener, Ont., 7/18/1943.

Season	Club	League	GP	G	A	Pts	AG	AA	APts	PIM	PP	SH	GW	S	%	TGF	PGF	TGA	PGA	+/-	GP	G	A	Pts	PIM	PP	SH	GW
1960-61	Waterloo Siskins	OHA-B	STATISTICS NOT AVAILABLE																									
	Niagara Falls Flyers	OHA-Jr.	3	0	0	0	....	....	....	11	....	....	....	....	....	....	....	....	....	....	....	....	....	....	....	....	....	....
1961-62	Niagara Falls Flyers	OHA-Jr.	41	6	12	18	....	....	....	90	....	....	....	....	....	....	....	....	....	....	10	0	3	3	15	....	....	....
1962-63	Niagara Falls Flyers	OHA-Jr.	50	7	23	30	....	....	....	111	....	....	....	....	....	....	....	....	....	....	9	4	9	13	*29	....	....	....
	Niagara Falls Flyers	Mem-Cup	16	4	8	12	....	....	....	58	....	....	....	....	....	....	....	....	....	....	....	....	....	....	....	....	....	....
1963-64	**Boston Bruins**	**NHL**	**16**	**1**	**0**	**1**	**1**	**0**	**1**	**4**	....	....	....	....	....	....	....	....	....	....	....	....	....	....	....	....	....	....
	Minneapolis Bruins	CPHL	54	4	15	19	....	....	....	136	....	....	....	....	....	....	....	....	....	....	5	0	0	0	9	....	....	....
1964-65	**Boston Bruins**	**NHL**	**47**	**2**	**3**	**5**	**2**	**3**	**5**	**41**	....	....	....	....	....	....	....	....	....	....	....	....	....	....	....	....	....	....
	Hershey Bears	AHL	23	2	4	6	....	....	....	38	....	....	....	....	....	....	....	....	....	....	15	0	1	1	29	....	....	....

			REGULAR SEASON																		PLAYOFFS							
Season	Club	League	GP	G	A	Pts	AG	AA	APts	PIM	PP	SH	GW	S	%	TGF	PGF	TGA	PGA	+/–	GP	G	A	Pts	PIM	PP	SH	GW
1965-66	**Boston Bruins**	**NHL**	**70**	**4**	**3**	**7**	**4**	**3**	**7**	**74**	....	....	....	....	....	....	....	....	....	....	....	....	....	....	....	....	....	....
1966-67	**Boston Bruins**	**NHL**	**4**	**1**	**0**	**1**	**1**	**0**	**1**	**6**	....	....	....	....	....	....	....	....	....	....	....	....	....	....	....	....	....	....
	Hershey Bears	AHL	63	1	13	14	....	....	....	153	....	....	....	....	....	....	....	....	....	....	5	0	0	0	19	....	....	....
1967-68	**Boston Bruins**	**NHL**	**74**	**3**	**12**	**15**	**3**	**12**	**15**	**150**	**0**	**0**	**0**	**92**	**3.3**	**95**	**2**	**104**	**29**	**18**	**4**	**0**	**1**	**1**	**4**	**0**	**0**	**0**
1968-69	**Boston Bruins**	**NHL**	**73**	**0**	**13**	**13**	**0**	**12**	**12**	**149**	**0**	**0**	**0**	**72**	**0.0**	**104**	**3**	**98**	**22**	**25**	**10**	**0**	**1**	**1**	**28**	**0**	**0**	**0**
1969-70♦	**Boston Bruins**	**NHL**	**73**	**3**	**10**	**13**	**3**	**9**	**12**	**120**	**0**	**0**	**0**	**96**	**3.1**	**85**	**0**	**100**	**42**	**27**	**14**	**0**	**5**	**5**	**32**	**0**	**0**	**0**
1970-71	**Boston Bruins**	**NHL**	**74**	**4**	**21**	**25**	**4**	**18**	**22**	**141**	**0**	**0**	**1**	**108**	**3.7**	**116**	**2**	**87**	**13**	**40**	**7**	**0**	**0**	**0**	**17**	**0**	**0**	**0**
1971-72♦	**Boston Bruins**	**NHL**	**34**	**1**	**8**	**9**	**1**	**7**	**8**	**52**	**0**	**0**	**0**	**53**	**1.9**	**57**	**2**	**44**	**9**	**20**	**15**	**0**	**4**	**4**	**45**	**0**	**0**	**0**
	Boston Braves	AHL	3	0	1	1	....	....	....	2	....	....	....	....	....	....	....	....	....	....	....	....	....	....	....	....	....	....
1972-73	Team Canada	Summit-72	2	0	0	0	....	....	....	0	....	....	....	....	....	....	....	....	....	....	....	....	....	....	....	....	....	....
	Boston Bruins	**NHL**	**78**	**2**	**17**	**19**	**2**	**13**	**15**	**90**	**0**	**0**	**0**	**110**	**1.8**	**120**	**0**	**104**	**13**	**29**	**4**	**0**	**0**	**0**	**6**	**0**	**0**	**0**
1973-74	**St. Louis Blues**	**NHL**	**75**	**5**	**16**	**21**	**5**	**13**	**18**	**51**	**1**	**0**	**0**	**94**	**5.3**	**85**	**7**	**114**	**29**	**–7**	....	....	....	....	....	....	....	....
1974-75	**St. Louis Blues**	**NHL**	**20**	**0**	**8**	**8**	**0**	**6**	**6**	**4**	**0**	**0**	**0**	**17**	**0.0**	**20**	**1**	**41**	**14**	**–8**	....	....	....	....	....	....	....	....
	Montreal Canadiens	**NHL**	**56**	**1**	**11**	**12**	**1**	**8**	**9**	**58**	**0**	**0**	**0**	**40**	**2.5**	**63**	**2**	**67**	**27**	**21**	**11**	**0**	**6**	**6**	**12**	**0**	**0**	**0**
1975-76♦	**Montreal Canadiens**	**NHL**	**72**	**0**	**12**	**12**	**0**	**9**	**9**	**29**	**0**	**0**	**0**	**60**	**0.0**	**73**	**2**	**57**	**16**	**30**	....	....	....	....	....	....	....	....
1976-77	**Pittsburgh Penguins**	**NHL**	**79**	**1**	**12**	**13**	**1**	**9**	**10**	**40**	**0**	**0**	**0**	**45**	**2.2**	**77**	**0**	**103**	**24**	**–2**	**3**	**0**	**1**	**1**	**0**	**0**	**0**	**0**
1977-78	**New York Rangers**	**NHL**	**78**	**2**	**8**	**10**	**2**	**6**	**8**	**38**	**0**	**0**	**1**	**40**	**5.0**	**68**	**2**	**95**	**15**	**–14**	**3**	**0**	**0**	**0**	**6**	**0**	**0**	**0**
1978-79	New Haven Nighthawks	AHL	6	2	1	3	....	....	....	6	....	....	....	....	....	....	....	....	....	....	....	....	....	....	....	....	....	....
	Colorado Rockies	**NHL**	**56**	**1**	**4**	**5**	**1**	**3**	**4**	**18**	**0**	**0**	**0**	**40**	**2.5**	**31**	**0**	**79**	**15**	**–33**	....	....	....	....	....	....	....	....
	NHL Totals		**979**	**31**	**158**	**189**	**31**	**131**	**162**	**1065**	....	....	....	....	....	....	....	....	....	....	**71**	**0**	**18**	**18**	**150**	....	....	....

Played in NHL All-Star Game (1974)

Traded to **St. Louis** by **Boston** for Jake Rathwell, St. Louis' 2nd round choice (Mark Howe) in 1974 Amateur Draft and cash, October 5, 1973. Traded to **Montreal** by **St. Louis** for Chuck Lefley, November 28, 1974. Traded to **Pittsburgh** by **Montreal** for Pittsburgh's 3rd round choice (Richard David) in 1978 Amateur Draft, August 11, 1976. Rights traded to **Washington** by **Pittsburgh** for Bob Paradise, October 1, 1977. Signed as a free agent by **NY Rangers**, October 4, 1977. Traded to **Colorado** by **NY Rangers** for cash, November, 1978.

• AXELSSON, P.J.

Anders Per-Johan LW – L. 6′1″, 174 lbs. b: Kungalv, Sweden, 2/26/1975. Boston's 7th, 177th overall, in 1995.

Season	Club	League	GP	G	A	Pts	AG	AA	APts	PIM	PP	SH	GW	S	%	TGF	PGF	TGA	PGA	+/–	GP	G	A	Pts	PIM	PP	SH	GW
1992-93	Vastra Frolunda	Sweden-Jr.	16	9	5	14	....	....	....	12	....	....	....	....	....	....	....	....	....	....	....	....	....	....	....	....	....	....
1993-94	Vastra Frolunda	Sweden	11	0	0	0	....	....	....	4	....	....	....	....	....	....	....	....	....	....	4	0	0	0	0	....	....	....
1994-95	Vastra Frolunda	Sweden-Jr.	19	16	9	25	....	....	....	22	....	....	....	....	....	....	....	....	....	....	....	....	....	....	....	....	....	....
	Vastra Frolunda	Sweden	8	2	1	3	....	....	....	6	....	....	....	....	....	....	....	....	....	....	....	....	....	....	....	....	....	....
	Sweden	WJC-A	7	2	3	5	....	....	....	2	....	....	....	....	....	....	....	....	....	....	....	....	....	....	....	....	....	....
1995-96	Vastra Frolunda	Sweden	36	15	5	20	....	....	....	10	....	....	....	....	....	....	....	....	....	....	13	3	0	3	10	....	....	....
1996-97	Vastra Frolunda	Sweden	50	19	15	34	....	....	....	34	....	....	....	....	....	....	....	....	....	....	3	0	2	2	0	....	....	....
	Vastra Frolunda	EuroHL	3	1	1	2	....	....	....	0	....	....	....	....	....	....	....	....	....	....	3	0	0	0	2	....	....	....
1997-98	**Boston Bruins**	**NHL**	**82**	**8**	**19**	**27**	**9**	**19**	**28**	**38**	**2**	**0**	**1**	**144**	**5.6**	**43**	**5**	**74**	**22**	**–14**	**6**	**1**	**0**	**1**	**0**	**0**	**0**	**0**
1998-99	**Boston Bruins**	**NHL**	**77**	**7**	**10**	**17**	**8**	**10**	**18**	**18**	**0**	**0**	**2**	**146**	**4.8**	**29**	**2**	**53**	**12**	**–14**	**12**	**1**	**1**	**2**	**4**	**0**	**0**	**0**
99-2000	**Boston Bruins**	**NHL**	**81**	**10**	**16**	**26**	**11**	**15**	**26**	**24**	**0**	**0**	**4**	**186**	**5.4**	**45**	**2**	**60**	**18**	**1**	....	....	....	....	....	....	....	....
	Sweden	WC-A	6	1	3	4	....	....	....	2	....	....	....	....	....	....	....	....	....	....	....	....	....	....	....	....	....	....
	NHL Totals		**240**	**25**	**45**	**70**	**28**	**44**	**72**	**80**	**2**	**0**	**7**	**476**	**5.3**	**117**	**9**	**187**	**52**		**18**	**2**	**1**	**3**	**4**	**0**	**0**	**0**

• BABCOCK, Bobby

D – L. 6′1″, 222 lbs. b: Agincourt, Ont., 8/3/1968. Washington's 11th, 208th overall, in 1986.

Season	Club	League	GP	G	A	Pts	AG	AA	APts	PIM	PP	SH	GW	S	%	TGF	PGF	TGA	PGA	+/–	GP	G	A	Pts	PIM	PP	SH	GW
1984-85	St. Michael's Buzzers	OJHL-B	40	8	30	38	....	....	....	140	....	....	....	....	....	....	....	....	....	....	....	....	....	....	....	....	....	....
1985-86	Sault Ste. Marie Greyhounds	OHL	50	1	7	8	....	....	....	188	....	....	....	....	....	....	....	....	....	....	....	....	....	....	....	....	....	....
1986-87	Sault Ste. Marie Greyhounds	OHL	62	7	8	15	....	....	....	243	....	....	....	....	....	....	....	....	....	....	4	0	0	0	11	....	....	....
1987-88	Sault Ste. Marie Greyhounds	OHL	8	0	2	2	....	....	....	30	....	....	....	....	....	....	....	....	....	....	....	....	....	....	....	....	....	....
	Cornwall Royals	OHL	42	0	16	16	....	....	....	120	....	....	....	....	....	....	....	....	....	....	....	....	....	....	....	....	....	....
1988-89	Cornwall Royals	OHL	42	0	9	9	....	....	....	163	....	....	....	....	....	....	....	....	....	....	18	1	3	4	29	....	....	....
1989-90	Baltimore Skipjacks	AHL	67	0	4	4	....	....	....	249	....	....	....	....	....	....	....	....	....	....	7	0	0	0	23	....	....	....
1990-91	**Washington Capitals**	**NHL**	**1**	**0**	**0**	**0**	**0**	**0**	**0**	**0**	**0**	**0**	**0**	**0**	**0.0**	**0**	**0**	**0**	**0**	**0**	....	....	....	....	....	....	....	....
	Baltimore Skipjacks	AHL	38	0	3	3	....	....	....	112	....	....	....	....	....	....	....	....	....	....	....	....	....	....	....	....	....	....
1991-92	Baltimore Skipjacks	AHL	26	0	2	2	....	....	....	55	....	....	....	....	....	....	....	....	....	....	....	....	....	....	....	....	....	....
1992-93	**Washington Capitals**	**NHL**	**1**	**0**	**0**	**0**	**0**	**0**	**0**	**2**	**0**	**0**	**0**	**0**	**0.0**	**0**	**0**	**0**	**0**	**0**	....	....	....	....	....	....	....	....
	Baltimore Skipjacks	AHL	26	0	2	2	....	....	....	93	....	....	....	....	....	....	....	....	....	....	....	....	....	....	....	....	....	....
	Hampton Roads Admirals	ECHL	26	3	13	16	....	....	....	96	....	....	....	....	....	....	....	....	....	....	1	0	0	0	10	....	....	....
1993-94	Binghamton Rangers	AHL	20	1	6	7	....	....	....	67	....	....	....	....	....	....	....	....	....	....	....	....	....	....	....	....	....	....
	NHL Totals		**2**	**0**	**0**	**0**	**0**	**0**	**0**	**2**	**0**	**0**	**0**	**0**	**0.0**	**0**	**0**	**0**	**0**		....	....	....	....	....	....	....	....

• BABE, Warren

LW – L. 6′2″, 190 lbs. b: Medicine Hat, Alta., 9/7/1968. Minnesota's 1st, 12th overall, in 1986.

Season	Club	League	GP	G	A	Pts	AG	AA	APts	PIM	PP	SH	GW	S	%	TGF	PGF	TGA	PGA	+/–	GP	G	A	Pts	PIM	PP	SH	GW
1983-84	Notre Dame Midget Hounds	SAHA	STATISTICS NOT AVAILABLE																									
1984-85	Lethbridge Broncos	WHL	70	7	14	21	....	....	....	117	....	....	....	....	....	....	....	....	....	....	....	....	....	....	....	....	....	....
1985-86	Lethbridge Broncos	WHL	63	33	24	57	....	....	....	125	....	....	....	....	....	....	....	....	....	....	....	....	....	....	....	....	....	....
1986-87	Swift Current Broncos	WHL	52	28	45	73	....	....	....	109	....	....	....	....	....	....	....	....	....	....	....	....	....	....	....	....	....	....
1987-88	Kamloops Blazers	WHL	32	17	19	36	....	....	....	73	....	....	....	....	....	....	....	....	....	....	18	5	12	17	42	....	....	....
	Canada	WJC-A	7	0	2	2	....	....	....	10	....	....	....	....	....	....	....	....	....	....	....	....	....	....	....	....	....	....
	Minnesota North Stars	**NHL**	**6**	**0**	**1**	**1**	**0**	**1**	**1**	**4**	**0**	**0**	**0**	**2**	**0.0**	**2**	**0**	**3**	**0**	**–1**	....	....	....	....	....	....	....	....
	Kalamazoo Wings	IHL	6	0	0	0	....	....	....	7	....	....	....	....	....	....	....	....	....	....	....	....	....	....	....	....	....	....
1988-89	**Minnesota North Stars**	**NHL**	**14**	**2**	**3**	**5**	**2**	**2**	**4**	**19**	**0**	**0**	**0**	**15**	**13.3**	**7**	**0**	**4**	**0**	**3**	**2**	**0**	**0**	**0**	**0**	**0**	**0**	**0**
	Kalamazoo Wings	IHL	62	18	24	42	....	....	....	102	....	....	....	....	....	....	....	....	....	....	6	1	4	5	24	....	....	....
1989-90	**Minnesota North Stars**	**NHL**	DID NOT PLAY – INJURED																									
1990-91	**Minnesota North Stars**	**NHL**	**1**	**0**	**1**	**1**	**0**	**1**	**1**	**0**	**0**	**0**	**0**	**0**	**0.0**	**1**	**0**	**0**	**0**	**1**	....	....	....	....	....	....	....	....
	Kalamazoo Wings	IHL	49	15	17	32	....	....	....	52	....	....	....	....	....	....	....	....	....	....	....	....	....	....	....	....	....	....
	NHL Totals		**21**	**2**	**5**	**7**	**2**	**4**	**6**	**23**	**0**	**0**	**0**	**17**	**11.8**	**10**	**0**	**7**	**0**		**2**	**0**	**0**	**0**	**0**	**0**	**0**	**0**

• Missed entire 1989-90 season recovering from head injury suffered during playoff game vs. Flint (IHL), April, 1990.

• BABIN, Mitch

C – L. 6′2″, 195 lbs. b: Kapuskasing, Ont., 11/1/1954. St. Louis' 10th, 180th overall, in 1974.

Season	Club	League	GP	G	A	Pts	AG	AA	APts	PIM	PP	SH	GW	S	%	TGF	PGF	TGA	PGA	+/–	GP	G	A	Pts	PIM	PP	SH	GW
1971-72	Kenora Muskies	MJHL	46	22	22	44	....	....	....	89	....	....	....	....	....	....	....	....	....	....	....	....	....	....	....	....	....	....
1972-73	North Bay Trappers	NOJHA	43	35	37	72	....	....	....	101	....	....	....	....	....	....	....	....	....	....	....	....	....	....	....	....	....	....
1973-74	North Bay Trappers	NOJHA	43	29	51	80	....	....	....	60	....	....	....	....	....	....	....	....	....	....	....	....	....	....	....	....	....	....
1974-75	Denver Spurs	CHL	70	30	43	73	....	....	....	48	....	....	....	....	....	....	....	....	....	....	2	0	2	2	4	....	....	....
1975-76	**St. Louis Blues**	**NHL**	**8**	**0**	**0**	**0**	**0**	**0**	**0**	**0**	**0**	**0**	**0**	**2**	**0.0**	**1**	**1**	**2**	**0**	**–2**	....	....	....	....	....	....	....	....
	Providence Reds	AHL	54	8	9	17	....	....	....	14	....	....	....	....	....	....	....	....	....	....	2	0	0	0	0	....	....	....
1976-77	Kansas City Blues	CHL	75	26	25	51	....	....	....	59	....	....	....	....	....	....	....	....	....	....	10	*4	4	8	6	....	....	....
1977-78	Salt Lake Golden Eagles	CHL	17	2	4	6	....	....	....	6	....	....	....	....	....	....	....	....	....	....	....	....	....	....	....	....	....	....
1978-79	VEU Feldkirch	Austria	29	28	23	51	....	....	....	62	....	....	....	....	....	....	....	....	....	....	....	....	....	....	....	....	....	....
	NHL Totals		**8**	**0**	**0**	**0**	**0**	**0**	**0**	**0**	**0**	**0**	**0**	**2**	**0.0**	**1**	**1**	**2**	**0**		....	....	....	....	....	....	....	....

• BABY, John

John George D – R. 6′, 195 lbs. b: Sudbury, Ont., 5/18/1957. Cleveland's 5th, 59th overall, in 1977.

Season	Club	League	GP	G	A	Pts	AG	AA	APts	PIM	PP	SH	GW	S	%	TGF	PGF	TGA	PGA	+/–	GP	G	A	Pts	PIM	PP	SH	GW
1973-74	North Bay Trappers	NOJHA	36	8	21	29	....	....	....	109	....	....	....	....	....	....	....	....	....	....	....	....	....	....	....	....	....	....
1974-75	Kitchener Rangers	OMJHL	70	13	26	39	....	....	....	112	....	....	....	....	....	....	....	....	....	....	....	....	....	....	....	....	....	....
1975-76	Sudbury Wolves	OMJHL	61	16	34	50	....	....	....	155	....	....	....	....	....	....	....	....	....	....	17	6	8	14	32	....	....	....
	Kitchener Rangers	OMJHL	3	0	0	0	....	....	....	0	....	....	....	....	....	....	....	....	....	....	....	....	....	....	....	....	....	....
1976-77	Sudbury Wolves	OMJHL	61	32	61	93	....	....	....	118	....	....	....	....	....	....	....	....	....	....	6	0	2	2	14	....	....	....
1977-78	**Cleveland Barons**	**NHL**	**24**	**2**	**7**	**9**	**2**	**5**	**7**	**26**	**0**	**0**	**0**	**42**	**4.8**	**23**	**6**	**28**	**1**	**–10**	....	....	....	....	....	....	....	....
	Phoenix Roadrunners	CHL	16	3	3	6	....	....	....	25	....	....	....	....	....	....	....	....	....	....	....	....	....	....	....	....	....	....
	Binghamton Whalers	AHL	25	3	1	4	....	....	....	16	....	....	....	....	....	....	....	....	....	....	....	....	....	....	....	....	....	....
1978-79	**Minnesota North Stars**	**NHL**	**2**	**0**	**1**	**1**	**0**	**1**	**1**	**0**	**0**	**0**	**0**	**6**	**0.0**	**1**	**0**	**4**	**1**	**–2**	....	....	....	....	....	....	....	....
	Oklahoma City Stars	CHL	76	18	22	40	....	....	....	114	....	....	....	....	....	....	....	....	....	....	....	....	....	....	....	....	....	....
1979-80	Syracuse Firebirds	AHL	73	3	24	27	....	....	....	73	....	....	....	....	....	....	....	....	....	....	....	....	....	....	....	....	....	....

			REGULAR SEASON																		PLAYOFFS							
Season	Club	League	GP	G	A	Pts	AG	AA	APts	PIM	PP	SH	GW	S	%	TGF	PGF	TGA	PGA	+/-	GP	G	A	Pts	PIM	PP	SH	GW
1980-81	Binghamton Whalers	AHL	66	9	25	34	....	....	....	80	....	....	....	....	....	....	....	....	....	....	2	0	0	0	2	....	....	....
1981-82	SC Rapperswil-Jona	Switz-2	STATISTICS NOT AVAILABLE																									
1982-83	SC Rapperswil-Jona	Switz-2	STATISTICS NOT AVAILABLE																									
1983-84	Kalamazoo Wings	IHL	46	2	14	16	....	....	....	35	....	....	....	....	....	....	....	....	....	....	3	0	0	0	4	....	....	....
	NHL Totals		**26**	**2**	**8**	**10**	**2**	**6**	**8**	**26**	**0**	**0**	**0**	**48**	**4.2**	**24**	**6**	**32**	**2**		....	....	....	....	....	....	....	....

OMJHL Second All-Star Team (1977)

Placed on **Minnesota** Reserve List after **Cleveland-Minnesota** Dispersal Draft, June 15, 1978. Claimed by **Quebec** from **Minnesota** in Expansion Draft, June 13, 1980.

• BABYCH, Dave

David Michael D – L. 6′2″, 215 lbs. b: Edmonton, Alta., 5/23/1961. Winnipeg's 1st, 2nd overall, in 1980.

Season	Club	League	GP	G	A	Pts	AG	AA	APts	PIM	PP	SH	GW	S	%	TGF	PGF	TGA	PGA	+/-	GP	G	A	Pts	PIM	PP	SH	GW
1977-78	Fort Saskatchewan Traders	AJHL	56	31	69	100	....	....	....	37	....	....	....	....	....	....	....	....	....	....	....	....	....	....	....	....	....	....
	Portland Winter Hawks	WCJHL	6	1	3	4	....	....	....	4	....	....	....	....	....	....	....	....	....	....	....	....	....	....	....	....	....	....
1978-79	Portland Winter Hawks	WHL	67	20	59	79	....	....	....	63	....	....	....	....	....	....	....	....	....	....	25	7	22	29	22	....	....	....
1979-80	Portland Winter Hawks	WHL	50	22	60	82	....	....	....	71	....	....	....	....	....	....	....	....	....	....	8	1	10	11	2	....	....	....
1980-81	**Winnipeg Jets**	**NHL**	**69**	**6**	**38**	**44**	**5**	**25**	**30**	**90**	**3**	**0**	**0**	**209**	**2.9**	**125**	**47**	**169**	**30**	**–61**	....	....	....	....	....	....	....	....
	Canada	WEC-A	7	0	2	2	....	....	....	8	....	....	....	....	....	....	....	....	....	....	....	....	....	....	....	....	....	....
1981-82	**Winnipeg Jets**	**NHL**	**79**	**19**	**49**	**68**	**15**	**33**	**48**	**92**	**11**	**0**	**2**	**262**	**7.3**	**188**	**70**	**151**	**22**	**–11**	**4**	**1**	**2**	**3**	**29**	**1**	**0**	**0**
1982-83	**Winnipeg Jets**	**NHL**	**79**	**13**	**61**	**74**	**11**	**42**	**53**	**56**	**7**	**0**	**1**	**253**	**5.1**	**184**	**70**	**146**	**22**	**–10**	**3**	**0**	**0**	**0**	**0**	**0**	**0**	**0**
1983-84	**Winnipeg Jets**	**NHL**	**66**	**18**	**39**	**57**	**14**	**27**	**41**	**62**	**10**	**0**	**4**	**233**	**7.7**	**156**	**56**	**167**	**36**	**–31**	**3**	**1**	**1**	**2**	**0**	**1**	**0**	**0**
1984-85	**Winnipeg Jets**	**NHL**	**78**	**13**	**49**	**62**	**11**	**33**	**44**	**78**	**6**	**0**	**1**	**239**	**5.4**	**159**	**54**	**142**	**21**	**–16**	**8**	**2**	**7**	**9**	**6**	**2**	**0**	**0**
1985-86	**Winnipeg Jets**	**NHL**	**19**	**4**	**12**	**16**	**3**	**8**	**11**	**14**	**2**	**0**	**0**	**53**	**7.5**	**37**	**13**	**35**	**10**	**–1**	....	....	....	....	....	....	....	....
	Hartford Whalers	**NHL**	**62**	**10**	**43**	**53**	**8**	**29**	**37**	**36**	**7**	**1**	**2**	**152**	**6.6**	**132**	**52**	**109**	**31**	**2**	**8**	**1**	**3**	**4**	**14**	**0**	**0**	**0**
1986-87	**Hartford Whalers**	**NHL**	**66**	**8**	**33**	**41**	**7**	**24**	**31**	**44**	**7**	**0**	**1**	**157**	**5.1**	**98**	**53**	**78**	**15**	**–18**	**6**	**1**	**1**	**2**	**14**	**1**	**0**	**0**
1987-88	**Hartford Whalers**	**NHL**	**71**	**14**	**36**	**50**	**12**	**26**	**38**	**54**	**10**	**0**	**2**	**233**	**6.0**	**108**	**68**	**67**	**2**	**–25**	**6**	**3**	**2**	**5**	**2**	**0**	**0**	**0**
1988-89	**Hartford Whalers**	**NHL**	**70**	**6**	**41**	**47**	**5**	**29**	**34**	**54**	**4**	**0**	**2**	**172**	**3.5**	**115**	**47**	**80**	**7**	**–5**	**4**	**1**	**5**	**6**	**2**	**0**	**0**	**0**
	Canada	WEC-A	10	2	0	2	....	....	....	4	....	....	....	....	....	....	....	....	....	....	....	....	....	....	....	....	....	....
1989-90	**Hartford Whalers**	**NHL**	**72**	**6**	**37**	**43**	**5**	**27**	**32**	**62**	**4**	**0**	**1**	**164**	**3.7**	**123**	**61**	**91**	**13**	**–16**	**7**	**1**	**2**	**3**	**0**	**0**	**0**	**0**
1990-91	**Hartford Whalers**	**NHL**	**8**	**0**	**6**	**6**	**0**	**5**	**5**	**4**	**0**	**0**	**0**	**15**	**0.0**	**13**	**9**	**8**	**0**	**–4**	....	....	....	....	....	....	....	....
1991-92	**Vancouver Canucks**	**NHL**	**75**	**5**	**24**	**29**	**5**	**18**	**23**	**63**	**4**	**0**	**1**	**148**	**3.4**	**85**	**29**	**75**	**17**	**–2**	**13**	**2**	**6**	**8**	**10**	**1**	**0**	**1**
1992-93	**Vancouver Canucks**	**NHL**	**43**	**3**	**16**	**19**	**2**	**11**	**13**	**44**	**3**	**0**	**0**	**78**	**3.8**	**63**	**22**	**52**	**17**	**6**	**12**	**2**	**5**	**7**	**6**	**1**	**0**	**0**
1993-94	**Vancouver Canucks**	**NHL**	**73**	**4**	**28**	**32**	**4**	**22**	**26**	**52**	**0**	**0**	**2**	**96**	**4.2**	**78**	**18**	**76**	**16**	**0**	**24**	**3**	**5**	**8**	**12**	**0**	**0**	**1**
1994-95	**Vancouver Canucks**	**NHL**	**40**	**3**	**11**	**14**	**5**	**16**	**21**	**18**	**1**	**0**	**0**	**58**	**5.2**	**42**	**12**	**58**	**15**	**–13**	**11**	**2**	**2**	**4**	**14**	**1**	**1**	**0**
1995-96	**Vancouver Canucks**	**NHL**	**53**	**3**	**21**	**24**	**3**	**17**	**20**	**38**	**3**	**0**	**0**	**69**	**4.3**	**65**	**15**	**72**	**17**	**–5**	....	....	....	....	....	....	....	....
1996-97	**Vancouver Canucks**	**NHL**	**78**	**5**	**22**	**27**	**5**	**20**	**25**	**38**	**2**	**0**	**1**	**105**	**4.8**	**75**	**7**	**87**	**17**	**–2**	....	....	....	....	....	....	....	....
1997-98	**Vancouver Canucks**	**NHL**	**47**	**0**	**9**	**9**	**0**	**9**	**9**	**37**	**0**	**0**	**0**	**40**	**0.0**	**35**	**2**	**61**	**17**	**–11**	....	....	....	....	....	....	....	....
	Philadelphia Flyers	**NHL**	**6**	**0**	**0**	**0**	**0**	**0**	**0**	**12**	**0**	**0**	**0**	**6**	**0.0**	**5**	**1**	**2**	**0**	**2**	**5**	**1**	**0**	**1**	**4**	**1**	**0**	**0**
1998-99	**Philadelphia Flyers**	**NHL**	**33**	**2**	**4**	**6**	**2**	**4**	**6**	**20**	**2**	**0**	**0**	**44**	**4.5**	**25**	**10**	**21**	**6**	**0**	....	....	....	....	....	....	....	....
	Los Angeles Kings	**NHL**	**8**	**0**	**2**	**2**	**0**	**2**	**2**	**2**	**0**	**0**	**0**	**5**	**0.0**	**4**	**0**	**7**	**1**	**–2**	....	....	....	....	....	....	....	....
99-2000	HC Ambri-Piotta	Switz.	1	0	0	0	....	....	....	0	....	....	....	....	....	....	....	....	....	....	2	0	0	0	0	....	....	....
	NHL Totals		**1195**	**142**	**581**	**723**	**122**	**427**	**549**	**970**	**86**	**1**	**20**	**2791**	**5.1**	**1915**	**716**	**1754**	**332**		**114**	**21**	**41**	**62**	**113**	**9**	**1**	**2**

• Brother of Wayne • WHL First All-Star Team (1980) • Played in NHL All-Star Game (1983, 1984)

Traded to **Hartford** by **Winnipeg** for Ray Neufeld, November 21, 1985. • Missed majority of 1990-91 season recovering from wrist surgery, October 29, 1990. Claimed by **Minnesota** from **Hartford** in Expansion Draft, May 30, 1991. Traded to **Vancouver** by **Minnesota** for Tom Kurvers, June 22, 1991. Traded to **Philadelphia** by **Vancouver** with Philadelphia's 5th round choice (previously acquired, Philadelphia selected Garrett Prosofsky) in 1998 Entry Draft for Philadelphia's 3rd round choice (Justin Morrison) in 1998 Entry Draft, March 24, 1998. Traded to **Los Angeles** by **Philadelphia** with Philadelphia's 5th round choice (Nathan Marsters) in 2000 Entry Draft for Steve Duchesne, March 23, 1999. Signed as a free agent by Ambri-Piotta (Switz), January 31, 2000.

• BABYCH, Wayne

Wayne Joseph RW – R. 5′11″, 191 lbs. b: Edmonton, Alta., 6/6/1958. St. Louis' 1st, 3rd overall, in 1978.

Season	Club	League	GP	G	A	Pts	AG	AA	APts	PIM	PP	SH	GW	S	%	TGF	PGF	TGA	PGA	+/-	GP	G	A	Pts	PIM	PP	SH	GW
1973-74	Spruce Grove Mets	AJHL	56	20	18	38	....	....	....	68	....	....	....	....	....	....	....	....	....	....	....	....	....	....	....	....	....	....
	Edmonton Oil Kings	WCJHL	1	0	1	1	....	....	....	0	....	....	....	....	....	....	....	....	....	....	3	0	0	0	0	....	....	....
1974-75	Edmonton Oil Kings	WCJHL	68	19	17	36	....	....	....	157	....	....	....	....	....	....	....	....	....	....	....	....	....	....	....	....	....	....
1975-76	Edmonton Oil Kings	WCJHL	61	32	46	78	....	....	....	98	....	....	....	....	....	....	....	....	....	....	5	2	1	3	23	....	....	....
1976-77	Portland Winter Hawks	WCJHL	71	50	62	112	....	....	....	76	....	....	....	....	....	....	....	....	....	....	10	2	6	8	10	....	....	....
1977-78	Portland Winter Hawks	WCJHL	68	50	71	121	....	....	....	218	....	....	....	....	....	....	....	....	....	....	8	4	4	8	19	....	....	....
	Canada	WJC-A	6	5	5	10	....	....	....	4	....	....	....	....	....	....	....	....	....	....	....	....	....	....	....	....	....	....
1978-79	**St. Louis Blues**	**NHL**	**67**	**27**	**36**	**63**	**23**	**26**	**49**	**75**	**11**	**0**	**0**	**196**	**13.8**	**101**	**34**	**80**	**2**	**–11**	....	....	....	....	....	....	....	....
	Canada	WEC-A	7	1	2	3	....	....	....	0	....	....	....	....	....	....	....	....	....	....	....	....	....	....	....	....	....	....
1979-80	**St. Louis Blues**	**NHL**	**59**	**26**	**35**	**61**	**22**	**26**	**48**	**49**	**7**	**0**	**3**	**159**	**16.4**	**81**	**22**	**48**	**0**	**11**	**3**	**1**	**2**	**3**	**2**	**0**	**0**	**0**
1980-81	**St. Louis Blues**	**NHL**	**78**	**54**	**42**	**96**	**42**	**28**	**70**	**93**	**14**	**0**	**7**	**306**	**17.6**	**142**	**45**	**83**	**0**	**14**	**11**	**2**	**0**	**2**	**8**	**1**	**0**	**0**
1981-82	**St. Louis Blues**	**NHL**	**51**	**19**	**25**	**44**	**15**	**17**	**32**	**51**	**4**	**0**	**3**	**142**	**13.4**	**57**	**16**	**53**	**0**	**–12**	**7**	**3**	**2**	**5**	**8**	**0**	**0**	**1**
1982-83	**St. Louis Blues**	**NHL**	**71**	**16**	**23**	**39**	**13**	**16**	**29**	**62**	**5**	**0**	**2**	**148**	**10.8**	**64**	**23**	**65**	**0**	**–24**	....	....	....	....	....	....	....	....
1983-84	**St. Louis Blues**	**NHL**	**70**	**13**	**29**	**42**	**10**	**20**	**30**	**52**	**3**	**0**	**0**	**115**	**11.3**	**63**	**13**	**50**	**1**	**1**	**10**	**1**	**4**	**5**	**4**	**0**	**0**	**0**
1984-85	**Pittsburgh Penguins**	**NHL**	**65**	**20**	**34**	**54**	**16**	**23**	**39**	**35**	**3**	**0**	**3**	**131**	**15.3**	**81**	**16**	**72**	**0**	**–7**	....	....	....	....	....	....	....	....
1985-86	**Pittsburgh Penguins**	**NHL**	**2**	**0**	**0**	**0**	**0**	**0**	**0**	**0**	**0**	**0**	**0**	**0**	**0.0**	**0**	**0**	**1**	**0**	**–1**	....	....	....	....	....	....	....	....
	Quebec Nordiques	**NHL**	**15**	**6**	**5**	**11**	**5**	**3**	**8**	**18**	**1**	**0**	**0**	**32**	**18.8**	**13**	**3**	**10**	**0**	**0**	....	....	....	....	....	....	....	....
	Hartford Whalers	**NHL**	**37**	**11**	**17**	**28**	**9**	**11**	**20**	**59**	**2**	**0**	**2**	**63**	**17.5**	**39**	**12**	**21**	**0**	**6**	**10**	**0**	**1**	**1**	**2**	**0**	**0**	**0**
1986-87	**Hartford Whalers**	**NHL**	**4**	**0**	**0**	**0**	**0**	**0**	**0**	**4**	**0**	**0**	**0**	**2**	**0.0**	**0**	**0**	**5**	**0**	**–5**	....	....	....	....	....	....	....	....
	Binghamton Whalers	AHL	6	2	5	7	....	....	....	6	....	....	....	....	....	....	....	....	....	....	....	....	....	....	....	....	....	....
	NHL Totals		**519**	**192**	**246**	**438**	**155**	**170**	**325**	**498**	**50**	**0**	**20**	**1294**	**14.8**	**641**	**184**	**488**	**3**		**41**	**7**	**9**	**16**	**24**	**1**	**0**	**1**

• Brother of Dave • WCJHL All-Star Team (1977, 1978) • Played in NHL All-Star Game (1981)

Claimed by **Pittsburgh** from **St. Louis** in Waiver Draft, October 9, 1984. Traded to **Quebec** by **Pittsburgh** for future considerations, October 20, 1985. Traded to **Hartford** by **Quebec** for Greg Malone, January 17, 1986.

• BACA, Jergus

D – L. 6′2″, 211 lbs. b: Liptovsky Mikulas, Czech., 1/4/1965. Hartford's 6th, 141st overall, in 1990.

Season	Club	League	GP	G	A	Pts	AG	AA	APts	PIM	PP	SH	GW	S	%	TGF	PGF	TGA	PGA	+/-	GP	G	A	Pts	PIM	PP	SH	GW
1987-88	VSZ Kosice	Czech.	40	5	5	10	....	....	....	32	....	....	....	....	....	....	....	....	....	....	....	....	....	....	....	....	....	....
1988-89	VSZ Kosice	Czech.	42	3	10	13	....	....	....	46	....	....	....	....	....	....	....	....	....	....	....	....	....	....	....	....	....	....
	Czechoslovakia	WEC-A	10	1	1	2	....	....	....	14	....	....	....	....	....	....	....	....	....	....	....	....	....	....	....	....	....	....
1989-90	VSZ Kosice	Czech.	44	9	15	24	....	....	....	....	....	....	....	....	....	....	....	....	....	....	3	0	1	1	....	....	....	....
	Czechoslovakia	WEC-A	8	0	0	0	....	....	....	16	....	....	....	....	....	....	....	....	....	....	....	....	....	....	....	....	....	....
1990-91	**Hartford Whalers**	**NHL**	**9**	**0**	**2**	**2**	**0**	**2**	**2**	**14**	**0**	**0**	**0**	**15**	**0.0**	**5**	**4**	**4**	**0**	**–3**	....	....	....	....	....	....	....	....
	Springfield Indians	AHL	57	6	23	29	....	....	....	89	....	....	....	....	....	....	....	....	....	....	18	3	13	16	18	....	....	....
1991-92	Czechoslovakia	Can-Cup	5	0	3	3	....	....	....	4	....	....	....	....	....	....	....	....	....	....	....	....	....	....	....	....	....	....
	Hartford Whalers	**NHL**	**1**	**0**	**0**	**0**	**0**	**0**	**0**	**0**	**0**	**0**	**0**	**1**	**0.0**	**0**	**0**	**1**	**0**	**–1**	....	....	....	....	....	....	....	....
	Springfield Indians	AHL	64	6	20	26	....	....	....	88	....	....	....	....	....	....	....	....	....	....	11	0	6	6	20	....	....	....
1992-93	Milwaukee Admirals	IHL	73	9	29	38	....	....	....	108	....	....	....	....	....	....	....	....	....	....	6	0	3	3	2	....	....	....
1993-94	Milwaukee Admirals	IHL	67	6	29	35	....	....	....	119	....	....	....	....	....	....	....	....	....	....	3	1	1	2	4	....	....	....
	Slovakia	Olympics	8	1	2	3	....	....	....	10	....	....	....	....	....	....	....	....	....	....	....	....	....	....	....	....	....	....
1994-95	Leksands IF	Sweden	38	2	5	7	....	....	....	50	....	....	....	....	....	....	....	....	....	....	4	1	1	2	6	....	....	....
1995-96	Milwaukee Admirals	IHL	74	3	12	15	....	....	....	130	....	....	....	....	....	....	....	....	....	....	5	1	3	4	8	....	....	....
1996-97	Slovakia	W-Cup	3	1	0	1	....	....	....	6	....	....	....	....	....	....	....	....	....	....	....	....	....	....	....	....	....	....
	HC Olomouc	Czech-Rep	52	4	9	13	....	....	....	109	....	....	....	....	....	....	....	....	....	....	....	....	....	....	....	....	....	....
	HC Kosice	Slovakia	....	....	....	....	....	....	....	....	....	....	....	....	....	....	....	....	....	....	7	2	2	4	....	....	....	....
	Slovakia	WC-A	8	0	2	2	....	....	....	4	....	....	....	....	....	....	....	....	....	....	....	....	....	....	....	....	....	....
1997-98	HC Kosice	Slovakia	33	6	12	18	....	....	....	12	....	....	....	....	....	....	....	....	....	....	11	4	3	7	4	....	....	....
	Slovakia	WC-A	6	0	0	0	....	....	....	4	....	....	....	....	....	....	....	....	....	....	....	....	....	....	....	....	....	....
1998-99	HC Kosice	Slovakia	42	4	15	19	....	....	....	64	....	....	....	....	....	....	....	....	....	....	11	1	4	5	12	....	....	....
99-2000	Revier Lowen	Germany	61	10	10	20	....	....	....	101	....	....	....	....	....	....	....	....	....	....	....	....	....	....	....	....	....	....
	NHL Totals		**10**	**0**	**2**	**2**	**0**	**2**	**2**	**14**	**0**	**0**	**0**	**16**	**0.0**	**5**	**4**	**5**	**0**		....	....	....	....	....	....	....	....

Czechoslovakian Rookie of the Year (1988) • Czechoslovakian First All-Star Team (1989, 1990)

• BACKMAN, Mike

Michael Charles RW – R. 5'10", 175 lbs. b: Halifax, N.S., 1/2/1955.

Season	Club	League	GP	G	A	Pts	AG	AA	APts	PIM	PP	SH	GW	S	%	TGF	PGF	TGA	PGA	+/–	GP	G	A	Pts	PIM	PP	SH	GW
			REGULAR SEASON																		PLAYOFFS							
1974-75	Montreal Red-White-Blue	QMJHL	38	13	20	33	....	....	....	85	....	....	....	....	....	....	....	....	....	....	....	....	....	....	....	....	....	....
	St. Mary's University	AUAA	6	0	8	8	....	....	....	8	....	....	....	....	....	....	....	....	....	....	....	....	....	....	....	....	....	....
1975-76	St. Mary's University	AUAA	19	13	10	23	....	....	....	49	....	....	....	....	....	....	....	....	....	....	....	....	....	....	....	....	....	....
1976-77	St. Mary's University	AUAA	19	13	15	28	....	....	....	59	....	....	....	....	....	....	....	....	....	....	....	....	....	....	....	....	....	....
1977-78	St. Mary's University	AUAA	17	7	12	19	....	....	....	47	....	....	....	....	....	....	....	....	....	....	....	....	....	....	....	....	....	....
1978-79	New Haven Nighthawks	AHL	6	2	1	3	....	....	....	0	....	....	....	....	....	....	....	....	....	....	6	3	1	4	15	....	....	....
	Toledo Goaldiggers	IHL	66	25	38	63	....	....	....	171	....	....	....	....	....	....	....	....	....	....	6	4	2	6	17	....	....	....
1979-80	New Haven Nighthawks	AHL	74	18	28	46	....	....	....	156	....	....	....	....	....	....	....	....	....	....	10	6	8	14	14	....	....	....
1980-81	New Haven Nighthawks	AHL	62	27	27	54	....	....	....	224	....	....	....	....	....	....	....	....	....	....	4	1	0	1	14	....	....	....
1981-82	New York Rangers	NHL	3	0	2	2	0	1	1	4	0	0	0	1	0.0	8	0	1	0	7	1	0	0	0	2	0	0	0
	Springfield Indians	AHL	74	24	27	51	....	....	....	147	....	....	....	....	....	....	....	....	....	....	....	....	....	....	....	....	....	....
1982-83	New York Rangers	NHL	7	1	3	4	1	2	3	6	0	0	0	9	11.1	6	0	11	0	–5	9	2	2	4	0	0	0	1
	Tulsa Oilers	CHL	71	29	47	76	....	....	....	170	....	....	....	....	....	....	....	....	....	....	....	....	....	....	....	....	....	....
1983-84	New York Rangers	NHL	8	0	1	1	0	1	1	8	0	0	0	6	0.0	1	0	2	0	–1	....	....	....	....	....	....	....	....
	Tulsa Oilers	CHL	50	12	28	40	....	....	....	103	....	....	....	....	....	....	....	....	....	....	9	4	2	6	22	....	....	....
1984-85	New Haven Nighthawks	AHL	72	10	36	46	....	....	....	120	....	....	....	....	....	....	....	....	....	....	....	....	....	....	....	....	....	....
1985-86	New Haven Nighthawks	AHL	4	0	0	0	....	....	....	4	....	....	....	....	....	....	....	....	....	....	....	....	....	....	....	....	....	....
	NHL Totals		18	1	6	7	1	4	5	18	0	0	0	16	6.3	15	0	14	0		10	2	2	4	2	0	0	1

CHL First All-Star Team (1983)

Signed as a free agent by **NY Rangers**, October 11, 1979.

• BACKSTROM, Ralph

Ralph Gerald C – L. 5'10", 165 lbs. b: Kirkland Lake, Ont., 9/18/1937.

Season	Club	League	GP	G	A	Pts	AG	AA	APts	PIM	PP	SH	GW	S	%	TGF	PGF	TGA	PGA	+/–	GP	G	A	Pts	PIM	PP	SH	GW
1953-54	Kirkland Lake Lion Cubs	NOHA	STATISTICS NOT AVAILABLE																									
1954-55	Montreal Jr. Canadiens	QJHL	21	7	6	13	....	....	....	2	....	....	....	....	....	....	....	....	....	....	5	2	1	3	4	....	....	....
1955-56	Montreal Jr. Canadiens	QJHL	18	10	8	18	....	....	....	4	....	....	....	....	....	....	....	....	....	....	....	....	....	....	....	....	....	....
	Montreal Jr. Canadiens	Mem-Cup	10	5	4	9	....	....	....	6	....	....	....	....	....	....	....	....	....	....	....	....	....	....	....	....	....	....
1956-57	Hull-Ottawa Jr. Canadiens	OHA-Jr.	18	10	8	18	....	....	....	4	....	....	....	....	....	....	....	....	....	....	....	....	....	....	....	....	....	....
	Montreal Canadiens	NHL	3	0	0	0	0	0	0	0	....	....	....	....	....	....	....	....	....	....	....	....	....	....	....	....	....	....
	Hull-Ottawa Canadiens	EOHL	18	7	10	17	....	....	....	4	....	....	....	....	....	....	....	....	....	....	....	....	....	....	....	....	....	....
	Hull-Ottawa Canadiens	Mem-Cup	15	17	11	28	....	....	....	19	....	....	....	....	....	....	....	....	....	....	....	....	....	....	....	....	....	....
1957-58	Hull-Ottawa Canadiens	OHA-Jr.	26	24	27	51	....	....	....	64	....	....	....	....	....	....	....	....	....	....	....	....	....	....	....	....	....	....
	Hull-Ottawa Canadiens	EOHL	33	21	25	46	....	....	....	13	....	....	....	....	....	....	....	....	....	....	....	....	....	....	....	....	....	....
	Montreal Royals	QHL	1	0	1	1	....	....	....	0	....	....	....	....	....	....	....	....	....	....	....	....	....	....	....	....	....	....
	Rochester Americans	AHL	2	0	0	0	....	....	....	0	....	....	....	....	....	....	....	....	....	....	....	....	....	....	....	....	....	....
	Montreal Canadiens	NHL	2	0	1	1	0	1	1	0	....	....	....	....	....	....	....	....	....	....	....	....	....	....	....	....	....	....
	Hull-Ottawa Canadiens	Mem-Cup	13	*17	9	26	....	....	....	24	....	....	....	....	....	....	....	....	....	....	....	....	....	....	....	....	....	....
1958-59♦	Montreal Canadiens	NHL	64	18	22	40	21	22	43	19	....	....	....	....	....	....	....	....	....	....	11	3	5	8	12	....	....	....
1959-60♦	Montreal Canadiens	NHL	64	13	15	28	15	15	30	24	....	....	....	....	....	....	....	....	....	....	7	0	3	3	2	....	....	....
1960-61	Montreal Canadiens	NHL	69	12	20	32	14	19	33	44	....	....	....	....	....	....	....	....	....	....	5	0	0	0	4	....	....	....
1961-62	Montreal Canadiens	NHL	66	27	38	65	31	37	68	29	....	....	....	....	....	....	....	....	....	....	5	0	1	1	6	....	....	....
1962-63	Montreal Canadiens	NHL	70	23	12	35	27	12	39	51	....	....	....	....	....	....	....	....	....	....	5	0	0	0	2	....	....	....
1963-64	Montreal Canadiens	NHL	70	8	21	29	10	22	32	41	....	....	....	....	....	....	....	....	....	....	7	2	1	3	8	....	....	....
1964-65♦	Montreal Canadiens	NHL	70	25	30	55	30	31	61	41	....	....	....	....	....	....	....	....	....	....	13	2	3	5	10	....	....	....
1965-66♦	Montreal Canadiens	NHL	67	22	20	42	25	19	44	10	....	....	....	....	....	....	....	....	....	....	10	3	4	7	4	....	....	....
1966-67	Montreal Canadiens	NHL	69	14	27	41	16	26	42	39	....	....	....	....	....	....	....	....	....	....	10	5	2	7	6	....	....	....
1967-68♦	Montreal Canadiens	NHL	70	20	25	45	23	25	48	14	3	0	5	198	10.1	55	12	39	0	4	13	4	3	7	4	0	0	2
1968-69♦	Montreal Canadiens	NHL	72	13	28	41	14	25	39	16	2	0	3	180	7.2	56	5	31	0	20	14	3	4	7	10	0	1	1
1969-70	Montreal Canadiens	NHL	72	19	24	43	21	22	43	20	1	0	2	187	10.2	57	9	44	0	4	....	....	....	....	....	....	....	....
1970-71	Montreal Canadiens	NHL	16	1	4	5	1	3	4	0	0	0	0	18	5.6	9	0	10	1	0	....	....	....	....	....	....	....	....
	Los Angeles Kings	NHL	33	14	13	27	14	11	25	8	2	1	1	108	13.0	37	10	46	12	–7	....	....	....	....	....	....	....	....
1971-72	Los Angeles Kings	NHL	76	23	29	52	23	25	48	22	7	1	4	181	12.7	64	15	95	24	–22	....	....	....	....	....	....	....	....
1972-73	Los Angeles Kings	NHL	63	20	29	49	19	23	42	6	1	1	6	132	15.2	70	10	79	7	–12	....	....	....	....	....	....	....	....
	Chicago Black Hawks	NHL	16	6	3	9	6	2	8	2	0	1	0	36	16.7	11	1	12	2	0	16	5	6	11	0	0	1	0
1973-74	Chicago Cougars	WHA	78	33	50	83	....	....	....	26	....	....	....	....	....	....	....	....	....	....	18	5	*14	19	4	....	....	....
1974-75	Team Canada	Summit-74	8	4	4	8	....	....	....	10	....	....	....	....	....	....	....	....	....	....	....	....	....	....	....	....	....	....
	Chicago Cougars	WHA	70	15	24	39	....	....	....	28	....	....	....	....	....	....	....	....	....	....	....	....	....	....	....	....	....	....
1975-76	Denver-Ottawa Civics	WHA	41	21	29	50	....	....	....	14	....	....	....	....	....	....	....	....	....	....	....	....	....	....	....	....	....	....
	New England Whalers	WHA	38	14	19	33	....	....	....	6	....	....	....	....	....	....	....	....	....	....	17	5	4	9	8	....	....	....
1976-77	New England Whalers	WHA	77	17	31	48	....	....	....	30	....	....	....	....	....	....	....	....	....	....	3	0	0	0	0	....	....	....
	NHL Totals		1032	278	361	639	310	340	650	386	....	....	....	....	....	....	....	....	....	....	116	27	32	59	68	....	....	....
	Other Major League Totals		304	100	153	253	....	....	....	104	....	....	....	....	....	....	....	....	....	....	38	10	18	28	12	....	....	....

Won Calder Memorial Trophy (1959) • Won Paul Daneau Trophy (WHA Most Gentlemanly Player) (1974) • Played in NHL All-Star Game (1958, 1959, 1960, 1962, 1965, 1967)

• **Hull-Ottawa** played partial schedule against OHA-Jr. teams that counted for opposition only. Traded to **LA Kings** by **Montreal** for Gord Labossiere and Ray Fortin, January 26, 1971. Selected by **New England** (WHA) in 1972 WHA General Player Draft, February 12, 1972. Traded to **Chicago** by **LA Kings** for Dan Maloney, February 26, 1973. WHA rights traded to **LA Sharks** (WHA) by **New England** (WHA) for cash, June, 1973. Traded to **Chicago** (WHA) by **LA Sharks** (WHA) for cash, July, 1973. Selected by **Denver** (WHA) from **Chicago** (WHA) in WHA Expansion Draft, May, 1975. Traded to **New England** (WHA) by **Denver-Ottawa** (WHA) with Don Borgeson for cash, January 20, 1976.

• BAILEY, Garnet

Garnet Edward "Ace" LW – L. 5'11", 192 lbs. b: Lloydminster, Sask., 6/13/1948. Boston's 3rd, 13th overall, in 1966.

Season	Club	League	GP	G	A	Pts	AG	AA	APts	PIM	PP	SH	GW	S	%	TGF	PGF	TGA	PGA	+/–	GP	G	A	Pts	PIM	PP	SH	GW
1964-65	Edmonton Oil Kings	CAHL	....	....	....	....	....	....	....	....	....	....	....	....	....	....	....	....	....	....	3	1	1	2	12	....	....	....
	Edmonton Oil Kings	Mem-Cup	19	2	5	7	....	....	....	35	....	....	....	....	....	....	....	....	....	....	....	....	....	....	....	....	....	....
1965-66	Edmonton Oil Kings	ASHL	25	14	18	32	....	....	....	27	....	....	....	....	....	....	....	....	....	....	8	1	3	4	10	....	....	....
	Edmonton Oil Kings	Mem-Cup	12	3	2	5	....	....	....	20	....	....	....	....	....	....	....	....	....	....	....	....	....	....	....	....	....	....
1966-67	Edmonton Oil Kings	CMJHL	56	47	46	93	....	....	....	177	....	....	....	....	....	....	....	....	....	....	9	7	6	13	16	....	....	....
1967-68	Oklahoma City Blazers	CPHL	34	8	13	21	....	....	....	67	....	....	....	....	....	....	....	....	....	....	7	0	5	5	36	....	....	....
1968-69	Boston Bruins	NHL	8	3	3	6	3	3	6	10	0	0	0	13	23.1	7	0	2	0	5	1	0	0	0	2	0	0	0
	Hershey Bears	AHL	60	24	32	56	....	....	....	104	....	....	....	....	....	....	....	....	....	....	9	4	*10	14	10	....	....	....
1969-70♦	Boston Bruins	NHL	58	11	11	22	12	10	22	82	2	0	2	78	14.1	35	1	18	1	17	....	....	....	....	....	....	....	....
1970-71	Boston Bruins	NHL	36	0	6	6	0	5	5	44	0	0	0	33	0.0	11	0	7	0	4	1	0	0	0	10	0	0	0
	Oklahoma City Blazers	CHL	11	3	8	11	....	....	....	28	....	....	....	....	....	....	....	....	....	....	....	....	....	....	....	....	....	....
1971-72♦	Boston Bruins	NHL	73	9	13	22	9	11	20	64	0	0	0	64	14.1	39	1	27	0	11	13	2	4	6	16	0	0	1
1972-73	Boston Bruins	NHL	57	8	13	21	7	10	17	89	0	3	1	76	10.5	31	1	35	12	7	....	....	....	....	....	....	....	....
	Detroit Red Wings	NHL	13	2	11	13	2	9	11	16	0	0	0	19	10.5	16	0	14	0	2	....	....	....	....	....	....	....	....
1973-74	Detroit Red Wings	NHL	45	9	14	23	9	12	21	33	3	0	2	70	12.9	37	14	36	1	–12	....	....	....	....	....	....	....	....
	St. Louis Blues	NHL	22	7	3	10	7	2	9	20	0	0	0	43	16.3	21	5	23	6	–1	....	....	....	....	....	....	....	....
1974-75	St. Louis Blues	NHL	49	15	26	41	13	19	32	113	4	0	1	102	14.7	57	15	47	1	–4	....	....	....	....	....	....	....	....
	Washington Capitals	NHL	22	4	13	17	3	10	13	8	1	0	0	46	8.7	23	9	44	1	–29	....	....	....	....	....	....	....	....
1975-76	Washington Capitals	NHL	67	13	19	32	11	14	25	75	2	0	2	131	9.9	59	21	84	4	–42	....	....	....	....	....	....	....	....
1976-77	Washington Capitals	NHL	78	19	27	46	17	21	38	51	2	0	2	154	12.3	74	15	94	14	–21	....	....	....	....	....	....	....	....
1977-78	Washington Capitals	NHL	40	7	12	19	6	9	15	28	0	0	2	58	12.1	33	5	44	4	–12	....	....	....	....	....	....	....	....
1978-79	Edmonton Oilers	WHA	38	5	4	9	....	....	....	22	....	....	....	....	....	....	....	....	....	....	2	0	0	0	4	....	....	....
1979-80	Houston Apollos	CHL	7	1	0	1	....	....	....	0	....	....	....	....	....	....	....	....	....	....	....	....	....	....	....	....	....	....
1980-81	Wichita Wind	CHL	1	0	0	0	....	....	....	2	....	....	....	....	....	....	....	....	....	....	....	....	....	....	....	....	....	....
	NHL Totals		568	107	171	278	99	135	234	633	14	3	12	887	12.1	443	87	475	44		15	2	4	6	28	0	0	1
	Other Major League Totals		38	5	4	9	....	....	....	22	....	....	....	....	....	....	....	....	....	....	2	0	0	0	4	....	....	....

• Regular season totals for **Edmonton** (CAHL) during 1964-65 unavailable. Selected by **Alberta** (WHA) in 1972 WHA General Player Draft, February 12, 1972. Traded to **Detroit** by **Boston** with future considerations (Murray Wing, June 4, 1974) for Gary Doak, March 1, 1973. Traded to **St. Louis** by **Detroit** with Ted Harris and Bill Collins for Chris Evans, Bryan Watson and Jean Hamel, February 14, 1974. Traded to **Washington** by **St. Louis** with Stan Gilbertson for Denis Dupere, February 10, 1975.

• BAILEY, Reid

D – L. 6'2", 200 lbs. b: Toronto, Ont., 5/28/1956.

Season	Club	League	GP	G	A	Pts	AG	AA	APts	PIM	PP	SH	GW	S	%	TGF	PGF	TGA	PGA	+/-	GP	G	A	Pts	PIM	PP	SH	GW
							REGULAR SEASON														PLAYOFFS							
1975-76	Sault Ste. Marie Greyhounds	OMJHL	9	0	2	2	....	....	....	47	....	....	....	....	....	....	....	....	....	....	....	....	....	....	....	....	....	....
	Kitchener Rangers	OMJHL	24	0	15	15	....	....	....	80	....	....	....	....	....	....	....	....	....	....	....	....	....	....	....	....	....	....
	Cornwall Royals	QMJHL	26	1	8	9	....	....	....	32	....	....	....	....	....	....	....	....	....	....	10	0	1	1	2	....	....	....
1976-77	Port Huron Flags	IHL	72	3	14	17	....	....	....	148	....	....	....	....	....	....	....	....	....	....	....	....	....	....	....	....	....	....
1977-78	Port Huron Flags	IHL	72	3	28	31	....	....	....	162	....	....	....	....	....	....	....	....	....	....	17	0	7	7	58	....	....	....
1978-79	Maine Mariners	AHL	56	6	8	14	....	....	....	127	....	....	....	....	....	....	....	....	....	....	6	0	0	0	10	....	....	....
1979-80	Maine Mariners	AHL	75	0	12	12	....	....	....	155	....	....	....	....	....	....	....	....	....	....	12	1	1	2	22	....	....	....
1980-81	**Philadelphia Flyers**	**NHL**	**17**	**1**	**3**	**4**	**1**	**2**	**3**	**55**	**0**	**0**	**0**	**16**	**6.3**	**16**	**0**	**14**	**6**	**8**	**12**	**0**	**2**	**2**	**23**	**0**	**0**	**0**
	Maine Mariners	AHL	59	6	29	35	....	....	....	155	....	....	....	....	....	....	....	....	....	....	....	....	....	....	....	....	....	....
1981-82	**Philadelphia Flyers**	**NHL**	**10**	**0**	**0**	**0**	**0**	**0**	**0**	**23**	**0**	**0**	**0**	**7**	**0.0**	**5**	**0**	**15**	**5**	**–5**	**2**	**0**	**0**	**0**	**0**	**0**	**0**	**0**
	Maine Mariners	AHL	54	4	26	30	....	....	....	55	....	....	....	....	....	....	....	....	....	....	2	0	1	1	2	....	....	....
1982-83	Moncton Alpines	AHL	21	0	9	9	....	....	....	22	....	....	....	....	....	....	....	....	....	....	....	....	....	....	....	....	....	....
	Toronto Maple Leafs	**NHL**	**1**	**0**	**0**	**0**	**0**	**0**	**0**	**2**	**0**	**0**	**0**	**0**	**0.0**	**1**	**0**	**4**	**1**	**–2**	**2**	**0**	**0**	**0**	**2**	**0**	**0**	**0**
	St. Catharines Saints	AHL	34	0	14	14	....	....	....	62	....	....	....	....	....	....	....	....	....	....	....	....	....	....	....	....	....	....
1983-84	St. Catharines Saints	AHL	25	0	8	8	....	....	....	73	....	....	....	....	....	....	....	....	....	....	....	....	....	....	....	....	....	....
	Hartford Whalers	**NHL**	**12**	**0**	**0**	**0**	**0**	**0**	**0**	**25**	**0**	**0**	**0**	**8**	**0.0**	**4**	**0**	**8**	**2**	**–2**	....	....	....	....	....	....	....	....
	Binghamton Whalers	AHL	33	2	11	13	....	....	....	95	....	....	....	....	....	....	....	....	....	....	....	....	....	....	....	....	....	....
	NHL Totals		**40**	**1**	**3**	**4**	**1**	**2**	**3**	**105**	**0**	**0**	**0**	**31**	**3.2**	**26**	**0**	**41**	**14**		**16**	**0**	**2**	**2**	**25**	**0**	**0**	**0**

Signed as a free agent by **Philadelphia**, November 20, 1978. Signed as free agent by **Edmonton**, October 27, 1982. Traded to **Toronto** by **Edmonton** for Serge Boisvert, January 15, 1983. Signed as a free agent by **Hartford**, December 9, 1983.

• BAILLARGEON, Joel

LW – L. 6'1", 205 lbs. b: Quebec City, Que., 10/6/1964. Winnipeg's 7th, 113th overall, in 1983.

Season	Club	League	GP	G	A	Pts	AG	AA	APts	PIM	PP	SH	GW	S	%	TGF	PGF	TGA	PGA	+/-	GP	G	A	Pts	PIM	PP	SH	GW
1981-82	Trois-Rivieres Draveurs	QMJHL	26	1	3	4	....	....	....	47	....	....	....	....	....	....	....	....	....	....	22	1	1	2	58	....	....	....
1982-83	Trois-Rivieres Draveurs	QMJHL	29	4	5	9	....	....	....	197	....	....	....	....	....	....	....	....	....	....	....	....	....	....	....	....	....	....
	Hull Olympiques	QMJHL	25	15	7	22	....	....	....	76	....	....	....	....	....	....	....	....	....	....	7	0	1	1	16	....	....	....
1983-84	Chicoutimi Sagueneens	QMJHL	60	48	35	83	....	....	....	184	....	....	....	....	....	....	....	....	....	....	....	....	....	....	....	....	....	....
	Sherbrooke Jets	AHL	8	0	0	0	....	....	....	26	....	....	....	....	....	....	....	....	....	....	....	....	....	....	....	....	....	....
1984-85	Granby Bisons	QMJHL	32	25	24	49	....	....	....	160	....	....	....	....	....	....	....	....	....	....	....	....	....	....	....	....	....	....
1985-86	Sherbrooke Canadiens	AHL	56	6	12	18	....	....	....	115	....	....	....	....	....	....	....	....	....	....	....	....	....	....	....	....	....	....
1986-87	**Winnipeg Jets**	**NHL**	**11**	**0**	**1**	**1**	**0**	**1**	**1**	**15**	**0**	**0**	**0**	**1**	**0.0**	**2**	**0**	**5**	**0**	**–3**	....	....	....	....	....	....	....	....
	Sherbrooke Canadiens	AHL	44	9	18	27	....	....	....	137	....	....	....	....	....	....	....	....	....	....	6	2	2	4	27	....	....	....
	Fort Wayne Komets	IHL	4	1	1	2	....	....	....	37	....	....	....	....	....	....	....	....	....	....	....	....	....	....	....	....	....	....
1987-88	**Winnipeg Jets**	**NHL**	**4**	**0**	**1**	**1**	**0**	**1**	**1**	**12**	**0**	**0**	**0**	**3**	**0.0**	**1**	**0**	**1**	**0**	**0**	....	....	....	....	....	....	....	....
	Moncton Hawks	AHL	48	8	14	22	....	....	....	133	....	....	....	....	....	....	....	....	....	....	....	....	....	....	....	....	....	....
1988-89	**Quebec Nordiques**	**NHL**	**5**	**0**	**0**	**0**	**0**	**0**	**0**	**4**	**0**	**0**	**0**	**2**	**0.0**	**2**	**0**	**5**	**0**	**–3**	....	....	....	....	....	....	....	....
	Halifax Citadels	AHL	53	11	19	30	....	....	....	122	....	....	....	....	....	....	....	....	....	....	4	1	0	1	26	....	....	....
1989-90	Halifax Citadels	AHL	21	0	3	3	....	....	....	39	....	....	....	....	....	....	....	....	....	....	....	....	....	....	....	....	....	....
1990-1996			OUT OF HOCKEY – RETIRED																									
1996-97	Vanier Voyageurs	QSPHL	23	4	5	9	....	....	....	41	....	....	....	....	....	....	....	....	....	....	....	....	....	....	....	....	....	....
	NHL Totals		**20**	**0**	**2**	**2**	**0**	**2**	**2**	**31**	**0**	**0**	**0**	**6**	**0.0**	**5**	**0**	**11**	**0**		....	....	....	....	....	....	....	....

Traded to **Quebec** by **Winnipeg** for future considerations, July 29, 1988.

• BAIRD, Ken

Kenneth Stewart D – L. 6', 190 lbs. b: Flin Flon, Man., 2/1/1951. California's 1st, 15th overall, in 1971.

Season	Club	League	GP	G	A	Pts	AG	AA	APts	PIM	PP	SH	GW	S	%	TGF	PGF	TGA	PGA	+/-	GP	G	A	Pts	PIM	PP	SH	GW
1969-70	Estevan Bruins	WCJHL	1	0	0	0	....	....	....	0	....	....	....	....	....	....	....	....	....	....	....	....	....	....	....	....	....	....
	Flin Flon Bombers	WCJHL	47	2	5	7	....	....	....	126	....	....	....	....	....	....	....	....	....	....	17	2	8	10	60	....	....	....
1970-71	Flin Flon Bombers	WCJHL	66	35	40	75	....	....	....	211	....	....	....	....	....	....	....	....	....	....	17	12	9	21	119	....	....	....
1971-72	**California Golden Seals**	**NHL**	**10**	**0**	**2**	**2**	**0**	**2**	**2**	**15**	**0**	**0**	**0**	**6**	**0.0**	**9**	**0**	**19**	**0**	**–10**	....	....	....	....	....	....	....	....
	Oklahoma City Blazers	CHL	59	5	11	16	....	....	....	196	....	....	....	....	....	....	....	....	....	....	6	0	2	2	29	....	....	....
1972-73	Alberta Oilers	WHA	75	14	15	29	....	....	....	112	....	....	....	....	....	....	....	....	....	....	....	....	....	....	....	....	....	....
1973-74	Edmonton Oilers	WHA	68	17	19	36	....	....	....	115	....	....	....	....	....	....	....	....	....	....	5	1	1	2	7	....	....	....
1974-75	Edmonton Oilers	WHA	77	30	28	58	....	....	....	151	....	....	....	....	....	....	....	....	....	....	....	....	....	....	....	....	....	....
1975-76	Edmonton Oilers	WHA	48	13	24	37	....	....	....	87	....	....	....	....	....	....	....	....	....	....	4	3	1	4	16	....	....	....
1976-77	Edmonton Oilers	WHA	2	1	2	3	....	....	....	0	....	....	....	....	....	....	....	....	....	....	....	....	....	....	....	....	....	....
	Calgary Cowboys	WHA	7	0	0	0	....	....	....	2	....	....	....	....	....	....	....	....	....	....	....	....	....	....	....	....	....	....
1977-78	Edmonton Oilers	WHA	6	2	4	6	....	....	....	2	....	....	....	....	....	....	....	....	....	....	....	....	....	....	....	....	....	....
	Winnipeg Jets	WHA	49	14	7	21	....	....	....	29	....	....	....	....	....	....	....	....	....	....	7	0	4	4	7	....	....	....
1978-79	Dusseldorfer EG	Germany-2	STATISTICS NOT AVAILABLE																									
1979-80	Dusseldorfer EG	Germany	47	32	28	60	....	....	....	141	....	....	....	....	....	....	....	....	....	....	....	....	....	....	....	....	....	....
1980-81	Dusseldorfer EG	Germany	39	31	40	71	....	....	....	108	....	....	....	....	....	....	....	....	....	....	6	2	6	8	23	....	....	....
	NHL Totals		**10**	**0**	**2**	**2**	**0**	**2**	**2**	**15**	**0**	**0**	**0**	**6**	**0.0**	**9**	**0**	**19**	**0**		....	....	....	....	....	....	....	....
	Other Major League Totals		332	91	99	190	....	....	....	498	....	....	....	....	....	....	....	....	....	....	16	4	6	10	30	....	....	....

Selected by **Alberta** (WHA) in 1972 WHA General Player Draft, February 12, 1972. Signed as a free agent by **Calgary** (WHA), November, 1976. Signed as a free agent by **Edmonton** (WHA) after **Calgary** (WHA) franchise folded, May 31, 1977. Signed as a free agent by **Winnipeg** (WHA) after being released by **Edmonton** (WHA), December, 1977.

• BAKER, Bill

William Robert D – L. 6'1", 195 lbs. b: Grand Rapids, MN, 11/29/1956. Montreal's 5th, 54th overall, in 1976.

Season	Club	League	GP	G	A	Pts	AG	AA	APts	PIM	PP	SH	GW	S	%	TGF	PGF	TGA	PGA	+/-	GP	G	A	Pts	PIM	PP	SH	GW
1972-1974	East Grand Rapids Pioneers	Hi-School	STATISTICS NOT AVAILABLE																									
1975-76	University of Minnesota	WCHA	44	8	15	23	....	....	....	28	....	....	....	....	....	....	....	....	....	....	....	....	....	....	....	....	....	....
1976-77	University of Minnesota	WCHA	28	0	8	8	....	....	....	42	....	....	....	....	....	....	....	....	....	....	....	....	....	....	....	....	....	....
1977-78	University of Minnesota	WCHA	38	10	23	33	....	....	....	24	....	....	....	....	....	....	....	....	....	....	....	....	....	....	....	....	....	....
1978-79	University of Minnesota	WCHA	44	12	42	54	....	....	....	38	....	....	....	....	....	....	....	....	....	....	....	....	....	....	....	....	....	....
	United States	WEC-A	7	2	1	3	....	....	....	2	....	....	....	....	....	....	....	....	....	....	....	....	....	....	....	....	....	....
1979-80	United States	Nat-Team	60	5	25	30	....	....	....	74	....	....	....	....	....	....	....	....	....	....	....	....	....	....	....	....	....	....
	United States	Olympics	7	1	0	1	....	....	....	4	....	....	....	....	....	....	....	....	....	....	....	....	....	....	....	....	....	....
	Nova Scotia Voyageurs	AHL	12	4	8	12	....	....	....	5	....	....	....	....	....	....	....	....	....	....	1	0	1	1	0	....	....	....
1980-81	**Montreal Canadiens**	**NHL**	**11**	**0**	**0**	**0**	**0**	**0**	**0**	**32**	**0**	**0**	**0**	**8**	**0.0**	**6**	**0**	**8**	**1**	**–1**	....	....	....	....	....	....	....	....
	Nova Scotia Voyageurs	AHL	18	5	12	17	....	....	....	42	....	....	....	....	....	....	....	....	....	....	....	....	....	....	....	....	....	....
	Colorado Rockies	**NHL**	**13**	**0**	**3**	**3**	**0**	**2**	**2**	**12**	**0**	**0**	**0**	**17**	**0.0**	**12**	**2**	**17**	**7**	**0**	....	....	....	....	....	....	....	....
	United States	WEC-A	7	0	1	1	....	....	....	8	....	....	....	....	....	....	....	....	....	....	....	....	....	....	....	....	....	....
1981-82	United States	Can-Cup	1	0	0	0	....	....	....	0	....	....	....	....	....	....	....	....	....	....	....	....	....	....	....	....	....	....
	Colorado Rockies	**NHL**	**14**	**0**	**3**	**3**	**0**	**2**	**2**	**17**	**0**	**0**	**0**	**11**	**0.0**	**7**	**1**	**25**	**6**	**–13**	....	....	....	....	....	....	....	....
	Fort Worth Texans	CHL	10	3	12	15	....	....	....	20	....	....	....	....	....	....	....	....	....	....	....	....	....	....	....	....	....	....
	St. Louis Blues	**NHL**	**35**	**3**	**5**	**8**	**2**	**3**	**5**	**50**	**1**	**0**	**0**	**44**	**6.8**	**43**	**6**	**51**	**6**	**–8**	**4**	**0**	**0**	**0**	**0**	**0**	**0**	**0**
1982-83	**New York Rangers**	**NHL**	**70**	**4**	**14**	**18**	**3**	**10**	**13**	**64**	**1**	**0**	**2**	**63**	**6.3**	**54**	**5**	**71**	**14**	**–8**	**2**	**0**	**0**	**0**	**0**	**0**	**0**	**0**
1983-84	Tulsa Oilers	CHL	59	11	22	33	....	....	....	47	....	....	....	....	....	....	....	....	....	....	....	....	....	....	....	....	....	....
	NHL Totals		**143**	**7**	**25**	**32**	**5**	**17**	**22**	**175**	**2**	**0**	**2**	**143**	**4.9**	**122**	**14**	**172**	**34**		**6**	**0**	**0**	**0**	**0**	**0**	**0**	**0**

WCHA First All-Star Team (1979) • NCAA West First All-American Team (1979)

Traded to **Colorado** by **Montreal** for Colorado's 3rd round choice (Daniel Letendre) in 1983 Entry Draft, March 10, 1981. Traded to **St. Louis** by **Colorado** for Joe Micheletti and Dick Lamby, December 4, 1981. Claimed by **NY Rangers** from **St. Louis** in Waiver Draft, October 4, 1982.

• BAKER, Jamie

James Patrick C – L. 6', 195 lbs. b: Ottawa, Ont., 8/31/1966. Quebec's 2nd, 8th overall, in 1988 Supplemental Draft.

Season	Club	League	GP	G	A	Pts	AG	AA	APts	PIM	PP	SH	GW	S	%	TGF	PGF	TGA	PGA	+/-	GP	G	A	Pts	PIM	PP	SH	GW
1983-84	Nepean Raiders	OJHL	49	21	35	56	....	....	....	41	....	....	....	....	....	....	....	....	....	....	....	....	....	....	....	....	....	....
1984-85	Nepean Raiders	OJHL	50	30	41	71	....	....	....		....	....	....	....	....	....	....	....	....	....	....	....	....	....	....	....	....	....
1985-86	St. Lawrence University	ECAC	31	9	16	25	....	....	....	52	....	....	....	....	....	....	....	....	....	....	....	....	....	....	....	....	....	....
1986-87	St. Lawrence University	ECAC	32	8	24	32	....	....	....	59	....	....	....	....	....	....	....	....	....	....	....	....	....	....	....	....	....	....
1987-88	St. Lawrence University	ECAC	34	26	24	50	....	....	....	38	....	....	....	....	....	....	....	....	....	....	....	....	....	....	....	....	....	....
1988-89	St. Lawrence University	ECAC	13	11	16	27	....	....	....	16	....	....	....	....	....	....	....	....	....	....	....	....	....	....	....	....	....	....

Season	Club	League	GP	G	A	Pts	AG	AA	APts	PIM	PP	SH	GW	S	%	TGF	PGF	TGA	PGA	+/–	GP	G	A	Pts	PIM	PP	SH	GW
			REGULAR SEASON																		PLAYOFFS							
1989-90	**Quebec Nordiques**	**NHL**	**1**	**0**	**0**	**0**	**0**	**0**	**0**	**0**	**0**	**0**	**0**	**0**	**0.0**	**0**	**0**	**1**	**0**	**–1**	....	....	....	....	....	....	....	....
	Halifax Citadels	AHL	74	17	43	60	....	....	....	47	....	....	....	....	....	....	....	....	....	....	6	0	0	0	7	....	....	....
1990-91	**Quebec Nordiques**	**NHL**	**18**	**2**	**0**	**2**	**2**	**0**	**2**	**8**	**0**	**1**	**0**	**18**	**11.1**	**6**	**0**	**15**	**5**	**–4**	....	....	....	....	....	....	....	....
	Halifax Citadels	AHL	50	14	22	36	....	....	....	85	....	....	....	....	....	....	....	....	....	....	....	....	....	....	....	....	....	....
1991-92	**Quebec Nordiques**	**NHL**	**52**	**7**	**10**	**17**	**6**	**8**	**14**	**32**	**3**	**0**	**1**	**77**	**9.1**	**28**	**9**	**33**	**9**	**–5**	....	....	....	....	....	....	....	....
	Halifax Citadels	AHL	9	5	0	5	....	....	....	12	....	....	....	....	....	....	....	....	....	....	....	....	....	....	....	....	....	....
1992-93	**Ottawa Senators**	**NHL**	**76**	**19**	**29**	**48**	**16**	**20**	**36**	**54**	**10**	**0**	**2**	**160**	**11.9**	**79**	**38**	**73**	**12**	**–20**	....	....	....	....	....	....	....	....
1993-94	**San Jose Sharks**	**NHL**	**65**	**12**	**5**	**17**	**11**	**4**	**15**	**38**	**0**	**0**	**2**	**68**	**17.6**	**31**	**1**	**55**	**27**	**2**	**14**	**3**	**2**	**5**	**30**	**0**	**0**	**1**
1994-95	**San Jose Sharks**	**NHL**	**43**	**7**	**4**	**11**	**12**	**6**	**18**	**22**	**0**	**1**	**0**	**60**	**11.7**	**16**	**0**	**39**	**16**	**–7**	**11**	**2**	**2**	**4**	**12**	**0**	**0**	**1**
1995-96	**San Jose Sharks**	**NHL**	**77**	**16**	**17**	**33**	**16**	**14**	**30**	**79**	**2**	**6**	**0**	**117**	**13.7**	**51**	**5**	**106**	**41**	**–19**	....	....	....	....	....	....	....	....
1996-97	**Toronto Maple Leafs**	**NHL**	**58**	**8**	**8**	**16**	**8**	**7**	**15**	**28**	**1**	**0**	**3**	**69**	**11.6**	**34**	**4**	**45**	**17**	**2**	....	....	....	....	....	....	....	....
1997-98	**Toronto Maple Leafs**	**NHL**	**13**	**0**	**5**	**5**	**0**	**5**	**5**	**10**	**0**	**0**	**0**	**16**	**0.0**	**8**	**0**	**11**	**4**	**1**	....	....	....	....	....	....	....	....
	Chicago Wolves	IHL	53	11	34	45	....	....	....	80	....	....	....	....	....	....	....	....	....	....	22	4	5	9	42	....	....	....
1998-99	**San Jose Sharks**	**NHL**	**1**	**0**	**1**	**1**	**0**	**1**	**1**	**0**	**0**	**0**	**0**	**1**	**0.0**	**1**	**0**	**0**	**0**	**1**	....	....	....	....	....	....	....	....
	HIFK Helsinki	Finland	11	1	5	6	....	....	....	22	....	....	....	....	....	....	....	....	....	....	6	0	3	3	35	....	....	....
	NHL Totals		**404**	**71**	**79**	**150**	**71**	**65**	**136**	**271**	**16**	**8**	**8**	**586**	**12.1**	**254**	**57**	**378**	**131**		**25**	**5**	**4**	**9**	**42**	**0**	**0**	**2**

Signed as a free agent by **Ottawa**, September 2, 1992. Signed as a free agent by **San Jose**, September 11, 1993. Traded to **Toronto** by **San Jose** with San Jose's 5th round choice (Peter Cava) in 1996 Entry Draft for Todd Gill, June 14, 1996. Signed as a free agent by **San Jose**, September 29, 1998.

• BAKOVIC, Peter

Peter George RW – R. 6'2", 200 lbs. b: Port Arthur, Ont., 1/31/1965.

Season	Club	League	GP	G	A	Pts	AG	AA	APts	PIM	PP	SH	GW	S	%	TGF	PGF	TGA	PGA	+/–	GP	G	A	Pts	PIM	PP	SH	GW
1982-83	Thunder Bay Flyers	TBJHL	40	30	29	59	....	....	....	159	....	....	....	....	....	....	....	....	....	....	....	....	....	....	....	....	....	....
1983-84	Dixie Beehives	OJHL	4	2	5	7	....	....	....	21	....	....	....	....	....	....	....	....	....	....	....	....	....	....	....	....	....	....
	Kitchener Rangers	OHL	28	2	6	8	....	....	....	87	....	....	....	....	....	....	....	....	....	....	....	....	....	....	....	....	....	....
	Windsor Spitfires	OHL	35	10	25	35	....	....	....	74	....	....	....	....	....	....	....	....	....	....	3	0	2	2	14	....	....	....
1984-85	Windsor Spitfires	OHL	58	26	48	74	....	....	....	*259	....	....	....	....	....	....	....	....	....	....	3	0	0	0	12	....	....	....
1985-86	Moncton Golden Flames	AHL	80	18	36	54	....	....	....	349	....	....	....	....	....	....	....	....	....	....	10	2	2	4	30	....	....	....
1986-87	Moncton Golden Flames	AHL	77	17	34	51	....	....	....	280	....	....	....	....	....	....	....	....	....	....	6	3	3	6	54	....	....	....
1987-88	Salt Lake Golden Eagles	IHL	39	16	27	43	....	....	....	221	....	....	....	....	....	....	....	....	....	....	....	....	....	....	....	....	....	....
	Vancouver Canucks	**NHL**	**10**	**2**	**0**	**2**	**2**	**0**	**2**	**48**	**0**	**0**	**0**	**7**	**28.6**	**4**	**0**	**5**	**0**	**–1**	....	....	....	....	....	....	....	....
1988-89	Milwaukee Admirals	IHL	40	16	14	30	....	....	....	211	....	....	....	....	....	....	....	....	....	....	11	4	4	8	46	....	....	....
1989-90	Milwaukee Admirals	IHL	56	19	30	49	....	....	....	230	....	....	....	....	....	....	....	....	....	....	6	4	1	5	52	....	....	....
1990-91	Milwaukee Admirals	IHL	69	17	45	62	....	....	....	220	....	....	....	....	....	....	....	....	....	....	6	0	4	4	16	....	....	....
1991-1996	Milwaukee Admirals	IHL	DID NOT PLAY – ASSISTANT COACH																									
	NHL Totals		**10**	**2**	**0**	**2**	**2**	**0**	**2**	**48**	**0**	**0**	**0**	**7**	**28.6**	**4**	**0**	**5**	**0**		....	....	....	....	....	....	....	....

Signed as a free agent by **Calgary**, October 10, 1985. Traded to **Vancouver** by **Calgary** with Brian Bradley and Kevan Guy for Craig Coxe, March 6, 1988.

• BALDERIS, Helmut

RW – R. 5'11", 190 lbs. b: Riga, Latvia, 6/30/1952. Minnesota's 13th, 238th overall, in 1989.

Season	Club	League	GP	G	A	Pts	AG	AA	APts	PIM	PP	SH	GW	S	%	TGF	PGF	TGA	PGA	+/–	GP	G	A	Pts	PIM	PP	SH	GW
1967-68	Dynamo Riga	USSR-2	STATISTICS NOT AVAILABLE																									
1968-69	Dynamo Riga	USSR-3	STATISTICS NOT AVAILABLE																									
1969-70	Dynamo Riga	USSR-3	....	12	....	12	....	....	....	....	....	....	....	....	....	....	....	....	....	....	....	....	....	....	....	....	....	....
1970-71	Dynamo Riga	USSR-2	....	10	....	10	....	....	....	....	....	....	....	....	....	....	....	....	....	....	....	....	....	....	....	....	....	....
	Soviet Union	EJC-A	5	10	1	11	....	....	....	4	....	....	....	....	....	....	....	....	....	....	....	....	....	....	....	....	....	....
1971-72	Dynamo Riga	USSR-2	....	14	9	23	....	....	....	....	....	....	....	....	....	....	....	....	....	....	....	....	....	....	....	....	....	....
1972-73	Dynamo Riga	USSR-2	....	27	15	42	....	....	....	....	....	....	....	....	....	....	....	....	....	....	....	....	....	....	....	....	....	....
1973-74	Dynamo Riga	USSR	24	9	6	15	....	....	....	13	....	....	....	....	....	....	....	....	....	....	....	....	....	....	....	....	....	....
1974-75	Dynamo Riga	USSR	36	34	14	48	....	....	....	20	....	....	....	....	....	....	....	....	....	....	....	....	....	....	....	....	....	....
1975-76	Dynamo Riga	USSR	36	31	14	45	....	....	....	18	....	....	....	....	....	....	....	....	....	....	....	....	....	....	....	....	....	....
	Soviet Union	WEC-A	10	3	7	10	....	....	....	6	....	....	....	....	....	....	....	....	....	....	....	....	....	....	....	....	....	....
1976-77	Soviet Union	Can-Cup	5	2	3	5	....	....	....	6	....	....	....	....	....	....	....	....	....	....	....	....	....	....	....	....	....	....
	Dynamo Riga	USSR	35	40	23	*63	....	....	....	57	....	....	....	....	....	....	....	....	....	....	....	....	....	....	....	....	....	....
	Soviet Union	WEC-A	9	8	7	15	....	....	....	4	....	....	....	....	....	....	....	....	....	....	....	....	....	....	....	....	....	....
1977-78	CSKA Moscow	USSR	36	17	17	*34	....	....	....	30	....	....	....	....	....	....	....	....	....	....	....	....	....	....	....	....	....	....
	Soviet Union	WEC-A	10	9	2	11	....	....	....	8	....	....	....	....	....	....	....	....	....	....	....	....	....	....	....	....	....	....
1978-79	CSKA Moscow	USSR	41	24	24	48	....	....	....	53	....	....	....	....	....	....	....	....	....	....	....	....	....	....	....	....	....	....
	USSR	Chal-Cup	3	1	1	2	....	....	....	0	....	....	....	....	....	....	....	....	....	....	....	....	....	....	....	....	....	....
	Soviet Union	WEC-A	8	4	5	9	....	....	....	9	....	....	....	....	....	....	....	....	....	....	....	....	....	....	....	....	....	....
1979-80	CSKA Moscow	USSR	42	26	35	61	....	....	....	21	....	....	....	....	....	....	....	....	....	....	....	....	....	....	....	....	....	....
	CSKA Moscow	Super-S	5	5	2	7	....	....	....	2	....	....	....	....	....	....	....	....	....	....	....	....	....	....	....	....	....	....
	Soviet Union	Olympics	7	5	4	9	....	....	....	5	....	....	....	....	....	....	....	....	....	....	....	....	....	....	....	....	....	....
1980-81	Dynamo Riga	USSR	44	26	24	50	....	....	....	28	....	....	....	....	....	....	....	....	....	....	....	....	....	....	....	....	....	....
1981-82	Dynamo Riga	USSR	41	24	19	43	....	....	....	48	....	....	....	....	....	....	....	....	....	....	9	*15	5	*20	2	....	....	....
1982-83	Dynamo Riga	USSR*	40	32	31	*63	....	....	....	39	....	....	....	....	....	....	....	....	....	....	....	....	....	....	....	....	....	....
	Soviet Union	WEC-A	10	4	5	9	....	....	....	22	....	....	....	....	....	....	....	....	....	....	....	....	....	....	....	....	....	....
1983-84	Dynamo Riga	USSR	39	24	15	39	....	....	....	18	....	....	....	....	....	....	....	....	....	....	....	....	....	....	....	....	....	....
1984-85	Dynamo Riga	USSR	39	31	20	51	....	....	....	52	....	....	....	....	....	....	....	....	....	....	....	....	....	....	....	....	....	....
1985-1989			OUT OF HOCKEY – RETIRED																									
1989-90	**Minnesota North Stars**	**NHL**	**26**	**3**	**6**	**9**	**3**	**4**	**7**	**2**	**2**	**0**	**0**	**30**	**10.0**	**15**	**5**	**10**	**0**	**0**	....	....	....	....	....	....	....	....
1990-91			OUT OF HOCKEY – RETIRED																									
1991-92	Vecmeistras Riga	Latvia	7	23	18	41	....	....	....	27	....	....	....	....	....	....	....	....	....	....	....	....	....	....	....	....	....	....
1992-93	Latvijas Zelts	Latvia	22	*76	*66	*142	....	....	....	16	....	....	....	....	....	....	....	....	....	....	....	....	....	....	....	....	....	....
1993-94			OUT OF HOCKEY – RETIRED																									
1994-95	Essamka Ogre	Latvia	1	0	1	1	....	....	....	0	....	....	....	....	....	....	....	....	....	....	....	....	....	....	....	....	....	....
1995-96	Essamka Ogre	Latvia	30	18	36	54	....	....	....	....	....	....	....	....	....	....	....	....	....	....	....	....	....	....	....	....	....	....
	NHL Totals		**26**	**3**	**6**	**9**	**3**	**4**	**7**	**2**	**2**	**0**	**0**	**30**	**10.0**	**15**	**5**	**10**	**0**		....	....	....	....	....	....	....	....

USSR First All-Star Team (1977) • Won Izvestia Trophy (USSR Top Scorer) (1977, 1983) • USSR Player of the Year (1977) • WEC-A All-Star Team (1977) • Named Best Forward at WEC-A (1977) • Only goals scored totals available for 1969-70 and 1970-71 seasons.

• BALL, Terry

Terrance James D – R. 5'9", 160 lbs. b: Selkirk, Man., 11/29/1944.

Season	Club	League	GP	G	A	Pts	AG	AA	APts	PIM	PP	SH	GW	S	%	TGF	PGF	TGA	PGA	+/–	GP	G	A	Pts	PIM	PP	SH	GW
1961-62	Winnipeg Rangers	MJHL	39	2	2	4	....	....	....	65	....	....	....	....	....	....	....	....	....	....	3	0	1	1	5	....	....	....
1962-63	Winnipeg Rangers	MJHL	39	8	23	31	....	....	....	104	....	....	....	....	....	....	....	....	....	....	....	....	....	....	....	....	....	....
	Brandon Wheat Kings	MJHL	....	....	....	....	....	....	....	....	....	....	....	....	....	....	....	....	....	....	5	0	0	0	12	....	....	....
	Brandon Wheat Kings	Mem-Cup	5	0	0	0	....	....	....	12	....	....	....	....	....	....	....	....	....	....	....	....	....	....	....	....	....	....
1963-64	Winnipeg Rangers	MJHL	29	6	16	22	....	....	....	110	....	....	....	....	....	....	....	....	....	....	4	0	2	2	11	....	....	....
	Vancouver Canucks	WHL	8	0	2	2	....	....	....	4	....	....	....	....	....	....	....	....	....	....	....	....	....	....	....	....	....	....
	Winnipeg Maroons	MHL-Sr.	....	....	....	....	....	....	....	....	....	....	....	....	....	....	....	....	....	....	3	1	0	1	0	....	....	....
1964-65	Kitchener Rangers	OHA-Jr.	55	6	47	53	....	....	....	153	....	....	....	....	....	....	....	....	....	....	....	....	....	....	....	....	....	....
	St. Paul Rangers	CPHL	....	....	....	....	....	....	....	....	....	....	....	....	....	....	....	....	....	....	1	0	0	0	0	....	....	....
1965-66	Minnesota Rangers	CPHL	68	0	10	10	....	....	....	98	....	....	....	....	....	....	....	....	....	....	7	1	0	1	17	....	....	....
1966-67	Omaha Knights	CPHL	70	5	15	20	....	....	....	78	....	....	....	....	....	....	....	....	....	....	5	1	0	1	2	....	....	....
1967-68	**Philadelphia Flyers**	**NHL**	**1**	**0**	**0**	**0**	**0**	**0**	**0**	**0**	**0**	**0**	**0**	**0**	**0.0**	**0**	**0**	**1**	**0**	**–1**	....	....	....	....	....	....	....	....
	Quebec Aces	AHL	72	3	39	42	....	....	....	99	....	....	....	....	....	....	....	....	....	....	15	1	7	8	22	....	....	....
1968-69	Quebec Aces	AHL	74	14	45	59	....	....	....	72	....	....	....	....	....	....	....	....	....	....	15	8	8	*16	8	....	....	....
1969-70	**Philadelphia Flyers**	**NHL**	**61**	**7**	**18**	**25**	**8**	**17**	**25**	**20**	**3**	**1**	**0**	**98**	**7.1**	**63**	**37**	**36**	**3**	**–7**	....	....	....	....	....	....	....	....
	Quebec Aces	AHL	10	3	5	8	....	....	....	8	....	....	....	....	....	....	....	....	....	....	....	....	....	....	....	....	....	....
1970-71	Amarillo Wranglers	CHL	41	5	30	35	....	....	....	24	....	....	....	....	....	....	....	....	....	....	....	....	....	....	....	....	....	....
	Buffalo Sabres	**NHL**	**2**	**0**	**0**	**0**	**0**	**0**	**0**	**0**	**0**	**0**	**0**	**2**	**0.0**	**1**	**0**	**1**	**0**	**0**	....	....	....	....	....	....	....	....
	Salt Lake Golden Eagles	WHL	22	2	12	14	....	....	....	20	....	....	....	....	....	....	....	....	....	....	....	....	....	....	....	....	....	....
1971-72	**Buffalo Sabres**	**NHL**	**10**	**0**	**1**	**1**	**0**	**1**	**1**	**6**	**0**	**0**	**0**	**8**	**0.0**	**10**	**4**	**13**	**0**	**–7**	....	....	....	....	....	....	....	....
	Cincinnati Swords	AHL	68	17	39	56	....	....	....	62	....	....	....	....	....	....	....	....	....	....	10	3	8	11	2	....	....	....
1972-73	Minnesota Fighting Saints	WHA	76	6	34	40	....	....	....	66	....	....	....	....	....	....	....	....	....	....	5	1	2	3	4	....	....	....

			REGULAR SEASON																		PLAYOFFS							
Season	Club	League	GP	G	A	Pts	AG	AA	APts	PIM	PP	SH	GW	S	%	TGF	PGF	TGA	PGA	+/-	GP	G	A	Pts	PIM	PP	SH	GW
1973-74	Minnesota Fighting Saints	WHA	71	8	28	36				34											11	1	2	3	6			
1974-75	Minnesota Fighting Saints	WHA	76	8	37	45				36											12	3	4	7	4			
1975-76	Cleveland Crusaders	WHA	23	2	15	17				18																		
	Cincinnati Stingers	WHA	36	3	14	17				12																		
1976-77	Birmingham Bulls	WHA	23	1	6	7				8																		
	Oklahoma City Blazers	CHL	15	0	4	4				4																		
1977-78	HIFK Helsinki	Finland	33	1	4	5				44																		
1978-79	HIFK Helsinki	Finland	6	0	2	2				4																		
	NHL Totals		**74**	**7**	**19**	**26**	**8**	**18**	**26**	**26**	**3**	**1**	**0**	**108**	**6.5**	**74**	**41**	**51**	**3**									
	Other Major League Totals		305	28	134	162				174											28	5	8	13	14			

AHL First All-Star Team (1972)

Claimed by **Philadelphia** from **NY Rangers** in Expansion Draft, June 6, 1967. Traded to **Pittsburgh** by **Philadelphia** for George Swarbrick, June 11, 1970. Traded to **Buffalo** by **Pittsburgh** for Jean-Guy Legace, January 24, 1971. Selected by **Minnesota** (WHA) in 1972 WHA General Player Draft, February 12, 1972. Claimed by **Cleveland** (WHA) from **Minnesota** (WHA) in WHA Intra-League Draft, June 19, 1975. Traded to **Cincinnati** (WHA) by **Cleveland** (WHA) for future considerations, January, 1976. Claimed on waivers by **Birmingham** (WHA) from **Cincinnati** (WHA), October, 1976.

• BALMOCHNYKH, Maxim

LW – L. 6', 185 lbs. b: Lipetsk, USSR, 3/7/1979. Anaheim's 2nd, 45th overall, in 1997.

Season	Club	League	GP	G	A	Pts	AG	AA	APts	PIM	PP	SH	GW	S	%	TGF	PGF	TGA	PGA	+/-	GP	G	A	Pts	PIM	PP	SH	GW
1994-95	HC Lipetsk	CIS 2	3	0	1	1				4																		
1995-96	HC Lipetsk	CIS 2	40	15	5	20				60																		
1996-97	Lada Togliatti	Russia	18	6	1	7				22																		
1997-98	Lada Togliatti	Russia	37	10	4	14				46																		
	Russia	WJC-A	7	2	6	8				4																		
	Traktor Chelyabinsk	Russia	2	0	0	0				2																		
1998-99	Quebec Remparts	QMJHL	21	9	22	31				38																		
	Lada Togliatti	Russia	15	2	1	3				10											4	0	1	1	8			
	Russia	WJC-A	7	3	5	8				4																		
99-2000	Mighty Ducks of Anaheim	NHL	6	0	1	1	0	1	1	2	0	0	0	6	0.0	3	1	0	0	2								
	Cincinnati Mighty Ducks	AHL	40	9	12	21				82																		
	NHL Totals		**6**	**0**	**1**	**1**	**0**	**1**	**1**	**2**	**0**	**0**	**0**	**6**	**0.0**	**3**	**1**	**0**	**0**									

WJC-A All-Star Team (1999)

• BALON, Dave

David Alexander LW – L. 5'10", 180 lbs. b: Wakaw, Sask., 8/2/1938.

Season	Club	League	GP	G	A	Pts	AG	AA	APts	PIM	PP	SH	GW	S	%	TGF	PGF	TGA	PGA	+/-	GP	G	A	Pts	PIM	PP	SH	GW
1955-56	Prince Albert Mintos	SJHL	14	5	5	10				14											12	3	2	5	14			
1956-57	Prince Albert Mintos	SJHL	40	29	30	59				112											13	5	5	10	15			
1957-58	Prince Albert Mintos	SJHL	51	35	44	79				113											6	3	1	4	10			
	Vancouver Canucks	WHL	4	0	2	2				8																		
	Regina Pats	Mem-Cup	16	6	4	10				23																		
1958-59	Saskatoon Quakers	WHL	57	12	25	37				80																		
1959-60	New York Rangers	NHL	3	0	0	0	0	0	0	0																		
	Vancouver Canucks	WHL	3	1	1	2				2																		
	Trois-Rivieres Lions	EPHL	61	28	42	70				104											7	2	2	4	19			
1960-61	New York Rangers	NHL	13	1	2	3	1	2	3	8																		
	Kitchener-Waterloo Beavers	EPHL	55	15	26	41				77											7	1	1	2	12			
1961-62	New York Rangers	NHL	30	4	11	15	5	10	15	11											6	2	3	5	2	0	0	2
	Kitchener-Waterloo Beavers	EPHL	37	23	19	42				87																		
1962-63	New York Rangers	NHL	70	11	13	24	13	13	26	72																		
1963-64	Montreal Canadiens	NHL	70	24	18	42	30	19	49	80											7	1	1	2	25	0	0	0
1964-65♦	Montreal Canadiens	NHL	63	18	23	41	22	24	46	61											10	0	0	0	10	0	0	0
1965-66♦	Montreal Canadiens	NHL	45	3	7	10	3	7	10	24											9	2	3	5	16	0	0	0
	Houston Apollos	CPHL	9	6	6	12				0																		
1966-67	Montreal Canadiens	NHL	48	11	8	19	13	8	21	31											9	0	2	2	6	0	0	0
1967-68	Minnesota North Stars	NHL	73	15	32	47	17	32	49	84	4	1	2	152	9.9	66	18	63	5	-10	14	4	*9	13	14	1	0	1
1968-69	New York Rangers	NHL	75	10	21	31	11	19	30	57	1	2	3	134	7.5	45	8	38	6	5	4	1	0	1	0	0	0	0
1969-70	New York Rangers	NHL	76	33	37	70	36	35	71	100	4	1	3	202	16.3	99	15	49	5	40	6	1	1	2	32	0	1	0
1970-71	New York Rangers	NHL	78	36	24	60	36	20	56	34	9	0	7	176	20.5	87	19	63	9	14	13	3	2	5	4	2	0	1
1971-72	New York Rangers	NHL	16	4	5	9	4	4	8	2	1	0	1	30	13.3	13	2	6	0	5								
	Vancouver Canucks	NHL	59	19	19	38	19	16	35	21	6	0	3	103	18.4	60	21	54	0	-15								
1972-73	Vancouver Canucks	NHL	57	3	2	5	3	2	5	22	1	0	0	23	13.0	13	3	26	0	-16								
1973-74	Quebec Nordiques	WHA	9	0	0	0				2																		
	Binghamton Dusters	AHL	7	0	1	1				0																		
	NHL Totals		**776**	**192**	**222**	**414**	**213**	**211**	**424**	**607**											**78**	**14**	**21**	**35**	**109**			
	Other Major League Totals		9	0	0	0				2																		

Played in NHL All-Star Game (1965, 1967, 1968, 1971)

Traded to **Montreal** by **NY Rangers** with Gump Worsley, Leon Rochefort and Len Ronson for Phil Goyette, Don Marshall and Jacques Plante, June 4, 1963. Selected by **Minnesota** from **Montreal** in Expansion Draft, June 6, 1967. Traded to **NY Rangers** by **Minnesota** for Wayne Hillman, Dan Seguin and Joey Johnston, June 12, 1968. Traded to **Vancouver** by **NY Rangers** with Wayne Connelly and Ron Stewart for Gary Doak and Jim Wiste, November 16, 1971. Selected by **Quebec** (WHA) in 1972 WHA General Player Draft, February 12, 1972.

• BALTIMORE, Bryon

Bryon Donald D – R. 6'2", 190 lbs. b: Whitehorse, Yukon, 8/26/1952.

Season	Club	League	GP	G	A	Pts	AG	AA	APts	PIM	PP	SH	GW	S	%	TGF	PGF	TGA	PGA	+/-	GP	G	A	Pts	PIM	PP	SH	GW
1970-71	University of Alberta	CWUAA	35	8	15	23				82																		
1971-72	University of Alberta	CWUAA	34	5	23	28				78																		
1972-73	Springfield Kings	AHL	73	15	12	27				36																		
1973-74	Springfield Kings	AHL	68	4	21	25				72																		
1974-75	Chicago Cougars	WHA	77	8	12	20				110																		
1975-76	Denver-Ottawa Civics	WHA	41	1	8	9				32																		
	Indianapolis Racers	WHA	37	1	10	11				30											7	0	1	1	4			
1976-77	Indianapolis Racers	WHA	55	0	15	15				63											9	0	0	0	5			
1977-78	Indianapolis Racers	WHA	22	1	7	8				23																		
	Cincinnati Stingers	WHA	28	2	9	11				47																		
1978-79	Indianapolis Racers	WHA	2	1	1	2				2																		
	Cincinnati Stingers	WHA	69	4	10	14				83											3	0	0	0	2			
1979-80	Edmonton Oilers	NHL	2	0	0	0	0	0	0	4	0	0	0	2	0.0	6	0	2	0	4								
	Houston Apollos	CHL	61	1	25	26				76											6	0	1	1	11			
1980-81	Wichita Wind	CHL	46	1	10	11				66											16	0	8	8	20			
	NHL Totals		**2**	**0**	**0**	**0**	**0**	**0**	**0**	**4**	**0**	**0**	**0**	**2**	**0.0**	**6**	**0**	**2**	**0**									
	Other Major League Totals		331	18	72	90				390											19	0	1	1	11			

Signed as a free agent by **Chicago** (WHA), July, 1974. Selected by **Denver** (WHA) from **Chicago** (WHA) in WHA Expansion Draft, May, 1975. Traded to **Indianapolis** (WHA) by **Denver-Ottawa** (WHA) with Darryl Maggs, Francois Rochon and Marl Lomenda for cash, January 20, 1976. Traded to **Cincinnati** (WHA) by **Indianapolis** (WHA) with Hugh Harris for Blaine Stoughton and Gilles Marotte, January, 1978. Claimed by **Edmonton** from **Cincinnati** (WHA) in WHA Dispersal Draft, June 9, 1979.

• BANCROFT, Steve

D – L. 6'1", 214 lbs. b: Toronto, Ont., 10/6/1970. Toronto's 3rd, 21st overall, in 1989.

Season	Club	League	GP	G	A	Pts	AG	AA	APts	PIM	PP	SH	GW	S	%	TGF	PGF	TGA	PGA	+/-	GP	G	A	Pts	PIM	PP	SH	GW
1985-86	Madoc MTM Hurricanes	OJHL-C	7	1	0	1				21																		
	Trenton Bobcats	OJHL-B	16	1	5	6				16																		
1986-87	Trenton Bobcats	OJHL-B	13	2	3	5				45																		
	St. Catharines Falcons	OJHL-B	11	5	8	13				20																		
1987-88	Belleville Bulls	OHL	56	1	8	9				42																		
1988-89	Belleville Bulls	OHL	66	7	30	37				99											5	0	2	2	10			
1989-90	Belleville Bulls	OHL	53	10	33	43				135											11	3	9	12	38			

Season	Club	League	GP	G	A	Pts	AG	AA	APts	PIM	PP	SH	GW	S	%	TGF	PGF	TGA	PGA	+/–	GP	G	A	Pts	PIM	PP	SH	GW
			REGULAR SEASON																		PLAYOFFS							
1990-91	Newmarket Saints	AHL	9	0	3	3	....	....	....	22	....	....	....	....	....	....	....	....	....	....	....	....	....	....	....	....	....	....
	Maine Mariners	AHL	53	2	12	14	....	....	....	46	....	....	....	....	....	....	....	....	....	....	2	0	0	0	2	....	....	....
1991-92	Maine Mariners	AHL	26	1	3	4	....	....	....	45	....	....	....	....	....	....	....	....	....	....	....	....	....	....	....	....	....	....
	Indianapolis Ice	IHL	36	8	23	31	....	....	....	49	....	....	....	....	....	....	....	....	....	....	....	....	....	....	....	....	....	....
1992-93	**Chicago Blackhawks**	**NHL**	**1**	**0**	**0**	**0**	**0**	**0**	**0**	**0**	**0**	**0**	**0**	**0**	**0.0**	**0**	**0**	**0**	**0**	**0**	....	....	....	....	....	....	....	....
	Indianapolis Ice	IHL	53	10	35	45	....	....	....	138	....	....	....	....	....	....	....	....	....	....	....	....	....	....	....	....	....	....
	Moncton Hawks	AHL	21	3	13	16	....	....	....	16	....	....	....	....	....	....	....	....	....	....	5	0	0	0	16	....	....	....
1993-94	Cleveland Lumberjacks	IHL	33	2	12	14	....	....	....	58	....	....	....	....	....	....	....	....	....	....	....	....	....	....	....	....	....	....
1994-95	Detroit Vipers	IHL	6	1	3	4	....	....	....	0	....	....	....	....	....	....	....	....	....	....	....	....	....	....	....	....	....	....
	Fort Wayne Komets	IHL	50	7	17	24	....	....	....	100	....	....	....	....	....	....	....	....	....	....	....	....	....	....	....	....	....	....
	St. John's Maple Leafs	AHL	4	2	0	2	....	....	....	2	....	....	....	....	....	....	....	....	....	....	5	0	3	3	8	....	....	....
1995-96	Los Angeles Ice Dogs	IHL	15	3	10	13	....	....	....	22	....	....	....	....	....	....	....	....	....	....	....	....	....	....	....	....	....	....
	Chicago Wolves	IHL	64	9	41	50	....	....	....	91	....	....	....	....	....	....	....	....	....	....	9	1	7	8	22	....	....	....
1996-97	Chicago Wolves	IHL	39	6	10	16	....	....	....	66	....	....	....	....	....	....	....	....	....	....	....	....	....	....	....	....	....	....
	Las Vegas Thunder	IHL	36	9	28	37	....	....	....	64	....	....	....	....	....	....	....	....	....	....	3	0	0	0	2	....	....	....
1997-98	Las Vegas Thunder	IHL	70	15	44	59	....	....	....	148	....	....	....	....	....	....	....	....	....	....	....	....	....	....	....	....	....	....
	Saint John Flames	AHL	9	0	4	4	....	....	....	12	....	....	....	....	....	....	....	....	....	....	19	2	11	13	30	....	....	....
1998-99	Saint John Flames	AHL	8	1	4	5	....	....	....	22	....	....	....	....	....	....	....	....	....	....	....	....	....	....	....	....	....	....
	Providence Bruins	AHL	62	7	34	41	....	....	....	78	....	....	....	....	....	....	....	....	....	....	15	0	6	6	28	....	....	....
99-2000	Cincinnati Cyclones	IHL	39	6	14	20	....	....	....	37	....	....	....	....	....	....	....	....	....	....	....	....	....	....	....	....	....	....
	Houston Aeros	IHL	37	2	18	20	....	....	....	47	....	....	....	....	....	....	....	....	....	....	10	2	6	8	40	....	....	....
	NHL Totals		**1**	**0**	**0**	**0**	**0**	**0**	**0**	**0**	**0**	**0**	**0**	**0**	**0.0**	**0**	**0**	**0**	**0**		....	....	....	....	....	....	....	....

Traded to **Boston** by **Toronto** for Rob Cimetta, November 9, 1990. Traded to **Chicago** by **Boston** with Boston's 11th round choice (later traded to Winnipeg — Winnipeg selected Russel Hewson) in 1993 Entry Draft for Chicago's 11th round choice (Eugene Pavlov) in 1992 Entry Draft, January 8, 1992. Traded to **Winnipeg** by **Chicago** with future considerations for Troy Murray, February 21, 1993. Claimed by **Florida** from **Winnipeg** in Expansion Draft, June 24, 1993. Signed as a free agent by **Pittsburgh**, August 2, 1993. Signed as a free agent by **Carolina**, August 4, 1999. Traded to **Houston** (IHL) by **Cincinnati** (IHL) with Carolina retaining NHL rights for Brian Felsner, January 19, 2000.

• BANDURA, Jeff

Jeff Joseph Mitchell D – R. 6'1", 195 lbs. b: White Rock, B.C., 2/4/1957. Vancouver's 2nd, 22nd overall, in 1977.

Season	Club	League	GP	G	A	Pts	AG	AA	APts	PIM	PP	SH	GW	S	%	TGF	PGF	TGA	PGA	+/–	GP	G	A	Pts	PIM	PP	SH	GW
1973-74	Merritt Centennials	BCJHL	40	1	14	15	....	....	....	35	....	....	....	....	....	....	....	....	....	....	....	....	....	....	....	....	....	....
1974-75	The Pas Blue Devils	AJHL	4	0	0	0	....	....	....	26	....	....	....	....	....	....	....	....	....	....	....	....	....	....	....	....	....	....
	Calgary Centennials	WCJHL	66	3	12	15	....	....	....	157	....	....	....	....	....	....	....	....	....	....	....	....	....	....	....	....	....	....
1975-76	Calgary Centennials	WCJHL	32	4	16	20	....	....	....	59	....	....	....	....	....	....	....	....	....	....	....	....	....	....	....	....	....	....
	Edmonton Oil Kings	WCJHL	35	6	21	27	....	....	....	64	....	....	....	....	....	....	....	....	....	....	5	0	3	3	14	....	....	....
1976-77	Portland Winter Hawks	WCJHL	71	3	28	31	....	....	....	224	....	....	....	....	....	....	....	....	....	....	10	4	3	7	18	....	....	....
1977-78	Tulsa Oilers	CHL	60	2	18	20	....	....	....	88	....	....	....	....	....	....	....	....	....	....	7	0	1	1	14	....	....	....
1978-79	Dallas Black Hawks	CHL	65	4	25	29	....	....	....	169	....	....	....	....	....	....	....	....	....	....	9	0	1	1	28	....	....	....
1979-80	Dallas Black Hawks	CHL	80	4	26	30	....	....	....	114	....	....	....	....	....	....	....	....	....	....	....	....	....	....	....	....	....	....
1980-81	Dallas Black Hawks	CHL	11	0	2	2	....	....	....	15	....	....	....	....	....	....	....	....	....	....	....	....	....	....	....	....	....	....
	New York Rangers	**NHL**	**2**	**0**	**1**	**1**	**0**	**1**	**1**	**0**	**0**	**0**	**0**	**2**	**0.0**	**1**	**0**	**4**	**0**	**–3**	....	....	....	....	....	....	....	....
	New Haven Nighthawks	AHL	55	1	14	15	....	....	....	131	....	....	....	....	....	....	....	....	....	....	4	0	0	0	13	....	....	....
	NHL Totals		**2**	**0**	**1**	**1**	**0**	**1**	**1**	**0**	**0**	**0**	**0**	**2**	**0.0**	**1**	**0**	**4**	**0**		....	....	....	....	....	....	....	....

CHL Second All-Star Team (1979)

Traded to **NY Rangers** by **Vancouver** with Jere Gillis for Mario Marois and Jim Mayer, November 11, 1980.

• BANHAM, Frank

RW – R. 6', 190 lbs. b: Calahoo, Alta., 4/14/1975. Washington's 4th, 147th overall, in 1993.

Season	Club	League	GP	G	A	Pts	AG	AA	APts	PIM	PP	SH	GW	S	%	TGF	PGF	TGA	PGA	+/–	GP	G	A	Pts	PIM	PP	SH	GW
1991-92	Fernie Ghostriders	RMJHL	47	45	45	90	....	....	....	120	....	....	....	....	....	....	....	....	....	....	....	....	....	....	....	....	....	....
1992-93	Saskatoon Blades	WHL	71	29	33	62	....	....	....	55	....	....	....	....	....	....	....	....	....	....	9	2	7	9	8	....	....	....
1993-94	Saskatoon Blades	WHL	65	28	39	67	....	....	....	99	....	....	....	....	....	....	....	....	....	....	16	8	11	19	36	....	....	....
1994-95	Saskatoon Blades	WHL	70	50	39	89	....	....	....	63	....	....	....	....	....	....	....	....	....	....	8	2	6	8	12	....	....	....
1995-96	Saskatoon Blades	WHL	72	*83	69	152	....	....	....	116	....	....	....	....	....	....	....	....	....	....	4	6	0	6	2	....	....	....
	Baltimore Bandits	AHL	9	1	4	5	....	....	....	0	....	....	....	....	....	....	....	....	....	....	7	1	1	2	2	....	....	....
1996-97	**Mighty Ducks of Anaheim**	**NHL**	**3**	**0**	**0**	**0**	**0**	**0**	**0**	**0**	**0**	**0**	**0**	**1**	**0.0**	**0**	**0**	**2**	**0**	**–2**	....	....	....	....	....	....	....	....
	Baltimore Bandits	AHL	21	11	13	24	....	....	....	4	....	....	....	....	....	....	....	....	....	....	....	....	....	....	....	....	....	....
1997-98	**Mighty Ducks of Anaheim**	**NHL**	**21**	**9**	**2**	**11**	**11**	**2**	**13**	**12**	**1**	**0**	**0**	**43**	**20.9**	**17**	**5**	**18**	**0**	**–6**	....	....	....	....	....	....	....	....
	Cincinnati Mighty Ducks	AHL	35	7	8	15	....	....	....	39	....	....	....	....	....	....	....	....	....	....	....	....	....	....	....	....	....	....
1998-99	Cincinnati Mighty Ducks	AHL	66	22	27	49	....	....	....	20	....	....	....	....	....	....	....	....	....	....	3	0	1	1	0	....	....	....
99-2000	**Mighty Ducks of Anaheim**	**NHL**	**3**	**0**	**0**	**0**	**0**	**0**	**0**	**2**	**0**	**0**	**0**	**4**	**0.0**	**0**	**0**	**0**	**0**	**0**	....	....	....	....	....	....	....	....
	Cincinnati Mighty Ducks	AHL	72	19	22	41	....	....	....	58	....	....	....	....	....	....	....	....	....	....	....	....	....	....	....	....	....	....
	NHL Totals		**27**	**9**	**2**	**11**	**11**	**2**	**13**	**14**	**1**	**0**	**0**	**48**	**18.8**	**17**	**5**	**20**	**0**		....	....	....	....	....	....	....	....

WHL East First All-Star Team (1996)

Signed as a free agent by **Anaheim**, January 27, 1996.

• BANKS, Darren

Darren Alexander LW – L. 6'2", 215 lbs. b: Toronto, Ont., 3/18/1966.

Season	Club	League	GP	G	A	Pts	AG	AA	APts	PIM	PP	SH	GW	S	%	TGF	PGF	TGA	PGA	+/–	GP	G	A	Pts	PIM	PP	SH	GW
1983-84	Leamington Flyers	OJHL-C	5	1	3	4	....	....	....	18	....	....	....	....	....	....	....	....	....	....	....	....	....	....	....	....	....	....
1984-1986			DID NOT PLAY																									
1986-87	Brock University	OUAA	24	5	3	8	....	....	....	82	....	....	....	....	....	....	....	....	....	....	....	....	....	....	....	....	....	....
1987-88	Brock University	OUAA	26	10	11	21	....	....	....	110	....	....	....	....	....	....	....	....	....	....	....	....	....	....	....	....	....	....
1988-89	Brock University	OUAA	26	19	14	33	....	....	....	88	....	....	....	....	....	....	....	....	....	....	....	....	....	....	....	....	....	....
1989-90	Salt Lake Golden Eagles	IHL	6	0	0	0	....	....	....	11	....	....	....	....	....	....	....	....	....	....	1	0	0	0	10	....	....	....
	Fort Wayne Komets	IHL	2	0	1	1	....	....	....	0	....	....	....	....	....	....	....	....	....	....	....	....	....	....	....	....	....	....
	Knoxville Cherokees	ECHL	52	25	22	47	....	....	....	258	....	....	....	....	....	....	....	....	....	....	....	....	....	....	....	....	....	....
1990-91	Salt Lake Golden Eagles	IHL	56	9	7	16	....	....	....	286	....	....	....	....	....	....	....	....	....	....	3	0	1	1	6	....	....	....
1991-92	Salt Lake Golden Eagles	IHL	55	5	5	10	....	....	....	303	....	....	....	....	....	....	....	....	....	....	....	....	....	....	....	....	....	....
1992-93	**Boston Bruins**	**NHL**	**16**	**2**	**1**	**3**	**2**	**1**	**3**	**64**	**0**	**0**	**0**	**15**	**13.3**	**6**	**0**	**1**	**0**	**5**	....	....	....	....	....	....	....	....
	Providence Bruins	AHL	43	9	5	14	....	....	....	199	....	....	....	....	....	....	....	....	....	....	1	0	0	0	0	....	....	....
1993-94	**Boston Bruins**	**NHL**	**4**	**0**	**1**	**1**	**0**	**1**	**1**	**9**	**0**	**0**	**0**	**3**	**0.0**	**1**	**0**	**1**	**0**	**0**	....	....	....	....	....	....	....	....
	Providence Bruins	AHL	41	6	3	9	....	....	....	189	....	....	....	....	....	....	....	....	....	....	....	....	....	....	....	....	....	....
1994-95	Adirondack Red Wings	AHL	20	3	2	5	....	....	....	65	....	....	....	....	....	....	....	....	....	....	....	....	....	....	....	....	....	....
	Portland Pirates	AHL	12	1	2	3	....	....	....	38	....	....	....	....	....	....	....	....	....	....	....	....	....	....	....	....	....	....
	Las Vegas Thunder	IHL	2	0	0	0	....	....	....	19	....	....	....	....	....	....	....	....	....	....	....	....	....	....	....	....	....	....
	Detroit Falcons	ColHL	22	9	10	19	....	....	....	51	....	....	....	....	....	....	....	....	....	....	12	3	5	8	59	....	....	....
1995-96	Detroit Falcons	ColHL	38	11	17	28	....	....	....	290	....	....	....	....	....	....	....	....	....	....	....	....	....	....	....	....	....	....
	Utica Blizzard	ColHL	6	1	2	3	....	....	....	22	....	....	....	....	....	....	....	....	....	....	....	....	....	....	....	....	....	....
	Las Vegas Thunder	IHL	5	0	2	2	....	....	....	10	....	....	....	....	....	....	....	....	....	....	10	0	0	0	54	....	....	....
1996-97	Detroit Vipers	IHL	64	10	13	23	....	....	....	306	....	....	....	....	....	....	....	....	....	....	20	4	5	9	40	....	....	....
1997-98	Quebec Rafales	IHL	4	0	1	1	....	....	....	9	....	....	....	....	....	....	....	....	....	....	....	....	....	....	....	....	....	....
	San Antonio Dragons	IHL	7	0	0	0	....	....	....	6	....	....	....	....	....	....	....	....	....	....	....	....	....	....	....	....	....	....
	Detroit Vipers	IHL	59	16	14	30	....	....	....	175	....	....	....	....	....	....	....	....	....	....	21	2	3	5	*97	....	....	....
1998-99	Detroit Vipers	IHL	58	6	12	18	....	....	....	296	....	....	....	....	....	....	....	....	....	....	3	0	0	0	35	....	....	....
99-2000	London Knights	BH-Cup	3	0	2	2	....	....	....	16	....	....	....	....	....	....	....	....	....	....	....	....	....	....	....	....	....	....
	London Knights	Britain	23	8	2	10	....	....	....	101	....	....	....	....	....	....	....	....	....	....	....	....	....	....	....	....	....	....
	Port Huron Border Cats	UHL	17	3	5	8	....	....	....	12	....	....	....	....	....	....	....	....	....	....	....	....	....	....	....	....	....	....
	NHL Totals		**20**	**2**	**2**	**4**	**2**	**2**	**4**	**73**	**0**	**0**	**0**	**18**	**11.1**	**7**	**0**	**2**	**0**		....	....	....	....	....	....	....	....

Signed as a free agent by **Calgary**, December 12, 1990. Signed as a free agent by **Boston**, July 16, 1992. • Played w/ RHI's Anaheim Bullfrogs in 1995 (17-13-8-21-86) and 1996 (9-1-4-5-46); Long Island Jawz in 1996 (4-2-1-3-21)

			REGULAR SEASON																		PLAYOFFS							
Season	Club	League	GP	G	A	Pts	AG	AA	APts	PIM	PP	SH	GW	S	%	TGF	PGF	TGA	PGA	+/-	GP	G	A	Pts	PIM	PP	SH	GW

• BANNISTER, Drew

D – R. 6'2", 200 lbs. b: Belleville, Ont., 9/4/1974. Tampa Bay's 2nd, 26th overall, in 1992.

Season	Club	League	GP	G	A	Pts	AG	AA	APts	PIM	PP	SH	GW	S	%	TGF	PGF	TGA	PGA	+/-	GP	G	A	Pts	PIM	PP	SH	GW
1989-90	Sudbury Legionaires	NOHA	26	13	14	27	....	....	....	98	....	....	....	....	....	....	....	....	....	....	....	....	....	....	....	....	....	....
1990-91	Sault Ste. Marie Greyhounds	OHL	41	2	8	10	....	....	....	51	....	....	....	....	....	....	....	....	....	....	4	0	0	0	0	....	....	....
	Sault Ste. Marie Greyhounds	Mem-Cup	1	0	0	0	....	....	....	0	....	....	....	....	....	....	....	....	....	....	....	....	....	....	....	....	....	....
1991-92	Sault Ste. Marie Greyhounds	OHL	64	4	21	25	....	....	....	122	....	....	....	....	....	....	....	....	....	....	16	3	10	13	36	....	....	....
	Sault Ste. Marie Greyhounds	Mem-Cup	4	1	1	2	....	....	....	8	....	....	....	....	....	....	....	....	....	....	....	....	....	....	....	....	....	....
1992-93	Sault Ste. Marie Greyhounds	OHL	59	5	28	33	....	....	....	114	....	....	....	....	....	....	....	....	....	....	18	2	7	9	12	....	....	....
	Sault Ste. Marie Greyhounds	Mem-Cup	4	0	5	5	....	....	....	2	....	....	....	....	....	....	....	....	....	....	....	....	....	....	....	....	....	....
1993-94	Sault Ste. Marie Greyhounds	OHL	58	7	43	50	....	....	....	108	....	....	....	....	....	....	....	....	....	....	14	6	9	15	20	....	....	....
	Canada	WJC-A	7	0	4	4	....	....	....	10	....	....	....	....	....	....	....	....	....	....	....	....	....	....	....	....	....	....
1994-95	Atlanta Knights	IHL	72	5	7	12	....	....	....	74	....	....	....	....	....	....	....	....	....	....	5	0	2	2	22	....	....	....
1995-96	**Tampa Bay Lightning**	**NHL**	**13**	**0**	**1**	**1**	**0**	**1**	**1**	**4**	**0**	**0**	**0**	**10**	**0.0**	**7**	**0**	**8**	**0**	**–1**	....	....	....	....	....	....	....	....
	Atlanta Knights	IHL	61	3	13	16	....	....	....	105	....	....	....	....	....	....	....	....	....	....	3	0	0	0	4	....	....	....
1996-97	**Tampa Bay Lightning**	**NHL**	**64**	**4**	**13**	**17**	**4**	**12**	**16**	**44**	**1**	**0**	**0**	**57**	**7.0**	**43**	**13**	**53**	**2**	**–21**	....	....	....	....	....	....	....	....
	Edmonton Oilers	**NHL**	**1**	**0**	**1**	**1**	**0**	**1**	**1**	**0**	**0**	**0**	**0**	**2**	**0.0**	**2**	**1**	**3**	**0**	**–2**	**12**	**0**	**0**	**0**	**30**	**0**	**0**	**0**
1997-98	**Edmonton Oilers**	**NHL**	**34**	**0**	**2**	**2**	**0**	**2**	**2**	**42**	**0**	**0**	**0**	**27**	**0.0**	**16**	**1**	**33**	**11**	**–7**	....	....	....	....	....	....	....	....
	Mighty Ducks of Anaheim	**NHL**	**27**	**0**	**6**	**6**	**0**	**6**	**6**	**47**	**0**	**0**	**0**	**23**	**0.0**	**14**	**0**	**24**	**8**	**–2**	....	....	....	....	....	....	....	....
1998-99	Las Vegas Thunder	IHL	16	2	1	3	....	....	....	73	....	....	....	....	....	....	....	....	....	....	....	....	....	....	....	....	....	....
	Tampa Bay Lighning	**NHL**	**21**	**1**	**2**	**3**	**1**	**2**	**3**	**24**	**0**	**0**	**0**	**29**	**3.4**	**12**	**3**	**17**	**4**	**–4**	....	....	....	....	....	....	....	....
99-2000	Hartford Wolf Pack	AHL	44	6	14	20	....	....	....	121	....	....	....	....	....	....	....	....	....	....	18	2	9	11	53	....	....	....
	NHL Totals		**160**	**5**	**25**	**30**	**5**	**24**	**29**	**161**	**1**	**0**	**0**	**148**	**3.4**	**94**	**18**	**138**	**25**		**12**	**0**	**0**	**0**	**30**	**0**	**0**	**0**

Memorial Cup All-Star Team (1993) • OHL Second All-Star Team (1994)

Traded to **Edmonton** by **Tampa Bay** with Tampa Bay's 6th round choice (Peter Sarno) in 1997 Entry Draft for Jeff Norton, March 18, 1997. Traded to **Anaheim** by **Edmonton** for Bobby Dollas, January 9, 1998. Traded to **Tampa Bay** by **Anaheim** for Tampa Bay's 5th round choice (Peter Podhradsky) in 2000 Entry Draft, December 10, 1998.

• BARAHONA, Ralph

Ralph J. C – L. 5'10", 180 lbs. b: Long Beach, CA, 11/16/1965.

Season	Club	League	GP	G	A	Pts	AG	AA	APts	PIM	PP	SH	GW	S	%	TGF	PGF	TGA	PGA	+/-	GP	G	A	Pts	PIM	PP	SH	GW
1984-85	Austin Mavericks	USHL	48	35	40	75	....	....	....	59	....	....	....	....	....	....	....	....	....	....	....	....	....	....	....	....	....	....
1985-86	Rochester Mustangs	USHL	40	22	36	58	....	....	....	16	....	....	....	....	....	....	....	....	....	....	....	....	....	....	....	....	....	....
1986-87	U. Wisconsin-Stevens Point	NCHA	29	21	21	42	....	....	....	8	....	....	....	....	....	....	....	....	....	....	....	....	....	....	....	....	....	....
1987-88	U. Wisconsin-Stevens Point	NCHA	31	25	26	51	....	....	....	16	....	....	....	....	....	....	....	....	....	....	....	....	....	....	....	....	....	....
1988-89	U. Wisconsin-Stevens Point	NCHA	41	33	47	80	....	....	....	40	....	....	....	....	....	....	....	....	....	....	....	....	....	....	....	....	....	....
1989-90	U. Wisconsin-Stevens Point	NCHA	35	17	26	43	....	....	....	20	....	....	....	....	....	....	....	....	....	....	....	....	....	....	....	....	....	....
1990-91	**Boston Bruins**	**NHL**	**3**	**2**	**1**	**3**	**2**	**1**	**3**	**0**	**0**	**0**	**0**	**5**	**40.0**	**3**	**1**	**0**	**0**	**2**	....	....	....	....	....	....	....	....
	Maine Mariners	AHL	72	24	33	57	....	....	....	14	....	....	....	....	....	....	....	....	....	....	2	1	1	2	0	....	....	....
1991-92	**Boston Bruins**	**NHL**	**3**	**0**	**1**	**1**	**0**	**1**	**1**	**0**	**0**	**0**	**0**	**0**	**0.0**	**2**	**0**	**1**	**0**	**1**	....	....	....	....	....	....	....	....
	Maine Mariners	AHL	74	27	32	59	....	....	....	39	....	....	....	....	....	....	....	....	....	....	....	....	....	....	....	....	....	....
1992-93	Utica Devils	AHL	2	0	0	0	....	....	....	0	....	....	....	....	....	....	....	....	....	....	....	....	....	....	....	....	....	....
	Cincinnati Cyclones	IHL	30	8	6	14	....	....	....	4	....	....	....	....	....	....	....	....	....	....	....	....	....	....	....	....	....	....
	Fort Wayne Komets	IHL	7	0	2	2	....	....	....	2	....	....	....	....	....	....	....	....	....	....	....	....	....	....	....	....	....	....
1993-94	Raleigh IceCaps	ECHL	36	14	21	35	....	....	....	12	....	....	....	....	....	....	....	....	....	....	....	....	....	....	....	....	....	....
	Hampton Roads Admirals	ECHL	27	13	20	33	....	....	....	12	....	....	....	....	....	....	....	....	....	....	7	3	5	8	4	....	....	....
1994-95			DID NOT PLAY																									
1995-96	San Diego Gulls	WCHL	56	31	56	87	....	....	....	36	....	....	....	....	....	....	....	....	....	....	....	....	....	....	....	....	....	....
1996-97			DID NOT PLAY																									
1997-98			DID NOT PLAY																									
1998-99	Phoenix Mustangs	WCHL	8	2	2	4	....	....	....	0	....	....	....	....	....	....	....	....	....	....	3	0	2	2	0	....	....	....
99-2000	Bakersfield Condors	WCHL	43	13	17	30	....	....	....	18	....	....	....	....	....	....	....	....	....	....	3	0	1	1	4	....	....	....
	NHL Totals		**6**	**2**	**2**	**4**	**2**	**2**	**4**	**0**	**0**	**0**	**0**	**5**	**40.0**	**5**	**1**	**1**	**0**		....	....	....	....	....	....	....	....

Signed as a free agent by **Boston**, September 26, 1990. • Spent 1996-97 and 1997-98 seasons playing w/ **Rapperswil-Jona** of the Swiss In-Line League. Signed as a free agent by **Phoenix Mustangs** (WCHL), March 9, 1999. Signed as a free agent by **Bakersfield** (WCHL), December 8, 1999.

• Played w/ RHI's LA Blades in 1993 (12-20-25-45-8); Phoenix Cobras in 1994 (19-24-27-51-4) and 1995 (21-16-16-32-18); San Diego Barracudas in 1996 (15-14-5-19-9); Tampa Bay Rolling Thunder in 1998 (16-16-31-47-0); Anaheim Bullfrogs (11-2-12-14-1) and San Jose Rhinos (2-0-1-1-0) in 1999.

• BARBER, Bill

William Charles LW – L. 6', 195 lbs. b: Callander, Ont., 7/11/1952. Philadelphia's 1st, 7th overall, in 1972. **HHOF**

Season	Club	League	GP	G	A	Pts	AG	AA	APts	PIM	PP	SH	GW	S	%	TGF	PGF	TGA	PGA	+/-	GP	G	A	Pts	PIM	PP	SH	GW
1967-68	North Bay Trappers	NOJHA	34	18	35	53	....	....	....	44	....	....	....	....	....	....	....	....	....	....	....	....	....	....	....	....	....	....
1968-69	North Bay Trappers	NOJHA	48	32	38	70	....	....	....	100	....	....	....	....	....	....	....	....	....	....	....	....	....	....	....	....	....	....
1969-70	Kitchener Rangers	OHA-Jr.	54	37	49	86	....	....	....	42	....	....	....	....	....	....	....	....	....	....	8	5	10	15	12	....	....	....
1970-71	Kitchener Rangers	OHA-Jr.	61	46	59	105	....	....	....	129	....	....	....	....	....	....	....	....	....	....	4	3	2	5	13	....	....	....
1971-72	Kitchener Rangers	OMJHL	62	44	63	107	....	....	....	89	....	....	....	....	....	....	....	....	....	....	5	2	7	9	6	....	....	....
1972-73	**Philadelphia Flyers**	**NHL**	**69**	**30**	**34**	**64**	**28**	**27**	**55**	**46**	**7**	**0**	**2**	**214**	**14.0**	**98**	**32**	**57**	**1**	**10**	**11**	**3**	**2**	**5**	**22**	**0**	**0**	**0**
	Richmond Robins	AHL	11	9	5	14	....	....	....	4	....	....	....	....	....	....	....	....	....	....	....	....	....	....	....	....	....	....
1973-74♦	**Philadelphia Flyers**	**NHL**	**75**	**34**	**35**	**69**	**33**	**29**	**62**	**54**	**9**	**2**	**5**	**290**	**11.7**	**108**	**38**	**52**	**16**	**34**	**17**	**3**	**6**	**9**	**18**	**0**	**0**	**1**
1974-75♦	**Philadelphia Flyers**	**NHL**	**79**	**34**	**37**	**71**	**30**	**28**	**58**	**66**	**8**	**5**	**4**	**276**	**12.3**	**120**	**43**	**55**	**24**	**46**	**17**	**6**	**9**	**15**	**8**	**0**	**0**	**0**
1975-76	**Philadelphia Flyers**	**NHL**	**80**	**50**	**62**	**112**	**44**	**46**	**90**	**104**	**15**	**4**	**10**	**380**	**13.2**	**162**	**57**	**57**	**26**	**74**	**16**	**6**	**7**	**13**	**18**	**3**	**0**	**0**
1976-77	Canada	Can-Cup	7	2	0	2	....	....	....	4	....	....	....	....	....	....	....	....	....	....	....	....	....	....	....	....	....	....
	Philadelphia Flyers	**NHL**	**73**	**20**	**35**	**55**	**18**	**27**	**45**	**62**	**3**	**0**	**3**	**245**	**8.2**	**91**	**27**	**51**	**19**	**32**	**10**	**1**	**4**	**5**	**2**	**0**	**0**	**0**
1977-78	**Philadelphia Flyers**	**NHL**	**80**	**41**	**31**	**72**	**37**	**24**	**61**	**34**	**8**	**4**	**9**	**262**	**15.6**	**107**	**34**	**66**	**24**	**31**	**12**	**6**	**3**	**9**	**2**	**1**	**0**	**0**
1978-79	**Philadelphia Flyers**	**NHL**	**79**	**34**	**46**	**80**	**29**	**33**	**62**	**22**	**10**	**6**	**4**	**258**	**13.2**	**122**	**50**	**79**	**26**	**19**	**8**	**3**	**4**	**7**	**10**	**0**	**0**	**0**
	NHL All-Stars	Chal-Cup	3	0	1	1	....	....	....	0	....	....	....	....	....	....	....	....	....	....	....	....	....	....	....	....	....	....
1979-80	**Philadelphia Flyers**	**NHL**	**79**	**40**	**32**	**72**	**34**	**23**	**57**	**17**	**7**	**2**	**7**	**265**	**15.1**	**119**	**30**	**85**	**35**	**39**	**19**	**12**	**9**	**21**	**23**	**1**	**3**	**4**
1980-81	**Philadelphia Flyers**	**NHL**	**80**	**43**	**42**	**85**	**34**	**28**	**62**	**69**	**16**	**2**	**2**	**292**	**14.7**	**129**	**57**	**95**	**29**	**6**	**12**	**11**	**5**	**16**	**0**	**3**	**1**	**1**
1981-82	**Philadelphia Flyers**	**NHL**	**80**	**45**	**44**	**89**	**36**	**29**	**65**	**85**	**13**	**4**	**6**	**350**	**12.9**	**136**	**64**	**122**	**54**	**4**	**4**	**1**	**5**	**6**	**4**	**0**	**1**	**0**
	Canada	WEC-A	10	8	1	9	....	....	....	10	....	....	....	....	....	....	....	....	....	....	....	....	....	....	....	....	....	....
1982-83	**Philadelphia Flyers**	**NHL**	**66**	**27**	**33**	**60**	**22**	**23**	**45**	**28**	**5**	**2**	**1**	**215**	**12.6**	**90**	**25**	**62**	**14**	**17**	**3**	**1**	**1**	**2**	**2**	**1**	**0**	**0**
1983-84	**Philadelphia Flyers**	**NHL**	**63**	**22**	**32**	**54**	**18**	**22**	**40**	**36**	**3**	**0**	**1**	**203**	**10.8**	**79**	**27**	**59**	**11**	**4**	....	....	....	....	....	....	....	....
1984-1985	Hershey Bears	AHL	DID NOT PLAY – COACHING																									
1985-1988	**Philadelphia Flyers**	**NHL**	DID NOT PLAY – ASSISTANT COACH																									
1988-1995	**Philadelphia Flyers**	**NHL**	DID NOT PLAY – SCOUTING																									
1995-1996	Hershey Bears	AHL	DID NOT PLAY – COACHING																									
1996-2000	Philadelphia Phantoms	AHL	DID NOT PLAY – COACHING																									
	NHL Totals		**903**	**420**	**463**	**883**	**363**	**339**	**702**	**623**	**104**	**31**	**54**	**3250**	**12.9**	**1361**	**484**	**840**	**279**		**129**	**53**	**55**	**108**	**109**	**9**	**5**	**6**

NHL First All-Star Team (1976) • NHL Second All-Star Team (1979, 1981) • WEC-A All-Star Team (1982) • Played in NHL All-Star Game (1975, 1976, 1978, 1980, 1981, 1982)

• BARBER, Don

"The Swan" W – L. 6'2", 205 lbs. b: Victoria, B.C., 12/2/1964. Edmonton's 5th, 124th overall, in 1983.

Season	Club	League	GP	G	A	Pts	AG	AA	APts	PIM	PP	SH	GW	S	%	TGF	PGF	TGA	PGA	+/-	GP	G	A	Pts	PIM	PP	SH	GW
1982-83	Kelowna Buckaroos	BCJHL	35	26	31	57	....	....	....	54	....	....	....	....	....	....	....	....	....	....	....	....	....	....	....	....	....	....
1983-84	St. Albert Saints	AJHL	53	42	38	80	....	....	....	74	....	....	....	....	....	....	....	....	....	....	....	....	....	....	....	....	....	....
1984-85	Bowling Green University	CCHA	39	15	22	37	....	....	....	44	....	....	....	....	....	....	....	....	....	....	....	....	....	....	....	....	....	....
1985-86	Bowling Green University	CCHA	35	21	22	43	....	....	....	64	....	....	....	....	....	....	....	....	....	....	....	....	....	....	....	....	....	....
1986-87	Bowling Green University	CCHA	43	29	34	63	....	....	....	107	....	....	....	....	....	....	....	....	....	....	....	....	....	....	....	....	....	....
1987-88	Bowling Green University	CCHA	38	18	47	65	....	....	....	62	....	....	....	....	....	....	....	....	....	....	....	....	....	....	....	....	....	....
1988-89	**Minnesota North Stars**	**NHL**	**23**	**8**	**5**	**13**	**7**	**4**	**11**	**8**	**3**	**0**	**2**	**42**	**19.0**	**19**	**9**	**9**	**1**	**2**	**4**	**1**	**1**	**2**	**2**	**0**	**0**	**1**
	Kalamazoo Wings	IHL	39	14	17	31	....	....	....	23	....	....	....	....	....	....	....	....	....	....	....	....	....	....	....	....	....	....
1989-90	**Minnesota North Stars**	**NHL**	**44**	**15**	**19**	**34**	**13**	**14**	**27**	**32**	**4**	**0**	**2**	**100**	**15.0**	**58**	**17**	**38**	**1**	**4**	**7**	**3**	**3**	**6**	**8**	**2**	**0**	**1**
	Kalamazoo Wings	IHL	10	4	4	8	....	....	....	38	....	....	....	....	....	....	....	....	....	....	....	....	....	....	....	....	....	....
1990-91	Minnesota North Stars	Fr-Tour	4	1	0	1	....	....	....	2	....	....	....	....	....	....	....	....	....	....	....	....	....	....	....	....	....	....
	Minnesota North Stars	**NHL**	**7**	**0**	**0**	**0**	**0**	**0**	**0**	**4**	**0**	**0**	**0**	**10**	**0.0**	**0**	**0**	**4**	**1**	**–3**	....	....	....	....	....	....	....	....
	Winnipeg Jets	**NHL**	**16**	**1**	**2**	**3**	**1**	**2**	**3**	**14**	**0**	**0**	**0**	**19**	**5.3**	**6**	**1**	**8**	**0**	**–3**	....	....	....	....	....	....	....	....
	Moncton Hawks	AHL	38	17	21	38	....	....	....	32	....	....	....	....	....	....	....	....	....	....	9	4	6	10	8	....	....	....

			REGULAR SEASON																		PLAYOFFS							
Season	Club	League	GP	G	A	Pts	AG	AA	APts	PIM	PP	SH	GW	S	%	TGF	PGF	TGA	PGA	+/-	GP	G	A	Pts	PIM	PP	SH	GW
1991-92	**Winnipeg Jets**	**NHL**	**11**	**0**	**3**	**3**	**0**	**2**	**2**	**4**	**0**	**0**	**0**	**6**	**0.0**	**8**	**5**	**1**	**0**	**2**	....	....	....	....	....	....	....	....
	Halifax Citadels	AHL	25	12	10	22	....	....	....	8	....	....	....	....	....	....	....	....	....	....	....	....	....	....	....	....	....	....
	Quebec Nordiques	**NHL**	**2**	**0**	**0**	**0**	**0**	**0**	**0**	**0**	**0**	**0**	**0**	**1**	**0.0**	**0**	**0**	**1**	**0**	**–1**	....	....	....	....	....	....	....	....
	San Jose Sharks	**NHL**	**12**	**1**	**3**	**4**	**1**	**2**	**3**	**2**	**0**	**0**	**0**	**17**	**5.9**	**8**	**3**	**12**	**0**	**–7**	....	....	....	....	....	....	....	....
1992-93	Kansas City Blades	IHL	9	3	1	4	....	....	....	4	....	....	....	....	....	....	....	....	....	....	....	....	....	....	....	....	....	....
	NHL Totals		**115**	**25**	**32**	**57**	**22**	**24**	**46**	**64**	**7**	**0**	**4**	**195**	**12.8**	**99**	**35**	**73**	**3**		**11**	**4**	**4**	**8**	**10**	**2**	**0**	**2**

Traded to **Minnesota** by **Edmonton** with Marc Habsheid and Emanuel Viveiros for Gord Sherven and Don Biggs, December 20, 1985. Traded to **Winnipeg** by **Minnesota** for Doug Smail, November 7, 1990. Claimed on waivers by **Quebec** from **Winnipeg**, November 12, 1991. Traded to **San Jose** by **Quebec** for Murray Garbutt, March 7, 1992.

• BARLOW, Bob

Robert George LW – L. 5'10", 165 lbs. b: Hamilton, Ont., 6/17/1935.

Season	Club	League	GP	G	A	Pts	AG	AA	APts	PIM	PP	SH	GW	S	%	TGF	PGF	TGA	PGA	+/-	GP	G	A	Pts	PIM	PP	SH	GW
1953-54	Barrie Flyers	OHA-Jr.	29	5	7	12	....	....	....	4	....	....	....	....	....	....	....	....	....	....	....	....	....	....	....	....	....	....
1954-55	Barrie Flyers	OHA-Jr.	46	33	27	60	....	....	....	41	....	....	....	....	....	....	....	....	....	....	....	....	....	....	....	....	....	....
	Cleveland Barons	AHL	3	0	0	0	....	....	....	0	....	....	....	....	....	....	....	....	....	....	....	....	....	....	....	....	....	....
1955-56	Cleveland Barons	AHL	2	1	0	1	....	....	....	0	....	....	....	....	....	....	....	....	....	....	....	....	....	....	....	....	....	....
	North Bay Trappers	NOHA	56	20	18	38	....	....	....	56	....	....	....	....	....	....	....	....	....	....	10	2	2	4	4	....	....	....
1956-57	Cleveland Barons	AHL	3	0	2	2	....	....	....	2	....	....	....	....	....	....	....	....	....	....	....	....	....	....	....	....	....	....
	North Bay Trappers	NOHA	56	21	20	41	....	....	....	27	....	....	....	....	....	....	....	....	....	....	13	7	5	12	8	....	....	....
1957-58	Cleveland Barons	AHL	6	4	0	4	....	....	....	2	....	....	....	....	....	....	....	....	....	....	7	2	2	4	4	....	....	....
	North Bay Trappers	NOHA	60	27	36	63	....	....	....	39	....	....	....	....	....	....	....	....	....	....	....	....	....	....	....	....	....	....
1958-59	Cleveland Barons	AHL	70	27	27	54	....	....	....	39	....	....	....	....	....	....	....	....	....	....	7	1	2	3	20	....	....	....
1959-60	Quebec Aces	AHL	72	28	32	60	....	....	....	50	....	....	....	....	....	....	....	....	....	....	....	....	....	....	....	....	....	....
1960-61	Quebec Aces	AHL	67	12	17	29	....	....	....	41	....	....	....	....	....	....	....	....	....	....	....	....	....	....	....	....	....	....
1961-62	Quebec Aces	AHL	61	11	12	23	....	....	....	25	....	....	....	....	....	....	....	....	....	....	....	....	....	....	....	....	....	....
1962-63	Seattle Totems	WHL	70	*47	30	77	....	....	....	17	....	....	....	....	....	....	....	....	....	....	17	8	9	17	10	....	....	....
1963-64	Seattle Totems	WHL	66	35	20	55	....	....	....	18	....	....	....	....	....	....	....	....	....	....	....	....	....	....	....	....	....	....
1964-65	Seattle Totems	WHL	70	30	17	47	....	....	....	50	....	....	....	....	....	....	....	....	....	....	7	3	2	5	10	....	....	....
1965-66	Victoria Maple Leafs	WHL	71	42	39	81	....	....	....	20	....	....	....	....	....	....	....	....	....	....	14	*10	9	19	21	....	....	....
1966-67	Victoria Maple Leafs	WHL	70	21	38	59	....	....	....	44	....	....	....	....	....	....	....	....	....	....	....	....	....	....	....	....	....	....
1967-68	Rochester Americans	AHL	72	43	52	95	....	....	....	72	....	....	....	....	....	....	....	....	....	....	11	*9	3	12	25	....	....	....
1968-69	Vancouver Canucks	WHL	74	36	48	84	....	....	....	50	....	....	....	....	....	....	....	....	....	....	8	4	6	10	11	....	....	....
1969-70	**Minnesota North Stars**	**NHL**	**70**	**16**	**17**	**33**	**17**	**16**	**33**	**10**	**6**	**1**	**1**	**157**	**10.2**	**54**	**18**	**40**	**1**	**–3**	**6**	**2**	**2**	**4**	**6**	**1**	**0**	**0**
1970-71	**Minnesota North Stars**	**NHL**	**7**	**0**	**0**	**0**	**0**	**0**	**0**	**0**	**0**	**0**	**0**	**7**	**0.0**	**0**	**0**	**0**	**0**	**0**	....	....	....	....	....	....	....	....
	Phoenix Roadrunners	WHL	44	19	26	45	....	....	....	21	....	....	....	....	....	....	....	....	....	....	10	3	3	6	26	....	....	....
1971-72	Phoenix Roadrunners	WHL	64	16	21	37	....	....	....	24	....	....	....	....	....	....	....	....	....	....	5	0	1	1	2	....	....	....
1972-73	Phoenix Roadrunners	WHL	51	26	42	68	....	....	....	41	....	....	....	....	....	....	....	....	....	....	10	4	7	11	28	....	....	....
1973-74	Phoenix Roadrunners	WHL	48	19	30	49	....	....	....	12	....	....	....	....	....	....	....	....	....	....	9	6	5	*11	6	....	....	....
1974-75	Phoenix Roadrunners	WHA	51	6	20	26	....	....	....	8	....	....	....	....	....	....	....	....	....	....	....	....	....	....	....	....	....	....
	Tulsa Oilers	CHL	25	7	12	19	....	....	....	10	....	....	....	....	....	....	....	....	....	....	2	0	1	1	2	....	....	....
1975-76	Tucson Mavericks	CHL	2	0	3	3	....	....	....	2	....	....	....	....	....	....	....	....	....	....	....	....	....	....	....	....	....	....
	NHL Totals		**77**	**16**	**17**	**33**	**17**	**16**	**33**	**10**	**6**	**1**	**1**	**164**	**9.8**	**54**	**18**	**40**	**1**		**6**	**2**	**2**	**4**	**6**	**1**	**0**	**0**
	Other Major League Totals		51	6	20	26	....	....	....	8	....	....	....	....	....	....	....	....	....	....	....	....	....	....	....	....	....	....

WHL Second All-Star Team (1963, 1969) • WHL First All-Star Team (1966) • AHL First All-Star Team (1968)

Loaned to **Quebec** (AHL) by **Cleveland** (AHL) for 1959-60 season for cash, July, 1959. Traded to **Quebec** (AHL) by **Cleveland** (AHL) for cash with Montreal retaining his NHL rights, May 6, 1960. Claimed by **Toronto** (Rochester-AHL) from **Montreal** in Reverse Draft, June 9, 1965. Rights transferred to **Vancouver** (WHL) after WHL club purchased **Rochester** (AHL) franchise, August 13, 1968. Claimed by **Philadelphia** from **Vancouver** (WHL) in Inter-League Draft, June 10, 1969. Traded to **Minnesota** by **Philadelphia** for cash, June 10, 1969. Selected by **Dayton-Houston** (WHA) in 1972 WHA General Player Draft, February 12, 1972. Traded to **Phoenix** (WHL) by **Minnesota** for cash, September, 1971. WHA rights transferred to **Phoenix** (WHA) after owners of Phoenix (WHL) franchise awarded WHA expansion team, September 14, 1973.

• BARNABY, Matthew

RW – L. 6', 188 lbs. b: Ottawa, Ont., 5/4/1973. Buffalo's 5th, 83rd overall, in 1992.

Season	Club	League	GP	G	A	Pts	AG	AA	APts	PIM	PP	SH	GW	S	%	TGF	PGF	TGA	PGA	+/-	GP	G	A	Pts	PIM	PP	SH	GW
1989-90	Hull Frontaliers	QAAA	50	43	50	93	....	....	....	149	....	....	....	....	....	....	....	....	....	....	....	....	....	....	....	....	....	....
1990-91	Beauport Harfangs	QMJHL	52	9	5	14	....	....	....	262	....	....	....	....	....	....	....	....	....	....	....	....	....	....	....	....	....	....
1991-92	Beauport Harfangs	QMJHL	63	29	37	66	....	....	....	*476	....	....	....	....	....	....	....	....	....	....	....	....	....	....	....	....	....	....
1992-93	Victoriaville Tigres	QMJHL	65	44	67	111	....	....	....	*448	....	....	....	....	....	....	....	....	....	....	6	2	4	6	44	....	....	....
	Buffalo Sabres	**NHL**	**2**	**1**	**0**	**1**	**1**	**0**	**1**	**10**	**1**	**0**	**0**	**8**	**12.5**	**1**	**1**	**0**	**0**	**0**	**1**	**0**	**1**	**1**	**4**	**0**	**0**	**0**
1993-94	**Buffalo Sabres**	**NHL**	**35**	**2**	**4**	**6**	**2**	**3**	**5**	**106**	**1**	**0**	**0**	**13**	**15.4**	**10**	**4**	**13**	**0**	**–7**	**3**	**0**	**0**	**0**	**17**	**0**	**0**	**0**
	Rochester Americans	AHL	42	10	32	42	....	....	....	153	....	....	....	....	....	....	....	....	....	....	....	....	....	....	....	....	....	....
1994-95	**Buffalo Sabres**	**NHL**	**23**	**1**	**1**	**2**	**2**	**1**	**3**	**116**	**0**	**0**	**0**	**27**	**3.7**	**5**	**1**	**7**	**1**	**–2**	....	....	....	....	....	....	....	....
	Rochester Americans	AHL	56	21	29	50	....	....	....	274	....	....	....	....	....	....	....	....	....	....	....	....	....	....	....	....	....	....
1995-96	**Buffalo Sabres**	**NHL**	**73**	**15**	**16**	**31**	**15**	**13**	**28**	***335**	**0**	**0**	**0**	**131**	**11.5**	**42**	**0**	**46**	**2**	**–2**	....	....	....	....	....	....	....	....
1996-97	**Buffalo Sabres**	**NHL**	**68**	**19**	**24**	**43**	**20**	**21**	**41**	**249**	**2**	**0**	**1**	**121**	**15.7**	**58**	**8**	**36**	**2**	**16**	**8**	**0**	**4**	**4**	**36**	**0**	**0**	**0**
1997-98	**Buffalo Sabres**	**NHL**	**72**	**5**	**20**	**25**	**6**	**20**	**26**	**289**	**0**	**0**	**2**	**96**	**5.2**	**36**	**4**	**26**	**2**	**8**	**15**	**7**	**6**	**13**	**22**	**3**	**0**	**1**
1998-99	**Buffalo Sabres**	**NHL**	**44**	**4**	**14**	**18**	**5**	**13**	**18**	**143**	**0**	**0**	**3**	**52**	**7.7**	**24**	**10**	**16**	**0**	**–2**	....	....	....	....	....	....	....	....
	Pittsburgh Penguins	**NHL**	**18**	**2**	**2**	**4**	**2**	**2**	**4**	**34**	**1**	**0**	**0**	**27**	**7.4**	**5**	**2**	**13**	**0**	**–10**	**13**	**0**	**0**	**0**	**35**	**0**	**0**	**0**
99-2000	**Pittsburgh Penguins**	**NHL**	**64**	**12**	**12**	**24**	**13**	**11**	**24**	**197**	**0**	**0**	**3**	**80**	**15.0**	**38**	**2**	**33**	**0**	**3**	**11**	**0**	**2**	**2**	**29**	**0**	**0**	**0**
	NHL Totals		**399**	**61**	**93**	**154**	**66**	**84**	**150**	**1479**	**5**	**0**	**9**	**555**	**11.0**	**219**	**32**	**190**	**7**		**51**	**7**	**13**	**20**	**143**	**3**	**0**	**1**

Traded to **Pittsburgh** by **Buffalo** for Stu Barnes, March 11, 1999.

• BARNES, Blair

RW – R. 5'11", 190 lbs. b: Windsor, Ont., 9/21/1960. Edmonton's 6th, 126th overall, in 1979.

Season	Club	League	GP	G	A	Pts	AG	AA	APts	PIM	PP	SH	GW	S	%	TGF	PGF	TGA	PGA	+/-	GP	G	A	Pts	PIM	PP	SH	GW
1976-77	Markham Waxers	OHA-B	46	32	34	66	....	....	....	....	....	....	....	....	....	....	....	....	....	....	....	....	....	....	....	....	....	....
1977-78	Windsor Spitfires	OMJHL	65	22	26	48	....	....	....	163	....	....	....	....	....	....	....	....	....	....	6	0	1	1	23	....	....	....
1978-79	Windsor Spitfires	OMJHL	67	42	76	118	....	....	....	195	....	....	....	....	....	....	....	....	....	....	7	4	5	9	6	....	....	....
1979-80	Windsor Spitfires	OMJHL	66	63	67	130	....	....	....	98	....	....	....	....	....	....	....	....	....	....	16	*17	12	*29	26	....	....	....
1980-81	Wichita Wind	CHL	30	10	14	24	....	....	....	49	....	....	....	....	....	....	....	....	....	....	....	....	....	....	....	....	....	....
1981-82	Wichita Wind	CHL	80	28	34	62	....	....	....	99	....	....	....	....	....	....	....	....	....	....	5	0	1	1	2	....	....	....
1982-83	**Los Angeles Kings**	**NHL**	**1**	**0**	**0**	**0**	**0**	**0**	**0**	**0**	**0**	**0**	**0**	**0**	**0.0**	**0**	**0**	**0**	**0**	**0**	....	....	....	....	....	....	....	....
	New Haven Nighthawks	AHL	72	29	34	63	....	....	....	80	....	....	....	....	....	....	....	....	....	....	1	0	0	0	0	....	....	....
1983-84	Nova Scotia Voyageurs	AHL	80	32	32	64	....	....	....	91	....	....	....	....	....	....	....	....	....	....	6	4	2	6	12	....	....	....
	NHL Totals		**1**	**0**	**0**	**0**	**0**	**0**	**0**	**0**	**0**	**0**	**0**	**0**	**0.0**	**0**	**0**	**0**	**0**		....	....	....	....	....	....	....	....

Traded to **LA Kings** by **Edmonton** for Paul Mulvey, June 22, 1982.

• BARNES, Norm

Norman Leonard D – L. 6', 190 lbs. b: Toronto, Ont., 8/24/1953. Philadelphia's 9th, 122nd overall, in 1973.

Season	Club	League	GP	G	A	Pts	AG	AA	APts	PIM	PP	SH	GW	S	%	TGF	PGF	TGA	PGA	+/-	GP	G	A	Pts	PIM	PP	SH	GW
1971-72	Michigan State Spartans	WCHA	33	5	16	21	....	....	....	68	....	....	....	....	....	....	....	....	....	....	....	....	....	....	....	....	....	....
1972-73	Michigan State Spartans	WCHA	34	9	26	35	....	....	....	74	....	....	....	....	....	....	....	....	....	....	....	....	....	....	....	....	....	....
1973-74	Michigan State Spartans	WCHA	37	8	56	64	....	....	....	107	....	....	....	....	....	....	....	....	....	....	....	....	....	....	....	....	....	....
1974-75	Philadelphia Firebirds	NAHL	18	4	6	10	....	....	....	38	....	....	....	....	....	....	....	....	....	....	....	....	....	....	....	....	....	....
	Richmond Robins	AHL	17	0	5	5	....	....	....	32	....	....	....	....	....	....	....	....	....	....	....	....	....	....	....	....	....	....
1975-76	Richmond Robins	AHL	67	2	7	9	....	....	....	74	....	....	....	....	....	....	....	....	....	....	8	0	0	0	2	....	....	....
1976-77	**Philadelphia Flyers**	**NHL**	**1**	**0**	**0**	**0**	**0**	**0**	**0**	**0**	**0**	**0**	**0**	**0**	**0.0**	**0**	**0**	**0**	**0**	**0**	....	....	....	....	....	....	....	....
	Baltimore Clippers	SHL	46	5	27	32	....	....	....	90	....	....	....	....	....	....	....	....	....	....	....	....	....	....	....	....	....	....
	Springfield Indians	AHL	2	0	0	0	....	....	....	0	....	....	....	....	....	....	....	....	....	....	....	....	....	....	....	....	....	....
	Philadelphia Firebirds	NAHL	22	3	18	21	....	....	....	27	....	....	....	....	....	....	....	....	....	....	4	1	1	2	7	....	....	....
1977-78	Maine Mariners	AHL	50	4	8	12	....	....	....	62	....	....	....	....	....	....	....	....	....	....	12	1	5	6	28	....	....	....
1978-79	Maine Mariners	AHL	67	9	21	30	....	....	....	108	....	....	....	....	....	....	....	....	....	....	10	3	3	6	19	....	....	....
	Philadelphia Flyers	**NHL**	....	....	....	....	....	....	....	....	....	....	....	....	....	....	....	....	....	....	**2**	**0**	**0**	**0**	**0**	**0**	**0**	**0**
1979-80	**Philadelphia Flyers**	**NHL**	**59**	**4**	**21**	**25**	**3**	**15**	**18**	**59**	**0**	**0**	**1**	**73**	**5.5**	**84**	**8**	**70**	**17**	**23**	**10**	**0**	**0**	**0**	**8**	**0**	**0**	**0**

Season	Club	League	REGULAR SEASON																		PLAYOFFS							
			GP	G	A	Pts	AG	AA	APts	PIM	PP	SH	GW	S	%	TGF	PGF	TGA	PGA	+/–	GP	G	A	Pts	PIM	PP	SH	GW
1980-81	**Philadelphia Flyers**	**NHL**	**22**	**0**	**3**	**3**	**0**	**2**	**2**	**18**	**0**	**0**	**0**	**12**	**0.0**	**16**	**1**	**26**	**8**	**–3**	....	....	....	....	....	....	....	....
	Hartford Whalers	**NHL**	**54**	**1**	**10**	**11**	**1**	**7**	**8**	**82**	**0**	**0**	**0**	**72**	**1.4**	**68**	**4**	**133**	**39**	**–30**	....	....	....	....	....	....	....	....
	Canada	WEC-A	6	0	1	1	....	....	....	6	....	....	....	....	....	....	....	....	....	....	....	....	....	....	....	....	....	....
1981-82	**Hartford Whalers**	**NHL**	**20**	**1**	**4**	**5**	**1**	**3**	**4**	**19**	**0**	**0**	**0**	**25**	**4.0**	**20**	**0**	**36**	**12**	**–4**	....	....	....	....	....	....	....	....
	Binghamton Whalers	AHL	56	4	17	21	....	....	....	58	....	....	....	....	....	....	....	....	....	....	15	1	4	5	16	....	....	....
	NHL Totals		**156**	**6**	**38**	**44**	**5**	**27**	**32**	**178**	**0**	**0**	**1**	**182**	**3.3**	**188**	**13**	**265**	**76**		**12**	**0**	**0**	**0**	**8**	**0**	**0**	**0**

WCHA First All-Star Team (1974) • NCAA West First All-American Team (1974) • AHL First All-Star Team (1982) • Played in NHL All-Star Game (1980)

Traded to **Hartford** by **Philadelphia** with Jack McIlhargey for Hartford's 2nd round choice (later traded to Toronto — Toronto selected Peter Ihnacak) in 1982 Entry Draft, November 21, 1980.

• BARNES, Stu

Stuart Douglas C – R. 5'11", 174 lbs. b: Spruce Grove, Alta., 12/25/1970. Winnipeg's 1st, 4th overall, in 1989.

1985-86	Spruce Grove Blades	AAHA	STATISTICS NOT AVAILABLE																									
1986-87	St. Albert Saints	AJHL	53	41	34	*75	....	....	....	103	....	....	....	....	....	....	....	....	....	....	19	7	15	22	....	....	....	....
1987-88	New Westminster Bruins	WHL	71	37	64	101	....	....	....	88	....	....	....	....	....	....	....	....	....	....	5	2	3	5	6	....	....	....
1988-89	Tri-City Americans	WHL	70	59	82	141	....	....	....	117	....	....	....	....	....	....	....	....	....	....	7	6	5	11	10	....	....	....
1989-90	Tri-City Americans	WHL	63	52	92	144	....	....	....	165	....	....	....	....	....	....	....	....	....	....	7	1	5	6	26	....	....	....
	Canada	WJC-A	7	2	4	6	....	....	....	6	....	....	....	....	....	....	....	....	....	....	....	....	....	....	....	....	....	....
1990-91	Canada	Nat-Team	53	22	27	49	....	....	....	68	....	....	....	....	....	....	....	....	....	....	....	....	....	....	....	....	....	....
1991-92	**Winnipeg Jets**	**NHL**	**46**	**8**	**9**	**17**	**7**	**7**	**14**	**26**	**4**	**0**	**0**	**75**	**10.7**	**33**	**14**	**21**	**0**	**–2**	....	....	....	....	....	....	....	....
	Moncton Hawks	AHL	30	13	19	32	....	....	....	10	....	....	....	....	....	....	....	....	....	....	11	3	9	12	6	....	....	....
1992-93	**Winnipeg Jets**	**NHL**	**38**	**12**	**10**	**22**	**10**	**7**	**17**	**10**	**3**	**0**	**3**	**73**	**16.4**	**34**	**5**	**32**	**0**	**–3**	**6**	**1**	**3**	**4**	**2**	**0**	**0**	**0**
	Moncton Hawks	AHL	42	23	31	54	....	....	....	58	....	....	....	....	....	....	....	....	....	....	....	....	....	....	....	....	....	....
1993-94	**Winnipeg Jets**	**NHL**	**18**	**5**	**4**	**9**	**5**	**3**	**8**	**8**	**2**	**0**	**0**	**24**	**20.8**	**12**	**4**	**9**	**0**	**–1**	....	....	....	....	....	....	....	....
	Florida Panthers	**NHL**	**59**	**18**	**20**	**38**	**17**	**16**	**33**	**30**	**6**	**1**	**3**	**148**	**12.2**	**57**	**19**	**36**	**3**	**5**	....	....	....	....	....	....	....	....
1994-95	**Florida Panthers**	**NHL**	**41**	**10**	**19**	**29**	**18**	**28**	**46**	**8**	**1**	**0**	**2**	**93**	**10.8**	**44**	**12**	**30**	**5**	**7**	....	....	....	....	....	....	....	....
1995-96	**Florida Panthers**	**NHL**	**72**	**19**	**25**	**44**	**19**	**20**	**39**	**46**	**8**	**0**	**5**	**158**	**12.0**	**67**	**32**	**53**	**6**	**–12**	**22**	**6**	**10**	**16**	**4**	**2**	**0**	**2**
1996-97	**Florida Panthers**	**NHL**	**19**	**2**	**8**	**10**	**2**	**7**	**9**	**10**	**1**	**0**	**0**	**44**	**4.5**	**15**	**8**	**11**	**1**	**–3**	....	....	....	....	....	....	....	....
	Pittsburgh Penguins	**NHL**	**62**	**17**	**22**	**39**	**18**	**20**	**38**	**16**	**4**	**0**	**3**	**132**	**12.9**	**53**	**14**	**67**	**8**	**–20**	**5**	**0**	**1**	**1**	**0**	**0**	**0**	**0**
1997-98	**Pittsburgh Penguins**	**NHL**	**78**	**30**	**35**	**65**	**35**	**34**	**69**	**30**	**15**	**1**	**5**	**196**	**15.3**	**101**	**40**	**61**	**15**	**15**	**6**	**3**	**3**	**6**	**2**	**0**	**0**	**1**
1998-99	**Pittsburgh Penguins**	**NHL**	**64**	**20**	**12**	**32**	**23**	**12**	**35**	**20**	**13**	**0**	**3**	**155**	**12.9**	**67**	**35**	**44**	**0**	**–12**	....	....	....	....	....	....	....	....
	Buffalo Sabres	**NHL**	**17**	**0**	**4**	**4**	**0**	**4**	**4**	**10**	**0**	**0**	**0**	**25**	**0.0**	**8**	**3**	**4**	**0**	**1**	**21**	**7**	**3**	**10**	**6**	**4**	**0**	**1**
99-2000	**Buffalo Sabres**	**NHL**	**82**	**20**	**25**	**45**	**22**	**23**	**45**	**16**	**8**	**2**	**2**	**137**	**14.6**	**58**	**22**	**57**	**18**	**–3**	**5**	**3**	**0**	**3**	**2**	**2**	**0**	**1**
	NHL Totals		**596**	**161**	**193**	**354**	**176**	**181**	**357**	**230**	**65**	**4**	**26**	**1260**	**12.8**	**549**	**208**	**425**	**56**		**65**	**20**	**20**	**40**	**16**	**8**	**0**	**5**

WHL West Second All-Star Team (1988, 1989)

Traded to **Florida** by **Winnipeg** with St. Louis' 6th round choice (previously acquired by Winnipeg — later traded to Edmonton — later traded to Winnipeg — Winnipeg selected Chris Kibermanis) in 1994 Entry Draft for Randy Gilhen, November 25, 1993. Traded to **Pittsburgh** by **Florida** with Jason Woolley for Chris Wells, November 19, 1996. Traded to **Buffalo** by **Pittsburgh** for Matthew Barnaby, March 11, 1999.

• BARON, Murray

"Bear" D – L. 6'3", 215 lbs. b: Prince George, B.C., 6/1/1967. Philadelphia's 7th, 167th overall, in 1986.

1984-85	Vernon Lakers	BCJHL	37	5	9	14	....	....	....	93	....	....	....	....	....	....	....	....	....	....	13	5	6	11	107	....	....	....
1985-86	Vernon Lakers	BCJHL	46	12	32	44	....	....	....	179	....	....	....	....	....	....	....	....	....	....	7	1	2	3	13	....	....	....
1986-87	University of North Dakota	WCHA	41	4	10	14	....	....	....	62	....	....	....	....	....	....	....	....	....	....	....	....	....	....	....	....	....	....
1987-88	University of North Dakota	WCHA	41	1	10	11	....	....	....	95	....	....	....	....	....	....	....	....	....	....	....	....	....	....	....	....	....	....
1988-89	University of North Dakota	WCHA	40	2	6	8	....	....	....	92	....	....	....	....	....	....	....	....	....	....	....	....	....	....	....	....	....	....
	Hershey Bears	AHL	9	0	3	3	....	....	....	8	....	....	....	....	....	....	....	....	....	....	....	....	....	....	....	....	....	....
1989-90	**Philadelphia Flyers**	**NHL**	**16**	**2**	**2**	**4**	**2**	**1**	**3**	**12**	**0**	**0**	**0**	**18**	**11.1**	**11**	**0**	**12**	**0**	**–1**	....	....	....	....	....	....	....	....
	Hershey Bears	AHL	50	0	10	10	....	....	....	101	....	....	....	....	....	....	....	....	....	....	....	....	....	....	....	....	....	....
1990-91	**Philadelphia Flyers**	**NHL**	**67**	**8**	**8**	**16**	**7**	**6**	**13**	**74**	**3**	**0**	**1**	**86**	**9.3**	**60**	**13**	**57**	**7**	**–3**	....	....	....	....	....	....	....	....
	Hershey Bears	AHL	6	2	3	5	....	....	....	0	....	....	....	....	....	....	....	....	....	....	....	....	....	....	....	....	....	....
1991-92	**St. Louis Blues**	**NHL**	**67**	**3**	**8**	**11**	**3**	**6**	**9**	**94**	**0**	**0**	**0**	**55**	**5.5**	**47**	**1**	**68**	**19**	**–3**	**2**	**0**	**0**	**0**	**2**	**0**	**0**	**0**
1992-93	**St. Louis Blues**	**NHL**	**53**	**2**	**2**	**4**	**2**	**1**	**3**	**59**	**0**	**0**	**1**	**42**	**4.8**	**41**	**1**	**56**	**11**	**–5**	**11**	**0**	**0**	**0**	**12**	**0**	**0**	**0**
1993-94	**St. Louis Blues**	**NHL**	**77**	**5**	**9**	**14**	**5**	**7**	**12**	**123**	**0**	**0**	**0**	**73**	**6.8**	**57**	**2**	**101**	**32**	**–14**	**4**	**0**	**0**	**0**	**10**	**0**	**0**	**0**
1994-95	**St. Louis Blues**	**NHL**	**39**	**0**	**5**	**5**	**0**	**7**	**7**	**93**	**0**	**0**	**0**	**28**	**0.0**	**38**	**0**	**52**	**23**	**9**	**7**	**1**	**1**	**2**	**2**	**0**	**0**	**0**
1995-96	**St. Louis Blues**	**NHL**	**82**	**2**	**9**	**11**	**2**	**7**	**9**	**190**	**0**	**0**	**0**	**86**	**2.3**	**61**	**3**	**98**	**43**	**3**	**13**	**1**	**0**	**1**	**20**	**0**	**1**	**0**
1996-97	**St. Louis Blues**	**NHL**	**11**	**0**	**2**	**2**	**0**	**2**	**2**	**11**	**0**	**0**	**0**	**7**	**0.0**	**8**	**0**	**15**	**3**	**–4**	....	....	....	....	....	....	....	....
	Montreal Canadiens	**NHL**	**60**	**1**	**5**	**6**	**1**	**4**	**5**	**107**	**0**	**0**	**0**	**52**	**1.9**	**44**	**1**	**78**	**19**	**–16**	....	....	....	....	....	....	....	....
	Phoenix Coyotes	**NHL**	**8**	**0**	**0**	**0**	**0**	**0**	**0**	**4**	**0**	**0**	**0**	**5**	**0.0**	**7**	**0**	**8**	**1**	**0**	**1**	**0**	**0**	**0**	**0**	**0**	**0**	**0**
1997-98	**Phoenix Coyotes**	**NHL**	**45**	**1**	**5**	**6**	**1**	**5**	**6**	**106**	**0**	**0**	**0**	**23**	**4.3**	**23**	**0**	**50**	**17**	**–10**	**6**	**0**	**2**	**2**	**6**	**0**	**0**	**0**
1998-99	**Vancouver Canucks**	**NHL**	**81**	**2**	**6**	**8**	**2**	**6**	**8**	**115**	**0**	**0**	**0**	**53**	**3.8**	**44**	**2**	**99**	**34**	**–23**	....	....	....	....	....	....	....	....
99-2000	**Vancouver Canucks**	**NHL**	**81**	**2**	**10**	**12**	**2**	**9**	**11**	**67**	**0**	**0**	**0**	**48**	**4.2**	**62**	**1**	**85**	**32**	**8**	....	....	....	....	....	....	....	....
	NHL Totals		**687**	**28**	**71**	**99**	**27**	**61**	**88**	**1055**	**3**	**0**	**2**	**576**	**4.9**	**503**	**24**	**779**	**241**		**44**	**2**	**3**	**5**	**52**	**0**	**1**	**0**

Traded to **St. Louis** by **Philadelphia** with Ron Sutter for Dan Quinn and Rod Brind'Amour, September 22, 1991. Traded to **Montreal** by **St. Louis** with Shayne Corson and St. Louis' 5th round choice (Gennady Razin) in 1997 Entry Draft for Pierre Turgeon, Rory Fitzpatrick and Craig Conroy, October 29, 1996. Traded to **Phoenix** by **Montreal** with Chris Murray for Dave Manson, March 18, 1997. Signed as a free agent by **Vancouver**, July 14, 1998.

• BARON, Normand

LW – L. 6', 205 lbs. b: Verdun, Que., 12/15/1957.

1976-77	Montreal Jr. Canadiens	QMJHL	7	1	1	2	....	....	....	0	....	....	....	....	....	....	....	....	....	....	....	....	....	....	....	....	....	....
1977-1983			DID NOT PLAY																									
1983-84	**Montreal Canadiens**	**NHL**	**4**	**0**	**0**	**0**	**0**	**0**	**0**	**12**	**0**	**0**	**0**	**2**	**0.0**	**0**	**0**	**2**	**0**	**–2**	**3**	**0**	**0**	**0**	**22**	**0**	**0**	**0**
	Nova Scotia Voyageurs	AHL	68	11	11	22	....	....	....	275	....	....	....	....	....	....	....	....	....	....	....	....	....	....	....	....	....	....
1984-85	Sherbrooke Canadiens	AHL	39	5	5	10	....	....	....	98	....	....	....	....	....	....	....	....	....	....	3	0	0	0	22	....	....	....
1985-86	**St. Louis Blues**	**NHL**	**23**	**2**	**0**	**2**	**2**	**0**	**2**	**39**	**0**	**0**	**0**	**13**	**15.4**	**5**	**0**	**12**	**0**	**–7**	....	....	....	....	....	....	....	....
	Peoria Rivermen	IHL	17	4	4	8	....	....	....	61	....	....	....	....	....	....	....	....	....	....	....	....	....	....	....	....	....	....
	Flint Spirits	IHL	11	1	7	8	....	....	....	43	....	....	....	....	....	....	....	....	....	....	....	....	....	....	....	....	....	....
	NHL Totals		**27**	**2**	**0**	**2**	**2**	**0**	**2**	**51**	**0**	**0**	**0**	**15**	**13.3**	**5**	**0**	**14**	**0**		**3**	**0**	**0**	**0**	**22**	**0**	**0**	**0**

• Worked as a professional weight-lifter and body builder from 1977 to 1983. Signed as a free agent by **Montreal**, March 15, 1984. Traded to **St. Louis** by **Montreal** for cash, September 30, 1985.

• BARR, Dave

David Angus RW – R. 6'1", 195 lbs. b: Toronto, Ont., 11/30/1960.

1977-78	Pincher Creek Pioneers	AJHL	60	16	32	48	....	....	....	53	....	....	....	....	....	....	....	....	....	....	....	....	....	....	....	....	....	....
	Billings Bighorns	WCJHL	2	0	1	1	....	....	....	0	....	....	....	....	....	....	....	....	....	....	....	....	....	....	....	....	....	....
1978-79	Edmonton Oil Kings	WHL	72	16	19	35	....	....	....	61	....	....	....	....	....	....	....	....	....	....	8	4	0	4	2	....	....	....
1979-80	Great Falls Americans	WHL	3	0	1	1	....	....	....	10	....	....	....	....	....	....	....	....	....	....	....	....	....	....	....	....	....	....
	Portland Winter Hawks	WHL	27	4	12	16	....	....	....	18	....	....	....	....	....	....	....	....	....	....	....	....	....	....	....	....	....	....
	Lethbridge Broncos	WHL	30	12	25	37	....	....	....	29	....	....	....	....	....	....	....	....	....	....	....	....	....	....	....	....	....	....
1980-81	Lethbridge Broncos	WHL	72	26	62	88	....	....	....	106	....	....	....	....	....	....	....	....	....	....	10	4	10	14	4	....	....	....
1981-82	**Boston Bruins**	**NHL**	**2**	**0**	**0**	**0**	**0**	**0**	**0**	**0**	**0**	**0**	**0**	**1**	**0.0**	**0**	**0**	**0**	**0**	**0**	**5**	**1**	**0**	**1**	**0**	**0**	**0**	**0**
	Erie Blades	AHL	76	18	48	66	....	....	....	29	....	....	....	....	....	....	....	....	....	....	....	....	....	....	....	....	....	....
1982-83	**Boston Bruins**	**NHL**	**10**	**1**	**1**	**2**	**1**	**1**	**2**	**7**	**0**	**0**	**0**	**11**	**9.1**	**3**	**0**	**2**	**0**	**1**	**10**	**0**	**0**	**0**	**2**	**0**	**0**	**0**
	Baltimore Skipjacks	AHL	72	27	51	78	....	....	....	67	....	....	....	....	....	....	....	....	....	....	....	....	....	....	....	....	....	....
1983-84	**New York Rangers**	**NHL**	**6**	**0**	**0**	**0**	**0**	**0**	**0**	**2**	**0**	**0**	**0**	**9**	**0.0**	**1**	**0**	**1**	**0**	**0**	....	....	....	....	....	....	....	....
	Tulsa Oilers	CHL	50	28	37	65	....	....	....	24	....	....	....	....	....	....	....	....	....	....	....	....	....	....	....	....	....	....
	St. Louis Blues	**NHL**	**1**	**0**	**0**	**0**	**0**	**0**	**0**	**0**	**0**	**0**	**0**	**0**	**0.0**	**0**	**0**	**1**	**0**	**–1**	....	....	....	....	....	....	....	....
1984-85	**St. Louis Blues**	**NHL**	**75**	**16**	**18**	**34**	**13**	**12**	**25**	**32**	**2**	**0**	**1**	**75**	**21.3**	**48**	**7**	**40**	**4**	**5**	**2**	**0**	**0**	**0**	**2**	**0**	**0**	**0**
1985-86	**St. Louis Blues**	**NHL**	**72**	**13**	**38**	**51**	**10**	**26**	**36**	**70**	**0**	**0**	**2**	**106**	**12.3**	**72**	**10**	**52**	**1**	**11**	**11**	**1**	**1**	**2**	**14**	**1**	**0**	**0**
1986-87	**St. Louis Blues**	**NHL**	**2**	**0**	**0**	**0**	**0**	**0**	**0**	**0**	**0**	**0**	**0**	**3**	**0.0**	**1**	**0**	**0**	**0**	**1**	....	....	....	....	....	....	....	....
	Hartford Whalers	**NHL**	**30**	**2**	**4**	**6**	**2**	**3**	**5**	**19**	**0**	**1**	**0**	**25**	**8.0**	**14**	**0**	**19**	**4**	**–1**	....	....	....	....	....	....	....	....
	Detroit Red Wings	**NHL**	**37**	**13**	**13**	**26**	**11**	**9**	**20**	**49**	**4**	**0**	**5**	**55**	**23.6**	**42**	**12**	**27**	**4**	**7**	**13**	**1**	**0**	**1**	**14**	**0**	**0**	**0**
1987-88	**Detroit Red Wings**	**NHL**	**51**	**14**	**26**	**40**	**12**	**19**	**31**	**58**	**3**	**1**	**0**	**64**	**21.9**	**67**	**11**	**43**	**7**	**20**	**16**	**5**	**7**	**12**	**22**	**2**	**0**	**0**

			REGULAR SEASON																		PLAYOFFS							
Season	Club	League	GP	G	A	Pts	AG	AA	APts	PIM	PP	SH	GW	S	%	TGF	PGF	TGA	PGA	+/–	GP	G	A	Pts	PIM	PP	SH	GW
1988-89	Detroit Red Wings	NHL	73	27	32	59	23	23	46	69	5	2	3	140	19.3	103	18	93	20	12	6	3	1	4	6	1	0	1
1989-90	Detroit Red Wings	NHL	62	10	25	35	9	18	27	45	2	3	0	96	10.4	55	5	68	23	5	....	....	....	....	....	....	....	....
	Adirondack Red Wings	AHL	9	1	14	15	....	....	....	17	....	....	....	....	....	....	....	....	....	....	....	....	....	....	....	....	....	....
1990-91	Detroit Red Wings	NHL	70	18	22	40	16	17	33	55	2	2	2	98	18.4	54	2	57	25	20	....	....	....	....	....	....	....	....
1991-92	New Jersey Devils	NHL	41	6	12	18	5	9	14	32	0	1	0	49	12.2	22	1	19	7	9	....	....	....	....	....	....	....	....
	Utica Devils	AHL	1	0	0	0	....	....	....	7	....	....	....	....	....	....	....	....	....	....	....	....	....	....	....	....	....	....
1992-93	New Jersey Devils	NHL	62	6	8	14	5	5	10	61	0	1	1	41	14.6	24	0	52	29	1	5	1	0	1	6	0	0	0
1993-94	Dallas Stars	NHL	20	2	5	7	2	4	6	21	0	0	0	20	10.0	8	0	14	0	–6	3	0	1	1	4	0	0	0
	Kalamazoo Wings	IHL	4	3	2	5	....	....	....	5	....	....	....	....	....	....	....	....	....	....	....	....	....	....	....	....	....	....
1994-95	Kalamazoo Wings	IHL	66	18	41	59	....	....	....	77	....	....	....	....	....	....	....	....	....	....	16	1	4	5	8	....	....	....
1995-96	Orlando Solar Bears	IHL	82	38	62	100	....	....	....	87	....	....	....	....	....	....	....	....	....	....	23	8	13	21	14	....	....	....
1996-97	Orlando Solar Bears	IHL	50	15	29	44	....	....	....	29	....	....	....	....	....	....	....	....	....	....	9	2	3	5	8	....	....	....
1997-2000	Houston Aeros	IHL	DID NOT PLAY – ASSISTANT COACH																									
	NHL Totals		614	128	204	332	109	146	255	520	18	11	14	793	16.1	514	66	488	124		71	12	10	22	70	4	0	1

Signed as a free agent by **Boston**, September 28, 1981. Traded to **NY Rangers** by **Boston** for Dave Silk, October 5, 1983. Traded to **St. Louis** by **NY Rangers** with NY Rangers' 3rd round choice (Alan Perry) in 1984 Entry Draft and cash for Larry Patey and Bob Brooke, March 5, 1984. Traded to **Hartford** by **St. Louis** for Tim Bothwell, October 21, 1986. Traded to **Detroit** by **Hartford** for Randy Ladouceur, January 12, 1987. Transferred to **New Jersey** from **Detroit** with Randy McKay as compensation for Detroit's signing of free agent Troy Crowder, September 9, 1991. Signed as a free agent by **Dallas**, August 28, 1993. • Missed majority of 1993-94 season recovering from arthroscopic elbow surgery, October 13, 1993. • Officially announced retirement and named Assistant Coach of **Houston** (IHL), July 15, 1997. • Also served as Assistant General Manager with **Houston** (IHL) in 1999-2000.

• BARRAULT, Doug

Douglas RW – R. 6'2", 205 lbs. b: Golden, B.C., 4/21/1970. Minnesota's 8th, 155th overall, in 1990.

Season	Club	League	GP	G	A	Pts	AG	AA	APts	PIM	PP	SH	GW	S	%	TGF	PGF	TGA	PGA	+/–	GP	G	A	Pts	PIM	PP	SH	GW
1988-89	Lethbridge Hurricanes	WHL	57	14	13	27	....	....	....	34	....	....	....	....	....	....	....	....	....	....	....	....	....	....	....	....	....	....
1989-90	Lethbridge Hurricanes	WHL	54	14	16	30	....	....	....	36	....	....	....	....	....	....	....	....	....	....	19	7	3	10	0	....	....	....
1990-91	Lethbridge Hurricanes	WHL	4	2	2	4	....	....	....	16	....	....	....	....	....	....	....	....	....	....	....	....	....	....	....	....	....	....
	Seattle Thunderbirds	WHL	61	42	42	84	....	....	....	69	....	....	....	....	....	....	....	....	....	....	6	5	3	8	4	....	....	....
1991-92	Kalamazoo Wings	IHL	60	5	14	19	....	....	....	26	....	....	....	....	....	....	....	....	....	....	....	....	....	....	....	....	....	....
1992-93	Minnesota North Stars	NHL	2	0	0	0	0	0	0	2	0	0	0	0	0.0	0	0	1	0	–1	....	....	....	....	....	....	....	....
	Kalamazoo Wings	IHL	78	32	34	66	....	....	....	74	....	....	....	....	....	....	....	....	....	....	....	....	....	....	....	....	....	....
1993-94	Florida Panthers	NHL	2	0	0	0	0	0	0	0	0	0	0	2	0.0	0	0	2	0	–2	....	....	....	....	....	....	....	....
	Cincinnati Cyclones	IHL	75	36	28	64	....	....	....	59	....	....	....	....	....	....	....	....	....	....	9	8	2	10	0	....	....	....
1994-95	Cincinnati Cyclones	IHL	74	20	40	60	....	....	....	57	....	....	....	....	....	....	....	....	....	....	10	2	6	8	20	....	....	....
1995-96	Atlanta Knights	IHL	19	5	9	14	....	....	....	16	....	....	....	....	....	....	....	....	....	....	....	....	....	....	....	....	....	....
	Chicago Wolves	IHL	54	12	18	30	....	....	....	39	....	....	....	....	....	....	....	....	....	....	9	2	3	5	6	....	....	....
1996-97	Chicago Wolves	IHL	16	3	5	8	....	....	....	12	....	....	....	....	....	....	....	....	....	....	....	....	....	....	....	....	....	....
1997-98	Chicago Wolves	IHL	63	9	16	25	....	....	....	26	....	....	....	....	....	....	....	....	....	....	1	0	0	0	0	....	....	....
	United States	WC-A	1	0	0	0	....	....	....	0	....	....	....	....	....	....	....	....	....	....	....	....	....	....	....	....	....	....
	NHL Totals		4	0	0	0	0	0	0	2	0	0	0	2	0.0	0	0	3	0		....	....	....	....	....	....	....	....

WHL West Second All-Star Team (1991)

Transferred to **Dallas** after **Minnesota** franchise relocated, June 9, 1993. Claimed by **Florida** from **Dallas** in Expansion Draft, June 24, 1993. • Suffered season-ending knee injury in December, 1996.

• BARRETT, Fred

Frederick William D – L. 5'11", 195 lbs. b: Ottawa, Ont., 1/26/1950. Minnesota's 2nd, 20th overall, in 1970.

Season	Club	League	GP	G	A	Pts	AG	AA	APts	PIM	PP	SH	GW	S	%	TGF	PGF	TGA	PGA	+/–	GP	G	A	Pts	PIM	PP	SH	GW
1965-66	South Ottawa Canadians	OMHA	STATISTICS NOT AVAILABLE																									
	Ottawa Capitals	OJHL	2	0	0	0	....	....	....	0	....	....	....	....	....	....	....	....	....	....	....	....	....	....	....	....	....	....
1966-67	Ottawa Capitals	OJHL	STATISTICS NOT AVAILABLE																									
	Toronto Marlboros	OHA-Jr.	2	0	0	0	....	....	....	2	....	....	....	....	....	....	....	....	....	....	9	0	0	0	2	....	....	....
1967-68	Toronto Marlboros	OHA-Jr.	51	5	8	13	....	....	....	98	....	....	....	....	....	....	....	....	....	....	5	0	0	0	22	....	....	....
1968-69	Toronto Marlboros	OHA-Jr.	52	3	17	20	....	....	....	113	....	....	....	....	....	....	....	....	....	....	6	1	2	3	15	....	....	....
1969-70	Toronto Marlboros	OHA-Jr.	48	8	20	28	....	....	....	146	....	....	....	....	....	....	....	....	....	....	15	3	5	8	45	....	....	....
1970-71	Minnesota North Stars	NHL	57	0	13	13	0	11	11	75	0	0	0	75	0.0	58	1	70	15	2	....	....	....	....	....	....	....	....
1971-72	Cleveland Barons	AHL	51	2	27	29	....	....	....	91	....	....	....	....	....	....	....	....	....	....	1	0	0	0	2	....	....	....
1972-73	Minnesota North Stars	NHL	46	2	4	6	2	3	5	21	0	0	0	51	3.9	49	0	51	16	14	6	0	0	0	4	0	0	0
1973-74	Minnesota North Stars	NHL	40	0	7	7	0	6	6	12	0	0	0	31	0.0	24	0	30	5	–1	....	....	....	....	....	....	....	....
1974-75	Minnesota North Stars	NHL	62	3	18	21	3	13	16	82	0	0	0	79	3.8	68	4	123	38	–21	....	....	....	....	....	....	....	....
1975-76	Minnesota North Stars	NHL	79	2	9	11	2	7	9	66	0	0	1	70	2.9	62	3	133	49	–25	....	....	....	....	....	....	....	....
1976-77	Minnesota North Stars	NHL	60	1	8	9	1	6	7	46	0	0	0	54	1.9	42	4	86	17	–31	2	0	0	0	2	0	0	0
1977-78	Minnesota North Stars	NHL	79	0	15	15	0	12	12	59	0	0	0	87	0.0	65	1	140	41	–35	....	....	....	....	....	....	....	....
1978-79	Minnesota North Stars	NHL	45	1	9	10	1	7	8	48	0	0	0	36	2.8	44	2	57	11	–4	....	....	....	....	....	....	....	....
1979-80	Minnesota North Stars	NHL	80	8	14	22	7	10	17	71	0	0	0	85	9.4	80	1	88	26	17	14	0	0	0	22	0	0	0
1980-81	Minnesota North Stars	DN-Cup	3	0	1	1	....	....	....	0	....	....	....	....	....	....	....	....	....	....	....	....	....	....	....	....	....	....
	Minnesota North Stars	NHL	62	4	8	12	3	5	8	72	0	0	1	73	5.5	56	2	74	21	1	14	0	1	1	16	0	0	0
1981-82	Minnesota North Stars	NHL	69	1	15	16	1	10	11	89	0	0	0	43	2.3	66	0	101	23	–12	4	0	1	1	16	0	0	0
1982-83	Minnesota North Stars	NHL	51	1	3	4	1	2	3	22	0	0	0	29	3.4	25	0	48	13	–10	4	0	0	0	0	0	0	0
1983-84	Los Angeles Kings	NHL	15	2	0	2	2	0	2	8	0	0	0	4	50.0	12	0	15	1	–2	....	....	....	....	....	....	....	....
	NHL Totals		745	25	123	148	23	92	115	671	0	0	2	717	3.5	651	18	1016	276		44	0	2	2	60	0	0	0

• Brother of John • Missed majority of 1965-66 season recovering from kneecap injury, November, 1965. • Missed majority of 1966-67 season recovering from ankle injury suffered in training camp, September, 1967. Traded to **LA Kings** by **Minnesota** with Steve Christoff for Dave Lewis, October 3, 1983.

• BARRETT, John

John David D – L. 6'1", 210 lbs. b: Ottawa, Ont., 7/1/1958. Detroit's 10th, 129th overall, in 1978.

Season	Club	League	GP	G	A	Pts	AG	AA	APts	PIM	PP	SH	GW	S	%	TGF	PGF	TGA	PGA	+/–	GP	G	A	Pts	PIM	PP	SH	GW
1975-76	Gloucester Rangers	OJHL	STATISTICS NOT AVAILABLE																									
1976-77	Windsor Spitfires	OMJHL	63	7	17	24	....	....	....	168	....	....	....	....	....	....	....	....	....	....	9	1	1	2	12	....	....	....
1977-78	Windsor Spitfires	OMJHL	67	8	18	26	....	....	....	133	....	....	....	....	....	....	....	....	....	....	6	2	1	3	30	....	....	....
1978-79	Milwaukee Admirals	IHL	42	8	13	21	....	....	....	117	....	....	....	....	....	....	....	....	....	....	....	....	....	....	....	....	....	....
	Kalamazoo Wings	IHL	31	1	12	13	....	....	....	54	....	....	....	....	....	....	....	....	....	....	15	2	11	13	48	....	....	....
1979-80	Kalamazoo Wings	IHL	52	8	33	41	....	....	....	63	....	....	....	....	....	....	....	....	....	....	....	....	....	....	....	....	....	....
	Adirondack Red Wings	AHL	28	0	4	4	....	....	....	59	....	....	....	....	....	....	....	....	....	....	5	1	2	3	6	....	....	....
1980-81	Detroit Red Wings	NHL	56	3	10	13	2	7	9	60	0	0	1	97	3.1	51	3	111	42	–21	....	....	....	....	....	....	....	....
	Adirondack Red Wings	AHL	21	4	11	15	....	....	....	63	....	....	....	....	....	....	....	....	....	....	....	....	....	....	....	....	....	....
1981-82	Detroit Red Wings	NHL	69	1	12	13	1	8	9	93	0	0	0	97	1.0	55	1	111	26	–31	....	....	....	....	....	....	....	....
1982-83	Detroit Red Wings	NHL	79	4	10	14	3	7	10	74	0	0	0	72	5.6	67	1	109	25	–18	....	....	....	....	....	....	....	....
1983-84	Detroit Red Wings	NHL	78	2	8	10	2	5	7	78	0	0	0	63	3.2	71	1	95	25	0	4	0	0	0	4	0	0	0
1984-85	Detroit Red Wings	NHL	71	6	19	25	5	13	18	117	0	0	1	72	8.3	63	1	106	29	–15	3	0	1	1	11	0	0	0
1985-86	Detroit Red Wings	NHL	65	2	12	14	2	8	10	125	0	0	0	60	3.3	57	2	122	38	–29	....	....	....	....	....	....	....	....
	Washington Capitals	NHL	14	0	3	3	0	2	2	12	0	0	0	7	0.0	10	0	7	0	3	9	2	1	3	35	0	0	1
1986-87	Washington Capitals	NHL	55	2	2	4	2	1	3	43	0	0	0	37	5.4	25	2	47	8	–16	....	....	....	....	....	....	....	....
1987-88	Binghamton Whalers	AHL	5	0	2	2	....	....	....	6	....	....	....	....	....	....	....	....	....	....	....	....	....	....	....	....	....	....
	Minnesota North Stars	NHL	1	0	1	1	0	1	1	2	0	0	0	0	0.0	0	0	3	0	–3	....	....	....	....	....	....	....	....
	Kalamazoo Wings	IHL	2	0	1	1	....	....	....	2	....	....	....	....	....	....	....	....	....	....	....	....	....	....	....	....	....	....
	NHL Totals		488	20	77	97	17	52	69	604	0	0	2	505	4.0	399	11	711	193		16	2	2	4	50	0	0	1

• Brother of Fred

Traded to **Washington** by **Detroit** with Greg Smith for Darren Veitch, March 10, 1986. • Suffered eventual career-ending knee injury in game vs. Vancouver, January 20, 1987. Traded to **Minnesota** by **Washington** for future considerations, February 22, 1988.

• BARRIE, Doug

Douglas Robert D – R. 5'9", 175 lbs. b: Edmonton, Alta., 10/2/1946.

Season	Club	League	GP	G	A	Pts	AG	AA	APts	PIM	PP	SH	GW	S	%	TGF	PGF	TGA	PGA	+/–	GP	G	A	Pts	PIM	PP	SH	GW
1965-66	Edmonton Oil Kings	ASHL	40	2	7	9	....	....	....	80	....	....	....	....	....	....	....	....	....	....	11	1	4	5	31	....	....	....
	Edmonton Oil Kings	Mem-Cup	19	3	3	6	....	....	....	66	....	....	....	....	....	....	....	....	....	....	....	....	....	....	....	....	....	....
1966-67	Memphis Wings	CPHL	11	1	5	6	....	....	....	14	....	....	....	....	....	....	....	....	....	....	....	....	....	....	....	....	....	....
	Pittsburgh Hornets	AHL	27	0	2	2	....	....	....	6	....	....	....	....	....	....	....	....	....	....	....	....	....	....	....	....	....	....

			REGULAR SEASON																		PLAYOFFS							
Season	Club	League	GP	G	A	Pts	AG	AA	APts	PIM	PP	SH	GW	S	%	TGF	PGF	TGA	PGA	+/–	GP	G	A	Pts	PIM	PP	SH	GW
1967-68	Kansas City Blues	CPHL	32	0	6	6	....	....	....	74	....	....	....	....	....	....	....	....	....	....	....	....	....	....	....	....	....	....
	Omaha Knights	CPHL	23	1	6	7	....	....	....	74	....	....	....	....	....	....	....	....	....	....	....	....	....	....	....	....	....	....
	Tulsa Oilers	CPHL	8	0	2	2	....	....	....	21	....	....	....	....	....	....	....	....	....	....	11	1	5	6	*55	....	....	....
1968-69	**Pittsburgh Penguins**	**NHL**	**8**	**1**	**1**	**2**	**1**	**1**	**2**	**8**	**0**	**0**	**0**	**10**	**10.0**	**4**	**1**	**6**	**1**	**–2**	....	....	....	....	....	....	....	....
	Amarillo Wranglers	CPHL	66	7	29	36	....	....	....	163	....	....	....	....	....	....	....	....	....	....	....	....	....	....	....	....	....	....
1969-70	Baltimore Clippers	AHL	70	5	9	14	....	....	....	139	....	....	....	....	....	....	....	....	....	....	5	2	6	8	10	....	....	....
1970-71	**Buffalo Sabres**	**NHL**	**75**	**4**	**23**	**27**	**4**	**19**	**23**	**168**	**0**	**0**	**0**	**128**	**3.1**	**82**	**7**	**117**	**23**	**–19**	....	....	....	....	....	....	....	....
1971-72	**Buffalo Sabres**	**NHL**	**27**	**2**	**5**	**7**	**2**	**4**	**6**	**45**	**0**	**0**	**1**	**24**	**8.3**	**17**	**1**	**44**	**7**	**–21**	....	....	....	....	....	....	....	....
	Los Angeles Kings	**NHL**	**48**	**3**	**13**	**16**	**3**	**11**	**14**	**47**	**1**	**0**	**0**	**69**	**4.3**	**56**	**11**	**61**	**6**	**–10**	....	....	....	....	....	....	....	....
1972-73	Alberta Oilers	WHA	54	9	22	31	....	....	....	111	....	....	....	....	....	....	....	....	....	....	....	....	....	....	....	....	....	....
1973-74	Edmonton Oilers	WHA	69	4	27	31	....	....	....	214	....	....	....	....	....	....	....	....	....	....	4	1	0	1	16	....	....	....
1974-75	Edmonton Oilers	WHA	78	12	33	45	....	....	....	122	....	....	....	....	....	....	....	....	....	....	....	....	....	....	....	....	....	....
1975-76	Edmonton Oilers	WHA	79	4	21	25	....	....	....	81	....	....	....	....	....	....	....	....	....	....	4	0	1	1	15	....	....	....
1976-77	Edmonton Oilers	WHA	70	8	19	27	....	....	....	92	....	....	....	....	....	....	....	....	....	....	4	0	0	0	0	....	....	....
	NHL Totals		**158**	**10**	**42**	**52**	**10**	**35**	**45**	**268**	**1**	**0**	**1**	**231**	**4.3**	**159**	**20**	**228**	**37**		....	....	....	....	....	....	....	....
	Other Major League Totals		350	37	122	159	....	....	....	620	....	....	....	....	....	....	....	....	....	....	12	1	1	2	31	....	....	....

CHL Second All-Star Team (1969)

Traded to **Toronto** by **Detroit** with Norm Ullman, Paul Henderson and Floyd Smith for Frank Mahovlich, Pete Stemkowski, Garry Unger and the rights to Carl Brewer, March 3, 1968. Traded to **Detroit** by **Toronto** for cash, June 6, 1968. Traded to **Pittsburgh** by **Detroit** for cash, October, 1968. Claimed by **Buffalo** from **Pittsburgh** in Expansion Draft, June 10, 1970. Traded to **LA Kings** by **Buffalo** with Mike Keeler for Mike Byers and Larry Hillman, December 16, 1971. Selected by **Alberta** (WHA) in 1972 WHA General Player Draft, February 12, 1972.

• BARRIE, Len

C – L. 6′, 200 lbs. b: Kimberley, B.C., 6/4/1969. Edmonton's 7th, 124th overall, in 1988.

Season	Club	League	GP	G	A	Pts	AG	AA	APts	PIM	PP	SH	GW	S	%	TGF	PGF	TGA	PGA	+/–	GP	G	A	Pts	PIM	PP	SH	GW
1984-85	Kelowna Midget Blazers	BCAHA	20	51	55	106	....	....	....	24	....	....	....	....	....	....	....	....	....	....	....	....	....	....	....	....	....	....
1985-86	Calgary Spurs	AJHL	23	7	14	21	....	....	....	86	....	....	....	....	....	....	....	....	....	....	....	....	....	....	....	....	....	....
	Calgary Wranglers	WHL	32	3	0	3	....	....	....	18	....	....	....	....	....	....	....	....	....	....	....	....	....	....	....	....	....	....
1986-87	Calgary Wranglers	WHL	34	13	13	26	....	....	....	81	....	....	....	....	....	....	....	....	....	....	....	....	....	....	....	....	....	....
	Victoria Cougars	WHL	34	7	6	13	....	....	....	92	....	....	....	....	....	....	....	....	....	....	5	0	1	1	15	....	....	....
1987-88	Victoria Cougars	WHL	70	37	49	86	....	....	....	192	....	....	....	....	....	....	....	....	....	....	8	2	0	2	29	....	....	....
1988-89	Victoria Cougars	WHL	67	39	48	87	....	....	....	157	....	....	....	....	....	....	....	....	....	....	7	5	2	7	23	....	....	....
1989-90	Kamloops Blazers	WHL	70	*85	*100	*185	....	....	....	108	....	....	....	....	....	....	....	....	....	....	17	*14	23	*37	24	....	....	....
	Philadelphia Flyers	**NHL**	**1**	**0**	**0**	**0**	**0**	**0**	**0**	**0**	**0**	**0**	**0**	**0**	**0.0**	**0**	**0**	**2**	**0**	**–2**	....	....	....	....	....	....	....	....
	Kamloops Blazers	Mem-Cup	3	2	4	6	....	....	....	6	....	....	....	....	....	....	....	....	....	....	....	....	....	....	....	....	....	....
1990-91	Hershey Bears	AHL	63	26	32	58	....	....	....	60	....	....	....	....	....	....	....	....	....	....	7	4	0	4	12	....	....	....
1991-92	Hershey Bears	AHL	75	42	43	85	....	....	....	78	....	....	....	....	....	....	....	....	....	....	3	0	2	2	32	....	....	....
1992-93	**Philadelphia Flyers**	**NHL**	**8**	**2**	**2**	**4**	**2**	**1**	**3**	**9**	**0**	**0**	**0**	**14**	**14.3**	**5**	**0**	**3**	**0**	**2**	....	....	....	....	....	....	....	....
	Hershey Bears	AHL	61	31	45	76	....	....	....	162	....	....	....	....	....	....	....	....	....	....	....	....	....	....	....	....	....	....
1993-94	**Florida Panthers**	**NHL**	**2**	**0**	**0**	**0**	**0**	**0**	**0**	**0**	**0**	**0**	**0**	**0**	**0.0**	**0**	**0**	**2**	**0**	**–2**	....	....	....	....	....	....	....	....
	Cincinnati Cyclones	IHL	77	45	71	116	....	....	....	246	....	....	....	....	....	....	....	....	....	....	11	8	13	21	60	....	....	....
1994-95	Cleveland Lumberjacks	IHL	28	13	30	43	....	....	....	137	....	....	....	....	....	....	....	....	....	....	....	....	....	....	....	....	....	....
	Pittsburgh Penguins	**NHL**	**48**	**3**	**11**	**14**	**5**	**16**	**21**	**66**	**0**	**0**	**1**	**37**	**8.1**	**19**	**4**	**21**	**2**	**–4**	**4**	**1**	**0**	**1**	**8**	**1**	**0**	**0**
1995-96	**Pittsburgh Penguins**	**NHL**	**5**	**0**	**0**	**0**	**0**	**0**	**0**	**18**	**0**	**0**	**0**	**5**	**0.0**	**0**	**0**	**1**	**0**	**–1**	....	....	....	....	....	....	....	....
	Cleveland Lumberjacks	IHL	55	29	43	72	....	....	....	178	....	....	....	....	....	....	....	....	....	....	3	2	3	5	6	....	....	....
1996-97	San Antonio Dragons	IHL	57	26	40	66	....	....	....	196	....	....	....	....	....	....	....	....	....	....	9	5	5	10	20	....	....	....
1997-98	San Antonio Dragons	IHL	32	7	13	20	....	....	....	90	....	....	....	....	....	....	....	....	....	....	....	....	....	....	....	....	....	....
	Frankfurt Lions	Germany	25	11	19	30	....	....	....	32	....	....	....	....	....	....	....	....	....	....	6	2	3	5	35	....	....	....
1998-99	Frankfurt Lions	Germany	41	24	35	59	....	....	....	105	....	....	....	....	....	....	....	....	....	....	8	2	4	6	43	....	....	....
	Frankfurt Lions	EuroHL	5	3	1	4	....	....	....	10	....	....	....	....	....	....	....	....	....	....	....	....	....	....	....	....	....	....
99-2000	**Los Angeles Kings**	**NHL**	**46**	**5**	**8**	**13**	**6**	**7**	**13**	**56**	**0**	**0**	**0**	**46**	**10.9**	**20**	**1**	**16**	**2**	**5**	....	....	....	....	....	....	....	....
	Long Beach Ice Dogs	IHL	17	10	10	20	....	....	....	16	....	....	....	....	....	....	....	....	....	....	....	....	....	....	....	....	....	....
	Florida Panthers	**NHL**	**14**	**4**	**6**	**10**	**4**	**6**	**10**	**6**	**0**	**0**	**0**	**15**	**26.7**	**13**	**1**	**11**	**3**	**4**	**4**	**0**	**0**	**0**	**0**	**0**	**0**	**0**
	NHL Totals		**124**	**14**	**27**	**41**	**17**	**30**	**47**	**155**	**0**	**0**	**1**	**117**	**12.0**	**57**	**6**	**56**	**7**		**8**	**1**	**0**	**1**	**8**	**1**	**0**	**0**

WHL West First All-Star Team (1990) • IHL Second All-Star Team (1994)

Signed as a free agent by **Philadelphia**, February 28, 1990. Signed as a free agent by **Florida**, July 20, 1993. Signed as a free agent by **Pittsburgh**, August 15, 1994. Signed as a free agent by **LA Kings**, July 9, 1999. Claimed on waivers by **Florida** from **LA Kings**, March 10, 2000.

• BARTECKO, Lubos

LW – L. 6′1″, 200 lbs. b: Kezmarok, Czech., 7/14/1976.

Season	Club	League	GP	G	A	Pts	AG	AA	APts	PIM	PP	SH	GW	S	%	TGF	PGF	TGA	PGA	+/–	GP	G	A	Pts	PIM	PP	SH	GW
1994-95	SKP Propad	Slovak-Jr.	STATISTICS NOT AVAILABLE																									
	SKP Propad	Slovakia	3	1	0	1	....	....	....	0	....	....	....	....	....	....	....	....	....	....	....	....	....	....	....	....	....	....
1995-96	Chicoutimi Sagueneens	QMJHL	70	32	41	73	....	....	....	50	....	....	....	....	....	....	....	....	....	....	17	8	15	23	10	....	....	....
1996-97	Drummondville Voltigeurs	QMJHL	58	40	51	91	....	....	....	49	....	....	....	....	....	....	....	....	....	....	8	1	8	9	4	....	....	....
1997-98	Worcester IceCats	AHL	34	10	12	22	....	....	....	24	....	....	....	....	....	....	....	....	....	....	10	4	2	6	2	....	....	....
1998-99	SKP Propad	Slovakia	1	1	0	1	....	....	....	0	....	....	....	....	....	....	....	....	....	....	....	....	....	....	....	....	....	....
	St. Louis Blues	**NHL**	**32**	**5**	**11**	**16**	**6**	**11**	**17**	**6**	**0**	**0**	**1**	**37**	**13.5**	**24**	**5**	**15**	**0**	**4**	**5**	**0**	**0**	**0**	**2**	**0**	**0**	**0**
	Worcester IceCats	AHL	49	14	24	38	....	....	....	22	....	....	....	....	....	....	....	....	....	....	....	....	....	....	....	....	....	....
99-2000	**St. Louis Blues**	**NHL**	**67**	**16**	**23**	**39**	**18**	**21**	**39**	**51**	**3**	**0**	**3**	**75**	**21.3**	**54**	**7**	**23**	**0**	**24**	**7**	**1**	**1**	**2**	**0**	**0**	**0**	**0**
	Worcester IceCats	AHL	12	4	7	11	....	....	....	4	....	....	....	....	....	....	....	....	....	....	....	....	....	....	....	....	....	....
	Slovakia	WC-A	7	2	3	5	....	....	....	14	....	....	....	....	....	....	....	....	....	....	....	....	....	....	....	....	....	....
	NHL Totals		**99**	**21**	**34**	**55**	**24**	**32**	**56**	**57**	**3**	**0**	**4**	**112**	**18.8**	**78**	**12**	**38**	**0**		**12**	**1**	**1**	**2**	**2**	**0**	**0**	**0**

Signed as a free agent by **St. Louis**, October 3, 1997.

• BARTEL, Robin

Robin Dale D – L. 6′, 200 lbs. b: Drake, Sask., 5/16/1961.

Season	Club	League	GP	G	A	Pts	AG	AA	APts	PIM	PP	SH	GW	S	%	TGF	PGF	TGA	PGA	+/–	GP	G	A	Pts	PIM	PP	SH	GW
1979-80	Prince Albert Raiders	SJHL	60	6	31	37	....	....	....	151	....	....	....	....	....	....	....	....	....	....	....	....	....	....	....	....	....	....
1980-81	Prince Albert Raiders	SJHL	60	11	41	52	....	....	....	165	....	....	....	....	....	....	....	....	....	....	26	11	22	33	....	....	....	....
	Prince Albert Raiders	Cen-Cup	STATISTICS NOT AVAILABLE																									
1981-82	Prince Albert Raiders	SJHL	60	12	45	57	....	....	....	166	....	....	....	....	....	....	....	....	....	....	23	5	28	33	....	....	....	....
1982-83	University of Saskatchewan	CWUAA	24	4	14	18	....	....	....	36	....	....	....	....	....	....	....	....	....	....	....	....	....	....	....	....	....	....
1983-84	Canada	Nat-Team	51	4	6	10	....	....	....	50	....	....	....	....	....	....	....	....	....	....	....	....	....	....	....	....	....	....
	Canada	Olympics	6	0	1	1	....	....	....	4	....	....	....	....	....	....	....	....	....	....	....	....	....	....	....	....	....	....
1984-85	EHC Wetzikon	Switz-2	STATISTICS NOT AVAILABLE																									
	Moncton Golden Flames	AHL	41	4	11	15	....	....	....	54	....	....	....	....	....	....	....	....	....	....	....	....	....	....	....	....	....	....
1985-86	**Calgary Flames**	**NHL**	**1**	**0**	**0**	**0**	**0**	**0**	**0**	**0**	**0**	**0**	**0**	**0**	**0.0**	**0**	**0**	**1**	**0**	**–1**	**6**	**0**	**0**	**0**	**16**	**0**	**0**	**0**
	Moncton Golden Flames	AHL	74	4	21	25	....	....	....	100	....	....	....	....	....	....	....	....	....	....	3	0	0	0	0	....	....	....
1986-87	**Vancouver Canucks**	**NHL**	**40**	**0**	**1**	**1**	**0**	**1**	**1**	**14**	**0**	**0**	**0**	**16**	**0.0**	**27**	**1**	**31**	**7**	**2**	....	....	....	....	....	....	....	....
	Fredericton Express	AHL	10	0	2	2	....	....	....	15	....	....	....	....	....	....	....	....	....	....	....	....	....	....	....	....	....	....
1987-88	Fredericton Express	AHL	37	1	10	11	....	....	....	54	....	....	....	....	....	....	....	....	....	....	3	0	0	0	9	....	....	....
1988-89	Moncton Hawks	AHL	23	0	4	4	....	....	....	19	....	....	....	....	....	....	....	....	....	....	10	0	1	1	18	....	....	....
	Milwaukee Admirals	IHL	26	1	5	6	....	....	....	59	....	....	....	....	....	....	....	....	....	....	....	....	....	....	....	....	....	....
1989-90	Medway Bears	Aut-Cup	8	4	6	10	....	....	....	26	....	....	....	....	....	....	....	....	....	....	....	....	....	....	....	....	....	....
	Medway Bears	Britain	16	8	19	27	....	....	....	32	....	....	....	....	....	....	....	....	....	....	....	....	....	....	....	....	....	....
	Canada	Nat-Team	23	1	1	2	....	....	....	10	....	....	....	....	....	....	....	....	....	....	....	....	....	....	....	....	....	....
	NHL Totals		**41**	**0**	**1**	**1**	**0**	**1**	**1**	**14**	**0**	**0**	**0**	**16**	**0.0**	**27**	**1**	**32**	**7**		**6**	**0**	**0**	**0**	**16**	**0**	**0**	**0**

Signed as a free agent by **Calgary**, July 1, 1985. Signed as a free agent by **Vancouver**, June 27, 1986.

• BASHKIROV, Andrei

LW – L. 6′, 198 lbs. b: Shelekhov, USSR, 6/22/1970. Montreal's 4th, 132nd overall, in 1998.

Season	Club	League	GP	G	A	Pts	AG	AA	APts	PIM	PP	SH	GW	S	%	TGF	PGF	TGA	PGA	+/–	GP	G	A	Pts	PIM	PP	SH	GW
1990-91	Yermak Angarsk	USSR-3	STATISTICS NOT AVAILABLE																									
1991-92	Khimik Voskresensk	CIS	11	2	0	2	....	....	....	4	....	....	....	....	....	....	....	....	....	....	....	....	....	....	....	....	....	....
1992-93	Yermak Angarsk	CIS-3	STATISTICS NOT AVAILABLE																									

			REGULAR SEASON																		PLAYOFFS							
Season	Club	League	GP	G	A	Pts	AG	AA	APts	PIM	PP	SH	GW	S	%	TGF	PGF	TGA	PGA	+/–	GP	G	A	Pts	PIM	PP	SH	GW
1993-94	Charlotte Checkers	ECHL	62	28	42	70	....	....	....	25	....	....	....	....	....	....	....	....	....	....	3	1	0	1	0	....	....	....
	Providence Bruins	AHL	1	0	0	0	....	....	....	2	....	....	....	....	....	....	....	....	....	....	....	....	....	....	....	....	....	....
1994-95	Charlotte Checkers	ECHL	61	19	27	46	....	....	....	20	....	....	....	....	....	....	....	....	....	....	3	0	0	0	0	....	....	....
1995-96	Huntington Blizzard	ECHL	55	19	39	58	....	....	....	35	....	....	....	....	....	....	....	....	....	....	....	....	....	....	....	....	....	....
1996-97	Huntington Blizzard	ECHL	47	29	41	70	....	....	....	12	....	....	....	....	....	....	....	....	....	....	....	....	....	....	....	....	....	....
	Detroit Vipers	IHL	2	0	0	0	....	....	....	0	....	....	....	....	....	....	....	....	....	....	....	....	....	....	....	....	....	....
	Las Vegas Thunder	IHL	27	10	12	22	....	....	....	0	....	....	....	....	....	....	....	....	....	....	2	0	0	0	0	....	....	....
1997-98	Las Vegas Thunder	IHL	15	2	3	5	....	....	....	5	....	....	....	....	....	....	....	....	....	....	....	....	....	....	....	....	....	....
	Port Huron Border Cats	UHL	3	1	3	4	....	....	....	0	....	....	....	....	....	....	....	....	....	....	....	....	....	....	....	....	....	....
	Fort Wayne Komets	IHL	65	28	48	76	....	....	....	16	....	....	....	....	....	....	....	....	....	....	4	2	2	4	2	....	....	....
1998-99	**Montreal Canadiens**	**NHL**	**10**	**0**	**0**	**0**	**0**	**0**	**0**	**0**	**0**	**0**	**0**	**4**	**0.0**	**1**	**0**	**4**	**0**	**–3**	....	....	....	....	....	....	....	....
	Fredericton Canadiens	AHL	13	7	5	12	....	....	....	4	....	....	....	....	....	....	....	....	....	....	....	....	....	....	....	....	....	....
	Fort Wayne Komets	IHL	34	11	25	36	....	....	....	10	....	....	....	....	....	....	....	....	....	....	....	....	....	....	....	....	....	....
99-2000	**Montreal Canadiens**	**NHL**	**2**	**0**	**0**	**0**	**0**	**0**	**0**	**0**	**0**	**0**	**0**	**0**	**0.0**	**0**	**0**	**0**	**0**	**0**	....	....	....	....	....	....	....	....
	Quebec Citadelles	AHL	78	28	33	61	....	....	....	17	....	....	....	....	....	....	....	....	....	....	3	0	3	3	0	....	....	....
	NHL Totals		**12**	**0**	**0**	**0**	**0**	**0**	**0**	**0**	**0**	**0**	**0**	**4**	**0.0**	**1**	**0**	**4**	**0**		....	....	....	....	....	....	....	....

• Played w/ RHI's Portland Rage in 1994 (17-12-25-37-20) and Sacramento River Rats in 1995 (9-6-18-24-0)

• BASSEN, Bob

Robert P. C – L. 5'10", 185 lbs. b: Calgary, Alta., 5/6/1965.

Season	Club	League	GP	G	A	Pts	AG	AA	APts	PIM	PP	SH	GW	S	%	TGF	PGF	TGA	PGA	+/–	GP	G	A	Pts	PIM	PP	SH	GW
1982-83	Calgary Spurs	AJHL	STATISTICS NOT AVAILABLE																									
	Medicine Hat Tigers	WHL	4	3	2	5	....	....	....	0	....	....	....	....	....	....	....	....	....	....	3	0	0	0	4	....	....	....
1983-84	Medicine Hat Tigers	WHL	72	29	29	58	....	....	....	93	....	....	....	....	....	....	....	....	....	....	14	5	11	16	12	....	....	....
1984-85	Medicine Hat Tigers	WHL	65	32	50	82	....	....	....	143	....	....	....	....	....	....	....	....	....	....	10	2	8	10	39	....	....	....
	Canada	WJC-A	7	2	0	2	....	....	....	8	....	....	....	....	....	....	....	....	....	....	....	....	....	....	....	....	....	....
1985-86	**New York Islanders**	**NHL**	**11**	**2**	**1**	**3**	**2**	**1**	**3**	**6**	**0**	**0**	**0**	**5**	**40.0**	**3**	**0**	**5**	**2**	**0**	**3**	**0**	**1**	**1**	**0**	**0**	**0**	**0**
	Springfield Indians	AHL	54	13	21	34	....	....	....	111	....	....	....	....	....	....	....	....	....	....	....	....	....	....	....	....	....	....
1986-87	**New York Islanders**	**NHL**	**77**	**7**	**10**	**17**	**6**	**7**	**13**	**89**	**0**	**0**	**1**	**59**	**11.9**	**23**	**0**	**54**	**14**	**–17**	**14**	**1**	**2**	**3**	**21**	**0**	**0**	**0**
1987-88	**New York Islanders**	**NHL**	**77**	**6**	**16**	**22**	**5**	**11**	**16**	**99**	**1**	**0**	**2**	**65**	**9.2**	**41**	**3**	**49**	**19**	**8**	**6**	**0**	**1**	**1**	**23**	**0**	**0**	**0**
1988-89	**New York Islanders**	**NHL**	**19**	**1**	**4**	**5**	**1**	**3**	**4**	**21**	**0**	**0**	**0**	**14**	**7.1**	**8**	**1**	**13**	**6**	**0**	....	....	....	....	....	....	....	....
	Chicago Blackhawks	**NHL**	**49**	**4**	**12**	**16**	**3**	**8**	**11**	**62**	**0**	**0**	**1**	**37**	**10.8**	**22**	**0**	**34**	**17**	**5**	**10**	**1**	**1**	**2**	**34**	**0**	**0**	**0**
1989-90	**Chicago Blackhawks**	**NHL**	**6**	**1**	**1**	**2**	**1**	**1**	**2**	**8**	**0**	**0**	**0**	**7**	**14.3**	**2**	**0**	**1**	**0**	**1**	**1**	**0**	**0**	**0**	**2**	**0**	**0**	**0**
	Indianapolis Ice	IHL	73	22	32	54	....	....	....	179	....	....	....	....	....	....	....	....	....	....	12	3	8	11	33	....	....	....
1990-91	**St. Louis Blues**	**NHL**	**79**	**16**	**18**	**34**	**15**	**14**	**29**	**183**	**0**	**2**	**1**	**117**	**13.7**	**56**	**1**	**65**	**27**	**17**	**13**	**1**	**3**	**4**	**24**	**0**	**0**	**0**
1991-92	**St. Louis Blues**	**NHL**	**79**	**7**	**25**	**32**	**6**	**19**	**25**	**167**	**0**	**0**	**1**	**101**	**6.9**	**53**	**2**	**57**	**18**	**12**	**6**	**0**	**2**	**2**	**4**	**0**	**0**	**0**
	Canada	WC-A	3	1	1	2	....	....	....	0	....	....	....	....	....	....	....	....	....	....	....	....	....	....	....	....	....	....
1992-93	**St. Louis Blues**	**NHL**	**53**	**9**	**10**	**19**	**7**	**7**	**14**	**63**	**0**	**1**	**0**	**61**	**14.8**	**34**	**1**	**54**	**21**	**0**	**11**	**0**	**0**	**0**	**10**	**0**	**0**	**0**
1993-94	**St. Louis Blues**	**NHL**	**46**	**2**	**7**	**9**	**2**	**5**	**7**	**44**	**0**	**1**	**0**	**73**	**2.7**	**18**	**0**	**50**	**18**	**–14**	....	....	....	....	....	....	....	....
	Quebec Nordiques	**NHL**	**37**	**11**	**8**	**19**	**10**	**6**	**16**	**55**	**1**	**0**	**0**	**56**	**19.6**	**28**	**4**	**41**	**14**	**–3**	....	....	....	....	....	....	....	....
1994-95	**Quebec Nordiques**	**NHL**	**47**	**12**	**15**	**27**	**21**	**22**	**43**	**33**	**0**	**1**	**1**	**66**	**18.2**	**37**	**0**	**33**	**10**	**14**	**5**	**2**	**4**	**6**	**0**	**0**	**0**	**0**
1995-96	**Dallas Stars**	**NHL**	**13**	**0**	**1**	**1**	**0**	**1**	**1**	**15**	**0**	**0**	**0**	**9**	**0.0**	**3**	**0**	**12**	**3**	**–6**	....	....	....	....	....	....	....	....
	Michigan K-Wings	IHL	1	0	0	0	....	....	....	4	....	....	....	....	....	....	....	....	....	....	....	....	....	....	....	....	....	....
1996-97	**Dallas Stars**	**NHL**	**46**	**5**	**7**	**12**	**5**	**6**	**11**	**41**	**0**	**0**	**2**	**50**	**10.0**	**22**	**0**	**19**	**2**	**5**	**7**	**3**	**1**	**4**	**4**	**0**	**0**	**0**
1997-98	**Dallas Stars**	**NHL**	**58**	**3**	**4**	**7**	**4**	**4**	**8**	**57**	**0**	**0**	**1**	**40**	**7.5**	**10**	**0**	**19**	**5**	**–4**	**17**	**1**	**0**	**1**	**12**	**0**	**0**	**0**
1998-99	**Calgary Flames**	**NHL**	**41**	**1**	**2**	**3**	**1**	**2**	**3**	**35**	**0**	**0**	**0**	**47**	**2.1**	**9**	**0**	**25**	**3**	**–13**	....	....	....	....	....	....	....	....
99-2000	Frankfurt Lions	Germany	14	2	9	11	....	....	....	6	....	....	....	....	....	....	....	....	....	....	....	....	....	....	....	....	....	....
	St. Louis Blues	**NHL**	**27**	**1**	**3**	**4**	**1**	**3**	**4**	**26**	**0**	**0**	**0**	**26**	**3.8**	**5**	**0**	**8**	**0**	**–3**	....	....	....	....	....	....	....	....
	NHL Totals		**765**	**88**	**144**	**232**	**90**	**120**	**210**	**1004**	**2**	**5**	**10**	**833**	**10.6**	**374**	**12**	**539**	**179**		**93**	**9**	**15**	**24**	**134**	**0**	**0**	**0**

• Son of Hank • WHL First All-Star Team (1985) • IHL First All-Star Team (1990)

Signed as a free agent by **NY Islanders**, October 19, 1984. Traded to **Chicago** by **NY Islanders** with Steve Konroyd for Marc Bergevin and Gary Nylund, November 25, 1988. Claimed by **St. Louis** from **Chicago** in NHL Waiver Draft, October 1, 1990. Traded to **Quebec** by **St. Louis** with Garth Butcher and Ron Sutter for Steve Duchesne and Denis Chasse, January 23, 1994. Signed as a free agent by **Dallas**, August 10, 1995. Traded to **Calgary** by **Dallas** for Aaron Gavey, July 14, 1998. Claimed on waivers by **St. Louis** from **Calgary**, December 9, 1999.

• BAST, Ryan

D – L. 6'2", 190 lbs. b: Spruce Grove, Alta., 8/27/1975.

Season	Club	League	GP	G	A	Pts	AG	AA	APts	PIM	PP	SH	GW	S	%	TGF	PGF	TGA	PGA	+/–	GP	G	A	Pts	PIM	PP	SH	GW
1992-93	St. Albert Raiders	AAHA	35	1	18	19	....	....	....	51	....	....	....	....	....	....	....	....	....	....	....	....	....	....	....	....	....	....
1993-94	Portland Winter Hawks	WHL	6	0	0	0	....	....	....	4	....	....	....	....	....	....	....	....	....	....	....	....	....	....	....	....	....	....
	Prince Albert Raiders	WHL	47	2	8	10	....	....	....	139	....	....	....	....	....	....	....	....	....	....	....	....	....	....	....	....	....	....
1994-95	Prince Albert Raiders	WHL	42	1	10	11	....	....	....	149	....	....	....	....	....	....	....	....	....	....	14	0	3	3	13	....	....	....
1995-96	Prince Albert Raiders	WHL	44	7	15	22	....	....	....	129	....	....	....	....	....	....	....	....	....	....	....	....	....	....	....	....	....	....
	Calgary Hitmen	WHL	3	0	0	0	....	....	....	24	....	....	....	....	....	....	....	....	....	....	....	....	....	....	....	....	....	....
	Swift Current Broncos	WHL	25	2	3	5	....	....	....	50	....	....	....	....	....	....	....	....	....	....	6	1	0	1	21	....	....	....
1996-97	Las Vegas Thunder	IHL	49	2	3	5	....	....	....	266	....	....	....	....	....	....	....	....	....	....	....	....	....	....	....	....	....	....
	Toledo Storm	ECHL	12	2	2	4	....	....	....	75	....	....	....	....	....	....	....	....	....	....	....	....	....	....	....	....	....	....
	Saint John Flames	AHL	12	0	0	0	....	....	....	21	....	....	....	....	....	....	....	....	....	....	5	0	0	0	4	....	....	....
1997-98	Saint John Flames	AHL	77	3	8	11	....	....	....	187	....	....	....	....	....	....	....	....	....	....	21	0	1	1	55	....	....	....
1998-99	Saint John Flames	AHL	2	0	0	0	....	....	....	5	....	....	....	....	....	....	....	....	....	....	....	....	....	....	....	....	....	....
	Philadelphia Flyers	**NHL**	**2**	**0**	**1**	**1**	**0**	**1**	**1**	**0**	**0**	**0**	**0**	**1**	**0.0**	**2**	**0**	**2**	**0**	**0**	....	....	....	....	....	....	....	....
	Philadelphia Phantoms	AHL	69	0	11	11	....	....	....	160	....	....	....	....	....	....	....	....	....	....	16	0	0	0	30	....	....	....
99-2000	Philadelphia Phantoms	AHL	71	1	9	10	....	....	....	198	....	....	....	....	....	....	....	....	....	....	5	0	0	0	6	....	....	....
	NHL Totals		**2**	**0**	**1**	**1**	**0**	**1**	**1**	**0**	**0**	**0**	**0**	**1**	**0.0**	**2**	**0**	**2**	**0**		....	....	....	....	....	....	....	....

AHL Second All-Star Team (1998)

Signed as a free agent by **Las Vegas** (IHL), September 30, 1996. Traded to **Saint John** (AHL) by **Las Vegas** (IHL) for loan of Sasha Lakovic, March 20, 1997. Signed as a free agent by **Philadelphia**, May 18, 1998. • Calgary Flames filed official protest to NHL contesting Philadelphia's signing of Bast under the contention that he was property of AHL's Saint John Flames, May 20, 1998. • NHL ruled that Bast was not under contract to Calgary since he was never drafted and had no NHL clause in contract, May 22, 1998. NHL also ruled that Bast was not property of Philadelphia because Flyers' contract offer exceeded NHL rookie salary cap, May 22, 1998. A compromise was reached that traded Bast to **Philadelphia** by **Calgary** with Calgary's 8th round choice (David Nystrom) in 1999 Entry Draft for Philadelphia's 3rd round choice (later traded to NY Rangers, NY Rangers selected Patrik Aufiero) in 1999 Entry Draft, October 13, 1998.

• BATES, Shawn

Shawn William C – R. 5'11", 205 lbs. b: Melrose, MA, 4/3/1975. Boston's 4th, 103rd overall, in 1993.

Season	Club	League	GP	G	A	Pts	AG	AA	APts	PIM	PP	SH	GW	S	%	TGF	PGF	TGA	PGA	+/–	GP	G	A	Pts	PIM	PP	SH	GW
1990-91	Medford Mustangs	Hi-School	22	18	43	61	....	....	....	6	....	....	....	....	....	....	....	....	....	....	....	....	....	....	....	....	....	....
1991-92	Medford Mustangs	Hi-School	22	38	41	79	....	....	....	10	....	....	....	....	....	....	....	....	....	....	....	....	....	....	....	....	....	....
1992-93	Medford Mustangs	Hi-School	25	49	46	95	....	....	....	20	....	....	....	....	....	....	....	....	....	....	....	....	....	....	....	....	....	....
1993-94	Boston University	H-East	41	10	19	29	....	....	....	24	....	....	....	....	....	....	....	....	....	....	....	....	....	....	....	....	....	....
1994-95	Boston University	H-East	38	18	12	30	....	....	....	48	....	....	....	....	....	....	....	....	....	....	....	....	....	....	....	....	....	....
	United States	WJC-A	7	5	1	6	....	....	....	2	....	....	....	....	....	....	....	....	....	....	....	....	....	....	....	....	....	....
1995-96	Boston University	H-East	40	28	22	50	....	....	....	54	....	....	....	....	....	....	....	....	....	....	....	....	....	....	....	....	....	....
1996-97	Boston University	H-East	41	17	18	35	....	....	....	64	....	....	....	....	....	....	....	....	....	....	....	....	....	....	....	....	....	....
1997-98	**Boston Bruins**	**NHL**	**13**	**2**	**0**	**2**	**2**	**0**	**2**	**2**	**0**	**0**	**0**	**12**	**16.7**	**3**	**1**	**6**	**1**	**–3**	....	....	....	....	....	....	....	....
	Providence Bruins	AHL	50	15	19	34	....	....	....	22	....	....	....	....	....	....	....	....	....	....	....	....	....	....	....	....	....	....
1998-99	**Boston Bruins**	**NHL**	**33**	**5**	**4**	**9**	**6**	**4**	**10**	**2**	**0**	**0**	**0**	**30**	**16.7**	**10**	**0**	**7**	**0**	**3**	**12**	**0**	**0**	**0**	**4**	**0**	**0**	**0**
	Providence Bruins	AHL	37	25	21	46	....	....	....	39	....	....	....	....	....	....	....	....	....	....	....	....	....	....	....	....	....	....
99-2000	**Boston Bruins**	**NHL**	**44**	**5**	**7**	**12**	**6**	**6**	**12**	**14**	**0**	**0**	**1**	**65**	**7.7**	**17**	**0**	**36**	**2**	**–17**	....	....	....	....	....	....	....	....
	NHL Totals		**90**	**12**	**11**	**23**	**14**	**10**	**24**	**18**	**0**	**0**	**1**	**107**	**11.2**	**30**	**1**	**49**	**3**		**12**	**0**	**0**	**0**	**4**	**0**	**0**	**0**

NCAA Championship All-Tournament Team (1995)

• BATHE, Frank

Francis Leonard D – L. 6'1", 185 lbs. b: Oshawa, Ont., 9/27/1954.

Season	Club	League	GP	G	A	Pts	AG	AA	APts	PIM	PP	SH	GW	S	%	TGF	PGF	TGA	PGA	+/–	GP	G	A	Pts	PIM	PP	SH	GW
1972-73	Windsor Spitfires	OJHL	59	10	25	35	....	....	....	232	....	....	....	....	....	....	....	....	....	....	....	....	....	....	....	....	....	....
1973-74	Windsor Spitfires	OJHL	58	19	34	53	....	....	....	306	....	....	....	....	....	....	....	....	....	....	....	....	....	....	....	....	....	....
1974-75	**Detroit Red Wings**	**NHL**	**19**	**0**	**3**	**3**	**0**	**2**	**2**	**31**	**0**	**0**	**0**	**7**	**0.0**	**12**	**1**	**16**	**0**	**–5**	....	....	....	....	....	....	....	....
	Virginia Wings	AHL	50	7	11	18	....	....	....	146	....	....	....	....	....	....	....	....	....	....	....	....	....	....	....	....	....	....

			REGULAR SEASON																		PLAYOFFS							
Season	Club	League	GP	G	A	Pts	AG	AA	APts	PIM	PP	SH	GW	S	%	TGF	PGF	TGA	PGA	+/–	GP	G	A	Pts	PIM	PP	SH	GW
1975-76	**Detroit Red Wings**	**NHL**	**7**	**0**	**1**	**1**	**0**	**1**	**1**	**9**	**0**	**0**	**0**	**6**	**0.0**	**2**	**0**	**7**	**4**	**–1**	....	....	....	....	....	....	....	....
	New Haven Nighthawks	AHL	7	0	1	1	....	....	....	24	....	....	....	....	....	....	....	....	....	....	....	....	....	....	....	....	....	....
	Kalamazoo Wings	IHL	14	0	5	5	....	....	....	46	....	....	....	....	....	....	....	....	....	....	....	....	....	....	....	....	....	....
	Port Huron Flags	IHL	43	2	3	5	....	....	....	148	....	....	....	....	....	....	....	....	....	....	15	0	4	4	54	....	....	....
1976-77	Port Huron Flags	IHL	71	7	30	37	....	....	....	250	....	....	....	....	....	....	....	....	....	....	....	....	....	....	....	....	....	....
1977-78	**Philadelphia Flyers**	**NHL**	**1**	**0**	**0**	**0**	**0**	**0**	**0**	**0**	**0**	**0**	**0**	**0**	**0.0**	**0**	**0**	**0**	**0**	**0**	....	....	....	....	....	....	....	....
	Maine Mariners	AHL	78	4	11	15	....	....	....	159	....	....	....	....	....	....	....	....	....	....	12	1	1	2	24	....	....	....
1978-79	**Philadelphia Flyers**	**NHL**	**21**	**1**	**3**	**4**	**1**	**2**	**3**	**76**	**0**	**0**	**0**	**10**	**10.0**	**15**	**0**	**12**	**6**	**9**	**6**	**1**	**0**	**1**	**12**	**0**	**0**	**0**
	Maine Mariners	AHL	26	3	3	6	....	....	....	106	....	....	....	....	....	....	....	....	....	....	....	....	....	....	....	....	....	....
1979-80	**Philadelphia Flyers**	**NHL**	**47**	**0**	**7**	**7**	**0**	**5**	**5**	**111**	**0**	**0**	**0**	**34**	**0.0**	**45**	**0**	**47**	**9**	**7**	**1**	**0**	**0**	**0**	**0**	**0**	**0**	**0**
1980-81	**Philadelphia Flyers**	**NHL**	**44**	**0**	**3**	**3**	**0**	**2**	**2**	**175**	**0**	**0**	**0**	**35**	**0.0**	**20**	**1**	**42**	**20**	**–3**	**12**	**0**	**3**	**3**	**16**	**0**	**0**	**0**
1981-82	**Philadelphia Flyers**	**NHL**	**28**	**1**	**3**	**4**	**1**	**2**	**3**	**68**	**0**	**0**	**0**	**36**	**2.8**	**31**	**1**	**33**	**14**	**11**	**4**	**0**	**0**	**0**	**2**	**0**	**0**	**0**
1982-83	**Philadelphia Flyers**	**NHL**	**57**	**1**	**8**	**9**	**1**	**6**	**7**	**72**	**0**	**0**	**0**	**60**	**1.7**	**37**	**0**	**49**	**16**	**4**	**3**	**0**	**0**	**0**	**12**	**0**	**0**	**0**
1983-84	Maine Mariners	AHL	4	1	0	1	....	....	....	2	....	....	....	....	....	....	....	....	....	....	....	....	....	....	....	....	....	....
	Philadelphia Flyers	**NHL**	....	....	....	....	....	....	....	....	....	....	....	....	....	....	....	....	....	....	**1**	**0**	**0**	**0**	**0**	**0**	**0**	**0**
	NHL Totals		**224**	**3**	**28**	**31**	**3**	**20**	**23**	**542**	**0**	**0**	**0**	**188**	**1.6**	**162**	**3**	**206**	**69**		**27**	**1**	**3**	**4**	**42**	**0**	**0**	**0**

Signed as a free agent by **Detroit**, October 10, 1974. Traded to **Port Huron** (IHL) by **Detroit** (Kalamazoo-IHL) for Henry Lehvonen, November, 1975. Signed as a free agent by **Philadelphia**, October 7, 1977. • Suffered eventual career-ending back injury in training camp, October 15, 1983.

• BATHGATE, Andy

Andrew James RW – R. 6′, 180 lbs. b: Winnipeg, Man., 8/28/1932. **HHOF**

Season	Club	League	GP	G	A	Pts	AG	AA	APts	PIM	PP	SH	GW	S	%	TGF	PGF	TGA	PGA	+/–	GP	G	A	Pts	PIM	PP	SH	GW
1948-49	Winnipeg Black Hawks	MJHL	1	0	0	0	....	....	....	0	....	....	....	....	....	....	....	....	....	....	....	....	....	....	....	....	....	....
1949-50	Guelph Biltmores	OHA-Jr.	41	21	25	46	....	....	....	28	....	....	....	....	....	....	....	....	....	....	15	6	9	15	12	....	....	....
	Guelph Biltmores	Mem-Cup	11	10	5	15	....	....	....	8	....	....	....	....	....	....	....	....	....	....	....	....	....	....	....	....	....	....
1950-51	Guelph Biltmores	OHA-Jr.	52	33	57	90	....	....	....	66	....	....	....	....	....	....	....	....	....	....	5	6	1	7	9	....	....	....
1951-52	Guelph Biltmores	OHA-Jr.	34	27	50	77	....	....	....	20	....	....	....	....	....	....	....	....	....	....	11	6	10	16	18	....	....	....
	Guelph Biltmores	Mem-Cup	12	8	12	20	....	....	....	21	....	....	....	....	....	....	....	....	....	....	....	....	....	....	....	....	....	....
1952-53	Guelph Biltmores	OHA-Jr.	2	2	1	3	....	....	....	0	....	....	....	....	....	....	....	....	....	....	....	....	....	....	....	....	....	....
	New York Rangers	**NHL**	**18**	**0**	**1**	**1**	**0**	**1**	**1**	**6**	....	....	....	....	....	....	....	....	....	....	....	....	....	....	....	....	....	....
	Vancouver Canucks	WHL	37	13	13	26	....	....	....	29	....	....	....	....	....	....	....	....	....	....	9	11	4	15	2	....	....	....
1953-54	**New York Rangers**	**NHL**	**20**	**2**	**2**	**4**	**3**	**2**	**5**	**18**	....	....	....	....	....	....	....	....	....	....	....	....	....	....	....	....	....	....
	Vancouver Canucks	WHL	17	12	10	22	....	....	....	6	....	....	....	....	....	....	....	....	....	....	....	....	....	....	....	....	....	....
	Cleveland Barons	AHL	36	13	19	32	....	....	....	44	....	....	....	....	....	....	....	....	....	....	9	3	5	8	8	....	....	....
1954-55	**New York Rangers**	**NHL**	**70**	**20**	**20**	**40**	**26**	**23**	**49**	**37**	....	....	....	....	....	....	....	....	....	....	....	....	....	....	....	....	....	....
1955-56	**New York Rangers**	**NHL**	**70**	**19**	**47**	**66**	**26**	**57**	**83**	**59**	....	....	....	....	....	....	....	....	....	....	**5**	**1**	**2**	**3**	**2**	....	....	....
1956-57	**New York Rangers**	**NHL**	**70**	**27**	**50**	**77**	**35**	**56**	**91**	**60**	....	....	....	....	....	....	....	....	....	....	**5**	**2**	**0**	**2**	**27**	....	....	....
1957-58	**New York Rangers**	**NHL**	**65**	**30**	**48**	**78**	**37**	**50**	**87**	**42**	....	....	....	....	....	....	....	....	....	....	**6**	**5**	**3**	**8**	**6**	....	....	....
1958-59	**New York Rangers**	**NHL**	**70**	**40**	**48**	**88**	**49**	**49**	**98**	**48**	....	....	....	....	....	....	....	....	....	....	....	....	....	....	....	....	....	....
1959-60	**New York Rangers**	**NHL**	**70**	**26**	**48**	**74**	**31**	**47**	**78**	**28**	....	....	....	....	....	....	....	....	....	....	....	....	....	....	....	....	....	....
1960-61	**New York Rangers**	**NHL**	**70**	**29**	**48**	**77**	**34**	**47**	**81**	**22**	....	....	....	....	....	....	....	....	....	....	....	....	....	....	....	....	....	....
1961-62	**New York Rangers**	**NHL**	**70**	**28**	***56**	***84**	**32**	**55**	**87**	**44**	....	....	....	....	....	....	....	....	....	....	**6**	**1**	**2**	**3**	**4**	....	....	....
1962-63	**New York Rangers**	**NHL**	**70**	**35**	**46**	**81**	**41**	**46**	**87**	**54**	....	....	....	....	....	....	....	....	....	....	....	....	....	....	....	....	....	....
1963-64	**New York Rangers**	**NHL**	**56**	**16**	***43**	**59**	**20**	**46**	**66**	**26**	....	....	....	....	....	....	....	....	....	....	....	....	....	....	....	....	....	....
♦	**Toronto Maple Leafs**	**NHL**	**15**	**3**	***15**	**18**	**4**	**16**	**20**	**8**	....	....	....	....	....	....	....	....	....	....	**14**	**5**	**4**	**9**	**25**	....	....	....
1964-65	**Toronto Maple Leafs**	**NHL**	**55**	**16**	**29**	**45**	**19**	**30**	**49**	**34**	....	....	....	....	....	....	....	....	....	....	**6**	**1**	**0**	**1**	**6**	....	....	....
1965-66	**Detroit Red Wings**	**NHL**	**70**	**15**	**32**	**47**	**17**	**31**	**48**	**25**	....	....	....	....	....	....	....	....	....	....	**12**	***6**	**3**	**9**	**6**	....	....	....
1966-67	**Detroit Red Wings**	**NHL**	**60**	**8**	**23**	**31**	**9**	**22**	**31**	**24**	....	....	....	....	....	....	....	....	....	....	....	....	....	....	....	....	....	....
	Pittsburgh Hornets	AHL	6	4	6	10	....	....	....	7	....	....	....	....	....	....	....	....	....	....	....	....	....	....	....	....	....	....
1967-68	**Pittsburgh Penguins**	**NHL**	**74**	**20**	**39**	**59**	**23**	**39**	**62**	**55**	**2**	**0**	**4**	**293**	**6.8**	**86**	**28**	**69**	**0**	**–11**	....	....	....	....	....	....	....	....
1968-69	Vancouver Canucks	WHL	71	37	36	73	....	....	....	44	....	....	....	....	....	....	....	....	....	....	8	3	5	8	5	....	....	....
1969-70	Vancouver Canucks	WHL	72	40	68	108	....	....	....	66	....	....	....	....	....	....	....	....	....	....	16	7	5	12	8	....	....	....
1970-71	**Pittsburgh Penguins**	**NHL**	**76**	**15**	**29**	**44**	**15**	**24**	**39**	**34**	**7**	**0**	**3**	**209**	**7.2**	**68**	**31**	**48**	**0**	**–11**	....	....	....	....	....	....	....	....
1971-1974	HC Ambri-Piotta	Switz.	PLAYER/COACH – STATISTICS UNAVAILABLE																									
1974-75	Vancouver Blazers	WHA	11	1	6	7				2																		
	NHL Totals		**1069**	**349**	**624**	**973**	**421**	**641**	**1062**	**624**	....	....	....	....	....	....	....	....	....	....	**54**	**21**	**14**	**35**	**76**	....	....	....
	Other Major League Totals		11	1	6	7	....	....	....	2	....	....	....	....	....	....	....	....	....	....								

• Brother of Frank • NHL Second All-Star Team (1958, 1963) • NHL First All-Star Team (1959, 1962) • Won Hart Trophy (1959) • WHL First All-Star Team (1970) • Won Leader Cup (WHL - MVP) (1970) • Played in NHL All-Star Game (1957, 1958, 1959, 1960, 1961, 1962, 1963, 1964)

Traded to **NY Rangers** by **Cleveland** (AHL) with Vic Howe for Glen Sonmor and Eric Pogue, November 15, 1954. Traded to **Toronto** by **NY Rangers** with Don McKenney for Dick Duff, Bob Nevin, Arnie Brown, Bill Collins and Rod Seiling, February 22, 1964. Traded to **Detroit** by **Toronto** with Billy Harris and Gary Jarrett for Marcel Pronovost, Ed Joyal, Larry Jeffrey, Lowell McDonald and Aut Erickson, May 20, 1965. Claimed by **Pittsburgh** from **Detroit** in Expansion Draft, June 6, 1967. Loaned to **Vancouver** (WHL) by **Pittsburgh** for the 1968-69 season for future considerations, October, 1968. Loaned to **Vancouver** (WHL) by **Pittsburgh** for the 1969-70 season with the trade of Paul Andrea and John Arbour for Bryan Hextall Jr., May 20, 1969. Selected by **Miami-Philadelphia** (WHA) in 1972 WHA General Player Draft, February 12, 1972. Transferred to **Vancouver** (WHA) after **Philadelphia** (WHA) franchise relocated, May, 1973.

• BATTAGLIA, Bates

Jonathan B. LW – L. 6′2″, 205 lbs. b: Chicago, IL, 12/13/1975. Anaheim's 6th, 132nd overall, in 1994.

Season	Club	League	GP	G	A	Pts	AG	AA	APts	PIM	PP	SH	GW	S	%	TGF	PGF	TGA	PGA	+/–	GP	G	A	Pts	PIM	PP	SH	GW
1992-93	Team Illinois	MNHL	60	42	42	84	....	....	....	68	....	....	....	....	....	....	....	....	....	....	....	....	....	....	....	....	....	....
1993-94	Caledon Canadians	OJHL	44	15	33	48	....	....	....	104	....	....	....	....	....	....	....	....	....	....	....	....	....	....	....	....	....	....
1994-95	Lake Superior State	CCHA	38	6	14	20	....	....	....	34	....	....	....	....	....	....	....	....	....	....	....	....	....	....	....	....	....	....
	Unites States	WJC-A	7	3	2	5	....	....	....	2	....	....	....	....	....	....	....	....	....	....	....	....	....	....	....	....	....	....
1995-96	Lake Superior State	CCHA	40	13	22	35	....	....	....	48	....	....	....	....	....	....	....	....	....	....	....	....	....	....	....	....	....	....
1996-97	Lake Superior State	CCHA	38	12	27	39	....	....	....	80	....	....	....	....	....	....	....	....	....	....	....	....	....	....	....	....	....	....
1997-98	**Carolina Hurricanes**	**NHL**	**33**	**2**	**4**	**6**	**2**	**4**	**6**	**10**	**0**	**0**	**1**	**21**	**9.5**	**8**	**0**	**11**	**2**	**–1**	....	....	....	....	....	....	....	....
	Beast of New Haven	AHL	48	15	21	36	....	....	....	48	....	....	....	....	....	....	....	....	....	....	1	0	0	0	0	....	....	....
	United States	WC-A	6	1	1	2	....	....	....	6	....	....	....	....	....	....	....	....	....	....	....	....	....	....	....	....	....	....
1998-99	**Carolina Hurricanes**	**NHL**	**60**	**7**	**11**	**18**	**8**	**11**	**19**	**97**	**0**	**0**	**0**	**52**	**13.5**	**30**	**0**	**25**	**2**	**7**	**6**	**0**	**3**	**3**	**8**	**0**	**0**	**0**
99-2000	**Carolina Hurricanes**	**NHL**	**77**	**16**	**18**	**34**	**18**	**17**	**35**	**39**	**3**	**0**	**3**	**86**	**18.6**	**53**	**8**	**25**	**0**	**20**	....	....	....	....	....	....	....	....
	NHL Totals		**170**	**25**	**33**	**58**	**28**	**32**	**60**	**146**	**3**	**0**	**4**	**159**	**15.7**	**91**	**8**	**61**	**4**		**6**	**0**	**3**	**3**	**8**	**0**	**0**	**0**

Traded to **Hartford** by **Anaheim** with Anaheim's 4th round choice (Josef Vasicek) in 1998 Entry Draft for Mark Janssens, March 18, 1997. Rights transferred to **Carolina** after **Hartford** franchise relocated, June 25, 1997.

• BATTERS, Jeff

D – R. 6′2″, 215 lbs. b: Victoria, B.C., 10/23/1970 d: 8/23/1996. St. Louis' 7th, 135th overall, in 1989.

Season	Club	League	GP	G	A	Pts	AG	AA	APts	PIM	PP	SH	GW	S	%	TGF	PGF	TGA	PGA	+/–	GP	G	A	Pts	PIM	PP	SH	GW
1987-88	Notre Dame Hounds	AJHL	STATISTICS NOT AVAILABLE																									
	Notre Dame Hounds	Cen-Cup	2	0	1	1	....	....	....	2	....	....	....	....	....	....	....	....	....	....	....	....	....	....	....	....	....	....
1988-89	U. of Alaska-Anchorage	NCAA-2	33	8	14	22	....	....	....	123	....	....	....	....	....	....	....	....	....	....	....	....	....	....	....	....	....	....
1989-90	U. of Alaska-Anchorage	NCAA-2	34	6	9	15	....	....	....	102	....	....	....	....	....	....	....	....	....	....	....	....	....	....	....	....	....	....
1990-91	U. of Alaska-Anchorage	NCAA-2	39	16	14	30	....	....	....	90	....	....	....	....	....	....	....	....	....	....	....	....	....	....	....	....	....	....
1991-92	U. of Alaska-Anchorage	NCAA-2	33	6	16	22	....	....	....	84	....	....	....	....	....	....	....	....	....	....	....	....	....	....	....	....	....	....
1992-93	Peoria Rivermen	IHL	74	5	18	23	....	....	....	113	....	....	....	....	....	....	....	....	....	....	4	0	0	0	10	....	....	....
1993-94	**St. Louis Blues**	**NHL**	**6**	**0**	**0**	**0**	**0**	**0**	**0**	**7**	**0**	**0**	**0**	**1**	**0.0**	**2**	**0**	**1**	**0**	**1**	....	....	....	....	....	....	....	....
	Peoria Rivermen	IHL	59	3	9	12	....	....	....	175	....	....	....	....	....	....	....	....	....	....	6	0	0	0	18	....	....	....
1994-95	Peoria Rivermen	IHL	42	0	11	11	....	....	....	128	....	....	....	....	....	....	....	....	....	....	5	0	1	1	18	....	....	....
	St. Louis Blues	**NHL**	**10**	**0**	**0**	**0**	**0**	**0**	**0**	**21**	**0**	**0**	**0**	**3**	**0.0**	**5**	**0**	**12**	**2**	**–5**	....	....	....	....	....	....	....	....
1995-96	Kansas City Blades	IHL	77	5	29	34	....	....	....	223	....	....	....	....	....	....	....	....	....	....	5	0	1	1	12	....	....	....
	NHL Totals		**16**	**0**	**0**	**0**	**0**	**0**	**0**	**28**	**0**	**0**	**0**	**4**	**0.0**	**7**	**0**	**13**	**2**		....	....	....	....	....	....	....	....

Signed as a free agent by **San Jose**, September 27, 1995. • Died from injuries suffered in automobile accicent, August 23, 1996.

• BATYRSHIN, Ruslan

D – L. 6'1", 185 lbs. b: Moscow, USSR, 2/19/1975. Winnipeg's 4th, 79th overall, in 1993.

			REGULAR SEASON																		PLAYOFFS							
Season	Club	League	GP	G	A	Pts	AG	AA	APts	PIM	PP	SH	GW	S	%	TGF	PGF	TGA	PGA	+/–	GP	G	A	Pts	PIM	PP	SH	GW
1991-92	Dynamo Moscow	CIS-3	40	0	2	2	....	....	....	52	....	....	....	....	....	....	....	....	....	....	....	....	....	....	....	....	....	....
1992-93	Dynamo Moscow	CIS-2	STATISTICS NOT AVAILABLE																									
	Russia	EJC-A	6	1	2	3	....	....	....	8	....	....	....	....	....	....	....	....	....	....	....	....	....	....	....	....	....	....
1993-94	Dynamo Moscow	CIS	10	0	0	0	....	....	....	10	....	....	....	....	....	....	....	....	....	....	3	0	0	0	22	....	....	....
1994-95	Dynamo Moscow	CIS	36	2	2	4	....	....	....	65	....	....	....	....	....	....	....	....	....	....	12	1	1	2	6	....	....	....
	Russia	WJC-A	7	1	4	5	....	....	....	10	....	....	....	....	....	....	....	....	....	....	....	....	....	....	....	....	....	....
1995-96	**Los Angeles Kings**	**NHL**	**2**	**0**	**0**	**0**	**0**	**0**	**0**	**6**	**0**	**0**	**0**	**0**	**0.0**	**0**	**0**	**0**	**0**	**0**	....	....	....	....	....	....	....	....
	Phoenix Roadrunners	IHL	71	1	9	10	....	....	....	144	....	....	....	....	....	....	....	....	....	....	2	0	0	0	2	....	....	....
1996-97	Phoenix Roadrunners	IHL	59	3	4	7	....	....	....	123	....	....	....	....	....	....	....	....	....	....	....	....	....	....	....	....	....	....
1997-98	Springfield Falcons	AHL	47	0	6	6	....	....	....	130	....	....	....	....	....	....	....	....	....	....	....	....	....	....	....	....	....	....
	Grand Rapids Griffins	IHL	22	0	2	2	....	....	....	54	....	....	....	....	....	....	....	....	....	....	....	....	....	....	....	....	....	....
1998-99	Dynamo Moscow	Russia	29	0	4	4	....	....	....	42	....	....	....	....	....	....	....	....	....	....	15	0	1	1	16	....	....	....
99-2000	Anchorage Aces	WCHL	61	5	17	22	....	....	....	243	....	....	....	....	....	....	....	....	....	....	4	0	1	1	10	....	....	....
	NHL Totals		**2**	**0**	**0**	**0**	**0**	**0**	**0**	**6**	**0**	**0**	**0**	**0**	**0.0**	**0**	**0**	**0**	**0**		....	....	....	....	....	....	....	....

Rights traded to **LA Kings** by **Winnipeg** with Winnipeg's 2nd round choice (Marian Cisar) in 1996 Entry Draft for Brent Thompson and future considerations, August 8, 1994. Signed as a free agent by **Anchorage** (WCHL), November 4, 1999.

• BAUMGARTNER, Ken

Kenneth James "Bomber" LW – L. 6'1", 205 lbs. b: Flin Flon, Man., 3/11/1966. Buffalo's 12th, 245th overall, in 1985.

Season	Club	League	GP	G	A	Pts	AG	AA	APts	PIM	PP	SH	GW	S	%	TGF	PGF	TGA	PGA	+/–	GP	G	A	Pts	PIM	PP	SH	GW
1982-83	Swift Current Broncos	SJHL	STATISTICS NOT AVAILABLE																									
1983-84	Prince Albert Raiders	WHL	57	1	6	7	....	....	....	203	....	....	....	....	....	....	....	....	....	....	4	0	0	0	23	....	....	....
1984-85	Prince Albert Raiders	WHL	60	3	9	12	....	....	....	252	....	....	....	....	....	....	....	....	....	....	13	1	3	4	89	....	....	....
	Prince Albert Raiders	Mem-Cup	4	0	0	0	....	....	....	*80	....	....	....	....	....	....	....	....	....	....	....	....	....	....	....	....	....	....
1985-86	Prince Albert Raiders	WHL	70	4	23	27	....	....	....	277	....	....	....	....	....	....	....	....	....	....	20	3	9	12	112	....	....	....
1986-87	EHC Chur	Switz.	36	2	3	5	....	....	....	85	....	....	....	....	....	....	....	....	....	....	....	....	....	....	....	....	....	....
	New Haven Nighthawks	AHL	13	0	3	3	....	....	....	99	....	....	....	....	....	....	....	....	....	....	6	0	0	0	60	....	....	....
1987-88	**Los Angeles Kings**	**NHL**	**30**	**2**	**3**	**5**	**2**	**2**	**4**	**189**	**0**	**0**	**0**	**17**	**11.8**	**24**	**0**	**19**	**0**	**5**	**5**	**0**	**1**	**1**	**28**	**0**	**0**	**0**
	New Haven Nighthawks	AHL	48	1	5	6	....	....	....	181	....	....	....	....	....	....	....	....	....	....	....	....	....	....	....	....	....	....
1988-89	**Los Angeles Kings**	**NHL**	**49**	**1**	**3**	**4**	**1**	**2**	**3**	**288**	**0**	**0**	**0**	**15**	**6.7**	**27**	**0**	**41**	**5**	**–9**	**5**	**0**	**0**	**0**	**8**	**0**	**0**	**0**
	New Haven Nighthawks	AHL	10	1	3	4	....	....	....	26	....	....	....	....	....	....	....	....	....	....	....	....	....	....	....	....	....	....
1989-90	**Los Angeles Kings**	**NHL**	**12**	**1**	**0**	**1**	**1**	**0**	**1**	**28**	**0**	**0**	**0**	**7**	**14.3**	**1**	**0**	**13**	**2**	**–10**	....	....	....	....	....	....	....	....
	New York Islanders	**NHL**	**53**	**0**	**5**	**5**	**0**	**4**	**4**	**194**	**0**	**0**	**0**	**41**	**0.0**	**40**	**0**	**34**	**0**	**6**	**4**	**0**	**0**	**0**	**27**	**0**	**0**	**0**
1990-91	**New York Islanders**	**NHL**	**78**	**1**	**6**	**7**	**1**	**5**	**6**	**282**	**0**	**0**	**0**	**41**	**2.4**	**28**	**0**	**43**	**1**	**–14**	....	....	....	....	....	....	....	....
1991-92	**New York Islanders**	**NHL**	**44**	**0**	**1**	**1**	**0**	**1**	**1**	**202**	**0**	**0**	**0**	**11**	**0.0**	**9**	**0**	**20**	**1**	**–10**	....	....	....	....	....	....	....	....
	Toronto Maple Leafs	**NHL**	**11**	**0**	**0**	**0**	**0**	**0**	**0**	**23**	**0**	**0**	**0**	**5**	**0.0**	**3**	**0**	**2**	**0**	**1**	....	....	....	....	....	....	....	....
1992-93	**Toronto Maple Leafs**	**NHL**	**63**	**1**	**0**	**1**	**1**	**0**	**1**	**155**	**0**	**0**	**0**	**23**	**4.3**	**2**	**0**	**14**	**1**	**–11**	**7**	**1**	**0**	**1**	**0**	**0**	**0**	**0**
1993-94	**Toronto Maple Leafs**	**NHL**	**64**	**4**	**4**	**8**	**4**	**3**	**7**	**185**	**0**	**0**	**0**	**34**	**11.8**	**13**	**0**	**19**	**0**	**–6**	**10**	**0**	**0**	**0**	**18**	**0**	**0**	**0**
1994-95	**Toronto Maple Leafs**	**NHL**	**2**	**0**	**0**	**0**	**0**	**0**	**0**	**5**	**0**	**0**	**0**	**1**	**0.0**	**0**	**0**	**0**	**0**	**0**	....	....	....	....	....	....	....	....
1995-96	**Toronto Maple Leafs**	**NHL**	**60**	**2**	**3**	**5**	**2**	**2**	**4**	**152**	**0**	**0**	**1**	**27**	**7.4**	**8**	**0**	**13**	**0**	**–5**	....	....	....	....	....	....	....	....
	Mighty Ducks of Anaheim	**NHL**	**12**	**0**	**1**	**1**	**0**	**1**	**1**	**41**	**0**	**0**	**0**	**5**	**0.0**	**2**	**0**	**2**	**0**	**0**	....	....	....	....	....	....	....	....
1996-97	**Mighty Ducks of Anaheim**	**NHL**	**67**	**0**	**11**	**11**	**0**	**10**	**10**	**182**	**0**	**0**	**0**	**20**	**0.0**	**16**	**0**	**16**	**0**	**0**	**11**	**0**	**1**	**1**	**11**	**0**	**0**	**0**
1997-98	**Boston Bruins**	**NHL**	**82**	**0**	**1**	**1**	**0**	**1**	**1**	**199**	**0**	**0**	**0**	**28**	**0.0**	**3**	**0**	**17**	**0**	**–14**	**6**	**0**	**0**	**0**	**14**	**0**	**0**	**0**
1998-99	**Boston Bruins**	**NHL**	**69**	**1**	**3**	**4**	**1**	**3**	**4**	**119**	**0**	**0**	**0**	**15**	**6.7**	**6**	**0**	**12**	**0**	**–6**	**3**	**0**	**0**	**0**	**0**	**0**	**0**	**0**
99-2000	**Boston Bruins**	**NHL**	DID NOT PLAY – ASSISTANT COACH																									
	NHL Totals		**696**	**13**	**41**	**54**	**13**	**34**	**47**	**2244**	**0**	**0**	**1**	**290**	**4.5**	**182**	**0**	**265**	**10**		**51**	**1**	**2**	**3**	**106**	**0**	**0**	**0**

Traded to **LA Kings** by **Buffalo** with Sean McKenna and Larry Playfair for Brian Engblom and Doug Smith, January 30, 1986. Traded to **NY Islanders** by **LA Kings** with Hubie McDonough for Mikko Makela, November 29, 1989. Traded to **Toronto** by **NY Islanders** with Dave McLlwain for Daniel Marois and Claude Loiselle, March 10, 1992. Traded to **Anaheim** by **Toronto** for Winnipeg's 4th round choice (previously acquired by Anaheim - later traded to Montreal - Montreal selected Kim Staal) in 1996 Entry Draft, March 20, 1996. Signed as a free agent by **Boston**, July 14, 1997.

• BAUMGARTNER, Mike

Michael Edward D – L. 6'2", 195 lbs. b: Roseau, MN, 1/30/1949. Chicago's 5th, 60th overall, in 1969.

Season	Club	League	GP	G	A	Pts	AG	AA	APts	PIM	PP	SH	GW	S	%	TGF	PGF	TGA	PGA	+/–	GP	G	A	Pts	PIM	PP	SH	GW
1966-67	Roseau Rams	Hi-School	STATISTICS NOT AVAILABLE																									
1967-68	University of North Dakota	WCHA	29	3	9	12	....	....	....		....	....	....	....	....	....	....	....	....	....	....	....	....	....	....	....	....	....
1968-69	University of North Dakota	WCHA	29	2	5	7	....	....	....	12	....	....	....	....	....	....	....	....	....	....	....	....	....	....	....	....	....	....
1969-70	University of North Dakota	WCHA	30	9	5	14	....	....	....	12	....	....	....	....	....	....	....	....	....	....	....	....	....	....	....	....	....	....
1970-71	University of North Dakota	WCHA	33	6	13	19	....	....	....	29	....	....	....	....	....	....	....	....	....	....	....	....	....	....	....	....	....	....
1971-72	Dallas Black Hawks	CHL	72	3	22	25	....	....	....	66	....	....	....	....	....	....	....	....	....	....	12	1	2	3	6	....	....	....
1972-73	Dallas Black Hawks	CHL	72	10	37	47	....	....	....	75	....	....	....	....	....	....	....	....	....	....	4	0	2	2	4	....	....	....
1973-74	Omaha Knights	CHL	70	7	36	43	....	....	....	28	....	....	....	....	....	....	....	....	....	....	5	0	1	1	6	....	....	....
1974-75	**Kansas City Scouts**	**NHL**	**17**	**0**	**0**	**0**	**0**	**0**	**0**	**0**	**0**	**0**	**0**	**12**	**0.0**	**6**	**0**	**18**	**3**	**–9**	....	....	....	....	....	....	....	....
1975-76	Springfield Indians	AHL	1	0	0	0	....	....	....	2	....	....	....	....	....	....	....	....	....	....	....	....	....	....	....	....	....	....
	NHL Totals		**17**	**0**	**0**	**0**	**0**	**0**	**0**	**0**	**0**	**0**	**0**	**12**	**0.0**	**6**	**0**	**18**	**3**		....	....	....	....	....	....	....	....

Traded to **Atlanta** by **Chicago** for Lynn Powis, August 30, 1973. Traded to **Montreal** by **Atlanta** for cash, May 27, 1974. Traded to **Kansas City** by **Montreal** for cash, August 22, 1974.
• Suffered eventual career-ending eye injury in game vs. Vancouver, December 14, 1974.

• BAUMGARTNER, Nolan

D – R. 6'2", 205 lbs. b: Calgary, Alta., 3/23/1976. Washington's 1st, 10th overall, in 1994.

Season	Club	League	GP	G	A	Pts	AG	AA	APts	PIM	PP	SH	GW	S	%	TGF	PGF	TGA	PGA	+/–	GP	G	A	Pts	PIM	PP	SH	GW
1991-92	Calgary Midget Flames	AMHL	39	11	29	40	....	....	....	40	....	....	....	....	....	....	....	....	....	....	....	....	....	....	....	....	....	....
1992-93	Kamloops Blazers	WHL	43	0	5	5	....	....	....	30	....	....	....	....	....	....	....	....	....	....	11	1	1	2	0	....	....	....
1993-94	Kamloops Blazers	WHL	69	13	42	55	....	....	....	109	....	....	....	....	....	....	....	....	....	....	19	3	14	17	33	....	....	....
	Kamloops Blazers	Mem-Cup	4	0	2	2	....	....	....	4	....	....	....	....	....	....	....	....	....	....	....	....	....	....	....	....	....	....
1994-95	Kamloops Blazers	WHL	62	8	36	44	....	....	....	71	....	....	....	....	....	....	....	....	....	....	21	4	13	17	16	....	....	....
	Canada	WJC-A	7	0	1	1	....	....	....	4	....	....	....	....	....	....	....	....	....	....	....	....	....	....	....	....	....	....
	Kamloops Blazers	Mem-Cup	4	0	*6	6	....	....	....	6	....	....	....	....	....	....	....	....	....	....	....	....	....	....	....	....	....	....
1995-96	Kamloops Blazers	WHL	28	13	15	28	....	....	....	45	....	....	....	....	....	....	....	....	....	....	16	1	9	10	26	....	....	....
	Canada	WJC-A	6	1	1	2	....	....	....	22	....	....	....	....	....	....	....	....	....	....	....	....	....	....	....	....	....	....
	Washington Capitals	**NHL**	**1**	**0**	**0**	**0**	**0**	**0**	**0**	**0**	**0**	**0**	**0**	**0**	**0.0**	**0**	**0**	**1**	**0**	**–1**	**1**	**0**	**0**	**0**	**10**	**0**	**0**	**0**
1996-97	Portland Pirates	AHL	8	2	2	4	....	....	....	4	....	....	....	....	....	....	....	....	....	....	....	....	....	....	....	....	....	....
1997-98	**Washington Capitals**	**NHL**	**4**	**0**	**1**	**1**	**0**	**1**	**1**	**0**	**0**	**0**	**0**	**4**	**0.0**	**4**	**2**	**3**	**1**	**0**	....	....	....	....	....	....	....	....
	Portland Pirates	AHL	70	2	24	26	....	....	....	70	....	....	....	....	....	....	....	....	....	....	10	1	4	5	10	....	....	....
1998-99	**Washington Capitals**	**NHL**	**5**	**0**	**0**	**0**	**0**	**0**	**0**	**0**	**0**	**0**	**0**	**1**	**0.0**	**1**	**0**	**4**	**0**	**–3**	....	....	....	....	....	....	....	....
	Portland Pirates	AHL	38	5	14	19	....	....	....	62	....	....	....	....	....	....	....	....	....	....	....	....	....	....	....	....	....	....
99-2000	**Washington Capitals**	**NHL**	**8**	**0**	**1**	**1**	**0**	**1**	**1**	**2**	**0**	**0**	**0**	**6**	**0.0**	**3**	**1**	**1**	**0**	**1**	....	....	....	....	....	....	....	....
	Portland Pirates	AHL	71	5	18	23	....	....	....	56	....	....	....	....	....	....	....	....	....	....	4	1	2	3	10	....	....	....
	NHL Totals		**18**	**0**	**2**	**2**	**0**	**2**	**2**	**2**	**0**	**0**	**0**	**11**	**0.0**	**8**	**3**	**9**	**1**		**1**	**0**	**0**	**0**	**10**	**0**	**0**	**0**

Memorial Cup All-Star Team (1994, 1995) • WHL West First All-Star Team (1995, 1996) • Canadian Major Junior First All-Star Team (1995) • Canadian Major Junior Defenseman of the Year (1995) • WJC-A All-Star Team (1996)

• BAUN, Bob

Robert Neil "Boomer" D – R. 5'9", 175 lbs. b: Lanigan, Sask., 9/9/1936.

Season	Club	League	GP	G	A	Pts	AG	AA	APts	PIM	PP	SH	GW	S	%	TGF	PGF	TGA	PGA	+/–	GP	G	A	Pts	PIM	PP	SH	GW
1952-53	Toronto Marlboros	OHA-Jr.	16	1	1	2	....	....	....	12	....	....	....	....	....	....	....	....	....	....	7	0	2	2	6	....	....	....
1953-54	Toronto Marlboros	OHA-Jr.	59	2	15	17	....	....	....	63	....	....	....	....	....	....	....	....	....	....	15	3	0	3	10	....	....	....
1954-55	Toronto Marlboros	OHA-Jr.	47	3	6	9	....	....	....	99	....	....	....	....	....	....	....	....	....	....	13	0	1	1	31	....	....	....
	Toronto Marlboros	Mem-Cup	11	0	2	2	....	....	....	32	....	....	....	....	....	....	....	....	....	....	....	....	....	....	....	....	....	....
1955-56	Toronto Marlboros	OHA-Jr.	48	5	14	19	....	....	....	93	....	....	....	....	....	....	....	....	....	....	11	3	2	5	38	....	....	....
	Toronto Marlboros	Mem-Cup	13	1	1	2	....	....	....	*39	....	....	....	....	....	....	....	....	....	....	....	....	....	....	....	....	....	....
1956-57	**Toronto Maple Leafs**	**NHL**	**20**	**0**	**5**	**5**	**0**	**5**	**5**	**37**	....	....	....	....	....	....	....	....	....	....	....	....	....	....	....	....	....	....
	Rochester Americans	AHL	46	2	13	15	....	....	....	117	....	....	....	....	....	....	....	....	....	....	....	....	....	....	....	....	....	....
1957-58	**Toronto Maple Leafs**	**NHL**	**67**	**1**	**9**	**10**	**1**	**9**	**10**	**91**	....	....	....	....	....	....	....	....	....	....	....	....	....	....	....	....	....	....
1958-59	**Toronto Maple Leafs**	**NHL**	**51**	**1**	**8**	**9**	**1**	**8**	**9**	**87**	....	....	....	....	....	....	....	....	....	....	**12**	**0**	**0**	**0**	**24**	**0**	**0**	**0**

			REGULAR SEASON																		PLAYOFFS							
Season	Club	League	GP	G	A	Pts	AG	AA	APts	PIM	PP	SH	GW	S	%	TGF	PGF	TGA	PGA	+/–	GP	G	A	Pts	PIM	PP	SH	GW
1959-60	**Toronto Maple Leafs**	**NHL**	**61**	**8**	**9**	**17**	**9**	**9**	**18**	**59**	....	....	....	....	....	....	....	....	....	....	**10**	**1**	**0**	**1**	**17**	**0**	**0**	**0**
1960-61	**Toronto Maple Leafs**	**NHL**	**70**	**1**	**14**	**15**	**1**	**13**	**14**	**70**	....	....	....	....	....	....	....	....	....	....	**3**	**0**	**0**	**0**	**8**	**0**	**0**	**0**
1961-62♦	**Toronto Maple Leafs**	**NHL**	**65**	**4**	**11**	**15**	**5**	**10**	**15**	**94**	....	....	....	....	....	....	....	....	....	....	**12**	**0**	**3**	**3**	**19**	**0**	**0**	**0**
1962-63♦	**Toronto Maple Leafs**	**NHL**	**48**	**4**	**8**	**12**	**5**	**8**	**13**	**65**	....	....	....	....	....	....	....	....	....	....	**10**	**0**	**3**	**3**	**6**	**0**	**0**	**0**
1963-64♦	**Toronto Maple Leafs**	**NHL**	**52**	**4**	**14**	**18**	**5**	**15**	**20**	**113**	....	....	....	....	....	....	....	....	....	....	**14**	**2**	**3**	**5**	***42**	**0**	**0**	**1**
1964-65	**Toronto Maple Leafs**	**NHL**	**70**	**0**	**18**	**18**	**0**	**18**	**18**	**160**	....	....	....	....	....	....	....	....	....	....	**6**	**0**	**1**	**1**	**14**	**0**	**0**	**0**
1965-66	**Toronto Maple Leafs**	**NHL**	**44**	**0**	**6**	**6**	**0**	**6**	**6**	**68**	....	....	....	....	....	....	....	....	....	....	**4**	**0**	**1**	**1**	**8**	**0**	**0**	**0**
1966-67♦	**Toronto Maple Leafs**	**NHL**	**54**	**2**	**8**	**10**	**2**	**8**	**10**	**83**	....	....	....	....	....	....	....	....	....	....	**10**	**0**	**0**	**0**	**4**	**0**	**0**	**0**
1967-68	**Oakland Seals**	**NHL**	**67**	**3**	**10**	**13**	**3**	**10**	**13**	**81**	**0**	**0**	**0**	**80**	**3.8**	**56**	**7**	**83**	**16**	**–18**	....	....	....	....	....	....	....	....
1968-69	**Detroit Red Wings**	**NHL**	**76**	**4**	**16**	**20**	**4**	**14**	**18**	**121**	**0**	**0**	**0**	**117**	**3.4**	**103**	**1**	**125**	**47**	**24**	....	....	....	....	....	....	....	....
1969-70	**Detroit Red Wings**	**NHL**	**71**	**1**	**18**	**19**	**1**	**17**	**18**	**112**	**0**	**0**	**0**	**112**	**0.9**	**84**	**3**	**110**	**36**	**7**	**4**	**0**	**0**	**0**	**6**	**0**	**0**	**0**
1970-71	**Detroit Red Wings**	**NHL**	**11**	**0**	**3**	**3**	**0**	**2**	**2**	**24**	**0**	**0**	**0**	**16**	**0.0**	**10**	**0**	**16**	**4**	**–2**	....	....	....	....	....	....	....	....
	Toronto Maple Leafs	**NHL**	**58**	**1**	**17**	**18**	**1**	**14**	**15**	**123**	**0**	**0**	**0**	**104**	**1.0**	**76**	**8**	**66**	**15**	**17**	**6**	**0**	**1**	**1**	**19**	**0**	**0**	**0**
1971-72	**Toronto Maple Leafs**	**NHL**	**74**	**2**	**12**	**14**	**2**	**10**	**12**	**101**	**0**	**0**	**0**	**158**	**1.3**	**68**	**9**	**82**	**31**	**8**	**5**	**0**	**0**	**0**	**4**	**0**	**0**	**0**
1972-73	**Toronto Maple Leafs**	**NHL**	**5**	**1**	**1**	**2**	**1**	**1**	**2**	**4**	**0**	**0**	**0**	**5**	**20.0**	**4**	**0**	**10**	**1**	**–5**	....	....	....	....	....	....	....	....
	NHL Totals		**964**	**37**	**187**	**224**	**41**	**177**	**218**	**1493**	....	....	....	....	....	....	....	....	....	....	**96**	**3**	**12**	**15**	**171**	....	....	....

Played in NHL All-Star Game (1962, 1963, 1964, 1965, 1968)

Claimed by **Oakland** from **Toronto** in Expansion Draft, June 6, 1967. Traded to **Detroit** by **Oakland** with Ron Harris for Gary Jarrett, Doug Roberts, Howie Young and Chris Worthy, May 27, 1968. Claimed on waivers by **Buffalo** from **Detroit**, November 3, 1970. Traded to **St. Louis** by **Buffalo** for Larry Keenan and Jean-Guy Talbot, November 4, 1970. Traded to **Toronto** by **St. Louis** for Brit Selby, November 13, 1970. • Suffered career-ending neck injury in game vs. Detroit, October 21, 1972.

• BAUTIN, Sergei

Sergei V. D – L. 6'3", 200 lbs. b: Rogachev, USSR, 3/11/1967. Winnipeg's 1st, 17th overall, in 1992.

Season	Club	League	GP	G	A	Pts	AG	AA	APts	PIM	PP	SH	GW	S	%	TGF	PGF	TGA	PGA	+/–	GP	G	A	Pts	PIM	PP	SH	GW
1990-91	Dynamo Moscow	USSR	33	2	0	2	....	....	....	28	....	....	....	....	....	....	....	....	....	....	....	....	....	....	....	....	....	....
	Dynamo Moscow	Super-S	4	0	0	0	....	....	....	5	....	....	....	....	....	....	....	....	....	....	....	....	....	....	....	....	....	....
1991-92	Dynamo Moscow	CIS	32	1	2	3	....	....	....	88	....	....	....	....	....	....	....	....	....	....	5	0	1	1	....	....	....	....
	Russia	Olympics	8	0	0	0	....	....	....	6	....	....	....	....	....	....	....	....	....	....	....	....	....	....	....	....	....	....
	Russia	WC-A	6	1	1	2	....	....	....	8	....	....	....	....	....	....	....	....	....	....	....	....	....	....	....	....	....	....
1992-93	**Winnipeg Jets**	**NHL**	**71**	**5**	**18**	**23**	**4**	**12**	**16**	**96**	**0**	**0**	**0**	**82**	**6.1**	**65**	**2**	**97**	**32**	**–2**	**6**	**0**	**0**	**0**	**2**	**0**	**0**	**0**
1993-94	**Winnipeg Jets**	**NHL**	**59**	**0**	**7**	**7**	**0**	**5**	**5**	**78**	**0**	**0**	**0**	**39**	**0.0**	**45**	**4**	**80**	**26**	**–13**	....	....	....	....	....	....	....	....
	Detroit Red Wings	**NHL**	**1**	**0**	**0**	**0**	**0**	**0**	**0**	**0**	**0**	**0**	**0**	**0**	**0.0**	**1**	**0**	**0**	**0**	**1**	....	....	....	....	....	....	....	....
	Adirondack Red Wings	AHL	9	1	5	6	....	....	....	6	....	....	....	....	....	....	....	....	....	....	....	....	....	....	....	....	....	....
1994-95	Adirondack Red Wings	AHL	32	0	10	10	....	....	....	57	....	....	....	....	....	....	....	....	....	....	1	0	0	0	4	....	....	....
1995-96	**San Jose Sharks**	**NHL**	**1**	**0**	**0**	**0**	**0**	**0**	**0**	**2**	**0**	**0**	**0**	**0**	**0.0**	**1**	**0**	**2**	**0**	**–1**	....	....	....	....	....	....	....	....
	Kansas City Blades	IHL	60	0	14	14	....	....	....	113	....	....	....	....	....	....	....	....	....	....	3	0	0	0	6	....	....	....
1996-97	Lulea HF	Sweden	36	1	0	1	....	....	....	*153	....	....	....	....	....	....	....	....	....	....	8	1	2	3	31	....	....	....
	Lulea HF	EuroHL	6	0	2	2	....	....	....	18	....	....	....	....	....	....	....	....	....	....	....	....	....	....	....	....	....	....
	Russia	WC-A	9	0	2	2	....	....	....	14	....	....	....	....	....	....	....	....	....	....	....	....	....	....	....	....	....	....
1997-98	Lulea HF	Sweden	43	3	5	8	....	....	....	21	....	....	....	....	....	....	....	....	....	....	2	0	0	0	4	....	....	....
	Lulea HF	EuroHL	6	0	1	1	....	....	....	29	....	....	....	....	....	....	....	....	....	....	....	....	....	....	....	....	....	....
1998-99	Ak Bars Kazan	Russia	41	0	5	5	....	....	....	76	....	....	....	....	....	....	....	....	....	....	9	0	3	3	18	....	....	....
	Ak Bars Kazan	EuroHL	6	0	0	0	....	....	....	12	....	....	....	....	....	....	....	....	....	....	2	0	1	1	25	....	....	....
	Russia	WC-A	4	0	2	2	....	....	....	8	....	....	....	....	....	....	....	....	....	....	....	....	....	....	....	....	....	....
99-2000	Nurnberg Ice Tigers	Germany	61	5	11	16	....	....	....	140	....	....	....	....	....	....	....	....	....	....	....	....	....	....	....	....	....	....
	Nurnberg Ice Tigers	EuroHL	6	0	1	1	....	....	....	6	....	....	....	....	....	....	....	....	....	....	2	0	0	0	29	....	....	....
	NHL Totals		**132**	**5**	**25**	**30**	**4**	**17**	**21**	**176**	**0**	**0**	**0**	**121**	**4.1**	**112**	**6**	**179**	**58**		**6**	**0**	**0**	**0**	**2**	**0**	**0**	**0**

Traded to **Detroit** by **Winnipeg** with Bob Essensa for Tim Cheveldae and Dallas Drake, March 8, 1994. Signed as a free agent by **San Jose**, October 12, 1995.

• BAWA, Robin

Robin N. RW – R. 6'2", 214 lbs. b: Chemainus, B.C., 3/26/1966.

Season	Club	League	GP	G	A	Pts	AG	AA	APts	PIM	PP	SH	GW	S	%	TGF	PGF	TGA	PGA	+/–	GP	G	A	Pts	PIM	PP	SH	GW
1981-82	Cowichan Valley Reps	BCAHA	STATISTICS NOT AVAILABLE																									
1982-83	Kamloops Jr. Oilers	WHL	66	10	24	34	....	....	....	17	....	....	....	....	....	....	....	....	....	....	7	1	2	3	0	....	....	....
1983-84	Kamloops Jr. Oilers	WHL	64	16	28	44	....	....	....	40	....	....	....	....	....	....	....	....	....	....	13	4	2	6	4	....	....	....
	Kamloops Jr. Oilers	Mem-Cup	4	0	0	0	....	....	....	0	....	....	....	....	....	....	....	....	....	....	....	....	....	....	....	....	....	....
1984-85	Kamloops Blazers	WHL	52	6	19	25	....	....	....	45	....	....	....	....	....	....	....	....	....	....	15	4	9	13	14	....	....	....
1985-86	Kamloops Blazers	WHL	63	29	43	72	....	....	....	78	....	....	....	....	....	....	....	....	....	....	16	5	13	18	4	....	....	....
	Kamloops Jr. Oilers	Mem-Cup	5	1	1	2	....	....	....	16	....	....	....	....	....	....	....	....	....	....	....	....	....	....	....	....	....	....
1986-87	Kamloops Blazers	WHL	62	57	56	113	....	....	....	91	....	....	....	....	....	....	....	....	....	....	13	6	7	13	22	....	....	....
1987-88	Fort Wayne Komets	IHL	55	12	27	39	....	....	....	239	....	....	....	....	....	....	....	....	....	....	6	1	3	4	24	....	....	....
1988-89	Baltimore Skipjacks	AHL	75	23	24	47	....	....	....	205	....	....	....	....	....	....	....	....	....	....	....	....	....	....	....	....	....	....
1989-90	**Washington Capitals**	**NHL**	**5**	**1**	**0**	**1**	**1**	**0**	**1**	**6**	**0**	**0**	**0**	**1**	**100.0**	**1**	**0**	**4**	**0**	**–3**	....	....	....	....	....	....	....	....
	Baltimore Skipjacks	AHL	61	7	18	25	....	....	....	189	....	....	....	....	....	....	....	....	....	....	11	1	2	3	49	....	....	....
1990-91	Fort Wayne Komets	IHL	72	21	26	47	....	....	....	381	....	....	....	....	....	....	....	....	....	....	18	4	4	8	87	....	....	....
1991-92	**Vancouver Canucks**	**NHL**	**2**	**0**	**0**	**0**	**0**	**0**	**0**	**0**	**0**	**0**	**0**	**1**	**0.0**	**1**	**1**	**0**	**0**	**0**	**1**	**0**	**0**	**0**	**0**	**0**	**0**	**0**
	Milwaukee Admirals	IHL	70	27	14	41	....	....	....	238	....	....	....	....	....	....	....	....	....	....	5	2	2	4	8	....	....	....
1992-93	Hamilton Canucks	AHL	23	3	4	7	....	....	....	58	....	....	....	....	....	....	....	....	....	....	....	....	....	....	....	....	....	....
	San Jose Sharks	**NHL**	**42**	**5**	**0**	**5**	**4**	**0**	**4**	**47**	**0**	**0**	**1**	**25**	**20.0**	**9**	**0**	**38**	**4**	**–25**	....	....	....	....	....	....	....	....
	Kansas City Blades	IHL	5	2	0	2	....	....	....	20	....	....	....	....	....	....	....	....	....	....	....	....	....	....	....	....	....	....
1993-94	**Mighty Ducks of Anaheim**	**NHL**	**12**	**0**	**1**	**1**	**0**	**1**	**1**	**7**	**0**	**0**	**0**	**1**	**0.0**	**1**	**0**	**4**	**0**	**–3**	....	....	....	....	....	....	....	....
	San Diego Gulls	IHL	25	6	15	21	....	....	....	54	....	....	....	....	....	....	....	....	....	....	6	0	0	0	52	....	....	....
1994-95	Kalamazoo Wings	IHL	71	22	12	34	....	....	....	184	....	....	....	....	....	....	....	....	....	....	....	....	....	....	....	....	....	....
	Milwaukee Admirals	IHL	4	1	1	2	....	....	....	19	....	....	....	....	....	....	....	....	....	....	15	1	5	6	48	....	....	....
1995-96	San Francisco Spiders	IHL	77	23	25	48	....	....	....	234	....	....	....	....	....	....	....	....	....	....	4	0	2	2	4	....	....	....
1996-97	Fort Wayne Komets	IHL	54	10	23	33	....	....	....	181	....	....	....	....	....	....	....	....	....	....	....	....	....	....	....	....	....	....
1997-98	Fort Wayne Komets	IHL	58	12	15	27	....	....	....	125	....	....	....	....	....	....	....	....	....	....	....	....	....	....	....	....	....	....
1998-99	Fort Wayne Komets	IHL	74	11	17	28	....	....	....	194	....	....	....	....	....	....	....	....	....	....	....	....	....	....	....	....	....	....
99-2000	Fort Wayne Komets	IHL	DID NOT PLAY – INJURED																									
	NHL Totals		**61**	**6**	**1**	**7**	**5**	**1**	**6**	**60**	**0**	**0**	**1**	**28**	**21.4**	**12**	**1**	**46**	**4**		**1**	**0**	**0**	**0**	**0**	**0**	**0**	**0**

WHL West All-Star Team (1987)

Signed as a free agent by **Washington**, May 22, 1987. Traded to **Vancouver** by **Washington** for cash, July 31, 1991. Traded to **San Jose** by **Vancouver** for Rick Lessard, December 15, 1992. Claimed by **Anaheim** from **San Jose** in Expansion Draft, June 24, 1993. Signed as a free agent by **Dallas**, July 22, 1994. • Missed remainder of 1998-99 and entire 1999-2000 seasons recovering from head injury suffered in game vs. Kansas City (IHL), April 14, 1999.

• BAXTER, Paul

Paul Gordon D – R. 5'11", 200 lbs. b: Winnipeg, Man., 10/28/1955. Pittsburgh's 3rd, 49th overall, in 1975.

Season	Club	League	GP	G	A	Pts	AG	AA	APts	PIM	PP	SH	GW	S	%	TGF	PGF	TGA	PGA	+/–	GP	G	A	Pts	PIM	PP	SH	GW
1972-73	Winnipeg Monarchs	MJHL	44	9	22	31	....	....	....	*359	....	....	....	....	....	....	....	....	....	....	....	....	....	....	....	....	....	....
1973-74	Winnipeg Clubs	WCJHL	63	10	30	40	....	....	....	384	....	....	....	....	....	....	....	....	....	....	....	....	....	....	....	....	....	....
1974-75	Cleveland Crusaders	WHA	5	0	0	0	....	....	....	37	....	....	....	....	....	....	....	....	....	....	....	....	....	....	....	....	....	....
	Cape Cod Codders	NAHL	2	1	0	1	....	....	....	2	....	....	....	....	....	....	....	....	....	....	....	....	....	....	....	....	....	....
1975-76	Cleveland Crusaders	WHA	67	3	7	10	....	....	....	201	....	....	....	....	....	....	....	....	....	....	3	0	0	0	10	....	....	....
	Syracuse Blazers	NAHL	3	1	2	3	....	....	....	9	....	....	....	....	....	....	....	....	....	....	....	....	....	....	....	....	....	....
1976-77	Quebec Nordiques	WHA	66	6	17	23	....	....	....	244	....	....	....	....	....	....	....	....	....	....	12	2	2	4	35	....	....	....
	Maine Nordiques	NAHL	6	1	4	5	....	....	....	52	....	....	....	....	....	....	....	....	....	....	....	....	....	....	....	....	....	....
1977-78	Quebec Nordiques	WHA	76	6	29	35	....	....	....	240	....	....	....	....	....	....	....	....	....	....	11	4	7	11	42	....	....	....
1978-79	Quebec Nordiques	WHA	76	10	36	46	....	....	....	240	....	....	....	....	....	....	....	....	....	....	4	0	2	2	7	....	....	....
1979-80	**Quebec Nordiques**	**NHL**	**61**	**7**	**13**	**20**	**6**	**9**	**15**	**145**	**4**	**0**	**1**	**90**	**7.8**	**67**	**22**	**81**	**9**	**–27**	....	....	....	....	....	....	....	....
1980-81	**Pittsburgh Penguins**	**NHL**	**51**	**5**	**14**	**19**	**4**	**9**	**13**	**204**	**1**	**0**	**0**	**62**	**8.1**	**51**	**5**	**79**	**22**	**–11**	**5**	**0**	**1**	**1**	**28**	**0**	**0**	**0**
1981-82	**Pittsburgh Penguins**	**NHL**	**76**	**9**	**34**	**43**	**7**	**23**	**30**	***409**	**4**	**0**	**2**	**177**	**5.1**	**114**	**30**	**129**	**36**	**–9**	**5**	**0**	**0**	**0**	**14**	**0**	**0**	**0**
1982-83	**Pittsburgh Penguins**	**NHL**	**75**	**11**	**21**	**32**	**9**	**15**	**24**	**238**	**5**	**0**	**0**	**159**	**6.9**	**94**	**28**	**147**	**32**	**–49**	....	....	....	....	....	....	....	....
1983-84	**Calgary Flames**	**NHL**	**74**	**7**	**20**	**27**	**6**	**14**	**20**	**182**	**1**	**0**	**1**	**87**	**8.0**	**80**	**2**	**85**	**6**	**–1**	**11**	**0**	**2**	**2**	**37**	**0**	**0**	**0**
1984-85	**Calgary Flames**	**NHL**	**70**	**5**	**14**	**19**	**4**	**10**	**14**	**126**	**0**	**0**	**1**	**83**	**6.0**	**96**	**1**	**73**	**17**	**39**	**4**	**0**	**1**	**1**	**18**	**0**	**0**	**0**
1985-86	**Calgary Flames**	**NHL**	**47**	**4**	**3**	**7**	**3**	**2**	**5**	**194**	**0**	**1**	**0**	**41**	**9.8**	**47**	**0**	**54**	**12**	**5**	**13**	**0**	**1**	**1**	**55**	**0**	**0**	**0**

Season	Club	League	GP	G	A	Pts	AG	AA	APts	PIM	PP	SH	GW	S	%	TGF	PGF	TGA	PGA	+/-	GP	G	A	Pts	PIM	PP	SH	GW
			REGULAR SEASON																		PLAYOFFS							
1986-87	**Calgary Flames**	**NHL**	**18**	**0**	**2**	**2**	**0**	**1**	**1**	**66**	**0**	**0**	**0**	**13**	**0.0**	**8**	**0**	**13**	**0**	**–5**	**2**	**0**	**0**	**0**	**10**	**0**	**0**	**0**
1987-1989	Salt Lake Golden Eagles	IHL	DID NOT PLAY – COACHING																									
1989-1992	**Calgary Flames**	**NHL**	DID NOT PLAY – ASSISTANT COACH																									
1992-1995	**Chicago Blackhawks**	**NHL**	DID NOT PLAY – ASSISTANT COACH																									
1995-1997	Saint John Flames	AHL	DID NOT PLAY – COACHING																									
1997-2000	**San Jose Sharks**	**NHL**	DID NOT PLAY – ASSISTANT COACH																									
	NHL Totals		**472**	**48**	**121**	**169**	**39**	**83**	**122**	**1564**	**15**	**1**	**5**	**712**	**6.7**	**557**	**88**	**661**	**134**		**40**	**0**	**5**	**5**	**162**	**0**	**0**	**0**
	Other Major League Totals		290	25	89	114	....	....	....	962	....	....	....	....	....	....	....	....	....	....	30	6	11	17	94	....	....	....

Selected by **Cleveland** (WHA) in 1974 WHA Amateur Draft, June, 1974. • Suffered eventual season-ending knee injury in game vs. Maine (NAHL), October 19, 1974. Signed as a free agent by **Quebec** (WHA) after **Cleveland** (WHA) franchise folded, June, 1976. Reclaimed by **Pittsburgh** from **Quebec** prior to Expansion Draft, June 9, 1979. Claimed as a priority selection by **Quebec** prior to Expansion Draft, June 9, 1979. Signed as a free agent by **Pittsburgh**, August 7, 1980. Signed as a free agent by **Calgary**, September 29, 1983.

• BEADLE, Sandy

Sandy James LW – L. 6'2", 185 lbs. b: Regina, Sask., 7/12/1960. Winnipeg's 9th, 149th overall, in 1980.

Season	Club	League	GP	G	A	Pts	AG	AA	APts	PIM	PP	SH	GW	S	%	TGF	PGF	TGA	PGA	+/-	GP	G	A	Pts	PIM	PP	SH	GW
1978-79	Regina Blues	SJHL	52	41	57	98	....	....	....	25	....	....	....	....	....	....	....	....	....	....	....	....	....	....	....	....	....	....
	Regina Pats	WHL	2	1	1	2	....	....	....	0	....	....	....	....	....	....	....	....	....	....	....	....	....	....	....	....	....	....
1979-80	Northeastern University	ECAC	23	11	16	27	....	....	....	6	....	....	....	....	....	....	....	....	....	....	....	....	....	....	....	....	....	....
1980-81	Northeastern University	ECAC	26	29	30	59	....	....	....	26	....	....	....	....	....	....	....	....	....	....	....	....	....	....	....	....	....	....
	Winnipeg Jets	**NHL**	**6**	**1**	**0**	**1**	**1**	**0**	**1**	**2**	**0**	**0**	**0**	**7**	**14.3**	**2**	**0**	**4**	**0**	**–2**	....	....	....	....	....	....	....	....
	Tulsa Oilers	CHL	....	....	....	....	....	....	....	....	....	....	....	....	....	....	....	....	....	....	6	0	1	1	2	....	....	....
1981-82	Tulsa Oilers	CHL	54	12	21	33	....	....	....	34	....	....	....	....	....	....	....	....	....	....	3	0	0	0	7	....	....	....
1982-83	Sherbrooke Jets	AHL	9	2	3	5	....	....	....	0	....	....	....	....	....	....	....	....	....	....	....	....	....	....	....	....	....	....
	Fort Wayne Komets	IHL	13	3	10	13	....	....	....	11	....	....	....	....	....	....	....	....	....	....	....	....	....	....	....	....	....	....
1983-84	Sherbrooke Jets	AHL	70	2	5	7	....	....	....	8	....	....	....	....	....	....	....	....	....	....	....	....	....	....	....	....	....	....
	NHL Totals		**6**	**1**	**0**	**1**	**1**	**0**	**1**	**2**	**0**	**0**	**0**	**7**	**14.3**	**2**	**0**	**4**	**0**		....	....	....	....	....	....	....	....

ECAC First All-Star Team (1981) • NCAA East First All-American Team (1981)

• BEATON, Frank

Alexander Francis "Seldom" LW – L. 5'10", 200 lbs. b: Antigonish, N.S., 4/28/1953.

Season	Club	League	GP	G	A	Pts	AG	AA	APts	PIM	PP	SH	GW	S	%	TGF	PGF	TGA	PGA	+/-	GP	G	A	Pts	PIM	PP	SH	GW
1969-70	Antigonish Midget Alpines	NSAHA	STATISTICS NOT AVAILABLE																									
	Dartmouth Lakers	MJrHL	....	....	....	....	....	....	....	....	....	....	....	....	....	....	....	....	....	....	4	1	0	1	2	....	....	....
1970-71	Dartmouth Lakers	MJrHL	STATISTICS NOT AVAILABLE																									
	Cape Breton Metros	MJrHL	1	0	1	1	....	....	....	0	....	....	....	....	....	....	....	....	....	....	....	....	....	....	....	....	....	....
	Antigonish Bulldogs	MJrHL	....	....	....	....	....	....	....	....	....	....	....	....	....	....	....	....	....	....	7	4	5	9	22	....	....	....
1971-72	Sarnia Bees	OHA-B	49	5	10	15	....	....	....	226	....	....	....	....	....	....	....	....	....	....	....	....	....	....	....	....	....	....
1972-73	Windsor Spitfires	OJHL	16	3	10	13	....	....	....	91	....	....	....	....	....	....	....	....	....	....	....	....	....	....	....	....	....	....
1973-74	Flint Generals	IHL	66	8	14	22	....	....	....	90	....	....	....	....	....	....	....	....	....	....	7	2	2	4	18	....	....	....
1974-75	Flint Generals	IHL	65	4	17	21	....	....	....	175	....	....	....	....	....	....	....	....	....	....	5	0	0	0	13	....	....	....
1975-76	Cincinnati Stingers	WHA	29	2	3	5	....	....	....	61	....	....	....	....	....	....	....	....	....	....	....	....	....	....	....	....	....	....
	Hampton Gulls	SHL	45	17	14	31	....	....	....	*276	....	....	....	....	....	....	....	....	....	....	1	1	1	2	0	....	....	....
1976-77	Hampton Gulls	SHL	7	2	3	5	....	....	....	14	....	....	....	....	....	....	....	....	....	....	....	....	....	....	....	....	....	....
	Edmonton Oilers	WHA	68	4	9	13	....	....	....	*274	....	....	....	....	....	....	....	....	....	....	5	0	2	2	21	....	....	....
1977-78	Hampton Gulls	AHL	6	0	2	2	....	....	....	33	....	....	....	....	....	....	....	....	....	....	....	....	....	....	....	....	....	....
	Birmingham Bulls	WHA	56	6	9	15	....	....	....	279	....	....	....	....	....	....	....	....	....	....	5	2	0	2	10	....	....	....
1978-79	**New York Rangers**	**NHL**	**2**	**0**	**0**	**0**	**0**	**0**	**0**	**0**	**0**	**0**	**0**	**0**	**0.0**	**0**	**0**	**1**	**0**	**–1**	....	....	....	....	....	....	....	....
	New Haven Nighthawks	AHL	74	6	23	29	....	....	....	319	....	....	....	....	....	....	....	....	....	....	10	2	0	2	40	....	....	....
1979-80	**New York Rangers**	**NHL**	**23**	**1**	**1**	**2**	**1**	**1**	**2**	**43**	**0**	**0**	**0**	**19**	**5.3**	**9**	**0**	**14**	**0**	**–5**	....	....	....	....	....	....	....	....
	New Haven Nighthawks	AHL	40	10	14	24	....	....	....	106	....	....	....	....	....	....	....	....	....	....	10	1	4	5	52	....	....	....
1980-81	New Haven Nighthawks	AHL	15	1	1	2	....	....	....	20	....	....	....	....	....	....	....	....	....	....	....	....	....	....	....	....	....	....
	Birmingham Bulls	CHL	41	8	5	13	....	....	....	143	....	....	....	....	....	....	....	....	....	....	....	....	....	....	....	....	....	....
1981-82	Indianapolis Checkers	CHL	77	13	28	41	....	....	....	270	....	....	....	....	....	....	....	....	....	....	13	3	6	9	36	....	....	....
1982-83	Birmingham South Stars	CHL	69	15	19	34	....	....	....	188	....	....	....	....	....	....	....	....	....	....	10	4	2	6	18	....	....	....
	NHL Totals		**25**	**1**	**1**	**2**	**1**	**1**	**2**	**43**	**0**	**0**	**0**	**19**	**5.3**	**9**	**0**	**15**	**0**		....	....	....	....	....	....	....	....
	Other Major League Totals		153	12	21	33	....	....	....	614	....	....	....	....	....	....	....	....	....	....	10	2	2	4	31	....	....	....

Signed as a free agent by **Cincinnati** (WHA), August, 1975. Traded to **Edmonton** (WHA) by **Cincinnati** (WHA) for cash, October, 1976. Signed as a free agent by **Birmingham** (WHA), November, 1977. Signed as a free agent by **NY Rangers**, July 28, 1978. Traded to **Calgary** by **NY Rangers** for Dale Lewis, November 18, 1980. Signed as a free agent by **NY Islanders**, August 25, 1981. Traded to **Minnesota** by **NY Islanders** for future considerations, September 27, 1982.

• BEAUDIN, Norm

Norman Joseph Andrew RW – R. 5'8", 165 lbs. b: Montmartre, Sask., 11/28/1941.

Season	Club	League	GP	G	A	Pts	AG	AA	APts	PIM	PP	SH	GW	S	%	TGF	PGF	TGA	PGA	+/-	GP	G	A	Pts	PIM	PP	SH	GW
1959-60	Regina Pats	SJHL	58	25	32	57	....	....	....	18	....	....	....	....	....	....	....	....	....	....	13	7	2	9	4	....	....	....
1960-61	Regina Pats	SJHL	60	39	40	79	....	....	....	23	....	....	....	....	....	....	....	....	....	....	16	12	6	18	6	....	....	....
	Regina Pats	Mem-Cup	6	*3	0	3	....	....	....	0	....	....	....	....	....	....	....	....	....	....	....	....	....	....	....	....	....	....
1961-62	Regina Pats	SJHL	54	*58	30	88	....	....	....	22	....	....	....	....	....	....	....	....	....	....	16	14	6	20	2	....	....	....
	Spokane Comets	WHL	....	....	....	....	....	....	....	....	....	....	....	....	....	....	....	....	....	....	4	1	3	4	0	....	....	....
	Edmonton Oil Kings	Mem-Cup	4	3	2	5	....	....	....	4	....	....	....	....	....	....	....	....	....	....	....	....	....	....	....	....	....	....
1962-63	Hull-Ottawa Canadiens	EPHL	72	19	22	41	....	....	....	16	....	....	....	....	....	....	....	....	....	....	3	1	0	1	2	....	....	....
1963-64	Cincinnati Wings	CPHL	54	19	30	49	....	....	....	14	....	....	....	....	....	....	....	....	....	....	....	....	....	....	....	....	....	....
	Pittsburgh Hornets	AHL	16	6	9	15	....	....	....	4	....	....	....	....	....	....	....	....	....	....	5	1	3	4	4	....	....	....
1964-65	Memphis Wings	CPHL	53	41	24	65	....	....	....	28	....	....	....	....	....	....	....	....	....	....	....	....	....	....	....	....	....	....
	Pittsburgh Hornets	AHL	13	4	2	6	....	....	....	2	....	....	....	....	....	....	....	....	....	....	2	1	0	1	0	....	....	....
1965-66	Pittsburgh Hornets	AHL	70	29	29	58	....	....	....	35	....	....	....	....	....	....	....	....	....	....	3	1	1	2	0	....	....	....
1966-67	Memphis Wings	CPHL	65	*39	37	76	....	....	....	32	....	....	....	....	....	....	....	....	....	....	7	4	3	7	0	....	....	....
1967-68	**St. Louis Blues**	**NHL**	**13**	**1**	**1**	**2**	**1**	**1**	**2**	**4**	**1**	**0**	**0**	**9**	**11.1**	**4**	**4**	**4**	**0**	**–4**	....	....	....	....	....	....	....	....
	Kansas City Blues	CPHL	59	22	23	45	....	....	....	26	....	....	....	....	....	....	....	....	....	....	7	5	7	12	5	....	....	....
1968-69	Buffalo Bisons	AHL	74	32	39	71	....	....	....	10	....	....	....	....	....	....	....	....	....	....	6	1	3	4	7	....	....	....
1969-70	Cleveland Barons	AHL	70	37	44	81	....	....	....	10	....	....	....	....	....	....	....	....	....	....	....	....	....	....	....	....	....	....
1970-71	**Minnesota North Stars**	**NHL**	**12**	**0**	**1**	**1**	**0**	**1**	**1**	**0**	**0**	**0**	**0**	**16**	**0.0**	**3**	**1**	**5**	**0**	**–3**	....	....	....	....	....	....	....	....
	Cleveland Barons	AHL	59	27	48	75	....	....	....	39	....	....	....	....	....	....	....	....	....	....	8	2	2	4	4	....	....	....
1971-72	Cleveland Barons	AHL	75	33	33	66	....	....	....	16	....	....	....	....	....	....	....	....	....	....	5	2	1	3	4	....	....	....
1972-73	Winnipeg Jets	WHA	78	38	65	103	....	....	....	15	....	....	....	....	....	....	....	....	....	....	14	*13	15	*28	2	....	....	....
1973-74	Winnipeg Jets	WHA	74	27	28	55	....	....	....	8	....	....	....	....	....	....	....	....	....	....	4	3	1	4	2	....	....	....
1974-75	Winnipeg Jets	WHA	79	16	31	47	....	....	....	8	....	....	....	....	....	....	....	....	....	....	....	....	....	....	....	....	....	....
1975-76	Winnipeg Jets	WHA	80	16	31	47	....	....	....	38	....	....	....	....	....	....	....	....	....	....	13	2	3	5	10	....	....	....
1976-77	SC Langnau	Switz.	28	27	11	38	....	....	....	....	....	....	....	....	....	....	....	....	....	....	....	....	....	....	....	....	....	....
1977-78	SC Langnau	Switz.	28	19	11	30	....	....	....	....	....	....	....	....	....	....	....	....	....	....	....	....	....	....	....	....	....	....
	NHL Totals		**25**	**1**	**2**	**3**	**1**	**2**	**3**	**4**	**1**	**0**	**0**	**25**	**4.0**	**7**	**5**	**9**	**0**		....	....	....	....	....	....	....	....
	Other Major League Totals		311	97	155	252	....	....	....	69	....	....	....	....	....	....	....	....	....	....	31	18	19	37	14	....	....	....

AHL Second All-Star Team (1970)

Claimed by **Detroit** from **Hull-Ottawa** (EPHL) in Inter-League Draft, June 4, 1963. Claimed by **St. Louis** from **Detroit** in Expansion Draft, June 6, 1967. Loaned to **Buffalo** (AHL) by **St. Louis** for the 1968-69 season for cash, September, 1968. Traded to **Buffalo** (AHL) by **St. Louis** with Norm Dennis for cash, May 13, 1969. Traded to **St. Louis** by **NY Rangers** (Buffalo-AHL) with Camille Henry for cash, June 27, 1969. Traded to **Montreal** by **St. Louis** with Bob Schmautz for Ernie Wakely, June 27, 1969. Traded to **Minnesota** by **Montreal** for cash, June, 1970. Selected by **Winnipeg** (WHA) in 1972 WHA General Player Draft, February 12, 1972.

• BEAUDOIN, Serge

D – L. 6'2", 215 lbs. b: Montreal, Que., 11/30/1952. Philadelphia's 7th, 103rd overall, in 1972.

Season	Club	League	GP	G	A	Pts	AG	AA	APts	PIM	PP	SH	GW	S	%	TGF	PGF	TGA	PGA	+/-	GP	G	A	Pts	PIM	PP	SH	GW
1968-69	Montreal North Beavers	MMJHL	STATISTICS NOT AVAILABLE																									
1969-70	Laval Saints	QJHL	38	2	15	17	....	....	....	178	....	....	....	....	....	....	....	....	....	....	....	....	....	....	....	....	....	....
1970-71	Trois-Rivieres Ducs	QMJHL	56	8	33	41	....	....	....	191	....	....	....	....	....	....	....	....	....	....	11	0	7	7	41	....	....	....
1971-72	Trois-Rivieres Ducs	QMJHL	61	17	50	67	....	....	....	244	....	....	....	....	....	....	....	....	....	....	5	0	1	1	59	....	....	....
1972-73	Roanoke Valley Rebels	EHL	76	10	43	53	....	....	....	221	....	....	....	....	....	....	....	....	....	....	16	1	10	11	43	....	....	....

Season	Club	League	REGULAR SEASON																		PLAYOFFS							
			GP	G	A	Pts	AG	AA	APts	PIM	PP	SH	GW	S	%	TGF	PGF	TGA	PGA	+/–	GP	G	A	Pts	PIM	PP	SH	GW
1973-74	Vancouver Blazers	WHA	26	1	11	12				37																		
	Roanoke Valley Rebels	SHL	37	8	20	28				179																		
1974-75	Tulsa Oilers	CHL	37	6	31	37				139											2	0	0	0	8			
	Vancouver Blazers	WHA	4	0	0	0				2																		
1975-76	Phoenix Roadrunners	WHA	76	0	21	21				102											5	1	0	1	10			
1976-77	Phoenix Roadrunners	WHA	77	6	24	30				136																		
1977-78	Cincinnati Stingers	WHA	13	0	1	1				10																		
	Birmingham Bulls	WHA	64	8	25	33				105											5	1	0	1	46			
1978-79	Binghamton Dusters	AHL	3	1	1	2				0																		
	Birmingham Bulls	WHA	72	5	21	26				127																		
1979-80	**Atlanta Flames**	**NHL**	**3**	**0**	**0**	**0**	**0**	**0**	**0**	**0**	**0**	**0**	**0**	**1**	**0.0**	**0**	**0**	**1**	**0**	**–1**								
	Birmingham Bulls	CHL	76	6	26	32				135											3	0	1	1	6			
1980-81	Birmingham Bulls	CHL	7	0	3	3				12																		
	NHL Totals		**3**	**0**	**0**	**0**	**0**	**0**	**0**	**0**	**0**	**0**	**0**	**1**	**0.0**	**0**	**0**	**1**	**0**									
	Other Major League Totals		332	20	103	123				519											10	2	0	2	56			

SHL Second All-Star Team (1974)

Selected by **Miami-Philadelphia** (WHA) in 1972 WHA General Player Draft, February 12, 1972. Transferred to **Vancouver** (WHA) when **Philadelphia** (WHA) franchise relocated, May, 1973. Traded to **Phoenix** (WHA) by **Vancouver** (WHA) with Pete McNamee and John Migneault for Hugh Harris, November, 1974. Signed as a free agent by **Cincinnati** (WHA) after **Phoenix** (WHA) franchise folded, September, 1977. Traded to **Birmingham** (WHA) by **Cincinnati** (WHA) for cash, November 5, 1977. Signed as a free agent by **Atlanta**, August 15, 1979.

• BEAUDOIN, Yves

D – R. 5'11", 180 lbs. b: Pointe-aux-Trembles, Que., 1/7/1965. Washington's 6th, 203rd overall, in 1983.

Season	Club	League	GP	G	A	Pts	AG	AA	APts	PIM	PP	SH	GW	S	%	TGF	PGF	TGA	PGA	+/–	GP	G	A	Pts	PIM	PP	SH	GW
1980-81	Bourasaa Angevins	QAAA	48	18	31	49																						
1981-82	Hull Olympiques	QMJHL	50	2	18	20				39																		
1982-83	Hull Olympiques	QMJHL	6	1	2	3				9																		
	Shawinigan Cataracts	QMJHL	56	11	23	34				51											10	2	2	4	18			
1983-84	Shawinigan Cataracts	QMJHL	68	14	43	57				93											6	1	6	7	2			
1984-85	Shawinigan Cataracts	QMJHL	58	20	38	58				78											9	4	3	7	31			
	Canada	WJC-A	7	0	3	3				4																		
	Shawinigan Cataracts	Mem-Cup	4	0	1	1				6																		
1985-86	**Washington Capitals**	**NHL**	**4**	**0**	**0**	**0**	**0**	**0**	**0**	**0**	**0**	**0**	**0**	**7**	**0.0**	**0**	**0**	**4**	**0**	**–4**								
	Binghamton Whalers	AHL	48	5	12	17				36											6	1	2	3	0			
1986-87	**Washington Capitals**	**NHL**	**6**	**0**	**0**	**0**	**0**	**0**	**0**	**5**	**0**	**0**	**0**	**4**	**0.0**	**1**	**0**	**5**	**0**	**–4**								
	Binghamton Whalers	AHL	63	11	25	36				35											11	0	1	1	6			
1987-88	**Washington Capitals**	**NHL**	**1**	**0**	**0**	**0**	**0**	**0**	**0**	**0**	**0**	**0**	**0**	**0**	**0.0**	**0**	**0**	**1**	**0**	**–1**								
	Binghamton Whalers	AHL	64	11	39	50				56											4	0	2	2	6			
1988-89	IEV Innsbruck	Austria	46	9	26	35																						
1989-90	Nottingham Panthers	Un-Cup	8	7	10	17				22																		
	Nottingham Panthers	Britain	14	11	15	26				12																		
1991-1997			OUT OF HOCKEY – RETIRED																									
1997-98	Lachute Rapides	QSPHL	32	5	22	27				33											25	5	20	25				
1998-99	Lachute Rapides	QSPHL	31	16	14	30				22																		
99-2000	LaSalle Rapides	QSPHL	35	7	30	37				32											19	6	19	25	12			
	NHL Totals		**11**	**0**	**0**	**0**	**0**	**0**	**0**	**5**	**0**	**0**	**0**	**11**	**0.0**	**1**	**0**	**10**	**0**									

QMJHL First All-Star Team (1985) • Memorial Cup All-Star Team (1985)

• BEAUFAIT, Mark

Mark David C – R. 5'9", 170 lbs. b: Livonia, MI, 5/13/1970. San Jose's 2nd, 7th overall, in 1991 Supplemental Draft.

Season	Club	League	GP	G	A	Pts	AG	AA	APts	PIM	PP	SH	GW	S	%	TGF	PGF	TGA	PGA	+/–	GP	G	A	Pts	PIM	PP	SH	GW
1987-88	Redford Royals	NAJHL	STATISTICS NOT AVAILABLE																									
1988-89	Northern Michigan University	WCHA	11	2	1	3				2																		
1989-90	Northern Michigan University	WCHA	34	10	14	24				12																		
1990-91	Northern Michigan University	WCHA	47	19	30	49				18																		
1991-92	Northern Michigan University	WCHA	39	31	44	75				43																		
1992-93	**San Jose Sharks**	**NHL**	**5**	**1**	**0**	**1**	**1**	**0**	**1**	**0**	**0**	**0**	**0**	**3**	**33.3**	**1**	**0**	**3**	**1**	**–1**								
	Kansas City Blades	IHL	66	19	40	59				22											9	1	1	2	8			
1993-94	United States	Nat-Team	51	22	29	51				36																		
	United States	Olympics	8	1	4	5				2																		
	Kansas City Blades	IHL	21	12	9	21				18																		
1994-95	San Diego Gulls	IHL	68	24	39	63				22											5	2	2	4	2			
1995-96	Orlando Solar Bears	IHL	77	30	79	109				87											22	9	*19	*28	22			
1996-97	Orlando Solar Bears	IHL	80	26	65	91				63											10	5	8	13	18			
1997-98	Orlando Solar Bears	IHL	76	24	61	85				56											17	6	16	22	10			
1998-99	Orlando Solar Bears	IHL	71	28	43	71				38											15	2	12	14	14			
99-2000	Orlando Solar Bears	IHL	78	28	49	77				87											6	2	0	2	4			
	NHL Totals		**5**	**1**	**0**	**1**	**1**	**0**	**1**	**0**	**0**	**0**	**0**	**3**	**33.3**	**1**	**0**	**3**	**1**									

IHL Second All-Star Team (1997)

Selected by **Orlando** (IHL) from **San Diego** (IHL) in 1995 IHL Expansion Draft, July 13, 1995.

• BECK, Barry

Barry David "Bubba" D – L. 6'3", 216 lbs. b: Vancouver, B.C., 6/3/1957. Colorado's 1st, 2nd overall, in 1977.

Season	Club	League	GP	G	A	Pts	AG	AA	APts	PIM	PP	SH	GW	S	%	TGF	PGF	TGA	PGA	+/–	GP	G	A	Pts	PIM	PP	SH	GW
1973-74	Langley Lords	BCJHL	63	8	28	36				329																		
	Kamloops Chiefs	WCJHL	1	0	0	0				0																		
1974-75	New Westminster Bruins	WCJHL	58	9	33	42				162											18	4	9	13	52			
	Kamloops Blazers	WCJHL	1	0	0	0				0																		
	New Westminster Bruins	Mem-Cup	3	0	3	3				11																		
1975-76	New Westminster Bruins	WCJHL	68	19	80	99				325											17	3	9	12	58			
	New Westminster Bruins	Mem-Cup	4	1	3	4				13																		
1976-77	New Westminster Bruins	WCJHL	61	16	46	62				167											12	4	6	10	39			
	New Westminster Bruins	Mem-Cup	5	3	5	8				13																		
1977-78	**Colorado Rockies**	**NHL**	**75**	**22**	**38**	**60**	**20**	**29**	**49**	**89**	**6**	**0**	**4**	**271**	**8.1**	**133**	**42**	**133**	**28**	**–14**	**2**	**0**	**1**	**1**	**0**	**0**	**0**	**0**
1978-79	**Colorado Rockies**	**NHL**	**63**	**14**	**28**	**42**	**12**	**20**	**32**	**91**	**5**	**0**	**0**	**217**	**6.5**	**102**	**36**	**124**	**28**	**–30**								
	NHL All-Stars	Chal-Cup	3	0	1	1				2																		
1979-80	**Colorado Rockies**	**NHL**	**10**	**1**	**5**	**6**	**1**	**4**	**5**	**8**	**0**	**0**	**0**	**20**	**5.0**	**11**	**3**	**16**	**6**	**–2**								
	New York Rangers	**NHL**	**61**	**14**	**45**	**59**	**12**	**33**	**45**	**98**	**5**	**0**	**4**	**150**	**9.3**	**124**	**46**	**80**	**18**	**16**	**9**	**1**	**4**	**5**	**6**	**1**	**0**	**0**
1980-81	**New York Rangers**	**NHL**	**75**	**11**	**23**	**34**	**9**	**15**	**24**	**231**	**6**	**1**	**0**	**182**	**6.0**	**114**	**30**	**111**	**36**	**9**	**14**	**5**	**8**	**13**	**32**	**1**	**1**	**0**
1981-82	Canada	Can-Cup	7	0	0	0				2																		
	New York Rangers	**NHL**	**60**	**9**	**29**	**38**	**7**	**19**	**26**	**111**	**5**	**0**	**0**	**160**	**5.6**	**125**	**40**	**99**	**33**	**19**	**10**	**1**	**5**	**6**	**14**	**1**	**0**	**0**
1982-83	**New York Rangers**	**NHL**	**66**	**12**	**22**	**34**	**10**	**15**	**25**	**112**	**4**	**0**	**1**	**162**	**7.4**	**120**	**22**	**116**	**40**	**22**	**9**	**2**	**4**	**6**	**8**	**0**	**0**	**0**
1983-84	**New York Rangers**	**NHL**	**72**	**9**	**27**	**36**	**7**	**18**	**25**	**134**	**2**	**1**	**0**	**159**	**5.7**	**103**	**10**	**132**	**51**	**12**	**4**	**1**	**0**	**1**	**6**	**0**	**0**	**0**
1984-85	**New York Rangers**	**NHL**	**56**	**7**	**19**	**26**	**6**	**13**	**19**	**65**	**2**	**2**	**0**	**70**	**10.0**	**90**	**18**	**110**	**27**	**–11**	**3**	**0**	**1**	**1**	**11**	**0**	**0**	**0**
1985-86	**New York Rangers**	**NHL**	**25**	**4**	**8**	**12**	**3**	**5**	**8**	**24**	**3**	**0**	**1**	**53**	**7.5**	**39**	**15**	**30**	**13**	**7**								
1986-1989			OUT OF HOCKEY – RETIRED																									
1989-90	**Los Angeles Kings**	**NHL**	**52**	**1**	**7**	**8**	**1**	**5**	**6**	**53**	**0**	**0**	**0**	**36**	**2.8**	**49**	**2**	**70**	**26**	**3**								
	NHL Totals		**615**	**104**	**251**	**355**	**88**	**176**	**264**	**1016**	**38**	**4**	**10**	**1480**	**7.0**	**1010**	**264**	**1021**	**306**		**51**	**10**	**23**	**33**	**77**	**3**	**1**	**0**

WCJHL First All-Star Team (1976, 1977) • Memorial Cup All-Star Team (1976, 1977) • Won Stafford Smythe Memorial Trophy (Memorial Cup Tournament MVP) (1977)

Played in NHL All-Star Game (1978, 1979, 1980, 1981, 1982)

Traded to **NY Rangers** by **Colorado** for Pat Hickey, Lucien Deblois, Mike McEwen, Dean Turner and future considerations (Bobby Crawford, January 15, 1980), November 2, 1979. Traded to **LA Kings** by **NY Rangers** for cash, September 1, 1989.

• BEDDOES, Clayton

C – L. 5'11", 190 lbs. b: Bentley, Alta., 11/10/1970.

Season	Club	League	GP	G	A	Pts	AG	AA	APts	PIM	PP	SH	GW	S	%	TGF	PGF	TGA	PGA	+/–	GP	G	A	Pts	PIM	PP	SH	GW
			REGULAR SEASON																		PLAYOFFS							
1989-90	Weyburn Red Wings	MJHL	63	34	60	94	....	....	....	69	....	....	....	....	....	....	....	....	....	....	13	7	6	13	....	....	....	....
1990-91	Lake Superior State	CCHA	45	14	28	42	....	....	....	26	....	....	....	....	....	....	....	....	....	....	....	....	....	....	....	....	....	....
1991-92	Lake Superior State	CCHA	38	14	26	40	....	....	....	24	....	....	....	....	....	....	....	....	....	....	....	....	....	....	....	....	....	....
1992-93	Lake Superior State	CCHA	43	18	40	58	....	....	....	30	....	....	....	....	....	....	....	....	....	....	....	....	....	....	....	....	....	....
1993-94	Lake Superior State	CCHA	44	23	31	54	....	....	....	56	....	....	....	....	....	....	....	....	....	....	....	....	....	....	....	....	....	....
1994-95	Providence Bruins	AHL	65	16	20	36	....	....	....	39	....	....	....	....	....	....	....	....	....	....	13	3	1	4	18	....	....	....
1995-96	**Boston Bruins**	**NHL**	**39**	**1**	**6**	**7**	**1**	**5**	**6**	**44**	**0**	**0**	**0**	**18**	**5.6**	**9**	**0**	**19**	**5**	**–5**	....	....	....	....	....	....	....	....
	Providence Bruins	AHL	32	10	15	25	....	....	....	24	....	....	....	....	....	....	....	....	....	....	4	2	3	5	0	....	....	....
1996-97	**Boston Bruins**	**NHL**	**21**	**1**	**2**	**3**	**1**	**2**	**3**	**13**	**0**	**0**	**0**	**11**	**9.1**	**5**	**0**	**7**	**1**	**–1**	....	....	....	....	....	....	....	....
	Providence Bruins	AHL	36	11	23	34	....	....	....	60	....	....	....	....	....	....	....	....	....	....	7	2	0	2	4	....	....	....
1997-98	Detroit Vipers	IHL	65	22	24	46	....	....	....	63	....	....	....	....	....	....	....	....	....	....	22	5	10	15	16	....	....	....
1998-99	Berlin Capitals	Germany	52	17	26	43	....	....	....	12	....	....	....	....	....	....	....	....	....	....	....	....	....	....	....	....	....	....
99-2000	Adler Mannheim	Germany	46	13	12	25	....	....	....	41	....	....	....	....	....	....	....	....	....	....	5	1	0	1	12	....	....	....
	Adler Mannheim	EuroHL	6	0	1	1	....	....	....	2	....	....	....	....	....	....	....	....	....	....	....	....	....	....	....	....	....	....
	NHL Totals		**60**	**2**	**8**	**10**	**2**	**7**	**9**	**57**	**0**	**0**	**0**	**29**	**6.9**	**14**	**0**	**26**	**6**		....	....	....	....	....	....	....	....

CCHA Second All-Star Team (1994) • NCAA West Second All-American Team (1994) • NCAA Championship All-Tournament Team (1994)

Signed as a free agent by **Boston**, June 2, 1994. Signed as a free agent by **Ottawa**, July 28, 1997.

• BEDNARSKI, John

John Severn D – L. 5'10", 195 lbs. b: Thunder Bay, Ont., 7/4/1952.

Season	Club	League	GP	G	A	Pts	AG	AA	APts	PIM	PP	SH	GW	S	%	TGF	PGF	TGA	PGA	+/–	GP	G	A	Pts	PIM	PP	SH	GW
1970-71	West Kildonan North Stars	MJHL	46	10	27	37	....	....	....	*229	....	....	....	....	....	....	....	....	....	....	....	....	....	....	....	....	....	....
	Winnipeg Jets	WCJHL	3	0	0	0	....	....	....	2	....	....	....	....	....	....	....	....	....	....	12	1	1	2	15	....	....	....
1971-72	Winnipeg Jets	WCJHL	65	4	17	21	....	....	....	212	....	....	....	....	....	....	....	....	....	....	....	....	....	....	....	....	....	....
1972-73	Rochester Americans	AHL	72	14	24	38	....	....	....	205	....	....	....	....	....	....	....	....	....	....	6	1	8	9	16	....	....	....
1973-74	Providence Reds	AHL	76	15	46	61	....	....	....	*222	....	....	....	....	....	....	....	....	....	....	15	3	11	14	35	....	....	....
1974-75	**New York Rangers**	**NHL**	**35**	**1**	**10**	**11**	**1**	**7**	**8**	**37**	**0**	**0**	**0**	**45**	**2.2**	**32**	**2**	**35**	**4**	**–1**	**1**	**0**	**0**	**0**	**17**	**0**	**0**	**0**
	Providence Reds	AHL	25	6	5	11	....	....	....	66	....	....	....	....	....	....	....	....	....	....	1	0	0	0	6	....	....	....
1975-76	**New York Rangers**	**NHL**	**59**	**1**	**8**	**9**	**1**	**6**	**7**	**77**	**0**	**0**	**0**	**62**	**1.6**	**41**	**1**	**62**	**7**	**–15**	....	....	....	....	....	....	....	....
1976-77	**New York Rangers**	**NHL**	**5**	**0**	**0**	**0**	**0**	**0**	**0**	**0**	**0**	**0**	**0**	**3**	**0.0**	**1**	**0**	**5**	**1**	**–3**	....	....	....	....	....	....	....	....
	New Haven Nighthawks	AHL	74	10	48	58	....	....	....	110	....	....	....	....	....	....	....	....	....	....	6	2	6	8	4	....	....	....
1977-78	New Haven Nighthawks	AHL	64	12	40	52	....	....	....	98	....	....	....	....	....	....	....	....	....	....	15	0	6	6	21	....	....	....
1978-79	New Haven Nighthawks	AHL	77	13	41	54	....	....	....	146	....	....	....	....	....	....	....	....	....	....	10	2	5	7	28	....	....	....
1979-80	**Edmonton Oilers**	**NHL**	**1**	**0**	**0**	**0**	**0**	**0**	**0**	**0**	**0**	**0**	**0**	**2**	**0.0**	**0**	**0**	**0**	**0**	**0**	....	....	....	....	....	....	....	....
	Cincinnati Stingers	CHL	28	6	18	24	....	....	....	53	....	....	....	....	....	....	....	....	....	....	....	....	....	....	....	....	....	....
	Adirondack Red Wings	AHL	46	11	33	44	....	....	....	54	....	....	....	....	....	....	....	....	....	....	5	0	4	4	16	....	....	....
1980-81	Rochester Americans	AHL	76	3	18	21	....	....	....	156	....	....	....	....	....	....	....	....	....	....	....	....	....	....	....	....	....	....
1981-82	Erie Blades	AHL	66	10	30	40	....	....	....	59	....	....	....	....	....	....	....	....	....	....	....	....	....	....	....	....	....	....
	NHL Totals		**100**	**2**	**18**	**20**	**2**	**13**	**15**	**114**	**0**	**0**	**0**	**112**	**1.8**	**74**	**3**	**102**	**12**		**1**	**0**	**0**	**0**	**17**	**0**	**0**	**0**

AHL Second All-Star Team (1974, 1978) • AHL First All-Star Team (1977, 1979)

Signed as a free agent by **NY Rangers**, September, 1972. Signed as a free agent by **Edmonton**, July 15, 1979. Signed as a free agent by **Buffalo**, June 26, 1980.

• BEERS, Bob

Robert Charles D – R. 6'2", 200 lbs. b: Pittsburgh, PA, 5/20/1967. Boston's 10th, 210th overall, in 1985.

Season	Club	League	GP	G	A	Pts	AG	AA	APts	PIM	PP	SH	GW	S	%	TGF	PGF	TGA	PGA	+/–	GP	G	A	Pts	PIM	PP	SH	GW
1985-86	Buffalo Jr. Sabres	NYJHL	47	11	39	50	....	....	....	96	....	....	....	....	....	....	....	....	....	....	....	....	....	....	....	....	....	....
1986-87	University of Maine	H-East	28	0	13	13	....	....	....	46	....	....	....	....	....	....	....	....	....	....	....	....	....	....	....	....	....	....
1987-88	University of Maine	H-East	41	3	11	14	....	....	....	72	....	....	....	....	....	....	....	....	....	....	....	....	....	....	....	....	....	....
1988-89	University of Maine	H-East	44	10	27	37	....	....	....	53	....	....	....	....	....	....	....	....	....	....	....	....	....	....	....	....	....	....
1989-90	**Boston Bruins**	**NHL**	**3**	**0**	**1**	**1**	**0**	**1**	**1**	**6**	**0**	**0**	**0**	**0**	**0.0**	**4**	**1**	**2**	**1**	**2**	**14**	**1**	**1**	**2**	**18**	**0**	**0**	**0**
	Maine Mariners	AHL	74	7	36	43	....	....	....	63	....	....	....	....	....	....	....	....	....	....	....	....	....	....	....	....	....	....
1990-91	**Boston Bruins**	**NHL**	**16**	**0**	**1**	**1**	**0**	**1**	**1**	**10**	**0**	**0**	**0**	**9**	**0.0**	**7**	**1**	**15**	**1**	**–8**	**6**	**0**	**0**	**0**	**4**	**0**	**0**	**0**
	Maine Mariners	AHL	36	2	16	18	....	....	....	21	....	....	....	....	....	....	....	....	....	....	....	....	....	....	....	....	....	....
1991-92	**Boston Bruins**	**NHL**	**31**	**0**	**5**	**5**	**0**	**4**	**4**	**29**	**0**	**0**	**0**	**25**	**0.0**	**14**	**2**	**27**	**2**	**–13**	**1**	**0**	**0**	**0**	**0**	**0**	**0**	**0**
	Maine Mariners	AHL	33	6	23	29	....	....	....	24	....	....	....	....	....	....	....	....	....	....	....	....	....	....	....	....	....	....
1992-93	Providence Bruins	AHL	6	1	2	3	....	....	....	10	....	....	....	....	....	....	....	....	....	....	....	....	....	....	....	....	....	....
	Tampa Bay Lightning	**NHL**	**64**	**12**	**24**	**36**	**10**	**17**	**27**	**70**	**7**	**0**	**0**	**138**	**8.7**	**87**	**38**	**106**	**32**	**–25**	....	....	....	....	....	....	....	....
	Atlanta Knights	IHL	1	0	0	0	....	....	....	0	....	....	....	....	....	....	....	....	....	....	....	....	....	....	....	....	....	....
	United States	WC-A	6	1	2	3	....	....	....	2	....	....	....	....	....	....	....	....	....	....	....	....	....	....	....	....	....	....
1993-94	**Tampa Bay Lightning**	**NHL**	**16**	**1**	**5**	**6**	**1**	**4**	**5**	**12**	**1**	**0**	**0**	**35**	**2.9**	**13**	**7**	**20**	**3**	**–11**	....	....	....	....	....	....	....	....
	Edmonton Oilers	**NHL**	**66**	**10**	**27**	**37**	**9**	**21**	**30**	**74**	**5**	**0**	**0**	**152**	**6.6**	**85**	**29**	**92**	**25**	**–11**	....	....	....	....	....	....	....	....
	United States	WC-A	8	2	0	2	....	....	....	4	....	....	....	....	....	....	....	....	....	....	....	....	....	....	....	....	....	....
1994-95	**New York Islanders**	**NHL**	**22**	**2**	**7**	**9**	**4**	**10**	**14**	**6**	**1**	**0**	**0**	**38**	**5.3**	**22**	**4**	**37**	**11**	**–8**	....	....	....	....	....	....	....	....
1995-96	**New York Islanders**	**NHL**	**13**	**0**	**5**	**5**	**0**	**4**	**4**	**10**	**0**	**0**	**0**	**9**	**0.0**	**16**	**7**	**14**	**3**	**–2**	....	....	....	....	....	....	....	....
	Utah Grizzlies	IHL	65	6	36	42	....	....	....	54	....	....	....	....	....	....	....	....	....	....	22	1	12	13	16	....	....	....
1996-97	**Boston Bruins**	**NHL**	**27**	**3**	**4**	**7**	**3**	**4**	**7**	**8**	**1**	**0**	**0**	**49**	**6.1**	**21**	**2**	**22**	**3**	**0**	....	....	....	....	....	....	....	....
	Providence Bruins	AHL	45	10	12	22	....	....	....	18	....	....	....	....	....	....	....	....	....	....	....	....	....	....	....	....	....	....
	United States	WC-A	8	1	0	1	....	....	....	8	....	....	....	....	....	....	....	....	....	....	....	....	....	....	....	....	....	....
1997-98			OUT OF HOCKEY – RETIRED																									
1998-99	Providence Bruins	AHL	10	1	2	3	....	....	....	4	....	....	....	....	....	....	....	....	....	....	5	0	1	1	2	....	....	....
99-2000	Providence Bruins	AHL	13	0	4	4	....	....	....	14	....	....	....	....	....	....	....	....	....	....	14	1	5	6	9	....	....	....
	NHL Totals		**258**	**28**	**79**	**107**	**27**	**66**	**93**	**225**	**15**	**0**	**0**	**455**	**6.2**	**269**	**91**	**335**	**81**		**21**	**1**	**1**	**2**	**22**	**0**	**0**	**0**

Hockey East Second All-Star Team (1989) • NCAA East Second All-American Team (1989)

Traded to **Tampa Bay** by **Boston** for Stephane J.G. Richer, October 28, 1992. Traded to **Edmonton** by **Tampa Bay** for Chris Joseph, November 11, 1993. Signed as a free agent by **NY Islanders**, August 29, 1994. Signed as a free agent by **Boston**, August 5, 1996. • Spent 1997-98 season working as the colour analyst on Providence Bruins (AHL) television broadcasts. Signed as a free agent by **Providence** (AHL), March 12, 1999.

• BEERS, Eddy

Edward Joseph LW – L. 6'2", 195 lbs. b: Merritt, B.C., 10/12/1959.

Season	Club	League	GP	G	A	Pts	AG	AA	APts	PIM	PP	SH	GW	S	%	TGF	PGF	TGA	PGA	+/–	GP	G	A	Pts	PIM	PP	SH	GW
1977-78	Merritt Centennials	BCJHL	63	55	60	115	....	....	....	100	....	....	....	....	....	....	....	....	....	....	....	....	....	....	....	....	....	....
1978-79	University of Denver	WCHA	17	7	5	12	....	....	....	23	....	....	....	....	....	....	....	....	....	....	....	....	....	....	....	....	....	....
1979-80	University of Denver	WCHA	36	13	20	33	....	....	....	24	....	....	....	....	....	....	....	....	....	....	....	....	....	....	....	....	....	....
1980-81	University of Denver	WCHA	39	24	15	39	....	....	....	63	....	....	....	....	....	....	....	....	....	....	....	....	....	....	....	....	....	....
1981-82	University of Denver	WCHA	42	50	34	84	....	....	....	59	....	....	....	....	....	....	....	....	....	....	....	....	....	....	....	....	....	....
	Calgary Flames	**NHL**	**5**	**1**	**1**	**2**	**1**	**1**	**2**	**21**	**0**	**0**	**0**	**7**	**14.3**	**3**	**0**	**3**	**0**	**0**	....	....	....	....	....	....	....	....
1982-83	**Calgary Flames**	**NHL**	**41**	**11**	**15**	**26**	**9**	**10**	**19**	**21**	**2**	**0**	**2**	**72**	**15.3**	**43**	**5**	**27**	**0**	**11**	**8**	**1**	**1**	**2**	**27**	**0**	**0**	**1**
	Colorado Flames	CHL	29	12	17	29	....	....	....	52	....	....	....	....	....	....	....	....	....	....	....	....	....	....	....	....	....	....
1983-84	**Calgary Flames**	**NHL**	**73**	**36**	**39**	**75**	**29**	**27**	**56**	**88**	**16**	**0**	**4**	**189**	**19.0**	**122**	**48**	**67**	**0**	**7**	**11**	**2**	**5**	**7**	**12**	**0**	**0**	**0**
1984-85	**Calgary Flames**	**NHL**	**74**	**28**	**40**	**68**	**23**	**27**	**50**	**94**	**13**	**0**	**0**	**171**	**16.4**	**104**	**38**	**59**	**0**	**7**	**3**	**1**	**0**	**1**	**0**	**1**	**0**	**0**
1985-86	**Calgary Flames**	**NHL**	**33**	**11**	**10**	**21**	**9**	**7**	**16**	**8**	**4**	**0**	**1**	**83**	**13.3**	**42**	**22**	**23**	**0**	**–3**	....	....	....	....	....	....	....	....
	St. Louis Blues	**NHL**	**24**	**7**	**11**	**18**	**6**	**7**	**13**	**24**	**4**	**0**	**0**	**53**	**13.2**	**25**	**8**	**20**	**0**	**–3**	**19**	**3**	**4**	**7**	**8**	**2**	**0**	**1**
1986-87	**St. Louis Blues**	**NHL**	DID NOT PLAY – INJURED																									
	NHL Totals		**250**	**94**	**116**	**210**	**77**	**79**	**156**	**256**	**39**	**0**	**7**	**575**	**16.3**	**339**	**121**	**199**	**0**		**41**	**7**	**10**	**17**	**47**	**3**	**0**	**2**

Signed as a free agent by **Calgary**, April 1, 1982. Traded to **St. Louis** by **Calgary** with Charlie Bourgeois and Gino Cavallini for Joe Mullen, Terry Johnson and Rik Wilson, February 1, 1986. • Suffered eventual career-ending back injury in training camp, September 23, 1986.

• BEGIN, Steve

C – L. 5'11", 190 lbs. b: Trois-Rivieres, Que., 6/14/1978. Calgary's 3rd, 40th overall, in 1996.

Season	Club	League	GP	G	A	Pts	AG	AA	APts	PIM	PP	SH	GW	S	%	TGF	PGF	TGA	PGA	+/–	GP	G	A	Pts	PIM	PP	SH	GW
1994-95	Cap-de-Madelane Estacades	QAAA	35	9	15	24	....	....	....	48	....	....	....	....	....	....	....	....	....	....	....	....	....	....	....	....	....	....
1995-96	Val d'Or Foreurs	QMJHL	64	13	23	36	....	....	....	218	....	....	....	....	....	....	....	....	....	....	13	1	3	4	33	....	....	....
1996-97	Val d'Or Foreurs	QMJHL	58	13	33	46	....	....	....	229	....	....	....	....	....	....	....	....	....	....	10	0	3	3	8	....	....	....
	Saint John Flames	AHL	....	....	....	....	....	....	....	....	....	....	....	....	....	....	....	....	....	....	4	0	2	2	6	....	....	....

Season	Club	League	GP	G	A	Pts	AG	AA	APts	PIM	PP	SH	GW	S	%	TGF	PGF	TGA	PGA	+/–	GP	G	A	Pts	PIM	PP	SH	GW
			REGULAR SEASON																		PLAYOFFS							
1997-98	Val d'Or Foreurs	QMJHL	35	18	17	35	....	....	....	73	....	....	....	....	....	....	....	....	....	....	15	2	12	14	34	....	....	....
	Canada	WJC-A	7	0	0	0	....	....	....	10	....	....	....	....	....	....	....	....	....	....	....	....	....	....	....	....	....	....
	Calgary Flames	**NHL**	**5**	**0**	**0**	**0**	**0**	**0**	**0**	**23**	**0**	**0**	**0**	**2**	**0.0**	**0**	**0**	**2**	**2**	**0**	....	....	....	....	....	....	....	....
	Val d'Or Foreurs	Mem-Cup	3	0	1	1	....	....	....	4	....	....	....	....	....	....	....	....	....	....	....	....	....	....	....	....	....	....
1998-99	Saint John Flames	AHL	73	11	9	20	....	....	....	156	....	....	....	....	....	....	....	....	....	....	7	2	0	2	18	....	....	....
99-2000	**Calgary Flames**	**NHL**	**13**	**1**	**1**	**2**	**1**	**1**	**2**	**18**	**0**	**0**	**0**	**3**	**33.3**	**4**	**1**	**6**	**0**	**–3**	....	....	....	....	....	....	....	....
	Saint John Flames	AHL	47	13	12	25	....	....	....	99	....	....	....	....	....	....	....	....	....	....	....	....	....	....	....	....	....	....
	NHL Totals		**18**	**1**	**1**	**2**	**1**	**1**	**2**	**41**	**0**	**0**	**0**	**5**	**20.0**	**4**	**1**	**8**	**2**		....	....	....	....	....	....	....	....

• BEKAR, Derek

LW – L. 6'3", 194 lbs. b: Burnaby, B.C., 9/15/1975. St. Louis' 7th, 205th overall, in 1995.

Season	Club	League	GP	G	A	Pts	AG	AA	APts	PIM	PP	SH	GW	S	%	TGF	PGF	TGA	PGA	+/–	GP	G	A	Pts	PIM	PP	SH	GW
1992-93	Notre Dame Midget Hounds	AAHA	29	25	24	49	....	....	....	68	....	....	....	....	....	....	....	....	....	....	....	....	....	....	....	....	....	....
1993-94	Notre Dame Hounds	SJHL	62	20	31	51	....	....	....	77	....	....	....	....	....	....	....	....	....	....	....	....	....	....	....	....	....	....
1994-95	Powell River Paper Kings	BCJHL	46	33	29	62	....	....	....	35	....	....	....	....	....	....	....	....	....	....	....	....	....	....	....	....	....	....
1995-96	University of New Hampshire	H-East	34	15	18	33	....	....	....	4	....	....	....	....	....	....	....	....	....	....	....	....	....	....	....	....	....	....
1996-97	University of New Hampshire	H-East	39	18	21	39	....	....	....	34	....	....	....	....	....	....	....	....	....	....	....	....	....	....	....	....	....	....
1997-98	University of New Hampshire	H-East	35	32	28	60	....	....	....	46	....	....	....	....	....	....	....	....	....	....	....	....	....	....	....	....	....	....
1998-99	Worcester IceCats	AHL	51	16	20	36	....	....	....	6	....	....	....	....	....	....	....	....	....	....	4	0	0	0	0	....	....	....
99-2000	**St. Louis Blues**	**NHL**	**1**	**0**	**0**	**0**	**0**	**0**	**0**	**0**	**0**	**0**	**0**	**0**	**0.0**	**0**	**0**	**0**	**0**	**0**	....	....	....	....	....	....	....	....
	Worcester IceCats	AHL	71	21	19	40	....	....	....	26	....	....	....	....	....	....	....	....	....	....	7	0	3	3	2	....	....	....
	NHL Totals		**1**	**0**	**0**	**0**	**0**	**0**	**0**	**0**	**0**	**0**	**0**	**0**	**0.0**	**0**	**0**	**0**	**0**		....	....	....	....	....	....	....	....

Hockey East Second All-Star Team (1998)

• BELAK, Wade

D – R. 6'5", 222 lbs. b: Saskatoon, Sask., 7/3/1976. Quebec's 1st, 12th overall, in 1994.

Season	Club	League	GP	G	A	Pts	AG	AA	APts	PIM	PP	SH	GW	S	%	TGF	PGF	TGA	PGA	+/–	GP	G	A	Pts	PIM	PP	SH	GW
1991-92	North Battleford North Stars	SAHA	57	6	20	26	....	....	....	186	....	....	....	....	....	....	....	....	....	....	....	....	....	....	....	....	....	....
1992-93	North Battleford Stars	SJHL	50	5	15	20	....	....	....	146	....	....	....	....	....	....	....	....	....	....	....	....	....	....	....	....	....	....
	Saskatoon Blades	WHL	7	0	0	0	....	....	....	23	....	....	....	....	....	....	....	....	....	....	7	0	0	0	0	....	....	....
1993-94	Saskatoon Blades	WHL	69	4	13	17	....	....	....	226	....	....	....	....	....	....	....	....	....	....	16	2	2	4	43	....	....	....
1994-95	Saskatoon Blades	WHL	72	4	14	18	....	....	....	290	....	....	....	....	....	....	....	....	....	....	9	0	0	0	36	....	....	....
	Cornwall Aces	AHL	....	....	....	....	....	....	....	....	....	....	....	....	....	....	....	....	....	....	11	1	2	3	40	....	....	....
1995-96	Saskatoon Blades	WHL	63	3	15	18	....	....	....	207	....	....	....	....	....	....	....	....	....	....	4	0	0	0	9	....	....	....
	Cornwall Aces	AHL	5	0	0	0	....	....	....	18	....	....	....	....	....	....	....	....	....	....	2	0	0	0	2	....	....	....
1996-97	**Colorado Avalanche**	**NHL**	**5**	**0**	**0**	**0**	**0**	**0**	**0**	**11**	**0**	**0**	**0**	**1**	**0.0**	**0**	**0**	**1**	**0**	**–1**	....	....	....	....	....	....	....	....
	Hershey Bears	AHL	65	1	7	8	....	....	....	320	....	....	....	....	....	....	....	....	....	....	16	0	1	1	61	....	....	....
1997-98	**Colorado Avalanche**	**NHL**	**8**	**1**	**1**	**2**	**1**	**1**	**2**	**27**	**0**	**0**	**1**	**2**	**50.0**	**2**	**0**	**5**	**0**	**–3**	....	....	....	....	....	....	....	....
	Hershey Bears	AHL	11	0	0	0	....	....	....	30	....	....	....	....	....	....	....	....	....	....	....	....	....	....	....	....	....	....
1998-99	**Colorado Avalanche**	**NHL**	**22**	**0**	**0**	**0**	**0**	**0**	**0**	**71**	**0**	**0**	**0**	**5**	**0.0**	**2**	**0**	**4**	**0**	**–2**	....	....	....	....	....	....	....	....
	Hershey Bears	AHL	17	0	1	1	....	....	....	49	....	....	....	....	....	....	....	....	....	....	....	....	....	....	....	....	....	....
	Calgary Flames	**NHL**	**9**	**0**	**1**	**1**	**0**	**1**	**1**	**23**	**0**	**0**	**0**	**2**	**0.0**	**4**	**0**	**1**	**0**	**3**	....	....	....	....	....	....	....	....
	Saint John Flames	AHL	12	0	2	2	....	....	....	43	....	....	....	....	....	....	....	....	....	....	6	0	1	1	23	....	....	....
99-2000	**Calgary Flames**	**NHL**	**40**	**0**	**2**	**2**	**0**	**2**	**2**	**122**	**0**	**0**	**0**	**11**	**0.0**	**12**	**0**	**17**	**1**	**–4**	....	....	....	....	....	....	....	....
	NHL Totals		**84**	**1**	**4**	**5**	**1**	**4**	**5**	**254**	**0**	**0**	**1**	**21**	**4.8**	**20**	**0**	**28**	**1**		....	....	....	....	....	....	....	....

Rights transferred to **Colorado** after **Quebec** franchise relocated, June 21, 1995. Traded to **Calgary** by **Colorado** with Rene Corbet, Robyn Regehr and Colorado's 2nd round compensatory choice (Jarret Stoll) in 2000 Entry Draft for Theoren Fleury and Chris Dingman, February 28, 1999. • Missed majority of 1999-2000 season recovering from shoulder injury suffered in game vs. Colorado, February 10, 2000.

• BELANGER, Alain

"Bam-Bam" RW – R. 6'1", 190 lbs. b: St. Janvier, Que., 1/18/1956. Toronto's 2nd, 48th overall, in 1976.

Season	Club	League	GP	G	A	Pts	AG	AA	APts	PIM	PP	SH	GW	S	%	TGF	PGF	TGA	PGA	+/–	GP	G	A	Pts	PIM	PP	SH	GW
1973-74	Ste-Theresa Volants	QJHL-B	STATISTICS NOT AVAILABLE																									
	Drummondville Rangers	QMJHL	28	1	2	3	....	....	....	104	....	....	....	....	....	....	....	....	....	....	....	....	....	....	....	....	....	....
1974-75	Sherbrooke Beavers	QMJHL	51	17	19	36	....	....	....	342	....	....	....	....	....	....	....	....	....	....	....	....	....	....	....	....	....	....
	Sherbrooke Beavers	Mem-Cup	3	0	0	0	....	....	....	*27	....	....	....	....	....	....	....	....	....	....	....	....	....	....	....	....	....	....
1975-76	Sherbrooke Beavers	QMJHL	65	26	25	51	....	....	....	274	....	....	....	....	....	....	....	....	....	....	....	....	....	....	....	....	....	....
1976-77	Dallas Black Hawks	CHL	30	16	10	26	....	....	....	149	....	....	....	....	....	....	....	....	....	....	....	....	....	....	....	....	....	....
1977-78	**Toronto Maple Leafs**	**NHL**	**9**	**0**	**1**	**1**	**0**	**1**	**1**	**6**	**0**	**0**	**0**	**2**	**0.0**	**2**	**0**	**2**	**0**	**0**	....	....	....	....	....	....	....	....
	Dallas Black Hawks	CHL	61	7	16	23	....	....	....	*262	....	....	....	....	....	....	....	....	....	....	12	1	4	5	44	....	....	....
1978-79	New Brunswick Hawks	AHL	57	8	12	20	....	....	....	197	....	....	....	....	....	....	....	....	....	....	5	1	0	1	2	....	....	....
1979-80	New Brunswick Hawks	AHL	49	4	16	20	....	....	....	120	....	....	....	....	....	....	....	....	....	....	....	....	....	....	....	....	....	....
1980-81			DID NOT PLAY																									
1981-82			DID NOT PLAY																									
1982-83	Sherbrooke Jets	AHL	21	0	0	0	....	....	....	79	....	....	....	....	....	....	....	....	....	....	....	....	....	....	....	....	....	....
	NHL Totals		**9**	**0**	**1**	**1**	**0**	**1**	**1**	**6**	**0**	**0**	**0**	**2**	**0.0**	**2**	**0**	**2**	**0**		....	....	....	....	....	....	....	....

• BELANGER, Jesse

C – R. 6'1", 190 lbs. b: St. Georges de Beauce, Que., 6/15/1969.

Season	Club	League	GP	G	A	Pts	AG	AA	APts	PIM	PP	SH	GW	S	%	TGF	PGF	TGA	PGA	+/–	GP	G	A	Pts	PIM	PP	SH	GW
1987-88	Granby Bisons	QMJHL	69	33	43	76	....	....	....	10	....	....	....	....	....	....	....	....	....	....	5	3	3	6	0	....	....	....
1988-89	Granby Bisons	QMJHL	67	40	63	103	....	....	....	26	....	....	....	....	....	....	....	....	....	....	4	0	5	5	0	....	....	....
1989-90	Granby Bisons	QMJHL	67	53	54	107	....	....	....	53	....	....	....	....	....	....	....	....	....	....	....	....	....	....	....	....	....	....
	Canada	Nat-Team	1	0	0	0	....	....	....	0	....	....	....	....	....	....	....	....	....	....	....	....	....	....	....	....	....	....
1990-91	Fredericton Canadiens	AHL	75	40	58	98	....	....	....	30	....	....	....	....	....	....	....	....	....	....	6	2	4	6	0	....	....	....
1991-92	**Montreal Canadiens**	**NHL**	**4**	**0**	**0**	**0**	**0**	**0**	**0**	**0**	**0**	**0**	**0**	**4**	**0.0**	**2**	**0**	**3**	**0**	**–1**	....	....	....	....	....	....	....	....
	Fredericton Canadiens	AHL	65	30	41	71	....	....	....	26	....	....	....	....	....	....	....	....	....	....	7	3	3	6	2	....	....	....
1992-93♦	**Montreal Canadiens**	**NHL**	**19**	**4**	**2**	**6**	**3**	**1**	**4**	**4**	**0**	**0**	**0**	**24**	**16.7**	**8**	**0**	**13**	**6**	**1**	**9**	**0**	**1**	**1**	**0**	**0**	**0**	**0**
	Fredericton Canadiens	AHL	39	19	32	51	....	....	....	24	....	....	....	....	....	....	....	....	....	....	....	....	....	....	....	....	....	....
1993-94	**Florida Panthers**	**NHL**	**70**	**17**	**33**	**50**	**16**	**26**	**42**	**16**	**11**	**0**	**3**	**104**	**16.3**	**69**	**34**	**42**	**3**	**–4**	....	....	....	....	....	....	....	....
1994-95	**Florida Panthers**	**NHL**	**47**	**15**	**14**	**29**	**27**	**21**	**48**	**18**	**6**	**0**	**3**	**89**	**16.9**	**38**	**18**	**25**	**0**	**–5**	....	....	....	....	....	....	....	....
1995-96	**Florida Panthers**	**NHL**	**63**	**17**	**21**	**38**	**17**	**17**	**34**	**10**	**7**	**0**	**1**	**140**	**12.1**	**65**	**41**	**30**	**1**	**–5**	....	....	....	....	....	....	....	....
	Vancouver Canucks	**NHL**	**9**	**3**	**0**	**3**	**3**	**0**	**3**	**4**	**1**	**0**	**1**	**11**	**27.3**	**3**	**1**	**2**	**0**	**0**	**3**	**0**	**2**	**2**	**2**	**0**	**0**	**0**
1996-97	**Edmonton Oilers**	**NHL**	**6**	**0**	**0**	**0**	**0**	**0**	**0**	**0**	**0**	**0**	**0**	**8**	**0.0**	**1**	**1**	**4**	**1**	**–3**	....	....	....	....	....	....	....	....
	Hamilton Bulldogs	AHL	6	4	3	7	....	....	....	0	....	....	....	....	....	....	....	....	....	....	....	....	....	....	....	....	....	....
	Quebec Rafales	IHL	47	34	28	62	....	....	....	18	....	....	....	....	....	....	....	....	....	....	9	3	5	8	13	....	....	....
1997-98	SC Herisau	Switz.	5	4	3	7	....	....	....	4	....	....	....	....	....	....	....	....	....	....	....	....	....	....	....	....	....	....
	Las Vegas Thunder	IHL	54	32	36	68	....	....	....	20	....	....	....	....	....	....	....	....	....	....	....	....	....	....	....	....	....	....
1998-99	Cleveland Lumberjacks	IHL	22	9	13	22	....	....	....	10	....	....	....	....	....	....	....	....	....	....	4	0	1	1	0	....	....	....
99-2000	**Montreal Canadiens**	**NHL**	**16**	**3**	**6**	**9**	**3**	**6**	**9**	**2**	**0**	**0**	**0**	**21**	**14.3**	**11**	**2**	**7**	**0**	**2**	....	....	....	....	....	....	....	....
	Quebec Citadelles	AHL	36	15	18	33	....	....	....	20	....	....	....	....	....	....	....	....	....	....	3	0	3	3	4	....	....	....
	NHL Totals		**234**	**59**	**76**	**135**	**69**	**71**	**140**	**54**	**25**	**0**	**8**	**401**	**14.7**	**197**	**97**	**126**	**11**		**12**	**0**	**3**	**3**	**2**	**0**	**0**	**0**

Signed as a free agent by **Montreal**, October 3, 1990. Claimed by **Florida** from **Montreal** in Expansion Draft, June 24, 1993. Traded to **Vancouver** by **Florida** for Vancouver's 3rd round choice (Oleg Kvasha) in 1996 Entry Draft and future considerations, March 20, 1996. Signed as a free agent by **Edmonton**, September 16, 1996. Signed as a free agent by **Tampa Bay**, August 18, 1998. Signed as a free agent by **Montreal**, July 23, 1999.

• BELANGER, Ken

LW – L. 6'4", 225 lbs. b: Sault Ste. Marie, Ont., 5/14/1974. Hartford's 7th, 153rd overall, in 1992.

Season	Club	League	GP	G	A	Pts	AG	AA	APts	PIM	PP	SH	GW	S	%	TGF	PGF	TGA	PGA	+/–	GP	G	A	Pts	PIM	PP	SH	GW
1990-91	Sault Ste. Marie Legionaires	OMHA	43	24	29	53	....	....	....	169	....	....	....	....	....	....	....	....	....	....	....	....	....	....	....	....	....	....
1991-92	Ottawa 67's	OHL	51	4	4	8	....	....	....	174	....	....	....	....	....	....	....	....	....	....	11	0	0	0	24	....	....	....
1992-93	Ottawa 67's	OHL	34	6	12	18	....	....	....	139	....	....	....	....	....	....	....	....	....	....	....	....	....	....	....	....	....	....
	Guelph Storm	OHL	29	10	14	24	....	....	....	86	....	....	....	....	....	....	....	....	....	....	5	2	1	3	14	....	....	....
1993-94	Guelph Storm	OHL	55	11	22	33	....	....	....	185	....	....	....	....	....	....	....	....	....	....	9	2	3	5	30	....	....	....
1994-95	St. John's Maple Leafs	AHL	47	5	5	10	....	....	....	246	....	....	....	....	....	....	....	....	....	....	4	0	0	0	30	....	....	....
	Toronto Maple Leafs	**NHL**	**3**	**0**	**0**	**0**	**0**	**0**	**0**	**9**	**0**	**0**	**0**	**1**	**0.0**	**0**	**0**	**0**	**0**	**0**	....	....	....	....	....	....	....	....
1995-96	St. John's Maple Leafs	AHL	40	16	14	30	....	....	....	222	....	....	....	....	....	....	....	....	....	....	....	....	....	....	....	....	....	....
	New York Islanders	**NHL**	**7**	**0**	**0**	**0**	**0**	**0**	**0**	**27**	**0**	**0**	**0**	**0**	**0.0**	**0**	**0**	**2**	**0**	**–2**	....	....	....	....	....	....	....	....

			REGULAR SEASON																		PLAYOFFS							
Season	Club	League	GP	G	A	Pts	AG	AA	APts	PIM	PP	SH	GW	S	%	TGF	PGF	TGA	PGA	+/–	GP	G	A	Pts	PIM	PP	SH	GW
1996-97	**New York Islanders**	**NHL**	**18**	**0**	**2**	**2**	**0**	**2**	**2**	**102**	**0**	**0**	**0**	**5**	**0.0**	**3**	**0**	**4**	**0**	**–1**	....	....	....	....	....	....	....	....
	Kentucky Thoroughblades	AHL	38	10	12	22	....	....	....	164	....	....	....	....	....	....	....	....	....	....	4	0	1	1	27	....	....	....
1997-98	**New York Islanders**	**NHL**	**37**	**3**	**1**	**4**	**4**	**1**	**5**	**101**	**0**	**0**	**1**	**10**	**30.0**	**6**	**0**	**5**	**0**	**1**	....	....	....	....	....	....	....	....
1998-99	**New York Islanders**	**NHL**	**9**	**1**	**1**	**2**	**1**	**1**	**2**	**30**	**0**	**0**	**0**	**3**	**33.3**	**3**	**0**	**2**	**0**	**1**	....	....	....	....	....	....	....	....
	Boston Bruins	**NHL**	**45**	**1**	**4**	**5**	**1**	**4**	**5**	**152**	**0**	**0**	**0**	**16**	**6.3**	**5**	**0**	**7**	**0**	**–2**	**12**	**1**	**0**	**1**	**16**	**0**	**0**	**0**
99-2000	**Boston Bruins**	**NHL**	**37**	**2**	**2**	**4**	**2**	**2**	**4**	**44**	**0**	**0**	**0**	**20**	**10.0**	**6**	**0**	**10**	**0**	**–4**	....	....	....	....	....	....	....	....
	NHL Totals		**156**	**7**	**10**	**17**	**8**	**10**	**18**	**465**	**0**	**0**	**1**	**55**	**12.7**	**23**	**0**	**30**	**0**		**12**	**1**	**0**	**1**	**16**	**0**	**0**	**0**

Traded to **Toronto** by **Hartford** for Toronto's 9th round choice (Matt Ball) in 1994 Entry Draft, March 18, 1994. Traded to **NY Islanders** by **Toronto** with Damian Rhodes for future considerations (Kirk Muller and Don Beaupre, January 23, 1996), January 23, 1996. Traded to **Boston** by **NY Islanders** for Ted Donato, November 7, 1998. • Missed majority of 1999-2000 season recovering from head injury suffered in game vs. Toronto, November 11, 1999.

• BELANGER, Roger

C – R. 6', 190 lbs. b: St. Catharines, Ont., 12/1/1965. Pittsburgh's 3rd, 16th overall, in 1984.

1981-82	Welland Maple Leafs	OMHA	25	20	21	41	....	....	....	....	....	....	....	....	....	....	....	....	....	....	....	....	....	....	....	....	....	....
1982-83	London Knights	OHL	68	17	14	31	....	....	....	53	....	....	....	....	....	....	....	....	....	....	1	0	0	0	5	....	....	....
1983-84	Kingston Canadians	OHL	67	44	46	90	....	....	....	66	....	....	....	....	....	....	....	....	....	....	....	....	....	....	....	....	....	....
1984-85	Hamilton Steelhawks	OHL	3	3	3	6	....	....	....	0	....	....	....	....	....	....	....	....	....	....	17	3	10	13	47	....	....	....
	Pittsburgh Penguins	**NHL**	**44**	**3**	**5**	**8**	**2**	**3**	**5**	**32**	**0**	**0**	**0**	**65**	**4.6**	**17**	**2**	**28**	**0**	**–13**	....	....	....	....	....	....	....	....
1985-86	Baltimore Skipjacks	AHL	69	17	21	38	....	....	....	61	....	....	....	....	....	....	....	....	....	....	....	....	....	....	....	....	....	....
1986-87	Baltimore Skipjacks	AHL	32	9	11	20	....	....	....	14	....	....	....	....	....	....	....	....	....	....	....	....	....	....	....	....	....	....
	Muskegon Lumberjacks	IHL	5	1	2	3	....	....	....	0	....	....	....	....	....	....	....	....	....	....	....	....	....	....	....	....	....	....
1987-88	Muskegon Lumberjacks	IHL	5	1	3	4	....	....	....	6	....	....	....	....	....	....	....	....	....	....	....	....	....	....	....	....	....	....
	New Haven Nighthawks	AHL	2	0	0	0	....	....	....	0	....	....	....	....	....	....	....	....	....	....	....	....	....	....	....	....	....	....
	NHL Totals		**44**	**3**	**5**	**8**	**2**	**3**	**5**	**32**	**0**	**0**	**0**	**65**	**4.6**	**17**	**2**	**28**	**0**		....	....	....	....	....	....	....	....

• BELIVEAU, Jean

Jean Arthur "Le Gros Bill" C – L. 6'3", 205 lbs. b: Trois Rivieres, Que., 8/31/1931. **HHOF**

1946-47	Victoriaville Panthers	QIHA	30	47	21	68	....	....	....	....	....	....	....	....	....	....	....	....	....	....	....	....	....	....	....	....	....	....
1947-48	Victoriaville Tigers	QJHL	42	46	21	67	....	....	....	....	....	....	....	....	....	....	....	....	....	....	....	....	....	....	....	....	....	....
1948-49	Victoriaville Tigers	QJHL	42	*48	27	75	....	....	....	54	....	....	....	....	....	....	....	....	....	....	4	4	2	6	2	....	....	....
1949-50	Quebec Citadelle	QJHL	35	36	44	80	....	....	....	47	....	....	....	....	....	....	....	....	....	....	14	*22	9	*31	15	....	....	....
1950-51	Quebec Citadelle	QJHL	46	*61	63	*124	....	....	....	120	....	....	....	....	....	....	....	....	....	....	22	*23	*31	*54	*76	....	....	....
	Quebec Aces	QMHL	1	2	1	3	....	....	....	0	....	....	....	....	....	....	....	....	....	....	....	....	....	....	....	....	....	....
	Montreal Canadiens	**NHL**	**2**	**1**	**1**	**2**	**1**	**1**	**2**	**0**	....	....	....	....	....	....	....	....	....	....	....	....	....	....	....	....	....	....
1951-52	Quebec Aces	QMHL	59	*45	38	*83	....	....	....	88	....	....	....	....	....	....	....	....	....	....	15	*14	10	24	14	....	....	....
	Quebec Aces	Alx-Cup	5	*9	2	*11	....	....	....	6	....	....	....	....	....	....	....	....	....	....	....	....	....	....	....	....	....	....
1952-53	Quebec Aces	QMHL	57	*50	39	*89	....	....	....	59	....	....	....	....	....	....	....	....	....	....	19	14	15	*29	*25	....	....	....
	Montreal Canadiens	**NHL**	**3**	**5**	**0**	**5**	**7**	**0**	**7**	**0**	....	....	....	....	....	....	....	....	....	....	....	....	....	....	....	....	....	....
1953-54	**Montreal Canadiens**	**NHL**	**44**	**13**	**21**	**34**	**18**	**26**	**44**	**22**	....	....	....	....	....	....	....	....	....	....	**10**	**2**	***8**	**10**	**4**	....	....	....
1954-55	**Montreal Canadiens**	**NHL**	**70**	**37**	**36**	**73**	**49**	**42**	**91**	**58**	....	....	....	....	....	....	....	....	....	....	**12**	**6**	**7**	**13**	**18**	....	....	....
1955-56♦	**Montreal Canadiens**	**NHL**	**70**	***47**	**41**	***88**	**66**	**49**	**115**	**143**	....	....	....	....	....	....	....	....	....	....	**10**	***12**	**7**	***19**	**22**	....	....	....
1956-57♦	**Montreal Canadiens**	**NHL**	**69**	**33**	**51**	**84**	**43**	**57**	**100**	**105**	....	....	....	....	....	....	....	....	....	....	**10**	**6**	**6**	**12**	**15**	....	....	....
1957-58♦	**Montreal Canadiens**	**NHL**	**55**	**27**	**32**	**59**	**34**	**33**	**67**	**93**	....	....	....	....	....	....	....	....	....	....	**10**	**4**	**8**	**12**	**10**	....	....	....
1958-59♦	**Montreal Canadiens**	**NHL**	**64**	***45**	**46**	**91**	**55**	**47**	**102**	**67**	....	....	....	....	....	....	....	....	....	....	**3**	**1**	**4**	**5**	**4**	....	....	....
1959-60♦	**Montreal Canadiens**	**NHL**	**60**	**34**	**40**	**74**	**40**	**39**	**79**	**57**	....	....	....	....	....	....	....	....	....	....	**8**	**5**	**2**	**7**	**6**	....	....	....
1960-61	**Montreal Canadiens**	**NHL**	**69**	**32**	***58**	**90**	**37**	**57**	**94**	**57**	....	....	....	....	....	....	....	....	....	....	**6**	**0**	**5**	**5**	**0**	....	....	....
1961-62	**Montreal Canadiens**	**NHL**	**43**	**18**	**23**	**41**	**21**	**22**	**43**	**36**	....	....	....	....	....	....	....	....	....	....	**6**	**2**	**1**	**3**	**4**	....	....	....
1962-63	**Montreal Canadiens**	**NHL**	**69**	**18**	**49**	**67**	**21**	**49**	**70**	**68**	....	....	....	....	....	....	....	....	....	....	**5**	**2**	**1**	**3**	**2**	....	....	....
1963-64	**Montreal Canadiens**	**NHL**	**68**	**28**	**50**	**78**	**35**	**53**	**88**	**42**	....	....	....	....	....	....	....	....	....	....	**5**	**2**	**0**	**2**	**18**	....	....	....
1964-65♦	**Montreal Canadiens**	**NHL**	**58**	**20**	**23**	**43**	**24**	**24**	**48**	**76**	....	....	....	....	....	....	....	....	....	....	**13**	**8**	**8**	**16**	**34**	....	....	....
1965-66♦	**Montreal Canadiens**	**NHL**	**67**	**29**	***48**	**77**	**33**	**46**	**79**	**50**	....	....	....	....	....	....	....	....	....	....	**10**	**5**	**5**	**10**	**6**	....	....	....
1966-67	**Montreal Canadiens**	**NHL**	**53**	**12**	**26**	**38**	**14**	**25**	**39**	**22**	....	....	....	....	....	....	....	....	....	....	**10**	**6**	**5**	**11**	***26**	....	....	....
1967-68♦	**Montreal Canadiens**	**NHL**	**59**	**31**	**37**	**68**	**36**	**37**	**73**	**28**	**9**	**0**	**3**	**206**	**15.0**	**86**	**27**	**32**	**0**	**27**	**10**	**7**	**4**	**11**	**6**	**3**	**0**	**1**
1968-69♦	**Montreal Canadiens**	**NHL**	**69**	**33**	**49**	**82**	**35**	**44**	**79**	**55**	**7**	**0**	**5**	**235**	**14.0**	**102**	**28**	**59**	**0**	**15**	**14**	**5**	***10**	**15**	**8**	**1**	**1**	**0**
1969-70	**Montreal Canadiens**	**NHL**	**63**	**19**	**30**	**49**	**21**	**28**	**49**	**10**	**3**	**0**	**1**	**169**	**11.2**	**61**	**28**	**32**	**0**	**1**	....	....	....	....	....	....	....	....
1970-71♦	**Montreal Canadiens**	**NHL**	**70**	**25**	**51**	**76**	**25**	**43**	**68**	**40**	**7**	**0**	**4**	**172**	**14.5**	**101**	**37**	**40**	**0**	**24**	**20**	**6**	***16**	**22**	**28**	**2**	**0**	**0**
	NHL Totals		**1125**	**507**	**712**	**1219**	**615**	**722**	**1337**	**1029**	....	....	....	....	....	....	....	....	....	....	**162**	**79**	**97**	**176**	**211**	....	....	....

QMHL First All-Star Team (1951 1953) • Won President's Cup (Scoring Champion - QMHL) (1953) • NHL First All-Star Team (1955, 1956, 1957, 1959, 1960, 1961) • Won Art Ross Trophy (1956) • Won Hart Trophy (1956, 1964) • NHL Second All-Star Team (1958, 1964, 1966, 1969) • Won Conn Smythe Trophy (1965) • Played in NHL All-Star Game (1953, 1954, 1955, 1956, 1957, 1958, 1959, 1960, 1963, 1964, 1965, 1968, 1969)

Signed as a free agent by **Montreal**, October 3, 1953. • Missed majority of 1961-62 season recovering from knee injury suffered in exhibition game vs. Spokane Flyers (OSHL), September 30, 1961.

• BELL, Bruce

Bruce W. D – L. 6'1", 190 lbs. b: Toronto, Ont., 2/15/1965. Quebec's 2nd, 53rd overall, in 1983.

1980-81	Toronto Young Nationals	MTHL	STATISTICS NOT AVAILABLE																									
1981-82	Sault Ste. Marie Greyhounds	OHL	67	11	18	29	....	....	....	63	....	....	....	....	....	....	....	....	....	....	12	0	2	2	24	....	....	....
1982-83	Sault Ste. Marie Greyhounds	OHL	5	0	2	2	....	....	....	2	....	....	....	....	....	....	....	....	....	....	....	....	....	....	....	....	....	....
	Windsor Spitfires	OHL	61	10	35	45	....	....	....	39	....	....	....	....	....	....	....	....	....	....	3	0	4	4	0	....	....	....
1983-84	Brantford Alexanders	OHL	63	7	41	48	....	....	....	55	....	....	....	....	....	....	....	....	....	....	6	0	3	3	16	....	....	....
1984-85	**Quebec Nordiques**	**NHL**	**75**	**6**	**31**	**37**	**5**	**21**	**26**	**44**	**2**	**0**	**1**	**116**	**5.2**	**110**	**23**	**60**	**5**	**32**	**16**	**2**	**2**	**4**	**21**	**1**	**0**	**0**
1985-86	**St. Louis Blues**	**NHL**	**75**	**2**	**18**	**20**	**2**	**12**	**14**	**43**	**2**	**0**	**0**	**96**	**2.1**	**99**	**33**	**67**	**3**	**2**	**14**	**0**	**2**	**2**	**13**	**0**	**0**	**0**
1986-87	**St. Louis Blues**	**NHL**	**45**	**3**	**13**	**16**	**3**	**9**	**12**	**18**	**1**	**0**	**0**	**50**	**6.0**	**48**	**12**	**33**	**0**	**3**	**4**	**1**	**1**	**2**	**7**	**0**	**0**	**0**
1987-88	**New York Rangers**	**NHL**	**13**	**1**	**2**	**3**	**1**	**1**	**2**	**8**	**0**	**0**	**1**	**12**	**8.3**	**14**	**6**	**19**	**1**	**–10**	....	....	....	....	....	....	....	....
	Colorado Rangers	IHL	65	11	34	45	....	....	....	107	....	....	....	....	....	....	....	....	....	....	4	2	3	5	0	....	....	....
1988-89	HC Bolzano	Italy	11	6	7	13	....	....	....	6	....	....	....	....	....	....	....	....	....	....	5	1	3	4	2	....	....	....
	Adirondack Red Wings	AHL	9	1	4	5	....	....	....	4	....	....	....	....	....	....	....	....	....	....	....	....	....	....	....	....	....	....
	Halifax Citadels	AHL	12	0	6	6	....	....	....	0	....	....	....	....	....	....	....	....	....	....	2	0	1	1	2	....	....	....
1989-90	**Edmonton Oilers**	**NHL**	**1**	**0**	**0**	**0**	**0**	**0**	**0**	**0**	**0**	**0**	**0**	**1**	**0.0**	**1**	**0**	**1**	**0**	**0**	....	....	....	....	....	....	....	....
	Cape Breton Oilers	AHL	52	8	26	34	....	....	....	64	....	....	....	....	....	....	....	....	....	....	6	3	4	7	2	....	....	....
1990-91	Cape Breton Oilers	AHL	14	2	5	7	....	....	....	7	....	....	....	....	....	....	....	....	....	....	....	....	....	....	....	....	....	....
	Kalamazoo Wings	IHL	48	5	21	26	....	....	....	32	....	....	....	....	....	....	....	....	....	....	3	0	0	0	8	....	....	....
1991-92	St. John's Maple Leafs	AHL	45	5	16	21	....	....	....	70	....	....	....	....	....	....	....	....	....	....	10	4	7	11	8	....	....	....
1992-93	Milwaukee Admirals	IHL	70	10	28	38	....	....	....	120	....	....	....	....	....	....	....	....	....	....	6	0	2	2	6	....	....	....
1993-94	Brantford Smoke	ColHL	51	10	38	48	....	....	....	22	....	....	....	....	....	....	....	....	....	....	....	....	....	....	....	....	....	....
	Binghamton Rangers	AHL	13	1	5	6	....	....	....	16	....	....	....	....	....	....	....	....	....	....	....	....	....	....	....	....	....	....
1994-95	Fort Worth Fire	CHL	48	12	50	62	....	....	....	77	....	....	....	....	....	....	....	....	....	....	....	....	....	....	....	....	....	....
1995-96	Durham Wasps	BH-Cup	4	0	2	2	....	....	....	8	....	....	....	....	....	....	....	....	....	....	....	....	....	....	....	....	....	....
	Durham Wasps	Britain	17	5	12	17	....	....	....	30	....	....	....	....	....	....	....	....	....	....	....	....	....	....	....	....	....	....
	Humberside Hawks	Britain	11	3	5	8	....	....	....	76	....	....	....	....	....	....	....	....	....	....	5	0	0	0	0	....	....	....
1996-97	VSV Villach	Alpenliga	42	5	30	35	....	....	....	76	....	....	....	....	....	....	....	....	....	....	....	....	....	....	....	....	....	....
	VSV Villach	Austria	6	1	4	5	....	....	....	36	....	....	....	....	....	....	....	....	....	....	....	....	....	....	....	....	....	....

Season	Club	League	GP	G	A	Pts	AG	AA	APts	PIM	PP	SH	GW	S	%	TGF	PGF	TGA	PGA	+/-	GP	G	A	Pts	PIM	PP	SH	GW
			REGULAR SEASON																		PLAYOFFS							
1997-98	Reno Renegades	WCHL	24	4	11	15	....	....	....	14	....	....	....	....	....	....	....	....	....	....	....	....	....	....	....	....	....	....
	Phoenix Mustangs	WCHL	9	1	2	3	....	....	....	8	....	....	....	....	....	....	....	....	....	....	....	....	....	....	....	....	....	....
	Houston Aeros	IHL	2	0	0	0	....	....	....	2	....	....	....	....	....	....	....	....	....	....	....	....	....	....	....	....	....	....
	Chicago Wolves	IHL	8	0	0	0	....	....	....	16	....	....	....	....	....	....	....	....	....	....	....	....	....	....	....	....	....	....
	NHL Totals		**209**	**12**	**64**	**76**	**11**	**43**	**54**	**113**	**5**	**0**	**2**	**275**	**4.4**	**272**	**74**	**180**	**9**		**34**	**3**	**5**	**8**	**41**	**1**	**0**	**0**

NHL All-Rookie Team (1985) • CHL Second All-Star Team (1995)

Traded to **St. Louis** by **Quebec** for Gilbert Delorme, October 2, 1985. Traded to **NY Rangers** by **St. Louis** with future considerations for Tony McKegney and Rob Whistle, May 28, 1987. Traded to **Quebec** by **NY Rangers** with Jari Gronstrand, Walt Poddubny and NY Rangers' 4th round choice (Eric Dubois) in 1989 Entry Draft for Jason Lafreniere and Normand Rochefort, August 1, 1988. Claimed on waivers by **Detroit** from **Quebec**, December 20, 1988. Signed as a free agent by **Edmonton**, February 1, 1990. Traded to **Minnesota** by **Edmonton** for Kari Takko, November, 22, 1990.

• Played w/ RHI's Sacramento River Rats in 1995 (22-10-10-20-36)

• BELLAND, Neil

Neil G. D – L. 5'11", 180 lbs. b: Parry Sound, Ont., 4/3/1961.

Season	Club	League	GP	G	A	Pts	AG	AA	APts	PIM	PP	SH	GW	S	%	TGF	PGF	TGA	PGA	+/-	GP	G	A	Pts	PIM	PP	SH	GW
1977-78	North Bay Trappers	NOJHA	50	25	36	61	....	....	....	30	....	....	....	....	....	....	....	....	....	....	....	....	....	....	....	....	....	....
1978-79	Kingston Canadians	OMJHL	64	8	41	49	....	....	....	14	....	....	....	....	....	....	....	....	....	....	8	3	2	5	2	....	....	....
1979-80	Kingston Canadians	OMJHL	54	7	44	51	....	....	....	44	....	....	....	....	....	....	....	....	....	....	3	0	0	0	12	....	....	....
1980-81	Kingston Canadians	OMJHL	53	28	54	82	....	....	....	54	....	....	....	....	....	....	....	....	....	....	14	5	6	11	23	....	....	....
1981-82	**Vancouver Canucks**	**NHL**	**28**	**3**	**6**	**9**	**2**	**4**	**6**	**16**	**1**	**0**	**0**	**33**	**9.1**	**27**	**9**	**19**	**0**	**–1**	**17**	**1**	**7**	**8**	**16**	**1**	**0**	**0**
	Dallas Black Hawks	CHL	27	2	20	22	....	....	....	18	....	....	....	....	....	....	....	....	....	....	....	....	....	....	....	....	....	....
1982-83	**Vancouver Canucks**	**NHL**	**14**	**2**	**4**	**6**	**2**	**3**	**5**	**4**	**0**	**0**	**0**	**13**	**15.4**	**13**	**5**	**12**	**0**	**–4**	....	....	....	....	....	....	....	....
	Fredericton Express	AHL	46	4	17	21	....	....	....	12	....	....	....	....	....	....	....	....	....	....	7	1	2	3	8	....	....	....
1983-84	**Vancouver Canucks**	**NHL**	**44**	**7**	**13**	**20**	**6**	**9**	**15**	**24**	**2**	**0**	**0**	**84**	**8.3**	**51**	**17**	**53**	**11**	**–8**	**4**	**1**	**2**	**3**	**7**	**0**	**0**	**1**
	Fredericton Express	AHL	17	3	15	18	....	....	....	2	....	....	....	....	....	....	....	....	....	....	....	....	....	....	....	....	....	....
1984-85	**Vancouver Canucks**	**NHL**	**13**	**0**	**6**	**6**	**0**	**4**	**4**	**6**	**0**	**0**	**0**	**22**	**0.0**	**14**	**5**	**14**	**1**	**–4**	....	....	....	....	....	....	....	....
	Fredericton Express	AHL	57	7	34	41	....	....	....	31	....	....	....	....	....	....	....	....	....	....	6	0	2	2	4	....	....	....
1985-86	**Vancouver Canucks**	**NHL**	**7**	**1**	**2**	**3**	**1**	**1**	**2**	**4**	**1**	**0**	**1**	**10**	**10.0**	**8**	**6**	**4**	**0**	**–2**	....	....	....	....	....	....	....	....
	Fredericton Express	AHL	36	6	18	24	....	....	....	10	....	....	....	....	....	....	....	....	....	....	6	1	6	7	2	....	....	....
1986-87	**Pittsburgh Penguins**	**NHL**	**3**	**0**	**1**	**1**	**0**	**1**	**1**	**0**	**0**	**0**	**0**	**4**	**0.0**	**1**	**1**	**0**	**0**	**0**	....	....	....	....	....	....	....	....
	Baltimore Skipjacks	AHL	61	6	18	24	....	....	....	12	....	....	....	....	....	....	....	....	....	....	....	....	....	....	....	....	....	....
1987-88	Lukko Rauma	Finland	44	8	14	22	....	....	....	36	....	....	....	....	....	....	....	....	....	....	8	0	0	0	6	....	....	....
	Hershey Bears	AHL	....	....	....	....	....	....	....	....	....	....	....	....	....	....	....	....	....	....	1	0	0	0	0	....	....	....
1988-89	IEV Innsbruck	Austria	46	17	39	56	....	....	....	....	....	....	....	....	....	....	....	....	....	....	....	....	....	....	....	....	....	....
1989-90	IEV Innsbruck	Austria	34	15	38	53	....	....	....	51	....	....	....	....	....	....	....	....	....	....	....	....	....	....	....	....	....	....
1990-91	Canada	Nat-Team	9	0	4	4	....	....	....	10	....	....	....	....	....	....	....	....	....	....	....	....	....	....	....	....	....	....
	IEV Innsbruck	Austria	17	5	7	12	....	....	....	....	....	....	....	....	....	....	....	....	....	....	....	....	....	....	....	....	....	....
1991-92	EC Graz	Austria	28	11	11	22	....	....	....	12	....	....	....	....	....	....	....	....	....	....	....	....	....	....	....	....	....	....
1992-93	EC Graz	Austria	1	0	0	0	....	....	....	....	....	....	....	....	....	....	....	....	....	....	....	....	....	....	....	....	....	....
1993-94	EC Graz	Austria	57	8	29	37	....	....	....	....	....	....	....	....	....	....	....	....	....	....	....	....	....	....	....	....	....	....
	NHL Totals		**109**	**13**	**32**	**45**	**11**	**22**	**33**	**54**	**4**	**0**	**1**	**166**	**7.8**	**114**	**43**	**102**	**12**		**21**	**2**	**9**	**11**	**23**	**1**	**0**	**1**

AHL Second All-Star Team (1985)

Signed as a free agent by **Vancouver**, October 1, 1980. Signed as a free agent by **Pittsburgh**, September 29, 1986.

• BELLOWS, Brian

LW – R. 5'11", 210 lbs. b: St. Catharines, Ont., 9/1/1964. Minnesota's 1st, 2nd overall, in 1982.

Season	Club	League	GP	G	A	Pts	AG	AA	APts	PIM	PP	SH	GW	S	%	TGF	PGF	TGA	PGA	+/-	GP	G	A	Pts	PIM	PP	SH	GW
1979-80	St. Catharines Falcons	OHA-B	44	*50	*80	*130	....	....	....	26	....	....	....	....	....	....	....	....	....	....	....	....	....	....	....	....	....	....
1980-81	Kitchener Rangers	OMJHL	66	49	67	116	....	....	....	23	....	....	....	....	....	....	....	....	....	....	16	14	13	27	13	....	....	....
	Kitchener Rangers	Mem-Cup	5	6	0	6	....	....	....	4	....	....	....	....	....	....	....	....	....	....	....	....	....	....	....	....	....	....
1981-82	Kitchener Rangers	OHL	47	45	52	97	....	....	....	23	....	....	....	....	....	....	....	....	....	....	15	16	13	29	11	....	....	....
	Kitchener Rangers	Mem-Cup	5	*6	6	12	....	....	....	4	....	....	....	....	....	....	....	....	....	....	....	....	....	....	....	....	....	....
1982-83	**Minnesota North Stars**	**NHL**	**78**	**35**	**30**	**65**	**29**	**21**	**50**	**27**	**15**	**1**	**3**	**184**	**19.0**	**99**	**44**	**74**	**7**	**–12**	**9**	**5**	**4**	**9**	**18**	**2**	**0**	**0**
1983-84	**Minnesota North Stars**	**NHL**	**78**	**41**	**42**	**83**	**33**	**29**	**62**	**66**	**14**	**5**	**5**	**236**	**17.4**	**115**	**41**	**104**	**28**	**–2**	**16**	**2**	**12**	**14**	**6**	**0**	**1**	**0**
1984-85	Canada	Can-Cup	5	0	1	1	....	....	....	0	....	....	....	....	....	....	....	....	....	....	....	....	....	....	....	....	....	....
	Minnesota North Stars	**NHL**	**78**	**26**	**36**	**62**	**21**	**24**	**45**	**72**	**8**	**1**	**3**	**211**	**12.3**	**92**	**39**	**87**	**16**	**–18**	**9**	**2**	**4**	**6**	**9**	**0**	**1**	**0**
1985-86	**Minnesota North Stars**	**NHL**	**77**	**31**	**48**	**79**	**25**	**32**	**57**	**46**	**11**	**2**	**2**	**256**	**12.1**	**112**	**36**	**78**	**18**	**16**	**5**	**5**	**0**	**5**	**16**	**3**	**0**	**0**
1986-87	**Minnesota North Stars**	**NHL**	**65**	**26**	**27**	**53**	**22**	**20**	**42**	**34**	**8**	**1**	**2**	**200**	**13.0**	**78**	**30**	**84**	**23**	**–13**	....	....	....	....	....	....	....	....
	Canada	WEC-A	10	1	3	4	....	....	....	8	....	....	....	....	....	....	....	....	....	....	....	....	....	....	....	....	....	....
1987-88	**Minnesota North Stars**	**NHL**	**77**	**40**	**41**	**81**	**34**	**29**	**63**	**81**	**21**	**1**	**4**	**283**	**14.1**	**111**	**49**	**88**	**18**	**–8**	....	....	....	....	....	....	....	....
1988-89	**Minnesota North Stars**	**NHL**	**60**	**23**	**27**	**50**	**19**	**19**	**38**	**55**	**7**	**0**	**4**	**196**	**11.7**	**75**	**40**	**55**	**6**	**–14**	**5**	**2**	**3**	**5**	**8**	**2**	**0**	**0**
	Canada	WEC-A	10	8	6	14	....	....	....	2	....	....	....	....	....	....	....	....	....	....	....	....	....	....	....	....	....	....
1989-90	**Minnesota North Stars**	**NHL**	**80**	**55**	**44**	**99**	**48**	**32**	**80**	**72**	**21**	**1**	**9**	**300**	**18.3**	**143**	**58**	**93**	**5**	**–3**	**7**	**4**	**3**	**7**	**10**	**3**	**0**	**1**
	Canada	WEC-A	8	3	6	9	....	....	....	8	....	....	....	....	....	....	....	....	....	....	....	....	....	....	....	....	....	....
1990-91	Minnesota North Stars	Fr-Tour	4	1	2	3	....	....	....	22	....	....	....	....	....	....	....	....	....	....	....	....	....	....	....	....	....	....
	Minnesota North Stars	**NHL**	**80**	**35**	**40**	**75**	**32**	**30**	**62**	**43**	**17**	**0**	**4**	**296**	**11.8**	**111**	**56**	**71**	**3**	**–13**	**23**	**10**	**19**	**29**	**30**	**6**	**0**	**1**
1991-92	**Minnesota North Stars**	**NHL**	**80**	**30**	**45**	**75**	**27**	**34**	**61**	**41**	**12**	**1**	**4**	**255**	**11.8**	**100**	**48**	**89**	**17**	**–20**	**7**	**4**	**4**	**8**	**14**	**2**	**0**	**1**
1992-93♦	**Montreal Canadiens**	**NHL**	**82**	**40**	**48**	**88**	**33**	**33**	**66**	**44**	**16**	**0**	**5**	**260**	**15.4**	**127**	**55**	**71**	**3**	**4**	**18**	**6**	**9**	**15**	**18**	**2**	**0**	**0**
1993-94	**Montreal Canadiens**	**NHL**	**77**	**33**	**38**	**71**	**31**	**30**	**61**	**36**	**13**	**0**	**2**	**251**	**13.1**	**110**	**49**	**53**	**1**	**9**	**6**	**1**	**2**	**3**	**2**	**0**	**0**	**0**
1994-95	**Montreal Canadiens**	**NHL**	**41**	**8**	**8**	**16**	**14**	**12**	**26**	**8**	**1**	**0**	**1**	**110**	**7.3**	**34**	**9**	**32**	**0**	**–7**	....	....	....	....	....	....	....	....
1995-96	**Tampa Bay Lightning**	**NHL**	**79**	**23**	**26**	**49**	**23**	**21**	**44**	**39**	**13**	**0**	**4**	**190**	**12.1**	**77**	**46**	**46**	**1**	**–14**	**6**	**2**	**0**	**2**	**4**	**0**	**0**	**1**
1996-97	**Tampa Bay Lightning**	**NHL**	**7**	**1**	**2**	**3**	**1**	**2**	**3**	**0**	**0**	**0**	**0**	**17**	**5.9**	**5**	**1**	**8**	**0**	**–4**	....	....	....	....	....	....	....	....
	Mighty Ducks of Anaheim	**NHL**	**62**	**15**	**13**	**28**	**16**	**12**	**28**	**22**	**8**	**0**	**1**	**151**	**9.9**	**44**	**19**	**37**	**1**	**–11**	**11**	**2**	**4**	**6**	**2**	**1**	**0**	**0**
1997-98	Berlin Capitals	Germany	31	15	17	32	....	....	....	18	....	....	....	....	....	....	....	....	....	....	....	....	....	....	....	....	....	....
	Washington Capitals	**NHL**	**11**	**6**	**3**	**9**	**7**	**3**	**10**	**6**	**5**	**0**	**2**	**26**	**23.1**	**9**	**5**	**7**	**0**	**–3**	**21**	**6**	**7**	**13**	**6**	**2**	**0**	**1**
1998-99	**Washington Capitals**	**NHL**	**76**	**17**	**19**	**36**	**20**	**18**	**38**	**26**	**8**	**0**	**3**	**166**	**10.2**	**56**	**22**	**46**	**0**	**–12**	....	....	....	....	....	....	....	....
	NHL Totals		**1188**	**485**	**537**	**1022**	**435**	**401**	**836**	**718**	**198**	**13**	**58**	**3588**	**13.5**	**1498**	**647**	**1123**	**147**		**143**	**51**	**71**	**122**	**143**	**23**	**2**	**5**

OHL First All-Star Team (1982) • Won George Parsons Trophy (Memorial Cup Tournament Most Sportsmanlike Player) (1982) • Named Best Forward at WEC-A (1989) • NHL Second All-Star Team (1990) • Played in NHL All-Star Game (1984, 1988, 1992)

Traded to **Montreal** by **Minnesota** for Russ Courtnall, August 31, 1992. Traded to **Tampa Bay** by **Montreal** for Marc Bureau, June 30, 1995. Traded to **Anaheim** by **Tampa Bay** for Anaheim's 6th round choice (Andrei Skopintsev) in 1997 Entry Draft, November 19, 1996. Signed as a free agent by **Washington**, March 21, 1998.

• BENDA, Jan

C – R. 6'2", 208 lbs. b: Reef, Belgium, 3/28/1972.

Season	Club	League	GP	G	A	Pts	AG	AA	APts	PIM	PP	SH	GW	S	%	TGF	PGF	TGA	PGA	+/-	GP	G	A	Pts	PIM	PP	SH	GW
1988-89	Henry Carr Crusaders	OJHL-B	18	0	3	3	....	....	....	22	....	....	....	....	....	....	....	....	....	....	....	....	....	....	....	....	....	....
1989-90	Oshawa Legionaires	OJHL-B	44	50	80	130	....	....	....	24	....	....	....	....	....	....	....	....	....	....	....	....	....	....	....	....	....	....
	Oshawa Generals	OHL	1	0	1	1	....	....	....	0	....	....	....	....	....	....	....	....	....	....	....	....	....	....	....	....	....	....
1990-91	Oshawa Generals	OHL	51	4	11	15	....	....	....	64	....	....	....	....	....	....	....	....	....	....	16	2	4	6	19	....	....	....
	Grefrather EC	Germany-3	13	0	0	0	....	....	....	2	....	....	....	....	....	....	....	....	....	....	....	....	....	....	....	....	....	....
1991-92	Oshawa Generals	OHL	61	12	23	35	....	....	....	68	....	....	....	....	....	....	....	....	....	....	7	1	1	2	12	....	....	....
1992-93	EHC Freiburg	Germany	41	6	11	17	....	....	....	49	....	....	....	....	....	....	....	....	....	....	9	3	3	6	12	....	....	....
1993-94	ECH Munich	Germany	43	16	11	27	....	....	....	67	....	....	....	....	....	....	....	....	....	....	10	3	2	5	21	....	....	....
	Germany	Olympics	8	0	1	1	....	....	....	6	....	....	....	....	....	....	....	....	....	....	....	....	....	....	....	....	....	....
	Germany	WC-A	5	0	0	0	....	....	....	24	....	....	....	....	....	....	....	....	....	....	....	....	....	....	....	....	....	....
1994-95	Binghamton Rangers	AHL	4	0	0	0	....	....	....	0	....	....	....	....	....	....	....	....	....	....	....	....	....	....	....	....	....	....
	Richmond Renegades	ECHL	62	21	39	60	....	....	....	187	....	....	....	....	....	....	....	....	....	....	17	8	5	13	50	....	....	....
1995-96	ESC Essen-West	Germany-2	2	1	0	1	....	....	....	6	....	....	....	....	....	....	....	....	....	....	....	....	....	....	....	....	....	....
	Slavia Praha	Czech-Rep	28	8	11	19	....	....	....	....	....	....	....	....	....	....	....	....	....	....	7	1	5	6	....	....	....	....
	Germany	WC-A	6	1	1	2	....	....	....	33	....	....	....	....	....	....	....	....	....	....	....	....	....	....	....	....	....	....
1996-97	Germany	W-Cup	4	2	1	3	....	....	....	0	....	....	....	....	....	....	....	....	....	....	....	....	....	....	....	....	....	....
	HC Sparta Praha	Czech-Rep	49	7	21	28	....	....	....	61	....	....	....	....	....	....	....	....	....	....	10	1	1	2	12	....	....	....
	HC Sparta Praha	EuroHL	5	1	0	1	....	....	....	4	....	....	....	....	....	....	....	....	....	....	4	0	1	1	2	....	....	....
	Germany	WC-A	8	0	2	2	....	....	....	18	....	....	....	....	....	....	....	....	....	....	....	....	....	....	....	....	....	....

			REGULAR SEASON																		PLAYOFFS							
Season	Club	League	GP	G	A	Pts	AG	AA	APts	PIM	PP	SH	GW	S	%	TGF	PGF	TGA	PGA	+/–	GP	G	A	Pts	PIM	PP	SH	GW
1997-98	HC Sparta Praha	Czech-Rep	1	0	1	1	....	....	....	4	....	....	....	....	....	....	....	....	....	....	....	....	....	....	....	....	....	....
	Washington Capitals	**NHL**	**9**	**0**	**3**	**3**	**0**	**3**	**3**	**6**	....	....	....	....	....	....	....	....	....	....	....	....	....	....	....	....	....	....
	Portland Pirates	AHL	62	25	29	54	....	....	....	90	....	....	....	....	....	....	....	....	....	....	8	0	7	7	6	....	....	....
	Germany	Olympics	4	3	0	3	....	....	....	8	....	....	....	....	....	....	....	....	....	....	....	....	....	....	....	....	....	....
1998-99	HC Assat-Pori	Finland	52	21	22	43	....	....	....	139	....	....	....	....	....	....	....	....	....	....	....	....	....	....	....	....	....	....
99-2000	Jokerit Helsinki	Finland	52	19	28	47	....	....	....	99	....	....	....	....	....	....	....	....	....	....	11	2	4	6	16	....	....	....
	NHL Totals		**9**	**0**	**3**	**3**	**0**	**3**	**3**	**6**	....	....	....	....	....	....	....	....	....	....	....	....	....	....	....	....	....	....

Signed as a free agent by **Washington**, October 1, 1997.

• BENNETT, Adam

D – R. 6'4", 206 lbs. b: Georgetown, Ont., 3/30/1971. Chicago's 1st, 6th overall, in 1989.

Season	Club	League	GP	G	A	Pts	AG	AA	APts	PIM	PP	SH	GW	S	%	TGF	PGF	TGA	PGA	+/–	GP	G	A	Pts	PIM	PP	SH	GW
1986-87	Georgetown Raiders	OMHA	STATISTICS NOT AVAILABLE																									
	Georgetown Geminis	OJHL-B	1	0	0	0	....	....	....	0	....	....	....	....	....	....	....	....	....	....	....	....	....	....	....	....	....	....
1987-88	Georgetown Geminis	OJHL-B	32	9	31	40	....	....	....	63	....	....	....	....	....	....	....	....	....	....	....	....	....	....	....	....	....	....
1988-89	Sudbury Wolves	OHL	66	7	22	29	....	....	....	133	....	....	....	....	....	....	....	....	....	....	....	....	....	....	....	....	....	....
1989-90	Sudbury Wolves	OHL	65	18	43	61	....	....	....	116	....	....	....	....	....	....	....	....	....	....	7	1	2	3	23	....	....	....
1990-91	Sudbury Wolves	OHL	54	21	29	50	....	....	....	123	....	....	....	....	....	....	....	....	....	....	5	1	2	3	11	....	....	....
	Indianapolis Ice	IHL	3	0	1	1	....	....	....	12	....	....	....	....	....	....	....	....	....	....	2	0	0	0	0	....	....	....
1991-92	**Chicago Blackhawks**	**NHL**	**5**	**0**	**0**	**0**	**0**	**0**	**0**	**12**	**0**	**0**	**0**	**6**	**0.0**	**2**	**0**	**2**	**1**	**1**	....	....	....	....	....	....	....	....
	Indianapolis Ice	IHL	59	4	10	14	....	....	....	89	....	....	....	....	....	....	....	....	....	....	....	....	....	....	....	....	....	....
1992-93	**Chicago Blackhawks**	**NHL**	**16**	**0**	**2**	**2**	**0**	**1**	**1**	**8**	**0**	**0**	**0**	**15**	**0.0**	**6**	**2**	**9**	**3**	**–2**	....	....	....	....	....	....	....	....
	Indianapolis Ice	IHL	39	8	16	24	....	....	....	69	....	....	....	....	....	....	....	....	....	....	2	0	0	0	2	....	....	....
1993-94	**Edmonton Oilers**	**NHL**	**48**	**3**	**6**	**9**	**3**	**5**	**8**	**49**	**1**	**0**	**0**	**57**	**5.3**	**36**	**7**	**42**	**5**	**–8**	....	....	....	....	....	....	....	....
	Cape Breton Oilers	AHL	7	2	5	7	....	....	....	7	....	....	....	....	....	....	....	....	....	....	....	....	....	....	....	....	....	....
1994-95	Cape Breton Oilers	AHL	10	0	3	3	....	....	....	6	....	....	....	....	....	....	....	....	....	....	....	....	....	....	....	....	....	....
1995-96	Richmond Renegades	ECHL	5	0	1	1	....	....	....	2	....	....	....	....	....	....	....	....	....	....	....	....	....	....	....	....	....	....
	NHL Totals		**69**	**3**	**8**	**11**	**3**	**6**	**9**	**69**	**1**	**0**	**0**	**78**	**3.8**	**44**	**9**	**53**	**9**		....	....	....	....	....	....	....	....

OHL Second All-Star Team (1991)

Traded to **Edmonton** by **Chicago** for Kevin Todd, October 7, 1993.

• BENNETT, Bill

William LW – L. 6'5", 235 lbs. b: Warwick, RI, 5/31/1953.

Season	Club	League	GP	G	A	Pts	AG	AA	APts	PIM	PP	SH	GW	S	%	TGF	PGF	TGA	PGA	+/–	GP	G	A	Pts	PIM	PP	SH	GW
1974-75	Waterloo Black Hawks	USHL	34	4	7	11	....	....	....	75	....	....	....	....	....	....	....	....	....	....	....	....	....	....	....	....	....	....
1975-76	Central Wisconsin Flyers	USHL	11	2	4	6	....	....	....	17	....	....	....	....	....	....	....	....	....	....	....	....	....	....	....	....	....	....
1976-77	Columbus Owls	IHL	70	27	30	57	....	....	....	131	....	....	....	....	....	....	....	....	....	....	7	1	2	3	2	....	....	....
	Rochester Americans	AHL	....	....	....	....	....	....	....	....	....	....	....	....	....	....	....	....	....	....	4	1	1	2	12	....	....	....
1977-78	Rochester Americans	AHL	67	11	19	30	....	....	....	107	....	....	....	....	....	....	....	....	....	....	6	0	4	4	14	....	....	....
1978-79	**Boston Bruins**	**NHL**	**7**	**1**	**4**	**5**	**1**	**3**	**4**	**2**	**0**	**0**	**0**	**4**	**25.0**	**6**	**0**	**2**	**0**	**4**	....	....	....	....	....	....	....	....
	Rochester Americans	AHL	72	33	38	71	....	....	....	89	....	....	....	....	....	....	....	....	....	....	....	....	....	....	....	....	....	....
1979-80	**Hartford Whalers**	**NHL**	**24**	**3**	**3**	**6**	**3**	**2**	**5**	**63**	**2**	**0**	**0**	**15**	**20.0**	**10**	**2**	**7**	**0**	**1**	....	....	....	....	....	....	....	....
	Springfield Indians	AHL	35	20	16	36	....	....	....	25	....	....	....	....	....	....	....	....	....	....	....	....	....	....	....	....	....	....
1980-81	Wichita Wind	CHL	28	6	4	10	....	....	....	39	....	....	....	....	....	....	....	....	....	....	9	2	1	3	68	....	....	....
1981-82	Hershey Bears	AHL	10	0	2	2	....	....	....	36	....	....	....	....	....	....	....	....	....	....	....	....	....	....	....	....	....	....
	Fort Wayne Komets	IHL	11	1	4	5	....	....	....	2	....	....	....	....	....	....	....	....	....	....	....	....	....	....	....	....	....	....
	NHL Totals		**31**	**4**	**7**	**11**	**4**	**5**	**9**	**65**	**2**	**0**	**0**	**19**	**21.1**	**16**	**2**	**9**	**0**		....	....	....	....	....	....	....	....

• Son of Harvey • Brother of Curt and Harvey Jr.

Signed as a free agent by **Boston**, October, 1976. Claimed by **Hartford** from **Boston** in Expansion Draft, June 13, 1979.

• BENNETT, Curt

Curt Alexander LW – L. 6'3", 195 lbs. b: Regina, Sask., 3/27/1948. St. Louis' 2nd, 16th overall, in 1968.

Season	Club	League	GP	G	A	Pts	AG	AA	APts	PIM	PP	SH	GW	S	%	TGF	PGF	TGA	PGA	+/–	GP	G	A	Pts	PIM	PP	SH	GW
1966-67	Cranston High School	Hi-School	STATISTICS NOT AVAILABLE																									
1967-68	Brown University	ECAC	20	15	28	43	....	....	....	34	....	....	....	....	....	....	....	....	....	....	....	....	....	....	....	....	....	....
1968-69	Brown University	ECAC	20	9	20	29	....	....	....	36	....	....	....	....	....	....	....	....	....	....	....	....	....	....	....	....	....	....
1969-70	Brown University	ECAC	20	26	37	63	....	....	....	22	....	....	....	....	....	....	....	....	....	....	....	....	....	....	....	....	....	....
1970-71	**St. Louis Blues**	**NHL**	**4**	**2**	**0**	**2**	**2**	**0**	**2**	**0**	**0**	**0**	**1**	**4**	**50.0**	**3**	**0**	**3**	**0**	**0**	**2**	**0**	**0**	**0**	**0**	**0**	**0**	**0**
	Kansas City Blues	CHL	63	19	23	42	....	....	....	63	....	....	....	....	....	....	....	....	....	....	....	....	....	....	....	....	....	....
1971-72	**St. Louis Blues**	**NHL**	**31**	**3**	**5**	**8**	**3**	**4**	**7**	**30**	**0**	**0**	**0**	**32**	**9.4**	**12**	**0**	**16**	**0**	**–4**	**10**	**0**	**0**	**0**	**12**	**0**	**0**	**0**
	Denver Spurs	WHL	32	13	19	32	....	....	....	52	....	....	....	....	....	....	....	....	....	....	....	....	....	....	....	....	....	....
1972-73	**New York Rangers**	**NHL**	**16**	**0**	**1**	**1**	**0**	**1**	**1**	**11**	**0**	**0**	**0**	**13**	**0.0**	**6**	**0**	**8**	**0**	**–2**	....	....	....	....	....	....	....	....
	Atlanta Flames	**NHL**	**52**	**18**	**17**	**35**	**17**	**13**	**30**	**9**	**1**	**0**	**2**	**135**	**13.3**	**44**	**7**	**58**	**8**	**–13**	....	....	....	....	....	....	....	....
1973-74	**Atlanta Flames**	**NHL**	**71**	**17**	**24**	**41**	**16**	**20**	**36**	**34**	**1**	**0**	**1**	**136**	**12.5**	**56**	**5**	**48**	**0**	**3**	**4**	**0**	**1**	**1**	**34**	**0**	**0**	**0**
1974-75	**Atlanta Flames**	**NHL**	**80**	**31**	**33**	**64**	**27**	**25**	**52**	**40**	**6**	**0**	**6**	**210**	**14.8**	**95**	**21**	**69**	**5**	**10**	....	....	....	....	....	....	....	....
1975-76	**Atlanta Flames**	**NHL**	**80**	**34**	**31**	**65**	**30**	**23**	**53**	**61**	**8**	**0**	**8**	**221**	**15.4**	**91**	**27**	**74**	**11**	**1**	**2**	**0**	**0**	**0**	**4**	**0**	**0**	**0**
1976-77	United States	Can-Cup	5	0	3	3	....	....	....	0	....	....	....	....	....	....	....	....	....	....	....	....	....	....	....	....	....	....
	Atlanta Flames	**NHL**	**76**	**22**	**25**	**47**	**20**	**19**	**39**	**36**	**5**	**1**	**5**	**183**	**12.0**	**74**	**15**	**84**	**11**	**–14**	**3**	**1**	**0**	**1**	**7**	**0**	**0**	**0**
1977-78	**Atlanta Flames**	**NHL**	**25**	**3**	**7**	**10**	**3**	**5**	**8**	**10**	**0**	**0**	**0**	**44**	**6.8**	**17**	**0**	**23**	**2**	**–4**	....	....	....	....	....	....	....	....
	St. Louis Blues	**NHL**	**50**	**7**	**17**	**24**	**6**	**13**	**19**	**54**	**1**	**0**	**1**	**92**	**7.6**	**34**	**6**	**53**	**3**	**–22**	....	....	....	....	....	....	....	....
	United States	WEC-A	10	3	0	3	....	....	....	0	....	....	....	....	....	....	....	....	....	....	....	....	....	....	....	....	....	....
1978-79	**St. Louis Blues**	**NHL**	**74**	**14**	**19**	**33**	**12**	**14**	**26**	**62**	**1**	**0**	**1**	**141**	**9.9**	**44**	**1**	**88**	**22**	**–23**	....	....	....	....	....	....	....	....
	United States	WEC-A	8	0	1	1	....	....	....	2	....	....	....	....	....	....	....	....	....	....	....	....	....	....	....	....	....	....
1979-80	**Atlanta Flames**	**NHL**	**21**	**1**	**3**	**4**	**1**	**2**	**3**	**0**	**0**	**0**	**0**	**21**	**4.8**	**6**	**0**	**15**	**3**	**–6**	....	....	....	....	....	....	....	....
	Birmingham Bulls	CHL	7	3	0	3	....	....	....	14	....	....	....	....	....	....	....	....	....	....	....	....	....	....	....	....	....	....
1980-81	Furukawa Denko	Japan	20	10	10	20	....	....	....	....	....	....	....	....	....	....	....	....	....	....	....	....	....	....	....	....	....	....
1981-82	Furukawa Denko	Japan	20	11	19	30	....	....	....	....	....	....	....	....	....	....	....	....	....	....	....	....	....	....	....	....	....	....
	NHL Totals		**580**	**152**	**182**	**334**	**137**	**139**	**276**	**347**	**23**	**1**	**25**	**1232**	**12.3**	**482**	**82**	**539**	**65**		**21**	**1**	**1**	**2**	**57**	**0**	**0**	**0**

• Son of Harvey • Brother of Harvey Jr. and Bill • ECAC Second All-Star Team (1969) • ECAC First All-Star Team (1970) • NCAA East First All-American Team (1970) • Played in NHL All-Star Game (1975, 1976)

Traded to **NY Rangers** by **St. Louis** with Peter McDuffe to complete transaction that sent Steve Durbano to St. Louis (May 24, 1972), June 7, 1972. Traded to **Atlanta** by **NY Rangers** for Ron Harris, November 28, 1972. Traded to **St. Louis** by **Atlanta** with Phil Myre and Barry Gibbs for Yves Belanger, Dick Redmond, Bob MacMillan and St. Louis' 2nd round choice (Mike Perovich) in 1979 Amateur Draft, December 12, 1977. Traded to **Atlanta** by **St. Louis** for Bobby Simpson, May 24, 1979.

• BENNETT, Harvey

C – L. 6'4", 215 lbs. b: Cranston, RI, 8/9/1952.

Season	Club	League	GP	G	A	Pts	AG	AA	APts	PIM	PP	SH	GW	S	%	TGF	PGF	TGA	PGA	+/–	GP	G	A	Pts	PIM	PP	SH	GW
1968-69	Cranston High School	Hi-School	STATISTICS NOT AVAILABLE																									
1969-70	Boston College JV Eagles	ECAC	21	7	15	22	....	....	....	17	....	....	....	....	....	....	....	....	....	....	....	....	....	....	....	....	....	....
1970-71	Boston College	ECAC	26	8	10	18	....	....	....	10	....	....	....	....	....	....	....	....	....	....	....	....	....	....	....	....	....	....
1971-72	Boston College	ECAC	29	8	9	17	....	....	....	27	....	....	....	....	....	....	....	....	....	....	....	....	....	....	....	....	....	....
1972-73	Boston College	ECAC	27	3	7	10	....	....	....	21	....	....	....	....	....	....	....	....	....	....	....	....	....	....	....	....	....	....
1973-74	Des Moines Capitols	IHL	74	31	50	81	....	....	....	93	....	....	....	....	....	....	....	....	....	....	10	3	6	9	17	....	....	....
1974-75	**Pittsburgh Penguins**	**NHL**	**7**	**0**	**0**	**0**	**0**	**0**	**0**	**0**	**0**	**0**	**0**	**2**	**0.0**	**0**	**0**	**2**	**0**	**–2**	....	....	....	....	....	....	....	....
	Hershey Bears	AHL	61	17	19	36	....	....	....	99	....	....	....	....	....	....	....	....	....	....	12	5	3	8	37	....	....	....
1975-76	**Pittsburgh Penguins**	**NHL**	**25**	**3**	**3**	**6**	**3**	**2**	**5**	**53**	**1**	**0**	**1**	**20**	**15.0**	**16**	**1**	**11**	**0**	**4**	....	....	....	....	....	....	....	....
	Washington Capitals	**NHL**	**49**	**12**	**10**	**22**	**11**	**7**	**18**	**39**	**1**	**0**	**1**	**72**	**16.7**	**43**	**7**	**63**	**0**	**–27**	....	....	....	....	....	....	....	....
1976-77	United States	Can-Cup	4	0	2	2	....	....	....	2	....	....	....	....	....	....	....	....	....	....	....	....	....	....	....	....	....	....
	Washington Capitals	**NHL**	**18**	**2**	**6**	**8**	**2**	**5**	**7**	**34**	**0**	**0**	**0**	**22**	**9.1**	**15**	**2**	**23**	**1**	**–9**	....	....	....	....	....	....	....	....
	Philadelphia Flyers	**NHL**	**51**	**12**	**8**	**20**	**11**	**6**	**17**	**60**	**0**	**0**	**2**	**53**	**22.6**	**30**	**4**	**35**	**0**	**–9**	**4**	**0**	**0**	**0**	**2**	**0**	**0**	**0**
1977-78	**Philadelphia Flyers**	**NHL**	**2**	**1**	**0**	**1**	**1**	**0**	**1**	**7**	**0**	**0**	**0**	**2**	**50.0**	**1**	**0**	**0**	**0**	**1**	....	....	....	....	....	....	....	....
	Minnesota North Stars	**NHL**	**64**	**11**	**10**	**21**	**10**	**8**	**18**	**91**	**1**	**0**	**0**	**67**	**16.4**	**27**	**5**	**54**	**0**	**–32**	....	....	....	....	....	....	....	....
	United States	WEC-A	8	3	0	3	....	....	....	19	....	....	....	....	....	....	....	....	....	....	....	....	....	....	....	....	....	....
1978-79	**St. Louis Blues**	**NHL**	**52**	**3**	**9**	**12**	**3**	**7**	**10**	**63**	**0**	**0**	**0**	**44**	**6.8**	**18**	**0**	**41**	**5**	**–18**	....	....	....	....	....	....	....	....
	Salt Lake Golden Eagles	CHL	1	0	0	0	....	....	....	0	....	....	....	....	....	....	....	....	....	....	....	....	....	....	....	....	....	....

Season	Club	League	GP	G	A	Pts	AG	AA	APts	PIM	PP	SH	GW	S	%	TGF	PGF	TGA	PGA	+/–	GP	G	A	Pts	PIM	PP	SH	GW
			REGULAR SEASON																		PLAYOFFS							
1979-80	Birmingham Bulls	CHL	69	15	22	37	....	....	....	96	....	....	....	....	....	....	....	....	....	....	4	0	2	2	2	....	....	....
1980-81	Furukawa Denko	Japan	STATISTICS NOT AVAILABLE																									
1981-82	Furukawa Denko	Japan	STATISTICS NOT AVAILABLE																									
	NHL Totals		**268**	**44**	**46**	**90**	**41**	**35**	**76**	**347**	**3**	**0**	**4**	**282**	**15.6**	**150**	**19**	**229**	**6**		**4**	**0**	**0**	**0**	**2**	**0**	**0**	**0**

• Son of Harvey Sr. • Brother of Curt and Bill

Signed as a free agent by **Pittsburgh**, June 25, 1974. Traded to **Washington** by **Pittsburgh** for Stan Gilbertson, December 16, 1975. Traded to **Philadelphia** by **Washington** for cash, November 24, 1976. Traded to **Minnesota** by **Philadelphia** for Blake Dunlop and Minnesota's 3rd round choice (Gord Salt) in 1978 Amateur Draft, October 28, 1977. Traded to **St. Louis** by **Minnesota** for St. Louis' 2nd round choice (Jali Wahlsten) in 1981 Entry Draft, August 28, 1978. Traded to **Atlanta** by **St. Louis** for cash, November 6, 1979.

• BENNETT, Rick

LW – L. 6'4", 215 lbs. b: Springfield, MA, 7/24/1967. Minnesota's 4th, 54th overall, in 1986.

Season	Club	League	GP	G	A	Pts	AG	AA	APts	PIM	PP	SH	GW	S	%	TGF	PGF	TGA	PGA	+/–	GP	G	A	Pts	PIM	PP	SH	GW
1985-86	Wilbraham Monson Academy	Hi-School	20	30	69	99	....	....	....	25	....	....	....	....	....	....	....	....	....	....	....	....	....	....	....	....	....	....
1986-87	Providence College	H-East	32	15	12	27	....	....	....	34	....	....	....	....	....	....	....	....	....	....	....	....	....	....	....	....	....	....
1987-88	Providence College	H-East	33	9	16	25	....	....	....	70	....	....	....	....	....	....	....	....	....	....	....	....	....	....	....	....	....	....
1988-89	Providence College	H-East	32	14	32	46	....	....	....	74	....	....	....	....	....	....	....	....	....	....	....	....	....	....	....	....	....	....
1989-90	Providence College	H-East	31	12	24	36	....	....	....	74	....	....	....	....	....	....	....	....	....	....	....	....	....	....	....	....	....	....
	New York Rangers	**NHL**	**6**	**1**	**0**	**1**	**1**	**0**	**1**	**5**	**0**	**0**	**0**	**6**	**16.7**	**1**	**0**	**6**	**1**	**–4**	....	....	....	....	....	....	....	....
1990-91	**New York Rangers**	**NHL**	**6**	**0**	**0**	**0**	**0**	**0**	**0**	**6**	**0**	**0**	**0**	**3**	**0.0**	**2**	**0**	**4**	**0**	**–2**	....	....	....	....	....	....	....	....
	Binghamton Rangers	AHL	71	27	32	59	....	....	....	206	....	....	....	....	....	....	....	....	....	....	10	2	1	3	27	....	....	....
1991-92	**New York Rangers**	**NHL**	**3**	**0**	**1**	**1**	**0**	**1**	**1**	**2**	**0**	**0**	**0**	**2**	**0.0**	**1**	**0**	**1**	**0**	**0**	....	....	....	....	....	....	....	....
	Binghamton Rangers	AHL	69	19	23	42	....	....	....	112	....	....	....	....	....	....	....	....	....	....	11	0	1	1	23	....	....	....
1992-93	Binghamton Rangers	AHL	76	15	22	37	....	....	....	114	....	....	....	....	....	....	....	....	....	....	10	0	0	0	30	....	....	....
1993-94	Springfield Indians	AHL	67	9	19	28	....	....	....	82	....	....	....	....	....	....	....	....	....	....	6	1	0	1	31	....	....	....
1994-95	Springfield Falcons	AHL	34	3	5	8	....	....	....	74	....	....	....	....	....	....	....	....	....	....	....	....	....	....	....	....	....	....
	Hershey Bears	AHL	30	3	4	7	....	....	....	40	....	....	....	....	....	....	....	....	....	....	3	2	1	3	14	....	....	....
1995-96	Jacksonville Lizard Kings	ECHL	67	28	34	62	....	....	....	182	....	....	....	....	....	....	....	....	....	....	18	5	10	15	30	....	....	....
	Cincinnati Cyclones	IHL	4	0	1	1	....	....	....	0	....	....	....	....	....	....	....	....	....	....	1	0	0	0	2	....	....	....
1996-97	Jacksonville Lizard Kings	ECHL	64	23	33	56	....	....	....	120	....	....	....	....	....	....	....	....	....	....	....	....	....	....	....	....	....	....
	Albany River Rats	AHL	4	0	0	0	....	....	....	0	....	....	....	....	....	....	....	....	....	....	....	....	....	....	....	....	....	....
1997-98	Pee Dee Pride	ECHL	68	12	30	42	....	....	....	137	....	....	....	....	....	....	....	....	....	....	8	3	2	5	14	....	....	....
1998-99	Pee Dee Pride	ECHL	66	21	18	39	....	....	....	103	....	....	....	....	....	....	....	....	....	....	11	3	1	4	33	....	....	....
	NHL Totals		**15**	**1**	**1**	**2**	**1**	**1**	**2**	**13**	**0**	**0**	**0**	**11**	**9.1**	**4**	**0**	**11**	**1**		....	....	....	....	....	....	....	....

Hockey East Second All-Star Team (1990)

Rights traded to **NY Rangers** by **Minnesota** with Brian Lawton and Igor Liba for Paul Jerrard, Mark Tinordi, Mike Sullivan, the rights to Bret Barnett and LA Kings' 3rd round choice (previously acquired, Minnesota selected Murray Garbutt) in 1989 Entry Draft, October 11, 1988. • • Played w/ RHI's New Jersey R@R in 1996 (28-2-20-22-46) and Orlanda Jackals in 1997 (22-6-17-23-24).

• BENNING, Brian

Brian A. D – L. 6', 195 lbs. b: Edmonton, Alta., 6/10/1966. St. Louis' 1st, 26th overall, in 1984.

Season	Club	League	GP	G	A	Pts	AG	AA	APts	PIM	PP	SH	GW	S	%	TGF	PGF	TGA	PGA	+/–	GP	G	A	Pts	PIM	PP	SH	GW
1982-83	St. Albert Saints	AJHL	57	8	38	46	....	....	....	81	....	....	....	....	....	....	....	....	....	....	....	....	....	....	....	....	....	....
1983-84	Portland Winter Hawks	WHL	38	6	41	47	....	....	....	108	....	....	....	....	....	....	....	....	....	....	....	....	....	....	....	....	....	....
1984-85	Kamloops Blazers	WHL	17	3	18	21	....	....	....	26	....	....	....	....	....	....	....	....	....	....	....	....	....	....	....	....	....	....
	St. Louis Blues	**NHL**	**4**	**0**	**2**	**2**	**0**	**1**	**1**	**0**	**0**	**0**	**0**	**1**	**0.0**	**2**	**2**	**6**	**0**	**–6**	....	....	....	....	....	....	....	....
1985-86	Canada	Nat-Team	60	6	13	19	....	....	....	43	....	....	....	....	....	....	....	....	....	....	....	....	....	....	....	....	....	....
	St. Louis Blues	**NHL**	....	....	....	....	....	....	....	....	**0**	**0**	**0**	**0**	**0.0**	**0**	**0**	**0**	**0**	**0**	**6**	**1**	**2**	**3**	**13**	**1**	**0**	**0**
1986-87	**St. Louis Blues**	**NHL**	**78**	**13**	**36**	**49**	**11**	**26**	**37**	**110**	**7**	**0**	**2**	**144**	**9.0**	**143**	**57**	**114**	**30**	**2**	**6**	**0**	**4**	**4**	**9**	**0**	**0**	**0**
1987-88	**St. Louis Blues**	**NHL**	**77**	**8**	**29**	**37**	**7**	**21**	**28**	**107**	**5**	**0**	**5**	**130**	**6.2**	**126**	**51**	**105**	**25**	**–5**	**10**	**1**	**6**	**7**	**25**	**1**	**0**	**0**
1988-89	**St. Louis Blues**	**NHL**	**66**	**8**	**26**	**34**	**7**	**18**	**25**	**102**	**3**	**0**	**0**	**91**	**8.8**	**94**	**44**	**76**	**3**	**–23**	**7**	**1**	**1**	**2**	**11**	**1**	**0**	**0**
1989-90	**St. Louis Blues**	**NHL**	**7**	**1**	**1**	**2**	**1**	**1**	**2**	**2**	**0**	**0**	**0**	**8**	**12.5**	**8**	**3**	**8**	**0**	**–3**								
	Los Angeles Kings	**NHL**	**48**	**5**	**18**	**23**	**4**	**13**	**17**	**104**	**3**	**0**	**0**	**114**	**4.4**	**78**	**21**	**62**	**6**	**1**	**7**	**0**	**2**	**2**	**10**	**0**	**0**	**0**
1990-91	**Los Angeles Kings**	**NHL**	**61**	**7**	**24**	**31**	**6**	**18**	**24**	**127**	**2**	**0**	**1**	**120**	**5.8**	**82**	**26**	**46**	**2**	**12**	**12**	**0**	**5**	**5**	**6**	**0**	**0**	**0**
1991-92	**Los Angeles Kings**	**NHL**	**53**	**2**	**30**	**32**	**2**	**23**	**25**	**99**	**0**	**0**	**0**	**102**	**2.0**	**83**	**29**	**58**	**8**	**4**	....	....	....	....	....	....	....	....
	Philadelphia Flyers	**NHL**	**22**	**2**	**12**	**14**	**2**	**9**	**11**	**35**	**2**	**0**	**0**	**50**	**4.0**	**27**	**12**	**31**	**7**	**–9**	....	....	....	....	....	....	....	....
1992-93	**Philadelphia Flyers**	**NHL**	**37**	**9**	**17**	**26**	**7**	**12**	**19**	**93**	**6**	**0**	**0**	**87**	**10.3**	**64**	**23**	**52**	**11**	**0**	....	....	....	....	....	....	....	....
	Edmonton Oilers	**NHL**	**18**	**1**	**7**	**8**	**1**	**5**	**6**	**59**	**0**	**0**	**0**	**28**	**3.6**	**19**	**4**	**22**	**6**	**–1**	....	....	....	....	....	....	....	....
	Canada	WC-A	8	1	2	3	....	....	....	0	....	....	....	....	....	....	....	....	....	....	....	....	....	....	....	....	....	....
1993-94	**Florida Panthers**	**NHL**	**73**	**6**	**24**	**30**	**6**	**19**	**25**	**107**	**2**	**0**	**0**	**112**	**5.4**	**81**	**27**	**76**	**15**	**–7**	....	....	....	....	....	....	....	....
1994-95	**Florida Panthers**	**NHL**	**24**	**1**	**7**	**8**	**2**	**10**	**12**	**18**	**1**	**0**	**0**	**26**	**3.8**	**20**	**5**	**25**	**4**	**–6**	....	....	....	....	....	....	....	....
	NHL Totals		**568**	**63**	**233**	**296**	**56**	**176**	**232**	**963**	**31**	**0**	**8**	**1013**	**6.2**	**827**	**304**	**681**	**117**		**48**	**3**	**20**	**23**	**74**	**3**	**0**	**0**

• Brother of Jim • NHL All-Rookie Team (1987)

Traded to **LA Kings** by **St. Louis** for LA Kings' 3rd round choice (Kyle Reeves) in 1991 Entry Draft, November 10, 1989. Traded to **Pittsburgh** by **LA Kings** with Jeff Chychrun and LA Kings' 1st round choice (later traded to Philadelphia — Philadelphia selected Jason Bowen) in 1992 Entry Draft for Paul Coffey, February 19, 1992. Traded to **Philadelphia** by **Pittsburgh** with Mark Recchi and LA Kings' 1st round choice (previously acquired, Philadelphia selected Jason Bowen) in 1992 Entry Draft for Rick Tocchet, Kjell Samuelsson, Ken Wregget and Philadelphia's 3rd round choice (Dave Roche) in 1993 Entry Draft, February 19, 1992. Traded to **Edmonton** by **Philadelphia** for Greg Hawgood and Josef Beranek, January 16, 1993. Signed as a free agent by **Florida**, July 13, 1993.

• BENNING, Jim

James Elmer D – L. 6', 180 lbs. b: Edmonton, Alta., 4/29/1963. Toronto's 1st, 6th overall, in 1981.

Season	Club	League	GP	G	A	Pts	AG	AA	APts	PIM	PP	SH	GW	S	%	TGF	PGF	TGA	PGA	+/–	GP	G	A	Pts	PIM	PP	SH	GW
1978-79	Fort Saskatchewan Traders	AJHL	45	14	57	71	....	....	....	10	....	....	....	....	....	....	....	....	....	....	....	....	....	....	....	....	....	....
	Portland Winter Hawks	WHL	....	....	....	....	....	....	....	....	....	....	....	....	....	....	....	....	....	....	3	0	0	0	0	....	....	....
1979-80	Portland Winter Hawks	WHL	71	11	60	71	....	....	....	42	....	....	....	....	....	....	....	....	....	....	8	3	9	12	6	....	....	....
1980-81	Portland Winter Hawks	WHL	72	28	*111	139	....	....	....	61	....	....	....	....	....	....	....	....	....	....	9	1	5	6	16	....	....	....
1981-82	**Toronto Maple Leafs**	**NHL**	**74**	**7**	**24**	**31**	**6**	**16**	**22**	**46**	**2**	**0**	**0**	**90**	**7.8**	**82**	**25**	**91**	**7**	**–27**	....	....	....	....	....	....	....	....
1982-83	**Toronto Maple Leafs**	**NHL**	**74**	**5**	**17**	**22**	**4**	**12**	**16**	**47**	**3**	**0**	**0**	**68**	**7.4**	**78**	**29**	**58**	**1**	**–8**	**4**	**1**	**1**	**2**	**2**	**0**	**0**	**0**
1983-84	**Toronto Maple Leafs**	**NHL**	**79**	**12**	**39**	**51**	**10**	**27**	**37**	**66**	**6**	**0**	**1**	**136**	**8.8**	**139**	**54**	**109**	**20**	**–4**	....	....	....	....	....	....	....	....
1984-85	**Toronto Maple Leafs**	**NHL**	**80**	**9**	**35**	**44**	**7**	**24**	**31**	**55**	**6**	**0**	**2**	**160**	**5.6**	**110**	**52**	**101**	**4**	**–39**	....	....	....	....	....	....	....	....
1985-86	**Toronto Maple Leafs**	**NHL**	**52**	**4**	**21**	**25**	**3**	**14**	**17**	**71**	**2**	**0**	**0**	**76**	**5.3**	**78**	**23**	**64**	**5**	**–4**	....	....	....	....	....	....	....	....
1986-87	**Toronto Maple Leafs**	**NHL**	**5**	**0**	**0**	**0**	**0**	**0**	**0**	**4**	**0**	**0**	**0**	**3**	**0.0**	**5**	**2**	**3**	**0**	**0**	....	....	....	....	....	....	....	....
	Newmarket Saints	AHL	10	1	5	6	....	....	....	0	....	....	....	....	....	....	....	....	....	....	....	....	....	....	....	....	....	....
	Vancouver Canucks	**NHL**	**54**	**2**	**11**	**13**	**2**	**8**	**10**	**40**	**0**	**0**	**1**	**60**	**3.3**	**57**	**11**	**40**	**3**	**9**	....	....	....	....	....	....	....	....
1987-88	**Vancouver Canucks**	**NHL**	**77**	**7**	**26**	**33**	**6**	**19**	**25**	**58**	**1**	**1**	**1**	**102**	**6.9**	**97**	**29**	**92**	**24**	**0**	....	....	....	....	....	....	....	....
1988-89	**Vancouver Canucks**	**NHL**	**65**	**3**	**9**	**12**	**3**	**6**	**9**	**48**	**1**	**0**	**0**	**55**	**5.5**	**45**	**10**	**43**	**4**	**–4**	**3**	**0**	**0**	**0**	**0**	**0**	**0**	**0**
1989-90	**Vancouver Canucks**	**NHL**	**45**	**3**	**9**	**12**	**3**	**6**	**9**	**26**	**0**	**1**	**0**	**49**	**6.1**	**42**	**6**	**41**	**9**	**4**	....	....	....	....	....	....	....	....
1990-91	Milwaukee Admirals	IHL	66	1	31	32	....	....	....	75	....	....	....	....	....	....	....	....	....	....	6	0	0	0	0	....	....	....
1991-92	HC Varese	Alpenliga	18	3	13	16	....	....	....	30	....	....	....	....	....	....	....	....	....	....	....	....	....	....	....	....	....	....
	HC Varese	Italy	18	0	12	12	....	....	....	14	....	....	....	....	....	....	....	....	....	....	7	0	2	2	50	....	....	....
	NHL Totals		**605**	**52**	**191**	**243**	**44**	**132**	**176**	**461**	**21**	**2**	**5**	**799**	**6.5**	**733**	**241**	**642**	**77**		**7**	**1**	**1**	**2**	**2**	**0**	**0**	**0**

• Brother of Brian • WHL First All-Star Team (1981)

Traded to **Vancouver** by **Toronto** with Dan Hodgson for Rick Lanz, December 2, 1986.

• BENYSEK, Ladislav

D – L. 6'2", 190 lbs. b: Olomouc, Czech., 3/24/1975. Edmonton's 16th, 266th overall, in 1994.

Season	Club	League	GP	G	A	Pts	AG	AA	APts	PIM	PP	SH	GW	S	%	TGF	PGF	TGA	PGA	+/–	GP	G	A	Pts	PIM	PP	SH	GW
1993-94	HC Olomouc	Czech-Jr.	STATISTICS NOT AVAILABLE																									
1994-95	Cape Breton Oilers	AHL	58	2	7	9	....	....	....	54	....	....	....	....	....	....	....	....	....	....	....	....	....	....	....	....	....	....
1995-96	HC Olomouc	Czech-Rep	33	1	4	5	....	....	....	....	....	....	....	....	....	....	....	....	....	....	4	0	0	0	....	....	....	....
1996-97	HC Olomouc	Czech-Rep	14	0	1	1	....	....	....	8	....	....	....	....	....	....	....	....	....	....	....	....	....	....	....	....	....	....
	HC Sparta Praha	Czech-Rep	36	5	5	10	....	....	....	28	....	....	....	....	....	....	....	....	....	....	5	0	1	1	2	....	....	....
	HC Sparta Praha	EuroHL	3	0	0	0	....	....	....	4	....	....	....	....	....	....	....	....	....	....	4	0	0	0	0	....	....	....
	Czech-Republic	WC-A	9	0	1	1	....	....	....	6	....	....	....	....	....	....	....	....	....	....	....	....	....	....	....	....	....	....

			REGULAR SEASON																		PLAYOFFS							
Season	**Club**	**League**	**GP**	**G**	**A**	**Pts**	**AG**	**AA**	**APts**	**PIM**	**PP**	**SH**	**GW**	**S**	**%**	**TGF**	**PGF**	**TGA**	**PGA**	**+/–**	**GP**	**G**	**A**	**Pts**	**PIM**	**PP**	**SH**	**GW**
1997-98	HC Sparta Praha	Czech-Rep	1	0	0	0	....	....	....	0	....	....	....	....	....	....	....	....	....	....	....	....	....	....	....	....	....	....
	Edmonton Oilers	**NHL**	**2**	**0**	**0**	**0**	**0**	**0**	**0**	**0**	....	....	....	....	....	....	....	....	....	....	....	....	....	....	....	....	....	....
	Hamilton Bulldogs	AHL	53	2	14	16	....	....	....	29	....	....	....	....	....	....	....	....	....	....	9	1	1	2	2	....	....	....
1998-99	HC Sparta Praha	Czech-Rep	52	8	11	19	....	....	....	47	....	....	....	....	....	....	....	....	....	....	8	0	1	1	....	....	....	....
	HC Sparta Praha	EuroHL	7	0	0	0	....	....	....	2	....	....	....	....	....	....	....	....	....	....	2	0	0	0	0	....	....	....
	Czech Rebublic	WC-A	12	0	0	0	....	....	....	0	....	....	....	....	....	....	....	....	....	....	....	....	....	....	....	....	....	....
99-2000	HC Sparta Praha	Czech-Rep	51	1	5	6	....	....	....	45	....	....	....	....	....	....	....	....	....	....	9	0	0	0	4	....	....	....
	HC Sparta Praha	EuroHL	5	1	1	2	....	....	....	6	....	....	....	....	....	....	....	....	....	....	4	0	0	0	4	....	....	....
	Czech Republic	WC-A	9	1	0	1	....	....	....	2	....	....	....	....	....	....	....	....	....	....	....	....	....	....	....	....	....	....
	NHL Totals		**2**	**0**	**0**	**0**	**0**	**0**	**0**	**0**	....	....	....	....	....	....	....	....	....		....	....	....	....	....	....	....	....

Selected by **Minnesota** from **Anaheim** in Expansion Draft, June 23, 2000.

• BERALDO, Paul

RW – R. 5'11", 175 lbs. b: Hamilton, Ont., 10/5/1967. Boston's 6th, 139th overall, in 1986.

Season	**Club**	**League**	**GP**	**G**	**A**	**Pts**	**AG**	**AA**	**APts**	**PIM**	**PP**	**SH**	**GW**	**S**	**%**	**TGF**	**PGF**	**TGA**	**PGA**	**+/–**	**GP**	**G**	**A**	**Pts**	**PIM**	**PP**	**SH**	**GW**
1983-84	Stoney Creek Warriors	OJHL-C	35	18	23	41	....	....	....	27	....	....	....	....	....	....	....	....	....	....	....	....	....	....	....	....	....	....
1984-85	Grimsby Peach Kings	OJHL-B	25	9	4	13	....	....	....	24	....	....	....	....	....	....	....	....	....	....	....	....	....	....	....	....	....	....
	Dixie Beehives	OJHL	2	0	0	0	....	....	....	2	....	....	....	....	....	....	....	....	....	....	....	....	....	....	....	....	....	....
1985-86	Sault Ste. Marie Greyhounds	OHL	61	15	13	28	....	....	....	48	....	....	....	....	....	....	....	....	....	....	....	....	....	....	....	....	....	....
1986-87	Sault Ste. Marie Greyhounds	OHL	63	39	51	90	....	....	....	117	....	....	....	....	....	....	....	....	....	....	4	3	2	5	6	....	....	....
1987-88	**Boston Bruins**	**NHL**	**3**	**0**	**0**	**0**	**0**	**0**	**0**	**0**	**0**	**0**	**0**	**1**	**0.0**	**1**	**0**	**4**	**0**	**–3**	....	....	....	....	....	....	....	....
	Maine Mariners	AHL	62	22	15	37	....	....	....	112	....	....	....	....	....	....	....	....	....	....	2	0	0	0	19	....	....	....
1988-89	**Boston Bruins**	**NHL**	**7**	**0**	**0**	**0**	**0**	**0**	**0**	**4**	**0**	**0**	**0**	**1**	**0.0**	**0**	**0**	**2**	**0**	**–2**	....	....	....	....	....	....	....	....
	Maine Mariners	AHL	73	25	28	53	....	....	....	134	....	....	....	....	....	....	....	....	....	....	....	....	....	....	....	....	....	....
1989-90	Canada	Nat-Team	9	2	8	10	....	....	....	20	....	....	....	....	....	....	....	....	....	....	....	....	....	....	....	....	....	....
	Maine Mariners	AHL	51	14	27	41	....	....	....	31	....	....	....	....	....	....	....	....	....	....	....	....	....	....	....	....	....	....
1990-91	HC Milano Saima	Italy	34	34	27	61	....	....	....	77	....	....	....	....	....	....	....	....	....	....	10	12	12	24	13	....	....	....
1991-92	HC Milano Saima	Alpenliga	10	5	7	12	....	....	....	33	....	....	....	....	....	....	....	....	....	....	....	....	....	....	....	....	....	....
	HC Milano Saima	Italy	16	23	13	36	....	....	....	24	....	....	....	....	....	....	....	....	....	....	12	10	5	15	11	....	....	....
1992-93	HC Milano Devils	Alpenliga	30	25	19	44	....	....	....	47	....	....	....	....	....	....	....	....	....	....	....	....	....	....	....	....	....	....
	HC Milano Devils	Italy	16	16	11	27	....	....	....	10	....	....	....	....	....	....	....	....	....	....	11	8	3	11	13	....	....	....
1993-94	BSC Preussen Berlin	Germany	12	6	10	16	....	....	....	14	....	....	....	....	....	....	....	....	....	....	2	1	1	2	0	....	....	....
	HC Milano Devils	Italy	....	....	....	....	....	....	....	....	....	....	....	....	....	....	....	....	....	....	3	0	2	2	10	....	....	....
	Italy	WC-A	6	2	1	3	....	....	....	6	....	....	....	....	....	....	....	....	....	....	....	....	....	....	....	....	....	....
1994-95	HC Milano Devils	Italy	1	0	0	0	....	....	....	0	....	....	....	....	....	....	....	....	....	....	....	....	....	....	....	....	....	....
	TuS Geretsried	Germany-2	18	28	30	58	....	....	....	56	....	....	....	....	....	....	....	....	....	....	....	....	....	....	....	....	....	....
	Brantford Smoke	ColHL	22	7	17	24	....	....	....	22	....	....	....	....	....	....	....	....	....	....	....	....	....	....	....	....	....	....
1995-96	Ratinger Lowen	Germany	16	14	7	21	....	....	....	56	....	....	....	....	....	....	....	....	....	....	....	....	....	....	....	....	....	....
1996-97	Adler Mannheim	Germany	50	23	25	48	....	....	....	71	....	....	....	....	....	....	....	....	....	....	9	3	2	5	22	....	....	....
1997-98	Kassel Huskies	Germany	18	8	8	16	....	....	....	18	....	....	....	....	....	....	....	....	....	....	....	....	....	....	....	....	....	....
	Star Bulls Rosenheim	Germany	43	5	5	10	....	....	....	12	....	....	....	....	....	....	....	....	....	....	....	....	....	....	....	....	....	....
1998-99	HC Fribourg-Gotteron	Switz.	21	5	12	17	....	....	....	83	....	....	....	....	....	....	....	....	....	....	....	....	....	....	....	....	....	....
	HC Fribourg-Gotteron	EuroHL	2	1	0	1	....	....	....	2	....	....	....	....	....	....	....	....	....	....	....	....	....	....	....	....	....	....
	NHL Totals		**10**	**0**	**0**	**0**	**0**	**0**	**0**	**4**	**0**	**0**	**0**	**2**	**0.0**	**1**	**0**	**6**	**0**		....	....	....	....	....	....	....	....

• Played w/ RHI's Buffalo Stampede in 1995 (9-11-7-18-3).

• BERANEK, Josef

LW/C – L. 6'2", 195 lbs. b: Litvinov, Czech., 10/25/1969. Edmonton's 3rd, 78th overall, in 1989.

Season	**Club**	**League**	**GP**	**G**	**A**	**Pts**	**AG**	**AA**	**APts**	**PIM**	**PP**	**SH**	**GW**	**S**	**%**	**TGF**	**PGF**	**TGA**	**PGA**	**+/–**	**GP**	**G**	**A**	**Pts**	**PIM**	**PP**	**SH**	**GW**
1987-88	CHZ Litvinov	Czech.	14	7	4	11	....	....	....	12	....	....	....	....	....	....	....	....	....	....	....	....	....	....	....	....	....	....
1988-89	CHZ Litvinov	Czech.	32	18	10	28	....	....	....	47	....	....	....	....	....	....	....	....	....	....	....	....	....	....	....	....	....	....
	Czechoslovakia	WJC-A	7	4	9	13	....	....	....	6	....	....	....	....	....	....	....	....	....	....	....	....	....	....	....	....	....	....
1989-90	Dukla Trencin	Czech.	40	16	21	37	....	....	....	....	....	....	....	....	....	....	....	....	....	....	9	3	2	5	....	....	....	....
1990-91	CHZ Litvinov	Czech.	58	29	31	60	....	....	....	98	....	....	....	....	....	....	....	....	....	....	....	....	....	....	....	....	....	....
	Czechoslovakia	WEC-A	8	2	2	4	....	....	....	6	....	....	....	....	....	....	....	....	....	....	....	....	....	....	....	....	....	....
1991-92	Czechoslovakia	Can-Cup	5	1	1	2	....	....	....	4	....	....	....	....	....	....	....	....	....	....	....	....	....	....	....	....	....	....
	Edmonton Oilers	**NHL**	**58**	**12**	**16**	**28**	**11**	**12**	**23**	**18**	**0**	**0**	**1**	**79**	**15.2**	**34**	**4**	**32**	**0**	**–2**	**12**	**2**	**1**	**3**	**0**	**1**	**0**	**1**
1992-93	**Edmonton Oilers**	**NHL**	**26**	**2**	**6**	**8**	**2**	**4**	**6**	**28**	**0**	**0**	**0**	**44**	**4.5**	**11**	**2**	**21**	**5**	**–7**	....	....	....	....	....	....	....	....
	Cape Breton Oilers	AHL	6	1	2	3	....	....	....	8	....	....	....	....	....	....	....	....	....	....	....	....	....	....	....	....	....	....
	Philadelphia Flyers	**NHL**	**40**	**13**	**12**	**25**	**11**	**8**	**19**	**50**	**1**	**0**	**0**	**86**	**15.1**	**36**	**5**	**32**	**0**	**–1**	....	....	....	....	....	....	....	....
	Czech-Republic	WC-A	8	3	3	6	....	....	....	22	....	....	....	....	....	....	....	....	....	....	....	....	....	....	....	....	....	....
1993-94	**Philadelphia Flyers**	**NHL**	**80**	**28**	**21**	**49**	**26**	**16**	**42**	**85**	**6**	**0**	**2**	**182**	**15.4**	**62**	**13**	**51**	**0**	**–2**	....	....	....	....	....	....	....	....
	Czech-Republic	WC-A	6	1	2	3	....	....	....	0	....	....	....	....	....	....	....	....	....	....	....	....	....	....	....	....	....	....
1994-95	HC Petra Vsetin	Czech-Rep	16	7	7	14	....	....	....	26	....	....	....	....	....	....	....	....	....	....	....	....	....	....	....	....	....	....
	Philadelphia Flyers	**NHL**	**14**	**5**	**5**	**10**	**9**	**7**	**16**	**2**	**1**	**0**	**0**	**39**	**12.8**	**13**	**4**	**6**	**0**	**3**	....	....	....	....	....	....	....	....
	Vancouver Canucks	**NHL**	**37**	**8**	**13**	**21**	**14**	**19**	**33**	**28**	**2**	**0**	**0**	**95**	**8.4**	**31**	**10**	**31**	**0**	**–10**	**11**	**1**	**1**	**2**	**12**	**0**	**0**	**0**
1995-96	**Vancouver Canucks**	**NHL**	**61**	**6**	**14**	**20**	**6**	**11**	**17**	**60**	**0**	**0**	**1**	**131**	**4.6**	**29**	**3**	**55**	**18**	**–11**	**3**	**2**	**1**	**3**	**0**	**0**	**0**	**0**
1996-97	Czech-Republic	W-Cup	3	0	0	0	....	....	....	4	....	....	....	....	....	....	....	....	....	....	....	....	....	....	....	....	....	....
	HC Petra Vsetin	Czech-Rep	39	19	24	43	....	....	....	115	....	....	....	....	....	....	....	....	....	....	3	3	2	5	4	....	....	....
	Pittsburgh Penguins	**NHL**	**8**	**3**	**1**	**4**	**3**	**1**	**4**	**4**	**1**	**0**	**0**	**15**	**20.0**	**5**	**1**	**7**	**2**	**–1**	**5**	**0**	**0**	**0**	**2**	**0**	**0**	**0**
1997-98	HC Petra Vsetin	Czech-Rep	45	24	27	51	....	....	....	92	....	....	....	....	....	....	....	....	....	....	10	2	8	10	14	....	....	....
	HC Petra Vsetin	EuroHL	8	5	4	9	....	....	....	10	....	....	....	....	....	....	....	....	....	....	....	....	....	....	....	....	....	....
	Czech-Republic	Olympics	6	1	0	1	....	....	....	4	....	....	....	....	....	....	....	....	....	....	....	....	....	....	....	....	....	....
	Czech-Republic	WC-A	9	0	3	3	....	....	....	12	....	....	....	....	....	....	....	....	....	....	....	....	....	....	....	....	....	....
1998-99	**Edmonton Oilers**	**NHL**	**66**	**19**	**30**	**49**	**22**	**29**	**51**	**23**	**7**	**0**	**2**	**160**	**11.9**	**68**	**25**	**37**	**0**	**6**	**2**	**0**	**0**	**0**	**4**	**0**	**0**	**0**
99-2000	**Edmonton Oilers**	**NHL**	**58**	**9**	**8**	**17**	**10**	**7**	**17**	**39**	**3**	**0**	**1**	**107**	**8.4**	**34**	**14**	**26**	**0**	**–6**	....	....	....	....	....	....	....	....
	Pittsburgh Penguins	**NHL**	**13**	**4**	**4**	**8**	**4**	**4**	**8**	**18**	**1**	**0**	**0**	**32**	**12.5**	**12**	**6**	**13**	**1**	**–6**	**11**	**0**	**3**	**3**	**4**	**0**	**0**	**0**
	NHL Totals		**461**	**109**	**130**	**239**	**118**	**118**	**236**	**355**	**22**	**0**	**7**	**970**	**11.2**	**335**	**87**	**311**	**26**		**44**	**5**	**6**	**11**	**22**	**1**	**0**	**1**

Traded to **Philadelphia** by **Edmonton** with Greg Hawgood for Brian Benning, January 16, 1993. Traded to **Vancouver** by **Philadelphia** for Shawn Antoski, February 15, 1995. Traded to **Pittsburgh** by **Vancouver** for future considerations, March 18, 1997. Traded to **Edmonton** by **Pittsburgh** for Bobby Dollas and Tony Hrkac, June 16, 1998. Traded to **Pittsburgh** by **Edmonton** for German Titov, March 14, 2000.

• BERARD, Bryan

"B.B." D – L. 6'1", 190 lbs. b: Woonsocket, RI, 3/5/1977. Ottawa's 1st, 1st overall, in 1995.

Season	**Club**	**League**	**GP**	**G**	**A**	**Pts**	**AG**	**AA**	**APts**	**PIM**	**PP**	**SH**	**GW**	**S**	**%**	**TGF**	**PGF**	**TGA**	**PGA**	**+/–**	**GP**	**G**	**A**	**Pts**	**PIM**	**PP**	**SH**	**GW**
1990-91	Mass Bay Chiefs	MAAA	STATISTICS NOT AVAILABLE																									
1991-92	Mount St. Charles Mounties	Hi-School	15	3	15	18	....	....	....	4	....	....	....	....	....	....	....	....	....	....	....	....	....	....	....	....	....	....
1992-93	Mount St. Charles Mounties	Hi-School	15	8	12	20	....	....	....	18	....	....	....	....	....	....	....	....	....	....	....	....	....	....	....	....	....	....
1993-94	Mount St. Charles Mounties	Hi-School	15	11	26	37	....	....	....	4.5	....	....	....	....	....	....	....	....	....	....	4	3	3	6	6	....	....	....
1994-95	Detroit Jr. Red Wings	OHL	58	20	55	75	....	....	....	97	....	....	....	....	....	....	....	....	....	....	21	4	20	24	38	....	....	....
	United States	WJC-A	7	0	1	1	....	....	....	36	....	....	....	....	....	....	....	....	....	....	....	....	....	....	....	....	....	....
	Detroit Jr. Red Wings	Mem-Cup	5	1	3	4	....	....	....	6	....	....	....	....	....	....	....	....	....	....	....	....	....	....	....	....	....	....
1995-96	Detroit Whalers	OHL	56	31	58	89	....	....	....	116	....	....	....	....	....	....	....	....	....	....	17	7	18	25	41	....	....	....
	United States	WJC-A	6	1	4	5	....	....	....	20	....	....	....	....	....	....	....	....	....	....	....	....	....	....	....	....	....	....
1996-97	**New York Islanders**	**NHL**	**82**	**8**	**40**	**48**	**8**	**36**	**44**	**86**	**3**	**0**	**1**	**172**	**4.7**	**105**	**33**	**73**	**2**	**1**	....	....	....	....	....	....	....	....
	United States	WC-A	1	1	0	1	....	....	....	0	....	....	....	....	....	....	....	....	....	....	....	....	....	....	....	....	....	....
1997-98	**New York Islanders**	**NHL**	**75**	**14**	**32**	**46**	**16**	**31**	**47**	**59**	**8**	**1**	**2**	**192**	**7.3**	**97**	**45**	**92**	**8**	**–32**	....	....	....	....	....	....	....	....
	United States	Olympics	2	0	0	0	....	....	....	0	....	....	....	....	....	....	....	....	....	....	....	....	....	....	....	....	....	....

Season	Club	League	REGULAR SEASON GP	G	A	Pts	AG	AA	APts	PIM	PP	SH	GW	S	%	TGF	PGF	TGA	PGA	+/–	PLAYOFFS GP	G	A	Pts	PIM	PP	SH	GW
1998-99	**New York Islanders**	**NHL**	**31**	**4**	**11**	**15**	**5**	**11**	**16**	**26**	**2**	**0**	**3**	**72**	**5.6**	**38**	**20**	**34**	**10**	**–6**	....	....	....	....	....	....	....	....
	Toronto Maple Leafs	**NHL**	**38**	**5**	**14**	**19**	**6**	**13**	**19**	**22**	**2**	**0**	**2**	**63**	**7.9**	**55**	**17**	**42**	**11**	**7**	....	....	....	....	....	....	....	....
99-2000	**Toronto Maple Leafs**	**NHL**	**64**	**3**	**27**	**30**	**3**	**25**	**28**	**42**	**1**	**0**	**0**	**98**	**3.1**	**76**	**23**	**45**	**3**	**11**	**17**	**1**	**8**	**9**	**8**	**1**	**0**	**0**
	NHL Totals		**290**	**34**	**124**	**158**	**38**	**116**	**154**	**235**	**16**	**1**	**8**	**597**	**5.7**	**371**	**138**	**286**	**34**		**17**	**1**	**8**	**9**	**8**	**1**	**0**	**0**

OHL First All-Star Team (1995, 1996) • Canadian Major Junior First All-Star Team (1995, 1996) • Canadian Major Junior Rookie of the Year (1995) • Canadian Major Junior Defenseman of the Year (1996) • NHL All-Rookie Team (1997) • Won Calder Memorial Trophy (1997)

Traded to **NY Islanders** by **Ottawa** with Don Beaupre and Martin Straka for Damian Rhodes and Wade Redden, January 23, 1996. Traded to **Toronto** by **NY Islanders** with NY Islanders' 6th round choice (Jan Socher) in 1999 Entry Draft for Felix Potvin and Toronto's 6th round choice (later traded to Tampa Bay - Tampa Bay selected Fedor Fedorov) in 1999 Entry Draft, January 9, 1999. • Suffered season-ending eye injury in game vs. Ottawa, March 11, 2000.

• BEREHOWSKY, Drake

D – R. 6', 212 lbs. b: Toronto, Ont., 1/3/1972. Toronto's 1st, 10th overall, in 1990.

Season	Club	League	GP	G	A	Pts	AG	AA	APts	PIM	PP	SH	GW	S	%	TGF	PGF	TGA	PGA	+/–	GP	G	A	Pts	PIM	PP	SH	GW
1987-88	Barrie Colts	OJHL-B	40	10	36	46	....	....	....	81	....	....	....	....	....	....	....	....	....	....	....	....	....	....	....	....	....	....
1988-89	Kingston Raiders	OHL	63	7	39	46	....	....	....	85	....	....	....	....	....	....	....	....	....	....	....	....	....	....	....	....	....	....
	Canada	Nat-Team	1	0	0	0	....	....	....	0	....	....	....	....	....	....	....	....	....	....	....	....	....	....	....	....	....	....
1989-90	Kingston Frontenacs	OHL	9	3	11	14	....	....	....	28	....	....	....	....	....	....	....	....	....	....	....	....	....	....	....	....	....	....
1990-91	Kingston Frontenacs	OHL	13	5	13	18	....	....	....	38	....	....	....	....	....	....	....	....	....	....	....	....	....	....	....	....	....	....
	North Bay Centennials	OHL	26	7	23	30	....	....	....	51	....	....	....	....	....	....	....	....	....	....	10	2	7	9	21	....	....	....
	Toronto Maple Leafs	**NHL**	**8**	**0**	**1**	**1**	**0**	**1**	**1**	**25**	**0**	**0**	**0**	**4**	**0.0**	**2**	**1**	**8**	**1**	**–6**	....	....	....	....	....	....	....	....
1991-92	North Bay Centennials	OHL	62	19	63	82	....	....	....	147	....	....	....	....	....	....	....	....	....	....	21	7	24	31	22	....	....	....
	Toronto Maple Leafs	**NHL**	**1**	**0**	**0**	**0**	**0**	**0**	**0**	**0**	**0**	**0**	**0**	**0**	**0.0**	**0**	**0**	**0**	**0**	**0**	....	....	....	....	....	....	....	....
	St. John's Maple Leafs	AHL	....	....	....	....	....	....	....	....	....	....	....	....	....	....	....	....	....	....	6	0	5	5	21	....	....	....
1992-93	**Toronto Maple Leafs**	**NHL**	**41**	**4**	**15**	**19**	**3**	**10**	**13**	**61**	**1**	**0**	**1**	**41**	**9.8**	**35**	**17**	**17**	**0**	**1**	....	....	....	....	....	....	....	....
	St. John's Maple Leafs	AHL	28	10	17	27	....	....	....	38	....	....	....	....	....	....	....	....	....	....	....	....	....	....	....	....	....	....
1993-94	**Toronto Maple Leafs**	**NHL**	**49**	**2**	**8**	**10**	**2**	**6**	**8**	**63**	**2**	**0**	**2**	**29**	**6.9**	**29**	**17**	**15**	**0**	**–3**	....	....	....	....	....	....	....	....
	St. John's Maple Leafs	AHL	18	3	12	15	....	....	....	40	....	....	....	....	....	....	....	....	....	....	....	....	....	....	....	....	....	....
1994-95	**Toronto Maple Leafs**	**NHL**	**25**	**0**	**2**	**2**	**0**	**3**	**3**	**15**	**0**	**0**	**0**	**12**	**0.0**	**10**	**2**	**18**	**0**	**–10**	....	....	....	....	....	....	....	....
	Pittsburgh Penguins	**NHL**	**4**	**0**	**0**	**0**	**0**	**0**	**0**	**13**	**0**	**0**	**0**	**2**	**0.0**	**3**	**0**	**2**	**0**	**1**	**1**	**0**	**0**	**0**	**0**	**0**	**0**	**0**
1995-96	**Pittsburgh Penguins**	**NHL**	**1**	**0**	**0**	**0**	**0**	**0**	**0**	**0**	**0**	**0**	**0**	**0**	**0.0**	**1**	**0**	**0**	**0**	**1**	....	....	....	....	....	....	....	....
	Cleveland Lumberjacks	IHL	74	6	28	34	....	....	....	141	....	....	....	....	....	....	....	....	....	....	3	0	3	3	6	....	....	....
1996-97	Carolina Monarchs	AHL	49	2	15	17	....	....	....	55	....	....	....	....	....	....	....	....	....	....	....	....	....	....	....	....	....	....
	San Antonio Dragons	IHL	16	3	4	7	....	....	....	36	....	....	....	....	....	....	....	....	....	....	....	....	....	....	....	....	....	....
1997-98	**Edmonton Oilers**	**NHL**	**67**	**1**	**6**	**7**	**1**	**6**	**7**	**169**	**1**	**0**	**1**	**58**	**1.7**	**39**	**8**	**33**	**3**	**1**	**12**	**1**	**2**	**3**	**14**	**0**	**0**	**1**
	Hamilton Bulldogs	AHL	8	2	0	2	....	....	....	21	....	....	....	....	....	....	....	....	....	....	....	....	....	....	....	....	....	....
1998-99	**Nashville Predators**	**NHL**	**74**	**2**	**15**	**17**	**2**	**14**	**16**	**140**	**0**	**0**	**0**	**79**	**2.5**	**59**	**12**	**85**	**29**	**–9**	....	....	....	....	....	....	....	....
99-2000	**Nashville Predators**	**NHL**	**79**	**12**	**20**	**32**	**13**	**19**	**32**	**87**	**5**	**0**	**1**	**102**	**11.8**	**76**	**16**	**91**	**27**	**–4**	....	....	....	....	....	....	....	....
	NHL Totals		**349**	**21**	**67**	**88**	**21**	**59**	**80**	**573**	**9**	**0**	**5**	**327**	**6.4**	**254**	**73**	**269**	**60**		**13**	**1**	**2**	**3**	**14**	**0**	**0**	**1**

OHL First All-Star Team (1992) • Canadian Major Junior Defenseman of the Year (1992)

• Missed majority of 1989-90 season recovering from knee injury suffered in game vs. Chicago, October 12, 1989. Traded to **Pittsburgh** by **Toronto** for Grant Jennings, April 7, 1995. Signed as a free agent by **Edmonton**, September 30, 1997. Traded to **Nashville** by **Edmonton** with Eric Fichaud and Greg de Vries for Mikhail Shtalenkov and Jim Dowd, October 1, 1998.

• BERENSON, Red

Gordon Arthur "The Red Baron" C – L. 6', 185 lbs. b: Regina, Sask., 12/8/1939.

Season	Club	League	GP	G	A	Pts	AG	AA	APts	PIM	PP	SH	GW	S	%	TGF	PGF	TGA	PGA	+/–	GP	G	A	Pts	PIM	PP	SH	GW
1955-56	Regina Pat Canadians	SJHL-B	STATISTICS NOT AVAILABLE																									
	Regina Pats	Mem-Cup	5	0	0	0	....	....	....	0	....	....	....	....	....	....	....	....	....	....	....	....	....	....	....	....	....	....
1956-57	Regina Pats	SJHL	51	21	23	44	....	....	....	86	....	....	....	....	....	....	....	....	....	....	7	4	3	7	4	....	....	....
1957-58	Regina Pats	SJHL	51	46	*49	95	....	....	....	62	....	....	....	....	....	....	....	....	....	....	27	11	20	31	*49	....	....	....
	Regina Pats	Mem-Cup	16	7	17	24	....	....	....	21	....	....	....	....	....	....	....	....	....	....	....	....	....	....	....	....	....	....
1958-59	Belleville McFarlands	EOHL	1	2	1	3	....	....	....	2	....	....	....	....	....	....	....	....	....	....	....	....	....	....	....	....	....	....
	Canada	WEC-A	8	9	4	*13	....	....	....	....	....	....	....	....	....	....	....	....	....	....	....	....	....	....	....	....	....	....
	Flin Flon Bombers	WCJHL	....	....	....	....	....	....	....	....	....	....	....	....	....	....	....	....	....	....	10	10	9	19	10	....	....	....
	Flin Flon Bombers	Mem-Cup	6	3	3	6	....	....	....	2	....	....	....	....	....	....	....	....	....	....	....	....	....	....	....	....	....	....
1959-60	University of Michigan	WCHA	28	12	7	19	....	....	....	12	....	....	....	....	....	....	....	....	....	....	....	....	....	....	....	....	....	....
1960-61	University of Michigan	WCHA	28	24	25	49	....	....	....	....	....	....	....	....	....	....	....	....	....	....	....	....	....	....	....	....	....	....
1961-62	University of Michigan	WCHA	28	*43	27	70	....	....	....	40	....	....	....	....	....	....	....	....	....	....	....	....	....	....	....	....	....	....
	Montreal Canadiens	**NHL**	**4**	**1**	**2**	**3**	**1**	**2**	**3**	**4**	....	....	....	....	....	....	....	....	....	....	**5**	**2**	**0**	**2**	**0**	**0**	**0**	**0**
1962-63	**Montreal Canadiens**	**NHL**	**37**	**2**	**6**	**8**	**2**	**6**	**8**	**15**	....	....	....	....	....	....	....	....	....	....	**5**	**0**	**0**	**0**	**0**	**0**	**0**	**0**
	Hull-Ottawa Canadiens	EPHL	30	23	25	48	....	....	....	28	....	....	....	....	....	....	....	....	....	....	....	....	....	....	....	....	....	....
1963-64	**Montreal Canadiens**	**NHL**	**69**	**7**	**9**	**16**	**9**	**9**	**18**	**12**	....	....	....	....	....	....	....	....	....	....	**7**	**0**	**0**	**0**	**4**	**0**	**0**	**0**
1964-65♦	**Montreal Canadiens**	**NHL**	**3**	**1**	**2**	**3**	**1**	**2**	**3**	**0**	....	....	....	....	....	....	....	....	....	....	**9**	**0**	**1**	**1**	**2**	**0**	**0**	**0**
	Quebec Aces	AHL	65	22	34	56	....	....	....	16	....	....	....	....	....	....	....	....	....	....	5	1	2	3	8	....	....	....
1965-66	**Montreal Canadiens**	**NHL**	**23**	**3**	**4**	**7**	**3**	**4**	**7**	**12**	....	....	....	....	....	....	....	....	....	....	....	....	....	....	....	....	....	....
	Quebec Aces	AHL	34	17	36	53	....	....	....	14	....	....	....	....	....	....	....	....	....	....	6	1	5	6	2	....	....	....
1966-67	**New York Rangers**	**NHL**	**30**	**0**	**5**	**5**	**0**	**5**	**5**	**2**	....	....	....	....	....	....	....	....	....	....	**4**	**0**	**1**	**1**	**2**	**0**	**0**	**0**
1967-68	**New York Rangers**	**NHL**	**19**	**2**	**1**	**3**	**2**	**1**	**3**	**2**	**0**	**0**	**0**	**25**	**8.0**	**3**	**0**	**8**	**4**	**–1**	....	....	....	....	....	....	....	....
	St. Louis Blues	**NHL**	**55**	**22**	**29**	**51**	**26**	**29**	**55**	**22**	**7**	**0**	**7**	**219**	**10.0**	**69**	**21**	**71**	**15**	**–8**	**18**	**5**	**2**	**7**	**9**	**1**	**1**	**0**
1968-69	**St. Louis Blues**	**NHL**	**76**	**35**	**47**	**82**	**37**	**42**	**79**	**43**	**7**	**1**	**6**	**288**	**12.2**	**106**	**30**	**62**	**12**	**26**	**12**	**7**	**3**	**10**	**20**	**2**	**1**	**0**
1969-70	**St. Louis Blues**	**NHL**	**67**	**33**	**39**	**72**	**36**	**37**	**73**	**38**	**16**	**0**	**8**	**282**	**11.7**	**105**	**61**	**56**	**9**	**–3**	**16**	**7**	**5**	**12**	**8**	**3**	**1**	**1**
1970-71	**St. Louis Blues**	**NHL**	**45**	**16**	**26**	**42**	**16**	**22**	**38**	**12**	**6**	**1**	**1**	**174**	**9.2**	**56**	**27**	**47**	**11**	**–7**	....	....	....	....	....	....	....	....
	Detroit Red Wings	**NHL**	**24**	**5**	**12**	**17**	**5**	**10**	**15**	**4**	**1**	**0**	**1**	**51**	**9.8**	**24**	**11**	**26**	**6**	**–7**	....	....	....	....	....	....	....	....
1971-72	**Detroit Red Wings**	**NHL**	**78**	**28**	**41**	**69**	**28**	**36**	**64**	**16**	**5**	**2**	**2**	**218**	**12.8**	**101**	**37**	**95**	**23**	**–8**	....	....	....	....	....	....	....	....
1972-73	Team Canada	Summit-72	2	0	1	1	....	....	....	0	....	....	....	....	....	....	....	....	....	....	....	....	....	....	....	....	....	....
	Detroit Red Wings	**NHL**	**78**	**13**	**30**	**43**	**12**	**24**	**36**	**8**	**5**	**0**	**1**	**180**	**7.2**	**68**	**19**	**68**	**5**	**–14**	....	....	....	....	....	....	....	....
1973-74	**Detroit Red Wings**	**NHL**	**76**	**24**	**42**	**66**	**23**	**35**	**58**	**28**	**6**	**1**	**2**	**179**	**13.4**	**98**	**36**	**106**	**22**	**–22**	....	....	....	....	....	....	....	....
1974-75	**Detroit Red Wings**	**NHL**	**27**	**3**	**3**	**6**	**3**	**2**	**5**	**8**	**1**	**0**	**0**	**40**	**7.5**	**9**	**5**	**31**	**17**	**–10**	....	....	....	....	....	....	....	....
	St. Louis Blues	**NHL**	**44**	**12**	**19**	**31**	**10**	**14**	**24**	**12**	**4**	**1**	**1**	**111**	**10.8**	**45**	**13**	**53**	**14**	**–7**	**2**	**1**	**0**	**1**	**0**	**1**	**0**	**0**
1975-76	**St. Louis Blues**	**NHL**	**72**	**20**	**27**	**47**	**18**	**20**	**38**	**47**	**9**	**2**	**1**	**171**	**11.7**	**72**	**40**	**80**	**37**	**–11**	**3**	**1**	**2**	**3**	**0**	**0**	**0**	**0**
1976-77	**St. Louis Blues**	**NHL**	**80**	**21**	**28**	**49**	**19**	**22**	**41**	**8**	**4**	**0**	**3**	**178**	**11.8**	**75**	**26**	**97**	**20**	**–28**	**4**	**0**	**0**	**0**	**4**	**0**	**0**	**0**
1977-78	**St. Louis Blues**	**NHL**	**80**	**13**	**25**	**38**	**12**	**19**	**31**	**12**	**0**	**1**	**2**	**140**	**9.3**	**54**	**17**	**89**	**32**	**–20**	....	....	....	....	....	....	....	....
1978-1979	**St. Louis Blues**	**NHL**	DID NOT PLAY – ASSISTANT COACH																									
1979-1980	**St. Louis Blues**	**NHL**	DID NOT PLAY – ASSISTANT COACH																									
	St. Louis Blues	**NHL**	DID NOT PLAY – COACHING																									
1980-1982	**St. Louis Blues**	**NHL**	DID NOT PLAY – COACHING																									
1982-1984	**Buffalo Sabres**	**NHL**	DID NOT PLAY – ASSISTANT COACH																									
1984-2000	University of Michigan	CCHA	DID NOT PLAY – COACHING																									
	NHL Totals		**987**	**261**	**397**	**658**	**263**	**341**	**604**	**305**	....	....	....	....	....	....	....	....	....	....	**85**	**23**	**14**	**37**	**49**	....	....	....

WCHA First All-Star Team (1961, 1962) • NCAA West First All-American Team (1961, 1962) • NCAA Championship All-Tournament Team (1962) • Won Jack Adams Award (1981)

Played in NHL All-Star Game (1965, 1969, 1970, 1971, 1972, 1974)

Traded to **NY Rangers** by **Montreal** for Ted Taylor and Garry Peters, June 13, 1966. Traded to **St. Louis** by **NY Rangers** with Barclay Plager for Ron Stewart and Ron Attwell, November 29, 1967. Traded to **Detroit** by **St. Louis** with Tim Ecclestone for Garry Unger and Wayne Connelly, February 6, 1971. Traded to **St. Louis** by **Detroit** for Phil Roberto and St. Louis' 3rd round choice (Blair Davidson) in 1975 Amateur Draft, December 30, 1974.

• BERENZWEIG, Andy

"Bubba" D – L. 6'2", 195 lbs. b: Arlington Heights, IL, 8/8/1977. NY Islanders' 5th, 109th overall, in 1996.

Season	Club	League	GP	G	A	Pts	AG	AA	APts	PIM	PP	SH	GW	S	%	TGF	PGF	TGA	PGA	+/–	GP	G	A	Pts	PIM	PP	SH	GW
1992-93	Loomis-Chaffee Prep School	Hi-School	22	5	13	18	....	....	....	....	....	....	....	....	....	....	....	....	....	....	....	....	....	....	....	....	....	....
1993-94	Loomis-Chaffee Prep School	Hi-School	22	12	27	39	....	....	....	....	....	....	....	....	....	....	....	....	....	....	....	....	....	....	....	....	....	....
1994-95	Loomis-Chaffee Prep School	Hi-School	23	19	23	42	....	....	....	10	....	....	....	....	....	....	....	....	....	....	....	....	....	....	....	....	....	....
1995-96	University of Michigan	CCHA	42	4	8	12	....	....	....	4	....	....	....	....	....	....	....	....	....	....	....	....	....	....	....	....	....	....
1996-97	University of Michigan	CCHA	38	7	12	19	....	....	....	49	....	....	....	....	....	....	....	....	....	....	....	....	....	....	....	....	....	....

Season	Club	League	REGULAR SEASON																		PLAYOFFS							
			GP	G	A	Pts	AG	AA	APts	PIM	PP	SH	GW	S	%	TGF	PGF	TGA	PGA	+/–	GP	G	A	Pts	PIM	PP	SH	GW
1997-98	University of Michigan	CCHA	45	8	11	19	....	....	....	32	....	....	....	....	....	....	....	....	....	....	....	....	....	....	....	....	....	....
1998-99	University of Michigan	CCHA	42	7	24	31	....	....	....	38	....	....	....	....	....	....	....	....	....	....	....	....	....	....	....	....	....	....
99-2000	**Nashville Predators**	**NHL**	**2**	**0**	**0**	**0**	**0**	**0**	**0**	**0**	**0**	**0**	**0**	**3**	**0.0**	**0**	**0**	**1**	**0**	**–1**	....	....	....	....	....	....	....	....
	Milwaukee Admirals	IHL	79	4	23	27	....	....	....	48	....	....	....	....	....	....	....	....	....	....	3	1	2	3	0	....	....	....
	NHL Totals		**2**	**0**	**0**	**0**	**0**	**0**	**0**	**0**	**0**	**0**	**0**	**3**	**0.0**	**0**	**0**	**1**	**0**		....	....	....	....	....	....	....	....

CCHA Second All-Star Team (1998) • NCAA Championship All-Tournament Team (1998)

Traded to **Nashville** by **NY Islanders** for Nashville's 4th round choice (Jonathon Halvarson) in 1999 Entry Draft, April 14, 1999.

• BEREZAN, Perry

Perry E. C – R. 6'2", 190 lbs. b: Edmonton, Alta., 12/5/1964. Calgary's 3rd, 56th overall, in 1983.

Season	Club	League	GP	G	A	Pts	AG	AA	APts	PIM	PP	SH	GW	S	%	TGF	PGF	TGA	PGA	+/–	GP	G	A	Pts	PIM	PP	SH	GW
1981-82	St. Albert Saints	AJHL	47	16	36	52	....	....	....	47	....	....	....	....	....	....	....	....	....	....	....	....	....	....	....	....	....	....
1982-83	St. Albert Saints	AJHL	57	37	40	77	....	....	....	110	....	....	....	....	....	....	....	....	....	....	....	....	....	....	....	....	....	....
1983-84	University of North Dakota	WCHA	44	28	24	52	....	....	....	29	....	....	....	....	....	....	....	....	....	....	....	....	....	....	....	....	....	....
1984-85	University of North Dakota	WCHA	42	23	35	58	....	....	....	32	....	....	....	....	....	....	....	....	....	....	....	....	....	....	....	....	....	....
	Calgary Flames	**NHL**	**9**	**3**	**2**	**5**	**2**	**1**	**3**	**4**	**0**	**0**	**1**	**13**	**23.1**	**7**	**0**	**2**	**0**	**5**	**2**	**1**	**0**	**1**	**4**	**1**	**0**	**0**
1985-86	**Calgary Flames**	**NHL**	**55**	**12**	**21**	**33**	**10**	**14**	**24**	**39**	**0**	**2**	**3**	**117**	**10.3**	**55**	**0**	**64**	**28**	**19**	**8**	**1**	**1**	**2**	**6**	**0**	**0**	**1**
1986-87	**Calgary Flames**	**NHL**	**24**	**5**	**3**	**8**	**4**	**2**	**6**	**24**	**0**	**1**	**0**	**31**	**16.1**	**14**	**0**	**20**	**10**	**4**	**2**	**0**	**2**	**2**	**7**	**0**	**0**	**0**
1987-88	**Calgary Flames**	**NHL**	**29**	**7**	**12**	**19**	**6**	**9**	**15**	**66**	**0**	**2**	**1**	**69**	**10.1**	**28**	**1**	**34**	**18**	**11**	**8**	**0**	**2**	**2**	**13**	**0**	**0**	**0**
1988-89	**Calgary Flames**	**NHL**	**35**	**4**	**4**	**8**	**3**	**3**	**6**	**23**	**0**	**1**	**0**	**49**	**8.2**	**16**	**0**	**19**	**8**	**5**	....	....	....	....	....	....	....	....
	Minnesota North Stars	**NHL**	**16**	**1**	**4**	**5**	**1**	**3**	**4**	**4**	**0**	**0**	**0**	**16**	**6.3**	**8**	**0**	**12**	**5**	**1**	**5**	**1**	**2**	**3**	**4**	**0**	**0**	**0**
1989-90	**Minnesota North Stars**	**NHL**	**64**	**3**	**12**	**15**	**3**	**9**	**12**	**31**	**0**	**0**	**0**	**75**	**4.0**	**20**	**0**	**50**	**26**	**–4**	**5**	**1**	**0**	**1**	**0**	**0**	**0**	**0**
1990-91	Minnesota North Stars	Fr-Tour	3	0	1	1	....	....	....	6	....	....	....	....	....	....	....	....	....	....	....	....	....	....	....	....	....	....
	Minnesota North Stars	**NHL**	**52**	**11**	**6**	**17**	**10**	**5**	**15**	**30**	**1**	**3**	**1**	**73**	**15.1**	**24**	**3**	**40**	**17**	**–2**	**1**	**0**	**0**	**0**	**0**	**0**	**0**	**0**
	Kalamazoo Wings	IHL	2	0	0	0	....	....	....	2	....	....	....	....	....	....	....	....	....	....	....	....	....	....	....	....	....	....
1991-92	**San Jose Sharks**	**NHL**	**66**	**12**	**7**	**19**	**11**	**5**	**16**	**30**	**4**	**1**	**2**	**112**	**10.7**	**43**	**9**	**91**	**31**	**–26**	....	....	....	....	....	....	....	....
1992-93	**San Jose Sharks**	**NHL**	**28**	**3**	**4**	**7**	**2**	**3**	**5**	**28**	**1**	**1**	**0**	**37**	**8.1**	**10**	**1**	**39**	**12**	**–18**	....	....	....	....	....	....	....	....
	Kansas City Blades	IHL	9	4	4	8	....	....	....	31	....	....	....	....	....	....	....	....	....	....	....	....	....	....	....	....	....	....
	NHL Totals		**378**	**61**	**75**	**136**	**52**	**54**	**106**	**279**	**6**	**11**	**8**	**592**	**10.3**	**225**	**14**	**371**	**155**		**31**	**4**	**7**	**11**	**34**	**1**	**0**	**1**

Traded to **Minnesota** by **Calgary** with Shane Churla for Brian MacLellan and Minnesota's 4th round choice (Robert Reichel) in 1989 Entry Draft, March 4, 1989. Signed as a free agent by **San Jose**, October 10, 1991.

• BEREZIN, Sergei

LW – R. 5'10", 200 lbs. b: Voskresensk, USSR, 11/5/1971. Toronto's 8th, 256th overall, in 1994.

Season	Club	League	GP	G	A	Pts	AG	AA	APts	PIM	PP	SH	GW	S	%	TGF	PGF	TGA	PGA	+/–	GP	G	A	Pts	PIM	PP	SH	GW
1990-91	Khimik Voskresensk	Fr-Tour	1	0	0	0	....	....	....	0	....	....	....	....	....	....	....	....	....	....	....	....	....	....	....	....	....	....
	Khimik Voskresensk	USSR	30	6	2	8	....	....	....	4	....	....	....	....	....	....	....	....	....	....	....	....	....	....	....	....	....	....
	Soviet Union	WJC-A	7	3	1	4	....	....	....	6	....	....	....	....	....	....	....	....	....	....	....	....	....	....	....	....	....	....
1991-92	Khimik Voskresensk	CIS	36	7	5	12	....	....	....	10	....	....	....	....	....	....	....	....	....	....	....	....	....	....	....	....	....	....
1992-93	Khimik Voskresensk	CIS	38	9	3	12	....	....	....	12	....	....	....	....	....	....	....	....	....	....	2	1	0	1	0	....	....	....
1993-94	Khimik Voskresensk	CIS	40	31	10	41	....	....	....	16	....	....	....	....	....	....	....	....	....	....	3	2	0	2	2	....	....	....
	Russia	Olympics	8	3	2	5	....	....	....	2	....	....	....	....	....	....	....	....	....	....	....	....	....	....	....	....	....	....
	Russia	WC-A	6	2	1	3	....	....	....	2	....	....	....	....	....	....	....	....	....	....	....	....	....	....	....	....	....	....
1994-95	Kolner Haie	Germany	43	*38	19	57	....	....	....	8	....	....	....	....	....	....	....	....	....	....	18	*17	8	25	14	....	....	....
	Russia	WC-A	6	7	1	8	....	....	....	4	....	....	....	....	....	....	....	....	....	....	....	....	....	....	....	....	....	....
1995-96	Kolner Haie	Germany	45	*49	31	80	....	....	....	8	....	....	....	....	....	....	....	....	....	....	14	*13	9	22	10	....	....	....
	Russia	WC-A	8	4	5	9	....	....	....	2	....	....	....	....	....	....	....	....	....	....	....	....	....	....	....	....	....	....
1996-97	Russia	W-Cup	2	1	0	1	....	....	....	0	....	....	....	....	....	....	....	....	....	....	....	....	....	....	....	....	....	....
	Toronto Maple Leafs	**NHL**	**73**	**25**	**16**	**41**	**26**	**14**	**40**	**2**	**7**	**0**	**2**	**177**	**14.1**	**64**	**20**	**47**	**0**	**–3**	....	....	....	....	....	....	....	....
1997-98	**Toronto Maple Leafs**	**NHL**	**68**	**16**	**15**	**31**	**19**	**15**	**34**	**10**	**3**	**0**	**3**	**167**	**9.6**	**47**	**11**	**40**	**1**	**–3**	....	....	....	....	....	....	....	....
	Russia	WC-A	6	6	2	8	....	....	....	2	....	....	....	....	....	....	....	....	....	....	....	....	....	....	....	....	....	....
1998-99	**Toronto Maple Leafs**	**NHL**	**76**	**37**	**22**	**59**	**44**	**21**	**65**	**12**	**9**	**1**	**4**	**263**	**14.1**	**82**	**18**	**50**	**2**	**16**	**17**	**6**	**6**	**12**	**4**	**2**	**0**	**2**
99-2000	**Toronto Maple Leafs**	**NHL**	**61**	**26**	**13**	**39**	**29**	**12**	**41**	**2**	**5**	**0**	**4**	**241**	**10.8**	**58**	**15**	**37**	**2**	**8**	**12**	**4**	**4**	**8**	**0**	**0**	**0**	**1**
	NHL Totals		**278**	**104**	**66**	**170**	**118**	**62**	**180**	**26**	**24**	**1**	**13**	**848**	**12.3**	**251**	**64**	**174**	**5**		**29**	**10**	**10**	**20**	**4**	**2**	**0**	**3**

NHL All-Rookie Team (1997)

• BERG, Aki

D – L. 6'3", 215 lbs. b: Turku, Finland, 7/28/1977. Los Angeles' 1st, 3rd overall, in 1995.

Season	Club	League	GP	G	A	Pts	AG	AA	APts	PIM	PP	SH	GW	S	%	TGF	PGF	TGA	PGA	+/–	GP	G	A	Pts	PIM	PP	SH	GW
1992-93	TPS Turku	Finland-Jr.	39	18	24	42	....	....	....	24	....	....	....	....	....	....	....	....	....	....	....	....	....	....	....	....	....	....
1993-94	TPS Turku	Finland-Jr.	21	3	11	14	....	....	....	24	....	....	....	....	....	....	....	....	....	....	7	0	0	0	10	....	....	....
	Kiekko-67 Turku	Finland-2	12	1	1	2	....	....	....	16	....	....	....	....	....	....	....	....	....	....	....	....	....	....	....	....	....	....
	TPS Turku	Finland	6	0	3	3	....	....	....	4	....	....	....	....	....	....	....	....	....	....	....	....	....	....	....	....	....	....
1994-95	TPS Turku	Finn-Jr.	8	1	0	1	....	....	....	30	....	....	....	....	....	....	....	....	....	....	....	....	....	....	....	....	....	....
	Kiekko-67 Turku	Finland-2	21	3	9	12	....	....	....	24	....	....	....	....	....	....	....	....	....	....	7	0	0	0	10	....	....	....
	TPS Turku	Finland	5	0	0	0	....	....	....	4	....	....	....	....	....	....	....	....	....	....	....	....	....	....	....	....	....	....
	Finland	EJC-A	5	0	1	1	....	....	....	10	....	....	....	....	....	....	....	....	....	....	....	....	....	....	....	....	....	....
1995-96	**Los Angeles Kings**	**NHL**	**51**	**0**	**7**	**7**	**0**	**6**	**6**	**29**	**0**	**0**	**0**	**56**	**0.0**	**34**	**3**	**50**	**6**	**–13**	....	....	....	....	....	....	....	....
	Phoenix Roadrunners	IHL	20	0	3	3	....	....	....	18	....	....	....	....	....	....	....	....	....	....	2	0	0	0	4	....	....	....
1996-97	**Los Angeles Kings**	**NHL**	**41**	**2**	**6**	**8**	**2**	**5**	**7**	**24**	**2**	**0**	**0**	**65**	**3.1**	**35**	**11**	**41**	**8**	**–9**	....	....	....	....	....	....	....	....
	Finland	WJC-A	6	0	2	2	....	....	....	8	....	....	....	....	....	....	....	....	....	....	....	....	....	....	....	....	....	....
	Phoenix Roadrunners	IHL	23	1	3	4	....	....	....	21	....	....	....	....	....	....	....	....	....	....	....	....	....	....	....	....	....	....
1997-98	**Los Angeles Kings**	**NHL**	**72**	**0**	**8**	**8**	**0**	**8**	**8**	**61**	**0**	**0**	**0**	**58**	**0.0**	**42**	**4**	**49**	**14**	**3**	**4**	**0**	**3**	**3**	**0**	**0**	**0**	**0**
	Finland	Olympics	6	0	0	0	....	....	....	6	....	....	....	....	....	....	....	....	....	....	....	....	....	....	....	....	....	....
1998-99	TPS Turku	Finland	48	8	7	15	....	....	....	137	....	....	....	....	....	....	....	....	....	....	9	1	1	2	45	....	....	....
	Finland	WC-A	12	0	0	0	....	....	....	29	....	....	....	....	....	....	....	....	....	....	....	....	....	....	....	....	....	....
99-2000	**Los Angeles Kings**	**NHL**	**70**	**3**	**13**	**16**	**3**	**12**	**15**	**45**	**0**	**0**	**0**	**70**	**4.3**	**55**	**9**	**60**	**13**	**–1**	**2**	**0**	**0**	**0**	**2**	**0**	**0**	**0**
	Finland	WC-A	9	1	0	1	....	....	....	6	....	....	....	....	....	....	....	....	....	....	....	....	....	....	....	....	....	....
	NHL Totals		**234**	**5**	**34**	**39**	**5**	**31**	**36**	**159**	**2**	**0**	**0**	**249**	**2.0**	**166**	**27**	**200**	**41**		**6**	**0**	**3**	**3**	**2**	**0**	**0**	**0**

• BERG, Bill

William Daniel LW – L. 6'1", 205 lbs. b: St. Catharines, Ont., 10/21/1967. NY Islanders' 3rd, 59th overall, in 1986.

Season	Club	League	GP	G	A	Pts	AG	AA	APts	PIM	PP	SH	GW	S	%	TGF	PGF	TGA	PGA	+/–	GP	G	A	Pts	PIM	PP	SH	GW
1982-83	Beamsville Blades	OJHL-C	19	3	5	8	....	....	....	24	....	....	....	....	....	....	....	....	....	....	....	....	....	....	....	....	....	....
1983-84	Grimsby Peach Kings	OJHL-B	39	5	20	25	....	....	....	107	....	....	....	....	....	....	....	....	....	....	....	....	....	....	....	....	....	....
1984-85	Grimsby Peach Kings	OJHL-B	42	10	22	32	....	....	....	153	....	....	....	....	....	....	....	....	....	....	....	....	....	....	....	....	....	....
1985-86	Toronto Marlboros	OHL	64	3	35	38	....	....	....	143	....	....	....	....	....	....	....	....	....	....	4	0	0	0	19	....	....	....
	Springfield Indians	AHL	4	1	1	2	....	....	....	4	....	....	....	....	....	....	....	....	....	....	....	....	....	....	....	....	....	....
1986-87	Toronto Marlboros	OHL	57	3	15	18	....	....	....	138	....	....	....	....	....	....	....	....	....	....	....	....	....	....	....	....	....	....
1987-88	Springfield Indians	AHL	76	6	26	32	....	....	....	148	....	....	....	....	....	....	....	....	....	....	....	....	....	....	....	....	....	....
	Peoria Rivermen	IHL	5	0	1	1	....	....	....	8	....	....	....	....	....	....	....	....	....	....	7	0	3	3	31	....	....	....
1988-89	**New York Islanders**	**NHL**	**7**	**1**	**2**	**3**	**1**	**1**	**2**	**10**	**1**	**0**	**0**	**10**	**10.0**	**11**	**7**	**7**	**1**	**–2**	....	....	....	....	....	....	....	....
	Springfield Indians	AHL	69	17	32	49	....	....	....	122	....	....	....	....	....	....	....	....	....	....	....	....	....	....	....	....	....	....
1989-90	Springfield Indians	AHL	74	12	42	54	....	....	....	74	....	....	....	....	....	....	....	....	....	....	15	5	12	17	35	....	....	....
1990-91	**New York Islanders**	**NHL**	**78**	**9**	**14**	**23**	**8**	**11**	**19**	**67**	**0**	**0**	**0**	**95**	**9.5**	**41**	**1**	**62**	**19**	**–3**	....	....	....	....	....	....	....	....
1991-92	**New York Islanders**	**NHL**	**47**	**5**	**9**	**14**	**5**	**7**	**12**	**28**	**1**	**0**	**1**	**60**	**8.3**	**21**	**3**	**49**	**13**	**–18**	....	....	....	....	....	....	....	....
	Capital District Islanders	AHL	3	0	2	2	....	....	....	16	....	....	....	....	....	....	....	....	....	....	....	....	....	....	....	....	....	....
1992-93	**New York Islanders**	**NHL**	**22**	**6**	**3**	**9**	**5**	**2**	**7**	**49**	**0**	**2**	**0**	**30**	**20.0**	**14**	**0**	**19**	**9**	**4**	....	....	....	....	....	....	....	....
	Toronto Maple Leafs	**NHL**	**58**	**7**	**8**	**15**	**6**	**5**	**11**	**54**	**0**	**1**	**2**	**83**	**8.4**	**29**	**0**	**40**	**10**	**–1**	**21**	**1**	**1**	**2**	**18**	**0**	**0**	**0**
1993-94	**Toronto Maple Leafs**	**NHL**	**83**	**8**	**11**	**19**	**7**	**9**	**16**	**93**	**0**	**0**	**1**	**99**	**8.1**	**31**	**0**	**58**	**24**	**–3**	**18**	**1**	**2**	**3**	**10**	**0**	**0**	**0**
1994-95	**Toronto Maple Leafs**	**NHL**	**32**	**5**	**1**	**6**	**9**	**1**	**10**	**26**	**0**	**0**	**2**	**57**	**8.8**	**7**	**0**	**21**	**3**	**–11**	**7**	**0**	**1**	**1**	**4**	**0**	**0**	**0**
1995-96	**Toronto Maple Leafs**	**NHL**	**23**	**1**	**1**	**2**	**1**	**1**	**2**	**33**	**0**	**0**	**0**	**33**	**3.0**	**6**	**0**	**18**	**6**	**–6**	....	....	....	....	....	....	....	....
	New York Rangers	**NHL**	**18**	**2**	**1**	**3**	**2**	**1**	**3**	**8**	**0**	**1**	**0**	**27**	**7.4**	**7**	**0**	**15**	**8**	**0**	**10**	**1**	**0**	**1**	**0**	**0**	**0**	**0**
1996-97	**New York Rangers**	**NHL**	**67**	**8**	**6**	**14**	**8**	**5**	**13**	**37**	**0**	**2**	**3**	**84**	**9.5**	**23**	**0**	**29**	**8**	**2**	**3**	**0**	**0**	**0**	**2**	**0**	**0**	**0**

Season	Club	League	REGULAR SEASON																		PLAYOFFS							
			GP	G	A	Pts	AG	AA	APts	PIM	PP	SH	GW	S	%	TGF	PGF	TGA	PGA	+/–	GP	G	A	Pts	PIM	PP	SH	GW
1997-98	**New York Rangers**	**NHL**	**67**	**1**	**9**	**10**	**1**	**9**	**10**	**55**	**0**	**0**	**0**	**74**	**1.4**	**15**	**1**	**47**	**18**	**–15**	....	....	....	....	....	....	....	....
1998-99	Hartford Wolf Pack	AHL	16	4	7	11	....	....	....	23	....	....	....	....	....	....	....	....	....	....	....	....	....	....	....	....	....	....
	Ottawa Senators	**NHL**	**44**	**2**	**2**	**4**	**2**	**2**	**4**	**28**	**0**	**0**	**0**	**40**	**5.0**	**9**	**0**	**10**	**5**	**4**	**2**	**0**	**0**	**0**	**0**	**0**	**0**	**0**
	NHL Totals		**546**	**55**	**67**	**122**	**55**	**54**	**109**	**488**	**2**	**6**	**9**	**692**	**7.9**	**214**	**12**	**375**	**124**		**61**	**3**	**4**	**7**	**34**	**0**	**0**	**0**

Claimed on waivers by **Toronto** from **NY Islanders**, December 3, 1992. Traded to **NY Rangers** by **Toronto** for Nick Kypreos, February 29, 1996. Traded to **Ottawa** by **NY Rangers** with NY Rangers' 2nd round choice (later traded to Anaheim, Anaheim selected Jordan Leopold) in 1999 Entry Draft for Stan Neckar, November 27, 1998.

• BERGEN, Todd

C – L. 6'3", 185 lbs. b: Prince Albert, Sask., 7/11/1963. Philadelphia's 5th, 98th overall, in 1982.

Season	Club	League	GP	G	A	Pts	AG	AA	APts	PIM	PP	SH	GW	S	%	TGF	PGF	TGA	PGA	+/–	GP	G	A	Pts	PIM	PP	SH	GW
1981-82	Prince Albert Raiders	SJHL	59	30	62	92	....	....	....	35	....	....	....	....	....	....	....	....	....	....	....	....	....	....	....	....	....	....
1982-83	Prince Albert Raiders	WHL	70	34	47	81	....	....	....	17	....	....	....	....	....	....	....	....	....	....	....	....	....	....	....	....	....	....
1983-84	Prince Albert Raiders	WHL	43	57	39	96	....	....	....	15	....	....	....	....	....	....	....	....	....	....	5	2	5	7	4	....	....	....
	Springfield Indians	AHL	1	0	0	0	....	....	....	0	....	....	....	....	....	....	....	....	....	....	....	....	....	....	....	....	....	....
1984-85	**Philadelphia Flyers**	**NHL**	**14**	**11**	**5**	**16**	**9**	**3**	**12**	**4**	**3**	**0**	**3**	**38**	**28.9**	**20**	**6**	**5**	**0**	**9**	**17**	**4**	**9**	**13**	**8**	**2**	**0**	**1**
	Hershey Bears	AHL	38	20	19	39	....	....	....	2	....	....	....	....	....	....	....	....	....	....	....	....	....	....	....	....	....	....
1985-86	**Philadelphia Flyers**	**NHL**	DID NOT PLAY – SUSPENDED																									
1986-87	Springfield Indians	AHL	27	12	11	23	....	....	....	14	....	....	....	....	....	....	....	....	....	....	....	....	....	....	....	....	....	....
	NHL Totals		**14**	**11**	**5**	**16**	**9**	**3**	**12**	**4**	**3**	**0**	**3**	**38**	**28.9**	**20**	**6**	**5**	**0**		**17**	**4**	**9**	**13**	**8**	**2**	**0**	**1**

• Suspended by **Philadelphia** for refusing to report to training camp, September, 1985. • Announced retirement to pursue career as professional golfer, September, 1985. Traded to **Minnesota** by **Philadelphia** with Ed Hospodar for Dave Richter and Bo Berglund, November 29, 1985.

• BERGER, Mike

Michael D – R. 6', 195 lbs. b: Edmonton, Alta., 6/2/1967. Minnesota's 2nd, 69th overall, in 1985.

Season	Club	League	GP	G	A	Pts	AG	AA	APts	PIM	PP	SH	GW	S	%	TGF	PGF	TGA	PGA	+/–	GP	G	A	Pts	PIM	PP	SH	GW
1982-83	Fort Saskatchewan Traders	AJHL	54	7	47	54	....	....	....	92	....	....	....	....	....	....	....	....	....	....	....	....	....	....	....	....	....	....
	Lethbridge Broncos	WHL	1	0	0	0	....	....	....	0	....	....	....	....	....	....	....	....	....	....	....	....	....	....	....	....	....	....
1983-84	Lethbridge Broncos	WHL	41	2	9	11	....	....	....	60	....	....	....	....	....	....	....	....	....	....	5	0	1	1	7	....	....	....
1984-85	Lethbridge Broncos	WHL	58	9	31	40	....	....	....	85	....	....	....	....	....	....	....	....	....	....	4	0	3	3	9	....	....	....
1985-86	Lethbridge Broncos	WHL	21	2	9	11	....	....	....	39	....	....	....	....	....	....	....	....	....	....	....	....	....	....	....	....	....	....
	Spokane Chiefs	WHL	36	7	31	38	....	....	....	56	....	....	....	....	....	....	....	....	....	....	9	1	5	6	14	....	....	....
1986-87	Spokane Chiefs	WHL	65	26	49	75	....	....	....	80	....	....	....	....	....	....	....	....	....	....	2	0	0	0	2	....	....	....
	Indianapolis Checkers	IHL	4	0	3	3	....	....	....	4	....	....	....	....	....	....	....	....	....	....	6	0	1	1	13	....	....	....
1987-88	**Minnesota North Stars**	**NHL**	**29**	**3**	**1**	**4**	**3**	**1**	**4**	**65**	**3**	**0**	**0**	**41**	**7.3**	**11**	**7**	**30**	**7**	**–19**	....	....	....	....	....	....	....	....
	Kalamazoo Wings	IHL	36	5	10	15	....	....	....	94	....	....	....	....	....	....	....	....	....	....	6	2	0	2	8	....	....	....
1988-89	**Minnesota North Stars**	**NHL**	**1**	**0**	**0**	**0**	**0**	**0**	**0**	**2**	**0**	**0**	**0**	**0**	**0.0**	**0**	**0**	**1**	**0**	**–1**	....	....	....	....	....	....	....	....
	Kalamazoo Wings	IHL	67	9	16	25	....	....	....	96	....	....	....	....	....	....	....	....	....	....	6	0	2	2	8	....	....	....
1989-90	Phoenix Roadrunners	IHL	51	5	12	17	....	....	....	75	....	....	....	....	....	....	....	....	....	....	....	....	....	....	....	....	....	....
	Binghamton Whalers	AHL	10	0	4	4	....	....	....	10	....	....	....	....	....	....	....	....	....	....	....	....	....	....	....	....	....	....
1990-91	Kansas City Blades	IHL	46	7	14	21	....	....	....	43	....	....	....	....	....	....	....	....	....	....	....	....	....	....	....	....	....	....
	Knoxville Cherokees	ECHL	7	1	7	8	....	....	....	31	....	....	....	....	....	....	....	....	....	....	....	....	....	....	....	....	....	....
1991-92	Thunder Bay Thunder Hawks	ColHL	54	17	27	44	....	....	....	127	....	....	....	....	....	....	....	....	....	....	10	6	7	13	16	....	....	....
1992-93	Tulsa Oilers	CHL	47	16	26	42	....	....	....	116	....	....	....	....	....	....	....	....	....	....	7	2	3	5	4	....	....	....
	Thunder Bay Thunder Hawks	ColHL	8	3	5	8	....	....	....	20	....	....	....	....	....	....	....	....	....	....	....	....	....	....	....	....	....	....
1993-94	Tulsa Oilers	CHL	58	15	19	34	....	....	....	134	....	....	....	....	....	....	....	....	....	....	11	7	4	11	22	....	....	....
1994-95	Tulsa Oilers	CHL	46	10	20	30	....	....	....	64	....	....	....	....	....	....	....	....	....	....	....	....	....	....	....	....	....	....
1995-96	Tulsa Oilers	CHL	45	9	18	27	....	....	....	110	....	....	....	....	....	....	....	....	....	....	6	0	1	1	22	....	....	....
1996-97	Tulsa Oilers	CHL	64	9	33	42	....	....	....	68	....	....	....	....	....	....	....	....	....	....	5	0	2	2	10	....	....	....
1997-98	Tulsa Oilers	CHL	63	11	28	39	....	....	....	121	....	....	....	....	....	....	....	....	....	....	3	2	1	3	2	....	....	....
1998-99	Tulsa Oilers	CHL	69	25	35	60	....	....	....	93	....	....	....	....	....	....	....	....	....	....	....	....	....	....	....	....	....	....
99-2000	Indianapolis Ice	CHL	67	10	26	36	....	....	....	72	....	....	....	....	....	....	....	....	....	....	9	2	0	2	38	....	....	....
	NHL Totals		**30**	**3**	**1**	**4**	**3**	**1**	**4**	**67**	**3**	**0**	**0**	**41**	**7.3**	**11**	**7**	**31**	**7**		....	....	....	....	....	....	....	....

WHL West Second All-Star Team (1986, 1987) • CHL Second All-Star Team (1993)

Traded to **Hartford** by **Minnesota** for Kevin Sullivan, October 7, 1989. Signed as a free agent by **Indianapolis** (CHL), September 9, 1999. • Played w/ RHI's Oakland Skates in 1994 (17-1-3-4-62).

• BERGERON, Michel

RW – R. 5'10", 170 lbs. b: Chicoutimi, Que., 11/11/1954. Detroit's 4th, 63rd overall, in 1974.

Season	Club	League	GP	G	A	Pts	AG	AA	APts	PIM	PP	SH	GW	S	%	TGF	PGF	TGA	PGA	+/–	GP	G	A	Pts	PIM	PP	SH	GW
1971-72	Sorel Black Hawks	QMJHL	24	23	21	44	....	....	....	11	....	....	....	....	....	....	....	....	....	....	4	0	1	1	29	....	....	....
1972-73	Sorel Black Hawks	QMJHL	63	40	62	102	....	....	....	54	....	....	....	....	....	....	....	....	....	....	....	....	....	....	....	....	....	....
1973-74	Sorel Black Hawks	QMJHL	70	62	81	143	....	....	....	120	....	....	....	....	....	....	....	....	....	....	....	....	....	....	....	....	....	....
1974-75	**Detroit Red Wings**	**NHL**	**25**	**10**	**7**	**17**	**9**	**5**	**14**	**10**	**1**	**0**	**0**	**51**	**19.6**	**23**	**1**	**17**	**0**	**5**	....	....	....	....	....	....	....	....
	Virginia Wings	AHL	49	9	13	22	....	....	....	14	....	....	....	....	....	....	....	....	....	....	....	....	....	....	....	....	....	....
1975-76	**Detroit Red Wings**	**NHL**	**72**	**32**	**27**	**59**	**28**	**20**	**48**	**48**	**12**	**0**	**4**	**190**	**16.8**	**73**	**24**	**47**	**0**	**2**	....	....	....	....	....	....	....	....
1976-77	**Detroit Red Wings**	**NHL**	**74**	**21**	**12**	**33**	**19**	**9**	**28**	**98**	**3**	**0**	**5**	**197**	**10.7**	**48**	**10**	**80**	**2**	**–40**	....	....	....	....	....	....	....	....
	Kansas City Blues	CHL	4	3	5	8	....	....	....	4	....	....	....	....	....	....	....	....	....	....	....	....	....	....	....	....	....	....
1977-78	**Detroit Red Wings**	**NHL**	**3**	**1**	**0**	**1**	**1**	**0**	**1**	**0**	**0**	**0**	**0**	**6**	**16.7**	**1**	**0**	**3**	**0**	**–2**	....	....	....	....	....	....	....	....
	New York Islanders	**NHL**	**25**	**9**	**6**	**15**	**8**	**5**	**13**	**2**	**0**	**0**	**2**	**40**	**22.5**	**22**	**0**	**6**	**0**	**16**	....	....	....	....	....	....	....	....
	Fort Worth Texans	CHL	9	2	1	3	....	....	....	4	....	....	....	....	....	....	....	....	....	....	....	....	....	....	....	....	....	....
1978-79	**Washington Capitals**	**NHL**	**30**	**7**	**6**	**13**	**6**	**4**	**10**	**7**	**1**	**0**	**1**	**53**	**13.2**	**16**	**2**	**32**	**0**	**–18**	....	....	....	....	....	....	....	....
	Milwaukee Admirals	IHL	15	3	5	8	....	....	....	2	....	....	....	....	....	....	....	....	....	....	8	7	4	11	2	....	....	....
1979-80	Nova Scotia Voyageurs	AHL	33	11	20	31	....	....	....	30	....	....	....	....	....	....	....	....	....	....	....	....	....	....	....	....	....	....
	Milwaukee Admirals	IHL	34	25	37	62	....	....	....	34	....	....	....	....	....	....	....	....	....	....	2	0	1	1	20	....	....	....
1980-81	Milwaukee Admirals	IHL	71	30	49	79	....	....	....	22	....	....	....	....	....	....	....	....	....	....	7	2	4	6	11	....	....	....
1981-82	Milwaukee Admirals	IHL	22	8	15	23	....	....	....	4	....	....	....	....	....	....	....	....	....	....	....	....	....	....	....	....	....	....
	Kalamazoo Wings	IHL	22	5	9	14	....	....	....	13	....	....	....	....	....	....	....	....	....	....	....	....	....	....	....	....	....	....
	NHL Totals		**229**	**80**	**58**	**138**	**71**	**43**	**114**	**165**	**17**	**0**	**12**	**537**	**14.9**	**183**	**37**	**185**	**2**		....	....	....	....	....	....	....	....

Traded to **NY Islanders** by **Detroit** for Andre St. Laurent, October 20, 1977. Traded to **Washington** by **NY Islanders** for Washington's 2nd round choice (Tomas Jonsson) in 1979 Entry Draft, October 19, 1978.

• BERGERON, Yves

RW – R. 5'9", 165 lbs. b: Malartic, Que., 1/11/1952. Pittsburgh's 8th, 120th overall, in 1972.

Season	Club	League	GP	G	A	Pts	AG	AA	APts	PIM	PP	SH	GW	S	%	TGF	PGF	TGA	PGA	+/–	GP	G	A	Pts	PIM	PP	SH	GW
1969-70	Shawinigan Bruins	QJHL	52	36	43	79	....	....	....	131	....	....	....	....	....	....	....	....	....	....	5	0	5	5	2	....	....	....
1970-71	Shawinigan Bruins	QJHL	62	35	54	89	....	....	....	87	....	....	....	....	....	....	....	....	....	....	15	3	14	17	6	....	....	....
1971-72	Shawinigan Bruins	QMJHL	57	31	60	91	....	....	....	54	....	....	....	....	....	....	....	....	....	....	9	1	3	4	15	....	....	....
1972-73	Quebec Nordiques	WHA	65	14	19	33	....	....	....	32	....	....	....	....	....	....	....	....	....	....	....	....	....	....	....	....	....	....
1973-74	Maine Nordiques	NAHL	73	27	52	79	....	....	....	54	....	....	....	....	....	....	....	....	....	....	8	2	1	3	11	....	....	....
1974-75	**Pittsburgh Penguins**	**NHL**	**2**	**0**	**0**	**0**	**0**	**0**	**0**	**0**	**0**	**0**	**0**	**0**	**0.0**	**0**	**0**	**3**	**0**	**–3**	....	....	....	....	....	....	....	....
	Hershey Bears	AHL	67	31	28	59	....	....	....	116	....	....	....	....	....	....	....	....	....	....	12	4	9	13	46	....	....	....
1975-76	Hershey Bears	AHL	67	26	23	49	....	....	....	87	....	....	....	....	....	....	....	....	....	....	10	2	4	6	14	....	....	....
1976-77	**Pittsburgh Penguins**	**NHL**	**1**	**0**	**0**	**0**	**0**	**0**	**0**	**0**	**0**	**0**	**0**	**2**	**0.0**	**0**	**0**	**0**	**0**	**0**	....	....	....	....	....	....	....	....
	Hershey Bears	AHL	72	23	27	50	....	....	....	90	....	....	....	....	....	....	....	....	....	....	6	1	1	2	0	....	....	....
1977-78			DID NOT PLAY																									
1978-79	Bathurst Alpines	NNBSL	....	....	....	....	....	....	....	....	....	....	....	....	....	....	....	....	....	....	4	1	3	4	51	....	....	....
1979-80	Bathurst Alpines	NNBSL	....	....	....	....	....	....	....	....	....	....	....	....	....	....	....	....	....	....	5	1	2	3	30	....	....	....
1980-81	Bathurst Alpines	NNBSL	....	....	....	....	....	....	....	....	....	....	....	....	....	....	....	....	....	....	8	1	2	3	19	....	....	....
1981-82	Bathurst Alpines	NNBSL	....	....	....	....	....	....	....	....	....	....	....	....	....	....	....	....	....	....	11	4	8	12	24	....	....	....

Season	Club	League	REGULAR SEASON																		PLAYOFFS							
			GP	G	A	Pts	AG	AA	APts	PIM	PP	SH	GW	S	%	TGF	PGF	TGA	PGA	+/-	GP	G	A	Pts	PIM	PP	SH	GW
1982-83	Bathurst Alpines	NNBSL	26	14	15	29	....	....	....	92	....	....	....	....	....	....	....	....	....	....	7	2	3	5	10	....	....	....
1983-84	Bathurst Alpines	NNBSL	19	6	6	12	....	....	....	40	....	....	....	....	....	....	....	....	....	....	5	3	1	4	6	....	....	....
1984-85	Bathurst Alpines	NNBSL	....	....	....	....	....	....	....	....	....	....	....	....	....	....	....	....	....	....	4	0	2	2	4	....	....	....
	NHL Totals		**3**	**0**	**0**	**0**	**0**	**0**	**0**	**0**	**0**	**0**	**0**	**2**	**0.0**	**0**	**0**	**3**	**0**		....	....	....	....	....	....	....	....
	Other Major League Totals		65	14	19	33	....	....	....	32	....	....	....	....	....	....	....	....	....	....	....	....	....	....	....	....	....	....

QJHL Second All-Star Team (1971)

Selected by **Quebec** (WHA) in 1972 WHA General Players Draft, February 12, 1972. • Served as playing/coach with **Bathurst Alpines** (NNBSL) from 1978-1985.

• BERGEVIN, Marc

D – L. 6'1", 214 lbs. b: Montreal, Que., 8/11/1965. Chicago's 3rd, 60th overall, in 1983.

Season	Club	League	GP	G	A	Pts	AG	AA	APts	PIM	PP	SH	GW	S	%	TGF	PGF	TGA	PGA	+/-	GP	G	A	Pts	PIM	PP	SH	GW
1981-82	Montreal Concordia	QAAA	44	10	20	30	....	....	....	....	....	....	....	....	....	....	....	....	....	....	....	....	....	....	....	....	....	....
1982-83	Chicoutimi Sagueneens	QMJHL	64	3	27	30	....	....	....	113	....	....	....	....	....	....	....	....	....	....	....	....	....	....	....	....	....	....
1983-84	Chicoutimi Sagueneens	QMJHL	70	10	35	45	....	....	....	125	....	....	....	....	....	....	....	....	....	....	....	....	....	....	....	....	....	....
	Springfield Indians	AHL	7	0	1	1	....	....	....	2	....	....	....	....	....	....	....	....	....	....	....	....	....	....	....	....	....	....
1984-85	**Chicago Black Hawks**	**NHL**	**60**	**0**	**6**	**6**	**0**	**4**	**4**	**54**	**0**	**0**	**0**	**41**	**0.0**	**36**	**0**	**46**	**1**	**–9**	**6**	**0**	**3**	**3**	**2**	**0**	**0**	**0**
	Springfield Indians	AHL	....	....	....	....	....	....	....	....	....	....	....	....	....	....	....	....	....	....	4	0	0	0	0	....	....	....
1985-86	**Chicago Black Hawks**	**NHL**	**71**	**7**	**7**	**14**	**6**	**5**	**11**	**60**	**0**	**0**	**1**	**50**	**14.0**	**47**	**0**	**49**	**2**	**0**	**3**	**0**	**0**	**0**	**0**	**0**	**0**	**0**
1986-87	**Chicago Blackhawks**	**NHL**	**66**	**4**	**10**	**14**	**3**	**7**	**10**	**66**	**0**	**0**	**0**	**56**	**7.1**	**48**	**0**	**53**	**9**	**4**	**3**	**1**	**0**	**1**	**2**	**0**	**0**	**0**
1987-88	**Chicago Blackhawks**	**NHL**	**58**	**1**	**6**	**7**	**1**	**4**	**5**	**85**	**0**	**0**	**0**	**51**	**2.0**	**32**	**2**	**67**	**18**	**–19**	....	....	....	....	....	....	....	....
	Saginaw Hawks	IHL	10	2	7	9	....	....	....	20	....	....	....	....	....	....	....	....	....	....	....	....	....	....	....	....	....	....
1988-89	**Chicago Blackhawks**	**NHL**	**11**	**0**	**0**	**0**	**0**	**0**	**0**	**18**	**0**	**0**	**0**	**9**	**0.0**	**7**	**0**	**15**	**5**	**–3**	....	....	....	....	....	....	....	....
	New York Islanders	**NHL**	**58**	**2**	**13**	**15**	**2**	**9**	**11**	**62**	**1**	**0**	**0**	**56**	**3.6**	**55**	**3**	**77**	**27**	**2**	....	....	....	....	....	....	....	....
1989-90	**New York Islanders**	**NHL**	**18**	**0**	**4**	**4**	**0**	**3**	**3**	**30**	**0**	**0**	**0**	**12**	**0.0**	**14**	**2**	**24**	**4**	**–8**	....	....	....	....	....	....	....	....
	Springfield Indians	AHL	47	7	16	23	....	....	....	66	....	....	....	....	....	....	....	....	....	....	17	2	11	13	16	....	....	....
1990-91	Capital District Islanders	AHL	7	0	5	5	....	....	....	6	....	....	....	....	....	....	....	....	....	....	....	....	....	....	....	....	....	....
	Hartford Whalers	**NHL**	**4**	**0**	**0**	**0**	**0**	**0**	**0**	**4**	**0**	**0**	**0**	**2**	**0.0**	**0**	**0**	**3**	**0**	**–3**	....	....	....	....	....	....	....	....
	Springfield Indians	AHL	58	4	23	27	....	....	....	85	....	....	....	....	....	....	....	....	....	....	18	0	7	7	26	....	....	....
1991-92	**Hartford Whalers**	**NHL**	**75**	**7**	**17**	**24**	**6**	**13**	**19**	**64**	**4**	**1**	**1**	**96**	**7.3**	**73**	**26**	**91**	**31**	**–13**	**5**	**0**	**0**	**0**	**2**	**0**	**0**	**0**
1992-93	**Tampa Bay Lightning**	**NHL**	**78**	**2**	**12**	**14**	**2**	**8**	**10**	**66**	**0**	**0**	**0**	**69**	**2.9**	**50**	**1**	**107**	**42**	**–16**	....	....	....	....	....	....	....	....
1993-94	**Tampa Bay Lightning**	**NHL**	**83**	**1**	**15**	**16**	**1**	**12**	**13**	**87**	**0**	**0**	**1**	**76**	**1.3**	**56**	**4**	**95**	**38**	**–5**	....	....	....	....	....	....	....	....
	Canada	WC-A	8	0	0	0	....	....	....	2	....	....	....	....	....	....	....	....	....	....	....	....	....	....	....	....	....	....
1994-95	**Tampa Bay Lightning**	**NHL**	**44**	**2**	**4**	**6**	**4**	**6**	**10**	**51**	**0**	**1**	**0**	**32**	**6.3**	**35**	**1**	**62**	**22**	**–6**	....	....	....	....	....	....	....	....
1995-96	**Detroit Red Wings**	**NHL**	**70**	**1**	**9**	**10**	**1**	**7**	**8**	**33**	**0**	**0**	**0**	**26**	**3.8**	**53**	**1**	**56**	**11**	**7**	**17**	**1**	**0**	**1**	**14**	**1**	**0**	**0**
1996-97	**St. Louis Blues**	**NHL**	**82**	**0**	**4**	**4**	**0**	**4**	**4**	**53**	**0**	**0**	**0**	**30**	**0.0**	**46**	**1**	**72**	**18**	**–9**	**6**	**1**	**0**	**1**	**8**	**0**	**0**	**0**
1997-98	**St. Louis Blues**	**NHL**	**81**	**3**	**7**	**10**	**4**	**7**	**11**	**90**	**0**	**0**	**0**	**40**	**7.5**	**58**	**0**	**86**	**26**	**–2**	**10**	**0**	**1**	**1**	**8**	**0**	**0**	**0**
1998-99	**St. Louis Blues**	**NHL**	**52**	**1**	**1**	**2**	**1**	**1**	**2**	**99**	**0**	**0**	**0**	**40**	**2.5**	**28**	**0**	**54**	**12**	**–14**	....	....	....	....	....	....	....	....
99-2000	**St. Louis Blues**	**NHL**	**81**	**1**	**8**	**9**	**1**	**7**	**8**	**75**	**0**	**0**	**0**	**54**	**1.9**	**64**	**2**	**61**	**26**	**27**	**7**	**0**	**1**	**1**	**6**	**0**	**0**	**0**
	NHL Totals		**992**	**32**	**123**	**155**	**32**	**97**	**129**	**997**	**5**	**2**	**3**	**740**	**4.3**	**702**	**43**	**1018**	**292**		**57**	**3**	**5**	**8**	**42**	**1**	**0**	**0**

Traded to **NY Islanders** by **Chicago** with Gary Nylund for Steve Konroyd and Bob Bassen, November 25, 1988. Traded to **Hartford** by **NY Islanders** for Hartford's 5th round choice (Ryan Duthie) in 1992 Entry Draft, October 30, 1990. Signed as a free agent by **Tampa Bay**, July 9, 1992. Traded to **Detroit** by **Tampa Bay** with Ben Hankinson for Shawn Burr and Detroit's 3rd round choice (later traded to Boston — Boston selected Jason Doyle) in 1996 Entry Draft, August 17, 1995. Signed as a free agent by **St. Louis**, July 31, 1996.

• BERGKVIST, Stefan

D – L. 6'2", 224 lbs. b: Leksand, Sweden, 3/10/1975. Pittsburgh's 1st, 26th overall, in 1993.

Season	Club	League	GP	G	A	Pts	AG	AA	APts	PIM	PP	SH	GW	S	%	TGF	PGF	TGA	PGA	+/-	GP	G	A	Pts	PIM	PP	SH	GW
1992-93	Leksands IF	Sweden-Jr.	2	0	0	0	....	....	....	0	....	....	....	....	....	....	....	....	....	....	....	....	....	....	....	....	....	....
	Leksands IF	Sweden	15	0	0	0	....	....	....	6	....	....	....	....	....	....	....	....	....	....	....	....	....	....	....	....	....	....
	Sweden	EJC-A	6	1	1	2	....	....	....	8	....	....	....	....	....	....	....	....	....	....	....	....	....	....	....	....	....	....
1993-94	Leksands IF	Sweden-Jr.	14	2	5	7	....	....	....	*60	....	....	....	....	....	....	....	....	....	....	....	....	....	....	....	....	....	....
	Leksands IF	Sweden	6	0	0	0	....	....	....	0	....	....	....	....	....	....	....	....	....	....	....	....	....	....	....	....	....	....
1994-95	London Knights	OHL	64	3	17	20	....	....	....	93	....	....	....	....	....	....	....	....	....	....	4	0	0	0	5	....	....	....
1995-96	**Pittsburgh Penguins**	**NHL**	**2**	**0**	**0**	**0**	**0**	**0**	**0**	**2**	**0**	**0**	**0**	**4**	**0.0**	**1**	**0**	**1**	**0**	**0**	**4**	**0**	**0**	**0**	**2**	**0**	**0**	**0**
	Cleveland Lumberjacks	IHL	61	2	8	10	....	....	....	58	....	....	....	....	....	....	....	....	....	....	3	0	0	0	14	....	....	....
1996-97	**Pittsburgh Penguins**	**NHL**	**5**	**0**	**0**	**0**	**0**	**0**	**0**	**7**	**0**	**0**	**0**	**0**	**0.0**	**1**	**0**	**2**	**0**	**–1**	....	....	....	....	....	....	....	....
	Cleveland Lumberjacks	IHL	33	0	1	1	....	....	....	54	....	....	....	....	....	....	....	....	....	....	4	0	0	0	0	....	....	....
1997-98	Cleveland Lumberjacks	IHL	71	3	6	9	....	....	....	129	....	....	....	....	....	....	....	....	....	....	10	0	2	2	24	....	....	....
1998-99	Leksands IF	Sweden	42	0	2	2	....	....	....	167	....	....	....	....	....	....	....	....	....	....	3	0	0	0	4	....	....	....
	Leksands IF	EuroHL	6	0	2	2	....	....	....	28	....	....	....	....	....	....	....	....	....	....	1	0	0	0	0	....	....	....
99-2000	Leksands IF	Sweden	27	0	3	3	....	....	....	61	....	....	....	....	....	....	....	....	....	....	....	....	....	....	....	....	....	....
	NHL Totals		**7**	**0**	**0**	**0**	**0**	**0**	**0**	**9**	**0**	**0**	**0**	**4**	**0.0**	**2**	**0**	**3**	**0**		**4**	**0**	**0**	**0**	**2**	**0**	**0**	**0**

• BERGLAND, Tim

Timothy Daniel RW – R. 6'3", 194 lbs. b: Crookston, MN, 1/11/1965. Washington's 1st, 77th overall, in 1983.

Season	Club	League	GP	G	A	Pts	AG	AA	APts	PIM	PP	SH	GW	S	%	TGF	PGF	TGA	PGA	+/-	GP	G	A	Pts	PIM	PP	SH	GW
1981-82	Lincoln High Prowlers	Hi-School	20	16	20	36	....	....	....	....	....	....	....	....	....	....	....	....	....	....	....	....	....	....	....	....	....	....
1982-83	Lincoln High Prowlers	Hi-School	20	30	23	53	....	....	....	....	....	....	....	....	....	....	....	....	....	....	....	....	....	....	....	....	....	....
1983-84	University of Minnesota	WCHA	24	4	11	15	....	....	....	4	....	....	....	....	....	....	....	....	....	....	....	....	....	....	....	....	....	....
1984-85	University of Minnesota	WCHA	34	5	9	14	....	....	....	8	....	....	....	....	....	....	....	....	....	....	....	....	....	....	....	....	....	....
1985-86	University of Minnesota	WCHA	48	11	16	27	....	....	....	26	....	....	....	....	....	....	....	....	....	....	....	....	....	....	....	....	....	....
1986-87	University of Minnesota	WCHA	49	18	17	35	....	....	....	48	....	....	....	....	....	....	....	....	....	....	....	....	....	....	....	....	....	....
1987-88	Fort Wayne Komets	IHL	13	2	1	3	....	....	....	9	....	....	....	....	....	....	....	....	....	....	....	....	....	....	....	....	....	....
	Binghamton Whalers	AHL	63	21	26	47	....	....	....	31	....	....	....	....	....	....	....	....	....	....	4	0	0	0	0	....	....	....
1988-89	Baltimore Skipjacks	AHL	78	24	29	53	....	....	....	39	....	....	....	....	....	....	....	....	....	....	....	....	....	....	....	....	....	....
1989-90	Washington Capitals	Fr-Tour	1	1	0	1	....	....	....	0	....	....	....	....	....	....	....	....	....	....	....	....	....	....	....	....	....	....
	Washington Capitals	**NHL**	**32**	**2**	**5**	**7**	**2**	**4**	**6**	**31**	**0**	**0**	**0**	**20**	**10.0**	**10**	**0**	**14**	**6**	**2**	**15**	**1**	**1**	**2**	**10**	**0**	**0**	**0**
	Baltimore Skipjacks	AHL	47	12	19	31	....	....	....	55	....	....	....	....	....	....	....	....	....	....	....	....	....	....	....	....	....	....
1990-91	**Washington Capitals**	**NHL**	**47**	**5**	**9**	**14**	**5**	**7**	**12**	**21**	**0**	**0**	**0**	**41**	**12.2**	**15**	**0**	**18**	**2**	**–1**	**11**	**1**	**1**	**2**	**12**	**0**	**0**	**0**
	Baltmore Skipjacks	AHL	15	8	9	17	....	....	....	16	....	....	....	....	....	....	....	....	....	....	....	....	....	....	....	....	....	....
1991-92	**Washington Capitals**	**NHL**	**22**	**1**	**4**	**5**	**1**	**3**	**4**	**2**	**0**	**0**	**0**	**18**	**5.6**	**9**	**0**	**15**	**3**	**–3**	....	....	....	....	....	....	....	....
	Baltimore Skipjacks	AHL	11	6	10	16	....	....	....	5	....	....	....	....	....	....	....	....	....	....	....	....	....	....	....	....	....	....
1992-93	**Tampa Bay Lightning**	**NHL**	**27**	**3**	**3**	**6**	**2**	**2**	**4**	**11**	**0**	**0**	**0**	**44**	**6.8**	**12**	**2**	**19**	**4**	**–5**	....	....	....	....	....	....	....	....
	Atlanta Knights	IHL	49	18	21	39	....	....	....	26	....	....	....	....	....	....	....	....	....	....	9	3	3	6	10	....	....	....
1993-94	**Tampa Bay Lightning**	**NHL**	**51**	**6**	**5**	**11**	**6**	**4**	**10**	**6**	**0**	**0**	**0**	**61**	**9.8**	**21**	**0**	**46**	**11**	**–14**	....	....	....	....	....	....	....	....
	Atlanta Knights	IHL	19	6	7	13	....	....	....	6	....	....	....	....	....	....	....	....	....	....	....	....	....	....	....	....	....	....
	Washington Capitals	**NHL**	**3**	**0**	**0**	**0**	**0**	**0**	**0**	**4**	**0**	**0**	**0**	**4**	**0.0**	**0**	**0**	**1**	**0**	**–1**	....	....	....	....	....	....	....	....
1994-95	Chicago Wolves	IHL	81	12	21	33	....	....	....	70	....	....	....	....	....	....	....	....	....	....	3	1	2	3	4	....	....	....
	United States	WC-A	5	2	1	3	....	....	....	2	....	....	....	....	....	....	....	....	....	....	....	....	....	....	....	....	....	....
1995-96	Chicago Wolves	IHL	81	9	19	28	....	....	....	45	....	....	....	....	....	....	....	....	....	....	9	0	1	1	4	....	....	....
1996-97	Chicago Wolves	IHL	82	20	22	42	....	....	....	68	....	....	....	....	....	....	....	....	....	....	4	1	1	2	0	....	....	....
1997-98	HIFK Helsinki	Finland	7	2	1	3	....	....	....	16	....	....	....	....	....	....	....	....	....	....	....	....	....	....	....	....	....	....
	Chicago Wolves	IHL	49	8	10	18	....	....	....	18	....	....	....	....	....	....	....	....	....	....	10	2	0	2	16	....	....	....
1998-99	Chicago Wolves	IHL	68	4	9	13	....	....	....	20	....	....	....	....	....	....	....	....	....	....	....	....	....	....	....	....	....	....
	NHL Totals		**182**	**17**	**26**	**43**	**16**	**20**	**36**	**75**	**0**	**0**	**0**	**188**	**9.0**	**67**	**2**	**113**	**26**		**26**	**2**	**2**	**4**	**22**	**0**	**0**	**0**

Claimed by **Tampa Bay** from **Washington** in Expansion Draft, June 18, 1992. Claimed on waivers by **Washington** from **Tampa Bay**, March 19, 1994. Signed as a free agent by **Chicago** (IHL), Septmeber 30, 1994.

• BERGLOFF, Bob

Robert D – R. 6'1", 185 lbs. b: Dickinson, ND, 7/26/1958. Minnesota's 6th, 87th overall, in 1978.

Season	Club	League	GP	G	A	Pts	AG	AA	APts	PIM	PP	SH	GW	S	%	TGF	PGF	TGA	PGA	+/-	GP	G	A	Pts	PIM	PP	SH	GW
1976-77	Bloomington Jr. Stars	MWJHL	40	21	21	42				64	....	....	....	....	....	....	....	....	....	....	....	....	....	....	....	....	....	....
1977-78	University of Minnesota	WCHA	DID NOT PLAY – FRESHMAN																									
1978-79	University of Minnesota	WCHA	STATISTICS NOT AVAILABLE																									
1979-80	University of Minnesota	WCHA	40	9	22	31	....	....	....	54	....	....	....	....	....	....	....	....	....	....	....	....	....	....	....	....	....	....
1980-81	University of Minnesota	WCHA	45	2	16	18	....	....	....	89	....	....	....	....	....	....	....	....	....	....	....	....	....	....	....	....	....	....
1981-82	Nashville South Stars	CHL	74	2	20	22	....	....	....	111	....	....	....	....	....	....	....	....	....	....	3	0	0	0	7	....	....	....
	Toledo Goaldiggers	IHL	3	1	1	2	....	....	....	11	....	....	....	....	....	....	....	....	....	....	....	....	....	....	....	....	....	....

Season	Club	League	REGULAR SEASON																		PLAYOFFS							
			GP	G	A	Pts	AG	AA	APts	PIM	PP	SH	GW	S	%	TGF	PGF	TGA	PGA	+/–	GP	G	A	Pts	PIM	PP	SH	GW
1982-83	**Minnesota North Stars**	**NHL**	**2**	**0**	**0**	**0**	**0**	**0**	**0**	**5**	**0**	**0**	**0**	**1**	**0.0**	**0**	**0**	**1**	**0**	**–1**	....	....	....	....	....	....	....	....
	Birmingham South Stars	CHL	78	6	20	26	....	....	....	156	....	....	....	....	....	....	....	....	....	....	13	0	4	4	10	....	....	....
1983-84	Salt Lake Golden Eagles	CHL	44	4	17	21	....	....	....	78	....	....	....	....	....	....	....	....	....	....	2	0	0	0	4	....	....	....
1984-85	Salt Lake Golden Eagles	IHL	9	0	4	4	....	....	....	15	....	....	....	....	....	....	....	....	....	....	....	....	....	....	....	....	....	....
1985-86	New Haven Nighthawks	AHL	7	0	1	1	....	....	....	7	....	....	....	....	....	....	....	....	....	....	4	0	2	2	2	....	....	....
1986-87	GIJS Groningen	Holland	STATISTICS NOT AVAILABLE																									
1987-88	Dundee Tigers	Un-Cup	6	6	5	11	....	....	....	13	....	....	....	....	....	....	....	....	....	....	....	....	....	....	....	....	....	....
	Dundee Tigers	Britain	36	14	44	58	....	....	....	103	....	....	....	....	....	....	....	....	....	....	....	....	....	....	....	....	....	....
	NHL Totals		**2**	**0**	**0**	**0**	**0**	**0**	**0**	**5**	**0**	**0**	**0**	**1**	**0.0**	**0**	**0**	**1**	**0**		....	....	....	....	....	....	....	....

• BERGLUND, Bo

RW – L. 5′10″, 175 lbs. b: Sjalevad, Sweden, 4/6/1955. Quebec's 10th, 242nd overall, in 1983.

Season	Club	League	GP	G	A	Pts	AG	AA	APts	PIM	PP	SH	GW	S	%	TGF	PGF	TGA	PGA	+/–	GP	G	A	Pts	PIM	PP	SH	GW
1973-74	MoDo AIK	Sweden-Jr.	14	6	4	10	....	....	....	12	....	....	....	....	....	....	....	....	....	....	14	5	6	11	14	....	....	....
	Sweden	WJC-A	5	1	4	5	....	....	....	0	....	....	....	....	....	....	....	....	....	....	....	....	....	....	....	....	....	....
1974-75	MoDo AIK	Sweden	26	15	17	32	....	....	....	16	....	....	....	....	....	....	....	....	....	....	2	2	2	4	*14	....	....	....
	Sweden	WJC-A	....	0	1	1	....	....	....	....	....	....	....	....	....	....	....	....	....	....	....	....	....	....	....	....	....	....
1975-76	MoDo AIK	Sweden	35	16	19	35	....	....	....	43	....	....	....	....	....	....	....	....	....	....	....	....	....	....	....	....	....	....
1976-77	MoDo AIK	Sweden	33	17	21	38	....	....	....	30	....	....	....	....	....	....	....	....	....	....	4	3	2	5	0	....	....	....
1977-78	Djurgardens IF Stockholm	Sweden	15	7	5	12	....	....	....	6	....	....	....	....	....	....	....	....	....	....	....	....	....	....	....	....	....	....
1978-79	Djurgardens IF Stockholm	Sweden	36	23	13	36	....	....	....	46	....	....	....	....	....	....	....	....	....	....	6	2	3	5	14	....	....	....
1979-80	Djurgardens IF Stockholm	Sweden	36	20	17	37	....	....	....	50	....	....	....	....	....	....	....	....	....	....	....	....	....	....	....	....	....	....
	Sweden	Olympics	7	1	3	4	....	....	....	4	....	....	....	....	....	....	....	....	....	....	....	....	....	....	....	....	....	....
1980-81	Djurgardens IF Stockholm	DN-Cup	3	0	0	0	....	....	....	2	....	....	....	....	....	....	....	....	....	....	....	....	....	....	....	....	....	....
	Djurgardens IF Stockholm	Sweden	31	13	9	22	....	....	....	64	....	....	....	....	....	....	....	....	....	....	....	....	....	....	....	....	....	....
1981-82	Djurgardens IF Stockholm	DN-Cup	4	2	1	3	....	....	....	....	....	....	....	....	....	....	....	....	....	....	....	....	....	....	....	....	....	....
	Djurgardens IF Stockholm	Sweden	34	16	36	52	....	....	....	58	....	....	....	....	....	....	....	....	....	....	....	....	....	....	....	....	....	....
1982-83	Djurgardens IF Stockholm	Sweden	32	19	13	32	....	....	....	66	....	....	....	....	....	....	....	....	....	....	8	5	1	6	8	....	....	....
1983-84	**Quebec Nordiques**	**NHL**	**75**	**16**	**27**	**43**	**13**	**18**	**31**	**20**	**1**	**0**	**1**	**83**	**19.3**	**64**	**17**	**41**	**0**	**6**	**7**	**2**	**0**	**2**	**4**	**0**	**0**	**1**
1984-85	**Quebec Nordiques**	**NHL**	**12**	**4**	**1**	**5**	**3**	**1**	**4**	**6**	**0**	**0**	**1**	**15**	**26.7**	**6**	**1**	**3**	**0**	**2**	....	....	....	....	....	....	....	....
	Minnesota North Stars	**NHL**	**33**	**6**	**9**	**15**	**5**	**6**	**11**	**8**	**1**	**0**	**1**	**38**	**15.8**	**20**	**2**	**21**	**0**	**–3**	**2**	**0**	**0**	**0**	**2**	**0**	**0**	**0**
	Springfield Indians	AHL	3	1	2	3	....	....	....	0	....	....	....	....	....	....	....	....	....	....	....	....	....	....	....	....	....	....
1985-86	**Minnesota North Stars**	**NHL**	**3**	**2**	**0**	**2**	**2**	**0**	**2**	**2**	**1**	**0**	**0**	**6**	**33.3**	**2**	**0**	**2**	**0**	**0**	....	....	....	....	....	....	....	....
	Springfield Indians	AHL	3	0	1	1	....	....	....	2	....	....	....	....	....	....	....	....	....	....	....	....	....	....	....	....	....	....
	Philadelphia Flyers	**NHL**	**7**	**0**	**2**	**2**	**0**	**1**	**1**	**4**	**0**	**0**	**0**	**5**	**0.0**	**2**	**0**	**2**	**0**	**0**	....	....	....	....	....	....	....	....
	Hershey Bears	AHL	43	17	28	45	....	....	....	40	....	....	....	....	....	....	....	....	....	....	16	7	10	17	17	....	....	....
1986-87	AIK Solna Stockholm	Sweden-2	28	26	24	50	....	....	....	36	....	....	....	....	....	....	....	....	....	....	....	....	....	....	....	....	....	....
1987-88	AIK Solna Stockholm	Sweden	39	25	31	*56	....	....	....	44	....	....	....	....	....	....	....	....	....	....	5	3	4	7	4	....	....	....
	Sweden	Olympics	8	4	4	8	....	....	....	4	....	....	....	....	....	....	....	....	....	....	....	....	....	....	....	....	....	....
1988-89	AIK Solna Stockholm	Sweden	33	11	17	28	....	....	....	42	....	....	....	....	....	....	....	....	....	....	1	0	0	0	0	....	....	....
	Sweden	WEC-A	9	4	0	4	....	....	....	4	....	....	....	....	....	....	....	....	....	....	....	....	....	....	....	....	....	....
1989-90	AIK Solna Stockholm	Sweden	24	5	11	16	....	....	....	20	....	....	....	....	....	....	....	....	....	....	....	....	....	....	....	....	....	....
	NHL Totals		**130**	**28**	**39**	**67**	**23**	**26**	**49**	**40**	**3**	**0**	**3**	**147**	**19.0**	**94**	**20**	**69**	**0**		**9**	**2**	**0**	**2**	**6**	**0**	**0**	**1**

Swedish World All-Star Team (1988) • Won Golden Puck Award as Swedish Player of the Year (1988)

Traded to **Minnesota** by **Quebec** with Tony McKegney for Brad Maxwell and Brent Ashton, December 14, 1984. Traded to **Philadelphia** by **Minnesota** with Dave Richter for Todd Bergen and Ed Hospodar, November 29, 1985.

• BERGMAN, Gary

Gary Gunnar D – L. 5′11″, 188 lbs. b: Kenora, Ont., 10/7/1938.

Season	Club	League	GP	G	A	Pts	AG	AA	APts	PIM	PP	SH	GW	S	%	TGF	PGF	TGA	PGA	+/–	GP	G	A	Pts	PIM	PP	SH	GW
1957-58	Winnipeg Braves	MJHL	30	4	2	6	....	....	....	73	....	....	....	....	....	....	....	....	....	....	5	1	2	3	14	....	....	....
	Winnipeg Warriors	WHL	2	0	0	0	....	....	....	0	....	....	....	....	....	....	....	....	....	....	....	....	....	....	....	....	....	....
1958-59	Winnipeg Braves	MJHL	29	15	15	30	....	....	....	114	....	....	....	....	....	....	....	....	....	....	24	4	*20	24	46	....	....	....
1959-60	Winnipeg Warriors	WHL	58	1	9	10	....	....	....	147	....	....	....	....	....	....	....	....	....	....	....	....	....	....	....	....	....	....
1960-61	Buffalo Bisons	AHL	67	5	14	19	....	....	....	104	....	....	....	....	....	....	....	....	....	....	4	0	0	0	12	....	....	....
1961-62	Cleveland Barons	AHL	68	10	30	40	....	....	....	164	....	....	....	....	....	....	....	....	....	....	6	1	2	3	14	....	....	....
1962-63	Quebec Aces	AHL	8	1	2	3	....	....	....	14	....	....	....	....	....	....	....	....	....	....	....	....	....	....	....	....	....	....
	Cleveland Barons	AHL	47	4	19	23	....	....	....	127	....	....	....	....	....	....	....	....	....	....	7	1	5	6	10	....	....	....
1963-64	Springfield Indians	AHL	60	13	24	37	....	....	....	106	....	....	....	....	....	....	....	....	....	....	....	....	....	....	....	....	....	....
1964-65	**Detroit Red Wings**	**NHL**	**58**	**4**	**7**	**11**	**5**	**7**	**12**	**85**	....	....	....	....	....	....	....	....	....	....	**5**	**0**	**1**	**1**	**4**	**0**	**0**	**0**
1965-66	**Detroit Red Wings**	**NHL**	**61**	**3**	**16**	**19**	**3**	**15**	**18**	**96**	....	....	....	....	....	....	....	....	....	....	**12**	**0**	**3**	**3**	**14**	**0**	**0**	**0**
	Memphis Wings	CPHL	5	2	3	5	....	....	....	4	....	....	....	....	....	....	....	....	....	....	....	....	....	....	....	....	....	....
1966-67	**Detroit Red Wings**	**NHL**	**70**	**5**	**30**	**35**	**6**	**29**	**35**	**129**	....	....	....	....	....	....	....	....	....	....	....	....	....	....	....	....	....	....
1967-68	**Detroit Red Wings**	**NHL**	**74**	**13**	**28**	**41**	**15**	**28**	**43**	**109**	**5**	**2**	**3**	**165**	**7.9**	**124**	**22**	**141**	**38**	**–1**	....	....	....	....	....	....	....	....
1968-69	**Detroit Red Wings**	**NHL**	**76**	**7**	**30**	**37**	**7**	**27**	**34**	**80**	**2**	**0**	**2**	**191**	**3.7**	**126**	**12**	**98**	**29**	**45**	....	....	....	....	....	....	....	....
1969-70	**Detroit Red Wings**	**NHL**	**69**	**6**	**17**	**23**	**6**	**16**	**22**	**122**	**1**	**0**	**1**	**146**	**4.1**	**84**	**14**	**94**	**28**	**4**	**4**	**0**	**1**	**1**	**2**	**0**	**0**	**0**
1970-71	**Detroit Red Wings**	**NHL**	**68**	**8**	**25**	**33**	**8**	**21**	**29**	**149**	**0**	**1**	**0**	**168**	**4.8**	**85**	**18**	**128**	**33**	**–28**	....	....	....	....	....	....	....	....
1971-72	**Detroit Red Wings**	**NHL**	**75**	**6**	**31**	**37**	**6**	**27**	**33**	**138**	**1**	**0**	**0**	**141**	**4.3**	**133**	**35**	**111**	**20**	**7**	....	....	....	....	....	....	....	....
1972-73	Team Canada	Summit-72	8	0	3	3	....	....	....	13	....	....	....	....	....	....	....	....	....	....	....	....	....	....	....	....	....	....
	Detroit Red Wings	**NHL**	**68**	**3**	**28**	**31**	**3**	**22**	**25**	**71**	**0**	**0**	**0**	**174**	**1.7**	**127**	**30**	**105**	**18**	**10**	....	....	....	....	....	....	....	....
1973-74	**Detroit Red Wings**	**NHL**	**11**	**0**	**6**	**6**	**0**	**5**	**5**	**18**	**0**	**0**	**0**	**10**	**0.0**	**14**	**1**	**24**	**5**	**–6**	....	....	....	....	....	....	....	....
	Minnesota North Stars	**NHL**	**57**	**3**	**23**	**26**	**3**	**19**	**22**	**66**	**1**	**0**	**1**	**87**	**3.4**	**66**	**8**	**79**	**9**	**–12**	....	....	....	....	....	....	....	....
1974-75	**Detroit Red Wings**	**NHL**	**76**	**5**	**25**	**30**	**4**	**19**	**23**	**104**	**2**	**1**	**0**	**100**	**5.0**	**95**	**27**	**119**	**26**	**–25**	....	....	....	....	....	....	....	....
1975-76	**Kansas City Scouts**	**NHL**	**75**	**5**	**33**	**38**	**4**	**25**	**29**	**82**	**1**	**0**	**1**	**125**	**4.0**	**85**	**27**	**143**	**33**	**–52**	....	....	....	....	....	....	....	....
	NHL Totals		**838**	**68**	**299**	**367**	**70**	**260**	**330**	**1249**	....	....	....	....	....	....	....	....	....		**21**	**0**	**5**	**5**	**20**	....	....	....

Played in NHL All-Star Game (1973)

Claimed by **Chicago** from **Winnipeg** (WHL) in Inter-League Draft, June 7, 1960. Traded to **Cleveland** (AHL) by **Chicago** (Buffalo-AHL) for cash, October, 1961. Traded to **Quebec** (AHL) by **Montreal** (Cleveland-AHL) for cash, July, 1962. Traded to **Montreal** (Cleveland-AHL) by **Quebec** (AHL) for Terry Gray with Boston retaining Gray's NHL rights, November 1, 1962. Loaned to **Springfield** (AHL) by **Montreal** with Brian D. Smith, Wayne Boddy, Fred Hilts, Lorne O'Donnell and John Rodger for Terry Gray, Bruce Cline, Wayne Larkin, John Chasczewski and Ted Harris, June, 1963. Claimed by **Detroit** from **Montreal** in Intra-League Draft, June 10, 1964. Traded to **Minnesota** by **Detroit** for Ted Harris, November 7, 1973. Traded to **Detroit** by **Minnesota** for Detroit's 3rd round choice (Alex Pirus) in 1975 Amateur Draft, October 1, 1974. Traded to **Kansas City** by **Detroit** with Bill McKenzie for Peter McDuffe and Glen Burdon, August 22, 1975.

• BERGMAN, Thommie

Lars Rudolf Thommie D – L. 6′2″, 200 lbs. b: Munkfors, Sweden, 12/10/1947.

Season	Club	League	GP	G	A	Pts	AG	AA	APts	PIM	PP	SH	GW	S	%	TGF	PGF	TGA	PGA	+/–	GP	G	A	Pts	PIM	PP	SH	GW
1964-1968	KB-63 Karlsloga	Sweden-2	STATISTICS NOT AVAILABLE																									
1968-69	IK Kaarlsoga	Sweden	20	4	2	6	....	....	....	22	....	....	....	....	....	....	....	....	....	....	....	....	....	....	....	....	....	....
1969-70	Sodertalje SK	Sweden	14	5	4	9	....	....	....	2	....	....	....	....	....	....	....	....	....	....	14	4	2	6	12	....	....	....
1970-71	Sodertalje SK	Sweden	12	8	2	10	....	....	....	18	....	....	....	....	....	....	....	....	....	....	14	3	6	9	14	....	....	....
	Sweden	WEC-A	10	1	0	1	....	....	....	4	....	....	....	....	....	....	....	....	....	....	....	....	....	....	....	....	....	....
1971-72	Vastra Frolunda	Sweden	26	9	9	18	....	....	....	36	....	....	....	....	....	....	....	....	....	....	8	2	4	6	8	....	....	....
	Sweden	Olympics	5	1	1	2	....	....	....	10	....	....	....	....	....	....	....	....	....	....	....	....	....	....	....	....	....	....
	Sweden	WEC-A	8	2	4	6	....	....	....	8	....	....	....	....	....	....	....	....	....	....	....	....	....	....	....	....	....	....
1972-73	**Detroit Red Wings**	**NHL**	**75**	**9**	**12**	**21**	**8**	**9**	**17**	**70**	**1**	**0**	**2**	**165**	**5.5**	**102**	**17**	**92**	**13**	**6**	....	....	....	....	....	....	....	....
1973-74	**Detroit Red Wings**	**NHL**	**43**	**0**	**3**	**3**	**0**	**2**	**2**	**21**	**0**	**0**	**0**	**49**	**0.0**	**24**	**1**	**45**	**7**	**–15**	....	....	....	....	....	....	....	....
	Virginia Wings	AHL	8	0	3	3	....	....	....	9	....	....	....	....	....	....	....	....	....	....	....	....	....	....	....	....	....	....
1974-75	**Detroit Red Wings**	**NHL**	**18**	**0**	**1**	**1**	**0**	**1**	**1**	**27**	**0**	**0**	**0**	**20**	**0.0**	**4**	**0**	**15**	**4**	**–7**	....	....	....	....	....	....	....	....
	Winnipeg Jets	WHA	49	4	15	19	....	....	....	70	....	....	....	....	....	....	....	....	....	....	....	....	....	....	....	....	....	....
1975-76	Winnipeg Jets	WHA	81	11	30	41	....	....	....	111	....	....	....	....	....	....	....	....	....	....	13	3	10	13	8	....	....	....
1976-77	Sweden	Can-Cup	3	0	2	2	....	....	....	6	....	....	....	....	....	....	....	....	....	....	....	....	....	....	....	....	....	....
	Winnipeg Jets	WHA	42	2	24	26	....	....	....	37	....	....	....	....	....	....	....	....	....	....	....	....	....	....	....	....	....	....
1977-78	Winnipeg Jets	WHA	62	5	28	33	....	....	....	43	....	....	....	....	....	....	....	....	....	....	....	....	....	....	....	....	....	....
	Detroit Red Wings	**NHL**	**14**	**1**	**6**	**7**	**1**	**5**	**6**	**16**	**0**	**0**	**0**	**18**	**5.6**	**17**	**1**	**21**	**6**	**1**	**7**	**0**	**2**	**2**	**2**	**0**	**0**	**0**
1978-79	**Detroit Red Wings**	**NHL**	**68**	**10**	**17**	**27**	**9**	**12**	**21**	**64**	**3**	**1**	**1**	**88**	**11.4**	**72**	**12**	**114**	**29**	**–25**	....	....	....	....	....	....	....	....

			REGULAR SEASON																		PLAYOFFS							
Season	Club	League	GP	G	A	Pts	AG	AA	APts	PIM	PP	SH	GW	S	%	TGF	PGF	TGA	PGA	+/–	GP	G	A	Pts	PIM	PP	SH	GW
1979-80	**Detroit Red Wings**	**NHL**	**28**	**1**	**5**	**6**	**1**	**4**	**5**	**45**	**0**	**0**	**0**	**39**	**2.6**	**29**	**3**	**31**	**9**	**4**								
	Adirondack Red Wings	AHL	15	0	2	2				7																		
1980-81	Vastra Frolunda	Sweden	33	9	8	17				*101											2	0	0	0	4			
1981-82	Sodertalje SK	Sweden-2	27	11	12	23				73																		
1982-83	Sodertalje SK	Sweden-2	20	9	7	16				44																		
	NHL Totals		**246**	**21**	**44**	**65**	**19**	**33**	**52**	**243**	**4**	**1**	**3**	**379**	**5.5**	**248**	**34**	**318**	**68**		**7**	**0**	**2**	**2**	**2**	**0**	**0**	**0**
	Other Major League Totals		234	22	97	119				261											13	3	10	13	8			

Signed as a free agent by **Detroit**, August 31, 1972. Traded to **Winnipeg** (WHA) by **Detroit** for cash, December, 1974. Signed as a free agent by **Detroit**, March 16, 1978.

• BERGQVIST, Jonas

RW – L. 6', 185 lbs. b: Hassleholm, Sweden, 9/26/1962. Calgary's 6th, 126th overall, in 1988.

Season	Club	League	GP	G	A	Pts	AG	AA	APts	PIM	PP	SH	GW	S	%	TGF	PGF	TGA	PGA	+/–	GP	G	A	Pts	PIM	PP	SH	GW
1978-79	Rogle BK Stockholm	Sweden-3	STATISTICS NOT AVAILABLE																									
1979-1981	Leksands IF	Sweden-Jr.	STATISTICS NOT AVAILABLE																									
1981-82	Leksands IF	Sweden	33	6	7	13				10																		
	Sweden	WJC-A	7	4	5	9				9																		
1982-83	Leksands IF	Sweden	35	8	11	19				20																		
1983-84	Leksands IF	Sweden	29	11	11	22				16																		
1984-85	Leksands IF	Sweden	35	11	11	22				26																		
1985-86	Leksands IF	Sweden	36	16	21	37				16																		
	Sweden	WEC-A	10	4	3	7				12																		
1986-87	Leksands IF	Sweden	36	9	11	20				26																		
	Sweden	WEC-A	9	1	3	4				4																		
1987-88	Sweden	Can-Cup	6	2	0	2				4																		
	Leksands IF	Sweden	37	19	12	31				32											3	0	0	0	0			
	Sweden	Olympics	8	3	0	3				4																		
1988-89	Leksands IF	Sweden	27	15	20	35				18											10	4	3	7	2			
	Sweden	WEC-A	10	3	2	5				4																		
1989-90	Calgary Flames	Fr-Tour	DID NOT PLAY																									
	Calgary Flames	**NHL**	**22**	**2**	**5**	**7**	**2**	**4**	**6**	**10**	**0**	**0**	**0**	**30**	**6.7**	**15**	**0**	**6**	**1**	**10**								
	Salt Lake Golden Eagles	IHL	13	6	10	16				4																		
1990-91	Mannheimer ERC	Germany	36	16	23	39				22											3	0	0	0	4			
	Sweden	WEC-A	9	4	2	6				8																		
1991-92	Sweden	Can-Cup	6	0	1	1				0																		
	Leksands IF	Sweden	22	11	10	21				4																		
1992-93	Leksands IF	Sweden	39	15	23	38				40											2	0	0	0	0			
	Sweden	WC-A	8	3	1	4				14																		
1993-94	Leksands IF	Sweden	35	12	23	35				29																		
	Sweden	Olympics	8	1	3	4				4																		
	Sweden	WC-A	8	3	5	8				4																		
1994-95	Leksands IF	Sweden	33	17	12	29				16											4	0	0	0	4			
	Sweden	WC-A	5	1	0	1				0																		
1995-96	Leksands IF	Sweden	37	16	14	30				30											5	2	1	3	0			
	Sweden	WC-A	6	4	0	4				0																		
1996-97	Sweden	W-Cup	4	1	0	1				2																		
	Leksands IF	Sweden	38	13	16	29				22											9	4	2	6	12			
1997-98	Leksands IF	Sweden	31	14	19	33				18											3	0	1	1	8			
	Sweden	WC-A	10	2	0	2				6																		
1998-99	VEU Feldkirch	Alpenliga	29	17	21	38				24																		
	VEU Feldkirch	Austria	17	5	5	10				4																		
99-2000	Leksands IF	Sweden	DID NOT PLAY – GENERAL MANAGER																									
	NHL Totals		**22**	**2**	**5**	**7**	**2**	**4**	**6**	**10**	**0**	**0**	**0**	**30**	**6.7**	**15**	**0**	**6**	**1**									

Swedish World All-Star Team (1989, 1996) • Swedish Player of the Year (1996)

• BERNIER, Serge

Serge Joseph RW – R. 6'1", 190 lbs. b: Padoue, Que., 4/29/1947. Philadelphia's 1st, 5th overall, in 1967.

Season	Club	League	GP	G	A	Pts	AG	AA	APts	PIM	PP	SH	GW	S	%	TGF	PGF	TGA	PGA	+/–	GP	G	A	Pts	PIM	PP	SH	GW
1966-67	Sorel Eperviers	QJHL	33	37	46	83				139											4	2	1	3	18			
1967-68	Quebec Aces	AHL	33	7	11	18				56											6	6	4	10	6			
1968-69	**Philadelphia Flyers**	**NHL**	**1**	**0**	**0**	**0**	**0**	**0**	**0**	**2**	**0**	**0**	**0**	**3**	**0.0**	**0**	**0**	**0**	**0**	**0**								
	Quebec Aces	AHL	70	27	32	59				118											12	1	6	7	2			
1969-70	**Philadelphia Flyers**	**NHL**	**1**	**0**	**1**	**1**	**0**	**1**	**1**	**0**	**0**	**0**	**0**	**2**	**0.0**	**1**	**0**	**2**	**0**	**–1**								
	Quebec Aces	AHL	70	22	48	70				88											5	2	3	5	36			
1970-71	**Philadelphia Flyers**	**NHL**	**77**	**23**	**28**	**51**	**23**	**23**	**46**	**77**	**2**	**0**	**1**	**205**	**11.2**	**67**	**11**	**65**	**2**	**–7**	**4**	**1**	**1**	**2**	**0**	**1**	**0**	**0**
1971-72	**Philadelphia Flyers**	**NHL**	**44**	**12**	**11**	**23**	**12**	**9**	**21**	**51**	**5**	**0**	**3**	**120**	**10.0**	**32**	**13**	**39**	**0**	**–20**								
	Los Angeles Kings	**NHL**	**26**	**11**	**11**	**22**	**11**	**9**	**20**	**12**	**1**	**0**	**1**	**97**	**11.3**	**33**	**10**	**20**	**0**	**3**								
1972-73	**Los Angeles Kings**	**NHL**	**75**	**22**	**46**	**68**	**21**	**37**	**58**	**43**	**6**	**0**	**3**	**255**	**8.6**	**104**	**46**	**78**	**0**	**–20**								
1973-74	Quebec Nordiques	WHA	74	37	49	86				107																		
1974-75	Team Canada	Summit-74	8	1	2	3				4																		
	Quebec Nordiques	WHA	76	54	68	122				75											16	8	8	16	6			
1975-76	Quebec Nordiques	WHA	70	34	68	102				91											5	2	6	8	6			
1976-77	Quebec Nordiques	WHA	74	43	53	96				94											17	*14	*22	*36	10			
1977-78	Quebec Nordiques	WHA	58	26	52	78				48											11	4	10	14	17			
1978-79	Quebec Nordiques	WHA	65	36	46	82				71											1	0	0	0	2			
1979-80	**Quebec Nordiques**	**NHL**	**32**	**8**	**14**	**22**	**7**	**10**	**17**	**31**	**3**	**0**	**3**	**76**	**10.5**	**38**	**17**	**33**	**7**	**–5**								
1980-81	**Quebec Nordiques**	**NHL**	**46**	**2**	**8**	**10**	**2**	**5**	**7**	**18**	**1**	**0**	**0**	**35**	**5.7**	**21**	**11**	**23**	**5**	**–8**	**1**	**0**	**0**	**0**	**0**	**0**	**0**	**0**
	NHL Totals		**302**	**78**	**119**	**197**	**76**	**94**	**170**	**234**	**18**	**0**	**11**	**793**	**9.8**	**296**	**108**	**260**	**14**		**5**	**1**	**1**	**2**	**0**	**1**	**0**	**0**
	Other Major League Totals		417	230	336	566				486											50	28	46	74	41			

WHA Second All-Star Team (1975) • Won WHA Playoff MVP Trophy (1977)

Traded to **LA Kings** by **Philadelphia** with Bill Lesuk and Jim Johnson for Bill Flett, Eddie Joyal, Jean Potvin and Ross Lonsberry, January 28, 1972. Selected by **Ontario-Ottawa** (WHA) in 1972 WHA General Player Draft, February 12, 1972. WHA rights traded to **Quebec** (WHA) by **Ottawa** (WHA) for future considerations, June, 1973. Rights retained by **Quebec** prior to Expansion Draft, June 9, 1979.

• BERRY, Bob

Robert Victor "Crease" LW – L. 6', 185 lbs. b: Montreal, Que., 11/29/1943.

Season	Club	League	GP	G	A	Pts	AG	AA	APts	PIM	PP	SH	GW	S	%	TGF	PGF	TGA	PGA	+/–	GP	G	A	Pts	PIM	PP	SH	GW
1962-63	Middlebury College	NCAA-2	STATISTICS NOT AVAILABLE																									
1963-64	Verdun Maple Leafs	MMJHL	25	38	27	65				93																		
	Peterborough Petes	OHA-Jr.	11	4	3	7				36											2	0	0	0	4			
1964-65	George Williams College	OQAA	17	13	27	40																						
1965-66	George Williams College	OQAA	27	36	48	84																						
1966-67	George Williams College	OQAA	31	48	41	89																						
	Canada	Nat-Team	5	1	1	2				0																		
1967-68	Hull Nationals	QSHL	39	32	23	55				80																		
1968-69	**Montreal Canadiens**	**NHL**	**2**	**0**	**0**	**0**	**0**	**0**	**0**	**0**	**0**	**0**	**0**	**0**	**0.0**	**0**	**0**	**0**	**0**	**0**								
	Cleveland Barons	AHL	68	24	29	53				104											5	0	3	3	10			
1969-70	Montreal Voyageurs	AHL	71	18	41	59				104											8	1	0	1	11			
1970-71	**Los Angeles Kings**	**NHL**	**77**	**25**	**38**	**63**	**25**	**32**	**57**	**52**	**4**	**0**	**2**	**149**	**16.8**	**87**	**16**	**77**	**1**	**–5**								
1971-72	**Los Angeles Kings**	**NHL**	**78**	**17**	**22**	**39**	**17**	**19**	**36**	**44**	**3**	**0**	**3**	**102**	**16.7**	**59**	**10**	**72**	**0**	**–23**								
1972-73	**Los Angeles Kings**	**NHL**	**78**	**36**	**28**	**64**	**34**	**22**	**56**	**75**	**14**	**0**	**2**	**176**	**20.5**	**94**	**33**	**74**	**0**	**–13**								
1973-74	**Los Angeles Kings**	**NHL**	**77**	**23**	**33**	**56**	**22**	**27**	**49**	**56**	**8**	**0**	**2**	**122**	**18.9**	**85**	**22**	**63**	**0**	**0**	**5**	**0**	**0**	**0**	**0**	**0**	**0**	**0**
1974-75	**Los Angeles Kings**	**NHL**	**80**	**25**	**23**	**48**	**22**	**17**	**39**	**60**	**7**	**0**	**7**	**136**	**18.4**	**75**	**18**	**38**	**2**	**21**	**3**	**1**	**2**	**3**	**2**	**0**	**0**	**0**
1975-76	**Los Angeles Kings**	**NHL**	**80**	**20**	**22**	**42**	**18**	**16**	**34**	**37**	**3**	**0**	**3**	**156**	**12.8**	**78**	**14**	**62**	**0**	**2**	**9**	**1**	**1**	**2**	**0**	**0**	**0**	**1**
1976-77	**Los Angeles Kings**	**NHL**	**69**	**13**	**25**	**38**	**12**	**19**	**31**	**20**	**2**	**0**	**1**	**85**	**15.3**	**58**	**8**	**39**	**1**	**12**	**9**	**0**	**3**	**3**	**4**	**0**	**0**	**0**
	Fort Worth Texans	CHL	7	4	4	8				0																		
1977-78	Springfield Indians	AHL	74	26	27	53				56											4	0	0	0	0			

Season	Club	League	GP	G	A	Pts	AG	AA	APts	PIM	PP	SH	GW	S	%	TGF	PGF	TGA	PGA	+/-	GP	G	A	Pts	PIM	PP	SH	GW
			REGULAR SEASON																		PLAYOFFS							
1978-1981	**Los Angeles Kings**	**NHL**	DID NOT PLAY – COACHING																									
1981-1984	**Montreal Canadiens**	**NHL**	DID NOT PLAY – COACHING																									
1984-1987	**Pittsburgh Penguins**	**NHL**	DID NOT PLAY – COACHING																									
1987-1988			OUT OF HOCKEY – RETIRED																									
1988-1992	**St. Louis Blues**	**NHL**	DID NOT PLAY – ASSISTANT COACH																									
1992-1994	**St. Louis Blues**	**NHL**	DID NOT PLAY – COACHING																									
1994-1996	**St. Louis Blues**	**NHL**	DID NOT PLAY – ASSISTANT COACH																									
1996-1997	**St. Louis Blues**	**NHL**	DID NOT PLAY – ASSISTANT GENERAL MANAGER																									
1997-2000	**San Jose Sharks**	**NHL**	DID NOT PLAY – ASSISTANT COACH																									
	NHL Totals		**541**	**159**	**191**	**350**	**150**	**152**	**302**	**344**	**41**	**0**	**19**	**926**	**17.2**	**536**	**121**	**425**	**4**		**26**	**2**	**6**	**8**	**6**	**0**	**0**	**1**

QSHL First All-Star Team (1968) • Played in NHL All-Star Game (1973, 1974)

• Played semi-pro football for Montreal Rifles, 1964-1965. Traded to **LA Kings** by **Montreal** for cash, October 8, 1970.

• BERRY, Brad

D – L. 6'2", 190 lbs. b: Bashaw, Alta., 4/1/1965. Winnipeg's 3rd, 29th overall, in 1983.

Season	Club	League	GP	G	A	Pts	AG	AA	APts	PIM	PP	SH	GW	S	%	TGF	PGF	TGA	PGA	+/-	GP	G	A	Pts	PIM	PP	SH	GW
1982-83	St. Albert Saints	AJHL	55	9	33	42	....	....	....	97	....	....	....	....	....	....	....	....	....	....	....	....	....	....	....	....	....	....
1983-84	University of North Dakota	WCHA	32	2	7	9	....	....	....	8	....	....	....	....	....	....	....	....	....	....	....	....	....	....	....	....	....	....
1984-85	University of North Dakota	WCHA	40	4	26	30	....	....	....	26	....	....	....	....	....	....	....	....	....	....	....	....	....	....	....	....	....	....
	Canada	WJC-A	7	0	1	1	....	....	....	2	....	....	....	....	....	....	....	....	....	....	....	....	....	....	....	....	....	....
1985-86	University of North Dakota	WCHA	40	6	29	35	....	....	....	26	....	....	....	....	....	....	....	....	....	....	....	....	....	....	....	....	....	....
	Winnipeg Jets	**NHL**	**13**	**1**	**0**	**1**	**1**	**0**	**1**	**10**	**0**	**0**	**0**	**16**	**6.3**	**14**	**0**	**15**	**2**	**1**	**3**	**0**	**0**	**0**	**0**	**0**	**0**	**0**
1986-87	**Winnipeg Jets**	**NHL**	**52**	**2**	**8**	**10**	**2**	**6**	**8**	**60**	**0**	**0**	**0**	**39**	**5.1**	**42**	**0**	**46**	**10**	**6**	**7**	**0**	**1**	**1**	**14**	**0**	**0**	**0**
1987-88	**Winnipeg Jets**	**NHL**	**48**	**0**	**6**	**6**	**0**	**4**	**4**	**75**	**0**	**0**	**0**	**31**	**0.0**	**35**	**0**	**59**	**13**	**-11**	....	....	....	....	....	....	....	....
	Moncton Hawks	AHL	10	1	3	4	....	....	....	14	....	....	....	....	....	....	....	....	....	....	....	....	....	....	....	....	....	....
1988-89	**Winnipeg Jets**	**NHL**	**38**	**0**	**9**	**9**	**0**	**6**	**6**	**45**	**0**	**0**	**0**	**21**	**0.0**	**21**	**0**	**33**	**4**	**-8**	....	....	....	....	....	....	....	....
	Moncton Hawks	AHL	38	3	16	19	....	....	....	39	....	....	....	....	....	....	....	....	....	....	....	....	....	....	....	....	....	....
1989-90	**Winnipeg Jets**	**NHL**	**12**	**1**	**2**	**3**	**1**	**1**	**2**	**6**	**0**	**0**	**0**	**7**	**14.3**	**11**	**1**	**12**	**0**	**-2**	**1**	**0**	**0**	**0**	**0**	**0**	**0**	**0**
	Moncton Hawks	AHL	38	1	9	10	....	....	....	58	....	....	....	....	....	....	....	....	....	....	....	....	....	....	....	....	....	....
1990-91	Brynas IF Gavle	Sweden	38	3	1	4	....	....	....	38	....	....	....	....	....	....	....	....	....	....	....	....	....	....	....	....	....	....
	Canada	Nat-Team	4	0	1	1	....	....	....	0	....	....	....	....	....	....	....	....	....	....	....	....	....	....	....	....	....	....
1991-92	**Minnesota North Stars**	**NHL**	**7**	**0**	**0**	**0**	**0**	**0**	**0**	**6**	**0**	**0**	**0**	**2**	**0.0**	**2**	**0**	**3**	**0**	**-1**	**2**	**0**	**0**	**0**	**2**	**0**	**0**	**0**
	Kalamazoo Wings	IHL	65	5	18	23	....	....	....	90	....	....	....	....	....	....	....	....	....	....	5	2	0	2	6	....	....	....
1992-93	**Minnesota North Stars**	**NHL**	**63**	**0**	**3**	**3**	**0**	**2**	**2**	**109**	**0**	**0**	**0**	**49**	**0.0**	**40**	**0**	**59**	**21**	**2**	....	....	....	....	....	....	....	....
1993-94	**Dallas Stars**	**NHL**	**8**	**0**	**0**	**0**	**0**	**0**	**0**	**12**	**0**	**0**	**0**	**4**	**0.0**	**2**	**0**	**4**	**0**	**-2**	....	....	....	....	....	....	....	....
	Kalamazoo Wings	IHL	45	3	19	22	....	....	....	91	....	....	....	....	....	....	....	....	....	....	1	0	0	0	0	....	....	....
1994-95	Kalamazoo Wings	IHL	65	4	11	15	....	....	....	146	....	....	....	....	....	....	....	....	....	....	1	0	0	0	0	....	....	....
1995-96	Michigan K-Wings	IHL	80	4	13	17	....	....	....	73	....	....	....	....	....	....	....	....	....	....	10	0	5	5	12	....	....	....
1996-97	Michigan K-Wings	IHL	77	4	7	11	....	....	....	68	....	....	....	....	....	....	....	....	....	....	4	0	0	0	4	....	....	....
1997-98	Michigan K-Wings	IHL	67	3	8	11	....	....	....	60	....	....	....	....	....	....	....	....	....	....	....	....	....	....	....	....	....	....
1998-99	Michigan K-Wings	IHL	5	0	1	1	....	....	....	10	....	....	....	....	....	....	....	....	....	....	....	....	....	....	....	....	....	....
99-2000	**Dallas Stars**	**NHL**	DID NOT PLAY – SCOUTING																									
	NHL Totals		**241**	**4**	**28**	**32**	**4**	**19**	**23**	**323**	**0**	**0**	**0**	**169**	**2.4**	**167**	**1**	**231**	**50**		**13**	**0**	**1**	**1**	**16**	**0**	**0**	**0**

Signed as a free agent by **Minnesota**, October 4, 1991. Transferred to **Dallas** after **Minnesota** franchise relocated, June 9, 1993. • Officially announced retirement, October 25, 1998.

• BERRY, Doug

Douglas Alan C – L. 6'1", 190 lbs. b: New Westminster, B.C., 6/3/1957. Colorado's 2nd, 38th overall, in 1977.

Season	Club	League	GP	G	A	Pts	AG	AA	APts	PIM	PP	SH	GW	S	%	TGF	PGF	TGA	PGA	+/-	GP	G	A	Pts	PIM	PP	SH	GW
1974-75	Kelowna Buckaroos	BCJHL	66	37	*103	140	....	....	....	45	....	....	....	....	....	....	....	....	....	....	....	....	....	....	....	....	....	....
1975-76	University of Denver	WCHA	39	12	28	40	....	....	....	32	....	....	....	....	....	....	....	....	....	....	....	....	....	....	....	....	....	....
1976-77	University of Denver	WCHA	40	17	41	58	....	....	....	42	....	....	....	....	....	....	....	....	....	....	....	....	....	....	....	....	....	....
1977-78	University of Denver	WCHA	32	25	39	64	....	....	....	34	....	....	....	....	....	....	....	....	....	....	....	....	....	....	....	....	....	....
1978-79	Edmonton Oilers	WHA	29	6	3	9	....	....	....	4	....	....	....	....	....	....	....	....	....	....	....	....	....	....	....	....	....	....
	Dallas Black Hawks	CHL	44	19	34	53	....	....	....	15	....	....	....	....	....	....	....	....	....	....	9	0	7	7	0	....	....	....
1979-80	**Colorado Rockies**	**NHL**	**75**	**7**	**23**	**30**	**6**	**17**	**23**	**16**	**0**	**1**	**1**	**66**	**10.6**	**46**	**10**	**60**	**1**	**-23**	....	....	....	....	....	....	....	....
1980-81	**Colorado Rockies**	**NHL**	**46**	**3**	**10**	**13**	**2**	**7**	**9**	**9**	**0**	**1**	**0**	**44**	**6.8**	**27**	**3**	**48**	**9**	**-15**	....	....	....	....	....	....	....	....
	Fort Worth Texans	CHL	23	8	7	15	....	....	....	2	....	....	....	....	....	....	....	....	....	....	5	1	3	4	4	....	....	....
1981-82	Wichita Wind	CHL	10	4	5	9	....	....	....	2	....	....	....	....	....	....	....	....	....	....	7	0	4	4	0	....	....	....
	Mannheimer ERC	Germany	44	19	37	56	....	....	....	30	....	....	....	....	....	....	....	....	....	....	....	....	....	....	....	....	....	....
1982-83	Mannheimer ERC	Germany	36	19	34	53	....	....	....	36	....	....	....	....	....	....	....	....	....	....	....	....	....	....	....	....	....	....
1983-84	Mannheimer ERC	Germany	47	26	47	73	....	....	....	36	....	....	....	....	....	....	....	....	....	....	....	....	....	....	....	....	....	....
1984-85	HC Geneve-Servette	Switz-2	26	24	18	42	....	....	....	14	....	....	....	....	....	....	....	....	....	....	14	14	15	29	....	....	....	....
1985-86	Kolner EC	Germany	36	25	24	49	....	....	....	8	....	....	....	....	....	....	....	....	....	....	10	6	7	13	2	....	....	....
1986-87	Kolner EC	Germany	33	11	38	49	....	....	....	28	....	....	....	....	....	....	....	....	....	....	9	8	12	20	10	....	....	....
1987-88	Kolner EC	Germany	36	15	33	48	....	....	....	24	....	....	....	....	....	....	....	....	....	....	11	7	7	14	6	....	....	....
1988-89	Kolner EC	Germany	29	9	23	32	....	....	....	23	....	....	....	....	....	....	....	....	....	....	9	1	4	5	6	....	....	....
1989-90	Kolner EC	Germany	36	15	24	39	....	....	....	26	....	....	....	....	....	....	....	....	....	....	8	3	7	10	4	....	....	....
1990-91	Kolner EC	Germany	44	13	40	53	....	....	....	39	....	....	....	....	....	....	....	....	....	....	14	3	8	11	6	....	....	....
1991-92	Kolner EC	Germany	32	13	25	38	....	....	....	18	....	....	....	....	....	....	....	....	....	....	3	0	0	0	4	....	....	....
	NHL Totals		**121**	**10**	**33**	**43**	**8**	**24**	**32**	**25**	**0**	**2**	**1**	**110**	**9.1**	**73**	**13**	**108**	**10**		....	....	....	....	....	....	....	....
	Other Major League Totals		29	6	3	9	....	....	....	4	....	....	....	....	....	....	....	....	....	....	....	....	....	....	....	....	....	....

• Brother of Ken • WCHA First All-Star Team (1978) • NCAA West First All-American Team (1978)

Selected by **Calgary** (WHA) in 1977 WHA Amateur Draft, May, 1977. Signed as a free agent by **Edmonton** (WHA) after **Calgary** (WHA) franchise folded, July, 1978. Reclaimed by **Colorado** from **Edmonton** (WHA) prior to Expansion Draft, June 9, 1979.

• BERRY, Fred

Frederick Allan C – L. 5'9", 175 lbs. b: Edmonton, Alta., 3/26/1956. Detroit's 3rd, 40th overall, in 1976.

Season	Club	League	GP	G	A	Pts	AG	AA	APts	PIM	PP	SH	GW	S	%	TGF	PGF	TGA	PGA	+/-	GP	G	A	Pts	PIM	PP	SH	GW
1973-74	Merritt Centennials	BCJHL	60	*60	*76	*136	....	....	....	91	....	....	....	....	....	....	....	....	....	....	....	....	....	....	....	....	....	....
	Victoria Cougars	WCJHL	1	0	1	1	....	....	....	0	....	....	....	....	....	....	....	....	....	....	....	....	....	....	....	....	....	....
1974-75	New Westminster Bruins	WCJHL	69	32	43	75	....	....	....	120	....	....	....	....	....	....	....	....	....	....	18	12	12	24	38	....	....	....
	New Westminster Bruins	Mem-Cup	3	2	1	3	....	....	....	2	....	....	....	....	....	....	....	....	....	....	....	....	....	....	....	....	....	....
1975-76	New Westminster Bruins	WCJHL	72	59	87	146	....	....	....	164	....	....	....	....	....	....	....	....	....	....	17	6	15	21	45	....	....	....
	New Westminster Bruins	Mem-Cup	4	0	3	3	....	....	....	0	....	....	....	....	....	....	....	....	....	....	....	....	....	....	....	....	....	....
1976-77	**Detroit Red Wings**	**NHL**	**3**	**0**	**0**	**0**	**0**	**0**	**0**	**0**	**0**	**0**	**0**	**4**	**0.0**	**0**	**0**	**3**	**0**	**-3**	....	....	....	....	....	....	....	....
	Kalamazoo Wings	IHL	66	17	42	59	....	....	....	146	....	....	....	....	....	....	....	....	....	....	10	9	8	17	12	....	....	....
1977-78	Kansas City Red Wings	CHL	65	11	14	25	....	....	....	79	....	....	....	....	....	....	....	....	....	....	....	....	....	....	....	....	....	....
1978-79	Kalamazoo Wings	IHL	19	7	11	18	....	....	....	43	....	....	....	....	....	....	....	....	....	....	....	....	....	....	....	....	....	....
	Toledo Goaldiggers	IHL	49	27	43	70	....	....	....	91	....	....	....	....	....	....	....	....	....	....	....	....	....	....	....	....	....	....
1979-80	Toledo Goaldiggers	IHL	33	11	29	40	....	....	....	33	....	....	....	....	....	....	....	....	....	....	....	....	....	....	....	....	....	....
	Milwaukee Admirals	IHL	26	9	22	31	....	....	....	29	....	....	....	....	....	....	....	....	....	....	2	1	1	2	5	....	....	....
	Hampton Aces	EHL	6	3	4	7	....	....	....	4	....	....	....	....	....	....	....	....	....	....	....	....	....	....	....	....	....	....
1980-81	Milwaukee Admirals	IHL	72	35	71	106	....	....	....	73	....	....	....	....	....	....	....	....	....	....	7	5	7	12	45	....	....	....
1981-82	Milwaukee Admirals	IHL	76	47	65	112	....	....	....	114	....	....	....	....	....	....	....	....	....	....	5	4	4	8	65	....	....	....
1982-83	Milwaukee Admirals	IHL	71	47	74	121	....	....	....	57	....	....	....	....	....	....	....	....	....	....	10	3	5	8	0	....	....	....
1983-84	Milwaukee Admirals	IHL	82	38	58	96	....	....	....	50	....	....	....	....	....	....	....	....	....	....	4	3	1	4	2	....	....	....
1984-85			OUT OF HOCKEY – RETIRED																									
1985-86	Milwaukee Admirals	IHL	81	31	58	89	....	....	....	51	....	....	....	....	....	....	....	....	....	....	5	3	2	5	2	....	....	....
1986-87	Milwaukee Admirals	IHL	57	18	31	49	....	....	....	50	....	....	....	....	....	....	....	....	....	....	....	....	....	....	....	....	....	....
	NHL Totals		**3**	**0**	**0**	**0**	**0**	**0**	**0**	**0**	**0**	**0**	**0**	**4**	**0.0**	**0**	**0**	**3**	**0**		....	....	....	....	....	....	....	....

IHL Second All-Star Team (1982)

Traded to **Toledo** (IHL) by **Detroit** (Kalamazoo (IHL) with Al Stoneman and Dean Willers for Pete Crawford and Randy Mohns, December, 1978.

Season	Club	League	GP	G	A	Pts	AG	AA	APts	PIM	PP	SH	GW	S	%	TGF	PGF	TGA	PGA	+/–	GP	G	A	Pts	PIM	PP	SH	GW
			REGULAR SEASON																		PLAYOFFS							

• BERRY, Ken

Kenneth Edward LW – L. 5'9", 175 lbs. b: Burnaby, B.C., 6/21/1960. Vancouver's 5th, 112th overall, in 1980.

Season	Club	League	GP	G	A	Pts	AG	AA	APts	PIM	PP	SH	GW	S	%	TGF	PGF	TGA	PGA	+/–	GP	G	A	Pts	PIM	PP	SH	GW
1977-78	Bellingham Blazers	BCJHL	65	57	73	130	....	....	....	124	....	....	....	....	....	....	....	....	....	....	....	....	....	....	....	....	....	....
	New Westminster Bruins	WCJHL	5	0	0	0	....	....	....	0	....	....	....	....	....	....	....	....	....	....	6	3	4	7	2	....	....	....
	New Westminster Bruins	Mem-Cup	5	2	3	5	....	....	....	2	....	....	....	....	....	....	....	....	....	....	....	....	....	....	....	....	....	....
1978-79	University of Denver	WCHA	39	17	20	37	....	....	....	52	....	....	....	....	....	....	....	....	....	....	....	....	....	....	....	....	....	....
1979-80	Canada	Nat-Team	57	19	20	39	....	....	....	48	....	....	....	....	....	....	....	....	....	....	....	....	....	....	....	....	....	....
	Canada	Olympics	6	4	1	5	....	....	....	8	....	....	....	....	....	....	....	....	....	....	....	....	....	....	....	....	....	....
1980-81	University of Denver	WCHA	40	22	34	56	....	....	....	74	....	....	....	....	....	....	....	....	....	....	....	....	....	....	....	....	....	....
	Wichita Wind	CHL	9	7	6	13	....	....	....	13	....	....	....	....	....	....	....	....	....	....	17	2	4	6	28	....	....	....
1981-82	Wichita Wind	CHL	58	28	29	57	....	....	....	70	....	....	....	....	....	....	....	....	....	....	....	....	....	....	....	....	....	....
	Edmonton Oilers	**NHL**	**15**	**2**	**3**	**5**	**2**	**2**	**4**	**9**	**0**	**0**	**0**	**9**	**22.2**	**5**	**1**	**11**	**1**	**–6**	....	....	....	....	....	....	....	....
1982-83	Moncton Alpines	AHL	76	24	26	50	....	....	....	80	....	....	....	....	....	....	....	....	....	....	....	....	....	....	....	....	....	....
1983-84	**Edmonton Oilers**	**NHL**	**13**	**2**	**3**	**5**	**2**	**2**	**4**	**10**	**0**	**1**	**0**	**18**	**11.1**	**12**	**0**	**6**	**0**	**6**	....	....	....	....	....	....	....	....
	Moncton Alpines	AHL	53	18	20	38	....	....	....	75	....	....	....	....	....	....	....	....	....	....	....	....	....	....	....	....	....	....
1984-85	Nova Scotia Voyageurs	AHL	71	30	27	57	....	....	....	40	....	....	....	....	....	....	....	....	....	....	6	2	2	4	2	....	....	....
1985-86	EV Bayreuth	Germany	33	27	25	52	....	....	....	88	....	....	....	....	....	....	....	....	....	....	....	....	....	....	....	....	....	....
	Canada	Nat-Team	8	1	2	3	....	....	....	20	....	....	....	....	....	....	....	....	....	....	....	....	....	....	....	....	....	....
1986-87	Canada	Nat-Team	52	17	27	44	....	....	....	60	....	....	....	....	....	....	....	....	....	....	....	....	....	....	....	....	....	....
1987-88	Canada	Nat-Team	59	18	15	33	....	....	....	47	....	....	....	....	....	....	....	....	....	....	....	....	....	....	....	....	....	....
	Canada	Olympics	8	2	4	6	....	....	....	4	....	....	....	....	....	....	....	....	....	....	....	....	....	....	....	....	....	....
	Vancouver Canucks	**NHL**	**14**	**2**	**3**	**5**	**2**	**2**	**4**	**6**	**1**	**0**	**0**	**26**	**7.7**	**9**	**1**	**11**	**2**	**–1**	....	....	....	....	....	....	....	....
1988-89	**Vancouver Canucks**	**NHL**	**13**	**2**	**1**	**3**	**2**	**1**	**3**	**5**	**0**	**0**	**0**	**10**	**20.0**	**7**	**1**	**7**	**3**	**2**	....	....	....	....	....	....	....	....
	Milwaukee Admirals	IHL	5	4	4	8	....	....	....	2	....	....	....	....	....	....	....	....	....	....	....	....	....	....	....	....	....	....
1989-90	EC Hedos Munich	Germany	36	24	33	57	....	....	....	70	....	....	....	....	....	....	....	....	....	....	3	2	0	2	2	....	....	....
1990-91	EC Hedos Munich	Germany	43	26	17	43	....	....	....	68	....	....	....	....	....	....	....	....	....	....	4	1	1	2	8	....	....	....
1991-92	EC Hedos Munich	Germany	39	17	15	32	....	....	....	71	....	....	....	....	....	....	....	....	....	....	....	....	....	....	....	....	....	....
1992-93	EC Hedos Munich	Germany	29	4	5	9	....	....	....	58	....	....	....	....	....	....	....	....	....	....	6	6	5	11	8	....	....	....
	NHL Totals		**55**	**8**	**10**	**18**	**8**	**7**	**15**	**30**	**1**	**1**	**0**	**63**	**12.7**	**33**	**3**	**35**	**6**		....	....	....	....	....	....	....	....

• Brother of Doug

Traded to **Edmonton** by **Vancouver** with Garry Lariviere for Blair MacDonald and the rights to Lars-Gunnar Petersson, March 10, 1981. Signed as a free agent by **Vancouver**, March 2, 1988.

• BERTRAND, Eric

LW – L. 6'1", 205 lbs. b: St. Ephrem, Que., 4/16/1975. New Jersey's 9th, 207th overall, in 1994.

Season	Club	League	GP	G	A	Pts	AG	AA	APts	PIM	PP	SH	GW	S	%	TGF	PGF	TGA	PGA	+/–	GP	G	A	Pts	PIM	PP	SH	GW
1991-92	Beauce-Amiante Beavers	QAAA	STATISTICS NOT AVAILABLE																									
1992-93	Granby Bisons	QMJHL	64	10	15	25	....	....	....	82	....	....	....	....	....	....	....	....	....	....	....	....	....	....	....	....	....	....
1993-94	Granby Bisons	QMJHL	60	11	15	26	....	....	....	151	....	....	....	....	....	....	....	....	....	....	6	1	0	1	18	....	....	....
1994-95	Granby Bisons	QMJHL	56	14	26	40	....	....	....	268	....	....	....	....	....	....	....	....	....	....	13	3	8	11	50	....	....	....
1995-96	Albany River Rats	AHL	70	16	13	29	....	....	....	199	....	....	....	....	....	....	....	....	....	....	4	0	0	0	6	....	....	....
1996-97	Albany River Rats	AHL	77	16	27	43	....	....	....	204	....	....	....	....	....	....	....	....	....	....	8	3	3	6	15	....	....	....
1997-98	Albany River Rats	AHL	76	20	29	49	....	....	....	256	....	....	....	....	....	....	....	....	....	....	13	5	5	10	4	....	....	....
1998-99	Albany River Rats	AHL	78	34	31	65	....	....	....	160	....	....	....	....	....	....	....	....	....	....	5	4	2	6	0	....	....	....
99-2000	**New Jersey Devils**	**NHL**	**4**	**0**	**0**	**0**	**0**	**0**	**0**	**0**	**0**	**0**	**0**	**1**	**0.0**	**1**	**0**	**2**	**0**	**–1**	....	....	....	....	....	....	....	....
	Atlanta Thrashers	**NHL**	**8**	**0**	**0**	**0**	**0**	**0**	**0**	**4**	**0**	**0**	**0**	**11**	**0.0**	**2**	**1**	**6**	**0**	**–5**	....	....	....	....	....	....	....	....
	Philadelphia Phantoms	AHL	15	3	6	9	....	....	....	67	....	....	....	....	....	....	....	....	....	....	....	....	....	....	....	....	....	....
	Milwaukee Admirals	IHL	27	7	9	16	....	....	....	56	....	....	....	....	....	....	....	....	....	....	3	0	0	0	2	....	....	....
	NHL Totals		**12**	**0**	**0**	**0**	**0**	**0**	**0**	**4**	**0**	**0**	**0**	**12**	**0.0**	**3**	**1**	**8**	**0**									

Traded to **Atlanta** by **New Jersey** with Wes Mason for Sylvain Cloutier, Jeff Williams and Atlanta's 7th round choice (Ken Magovan) in 2000 Entry Draft, November 1, 1999. Traded to **Philadelphia** by **Atlanta** for Brian Wesenberg, December 9, 1999. Traded to **Nashville** by **Philadelphia** for future considerations, February 14, 2000. Signed as a free agent by **Montreal**, July 7, 2000.

• BERTUZZI, Todd

C – L. 6'3", 224 lbs. b: Sudbury, Ont., 2/2/1975. NY Islanders' 1st, 23rd overall, in 1993.

Season	Club	League	GP	G	A	Pts	AG	AA	APts	PIM	PP	SH	GW	S	%	TGF	PGF	TGA	PGA	+/–	GP	G	A	Pts	PIM	PP	SH	GW
1990-91	Sudbury Legionaires	OMHA	48	25	46	71	....	....	....	247	....	....	....	....	....	....	....	....	....	....	....	....	....	....	....	....	....	....
	Sudbury Cubs	OJHL	3	3	2	5	....	....	....	10	....	....	....	....	....	....	....	....	....	....	....	....	....	....	....	....	....	....
1991-92	Guelph Storm	OHL	47	7	14	21	....	....	....	145	....	....	....	....	....	....	....	....	....	....	....	....	....	....	....	....	....	....
1992-93	Guelph Storm	OHL	59	27	32	59	....	....	....	164	....	....	....	....	....	....	....	....	....	....	5	2	2	4	6	....	....	....
1993-94	Guelph Storm	OHL	61	28	54	82	....	....	....	165	....	....	....	....	....	....	....	....	....	....	9	2	6	8	30	....	....	....
1994-95	Guelph Storm	OHL	62	54	65	119	....	....	....	58	....	....	....	....	....	....	....	....	....	....	14	*15	18	33	41	....	....	....
1995-96	**New York Islanders**	**NHL**	**76**	**18**	**21**	**39**	**18**	**17**	**35**	**83**	**4**	**0**	**2**	**127**	**14.2**	**69**	**23**	**60**	**0**	**–14**	....	....	....	....	....	....	....	....
1996-97	**New York Islanders**	**NHL**	**64**	**10**	**13**	**23**	**11**	**12**	**23**	**68**	**3**	**0**	**1**	**79**	**12.7**	**43**	**10**	**36**	**0**	**–3**	....	....	....	....	....	....	....	....
	Utah Grizzlies	IHL	13	5	5	10	....	....	....	16	....	....	....	....	....	....	....	....	....	....	....	....	....	....	....	....	....	....
1997-98	**New York Islanders**	**NHL**	**52**	**7**	**11**	**18**	**8**	**11**	**19**	**58**	**1**	**0**	**1**	**63**	**11.1**	**22**	**5**	**36**	**0**	**–19**	....	....	....	....	....	....	....	....
	Vancouver Canucks	**NHL**	**22**	**6**	**9**	**15**	**7**	**9**	**16**	**63**	**1**	**1**	**1**	**39**	**15.4**	**22**	**4**	**19**	**3**	**2**	....	....	....	....	....	....	....	....
	Canada	WC-A	6	1	2	3	....	....	....	16	....	....	....	....	....	....	....	....	....	....	....	....	....	....	....	....	....	....
1998-99	**Vancouver Canucks**	**NHL**	**32**	**8**	**8**	**16**	**9**	**8**	**17**	**44**	**1**	**0**	**3**	**72**	**11.1**	**27**	**8**	**29**	**4**	**–6**	....	....	....	....	....	....	....	....
99-2000	**Vancouver Canucks**	**NHL**	**80**	**25**	**25**	**50**	**28**	**23**	**51**	**126**	**4**	**0**	**2**	**173**	**14.5**	**63**	**18**	**47**	**0**	**–2**	....	....	....	....	....	....	....	....
	Canada	WC-A	9	5	4	9	....	....	....	47	....	....	....	....	....	....	....	....	....	....	....	....	....	....	....	....	....	....
	NHL Totals		**326**	**74**	**87**	**161**	**81**	**80**	**161**	**442**	**14**	**1**	**10**	**553**	**13.4**	**246**	**68**	**227**	**7**		....	....	....	....	....	....	....	....

OHL Second All-Star team (1995)

Traded to **Vancouver** by **NY Islanders** with Bryan McCabe and NY Islanders' 3rd round choice (Jarkko Ruutu) in 1998 Entry Draft for Trevor Linden, February 6, 1998. • Missed majority of 1998-99 season recovering from broken leg suffered in game vs. Washington, November 1, 1998.

• BERUBE, Craig

LW – L. 6'1", 205 lbs. b: Calahoo, Alta., 12/17/1965.

Season	Club	League	GP	G	A	Pts	AG	AA	APts	PIM	PP	SH	GW	S	%	TGF	PGF	TGA	PGA	+/–	GP	G	A	Pts	PIM	PP	SH	GW
1982-83	Williams Lake Mustangs	PCJHL	33	9	24	33	....	....	....	99	....	....	....	....	....	....	....	....	....	....	....	....	....	....	....	....	....	....
	Kamloops Jr. Oilers	WHL	4	0	0	0	....	....	....	0	....	....	....	....	....	....	....	....	....	....	....	....	....	....	....	....	....	....
1983-84	New Westminster Bruins	WHL	70	11	20	31	....	....	....	104	....	....	....	....	....	....	....	....	....	....	8	1	2	3	5	....	....	....
1984-85	New Westminster Royals	WHL	70	25	44	69	....	....	....	191	....	....	....	....	....	....	....	....	....	....	10	3	2	5	4	....	....	....
1985-86	Kamloops Blazers	WHL	32	17	14	31	....	....	....	119	....	....	....	....	....	....	....	....	....	....	....	....	....	....	....	....	....	....
	Medicine Hat Tigers	WHL	34	14	16	30	....	....	....	95	....	....	....	....	....	....	....	....	....	....	25	7	8	15	102	....	....	....
1986-87	**Philadelphia Flyers**	**NHL**	**7**	**0**	**0**	**0**	**0**	**0**	**0**	**57**	**0**	**0**	**0**	**4**	**0.0**	**2**	**0**	**0**	**0**	**2**	**5**	**0**	**0**	**0**	**17**	**0**	**0**	**0**
	Hershey Bears	AHL	63	7	17	24	....	....	....	325	....	....	....	....	....	....	....	....	....	....	....	....	....	....	....	....	....	....
1987-88	**Philadelphia Flyers**	**NHL**	**27**	**3**	**2**	**5**	**3**	**1**	**4**	**108**	**0**	**0**	**2**	**13**	**23.1**	**7**	**0**	**7**	**1**	**1**	....	....	....	....	....	....	....	....
	Hershey Bears	AHL	31	5	9	14	....	....	....	119	....	....	....	....	....	....	....	....	....	....	....	....	....	....	....	....	....	....
1988-89	**Philadelphia Flyers**	**NHL**	**53**	**1**	**1**	**2**	**1**	**1**	**2**	**199**	**0**	**0**	**0**	**31**	**3.2**	**6**	**0**	**21**	**0**	**–15**	**16**	**0**	**0**	**0**	**56**	**0**	**0**	**0**
	Hershey Bears	AHL	7	0	2	2	....	....	....	19	....	....	....	....	....	....	....	....	....	....	....	....	....	....	....	....	....	....
1989-90	**Philadelphia Flyers**	**NHL**	**74**	**4**	**14**	**18**	**3**	**10**	**13**	**291**	**0**	**0**	**0**	**52**	**7.7**	**28**	**0**	**35**	**0**	**–7**	....	....	....	....	....	....	....	....
1990-91	**Philadelphia Flyers**	**NHL**	**74**	**8**	**9**	**17**	**7**	**7**	**14**	**293**	**0**	**0**	**0**	**46**	**17.4**	**25**	**1**	**30**	**0**	**–6**	....	....	....	....	....	....	....	....
1991-92	**Toronto Maple Leafs**	**NHL**	**40**	**5**	**7**	**12**	**5**	**5**	**10**	**109**	**1**	**0**	**1**	**42**	**11.9**	**21**	**3**	**20**	**0**	**–2**	....	....	....	....	....	....	....	....
	Calgary Flames	**NHL**	**36**	**1**	**4**	**5**	**1**	**3**	**4**	**155**	**0**	**0**	**0**	**27**	**3.7**	**16**	**0**	**19**	**0**	**–3**	....	....	....	....	....	....	....	....
1992-93	**Calgary Flames**	**NHL**	**77**	**4**	**8**	**12**	**3**	**5**	**8**	**209**	**0**	**0**	**2**	**58**	**6.9**	**27**	**0**	**33**	**0**	**–6**	**6**	**0**	**1**	**1**	**21**	**0**	**0**	**0**
1993-94	**Washington Capitals**	**NHL**	**84**	**7**	**7**	**14**	**6**	**5**	**11**	**305**	**0**	**0**	**0**	**48**	**14.6**	**23**	**2**	**25**	**0**	**–4**	**8**	**0**	**0**	**0**	**21**	**0**	**0**	**0**
1994-95	**Washington Capitals**	**NHL**	**43**	**2**	**4**	**6**	**4**	**6**	**10**	**173**	**0**	**0**	**0**	**22**	**9.1**	**7**	**0**	**12**	**0**	**–5**	**7**	**0**	**0**	**0**	**29**	**0**	**0**	**0**
1995-96	**Washington Capitals**	**NHL**	**50**	**2**	**10**	**12**	**2**	**8**	**10**	**151**	**1**	**0**	**1**	**28**	**7.1**	**17**	**2**	**15**	**1**	**1**	**2**	**0**	**0**	**0**	**19**	**0**	**0**	**0**
1996-97	**Washington Capitals**	**NHL**	**80**	**4**	**3**	**7**	**4**	**3**	**7**	**218**	**0**	**0**	**1**	**55**	**7.3**	**10**	**1**	**20**	**0**	**–11**	....	....	....	....	....	....	....	....
1997-98	**Washington Capitals**	**NHL**	**74**	**6**	**9**	**15**	**7**	**9**	**16**	**189**	**0**	**0**	**0**	**68**	**8.8**	**20**	**0**	**23**	**0**	**–3**	**21**	**1**	**0**	**1**	**21**	**0**	**0**	**1**

Season	Club	League	GP	G	A	Pts	AG	AA	APts	PIM	PP	SH	GW	S	%	TGF	PGF	TGA	PGA	+/–	GP	G	A	Pts	PIM	PP	SH	GW
			REGULAR SEASON																		PLAYOFFS							
1998-99	**Washington Capitals**	**NHL**	**66**	**5**	**4**	**9**	**6**	**4**	**10**	**166**	**0**	**0**	**0**	**45**	**11.1**	**11**	**0**	**18**	**0**	**–7**	....	....	....	....	....	....	....	....
	Philadelphia Flyers	**NHL**	**11**	**0**	**0**	**0**	**0**	**0**	**0**	**28**	**0**	**0**	**0**	**7**	**0.0**	**0**	**0**	**3**	**0**	**–3**	**6**	**1**	**0**	**1**	**4**	**0**	**0**	**0**
99-2000	**Philadelphia Flyers**	**NHL**	**77**	**4**	**8**	**12**	**4**	**7**	**11**	**162**	**0**	**0**	**0**	**63**	**6.3**	**16**	**0**	**13**	**0**	**3**	**18**	**1**	**0**	**1**	**23**	**0**	**0**	**1**
	NHL Totals		**873**	**56**	**90**	**146**	**56**	**74**	**130**	**2813**	**2**	**0**	**7**	**609**	**9.2**	**236**	**9**	**294**	**2**		**89**	**3**	**1**	**4**	**211**	**0**	**0**	**2**

Signed as a free agent by **Philadelphia**, March 19, 1986. Traded to **Edmonton** by **Philadelphia** with Craig Fisher and Scott Mellanby for Dave Brown, Corey Foster and Jari Kurri, May 30, 1991. Traded to **Toronto** by **Edmonton** with Grant Fuhr and Glenn Anderson for Vincent Damphousse, Peter Ing, Scott Thornton, Luke Richardson, future considerations and cash, September 19, 1991. Traded to **Calgary** by **Toronto** with Alexander Godynyuk, Gary Leeman, Michel Petit and Jeff Reese for Doug Gilmour, Jamie Macoun, Ric Nattress, Rick Wamsley and Kent Manderville, January 2, 1992. Traded to **Washington** by **Calgary** for Washington's 5th round choice (Darryl Lafrance) in 1993 Entry Draft, June 26, 1993. Traded to **Philadelphia** by **Washington** for cash, March 23, 1999. Signed as a free agent by **Washington**, July 7, 2000.

• BETHEL, John

John Charles LW – L. 5'11", 185 lbs. b: Montreal, Que., 1/15/1957. NY Rangers' 7th, 98th overall, in 1977.

Season	Club	League	GP	G	A	Pts	AG	AA	APts	PIM	PP	SH	GW	S	%	TGF	PGF	TGA	PGA	+/–	GP	G	A	Pts	PIM	PP	SH	GW
1974-75	Pierrefonds Pirates	QJHL	STATISTICS NOT AVAILABLE																									
1975-76	Pierrefonds Pirates	QJHL	15	17	21	38	....	....	....	....	....	....	....	....	....	....	....	....	....	....	....	....	....	....	....	....	....	....
1976-77	Boston University	ECAC	33	14	12	26	....	....	....	30	....	....	....	....	....	....	....	....	....	....	....	....	....	....	....	....	....	....
1977-78	Boston University	ECAC	30	25	38	63	....	....	....	53	....	....	....	....	....	....	....	....	....	....	....	....	....	....	....	....	....	....
1978-79	Boston University	ECAC	19	5	10	15	....	....	....	28	....	....	....	....	....	....	....	....	....	....	....	....	....	....	....	....	....	....
1979-80	**Winnipeg Jets**	**NHL**	**17**	**0**	**2**	**2**	**0**	**1**	**1**	**4**	**0**	**0**	**0**	**12**	**0.0**	**4**	**1**	**6**	**0**	**–3**	....	....	....	....	....	....	....	....
	Tulsa Oilers	CHL	45	17	11	28	....	....	....	50	....	....	....	....	....	....	....	....	....	....	....	....	....	....	....	....	....	....
1980-81	Tulsa Oilers	CHL	58	23	35	58	....	....	....	51	....	....	....	....	....	....	....	....	....	....	....	....	....	....	....	....	....	....
1981-82	Tulsa Oilers	CHL	74	19	51	70	....	....	....	83	....	....	....	....	....	....	....	....	....	....	3	0	0	0	2	....	....	....
1982-83	Sherbrooke Jets	AHL	63	24	26	50	....	....	....	26	....	....	....	....	....	....	....	....	....	....	....	....	....	....	....	....	....	....
	NHL Totals		**17**	**0**	**2**	**2**	**0**	**1**	**1**	**4**	**0**	**0**	**0**	**12**	**0.0**	**4**	**1**	**6**	**0**		....	....	....	....	....	....	....	....

Signed as a free agent by **Winnipeg**, September, 1979.

• BETIK, Karel

D – L. 6'2", 208 lbs. b: Karvina, Czech., 10/28/1978. Tampa Bay's 6th, 112th overall, in 1997.

Season	Club	League	GP	G	A	Pts	AG	AA	APts	PIM	PP	SH	GW	S	%	TGF	PGF	TGA	PGA	+/–	GP	G	A	Pts	PIM	PP	SH	GW
1995-96	HC Vitkovice	Czech-Jr.	48	3	12	15	....	....	....	88	....	....	....	....	....	....	....	....	....	....	....	....	....	....	....	....	....	....
1996-97	Kelowna Rockets	WHL	56	3	10	13	....	....	....	76	....	....	....	....	....	....	....	....	....	....	6	1	1	2	2	....	....	....
1997-98	Kelowna Rockets	WHL	61	5	25	30	....	....	....	121	....	....	....	....	....	....	....	....	....	....	7	1	2	3	8	....	....	....
1998-99	**Tampa Bay Lightning**	**NHL**	**3**	**0**	**2**	**2**	**0**	**2**	**2**	**2**	**0**	**0**	**0**	**2**	**0.0**	**3**	**0**	**6**	**0**	**–3**	....	....	....	....	....	....	....	....
	Cleveland Lumberjacks	IHL	74	5	11	16	....	....	....	97	....	....	....	....	....	....	....	....	....	....	....	....	....	....	....	....	....	....
99-2000	Detroit Vipers	IHL	17	0	0	0	....	....	....	22	....	....	....	....	....	....	....	....	....	....	....	....	....	....	....	....	....	....
	Toledo Storm	ECHL	22	0	7	7	....	....	....	42	....	....	....	....	....	....	....	....	....	....	....	....	....	....	....	....	....	....
	NHL Totals		**3**	**0**	**2**	**2**	**0**	**2**	**2**	**2**	**0**	**0**	**0**	**2**	**0.0**	**3**	**0**	**6**	**0**		....	....	....	....	....	....	....	....

• BETS, Maxim

LW – L. 6'1", 185 lbs. b: Chelyabinsk, USSR, 1/31/1974. St. Louis' 1st, 37th overall, in 1993.

Season	Club	League	GP	G	A	Pts	AG	AA	APts	PIM	PP	SH	GW	S	%	TGF	PGF	TGA	PGA	+/–	GP	G	A	Pts	PIM	PP	SH	GW
1990-91	Traktor Chelyabinsk	CIS-Jr.	60	71	37	108	....	....	....	....	....	....	....	....	....	....	....	....	....	....	....	....	....	....	....	....	....	....
1991-92	Traktor Chelyabinsk	CIS	25	1	1	2	....	....	....	8	....	....	....	....	....	....	....	....	....	....	....	....	....	....	....	....	....	....
	Russia	EJC-A	6	3	4	7	....	....	....	0	....	....	....	....	....	....	....	....	....	....	....	....	....	....	....	....	....	....
1992-93	Spokane Chiefs	WHL	54	49	57	106	....	....	....	130	....	....	....	....	....	....	....	....	....	....	9	5	6	11	20	....	....	....
1993-94	Spokane Chiefs	WHL	63	46	70	116	....	....	....	111	....	....	....	....	....	....	....	....	....	....	3	1	1	2	12	....	....	....
	Russia	WJC-A	7	0	0	0	....	....	....	8	....	....	....	....	....	....	....	....	....	....	....	....	....	....	....	....	....	....
	Mighty Ducks of Anaheim	**NHL**	**3**	**0**	**0**	**0**	**0**	**0**	**0**	**0**	**0**	**0**	**0**	**1**	**0.0**	**0**	**0**	**3**	**0**	**–3**	....	....	....	....	....	....	....	....
	San Diego Gulls	IHL	....	....	....	....	....	....	....	....	....	....	....	....	....	....	....	....	....	....	9	0	2	2	0	....	....	....
1994-95	San Diego Gulls	IHL	36	2	6	8	....	....	....	31	....	....	....	....	....	....	....	....	....	....	....	....	....	....	....	....	....	....
	Worcester IceCats	AHL	9	1	1	2	....	....	....	6	....	....	....	....	....	....	....	....	....	....	....	....	....	....	....	....	....	....
1995-96	Baltimore Bandits	AHL	34	5	5	10	....	....	....	18	....	....	....	....	....	....	....	....	....	....	....	....	....	....	....	....	....	....
	Raleigh IceCaps	ECHL	9	0	4	4	....	....	....	6	....	....	....	....	....	....	....	....	....	....	4	0	0	0	0	....	....	....
1996-97	CSKA Moscow	Russia	16	3	2	5	....	....	....	12	....	....	....	....	....	....	....	....	....	....	....	....	....	....	....	....	....	....
	CSKA Moscow	EuroHL	3	1	2	3	....	....	....	2	....	....	....	....	....	....	....	....	....	....	....	....	....	....	....	....	....	....
1997-98	Traktor Chelyabinsk	Russia	35	12	9	21	....	....	....	16	....	....	....	....	....	....	....	....	....	....	....	....	....	....	....	....	....	....
1998-99	Mechel Chelyabinsk	Russia	41	12	19	31	....	....	....	57	....	....	....	....	....	....	....	....	....	....	3	0	1	1	2	....	....	....
99-2000	Metallurg Magnitogorsk	Russia	36	3	5	8	....	....	....	26	....	....	....	....	....	....	....	....	....	....	12	4	2	6	2	....	....	....
	Metallurg Magnitogorsk	EuroHL	6	3	1	4	....	....	....	2	....	....	....	....	....	....	....	....	....	....	5	1	0	1	0	....	....	....
	NHL Totals		**3**	**0**	**0**	**0**	**0**	**0**	**0**	**0**	**0**	**0**	**0**	**1**	**0.0**	**0**	**0**	**3**	**0**		....	....	....	....	....	....	....	....

Rights traded to **Anaheim** by **St. Louis** with St. Louis' 6th round choice (later traded back to St. Louis — St. Louis selected Denis Hamel) in 1995 Entry Draft for Alexei Kasatonov, March 21, 1994.

• BEUKEBOOM, Jeff

D – R. 6'5", 230 lbs. b: Ajax, Ont., 3/28/1965. Edmonton's 1st, 19th overall, in 1983.

Season	Club	League	GP	G	A	Pts	AG	AA	APts	PIM	PP	SH	GW	S	%	TGF	PGF	TGA	PGA	+/–	GP	G	A	Pts	PIM	PP	SH	GW
1981-82	Newmarket Royals	OJHL-B	49	5	30	35	....	....	....	218	....	....	....	....	....	....	....	....	....	....	....	....	....	....	....	....	....	....
1982-83	Sault Ste. Marie Greyhounds	OHL	70	0	25	25	....	....	....	143	....	....	....	....	....	....	....	....	....	....	16	1	4	5	46	....	....	....
1983-84	Sault Ste. Marie Greyhounds	OHL	61	6	30	36	....	....	....	178	....	....	....	....	....	....	....	....	....	....	16	1	7	8	43	....	....	....
1984-85	Sault Ste. Marie Greyhounds	OHL	37	4	20	24	....	....	....	85	....	....	....	....	....	....	....	....	....	....	16	4	6	10	47	....	....	....
	Canada	WJC-A	3	1	0	1	....	....	....	4	....	....	....	....	....	....	....	....	....	....	....	....	....	....	....	....	....	....
	Sault Ste. Marie Greyhounds	Mem-Cup	4	1	1	2	....	....	....	13	....	....	....	....	....	....	....	....	....	....	....	....	....	....	....	....	....	....
1985-86	Nova Scotia Oilers	AHL	77	9	20	29	....	....	....	175	....	....	....	....	....	....	....	....	....	....	....	....	....	....	....	....	....	....
	Edmonton Oilers	**NHL**	....	....	....	....	....	....	....	....	....	....	....	....	....	....	....	....	....	....	**1**	**0**	**0**	**0**	**4**	**0**	**0**	**0**
1986-87♦	**Edmonton Oilers**	**NHL**	**44**	**3**	**8**	**11**	**3**	**6**	**9**	**124**	**1**	**0**	**1**	**24**	**12.5**	**49**	**1**	**44**	**3**	**7**	....	....	....	....	....	....	....	....
	Nova Scotia Oilers	AHL	14	1	7	8	....	....	....	35	....	....	....	....	....	....	....	....	....	....	....	....	....	....	....	....	....	....
1987-88♦	**Edmonton Oilers**	**NHL**	**73**	**5**	**20**	**25**	**4**	**14**	**18**	**201**	**1**	**0**	**1**	**76**	**6.6**	**94**	**16**	**73**	**22**	**27**	**7**	**0**	**0**	**0**	**16**	**0**	**0**	**0**
1988-89	**Edmonton Oilers**	**NHL**	**36**	**0**	**5**	**5**	**0**	**4**	**4**	**94**	**0**	**0**	**0**	**26**	**0.0**	**28**	**2**	**35**	**11**	**2**	**1**	**0**	**0**	**0**	**2**	**0**	**0**	**0**
	Cape Breton Oilers	AHL	8	0	4	4	....	....	....	36	....	....	....	....	....	....	....	....	....	....	....	....	....	....	....	....	....	....
1989-90♦	**Edmonton Oilers**	**NHL**	**46**	**1**	**12**	**13**	**1**	**9**	**10**	**86**	**0**	**0**	**0**	**36**	**2.8**	**43**	**6**	**46**	**14**	**5**	**2**	**0**	**0**	**0**	**0**	**0**	**0**	**0**
1990-91	**Edmonton Oilers**	**NHL**	**67**	**3**	**7**	**10**	**3**	**5**	**8**	**150**	**0**	**0**	**0**	**48**	**6.3**	**65**	**4**	**82**	**27**	**6**	**18**	**1**	**3**	**4**	**28**	**0**	**0**	**0**
1991-92	**Edmonton Oilers**	**NHL**	**18**	**0**	**5**	**5**	**0**	**4**	**4**	**78**	**0**	**0**	**0**	**7**	**0.0**	**17**	**0**	**23**	**10**	**4**	....	....	....	....	....	....	....	....
	New York Rangers	**NHL**	**56**	**1**	**10**	**11**	**1**	**8**	**9**	**122**	**0**	**0**	**0**	**41**	**2.4**	**73**	**0**	**74**	**20**	**19**	**13**	**2**	**3**	**5**	**47**	**0**	**0**	**0**
1992-93	**New York Rangers**	**NHL**	**82**	**2**	**17**	**19**	**2**	**12**	**14**	**153**	**0**	**0**	**0**	**54**	**3.7**	**91**	**2**	**112**	**32**	**9**	....	....	....	....	....	....	....	....
1993-94♦	**New York Rangers**	**NHL**	**68**	**8**	**8**	**16**	**7**	**6**	**13**	**170**	**1**	**0**	**0**	**58**	**13.8**	**63**	**1**	**75**	**31**	**18**	**22**	**0**	**6**	**6**	**50**	**0**	**0**	**0**
1994-95	**New York Rangers**	**NHL**	**44**	**1**	**3**	**4**	**2**	**4**	**6**	**70**	**0**	**0**	**0**	**29**	**3.4**	**34**	**0**	**49**	**18**	**3**	**9**	**0**	**0**	**0**	**10**	**0**	**0**	**0**
1995-96	**New York Rangers**	**NHL**	**82**	**3**	**11**	**14**	**3**	**9**	**12**	**220**	**0**	**0**	**1**	**65**	**4.6**	**67**	**1**	**87**	**40**	**19**	**11**	**0**	**3**	**3**	**6**	**0**	**0**	**0**
1996-97	**New York Rangers**	**NHL**	**80**	**3**	**9**	**12**	**3**	**8**	**11**	**167**	**0**	**0**	**0**	**55**	**5.5**	**80**	**4**	**82**	**28**	**22**	**15**	**0**	**1**	**1**	**34**	**0**	**0**	**0**
1997-98	**New York Rangers**	**NHL**	**63**	**0**	**5**	**5**	**0**	**5**	**5**	**195**	**0**	**0**	**0**	**23**	**0.0**	**30**	**1**	**71**	**17**	**–25**	....	....	....	....	....	....	....	....
1998-99	**New York Rangers**	**NHL**	**45**	**0**	**9**	**9**	**0**	**9**	**9**	**60**	**0**	**0**	**0**	**8**	**0.0**	**18**	**0**	**26**	**6**	**–2**	....	....	....	....	....	....	....	....
	NHL Totals		**804**	**30**	**129**	**159**	**29**	**103**	**132**	**1890**	**3**	**0**	**3**	**550**	**5.5**	**752**	**38**	**879**	**279**		**99**	**3**	**16**	**19**	**197**	**0**	**0**	**0**

OHL First All-Star Team (1985)

Traded to **NY Rangers** by **Edmonton** for David Shaw to complete transaction that sent Mark Messier to NY Rangers for Bernie Nicholls, Steven Rice and Louie DeBrusk (October 4, 1991), November 12, 1991. • Suffered eventual career-ending head injury in game vs. LA Kings, November 19, 1998. • Announced retirement July 15, 1999.

• BEVERLEY, Nick

Nicholas Gerald D – R. 6'2", 185 lbs. b: Toronto, Ont., 4/21/1947.

Season	Club	League	GP	G	A	Pts	AG	AA	APts	PIM	PP	SH	GW	S	%	TGF	PGF	TGA	PGA	+/–	GP	G	A	Pts	PIM	PP	SH	GW
1963-64	Oshawa Generals	OHA-Jr.	3	0	1	1	....	....	....	4	....	....	....	....	....	....	....	....	....	....	6	0	0	0	0	....	....	....
1964-65	Oshawa Generals	OHA-Jr.	56	0	10	10	....	....	....	42	....	....	....	....	....	....	....	....	....	....	6	0	1	1	19	....	....	....
1965-66	Oshawa Generals	OHA-Jr.	47	0	10	10	....	....	....	41	....	....	....	....	....	....	....	....	....	....	17	1	4	5	18	....	....	....
	Oshawa Generals	Mem-Cup	14	2	5	7	....	....	....	6	....	....	....	....	....	....	....	....	....	....	....	....	....	....	....	....	....	....
1966-67	Oshawa Generals	OHA-Jr.	48	8	14	22	....	....	....	57	....	....	....	....	....	....	....	....	....	....	....	....	....	....	....	....	....	....
	Boston Bruins	**NHL**	**2**	**0**	**0**	**0**	**0**	**0**	**0**	**0**	....	....	....	....	....	....	....	....	....	....	....	....	....	....	....	....	....	....
1967-68	Oklahoma City Blazers	CPHL	70	7	20	27	....	....	....	60	....	....	....	....	....	....	....	....	....	....	4	0	0	0	17	....	....	....
1968-69	Oklahoma City Blazers	CPHL	62	3	22	25	....	....	....	32	....	....	....	....	....	....	....	....	....	....	12	0	4	4	4	....	....	....

			REGULAR SEASON																		PLAYOFFS							
Season	Club	League	GP	G	A	Pts	AG	AA	APts	PIM	PP	SH	GW	S	%	TGF	PGF	TGA	PGA	+/–	GP	G	A	Pts	PIM	PP	SH	GW
1969-70	**Boston Bruins**	**NHL**	**2**	**0**	**0**	**0**	**0**	**0**	**0**	**2**	**0**	**0**	**0**	**0**	**0.0**	**0**	**0**	**0**	**0**	**0**	....	....	....	....	....	....	....	....
	Oklahoma City Blazers	CHL	58	6	24	30	....	....	....	26	....	....	....	....	....	....	....	....	....	....	....	....	....	....	....	....	....	....
1970-71	Hershey Bears	AHL	70	3	23	26	....	....	....	46	....	....	....	....	....	....	....	....	....	....	4	0	0	0	2	....	....	....
1971-72	**Boston Bruins**	**NHL**	**1**	**0**	**0**	**0**	**0**	**0**	**0**	**0**	**0**	**0**	**0**	**0**	**0.0**	**0**	**0**	**0**	**0**	**0**	....	....	....	....	....	....	....	....
	Boston Braves	AHL	73	9	31	40	....	....	....	36	....	....	....	....	....	....	....	....	....	....	9	0	5	5	2	....	....	....
1972-73	**Boston Bruins**	**NHL**	**76**	**1**	**10**	**11**	**1**	**8**	**9**	**26**	**0**	**0**	**0**	**57**	**1.8**	**55**	**0**	**58**	**10**	**7**	**4**	**0**	**0**	**0**	**0**	**0**	**0**	**0**
1973-74	**Boston Bruins**	**NHL**	**1**	**0**	**0**	**0**	**0**	**0**	**0**	**0**	**0**	**0**	**0**	**0**	**0.0**	**0**	**0**	**1**	**0**	**–1**	....	....	....	....	....	....	....	....
	Pittsburgh Penguins	**NHL**	**67**	**2**	**14**	**16**	**2**	**12**	**14**	**21**	**0**	**0**	**1**	**74**	**2.7**	**69**	**3**	**98**	**16**	**–16**	....	....	....	....	....	....	....	....
1974-75	**New York Rangers**	**NHL**	**67**	**3**	**15**	**18**	**3**	**11**	**14**	**19**	**0**	**0**	**0**	**79**	**3.8**	**66**	**2**	**64**	**13**	**13**	**3**	**0**	**1**	**1**	**0**	**0**	**0**	**0**
1975-76	**New York Rangers**	**NHL**	**63**	**1**	**8**	**9**	**1**	**6**	**7**	**46**	**0**	**0**	**0**	**75**	**1.3**	**56**	**0**	**87**	**22**	**–9**	....	....	....	....	....	....	....	....
1976-77	**New York Rangers**	**NHL**	**9**	**0**	**0**	**0**	**0**	**0**	**0**	**2**	**0**	**0**	**0**	**1**	**0.0**	**5**	**0**	**10**	**5**	**0**	....	....	....	....	....	....	....	....
	Minnesota North Stars	**NHL**	**52**	**2**	**17**	**19**	**2**	**13**	**15**	**6**	**0**	**0**	**0**	**59**	**3.4**	**62**	**2**	**77**	**17**	**0**	....	....	....	....	....	....	....	....
1977-78	**Minnesota North Stars**	**NHL**	**57**	**7**	**14**	**21**	**6**	**11**	**17**	**18**	**0**	**0**	**1**	**87**	**8.0**	**52**	**5**	**69**	**21**	**–1**	....	....	....	....	....	....	....	....
1978-79	**Los Angeles Kings**	**NHL**	**7**	**0**	**3**	**3**	**0**	**2**	**2**	**0**	**0**	**0**	**0**	**2**	**0.0**	**7**	**2**	**4**	**1**	**2**	....	....	....	....	....	....	....	....
	Colorado Rockies	**NHL**	**52**	**2**	**4**	**6**	**2**	**3**	**5**	**6**	**0**	**1**	**0**	**42**	**4.8**	**28**	**2**	**53**	**11**	**–16**	....	....	....	....	....	....	....	....
1979-80	**Colorado Rockies**	**NHL**	**46**	**0**	**9**	**9**	**0**	**7**	**7**	**10**	**0**	**0**	**0**	**23**	**0.0**	**43**	**0**	**68**	**21**	**–4**	....	....	....	....	....	....	....	....
	Fort Worth Texans	CHL	12	0	6	6	....	....	....	4	....	....	....	....	....	....	....	....	....	....	....	....	....	....	....	....	....	....
1980-1981	Houston Apollos	AHL	DID NOT PLAY – COACHING																									
1981-1983	New Haven Nighthawks	AHL	DID NOT PLAY – COACHING																									
1983-1984	New Haven Nighthawks	AHL	DID NOT PLAY – COACHING																									
	New Haven Nighthawks	AHL	2	0	1	1	....	....	....	0	....	....	....	....	....	....	....	....	....	....	....	....	....	....	....	....	....	....
1984-1985	New Haven Nighthawks	AHL	DID NOT PLAY – COACHING																									
1985-1988	**Los Angeles Kings**	**NHL**	DID NOT PLAY – SCOUTING																									
1988-1990	**Los Angeles Kings**	**NHL**	DID NOT PLAY – FRONT OFFICE STAFF																									
1990-1992	**Los Angeles Kings**	**NHL**	DID NOT PLAY – ASSISTANT GENERAL MANAGER																									
1992-1994	**Los Angeles Kings**	**NHL**	DID NOT PLAY – GENERAL MANAGER																									
1994-1996	**Toronto Maple Leafs**	**NHL**	DID NOT PLAY – SCOUTING																									
1996-2000	**Toronto Maple Leafs**	**NHL**	DID NOT PLAY – FRONT OFFICE STAFF																									
	NHL Totals		**502**	**18**	**94**	**112**	**17**	**73**	**90**	**156**	....	....	....	....	....	....	....	....	....	....	**7**	**0**	**1**	**1**	**0**	....	....	....

Traded to **Pittsburgh** by **Boston** for Darryl Edestrand, October 25, 1973. Traded to **NY Rangers** by **Pittsburgh** for Vic Hadfield, May 27, 1974. Traded to **Minnesota** by **NY Rangers** with Bill Fairbairn for Bill Goldsworthy, November 11, 1976. Claimed on waivers by **LA Kings** from **Minnesota**, September 5, 1978. Traded to **Colorado** by **LA Kings** for Colorado's (New Jersey's) 4th round choice (Dave Gans) in 1982 Entry Draft, November 18, 1978. Claimed by **Hartford** from **Colorado** in Expansion Draft, June 13, 1979. Signed as a free agent by **Colorado**, September 15, 1979. • Played w/ **New Haven** as emergency injury replacement, February 8, 1984. • Served as interim Head Coach of **Toronto**, March 5, 1996 to April 27, 1996.

• BIALOWAS, Dwight

Dwight Joseph D – R. 6', 185 lbs. b: Regina, Sask., 9/8/1952. Atlanta's 2nd, 18th overall, in 1972.

Season	Club	League	GP	G	A	Pts	AG	AA	APts	PIM	PP	SH	GW	S	%	TGF	PGF	TGA	PGA	+/–	GP	G	A	Pts	PIM	PP	SH	GW
1969-70	Regina Pats	SJHL	....	5	18	23	....	....	....	18	....	....	....	....	....	....	....	....	....	....	....	....	....	....	....	....	....	....
1970-71	Regina Pats	WCJHL	63	12	29	41	....	....	....	40	....	....	....	....	....	....	....	....	....	....	6	2	6	8	4	....	....	....
1971-72	Regina Pats	WCJHL	61	12	39	51	....	....	....	45	....	....	....	....	....	....	....	....	....	....	15	1	8	9	24	....	....	....
1972-73	Omaha Knights	CHL	70	11	24	35	....	....	....	58	....	....	....	....	....	....	....	....	....	....	11	0	6	6	16	....	....	....
1973-74	**Atlanta Flames**	**NHL**	**11**	**0**	**0**	**0**	**0**	**0**	**0**	**2**	**0**	**0**	**0**	**3**	**0.0**	**2**	**0**	**8**	**0**	**–6**	....	....	....	....	....	....	....	....
	Omaha Knights	CHL	30	6	12	18	....	....	....	22	....	....	....	....	....	....	....	....	....	....	....	....	....	....	....	....	....	....
	Nova Scotia Voyageurs	AHL	4	1	0	1	....	....	....	4	....	....	....	....	....	....	....	....	....	....	6	0	1	1	4	....	....	....
1974-75	**Atlanta Flames**	**NHL**	**37**	**3**	**9**	**12**	**3**	**7**	**10**	**20**	**2**	**0**	**0**	**42**	**7.1**	**30**	**9**	**25**	**7**	**3**	....	....	....	....	....	....	....	....
	Minnesota North Stars	**NHL**	**40**	**2**	**10**	**12**	**2**	**7**	**9**	**2**	**1**	**0**	**0**	**62**	**3.2**	**41**	**6**	**50**	**10**	**–5**	....	....	....	....	....	....	....	....
1975-76	**Minnesota North Stars**	**NHL**	**58**	**5**	**18**	**23**	**4**	**13**	**17**	**22**	**5**	**0**	**1**	**87**	**5.7**	**64**	**20**	**56**	**3**	**–9**	....	....	....	....	....	....	....	....
	New Haven Nighthawks	AHL	17	1	6	7	....	....	....	15	....	....	....	....	....	....	....	....	....	....	....	....	....	....	....	....	....	....
1976-77	**Minnesota North Stars**	**NHL**	**18**	**1**	**9**	**10**	**1**	**7**	**8**	**0**	**1**	**0**	**0**	**21**	**4.8**	**18**	**12**	**9**	**0**	**–3**	....	....	....	....	....	....	....	....
	New Haven Nighthawks	AHL	39	4	20	24	....	....	....	25	....	....	....	....	....	....	....	....	....	....	6	0	1	1	0	....	....	....
1977-78	Fort Worth Texans	CHL	62	6	21	27	....	....	....	24	....	....	....	....	....	....	....	....	....	....	3	0	0	0	2	....	....	....
	NHL Totals		**164**	**11**	**46**	**57**	**10**	**34**	**44**	**46**	**9**	**0**	**1**	**215**	**5.1**	**155**	**47**	**148**	**20**		....	....	....	....	....	....	....	....

Traded to **Minnesota** by **Atlanta** with Dean Talafous for Barry Gibbs, January 3, 1975.

• BIALOWAS, Frank

Francis Michael "The Animal" LW – L. 5'11", 220 lbs. b: Winnipeg, Man., 9/25/1969.

Season	Club	League	GP	G	A	Pts	AG	AA	APts	PIM	PP	SH	GW	S	%	TGF	PGF	TGA	PGA	+/–	GP	G	A	Pts	PIM	PP	SH	GW
1987-88	Estevan Bruins	MJHL	58	8	12	20	....	....	....	161	....	....	....	....	....	....	....	....	....	....	....	....	....	....	....	....	....	....
1988-1990	Winkler Flyers	MJHL	STATISTICS NOT AVAILABLE																									
1990-91			DID NOT PLAY																									
1991-92	Roanoke Valley Rebels	ECHL	23	4	2	6	....	....	....	150	....	....	....	....	....	....	....	....	....	....	3	0	0	0	4	....	....	....
1992-93	Richmond Renegades	ECHL	60	3	18	21	....	....	....	261	....	....	....	....	....	....	....	....	....	....	1	0	0	0	2	....	....	....
	St. John's Maple Leafs	AHL	7	1	0	1	....	....	....	28	....	....	....	....	....	....	....	....	....	....	1	0	0	0	0	....	....	....
1993-94	**Toronto Maple Leafs**	**NHL**	**3**	**0**	**0**	**0**	**0**	**0**	**0**	**12**	**0**	**0**	**0**	**1**	**0.0**	**0**	**0**	**0**	**0**	**0**	....	....	....	....	....	....	....	....
	St. John's Maple Leafs	AHL	69	2	8	10	....	....	....	352	....	....	....	....	....	....	....	....	....	....	7	0	3	3	25	....	....	....
1994-95	St. John's Maple Leafs	AHL	51	2	3	5	....	....	....	277	....	....	....	....	....	....	....	....	....	....	4	0	0	0	12	....	....	....
1995-96	Portland Pirates	AHL	65	4	3	7	....	....	....	211	....	....	....	....	....	....	....	....	....	....	7	0	0	0	42	....	....	....
1996-97	Philadelphia Phantoms	AHL	67	7	6	13	....	....	....	254	....	....	....	....	....	....	....	....	....	....	6	0	2	2	41	....	....	....
1997-98	Philadelphia Phantoms	AHL	65	5	7	12	....	....	....	259	....	....	....	....	....	....	....	....	....	....	19	0	0	0	26	....	....	....
1998-99	Philadelphia Phantoms	AHL	24	0	3	3	....	....	....	42	....	....	....	....	....	....	....	....	....	....	....	....	....	....	....	....	....	....
	Portland Pirates	AHL	6	0	0	0	....	....	....	10	....	....	....	....	....	....	....	....	....	....	....	....	....	....	....	....	....	....
	Indianapolis Ice	IHL	16	1	0	1	....	....	....	27	....	....	....	....	....	....	....	....	....	....	2	0	0	0	6	....	....	....
99-2000	Hershey Bears	AHL	40	4	3	7	....	....	....	65	....	....	....	....	....	....	....	....	....	....	8	1	0	1	32	....	....	....
	NHL Totals		**3**	**0**	**0**	**0**	**0**	**0**	**0**	**12**	**0**	**0**	**0**	**1**	**0.0**	**0**	**0**	**0**	**0**		....	....	....	....	....	....	....	....

Signed as a free agent by **Toronto**, March 20, 1994. Signed as a free agent by **Washington**, September 8, 1995. Traded to **Philadelphia** by **Washington** for future considerations, July 18, 1996. Traded to **Chicago** by **Philadelphia** for Dennis Bonvie, January 8, 1999. Signed as a free agent by **Hershey** (AHL), September 9, 1999.

• BIANCHIN, Wayne

Wayne Richard LW – L. 5'10", 180 lbs. b: Nanaimo, B.C., 9/6/1953. Pittsburgh's 2nd, 23rd overall, in 1973.

Season	Club	League	GP	G	A	Pts	AG	AA	APts	PIM	PP	SH	GW	S	%	TGF	PGF	TGA	PGA	+/–	GP	G	A	Pts	PIM	PP	SH	GW
1970-71	Kamloops Buckaroos	BCJHL	57	30	42	72	....	....	....	2	....	....	....	....	....	....	....	....	....	....	....	....	....	....	....	....	....	....
1971-72	Calgary Centennials	WCJHL	7	1	5	6	....	....	....	7	....	....	....	....	....	....	....	....	....	....	....	....	....	....	....	....	....	....
	Victoria Cougars	WCJHL	22	7	3	10	....	....	....	57	....	....	....	....	....	....	....	....	....	....	....	....	....	....	....	....	....	....
	Flin Flon Bombers	WCJHL	27	12	15	27	....	....	....	8	....	....	....	....	....	....	....	....	....	....	7	3	0	3	28	....	....	....
1972-73	Flin Flon Bombers	WCJHL	68	60	54	114	....	....	....	90	....	....	....	....	....	....	....	....	....	....	9	5	7	12	28	....	....	....
1973-74	**Pittsburgh Penguins**	**NHL**	**69**	**12**	**13**	**25**	**12**	**11**	**23**	**38**	**1**	**0**	**1**	**118**	**10.2**	**35**	**4**	**47**	**1**	**–15**	....	....	....	....	....	....	....	....
	Hershey Bears	AHL	4	1	2	3	....	....	....	2	....	....	....	....	....	....	....	....	....	....	....	....	....	....	....	....	....	....
1974-75	**Pittsburgh Penguins**	**NHL**	**2**	**0**	**0**	**0**	**0**	**0**	**0**	**0**	**0**	**0**	**0**	**0**	**0.0**	**0**	**0**	**1**	**0**	**–1**	....	....	....	....	....	....	....	....
	Syracuse Eagles	AHL	12	5	4	9	....	....	....	26	....	....	....	....	....	....	....	....	....	....	....	....	....	....	....	....	....	....
	Hershey Bears	AHL	3	0	1	1	....	....	....	0	....	....	....	....	....	....	....	....	....	....	....	....	....	....	....	....	....	....
	Johnstown Jets	NAHL	8	8	2	10	....	....	....	4	....	....	....	....	....	....	....	....	....	....	....	....	....	....	....	....	....	....
1975-76	**Pittsburgh Penguins**	**NHL**	**14**	**1**	**5**	**6**	**1**	**4**	**5**	**4**	**0**	**0**	**1**	**26**	**3.8**	**9**	**0**	**13**	**0**	**–4**	....	....	....	....	....	....	....	....
	Hershey Bears	AHL	54	22	24	46	....	....	....	17	....	....	....	....	....	....	....	....	....	....	6	1	3	4	4	....	....	....
1976-77	**Pittsburgh Penguins**	**NHL**	**79**	**28**	**6**	**34**	**25**	**5**	**30**	**28**	**4**	**0**	**3**	**130**	**21.5**	**56**	**10**	**48**	**1**	**–1**	**3**	**0**	**1**	**1**	**6**	**0**	**0**	**0**
1977-78	**Pittsburgh Penguins**	**NHL**	**61**	**20**	**13**	**33**	**18**	**10**	**28**	**40**	**3**	**1**	**2**	**95**	**21.1**	**50**	**10**	**55**	**1**	**–14**	....	....	....	....	....	....	....	....
1978-79	**Pittsburgh Penguins**	**NHL**	**40**	**7**	**4**	**11**	**6**	**3**	**9**	**20**	**1**	**0**	**3**	**57**	**12.3**	**24**	**5**	**21**	**0**	**–2**	....	....	....	....	....	....	....	....
1979-80	**Edmonton Oilers**	**NHL**	**11**	**0**	**0**	**0**	**0**	**0**	**0**	**7**	**0**	**0**	**0**	**7**	**0.0**	**0**	**0**	**4**	**0**	**–4**	....	....	....	....	....	....	....	....
	Houston Apollos	CHL	57	20	19	39	....	....	....	20	....	....	....	....	....	....	....	....	....	....	6	2	5	7	4	....	....	....

Season	Club	League	GP	G	A	Pts	AG	AA	APts	PIM	PP	SH	GW	S	%	TGF	PGF	TGA	PGA	+/–	GP	G	A	Pts	PIM	PP	SH	GW
			REGULAR SEASON																		PLAYOFFS							
1980-81	HC Asiago	Italy	28	34	24	58	....	....	....	29	....	....	....	....	....	....	....	....	....	....	14	6	9	*15	6	....	....	....
	Italy	WEC-B	7	3	*9	12	....	....	....	2	....	....	....	....	....	....	....	....	....	....	....	....	....	....	....	....	....	....
1981-82	HC Varese	Italy	20	13	14	27	....	....	....	....	....	....	....	....	....	....	....	....	....	....	....	....	....	....	....	....	....	....
	Italy	Nat-Team	6	0	1	1	....	....	....	8	....	....	....	....	....	....	....	....	....	....	....	....	....	....	....	....	....	....
	NHL Totals		**276**	**68**	**41**	**109**	**62**	**33**	**95**	**137**	**9**	**1**	**10**	**433**	**15.7**	**174**	**29**	**189**	**3**		**3**	**0**	**1**	**1**	**6**	**0**	**0**	**0**

WEC-B All-Star Team (1981)

• Missed majority of 1974-75 recovering from neck surgery, April, 1974. Claimed by **Edmonton** from **Pittsburgh** in Expansion Draft, June 13, 1979.

• BICANEK, Radim

D – L. 6'1", 195 lbs. b: Uherske Hradiste, Czech., 1/18/1975. Ottawa's 2nd, 27th overall, in 1993.

Season	Club	League	GP	G	A	Pts	AG	AA	APts	PIM	PP	SH	GW	S	%	TGF	PGF	TGA	PGA	+/–	GP	G	A	Pts	PIM	PP	SH	GW
1992-93	Dukla Jihlava	Czech.	43	2	3	5	....	....	....	....	....	....	....	....	....	....	....	....	....	....	....	....	....	....	....	....	....	....
	Czech-Republic	WJC-A	7	1	0	1	....	....	....	0	....	....	....	....	....	....	....	....	....	....	....	....	....	....	....	....	....	....
	Czech-Republic	EJC-A	6	3	1	4	....	....	....	10	....	....	....	....	....	....	....	....	....	....	....	....	....	....	....	....	....	....
1993-94	Belleville Bulls	OHL	63	16	27	43	....	....	....	49	....	....	....	....	....	....	....	....	....	....	12	2	8	10	21	....	....	....
1994-95	Belleville Bulls	OHL	49	13	26	39	....	....	....	61	....	....	....	....	....	....	....	....	....	....	16	6	5	11	30	....	....	....
	Ottawa Senators	**NHL**	**6**	**0**	**0**	**0**	**0**	**0**	**0**	**0**	**0**	**0**	**0**	**6**	**0.0**	**3**	**0**	**0**	**0**	**3**	....	....	....	....	....	....	....	....
	P.E.I. Senators	AHL	....	....	....	....	....	....	....	....	....	....	....	....	....	....	....	....	....	....	3	0	1	1	0	....	....	....
1995-96	P.E.I. Senators	AHL	74	7	19	26	....	....	....	87	....	....	....	....	....	....	....	....	....	....	5	0	2	2	6	....	....	....
1996-97	**Ottawa Senators**	**NHL**	**21**	**0**	**1**	**1**	**0**	**1**	**1**	**8**	**0**	**0**	**0**	**27**	**0.0**	**11**	**1**	**17**	**3**	**–4**	**7**	**0**	**0**	**0**	**8**	**0**	**0**	**0**
	Worcester IceCats	AHL	44	1	15	16	....	....	....	22	....	....	....	....	....	....	....	....	....	....	....	....	....	....	....	....	....	....
1997-98	**Ottawa Senators**	**NHL**	**1**	**0**	**0**	**0**	**0**	**0**	**0**	**0**	**0**	**0**	**0**	**0**	**0.0**	**0**	**0**	**0**	**0**	**0**	....	....	....	....	....	....	....	....
	Detroit Vipers	IHL	9	1	3	4	....	....	....	16	....	....	....	....	....	....	....	....	....	....	....	....	....	....	....	....	....	....
	Manitoba Moose	IHL	42	1	7	8	....	....	....	52	....	....	....	....	....	....	....	....	....	....	....	....	....	....	....	....	....	....
1998-99	**Ottawa Senators**	**NHL**	**7**	**0**	**0**	**0**	**0**	**0**	**0**	**4**	**0**	**0**	**0**	**6**	**0.0**	**2**	**0**	**3**	**0**	**–1**	....	....	....	....	....	....	....	....
	Grand Rapids Griffins	IHL	46	8	17	25	....	....	....	48	....	....	....	....	....	....	....	....	....	....	....	....	....	....	....	....	....	....
	Chicago Blackhawks	**NHL**	**7**	**0**	**0**	**0**	**0**	**0**	**0**	**6**	**0**	**0**	**0**	**7**	**0.0**	**3**	**1**	**5**	**0**	**–3**	....	....	....	....	....	....	....	....
99-2000	**Chicago Blackhawks**	**NHL**	**11**	**0**	**3**	**3**	**0**	**3**	**3**	**4**	**0**	**0**	**0**	**8**	**0.0**	**15**	**1**	**10**	**3**	**7**	....	....	....	....	....	....	....	....
	Cleveland Lumberjacks	IHL	70	5	27	32	....	....	....	125	....	....	....	....	....	....	....	....	....	....	9	2	2	4	8	....	....	....
	NHL Totals		**53**	**0**	**4**	**4**	**0**	**4**	**4**	**22**	**0**	**0**	**0**	**54**	**0.0**	**34**	**3**	**35**	**6**		**7**	**0**	**0**	**0**	**8**	**0**	**0**	**0**

Traded to **Chicago** by **Ottawa** for Los Angeles' 6th round choice (previously acquired, Ottawa selected Martin Prusek) in 1999 Entry Draft, March 12, 1999. Selected by **Columbus** from **Chicago** in Expansion Draft, June 23, 2000.

• BIDNER, Todd

Richard Todd LW – L. 6'2", 205 lbs. b: Petrolia, Ont., 7/5/1961. Washington's 5th, 110th overall, in 1980.

Season	Club	League	GP	G	A	Pts	AG	AA	APts	PIM	PP	SH	GW	S	%	TGF	PGF	TGA	PGA	+/–	GP	G	A	Pts	PIM	PP	SH	GW
1977-78	Petrolia Jets	OHA-B	44	10	33	43	....	....	....	50	....	....	....	....	....	....	....	....	....	....	....	....	....	....	....	....	....	....
1978-79	Toronto Marlboros	OMJHL	64	10	12	22	....	....	....	64	....	....	....	....	....	....	....	....	....	....	3	0	0	0	0	....	....	....
1979-80	Toronto Marlboros	OMJHL	68	22	26	48	....	....	....	69	....	....	....	....	....	....	....	....	....	....	4	0	0	0	2	....	....	....
1980-81	Toronto Marlboros	OMJHL	67	34	43	77	....	....	....	124	....	....	....	....	....	....	....	....	....	....	5	2	4	6	6	....	....	....
	Hershey Bears	AHL	1	0	0	0	....	....	....	0	....	....	....	....	....	....	....	....	....	....	....	....	....	....	....	....	....	....
1981-82	**Washington Capitals**	**NHL**	**12**	**2**	**1**	**3**	**2**	**1**	**3**	**7**	**0**	**0**	**1**	**5**	**40.0**	**5**	**0**	**7**	**2**	**0**	....	....	....	....	....	....	....	....
	Hershey Bears	AHL	30	6	12	18	....	....	....	28	....	....	....	....	....	....	....	....	....	....	....	....	....	....	....	....	....	....
	Wichita Wind	CHL	15	2	9	11	....	....	....	17	....	....	....	....	....	....	....	....	....	....	7	1	2	3	9	....	....	....
1982-83	Moncton Alpines	AHL	59	15	12	27	....	....	....	64	....	....	....	....	....	....	....	....	....	....	....	....	....	....	....	....	....	....
1983-84	Moncton Alpines	AHL	60	17	16	33	....	....	....	75	....	....	....	....	....	....	....	....	....	....	....	....	....	....	....	....	....	....
1984-85	Nova Scotia Voyageurs	AHL	4	2	2	4	....	....	....	4	....	....	....	....	....	....	....	....	....	....	....	....	....	....	....	....	....	....
	Adirondack Red Wings	AHL	74	22	35	57	....	....	....	61	....	....	....	....	....	....	....	....	....	....	....	....	....	....	....	....	....	....
1985-86	Fife Flyers	Aut-Cup	8	18	10	28	....	....	....	22	....	....	....	....	....	....	....	....	....	....	....	....	....	....	....	....	....	....
	Fife Flyers	Britain	31	71	52	123	....	....	....	116	....	....	....	....	....	....	....	....	....	....	5	7	10	17	10	....	....	....
1986-87	Peterborough Pirates	Aut-Cup	8	21	18	39	....	....	....	30	....	....	....	....	....	....	....	....	....	....	....	....	....	....	....	....	....	....
	Peterborough Pirates	Britain	29	79	112	191	....	....	....	95	....	....	....	....	....	....	....	....	....	....	8	21	18	39	30	....	....	....
1987-88	Peterborough Pirates	Aut-Cup	7	13	16	29	....	....	....	28	....	....	....	....	....	....	....	....	....	....	....	....	....	....	....	....	....	....
	Peterborough Pirates	Britain	30	50	52	102	....	....	....	86	....	....	....	....	....	....	....	....	....	....	....	....	....	....	....	....	....	....
1988-89	Peterborough Pirates	Aut-Cup	10	24	29	53	....	....	....	10	....	....	....	....	....	....	....	....	....	....	....	....	....	....	....	....	....	....
	Peterborough Pirates	Britain	33	76	67	143	....	....	....	70	....	....	....	....	....	....	....	....	....	....	....	....	....	....	....	....	....	....
1989-90	Peterborough Pirates	Aut-Cup	7	11	8	19	....	....	....	8	....	....	....	....	....	....	....	....	....	....	....	....	....	....	....	....	....	....
	Peterborough Pirates	Britain	13	21	17	38	....	....	....	16	....	....	....	....	....	....	....	....	....	....	....	....	....	....	....	....	....	....
	Telford Tigers	Britain-2	13	23	42	65	....	....	....	32	....	....	....	....	....	....	....	....	....	....	....	....	....	....	....	....	....	....
1990-91	Telford Tigers	Aut-Cup	8	13	13	26	....	....	....	12	....	....	....	....	....	....	....	....	....	....	....	....	....	....	....	....	....	....
	Telford Tigers	Britain-2	16	25	24	49	....	....	....	42	....	....	....	....	....	....	....	....	....	....	....	....	....	....	....	....	....	....
	Nottingham Panthers	Britain	20	20	28	48	....	....	....	67	....	....	....	....	....	....	....	....	....	....	6	4	4	8	10	....	....	....
1991-92	Bracknell Bees	Aut-Cup	8	10	10	20	....	....	....	10	....	....	....	....	....	....	....	....	....	....	....	....	....	....	....	....	....	....
	Bracknell Bees	Britain	19	20	20	40	....	....	....	70	....	....	....	....	....	....	....	....	....	....	....	....	....	....	....	....	....	....
	Humberside Seahawks	Britain	17	21	21	42	....	....	....	50	....	....	....	....	....	....	....	....	....	....	4	4	3	7	12	....	....	....
1992-93	Humberside Seahawks	BH-Cup	6	6	7	13	....	....	....	47	....	....	....	....	....	....	....	....	....	....	....	....	....	....	....	....	....	....
	Humberside Seahawks	Britain	13	15	18	33	....	....	....	26	....	....	....	....	....	....	....	....	....	....	....	....	....	....	....	....	....	....
	Telford Tigers	Britain-2	15	22	26	48	....	....	....	92	....	....	....	....	....	....	....	....	....	....	....	....	....	....	....	....	....	....
	Sheffield Steelers	Britain	....	....	....	....	....	....	....	....	....	....	....	....	....	....	....	....	....	....	6	7	11	18	10	....	....	....
1993-94	Teeside Bombers	Britain	36	49	31	80	....	....	....	108	....	....	....	....	....	....	....	....	....	....	....	....	....	....	....	....	....	....
1994-95	Teeside Bombers	BH-Cup	8	7	7	14	....	....	....	57	....	....	....	....	....	....	....	....	....	....	....	....	....	....	....	....	....	....
	Durham Wasps	Britain	30	30	27	57	....	....	....	141	....	....	....	....	....	....	....	....	....	....	....	....	....	....	....	....	....	....
1995-96	Humberside Hawks	BH-Cup	10	8	10	18	....	....	....	56	....	....	....	....	....	....	....	....	....	....	....	....	....	....	....	....	....	....
	Humberside Hawks	Britain	4	4	4	8	....	....	....	4	....	....	....	....	....	....	....	....	....	....	....	....	....	....	....	....	....	....
	Durham Wasps	Britain	21	9	12	21	....	....	....	72	....	....	....	....	....	....	....	....	....	....	1	0	0	0	0	....	....	....
1996-97	Guildford Flames	BH-Cup	6	0	4	4	....	....	....	20	....	....	....	....	....	....	....	....	....	....	....	....	....	....	....	....	....	....
	Guildford Flames	Britain-2	5	2	3	5	....	....	....	2	....	....	....	....	....	....	....	....	....	....	....	....	....	....	....	....	....	....
	Blackburn Black Hawks	Britain-2	8	14	17	31	....	....	....	6	....	....	....	....	....	....	....	....	....	....	10	9	17	26	22	....	....	....
1997-98	Amarillo Rattlers	WPHL	6	1	2	3	....	....	....	7	....	....	....	....	....	....	....	....	....	....	....	....	....	....	....	....	....	....
	NHL Totals		**12**	**2**	**1**	**3**	**2**	**1**	**3**	**7**	**0**	**0**	**1**	**5**	**40.0**	**5**	**0**	**7**	**2**		....	....	....	....	....	....	....	....

Traded to **Edmonton** by **Washington** for Doug Hicks, March 9, 1982. Traded to **Detroit** by **Edmonton** for Rejean Cloutier, October 17, 1984.

• BIGGS, Don

Donald R. C – R. 5'8", 185 lbs. b: Mississauga, Ont., 4/7/1965. Minnesota's 9th, 162nd overall, in 1983.

Season	Club	League	GP	G	A	Pts	AG	AA	APts	PIM	PP	SH	GW	S	%	TGF	PGF	TGA	PGA	+/–	GP	G	A	Pts	PIM	PP	SH	GW
1981-82	Mississaugua Reps	MTHL	54	49	67	116	....	....	....	125	....	....	....	....	....	....	....	....	....	....	....	....	....	....	....	....	....	....
1982-83	Oshawa Generals	OHL	70	22	53	75	....	....	....	145	....	....	....	....	....	....	....	....	....	....	16	3	6	9	17	....	....	....
	Oshawa Generals	Mem-Cup	4	1	3	4	....	....	....	27	....	....	....	....	....	....	....	....	....	....	....	....	....	....	....	....	....	....
1983-84	Oshawa Generals	OHL	58	31	60	91	....	....	....	149	....	....	....	....	....	....	....	....	....	....	7	4	4	8	18	....	....	....
1984-85	Oshawa Generals	OHL	60	48	69	117	....	....	....	105	....	....	....	....	....	....	....	....	....	....	5	3	4	7	6	....	....	....
	Minnesota North Stars	**NHL**	**1**	**0**	**0**	**0**	**0**	**0**	**0**	**0**	**0**	**0**	**0**	**0**	**0.0**	**0**	**0**	**0**	**0**	**0**	....	....	....	....	....	....	....	....
	Springfield Indians	AHL	6	0	3	3	....	....	....	0	....	....	....	....	....	....	....	....	....	....	2	1	0	1	0	....	....	....
1985-86	Springfield Indians	AHL	28	15	16	31	....	....	....	46	....	....	....	....	....	....	....	....	....	....	....	....	....	....	....	....	....	....
	Nova Scotia Oilers	AHL	47	6	23	29	....	....	....	36	....	....	....	....	....	....	....	....	....	....	....	....	....	....	....	....	....	....
1986-87	Nova Scotia Oilers	AHL	80	22	25	47	....	....	....	165	....	....	....	....	....	....	....	....	....	....	5	1	2	3	4	....	....	....
1987-88	Hershey Bears	AHL	77	38	41	79	....	....	....	151	....	....	....	....	....	....	....	....	....	....	12	5	11	*16	*22	....	....	....
1988-89	Hershey Bears	AHL	76	36	67	103	....	....	....	158	....	....	....	....	....	....	....	....	....	....	11	5	9	14	30	....	....	....
1989-90	**Philadelphia Flyers**	**NHL**	**11**	**2**	**0**	**2**	**2**	**0**	**2**	**8**	**1**	**0**	**0**	**14**	**14.3**	**2**	**1**	**5**	**0**	**–4**	....	....	....	....	....	....	....	....
	Hershey Bears	AHL	66	39	53	92	....	....	....	125	....	....	....	....	....	....	....	....	....	....	....	....	....	....	....	....	....	....
1990-91	Rochester Americans	AHL	65	31	57	88	....	....	....	115	....	....	....	....	....	....	....	....	....	....	15	9	*14	*23	14	....	....	....
1991-92	Binghamton Rangers	AHL	74	32	50	82	....	....	....	122	....	....	....	....	....	....	....	....	....	....	11	3	7	10	8	....	....	....
1992-93	Binghamton Rangers	AHL	78	54	*84	*138	....	....	....	112	....	....	....	....	....	....	....	....	....	....	14	3	9	12	32	....	....	....
1993-94	Cincinnati Cyclones	IHL	80	30	59	89	....	....	....	128	....	....	....	....	....	....	....	....	....	....	11	8	9	17	29	....	....	....
1994-95	Cincinnati Cyclones	IHL	77	27	49	76	....	....	....	152	....	....	....	....	....	....	....	....	....	....	10	1	9	10	29	....	....	....
1995-96	Cincinnati Cyclones	IHL	82	27	57	84	....	....	....	160	....	....	....	....	....	....	....	....	....	....	17	9	10	19	24	....	....	....
1996-97	Cincinnati Cyclones	IHL	82	25	41	66	....	....	....	128	....	....	....	....	....	....	....	....	....	....	3	1	2	3	19	....	....	....

			REGULAR SEASON																		PLAYOFFS							
Season	Club	League	GP	G	A	Pts	AG	AA	APts	PIM	PP	SH	GW	S	%	TGF	PGF	TGA	PGA	+/–	GP	G	A	Pts	PIM	PP	SH	GW
1997-98	Cincinnati Cyclones	IHL	82	25	52	77	....	....	....	88	....	....	....	....	....	....	....	....	....	....	9	5	4	9	27	....	....	....
1998-99	Cincinnati Cyclones	IHL	23	3	17	20	....	....	....	33	....	....	....	....	....	....	....	....	....	....	....	....	....	....	....	....	....	....
	Utah Grizzlies	IHL	60	19	36	55	....	....	....	73	....	....	....	....	....	....	....	....	....	....	....	....	....	....	....	....	....	....
	NHL Totals		**12**	**2**	**0**	**2**	**2**	**0**	**2**	**8**	**1**	**0**	**0**	**14**	**14.3**	**2**	**1**	**5**	**0**		....	....	....	....	....	....	....	....

AHL First All-Star Team (1993) • Won John B. Sollenberger Trophy (Top Scorer - AHL) • (1993) Won Les Cunningham Award (MVP - AHL) (193)

Traded to **Edmonton** by **Minnesota** with Gord Sherven for Marc Habscheid, Don Barber and Emanuel Viveiros, December 20, 1985. Signed as a free agent by **Philadelphia**, July 17, 1987. Traded to **NY Rangers** by **Philadelphia** for future considerations, August 8, 1991. Signed as a free agent by **Cincinnati** (IHL), July 22, 1993. Traded to **Utah** (IHL) by **Cincinnati** (IHL) for Fred Knipscheer, December 3, 1998.

• BIGNELL, Larry

Larry Irvin D – L. 6', 175 lbs. b: Edmonton, Alta., 1/7/1950. Pittsburgh's 3rd, 35th overall, in 1970.

Season	Club	League	GP	G	A	Pts	AG	AA	APts	PIM	PP	SH	GW	S	%	TGF	PGF	TGA	PGA	+/–	GP	G	A	Pts	PIM	PP	SH	GW
1968-69	Edmonton Movers	AJHL	STATISTICS NOT AVAILABLE																									
1969-70	Edmonton Oil Kings	WCJHL	58	5	22	27	....	....	....	91	....	....	....	....	....	....	....	....	....	....	....	....	....	....	....	....	....	....
1970-71	Amarillo Wranglers	CHL	63	3	16	19	....	....	....	64	....	....	....	....	....	....	....	....	....	....	....	....	....	....	....	....	....	....
1971-72	Hershey Bears	AHL	58	4	10	14	....	....	....	59	....	....	....	....	....	....	....	....	....	....	3	0	0	0	4	....	....	....
1972-73	Hershey Bears	AHL	65	6	15	21	....	....	....	94	....	....	....	....	....	....	....	....	....	....	7	1	1	2	16	....	....	....
1973-74	**Pittsburgh Penguins**	**NHL**	**20**	**0**	**3**	**3**	**0**	**2**	**2**	**2**	**0**	**0**	**0**	**13**	**0.0**	**17**	**2**	**23**	**5**	**–3**	....	....	....	....	....	....	....	....
	Hershey Bears	AHL	17	2	2	4	....	....	....	40	....	....	....	....	....	....	....	....	....	....	....	....	....	....	....	....	....	....
	Richmond Robins	AHL	35	7	10	17	....	....	....	103	....	....	....	....	....	....	....	....	....	....	5	4	3	7	6	....	....	....
1974-75	Baltimore Clippers	AHL	44	8	18	26	....	....	....	139	....	....	....	....	....	....	....	....	....	....	....	....	....	....	....	....	....	....
	Hershey Bears	AHL	30	0	8	8	....	....	....	67	....	....	....	....	....	....	....	....	....	....	8	2	5	7	27	....	....	....
	Pittsburgh Penguins	**NHL**	....	....	....	....	....	....	....	....	....	....	....	....	....	....	....	....	....	....	**3**	**0**	**0**	**0**	**2**	**0**	**0**	**0**
1975-76	Hershey Bears	AHL	29	1	9	10	....	....	....	85	....	....	....	....	....	....	....	....	....	....	10	0	1	1	29	....	....	....
	Denver-Ottawa Civics	WHA	41	5	5	10	....	....	....	43	....	....	....	....	....	....	....	....	....	....	....	....	....	....	....	....	....	....
1976-77	Hershey Bears	AHL	72	7	19	26	....	....	....	135	....	....	....	....	....	....	....	....	....	....	6	0	1	1	11	....	....	....
	NHL Totals		**20**	**0**	**3**	**3**	**0**	**2**	**2**	**2**	**0**	**0**	**0**	**13**	**0.0**	**17**	**2**	**23**	**5**		**3**	**0**	**0**	**0**	**2**	**0**	**0**	**0**
	Other Major League Totals		41	5	5	10	....	....	....	43	....	....	....	....	....	....	....	....	....	....	....	....	....	....	....	....	....	....

Selected by **Vancouver** (WHA) in 1973 WHA Professional Player Draft, June, 1973. WHA rights traded to **Denver** (WHA) by **Calgary** (WHA) for cash, July, 1975. Signed as a free agent by **Hershey** (AHL) after **Denver-Ottawa** (WHA) franchise folded, January 17, 1976.

• BILODEAU, Gilles

"Bad News" LW – L. 6'1", 220 lbs. b: St. Prime, Que., 7/31/1955.

Season	Club	League	GP	G	A	Pts	AG	AA	APts	PIM	PP	SH	GW	S	%	TGF	PGF	TGA	PGA	+/–	GP	G	A	Pts	PIM	PP	SH	GW
1974-75	Sorel Eperviers	QMJHL	66	6	9	15	....	....	....	377	....	....	....	....	....	....	....	....	....	....	....	....	....	....	....	....	....	....
1975-76	Toronto Toros	WHA	14	0	1	1	....	....	....	38	....	....	....	....	....	....	....	....	....	....	....	....	....	....	....	....	....	....
	Beauce Jaros	NAHL	58	8	17	25	....	....	....	*451	....	....	....	....	....	....	....	....	....	....	5	0	1	1	46	....	....	....
1976-77	Birmingham Bulls	WHA	34	2	6	8	....	....	....	133	....	....	....	....	....	....	....	....	....	....	....	....	....	....	....	....	....	....
	Charlotte Checkers	SHL	28	3	6	9	....	....	....	*242	....	....	....	....	....	....	....	....	....	....	....	....	....	....	....	....	....	....
1977-78	Birmingham Bulls	WHA	59	2	2	4	....	....	....	258	....	....	....	....	....	....	....	....	....	....	3	0	0	0	27	....	....	....
	Binghamton Dusters	AHL	4	1	2	3	....	....	....	7	....	....	....	....	....	....	....	....	....	....	....	....	....	....	....	....	....	....
1978-79	Quebec Nordiques	WHA	36	3	6	9	....	....	....	141	....	....	....	....	....	....	....	....	....	....	3	0	0	0	25	....	....	....
	Binghamton Dusters	AHL	30	2	1	3	....	....	....	114	....	....	....	....	....	....	....	....	....	....	....	....	....	....	....	....	....	....
1979-80	**Quebec Nordiques**	**NHL**	**9**	**0**	**1**	**1**	**0**	**1**	**1**	**25**	**0**	**0**	**0**	**1**	**0.0**	**1**	**0**	**2**	**0**	**–1**	....	....	....	....	....	....	....	....
	Syracuse Firebirds	AHL	61	1	6	7	....	....	....	131	....	....	....	....	....	....	....	....	....	....	3	0	1	1	25	....	....	....
1980-81	Richmond Rifles	EHL	39	6	6	12	....	....	....	207	....	....	....	....	....	....	....	....	....	....	8	0	2	2	30	....	....	....
1981-82			OUT OF HOCKEY – RETIRED																									
1982-83			OUT OF HOCKEY – RETIRED																									
1983-84	Birmingham Bulls	ACHL	2	1	2	3	....	....	....	16	....	....	....	....	....	....	....	....	....	....	....	....	....	....	....	....	....	....
	NHL Totals		**9**	**0**	**1**	**1**	**0**	**1**	**1**	**25**	**0**	**0**	**0**	**1**	**0.0**	**1**	**0**	**2**	**0**		....	....	....	....	....	....	....	....
	Other Major League Totals		143	7	15	22	....	....	....	570	....	....	....	....	....	....	....	....	....	....	6	0	0	0	52	....	....	....

Selected by **Toronto** (WHA) in 1975 WHA Amateur Draft, May, 1975. Transferred to **Birmingham** (WHA) after **Toronto** (WHA) franchise relocated, June 30, 1976. Signed as a free agent by **Quebec** (WHA), September 29, 1978. Rights retained by **Quebec** prior to Expansion Draft, June 9, 1979.

• BIRON, Mathieu

D – R. 6'6", 212 lbs. b: Lac St. Charles, Que., 4/29/1980. Los Angeles' 1st, 21st overall, in 1998.

Season	Club	League	GP	G	A	Pts	AG	AA	APts	PIM	PP	SH	GW	S	%	TGF	PGF	TGA	PGA	+/–	GP	G	A	Pts	PIM	PP	SH	GW
1996-97	Ste-Foy Gouverneurs	QAAA	40	4	22	26	....	....	....	49	....	....	....	....	....	....	....	....	....	....	....	....	....	....	....	....	....	....
1997-98	Shawinigan Cataractes	QMJHL	59	8	28	36	....	....	....	60	....	....	....	....	....	....	....	....	....	....	....	....	....	....	....	....	....	....
1998-99	Shawinigan Cataractes	QMJHL	69	13	32	45	....	....	....	116	....	....	....	....	....	....	....	....	....	....	6	0	2	2	6	....	....	....
99-2000	**New York Islanders**	**NHL**	**60**	**4**	**4**	**8**	**4**	**4**	**8**	**38**	**2**	**0**	**2**	**70**	**5.7**	**39**	**7**	**46**	**1**	**–13**	....	....	....	....	....	....	....	....
	Canada	WJC-A	7	0	0	0	....	....	....	8	....	....	....	....	....	....	....	....	....	....	....	....	....	....	....	....	....	....
	NHL Totals		**60**	**4**	**4**	**8**	**4**	**4**	**8**	**38**	**2**	**0**	**2**	**70**	**5.7**	**39**	**7**	**46**	**1**		....	....	....	....	....	....	....	....

• Brother of Martin • WJC-A All-Star Team (2000)

Traded to **NY Islanders** by **LA Kings** with Olli Jokinen, Josh Green and LA Kings' 1st round choice (Taylor Pyatt) in 1999 Entry Draft for Zigmund Palffy, Brian Smolinski, Marcel Cousineau and New Jersey's 4th round choice (previously acquired, LA Kings selected Daniel Johanssen) in 1999 Entry Draft, June 20, 1999.

• BISSETT, Tom

"Mahoney" C – L. 6', 180 lbs. b: Seattle, WA, 3/13/1966. Detroit's 11th, 211th overall, in 1986.

Season	Club	League	GP	G	A	Pts	AG	AA	APts	PIM	PP	SH	GW	S	%	TGF	PGF	TGA	PGA	+/–	GP	G	A	Pts	PIM	PP	SH	GW
1984-85	Waterloo Black Hawks	USHL	48	38	*65	103	....	....	....	24	....	....	....	....	....	....	....	....	....	....	....	....	....	....	....	....	....	....
1985-86	Michigan Tech Huskies	WCHA	40	12	21	33	....	....	....	18	....	....	....	....	....	....	....	....	....	....	....	....	....	....	....	....	....	....
1986-87	Michigan Tech Huskies	WCHA	40	16	19	35	....	....	....	12	....	....	....	....	....	....	....	....	....	....	....	....	....	....	....	....	....	....
1987-88	Michigan Tech Huskies	WCHA	41	18	26	44	....	....	....	20	....	....	....	....	....	....	....	....	....	....	....	....	....	....	....	....	....	....
1988-89	Michigan Tech Huskies	WCHA	42	19	28	47	....	....	....	16	....	....	....	....	....	....	....	....	....	....	....	....	....	....	....	....	....	....
	Adirondack Red Wings	AHL	5	0	1	1	....	....	....	0	....	....	....	....	....	....	....	....	....	....	....	....	....	....	....	....	....	....
1989-90	Adirondack Red Wings	AHL	16	11	4	15	....	....	....	4	....	....	....	....	....	....	....	....	....	....	....	....	....	....	....	....	....	....
	Hampton Roads Admirals	ECHL	5	7	7	14	....	....	....	2	....	....	....	....	....	....	....	....	....	....	....	....	....	....	....	....	....	....
1990-91	**Detroit Red Wings**	**NHL**	**5**	**0**	**0**	**0**	**0**	**0**	**0**	**0**	**0**	**0**	**0**	**2**	**0.0**	**1**	**0**	**5**	**0**	**–4**	....	....	....	....	....	....	....	....
	Adirondack Red Wings	AHL	73	44	38	82	....	....	....	12	....	....	....	....	....	....	....	....	....	....	2	0	0	0	0	....	....	....
1991-92	Brynas IF Gavle	Sweden	40	25	15	40	....	....	....	32	....	....	....	....	....	....	....	....	....	....	....	....	....	....	....	....	....	....
	United States	WC-A	6	1	0	1	....	....	....	0	....	....	....	....	....	....	....	....	....	....	....	....	....	....	....	....	....	....
1992-93	Brynas IF Gavle	Sweden	40	21	11	32	....	....	....	20	....	....	....	....	....	....	....	....	....	....	10	*7	1	8	8	....	....	....
1993-94	SC Rapperswil-Jona	Switz-2	36	24	24	48	....	....	....	....	....	....	....	....	....	....	....	....	....	....	....	....	....	....	....	....	....	....
1994-95	SC Rapperswil-Jona	Switz.	33	12	15	27	....	....	....	18	....	....	....	....	....	....	....	....	....	....	6	4	3	7	2	....	....	....
1995-96	TuS Geretsried	Germany-2	31	26	37	63	....	....	....	18	....	....	....	....	....	....	....	....	....	....	....	....	....	....	....	....	....	....
	ESV Kaufbeuren	Germany	1	0	1	1	....	....	....	0	....	....	....	....	....	....	....	....	....	....	....	....	....	....	....	....	....	....
	HC Chaux-de-Fonds	Switz-2	5	1	4	5	....	....	....	6	....	....	....	....	....	....	....	....	....	....	....	....	....	....	....	....	....	....
	Houston Aeros	IHL	3	0	0	0	....	....	....	0	....	....	....	....	....	....	....	....	....	....	....	....	....	....	....	....	....	....
1996-97	HIFK Helsinki	Finland	50	14	9	23	....	....	....	26	....	....	....	....	....	....	....	....	....	....	....	....	....	....	....	....	....	....
1997-98	Star Bulls Rosenheim	Germany	34	10	14	24	....	....	....	20	....	....	....	....	....	....	....	....	....	....	....	....	....	....	....	....	....	....
	SC Rapperswil-Jona	Switz.	9	2	3	5	....	....	....	4	....	....	....	....	....	....	....	....	....	....	2	0	2	2	2	....	....	....
1998-99	Brynas IF Gavle	Sweden	50	*40	12	52	....	....	....	30	....	....	....	....	....	....	....	....	....	....	14	6	2	8	4	....	....	....
	United States	WC-A	6	3	0	3	....	....	....	0	....	....	....	....	....	....	....	....	....	....	....	....	....	....	....	....	....	....
99-2000	Brynas IF Gavle	Sweden	50	15	37	52	....	....	....	55	....	....	....	....	....	....	....	....	....	....	11	3	2	5	0	....	....	....
	Brynas IF Gavle	EuroHL	6	0	2	2	....	....	....	2	....	....	....	....	....	....	....	....	....	....	....	....	....	....	....	....	....	....
	NHL Totals		**5**	**0**	**0**	**0**	**0**	**0**	**0**	**0**	**0**	**0**	**0**	**2**	**0.0**	**1**	**0**	**5**	**0**		....	....	....	....	....	....	....	....

• BJUGSTAD, Scott

Barry Scott RW – L. 6'1", 185 lbs. b: St. Paul, MN, 6/2/1961. Minnesota's 13th, 181st overall, in 1981.

Season	Club	League	GP	G	A	Pts	AG	AA	APts	PIM	PP	SH	GW	S	%	TGF	PGF	TGA	PGA	+/–	GP	G	A	Pts	PIM	PP	SH	GW
1978-79	Irondale Knights	Hi-School	STATISTICS NOT AVAILABLE																									
1979-80	University of Minnesota	WCHA	18	2	2	4	....	....	....	2	....	....	....	....	....	....	....	....	....	....	....	....	....	....	....	....	....	....
1980-81	University of Minnesota	WCHA	35	12	13	25	....	....	....	34	....	....	....	....	....	....	....	....	....	....	....	....	....	....	....	....	....	....
1981-82	University of Minnesota	WCHA	36	29	14	43	....	....	....	24	....	....	....	....	....	....	....	....	....	....	....	....	....	....	....	....	....	....
1982-83	University of Minnesota	WCHA	26	21	35	56	....	....	....	12	....	....	....	....	....	....	....	....	....	....	....	....	....	....	....	....	....	....

			REGULAR SEASON																		PLAYOFFS							
Season	Club	League	GP	G	A	Pts	AG	AA	APts	PIM	PP	SH	GW	S	%	TGF	PGF	TGA	PGA	+/–	GP	G	A	Pts	PIM	PP	SH	GW
1983-84	United States	Nat-Team	54	31	20	51	....	....	....	28	....	....	....	....	....	....	....	....	....	....	....	....	....	....	....	....	....	....
	United States	Olympics	6	3	1	4	....	....	....	6	....	....	....	....	....	....	....	....	....	....	....	....	....	....	....	....	....	....
	Minnesota North Stars	**NHL**	**5**	**0**	**0**	**0**	**0**	**0**	**0**	**2**	**0**	**0**	**0**	**5**	**0.0**	**0**	**0**	**1**	**0**	**–1**	....	....	....	....	....	....	....	....
	Salt Lake Golden Eagles	CHL	15	10	8	18	....	....	....	6	....	....	....	....	....	....	....	....	....	....	5	3	4	7	0	....	....	....
1984-85	**Minnesota North Stars**	**NHL**	**72**	**11**	**4**	**15**	**9**	**3**	**12**	**32**	**1**	**0**	**1**	**108**	**10.2**	**22**	**3**	**72**	**32**	**–21**	....	....	....	....	....	....	....	....
	Springfield Indians	AHL	5	2	3	5	....	....	....	2	....	....	....	....	....	....	....	....	....	....	....	....	....	....	....	....	....	....
1985-86	**Minnesota North Stars**	**NHL**	**80**	**43**	**33**	**76**	**34**	**22**	**56**	**24**	**14**	**2**	**6**	**217**	**19.8**	**109**	**40**	**89**	**25**	**5**	**5**	**0**	**1**	**1**	**0**	**0**	**0**	**0**
1986-87	**Minnesota North Stars**	**NHL**	**39**	**4**	**9**	**13**	**3**	**7**	**10**	**43**	**0**	**0**	**0**	**58**	**6.9**	**20**	**7**	**27**	**8**	**–6**	....	....	....	....	....	....	....	....
	Springfield Indians	AHL	11	6	4	10	....	....	....	7	....	....	....	....	....	....	....	....	....	....	....	....	....	....	....	....	....	....
1987-88	**Minnesota North Stars**	**NHL**	**33**	**10**	**12**	**22**	**9**	**9**	**18**	**15**	**3**	**0**	**3**	**72**	**13.9**	**36**	**11**	**23**	**0**	**2**	....	....	....	....	....	....	....	....
1988-89	Kalamazoo Wings	IHL	4	5	0	5	....	....	....	4	....	....	....	....	....	....	....	....	....	....	....	....	....	....	....	....	....	....
	Pittsburgh Penguins	**NHL**	**24**	**3**	**0**	**3**	**3**	**0**	**3**	**4**	**0**	**0**	**1**	**21**	**14.3**	**4**	**0**	**16**	**0**	**–12**	....	....	....	....	....	....	....	....
1989-90	**Los Angeles Kings**	**NHL**	**11**	**1**	**2**	**3**	**1**	**1**	**2**	**2**	**0**	**0**	**1**	**10**	**10.0**	**6**	**0**	**4**	**0**	**2**	**2**	**0**	**0**	**0**	**2**	**0**	**0**	**0**
	New Haven Nighthawks	AHL	47	45	21	66	....	....	....	40	....	....	....	....	....	....	....	....	....	....	....	....	....	....	....	....	....	....
1990-91	**Los Angeles Kings**	**NHL**	**31**	**2**	**4**	**6**	**2**	**3**	**5**	**12**	**0**	**0**	**1**	**39**	**5.1**	**12**	**1**	**21**	**5**	**–5**	**2**	**0**	**0**	**0**	**0**	**0**	**0**	**0**
	Phoenix Roadrunners	IHL	3	7	2	9	....	....	....	2	....	....	....	....	....	....	....	....	....	....	....	....	....	....	....	....	....	....
1991-92	**Los Angeles Kings**	**NHL**	**22**	**2**	**4**	**6**	**2**	**3**	**5**	**10**	**0**	**0**	**0**	**25**	**8.0**	**9**	**0**	**11**	**1**	**–1**	....	....	....	....	....	....	....	....
	Phoenix Roadrunners	IHL	28	14	14	28	....	....	....	12	....	....	....	....	....	....	....	....	....	....	....	....	....	....	....	....	....	....
1992-93	Phoenix Roadrunners	IHL	7	5	4	9	....	....	....	4	....	....	....	....	....	....	....	....	....	....	....	....	....	....	....	....	....	....
	NHL Totals		**317**	**76**	**68**	**144**	**63**	**48**	**111**	**144**	**18**	**2**	**13**	**555**	**13.7**	**218**	**62**	**264**	**71**		**9**	**0**	**1**	**1**	**2**	**0**	**0**	**0**

WCHA First All-Star Team (1983)

Traded to **Pittsburgh** by **Minnesota** with Gord Dineen for Ville Siren and Steve Gotaas, December 17, 1988. Signed as a free agent by **LA Kings**, August 24, 1989.

• BLACK, James

LW – L. 6', 202 lbs. b: Regina, Sask., 8/15/1969. Hartford's 4th, 94th overall, in 1989.

Season	Club	League	GP	G	A	Pts	AG	AA	APts	PIM	PP	SH	GW	S	%	TGF	PGF	TGA	PGA	+/–	GP	G	A	Pts	PIM	PP	SH	GW
1986-87	Edmonton Mets	AJHL	41	36	48	84	....	....	....	58	....	....	....	....	....	....	....	....	....	....	....	....	....	....	....	....	....	....
1987-88	Portland Winter Hawks	WHL	72	30	50	80	....	....	....	50	....	....	....	....	....	....	....	....	....	....	....	....	....	....	....	....	....	....
1988-89	Portland Winter Hawks	WHL	71	45	51	96	....	....	....	57	....	....	....	....	....	....	....	....	....	....	19	13	6	19	28	....	....	....
1989-90	**Hartford Whalers**	**NHL**	**1**	**0**	**0**	**0**	**0**	**0**	**0**	**0**	**0**	**0**	**0**	**0**	**0.0**	**0**	**0**	**0**	**0**	**0**	....	....	....	....	....	....	....	....
	Binghamton Whalers	AHL	80	37	35	72	....	....	....	34	....	....	....	....	....	....	....	....	....	....	....	....	....	....	....	....	....	....
1990-91	**Hartford Whalers**	**NHL**	**1**	**0**	**0**	**0**	**0**	**0**	**0**	**0**	**0**	**0**	**0**	**0**	**0.0**	**0**	**0**	**0**	**0**	**0**	....	....	....	....	....	....	....	....
	Springfield Indians	AHL	79	35	61	96	....	....	....	34	....	....	....	....	....	....	....	....	....	....	18	9	9	18	6	....	....	....
1991-92	**Hartford Whalers**	**NHL**	**30**	**4**	**6**	**10**	**4**	**5**	**9**	**10**	**1**	**0**	**1**	**54**	**7.4**	**16**	**6**	**27**	**13**	**–4**	....	....	....	....	....	....	....	....
	Springfield Indians	AHL	47	15	25	40	....	....	....	33	....	....	....	....	....	....	....	....	....	....	10	3	2	5	18	....	....	....
1992-93	**Minnesota North Stars**	**NHL**	**10**	**2**	**1**	**3**	**2**	**1**	**3**	**4**	**0**	**0**	**0**	**10**	**20.0**	**4**	**0**	**4**	**0**	**0**	....	....	....	....	....	....	....	....
	Kalamazoo Wings	IHL	63	25	45	70	....	....	....	40	....	....	....	....	....	....	....	....	....	....	....	....	....	....	....	....	....	....
1993-94	**Dallas Stars**	**NHL**	**13**	**2**	**3**	**5**	**2**	**2**	**4**	**2**	**2**	**0**	**0**	**16**	**12.5**	**6**	**2**	**8**	**0**	**–4**	....	....	....	....	....	....	....	....
	Buffalo Sabres	**NHL**	**2**	**0**	**0**	**0**	**0**	**0**	**0**	**0**	**2**	**0**	**0**	**2**	**0.0**	**0**	**0**	**0**	**0**	**0**	....	....	....	....	....	....	....	....
	Rochester Americans	AHL	45	19	32	51	....	....	....	28	....	....	....	....	....	....	....	....	....	....	4	2	3	5	0	....	....	....
1994-95	Las Vegas Thunder	IHL	78	29	44	73	....	....	....	54	....	....	....	....	....	....	....	....	....	....	10	1	6	7	4	....	....	....
1995-96	**Chicago Blackhawks**	**NHL**	**13**	**3**	**3**	**6**	**3**	**2**	**5**	**16**	**0**	**0**	**1**	**23**	**13.0**	**7**	**0**	**6**	**0**	**1**	**8**	**1**	**0**	**1**	**2**	**0**	**0**	**0**
	Indianapolis Ice	IHL	67	32	50	82	....	....	....	56	....	....	....	....	....	....	....	....	....	....	....	....	....	....	....	....	....	....
1996-97	**Chicago Blackhawks**	**NHL**	**64**	**12**	**11**	**23**	**13**	**10**	**23**	**20**	**0**	**0**	**3**	**122**	**9.8**	**32**	**1**	**33**	**8**	**6**	**5**	**1**	**1**	**2**	**2**	**0**	**0**	**0**
1997-98	**Chicago Blackhawks**	**NHL**	**52**	**10**	**5**	**15**	**12**	**5**	**17**	**8**	**2**	**1**	**3**	**90**	**11.1**	**18**	**4**	**31**	**9**	**–8**	....	....	....	....	....	....	....	....
1998-99	Chicago Wolves	IHL	5	6	0	6	....	....	....	0	....	....	....	....	....	....	....	....	....	....	....	....	....	....	....	....	....	....
	Washington Capitals	**NHL**	**75**	**16**	**14**	**30**	**19**	**13**	**32**	**14**	**1**	**1**	**3**	**135**	**11.9**	**47**	**7**	**45**	**10**	**5**	....	....	....	....	....	....	....	....
99-2000	**Washington Capitals**	**NHL**	**49**	**8**	**9**	**17**	**9**	**8**	**17**	**6**	**1**	**0**	**1**	**71**	**11.3**	**21**	**3**	**21**	**2**	**–1**	....	....	....	....	....	....	....	....
	NHL Totals		**310**	**57**	**52**	**109**	**64**	**46**	**110**	**80**	**9**	**2**	**12**	**523**	**10.9**	**151**	**23**	**175**	**42**		**13**	**2**	**1**	**3**	**4**	**0**	**0**	**0**

Traded to **Minnesota** by **Hartford** for Mark Janssens, September 3, 1992. Transferred to **Dallas** after **Minnesota** franchise relocated, June 9, 1993. Traded to **Buffalo** by **Dallas** with Dallas' 7th round choice (Steve Webb) in 1994 Entry Draft for Gord Donnelly, December 15, 1993. Signed as a free agent by **Chicago**, September 18, 1995. Traded to **Washington** by **Chicago** for future considerations, October 15, 1998.

• BLACKBURN, Bob

Robert John D – L. 5'11", 198 lbs. b: Rouyn, Que., 2/1/1938.

Season	Club	League	GP	G	A	Pts	AG	AA	APts	PIM	PP	SH	GW	S	%	TGF	PGF	TGA	PGA	+/–	GP	G	A	Pts	PIM	PP	SH	GW
1956-57	Barrie Flyers	OHA-Jr.	21	0	0	0	....	....	....	7	....	....	....	....	....	....	....	....	....	....	1	0	0	0	0	....	....	....
1957-58	Barrie Flyers	OHA-Jr.	51	13	26	39	....	....	....	171	....	....	....	....	....	....	....	....	....	....	4	3	0	3	23	....	....	....
1958-59	Quebec Aces	QHL	29	1	1	2	....	....	....	36	....	....	....	....	....	....	....	....	....	....	....	....	....	....	....	....	....	....
	Washington Presidents	EHL	21	1	10	11	....	....	....	44	....	....	....	....	....	....	....	....	....	....	....	....	....	....	....	....	....	....
1959-60	Kingston Frontenacs	EPHL	27	0	7	7	....	....	....	41	....	....	....	....	....	....	....	....	....	....	....	....	....	....	....	....	....	....
	Providence Reds	AHL	37	0	2	2	....	....	....	8	....	....	....	....	....	....	....	....	....	....	....	....	....	....	....	....	....	....
1960-61	Providence Reds	AHL	50	1	5	6	....	....	....	53	....	....	....	....	....	....	....	....	....	....	....	....	....	....	....	....	....	....
1961-62	Providence Reds	AHL	64	1	11	12	....	....	....	157	....	....	....	....	....	....	....	....	....	....	3	0	1	1	2	....	....	....
1962-63	Providence Reds	AHL	47	2	7	9	....	....	....	56	....	....	....	....	....	....	....	....	....	....	6	0	0	0	4	....	....	....
1963-64	Providence Reds	AHL	70	2	20	22	....	....	....	175	....	....	....	....	....	....	....	....	....	....	3	0	2	2	4	....	....	....
1964-65	Providence Reds	AHL	67	1	17	18	....	....	....	162	....	....	....	....	....	....	....	....	....	....	....	....	....	....	....	....	....	....
1965-66	Providence Reds	AHL	27	0	4	4	....	....	....	52	....	....	....	....	....	....	....	....	....	....	....	....	....	....	....	....	....	....
	Vancouver Canucks	WHL	28	1	5	6	....	....	....	44	....	....	....	....	....	....	....	....	....	....	7	0	0	0	12	....	....	....
1966-67	Vancouver Canucks	WHL	69	2	11	13	....	....	....	120	....	....	....	....	....	....	....	....	....	....	8	0	4	4	16	....	....	....
1967-68	Buffalo Bisons	AHL	69	2	15	17	....	....	....	116	....	....	....	....	....	....	....	....	....	....	5	1	1	2	14	....	....	....
1968-69	**New York Rangers**	**NHL**	**11**	**0**	**0**	**0**	**0**	**0**	**0**	**0**	**0**	**0**	**0**	**6**	**0.0**	**5**	**0**	**2**	**1**	**4**	....	....	....	....	....	....	....	....
	Buffalo Bisons	AHL	58	3	15	18	....	....	....	73	....	....	....	....	....	....	....	....	....	....	6	0	1	1	14	....	....	....
1969-70	Baltimore Clippers	AHL	6	0	0	0	....	....	....	0	....	....	....	....	....	....	....	....	....	....	....	....	....	....	....	....	....	....
	Pittsburgh Penguins	**NHL**	**60**	**4**	**7**	**11**	**4**	**7**	**11**	**51**	**0**	**0**	**1**	**49**	**8.2**	**38**	**2**	**69**	**19**	**–14**	**6**	**0**	**0**	**0**	**4**	**0**	**0**	**0**
1970-71	**Pittsburgh Penguins**	**NHL**	**64**	**4**	**5**	**9**	**4**	**4**	**8**	**54**	**0**	**0**	**1**	**87**	**4.6**	**56**	**0**	**68**	**12**	**0**	....	....	....	....	....	....	....	....
1971-72	Rochester Americans	AHL	64	7	11	18	....	....	....	72	....	....	....	....	....	....	....	....	....	....	....	....	....	....	....	....	....	....
	NHL Totals		**135**	**8**	**12**	**20**	**8**	**11**	**19**	**105**	**0**	**0**	**2**	**142**	**5.6**	**99**	**2**	**139**	**32**		**6**	**0**	**0**	**0**	**4**	**0**	**0**	**0**

AHL First All-Star Team (1969) • Won Eddie Shore Award (Outstanding Defenseman - AHL) (1969)

Traded to **Vancouver** (WHL) by **Providence** (AHL) for Wayne Muloin and Ron Hutchinson, February 3, 1966. • Hutchinson failed to report to Providence (AHL). Claimed by **Buffalo** (AHL) from **NY Rangers** in Reverse Draft, June 6, 1967. Traded to **NY Rangers** by **Buffalo** (AHL) for cash, August, 1968. Claimed by **Pittsburgh** from **NY Rangers** in Intra-League Draft, June 11, 1969. Traded to **Vancouver** by **Pittsburgh** for cash, October 3, 1971.

• BLACKBURN, Don

John Donald LW – L. 6', 190 lbs. b: Kirkland Lake, Ont., 5/14/1938.

Season	Club	League	GP	G	A	Pts	AG	AA	APts	PIM	PP	SH	GW	S	%	TGF	PGF	TGA	PGA	+/–	GP	G	A	Pts	PIM	PP	SH	GW
1956-57	Hamilton Tiger Cubs	OHA-Jr.	52	9	8	17	....	....	....	17	....	....	....	....	....	....	....	....	....	....	4	0	2	2	0	....	....	....
1957-58	Hamilton Tiger Cubs	OHA-Jr.	52	15	18	33	....	....	....	37	....	....	....	....	....	....	....	....	....	....	15	4	3	7	16	....	....	....
1958-59	Victoria Cougars	WHL	50	15	16	31	....	....	....	14	....	....	....	....	....	....	....	....	....	....	....	....	....	....	....	....	....	....
1959-60	Victoria Cougars	WHL	41	8	7	15	....	....	....	8	....	....	....	....	....	....	....	....	....	....	11	1	1	2	2	....	....	....
	Providence Reds	AHL	16	1	1	2	....	....	....	8	....	....	....	....	....	....	....	....	....	....	....	....	....	....	....	....	....	....
1960-61	Kingston Frontenacs	EPHL	59	14	31	45	....	....	....	27	....	....	....	....	....	....	....	....	....	....	5	1	0	1	0	....	....	....
1961-62	Kingston Frontenacs	EPHL	51	13	24	37	....	....	....	30	....	....	....	....	....	....	....	....	....	....	11	2	*12	14	5	....	....	....
1962-63	**Boston Bruins**	**NHL**	**6**	**0**	**5**	**5**	**0**	**5**	**5**	**4**	....	....	....	....	....	....	....	....	....	....	....	....	....	....	....	....	....	....
	Kingston Frontenacs	EPHL	67	42	54	96	....	....	....	22	....	....	....	....	....	....	....	....	....	....	5	4	4	8	0	....	....	....
1963-64	Quebec Aces	AHL	63	19	19	38	....	....	....	39	....	....	....	....	....	....	....	....	....	....	9	1	1	2	9	....	....	....
1964-65	Quebec Aces	AHL	70	19	42	61	....	....	....	34	....	....	....	....	....	....	....	....	....	....	5	0	2	2	0	....	....	....
1965-66	Quebec Aces	AHL	72	36	42	78	....	....	....	51	....	....	....	....	....	....	....	....	....	....	6	1	4	5	4	....	....	....
1966-67	Rochester Americans	AHL	70	20	37	57	....	....	....	24	....	....	....	....	....	....	....	....	....	....	13	3	3	6	10	....	....	....
1967-68	**Philadelphia Flyers**	**NHL**	**67**	**9**	**20**	**29**	**10**	**20**	**30**	**23**	**1**	**0**	**2**	**157**	**5.7**	**43**	**8**	**37**	**0**	**–2**	**7**	**3**	**0**	**3**	**8**	**1**	**0**	**1**
1968-69	**Philadelphia Flyers**	**NHL**	**48**	**7**	**9**	**16**	**7**	**8**	**15**	**36**	**0**	**0**	**2**	**94**	**7.4**	**20**	**0**	**33**	**0**	**–13**	**4**	**0**	**0**	**0**	**2**	**0**	**0**	**0**
	Baltimore Clippers	AHL	12	6	13	19	....	....	....	10	....	....	....	....	....	....	....	....	....	....	....	....	....	....	....	....	....	....
1969-70	**New York Rangers**	**NHL**	**3**	**0**	**0**	**0**	**0**	**0**	**0**	**0**	**0**	**0**	**0**	**1**	**0.0**	**0**	**0**	**0**	**0**	**0**	**1**	**0**	**0**	**0**	**0**	**0**	**0**	**0**
	Buffalo Bisons	AHL	68	27	44	71	....	....	....	40	....	....	....	....	....	....	....	....	....	....	13	5	7	12	6	....	....	....

Season	Club	League	GP	G	A	Pts	AG	AA	APts	PIM	PP	SH	GW	S	%	TGF	PGF	TGA	PGA	+/–	GP	G	A	Pts	PIM	PP	SH	GW
			REGULAR SEASON																		PLAYOFFS							
1970-71	Rochester Americans	AHL	62	25	44	69	....	....	....	22	....	....	....	....	....	....	....	....	....	....	....	....	....	....	....	....	....	....
	New York Rangers	**NHL**	**1**	**0**	**0**	**0**	**0**	**0**	**0**	**0**	**0**	**0**	**0**	**0**	**0.0**	**0**	**0**	**0**	**0**	**0**	....	....	....	....	....	....	....	....
1971-72	Providence Reds	AHL	76	34	65	*99	....	....	....	12	....	....	....	....	....	....	....	....	....	....	5	1	3	4	2	....	....	....
1972-73	**New York Islanders**	**NHL**	**56**	**7**	**10**	**17**	**7**	**8**	**15**	**20**	**1**	**0**	**1**	**65**	**10.8**	**29**	**4**	**58**	**0**	**–33**	....	....	....	....	....	....	....	....
	Minnesota North Stars	**NHL**	**4**	**0**	**0**	**0**	**0**	**0**	**0**	**4**	**0**	**0**	**0**	**0**	**0.0**	**0**	**0**	**0**	**0**	**0**	....	....	....	....	....	....	....	....
1973-74	New England Whalers	WHA	75	20	39	59	....	....	....	18	....	....	....	....	....	....	....	....	....	....	7	2	4	6	4	....	....	....
1974-75	New England Whalers	WHA	50	18	32	50	....	....	....	16	....	....	....	....	....	....	....	....	....	....	5	1	2	3	2	....	....	....
	Cape Cod Codders	NAHL	2	2	2	4	....	....	....	0	....	....	....	....	....	....	....	....	....	....	....	....	....	....	....	....	....	....
1975-76	New England Whalers	WHA	21	2	3	5	....	....	....	6	....	....	....	....	....	....	....	....	....	....	....	....	....	....	....	....	....	....
	Cape Cod Codders	NAHL	8	4	4	8	....	....	....	0	....	....	....	....	....	....	....	....	....	....	....	....	....	....	....	....	....	....
	NHL Totals		**185**	**23**	**44**	**67**	**24**	**41**	**65**	**87**	....	....	....	....	....	....	....	....	....	....	**12**	**3**	**0**	**3**	**10**	....	....	....
	Other Major League Totals		146	40	74	114				40	....	....	....	....	....	....	....	....	....	....	12	3	6	9	6	....	....	....

EPHL First All-Star Team (1963) • AHL Second All-Star Team (1970, 1972) • AHL First All-Star Team (1971) • Won John B. Sollenberger Trophy (Top Scorer - AHL) (1972)

Claimed by **Montreal** from **Boston** (Kingston-EPHL) in Inter-League Draft, June 4, 1963. Claimed by **Toronto** from **Montreal** in Intra-League Draft, June 15, 1966. Claimed by **Philadelphia** from **Toronto** in Expansion Draft, June 6, 1967. Traded to **NY Rangers** by **Philadelphia** with Leon Rochefort for Reggie Fleming, June 6, 1969. Loaned to **Rochester** (AHL) by **NY Rangers**, September 30, 1970. Selected by **NY Raiders** (WHA) in 1972 WHA General Player Draft, February 12, 1972. Claimed by **NY Islanders** from **NY Rangers** in Intra-League Draft, June 6, 1972. Traded to **Minnesota** by **NY Islanders** for cash, March 1, 1973. WHA rights traded to **New England** (WHA) by **NY Raiders** (WHA) for future considerations, September, 1973.

• BLADON, Tom

Thomas George "Bomber" D – R. 6'1", 195 lbs. b: Edmonton, Alta., 12/29/1952. Philadelphia's 2nd, 23rd overall, in 1972.

Season	Club	League	GP	G	A	Pts	AG	AA	APts	PIM	PP	SH	GW	S	%	TGF	PGF	TGA	PGA	+/–	GP	G	A	Pts	PIM	PP	SH	GW
1969-70	Edmonton Maple Leafs	AJHL	46	12	17	29	....	....	....	115	....	....	....	....	....	....	....	....	....	....	....	....	....	....	....	....	....	....
1970-71	Edmonton Oil Kings	WCJHL	66	13	25	38	....	....	....	124	....	....	....	....	....	....	....	....	....	....	14	5	6	11	46	....	....	....
1971-72	Edmonton Oil Kings	WCJHL	65	11	44	55	....	....	....	90	....	....	....	....	....	....	....	....	....	....	16	6	7	13	10	....	....	....
	Edmonton Oil Kings	Mem-Cup	2	0	1	1	....	....	....	4	....	....	....	....	....	....	....	....	....	....	....	....	....	....	....	....	....	....
1972-73	**Philadelphia Flyers**	**NHL**	**78**	**11**	**31**	**42**	**10**	**25**	**35**	**26**	**7**	**0**	**0**	**151**	**7.3**	**116**	**48**	**64**	**5**	**9**	**11**	**0**	**4**	**4**	**2**	**0**	**0**	**0**
1973-74♦	**Philadelphia Flyers**	**NHL**	**70**	**12**	**22**	**34**	**12**	**18**	**30**	**37**	**6**	**0**	**2**	**159**	**7.5**	**97**	**35**	**45**	**7**	**24**	**16**	**4**	**6**	**10**	**25**	**3**	**0**	**1**
1974-75♦	**Philadelphia Flyers**	**NHL**	**76**	**9**	**20**	**29**	**8**	**15**	**23**	**54**	**5**	**0**	**3**	**174**	**5.2**	**108**	**35**	**42**	**11**	**42**	**13**	**1**	**3**	**4**	**12**	**1**	**0**	**0**
1975-76	**Philadelphia Flyers**	**NHL**	**80**	**14**	**23**	**37**	**12**	**17**	**29**	**68**	**5**	**0**	**0**	**182**	**7.7**	**124**	**30**	**70**	**21**	**45**	**16**	**2**	**6**	**8**	**14**	**1**	**0**	**0**
1976-77	**Philadelphia Flyers**	**NHL**	**80**	**10**	**43**	**53**	**9**	**33**	**42**	**39**	**2**	**0**	**2**	**158**	**6.3**	**118**	**22**	**95**	**33**	**34**	**10**	**1**	**3**	**4**	**4**	**0**	**0**	**0**
1977-78	**Philadelphia Flyers**	**NHL**	**79**	**11**	**24**	**35**	**10**	**19**	**29**	**57**	**1**	**1**	**1**	**153**	**7.2**	**92**	**13**	**73**	**26**	**32**	**12**	**0**	**2**	**2**	**11**	**0**	**0**	**0**
1978-79	**Pittsburgh Penguins**	**NHL**	**78**	**4**	**23**	**27**	**3**	**17**	**20**	**64**	**1**	**0**	**0**	**135**	**3.0**	**105**	**23**	**124**	**25**	**–17**	**7**	**0**	**4**	**4**	**2**	**0**	**0**	**0**
1979-80	**Pittsburgh Penguins**	**NHL**	**57**	**2**	**6**	**8**	**2**	**4**	**6**	**35**	**1**	**0**	**1**	**69**	**2.9**	**48**	**11**	**79**	**17**	**–25**	**1**	**0**	**1**	**1**	**0**	**0**	**0**	**0**
1980-81	**Edmonton Oilers**	**NHL**	**1**	**0**	**0**	**0**	**0**	**0**	**0**	**0**	**0**	**0**	**0**	**0**	**0.0**	**0**	**0**	**1**	**0**	**–1**	....	....	....	....	....	....	....	....
	Winnipeg Jets	**NHL**	**9**	**0**	**5**	**5**	**0**	**3**	**3**	**10**	**0**	**0**	**0**	**13**	**0.0**	**12**	**5**	**19**	**2**	**–10**	....	....	....	....	....	....	....	....
	Detroit Red Wings	**NHL**	**2**	**0**	**0**	**0**	**0**	**0**	**0**	**2**	**0**	**0**	**0**	**1**	**0.0**	**2**	**0**	**2**	**0**	**0**	....	....	....	....	....	....	....	....
	Adirondack Red Wings	AHL	41	3	15	18	....	....	....	28	....	....	....	....	....	....	....	....	....	....	18	3	3	6	16	....	....	....
	NHL Totals		**610**	**73**	**197**	**270**	**66**	**151**	**217**	**392**	**28**	**1**	**9**	**1195**	**6.1**	**822**	**222**	**614**	**147**		**86**	**8**	**29**	**37**	**70**	**5**	**0**	**1**

WCJHL Second All-Star Team (1972) • Played in NHL All-Star Game (1977, 1978)

Traded to **Pittsburgh** by **Philadelphia** with Ross Lonsberry and Orest Kindrachuk for Pittsburgh's 1st round choice (Behn Wilson) in 1978 Amateur Draft, June 14, 1978. Signed as a free agent by **Edmonton**, July 10, 1980. Signed as a free agent by **Winnipeg**, December 13, 1980. Signed as a free agent by **Detroit**, January 14, 1981.

• BLAISDELL, Mike

Michael Walter "Wally" RW – R. 6'1", 196 lbs. b: Moose Jaw, Sask., 1/18/1960. Detroit's 1st, 11th overall, in 1980.

Season	Club	League	GP	G	A	Pts	AG	AA	APts	PIM	PP	SH	GW	S	%	TGF	PGF	TGA	PGA	+/–	GP	G	A	Pts	PIM	PP	SH	GW
1977-78	Regina Blues	SJHL	60	70	46	116	....	....	....	43	....	....	....	....	....	....	....	....	....	....	....	....	....	....	....	....	....	....
	Regina Pats	WCJHL	6	5	5	10	....	....	....	2	....	....	....	....	....	....	....	....	....	....	13	4	7	11	0	....	....	....
1978-79	University of Wisconsin	WCHA	20	7	1	8	....	....	....	4	....	....	....	....	....	....	....	....	....	....	....	....	....	....	....	....	....	....
1979-80	Regina Pats	WHL	63	71	38	109	....	....	....	62	....	....	....	....	....	....	....	....	....	....	18	*16	9	25	26	....	....	....
	Regina Pats	Mem-Cup	4	4	5	*9	....	....	....	0	....	....	....	....	....	....	....	....	....	....	....	....	....	....	....	....	....	....
1980-81	**Detroit Red Wings**	**NHL**	**32**	**3**	**6**	**9**	**2**	**4**	**6**	**10**	**0**	**0**	**0**	**45**	**6.7**	**18**	**3**	**22**	**0**	**–7**	....	....	....	....	....	....	....	....
	Adirondack Red Wings	AHL	41	10	4	14	....	....	....	8	....	....	....	....	....	....	....	....	....	....	12	2	2	4	5	....	....	....
1981-82	**Detroit Red Wings**	**NHL**	**80**	**23**	**32**	**55**	**18**	**21**	**39**	**48**	**5**	**0**	**3**	**165**	**13.9**	**75**	**9**	**83**	**2**	**–15**	....	....	....	....	....	....	....	....
1982-83	**Detroit Red Wings**	**NHL**	**80**	**18**	**23**	**41**	**15**	**16**	**31**	**22**	**0**	**0**	**2**	**171**	**10.5**	**72**	**7**	**72**	**1**	**–6**	....	....	....	....	....	....	....	....
1983-84	**New York Rangers**	**NHL**	**36**	**5**	**6**	**11**	**4**	**4**	**8**	**31**	**0**	**0**	**1**	**63**	**7.9**	**22**	**1**	**21**	**0**	**0**	....	....	....	....	....	....	....	....
	Tulsa Oilers	CHL	32	10	8	18	....	....	....	23	....	....	....	....	....	....	....	....	....	....	9	6	6	12	6	....	....	....
1984-85	**New York Rangers**	**NHL**	**12**	**1**	**0**	**1**	**1**	**0**	**1**	**11**	**0**	**0**	**0**	**20**	**5.0**	**3**	**1**	**6**	**0**	**–4**	....	....	....	....	....	....	....	....
	New Haven Nighthawks	AHL	64	21	23	44	....	....	....	41	....	....	....	....	....	....	....	....	....	....	....	....	....	....	....	....	....	....
1985-86	**Pittsburgh Penguins**	**NHL**	**66**	**15**	**14**	**29**	**12**	**9**	**21**	**36**	**0**	**0**	**0**	**125**	**12.0**	**51**	**3**	**33**	**0**	**15**	....	....	....	....	....	....	....	....
1986-87	**Pittsburgh Penguins**	**NHL**	**10**	**1**	**1**	**2**	**1**	**1**	**2**	**2**	**0**	**0**	**0**	**12**	**8.3**	**4**	**0**	**2**	**0**	**2**	....	....	....	....	....	....	....	....
	Baltimore Skipjacks	AHL	43	12	12	24	....	....	....	47	....	....	....	....	....	....	....	....	....	....	....	....	....	....	....	....	....	....
1987-88	**Toronto Maple Leafs**	**NHL**	**18**	**3**	**2**	**5**	**3**	**1**	**4**	**2**	**0**	**0**	**1**	**32**	**9.4**	**8**	**0**	**13**	**0**	**–5**	**6**	**1**	**2**	**3**	**10**	**0**	**0**	**0**
	Newmarket Saints	AHL	57	25	28	53	....	....	....	30	....	....	....	....	....	....	....	....	....	....	....	....	....	....	....	....	....	....
1988-89	**Toronto Maple Leafs**	**NHL**	**9**	**1**	**0**	**1**	**1**	**0**	**1**	**4**	**0**	**0**	**0**	**8**	**12.5**	**2**	**1**	**6**	**0**	**–5**	....	....	....	....	....	....	....	....
	Newmarket Saints	AHL	40	16	7	23	....	....	....	48	....	....	....	....	....	....	....	....	....	....	....	....	....	....	....	....	....	....
1989-90	Canada	Nat-Team	50	12	18	30	....	....	....	40	....	....	....	....	....	....	....	....	....	....	....	....	....	....	....	....	....	....
	Schwenniger ERC	Germany	3	1	0	1	....	....	....	0	....	....	....	....	....	....	....	....	....	....	....	....	....	....	....	....	....	....
1990-91	Albany Choppers	IHL	6	2	0	2	....	....	....	0	....	....	....	....	....	....	....	....	....	....	....	....	....	....	....	....	....	....
	Durham Wasps	Britain	18	36	35	71	....	....	....	114	....	....	....	....	....	....	....	....	....	....	8	24	14	38	18	....	....	....
1991-92	Durham Wasps	Aut-Cup	9	10	20	30	....	....	....	54	....	....	....	....	....	....	....	....	....	....	....	....	....	....	....	....	....	....
	Durham Wasps	Britain	36	74	52	126	....	....	....	86	....	....	....	....	....	....	....	....	....	....	8	11	13	24	22	....	....	....
1992-93	Durham Wasps	BH-Cup	9	18	10	28	....	....	....	22	....	....	....	....	....	....	....	....	....	....	....	....	....	....	....	....	....	....
	Durham Wasps	Britain	13	24	18	42	....	....	....	46	....	....	....	....	....	....	....	....	....	....	....	....	....	....	....	....	....	....
1993-1994	Nottingham Panthers	Britain	DID NOT PLAY – COACHING																									
1994-1995	Nottingham Panthers	BH-Cup	3	4	4	8	....	....	....	6	....	....	....	....	....	....	....	....	....	....	....	....	....	....	....	....	....	....
	Nottingham Panthers	Britain	DID NOT PLAY – COACHING																									
	Nottingham Panthers	Britain	11	7	10	17	....	....	....	60	....	....	....	....	....	....	....	....	....	....	....	....	....	....	....	....	....	....
1995-96	Nottingham Panthers	BH-Cup	11	8	7	15	....	....	....	43	....	....	....	....	....	....	....	....	....	....	....	....	....	....	....	....	....	....
	Nottingham Panthers	Britain	33	26	33	59	....	....	....	77	....	....	....	....	....	....	....	....	....	....	8	1	6	7	4	....	....	....
1996-1997	Nottingham Panthers	Brirain	DID NOT PLAY – COACHING																									
	Nottingham Panthers	Britain	7	2	2	4	....	....	....	6	....	....	....	....	....	....	....	....	....	....	....	....	....	....	....	....	....	....
1997-1998	Nottingham Panthers	Britain	DID NOT PLAY – COACHING																									
1998-1999	Nottingham Panthers	BH-Cup	3	0	1	1	....	....	....	0	....	....	....	....	....	....	....	....	....	....	....	....	....	....	....	....	....	....
	Nottingham Panthers	Britain	DID NOT PLAY – COACHING																									
	Nottingham Panthers	Britain	3	0	1	1	....	....	....	2	....	....	....	....	....	....	....	....	....	....	....	....	....	....	....	....	....	....
1999-2000	Nottingham Panthers	Britain	DID NOT PLAY – COACHING																									
	Sheffield Steelers	Britain	DID NOT PLAY – COACHING																									
	NHL Totals		**343**	**70**	**84**	**154**	**57**	**56**	**113**	**166**	**5**	**0**	**7**	**641**	**10.9**	**255**	**25**	**258**	**3**		**6**	**1**	**2**	**3**	**10**	**0**	**0**	**0**

Traded to **NY Rangers** by **Detroit** with Willie Huber and Mark Osborne for Ron Duguay, Eddie Mio and Eddie Johnstone, June 13, 1983. Claimed by **Pittsburgh** from **NY Rangers** in Waiver Draft, October 7, 1985. Signed as a free agent by **Toronto**, July 10, 1987.

• BLAKE, Jason

C – L. 5'10", 185 lbs. b: Moorhead, MN, 9/2/1973.

Season	Club	League	GP	G	A	Pts	AG	AA	APts	PIM	PP	SH	GW	S	%	TGF	PGF	TGA	PGA	+/–	GP	G	A	Pts	PIM	PP	SH	GW
1991-92	Moorehead Spuds	Hi-School	25	30	30	60	....	....	....	....	....	....	....	....	....	....	....	....	....	....	....	....	....	....	....	....	....	....
1992-93	Waterloo Black Hawks	USHL	STATISTICS NOT AVAILABLE																									
1993-94	Waterloo Black Hawks	USHL	47	50	50	100	....	....	....	76	....	....	....	....	....	....	....	....	....	....	....	....	....	....	....	....	....	....
1994-95	Ferris State University	CCHA	36	16	16	32	....	....	....	46	....	....	....	....	....	....	....	....	....	....	....	....	....	....	....	....	....	....
1995-96			DID NOT PLAY – TRANSFERRED COLLEGES																									
1996-97	University of North Dakota	WCHA	43	19	32	51	....	....	....	44	....	....	....	....	....	....	....	....	....	....	....	....	....	....	....	....	....	....
1997-98	University of North Dakota	WCHA	38	24	27	51	....	....	....	62	....	....	....	....	....	....	....	....	....	....	....	....	....	....	....	....	....	....
1998-99	University of North Dakota	WCHA	38	*28	*41	*69	....	....	....	49	....	....	....	....	....	....	....	....	....	....	....	....	....	....	....	....	....	....
	United States	WC-Q	2	0	1	1	....	....	....	2	....	....	....	....	....	....	....	....	....	....	....	....	....	....	....	....	....	....
	Los Angeles Kings	**NHL**	**1**	**1**	**0**	**1**	**1**	**0**	**1**	**0**	**0**	**0**	**0**	**5**	**20.0**	**1**	**0**	**0**	**0**	**1**	....	....	....	....	....	....	....	....
	Orlando Solar Bears	IHL	5	3	5	8	....	....	....	6	....	....	....	....	....	....	....	....	....	....	13	3	4	7	20	....	....	....

			REGULAR SEASON																		PLAYOFFS							
Season	Club	League	GP	G	A	Pts	AG	AA	APts	PIM	PP	SH	GW	S	%	TGF	PGF	TGA	PGA	+/-	GP	G	A	Pts	PIM	PP	SH	GW
99-2000	**Los Angeles Kings**	**NHL**	**64**	**5**	**18**	**23**	**6**	**17**	**23**	**26**	**0**	**0**	**1**	**131**	**3.8**	**36**	**6**	**30**	**4**	**4**	**3**	**0**	**0**	**0**	**0**	**0**	**0**	**0**
	Long Beach Ice Dogs	IHL	7	3	6	9	....	....	....	2	....	....	....	....	....	....	....	....	....	....	....	....	....	....	....	....	....	....
	United States	WC-A	7	1	1	2	....	....	....	2	....	....	....	....	....	....	....	....	....	....	....	....	....	....	....	....	....	....
	NHL Totals		**65**	**6**	**18**	**24**	**7**	**17**	**24**	**26**	**0**	**0**	**1**	**136**	**4.4**	**37**	**6**	**30**	**4**		**3**	**0**	**0**	**0**	**0**	**0**	**0**	**0**

WCHA First All-Star Team (1997, 1998, 1999) • NCAA West Second All-American Team (1998) • NCAA West First All-American Team (1999)

Signed as a free agent by **LA Kings**, April 20, 1999.

• BLAKE, Rob

D – R. 6'4", 227 lbs. b: Simcoe, Ont., 12/10/1969. Los Angeles' 4th, 70th overall, in 1988.

Season	Club	League	GP	G	A	Pts	AG	AA	APts	PIM	PP	SH	GW	S	%	TGF	PGF	TGA	PGA	+/-	GP	G	A	Pts	PIM	PP	SH	GW
1986-87	Stratford Cullitons	OJHL-B	31	11	20	31	....	....	....	115	....	....	....	....	....	....	....	....	....	....	....	....	....	....	....	....	....	....
1987-88	Bowling Green University	CCHA	43	5	8	13	....	....	....	88	....	....	....	....	....	....	....	....	....	....	....	....	....	....	....	....	....	....
1988-89	Bowling Green University	CCHA	46	11	21	32	....	....	....	140	....	....	....	....	....	....	....	....	....	....	....	....	....	....	....	....	....	....
1989-90	Bowling Green University	CCHA	42	23	36	59	....	....	....	140	....	....	....	....	....	....	....	....	....	....	....	....	....	....	....	....	....	....
	Los Angeles Kings	**NHL**	**4**	**0**	**0**	**0**	**0**	**0**	**0**	**4**	**0**	**0**	**0**	**3**	**0.0**	**4**	**1**	**6**	**3**	**0**	**8**	**1**	**3**	**4**	**4**	**1**	**0**	**0**
1990-91	**Los Angeles Kings**	**NHL**	**75**	**12**	**34**	**46**	**11**	**26**	**37**	**125**	**9**	**0**	**2**	**150**	**8.0**	**110**	**46**	**84**	**23**	**3**	**12**	**1**	**4**	**5**	**26**	**1**	**0**	**0**
	Canada	WEC-A	2	0	2	2	....	....	....	0	....	....	....	....	....	....	....	....	....	....	....	....	....	....	....	....	....	....
1991-92	**Los Angeles Kings**	**NHL**	**57**	**7**	**13**	**20**	**6**	**10**	**16**	**102**	**5**	**0**	**0**	**131**	**5.3**	**96**	**35**	**81**	**15**	**–5**	**6**	**2**	**1**	**3**	**12**	**0**	**0**	**0**
1992-93	**Los Angeles Kings**	**NHL**	**76**	**16**	**43**	**59**	**13**	**30**	**43**	**152**	**10**	**0**	**4**	**243**	**6.6**	**145**	**56**	**103**	**32**	**18**	**23**	**4**	**6**	**10**	**46**	**1**	**1**	**0**
1993-94	**Los Angeles Kings**	**NHL**	**84**	**20**	**48**	**68**	**19**	**37**	**56**	**137**	**7**	**0**	**6**	**304**	**6.6**	**157**	**67**	**141**	**44**	**–7**	....	....	....	....	....	....	....	....
	Canada	WC-A	8	0	2	2	....	....	....	6	....	....	....	....	....	....	....	....	....	....	....	....	....	....	....	....	....	....
1994-95	**Los Angeles Kings**	**NHL**	**24**	**4**	**7**	**11**	**7**	**10**	**17**	**38**	**4**	**0**	**1**	**76**	**5.3**	**23**	**12**	**38**	**11**	**–16**	....	....	....	....	....	....	....	....
1995-96	**Los Angeles Kings**	**NHL**	**6**	**1**	**2**	**3**	**1**	**2**	**3**	**8**	**0**	**0**	**0**	**13**	**7.7**	**11**	**7**	**7**	**3**	**0**	....	....	....	....	....	....	....	....
1996-97	Canada	W-Cup	4	0	1	1	....	....	....	0	....	....	....	....	....	....	....	....	....	....	....	....	....	....	....	....	....	....
	Los Angeles Kings	**NHL**	**62**	**8**	**23**	**31**	**8**	**20**	**28**	**82**	**4**	**0**	**1**	**169**	**4.7**	**69**	**20**	**97**	**20**	**–28**	....	....	....	....	....	....	....	....
	Canada	WC-A	11	2	2	4	....	....	....	22	....	....	....	....	....	....	....	....	....	....	....	....	....	....	....	....	....	....
1997-98	**Los Angeles Kings**	**NHL**	**81**	**23**	**27**	**50**	**27**	**26**	**53**	**94**	**11**	**0**	**4**	**261**	**8.8**	**113**	**41**	**111**	**36**	**–3**	**4**	**0**	**0**	**0**	**6**	**0**	**0**	**0**
	Canada	Olympics	6	1	1	2	....	....	....	2	....	....	....	....	....	....	....	....	....	....	....	....	....	....	....	....	....	....
	Canada	WC-A	5	1	0	1	....	....	....	6	....	....	....	....	....	....	....	....	....	....	....	....	....	....	....	....	....	....
1998-99	**Los Angeles Kings**	**NHL**	**62**	**12**	**23**	**35**	**14**	**22**	**36**	**128**	**5**	**1**	**2**	**216**	**5.6**	**73**	**23**	**67**	**10**	**–7**	....	....	....	....	....	....	....	....
	Canada	WC-A	10	2	5	7	....	....	....	12	....	....	....	....	....	....	....	....	....	....	....	....	....	....	....	....	....	....
99-2000	**Los Angeles Kings**	**NHL**	**77**	**18**	**39**	**57**	**20**	**36**	**56**	**112**	**12**	**0**	**5**	**327**	**5.5**	**125**	**48**	**100**	**33**	**10**	**4**	**0**	**2**	**2**	**4**	**0**	**0**	**0**
	NHL Totals		**608**	**121**	**259**	**380**	**126**	**219**	**345**	**982**	**67**	**1**	**25**	**1893**	**6.4**	**926**	**356**	**835**	**230**		**57**	**8**	**16**	**24**	**98**	**3**	**1**	**0**

CCHA Second All-Star Team (1989) • CCHA First All-Star Team (1990) • NCAA West First All-American Team (1990) • NHL All-Rookie Team (1991) • WC-A All-Star Team (1997) • Named Best Defenseman at WC-A (1997) • Named Best Defenseman at Olympic Games (1998) • NHL First All-Star Team (1998) • Won James Norris Memorial Trophy (1998) • NHL Second All-Star Team (2000) • Played in NHL All-Star Game (1994, 1999, 2000)

• Suffered season-ending knee injury in game vs. Washington, October 20, 1995.

• BLIGHT, Rick

Richard Derek RW – R. 6'2", 195 lbs. b: Portage La Prairie, Man., 10/17/1955. Vancouver's 1st, 10th overall, in 1975.

Season	Club	League	GP	G	A	Pts	AG	AA	APts	PIM	PP	SH	GW	S	%	TGF	PGF	TGA	PGA	+/-	GP	G	A	Pts	PIM	PP	SH	GW
1970-71	Portage Terriers	MJHL	47	20	19	39	....	....	....	33	....	....	....	....	....	....	....	....	....	....	....	....	....	....	....	....	....	....
1971-72	Portage Terriers	MJHL	45	32	35	67	....	....	....	73	....	....	....	....	....	....	....	....	....	....	....	....	....	....	....	....	....	....
	Brandon Wheat Kings	WCJHL	1	1	0	1	....	....	....	0	....	....	....	....	....	....	....	....	....	....	11	3	1	4	8	....	....	....
1972-73	Brandon Wheat Kings	WCJHL	68	31	62	93	....	....	....	70	....	....	....	....	....	....	....	....	....	....	6	0	1	1	0	....	....	....
1973-74	Brandon Wheat Kings	WCJHL	67	49	81	130	....	....	....	122	....	....	....	....	....	....	....	....	....	....	6	0	1	1	0	....	....	....
1974-75	Brandon Wheat Kings	WCJHL	65	60	52	112	....	....	....	65	....	....	....	....	....	....	....	....	....	....	5	2	3	5	6	....	....	....
	Canada	WJC-A	6	2	2	4	....	....	....	4	....	....	....	....	....	....	....	....	....	....	....	....	....	....	....	....	....	....
1975-76	**Vancouver Canucks**	**NHL**	**74**	**25**	**31**	**56**	**22**	**23**	**45**	**29**	**10**	**0**	**3**	**212**	**11.8**	**79**	**27**	**57**	**1**	**–4**	**2**	**0**	**1**	**1**	**0**	**0**	**0**	**0**
1976-77	**Vancouver Canucks**	**NHL**	**78**	**28**	**40**	**68**	**25**	**31**	**56**	**32**	**11**	**0**	**5**	**197**	**14.2**	**102**	**41**	**62**	**1**	**0**	....	....	....	....	....	....	....	....
1977-78	**Vancouver Canucks**	**NHL**	**80**	**25**	**38**	**63**	**23**	**29**	**52**	**33**	**11**	**0**	**2**	**238**	**10.5**	**93**	**41**	**84**	**0**	**–32**	....	....	....	....	....	....	....	....
1978-79	**Vancouver Canucks**	**NHL**	**56**	**5**	**10**	**15**	**4**	**7**	**11**	**16**	**1**	**0**	**1**	**91**	**5.5**	**26**	**9**	**45**	**0**	**–28**	**3**	**0**	**4**	**4**	**2**	**0**	**0**	**0**
	Dallas Black Hawks	CHL	15	8	7	15	....	....	....	7	....	....	....	....	....	....	....	....	....	....	....	....	....	....	....	....	....	....
1979-80	**Vancouver Canucks**	**NHL**	**33**	**12**	**6**	**18**	**10**	**4**	**14**	**54**	**1**	**0**	**0**	**82**	**14.6**	**28**	**5**	**16**	**0**	**7**	....	....	....	....	....	....	....	....
1980-81	**Vancouver Canucks**	**NHL**	**3**	**1**	**0**	**1**	**1**	**0**	**1**	**4**	**0**	**0**	**0**	**9**	**11.1**	**1**	**0**	**2**	**0**	**–1**	....	....	....	....	....	....	....	....
	Dallas Black Hawks	CHL	74	46	49	95	....	....	....	122	....	....	....	....	....	....	....	....	....	....	6	0	3	3	9	....	....	....
1981-82	Cincinnati Tigers	CHL	37	16	23	39	....	....	....	21	....	....	....	....	....	....	....	....	....	....	....	....	....	....	....	....	....	....
	Wichita Wind	CHL	16	18	14	32	....	....	....	18	....	....	....	....	....	....	....	....	....	....	7	3	0	3	6	....	....	....
1982-83	Moncton Alpines	AHL	19	8	7	15	....	....	....	6	....	....	....	....	....	....	....	....	....	....	....	....	....	....	....	....	....	....
	Los Angeles Kings	**NHL**	**2**	**0**	**0**	**0**	**0**	**0**	**0**	**2**	**0**	**0**	**0**	**2**	**0.0**	**2**	**1**	**5**	**1**	**–3**	....	....	....	....	....	....	....	....
	New Haven Nighthawks	AHL	47	17	24	41	....	....	....	8	....	....	....	....	....	....	....	....	....	....	12	2	3	5	4	....	....	....
	NHL Totals		**326**	**96**	**125**	**221**	**85**	**94**	**179**	**170**	**34**	**0**	**11**	**831**	**11.6**	**331**	**124**	**271**	**3**		**5**	**0**	**5**	**5**	**2**	**0**	**0**	**0**

CHL Second All-Star Team (1981)

Signed as a free agent by **Toronto**, August 31, 1981. Signed as a free agent by **Edmonton**, October 25, 1982. Traded to **LA Kings** by **Edmonton** for Alan Hangsleben, December 7, 1982.

• BLOCK, Ken

Kenneth Richard D – L. 5'10", 191 lbs. b: Steinbach, Man., 3/18/1944.

Season	Club	League	GP	G	A	Pts	AG	AA	APts	PIM	PP	SH	GW	S	%	TGF	PGF	TGA	PGA	+/-	GP	G	A	Pts	PIM	PP	SH	GW
1962-63	Flin Flon Bombers	SJHL	54	5	11	16	....	....	....	34	....	....	....	....	....	....	....	....	....	....	6	2	5	7	4	....	....	....
1963-64	Flin Flon Bombers	MJHL	62	14	43	57	....	....	....	59	....	....	....	....	....	....	....	....	....	....	2	1	3	4	0	....	....	....
1964-65	New York Rovers	EHL	70	5	31	36	....	....	....	51	....	....	....	....	....	....	....	....	....	....	....	....	....	....	....	....	....	....
	Baltimore Clippers	AHL	5	0	2	2	....	....	....	2	....	....	....	....	....	....	....	....	....	....	5	1	0	1	2	....	....	....
1965-66	Baltimore Clippers	AHL	37	2	8	10	....	....	....	6	....	....	....	....	....	....	....	....	....	....	....	....	....	....	....	....	....	....
	Minnesota Rangers	CPHL	30	0	6	6	....	....	....	8	....	....	....	....	....	....	....	....	....	....	....	....	....	....	....	....	....	....
1966-67	Omaha Knights	CPHL	10	0	4	4	....	....	....	6	....	....	....	....	....	....	....	....	....	....	....	....	....	....	....	....	....	....
	Vancouver Canucks	WHL	62	8	22	30	....	....	....	18	....	....	....	....	....	....	....	....	....	....	8	1	3	4	0	....	....	....
1967-68	Memphis South Stars	CPHL	18	5	5	10	....	....	....	24	....	....	....	....	....	....	....	....	....	....	....	....	....	....	....	....	....	....
	Vancouver Canucks	WHL	17	2	6	8	....	....	....	4	....	....	....	....	....	....	....	....	....	....	....	....	....	....	....	....	....	....
	Rochester Americans	AHL	24	1	1	2	....	....	....	0	....	....	....	....	....	....	....	....	....	....	....	....	....	....	....	....	....	....
1968-69	Vancouver Canucks	WHL	22	1	2	3	....	....	....	6	....	....	....	....	....	....	....	....	....	....	....	....	....	....	....	....	....	....
	Rochester Americans	AHL	45	4	15	19	....	....	....	10	....	....	....	....	....	....	....	....	....	....	....	....	....	....	....	....	....	....
1969-70	Rochester Americans	AHL	69	9	35	44	....	....	....	51	....	....	....	....	....	....	....	....	....	....	....	....	....	....	....	....	....	....
1970-71	**Vancouver Canucks**	**NHL**	**1**	**0**	**0**	**0**	**0**	**0**	**0**	**0**	**0**	**0**	**0**	**0**	**0.0**	**0**	**0**	**1**	**0**	**–1**	....	....	....	....	....	....	....	....
	Rochester Americans	AHL	71	5	33	38	....	....	....	38	....	....	....	....	....	....	....	....	....	....	....	....	....	....	....	....	....	....
1971-72	Rochester Americans	AHL	71	4	29	33	....	....	....	69	....	....	....	....	....	....	....	....	....	....	....	....	....	....	....	....	....	....
1972-73	New York Raiders	WHA	78	5	53	58	....	....	....	43	....	....	....	....	....	....	....	....	....	....	....	....	....	....	....	....	....	....
1973-74	New York-Jersey Knights	WHA	74	3	43	46	....	....	....	22	....	....	....	....	....	....	....	....	....	....	....	....	....	....	....	....	....	....
1974-75	San Diego Mariners	WHA	36	1	11	12	....	....	....	12	....	....	....	....	....	....	....	....	....	....	....	....	....	....	....	....	....	....
	Indianapolis Racers	WHA	37	0	17	17	....	....	....	18	....	....	....	....	....	....	....	....	....	....	....	....	....	....	....	....	....	....
1975-76	Indianapolis Racers	WHA	79	1	25	26	....	....	....	28	....	....	....	....	....	....	....	....	....	....	7	0	4	4	2	....	....	....
1976-77	Indianapolis Racers	WHA	52	3	10	13	....	....	....	25	....	....	....	....	....	....	....	....	....	....	9	0	2	2	6	....	....	....
1977-78	Indianapolis Racers	WHA	77	1	25	26	....	....	....	34	....	....	....	....	....	....	....	....	....	....	....	....	....	....	....	....	....	....
1978-79	Indianapolis Racers	WHA	22	2	3	5	....	....	....	10	....	....	....	....	....	....	....	....	....	....	....	....	....	....	....	....	....	....
	NHL Totals		**1**	**0**	**0**	**0**	**0**	**0**	**0**	**0**	**0**	**0**	**0**	**0**	**0.0**	**0**	**0**	**1**	**0**		....	....	....	....	....	....	....	....
	Other Major League Totals		455	16	187	203	....	....	....	192	....	....	....	....	....	....	....	....	....	....	16	0	6	6	8	....	....	....

Claimed by **LA Kings** from **NY Rangers** in Expansion Draft, June 6, 1967. Traded to **Toronto** by **LA Kings** for the rights to Red Kelly, June 8, 1967. Rights transferred to **Vancouver** (WHL) after WHL club purchased **Rochester** (AHL) franchise, August 13, 1968. NHL rights transferred to **Vancouver** after NHL club purchased **Vancouver** (WHL) franchise, December 19, 1969. Selected by **NY Raiders** (WHA) in 1972 WHA General Player Draft, February 13, 1972. Transferred to **San Diego** (WHA) after **New York-Jersey** (WHA) franchise relocated, April 30, 1974. Traded to **Indianapolis** (WHA) by **San Diego** (WHA) for Jim Hargreaves, January, 1975.

• BLOEMBERG, Jeff

D – R. 6'2", 205 lbs. b: Listowel, Ont., 1/31/1968. NY Rangers' 5th, 93rd overall, in 1986.

Season	Club	League	GP	G	A	Pts	AG	AA	APts	PIM	PP	SH	GW	S	%	TGF	PGF	TGA	PGA	+/-	GP	G	A	Pts	PIM	PP	SH	GW
1984-85	Listowel Cyclones	OJHL-B	31	7	14	21	....	....	....	73	....	....	....	....	....	....	....	....	....	....	....	....	....	....	....	....	....	....
1985-86	North Bay Centennials	OHL	60	2	11	13	....	....	....	76	....	....	....	....	....	....	....	....	....	....	8	1	2	3	9	....	....	....
1986-87	North Bay Centennials	OHL	60	5	13	18	....	....	....	91	....	....	....	....	....	....	....	....	....	....	21	1	6	7	13	....	....	....

			REGULAR SEASON																		PLAYOFFS							
Season	Club	League	GP	G	A	Pts	AG	AA	APts	PIM	PP	SH	GW	S	%	TGF	PGF	TGA	PGA	+/-	GP	G	A	Pts	PIM	PP	SH	GW
1987-88	North Bay Centennials	OHL	46	9	26	35	....	....	....	60	....	....	....	....	....	....	....	....	....	....	4	1	4	5	2	....	....	....
	Colorado Rangers	IHL	5	0	0	0	....	....	....	0	....	....	....	....	....	....	....	....	....	....	11	1	0	1	8	....	....	....
1988-89	**New York Rangers**	**NHL**	**9**	**0**	**0**	**0**	**0**	**0**	**0**	**0**	**0**	**0**	**0**	**9**	**0.0**	**6**	**0**	**6**	**2**	**2**	....	....	....	....	....	....	....	....
	Denver Rangers	IHL	64	7	22	29	....	....	....	55	....	....	....	....	....	....	....	....	....	....	1	0	0	0	0	....	....	....
1989-90	**New York Rangers**	**NHL**	**28**	**3**	**3**	**6**	**3**	**2**	**5**	**25**	**2**	**0**	**1**	**20**	**15.0**	**21**	**8**	**33**	**12**	**–8**	**7**	**0**	**3**	**3**	**5**	**0**	**0**	**0**
	Flint Spirits	IHL	41	7	21	28	....	....	....	24	....	....	....	....	....	....	....	....	....	....	....	....	....	....	....	....	....	....
1990-91	**New York Rangers**	**NHL**	**3**	**0**	**2**	**2**	**0**	**2**	**2**	**0**	**0**	**0**	**0**	**4**	**0.0**	**5**	**2**	**0**	**0**	**3**	....	....	....	....	....	....	....	....
	Binghamton Rangers	AHL	77	16	46	62	....	....	....	28	....	....	....	....	....	....	....	....	....	....	10	0	6	6	10	....	....	....
1991-92	**New York Rangers**	**NHL**	**3**	**0**	**1**	**1**	**0**	**1**	**1**	**0**	**0**	**0**	**0**	**5**	**0.0**	**2**	**0**	**1**	**0**	**1**	....	....	....	....	....	....	....	....
	Binghamton Rangers	AHL	66	6	41	47	....	....	....	22	....	....	....	....	....	....	....	....	....	....	11	1	10	11	10	....	....	....
1992-93	Cape Breton Oilers	AHL	76	6	45	51	....	....	....	34	....	....	....	....	....	....	....	....	....	....	16	5	10	15	10	....	....	....
1993-94	Springfield Indians	AHL	78	8	28	36	....	....	....	36	....	....	....	....	....	....	....	....	....	....	6	0	3	3	8	....	....	....
1994-95	Adirondack Red Wings	AHL	44	5	19	24	....	....	....	10	....	....	....	....	....	....	....	....	....	....	4	0	0	0	0	....	....	....
1995-96	Adirondack Red Wings	AHL	72	10	28	38	....	....	....	32	....	....	....	....	....	....	....	....	....	....	3	0	1	1	4	....	....	....
1996-97	Adirondack Red Wings	AHL	69	5	31	36	....	....	....	24	....	....	....	....	....	....	....	....	....	....	4	0	3	3	2	....	....	....
1997-98	Berlin Capitals	Germany	27	3	7	10	....	....	....	16	....	....	....	....	....	....	....	....	....	....	....	....	....	....	....	....	....	....
1998-99	Revier Lowen	Germany	52	3	17	20	....	....	....	54	....	....	....	....	....	....	....	....	....	....	....	....	....	....	....	....	....	....
	NHL Totals		**43**	**3**	**6**	**9**	**3**	**5**	**8**	**25**	**2**	**0**	**1**	**38**	**7.9**	**34**	**10**	**40**	**14**		**7**	**0**	**3**	**3**	**5**	**0**	**0**	**0**

AHL Second All-Star Team (1991)

Claimed by **Tampa Bay** from **NY Rangers** in Expansion Draft, June 18, 1992. Traded to **Edmonton** by **Tampa Bay** for future considerations, September 25, 1992. Signed as a free agent by **Hartford**, August 9, 1993. Signed as a free agent by **Detroit**, May 9, 1995.

• BLOMQVIST, Timo

Timo P. D – R. 6', 200 lbs. b: Helsinki, Finland, 1/23/1961. Washington's 4th, 89th overall, in 1980.

Season	Club	League	GP	G	A	Pts	AG	AA	APts	PIM	PP	SH	GW	S	%	TGF	PGF	TGA	PGA	+/-	GP	G	A	Pts	PIM	PP	SH	GW
1976-77	Jokerit Helsinki	Finland-Jr.	19	2	3	5	....	....	....	13	....	....	....	....	....	....	....	....	....	....	....	....	....	....	....	....	....	....
1977-78	Jokerit Helsinki	Finland-Jr.	14	3	2	5	....	....	....	24	....	....	....	....	....	....	....	....	....	....	....	....	....	....	....	....	....	....
	Jokerit Helsinki	Finland	22	1	0	1	....	....	....	2	....	....	....	....	....	....	....	....	....	....	....	....	....	....	....	....	....	....
1978-79	Jokerit Helsinki	Finland-Jr.	2	1	0	1	....	....	....	2	....	....	....	....	....	....	....	....	....	....	....	....	....	....	....	....	....	....
	Jokerit Helsinki	Finland	36	4	2	6	....	....	....	35	....	....	....	....	....	....	....	....	....	....	....	....	....	....	....	....	....	....
	Finland	WJC-A	6	1	1	2	....	....	....	34	....	....	....	....	....	....	....	....	....	....	....	....	....	....	....	....	....	....
1979-80	Jokerit Helsinki	Finland	32	3	1	4	....	....	....	52	....	....	....	....	....	....	....	....	....	....	....	....	....	....	....	....	....	....
	Finland	WJC-A	5	2	0	2	....	....	....	2	....	....	....	....	....	....	....	....	....	....	....	....	....	....	....	....	....	....
1980-81	Kiekko Reipas	Finland	30	6	7	13	....	....	....	14	....	....	....	....	....	....	....	....	....	....	....	....	....	....	....	....	....	....
	Finland	WJC-A	5	1	3	4	....	....	....	14	....	....	....	....	....	....	....	....	....	....	....	....	....	....	....	....	....	....
	Finland	Nat-Team	2	0	0	0	....	....	....	0	....	....	....	....	....	....	....	....	....	....	....	....	....	....	....	....	....	....
1981-82	**Washington Capitals**	**NHL**	**44**	**1**	**11**	**12**	**1**	**7**	**8**	**62**	**0**	**0**	**0**	**53**	**1.9**	**36**	**9**	**50**	**6**	**–17**	....	....	....	....	....	....	....	....
	Hershey Bears	AHL	13	0	8	8	....	....	....	14	....	....	....	....	....	....	....	....	....	....	....	....	....	....	....	....	....	....
1982-83	**Washington Capitals**	**NHL**	**61**	**1**	**17**	**18**	**1**	**12**	**13**	**67**	**1**	**0**	**1**	**70**	**1.4**	**85**	**13**	**68**	**11**	**15**	**3**	**0**	**0**	**0**	**16**	**0**	**0**	**0**
	Hershey Bears	AHL	8	2	7	9	....	....	....	16	....	....	....	....	....	....	....	....	....	....	....	....	....	....	....	....	....	....
1983-84	**Washington Capitals**	**NHL**	**65**	**1**	**19**	**20**	**1**	**13**	**14**	**84**	**0**	**0**	**0**	**69**	**1.4**	**63**	**4**	**51**	**9**	**17**	**8**	**0**	**0**	**0**	**8**	**0**	**0**	**0**
1984-85	**Washington Capitals**	**NHL**	**53**	**1**	**4**	**5**	**1**	**3**	**4**	**51**	**0**	**0**	**0**	**59**	**1.7**	**42**	**0**	**39**	**8**	**11**	**2**	**0**	**0**	**0**	**0**	**0**	**0**	**0**
	Finland	WEC-A	9	0	3	3	....	....	....	6	....	....	....	....	....	....	....	....	....	....	....	....	....	....	....	....	....	....
1985-86	Binghamton Whalers	AHL	71	6	18	24	....	....	....	76	....	....	....	....	....	....	....	....	....	....	6	0	4	4	6	....	....	....
1986-87	**New Jersey Devils**	**NHL**	**20**	**0**	**2**	**2**	**0**	**1**	**1**	**29**	**0**	**0**	**0**	**16**	**0.0**	**19**	**3**	**27**	**8**	**–3**	....	....	....	....	....	....	....	....
1987-88	Finland	Can-Cup	4	0	0	0	....	....	....	0	....	....	....	....	....	....	....	....	....	....	....	....	....	....	....	....	....	....
	MoDo AIK	Sweden	36	6	10	16	....	....	....	64	....	....	....	....	....	....	....	....	....	....	4	0	2	2	10	....	....	....
	Finland	Nat-Team	18	1	1	2	....	....	....	14	....	....	....	....	....	....	....	....	....	....	....	....	....	....	....	....	....	....
	Finland	Olympics	8	1	1	2	....	....	....	10	....	....	....	....	....	....	....	....	....	....	....	....	....	....	....	....	....	....
1988-89	MoDo AIK	Sweden	39	4	8	12	....	....	....	92	....	....	....	....	....	....	....	....	....	....	....	....	....	....	....	....	....	....
	Finland	Nat-Team	13	0	0	0	....	....	....	10	....	....	....	....	....	....	....	....	....	....	....	....	....	....	....	....	....	....
	Finland	WEC-A	7	0	1	1	....	....	....	8	....	....	....	....	....	....	....	....	....	....	....	....	....	....	....	....	....	....
1989-90	MoDo AIK	Sweden	17	3	4	7	....	....	....	38	....	....	....	....	....	....	....	....	....	....	9	1	3	4	*38	....	....	....
1990-91	Malmo IF	Sweden	40	5	3	8	....	....	....	59	....	....	....	....	....	....	....	....	....	....	2	0	0	0	2	....	....	....
	Finland	Nat-Team	4	0	0	0	....	....	....	4	....	....	....	....	....	....	....	....	....	....	....	....	....	....	....	....	....	....
1991-92	Malmo IF	Sweden	39	5	8	13	....	....	....	36	....	....	....	....	....	....	....	....	....	....	10	0	2	2	8	....	....	....
	Finland	Nat-Team	4	0	0	0	....	....	....	2	....	....	....	....	....	....	....	....	....	....	....	....	....	....	....	....	....	....
	Finland	Olympics	8	0	1	1	....	....	....	8	....	....	....	....	....	....	....	....	....	....	....	....	....	....	....	....	....	....
1992-93	Malmo IF	Sweden	35	2	4	6	....	....	....	46	....	....	....	....	....	....	....	....	....	....	6	0	0	0	4	....	....	....
1993-94	IHK Sparta Sarpsborg	Norway	30	3	12	15	....	....	....	63	....	....	....	....	....	....	....	....	....	....	2	0	0	0	6	....	....	....
1994-95	Kiekko-Espoo	Finland	34	6	4	10	....	....	....	46	....	....	....	....	....	....	....	....	....	....	4	0	1	1	6	....	....	....
1995-96	Kiekko-Espoo	Finland	48	4	4	8	....	....	....	68	....	....	....	....	....	....	....	....	....	....	....	....	....	....	....	....	....	....
1996-97	WEV Wien	Alpenliga	37	2	7	9	....	....	....	84	....	....	....	....	....	....	....	....	....	....	....	....	....	....	....	....	....	....
	WEV Wien	EuroHL	6	1	1	2	....	....	....	8	....	....	....	....	....	....	....	....	....	....	....	....	....	....	....	....	....	....
1997-98	ES Weisswasser	Germany-2	15	0	5	5	....	....	....	43	....	....	....	....	....	....	....	....	....	....	....	....	....	....	....	....	....	....
	EPS Espoo	Finland-3	6	1	3	4	....	....	....	12	....	....	....	....	....	....	....	....	....	....	....	....	....	....	....	....	....	....
	Ahmat Hyvinkaa	Finland-2	18	0	3	3	....	....	....	24	....	....	....	....	....	....	....	....	....	....	....	....	....	....	....	....	....	....
	Ahmat Hyvinkaa	Finland-Q	5	0	2	2	....	....	....	4	....	....	....	....	....	....	....	....	....	....	....	....	....	....	....	....	....	....
1998-99	HIFK Helsinki	Finland	DID NOT PLAY – ASSISTANT COACH																									
	NHL Totals		**243**	**4**	**53**	**57**	**4**	**36**	**40**	**293**	**1**	**0**	**1**	**267**	**1.5**	**245**	**29**	**235**	**42**		**13**	**0**	**0**	**0**	**24**	**0**	**0**	**0**

Signed as a free agent by **New Jersey**, July 2, 1986.

• BLOMSTEN, Arto

D – L. 6'3", 210 lbs. b: Vaasa, Finland, 3/16/1965. Winnipeg's 11th, 239th overall, in 1986.

Season	Club	League	GP	G	A	Pts	AG	AA	APts	PIM	PP	SH	GW	S	%	TGF	PGF	TGA	PGA	+/-	GP	G	A	Pts	PIM	PP	SH	GW
1983-84	Djurgardens IF Stockholm	Sweden	3	0	0	0	....	....	....	4	....	....	....	....	....	....	....	....	....	....	....	....	....	....	....	....	....	....
1984-85	Djurgardens IF Stockholm	Sweden	19	3	1	4	....	....	....	22	....	....	....	....	....	....	....	....	....	....	8	0	0	0	8	....	....	....
	Sweden	WJC-A	6	0	0	0	....	....	....	6	....	....	....	....	....	....	....	....	....	....	....	....	....	....	....	....	....	....
1985-86	Djurgardens IF Stockholm	Sweden	8	0	3	3	....	....	....	6	....	....	....	....	....	....	....	....	....	....	....	....	....	....	....	....	....	....
1986-87	Djurgardens IF Stockholm	Sweden	29	2	4	6	....	....	....	28	....	....	....	....	....	....	....	....	....	....	....	....	....	....	....	....	....	....
1987-88	Djurgardens IF Stockholm	Sweden	39	12	6	18	....	....	....	36	....	....	....	....	....	....	....	....	....	....	2	1	0	1	0	....	....	....
1988-89	Djurgardens IF Stockholm	Sweden	40	10	9	19	....	....	....	38	....	....	....	....	....	....	....	....	....	....	....	....	....	....	....	....	....	....
1989-90	Djurgardens IF Stockholm	Sweden	36	5	21	26	....	....	....	28	....	....	....	....	....	....	....	....	....	....	8	0	1	1	6	....	....	....
1990-91	Djurgardens IF Stockholm	Sweden	38	2	9	11	....	....	....	38	....	....	....	....	....	....	....	....	....	....	7	2	1	3	12	....	....	....
1991-92	Djurgardens IF Stockholm	Sweden	39	6	8	14	....	....	....	34	....	....	....	....	....	....	....	....	....	....	10	2	0	2	8	....	....	....
	Sweden	WC-A	8	4	0	4	....	....	....	6	....	....	....	....	....	....	....	....	....	....	....	....	....	....	....	....	....	....
1992-93	Djurgardens IF Stockholm	Sweden	40	4	16	20	....	....	....	52	....	....	....	....	....	....	....	....	....	....	....	....	....	....	....	....	....	....
	Sweden	WC-A	8	0	0	0	....	....	....	16	....	....	....	....	....	....	....	....	....	....	....	....	....	....	....	....	....	....
1993-94	**Winnipeg Jets**	**NHL**	**18**	**0**	**2**	**2**	**0**	**2**	**2**	**6**	**0**	**0**	**0**	**15**	**0.0**	**6**	**1**	**15**	**4**	**–6**	....	....	....	....	....	....	....	....
	Moncton Hawks	AHL	44	6	27	33	....	....	....	25	....	....	....	....	....	....	....	....	....	....	20	4	10	14	8	....	....	....
1994-95	**Winnipeg Jets**	**NHL**	**1**	**0**	**0**	**0**	**0**	**0**	**0**	**2**	**0**	**0**	**0**	**0**	**0.0**	**0**	**0**	**0**	**0**	**0**	....	....	....	....	....	....	....	....
	Springfield Falcons	AHL	27	3	16	19	....	....	....	20	....	....	....	....	....	....	....	....	....	....	....	....	....	....	....	....	....	....
	Los Angeles Kings	**NHL**	**4**	**0**	**1**	**1**	**0**	**1**	**1**	**0**	**0**	**0**	**0**	**1**	**0.0**	**3**	**0**	**2**	**1**	**2**	....	....	....	....	....	....	....	....
	Phoenix Roadrunners	IHL	2	1	2	3	....	....	....	0	....	....	....	....	....	....	....	....	....	....	8	3	6	9	6	....	....	....
1995-96	**Los Angeles Kings**	**NHL**	**2**	**0**	**1**	**1**	**0**	**1**	**1**	**0**	**0**	**0**	**0**	**1**	**0.0**	**2**	**0**	**2**	**1**	**1**	....	....	....	....	....	....	....	....
	Phoenix Roadrunners	IHL	47	4	15	19	....	....	....	10	....	....	....	....	....	....	....	....	....	....	4	0	4	4	2	....	....	....
1996-97	Vastra Frolunda	Sweden	41	4	10	14	....	....	....	45	....	....	....	....	....	....	....	....	....	....	3	0	0	0	0	....	....	....
	Vastra Frolunda	EuroHL	4	0	3	3	....	....	....	2	....	....	....	....	....	....	....	....	....	....	4	0	0	0	0	....	....	....
1997-98	Vastra Frolunda	Sweden	24	3	1	4	....	....	....	18	....	....	....	....	....	....	....	....	....	....	7	0	0	0	10	....	....	....
1998-99	Vasteras IK	Sweden-2	9	0	1	1	....	....	....	6	....	....	....	....	....	....	....	....	....	....	....	....	....	....	....	....	....	....
	Vasteras IK	Sweden	47	2	2	4	....	....	....	42	....	....	....	....	....	....	....	....	....	....	....	....	....	....	....	....	....	....
99-2000	Vasteras IK	Sweden	11	0	0	0	....	....	....	6	....	....	....	....	....	....	....	....	....	....	....	....	....	....	....	....	....	....
	NHL Totals		**25**	**0**	**4**	**4**	**0**	**4**	**4**	**8**	**0**	**0**	**0**	**17**	**0.0**	**11**	**1**	**19**	**6**		....	....	....	....	....	....	....	....

Traded to **LA Kings** by **Winnipeg** for LA Kings' 8th round choice (Frederik Loven) in 1995 Entry Draft, March 27, 1995.

• BLOOM, Mike

Michael Carroll LW – L. 6'3", 206 lbs. b: Ottawa, Ont., 4/12/1952. Boston's 1st, 16th overall, in 1972.

			REGULAR SEASON																		PLAYOFFS							
Season	Club	League	GP	G	A	Pts	AG	AA	APts	PIM	PP	SH	GW	S	%	TGF	PGF	TGA	PGA	+/-	GP	G	A	Pts	PIM	PP	SH	GW
1969-70	St. Catharines Black Hawks	OHA-Jr.	42	20	14	34	....	....	....	94	....	....	....	....	....	....	....	....	....	....	10	2	5	7	14	....	....	....
1970-71	St. Catharines Black Hawks	OHA-Jr.	58	20	33	53	....	....	....	117	....	....	....	....	....	....	....	....	....	....	15	9	14	23	24	....	....	....
1971-72	St. Catharines Black Hawks	OMJHL	50	25	40	65	....	....	....	116	....	....	....	....	....	....	....	....	....	....	5	1	3	4	11	....	....	....
1972-73	Boston Braves	AHL	32	4	5	9	....	....	....	41	....	....	....	....	....	....	....	....	....	....	....	....	....	....	....	....	....	....
	San Diego Gulls	WHL	39	14	15	29	....	....	....	54	....	....	....	....	....	....	....	....	....	....	6	2	1	3	19	....	....	....
1973-74	San Diego Gulls	WHL	76	25	44	69	....	....	....	108	....	....	....	....	....	....	....	....	....	....	4	1	3	4	7	....	....	....
1974-75	**Washington Capitals**	**NHL**	**67**	**7**	**19**	**26**	**6**	**14**	**20**	**84**	**0**	**0**	**0**	**88**	**8.0**	**39**	**7**	**86**	**0**	**−54**	....	....	....	....	....	....	....	....
	Detroit Red Wings	**NHL**	**13**	**4**	**8**	**12**	**3**	**6**	**9**	**10**	**1**	**0**	**1**	**20**	**20.0**	**19**	**1**	**17**	**1**	**2**	....	....	....	....	....	....	....	....
1975-76	**Detroit Red Wings**	**NHL**	**76**	**13**	**17**	**30**	**11**	**13**	**24**	**99**	**1**	**0**	**1**	**130**	**10.0**	**39**	**5**	**58**	**5**	**−19**	....	....	....	....	....	....	....	....
1976-77	**Detroit Red Wings**	**NHL**	**45**	**6**	**3**	**9**	**5**	**2**	**7**	**22**	**0**	**0**	**0**	**40**	**15.0**	**13**	**0**	**23**	**0**	**−10**	....	....	....	....	....	....	....	....
	Rhode Island Reds	AHL	12	8	2	10	....	....	....	12	....	....	....	....	....	....	....	....	....	....	....	....	....	....	....	....	....	....
	Kansas City Blues	CHL	21	14	13	27	....	....	....	33	....	....	....	....	....	....	....	....	....	....	10	2	5	7	14	....	....	....
1977-78	Kansas City Red Wings	CHL	76	23	54	77	....	....	....	155	....	....	....	....	....	....	....	....	....	....	....	....	....	....	....	....	....	....
1978-79	San Diego Hawks	PHL	52	25	27	52	....	....	....	60	....	....	....	....	....	....	....	....	....	....	....	....	....	....	....	....	....	....
1979-80	SIJ Rheem Utrecht	Holland	14	4	9	13	....	....	....	....	....	....	....	....	....	....	....	....	....	....	....	....	....	....	....	....	....	....
	NHL Totals		**201**	**30**	**47**	**77**	**25**	**35**	**60**	**215**	**2**	**0**	**2**	**278**	**10.8**	**110**	**13**	**184**	**6**		....	....	....	....	....	....	....	....

Claimed by **Washington** from **Boston** in Expansion Draft, June 12, 1974. Traded to **Detroit** by **Washington** for Blair Stewart, March 9, 1975.

• BLOUIN, Sylvain

Sylvain Lucien LW – L. 6'2", 207 lbs. b: Montreal, Que., 5/21/1974. NY Rangers' 5th, 104th overall, in 1994.

Season	Club	League	GP	G	A	Pts	AG	AA	APts	PIM	PP	SH	GW	S	%	TGF	PGF	TGA	PGA	+/-	GP	G	A	Pts	PIM	PP	SH	GW
1991-92	Laval Titan	QMJHL	28	0	0	0	....	....	....	23	....	....	....	....	....	....	....	....	....	....	9	0	0	0	35	....	....	....
1992-93	Laval Titan	QMJHL	68	0	10	10	....	....	....	373	....	....	....	....	....	....	....	....	....	....	13	1	0	1	*66	....	....	....
	Laval Titan	Mem-Cup	5	0	2	2	....	....	....	14	....	....	....	....	....	....	....	....	....	....	....	....	....	....	....	....	....	....
1993-94	Laval Titan	QMJHL	62	18	22	40	....	....	....	*492	....	....	....	....	....	....	....	....	....	....	21	4	13	17	*177	....	....	....
	Laval Titan	Mem-Cup	5	0	2	2	....	....	....	*30	....	....	....	....	....	....	....	....	....	....	....	....	....	....	....	....	....	....
1994-95	Chicago Wolves	IHL	1	0	0	0	....	....	....	2	....	....	....	....	....	....	....	....	....	....	....	....	....	....	....	....	....	....
	Charlotte Checkers	ECHL	50	5	7	12	....	....	....	280	....	....	....	....	....	....	....	....	....	....	3	0	0	0	6	....	....	....
	Binghamton Rangers	AHL	10	1	0	1	....	....	....	46	....	....	....	....	....	....	....	....	....	....	2	0	0	0	24	....	....	....
1995-96	Binghamton Rangers	AHL	71	5	8	13	....	....	....	*352	....	....	....	....	....	....	....	....	....	....	4	0	3	3	4	....	....	....
1996-97	**New York Rangers**	**NHL**	**6**	**0**	**0**	**0**	**0**	**0**	**0**	**18**	**0**	**0**	**0**	**1**	**0.0**	**0**	**0**	**1**	**0**	**−1**	....	....	....	....	....	....	....	....
	Binghamton Rangers	AHL	62	13	17	30	....	....	....	301	....	....	....	....	....	....	....	....	....	....	4	2	1	3	16	....	....	....
1997-98	**New York Rangers**	**NHL**	**1**	**0**	**0**	**0**	**0**	**0**	**0**	**5**	**0**	**0**	**0**	**0**	**0.0**	**0**	**0**	**0**	**0**	**0**	....	....	....	....	....	....	....	....
	Hartford Wolf Pack	AHL	53	8	9	17	....	....	....	286	....	....	....	....	....	....	....	....	....	....	9	0	1	1	63	....	....	....
1998-99	**Montreal Canadiens**	**NHL**	**5**	**0**	**0**	**0**	**0**	**0**	**0**	**19**	**0**	**0**	**0**	**1**	**0.0**	**0**	**0**	**0**	**0**	**0**	....	....	....	....	....	....	....	....
	Fredericton Canadiens	AHL	67	6	10	16	....	....	....	333	....	....	....	....	....	....	....	....	....	....	15	2	0	2	*87	....	....	....
99-2000	Worcester IceCats	AHL	70	16	18	34	....	....	....	337	....	....	....	....	....	....	....	....	....	....	8	3	5	8	30	....	....	....
	NHL Totals		**12**	**0**	**0**	**0**	**0**	**0**	**0**	**42**	**0**	**0**	**0**	**2**	**0.0**	**0**	**0**	**1**	**0**		....	....	....	....	....	....	....	....

Traded to **Montreal** by **NY Rangers** with NY Rangers' 6th round choice (later traded to Phoenix, Phoenix selected Erik Leverstrom) in 1999 Entry Draft for Peter Popovic, June 30, 1998. Signed as a free agent by **St. Louis**, August 25, 1999. Signed as a free agent by **Montreal**, July 7, 2000.

• BLUM, John

John Joseph D – R. 6'3", 205 lbs. b: Detroit, MI, 10/8/1959.

Season	Club	League	GP	G	A	Pts	AG	AA	APts	PIM	PP	SH	GW	S	%	TGF	PGF	TGA	PGA	+/-	GP	G	A	Pts	PIM	PP	SH	GW
1976-77	Notre Dame High School	Hi-School	STATISTICS NOT AVAILABLE																									
1977-78	University of Michigan	WCHA	7	0	0	0	....	....	....	4	....	....	....	....	....	....	....	....	....	....	....	....	....	....	....	....	....	....
1978-79	University of Michigan	WCHA	35	1	11	12	....	....	....	87	....	....	....	....	....	....	....	....	....	....	....	....	....	....	....	....	....	....
1979-80	University of Michigan	WCHA	37	9	41	50	....	....	....	79	....	....	....	....	....	....	....	....	....	....	....	....	....	....	....	....	....	....
1980-81	University of Michigan	WCHA	38	9	43	52	....	....	....	93	....	....	....	....	....	....	....	....	....	....	....	....	....	....	....	....	....	....
1981-82	Wichita Wind	CHL	78	8	33	41	....	....	....	247	....	....	....	....	....	....	....	....	....	....	7	0	3	3	24	....	....	....
1982-83	**Edmonton Oilers**	**NHL**	**5**	**0**	**3**	**3**	**0**	**2**	**2**	**24**	**0**	**0**	**0**	**0**	**0.0**	**5**	**0**	**3**	**0**	**2**	....	....	....	....	....	....	....	....
	Moncton Alpines	AHL	76	10	30	40	....	....	....	219	....	....	....	....	....	....	....	....	....	....	....	....	....	....	....	....	....	....
1983-84	**Edmonton Oilers**	**NHL**	**4**	**0**	**1**	**1**	**0**	**1**	**1**	**2**	**0**	**0**	**0**	**3**	**0.0**	**2**	**0**	**2**	**0**	**0**	....	....	....	....	....	....	....	....
	Moncton Alpines	AHL	57	3	22	25	....	....	....	202	....	....	....	....	....	....	....	....	....	....	....	....	....	....	....	....	....	....
	Boston Bruins	**NHL**	**12**	**1**	**1**	**2**	**1**	**1**	**2**	**30**	**0**	**0**	**1**	**9**	**11.1**	**16**	**1**	**11**	**1**	**5**	**3**	**0**	**0**	**0**	**4**	**0**	**0**	**0**
1984-85	**Boston Bruins**	**NHL**	**75**	**3**	**13**	**16**	**2**	**9**	**11**	**263**	**0**	**0**	**0**	**36**	**8.3**	**56**	**0**	**69**	**13**	**0**	**5**	**0**	**0**	**0**	**13**	**0**	**0**	**0**
1985-86	**Boston Bruins**	**NHL**	**61**	**1**	**7**	**8**	**1**	**5**	**6**	**80**	**0**	**0**	**0**	**34**	**2.9**	**45**	**0**	**65**	**28**	**8**	**3**	**0**	**0**	**0**	**6**	**0**	**0**	**0**
	Moncton Golden Flames	AHL	12	1	5	6	....	....	....	37	....	....	....	....	....	....	....	....	....	....	....	....	....	....	....	....	....	....
1986-87	**Washington Capitals**	**NHL**	**66**	**2**	**8**	**10**	**2**	**6**	**8**	**133**	**0**	**0**	**0**	**32**	**6.3**	**25**	**0**	**34**	**10**	**1**	**6**	**0**	**1**	**1**	**4**	**0**	**0**	**0**
1987-88	**Boston Bruins**	**NHL**	**19**	**0**	**1**	**1**	**0**	**1**	**1**	**70**	**0**	**0**	**0**	**6**	**0.0**	**10**	**0**	**17**	**2**	**−5**	**3**	**0**	**1**	**1**	**0**	**0**	**0**	**0**
	Maine Mariners	AHL	43	5	18	23	....	....	....	136	....	....	....	....	....	....	....	....	....	....	8	0	6	6	35	....	....	....
1988-89	**Detroit Red Wings**	**NHL**	**6**	**0**	**0**	**0**	**0**	**0**	**0**	**8**	**0**	**0**	**0**	**3**	**0.0**	**2**	**0**	**5**	**1**	**−2**	....	....	....	....	....	....	....	....
	Adirondack Red Wings	AHL	56	1	19	20	....	....	....	168	....	....	....	....	....	....	....	....	....	....	12	0	1	1	18	....	....	....
1989-90	**Boston Bruins**	**NHL**	**2**	**0**	**0**	**0**	**0**	**0**	**0**	**0**	**0**	**0**	**0**	**0**	**0.0**	**0**	**0**	**2**	**1**	**−1**	....	....	....	....	....	....	....	....
	Maine Mariners	AHL	77	1	20	21	....	....	....	134	....	....	....	....	....	....	....	....	....	....	....	....	....	....	....	....	....	....
1990-91	Maine Mariners	AHL	57	4	8	12	....	....	....	75	....	....	....	....	....	....	....	....	....	....	1	0	0	0	2	....	....	....
1991-92	Capital District Islanders	AHL	51	0	6	6	....	....	....	76	....	....	....	....	....	....	....	....	....	....	1	0	0	0	2	....	....	....
1992-93			DID NOT PLAY																									
1993-94	Daytona Beach Sun Devils	SunHL	12	0	2	2	....	....	....	67	....	....	....	....	....	....	....	....	....	....	....	....	....	....	....	....	....	....
1994-95	Detroit Falcons	ColHL	71	1	14	15	....	....	....	98	....	....	....	....	....	....	....	....	....	....	12	0	2	2	20	....	....	....
	NHL Totals		**250**	**7**	**34**	**41**	**6**	**25**	**31**	**610**	**0**	**0**	**1**	**123**	**5.7**	**161**	**1**	**208**	**56**		**20**	**0**	**2**	**2**	**27**	**0**	**0**	**0**

WCHA Second All-Star Team (1981)

Signed as a free agent by **Edmonton**, May 5, 1981. Traded to **Boston** by **Edmonton** for Larry Melnyk, March 6, 1984. Claimed by **Washington** from **Boston** in Waiver Draft, October 6, 1986. Traded to **Boston** by **Washington** for Boston's 7th round choice (Brad Schlegel) in 1988 Entry Draft, June 1, 1987. Signed as a free agent by **Detroit**, August 12, 1988. Signed as a free agent by **Boston**, July 6, 1989.

• BODAK, Bob

Robert Peter LW – L. 6'2", 200 lbs. b: Thunder Bay, Ont., 5/28/1961.

Season	Club	League	GP	G	A	Pts	AG	AA	APts	PIM	PP	SH	GW	S	%	TGF	PGF	TGA	PGA	+/-	GP	G	A	Pts	PIM	PP	SH	GW
1979-80	Thunder Bay North Stars	TBJHL	34	20	19	39	....	....	....	25	....	....	....	....	....	....	....	....	....	....	....	....	....	....	....	....	....	....
1980-81	Belleville Bulls	OJHL	2	1	0	1	....	....	....	4	....	....	....	....	....	....	....	....	....	....	....	....	....	....	....	....	....	....
1981-82	Lakehead University	GPAC	STATISTICS NOT AVAILABLE																									
1982-83	Lakehead University	GPAC	STATISTICS NOT AVAILABLE																									
1983-84	Lakehead University	GPAC	22	23	24	47	....	....	....	18	....	....	....	....	....	....	....	....	....	....	....	....	....	....	....	....	....	....
1984-85	Springfield Indians	AHL	79	20	25	45	....	....	....	52	....	....	....	....	....	....	....	....	....	....	4	1	0	1	2	....	....	....
1985-86	Springfield Indians	AHL	4	0	0	0	....	....	....	4	....	....	....	....	....	....	....	....	....	....	....	....	....	....	....	....	....	....
	Moncton Golden Flames	AHL	58	27	15	42	....	....	....	114	....	....	....	....	....	....	....	....	....	....	10	3	3	6	0	....	....	....
1986-87	Moncton Golden Flames	AHL	48	11	20	31	....	....	....	75	....	....	....	....	....	....	....	....	....	....	6	1	1	2	18	....	....	....
1987-88	**Calgary Flames**	**NHL**	**3**	**0**	**0**	**0**	**0**	**0**	**0**	**22**	**0**	**0**	**0**	**0**	**0.0**	**0**	**0**	**2**	**0**	**−2**	....	....	....	....	....	....	....	....
	Salt Lake Golden Eagles	IHL	44	12	10	22	....	....	....	117	....	....	....	....	....	....	....	....	....	....	18	1	3	4	74	....	....	....
1988-89	Salt Lake Golden Eagles	IHL	4	0	0	0	....	....	....	2	....	....	....	....	....	....	....	....	....	....	....	....	....	....	....	....	....	....
	Binghamton Whalers	AHL	44	15	25	40	....	....	....	135	....	....	....	....	....	....	....	....	....	....	....	....	....	....	....	....	....	....
1989-90	**Hartford Whalers**	**NHL**	**1**	**0**	**0**	**0**	**0**	**0**	**0**	**7**	**0**	**0**	**0**	**1**	**0.0**	**0**	**0**	**0**	**0**	**0**	....	....	....	....	....	....	....	....
	Binghamton Whalers	AHL	79	32	25	57	....	....	....	59	....	....	....	....	....	....	....	....	....	....	....	....	....	....	....	....	....	....
1990-91	Binghamton Rangers	AHL	27	2	11	13	....	....	....	36	....	....	....	....	....	....	....	....	....	....	....	....	....	....	....	....	....	....
	San Diego Gulls	IHL	17	1	5	6	....	....	....	18	....	....	....	....	....	....	....	....	....	....	....	....	....	....	....	....	....	....
	Albany Choppers	IHL	5	1	1	2	....	....	....	13	....	....	....	....	....	....	....	....	....	....	....	....	....	....	....	....	....	....
1991-92	Erie Panthers	ECHL	28	9	11	20	....	....	....	48	....	....	....	....	....	....	....	....	....	....	....	....	....	....	....	....	....	....
	NHL Totals		**4**	**0**	**0**	**0**	**0**	**0**	**0**	**29**	**0**	**0**	**0**	**1**	**0.0**	**0**	**0**	**2**	**0**		....	....	....	....	....	....	....	....

Signed as a free agent by **Calgary**, January 28, 1986. Signed as a free agent by **Hartford**, May 10, 1989.

• **BODDY, Gregg** Gregg Allan D – L. 6'2", 200 lbs. b: Ponoka, Alta., 3/19/1949. Los Angeles' 2nd, 27th overall, in 1969.

Season	Club	League	GP	G	A	Pts	AG	AA	APts	PIM	PP	SH	GW	S	%	TGF	PGF	TGA	PGA	+/–	Playoffs GP	G	A	Pts	PIM	PP	SH	GW
1966-67	Edmonton Oil Kings	CMJHL	55	1	5	6	....	....	....	42	....	....	....	....	....	....	....	....	....	....	9	0	1	1	12	....	....	....
1967-68	Edmonton Oil Kings	WCJHL	59	3	14	17	....	....	....	101	....	....	....	....	....	....	....	....	....	....	13	1	1	2	20	....	....	....
1968-69	Edmonton Oil Kings	WCJHL	59	1	21	22	....	....	....	119	....	....	....	....	....	....	....	....	....	....	17	0	7	7	17	....	....	....
1969-70	Springfield Kings	AHL	68	2	9	11	....	....	....	70	....	....	....	....	....	....	....	....	....	....	14	0	3	3	14	....	....	....
1970-71	Montreal Voyageurs	AHL	63	0	17	17	....	....	....	108	....	....	....	....	....	....	....	....	....	....	3	0	0	0	0	....	....	....
1971-72	**Vancouver Canucks**	**NHL**	**40**	**2**	**5**	**7**	**2**	**4**	**6**	**45**	**0**	**0**	**1**	**29**	**6.9**	**28**	**0**	**35**	**9**	**2**	....	....	....	....	....	....	....	....
	Rochester Americans	AHL	28	2	6	8	....	....	....	77	....	....	....	....	....	....	....	....	....	....	....	....	....	....	....	....	....	....
1972-73	**Vancouver Canucks**	**NHL**	**74**	**3**	**11**	**14**	**3**	**9**	**12**	**70**	**1**	**0**	**0**	**54**	**5.6**	**44**	**4**	**87**	**12**	**–35**	....	....	....	....	....	....	....	....
1973-74	**Vancouver Canucks**	**NHL**	**53**	**2**	**10**	**12**	**2**	**8**	**10**	**59**	**0**	**0**	**1**	**52**	**3.8**	**34**	**3**	**48**	**13**	**–4**	....	....	....	....	....	....	....	....
	Seattle Totems	WHL	4	0	1	1	....	....	....	0	....	....	....	....	....	....	....	....	....	....	....	....	....	....	....	....	....	....
1974-75	**Vancouver Canucks**	**NHL**	**72**	**11**	**12**	**23**	**10**	**9**	**19**	**56**	**2**	**1**	**1**	**83**	**13.3**	**50**	**7**	**63**	**15**	**–5**	**3**	**0**	**0**	**0**	**0**	**0**	**0**	**0**
1975-76	**Vancouver Canucks**	**NHL**	**34**	**5**	**6**	**11**	**4**	**4**	**8**	**33**	**0**	**0**	**1**	**28**	**17.9**	**17**	**2**	**17**	**0**	**–2**	....	....	....	....	....	....	....	....
	Tulsa Oilers	CHL	24	0	9	9	....	....	....	29	....	....	....	....	....	....	....	....	....	....	9	0	2	2	19	....	....	....
1976-77	San Diego Mariners	WHA	18	1	2	3	....	....	....	19	....	....	....	....	....	....	....	....	....	....	....	....	....	....	....	....	....	....
	Edmonton Oilers	WHA	46	1	17	18	....	....	....	41	....	....	....	....	....	....	....	....	....	....	4	1	2	3	14	....	....	....
1977-78	Jujyo-Seishi	Japan	STATISTICS NOT AVAILABLE																									
1978-79	Jujyo-Seishi	Japan	20	6	10	16	....	....	....	44	....	....	....	....	....	....	....	....	....	....	....	....	....	....	....	....	....	....
	NHL Totals		**273**	**23**	**44**	**67**	**21**	**34**	**55**	**263**	**3**	**1**	**4**	**246**	**9.3**	**173**	**16**	**250**	**49**		**3**	**0**	**0**	**0**	**0**	**0**	**0**	**0**
	Other Major League Totals		64	2	19	21				60	....	....	....	....	....	....	....	....	....	....	4	1	2	3	14	....	....	....

Traded to **Montreal** by **LA Kings** with Leon Rochefort and Wayne Thomas for Larry Mickey, Lucien Grenier and Jack Norris, May 22, 1970. Traded to **Vancouver** by **Montreal** for cash and Vancouver's 3rd round choice (Jim Cahoon) in 1971 Amateur Draft, May 25, 1971. Selected by **New England** (WHA) in 1972 WHA General Player Draft, February 12, 1972. WHA rights traded to **San Diego** (WHA) by **New England** (WHA) for cash, September, 1976. Traded to **Edmonton** (WHA) by **San Diego** (WHA) for Larry Hornung, November, 1976.

• **BODGER, Doug** D – L. 6'2", 210 lbs. b: Chemainus, B.C., 6/18/1966. Pittsburgh's 2nd, 9th overall, in 1984.

Season	Club	League	GP	G	A	Pts	AG	AA	APts	PIM	PP	SH	GW	S	%	TGF	PGF	TGA	PGA	+/–	Playoffs GP	G	A	Pts	PIM	PP	SH	GW
1981-82	Cowichan Valley Reps	BCAHA	STATISTICS NOT AVAILABLE																									
1982-83	Kamloops Jr. Oilers	WHL	72	26	66	92	....	....	....	98	....	....	....	....	....	....	....	....	....	....	7	0	5	5	2	....	....	....
1983-84	Kamloops Jr. Oilers	WHL	70	21	77	98	....	....	....	90	....	....	....	....	....	....	....	....	....	....	17	2	15	17	12	....	....	....
	Kamloops Jr. Oilers	Mem-Cup	4	0	1	1	....	....	....	2	....	....	....	....	....	....	....	....	....	....	....	....	....	....	....	....	....	....
1984-85	**Pittsburgh Penguins**	**NHL**	**65**	**5**	**26**	**31**	**4**	**18**	**22**	**67**	**3**	**0**	**1**	**119**	**4.2**	**93**	**23**	**115**	**21**	**–24**	....	....	....	....	....	....	....	....
1985-86	**Pittsburgh Penguins**	**NHL**	**79**	**4**	**33**	**37**	**3**	**22**	**25**	**63**	**1**	**0**	**1**	**140**	**2.9**	**120**	**45**	**108**	**36**	**3**	....	....	....	....	....	....	....	....
1986-87	**Pittsburgh Penguins**	**NHL**	**76**	**11**	**38**	**49**	**9**	**28**	**37**	**52**	**5**	**0**	**1**	**176**	**6.3**	**118**	**43**	**95**	**26**	**6**	....	....	....	....	....	....	....	....
	Canada	WEC-A	10	1	1	2	....	....	....	4	....	....	....	....	....	....	....	....	....	....	....	....	....	....	....	....	....	....
1987-88	**Pittsburgh Penguins**	**NHL**	**69**	**14**	**31**	**45**	**12**	**22**	**34**	**103**	**13**	**0**	**1**	**184**	**7.6**	**120**	**69**	**108**	**53**	**–4**	....	....	....	....	....	....	....	....
1988-89	**Pittsburgh Penguins**	**NHL**	**10**	**1**	**4**	**5**	**1**	**3**	**4**	**7**	**0**	**0**	**0**	**22**	**4.5**	**17**	**8**	**3**	**0**	**6**	....	....	....	....	....	....	....	....
	Buffalo Sabres	**NHL**	**61**	**7**	**40**	**47**	**6**	**28**	**34**	**52**	**6**	**0**	**1**	**134**	**5.2**	**111**	**47**	**77**	**22**	**9**	**5**	**1**	**1**	**2**	**11**	**1**	**0**	**0**
1989-90	**Buffalo Sabres**	**NHL**	**71**	**12**	**36**	**48**	**10**	**26**	**36**	**64**	**8**	**0**	**1**	**167**	**7.2**	**120**	**56**	**86**	**22**	**0**	**6**	**1**	**5**	**6**	**6**	**0**	**0**	**0**
1990-91	**Buffalo Sabres**	**NHL**	**58**	**5**	**23**	**28**	**5**	**17**	**22**	**54**	**2**	**0**	**0**	**139**	**3.6**	**92**	**34**	**84**	**18**	**–8**	**4**	**0**	**1**	**1**	**0**	**0**	**0**	**0**
1991-92	**Buffalo Sabres**	**NHL**	**73**	**11**	**35**	**46**	**10**	**26**	**36**	**108**	**4**	**0**	**1**	**180**	**6.1**	**142**	**71**	**101**	**31**	**1**	**7**	**2**	**1**	**3**	**2**	**2**	**0**	**1**
1992-93	**Buffalo Sabres**	**NHL**	**81**	**9**	**45**	**54**	**7**	**31**	**38**	**87**	**6**	**0**	**0**	**154**	**5.8**	**158**	**64**	**122**	**42**	**14**	**8**	**2**	**3**	**5**	**0**	**2**	**0**	**0**
1993-94	**Buffalo Sabres**	**NHL**	**75**	**7**	**32**	**39**	**6**	**25**	**31**	**76**	**5**	**1**	**1**	**144**	**4.9**	**110**	**50**	**80**	**28**	**8**	**7**	**0**	**3**	**3**	**6**	**0**	**0**	**0**
1994-95	**Buffalo Sabres**	**NHL**	**44**	**3**	**17**	**20**	**5**	**25**	**30**	**47**	**2**	**0**	**0**	**87**	**3.4**	**50**	**30**	**38**	**15**	**–3**	**5**	**0**	**4**	**4**	**0**	**0**	**0**	**0**
1995-96	**Buffalo Sabres**	**NHL**	**16**	**0**	**5**	**5**	**0**	**4**	**4**	**18**	**0**	**0**	**0**	**27**	**0.0**	**16**	**9**	**23**	**10**	**–6**	....	....	....	....	....	....	....	....
	San Jose Sharks	**NHL**	**57**	**4**	**19**	**23**	**4**	**16**	**20**	**50**	**3**	**0**	**0**	**94**	**4.3**	**68**	**27**	**85**	**26**	**–18**	....	....	....	....	....	....	....	....
	Canada	WC-A	8	0	3	3	....	....	....	0	....	....	....	....	....	....	....	....	....	....	....	....	....	....	....	....	....	....
1996-97	**San Jose Sharks**	**NHL**	**81**	**1**	**15**	**16**	**1**	**13**	**14**	**64**	**0**	**0**	**1**	**96**	**1.0**	**66**	**18**	**94**	**32**	**–14**	....	....	....	....	....	....	....	....
1997-98	**San Jose Sharks**	**NHL**	**28**	**4**	**6**	**10**	**5**	**6**	**11**	**32**	**0**	**0**	**1**	**41**	**9.8**	**29**	**9**	**33**	**13**	**0**	....	....	....	....	....	....	....	....
	New Jersey Devils	**NHL**	**49**	**5**	**5**	**10**	**6**	**5**	**11**	**25**	**3**	**0**	**0**	**55**	**9.1**	**31**	**9**	**25**	**2**	**–1**	**5**	**0**	**0**	**0**	**0**	**0**	**0**	**0**
1998-99	**Los Angeles Kings**	**NHL**	**65**	**3**	**11**	**14**	**4**	**11**	**15**	**34**	**0**	**0**	**0**	**67**	**4.5**	**48**	**9**	**53**	**15**	**1**	....	....	....	....	....	....	....	....
	Canada	WC-A	10	0	2	2	....	....	....	4	....	....	....	....	....	....	....	....	....	....	....	....	....	....	....	....	....	....
99-2000	**Vancouver Canucks**	**NHL**	**13**	**0**	**1**	**1**	**0**	**1**	**1**	**4**	**0**	**0**	**0**	**11**	**0.0**	**4**	**0**	**15**	**5**	**–6**	....	....	....	....	....	....	....	....
	NHL Totals		**1071**	**106**	**422**	**528**	**98**	**327**	**425**	**1007**	**61**	**1**	**10**	**2037**	**5.2**	**1513**	**621**	**1345**	**417**		**47**	**6**	**18**	**24**	**25**	**5**	**0**	**1**

WHL Second All-Star Team (1983) • WHL West First All-Star Team (1984)

Traded to **Buffalo** by **Pittsburgh** wih Darrin Shannon for Tom Barrasso and Buffalo's 3rd round choice (Joe Dziedzic) in 1990 Entry Draft, November 12, 1988. Traded to **San Jose** by **Buffalo** for Vaclav Varada, Martin Spanhel and Philadelphia's 1st (previously acquired by San Jose — later traded to Phoenix — Phoenix selected Daniel Briere) and 4th (previously acquired, Buffalo selected Mike Martone) round choices in 1996 Entry Draft, November 16, 1995. Traded to **New Jersey** by **San Jose** with Dody Wood for John MacLean and Ken Sutton, December 7, 1997. Traded to **LA Kings** by **New Jersey** for Boston's 4th round choice (previously acquired, New Jersey selected Pierre Dagenais) in 1998 Entry Draft, June 18, 1998. Signed as a free agent by **Vancouver**, August 18, 1999. • Officially announced retirement, December 14, 1999.

• **BOEHM, Ron** Ronald John LW – L. 5'8", 160 lbs. b: Saskatoon, Sask., 8/14/1943.

Season	Club	League	GP	G	A	Pts	AG	AA	APts	PIM	PP	SH	GW	S	%	TGF	PGF	TGA	PGA	+/–	Playoffs GP	G	A	Pts	PIM	PP	SH	GW
1960-61	Estevan Bruins	SJHL	7	0	1	1	....	....	....	0	....	....	....	....	....	....	....	....	....	....	....	....	....	....	....	....	....	....
1961-62	Weyburn Elks	SJHL-B	STATISTICS NOT AVAILABLE																									
1962-63	Estevan Bruins	SJHL	54	15	31	46	....	....	....	42	....	....	....	....	....	....	....	....	....	....	17	3	6	9	10	....	....	....
	Estevan Bruins	Mem-Cup	6	1	1	2	....	....	....	6	....	....	....	....	....	....	....	....	....	....	....	....	....	....	....	....	....	....
1963-64	Estevan Bruins	SJHL	61	35	53	88	....	....	....	80	....	....	....	....	....	....	....	....	....	....	11	7	11	18	18	....	....	....
	Estevan Bruins	Mem-Cup	5	2	0	2	....	....	....	0	....	....	....	....	....	....	....	....	....	....	....	....	....	....	....	....	....	....
	Edmonton Oil Kings	Mem-Cup	4	1	0	1	....	....	....	0	....	....	....	....	....	....	....	....	....	....	....	....	....	....	....	....	....	....
1964-65	Minneapolis Bruins	CPHL	49	12	19	31	....	....	....	42	....	....	....	....	....	....	....	....	....	....	4	0	1	1	2	....	....	....
1965-66	Minnesota Rangers	CPHL	70	8	20	28	....	....	....	37	....	....	....	....	....	....	....	....	....	....	7	0	5	5	4	....	....	....
1966-67	Vancouver Canucks	WHL	71	18	24	42	....	....	....	49	....	....	....	....	....	....	....	....	....	....	8	2	0	2	2	....	....	....
1967-68	**Oakland Seals**	**NHL**	**16**	**2**	**1**	**3**	**2**	**1**	**3**	**10**	**1**	**0**	**0**	**18**	**11.1**	**6**	**1**	**14**	**4**	**–5**	....	....	....	....	....	....	....	....
	Vancouver Canucks	WHL	43	5	11	16	....	....	....	34	....	....	....	....	....	....	....	....	....	....	....	....	....	....	....	....	....	....
1968-69	Omaha Knights	CHL	67	12	16	28	....	....	....	41	....	....	....	....	....	....	....	....	....	....	7	3	1	4	7	....	....	....
1969-70	Omaha Knights	CHL	65	18	25	43	....	....	....	55	....	....	....	....	....	....	....	....	....	....	7	1	4	5	2	....	....	....
1970-71	Seattle Totems	WHL	72	10	26	36	....	....	....	39	....	....	....	....	....	....	....	....	....	....	....	....	....	....	....	....	....	....
1971-72	Boston Braves	AHL	74	18	37	55	....	....	....	61	....	....	....	....	....	....	....	....	....	....	9	2	3	5	4	....	....	....
1972-73	Boston Braves	AHL	28	6	16	22	....	....	....	28	....	....	....	....	....	....	....	....	....	....	4	1	0	1	4	....	....	....
1973-74	Boston Braves	AHL	76	18	23	41	....	....	....	60	....	....	....	....	....	....	....	....	....	....	....	....	....	....	....	....	....	....
1974-75	Binghamton Dusters	NAHL	39	9	23	32	....	....	....	61	....	....	....	....	....	....	....	....	....	....	15	3	4	7	4	....	....	....
	NHL Totals		**16**	**2**	**1**	**3**	**2**	**1**	**3**	**10**	**1**	**0**	**0**	**18**	**11.1**	**6**	**1**	**14**	**4**		....	....	....	....	....	....	....	....

Won WHL Rookie of the Year Award (1967)

• Loaned to **Edmonton** (CAHL) by **Estevan** (SJHL) for Memorial Cup playoffs, April, 1964. Claimed by **NY Rangers** (Vancouver-WHL) from **Boston** in Inter-League Draft, June 9, 1965. Claimed by **Oakland** from **NY Rangers** in Expansion Draft, June 6, 1967. Traded to **NY Rangers** by **Oakland** for cash, September 13, 1968. Claimed by **Cleveland** (AHL) from **NY Rangers** in Reverse Draft, June, 1971. Traded to **Boston** by **Cleveland** (AHL) for cash, June, 1971.

• **BOGUNIECKI, Eric** C – R. 5'8", 192 lbs. b: New Haven, CT, 5/6/1975. St. Louis' 6th, 193rd overall, in 1993.

Season	Club	League	GP	G	A	Pts	AG	AA	APts	PIM	PP	SH	GW	S	%	TGF	PGF	TGA	PGA	+/–	Playoffs GP	G	A	Pts	PIM	PP	SH	GW
1992-93	Westminster Prep School	Hi-School	24	30	24	54	....	....	....	55	....	....	....	....	....	....	....	....	....	....	....	....	....	....	....	....	....	....
1993-94	University of New Hampshire	H-East	40	17	16	33	....	....	....	66	....	....	....	....	....	....	....	....	....	....	....	....	....	....	....	....	....	....
1994-95	University of New Hampshire	H-East	34	12	16	28	....	....	....	62	....	....	....	....	....	....	....	....	....	....	....	....	....	....	....	....	....	....
1995-96	University of New Hampshire	H-East	32	23	28	51	....	....	....	46	....	....	....	....	....	....	....	....	....	....	....	....	....	....	....	....	....	....
1996-97	University of New Hampshire	H-East	36	26	31	57	....	....	....	58	....	....	....	....	....	....	....	....	....	....	....	....	....	....	....	....	....	....
1997-98	Dayton Bombers	ECHL	26	19	18	37	....	....	....	36	....	....	....	....	....	....	....	....	....	....	....	....	....	....	....	....	....	....
	Fort Wayne Komets	IHL	35	4	8	12	....	....	....	29	....	....	....	....	....	....	....	....	....	....	4	1	2	3	10	....	....	....
1998-99	Fort Wayne Komets	IHL	72	32	34	66	....	....	....	100	....	....	....	....	....	....	....	....	....	....	2	0	1	1	2	....	....	....

			REGULAR SEASON																		PLAYOFFS							
Season	Club	League	GP	G	A	Pts	AG	AA	APts	PIM	PP	SH	GW	S	%	TGF	PGF	TGA	PGA	+/-	GP	G	A	Pts	PIM	PP	SH	GW
99-2000	**Florida Panthers**	**NHL**	**4**	**0**	**0**	**0**	**0**	**0**	**0**	**2**	**0**	**0**	**0**	**5**	**0.0**	**0**	**0**	**1**	**0**	**–1**	....	....	....	....	....	....	....	....
	Louisville Panthers	AHL	57	33	42	75	....	....	....	148	....	....	....	....	....	....	....	....	....	....	4	3	2	5	20	....	....	....
	United States	WC-A	7	0	1	1	....	....	....	2	....	....	....	....	....	....	....	....	....	....	....	....	....	....	....	....	....	....
	NHL Totals		**4**	**0**	**0**	**0**	**0**	**0**	**0**	**2**	**0**	**0**	**0**	**5**	**0.0**	**0**	**0**	**1**	**0**		....	....	....	....	....	....	....	....

Hockey East Second All-Star Team (1997)

Signed as a free agent by **Florida**, July 7, 1999.

• BOH, Rick

Richard C – R. 5'10", 185 lbs. b: Kamloops, B.C., 5/18/1964. Minnesota's 2nd, 9th overall, in 1987 Supplemental Draft.

Season	Club	League	GP	G	A	Pts	AG	AA	APts	PIM	PP	SH	GW	S	%	TGF	PGF	TGA	PGA	+/-	GP	G	A	Pts	PIM	PP	SH	GW
1982-83	Penticton Knights	BCJHL	41	18	49	67	....	....	....	139	....	....	....	....	....	....	....	....	....	....	....	....	....	....	....	....	....	....
1983-84	Colorado College	WCHA	27	1	5	6	....	....	....	12	....	....	....	....	....	....	....	....	....	....	....	....	....	....	....	....	....	....
1984-85	Colorado College	WCHA	38	10	18	28	....	....	....	24	....	....	....	....	....	....	....	....	....	....	....	....	....	....	....	....	....	....
1985-86	Colorado College	WCHA	40	30	29	59	....	....	....	14	....	....	....	....	....	....	....	....	....	....	....	....	....	....	....	....	....	....
1986-87	Colorado College	WCHA	38	22	42	64	....	....	....	37	....	....	....	....	....	....	....	....	....	....	....	....	....	....	....	....	....	....
	Canada	Nat-Team	10	3	3	6	....	....	....	0	....	....	....	....	....	....	....	....	....	....	....	....	....	....	....	....	....	....
1987-88	**Minnesota North Stars**	**NHL**	**8**	**2**	**1**	**3**	**2**	**1**	**3**	**4**	**0**	**0**	**0**	**8**	**25.0**	**5**	**0**	**4**	**0**	**1**	....	....	....	....	....	....	....	....
	Kalamazoo Wings	IHL	75	26	41	67	....	....	....	45	....	....	....	....	....	....	....	....	....	....	7	2	1	3	5	....	....	....
1988-89	HC Fiemme	Italy	31	29	37	66	....	....	....	34	....	....	....	....	....	....	....	....	....	....	....	....	....	....	....	....	....	....
1989-90			STATISTICS NOT AVAILABLE																									
1990-91	STIJ Geleen	Holland	34	32	45	77	....	....	....	14	....	....	....	....	....	....	....	....	....	....	4	2	2	4	4	....	....	....
1991-92	STIJ Geleen	Holland	38	*37	49	*86	....	....	....	....	....	....	....	....	....	....	....	....	....	....	....	....	....	....	....	....	....	....
1992-93	STIJ Geleen	Holland	24	21	25	46	....	....	....	....	....	....	....	....	....	....	....	....	....	....	6	6	5	*11	....	....	....	....
	NHL Totals		**8**	**2**	**1**	**3**	**2**	**1**	**3**	**4**	**0**	**0**	**0**	**8**	**25.0**	**5**	**0**	**4**	**0**		....	....	....	....	....	....	....	....

WCHA Second All-Star Team (1987)

• BOHONOS, Lonny

Lonny W. RW – R. 5'11", 190 lbs. b: Winnipeg, Man., 5/20/1973.

Season	Club	League	GP	G	A	Pts	AG	AA	APts	PIM	PP	SH	GW	S	%	TGF	PGF	TGA	PGA	+/-	GP	G	A	Pts	PIM	PP	SH	GW
1990-91	Winnipeg South Blues	MJHL	46	33	22	55	....	....	....	70	....	....	....	....	....	....	....	....	....	....	....	....	....	....	....	....	....	....
1991-92	Winnipeg South Blues	MJHL	40	53	36	89	....	....	....	42	....	....	....	....	....	....	....	....	....	....	....	....	....	....	....	....	....	....
	Moose Jaw Warriors	WHL	8	1	1	2	....	....	....	0	....	....	....	....	....	....	....	....	....	....	....	....	....	....	....	....	....	....
1992-93	Seattle Thunderbirds	WHL	46	13	13	26	....	....	....	27	....	....	....	....	....	....	....	....	....	....	....	....	....	....	....	....	....	....
	Portland Winter Hawks	WHL	27	20	17	37	....	....	....	16	....	....	....	....	....	....	....	....	....	....	15	8	13	21	19	....	....	....
1993-94	Portland Winter Hawks	WHL	70	*62	*90	*152	....	....	....	80	....	....	....	....	....	....	....	....	....	....	10	8	11	19	13	....	....	....
1994-95	Syracuse Crunch	AHL	67	30	45	75	....	....	....	71	....	....	....	....	....	....	....	....	....	....	....	....	....	....	....	....	....	....
1995-96	**Vancouver Canucks**	**NHL**	**3**	**0**	**1**	**1**	**0**	**1**	**1**	**0**	**0**	**0**	**0**	**3**	**0.0**	**1**	**0**	**0**	**0**	**1**	....	....	....	....	....	....	....	....
	Syracuse Crunch	AHL	74	40	39	79	....	....	....	82	....	....	....	....	....	....	....	....	....	....	16	14	8	22	16	....	....	....
1996-97	**Vancouver Canucks**	**NHL**	**36**	**11**	**11**	**22**	**12**	**10**	**22**	**10**	**2**	**0**	**1**	**67**	**16.4**	**28**	**9**	**22**	**0**	**–3**	....	....	....	....	....	....	....	....
	Syracuse Crunch	AHL	41	22	30	52	....	....	....	28	....	....	....	....	....	....	....	....	....	....	3	2	2	4	4	....	....	....
1997-98	**Vancouver Canucks**	**NHL**	**31**	**2**	**1**	**3**	**2**	**1**	**3**	**4**	**0**	**0**	**0**	**37**	**5.4**	**3**	**0**	**12**	**0**	**–9**	....	....	....	....	....	....	....	....
	Syracuse Crunch	AHL	17	12	12	24	....	....	....	8	....	....	....	....	....	....	....	....	....	....	....	....	....	....	....	....	....	....
	Toronto Maple Leafs	**NHL**	**6**	**3**	**3**	**6**	**4**	**3**	**7**	**4**	**0**	**0**	**0**	**13**	**23.1**	**7**	**1**	**5**	**0**	**1**	....	....	....	....	....	....	....	....
	St. John's Maple Leafs	AHL	11	7	9	16	....	....	....	10	....	....	....	....	....	....	....	....	....	....	2	1	1	2	2	....	....	....
1998-99	**Toronto Maple Leafs**	**NHL**	**7**	**3**	**0**	**3**	**4**	**0**	**4**	**4**	**0**	**0**	**0**	**13**	**23.1**	**5**	**1**	**2**	**1**	**3**	**9**	**3**	**6**	**9**	**2**	**0**	**0**	**0**
	St. John's Maple Leafs	AHL	70	34	48	82	....	....	....	40	....	....	....	....	....	....	....	....	....	....	5	2	4	6	2	....	....	....
99-2000	Manitoba Moose	IHL	63	18	33	51	....	....	....	45	....	....	....	....	....	....	....	....	....	....	2	0	0	0	2	....	....	....
	NHL Totals		**83**	**19**	**16**	**35**	**22**	**15**	**37**	**22**	**2**	**0**	**1**	**133**	**14.3**	**44**	**11**	**41**	**1**		**9**	**3**	**6**	**9**	**2**	**0**	**0**	**0**

WHL West First All-Star Team (1994) • Canadian Major Junior First All-Star Team (1994)

Signed as a free agent by **Vancouver**, May 31, 1994. Traded to **Toronto** by **Vancouver** for Brandon Convery, March 7, 1998.

• BOIKOV, Alexander

D – L. 6', 180 lbs. b: Chelyabinsk, USSR, 2/7/1975.

Season	Club	League	GP	G	A	Pts	AG	AA	APts	PIM	PP	SH	GW	S	%	TGF	PGF	TGA	PGA	+/-	GP	G	A	Pts	PIM	PP	SH	GW
1993-94	Victoria Cougars	WHL	70	4	31	35	....	....	....	250	....	....	....	....	....	....	....	....	....	....	....	....	....	....	....	....	....	....
1994-95	Prince George Cougars	WHL	46	5	23	28	....	....	....	115	....	....	....	....	....	....	....	....	....	....	....	....	....	....	....	....	....	....
	Russia	WJC-A	7	0	0	0	....	....	....	0	....	....	....	....	....	....	....	....	....	....	....	....	....	....	....	....	....	....
	Tri-City Americans	WHL	24	3	13	16	....	....	....	63	....	....	....	....	....	....	....	....	....	....	17	1	7	8	30	....	....	....
1995-96	Tri-City Americans	WHL	71	3	49	52	....	....	....	230	....	....	....	....	....	....	....	....	....	....	11	2	4	6	28	....	....	....
1996-97	Kentucky Thoroughblades	AHL	61	1	19	20	....	....	....	182	....	....	....	....	....	....	....	....	....	....	4	0	1	1	4	....	....	....
1997-98	Kentucky Thoroughblades	AHL	69	5	14	19	....	....	....	153	....	....	....	....	....	....	....	....	....	....	3	0	1	1	8	....	....	....
1998-99	Kentucky Thoroughblades	AHL	55	5	13	18	....	....	....	116	....	....	....	....	....	....	....	....	....	....	....	....	....	....	....	....	....	....
	Rochester Americans	AHL	13	0	1	1	....	....	....	15	....	....	....	....	....	....	....	....	....	....	17	1	3	4	24	....	....	....
99-2000	**Nashville Predators**	**NHL**	**2**	**0**	**0**	**0**	**0**	**0**	**0**	**2**	**0**	**0**	**0**	**1**	**0.0**	**0**	**0**	**0**	**0**	**0**	....	....	....	....	....	....	....	....
	Milwaukee Admirals	IHL	58	1	6	7	....	....	....	120	....	....	....	....	....	....	....	....	....	....	....	....	....	....	....	....	....	....
	NHL Totals		**2**	**0**	**0**	**0**	**0**	**0**	**0**	**2**	**0**	**0**	**0**	**1**	**0.0**	**0**	**0**	**0**	**0**		....	....	....	....	....	....	....	....

Signed as a free agent by **San Jose**, April 22, 1996. Signed as a free agent by **Nashville**, July 24, 1999.

• BOILEAU, Patrick

D – R. 6', 202 lbs. b: Montreal, Que., 2/22/1975. Washington's 3rd, 69th overall, in 1993.

Season	Club	League	GP	G	A	Pts	AG	AA	APts	PIM	PP	SH	GW	S	%	TGF	PGF	TGA	PGA	+/-	GP	G	A	Pts	PIM	PP	SH	GW
1991-92	Laval Regents	QAAA	42	9	36	45	....	....	....	94	....	....	....	....	....	....	....	....	....	....	....	....	....	....	....	....	....	....
1992-93	Laval Titan	QMJHL	69	4	19	23	....	....	....	73	....	....	....	....	....	....	....	....	....	....	13	1	2	3	10	....	....	....
	Laval Titan	Mem-Cup	5	0	1	1	....	....	....	4	....	....	....	....	....	....	....	....	....	....	....	....	....	....	....	....	....	....
1993-94	Laval Titan	QMJHL	64	13	57	70	....	....	....	56	....	....	....	....	....	....	....	....	....	....	21	1	7	8	24	....	....	....
	Laval Titan	Mem-Cup	5	0	0	0	....	....	....	6	....	....	....	....	....	....	....	....	....	....	....	....	....	....	....	....	....	....
1994-95	Laval Titan	QMJHL	38	8	25	33	....	....	....	46	....	....	....	....	....	....	....	....	....	....	20	4	16	20	24	....	....	....
1995-96	Portland Pirates	AHL	78	10	28	38	....	....	....	41	....	....	....	....	....	....	....	....	....	....	19	1	3	4	12	....	....	....
1996-97	**Washington Capitals**	**NHL**	**1**	**0**	**0**	**0**	**0**	**0**	**0**	**0**	**0**	**0**	**0**	**0**	**0.0**	**0**	**0**	**0**	**0**	**0**	....	....	....	....	....	....	....	....
	Portland Pirates	AHL	67	16	28	44	....	....	....	63	....	....	....	....	....	....	....	....	....	....	5	1	1	2	4	....	....	....
1997-98	Portland Pirates	AHL	47	6	21	27	....	....	....	53	....	....	....	....	....	....	....	....	....	....	10	0	1	1	8	....	....	....
1998-99	**Washington Capitals**	**NHL**	**4**	**0**	**1**	**1**	**0**	**1**	**1**	**2**	**0**	**0**	**0**	**7**	**0.0**	**2**	**1**	**5**	**0**	**–4**	....	....	....	....	....	....	....	....
	Portland Pirates	AHL	52	6	18	24	....	....	....	52	....	....	....	....	....	....	....	....	....	....	....	....	....	....	....	....	....	....
	Indianapolis Ice	IHL	29	8	13	21	....	....	....	27	....	....	....	....	....	....	....	....	....	....	4	0	1	1	2	....	....	....
99-2000	Portland Pirates	AHL	63	2	15	17	....	....	....	61	....	....	....	....	....	....	....	....	....	....	4	0	0	0	4	....	....	....
	NHL Totals		**5**	**0**	**1**	**1**	**0**	**1**	**1**	**2**	**0**	**0**	**0**	**7**	**0.0**	**2**	**1**	**5**	**0**		....	....	....	....	....	....	....	....

Canadian Major Junior Scholastic Player of the Year (1994)

Loaned to **Indianapolis** (IHL) by **Portland** (AHL), February 4, 1999.

• BOIMISTRUCK, Fred

"Broomstick" D – R. 5'11", 190 lbs. b: Sudbury, Ont., 1/14/1962. Toronto's 3rd, 43rd overall, in 1980.

Season	Club	League	GP	G	A	Pts	AG	AA	APts	PIM	PP	SH	GW	S	%	TGF	PGF	TGA	PGA	+/-	GP	G	A	Pts	PIM	PP	SH	GW
1978-79	Streetsville Derbys	OHA-B	STATISTICS NOT AVAILABLE																									
1979-80	Cornwall Royals	QMJHL	70	12	34	46	....	....	....	99	....	....	....	....	....	....	....	....	....	....	11	0	8	8	6	....	....	....
	Cornwall Royals	Mem-Cup	5	3	2	5	....	....	....	2	....	....	....	....	....	....	....	....	....	....	....	....	....	....	....	....	....	....
1980-81	Cornwall Royals	QMJHL	68	22	48	70	....	....	....	158	....	....	....	....	....	....	....	....	....	....	18	4	11	15	61	....	....	....
	Canada	WJC-A	5	3	0	3	....	....	....	8	....	....	....	....	....	....	....	....	....	....	....	....	....	....	....	....	....	....
	Cornwall Royals	Mem-Cup	5	0	3	3	....	....	....	6	....	....	....	....	....	....	....	....	....	....	....	....	....	....	....	....	....	....
1981-82	**Toronto Maple Leafs**	**NHL**	**57**	**2**	**11**	**13**	**2**	**7**	**9**	**32**	**0**	**0**	**1**	**48**	**4.2**	**67**	**1**	**70**	**13**	**9**	....	....	....	....	....	....	....	....
1982-83	**Toronto Maple Leafs**	**NHL**	**26**	**2**	**3**	**5**	**2**	**2**	**4**	**13**	**0**	**0**	**0**	**26**	**7.7**	**28**	**3**	**35**	**7**	**–3**	....	....	....	....	....	....	....	....
	St. Catharines Saints	AHL	50	6	23	29	....	....	....	32	....	....	....	....	....	....	....	....	....	....	....	....	....	....	....	....	....	....
1983-84	St. Catharines Saints	AHL	80	2	28	30	....	....	....	68	....	....	....	....	....	....	....	....	....	....	7	1	0	1	19	....	....	....

			REGULAR SEASON																		PLAYOFFS							
Season	**Club**	**League**	**GP**	**G**	**A**	**Pts**	**AG**	**AA**	**APts**	**PIM**	**PP**	**SH**	**GW**	**S**	**%**	**TGF**	**PGF**	**TGA**	**PGA**	**+/–**	**GP**	**G**	**A**	**Pts**	**PIM**	**PP**	**SH**	**GW**
1984-85	Fort Wayne Komets	IHL	2	0	1	1	....	....	....	5	....	....	....	....	....	....	....	....	....	....	....	....	....	....	....	....	....	....
	HC Langnau	Switz.	6	1	2	3	....	....	....	....	....	....	....	....	....	....	....	....	....	....	....	....	....	....	....	....	....	....
1985-86	Flint Spirit	IHL	17	3	6	9	....	....	....	15	....	....	....	....	....	....	....	....	....	....	....	....	....	....	....	....	....	....
1986-87	Brantford Mott's Clamatos	OHA-Sr.	32	1	8	9	....	....	....	51	....	....	....	....	....	....	....	....	....	....	....	....	....	....	....	....	....	....
	NHL Totals		**83**	**4**	**14**	**18**	**4**	**9**	**13**	**45**	**0**	**0**	**1**	**74**	**5.4**	**95**	**4**	**105**	**20**		....	....	....	....	....	....	....	....

QMJHL First All-Star Team (1981)

• BOISVERT, Serge

Pierre Serge RW – R. 5'9", 172 lbs. b: Drummondville, Que., 6/1/1959.

Season	**Club**	**League**	**GP**	**G**	**A**	**Pts**	**AG**	**AA**	**APts**	**PIM**	**PP**	**SH**	**GW**	**S**	**%**	**TGF**	**PGF**	**TGA**	**PGA**	**+/–**	**GP**	**G**	**A**	**Pts**	**PIM**	**PP**	**SH**	**GW**
1977-78	Sherbrooke Castors	QMJHL	55	17	33	50	....	....	....	19	....	....	....	....	....	....	....	....	....	....	10	2	2	4	2	....	....	....
1978-79	Sherbrooke Castors	QMJHL	72	50	72	122	....	....	....	45	....	....	....	....	....	....	....	....	....	....	12	11	17	28	2	....	....	....
1979-80	Sherbrooke Castors	QMJHL	70	52	72	124	....	....	....	47	....	....	....	....	....	....	....	....	....	....	15	14	18	32	4	....	....	....
	New Brunswick Hawks	AHL	....	....	....	....	....	....	....	....	....	....	....	....	....	....	....	....	....	....	7	4	0	4	4	....	....	....
1980-81	New Brunswick Hawks	AHL	60	19	27	46	....	....	....	31	....	....	....	....	....	....	....	....	....	....	5	0	0	0	2	....	....	....
1981-82	Yukijirushi Sopporo	Japan	30	29	20	49	....	....	....	....	....	....	....	....	....	....	....	....	....	....	....	....	....	....	....	....	....	....
1982-83	**Toronto Maple Leafs**	**NHL**	**17**	**0**	**2**	**2**	**0**	**1**	**1**	**4**	**0**	**0**	**0**	**18**	**0.0**	**4**	**0**	**14**	**0**	**–10**	....	....	....	....	....	....	....	....
	St. Catharines Saints	AHL	19	10	9	19	....	....	....	2	....	....	....	....	....	....	....	....	....	....	....	....	....	....	....	....	....	....
	Moncton Alpines	AHL	29	6	12	18	....	....	....	7	....	....	....	....	....	....	....	....	....	....	....	....	....	....	....	....	....	....
1983-84	Moncton Alpines	AHL	66	15	13	28	....	....	....	34	....	....	....	....	....	....	....	....	....	....	....	....	....	....	....	....	....	....
1984-85	**Montreal Canadiens**	**NHL**	**14**	**2**	**2**	**4**	**2**	**1**	**3**	**0**	**0**	**0**	**0**	**18**	**11.1**	**7**	**1**	**9**	**0**	**–3**	**12**	**3**	**5**	**8**	**2**	**1**	**0**	**0**
	Sherbrooke Canadiens	AHL	63	38	41	79	....	....	....	8	....	....	....	....	....	....	....	....	....	....	10	1	9	10	12	....	....	....
1985-86 ♦	**Montreal Canadiens**	**NHL**	**9**	**2**	**2**	**4**	**2**	**1**	**3**	**2**	**0**	**0**	**0**	**18**	**11.1**	**5**	**0**	**7**	**3**	**1**	**8**	**0**	**1**	**1**	**0**	**0**	**0**	**0**
	Sherbrooke Canadiens	AHL	69	40	48	88	....	....	....	18	....	....	....	....	....	....	....	....	....	....	....	....	....	....	....	....	....	....
1986-87	**Montreal Canadiens**	**NHL**	**1**	**0**	**0**	**0**	**0**	**0**	**0**	**0**	**0**	**0**	**0**	**0**	**0.0**	**0**	**0**	**0**	**0**	**0**	....	....	....	....	....	....	....	....
	Sherbrooke Canadiens	AHL	78	27	54	81	....	....	....	29	....	....	....	....	....	....	....	....	....	....	15	8	10	18	15	....	....	....
1987-88	**Montreal Canadiens**	**NHL**	**5**	**1**	**1**	**2**	**1**	**1**	**2**	**2**	**0**	**0**	**0**	**5**	**20.0**	**3**	**0**	**3**	**0**	**0**	**3**	**0**	**1**	**1**	**2**	**0**	**0**	**0**
	Canada	Nat-Team	63	22	26	48	....	....	....	34	....	....	....	....	....	....	....	....	....	....	....	....	....	....	....	....	....	....
	Canada	Olympics	8	7	2	9	....	....	....	2	....	....	....	....	....	....	....	....	....	....	....	....	....	....	....	....	....	....
1988-89	HC Davos	Switz.	36	20	14	34	....	....	....	....	....	....	....	....	....	....	....	....	....	....	7	6	7	13	....	....	....	....
1989-90	Canada	Nat-Team	5	1	0	1	....	....	....	0	....	....	....	....	....	....	....	....	....	....	....	....	....	....	....	....	....	....
	Vastra Frolunda	Sweden	39	18	14	32	....	....	....	24	....	....	....	....	....	....	....	....	....	....	....	....	....	....	....	....	....	....
1990-91	Vastra Frolunda	Sweden	22	4	4	8	....	....	....	10	....	....	....	....	....	....	....	....	....	....	....	....	....	....	....	....	....	....
1991-92	Vastra Frolunda	Sweden	40	12	16	28	....	....	....	30	....	....	....	....	....	....	....	....	....	....	....	....	....	....	....	....	....	....
1992-93	Vastra Frolunda	Sweden	36	20	21	41	....	....	....	52	....	....	....	....	....	....	....	....	....	....	3	2	1	3	0	....	....	....
	Canada	Nat-Team	3	3	1	4	....	....	....	0	....	....	....	....	....	....	....	....	....	....	....	....	....	....	....	....	....	....
1993-94	Vastra Frolunda	Sweden	36	6	9	15	....	....	....	26	....	....	....	....	....	....	....	....	....	....	4	1	1	2	....	....	....	....
1994-95	Valerenga IF Oslo	Norway	27	15	17	32	....	....	....	24	....	....	....	....	....	....	....	....	....	....	2	1	1	2	0	....	....	....
	Canada	Nat-Team	2	0	0	0	....	....	....	2	....	....	....	....	....	....	....	....	....	....	....	....	....	....	....	....	....	....
1995-96	Valerenga IF Oslo	Norway	28	23	21	44	....	....	....	....	....	....	....	....	....	....	....	....	....	....	4	2	2	4	....	....	....	....
1996-97	Valerenga IF Oslo	Norway	33	21	20	41	....	....	....	32	....	....	....	....	....	....	....	....	....	....	9	5	5	10	....	....	....	....
	Valerenga IF Oslo	EuroHL	6	3	0	3	....	....	....	2	....	....	....	....	....	....	....	....	....	....	....	....	....	....	....	....	....	....
1997-98	Valerenga IF Oslo	Norway	40	21	24	45	....	....	....	51	....	....	....	....	....	....	....	....	....	....	....	....	....	....	....	....	....	....
1998-99	Valerenga IF Oslo	Norway	6	2	4	6	....	....	....	4	....	....	....	....	....	....	....	....	....	....	....	....	....	....	....	....	....	....
	Valerenga IF Oslo	EuroHL	2	0	2	2	....	....	....	2	....	....	....	....	....	....	....	....	....	....	....	....	....	....	....	....	....	....
	IF Frisk Asker	Norway	DID NOT PLAY – COACHING																									
	NHL Totals		**46**	**5**	**7**	**12**	**5**	**4**	**9**	**8**	**0**	**0**	**0**	**59**	**8.5**	**19**	**1**	**33**	**3**		**23**	**3**	**7**	**10**	**4**	**1**	**0**	**0**

AHL Second All-Star Team (1986, 1987)

Signed as a free agent by **Toronto**, October 9, 1980. Traded to **Edmonton** by **Toronto** for Reid Bailey, January 15, 1983. Signed as a free agent by **Montreal**, February 8, 1985.

• BOIVIN, Claude

LW – L. 6'2", 200 lbs. b: Ste. Foy, Que., 3/1/1970. Philadelphia's 1st, 14th overall, in 1988.

Season	**Club**	**League**	**GP**	**G**	**A**	**Pts**	**AG**	**AA**	**APts**	**PIM**	**PP**	**SH**	**GW**	**S**	**%**	**TGF**	**PGF**	**TGA**	**PGA**	**+/–**	**GP**	**G**	**A**	**Pts**	**PIM**	**PP**	**SH**	**GW**
1986-87	Ste-Foy Gouverneurs	QAAA	39	12	27	39	....	....	....	90	....	....	....	....	....	....	....	....	....	....	....	....	....	....	....	....	....	....
1987-88	Drummondville Voltigeurs	QMJHL	63	23	26	49	....	....	....	233	....	....	....	....	....	....	....	....	....	....	17	5	3	8	74	....	....	....
	Drummondville Voltigeurs	Mem-Cup	3	0	1	1	....	....	....	6	....	....	....	....	....	....	....	....	....	....	....	....	....	....	....	....	....	....
1988-89	Drummondville Voltigeurs	QMJHL	63	20	36	56	....	....	....	218	....	....	....	....	....	....	....	....	....	....	4	0	2	2	27	....	....	....
1989-90	Laval Titan	QMJHL	59	24	51	75	....	....	....	309	....	....	....	....	....	....	....	....	....	....	13	7	13	20	59	....	....	....
	Laval Titan	Mem-Cup	4	3	2	5	....	....	....	12	....	....	....	....	....	....	....	....	....	....	....	....	....	....	....	....	....	....
1990-91	Hershey Bears	AHL	65	13	32	45	....	....	....	159	....	....	....	....	....	....	....	....	....	....	7	1	5	6	28	....	....	....
1991-92	**Philadelphia Flyers**	**NHL**	**58**	**5**	**13**	**18**	**5**	**10**	**15**	**187**	**0**	**0**	**0**	**46**	**10.9**	**26**	**0**	**28**	**0**	**–2**	....	....	....	....	....	....	....	....
	Hershey Bears	AHL	20	4	5	9	....	....	....	96	....	....	....	....	....	....	....	....	....	....	....	....	....	....	....	....	....	....
1992-93	**Philadelphia Flyers**	**NHL**	**30**	**5**	**4**	**9**	**4**	**3**	**7**	**76**	**0**	**0**	**1**	**21**	**23.8**	**13**	**0**	**18**	**0**	**–5**	....	....	....	....	....	....	....	....
1993-94	**Philadelphia Flyers**	**NHL**	**26**	**1**	**1**	**2**	**1**	**1**	**2**	**57**	**0**	**0**	**0**	**11**	**9.1**	**3**	**1**	**14**	**1**	**–11**	....	....	....	....	....	....	....	....
	Hershey Bears	AHL	4	1	6	7	....	....	....	6	....	....	....	....	....	....	....	....	....	....	....	....	....	....	....	....	....	....
	Ottawa Senators	**NHL**	**15**	**1**	**0**	**1**	**1**	**0**	**1**	**38**	**0**	**0**	**0**	**6**	**16.7**	**2**	**0**	**8**	**0**	**–6**	....	....	....	....	....	....	....	....
1994-95	**Ottawa Senators**	**NHL**	**3**	**0**	**1**	**1**	**0**	**1**	**1**	**6**	**0**	**0**	**0**	**0**	**0.0**	**1**	**0**	**2**	**0**	**–1**	....	....	....	....	....	....	....	....
	P.E.I. Senators	AHL	22	10	9	19	....	....	....	89	....	....	....	....	....	....	....	....	....	....	9	1	2	3	32	....	....	....
1995-96			DID NOT PLAY – INJURED																									
1996-97			DID NOT PLAY – INJURED																									
1997-98	Pensacola Ice Pilots	ECHL	10	0	1	1	....	....	....	45	....	....	....	....	....	....	....	....	....	....	....	....	....	....	....	....	....	....
	Quebec Rafales	IHL	13	2	3	5	....	....	....	46	....	....	....	....	....	....	....	....	....	....	....	....	....	....	....	....	....	....
	Grand Rapids Griffins	IHL	31	12	5	17	....	....	....	69	....	....	....	....	....	....	....	....	....	....	3	0	0	0	0	....	....	....
1998-99	WSV Sterzing	Alpenliga	33	11	18	29	....	....	....	120	....	....	....	....	....	....	....	....	....	....	....	....	....	....	....	....	....	....
	WSV Sterzing	Italy	12	3	10	13	....	....	....	73	....	....	....	....	....	....	....	....	....	....	6	4	2	6	56	....	....	....
99-2000	Long Beach Ice Dogs	IHL	42	2	6	8	....	....	....	147	....	....	....	....	....	....	....	....	....	....	4	0	0	0	12	....	....	....
	NHL Totals		**132**	**12**	**19**	**31**	**11**	**15**	**26**	**364**	**0**	**0**	**1**	**84**	**14.3**	**45**	**1**	**70**	**1**		....	....	....	....	....	....	....	....

• Missed majority of 1993-94 and entire 1995-96 and 1996-97 seasons recovering from knee surgery originally performed in September, 1992. Traded to **Ottawa** by **Philadelphia** with Kirk Daubenspeck for Mark Lamb, March 5, 1994. • Signed as a free agent by **Long Beach** (IHL) August 5, 1999.

• BOIVIN, Leo

Leo Joseph D – L. 5'8", 183 lbs. b: Prescott, Ont., 8/2/1932. **HHOF**

Season	**Club**	**League**	**GP**	**G**	**A**	**Pts**	**AG**	**AA**	**APts**	**PIM**	**PP**	**SH**	**GW**	**S**	**%**	**TGF**	**PGF**	**TGA**	**PGA**	**+/–**	**GP**	**G**	**A**	**Pts**	**PIM**	**PP**	**SH**	**GW**
1948-49	Inkerman Rockets	OVJHL	STATISTICS NOT AVAILABLE																									
	Inkerman Rockets	Mem-Cup	4	2	0	2	....	....	....	0	....	....	....	....	....	....	....	....	....	....	....	....	....	....	....	....	....	....
1949-50	Port Arthur Bruins	TBJHL	18	4	4	8	....	....	....	32	....	....	....	....	....	....	....	....	....	....	5	0	3	3	10	....	....	....
	Port Arthur Bruins	Mem-Cup	16	6	4	10	....	....	....	12	....	....	....	....	....	....	....	....	....	....	....	....	....	....	....	....	....	....
1950-51	Port Arthur Bruins	TBJHL	20	16	11	27	....	....	....	37	....	....	....	....	....	....	....	....	....	....	13	3	6	9	28	....	....	....
	Port Arthur Bruins	Mem-Cup	7	1	3	4	....	....	....	16	....	....	....	....	....	....	....	....	....	....	....	....	....	....	....	....	....	....
1951-52	**Toronto Maple Leafs**	**NHL**	**2**	**0**	**1**	**1**	**0**	**1**	**1**	**0**	....	....	....	....	....	....	....	....	....	....	....	....	....	....	....	....	....	....
	Pittsburgh Hornets	AHL	30	2	3	5	....	....	....	32	....	....	....	....	....	....	....	....	....	....	10	0	1	1	16	....	....	....
1952-53	**Toronto Maple Leafs**	**NHL**	**70**	**2**	**13**	**15**	**3**	**16**	**19**	**97**	....	....	....	....	....	....	....	....	....	....	....	....	....	....	....	....	....	....
1953-54	**Toronto Maple Leafs**	**NHL**	**58**	**1**	**6**	**7**	**1**	**7**	**8**	**81**	....	....	....	....	....	....	....	....	....	....	**5**	**0**	**0**	**0**	**2**	**0**	**0**	**0**
1954-55	**Toronto Maple Leafs**	**NHL**	**7**	**0**	**0**	**0**	**0**	**0**	**0**	**8**	....	....	....	....	....	....	....	....	....	....	....	....	....	....	....	....	....	....
	Boston Bruins	**NHL**	**59**	**6**	**11**	**17**	**8**	**13**	**21**	**105**	....	....	....	....	....	....	....	....	....	....	**5**	**0**	**1**	**1**	**4**	**0**	**0**	**0**
1955-56	**Boston Bruins**	**NHL**	**68**	**4**	**16**	**20**	**5**	**19**	**24**	**80**	....	....	....	....	....	....	....	....	....	....	....	....	....	....	....	....	....	....
1956-57	**Boston Bruins**	**NHL**	**55**	**2**	**8**	**10**	**3**	**9**	**12**	**55**	....	....	....	....	....	....	....	....	....	....	**10**	**2**	**3**	**5**	**12**	**0**	**0**	**0**
1957-58	**Boston Bruins**	**NHL**	**33**	**0**	**4**	**4**	**0**	**4**	**4**	**54**	....	....	....	....	....	....	....	....	....	....	**12**	**0**	**3**	**3**	**21**	**0**	**0**	**0**
1958-59	**Boston Bruins**	**NHL**	**70**	**5**	**16**	**21**	**6**	**16**	**22**	**94**	....	....	....	....	....	....	....	....	....	....	**7**	**1**	**2**	**3**	**4**	**0**	**0**	**0**
1959-60	**Boston Bruins**	**NHL**	**70**	**4**	**21**	**25**	**5**	**20**	**25**	**66**	....	....	....	....	....	....	....	....	....	....	....	....	....	....	....	....	....	....
1960-61	**Boston Bruins**	**NHL**	**57**	**6**	**17**	**23**	**7**	**16**	**23**	**50**	....	....	....	....	....	....	....	....	....	....	....	....	....	....	....	....	....	....
1961-62	**Boston Bruins**	**NHL**	**65**	**5**	**18**	**23**	**6**	**17**	**23**	**70**	....	....	....	....	....	....	....	....	....	....	....	....	....	....	....	....	....	....
1962-63	**Boston Bruins**	**NHL**	**62**	**2**	**24**	**26**	**2**	**24**	**26**	**48**	....	....	....	....	....	....	....	....	....	....	....	....	....	....	....	....	....	....
1963-64	**Boston Bruins**	**NHL**	**65**	**10**	**14**	**24**	**12**	**15**	**27**	**42**	....	....	....	....	....	....	....	....	....	....	....	....	....	....	....	....	....	....

			REGULAR SEASON																		PLAYOFFS							
Season	Club	League	GP	G	A	Pts	AG	AA	APts	PIM	PP	SH	GW	S	%	TGF	PGF	TGA	PGA	+/–	GP	G	A	Pts	PIM	PP	SH	GW
1964-65	Boston Bruins	NHL	67	3	10	13	4	10	14	68	....	....	....	....	....	....	....	....	....	....	....	....	....	....	....	....	....	....
1965-66	Boston Bruins	NHL	46	0	5	5	0	5	5	34	....	....	....	....	....	....	....	....	....	....	....	....	....	....	....	....	....	....
	Detroit Red Wings	NHL	16	0	5	5	0	5	5	16	....	....	....	....	....	....	....	....	....	....	12	0	1	1	16	0	0	0
1966-67	Detroit Red Wings	NHL	69	4	17	21	5	17	22	78	....	....	....	....	....	....	....	....	....	....	....	....	....	....	....	....	....	....
1967-68	Pittsburgh Penguins	NHL	73	9	13	22	10	13	23	74	4	0	1	163	5.5	99	14	117	17	–15	....	....	....	....	....	....	....	....
1968-69	Pittsburgh Penguins	NHL	41	5	13	18	5	12	17	26	2	0	1	74	6.8	51	15	47	5	–6	....	....	....	....	....	....	....	....
	Minnesota North Stars	NHL	28	1	6	7	1	5	6	16	1	0	0	64	1.6	29	5	48	5	–19	....	....	....	....	....	....	....	....
1969-70	Minnesota North Stars	NHL	69	3	12	15	3	11	14	30	0	0	0	95	3.2	70	1	111	40	–2	3	0	0	0	0	0	0	0
	NHL Totals		1150	72	250	322	86	255	341	1192	....	....	....	....	....	....	....	....	....		54	3	10	13	59	....	....	....

Played in NHL All-Star Game (1961, 1962, 1964)

Traded to **Toronto** by **Boston** with Fern Flaman, Ken Smith and Phil Maloney for Bill Ezinicki and Vic Lynn, November 16, 1950. Traded to **Boston** by **Toronto** for Joe Klukay, November 9, 1954. Traded to **Detroit** by **Boston** with Dean Prentice for Gary Doak, Ron Murphy, Bill Lesuk and future considerations (Steve Atkinson, June 6, 1966), February 16, 1966. Claimed by **Pittsburgh** from **Detroit** in Expansion Draft, June 6, 1967. Traded to **Minnesota** by **Pittsburgh** for Duane Rupp, January 24, 1969.

• BOLAND, Mike

Michael Anthony RW – R. 5'10", 183 lbs. b: Montreal, Que., 12/16/1949.

Season	Club	League	GP	G	A	Pts	AG	AA	APts	PIM	PP	SH	GW	S	%	TGF	PGF	TGA	PGA	+/–	GP	G	A	Pts	PIM	PP	SH	GW
1966-67	St. Michael's Buzzers	OHA-B	STATISTICS NOT AVAILABLE																									
1967-68	University of Toronto	OQAA	STATISTICS NOT AVAILABLE																									
1968-69	University of Toronto	OQAA	10	5	5	10	....	....	....	4	....	....	....	....	....	....	....	....	....	....	....	....	....	....	....	....	....	....
1969-70	University of Toronto	OQAA	10	3	13	16	....	....	....	22	....	....	....	....	....	....	....	....	....	....	....	....	....	....	....	....	....	....
1970-71	University of Toronto	OQAA	1	1	0	1	....	....	....	0	....	....	....	....	....	....	....	....	....	....	....	....	....	....	....	....	....	....
	Springfield Kings	AHL	34	7	5	12	....	....	....	33	....	....	....	....	....	....	....	....	....	....	12	2	6	8	4	....	....	....
1971-72	Springfield Kings	AHL	48	4	20	24	....	....	....	47	....	....	....	....	....	....	....	....	....	....	5	1	0	1	2	....	....	....
1972-73	Ottawa Nationals	WHA	41	1	15	16	....	....	....	44	....	....	....	....	....	....	....	....	....	....	1	0	0	0	12	....	....	....
1973-74	Richmond Robins	AHL	38	10	19	29	....	....	....	49	....	....	....	....	....	....	....	....	....	....	5	3	1	4	8	....	....	....
1974-75	**Philadelphia Flyers**	**NHL**	2	0	0	0	0	0	0	0	0	0	0	0	0.0	0	0	0	0	0	....	....	....	....	....	....	....	....
	Richmond Robins	AHL	5	0	1	1	....	....	....	21	....	....	....	....	....	....	....	....	....	....	....	....	....	....	....	....	....	....
	Philadelphia Firebirds	NAHL	59	31	55	86	....	....	....	49	....	....	....	....	....	....	....	....	....	....	3	2	1	3	0	....	....	....
1975-76	Philadelphia Firebirds	NAHL	13	4	8	12	....	....	....	9	....	....	....	....	....	....	....	....	....	....	....	....	....	....	....	....	....	....
	Cape Cod Codders	NAHL	35	13	23	36	....	....	....	24	....	....	....	....	....	....	....	....	....	....	....	....	....	....	....	....	....	....
1976-77	HIFK Helsinki	Finland	35	11	16	27	....	....	....	58	....	....	....	....	....	....	....	....	....	....	4	0	0	0	0	....	....	....
1977-78			OUT OF HOCKEY – RETIRED																									
1978-79	Philadelphia Firebirds	AHL	3	0	0	0	....	....	....	0	....	....	....	....	....	....	....	....	....	....	....	....	....	....	....	....	....	....
	NHL Totals		2	0	0	0	0	0	0	0	0	0	0	0	0.0	0	0	0	0		....	....	....	....	....	....	....	....
	Other Major League Totals		41	1	15	16	....	....	....	44	....	....	....	....	....	....	....	....	....	....	1	0	0	0	12	....	....	....

NAHL Second All-Star Team (1975)

Selected by **Ontario-Ottawa** (WHA) in 1972 WHA General Player Draft, February 13, 1972. Signed as a free agent by **Philadelphia**, September, 1973. Traded to **Cape Cod** (NAHL) by **Philadelphia** (NAHL) for Mike Penasse, November, 1975.

• BOLAND, Mike J.

Mike J. John D – R. 6', 190 lbs. b: London, Ont., 10/29/1954. Kansas City's 7th, 110th overall, in 1974.

Season	Club	League	GP	G	A	Pts	AG	AA	APts	PIM	PP	SH	GW	S	%	TGF	PGF	TGA	PGA	+/–	GP	G	A	Pts	PIM	PP	SH	GW
1972-73	Sault Ste. Marie Greyhounds	OMJHL	55	4	15	19	....	....	....	139	....	....	....	....	....	....	....	....	....	....	....	....	....	....	....	....	....	....
1973-74	Sault Ste. Marie Greyhounds	OMJHL	67	11	39	50	....	....	....	200	....	....	....	....	....	....	....	....	....	....	....	....	....	....	....	....	....	....
1974-75	**Kansas City Scouts**	**NHL**	1	0	0	0	0	0	0	0	0	0	0	0	0.0	0	0	0	0	0	....	....	....	....	....	....	....	....
	Port Huron Flags	IHL	71	2	12	14	....	....	....	172	....	....	....	....	....	....	....	....	....	....	5	2	1	3	14	....	....	....
1975-76	Port Huron Flags	IHL	75	8	16	24	....	....	....	208	....	....	....	....	....	....	....	....	....	....	15	0	6	6	51	....	....	....
1976-77	Port Huron Flags	IHL	66	7	37	44	....	....	....	306	....	....	....	....	....	....	....	....	....	....	....	....	....	....	....	....	....	....
1977-78	Port Huron Flags	IHL	2	0	0	0	....	....	....	4	....	....	....	....	....	....	....	....	....	....	....	....	....	....	....	....	....	....
	Fort Wayne Komets	IHL	74	7	39	46	....	....	....	228	....	....	....	....	....	....	....	....	....	....	11	3	3	6	40	....	....	....
1978-79	**Buffalo Sabres**	**NHL**	22	1	2	3	1	1	2	29	0	0	0	17	5.9	21	0	16	1	6	3	1	0	1	2	0	0	0
	Hershey Bears	AHL	46	3	17	20	....	....	....	86	....	....	....	....	....	....	....	....	....	....	....	....	....	....	....	....	....	....
1979-80	Rochester Americans	AHL	80	4	28	32	....	....	....	178	....	....	....	....	....	....	....	....	....	....	4	1	1	2	6	....	....	....
1980-81	Rochester Americans	AHL	5	0	1	1	....	....	....	8	....	....	....	....	....	....	....	....	....	....	....	....	....	....	....	....	....	....
	Salt Lake Golden Eagles	CHL	69	5	21	26	....	....	....	188	....	....	....	....	....	....	....	....	....	....	17	2	1	3	*70	....	....	....
1981-82	Salt Lake Golden Eagles	CHL	64	1	13	14	....	....	....	161	....	....	....	....	....	....	....	....	....	....	10	1	2	3	45	....	....	....
1982-83	Fort Wayne Komets	IHL	1	0	0	0	....	....	....	0	....	....	....	....	....	....	....	....	....	....	....	....	....	....	....	....	....	....
	Hershey Bears	AHL	57	0	11	11	....	....	....	68	....	....	....	....	....	....	....	....	....	....	5	0	0	0	6	....	....	....
1983-84	Fort Wayne Komets	IHL	81	8	49	57	....	....	....	161	....	....	....	....	....	....	....	....	....	....	6	0	3	3	35	....	....	....
	NHL Totals		23	1	2	3	1	1	2	29	0	0	0	17	5.9	21	0	16	1		3	1	0	1	2	0	0	0

Signed as a free agent by **Buffalo**, January 5, 1979.

• BOLDIREV, Ivan

"Ike" C – L. 6', 190 lbs. b: Zranjanin, Yugoslavia, 8/15/1949. Boston's 3rd, 11th overall, in 1969.

Season	Club	League	GP	G	A	Pts	AG	AA	APts	PIM	PP	SH	GW	S	%	TGF	PGF	TGA	PGA	+/–	GP	G	A	Pts	PIM	PP	SH	GW
1966-67	Sault Ste. Marie Greyhounds	NOJHA	40	26	42	68	....	....	....	35	....	....	....	....	....	....	....	....	....	....	....	....	....	....	....	....	....	....
1967-68	Oshawa Generals	OHA-Jr.	50	18	26	44	....	....	....	76	....	....	....	....	....	....	....	....	....	....	....	....	....	....	....	....	....	....
1968-69	Oshawa Generals	OHA-Jr.	54	25	34	59	....	....	....	101	....	....	....	....	....	....	....	....	....	....	....	....	....	....	....	....	....	....
1969-70	Oklahoma City Blazers	CHL	65	18	49	67	....	....	....	114	....	....	....	....	....	....	....	....	....	....	....	....	....	....	....	....	....	....
1970-71	**Boston Bruins**	**NHL**	2	0	0	0	0	0	0	0	0	0	0	1	0.0	0	0	0	0	0	....	....	....	....	....	....	....	....
	Oklahoma City Blazers	CHL	68	19	52	71	....	....	....	98	....	....	....	....	....	....	....	....	....	....	5	1	4	5	9	....	....	....
1971-72	**Boston Bruins**	**NHL**	11	0	2	2	0	2	2	6	0	0	0	2	0.0	3	0	1	0	2	....	....	....	....	....	....	....	....
	California Golden Seals	**NHL**	57	16	23	39	16	20	36	54	4	2	2	109	14.7	55	21	66	18	–14	....	....	....	....	....	....	....	....
1972-73	**California Golden Seals**	**NHL**	56	11	23	34	10	18	28	58	3	0	3	157	7.0	46	11	66	8	–23	....	....	....	....	....	....	....	....
1973-74	**California Golden Seals**	**NHL**	78	25	31	56	24	26	50	22	2	0	2	220	11.4	77	18	115	5	–51	....	....	....	....	....	....	....	....
1974-75	**Chicago Black Hawks**	**NHL**	80	24	43	67	21	32	53	54	6	0	1	195	12.3	87	15	75	0	–3	8	4	2	6	2	1	0	1
1975-76	**Chicago Black Hawks**	**NHL**	78	28	34	62	25	25	50	33	5	0	4	178	15.7	76	18	82	1	–23	4	0	1	1	0	0	0	0
1976-77	**Chicago Black Hawks**	**NHL**	80	24	38	62	22	29	51	40	4	0	4	164	14.6	72	17	73	3	–15	2	0	1	1	0	0	0	0
1977-78	**Chicago Black Hawks**	**NHL**	80	35	45	80	32	35	67	34	10	0	2	242	14.5	95	33	65	0	–3	4	0	2	2	2	0	0	0
1978-79	**Chicago Black Hawks**	**NHL**	66	29	35	64	25	25	50	25	10	0	4	192	15.1	91	24	60	0	7	....	....	....	....	....	....	....	....
	Atlanta Flames	**NHL**	13	6	8	14	5	6	11	6	4	0	0	33	18.2	23	11	11	0	1	2	0	2	2	2	0	0	0
1979-80	**Atlanta Flames**	**NHL**	52	16	24	40	14	17	31	20	1	0	2	121	13.2	65	13	53	0	–1	....	....	....	....	....	....	....	....
	Vancouver Canucks	**NHL**	27	16	11	27	14	8	22	14	5	0	3	82	19.5	38	13	28	2	–1	4	0	2	2	0	0	0	0
1980-81	**Vancouver Canucks**	**NHL**	72	26	33	59	20	22	42	34	9	0	3	195	13.3	92	31	75	2	–12	1	1	1	2	0	0	0	0
1981-82	**Vancouver Canucks**	**NHL**	78	33	40	73	26	27	53	45	10	0	4	202	16.3	89	32	77	3	–17	17	8	3	11	4	3	0	1
1982-83	**Vancouver Canucks**	**NHL**	39	5	20	25	4	14	18	12	3	0	1	74	6.8	42	14	37	0	–9	....	....	....	....	....	....	....	....
	Detroit Red Wings	**NHL**	33	13	17	30	11	12	23	14	3	1	0	62	21.0	39	7	46	8	–6	....	....	....	....	....	....	....	....
1983-84	**Detroit Red Wings**	**NHL**	75	35	48	83	28	33	61	20	12	0	4	185	18.9	114	43	71	3	3	4	0	5	5	4	0	0	0
1984-85	**Detroit Red Wings**	**NHL**	75	19	30	49	15	20	35	16	11	0	3	104	18.3	77	35	67	0	–25	2	0	1	1	0	0	0	0
	NHL Totals		1052	361	505	866	312	371	683	507	102	3	42	2518	14.3	1181	356	1068	53		48	13	20	33	14	4	0	2

CHL Second All-Star Team (1971) • Played in NHL All-Star Game (1978)

Traded to **California** by **Boston** for Rich Leduc and Chris Oddleifson, November 17, 1971. Traded to **Chicago** by **California** for Len Frig and Mike Christie, May 24, 1974. Traded to **Atlanta** by **Chicago** with Phil Russell and Darcy Rota for Tom Lysiak, Pat Ribble, Greg Fox, Harold Phillipoff and Miles Zaharko, March 13, 1979. Traded to **Vancouver** by **Atlanta** with Darcy Rota for Don Lever and Brad Smith, February 8, 1980. Traded to **Detroit** by **Vancouver** for Mark Kirton, January 17, 1983.

• BOLDUC, Danny

Daniel George LW – L. 5'9", 180 lbs. b: Waterville, ME, 4/6/1953.

Season	Club	League	GP	G	A	Pts	AG	AA	APts	PIM	PP	SH	GW	S	%	TGF	PGF	TGA	PGA	+/–	GP	G	A	Pts	PIM	PP	SH	GW
1972-73	Harvard University	ECAC	13	15	17	32	....	....	....	17	....	....	....	....	....	....	....	....	....	....	....	....	....	....	....	....	....	....
1973-74	Harvard University	ECAC	29	15	9	24	....	....	....	24	....	....	....	....	....	....	....	....	....	....	....	....	....	....	....	....	....	....
1974-75	Harvard University	ECAC	29	13	11	24	....	....	....	18	....	....	....	....	....	....	....	....	....	....	....	....	....	....	....	....	....	....
1975-76	United States	Nat-Team	54	39	31	70	....	....	....	46	....	....	....	....	....	....	....	....	....	....	....	....	....	....	....	....	....	....
	United States	Olympics	6	2	0	2	....	....	....	6	....	....	....	....	....	....	....	....	....	....	....	....	....	....	....	....	....	....
	New England Whalers	WHA	14	2	5	7	....	....	....	14	....	....	....	....	....	....	....	....	....	....	16	1	6	7	4	....	....	....

			REGULAR SEASON																		PLAYOFFS							
Season	Club	League	GP	G	A	Pts	AG	AA	APts	PIM	PP	SH	GW	S	%	TGF	PGF	TGA	PGA	+/-	GP	G	A	Pts	PIM	PP	SH	GW
1976-77	New England Whalers	WHA	33	8	3	11	....	....	....	15	....	....	....	....	....	....	....	....	....	....	....	....	....	....	....	....	....	....
	Rhode Island Reds	AHL	44	11	22	33	....	....	....	23	....	....	....	....	....	....	....	....	....	....	....	....	....	....	....	....	....	....
1977-78	New England Whalers	WHA	41	5	5	10	....	....	....	22	....	....	....	....	....	....	....	....	....	....	14	2	4	6	4	....	....	....
	Springfield Indians	AHL	35	14	9	23	....	....	....	35	....	....	....	....	....	....	....	....	....	....	....	....	....	....	....	....	....	....
1978-79	**Detroit Red Wings**	**NHL**	**56**	**16**	**13**	**29**	**14**	**9**	**23**	**14**	**3**	**0**	**4**	**81**	**19.8**	**36**	**7**	**38**	**0**	**–9**	....	....	....	....	....	....	....	....
	Kansas City Red Wings	CHL	23	21	11	32	....	....	....	11	....	....	....	....	....	....	....	....	....	....	....	....	....	....	....	....	....	....
1979-80	**Detroit Red Wings**	**NHL**	**44**	**6**	**5**	**11**	**5**	**4**	**9**	**19**	**2**	**0**	**0**	**52**	**11.5**	**16**	**2**	**28**	**0**	**–14**	....	....	....	....	....	....	....	....
	Adirondack Red Wings	AHL	13	1	3	4	....	....	....	4	....	....	....	....	....	....	....	....	....	....	5	0	0	0	0	....	....	....
1980-81	Adirondack Red Wings	AHL	77	23	25	48	....	....	....	58	....	....	....	....	....	....	....	....	....	....	18	4	6	10	36	....	....	....
1981-82	Nova Scotia Voyageurs	AHL	74	39	40	79	....	....	....	60	....	....	....	....	....	....	....	....	....	....	5	2	0	2	0	....	....	....
1982-83	Colorado Flames	CHL	79	27	45	72	....	....	....	39	....	....	....	....	....	....	....	....	....	....	6	2	3	5	2	....	....	....
1983-84	**Calgary Flames**	**NHL**	**2**	**0**	**1**	**1**	**0**	**1**	**1**	**0**	**0**	**0**	**0**	**4**	**0.0**	**2**	**0**	**1**	**0**	**1**	**1**	**0**	**0**	**0**	**0**	**0**	**0**	**0**
	Colorado Flames	CHL	60	37	17	54	....	....	....	34	....	....	....	....	....	....	....	....	....	....	6	2	1	3	4	....	....	....
1984-85	Moncton Golden Flames	AHL	45	7	8	15	....	....	....	22	....	....	....	....	....	....	....	....	....	....	....	....	....	....	....	....	....	....
	NHL Totals		**102**	**22**	**19**	**41**	**19**	**14**	**33**	**33**	**5**	**0**	**4**	**137**	**16.1**	**54**	**9**	**67**	**0**		**1**	**0**	**0**	**0**	**0**	**0**	**0**	**0**
	Other Major League Totals		88	15	13	28	....	....	....	51	....	....	....	....	....	....	....	....	....	....	30	3	10	13	8	....	....	....

CHL Second All-Star Team (1983)

Signed as a free agent by **New England** (WHA), March, 1976. Signed as a free agent by **Detroit**, August 24, 1978. Signed as a free agent by **Montreal**, March 9, 1982. Signed as a free agent by **Calgary**, September 1, 1982.

• BOLDUC, Michel

D – L. 6'2", 190 lbs. b: Angegardien, Que., 3/13/1961. Quebec's 6th, 150th overall, in 1980.

Season	Club	League	GP	G	A	Pts	AG	AA	APts	PIM	PP	SH	GW	S	%	TGF	PGF	TGA	PGA	+/-	GP	G	A	Pts	PIM	PP	SH	GW
1977-78	Hull Olympiques	QMJHL	60	1	5	6	....	....	....	36	....	....	....	....	....	....	....	....	....	....	....	....	....	....	....	....	....	....
1978-79	Hull Olympiques	QMJHL	6	0	1	1	....	....	....	5	....	....	....	....	....	....	....	....	....	....	....	....	....	....	....	....	....	....
	Chicoutimi Sagueneens	QMJHL	66	1	23	24	....	....	....	142	....	....	....	....	....	....	....	....	....	....	....	....	....	....	....	....	....	....
1979-80	Chicoutimi Sagueneens	QMJHL	65	3	29	32	....	....	....	219	....	....	....	....	....	....	....	....	....	....	12	1	3	4	44	....	....	....
1980-81	Chicoutimi Sagueneens	QMJHL	67	11	35	46	....	....	....	244	....	....	....	....	....	....	....	....	....	....	12	0	4	4	34	....	....	....
1981-82	**Quebec Nordiques**	**NHL**	**3**	**0**	**0**	**0**	**0**	**0**	**0**	**0**	**0**	**0**	**0**	**1**	**0.0**	**0**	**0**	**0**	**0**	**0**	....	....	....	....	....	....	....	....
	Fredericton Express	AHL	69	4	9	13	....	....	....	130	....	....	....	....	....	....	....	....	....	....	....	....	....	....	....	....	....	....
1982-83	**Quebec Nordiques**	**NHL**	**7**	**0**	**0**	**0**	**0**	**0**	**0**	**6**	**0**	**0**	**0**	**4**	**0.0**	**6**	**0**	**5**	**1**	**2**	....	....	....	....	....	....	....	....
	Fredericton Express	AHL	68	4	18	22	....	....	....	165	....	....	....	....	....	....	....	....	....	....	11	1	1	2	50	....	....	....
1983-84	Fredericton Express	AHL	70	2	15	17	....	....	....	96	....	....	....	....	....	....	....	....	....	....	7	0	1	1	19	....	....	....
1984-85	Fredericton Express	AHL	29	0	9	9	....	....	....	74	....	....	....	....	....	....	....	....	....	....	....	....	....	....	....	....	....	....
	Maine Mariners	AHL	31	1	7	8	....	....	....	86	....	....	....	....	....	....	....	....	....	....	11	1	1	2	23	....	....	....
1985-86	Maine Mariners	AHL	66	1	6	7	....	....	....	29	....	....	....	....	....	....	....	....	....	....	5	0	1	1	6	....	....	....
1986-87	Riviere-du-Loup 3 L's	RHL	29	2	19	21	....	....	....	105	....	....	....	....	....	....	....	....	....	....	....	1	3	4	6	....	....	....
	NHL Totals		**10**	**0**	**0**	**0**	**0**	**0**	**0**	**6**	**0**	**0**	**0**	**5**	**0.0**	**6**	**0**	**5**	**1**		....	....	....	....	....	....	....	....

Claimed on waivers by **New Jersey** from **Quebec**, January 25, 1985.

• BOLONCHUK, Larry

Kenneth Lawrence D – L. 5'10", 190 lbs. b: Winnipeg, Man., 2/26/1952. Vancouver's 5th, 67th overall, in 1972.

Season	Club	League	GP	G	A	Pts	AG	AA	APts	PIM	PP	SH	GW	S	%	TGF	PGF	TGA	PGA	+/-	GP	G	A	Pts	PIM	PP	SH	GW
1970-71	Winnipeg Jets	WCJHL	66	4	31	35	....	....	....	140	....	....	....	....	....	....	....	....	....	....	12	1	1	2	66	....	....	....
1971-72	Winnipeg Jets	WCJHL	67	7	32	39	....	....	....	175	....	....	....	....	....	....	....	....	....	....	....	....	....	....	....	....	....	....
1972-73	**Vancouver Canucks**	**NHL**	**15**	**0**	**0**	**0**	**0**	**0**	**0**	**6**	**0**	**0**	**0**	**11**	**0.0**	**9**	**0**	**24**	**4**	**–11**	....	....	....	....	....	....	....	....
	Seattle Totems	WHL	59	2	9	11	....	....	....	97	....	....	....	....	....	....	....	....	....	....	....	....	....	....	....	....	....	....
1973-74	Des Moines Capitols	IHL	71	6	27	33	....	....	....	166	....	....	....	....	....	....	....	....	....	....	10	2	4	6	37	....	....	....
	Seattle Totems	WHL	3	0	2	2	....	....	....	4	....	....	....	....	....	....	....	....	....	....	....	....	....	....	....	....	....	....
1974-75	Dayton Gems	IHL	58	9	21	30	....	....	....	139	....	....	....	....	....	....	....	....	....	....	14	0	13	13	31	....	....	....
1975-76	**Washington Capitals**	**NHL**	**1**	**0**	**1**	**1**	**0**	**1**	**1**	**0**	**0**	**0**	**0**	**1**	**0.0**	**1**	**0**	**2**	**0**	**–1**	....	....	....	....	....	....	....	....
	Dayton Gems	IHL	77	4	39	43	....	....	....	174	....	....	....	....	....	....	....	....	....	....	15	0	11	11	59	....	....	....
1976-77	**Washington Capitals**	**NHL**	**9**	**0**	**0**	**0**	**0**	**0**	**0**	**12**	**0**	**0**	**0**	**3**	**0.0**	**2**	**0**	**17**	**3**	**–12**	....	....	....	....	....	....	....	....
	Dayton Gems	IHL	71	2	21	23	....	....	....	124	....	....	....	....	....	....	....	....	....	....	4	0	2	2	6	....	....	....
1977-78	**Washington Capitals**	**NHL**	**49**	**3**	**8**	**11**	**3**	**6**	**9**	**79**	**0**	**0**	**0**	**41**	**7.3**	**30**	**0**	**66**	**17**	**–19**	....	....	....	....	....	....	....	....
	Hampton Gulls	AHL	14	1	1	2	....	....	....	38	....	....	....	....	....	....	....	....	....	....	....	....	....	....	....	....	....	....
	Hershey Bears	AHL	19	0	7	7	....	....	....	12	....	....	....	....	....	....	....	....	....	....	....	....	....	....	....	....	....	....
1978-79	Binghamton Dusters	AHL	75	2	28	30	....	....	....	108	....	....	....	....	....	....	....	....	....	....	10	0	1	1	18	....	....	....
1979-80	Cincinnati Stingers	CHL	1	0	0	0	....	....	....	4	....	....	....	....	....	....	....	....	....	....	....	....	....	....	....	....	....	....
	Dayton Gems	IHL	73	7	32	39	....	....	....	139	....	....	....	....	....	....	....	....	....	....	....	....	....	....	....	....	....	....
	NHL Totals		**74**	**3**	**9**	**12**	**3**	**7**	**10**	**97**	**0**	**0**	**0**	**56**	**5.4**	**42**	**0**	**109**	**24**		....	....	....	....	....	....	....	....

IHL Second All-Star Team (1977)

Claimed by **Washington** from **Vancouver** in Expansion Draft, June 12, 1974.

• BOMBARDIR, Brad

Luke Bradley D – L. 6'1", 205 lbs. b: Powell River, B.C., 5/5/1972. New Jersey's 5th, 56th overall, in 1990.

Season	Club	League	GP	G	A	Pts	AG	AA	APts	PIM	PP	SH	GW	S	%	TGF	PGF	TGA	PGA	+/-	GP	G	A	Pts	PIM	PP	SH	GW
1988-89	Powell River Paper Kings	BCJHL	30	6	5	11	....	....	....	24	....	....	....	....	....	....	....	....	....	....	6	0	0	0	0	....	....	....
1989-90	Powell River Paper Kings	BCJHL	60	10	35	45	....	....	....	93	....	....	....	....	....	....	....	....	....	....	8	2	3	5	4	....	....	....
1990-91	University of North Dakota	WCHA	33	3	6	9	....	....	....	18	....	....	....	....	....	....	....	....	....	....	....	....	....	....	....	....	....	....
1991-92	University of North Dakota	WCHA	35	3	14	17	....	....	....	54	....	....	....	....	....	....	....	....	....	....	....	....	....	....	....	....	....	....
	Canada	WJC-A	7	0	3	3	....	....	....	4	....	....	....	....	....	....	....	....	....	....	....	....	....	....	....	....	....	....
1992-93	University of North Dakota	WCHA	38	8	15	23	....	....	....	34	....	....	....	....	....	....	....	....	....	....	....	....	....	....	....	....	....	....
1993-94	University of North Dakota	WCHA	38	5	17	22	....	....	....	38	....	....	....	....	....	....	....	....	....	....	....	....	....	....	....	....	....	....
1994-95	Albany River Rats	AHL	77	5	22	27	....	....	....	22	....	....	....	....	....	....	....	....	....	....	14	0	3	3	6	....	....	....
1995-96	Albany River Rats	AHL	80	6	25	31	....	....	....	63	....	....	....	....	....	....	....	....	....	....	3	0	1	1	4	....	....	....
1996-97	Albany River Rats	AHL	32	0	8	8	....	....	....	6	....	....	....	....	....	....	....	....	....	....	16	1	3	4	8	....	....	....
1997-98	**New Jersey Devils**	**NHL**	**43**	**1**	**5**	**6**	**1**	**5**	**6**	**8**	**0**	**0**	**0**	**16**	**6.3**	**29**	**0**	**19**	**1**	**11**	....	....	....	....	....	....	....	....
	Albany River Rats	AHL	5	0	0	0	....	....	....	0	....	....	....	....	....	....	....	....	....	....	....	....	....	....	....	....	....	....
1998-99	**New Jersey Devils**	**NHL**	**56**	**1**	**7**	**8**	**1**	**7**	**8**	**16**	**0**	**0**	**0**	**47**	**2.1**	**32**	**2**	**35**	**1**	**–4**	**5**	**0**	**0**	**0**	**0**	**0**	**0**	**0**
99-2000	**New Jersey Devils**	**NHL**	**32**	**3**	**1**	**4**	**3**	**1**	**4**	**6**	**0**	**0**	**0**	**24**	**12.5**	**17**	**1**	**25**	**3**	**–6**	**1**	**0**	**0**	**0**	**0**	**0**	**0**	**0**
	NHL Totals		**131**	**5**	**13**	**18**	**5**	**13**	**18**	**30**	**0**	**0**	**0**	**87**	**5.7**	**78**	**3**	**79**	**5**		**6**	**0**	**0**	**0**	**0**	**0**	**0**	**0**

AHL Second All-Star Team (1996)

Traded to **Minnesota** by **New Jersey** for Chris Terreri and Minnesota's 9th round choice (later traded to Tampa Bay - Tampa Bay selected Thomas Ziegler) in 2000 Entry Draft, June 23, 2000.

• BONAR, Dan

Daniel Gordon C – R. 5'9", 175 lbs. b: Brandon, Man., 9/23/1956.

Season	Club	League	GP	G	A	Pts	AG	AA	APts	PIM	PP	SH	GW	S	%	TGF	PGF	TGA	PGA	+/-	GP	G	A	Pts	PIM	PP	SH	GW
1973-74	Portage Terriers	MJHL	48	39	41	80	....	....	....	81	....	....	....	....	....	....	....	....	....	....	....	....	....	....	....	....	....	....
1974-75	Brandon Wheat Kings	WCJHL	70	43	41	84	....	....	....	62	....	....	....	....	....	....	....	....	....	....	5	2	4	6	10	....	....	....
1975-76	Brandon Wheat Kings	WCJHL	69	44	59	103	....	....	....	49	....	....	....	....	....	....	....	....	....	....	5	2	3	5	0	....	....	....
1976-77	Brandon Wheat Kings	WCJHL	72	75	50	125	....	....	....	70	....	....	....	....	....	....	....	....	....	....	16	6	14	20	44	....	....	....
1977-78	Fort Wayne Komets	IHL	79	47	61	108	....	....	....	43	....	....	....	....	....	....	....	....	....	....	11	6	9	15	6	....	....	....
1978-79	Springfield Indians	AHL	80	33	39	72	....	....	....	30	....	....	....	....	....	....	....	....	....	....	....	....	....	....	....	....	....	....
1979-80	Binghamton Dusters	AHL	64	29	32	61	....	....	....	91	....	....	....	....	....	....	....	....	....	....	....	....	....	....	....	....	....	....
1980-81	**Los Angeles Kings**	**NHL**	**71**	**11**	**15**	**26**	**9**	**10**	**19**	**57**	**3**	**1**	**3**	**64**	**17.2**	**41**	**6**	**69**	**34**	**0**	**4**	**1**	**1**	**2**	**11**	**0**	**1**	**0**
1981-82	**Los Angeles Kings**	**NHL**	**79**	**13**	**23**	**36**	**10**	**15**	**25**	**111**	**1**	**0**	**0**	**123**	**10.6**	**48**	**1**	**92**	**41**	**–4**	**10**	**2**	**3**	**5**	**11**	**0**	**0**	**0**
1982-83	**Los Angeles Kings**	**NHL**	**20**	**1**	**1**	**2**	**1**	**1**	**2**	**40**	**0**	**0**	**0**	**16**	**6.3**	**2**	**0**	**18**	**9**	**–7**	....	....	....	....	....	....	....	....
	New Haven Nighthawks	AHL	22	10	13	23	....	....	....	29	....	....	....	....	....	....	....	....	....	....	11	1	7	8	13	....	....	....

Season	Club	League	GP	G	A	Pts	AG	AA	APts	PIM	PP	SH	GW	S	%	TGF	PGF	TGA	PGA	+/-	GP	G	A	Pts	PIM	PP	SH	GW
			REGULAR SEASON																		PLAYOFFS							
1983-84	New Haven Nighthawks	AHL	35	9	14	23	....	....	....	27	....	....	....	....	....	....	....	....	....	....	....	....	....	....	....	....	....	....
	Nova Scotia Voyageurs	AHL	44	13	23	36	....	....	....	75	....	....	....	....	....	....	....	....	....	....	12	4	7	11	38	....	....	....
1984-85	Adirondack Red Wings	AHL	31	3	13	16	....	....	....	43	....	....	....	....	....	....	....	....	....	....	....	....	....	....	....	....	....	....
	NHL Totals		**170**	**25**	**39**	**64**	**20**	**26**	**46**	**208**	**4**	**1**	**3**	**203**	**12.3**	**91**	**7**	**179**	**84**		**14**	**3**	**4**	**7**	**22**	**0**	**1**	**0**

IHL First All-Star Team (1978) • Won Garry F. Longman Memorial Trophy (Top Rookie - IHL) (1978) • Won James Gatschene Memorial Trophy (MVP - IHL) (1978)

Signed as a free agent by **LA Kings**, August 7, 1978. Traded to **Montreal** by **LA Kings** for cash, December 20, 1983.

• BONDRA, Peter

RW – L. 6′1″, 205 lbs. b: Luck, USSR, 2/7/1968. Washington's 9th, 156th overall, in 1990.

Season	Club	League	GP	G	A	Pts	AG	AA	APts	PIM	PP	SH	GW	S	%	TGF	PGF	TGA	PGA	+/-	GP	G	A	Pts	PIM	PP	SH	GW
1986-87	VSZ Kosice	Czech.	32	4	5	9	....	....	....	24	....	....	....	....	....	....	....	....	....	....	....	....	....	....	....	....	....	....
1987-88	VSZ Kosice	Czech.	45	27	11	38	....	....	....	20	....	....	....	....	....	....	....	....	....	....	....	....	....	....	....	....	....	....
1988-89	VSZ Kosice	Czech.	40	30	10	40	....	....	....	20	....	....	....	....	....	....	....	....	....	....	....	....	....	....	....	....	....	....
1989-90	VSZ Kosice	Czech.	44	29	17	46	....	....	....	....	....	....	....	....	....	....	....	....	....	....	5	7	2	9	....	....	....	....
1990-91	**Washington Capitals**	**NHL**	**54**	**12**	**16**	**28**	**11**	**12**	**23**	**47**	**4**	**0**	**1**	**95**	**12.6**	**36**	**6**	**40**	**0**	**–10**	**4**	**0**	**1**	**1**	**2**	**0**	**0**	**0**
1991-92	**Washington Capitals**	**NHL**	**71**	**28**	**28**	**56**	**25**	**21**	**46**	**42**	**4**	**0**	**3**	**158**	**17.7**	**73**	**13**	**47**	**3**	**16**	**7**	**6**	**2**	**8**	**4**	**1**	**0**	**0**
1992-93	**Washington Capitals**	**NHL**	**83**	**37**	**48**	**85**	**31**	**33**	**64**	**70**	**10**	**0**	**7**	**239**	**15.5**	**116**	**35**	**75**	**2**	**8**	**6**	**0**	**6**	**6**	**0**	**0**	**0**	**0**
1993-94	**Washington Capitals**	**NHL**	**69**	**24**	**19**	**43**	**22**	**15**	**37**	**40**	**4**	**0**	**2**	**200**	**12.0**	**69**	**12**	**36**	**1**	**22**	**9**	**2**	**4**	**6**	**4**	**0**	**0**	**1**
1994-95	HC Kosice	Slovakia	2	1	0	1	....	....	....	0	....	....	....	....	....	....	....	....	....	....	....	....	....	....	....	....	....	....
	Washington Capitals	**NHL**	**47**	***34**	**9**	**43**	**60**	**13**	**73**	**24**	**12**	**6**	**3**	**177**	**19.2**	**60**	**28**	**33**	**10**	**9**	**7**	**5**	**3**	**8**	**10**	**2**	**0**	**1**
1995-96	Detroit Vipers	IHL	7	8	1	9	....	....	....	0	....	....	....	....	....	....	....	....	....	....	....	....	....	....	....	....	....	....
	Washington Capitals	**NHL**	**67**	**52**	**28**	**80**	**51**	**23**	**74**	**40**	**11**	**4**	**7**	**322**	**16.1**	**102**	**32**	**60**	**8**	**18**	**6**	**3**	**2**	**5**	**8**	**2**	**0**	**1**
1996-97	Slovakia	W-Cup	3	3	0	3	....	....	....	2	....	....	....	....	....	....	....	....	....	....	....	....	....	....	....	....	....	....
	Washington Capitals	**NHL**	**77**	**46**	**31**	**77**	**49**	**28**	**77**	**72**	**10**	**4**	**3**	**314**	**14.6**	**99**	**30**	**65**	**3**	**7**	....	....	....	....	....	....	....	....
1997-98	**Washington Capitals**	**NHL**	**76**	***52**	**26**	**78**	**61**	**25**	**86**	**44**	**11**	**5**	**13**	**284**	**18.3**	**103**	**34**	**64**	**9**	**14**	**17**	**7**	**5**	**12**	**12**	**3**	**0**	**2**
	Slovakia	Olympics	2	1	0	1	....	....	....	25	....	....	....	....	....	....	....	....	....	....	....	....	....	....	....	....	....	....
1998-99	**Washington Capitals**	**NHL**	**66**	**31**	**24**	**55**	**36**	**23**	**59**	**56**	**6**	**3**	**5**	**284**	**10.9**	**81**	**29**	**64**	**11**	**–1**	....	....	....	....	....	....	....	....
99-2000	**Washington Capitals**	**NHL**	**62**	**21**	**17**	**38**	**24**	**16**	**40**	**30**	**5**	**3**	**5**	**187**	**11.2**	**59**	**19**	**42**	**7**	**5**	**5**	**1**	**1**	**2**	**4**	**1**	**0**	**0**
	NHL Totals		**672**	**337**	**246**	**583**	**370**	**209**	**579**	**465**	**77**	**25**	**49**	**2260**	**14.9**	**798**	**238**	**526**	**54**		**61**	**24**	**24**	**48**	**44**	**9**	**0**	**5**

Played in NHL All-Star Game (1993, 1996, 1997, 1998, 1999)

• BONIN, Brian

C – L. 5′10″, 185 lbs. b: St. Paul, MN, 11/28/1973. Pittsburgh's 9th, 211th overall, in 1992.

Season	Club	League	GP	G	A	Pts	AG	AA	APts	PIM	PP	SH	GW	S	%	TGF	PGF	TGA	PGA	+/-	GP	G	A	Pts	PIM	PP	SH	GW
1991-92	White Bear Lake Bears	Hi-School	23	22	35	57	....	....	....	8	....	....	....	....	....	....	....	....	....	....	....	....	....	....	....	....	....	....
1992-93	University of Minnesota	WCHA	38	10	18	28	....	....	....	10	....	....	....	....	....	....	....	....	....	....	....	....	....	....	....	....	....	....
1993-94	University of Minnesota	WCHA	42	24	20	44	....	....	....	14	....	....	....	....	....	....	....	....	....	....	....	....	....	....	....	....	....	....
1994-95	University of Minnesota	WCHA	44	32	31	*63	....	....	....	28	....	....	....	....	....	....	....	....	....	....	....	....	....	....	....	....	....	....
1995-96	University of Minnesota	WCHA	42	34	*47	*81	....	....	....	30	....	....	....	....	....	....	....	....	....	....	....	....	....	....	....	....	....	....
	United States	WC-A	8	1	0	1	....	....	....	2	....	....	....	....	....	....	....	....	....	....	....	....	....	....	....	....	....	....
1996-97	Cleveland Lumberjacks	IHL	60	13	26	39	....	....	....	18	....	....	....	....	....	....	....	....	....	....	1	1	0	1	0	....	....	....
1997-98	Syracuse Crunch	AHL	67	31	38	69	....	....	....	46	....	....	....	....	....	....	....	....	....	....	5	1	3	4	6	....	....	....
1998-99	**Pittsburgh Penguins**	**NHL**	**5**	**0**	**0**	**0**	**0**	**0**	**0**	**0**	**0**	**0**	**0**	**2**	**0.0**	**0**	**0**	**2**	**0**	**–2**	**3**	**0**	**0**	**0**	**0**	**0**	**0**	**0**
	Kansas City Blades	IHL	19	2	5	7	....	....	....	10	....	....	....	....	....	....	....	....	....	....	....	....	....	....	....	....	....	....
	Adirondack Red Wings	AHL	54	19	16	35	....	....	....	31	....	....	....	....	....	....	....	....	....	....	2	0	0	0	0	....	....	....
99-2000	Syracuse Crunch	AHL	67	19	28	47	....	....	....	20	....	....	....	....	....	....	....	....	....	....	4	0	1	1	0	....	....	....
	NHL Totals		**5**	**0**	**0**	**0**	**0**	**0**	**0**	**0**	**0**	**0**	**0**	**2**	**0.0**	**0**	**0**	**2**	**0**		**3**	**0**	**0**	**0**	**0**	**0**	**0**	**0**

WCHA First All-Star Team (1995, 1996) • NCAA West First All-American Team (1995, 1996) • Won Hobey Baker Memorial Award (Top U.S. Collegiate Player) (1996)

Signed as a free agent by **Vancouver**, September 9, 1999. Signed as a free agent by **Minnesota**, July 6, 2000.

• BONK, Radek

C – L. 6′3″, 210 lbs. b: Krnov, Czech., 1/9/1976. Ottawa's 1st, 3rd overall, in 1994.

Season	Club	League	GP	G	A	Pts	AG	AA	APts	PIM	PP	SH	GW	S	%	TGF	PGF	TGA	PGA	+/-	GP	G	A	Pts	PIM	PP	SH	GW
1990-91	HC Opava	Czech-Jr.	35	47	42	89	....	....	....	25	....	....	....	....	....	....	....	....	....	....	....	....	....	....	....	....	....	....
1991-92	ZPS Zlin	Czech-Jr.	45	47	36	83	....	....	....	30	....	....	....	....	....	....	....	....	....	....	....	....	....	....	....	....	....	....
1992-93	ZPS Zlin	Czech.	30	5	5	10	....	....	....	10	....	....	....	....	....	....	....	....	....	....	....	....	....	....	....	....	....	....
	Czech-Republic	EJC-A	6	4	2	6	....	....	....	6	....	....	....	....	....	....	....	....	....	....	....	....	....	....	....	....	....	....
1993-94	Las Vegas Thunder	IHL	76	42	45	87	....	....	....	208	....	....	....	....	....	....	....	....	....	....	5	1	2	3	10	....	....	....
1994-95	Las Vegas Thunder	IHL	33	7	13	20	....	....	....	62	....	....	....	....	....	....	....	....	....	....	....	....	....	....	....	....	....	....
	Ottawa Senators	**NHL**	**42**	**3**	**8**	**11**	**5**	**12**	**17**	**28**	**1**	**0**	**0**	**40**	**7.5**	**15**	**6**	**14**	**0**	**–5**	....	....	....	....	....	....	....	....
	P.E.I. Senators	AHL	....	....	....	....	....	....	....	....	....	....	....	....	....	....	....	....	....	....	1	0	0	0	0	....	....	....
1995-96	**Ottawa Senators**	**NHL**	**76**	**16**	**19**	**35**	**16**	**16**	**32**	**36**	**5**	**0**	**1**	**161**	**9.9**	**59**	**19**	**63**	**18**	**–5**	....	....	....	....	....	....	....	....
	Czech-Republic	WC-A	8	2	2	4	....	....	....	14	....	....	....	....	....	....	....	....	....	....	....	....	....	....	....	....	....	....
1996-97	Czech-Republic	W-Cup	3	1	0	1	....	....	....	0	....	....	....	....	....	....	....	....	....	....	....	....	....	....	....	....	....	....
	Ottawa Senators	**NHL**	**53**	**5**	**13**	**18**	**5**	**12**	**17**	**14**	**0**	**1**	**0**	**82**	**6.1**	**34**	**2**	**45**	**9**	**–4**	**7**	**0**	**1**	**1**	**4**	**0**	**0**	**0**
1997-98	**Ottawa Senators**	**NHL**	**65**	**7**	**9**	**16**	**8**	**9**	**17**	**16**	**1**	**0**	**0**	**93**	**7.5**	**27**	**7**	**35**	**2**	**–13**	**5**	**0**	**0**	**0**	**2**	**0**	**0**	**0**
1998-99	**Ottawa Senators**	**NHL**	**81**	**16**	**16**	**32**	**19**	**15**	**34**	**48**	**0**	**1**	**6**	**110**	**14.5**	**46**	**0**	**46**	**15**	**15**	**4**	**0**	**0**	**0**	**6**	**0**	**0**	**0**
99-2000	HC Pardubice	Czech-Rep	3	1	0	1	....	....	....	4	....	....	....	....	....	....	....	....	....	....	....	....	....	....	....	....	....	....
	Ottawa Senators	**NHL**	**80**	**23**	**37**	**60**	**26**	**34**	**60**	**53**	**10**	**0**	**5**	**167**	**13.8**	**73**	**24**	**56**	**5**	**–2**	**6**	**0**	**0**	**0**	**8**	**0**	**0**	**0**
	NHL Totals		**397**	**70**	**102**	**172**	**79**	**98**	**177**	**195**	**17**	**2**	**12**	**653**	**10.7**	**254**	**58**	**259**	**49**		**22**	**0**	**1**	**1**	**20**	**0**	**0**	**0**

Won Garry F. Longman Memorial Trophy (Top Rookie - IHL) (1994) • Played in NHL All-Star Game (2000)

• BONNI, Ryan

D – L. 6′4″, 190 lbs. b: Winnipeg, Man., 2/18/1979. Vancouver's 2nd, 34th overall, in 1997.

Season	Club	League	GP	G	A	Pts	AG	AA	APts	PIM	PP	SH	GW	S	%	TGF	PGF	TGA	PGA	+/-	GP	G	A	Pts	PIM	PP	SH	GW
1994-95	Winnipeg Sharks	MAHA	24	3	19	22	....	....	....	59	....	....	....	....	....	....	....	....	....	....	....	....	....	....	....	....	....	....
1995-96	Saskatoon Blades	WHL	63	1	7	8	....	....	....	78	....	....	....	....	....	....	....	....	....	....	3	0	0	0	0	....	....	....
1996-97	Saskatoon Blades	WHL	69	11	19	30	....	....	....	219	....	....	....	....	....	....	....	....	....	....	....	....	....	....	....	....	....	....
1997-98	Saskatoon Blades	WHL	42	5	14	19	....	....	....	100	....	....	....	....	....	....	....	....	....	....	0	0	0	0	0	....	....	....
1998-99	Saskatoon Blades	WHL	51	6	26	32	....	....	....	211	....	....	....	....	....	....	....	....	....	....	....	....	....	....	....	....	....	....
	Red Deer Rebels	WHL	20	3	10	13	....	....	....	41	....	....	....	....	....	....	....	....	....	....	9	0	4	4	25	....	....	....
99-2000	**Vancouver Canucks**	**NHL**	**3**	**0**	**0**	**0**	**0**	**0**	**0**	**0**	**0**	**0**	**0**	**1**	**0.0**	**1**	**0**	**3**	**1**	**–1**	....	....	....	....	....	....	....	....
	Syracuse Crunch	AHL	71	5	13	18	....	....	....	125	....	....	....	....	....	....	....	....	....	....	2	0	1	1	2	....	....	....
	NHL Totals		**3**	**0**	**0**	**0**	**0**	**0**	**0**	**0**	**0**	**0**	**0**	**1**	**0.0**	**1**	**0**	**3**	**1**		....	....	....	....	....	....	....	....

• BONSIGNORE, Jason

C – R. 6′4″, 220 lbs. b: Rochester, NY, 4/15/1976. Edmonton's 1st, 4th overall, in 1994.

Season	Club	League	GP	G	A	Pts	AG	AA	APts	PIM	PP	SH	GW	S	%	TGF	PGF	TGA	PGA	+/-	GP	G	A	Pts	PIM	PP	SH	GW
1989-90	Greece Lightning	Hi-School	18	33	33	66	....	....	....	....	....	....	....	....	....	....	....	....	....	....	....	....	....	....	....	....	....	....
1990-91	Greece Lightning	Hi-School	18	24	18	42	....	....	....	....	....	....	....	....	....	....	....	....	....	....	....	....	....	....	....	....	....	....
1991-92	Rochester Jr. Americans	NAJHL	60	31	29	60	....	....	....	42	....	....	....	....	....	....	....	....	....	....	....	....	....	....	....	....	....	....
1992-93	Newmarket Royals	OHL	66	22	20	42	....	....	....	6	....	....	....	....	....	....	....	....	....	....	7	0	3	3	0	....	....	....
1993-94	Newmarket Royals	OHL	17	7	17	24	....	....	....	22	....	....	....	....	....	....	....	....	....	....	....	....	....	....	....	....	....	....
	United States	Nat-Team	5	0	2	2	....	....	....	0	....	....	....	....	....	....	....	....	....	....	....	....	....	....	....	....	....	....
	United States	WJC-A	7	0	0	0	....	....	....	26	....	....	....	....	....	....	....	....	....	....	....	....	....	....	....	....	....	....
	Niagara Falls Thunder	OHL	41	15	47	62	....	....	....	41	....	....	....	....	....	....	....	....	....	....	....	....	....	....	....	....	....	....
1994-95	Niagara Falls Thunder	OHL	26	12	21	33	....	....	....	51	....	....	....	....	....	....	....	....	....	....	....	....	....	....	....	....	....	....
	United States	WJC-A	7	2	2	4	....	....	....	6	....	....	....	....	....	....	....	....	....	....	....	....	....	....	....	....	....	....
	Sudbury Wolves	OHL	23	15	14	29	....	....	....	45	....	....	....	....	....	....	....	....	....	....	17	13	10	23	12	....	....	....
	Edmonton Oilers	**NHL**	**1**	**1**	**0**	**1**	**2**	**0**	**2**	**0**	**0**	**0**	**0**	**3**	**33.3**	**2**	**1**	**2**	**0**	**–1**	....	....	....	....	....	....	....	....
1995-96	Sudbury Wolves	OHL	18	10	16	26	....	....	....	37	....	....	....	....	....	....	....	....	....	....	....	....	....	....	....	....	....	....
	Edmonton Oilers	**NHL**	**20**	**0**	**2**	**2**	**0**	**2**	**2**	**4**	**0**	**0**	**0**	**13**	**0.0**	**5**	**1**	**11**	**1**	**–6**	....	....	....	....	....	....	....	....
	Cape Breton Oilers	AHL	12	1	4	5	....	....	....	12	....	....	....	....	....	....	....	....	....	....	....	....	....	....	....	....	....	....
1996-97	Hamilton Bulldogs	AHL	78	21	33	54	....	....	....	78	....	....	....	....	....	....	....	....	....	....	7	0	0	0	4	....	....	....

			REGULAR SEASON																		PLAYOFFS							
Season	**Club**	**League**	**GP**	**G**	**A**	**Pts**	**AG**	**AA**	**APts**	**PIM**	**PP**	**SH**	**GW**	**S**	**%**	**TGF**	**PGF**	**TGA**	**PGA**	**+/–**	**GP**	**G**	**A**	**Pts**	**PIM**	**PP**	**SH**	**GW**
1997-98	Hamilton Bulldogs	AHL	8	0	2	2	....	....	....	14	....	....	....	....	....	....	....	....	....	....	....	....	....	....	....	....	....	....
	San Antonio Dragons	IHL	22	3	8	11	....	....	....	34	....	....	....	....	....	....	....	....	....	....	....	....	....	....	....	....	....	....
	Tampa Bay Lightning	**NHL**	**35**	**2**	**8**	**10**	**2**	**8**	**10**	**22**	**0**	**0**	**0**	**29**	**6.9**	**12**	**2**	**22**	**1**	**–11**	....	....	....	....	....	....	....	....
	Cleveland Lumberjacks	IHL	6	4	0	4	....	....	....	32	....	....	....	....	....	....	....	....	....	....	8	1	1	2	20	....	....	....
1998-99	**Tampa Bay Lighning**	**NHL**	**23**	**0**	**3**	**3**	**0**	**3**	**3**	**8**	**0**	**0**	**0**	**12**	**0.0**	**5**	**0**	**9**	**0**	**–4**	....	....	....	....	....	....	....	....
	Cleveland Lumberjacks	IHL	48	14	19	33	....	....	....	68	....	....	....	....	....	....	....	....	....	....	....	....	....	....	....	....	....	....
99-2000	St. John's Maple Leafs	AHL	29	6	13	19	....	....	....	30	....	....	....	....	....	....	....	....	....	....	....	....	....	....	....	....	....	....
	NHL Totals		**79**	**3**	**13**	**16**	**4**	**13**	**17**	**34**	**0**	**0**	**0**	**57**	**5.3**	**24**	**4**	**44**	**2**		....	....	....	....	....	....	....	....

Traded to **Tampa Bay** by **Edmonton** with Bryan Marchment and Steve Kelly for Roman Hamrlik and Paul Comrie, December 30, 1997. Signed as a free agent by **Toronto**, July 15, 1999.

• BONVIE, Dennis

Dennis Kevin RW/D – R. 5'11", 205 lbs. b: Antigonish, N.S., 7/23/1973.

Season	Club	League	GP	G	A	Pts	AG	AA	APts	PIM	PP	SH	GW	S	%	TGF	PGF	TGA	PGA	+/–	GP	G	A	Pts	PIM	PP	SH	GW
1989-90	Antigonish Bulldogs	NSAHA	50	15	30	45	....	....	....	52	....	....	....	....	....	....	....	....	....	....	....	....	....	....	....	....	....	....
1990-91	Antigonish Bulldogs	MJrHL	40	1	8	9	....	....	....	347	....	....	....	....	....	....	....	....	....	....	....	....	....	....	....	....	....	....
1991-92	Kitchener Rangers	OHL	7	1	1	2	....	....	....	23	....	....	....	....	....	....	....	....	....	....	....	....	....	....	....	....	....	....
	North Bay Centennials	OHL	49	0	12	12	....	....	....	261	....	....	....	....	....	....	....	....	....	....	21	0	1	1	91	....	....	....
1992-93	North Bay Centennials	OHL	64	3	21	24	....	....	....	*316	....	....	....	....	....	....	....	....	....	....	5	0	0	0	34	....	....	....
1993-94	Cape Breton Oilers	AHL	63	1	10	11	....	....	....	278	....	....	....	....	....	....	....	....	....	....	4	0	0	0	11	....	....	....
1994-95	**Edmonton Oilers**	**NHL**	**2**	**0**	**0**	**0**	**0**	**0**	**0**	**0**	**0**	**0**	**0**	**0**	**0.0**	**0**	**0**	**0**	**0**	**0**	....	....	....	....	....	....	....	....
	Cape Breton Oilers	AHL	74	5	15	20	....	....	....	422	....	....	....	....	....	....	....	....	....	....	....	....	....	....	....	....	....	....
1995-96	**Edmonton Oilers**	**NHL**	**8**	**0**	**0**	**0**	**0**	**0**	**0**	**47**	**0**	**0**	**0**	**0**	**0.0**	**0**	**0**	**3**	**0**	**–3**	....	....	....	....	....	....	....	....
	Cape Breton Oilers	AHL	38	13	14	27	....	....	....	269	....	....	....	....	....	....	....	....	....	....	....	....	....	....	....	....	....	....
1996-97	Hamilton Bulldogs	AHL	73	9	20	29	....	....	....	*522	....	....	....	....	....	....	....	....	....	....	22	3	11	14	*91	....	....	....
1997-98	**Edmonton Oilers**	**NHL**	**4**	**0**	**0**	**0**	**0**	**0**	**0**	**27**	**0**	**0**	**0**	**0**	**0.0**	**0**	**0**	**0**	**0**	**0**	....	....	....	....	....	....	....	....
	Hamilton Bulldogs	AHL	57	11	19	30	....	....	....	295	....	....	....	....	....	....	....	....	....	....	9	0	5	5	18	....	....	....
1998-99	**Chicago Blackhawks**	**NHL**	**11**	**0**	**0**	**0**	**0**	**0**	**0**	**44**	**0**	**0**	**0**	**1**	**0.0**	**0**	**0**	**4**	**0**	**–4**	....	....	....	....	....	....	....	....
	Portland Pirates	AHL	3	1	0	1	....	....	....	16	....	....	....	....	....	....	....	....	....	....	....	....	....	....	....	....	....	....
	Philadelphia Phantoms	AHL	37	4	10	14	....	....	....	158	....	....	....	....	....	....	....	....	....	....	14	3	3	6	26	....	....	....
99-2000	**Pittsburgh Penguins**	**NHL**	**28**	**0**	**0**	**0**	**0**	**0**	**0**	**80**	**0**	**0**	**0**	**6**	**0.0**	**2**	**0**	**4**	**0**	**–2**	....	....	....	....	....	....	....	....
	Wilkes-Barre Penguins	AHL	42	5	26	31	....	....	....	243	....	....	....	....	....	....	....	....	....	....	....	....	....	....	....	....	....	....
	NHL Totals		**53**	**0**	**0**	**0**	**0**	**0**	**0**	**198**	**0**	**0**	**0**	**7**	**0.0**	**2**	**0**	**11**	**0**		....	....	....	....	....	....	....	....

Signed as a free agent by **Edmonton**, August 25, 1994. Claimed by **Chicago** from **Edmonton** in NHL Waiver Draft, October 5, 1998. Traded to **Philadelphia** by **Chicago** for Frank Bialowas, January 8, 1999. Signed as a free agent by **Pittsburgh**, September 20, 1999.

• BOO, Jim

James McQuaid D – R. 6'1", 200 lbs. b: Rolla, MO, 11/12/1954.

Season	Club	League	GP	G	A	Pts	AG	AA	APts	PIM	PP	SH	GW	S	%	TGF	PGF	TGA	PGA	+/–	GP	G	A	Pts	PIM	PP	SH	GW
1973-74	St. Paul Vulcans	MWJHL	STATISTICS NOT AVAILABLE																									
1974-75	University of Minnesota	WCHA	DID NOT PLAY – FRESHMAN																									
1975-76	University of Minnesota	WCHA	19	0	1	1	....	....	....	21	....	....	....	....	....	....	....	....	....	....	....	....	....	....	....	....	....	....
1976-77	University of Minnesota	WCHA	37	2	10	12	....	....	....	66	....	....	....	....	....	....	....	....	....	....	....	....	....	....	....	....	....	....
1977-78	University of Minnesota	WCHA	37	4	17	21	....	....	....	63	....	....	....	....	....	....	....	....	....	....	....	....	....	....	....	....	....	....
	Minnesota North Stars	**NHL**	**6**	**0**	**0**	**0**	**0**	**0**	**0**	**22**	**0**	**0**	**0**	**2**	**0.0**	**0**	**0**	**6**	**0**	**–6**	....	....	....	....	....	....	....	....
	Fort Worth Texans	CHL	9	0	2	2	....	....	....	17	....	....	....	....	....	....	....	....	....	....	9	0	1	1	23	....	....	....
1978-79	Oklahoma City Stars	CHL	71	2	19	21	....	....	....	170	....	....	....	....	....	....	....	....	....	....	....	....	....	....	....	....	....	....
1979-80	Oklahoma City Stars	CHL	54	3	14	17	....	....	....	24	....	....	....	....	....	....	....	....	....	....	....	....	....	....	....	....	....	....
	NHL Totals		**6**	**0**	**0**	**0**	**0**	**0**	**0**	**22**	**0**	**0**	**0**	**2**	**0.0**	**0**	**0**	**6**	**0**		....	....	....	....	....	....	....	....

Signed as a free agent by **Minnesota**, March 1, 1978.

• BORDELEAU, Christian

Christian Gerrard C – L. 5'8", 172 lbs. b: Noranda, Que., 9/23/1947.

Season	Club	League	GP	G	A	Pts	AG	AA	APts	PIM	PP	SH	GW	S	%	TGF	PGF	TGA	PGA	+/–	GP	G	A	Pts	PIM	PP	SH	GW
1962-63	Noranda Copper Kings	NOJHA	40	42	36	*78	....	....	....	....	....	....	....	....	....	....	....	....	....	....	....	....	....	....	....	....	....	....
1963-64	Montreal Jr. Canadiens	OHA-Jr.	49	16	18	34	....	....	....	10	....	....	....	....	....	....	....	....	....	....	17	3	2	5	2	....	....	....
1964-65	Montreal Jr. Canadiens	OHA-Jr.	50	28	28	56	....	....	....	46	....	....	....	....	....	....	....	....	....	....	7	6	2	8	8	....	....	....
1965-66	Montreal Jr. Canadiens	OHA-Jr.	43	15	48	63	....	....	....	57	....	....	....	....	....	....	....	....	....	....	10	9	5	14	13	....	....	....
1966-67	Montreal Jr. Canadiens	OHA-Jr.	33	8	19	27	....	....	....	30	....	....	....	....	....	....	....	....	....	....	....	....	....	....	....	....	....	....
1967-68	Houston Apollos	CPHL	68	23	28	51	....	....	....	22	....	....	....	....	....	....	....	....	....	....	....	....	....	....	....	....	....	....
1968-69♦	**Montreal Canadiens**	**NHL**	**13**	**1**	**3**	**4**	**1**	**3**	**4**	**4**	**0**	**0**	**0**	**14**	**7.1**	**4**	**0**	**4**	**1**	**1**	**6**	**1**	**0**	**1**	**0**	**0**	**0**	**1**
	Houston Apollos	CHL	54	21	36	57	....	....	....	33	....	....	....	....	....	....	....	....	....	....	....	....	....	....	....	....	....	....
1969-70	**Montreal Canadiens**	**NHL**	**48**	**2**	**13**	**15**	**2**	**12**	**14**	**18**	**0**	**0**	**0**	**51**	**3.9**	**23**	**0**	**29**	**8**	**2**	....	....	....	....	....	....	....	....
	Montreal Canadiens	Mem-Cup	12	5	8	13	....	....	....	4	....	....	....	....	....	....	....	....	....	....	....	....	....	....	....	....	....	....
1970-71	**St. Louis Blues**	**NHL**	**78**	**21**	**32**	**53**	**21**	**27**	**48**	**48**	**3**	**2**	**7**	**187**	**11.2**	**71**	**16**	**52**	**11**	**14**	**5**	**0**	**1**	**1**	**17**	**0**	**0**	**0**
1971-72	**St. Louis Blues**	**NHL**	**41**	**8**	**9**	**17**	**8**	**8**	**16**	**6**	**1**	**0**	**1**	**123**	**6.5**	**27**	**7**	**47**	**14**	**–13**	....	....	....	....	....	....	....	....
	Chicago Black Hawks	**NHL**	**25**	**6**	**8**	**14**	**6**	**7**	**13**	**6**	**1**	**0**	**1**	**35**	**17.1**	**18**	**2**	**11**	**0**	**5**	**8**	**3**	**6**	**9**	**0**	**0**	**0**	**1**
1972-73	Winnipeg Jets	WHA	78	47	54	101	....	....	....	12	....	....	....	....	....	....	....	....	....	....	12	5	8	13	4	....	....	....
1973-74	Winnipeg Jets	WHA	75	26	49	75	....	....	....	22	....	....	....	....	....	....	....	....	....	....	3	3	2	5	0	....	....	....
1974-75	Winnipeg Jets	WHA	18	8	8	16	....	....	....	0	....	....	....	....	....	....	....	....	....	....	....	....	....	....	....	....	....	....
	Quebec Nordiques	WHA	53	15	33	48	....	....	....	24	....	....	....	....	....	....	....	....	....	....	15	2	*13	15	2	....	....	....
1975-76	Quebec Nordiques	WHA	74	37	72	109	....	....	....	42	....	....	....	....	....	....	....	....	....	....	5	1	1	2	4	....	....	....
1976-77	Quebec Nordiques	WHA	72	32	75	107	....	....	....	34	....	....	....	....	....	....	....	....	....	....	8	4	5	9	0	....	....	....
1977-78	Quebec Nordiques	WHA	26	9	22	31	....	....	....	28	....	....	....	....	....	....	....	....	....	....	10	1	5	6	6	....	....	....
1978-79	Quebec Nordiques	WHA	16	5	12	17	....	....	....	0	....	....	....	....	....	....	....	....	....	....	....	....	....	....	....	....	....	....
1979-80	Salt Lake Golden Eagles	CHL	11	3	6	9	....	....	....	4	....	....	....	....	....	....	....	....	....	....	....	....	....	....	....	....	....	....
	NHL Totals		**205**	**38**	**65**	**103**	**38**	**57**	**95**	**82**	**5**	**2**	**9**	**410**	**9.3**	**143**	**25**	**143**	**34**		**19**	**4**	**7**	**11**	**17**	**0**	**0**	**2**
	Other Major League Totals		412	179	325	504	....	....	....	162	....	....	....	....	....	....	....	....	....	....	53	16	34	50	16	....	....	....

Brother of J.P. and Paulin

Traded to **St. Louis** by **Montreal** for cash, May 22, 1970. Traded to **Chicago** by **St. Louis** with future considerations (John Garrett, September 19, 1972) for Danny O'Shea, February 8, 1972. Selected by **LA Sharks** (WHA) in 1972 WHA General Player Draft, February 12, 1972. WHA rights traded to **Winnipeg** (WHA) by **LA Sharks** (WHA) for cash, August 25, 1972. Traded to **St. Louis** by **Chicago** for rights to John Garrett, September 15, 1972. Traded to **Quebec** (WHA) by **Winnipeg** (WHA) for Alain Beaule, December 5, 1974. Reclaimed by **St. Louis** from **Quebec** prior to Expansion Draft, June 9, 1979.

• BORDELEAU, J.P.

Jean-Pierre RW – R. 6'1", 175 lbs. b: Noranda, Que., 6/13/1949. Chicago's 1st, 13th overall, in 1969.

Season	Club	League	GP	G	A	Pts	AG	AA	APts	PIM	PP	SH	GW	S	%	TGF	PGF	TGA	PGA	+/–	GP	G	A	Pts	PIM	PP	SH	GW
1967-68	Montreal Jr. Canadiens	OHA-Jr.	54	22	21	43	....	....	....	96	....	....	....	....	....	....	....	....	....	....	11	2	4	6	8	....	....	....
1968-69	Montreal Jr. Canadiens	OHA-Jr.	51	17	36	53	....	....	....	150	....	....	....	....	....	....	....	....	....	....	14	2	11	13	8	....	....	....
	Montreal Jr. Canadiens	Mem-Cup	4	4	1	5	....	....	....	10	....	....	....	....	....	....	....	....	....	....	....	....	....	....	....	....	....	....
1969-70	Dallas Black Hawks	CHL	62	14	15	29	....	....	....	44	....	....	....	....	....	....	....	....	....	....	....	....	....	....	....	....	....	....
	Chicago Black Hawks	**NHL**	....	....	....	....	....	....	....	....	....	....	....	....	....	....	....	....	....	....	**1**	**0**	**0**	**0**	**0**	**0**	**0**	**0**
1970-71	Dallas Black Hawks	CHL	35	15	15	30	....	....	....	48	....	....	....	....	....	....	....	....	....	....	6	2	0	2	4	....	....	....
1971-72	**Chicago Black Hawks**	**NHL**	**3**	**0**	**2**	**2**	**0**	**2**	**2**	**2**	**0**	**0**	**0**	**4**	**0.0**	**2**	**0**	**2**	**1**	**1**	....	....	....	....	....	....	....	....
	Dallas Black Hawks	CHL	70	*41	31	72	....	....	....	72	....	....	....	....	....	....	....	....	....	....	12	*10	2	12	0	....	....	....
1972-73	**Chicago Black Hawks**	**NHL**	**73**	**15**	**15**	**30**	**14**	**12**	**26**	**6**	**0**	**1**	**2**	**113**	**13.3**	**44**	**6**	**35**	**4**	**7**	**14**	**1**	**0**	**1**	**4**	**1**	**0**	**0**
1973-74	**Chicago Black Hawks**	**NHL**	**64**	**11**	**9**	**20**	**11**	**7**	**18**	**11**	**0**	**0**	**3**	**50**	**22.0**	**34**	**1**	**24**	**2**	**11**	**11**	**0**	**2**	**2**	**2**	**0**	**0**	**0**
1974-75	**Chicago Black Hawks**	**NHL**	**59**	**7**	**8**	**15**	**6**	**6**	**12**	**4**	**0**	**0**	**1**	**42**	**16.7**	**18**	**1**	**26**	**4**	**–5**	**7**	**2**	**2**	**4**	**2**	**0**	**0**	**0**
1975-76	**Chicago Black Hawks**	**NHL**	**76**	**12**	**18**	**30**	**11**	**13**	**24**	**6**	**1**	**0**	**2**	**71**	**16.9**	**48**	**12**	**46**	**1**	**–9**	**4**	**0**	**0**	**0**	**0**	**0**	**0**	**0**
1976-77	**Chicago Black Hawks**	**NHL**	**60**	**15**	**14**	**29**	**13**	**11**	**24**	**20**	**2**	**0**	**1**	**84**	**17.9**	**46**	**8**	**56**	**4**	**–14**	**2**	**0**	**0**	**0**	**2**	**0**	**0**	**0**
1977-78	**Chicago Black Hawks**	**NHL**	**76**	**15**	**25**	**40**	**14**	**19**	**33**	**32**	**0**	**2**	**3**	**103**	**14.6**	**67**	**12**	**52**	**6**	**9**	**4**	**0**	**1**	**1**	**0**	**0**	**0**	**0**
1978-79	**Chicago Black Hawks**	**NHL**	**63**	**15**	**21**	**36**	**13**	**15**	**28**	**34**	**2**	**1**	**2**	**101**	**14.9**	**51**	**12**	**54**	**8**	**–7**	**4**	**0**	**1**	**1**	**2**	**0**	**0**	**0**
1979-80	**Chicago Black Hawks**	**NHL**	**45**	**7**	**14**	**21**	**6**	**10**	**16**	**28**	**1**	**0**	**0**	**53**	**13.2**	**28**	**2**	**28**	**5**	**3**	**1**	**0**	**0**	**0**	**0**	**0**	**0**	**0**
1980-81	New Brunswick Hawks	AHL	64	24	28	52	....	....	....	71	....	....	....	....	....	....	....	....	....	....	13	4	9	13	6	....	....	....

Season	Club	League	GP	G	A	Pts	AG	AA	APts	PIM	PP	SH	GW	S	%	TGF	PGF	TGA	PGA	+/-	GP	G	A	Pts	PIM	PP	SH	GW
			REGULAR SEASON																		PLAYOFFS							
1981-82	New Brunswick Hawks	AHL	15	5	8	13	....	....	....	10	....	....	....	....	....	....	....	....	....	....	....	....	....	....	....	....	....	....
1982-83	Riverview Trappers	NBSHL	....	44	28	72	....	....	....	....	....	....	....	....	....	....	....	....	....	....	....	....	....	....	....	....	....	....
1983-84	Riverview Trappers	NBSHL	2	0	3	3	....	....	....	2	....	....	....	....	....	....	....	....	....	....	....	....	....	....	....	....	....	....
	NHL Totals		**519**	**97**	**126**	**223**	**88**	**95**	**183**	**143**	**6**	**4**	**14**	**621**	**15.6**	**338**	**54**	**323**	**35**		**48**	**3**	**6**	**9**	**12**	**1**	**0**	**0**

• Brother of Paulin and Christian • CHL First All-Star Team (1972)

• BORDELEAU, Paulin

Paulin Joseph RW – R. 5'9", 162 lbs. b: Noranda, Que., 1/29/1953. Vancouver's 3rd, 19th overall, in 1973.

Season	Club	League	GP	G	A	Pts	AG	AA	APts	PIM	PP	SH	GW	S	%	TGF	PGF	TGA	PGA	+/-	GP	G	A	Pts	PIM	PP	SH	GW
1969-70	Montreal Jr. Canadiens	OHA-Jr.	41	18	29	47	....	....	....	48	....	....	....	....	....	....	....	....	....	....	16	3	6	9	6	....	....	....
	Montreal Jr. Canadiens	Mem-Cup	12	5	8	13	....	....	....	4	....	....	....	....	....	....	....	....	....	....	....	....	....	....	....	....	....	....
1970-71	Toronto Marlboros	OHA-Jr.	45	27	42	69	....	....	....	69	....	....	....	....	....	....	....	....	....	....	13	13	11	24	24	....	....	....
1971-72	Toronto Marlboros	OMJHL	34	34	33	67	....	....	....	37	....	....	....	....	....	....	....	....	....	....	10	9	7	16	7	....	....	....
1972-73	Toronto Marlboros	OMJHL	56	54	43	97	....	....	....	26	....	....	....	....	....	....	....	....	....	....	....	7	9	16	5	....	....	....
	Toronto Marlboros	Mem-Cup	3	*4	*4	*8	....	....	....	2	....	....	....	....	....	....	....	....	....	....	....	....	....	....	....	....	....	....
1973-74	**Vancouver Canucks**	**NHL**	**68**	**11**	**13**	**24**	**11**	**11**	**22**	**20**	**4**	**0**	**1**	**77**	**14.3**	**38**	**14**	**40**	**0**	**-16**	....	....	....	....	....	....	....	....
1974-75	**Vancouver Canucks**	**NHL**	**67**	**17**	**31**	**48**	**15**	**23**	**38**	**21**	**3**	**0**	**6**	**101**	**16.8**	**70**	**21**	**41**	**1**	**9**	**5**	**2**	**1**	**3**	**0**	**1**	**0**	**0**
1975-76	**Vancouver Canucks**	**NHL**	**48**	**5**	**12**	**17**	**4**	**9**	**13**	**6**	**0**	**0**	**1**	**35**	**14.3**	**26**	**5**	**24**	**2**	**-1**	....	....	....	....	....	....	....	....
	Tulsa Oilers	CHL	14	5	9	14	....	....	....	11	....	....	....	....	....	....	....	....	....	....	....	....	....	....	....	....	....	....
1976-77	Quebec Nordiques	WHA	80	42	41	83	....	....	....	52	....	....	....	....	....	....	....	....	....	....	16	12	9	21	12	....	....	....
1977-78	Quebec Nordiques	WHA	77	42	23	65	....	....	....	29	....	....	....	....	....	....	....	....	....	....	11	4	6	10	2	....	....	....
1978-79	Quebec Nordiques	WHA	77	17	12	29	....	....	....	44	....	....	....	....	....	....	....	....	....	....	4	1	0	1	0	....	....	....
1979-80			STATISTICS NOT AVAILABLE																									
1980-81	HC Tours	France	26	26	14	40	....	....	....		....	....	....	....	....	....	....	....	....	....	10	17	9	26	....	....	....	....
1981-82	HC Megeve	France	26	33	20	53	....	....	....	....	....	....	....	....	....	....	....	....	....	....	....	....	....	....	....	....	....	....
1982-83	HC Megeve	France	28	44	28	72	....	....	....	....	....	....	....	....	....	....	....	....	....	....	....	....	....	....	....	....	....	....
1983-84	HC Megeve	France	32	39	29	68	....	....	....	....	....	....	....	....	....	....	....	....	....	....	....	....	....	....	....	....	....	....
1984-85	HC Megeve	France	32	16	10	26	....	....	....	....	....	....	....	....	....	....	....	....	....	....	....	....	....	....	....	....	....	....
1985-86	HC Megeve	France	32	22	44	66	....	....	....	....	....	....	....	....	....	....	....	....	....	....	....	....	....	....	....	....	....	....
	France	WEC-B	7	2	1	3	....	....	....	4	....	....	....	....	....	....	....	....	....	....	....	....	....	....	....	....	....	....
1986-87	HC Mont-Blanc	France	37	57	47	104	....	....	....	....	....	....	....	....	....	....	....	....	....	....	....	....	....	....	....	....	....	....
	France	WEC-B	7	9	6	15	....	....	....	15	....	....	....	....	....	....	....	....	....	....	....	....	....	....	....	....	....	....
1987-88	HC Mont-Blanc	France	28	20	22	42	....	....	....	63	....	....	....	....	....	....	....	....	....	....	....	....	....	....	....	....	....	....
	France	Olympics	6	2	2	4	....	....	....	24	....	....	....	....	....	....	....	....	....	....	....	....	....	....	....	....	....	....
1988-1989	Laval Titan	QMJHL	DID NOT PLAY – COACHING																									
1989-1990	Laval Titan	QMJHL	DID NOT PLAY – COACHING																									
	Halifax Citadels	AHL	DID NOT PLAY – COACHING																									
1990-1996	Fredericton Canadiens	AHL	DID NOT PLAY – COACHING																									
1996-1997	Fredericton Canadiens	AHL	DID NOT PLAY – COACHING																									
	Fredericton Canadiens	AHL	1	0	2	2	....	....	....	2	....	....	....	....	....	....	....	....	....	....	....	....	....	....	....	....	....	....
1997-1998	Laval College-Francais	QMJHL	DID NOT PLAY – COACHING																									
1998-1999	**Tampa Bay Lightning**	**NHL**	DID NOT PLAY – ASSISTANT COACH																									
1999-2000	Detroit Vipers	IHL	DID NOT PLAY – COACHING																									
	NHL Totals		**183**	**33**	**56**	**89**	**30**	**43**	**73**	**47**	**7**	**0**	**8**	**213**	**15.5**	**134**	**40**	**105**	**3**		**5**	**2**	**1**	**3**	**0**	**1**	**0**	**0**
	Other Major League Totals		234	101	76	177	....	....	....	125	....	....	....	....	....	....	....	....	....	....	31	17	15	32	14	....	....	....

• Brother of Christian and Jean-Pierre (J.P.) • Father of Sebastien

Selected by **Toronto** (WHA) in 1973 WHA Amateur Draft, June, 1973. WHA rights traded to **Quebec** (WHA) by **Birmingham** (WHA) for future considerations, August, 1976. • Played one game as injury replacement while coaching **Fredericton** (AHL), February, 1996.

• BORDELEAU, Sebastien

C – R. 5'11", 187 lbs. b: Vancouver, B.C., 2/15/1975. Montreal's 3rd, 73rd overall, in 1993.

Season	Club	League	GP	G	A	Pts	AG	AA	APts	PIM	PP	SH	GW	S	%	TGF	PGF	TGA	PGA	+/-	GP	G	A	Pts	PIM	PP	SH	GW
1990-91	Laval-Laurentides Regents	QAAA	39	27	36	63	....	....	....	....	....	....	....	....	....	....	....	....	....	....	....	....	....	....	....	....	....	....
1991-92	Hull Olympiques	QMJHL	62	26	32	58	....	....	....	91	....	....	....	....	....	....	....	....	....	....	5	0	3	3	23	....	....	....
1992-93	Hull Olympiques	QMJHL	60	18	39	57	....	....	....	95	....	....	....	....	....	....	....	....	....	....	10	3	8	11	20	....	....	....
1993-94	Hull Olympiques	QMJHL	60	26	57	83	....	....	....	147	....	....	....	....	....	....	....	....	....	....	17	6	14	20	26	....	....	....
1994-95	Hull Olympiques	QMJHL	68	52	76	128	....	....	....	142	....	....	....	....	....	....	....	....	....	....	18	*13	19	*32	25	....	....	....
	Fredericton Canadiens	AHL	....	....	....	....	....	....	....	....	....	....	....	....	....	....	....	....	....	....	1	0	0	0	0	....	....	....
	Hull Olympiques	Mem-Cup	3	1	0	1	....	....	....	4	....	....	....	....	....	....	....	....	....	....	....	....	....	....	....	....	....	....
1995-96	**Montreal Canadiens**	**NHL**	**4**	**0**	**0**	**0**	**0**	**0**	**0**	**0**	**0**	**0**	**0**	**0**	**0.0**	**0**	**0**	**1**	**0**	**-1**	....	....	....	....	....	....	....	....
	Fredericton Canadiens	AHL	43	17	29	46	....	....	....	68	....	....	....	....	....	....	....	....	....	....	7	0	2	2	8	....	....	....
1996-97	**Montreal Canadiens**	**NHL**	**28**	**2**	**9**	**11**	**2**	**8**	**10**	**2**	**0**	**0**	**0**	**27**	**7.4**	**13**	**0**	**23**	**7**	**-3**	....	....	....	....	....	....	....	....
	Fredericton Canadiens	AHL	34	18	22	40	....	....	....	50	....	....	....	....	....	....	....	....	....	....	....	....	....	....	....	....	....	....
1997-98	**Montreal Canadiens**	**NHL**	**53**	**6**	**8**	**14**	**7**	**8**	**15**	**36**	**2**	**1**	**0**	**55**	**10.9**	**23**	**10**	**13**	**5**	**5**	**5**	**0**	**0**	**0**	**2**	**0**	**0**	**0**
1998-99	**Nashville Predators**	**NHL**	**72**	**16**	**24**	**40**	**19**	**23**	**42**	**26**	**1**	**2**	**3**	**168**	**9.5**	**45**	**5**	**75**	**21**	**-14**	....	....	....	....	....	....	....	....
99-2000	**Nashville Predators**	**NHL**	**60**	**10**	**13**	**23**	**11**	**12**	**23**	**30**	**0**	**2**	**1**	**127**	**7.9**	**32**	**0**	**51**	**7**	**-12**	....	....	....	....	....	....	....	....
	NHL Totals		**217**	**34**	**54**	**88**	**39**	**51**	**90**	**94**	**3**	**5**	**4**	**377**	**9.0**	**113**	**15**	**163**	**40**		**5**	**0**	**0**	**0**	**2**	**0**	**0**	**0**

• Son of Paulin • QMJHL First All-Star Team (1995)

Traded to **Nashville** by **Montreal** for future considerations, June 26, 1998.

• BOROTSIK, Jack

Jack Nicolas C – L. 5'9", 180 lbs. b: Brandon, Man., 11/26/1949.

Season	Club	League	GP	G	A	Pts	AG	AA	APts	PIM	PP	SH	GW	S	%	TGF	PGF	TGA	PGA	+/-	GP	G	A	Pts	PIM	PP	SH	GW
1967-68	Brandon Wheat Kings	WCJHL	60	36	49	85	....	....	....	37	....	....	....	....	....	....	....	....	....	....	....	....	....	....	....	....	....	....
1968-69	Brandon Wheat Kings	WCJHL	59	24	40	64	....	....	....	2	....	....	....	....	....	....	....	....	....	....	....	....	....	....	....	....	....	....
1969-70	Brandon University	WCIAA	20	14	10	24	....	....	....	....	....	....	....	....	....	....	....	....	....	....	....	....	....	....	....	....	....	....
1970-71	Dayton Gems	IHL	71	15	38	53	....	....	....	4	....	....	....	....	....	....	....	....	....	....	10	3	4	7	5	....	....	....
1971-72	Dayton Gems	IHL	67	29	41	70	....	....	....	6	....	....	....	....	....	....	....	....	....	....	5	0	5	5	2	....	....	....
1972-73	Denver Spurs	WHL	71	24	38	62	....	....	....	15	....	....	....	....	....	....	....	....	....	....	5	1	1	2	0	....	....	....
1973-74	Denver Spurs	WHL	58	7	17	24	....	....	....	2	....	....	....	....	....	....	....	....	....	....	....	....	....	....	....	....	....	....
1974-75	**St. Louis Blues**	**NHL**	**1**	**0**	**0**	**0**	**0**	**0**	**0**	**0**	**0**	**0**	**0**	**0**	**0.0**	**0**	**0**	**0**	**0**	**0**	....	....	....	....	....	....	....	....
	Denver Spurs	CHL	76	13	42	55	....	....	....	10	....	....	....	....	....	....	....	....	....	....	2	0	0	0	0	....	....	....
1975-76	Brandon Elks	WCSHL	PLAYER/COACH – STATISTICS UNAVAILABLE																									
1976-77	Brandon Elks	WCSHL	PLAYER/COACH – STATISTICS UNAVAILABLE																									
1977-78	Brandon Elks	CSHL	30	11	36	47	....	....	....	6	....	....	....	....	....	....	....	....	....	....	....	....	....	....	....	....	....	....
	NHL Totals		**1**	**0**	**0**	**0**	**0**	**0**	**0**	**0**	**0**	**0**	**0**	**0**	**0.0**	**0**	**0**	**0**	**0**		....	....	....	....	....	....	....	....

Signed as a free agent by **St. Louis**, October 12, 1972.

• BORSATO, Luciano

Luciano Roberto C – R. 5'11", 190 lbs. b: Richmond Hill, Ont., 1/7/1966. Winnipeg's 7th, 135th overall, in 1984.

Season	Club	League	GP	G	A	Pts	AG	AA	APts	PIM	PP	SH	GW	S	%	TGF	PGF	TGA	PGA	+/-	GP	G	A	Pts	PIM	PP	SH	GW
1983-84	Bramelea Blues	OJHL	37	20	36	56	....	....	....	49	....	....	....	....	....	....	....	....	....	....	....	....	....	....	....	....	....	....
1984-85	Clarkson University	ECAC	33	15	17	32	....	....	....	37	....	....	....	....	....	....	....	....	....	....	....	....	....	....	....	....	....	....
1985-86	Clarkson University	ECAC	28	14	17	31	....	....	....	44	....	....	....	....	....	....	....	....	....	....	....	....	....	....	....	....	....	....
1986-87	Clarkson University	ECAC	31	16	41	57	....	....	....	55	....	....	....	....	....	....	....	....	....	....	....	....	....	....	....	....	....	....
1987-88	Clarkson University	ECAC	33	15	29	44	....	....	....	38	....	....	....	....	....	....	....	....	....	....	....	....	....	....	....	....	....	....
	Moncton Hawks	AHL	3	1	1	2	....	....	....	0	....	....	....	....	....	....	....	....	....	....	....	....	....	....	....	....	....	....
1988-89	Tappara Tampere	Finland	44	31	36	67	....	....	....	69	....	....	....	....	....	....	....	....	....	....	7	0	3	3	4	....	....	....
	Moncton Hawks	AHL	6	2	5	7	....	....	....	4	....	....	....	....	....	....	....	....	....	....	....	....	....	....	....	....	....	....
1989-90	Moncton Hawks	AHL	1	1	0	1	....	....	....	0	....	....	....	....	....	....	....	....	....	....	....	....	....	....	....	....	....	....
1990-91	**Winnipeg Jets**	**NHL**	**1**	**0**	**1**	**1**	**0**	**1**	**1**	**2**	**0**	**0**	**0**	**1**	**0.0**	**1**	**0**	**1**	**0**	**0**	....	....	....	....	....	....	....	....
	Moncton Hawks	AHL	41	14	24	38	....	....	....	40	....	....	....	....	....	....	....	....	....	....	9	3	7	10	22	....	....	....
1991-92	**Winnipeg Jets**	**NHL**	**56**	**15**	**21**	**36**	**14**	**16**	**30**	**45**	**5**	**0**	**1**	**81**	**18.5**	**50**	**22**	**34**	**0**	**-6**	**1**	**0**	**0**	**0**	**0**	**0**	**0**	**0**
	Moncton Hawks	AHL	14	2	7	9	....	....	....	39	....	....	....	....	....	....	....	....	....	....	....	....	....	....	....	....	....	....
1992-93	**Winnipeg Jets**	**NHL**	**67**	**15**	**20**	**35**	**12**	**14**	**26**	**38**	**1**	**1**	**3**	**101**	**14.9**	**47**	**6**	**58**	**16**	**-1**	**6**	**1**	**0**	**1**	**4**	**0**	**1**	**0**
1993-94	**Winnipeg Jets**	**NHL**	**75**	**5**	**13**	**18**	**5**	**10**	**15**	**28**	**1**	**1**	**2**	**65**	**7.7**	**28**	**6**	**56**	**23**	**-11**	....	....	....	....	....	....	....	....

			REGULAR SEASON																		PLAYOFFS							
Season	Club	League	GP	G	A	Pts	AG	AA	APts	PIM	PP	SH	GW	S	%	TGF	PGF	TGA	PGA	+/–	GP	G	A	Pts	PIM	PP	SH	GW
1994-95	**Winnipeg Jets**	**NHL**	**4**	**0**	**0**	**0**	**0**	**0**	**0**	**0**	**0**	**0**	**0**	**2**	**0.0**	**0**	**0**	**1**	**0**	**–1**	....	....	....	....	....	....	....	....
	Springfield Falcons	AHL	22	9	11	20	....	....	....	14	....	....	....	....	....	....	....	....	....	....	....	....	....	....	....	....	....	....
	Canada	WC-A	7	3	1	4	....	....	....	18	....	....	....	....	....	....	....	....	....	....	....	....	....	....	....	....	....	....
1995-96	Kolner Haie	Germany	49	25	36	61	....	....	....	52	....	....	....	....	....	....	....	....	....	....	12	6	8	14	28	....	....	....
1996-97	Kolner Haie	Germany	23	13	21	34	....	....	....	32	....	....	....	....	....	....	....	....	....	....	4	2	3	5	0	....	....	....
	Kolner Haie	EuroHL	4	0	0	0	....	....	....	10	....	....	....	....	....	....	....	....	....	....	....	....	....	....	....	....	....	....
1997-98	Kolner Haie	Germany	29	12	15	27	....	....	....	77	....	....	....	....	....	....	....	....	....	....	3	0	1	1	27	....	....	....
	Kolner Haie	EuroHL	5	1	2	3	....	....	....	14	....	....	....	....	....	....	....	....	....	....	....	....	....	....	....	....	....	....
1998-99	HIFK Helsinki	Finland	8	4	7	11	....	....	....	0	....	....	....	....	....	....	....	....	....	....	11	4	3	7	20	....	....	....
	HIFK Helsinki	EuroHL	2	2	0	2	....	....	....	6	....	....	....	....	....	....	....	....	....	....	4	0	1	1	12	....	....	....
99-2000	HIFK Helsinki	Finland	1	0	0	0	....	....	....	0	....	....	....	....	....	....	....	....	....	....	....	....	....	....	....	....	....	....
	HC Davos	Switz.	7	0	1	1	....	....	....	6	....	....	....	....	....	....	....	....	....	....	....	....	....	....	....	....	....	....
	NHL Totals		**203**	**35**	**55**	**90**	**31**	**41**	**72**	**113**	**7**	**2**	**6**	**250**	**14.0**	**126**	**34**	**150**	**39**		**7**	**1**	**0**	**1**	**4**	**0**	**1**	**0**

ECAC Second All-Star Team (1988) • NCAA East Second All-American Team (1988)

• BORSCHEVSKY, Nikolai

"Stick" RW – L. 5'9", 180 lbs. b: Tomsk, USSR, 1/12/1965. Toronto's 3rd, 77th overall, in 1992.

Season	Club	League	GP	G	A	Pts	AG	AA	APts	PIM	PP	SH	GW	S	%	TGF	PGF	TGA	PGA	+/–	GP	G	A	Pts	PIM	PP	SH	GW
1981-82	Dynamo Moscow	USSR-Jr.	STATISTICS NOT AVAILABLE																									
	Soviet Union	EJC-A	5	3	1	4	....	....	....	8	....	....	....	....	....	....	....	....	....	....	....	....	....	....	....	....	....	....
1982-83	Dynamo Moscow	USSR-Jr.	STATISTICS NOT AVAILABLE																									
	Soviet Union	EJC-A	5	6	5	11	....	....	....	8	....	....	....	....	....	....	....	....	....	....	....	....	....	....	....	....	....	....
1983-84	Dynamo Moscow	USSR	34	4	5	9	....	....	....	4	....	....	....	....	....	....	....	....	....	....	....	....	....	....	....	....	....	....
	Soviet Union	WJC-A	7	6	7	13	....	....	....	4	....	....	....	....	....	....	....	....	....	....	....	....	....	....	....	....	....	....
1984-85	Dynamo Moscow	USSR	34	5	9	14	....	....	....	6	....	....	....	....	....	....	....	....	....	....	....	....	....	....	....	....	....	....
1985-86	Dynamo Moscow	USSR	31	6	4	10	....	....	....	4	....	....	....	....	....	....	....	....	....	....	....	....	....	....	....	....	....	....
	Dynamo Moscow	Super-S	4	0	0	0	....	....	....	0	....	....	....	....	....	....	....	....	....	....	....	....	....	....	....	....	....	....
1986-87	Dynamo Moscow	USSR	28	1	4	5	....	....	....	8	....	....	....	....	....	....	....	....	....	....	....	....	....	....	....	....	....	....
1987-88	Dynamo Moscow	USSR	37	11	7	18	....	....	....	6	....	....	....	....	....	....	....	....	....	....	....	....	....	....	....	....	....	....
1988-89	Dynamo Moscow	USSR	43	7	8	15	....	....	....	18	....	....	....	....	....	....	....	....	....	....	....	....	....	....	....	....	....	....
1989-90	Spartak Moscow	Fr-Tour	1	1	1	2	....	....	....	0	....	....	....	....	....	....	....	....	....	....	....	....	....	....	....	....	....	....
	Spartak Moscow	USSR	48	17	25	42	....	....	....	8	....	....	....	....	....	....	....	....	....	....	....	....	....	....	....	....	....	....
1990-91	Spartak Moscow	Fr-Tour	1	0	2	2	....	....	....	0	....	....	....	....	....	....	....	....	....	....	....	....	....	....	....	....	....	....
	Spartak Moscow	USSR	45	19	16	35	....	....	....	16	....	....	....	....	....	....	....	....	....	....	....	....	....	....	....	....	....	....
1991-92	Spartak Moscow	CIS	40	25	14	39	....	....	....	16	....	....	....	....	....	....	....	....	....	....	....	....	....	....	....	....	....	....
	Team United	Olympics	8	7	2	9	....	....	....	0	....	....	....	....	....	....	....	....	....	....	....	....	....	....	....	....	....	....
	Russia	WC-A	6	1	3	4	....	....	....	2	....	....	....	....	....	....	....	....	....	....	....	....	....	....	....	....	....	....
1992-93	**Toronto Maple Leafs**	**NHL**	**78**	**34**	**40**	**74**	**28**	**28**	**56**	**28**	**12**	**0**	**4**	**204**	**16.7**	**111**	**45**	**33**	**0**	**33**	**16**	**2**	**7**	**9**	**0**	**0**	**0**	**1**
1993-94	**Toronto Maple Leafs**	**NHL**	**45**	**14**	**20**	**34**	**13**	**16**	**29**	**10**	**7**	**0**	**1**	**105**	**13.3**	**52**	**27**	**19**	**0**	**6**	**15**	**2**	**2**	**4**	**4**	**1**	**0**	**0**
1994-95	Spartak Moscow	CIS	9	5	1	6	....	....	....	14	....	....	....	....	....	....	....	....	....	....	....	....	....	....	....	....	....	....
	Toronto Maple Leafs	**NHL**	**19**	**0**	**5**	**5**	**0**	**7**	**7**	**0**	**0**	**0**	**0**	**28**	**0.0**	**12**	**1**	**9**	**1**	**3**	....	....	....	....	....	....	....	....
	Calgary Flames	**NHL**	**8**	**0**	**5**	**5**	**0**	**7**	**7**	**0**	**0**	**0**	**0**	**12**	**0.0**	**12**	**3**	**2**	**0**	**7**	....	....	....	....	....	....	....	....
1995-96	**Dallas Stars**	**NHL**	**12**	**1**	**3**	**4**	**1**	**2**	**3**	**6**	**0**	**0**	**1**	**22**	**4.5**	**7**	**1**	**13**	**0**	**–7**	....	....	....	....	....	....	....	....
	Kolner EC	Germany	8	0	4	4	....	....	....	27	....	....	....	....	....	....	....	....	....	....	8	2	2	4	4	....	....	....
1996-97	Spartak Moscow	Russia	42	15	*29	*44	....	....	....	52	....	....	....	....	....	....	....	....	....	....	....	....	....	....	....	....	....	....
1997-98	Spartak Moscow	Russia	46	10	17	27	....	....	....	30	....	....	....	....	....	....	....	....	....	....	....	....	....	....	....	....	....	....
	NHL Totals		**162**	**49**	**73**	**122**	**42**	**60**	**102**	**44**	**19**	**0**	**6**	**371**	**13.2**	**194**	**77**	**76**	**1**		**31**	**4**	**9**	**13**	**4**	**1**	**0**	**1**

EJC-A All-Star Team (1983) • WJC-A All-Star Team (1984) • Won Izvestia Trophy (Russian Top Scorer) (1997)

Traded to **Calgary** by **Toronto** for Calgary's 6th round choice (Chris Bogas) in 1996 Entry Draft, April 6, 1995. Signed as a free agent by **Dallas**, September 13, 1995.

• BOSCHMAN, Laurie

Lawrence Joseph C – L. 6', 185 lbs. b: Major, Sask., 6/4/1960. Toronto's 1st, 9th overall, in 1979.

Season	Club	League	GP	G	A	Pts	AG	AA	APts	PIM	PP	SH	GW	S	%	TGF	PGF	TGA	PGA	+/–	GP	G	A	Pts	PIM	PP	SH	GW
1975-76	Brandon Bobcats	MJHL	2	1	3	4	....	....	....	2	....	....	....	....	....	....	....	....	....	....	....	....	....	....	....	....	....	....
1976-77	Brandon Bobcats	MJHL	47	17	40	57	....	....	....	139	....	....	....	....	....	....	....	....	....	....	....	....	....	....	....	....	....	....
	Brandon Wheat Kings	WCJHL	3	0	1	1	....	....	....	0	....	....	....	....	....	....	....	....	....	....	12	1	1	2	17	....	....	....
1977-78	Brandon Wheat Kings	WCJHL	72	42	57	99	....	....	....	227	....	....	....	....	....	....	....	....	....	....	6	2	5	7	45	....	....	....
1978-79	Brandon Wheat Kings	WHL	65	66	83	149	....	....	....	215	....	....	....	....	....	....	....	....	....	....	22	11	23	34	56	....	....	....
	Brandon Wheat Kings	Mem-Cup	5	3	4	7	....	....	....	10	....	....	....	....	....	....	....	....	....	....	....	....	....	....	....	....	....	....
1979-80	**Toronto Maple Leafs**	**NHL**	**80**	**16**	**32**	**48**	**14**	**23**	**37**	**78**	**2**	**0**	**4**	**99**	**16.2**	**73**	**9**	**62**	**0**	**2**	**3**	**1**	**1**	**2**	**18**	**1**	**0**	**0**
1980-81	**Toronto Maple Leafs**	**NHL**	**53**	**14**	**19**	**33**	**11**	**13**	**24**	**178**	**3**	**0**	**4**	**70**	**20.0**	**47**	**7**	**55**	**5**	**–10**	**3**	**0**	**0**	**0**	**7**	**0**	**0**	**0**
	New Brunswick Hawks	AHL	4	4	1	5	....	....	....	47	....	....	....	....	....	....	....	....	....	....	....	....	....	....	....	....	....	....
1981-82	**Toronto Maple Leafs**	**NHL**	**54**	**9**	**19**	**28**	**7**	**13**	**20**	**150**	**1**	**0**	**1**	**64**	**14.1**	**50**	**3**	**62**	**12**	**–3**	....	....	....	....	....	....	....	....
	Edmonton Oilers	**NHL**	**11**	**2**	**3**	**5**	**2**	**2**	**4**	**37**	**0**	**0**	**0**	**4**	**50.0**	**8**	**0**	**6**	**0**	**2**	**3**	**0**	**1**	**1**	**4**	**0**	**0**	**0**
1982-83	**Edmonton Oilers**	**NHL**	**62**	**8**	**12**	**20**	**7**	**8**	**15**	**183**	**0**	**0**	**0**	**59**	**13.6**	**30**	**0**	**30**	**3**	**3**	....	....	....	....	....	....	....	....
	Winnipeg Jets	**NHL**	**12**	**3**	**5**	**8**	**2**	**3**	**5**	**36**	**1**	**0**	**0**	**25**	**12.0**	**16**	**3**	**10**	**0**	**3**	**3**	**0**	**1**	**1**	**12**	**0**	**0**	**0**
1983-84	**Winnipeg Jets**	**NHL**	**61**	**28**	**46**	**74**	**22**	**31**	**53**	**234**	**9**	**0**	**3**	**138**	**20.3**	**95**	**26**	**93**	**20**	**–4**	**3**	**0**	**1**	**1**	**5**	**0**	**0**	**0**
1984-85	**Winnipeg Jets**	**NHL**	**80**	**32**	**44**	**76**	**26**	**30**	**56**	**180**	**5**	**2**	**4**	**167**	**19.2**	**105**	**19**	**126**	**32**	**–8**	**8**	**2**	**1**	**3**	**21**	**0**	**1**	**0**
1985-86	**Winnipeg Jets**	**NHL**	**77**	**27**	**42**	**69**	**22**	**28**	**50**	**241**	**3**	**2**	**2**	**158**	**17.1**	**94**	**20**	**122**	**19**	**–29**	**3**	**0**	**1**	**1**	**6**	**0**	**0**	**0**
1986-87	**Winnipeg Jets**	**NHL**	**80**	**17**	**24**	**41**	**15**	**17**	**32**	**152**	**1**	**1**	**2**	**161**	**10.6**	**69**	**11**	**82**	**7**	**–17**	**10**	**2**	**3**	**5**	**32**	**1**	**0**	**0**
1987-88	**Winnipeg Jets**	**NHL**	**80**	**25**	**23**	**48**	**21**	**16**	**37**	**229**	**10**	**1**	**3**	**166**	**15.1**	**71**	**31**	**80**	**16**	**–24**	**5**	**1**	**3**	**4**	**9**	**0**	**0**	**0**
1988-89	**Winnipeg Jets**	**NHL**	**70**	**10**	**26**	**36**	**8**	**18**	**26**	**163**	**3**	**0**	**1**	**113**	**8.8**	**58**	**12**	**73**	**10**	**–17**	....	....	....	....	....	....	....	....
1989-90	**Winnipeg Jets**	**NHL**	**66**	**10**	**17**	**27**	**9**	**12**	**21**	**103**	**3**	**1**	**1**	**87**	**11.5**	**39**	**4**	**55**	**9**	**–11**	**2**	**0**	**0**	**0**	**2**	**0**	**0**	**0**
1990-91	**New Jersey Devils**	**NHL**	**78**	**11**	**9**	**20**	**10**	**7**	**17**	**79**	**0**	**1**	**1**	**91**	**12.1**	**37**	**1**	**67**	**30**	**–1**	**7**	**1**	**1**	**2**	**16**	**0**	**0**	**0**
1991-92	**New Jersey Devils**	**NHL**	**75**	**8**	**20**	**28**	**7**	**15**	**22**	**121**	**0**	**0**	**2**	**89**	**9.0**	**44**	**1**	**69**	**35**	**9**	**7**	**1**	**0**	**1**	**8**	**0**	**0**	**1**
1992-93	**Ottawa Senators**	**NHL**	**70**	**9**	**7**	**16**	**7**	**5**	**12**	**101**	**0**	**1**	**1**	**84**	**10.7**	**26**	**3**	**85**	**36**	**–26**	....	....	....	....	....	....	....	....
1993-94			OUT OF HOCKEY – RETIRED																									
1994-95	Fife Flyers	Britain	7	9	9	18	....	....	....	6	....	....	....	....	....	....	....	....	....	....	6	5	8	13	12	....	....	....
	NHL Totals		**1009**	**229**	**348**	**577**	**190**	**241**	**431**	**2265**	**41**	**9**	**29**	**1575**	**14.5**	**862**	**150**	**1077**	**234**		**57**	**8**	**13**	**21**	**140**	**2**	**1**	**1**

WHL All-Star Team (1979) • Memorial Cup All-Star Team (1979)

Traded to **Edmonton** by **Toronto** for Walt Poddubny and Phil Drouillard, March 9, 1982. Traded to **Winnipeg** by **Edmonton** for Willy Lindstrom, March 7, 1983. Traded to **New Jersey** by **Winnipeg** for Bob Brooke, September 6, 1990. • Brooke retired and Winnipeg received New Jersey's 5th round choice (Jan Kaminsky) in 1991 Entry Draft as compensation. Claimed by **Ottawa** from **New Jersey** in Expansion Draft, June 18, 1992.

• BOSSY, Mike

Michael Jean RW – R. 6', 186 lbs. b: Montreal, Que., 1/22/1957. NY Islanders' 1st, 15th overall, in 1977. **HHOF**

Season	Club	League	GP	G	A	Pts	AG	AA	APts	PIM	PP	SH	GW	S	%	TGF	PGF	TGA	PGA	+/–	GP	G	A	Pts	PIM	PP	SH	GW
1972-73	Montreal-Bourassa	QAAA	STATISTICS NOT AVAILABLE																									
	Laval National	QMJHL	4	1	2	3	....	....	....	0	....	....	....	....	....	....	....	....	....	....	....	....	....	....	....	....	....	....
1973-74	Laval National	QMJHL	68	70	48	118	....	....	....	45	....	....	....	....	....	....	....	....	....	....	11	6	16	22	2	....	....	....
1974-75	Laval National	QMJHL	67	*84	65	149	....	....	....	42	....	....	....	....	....	....	....	....	....	....	16	18	20	38	2	....	....	....
1975-76	Laval National	QMJHL	64	79	57	136	....	....	....	25	....	....	....	....	....	....	....	....	....	....	....	....	....	....	....	....	....	....
1976-77	Laval National	QMJHL	61	75	51	126	....	....	....	12	....	....	....	....	....	....	....	....	....	....	7	5	5	10	12	....	....	....
1977-78	**New York Islanders**	**NHL**	**73**	**53**	**38**	**91**	**48**	**29**	**77**	**6**	**25**	**0**	**5**	**235**	**22.6**	**130**	**57**	**42**	**0**	**31**	**7**	**2**	**2**	**4**	**2**	**0**	**0**	**1**
1978-79	**New York Islanders**	**NHL**	**80**	***69**	**57**	**126**	**60**	**41**	**101**	**25**	**27**	**0**	**9**	**279**	**24.7**	**174**	**70**	**41**	**0**	**63**	**10**	**6**	**2**	**8**	**2**	**2**	**0**	**1**
	NHL All-Stars	Chal-Cup	3	2	2	4	....	....	....	0	....	....	....	....	....	....	....	....	....	....	....	....	....	....	....	....	....	....
1979-80♦	**New York Islanders**	**NHL**	**75**	**51**	**41**	**92**	**44**	**30**	**74**	**12**	**16**	**0**	**8**	**244**	**20.9**	**126**	**47**	**51**	**0**	**28**	**16**	**10**	**13**	**23**	**8**	**6**	**0**	**1**
1980-81♦	**New York Islanders**	**NHL**	**79**	***68**	**51**	**119**	**53**	**34**	**87**	**32**	**28**	**2**	**10**	**315**	**21.6**	**161**	**64**	**65**	**5**	**37**	**18**	***17**	***18**	***35**	**4**	**9**	**0**	**3**
1981-82	Canada	Can-Cup	7	*8	3	11	....	....	....	2	....	....	....	....	....	....	....	....	....	....	....	....	....	....	....	....	....	....
♦	**New York Islanders**	**NHL**	**80**	**64**	**83**	**147**	**51**	**55**	**106**	**22**	**17**	**0**	**10**	**301**	**21.3**	**178**	**58**	**54**	**3**	**69**	**19**	***17**	**10**	**27**	**0**	**6**	**0**	**3**
1982-83♦	**New York Islanders**	**NHL**	**79**	**60**	**58**	**118**	**49**	**40**	**89**	**20**	**19**	**0**	**8**	**272**	**22.1**	**141**	**48**	**66**	**0**	**27**	**19**	***17**	**9**	**26**	**10**	**6**	**0**	**5**
1983-84	**New York Islanders**	**NHL**	**67**	**51**	**67**	**118**	**41**	**46**	**87**	**8**	**6**	**0**	**11**	**246**	**20.7**	**147**	**35**	**46**	**0**	**66**	**21**	**8**	**10**	**18**	**4**	**2**	**0**	**3**

Season	Club	League	GP	G	A	Pts	AG	AA	APts	PIM	PP	SH	GW	S	%	TGF	PGF	TGA	PGA	+/–	GP	G	A	Pts	PIM	PP	SH	GW
			REGULAR SEASON																		PLAYOFFS							
1984-85	Canada	Can-Cup	8	5	4	9	....	....	....	2	....	....	....	....	....	....	....	....	....	....	....	....	....	....	....	....	....	....
	New York Islanders	**NHL**	76	58	59	117	47	40	87	38	14	4	7	285	20.4	151	49	74	9	37	10	5	6	11	4	2	0	0
1985-86	**New York Islanders**	**NHL**	80	61	62	123	49	42	91	14	21	1	9	302	20.2	155	50	87	12	30	3	1	2	3	4	0	0	0
1986-87	**New York Islanders**	**NHL**	63	38	37	75	33	27	60	33	8	1	5	226	16.8	105	53	62	3	–7	6	2	3	5	0	2	0	0
	NHL Totals		752	573	553	1126	475	384	859	210	181	8	82	2705	21.2	1468	531	588	32		129	85	75	160	38	35	0	17

QMJHL First All-Star Team (1975) • QMJHL West First All-Star Team (1976) • QMJHL Second All-Star Team (1977) • NHL Second All-Star Team (1978, 1979, 1985) • Won Calder Memorial Trophy (1978) • NHL First All-Star Team (1981, 1982, 1983, 1984, 1986) • Canada Cup All-Star Team (1981) • Won Conn Smythe Trophy (1982) • Won Lady Byng Trophy (1983, 1984, 1986) • Played in NHL All-Star Game (1978, 1980, 1981, 1982, 1983, 1985, 1986)

• BOTELL, Mark

D – L. 6'4", 220 lbs. b: Scarborough, Ont., 8/27/1961. Philadelphia's 8th, 168th overall, in 1980.

Season	Club	League	GP	G	A	Pts	AG	AA	APts	PIM	PP	SH	GW	S	%	TGF	PGF	TGA	PGA	+/–	GP	G	A	Pts	PIM	PP	SH	GW
1977-78	Wexford Raiders	MTHL	73	15	28	43	....	....	....	168	....	....	....	....	....	....	....	....	....	....	....	....	....	....	....	....	....	....
1978-79	Niagara Falls Flyers	OMJHL	55	2	8	10	....	....	....	122	....	....	....	....	....	....	....	....	....	....	14	2	1	3	6	....	....	....
1979-80	Niagara Falls Flyers	OMJHL	20	2	5	7	....	....	....	11	....	....	....	....	....	....	....	....	....	....	....	....	....	....	....	....	....	....
	Windsor Spitfires	OMJHL	2	0	0	0	....	....	....	0	....	....	....	....	....	....	....	....	....	....	....	....	....	....	....	....	....	....
	Brantford Alexanders	OMJHL	15	2	3	5	....	....	....	24	....	....	....	....	....	....	....	....	....	....	11	1	5	6	10	....	....	....
1980-81	Brantford Alexanders	OMJHL	58	11	20	31	....	....	....	143	....	....	....	....	....	....	....	....	....	....	4	0	2	2	12	....	....	....
	Maine Mariners	AHL	2	0	1	1	....	....	....	0	....	....	....	....	....	....	....	....	....	....	20	4	4	8	36	....	....	....
1981-82	**Philadelphia Flyers**	**NHL**	32	4	10	14	3	7	10	31	0	0	1	50	8.0	43	11	27	3	8	....	....	....	....	....	....	....	....
	Maine Mariners	AHL	42	3	14	17	....	....	....	41	....	....	....	....	....	....	....	....	....	....	3	0	1	1	4	....	....	....
1982-83	Toledo Goaldiggers	IHL	24	6	14	20	....	....	....	43	....	....	....	....	....	....	....	....	....	....	....	....	....	....	....	....	....	....
	Maine Mariners	AHL	30	1	4	5	....	....	....	26	....	....	....	....	....	....	....	....	....	....	....	....	....	....	....	....	....	....
1983-84	Montana Magic	CHL	2	0	0	0	....	....	....	2	....	....	....	....	....	....	....	....	....	....	....	....	....	....	....	....	....	....
	Toledo Goaldiggers	IHL	78	16	27	43	....	....	....	164	....	....	....	....	....	....	....	....	....	....	9	2	1	3	6	....	....	....
1984-85	Peoria Rivermen	IHL	70	6	21	27	....	....	....	77	....	....	....	....	....	....	....	....	....	....	20	1	3	4	35	....	....	....
1985-86	SIJ Hertogenbosch	Holland	STATISTICS NOT AVAILABLE																									
	St. Catharines Saints	AHL	11	1	3	4	....	....	....	17	....	....	....	....	....	....	....	....	....	....	12	1	3	4	8	....	....	....
	NHL Totals		32	4	10	14	3	7	10	31	0	0	1	50	8.0	43	11	27	3		....	....	....	....	....	....	....	....

• BOTHWELL, Tim

Timothy John D – L. 6'3", 190 lbs. b: Vancouver, B.C., 5/6/1955.

Season	Club	League	GP	G	A	Pts	AG	AA	APts	PIM	PP	SH	GW	S	%	TGF	PGF	TGA	PGA	+/–	GP	G	A	Pts	PIM	PP	SH	GW
1973-74	Burlington Mohawks	OHA-B	42	22	41	63	....	....	....	59	....	....	....	....	....	....	....	....	....	....	....	....	....	....	....	....	....	....
1974-75	Brown University	ECAC	9	6	9	15	....	....	....	14	....	....	....	....	....	....	....	....	....	....	....	....	....	....	....	....	....	....
1975-76	Brown University	ECAC	29	12	22	34	....	....	....	30	....	....	....	....	....	....	....	....	....	....	....	....	....	....	....	....	....	....
1976-77	Brown University	ECAC	27	7	27	34	....	....	....	40	....	....	....	....	....	....	....	....	....	....	....	....	....	....	....	....	....	....
1977-78	Brown University	ECAC	29	9	26	35	....	....	....	48	....	....	....	....	....	....	....	....	....	....	....	....	....	....	....	....	....	....
1978-79	**New York Rangers**	**NHL**	1	0	0	0	0	0	0	2	0	0	0	2	0.0	0	0	2	1	–1	....	....	....	....	....	....	....	....
	New Haven Nighthawks	AHL	66	15	33	48	....	....	....	44	....	....	....	....	....	....	....	....	....	....	10	4	6	10	8	....	....	....
1979-80	**New York Rangers**	**NHL**	45	4	6	10	3	4	7	20	0	0	2	37	10.8	36	1	45	7	–3	9	0	0	0	8	0	0	0
	New Haven Nighthawks	AHL	22	6	7	13	....	....	....	25	....	....	....	....	....	....	....	....	....	....	....	....	....	....	....	....	....	....
1980-81	**New York Rangers**	**NHL**	3	0	1	1	0	1	1	0	0	0	0	0	0.0	3	0	3	0	0	....	....	....	....	....	....	....	....
	New Haven Nighthawks	AHL	73	10	53	63	....	....	....	98	....	....	....	....	....	....	....	....	....	....	4	1	2	3	6	....	....	....
1981-82	**New York Rangers**	**NHL**	13	0	3	3	0	2	2	10	0	0	0	6	0.0	9	1	13	0	–5	....	....	....	....	....	....	....	....
	Springfield Indians	AHL	10	0	4	4	....	....	....	7	....	....	....	....	....	....	....	....	....	....	....	....	....	....	....	....	....	....
1982-83	**St. Louis Blues**	**NHL**	61	4	11	15	3	8	11	34	0	1	1	62	6.5	73	9	93	21	–8	....	....	....	....	....	....	....	....
1983-84	**St. Louis Blues**	**NHL**	62	2	13	15	2	9	11	65	1	0	0	59	3.4	69	1	71	25	22	11	0	2	2	14	0	0	0
	Montana Magic	CHL	4	0	3	3	....	....	....	0	....	....	....	....	....	....	....	....	....	....	....	....	....	....	....	....	....	....
1984-85	**St. Louis Blues**	**NHL**	79	4	22	26	3	15	18	62	1	0	0	102	3.9	113	9	112	35	27	3	0	0	0	2	0	0	0
1985-86	**Hartford Whalers**	**NHL**	62	2	8	10	2	5	7	53	0	0	0	50	4.0	68	2	72	19	13	10	0	0	0	8	0	0	0
1986-87	**Hartford Whalers**	**NHL**	4	1	0	1	1	0	1	0	0	0	0	3	33.3	2	0	8	1	–5	....	....	....	....	....	....	....	....
	St. Louis Blues	**NHL**	72	5	16	21	4	12	16	46	0	0	1	75	6.7	68	9	89	16	–14	6	0	0	0	6	0	0	0
1987-88	**St. Louis Blues**	**NHL**	78	6	13	19	5	9	14	76	0	0	1	88	6.8	76	0	125	55	6	10	0	1	1	18	0	0	0
1988-89	**St. Louis Blues**	**NHL**	22	0	0	0	0	0	0	14	0	0	0	10	0.0	14	0	17	7	4	....	....	....	....	....	....	....	....
	Peoria Rivermen	IHL	14	0	7	7	....	....	....	14	....	....	....	....	....	....	....	....	....	....	....	....	....	....	....	....	....	....
1989-90	New Haven Nighthawks	AHL	75	3	26	29	....	....	....	56	....	....	....	....	....	....	....	....	....	....	....	....	....	....	....	....	....	....
	NHL Totals		502	28	93	121	23	65	88	382	2	1	5	494	5.7	531	32	650	187		49	0	3	3	56	0	0	0

ECAC First All-Star Team (1977)

Signed as a free agent by **NY Rangers**, June 8, 1978. Claimed by **St. Louis** from **NY Rangers** in Waiver Draft, October 4, 1982. Rights traded to **Hartford** by **St. Louis** for cash, October 4, 1985. Traded to **St. Louis** by **Hartford** for Dave Barr, October 21, 1986.

• BOTTERILL, Jason

Jason N. LW – L. 6'4", 220 lbs. b: Edmonton, Alta., 5/19/1976. Dallas' 1st, 20th overall, in 1994.

Season	Club	League	GP	G	A	Pts	AG	AA	APts	PIM	PP	SH	GW	S	%	TGF	PGF	TGA	PGA	+/–	GP	G	A	Pts	PIM	PP	SH	GW
1991-92	Victoria Warriors	BCAHA	STATISTICS NOT AVAILABLE																									
1992-93	St. Paul's High School	Hi-School	22	22	26	48	....	....	....	....	....	....	....	....	....	....	....	....	....	....	....	....	....	....	....	....	....	....
1993-94	University of Michigan	CCHA	36	20	19	39	....	....	....	94	....	....	....	....	....	....	....	....	....	....	....	....	....	....	....	....	....	....
	Canada	WJC-A	7	1	0	1	....	....	....	8	....	....	....	....	....	....	....	....	....	....	....	....	....	....	....	....	....	....
1994-95	University of Michigan	CCHA	34	14	14	28	....	....	....	117	....	....	....	....	....	....	....	....	....	....	....	....	....	....	....	....	....	....
	Canada	WJC-A	7	0	4	4	....	....	....	6	....	....	....	....	....	....	....	....	....	....	....	....	....	....	....	....	....	....
1995-96	University of Michigan	CCHA	37	*32	25	57	....	....	....	*143	....	....	....	....	....	....	....	....	....	....	....	....	....	....	....	....	....	....
	Canada	WJC-A	6	1	3	4	....	....	....	6	....	....	....	....	....	....	....	....	....	....	....	....	....	....	....	....	....	....
1996-97	University of Michigan	CCHA	42	*37	24	61	....	....	....	129	....	....	....	....	....	....	....	....	....	....	....	....	....	....	....	....	....	....
1997-98	**Dallas Stars**	**NHL**	4	0	0	0	0	0	0	19	0	0	0	2	0.0	0	0	1	0	–1	....	....	....	....	....	....	....	....
	Michigan K-Wings	IHL	50	11	11	22	....	....	....	82	....	....	....	....	....	....	....	....	....	....	4	0	0	0	5	....	....	....
1998-99	**Dallas Stars**	**NHL**	17	0	0	0	0	0	0	23	0	0	0	8	0.0	1	0	3	0	–2	....	....	....	....	....	....	....	....
	Michigan K-Wings	IHL	56	13	25	38	....	....	....	106	....	....	....	....	....	....	....	....	....	....	5	2	1	3	4	....	....	....
99-2000	**Atlanta Thrashers**	**NHL**	25	1	4	5	1	4	5	17	0	0	1	17	5.9	7	0	14	0	–7	....	....	....	....	....	....	....	....
	Orlando Solar Bears	IHL	17	7	8	15	....	....	....	27	....	....	....	....	....	....	....	....	....	....	....	....	....	....	....	....	....	....
	Calgary Flames	**NHL**	2	0	0	0	0	0	0	0	0	0	0	2	0.0	0	0	4	0	–4	....	....	....	....	....	....	....	....
	Saint John Flames	AHL	21	3	4	7	....	....	....	39	....	....	....	....	....	....	....	....	....	....	3	0	0	0	19	....	....	....
	NHL Totals		48	1	4	5	1	4	5	59	0	0	1	29	3.4	8	0	22	0		....	....	....	....	....	....	....	....

CCHA Second All-Star Team (1996) • NCAA West Second All-American Team (1997)

Traded to **Atlanta** by **Dallas** for Jamie Pushor, July 15, 1999. Traded to **Calgary** by **Atlanta** with Darryl Shannon for Hnat Domenichelli and Dmitri Vlasenkov, February 11, 2000.

• BOTTING, Cam

Cameron Allan RW – R. 6'2", 205 lbs. b: Kingston, Ont., 3/10/1954. Atlanta's 4th, 64th overall, in 1974.

Season	Club	League	GP	G	A	Pts	AG	AA	APts	PIM	PP	SH	GW	S	%	TGF	PGF	TGA	PGA	+/–	GP	G	A	Pts	PIM	PP	SH	GW
1971-72	Hamilton Red Wings	OMJHL	27	1	6	7	....	....	....	17	....	....	....	....	....	....	....	....	....	....	....	....	....	....	....	....	....	....
1972-73	Niagara Falls Flyers	OHA-B	48	30	23	53	....	....	....	113	....	....	....	....	....	....	....	....	....	....	....	....	....	....	....	....	....	....
	Hamilton Red Wings	OMJHL	8	1	3	4	....	....	....	7	....	....	....	....	....	....	....	....	....	....	....	....	....	....	....	....	....	....
1973-74	Niagara Falls Flyers	OJHL	48	40	56	96	....	....	....	210	....	....	....	....	....	....	....	....	....	....	....	....	....	....	....	....	....	....
1974-75	Omaha Knights	CHL	15	2	3	5	....	....	....	9	....	....	....	....	....	....	....	....	....	....	....	....	....	....	....	....	....	....
	Des Moines Capitols	IHL	49	8	5	13	....	....	....	30	....	....	....	....	....	....	....	....	....	....	7	0	3	3	9	....	....	....
1975-76	**Atlanta Flames**	**NHL**	2	0	1	1	0	1	1	0	0	0	0	0	0.0	1	0	0	0	1	....	....	....	....	....	....	....	....
	Tulsa Oilers	CHL	73	22	29	51	....	....	....	68	....	....	....	....	....	....	....	....	....	....	9	2	5	7	6	....	....	....
1976-77	Tulsa Oilers	CHL	74	26	23	49	....	....	....	74	....	....	....	....	....	....	....	....	....	....	9	3	1	4	0	....	....	....
1977-78	Tulsa Oilers	CHL	76	17	26	43	....	....	....	52	....	....	....	....	....	....	....	....	....	....	7	0	2	2	4	....	....	....
1979-80	Dundas Blues	GBSHL	STATISTICS NOT AVAILABLE																									
1980-1982	Dundas Blues	OHA-Sr.	STATISTICS NOT AVAILABLE																									
1982-83	Flint Generals	IHL	12	2	4	6	....	....	....	9	....	....	....	....	....	....	....	....	....	....	....	....	....	....	....	....	....	....
	Erie Golden Blades	ACHL	49	9	27	36	....	....	....	13	....	....	....	....	....	....	....	....	....	....	5	2	3	5	0	....	....	....
1983-84	Erie Golden Blades	ACHL	13	2	2	4	....	....	....	22	....	....	....	....	....	....	....	....	....	....	....	....	....	....	....	....	....	....
	NHL Totals		2	0	1	1	0	1	1	0	0	0	0	0	0.0	1	0	0	0		....	....	....	....	....	....	....	....

Season	Club	League	GP	G	A	Pts	AG	AA	APts	PIM	PP	SH	GW	S	%	TGF	PGF	TGA	PGA	+/–	GP	G	A	Pts	PIM	PP	SH	GW
			REGULAR SEASON																		PLAYOFFS							

• BOUCHA, Henry Henry Charles C – R. 6′, 185 lbs. b: Warroad, MN, 6/1/1951. Detroit's 2nd, 16th overall, in 1971. **USHOF**

Season	Club	League	GP	G	A	Pts	AG	AA	APts	PIM	PP	SH	GW	S	%	TGF	PGF	TGA	PGA	+/–	GP	G	A	Pts	PIM	PP	SH	GW
1965-1968	Warroad Warriors	Hi-School	STATISTICS NOT AVAILABLE																									
1968-69	Warroad Warriors	Hi-School	25	60	35	95	....	....	....	....	....	....	....	....	....	....	....	....	....	....	....	....	....	....	....	....	....	....
1969-70	Winnipeg Jets	WCJHL	51	27	26	53	....	....	....	37	....	....	....	....	....	....	....	....	....	....	14	6	3	9	37	....	....	....
	United States	Mat-Team	6	0	2	2	....	....	....	4	....	....	....	....	....	....	....	....	....	....	....	....	....	....	....	....	....	....
	United States	WEC-B	7	4	1	5	....	....	....	4	....	....	....	....	....	....	....	....	....	....	....	....	....	....	....	....	....	....
1970-71	United States	Nat-Team	STATISTICS NOT AVAILABLE																									
	United States	WEC-A	10	7	1	8	....	....	....	2	....	....	....	....	....	....	....	....	....	....	....	....	....	....	....	....	....	....
1971-72	United States	Nat-Team	STATISTICS NOT AVAILABLE																									
	United States	Olympics	6	2	4	6	....	....	....	6	....	....	....	....	....	....	....	....	....	....	....	....	....	....	....	....	....	....
	Detroit Red Wings	**NHL**	16	1	0	1	1	0	1	2	0	0	0	11	9.1	5	1	7	0	–3	....	....	....	....	....	....	....	....
1972-73	**Detroit Red Wings**	**NHL**	73	14	14	28	13	11	24	82	0	1	0	136	10.3	44	1	63	18	–2	....	....	....	....	....	....	....	....
	Virginia Wings	AHL	7	3	2	5	....	....	....	9	....	....	....	....	....	....	....	....	....	....	....	....	....	....	....	....	....	....
1973-74	**Detroit Red Wings**	**NHL**	70	19	12	31	18	10	28	32	2	3	5	132	14.4	51	7	92	26	–22	....	....	....	....	....	....	....	....
1974-75	**Minnesota North Stars**	**NHL**	51	15	14	29	13	10	23	23	1	0	1	129	11.6	52	13	81	30	–12	....	....	....	....	....	....	....	....
1975-76	Minnesota Fighting Saints	WHA	36	15	20	35	....	....	....	47	....	....	....	....	....	....	....	....	....	....	....	....	....	....	....	....	....	....
	Kansas City Scouts	**NHL**	28	4	7	11	3	5	8	14	2	0	0	42	9.5	23	8	33	5	–13	....	....	....	....	....	....	....	....
1976-77	**Colorado Rockies**	**NHL**	9	0	2	2	0	2	2	4	0	0	0	10	0.0	2	0	5	3	0	....	....	....	....	....	....	....	....
	NHL Totals		**247**	**53**	**49**	**102**	**48**	**38**	**86**	**157**	**5**	**4**	**6**	**460**	**11.5**	**177**	**30**	**281**	**82**		....	....	....	....	....	....	....	....
	Other Major League Totals		36	15	20	35	....	....	....	47	....	....	....	....	....	....	....	....	....	....	....	....	....	....	....	....	....	....

Selected by **Minnesota** (WHA) in 1972 WHA General Player Draft, February 12, 1972. Traded to **Minnesota** by **Detroit** for Danny Grant, August 27, 1974. • Suffered eventual career-ending eye-injury in game vs. Boston, January 4, 1975. Signed as a free agent by **Minnesota** (WHA), June 6, 1975. Rights traded to **Kansas City** by **Minnesota** for Kansas City's 2nd round choice (Steve Christoff) in 1978 Amateur Draft, December 9, 1975. Transferred to **Colorado** after **Kansas City** franchise relocated, July 15, 1976.

• BOUCHARD, Joel D – L. 6′, 200 lbs. b: Montreal, Que., 1/23/1974. Calgary's 7th, 129th overall, in 1992.

Season	Club	League	GP	G	A	Pts	AG	AA	APts	PIM	PP	SH	GW	S	%	TGF	PGF	TGA	PGA	+/–	GP	G	A	Pts	PIM	PP	SH	GW
1989-90	Montreal Bourassa	QAAA	41	7	17	24	....	....	....	10	....	....	....	....	....	....	....	....	....	....	1	1	0	1	0	....	....	....
1990-91	Longueuil College-Francais	QMJHL	53	3	19	22	....	....	....	34	....	....	....	....	....	....	....	....	....	....	8	1	0	1	11	....	....	....
1991-92	Verdun College Francais	QMJHL	70	9	20	29	....	....	....	55	....	....	....	....	....	....	....	....	....	....	19	1	7	8	20	....	....	....
	Verdun College Francais	Mem-Cup	2	0	0	0	....	....	....	0	....	....	....	....	....	....	....	....	....	....	....	....	....	....	....	....	....	....
1992-93	Verdun College Francais	QMJHL	60	10	49	59	....	....	....	126	....	....	....	....	....	....	....	....	....	....	4	0	2	2	4	....	....	....
	Canada	WJC-A	7	0	0	0	....	....	....	0	....	....	....	....	....	....	....	....	....	....	....	....	....	....	....	....	....	....
1993-94	Verdun College Francais	QMJHL	60	15	55	70	....	....	....	62	....	....	....	....	....	....	....	....	....	....	4	1	0	1	6	....	....	....
	Canada	WJC-A	7	0	1	1	....	....	....	10	....	....	....	....	....	....	....	....	....	....	....	....	....	....	....	....	....	....
	Saint John Flames	AHL	1	0	0	0	....	....	....	0	....	....	....	....	....	....	....	....	....	....	2	0	0	0	0	....	....	....
1994-95	**Calgary Flames**	**NHL**	2	0	0	0	0	0	0	0	0	0	0	0	0.0	0	0	0	0	0	....	....	....	....	....	....	....	....
	Saint John Flames	AHL	77	6	25	31	....	....	....	63	....	....	....	....	....	....	....	....	....	....	5	1	0	1	4	....	....	....
1995-96	**Calgary Flames**	**NHL**	4	0	0	0	0	0	0	4	0	0	0	0	0.0	1	0	1	0	0	....	....	....	....	....	....	....	....
	Saint John Flames	AHL	74	8	25	33	....	....	....	104	....	....	....	....	....	....	....	....	....	....	16	1	4	5	10	....	....	....
1996-97	**Calgary Flames**	**NHL**	76	4	5	9	4	4	8	49	0	1	0	61	6.6	50	3	97	27	–23	....	....	....	....	....	....	....	....
	Canada	WC-A	11	0	1	1	....	....	....	2	....	....	....	....	....	....	....	....	....	....	....	....	....	....	....	....	....	....
1997-98	**Calgary Flames**	**NHL**	44	5	7	12	6	7	13	57	0	1	1	51	9.8	28	1	41	14	0	....	....	....	....	....	....	....	....
	Saint John Flames	AHL	3	2	1	3	....	....	....	6	....	....	....	....	....	....	....	....	....	....	....	....	....	....	....	....	....	....
1998-99	**Nashville Predators**	**NHL**	64	4	11	15	5	11	16	60	0	0	0	78	5.1	48	4	82	28	–10	....	....	....	....	....	....	....	....
99-2000	**Nashville Predators**	**NHL**	52	1	4	5	1	4	5	23	0	0	0	60	1.7	29	0	45	5	–11	....	....	....	....	....	....	....	....
	Dallas Stars	**NHL**	2	0	0	0	0	0	0	2	0	0	0	1	0.0	1	0	1	1	1	....	....	....	....	....	....	....	....
	NHL Totals		**244**	**14**	**27**	**41**	**16**	**26**	**42**	**195**	**0**	**2**	**1**	**251**	**5.6**	**157**	**8**	**267**	**75**		....	....	....	....	....	....	....	....

QMJHL First All-Star Team (1994)

Claimed by **Nashville** from **Calgary** in Expansion Draft, June 26, 1998. Claimed on waivers by **Dallas** from **Nashville**, March 14, 2000.

• BOUCHARD, Pierre Pierre Emile D – L. 6′2″, 205 lbs. b: Montreal, Que., 2/20/1948. Montreal's 1st, 5th overall, in 1965.

Season	Club	League	GP	G	A	Pts	AG	AA	APts	PIM	PP	SH	GW	S	%	TGF	PGF	TGA	PGA	+/–	GP	G	A	Pts	PIM	PP	SH	GW
1964-65	Laval College	Hi-School	STATISTICS NOT AVAILABLE																									
1965-66	Montreal Nationale	MMJHL	40	6	19	25	....	....	....	53	....	....	....	....	....	....	....	....	....	....	....	....	....	....	....	....	....	....
1966-67	Montreal Jr. Canadiens	OHA-Jr.	48	4	9	13	....	....	....	105	....	....	....	....	....	....	....	....	....	....	6	0	0	0	2	....	....	....
1967-68	Montreal Jr. Canadiens	OHA-Jr.	54	10	18	28	....	....	....	134	....	....	....	....	....	....	....	....	....	....	11	2	2	4	20	....	....	....
1968-69	Cleveland Barons	AHL	69	6	16	22	....	....	....	32	....	....	....	....	....	....	....	....	....	....	5	1	1	2	4	....	....	....
1969-70	Montreal Voyageurs	AHL	65	5	13	18	....	....	....	124	....	....	....	....	....	....	....	....	....	....	8	1	3	4	24	....	....	....
1970-71♦	**Montreal Canadiens**	**NHL**	51	0	3	3	0	2	2	50	0	0	0	33	0.0	34	0	31	0	3	13	0	1	1	10	0	0	0
1971-72	**Montreal Canadiens**	**NHL**	60	3	5	8	3	4	7	39	0	0	0	42	7.1	39	0	30	1	10	1	0	0	0	0	0	0	0
1972-73♦	**Montreal Canadiens**	**NHL**	41	0	7	7	0	6	6	69	0	0	0	31	0.0	38	0	27	0	11	17	1	3	4	13	0	0	0
1973-74	**Montreal Canadiens**	**NHL**	60	1	14	15	1	12	13	25	0	0	0	53	1.9	60	0	60	8	8	6	0	2	2	4	0	0	0
1974-75	**Montreal Canadiens**	**NHL**	79	3	9	12	3	7	10	65	0	0	0	67	4.5	72	0	51	3	24	10	0	2	2	10	0	0	0
1975-76♦	**Montreal Canadiens**	**NHL**	66	1	11	12	1	8	9	50	0	0	1	72	1.4	54	0	44	10	20	13	2	0	2	8	1	0	1
1976-77♦	**Montreal Canadiens**	**NHL**	73	4	11	15	4	8	12	52	0	1	0	73	5.5	68	0	38	3	33	6	0	1	1	6	0	0	0
1977-78♦	**Montreal Canadiens**	**NHL**	59	4	6	10	4	5	9	29	0	0	1	55	7.3	42	0	17	2	27	10	0	1	1	5	0	0	0
1978-79	**Washington Capitals**	**NHL**	1	0	0	0	0	0	0	0	0	0	0	0	0.0	1	0	0	0	1	....	....	....	....	....	....	....	....
1979-80	**Washington Capitals**	**NHL**	54	5	9	14	4	7	11	16	0	0	0	59	8.5	64	1	87	17	–7	....	....	....	....	....	....	....	....
1980-81	**Washington Capitals**	**NHL**	50	3	7	10	2	5	7	28	0	0	0	36	8.3	39	1	73	17	–18	....	....	....	....	....	....	....	....
1981-82	**Washington Capitals**	**NHL**	1	0	0	0	0	0	0	10	0	0	0	1	0.0	0	0	2	0	–2	....	....	....	....	....	....	....	....
	Hershey Bears	AHL	62	2	10	12	....	....	....	26	....	....	....	....	....	....	....	....	....	....	5	0	0	0	6	....	....	....
	NHL Totals		**595**	**24**	**82**	**106**	**22**	**64**	**86**	**433**	**0**	**1**	**2**	**522**	**4.6**	**511**	**2**	**460**	**61**		**76**	**3**	**10**	**13**	**56**	**1**	**0**	**1**

• Son of Butch • Claimed by Washington from Montreal in waiver Draft, October 9, 1978

• BOUCHER, Philippe D – R. 6′2″, 221 lbs. b: St. Apollinaire, Que., 3/24/1973. Buffalo's 1st, 13th overall, in 1991.

Season	Club	League	GP	G	A	Pts	AG	AA	APts	PIM	PP	SH	GW	S	%	TGF	PGF	TGA	PGA	+/–	GP	G	A	Pts	PIM	PP	SH	GW
1989-90	Ste-Foy Gouverneurs	QAAA	33	18	47	65	....	....	....	64	....	....	....	....	....	....	....	....	....	....	9	8	13	21	12	....	....	....
1990-91	Granby Bisons	QMJHL	69	21	46	67	....	....	....	92	....	....	....	....	....	....	....	....	....	....	....	....	....	....	....	....	....	....
1991-92	Granby Bisons	QMJHL	49	22	37	59	....	....	....	47	....	....	....	....	....	....	....	....	....	....	....	....	....	....	....	....	....	....
	Laval Titans	QMJHL	16	7	11	18	....	....	....	36	....	....	....	....	....	....	....	....	....	....	10	5	6	11	8	....	....	....
1992-93	Laval Titans	QMJHL	16	12	15	27	....	....	....	37	....	....	....	....	....	....	....	....	....	....	13	6	15	21	12	....	....	....
	Buffalo Sabres	**NHL**	18	0	4	4	0	3	3	14	0	0	0	28	0.0	23	1	23	2	1	....	....	....	....	....	....	....	....
	Rochester Americans	AHL	5	4	3	7	....	....	....	8	....	....	....	....	....	....	....	....	....	....	3	0	1	1	2	....	....	....
	Laval Titans	Mem-Cup	5	2	2	4	....	....	....	15	....	....	....	....	....	....	....	....	....	....	....	....	....	....	....	....	....	....
1993-94	**Buffalo Sabres**	**NHL**	38	6	8	14	6	6	12	29	4	0	1	67	9.0	45	25	21	0	–1	7	1	1	2	2	1	0	0
	Rochester Americans	AHL	31	10	22	32	....	....	....	51	....	....	....	....	....	....	....	....	....	....	....	....	....	....	....	....	....	....
1994-95	**Buffalo Sabres**	**NHL**	9	1	4	5	2	6	8	0	0	0	0	15	6.7	12	5	1	0	6	....	....	....	....	....	....	....	....
	Rochester Americans	AHL	43	14	27	41	....	....	....	26	....	....	....	....	....	....	....	....	....	....	....	....	....	....	....	....	....	....
	Los Angeles Kings	**NHL**	6	1	0	1	2	0	2	4	0	0	0	15	6.7	4	1	8	2	–3	....	....	....	....	....	....	....	....
1995-96	**Los Angeles Kings**	**NHL**	53	7	16	23	7	13	20	31	5	0	1	145	4.8	61	24	76	13	–26	....	....	....	....	....	....	....	....
	Phoenix Roadrunners	IHL	10	4	3	7	....	....	....	4	....	....	....	....	....	....	....	....	....	....	....	....	....	....	....	....	....	....
1996-97	**Los Angeles Kings**	**NHL**	60	7	18	25	7	16	23	25	2	0	1	159	4.4	63	14	57	8	0	....	....	....	....	....	....	....	....
1997-98	**Los Angeles Kings**	**NHL**	45	6	10	16	7	10	17	49	1	0	0	80	7.5	42	9	35	8	6	....	....	....	....	....	....	....	....
	Long Beach Ice Dogs	IHL	2	0	1	1	....	....	....	4	....	....	....	....	....	....	....	....	....	....	....	....	....	....	....	....	....	....

Season	Club	League	REGULAR SEASON																		PLAYOFFS							
			GP	G	A	Pts	AG	AA	APts	PIM	PP	SH	GW	S	%	TGF	PGF	TGA	PGA	+/-	GP	G	A	Pts	PIM	PP	SH	GW
1998-99	**Los Angeles Kings**	**NHL**	45	2	6	8	2	6	8	32	1	0	0	87	2.3	28	11	35	6	–12	....	....	....	....	....	....	....	....
99-2000	**Los Angeles Kings**	**NHL**	1	0	0	0	0	0	0	0	0	0	0	3	0.0	0	0	0	0	0	....	....	....	....	....	....	....	....
	Long Beach Ice Dogs	IHL	14	4	11	15	....	....	....	8	....	....	....	....	....	....	....	....	....	....	6	0	9	9	8	....	....	....
	NHL Totals		275	30	66	96	33	60	93	184	13	0	3	599	5.0	278	90	256	39		7	1	1	2	2	1	0	0

Canadian Major Junior Rookie of the Year (1991) • QMJHL Second All-Star Team (1991, 1992)

Traded to **LA Kings** by **Buffalo** with Denis Tsygurov and Grant Fuhr for Alexei Zhitnik, Robb Stauber, Charlie Huddy and LA Kings' 5th round choice (Marian Menhart) in 1995 Entry Draft, February 14, 1995. • Missed majority of 1999-2000 season recovering from foot injury that required surgery, September, 1999.

• BOUDREAU, Bruce

Bruce Allan "Gabby"   C – L. 5'9", 170 lbs.   b: Toronto, Ont., 1/9/1955. Toronto's 3rd, 42nd overall, in 1975.

Season	Club	League	GP	G	A	Pts	AG	AA	APts	PIM	PP	SH	GW	S	%	TGF	PGF	TGA	PGA	+/-	GP	G	A	Pts	PIM	PP	SH	GW
1972-73	Toronto Marlboros	OMJHL	61	38	49	87	....	....	....	22	....	....	....	....	....	....	....	....	....	....	....	....	....	....	....	....	....	....
1973-74	Toronto Marlboros	OMJHL	53	46	67	113	....	....	....	51	....	....	....	....	....	....	....	....	....	....	....	....	....	....	....	....	....	....
1974-75	Toronto Marlboros	OMJHL	69	*68	97	*165	....	....	....	52	....	....	....	....	....	....	....	....	....	....	22	12	*28	40	26	....	....	....
	Toronto Marlboros	Mem-Cup	5	2	2	4	....	....	....	15	....	....	....	....	....	....	....	....	....	....	....	....	....	....	....	....	....	....
1975-76	Minnesota Fighting Saints	WHA	30	3	6	9	....	....	....	4	....	....	....	....	....	....	....	....	....	....	....	....	....	....	....	....	....	....
	Johnstown Jets	NAHL	34	25	35	60	....	....	....	14	....	....	....	....	....	....	....	....	....	....	....	....	....	....	....	....	....	....
1976-77	**Toronto Maple Leafs**	**NHL**	15	2	5	7	2	4	6	4	0	0	1	17	11.8	8	2	4	0	2	3	0	0	0	0	0	0	0
	Dallas Black Hawks	CHL	58	*37	34	71	....	....	....	40	....	....	....	....	....	....	....	....	....	....	1	1	1	2	0	....	....	....
1977-78	**Toronto Maple Leafs**	**NHL**	40	11	18	29	10	14	24	12	1	0	2	71	15.5	36	5	23	0	8	....	....	....	....	....	....	....	....
	Dallas Black Hawks	CHL	22	13	9	22	....	....	....	11	....	....	....	....	....	....	....	....	....	....	....	....	....	....	....	....	....	....
1978-79	**Toronto Maple Leafs**	**NHL**	26	4	3	7	3	2	5	2	0	0	0	30	13.3	10	1	12	0	–3	....	....	....	....	....	....	....	....
	New Brunswick Hawks	AHL	49	20	38	58	....	....	....	20	....	....	....	....	....	....	....	....	....	....	5	1	1	2	8	....	....	....
1979-80	**Toronto Maple Leafs**	**NHL**	2	0	0	0	0	0	0	2	0	0	0	0	0.0	0	0	0	0	0	....	....	....	....	....	....	....	....
	New Brunswick Hawks	AHL	75	36	54	90	....	....	....	47	....	....	....	....	....	....	....	....	....	....	17	6	7	13	23	....	....	....
1980-81	**Toronto Maple Leafs**	**NHL**	39	10	14	24	8	9	17	18	0	0	0	47	21.3	31	1	39	2	–7	2	1	0	1	0	0	0	0
	New Brunswick Hawks	AHL	40	17	41	58	....	....	....	22	....	....	....	....	....	....	....	....	....	....	8	6	5	11	14	....	....	....
1981-82	**Toronto Maple Leafs**	**NHL**	12	0	2	2	0	1	1	6	0	0	0	5	0.0	2	0	8	0	–6	....	....	....	....	....	....	....	....
	Cincinnati Tigers	CHL	65	42	61	103	....	....	....	42	....	....	....	....	....	....	....	....	....	....	4	3	1	4	8	....	....	....
1982-83	St. Catharines Saints	AHL	80	50	72	122	....	....	....	65	....	....	....	....	....	....	....	....	....	....	....	....	....	....	....	....	....	....
	Toronto Maple Leafs	**NHL**	....	....	....	....	....	....	....	....	....	....	....	....	....	....	....	....	....	....	4	1	0	1	0	0	0	0
1983-84	St. Catharines Saints	AHL	80	47	62	109	....	....	....	44	....	....	....	....	....	....	....	....	....	....	7	0	5	5	11	....	....	....
1984-85	ECD Iserlohn	Germany	30	20	28	48	....	....	....	41	....	....	....	....	....	....	....	....	....	....	3	2	1	3	4	....	....	....
	Baltimore Skipjacks	AHL	17	4	7	11	....	....	....	4	....	....	....	....	....	....	....	....	....	....	15	3	9	12	4	....	....	....
1985-86	**Chicago Black Hawks**	**NHL**	7	1	0	1	1	0	1	2	0	0	0	3	33.3	1	0	0	0	1	....	....	....	....	....	....	....	....
	Nova Scotia Oilers	AHL	65	30	36	66	....	....	....	36	....	....	....	....	....	....	....	....	....	....	....	....	....	....	....	....	....	....
1986-87	Nova Scotia Oilers	AHL	78	35	47	82	....	....	....	40	....	....	....	....	....	....	....	....	....	....	5	3	3	6	4	....	....	....
1987-88	Springfield Indians	AHL	80	42	*74	*116	....	....	....	84	....	....	....	....	....	....	....	....	....	....	....	....	....	....	....	....	....	....
1988-89	Springfield Indians	AHL	50	28	36	64	....	....	....	42	....	....	....	....	....	....	....	....	....	....	....	....	....	....	....	....	....	....
	Newmarket Saints	AHL	20	7	16	23	....	....	....	12	....	....	....	....	....	....	....	....	....	....	4	0	1	1	6	....	....	....
1989-90	Phoenix Roadrunners	IHL	82	41	68	109	....	....	....	89	....	....	....	....	....	....	....	....	....	....	....	....	....	....	....	....	....	....
1990-91	Fort Wayne Komets	IHL	81	40	*80	120	....	....	....	111	....	....	....	....	....	....	....	....	....	....	19	11	7	18	30	....	....	....
1991-92	Fort Wayne Komets	IHL	77	34	50	84	....	....	....	100	....	....	....	....	....	....	....	....	....	....	7	3	4	7	10	....	....	....
	Adirondack Red Wings	AHL	....	....	....	....	....	....	....	....	....	....	....	....	....	....	....	....	....	....	4	1	1	2	2	....	....	....
1992-1993	Muskegon Fury	ColHL	DID NOT PLAY – COACHING																									
1993-1995	Muskegon Fury	IHL	DID NOT PLAY – COACHING																									
1995-1996	San Francisco Spiders	IHL	DID NOT PLAY – ASSISTANT COACH																									
1996-1999	Mississippi Sea Wolves	ECHL	DID NOT PLAY – COACHING																									
1999-2000	Lowell Lock Monsters	AHL	DID NOT PLAY – COACHING																									
	NHL Totals		141	28	42	70	24	30	54	46	1	0	3	173	16.2	88	9	86	2		9	2	0	2	0	0	0	0
	Other Major League Totals		30	3	6	9	....	....	....	4	....	....	....	....	....	....	....	....	....	....	....	....	....	....	....	....	....	....

OMJHL Second All-Star Team (1974) • CHL Second All-Star Team (1982) • AHL First All-Star Team (1988) • Won Fred T. Hunt Memorial Trophy (Sportsmanship - AHL) (1988) • Won John B. Sollenberger Trophy (Top Scorer - AHL) (1988)

Selected by **Minnesota** (WHA) in 1974 WHA Amateur Draft, June, 1974. Claimed by **Toronto** as a fill-in during Expansion Draft, June 13, 1979. Signed as a free agent by **Baltimore** (AHL), March 5, 1985. Signed as a free agent by **Chicago**, October 10, 1985.

• BOUDRIAS, Andre

Andre Gerard   LW – L. 5'8", 165 lbs.   b: Montreal, Que., 9/19/1943.

Season	Club	League	GP	G	A	Pts	AG	AA	APts	PIM	PP	SH	GW	S	%	TGF	PGF	TGA	PGA	+/-	GP	G	A	Pts	PIM	PP	SH	GW
1958-59	St-Jerome Alouettes	MMJHL	STATISTICS NOT AVAILABLE																									
1959-60	Montreal NDG Monarchs	MMJHL	STATISTICS NOT AVAILABLE																									
1960-61	Hull Canadiens	IPSHL	....	15	17	32	....	....	....	....	....	....	....	....	....	....	....	....	....	....	....	....	....	....	....	....	....	....
	Hull Canadiens	Al-Cup	3	0	0	0	....	....	....	0	....	....	....	....	....	....	....	....	....	....	....	....	....	....	....	....	....	....
1961-62	Montreal Jr. Canadiens	OHA-Jr.	50	34	*63	*97	....	....	....	54	....	....	....	....	....	....	....	....	....	....	6	2	3	5	4	....	....	....
	Hull-Ottawa Canadiens	EPHL	1	0	0	0	....	....	....	0	....	....	....	....	....	....	....	....	....	....	....	....	....	....	....	....	....	....
	North Bay Trappers	EPHL	1	0	3	3	....	....	....	2	....	....	....	....	....	....	....	....	....	....	1	0	0	0	0	....	....	....
1962-63	Montreal Jr. Canadiens	OHA-Jr.	50	12	43	55	....	....	....	72	....	....	....	....	....	....	....	....	....	....	10	3	4	7	18	....	....	....
	Hull-Ottawa Canadiens	EPHL	3	0	1	1	....	....	....	0	....	....	....	....	....	....	....	....	....	....	....	....	....	....	....	....	....	....
1963-64	Montreal Jr. Canadiens	OHA-Jr.	55	38	*97	*135	....	....	....	48	....	....	....	....	....	....	....	....	....	....	16	11	*26	*37	18	....	....	....
	Montreal Canadiens	**NHL**	4	1	4	5	1	4	5	2	....	....	....	....	....	....	....	....	....	....	....	....	....	....	....	....	....	....
1964-65	**Montreal Canadiens**	**NHL**	1	0	0	0	0	0	0	2	....	....	....	....	....	....	....	....	....	....	....	....	....	....	....	....	....	....
	Quebec Aces	AHL	14	4	9	13	....	....	....	4	....	....	....	....	....	....	....	....	....	....	....	....	....	....	....	....	....	....
	Omaha Knights	CPHL	52	15	49	64	....	....	....	10	....	....	....	....	....	....	....	....	....	....	6	1	7	8	2	....	....	....
1965-66	Quebec Aces	AHL	1	2	0	2	....	....	....	0	....	....	....	....	....	....	....	....	....	....	....	....	....	....	....	....	....	....
	Houston Apollos	CPHL	70	27	46	73	....	....	....	53	....	....	....	....	....	....	....	....	....	....	....	....	....	....	....	....	....	....
1966-67	**Montreal Canadiens**	**NHL**	2	0	1	1	0	1	1	0	....	....	....	....	....	....	....	....	....	....	....	....	....	....	....	....	....	....
	Houston Apollos	CPHL	67	16	48	64	....	....	....	58	....	....	....	....	....	....	....	....	....	....	6	1	2	3	6	....	....	....
1967-68	**Minnesota North Stars**	**NHL**	74	18	35	53	21	35	56	42	4	0	3	183	9.8	80	19	90	26	–3	14	3	6	9	8	0	0	1
1968-69	**Minnesota North Stars**	**NHL**	53	4	9	13	4	8	12	6	1	0	0	87	4.6	16	3	69	26	–30	....	....	....	....	....	....	....	....
	Chicago Black Hawks	**NHL**	20	4	10	14	4	9	13	4	1	0	1	40	10.0	22	2	10	1	11	....	....	....	....	....	....	....	....
1969-70	**St. Louis Blues**	**NHL**	50	3	14	17	3	13	16	20	1	0	2	95	3.2	29	7	20	5	7	14	2	4	6	4	1	0	0
	Kansas City Blues	CHL	19	7	16	23	....	....	....	16	....	....	....	....	....	....	....	....	....	....	....	....	....	....	....	....	....	....
1970-71	**Vancouver Canucks**	**NHL**	77	25	41	66	25	34	59	16	7	1	2	254	9.8	86	19	91	39	15	....	....	....	....	....	....	....	....
1971-72	**Vancouver Canucks**	**NHL**	78	27	34	61	27	29	56	26	6	0	5	224	12.1	82	27	96	7	–34	....	....	....	....	....	....	....	....
1972-73	**Vancouver Canucks**	**NHL**	77	30	40	70	28	32	60	24	8	0	2	194	15.5	97	29	89	1	–20	....	....	....	....	....	....	....	....
1973-74	**Vancouver Canucks**	**NHL**	78	16	59	75	15	49	64	18	3	1	1	180	8.9	96	31	90	19	–6	....	....	....	....	....	....	....	....
1974-75	**Vancouver Canucks**	**NHL**	77	16	62	78	14	47	61	46	9	0	2	167	9.6	95	41	47	1	8	5	1	0	1	0	0	0	0
1975-76	**Vancouver Canucks**	**NHL**	71	7	31	38	6	23	29	10	2	0	0	69	10.1	52	19	49	9	–7	1	0	0	0	0	0	0	0
1976-77	Quebec Nordiques	WHA	74	12	31	43	....	....	....	12	....	....	....	....	....	....	....	....	....	....	17	3	12	15	6	....	....	....
1977-78	Quebec Nordiques	WHA	66	10	17	27	....	....	....	22	....	....	....	....	....	....	....	....	....	....	11	0	2	2	4	....	....	....
	NHL Totals		662	151	340	491	148	284	432	216	....	....	....	....	....	....	....	....	....	....	34	6	10	16	12	....	....	....
	Other Major League Totals		140	22	48	70	....	....	....	34	....	....	....	....	....	....	....	....	....	....	28	3	14	17	10	....	....	....

Played in NHL All-Star Game (1967)

Traded to **Minnesota** by **Montreal** with Bob Charlebois and Bernard Cote for Minnesota's 1st round choice (Chuck Arnason) in 1971 Amateur Draft, June 6, 1967. Traded to **Chicago** by **Minnesota** with Mike McMahon Jr. for Tom Reid and Bill Orban, February 14, 1969. Claimed by **St. Louis** from **Chicago** in Intra-League Draft, June 11, 1969. Traded to **Vancouver** by **St. Louis** for Vancouver's 7th (Jack Taggart) and 9th (Bob Winogard) round choices in 1970 Amateur Draft and cash, June 10, 1970. Selected by **Minnesota** (WHA) in 1972 WHA General Player Draft, February 12, 1972. WHA rights traded to **Quebec** (WHA) by **Minnesota** (WHA) for Gordie Gallant, September, 1976.

• BOUGHNER, Barry

Barry Michael   LW – L. 5'10", 180 lbs.   b: Delhi, Ont., 1/29/1948.

Season	Club	League	GP	G	A	Pts	AG	AA	APts	PIM	PP	SH	GW	S	%	TGF	PGF	TGA	PGA	+/-	GP	G	A	Pts	PIM	PP	SH	GW
1966-67	London Nationals	OHA-Jr.	42	1	7	8	....	....	....	11	....	....	....	....	....	....	....	....	....	....	6	1	2	3	6	....	....	....
1967-68	London Nationals/Knights	OHA-Jr.	52	15	19	34	....	....	....	43	....	....	....	....	....	....	....	....	....	....	5	2	1	3	0	....	....	....
1968-69	Des Moines Oak Leafs	IHL	58	19	13	32	....	....	....	34	....	....	....	....	....	....	....	....	....	....	....	....	....	....	....	....	....	....

			REGULAR SEASON																		PLAYOFFS							
Season	Club	League	GP	G	A	Pts	AG	AA	APts	PIM	PP	SH	GW	S	%	TGF	PGF	TGA	PGA	+/–	GP	G	A	Pts	PIM	PP	SH	GW
1969-70	**Oakland Seals**	**NHL**	**4**	**0**	**0**	**0**	**0**	**0**	**0**	**2**	**0**	**0**	**0**	**5**	**0.0**	**1**	**0**	**1**	**0**	**0**	....	....	....	....	....	....	....	....
	Providence Reds	AHL	71	9	13	22	....	....	....	16	....	....	....	....	....	....	....	....	....	....	....	....	....	....	....	....	....	....
1970-71	**California Golden Seals**	**NHL**	**16**	**0**	**0**	**0**	**0**	**0**	**0**	**9**	**0**	**0**	**0**	**7**	**0.0**	**0**	**0**	**3**	**0**	**–3**	....	....	....	....	....	....	....	....
	Providence Reds	AHL	21	1	0	1	....	....	....	4	....	....	....	....	....	....	....	....	....	....	....	....	....	....	....	....	....	....
1971-72	Des Moines Oak Leafs	IHL	66	14	19	33	....	....	....	83	....	....	....	....	....	....	....	....	....	....	3	1	1	2	2	....	....	....
1972-73	New Haven Nighthawks	AHL	63	9	17	26	....	....	....	14	....	....	....	....	....	....	....	....	....	....	....	....	....	....	....	....	....	....
1973-74	Albuquerque 6-Guns	CHL	62	11	14	25	....	....	....	19	....	....	....	....	....	....	....	....	....	....	....	....	....	....	....	....	....	....
1974-75	Brantford Foresters	OHA-Sr.	12	3	4	7	....	....	....	15	....	....	....	....	....	....	....	....	....	....	....	....	....	....	....	....	....	....
	NHL Totals		**20**	**0**	**0**	**0**	**0**	**0**	**0**	**11**	**0**	**0**	**0**	**12**	**0.0**	**1**	**0**	**4**	**0**		....	....	....	....	....	....	....	....

Signed as a free agent by **Port Huron** (IHL), September, 1968. Traded to **Des Moines** (IHL) by **Port Huron** with Ron Schwindt for Reg Bechtold and Joe Cooper, November, 1968. Signed as a free agent by **Oakland** , October, 1969.

• BOUGHNER, Bob

D – R. 6′, 206 lbs. b: Windsor, Ont., 3/8/1971. Detroit's 2nd, 32nd overall, in 1989.

Season	Club	League	GP	G	A	Pts	AG	AA	APts	PIM	PP	SH	GW	S	%	TGF	PGF	TGA	PGA	+/–	GP	G	A	Pts	PIM	PP	SH	GW
1986-87	Belle River Canadians	OJHL-C	37	3	11	14	....	....	....	88	....	....	....	....	....	....	....	....	....	....	....	....	....	....	....	....	....	....
1987-88	St. Mary's Lincolns	OJHL-B	36	4	18	22	....	....	....	177	....	....	....	....	....	....	....	....	....	....	....	....	....	....	....	....	....	....
1988-89	Sault Ste. Marie Greyhounds	OHL	64	6	15	21	....	....	....	182	....	....	....	....	....	....	....	....	....	....	....	....	....	....	....	....	....	....
1989-90	Sault Ste. Marie Greyhounds	OHL	49	7	23	30	....	....	....	122	....	....	....	....	....	....	....	....	....	....	....	....	....	....	....	....	....	....
1990-91	Sault Ste. Marie Greyhounds	OHL	64	13	33	46	....	....	....	156	....	....	....	....	....	....	....	....	....	....	14	2	9	11	35	....	....	....
	Sault Ste. Marie Greyhounds	Mem-Cup	4	*6	3	9	....	....	....	0	....	....	....	....	....	....	....	....	....	....	....	....	....	....	....	....	....	....
1991-92	Toledo Storm	ECHL	28	3	10	13	....	....	....	79	....	....	....	....	....	....	....	....	....	....	5	2	0	2	15	....	....	....
	Adirondack Red Wings	AHL	1	0	0	0	....	....	....	7	....	....	....	....	....	....	....	....	....	....	....	....	....	....	....	....	....	....
1992-93	Adirondack Red Wings	AHL	69	1	16	17	....	....	....	190	....	....	....	....	....	....	....	....	....	....	....	....	....	....	....	....	....	....
1993-94	Adirondack Red Wings	AHL	72	8	14	22	....	....	....	292	....	....	....	....	....	....	....	....	....	....	10	1	1	2	18	....	....	....
1994-95	Cincinnati Cyclones	IHL	81	2	14	16	....	....	....	192	....	....	....	....	....	....	....	....	....	....	10	0	0	0	18	....	....	....
1995-96	Carolina Monarchs	AHL	46	2	15	17	....	....	....	127	....	....	....	....	....	....	....	....	....	....	....	....	....	....	....	....	....	....
	Buffalo Sabres	**NHL**	**31**	**0**	**1**	**1**	**0**	**1**	**1**	**104**	**0**	**0**	**0**	**14**	**0.0**	**10**	**0**	**9**	**2**	**3**	....	....	....	....	....	....	....	....
1996-97	**Buffalo Sabres**	**NHL**	**77**	**1**	**7**	**8**	**1**	**6**	**7**	**225**	**0**	**0**	**0**	**34**	**2.9**	**41**	**0**	**38**	**9**	**12**	**11**	**0**	**1**	**1**	**9**	**0**	**0**	**0**
1997-98	**Buffalo Sabres**	**NHL**	**69**	**1**	**3**	**4**	**1**	**3**	**4**	**165**	**0**	**0**	**0**	**26**	**3.8**	**29**	**0**	**35**	**11**	**5**	**14**	**0**	**4**	**4**	**15**	**0**	**0**	**0**
1998-99	**Nashville Predators**	**NHL**	**79**	**3**	**10**	**13**	**4**	**10**	**14**	**137**	**0**	**0**	**1**	**59**	**5.1**	**54**	**0**	**89**	**29**	**–6**	....	....	....	....	....	....	....	....
99-2000	**Nashville Predators**	**NHL**	**62**	**2**	**4**	**6**	**2**	**4**	**6**	**97**	**0**	**0**	**0**	**32**	**6.3**	**33**	**0**	**54**	**8**	**–13**	....	....	....	....	....	....	....	....
	Pittsburgh Penguins	**NHL**	**11**	**1**	**0**	**1**	**1**	**0**	**1**	**69**	**1**	**0**	**1**	**8**	**12.5**	**11**	**1**	**9**	**1**	**2**	**11**	**0**	**2**	**2**	**15**	**0**	**0**	**0**
	NHL Totals		**329**	**8**	**25**	**33**	**9**	**24**	**33**	**797**	**1**	**0**	**2**	**173**	**4.6**	**178**	**1**	**234**	**60**		**36**	**0**	**7**	**7**	**39**	**0**	**0**	**0**

Signed as a free agent by **Florida**, July 25, 1994. Traded to **Buffalo** by **Florida** for Buffalo's 3rd round choice (Chris Allen) in 1996 Entry Draft, February 1, 1996. Claimed by **Nashville** from **Buffalo** in Expansion Draft, June 26, 1998. Traded to **Pittsburgh** by **Buffalo** for Pavel Skrbek, March 13, 2000.

• BOUILLON, Francis

D – L. 5′8″, 186 lbs. b: New York, NY, 10/17/1975.

Season	Club	League	GP	G	A	Pts	AG	AA	APts	PIM	PP	SH	GW	S	%	TGF	PGF	TGA	PGA	+/–	GP	G	A	Pts	PIM	PP	SH	GW
1992-93	Laval Titan	QMJHL	46	0	7	7	....	....	....	45	....	....	....	....	....	....	....	....	....	....	....	....	....	....	....	....	....	....
1993-94	Laval Titan	QMJHL	68	3	15	18	....	....	....	129	....	....	....	....	....	....	....	....	....	....	19	2	9	11	48	....	....	....
1994-95	Laval Titan	QMJHL	72	8	25	33	....	....	....	115	....	....	....	....	....	....	....	....	....	....	20	3	11	14	21	....	....	....
1995-96	Granby Predateurs	QMJHL	68	11	35	46	....	....	....	156	....	....	....	....	....	....	....	....	....	....	21	2	12	14	30	....	....	....
1996-97	Wheeling Nailers	ECHL	69	10	32	42	....	....	....	77	....	....	....	....	....	....	....	....	....	....	3	0	2	2	10	....	....	....
1997-98	Quebec Rafales	IHL	71	8	27	35	....	....	....	76	....	....	....	....	....	....	....	....	....	....	....	....	....	....	....	....	....	....
1998-99	Fredericton Canadiens	AHL	79	19	36	55	....	....	....	174	....	....	....	....	....	....	....	....	....	....	5	2	1	3	0	....	....	....
99-2000	**Montreal Canadiens**	**NHL**	**74**	**3**	**13**	**16**	**3**	**12**	**15**	**38**	**2**	**0**	**1**	**76**	**3.9**	**49**	**14**	**47**	**5**	**–7**	....	....	....	....	....	....	....	....
	NHL Totals		**74**	**3**	**13**	**16**	**3**	**12**	**15**	**38**	**2**	**0**	**1**	**76**	**3.9**	**49**	**14**	**47**	**5**		....	....	....	....	....	....	....	....

Signed as a free agent by **Montreal**, June 28, 1998 • Played w/ RHI's Montreal Roadrunners in 1996 (23-4-9-13-63).

• BOURBONNAIS, Dan

Daniel Richard LW – L. 5′10″, 185 lbs. b: Winnipeg, Man., 3/6/1962. Hartford's 5th, 103rd overall, in 1981.

Season	Club	League	GP	G	A	Pts	AG	AA	APts	PIM	PP	SH	GW	S	%	TGF	PGF	TGA	PGA	+/–	GP	G	A	Pts	PIM	PP	SH	GW
1978-79	Pincher Creek Panthers	AJHL	60	17	41	58	....	....	....	36	....	....	....	....	....	....	....	....	....	....	....	....	....	....	....	....	....	....
	Calgary Wranglers	WHL	2	0	2	2	....	....	....	0	....	....	....	....	....	....	....	....	....	....	....	....	....	....	....	....	....	....
1979-80	Calgary Wranglers	WHL	66	14	29	43	....	....	....	41	....	....	....	....	....	....	....	....	....	....	6	2	2	4	0	....	....	....
1980-81	Calgary Wranglers	WHL	72	41	62	103	....	....	....	34	....	....	....	....	....	....	....	....	....	....	22	5	10	15	28	....	....	....
1981-82	Calgary Wranglers	WHL	50	27	32	59	....	....	....	175	....	....	....	....	....	....	....	....	....	....	9	6	4	10	17	....	....	....
	Hartford Whalers	**NHL**	**24**	**3**	**9**	**12**	**2**	**6**	**8**	**11**	**0**	**0**	**0**	**30**	**10.0**	**17**	**3**	**22**	**0**	**–8**	....	....	....	....	....	....	....	....
1982-83	Binghamton Whalers	AHL	75	31	33	64	....	....	....	24	....	....	....	....	....	....	....	....	....	....	5	4	0	4	0	....	....	....
1983-84	**Hartford Whalers**	**NHL**	**35**	**0**	**16**	**16**	**0**	**11**	**11**	**0**	**0**	**0**	**0**	**42**	**0.0**	**23**	**4**	**19**	**3**	**3**	....	....	....	....	....	....	....	....
	Binghamton Whalers	AHL	39	16	32	48	....	....	....	40	....	....	....	....	....	....	....	....	....	....	....	....	....	....	....	....	....	....
1984-85	Binghamton Whalers	AHL	56	13	22	35	....	....	....	17	....	....	....	....	....	....	....	....	....	....	....	....	....	....	....	....	....	....
1985-86			STATISTICS NOT AVAILABLE																									
1986-87			STATISTICS NOT AVAILABLE																									
1987-88	SIJ Heerenveen	Holland	46	46	63	109	....	....	....	....	....	....	....	....	....	....	....	....	....	....	....	....	....	....	....	....	....	....
1988-89	EC Westfalen-Dortmund	Germany-2	32	34	41	75	....	....	....	30	....	....	....	....	....	....	....	....	....	....	....	....	....	....	....	....	....	....
1989-90	HC Caen	France	11	5	4	9	....	....	....	18	....	....	....	....	....	....	....	....	....	....	....	....	....	....	....	....	....	....
	NHL Totals		**59**	**3**	**25**	**28**	**2**	**17**	**19**	**11**	**0**	**0**	**0**	**72**	**4.2**	**40**	**7**	**41**	**3**		....	....	....	....	....	....	....	....

• BOURBONNAIS, Rick

Richard Ronald RW – R. 6′, 186 lbs. b: Toronto, Ont., 4/20/1955. St. Louis' 3rd, 63rd overall, in 1975.

Season	Club	League	GP	G	A	Pts	AG	AA	APts	PIM	PP	SH	GW	S	%	TGF	PGF	TGA	PGA	+/–	GP	G	A	Pts	PIM	PP	SH	GW
1972-73	Kitchener Rangers	OMJHL	56	7	13	20	....	....	....	53	....	....	....	....	....	....	....	....	....	....	....	....	....	....	....	....	....	....
1973-74	Kitchener Rangers	OMJHL	70	30	35	65	....	....	....	40	....	....	....	....	....	....	....	....	....	....	....	....	....	....	....	....	....	....
1974-75	Kitchener–Ottawa	OMJHL	64	21	37	58	....	....	....	79	....	....	....	....	....	....	....	....	....	....	7	1	2	3	6	....	....	....
1975-76	**St. Louis Blues**	**NHL**	**7**	**0**	**0**	**0**	**0**	**0**	**0**	**8**	**0**	**0**	**0**	**5**	**0.0**	**1**	**0**	**2**	**0**	**–1**	....	....	....	....	....	....	....	....
	Providence Reds	AHL	64	18	17	35	....	....	....	96	....	....	....	....	....	....	....	....	....	....	2	1	0	1	6	....	....	....
1976-77	**St. Louis Blues**	**NHL**	**33**	**6**	**8**	**14**	**5**	**6**	**11**	**10**	**2**	**0**	**1**	**44**	**13.6**	**27**	**9**	**24**	**0**	**–6**	**4**	**0**	**1**	**1**	**0**	**0**	**0**	**0**
	Kansas City Blues	CHL	39	20	24	44	....	....	....	19	....	....	....	....	....	....	....	....	....	....	....	....	....	....	....	....	....	....
1977-78	**St. Louis Blues**	**NHL**	**31**	**3**	**7**	**10**	**3**	**5**	**8**	**11**	**1**	**0**	**0**	**56**	**5.4**	**19**	**5**	**26**	**0**	**–12**	....	....	....	....	....	....	....	....
	Salt Lake Golden Eagles	CHL	40	18	21	39	....	....	....	12	....	....	....	....	....	....	....	....	....	....	6	3	2	5	2	....	....	....
1978-79	Salt Lake Golden Eagles	CHL	74	15	22	37	....	....	....	35	....	....	....	....	....	....	....	....	....	....	4	0	0	0	2	....	....	....
1979-80	Binghamton Dusters	AHL	49	8	11	19	....	....	....	20	....	....	....	....	....	....	....	....	....	....	....	....	....	....	....	....	....	....
	Salt Lake Golden Eagles	CHL	6	1	0	1	....	....	....	0	....	....	....	....	....	....	....	....	....	....	....	....	....	....	....	....	....	....
1980-81			STATISTICS NOT AVAILABLE																									
1981-82	HC Chamonix	France	32	15	13	28	....	....	....	....	....	....	....	....	....	....	....	....	....	....	....	....	....	....	....	....	....	....
1982-83	SB Rosenheim	Germany	36	31	31	62	....	....	....	26	....	....	....	....	....	....	....	....	....	....	....	....	....	....	....	....	....	....
1983-84	SB Rosenheim	Germany	29	13	14	27	....	....	....	8	....	....	....	....	....	....	....	....	....	....	....	....	....	....	....	....	....	....
1984-85	IEV Innsbruck	Austria	5	2	2	4	....	....	....	6	....	....	....	....	....	....	....	....	....	....	....	....	....	....	....	....	....	....
	EA Kempten	Germany-2	15	22	7	29	....	....	....	20	....	....	....	....	....	....	....	....	....	....	12	16	17	33	50	....	....	....
1985-86	EA Kempten	Germany-2	14	21	13	34	....	....	....	....	....	....	....	....	....	....	....	....	....	....	....	....	....	....	....	....	....	....
1986-87	EC Deggendorf	Germany-3	10	20	23	43	....	....	....	....	....	....	....	....	....	....	....	....	....	....	....	....	....	....	....	....	....	....
1987-88	Sun Valley Suns	X-Games	STATISTICS NOT AVAILABLE																									
1988-89	EA Kempten	Germany-2	32	34	41	75	....	....	....	30	....	....	....	....	....	....	....	....	....	....	....	....	....	....	....	....	....	....
1989-1992	Sun Valley Suns	X-Games	56	54	51	105	....	....	....	24	....	....	....	....	....	....	....	....	....	....	....	....	....	....	....	....	....	....
	NHL Totals		**71**	**9**	**15**	**24**	**8**	**11**	**19**	**29**	**3**	**0**	**1**	**105**	**8.6**	**47**	**14**	**52**	**0**		**4**	**0**	**1**	**1**	**0**	**0**	**0**	**0**

• Statistics for Sun Valley Suns (X-Games) represent totals for entire career - 1987-88 and 1989-1992 - with team.

• BOURGEOIS, Charlie

Charles Marc "Boo-Boo" D – R. 6′4″, 220 lbs. b: Moncton, N.B., 11/19/1959.

Season	Club	League	GP	G	A	Pts	AG	AA	APts	PIM	PP	SH	GW	S	%	TGF	PGF	TGA	PGA	+/–	GP	G	A	Pts	PIM	PP	SH	GW
1977-78	Dieppe Voyageurs	SNBHL	STATISTICS NOT AVAILABLE																									
1978-79	University of Moncton	AUAA	18	3	3	6	....	....	....	8	....	....	....	....	....	....	....	....	....	....	....	....	....	....	....	....	....	....
1979-80	Cap Pele Fishermen	MJrHL	STATISTICS NOT AVAILABLE																									
1980-81	University of Moncton	AUAA	24	10	21	31	....	....	....	44	....	....	....	....	....	....	....	....	....	....	6	4	6	10	....	....	....	....

Season	Club	League	REGULAR SEASON GP	G	A	Pts	AG	AA	APts	PIM	PP	SH	GW	S	%	TGF	PGF	TGA	PGA	+/–	PLAYOFFS GP	G	A	Pts	PIM	PP	SH	GW
1981-82	**Calgary Flames**	**NHL**	**54**	**2**	**13**	**15**	**2**	**9**	**11**	**112**	**0**	**0**	**0**	**33**	**6.1**	**50**	**0**	**47**	**2**	**5**	**3**	**0**	**0**	**0**	**7**	**0**	**0**	**0**
	Oklahoma City Stars	CHL	13	2	2	4	....	....	....	17	....	....	....	....	....	....	....	....	....	....	....	....	....	....	....	....	....	....
1982-83	**Calgary Flames**	**NHL**	**15**	**2**	**3**	**5**	**2**	**2**	**4**	**21**	**0**	**0**	**0**	**11**	**18.2**	**10**	**0**	**16**	**2**	**–4**	....	....	....	....	....	....	....	....
	Colorado Flames	CHL	51	10	18	28	....	....	....	128	....	....	....	....	....	....	....	....	....	....	6	2	3	5	30	....	....	....
1983-84	**Calgary Flames**	**NHL**	**17**	**1**	**3**	**4**	**1**	**2**	**3**	**35**	**0**	**0**	**0**	**20**	**5.0**	**15**	**0**	**18**	**3**	**0**	**8**	**0**	**1**	**1**	**27**	**0**	**0**	**0**
	Colorado Flames	CHL	54	12	32	44	....	....	....	133	....	....	....	....	....	....	....	....	....	....	....	....	....	....	....	....	....	....
1984-85	**Calgary Flames**	**NHL**	**47**	**2**	**10**	**12**	**2**	**7**	**9**	**134**	**0**	**0**	**0**	**38**	**5.3**	**45**	**3**	**31**	**3**	**14**	**4**	**0**	**0**	**0**	**17**	**0**	**0**	**0**
1985-86	**Calgary Flames**	**NHL**	**29**	**5**	**5**	**10**	**4**	**3**	**7**	**128**	**0**	**0**	**0**	**30**	**16.7**	**29**	**0**	**28**	**8**	**9**	....	....	....	....	....	....	....	....
	St. Louis Blues	**NHL**	**31**	**2**	**7**	**9**	**2**	**5**	**7**	**116**	**1**	**0**	**1**	**34**	**5.9**	**30**	**1**	**31**	**11**	**9**	**19**	**2**	**2**	**4**	**116**	**1**	**0**	**0**
1986-87	**St. Louis Blues**	**NHL**	**66**	**2**	**12**	**14**	**2**	**9**	**11**	**164**	**0**	**0**	**1**	**54**	**3.7**	**61**	**4**	**47**	**6**	**16**	**6**	**0**	**0**	**0**	**27**	**0**	**0**	**0**
1987-88	**St. Louis Blues**	**NHL**	**30**	**0**	**1**	**1**	**0**	**1**	**1**	**78**	**0**	**0**	**0**	**9**	**0.0**	**16**	**0**	**26**	**8**	**–2**	....	....	....	....	....	....	....	....
	Hartford Whalers	**NHL**	**1**	**0**	**0**	**0**	**0**	**0**	**0**	**0**	**0**	**0**	**0**	**0**	**0.0**	**0**	**0**	**1**	**0**	**–1**	....	....	....	....	....	....	....	....
1988-89	Binghamton Whalers	AHL	76	9	35	44	....	....	....	239	....	....	....	....	....	....	....	....	....	....	....	....	....	....	....	....	....	....
1989-90	Paris Francais Volants	France	36	17	21	38	....	....	....	122	....	....	....	....	....	....	....	....	....	....	4	2	1	3	10	....	....	....
1990-91	HC Chamonix	France	PLAYER/COACH – STATISTICS UNAVAILABLE																									
1991-92	HC Chamonix	France	11	3	7	10	....	....	....	36	....	....	....	....	....	....	....	....	....	....	....	....	....	....	....	....	....	....
	Moncton Hawks	AHL	3	0	1	1	....	....	....	6	....	....	....	....	....	....	....	....	....	....	....	....	....	....	....	....	....	....
	Saint John Vitos	NBSHL	STATISTICS NOT AVAILABLE																									
	Saint John Vitos	Al-Cup	STATISTICS NOT AVAILABLE																									
	NHL Totals		**290**	**16**	**54**	**70**	**15**	**38**	**53**	**788**	**1**	**0**	**2**	**229**	**7.0**	**256**	**8**	**245**	**43**		**40**	**2**	**3**	**5**	**194**	**1**	**0**	**0**

CHL First All-Star Team (1984)

Signed as a free agent by **Calgary**, April 19, 1981. Traded to **St. Louis** by **Calgary** with Eddie Beers and Gino Cavallini for Joe Mullen, Terry Johnson and Rik Wilson, February 1, 1986. Traded to **Hartford** by **St. Louis** with Hartford's 3rd round choice (Blair Atcheynum) in 1989 Entry Draft (previously acquired, Hartford selected Rick Corriveau) in 1989 Entry Draft, March 8, 1988.

• BOURNE, Bob

Robert Glen C – L. 6'3", 200 lbs. b: Kindersley, Sask., 6/21/1954. Kansas City's 3rd, 38th overall, in 1974.

Season	Club	League	GP	G	A	Pts	AG	AA	APts	PIM	PP	SH	GW	S	%	TGF	PGF	TGA	PGA	+/–	GP	G	A	Pts	PIM	PP	SH	GW
1971-72	Saskatoon Blades	WCJHL	63	28	32	60	....	....	....	36	....	....	....	....	....	....	....	....	....	....	8	3	7	10	2	....	....	....
1972-73	Saskatoon Blades	WCJHL	66	40	53	93	....	....	....	74	....	....	....	....	....	....	....	....	....	....	16	7	10	17	30	....	....	....
1973-74	Saskatoon Blades	WCJHL	63	29	42	71	....	....	....	41	....	....	....	....	....	....	....	....	....	....	6	3	2	5	12	....	....	....
1974-75	**New York Islanders**	**NHL**	**77**	**16**	**23**	**39**	**14**	**17**	**31**	**12**	**2**	**0**	**2**	**127**	**12.6**	**55**	**10**	**36**	**0**	**9**	**9**	**1**	**2**	**3**	**4**	**1**	**0**	**0**
1975-76	**New York Islanders**	**NHL**	**14**	**2**	**3**	**5**	**2**	**2**	**4**	**13**	**0**	**0**	**1**	**16**	**12.5**	**5**	**1**	**6**	**0**	**–2**	....	....	....	....	....	....	....	....
	Fort Worth Texans	CHL	62	29	44	73	....	....	....	80	....	....	....	....	....	....	....	....	....	....	....	....	....	....	....	....	....	....
1976-77	**New York Islanders**	**NHL**	**75**	**16**	**19**	**35**	**14**	**15**	**29**	**30**	**0**	**0**	**5**	**137**	**11.7**	**47**	**0**	**20**	**0**	**27**	**8**	**2**	**0**	**2**	**4**	**0**	**0**	**0**
1977-78	**New York Islanders**	**NHL**	**80**	**30**	**33**	**63**	**27**	**26**	**53**	**31**	**2**	**0**	**8**	**178**	**16.9**	**81**	**10**	**56**	**0**	**15**	**7**	**2**	**3**	**5**	**2**	**1**	**0**	**0**
1978-79	**New York Islanders**	**NHL**	**80**	**30**	**31**	**61**	**26**	**22**	**48**	**48**	**4**	**1**	**2**	**148**	**20.3**	**88**	**16**	**64**	**26**	**34**	**10**	**1**	**3**	**4**	**6**	**0**	**0**	**0**
1979-80♦	**New York Islanders**	**NHL**	**73**	**15**	**25**	**40**	**13**	**18**	**31**	**52**	**3**	**0**	**1**	**155**	**9.7**	**67**	**22**	**75**	**35**	**5**	**21**	**10**	**10**	**20**	**10**	**5**	**2**	**1**
1980-81♦	**New York Islanders**	**NHL**	**78**	**35**	**41**	**76**	**27**	**27**	**54**	**62**	**9**	**7**	**5**	**195**	**17.9**	**105**	**28**	**77**	**34**	**34**	**14**	**4**	**6**	**10**	**19**	**1**	**1**	**1**
1981-82♦	**New York Islanders**	**NHL**	**76**	**27**	**26**	**53**	**21**	**17**	**38**	**77**	**5**	**2**	**2**	**173**	**15.6**	**82**	**11**	**73**	**29**	**27**	**19**	**9**	**7**	**16**	**36**	**3**	**1**	**0**
1982-83♦	**New York Islanders**	**NHL**	**77**	**20**	**42**	**62**	**16**	**29**	**45**	**55**	**5**	**1**	**3**	**147**	**13.6**	**85**	**22**	**72**	**23**	**14**	**20**	**8**	**20**	**28**	**14**	**0**	**1**	**2**
1983-84	**New York Islanders**	**NHL**	**78**	**22**	**34**	**56**	**18**	**23**	**41**	**75**	**5**	**5**	**2**	**140**	**15.7**	**82**	**16**	**83**	**29**	**12**	**8**	**1**	**1**	**2**	**7**	**0**	**0**	**1**
1984-85	Canada	Can-Cup	8	0	3	3	....	....	....	0	....	....	....	....	....	....	....	....	....	....	....	....	....	....	....	....	....	....
	New York Islanders	**NHL**	**44**	**8**	**12**	**20**	**6**	**8**	**14**	**51**	**1**	**0**	**1**	**56**	**14.3**	**31**	**2**	**53**	**16**	**–8**	**10**	**0**	**2**	**2**	**6**	**0**	**0**	**0**
1985-86	**New York Islanders**	**NHL**	**62**	**17**	**15**	**32**	**14**	**10**	**24**	**36**	**2**	**0**	**5**	**100**	**17.0**	**40**	**5**	**66**	**24**	**–7**	**3**	**0**	**0**	**0**	**0**	**0**	**0**	**0**
1986-87	**Los Angeles Kings**	**NHL**	**78**	**13**	**9**	**22**	**11**	**7**	**18**	**35**	**0**	**3**	**0**	**93**	**14.0**	**32**	**0**	**100**	**55**	**–13**	**5**	**2**	**1**	**3**	**0**	**0**	**0**	**0**
1987-88	**Los Angeles Kings**	**NHL**	**72**	**7**	**11**	**18**	**6**	**8**	**14**	**28**	**1**	**0**	**1**	**75**	**9.3**	**25**	**8**	**98**	**50**	**–31**	**5**	**0**	**1**	**1**	**0**	**0**	**0**	**0**
1988-1993			OUT OF HOCKEY – RETIRED																									
1993-1994	Las Vegas Thunder	IHL	DID NOT PLAY – ASSISTANT COACH																									
1994-1996			OUT OF HOCKEY – RETIRED																									
1996-1997	Central Texas Stampede	WPHL	DID NOT PLAY – COACHING																									
1997-1998	Utah Grizzlies	IHL	DID NOT PLAY – ASSISTANT COACH																									
1998-2000	Utah Grizzlies	IHL	DID NOT PLAY – COACHING																									
	NHL Totals		**964**	**258**	**324**	**582**	**215**	**229**	**444**	**605**	**39**	**19**	**38**	**1740**	**14.8**	**825**	**151**	**879**	**321**		**139**	**40**	**56**	**96**	**108**	**11**	**5**	**5**

CHL Second All-Star Team (1976) • Won Bill Masterton Trophy (1988) • Played in NHL All-Star Game (1981)

Traded to **NY Islanders** by **Kansas City** for the rights to Larry Hornung and future considerations (Bart Crashley, September 16, 1974), September 10, 1974. Claimed by **LA Kings** from **NY Islanders** in Waiver Draft, October 6, 1986.

• BOURQUE, Phil

Phillipe Raymond LW – L. 6'1", 196 lbs. b: Chelmsford, MA, 6/8/1962.

Season	Club	League	GP	G	A	Pts	AG	AA	APts	PIM	PP	SH	GW	S	%	TGF	PGF	TGA	PGA	+/–	GP	G	A	Pts	PIM	PP	SH	GW
1979-80	Flitchburg Wallopers	NEJHL	23	12	3	15	....	....	....	....	....	....	....	....	....	....	....	....	....	....	....	12	3	15	....	....	....	....
1980-81	Kingston Canadians	OMJHL	47	4	4	8	....	....	....	46	....	....	....	....	....	....	....	....	....	....	6	0	0	0	10	....	....	....
1981-82	Kingston Canadians	OHL	67	11	40	51	....	....	....	111	....	....	....	....	....	....	....	....	....	....	4	0	0	0	0	....	....	....
1982-83	Baltimore Skipjacks	AHL	65	1	15	16	....	....	....	93	....	....	....	....	....	....	....	....	....	....	....	....	....	....	....	....	....	....
1983-84	**Pittsburgh Penguins**	**NHL**	**5**	**0**	**1**	**1**	**0**	**1**	**1**	**12**	**0**	**0**	**0**	**6**	**0.0**	**2**	**0**	**4**	**0**	**–2**	....	....	....	....	....	....	....	....
	Baltimore Skipjacks	AHL	58	5	17	22	....	....	....	96	....	....	....	....	....	....	....	....	....	....	....	....	....	....	....	....	....	....
1984-85	Baltimore Skipjacks	AHL	79	6	15	21	....	....	....	164	....	....	....	....	....	....	....	....	....	....	13	2	5	7	23	....	....	....
1985-86	**Pittsburgh Penguins**	**NHL**	**4**	**0**	**0**	**0**	**0**	**0**	**0**	**2**	**0**	**0**	**0**	**0**	**0.0**	**1**	**0**	**3**	**0**	**–2**	....	....	....	....	....	....	....	....
	Baltimore Skipjacks	AHL	74	8	18	26	....	....	....	226	....	....	....	....	....	....	....	....	....	....	....	....	....	....	....	....	....	....
1986-87	**Pittsburgh Penguins**	**NHL**	**22**	**2**	**3**	**5**	**2**	**2**	**4**	**32**	**0**	**0**	**1**	**23**	**8.7**	**8**	**2**	**8**	**0**	**–2**	....	....	....	....	....	....	....	....
	Baltimore Skipjacks	AHL	49	15	16	31	....	....	....	183	....	....	....	....	....	....	....	....	....	....	....	....	....	....	....	....	....	....
1987-88	**Pittsburgh Penguins**	**NHL**	**21**	**4**	**12**	**16**	**3**	**9**	**12**	**20**	**2**	**0**	**1**	**56**	**7.1**	**39**	**19**	**19**	**2**	**3**	....	....	....	....	....	....	....	....
	Muskegon Lumberjacks	IHL	52	16	36	52	....	....	....	66	....	....	....	....	....	....	....	....	....	....	6	1	2	3	16	....	....	....
1988-89	**Pittsburgh Penguins**	**NHL**	**80**	**17**	**26**	**43**	**14**	**18**	**32**	**97**	**5**	**2**	**3**	**153**	**11.1**	**97**	**47**	**100**	**28**	**–22**	**11**	**4**	**1**	**5**	**66**	**0**	**0**	**1**
1989-90	**Pittsburgh Penguins**	**NHL**	**76**	**22**	**17**	**39**	**19**	**12**	**31**	**108**	**2**	**1**	**3**	**110**	**20.0**	**70**	**20**	**73**	**16**	**–7**	....	....	....	....	....	....	....	....
1990-91♦	**Pittsburgh Penguins**	**NHL**	**78**	**20**	**14**	**34**	**18**	**11**	**29**	**106**	**1**	**4**	**0**	**122**	**16.4**	**65**	**3**	**81**	**26**	**7**	**24**	**6**	**7**	**13**	**16**	**0**	**0**	**0**
1991-92♦	**Pittsburgh Penguins**	**NHL**	**58**	**10**	**16**	**26**	**9**	**12**	**21**	**58**	**0**	**1**	**3**	**51**	**19.6**	**35**	**2**	**55**	**16**	**–6**	**21**	**3**	**4**	**7**	**25**	**2**	**0**	**0**
1992-93	**New York Rangers**	**NHL**	**55**	**6**	**14**	**20**	**5**	**10**	**15**	**39**	**0**	**0**	**2**	**71**	**8.5**	**27**	**3**	**35**	**2**	**–9**	....	....	....	....	....	....	....	....
1993-94	**New York Rangers**	**NHL**	**16**	**0**	**1**	**1**	**0**	**1**	**1**	**8**	**0**	**0**	**0**	**2**	**0.0**	**1**	**0**	**3**	**0**	**–2**	....	....	....	....	....	....	....	....
	Ottawa Senators	**NHL**	**11**	**2**	**3**	**5**	**2**	**2**	**4**	**0**	**0**	**2**	**0**	**19**	**10.5**	**9**	**1**	**14**	**4**	**–2**	....	....	....	....	....	....	....	....
	United States	WC-A	8	0	1	1	....	....	....	6	....	....	....	....	....	....	....	....	....	....	....	....	....	....	....	....	....	....
1994-95	**Ottawa Senators**	**NHL**	**38**	**4**	**3**	**7**	**7**	**4**	**11**	**20**	**0**	**0**	**0**	**34**	**11.8**	**11**	**0**	**44**	**16**	**–17**	....	....	....	....	....	....	....	....
1995-96	**Ottawa Senators**	**NHL**	**13**	**1**	**1**	**2**	**1**	**1**	**2**	**14**	**0**	**0**	**0**	**12**	**8.3**	**4**	**0**	**14**	**7**	**–3**	....	....	....	....	....	....	....	....
	Detroit Vipers	IHL	36	4	13	17	....	....	....	70	....	....	....	....	....	....	....	....	....	....	10	1	3	4	10	....	....	....
1996-97	Chicago Wolves	IHL	77	7	14	21	....	....	....	50	....	....	....	....	....	....	....	....	....	....	4	0	2	2	2	....	....	....
1997-98	Star Bulls Rosenheim	Germany	40	4	7	11	....	....	....	60	....	....	....	....	....	....	....	....	....	....	....	....	....	....	....	....	....	....
1998-99	EHC Hamburg	Germany-2	22	5	12	17	....	....	....	78	....	....	....	....	....	....	....	....	....	....	13	3	7	10	20	....	....	....
99-2000	EHC Hamburg	Germany-2	23	0	6	6	....	....	....	47	....	....	....	....	....	....	....	....	....	....	13	1	1	2	10	....	....	....
	NHL Totals		**477**	**88**	**111**	**199**	**80**	**83**	**163**	**516**	**10**	**10**	**13**	**659**	**13.4**	**369**	**97**	**453**	**117**		**56**	**13**	**12**	**25**	**107**	**2**	**0**	**1**

IHL First All-Star Team (1988) • Won Governor's Trophy (Outstanding Defenseman - IHL) (1988)

Signed as a free agent by **Pittsburgh**, October 4, 1982. Signed as a free agent by **NY Rangers**, August 31, 1992. Traded to **Ottawa** by **NY Rangers** for future considerations, March 21, 1994.

• BOURQUE, Ray

Raymond Jean D – L. 5'11", 219 lbs. b: Montreal, Que., 12/28/1960. Boston's 1st, 8th overall, in 1979.

Season	Club	League	GP	G	A	Pts	AG	AA	APts	PIM	PP	SH	GW	S	%	TGF	PGF	TGA	PGA	+/–	GP	G	A	Pts	PIM	PP	SH	GW
1976-77	Sorel Eperviers	QMJHL	69	12	36	48	....	....	....	61	....	....	....	....	....	....	....	....	....	....	....	....	....	....	....	....	....	....
1977-78	Verdun Eperviers	QMJHL	72	22	57	79	....	....	....	90	....	....	....	....	....	....	....	....	....	....	4	2	1	3	0	....	....	....
1978-79	Verdun Eperviers	QMJHL	63	22	71	93	....	....	....	44	....	....	....	....	....	....	....	....	....	....	11	3	16	19	18	....	....	....
1979-80	**Boston Bruins**	**NHL**	**80**	**17**	**48**	**65**	**14**	**35**	**49**	**73**	**3**	**2**	**1**	**185**	**9.2**	**162**	**50**	**82**	**22**	**52**	**10**	**2**	**9**	**11**	**27**	**0**	**0**	**0**
1980-81	**Boston Bruins**	**NHL**	**67**	**27**	**29**	**56**	**21**	**19**	**40**	**96**	**9**	**1**	**6**	**207**	**13.0**	**128**	**47**	**87**	**35**	**29**	**3**	**0**	**1**	**1**	**2**	**0**	**0**	**0**
1981-82	Canada	Can-Cup	7	1	4	5	....	....	....	6	....	....	....	....	....	....	....	....	....	....	....	....	....	....	....	....	....	....
	Boston Bruins	**NHL**	**65**	**17**	**49**	**66**	**13**	**33**	**46**	**51**	**4**	**0**	**2**	**211**	**8.1**	**139**	**43**	**96**	**22**	**22**	**9**	**1**	**5**	**6**	**16**	**0**	**0**	**1**
1982-83	**Boston Bruins**	**NHL**	**65**	**22**	**51**	**73**	**18**	**35**	**53**	**20**	**7**	**0**	**5**	**205**	**10.7**	**150**	**53**	**73**	**25**	**49**	**17**	**8**	**15**	**23**	**10**	**2**	**0**	**1**
1983-84	**Boston Bruins**	**NHL**	**78**	**31**	**65**	**96**	**25**	**44**	**69**	**57**	**12**	**1**	**5**	**340**	**9.1**	**187**	**66**	**92**	**22**	**51**	**3**	**0**	**2**	**2**	**0**	**0**	**0**	**0**

			REGULAR SEASON																		PLAYOFFS							
Season	Club	League	GP	G	A	Pts	AG	AA	APts	PIM	PP	SH	GW	S	%	TGF	PGF	TGA	PGA	+/–	GP	G	A	Pts	PIM	PP	SH	GW
1984-85	Canada	Can-Cup	8	0	4	4	....	....	....	8	....	....	....	....	....	....	....	....	....	....	....	....	....	....	....	....	....	....
	Boston Bruins	NHL	73	20	66	86	16	45	61	53	10	1	1	333	6.0	167	58	114	35	30	5	0	3	3	4	0	0	0
1985-86	Boston Bruins	NHL	74	19	58	77	15	39	54	68	11	0	3	289	6.6	169	76	122	46	17	3	0	0	0	0	0	0	0
1986-87	Boston Bruins	NHL	78	23	72	95	20	53	73	36	6	1	3	334	6.9	168	59	98	33	44	4	1	2	3	0	0	0	0
	NHL All-Stars	RV-87	2	1	0	1	....	....	....	2	....	....	....	....	....	....	....	....	....	....	....	....	....	....	....	....	....	....
1987-88	Canada	Can-Cup	9	2	6	8	....	....	....	10	....	....	....	....	....	....	....	....	....	....	....	....	....	....	....	....	....	....
	Boston Bruins	NHL	78	17	64	81	14	46	60	72	7	1	5	344	4.9	163	54	109	34	34	23	3	18	21	26	0	0	1
1988-89	Boston Bruins	NHL	60	18	43	61	15	30	45	52	6	0	0	243	7.4	120	46	83	29	20	10	0	4	4	6	0	0	0
1989-90	Boston Bruins	NHL	76	19	65	84	16	47	63	50	8	0	3	310	6.1	170	75	97	33	31	17	5	12	17	16	1	0	0
1990-91	Boston Bruins	NHL	76	21	73	94	19	56	75	75	7	0	3	323	6.5	173	66	106	32	33	19	7	18	25	12	3	0	0
1991-92	Boston Bruins	NHL	80	21	60	81	19	45	64	56	7	1	2	334	6.3	160	68	122	41	11	12	3	6	9	12	2	0	0
1992-93	Boston Bruins	NHL	78	19	63	82	16	43	59	40	8	0	7	330	5.8	187	76	114	41	38	4	1	0	1	2	1	0	0
1993-94	Boston Bruins	NHL	72	20	71	91	19	55	74	58	10	3	1	386	5.2	171	79	97	31	26	13	2	8	10	0	1	0	0
1994-95	Boston Bruins	NHL	46	12	31	43	21	46	67	20	9	0	2	210	5.7	82	42	56	19	3	5	0	3	3	0	0	0	0
1995-96	Boston Bruins	NHL	82	20	62	82	20	51	71	58	9	2	2	390	5.1	176	61	127	43	31	5	1	6	7	2	1	0	0
1996-97	Boston Bruins	NHL	62	19	31	50	20	28	48	18	8	1	3	230	8.3	101	29	111	28	–11	....	....	....	....	....	....	....	....
1997-98	Boston Bruins	NHL	82	13	35	48	15	34	49	80	9	0	3	264	4.9	117	54	87	26	2	6	1	4	5	2	1	0	0
	Canada	Olympics	6	1	2	3	....	....	....	4	....	....	....	....	....	....	....	....	....	....	....	....	....	....	....	....	....	....
1998-99	Boston Bruins	NHL	81	10	47	57	12	45	57	34	8	0	3	262	3.8	115	59	84	21	–7	12	1	9	10	14	0	0	0
99-2000	Boston Bruins	NHL	65	10	28	38	11	26	37	20	6	0	0	217	4.6	86	36	85	24	–11	....	....	....	....	....	....	....	....
	Colorado Avalanche	NHL	14	8	6	14	9	6	15	6	7	0	0	43	18.6	24	11	12	8	9	13	1	8	9	8	0	0	0
	NHL Totals		1532	403	1117	1520	368	861	1229	1093	171	14	60	5990	6.7	3115	1208	2054	650		193	37	133	170	159	12	0	3

QMJHL First All-Star Team (1978, 1979) • Won Calder Memorial Trophy (1980) • NHL First All-Star Team (1980, 1982, 1984, 1985, 1987, 1988, 1990, 1991, 1992, 1993, 1994, 1996) • NHL Second All-Star Team (1981, 1983, 1986, 1989, 1995, 1999) • Won James Norris Memorial Trophy (1987, 1988, 1990, 1991, 1994) • Canada Cup All-Star Team (1987) • Won King Clancy Memorial Trophy (1992) • Played in NHL All-Star Game (1981, 1982, 1983, 1984, 1985, 1986, 1988, 1989, 1990, 1991, 1992, 1993, 1994, 1996, 1997, 1998, 1999, 2000)

Traded to **Colorado** by **Boston** with Dave Andreychuk for Brian Rolston, Martin Grenier, Sami Pahlsson and New Jersey's 1st round choice (previously acquired, Boston selected Martin Samuelsson) in 2000 Entry Draft, March 6, 2000.

• BOUTETTE, Pat

Patrick Michael "Booter" C/RW – L. 5'8", 175 lbs. b: Windsor, Ont., 3/1/1952. Toronto's 9th, 139th overall, in 1972.

1968-69	Riverside Cement	OMHA	STATISTICS NOT AVAILABLE																									
1969-70	London Knights	OHA-Jr.	53	11	17	28	....	....	....	87	....	....	....	....	....	....	....	....	....	....	10	1	4	5	66	....	....	....
1970-71	University of Minnesota-Duluth	WCHA	33	18	13	31	....	....	....	86	....	....	....	....	....	....	....	....	....	....	....	....	....	....	....	....	....	....
1971-72	University of Minnesota-Duluth	WCHA	34	17	20	37	....	....	....	71	....	....	....	....	....	....	....	....	....	....	....	....	....	....	....	....	....	....
1972-73	University of Minnesota-Duluth	WCHA	34	18	45	63	....	....	....	91	....	....	....	....	....	....	....	....	....	....	....	....	....	....	....	....	....	....
1973-74	Oklahoma City Blazers	CHL	70	17	34	51	....	....	....	118	....	....	....	....	....	....	....	....	....	....	10	0	*7	7	35	....	....	....
1974-75	Oklahoma City Blazers	CHL	77	26	42	68	....	....	....	163	....	....	....	....	....	....	....	....	....	....	5	2	4	6	4	....	....	....
1975-76	Toronto Maple Leafs	NHL	77	10	22	32	9	16	25	140	2	0	2	92	10.9	51	9	45	2	–1	10	1	4	5	16	0	0	0
1976-77	Toronto Maple Leafs	NHL	80	18	18	36	16	14	30	107	3	0	1	104	17.3	71	4	54	0	13	9	0	4	4	17	0	0	0
1977-78	Toronto Maple Leafs	NHL	80	17	19	36	15	15	30	120	2	0	1	130	13.1	54	5	49	0	0	13	3	3	6	40	0	0	0
1978-79	Toronto Maple Leafs	NHL	80	14	19	33	12	14	26	136	0	0	2	89	15.7	53	1	51	2	3	6	2	2	4	22	0	0	0
1979-80	Toronto Maple Leafs	NHL	32	0	4	4	0	3	3	17	0	0	0	11	0.0	7	0	21	8	–6	....	....	....	....	....	....	....	....
	Hartford Whalers	NHL	47	13	31	44	11	23	34	75	3	0	0	72	18.1	77	16	62	18	17	3	1	0	1	6	0	1	0
1980-81	Hartford Whalers	NHL	80	28	52	80	22	35	57	160	8	2	3	182	15.4	130	37	132	26	–13	....	....	....	....	....	....	....	....
	Canada	WEC-A	8	1	1	2	....	....	....	16	....	....	....	....	....	....	....	....	....	....	....	....	....	....	....	....	....	....
1981-82	Pittsburgh Penguins	NHL	80	23	51	74	18	34	52	230	14	1	2	140	16.4	131	72	113	31	–23	5	3	1	4	8	2	0	0
1982-83	Pittsburgh Penguins	NHL	80	27	29	56	22	20	42	152	13	1	4	142	19.0	118	65	143	57	–33	....	....	....	....	....	....	....	....
1983-84	Pittsburgh Penguins	NHL	73	14	26	40	11	18	29	142	10	0	1	107	13.1	69	33	153	59	–58	....	....	....	....	....	....	....	....
1984-85	Pittsburgh Penguins	NHL	14	1	3	4	1	2	3	24	0	1	0	11	9.1	9	3	24	13	–5	....	....	....	....	....	....	....	....
	Hartford Whalers	NHL	33	6	8	14	5	5	10	51	0	0	2	43	14.0	29	4	37	6	–6	....	....	....	....	....	....	....	....
	Binghamton Whalers	AHL	27	8	17	25	....	....	....	10	....	....	....	....	....	....	....	....	....	....	7	0	2	2	0	....	....	....
	NHL Totals		756	171	282	453	142	199	341	1354	55	5	18	1123	15.2	799	249	884	222		46	10	14	24	109	2	1	0

WCHA Second All-Star Team (1973) • NCAA West First All-American Team (1973)

Traded to **Hartford** by **Toronto** for Bob Stephenson, December 24, 1979. Transferred to **Pittsburgh** by **Hartford** with Kevin McClelland as compensation for Hartford's signing of free agent Greg Millen, June 29, 1981. Traded to **Hartford** by **Pittsburgh** for the rights to Ville Siren, November 16, 1984.

• BOUTILIER, Paul

Paul Andre D – L. 6', 200 lbs. b: Sydney, N.S., 5/3/1963. NY Islanders' 1st, 21st overall, in 1981.

1979-80	Cape Breton Miners	NSAHA	56	30	43	73	....	....	....	....	....	....	....	....	....	....	....	....	....	....	....	....	....	....	....	....	....	....
1980-81	Sherbrooke Beavers	QMJHL	72	10	29	39	....	....	....	95	....	....	....	....	....	....	....	....	....	....	14	3	7	10	10	....	....	....
1981-82	Sherbrooke Beavers	QMJHL	57	20	60	80	....	....	....	62	....	....	....	....	....	....	....	....	....	....	21	7	31	38	12	....	....	....
	New York Islanders	NHL	1	0	0	0	0	0	0	0	0	0	0	0	0.0	0	0	0	0	0	....	....	....	....	....	....	....	....
	Sherbrooke Beavers	Mem-Cup	5	2	8	10	....	....	....	2	....	....	....	....	....	....	....	....	....	....	....	....	....	....	....	....	....	....
1982-83	St-Jean Castors	QMJHL	22	5	14	19	....	....	....	30	....	....	....	....	....	....	....	....	....	....	....	....	....	....	....	....	....	....
♦	New York Islanders	NHL	29	4	5	9	3	3	6	24	3	0	1	52	7.7	25	5	25	0	–5	2	0	0	0	2	0	0	0
1983-84	New York Islanders	NHL	28	0	11	11	0	7	7	36	0	0	0	31	0.0	33	1	14	0	18	21	1	7	8	10	0	0	1
	Indianapolis Checkers	CHL	50	6	17	23	....	....	....	56	....	....	....	....	....	....	....	....	....	....	....	....	....	....	....	....	....	....
1984-85	New York Islanders	NHL	78	12	23	35	10	16	26	90	2	1	3	137	8.8	109	20	111	22	0	10	0	2	2	16	0	0	0
1985-86	New York Islanders	NHL	77	4	30	34	3	20	23	100	0	0	0	124	3.2	94	22	107	30	–5	3	0	0	0	2	0	0	0
1986-87	Boston Bruins	NHL	52	5	9	14	4	7	11	84	1	1	0	68	7.4	60	14	58	10	–2	....	....	....	....	....	....	....	....
	Minnesota North Stars	NHL	10	2	4	6	2	3	5	8	0	0	0	21	9.5	13	2	12	2	1	....	....	....	....	....	....	....	....
1987-88	New York Rangers	NHL	4	0	1	1	0	1	1	6	0	0	0	3	0.0	3	1	3	0	–1	....	....	....	....	....	....	....	....
	New Haven Nighthawks	AHL	9	0	3	3	....	....	....	10	....	....	....	....	....	....	....	....	....	....	....	....	....	....	....	....	....	....
	Colorado Rangers	IHL	9	2	6	8	....	....	....	4	....	....	....	....	....	....	....	....	....	....	....	....	....	....	....	....	....	....
	Winnipeg Jets	NHL	6	0	0	0	0	0	0	6	0	0	0	6	0.0	3	0	8	3	–2	5	0	0	0	15	0	0	0
	Moncton Hawks	AHL	41	9	29	38	....	....	....	40	....	....	....	....	....	....	....	....	....	....	....	....	....	....	....	....	....	....
1988-89	Winnipeg Jets	NHL	3	0	0	0	0	0	0	4	0	0	0	4	0.0	5	0	3	0	2	....	....	....	....	....	....	....	....
	Moncton Hawks	AHL	77	6	54	60	....	....	....	101	....	....	....	....	....	....	....	....	....	....	10	2	7	9	4	....	....	....
1989-90	Canada	Nat-Team	4	0	2	2	....	....	....	0	....	....	....	....	....	....	....	....	....	....	....	....	....	....	....	....	....	....
	SC Bern	Switz.	36	12	28	40	....	....	....	....	....	....	....	....	....	....	....	....	....	....	....	....	....	....	....	....	....	....
	Maine Mariners	AHL	12	0	4	4	....	....	....	21	....	....	....	....	....	....	....	....	....	....	....	....	....	....	....	....	....	....
1990-91	ZSC Zurich	Switz-2	20	3	8	11	....	....	....	....	....	....	....	....	....	....	....	....	....	....	....	....	....	....	....	....	....	....
	NHL Totals		288	27	83	110	22	57	79	358	6	2	4	446	6.1	345	65	341	67		41	1	9	10	45	0	0	1

QMJHL First All-Star Team (1982) • Memorial Cup All-Star Team (1982) • AHL First All-Star Team (1989)

Transferred to **Boston** by **NY Islanders** as compensation for the NY Islanders' signing of free agent Brian Curran, August 6, 1987. Traded to **Minnesota** by **Boston** for Minnesota's 4th round choice (Darwin MacPherson) in 1987 Entry Draft, March 10, 1987. Traded to **NY Rangers** by **Minnesota** with Jari Gronstrand for Jay Caufield and Dave Gagner, October 8, 1987. Traded to **Winnipeg** by **NY Rangers** for future considerations, December 16, 1987.

• BOWEN, Jason

D – L. 6'4", 220 lbs. b: Port Alice, B.C., 11/9/1973. Philadelphia's 2nd, 15th overall, in 1992.

1988-89	Notre Dame Midget Hounds	AAHA	56	10	29	39	....	....	....	40	....	....	....	....	....	....	....	....	....	....	....	....	....	....	....	....	....	....
1989-90	Tri-City Americans	WHL	61	8	5	13	....	....	....	129	....	....	....	....	....	....	....	....	....	....	7	0	3	3	4	....	....	....
1990-91	Tri-City Americans	WHL	60	7	13	20	....	....	....	252	....	....	....	....	....	....	....	....	....	....	6	2	2	4	18	....	....	....
1991-92	Tri-City Americans	WHL	19	5	3	8	....	....	....	135	....	....	....	....	....	....	....	....	....	....	5	0	1	1	42	....	....	....
1992-93	Tri-City Americans	WHL	62	10	12	22	....	....	....	219	....	....	....	....	....	....	....	....	....	....	3	1	1	2	18	....	....	....
	Philadelphia Flyers	NHL	7	1	0	1	1	0	1	2	0	0	0	3	33.3	1	0	0	0	1	....	....	....	....	....	....	....	....
1993-94	Philadelphia Flyers	NHL	56	1	5	6	1	4	5	87	0	0	1	50	2.0	35	0	31	8	12	....	....	....	....	....	....	....	....
1994-95	Philadelphia Flyers	NHL	4	0	0	0	0	0	0	0	0	0	0	2	0.0	0	0	2	0	–2	....	....	....	....	....	....	....	....
	Hershey Bears	AHL	55	5	5	10	....	....	....	116	....	....	....	....	....	....	....	....	....	....	6	0	0	0	46	....	....	....
1995-96	Philadelphia Flyers	NHL	2	0	0	0	0	0	0	2	0	0	0	2	0.0	0	0	0	0	0	....	....	....	....	....	....	....	....
	Hershey Bears	AHL	72	6	7	13	....	....	....	128	....	....	....	....	....	....	....	....	....	....	4	2	0	2	13	....	....	....

Season	Club	League	REGULAR SEASON GP	G	A	Pts	AG	AA	APts	PIM	PP	SH	GW	S	%	TGF	PGF	TGA	PGA	+/–	PLAYOFFS GP	G	A	Pts	PIM	PP	SH	GW
1996-97	**Philadelphia Flyers**	**NHL**	**4**	**0**	**1**	**1**	**0**	**1**	**1**	**8**	**0**	**0**	**0**	**1**	**0.0**	**2**	**0**	**1**	**0**	**1**	....	....	....	....	....	....	....	....
	Philadelphia Phantoms	AHL	61	10	12	22	....	....	....	160	....	....	....	....	....	....	....	....	....	....	6	0	1	1	10	....	....	....
1997-98	Philadelphia Phantoms	AHL	3	0	0	0	....	....	....	19	....	....	....	....	....	....	....	....	....	....	....	....	....	....	....	....	....	....
	Edmonton Oilers	**NHL**	**4**	**0**	**0**	**0**	**0**	**0**	**0**	**10**	**0**	**0**	**0**	**3**	**0.0**	**0**	**0**	**0**	**0**	**0**	....	....	....	....	....	....	....	....
	Hamilton Bulldogs	AHL	51	5	14	19	....	....	....	108	....	....	....	....	....	....	....	....	....	....	7	1	1	2	22	....	....	....
	Canada	WC-A	4	0	0	0	....	....	....	0	....	....	....	....	....	....	....	....	....	....	....	....	....	....	....	....	....	....
1998-99	Hamilton Bulldogs	AHL	58	3	3	6	....	....	....	178	....	....	....	....	....	....	....	....	....	....	11	0	1	1	16	....	....	....
99-2000	Hershey Bears	AHL	54	2	8	10	....	....	....	152	....	....	....	....	....	....	....	....	....	....	....	....	....	....	....	....	....	....
	Saint John Flames	AHL	11	0	1	1	....	....	....	28	....	....	....	....	....	....	....	....	....	....	2	0	0	0	4	....	....	....
	NHL Totals		**77**	**2**	**6**	**8**	**2**	**5**	**7**	**109**	**0**	**0**	**1**	**61**	**3.3**	**38**	**0**	**34**	**8**		....	....	....	....	....	....	....	....

Traded to **Edmonton** by **Philadelphia** for Brantt Myhres, October 15, 1997. Signed as a free agent by **Colorado**, August 26, 1999. Loaned to **Saint John** (AHL) by **Colorado**, March 15, 2000.

• BOWMAN, Kirk

Robert Kirk LW – L. 5'9", 178 lbs. b: Leamington, Ont., 9/30/1952.

Season	Club	League	GP	G	A	Pts	AG	AA	APts	PIM	PP	SH	GW	S	%	TGF	PGF	TGA	PGA	+/–	GP	G	A	Pts	PIM	PP	SH	GW
1970-71	Guelph GMC's	OJHL	44	42	29	71	....	....	....	....	....	....	....	....	....	....	....	....	....	....	....	....	....	....	....	....	....	....
1971-72	Columbus Golden Seals	IHL	19	10	8	18	....	....	....	9	....	....	....	....	....	....	....	....	....	....	....	....	....	....	....	....	....	....
	Greensboro Generals	EHL	46	15	15	30	....	....	....	19	....	....	....	....	....	....	....	....	....	....	11	4	5	9	6	....	....	....
1972-73	Greensboro Generals	EHL	70	27	51	78	....	....	....	23	....	....	....	....	....	....	....	....	....	....	7	1	8	9	0	....	....	....
	Flint Generals	IHL	....	....	....	....	....	....	....	....	....	....	....	....	....	....	....	....	....	....	1	1	2	3	0	....	....	....
1973-74	Los Angeles Sharks	WHA	10	0	2	2	....	....	....	0	....	....	....	....	....	....	....	....	....	....	....	....	....	....	....	....	....	....
	Greensboro Generals	SHL	58	23	55	78	....	....	....	20	....	....	....	....	....	....	....	....	....	....	6	1	8	9	0	....	....	....
1974-75	Dallas Black Hawks	CHL	....	....	....	....	....	....	....	....	....	....	....	....	....	....	....	....	....	....	4	0	3	3	0	....	....	....
	Flint Generals	IHL	75	29	*79	108	....	....	....	62	....	....	....	....	....	....	....	....	....	....	5	2	5	7	2	....	....	....
1975-76	Dallas Black Hawks	CHL	....	....	....	....	....	....	....	....	....	....	....	....	....	....	....	....	....	....	10	3	*8	*11	4	....	....	....
	Flint Generals	IHL	78	44	*63	107	....	....	....	12	....	....	....	....	....	....	....	....	....	....	4	2	3	5	5	....	....	....
1976-77	**Chicago Black Hawks**	**NHL**	**55**	**10**	**13**	**23**	**9**	**10**	**19**	**6**	**2**	**0**	**2**	**64**	**15.6**	**36**	**8**	**45**	**10**	**–7**	**2**	**1**	**0**	**1**	**0**	**1**	**0**	**0**
	Flint Generals	IHL	11	5	14	19	....	....	....	2	....	....	....	....	....	....	....	....	....	....	....	....	....	....	....	....	....	....
1977-78	**Chicago Black Hawks**	**NHL**	**33**	**1**	**4**	**5**	**1**	**3**	**4**	**13**	**0**	**0**	**0**	**41**	**2.4**	**13**	**1**	**17**	**5**	**0**	**3**	**0**	**0**	**0**	**0**	**0**	**0**	**0**
	Dallas Black Hawks	CHL	39	10	23	33	....	....	....	6	....	....	....	....	....	....	....	....	....	....	....	....	....	....	....	....	....	....
1978-79	New Brunswick Hawks	AHL	80	26	56	82	....	....	....	44	....	....	....	....	....	....	....	....	....	....	5	2	3	5	2	....	....	....
	Chicago Black Hawks	**NHL**	....	....	....	....	....	....	....	....	....	....	....	....	....	....	....	....	....	....	**2**	**0**	**0**	**0**	**0**	**0**	**0**	**0**
1979-80	Schwenninger ERC	Germany-2	44	48	46	94	....	....	....	....	....	....	....	....	....	....	....	....	....	....	....	....	....	....	....	....	....	....
1980-81	Krefelder EV	Germany-2	STATISTICS NOT AVAILABLE																									
1981-82	Schwenninger ERC	Germany	44	35	36	71	....	....	....	33	....	....	....	....	....	....	....	....	....	....	....	....	....	....	....	....	....	....
1982-83	Schwenninger ERC	Germany	36	21	16	37	....	....	....	14	....	....	....	....	....	....	....	....	....	....	....	....	....	....	....	....	....	....
1983-84	Schwenninger ERC	Germany	45	28	33	61	....	....	....	34	....	....	....	....	....	....	....	....	....	....	....	....	....	....	....	....	....	....
1984-85	SC Bern	Switz.	36	31	18	49	....	....	....	....	....	....	....	....	....	....	....	....	....	....	14	14	8	22	....	....	....	....
1985-86	SC Bern	Switz.	36	38	40	78	....	....	....	....	....	....	....	....	....	....	....	....	....	....	5	3	2	5	....	....	....	....
1986-87	SC Bern	Switz.	36	30	45	75	....	....	....	....	....	....	....	....	....	....	....	....	....	....	....	....	....	....	....	....	....	....
1987-88	SC Bern	Switz.	36	12	27	39	....	....	....	....	....	....	....	....	....	....	....	....	....	....	....	....	....	....	....	....	....	....
	NHL Totals		**88**	**11**	**17**	**28**	**10**	**13**	**23**	**19**	**2**	**0**	**2**	**105**	**10.5**	**49**	**9**	**62**	**15**		**7**	**1**	**0**	**1**	**0**	**1**	**0**	**0**
	Other Major League Totals		10	0	2	2	....	....	....	0	....	....	....	....	....	....	....	....	....	....	....	....	....	....	....	....	....	....

IHL Second All-Star Team (1976)

Signed as a free agent by **Columbus** (IHL), September, 1971. Claimed on waivers by **Greensboro** (SHL) from **Columbus** (IHL), December, 1971. Rights transferred to **LA Sharks** (WHA) after WHA club signed **Greensboro** (SHL) as a minor league affiliate, June, 1973. Signed as a free agent by **Chicago**, September, 1974.

• BOWNESS, Rick

Richard Gary RW – R. 6'1", 185 lbs. b: Moncton, N.B., 1/25/1955. Atlanta's 2nd, 26th overall, in 1975.

Season	Club	League	GP	G	A	Pts	AG	AA	APts	PIM	PP	SH	GW	S	%	TGF	PGF	TGA	PGA	+/–	GP	G	A	Pts	PIM	PP	SH	GW
1972-73	Quebec Remparts	QMJHL	30	2	7	9	....	....	....	2	....	....	....	....	....	....	....	....	....	....	....	....	....	....	....	....	....	....
1973-74	St. Mary's University	AUAA	1	0	0	0	....	....	....	0	....	....	....	....	....	....	....	....	....	....	....	....	....	....	....	....	....	....
	Quebec Remparts	QMJHL	34	16	29	45	....	....	....	64	....	....	....	....	....	....	....	....	....	....	....	....	....	....	....	....	....	....
	Montreal Red-White-Blue	QMJHL	33	9	17	26	....	....	....	31	....	....	....	....	....	....	....	....	....	....	9	4	4	8	4	....	....	....
1974-75	Montreal Red-White-Blue	QMJHL	71	24	76	100	....	....	....	130	....	....	....	....	....	....	....	....	....	....	8	5	3	8	29	....	....	....
1975-76	**Atlanta Flames**	**NHL**	**5**	**0**	**0**	**0**	**0**	**0**	**0**	**0**	**0**	**0**	**0**	**6**	**0.0**	**0**	**0**	**5**	**0**	**–5**	....	....	....	....	....	....	....	....
	Nova Scotia Voyageurs	AHL	2	0	1	1	....	....	....	0	....	....	....	....	....	....	....	....	....	....	....	....	....	....	....	....	....	....
	Tulsa Oilers	CHL	64	25	38	63	....	....	....	160	....	....	....	....	....	....	....	....	....	....	9	4	3	7	12	....	....	....
1976-77	**Atlanta Flames**	**NHL**	**28**	**0**	**4**	**4**	**0**	**3**	**3**	**29**	**0**	**0**	**0**	**21**	**0.0**	**8**	**0**	**18**	**1**	**–9**	....	....	....	....	....	....	....	....
	Tulsa Oilers	CHL	39	15	15	30	....	....	....	72	....	....	....	....	....	....	....	....	....	....	8	0	1	1	20	....	....	....
1977-78	**Detroit Red Wings**	**NHL**	**61**	**8**	**11**	**19**	**7**	**8**	**15**	**76**	**2**	**0**	**2**	**46**	**17.4**	**29**	**4**	**33**	**0**	**–8**	**4**	**0**	**0**	**0**	**2**	**0**	**0**	**0**
1978-79	**St. Louis Blues**	**NHL**	**24**	**1**	**3**	**4**	**1**	**2**	**3**	**30**	**0**	**0**	**0**	**18**	**5.6**	**9**	**0**	**27**	**1**	**–17**	....	....	....	....	....	....	....	....
	Salt Lake Golden Eagles	CHL	48	25	28	53	....	....	....	92	....	....	....	....	....	....	....	....	....	....	10	5	4	9	27	....	....	....
1979-80	**St. Louis Blues**	**NHL**	**10**	**1**	**2**	**3**	**1**	**1**	**2**	**11**	**0**	**0**	**0**	**4**	**25.0**	**4**	**0**	**6**	**0**	**–2**	....	....	....	....	....	....	....	....
	Salt Lake Golden Eagles	CHL	71	25	46	71	....	....	....	135	....	....	....	....	....	....	....	....	....	....	13	5	9	14	39	....	....	....
1980-81	**Winnipeg Jets**	**NHL**	**45**	**8**	**17**	**25**	**6**	**11**	**17**	**45**	**0**	**0**	**1**	**55**	**14.5**	**32**	**2**	**65**	**0**	**–35**	....	....	....	....	....	....	....	....
	Tulsa Oilers	CHL	35	12	20	32	....	....	....	82	....	....	....	....	....	....	....	....	....	....	....	....	....	....	....	....	....	....
1981-82	Tulsa Oilers	CHL	79	34	53	87	....	....	....	201	....	....	....	....	....	....	....	....	....	....	3	0	2	2	2	....	....	....
	Winnipeg Jets	**NHL**	....	....	....	....	....	....	....	....	....	....	....	....	....	....	....	....	....	....	**1**	**0**	**0**	**0**	**0**	**0**	**0**	**0**
1982-83	Sherbrooke Jets	AHL	65	17	31	48	....	....	....	117	....	....	....	....	....	....	....	....	....	....	....	....	....	....	....	....	....	....
1983-1984	Sherbrooke Jets	AHL	21	9	11	20	....	....	....	44	....	....	....	....	....	....	....	....	....	....	....	....	....	....	....	....	....	....
	Winnipeg Jets	**NHL**	DID NOT PLAY – ASSISTANT COACH																									
1984-1987	**Winnipeg Jets**	**NHL**	DID NOT PLAY – ASSISTANT COACH																									
1987-1988	Moncton Hawks	AHL	DID NOT PLAY – COACHING																									
1988-1989	Moncton Hawks	AHL	DID NOT PLAY – COACHING																									
	Winnipeg Jets	**NHL**	DID NOT PLAY – COACHING																									
1989-1991	Maine Mariners	AHL	DID NOT PLAY – COACHING																									
1991-1992	**Boston Bruins**	**NHL**	DID NOT PLAY – COACHING																									
1992-1995	**Ottawa Senators**	**NHL**	DID NOT PLAY – COACHING																									
1995-1997	**New York Islanders**	**NHL**	DID NOT PLAY – ASSISTANT COACH																									
1997-1998	**New York Islanders**	**NHL**	DID NOT PLAY – COACHING																									
1998-1999			OUT OF HOCKEY – RETIRED																									
1999-2000	**Phoenix Coyotes**	**NHL**	DID NOT PLAY – ASSISTANT COACH																									
	NHL Totals		**173**	**18**	**37**	**55**	**15**	**25**	**40**	**191**	**2**	**0**	**3**	**150**	**12.0**	**82**	**6**	**154**	**2**		**5**	**0**	**0**	**0**	**2**	**0**	**0**	**0**

Traded to **Detroit** by **Atlanta** for cash, August 18, 1977. Traded to **St. Louis** by **Detroit** for cash, October 10, 1978. Traded to **Winnipeg** by **St. Louis** for Craig Norwich, June 19, 1980.

• BOYD, Randy

Randall Keith Joseph D – L. 5'11", 190 lbs. b: Coniston, Ont., 1/23/1962. Pittsburgh's 2nd, 51st overall, in 1980.

Season	Club	League	GP	G	A	Pts	AG	AA	APts	PIM	PP	SH	GW	S	%	TGF	PGF	TGA	PGA	+/–	GP	G	A	Pts	PIM	PP	SH	GW
1978-79	North Bay Centennials	OJHL	42	10	35	45	....	....	....	121	....	....	....	....	....	....	....	....	....	....	....	....	....	....	....	....	....	....
1979-80	Ottawa 67's	OMJHL	65	3	21	24	....	....	....	148	....	....	....	....	....	....	....	....	....	....	11	0	2	2	13	....	....	....
1980-81	Ottawa 67's	OMJHL	64	11	43	54	....	....	....	225	....	....	....	....	....	....	....	....	....	....	7	2	3	5	35	....	....	....
1981-82	Ottawa 67's	OHL	26	9	29	38	....	....	....	51	....	....	....	....	....	....	....	....	....	....	....	....	....	....	....	....	....	....
	Pittsburgh Penguins	**NHL**	**23**	**0**	**2**	**2**	**0**	**1**	**1**	**49**	**0**	**0**	**0**	**26**	**0.0**	**16**	**1**	**22**	**2**	**–5**	**3**	**0**	**0**	**0**	**11**	**0**	**0**	**0**
1982-83	**Pittsburgh Penguins**	**NHL**	**56**	**4**	**14**	**18**	**3**	**10**	**13**	**71**	**1**	**0**	**0**	**102**	**3.9**	**48**	**12**	**100**	**28**	**–36**	....	....	....	....	....	....	....	....
	Baltimore Skipjacks	AHL	21	5	10	15	....	....	....	43	....	....	....	....	....	....	....	....	....	....	....	....	....	....	....	....	....	....
1983-84	**Pittsburgh Penguins**	**NHL**	**5**	**0**	**1**	**1**	**0**	**1**	**1**	**6**	**0**	**0**	**0**	**14**	**0.0**	**4**	**0**	**8**	**2**	**–2**	....	....	....	....	....	....	....	....
	Baltimore Skipjacks	AHL	20	6	13	19	....	....	....	69	....	....	....	....	....	....	....	....	....	....	....	....	....	....	....	....	....	....
	Chicago Black Hawks	**NHL**	**23**	**0**	**4**	**4**	**0**	**3**	**3**	**16**	**0**	**0**	**0**	**21**	**0.0**	**10**	**0**	**15**	**5**	**0**	....	....	....	....	....	....	....	....
	Springfield Indians	AHL	27	2	11	13	....	....	....	48	....	....	....	....	....	....	....	....	....	....	4	0	2	2	34	....	....	....
1984-85	**Chicago Black Hawks**	**NHL**	**3**	**0**	**0**	**0**	**0**	**0**	**0**	**6**	**0**	**0**	**0**	**2**	**0.0**	**1**	**0**	**1**	**0**	**0**	**3**	**0**	**1**	**1**	**7**	**0**	**0**	**0**
	Milwaukee Admirals	IHL	68	18	55	73	....	....	....	162	....	....	....	....	....	....	....	....	....	....	....	....	....	....	....	....	....	....
1985-86	**New York Islanders**	**NHL**	**55**	**2**	**12**	**14**	**2**	**8**	**10**	**79**	**0**	**0**	**0**	**52**	**3.8**	**52**	**7**	**43**	**7**	**9**	**3**	**0**	**0**	**0**	**2**	**0**	**0**	**0**
1986-87	**New York Islanders**	**NHL**	**30**	**7**	**17**	**24**	**6**	**12**	**18**	**37**	**3**	**1**	**0**	**69**	**10.1**	**50**	**22**	**30**	**2**	**0**	**4**	**0**	**1**	**1**	**6**	**0**	**0**	**0**
	Springfield Indians	AHL	48	9	30	39	....	....	....	96	....	....	....	....	....	....	....	....	....	....	....	....	....	....	....	....	....	....
1987-88	**Vancouver Canucks**	**NHL**	**60**	**7**	**16**	**23**	**6**	**11**	**17**	**64**	**2**	**0**	**1**	**85**	**8.2**	**71**	**21**	**65**	**6**	**–9**	....	....	....	....	....	....	....	....

			REGULAR SEASON																		PLAYOFFS							
Season	Club	League	GP	G	A	Pts	AG	AA	APts	PIM	PP	SH	GW	S	%	TGF	PGF	TGA	PGA	+/–	GP	G	A	Pts	PIM	PP	SH	GW
1988-89	**Vancouver Canucks**	**NHL**	**2**	**0**	**1**	**1**	**0**	**1**	**1**	**0**	**0**	**0**	**0**	**6**	**0.0**	**1**	**1**	**1**	**0**	**–1**	....	....	....	....	....	....	....	....
	Milwaukee Admirals	IHL	73	24	55	79	....	....	....	218	....	....	....	....	....	....	....	....	....	....	9	0	6	6	26	....	....	....
1989-90	WEV Wien	Austria	16	4	16	20	....	....	....	75	....	....	....	....	....	....	....	....	....	....	....	....	....	....	....	....	....	....
1990-91	WEV Wien	Austria	31	6	14	20	....	....	....	121	....	....	....	....	....	....	....	....	....	....	....	....	....	....	....	....	....	....
1991-92	Milwaukee Admirals	IHL	42	7	9	16	....	....	....	80	....	....	....	....	....	....	....	....	....	....	2	0	1	1	2	....	....	....
1992-93	Milwaukee Admirals	IHL	8	1	4	5	....	....	....	8	....	....	....	....	....	....	....	....	....	....	....	....	....	....	....	....	....	....
	Wichita Thunder	CHL	22	10	26	36	....	....	....	92	....	....	....	....	....	....	....	....	....	....	....	....	....	....	....	....	....	....
1993-94	Memphis RiverKings	ECHL	DID NOT PLAY – COACHING																									
	NHL Totals		**257**	**20**	**67**	**87**	**17**	**47**	**64**	**328**	**6**	**1**	**1**	**377**	**5.3**	**253**	**64**	**285**	**52**		**13**	**0**	**2**	**2**	**26**	**0**	**0**	**0**

OMJHL First All-Star Team (1981) • IHL First All-Star Team (1985, 1989) • Won Governors' Trophy (Top Defenseman - IHL) (1989)

Traded to **Chicago** by **Pittsburgh** for Greg Fox, December 6, 1983. Claimed by **NY Islanders** from **Chicago** in Waiver Draft, October 7, 1985. Claimed by **Vancouver** from **NY Islanders** in Waiver Draft, October 5, 1987. • Played w/ RHI's Chicago Cheetahs in 1995 (3-2-9-11-0).

• BOYER, Wally

Walter C – L. 5'8", 165 lbs. b: Cowan, Man., 9/27/1937.

Season	Club	League	GP	G	A	Pts	AG	AA	APts	PIM	PP	SH	GW	S	%	TGF	PGF	TGA	PGA	+/–	GP	G	A	Pts	PIM	PP	SH	GW
1955-56	Toronto Marlboros	OHA-Jr.	48	14	19	33	....	....	....	51	....	....	....	....	....	....	....	....	....	....	11	2	2	4	4	....	....	....
	Toronto Marlboros	Mem-Cup	13	3	7	10	....	....	....	2	....	....	....	....	....	....	....	....	....	....	....	....	....	....	....	....	....	....
1956-57	Toronto Marlboros	OHA-Jr.	40	17	17	34	....	....	....	21	....	....	....	....	....	....	....	....	....	....	8	2	6	8	19	....	....	....
1957-58	Toronto Marlboros	OHA-Jr.	27	11	11	22	....	....	....	17	....	....	....	....	....	....	....	....	....	....	12	6	*14	20	17	....	....	....
	Toronto Marlboros	Mem-Cup	5	0	2	2	....	....	....	2	....	....	....	....	....	....	....	....	....	....	....	....	....	....	....	....	....	....
1958-59	Hershey Bears	AHL	4	0	1	1	....	....	....	2	....	....	....	....	....	....	....	....	....	....	....	....	....	....	....	....	....	....
	New Westminster Royals	WHL	27	5	5	10	....	....	....	0	....	....	....	....	....	....	....	....	....	....	....	....	....	....	....	....	....	....
	Chicoutimi–Montreal	QHL	28	3	7	10	....	....	....	8	....	....	....	....	....	....	....	....	....	....	4	0	0	0	0	....	....	....
1959-60	Sudbury Wolves	EPHL	70	23	42	65	....	....	....	36	....	....	....	....	....	....	....	....	....	....	11	2	4	6	4	....	....	....
1960-61	Rochester Americans	AHL	70	24	33	57	....	....	....	31	....	....	....	....	....	....	....	....	....	....	....	....	....	....	....	....	....	....
1961-62	Rochester Americans	AHL	67	20	21	41	....	....	....	67	....	....	....	....	....	....	....	....	....	....	2	0	0	0	0	....	....	....
1962-63	Springfield Indians	AHL	66	28	45	73	....	....	....	59	....	....	....	....	....	....	....	....	....	....	....	....	....	....	....	....	....	....
1963-64	Rochester Americans	AHL	52	20	19	39	....	....	....	35	....	....	....	....	....	....	....	....	....	....	2	1	0	1	2	....	....	....
1964-65	Rochester Americans	AHL	70	20	41	61	....	....	....	28	....	....	....	....	....	....	....	....	....	....	10	2	4	6	4	....	....	....
1965-66	**Toronto Maple Leafs**	**NHL**	**46**	**4**	**17**	**21**	**4**	**16**	**20**	**23**	....	....	....	....	....	....	....	....	....	....	**4**	**0**	**1**	**1**	**0**	**0**	**0**	**0**
	Rochester Americans	AHL	19	3	10	13	....	....	....	13	....	....	....	....	....	....	....	....	....	....	....	....	....	....	....	....	....	....
1966-67	**Chicago Black Hawks**	**NHL**	**42**	**5**	**6**	**11**	**6**	**6**	**12**	**15**	....	....	....	....	....	....	....	....	....	....	**1**	**0**	**0**	**0**	**0**	**0**	**0**	**0**
	Portland Buckaroos	WHL	17	7	6	13	....	....	....	10	....	....	....	....	....	....	....	....	....	....	....	....	....	....	....	....	....	....
1967-68	**Oakland Seals**	**NHL**	**74**	**13**	**20**	**33**	**15**	**20**	**35**	**44**	**1**	**0**	**0**	**142**	**9.2**	**52**	**11**	**44**	**3**	**0**	....	....	....	....	....	....	....	....
1968-69	**Pittsburgh Penguins**	**NHL**	**62**	**10**	**19**	**29**	**11**	**17**	**28**	**17**	**2**	**0**	**0**	**127**	**7.9**	**46**	**21**	**50**	**4**	**–21**	....	....	....	....	....	....	....	....
1969-70	**Pittsburgh Penguins**	**NHL**	**72**	**11**	**12**	**23**	**12**	**11**	**23**	**34**	**2**	**0**	**1**	**112**	**9.8**	**41**	**14**	**55**	**23**	**–5**	**10**	**1**	**2**	**3**	**0**	**0**	**1**	**0**
1970-71	**Pittsburgh Penguins**	**NHL**	**68**	**11**	**30**	**41**	**11**	**25**	**36**	**30**	**4**	**0**	**0**	**111**	**9.9**	**55**	**11**	**45**	**11**	**10**	....	....	....	....	....	....	....	....
1971-72	**Pittsburgh Penguins**	**NHL**	**1**	**0**	**1**	**1**	**0**	**1**	**1**	**0**	**0**	**0**	**0**	**0**	**0.0**	**1**	**0**	**2**	**0**	**–1**	....	....	....	....	....	....	....	....
	Hershey Bears	AHL	64	18	30	48	....	....	....	43	....	....	....	....	....	....	....	....	....	....	3	1	0	1	2	....	....	....
1972-73	Winnipeg Jets	WHA	69	6	28	34	....	....	....	27	....	....	....	....	....	....	....	....	....	....	14	4	2	6	4	....	....	....
	NHL Totals		**365**	**54**	**105**	**159**	**59**	**96**	**155**	**163**	....	....	....	....	....	....	....	....	....	....	**15**	**1**	**3**	**4**	**0**	....	....	....
	Other Major League Totals		69	6	28	34	....	....	....	27	....	....	....	....	....	....	....	....	....	....	14	4	2	6	4	....	....	....

Loaned to **Hershey** (AHL) by **Toronto** for the 1958-59 and 1959-60 seasons with the trade of Mike Nykolyk and Ron Hurst for Willie Marshall, April 29, 1958. Toronto retains right of recall. Rights traded to **Springfield** (AHL) by **Toronto** with Jim Wilcox, Roger Cote, Bill White and Dick Mattiussi for Kent Douglas, June 7, 1962. Toronto retains right of recall. Claimed by **Montreal** from **Toronto** in Intra-League Draft, June 15, 1966. Claimed by **Chicago** from **Montreal** in Intra-League Draft, June 15, 1966. Claimed by **Oakland** from **Chicago** in Expansion Draft, June 6, 1967. Traded to **Montreal** by **Oakland** with Alain Caron, Oakland's 1st round choices in 1968 (Jim Pritchard) and 1970 (Ray Martynuik) Amateur Drafts and future considerations (Lyle Bradley, June, 1968) for Norm Ferguson, Stan Fuller and future considerations (Francois Lacombe and Michel Jacques, June, 1968), May 21, 1968. Traded to **Pittsburgh** by **Montreal** for Al MacNeil, June 12, 1968. Selected by **Winnipeg** (WHA) in 1972 WHA General Player Draft, February 12, 1972. Traded to **Toronto** (WHA) by **Winnipeg** (WHA) with Steve Cuddie for Ken Stephenson, June, 1973.

• BOYER, Zac

RW – R. 6'1", 199 lbs. b: Inuvik, N.W.T., 10/25/1971. Chicago's 6th, 88th overall, in 1991.

Season	Club	League	GP	G	A	Pts	AG	AA	APts	PIM	PP	SH	GW	S	%	TGF	PGF	TGA	PGA	+/–	GP	G	A	Pts	PIM	PP	SH	GW
1985-86	Edmonton Shamrocks	AAHA	35	40	64	104	....	....	....	40	....	....	....	....	....	....	....	....	....	....	....	....	....	....	....	....	....	....
1986-87	Edmonton Pats	AAHA	35	30	41	71	....	....	....	60	....	....	....	....	....	....	....	....	....	....	....	....	....	....	....	....	....	....
1987-88	St. Albert Saints	AJHL	55	16	31	47	....	....	....	258	....	....	....	....	....	....	....	....	....	....	....	....	....	....	....	....	....	....
1988-89	Kamloops Blazers	WHL	42	10	17	27	....	....	....	22	....	....	....	....	....	....	....	....	....	....	16	9	8	17	10	....	....	....
1989-90	Kamloops Blazers	WHL	71	24	47	71	....	....	....	63	....	....	....	....	....	....	....	....	....	....	17	4	4	8	8	....	....	....
	Kamloops Blazers	Mem-Cup	3	0	4	4	....	....	....	0	....	....	....	....	....	....	....	....	....	....	....	....	....	....	....	....	....	....
1990-91	Kamloops Blazers	WHL	64	45	60	105	....	....	....	58	....	....	....	....	....	....	....	....	....	....	12	6	10	16	8	....	....	....
1991-92	Kamloops Blazers	WHL	70	40	69	109	....	....	....	90	....	....	....	....	....	....	....	....	....	....	17	9	*20	*29	16	....	....	....
	Kamloops Blazers	Mem-Cup	5	*5	4	9	....	....	....	4	....	....	....	....	....	....	....	....	....	....	....	....	....	....	....	....	....	....
1992-93	Indianapolis Ice	IHL	59	7	14	21	....	....	....	26	....	....	....	....	....	....	....	....	....	....	....	....	....	....	....	....	....	....
1993-94	Indianapolis Ice	IHL	54	13	12	25	....	....	....	67	....	....	....	....	....	....	....	....	....	....	....	....	....	....	....	....	....	....
1994-95	**Dallas Stars**	**NHL**	**1**	**0**	**0**	**0**	**0**	**0**	**0**	**0**	**0**	**0**	**0**	**1**	**0.0**	**0**	**0**	**0**	**0**	**0**	**2**	**0**	**0**	**0**	**0**	**0**	**0**	**0**
	Kalamazoo Wings	IHL	22	9	7	16	....	....	....	22	....	....	....	....	....	....	....	....	....	....	15	3	9	12	8	....	....	....
1995-96	**Dallas Stars**	**NHL**	**2**	**0**	**0**	**0**	**0**	**0**	**0**	**0**	**0**	**0**	**0**	**3**	**0.0**	**0**	**0**	**0**	**0**	**0**	....	....	....	....	....	....	....	....
	Michigan K-Wings	IHL	67	24	27	51	....	....	....	58	....	....	....	....	....	....	....	....	....	....	10	11	6	17	0	....	....	....
1996-97	Orlando Solar Bears	IHL	80	25	49	74	....	....	....	63	....	....	....	....	....	....	....	....	....	....	3	0	1	1	2	....	....	....
1997-98	SC Herisau	Switz.	19	7	16	23	....	....	....	77	....	....	....	....	....	....	....	....	....	....	....	....	....	....	....	....	....	....
	VSV Villach	Alpenliga	6	3	5	8	....	....	....	4	....	....	....	....	....	....	....	....	....	....	....	....	....	....	....	....	....	....
	Dusseldorfer EG	Germany	15	2	0	2	....	....	....	8	....	....	....	....	....	....	....	....	....	....	2	0	0	0	0	....	....	....
1998-99	Houston Aeros	IHL	61	16	23	39	....	....	....	40	....	....	....	....	....	....	....	....	....	....	1	0	0	0	0	....	....	....
	NHL Totals		**3**	**0**	**0**	**0**	**0**	**0**	**0**	**0**	**0**	**0**	**0**	**4**	**0.0**	**0**	**0**	**0**	**0**		**2**	**0**	**0**	**0**	**0**	**0**	**0**	**0**

Signed as a free agent by **Dallas**, July 25, 1994. • Suffered eventual career-ending head injury in game vs. Manitoba (IHL), March 27, 1999. • Officially announced retirement, September 24, 1999.

• BOYKO, Darren

C – R. 5'9", 169 lbs. b: Winnipeg, Man., 1/16/1964.

Season	Club	League	GP	G	A	Pts	AG	AA	APts	PIM	PP	SH	GW	S	%	TGF	PGF	TGA	PGA	+/–	GP	G	A	Pts	PIM	PP	SH	GW
1980-81	St. Boniface Saints	MJHL	48	48	68	*116	....	....	....	....	....	....	....	....	....	....	....	....	....	....	....	....	....	....	....	....	....	....
1981-82	Winnipeg Warriors	WHL	65	35	37	72	....	....	....	14	....	....	....	....	....	....	....	....	....	....	....	....	....	....	....	....	....	....
1982-83	Winnipeg Warriors	WHL	72	49	81	130	....	....	....	8	....	....	....	....	....	....	....	....	....	....	3	0	2	2	0	....	....	....
1983-84	University of Toronto	OUAA	40	33	51	84	....	....	....	24	....	....	....	....	....	....	....	....	....	....	9	7	10	17	4	....	....	....
1984-85	University of Toronto	OUAA	39	31	53	84	....	....	....	42	....	....	....	....	....	....	....	....	....	....	2	1	0	1	6	....	....	....
1985-86	HIFK Helsinki	Finland	36	18	26	44	....	....	....	8	....	....	....	....	....	....	....	....	....	....	8	1	3	4	2	....	....	....
1986-87	HIFK Helsinki	Finland	44	22	13	35	....	....	....	44	....	....	....	....	....	....	....	....	....	....	5	1	3	4	0	....	....	....
1987-88	HIFK Helsinki	Finland	44	14	40	54	....	....	....	16	....	....	....	....	....	....	....	....	....	....	6	1	3	4	0	....	....	....
1988-89	HIFK Helsinki	Finland	34	15	15	30	....	....	....	10	....	....	....	....	....	....	....	....	....	....	2	0	0	0	0	....	....	....
	Winnipeg Jets	**NHL**	**1**	**0**	**0**	**0**	**0**	**0**	**0**	**0**	**0**	**0**	**0**	**0**	**0.0**	**0**	**0**	**1**	**0**	**–1**	....	....	....	....	....	....	....	....
	Moncton Hawks	AHL	18	3	7	10	....	....	....	2	....	....	....	....	....	....	....	....	....	....	4	0	0	0	0	....	....	....
1989-90	HIFK Helsinki	Finland	42	12	20	32	....	....	....	36	....	....	....	....	....	....	....	....	....	....	2	1	0	1	2	....	....	....
1990-91	HIFK Helsinki	Finland	42	16	22	38	....	....	....	20	....	....	....	....	....	....	....	....	....	....	3	0	3	3	4	....	....	....
1991-92	HIFK Helsinki	Finland	44	14	23	37	....	....	....	18	....	....	....	....	....	....	....	....	....	....	9	2	3	5	0	....	....	....
1992-93	HIFK Helsinki	Finland	47	15	16	31	....	....	....	6	....	....	....	....	....	....	....	....	....	....	4	0	0	0	0	....	....	....
1993-94	HIFK Helsinki	Finland	48	18	20	38	....	....	....	14	....	....	....	....	....	....	....	....	....	....	3	0	0	0	0	....	....	....
1994-95	HIFK Helsinki	Finland	48	15	20	35	....	....	....	24	....	....	....	....	....	....	....	....	....	....	3	0	0	0	2	....	....	....
1995-96	HIFK Helsinki	Finland	47	12	20	32	....	....	....	30	....	....	....	....	....	....	....	....	....	....	....	....	....	....	....	....	....	....
1996-97	Berlin Capitals	Germany	32	4	18	22	....	....	....	8	....	....	....	....	....	....	....	....	....	....	4	0	2	2	2	....	....	....
	Berlin Capitals	EuroHL	1	0	0	0	....	....	....	0	....	....	....	....	....	....	....	....	....	....	....	....	....	....	....	....	....	....
	Vastra Frolunda	Sweden	1	0	0	0	....	....	....	0	....	....	....	....	....	....	....	....	....	....	....	....	....	....	....	....	....	....
	Vastra Frolunda	EuroHL	2	0	0	0	....	....	....	0	....	....	....	....	....	....	....	....	....	....	....	....	....	....	....	....	....	....
	NHL Totals		**1**	**0**	**0**	**0**	**0**	**0**	**0**	**0**	**0**	**0**	**0**	**0**	**0.0**	**0**	**0**	**1**	**0**		....	....	....	....	....	....	....	....

Signed as a free agent by **Winnipeg**, May 16, 1988.

• BOYLE, Dan

D – R. 5′11″, 190 lbs. b: Ottawa, Ont., 7/12/1976.

			REGULAR SEASON																		PLAYOFFS							
Season	Club	League	GP	G	A	Pts	AG	AA	APts	PIM	PP	SH	GW	S	%	TGF	PGF	TGA	PGA	+/–	GP	G	A	Pts	PIM	PP	SH	GW
1991-92	Ottawa South Canadians	OMHA	STATISTICS NOT AVAILABLE																									
	Gloucester Rangers	OJHL	4	0	1	1	....	....	....	0	....	....	....	....	....	....	....	....	....	....	....	....	....	....	....	....	....	....
1992-93	Gloucester Rangers	OJHL	55	22	51	73	....	....	....	60	....	....	....	....	....	....	....	....	....	....	....	....	....	....	....	....	....	....
1993-94	Gloucester Rangers	OJHL	53	27	54	81	....	....	....	155	....	....	....	....	....	....	....	....	....	....	....	....	....	....	....	....	....	....
1994-95	University of Miami-Ohio	CCHA	35	8	18	26	....	....	....	24	....	....	....	....	....	....	....	....	....	....	....	....	....	....	....	....	....	....
1995-96	University of Miami-Ohio	CCHA	36	7	20	27	....	....	....	70	....	....	....	....	....	....	....	....	....	....	....	....	....	....	....	....	....	....
1996-97	University of Miami-Ohio	CCHA	40	11	43	54	....	....	....	52	....	....	....	....	....	....	....	....	....	....	....	....	....	....	....	....	....	....
1997-98	University of Miami-Ohio	CCHA	37	14	26	40	....	....	....	58	....	....	....	....	....	....	....	....	....	....	....	....	....	....	....	....	....	....
1998-99	**Florida Panthers**	**NHL**	**22**	**3**	**5**	**8**	**4**	**5**	**9**	**6**	**1**	**0**	**1**	**31**	**9.7**	**21**	**5**	**18**	**2**	**0**	....	....	....	....	....	....	....	....
	Kentucky Thoroughblades	AHL	53	8	34	42	....	....	....	87	....	....	....	....	....	....	....	....	....	....	12	3	5	8	16	....	....	....
99-2000	**Florida Panthers**	**NHL**	**13**	**0**	**3**	**3**	**0**	**3**	**3**	**4**	**0**	**0**	**0**	**9**	**0.0**	**7**	**1**	**9**	**1**	**–2**	....	....	....	....	....	....	....	....
	Louisville Panthers	AHL	58	14	38	52	....	....	....	75	....	....	....	....	....	....	....	....	....	....	4	0	2	2	8	....	....	....
	NHL Totals		**35**	**3**	**8**	**11**	**4**	**8**	**12**	**10**	**1**	**0**	**1**	**40**	**7.5**	**28**	**6**	**27**	**3**		....	....	....	....	....	....	....	....

CCHA First All-Star Team (1997, 1998) • NCAA West First All-American Team (1997, 1998) • AHL Second All-Star Team (1999, 2000)

Signed as a free agent by **Florida**, March 30, 1998.

• BOYNTON, Nick

Nicholas Carl D – R. 6′2″, 210 lbs. b: Nobleton, Ont., 1/14/1979. Boston's 1st, 21st overall, in 1999.

Season	Club	League	GP	G	A	Pts	AG	AA	APts	PIM	PP	SH	GW	S	%	TGF	PGF	TGA	PGA	+/–	GP	G	A	Pts	PIM	PP	SH	GW
1993-94	Caledon Canadians	OJHL	4	0	1	1	....	....	....	0	....	....	....	....	....	....	....	....	....	....	....	....	....	....	....	....	....	....
1994-95	Caledon Canadians	OJHL	44	10	35	45	....	....	....	139	....	....	....	....	....	....	....	....	....	....	....	....	....	....	....	....	....	....
1995-96	Ottawa 67's	OHL	64	10	14	24	....	....	....	90	....	....	....	....	....	....	....	....	....	....	4	0	3	3	10	....	....	....
1996-97	Ottawa 67's	OHL	63	13	51	64	....	....	....	143	....	....	....	....	....	....	....	....	....	....	24	4	*24	28	38	....	....	....
1997-98	Ottawa 67's	OHL	40	7	31	38	....	....	....	94	....	....	....	....	....	....	....	....	....	....	13	0	4	4	24	....	....	....
1998-99	Ottawa 67's	OHL	51	11	48	59	....	....	....	83	....	....	....	....	....	....	....	....	....	....	9	1	9	10	18	....	....	....
	Ottawa 67's	Mem-Cup	5	1	6	7	....	....	....	4	....	....	....	....	....	....	....	....	....	....	....	....	....	....	....	....	....	....
99-2000	**Boston Bruins**	**NHL**	**5**	**0**	**0**	**0**	**0**	**0**	**0**	**0**	**0**	**0**	**0**	**6**	**0.0**	**2**	**0**	**7**	**0**	**–5**	....	....	....	....	....	....	....	....
	Providence Bruins	AHL	53	5	14	19	....	....	....	66	....	....	....	....	....	....	....	....	....	....	12	1	0	1	6	....	....	....
	NHL Totals		**5**	**0**	**0**	**0**	**0**	**0**	**0**	**0**	**0**	**0**	**0**	**6**	**0.0**	**2**	**0**	**7**	**0**		....	....	....	....	....	....	....	....

Memorial Cup All-Star Team (1999) • Won Stafford Smythe Memorial Trophy (Memorial Cup Tournament MVP) (1999)

• Re-entered NHL draft. Originally Washington's 1st choice, 9th overall, in 1997 Entry Draft.

• BOZEK, Steve

Steven Michael LW – L. 5′11″, 180 lbs. b: Kelowna, B.C., 11/26/1960. Los Angeles' 5th, 52nd overall, in 1980.

Season	Club	League	GP	G	A	Pts	AG	AA	APts	PIM	PP	SH	GW	S	%	TGF	PGF	TGA	PGA	+/–	GP	G	A	Pts	PIM	PP	SH	GW
1977-78	Castlegar Rebels	BCJHL	STATISTICS NOT AVAILABLE																									
1978-79	Northern Michigan University	CCHA	33	12	12	24	....	....	....	21	....	....	....	....	....	....	....	....	....	....	....	....	....	....	....	....	....	....
1979-80	Northern Michigan University	CCHA	41	42	47	89	....	....	....	32	....	....	....	....	....	....	....	....	....	....	....	....	....	....	....	....	....	....
1980-81	Northern Michigan University	CCHA	44	35	55	90	....	....	....	0	....	....	....	....	....	....	....	....	....	....	....	....	....	....	....	....	....	....
1981-82	**Los Angeles Kings**	**NHL**	**71**	**33**	**23**	**56**	**26**	**15**	**41**	**68**	**10**	**0**	**5**	**182**	**18.1**	**93**	**27**	**73**	**1**	**–6**	**10**	**4**	**1**	**5**	**6**	**2**	**0**	**1**
1982-83	**Los Angeles Kings**	**NHL**	**53**	**13**	**13**	**26**	**11**	**9**	**20**	**14**	**3**	**0**	**1**	**104**	**12.5**	**33**	**5**	**61**	**15**	**–18**	....	....	....	....	....	....	....	....
1983-84	**Calgary Flames**	**NHL**	**46**	**10**	**10**	**20**	**8**	**7**	**15**	**16**	**0**	**0**	**2**	**76**	**13.2**	**28**	**0**	**44**	**0**	**–16**	**10**	**3**	**1**	**4**	**15**	**1**	**0**	**0**
1984-85	**Calgary Flames**	**NHL**	**54**	**13**	**22**	**35**	**11**	**15**	**26**	**6**	**0**	**0**	**1**	**93**	**14.0**	**48**	**1**	**46**	**10**	**11**	**3**	**1**	**0**	**1**	**4**	**1**	**0**	**0**
1985-86	**Calgary Flames**	**NHL**	**64**	**21**	**22**	**43**	**17**	**15**	**32**	**24**	**5**	**4**	**3**	**147**	**14.3**	**77**	**16**	**61**	**24**	**24**	**14**	**2**	**6**	**8**	**32**	**0**	**0**	**0**
1986-87	**Calgary Flames**	**NHL**	**71**	**17**	**18**	**35**	**15**	**13**	**28**	**22**	**2**	**2**	**4**	**139**	**12.2**	**47**	**5**	**71**	**32**	**3**	**4**	**1**	**0**	**1**	**2**	**0**	**0**	**0**
1987-88	**Calgary Flames**	**NHL**	**26**	**3**	**7**	**10**	**3**	**5**	**8**	**12**	**0**	**1**	**0**	**37**	**8.1**	**14**	**0**	**24**	**7**	**–3**	....	....	....	....	....	....	....	....
	St. Louis Blues	**NHL**	**7**	**0**	**0**	**0**	**0**	**0**	**0**	**2**	**0**	**0**	**0**	**6**	**0.0**	**1**	**0**	**6**	**3**	**–2**	**7**	**1**	**1**	**2**	**6**	**0**	**0**	**0**
1988-89	**Vancouver Canucks**	**NHL**	**71**	**17**	**18**	**35**	**14**	**13**	**27**	**64**	**0**	**2**	**2**	**138**	**12.3**	**44**	**2**	**72**	**31**	**1**	**7**	**0**	**2**	**2**	**4**	**0**	**0**	**0**
1989-90	**Vancouver Canucks**	**NHL**	**58**	**14**	**9**	**23**	**12**	**6**	**18**	**32**	**0**	**1**	**2**	**105**	**13.3**	**35**	**0**	**64**	**26**	**–3**	....	....	....	....	....	....	....	....
1990-91	**Vancouver Canucks**	**NHL**	**62**	**15**	**17**	**32**	**14**	**13**	**27**	**22**	**0**	**1**	**2**	**126**	**11.9**	**44**	**2**	**75**	**27**	**–6**	**3**	**0**	**0**	**0**	**0**	**0**	**0**	**0**
	Canada	WEC-A	8	1	1	2	....	....	....	4	....	....	....	....	....	....	....	....	....	....	....	....	....	....	....	....	....	....
1991-92	**San Jose Sharks**	**NHL**	**58**	**8**	**8**	**16**	**7**	**6**	**13**	**27**	**2**	**0**	**0**	**105**	**7.6**	**26**	**5**	**77**	**26**	**–30**	....	....	....	....	....	....	....	....
1992-93	HC Bolzano	Alpenliga	17	13	11	24	....	....	....	6	....	....	....	....	....	....	....	....	....	....	....	....	....	....	....	....	....	....
	HC Bolzano	Italy	9	4	3	7	....	....	....	8	....	....	....	....	....	....	....	....	....	....	6	2	2	4	11	....	....	....
1993-94	HK Olimpija Ljubljana	Alpenliga	1	0	0	0	....	....	....	0	....	....	....	....	....	....	....	....	....	....	....	....	....	....	....	....	....	....
	NHL Totals		**641**	**164**	**167**	**331**	**138**	**117**	**255**	**309**	**22**	**11**	**22**	**1258**	**13.0**	**490**	**63**	**674**	**202**		**58**	**12**	**11**	**23**	**69**	**4**	**0**	**1**

CCHA First All-Star Team (1980, 1981) • NCAA West First All-American Team (1981) • NCAA Championship All-Tournament Team (1981)

Traded to **Calgary** by **LA Kings** for Carl Mokosak and Kevin LaVallee, June 20, 1983. • Missed majority of 1987-88 season due to knee injury, October, 1987. Traded to **St. Louis** by **Calgary** with Brett Hull for Rob Ramage and Rick Wamsley, March 7, 1988. Traded to **Calgary** by **St. Louis** with Mark Hunter, Doug Gilmour and Michael Dark for Craig Coxe, Mike Bullard and Tim Corkery, September 6, 1988. Traded to **Vancouver** by **Calgary** with Paul Reinhart for Vancouver's 3rd round choice (Veli-Pekka Kautonen) in 1989 Entry Draft, September 6, 1988. Signed as a free agent by **San Jose**, August 9, 1991.

• BOZON, Philippe

LW – L. 5′10″, 185 lbs. b: Chamonix, France, 11/30/1966.

Season	Club	League	GP	G	A	Pts	AG	AA	APts	PIM	PP	SH	GW	S	%	TGF	PGF	TGA	PGA	+/–	GP	G	A	Pts	PIM	PP	SH	GW
1984-85	St-Jean Beavers	QMJHL	67	32	50	82	....	....	....	82	....	....	....	....	....	....	....	....	....	....	5	0	5	5	4	....	....	....
1985-86	St-Jean Beavers	QMJHL	65	59	52	111	....	....	....	72	....	....	....	....	....	....	....	....	....	....	10	10	6	16	16	....	....	....
	Peoria Rivermen	IHL	....	....	....	....	....	....	....	....	....	....	....	....	....	....	....	....	....	....	5	1	0	1	0	....	....	....
1986-87	St-Jean Beavers	QMJHL	25	20	21	41	....	....	....	75	....	....	....	....	....	....	....	....	....	....	8	5	5	10	30	....	....	....
	Peoria Rivermen	IHL	28	4	11	15	....	....	....	17	....	....	....	....	....	....	....	....	....	....	....	....	....	....	....	....	....	....
1987-88	HC Mont-Blanc	France	18	11	15	26	....	....	....	34	....	....	....	....	....	....	....	....	....	....	10	15	6	21	6	....	....	....
	France	Olympics	6	3	2	5	....	....	....	0	....	....	....	....	....	....	....	....	....	....	....	....	....	....	....	....	....	....
1988-89	HC Mont-Blanc	France-2	18	11	18	29	....	....	....	18	....	....	....	....	....	....	....	....	....	....	11	11	17	28	38	....	....	....
	France	WEC-B	7	*8	3	11	....	....	....	10	....	....	....	....	....	....	....	....	....	....	....	....	....	....	....	....	....	....
1989-90	CSG Grenoble	France	36	*45	38	83	....	....	....	34	....	....	....	....	....	....	....	....	....	....	6	4	3	7	2	....	....	....
	France	WEC-B	7	4	2	6	....	....	....	4	....	....	....	....	....	....	....	....	....	....	....	....	....	....	....	....	....	....
1990-91	CSG Grenoble	France	26	22	16	38	....	....	....	16	....	....	....	....	....	....	....	....	....	....	10	7	8	15	8	....	....	....
	France	WEC-B	7	5	5	10	....	....	....	0	....	....	....	....	....	....	....	....	....	....	....	....	....	....	....	....	....	....
1991-92	HC Chamonix	France	10	12	8	20	....	....	....	20	....	....	....	....	....	....	....	....	....	....	12	18	11	29	....	....	....	....
	France	Olympics	7	3	2	5	....	....	....	4	....	....	....	....	....	....	....	....	....	....	....	....	....	....	....	....	....	....
	France	WC-A	3	1	1	2	....	....	....	4	....	....	....	....	....	....	....	....	....	....	....	....	....	....	....	....	....	....
	St. Louis Blues	**NHL**	**9**	**1**	**3**	**4**	**1**	**2**	**3**	**4**	**0**	**0**	**0**	**19**	**5.3**	**12**	**4**	**3**	**0**	**5**	**6**	**1**	**0**	**1**	**27**	**0**	**0**	**0**
1992-93	**St. Louis Blues**	**NHL**	**54**	**6**	**6**	**12**	**5**	**4**	**9**	**55**	**0**	**0**	**0**	**90**	**6.7**	**22**	**0**	**26**	**1**	**–3**	**9**	**1**	**0**	**1**	**0**	**0**	**0**	**0**
	Peoria Rivermen	IHL	4	3	2	5	....	....	....	2	....	....	....	....	....	....	....	....	....	....	....	....	....	....	....	....	....	....
1993-94	**St. Louis Blues**	**NHL**	**80**	**9**	**16**	**25**	**8**	**12**	**20**	**42**	**0**	**1**	**1**	**118**	**7.6**	**43**	**1**	**60**	**22**	**4**	**4**	**0**	**0**	**0**	**4**	**0**	**0**	**0**
	France	WC-A	3	0	0	0	....	....	....	2	....	....	....	....	....	....	....	....	....	....	....	....	....	....	....	....	....	....
1994-95	CSG Grenoble	France	21	8	20	28	....	....	....	38	....	....	....	....	....	....	....	....	....	....	....	....	....	....	....	....	....	....
	France	WC-A	6	2	3	5	....	....	....	0	....	....	....	....	....	....	....	....	....	....	....	....	....	....	....	....	....	....
	St. Louis Blues	**NHL**	**1**	**0**	**0**	**0**	**0**	**0**	**0**	**0**	**0**	**0**	**0**	**0**	**0.0**	**0**	**0**	**0**	**0**	**0**	....	....	....	....	....	....	....	....
1995-96	HC La Chaux-de-Fonds	Switz.	29	31	28	59	....	....	....	48	....	....	....	....	....	....	....	....	....	....	7	8	5	13	6	....	....	....
	France	WC-A	7	4	2	6	....	....	....	4	....	....	....	....	....	....	....	....	....	....	....	....	....	....	....	....	....	....
1996-97	HC Lausanne	Switz-2	23	17	15	32	....	....	....	89	....	....	....	....	....	....	....	....	....	....	....	....	....	....	....	....	....	....
	Adler Mannheim	Germany	22	11	7	18	....	....	....	6	....	....	....	....	....	....	....	....	....	....	9	6	9	*15	2	....	....	....
	France	WC-A	8	2	4	6	....	....	....	27	....	....	....	....	....	....	....	....	....	....	....	....	....	....	....	....	....	....
1997-98	Adler Mannheim	Germany	41	20	17	37	....	....	....	36	....	....	....	....	....	....	....	....	....	....	10	5	5	10	16	....	....	....
	Adler Mannheim	EuroHL	5	2	4	6	....	....	....	14	....	....	....	....	....	....	....	....	....	....	....	....	....	....	....	....	....	....
	France	Olympics	4	5	2	7	....	....	....	4	....	....	....	....	....	....	....	....	....	....	....	....	....	....	....	....	....	....
	France	WC-A	3	2	1	3	....	....	....	2	....	....	....	....	....	....	....	....	....	....	....	....	....	....	....	....	....	....
1998-99	Adler Mannheim	Germany	51	17	30	47	....	....	....	66	....	....	....	....	....	....	....	....	....	....	12	4	5	9	30	....	....	....
	Adler Mannheim	EuroHL	6	1	3	4	....	....	....	4	....	....	....	....	....	....	....	....	....	....	4	0	2	2	2	....	....	....
	France	WC-A	3	1	0	1	....	....	....	4	....	....	....	....	....	....	....	....	....	....	....	....	....	....	....	....	....	....

			REGULAR SEASON																		PLAYOFFS							
Season	Club	League	GP	G	A	Pts	AG	AA	APts	PIM	PP	SH	GW	S	%	TGF	PGF	TGA	PGA	+/–	GP	G	A	Pts	PIM	PP	SH	GW
99-2000	HC Lugano	Switz.	44	13	31	44	....	....	....	73	....	....	....	....	....	....	....	....	....	....	12	*9	6	15	37	....	....	....
	HC Lugano	EuroHL	6	3	2	5	....	....	....	10	....	....	....	....	....	....	....	....	....	....	4	1	6	7	2	....	....	....
	France	WC-A	6	1	2	3	....	....	....	6	....	....	....	....	....	....	....	....	....	....	....	....	....	....	....	....	....	....
	NHL Totals		**144**	**16**	**25**	**41**	**14**	**18**	**32**	**101**	**0**	**1**	**1**	**227**	**7.0**	**77**	**5**	**89**	**23**		**19**	**2**	**0**	**2**	**31**	**0**	**0**	**0**

QMJHL Second All-Star Team (1986) • WEC-B All-Star Team (1989, 1991) • Named Best Forward at WEC-B (1991)

Signed as a free agent by **St. Louis**, September 29, 1985.

• BRACKENBURY, Curt

John Curtis RW – R. 5'10", 200 lbs. b: Kapuskasing, Ont., 1/31/1952.

Season	Club	League	GP	G	A	Pts	AG	AA	APts	PIM	PP	SH	GW	S	%	TGF	PGF	TGA	PGA	+/–	GP	G	A	Pts	PIM	PP	SH	GW
1971-72	Sudbury Wolves	NOJHA	STATISTICS NOT AVAILABLE																									
1972-73	Jersey Devils	EHL	68	17	27	44	....	....	....	66	....	....	....	....	....	....	....	....	....	....	....	....	....	....	....	....	....	....
1973-74	Chicago Cougars	WHA	4	0	1	1	....	....	....	11	....	....	....	....	....	....	....	....	....	....	....	....	....	....	....	....	....	....
	Des Moines Capitols	IHL	13	1	5	6	....	....	....	4	....	....	....	....	....	....	....	....	....	....	....	....	....	....	....	....	....	....
	Long Island Cougars	NAHL	45	8	20	28	....	....	....	194	....	....	....	....	....	....	....	....	....	....	17	5	1	6	51	....	....	....
1974-75	Hampton Gulls	SHL	46	19	24	43	....	....	....	212	....	....	....	....	....	....	....	....	....	....	13	5	5	10	48	....	....	....
	Minnesota Fighting Saints	WHA	7	0	0	0	....	....	....	22	....	....	....	....	....	....	....	....	....	....	12	0	2	2	59	....	....	....
1975-76	Minnesota Fighting Saints	WHA	59	4	9	13	....	....	....	*255	....	....	....	....	....	....	....	....	....	....	....	....	....	....	....	....	....	....
	Quebec Nordiques	WHA	15	4	5	9	....	....	....	*110	....	....	....	....	....	....	....	....	....	....	5	0	0	0	18	....	....	....
1976-77	Quebec Nordiques	WHA	77	16	13	29	....	....	....	146	....	....	....	....	....	....	....	....	....	....	17	3	5	8	51	....	....	....
1977-78	Quebec Nordiques	WHA	33	4	9	13	....	....	....	54	....	....	....	....	....	....	....	....	....	....	10	1	1	2	31	....	....	....
1978-79	Quebec Nordiques	WHA	70	13	13	26	....	....	....	155	....	....	....	....	....	....	....	....	....	....	4	1	1	2	2	....	....	....
1979-80	**Quebec Nordiques**	**NHL**	**63**	**6**	**8**	**14**	**5**	**6**	**11**	**55**	**0**	**0**	**1**	**42**	**14.3**	**27**	**3**	**53**	**8**	**–21**	....	....	....	....	....	....	....	....
1980-81	**Edmonton Oilers**	**NHL**	**58**	**2**	**7**	**9**	**2**	**5**	**7**	**153**	**0**	**0**	**0**	**20**	**10.0**	**19**	**1**	**25**	**4**	**–3**	**2**	**0**	**0**	**0**	**0**	**0**	**0**	**0**
1981-82	**Edmonton Oilers**	**NHL**	**14**	**0**	**2**	**2**	**0**	**1**	**1**	**12**	**0**	**0**	**0**	**2**	**0.0**	**5**	**0**	**3**	**0**	**2**	....	....	....	....	....	....	....	....
	Wichita Wind	CHL	47	11	27	38	....	....	....	99	....	....	....	....	....	....	....	....	....	....	7	0	7	7	13	....	....	....
1982-83	**St. Louis Blues**	**NHL**	**6**	**1**	**0**	**1**	**1**	**0**	**1**	**6**	**0**	**0**	**0**	**2**	**50.0**	**1**	**0**	**9**	**0**	**–8**	....	....	....	....	....	....	....	....
	Salt Lake Golden Eagles	CHL	44	4	19	23	....	....	....	137	....	....	....	....	....	....	....	....	....	....	5	0	1	1	2	....	....	....
	NHL Totals		**141**	**9**	**17**	**26**	**8**	**12**	**20**	**226**	**0**	**0**	**1**	**66**	**13.6**	**52**	**4**	**90**	**12**		**2**	**0**	**0**	**0**	**0**	**0**	**0**	**0**
	Other Major League Totals		265	41	50	91	....	....	....	753	....	....	....	....	....	....	....	....	....	....	48	5	9	14	161	....	....	....

Signed as a free agent by **Chicago** (WHA), October, 1973. Traded to **Minnesota** (WHA) by **Chicago** (WHA) for cash, November, 1974. Signed as a free agent by **Quebec** (WHA) after **Minnesota** (WHA) franchise folded, March 10, 1976. Claimed by **Edmonton** from **Quebec** in Waiver Draft, October 10, 1980. Signed as a free agent by **St. Louis**, October 1, 1982.

• BRADLEY, Brian

Brian Richard Walter C – R. 5'10", 180 lbs. b: Kitchener, Ont., 1/21/1965. Calgary's 2nd, 52nd overall, in 1983.

Season	Club	League	GP	G	A	Pts	AG	AA	APts	PIM	PP	SH	GW	S	%	TGF	PGF	TGA	PGA	+/–	GP	G	A	Pts	PIM	PP	SH	GW
1980-81	Guelph Platers	OJHL	42	31	40	71	....	....	....	59	....	....	....	....	....	....	....	....	....	....	....	....	....	....	....	....	....	....
	Wexford Raiders	OJHL	4	1	1	2	....	....	....	2	....	....	....	....	....	....	....	....	....	....	....	....	....	....	....	....	....	....
1981-82	London Knights	OHL	62	34	44	78	....	....	....	34	....	....	....	....	....	....	....	....	....	....	....	....	....	....	....	....	....	....
1982-83	London Knights	OHL	67	37	82	119	....	....	....	37	....	....	....	....	....	....	....	....	....	....	3	1	0	1	0	....	....	....
1983-84	London Knights	OHL	49	40	60	100	....	....	....	24	....	....	....	....	....	....	....	....	....	....	4	2	4	6	0	....	....	....
1984-85	London Knights	OHL	32	27	49	76	....	....	....	22	....	....	....	....	....	....	....	....	....	....	8	5	10	15	4	....	....	....
	Canada	WJC-A	7	9	5	14	....	....	....	2	....	....	....	....	....	....	....	....	....	....	....	....	....	....	....	....	....	....
1985-86	**Calgary Flames**	**NHL**	**5**	**0**	**1**	**1**	**0**	**1**	**1**	**0**	**0**	**0**	**0**	**4**	**0.0**	**1**	**0**	**5**	**1**	**–3**	**1**	**0**	**0**	**0**	**0**	**0**	**0**	**0**
	Moncton Golden Flames	AHL	59	23	42	65	....	....	....	40	....	....	....	....	....	....	....	....	....	....	10	6	9	15	4	....	....	....
1986-87	**Calgary Flames**	**NHL**	**40**	**10**	**18**	**28**	**9**	**13**	**22**	**16**	**2**	**0**	**2**	**64**	**15.6**	**42**	**13**	**32**	**9**	**6**	....	....	....	....	....	....	....	....
	Moncton Golden Flames	AHL	20	12	16	28	....	....	....	8	....	....	....	....	....	....	....	....	....	....	....	....	....	....	....	....	....	....
1987-88	Canada	Nat-Team	47	18	19	37	....	....	....	42	....	....	....	....	....	....	....	....	....	....	....	....	....	....	....	....	....	....
	Canada	Olympics	7	0	4	4	....	....	....	0	....	....	....	....	....	....	....	....	....	....	....	....	....	....	....	....	....	....
	Vancouver Canucks	**NHL**	**11**	**3**	**5**	**8**	**3**	**4**	**7**	**6**	**0**	**0**	**0**	**26**	**11.5**	**12**	**5**	**15**	**5**	**–3**	....	....	....	....	....	....	....	....
1988-89	**Vancouver Canucks**	**NHL**	**71**	**18**	**27**	**45**	**15**	**19**	**34**	**42**	**6**	**0**	**3**	**151**	**11.9**	**56**	**13**	**51**	**3**	**–5**	**7**	**3**	**4**	**7**	**10**	**1**	**0**	**0**
1989-90	**Vancouver Canucks**	**NHL**	**67**	**19**	**29**	**48**	**16**	**21**	**37**	**65**	**2**	**0**	**0**	**121**	**15.7**	**74**	**19**	**60**	**10**	**5**	....	....	....	....	....	....	....	....
1990-91	**Vancouver Canucks**	**NHL**	**44**	**11**	**20**	**31**	**10**	**15**	**25**	**42**	**3**	**0**	**3**	**84**	**13.1**	**47**	**11**	**39**	**1**	**–2**	....	....	....	....	....	....	....	....
	Toronto Maple Leafs	**NHL**	**26**	**0**	**11**	**11**	**0**	**8**	**8**	**20**	**0**	**0**	**0**	**32**	**0.0**	**18**	**8**	**17**	**0**	**–7**	....	....	....	....	....	....	....	....
1991-92	**Toronto Maple Leafs**	**NHL**	**59**	**10**	**21**	**31**	**9**	**16**	**25**	**48**	**4**	**0**	**3**	**78**	**12.8**	**48**	**23**	**30**	**2**	**–3**	....	....	....	....	....	....	....	....
1992-93	**Tampa Bay Lightning**	**NHL**	**80**	**42**	**44**	**86**	**35**	**30**	**65**	**92**	**16**	**0**	**6**	**205**	**20.5**	**113**	**53**	**86**	**2**	**–24**	....	....	....	....	....	....	....	....
1993-94	**Tampa Bay Lightning**	**NHL**	**78**	**24**	**40**	**64**	**22**	**31**	**53**	**56**	**6**	**0**	**2**	**180**	**13.3**	**88**	**34**	**65**	**3**	**–8**	....	....	....	....	....	....	....	....
1994-95	**Tampa Bay Lightning**	**NHL**	**46**	**13**	**27**	**40**	**23**	**40**	**63**	**42**	**3**	**0**	**2**	**111**	**11.7**	**56**	**19**	**43**	**0**	**–6**	....	....	....	....	....	....	....	....
1995-96	**Tampa Bay Lightning**	**NHL**	**75**	**23**	**56**	**79**	**23**	**46**	**69**	**77**	**9**	**0**	**5**	**189**	**12.2**	**103**	**53**	**63**	**2**	**–11**	**5**	**0**	**3**	**3**	**6**	**0**	**0**	**0**
1996-97	**Tampa Bay Lightning**	**NHL**	**35**	**7**	**17**	**24**	**7**	**15**	**22**	**16**	**1**	**2**	**1**	**93**	**7.5**	**41**	**13**	**29**	**3**	**2**	....	....	....	....	....	....	....	....
1997-98	**Tampa Bay Lightning**	**NHL**	**14**	**2**	**5**	**7**	**2**	**5**	**7**	**6**	**2**	**0**	**0**	**24**	**8.3**	**12**	**5**	**16**	**0**	**–9**	....	....	....	....	....	....	....	....
1998-99	**Tampa Bay Lightning**	**NHL**	DID NOT PLAY – INJURED																		....	....	....	....	....	....	....	....
	NHL Totals		**651**	**182**	**321**	**503**	**174**	**264**	**438**	**528**	**54**	**2**	**27**	**1362**	**13.4**	**711**	**269**	**551**	**41**		**13**	**3**	**7**	**10**	**16**	**1**	**0**	**0**

Played in NHL All-Star Game (1993, 1994)

Traded to **Vancouver** by **Calgary** with Peter Bakovic and Kevan Guy for Craig Coxe, March 6, 1988. Traded to **Toronto** by **Vancouver** for Tom Kurvers, January 12, 1991. Claimed by **Tampa Bay** from **Toronto** in Expansion Draft, June 18, 1992. • Missed majority of 1997-98 and entire 1998-99 seasons recovering from head injury suffered in game vs. LA Kings, November 11, 1997. • Officially announced retirement, October 23, 1999.

• BRADLEY, Lyle

Walter Lyle C/RW – R. 5'9", 160 lbs. b: Lloydminster, Sask., 7/31/1943.

Season	Club	League	GP	G	A	Pts	AG	AA	APts	PIM	PP	SH	GW	S	%	TGF	PGF	TGA	PGA	+/–	GP	G	A	Pts	PIM	PP	SH	GW
1960-61	Estevan Bruins	SJHL	2	0	0	0	....	....	....	2	....	....	....	....	....	....	....	....	....	....	....	....	....	....	....	....	....	....
1961-62	Estevan Bruins	SJHL	47	16	25	41	....	....	....	40	....	....	....	....	....	....	....	....	....	....	10	3	2	5	0	....	....	....
1962-63	Estevan Bruins	SJHL	54	23	45	68	....	....	....	54	....	....	....	....	....	....	....	....	....	....	11	10	8	18	14	....	....	....
	Estevan Bruins	Mem-Cup	6	2	5	7	....	....	....	2	....	....	....	....	....	....	....	....	....	....	....	....	....	....	....	....	....	....
1963-64	University of Denver	WCHA	DID NOT PLAY – FRESHMAN																									
1964-65	University of Denver	WCHA	12	3	7	10	....	....	....	16	....	....	....	....	....	....	....	....	....	....	....	....	....	....	....	....	....	....
1965-66	University of Denver	WCHA	32	12	34	46	....	....	....	43	....	....	....	....	....	....	....	....	....	....	....	....	....	....	....	....	....	....
1966-67	Des Moines Oak Leafs	IHL	69	28	63	91	....	....	....	113	....	....	....	....	....	....	....	....	....	....	7	2	3	5	8	....	....	....
1967-68	Des Moines Oak Leafs	IHL	72	27	54	81	....	....	....	98	....	....	....	....	....	....	....	....	....	....	....	....	....	....	....	....	....	....
1968-69	Houston Apollos	CHL	26	1	5	6	....	....	....	12	....	....	....	....	....	....	....	....	....	....	....	....	....	....	....	....	....	....
	Quebec Aces	AHL	22	6	7	13	....	....	....	38	....	....	....	....	....	....	....	....	....	....	15	3	4	7	6	....	....	....
1969-70	Salt Lake Golden Eagles	WHL	16	3	2	5	....	....	....	10	....	....	....	....	....	....	....	....	....	....	....	....	....	....	....	....	....	....
	Denver Spurs	WHL	24	7	11	18	....	....	....	25	....	....	....	....	....	....	....	....	....	....	....	....	....	....	....	....	....	....
1970-71	Denver Spurs	WHL	71	25	43	68	....	....	....	74	....	....	....	....	....	....	....	....	....	....	5	1	2	3	2	....	....	....
1971-72	Portland Buckaroos	WHL	28	7	12	19	....	....	....	20	....	....	....	....	....	....	....	....	....	....	....	....	....	....	....	....	....	....
	Salt Lake Golden Eagles	WHL	40	16	24	40	....	....	....	25	....	....	....	....	....	....	....	....	....	....	....	....	....	....	....	....	....	....
1972-73	Salt Lake Golden Eagles	WHL	71	29	58	87	....	....	....	83	....	....	....	....	....	....	....	....	....	....	9	1	4	5	15	....	....	....
1973-74	**California Golden Seals**	**NHL**	**4**	**1**	**0**	**1**	**1**	**0**	**1**	**2**	**1**	**0**	**0**	**8**	**12.5**	**3**	**2**	**3**	**0**	**–2**	....	....	....	....	....	....	....	....
	Salt Lake Golden Eagles	WHL	76	34	*81	*115	....	....	....	29	....	....	....	....	....	....	....	....	....	....	5	1	1	2	4	....	....	....
1974-75	Salt Lake Golden Eagles	CHL	55	20	32	52	....	....	....	28	....	....	....	....	....	....	....	....	....	....	11	3	*12	*15	11	....	....	....
1975-76	Salt Lake Golden Eagles	CHL	76	17	57	74	....	....	....	65	....	....	....	....	....	....	....	....	....	....	5	1	3	4	2	....	....	....
1976-77	**Cleveland Barons**	**NHL**	**2**	**0**	**0**	**0**	**0**	**0**	**0**	**0**	**0**	**0**	**0**	**2**	**0.0**	**1**	**0**	**1**	**0**	**0**	....	....	....	....	....	....	....	....
	Salt Lake Golden Eagles	CHL	67	24	44	68	....	....	....	43	....	....	....	....	....	....	....	....	....	....	....	....	....	....	....	....	....	....
1977-78	Salt Lake Golden Eagles	CHL	62	16	41	57	....	....	....	50	....	....	....	....	....	....	....	....	....	....	6	1	2	3	2	....	....	....
	NHL Totals		**6**	**1**	**0**	**1**	**1**	**0**	**1**	**2**	**1**	**0**	**0**	**10**	**10.0**	**4**	**2**	**4**	**0**		....	....	....	....	....	....	....	....

WHL First All-Star Team (1974) • Won Leader Cup (WHL - MVP) (1974)

Traded to **Montreal** by **Oakland** to complete transaction that sent Norm Ferguson to Oakland (May 21, 1968), June, 1968. Loaned to **Quebec** (AHL) by **Montreal**, February, 1969. Traded to **Portland** (WHL) by **Montreal** for cash, June, 1971. Traded to **California** (Salt Lake-WHL) by **Portland) (WHL) with Fred Hilts for Guyle Fielder and John Rathwell, January, 1972. Transferred to Cleveland** after **California** franchise relocated, August 26, 1976.

• BRADY, Neil

Neil Patrick C – L. 6'2", 200 lbs. b: Montreal, Que., 4/12/1968. New Jersey's 1st, 3rd overall, in 1986.

Season	Club	League	GP	G	A	Pts	AG	AA	APts	PIM	PP	SH	GW	S	%	TGF	PGF	TGA	PGA	+/–	GP	G	A	Pts	PIM	PP	SH	GW
			REGULAR SEASON																		PLAYOFFS							
1984-85	Calgary North Stars	AAHA	37	25	50	75	....	....	....	75	....	....	....	....	....	....	....	....	....	....	....	....	....	....	....	....	....	....
	Medicine Hat Tigers	WHL	....	....	....	....	....	....	....	....	....	....	....	....	....	....	....	....	....	....	3	0	0	0	2	....	....	....
1985-86	Medicine Hat Tigers	WHL	72	21	60	81	....	....	....	104	....	....	....	....	....	....	....	....	....	....	21	9	11	20	23	....	....	....
1986-87	Medicine Hat Tigers	WHL	57	19	64	83	....	....	....	126	....	....	....	....	....	....	....	....	....	....	18	1	4	5	25	....	....	....
	Medicine Hat Tigers	Mem-Cup	5	0	1	1	....	....	....	23	....	....	....	....	....	....	....	....	....	....	....	....	....	....	....	....	....	....
1987-88	Medicine Hat Tigers	WHL	61	16	35	51	....	....	....	110	....	....	....	....	....	....	....	....	....	....	15	0	3	3	19	....	....	....
	Medicine Hat Tigers	Mem-Cup	5	1	1	2	....	....	....	6	....	....	....	....	....	....	....	....	....	....	....	....	....	....	....	....	....	....
1988-89	Utica Devils	AHL	75	16	21	37	....	....	....	56	....	....	....	....	....	....	....	....	....	....	4	0	3	3	0	....	....	....
1989-90	**New Jersey Devils**	**NHL**	**19**	**1**	**4**	**5**	**1**	**3**	**4**	**13**	**0**	**0**	**0**	**10**	**10.0**	**7**	**0**	**11**	**3**	**–1**	....	....	....	....	....	....	....	....
	Utica Devils	AHL	38	10	13	23	....	....	....	21	....	....	....	....	....	....	....	....	....	....	5	0	1	1	10	....	....	....
1990-91	**New Jersey Devils**	**NHL**	**3**	**0**	**0**	**0**	**0**	**0**	**0**	**0**	**0**	**0**	**0**	**6**	**0.0**	**0**	**0**	**0**	**0**	**0**	....	....	....	....	....	....	....	....
	Utica Devils	AHL	77	33	63	96	....	....	....	91	....	....	....	....	....	....	....	....	....	....	....	....	....	....	....	....	....	....
1991-92	**New Jersey Devils**	**NHL**	**7**	**1**	**0**	**1**	**1**	**0**	**1**	**4**	**0**	**0**	**0**	**3**	**33.3**	**1**	**0**	**0**	**0**	**1**	....	....	....	....	....	....	....	....
	Utica Devils	AHL	33	12	30	42	....	....	....	28	....	....	....	....	....	....	....	....	....	....	....	....	....	....	....	....	....	....
1992-93	**Ottawa Senators**	**NHL**	**55**	**7**	**17**	**24**	**6**	**12**	**18**	**57**	**5**	**0**	**0**	**68**	**10.3**	**37**	**19**	**45**	**2**	**–25**	....	....	....	....	....	....	....	....
	New Haven Senators	AHL	8	6	3	9	....	....	....	2	....	....	....	....	....	....	....	....	....	....	....	....	....	....	....	....	....	....
1993-94	**Dallas Stars**	**NHL**	**5**	**0**	**1**	**1**	**0**	**1**	**1**	**21**	**0**	**0**	**0**	**1**	**0.0**	**1**	**0**	**2**	**0**	**–1**	....	....	....	....	....	....	....	....
	Kalamazoo Wings	IHL	43	10	16	26	....	....	....	188	....	....	....	....	....	....	....	....	....	....	5	1	1	2	10	....	....	....
1994-95	Kalamazoo Wings	IHL	70	13	45	58	....	....	....	140	....	....	....	....	....	....	....	....	....	....	15	5	14	19	22	....	....	....
1995-96	Michigan K-Wings	IHL	61	14	20	34	....	....	....	127	....	....	....	....	....	....	....	....	....	....	10	1	4	5	8	....	....	....
1996-97	Michigan K-Wings	IHL	76	13	20	33	....	....	....	62	....	....	....	....	....	....	....	....	....	....	4	1	0	1	0	....	....	....
1997-98	Houston Aeros	IHL	65	9	26	35	....	....	....	56	....	....	....	....	....	....	....	....	....	....	4	2	0	2	34	....	....	....
1998-99	Manitoba Moose	IHL	13	1	5	6	....	....	....	8	....	....	....	....	....	....	....	....	....	....	....	....	....	....	....	....	....	....
99-2000	Utah Grizzlies	IHL	82	14	36	50	....	....	....	129	....	....	....	....	....	....	....	....	....	....	3	0	0	0	2	....	....	....
	NHL Totals		**89**	**9**	**22**	**31**	**8**	**16**	**24**	**95**	**5**	**0**	**0**	**88**	**10.2**	**46**	**19**	**58**	**5**		....	....	....	....	....	....	....	....

Traded to **Ottawa** by **New Jersey** for future considerations, September 3, 1992. Signed as a free agent by **Dallas**, December 3, 1993. Signed as a free agent by **Utah** (IHL), August 18, 1999.

• BRAGNALO, Rick

Rick James C – L. 5'8", 160 lbs. b: Fort William, Ont., 12/1/1951.

Season	Club	League	GP	G	A	Pts	AG	AA	APts	PIM	PP	SH	GW	S	%	TGF	PGF	TGA	PGA	+/–	GP	G	A	Pts	PIM	PP	SH	GW
1968-69	Fort William Canadiens	TBJHL	36	*35	37	*72	....	....	....	17	....	....	....	....	....	....	....	....	....	....	5	4	3	7	11	....	....	....
	Fort William Beavers	TBSHL	2	0	0	0	....	....	....	2	....	....	....	....	....	....	....	....	....	....	....	....	....	....	....	....	....	....
1969-70	Fort William Canadiens	TBJHL	23	15	16	31	....	....	....	23	....	....	....	....	....	....	....	....	....	....	....	....	....	....	....	....	....	....
	Fort William Canadiens	Mem-Cup	12	4	8	12	....	....	....	11	....	....	....	....	....	....	....	....	....	....	....	....	....	....	....	....	....	....
1970-71	University of Denver	WCHA	36	13	16	29	....	....	....	20	....	....	....	....	....	....	....	....	....	....	....	....	....	....	....	....	....	....
1971-72	University of Denver	WCHA	38	11	7	18	....	....	....	24	....	....	....	....	....	....	....	....	....	....	....	....	....	....	....	....	....	....
1972-73	University of Denver	WCHA	34	12	21	33	....	....	....	52	....	....	....	....	....	....	....	....	....	....	....	....	....	....	....	....	....	....
1973-74	University of Denver	WCHA	29	24	22	46	....	....	....	22	....	....	....	....	....	....	....	....	....	....	....	....	....	....	....	....	....	....
1974-75	Dayton Gems	IHL	75	41	72	*113	....	....	....	50	....	....	....	....	....	....	....	....	....	....	14	10	7	17	36	....	....	....
1975-76	Dayton Gems	IHL	48	29	34	63	....	....	....	55	....	....	....	....	....	....	....	....	....	....	....	....	....	....	....	....	....	....
	Washington Capitals	**NHL**	**19**	**2**	**10**	**12**	**2**	**7**	**9**	**8**	**0**	**0**	**0**	**28**	**7.1**	**15**	**7**	**13**	**1**	**–4**	....	....	....	....	....	....	....	....
1976-77	**Washington Capitals**	**NHL**	**80**	**11**	**12**	**23**	**10**	**9**	**19**	**16**	**1**	**2**	**1**	**89**	**12.4**	**31**	**3**	**51**	**7**	**–16**	....	....	....	....	....	....	....	....
1977-78	**Washington Capitals**	**NHL**	**44**	**2**	**13**	**15**	**2**	**10**	**12**	**22**	**0**	**0**	**0**	**60**	**3.3**	**25**	**4**	**50**	**23**	**–6**	....	....	....	....	....	....	....	....
	Hershey Bears	AHL	30	11	17	28	....	....	....	15	....	....	....	....	....	....	....	....	....	....	....	....	....	....	....	....	....	....
1978-79	**Washington Capitals**	**NHL**	**2**	**0**	**0**	**0**	**0**	**0**	**0**	**0**	**0**	**0**	**0**	**0**	**0.0**	**0**	**0**	**1**	**0**	**–1**	....	....	....	....	....	....	....	....
	Hershey Bears	AHL	77	21	39	60	....	....	....	41	....	....	....	....	....	....	....	....	....	....	4	0	1	1	2	....	....	....
1979-80	Hershey Bears	AHL	1	0	0	0	....	....	....	0	....	....	....	....	....	....	....	....	....	....	....	....	....	....	....	....	....	....
	Port Huron Flags	IHL	67	22	61	83	....	....	....	26	....	....	....	....	....	....	....	....	....	....	11	3	10	13	12	....	....	....
1980-81	SG Brunico	Italy	28	29	43	72	....	....	....	24	....	....	....	....	....	....	....	....	....	....	15	6	10	16	45	....	....	....
	Italy	WEC-B	7	4	7	11	....	....	....	22	....	....	....	....	....	....	....	....	....	....	....	....	....	....	....	....	....	....
1981-82	SG Brunico	Italy	32	33	48	81	....	....	....	63	....	....	....	....	....	....	....	....	....	....	6	7	*8	15	2	....	....	....
	Italy	WEC-A	7	3	2	5	....	....	....	8	....	....	....	....	....	....	....	....	....	....	....	....	....	....	....	....	....	....
1982-83	SG Brunico	Italy	32	49	59	108	....	....	....	21	....	....	....	....	....	....	....	....	....	....	....	....	....	....	....	....	....	....
	Italy	WEC-A	10	1	2	3	....	....	....	6	....	....	....	....	....	....	....	....	....	....	....	....	....	....	....	....	....	....
1983-84	SG Brunico	Italy	26	26	42	68	....	....	....	44	....	....	....	....	....	....	....	....	....	....	7	7	8	15	20	....	....	....
1984-85	SG Brunico	Italy	18	18	27	45	....	....	....	12	....	....	....	....	....	....	....	....	....	....	6	4	8	12	4	....	....	....
	Italy	WEC-B	7	1	2	3	....	....	....	10	....	....	....	....	....	....	....	....	....	....	....	....	....	....	....	....	....	....
1985-86	SG Brunico	Italy	36	23	43	66	....	....	....	36	....	....	....	....	....	....	....	....	....	....	5	4	7	11	2	....	....	....
	Italy	WEC-B	7	1	1	2	....	....	....	0	....	....	....	....	....	....	....	....	....	....	....	....	....	....	....	....	....	....
1986-87	SG Brunico	Italy	42	25	37	62	....	....	....	38	....	....	....	....	....	....	....	....	....	....	....	....	....	....	....	....	....	....
	Italy	WEC-B	7	3	5	8	....	....	....	10	....	....	....	....	....	....	....	....	....	....	....	....	....	....	....	....	....	....
1987-88	SG Brunico	Italy	35	21	30	51	....	....	....	38	....	....	....	....	....	....	....	....	....	....	8	4	14	18	8	....	....	....
1988-89	SG Brunico	Italy	41	27	30	57	....	....	....	40	....	....	....	....	....	....	....	....	....	....	....	....	....	....	....	....	....	....
1989-90	SG Brunico	Italy	PLAYER/COACH – STATISTICS UNAVAILABLE																									
1990-91	HC Milano Saima	Italy	35	10	23	33	....	....	....	8	....	....	....	....	....	....	....	....	....	....	10	2	8	10	6	....	....	....
1991-92	HC Milano Saima	Alpenliga	20	4	3	7	....	....	....	2	....	....	....	....	....	....	....	....	....	....	....	....	....	....	....	....	....	....
	HC Milano Saima	Italy	15	4	10	14	....	....	....	2	....	....	....	....	....	....	....	....	....	....	7	2	5	7	6	....	....	....
	NHL Totals		**145**	**15**	**35**	**50**	**14**	**26**	**40**	**46**	**1**	**2**	**1**	**177**	**8.5**	**71**	**14**	**115**	**31**		....	....	....	....	....	....	....	....

IHL First All-Star Team (1975) • Won Garry F. Longman Memorial Trophy (Top Rookie - IHL) (1975) • Won Leo P. Lamoureux Memorial Trophy (Top Scorer - IHL) (1975) • WEC-B All-Star Team (1981)

Signed as a free agent by **Washington**, March 1, 1976.

• BRASAR, Per-Olov

LW – L. 5'8", 172 lbs. b: Falun, Sweden, 9/30/1950.

Season	Club	League	GP	G	A	Pts	AG	AA	APts	PIM	PP	SH	GW	S	%	TGF	PGF	TGA	PGA	+/–	GP	G	A	Pts	PIM	PP	SH	GW
1969-70	Leksands IF	Sweden	13	3	3	6	....	....	....	0	....	....	....	....	....	....	....	....	....	....	14	4	4	8	2	....	....	....
1970-71	Leksands IF	Sweden	13	2	3	5	....	....	....	0	....	....	....	....	....	....	....	....	....	....	14	9	5	14	0	....	....	....
1971-72	Leksands IF	Sweden	28	11	7	18	....	....	....	2	....	....	....	....	....	....	....	....	....	....	....	....	....	....	....	....	....	....
1972-73	Leksands IF	Sweden	14	6	2	8	....	....	....	2	....	....	....	....	....	....	....	....	....	....	14	9	5	14	2	....	....	....
1973-74	Sweden	Nat-Team	10	4	5	9	....	....	....	0	....	....	....	....	....	....	....	....	....	....	....	....	....	....	....	....	....	....
	Sweden	WEC-A	9	4	5	9	....	....	....	0	....	....	....	....	....	....	....	....	....	....	....	....	....	....	....	....	....	....
1974-75	Leksands IF	Sweden	30	19	23	42	....	....	....	4	....	....	....	....	....	....	....	....	....	....	5	0	5	5	0	....	....	....
	Sweden	WEC-A	9	0	1	1	....	....	....	0	....	....	....	....	....	....	....	....	....	....	....	....	....	....	....	....	....	....
1975-76	Leksands IF	Sweden	34	11	12	23	....	....	....	4	....	....	....	....	....	....	....	....	....	....	4	1	4	5	8	....	....	....
	Sweden	WEC-A	10	0	0	0	....	....	....	6	....	....	....	....	....	....	....	....	....	....	....	....	....	....	....	....	....	....
1976-77	Sweden	Can-Cup	5	0	1	1	....	....	....	2	....	....	....	....	....	....	....	....	....	....	....	....	....	....	....	....	....	....
	Leksands IF	Sweden	30	23	18	41	....	....	....	14	....	....	....	....	....	....	....	....	....	....	5	3	2	5	0	....	....	....
	Sweden	WEC-A	10	3	8	11	....	....	....	2	....	....	....	....	....	....	....	....	....	....	....	....	....	....	....	....	....	....
1977-78	**Minnesota North Stars**	**NHL**	**77**	**20**	**37**	**57**	**18**	**29**	**47**	**6**	**7**	**2**	**2**	**170**	**11.8**	**81**	**30**	**86**	**28**	**–7**	....	....	....	....	....	....	....	....
	Sweden	WEC-A	10	1	4	5	....	....	....	18	....	....	....	....	....	....	....	....	....	....	....	....	....	....	....	....	....	....
1978-79	**Minnesota North Stars**	**NHL**	**68**	**6**	**28**	**34**	**5**	**20**	**25**	**6**	**2**	**0**	**0**	**126**	**4.8**	**60**	**20**	**58**	**14**	**–4**	....	....	....	....	....	....	....	....
1979-80	**Minnesota North Stars**	**NHL**	**22**	**1**	**14**	**15**	**1**	**10**	**11**	**0**	**0**	**0**	**1**	**38**	**2.6**	**20**	**7**	**13**	**1**	**1**	....	....	....	....	....	....	....	....
	Vancouver Canucks	**NHL**	**48**	**9**	**10**	**19**	**8**	**7**	**15**	**7**	**1**	**0**	**0**	**101**	**8.9**	**44**	**17**	**41**	**10**	**–4**	**4**	**1**	**2**	**3**	**0**	**0**	**0**	**1**
1980-81	**Vancouver Canucks**	**NHL**	**80**	**22**	**41**	**63**	**17**	**27**	**44**	**8**	**3**	**0**	**1**	**167**	**13.2**	**103**	**31**	**81**	**21**	**12**	**3**	**0**	**0**	**0**	**0**	**0**	**0**	**0**
1981-82	**Vancouver Canucks**	**NHL**	**53**	**6**	**12**	**18**	**5**	**8**	**13**	**6**	**0**	**0**	**1**	**90**	**6.7**	**31**	**9**	**49**	**18**	**–9**	**6**	**0**	**0**	**0**	**0**	**0**	**0**	**0**
1982-83	Leksands IF	Sweden	35	6	9	15	....	....	....	8	....	....	....	....	....	....	....	....	....	....	....	....	....	....	....	....	....	....
1983-84	Mora IK	Sweden-2	26	5	12	17	....	....	....	2	....	....	....	....	....	....	....	....	....	....	....	....	....	....	....	....	....	....
	NHL Totals		**348**	**64**	**142**	**206**	**54**	**101**	**155**	**33**	**13**	**2**	**5**	**692**	**9.2**	**339**	**114**	**328**	**92**		**13**	**1**	**2**	**3**	**0**	**0**	**0**	**1**

Signed as a free agent by **Minnesota**, August, 1977. Traded to **Vancouver** by **Minnesota** for Vancouver's 2nd round choice (Mike Sands) in 1981 Entry Draft, December 10, 1979.

• BRASHEAR, Donald

LW – L. 6'2", 225 lbs. b: Bedford, IN, 1/7/1972.

Season	Club	League	GP	G	A	Pts	AG	AA	APts	PIM	PP	SH	GW	S	%	TGF	PGF	TGA	PGA	+/-	GP	G	A	Pts	PIM	PP	SH	GW
			REGULAR SEASON																		PLAYOFFS							
1988-89	Ste-Foy Gouverneurs	QAAA	10	1	2	3	....	....	....	10	....	....	....	....	....	....	....	....	....	....	....	....	....	....	....	....	....	....
1989-90	Longueuil College-Francais	QMJHL	64	12	14	26	....	....	....	169	....	....	....	....	....	....	....	....	....	....	7	0	0	0	11	....	....	....
1990-91	Longueuil College-Francais	QMJHL	68	12	26	38	....	....	....	195	....	....	....	....	....	....	....	....	....	....	8	0	3	3	33	....	....	....
1991-92	Verdun College-Francais	QMJHL	65	18	24	42	....	....	....	283	....	....	....	....	....	....	....	....	....	....	18	4	2	6	98	....	....	....
	Verdun College-Francais	Mem-Cup	3	0	0	0	....	....	....	15	....	....	....	....	....	....	....	....	....	....	....	....	....	....	....	....	....	....
1992-93	Fredericton Canadiens	AHL	76	11	3	14	....	....	....	261	....	....	....	....	....	....	....	....	....	....	5	0	0	0	8	....	....	....
1993-94	**Montreal Canadiens**	**NHL**	**14**	**2**	**2**	**4**	**2**	**2**	**4**	**34**	**0**	**0**	**0**	**15**	**13.3**	**4**	**0**	**5**	**1**	**0**	**2**	**0**	**0**	**0**	**0**	**0**	**0**	**0**
	Fredericton Canadiens	AHL	62	38	28	66	....	....	....	250	....	....	....	....	....	....	....	....	....	....	....	....	....	....	....	....	....	....
1994-95	Fredericton Canadiens	AHL	29	10	9	19	....	....	....	182	....	....	....	....	....	....	....	....	....	....	17	7	5	12	77	....	....	....
	Montreal Canadiens	**NHL**	**20**	**1**	**1**	**2**	**2**	**1**	**3**	**63**	**0**	**0**	**1**	**10**	**10.0**	**2**	**0**	**7**	**0**	**–5**	....	....	....	....	....	....	....	....
1995-96	**Montreal Canadiens**	**NHL**	**67**	**0**	**4**	**4**	**0**	**3**	**3**	**223**	**0**	**0**	**0**	**25**	**0.0**	**12**	**2**	**20**	**0**	**–10**	**6**	**0**	**0**	**0**	**2**	**0**	**0**	**0**
1996-97	**Montreal Canadiens**	**NHL**	**10**	**0**	**0**	**0**	**0**	**0**	**0**	**38**	**0**	**0**	**0**	**6**	**0.0**	**0**	**0**	**2**	**0**	**–2**	....	....	....	....	....	....	....	....
	Vancouver Canucks	**NHL**	**59**	**8**	**5**	**13**	**8**	**4**	**12**	**207**	**0**	**0**	**2**	**55**	**14.5**	**20**	**4**	**22**	**0**	**–6**	....	....	....	....	....	....	....	....
	United States	WC-A	8	2	3	5	....	....	....	8	....	....	....	....	....	....	....	....	....	....	....	....	....	....	....	....	....	....
1997-98	**Vancouver Canucks**	**NHL**	**77**	**9**	**9**	**18**	**11**	**9**	**20**	***372**	**0**	**0**	**1**	**64**	**14.1**	**29**	**1**	**37**	**0**	**–9**	....	....	....	....	....	....	....	....
	United States	WC-A	6	0	0	0	....	....	....	10	....	....	....	....	....	....	....	....	....	....	....	....	....	....	....	....	....	....
1998-99	**Vancouver Canucks**	**NHL**	**82**	**8**	**10**	**18**	**9**	**10**	**19**	**209**	**2**	**0**	**1**	**112**	**7.1**	**36**	**10**	**52**	**1**	**–25**	....	....	....	....	....	....	....	....
99-2000	**Vancouver Canucks**	**NHL**	**60**	**11**	**2**	**13**	**12**	**2**	**14**	**136**	**1**	**0**	**3**	**83**	**13.3**	**26**	**3**	**35**	**3**	**–9**	....	....	....	....	....	....	....	....
	NHL Totals		**389**	**39**	**33**	**72**	**44**	**31**	**75**	**1282**	**3**	**0**	**8**	**370**	**10.5**	**129**	**20**	**180**	**5**		**8**	**0**	**0**	**0**	**2**	**0**	**0**	**0**

Signed as a free agent by **Montreal**, July 28, 1992. Traded to **Vancouver** by **Montreal** for Jassen Cullimore, November 13, 1996.

• BREAULT, Francois

"Frank" RW – L. 5'11", 185 lbs. b: Acton Vale, Que., 5/11/1967.

Season	Club	League	GP	G	A	Pts	AG	AA	APts	PIM	PP	SH	GW	S	%	TGF	PGF	TGA	PGA	+/-	GP	G	A	Pts	PIM	PP	SH	GW
1983-84	Montreal L'est Cantonniers	QAAA	36	15	13	28	....	....	....	....	....	....	....	....	....	....	....	....	....	....	....	....	....	....	....	....	....	....
1984-85	Chicoutimi Sagueneens	QMJHL	68	8	6	14	....	....	....	50	....	....	....	....	....	....	....	....	....	....	14	2	1	3	40	....	....	....
1985-86	Chicoutimi Sagueneens	QMJHL	9	0	0	0	....	....	....	17	....	....	....	....	....	....	....	....	....	....	....	....	....	....	....	....	....	....
	Trois-Rivieres Draveurs	QMJHL	51	15	11	26	....	....	....	56	....	....	....	....	....	....	....	....	....	....	5	0	1	1	18	....	....	....
1986-87	Trois-Rivieres Draveurs	QMJHL	45	20	24	44	....	....	....	89	....	....	....	....	....	....	....	....	....	....	....	....	....	....	....	....	....	....
	Granby Bisons	QMJHL	15	4	9	13	....	....	....	45	....	....	....	....	....	....	....	....	....	....	8	3	2	5	50	....	....	....
1987-88	Trois-Rivieres Draveurs	QMJHL	28	16	19	35	....	....	....	108	....	....	....	....	....	....	....	....	....	....	5	0	1	1	14	....	....	....
	Maine Mariners	AHL	11	0	1	1	....	....	....	37	....	....	....	....	....	....	....	....	....	....	....	....	....	....	....	....	....	....
1988-89	New Haven Nighthawks	AHL	68	21	24	45	....	....	....	51	....	....	....	....	....	....	....	....	....	....	....	....	....	....	....	....	....	....
1989-90	New Haven Nighthawks	AHL	37	17	21	38	....	....	....	33	....	....	....	....	....	....	....	....	....	....	....	....	....	....	....	....	....	....
1990-91	**Los Angeles Kings**	**NHL**	**17**	**1**	**4**	**5**	**1**	**3**	**4**	**6**	**0**	**0**	**0**	**12**	**8.3**	**5**	**0**	**6**	**0**	**–1**	....	....	....	....	....	....	....	....
1991-92	**Los Angeles Kings**	**NHL**	**6**	**1**	**0**	**1**	**1**	**0**	**1**	**30**	**0**	**0**	**0**	**6**	**16.7**	**1**	**0**	**1**	**0**	**0**	....	....	....	....	....	....	....	....
	Phoenix Roadrunners	IHL	54	14	19	33	....	....	....	40	....	....	....	....	....	....	....	....	....	....	....	....	....	....	....	....	....	....
1992-93	**Los Angeles Kings**	**NHL**	**4**	**0**	**0**	**0**	**0**	**0**	**0**	**6**	**0**	**0**	**0**	**0**	**0.0**	**0**	**0**	**1**	**0**	**–1**	....	....	....	....	....	....	....	....
	Phoenix Roadrunners	IHL	31	5	11	16	....	....	....	26	....	....	....	....	....	....	....	....	....	....	....	....	....	....	....	....	....	....
	Utica Devils	AHL	32	8	20	28	....	....	....	56	....	....	....	....	....	....	....	....	....	....	4	2	0	2	0	....	....	....
1993-94	Durham Wasps	Britain	14	23	17	40	....	....	....	20	....	....	....	....	....	....	....	....	....	....	6	6	4	10	2	....	....	....
	NHL Totals		**27**	**2**	**4**	**6**	**2**	**3**	**5**	**42**	**0**	**0**	**0**	**18**	**11.1**	**6**	**0**	**8**	**0**		....	....	....	....	....	....	....	....

Signed as a free agent by **LA Kings**, July, 1988. • Missed remainder of 1990-91 season recovering from knee injury suffered in game vs. Calgary, December 13, 1990.

• BREITENBACH, Ken

D – L. 6'1", 190 lbs. b: Welland, Ont., 1/9/1955. Buffalo's 2nd, 35th overall, in 1975.

Season	Club	League	GP	G	A	Pts	AG	AA	APts	PIM	PP	SH	GW	S	%	TGF	PGF	TGA	PGA	+/-	GP	G	A	Pts	PIM	PP	SH	GW
1971-72	Welland Sabres	OHA-B	34	6	18	24	....	....	....	44	....	....	....	....	....	....	....	....	....	....	....	....	....	....	....	....	....	....
1972-73	St. Catharines Black Hawks	OMJHL	37	1	8	9	....	....	....	0	....	....	....	....	....	....	....	....	....	....	....	....	....	....	....	....	....	....
1973-74	St. Catharines Black Hawks	OMJHL	68	4	34	38	....	....	....	46	....	....	....	....	....	....	....	....	....	....	....	....	....	....	....	....	....	....
1974-75	St. Catharines Black Hawks	OMJHL	65	7	30	37	....	....	....	143	....	....	....	....	....	....	....	....	....	....	4	0	1	1	9	....	....	....
1975-76	**Buffalo Sabres**	**NHL**	**7**	**0**	**0**	**0**	**0**	**0**	**0**	**6**	**0**	**0**	**0**	**0**	**0.0**	**5**	**1**	**0**	**0**	**4**	**1**	**0**	**0**	**0**	**0**	**0**	**0**	**0**
	Hershey Bears	AHL	57	1	19	20	....	....	....	58	....	....	....	....	....	....	....	....	....	....	10	1	2	3	6	....	....	....
1976-77	**Buffalo Sabres**	**NHL**	**31**	**0**	**5**	**5**	**0**	**4**	**4**	**18**	**0**	**0**	**0**	**11**	**0.0**	**10**	**0**	**14**	**2**	**–2**	**4**	**0**	**0**	**0**	**0**	**0**	**0**	**0**
	Hershey Bears	AHL	37	3	8	11	....	....	....	29	....	....	....	....	....	....	....	....	....	....	....	....	....	....	....	....	....	....
1977-78	**Buffalo Sabres**	**NHL**	DID NOT PLAY – INJURED																									
1978-79	**Buffalo Sabres**	**NHL**	**30**	**1**	**8**	**9**	**1**	**6**	**7**	**25**	**0**	**0**	**0**	**41**	**2.4**	**34**	**0**	**33**	**4**	**5**	**3**	**0**	**1**	**1**	**4**	**0**	**0**	**0**
	Hershey Bears	AHL	17	3	2	5	....	....	....	14	....	....	....	....	....	....	....	....	....	....	....	....	....	....	....	....	....	....
	NHL Totals		**68**	**1**	**13**	**14**	**1**	**10**	**11**	**49**	**0**	**0**	**0**	**52**	**1.9**	**49**	**1**	**47**	**6**		**8**	**0**	**1**	**1**	**4**	**0**	**0**	**0**

OMJHL Second All-Star Team (1975)

• Missed entire 1977-78 season recovering from broken leg suffered in training camp, September, 1977.

• BRENNAN, Dan

LW – L. 6'3", 210 lbs. b: Dawson Creek, B.C., 10/1/1962. Los Angeles' 7th, 165th overall, in 1981.

Season	Club	League	GP	G	A	Pts	AG	AA	APts	PIM	PP	SH	GW	S	%	TGF	PGF	TGA	PGA	+/-	GP	G	A	Pts	PIM	PP	SH	GW
1980-81	University of North Dakota	WCHA	37	3	9	12	....	....	....	66	....	....	....	....	....	....	....	....	....	....	....	....	....	....	....	....	....	....
1981-82	University of North Dakota	WCHA	42	10	17	27	....	....	....	78	....	....	....	....	....	....	....	....	....	....	....	....	....	....	....	....	....	....
1982-83	University of North Dakota	WCHA	31	9	11	20	....	....	....	60	....	....	....	....	....	....	....	....	....	....	....	....	....	....	....	....	....	....
1983-84	University of North Dakota	WCHA	45	28	37	65	....	....	....	36	....	....	....	....	....	....	....	....	....	....	....	....	....	....	....	....	....	....
	Los Angeles Kings	**NHL**	**2**	**0**	**0**	**0**	**0**	**0**	**0**	**0**	**0**	**0**	**0**	**1**	**0.0**	**0**	**0**	**1**	**0**	**–1**	....	....	....	....	....	....	....	....
1984-85	New Haven Nighthawks	AHL	80	25	33	58	....	....	....	56	....	....	....	....	....	....	....	....	....	....	....	....	....	....	....	....	....	....
1985-86	**Los Angeles Kings**	**NHL**	**6**	**0**	**1**	**1**	**0**	**1**	**1**	**9**	**0**	**0**	**0**	**6**	**0.0**	**2**	**0**	**3**	**0**	**–1**	....	....	....	....	....	....	....	....
	New Haven Nighthawks	AHL	62	8	22	30	....	....	....	76	....	....	....	....	....	....	....	....	....	....	2	0	0	0	10	....	....	....
	NHL Totals		**8**	**0**	**1**	**1**	**0**	**1**	**1**	**9**	**0**	**0**	**0**	**7**	**0.0**	**2**	**0**	**4**	**0**		....	....	....	....	....	....	....	....

WCHA First All-Star Team (1984)

• BRENNAN, Rich

D – R. 6'2", 200 lbs. b: Schenectady, NY, 11/26/1972. Quebec's 3rd, 46th overall, in 1991.

Season	Club	League	GP	G	A	Pts	AG	AA	APts	PIM	PP	SH	GW	S	%	TGF	PGF	TGA	PGA	+/-	GP	G	A	Pts	PIM	PP	SH	GW
1988-89	Albany Academy	Hi-School	25	17	30	47	....	....	....	57	....	....	....	....	....	....	....	....	....	....	....	....	....	....	....	....	....	....
1989-90	Tabor Academy Seawolves	Hi-School	33	12	14	26	....	....	....	68	....	....	....	....	....	....	....	....	....	....	....	....	....	....	....	....	....	....
1990-91	Tabor Academy Seawolves	Hi-School	34	13	37	50	....	....	....	91	....	....	....	....	....	....	....	....	....	....	....	....	....	....	....	....	....	....
1991-92	Boston University	H-East	30	4	13	17	....	....	....	50	....	....	....	....	....	....	....	....	....	....	....	....	....	....	....	....	....	....
	United States	WJC-A	7	0	2	2	....	....	....	4	....	....	....	....	....	....	....	....	....	....	....	....	....	....	....	....	....	....
1992-93	Boston University	H-East	40	9	11	20	....	....	....	68	....	....	....	....	....	....	....	....	....	....	....	....	....	....	....	....	....	....
1993-94	Boston University	H-East	41	8	27	35	....	....	....	82	....	....	....	....	....	....	....	....	....	....	....	....	....	....	....	....	....	....
1994-95	Boston University	H-East	31	5	22	27	....	....	....	56	....	....	....	....	....	....	....	....	....	....	....	....	....	....	....	....	....	....
1995-96	Brantford Smoke	ColHL	5	1	2	3	....	....	....	2	....	....	....	....	....	....	....	....	....	....	....	....	....	....	....	....	....	....
	Cornwall Aces	AHL	36	4	8	12	....	....	....	61	....	....	....	....	....	....	....	....	....	....	7	0	0	0	6	....	....	....
1996-97	**Colorado Avalanche**	**NHL**	**2**	**0**	**0**	**0**	**0**	**0**	**0**	**0**	**0**	**0**	**0**	**0**	**0.0**	**0**	**0**	**0**	**0**	**0**	....	....	....	....	....	....	....	....
	Hershey Bears	AHL	74	11	45	56	....	....	....	88	....	....	....	....	....	....	....	....	....	....	23	2	*16	18	22	....	....	....
1997-98	**San Jose Sharks**	**NHL**	**11**	**1**	**2**	**3**	**1**	**2**	**3**	**2**	**1**	**0**	**0**	**24**	**4.2**	**9**	**5**	**8**	**0**	**–4**	....	....	....	....	....	....	....	....
	Kentucky Thoroughblades	AHL	42	11	17	28	....	....	....	71	....	....	....	....	....	....	....	....	....	....	....	....	....	....	....	....	....	....
	Hartford Wolf Pack	AHL	9	2	4	6	....	....	....	12	....	....	....	....	....	....	....	....	....	....	15	4	5	9	14	....	....	....
1998-99	**New York Rangers**	**NHL**	**24**	**1**	**3**	**4**	**1**	**3**	**4**	**23**	**0**	**0**	**0**	**36**	**2.8**	**12**	**5**	**13**	**2**	**–4**	....	....	....	....	....	....	....	....
	Hartford Wolf Pack	AHL	47	4	24	28	....	....	....	42	....	....	....	....	....	....	....	....	....	....	....	....	....	....	....	....	....	....
99-2000	Lowell Lock Monsters	AHL	67	15	30	45	....	....	....	110	....	....	....	....	....	....	....	....	....	....	7	1	5	6	0	....	....	....
	NHL Totals		**37**	**2**	**5**	**7**	**2**	**5**	**7**	**25**	**1**	**0**	**0**	**60**	**3.3**	**21**	**10**	**21**	**2**		....	....	....	....	....	....	....	....

Hockey East First All-Star Team (1994) • NCAA East Second All-American Team (1994)

• Rights transferred to **Colorado** after **Quebec** franchise relocated, June 21, 1995. Signed as a free agent by **San Jose**, July 9, 1997. Traded to **NY Rangers** by **San Jose** for Jason Muzzatti, March 24, 1998.

• BRENNEMAN, John John Gary LW – L. 5'10", 175 lbs. b: Fort Erie, Ont., 1/5/1943.

			REGULAR SEASON																		PLAYOFFS							
Season	Club	League	GP	G	A	Pts	AG	AA	APts	PIM	PP	SH	GW	S	%	TGF	PGF	TGA	PGA	+/–	GP	G	A	Pts	PIM	PP	SH	GW
1959-60	St. Catharines Teepees	OHA-Jr.	48	11	18	29	....	....	....	17	....	....	....	....	....	....	....	....	....	....	17	5	3	8	8	....	....	....
	St. Catharines Teepees	Mem-Cup	14	5	8	13	....	....	....	2	....	....	....	....	....	....	....	....	....	....	....	....	....	....	....	....	....	....
1960-61	St. Catharines Teepees	OHA-Jr.	48	12	13	25	....	....	....	26	....	....	....	....	....	....	....	....	....	....	6	2	4	6	2	....	....	....
1961-62	St. Catharines Teepees	OHA-Jr.	49	12	30	42	....	....	....	10	....	....	....	....	....	....	....	....	....	....	6	2	4	6	4	....	....	....
1962-63	St. Catharines Teepees	OHA-Jr.	48	31	27	58	....	....	....	38	....	....	....	....	....	....	....	....	....	....	....	....	....	....	....	....	....	....
	Buffalo Bisons	AHL	4	1	0	1	....	....	....	0	....	....	....	....	....	....	....	....	....	....	....	....	....	....	....	....	....	....
1963-64	St. Louis Braves	CPHL	70	28	47	75	....	....	....	28	....	....	....	....	....	....	....	....	....	....	6	2	1	3	11	....	....	....
1964-65	**Chicago Black Hawks**	**NHL**	**17**	**1**	**0**	**1**	**1**	**0**	**1**	**2**	....	....	....	....	....	....	....	....	....	....	....	....	....	....	....	....	....	....
	St. Louis Braves	CPHL	27	7	17	24	....	....	....	20	....	....	....	....	....	....	....	....	....	....	....	....	....	....	....	....	....	....
	New York Rangers	**NHL**	**22**	**3**	**3**	**6**	**4**	**3**	**7**	**6**	....	....	....	....	....	....	....	....	....	....	....	....	....	....	....	....	....	....
1965-66	**New York Rangers**	**NHL**	**11**	**0**	**0**	**0**	**0**	**0**	**0**	**14**	....	....	....	....	....	....	....	....	....	....	....	....	....	....	....	....	....	....
	Baltimore Clippers	AHL	33	5	8	13	....	....	....	16	....	....	....	....	....	....	....	....	....	....	....	....	....	....	....	....	....	....
	Minnesota Rangers	CPHL	20	10	7	17	....	....	....	16	....	....	....	....	....	....	....	....	....	....	7	0	2	2	0	....	....	....
1966-67♦	**Toronto Maple Leafs**	**NHL**	**41**	**6**	**4**	**10**	**7**	**4**	**11**	**4**	....	....	....	....	....	....	....	....	....	....	....	....	....	....	....	....	....	....
	Rochester Americans	AHL	13	3	10	13	....	....	....	4	....	....	....	....	....	....	....	....	....	....	13	0	3	3	0	....	....	....
1967-68	**Detroit Red Wings**	**NHL**	**9**	**0**	**2**	**2**	**0**	**2**	**2**	**0**	**0**	**0**	**0**	**12**	**0.0**	**3**	**0**	**1**	**0**	**2**	....	....	....	....	....	....	....	....
	Fort Worth Wings	CPHL	14	5	2	7	....	....	....	10	....	....	....	....	....	....	....	....	....	....	....	....	....	....	....	....	....	....
	Oakland Seals	**NHL**	**31**	**10**	**8**	**18**	**12**	**8**	**20**	**14**	**2**	**0**	**0**	**61**	**16.4**	**27**	**7**	**31**	**2**	**–9**	....	....	....	....	....	....	....	....
	San Diego Gulls	WHL	5	2	2	4	....	....	....	4	....	....	....	....	....	....	....	....	....	....	....	....	....	....	....	....	....	....
1968-69	**Oakland Seals**	**NHL**	**21**	**1**	**2**	**3**	**1**	**2**	**3**	**6**	**0**	**0**	**0**	**16**	**6.3**	**6**	**1**	**9**	**0**	**–4**	....	....	....	....	....	....	....	....
	Cleveland Barons	AHL	49	14	13	27	....	....	....	41	....	....	....	....	....	....	....	....	....	....	5	1	0	1	0	....	....	....
1969-70			OUT OF HOCKEY – RETIRED																									
1970-71	Dayton Gems	IHL	50	23	18	41	....	....	....	20	....	....	....	....	....	....	....	....	....	....	10	3	4	7	4	....	....	....
1971-72			OUT OF HOCKEY – RETIRED																									
1972-73			OUT OF HOCKEY – RETIRED																									
1973-74	Cambridge Hornets	OHA-Sr.	16	7	5	12	....	....	....	12	....	....	....	....	....	....	....	....	....	....	....	....	....	....	....	....	....	....
1974-75	IEV Innsbruck	Austria	28	18	13	31	....	....	....	16	....	....	....	....	....	....	....	....	....	....	....	....	....	....	....	....	....	....
	NHL Totals		**152**	**21**	**19**	**40**	**25**	**19**	**44**	**46**	....	....	....	....	....	....	....	....	....	....	....	....	....	....	....	....	....	....

CPHL First All-Star Team (1964)

Traded to **NY Rangers** by **Chicago** with Doug Robinson and Wayne Hillman for Camille Henry, Don Johns, Billy Taylor and Wally Chevrier, February 4, 1965. Claimed by **Toronto** from **NY Rangers** in Intra-League Draft, June 15, 1966. Claimed by **St. Louis** from **Toronto** in Expansion Draft, June 6, 1967. Traded to **Detroit** by **St. Louis** for Craig Cameron, Larry Hornung and Don Giesebrecht, October 9, 1967. Traded to **Oakland** by **Detroit** with Ted Hampson and Bert Marshall for Kent Douglas, January 9, 1968.

• BREWER, Carl Carl Thomas D – L. 5'9", 180 lbs. b: Toronto, Ont., 10/21/1938.

Season	Club	League	GP	G	A	Pts	AG	AA	APts	PIM	PP	SH	GW	S	%	TGF	PGF	TGA	PGA	+/–	GP	G	A	Pts	PIM	PP	SH	GW
1955-56	Westen Dukes	OHA-B	STATISTICS NOT AVAILABLE																									
	Toronto Marlboros	OHA-Jr.	10	1	3	4	....	....	....	6	....	....	....	....	....	....	....	....	....	....	11	3	5	8	10	....	....	....
	Toronto Marlboros	Mem-Cup	13	1	2	3	....	....	....	12	....	....	....	....	....	....	....	....	....	....	....	....	....	....	....	....	....	....
1956-57	Toronto Marlboros	OHA-Jr.	48	8	24	32	....	....	....	154	....	....	....	....	....	....	....	....	....	....	9	4	3	7	33	....	....	....
1957-58	Toronto Marlboros	OHA-Jr.	50	10	37	47	....	....	....	212	....	....	....	....	....	....	....	....	....	....	13	3	9	12	*75	....	....	....
	Toronto Maple Leafs	**NHL**	**2**	**0**	**0**	**0**	**0**	**0**	**0**	**0**	....	....	....	....	....	....	....	....	....	....	....	....	....	....	....	....	....	....
	Toronto Marlboros	Mem-Cup	5	1	1	2	....	....	....	12	....	....	....	....	....	....	....	....	....	....	....	....	....	....	....	....	....	....
1958-59	**Toronto Maple Leafs**	**NHL**	**69**	**3**	**21**	**24**	**4**	**21**	**25**	**125**	....	....	....	....	....	....	....	....	....	....	**12**	**0**	**6**	**6**	***40**	**0**	**0**	**0**
	Rochester Americans	AHL	1	0	1	1	....	....	....	2	....	....	....	....	....	....	....	....	....	....	....	....	....	....	....	....	....	....
1959-60	**Toronto Maple Leafs**	**NHL**	**67**	**4**	**19**	**23**	**5**	**18**	**23**	***150**	....	....	....	....	....	....	....	....	....	....	**10**	**2**	**3**	**5**	**16**	**0**	**0**	**0**
1960-61	**Toronto Maple Leafs**	**NHL**	**51**	**1**	**14**	**15**	**1**	**13**	**14**	**92**	....	....	....	....	....	....	....	....	....	....	**5**	**0**	**0**	**0**	**4**	**0**	**0**	**0**
1961-62♦	**Toronto Maple Leafs**	**NHL**	**67**	**1**	**22**	**23**	**1**	**21**	**22**	**89**	....	....	....	....	....	....	....	....	....	....	**8**	**0**	**2**	**2**	**22**	**0**	**0**	**0**
1962-63♦	**Toronto Maple Leafs**	**NHL**	**70**	**2**	**23**	**25**	**2**	**23**	**25**	**168**	....	....	....	....	....	....	....	....	....	....	**10**	**0**	**1**	**1**	**12**	**0**	**0**	**0**
1963-64♦	**Toronto Maple Leafs**	**NHL**	**57**	**4**	**9**	**13**	**5**	**9**	**14**	**114**	....	....	....	....	....	....	....	....	....	....	**12**	**0**	**1**	**1**	**30**	**0**	**0**	**0**
1964-65	**Toronto Maple Leafs**	**NHL**	**70**	**4**	**23**	**27**	**5**	**24**	**29**	***177**	....	....	....	....	....	....	....	....	....	....	**6**	**1**	**2**	**3**	**12**	**0**	**0**	**0**
1965-66			OUT OF HOCKEY – RETIRED																									
1966-67	Canada	Nat-Team	STATISTICS NOT AVAILABLE																									
	Canada	WEC-A	7	1	6	7	....	....	....	10	....	....	....	....	....	....	....	....	....	....	....	....	....	....	....	....	....	....
1967-68	Muskegon Mohawks	IHL	63	13	55	68	....	....	....	82	....	....	....	....	....	....	....	....	....	....	9	3	9	12	4	....	....	....
1968-69	HIFK Helsinki	Finland	20	4	14	18	....	....	....	53	....	....	....	....	....	....	....	....	....	....	....	....	....	....	....	....	....	....
1969-70	**Detroit Red Wings**	**NHL**	**70**	**2**	**37**	**39**	**2**	**35**	**37**	**51**	**0**	**0**	**0**	**109**	**1.8**	**128**	**33**	**80**	**29**	**44**	**4**	**0**	**0**	**0**	**2**	**0**	**0**	**0**
1970-71	**St. Louis Blues**	**NHL**	**19**	**2**	**9**	**11**	**2**	**7**	**9**	**29**	**0**	**0**	**0**	**35**	**5.7**	**31**	**16**	**21**	**5**	**–1**	**5**	**0**	**2**	**2**	**8**	**0**	**0**	**0**
1971-72	**St. Louis Blues**	**NHL**	**42**	**2**	**16**	**18**	**2**	**14**	**16**	**40**	**0**	**0**	**1**	**58**	**3.4**	**54**	**12**	**62**	**14**	**–6**	....	....	....	....	....	....	....	....
1972-73			OUT OF HOCKEY – RETIRED																									
1973-74	Toronto Toros	WHA	77	2	23	25	....	....	....	42	....	....	....	....	....	....	....	....	....	....	12	0	4	4	11	....	....	....
1974-1979			OUT OF HOCKEY – RETIRED																									
1979-80	New Brunswick Hawks	AHL	3	0	0	0	....	....	....	0	....	....	....	....	....	....	....	....	....	....	....	....	....	....	....	....	....	....
	Toronto Maple Leafs	**NHL**	**20**	**0**	**5**	**5**	**0**	**4**	**4**	**2**	**0**	**0**	**0**	**11**	**0.0**	**19**	**1**	**28**	**5**	**–5**	....	....	....	....	....	....	....	....
	NHL Totals		**604**	**25**	**198**	**223**	**29**	**189**	**218**	**1037**	....	....	....	....	....	....	....	....	....	....	**72**	**3**	**17**	**20**	**146**	....	....	....
	Other Major League Totals		77	2	23	25	....	....	....	42	....	....	....	....	....	....	....	....	....	....	12	0	4	4	11	....	....	....

NHL Second All-Star Team (1962, 1965, 1970) • NHL First All-Star Team (1963) • WEC-A All-Star Team (1967) • IHL First All-Star Team (1968) • Won Governors' Trophy (Top Defenseman - IHL) (1968) • Played in NHL All-Star Game (1959, 1962, 1964, 1970)

Signed as a free agent by **Muskegon** (IHL), July, 1967. Rights traded to **Detroit** by **Toronto** with Frank Mahovlich, Pete Stemkowski and Garry Unger for Norm Ullman, Floyd Smith, Paul Henderson and Doug Barrie, March 3, 1968. • Left Detroit's training camp on September 4, 1970 to concentrate on job with the KOHO hockey stick company. Traded to **St. Louis** by **Detroit** for future considerations (Mike Lowe, Ab McDonald and Bob Wall, May 12, 1971), February 22, 1971. Selected by **LA Sharks** (WHA) in 1972 WHA General Player Draft, February 12, 1972. WHA rights traded to **Toronto** (WHA) by **LA Sharks** (WHA) for cash, October, 1973. Signed as a free agent by **Toronto**, January 2, 1980.

• BREWER, Eric D – L. 6'3", 195 lbs. b: Vernon, B.C., 4/17/1979. NY Islanders' 2nd, 5th overall, in 1997.

Season	Club	League	GP	G	A	Pts	AG	AA	APts	PIM	PP	SH	GW	S	%	TGF	PGF	TGA	PGA	+/–	GP	G	A	Pts	PIM	PP	SH	GW
1994-95	Kamloops Bantam Chiefs	BCAHA	40	19	19	38	....	....	....	62	....	....	....	....	....	....	....	....	....	....	....	....	....	....	....	....	....	....
1995-96	Prince George Cougars	WHL	63	4	10	14	....	....	....	25	....	....	....	....	....	....	....	....	....	....	....	....	....	....	....	....	....	....
1996-97	Prince George Cougars	WHL	71	5	24	29	....	....	....	81	....	....	....	....	....	....	....	....	....	....	15	2	4	6	16	....	....	....
1997-98	Prince George Cougars	WHL	34	5	28	33	....	....	....	45	....	....	....	....	....	....	....	....	....	....	11	4	2	6	19	....	....	....
	Canada	WJC-A	7	0	2	2	....	....	....	8	....	....	....	....	....	....	....	....	....	....	....	....	....	....	....	....	....	....
1998-99	**New York Islanders**	**NHL**	**63**	**5**	**6**	**11**	**6**	**6**	**12**	**32**	**2**	**0**	**0**	**63**	**7.9**	**44**	**9**	**52**	**3**	**–14**	....	....	....	....	....	....	....	....
99-2000	**New York Islanders**	**NHL**	**26**	**0**	**2**	**2**	**0**	**2**	**2**	**20**	**0**	**0**	**0**	**30**	**0.0**	**14**	**0**	**32**	**7**	**–11**	....	....	....	....	....	....	....	....
	Lowell Lock Monsters	AHL	25	2	2	4	....	....	....	26	....	....	....	....	....	....	....	....	....	....	7	0	0	0	0	....	....	....
	NHL Totals		**89**	**5**	**8**	**13**	**6**	**8**	**14**	**52**	**2**	**0**	**0**	**93**	**5.4**	**58**	**9**	**84**	**10**		....	....	....	....	....	....	....	....

WHL West Second All-Star Team (1998)

Traded to **Edmonton** by **NY Islanders** with Josh Green and NY Islanders' 2nd round choice (Brad Winchester) in 2000 Entry Draft for Roman Hamrlik, June 24, 2000.

• BRICKLEY, Andy LW/C – L. 5'11", 200 lbs. b: Melrose, MA, 8/9/1961. Philadelphia's 11th, 210th overall, in 1980.

Season	Club	League	GP	G	A	Pts	AG	AA	APts	PIM	PP	SH	GW	S	%	TGF	PGF	TGA	PGA	+/–	GP	G	A	Pts	PIM	PP	SH	GW
1979-80	University of New Hampshire	ECAC	27	15	17	32	....	....	....	8	....	....	....	....	....	....	....	....	....	....	....	....	....	....	....	....	....	....
1980-81	University of New Hampshire	ECAC	31	27	25	52	....	....	....	16	....	....	....	....	....	....	....	....	....	....	....	....	....	....	....	....	....	....
	United States	WJC-A	5	1	1	2	....	....	....	4	....	....	....	....	....	....	....	....	....	....	....	....	....	....	....	....	....	....
1981-82	University of New Hampshire	ECAC	35	26	27	53	....	....	....	6	....	....	....	....	....	....	....	....	....	....	....	....	....	....	....	....	....	....
1982-83	**Philadelphia Flyers**	**NHL**	**3**	**1**	**1**	**2**	**1**	**1**	**2**	**0**	**1**	**0**	**0**	**7**	**14.3**	**5**	**3**	**3**	**0**	**–1**	....	....	....	....	....	....	....	....
	Maine Mariners	AHL	76	29	54	83	....	....	....	10	....	....	....	....	....	....	....	....	....	....	17	9	5	14	0	....	....	....
1983-84	Springfield Indians	AHL	7	1	5	6	....	....	....	2	....	....	....	....	....	....	....	....	....	....	....	....	....	....	....	....	....	....
	Pittsburgh Penguins	**NHL**	**50**	**18**	**20**	**38**	**14**	**14**	**28**	**9**	**7**	**1**	**2**	**75**	**24.0**	**62**	**21**	**57**	**9**	**–7**	....	....	....	....	....	....	....	....
	Baltimore Skipjacks	AHL	4	0	5	5	....	....	....	2	....	....	....	....	....	....	....	....	....	....	....	....	....	....	....	....	....	....
1984-85	**Pittsburgh Penguins**	**NHL**	**45**	**7**	**15**	**22**	**6**	**10**	**16**	**10**	**1**	**0**	**1**	**58**	**12.1**	**38**	**7**	**45**	**0**	**–14**	....	....	....	....	....	....	....	....
	Baltimore Skipjacks	AHL	31	13	14	27	....	....	....	8	....	....	....	....	....	....	....	....	....	....	15	*10	8	18	0	....	....	....
1985-86	Maine Mariners	AHL	60	26	34	60	....	....	....	20	....	....	....	....	....	....	....	....	....	....	5	0	4	4	0	....	....	....

Season	Club	League	GP	G	A	Pts	AG	AA	APts	PIM	PP	SH	GW	S	%	TGF	PGF	TGA	PGA	+/–	GP	G	A	Pts	PIM	PP	SH	GW
			REGULAR SEASON																		PLAYOFFS							
1986-87	**New Jersey Devils**	**NHL**	**51**	**11**	**12**	**23**	**9**	**9**	**18**	**8**	**1**	**3**	**0**	**55**	**20.0**	**33**	**3**	**62**	**17**	**–15**	....	....	....	....	....	....	....	....
1987-88	**New Jersey Devils**	**NHL**	**45**	**8**	**14**	**22**	**7**	**10**	**17**	**14**	**2**	**1**	**3**	**61**	**13.1**	**33**	**5**	**42**	**15**	**1**	**4**	**0**	**1**	**1**	**4**	**0**	**0**	**0**
	Utica Devils	AHL	9	5	8	13	....	....	....	4	....	....	....	....	....	....	....	....	....	....	....	....	....	....	....	....	....	....
1988-89	**Boston Bruins**	**NHL**	**71**	**13**	**22**	**35**	**11**	**16**	**27**	**20**	**2**	**0**	**3**	**98**	**13.3**	**63**	**16**	**59**	**16**	**4**	**10**	**0**	**2**	**2**	**0**	**0**	**0**	**0**
1989-90	**Boston Bruins**	**NHL**	**43**	**12**	**28**	**40**	**10**	**20**	**30**	**8**	**6**	**0**	**1**	**69**	**17.4**	**61**	**19**	**35**	**4**	**11**	**2**	**0**	**0**	**0**	**0**	**0**	**0**	**0**
1990-91	**Boston Bruins**	**NHL**	**40**	**2**	**9**	**11**	**2**	**7**	**9**	**8**	**0**	**0**	**0**	**28**	**7.1**	**27**	**5**	**26**	**0**	**–4**	....	....	....	....	....	....	....	....
	Maine Mariners	AHL	17	8	17	25	....	....	....	2	....	....	....	....	....	....	....	....	....	....	1	0	0	0	0	....	....	....
1991-92	**Boston Bruins**	**NHL**	**23**	**10**	**17**	**27**	**9**	**13**	**22**	**2**	**5**	**0**	**1**	**28**	**35.7**	**38**	**15**	**18**	**1**	**6**	....	....	....	....	....	....	....	....
	Maine Mariners	AHL	14	5	15	20	....	....	....	2	....	....	....	....	....	....	....	....	....	....	....	....	....	....	....	....	....	....
	United States	WC-A	6	1	1	2	....	....	....	0	....	....	....	....	....	....	....	....	....	....	....	....	....	....	....	....	....	....
1992-93	**Winnipeg Jets**	**NHL**	**12**	**0**	**2**	**2**	**0**	**1**	**1**	**2**	**0**	**0**	**0**	**5**	**0.0**	**4**	**0**	**6**	**2**	**0**	**1**	**1**	**1**	**2**	**0**	**0**	**0**	**0**
	Moncton Hawks	AHL	38	15	36	51	....	....	....	10	....	....	....	....	....	....	....	....	....	....	5	4	2	6	0	....	....	....
1993-94	**Winnipeg Jets**	**NHL**	**2**	**0**	**0**	**0**	**0**	**0**	**0**	**0**	**0**	**0**	**0**	**0**	**0.0**	**0**	**0**	**2**	**0**	**–2**	....	....	....	....	....	....	....	....
	Moncton Hawks	AHL	53	20	39	59	....	....	....	20	....	....	....	....	....	....	....	....	....	....	19	8	*19	*27	4	....	....	....
1994-95	Denver Grizzlies	IHL	58	15	35	50	....	....	....	16	....	....	....	....	....	....	....	....	....	....	16	5	*25	*30	2	....	....	....
1995-96	Utah Grizzlies	IHL	36	12	34	46	....	....	....	24	....	....	....	....	....	....	....	....	....	....	16	6	13	19	8	....	....	....
1996-97	Utah Grizzlies	IHL	1	1	0	1	....	....	....	0	....	....	....	....	....	....	....	....	....	....	7	1	0	1	0	....	....	....
	NHL Totals		**385**	**82**	**140**	**222**	**69**	**101**	**170**	**81**	**25**	**5**	**11**	**484**	**16.9**	**364**	**94**	**355**	**64**		**17**	**1**	**4**	**5**	**4**	**0**	**0**	**0**

ECAC First All-Star Team (1982) • NCAA East First All-American Team (1982) • AHL Second All-Star Team (1983)

Traded to **Pittsburgh** by **Philadelphia** with Ron Flockhart, Mark Taylor and Philadelphia's 1st (Roger Belanger) and 3rd (later traded to Vancouver - Vancouver selected Mike Stevens) round choices in 1984 Entry Draft for Rich Sutter and Pittsburgh's 2nd (Greg Smyth) and 3rd (David McLay) round choices in 1984 Entry Draft, October 23, 1983. Signed as a free agent by **New Jersey**, July 8, 1986. Claimed by **Boston** from **New Jersey** in Waiver Draft, October 3, 1988. Signed as a free agent by **Winnipeg**, November 11, 1992. Signed as a free agent by **NY Islanders**, July 27, 1994. • Retired following 1995-96 season to serve as colour commentater for Boston Bruins radio broadcasts. Signed as a free agent by **Utah** (IHL), March 20, 1996.

• BRIDGMAN, Mel

Melvin John C – L. 6′, 190 lbs. b: Trenton, Ont., 4/28/1955. Philadelphia's 1st, 1st overall, in 1975.

Season	Club	League	GP	G	A	Pts	AG	AA	APts	PIM	PP	SH	GW	S	%	TGF	PGF	TGA	PGA	+/–	GP	G	A	Pts	PIM	PP	SH	GW
1971-72	Nanaimo Clippers	BCJHL	STATISTICS NOT AVAILABLE																									
	Victoria Cougars	WCJHL	4	0	0	0	....	....	....	0	....	....	....	....	....	....	....	....	....	....	....	....	....	....	....	....	....	....
1972-73	Nanaimo Clippers	BCJHL	49	37	50	87	....	....	....	31	....	....	....	....	....	....	....	....	....	....	....	....	....	....	....	....	....	....
	Victoria Cougars	WCJHL	4	1	1	2	....	....	....	0	....	....	....	....	....	....	....	....	....	....	....	....	....	....	....	....	....	....
1973-74	Victoria Cougars	WCJHL	62	26	39	65	....	....	....	149	....	....	....	....	....	....	....	....	....	....	....	....	....	....	....	....	....	....
1974-75	Victoria Cougars	WCJHL	66	66	91	*157	....	....	....	175	....	....	....	....	....	....	....	....	....	....	12	12	6	18	34	....	....	....
	Canada	WJC-A	5	4	1	5	....	....	....	9	....	....	....	....	....	....	....	....	....	....	....	....	....	....	....	....	....	....
1975-76	**Philadelphia Flyers**	**NHL**	**80**	**23**	**27**	**50**	**20**	**20**	**40**	**86**	**5**	**1**	**2**	**166**	**13.9**	**64**	**10**	**34**	**2**	**22**	**16**	**6**	**8**	**14**	**31**	**0**	**0**	**2**
1976-77	**Philadelphia Flyers**	**NHL**	**70**	**19**	**38**	**57**	**17**	**29**	**46**	**120**	**4**	**0**	**2**	**136**	**14.0**	**77**	**10**	**39**	**7**	**35**	**7**	**1**	**0**	**1**	**8**	**0**	**1**	**0**
1977-78	**Philadelphia Flyers**	**NHL**	**76**	**16**	**32**	**48**	**15**	**25**	**40**	**203**	**3**	**1**	**2**	**154**	**10.4**	**71**	**11**	**51**	**17**	**26**	**12**	**1**	**7**	**8**	**36**	**0**	**0**	**1**
1978-79	**Philadelphia Flyers**	**NHL**	**76**	**24**	**35**	**59**	**21**	**25**	**46**	**184**	**0**	**0**	**3**	**157**	**15.3**	**77**	**12**	**65**	**14**	**14**	**8**	**1**	**2**	**3**	**17**	**0**	**0**	**0**
1979-80	**Philadelphia Flyers**	**NHL**	**74**	**16**	**31**	**47**	**14**	**23**	**37**	**136**	**2**	**2**	**2**	**145**	**11.0**	**60**	**9**	**61**	**23**	**13**	**19**	**2**	**9**	**11**	**70**	**0**	**0**	**0**
1980-81	**Philadelphia Flyers**	**NHL**	**77**	**14**	**37**	**51**	**11**	**25**	**36**	**195**	**1**	**0**	**3**	**138**	**10.1**	**73**	**10**	**68**	**33**	**28**	**12**	**2**	**4**	**6**	**39**	**0**	**0**	**0**
1981-82	**Philadelphia Flyers**	**NHL**	**9**	**7**	**5**	**12**	**6**	**3**	**9**	**47**	**3**	**0**	**1**	**22**	**31.8**	**14**	**4**	**18**	**8**	**0**	....	....	....	....	....	....	....	....
	Calgary Flames	**NHL**	**63**	**26**	**49**	**75**	**21**	**33**	**54**	**94**	**6**	**2**	**3**	**141**	**18.4**	**123**	**46**	**80**	**19**	**16**	**3**	**2**	**0**	**2**	**14**	**0**	**0**	**0**
1982-83	**Calgary Flames**	**NHL**	**79**	**19**	**31**	**50**	**16**	**21**	**37**	**103**	**9**	**0**	**1**	**131**	**14.5**	**93**	**38**	**68**	**12**	**–1**	**9**	**3**	**4**	**7**	**33**	**2**	**0**	**0**
1983-84	**New Jersey Devils**	**NHL**	**79**	**23**	**38**	**61**	**18**	**26**	**44**	**121**	**9**	**1**	**0**	**127**	**18.1**	**93**	**27**	**130**	**37**	**–27**	....	....	....	....	....	....	....	....
1984-85	**New Jersey Devils**	**NHL**	**80**	**22**	**39**	**61**	**18**	**27**	**45**	**105**	**5**	**3**	**3**	**143**	**15.4**	**92**	**29**	**117**	**38**	**–16**	....	....	....	....	....	....	....	....
1985-86	**New Jersey Devils**	**NHL**	**78**	**23**	**40**	**63**	**18**	**27**	**45**	**80**	**5**	**1**	**1**	**136**	**16.9**	**91**	**25**	**110**	**43**	**–1**	....	....	....	....	....	....	....	....
1986-87	**New Jersey Devils**	**NHL**	**51**	**8**	**31**	**39**	**7**	**23**	**30**	**80**	**1**	**1**	**1**	**73**	**11.0**	**56**	**11**	**68**	**15**	**–8**	....	....	....	....	....	....	....	....
	Detroit Red Wings	**NHL**	**13**	**2**	**2**	**4**	**2**	**1**	**3**	**19**	**0**	**1**	**1**	**13**	**15.4**	**8**	**0**	**14**	**7**	**1**	**16**	**5**	**2**	**7**	**28**	**0**	**1**	**1**
1987-88	**Detroit Red Wings**	**NHL**	**57**	**6**	**11**	**17**	**5**	**8**	**13**	**42**	**0**	**0**	**1**	**40**	**15.0**	**26**	**1**	**25**	**4**	**4**	**16**	**4**	**1**	**5**	**12**	**0**	**0**	**0**
	Adirondack Red Wings	AHL	2	1	2	3	....	....	....	0	....	....	....	....	....	....	....	....	....	....	....	....	....	....	....	....	....	....
1988-89	HC Sierre	Switz-2	STATISTICS NOT AVAILABLE																									
	Vancouver Canucks	**NHL**	**15**	**4**	**3**	**7**	**3**	**2**	**5**	**10**	**2**	**0**	**0**	**17**	**23.5**	**10**	**5**	**11**	**2**	**–4**	**7**	**1**	**2**	**3**	**10**	**1**	**0**	**0**
	NHL Totals		**977**	**252**	**449**	**701**	**212**	**318**	**530**	**1625**	**55**	**13**	**26**	**1739**	**14.5**	**1028**	**248**	**959**	**281**		**125**	**28**	**39**	**67**	**298**	**3**	**2**	**4**

WCJHL First All-Star Team (1975)

Traded to **Calgary** by **Philadelphia** for Brad Marsh, November 11, 1981. Traded to **New Jersey** by **Calgary** with Phil Russell for Steve Tambellini and Joel Quenneville, June 20, 1983. Traded to **Detroit** by **New Jersey** for Chris Cichocki and Detroit's 3rd round choice (later traded to Buffalo — Buffalo selected Andrew McVicar) in 1987 Entry Draft, March 9, 1987. Signed as a free agent by **Vancouver**, October 4, 1988.

• BRIERE, Daniel

C – R. 5′9″, 185 lbs. b: Gatineau, Que., 10/6/1977. Phoenix's 2nd, 24th overall, in 1996.

Season	Club	League	GP	G	A	Pts	AG	AA	APts	PIM	PP	SH	GW	S	%	TGF	PGF	TGA	PGA	+/–	GP	G	A	Pts	PIM	PP	SH	GW
1992-93	D'Abitiibi Forestiers	QAAA	42	24	30	54	....	....	....		....	....	....	....	....	....	....	....	....	....	....	....	....	....	....	....	....	....
1993-94	Gatineau L'intrepide	QAAA	44	56	47	103	....	....	....	56	....	....	....	....	....	....	....	....	....	....	....	....	....	....	....	....	....	....
1994-95	Drummondville Voltigeurs	QMJHL	72	51	72	123	....	....	....	54	....	....	....	....	....	....	....	....	....	....	4	2	3	5	2	....	....	....
1995-96	Drummondville Voltigeurs	QMJHL	67	*67	*96	*163	....	....	....	84	....	....	....	....	....	....	....	....	....	....	6	6	12	18	8	....	....	....
1996-97	Drummondville Voltigeurs	QMJHL	59	52	78	130	....	....	....	94	....	....	....	....	....	....	....	....	....	....	8	7	7	14	14	....	....	....
	Canada	WJC-A	7	2	4	6	....	....	....	4	....	....	....	....	....	....	....	....	....	....	....	....	....	....	....	....	....	....
1997-98	**Phoenix Coyotes**	**NHL**	**5**	**1**	**0**	**1**	**1**	**0**	**1**	**2**	**0**	**0**	**0**	**4**	**25.0**	**1**	**0**	**0**	**0**	**1**	....	....	....	....	....	....	....	....
	Springfield Falcons	AHL	68	36	56	92	....	....	....	42	....	....	....	....	....	....	....	....	....	....	4	1	2	3	4	....	....	....
1998-99	**Phoenix Coyotes**	**NHL**	**64**	**8**	**14**	**22**	**9**	**13**	**22**	**30**	**2**	**0**	**2**	**90**	**8.9**	**30**	**6**	**27**	**0**	**–3**	....	....	....	....	....	....	....	....
	Las Vegas Thunder	IHL	1	1	1	2	....	....	....	0	....	....	....	....	....	....	....	....	....	....	....	....	....	....	....	....	....	....
	Springfield Falcons	AHL	13	2	6	8	....	....	....	20	....	....	....	....	....	....	....	....	....	....	3	0	1	1	2	....	....	....
99-2000	**Phoenix Coyotes**	**NHL**	**13**	**1**	**1**	**2**	**1**	**1**	**2**	**0**	**0**	**0**	**0**	**9**	**11.1**	**4**	**1**	**3**	**0**	**0**	**1**	**0**	**0**	**0**	**0**	**0**	**0**	**0**
	Springfield Falcons	AHL	58	29	42	71	....	....	....	56	....	....	....	....	....	....	....	....	....	....	....	....	....	....	....	....	....	....
	NHL Totals		**82**	**10**	**15**	**25**	**11**	**14**	**25**	**32**	**2**	**0**	**2**	**103**	**9.7**	**35**	**7**	**30**	**0**		**1**	**0**	**0**	**0**	**0**	**0**	**0**	**0**

QMJHL Second All-Star Team (1996, 1997) • AHL First All-Star Team (1998) • Won Dudley "Red" Garrett Memorial Trophy (Top Rookie - AHL) (1998)

• BRIERE, Michel

Michel Edouard C – L. 5′10″, 165 lbs. b: Shawinigan Falls, Que., 10/21/1949 d: 4/13/1971. Pittsburgh's 2nd, 26th overall, in 1969.

Season	Club	League	GP	G	A	Pts	AG	AA	APts	PIM	PP	SH	GW	S	%	TGF	PGF	TGA	PGA	+/–	GP	G	A	Pts	PIM	PP	SH	GW
1967-68	Shawinigan Bruins	QJHL	50	54	*105	*159	....	....	....	....	....	....	....	....	....	....	....	....	....	....	12	11	16	27	8	....	....	....
1968-69	Shawinigan Bruins	QJHL	50	75	86	*161	....	....	....	31	....	....	....	....	....	....	....	....	....	....	....	....	....	....	....	....	....	....
	Sorel Black Hawks	Mem-Cup	....	....	....	....	....	....	....	....	....	....	....	....	....	....	....	....	....	....	....	....	....	....	....	....	....	....
1969-70	**Pittsburgh Penguins**	**NHL**	**76**	**12**	**32**	**44**	**13**	**30**	**43**	**20**	**4**	**0**	**3**	**223**	**5.4**	**56**	**21**	**52**	**2**	**–15**	**10**	**5**	**3**	**8**	**17**	**1**	**3**	**0**
	NHL Totals		**76**	**12**	**32**	**44**	**13**	**30**	**43**	**20**	**4**	**0**	**3**	**223**	**5.4**	**56**	**21**	**52**	**2**		**10**	**5**	**3**	**8**	**17**	**1**	**3**	**0**

QJHL Second All-Star Team (1968) • QJHL First All-Star Team (1969) • Died on April 13, 1971 of injuries suffered in automobile accident originally suffered on May 15, 1970 .

• BRIGLEY, Travis

LW – L. 6′1″, 195 lbs. b: Coronation, Alta., 6/16/1977. Calgary's 2nd, 39th overall, in 1996.

Season	Club	League	GP	G	A	Pts	AG	AA	APts	PIM	PP	SH	GW	S	%	TGF	PGF	TGA	PGA	+/–	GP	G	A	Pts	PIM	PP	SH	GW
1992-93	Leduc Oil Barons	AAHA	32	36	24	60	....	....	....	56	....	....	....	....	....	....	....	....	....	....	....	....	....	....	....	....	....	....
1993-94	Leduc Oil Barons	AAHA	34	29	44	73	....	....	....	141	....	....	....	....	....	....	....	....	....	....	....	....	....	....	....	....	....	....
	Lethbridge Hurricanes	WHL	1	0	0	0	....	....	....	0	....	....	....	....	....	....	....	....	....	....	....	....	....	....	....	....	....	....
1994-95	Lethbridge Hurricanes	WHL	64	14	18	32	....	....	....	14	....	....	....	....	....	....	....	....	....	....	....	....	....	....	....	....	....	....
1995-96	Lethbridge Hurricanes	WHL	69	34	43	77	....	....	....	94	....	....	....	....	....	....	....	....	....	....	4	2	3	5	8	....	....	....
1996-97	Lethbridge Hurricanes	WHL	71	43	47	90	....	....	....	56	....	....	....	....	....	....	....	....	....	....	19	9	9	18	31	....	....	....
	Lethbridge Hurricanes	Mem-Cup	5	1	3	4	....	....	....	4	....	....	....	....	....	....	....	....	....	....	....	....	....	....	....	....	....	....
1997-98	**Calgary Flames**	**NHL**	**2**	**0**	**0**	**0**	**0**	**0**	**0**	**2**	**0**	**0**	**0**	**1**	**0.0**	**0**	**0**	**1**	**1**	**0**	....	....	....	....	....	....	....	....
	Saint John Flames	AHL	79	17	15	32	....	....	....	28	....	....	....	....	....	....	....	....	....	....	8	0	0	0	0	....	....	....
1998-99	Saint John Flames	AHL	74	15	35	50	....	....	....	48	....	....	....	....	....	....	....	....	....	....	7	3	1	4	2	....	....	....

			REGULAR SEASON																		PLAYOFFS							
Season	Club	League	GP	G	A	Pts	AG	AA	APts	PIM	PP	SH	GW	S	%	TGF	PGF	TGA	PGA	+/–	GP	G	A	Pts	PIM	PP	SH	GW
99-2000	**Calgary Flames**	**NHL**	**17**	**0**	**2**	**2**	**0**	**2**	**2**	**4**	**0**	**0**	**0**	**17**	**0.0**	**2**	**0**	**12**	**4**	**–6**	....	....	....	....	....	....	....	....
	Saint John Flames	AHL	9	3	1	4	....	....	....	4	....	....	....	....	....	....	....	....	....	....	....	....	....	....	....	....	....	....
	Detroit Vipers	IHL	29	6	10	16	....	....	....	24	....	....	....	....	....	....	....	....	....	....	....	....	....	....	....	....	....	....
	Philadelphia Phantoms	AHL	15	2	2	4	....	....	....	15	....	....	....	....	....	....	....	....	....	....	5	1	0	1	4	....	....	....
	NHL Totals		**19**	**0**	**2**	**2**	**0**	**2**	**2**	**6**	**0**	**0**	**0**	**18**	**0.0**	**2**	**0**	**13**	**5**		....	....	....	....	....	....	....	....

Traded to **Philadelphia** by **Calgary** with Calgary's 6th round choice in 2001 Entry Draft for Marc Bureau, March 6, 2000.

• BRIMANIS, Aris

Aris A. D – R. 6'3", 210 lbs. b: Cleveland, OH, 3/14/1972. Philadelphia's 3rd, 86th overall, in 1991.

Season	Club	League	GP	G	A	Pts	AG	AA	APts	PIM	PP	SH	GW	S	%	TGF	PGF	TGA	PGA	+/–	GP	G	A	Pts	PIM	PP	SH	GW
1988-89	Culver Academy Eagles	Hi-School	38	10	13	23	....	....	....	24	....	....	....	....	....	....	....	....	....	....	....	....	....	....	....	....	....	....
1989-90	Culver Academy Eagles	Hi-School	37	15	10	25	....	....	....	52	....	....	....	....	....	....	....	....	....	....	....	....	....	....	....	....	....	....
1990-91	Bowling Green University	CCHA	38	3	6	9	....	....	....	42	....	....	....	....	....	....	....	....	....	....	....	....	....	....	....	....	....	....
1991-92	Bowling Green University	CCHA	32	2	9	11	....	....	....	38	....	....	....	....	....	....	....	....	....	....	....	....	....	....	....	....	....	....
1992-93	Brandon Wheat Kings	WHL	71	8	50	58	....	....	....	110	....	....	....	....	....	....	....	....	....	....	4	2	1	3	7	....	....	....
1993-94	**Philadelphia Flyers**	**NHL**	**1**	**0**	**0**	**0**	**0**	**0**	**0**	**0**	**0**	**0**	**0**	**1**	**0.0**	**1**	**0**	**2**	**0**	**–1**	....	....	....	....	....	....	....	....
	Hershey Bears	AHL	75	8	15	23	....	....	....	65	....	....	....	....	....	....	....	....	....	....	11	2	3	5	12	....	....	....
1994-95	Hershey Bears	AHL	76	8	17	25	....	....	....	68	....	....	....	....	....	....	....	....	....	....	6	1	1	2	14	....	....	....
1995-96	**Philadelphia Flyers**	**NHL**	**17**	**0**	**2**	**2**	**0**	**2**	**2**	**12**	**0**	**0**	**0**	**11**	**0.0**	**7**	**0**	**10**	**2**	**–1**	....	....	....	....	....	....	....	....
	Hershey Bears	AHL	54	9	22	31	....	....	....	64	....	....	....	....	....	....	....	....	....	....	5	1	2	3	4	....	....	....
1996-97	**Philadelphia Flyers**	**NHL**	**3**	**0**	**1**	**1**	**0**	**1**	**1**	**0**	**0**	**0**	**0**	**1**	**0.0**	**3**	**0**	**3**	**0**	**0**	....	....	....	....	....	....	....	....
	Philadelphia Phantoms	AHL	65	14	18	32	....	....	....	69	....	....	....	....	....	....	....	....	....	....	10	2	2	4	13	....	....	....
1997-98	Philadelphia Phantoms	AHL	30	1	11	12	....	....	....	26	....	....	....	....	....	....	....	....	....	....	....	....	....	....	....	....	....	....
	Michigan K-Wings	IHL	35	3	9	12	....	....	....	24	....	....	....	....	....	....	....	....	....	....	4	1	0	1	4	....	....	....
1998-99	Grand Rapids Griffins	IHL	66	16	21	37	....	....	....	70	....	....	....	....	....	....	....	....	....	....	....	....	....	....	....	....	....	....
	Fredericton Canadiens	AHL	8	2	4	6	....	....	....	6	....	....	....	....	....	....	....	....	....	....	15	3	10	13	18	....	....	....
99-2000	**New York Islanders**	**NHL**	**18**	**2**	**1**	**3**	**2**	**1**	**3**	**6**	**2**	**0**	**0**	**16**	**12.5**	**13**	**3**	**19**	**4**	**–5**	....	....	....	....	....	....	....	....
	Kansas City Blades	IHL	46	5	17	22	....	....	....	28	....	....	....	....	....	....	....	....	....	....	....	....	....	....	....	....	....	....
	Providence Bruins	AHL	7	0	2	2	....	....	....	2	....	....	....	....	....	....	....	....	....	....	14	3	4	7	10	....	....	....
	NHL Totals		**39**	**2**	**4**	**6**	**2**	**4**	**6**	**18**	**2**	**0**	**0**	**29**	**6.9**	**24**	**3**	**34**	**6**		....	....	....	....	....	....	....	....

Signed as a free agent by **NY Islanders**, August 16, 1999. Loaned to **Providence** (AHL) by **NY Islanders**, March 14, 2000.

• BRIND'AMOUR, Rod

Rod J. C – L. 6'1", 202 lbs. b: Ottawa, Ont., 8/9/1970. St. Louis' 1st, 9th overall, in 1988.

Season	Club	League	GP	G	A	Pts	AG	AA	APts	PIM	PP	SH	GW	S	%	TGF	PGF	TGA	PGA	+/–	GP	G	A	Pts	PIM	PP	SH	GW
1986-87	Notre Dame Midget Hounds	AAHA	33	38	50	88	....	....	....	66	....	....	....	....	....	....	....	....	....	....	....	....	....	....	....	....	....	....
1987-88	Notre Dame Hounds	SJHL	56	46	61	107	....	....	....	136	....	....	....	....	....	....	....	....	....	....	....	....	....	....	....	....	....	....
	Notre Dame Hounds	Cen-Cup	5	*5	*9	*14	....	....	....	4	....	....	....	....	....	....	....	....	....	....	....	....	....	....	....	....	....	....
1988-89	Michigan State Spartans	CCHA	42	27	32	59	....	....	....	63	....	....	....	....	....	....	....	....	....	....	....	....	....	....	....	....	....	....
	Canada	WJC-A	7	2	3	5	....	....	....	4	....	....	....	....	....	....	....	....	....	....	....	....	....	....	....	....	....	....
	St. Louis Blues	**NHL**	....	....	....	....	....	....	....	....	....	....	....	....	....	....	....	....	....	....	**5**	**2**	**0**	**2**	**4**	**0**	**0**	**0**
1989-90	**St. Louis Blues**	**NHL**	**79**	**26**	**35**	**61**	**22**	**25**	**47**	**46**	**10**	**0**	**1**	**160**	**16.3**	**103**	**29**	**59**	**8**	**23**	**12**	**5**	**8**	**13**	**6**	**1**	**0**	**0**
1990-91	**St. Louis Blues**	**NHL**	**78**	**17**	**32**	**49**	**16**	**24**	**40**	**93**	**4**	**0**	**3**	**169**	**10.1**	**97**	**32**	**65**	**2**	**2**	**13**	**2**	**5**	**7**	**10**	**1**	**0**	**0**
1991-92	**Philadelphia Flyers**	**NHL**	**80**	**33**	**44**	**77**	**30**	**33**	**63**	**100**	**8**	**4**	**5**	**202**	**16.3**	**112**	**35**	**116**	**36**	**–3**	....	....	....	....	....	....	....	....
	Canada	WC-A	6	1	1	2	....	....	....	4	....	....	....	....	....	....	....	....	....	....	....	....	....	....	....	....	....	....
1992-93	**Philadelphia Flyers**	**NHL**	**81**	**37**	**49**	**86**	**31**	**34**	**65**	**89**	**13**	**4**	**4**	**206**	**18.0**	**123**	**45**	**121**	**35**	**–8**	....	....	....	....	....	....	....	....
	Canada	WC-A	8	3	1	4	....	....	....	6	....	....	....	....	....	....	....	....	....	....	....	....	....	....	....	....	....	....
1993-94	**Philadelphia Flyers**	**NHL**	**84**	**35**	**62**	**97**	**33**	**48**	**81**	**85**	**14**	**1**	**4**	**230**	**15.2**	**131**	**42**	**137**	**39**	**–9**	....	....	....	....	....	....	....	....
	Canada	WC-A	8	4	2	6	....	....	....	2	....	....	....	....	....	....	....	....	....	....	....	....	....	....	....	....	....	....
1994-95	**Philadelphia Flyers**	**NHL**	**48**	**12**	**27**	**39**	**21**	**40**	**61**	**33**	**4**	**1**	**2**	**86**	**14.0**	**56**	**26**	**52**	**18**	**–4**	**15**	**6**	**9**	**15**	**8**	**2**	**1**	**1**
1995-96	**Philadelphia Flyers**	**NHL**	**82**	**26**	**61**	**87**	**26**	**50**	**76**	**110**	**4**	**4**	**5**	**213**	**12.2**	**114**	**43**	**94**	**43**	**20**	**12**	**2**	**5**	**7**	**6**	**1**	**0**	**0**
1996-97	Canada	W-Cup	7	1	2	3	....	....	....	0	....	....	....	....	....	....	....	....	....	....	....	....	....	....	....	....	....	....
	Philadelphia Flyers	**NHL**	**82**	**27**	**32**	**59**	**29**	**28**	**57**	**41**	**8**	**2**	**3**	**205**	**13.2**	**93**	**21**	**100**	**30**	**2**	**19**	***13**	**8**	**21**	**10**	**4**	**2**	**1**
1997-98	**Philadelphia Flyers**	**NHL**	**82**	**36**	**38**	**74**	**42**	**37**	**79**	**54**	**10**	**2**	**8**	**205**	**17.6**	**96**	**39**	**85**	**26**	**–2**	**5**	**2**	**2**	**4**	**7**	**0**	**0**	**0**
	Canada	Olympics	6	1	2	3	....	....	....	0	....	....	....	....	....	....	....	....	....	....	....	....	....	....	....	....	....	....
1998-99	**Philadelphia Flyers**	**NHL**	**82**	**24**	**50**	**74**	**28**	**48**	**76**	**47**	**10**	**0**	**3**	**191**	**12.6**	**95**	**46**	**70**	**24**	**3**	**6**	**1**	**3**	**4**	**0**	**0**	**0**	**0**
99-2000	**Philadelphia Flyers**	**NHL**	**12**	**5**	**3**	**8**	**6**	**3**	**9**	**4**	**4**	**0**	**0**	**26**	**19.2**	**12**	**7**	**9**	**3**	**–1**	....	....	....	....	....	....	....	....
	Carolina Hurricanes	**NHL**	**33**	**4**	**10**	**14**	**4**	**9**	**13**	**22**	**0**	**1**	**1**	**61**	**6.6**	**21**	**5**	**35**	**7**	**–12**	....	....	....	....	....	....	....	....
	NHL Totals		**823**	**282**	**443**	**725**	**288**	**379**	**667**	**724**	**89**	**19**	**39**	**1954**	**14.4**	**1053**	**370**	**943**	**271**		**87**	**33**	**40**	**73**	**51**	**9**	**3**	**2**

Centennial Cup All-Star Team (1988) • NHL All-Rookie Team (1990) • Played in NHL All-Star Game (1992)

Traded to **Philadelphia** by **St. Louis** with Dan Quinn for Ron Sutter and Murray Baron, September 22, 1991. Traded to **Carolina** by **Philadelphia** with Jean-Marc Pelletier and Philadelphia's 2nd round choice (later traded to Colorado - Colorado selected Argis Saviels) in 2000 Entry Draft for Keith Primeau and Carolina's 5th round choice (later traded to NY Islanders - NY Islanders selected Kristofer Ottoson) in 2000 Entry Draft, January 23, 2000.

• BRINDLEY, Doug

Douglas Allen LW/C – L. 6'1", 175 lbs. b: Walkerton, Ont., 6/8/1949. Toronto's 2nd, 20th overall, in 1969.

Season	Club	League	GP	G	A	Pts	AG	AA	APts	PIM	PP	SH	GW	S	%	TGF	PGF	TGA	PGA	+/–	GP	G	A	Pts	PIM	PP	SH	GW
1967-68	Niagara Falls Flyers	OHA-Jr.	54	15	28	43	....	....	....	20	....	....	....	....	....	....	....	....	....	....	19	15	7	22	18	....	....	....
	Niagara Falls Flyers	Mem-Cup	10	6	2	8	....	....	....	6	....	....	....	....	....	....	....	....	....	....	....	....	....	....	....	....	....	....
1968-69	Niagara Falls Flyers	OHA-Jr.	54	40	37	77	....	....	....	62	....	....	....	....	....	....	....	....	....	....	14	12	6	22	16	....	....	....
1969-70	Tulsa Oilers	CHL	65	22	25	47	....	....	....	14	....	....	....	....	....	....	....	....	....	....	6	0	6	6	0	....	....	....
	Buffalo Bisons	AHL	....	....	....	....	....	....	....	....	....	....	....	....	....	....	....	....	....	....	1	0	1	1	0	....	....	....
1970-71	**Toronto Maple Leafs**	**NHL**	**3**	**0**	**0**	**0**	**0**	**0**	**0**	**0**	**0**	**0**	**0**	**0**	**0.0**	**0**	**0**	**0**	**0**	**0**	....	....	....	....	....	....	....	....
	Tulsa Oilers	CHL	65	29	38	67	....	....	....	17	....	....	....	....	....	....	....	....	....	....	....	....	....	....	....	....	....	....
1971-72	Rochester Americans	AHL	74	20	27	47	....	....	....	12	....	....	....	....	....	....	....	....	....	....	....	....	....	....	....	....	....	....
1972-73	Cleveland Crusaders	WHA	73	15	11	26	....	....	....	6	....	....	....	....	....	....	....	....	....	....	9	0	0	0	6	....	....	....
1973-74	Cleveland Crusaders	WHA	30	13	9	22	....	....	....	13	....	....	....	....	....	....	....	....	....	....	5	0	1	1	2	....	....	....
	Jacksonville Barons	AHL	50	19	14	33	....	....	....	65	....	....	....	....	....	....	....	....	....	....	....	....	....	....	....	....	....	....
1974-75	Mohawk Valley Comets	NAHL	71	28	44	72	....	....	....	26	....	....	....	....	....	....	....	....	....	....	....	....	....	....	....	....	....	....
1975-76	Syracuse Blazers	NAHL	70	43	58	101	....	....	....	34	....	....	....	....	....	....	....	....	....	....	8	0	8	8	4	....	....	....
	NHL Totals		**3**	**0**	**0**	**0**	**0**	**0**	**0**	**0**	**0**	**0**	**0**	**0**	**0.0**	**0**	**0**	**0**	**0**		....	....	....	....	....	....	....	....
	Other Major League Totals		103	28	20	48				19											14	0	1	1	8			

Traded to **Vancouver** by **Toronto** for Andre Hinse, September 27, 1971. Selected by **Alberta** (WHA) in 1972 WHA General Player Draft, February 12, 1972. WHA rights traded to **Cleveland** (WHA) by **Alberta** (WHA) for cash, August, 1972. Traded to **Indianapolis** (WHA) by **Cleveland** (WHA) for cash, August, 1974. Claimed by **Cleveland** (WHA) from **Indianapolis** (WHA) in WHA Intra-League Draft, June 19, 1975.

• BRISEBOIS, Patrice

D – R. 6'2", 204 lbs. b: Montreal, Que., 1/27/1971. Montreal's 2nd, 30th overall, in 1989.

Season	Club	League	GP	G	A	Pts	AG	AA	APts	PIM	PP	SH	GW	S	%	TGF	PGF	TGA	PGA	+/–	GP	G	A	Pts	PIM	PP	SH	GW
1986-87	Montreal Bourassa	QAAA	39	15	19	34	....	....	....	66	....	....	....	....	....	....	....	....	....	....	....	....	....	....	....	....	....	....
1987-88	Laval Titan	QMJHL	48	10	34	44	....	....	....	95	....	....	....	....	....	....	....	....	....	....	6	0	2	2	2	....	....	....
1988-89	Laval Titan	QMJHL	50	20	45	65	....	....	....	95	....	....	....	....	....	....	....	....	....	....	17	8	14	22	45	....	....	....
	Laval Titan	Mem-Cup	4	2	2	4	....	....	....	6	....	....	....	....	....	....	....	....	....	....	....	....	....	....	....	....	....	....
1989-90	Laval Titan	QMJHL	56	18	70	88	....	....	....	108	....	....	....	....	....	....	....	....	....	....	13	7	9	16	26	....	....	....
	Canada	WJC-A	7	2	2	4	....	....	....	6	....	....	....	....	....	....	....	....	....	....	....	....	....	....	....	....	....	....
	Laval Titan	Mem-Cup	4	0	4	4	....	....	....	6	....	....	....	....	....	....	....	....	....	....	....	....	....	....	....	....	....	....
1990-91	Drummondville Voltigeurs	QMJHL	54	17	44	61	....	....	....	72	....	....	....	....	....	....	....	....	....	....	14	6	18	24	49	....	....	....
	Canada	WJC-A	7	1	6	7	....	....	....	2	....	....	....	....	....	....	....	....	....	....	....	....	....	....	....	....	....	....
	Montreal Canadiens	**NHL**	**10**	**0**	**2**	**2**	**0**	**2**	**2**	**4**	**0**	**0**	**0**	**11**	**0.0**	**13**	**5**	**7**	**0**	**1**	....	....	....	....	....	....	....	....
	Drummondville Voltigeurs	Mem-Cup	5	2	1	3	....	....	....	10	....	....	....	....	....	....	....	....	....	....	....	....	....	....	....	....	....	....
1991-92	**Montreal Canadiens**	**NHL**	**26**	**2**	**8**	**10**	**2**	**6**	**8**	**20**	**0**	**0**	**1**	**37**	**5.4**	**41**	**16**	**22**	**6**	**9**	**11**	**2**	**4**	**6**	**6**	**1**	**0**	**1**
	Fredericton Canadiens	AHL	53	12	27	39	....	....	....	51	....	....	....	....	....	....	....	....	....	....	....	....	....	....	....	....	....	....
1992-93♦	**Montreal Canadiens**	**NHL**	**70**	**10**	**21**	**31**	**8**	**14**	**22**	**79**	**4**	**0**	**2**	**123**	**8.1**	**89**	**33**	**60**	**10**	**6**	**20**	**0**	**4**	**4**	**18**	**0**	**0**	**0**
1993-94	**Montreal Canadiens**	**NHL**	**53**	**2**	**21**	**23**	**2**	**16**	**18**	**63**	**1**	**0**	**0**	**71**	**2.8**	**55**	**17**	**41**	**8**	**5**	**7**	**0**	**4**	**4**	**6**	**0**	**0**	**0**
1994-95	**Montreal Canadiens**	**NHL**	**35**	**4**	**8**	**12**	**7**	**12**	**19**	**26**	**0**	**0**	**2**	**67**	**6.0**	**36**	**7**	**37**	**6**	**–2**	....	....	....	....	....	....	....	....
1995-96	**Montreal Canadiens**	**NHL**	**69**	**9**	**27**	**36**	**9**	**22**	**31**	**65**	**3**	**0**	**1**	**127**	**7.1**	**104**	**41**	**80**	**27**	**10**	**6**	**1**	**2**	**3**	**6**	**0**	**0**	**0**

			REGULAR SEASON																		PLAYOFFS							
Season	Club	League	GP	G	A	Pts	AG	AA	APts	PIM	PP	SH	GW	S	%	TGF	PGF	TGA	PGA	+/–	GP	G	A	Pts	PIM	PP	SH	GW
1996-97	**Montreal Canadiens**	**NHL**	49	2	13	15	2	12	14	24	0	0	1	72	2.8	49	13	58	15	–7	3	1	1	2	24	0	0	1
1997-98	**Montreal Canadiens**	**NHL**	79	10	27	37	12	26	38	67	5	0	1	125	8.0	92	27	71	22	16	10	1	0	1	0	0	0	0
1998-99	**Montreal Canadiens**	**NHL**	54	3	9	12	4	9	13	28	1	0	1	90	3.3	37	9	49	13	–8	....	....	....	....	....	....	....	....
99-2000	**Montreal Canadiens**	**NHL**	54	10	25	35	11	23	34	18	5	0	2	88	11.4	66	29	46	8	–1	....	....	....	....	....	....	....	....
	NHL Totals		499	52	161	213	57	142	199	394	19	0	11	811	6.4	582	197	471	115		57	5	15	20	60	1	0	2

QMJHL Second All-Star Team (1990) • Canadian Major Junior Defenseman of the Year (1991) • QMJHL First All-Star Team (1991) • Memorial Cup All-Star Team (1991)

• BRITZ, Greg

Gregory RW – L. 6′, 190 lbs. b: Buffalo, NY, 1/3/1961.

Season	Club	League	GP	G	A	Pts	AG	AA	APts	PIM	PP	SH	GW	S	%	TGF	PGF	TGA	PGA	+/–	GP	G	A	Pts	PIM	PP	SH	GW
1978-79	St. Michael's Buzzers	OHA-B	42	26	26	52	....	....	....	50	....	....	....	....	....	....	....	....	....	....	....	....	....	....	....	....	....	....
1979-80	Harvard University	ECAC	26	8	5	13	....	....	....	17	....	....	....	....	....	....	....	....	....	....	....	....	....	....	....	....	....	....
1980-81	Harvard University	ECAC	24	3	4	7	....	....	....	10	....	....	....	....	....	....	....	....	....	....	....	....	....	....	....	....	....	....
1981-82	Harvard University	ECAC	24	11	13	24	....	....	....	12	....	....	....	....	....	....	....	....	....	....	....	....	....	....	....	....	....	....
1982-83	Harvard University	ECAC	33	16	23	39	....	....	....	25	....	....	....	....	....	....	....	....	....	....	....	....	....	....	....	....	....	....
1983-84	**Toronto Maple Leafs**	**NHL**	6	0	0	0	0	0	0	2	0	0	0	1	0.0	1	0	2	0	–1	....	....	....	....	....	....	....	....
	St. Catharines Saints	AHL	44	23	16	39	....	....	....	25	....	....	....	....	....	....	....	....	....	....	7	1	0	1	0	....	....	....
1984-85	**Toronto Maple Leafs**	**NHL**	1	0	0	0	0	0	0	2	0	0	0	0	0.0	0	0	0	0	0	....	....	....	....	....	....	....	....
	St. Catharines Saints	AHL	74	15	17	32	....	....	....	31	....	....	....	....	....	....	....	....	....	....	....	....	....	....	....	....	....	....
1985-86	St. Catharines Saints	AHL	72	17	19	36	....	....	....	52	....	....	....	....	....	....	....	....	....	....	13	3	3	6	7	....	....	....
1986-87	**Hartford Whalers**	**NHL**	1	0	0	0	0	0	0	0	0	0	0	0	0.0	0	0	1	1	0	....	....	....	....	....	....	....	....
	Binghamton Whalers	AHL	74	25	16	41	....	....	....	66	....	....	....	....	....	....	....	....	....	....	13	3	3	6	6	....	....	....
	NHL Totals		8	0	0	0	0	0	0	4	0	0	0	1	0.0	1	0	3	1		....	....	....	....	....	....	....	....

Signed as a free agent by **Toronto**, November 2, 1983. Signed as a free agent by **Hartford**, November, 1986.

• BROCHU, Stephane

D – L. 6′, 185 lbs. b: Sherbrooke, Que., 8/15/1967. NY Rangers' 9th, 175th overall, in 1985.

Season	Club	League	GP	G	A	Pts	AG	AA	APts	PIM	PP	SH	GW	S	%	TGF	PGF	TGA	PGA	+/–	GP	G	A	Pts	PIM	PP	SH	GW
1983-84	Montreal L'est Cantonniers	QAAA	38	7	24	31	....	....	....	36	....	....	....	....	....	....	....	....	....	....	....	....	....	....	....	....	....	....
1984-85	Quebec Remparts	QMJHL	59	2	16	18	....	....	....	56	....	....	....	....	....	....	....	....	....	....	4	0	2	2	2	....	....	....
1985-86	St-Jean Castors	QMJHL	63	14	27	41	....	....	....	121	....	....	....	....	....	....	....	....	....	....	3	1	0	1	2	....	....	....
1986-87	St-Jean Castors	QMJHL	10	0	1	1	....	....	....	17	....	....	....	....	....	....	....	....	....	....	8	0	2	2	11	....	....	....
1987-88	St-Jean Castors	QMJHL	29	4	35	39	....	....	....	88	....	....	....	....	....	....	....	....	....	....	....	....	....	....	....	....	....	....
	Colorado Rangers	IHL	52	4	10	14	....	....	....	70	....	....	....	....	....	....	....	....	....	....	12	3	3	6	13	....	....	....
1988-89	**New York Rangers**	**NHL**	1	0	0	0	0	0	0	0	0	0	0	1	0.0	1	0	0	0	1	....	....	....	....	....	....	....	....
	Denver Rangers	IHL	67	5	14	19	....	....	....	109	....	....	....	....	....	....	....	....	....	....	3	0	0	0	0	....	....	....
1989-90	Flint Spirits	IHL	5	0	0	0	....	....	....	2	....	....	....	....	....	....	....	....	....	....	....	....	....	....	....	....	....	....
	Fort Wayne Komets	IHL	63	9	19	28	....	....	....	98	....	....	....	....	....	....	....	....	....	....	5	0	2	2	6	....	....	....
1990-91	Fort Wayne Komets	IHL	73	14	29	43	....	....	....	49	....	....	....	....	....	....	....	....	....	....	14	1	3	4	31	....	....	....
1991-92	Kansas City Blades	IHL	3	0	0	0	....	....	....	0	....	....	....	....	....	....	....	....	....	....	....	....	....	....	....	....	....	....
	Flint Bulldogs	ColHL	53	13	27	40	....	....	....	80	....	....	....	....	....	....	....	....	....	....	....	....	....	....	....	....	....	....
1992-93	Flint Bulldogs	ColHL	44	6	28	34	....	....	....	77	....	....	....	....	....	....	....	....	....	....	6	4	8	12	22	....	....	....
1993-94	Flint Generals	ColHL	54	8	32	40	....	....	....	116	....	....	....	....	....	....	....	....	....	....	10	1	4	5	2	....	....	....
1994-95	Flint Generals	ColHL	60	12	37	49	....	....	....	39	....	....	....	....	....	....	....	....	....	....	6	0	9	9	8	....	....	....
1995-96	Flint Generals	ColHL	68	4	41	45	....	....	....	68	....	....	....	....	....	....	....	....	....	....	15	5	12	17	18	....	....	....
1996-97	Detroit Vipers	IHL	1	0	0	0	....	....	....	2	....	....	....	....	....	....	....	....	....	....	....	....	....	....	....	....	....	....
	Adirondack Red Wings	AHL	18	0	8	8	....	....	....	12	....	....	....	....	....	....	....	....	....	....	....	....	....	....	....	....	....	....
	Flint Generals	ColHL	42	8	45	53	....	....	....	32	....	....	....	....	....	....	....	....	....	....	14	5	*20	*25	14	....	....	....
1997-98	Chicago Wolves	IHL	1	0	0	0	....	....	....	0	....	....	....	....	....	....	....	....	....	....	....	....	....	....	....	....	....	....
	Detroit Vipers	IHL	3	0	0	0	....	....	....	2	....	....	....	....	....	....	....	....	....	....	....	....	....	....	....	....	....	....
	Fort Wayne Komets	IHL	2	1	0	1	....	....	....	0	....	....	....	....	....	....	....	....	....	....	....	....	....	....	....	....	....	....
	Flint Generals	UHL	54	10	62	72	....	....	....	52	....	....	....	....	....	....	....	....	....	....	17	2	18	20	12	....	....	....
1998-99	Flint Generals	UHL	58	12	55	67	....	....	....	39	....	....	....	....	....	....	....	....	....	....	8	1	3	4	8	....	....	....
99-2000	Adirondack IceHawks	UHL	55	8	34	42	....	....	....	41	....	....	....	....	....	....	....	....	....	....	2	0	0	0	4	....	....	....
	NHL Totals		1	0	0	0	0	0	0	0	0	0	0	1	0.0	1	0	0	0		....	....	....	....	....	....	....	....

• BROOKE, Bob

Robert William C – R. 5′11″, 195 lbs. b: Melrose, MA, 12/18/1960. St. Louis' 3rd, 75th overall, in 1980.

Season	Club	League	GP	G	A	Pts	AG	AA	APts	PIM	PP	SH	GW	S	%	TGF	PGF	TGA	PGA	+/–	GP	G	A	Pts	PIM	PP	SH	GW
1978-79	Acton-Boxborough High	Hi-School	STATISTICS NOT AVAILABLE																									
1979-80	Yale University	ECAC	24	7	22	29	....	....	....	38	....	....	....	....	....	....	....	....	....	....	....	....	....	....	....	....	....	....
	United States	WJC-A	5	3	2	5	....	....	....	8	....	....	....	....	....	....	....	....	....	....	....	....	....	....	....	....	....	....
1980-81	Yale University	ECAC	27	12	30	42	....	....	....	59	....	....	....	....	....	....	....	....	....	....	....	....	....	....	....	....	....	....
1981-82	Yale University	ECAC	25	12	30	42	....	....	....	60	....	....	....	....	....	....	....	....	....	....	....	....	....	....	....	....	....	....
1982-83	Yale University	ECAC	21	10	27	37	....	....	....	48	....	....	....	....	....	....	....	....	....	....	....	....	....	....	....	....	....	....
1983-84	United States	Nat-Team	54	7	18	25	....	....	....	75	....	....	....	....	....	....	....	....	....	....	....	....	....	....	....	....	....	....
	United States	Olympics	6	1	1	2	....	....	....	10	....	....	....	....	....	....	....	....	....	....	....	....	....	....	....	....	....	....
	New York Rangers	**NHL**	9	1	2	3	1	1	2	4	0	0	0	10	10.0	5	0	5	1	1	5	0	0	0	7	0	0	0
1984-85	United States	Can-Cup	5	0	1	1	....	....	....	4	....	....	....	....	....	....	....	....	....	....	....	....	....	....	....	....	....	....
	New York Rangers	**NHL**	72	7	9	16	6	6	12	79	0	0	2	93	7.5	35	1	66	14	–18	3	0	0	0	8	0	0	0
	United States	WEC-A	10	0	1	1	....	....	....	14	....	....	....	....	....	....	....	....	....	....	....	....	....	....	....	....	....	....
1985-86	**New York Rangers**	**NHL**	79	24	20	44	19	13	32	111	6	2	1	178	13.5	75	18	92	41	6	16	6	9	15	28	0	2	2
1986-87	**New York Rangers**	**NHL**	15	3	5	8	3	4	7	20	0	0	0	24	12.5	17	6	22	8	–3	....	....	....	....	....	....	....	....
	Minnesota North Stars	**NHL**	65	10	18	28	9	13	22	78	1	1	0	114	8.8	45	6	75	30	–6	....	....	....	....	....	....	....	....
	United States	WEC-A	10	2	1	3	....	....	....	10	....	....	....	....	....	....	....	....	....	....	....	....	....	....	....	....	....	....
1987-88	United States	Can-Cup	5	1	0	1	....	....	....	4	....	....	....	....	....	....	....	....	....	....	....	....	....	....	....	....	....	....
	Minnesota North Stars	**NHL**	77	5	20	25	4	14	18	108	1	1	1	127	3.9	73	21	105	47	–6	....	....	....	....	....	....	....	....
1988-89	**Minnesota North Stars**	**NHL**	57	7	9	16	6	6	12	57	0	1	2	77	9.1	24	0	46	10	–12	5	3	0	3	2	0	0	0
1989-90	**Minnesota North Stars**	**NHL**	38	4	4	8	3	3	6	33	0	3	0	65	6.2	16	4	27	10	–5	....	....	....	....	....	....	....	....
	New Jersey Devils	**NHL**	35	8	10	18	7	7	14	30	0	0	1	44	18.2	26	0	34	11	3	5	0	0	0	14	0	0	0
	NHL Totals		447	69	97	166	58	67	125	520	8	8	7	732	9.4	316	56	472	172		34	9	9	18	59	0	2	2

ECAC First All-Star Team (1983) • NCAA East First All-American Team (1983)

Rights traded to **NY Rangers** by **St. Louis** with Larry Patey for Dave Barr, NY Rangers' 3rd round choice (Alan Perry) in 1984 Entry Draft and cash, March 5, 1984. Traded to **Minnesota** by **NY Rangers** with Minnesota's 4th round choice (previously acquired, Minnesota selected Jeffrey Stolp) in 1988 Entry Draft for Curt Giles, Tony McKegney and Minnesota's 2nd round choice (Troy Mallette) in 1988 Entry Draft, November 13, 1986. Traded to **New Jersey** by **Minnesota** for Aaron Broten, January 5, 1990. Traded to **Winnipeg** by **New Jersey** for Laurie Boschman, September 6, 1990. • Officially announced retirement on September 7, 1990.

• BROOKS, Gord

Gordon John RW – R. 5′8″, 168 lbs. b: Cobourg, Ont., 9/11/1950. St. Louis' 3rd, 51st overall, in 1970.

Season	Club	League	GP	G	A	Pts	AG	AA	APts	PIM	PP	SH	GW	S	%	TGF	PGF	TGA	PGA	+/–	GP	G	A	Pts	PIM	PP	SH	GW
1967-68	Cobourg Cougars	OHA-B	STATISTICS NOT AVAILABLE																									
1968-69	Hamilton Red Wings	OHA-Jr.	54	9	7	16	....	....	....	47	....	....	....	....	....	....	....	....	....	....	5	1	1	2	5	....	....	....
1969-70	Hamilton Red Wings	OHA-Jr.	21	6	5	11	....	....	....	32	....	....	....	....	....	....	....	....	....	....	....	....	....	....	....	....	....	....
	London Knights	OHA-Jr.	31	9	23	32	....	....	....	47	....	....	....	....	....	....	....	....	....	....	12	5	11	16	14	....	....	....
1970-71	Kansas City Blues	CHL	67	16	16	32	....	....	....	44	....	....	....	....	....	....	....	....	....	....	....	....	....	....	....	....	....	....
1971-72	**St. Louis Blues**	**NHL**	2	0	0	0	0	0	0	0	0	0	0	2	0.0	2	0	2	0	0	....	....	....	....	....	....	....	....
	Kansas City Blues	CHL	62	21	18	39	....	....	....	34	....	....	....	....	....	....	....	....	....	....	....	....	....	....	....	....	....	....
1972-73	Fort Worth Wings	CHL	23	10	16	26	....	....	....	22	....	....	....	....	....	....	....	....	....	....	3	0	0	0	0	....	....	....
1973-74	**St. Louis Blues**	**NHL**	30	6	8	14	6	7	13	12	0	0	1	51	11.8	18	1	18	1	0	....	....	....	....	....	....	....	....
	Denver Spurs	WHL	41	20	20	40	....	....	....	34	....	....	....	....	....	....	....	....	....	....	....	....	....	....	....	....	....	....
1974-75	**Washington Capitals**	**NHL**	38	1	10	11	1	7	8	25	1	0	0	79	1.3	15	5	33	4	–19	....	....	....	....	....	....	....	....
	Richmond Robins	AHL	15	3	4	7	....	....	....	8	....	....	....	....	....	....	....	....	....	....	3	0	0	0	2	....	....	....
1975-76	Philadelphia Firebirds	NAHL	66	39	54	93	....	....	....	46	....	....	....	....	....	....	....	....	....	....	16	15	17	32	4	....	....	....
1976-77	Philadelphia Firebirds	NAHL	74	65	59	124	....	....	....	37	....	....	....	....	....	....	....	....	....	....	4	1	5	6	4	....	....	....
1977-78	Philadelphia Firebirds	AHL	81	42	56	*98	....	....	....	40	....	....	....	....	....	....	....	....	....	....	4	0	0	0	2	....	....	....
1978-79	Philadelphia Firebirds	AHL	80	43	31	74	....	....	....	27	....	....	....	....	....	....	....	....	....	....	....	....	....	....	....	....	....	....
1979-80	Syracuse Firebirds	AHL	77	34	41	75	....	....	....	38	....	....	....	....	....	....	....	....	....	....	4	1	1	2	0	....	....	....

Season	Club	League	REGULAR SEASON																		PLAYOFFS							
			GP	G	A	Pts	AG	AA	APts	PIM	PP	SH	GW	S	%	TGF	PGF	TGA	PGA	+/–	GP	G	A	Pts	PIM	PP	SH	GW
1980-81	KAC Klagenfurt	Austria	13	13	13	26	....	....	....	12	....	....	....	....	....	....	....	....	....	....	....	....	....	....	....	....	....	....
	Saginaw Gears	IHL	39	17	25	42	....	....	....	4	....	....	....	....	....	....	....	....	....	....	13	8	9	17	6	....	....	....
1981-82	Saginaw Gears	IHL	82	49	64	113	....	....	....	35	....	....	....	....	....	....	....	....	....	....	14	*12	9	*21	0	....	....	....
1982-83	Saginaw Gears	IHL	21	15	9	24	....	....	....	6	....	....	....	....	....	....	....	....	....	....	....	....	....	....	....	....	....	....
1983-84	Toledo Goaldiggers	IHL	5	0	3	3	....	....	....	0	....	....	....	....	....	....	....	....	....	....	....	....	....	....	....	....	....	....
1984-85			OUT OF HOCKEY – RETIRED																									
1985-86	Petrolia Aces	OHA-Sr.	36	22	31	53	....	....	....	....	....	....	....	....	....	....	....	....	....	....	....	....	....	....	....	....	....	....
1986-87	Brantford Mott's Clamatos	OHA-Sr.	33	4	16	20	....	....	....	8	....	....	....	....	....	....	....	....	....	....	....	....	....	....	....	....	....	....
	NHL Totals		**70**	**7**	**18**	**25**	**7**	**14**	**21**	**37**	**1**	**0**	**1**	**132**	**5.3**	**35**	**6**	**53**	**5**		....	....	....	....	....	....	....	....

NAHL Second All-Star Team (1977) • AHL First All-Star Team (1978) • Won John B. Sollenberger Trophy (Top Scorer - AHL) (1978) • IHL First All-Star Team (1982)

Claimed by **Washington** from **St. Louis** in Expansion Draft, June 12, 1974.

• BROSSART, Willie

Wilfrid James D – L. 6', 190 lbs. b: Allan, Sask., 5/29/1949. Philadelphia's 3rd, 28th overall, in 1969.

Season	Club	League	GP	G	A	Pts	AG	AA	APts	PIM	PP	SH	GW	S	%	TGF	PGF	TGA	PGA	+/–	GP	G	A	Pts	PIM	PP	SH	GW
1966-67	Swift Current Broncos	X-Games	26	13	10	23	....	....	....	....	....	....	....	....	....	....	....	....	....	....	....	....	....	....	....	....	....	....
1967-68	Swift Current Broncos	WCJHL	59	12	34	46	....	....	....	199	....	....	....	....	....	....	....	....	....	....	....	....	....	....	....	....	....	....
1968-69	Swift Current–Estevan	WCJHL	62	8	27	35	....	....	....	94	....	....	....	....	....	....	....	....	....	....	10	1	3	4	14	....	....	....
1969-70	Quebec Aces	AHL	57	5	9	14	....	....	....	67	....	....	....	....	....	....	....	....	....	....	6	0	0	0	0	....	....	....
1970-71	**Philadelphia Flyers**	**NHL**	**1**	**0**	**0**	**0**	**0**	**0**	**0**	**0**	**0**	**0**	**0**	**3**	**0.0**	**1**	**1**	**2**	**0**	**–2**	....	....	....	....	....	....	....	....
	Quebec Aces	AHL	62	8	17	25	....	....	....	182	....	....	....	....	....	....	....	....	....	....	1	0	2	2	0	....	....	....
1971-72	**Philadelphia Flyers**	**NHL**	**42**	**0**	**4**	**4**	**0**	**3**	**3**	**12**	**0**	**0**	**0**	**42**	**0.0**	**18**	**1**	**29**	**5**	**–7**	....	....	....	....	....	....	....	....
	Richmond Robins	AHL	29	3	14	17	....	....	....	76	....	....	....	....	....	....	....	....	....	....	....	....	....	....	....	....	....	....
1972-73	**Philadelphia Flyers**	**NHL**	**4**	**0**	**1**	**1**	**0**	**1**	**1**	**0**	**0**	**0**	**0**	**6**	**0.0**	**2**	**1**	**7**	**1**	**–5**	....	....	....	....	....	....	....	....
	Richmond Robins	AHL	54	1	29	30	....	....	....	66	....	....	....	....	....	....	....	....	....	....	3	0	0	0	0	....	....	....
1973-74	**Toronto Maple Leafs**	**NHL**	**17**	**0**	**1**	**1**	**0**	**1**	**1**	**20**	**0**	**0**	**0**	**9**	**0.0**	**14**	**0**	**13**	**1**	**2**	**1**	**0**	**0**	**0**	**0**	**0**	**0**	**0**
1974-75	**Toronto Maple Leafs**	**NHL**	**4**	**0**	**0**	**0**	**0**	**0**	**0**	**2**	**0**	**0**	**0**	**1**	**0.0**	**2**	**0**	**3**	**1**	**0**	....	....	....	....	....	....	....	....
	Washington Capitals	**NHL**	**12**	**1**	**0**	**1**	**1**	**0**	**1**	**14**	**0**	**0**	**0**	**12**	**8.3**	**13**	**3**	**28**	**4**	**–14**	....	....	....	....	....	....	....	....
1975-76	**Washington Capitals**	**NHL**	**49**	**0**	**8**	**8**	**0**	**6**	**6**	**40**	**0**	**0**	**0**	**36**	**0.0**	**36**	**3**	**101**	**19**	**–49**	....	....	....	....	....	....	....	....
	Richmond Robins	AHL	30	2	7	9	....	....	....	22	....	....	....	....	....	....	....	....	....	....	8	0	3	3	2	....	....	....
1976-77	Richmond Wildcats	SHL	36	4	20	24	....	....	....	24	....	....	....	....	....	....	....	....	....	....	....	....	....	....	....	....	....	....
	Baltimore Clippers	SHL	8	0	4	4	....	....	....	0	....	....	....	....	....	....	....	....	....	....	....	....	....	....	....	....	....	....
	NHL Totals		**129**	**1**	**14**	**15**	**1**	**11**	**12**	**88**	**0**	**0**	**0**	**109**	**0.9**	**86**	**9**	**183**	**31**		**1**	**0**	**0**	**0**	**0**	**0**	**0**	**0**

Traded to **Toronto** by **Philadelphia** for cash, May 23, 1973. Traded to **Washington** by **Toronto** with Tim Ecclestone for Rod Seiling, November 2, 1974.

• BROTEN, Aaron

LW/C – L. 5'10", 180 lbs. b: Roseau, MN, 11/14/1960. Colorado's 5th, 106th overall, in 1980.

Season	Club	League	GP	G	A	Pts	AG	AA	APts	PIM	PP	SH	GW	S	%	TGF	PGF	TGA	PGA	+/–	GP	G	A	Pts	PIM	PP	SH	GW
1978-79	Roseau Rams	Hi-School	STATISTICS NOT AVAILABLE																									
	United States	WJC-A	5	4	3	7	....	....	....	0	....	....	....	....	....	....	....	....	....	....	....	....	....	....	....	....	....	....
1979-80	University of Minnesota	WCHA	41	25	47	72	....	....	....	8	....	....	....	....	....	....	....	....	....	....	....	....	....	....	....	....	....	....
1980-81	University of Minnesota	WCHA	45	*47	*59	*106	....	....	....	24	....	....	....	....	....	....	....	....	....	....	....	....	....	....	....	....	....	....
	United States	WEC-A	8	2	2	4	....	....	....	0	....	....	....	....	....	....	....	....	....	....	....	....	....	....	....	....	....	....
	Colorado Rockies	**NHL**	**2**	**0**	**0**	**0**	**0**	**0**	**0**	**0**	**0**	**0**	**0**	**1**	**0.0**	**0**	**0**	**0**	**0**	**0**	....	....	....	....	....	....	....	....
1981-82	**Colorado Rockies**	**NHL**	**58**	**15**	**24**	**39**	**12**	**16**	**28**	**6**	**5**	**1**	**5**	**67**	**22.4**	**61**	**21**	**53**	**2**	**–11**	....	....	....	....	....	....	....	....
	Fort Worth Texans	CHL	19	15	21	36	....	....	....	11	....	....	....	....	....	....	....	....	....	....	....	....	....	....	....	....	....	....
	United States	WEC-A	7	2	2	4	....	....	....	8	....	....	....	....	....	....	....	....	....	....	....	....	....	....	....	....	....	....
1982-83	**New Jersey Devils**	**NHL**	**73**	**16**	**39**	**55**	**13**	**27**	**40**	**28**	**5**	**1**	**1**	**126**	**12.7**	**87**	**44**	**83**	**20**	**–20**	....	....	....	....	....	....	....	....
	Wichita Wind	CHL	4	0	4	4	....	....	....	0	....	....	....	....	....	....	....	....	....	....	....	....	....	....	....	....	....	....
1983-84	**New Jersey Devils**	**NHL**	**80**	**13**	**23**	**36**	**10**	**16**	**26**	**36**	**3**	**0**	**1**	**102**	**12.7**	**60**	**19**	**73**	**4**	**–28**	....	....	....	....	....	....	....	....
1984-85	United States	Can-Cup	5	0	4	4	....	....	....	2	....	....	....	....	....	....	....	....	....	....	....	....	....	....	....	....	....	....
	New Jersey Devils	**NHL**	**80**	**22**	**35**	**57**	**18**	**24**	**42**	**38**	**10**	**0**	**2**	**170**	**12.9**	**75**	**28**	**68**	**3**	**–18**	....	....	....	....	....	....	....	....
	United States	WEC-A	10	0	1	1	....	....	....	8	....	....	....	....	....	....	....	....	....	....	....	....	....	....	....	....	....	....
1985-86	**New Jersey Devils**	**NHL**	**66**	**18**	**25**	**43**	**14**	**17**	**31**	**26**	**4**	**0**	**1**	**157**	**11.5**	**67**	**16**	**77**	**28**	**2**	....	....	....	....	....	....	....	....
	United States	WEC-A	10	2	6	8	....	....	....	14	....	....	....	....	....	....	....	....	....	....	....	....	....	....	....	....	....	....
1986-87	**New Jersey Devils**	**NHL**	**80**	**26**	**53**	**79**	**22**	**39**	**61**	**36**	**6**	**0**	**3**	**179**	**14.5**	**107**	**40**	**83**	**21**	**5**	....	....	....	....	....	....	....	....
	United States	WEC-A	10	5	6	11	....	....	....	6	....	....	....	....	....	....	....	....	....	....	....	....	....	....	....	....	....	....
1987-88	United States	Can-Cup	5	0	2	2	....	....	....	2	....	....	....	....	....	....	....	....	....	....	....	....	....	....	....	....	....	....
	New Jersey Devils	**NHL**	**80**	**26**	**57**	**83**	**22**	**41**	**63**	**80**	**7**	**2**	**4**	**180**	**14.4**	**125**	**49**	**67**	**11**	**20**	**20**	**5**	**11**	**16**	**20**	**3**	**0**	**1**
1988-89	**New Jersey Devils**	**NHL**	**80**	**16**	**43**	**59**	**14**	**30**	**44**	**81**	**4**	**0**	**2**	**178**	**9.0**	**99**	**40**	**98**	**32**	**–7**	....	....	....	....	....	....	....	....
1989-90	**New Jersey Devils**	**NHL**	**42**	**10**	**8**	**18**	**9**	**6**	**15**	**36**	**1**	**2**	**0**	**83**	**12.0**	**24**	**4**	**46**	**11**	**–15**	....	....	....	....	....	....	....	....
	Minnesota North Stars	**NHL**	**35**	**9**	**9**	**18**	**8**	**6**	**14**	**22**	**0**	**0**	**2**	**65**	**13.8**	**26**	**4**	**31**	**1**	**–8**	**7**	**0**	**5**	**5**	**8**	**0**	**0**	**0**
1990-91	Minnesota North Stars	Fr-Tour	3	1	0	1	....	....	....	2	....	....	....	....	....	....	....	....	....	....	....	....	....	....	....	....	....	....
	Quebec Nordiques	**NHL**	**20**	**5**	**4**	**9**	**5**	**3**	**8**	**6**	**1**	**0**	**0**	**40**	**12.5**	**13**	**2**	**30**	**16**	**–3**	....	....	....	....	....	....	....	....
	Toronto Maple Leafs	**NHL**	**27**	**6**	**4**	**10**	**5**	**3**	**8**	**32**	**0**	**0**	**1**	**45**	**13.3**	**16**	**1**	**10**	**7**	**12**	....	....	....	....	....	....	....	....
1991-92	**Winnipeg Jets**	**NHL**	**25**	**4**	**5**	**9**	**4**	**4**	**8**	**14**	**0**	**0**	**3**	**29**	**13.8**	**12**	**1**	**11**	**2**	**2**	**7**	**2**	**2**	**4**	**12**	**0**	**0**	**0**
	Moncton Hawks	AHL	4	0	2	2	....	....	....	0	....	....	....	....	....	....	....	....	....	....	....	....	....	....	....	....	....	....
1992-1998			OUT OF HOCKEY – RETIRED																									
1998-99	United States	WC-Q	3	0	0	0	....	....	....	0	....	....	....	....	....					....	....	....	....	....	....	....	....	....
99-2000	Roseau Rams	Hi-School	DID NOT PLAY – COACHING																									
	NHL Totals		**748**	**186**	**329**	**515**	**156**	**232**	**388**	**441**	**46**	**6**	**25**	**1422**	**13.1**	**772**	**269**	**730**	**158**		**34**	**7**	**18**	**25**	**40**	**3**	**0**	**1**

• Brother of Neal and Paul • WCHA First All-Star Team (1981) • NCAA Championship All-Tournament Team (1981)

Transferred to **New Jersey** after **Colorado** franchise relocated, June 30, 1982. Traded to **Minnesota** by **New Jersey** for Bob Brooke, January 5, 1990. Claimed by **Quebec** from **Minnesota** in Waiver Draft, October 1, 1990. Traded to **Toronto** by **Quebec** with Lucien DeBlois and Michel Petit for Scott Pearson and Toronto's 2nd round choices in 1991 (later traded to Washington—Washington selected Eric Lavigne) and 1992 (Toumas Gronman) Entry Drafts, November 17, 1990. Signed as a free agent by **Winnipeg**, January 21, 1992.

• BROTEN, Neal

Neal LaMoy C – L. 5'9", 175 lbs. b: Roseau, MN, 11/29/1959. Minnesota's 3rd, 42nd overall, in 1979.

Season	Club	League	GP	G	A	Pts	AG	AA	APts	PIM	PP	SH	GW	S	%	TGF	PGF	TGA	PGA	+/–	GP	G	A	Pts	PIM	PP	SH	GW
1977-78	Roseau Rams	Hi-School	STATISTICS NOT AVAILABLE																									
1978-79	University of Minnesota	WCHA	40	21	50	71	....	....	....	18	....	....	....	....	....	....	....	....	....	....	....	....	....	....	....	....	....	....
	United States	WJC-A	5	2	4	6	....	....	....	10	....	....	....	....	....	....	....	....	....	....	....	....	....	....	....	....	....	....
1979-80	United States	Nat-Team	55	25	30	55	....	....	....	20	....	....	....	....	....	....	....	....	....	....	....	....	....	....	....	....	....	....
	United States	Olympics	7	2	1	3	....	....	....	2	....	....	....	....	....	....	....	....	....	....	....	....	....	....	....	....	....	....
1980-81	University of Minnesota	WCHA	36	17	54	71	....	....	....	56	....	....	....	....	....	....	....	....	....	....	....	....	....	....	....	....	....	....
	Minnesota North Stars	**NHL**	**3**	**2**	**0**	**2**	**2**	**0**	**2**	**12**	**0**	**0**	**0**	**6**	**33.3**	**3**	**0**	**2**	**0**	**1**	**19**	**1**	**7**	**8**	**9**	**0**	**0**	**1**
1981-82	United States	Can-Cup	6	3	2	5	....	....	....	0	....	....	....	....	....	....	....	....	....	....	....	....	....	....	....	....	....	....
	Minnesota North Stars	**NHL**	**73**	**38**	**60**	**98**	**30**	**40**	**70**	**42**	**7**	**2**	**4**	**188**	**20.2**	**123**	**38**	**91**	**20**	**14**	**4**	**0**	**2**	**2**	**0**	**0**	**0**	**0**
1982-83	**Minnesota North Stars**	**NHL**	**79**	**32**	**45**	**77**	**26**	**31**	**57**	**43**	**8**	**2**	**4**	**165**	**19.4**	**115**	**37**	**62**	**8**	**24**	**9**	**1**	**6**	**7**	**10**	**1**	**0**	**0**
1983-84	**Minnesota North Stars**	**NHL**	**76**	**28**	**61**	**89**	**22**	**42**	**64**	**43**	**8**	**3**	**5**	**185**	**15.1**	**132**	**53**	**90**	**27**	**16**	**16**	**5**	**5**	**10**	**4**	**2**	**0**	**1**
1984-85	United States	Can-Cup	6	3	1	4	....	....	....	4	....	....	....	....	....	....	....	....	....	....	....	....	....	....	....	....	....	....
	Minnesota North Stars	**NHL**	**80**	**19**	**37**	**56**	**15**	**25**	**40**	**39**	**5**	**1**	**1**	**188**	**10.1**	**93**	**39**	**98**	**26**	**–18**	**9**	**2**	**5**	**7**	**10**	**0**	**0**	**0**
1985-86	**Minnesota North Stars**	**NHL**	**80**	**29**	**76**	**105**	**23**	**51**	**74**	**47**	**6**	**0**	**0**	**193**	**15.0**	**150**	**60**	**81**	**5**	**14**	**5**	**3**	**2**	**5**	**2**	**1**	**0**	**0**
1986-87	**Minnesota North Stars**	**NHL**	**46**	**18**	**35**	**53**	**16**	**25**	**41**	**33**	**5**	**1**	**4**	**112**	**16.1**	**85**	**37**	**47**	**11**	**12**	....	....	....	....	....	....	....	....
1987-88	**Minnesota North Stars**	**NHL**	**54**	**9**	**30**	**39**	**8**	**21**	**29**	**32**	**4**	**1**	**0**	**121**	**7.4**	**70**	**36**	**73**	**16**	**–23**	....	....	....	....	....	....	....	....
1988-89	**Minnesota North Stars**	**NHL**	**68**	**18**	**38**	**56**	**15**	**27**	**42**	**57**	**4**	**5**	**1**	**160**	**11.3**	**75**	**28**	**65**	**19**	**1**	**5**	**2**	**2**	**4**	**4**	**1**	**1**	**0**
1989-90	**Minnesota North Stars**	**NHL**	**80**	**23**	**62**	**85**	**20**	**45**	**65**	**45**	**9**	**1**	**4**	**212**	**10.8**	**123**	**55**	**111**	**27**	**–16**	**7**	**2**	**2**	**4**	**18**	**1**	**0**	**0**
	United States	WEC-A	8	1	5	6	....	....	....	4	....	....	....	....	....	....	....	....	....	....	....	....	....	....	....	....	....	....
1990-91	Minnesota North Stars	Fr-Tour	3	0	3	3	....	....	....	2	....	....	....	....	....	....	....	....	....	....	....	....	....	....	....	....	....	....
	Minnesota North Stars	**NHL**	**79**	**13**	**56**	**69**	**12**	**43**	**55**	**26**	**1**	**2**	**0**	**191**	**6.8**	**104**	**50**	**89**	**32**	**–3**	**23**	**9**	**13**	**22**	**6**	**2**	**1**	**0**
1991-92	BSC Preussen Berlin	Germany	8	3	5	8	....	....	....	2	....	....	....	....	....	....	....	....	....	....	....	....	....	....	....	....	....	....
	Minnesota North Stars	**NHL**	**76**	**8**	**26**	**34**	**7**	**20**	**27**	**16**	**4**	**1**	**1**	**119**	**6.7**	**62**	**32**	**82**	**37**	**–15**	**7**	**1**	**5**	**6**	**2**	**0**	**0**	**0**
1992-93	**Minnesota North Stars**	**NHL**	**82**	**12**	**21**	**33**	**10**	**14**	**24**	**22**	**0**	**3**	**3**	**123**	**9.8**	**57**	**5**	**94**	**49**	**7**	....	....	....	....	....	....	....	....
1993-94	**Dallas Stars**	**NHL**	**79**	**17**	**35**	**52**	**16**	**27**	**43**	**62**	**2**	**1**	**1**	**153**	**11.1**	**85**	**21**	**85**	**31**	**10**	**9**	**2**	**1**	**3**	**6**	**0**	**0**	**1**

			REGULAR SEASON																		PLAYOFFS							
Season	**Club**	**League**	**GP**	**G**	**A**	**Pts**	**AG**	**AA**	**APts**	**PIM**	**PP**	**SH**	**GW**	**S**	**%**	**TGF**	**PGF**	**TGA**	**PGA**	**+/–**	**GP**	**G**	**A**	**Pts**	**PIM**	**PP**	**SH**	**GW**
1994-95	**Dallas Stars**	**NHL**	**17**	**0**	**4**	**4**	**0**	**6**	**6**	**4**	**0**	**0**	**0**	**29**	**0.0**	**6**	**1**	**21**	**8**	**–8**	....	....	....	....	....	....	....	....
♦	**New Jersey Devils**	**NHL**	**30**	**8**	**20**	**28**	**14**	**30**	**44**	**20**	**2**	**0**	**3**	**43**	**18.6**	**34**	**7**	**26**	**8**	**9**	**20**	**7**	**12**	**19**	**6**	**1**	**0**	**4**
1995-96	**New Jersey Devils**	**NHL**	**55**	**7**	**16**	**23**	**7**	**13**	**20**	**14**	**1**	**1**	**1**	**73**	**9.6**	**42**	**15**	**53**	**23**	**–3**	....	....	....	....	....	....	....	....
1996-97	**New Jersey Devils**	**NHL**	**3**	**0**	**1**	**1**	**0**	**1**	**1**	**0**	**0**	**0**	**0**	**3**	**0.0**	**2**	**1**	**2**	**0**	**–1**	....	....	....	....	....	....	....	....
	Los Angeles Kings	**NHL**	**19**	**0**	**4**	**4**	**0**	**4**	**4**	**0**	**0**	**0**	**0**	**17**	**0.0**	**10**	**3**	**18**	**2**	**–9**	....	....	....	....	....	....	....	....
	Phoenix Roadrunners	IHL	11	3	3	6	....	....	....	4	....	....	....	....	....	....	....	....	....	....	....	....	....	....	....	....	....	....
	Dallas Stars	**NHL**	**20**	**8**	**7**	**15**	**8**	**6**	**14**	**12**	**1**	**1**	**2**	**35**	**22.9**	**15**	**1**	**13**	**5**	**6**	**2**	**0**	**1**	**1**	**0**	**0**	**0**	**0**
1997-98			OUT OF HOCKEY – RETIRED																									
1998-99	United States	WC-Q	3	3	3	6	....	....	....	2	....	....	....	....	....	....	....	....	....	....	....	....	....	....	....	....	....	....
	NHL Totals		**1099**	**289**	**634**	**923**	**251**	**471**	**722**	**569**	**67**	**25**	**34**	**2316**	**12.5**	**1386**	**519**	**1203**	**354**		**135**	**35**	**63**	**98**	**77**	**9**	**2**	**7**

• Brother of Aaron and Paul • WCHA First All-Star Team (1981) • NCAA West First All-American Team (1981) • Won Hobey Baker Memorial Award (Top U.S. Collegiate Player) (1981) • Won Lester Patrick Trophy (1998) • Played in NHL All-Star Game (1983, 1986)

Transferred to **Dallas** after **Minnesota** franchise relocated, June 9, 1993. Traded to **New Jersey** by **Dallas** for Corey Millen, February 27, 1995. Traded to **LA Kings** by **New Jersey** for future considerations, November 22, 1996. Claimed on waivers by **Dallas** from **LA Kings**, January 28, 1997.

• BROTEN, Paul

RW – R. 5'11", 188 lbs. b: Roseau, MN, 10/27/1965. NY Rangers' 3rd, 77th overall, in 1984.

Season	Club	League	GP	G	A	Pts	AG	AA	APts	PIM	PP	SH	GW	S	%	TGF	PGF	TGA	PGA	+/–	GP	G	A	Pts	PIM	PP	SH	GW
1983-84	Roseau Rams	Hi-School	26	26	29	55	....	....	....	4	....	....	....	....	....	....	....	....	....	....	....	....	....	....	....	....	....	....
1984-85	University of Minnesota	WCHA	44	8	8	16	....	....	....	26	....	....	....	....	....	....	....	....	....	....	....	....	....	....	....	....	....	....
1985-86	University of Minnesota	WCHA	38	6	16	22	....	....	....	24	....	....	....	....	....	....	....	....	....	....	....	....	....	....	....	....	....	....
1986-87	University of Minnesota	WCHA	48	17	22	39	....	....	....	52	....	....	....	....	....	....	....	....	....	....	....	....	....	....	....	....	....	....
1987-88	University of Minnesota	WCHA	38	18	21	39	....	....	....	42	....	....	....	....	....	....	....	....	....	....	....	....	....	....	....	....	....	....
1988-89	Denver Rangers	IHL	77	28	31	59	....	....	....	133	....	....	....	....	....	....	....	....	....	....	4	0	2	2	6	....	....	....
1989-90	**New York Rangers**	**NHL**	**32**	**5**	**3**	**8**	**4**	**2**	**6**	**26**	**0**	**0**	**0**	**43**	**11.6**	**10**	**0**	**23**	**9**	**–4**	**6**	**1**	**1**	**2**	**2**	**0**	**1**	**0**
	Flint Spirits	IHL	28	17	9	26	....	....	....	55	....	....	....	....	....	....	....	....	....	....	....	....	....	....	....	....	....	....
1990-91	**New York Rangers**	**NHL**	**28**	**4**	**6**	**10**	**4**	**5**	**9**	**18**	**0**	**0**	**0**	**34**	**11.8**	**15**	**0**	**13**	**5**	**7**	**5**	**0**	**0**	**0**	**2**	**0**	**0**	**0**
	Binghamton Rangers	AHL	8	2	2	4	....	....	....	4	....	....	....	....	....	....	....	....	....	....	....	....	....	....	....	....	....	....
1991-92	**New York Rangers**	**NHL**	**74**	**13**	**15**	**28**	**12**	**11**	**23**	**102**	**0**	**3**	**1**	**96**	**13.5**	**46**	**0**	**52**	**20**	**14**	**13**	**1**	**2**	**3**	**10**	**0**	**0**	**0**
1992-93	**New York Rangers**	**NHL**	**60**	**5**	**9**	**14**	**4**	**6**	**10**	**48**	**0**	**1**	**0**	**57**	**8.8**	**19**	**0**	**52**	**27**	**–6**	....	....	....	....	....	....	....	....
1993-94	**Dallas Stars**	**NHL**	**64**	**12**	**12**	**24**	**11**	**9**	**20**	**30**	**0**	**0**	**3**	**76**	**15.8**	**39**	**1**	**26**	**6**	**18**	**9**	**1**	**1**	**2**	**2**	**0**	**0**	**0**
1994-95	**Dallas Stars**	**NHL**	**47**	**7**	**9**	**16**	**12**	**13**	**25**	**36**	**0**	**0**	**0**	**67**	**10.4**	**27**	**2**	**37**	**5**	**–7**	**5**	**1**	**2**	**3**	**2**	**0**	**0**	**0**
1995-96	**St. Louis Blues**	**NHL**	**17**	**0**	**1**	**1**	**0**	**1**	**1**	**4**	**0**	**0**	**0**	**11**	**0.0**	**3**	**0**	**4**	**0**	**–1**	....	....	....	....	....	....	....	....
	Worcester IceCats	AHL	50	22	21	43	....	....	....	42	....	....	....	....	....	....	....	....	....	....	3	0	0	0	0	....	....	....
1996-97	Fort Wayne Komets	IHL	59	19	28	47	....	....	....	82	....	....	....	....	....	....	....	....	....	....	....	....	....	....	....	....	....	....
1997-98	Cincinnati Cyclones	IHL	81	9	12	21	....	....	....	80	....	....	....	....	....	....	....	....	....	....	9	3	1	4	8	....	....	....
1998-99	Berlin Capitals	Germany	50	8	15	23	....	....	....	100	....	....	....	....	....	....	....	....	....	....	....	....	....	....	....	....	....	....
	United States	WC-Q	3	0	0	0	....	....	....	2	....	....	....	....	....	....	....	....	....	....	....	....	....	....	....	....	....	....
	NHL Totals		**322**	**46**	**55**	**101**	**47**	**47**	**94**	**264**	**0**	**4**	**4**	**384**	**12.0**	**159**	**3**	**207**	**72**		**38**	**4**	**6**	**10**	**18**	**0**	**1**	**0**

Brother of Neal and Aaron

Claimed by **Dallas** from **NY Rangers** in Waiver Draft, October 3, 1993. Traded to **St. Louis** by **Dallas** for Guy Carbonneau, October 2, 1995. Signed as a free agent by **Cincinnati** (IHL), August 25, 1997.

• BROUSSEAU, Paul

RW – R. 6'2", 203 lbs. b: Pierrefonds, Que., 9/18/1973. Quebec's 2nd, 28th overall, in 1992.

Season	Club	League	GP	G	A	Pts	AG	AA	APts	PIM	PP	SH	GW	S	%	TGF	PGF	TGA	PGA	+/–	GP	G	A	Pts	PIM	PP	SH	GW
1988-89	Lac St-Louis Lions	QAAA	37	6	17	23	....	....	....	....	....	....	....	....	....	....	....	....	....	....	....	....	....	....	....	....	....	....
1989-90	Chicoutimi Sagueneens	QMJHL	57	17	24	41	....	....	....	32	....	....	....	....	....	....	....	....	....	....	7	0	3	3	0	....	....	....
1990-91	Trois-Rivieres Draveurs	QMJHL	67	30	66	96	....	....	....	48	....	....	....	....	....	....	....	....	....	....	6	3	2	5	2	....	....	....
1991-92	Hull Olympiques	QMJHL	57	35	61	96	....	....	....	54	....	....	....	....	....	....	....	....	....	....	6	3	5	8	10	....	....	....
1992-93	Hull Olympiques	QMJHL	59	27	48	75	....	....	....	49	....	....	....	....	....	....	....	....	....	....	10	7	8	15	6	....	....	....
1993-94	Cornwall Aces	AHL	69	18	26	44	....	....	....	35	....	....	....	....	....	....	....	....	....	....	1	0	0	0	0	....	....	....
1994-95	Cornwall Aces	AHL	57	19	17	36	....	....	....	29	....	....	....	....	....	....	....	....	....	....	7	2	1	3	10	....	....	....
1995-96	**Colorado Avalanche**	**NHL**	**8**	**1**	**1**	**2**	**1**	**1**	**2**	**2**	**0**	**0**	**0**	**10**	**10.0**	**4**	**0**	**3**	**0**	**1**	....	....	....	....	....	....	....	....
	Cornwall Aces	AHL	63	21	22	43	....	....	....	60	....	....	....	....	....	....	....	....	....	....	8	4	0	4	2	....	....	....
1996-97	**Tampa Bay Lightning**	**NHL**	**6**	**0**	**0**	**0**	**0**	**0**	**0**	**0**	**0**	**0**	**0**	**3**	**0.0**	**0**	**0**	**4**	**0**	**–4**	....	....	....	....	....	....	....	....
	Adirondack Red Wings	AHL	66	35	31	66	....	....	....	25	....	....	....	....	....	....	....	....	....	....	4	1	2	3	0	....	....	....
1997-98	**Tampa Bay Lightning**	**NHL**	**11**	**0**	**2**	**2**	**0**	**2**	**2**	**27**	**0**	**0**	**0**	**6**	**0.0**	**4**	**0**	**4**	**0**	**0**	....	....	....	....	....	....	....	....
	Adirondack Red Wings	AHL	67	45	20	65	....	....	....	18	....	....	....	....	....	....	....	....	....	....	3	1	1	2	0	....	....	....
1998-99	Milwaukee Admirals	IHL	5	1	1	2	....	....	....	2	....	....	....	....	....	....	....	....	....	....	....	....	....	....	....	....	....	....
	Hershey Bears	AHL	39	11	21	32	....	....	....	15	....	....	....	....	....	....	....	....	....	....	5	1	1	2	0	....	....	....
99-2000	Louisville Panthers	AHL	36	19	24	43	....	....	....	10	....	....	....	....	....	....	....	....	....	....	4	1	1	2	12	....	....	....
	NHL Totals		**25**	**1**	**3**	**4**	**1**	**3**	**4**	**29**	**0**	**0**	**0**	**19**	**5.3**	**8**	**0**	**11**	**0**		....	....	....	....	....	....	....	....

AHL Second All-Star Team (1998)

Rights transferred to **Colorado** after **Quebec** franchise relocated, June 21, 1995. Signed as a free agent by **Tampa Bay**, September 10, 1996. Claimed by **Nashville** from **Tampa Bay** in Expansion Draft, June 26, 1998. Signed as a free agent by **Florida**, September 20, 1999. • Missed majority of the 1999-2000 season recovering from knee injury suffered in game vs. Rochester (AHL), January 8, 2000.

• BROWN, Arnie

Stewart Arnold D – L. 6'1", 185 lbs. b: Oshawa, Ont., 1/28/1942.

Season	Club	League	GP	G	A	Pts	AG	AA	APts	PIM	PP	SH	GW	S	%	TGF	PGF	TGA	PGA	+/–	GP	G	A	Pts	PIM	PP	SH	GW
1959-60	St. Michael's Majors	OHA-Jr.	48	2	5	7	....	....	....	112	....	....	....	....	....	....	....	....	....	....	10	0	2	2	14	....	....	....
1960-61	St. Michael's Majors	OHA-Jr.	47	7	11	18	....	....	....	110	....	....	....	....	....	....	....	....	....	....	20	6	9	15	60	....	....	....
	St. Michael's Majors	Mem-Cup	9	0	4	4	....	....	....	26	....	....	....	....	....	....	....	....	....	....	....	....	....	....	....	....	....	....
1961-62	Toronto Marlboros	MTJHL	19	7	10	17	....	....	....	70	....	....	....	....	....	....	....	....	....	....	7	0	8	8	23	....	....	....
	Rochester Americans	AHL	3	0	3	3	....	....	....	2	....	....	....	....	....	....	....	....	....	....	....	....	....	....	....	....	....	....
	Toronto Maple Leafs	**NHL**	**2**	**0**	**0**	**0**	**0**	**0**	**0**	**0**	....	....	....	....	....	....	....	....	....	....	....	....	....	....	....	....	....	....
1962-63	Rochester Americans	AHL	71	4	24	28	....	....	....	143	....	....	....	....	....	....	....	....	....	....	2	0	0	0	6	....	....	....
1963-64	**Toronto Maple Leafs**	**NHL**	**4**	**0**	**0**	**0**	**0**	**0**	**0**	**6**	....	....	....	....	....	....	....	....	....	....	....	....	....	....	....	....	....	....
	Rochester Americans	AHL	47	4	23	27	....	....	....	119	....	....	....	....	....	....	....	....	....	....	....	....	....	....	....	....	....	....
	Baltimore Clippers	AHL	11	0	3	3	....	....	....	8	....	....	....	....	....	....	....	....	....	....	....	....	....	....	....	....	....	....
1964-65	**New York Rangers**	**NHL**	**58**	**1**	**11**	**12**	**1**	**11**	**12**	**145**	....	....	....	....	....	....	....	....	....	....	....	....	....	....	....	....	....	....
1965-66	**New York Rangers**	**NHL**	**64**	**1**	**7**	**8**	**1**	**7**	**8**	**106**	....	....	....	....	....	....	....	....	....	....	....	....	....	....	....	....	....	....
1966-67	**New York Rangers**	**NHL**	**69**	**2**	**10**	**12**	**2**	**10**	**12**	**61**	....	....	....	....	....	....	....	....	....	....	**4**	**0**	**0**	**0**	**6**	**0**	**0**	**0**
1967-68	**New York Rangers**	**NHL**	**74**	**1**	**25**	**26**	**1**	**25**	**26**	**83**	**0**	**0**	**0**	**116**	**0.9**	**84**	**1**	**90**	**24**	**17**	**6**	**0**	**1**	**1**	**8**	**0**	**0**	**0**
1968-69	**New York Rangers**	**NHL**	**74**	**10**	**12**	**22**	**11**	**11**	**22**	**48**	**0**	**0**	**1**	**189**	**5.3**	**74**	**4**	**91**	**22**	**1**	**4**	**0**	**1**	**1**	**0**	**0**	**0**	**0**
1969-70	**New York Rangers**	**NHL**	**73**	**15**	**21**	**36**	**16**	**20**	**36**	**78**	**3**	**0**	**2**	**220**	**6.8**	**118**	**18**	**91**	**19**	**28**	**4**	**0**	**4**	**4**	**9**	**0**	**0**	**0**
1970-71	**New York Rangers**	**NHL**	**48**	**3**	**12**	**15**	**3**	**10**	**13**	**24**	**0**	**0**	**2**	**114**	**2.6**	**53**	**11**	**52**	**10**	**0**	....	....	....	....	....	....	....	....
	Detroit Red Wings	**NHL**	**27**	**2**	**6**	**8**	**2**	**5**	**7**	**30**	**0**	**0**	**1**	**57**	**3.5**	....	....	....	....	....	....	....	....	....	....	....	....	....
1971-72	**Detroit Red Wings**	**NHL**	**77**	**2**	**23**	**25**	**2**	**20**	**22**	**84**	**0**	**0**	**0**	**107**	**1.8**	**0**	**0**	**0**	**0**	**0**	....	....	....	....	....	....	....	....
1972-73	**New York Islanders**	**NHL**	**48**	**4**	**8**	**12**	**4**	**6**	**10**	**27**	**1**	**0**	**0**	**50**	**8.0**	**40**	**6**	**101**	**20**	**–47**	....	....	....	....	....	....	....	....
	Atlanta Flames	**NHL**	**15**	**1**	**0**	**1**	**1**	**0**	**1**	**17**	**0**	**0**	**0**	**13**	**7.7**	**6**	**0**	**17**	**1**	**–10**	....	....	....	....	....	....	....	....
1973-74	**Atlanta Flames**	**NHL**	**48**	**2**	**6**	**8**	**2**	**5**	**7**	**29**	**0**	**0**	**0**	**58**	**3.4**	**35**	**0**	**52**	**3**	**–14**	**4**	**0**	**0**	**0**	**0**	**0**	**0**	**0**
1974-75	Michigan-Baltimore Blades	WHA	50	3	4	7	....	....	....	27	....	....	....	....	....	....	....	....	....	....	....	....	....	....	....	....	....	....
	Vancouver Blazers	WHA	10	0	1	1	....	....	....	13	....	....	....	....	....	....	....	....	....	....	....	....	....	....	....	....	....	....
	NHL Totals		**681**	**44**	**141**	**185**	**46**	**130**	**176**	**738**	....	....	....	....	....	....	....	....	....	....	**22**	**0**	**6**	**6**	**23**	....	....	....
	Other Major League Totals		60	3	5	8	....	....	....	40	....	....	....	....	....	....	....	....	....	....	....	....	....	....	....	....	....	....

Traded to **NY Rangers** by **Toronto** with Rod Seiling, Dick Duff, Bob Nevin and Bill Collins for Andy Bathgate and Don McKenney, February 22, 1964. Traded to **Detroit** by **NY Rangers** with Mike Robitaille and Tom Miller for Bruce MacGregor and Larry Brown, February 2, 1971. Selected by **Chicago** (WHA) in 1972 WHA General Player Draft, February 12, 1972. Traded to **NY Islanders** by **Detroit** with Gerry Gray for Denis Dejordy and Don McLaughlin, October 4, 1972. Traded to **Atlanta** by **NY Islanders** for Ernie Hicke and future considerations (Billy MacMillan, May 29, 1973), February 13, 1973. WHA rights traded to **Michigan** (WHA) by **Chicago** (WHA) for cash, October, 1974. Signed as a free agent by **Vancouver** (WHA) after **Michigan-Baltimore** (WHA) franchise folded, March, 1975.

			REGULAR SEASON																		PLAYOFFS							
Season	Club	League	GP	G	A	Pts	AG	AA	APts	PIM	PP	SH	GW	S	%	TGF	PGF	TGA	PGA	+/–	GP	G	A	Pts	PIM	PP	SH	GW

• BROWN, Brad

D – R. 6'4", 218 lbs. b: Baie Verte, Nfld., 12/27/1975. Montreal's 1st, 18th overall, in 1994.

Season	Club	League	GP	G	A	Pts	AG	AA	APts	PIM	PP	SH	GW	S	%	TGF	PGF	TGA	PGA	+/–	GP	G	A	Pts	PIM	PP	SH	GW
1990-91	Toronto Red Wings	MTHL	80	15	45	60	....	....	....	105	....	....	....	....	....	....	....	....	....	....	....	....	....	....	....	....	....	....
	St. Michael's Buzzers	OJHL-B	2	0	0	0	....	....	....	0	....	....	....	....	....	....	....	....	....	....	....	....	....	....	....	....	....	....
1991-92	North Bay Centennials	OHL	49	2	9	11	....	....	....	170	....	....	....	....	....	....	....	....	....	....	18	0	6	6	43	....	....	....
1992-93	North Bay Centennials	OHL	61	4	9	13	....	....	....	228	....	....	....	....	....	....	....	....	....	....	2	0	2	2	13	....	....	....
1993-94	North Bay Centennials	OHL	66	8	24	32	....	....	....	196	....	....	....	....	....	....	....	....	....	....	18	3	12	15	33	....	....	....
	North Bay Centennials	Mem-Cup	3	0	0	0	....	....	....	21	....	....	....	....	....	....	....	....	....	....	....	....	....	....	....	....	....	....
1994-95	North Bay Centennials	OHL	64	8	38	46	....	....	....	172	....	....	....	....	....	....	....	....	....	....	6	1	4	5	8	....	....	....
1995-96	Barrie Colts	OHL	27	3	13	16	....	....	....	82	....	....	....	....	....	....	....	....	....	....	....	....	....	....	....	....	....	....
	Fredericton Canadiens	AHL	38	0	3	3	....	....	....	148	....	....	....	....	....	....	....	....	....	....	10	2	1	3	6	....	....	....
1996-97	**Montreal Canadiens**	**NHL**	**8**	**0**	**0**	**0**	**0**	**0**	**0**	**22**	**0**	**0**	**0**	**0**	**0.0**	**2**	**0**	**3**	**0**	**–1**	....	....	....	....	....	....	....	....
	Fredericton Canadiens	AHL	64	3	7	10	....	....	....	368	....	....	....	....	....	....	....	....	....	....	....	....	....	....	....	....	....	....
1997-98	Fredericton Canadiens	AHL	64	1	8	9	....	....	....	297	....	....	....	....	....	....	....	....	....	....	4	0	0	0	29	....	....	....
1998-99	**Montreal Canadiens**	**NHL**	**5**	**0**	**0**	**0**	**0**	**0**	**0**	**21**	**0**	**0**	**0**	**0**	**0.0**	**0**	**0**	**0**	**0**	**0**	....	....	....	....	....	....	....	....
	Chicago Blackhawks	**NHL**	**61**	**1**	**7**	**8**	**1**	**7**	**8**	**184**	**0**	**0**	**0**	**26**	**3.8**	**33**	**0**	**46**	**9**	**–4**	....	....	....	....	....	....	....	....
99-2000	**Chicago Blackhawks**	**NHL**	**57**	**0**	**9**	**9**	**0**	**8**	**8**	**134**	**0**	**0**	**0**	**15**	**0.0**	**27**	**1**	**37**	**10**	**–1**	....	....	....	....	....	....	....	....
	NHL Totals		**131**	**1**	**16**	**17**	**1**	**15**	**16**	**361**	**0**	**0**	**0**	**41**	**2.4**	**62**	**1**	**86**	**19**		....	....	....	....	....	....	....	....

Traded to **Chicago** by **Montreal** with Jocelyn Thibault and Dave Manson for Jeff Hackett, Eric Weinrich, Alain Nasreddine and Tampa Bay's 4th round choice (previously acquired, Montreal selected Chris Dyment) in 1999 Entry Draft, November 16, 1998.

• BROWN, Cam

Richard Cameron LW – L. 6'1", 210 lbs. b: Saskatoon, Sask., 5/15/1969.

Season	Club	League	GP	G	A	Pts	AG	AA	APts	PIM	PP	SH	GW	S	%	TGF	PGF	TGA	PGA	+/–	GP	G	A	Pts	PIM	PP	SH	GW
1986-87	Weyburn Red Wings	MJHL	64	8	19	27	....	....	....	183	....	....	....	....	....	....	....	....	....	....	....	....	....	....	....	....	....	....
1987-88	Brandon Wheat Kings	WHL	69	2	13	15	....	....	....	185	....	....	....	....	....	....	....	....	....	....	4	1	1	2	15	....	....	....
1988-89	Brandon Wheat Kings	WHL	72	17	42	59	....	....	....	225	....	....	....	....	....	....	....	....	....	....	....	....	....	....	....	....	....	....
1989-90	Brandon Wheat Kings	WHL	68	34	41	75	....	....	....	182	....	....	....	....	....	....	....	....	....	....	....	....	....	....	....	....	....	....
1990-91	**Vancouver Canucks**	**NHL**	**1**	**0**	**0**	**0**	**0**	**0**	**0**	**7**	**0**	**0**	**0**	**0**	**0.0**	**0**	**0**	**0**	**0**	**0**	....	....	....	....	....	....	....	....
	Milwaukee Admirals	IHL	74	11	13	24	....	....	....	218	....	....	....	....	....	....	....	....	....	....	3	0	0	0	0	....	....	....
1991-92	Milwaukee Admirals	IHL	51	6	8	14	....	....	....	179	....	....	....	....	....	....	....	....	....	....	1	0	0	0	0	....	....	....
	Columbus Chill	ECHL	10	11	6	17	....	....	....	64	....	....	....	....	....	....	....	....	....	....	....	....	....	....	....	....	....	....
1992-93	Hamilton Canucks	AHL	1	0	0	0	....	....	....	2	....	....	....	....	....	....	....	....	....	....	....	....	....	....	....	....	....	....
	Rochester Americans	AHL	4	0	0	0	....	....	....	26	....	....	....	....	....	....	....	....	....	....	....	....	....	....	....	....	....	....
	Columbus Chill	ECHL	36	13	18	31	....	....	....	218	....	....	....	....	....	....	....	....	....	....	....	....	....	....	....	....	....	....
	Erie Panthers	ECHL	15	4	3	7	....	....	....	50	....	....	....	....	....	....	....	....	....	....	5	0	1	1	62	....	....	....
1993-94			STATISTICS NOT AVAILABLE																									
1994-95	Erie Panthers	ECHL	60	14	28	42	....	....	....	341	....	....	....	....	....	....	....	....	....	....	....	....	....	....	....	....	....	....
1995-96	Erie Panthers	ECHL	64	18	26	44	....	....	....	307	....	....	....	....	....	....	....	....	....	....	....	....	....	....	....	....	....	....
1996-97	Baton Rouge Kingfish	ECHL	57	10	13	23	....	....	....	220	....	....	....	....	....	....	....	....	....	....	....	....	....	....	....	....	....	....
1997-98	Baton Rouge Kingfish	ECHL	62	18	19	37	....	....	....	205	....	....	....	....	....	....	....	....	....	....	....	....	....	....	....	....	....	....
1998-99	Baton Rouge Kingfish	ECHL	68	17	23	40	....	....	....	213	....	....	....	....	....	....	....	....	....	....	6	6	1	7	42	....	....	....
99-2000	Baton Rouge Kingfish	ECHL	70	23	38	61	....	....	....	194	....	....	....	....	....	....	....	....	....	....	2	2	0	2	9	....	....	....
	NHL Totals		**1**	**0**	**0**	**0**	**0**	**0**	**0**	**7**	**0**	**0**	**0**	**0**	**0.0**	**0**	**0**	**0**	**0**		....	....	....	....	....	....	....	....

Signed as a free agent by **Vancouver**, April 6, 1990.

• BROWN, Curtis

Curtis Dean C – L. 6', 190 lbs. b: Unity, Sask., 2/12/1976. Buffalo's 2nd, 43rd overall, in 1994.

Season	Club	League	GP	G	A	Pts	AG	AA	APts	PIM	PP	SH	GW	S	%	TGF	PGF	TGA	PGA	+/–	GP	G	A	Pts	PIM	PP	SH	GW
1990-91	Unity Bantams	SAHA	60	93	104	197	....	....	....	55	....	....	....	....	....	....	....	....	....	....	....	....	....	....	....	....	....	....
1991-92	Moose Jaw Midget Warriors	SAHA	36	35	30	65	....	....	....	44	....	....	....	....	....	....	....	....	....	....	....	....	....	....	....	....	....	....
1992-93	Moose Jaw Warriors	WHL	71	13	16	29	....	....	....	30	....	....	....	....	....	....	....	....	....	....	....	....	....	....	....	....	....	....
1993-94	Moose Jaw Warriors	WHL	72	27	38	65	....	....	....	82	....	....	....	....	....	....	....	....	....	....	....	....	....	....	....	....	....	....
1994-95	Moose Jaw Warriors	WHL	70	51	53	104	....	....	....	63	....	....	....	....	....	....	....	....	....	....	10	8	7	15	20	....	....	....
	Buffalo Sabres	**NHL**	**1**	**1**	**1**	**2**	**2**	**1**	**3**	**2**	**0**	**0**	**0**	**4**	**25.0**	**3**	**0**	**1**	**0**	**2**	....	....	....	....	....	....	....	....
1995-96	Moose Jaw Warriors	WHL	25	20	18	38	....	....	....	30	....	....	....	....	....	....	....	....	....	....	....	....	....	....	....	....	....	....
	Canada	WJC-A	5	0	1	1	....	....	....	2	....	....	....	....	....	....	....	....	....	....	....	....	....	....	....	....	....	....
	Prince Albert Raiders	WHL	19	12	21	33	....	....	....	8	....	....	....	....	....	....	....	....	....	....	18	10	15	25	18	....	....	....
	Buffalo Sabres	**NHL**	**4**	**0**	**0**	**0**	**0**	**0**	**0**	**0**	**0**	**0**	**0**	**1**	**0.0**	**0**	**0**	**0**	**0**	**0**	....	....	....	....	....	....	....	....
	Rochester Americans	AHL	....	....	....	....	....	....	....	....	....	....	....	....	....	....	....	....	....	....	12	0	1	1	2	....	....	....
1996-97	**Buffalo Sabres**	**NHL**	**28**	**4**	**3**	**7**	**4**	**3**	**7**	**18**	**0**	**0**	**1**	**31**	**12.9**	**12**	**0**	**8**	**0**	**4**	....	....	....	....	....	....	....	....
	Rochester Americans	AHL	51	22	21	43	....	....	....	30	....	....	....	....	....	....	....	....	....	....	10	4	6	10	4	....	....	....
1997-98	**Buffalo Sabres**	**NHL**	**63**	**12**	**12**	**24**	**14**	**12**	**26**	**34**	**1**	**1**	**2**	**91**	**13.2**	**41**	**8**	**29**	**7**	**11**	**13**	**1**	**2**	**3**	**10**	**1**	**0**	**0**
1998-99	**Buffalo Sabres**	**NHL**	**78**	**16**	**31**	**47**	**19**	**30**	**49**	**56**	**5**	**1**	**3**	**128**	**12.5**	**65**	**14**	**37**	**9**	**23**	**21**	**7**	**6**	**13**	**10**	**3**	**0**	**3**
99-2000	**Buffalo Sabres**	**NHL**	**74**	**22**	**29**	**51**	**25**	**27**	**52**	**42**	**5**	**0**	**4**	**149**	**14.8**	**77**	**15**	**58**	**15**	**19**	**5**	**1**	**3**	**4**	**6**	**1**	**0**	**0**
	Canada	WC-A	9	1	3	4	....	....	....	8	....	....	....	....	....	....	....	....	....	....	....	....	....	....	....	....	....	....
	NHL Totals		**248**	**55**	**76**	**131**	**64**	**73**	**137**	**152**	**11**	**2**	**10**	**404**	**13.6**	**198**	**37**	**133**	**31**		**39**	**9**	**11**	**20**	**26**	**5**	**0**	**3**

WHL East First All-Star Team (1995) • WHL East Second All-Star Team (1996)

• BROWN, David

David James RW – R. 6'5", 222 lbs. b: Saskatoon, Sask., 10/12/1962. Philadelphia's 7th, 140th overall, in 1982.

Season	Club	League	GP	G	A	Pts	AG	AA	APts	PIM	PP	SH	GW	S	%	TGF	PGF	TGA	PGA	+/–	GP	G	A	Pts	PIM	PP	SH	GW
1980-81	Yorkton Terriers	SJHL	STATISTICS NOT AVAILABLE																									
	Spokane Flyers	WHL	9	2	2	4	....	....	....	21	....	....	....	....	....	....	....	....	....	....	....	....	....	....	....	....	....	....
1981-82	Saskatoon Blades	WHL	62	11	33	44	....	....	....	344	....	....	....	....	....	....	....	....	....	....	5	1	0	1	4	....	....	....
1982-83	**Philadelphia Flyers**	**NHL**	**2**	**0**	**0**	**0**	**0**	**0**	**0**	**5**	**0**	**0**	**0**	**2**	**0.0**	**0**	**0**	**1**	**0**	**–1**	....	....	....	....	....	....	....	....
	Maine Mariners	AHL	71	8	6	14	....	....	....	*418	....	....	....	....	....	....	....	....	....	....	16	0	0	0	*107	....	....	....
1983-84	**Philadelphia Flyers**	**NHL**	**19**	**1**	**5**	**6**	**1**	**3**	**4**	**98**	**0**	**0**	**0**	**9**	**11.1**	**8**	**1**	**3**	**0**	**4**	**2**	**0**	**0**	**0**	**12**	**0**	**0**	**0**
	Springfield Indians	AHL	59	17	14	31	....	....	....	150	....	....	....	....	....	....	....	....	....	....	....	....	....	....	....	....	....	....
1984-85	**Philadelphia Flyers**	**NHL**	**57**	**3**	**6**	**9**	**2**	**4**	**6**	**165**	**0**	**0**	**1**	**53**	**5.7**	**15**	**0**	**18**	**0**	**–3**	**11**	**0**	**0**	**0**	**59**	**0**	**0**	**0**
1985-86	**Philadelphia Flyers**	**NHL**	**76**	**10**	**7**	**17**	**8**	**5**	**13**	**277**	**0**	**0**	**1**	**73**	**13.7**	**23**	**1**	**16**	**1**	**7**	**5**	**0**	**0**	**0**	**16**	**0**	**0**	**0**
1986-87	**Philadelphia Flyers**	**NHL**	**62**	**7**	**3**	**10**	**6**	**2**	**8**	**274**	**0**	**0**	**0**	**53**	**13.2**	**17**	**0**	**24**	**0**	**–7**	**26**	**1**	**2**	**3**	**59**	**0**	**0**	**0**
1987-88	**Philadelphia Flyers**	**NHL**	**47**	**12**	**5**	**17**	**10**	**4**	**14**	**114**	**0**	**0**	**4**	**41**	**29.3**	**26**	**0**	**16**	**0**	**10**	**7**	**1**	**0**	**1**	**27**	**0**	**0**	**0**
1988-89	**Philadelphia Flyers**	**NHL**	**50**	**0**	**3**	**3**	**0**	**2**	**2**	**100**	**0**	**0**	**0**	**28**	**0.0**	**6**	**0**	**14**	**0**	**–8**	....	....	....	....	....	....	....	....
	Edmonton Oilers	**NHL**	**22**	**0**	**2**	**2**	**0**	**1**	**1**	**56**	**0**	**0**	**0**	**14**	**0.0**	**5**	**0**	**9**	**0**	**–4**	**7**	**0**	**0**	**0**	**6**	**0**	**0**	**0**
1989-90 ♦	**Edmonton Oilers**	**NHL**	**60**	**0**	**6**	**6**	**0**	**4**	**4**	**145**	**0**	**0**	**0**	**32**	**0.0**	**9**	**0**	**12**	**0**	**–3**	**3**	**0**	**0**	**0**	**0**	**0**	**0**	**0**
1990-91	**Edmonton Oilers**	**NHL**	**58**	**3**	**4**	**7**	**3**	**3**	**6**	**160**	**0**	**0**	**0**	**32**	**9.4**	**10**	**0**	**17**	**0**	**–7**	**16**	**0**	**1**	**1**	**30**	**0**	**0**	**0**
1991-92	**Philadelphia Flyers**	**NHL**	**70**	**4**	**2**	**6**	**4**	**2**	**6**	**81**	**0**	**0**	**0**	**50**	**8.0**	**15**	**0**	**26**	**0**	**–11**	....	....	....	....	....	....	....	....
1992-93	**Philadelphia Flyers**	**NHL**	**70**	**0**	**2**	**2**	**0**	**1**	**1**	**78**	**0**	**0**	**0**	**19**	**0.0**	**8**	**1**	**12**	**0**	**–5**	....	....	....	....	....	....	....	....
1993-94	**Philadelphia Flyers**	**NHL**	**71**	**1**	**4**	**5**	**1**	**3**	**4**	**137**	**0**	**0**	**0**	**16**	**6.3**	**10**	**1**	**21**	**0**	**–12**	....	....	....	....	....	....	....	....
1994-95	**Philadelphia Flyers**	**NHL**	**28**	**1**	**2**	**3**	**2**	**3**	**5**	**53**	**0**	**0**	**0**	**8**	**12.5**	**4**	**1**	**4**	**0**	**–1**	**3**	**0**	**0**	**0**	**0**	**0**	**0**	**0**
1995-96	**San Jose Sharks**	**NHL**	**37**	**3**	**1**	**4**	**3**	**1**	**4**	**46**	**0**	**0**	**0**	**8**	**37.5**	**8**	**0**	**4**	**0**	**4**	....	....	....	....	....	....	....	....
	NHL Totals		**729**	**45**	**52**	**97**	**40**	**38**	**78**	**1789**	**0**	**0**	**6**	**438**	**10.3**	**164**	**5**	**197**	**1**		**80**	**2**	**3**	**5**	**209**	**0**	**0**	**0**

Traded to **Edmonton** by **Philadelphia** for Keith Acton and Edmonton's 6th round choice (Dimitri Yushkevich) in 1991 Entry Draft, February 7, 1989. Traded to **Philadelphia** by **Edmonton** with Jari Kurri and Corey Foster for Craig Fisher, Scott Mellanby and Craig Berube, May 30, 1991. Signed as a free agent by **San Jose**, August 10, 1995.

• BROWN, Doug

RW – R. 5'10", 185 lbs. b: Southborough, MA, 6/12/1964.

Season	Club	League	GP	G	A	Pts	AG	AA	APts	PIM	PP	SH	GW	S	%	TGF	PGF	TGA	PGA	+/–	GP	G	A	Pts	PIM	PP	SH	GW
1981-82	St. Mark's Spartans	Hi-School	STATISTICS NOT AVAILABLE																									
1982-83	Boston College	ECAC	22	9	8	17	....	....	....	0	....	....	....	....	....	....	....	....	....	....	....	....	....	....	....	....	....	....
1983-84	Boston College	ECAC	38	11	10	21	....	....	....	6	....	....	....	....	....	....	....	....	....	....	....	....	....	....	....	....	....	....
1984-85	Boston College	H-East	45	37	31	68	....	....	....	10	....	....	....	....	....	....	....	....	....	....	....	....	....	....	....	....	....	....
1985-86	Boston College	H-East	38	16	40	56	....	....	....	16	....	....	....	....	....	....	....	....	....	....	....	....	....	....	....	....	....	....
	United States	WEC-A	10	2	1	3	....	....	....	2	....	....	....	....	....	....	....	....	....	....	....	....	....	....	....	....	....	....
1986-87	**New Jersey Devils**	**NHL**	**4**	**0**	**1**	**1**	**0**	**1**	**1**	**0**	**0**	**0**	**0**	**10**	**0.0**	**1**	**0**	**6**	**1**	**–4**	....	....	....	....	....	....	....	....
	Maine Mariners	AHL	73	24	34	58	....	....	....	15	....	....	....	....	....	....	....	....	....	....	....	....	....	....	....	....	....	....

Season	Club	League	GP	G	A	Pts	AG	AA	APts	PIM	PP	SH	GW	S	%	TGF	PGF	TGA	PGA	+/–	GP	G	A	Pts	PIM	PP	SH	GW
			REGULAR SEASON																		PLAYOFFS							
1987-88	**New Jersey Devils**	**NHL**	**70**	**14**	**11**	**25**	**12**	**8**	**20**	**20**	**1**	**4**	**2**	**112**	**12.5**	**46**	**4**	**63**	**28**	**7**	**19**	**5**	**1**	**6**	**6**	**0**	**1**	**1**
	Utica Devils	AHL	2	0	2	2	....	....	....	2	....	....	....	....	....	....	....	....	....	....	....	....	....	....	....	....	....	....
1988-89	**New Jersey Devils**	**NHL**	**63**	**15**	**10**	**25**	**13**	**7**	**20**	**15**	**4**	**0**	**2**	**110**	**13.6**	**38**	**10**	**67**	**32**	**–7**	....	....	....	....	....	....	....	....
	Utica Devils	AHL	4	1	4	5	....	....	....	0	....	....	....	....	....	....	....	....	....	....	....	....	....	....	....	....	....	....
	United States	WEC-A	10	1	2	3	....	....	....	0	....	....	....	....	....	....	....	....	....	....	....	....	....	....	....	....	....	....
1989-90	**New Jersey Devils**	**NHL**	**69**	**14**	**20**	**34**	**12**	**14**	**26**	**16**	**1**	**3**	**3**	**135**	**10.4**	**48**	**5**	**56**	**20**	**7**	**6**	**0**	**1**	**1**	**2**	**0**	**0**	**0**
1990-91	**New Jersey Devils**	**NHL**	**58**	**14**	**16**	**30**	**13**	**12**	**25**	**4**	**0**	**2**	**2**	**122**	**11.5**	**41**	**0**	**47**	**24**	**18**	**7**	**2**	**2**	**4**	**2**	**0**	**1**	**0**
	United States	WEC-A	10	0	1	1	....	....	....	0	....	....	....	....	....	....	....	....	....	....	....	....	....	....	....	....	....	....
1991-92	United States	Can-Cup	8	1	2	3	....	....	....	0	....	....	....	....	....	....	....	....	....	....	....	....	....	....	....	....	....	....
	New Jersey Devils	**NHL**	**71**	**11**	**17**	**28**	**10**	**13**	**23**	**27**	**1**	**2**	**1**	**140**	**7.9**	**42**	**1**	**45**	**21**	**17**	....	....	....	....	....	....	....	....
1992-93	**New Jersey Devils**	**NHL**	**15**	**0**	**5**	**5**	**0**	**3**	**3**	**2**	**0**	**0**	**0**	**17**	**0.0**	**6**	**0**	**10**	**7**	**3**	....	....	....	....	....	....	....	....
	Utica Devils	AHL	25	11	17	28	....	....	....	8	....	....	....	....	....	....	....	....	....	....	....	....	....	....	....	....	....	....
1993-94	**Pittsburgh Penguins**	**NHL**	**77**	**18**	**37**	**55**	**17**	**29**	**46**	**18**	**2**	**0**	**1**	**152**	**11.8**	**71**	**4**	**61**	**13**	**19**	**6**	**0**	**0**	**0**	**2**	**0**	**0**	**0**
1994-95	**Detroit Red Wings**	**NHL**	**45**	**9**	**12**	**21**	**16**	**18**	**34**	**16**	**1**	**1**	**2**	**69**	**13.0**	**33**	**3**	**22**	**6**	**14**	**18**	**4**	**8**	**12**	**2**	**0**	**1**	**1**
1995-96	**Detroit Red Wings**	**NHL**	**62**	**12**	**15**	**27**	**12**	**12**	**24**	**4**	**0**	**1**	**1**	**115**	**10.4**	**41**	**4**	**37**	**11**	**11**	**13**	**3**	**3**	**6**	**4**	**0**	**1**	**0**
1996-97♦	**Detroit Red Wings**	**NHL**	**49**	**6**	**7**	**13**	**6**	**6**	**12**	**8**	**1**	**0**	**0**	**69**	**8.7**	**17**	**2**	**26**	**8**	**–3**	**14**	**3**	**3**	**6**	**2**	**0**	**0**	**0**
1997-98♦	**Detroit Red Wings**	**NHL**	**80**	**19**	**23**	**42**	**22**	**23**	**45**	**12**	**6**	**1**	**5**	**145**	**13.1**	**63**	**19**	**36**	**9**	**17**	**9**	**4**	**2**	**6**	**0**	**3**	**0**	**1**
1998-99	**Detroit Red Wings**	**NHL**	**80**	**9**	**19**	**28**	**11**	**18**	**29**	**42**	**3**	**1**	**1**	**180**	**5.0**	**52**	**13**	**45**	**11**	**5**	**10**	**2**	**2**	**4**	**4**	**1**	**0**	**1**
99-2000	**Detroit Red Wings**	**NHL**	**51**	**10**	**8**	**18**	**11**	**7**	**18**	**12**	**0**	**1**	**0**	**67**	**14.9**	**34**	**1**	**30**	**5**	**8**	**3**	**0**	**1**	**1**	**0**	**0**	**0**	**0**
	NHL Totals		**794**	**151**	**201**	**352**	**155**	**171**	**326**	**196**	**20**	**16**	**20**	**1443**	**10.5**	**533**	**66**	**551**	**196**		**105**	**23**	**23**	**46**	**24**	**4**	**4**	**4**

• Brother of Greg • Hockey East Second All-Star Team (1985, 1986)

Signed as a free agent by **New Jersey**, August 6, 1986. Signed as a free agent by **Pittsburgh**, September 28, 1993. Claimed by **Detroit** from **Pittsburgh** in NHL Waiver Draft, January 18, 1995. Claimed by **Nashville** from **Detroit** in Expansion Draft, June 26, 1998. Traded to **Detroit** by **Nashville** for Petr Sykora, Detroit's 3rd round choice (later traded to Edmonton, Edmonton selected Mike Comrie) in 1999 Entry Draft and Detroit's compensatory 4th round choice (Alexander Krevsun) in 1999 Entry Draft), July 14, 1998.

• BROWN, Greg

D – R. 6', 185 lbs. b: Hartford, CT, 3/7/1968. Buffalo's 2nd, 26th overall, in 1986.

Season	Club	League	GP	G	A	Pts	AG	AA	APts	PIM	PP	SH	GW	S	%	TGF	PGF	TGA	PGA	+/–	GP	G	A	Pts	PIM	PP	SH	GW
1984-85	St. Mark's Spartans	Hi-School	24	16	24	40	....	....	....	12	....	....	....	....	....	....	....	....	....	....	....	....	....	....	....	....	....	....
1985-86	St. Mark's Spartans	Hi-School	19	22	28	50	....	....	....	30	....	....	....	....	....	....	....	....	....	....	....	....	....	....	....	....	....	....
	United States	WJC-A	7	0	2	2	....	....	....	6	....	....	....	....	....	....	....	....	....	....	....	....	....	....	....	....	....	....
1986-87	Boston College	H-East	37	10	27	37	....	....	....	22	....	....	....	....	....	....	....	....	....	....	....	....	....	....	....	....	....	....
1987-88	United States	Nat-Team	55	6	29	35	....	....	....	22	....	....	....	....	....	....	....	....	....	....	....	....	....	....	....	....	....	....
	United States	Olympics	6	0	4	4	....	....	....	2	....	....	....	....	....	....	....	....	....	....	....	....	....	....	....	....	....	....
1988-89	Boston College	H-East	40	9	34	43	....	....	....	24	....	....	....	....	....	....	....	....	....	....	....	....	....	....	....	....	....	....
	United States	WEC-A	10	0	1	1	....	....	....	4	....	....	....	....	....	....	....	....	....	....	....	....	....	....	....	....	....	....
1989-90	Boston College	H-East	42	5	35	40	....	....	....	42	....	....	....	....	....	....	....	....	....	....	....	....	....	....	....	....	....	....
	United States	WEC-A	10	2	3	5	....	....	....	0	....	....	....	....	....	....	....	....	....	....	....	....	....	....	....	....	....	....
1990-91	**Buffalo Sabres**	**NHL**	**39**	**1**	**2**	**3**	**1**	**2**	**3**	**35**	**0**	**0**	**0**	**26**	**3.8**	**22**	**3**	**39**	**0**	**–20**	....	....	....	....	....	....	....	....
	Rochester Americans	AHL	31	6	17	23	....	....	....	16	....	....	....	....	....	....	....	....	....	....	14	1	4	5	8	....	....	....
1991-92	Rochester Americans	AHL	56	8	30	38	....	....	....	25	....	....	....	....	....	....	....	....	....	....	16	1	5	6	4	....	....	....
	United States	Nat-Team	8	0	0	0	....	....	....	5	....	....	....	....	....	....	....	....	....	....	....	....	....	....	....	....	....	....
	United States	Olympics	7	0	0	0	....	....	....	2	....	....	....	....	....	....	....	....	....	....	....	....	....	....	....	....	....	....
1992-93	**Buffalo Sabres**	**NHL**	**10**	**0**	**1**	**1**	**0**	**1**	**1**	**6**	**0**	**0**	**0**	**10**	**0.0**	**4**	**0**	**11**	**2**	**–5**	....	....	....	....	....	....	....	....
	Rochester Americans	AHL	61	11	38	49	....	....	....	46	....	....	....	....	....	....	....	....	....	....	16	3	8	11	14	....	....	....
1993-94	**Pittsburgh Penguins**	**NHL**	**36**	**3**	**8**	**11**	**3**	**6**	**9**	**28**	....	....	....	....	....	....	....	....	....	....	**6**	**0**	**1**	**1**	**4**	**0**	**0**	**0**
	San Diego Gulls	IHL	42	8	25	33	....	....	....	26	....	....	....	....	....	....	....	....	....	....	....	....	....	....	....	....	....	....
1994-95	Cleveland Lumberjacks	IHL	28	5	14	19	....	....	....	22	....	....	....	....	....	....	....	....	....	....	....	....	....	....	....	....	....	....
	Winnipeg Jets	**NHL**	**9**	**0**	**3**	**3**	**0**	**4**	**4**	**17**	**0**	**0**	**0**	**12**	**0.0**	**11**	**3**	**7**	**0**	**1**	....	....	....	....	....	....	....	....
1995-96	Rogle BK Angelholm	Sweden	22	4	7	11	....	....	....	32	....	....	....	....	....	....	....	....	....	....	12	1	3	4	8	....	....	....
1996-97	VEU Feldkirch	Alpenliga	6	0	2	2	....	....	....	8	....	....	....	....	....	....	....	....	....	....	....	....	....	....	....	....	....	....
	EHC Kloten	Switz.	46	3	12	15	....	....	....	36	....	....	....	....	....	....	....	....	....	....	4	1	1	2	2	....	....	....
1997-98	EV Landshut	Germany	48	3	19	22	....	....	....	12	....	....	....	....	....	....	....	....	....	....	6	2	4	6	12	....	....	....
	United States	WC-A	6	0	0	0	....	....	....	0	....	....	....	....	....	....	....	....	....	....	....	....	....	....	....	....	....	....
1998-99	Kolner Haie	Germany	41	4	20	24	....	....	....	30	....	....	....	....	....	....	....	....	....	....	....	....	....	....	....	....	....	....
	United States	WC-Q	3	0	1	1	....	....	....	0	....	....	....	....	....	....	....	....	....	....	....	....	....	....	....	....	....	....
99-2000	Kolner Haie	Germany	56	2	12	14	....	....	....	32	....	....	....	....	....	....	....	....	....	....	10	0	4	4	8	....	....	....
	NHL Totals		**94**	**4**	**14**	**18**	**4**	**13**	**17**	**86**	**0**	**0**	**0**	**48**	**8.3**	**37**	**6**	**57**	**2**		**6**	**0**	**1**	**1**	**4**	**0**	**0**	**0**

• Brother of Doug • Hockey East First All-Star Team (1989, 1990)

Signed as a free agent by **Pittsburgh**, September 29, 1993. Traded to **Winnipeg** by **Pittsburgh** for cash, April 7, 1995.

• BROWN, Jeff

D – R. 6'1", 204 lbs. b: Ottawa, Ont., 4/30/1966. Quebec's 2nd, 36th overall, in 1984.

Season	Club	League	GP	G	A	Pts	AG	AA	APts	PIM	PP	SH	GW	S	%	TGF	PGF	TGA	PGA	+/–	GP	G	A	Pts	PIM	PP	SH	GW
1981-82	Hawkesbury Hawks	OJHL	49	12	47	59	....	....	....	72	....	....	....	....	....	....	....	....	....	....	....	....	....	....	....	....	....	....
1982-83	Sudbury Wolves	OHL	65	9	37	46	....	....	....	39	....	....	....	....	....	....	....	....	....	....	....	....	....	....	....	....	....	....
1983-84	Sudbury Wolves	OHL	68	17	60	77	....	....	....	39	....	....	....	....	....	....	....	....	....	....	....	....	....	....	....	....	....	....
1984-85	Sudbury Wolves	OHL	56	16	48	64	....	....	....	26	....	....	....	....	....	....	....	....	....	....	....	....	....	....	....	....	....	....
1985-86	Sudbury Wolves	OHL	45	22	28	50	....	....	....	24	....	....	....	....	....	....	....	....	....	....	4	0	2	2	11	....	....	....
	Quebec Nordiques	**NHL**	**8**	**3**	**2**	**5**	**2**	**1**	**3**	**6**	**0**	**0**	**0**	**16**	**18.8**	**15**	**4**	**6**	**0**	**5**	**1**	**0**	**0**	**0**	**0**	**0**	**0**	**0**
	Fredericton Express	AHL	....	....	....	....	....	....	....	....	....	....	....	....	....	....	....	....	....	....	1	0	1	1	0	....	....	....
1986-87	**Quebec Nordiques**	**NHL**	**44**	**7**	**22**	**29**	**6**	**16**	**22**	**16**	**3**	**0**	**0**	**99**	**7.1**	**70**	**32**	**29**	**2**	**11**	**13**	**3**	**3**	**6**	**2**	**2**	**0**	**0**
	Fredericton Express	AHL	26	2	14	16	....	....	....	16	....	....	....	....	....	....	....	....	....	....	....	....	....	....	....	....	....	....
1987-88	**Quebec Nordiques**	**NHL**	**78**	**16**	**36**	**52**	**14**	**26**	**40**	**64**	**9**	**0**	**4**	**208**	**7.7**	**126**	**73**	**95**	**17**	**–25**	....	....	....	....	....	....	....	....
1988-89	**Quebec Nordiques**	**NHL**	**78**	**21**	**47**	**68**	**18**	**33**	**51**	**62**	**13**	**1**	**1**	**276**	**7.6**	**135**	**69**	**116**	**28**	**–22**	....	....	....	....	....	....	....	....
1989-90	**Quebec Nordiques**	**NHL**	**29**	**6**	**10**	**16**	**5**	**7**	**12**	**18**	**2**	**0**	**3**	**104**	**5.8**	**43**	**20**	**42**	**5**	**–14**	....	....	....	....	....	....	....	....
	St. Louis Blues	**NHL**	**48**	**10**	**28**	**38**	**9**	**20**	**29**	**37**	**6**	**1**	**0**	**180**	**5.6**	**88**	**44**	**69**	**13**	**–12**	**12**	**2**	**10**	**12**	**4**	**1**	**0**	**1**
1990-91	**St. Louis Blues**	**NHL**	**67**	**12**	**47**	**59**	**11**	**36**	**47**	**39**	**6**	**1**	**0**	**176**	**6.8**	**120**	**50**	**86**	**20**	**4**	**13**	**3**	**9**	**12**	**6**	**0**	**0**	**0**
1991-92	**St. Louis Blues**	**NHL**	**80**	**20**	**39**	**59**	**18**	**29**	**47**	**38**	**10**	**0**	**2**	**214**	**9.3**	**135**	**52**	**97**	**22**	**8**	**6**	**2**	**1**	**3**	**2**	**0**	**0**	**1**
1992-93	**St. Louis Blues**	**NHL**	**71**	**25**	**53**	**78**	**21**	**37**	**58**	**58**	**12**	**2**	**3**	**220**	**11.4**	**146**	**75**	**95**	**18**	**–6**	**11**	**3**	**8**	**11**	**6**	**1**	**0**	**2**
1993-94	**St. Louis Blues**	**NHL**	**63**	**13**	**47**	**60**	**12**	**37**	**49**	**46**	**7**	**0**	**3**	**196**	**6.6**	**117**	**60**	**91**	**21**	**–13**	....	....	....	....	....	....	....	....
	Vancouver Canucks	**NHL**	**11**	**1**	**5**	**6**	**1**	**4**	**5**	**10**	**0**	**0**	**0**	**41**	**2.4**	**14**	**6**	**8**	**2**	**2**	**24**	**6**	**9**	**15**	**37**	**3**	**0**	**0**
1994-95	**Vancouver Canucks**	**NHL**	**33**	**8**	**23**	**31**	**14**	**34**	**48**	**16**	**3**	**0**	**0**	**111**	**7.2**	**51**	**30**	**34**	**11**	**–2**	**5**	**1**	**3**	**4**	**2**	**0**	**0**	**0**
1995-96	**Vancouver Canucks**	**NHL**	**28**	**1**	**16**	**17**	**1**	**13**	**14**	**18**	**0**	**0**	**0**	**62**	**1.6**	**47**	**14**	**35**	**8**	**6**	....	....	....	....	....	....	....	....
	Hartford Whalers	**NHL**	**48**	**7**	**31**	**38**	**7**	**25**	**32**	**38**	**5**	**0**	**0**	**115**	**6.1**	**80**	**36**	**62**	**20**	**2**	....	....	....	....	....	....	....	....
1996-97	**Hartford Whalers**	**NHL**	**1**	**0**	**0**	**0**	**0**	**0**	**0**	**0**	**0**	**0**	**0**	**0**	**0.0**	**0**	**0**	**0**	**0**	**0**	....	....	....	....	....	....	....	....
1997-98	**Carolina Hurricanes**	**NHL**	**32**	**3**	**10**	**13**	**4**	**10**	**14**	**16**	**3**	**0**	**0**	**57**	**5.3**	**39**	**18**	**30**	**8**	**–1**	....	....	....	....	....	....	....	....
	Toronto Maple Leafs	**NHL**	**19**	**1**	**8**	**9**	**1**	**8**	**9**	**10**	**1**	**0**	**0**	**30**	**3.3**	**21**	**10**	**12**	**3**	**2**	....	....	....	....	....	....	....	....
	Washington Capitals	**NHL**	**9**	**0**	**6**	**6**	**0**	**6**	**6**	**6**	**0**	**0**	**0**	**15**	**0.0**	**13**	**6**	**4**	**1**	**4**	**2**	**0**	**2**	**2**	**0**	**0**	**0**	**0**
	NHL Totals		**747**	**154**	**430**	**584**	**144**	**342**	**486**	**498**	**80**	**5**	**16**	**2120**	**7.3**	**1260**	**599**	**911**	**199**		**87**	**20**	**45**	**65**	**59**	**7**	**0**	**4**

OHL First All-Star Team (1986)

Traded to **St. Louis** by **Quebec** for Tony Hrkac and Greg Millen, December 13, 1989. Traded to **Vancouver** by **St. Louis** with Bret Hedican and Nathan Lafayette fro Craig Janney, March 21, 1994. Traded to **Hartford** by **Vancouver** with Vancouver's 3rd round choice (later traded to Calgary - Calgary selected Paul Manning) in 1998 Entry Draft for Jim Dowd, Frantisek Kucera and Hartford's 2nd round choice (Ryan Bonni) in 1997 Entry Draft, December 19, 1995. Transferred to **Carolina** after **Hartford** franchise relocated, June 25, 1997. Traded to **Toronto** by **Carolina** for Toronto's 4th round choice (later traded to Nashville - Nashville selected Yevgeny Pavlov) in 1999 Entry Draft, January 2, 1998. Traded to **Washington** by **Toronto** for Sylvain Cote, March 24, 1998.

• BROWN, Jim

D – R. 6'4", 210 lbs. b: Phoenix, AZ, 3/1/1960. Los Angeles' 6th, 92nd overall, in 1979.

Season	Club	League	GP	G	A	Pts	AG	AA	APts	PIM	PP	SH	GW	S	%	TGF	PGF	TGA	PGA	+/–	GP	G	A	Pts	PIM	PP	SH	GW
1976-77	Rochester Monarchs	NYJHL	48	13	19	32	....	....	....	....	....	....	....	....	....	....	....	....	....	....	....	....	....	....	....	....	....	....
1977-78	Rochester Monarchs	NYJHL	48	16	27	43	....	....	....	....	....	....	....	....	....	....	....	....	....	....	....	....	....	....	....	....	....	....
1978-79	University of Notre Dame	CCHA	37	4	8	12	....	....	....	....	....	....	....	....	....	....	....	....	....	....	....	....	....	....	....	....	....	....
1979-80	University of Notre Dame	CCHA	36	5	13	18	....	....	....	40	....	....	....	....	....	....	....	....	....	....	....	....	....	....	....	....	....	....
1980-81	University of Notre Dame	CCHA	27	2	7	9	....	....	....	45	....	....	....	....	....	....	....	....	....	....	....	....	....	....	....	....	....	....

			REGULAR SEASON																		PLAYOFFS							
Season	Club	League	GP	G	A	Pts	AG	AA	APts	PIM	PP	SH	GW	S	%	TGF	PGF	TGA	PGA	+/-	GP	G	A	Pts	PIM	PP	SH	GW
1981-82	University of Notre Dame	CCHA	39	8	19	27	....	....	....	101	....	....	....	....	....	....	....	....	....	....	....	....	....	....	....	....	....	....
1982-83	**Los Angeles Kings**	**NHL**	3	0	1	1	0	1	1	5	0	0	0	0	0.0	2	0	4	0	–2	....	....	....	....	....	....	....	....
	New Haven Nighthawks	AHL	75	3	12	15	....	....	....	120	....	....	....	....	....	....	....	....	....	....	12	2	4	6	8	....	....	....
1983-84	New Haven Nighthawks	AHL	39	2	4	6	....	....	....	18	....	....	....	....	....	....	....	....	....	....	....	....	....	....	....	....	....	....
	NHL Totals		3	0	1	1	0	1	1	5	0	0	0	0	0.0	2	0	4	0		....	....	....	....	....	....	....	....

NYJHL First All-Star team (1977, 1978)

• BROWN, Keith

Keith Jeffrey　D – R. 6'1", 196 lbs.　b: Corner Brook, Nfld., 5/6/1960. Chicago's 1st, 7th overall, in 1979.

Season	Club	League	GP	G	A	Pts	AG	AA	APts	PIM	PP	SH	GW	S	%	TGF	PGF	TGA	PGA	+/-	GP	G	A	Pts	PIM	PP	SH	GW
1976-77	Fort Saskatchewan Traders	AJHL	59	14	61	75	....	....	....	14	....	....	....	....	....	....	....	....	....	....	....	....	....	....	....	....	....	....
	Portland Winter Hawks	WCJHL	2	0	0	0	....	....	....	0	....	....	....	....	....	....	....	....	....	....	....	....	....	....	....	....	....	....
1977-78	Portland Winter Hawks	WCJHL	72	11	53	64	....	....	....	51	....	....	....	....	....	....	....	....	....	....	8	0	3	3	2	....	....	....
1978-79	Portland Winter Hawks	WHL	70	11	85	96	....	....	....	75	....	....	....	....	....	....	....	....	....	....	25	3	*30	33	21	....	....	....
	Canada	WJC-A	5	0	2	2	....	....	....	0	....	....	....	....	....	....	....	....	....	....	....	....	....	....	....	....	....	....
1979-80	**Chicago Black Hawks**	**NHL**	76	2	18	20	2	13	15	27	0	0	2	105	1.9	63	3	69	16	7	6	0	0	0	4	0	0	0
1980-81	**Chicago Black Hawks**	**NHL**	80	9	34	43	7	23	30	80	0	1	1	130	6.9	99	7	122	35	5	3	0	2	2	2	0	0	0
1981-82	**Chicago Black Hawks**	**NHL**	33	4	20	24	3	13	16	26	2	0	0	87	4.6	66	16	58	12	4	4	0	2	2	5	0	0	0
1982-83	**Chicago Black Hawks**	**NHL**	50	4	27	31	3	19	22	20	2	0	0	116	3.4	90	27	79	24	8	7	0	0	0	11	0	0	0
1983-84	**Chicago Black Hawks**	**NHL**	74	10	25	35	8	17	25	94	3	0	0	148	6.8	91	18	119	28	–18	5	0	1	1	10	0	0	0
1984-85	**Chicago Black Hawks**	**NHL**	56	1	22	23	1	15	16	55	0	0	0	100	1.0	76	15	80	21	2	11	2	7	9	31	1	0	0
1985-86	**Chicago Black Hawks**	**NHL**	70	11	29	40	9	19	28	87	1	1	0	151	7.3	112	37	103	22	–6	3	0	1	1	9	0	0	0
1986-87	**Chicago Blackhawks**	**NHL**	73	4	23	27	3	17	20	86	2	0	0	100	4.0	85	8	108	36	5	4	0	1	1	6	0	0	0
1987-88	**Chicago Blackhawks**	**NHL**	24	3	6	9	3	4	7	45	0	0	1	39	7.7	31	5	34	13	5	5	0	2	2	10	0	0	0
1988-89	**Chicago Blackhawks**	**NHL**	74	2	16	18	2	11	13	84	1	0	0	105	1.9	67	13	100	41	–5	13	1	3	4	25	0	0	0
1989-90	**Chicago Blackhawks**	**NHL**	67	5	20	25	4	14	18	87	2	0	0	111	4.5	98	16	88	32	26	18	0	4	4	43	0	0	0
1990-91	**Chicago Blackhawks**	**NHL**	45	1	10	11	1	8	9	55	0	0	0	71	1.4	39	13	25	8	9	6	1	0	1	8	0	0	0
1991-92	**Chicago Blackhawks**	**NHL**	57	6	10	16	5	8	13	69	2	1	1	105	5.7	54	16	47	16	7	14	0	8	8	18	0	0	0
1992-93	**Chicago Blackhawks**	**NHL**	33	2	6	8	2	4	6	39	0	0	0	47	4.3	29	3	28	5	3	4	0	1	1	2	0	0	0
1993-94	**Florida Panthers**	**NHL**	51	4	8	12	4	6	10	60	1	0	0	52	7.7	50	7	54	22	11	....	....	....	....	....	....	....	....
1994-95	**Florida Panthers**	**NHL**	13	0	0	0	0	0	0	2	0	0	0	10	0.0	9	2	11	5	1	....	....	....	....	....	....	....	....
	NHL Totals		876	68	274	342	57	191	248	916	16	3	5	1477	4.6	1059	206	1125	336		103	4	32	36	184	1	0	0

AJHL Rookie-of-the-Year (1977) • AJHL Top Defenseman (1977) • WHL All-Star Team (1979) • Shared WHL Rookie-of-the-Year Award with John Ogrodnick (1978)

• Missed majority of 1981-82 season recovering from knee injury suffered in game vs. Philadelphia, December 23, 1981. • Missed majority of 1987-88 season recovering from knee injury suffered in training camp, October, 1987. • Missed majority of 1992-93 season recovering from shoulder surgery, September 27, 1992. Traded to **Florida** by **Chicago** for Darin Kimble, September 30, 1993.

• BROWN, Kevin

Kevin J.　RW – R. 6'1", 212 lbs.　b: Birmingham, England, 5/11/1974. Los Angeles' 3rd, 87th overall, in 1992.

Season	Club	League	GP	G	A	Pts	AG	AA	APts	PIM	PP	SH	GW	S	%	TGF	PGF	TGA	PGA	+/-	GP	G	A	Pts	PIM	PP	SH	GW
1989-90	Georgetown Raiders	OJHL-B	31	3	8	11	....	....	....	59	....	....	....	....	....	....	....	....	....	....	....	....	....	....	....	....	....	....
1990-91	Waterloo Black Hawks	OJHL-B	46	25	33	58	....	....	....	116	....	....	....	....	....	....	....	....	....	....	....	....	....	....	....	....	....	....
1991-92	Belleville Bulls	OHL	66	24	24	48	....	....	....	52	....	....	....	....	....	....	....	....	....	....	5	1	4	5	8	....	....	....
1992-93	Belleville Bulls	OHL	6	2	5	7	....	....	....	4	....	....	....	....	....	....	....	....	....	....	....	....	....	....	....	....	....	....
	Detroit Jr. Red Wings	OHL	56	48	86	134	....	....	....	76	....	....	....	....	....	....	....	....	....	....	15	10	18	28	18	....	....	....
1993-94	Detroit Jr. Red Wings	OHL	57	54	81	135	....	....	....	85	....	....	....	....	....	....	....	....	....	....	17	14	*26	*40	28	....	....	....
1994-95	**Los Angeles Kings**	**NHL**	23	2	3	5	4	4	8	18	0	0	0	25	8.0	9	2	14	0	–7	....	....	....	....	....	....	....	....
	Phoenix Roadrunners	IHL	48	19	31	50	....	....	....	64	....	....	....	....	....	....	....	....	....	....	....	....	....	....	....	....	....	....
1995-96	**Los Angeles Kings**	**NHL**	7	1	0	1	1	0	1	4	0	0	0	9	11.1	2	0	4	0	–2	....	....	....	....	....	....	....	....
	Phoenix Roadrunners	IHL	45	10	16	26	....	....	....	39	....	....	....	....	....	....	....	....	....	....	....	....	....	....	....	....	....	....
	P.E.I. Senators	AHL	8	3	6	9	....	....	....	2	....	....	....	....	....	....	....	....	....	....	3	1	3	4	0	....	....	....
1996-97	**Hartford Whalers**	**NHL**	11	0	4	4	0	4	4	6	0	0	0	12	0.0	5	2	9	0	–6	....	....	....	....	....	....	....	....
	Springfield Falcons	AHL	48	32	16	48	....	....	....	45	....	....	....	....	....	....	....	....	....	....	17	*11	6	17	24	....	....	....
1997-98	**Carolina Hurricanes**	**NHL**	4	0	0	0	0	0	0	0	0	0	0	0	0.0	1	1	2	0	–2	....	....	....	....	....	....	....	....
	Beast of New Haven	AHL	67	28	44	72	....	....	....	65	....	....	....	....	....	....	....	....	....	....	3	0	2	2	0	....	....	....
1998-99	**Edmonton Oilers**	**NHL**	12	4	2	6	5	2	7	0	2	0	0	13	30.8	6	3	5	0	–2	....	....	....	....	....	....	....	....
	Hamilton Bulldogs	AHL	32	9	14	23	....	....	....	47	....	....	....	....	....	....	....	....	....	....	....	....	....	....	....	....	....	....
	Hartford Wolf Pack	AHL	9	3	2	5	....	....	....	14	....	....	....	....	....	....	....	....	....	....	5	1	3	4	4	....	....	....
99-2000	Hamilton Bulldogs	AHL	54	21	38	59	....	....	....	53	....	....	....	....	....	....	....	....	....	....	4	2	2	4	8	....	....	....
	Louisville Panthers	AHL	1	0	0	0	....	....	....	2	....	....	....	....	....	....	....	....	....	....	....	....	....	....	....	....	....	....
	Edmonton Oilers	**NHL**	7	0	0	0	0	0	0	0	0	0	0	5	0.0	1	0	1	0	0	1	0	0	0	0	0	0	0
	NHL Totals		64	7	9	16	10	10	20	28	2	0	0	64	10.9	24	8	35	0		1	0	0	0	0	0	0	0

OHL Second All-Star Team (1993) • OHL First All-Star Team (1994) • Canadian Major Junior Second All-Star Team (1994)

Traded to **Ottawa** by **LA Kings** for Jaroslav Modry and Ottawa's 8th round choice (Stephen Valiquette) in 1996 Entry Draft, March 20, 1996. Traded to **Anaheim** by **Ottawa** for Mike Maneluk, July 1, 1996. Traded to **Hartford** by **Anaheim** for the rights to Espen Knutsen, October 1, 1996. Transferred to **Carolina** after **Hartford** franchise relocated, June 25, 1997. Signed as a free agent by **Edmonton**, August 14, 1998. Traded to **NY Rangers** by **Edmonton** for Vladimir Vorobiev, March 23, 1999. Signed as a free agent by **Edmonton**, March 7, 2000.

• BROWN, Larry

Larry Wayne　D – L. 6'2", 210 lbs.　b: Brandon, Man., 4/14/1947.

Season	Club	League	GP	G	A	Pts	AG	AA	APts	PIM	PP	SH	GW	S	%	TGF	PGF	TGA	PGA	+/-	GP	G	A	Pts	PIM	PP	SH	GW
1963-64	Brandon Wheat Kings	MJHL	....	....	....	....	....	....	....	....	....	....	....	....	....	....	....	....	....	....	2	0	0	0	0	....	....	....
1964-65	Brandon Wheat Kings	SJHL	54	2	11	13	....	....	....	12	....	....	....	....	....	....	....	....	....	....	2	0	0	0	0	....	....	....
1965-66	Brandon Wheat Kings	SJHL	59	6	18	24	....	....	....	19	....	....	....	....	....	....	....	....	....	....	11	0	4	4	0	....	....	....
1966-67	Brandon Wheat Kings	MJHL	STATISTICS NOT AVAILABLE																									
1967-68	New Haven Blades	EHL	71	6	21	27	....	....	....	39	....	....	....	....	....	....	....	....	....	....	10	1	7	8	8	....	....	....
1968-69	Omaha Knights	CHL	69	5	14	19	....	....	....	14	....	....	....	....	....	....	....	....	....	....	7	4	1	5	6	....	....	....
1969-70	**New York Rangers**	**NHL**	15	0	3	3	0	3	3	8	0	0	0	17	0.0	11	1	7	3	6	....	....	....	....	....	....	....	....
	Buffalo Bisons	AHL	41	2	8	10	....	....	....	46	....	....	....	....	....	....	....	....	....	....	....	....	....	....	....	....	....	....
1970-71	**Detroit Red Wings**	**NHL**	33	1	4	5	1	3	4	8	0	0	1	52	1.9	18	2	40	9	–15	....	....	....	....	....	....	....	....
	New York Rangers	**NHL**	31	1	1	2	1	1	2	10	1	0	0	56	1.8	25	3	16	2	8	11	0	1	1	0	0	0	0
1971-72	**Philadelphia Flyers**	**NHL**	12	0	0	0	0	0	0	2	0	0	0	9	0.0	4	0	12	5	–3	....	....	....	....	....	....	....	....
	Richmond Robins	AHL	9	1	1	2	....	....	....	10	....	....	....	....	....	....	....	....	....	....	....	....	....	....	....	....	....	....
1972-73	**Los Angeles Kings**	**NHL**	55	0	7	7	0	6	6	8	0	0	0	46	0.0	36	0	44	4	–4	....	....	....	....	....	....	....	....
1973-74	**Los Angeles Kings**	**NHL**	45	0	4	4	0	3	3	14	0	0	0	31	0.0	35	1	37	7	4	2	0	0	0	0	0	0	0
	Springfield Kings	AHL	8	0	4	4	....	....	....	6	....	....	....	....	....	....	....	....	....	....	....	....	....	....	....	....	....	....
1974-75	**Los Angeles Kings**	**NHL**	78	1	15	16	1	11	12	50	0	0	0	83	1.2	87	1	79	24	31	3	0	2	2	0	0	0	0
1975-76	**Los Angeles Kings**	**NHL**	74	2	5	7	2	4	6	33	0	0	0	49	4.1	47	1	91	18	–27	9	0	0	0	2	0	0	0
1976-77	**Los Angeles Kings**	**NHL**	55	1	6	7	1	5	6	24	0	0	0	59	1.7	39	2	68	14	–17	9	0	1	1	6	0	0	0
	Fort Worth Texans	CHL	14	0	2	2	....	....	....	8	....	....	....	....	....	....	....	....	....	....	....	....	....	....	....	....	....	....
1977-78	**Los Angeles Kings**	**NHL**	57	1	8	9	1	6	7	23	0	0	0	24	4.2	40	3	65	15	–13	1	0	0	0	2	0	0	0
1978-79	Springfield Indians	AHL	65	3	6	9	....	....	....	20	....	....	....	....	....	....	....	....	....	....	....	....	....	....	....	....	....	....
1979-80	Cincinnati Stingers	CHL	31	0	5	5	....	....	....	41	....	....	....	....	....	....	....	....	....	....	....	....	....	....	....	....	....	....
	Houston Apollos	CHL	39	1	4	5	....	....	....	14	....	....	....	....	....	....	....	....	....	....	4	1	1	2	0	....	....	....
	NHL Totals		455	7	53	60	7	42	49	180	1	0	1	426	1.6	342	14	459	101		35	0	4	4	10	0	0	0

Traded to **Detroit** by **NY Rangers** for Pete Stemkowski, October 31, 1970. Traded to **NY Rangers** by **Detroit** with Bruce MacGregor for Arnie Brown, Mike Robitaille and Tom Miller, February 2, 1971. Claimed by **Philadelphia** from **NY Rangers** in Intra-League Draft, June 8, 1971. • Missed majority of 1971-72 season recovering from monoucleosis. Claimed on waivers by **LA Kings** from **Philadelphia**, January 28, 1972. Claimed by **Edmonton** from **LA Kings** in Expansion Draft, June 13, 1979.

• BROWN, Rob

RW – L. 5'10", 177 lbs.　b: Kingston, Ont., 4/10/1968. Pittsburgh's 4th, 67th overall, in 1986.

Season	Club	League	GP	G	A	Pts	AG	AA	APts	PIM	PP	SH	GW	S	%	TGF	PGF	TGA	PGA	+/-	GP	G	A	Pts	PIM	PP	SH	GW
1982-83	St. Albert Royals	AAHA	61	137	122	259	....	....	....	200	....	....	....	....	....	....	....	....	....	....	....	....	....	....	....	....	....	....
1983-84	St. Albert Saints	AJHL	1	0	0	0	....	....	....	0	....	....	....	....	....	....	....	....	....	....	....	....	....	....	....	....	....	....
	Kamloops Jr. Oilers	WHL	50	16	42	58	....	....	....	80	....	....	....	....	....	....	....	....	....	....	15	1	2	3	17	....	....	....
	Kamloops Jr. Oilers	Mem-Cup	4	1	3	4	....	....	....	2	....	....	....	....	....	....	....	....	....	....	....	....	....	....	....	....	....	....
1984-85	Kamloops Blazers	WHL	60	29	50	79	....	....	....	95	....	....	....	....	....	....	....	....	....	....	15	8	8	26	28	....	....	....

			REGULAR SEASON																		PLAYOFFS							
Season	Club	League	GP	G	A	Pts	AG	AA	APts	PIM	PP	SH	GW	S	%	TGF	PGF	TGA	PGA	+/–	GP	G	A	Pts	PIM	PP	SH	GW
1985-86	Kamloops Blazers	WHL	69	58	*115	*173	....	....	....	171	....	....	....	....	....	....	....	....	....	....	16	*18	*28	*46	14	....	....	....
	Kamloops Blazers	Mem-Cup	5	5	6	11	....	....	....	20	....	....	....	....	....	....	....	....	....	....	....	....	....	....	....	....	....	....
1986-87	Kamloops Blazers	WHL	63	*76	*136	*212	....	....	....	101	....	....	....	....	....	....	....	....	....	....	5	6	5	11	6	....	....	....
1987-88	**Pittsburgh Penguins**	**NHL**	51	24	20	44	20	14	34	56	13	0	1	80	30.0	66	28	30	0	8	....	....	....	....	....	....	....	....
	Canada	WJC-A	7	6	2	8	....	....	....	2	....	....	....	....	....	....	....	....	....	....	....	....	....	....	....	....	....	....
1988-89	**Pittsburgh Penguins**	**NHL**	68	49	66	115	42	47	89	118	24	0	6	169	29.0	164	77	63	3	27	11	5	3	8	22	1	0	3
1989-90	**Pittsburgh Penguins**	**NHL**	80	33	47	80	28	34	62	102	12	0	3	157	21.0	119	41	88	0	–10	....	....	....	....	....	....	....	....
1990-91	**Pittsburgh Penguins**	**NHL**	25	6	10	16	5	8	13	31	2	0	0	32	18.8	21	8	13	0	0	....	....	....	....	....	....	....	....
	Hartford Whalers	**NHL**	44	18	24	42	16	18	34	101	10	0	2	94	19.1	68	35	40	0	–7	5	1	0	1	7	1	0	1
1991-92	**Hartford Whalers**	**NHL**	42	16	15	31	15	11	26	39	13	0	2	65	24.6	42	29	27	0	–14	....	....	....	....	....	....	....	....
	Chicago Blackhawks	**NHL**	25	5	11	16	5	8	13	34	3	0	1	41	12.2	23	9	16	1	–1	8	2	4	6	4	1	0	0
1992-93	**Chicago Blackhawks**	**NHL**	15	1	6	7	1	4	5	33	0	0	0	16	6.3	11	1	4	0	6	....	....	....	....	....	....	....	....
	Indianapolis Ice	IHL	19	14	19	33	....	....	....	32	....	....	....	....	....	....	....	....	....	....	2	0	1	1	2	....	....	....
1993-94	**Dallas Stars**	**NHL**	1	0	0	0	0	0	0	0	0	0	0	1	0.0	0	0	1	0	–1	....	....	....	....	....	....	....	....
	Kalamazoo Wings	IHL	79	42	*113	*155	....	....	....	188	....	....	....	....	....	....	....	....	....	....	5	1	3	4	6	....	....	....
1994-95	Phoenix Roadrunners	IHL	69	34	73	107	....	....	....	135	....	....	....	....	....	....	....	....	....	....	9	4	12	16	0	....	....	....
	Los Angeles Kings	**NHL**	2	0	0	0	0	0	0	0	0	0	0	1	0.0	0	0	2	0	–2	....	....	....	....	....	....	....	....
1995-96	Chicago Wolves	IHL	79	52	*91	*143	....	....	....	100	....	....	....	....	....	....	....	....	....	....	9	4	11	15	6	....	....	....
1996-97	Chicago Wolves	IHL	76	37	*80	*117	....	....	....	98	....	....	....	....	....	....	....	....	....	....	4	2	4	6	16	....	....	....
1997-98	**Pittsburgh Penguins**	**NHL**	82	15	25	40	18	24	42	59	4	0	4	172	8.7	62	27	36	0	–1	6	1	0	1	4	1	0	0
1998-99	**Pittsburgh Penguins**	**NHL**	58	13	11	24	15	11	26	16	9	0	1	78	16.7	31	18	28	0	–15	13	2	5	7	8	2	0	0
99-2000	**Pittsburgh Penguins**	**NHL**	50	10	13	23	11	12	23	10	4	0	3	73	....	18	19	22	0	....	11	1	2	3	0	0	0	0
	NHL Totals		543	190	248	438	176	191	367	599	94	0	23	979	19.4	625	292	370	4		54	12	14	26	45	6	0	4

WHL West First All-Star Team (1986, 1987) • Canadian Major Junior Player of the Year (1987) • IHL First All-Star Team (1994, 1996, 1997) • Won Leo P. Lamoureux Memorial Trophy (Top Scorer - IHL) (1994, 1996, 1997) • Won James Gatschene Memorial Trophy (MVP - IHL) (1994) • IHL Second All-Star Team (1995) • Played in NHL All-Star Game (1989)

Traded to **Hartford** by **Pittsburgh** for Scott Young, December 21, 1990. Traded to **Chicago** by **Hartford** for Steve Konroyd, January 24, 1992. Signed as a free agent by **Dallas**, August 12, 1993. Signed as a free agent by **LA Kings**, June 14, 1994. Signed as a free agent by **Pittsburgh**, October 1, 1997.

• BROWN, Sean

Sean P. D – L. 6'3", 205 lbs. b: Oshawa, Ont., 11/5/1976. Boston's 2nd, 21st overall, in 1995.

Season	Club	League	GP	G	A	Pts	AG	AA	APts	PIM	PP	SH	GW	S	%	TGF	PGF	TGA	PGA	+/–	GP	G	A	Pts	PIM	PP	SH	GW
1992-93	Oshawa Legionaires	OMHA	15	0	1	1	....	....	....	9	....	....	....	....	....	....	....	....	....	....	....	....	....	....	....	....	....	....
1993-94	Wellington Dukes	OJHL	32	5	14	19	....	....	....	165	....	....	....	....	....	....	....	....	....	....	....	....	....	....	....	....	....	....
	Belleville Bulls	OHL	28	1	2	3	....	....	....	53	....	....	....	....	....	....	....	....	....	....	8	0	0	0	17	....	....	....
1994-95	Belleville Bulls	OHL	58	2	16	18	....	....	....	200	....	....	....	....	....	....	....	....	....	....	16	4	2	6	*67	....	....	....
1995-96	Belleville Bulls	OHL	37	10	23	33	....	....	....	150	....	....	....	....	....	....	....	....	....	....	....	....	....	....	....	....	....	....
	Sarnia Sting	OHL	26	8	17	25	....	....	....	112	....	....	....	....	....	....	....	....	....	....	10	1	0	1	38	....	....	....
1996-97	**Edmonton Oilers**	**NHL**	5	0	0	0	0	0	0	4	0	0	0	2	0.0	1	1	1	0	–1	....	....	....	....	....	....	....	....
	Hamilton Bulldogs	AHL	61	1	7	8	....	....	....	238	....	....	....	....	....	....	....	....	....	....	19	1	0	1	47	....	....	....
1997-98	**Edmonton Oilers**	**NHL**	18	0	1	1	0	1	1	43	0	0	0	9	0.0	7	0	11	3	–1	....	....	....	....	....	....	....	....
	Hamilton Bulldogs	AHL	43	4	6	10	....	....	....	166	....	....	....	....	....	....	....	....	....	....	6	0	2	2	38	....	....	....
1998-99	**Edmonton Oilers**	**NHL**	51	0	7	7	0	7	7	188	0	0	0	27	0.0	23	2	22	2	1	1	0	0	0	10	0	0	0
99-2000	**Edmonton Oilers**	**NHL**	72	4	8	12	4	7	11	192	0	0	2	36	11.1	43	1	44	3	1	3	0	0	0	23	0	0	0
	NHL Totals		146	4	16	20	4	15	19	427	0	0	2	74	5.4	74	4	78	8		4	0	0	0	33	0	0	0

OHL Second All-Star Team (1996)

Rights traded to **Edmonton** by **Boston** with Mariusz Czerkawski and Boston's 1st round choice (Matthieu Descoteaux) in 1996 Entry Draft for Bill Ranford, January 11, 1996.

• BROWNSCHIDLE, Jack

John J. D – L. 6'2", 195 lbs. b: Buffalo, N.Y., 10/2/1955. St. Louis' 5th, 99th overall, in 1975.

Season	Club	League	GP	G	A	Pts	AG	AA	APts	PIM	PP	SH	GW	S	%	TGF	PGF	TGA	PGA	+/–	GP	G	A	Pts	PIM	PP	SH	GW
1972-73	Niagara Falls Flyers	OJHL	32	9	19	28	....	....	....	20	....	....	....	....	....	....	....	....	....	....	....	....	....	....	....	....	....	....
1973-74	University of Notre Dame	WCHA	36	2	7	9	....	....	....	24	....	....	....	....	....	....	....	....	....	....	....	....	....	....	....	....	....	....
	United States	Nat-Team	18	2	3	5	....	....	....	....	....	....	....	....	....	....	....	....	....	....	....	....	....	....	....	....	....	....
1974-75	University of Notre Dame	WCHA	38	3	10	13	....	....	....	20	....	....	....	....	....	....	....	....	....	....	....	....	....	....	....	....	....	....
	United States	WEC-A	10	1	1	2	....	....	....	4	....	....	....	....	....	....	....	....	....	....	....	....	....	....	....	....	....	....
1975-76	University of Notre Dame	WCHA	38	12	24	36	....	....	....	24	....	....	....	....	....	....	....	....	....	....	....	....	....	....	....	....	....	....
1976-77	University of Notre Dame	WCHA	38	13	35	48	....	....	....	30	....	....	....	....	....	....	....	....	....	....	....	....	....	....	....	....	....	....
1977-78	**St. Louis Blues**	**NHL**	40	2	15	17	2	12	14	23	1	0	0	62	3.2	40	13	47	9	–11	....	....	....	....	....	....	....	....
	Salt Lake Golden Eagles	CHL	25	4	12	16	....	....	....	0	....	....	....	....	....	....	....	....	....	....	....	....	....	....	....	....	....	....
1978-79	**St. Louis Blues**	**NHL**	64	10	24	34	9	17	26	14	5	0	1	101	9.9	82	27	86	10	–21	....	....	....	....	....	....	....	....
	Salt Lake Golden Eagles	CHL	11	0	10	10	....	....	....	0	....	....	....	....	....	....	....	....	....	....	....	....	....	....	....	....	....	....
	United States	WEC-A	8	1	1	2	....	....	....	5	....	....	....	....	....	....	....	....	....	....	....	....	....	....	....	....	....	....
1979-80	**St. Louis Blues**	**NHL**	77	12	32	44	10	23	33	8	3	0	2	130	9.2	110	34	74	14	16	3	0	0	0	0	0	0	0
1980-81	**St. Louis Blues**	**NHL**	71	5	23	28	4	15	19	12	3	1	1	96	5.2	109	43	89	28	5	11	0	3	3	2	0	0	0
1981-82	**St. Louis Blues**	**NHL**	80	5	33	38	4	22	26	26	3	0	1	149	3.4	129	48	128	42	–5	8	0	2	2	14	0	0	0
1982-83	**St. Louis Blues**	**NHL**	72	1	22	23	1	15	16	30	1	0	0	127	0.8	99	20	105	23	–3	4	0	0	0	2	0	0	0
1983-84	**St. Louis Blues**	**NHL**	51	1	7	8	1	5	6	19	1	0	0	50	2.0	37	8	75	25	–21	....	....	....	....	....	....	....	....
	Hartford Whalers	**NHL**	13	2	2	4	2	1	3	10	0	0	1	17	11.8	8	0	13	0	–5	....	....	....	....	....	....	....	....
1984-85	**Hartford Whalers**	**NHL**	17	1	4	5	1	3	4	5	1	0	0	27	3.7	16	4	13	1	0	....	....	....	....	....	....	....	....
	Binghamton Whalers	AHL	56	4	17	21	....	....	....	8	....	....	....	....	....	....	....	....	....	....	....	....	....	....	....	....	....	....
1985-86	**Hartford Whalers**	**NHL**	9	0	0	0	0	0	0	4	0	0	0	7	0.0	2	0	11	5	–4	....	....	....	....	....	....	....	....
	Binghamton Whalers	AHL	58	5	26	31	....	....	....	18	....	....	....	....	....	....	....	....	....	....	6	0	3	3	0	....	....	....
1986-87	Rochester Americans	AHL	74	8	22	30	....	....	....	13	....	....	....	....	....	....	....	....	....	....	12	1	3	4	0	....	....	....
	NHL Totals		494	39	162	201	34	113	147	151	18	1	6	766	5.1	632	197	641	157		26	0	5	5	18	0	0	0

• Brother of Jeff • WCHA First All-Star Team (1976, 1977) • NCAA West First All-American Team (1976, 1977) • AHL Second All-Star Team (1986, 1987)

Claimed on waivers by **Hartford** from **St. Louis**, March 2, 1984.

• BROWNSCHIDLE, Jeff

Jeffrey Paul D – R. 6'2", 200 lbs. b: Buffalo, NY, 3/1/1959.

Season	Club	League	GP	G	A	Pts	AG	AA	APts	PIM	PP	SH	GW	S	%	TGF	PGF	TGA	PGA	+/–	GP	G	A	Pts	PIM	PP	SH	GW
1975-76	Amherst Knights	NYJHL	31	27	30	57	....	....	....	....	....	....	....	....	....	....	....	....	....	....	....	....	....	....	....	....	....	....
1976-77	Amherst Knights	NYJHL	34	31	29	60	....	....	....	....	....	....	....	....	....	....	....	....	....	....	....	....	....	....	....	....	....	....
1977-78	University of Notre Dame	WCHA	35	6	10	16	....	....	....	30	....	....	....	....	....	....	....	....	....	....	....	....	....	....	....	....	....	....
1978-79	University of Notre Dame	WCHA	32	5	15	20	....	....	....	40	....	....	....	....	....	....	....	....	....	....	....	....	....	....	....	....	....	....
	United States	WJC-A	5	1	2	3	....	....	....	2	....	....	....	....	....	....	....	....	....	....	....	....	....	....	....	....	....	....
1979-80	University of Notre Dame	WCHA	39	14	37	51	....	....	....	50	....	....	....	....	....	....	....	....	....	....	....	....	....	....	....	....	....	....
1980-81	University of Notre Dame	WCHA	36	4	28	32	....	....	....	56	....	....	....	....	....	....	....	....	....	....	....	....	....	....	....	....	....	....
1981-82	**Hartford Whalers**	**NHL**	3	0	1	1	0	1	1	2	0	0	0	4	0.0	3	1	6	1	–3	....	....	....	....	....	....	....	....
	Binghamton Whalers	AHL	52	4	23	27	....	....	....	24	....	....	....	....	....	....	....	....	....	....	15	2	4	6	6	....	....	....
1982-83	**Hartford Whalers**	**NHL**	4	0	0	0	0	0	0	0	0	0	0	0	0.0	1	0	7	0	–6	....	....	....	....	....	....	....	....
	Binghamton Whalers	AHL	64	9	18	27	....	....	....	52	....	....	....	....	....	....	....	....	....	....	5	0	1	1	23	....	....	....
1983-84	Binghamton Whalers	AHL	29	2	7	9	....	....	....	50	....	....	....	....	....	....	....	....	....	....	....	....	....	....	....	....	....	....
	Salt Lake Golden Eagles	CHL	11	1	7	8	....	....	....	12	....	....	....	....	....	....	....	....	....	....	....	....	....	....	....	....	....	....
	NHL Totals		7	0	1	1	0	1	1	2	0	0	0	4	0.0	4	1	13	1		....	....	....	....	....	....	....	....

Brother of Jack

Signed as a free agent by **Hartford**, June 9, 1981.

• BRUBAKER, Jeff

Jeffrey Joseph LW – L. 6'2", 207 lbs. b: Frederick, MD, 2/24/1958. Boston's 6th, 102nd overall, in 1978.

Season	Club	League	GP	G	A	Pts	AG	AA	APts	PIM	PP	SH	GW	S	%	TGF	PGF	TGA	PGA	+/–	GP	G	A	Pts	PIM	PP	SH	GW
1974-75	St. Paul Vulcans	MWJHL	57	13	14	27	....	....	....	130	....	....	....	....	....	....	....	....	....	....	....	....	....	....	....	....	....	....
1975-76	St. Paul Vulcans	MWJHL	47	6	34	40	....	....	....	152	....	....	....	....	....	....	....	....	....	....	....	....	....	....	....	....	....	....
1976-77	Michigan State Spartans	WCHA	18	0	3	3	....	....	....	30	....	....	....	....	....	....	....	....	....	....	....	....	....	....	....	....	....	....
	Peterborough Petes	OMJHL	26	0	5	5	....	....	....	143	....	....	....	....	....	....	....	....	....	....	4	0	2	2	7	....	....	....

Season	Club	League	GP	G	A	Pts	AG	AA	APts	PIM	PP	SH	GW	S	%	TGF	PGF	TGA	PGA	+/–	GP	G	A	Pts	PIM	PP	SH	GW
			REGULAR SEASON																		PLAYOFFS							
1977-78	Peterborough Petes	OMJHL	68	20	24	44	....	....	....	307	....	....	....	....	....	....	....	....	....	....	21	6	5	11	52	....	....	....
	Peterborough Petes	Mem-Cup	5	0	5	5	....	....	....	4	....	....	....	....	....	....	....	....	....	....	....	....	....	....	....	....	....	....
1978-79	New England Whalers	WHA	12	0	0	0	....	....	....	19	....	....	....	....	....	....	....	....	....	....	3	0	0	0	12	....	....	....
	Rochester Americans	AHL	57	4	10	14	....	....	....	253	....	....	....	....	....	....	....	....	....	....	....	....	....	....	....	....	....	....
1979-80	**Hartford Whalers**	**NHL**	**3**	**0**	**1**	**1**	**0**	**1**	**1**	**2**	**0**	**0**	**0**	**2**	**0.0**	**1**	**1**	**2**	**0**	**–2**	....	....	....	....	....	....	....	....
	Springfield Indians	AHL	50	12	13	25	....	....	....	165	....	....	....	....	....	....	....	....	....	....	....	....	....	....	....	....	....	....
1980-81	**Hartford Whalers**	**NHL**	**43**	**5**	**3**	**8**	**4**	**2**	**6**	**93**	**0**	**0**	**0**	**29**	**17.2**	**14**	**0**	**19**	**0**	**–5**	....	....	....	....	....	....	....	....
	Binghamton Whalers	AHL	33	18	11	29	....	....	....	138	....	....	....	....	....	....	....	....	....	....	....	....	....	....	....	....	....	....
1981-82	**Montreal Canadiens**	**NHL**	**3**	**0**	**1**	**1**	**0**	**1**	**1**	**32**	**0**	**0**	**0**	**3**	**0.0**	**1**	**0**	**0**	**0**	**1**	**2**	**0**	**0**	**0**	**27**	**0**	**0**	**0**
	Nova Scotia Voyageurs	AHL	60	28	12	40	....	....	....	256	....	....	....	....	....	....	....	....	....	....	6	2	1	3	32	....	....	....
1982-83	Nova Scotia Voyageurs	AHL	78	31	27	58	....	....	....	183	....	....	....	....	....	....	....	....	....	....	7	1	1	2	25	....	....	....
1983-84	**Calgary Flames**	**NHL**	**4**	**0**	**0**	**0**	**0**	**0**	**0**	**19**	**0**	**0**	**0**	**2**	**0.0**	**0**	**0**	**1**	**0**	**–1**	....	....	....	....	....	....	....	....
	Colorado Flames	CHL	57	16	19	35	....	....	....	218	....	....	....	....	....	....	....	....	....	....	6	3	1	4	15	....	....	....
1984-85	**Toronto Maple Leafs**	**NHL**	**68**	**8**	**4**	**12**	**6**	**3**	**9**	**209**	**2**	**0**	**1**	**39**	**20.5**	**17**	**3**	**32**	**0**	**–18**	....	....	....	....	....	....	....	....
1985-86	**Toronto Maple Leafs**	**NHL**	**21**	**0**	**0**	**0**	**0**	**0**	**0**	**67**	**0**	**0**	**0**	**8**	**0.0**	**2**	**0**	**2**	**0**	**0**	....	....	....	....	....	....	....	....
	Edmonton Oilers	**NHL**	**4**	**1**	**0**	**1**	**1**	**0**	**1**	**12**	**0**	**0**	**0**	**4**	**25.0**	**1**	**0**	**0**	**0**	**1**	....	....	....	....	....	....	....	....
	Nova Scotia Oilers	AHL	19	4	3	7	....	....	....	41	....	....	....	....	....	....	....	....	....	....	....	....	....	....	....	....	....	....
1986-87	Nova Scotia Oilers	AHL	47	10	16	26	....	....	....	80	....	....	....	....	....	....	....	....	....	....	....	....	....	....	....	....	....	....
	Hershey Bears	AHL	12	1	2	3	....	....	....	30	....	....	....	....	....	....	....	....	....	....	3	2	0	2	10	....	....	....
1987-88	**New York Rangers**	**NHL**	**31**	**2**	**0**	**2**	**2**	**0**	**2**	**78**	**0**	**0**	**0**	**9**	**22.2**	**4**	**0**	**4**	**0**	**0**	....	....	....	....	....	....	....	....
	Colorado Rangers	IHL	30	12	10	22	....	....	....	53	....	....	....	....	....	....	....	....	....	....	13	2	2	4	21	....	....	....
1988-89	**Detroit Red Wings**	**NHL**	**1**	**0**	**0**	**0**	**0**	**0**	**0**	**0**	**0**	**0**	**0**	**0**	**0.0**	**0**	**0**	**0**	**0**	**0**	....	....	....	....	....	....	....	....
	Adirondack Red Wings	AHL	63	3	10	13	....	....	....	137	....	....	....	....	....	....	....	....	....	....	....	....	....	....	....	....	....	....
	NHL Totals		**178**	**16**	**9**	**25**	**13**	**7**	**20**	**512**	**2**	**0**	**1**	**96**	**16.7**	**40**	**4**	**60**	**0**		**2**	**0**	**0**	**0**	**27**	**0**	**0**	**0**
	Other Major League Totals		12	0	0	0	....	....	....	19	....	....	....	....	....	....	....	....	....	....	3	0	0	0	12	....	....	....

Selected by **New England** (WHA) in 1978 WHA Amateur Draft, June, 1978. NHL rights retained by **Hartford** prior to Expansion Draft, June 9, 1979. Claimed by **Montreal** from **Hartford** in Waiver Draft, October 5, 1981. Claimed by **Quebec** from **Montreal** in Waiver Draft, October 3, 1983. Claimed by **Calgary** from **Quebec** in Waiver Draft, October 3, 1983. Signed as a free agent by **Edmonton**, June 21, 1984. Claimed by **Toronto** from **Edmonton** in Waiver Draft, October 9, 1984. Claimed on waivers by **Edmonton** from **Toronto**, December 5, 1985. Traded to **Philadelphia** by **Edmonton** for Dom Campedelli, March 9, 1987. Traded to **NY Rangers** by **Philadelphia** for cash, July 21, 1987. Signed as a free agent by **Detroit**, October, 1988.

• BRUCE, David

LW – R. 5'11", 190 lbs. b: Thunder Bay, Ont., 10/7/1964. Vancouver's 2nd, 30th overall, in 1983.

Season	Club	League	GP	G	A	Pts	AG	AA	APts	PIM	PP	SH	GW	S	%	TGF	PGF	TGA	PGA	+/–	GP	G	A	Pts	PIM	PP	SH	GW
1981-82	Thunder Bay Flyers	TBJHL	35	27	31	58	....	....	....	74	....	....	....	....	....	....	....	....	....	....	....	....	....	....	....	....	....	....
1982-83	Kitchener Rangers	OHL	67	36	35	71	....	....	....	199	....	....	....	....	....	....	....	....	....	....	12	7	9	16	27	....	....	....
1983-84	Kitchener Rangers	OHL	62	52	40	92	....	....	....	203	....	....	....	....	....	....	....	....	....	....	10	5	8	13	20	....	....	....
	Kitchener Rangers	Mem-Cup	4	2	4	6	....	....	....	18	....	....	....	....	....	....	....	....	....	....	....	....	....	....	....	....	....	....
1984-85	Fredericton Express	AHL	56	14	11	25	....	....	....	104	....	....	....	....	....	....	....	....	....	....	5	0	0	0	37	....	....	....
1985-86	**Vancouver Canucks**	**NHL**	**12**	**0**	**1**	**1**	**0**	**1**	**1**	**14**	**0**	**0**	**0**	**17**	**0.0**	**4**	**0**	**6**	**0**	**–2**	**1**	**0**	**0**	**0**	**0**	**0**	**0**	**0**
	Fredericton Express	AHL	66	25	16	41	....	....	....	151	....	....	....	....	....	....	....	....	....	....	2	0	1	1	12	....	....	....
1986-87	**Vancouver Canucks**	**NHL**	**50**	**9**	**7**	**16**	**8**	**5**	**13**	**109**	**0**	**0**	**2**	**76**	**11.8**	**27**	**0**	**26**	**1**	**2**	....	....	....	....	....	....	....	....
	Fredericton Express	AHL	17	7	6	13	....	....	....	73	....	....	....	....	....	....	....	....	....	....	....	....	....	....	....	....	....	....
1987-88	**Vancouver Canucks**	**NHL**	**28**	**7**	**3**	**10**	**6**	**2**	**8**	**57**	**1**	**0**	**0**	**46**	**15.2**	**16**	**6**	**17**	**1**	**–6**	....	....	....	....	....	....	....	....
	Fredericton Express	AHL	30	27	18	45	....	....	....	115	....	....	....	....	....	....	....	....	....	....	....	....	....	....	....	....	....	....
1988-89	**Vancouver Canucks**	**NHL**	**53**	**7**	**7**	**14**	**6**	**5**	**11**	**65**	**1**	**0**	**2**	**86**	**8.1**	**24**	**6**	**36**	**2**	**–16**	....	....	....	....	....	....	....	....
1989-90	Milwaukee Admirals	IHL	68	40	35	75	....	....	....	148	....	....	....	....	....	....	....	....	....	....	6	5	3	8	0	....	....	....
1990-91	**St. Louis Blues**	**NHL**	**12**	**1**	**2**	**3**	**1**	**2**	**3**	**14**	**0**	**0**	**0**	**23**	**4.3**	**7**	**1**	**5**	**0**	**1**	**2**	**0**	**0**	**0**	**2**	**0**	**0**	**0**
	Peoria Rivermen	IHL	60	*64	52	116	....	....	....	78	....	....	....	....	....	....	....	....	....	....	18	*18	11	*29	40	....	....	....
1991-92	**San Jose Sharks**	**NHL**	**60**	**22**	**16**	**38**	**20**	**12**	**32**	**46**	**10**	**1**	**1**	**137**	**16.1**	**50**	**17**	**59**	**6**	**–20**	....	....	....	....	....	....	....	....
	Kansas City Blades	IHL	7	5	5	10	....	....	....	6	....	....	....	....	....	....	....	....	....	....	....	....	....	....	....	....	....	....
1992-93	**San Jose Sharks**	**NHL**	**17**	**2**	**3**	**5**	**2**	**2**	**4**	**33**	**2**	**0**	**0**	**36**	**5.6**	**11**	**9**	**20**	**4**	**–14**	....	....	....	....	....	....	....	....
1993-94	**San Jose Sharks**	**NHL**	**2**	**0**	**0**	**0**	**0**	**0**	**0**	**0**	**0**	**0**	**0**	**5**	**0.0**	**0**	**0**	**2**	**0**	**–2**	....	....	....	....	....	....	....	....
	Kansas City Blades	IHL	72	40	24	64	....	....	....	115	....	....	....	....	....	....	....	....	....	....	....	....	....	....	....	....	....	....
1994-95	Kansas City Blades	IHL	63	33	25	58	....	....	....	80	....	....	....	....	....	....	....	....	....	....	....	....	....	....	....	....	....	....
1995-96	Kansas City Blades	IHL	62	27	26	53	....	....	....	84	....	....	....	....	....	....	....	....	....	....	1	0	0	0	8	....	....	....
1996-97	Kansas City Blades	IHL	79	45	24	69	....	....	....	90	....	....	....	....	....	....	....	....	....	....	3	0	0	0	2	....	....	....
1997-98	Kansas City Blades	IHL	54	20	12	32	....	....	....	58	....	....	....	....	....	....	....	....	....	....	11	3	2	5	21	....	....	....
1998-99	EV Landshut	Germany	43	4	9	13	....	....	....	20	....	....	....	....	....	....	....	....	....	....	2	0	0	0	2	....	....	....
	NHL Totals		**234**	**48**	**39**	**87**	**43**	**29**	**72**	**338**	**14**	**1**	**5**	**426**	**11.3**	**139**	**39**	**171**	**14**		**3**	**0**	**0**	**0**	**2**	**0**	**0**	**0**

IHL First All-Star Team (1990, 1991) • Won James Gatschene Memorial Trophy (MVP - IHL) (1991)

Signed as a free agent by **St. Louis**, July 6, 1990. Claimed by **San Jose** from **St. Louis** in Expansion Draft, May 30, 1991.

• BRULE, Steve

RW – R. 6', 200 lbs. b: Montreal, Que., 1/15/1975. New Jersey's 6th, 143rd overall, in 1993.

Season	Club	League	GP	G	A	Pts	AG	AA	APts	PIM	PP	SH	GW	S	%	TGF	PGF	TGA	PGA	+/–	GP	G	A	Pts	PIM	PP	SH	GW
1991-92	Montreal-Bourassa	QAAA	38	41	26	67	....	....	....	14	....	....	....	....	....	....	....	....	....	....	....	....	....	....	....	....	....	....
1992-93	St-Jean Lynx	QMJHL	70	33	47	80	....	....	....	46	....	....	....	....	....	....	....	....	....	....	4	0	0	0	9	....	....	....
1993-94	St-Jean Lynx	QMJHL	66	41	64	105	....	....	....	46	....	....	....	....	....	....	....	....	....	....	5	2	1	3	0	....	....	....
1994-95	St-Jean Lynx	QMJHL	69	44	64	108	....	....	....	42	....	....	....	....	....	....	....	....	....	....	7	3	4	7	8	....	....	....
	Albany River Rats	AHL	3	1	4	5	....	....	....	0	....	....	....	....	....	....	....	....	....	....	14	9	5	14	4	....	....	....
1995-96	Albany River Rats	AHL	80	30	21	51	....	....	....	37	....	....	....	....	....	....	....	....	....	....	4	0	0	0	17	....	....	....
1996-97	Albany River Rats	AHL	79	28	48	76	....	....	....	27	....	....	....	....	....	....	....	....	....	....	16	7	7	14	12	....	....	....
1997-98	Albany River Rats	AHL	80	34	43	77	....	....	....	34	....	....	....	....	....	....	....	....	....	....	13	8	3	11	4	....	....	....
1998-99	Albany River Rats	AHL	78	32	52	84	....	....	....	35	....	....	....	....	....	....	....	....	....	....	5	3	1	4	4	....	....	....
99-2000	Albany River Rats	AHL	75	30	46	76	....	....	....	18	....	....	....	....	....	....	....	....	....	....	5	1	2	3	0	....	....	....
	New Jersey Devils	**NHL**	....	....	....	....	....	....	....	....	....	....	....	....	....	....	....	....	....	....	**1**	**0**	**0**	**0**	**0**	**0**	**0**	**0**
	NHL Totals		....	....	....	....	....	....	....	....	....	....	....	....	....	....	....	....	....	....	**1**	**0**	**0**	**0**	**0**	**0**	**0**	**0**

QMJHL Second All-Star Team (1995)

• BRUMWELL, Murray

James Murray D – L. 6'2", 190 lbs. b: Calgary, Alta., 3/31/1960.

Season	Club	League	GP	G	A	Pts	AG	AA	APts	PIM	PP	SH	GW	S	%	TGF	PGF	TGA	PGA	+/–	GP	G	A	Pts	PIM	PP	SH	GW
1977-78	Calgary Canucks	AJHL	59	4	40	44	....	....	....	79	....	....	....	....	....	....	....	....	....	....	....	....	....	....	....	....	....	....
	Calgary Wranglers	WCJHL	1	0	0	0	....	....	....	2	....	....	....	....	....	....	....	....	....	....	....	....	....	....	....	....	....	....
	Saskatoon Blades	WCJHL	1	0	2	2	....	....	....	0	....	....	....	....	....	....	....	....	....	....	....	....	....	....	....	....	....	....
1978-79	Billings Bighorns	WHL	61	11	32	43	....	....	....	62	....	....	....	....	....	....	....	....	....	....	....	....	....	....	....	....	....	....
1979-80	Billings Bighorns	WHL	67	18	54	72	....	....	....	50	....	....	....	....	....	....	....	....	....	....	....	....	....	....	....	....	....	....
1980-81	**Minnesota North Stars**	**NHL**	**1**	**0**	**0**	**0**	**0**	**0**	**0**	**0**	**0**	**0**	**0**	**0**	**0.0**	**1**	**0**	**0**	**0**	**1**	....	....	....	....	....	....	....	....
	Oklahoma City Stars	CHL	79	12	43	55	....	....	....	79	....	....	....	....	....	....	....	....	....	....	3	0	0	0	4	....	....	....
1981-82	**Minnesota North Stars**	**NHL**	**21**	**0**	**3**	**3**	**0**	**2**	**2**	**18**	**0**	**0**	**0**	**12**	**0.0**	**19**	**1**	**23**	**5**	**0**	**2**	**0**	**0**	**0**	**2**	**0**	**0**	**0**
	Nashville South Stars	CHL	55	4	21	25	....	....	....	66	....	....	....	....	....	....	....	....	....	....	....	....	....	....	....	....	....	....
1982-83	**New Jersey Devils**	**NHL**	**59**	**5**	**14**	**19**	**4**	**10**	**14**	**34**	**1**	**0**	**0**	**61**	**8.2**	**60**	**19**	**73**	**12**	**–20**	....	....	....	....	....	....	....	....
	Wichita Wind	CHL	11	4	1	5	....	....	....	4	....	....	....	....	....	....	....	....	....	....	....	....	....	....	....	....	....	....
1983-84	**New Jersey Devils**	**NHL**	**42**	**7**	**13**	**20**	**6**	**9**	**15**	**14**	**5**	**0**	**0**	**55**	**12.7**	**48**	**15**	**48**	**10**	**–5**	....	....	....	....	....	....	....	....
	Maine Mariners	AHL	35	4	25	29	....	....	....	16	....	....	....	....	....	....	....	....	....	....	17	1	5	6	15	....	....	....
1984-85	Maine Mariners	AHL	64	8	31	39	....	....	....	12	....	....	....	....	....	....	....	....	....	....	10	4	5	9	19	....	....	....
1985-86	**New Jersey Devils**	**NHL**	**1**	**0**	**0**	**0**	**0**	**0**	**0**	**0**	**0**	**0**	**0**	**3**	**0.0**	**0**	**0**	**2**	**1**	**–1**	....	....	....	....	....	....	....	....
	Maine Mariners	AHL	66	9	28	37	....	....	....	35	....	....	....	....	....	....	....	....	....	....	5	0	3	3	2	....	....	....
1986-87	**New Jersey Devils**	**NHL**	**1**	**0**	**0**	**0**	**0**	**0**	**0**	**2**	**0**	**0**	**0**	**2**	**0.0**	**1**	**0**	**1**	**1**	**1**	....	....	....	....	....	....	....	....
	Maine Mariners	AHL	69	10	38	48	....	....	....	30	....	....	....	....	....	....	....	....	....	....	....	....	....	....	....	....	....	....
1987-88	**New Jersey Devils**	**NHL**	**3**	**0**	**1**	**1**	**0**	**1**	**1**	**2**	**0**	**0**	**0**	**4**	**0.0**	**2**	**0**	**2**	**0**	**0**	....	....	....	....	....	....	....	....
	Utica Devils	AHL	77	13	53	66	....	....	....	44	....	....	....	....	....	....	....	....	....	....	....	....	....	....	....	....	....	....

Season	Club	League	GP	G	A	Pts	AG	AA	APts	PIM	PP	SH	GW	S	%	TGF	PGF	TGA	PGA	+/–	GP	G	A	Pts	PIM	PP	SH	GW
			REGULAR SEASON																		PLAYOFFS							
1988-89	Utica Devils	AHL	73	5	29	34	....	....	....	29	....	....	....	....	....	....	....	....	....	....	5	0	0	0	2	....	....	....
1989-90	New Haven Nighthawks	AHL	62	7	29	36	....	....	....	24	....	....	....	....	....	....	....	....	....	....	....	....	....	....	....	....	....	....
1990-91	New Haven Nighthawks	AHL	67	8	18	26	....	....	....	27	....	....	....	....	....	....	....	....	....	....	....	....	....	....	....	....	....	....
	NHL Totals		**128**	**12**	**31**	**43**	**10**	**22**	**32**	**70**	**6**	**0**	**0**	**137**	**8.8**	**131**	**35**	**149**	**29**		**2**	**0**	**0**	**0**	**2**	**0**	**0**	**0**

AHL Second All-Star Team (1988)

Signed as a free agent by **Minnesota**, August 7, 1980. Claimed by **New Jersey** from **Minnesota** in Waiver Draft, October 4, 1982.

• BRUNET, Benoit

LW – L. 6', 198 lbs. b: Ste-Anne-de-Bellevue, Que., 8/24/1968. Montreal's 2nd, 27th overall, in 1986.

Season	Club	League	GP	G	A	Pts	AG	AA	APts	PIM	PP	SH	GW	S	%	TGF	PGF	TGA	PGA	+/–	GP	G	A	Pts	PIM	PP	SH	GW
1985-86	Hull Olympiques	QMJHL	71	33	37	70	....	....	....	81	....	....	....	....	....	....	....	....	....	....	....	....	....	....	....	....	....	....
	Hull Olympiques	Mem-Cup	5	1	2	3	....	....	....	2	....	....	....	....	....	....	....	....	....	....	....	....	....	....	....	....	....	....
1986-87	Hull Olympiques	QMJHL	60	43	67	110	....	....	....	105	....	....	....	....	....	....	....	....	....	....	6	7	5	12	8	....	....	....
1987-88	Hull Olympiques	QMJHL	62	54	89	143	....	....	....	131	....	....	....	....	....	....	....	....	....	....	10	3	10	13	11	....	....	....
	Hull Olympiques	Mem-Cup	4	1	3	4	....	....	....	0	....	....	....	....	....	....	....	....	....	....	....	....	....	....	....	....	....	....
1988-89	**Montreal Canadiens**	**NHL**	**2**	**0**	**1**	**1**	**0**	**1**	**1**	**0**	**0**	**0**	**0**	**1**	**0.0**	**2**	**0**	**2**	**0**	**0**	....	....	....	....	....	....	....	....
	Sherbrooke Canadiens	AHL	73	41	*76	117	....	....	....	95	....	....	....	....	....	....	....	....	....	....	6	2	0	2	4	....	....	....
1989-90	Sherbrooke Canadiens	AHL	72	32	35	67	....	....	....	82	....	....	....	....	....	....	....	....	....	....	12	8	7	15	20	....	....	....
1990-91	Montreal Canadiens	Fr-Tour	1	0	0	0	....	....	....	0	....	....	....	....	....	....	....	....	....	....	....	....	....	....	....	....	....	....
	Montreal Canadiens	**NHL**	**17**	**1**	**3**	**4**	**1**	**2**	**3**	**0**	**0**	**0**	**0**	**12**	**8.3**	**7**	**1**	**7**	**0**	**–1**	....	....	....	....	....	....	....	....
	Fredericton Canadiens	AHL	24	13	18	31	....	....	....	16	....	....	....	....	....	....	....	....	....	....	6	5	6	11	2	....	....	....
1991-92	**Montreal Canadiens**	**NHL**	**18**	**4**	**6**	**10**	**4**	**5**	**9**	**14**	**0**	**0**	**0**	**37**	**10.8**	**15**	**6**	**5**	**0**	**4**	....	....	....	....	....	....	....	....
	Fredericton Canadiens	AHL	6	7	9	16	....	....	....	27	....	....	....	....	....	....	....	....	....	....	....	....	....	....	....	....	....	....
1992-93♦	**Montreal Canadiens**	**NHL**	**47**	**10**	**15**	**25**	**8**	**10**	**18**	**19**	**0**	**0**	**1**	**71**	**14.1**	**39**	**4**	**23**	**1**	**13**	**20**	**2**	**8**	**10**	**8**	**1**	**0**	**1**
1993-94	**Montreal Canadiens**	**NHL**	**71**	**10**	**20**	**30**	**9**	**16**	**25**	**20**	**0**	**3**	**1**	**92**	**10.9**	**42**	**0**	**44**	**16**	**14**	**7**	**1**	**4**	**5**	**16**	**0**	**0**	**0**
1994-95	**Montreal Canadiens**	**NHL**	**45**	**7**	**18**	**25**	**12**	**27**	**39**	**16**	**1**	**1**	**2**	**80**	**8.8**	**34**	**4**	**32**	**9**	**7**	....	....	....	....	....	....	....	....
1995-96	**Montreal Canadiens**	**NHL**	**26**	**7**	**8**	**15**	**7**	**7**	**14**	**17**	**3**	**1**	**4**	**48**	**14.6**	**19**	**6**	**27**	**10**	**–4**	**3**	**0**	**2**	**2**	**0**	**0**	**0**	**0**
	Fredericton Canadiens	AHL	3	2	1	3	....	....	....	6	....	....	....	....	....	....	....	....	....	....	....	....	....	....	....	....	....	....
1996-97	**Montreal Canadiens**	**NHL**	**39**	**10**	**13**	**23**	**11**	**12**	**23**	**14**	**2**	**0**	**2**	**63**	**15.9**	**36**	**5**	**36**	**11**	**6**	**4**	**1**	**3**	**4**	**4**	**0**	**1**	**0**
1997-98	**Montreal Canadiens**	**NHL**	**68**	**12**	**20**	**32**	**14**	**20**	**34**	**61**	**1**	**2**	**2**	**87**	**13.8**	**51**	**13**	**41**	**14**	**11**	**8**	**1**	**0**	**1**	**4**	**0**	**0**	**1**
1998-99	**Montreal Canadiens**	**NHL**	**60**	**14**	**17**	**31**	**16**	**16**	**32**	**31**	**4**	**2**	**0**	**115**	**12.2**	**43**	**10**	**46**	**12**	**–1**	....	....	....	....	....	....	....	....
99-2000	**Montreal Canadiens**	**NHL**	**50**	**14**	**15**	**29**	**16**	**14**	**30**	**13**	**6**	**1**	**2**	**103**	**13.6**	**41**	**18**	**30**	**10**	**3**	....	....	....	....	....	....	....	....
	NHL Totals		**443**	**89**	**136**	**225**	**98**	**130**	**228**	**205**	**17**	**10**	**14**	**709**	**12.6**	**329**	**67**	**293**	**83**		**42**	**5**	**17**	**22**	**32**	**1**	**1**	**2**

QMJHL Second All-Star Team (1987) • AHL First All-Star Team (1989)

• BRUNETTE, Andrew

LW – L. 6'1", 210 lbs. b: Sudbury, Ont., 8/24/1973. Washington's 6th, 174th overall, in 1993.

Season	Club	League	GP	G	A	Pts	AG	AA	APts	PIM	PP	SH	GW	S	%	TGF	PGF	TGA	PGA	+/–	GP	G	A	Pts	PIM	PP	SH	GW
1989-90	Rayside-Balfour Sabrecats	OMHA	32	38	*65	*103	....	....	....	....	....	....	....	....	....	....	....	....	....	....	....	....	....	....	....	....	....	....
	Rayside-Balfour Canadians	OJHL	4	1	1	2	....	....	....	0	....	....	....	....	....	....	....	....	....	....	....	....	....	....	....	....	....	....
1990-91	Owen Sound Platers	OHL	63	15	20	35	....	....	....	15	....	....	....	....	....	....	....	....	....	....	....	....	....	....	....	....	....	....
1991-92	Owen Sound Platers	OHL	66	51	47	98	....	....	....	42	....	....	....	....	....	....	....	....	....	....	5	5	0	5	8	....	....	....
1992-93	Owen Sound Platers	OHL	66	*62	*100	*162	....	....	....	91	....	....	....	....	....	....	....	....	....	....	8	8	6	14	16	....	....	....
1993-94	Portland Pirates	AHL	23	9	11	20	....	....	....	10	....	....	....	....	....	....	....	....	....	....	2	0	1	1	0	....	....	....
	Providence Bruins	AHL	3	0	0	0	....	....	....	0	....	....	....	....	....	....	....	....	....	....	....	....	....	....	....	....	....	....
	Hampton Roads Admirals	ECHL	20	12	18	30	....	....	....	32	....	....	....	....	....	....	....	....	....	....	7	7	6	13	18	....	....	....
1994-95	Portland Pirates	AHL	79	30	50	80	....	....	....	53	....	....	....	....	....	....	....	....	....	....	7	3	3	6	10	....	....	....
1995-96	**Washington Capitals**	**NHL**	**11**	**3**	**3**	**6**	**3**	**2**	**5**	**0**	**0**	**0**	**1**	**16**	**18.8**	**10**	**1**	**4**	**0**	**5**	**6**	**1**	**3**	**4**	**0**	**0**	**0**	**0**
	Portland Pirates	AHL	69	28	66	94	....	....	....	125	....	....	....	....	....	....	....	....	....	....	20	11	18	29	15	....	....	....
1996-97	**Washington Capitals**	**NHL**	**23**	**4**	**7**	**11**	**4**	**6**	**10**	**12**	**2**	**0**	**0**	**23**	**17.4**	**15**	**7**	**11**	**0**	**–3**	....	....	....	....	....	....	....	....
	Portland Pirates	AHL	50	22	51	73	....	....	....	48	....	....	....	....	....	....	....	....	....	....	5	1	2	3	0	....	....	....
1997-98	**Washington Capitals**	**NHL**	**28**	**11**	**12**	**23**	**13**	**12**	**25**	**12**	**4**	**0**	**2**	**42**	**26.2**	**27**	**9**	**16**	**0**	**2**	....	....	....	....	....	....	....	....
	Portland Pirates	AHL	43	21	46	67	....	....	....	64	....	....	....	....	....	....	....	....	....	....	10	1	11	12	12	....	....	....
1998-99	**Nashville Predators**	**NHL**	**77**	**11**	**20**	**31**	**13**	**19**	**32**	**26**	**7**	**0**	**1**	**65**	**16.9**	**48**	**20**	**38**	**0**	**–10**	....	....	....	....	....	....	....	....
99-2000	**Atlanta Thrashers**	**NHL**	**81**	**23**	**27**	**50**	**26**	**25**	**51**	**30**	**9**	**0**	**2**	**107**	**21.5**	**68**	**26**	**76**	**2**	**–32**	....	....	....	....	....	....	....	....
	NHL Totals		**220**	**52**	**69**	**121**	**59**	**64**	**123**	**80**	**22**	**0**	**6**	**253**	**20.6**	**168**	**63**	**145**	**2**		**6**	**1**	**3**	**4**	**0**	**0**	**0**	**0**

OHL First All-Star Team (1993) • Canadian Major Junior Second All-Star Team (1993) • AHL Second All-Star Team (1995)

Claimed by **Nashville** from **Washington** in Expansion Draft, June 26, 1998. Traded to **Atlanta** by **Nashville** for Atlanta's 5th round choice (Matt Hendricks) in 2000 Entry Draft, June 21, 1999.

• BRYDGES, Paul

C – R. 5'11", 180 lbs. b: Guelph, Ont., 6/21/1965.

Season	Club	League	GP	G	A	Pts	AG	AA	APts	PIM	PP	SH	GW	S	%	TGF	PGF	TGA	PGA	+/–	GP	G	A	Pts	PIM	PP	SH	GW
1981-82	Guelph Midget Majors	OMHA	45	16	15	31	....	....	....	30	....	....	....	....	....	....	....	....	....	....	....	....	....	....	....	....	....	....
1982-83	Guelph Platers	OHL	56	13	13	26	....	....	....	27	....	....	....	....	....	....	....	....	....	....	....	....	....	....	....	....	....	....
1983-84	Guelph Platers	OHL	68	27	23	50	....	....	....	37	....	....	....	....	....	....	....	....	....	....	....	....	....	....	....	....	....	....
1984-85	Guelph Platers	OHL	57	22	24	46	....	....	....	39	....	....	....	....	....	....	....	....	....	....	....	....	....	....	....	....	....	....
1985-86	Guelph Platers	OHL	62	17	40	57	....	....	....	88	....	....	....	....	....	....	....	....	....	....	19	10	15	25	22	....	....	....
	Guelph Platers	Mem-Cup	4	0	2	2	....	....	....	8	....	....	....	....	....	....	....	....	....	....	....	....	....	....	....	....	....	....
1986-87	**Buffalo Sabres**	**NHL**	**15**	**2**	**2**	**4**	**2**	**1**	**3**	**6**	**0**	**0**	**0**	**8**	**25.0**	**9**	**0**	**9**	**4**	**4**	....	....	....	....	....	....	....	....
	Rochester Americans	AHL	54	13	17	30	....	....	....	54	....	....	....	....	....	....	....	....	....	....	1	0	0	0	0	....	....	....
1987-88	Rochester Americans	AHL	69	15	16	31	....	....	....	86	....	....	....	....	....	....	....	....	....	....	7	1	1	2	4	....	....	....
1988-89	Rochester Americans	AHL	51	8	3	11	....	....	....	36	....	....	....	....	....	....	....	....	....	....	....	....	....	....	....	....	....	....
1989-90	New Haven Nighthawks	AHL	37	6	7	13	....	....	....	38	....	....	....	....	....	....	....	....	....	....	....	....	....	....	....	....	....	....
	NHL Totals		**15**	**2**	**2**	**4**	**2**	**1**	**3**	**6**	**0**	**0**	**0**	**8**	**25.0**	**9**	**0**	**9**	**4**		....	....	....	....	....	....	....	....

Signed as a free agent by **Buffalo**, June 11, 1986.

• BRYLIN, Sergei

Sergei Vladimirovich C – L. 5'10", 190 lbs. b: Moscow, USSR, 1/13/1974. New Jersey's 2nd, 42nd overall, in 1992.

Season	Club	League	GP	G	A	Pts	AG	AA	APts	PIM	PP	SH	GW	S	%	TGF	PGF	TGA	PGA	+/–	GP	G	A	Pts	PIM	PP	SH	GW
1991-92	CSKA Moscow	CIS	44	1	6	7	....	....	....	4	....	....	....	....	....	....	....	....	....	....	....	....	....	....	....	....	....	....
	Russia	EJC-A	6	1	1	2	....	....	....	4	....	....	....	....	....	....	....	....	....	....	....	....	....	....	....	....	....	....
1992-93	CSKA Moscow	CIS	42	5	4	9	....	....	....	36	....	....	....	....	....	....	....	....	....	....	....	....	....	....	....	....	....	....
	Russia	WJC-A	7	3	3	6	....	....	....	6	....	....	....	....	....	....	....	....	....	....	....	....	....	....	....	....	....	....
1993-94	CSKA Moscow	CIS	39	4	6	10	....	....	....	36	....	....	....	....	....	....	....	....	....	....	3	1	0	1	2	....	....	....
	Russia	WJC-A	7	1	5	6	....	....	....	0	....	....	....	....	....	....	....	....	....	....	....	....	....	....	....	....	....	....
	Russian Penguins	IHL	13	4	5	9	....	....	....	18	....	....	....	....	....	....	....	....	....	....	....	....	....	....	....	....	....	....
1994-95♦	**New Jersey Devils**	**NHL**	**26**	**6**	**8**	**14**	**11**	**12**	**23**	**8**	**0**	**0**	**0**	**41**	**14.6**	**20**	**5**	**3**	**0**	**12**	**12**	**1**	**2**	**3**	**4**	**0**	**0**	**0**
	Albany River Rats	AHL	63	19	35	54	....	....	....	78	....	....	....	....	....	....	....	....	....	....	....	....	....	....	....	....	....	....
1995-96	**New Jersey Devils**	**NHL**	**50**	**4**	**5**	**9**	**4**	**4**	**8**	**26**	**0**	**0**	**1**	**51**	**7.8**	**19**	**2**	**21**	**2**	**–2**	....	....	....	....	....	....	....	....
	Russia	WC-A	8	3	2	5	....	....	....	12	....	....	....	....	....	....	....	....	....	....	....	....	....	....	....	....	....	....
1996-97	**New Jersey Devils**	**NHL**	**29**	**2**	**2**	**4**	**2**	**2**	**4**	**20**	**0**	**0**	**0**	**34**	**5.9**	**9**	**2**	**20**	**0**	**–13**	....	....	....	....	....	....	....	....
	Albany River Rats	AHL	43	17	24	41	....	....	....	38	....	....	....	....	....	....	....	....	....	....	16	4	8	12	12	....	....	....
1997-98	**New Jersey Devils**	**NHL**	**18**	**2**	**3**	**5**	**2**	**3**	**5**	**0**	**0**	**0**	**0**	**20**	**10.0**	**5**	**0**	**1**	**0**	**4**	....	....	....	....	....	....	....	....
	Albany River Rats	AHL	44	21	22	43	....	....	....	60	....	....	....	....	....	....	....	....	....	....	....	....	....	....	....	....	....	....
1998-99	**New Jersey Devils**	**NHL**	**47**	**5**	**10**	**15**	**6**	**10**	**16**	**28**	**3**	**0**	**1**	**51**	**9.8**	**28**	**6**	**14**	**0**	**8**	**5**	**3**	**1**	**4**	**4**	**1**	**0**	**1**
99-2000♦	**New Jersey Devils**	**NHL**	**64**	**9**	**11**	**20**	**10**	**10**	**20**	**20**	**1**	**0**	**1**	**84**	**10.7**	**32**	**4**	**33**	**5**	**0**	**17**	**3**	**5**	**8**	**0**	**0**	**0**	**0**
	NHL Totals		**234**	**28**	**39**	**67**	**35**	**41**	**76**	**102**	**4**	**0**	**3**	**281**	**10.0**	**113**	**19**	**92**	**7**		**34**	**7**	**8**	**15**	**8**	**1**	**0**	**1**

• BUBLA, Jiri

D – L. 5'11", 200 lbs. b: Usti nad Labem, CSSR, 1/27/1950.

Season	Club	League	GP	G	A	Pts	AG	AA	APts	PIM	PP	SH	GW	S	%	TGF	PGF	TGA	PGA	+/–	GP	G	A	Pts	PIM	PP	SH	GW
1967-68	CHZ Litvinov	Czech.	3	0	0	0	....	....	....	0	....	....	....	....	....	....	....	....	....	....	....	....	....	....	....	....	....	....
1968-69	CHZ Litvinov	Czech.	36	4	5	9	....	....	....	....	....	....	....	....	....	....	....	....	....	....	....	....	....	....	....	....	....	....
1969-70	CHZ Litvinov	Czech.	STATISTICS NOT AVAILABLE																									
1970-71	CHZ Litvinov	Czech-Jr.	36	3	9	12	....	....	....		....	....	....	....	....	....	....	....	....	....	....	....	....	....	....	....	....	....
	Czechoslovakia	WEC-A	9	1	0	1	....	....	....	2	....	....	....	....	....	....	....	....	....	....	....	....	....	....	....	....	....	....

			REGULAR SEASON																		PLAYOFFS							
Season	Club	League	GP	G	A	Pts	AG	AA	APts	PIM	PP	SH	GW	S	%	TGF	PGF	TGA	PGA	+/–	GP	G	A	Pts	PIM	PP	SH	GW
1971-72	CHZ Litvinov	Czech.	36	5	9	14	....	....	....	....	....	....	....	....	....	....	....	....	....	....	....	....	....	....	....	....	....	....
	Czechoslovakia	WEC-A	10	0	1	1	....	....	....	8	....	....	....	....	....	....	....	....	....	....	....	....	....	....	....	....	....	....
1972-73	CHZ Litvinov	Czech.	36	3	9	12	....	....	....	....	....	....	....	....	....	....	....	....	....	....	....	....	....	....	....	....	....	....
	Czechoslovakia	WEC-A	10	1	2	3	....	....	....	6	....	....	....	....	....	....	....	....	....	....	....	....	....	....	....	....	....	....
1973-74	CHZ Litvinov	Czech.	40	9	8	17	....	....	....	....	....	....	....	....	....	....	....	....	....	....	....	....	....	....	....	....	....	....
	Czechoslovakia	WEC-A	10	1	3	4	....	....	....	2	....	....	....	....	....	....	....	....	....	....	....	....	....	....	....	....	....	....
1974-75	CHZ Litvinov	Czech.	30	5	20	25	....	....	....	....	....	....	....	....	....	....	....	....	....	....	....	....	....	....	....	....	....	....
	Czechoslovakia	WEC-A	10	1	2	3	....	....	....	6	....	....	....	....	....	....	....	....	....	....	....	....	....	....	....	....	....	....
1975-76	CHZ Litvinov	Czech.	31	11	18	29	....	....	....	....	....	....	....	....	....	....	....	....	....	....	....	....	....	....	....	....	....	....
	Czechoslovakia	Olympics	5	1	3	4	....	....	....	6	....	....	....	....	....	....	....	....	....	....	....	....	....	....	....	....	....	....
	Czechoslovakia	WEC-A	10	4	3	7	....	....	....	2	....	....	....	....	....	....	....	....	....	....	....	....	....	....	....	....	....	....
1976-77	Czechoslovakia	Can-Cup	7	3	2	5	....	....	....	4	....	....	....	....	....	....	....	....	....	....	....	....	....	....	....	....	....	....
	CHZ Litvinov	Czech.	40	9	28	37	....	....	....	....	....	....	....	....	....	....	....	....	....	....	....	....	....	....	....	....	....	....
	Czechoslovakia	WEC-A	10	0	4	4	....	....	....	6	....	....	....	....	....	....	....	....	....	....	....	....	....	....	....	....	....	....
1977-78	CHZ Litvinov	Czech.	44	21	35	56	....	....	....	49	....	....	....	....	....	....	....	....	....	....	....	....	....	....	....	....	....	....
	Czechoslovakia	WEC-A	9	1	2	3	....	....	....	8	....	....	....	....	....	....	....	....	....	....	....	....	....	....	....	....	....	....
1978-79	CHZ Litvinov	Czech.	44	12	25	37	....	....	....	30	....	....	....	....	....	....	....	....	....	....	....	....	....	....	....	....	....	....
	Czechoslovakia	WEC-A	8	2	2	4	....	....	....	8	....	....	....	....	....	....	....	....	....	....	....	....	....	....	....	....	....	....
1979-80	CHZ Litvinov	Czech.	17	5	11	16	....	....	....	8	....	....	....	....	....	....	....	....	....	....	....	....	....	....	....	....	....	....
	Sparta CKD Praha	Czech.	14	1	6	7	....	....	....	10	....	....	....	....	....	....	....	....	....	....	....	....	....	....	....	....	....	....
	Czechoslovakia	Nat-Team	14	3	4	7	....	....	....	15	....	....	....	....	....	....	....	....	....	....	....	....	....	....	....	....	....	....
	Czechoslovakia	Olympics	6	0	3	3	....	....	....	2	....	....	....	....	....	....	....	....	....	....	....	....	....	....	....	....	....	....
1980-81	Sparta CKD Praha	Czech.	40	4	16	20	....	....	....	14	....	....	....	....	....	....	....	....	....	....	....	....	....	....	....	....	....	....
1981-82	**Vancouver Canucks**	**NHL**	**23**	**1**	**1**	**2**	**1**	**1**	**2**	**16**	**0**	**0**	**0**	**23**	**4.3**	**27**	**1**	**21**	**3**	**8**	....	....	....	....	....	....	....	....
1982-83	**Vancouver Canucks**	**NHL**	**72**	**2**	**28**	**30**	**2**	**19**	**21**	**59**	**1**	**0**	**0**	**92**	**2.2**	**96**	**31**	**82**	**8**	**–9**	**1**	**0**	**0**	**0**	**5**	**0**	**0**	**0**
1983-84	**Vancouver Canucks**	**NHL**	**62**	**6**	**33**	**39**	**5**	**22**	**27**	**43**	**2**	**0**	**1**	**84**	**7.1**	**107**	**39**	**97**	**19**	**–10**	**2**	**0**	**0**	**0**	**0**	**0**	**0**	**0**
1984-85	**Vancouver Canucks**	**NHL**	**56**	**2**	**15**	**17**	**2**	**10**	**12**	**54**	**0**	**0**	**0**	**73**	**2.7**	**50**	**5**	**88**	**28**	**–15**	....	....	....	....	....	....	....	....
1985-86	**Vancouver Canucks**	**NHL**	**43**	**6**	**24**	**30**	**5**	**16**	**21**	**30**	**4**	**0**	**1**	**62**	**9.7**	**78**	**32**	**88**	**17**	**–25**	**3**	**0**	**0**	**0**	**2**	**0**	**0**	**0**
	NHL Totals		**256**	**17**	**101**	**118**	**15**	**68**	**83**	**202**	**7**	**0**	**2**	**334**	**5.1**	**358**	**108**	**376**	**75**		**6**	**0**	**0**	**0**	**7**	**0**	**0**	**0**

• Father of Jiri Slegr • WEC-A All-Star Team (1978, 1979) • Named Best Defenseman at WEC-A (1979)

Claimed in Special Czechoslovakian Entry Draft by **Colorado**, May 28, 1981. Signed to a contract by **Vancouver**, June, 1981. • Colorado received Brent Ashton and Vancouver's 4th round choice (Tom Martin) in 1982 Entry Draft as compensation via earlier Vancouver/Winnipeg transaction involving Lucien Deblois, July 15, 1981.

• BUCHANAN, Jeff

D – R. 6'2", 200 lbs. b: Swift Current, Sask., 5/23/1971.

Season	Club	League	GP	G	A	Pts	AG	AA	APts	PIM	PP	SH	GW	S	%	TGF	PGF	TGA	PGA	+/–	GP	G	A	Pts	PIM	PP	SH	GW
1989-90	Saskatoon Blades	WHL	66	7	12	19	....	....	....	96	....	....	....	....	....	....	....	....	....	....	9	0	2	2	2	....	....	....
1990-91	Saskatoon Blades	WHL	69	10	26	36	....	....	....	123	....	....	....	....	....	....	....	....	....	....	....	....	....	....	....	....	....	....
1991-92	Saskatoon Blades	WHL	72	17	37	54	....	....	....	145	....	....	....	....	....	....	....	....	....	....	22	10	14	24	39	....	....	....
1992-93	Atlanta Knights	IHL	68	4	18	22	....	....	....	282	....	....	....	....	....	....	....	....	....	....	9	0	0	0	26	....	....	....
1993-94	Atlanta Knights	IHL	76	5	24	29	....	....	....	253	....	....	....	....	....	....	....	....	....	....	14	0	1	1	20	....	....	....
1994-95	Atlanta Knights	IHL	4	0	1	1	....	....	....	9	....	....	....	....	....	....	....	....	....	....	....	....	....	....	....	....	....	....
	Detroit Vipers	IHL	50	4	6	10	....	....	....	125	....	....	....	....	....	....	....	....	....	....	....	....	....	....	....	....	....	....
	Indianapolis Ice	IHL	25	3	9	12	....	....	....	63	....	....	....	....	....	....	....	....	....	....	....	....	....	....	....	....	....	....
1995-96	Indianapolis Ice	IHL	77	4	14	18	....	....	....	277	....	....	....	....	....	....	....	....	....	....	5	0	1	1	9	....	....	....
1996-97	Orlando Solar Bears	IHL	81	11	27	38	....	....	....	246	....	....	....	....	....	....	....	....	....	....	....	....	....	....	....	....	....	....
1997-98	Orlando Solar Bears	IHL	61	5	20	25	....	....	....	131	....	....	....	....	....	....	....	....	....	....	....	....	....	....	....	....	....	....
	Kansas City Blades	IHL	7	2	3	5	....	....	....	6	....	....	....	....	....	....	....	....	....	....	11	0	2	2	40	....	....	....
1998-99	**Colorado Avalanche**	**NHL**	**6**	**0**	**0**	**0**	**0**	**0**	**0**	**6**	**0**	**0**	**0**	**1**	**0.0**	**1**	**0**	**0**	**0**	**1**	....	....	....	....	....	....	....	....
	Hershey Bears	AHL	38	4	6	10	....	....	....	102	....	....	....	....	....	....	....	....	....	....	5	0	1	1	4	....	....	....
	NHL Totals		**6**	**0**	**0**	**0**	**0**	**0**	**0**	**6**	**0**	**0**	**0**	**1**	**0.0**	**1**	**0**	**0**	**0**		....	....	....	....	....	....	....	....

Signed as a free agent by **Tampa Bay**, July 13, 1992. Traded to **Chicago** by **Tampa Bay** with Jim Cummins and Tom Tilley for Paul Ysebaert and Rich Sutter, February 22, 1995. Signed as a free agent by **Colorado**, August 25, 1998.

• BUCHANAN, Ron

Ronald Leonard "Senior" C – L. 6'3", 170 lbs. b: Montreal, Que., 11/15/1944.

Season	Club	League	GP	G	A	Pts	AG	AA	APts	PIM	PP	SH	GW	S	%	TGF	PGF	TGA	PGA	+/–	GP	G	A	Pts	PIM	PP	SH	GW
1962-63	Oshawa Generals	OHA-Jr.	39	13	25	38	....	....	....	18	....	....	....	....	....	....	....	....	....	....	....	....	....	....	....	....	....	....
1963-64	Oshawa Generals	OHA-Jr.	56	52	47	99	....	....	....	38	....	....	....	....	....	....	....	....	....	....	4	4	3	7	12	....	....	....
1964-65	Oshawa Generals	OHA-Jr.	49	50	53	103	....	....	....	21	....	....	....	....	....	....	....	....	....	....	6	5	3	8	0	....	....	....
	Minneapolis Bruins	CPHL	....	....	....	....	....	....	....	....	....	....	....	....	....	....	....	....	....	....	4	0	0	0	0	....	....	....
1965-66	Oklahoma City Blazers	CPHL	70	27	16	43	....	....	....	33	....	....	....	....	....	....	....	....	....	....	9	5	5	10	0	....	....	....
1966-67	**Boston Bruins**	**NHL**	**3**	**0**	**0**	**0**	**0**	**0**	**0**	**0**	....	....	....	....	....	....	....	....	....	....	....	....	....	....	....	....	....	....
	Oklahoma City Blazers	CPHL	56	34	35	69	....	....	....	23	....	....	....	....	....	....	....	....	....	....	11	5	5	10	6	....	....	....
1967-68	Oklahoma City Blazers	CPHL	64	26	48	74	....	....	....	41	....	....	....	....	....	....	....	....	....	....	....	....	....	....	....	....	....	....
1968-69	Quebec Aces	AHL	11	3	1	4	....	....	....	2	....	....	....	....	....	....	....	....	....	....	....	....	....	....	....	....	....	....
	Kansas City Blues	CHL	50	16	45	61	....	....	....	16	....	....	....	....	....	....	....	....	....	....	....	....	....	....	....	....	....	....
1969-70	**St. Louis Blues**	**NHL**	**2**	**0**	**0**	**0**	**0**	**0**	**0**	**0**	**0**	**0**	**0**	**4**	**0.0**	**0**	**0**	**1**	**0**	**–1**	....	....	....	....	....	....	....	....
	Kansas City Blues	CHL	66	26	48	74	....	....	....	79	....	....	....	....	....	....	....	....	....	....	....	....	....	....	....	....	....	....
	Buffalo Bisons	AHL	....	....	....	....	....	....	....	....	....	....	....	....	....	....	....	....	....	....	1	0	0	0	0	....	....	....
1970-71	Kansas City Blues	CHL	63	23	33	56	....	....	....	31	....	....	....	....	....	....	....	....	....	....	....	....	....	....	....	....	....	....
1971-72	Denver Spurs	WHL	69	38	42	80	....	....	....	10	....	....	....	....	....	....	....	....	....	....	9	5	6	11	8	....	....	....
1972-73	Cleveland Crusaders	WHA	75	37	44	81	....	....	....	20	....	....	....	....	....	....	....	....	....	....	9	7	3	10	0	....	....	....
1973-74	Cleveland Crusaders	WHA	49	18	27	45	....	....	....	2	....	....	....	....	....	....	....	....	....	....	5	0	0	0	2	....	....	....
1974-75	Cleveland Crusaders	WHA	4	2	0	2	....	....	....	2	....	....	....	....	....	....	....	....	....	....	....	....	....	....	....	....	....	....
	Edmonton Oilers	WHA	22	6	9	15	....	....	....	4	....	....	....	....	....	....	....	....	....	....	....	....	....	....	....	....	....	....
	Indianapolis Racers	WHA	32	16	15	31	....	....	....	16	....	....	....	....	....	....	....	....	....	....	....	....	....	....	....	....	....	....
1975-76	Indianapolis Racers	WHA	23	4	7	11	....	....	....	4	....	....	....	....	....	....	....	....	....	....	....	....	....	....	....	....	....	....
	NHL Totals		**5**	**0**	**0**	**0**	**0**	**0**	**0**	**0**	....	....	....	....	....	....	....	....	....	....	....	....	....	....	....	....	....	....
	Other Major League Totals		205	83	102	185	....	....	....	48	....	....	....	....	....	....	....	....	....	....	14	7	3	10	2	....	....	....

• Son of Ralph (Bucky) • OHA-Jr. Second All-Star Team (1965) • CPHL Second All-Star Team (1968)

Claimed by **Philadelphia** from **Boston** in Intra-League Draft, June 12, 1968. Traded to **St. Louis** by **Philadelphia** for cash, May 14, 1969. Selected by **Minnesota** (WHA) in 1972 WHA General Player Draft, February 12, 1972. WHA rights traded to **Cleveland** (WHA) by **Minnesota** (WHA), July, 1972. Traded to **Edmonton** (WHA) by **Cleveland** (WHA) for Jim Harrison, October 14, 1974. Traded to **Indianapolis** (WHA) by **Edmonton** (WHA) for Murray Kennett, January, 1975.

• BUCHBERGER, Kelly

RW – L. 6'2", 210 lbs. b: Langenburg, Sask., 12/2/1966. Edmonton's 8th, 188th overall, in 1985.

Season	Club	League	GP	G	A	Pts	AG	AA	APts	PIM	PP	SH	GW	S	%	TGF	PGF	TGA	PGA	+/–	GP	G	A	Pts	PIM	PP	SH	GW
1983-84	Melville Millionaires	SJHL	60	14	11	25	....	....	....	139	....	....	....	....	....	....	....	....	....	....	....	....	....	....	....	....	....	....
1984-85	Moose Jaw Warriors	WHL	51	12	17	29	....	....	....	114	....	....	....	....	....	....	....	....	....	....	....	....	....	....	....	....	....	....
1985-86	Moose Jaw Warriors	WHL	72	14	22	36	....	....	....	206	....	....	....	....	....	....	....	....	....	....	13	11	4	15	37	....	....	....
1986-87	Nova Scotia Oilers	AHL	70	12	20	32	....	....	....	257	....	....	....	....	....	....	....	....	....	....	5	0	1	1	23	....	....	....
◆	**Edmonton Oilers**	**NHL**	....	....	....	....	....	....	....	....	....	....	....	....	....	....	....	....	....	....	**3**	**0**	**1**	**1**	**5**	**0**	**0**	**0**
1987-88	**Edmonton Oilers**	**NHL**	**19**	**1**	**0**	**1**	**1**	**0**	**1**	**81**	**0**	**0**	**0**	**10**	**10.0**	**4**	**0**	**5**	**0**	**–1**	....	....	....	....	....	....	....	....
	Nova Scotia Oilers	AHL	49	21	23	44	....	....	....	206	....	....	....	....	....	....	....	....	....	....	2	0	0	0	11	....	....	....
1988-89	**Edmonton Oilers**	**NHL**	**66**	**5**	**9**	**14**	**4**	**6**	**10**	**234**	**1**	**0**	**1**	**57**	**8.8**	**27**	**8**	**33**	**0**	**–14**	....	....	....	....	....	....	....	....
1989-90◆	**Edmonton Oilers**	**NHL**	**55**	**2**	**6**	**8**	**2**	**4**	**6**	**168**	**0**	**0**	**2**	**35**	**5.7**	**12**	**0**	**20**	**0**	**–8**	**19**	**0**	**5**	**5**	**13**	**0**	**0**	**0**
1990-91	**Edmonton Oilers**	**NHL**	**64**	**3**	**1**	**4**	**3**	**1**	**4**	**160**	**0**	**0**	**2**	**54**	**5.6**	**14**	**0**	**20**	**0**	**–6**	**12**	**2**	**1**	**3**	**25**	**0**	**0**	**0**
1991-92	**Edmonton Oilers**	**NHL**	**79**	**20**	**24**	**44**	**18**	**18**	**36**	**157**	**0**	**4**	**3**	**90**	**22.2**	**52**	**2**	**74**	**33**	**9**	**16**	**1**	**4**	**5**	**32**	**0**	**0**	**0**
1992-93	**Edmonton Oilers**	**NHL**	**83**	**12**	**18**	**30**	**10**	**12**	**22**	**133**	**1**	**2**	**3**	**92**	**13.0**	**42**	**4**	**113**	**48**	**–27**	....	....	....	....	....	....	....	....
	Canada	WC-A	8	0	2	2	....	....	....	6	....	....	....	....	....	....	....	....	....	....	....	....	....	....	....	....	....	....
1993-94	**Edmonton Oilers**	**NHL**	**84**	**3**	**18**	**21**	**3**	**14**	**17**	**199**	**0**	**0**	**0**	**93**	**3.2**	**33**	**3**	**82**	**32**	**–20**	....	....	....	....	....	....	....	....
	Canada	WC-A	8	0	0	0	....	....	....	8	....	....	....	....	....	....	....	....	....	....	....	....	....	....	....	....	....	....
1994-95	**Edmonton Oilers**	**NHL**	**48**	**7**	**17**	**24**	**12**	**25**	**37**	**82**	**2**	**1**	**5**	**73**	**9.6**	**37**	**3**	**67**	**33**	**0**	....	....	....	....	....	....	....	....

			REGULAR SEASON																		PLAYOFFS							
Season	Club	League	GP	G	A	Pts	AG	AA	APts	PIM	PP	SH	GW	S	%	TGF	PGF	TGA	PGA	+/–	GP	G	A	Pts	PIM	PP	SH	GW
1995-96	**Edmonton Oilers**	NHL	82	11	14	25	11	11	22	184	0	2	3	119	9.2	44	3	104	43	–20	....	....	....	....	....	....	....	....
	Canada	WC-A	4	0	0	0	....	....	....	6	....	....	....	....	....	....	....	....	....	....	....	....	....	....	....	....	....	....
1996-97	**Edmonton Oilers**	NHL	81	8	30	38	8	27	35	159	0	0	3	78	10.3	51	1	70	24	4	12	5	2	7	16	0	0	1
1997-98	**Edmonton Oilers**	NHL	82	6	17	23	7	17	24	122	1	1	1	86	7.0	37	3	79	35	–10	12	1	2	3	25	0	0	0
1998-99	**Edmonton Oilers**	NHL	52	4	4	8	5	4	9	68	0	2	1	29	13.8	11	0	32	15	–6	4	0	0	0	0	0	0	0
99-2000	**Atlanta Thrashers**	NHL	68	5	12	17	6	11	17	139	0	0	0	56	8.9	24	1	81	24	–34	....	....	....	....	....	....	....	....
	Los Angeles Kings	NHL	13	2	1	3	2	1	3	13	0	0	0	20	10.0	3	0	8	3	–2	4	0	0	0	4	0	0	0
	NHL Totals		876	89	171	260	92	151	243	1899	5	12	24	892	10.0	391	28	788	290		82	9	15	24	120	0	0	1

Claimed by **Atlanta** from **Edmonton** in Expansion Draft, June 25, 1999. Traded to **Los Angeles** by **Atlanta** with Nelson Emerson for Donald Audette and Frantisek Kaberle, March 13, 2000.

• BUCYK, John

John Paul "Chief" LW – L. 6', 215 lbs. b: Edmonton, Alta., 5/12/1935. **HHOF**

Season	Club	League	GP	G	A	Pts	AG	AA	APts	PIM	PP	SH	GW	S	%	TGF	PGF	TGA	PGA	+/–	GP	G	A	Pts	PIM	PP	SH	GW
1951-52	Edmonton Maple Leafs	AJHL	STATISTICS NOT AVAILABLE																									
	Edmonton Oil Kings	WCJHL	....	....	....	....	....	....	....	....	....	....	....	....	....	....	....	....	....	....	1	0	0	0	0	....	....	....
1952-53	Edmonton Oil Kings	WCJHL	39	19	12	31	....	....	....	24	....	....	....	....	....	....	....	....	....	....	12	5	1	6	14	....	....	....
1953-54	Edmonton Oil Kings	WCJHL	33	29	38	67	....	....	....	38	....	....	....	....	....	....	....	....	....	....	21	28	17	45	30	....	....	....
	Edmonton Flyers	WHL	2	2	0	2	....	....	....	2	....	....	....	....	....	....	....	....	....	....	....	....	....	....	....	....	....	....
	Edmonton Oil Kings	Mem-Cup	14	14	10	24	....	....	....	10	....	....	....	....	....	....	....	....	....	....	....	....	....	....	....	....	....	....
1954-55	Edmonton Flyers	WHL	70	30	58	88	....	....	....	57	....	....	....	....	....	....	....	....	....	....	9	1	*6	7	7	....	....	....
	Edmonton Flyers	Ed-Cup	7	2	3	5	....	....	....	22	....	....	....	....	....	....	....	....	....	....	....	....	....	....	....	....	....	....
1955-56	**Detroit Red Wings**	NHL	38	1	8	9	1	9	10	20	....	....	....	....	....	....	....	....	....	....	10	1	1	2	8	0	0	0
	Edmonton Flyers	WHL	6	0	0	0	....	....	....	9	....	....	....	....	....	....	....	....	....	....	....	....	....	....	....	....	....	....
1956-57	**Detroit Red Wings**	NHL	66	10	11	21	13	12	25	41	....	....	....	....	....	....	....	....	....	....	5	0	1	1	0	0	0	0
1957-58	**Boston Bruins**	NHL	68	21	31	52	26	32	58	57	....	....	....	....	....	....	....	....	....	....	12	0	4	4	16	0	0	0
1958-59	**Boston Bruins**	NHL	69	24	36	60	29	37	66	36	....	....	....	....	....	....	....	....	....	....	7	2	4	6	6	0	0	0
1959-60	**Boston Bruins**	NHL	56	16	36	52	19	35	54	26	....	....	....	....	....	....	....	....	....	....	....	....	....	....	....	....	....	....
1960-61	**Boston Bruins**	NHL	70	19	20	39	22	19	41	48	....	....	....	....	....	....	....	....	....	....	....	....	....	....	....	....	....	....
1961-62	**Boston Bruins**	NHL	67	20	40	60	23	39	62	32	....	....	....	....	....	....	....	....	....	....	....	....	....	....	....	....	....	....
1962-63	**Boston Bruins**	NHL	69	27	39	66	32	39	71	36	....	....	....	....	....	....	....	....	....	....	....	....	....	....	....	....	....	....
1963-64	**Boston Bruins**	NHL	62	18	36	54	22	38	60	36	....	....	....	....	....	....	....	....	....	....	....	....	....	....	....	....	....	....
1964-65	**Boston Bruins**	NHL	68	26	29	55	31	30	61	24	....	....	....	....	....	....	....	....	....	....	....	....	....	....	....	....	....	....
1965-66	**Boston Bruins**	NHL	63	27	30	57	31	29	60	12	....	....	....	....	....	....	....	....	....	....	....	....	....	....	....	....	....	....
1966-67	**Boston Bruins**	NHL	59	18	30	48	21	29	50	12	....	....	....	....	....	....	....	....	....	....	....	....	....	....	....	....	....	....
1967-68	**Boston Bruins**	NHL	72	30	39	69	35	39	74	8	6	1	4	172	17.4	101	29	54	0	18	3	0	2	2	0	0	0	0
1968-69	**Boston Bruins**	NHL	70	24	42	66	25	38	63	18	11	0	3	192	12.5	95	36	62	0	–3	10	5	6	11	0	2	1	0
1969-70♦	**Boston Bruins**	NHL	76	31	38	69	34	36	70	13	14	0	6	190	16.3	116	61	38	2	19	14	11	8	19	2	4	1	0
1970-71	**Boston Bruins**	NHL	78	51	65	116	51	55	106	8	22	0	5	225	22.7	154	70	48	0	36	7	2	5	7	0	0	0	0
1971-72♦	**Boston Bruins**	NHL	78	32	51	83	32	44	76	4	13	0	7	174	18.4	123	65	42	0	16	15	9	*11	20	6	0	0	0
1972-73	**Boston Bruins**	NHL	78	40	53	93	38	42	80	12	10	0	10	168	23.8	133	53	62	0	18	5	0	3	3	0	0	0	0
1973-74	**Boston Bruins**	NHL	76	31	44	75	30	36	66	8	12	0	9	139	22.3	115	47	55	0	13	16	8	10	18	4	3	0	1
1974-75	**Boston Bruins**	NHL	78	29	52	81	25	39	64	10	9	0	4	167	17.4	133	63	60	1	11	3	1	0	1	0	0	0	0
1975-76	**Boston Bruins**	NHL	77	36	47	83	32	35	67	20	13	0	9	151	23.8	129	56	51	0	22	12	2	7	9	0	2	0	0
1976-77	**Boston Bruins**	NHL	49	20	23	43	18	18	36	12	6	0	2	98	20.4	58	21	39	0	–2	5	0	0	0	0	0	0	0
1977-78	**Boston Bruins**	NHL	53	5	13	18	5	10	15	4	5	0	0	47	10.6	28	15	15	0	–2	....	....	....	....	....	....	....	....
	NHL Totals		1540	556	813	1369	595	740	1335	497	....	....	....	....	....	....	....	....	....	....	124	41	62	103	42	....	....	....

Won WHL Rookie of the Year Award (1955) • WHL Second All-Star Team (1955) • NHL Second All-Star Team (1968) • NHL First All-Star Team (1971) • Won Lady Byng Trophy (1971, 1974) • Won Lester Patrick Trophy (1977) • Played in NHL All-Star Game (1955, 1963, 1964, 1965, 1968, 1970, 1971)

Traded to **Boston** by **Detroit** with cash for Terry Sawchuk, June 10, 1957.

• BUCYK, Randy

C – L. 5'11", 185 lbs. b: Edmonton, Alta., 11/9/1962.

Season	Club	League	GP	G	A	Pts	AG	AA	APts	PIM	PP	SH	GW	S	%	TGF	PGF	TGA	PGA	+/–	GP	G	A	Pts	PIM	PP	SH	GW
1980-81	Northeastern University	ECAC	31	18	17	35	....	....	....	18	....	....	....	....	....	....	....	....	....	....	....	....	....	....	....	....	....	....
1981-82	Northeastern University	ECAC	33	19	17	36	....	....	....	10	....	....	....	....	....	....	....	....	....	....	....	....	....	....	....	....	....	....
1982-83	Northeastern University	ECAC	28	16	20	36	....	....	....	16	....	....	....	....	....	....	....	....	....	....	....	....	....	....	....	....	....	....
1983-84	Northeastern University	ECAC	29	16	13	29	....	....	....	11	....	....	....	....	....	....	....	....	....	....	....	....	....	....	....	....	....	....
1984-85	Sherbrooke Canadiens	AHL	62	21	26	47	....	....	....	20	....	....	....	....	....	....	....	....	....	....	8	0	0	0	20	....	....	....
1985-86♦	**Montreal Canadiens**	NHL	17	4	2	6	3	1	4	8	0	0	0	21	19.0	8	0	4	1	5	2	0	0	0	0	0	0	0
	Sherbrooke Canadiens	AHL	43	18	33	51	....	....	....	22	....	....	....	....	....	....	....	....	....	....	....	....	....	....	....	....	....	....
1986-87	Sherbrooke Canadiens	AHL	70	24	39	63	....	....	....	28	....	....	....	....	....	....	....	....	....	....	17	3	11	14	2	....	....	....
1987-88	**Calgary Flames**	NHL	2	0	0	0	0	0	0	0	0	0	0	2	0.0	1	0	2	0	–1	....	....	....	....	....	....	....	....
	Salt Lake Golden Eagles	IHL	75	37	45	82	....	....	....	68	....	....	....	....	....	....	....	....	....	....	19	7	8	15	12	....	....	....
1988-89	Salt Lake Golden Eagles	IHL	79	28	59	87	....	....	....	24	....	....	....	....	....	....	....	....	....	....	14	5	5	10	4	....	....	....
	Canada	Nat-Team	4	0	0	0	....	....	....	2	....	....	....	....	....	....	....	....	....	....	....	....	....	....	....	....	....	....
1989-90	Salt Lake Golden Eagles	IHL	67	22	41	63	....	....	....	16	....	....	....	....	....	....	....	....	....	....	11	2	6	8	10	....	....	....
1990-91	Salt Lake Golden Eagles	IHL	18	4	4	8	....	....	....	2	....	....	....	....	....	....	....	....	....	....	....	....	....	....	....	....	....	....
	NHL Totals		19	4	2	6	3	1	4	8	0	0	0	23	17.4	9	0	6	1		2	0	0	0	0	0	0	0

Signed as a free agent by **Montreal**, January 15, 1986. Signed as a free agent by **Calgary**, June 29, 1987.

• BUHR, Doug

Douglas Leonard LW – L. 6'3", 215 lbs. b: Vancouver, B.C., 6/29/1949.

Season	Club	League	GP	G	A	Pts	AG	AA	APts	PIM	PP	SH	GW	S	%	TGF	PGF	TGA	PGA	+/–	GP	G	A	Pts	PIM	PP	SH	GW
1968-69	Nor-West Caps	BCAHA	STATISTICS NOT AVAILABLE																									
	Victoria Cougars	BCJHL	STATISTICS NOT AVAILABLE																									
1969-1972	University of British Columbia	WUAA	STATISTICS NOT AVAILABLE																									
1972-73	Springfield Kings	AHL	71	10	12	22	....	....	....	152	....	....	....	....	....	....	....	....	....	....	....	....	....	....	....	....	....	....
1973-74	Springfield Kings	AHL	29	2	4	6	....	....	....	42	....	....	....	....	....	....	....	....	....	....	....	....	....	....	....	....	....	....
	Portland Buckaroos	WHL	37	1	4	5	....	....	....	117	....	....	....	....	....	....	....	....	....	....	10	1	0	1	27	....	....	....
1974-75	Springfield Indians	AHL	44	5	6	11	....	....	....	81	....	....	....	....	....	....	....	....	....	....	....	....	....	....	....	....	....	....
	Kansas City Scouts	NHL	6	0	2	2	0	1	1	4	0	0	0	3	0.0	2	0	2	0	0	....	....	....	....	....	....	....	....
	Oklahoma City Blazers	CHL	15	3	0	3	....	....	....	48	....	....	....	....	....	....	....	....	....	....	4	0	0	0	2	....	....	....
1975-76	Trail Smoke Eaters	WIHL	STATISTICS NOT AVAILABLE																									
1976-77	Trail Smoke Eaters	WIHL	56	12	13	25	....	....	....	162	....	....	....	....	....	....	....	....	....	....	....	....	....	....	....	....	....	....
1977-78	Trail Smoke Eaters	WIHL	56	11	15	26	....	....	....	76	....	....	....	....	....	....	....	....	....	....	....	....	....	....	....	....	....	....
	NHL Totals		6	0	2	2	0	1	1	4	0	0	0	3	0.0	2	0	2	0		....	....	....	....	....	....	....	....

Signed as a free agent by **LA Kings**, October 2, 1972. Traded to **Kansas City** by **LA Kings** for cash, February, 1975.

• BULIS, Jan

C – L. 6'1", 208 lbs. b: Pardubice, Czech., 3/18/1978. Washington's 3rd, 43rd overall, in 1996.

Season	Club	League	GP	G	A	Pts	AG	AA	APts	PIM	PP	SH	GW	S	%	TGF	PGF	TGA	PGA	+/–	GP	G	A	Pts	PIM	PP	SH	GW
1993-94	HC Pardubice	Czech-Jr.	25	16	11	27	....	....	....	....	....	....	....	....	....	....	....	....	....	....	....	....	....	....	....	....	....	....
1994-95	Kelowna Spartans	BCJHL	51	23	25	48	....	....	....	36	....	....	....	....	....	....	....	....	....	....	17	7	9	16	0	....	....	....
1995-96	Barrie Colts	OHL	59	29	30	59	....	....	....	22	....	....	....	....	....	....	....	....	....	....	7	2	3	5	2	....	....	....
1996-97	Barrie Colts	OHL	64	42	61	103	....	....	....	42	....	....	....	....	....	....	....	....	....	....	9	3	7	10	10	....	....	....
1997-98	Kingston Fronteancs	OHL	2	0	1	1	....	....	....	0	....	....	....	....	....	....	....	....	....	....	12	8	10	18	12	....	....	....
	Washington Capitals	NHL	48	5	11	16	6	11	17	18	0	0	0	37	13.5	24	2	27	0	–5	....	....	....	....	....	....	....	....
	Portland Pirates	AHL	3	1	4	5	....	....	....	12	....	....	....	....	....	....	....	....	....	....	....	....	....	....	....	....	....	....
1998-99	**Washington Capitals**	NHL	38	7	16	23	8	15	23	6	3	0	3	57	12.3	29	10	17	1	3	....	....	....	....	....	....	....	....
	Cincinnati Cyclones	IHL	10	2	2	4	....	....	....	14	....	....	....	....	....	....	....	....	....	....	....	....	....	....	....	....	....	....
99-2000	**Washington Capitals**	NHL	56	9	22	31	10	20	30	30	0	0	1	92	9.8	38	4	28	1	7	....	....	....	....	....	....	....	....
	NHL Totals		142	21	49	70	24	46	70	54	3	0	4	186	11.3	91	16	72	2		....	....	....	....	....	....	....	....

			REGULAR SEASON																		PLAYOFFS							
Season	Club	League	GP	G	A	Pts	AG	AA	APts	PIM	PP	SH	GW	S	%	TGF	PGF	TGA	PGA	+/–	GP	G	A	Pts	PIM	PP	SH	GW

• BULLARD, Mike

Michael Brian C – L. 6', 195 lbs. b: Ottawa, Ont., 3/10/1961. Pittsburgh's 1st, 9th overall, in 1980.

Season	Club	League	GP	G	A	Pts	AG	AA	APts	PIM	PP	SH	GW	S	%	TGF	PGF	TGA	PGA	+/–	GP	G	A	Pts	PIM	PP	SH	GW
1977-78	East Ottawa Voyageurs	OMHA	90	89	114	203	....	....	....	....	....	....	....	....	....	....	....	....	....	....	....	....	....	....	....	....	....	....
1978-79	Brantford Alexanders	OMJHL	66	43	56	99	....	....	....	66	....	....	....	....	....	....	....	....	....	....	....	....	....	....	....	....	....	....
1979-80	Brantford Alexanders	OMJHL	66	*66	84	150	....	....	....	86	....	....	....	....	....	....	....	....	....	....	11	10	6	16	29	....	....	....
1980-81	Brantford Alexanders	OMJHL	42	47	60	107	....	....	....	55	....	....	....	....	....	....	....	....	....	....	6	4	5	9	10	....	....	....
	Pittsburgh Penguins	**NHL**	**15**	**1**	**2**	**3**	**1**	**1**	**2**	**19**	**0**	**0**	**0**	**18**	**5.6**	**8**	**1**	**8**	**0**	**–1**	**4**	**3**	**3**	**6**	**0**	**1**	**0**	**1**
1981-82	**Pittsburgh Penguins**	**NHL**	**75**	**36**	**27**	**63**	**28**	**18**	**46**	**91**	**10**	**0**	**5**	**145**	**24.8**	**82**	**26**	**58**	**1**	**–1**	**5**	**1**	**1**	**2**	**4**	**0**	**0**	**0**
1982-83	**Pittsburgh Penguins**	**NHL**	**57**	**22**	**22**	**44**	**18**	**15**	**33**	**60**	**3**	**0**	**2**	**148**	**14.9**	**61**	**15**	**68**	**1**	**–21**	....	....	....	....	....	....	....	....
1983-84	**Pittsburgh Penguins**	**NHL**	**76**	**51**	**41**	**92**	**41**	**28**	**69**	**57**	**15**	**0**	**0**	**213**	**23.9**	**119**	**43**	**112**	**3**	**–33**	....	....	....	....	....	....	....	....
1984-85	**Pittsburgh Penguins**	**NHL**	**68**	**32**	**31**	**63**	**26**	**21**	**47**	**75**	**14**	**0**	**3**	**185**	**17.3**	**88**	**36**	**97**	**2**	**–43**	....	....	....	....	....	....	....	....
1985-86	**Pittsburgh Penguins**	**NHL**	**77**	**41**	**42**	**83**	**33**	**28**	**61**	**69**	**16**	**2**	**5**	**213**	**19.2**	**114**	**51**	**97**	**18**	**–16**	....	....	....	....	....	....	....	....
	Canada	WEC-A	10	2	1	3	....	....	....	2	....	....	....	....	....	....	....	....	....	....	....	....	....	....	....	....	....	....
1986-87	**Pittsburgh Penguins**	**NHL**	**14**	**2**	**10**	**12**	**2**	**7**	**9**	**17**	**0**	**0**	**0**	**49**	**4.1**	**13**	**0**	**48**	**30**	**–5**	....	....	....	....	....	....	....	....
	Calgary Flames	**NHL**	**57**	**28**	**26**	**54**	**24**	**19**	**43**	**34**	**10**	**0**	**3**	**138**	**20.3**	**75**	**21**	**47**	**3**	**10**	**6**	**4**	**3**	**7**	**2**	**3**	**0**	**1**
1987-88	**Calgary Flames**	**NHL**	**79**	**48**	**55**	**103**	**41**	**39**	**80**	**68**	**21**	**0**	**3**	**230**	**20.9**	**153**	**71**	**57**	**0**	**25**	**6**	**0**	**2**	**2**	**6**	**0**	**0**	**0**
1988-89	**St. Louis Blues**	**NHL**	**20**	**4**	**12**	**16**	**3**	**8**	**11**	**46**	**2**	**0**	**0**	**52**	**7.7**	**23**	**8**	**14**	**0**	**1**	....	....	....	....	....	....	....	....
	Philadelphia Flyers	**NHL**	**54**	**23**	**26**	**49**	**19**	**18**	**37**	**60**	**8**	**0**	**3**	**137**	**16.8**	**68**	**26**	**42**	**1**	**1**	**19**	**3**	**9**	**12**	**32**	**1**	**0**	**0**
1989-90	**Philadelphia Flyers**	**NHL**	**70**	**27**	**37**	**64**	**23**	**27**	**50**	**67**	**6**	**0**	**4**	**181**	**14.9**	**86**	**31**	**55**	**0**	**0**	....	....	....	....	....	....	....	....
1990-91	HC Ambri-Piotta	Switz.	36	36	33	69	....	....	....	39	....	....	....	....	....	....	....	....	....	....	5	6	4	10	....	....	....	....
1991-92	**Toronto Maple Leafs**	**NHL**	**65**	**14**	**14**	**28**	**13**	**11**	**24**	**40**	**7**	**0**	**0**	**140**	**10.0**	**51**	**30**	**40**	**0**	**–19**	....	....	....	....	....	....	....	....
1992-93	SC Rapperswil-Jona	Switz-2	36	51	32	83	....	....	....	39	....	....	....	....	....	....	....	....	....	....	7	6	7	13	4	....	....	....
1993-94	EV Landshut	Germany	44	*37	26	*63	....	....	....	45	....	....	....	....	....	....	....	....	....	....	....	....	....	....	....	....	....	....
1994-95	EV Landshut	Germany	38	22	43	65	....	....	....	83	....	....	....	....	....	....	....	....	....	....	18	*17	10	*27	28	....	....	....
1995-96	EV Landshut	Germany	50	29	41	70	....	....	....	56	....	....	....	....	....	....	....	....	....	....	11	6	11	17	20	....	....	....
1996-97	EV Landshut	Germany	47	19	*51	70	....	....	....	69	....	....	....	....	....	....	....	....	....	....	7	6	4	10	40	....	....	....
1997-98	EV Landshut	Germany	45	12	24	36	....	....	....	63	....	....	....	....	....	....	....	....	....	....	6	5	5	10	8	....	....	....
1998-99	Eisbaren Berlin	Germany	50	21	29	50	....	....	....	58	....	....	....	....	....	....	....	....	....	....	8	1	4	5	6	....	....	....
	Eisbaren Berlin	EuroHL	6	0	2	2	....	....	....	6	....	....	....	....	....	....	....	....	....	....	6	4	1	5	6	....	....	....
99-2000	Eisbaren Berlin	Germany	65	28	31	59	....	....	....	95	....	....	....	....	....	....	....	....	....	....	....	....	....	....	....	....	....	....
	NHL Totals		**727**	**329**	**345**	**674**	**272**	**240**	**512**	**703**	**112**	**2**	**28**	**1849**	**17.8**	**941**	**359**	**743**	**59**		**40**	**11**	**18**	**29**	**44**	**5**	**0**	**2**

OMJHL Second All-Star Team (1980) • Played in NHL All-Star Game (1984)

Traded to **Calgary** by **Pittsburgh** for Dan Quinn, November 12, 1986. Traded to **St. Louis** by **Calgary** with Craig Coxe and Tim Corkery for Mark Hunter, Doug Gilmour, Steve Bozek and Michael Dark, September 6, 1988. Traded to **Philadelphia** by **St. Louis** for Peter Zezel, November 29, 1988. Rights traded to **Toronto** by **Philadelphia** for Toronto's 3rd round choice (Vaclav Prospal) in 1993 Entry Draft, July 29, 1991.

• BULLEY, Ted

Edward Harold LW – L. 6'1", 192 lbs. b: Windsor, Ont., 3/25/1955. Chicago's 7th, 115th overall, in 1975.

Season	Club	League	GP	G	A	Pts	AG	AA	APts	PIM	PP	SH	GW	S	%	TGF	PGF	TGA	PGA	+/–	GP	G	A	Pts	PIM	PP	SH	GW
1972-73	Windsor Spitfires	OJHL	35	9	10	19	....	....	....	....	....	....	....	....	....	....	....	....	....	....	....	....	....	....	....	....	....	....
1973-74	Hull Festivals	QMJHL	67	28	37	65	....	....	....	116	....	....	....	....	....	....	....	....	....	....	....	....	....	....	....	....	....	....
1974-75	Hull Festivals	QMJHL	70	48	61	109	....	....	....	124	....	....	....	....	....	....	....	....	....	....	4	1	2	3	9	....	....	....
1975-76	Flint Generals	IHL	38	15	13	28	....	....	....	123	....	....	....	....	....	....	....	....	....	....	....	....	....	....	....	....	....	....
	Dallas Black Hawks	CHL	2	0	0	0	....	....	....	0	....	....	....	....	....	....	....	....	....	....	7	0	1	1	4	....	....	....
1976-77	**Chicago Black Hawks**	**NHL**	**2**	**0**	**0**	**0**	**0**	**0**	**0**	**0**	**0**	**0**	**0**	**0**	**0.0**	**0**	**0**	**2**	**0**	**–2**	....	....	....	....	....	....	....	....
	Dallas Black Hawks	CHL	2	2	2	4	....	....	....	10	....	....	....	....	....	....	....	....	....	....	....	....	....	....	....	....	....	....
	Flint Generals	IHL	70	46	46	92	....	....	....	122	....	....	....	....	....	....	....	....	....	....	2	0	0	0	0	....	....	....
1977-78	**Chicago Black Hawks**	**NHL**	**79**	**23**	**28**	**51**	**21**	**22**	**43**	**141**	**6**	**0**	**5**	**150**	**15.3**	**81**	**25**	**53**	**1**	**4**	**4**	**1**	**1**	**2**	**2**	**0**	**0**	**0**
1978-79	**Chicago Black Hawks**	**NHL**	**75**	**27**	**23**	**50**	**23**	**17**	**40**	**153**	**1**	**0**	**8**	**105**	**25.7**	**85**	**15**	**52**	**0**	**18**	**2**	**0**	**0**	**0**	**0**	**0**	**0**	**0**
1979-80	**Chicago Black Hawks**	**NHL**	**66**	**14**	**17**	**31**	**12**	**12**	**24**	**136**	**1**	**0**	**1**	**125**	**11.2**	**48**	**12**	**48**	**0**	**–12**	**7**	**2**	**3**	**5**	**10**	**0**	**0**	**0**
1980-81	**Chicago Black Hawks**	**NHL**	**68**	**18**	**16**	**34**	**14**	**11**	**25**	**95**	**3**	**0**	**2**	**112**	**16.1**	**60**	**9**	**33**	**0**	**18**	....	....	....	....	....	....	....	....
1981-82	**Chicago Black Hawks**	**NHL**	**59**	**12**	**18**	**30**	**9**	**12**	**21**	**120**	**2**	**0**	**2**	**83**	**14.5**	**47**	**5**	**43**	**0**	**–1**	**15**	**2**	**1**	**3**	**12**	**0**	**0**	**1**
1982-83	**Washington Capitals**	**NHL**	**39**	**4**	**9**	**13**	**3**	**6**	**9**	**47**	**0**	**0**	**1**	**35**	**11.4**	**19**	**1**	**22**	**1**	**–3**	**1**	**0**	**0**	**0**	**0**	**0**	**0**	**0**
1983-84	**Pittsburgh Penguins**	**NHL**	**26**	**3**	**2**	**5**	**2**	**1**	**3**	**12**	**0**	**0**	**1**	**27**	**11.1**	**5**	**0**	**20**	**1**	**–14**	....	....	....	....	....	....	....	....
	Baltimore Skipjacks	AHL	49	16	19	35	....	....	....	82	....	....	....	....	....	....	....	....	....	....	10	2	5	7	2	....	....	....
1984-85	Baltimore Skipjacks	AHL	57	9	11	20	....	....	....	125	....	....	....	....	....	....	....	....	....	....	14	1	1	2	25	....	....	....
	NHL Totals		**414**	**101**	**113**	**214**	**84**	**81**	**165**	**704**	**13**	**0**	**20**	**637**	**15.9**	**345**	**67**	**273**	**3**		**29**	**5**	**5**	**10**	**24**	**0**	**0**	**1**

Traded to **Washington** by **Chicago** with Dave Hutchinson for Washington's 6th round choice (Jari Torkki) in 1983 Entry Draft and 5th round choice (Darin Sceviour) in 1984 Entry Draft, August 24, 1982. Signed as a free agent by **Pittsburgh**, September 30, 1983.

• BURAKOVSKY, Robert

RW – R. 5'10", 185 lbs. b: Malmo, Sweden, 11/24/1966. NY Rangers' 11th, 217th overall, in 1985.

Season	Club	League	GP	G	A	Pts	AG	AA	APts	PIM	PP	SH	GW	S	%	TGF	PGF	TGA	PGA	+/–	GP	G	A	Pts	PIM	PP	SH	GW
1985-86	Leksands IF	Sweden	19	4	3	7	....	....	....	4	....	....	....	....	....	....	....	....	....	....	....	....	....	....	....	....	....	....
	Sweden	WJC-A	7	1	1	2	....	....	....	0	....	....	....	....	....	....	....	....	....	....	....	....	....	....	....	....	....	....
1986-87	Leksands IF	Sweden	36	21	15	36	....	....	....	26	....	....	....	....	....	....	....	....	....	....	....	....	....	....	....	....	....	....
1987-88	Leksands IF	Sweden	36	10	11	21	....	....	....	10	....	....	....	....	....	....	....	....	....	....	1	0	0	0	2	....	....	....
1988-89	Leksands IF	Sweden	40	23	20	43	....	....	....	44	....	....	....	....	....	....	....	....	....	....	10	6	7	13	4	....	....	....
1989-90	AIK Solna Stockholm	Sweden	37	28	29	*57	....	....	....	32	....	....	....	....	....	....	....	....	....	....	3	0	2	2	12	....	....	....
1990-91	AIK Solna Stockholm	Sweden	30	8	15	23	....	....	....	26	....	....	....	....	....	....	....	....	....	....	....	....	....	....	....	....	....	....
1991-92	Malmo IF	Sweden	40	19	22	41	....	....	....	42	....	....	....	....	....	....	....	....	....	....	9	5	0	5	4	....	....	....
1992-93	Malmo IF	Sweden	32	8	10	18	....	....	....	40	....	....	....	....	....	....	....	....	....	....	6	4	4	8	9	....	....	....
1993-94	**Ottawa Senators**	**NHL**	**23**	**2**	**3**	**5**	**2**	**2**	**4**	**6**	**0**	**0**	**0**	**40**	**5.0**	**8**	**0**	**15**	**0**	**–7**	....	....	....	....	....	....	....	....
	P.E.I. Senators	AHL	52	29	38	67	....	....	....	28	....	....	....	....	....	....	....	....	....	....	....	....	....	....	....	....	....	....
1994-95	KAC Klagenfurt	EuroHL	23	18	15	33	....	....	....	....	....	....	....	....	....	....	....	....	....	....	....	....	....	....	....	....	....	....
	KAC Klagenfurt	Austria	28	28	36	64	....	....	....	40	....	....	....	....	....	....	....	....	....	....	3	2	2	4	2	....	....	....
1995-96	Malmo IF	Sweden	40	23	21	44	....	....	....	34	....	....	....	....	....	....	....	....	....	....	5	2	1	3	6	....	....	....
1996-97	Malmo IF	Sweden	33	19	17	36	....	....	....	44	....	....	....	....	....	....	....	....	....	....	....	....	....	....	....	....	....	....
	Kassel Huskies	Germany	11	5	7	12	....	....	....	4	....	....	....	....	....	....	....	....	....	....	10	4	6	10	6	....	....	....
1997-98	Kassel Huskies	Germany	17	7	6	13	....	....	....	0	....	....	....	....	....	....	....	....	....	....	....	....	....	....	....	....	....	....
	Kassel Huskies	EuroHL	5	0	2	2	....	....	....	4	....	....	....	....	....	....	....	....	....	....	....	....	....	....	....	....	....	....
	JyP Jyvaskyla	Finland	14	14	7	21	....	....	....	16	....	....	....	....	....	....	....	....	....	....	....	....	....	....	....	....	....	....
	Ilves Tampere	Finland	11	5	4	9	....	....	....	40	....	....	....	....	....	....	....	....	....	....	9	7	3	10	0	....	....	....
1998-99	HC Fribourg-Gotteron	Switz.	5	4	2	6	....	....	....	4	....	....	....	....	....	....	....	....	....	....	....	....	....	....	....	....	....	....
	SC Herisau	Switz-2	35	38	32	70	....	....	....	10	....	....	....	....	....	....	....	....	....	....	....	....	....	....	....	....	....	....
99-2000	HC Fribourg-Gotteron	Switz.	45	16	33	49	....	....	....	49	....	....	....	....	....	....	....	....	....	....	....	....	....	....	....	....	....	....
	HC Ambri-Piotta	Switz.	1	0	0	0	....	....	....	0	....	....	....	....	....	....	....	....	....	....	....	....	....	....	....	....	....	....
	NHL Totals		**23**	**2**	**3**	**5**	**2**	**2**	**4**	**6**	**0**	**0**	**0**	**40**	**5.0**	**8**	**0**	**15**	**0**		....	....	....	....	....	....	....	....

Rights traded to **Ottawa** by **NY Rangers** for future considerations, May 7, 1993.

• BURDON, Glen

Glen William C – L. 6'2", 178 lbs. b: Regina, Sask., 8/4/1954. Kansas City's 2nd, 20th overall, in 1974.

Season	Club	League	GP	G	A	Pts	AG	AA	APts	PIM	PP	SH	GW	S	%	TGF	PGF	TGA	PGA	+/–	GP	G	A	Pts	PIM	PP	SH	GW
1970-71	Fort Qu'Appelle Silver Foxes	SJHL	STATISTICS NOT AVAILABLE																									
1971-72	Regina Pats	WCJHL	60	17	36	53	....	....	....	78	....	....	....	....	....	....	....	....	....	....	14	1	8	9	14	....	....	....
1972-73	Regina Pats	WCJHL	46	21	28	49	....	....	....	13	....	....	....	....	....	....	....	....	....	....	16	6	11	17	25	....	....	....
1973-74	Regina Pats	WCJHL	68	19	56	75	....	....	....	44	....	....	....	....	....	....	....	....	....	....	....	....	....	....	....	....	....	....
	Regina Pats	Mem-Cup	3	2	0	2	....	....	....	6	....	....	....	....	....	....	....	....	....	....	....	....	....	....	....	....	....	....
1974-75	**Kansas City Scouts**	**NHL**	**11**	**0**	**2**	**2**	**0**	**1**	**1**	**0**	**0**	**0**	**0**	**2**	**0.0**	**2**	**0**	**5**	**0**	**–3**	....	....	....	....	....	....	....	....
	Baltimore Clippers	AHL	5	0	0	0	....	....	....	0	....	....	....	....	....	....	....	....	....	....	....	....	....	....	....	....	....	....
	Providence Reds	AHL	25	1	2	3	....	....	....	12	....	....	....	....	....	....	....	....	....	....	....	....	....	....	....	....	....	....
1975-76	New Haven Nighthawks	AHL	23	1	5	6	....	....	....	6	....	....	....	....	....	....	....	....	....	....	....	....	....	....	....	....	....	....
1976-77	Kansas City Blues	CHL	3	0	0	0	....	....	....	0	....	....	....	....	....	....	....	....	....	....	....	....	....	....	....	....	....	....
1977-78	Regina Steelers	SIHA	STATISTICS NOT AVAILABLE																									

			REGULAR SEASON																		PLAYOFFS							
Season	Club	League	GP	G	A	Pts	AG	AA	APts	PIM	PP	SH	GW	S	%	TGF	PGF	TGA	PGA	+/-	GP	G	A	Pts	PIM	PP	SH	GW
1978-79	Fort Wayne Komets	IHL	5	0	2	2	....	....	....	7	....	....	....	....	....	....	....	....	....	....	....	....	....	....	....	....	....	....
1979-80			DID NOT PLAY																									
1980-81	Regina Bruins	SIHA	STATISTICS NOT AVAILABLE																									
	NHL Totals		**11**	**0**	**2**	**2**	**0**	**1**	**1**	**0**	**0**	**0**	**0**	**2**	**0.0**	**2**	**0**	**5**	**0**		....	....	....	....	....	....	....	....

Traded to **Detroit** by **Kansas City** with Peter McDuffe for Bill McKenzie and Gary Bergman, August 22, 1975.

• BURE, Pavel

Pavel V. "The Russian Rocket" RW – L. 5'10", 189 lbs. b: Moscow, USSR, 3/31/1971. Vancouver's 4th, 113th overall, in 1989.

Season	Club	League	GP	G	A	Pts	AG	AA	APts	PIM	PP	SH	GW	S	%	TGF	PGF	TGA	PGA	+/-	GP	G	A	Pts	PIM	PP	SH	GW
1987-88	CSKA Moscow	USSR	5	1	1	2	....	....	....	0	....	....	....	....	....	....	....	....	....	....	....	....	....	....	....	....	....	....
	Soviet Union	EJC-A	6	10	0	10	....	....	....	2	....	....	....	....	....	....	....	....	....	....	....	....	....	....	....	....	....	....
1988-89	CSKA Moscow	USSR	32	17	9	26	....	....	....	8	....	....	....	....	....	....	....	....	....	....	....	....	....	....	....	....	....	....
	Soviet Union	WJC-A	7	8	6	14	....	....	....	4	....	....	....	....	....	....	....	....	....	....	....	....	....	....	....	....	....	....
	Soviet Union	EJC-A	6	5	6	11	....	....	....	4	....	....	....	....	....	....	....	....	....	....	....	....	....	....	....	....	....	....
1989-90	CSKA Moscow	Fr-Tour	1	0	0	0	....	....	....	0	....	....	....	....	....	....	....	....	....	....	....	....	....	....	....	....	....	....
	CSKA Moscow	USSR	46	14	10	24	....	....	....	20	....	....	....	....	....	....	....	....	....	....	....	....	....	....	....	....	....	....
	Soviet Union	WJC-A	7	7	3	10	....	....	....	10	....	....	....	....	....	....	....	....	....	....	....	....	....	....	....	....	....	....
	Soviet Union	WEC-A	10	2	4	6	....	....	....	10	....	....	....	....	....	....	....	....	....	....	....	....	....	....	....	....	....	....
1990-91	CSKA Moscow	Fr-Tour	1	1	0	1	....	....	....	2	....	....	....	....	....	....	....	....	....	....	....	....	....	....	....	....	....	....
	CSKA Moscow	USSR	44	35	11	46	....	....	....	24	....	....	....	....	....	....	....	....	....	....	....	....	....	....	....	....	....	....
	Soviet Union	WJC-A	7	*12	3	15	....	....	....	*31	....	....	....	....	....	....	....	....	....	....	....	....	....	....	....	....	....	....
	Soviet Union	WEC-A	10	3	8	11	....	....	....	2	....	....	....	....	....	....	....	....	....	....	....	....	....	....	....	....	....	....
1991-92	**Vancouver Canucks**	**NHL**	**65**	**34**	**26**	**60**	**31**	**20**	**51**	**30**	**7**	**3**	**6**	**268**	**12.7**	**84**	**29**	**69**	**14**	**0**	**13**	**6**	**4**	**10**	**14**	**0**	**0**	**0**
1992-93	**Vancouver Canucks**	**NHL**	**83**	**60**	**50**	**110**	**50**	**34**	**84**	**69**	**13**	**7**	**9**	**407**	**14.7**	**140**	**48**	**80**	**23**	**35**	**12**	**5**	**7**	**12**	**8**	**0**	**0**	**1**
1993-94	**Vancouver Canucks**	**NHL**	**76**	***60**	**47**	**107**	**56**	**37**	**93**	**86**	**25**	**4**	**9**	**374**	**16.0**	**131**	**55**	**85**	**10**	**1**	**24**	***16**	**15**	**31**	**40**	**3**	**0**	**2**
1994-95	EV Landshut	Germany	1	3	0	3	....	....	....	2	....	....	....	....	....	....	....	....	....	....	....	....	....	....	....	....	....	....
	Spartak Moscow	CIS	1	2	0	2	....	....	....	2	....	....	....	....	....	....	....	....	....	....	....	....	....	....	....	....	....	....
	Vancouver Canucks	**NHL**	**44**	**20**	**23**	**43**	**35**	**34**	**69**	**47**	**6**	**2**	**2**	**198**	**10.1**	**73**	**36**	**58**	**13**	**–8**	**11**	**7**	**6**	**13**	**10**	**2**	**2**	**0**
1995-96	**Vancouver Canucks**	**NHL**	**15**	**6**	**7**	**13**	**6**	**6**	**12**	**8**	**1**	**1**	**0**	**78**	**7.7**	**20**	**8**	**19**	**5**	**–2**	....	....	....	....	....	....	....	....
1996-97	**Vancouver Canucks**	**NHL**	**63**	**23**	**32**	**55**	**24**	**28**	**52**	**40**	**4**	**1**	**2**	**265**	**8.7**	**82**	**30**	**86**	**20**	**–14**	....	....	....	....	....	....	....	....
1997-98	**Vancouver Canucks**	**NHL**	**82**	**51**	**39**	**90**	**60**	**38**	**98**	**48**	**13**	**6**	**4**	**329**	**15.5**	**118**	**40**	**107**	**34**	**5**	....	....	....	....	....	....	....	....
	Russia	Olympics	6	*9	0	9	....	....	....	2	....	....	....	....	....	....	....	....	....	....	....	....	....	....	....	....	....	....
1998-99	**Florida Panthers**	**NHL**	**11**	**13**	**3**	**16**	**15**	**3**	**18**	**4**	**5**	**1**	**0**	**44**	**29.5**	**18**	**6**	**12**	**3**	**3**	....	....	....	....	....	....	....	....
99-2000	**Florida Panthers**	**NHL**	**74**	***58**	**36**	**94**	**66**	**33**	**99**	**16**	**11**	**2**	**14**	**360**	**16.1**	**118**	**29**	**73**	**9**	**25**	**4**	**1**	**3**	**4**	**2**	**1**	**0**	**0**
	Russia	WC-A	6	4	1	5	....	....	....	10	....	....	....	....	....	....	....	....	....	....	....	....	....	....	....	....	....	....
	NHL Totals		**513**	**325**	**263**	**588**	**343**	**233**	**576**	**348**	**85**	**27**	**46**	**2323**	**14.0**	**784**	**281**	**589**	**131**		**64**	**35**	**35**	**70**	**74**	**6**	**2**	**3**

• Brother of Valeri • WJC-A All-Star Team (1989) • Named Best Forward at WJC-A (1989) • Named Soviet National League Rookie-of-the-Year (1989) • Won Calder Memorial Trophy (1992) • NHL First All-Star Team (1994) • Named Best Forward at Olympic Games (1998) • NHL Second All-Star Team (2000) • Won Maurice Richard Trophy (2000) • Played in NHL All-Star Game (1993, 1994, 1997, 1998, 2000)

Traded to **Florida** by **Vancouver** with Bret Hedican, Brad Ference and Vancouver's 3rd round choice (Robert Fried) in 2000 Entry Draft for Ed Jovanovski, Dave Gagner, Mike Brown, Kevin Weekes and Florida's 1st round choice (Nathan Smith) in 2000 Entry Draft, January 17, 1999. • Missed majority of 1998-99 season after demanding trade (August 10, 1998) and recovering from knee injury suffered in game vs. Pittsburgh, February 5, 1999.

• BURE, Valeri

RW – R. 5'10", 185 lbs. b: Moscow, USSR, 6/13/1974. Montreal's 2nd, 33rd overall, in 1992.

Season	Club	League	GP	G	A	Pts	AG	AA	APts	PIM	PP	SH	GW	S	%	TGF	PGF	TGA	PGA	+/-	GP	G	A	Pts	PIM	PP	SH	GW
1990-91	CSKA Moscow	USSR	3	0	0	0	....	....	....	0	....	....	....	....	....	....	....	....	....	....	....	....	....	....	....	....	....	....
1991-92	Spokane Chiefs	WHL	53	27	22	49	....	....	....	78	....	....	....	....	....	....	....	....	....	....	10	11	6	17	10	....	....	....
1992-93	Spokane Chiefs	WHL	66	68	79	147	....	....	....	49	....	....	....	....	....	....	....	....	....	....	9	6	11	17	14	....	....	....
1993-94	Spokane Chiefs	WHL	59	40	62	102	....	....	....	48	....	....	....	....	....	....	....	....	....	....	3	5	3	8	2	....	....	....
	Russia	WJC-A	7	5	3	8	....	....	....	4	....	....	....	....	....	....	....	....	....	....	....	....	....	....	....	....	....	....
	Russia	WC-A	6	3	0	3	....	....	....	2	....	....	....	....	....	....	....	....	....	....	....	....	....	....	....	....	....	....
1994-95	**Montreal Canadiens**	**NHL**	**24**	**3**	**1**	**4**	**5**	**1**	**6**	**6**	**0**	**0**	**1**	**39**	**7.7**	**7**	**0**	**8**	**0**	**–1**	....	....	....	....	....	....	....	....
	Fredericton Canadiens	AHL	45	23	25	48	....	....	....	32	....	....	....	....	....	....	....	....	....	....	....	....	....	....	....	....	....	....
1995-96	**Montreal Canadiens**	**NHL**	**77**	**22**	**20**	**42**	**22**	**16**	**38**	**28**	**5**	**0**	**1**	**143**	**15.4**	**69**	**24**	**35**	**0**	**10**	**6**	**0**	**1**	**1**	**6**	**0**	**0**	**0**
1996-97	Russia	W-Cup	1	0	0	0	....	....	....	2	....	....	....	....	....	....	....	....	....	....	....	....	....	....	....	....	....	....
	Montreal Canadiens	**NHL**	**64**	**14**	**21**	**35**	**15**	**19**	**34**	**6**	**4**	**0**	**2**	**131**	**10.7**	**46**	**16**	**27**	**1**	**4**	**5**	**0**	**1**	**1**	**2**	**0**	**0**	**0**
1997-98	**Montreal Canadiens**	**NHL**	**50**	**7**	**22**	**29**	**8**	**22**	**30**	**33**	**2**	**0**	**1**	**134**	**5.2**	**38**	**17**	**26**	**0**	**–5**	....	....	....	....	....	....	....	....
	Calgary Flames	**NHL**	**16**	**5**	**4**	**9**	**6**	**4**	**10**	**2**	**0**	**0**	**1**	**45**	**11.1**	**14**	**1**	**13**	**0**	**0**	....	....	....	....	....	....	....	....
	Russia	Olympics	6	1	0	1	....	....	....	0	....	....	....	....	....	....	....	....	....	....	....	....	....	....	....	....	....	....
1998-99	**Calgary Flames**	**NHL**	**80**	**26**	**27**	**53**	**31**	**26**	**57**	**22**	**7**	**0**	**4**	**260**	**10.0**	**85**	**35**	**52**	**2**	**0**	....	....	....	....	....	....	....	....
99-2000	**Calgary Flames**	**NHL**	**82**	**35**	**40**	**75**	**39**	**37**	**76**	**50**	**13**	**0**	**6**	**308**	**11.4**	**95**	**41**	**61**	**0**	**–7**	....	....	....	....	....	....	....	....
	NHL Totals		**393**	**112**	**135**	**247**	**126**	**125**	**251**	**147**	**31**	**0**	**16**	**1060**	**10.6**	**354**	**134**	**222**	**3**		**11**	**0**	**2**	**2**	**8**	**0**	**0**	**0**

• Brother of Pavel • WHL West First All-Star Team (1993) • WJC-A All-Star Team (1994) • WHL West Second All-Star Team (1994) • Played in NHL All-Star Game (2000)

Traded to **Calgary** by **Montreal** with Montreal's 4th round choice (Shaun Sutter) in 1998 Entry Draft for Jonas Hoglund and Zarley Zalapski, February 1, 1998.

• BUREAU, Marc

C – R. 6'1", 203 lbs. b: Trois-Rivières, Que., 5/19/1966.

Season	Club	League	GP	G	A	Pts	AG	AA	APts	PIM	PP	SH	GW	S	%	TGF	PGF	TGA	PGA	+/-	GP	G	A	Pts	PIM	PP	SH	GW
1983-84	Chicoutimi Sagueneens	QMJHL	56	6	16	22	....	....	....	14	....	....	....	....	....	....	....	....	....	....	....	....	....	....	....	....	....	....
1984-85	Chicoutimi Sagueneens	QMJHL	41	30	25	55	....	....	....	15	....	....	....	....	....	....	....	....	....	....	....	....	....	....	....	....	....	....
	Granby Predateurs	QMJHL	27	20	45	65	....	....	....	14	....	....	....	....	....	....	....	....	....	....	....	....	....	....	....	....	....	....
1985-86	Granby Predateurs	QMJHL	19	6	17	23	....	....	....	36	....	....	....	....	....	....	....	....	....	....	....	....	....	....	....	....	....	....
	Chicoutimi Sagueneens	QMJHL	44	30	45	75	....	....	....	33	....	....	....	....	....	....	....	....	....	....	9	3	7	10	10	....	....	....
1986-87	Longueuil Chevaliers	QMJHL	66	54	58	112	....	....	....	68	....	....	....	....	....	....	....	....	....	....	20	17	20	37	12	....	....	....
	Longueuil Chevaliers	Mem-Cup	5	1	2	3	....	....	....	4	....	....	....	....	....	....	....	....	....	....	....	....	....	....	....	....	....	....
1987-88	Salt Lake Golden Eagles	IHL	69	7	20	27	....	....	....	86	....	....	....	....	....	....	....	....	....	....	7	0	3	3	8	....	....	....
1988-89	Salt Lake Golden Eagles	IHL	76	28	36	64	....	....	....	119	....	....	....	....	....	....	....	....	....	....	14	7	5	12	31	....	....	....
1989-90	**Calgary Flames**	**NHL**	**5**	**0**	**0**	**0**	**0**	**0**	**0**	**4**	**0**	**0**	**0**	**3**	**0.0**	**1**	**0**	**2**	**0**	**–1**	....	....	....	....	....	....	....	....
	Salt Lake Golden Eagles	IHL	67	43	48	91	....	....	....	173	....	....	....	....	....	....	....	....	....	....	11	4	8	12	0	....	....	....
1990-91	**Calgary Flames**	**NHL**	**5**	**0**	**0**	**0**	**0**	**0**	**0**	**2**	**0**	**0**	**0**	**4**	**0.0**	**0**	**0**	**6**	**2**	**–4**	....	....	....	....	....	....	....	....
	Salt Lake Golden Eagles	IHL	54	40	48	88	....	....	....	101	....	....	....	....	....	....	....	....	....	....	....	....	....	....	....	....	....	....
	Minnesota North Stars	**NHL**	**9**	**0**	**6**	**6**	**0**	**5**	**5**	**4**	**0**	**0**	**0**	**8**	**0.0**	**6**	**2**	**8**	**1**	**–3**	**23**	**3**	**2**	**5**	**20**	**0**	**1**	**0**
1991-92	**Minnesota North Stars**	**NHL**	**46**	**6**	**4**	**10**	**5**	**3**	**8**	**50**	**0**	**0**	**0**	**53**	**11.3**	**18**	**6**	**34**	**17**	**–5**	**5**	**0**	**0**	**0**	**14**	**0**	**0**	**0**
	Kalamazoo Wings	IHL	7	2	8	10	....	....	....	2	....	....	....	....	....	....	....	....	....	....	....	....	....	....	....	....	....	....
1992-93	**Tampa Bay Lightning**	**NHL**	**63**	**10**	**21**	**31**	**8**	**14**	**22**	**111**	**1**	**2**	**1**	**132**	**7.6**	**42**	**11**	**74**	**31**	**–12**	....	....	....	....	....	....	....	....
1993-94	**Tampa Bay Lightning**	**NHL**	**75**	**8**	**7**	**15**	**7**	**5**	**12**	**30**	**0**	**1**	**1**	**110**	**7.3**	**27**	**1**	**48**	**13**	**–9**	....	....	....	....	....	....	....	....
1994-95	**Tampa Bay Lightning**	**NHL**	**48**	**2**	**12**	**14**	**4**	**18**	**22**	**30**	**0**	**1**	**0**	**72**	**2.8**	**18**	**1**	**46**	**21**	**–8**	....	....	....	....	....	....	....	....
1995-96	**Montreal Canadiens**	**NHL**	**65**	**3**	**7**	**10**	**3**	**6**	**9**	**46**	**0**	**0**	**1**	**43**	**7.0**	**15**	**1**	**36**	**19**	**–3**	**6**	**1**	**1**	**2**	**4**	**0**	**0**	**0**
1996-97	**Montreal Canadiens**	**NHL**	**43**	**6**	**9**	**15**	**6**	**8**	**14**	**16**	**1**	**1**	**2**	**56**	**10.7**	**20**	**1**	**28**	**13**	**4**	....	....	....	....	....	....	....	....
1997-98	**Montreal Canadiens**	**NHL**	**74**	**13**	**6**	**19**	**15**	**6**	**21**	**12**	**0**	**0**	**2**	**82**	**15.9**	**27**	**0**	**48**	**21**	**0**	**10**	**1**	**2**	**3**	**6**	**0**	**0**	**0**
1998-99	**Philadelphia Flyers**	**NHL**	**71**	**4**	**6**	**10**	**5**	**6**	**11**	**10**	**0**	**0**	**0**	**52**	**7.7**	**16**	**0**	**35**	**17**	**–2**	**6**	**0**	**2**	**2**	**2**	**0**	**0**	**0**
99-2000	**Philadelphia Flyers**	**NHL**	**54**	**2**	**2**	**4**	**2**	**2**	**4**	**10**	**0**	**1**	**0**	**46**	**4.3**	**9**	**0**	**25**	**15**	**–1**	....	....	....	....	....	....	....	....
	Calgary Flames	**NHL**	**9**	**1**	**3**	**4**	**1**	**3**	**4**	**2**	**0**	**0**	**0**	**5**	**20.0**	**5**	**0**	**12**	**4**	**–3**	....	....	....	....	....	....	....	....
	NHL Totals		**567**	**55**	**83**	**138**	**56**	**76**	**132**	**327**	**2**	**6**	**7**	**666**	**8.3**	**204**	**23**	**402**	**174**		**50**	**5**	**7**	**12**	**46**	**0**	**1**	**0**

IHL Second All-Star Team (1990, 1991)

Signed as a free agent by **Calgary**, May 19, 1987. Traded to **Minnesota** by **Calgary** for Minnesota's 3rd round choice (Sandy McCarthy) in 1991 Entry Draft, March 5, 1991. Claimed on waivers by **Tampa Bay** from **Minnesota**, October 16, 1992. Traded to **Montreal** by **Tampa Bay** for Brian Bellows, June 30, 1995. Signed as a free agent by **Philadelphia**, July 20, 1998. Traded to **Calgary** by **Philadelphia** for Travis Brigley and Calgary's 6th round choice in 2001 Entry Draft, March 6, 2000.

• BURNS, Charlie
Charles Frederick C – L. 5'11", 170 lbs. b: Detroit, MI, 2/14/1936.

			REGULAR SEASON																		PLAYOFFS							
Season	Club	League	GP	G	A	Pts	AG	AA	APts	PIM	PP	SH	GW	S	%	TGF	PGF	TGA	PGA	+/–	GP	G	A	Pts	PIM	PP	SH	GW
1951-52	St. Michael's Buzzers	OHA-B	STATISTICS NOT AVAILABLE																									
1952-53	Toronto Marlboros	OHA-Jr.	33	5	7	12	....	....	....	17	....	....	....	....	....	....	....	....	....	....	7	4	1	5	2	....	....	....
1953-54	Toronto Marlboros	OHA-Jr.	59	17	14	31	....	....	....	45	....	....	....	....	....	....	....	....	....	....	7	2	3	5	0	....	....	....
1954-55	Toronto Marlboros	OHA-Jr.	3	0	0	0	....	....	....	0	....	....	....	....	....	....	....	....	....	....	1	0	0	0	0	....	....	....
1955-56	Toronto Marlboros	OHA-Jr.	20	5	8	13	....	....	....	16	....	....	....	....	....	....	....	....	....	....	11	5	4	9	12	....	....	....
	Toronto Marlboros	Mem-Cup	13	2	2	4	....	....	....	8	....	....	....	....	....	....	....	....	....	....	....	....	....	....	....	....	....	....
1956-57	Whitby Dunlops	EOHL	40	16	25	41	....	....	....	29	....	....	....	....	....	....	....	....	....	....	5	4	6	10	2	....	....	....
	Whitby Dunlops	Al-Cup	16	4	9	13	....	....	....	25	....	....	....	....	....	....	....	....	....	....	....	....	....	....	....	....	....	....
1957-58	Whitby Dunlops	EOHL	31	24	28	52	....	....	....	32	....	....	....	....	....	....	....	....	....	....	....	....	....	....	....	....	....	....
	Canada	WEC-A	7	3	4	7	....	....	....	0	....	....	....	....	....	....	....	....	....	....	....	....	....	....	....	....	....	....
1958-59	**Detroit Red Wings**	**NHL**	70	9	11	20	11	11	22	32	....	....	....	....	....	....	....	....	....	....	....	....	....	....	....	....	....	....
1959-60	**Boston Bruins**	**NHL**	62	10	17	27	12	16	28	46	....	....	....	....	....	....	....	....	....	....	....	....	....	....	....	....	....	....
1960-61	**Boston Bruins**	**NHL**	62	15	26	41	17	25	42	16	....	....	....	....	....	....	....	....	....	....	....	....	....	....	....	....	....	....
	Kingston Frontenacs	EPHL	8	3	6	9	....	....	....	4	....	....	....	....	....	....	....	....	....	....	....	....	....	....	....	....	....	....
1961-62	**Boston Bruins**	**NHL**	70	11	17	28	13	16	29	43	....	....	....	....	....	....	....	....	....	....	....	....	....	....	....	....	....	....
1962-63	**Boston Bruins**	**NHL**	68	12	10	22	14	10	24	13	....	....	....	....	....	....	....	....	....	....	....	....	....	....	....	....	....	....
1963-64	San Francisco Seals	WHL	68	33	36	69	....	....	....	27	....	....	....	....	....	....	....	....	....	....	11	1	3	4	2	....	....	....
1964-65	San Francisco Seals	WHL	51	27	36	63	....	....	....	19	....	....	....	....	....	....	....	....	....	....	....	....	....	....	....	....	....	....
1965-66	San Francisco Seals	WHL	40	10	35	45	....	....	....	26	....	....	....	....	....	....	....	....	....	....	7	1	5	6	0	....	....	....
1966-67	California Seals	WHL	71	22	38	60	....	....	....	29	....	....	....	....	....	....	....	....	....	....	6	0	0	0	9	....	....	....
1967-68	**Oakland Seals**	**NHL**	73	9	26	35	10	26	36	20	1	2	1	119	7.6	48	8	80	26	–14	....	....	....	....	....	....	....	....
1968-69	**Pittsburgh Penguins**	**NHL**	76	13	38	51	14	34	48	22	1	1	1	133	9.8	72	12	98	29	–9	....	....	....	....	....	....	....	....
1969-70	**Minnesota North Stars**	**NHL**	50	3	13	16	3	12	15	10	0	1	0	61	4.9	25	1	67	39	–4	6	1	0	1	2	0	0	0
1970-71	**Minnesota North Stars**	**NHL**	76	9	19	28	9	16	25	13	0	0	1	110	8.2	41	1	89	49	0	12	3	3	6	2	0	0	1
1971-72	**Minnesota North Stars**	**NHL**	77	11	14	25	11	12	23	24	0	1	2	88	12.5	31	3	61	38	5	7	1	1	2	2	0	0	0
1972-73	**Minnesota North Stars**	**NHL**	65	4	7	11	4	6	10	13	0	1	0	41	9.8	16	2	59	42	–3	6	0	0	0	0	0	0	0
1973-74	New Haven Nighthawks	AHL	64	10	19	29	....	....	....	73	....	....	....	....	....	....	....	....	....	....	10	1	3	4	16	....	....	....
	NHL Totals		749	106	198	304	118	184	302	252	....	....	....	....	....	....	....	....	....	....	31	5	4	9	6	....	....	....

Named Best Forward at WEC-A (1958)

• Missed majority of 1954-55 season recovering from head injury, November, 1954. Claimed by **Boston** from **Detroit** in Intra-League Draft, June 10, 1959. NHL rights transferred to **Oakland** after owners of **San Francisco** (WHL) franchise granted NHL expansion team, April 26, 1966. Claimed by **Pittsburgh** from **Oakland** in Intra-League Draft, June 12, 1968. Claimed by **Minnesota** from **Pittsburgh** in Intra-League Draft, June 11, 1969. • Named playing-coach of **Minnesota**, December 28, 1969.

• BURNS, Gary
LW/C – L. 6'1", 190 lbs. b: Cambridge, MA, 1/16/1955. Toronto's 15th, 191st overall, in 1975.

Season	Club	League	GP	G	A	Pts	AG	AA	APts	PIM	PP	SH	GW	S	%	TGF	PGF	TGA	PGA	+/–	GP	G	A	Pts	PIM	PP	SH	GW
1973-74	Arlington North Shore High	Hi-School	STATISTICS NOT AVAILABLE																									
1974-75	University of New Hampshire	ECAC	31	17	15	32	....	....	....	42	....	....	....	....	....	....	....	....	....	....	....	....	....	....	....	....	....	....
1975-76	University of New Hampshire	ECAC	31	6	12	18	....	....	....	36	....	....	....	....	....	....	....	....	....	....	....	....	....	....	....	....	....	....
1976-77	University of New Hampshire	ECAC	38	9	6	15	....	....	....	24	....	....	....	....	....	....	....	....	....	....	....	....	....	....	....	....	....	....
1977-78	University of New Hampshire	ECAC	29	9	19	28	....	....	....	55	....	....	....	....	....	....	....	....	....	....	....	....	....	....	....	....	....	....
1978-79	Rochester Americans	AHL	79	16	30	46	....	....	....	99	....	....	....	....	....	....	....	....	....	....	....	....	....	....	....	....	....	....
1979-80	Binghamton Dusters	AHL	79	30	29	59	....	....	....	105	....	....	....	....	....	....	....	....	....	....	....	....	....	....	....	....	....	....
1980-81	**New York Rangers**	**NHL**	11	2	2	4	2	1	3	18	0	0	1	13	15.4	5	1	16	3	–9	1	0	0	0	2	0	0	0
	New Haven Nighthawks	AHL	69	25	29	54	....	....	....	137	....	....	....	....	....	....	....	....	....	....	4	1	0	1	2	....	....	....
1981-82	Springfield Indians	AHL	78	27	39	66	....	....	....	71	....	....	....	....	....	....	....	....	....	....	....	....	....	....	....	....	....	....
	New York Rangers	**NHL**	....	....	....	....	....	....	....	....	....	....	....	....	....	....	....	....	....	....	4	0	0	0	0	0	0	0
1982-83	Tulsa Oilers	CHL	80	21	33	54	....	....	....	61	....	....	....	....	....	....	....	....	....	....	....	....	....	....	....	....	....	....
1983-84	Tulsa Oilers	CHL	68	28	30	58	....	....	....	95	....	....	....	....	....	....	....	....	....	....	9	3	*9	12	2	....	....	....
1984-85	Rochester Americans	AHL	76	22	27	49	....	....	....	64	....	....	....	....	....	....	....	....	....	....	2	0	1	1	6	....	....	....
1985-86	Salt Lake Golden Eagles	IHL	78	23	35	58	....	....	....	85	....	....	....	....	....	....	....	....	....	....	4	1	0	1	6	....	....	....
	NHL Totals		11	2	2	4	2	1	3	18	0	0	1	13	15.4	5	1	16	3		5	0	0	0	2	0	0	0

Signed as a free agent by **Boston**, October 10, 1978. Signed as a free agent by **NY Rangers**, September 16, 1980.

• BURNS, Robin
Robert Arthur LW – L. 6', 195 lbs. b: Montreal, Que., 8/27/1946.

Season	Club	League	GP	G	A	Pts	AG	AA	APts	PIM	PP	SH	GW	S	%	TGF	PGF	TGA	PGA	+/–	GP	G	A	Pts	PIM	PP	SH	GW
1963-64	Montreal NDG Monarchs	MMJHL	44	13	16	29	....	....	....	50	....	....	....	....	....	....	....	....	....	....	18	3	5	8	27	....	....	....
	Montreal NDG Monarchs	Mem-Cup	13	3	5	8	....	....	....	14	....	....	....	....	....	....	....	....	....	....	....	....	....	....	....	....	....	....
1964-65	Montreal Jr. Canadiens	OHA-Jr.	39	1	5	6	....	....	....	66	....	....	....	....	....	....	....	....	....	....	7	2	1	3	8	....	....	....
1965-66	Montreal Jr. Canadiens	OHA-Jr.	42	6	2	8	....	....	....	97	....	....	....	....	....	....	....	....	....	....	10	0	4	4	20	....	....	....
1966-67	Montreal Jr. Canadiens	OHA-Jr.	46	11	12	23	....	....	....	99	....	....	....	....	....	....	....	....	....	....	4	1	2	3	6	....	....	....
1967-68	Houston Apollos	CPHL	65	21	25	46	....	....	....	41	....	....	....	....	....	....	....	....	....	....	....	....	....	....	....	....	....	....
1968-69	Houston Apollos	CHL	61	12	18	30	....	....	....	63	....	....	....	....	....	....	....	....	....	....	3	0	0	0	0	....	....	....
1969-70	Montreal Voyageurs	AHL	62	13	7	20	....	....	....	33	....	....	....	....	....	....	....	....	....	....	8	0	1	1	0	....	....	....
1970-71	**Pittsburgh Penguins**	**NHL**	10	0	3	3	0	2	2	4	0	0	0	10	0.0	6	0	5	0	1	....	....	....	....	....	....	....	....
	Amarillo Wranglers	CHL	46	16	24	40	....	....	....	49	....	....	....	....	....	....	....	....	....	....	....	....	....	....	....	....	....	....
1971-72	**Pittsburgh Penguins**	**NHL**	5	0	0	0	0	0	0	8	0	0	0	4	0.0	1	1	4	0	–4	....	....	....	....	....	....	....	....
	Hershey Bears	AHL	65	18	15	33	....	....	....	58	....	....	....	....	....	....	....	....	....	....	4	1	1	2	10	....	....	....
1972-73	**Pittsburgh Penguins**	**NHL**	26	0	2	2	0	2	2	20	0	0	0	26	0.0	3	0	9	0	–6	....	....	....	....	....	....	....	....
	Hershey Bears	AHL	39	22	25	47	....	....	....	51	....	....	....	....	....	....	....	....	....	....	....	....	....	....	....	....	....	....
1973-74	Hershey Bears	AHL	74	31	35	66	....	....	....	77	....	....	....	....	....	....	....	....	....	....	14	*10	4	14	6	....	....	....
1974-75	**Kansas City Scouts**	**NHL**	71	18	15	33	16	11	27	70	7	0	1	126	14.3	50	17	73	0	–40	....	....	....	....	....	....	....	....
1975-76	**Kansas City Scouts**	**NHL**	78	13	18	31	11	13	24	37	2	0	0	145	9.0	39	10	69	0	–40	....	....	....	....	....	....	....	....
	NHL Totals		190	31	38	69	27	28	55	139	9	0	1	311	10.0	99	28	160	0		....	....	....	....	....	....	....	....

Traded to **Pittsburgh** by **Montreal** for cash, October 2, 1970. Claimed by **Kansas City** from **Pittsburgh** in Expansion Draft, June 12, 1974.

• BURR, Shawn
Shawn Christopher LW/C – L. 6'1", 205 lbs. b: Sarnia, Ont., 7/1/1966. Detroit's 1st, 7th overall, in 1984.

Season	Club	League	GP	G	A	Pts	AG	AA	APts	PIM	PP	SH	GW	S	%	TGF	PGF	TGA	PGA	+/–	GP	G	A	Pts	PIM	PP	SH	GW
1982-83	Sarnia Black Hawks	OMHA	52	50	85	135	....	....	....	125	....	....	....	....	....	....	....	....	....	....	....	....	....	....	....	....	....	....
1983-84	Kitchener Rangers	OHL	68	41	44	85	....	....	....	50	....	....	....	....	....	....	....	....	....	....	16	5	12	17	22	....	....	....
	Kitchener Rangers	Mem-Cup	4	2	3	5	....	....	....	4	....	....	....	....	....	....	....	....	....	....	....	....	....	....	....	....	....	....
1984-85	Kitchener Rangers	OHL	48	24	42	66	....	....	....	50	....	....	....	....	....	....	....	....	....	....	4	3	3	6	2	....	....	....
	Detroit Red Wings	**NHL**	9	0	0	0	0	0	0	2	0	0	0	4	0.0	1	0	5	0	–4	....	....	....	....	....	....	....	....
	Adirondack Red Wings	AHL	4	0	0	0	....	....	....	2	....	....	....	....	....	....	....	....	....	....	....	....	....	....	....	....	....	....
1985-86	Kitchener Rangers	OHL	59	60	67	127	....	....	....	104	....	....	....	....	....	....	....	....	....	....	5	2	3	5	8	....	....	....
	Detroit Red Wings	**NHL**	5	1	0	1	1	0	1	4	1	0	0	6	16.7	4	2	1	0	1	....	....	....	....	....	....	....	....
	Adirondack Red Wings	AHL	3	2	2	4	....	....	....	2	....	....	....	....	....	....	....	....	....	....	17	5	7	12	32	....	....	....
1986-87	**Detroit Red Wings**	**NHL**	80	22	25	47	19	18	37	107	1	2	1	153	14.4	61	4	81	26	2	16	7	2	9	20	0	0	2
1987-88	**Detroit Red Wings**	**NHL**	78	17	23	40	14	16	30	97	5	3	3	124	13.7	58	8	68	25	7	9	3	1	4	14	0	0	1
1988-89	**Detroit Red Wings**	**NHL**	79	19	27	46	16	19	35	78	1	4	2	149	12.8	59	5	71	22	5	6	1	2	3	6	0	0	0
1989-90	**Detroit Red Wings**	**NHL**	76	24	32	56	21	23	44	82	4	3	2	173	13.9	86	18	83	29	14	....	....	....	....	....	....	....	....
	Adirondack Red Wings	AHL	3	4	2	6	....	....	....	2	....	....	....	....	....	....	....	....	....	....	....	....	....	....	....	....	....	....
	Canada	WEC-A	10	4	1	5	....	....	....	14	....	....	....	....	....	....	....	....	....	....	....	....	....	....	....	....	....	....
1990-91	**Detroit Red Wings**	**NHL**	80	20	30	50	18	23	41	112	6	0	4	164	12.2	70	11	64	19	14	7	0	4	4	15	0	0	0
1991-92	**Detroit Red Wings**	**NHL**	79	19	32	51	17	24	41	118	2	0	3	140	13.6	76	5	67	22	26	11	1	5	6	10	0	0	0
1992-93	**Detroit Red Wings**	**NHL**	80	10	25	35	8	17	25	74	1	1	2	99	10.1	53	1	68	34	18	7	2	1	3	2	0	1	0
1993-94	**Detroit Red Wings**	**NHL**	51	10	12	22	9	9	18	31	0	1	1	64	15.6	32	0	32	12	12	7	2	0	2	6	0	0	2
1994-95	**Detroit Red Wings**	**NHL**	42	6	8	14	11	12	23	60	0	0	3	65	9.2	29	1	23	8	13	16	0	2	2	6	0	0	0
1995-96	**Tampa Bay Lightning**	**NHL**	81	13	15	28	13	12	25	119	1	0	2	122	10.7	48	1	67	24	4	6	0	2	2	8	0	0	0
1996-97	**Tampa Bay Lightning**	**NHL**	74	14	21	35	15	19	34	106	1	0	3	128	10.9	53	7	51	10	5	....	....	....	....	....	....	....	....
1997-98	**San Jose Sharks**	**NHL**	42	6	6	12	7	6	13	50	0	0	0	63	9.5	16	0	18	4	2	6	0	0	0	8	0	0	0

			REGULAR SEASON																		PLAYOFFS							
Season	**Club**	**League**	**GP**	**G**	**A**	**Pts**	**AG**	**AA**	**APts**	**PIM**	**PP**	**SH**	**GW**	**S**	**%**	**TGF**	**PGF**	**TGA**	**PGA**	**+/–**	**GP**	**G**	**A**	**Pts**	**PIM**	**PP**	**SH**	**GW**
1998-99	**San Jose Sharks**	**NHL**	**18**	**0**	**1**	**1**	**0**	**1**	**1**	**29**	**0**	**0**	**0**	**22**	**0.0**	**2**	**1**	**4**	**0**	**–3**	....	....	....	....	....	....	....	....
	Kentucky Thoroughblades	AHL	26	10	14	24	....	....	....	29	....	....	....	....	....	....	....	....	....	....	12	4	9	13	10	....	....	....
99-2000	**Tampa Bay Lightning**	**NHL**	**4**	**0**	**2**	**2**	**0**	**2**	**2**	**0**	**0**	**0**	**0**	**6**	**0.0**	**2**	**0**	**3**	**3**	**2**	....	....	....	....	....	....	....	....
	Detroit Vipers	IHL	10	2	4	6	....	....	....	10	....	....	....	....	....	....	....	....	....	....	....	....	....	....	....	....	....	....
	Manitoba Moose	IHL	18	3	2	5	....	....	....	6	....	....	....	....	....	....	....	....	....	....	2	1	0	1	6	....	....	....
	NHL Totals		**878**	**181**	**259**	**440**	**169**	**201**	**370**	**1069**	**23**	**14**	**26**	**1482**	**12.2**	**650**	**64**	**706**	**238**		**91**	**16**	**19**	**35**	**95**	**0**	**1**	**5**

OHL Second All-Star Team (1986)

Traded to **Tampa Bay** by **Detroit** with Detroit's 3rd round choice (later traded to Boston — Boston selected Jason Doyle) in 1996 Entry Draft for Marc Bergevin and Ben Hankinson, August 17, 1995. Traded to **San Jose** by **Tampa Bay** for San Jose's 5th round choice (Mark Thompson) in 1997 Entry Draft, June 21, 1997. Traded to **Tampa Bay** by **San Jose** with Andrei Zyuzin, Bill Houlder and Steve Guolla for Niklas Sundstrom and NY Rangers' 3rd round choice (previously acquired, later traded to Chicago - Chicago selected Igor Radulov) in 2000 Entry Draft, August 4, 1999.

• BURRIDGE, Randy

"Stump" LW – L. 5'9", 188 lbs. b: Fort Erie, Ont., 1/7/1966. Boston's 7th, 157th overall, in 1985.

Season	Club	League	GP	G	A	Pts	AG	AA	APts	PIM	PP	SH	GW	S	%	TGF	PGF	TGA	PGA	+/–	GP	G	A	Pts	PIM	PP	SH	GW
1982-83	Fort Erie Meteors	OJHL-B	42	32	56	88	....	....	....	32	....	....	....	....	....	....	....	....	....	....	....	....	....	....	....	....	....	....
1983-84	Peterborough Petes	OHL	55	6	7	13	....	....	....	44	....	....	....	....	....	....	....	....	....	....	8	3	2	5	7	....	....	....
1984-85	Peterborough Petes	OHL	66	49	57	106	....	....	....	88	....	....	....	....	....	....	....	....	....	....	17	9	16	25	18	....	....	....
1985-86	Peterborough Petes	OHL	17	15	11	26	....	....	....	23	....	....	....	....	....	....	....	....	....	....	3	1	3	4	2	....	....	....
	Boston Bruins	**NHL**	**52**	**17**	**25**	**42**	**14**	**17**	**31**	**28**	**1**	**0**	**2**	**90**	**18.9**	**58**	**14**	**34**	**7**	**17**	**3**	**0**	**4**	**4**	**12**	**0**	**0**	**0**
	Moncton Golden Flames	AHL	....	....	....	....	....	....	....	....	....	....	....	....	....	....	....	....	....	....	3	0	2	2	2	....	....	....
1986-87	**Boston Bruins**	**NHL**	**23**	**1**	**4**	**5**	**1**	**3**	**4**	**16**	**0**	**0**	**1**	**27**	**3.7**	**12**	**0**	**23**	**5**	**–6**	**2**	**1**	**0**	**1**	**2**	**0**	**0**	**0**
	Moncton Golden Flames	AHL	47	26	41	67	....	....	....	139	....	....	....	....	....	....	....	....	....	....	3	1	2	3	30	....	....	....
1987-88	**Boston Bruins**	**NHL**	**79**	**27**	**28**	**55**	**23**	**20**	**43**	**105**	**5**	**3**	**3**	**159**	**17.0**	**85**	**21**	**92**	**28**	**0**	**23**	**2**	**10**	**12**	**16**	**0**	**0**	**0**
1988-89	**Boston Bruins**	**NHL**	**80**	**31**	**30**	**61**	**26**	**21**	**47**	**39**	**6**	**2**	**6**	**189**	**16.4**	**89**	**22**	**79**	**31**	**19**	**10**	**5**	**2**	**7**	**6**	**1**	**1**	**0**
1989-90	**Boston Bruins**	**NHL**	**63**	**17**	**15**	**32**	**15**	**11**	**26**	**47**	**7**	**0**	**1**	**118**	**14.4**	**66**	**20**	**47**	**10**	**9**	**21**	**4**	**11**	**15**	**14**	**0**	**1**	**0**
1990-91	**Boston Bruins**	**NHL**	**62**	**15**	**13**	**28**	**14**	**10**	**24**	**40**	**1**	**0**	**4**	**108**	**13.9**	**55**	**5**	**50**	**17**	**17**	**19**	**0**	**3**	**3**	**39**	**0**	**0**	**0**
1991-92	**Washington Capitals**	**NHL**	**66**	**23**	**44**	**67**	**21**	**33**	**54**	**50**	**9**	**0**	**3**	**131**	**17.6**	**98**	**43**	**69**	**10**	**–4**	**2**	**0**	**1**	**1**	**0**	**0**	**0**	**0**
1992-93	**Washington Capitals**	**NHL**	**4**	**0**	**0**	**0**	**0**	**0**	**0**	**0**	**0**	**0**	**0**	**7**	**0.0**	**1**	**0**	**0**	**0**	**1**	**4**	**1**	**0**	**1**	**0**	**0**	**0**	**0**
	Baltimore Skipjacks	AHL	2	0	1	1	....	....	....	2	....	....	....	....	....	....	....	....	....	....	....	....	....	....	....	....	....	....
1993-94	**Washington Capitals**	**NHL**	**78**	**25**	**17**	**42**	**23**	**13**	**36**	**73**	**8**	**1**	**5**	**150**	**16.7**	**78**	**34**	**52**	**7**	**–1**	**11**	**0**	**2**	**2**	**12**	**0**	**0**	**0**
1994-95	**Washington Capitals**	**NHL**	**2**	**0**	**0**	**0**	**0**	**0**	**0**	**2**	**0**	**0**	**0**	**2**	**0.0**	**0**	**0**	**0**	**0**	**0**	....	....	....	....	....	....	....	....
	Los Angeles Kings	**NHL**	**38**	**4**	**15**	**19**	**7**	**22**	**29**	**8**	**2**	**0**	**0**	**50**	**8.0**	**27**	**6**	**26**	**1**	**–4**	....	....	....	....	....	....	....	....
1995-96	**Buffalo Sabres**	**NHL**	**74**	**25**	**33**	**58**	**25**	**27**	**52**	**30**	**6**	**0**	**3**	**154**	**16.2**	**89**	**40**	**52**	**3**	**0**	....	....	....	....	....	....	....	....
1996-97	**Buffalo Sabres**	**NHL**	**55**	**10**	**21**	**31**	**11**	**19**	**30**	**20**	**1**	**3**	**0**	**85**	**11.8**	**48**	**11**	**28**	**8**	**17**	**12**	**5**	**1**	**6**	**2**	**3**	**0**	**0**
1997-98	**Buffalo Sabres**	**NHL**	**30**	**4**	**6**	**10**	**5**	**6**	**11**	**0**	**1**	**0**	**1**	**40**	**10.0**	**12**	**1**	**14**	**3**	**0**	....	....	....	....	....	....	....	....
	Rochester Americans	AHL	6	0	1	1	....	....	....	19	....	....	....	....	....	....	....	....	....	....	1	0	1	1	0	....	....	....
1998-99	Hannover Scorpions	Germany	14	7	6	13	....	....	....	35	....	....	....	....	....	....	....	....	....	....	....	....	....	....	....	....	....	....
	Las Vegas Thunder	IHL	25	7	12	19	....	....	....	8	....	....	....	....	....	....	....	....	....	....	....	....	....	....	....	....	....	....
	NHL Totals		**706**	**199**	**251**	**450**	**185**	**202**	**387**	**458**	**47**	**9**	**29**	**1310**	**15.2**	**718**	**217**	**566**	**130**		**107**	**18**	**34**	**52**	**103**	**4**	**2**	**0**

Played in NHL All-Star Game (1992)

Traded to **Washington** by **Boston** for Stephen Leach, June 21, 1991. • Missed majority of 1992-93 season recovering from knee injury suffered in training camp, September 5, 1992. Traded to **LA Kings** by **Washington** for Warren Rychel, February 10, 1995. Signed as a free agent by **Buffalo**, October 5, 1995. Signed as a free agent by **Las Vegas** (IHL), October 15, 1998. Signed as a free agent by EHC Hannover after release by Las Vegas, January 19, 1999.

• BURROWS, Dave

David James D – L. 6'1", 190 lbs. b: Toronto, Ont., 1/11/1949.

Season	Club	League	GP	G	A	Pts	AG	AA	APts	PIM	PP	SH	GW	S	%	TGF	PGF	TGA	PGA	+/–	GP	G	A	Pts	PIM	PP	SH	GW
1967-68	Dixie Beehives	OHA-B	STATISTICS NOT AVAILABLE																									
	St. Catharines Black Hawks	OHA-Jr.	9	0	3	3	....	....	....	4	....	....	....	....	....	....	....	....	....	....	5	0	0	0	0	....	....	....
1968-69	St. Catharines Black Hawks	OHA-Jr.	54	3	16	19	....	....	....	36	....	....	....	....	....	....	....	....	....	....	18	1	4	5	12	....	....	....
1969-70	Dallas Black Hawks	CHL	69	4	9	13	....	....	....	45	....	....	....	....	....	....	....	....	....	....	....	....	....	....	....	....	....	....
	Portland Buckaroos	WHL	....	....	....	....	....	....	....	....	....	....	....	....	....	....	....	....	....	....	11	1	2	3	6	....	....	....
1970-71	Dallas Black Hawks	CHL	67	1	11	12	....	....	....	49	....	....	....	....	....	....	....	....	....	....	10	0	2	2	4	....	....	....
1971-72	**Pittsburgh Penguins**	**NHL**	**77**	**2**	**10**	**12**	**2**	**9**	**11**	**48**	**0**	**0**	**0**	**100**	**2.0**	**77**	**7**	**104**	**27**	**–7**	**4**	**0**	**0**	**0**	**4**	**0**	**0**	**0**
1972-73	**Pittsburgh Penguins**	**NHL**	**78**	**3**	**24**	**27**	**3**	**19**	**22**	**42**	**0**	**0**	**0**	**132**	**2.3**	**99**	**5**	**118**	**20**	**–4**	....	....	....	....	....	....	....	....
1973-74	**Pittsburgh Penguins**	**NHL**	**71**	**3**	**14**	**17**	**3**	**12**	**15**	**30**	**2**	**0**	**0**	**123**	**2.4**	**87**	**15**	**112**	**27**	**–13**	....	....	....	....	....	....	....	....
1974-75	**Pittsburgh Penguins**	**NHL**	**78**	**2**	**15**	**17**	**2**	**11**	**13**	**49**	**0**	**0**	**1**	**126**	**1.6**	**99**	**7**	**127**	**38**	**3**	**9**	**1**	**1**	**2**	**12**	**0**	**0**	**1**
1975-76	**Pittsburgh Penguins**	**NHL**	**80**	**7**	**22**	**29**	**6**	**16**	**22**	**51**	**1**	**1**	**1**	**125**	**5.6**	**152**	**15**	**155**	**45**	**27**	**3**	**0**	**0**	**0**	**0**	**0**	**0**	**0**
1976-77	**Pittsburgh Penguins**	**NHL**	**69**	**3**	**6**	**9**	**3**	**5**	**8**	**29**	**1**	**0**	**1**	**92**	**3.3**	**84**	**11**	**106**	**18**	**–15**	**3**	**0**	**2**	**2**	**0**	**0**	**0**	**0**
1977-78	**Pittsburgh Penguins**	**NHL**	**67**	**4**	**15**	**19**	**4**	**12**	**16**	**24**	**0**	**0**	**1**	**92**	**4.3**	**79**	**2**	**139**	**32**	**–30**	....	....	....	....	....	....	....	....
1978-79	**Toronto Maple Leafs**	**NHL**	**65**	**2**	**11**	**13**	**2**	**8**	**10**	**28**	**0**	**0**	**0**	**70**	**2.9**	**65**	**1**	**99**	**25**	**–10**	**6**	**0**	**1**	**1**	**7**	**0**	**0**	**0**
1979-80	**Toronto Maple Leafs**	**NHL**	**80**	**3**	**16**	**19**	**3**	**12**	**15**	**42**	**0**	**0**	**0**	**102**	**2.9**	**94**	**2**	**132**	**40**	**0**	**3**	**0**	**1**	**1**	**2**	**0**	**0**	**0**
1980-81	**Toronto Maple Leafs**	**NHL**	**6**	**0**	**0**	**0**	**0**	**0**	**0**	**2**	**0**	**0**	**0**	**3**	**0.0**	**1**	**0**	**7**	**2**	**–4**	....	....	....	....	....	....	....	....
	Pittsburgh Penguins	**NHL**	**53**	**0**	**2**	**2**	**0**	**1**	**1**	**28**	**0**	**0**	**0**	**32**	**0.0**	**37**	**0**	**72**	**22**	**–13**	**1**	**0**	**0**	**0**	**0**	**0**	**0**	**0**
	NHL Totals		**724**	**29**	**135**	**164**	**28**	**105**	**133**	**373**	**4**	**1**	**4**	**997**	**2.9**	**874**	**65**	**1171**	**296**		**29**	**1**	**5**	**6**	**25**	**0**	**0**	**1**

Played in NHL All-Star Game (1974, 1976, 1980)

Claimed by **Pittsburgh** from **Chicago** in Intra-League Draft, June 8, 1971. Traded to **Toronto** by **Pittsburgh** for Randy Carlyle and George Ferguson, June 14, 1978. Traded to **Pittsburgh** by **Toronto** with Paul Gardner for Kim Davis and Paul Marshall, November 18, 1980.

• BURT, Adam

D – L. 6'2", 205 lbs. b: Detroit, MI, 1/15/1969. Hartford's 2nd, 39th overall, in 1987.

Season	Club	League	GP	G	A	Pts	AG	AA	APts	PIM	PP	SH	GW	S	%	TGF	PGF	TGA	PGA	+/–	GP	G	A	Pts	PIM	PP	SH	GW
1983-84	North Bay Hoppers	NOHA	15	5	7	12	....	....	....	48	....	....	....	....	....	....	....	....	....	....	....	....	....	....	....	....	....	....
1984-85	Detroit Compuware	MNHL	STATISTICS NOT AVAILABLE																									
1985-86	North Bay Centennials	OHL	49	0	11	11	....	....	....	81	....	....	....	....	....	....	....	....	....	....	10	0	0	0	24	....	....	....
1986-87	North Bay Centennials	OHL	57	4	27	31	....	....	....	138	....	....	....	....	....	....	....	....	....	....	24	1	6	7	68	....	....	....
	United States	WJC-A	7	0	1	1	....	....	....	8	....	....	....	....	....	....	....	....	....	....	....	....	....	....	....	....	....	....
1987-88	North Bay Centennials	OHL	66	17	53	70	....	....	....	176	....	....	....	....	....	....	....	....	....	....	2	0	3	3	6	....	....	....
	Binghamton Whalers	AHL	....	....	....	....	....	....	....	....	....	....	....	....	....	....	....	....	....	....	2	1	1	2	0	....	....	....
1988-89	North Bay Centennials	OHL	23	4	11	15	....	....	....	45	....	....	....	....	....	....	....	....	....	....	12	2	12	14	12	....	....	....
	United States	WJC-A	7	1	6	7	....	....	....	2	....	....	....	....	....	....	....	....	....	....	....	....	....	....	....	....	....	....
	Hartford Whalers	**NHL**	**5**	**0**	**0**	**0**	**0**	**0**	**0**	**6**	**0**	**0**	**0**	**1**	**0.0**	**0**	**0**	**1**	**0**	**–1**	....	....	....	....	....	....	....	....
	Binghamton Whalers	AHL	5	0	2	2	....	....	....	13	....	....	....	....	....	....	....	....	....	....	....	....	....	....	....	....	....	....
1989-90	**Hartford Whalers**	**NHL**	**63**	**4**	**8**	**12**	**3**	**6**	**9**	**105**	**1**	**0**	**0**	**83**	**4.8**	**63**	**3**	**71**	**14**	**3**	**2**	**0**	**0**	**0**	**0**	**0**	**0**	**0**
1990-91	**Hartford Whalers**	**NHL**	**42**	**2**	**7**	**9**	**2**	**5**	**7**	**63**	**1**	**0**	**1**	**43**	**4.7**	**46**	**11**	**49**	**10**	**–4**	....	....	....	....	....	....	....	....
	Springfield Indians	AHL	9	1	3	4	....	....	....	22	....	....	....	....	....	....	....	....	....	....	....	....	....	....	....	....	....	....
1991-92	**Hartford Whalers**	**NHL**	**66**	**9**	**15**	**24**	**8**	**11**	**19**	**93**	**4**	**0**	**1**	**89**	**10.1**	**66**	**20**	**79**	**17**	**–16**	**2**	**0**	**0**	**0**	**0**	**0**	**0**	**0**
1992-93	**Hartford Whalers**	**NHL**	**65**	**6**	**14**	**20**	**5**	**10**	**15**	**116**	**0**	**0**	**0**	**81**	**7.4**	**60**	**8**	**77**	**14**	**–11**	....	....	....	....	....	....	....	....
	United States	WC-A	6	2	1	3	....	....	....	6	....	....	....	....	....	....	....	....	....	....	....	....	....	....	....	....	....	....
1993-94	**Hartford Whalers**	**NHL**	**63**	**1**	**17**	**18**	**1**	**13**	**14**	**75**	**0**	**0**	**0**	**91**	**1.1**	**56**	**7**	**80**	**27**	**–4**	....	....	....	....	....	....	....	....
1994-95	**Hartford Whalers**	**NHL**	**46**	**7**	**11**	**18**	**12**	**16**	**28**	**65**	**3**	**0**	**1**	**73**	**9.6**	**54**	**14**	**53**	**13**	**0**	....	....	....	....	....	....	....	....
1995-96	**Hartford Whalers**	**NHL**	**78**	**4**	**9**	**13**	**4**	**7**	**11**	**121**	**0**	**0**	**1**	**90**	**4.4**	**57**	**7**	**77**	**23**	**–4**	....	....	....	....	....	....	....	....
1996-97	**Hartford Whalers**	**NHL**	**71**	**2**	**11**	**13**	**2**	**10**	**12**	**79**	**0**	**0**	**0**	**85**	**2.4**	**68**	**13**	**84**	**16**	**–13**	....	....	....	....	....	....	....	....
1997-98	**Carolina Hurricanes**	**NHL**	**76**	**1**	**11**	**12**	**1**	**11**	**12**	**106**	**0**	**1**	**0**	**51**	**2.0**	**48**	**1**	**75**	**22**	**–6**	....	....	....	....	....	....	....	....
	United States	WC-A	6	0	0	0	....	....	....	4	....	....	....	....	....	....	....	....	....	....	....	....	....	....	....	....	....	....
1998-99	**Carolina Hurricanes**	**NHL**	**51**	**0**	**3**	**3**	**0**	**3**	**3**	**46**	**0**	**0**	**0**	**37**	**0.0**	**36**	**0**	**44**	**11**	**3**	....	....	....	....	....	....	....	....
	Philadelphia Flyers	**NHL**	**17**	**0**	**1**	**1**	**0**	**1**	**1**	**14**	**0**	**0**	**0**	**24**	**0.0**	**7**	**0**	**8**	**2**	**1**	**6**	**0**	**0**	**0**	**4**	**0**	**0**	**0**
99-2000	**Philadelphia Flyers**	**NHL**	**67**	**1**	**6**	**7**	**1**	**6**	**7**	**45**	**0**	**0**	**1**	**49**	**2.0**	**36**	**3**	**44**	**9**	**–2**	**11**	**0**	**1**	**1**	**4**	**0**	**0**	**0**
	NHL Totals		**710**	**37**	**113**	**150**	**39**	**99**	**138**	**934**	**9**	**1**	**5**	**797**	**4.6**	**597**	**87**	**742**	**178**		**21**	**0**	**1**	**1**	**8**	**0**	**0**	**0**

OHL Second All-Star Team (1988)

Transferred to **Carolina** after **Hartford** franchise relocated, June 25, 1997. Traded to **Philadelphia** by **Carolina** for Andrei Kovalenko, March 6, 1999.

• BURTON, Nelson

Keith Nelson LW – L. 6', 205 lbs. b: Sydney, N.S., 11/6/1957. Washington's 4th, 57th overall, in 1977.

Season	Club	League	REGULAR SEASON																		PLAYOFFS							
			GP	G	A	Pts	AG	AA	APts	PIM	PP	SH	GW	S	%	TGF	PGF	TGA	PGA	+/–	GP	G	A	Pts	PIM	PP	SH	GW
1974-75	Hull Festivals	QMJHL	67	20	19	39	....	....	....	333	....	....	....	....	....	....	....	....	....	....	....	....	....	....	....	....	....	....
1975-76	Quebec Remparts	QMJHL	71	26	25	51	....	....	....	322	....	....	....	....	....	....	....	....	....	....	13	0	3	3	*90	....	....	....
	Quebec Remparts	Mem-Cup	3	0	0	0	....	....	....	13	....	....	....	....	....	....	....	....	....	....	....	....	....	....	....	....	....	....
1976-77	Quebec Remparts	QMJHL	67	22	28	50	....	....	....	398	....	....	....	....	....	....	....	....	....	....	9	1	5	6	70	....	....	....
1977-78	**Washington Capitals**	**NHL**	**5**	**1**	**0**	**1**	**1**	**0**	**1**	**8**	**0**	**0**	**0**	**3**	**33.3**	**1**	**0**	**4**	**0**	**–3**	....	....	....	....	....	....	....	....
	Hershey Bears	AHL	57	4	7	11	....	....	....	*323	....	....	....	....	....	....	....	....	....	....	....	....	....	....	....	....	....	....
1978-79	**Washington Capitals**	**NHL**	**3**	**0**	**0**	**0**	**0**	**0**	**0**	**13**	**0**	**0**	**0**	**0**	**0.0**	**1**	**0**	**4**	**1**	**–2**	....	....	....	....	....	....	....	....
	Hershey Bears	AHL	51	6	19	25	....	....	....	204	....	....	....	....	....	....	....	....	....	....	....	....	....	....	....	....	....	....
1979-80	Syracuse Firebirds	AHL	2	0	1	1	....	....	....	0	....	....	....	....	....	....	....	....	....	....	....	....	....	....	....	....	....	....
	Nova Scotia Voyageurs	AHL	70	3	10	13	....	....	....	190	....	....	....	....	....	....	....	....	....	....	3	0	0	0	37	....	....	....
1980-81	Erie Blades	EHL	68	20	24	44	....	....	....	*385	....	....	....	....	....	....	....	....	....	....	8	0	0	0	60	....	....	....
1981-82	Nashville South Stars	CHL	49	1	4	5	....	....	....	128	....	....	....	....	....	....	....	....	....	....	3	0	0	0	0	....	....	....
1982-83	Baltimore Skipjacks	AHL	60	3	8	11	....	....	....	71	....	....	....	....	....	....	....	....	....	....	....	....	....	....	....	....	....	....
1983-84	Erie Golden Blades	ACHL	65	10	12	22	....	....	....	156	....	....	....	....	....	....	....	....	....	....	9	0	1	1	79	....	....	....
	NHL Totals		**8**	**1**	**0**	**1**	**1**	**0**	**1**	**21**	**0**	**0**	**0**	**3**	**33.3**	**2**	**0**	**8**	**1**		....	....	....	....	....	....	....	....

Traded to **Quebec** by **Washington** for Dave Parro, June 15, 1979. Traded to **Minnesota** by **Quebec** for Dan Chicoine, June 9, 1981.

• BUSKAS, Rod

Rod Dale D – R. 6'1", 206 lbs. b: Wetaskiwin, Alta., 1/7/1961. Pittsburgh's 5th, 112th overall, in 1981.

Season	Club	League	GP	G	A	Pts	AG	AA	APts	PIM	PP	SH	GW	S	%	TGF	PGF	TGA	PGA	+/–	GP	G	A	Pts	PIM	PP	SH	GW
1977-78	Red Deer Rustlers	AJHL	60	5	2	7	....	....	....	36	....	....	....	....	....	....	....	....	....	....	....	....	....	....	....	....	....	....
1978-79	Red Deer Rustlers	AJHL	37	13	22	35	....	....	....	63	....	....	....	....	....	....	....	....	....	....	....	....	....	....	....	....	....	....
	Billings Bighorns	WHL	1	0	0	0	....	....	....	0	....	....	....	....	....	....	....	....	....	....	....	....	....	....	....	....	....	....
	Medicine Hat Tigers	WHL	34	1	12	13	....	....	....	60	....	....	....	....	....	....	....	....	....	....	....	....	....	....	....	....	....	....
1979-80	Medicine Hat Tigers	WHL	72	7	40	47	....	....	....	284	....	....	....	....	....	....	....	....	....	....	16	1	6	7	31	....	....	....
1980-81	Medicine Hat Tigers	WHL	72	14	46	60	....	....	....	164	....	....	....	....	....	....	....	....	....	....	5	1	1	2	8	....	....	....
1981-82	Erie Blades	AHL	69	1	18	19	....	....	....	78	....	....	....	....	....	....	....	....	....	....	....	....	....	....	....	....	....	....
1982-83	**Pittsburgh Penguins**	**NHL**	**41**	**2**	**2**	**4**	**2**	**1**	**3**	**102**	**1**	**0**	**0**	**27**	**7.4**	**18**	**1**	**43**	**11**	**–15**	....	....	....	....	....	....	....	....
	Muskegon Mohawks	IHL	1	0	0	0	....	....	....	9	....	....	....	....	....	....	....	....	....	....	....	....	....	....	....	....	....	....
	Baltimore Skipjacks	AHL	31	2	8	10	....	....	....	45	....	....	....	....	....	....	....	....	....	....	....	....	....	....	....	....	....	....
1983-84	**Pittsburgh Penguins**	**NHL**	**47**	**2**	**4**	**6**	**2**	**3**	**5**	**60**	**1**	**0**	**0**	**39**	**5.1**	**30**	**4**	**57**	**13**	**–18**	....	....	....	....	....	....	....	....
	Baltimore Skipjacks	AHL	33	2	12	14	....	....	....	100	....	....	....	....	....	....	....	....	....	....	10	1	3	4	22	....	....	....
1984-85	**Pittsburgh Penguins**	**NHL**	**69**	**2**	**7**	**9**	**2**	**5**	**7**	**191**	**0**	**0**	**0**	**53**	**3.8**	**67**	**6**	**103**	**21**	**–21**	....	....	....	....	....	....	....	....
1985-86	**Pittsburgh Penguins**	**NHL**	**72**	**2**	**7**	**9**	**2**	**5**	**7**	**159**	**1**	**0**	**0**	**50**	**4.0**	**49**	**2**	**73**	**17**	**–9**	....	....	....	....	....	....	....	....
1986-87	**Pittsburgh Penguins**	**NHL**	**68**	**3**	**15**	**18**	**3**	**11**	**14**	**123**	**1**	**0**	**0**	**90**	**3.3**	**73**	**7**	**81**	**17**	**2**	....	....	....	....	....	....	....	....
1987-88	**Pittsburgh Penguins**	**NHL**	**76**	**4**	**8**	**12**	**3**	**6**	**9**	**206**	**0**	**0**	**1**	**53**	**7.5**	**56**	**1**	**91**	**42**	**6**	....	....	....	....	....	....	....	....
1988-89	**Pittsburgh Penguins**	**NHL**	**52**	**1**	**5**	**6**	**1**	**4**	**5**	**105**	**0**	**0**	**0**	**15**	**6.7**	**28**	**0**	**52**	**22**	**–2**	**10**	**0**	**0**	**0**	**23**	**0**	**0**	**0**
1989-90	**Vancouver Canucks**	**NHL**	**17**	**0**	**3**	**3**	**0**	**2**	**2**	**36**	**0**	**0**	**0**	**11**	**0.0**	**14**	**0**	**14**	**1**	**1**	....	....	....	....	....	....	....	....
	Pittsburgh Penguins	**NHL**	**6**	**0**	**0**	**0**	**0**	**0**	**0**	**13**	**0**	**0**	**0**	**1**	**0.0**	**2**	**0**	**9**	**3**	**–4**	....	....	....	....	....	....	....	....
1990-91	**Los Angeles Kings**	**NHL**	**57**	**3**	**8**	**11**	**3**	**6**	**9**	**182**	**0**	**0**	**0**	**60**	**5.0**	**62**	**1**	**62**	**15**	**14**	**2**	**0**	**2**	**2**	**22**	**0**	**0**	**0**
1991-92	**Los Angeles Kings**	**NHL**	**5**	**0**	**0**	**0**	**0**	**0**	**0**	**11**	**0**	**0**	**0**	**1**	**0.0**	**4**	**0**	**6**	**1**	**–1**	....	....	....	....	....	....	....	....
	Chicago Blackhawks	**NHL**	**42**	**0**	**4**	**4**	**0**	**3**	**3**	**80**	**0**	**0**	**0**	**22**	**0.0**	**14**	**0**	**29**	**3**	**–12**	**6**	**0**	**1**	**1**	**0**	**0**	**0**	**0**
1992-93	**Chicago Blackhawks**	**NHL**	**4**	**0**	**0**	**0**	**0**	**0**	**0**	**26**	**0**	**0**	**0**	**3**	**0.0**	**2**	**0**	**0**	**0**	**2**	....	....	....	....	....	....	....	....
	Indianapolis Ice	IHL	15	0	3	3	....	....	....	40	....	....	....	....	....	....	....	....	....	....	....	....	....	....	....	....	....	....
	Salt Lake Golden Eagles	IHL	31	0	2	2	....	....	....	52	....	....	....	....	....	....	....	....	....	....	....	....	....	....	....	....	....	....
1993-94	Las Vegas Thunder	IHL	69	2	9	11	....	....	....	131	....	....	....	....	....	....	....	....	....	....	5	0	2	2	2	....	....	....
1994-95	Las Vegas Thunder	IHL	27	2	3	5	....	....	....	53	....	....	....	....	....	....	....	....	....	....	10	1	0	1	19	....	....	....
	NHL Totals		**556**	**19**	**63**	**82**	**18**	**46**	**64**	**1294**	**4**	**0**	**1**	**425**	**4.5**	**419**	**22**	**620**	**166**		**18**	**0**	**3**	**3**	**45**	**0**	**0**	**0**

Traded to **Vancouver** by **Pittsburgh** for Vancouver's 6th round choice (Ian Moran) in 1990 Entry Draft, October 24, 1989. Traded to **Pittsburgh** by **Vancouver** with Barry Pederson and Tony Tanti for Dave Capuano, Andrew McBain and Dan Quinn, January 8, 1990. Claimed by **LA Kings** from **Pittsburgh** in Waiver Draft, October 1, 1990. Traded to **Chicago** by **LA Kings** for Chris Norton and future considerations, October 28, 1991.

• BUSNIUK, Mike

Michael D – R. 6'3", 200 lbs. b: Thunder Bay, Ont., 12/13/1951. Montreal's 10th, 67th overall, in 1971.

Season	Club	League	GP	G	A	Pts	AG	AA	APts	PIM	PP	SH	GW	S	%	TGF	PGF	TGA	PGA	+/–	GP	G	A	Pts	PIM	PP	SH	GW
1967-68	Fort William Canadiens	TBJHL	24	11	11	22	....	....	....	27	....	....	....	....	....	....	....	....	....	....	....	....	....	....	....	....	....	....
1968-69	Fort William Canadiens	TBJHL	....	....	....	....	....	....	....	....	....	....	....	....	....	....	....	....	....	....	13	3	6	9	16	....	....	....
1969-70	Fort William Canadiens	TBJHL	STATISTICS NOT AVAILABLE																									
	Fort William Hurricanes	Mem-Cup	12	2	2	4	....	....	....	25	....	....	....	....	....	....	....	....	....	....	....	....	....	....	....	....	....	....
1970-71	University of Denver	WCHA	36	1	10	11	....	....	....	46	....	....	....	....	....	....	....	....	....	....	....	....	....	....	....	....	....	....
1971-72	University of Denver	WCHA	38	1	19	20	....	....	....	77	....	....	....	....	....	....	....	....	....	....	....	....	....	....	....	....	....	....
1972-73	University of Denver	WCHA	39	20	17	37	....	....	....	70	....	....	....	....	....	....	....	....	....	....	....	....	....	....	....	....	....	....
1973-74	University of Denver	WCHA	32	17	18	35	....	....	....	14	....	....	....	....	....	....	....	....	....	....	....	....	....	....	....	....	....	....
1974-75	Nova Scotia Voyageurs	AHL	69	15	17	32	....	....	....	94	....	....	....	....	....	....	....	....	....	....	6	1	0	1	2	....	....	....
1975-76	Beauce Jaros	NAHL	65	14	52	66	....	....	....	179	....	....	....	....	....	....	....	....	....	....	14	1	12	13	61	....	....	....
	Nova Scotia Voyageurs	AHL	....	....	....	....	....	....	....	....	....	....	....	....	....	....	....	....	....	....	1	0	0	0	4	....	....	....
1976-77	Nova Scotia Voyageurs	AHL	80	1	15	16	....	....	....	160	....	....	....	....	....	....	....	....	....	....	12	0	0	0	4	....	....	....
1977-78	Maine Mariners	AHL	75	5	15	20	....	....	....	72	....	....	....	....	....	....	....	....	....	....	12	0	1	1	44	....	....	....
1978-79	Maine Mariners	AHL	79	10	34	44	....	....	....	215	....	....	....	....	....	....	....	....	....	....	10	0	5	5	4	....	....	....
1979-80	**Philadelphia Flyers**	**NHL**	**71**	**2**	**18**	**20**	**2**	**13**	**15**	**93**	**0**	**0**	**1**	**56**	**3.6**	**83**	**0**	**66**	**22**	**39**	**19**	**2**	**4**	**6**	**23**	**0**	**0**	**0**
	Maine Mariners	AHL	3	2	1	3	....	....	....	7	....	....	....	....	....	....	....	....	....	....	....	....	....	....	....	....	....	....
1980-81	**Philadelphia Flyers**	**NHL**	**72**	**1**	**5**	**6**	**1**	**3**	**4**	**204**	**0**	**0**	**0**	**33**	**3.0**	**64**	**1**	**57**	**21**	**27**	**6**	**0**	**1**	**1**	**11**	**0**	**0**	**0**
1981-82	Maine Mariners	AHL	78	12	26	38	....	....	....	203	....	....	....	....	....	....	....	....	....	....	4	1	0	1	20	....	....	....
1982-83	HC Brunico	Italty	29	16	33	49	....	....	....	43	....	....	....	....	....	....	....	....	....	....	....	....	....	....	....	....	....	....
	Maine Mariners	AHL	11	0	5	5	....	....	....	14	....	....	....	....	....	....	....	....	....	....	17	1	5	6	52	....	....	....
1983-84	SG Brunico	Italy	27	16	30	46	....	....	....	28	....	....	....	....	....	....	....	....	....	....	7	3	5	8	6	....	....	....
	Maine Mariners	AHL	2	0	1	1	....	....	....	2	....	....	....	....	....	....	....	....	....	....	16	1	1	2	*105	....	....	....
1984-85	SG Brunico	Italy	26	9	16	25	....	....	....	29	....	....	....	....	....	....	....	....	....	....	6	4	4	8	14	....	....	....
1985-86	Thunder Bay Twins	CASH	STATISTICS NOT AVAILABLE																									
1986-87	Thunder Bay Twins	CASH	8	0	3	3	....	....	....	36	....	....	....	....	....	....	....	....	....	....	....	....	....	....	....	....	....	....
1987-1990	Thunder Bay Twins	CASH	PLAYER/COACH – STATISTICS UNAVAILABLE																									
1990-1993	Tri-City Americans	WHL	DID NOT PLAY – ASSISTANT COACH																									
1993-1997	Binghamton Rangers	AHL	DID NOT PLAY – ASSISTANT COACH																									
1997-2000	Hartford Wolf Pack	AHL	DID NOT PLAY – ASSISTANT COACH																									
	NHL Totals		**143**	**3**	**23**	**26**	**3**	**16**	**19**	**297**	**0**	**0**	**1**	**89**	**3.4**	**147**	**1**	**123**	**43**		**25**	**2**	**5**	**7**	**34**	**0**	**0**	**0**

• Brother of Ron

Signed as a free agent by **Philadelphia**, October 23, 1977. • Only player in AHL history to be a member of four consecutive championship teams (1976-1979). • Named Assistanr Coach of **Binghamton** (AHL), September 2, 1993.

• BUSNIUK, Ron

Ronald Edward RW – R. 5'11", 180 lbs. b: Fort William, Ont., 8/13/1948.

Season	Club	League	GP	G	A	Pts	AG	AA	APts	PIM	PP	SH	GW	S	%	TGF	PGF	TGA	PGA	+/–	GP	G	A	Pts	PIM	PP	SH	GW
1964-65	Fort William Kings	TBAHA	STATISTICS NOT AVAILABLE																									
	Fort William Canadiens	TBJHL	4	1	0	1	....	....	....	0	....	....	....	....	....	....	....	....	....	....	....	....	....	....	....	....	....	....
1965-66	Fort William Canadiens	TBJHL	30	15	27	42	....	....	....	28	....	....	....	....	....	....	....	....	....	....	....	....	....	....	....	....	....	....
1966-67	University of Minnesota-Duluth	WCHA	DID NOT PLAY – FRESHMAN																									
	Fort William Canadiens	Mem-Cup	16	9	11	20	....	....	....	41	....	....	....	....	....	....	....	....	....	....	....	....	....	....	....	....	....	....
1967-68	University of Minnesota-Duluth	WCHA	27	10	10	20	....	....	....	....	....	....	....	....	....	....	....	....	....	....	....	....	....	....	....	....	....	....
1968-69	University of Minnesota-Duluth	WCHA	29	7	20	27	....	....	....	....	....	....	....	....	....	....	....	....	....	....	....	....	....	....	....	....	....	....
1969-70	University of Minnesota-Duluth	WCHA	40	14	32	46	....	....	....	73	....	....	....	....	....	....	....	....	....	....	....	....	....	....	....	....	....	....
1970-71	Montreal Voyageurs	AHL	59	11	9	20	....	....	....	136	....	....	....	....	....	....	....	....	....	....	3	0	1	1	10	....	....	....
1971-72	Nova Scotia Voyageurs	AHL	67	13	13	26	....	....	....	133	....	....	....	....	....	....	....	....	....	....	15	3	5	8	*74	....	....	....
1972-73	**Buffalo Sabres**	**NHL**	**1**	**0**	**0**	**0**	**0**	**0**	**0**	**9**	**0**	**0**	**0**	**1**	**0.0**	**1**	**0**	**1**	**0**	**0**	....	....	....	....	....	....	....	....
	Cincinnati Swords	AHL	71	5	34	39	....	....	....	205	....	....	....	....	....	....	....	....	....	....	15	1	7	8	39	....	....	....

			REGULAR SEASON																		PLAYOFFS							
Season	Club	League	GP	G	A	Pts	AG	AA	APts	PIM	PP	SH	GW	S	%	TGF	PGF	TGA	PGA	+/-	GP	G	A	Pts	PIM	PP	SH	GW
1973-74	**Buffalo Sabres**	**NHL**	**5**	**0**	**3**	**3**	**0**	**2**	**2**	**4**	**0**	**0**	**0**	**3**	**0.0**	**4**	**2**	**3**	**0**	**–1**	....	....	....	....	....	....	....	....
	Cincinnati Swords	AHL	68	7	24	31	....	....	....	146	....	....	....	....	....	....	....	....	....	....	5	1	1	2	8	....	....	....
1974-75	Minnesota Fighting Saints	WHA	73	2	21	23	....	....	....	176	....	....	....	....	....	....	....	....	....	....	12	2	1	3	*63	....	....	....
1975-76	Minnesota Fighting Saints	WHA	59	2	11	13	....	....	....	150	....	....	....	....	....	....	....	....	....	....	....	....	....	....	....	....	....	....
	New England Whalers	WHA	11	0	3	3	....	....	....	55	....	....	....	....	....	....	....	....	....	....	17	0	2	2	14	....	....	....
1976-77	New England Whalers	WHA	55	1	9	10	....	....	....	141	....	....	....	....	....	....	....	....	....	....	....	....	....	....	....	....	....	....
	Edmonton Oilers	WHA	29	2	2	4	....	....	....	83	....	....	....	....	....	....	....	....	....	....	5	0	2	2	37	....	....	....
1977-78	Edmonton Oilers	WHA	59	2	18	20	....	....	....	157	....	....	....	....	....	....	....	....	....	....	5	0	0	0	18	....	....	....
	NHL Totals		**6**	**0**	**3**	**3**	**0**	**2**	**2**	**13**	**0**	**0**	**0**	**4**	**0.0**	**5**	**2**	**4**	**0**		....	....	....	....	....	....	....	....
	Other Major League Totals		286	9	64	73	....	....	....	762	....	....	....	....	....	....	....	....	....	....	39	2	5	7	132	....	....	....

• Brother of Mike • AHL First All-Star Team (1974) • WCHA First All-Star Team (1970) • NCAA West First All-American Team (1970)

Traded to **Buffalo** by **Montreal** for cash, June 8, 1972. Selected by **Minnesota** (WHA) in 1973 WHA Professional Draft, June, 1973. Claimed by **Detroit** from **Buffalo** in Intra-League Draft, June 10, 1974. Signed as a free agent by **New England** (WHA) after **Minnesota** (WHA) franchise folded, March, 1976. Traded to **Edmonton** (WHA) by **New England** (WHA) with Brett Callighen for Mike Antonovich and Bill Butters, February, 1977.

• BUTCHER, Garth

"Strangler" D – R. 6', 204 lbs. b: Regina, Sask., 1/8/1963. Vancouver's 1st, 10th overall, in 1981.

Season	Club	League	GP	G	A	Pts	AG	AA	APts	PIM	PP	SH	GW	S	%	TGF	PGF	TGA	PGA	+/-	GP	G	A	Pts	PIM	PP	SH	GW
1978-79	Regina Pat Canadians	AAHA	22	4	22	26	....	....	....	72	....	....	....	....	....	....	....	....	....	....	....	....	....	....	....	....	....	....
1979-80	Regina Blues	SJHL	51	15	31	46	....	....	....	236	....	....	....	....	....	....	....	....	....	....	....	....	....	....	....	....	....	....
	Regina Pats	WHL	13	0	4	4	....	....	....	20	....	....	....	....	....	....	....	....	....	....	9	0	0	0	45	....	....	....
	Regina Pats	Mem-Cup	3	0	1	1	....	....	....	0	....	....	....	....	....	....	....	....	....	....	....	....	....	....	....	....	....	....
1980-81	Regina Pats	WHL	69	9	77	86	....	....	....	230	....	....	....	....	....	....	....	....	....	....	11	5	17	22	60	....	....	....
1981-82	Regina Pats	WHL	65	24	68	92	....	....	....	318	....	....	....	....	....	....	....	....	....	....	19	3	17	20	95	....	....	....
	Canada	WJC-A	7	1	3	4	....	....	....	0	....	....	....	....	....	....	....	....	....	....	....	....	....	....	....	....	....	....
	Vancouver Canucks	**NHL**	**5**	**0**	**0**	**0**	**0**	**0**	**0**	**9**	**0**	**0**	**0**	**7**	**0.0**	**5**	**0**	**2**	**1**	**4**	**1**	**0**	**0**	**0**	**0**	**0**	**0**	**0**
1982-83	Kamloops Blazers	WHL	5	4	2	6	....	....	....	4	....	....	....	....	....	....	....	....	....	....	6	4	8	12	16	....	....	....
	Vancouver Canucks	**NHL**	**55**	**1**	**13**	**14**	**1**	**9**	**10**	**104**	**0**	**0**	**0**	**60**	**1.7**	**50**	**3**	**58**	**4**	**–7**	**3**	**1**	**0**	**1**	**2**	**0**	**0**	**0**
1983-84	**Vancouver Canucks**	**NHL**	**28**	**2**	**0**	**2**	**2**	**0**	**2**	**34**	**0**	**0**	**0**	**33**	**6.1**	**21**	**0**	**42**	**9**	**–12**	....	....	....	....	....	....	....	....
	Fredericton Express	AHL	25	4	13	17	....	....	....	43	....	....	....	....	....	....	....	....	....	....	6	0	2	2	19	....	....	....
1984-85	**Vancouver Canucks**	**NHL**	**75**	**3**	**9**	**12**	**2**	**6**	**8**	**152**	**0**	**0**	**1**	**59**	**5.1**	**68**	**1**	**131**	**33**	**–31**	....	....	....	....	....	....	....	....
	Fredericton Express	AHL	3	1	0	1	....	....	....	11	....	....	....	....	....	....	....	....	....	....	....	....	....	....	....	....	....	....
1985-86	**Vancouver Canucks**	**NHL**	**70**	**4**	**7**	**11**	**3**	**5**	**8**	**188**	**0**	**0**	**0**	**57**	**7.0**	**42**	**1**	**87**	**21**	**–25**	**3**	**0**	**0**	**0**	**0**	**0**	**0**	**0**
1986-87	**Vancouver Canucks**	**NHL**	**70**	**5**	**15**	**20**	**4**	**11**	**15**	**207**	**0**	**0**	**0**	**95**	**5.3**	**56**	**2**	**97**	**31**	**–12**	....	....	....	....	....	....	....	....
1987-88	**Vancouver Canucks**	**NHL**	**80**	**6**	**17**	**23**	**5**	**12**	**17**	**285**	**1**	**0**	**0**	**77**	**7.8**	**66**	**10**	**95**	**25**	**–14**	....	....	....	....	....	....	....	....
1988-89	**Vancouver Canucks**	**NHL**	**78**	**0**	**20**	**20**	**0**	**14**	**14**	**227**	**0**	**0**	**0**	**101**	**0.0**	**70**	**3**	**87**	**24**	**4**	**7**	**1**	**1**	**2**	**22**	**0**	**0**	**1**
1989-90	**Vancouver Canucks**	**NHL**	**80**	**6**	**14**	**20**	**5**	**10**	**15**	**205**	**1**	**0**	**1**	**87**	**6.9**	**71**	**3**	**114**	**36**	**–10**	....	....	....	....	....	....	....	....
1990-91	**Vancouver Canucks**	**NHL**	**69**	**6**	**12**	**18**	**5**	**9**	**14**	**257**	**1**	**0**	**1**	**70**	**8.6**	**63**	**6**	**118**	**43**	**–18**	....	....	....	....	....	....	....	....
	St. Louis Blues	**NHL**	**13**	**0**	**4**	**4**	**0**	**3**	**3**	**32**	**0**	**0**	**0**	**5**	**0.0**	**11**	**0**	**12**	**5**	**4**	**13**	**2**	**1**	**3**	**54**	**0**	**0**	**0**
1991-92	**St. Louis Blues**	**NHL**	**68**	**5**	**15**	**20**	**5**	**11**	**16**	**189**	**0**	**0**	**0**	**50**	**10.0**	**70**	**1**	**83**	**19**	**5**	**5**	**1**	**2**	**3**	**16**	**0**	**0**	**0**
	Canada	WC-A	3	1	0	1	....	....	....	4	....	....	....	....	....	....	....	....	....	....	....	....	....	....	....	....	....	....
1992-93	**St. Louis Blues**	**NHL**	**84**	**5**	**10**	**15**	**4**	**7**	**11**	**211**	**0**	**0**	**2**	**83**	**6.0**	**74**	**4**	**92**	**22**	**0**	**11**	**1**	**1**	**2**	**20**	**0**	**0**	**1**
1993-94	**St. Louis Blues**	**NHL**	**43**	**1**	**6**	**7**	**1**	**5**	**6**	**76**	**0**	**1**	**0**	**37**	**2.7**	**41**	**1**	**64**	**18**	**–6**	....	....	....	....	....	....	....	....
	Quebec Nordiques	**NHL**	**34**	**3**	**9**	**12**	**3**	**7**	**10**	**67**	**0**	**1**	**1**	**29**	**10.3**	**33**	**0**	**55**	**21**	**–1**	....	....	....	....	....	....	....	....
1994-95	**Toronto Maple Leafs**	**NHL**	**45**	**1**	**7**	**8**	**2**	**10**	**12**	**59**	**0**	**0**	**0**	**24**	**4.2**	**36**	**0**	**51**	**10**	**–5**	**7**	**0**	**0**	**0**	**8**	**0**	**0**	**0**
	NHL Totals		**897**	**48**	**158**	**206**	**42**	**119**	**161**	**2302**	**3**	**2**	**6**	**874**	**5.5**	**777**	**35**	**1188**	**322**		**50**	**6**	**5**	**11**	**122**	**0**	**0**	**2**

WHL First All-Star Team (1981, 1982) • Played in NHL All-Star Game (1993)

Traded to **St. Louis** by **Vancouver** with Dan Quinn for Geoff Courtnall, Robert Dirk, Sergio Momesso, Cliff Ronning and St. Louis' 5th round choice (Brian Loney) in 1992 Entry Draft, March 5, 1991. Traded to **Quebec** by **St. Louis** with Ron Sutter and Bob Bassen for Steve Duchesne and Denis Chase, January 23, 1994. Traded to **Toronto** by **Quebec** with Mats Sundin, Todd Warriner and Philadelphia's 1st round choice (previously acquired by Quebec — later traded to Washington — Washington selected Nolan Baumgartner) in 1994 Entry Draft for Wendel Clark, Sylvain Lefebvre, Landon Wilson and Toronto's 1st round choice (Jeffrey Kealty) in 1994 Entry Draft, June 28, 1994.

• BUTENSCHON, Sven

D – L. 6'4", 215 lbs. b: Itzehoe, West Germany, 3/22/1976. Pittsburgh's 3rd, 57th overall, in 1994.

Season	Club	League	GP	G	A	Pts	AG	AA	APts	PIM	PP	SH	GW	S	%	TGF	PGF	TGA	PGA	+/-	GP	G	A	Pts	PIM	PP	SH	GW
1991-92	Eastman Selects	MAHA	36	2	10	12	....	....	....	110	....	....	....	....	....	....	....	....	....	....	....	....	....	....	....	....	....	....
1992-93	Eastman Selects	MAHA	35	14	22	36	....	....	....	101	....	....	....	....	....	....	....	....	....	....	....	....	....	....	....	....	....	....
1993-94	Brandon Wheat Kings	WHL	70	3	19	22	....	....	....	51	....	....	....	....	....	....	....	....	....	....	4	0	0	0	6	....	....	....
1994-95	Brandon Wheat Kings	WHL	21	1	5	6	....	....	....	44	....	....	....	....	....	....	....	....	....	....	18	1	2	3	11	....	....	....
	Brandon Wheat Kings	Mem-Cup	4	0	0	0	....	....	....	0	....	....	....	....	....	....	....	....	....	....	....	....	....	....	....	....	....	....
1995-96	Brandon Wheat Kings	WHL	70	4	37	41	....	....	....	99	....	....	....	....	....	....	....	....	....	....	19	1	12	13	18	....	....	....
	Brandon Wheat Kings	Mem-Cup	4	0	0	0	....	....	....	4	....	....	....	....	....	....	....	....	....	....	....	....	....	....	....	....	....	....
1996-97	Cleveland Lumberjacks	IHL	75	3	12	15	....	....	....	68	....	....	....	....	....	....	....	....	....	....	10	0	1	1	4	....	....	....
1997-98	**Pittsburgh Penguins**	**NHL**	**8**	**0**	**0**	**0**	**0**	**0**	**0**	**6**	**0**	**0**	**0**	**4**	**0.0**	**5**	**1**	**6**	**1**	**–1**	....	....	....	....	....	....	....	....
	Syracuse Crunch	AHL	65	14	23	37	....	....	....	66	....	....	....	....	....	....	....	....	....	....	5	1	2	3	0	....	....	....
1998-99	**Pittsburgh Penguins**	**NHL**	**17**	**0**	**0**	**0**	**0**	**0**	**0**	**6**	**0**	**0**	**0**	**8**	**0.0**	**6**	**0**	**15**	**2**	**–7**	....	....	....	....	....	....	....	....
	Houston Aeros	IHL	57	1	4	5	....	....	....	81	....	....	....	....	....	....	....	....	....	....	....	....	....	....	....	....	....	....
99-2000	**Pittsburgh Penguins**	**NHL**	**3**	**0**	**0**	**0**	**0**	**0**	**0**	**0**	**0**	**0**	**0**	**2**	**0.0**	**3**	**0**	**1**	**1**	**3**	....	....	....	....	....	....	....	....
	Wilkes-Barre Penguins	AHL	75	19	21	40	....	....	....	101	....	....	....	....	....	....	....	....	....	....	....	....	....	....	....	....	....	....
	NHL Totals		**28**	**0**	**0**	**0**	**0**	**0**	**0**	**12**	**0**	**0**	**0**	**14**	**0.0**	**14**	**1**	**22**	**4**									

• BUTLER, Jerry

Jerry Patrick "Bugsy" RW – R. 6', 180 lbs. b: Sarnia, Ont., 2/27/1951. NY Rangers' 5th, 55th overall, in 1971.

Season	Club	League	GP	G	A	Pts	AG	AA	APts	PIM	PP	SH	GW	S	%	TGF	PGF	TGA	PGA	+/-	GP	G	A	Pts	PIM	PP	SH	GW
1969-70	Sarnia Bees	OHA-B	STATISTICS NOT AVAILABLE																									
1970-71	Hamilton Red Wings	OHA-Jr.	59	6	20	26	....	....	....	131	....	....	....	....	....	....	....	....	....	....	7	0	1	1	31	....	....	....
1971-72	Omaha Knights	CHL	72	19	18	37	....	....	....	173	....	....	....	....	....	....	....	....	....	....	....	....	....	....	....	....	....	....
1972-73	**New York Rangers**	**NHL**	**8**	**1**	**0**	**1**	**1**	**0**	**1**	**4**	**0**	**0**	**0**	**11**	**9.1**	**2**	**0**	**1**	**0**	**1**	....	....	....	....	....	....	....	....
	Providence Reds	AHL	64	29	30	59	....	....	....	97	....	....	....	....	....	....	....	....	....	....	4	1	2	3	11	....	....	....
1973-74	**New York Rangers**	**NHL**	**26**	**6**	**10**	**16**	**6**	**8**	**14**	**24**	**1**	**0**	**1**	**60**	**10.0**	**28**	**3**	**21**	**3**	**7**	**12**	**0**	**2**	**2**	**25**	**0**	**0**	**0**
	Providence Reds	AHL	48	20	22	42	....	....	....	114	....	....	....	....	....	....	....	....	....	....	....	....	....	....	....	....	....	....
1974-75	**New York Rangers**	**NHL**	**78**	**17**	**16**	**33**	**15**	**12**	**27**	**102**	**1**	**2**	**1**	**157**	**10.8**	**52**	**6**	**65**	**14**	**–5**	**3**	**1**	**0**	**1**	**16**	**0**	**0**	**0**
1975-76	**St. Louis Blues**	**NHL**	**66**	**17**	**24**	**41**	**15**	**18**	**33**	**75**	**1**	**0**	**3**	**154**	**11.0**	**56**	**9**	**56**	**9**	**0**	**3**	**0**	**0**	**0**	**0**	**0**	**0**	**0**
1976-77	**St. Louis Blues**	**NHL**	**80**	**12**	**20**	**32**	**11**	**15**	**26**	**65**	**0**	**0**	**0**	**152**	**7.9**	**50**	**2**	**98**	**19**	**–31**	**4**	**0**	**0**	**0**	**14**	**0**	**0**	**0**
1977-78	**St. Louis Blues**	**NHL**	**9**	**0**	**2**	**2**	**0**	**2**	**2**	**5**	**0**	**0**	**0**	**15**	**0.0**	**5**	**1**	**10**	**0**	**–6**	....	....	....	....	....	....	....	....
	Toronto Maple Leafs	**NHL**	**73**	**9**	**7**	**16**	**8**	**5**	**13**	**49**	**1**	**1**	**1**	**99**	**9.1**	**34**	**2**	**67**	**25**	**–10**	**13**	**1**	**1**	**2**	**18**	**0**	**0**	**0**
1978-79	**Toronto Maple Leafs**	**NHL**	**76**	**8**	**7**	**15**	**7**	**5**	**12**	**52**	**0**	**2**	**2**	**77**	**10.4**	**30**	**0**	**66**	**34**	**–2**	**6**	**0**	**0**	**0**	**4**	**0**	**0**	**0**
1979-80	**Toronto Maple Leafs**	**NHL**	**55**	**7**	**8**	**15**	**6**	**6**	**12**	**29**	**0**	**0**	**1**	**60**	**11.7**	**24**	**1**	**53**	**27**	**–3**	....	....	....	....	....	....	....	....
	Vancouver Canucks	**NHL**	**23**	**4**	**4**	**8**	**3**	**3**	**6**	**21**	**1**	**0**	**1**	**24**	**16.7**	**11**	**1**	**23**	**8**	**–5**	**4**	**0**	**0**	**0**	**2**	**0**	**0**	**0**
1980-81	**Vancouver Canucks**	**NHL**	**80**	**12**	**15**	**27**	**9**	**10**	**19**	**60**	**0**	**2**	**2**	**99**	**12.1**	**42**	**0**	**83**	**43**	**2**	**3**	**1**	**0**	**1**	**0**	**0**	**0**	**0**
1981-82	**Vancouver Canucks**	**NHL**	**25**	**3**	**1**	**4**	**2**	**1**	**3**	**15**	**0**	**0**	**0**	**21**	**14.3**	**10**	**0**	**29**	**14**	**–5**	....	....	....	....	....	....	....	....
	Dallas Black Hawks	CHL	47	6	24	30	....	....	....	30	....	....	....	....	....	....	....	....	....	....	16	4	5	9	36	....	....	....
1982-83	**Winnipeg Jets**	**NHL**	**42**	**3**	**6**	**9**	**2**	**4**	**6**	**14**	**0**	**1**	**1**	**24**	**12.5**	**13**	**1**	**29**	**12**	**–5**	....	....	....	....	....	....	....	....
	NHL Totals		**641**	**99**	**120**	**219**	**85**	**89**	**174**	**515**	**5**	**8**	**13**	**953**	**10.4**	**357**	**26**	**601**	**208**		**48**	**3**	**3**	**6**	**79**	**0**	**0**	**0**

Traded to **St. Louis** by **NY Rangers** with Ted Irvine and Bert Wilson for Bill Collins and John Davidson, June 18, 1975. Traded to **Toronto** by **St. Louis** for Inge Hammarstrom, November 1, 1977. Traded to **Vancouver** by **Toronto** with Tiger Williams for Bill Derlago and Rick Vaive, February 18, 1980. Signed as a free agent by **Winnipeg**, October 8, 1982.

• BUTSAYEV, Viacheslav

Viacheslav G. C – L. 6'2", 228 lbs. b: Togliatti, USSR, 6/13/1970. Philadelphia's 10th, 109th overall, in 1990.

Season	Club	League	GP	G	A	Pts	AG	AA	APts	PIM	PP	SH	GW	S	%	TGF	PGF	TGA	PGA	+/-	GP	G	A	Pts	PIM	PP	SH	GW
1987-88	Lada Togliatti	USSR-2	10	1	7	8	....	....	....	....	....	....	....	....	....	....	....	....	....	....	....	....	....	....	....	....	....	....
1988-89	Lada Togliatti	USSR-3	60	14	7	21	....	....	....	32	....	....	....	....	....	....	....	....	....	....	....	....	....	....	....	....	....	....
1989-90	CSKA Moscow	USSR	48	14	4	18	....	....	....	30	....	....	....	....	....	....	....	....	....	....	....	....	....	....	....	....	....	....
	Soviet Union	WJC-A	7	3	4	7	....	....	....	14	....	....	....	....	....	....	....	....	....	....	....	....	....	....	....	....	....	....
1990-91	CSKA Moscow	USSR	46	14	9	23	....	....	....	32	....	....	....	....	....	....	....	....	....	....	....	....	....	....	....	....	....	....
	Soviet Union	WEC-A	10	4	1	5	....	....	....	10	....	....	....	....	....	....	....	....	....	....	....	....	....	....	....	....	....	....

Season	Club	League	REGULAR SEASON																		PLAYOFFS							
			GP	G	A	Pts	AG	AA	APts	PIM	PP	SH	GW	S	%	TGF	PGF	TGA	PGA	+/–	GP	G	A	Pts	PIM	PP	SH	GW
1991-92	CSKA Moscow	CIS	36	12	13	25	....	....	....	26	....	....	....	....	....	....	....	....	....	....	....	....	....	....	....	....	....	....
	Russia	Olympics	8	1	1	2	....	....	....	4	....	....	....	....	....	....	....	....	....	....	....	....	....	....	....	....	....	....
	Russia	WC-A	6	0	1	1	....	....	....	10	....	....	....	....	....	....	....	....	....	....	....	....	....	....	....	....	....	....
1992-93	CSKA Moscow	CIS	5	3	4	7	....	....	....	6	....	....	....	....	....	....	....	....	....	....	....	....	....	....	....	....	....	....
	Philadelphia Flyers	**NHL**	**52**	**2**	**14**	**16**	**2**	**10**	**12**	**61**	**0**	**0**	**0**	**58**	**3.4**	**34**	**3**	**28**	**0**	**3**	....	....	....	....	....	....	....	....
	Hershey Bears	AHL	24	8	10	18	....	....	....	51	....	....	....	....	....	....	....	....	....	....	....	....	....	....	....	....	....	....
	Russia	WC-A	8	1	2	3	....	....	....	8	....	....	....	....	....	....	....	....	....	....	....	....	....	....	....	....	....	....
1993-94	**Philadelphia Flyers**	**NHL**	**47**	**12**	**9**	**21**	**11**	**7**	**18**	**58**	**0**	**0**	**3**	**79**	**15.2**	**30**	**5**	**25**	**2**	**2**	....	....	....	....	....	....	....	....
	San Jose Sharks	**NHL**	**12**	**0**	**2**	**2**	**0**	**2**	**2**	**10**	**2**	**0**	**0**	**6**	**0.0**	**2**	**1**	**3**	**0**	**–2**	....	....	....	....	....	....	....	....
1994-95	Lada Togliatti	CIS	9	2	6	8	....	....	....	6	....	....	....	....	....	....	....	....	....	....	....	....	....	....	....	....	....	....
	San Jose Sharks	**NHL**	**6**	**2**	**0**	**2**	**4**	**0**	**4**	**0**	**0**	**0**	**0**	**6**	**33.3**	**2**	**0**	**4**	**0**	**–2**	....	....	....	....	....	....	....	....
	Kansas City Blades	IHL	13	3	4	7	....	....	....	12	....	....	....	....	....	....	....	....	....	....	3	0	0	0	2	....	....	....
1995-96	**Mighty Ducks of Anaheim**	**NHL**	**7**	**1**	**0**	**1**	**1**	**0**	**1**	**0**	**0**	**0**	**0**	**9**	**11.1**	**1**	**0**	**5**	**0**	**–4**	....	....	....	....	....	....	....	....
	Baltimore Bandits	AHL	62	23	42	65	....	....	....	70	....	....	....	....	....	....	....	....	....	....	12	4	8	12	28	....	....	....
1996-97	Sodertalje SK	Sweden	16	2	4	6	....	....	....	61	....	....	....	....	....	....	....	....	....	....	....	....	....	....	....	....	....	....
	Farjestads BK Karlstad	Sweden	24	4	3	7	....	....	....	47	....	....	....	....	....	....	....	....	....	....	8	3	4	7	41	....	....	....
	Farjestads BK Karlstad	EuroHL	1	0	0	0	....	....	....	0	....	....	....	....	....	....	....	....	....	....	....	....	....	....	....	....	....	....
	Russia	WC-A	9	2	2	4	....	....	....	8	....	....	....	....	....	....	....	....	....	....	....	....	....	....	....	....	....	....
1997-98	Fort Wayne Komets	IHL	76	36	51	87	....	....	....	128	....	....	....	....	....	....	....	....	....	....	4	2	2	4	4	....	....	....
1998-99	**Florida Panthers**	**NHL**	**1**	**0**	**0**	**0**	**0**	**0**	**0**	**2**	**0**	**0**	**0**	**0**	**0.0**	**0**	**0**	**1**	**0**	**–1**	....	....	....	....	....	....	....	....
	Fort Wayne Komets	IHL	71	28	44	72	....	....	....	123	....	....	....	....	....	....	....	....	....	....	2	1	0	1	4	....	....	....
	Ottawa Senators	**NHL**	**2**	**0**	**1**	**1**	**0**	**1**	**1**	**2**	**0**	**0**	**0**	**5**	**0.0**	**1**	**0**	**1**	**0**	**0**	....	....	....	....	....	....	....	....
99-2000	**Tampa Bay Lightning**	**NHL**	**2**	**0**	**0**	**0**	**0**	**0**	**0**	**0**	**0**	**0**	**0**	**1**	**0.0**	**0**	**0**	**2**	**0**	**–2**	....	....	....	....	....	....	....	....
	Ottawa Senators	**NHL**	**3**	**0**	**0**	**0**	**0**	**0**	**0**	**0**	**0**	**0**	**0**	**1**	**0.0**	**0**	**0**	**2**	**0**	**–2**	....	....	....	....	....	....	....	....
	Grand Rapids Griffins	IHL	68	28	35	63	....	....	....	85	....	....	....	....	....	....	....	....	....	....	17	4	*12	16	24	....	....	....
	NHL Totals		**132**	**17**	**26**	**43**	**18**	**20**	**38**	**133**	**2**	**0**	**3**	**165**	**10.3**	**70**	**9**	**71**	**2**		....	....	....	....	....	....	....	....

• Brother of Yuri • IHL Second All-Star Team (1998)

Traded to **San Jose** by **Philadelphia** for Rob Zettler, February 1, 1994. Signed as a free agent by **Anaheim**, October 19, 1995. Signed as a free agent by **Florida**, August 1, 1998. Traded to **Ottawa** by **Florida** for Ottawa's 6th round choice (later traded to Dallas, Dallas selected Justin Cox) in 1999 Entry Draft, March 8, 1999. Claimed by **Tampa Bay** from **Ottawa** in Waiver Draft, September 27, 1999. Claimed on waivers by **Ottawa** from **Tampa Bay**, October 28, 1999.

• BUTSAYEV, Yuri

C – L. 6'1", 183 lbs. b: Togliatti, USSR, 10/11/1978. Detroit's 1st, 49th overall, in 1997.

Season	Club	League	GP	G	A	Pts	AG	AA	APts	PIM	PP	SH	GW	S	%	TGF	PGF	TGA	PGA	+/–	GP	G	A	Pts	PIM	PP	SH	GW
1995-96	Lada Togliatti-2	CIS-2	35	19	7	26	....	....	....	....	....	....	....	....	....	....	....	....	....	....	....	....	....	....	....	....	....	....
	Lada Togliatti	CIS	1	0	0	0	....	....	....	0	....	....	....	....	....	....	....	....	....	....	....	....	....	....	....	....	....	....
1996-97	Lada Togliatti	Russia	42	13	11	24	....	....	....	38	....	....	....	....	....	....	....	....	....	....	11	2	2	4	8	....	....	....
	Russia	WJC-A	6	1	0	1	....	....	....	0	....	....	....	....	....	....	....	....	....	....	....	....	....	....	....	....	....	....
1997-98	Lada Togliatti	EuroHL	6	2	0	2	....	....	....	8	....	....	....	....	....	....	....	....	....	....	....	....	....	....	....	....	....	....
	Lada Togliatti	Russia	44	8	9	17	....	....	....	63	....	....	....	....	....	....	....	....	....	....	....	....	....	....	....	....	....	....
1998-99	Dynamo Moscow	Russia	1	0	1	1	....	....	....	0	....	....	....	....	....	....	....	....	....	....	....	....	....	....	....	....	....	....
	Lada Togliatti	Russia	39	10	7	17	....	....	....	55	....	....	....	....	....	....	....	....	....	....	7	1	2	3	14	....	....	....
99-2000	**Detroit Red Wings**	**NHL**	**57**	**5**	**3**	**8**	**6**	**3**	**9**	**12**	**0**	**0**	**0**	**46**	**10.9**	**15**	**0**	**21**	**0**	**–6**	....	....	....	....	....	....	....	....
	Cincinnati Mighty Ducks	AHL	9	0	1	1	....	....	....	0	....	....	....	....	....	....	....	....	....	....	....	....	....	....	....	....	....	....
	NHL Totals		**57**	**5**	**3**	**8**	**6**	**3**	**9**	**12**	**0**	**0**	**0**	**46**	**10.9**	**15**	**0**	**21**	**0**		....	....	....	....	....	....	....	....

• Brother of Viacheslav

• BUTTERS, Bill

William Joseph D – R. 5'10", 185 lbs. b: St. Paul, MN, 1/10/1951.

Season	Club	League	GP	G	A	Pts	AG	AA	APts	PIM	PP	SH	GW	S	%	TGF	PGF	TGA	PGA	+/–	GP	G	A	Pts	PIM	PP	SH	GW
1970-71	University of Minnesota	WCHA	27	0	1	1	....	....	....	52	....	....	....	....	....	....	....	....	....	....	....	....	....	....	....	....	....	....
1971-72	University of Minnesota	WCHA	29	1	9	10	....	....	....	100	....	....	....	....	....	....	....	....	....	....	....	....	....	....	....	....	....	....
1972-73	University of Minnesota	WCHA	33	3	6	9	....	....	....	110	....	....	....	....	....	....	....	....	....	....	....	....	....	....	....	....	....	....
1973-74	Oklahoma City Blazers	CHL	71	7	18	25	....	....	....	174	....	....	....	....	....	....	....	....	....	....	10	2	4	6	37	....	....	....
1974-75	Oklahoma City Blazers	CHL	32	5	9	14	....	....	....	192	....	....	....	....	....	....	....	....	....	....	....	....	....	....	....	....	....	....
	Minnesota Fighting Saints	WHA	24	2	2	4	....	....	....	58	....	....	....	....	....	....	....	....	....	....	12	1	0	1	21	....	....	....
1975-76	Minnesota Fighting Saints	WHA	59	0	15	15	....	....	....	170	....	....	....	....	....	....	....	....	....	....	....	....	....	....	....	....	....	....
	Houston Aeros	WHA	14	0	4	4	....	....	....	18	....	....	....	....	....	....	....	....	....	....	17	0	3	3	51	....	....	....
1976-77	Minnesota Fighting Saints	WHA	42	0	7	7	....	....	....	133	....	....	....	....	....	....	....	....	....	....	....	....	....	....	....	....	....	....
	Edmonton Oilers	WHA	7	0	2	2	....	....	....	17	....	....	....	....	....	....	....	....	....	....	....	....	....	....	....	....	....	....
	New England Whalers	WHA	26	1	8	9	....	....	....	65	....	....	....	....	....	....	....	....	....	....	5	0	1	1	15	....	....	....
1977-78	New England Whalers	WHA	45	1	13	14	....	....	....	69	....	....	....	....	....	....	....	....	....	....	....	....	....	....	....	....	....	....
	Minnesota North Stars	**NHL**	**23**	**1**	**0**	**1**	**1**	**0**	**1**	**30**	**0**	**0**	**0**	**18**	**5.6**	**19**	**0**	**31**	**9**	**–3**	....	....	....	....	....	....	....	....
1978-79	**Minnesota North Stars**	**NHL**	**49**	**0**	**4**	**4**	**0**	**3**	**3**	**47**	**0**	**0**	**0**	**17**	**0.0**	**22**	**0**	**46**	**12**	**–12**	....	....	....	....	....	....	....	....
	Oklahoma City Stars	CHL	14	1	2	3	....	....	....	31	....	....	....	....	....	....	....	....	....	....	....	....	....	....	....	....	....	....
1979-80	Oklahoma City Stars	CHL	73	3	8	11	....	....	....	134	....	....	....	....	....	....	....	....	....	....	....	....	....	....	....	....	....	....
	NHL Totals		**72**	**1**	**4**	**5**	**1**	**3**	**4**	**77**	**0**	**0**	**0**	**35**	**2.9**	**41**	**0**	**77**	**21**		....	....	....	....	....	....	....	....
	Other Major League Totals		217	4	51	55	....	....	....	530	....	....	....	....	....	....	....	....	....	....	34	1	4	5	87	....	....	....

Signed as a free agent by **Toronto**, September 27, 1973. Rights traded to **Minnesota** (WHA) by **Toronto** for cash, February, 1975. Signed as a free agent by **Toronto** (WHA) after **Minnesota** (WHA) franchise folded, February 27, 1976. Traded to **Houston** (WHA) by **Toronto** (WHA) for Paul Crowley and future considerations, February 27, 1976. Claimed by **Birmingham** (WHA) from **Houston** (WHA) in 1976 WHA Intra-League Draft, June, 1976. Traded to **Minnesota** (WHA) by **Birmingham** (WHA) for cash, September, 1976. Traded to **Edmonton** (WHA) by **Minnesota** (WHA) with Mike Antonovich, Jean-Louis Levasseur, Dave Keon, Jack Carlson, Steve Carlson and John McKenzie for cash, January, 1977. Traded to **New England** (WHA) by **Edmonton** (WHA) with Mike Antonovich for Brett Callighen and Ron Busniuk, February, 1977. Signed as a free agent by **Minnesota** after clearing WHA waivers, February 16, 1978.

• BUYNAK, Gord

Gordon D – L. 6'1", 180 lbs. b: Detroit, MI, 3/19/1954. St. Louis' 2nd, 43rd overall, in 1974.

Season	Club	League	GP	G	A	Pts	AG	AA	APts	PIM	PP	SH	GW	S	%	TGF	PGF	TGA	PGA	+/–	GP	G	A	Pts	PIM	PP	SH	GW
1971-72	Detroit Jr. Red Wings	OJHL	53	2	17	19	....	....	....	132	....	....	....	....	....	....	....	....	....	....	....	....	....	....	....	....	....	....
1972-73	Detroit Jr. Red Wings	OJHL	57	10	14	24	....	....	....	150	....	....	....	....	....	....	....	....	....	....	....	....	....	....	....	....	....	....
1973-74	Kingston Canadians	OMJHL	70	9	35	44	....	....	....	187	....	....	....	....	....	....	....	....	....	....	....	....	....	....	....	....	....	....
1974-75	**St. Louis Blues**	**NHL**	**4**	**0**	**0**	**0**	**0**	**0**	**0**	**2**	**0**	**0**	**0**	**3**	**0.0**	**3**	**0**	**5**	**5**	**3**	....	....	....	....	....	....	....	....
	Denver Spurs	CHL	56	1	16	17	....	....	....	102	....	....	....	....	....	....	....	....	....	....	2	0	1	1	2	....	....	....
1975-76	Providence Reds	AHL	70	3	14	17	....	....	....	79	....	....	....	....	....	....	....	....	....	....	3	0	0	0	4	....	....	....
1976-77	Kansas City Blues	CHL	43	0	11	11	....	....	....	34	....	....	....	....	....	....	....	....	....	....	....	....	....	....	....	....	....	....
	Salt Lake Golden Eagles	CHL	20	2	6	8	....	....	....	10	....	....	....	....	....	....	....	....	....	....	....	....	....	....	....	....	....	....
1977-78	Salt Lake Golden Eagles	CHL	65	1	9	10	....	....	....	76	....	....	....	....	....	....	....	....	....	....	6	0	0	0	8	....	....	....
1978-79	Tulsa Oilers	CHL	72	4	12	16	....	....	....	88	....	....	....	....	....	....	....	....	....	....	....	....	....	....	....	....	....	....
1979-80	Dallas Black Hawks	CHL	42	2	6	8	....	....	....	33	....	....	....	....	....	....	....	....	....	....	....	....	....	....	....	....	....	....
	Salt Lake Golden Eagles	CHL	16	0	4	4	....	....	....	25	....	....	....	....	....	....	....	....	....	....	6	0	1	1	0	....	....	....
	NHL Totals		**4**	**0**	**0**	**0**	**0**	**0**	**0**	**2**	**0**	**0**	**0**	**3**	**0.0**	**3**	**0**	**5**	**5**		....	....	....	....	....	....	....	....

Traded to **Vancouver** by **St. Louis** with Bruce Affleck for cash, November 6, 1979. Traded to **St. Louis** by **Vancouver** with Bruce Affleck for cash, February 28, 1980.

• BUZEK, Petr

D – L. 6', 205 lbs. b: Jihlava, Czech., 4/26/1977. Dallas' 3rd, 63rd overall, in 1995.

Season	Club	League	GP	G	A	Pts	AG	AA	APts	PIM	PP	SH	GW	S	%	TGF	PGF	TGA	PGA	+/–	GP	G	A	Pts	PIM	PP	SH	GW
1993-94	Dukla Jihlava-Jr.	Czech-Rep	3	0	0	0	....	....	....	....	....	....	....	....	....	....	....	....	....	....	....	....	....	....	....	....	....	....
	Czech-Republic	EJC-A	5	0	0	0	....	....	....	4	....	....	....	....	....	....	....	....	....	....	....	....	....	....	....	....	....	....
1994-95	Dukla Jihlava	Czech-Rep	43	2	5	7	....	....	....	47	....	....	....	....	....	....	....	....	....	....	2	0	0	0	2	....	....	....
	Czech-Republic	WJC-A	7	2	2	4	....	....	....	10	....	....	....	....	....	....	....	....	....	....	....	....	....	....	....	....	....	....
1995-96	Michigan K-Wings	IHL	DID NOT PLAY – INJURED																									
1996-97	Michigan K-Wings	IHL	67	4	6	10	....	....	....	48	....	....	....	....	....	....	....	....	....	....	....	....	....	....	....	....	....	....
1997-98	**Dallas Stars**	**NHL**	**2**	**0**	**0**	**0**	**0**	**0**	**0**	**2**	**0**	**0**	**0**	**0**	**0.0**	**1**	**0**	**0**	**0**	**1**	....	....	....	....	....	....	....	....
	Michigan K-Wings	IHL	60	10	15	25	....	....	....	58	....	....	....	....	....	....	....	....	....	....	2	0	1	1	17	....	....	....

			REGULAR SEASON																		PLAYOFFS							
Season	Club	League	GP	G	A	Pts	AG	AA	APts	PIM	PP	SH	GW	S	%	TGF	PGF	TGA	PGA	+/–	GP	G	A	Pts	PIM	PP	SH	GW
1998-99	**Dallas Stars**	**NHL**	**2**	**0**	**0**	**0**	**0**	**0**	**0**	**2**	**0**	**0**	**0**	**0**	**0.0**	**0**	**0**	**0**	**0**	**0**	....	....	....	....	....	....	....	....
	Michigan K-Wings	IHL	74	5	14	19	....	....	....	68	....	....	....	....	....	....	....	....	....	....	5	0	0	0	10	....	....	....
99-2000	**Atlanta Thrashers**	**NHL**	**63**	**5**	**14**	**19**	**6**	**13**	**19**	**41**	**3**	**0**	**0**	**90**	**5.6**	**45**	**13**	**69**	**15**	**–22**	....	....	....	....	....	....	....	....
	Czech Republic	WC-A	9	1	3	4	....	....	....	24	....	....	....	....	....	....	....	....	....	....	....	....	....	....	....	....	....	....
	NHL Totals		**67**	**5**	**14**	**19**	**6**	**13**	**19**	**45**	**3**	**0**	**0**	**90**	**5.6**	**46**	**13**	**69**	**15**		....	....	....	....	....	....	....	....

Played in NHL All-Star Game (2000)

• Missed entire 1995-96 season recovering from injuries suffered in automobile accident, July, 1995. Claimed by **Atlanta** from **Dallas** in Expansion Draft, June 25, 1999.

• BYAKIN, Ilja

D – L. 5'9", 185 lbs. b: Sverdlovsk, USSR, 2/2/1963. Edmonton's 11th, 267th overall, in 1993.

Season	Club	League	GP	G	A	Pts	AG	AA	APts	PIM	PP	SH	GW	S	%	TGF	PGF	TGA	PGA	+/–	GP	G	A	Pts	PIM	PP	SH	GW
1980-81	Automobilist Sverdlovsk	USSR-Jr.	STATISTICS NOT AVAILABLE																									
	Soviet Union	EJC-A	5	1	0	1	....	....	....	8	....	....	....	....	....	....	....	....	....	....	....	....	....	....	....	....	....	....
1981-82	Automobilist Sverdlovsk	USSR-2	STATISTICS NOT AVAILABLE																									
	Soviet Union	WJC-A	7	0	4	4	....	....	....	10	....	....	....	....	....	....	....	....	....	....	....	....	....	....	....	....	....	....
	Soviet Union	WEC-A	7	0	4	4	....	....	....	10	....	....	....	....	....	....	....	....	....	....	....	....	....	....	....	....	....	....
1982-83	Automobilist Sverdlovsk	USSR-2	STATISTICS NOT AVAILABLE																									
	Soviet Union	WJC-A	7	1	5	6	....	....	....	6	....	....	....	....	....	....	....	....	....	....	....	....	....	....	....	....	....	....
	Soviet Union	WEC-A	7	1	5	6	....	....	....	6	....	....	....	....	....	....	....	....	....	....	....	....	....	....	....	....	....	....
1983-84	Spartak Moscow	USSR	44	9	12	21	....	....	....	26	....	....	....	....	....	....	....	....	....	....	....	....	....	....	....	....	....	....
1984-85	Spartak Moscow	USSR	46	7	11	18	....	....	....	56	....	....	....	....	....	....	....	....	....	....	....	....	....	....	....	....	....	....
1985-86	Spartak Moscow	USSR	34	8	7	15	....	....	....	41	....	....	....	....	....	....	....	....	....	....	....	....	....	....	....	....	....	....
1986-87	Automobilist Sverdlovsk	USSR	28	7	11	18	....	....	....	28	....	....	....	....	....	....	....	....	....	....	....	....	....	....	....	....	....	....
1987-88	Automobilist Sverdlovsk	USSR	30	10	10	20	....	....	....	37	....	....	....	....	....	....	....	....	....	....	....	....	....	....	....	....	....	....
	Soviet Union	Olympics	8	1	4	5	....	....	....	4	....	....	....	....	....	....	....	....	....	....	....	....	....	....	....	....	....	....
1988-89	Automobilist Sverdlovsk	USSR	40	11	9	20	....	....	....	53	....	....	....	....	....	....	....	....	....	....	....	....	....	....	....	....	....	....
	Soviet Union	WEC-A	9	0	2	2	....	....	....	4	....	....	....	....	....	....	....	....	....	....	....	....	....	....	....	....	....	....
1989-90	Automobilist Sverdlovsk	USSR	27	14	7	21	....	....	....	20	....	....	....	....	....	....	....	....	....	....	....	....	....	....	....	....	....	....
	Soviet Union	WEC-A	10	0	3	3	....	....	....	8	....	....	....	....	....	....	....	....	....	....	....	....	....	....	....	....	....	....
1990-91	CSKA Moscow	USSR	29	4	7	11	....	....	....	20	....	....	....	....	....	....	....	....	....	....	....	....	....	....	....	....	....	....
	Soviet Union	WEC-A	10	2	1	3	....	....	....	4	....	....	....	....	....	....	....	....	....	....	....	....	....	....	....	....	....	....
1991-92	SC Rapperswil-Jona	Switz.2	36	27	40	67	....	....	....	36	....	....	....	....	....	....	....	....	....	....	....	....	....	....	....	....	....	....
	Russia	WC-A	6	3	1	4	....	....	....	2	....	....	....	....	....	....	....	....	....	....	....	....	....	....	....	....	....	....
1992-93	EV Landshut	Germany	44	12	19	31	....	....	....	43	....	....	....	....	....	....	....	....	....	....	6	5	6	11	6	....	....	....
	Russia	WC-A	8	3	4	7	....	....	....	6	....	....	....	....	....	....	....	....	....	....	....	....	....	....	....	....	....	....
1993-94	**Edmonton Oilers**	**NHL**	**44**	**8**	**20**	**28**	**7**	**16**	**23**	**30**	**6**	**0**	**3**	**51**	**15.7**	**52**	**21**	**36**	**2**	**–3**	....	....	....	....	....	....	....	....
	Cape Breton Oilers	AHL	12	2	9	11	....	....	....	8	....	....	....	....	....	....	....	....	....	....	....	....	....	....	....	....	....	....
	Russia	WC-A	6	2	3	5	....	....	....	2	....	....	....	....	....	....	....	....	....	....	....	....	....	....	....	....	....	....
1994-95	Avtomobilist Yekaterinburg	CIS	4	3	2	5	....	....	....	14	....	....	....	....	....	....	....	....	....	....	....	....	....	....	....	....	....	....
	San Jose Sharks	**NHL**	**13**	**0**	**5**	**5**	**0**	**7**	**7**	**14**	**0**	**0**	**0**	**19**	**0.0**	**13**	**7**	**16**	**1**	**–9**	....	....	....	....	....	....	....	....
	Kansas City Blades	IHL	1	0	2	2	....	....	....	0	....	....	....	....	....	....	....	....	....	....	16	4	10	14	43	....	....	....
1995-96	Malmo IF	Sweden	36	10	15	25	....	....	....	52	....	....	....	....	....	....	....	....	....	....	3	1	0	1	19	....	....	....
1996-97	Malmo IF	Sweden	47	11	14	25	....	....	....	78	....	....	....	....	....	....	....	....	....	....	4	0	1	1	0	....	....	....
1997-98	San Antonio Dragons	IHL	6	0	1	1	....	....	....	10	....	....	....	....	....	....	....	....	....	....	....	....	....	....	....	....	....	....
	Las Vegas Thunder	IHL	52	3	7	10	....	....	....	40	....	....	....	....	....	....	....	....	....	....	....	....	....	....	....	....	....	....
1998-99	Spartak Moscow	Russia	21	3	6	9	....	....	....	24	....	....	....	....	....	....	....	....	....	....	....	....	....	....	....	....	....	....
99-2000	Lada Togliatti	Russia	37	9	13	22	....	....	....	*83	....	....	....	....	....	....	....	....	....	....	7	0	2	2	18	....	....	....
	NHL Totals		**57**	**8**	**25**	**33**	**7**	**23**	**30**	**44**	**6**	**0**	**3**	**70**	**11.4**	**65**	**28**	**52**	**3**		....	....	....	....	....	....	....	....

WC-A All-tar Team (1993)

Signed as a free agent by **San Jose**, September 18, 1994.

• BYCE, John

C – L. 6'1", 180 lbs. b: Madison, WI, 8/9/1967. Boston's 11th, 220th overall, in 1985.

Season	Club	League	GP	G	A	Pts	AG	AA	APts	PIM	PP	SH	GW	S	%	TGF	PGF	TGA	PGA	+/–	GP	G	A	Pts	PIM	PP	SH	GW
1984-85	Madison Bulldogs	Hi-School	24	39	47	86	....	....	....	32	....	....	....	....	....	....	....	....	....	....	....	....	....	....	....	....	....	....
1985-86	Madison Capitols	USHL	STATISTICS NOT AVAILABLE																									
1986-87	University of Wisconsin	WCHA	40	1	4	5	....	....	....	12	....	....	....	....	....	....	....	....	....	....	....	....	....	....	....	....	....	....
1987-88	University of Wisconsin	WCHA	41	22	12	34	....	....	....	18	....	....	....	....	....	....	....	....	....	....	....	....	....	....	....	....	....	....
1988-89	University of Wisconsin	WCHA	42	27	28	55	....	....	....	16	....	....	....	....	....	....	....	....	....	....	....	....	....	....	....	....	....	....
1989-90	University of Wisconsin	WCHA	46	27	44	71	....	....	....	20	....	....	....	....	....	....	....	....	....	....	....	....	....	....	....	....	....	....
	Boston Bruins	**NHL**	....	....	....	....	....	....	....	....	....	....	....	....	....	....	....	....	....	....	**8**	**2**	**0**	**2**	**2**	**0**	**0**	**0**
1990-91	**Boston Bruins**	**NHL**	**18**	**1**	**3**	**4**	**1**	**2**	**3**	**6**	**0**	**0**	**0**	**13**	**7.7**	**6**	**1**	**4**	**0**	**1**	....	....	....	....	....	....	....	....
	Maine Mariners	AHL	53	19	29	48	....	....	....	20	....	....	....	....	....	....	....	....	....	....	....	....	....	....	....	....	....	....
1991-92	**Boston Bruins**	**NHL**	**3**	**1**	**0**	**1**	**1**	**0**	**1**	**0**	**1**	**0**	**0**	**2**	**50.0**	**2**	**1**	**2**	**0**	**–1**	....	....	....	....	....	....	....	....
	Maine Mariners	AHL	55	29	21	50	....	....	....	41	....	....	....	....	....	....	....	....	....	....	....	....	....	....	....	....	....	....
	Baltimore Skipjacks	AHL	20	9	5	14	....	....	....	4	....	....	....	....	....	....	....	....	....	....	....	....	....	....	....	....	....	....
	United States	WC-A	6	0	2	2	....	....	....	2	....	....	....	....	....	....	....	....	....	....	....	....	....	....	....	....	....	....
1992-93	Baltimore Skipjacks	AHL	62	35	44	79	....	....	....	26	....	....	....	....	....	....	....	....	....	....	7	4	5	9	4	....	....	....
1993-94	HV-71 Jonkoping	Sweden	33	8	4	12	....	....	....	8	....	....	....	....	....	....	....	....	....	....	....	....	....	....	....	....	....	....
	Milwaukee Admirals	IHL	28	7	4	11	....	....	....	10	....	....	....	....	....	....	....	....	....	....	3	2	1	3	0	....	....	....
1994-95	Portland Pirates	AHL	6	1	1	2	....	....	....	2	....	....	....	....	....	....	....	....	....	....	....	....	....	....	....	....	....	....
	San Diego Gulls	IHL	5	2	3	5	....	....	....	2	....	....	....	....	....	....	....	....	....	....	....	....	....	....	....	....	....	....
	Milwaukee Admirals	IHL	30	9	11	20	....	....	....	10	....	....	....	....	....	....	....	....	....	....	15	4	5	9	4	....	....	....
1995-96	Los Angeles Ice Dogs	IHL	82	39	46	85	....	....	....	40	....	....	....	....	....	....	....	....	....	....	....	....	....	....	....	....	....	....
1996-97	Long Beach Ice Dogs	IHL	80	29	29	58	....	....	....	14	....	....	....	....	....	....	....	....	....	....	14	4	7	11	0	....	....	....
1997-98	Long Beach Ice Dogs	IHL	17	9	8	17	....	....	....	10	....	....	....	....	....	....	....	....	....	....	12	4	1	5	4	....	....	....
1998-99	Long Beach Ice Dogs	IHL	37	8	11	19	....	....	....	8	....	....	....	....	....	....	....	....	....	....	....	....	....	....	....	....	....	....
	Utah Grizzlies	IHL	35	11	20	31	....	....	....	18	....	....	....	....	....	....	....	....	....	....	....	....	....	....	....	....	....	....
99-2000	London Knights	BH-Cup	4	2	3	5	....	....	....	0	....	....	....	....	....	....	....	....	....	....	....	....	....	....	....	....	....	....
	London Knights	Britain	28	11	18	29	....	....	....	6	....	....	....	....	....	....	....	....	....	....	6	1	4	5	4	....	....	....
	NHL Totals		**21**	**2**	**3**	**5**	**2**	**2**	**4**	**6**	**1**	**0**	**0**	**15**	**13.3**	**8**	**2**	**6**	**0**		**8**	**2**	**0**	**2**	**2**	**0**	**0**	**0**

WCHA Second All-Star Team (1989, 1990) • NCAA All-Tournament Team (1990)

Traded to **Washington** by **Boston** with Dennis Smith for Brent Hughes and future considerations, February 24, 1992.

• BYERS, Jerry

Jerry William LW – L. 5'11", 170 lbs. b: Kentville, N.S., 3/29/1952. Minnesota's 1st, 12th overall, in 1972.

Season	Club	League	GP	G	A	Pts	AG	AA	APts	PIM	PP	SH	GW	S	%	TGF	PGF	TGA	PGA	+/–	GP	G	A	Pts	PIM	PP	SH	GW
1969-70	Kitchener Greenshirts	OHA-B	20	19	11	30	....	....	....	20	....	....	....	....	....	....	....	....	....	....	....	....	....	....	....	....	....	....
	Kitchener Rangers	OHA-Jr.	36	18	24	42	....	....	....	8	....	....	....	....	....	....	....	....	....	....	6	2	3	5	2	....	....	....
1970-71	Kitchener Rangers	OHA-Jr.	62	41	39	80	....	....	....	46	....	....	....	....	....	....	....	....	....	....	4	2	5	7	14	....	....	....
1971-72	Kitchener Rangers	OMJHL	60	41	60	101	....	....	....	49	....	....	....	....	....	....	....	....	....	....	5	3	5	8	2	....	....	....
1972-73	**Minnesota North Stars**	**NHL**	**14**	**0**	**2**	**2**	**0**	**2**	**2**	**6**	**0**	**0**	**0**	**17**	**0.0**	**3**	**1**	**4**	**0**	**–2**	....	....	....	....	....	....	....	....
	Jacksonville Barons	AHL	59	20	17	37	....	....	....	12	....	....	....	....	....	....	....	....	....	....	....	....	....	....	....	....	....	....
1973-74	**Minnesota North Stars**	**NHL**	**10**	**0**	**0**	**0**	**0**	**0**	**0**	**0**	**0**	**0**	**0**	**11**	**0.0**	**1**	**1**	**5**	**0**	**–5**	....	....	....	....	....	....	....	....
	New Haven Nighthawks	AHL	62	31	47	78	....	....	....	37	....	....	....	....	....	....	....	....	....	....	10	4	6	10	4	....	....	....
1974-75	**Atlanta Flames**	**NHL**	**12**	**1**	**1**	**2**	**1**	**1**	**2**	**9**	**0**	**0**	**0**	**10**	**10.0**	**2**	**0**	**6**	**0**	**–4**	....	....	....	....	....	....	....	....
	Omaha Knights	CHL	58	21	31	52	....	....	....	29	....	....	....	....	....	....	....	....	....	....	6	*9	2	11	2	....	....	....
1975-76	Providence Reds	AHL	74	27	34	61	....	....	....	28	....	....	....	....	....	....	....	....	....	....	3	0	2	2	2	....	....	....
1976-77	New Haven Nighthawks	AHL	77	31	34	65	....	....	....	18	....	....	....	....	....	....	....	....	....	....	6	1	3	4	0	....	....	....
1977-78	**New York Rangers**	**NHL**	**7**	**2**	**1**	**3**	**2**	**1**	**3**	**0**	**0**	**0**	**1**	**7**	**28.6**	**5**	**0**	**6**	**0**	**–1**	....	....	....	....	....	....	....	....
	New Haven Nighthawks	AHL	74	32	31	63	....	....	....	13	....	....	....	....	....	....	....	....	....	....	15	7	3	10	4	....	....	....
1978-79	Nova Scotia Voyageurs	AHL	78	33	42	75	....	....	....	28	....	....	....	....	....	....	....	....	....	....	10	0	5	5	4	....	....	....
1979-80	Nova Scotia Voyageurs	AHL	74	23	36	59	....	....	....	16	....	....	....	....	....	....	....	....	....	....	6	1	2	3	2	....	....	....
1980-81	HC Salzburg	Austria	23	20	15	35	....	....	....	27	....	....	....	....	....	....	....	....	....	....	....	....	....	....	....	....	....	....

			REGULAR SEASON																		PLAYOFFS							
Season	Club	League	GP	G	A	Pts	AG	AA	APts	PIM	PP	SH	GW	S	%	TGF	PGF	TGA	PGA	+/-	GP	G	A	Pts	PIM	PP	SH	GW
1981-82	EHC Grindelwald	Switz-2	STATISTICS NOT AVAILABLE																									
1982-83	EHC Grindelwald	Switz-2	28	38	14	52	....	....	....	....	....	....	....	....	....	....	....	....	....	....	....	....	....	....	....	....	....	....
1983-84	Jujo-Seishi Kusiro	Japan	30	25	14	39	....	....	....	....	....	....	....	....	....	....	....	....	....	....	....	....	....	....	....	....	....	....
	NHL Totals		**43**	**3**	**4**	**7**	**3**	**4**	**7**	**15**	**0**	**0**	**1**	**45**	**6.7**	**11**	**2**	**21**	**0**		....	....	....	....	....	....	....	....

AHL Second All-Star Team (1974, 1979)

Traded to **Atlanta** by **Minnesota** with Buster Harvey for John Flesch and Don Martineau, May 27, 1974. Traded to **NY Rangers** by **Atlanta** for Curt Ridley, September 9, 1975.

• BYERS, Lyndon

Lyndon Svi RW – R. 6'1", 200 lbs. b: Nipawin, Sask., 2/29/1964. Boston's 3rd, 39th overall, in 1982.

Season	Club	League	GP	G	A	Pts	AG	AA	APts	PIM	PP	SH	GW	S	%	TGF	PGF	TGA	PGA	+/-	GP	G	A	Pts	PIM	PP	SH	GW
1980-81	Notre Dame Midget Hounds	SAHA	37	35	42	77	....	....	....	106	....	....	....	....	....	....	....	....	....	....	....	....	....	....	....	....	....	....
1981-82	Regina Pats	WHL	57	18	25	43	....	....	....	169	....	....	....	....	....	....	....	....	....	....	20	5	6	11	48	....	....	....
1982-83	Regina Pats	WHL	70	32	38	70	....	....	....	153	....	....	....	....	....	....	....	....	....	....	5	1	1	2	16	....	....	....
1983-84	Regina Pats	WHL	58	32	57	89	....	....	....	154	....	....	....	....	....	....	....	....	....	....	23	17	18	35	78	....	....	....
	Canada	WJC-A	6	1	1	2	....	....	....	4	....	....	....	....	....	....	....	....	....	....	....	....	....	....	....	....	....	....
	Boston Bruins	**NHL**	**10**	**2**	**4**	**6**	**2**	**3**	**5**	**32**	**0**	**0**	**0**	**11**	**18.2**	**8**	**0**	**5**	**0**	**3**	....	....	....	....	....	....	....	....
1984-85	**Boston Bruins**	**NHL**	**33**	**3**	**8**	**11**	**2**	**5**	**7**	**41**	**0**	**0**	**0**	**25**	**12.0**	**18**	**1**	**17**	**0**	**0**	....	....	....	....	....	....	....	....
	Hershey Bears	AHL	27	4	6	10	....	....	....	55	....	....	....	....	....	....	....	....	....	....	....	....	....	....	....	....	....	....
1985-86	**Boston Bruins**	**NHL**	**5**	**0**	**2**	**2**	**0**	**1**	**1**	**9**	**0**	**0**	**0**	**1**	**0.0**	**3**	**0**	**2**	**0**	**1**	....	....	....	....	....	....	....	....
	Moncton Golden Flames	AHL	14	2	4	6	....	....	....	26	....	....	....	....	....	....	....	....	....	....	....	....	....	....	....	....	....	....
	Milwaukee Admirals	IHL	8	0	2	2	....	....	....	22	....	....	....	....	....	....	....	....	....	....	....	....	....	....	....	....	....	....
1986-87	**Boston Bruins**	**NHL**	**18**	**2**	**3**	**5**	**2**	**2**	**4**	**53**	**0**	**0**	**0**	**14**	**14.3**	**5**	**0**	**6**	**0**	**–1**	**1**	**0**	**0**	**0**	**0**	**0**	**0**	**0**
	Moncton Golden Flames	AHL	27	5	5	10	....	....	....	63	....	....	....	....	....	....	....	....	....	....	....	....	....	....	....	....	....	....
1987-88	**Boston Bruins**	**NHL**	**53**	**10**	**14**	**24**	**9**	**10**	**19**	**236**	**0**	**0**	**2**	**69**	**14.5**	**39**	**2**	**27**	**0**	**10**	**11**	**1**	**2**	**3**	**62**	**0**	**0**	**0**
	Maine Mariners	AHL	2	0	1	1	....	....	....	18	....	....	....	....	....	....	....	....	....	....	....	....	....	....	....	....	....	....
1988-89	**Boston Bruins**	**NHL**	**49**	**0**	**4**	**4**	**0**	**3**	**3**	**218**	**0**	**0**	**0**	**25**	**0.0**	**9**	**0**	**18**	**1**	**–8**	**2**	**0**	**0**	**0**	**0**	**0**	**0**	**0**
	Maine Mariners	AHL	4	1	3	4	....	....	....	2	....	....	....	....	....	....	....	....	....	....	....	....	....	....	....	....	....	....
1989-90	**Boston Bruins**	**NHL**	**43**	**4**	**4**	**8**	**3**	**3**	**6**	**159**	**0**	**0**	**0**	**43**	**9.3**	**10**	**0**	**10**	**0**	**0**	**17**	**1**	**0**	**1**	**12**	**0**	**0**	**0**
1990-91	**Boston Bruins**	**NHL**	**19**	**2**	**2**	**4**	**2**	**2**	**4**	**82**	**0**	**0**	**0**	**20**	**10.0**	**6**	**0**	**8**	**0**	**–2**	**1**	**0**	**0**	**0**	**10**	**0**	**0**	**0**
1991-92	**Boston Bruins**	**NHL**	**31**	**1**	**1**	**2**	**1**	**1**	**2**	**129**	**0**	**0**	**0**	**12**	**8.3**	**4**	**0**	**9**	**0**	**–5**	**5**	**0**	**0**	**0**	**12**	**0**	**0**	**0**
	Maine Mariners	AHL	11	5	4	9	....	....	....	47	....	....	....	....	....	....	....	....	....	....	....	....	....	....	....	....	....	....
1992-93	**San Jose Sharks**	**NHL**	**18**	**4**	**1**	**5**	**3**	**1**	**4**	**122**	**0**	**0**	**0**	**18**	**22.2**	**6**	**0**	**8**	**0**	**–2**	....	....	....	....	....	....	....	....
	Kansas City Blades	IHL	4	1	1	2	....	....	....	22	....	....	....	....	....	....	....	....	....	....	....	....	....	....	....	....	....	....
	San Diego Gulls	IHL	9	0	3	3	....	....	....	35	....	....	....	....	....	....	....	....	....	....	....	....	....	....	....	....	....	....
1993-94	Las Vegas Thunder	IHL	31	3	5	8	....	....	....	176	....	....	....	....	....	....	....	....	....	....	1	0	0	0	4	....	....	....
1994-95	Minnesota Moose	IHL	7	1	0	1	....	....	....	16	....	....	....	....	....	....	....	....	....	....	....	....	....	....	....	....	....	....
	NHL Totals		**279**	**28**	**43**	**71**	**24**	**31**	**55**	**1081**	**0**	**0**	**2**	**238**	**11.8**	**108**	**3**	**110**	**1**		**37**	**2**	**2**	**4**	**96**	**0**	**0**	**0**

SJHL Second Team All-Star (1981)

• Missed majority of 1990-91 season recovering from foot injury suffered in game vs. Soviet Khimyk, December 16, 1990. Signed as a free agent by **San Jose**, November 7, 1992. Signed as a free agent by **San Diego** (IHL) following release by San Jose, March 10, 1993.

• BYERS, Mike

Michael Arthur RW – R. 5'10", 185 lbs. b: Toronto, Ont., 9/11/1946.

Season	Club	League	GP	G	A	Pts	AG	AA	APts	PIM	PP	SH	GW	S	%	TGF	PGF	TGA	PGA	+/-	GP	G	A	Pts	PIM	PP	SH	GW
1962-63	Toronto Midget Marlboros	MTHL	STATISTICS NOT AVAILABLE																									
	Toronto Marlboros	OHA-Jr.	2	4	1	5	....	....	....	0	....	....	....	....	....	....	....	....	....	....	9	3	5	8	6	....	....	....
1963-64	Toronto Marlboros	OHA-Jr.	2	0	0	0	....	....	....	0	....	....	....	....	....	....	....	....	....	....	....	....	....	....	....	....	....	....
1964-65	Toronto Marlboros	OHA-Jr.	56	22	18	40	....	....	....	37	....	....	....	....	....	....	....	....	....	....	19	1	4	5	8	....	....	....
1965-66	Toronto Marlboros	OHA-Jr.	47	21	21	42	....	....	....	45	....	....	....	....	....	....	....	....	....	....	14	4	2	6	4	....	....	....
1966-67	Toronto Marlboros	OHA-Jr.	41	25	19	44	....	....	....	20	....	....	....	....	....	....	....	....	....	....	17	3	3	6	15	....	....	....
	Toronto Marlboros	Mem-Cup	9	3	3	6	....	....	....	14	....	....	....	....	....	....	....	....	....	....	....	....	....	....	....	....	....	....
1967-68	**Toronto Maple Leafs**	**NHL**	**10**	**2**	**2**	**4**	**2**	**2**	**4**	**0**	**1**	**0**	**0**	**16**	**12.5**	**5**	**1**	**2**	**0**	**2**	....	....	....	....	....	....	....	....
	Tulsa Oilers	CPHL	27	14	5	19	....	....	....	32	....	....	....	....	....	....	....	....	....	....	11	1	3	4	2	....	....	....
	Rochester Americans	AHL	31	7	8	15	....	....	....	0	....	....	....	....	....	....	....	....	....	....	....	....	....	....	....	....	....	....
1968-69	**Toronto Maple Leafs**	**NHL**	**5**	**0**	**0**	**0**	**0**	**0**	**0**	**2**	**0**	**0**	**0**	**8**	**0.0**	**1**	**0**	**1**	**0**	**0**	....	....	....	....	....	....	....	....
	Tulsa Oilers	CHL	51	17	17	34	....	....	....	6	....	....	....	....	....	....	....	....	....	....	....	....	....	....	....	....	....	....
	Philadelphia Flyers	**NHL**	**5**	**0**	**2**	**2**	**0**	**2**	**2**	**0**	**0**	**0**	**0**	**8**	**0.0**	**2**	**2**	**1**	**0**	**–1**	**4**	**0**	**1**	**1**	**0**	**0**	**0**	**0**
1969-70	Quebec Aces	AHL	62	15	23	38	....	....	....	11	....	....	....	....	....	....	....	....	....	....	6	1	0	1	0	....	....	....
1970-71	**Los Angeles Kings**	**NHL**	**72**	**27**	**18**	**45**	**27**	**15**	**42**	**14**	**4**	**0**	**5**	**179**	**15.1**	**73**	**12**	**68**	**2**	**–5**	....	....	....	....	....	....	....	....
1971-72	**Los Angeles Kings**	**NHL**	**28**	**4**	**5**	**9**	**4**	**4**	**8**	**11**	**0**	**0**	**1**	**48**	**8.3**	**20**	**4**	**30**	**1**	**–13**	....	....	....	....	....	....	....	....
	Buffalo Sabres	**NHL**	**46**	**9**	**7**	**16**	**9**	**6**	**15**	**12**	**3**	**0**	**1**	**69**	**13.0**	**43**	**13**	**51**	**1**	**–20**	....	....	....	....	....	....	....	....
1972-73	Los Angeles Sharks	WHA	56	19	17	36	....	....	....	20	....	....	....	....	....	....	....	....	....	....	....	....	....	....	....	....	....	....
	New England Whalers	WHA	19	6	4	10	....	....	....	4	....	....	....	....	....	....	....	....	....	....	12	6	5	11	6	....	....	....
1973-74	New England Whalers	WHA	78	29	21	50	....	....	....	6	....	....	....	....	....	....	....	....	....	....	7	2	4	6	12	....	....	....
1974-75	New England Whalers	WHA	72	22	26	48	....	....	....	10	....	....	....	....	....	....	....	....	....	....	6	2	2	4	2	....	....	....
1975-76	New England Whalers	WHA	21	4	3	7	....	....	....	0	....	....	....	....	....	....	....	....	....	....	....	....	....	....	....	....	....	....
	Cincinnati Stingers	WHA	20	3	3	6	....	....	....	0	....	....	....	....	....	....	....	....	....	....	....	....	....	....	....	....	....	....
1976-77	Rochester Americans	AHL	66	25	29	54	....	....	....	10	....	....	....	....	....	....	....	....	....	....	8	2	4	6	0	....	....	....
	NHL Totals		**166**	**42**	**34**	**76**	**42**	**29**	**71**	**39**	**8**	**0**	**7**	**328**	**12.8**	**144**	**32**	**153**	**4**		**4**	**0**	**1**	**1**	**0**	**0**	**0**	**0**
	Other Major League Totals		266	83	74	157	....	....	....	40	....	....	....	....	....	....	....	....	....	....	25	10	11	21	20	....	....	....

Traded to **Philadelphia** by **Toronto** with Bill Sutherland and Gerry Meehan for Brit Selby and Forbes Kennedy, March 2, 1969. Traded to **LA Kings** by **Philadelphia** for Brent Hughes, May 20, 1970. Traded to **Buffalo** by **LA Kings** with Larry Hillman for Doug Barrie and Mike Keeler, December 16, 1971. Selected by **LA Sharks** (WHA) in 1972 WHA General Player Draft, February 12, 1972. Traded to **New England** (WHA) by **LA Sharks** (WHA) for Mike Hyndman, February, 1973. Signed as a free agent by **Cincinnati** (WHA) following release by **New England** (WHA), February, 1976.

• BYLSMA, Dan

Dan Brian "Disco" RW – R. 6'2", 212 lbs. b: Grand Haven, MI, 9/19/1970. Winnipeg's 7th, 109th overall, in 1989.

Season	Club	League	GP	G	A	Pts	AG	AA	APts	PIM	PP	SH	GW	S	%	TGF	PGF	TGA	PGA	+/-	GP	G	A	Pts	PIM	PP	SH	GW
1986-87	Oakville Blades	OJHL-B	10	4	9	13	....	....	....	21	....	....	....	....	....	....	....	....	....	....	....	....	....	....	....	....	....	....
	St. Mary's Lincolns	OJHL-B	27	14	28	42	....	....	....	21	....	....	....	....	....	....	....	....	....	....	....	....	....	....	....	....	....	....
1987-88	St. Mary's Lincolns	OJHL-B	40	30	39	69	....	....	....	33	....	....	....	....	....	....	....	....	....	....	8	8	18	26	....	....	....	....
1988-89	Bowling Green University	CCHA	32	3	7	10	....	....	....	10	....	....	....	....	....	....	....	....	....	....	....	....	....	....	....	....	....	....
1989-90	Bowling Green University	CCHA	44	13	17	30	....	....	....	30	....	....	....	....	....	....	....	....	....	....	....	....	....	....	....	....	....	....
1990-91	Bowling Green University	CCHA	40	9	12	21	....	....	....	48	....	....	....	....	....	....	....	....	....	....	....	....	....	....	....	....	....	....
1991-92	Bowling Green University	CCHA	34	11	14	25	....	....	....	24	....	....	....	....	....	....	....	....	....	....	....	....	....	....	....	....	....	....
1992-93	Greensboro Monarchs	ECHL	60	25	35	60	....	....	....	66	....	....	....	....	....	....	....	....	....	....	1	0	1	1	10	....	....	....
	Rochester Americans	AHL	2	0	1	1	....	....	....	0	....	....	....	....	....	....	....	....	....	....	....	....	....	....	....	....	....	....
1993-94	Greensboro Monarchs	ECHL	25	14	16	30	....	....	....	52	....	....	....	....	....	....	....	....	....	....	....	....	....	....	....	....	....	....
	Albany River Rats	AHL	3	0	1	1	....	....	....	2	....	....	....	....	....	....	....	....	....	....	....	....	....	....	....	....	....	....
	Moncton Hawks	AHL	50	12	16	28	....	....	....	25	....	....	....	....	....	....	....	....	....	....	21	3	4	7	31	....	....	....
1994-95	Phoenix Roadrunners	IHL	81	19	23	42	....	....	....	41	....	....	....	....	....	....	....	....	....	....	9	4	4	8	4	....	....	....
1995-96	**Los Angeles Kings**	**NHL**	**4**	**0**	**0**	**0**	**0**	**0**	**0**	**0**	**0**	**0**	**0**	**6**	**0.0**	**2**	**0**	**4**	**2**	**0**	....	....	....	....	....	....	....	....
	Phoenix Roadrunners	IHL	78	22	20	42	....	....	....	48	....	....	....	....	....	....	....	....	....	....	4	1	0	1	2	....	....	....
1996-97	**Los Angeles Kings**	**NHL**	**79**	**3**	**6**	**9**	**3**	**5**	**8**	**32**	**0**	**0**	**0**	**86**	**3.5**	**16**	**1**	**55**	**25**	**–15**	....	....	....	....	....	....	....	....
1997-98	**Los Angeles Kings**	**NHL**	**65**	**3**	**9**	**12**	**4**	**9**	**13**	**33**	**0**	**0**	**0**	**57**	**5.3**	**23**	**0**	**28**	**14**	**9**	**2**	**0**	**0**	**0**	**0**	**0**	**0**	**0**
	Long Beach Ice Dogs	IHL	8	2	3	5	....	....	....	0	....	....	....	....	....	....	....	....	....	....	....	....	....	....	....	....	....	....
1998-99	**Los Angeles Kings**	**NHL**	**8**	**0**	**0**	**0**	**0**	**0**	**0**	**2**	**0**	**0**	**0**	**3**	**0.0**	**0**	**0**	**2**	**1**	**–1**	....	....	....	....	....	....	....	....
	Springfield Falcons	AHL	2	0	2	2	....	....	....	2	....	....	....	....	....	....	....	....	....	....	....	....	....	....	....	....	....	....
	Long Beach Ice Dogs	IHL	58	10	8	18	....	....	....	53	....	....	....	....	....	....	....	....	....	....	4	0	0	0	8	....	....	....
99-2000	**Los Angeles Kings**	**NHL**	**64**	**3**	**6**	**9**	**3**	**6**	**9**	**55**	**0**	**1**	**0**	**43**	**7.0**	**14**	**0**	**29**	**13**	**–2**	**3**	**0**	**0**	**0**	**0**	**0**	**0**	**0**
	Long Beach Ice Dogs	IHL	6	0	3	3	....	....	....	2	....	....	....	....	....	....	....	....	....	....	....	....	....	....	....	....	....	....
	Lowell Lock Monsters	AHL	2	1	1	2	....	....	....	2	....	....	....	....	....	....	....	....	....	....	....	....	....	....	....	....	....	....
	NHL Totals		**220**	**9**	**21**	**30**	**10**	**20**	**30**	**122**	**0**	**1**	**0**	**195**	**4.6**	**55**	**1**	**118**	**55**		**5**	**0**	**0**	**0**	**0**	**0**	**0**	**0**

Signed as a free agent by **LA Kings**, July 7, 1994. Signed as a free agent by **Anaheim**, July 13, 2000.

Season	Club	League	REGULAR SEASON GP	G	A	Pts	AG	AA	APts	PIM	PP	SH	GW	S	%	TGF	PGF	TGA	PGA	+/–	PLAYOFFS GP	G	A	Pts	PIM	PP	SH	GW

● **BYRAM, Shawn** Shawn D. LW – L. 6'2", 204 lbs. b: Neepawa, Man., 9/12/1968. NY Islanders' 4th, 80th overall, in 1986.

Season	Club	League	GP	G	A	Pts	AG	AA	APts	PIM	PP	SH	GW	S	%	TGF	PGF	TGA	PGA	+/–	GP	G	A	Pts	PIM	PP	SH	GW
1984-85	Regina Pat Canadians	SAHA	25	12	21	33	....	....	....	38	....	....	....	....	....	....	....	....	....	....	....	....	....	....	....	....	....	....
	Regina Pats	WHL	4	0	1	1	....	....	....	0	....	....	....	....	....	....	....	....	....	....	1	0	0	0	0	....	....	....
1985-86	Regina Pats	WHL	46	7	6	13	....	....	....	45	....	....	....	....	....	....	....	....	....	....	9	0	1	1	11	....	....	....
1986-87	Regina Pats	WHL	12	3	3	6	....	....	....	25	....	....	....	....	....	....	....	....	....	....	....	....	....	....	....	....	....	....
	Prince Albert Raiders	WHL	55	16	18	34	....	....	....	122	....	....	....	....	....	....	....	....	....	....	7	1	1	2	10	....	....	....
1987-88	Prince Albert Raiders	WHL	61	23	28	51	....	....	....	178	....	....	....	....	....	....	....	....	....	....	10	5	2	7	27	....	....	....
1988-89	Springfield Indians	AHL	45	5	11	16	....	....	....	195	....	....	....	....	....	....	....	....	....	....	....	....	....	....	....	....	....	....
	Indianapolis Ice	IHL	1	0	0	0	....	....	....	2	....	....	....	....	....	....	....	....	....	....	....	....	....	....	....	....	....	....
1989-90	Springfield Indians	AHL	31	4	4	8	....	....	....	30	....	....	....	....	....	....	....	....	....	....	....	....	....	....	....	....	....	....
	Johnstown Chiefs	ECHL	8	5	5	10	....	....	....	35	....	....	....	....	....	....	....	....	....	....	....	....	....	....	....	....	....	....
1990-91	**New York Islanders**	**NHL**	**4**	**0**	**0**	**0**	**0**	**0**	**0**	**14**	**0**	**0**	**0**	**2**	**0.0**	**2**	**1**	**3**	**0**	**–2**	....	....	....	....	....	....	....	....
	Capital District Islanders	AHL	62	28	35	63	....	....	....	162	....	....	....	....	....	....	....	....	....	....	....	....	....	....	....	....	....	....
1991-92	**Chicago Blackhawks**	**NHL**	**1**	**0**	**0**	**0**	**0**	**0**	**0**	**0**	**0**	**0**	**0**	**1**	**0.0**	**1**	**0**	**1**	**0**	**0**	....	....	....	....	....	....	....	....
	Indianapolis Ice	IHL	69	18	21	39	....	....	....	154	....	....	....	....	....	....	....	....	....	....	....	....	....	....	....	....	....	....
1992-93	Indianapolis Ice	IHL	41	2	13	15	....	....	....	123	....	....	....	....	....	....	....	....	....	....	5	1	2	3	8	....	....	....
1993-94	Indianapolis Ice	IHL	77	23	24	47	....	....	....	170	....	....	....	....	....	....	....	....	....	....	....	....	....	....	....	....	....	....
1994-95	HC Fassa	Italy	15	15	16	31	....	....	....	43	....	....	....	....	....	....	....	....	....	....	....	....	....	....	....	....	....	....
	Bracknell Bees	Britain	24	24	24	48	....	....	....	97	....	....	....	....	....	....	....	....	....	....	....	....	....	....	....	....	....	....
1995-96	HC Bolzano	Alpenliga	7	3	3	6	....	....	....	16	....	....	....	....	....	....	....	....	....	....	....	....	....	....	....	....	....	....
	Manchester Storm	Britain-2	42	70	120	190	....	....	....	135	....	....	....	....	....	....	....	....	....	....	6	4	16	20	12	....	....	....
1996-97	Manchester Storm	BH-Cup	8	1	5	6	....	....	....	6	....	....	....	....	....	....	....	....	....	....	....	....	....	....	....	....	....	....
	Manchester Storm	Britain	23	8	12	20	....	....	....	38	....	....	....	....	....	....	....	....	....	....	....	....	....	....	....	....	....	....
	Manchester Storm	EuroHL	5	0	1	1	....	....	....	12	....	....	....	....	....	....	....	....	....	....	....	....	....	....	....	....	....	....
	WEV Wien	Alpenliga	2	0	2	2	....	....	....	2	....	....	....	....	....	....	....	....	....	....	....	....	....	....	....	....	....	....
	WEV Wien	Austria	6	1	13	14	....	....	....	2	....	....	....	....	....	....	....	....	....	....	....	....	....	....	....	....	....	....
	Fresno Fighting Falcons	WCHL	6	3	5	8	....	....	....	13	....	....	....	....	....	....	....	....	....	....	5	2	5	7	67	....	....	....
1997-98	Ayr Scottish Eagles	BH-Cup	14	3	6	9	....	....	....	16	....	....	....	....	....	....	....	....	....	....	....	....	....	....	....	....	....	....
	Ayr Scottish Eagles	Britain	45	18	31	49	....	....	....	101	....	....	....	....	....	....	....	....	....	....	9	5	3	8	4	....	....	....
1998-99	Ayr Scottish Eagles	BH-Cup	13	8	15	23	....	....	....	4	....	....	....	....	....	....	....	....	....	....	....	....	....	....	....	....	....	....
	Ayr Scottish Eagles	Britain	23	9	12	21	....	....	....	30	....	....	....	....	....	....	....	....	....	....	13	8	15	23	4	....	....	....
	Ayr Scottish Eagles	EuroHL	6	2	1	3	....	....	....	10	....	....	....	....	....	....	....	....	....	....	....	....	....	....	....	....	....	....
99-2000	Ayr Scottish Eagles	BH-Cup	8	1	3	4	....	....	....	8	....	....	....	....	....	....	....	....	....	....	....	....	....	....	....	....	....	....
	Ayr Scottish Eagles	Britain	37	14	28	42	....	....	....	102	....	....	....	....	....	....	....	....	....	....	7	2	2	4	27	....	....	....
	NHL Totals		**5**	**0**	**0**	**0**	**0**	**0**	**0**	**14**	**0**	**0**	**0**	**3**	**0.0**	**3**	**1**	**4**	**0**		....	....	....	....	....	....	....	....

Signed as a free agent by **Chicago**, August 15, 1991.

● **CAFFERY, Terry** Terrance Michael C – R. 5'9", 165 lbs. b: Toronto, Ont., 4/1/1949. Chicago's 1st, 3rd overall, in 1966.

Season	Club	League	GP	G	A	Pts	AG	AA	APts	PIM	PP	SH	GW	S	%	TGF	PGF	TGA	PGA	+/–	GP	G	A	Pts	PIM	PP	SH	GW
1965-66	Toronto Marlboros	OHA-Jr.	43	14	25	39	....	....	....	36	....	....	....	....	....	....	....	....	....	....	13	3	6	9	18	....	....	....
1966-67	Toronto Marlboros	OHA-Jr.	39	16	29	45	....	....	....	29	....	....	....	....	....	....	....	....	....	....	17	10	15	25	10	....	....	....
	Toronto Marlboros	Mem-Cup	9	4	*13	17	....	....	....	4	....	....	....	....	....	....	....	....	....	....	....	....	....	....	....	....	....	....
1967-68	Toronto Marlboros	OHA-Jr.	48	36	47	83	....	....	....	64	....	....	....	....	....	....	....	....	....	....	2	0	0	0	0	....	....	....
1968-69	Ottawa Nationals	OHA-Sr.	5	4	8	12	....	....	....	0	....	....	....	....	....	....	....	....	....	....	....	....	....	....	....	....	....	....
	Canada	Nat-Team	STATISTICS NOT AVAILABLE																									
	Canada	WEC-A	10	4	4	8	....	....	....	8	....	....	....	....	....	....	....	....	....	....	....	....	....	....	....	....	....	....
1969-70	**Chicago Black Hawks**	**NHL**	**6**	**0**	**0**	**0**	**0**	**0**	**0**	**0**	**0**	**0**	**0**	**2**	**0.0**	**1**	**1**	**0**	**0**	**0**	....	....	....	....	....	....	....	....
	Dallas Black Hawks	CHL	42	12	28	40	....	....	....	4	....	....	....	....	....	....	....	....	....	....	....	....	....	....	....	....	....	....
1970-71	**Minnesota North Stars**	**NHL**	**8**	**0**	**0**	**0**	**0**	**0**	**0**	**0**	**0**	**0**	**0**	**1**	**0.0**	**0**	**0**	**2**	**0**	**–2**	**1**	**0**	**0**	**0**	**0**	**0**	**0**	**0**
	Dallas Black Hawks	CHL	40	13	34	47	....	....	....	22	....	....	....	....	....	....	....	....	....	....	....	....	....	....	....	....	....	....
1971-72	Cleveland Barons	AHL	65	29	59	88	....	....	....	18	....	....	....	....	....	....	....	....	....	....	6	1	3	4	0	....	....	....
1972-73	New England Whalers	WHA	74	39	61	100	....	....	....	14	....	....	....	....	....	....	....	....	....	....	8	3	7	10	0	....	....	....
1973-74	New England Whalers	WHA	DID NOT PLAY – INJURED																									
1974-75	New England Whalers	WHA	67	15	37	52	....	....	....	12	....	....	....	....	....	....	....	....	....	....	....	....	....	....	....	....	....	....
1975-76	New England Whalers	WHA	4	0	0	0	....	....	....	0	....	....	....	....	....	....	....	....	....	....	....	....	....	....	....	....	....	....
	Calgary Cowboys	WHA	21	5	13	18	....	....	....	4	....	....	....	....	....	....	....	....	....	....	....	....	....	....	....	....	....	....
	NHL Totals		**14**	**0**	**0**	**0**	**0**	**0**	**0**	**0**	**0**	**0**	**0**	**3**	**0.0**	**1**	**1**	**2**	**0**		**1**	**0**	**0**	**0**	**0**	**0**	**0**	**0**
	Other Major League Totals		166	59	111	170	....	....	....	30	....	....	....	....	....	....	....	....	....	....	8	3	7	10	0	....	....	....

Brother of Jack • OHA-Jr. Second All-Star Team (1968) • Won Dudley "Red" Garrett Memorial Award (Top Rookie - AHL) (1972) • Won Lou Kaplan Trophy (WHA Rookie of the Year) (1973)

Traded to **Minnesota** by **Chicago** with Doug Mohns for Danny O'Shea, February 22, 1971. Selected by **Miami-Philadelphia** (WHA) in 1972 WHA General Player Draft, February 12, 1972. WHA rights traded to **New England** (WHA) by **Philadelphia** (WHA) for future considerations, June, 1972. • Missed entire 1973-74 season recovering from knee surgery, September, 1973. Traded to **Calgary** (WHA) by **New England** (WHA) for future considerations, October 25, 1975.

● **CAHAN, Larry** Lawrence Henry "Hank" D – R. 6'2", 222 lbs. b: Fort William, Ont., 12/25/1933 d: 6/25/1992.

Season	Club	League	GP	G	A	Pts	AG	AA	APts	PIM	PP	SH	GW	S	%	TGF	PGF	TGA	PGA	+/–	GP	G	A	Pts	PIM	PP	SH	GW
1949-50	Fort William Hurricanes	TBJHL	STATISTICS NOT AVAILABLE																									
	Fort William Hurricanes	Mem-Cup	12	1	1	2	....	....	....	27	....	....	....	....	....	....	....	....	....	....	....	....	....	....	....	....	....	....
1950-51	Fort William Hurricanes	TBJHL	STATISTICS NOT AVAILABLE																									
1951-52	Fort William Hurricanes	TBJHL	29	6	17	23	....	....	....	82	....	....	....	....	....	....	....	....	....	....	9	2	6	8	32	....	....	....
	Fort William Hurricanes	mem-Cup	12	1	1	2	....	....	....	25	....	....	....	....	....	....	....	....	....	....	....	....	....	....	....	....	....	....
1952-53	Fort William Hurricanes	TBJHL	30	12	17	29	....	....	....	98	....	....	....	....	....	....	....	....	....	....	4	1	2	3	10	....	....	....
1953-54	Pittsburgh Hornets	AHL	70	1	25	26	....	....	....	*179	....	....	....	....	....	....	....	....	....	....	5	1	0	1	2	....	....	....
1954-55	**Toronto Maple Leafs**	**NHL**	**59**	**0**	**6**	**6**	**0**	**7**	**7**	**64**	....	....	....	....	....	....	....	....	....	....	**4**	**0**	**0**	**0**	**0**	**0**	**0**	**0**
1955-56	**Toronto Maple Leafs**	**NHL**	**21**	**0**	**2**	**2**	**0**	**2**	**2**	**46**	....	....	....	....	....	....	....	....	....	....	....	....	....	....	....	....	....	....
	Pittsburgh Hornets	AHL	39	6	9	15	....	....	....	160	....	....	....	....	....	....	....	....	....	....	4	0	1	1	12	....	....	....
1956-57	**New York Rangers**	**NHL**	**61**	**5**	**4**	**9**	**6**	**4**	**10**	**65**	....	....	....	....	....	....	....	....	....	....	**3**	**0**	**0**	**0**	**2**	**0**	**0**	**0**
1957-58	**New York Rangers**	**NHL**	**34**	**1**	**1**	**2**	**1**	**1**	**2**	**20**	....	....	....	....	....	....	....	....	....	....	**5**	**0**	**0**	**0**	**4**	**0**	**0**	**0**
1958-59	**New York Rangers**	**NHL**	**16**	**1**	**0**	**1**	**1**	**0**	**1**	**8**	....	....	....	....	....	....	....	....	....	....	....	....	....	....	....	....	....	....
	Vancouver Canucks	WHL	9	2	6	8	....	....	....	22	....	....	....	....	....	....	....	....	....	....	9	1	2	3	18	....	....	....
	Springfield Indians	AHL	33	3	11	14	....	....	....	75	....	....	....	....	....	....	....	....	....	....	....	....	....	....	....	....	....	....
	Buffalo Bisons	AHL	....	....	....	....	....	....	....	....	....	....	....	....	....	....	....	....	....	....	3	0	0	0	0	....	....	....
1959-60	Vancouver Canucks	WHL	70	11	22	33	....	....	....	116	....	....	....	....	....	....	....	....	....	....	11	0	4	4	*19	....	....	....
1960-61	Vancouver Canucks	WHL	70	13	15	28	....	....	....	81	....	....	....	....	....	....	....	....	....	....	9	2	2	4	12	....	....	....
1961-62	**New York Rangers**	**NHL**	**57**	**2**	**7**	**9**	**2**	**7**	**9**	**85**	....	....	....	....	....	....	....	....	....	....	**6**	**0**	**0**	**0**	**10**	**0**	**0**	**0**
1962-63	**New York Rangers**	**NHL**	**56**	**6**	**14**	**20**	**7**	**14**	**21**	**47**	....	....	....	....	....	....	....	....	....	....	....	....	....	....	....	....	....	....
1963-64	**New York Rangers**	**NHL**	**53**	**4**	**8**	**12**	**5**	**8**	**13**	**80**	....	....	....	....	....	....	....	....	....	....	....	....	....	....	....	....	....	....
	Baltimore Clippers	AHL	12	2	8	10	....	....	....	16	....	....	....	....	....	....	....	....	....	....	....	....	....	....	....	....	....	....
1964-65	**New York Rangers**	**NHL**	**26**	**0**	**5**	**5**	**0**	**5**	**5**	**32**	....	....	....	....	....	....	....	....	....	....	....	....	....	....	....	....	....	....
	Baltimore Clippers	AHL	16	1	6	7	....	....	....	34	....	....	....	....	....	....	....	....	....	....	....	....	....	....	....	....	....	....
	Vancouver Canucks	WHL	26	2	15	17	....	....	....	67	....	....	....	....	....	....	....	....	....	....	5	0	3	3	28	....	....	....
1965-66	Vancouver Canucks	WHL	72	14	34	48	....	....	....	156	....	....	....	....	....	....	....	....	....	....	7	4	12	16	4	....	....	....
1966-67	Vancouver Canucks	WHL	72	18	36	54	....	....	....	88	....	....	....	....	....	....	....	....	....	....	8	1	4	5	6	....	....	....
1967-68	**Oakland Seals**	**NHL**	**74**	**9**	**15**	**24**	**10**	**15**	**25**	**80**	**5**	**0**	**1**	**161**	**5.6**	**80**	**21**	**112**	**24**	**–29**	....	....	....	....	....	....	....	....
1968-69	**Los Angeles Kings**	**NHL**	**72**	**3**	**11**	**14**	**3**	**10**	**13**	**76**	**0**	**0**	**1**	**129**	**2.3**	**59**	**5**	**94**	**20**	**–20**	**11**	**1**	**1**	**2**	**22**	**0**	**1**	**0**
1969-70	**Los Angeles Kings**	**NHL**	**70**	**4**	**8**	**12**	**4**	**7**	**11**	**52**	**2**	**0**	**0**	**95**	**4.2**	**56**	**3**	**123**	**45**	**–25**	....	....	....	....	....	....	....	....
1970-71	**Los Angeles Kings**	**NHL**	**67**	**3**	**11**	**14**	**3**	**9**	**12**	**45**	**1**	**0**	**0**	**113**	**2.7**	**60**	**4**	**103**	**18**	**–29**	....	....	....	....	....	....	....	....

			REGULAR SEASON																		PLAYOFFS							
Season	**Club**	**League**	**GP**	**G**	**A**	**Pts**	**AG**	**AA**	**APts**	**PIM**	**PP**	**SH**	**GW**	**S**	**%**	**TGF**	**PGF**	**TGA**	**PGA**	**+/–**	**GP**	**G**	**A**	**Pts**	**PIM**	**PP**	**SH**	**GW**
1971-72	Seattle Totems	WHL	50	4	12	16	....	....	....	44	....	....	....	....	....	....	....	....	....	....	....	....	....	....	....	....	....	....
1972-73	Chicago Cougars	WHA	75	1	10	11	....	....	....	44	....	....	....	....	....	....	....	....	....	....	....	....	....	....	....	....	....	....
1973-74	Chicago Cougars	WHA	3	0	0	0	....	....	....	2	....	....	....	....	....	....	....	....	....	....	....	....	....	....	....	....	....	....
	NHL Totals		**666**	**38**	**92**	**130**	**42**	**89**	**131**	**700**	....	....	....	....	....	....	....	....	....		**29**	**1**	**1**	**2**	**38**	....	....	....
	Other Major League Totals		78	1	10	11	....	....	....	46	....	....	....	....	....	....	....	....	....	....	....	....	....	....	....	....	....	....

WHL Second All-Star Team (1960, 1966) • WHL First All-Star Team (1961, 1967) • Won Hal Laycoe Cup (WHL Top Defenseman) (1967)

Claimed by**NY Rangers** from **Toronto** in Intra-League Draft, September, 1956. Loaned to **Vancouver** (WHL) by **NY Rangers** for the loan of Milan Marcetta, January 10, 1959. Claimed by **Oakland** from **NY Rangers** in Expansion Draft, June 6, 1967. Claimed by **Montreal** from **Oakland** in Intra-League Draft, June 12, 1968. Traded to **LA Kings** by **Montreal** for Brian D. Smith and Yves Locas, July 1, 1968. Selected by **LA Sharks** (WHA) in 1972 WHA General Player Draft, February 12, 1972. WHA rights traded to **Chicago** (WHA) by **LA Sharks** (WHA) with Bob Liddington and Bob Whitlock for Bill Young and future considerations, July, 1972.

• CAIRNS, Don

LW – L. 6′1″, 195 lbs. b: Calgary, Alta., 10/8/1955. Kansas City's 2nd, 20th overall, in 1975.

Season	Club	League	GP	G	A	Pts	AG	AA	APts	PIM	PP	SH	GW	S	%	TGF	PGF	TGA	PGA	+/–	GP	G	A	Pts	PIM	PP	SH	GW
1973-74	Calgary Canucks	AJHL	54	30	31	61	....	....	....	180	....	....	....	....	....	....	....	....	....	....	....	....	....	....	....	....	....	....
1974-75	Victoria Cougars	WCJHL	68	32	37	69	....	....	....	214	....	....	....	....	....	....	....	....	....	....	12	5	4	9	10	....	....	....
1975-76	**Kansas City Scouts**	**NHL**	**7**	**0**	**0**	**0**	**0**	**0**	**0**	**0**	**0**	**0**	**0**	**2**	**0.0**	**0**	**0**	**1**	**0**	**–1**	....	....	....	....	....	....	....	....
	Springfield Indians	AHL	15	4	2	6	....	....	....	13	....	....	....	....	....	....	....	....	....	....	....	....	....	....	....	....	....	....
	Port Huron Flags	IHL	18	6	8	14	....	....	....	13	....	....	....	....	....	....	....	....	....	....	15	3	8	11	19	....	....	....
1976-77	**Colorado Rockies**	**NHL**	**2**	**0**	**1**	**1**	**0**	**1**	**1**	**2**	**0**	**0**	**0**	**3**	**0.0**	**1**	**0**	**0**	**0**	**1**	....	....	....	....	....	....	....	....
	Flint Generals	IHL	10	3	5	8	....	....	....	13	....	....	....	....	....	....	....	....	....	....	....	....	....	....	....	....	....	....
	Oklahoma City Blazers	CHL	21	1	2	3	....	....	....	34	....	....	....	....	....	....	....	....	....	....	....	....	....	....	....	....	....	....
1977-78	Phoenix Roadrunners	CHL	9	1	3	4	....	....	....	2	....	....	....	....	....	....	....	....	....	....	....	....	....	....	....	....	....	....
	NHL Totals		**9**	**0**	**1**	**1**	**0**	**1**	**1**	**2**	**0**	**0**	**0**	**5**	**0.0**	**1**	**0**	**1**	**0**		....	....	....	....	....	....	....	....

Transferred to **Colorado** after **Kansas City** franchise relocated, July 15, 1976.

• CAIRNS, Eric

D – L. 6′6″, 230 lbs. b: Oakville, Ont., 6/27/1974. NY Rangers' 3rd, 72nd overall, in 1992.

Season	Club	League	GP	G	A	Pts	AG	AA	APts	PIM	PP	SH	GW	S	%	TGF	PGF	TGA	PGA	+/–	GP	G	A	Pts	PIM	PP	SH	GW
1990-91	Burlington Cougars	OJHL-B	37	5	16	21	....	....	....	120	....	....	....	....	....	....	....	....	....	....	....	....	....	....	....	....	....	....
1991-92	Detroit Ambassadors	OHL	64	1	11	12	....	....	....	237	....	....	....	....	....	....	....	....	....	....	7	0	0	0	31	....	....	....
1992-93	Detroit Jr. Red Wings	OHL	64	3	13	16	....	....	....	194	....	....	....	....	....	....	....	....	....	....	15	0	3	3	24	....	....	....
1993-94	Detroit Jr. Red Wings	OHL	59	7	35	42	....	....	....	204	....	....	....	....	....	....	....	....	....	....	17	0	4	4	46	....	....	....
1994-95	Birmingham Bulls	ECHL	11	1	3	4	....	....	....	49	....	....	....	....	....	....	....	....	....	....	....	....	....	....	....	....	....	....
	Binghamton Rangers	AHL	27	0	3	3	....	....	....	134	....	....	....	....	....	....	....	....	....	....	9	1	1	2	28	....	....	....
1995-96	Binghamton Rangers	AHL	46	1	13	14	....	....	....	192	....	....	....	....	....	....	....	....	....	....	4	0	0	0	37	....	....	....
	Charlotte Checkers	ECHL	6	0	1	1	....	....	....	34	....	....	....	....	....	....	....	....	....	....	....	....	....	....	....	....	....	....
1996-97	**New York Rangers**	**NHL**	**40**	**0**	**1**	**1**	**0**	**1**	**1**	**147**	**0**	**0**	**0**	**17**	**0.0**	**9**	**1**	**15**	**0**	**–7**	**3**	**0**	**0**	**0**	**0**	**0**	**0**	**0**
	Binghamton Rangers	AHL	10	1	1	2	....	....	....	96	....	....	....	....	....	....	....	....	....	....	....	....	....	....	....	....	....	....
1997-98	**New York Rangers**	**NHL**	**39**	**0**	**3**	**3**	**0**	**3**	**3**	**92**	**0**	**0**	**0**	**17**	**0.0**	**13**	**0**	**18**	**2**	**–3**	....	....	....	....	....	....	....	....
	Hartford Wolf Pack	AHL	7	1	2	3	....	....	....	43	....	....	....	....	....	....	....	....	....	....	....	....	....	....	....	....	....	....
1998-99	Hartford Wolf Pack	AHL	11	0	2	2	....	....	....	49	....	....	....	....	....	....	....	....	....	....	....	....	....	....	....	....	....	....
	New York Islanders	**NHL**	**9**	**0**	**3**	**3**	**0**	**3**	**3**	**23**	**0**	**0**	**0**	**2**	**0.0**	**6**	**0**	**6**	**1**	**1**	....	....	....	....	....	....	....	....
	Lowell Lock Monsters	AHL	24	0	0	0	....	....	....	91	....	....	....	....	....	....	....	....	....	....	3	1	0	1	32	....	....	....
99-2000	**New York Islanders**	**NHL**	**67**	**2**	**7**	**9**	**2**	**6**	**8**	**196**	**0**	**0**	**0**	**55**	**3.6**	**37**	**1**	**70**	**29**	**–5**	....	....	....	....	....	....	....	....
	Providence Bruins	AHL	4	1	1	2	....	....	....	14	....	....	....	....	....	....	....	....	....	....	....	....	....	....	....	....	....	....
	NHL Totals		**155**	**2**	**14**	**16**	**2**	**13**	**15**	**458**	**0**	**0**	**0**	**91**	**2.2**	**65**	**2**	**109**	**32**		**3**	**0**	**0**	**0**	**0**	**0**	**0**	**0**

Claimed on waivers by **NY Islanders** from **NY Rangers**, December 22, 1998. Loaned to **Providence** (AHL) by **NY Islanders**, October 6, 1999 and recalled october 13, 1999.

• CALDER, Eric

D – R. 6′1″, 180 lbs. b: Kitchener, Ont., 7/26/1963. Washington's 2nd, 45th overall, in 1981.

Season	Club	League	GP	G	A	Pts	AG	AA	APts	PIM	PP	SH	GW	S	%	TGF	PGF	TGA	PGA	+/–	GP	G	A	Pts	PIM	PP	SH	GW
1979-80	Waterloo Siskins	OHA-B	42	13	36	49	....	....	....	33	....	....	....	....	....	....	....	....	....	....	....	....	....	....	....	....	....	....
1980-81	Waterloo Siskins	OJHL	4	2	0	2	....	....	....	13	....	....	....	....	....	....	....	....	....	....	....	....	....	....	....	....	....	....
	Cornwall Royals	QMJHL	66	9	34	43	....	....	....	39	....	....	....	....	....	....	....	....	....	....	14	0	6	6	25	....	....	....
	Canada	WJC-A	5	1	0	1	....	....	....	4	....	....	....	....	....	....	....	....	....	....	....	....	....	....	....	....	....	....
	Cornwall Royals	Mem-Cup	5	3	1	4	....	....	....	8	....	....	....	....	....	....	....	....	....	....	....	....	....	....	....	....	....	....
1981-82	Cornwall Royals	OHL	65	12	36	48	....	....	....	95	....	....	....	....	....	....	....	....	....	....	....	....	....	....	....	....	....	....
	Washington Capitals	**NHL**	**1**	**0**	**0**	**0**	**0**	**0**	**0**	**0**	**0**	**0**	**0**	**0**	**0.0**	**0**	**0**	**0**	**0**	**0**	....	....	....	....	....	....	....	....
1982-83	Cornwall Royals	OHL	66	5	30	35	....	....	....	72	....	....	....	....	....	....	....	....	....	....	8	0	5	5	6	....	....	....
	Washington Capitals	**NHL**	**1**	**0**	**0**	**0**	**0**	**0**	**0**	**0**	**0**	**0**	**0**	**0**	**0.0**	**0**	**0**	**0**	**0**	**0**	....	....	....	....	....	....	....	....
1983-84	Fort Wayne Komets	IHL	3	0	2	2	....	....	....	0	....	....	....	....	....	....	....	....	....	....	....	....	....	....	....	....	....	....
	Hershey Bears	AHL	68	2	6	8	....	....	....	50	....	....	....	....	....	....	....	....	....	....	....	....	....	....	....	....	....	....
1984-85	Sir Wilfred Laurier University	OUAA	REINSTATED AS AN AMATEUR																									
1985-86	Sir Wilfred Laurier University	OUAA	24	5	21	26	....	....	....	41	....	....	....	....	....	....	....	....	....	....	....	....	....	....	....	....	....	....
1986-87	Sir Wilfred Laurier University	OUAA	26	5	26	31	....	....	....	36	....	....	....	....	....	....	....	....	....	....	....	....	....	....	....	....	....	....
1987-88	Sir Wilfred Laurier University	OUAA	26	10	26	36	....	....	....	28	....	....	....	....	....	....	....	....	....	....	....	....	....	....	....	....	....	....
1988-89	TSV Peissenberg	Germany-3	25	14	27	41	....	....	....	56	....	....	....	....	....	....	....	....	....	....	12	5	6	11	24	....	....	....
1989-90	HC Rouen	France	8	0	4	4	....	....	....	16	....	....	....	....	....	....	....	....	....	....	....	....	....	....	....	....	....	....
1990-91	HC Chamonix	France-2	20	9	6	15	....	....	....	40	....	....	....	....	....	....	....	....	....	....	2	1	0	1	2	....	....	....
1991-92	HC Rouen	France	19	4	5	9	....	....	....	18	....	....	....	....	....	....	....	....	....	....	....	....	....	....	....	....	....	....
1992-93	HC Rouen	France	33	12	18	30	....	....	....	52	....	....	....	....	....	....	....	....	....	....	....	....	....	....	....	....	....	....
1993-94	HC Rouen	France	26	7	21	28	....	....	....	24	....	....	....	....	....	....	....	....	....	....	5	1	5	6	6	....	....	....
1994-95	HC Brest	France	28	4	6	10	....	....	....	42	....	....	....	....	....	....	....	....	....	....	9	0	3	3	27	....	....	....
1995-96	HC Brest	France	28	0	7	7	....	....	....	61	....	....	....	....	....	....	....	....	....	....	12	3	3	6	36	....	....	....
1996-97	Schwennigen Wild Wings	Germany	4	1	1	2	....	....	....	0	....	....	....	....	....	....	....	....	....	....	....	....	....	....	....	....	....	....
	Manchester Storm	BH-Cup	1	0	0	0	....	....	....	0	....	....	....	....	....	....	....	....	....	....	....	....	....	....	....	....	....	....
	Manchester Storm	Britain	39	4	6	10	....	....	....	62	....	....	....	....	....	....	....	....	....	....	....	....	....	....	....	....	....	....
	Manchester Storm	EuroHL	4	0	0	0	....	....	....	0	....	....	....	....	....	....	....	....	....	....	....	....	....	....	....	....	....	....
1997-98			OUT OF HOCKEY – RETIRED																									
1998-2000	University of Waterloo	OUAA	DID NOT PLAY – ASSISTANT COACH																									
	NHL Totals		**2**	**0**	**0**	**0**	**0**	**0**	**0**	**0**	**0**	**0**	**0**	**0**	**0.0**	**0**	**0**	**0**	**0**		....	....	....	....	....	....	....	....

OUAA First All-Star Team (1986, 1987, 1988) • CIAU All-Canadian (1988)

• CALDER, Kyle

C – L. 5′11″, 180 lbs. b: Mannville, Alta., 1/5/1979. Chicago's 7th, 130th overall, in 1997.

Season	Club	League	GP	G	A	Pts	AG	AA	APts	PIM	PP	SH	GW	S	%	TGF	PGF	TGA	PGA	+/–	GP	G	A	Pts	PIM	PP	SH	GW
1994-95	Leduc Oil Barons	AAHA	27	25	32	57	....	....	....	22	....	....	....	....	....	....	....	....	....	....	....	....	....	....	....	....	....	....
1995-96	Regina Pats	WHL	27	1	7	8	....	....	....	10	....	....	....	....	....	....	....	....	....	....	11	0	0	0	0	....	....	....
1996-97	Regina Pats	WHL	62	25	34	59	....	....	....	17	....	....	....	....	....	....	....	....	....	....	5	3	0	3	6	....	....	....
1997-98	Regina Pats	WHL	62	27	50	77	....	....	....	58	....	....	....	....	....	....	....	....	....	....	2	0	1	1	0	....	....	....
1998-99	Regina Pats	WHL	34	23	28	51	....	....	....	29	....	....	....	....	....	....	....	....	....	....	....	....	....	....	....	....	....	....
	Kamloops Blazers	WHL	27	19	18	37	....	....	....	30	....	....	....	....	....	....	....	....	....	....	15	6	10	16	6	....	....	....
	Canada	WJC-A	7	2	6	8	....	....	....	2	....	....	....	....	....	....	....	....	....	....	....	....	....	....	....	....	....	....
99-2000	**Chicago Blackhawks**	**NHL**	**8**	**1**	**1**	**2**	**1**	**1**	**2**	**2**	**0**	**0**	**0**	**5**	**20.0**	**4**	**0**	**7**	**0**	**–3**	....	....	....	....	....	....	....	....
	Cleveland Lumberjacks	IHL	74	14	22	36	....	....	....	43	....	....	....	....	....	....	....	....	....	....	9	2	2	4	14	....	....	....
	NHL Totals		**8**	**1**	**1**	**2**	**1**	**1**	**2**	**2**	**0**	**0**	**0**	**5**	**20.0**	**4**	**0**	**7**	**0**		....	....	....	....	....	....	....	....

• CALLANDER, Drew

Leonard Andrew C/RW – R. 6′2″, 185 lbs. b: Regina, Sask., 8/17/1956. Philadelphia's 2nd, 35th overall, in 1976.

Season	Club	League	GP	G	A	Pts	AG	AA	APts	PIM	PP	SH	GW	S	%	TGF	PGF	TGA	PGA	+/–	GP	G	A	Pts	PIM	PP	SH	GW
1972-73	Regina Pat Blues	SJHL	STATISTICS NOT AVAILABLE																									
1973-74	Regina Pats	WCJHL	68	9	7	16	....	....	....	7	....	....	....	....	....	....	....	....	....	....	16	0	0	0	0	....	....	....
1974-75	Regina Pats	WCJHL	51	17	15	32	....	....	....	36	....	....	....	....	....	....	....	....	....	....	11	9	10	19	16	....	....	....
1975-76	Regina Pats	WCJHL	72	49	56	105	....	....	....	64	....	....	....	....	....	....	....	....	....	....	6	4	6	10	16	....	....	....
1976-77	**Philadelphia Flyers**	**NHL**	**2**	**1**	**0**	**1**	**1**	**0**	**1**	**0**	**0**	**0**	**0**	**1**	**100.0**	**1**	**0**	**0**	**0**	**1**	....	....	....	....	....	....	....	....
	Springfield Indians	AHL	59	18	22	40	....	....	....	41	....	....	....	....	....	....	....	....	....	....	....	....	....	....	....	....	....	....

			REGULAR SEASON																		PLAYOFFS							
Season	Club	League	GP	G	A	Pts	AG	AA	APts	PIM	PP	SH	GW	S	%	TGF	PGF	TGA	PGA	+/–	GP	G	A	Pts	PIM	PP	SH	GW
1977-78	**Philadelphia Flyers**	**NHL**	1	0	0	0	0	0	0	0	0	0	0	0	0.0	0	0	0	0	0	....	....	....	....	....	....	....	....
	Maine Mariners	AHL	78	40	42	82	....	....	....	72	....	....	....	....	....	....	....	....	....	....	12	6	4	10	30	....	....	....
1978-79	**Philadelphia Flyers**	**NHL**	15	2	1	3	2	1	3	5	0	0	0	22	9.1	7	1	7	0	–1	....	....	....	....	....	....	....	....
	Maine Mariners	AHL	9	1	4	5	....	....	....	9	....	....	....	....	....	....	....	....	....	....	....	....	....	....	....	....	....	....
	Vancouver Canucks	**NHL**	17	2	0	2	2	0	2	2	0	0	0	19	10.5	3	0	12	0	–9	....	....	....	....	....	....	....	....
	Dallas Black Hawks	CHL	26	12	10	22	....	....	....	23	....	....	....	....	....	....	....	....	....	....	9	4	6	10	12	....	....	....
1979-80	**Vancouver Canucks**	**NHL**	4	1	1	2	1	1	2	0	0	0	0	3	33.3	2	0	4	0	–2	....	....	....	....	....	....	....	....
	Dallas Black Hawks	CHL	33	15	10	25	....	....	....	20	....	....	....	....	....	....	....	....	....	....	....	....	....	....	....	....	....	....
1980-81	Dallas Black Hawks	CHL	77	43	29	72	....	....	....	51	....	....	....	....	....	....	....	....	....	....	6	0	2	2	2	....	....	....
1981-82	Dallas Black Hawks	CHL	80	40	47	87	....	....	....	79	....	....	....	....	....	....	....	....	....	....	16	8	15	23	34	....	....	....
1982-83	EV Duisburg	Germany-2	40	55	58	113	....	....	....	....	....	....	....	....	....	....	....	....	....	....	....	....	....	....	....	....	....	....
1983-84	Kolner EC	Germany	42	19	7	26	....	....	....	44	....	....	....	....	....	....	....	....	....	....	....	....	....	....	....	....	....	....
1984-85	Kolner EC	Germany	38	16	20	36	....	....	....	36	....	....	....	....	....	....	....	....	....	....	7	3	8	11	10	....	....	....
1985-86	SV Bayreuth	Germany	36	12	17	29	....	....	....	22	....	....	....	....	....	....	....	....	....	....	17	15	13	28	31	....	....	....
1986-87	Muskegon Lumberjacks	IHL	80	34	52	86	....	....	....	92	....	....	....	....	....	....	....	....	....	....	10	5	5	10	0	....	....	....
	NHL Totals		**39**	**6**	**2**	**8**	**6**	**2**	**8**	**7**	**0**	**0**	**0**	**45**	**13.3**	**13**	**1**	**23**	**0**		....	....	....	....	....	....	....	....

• Brother of Jock

Traded to **Vancouver** by **Philadelphia** with Kevin McCarthy for Dennis Ververgaert, December 29, 1978.

• CALLANDER, Jock William Darren RW – R. 6'1", 188 lbs. b: Regina, Sask., 4/23/1961.

Season	Club	League	GP	G	A	Pts	AG	AA	APts	PIM	PP	SH	GW	S	%	TGF	PGF	TGA	PGA	+/–	GP	G	A	Pts	PIM	PP	SH	GW
1978-79	Regina Blues	SJHL	42	44	42	86	....	....	....	24	....	....	....	....	....	....	....	....	....	....	....	....	....	....	....	....	....	....
	Regina Pats	WHL	19	3	2	5	....	....	....	0	....	....	....	....	....	....	....	....	....	....	....	....	....	....	....	....	....	....
1979-80	Regina Pats	WHL	39	9	11	20	....	....	....	25	....	....	....	....	....	....	....	....	....	....	18	8	5	13	0	....	....	....
	Regina Pats	Mem-Cup	4	1	2	3	....	....	....	0	....	....	....	....	....	....	....	....	....	....	....	....	....	....	....	....	....	....
1980-81	Regina Pats	WHL	72	67	86	153	....	....	....	37	....	....	....	....	....	....	....	....	....	....	11	6	7	13	14	....	....	....
1981-82	Regina Pats	WHL	71	79	111	*190	....	....	....	59	....	....	....	....	....	....	....	....	....	....	20	13	*26	39	37	....	....	....
1982-83	Salt Lake Golden Eagles	CHL	68	20	27	47	....	....	....	26	....	....	....	....	....	....	....	....	....	....	6	0	1	1	9	....	....	....
1983-84	Montana Magic	CHL	72	27	32	59	....	....	....	69	....	....	....	....	....	....	....	....	....	....	....	....	....	....	....	....	....	....
	Toledo Goaldiggers	IHL	2	0	0	0	....	....	....	0	....	....	....	....	....	....	....	....	....	....	....	....	....	....	....	....	....	....
1984-85	Muskegon Mohawks	IHL	82	39	68	107	....	....	....	86	....	....	....	....	....	....	....	....	....	....	17	8	*13	*21	33	....	....	....
1985-86	Muskegon Lumberjacks	IHL	82	39	72	111	....	....	....	121	....	....	....	....	....	....	....	....	....	....	14	*12	11	*23	12	....	....	....
1986-87	Muskegon Lumberjacks	IHL	82	54	82	*136	....	....	....	110	....	....	....	....	....	....	....	....	....	....	15	13	7	20	23	....	....	....
1987-88	**Pittsburgh Penguins**	**NHL**	41	11	16	27	9	11	20	45	4	0	1	59	18.6	57	29	42	1	–13	....	....	....	....	....	....	....	....
	Muskegon Lumberjacks	IHL	31	20	36	56	....	....	....	49	....	....	....	....	....	....	....	....	....	....	6	2	3	5	25	....	....	....
1988-89	**Pittsburgh Penguins**	**NHL**	30	6	5	11	5	4	9	20	2	0	0	35	17.1	24	8	19	0	–3	10	2	5	7	10	0	0	0
	Muskegon Lumberjacks	IHL	48	25	39	64	....	....	....	40	....	....	....	....	....	....	....	....	....	....	7	5	5	10	30	....	....	....
1989-90	**Pittsburgh Penguins**	**NHL**	30	4	7	11	3	5	8	49	0	0	1	22	18.2	20	1	19	0	0	....	....	....	....	....	....	....	....
	Muskegon Lumberjacks	IHL	46	29	49	78	....	....	....	118	....	....	....	....	....	....	....	....	....	....	15	6	*14	20	54	....	....	....
1990-91	Muskegon Lumberjacks	IHL	30	14	20	34	....	....	....	102	....	....	....	....	....	....	....	....	....	....	....	....	....	....	....	....	....	....
1991-92	Muskegon Lumberjacks	IHL	81	42	70	112	....	....	....	160	....	....	....	....	....	....	....	....	....	....	10	4	10	14	13	....	....	....
♦	**Pittsburgh Penguins**	**NHL**	....	....	....	....	....	....	....	....	....	....	....	....	....	....	....	....	....	....	12	1	3	4	2	0	0	0
1992-93	**Tampa Bay Lightning**	**NHL**	8	1	1	2	1	1	2	2	0	0	0	12	8.3	2	0	7	0	–5	....	....	....	....	....	....	....	....
	Atlanta Knights	IHL	69	34	50	84	....	....	....	172	....	....	....	....	....	....	....	....	....	....	9	*7	5	12	25	....	....	....
1993-94	Cleveland Lumberjacks	IHL	81	31	70	101	....	....	....	126	....	....	....	....	....	....	....	....	....	....	....	....	....	....	....	....	....	....
1994-95	Cleveland Lumberjacks	IHL	61	24	36	60	....	....	....	90	....	....	....	....	....	....	....	....	....	....	4	2	2	4	6	....	....	....
1995-96	Cleveland Lumberjacks	IHL	81	42	53	95	....	....	....	150	....	....	....	....	....	....	....	....	....	....	3	1	0	1	8	....	....	....
1996-97	Cleveland Lumberjacks	IHL	61	20	34	54	....	....	....	56	....	....	....	....	....	....	....	....	....	....	14	7	6	13	10	....	....	....
1997-98	Cleveland Lumberjacks	IHL	72	20	33	53	....	....	....	105	....	....	....	....	....	....	....	....	....	....	10	5	6	11	6	....	....	....
1998-99	Cleveland Lumberjacks	IHL	81	28	26	54	....	....	....	121	....	....	....	....	....	....	....	....	....	....	....	....	....	....	....	....	....	....
99-2000	Cleveland Lumberjacks	IHL	64	16	27	43	....	....	....	83	....	....	....	....	....	....	....	....	....	....	9	1	5	6	6	....	....	....
	NHL Totals		**109**	**22**	**29**	**51**	**18**	**21**	**39**	**116**	**6**	**0**	**2**	**128**	**17.2**	**103**	**38**	**87**	**1**		**22**	**3**	**8**	**11**	**12**	**0**	**0**	**0**

• Brother of Drew • IHL First All-Star Team (1987, 1992) • Won Leo P. Lamoureux Memorial Trophy (Top Scorer - IHL) (Tied with Jeff Pyle) (1987) • Won James Gatschene Memorial Trophy (MVP - IHL) (Tied with Jeff Pyle) (1987) • Became IHL's All-Time leading scorer (1383 points) in game vs. Cincinnati (IHL), February 23, 2000.

Signed as a free agent by **St. Louis**, September 28, 1981. Signed as a free agent by **Pittsburgh**, July 31, 1987. Signed as a free agent by **Tampa Bay**, July 29, 1992.

• CALLIGHEN, Brett Brett Charles "Key" C – L. 5'11", 182 lbs. b: Toronto, Ont., 5/15/1953.

Season	Club	League	GP	G	A	Pts	AG	AA	APts	PIM	PP	SH	GW	S	%	TGF	PGF	TGA	PGA	+/–	GP	G	A	Pts	PIM	PP	SH	GW
1973-74	Centennial College	OCAA	STATISTICS NOT AVAILABLE																									
1974-75	Dallas Black Hawks	CHL	5	0	1	1	....	....	....	2	....	....	....	....	....	....	....	....	....	....	....	....	....	....	....	....	....	....
	Flint Generals	IHL	50	6	20	26	....	....	....	80	....	....	....	....	....	....	....	....	....	....	....	....	....	....	....	....	....	....
	Kalamazoo Wings	IHL	21	3	11	14	....	....	....	40	....	....	....	....	....	....	....	....	....	....	....	....	....	....	....	....	....	....
1975-76	Kalamazoo Wings	IHL	72	25	33	58	....	....	....	104	....	....	....	....	....	....	....	....	....	....	6	2	2	4	21	....	....	....
1976-77	New England Whalers	WHA	33	6	10	16	....	....	....	41	....	....	....	....	....	....	....	....	....	....	....	....	....	....	....	....	....	....
	Rhode Island Reds	AHL	22	4	8	12	....	....	....	32	....	....	....	....	....	....	....	....	....	....	....	....	....	....	....	....	....	....
	Edmonton Oilers	WHA	29	9	16	25	....	....	....	48	....	....	....	....	....	....	....	....	....	....	5	4	1	5	7	....	....	....
1977-78	Edmonton Oilers	WHA	80	20	30	50	....	....	....	112	....	....	....	....	....	....	....	....	....	....	5	0	2	2	16	....	....	....
1978-79	Edmonton Oilers	WHA	71	31	39	70	....	....	....	79	....	....	....	....	....	....	....	....	....	....	13	5	10	15	15	....	....	....
1979-80	**Edmonton Oilers**	**NHL**	59	23	35	58	20	26	46	72	7	0	0	159	14.5	94	34	66	5	–1	3	0	2	2	0	0	0	0
1980-81	**Edmonton Oilers**	**NHL**	55	25	35	60	19	23	42	32	6	0	1	127	19.7	96	25	61	3	13	9	4	4	8	6	1	0	1
1981-82	**Edmonton Oilers**	**NHL**	46	8	19	27	6	13	19	28	3	0	1	87	9.2	54	9	30	1	16	2	0	0	0	2	0	0	0
1982-83	SC Herisau	Switz-2	STATISTICS NOT AVAILABLE																									
1983-84	WEV Wien	Austria	23	26	13	39	....	....	....	38	....	....	....	....	....	....	....	....	....	....	....	....	....	....	....	....	....	....
1984-85			OUT OF HOCKEY – RETIRED																									
1985-86	Adirondack Red Wings	AHL	11	0	2	2	....	....	....	6	....	....	....	....	....	....	....	....	....	....	....	....	....	....	....	....	....	....
	NHL Totals		**160**	**56**	**89**	**145**	**45**	**62**	**107**	**132**	**16**	**0**	**2**	**373**	**15.0**	**244**	**68**	**157**	**9**		**14**	**4**	**6**	**10**	**8**	**1**	**0**	**1**
	Other Major League Totals		213	66	95	161	....	....	....	280	....	....	....	....	....	....	....	....	....	....	23	9	13	22	38	....	....	....

Signed as a free agent by **New England** (WHA), October, 1976. Traded to **Edmonton** (WHA) by **New England** (WHA) with Ron Busniuk for Mike Antonovich and Bill Butters, February, 1977. Traded to **New England** (WHA) by **Edmonton** (WHA) for future considerations, June, 1977. Traded to **Edmonton** (WHA) by **New England** (WHA) with Dave Dryden and future considerations for Jean-Louis Levasseur, September, 1977. NHL rights retained by **Edmonton** prior to Expansion Draft, June 9, 1979. • Missed remainder of 1979-80 regular season and start of 1980-81 season recovering from an eye injury suffered in game vs. Boston, February 24, 1980. Signed as a free agent by **Adirondack** (AHL), January 11, 1986.

• CALOUN, Jan RW – R. 5'10", 190 lbs. b: Usti-Nad-Labem, Czech., 12/20/1972. San Jose's 4th, 75th overall, in 1992.

Season	Club	League	GP	G	A	Pts	AG	AA	APts	PIM	PP	SH	GW	S	%	TGF	PGF	TGA	PGA	+/–	GP	G	A	Pts	PIM	PP	SH	GW
1989-90	CHZ Litvinov	Czech-Jr.	STATISTICS NOT AVAILABLE																									
	Czechoslovakia	EJC-A	6	4	3	7	....	....	....	16	....	....	....	....	....	....	....	....	....	....	....	....	....	....	....	....	....	....
1990-91	CHZ Litvinov	Czech.	50	28	19	47	....	....	....	12	....	....	....	....	....	....	....	....	....	....	....	....	....	....	....	....	....	....
1991-92	CHZ Litvinov	Czech.	46	39	13	52	....	....	....	24	....	....	....	....	....	....	....	....	....	....	....	....	....	....	....	....	....	....
	Czechoslovakia	WJC-A	7	8	1	9	....	....	....	20	....	....	....	....	....	....	....	....	....	....	....	....	....	....	....	....	....	....
1992-93	CHZ Litvinov	Czech.	47	45	22	67	....	....	....	....	....	....	....	....	....	....	....	....	....	....	....	....	....	....	....	....	....	....
	Czech-Republic	WC-A	8	0	2	2	....	....	....	8	....	....	....	....	....	....	....	....	....	....	....	....	....	....	....	....	....	....
1993-94	CHZ Chemopetrol Litvinov	Czech-Rep	38	25	17	42	....	....	....	....	....	....	....	....	....	....	....	....	....	....	4	2	2	4	....	....	....	....
1994-95	Kansas City Blades	IHL	76	34	39	73	....	....	....	50	....	....	....	....	....	....	....	....	....	....	21	13	10	23	18	....	....	....
1995-96	**San Jose Sharks**	**NHL**	11	8	3	11	8	2	10	0	2	0	0	20	40.0	13	3	6	0	4	....	....	....	....	....	....	....	....
	Kansas City Blades	IHL	61	38	30	68	....	....	....	58	....	....	....	....	....	....	....	....	....	....	5	0	1	1	6	....	....	....
1996-97	**San Jose Sharks**	**NHL**	2	0	0	0	0	0	0	0	0	0	0	3	0.0	0	0	2	0	–2	....	....	....	....	....	....	....	....
	Kentucky Thoroughblades	AHL	66	43	43	86	....	....	....	68	....	....	....	....	....	....	....	....	....	....	4	0	1	1	4	....	....	....
1997-98	HIFK Helsinki	Finland	41	22	26	48	....	....	....	73	....	....	....	....	....	....	....	....	....	....	9	6	*11	*17	6	....	....	....
	Czech-Republic	Olympics	3	0	0	0	....	....	....	6	....	....	....	....	....	....	....	....	....	....	....	....	....	....	....	....	....	....

Season	Club	League	GP	G	A	Pts	AG	AA	APts	PIM	PP	SH	GW	S	%	TGF	PGF	TGA	PGA	+/-	GP	G	A	Pts	PIM	PP	SH	GW
			REGULAR SEASON																		PLAYOFFS							
1998-99	HIFK Helsinki	Finland	51	24	*57	*81	....	....	....	95	....	....	....	....	....	....	....	....	....	....	8	*8	6	*14	31	....	....	....
	HIFK Helsinki	EuroHL	5	4	2	6	....	....	....	26	....	....	....	....	....	....	....	....	....	....	3	1	1	2	30	....	....	....
	Czech-Republic	WC-A	6	4	2	6	....	....	....	4	....	....	....	....	....	....	....	....	....	....	....	....	....	....	....	....	....	....
99-2000	HIFK Helsinki	Finland	44	38	34	72	....	....	....	94	....	....	....	....	....	....	....	....	....	....	9	3	6	9	10	....	....	....
	HIFK Helsinki	EuroHL	4	1	3	4	....	....	....	6	....	....	....	....	....	....	....	....	....	....	1	0	1	1	0	....	....	....
	NHL Totals		**13**	**8**	**3**	**11**	**8**	**2**	**10**	**0**	**2**	**0**	**0**	**23**	**34.8**	**13**	**3**	**8**	**0**		....	....	....	....	....	....	....	....

AHL Second All-Star Team (1997) • Finnish First All-Star Team (1999, 2000)

Traded to **Columbus** by **San Jose** with San Jose's 9th round choice (Martin Paroulek) in 2000 Entry Draft for future considerations, June 12, 2000.

• CAMAZZOLA, James

LW – L. 5'11", 190 lbs. b: Vancouver, B.C., 1/5/1964. Chicago's 10th, 196th overall, in 1982.

Season	Club	League	GP	G	A	Pts	AG	AA	APts	PIM	PP	SH	GW	S	%	TGF	PGF	TGA	PGA	+/-	GP	G	A	Pts	PIM	PP	SH	GW
1981-82	Penticton Knights	BCJHL	STATISTICS NOT AVAILABLE																									
1982-83	Kamloops Jr. Oilers	WHL	66	57	58	115	....	....	....	54	....	....	....	....	....	....	....	....	....	....	....	....	....	....	....	....	....	....
1983-84	Seattle Breakers	WHL	3	1	1	2	....	....	....	0	....	....	....	....	....	....	....	....	....	....	....	....	....	....	....	....	....	....
	Kamloops Jr. Oilers	WHL	29	26	24	50	....	....	....	25	....	....	....	....	....	....	....	....	....	....	17	12	19	31	44	....	....	....
	Chicago Black Hawks	**NHL**	**1**	**0**	**0**	**0**	**0**	**0**	**0**	**0**	**0**	**0**	**0**	**1**	**0.0**	**0**	**0**	**0**	**0**	**0**	....	....	....	....	....	....	....	....
	Kamloops Jr. Oilers	Mem-Cup	4	3	3	6	....	....	....	0	....	....	....	....	....	....	....	....	....	....	....	....	....	....	....	....	....	....
1984-85	New Westminster Bruins	WHL	25	19	29	48	....	....	....	25	....	....	....	....	....	....	....	....	....	....	11	10	12	22	4	....	....	....
1985-86	Nova Scotia Oilers	AHL	3	0	0	0	....	....	....	0	....	....	....	....	....	....	....	....	....	....	....	....	....	....	....	....	....	....
	Saginaw Generals	IHL	42	16	22	38	....	....	....	10	....	....	....	....	....	....	....	....	....	....	8	0	3	3	15	....	....	....
1986-87	**Chicago Blackhawks**	**NHL**	**2**	**0**	**0**	**0**	**0**	**0**	**0**	**0**	**0**	**0**	**0**	**2**	**0.0**	**0**	**0**	**0**	**0**	**0**	....	....	....	....	....	....	....	....
	Nova Scotia Oilers	AHL	48	13	18	31	....	....	....	31	....	....	....	....	....	....	....	....	....	....	3	0	0	0	0	....	....	....
1987-88	Maine Mariners	AHL	62	13	23	36	....	....	....	80	....	....	....	....	....	....	....	....	....	....	10	1	7	8	8	....	....	....
1988-89	HC Asiago	Italy	33	8	29	37	....	....	....	58	....	....	....	....	....	....	....	....	....	....	11	6	8	14	....	....	....	....
1989-90	HC Asiago	Italy	34	11	49	60	....	....	....	12	....	....	....	....	....	....	....	....	....	....	6	2	5	7	6	....	....	....
1990-91	HC Asiago	Italy	24	11	19	30	....	....	....	51	....	....	....	....	....	....	....	....	....	....	5	2	2	4	0	....	....	....
1991-92	HC Asiago	Alpenliga	11	7	15	22	....	....	....	24	....	....	....	....	....	....	....	....	....	....	....	....	....	....	....	....	....	....
	HC Asiago	Italy	16	6	10	16	....	....	....	9	....	....	....	....	....	....	....	....	....	....	11	6	9	15	2	....	....	....
	Italy	Olympics	7	0	2	2	....	....	....	18	....	....	....	....	....	....	....	....	....	....	....	....	....	....	....	....	....	....
	Italy	WC-A	5	1	1	2	....	....	....	10	....	....	....	....	....	....	....	....	....	....	....	....	....	....	....	....	....	....
1992-93	HC Asiago	Alpenliga	29	10	16	26	....	....	....	26	....	....	....	....	....	....	....	....	....	....	....	....	....	....	....	....	....	....
	HC Asiago	Italy	11	5	6	11	....	....	....	2	....	....	....	....	....	....	....	....	....	....	3	0	6	6	0	....	....	....
1993-94	HC Courmaosta	Alpenliga	28	8	31	39	....	....	....	6	....	....	....	....	....	....	....	....	....	....	....	....	....	....	....	....	....	....
	HC Courmaosta	Italy	18	9	12	21	....	....	....	6	....	....	....	....	....	....	....	....	....	....	6	3	5	8	8	....	....	....
	Italy	Olympics	7	2	2	4	....	....	....	4	....	....	....	....	....	....	....	....	....	....	....	....	....	....	....	....	....	....
1994-95	HC Courmaosta	Alpenliga	13	7	13	20	....	....	....	28	....	....	....	....	....	....	....	....	....	....	....	....	....	....	....	....	....	....
	HC Courmaosta	Italy	28	18	16	34	....	....	....	41	....	....	....	....	....	....	....	....	....	....	6	2	6	8	8	....	....	....
1995-96	HC Varese	Alpenliga	8	1	4	5	....	....	....	6	....	....	....	....	....	....	....	....	....	....	....	....	....	....	....	....	....	....
	HC Varese	Italy	22	3	12	15	....	....	....	6	....	....	....	....	....	....	....	....	....	....	8	2	6	8	6	....	....	....
1996-97	Berlin Capitals	Germany	42	8	13	21	....	....	....	56	....	....	....	....	....	....	....	....	....	....	....	....	....	....	....	....	....	....
	Berlin Capitals	EuroHL	5	1	1	2	....	....	....	6	....	....	....	....	....	....	....	....	....	....	....	....	....	....	....	....	....	....
1997-98	Augsburger Panther	Germany	50	5	14	19	....	....	....	34	....	....	....	....	....	....	....	....	....	....	....	....	....	....	....	....	....	....
1998-99	Augsburger Panther	Germany	44	6	7	13	....	....	....	59	....	....	....	....	....	....	....	....	....	....	5	1	0	1	2	....	....	....
99-2000	Augsburger Panther	Germany	49	8	10	18	....	....	....	50	....	....	....	....	....	....	....	....	....	....	3	1	1	2	2	....	....	....
	NHL Totals		**3**	**0**	**0**	**0**	**0**	**0**	**0**	**0**	**0**	**0**	**0**	**3**	**0.0**	**0**	**0**	**0**	**0**		....	....	....	....	....	....	....	....

• Brother of Tony • Memorial Cup All-Star Team (1984)

• CAMAZZOLA, Tony

Anthony Bert D – L. 6'2", 210 lbs. b: Vancouver, B.C., 9/11/1962. Washington's 9th, 194th overall, in 1980.

Season	Club	League	GP	G	A	Pts	AG	AA	APts	PIM	PP	SH	GW	S	%	TGF	PGF	TGA	PGA	+/-	GP	G	A	Pts	PIM	PP	SH	GW
1979-80	Brandon Wheat Kings	WHL	7	0	2	2	....	....	....	21	....	....	....	....	....	....	....	....	....	....	7	0	0	0	2	....	....	....
1980-81	Brandon Wheat Kings	WHL	69	4	20	24	....	....	....	144	....	....	....	....	....	....	....	....	....	....	5	0	1	1	10	....	....	....
1981-82	Brandon Wheat Kings	WHL	64	6	23	29	....	....	....	210	....	....	....	....	....	....	....	....	....	....	4	1	1	2	26	....	....	....
	Washington Capitals	**NHL**	**3**	**0**	**0**	**0**	**0**	**0**	**0**	**4**	**0**	**0**	**0**	**0**	**0.0**	**0**	**0**	**0**	**0**	**0**	....	....	....	....	....	....	....	....
1982-83	Hershey Bears	AHL	52	3	8	11	....	....	....	106	....	....	....	....	....	....	....	....	....	....	....	....	....	....	....	....	....	....
1983-84	Hershey Bears	AHL	63	6	10	16	....	....	....	138	....	....	....	....	....	....	....	....	....	....	....	....	....	....	....	....	....	....
1984-85	Fort Wayne Komets	IHL	15	0	3	3	....	....	....	56	....	....	....	....	....	....	....	....	....	....	....	....	....	....	....	....	....	....
	Toledo Goaldiggers	IHL	28	2	8	10	....	....	....	84	....	....	....	....	....	....	....	....	....	....	6	0	1	1	9	....	....	....
1985-86	Fort Wayne Komets	IHL	54	5	7	12	....	....	....	144	....	....	....	....	....	....	....	....	....	....	14	6	0	6	7	....	....	....
1986-87	Fort Wayne Komets	IHL	74	21	16	37	....	....	....	137	....	....	....	....	....	....	....	....	....	....	11	4	1	5	44	....	....	....
1987-88	Fort Wayne Komets	IHL	46	10	6	16	....	....	....	140	....	....	....	....	....	....	....	....	....	....	5	2	0	2	19	....	....	....
1988-89	Fort Wayne Komets	IHL	12	2	3	5	....	....	....	26	....	....	....	....	....	....	....	....	....	....	....	....	....	....	....	....	....	....
1989-90	Fort Wayne Komets	IHL	2	0	0	0	....	....	....	15	....	....	....	....	....	....	....	....	....	....	....	....	....	....	....	....	....	....
	NHL Totals		**3**	**0**	**0**	**0**	**0**	**0**	**0**	**4**	**0**	**0**	**0**	**0**	**0.0**	**0**	**0**	**0**	**0**		....	....	....	....	....	....	....	....

• Brother of James

• CAMERON, Al

Alan Richard D – L. 6'1", 205 lbs. b: Edmonton, Alta., 10/21/1955. Detroit's 3rd, 37th overall, in 1975.

Season	Club	League	GP	G	A	Pts	AG	AA	APts	PIM	PP	SH	GW	S	%	TGF	PGF	TGA	PGA	+/-	GP	G	A	Pts	PIM	PP	SH	GW
1972-73	Chilliwack Bruins	BCJHL	STATISTICS NOT AVAILABLE																									
	New Westminster Bruins	WCJHL	1	0	0	0	....	....	....	0	....	....	....	....	....	....	....	....	....	....	....	....	....	....	....	....	....	....
1973-74	New Westminster Bruins	WCJHL	67	4	17	21	....	....	....	90	....	....	....	....	....	....	....	....	....	....	11	0	2	2	24	....	....	....
1974-75	New Westminster Bruins	WCJHL	69	10	26	36	....	....	....	184	....	....	....	....	....	....	....	....	....	....	16	2	3	5	54	....	....	....
	New Westminster Bruins	Mem-Cup	3	0	0	0	....	....	....	0	....	....	....	....	....	....	....	....	....	....	....	....	....	....	....	....	....	....
1975-76	**Detroit Red Wings**	**NHL**	**38**	**2**	**8**	**10**	**2**	**6**	**8**	**49**	**1**	**0**	**0**	**59**	**3.4**	**34**	**4**	**51**	**14**	**–7**	....	....	....	....	....	....	....	....
	Kalamazoo Wings	IHL	43	3	17	20	....	....	....	71	....	....	....	....	....	....	....	....	....	....	....	....	....	....	....	....	....	....
1976-77	**Detroit Red Wings**	**NHL**	**80**	**3**	**13**	**16**	**3**	**10**	**13**	**112**	**1**	**0**	**0**	**139**	**2.2**	**62**	**16**	**121**	**32**	**–43**	....	....	....	....	....	....	....	....
1977-78	**Detroit Red Wings**	**NHL**	**63**	**2**	**7**	**9**	**2**	**5**	**7**	**94**	**1**	**0**	**0**	**71**	**2.8**	**35**	**3**	**44**	**0**	**–12**	**7**	**0**	**1**	**1**	**2**	**0**	**0**	**0**
	Kansas City Red Wings	CHL	6	1	6	7	....	....	....	4	....	....	....	....	....	....	....	....	....	....	....	....	....	....	....	....	....	....
1978-79	**Detroit Red Wings**	**NHL**	**9**	**0**	**3**	**3**	**0**	**2**	**2**	**8**	**0**	**0**	**0**	**7**	**0.0**	**8**	**0**	**7**	**0**	**1**	....	....	....	....	....	....	....	....
	Kansas City Red Wings	CHL	64	5	25	30	....	....	....	89	....	....	....	....	....	....	....	....	....	....	4	0	1	1	2	....	....	....
1979-80	**Winnipeg Jets**	**NHL**	**63**	**3**	**11**	**14**	**3**	**8**	**11**	**72**	**0**	**0**	**0**	**79**	**3.8**	**59**	**5**	**106**	**26**	**–26**	....	....	....	....	....	....	....	....
	Tulsa Oilers	CHL	15	1	2	3	....	....	....	20	....	....	....	....	....	....	....	....	....	....	....	....	....	....	....	....	....	....
1980-81	**Winnipeg Jets**	**NHL**	**29**	**1**	**2**	**3**	**1**	**1**	**2**	**21**	**0**	**0**	**0**	**16**	**6.3**	**19**	**1**	**46**	**9**	**–19**	....	....	....	....	....	....	....	....
	Tulsa Oilers	CHL	42	6	26	32	....	....	....	38	....	....	....	....	....	....	....	....	....	....	3	0	0	0	2	....	....	....
	NHL Totals		**282**	**11**	**44**	**55**	**11**	**32**	**43**	**356**	**3**	**0**	**0**	**371**	**3.0**	**217**	**29**	**375**	**81**		**7**	**0**	**1**	**1**	**2**	**0**	**0**	**0**

Claimed by **Winnipeg** from **Detroit** in Expansion Draft, June 13, 1979.

• CAMERON, Craig

Craig Lauder RW – R. 6', 200 lbs. b: Edmonton, Alta., 7/19/1945.

Season	Club	League	GP	G	A	Pts	AG	AA	APts	PIM	PP	SH	GW	S	%	TGF	PGF	TGA	PGA	+/-	GP	G	A	Pts	PIM	PP	SH	GW
1964-65	Edmonton Oil Kings	CAHL	....	....	....	....	....	....	....	....	....	....	....	....	....	....	....	....	....	....	5	1	0	1	5	....	....	....
	Edmonton Oil Kings	Mem-Cup	21	5	6	11	....	....	....	20	....	....	....	....	....	....	....	....	....	....	....	....	....	....	....	....	....	....
1965-66	Edmonton Oil Kings	ASHL	40	17	15	32	....	....	....	19	....	....	....	....	....	....	....	....	....	....	11	6	2	8	14	....	....	....
	Edmonton Oil Kings	Mem-Cup	19	7	14	21	....	....	....	19	....	....	....	....	....	....	....	....	....	....	....	....	....	....	....	....	....	....
1966-67	**Detroit Red Wings**	**NHL**	**1**	**0**	**0**	**0**	**0**	**0**	**0**	**0**	....	....	....	....	....	....	....	....	....	....	....	....	....	....	....	....	....	....
	Memphis Wings	CPHL	1	0	0	0	....	....	....	2	....	....	....	....	....	....	....	....	....	....	....	....	....	....	....	....	....	....
	Pittsburgh Hornets	AHL	50	9	11	20	....	....	....	12	....	....	....	....	....	....	....	....	....	....	....	....	....	....	....	....	....	....
1967-68	**St. Louis Blues**	**NHL**	**32**	**7**	**2**	**9**	**8**	**2**	**10**	**8**	**0**	**0**	**1**	**43**	**16.3**	**15**	**2**	**11**	**0**	**2**	**14**	**1**	**0**	**1**	**11**	**0**	**0**	**0**
	Kansas City Blues	CPHL	32	12	12	24	....	....	....	27	....	....	....	....	....	....	....	....	....	....	....	....	....	....	....	....	....	....
1968-69	**St. Louis Blues**	**NHL**	**72**	**11**	**5**	**16**	**12**	**4**	**16**	**40**	**2**	**0**	**1**	**123**	**8.9**	**33**	**3**	**40**	**2**	**–8**	**2**	**0**	**0**	**0**	**0**	**0**	**0**	**0**
1969-70	Baltimore Clippers	AHL	67	10	18	28	....	....	....	40	....	....	....	....	....	....	....	....	....	....	5	2	2	4	0	....	....	....
1970-71	**St. Louis Blues**	**NHL**	**78**	**14**	**6**	**20**	**14**	**5**	**19**	**32**	**0**	**1**	**2**	**86**	**16.3**	**33**	**0**	**47**	**3**	**–11**	**6**	**2**	**0**	**2**	**4**	**0**	**0**	**0**
1971-72	**Minnesota North Stars**	**NHL**	**64**	**2**	**1**	**3**	**2**	**1**	**3**	**11**	**0**	**0**	**0**	**32**	**6.3**	**6**	**0**	**13**	**6**	**–1**	**5**	**0**	**1**	**1**	**2**	**0**	**0**	**0**
1972-73	**New York Islanders**	**NHL**	**72**	**19**	**14**	**33**	**18**	**11**	**29**	**27**	**2**	**0**	**2**	**144**	**13.2**	**43**	**4**	**97**	**20**	**–38**	....	....	....	....	....	....	....	....

			REGULAR SEASON																		PLAYOFFS							
Season	Club	League	GP	G	A	Pts	AG	AA	APts	PIM	PP	SH	GW	S	%	TGF	PGF	TGA	PGA	+/–	GP	G	A	Pts	PIM	PP	SH	GW
1973-74	**New York Islanders**	**NHL**	**78**	**15**	**14**	**29**	**14**	**12**	**26**	**28**	**2**	**0**	**2**	**121**	**12.4**	**50**	**8**	**82**	**25**	**–15**	....	....	....	....	....	....	....	....
1974-75	**New York Islanders**	**NHL**	**37**	**1**	**6**	**7**	**1**	**4**	**5**	**4**	**0**	**0**	**0**	**52**	**1.9**	**0**	**0**	**0**	**0**	**0**	....	....	....	....	....	....	....	....
	Minnesota North Stars	**NHL**	**40**	**10**	**7**	**17**	**9**	**5**	**14**	**12**	**1**	**0**	**1**	**65**	**15.4**	**26**	**3**	**33**	**15**	**5**	....	....	....	....	....	....	....	....
1975-76	**Minnesota North Stars**	**NHL**	**78**	**8**	**10**	**18**	**7**	**7**	**14**	**34**	**1**	**0**	**0**	**73**	**11.0**	**30**	**3**	**96**	**42**	**–27**	....	....	....	....	....	....	....	....
1976-77	New Haven Nighthawks	AHL	79	14	26	40	....	....	....	33	....	....	....	....	....	....	....	....	....	....	6	0	0	0	2	....	....	....
	NHL Totals		**552**	**87**	**65**	**152**	**85**	**51**	**136**	**196**	....	....	....	....	....	....	....	....	....		**27**	**3**	**1**	**4**	**17**	....	....	....

Traded to **St. Louis** by **Detroit** with Larry Hornung and Don Giesebrecht for John Brenneman, October 9, 1967. Traded to **Pittsburgh** by **St. Louis** with Ron Schock for Lou Angotti and Pittsburgh's 1st round choice (Gene Carr) in 1971 Amateur Draft, June 6, 1969. Claimed by **LA Kings** from **Pittsburgh** in Intra-League Draft, June 9, 1970. Claimed by **Buffalo** from **LA Kings** in Expansion Draft, June 10, 1970. Traded to **St. Louis** by **Buffalo** for Ron C. Anderson, October 2, 1970. Claimed on waivers by **Minnesota** from **St. Louis**, October 1, 1971. Claimed by **NY Islanders** from **Minnesota** in Expansion Draft, June 6, 1972. Traded to **Minnesota** by **NY Islanders** for Jude Drouin, January 7, 1975.

• CAMERON, Dave

C – L. 6′, 185 lbs. b: Charlottetown, P.E.I., 7/29/1958. NY Islanders' 7th, 135th overall, in 1978.

Season	Club	League	GP	G	A	Pts	AG	AA	APts	PIM	PP	SH	GW	S	%	TGF	PGF	TGA	PGA	+/–	GP	G	A	Pts	PIM	PP	SH	GW
1976-77	University of P.E.I.	AUAA	20	7	10	17	....	....	....	12	....	....	....	....	....	....	....	....	....	....	....	....	....	....	....	....	....	....
1977-78	University of P.E.I.	AUAA	16	13	*30	43	....	....	....	26	....	....	....	....	....	....	....	....	....	....	....	....	....	....	....	....	....	....
1978-79	University of P.E.I.	AUAA	13	7	22	29	....	....	....	39	....	....	....	....	....	....	....	....	....	....	....	....	....	....	....	....	....	....
1979-80	Fort Wayne Komets	IHL	6	3	6	9	....	....	....	9	....	....	....	....	....	....	....	....	....	....	....	....	....	....	....	....	....	....
	Indianapolis Checkers	CHL	70	15	21	36	....	....	....	101	....	....	....	....	....	....	....	....	....	....	7	0	0	0	16	....	....	....
1980-81	Indianapolis Checkers	CHL	78	40	30	70	....	....	....	156	....	....	....	....	....	....	....	....	....	....	5	2	3	5	4	....	....	....
1981-82	**Colorado Rockies**	**NHL**	**66**	**11**	**12**	**23**	**9**	**8**	**17**	**103**	**0**	**1**	**0**	**65**	**16.9**	**38**	**5**	**63**	**16**	**–14**	....	....	....	....	....	....	....	....
	Fort Worth Texans	CHL	2	0	0	0	....	....	....	0	....	....	....	....	....	....	....	....	....	....	....	....	....	....	....	....	....	....
1982-83	**New Jersey Devils**	**NHL**	**35**	**5**	**4**	**9**	**4**	**3**	**7**	**50**	**1**	**0**	**0**	**29**	**17.2**	**16**	**3**	**28**	**7**	**–8**	....	....	....	....	....	....	....	....
	Wichita Wind	CHL	25	6	9	15	....	....	....	40	....	....	....	....	....	....	....	....	....	....	....	....	....	....	....	....	....	....
1983-84	**New Jersey Devils**	**NHL**	**67**	**9**	**12**	**21**	**7**	**8**	**15**	**85**	**2**	**0**	**0**	**79**	**11.4**	**37**	**7**	**69**	**28**	**–11**	....	....	....	....	....	....	....	....
1984-85	Maine Mariners	AHL	12	0	1	1	....	....	....	32	....	....	....	....	....	....	....	....	....	....	....	....	....	....	....	....	....	....
	Moncton Golden Flames	AHL	37	8	16	24	....	....	....	82	....	....	....	....	....	....	....	....	....	....	....	....	....	....	....	....	....	....
1985-86	Charlottetown Islanders	NBSHL	15	9	16	25	....	....	....	54	....	....	....	....	....	....	....	....	....	....	....	....	....	....	....	....	....	....
1986-87	Charlottetown Islanders	NBSHL	11	5	17	22	....	....	....	69	....	....	....	....	....	....	....	....	....	....	....	....	....	....	....	....	....	....
1987-88	Summerside Capitals	MJrHL	DID NOT PLAY – COACHING																									
1988-89	Summerside Capitals	MJrHL	DID NOT PLAY – COACHING																									
1989-90	Fredericton Alpines	NBSHL	14	0	8	8	....	....	....	30	....	....	....	....	....	....	....	....	....	....	6	1	6	7	....	....	....	....
1990-91	Charlottetown Islanders	NBSHL	25	23	21	44	....	....	....	69	....	....	....	....	....	....	....	....	....	....	....	....	....	....	....	....	....	....
	NHL Totals		**168**	**25**	**28**	**53**	**20**	**19**	**39**	**238**	**3**	**1**	**0**	**173**	**14.5**	**91**	**15**	**160**	**51**		....	....	....	....	....	....	....	....

CHL Second All-Star Team (1981)

Traded to **Colorado** by **NY Islanders** with Bob Lorimer for Colorado's 1st round choice (Pat LaFontaine) in 1983 Entry Draft, October 1, 1981. Transferred to **New Jersey** after **Colorado** franchise relocated, June 30, 1982.

• CAMPBELL, Brian

Brian Wesley D – L. 5′11″, 185 lbs. b: Strathroy, Ont., 5/23/1979. Buffalo's 7th, 156th overall, in 1997.

Season	Club	League	GP	G	A	Pts	AG	AA	APts	PIM	PP	SH	GW	S	%	TGF	PGF	TGA	PGA	+/–	GP	G	A	Pts	PIM	PP	SH	GW
1994-95	Petrolia Oil Barons	OJHL	49	11	27	38	....	....	....	43	....	....	....	....	....	....	....	....	....	....	....	....	....	....	....	....	....	....
1995-96	Ottawa 67's	OHL	66	5	22	27	....	....	....	23	....	....	....	....	....	....	....	....	....	....	4	0	1	1	2	....	....	....
1996-97	Ottawa 67's	OHL	66	7	36	43	....	....	....	12	....	....	....	....	....	....	....	....	....	....	24	2	11	13	8	....	....	....
1997-98	Ottawa 67's	OHL	66	14	39	53	....	....	....	31	....	....	....	....	....	....	....	....	....	....	13	1	14	15	0	....	....	....
1998-99	Ottawa 67's	OHL	62	12	75	87	....	....	....	27	....	....	....	....	....	....	....	....	....	....	9	2	10	12	6	....	....	....
	Rochester Americans	AHL	....	....	....	....	....	....	....	....	....	....	....	....	....	....	....	....	....	....	2	0	0	0	0	....	....	....
	Canada	WJC-A	7	1	1	2	....	....	....	4	....	....	....	....	....	....	....	....	....	....	....	....	....	....	....	....	....	....
99-2000	**Buffalo Sabres**	**NHL**	**12**	**1**	**4**	**5**	**1**	**4**	**5**	**4**	**0**	**0**	**0**	**10**	**10.0**	**11**	**3**	**10**	**0**	**–2**	....	....	....	....	....	....	....	....
	Rochester Americans	AHL	67	2	24	26	....	....	....	22	....	....	....	....	....	....	....	....	....	....	21	0	3	3	0	....	....	....
	NHL Totals		**12**	**1**	**4**	**5**	**1**	**4**	**5**	**4**	**0**	**0**	**0**	**10**	**10.0**	**11**	**3**	**10**	**0**		....	....	....	....	....	....	....	....

WJC-A All-Star Team (1999) • OHL First All-Star Team (1999) • Canadian Major Junior First All-Star Team (1999) • Won George Parsons Trophy (Memorial Cup Tournament Most Sportsmanlike Player) (1999) • Canadian Major Junior Player of the Year (1999)

• CAMPBELL, Bryan

Bryan Albert C – L. 6′, 175 lbs. b: Sudbury, Ont., 3/27/1944.

Season	Club	League	GP	G	A	Pts	AG	AA	APts	PIM	PP	SH	GW	S	%	TGF	PGF	TGA	PGA	+/–	GP	G	A	Pts	PIM	PP	SH	GW
1961-62	Hamilton Red Wings	OHA-Jr.	23	5	3	8	....	....	....	0	....	....	....	....	....	....	....	....	....	....	9	0	0	0	0	....	....	....
	Hamilton Red Wings	Mem-Cup	9	1	3	4	....	....	....	2	....	....	....	....	....	....	....	....	....	....	....	....	....	....	....	....	....	....
1962-63	Hamilton Red Wings	OHA-Jr.	49	21	40	61	....	....	....	19	....	....	....	....	....	....	....	....	....	....	5	2	2	4	2	....	....	....
1963-64	Hamilton Red Wings	OHA-Jr.	39	13	25	38	....	....	....	32	....	....	....	....	....	....	....	....	....	....	....	....	....	....	....	....	....	....
	Cincinnati Wings	CPHL	5	1	3	4	....	....	....	2	....	....	....	....	....	....	....	....	....	....	....	....	....	....	....	....	....	....
	Edmonton Oil Kings	CAHL	....	....	....	....	....	....	....	....	....	....	....	....	....	....	....	....	....	....	5	2	0	2	0	....	....	....
	Edmonton Oil Kings	Mem-Cup	5	9	8	17	....	....	....	2	....	....	....	....	....	....	....	....	....	....	....	....	....	....	....	....	....	....
1964-65	Memphis Wings	CPHL	69	23	39	62	....	....	....	54	....	....	....	....	....	....	....	....	....	....	....	....	....	....	....	....	....	....
1965-66	Memphis Wings	CPHL	56	24	31	55	....	....	....	32	....	....	....	....	....	....	....	....	....	....	....	....	....	....	....	....	....	....
1966-67	Omaha Knights	CPHL	65	26	42	68	....	....	....	46	....	....	....	....	....	....	....	....	....	....	12	1	9	10	4	....	....	....
1967-68	**Los Angeles Kings**	**NHL**	**44**	**6**	**15**	**21**	**7**	**15**	**22**	**16**	**0**	**0**	**1**	**55**	**10.9**	**26**	**4**	**23**	**3**	**2**	....	....	....	....	....	....	....	....
1968-69	**Los Angeles Kings**	**NHL**	**18**	**2**	**1**	**3**	**2**	**1**	**3**	**4**	**0**	**0**	**0**	**37**	**5.4**	**5**	**2**	**10**	**0**	**–7**	**6**	**2**	**1**	**3**	**0**	**0**	**0**	**1**
	Springfield Kings	AHL	53	27	28	55	....	....	....	24	....	....	....	....	....	....	....	....	....	....	....	....	....	....	....	....	....	....
1969-70	**Los Angeles Kings**	**NHL**	**31**	**4**	**4**	**8**	**4**	**4**	**8**	**4**	**0**	**0**	**0**	**54**	**7.4**	**10**	**2**	**28**	**5**	**–15**	....	....	....	....	....	....	....	....
	Springfield Kings	AHL	15	7	14	21	....	....	....	2	....	....	....	....	....	....	....	....	....	....	....	....	....	....	....	....	....	....
	Chicago Black Hawks	**NHL**	**14**	**1**	**1**	**2**	**1**	**1**	**2**	**2**	**0**	**0**	**0**	**7**	**14.3**	**2**	**0**	**0**	**0**	**2**	**8**	**1**	**2**	**3**	**0**	**1**	**0**	**0**
1970-71	**Chicago Black Hawks**	**NHL**	**78**	**17**	**37**	**54**	**17**	**31**	**48**	**26**	**3**	**0**	**1**	**155**	**11.0**	**74**	**12**	**36**	**0**	**26**	**4**	**0**	**1**	**1**	**0**	**0**	**0**	**0**
1971-72	**Chicago Black Hawks**	**NHL**	**75**	**5**	**13**	**18**	**5**	**11**	**16**	**22**	**0**	**0**	**1**	**87**	**5.7**	**28**	**0**	**27**	**1**	**2**	**4**	**0**	**0**	**0**	**2**	**0**	**0**	**0**
1972-73	Philadelphia Blazers	WHA	75	25	48	73	....	....	....	85	....	....	....	....	....	....	....	....	....	....	3	0	1	1	8	....	....	....
1973-74	Vancouver Blazers	WHA	76	27	62	89	....	....	....	50	....	....	....	....	....	....	....	....	....	....	....	....	....	....	....	....	....	....
1974-75	Vancouver Blazers	WHA	78	29	34	63	....	....	....	24	....	....	....	....	....	....	....	....	....	....	....	....	....	....	....	....	....	....
1975-76	Cincinnati Stingers	WHA	77	22	50	72	....	....	....	24	....	....	....	....	....	....	....	....	....	....	....	....	....	....	....	....	....	....
1976-77	Indianapolis Racers	WHA	8	1	4	5	....	....	....	6	....	....	....	....	....	....	....	....	....	....	....	....	....	....	....	....	....	....
	Edmonton Oilers	WHA	66	12	42	54	....	....	....	18	....	....	....	....	....	....	....	....	....	....	5	3	1	4	0	....	....	....
1977-78	Edmonton Oilers	WHA	53	7	13	20	....	....	....	12	....	....	....	....	....	....	....	....	....	....	....	....	....	....	....	....	....	....
	NHL Totals		**260**	**35**	**71**	**106**	**36**	**63**	**99**	**74**	**3**	**0**	**3**	**395**	**8.9**	**145**	**20**	**124**	**9**		**22**	**3**	**4**	**7**	**2**	**1**	**0**	**1**
	Other Major League Totals		433	123	253	376	....	....	....	219	....	....	....	....	....	....	....	....	....	....	8	3	2	5	8	....	....	....

Claimed by **NY Rangers** from **Detroit** in Intra-League Draft, June 15, 1966. Claimed by **LA Kings** from **NY Rangers** in Expansion Draft, June 6, 1967. Traded to **Chicago** by **LA Kings** with Bill White and Gerry Desjardins for Gilles Marotte, Jim Stanfield and Denis DeJordy, February 20, 1970. Selected by **Chicago** (WHA) in 1972 WHA General Player Draft, February 12, 1972. WHA rights traded to **Philadelphia** (WHA) by **Chicago** (WHA) for cash, May, 1972. Traded to **Cincinnati** (WHA) by **Calgary** (WHA) for cash, September, 1975. Traded to **Indianapolis** (WHA) by **Cincinnati** (WHA) for future considerations, August 2, 1976. Traded to **Edmonton** (WHA) by **Indianapolis** (WHA) for Gene Peacosh, November, 1976.

• CAMPBELL, Colin

Colin John "Colie" D – L. 5′9″, 190 lbs. b: London, Ont., 1/28/1953. Pittsburgh's 3rd, 27th overall, in 1973.

Season	Club	League	GP	G	A	Pts	AG	AA	APts	PIM	PP	SH	GW	S	%	TGF	PGF	TGA	PGA	+/–	GP	G	A	Pts	PIM	PP	SH	GW
1969-70	Tillsonburg Tigers	OHA-C	STATISTICS NOT AVAILABLE																									
1970-71	Peterborough Petes	OHA-Jr.	59	5	18	23	....	....	....	160	....	....	....	....	....	....	....	....	....	....	5	0	2	2	22	....	....	....
1971-72	Peterborough Petes	OMJHL	50	2	23	25	....	....	....	158	....	....	....	....	....	....	....	....	....	....	15	2	9	11	59	....	....	....
	Peterborough Petes	Mem-Cup	3	0	2	2	....	....	....	6	....	....	....	....	....	....	....	....	....	....	....	....	....	....	....	....	....	....
1972-73	Peterborough Petes	OMJHL	60	7	40	47	....	....	....	189	....	....	....	....	....	....	....	....	....	....	....	....	....	....	....	....	....	....
1973-74	Vancouver Blazers	WHA	78	3	20	23	....	....	....	191	....	....	....	....	....	....	....	....	....	....	....	....	....	....	....	....	....	....
1974-75	**Pittsburgh Penguins**	**NHL**	**59**	**4**	**15**	**19**	**3**	**11**	**14**	**172**	**0**	**1**	**0**	**84**	**4.8**	**78**	**2**	**62**	**14**	**28**	**9**	**1**	**3**	**4**	**21**	**0**	**1**	**1**
	Hershey Bears	AHL	15	1	3	4	....	....	....	55	....	....	....	....	....	....	....	....	....	....	....	....	....	....	....	....	....	....
1975-76	**Pittsburgh Penguins**	**NHL**	**64**	**7**	**10**	**17**	**6**	**7**	**13**	**105**	**1**	**0**	**2**	**64**	**10.9**	**60**	**2**	**77**	**15**	**–4**	**3**	**0**	**0**	**0**	**0**	**0**	**0**	**0**
1976-77	**Colorado Rockies**	**NHL**	**54**	**3**	**8**	**11**	**3**	**6**	**9**	**67**	**0**	**0**	**0**	**87**	**3.4**	**34**	**3**	**63**	**10**	**–22**	....	....	....	....	....	....	....	....
	Oklahoma City Blazers	CHL	7	1	2	3	....	....	....	9	....	....	....	....	....	....	....	....	....	....	....	....	....	....	....	....	....	....
1977-78	**Pittsburgh Penguins**	**NHL**	**55**	**1**	**9**	**10**	**1**	**7**	**8**	**103**	**1**	**0**	**1**	**54**	**1.9**	**33**	**5**	**57**	**10**	**–19**	....	....	....	....	....	....	....	....
1978-79	**Pittsburgh Penguins**	**NHL**	**65**	**2**	**18**	**20**	**2**	**13**	**15**	**137**	**0**	**0**	**1**	**52**	**3.8**	**58**	**1**	**52**	**9**	**14**	**7**	**1**	**4**	**5**	**30**	**0**	**0**	**0**

Season	Club	League	REGULAR SEASON GP	G	A	Pts	AG	AA	APts	PIM	PP	SH	GW	S	%	TGF	PGF	TGA	PGA	+/-	PLAYOFFS GP	G	A	Pts	PIM	PP	SH	GW
1979-80	**Edmonton Oilers**	**NHL**	**72**	**2**	**11**	**13**	**2**	**8**	**10**	**196**	**0**	**0**	**0**	**80**	**2.5**	**61**	**1**	**97**	**19**	**–18**	**3**	**0**	**0**	**0**	**11**	**0**	**0**	**0**
1980-81	**Vancouver Canucks**	**NHL**	**42**	**1**	**8**	**9**	**1**	**5**	**6**	**75**	**0**	**0**	**0**	**37**	**2.7**	**39**	**0**	**34**	**5**	**10**	**3**	**0**	**1**	**1**	**9**	**0**	**0**	**0**
1981-82	**Vancouver Canucks**	**NHL**	**47**	**0**	**8**	**8**	**0**	**5**	**5**	**131**	**0**	**0**	**0**	**35**	**0.0**	**45**	**2**	**56**	**17**	**4**	**16**	**2**	**2**	**4**	**89**	**0**	**0**	**1**
1982-83	**Detroit Red Wings**	**NHL**	**53**	**1**	**7**	**8**	**1**	**5**	**6**	**74**	**0**	**0**	**0**	**30**	**3.3**	**38**	**1**	**49**	**14**	**2**	....	....	....	....	....	....	....	....
1983-84	**Detroit Red Wings**	**NHL**	**68**	**3**	**4**	**7**	**2**	**3**	**5**	**108**	**0**	**0**	**1**	**48**	**6.3**	**50**	**0**	**69**	**19**	**0**	**4**	**0**	**0**	**0**	**21**	**0**	**0**	**0**
1984-85	**Detroit Red Wings**	**NHL**	**57**	**1**	**5**	**6**	**1**	**3**	**4**	**124**	**0**	**0**	**0**	**36**	**2.8**	**49**	**0**	**88**	**25**	**–14**	....	....	....	....	....	....	....	....
	NHL Totals		**636**	**25**	**103**	**128**	**22**	**73**	**95**	**1292**	**2**	**1**	**5**	**607**	**4.1**	**545**	**17**	**704**	**157**		**45**	**4**	**10**	**14**	**181**	**0**	**1**	**2**
	Other Major League Totals		78	3	20	23	....	....	....	191	....	....	....	....	....	....	....	....	....	....	....	....	....	....	....	....	....	....

Selected by **Vancouver** (WHA) in 1973 WHA Amateur Draft, June, 1973. Loaned to **Colorado** by **Pittsburgh** for the 1976-77 season to complete transaction that sent Simon Nolet and Michel Plasse to Colorado as compensation for Pittsburgh's signing of free agent Dennis Herron, September 1, 1976. Loaned to **Oklahoma City** (CHL) by **Pittsburgh**, January, 1977. Claimed by **Edmonton** from **Pittsburgh** in Expansion Draft, June 13, 1979. Claimed by **Vancouver** from **Edmonton** in Waiver Draft, October 10, 1980. Signed as a free agent by **Detroit**, June 26, 1982.

• CAMPBELL, Jim

James Tower "Soup" RW – R. 6'2", 205 lbs. b: Worcester, MA, 4/3/1973. Montreal's 2nd, 28th overall, in 1991.

Season	Club	League	GP	G	A	Pts	AG	AA	APts	PIM	PP	SH	GW	S	%	TGF	PGF	TGA	PGA	+/-	GP	G	A	Pts	PIM	PP	SH	GW
1988-89	Northwood Huskies	Hi-School	12	12	8	20	....	....	....	6	....	....	....	....	....	....	....	....	....	....	....	....	....	....	....	....	....	....
1989-90	Northwood Huskies	Hi-School	8	14	7	21	....	....	....	8	....	....	....	....	....	....	....	....	....	....	....	....	....	....	....	....	....	....
1990-91	Lawrence Academy	Hi-School	26	36	47	83	....	....	....	26	....	....	....	....	....	....	....	....	....	....	....	....	....	....	....	....	....	....
1991-92	Hull Olympiques	QMJHL	64	41	44	85	....	....	....	51	....	....	....	....	....	....	....	....	....	....	6	7	3	10	8	....	....	....
	United States	WJC-A	7	2	4	6	....	....	....	4	....	....	....	....	....	....	....	....	....	....	....	....	....	....	....	....	....	....
1992-93	Hull Olympiques	QMJHL	50	42	29	71	....	....	....	66	....	....	....	....	....	....	....	....	....	....	8	11	4	15	43	....	....	....
	United States	WJC-A	7	5	2	7	....	....	....	2	....	....	....	....	....	....	....	....	....	....	....	....	....	....	....	....	....	....
1993-94	United States	Nat-Team	56	24	33	57	....	....	....	59	....	....	....	....	....	....	....	....	....	....	....	....	....	....	....	....	....	....
	United States	Olympics	8	0	0	0	....	....	....	6	....	....	....	....	....	....	....	....	....	....	....	....	....	....	....	....	....	....
	Fredericton Canadiens	AHL	19	6	17	23	....	....	....	6	....	....	....	....	....	....	....	....	....	....	....	....	....	....	....	....	....	....
1994-95	Fredericton Canadiens	AHL	77	27	24	51	....	....	....	103	....	....	....	....	....	....	....	....	....	....	12	0	7	7	8	....	....	....
1995-96	Fredericton Canadiens	AHL	44	28	23	51	....	....	....	24	....	....	....	....	....	....	....	....	....	....	....	....	....	....	....	....	....	....
	Mighty Ducks of Anaheim	**NHL**	**16**	**2**	**3**	**5**	**2**	**2**	**4**	**36**	**1**	**0**	**0**	**25**	**8.0**	**6**	**2**	**4**	**0**	**0**	....	....	....	....	....	....	....	....
	Baltimore Bandits	AHL	16	13	7	20	....	....	....	8	....	....	....	....	....	....	....	....	....	....	12	7	5	12	10	....	....	....
1996-97	**St. Louis Blues**	**NHL**	**68**	**23**	**20**	**43**	**24**	**18**	**42**	**68**	**5**	**0**	**6**	**169**	**13.6**	**61**	**16**	**50**	**8**	**3**	**4**	**1**	**0**	**1**	**6**	**1**	**0**	**0**
	United States	WC-A	4	0	0	0	....	....	....	2	....	....	....	....	....	....	....	....	....	....	....	....	....	....	....	....	....	....
1997-98	**St. Louis Blues**	**NHL**	**76**	**22**	**19**	**41**	**26**	**19**	**45**	**55**	**7**	**0**	**6**	**147**	**15.0**	**72**	**28**	**45**	**1**	**0**	**10**	**7**	**3**	**10**	**12**	**4**	**0**	**2**
1998-99	**St. Louis Blues**	**NHL**	**55**	**4**	**21**	**25**	**5**	**20**	**25**	**41**	**1**	**0**	**0**	**99**	**4.0**	**32**	**13**	**27**	**0**	**–8**	....	....	....	....	....	....	....	....
99-2000	**St. Louis Blues**	**NHL**	**2**	**0**	**0**	**0**	**0**	**0**	**0**	**9**	**0**	**0**	**0**	**6**	**0.0**	**0**	**0**	**0**	**0**	**0**	....	....	....	....	....	....	....	....
	Manitoba Moose	IHL	10	1	3	4	....	....	....	10	....	....	....	....	....	....	....	....	....	....	....	....	....	....	....	....	....	....
	Worcester IceCats	AHL	66	31	34	65	....	....	....	88	....	....	....	....	....	....	....	....	....	....	9	1	2	3	6	....	....	....
	NHL Totals		**217**	**51**	**63**	**114**	**57**	**59**	**116**	**209**	**14**	**0**	**12**	**446**	**11.4**	**171**	**59**	**126**	**9**		**14**	**8**	**3**	**11**	**18**	**5**	**0**	**2**

NHL All-Rookie Team (1997)

Traded to **Anaheim** by **Montreal** for Robert Dirk, January 21, 1996. Signed as a free agent by **St. Louis**, July 11, 1996. Loaned to **Manitoba** (IHL) by **St. Louis**, October 4, 1999 and recalled November 1, 1999.

• CAMPBELL, Scott

Scott Gary D – L. 6'3", 205 lbs. b: Toronto, Ont., 6/22/1957. St. Louis' 1st, 9th overall, in 1977.

Season	Club	League	GP	G	A	Pts	AG	AA	APts	PIM	PP	SH	GW	S	%	TGF	PGF	TGA	PGA	+/-	GP	G	A	Pts	PIM	PP	SH	GW
1973-74	Guelph Mad Hatters	OJHL	STATISTICS NOT AVAILABLE																									
1974-75	London Knights	OMJHL	68	4	15	19	....	....	....	52	....	....	....	....	....	....	....	....	....	....	....	....	....	....	....	....	....	....
1975-76	London Knights	OMJHL	62	6	25	31	....	....	....	66	....	....	....	....	....	....	....	....	....	....	5	0	0	0	13	....	....	....
1976-77	London Knights	OMJHL	60	23	44	67	....	....	....	86	....	....	....	....	....	....	....	....	....	....	20	5	8	13	18	....	....	....
1977-78	Houston Aeros	WHA	75	8	29	37	....	....	....	116	....	....	....	....	....	....	....	....	....	....	6	1	1	2	8	....	....	....
1978-79	Winnipeg Jets	WHA	74	3	15	18	....	....	....	248	....	....	....	....	....	....	....	....	....	....	10	0	2	2	25	....	....	....
1979-80	**Winnipeg Jets**	**NHL**	**63**	**3**	**17**	**20**	**3**	**12**	**15**	**136**	**0**	**0**	**2**	**92**	**3.3**	**61**	**14**	**109**	**23**	**–39**	....	....	....	....	....	....	....	....
1980-81	**Winnipeg Jets**	**NHL**	**14**	**1**	**4**	**5**	**1**	**3**	**4**	**55**	**0**	**0**	**0**	**12**	**8.3**	**14**	**0**	**20**	**9**	**3**	....	....	....	....	....	....	....	....
	Tulsa Oilers	CHL	3	0	0	0	....	....	....	9	....	....	....	....	....	....	....	....	....	....	....	....	....	....	....	....	....	....
1981-82	**St. Louis Blues**	**NHL**	**3**	**0**	**0**	**0**	**0**	**0**	**0**	**52**	**0**	**0**	**0**	**4**	**0.0**	**1**	**0**	**2**	**0**	**–1**	....	....	....	....	....	....	....	....
	Salt Lake Golden Eagles	CHL	3	0	1	1	....	....	....	31	....	....	....	....	....	....	....	....	....	....	....	....	....	....	....	....	....	....
	NHL Totals		**80**	**4**	**21**	**25**	**4**	**15**	**19**	**243**	**0**	**0**	**2**	**108**	**3.7**	**76**	**14**	**131**	**32**		....	....	....	....	....	....	....	....
	Other Major League Totals		149	11	44	55	....	....	....	364	....	....	....	....	....	....	....	....	....	....	16	1	3	4	33	....	....	....

Selected by **Houston** (WHA) in 1977 WHA Amateur Draft, June, 1977. Signed as a free agent by **Winnipeg** (WHA) after **Houston** (WHA) franchise folded, July, 1978. Reclaimed by **St. Louis** from **Winnipeg** prior to Expansion Draft, June 9, 1979. Claimed as a priority selection by **Winnipeg**, June 9, 1979. • Missed majority of 1980-81 season recovering from shoulder injury suffered in game vs. Philadelphia, November 24, 1980. Traded to **St. Louis** by **Winnipeg** with John Markell for Bryan Maxwell, Ed Staniowski and Paul MacLean, July 3, 1981. • Retired following the 1981-82 season because of recurring headaches and asthma, July, 1982.

• CAMPBELL, Wade

Wade Allan D – R. 6'4", 220 lbs. b: Peace River, Alta., 1/2/1961.

Season	Club	League	GP	G	A	Pts	AG	AA	APts	PIM	PP	SH	GW	S	%	TGF	PGF	TGA	PGA	+/-	GP	G	A	Pts	PIM	PP	SH	GW
1979-80	Langley Canadians	BCJHL	59	12	36	48	....	....	....	61	....	....	....	....	....	....	....	....	....	....	....	....	....	....	....	....	....	....
1980-81	University of Alberta	CWUAA	24	3	15	18	....	....	....	46	....	....	....	....	....	....	....	....	....	....	....	....	....	....	....	....	....	....
1981-82	University of Alberta	CWUAA	24	8	26	34	....	....	....	85	....	....	....	....	....	....	....	....	....	....	....	....	....	....	....	....	....	....
1982-83	**Winnipeg Jets**	**NHL**	**42**	**1**	**2**	**3**	**1**	**1**	**2**	**50**	**0**	**0**	**0**	**36**	**2.8**	**27**	**0**	**40**	**1**	**–12**	....	....	....	....	....	....	....	....
	Sherbrooke Jets	AHL	18	4	2	6	....	....	....	23	....	....	....	....	....	....	....	....	....	....	....	....	....	....	....	....	....	....
1983-84	**Winnipeg Jets**	**NHL**	**79**	**7**	**14**	**21**	**6**	**10**	**16**	**147**	**0**	**0**	**0**	**89**	**7.9**	**87**	**3**	**123**	**37**	**–2**	**3**	**0**	**0**	**0**	**7**	**0**	**0**	**0**
1984-85	**Winnipeg Jets**	**NHL**	**40**	**1**	**6**	**7**	**1**	**4**	**5**	**21**	**0**	**1**	**0**	**28**	**3.6**	**26**	**0**	**31**	**6**	**1**	**3**	**0**	**0**	**0**	**2**	**0**	**0**	**0**
	Sherbrooke Canadiens	AHL	28	2	6	8	....	....	....	70	....	....	....	....	....	....	....	....	....	....	....	....	....	....	....	....	....	....
1985-86	**Winnipeg Jets**	**NHL**	**24**	**0**	**1**	**1**	**0**	**1**	**1**	**27**	**0**	**0**	**0**	**13**	**0.0**	**9**	**0**	**31**	**10**	**–12**	....	....	....	....	....	....	....	....
	Sherbrooke Canadiens	AHL	9	0	2	2	....	....	....	26	....	....	....	....	....	....	....	....	....	....	....	....	....	....	....	....	....	....
	Boston Bruins	**NHL**	**8**	**0**	**0**	**0**	**0**	**0**	**0**	**15**	**0**	**0**	**0**	**0**	**0.0**	**1**	**0**	**2**	**2**	**1**	....	....	....	....	....	....	....	....
	Moncton Golden Flames	AHL	17	2	2	4	....	....	....	21	....	....	....	....	....	....	....	....	....	....	10	0	0	0	16	....	....	....
1986-87	**Boston Bruins**	**NHL**	**14**	**0**	**3**	**3**	**0**	**2**	**2**	**24**	**0**	**0**	**0**	**20**	**0.0**	**14**	**0**	**16**	**1**	**–1**	**4**	**0**	**0**	**0**	**11**	**0**	**0**	**0**
	Moncton Golden Flames	AHL	64	12	23	35	....	....	....	34	....	....	....	....	....	....	....	....	....	....	....	....	....	....	....	....	....	....
1987-88	**Boston Bruins**	**NHL**	**6**	**0**	**1**	**1**	**0**	**1**	**1**	**21**	**0**	**0**	**0**	**3**	**0.0**	**3**	**0**	**3**	**1**	**1**	....	....	....	....	....	....	....	....
	Maine Mariners	AHL	69	11	29	40	....	....	....	118	....	....	....	....	....	....	....	....	....	....	10	2	4	6	29	....	....	....
1988-89	HC Bordeaux	France	30	8	12	20	....	....	....	79	....	....	....	....	....	....	....	....	....	....	....	....	....	....	....	....	....	....
1989-90	Cape Breton Oilers	AHL	77	4	31	35	....	....	....	84	....	....	....	....	....	....	....	....	....	....	6	2	3	5	6	....	....	....
1990-91	Cape Breton Oilers	AHL	66	8	13	21	....	....	....	54	....	....	....	....	....	....	....	....	....	....	4	1	1	2	4	....	....	....
	NHL Totals		**213**	**9**	**27**	**36**	**8**	**19**	**27**	**305**	**0**	**1**	**0**	**189**	**4.8**	**167**	**3**	**246**	**58**		**10**	**0**	**0**	**0**	**20**	**0**	**0**	**0**

Signed as a free agent by **Winnipeg**, October 5, 1982. Traded to **Boston** by **Winnipeg** for Bill Derlago, January 31, 1986.

• CAMPEDELLI, Dom

Dominic Joseph D – R. 6'1", 185 lbs. b: Cohasset, MA, 4/3/1964. Toronto's 10th, 129th overall, in 1982.

Season	Club	League	GP	G	A	Pts	AG	AA	APts	PIM	PP	SH	GW	S	%	TGF	PGF	TGA	PGA	+/-	GP	G	A	Pts	PIM	PP	SH	GW
1981-82	Bridgeport Bruins	NEJHL	18	12	8	20	....	....	....	....	....	....	....	....	....	....	....	....	....	....	....	....	....	....	....	....	....	....
1982-83	Boston College	ECAC	26	1	10	11	....	....	....	26	....	....	....	....	....	....	....	....	....	....	....	....	....	....	....	....	....	....
1983-84	Boston College	ECAC	37	10	19	29	....	....	....	24	....	....	....	....	....	....	....	....	....	....	....	....	....	....	....	....	....	....
1984-85	Boston College	H-East	44	5	44	49	....	....	....	74	....	....	....	....	....	....	....	....	....	....	....	....	....	....	....	....	....	....
1985-86	**Montreal Canadiens**	**NHL**	**2**	**0**	**0**	**0**	**0**	**0**	**0**	**0**	**0**	**0**	**0**	**1**	**0.0**	**0**	**0**	**2**	**0**	**–2**	....	....	....	....	....	....	....	....
	Sherbrooke Canadiens	AHL	38	4	10	14	....	....	....	27	....	....	....	....	....	....	....	....	....	....	....	....	....	....	....	....	....	....
1986-87	Sherbrooke Canadiens	AHL	7	3	2	5	....	....	....	2	....	....	....	....	....	....	....	....	....	....	....	....	....	....	....	....	....	....
	Hershey Bears	AHL	45	7	15	22	....	....	....	70	....	....	....	....	....	....	....	....	....	....	....	....	....	....	....	....	....	....
	Nova Scotia Oilers	AHL	12	0	4	4	....	....	....	7	....	....	....	....	....	....	....	....	....	....	5	0	0	0	17	....	....	....
1987-88	Nova Scotia Oilers	AHL	70	5	17	22	....	....	....	117	....	....	....	....	....	....	....	....	....	....	3	1	1	2	2	....	....	....
	NHL Totals		**2**	**0**	**0**	**0**	**0**	**0**	**0**	**0**	**0**	**0**	**0**	**1**	**0.0**	**0**	**0**	**2**	**0**		....	....	....	....	....	....	....	....

Traded to **Montreal** by **Toronto** for Montreal's 2nd round choice (Darryl Shannon) in 1986 Entry Draft and Toronto's 4th round choice (previously acquired, Toronto selected Kent Hulst) in 1986 Entry Draft, September 18, 1985. Traded to **Philadelphia** by **Montreal** for Andre Villeneuve, October 30, 1986. Traded to **Edmonton** by **Philadelphia** for Jeff Brubaker, March 9, 1987.

• CAPUANO, Dave

Dave Alan LW – L. 6'2", 190 lbs. b: Warwick, RI, 7/27/1968. Pittsburgh's 2nd, 25th overall, in 1986.

Season	Club	League	GP (Regular Season)	G	A	Pts	AG	AA	APts	PIM	PP	SH	GW	S	%	TGF	PGF	TGA	PGA	+/–	GP (Playoffs)	G	A	Pts	PIM	PP	SH	GW
1984-85	Mount St. Charles Mounties	Hi-School	22	41	38	79	....	....	....	18	....	....	....	....	....	....	....	....	....	....	....	....	....	....	....	....	....	....
1985-86	Mount St. Charles Mounties	Hi-School	22	39	48	87	....	....	....	20	....	....	....	....	....	....	....	....	....	....	....	....	....	....	....	....	....	....
1986-87	University of Maine	H-East	38	18	41	59	....	....	....	14	....	....	....	....	....	....	....	....	....	....	....	....	....	....	....	....	....	....
	United States	WJC-A	7	1	1	2	....	....	....	2	....	....	....	....	....	....	....	....	....	....	....	....	....	....	....	....	....	....
1987-88	University of Maine	H-East	42	*34	*51	*85	....	....	....	51	....	....	....	....	....	....	....	....	....	....	....	....	....	....	....	....	....	....
1988-89	University of Maine	H-East	41	37	30	67	....	....	....	38	....	....	....	....	....	....	....	....	....	....	....	....	....	....	....	....	....	....
1989-90	**Pittsburgh Penguins**	**NHL**	6	0	0	0	0	0	0	2	0	0	0	1	0.0	1	0	1	0	0	....	....	....	....	....	....	....	....
	Muskegon Lumberjacks	IHL	27	15	15	30	....	....	....	22	....	....	....	....	....	....	....	....	....	....	....	....	....	....	....	....	....	....
	Vancouver Canucks	**NHL**	27	3	5	8	3	4	7	10	0	0	1	25	12.0	10	1	16	0	–7	....	....	....	....	....	....	....	....
	Milwaukee Admirals	IHL	2	0	4	4	....	....	....	0	....	....	....	....	....	....	....	....	....	....	6	1	5	6	0	....	....	....
1990-91	**Vancouver Canucks**	**NHL**	61	13	31	44	12	24	36	42	5	0	1	77	16.9	56	17	38	0	1	6	1	1	2	5	0	0	0
1991-92	Milwaukee Admirals	IHL	9	2	6	8	....	....	....	8	....	....	....	....	....	....	....	....	....	....	....	....	....	....	....	....	....	....
1992-93	Hamilton Canucks	AHL	4	0	1	1	....	....	....	0	....	....	....	....	....	....	....	....	....	....	....	....	....	....	....	....	....	....
	Tampa Bay Lightning	**NHL**	6	1	1	2	1	1	2	2	1	0	0	10	10.0	3	3	4	0	–4	....	....	....	....	....	....	....	....
	Atlanta Knights	IHL	58	19	40	59	....	....	....	50	....	....	....	....	....	....	....	....	....	....	8	2	2	4	9	....	....	....
1993-94	**San Jose Sharks**	**NHL**	4	0	1	1	0	1	1	0	0	0	0	5	0.0	2	2	5	0	–5	....	....	....	....	....	....	....	....
	Providence Bruins	AHL	51	24	29	53	....	....	....	64	....	....	....	....	....	....	....	....	....	....	....	....	....	....	....	....	....	....
	NHL Totals		**104**	**17**	**38**	**55**	**16**	**30**	**46**	**56**	**6**	**0**	**2**	**118**	**14.4**	**72**	**23**	**64**	**0**		**6**	**1**	**1**	**2**	**5**	**0**	**0**	**0**

• Brother of Jack • Hockey East First All-Star Team (1988, 1989) • NCAA Championship All-Tournament Team (1988)

Traded to **Vancouver** by **Pittsburgh** with Andrew McBain and Dan Quinn for Rod Buskas, Barry Pederson and Tony Tanti, January 8, 1990. • Missed majority of 1991-92 season recovering from knee injury originally suffered in game vs. Minnesota, November 27, 1990. Traded to **Tampa Bay** by **Vancouver** with Vancouver's 4th round choice (later traded to New Jersey —later traded to Calgary — Calgary selected Ryan Duthie) in 1994 Entry Draft for Anatoli Semenov, November 3, 1992. Traded to **San Jose** by **Tampa Bay** for Peter Ahola, June 19, 1993. Traded to **Boston** by **San Jose** for cash, November 5, 1993.

• CAPUANO, Jack

D – L. 6'2", 210 lbs. b: Cranston, RI, 7/7/1966. Toronto's 4th, 88th overall, in 1984.

Season	Club	League	GP (Regular Season)	G	A	Pts	AG	AA	APts	PIM	PP	SH	GW	S	%	TGF	PGF	TGA	PGA	+/–	GP (Playoffs)	G	A	Pts	PIM	PP	SH	GW
1983-84	Kent Prep School	Hi-School	21	10	8	18	....	....	....	....	....	....	....	....	....	....	....	....	....	....	....	....	....	....	....	....	....	....
1984-85	University of Maine	H-East	DID NOT PLAY – FRESHMAN																									
1985-86	University of Maine	H-East	39	9	18	27	....	....	....	51	....	....	....	....	....	....	....	....	....	....	....	....	....	....	....	....	....	....
1986-87	University of Maine	H-East	42	10	34	44	....	....	....	20	....	....	....	....	....	....	....	....	....	....	....	....	....	....	....	....	....	....
1987-88	University of Maine	H-East	43	13	37	50	....	....	....	87	....	....	....	....	....	....	....	....	....	....	....	....	....	....	....	....	....	....
1988-89	Newmarket Saints	AHL	74	5	16	21	....	....	....	52	....	....	....	....	....	....	....	....	....	....	1	0	0	0	0	....	....	....
1989-90	**Toronto Maple Leafs**	**NHL**	1	0	0	0	0	0	0	0	0	0	0	1	0.0	0	0	1	0	–1	....	....	....	....	....	....	....	....
	Newmarket Saints	AHL	8	0	2	2	....	....	....	7	....	....	....	....	....	....	....	....	....	....	....	....	....	....	....	....	....	....
	Springfield Indians	AHL	14	0	4	4	....	....	....	8	....	....	....	....	....	....	....	....	....	....	....	....	....	....	....	....	....	....
	Milwaukee Admirals	IHL	17	3	10	13	....	....	....	60	....	....	....	....	....	....	....	....	....	....	6	0	1	1	12	....	....	....
1990-91	**Vancouver Canucks**	**NHL**	3	0	0	0	0	0	0	0	0	0	0	4	0.0	1	0	1	0	0	....	....	....	....	....	....	....	....
	Milwaukee Admirals	IHL	80	20	30	50	....	....	....	76	....	....	....	....	....	....	....	....	....	....	6	0	1	1	2	....	....	....
1991-92	**Boston Bruins**	**NHL**	2	0	0	0	0	0	0	0	0	0	0	1	0.0	1	0	2	0	–1	....	....	....	....	....	....	....	....
	Maine Mariners	AHL	74	14	26	40	....	....	....	35	....	....	....	....	....	....	....	....	....	....	....	....	....	....	....	....	....	....
1992-93			OUT OF HOCKEY – RETIRED																									
1993-1996	Tallahasse Tiger Sharks	ECHL	DID NOT PLAY – ASSISTANT COACH																									
1996-1997	Tallahasse Tiger Sharks	ECHL	DID NOT PLAY – ASSISTANT COACH																									
	Knoxville Speed	ECHL	DID NOT PLAY – COACHING																									
1997-2000	Pee Dee Pride	ECHL	DID NOT PLAY – COACHING																									
	NHL Totals		**6**	**0**	**0**	**0**	**0**	**0**	**0**	**0**	**0**	**0**	**0**	**6**	**0.0**	**2**	**0**	**4**	**0**		....	....	....	....	....	....	....	....

• Brother of Dave • Hockey East Second All-Star Team (1987) • Hockey East First All-Star Team (1988) • IHL Second All-Star Team (1991)

Traded to **NY Islanders** by **Toronto** with Paul Gagne and Derek Laxdal for Mike Stevens and Gilles Thibaudeau, December 20, 1989. Traded to **Vancouver** by **NY Islanders** for Jeff Rohlicek, March 6, 1990. Signed as a free agent by **Boston**, August 1, 1991.

• CARBONNEAU, Guy

C – R. 5'11", 186 lbs. b: Sept-Iles, Que., 3/18/1960. Montreal's 4th, 44th overall, in 1979.

Season	Club	League	GP (Regular Season)	G	A	Pts	AG	AA	APts	PIM	PP	SH	GW	S	%	TGF	PGF	TGA	PGA	+/–	GP (Playoffs)	G	A	Pts	PIM	PP	SH	GW
1976-77	Chicoutimi Sagueneens	QMJHL	59	9	20	29	....	....	....	8	....	....	....	....	....	....	....	....	....	....	4	1	0	1	0	....	....	....
1977-78	Chicoutimi Sagueneens	QMJHL	70	28	55	83	....	....	....	60	....	....	....	....	....	....	....	....	....	....	....	....	....	....	....	....	....	....
1978-79	Chicoutimi Sagueneens	QMJHL	72	62	79	141	....	....	....	47	....	....	....	....	....	....	....	....	....	....	4	2	1	3	4	....	....	....
1979-80	Chicoutimi Sagueneens	QMJHL	72	72	110	182	....	....	....	66	....	....	....	....	....	....	....	....	....	....	12	9	15	24	28	....	....	....
	Nova Scotia Voyageurs	AHL	....	....	....	....	....	....	....	....	....	....	....	....	....	....	....	....	....	....	2	1	1	2	2	....	....	....
1980-81	**Montreal Canadiens**	**NHL**	2	0	1	1	0	1	1	0	0	0	0	1	0.0	1	1	0	0	0	....	....	....	....	....	....	....	....
	Nova Scotia Voyageurs	AHL	78	35	53	88	....	....	....	87	....	....	....	....	....	....	....	....	....	....	6	1	3	4	9	....	....	....
1981-82	Nova Scotia Voyageurs	AHL	77	27	67	94	....	....	....	124	....	....	....	....	....	....	....	....	....	....	9	2	7	9	8	....	....	....
1982-83	**Montreal Canadiens**	**NHL**	77	18	29	47	15	20	35	68	0	5	2	109	16.5	69	4	78	31	18	3	0	0	0	2	0	0	0
1983-84	**Montreal Canadiens**	**NHL**	78	24	30	54	19	20	39	75	3	7	2	166	14.5	72	13	83	29	5	15	4	3	7	12	0	0	1
1984-85	**Montreal Canadiens**	**NHL**	79	23	34	57	19	23	42	43	0	4	2	163	14.1	83	2	86	33	28	12	4	3	7	8	0	1	1
1985-86♦	**Montreal Canadiens**	**NHL**	80	20	36	56	16	24	40	57	1	2	3	147	13.6	84	5	109	48	18	20	7	5	12	35	0	2	1
1986-87	**Montreal Canadiens**	**NHL**	79	18	27	45	16	20	36	68	0	0	2	120	15.0	61	1	78	27	9	17	3	8	11	20	0	0	0
1987-88	**Montreal Canadiens**	**NHL**	80	17	21	38	14	15	29	61	0	3	1	109	15.6	47	0	71	38	14	11	0	4	4	2	0	0	0
1988-89	**Montreal Canadiens**	**NHL**	79	26	30	56	22	21	43	44	1	2	10	142	18.3	72	5	61	31	37	21	4	5	9	10	0	1	0
1989-90	**Montreal Canadiens**	**NHL**	68	19	36	55	16	26	42	37	1	1	3	125	15.2	74	5	79	31	21	11	2	3	5	6	0	0	0
1990-91	Montreal Canadiens	Fr-Tour	3	0	0	0	....	....	....	2	....	....	....	....	....	....	....	....	....	....	....	....	....	....	....	....	....	....
	Montreal Canadiens	**NHL**	78	20	24	44	18	18	36	63	4	1	3	131	15.3	72	10	95	32	–1	13	1	5	6	10	0	0	1
1991-92	**Montreal Canadiens**	**NHL**	72	18	21	39	16	16	32	39	1	1	4	120	15.0	50	1	68	21	2	11	1	1	2	6	0	0	0
1992-93♦	**Montreal Canadiens**	**NHL**	61	4	13	17	3	9	12	20	0	1	0	73	5.5	24	0	68	35	–9	20	3	3	6	10	0	1	2
1993-94	**Montreal Canadiens**	**NHL**	79	14	24	38	13	19	32	48	0	0	1	120	11.7	57	4	67	30	16	7	1	3	4	4	0	0	0
1994-95	**St. Louis Blues**	**NHL**	42	5	11	16	9	16	25	16	1	0	1	33	15.2	28	1	24	8	11	7	1	2	3	6	0	0	0
1995-96	**Dallas Stars**	**NHL**	71	8	15	23	8	12	20	38	0	2	1	54	14.8	32	0	63	29	–2	....	....	....	....	....	....	....	....
1996-97	**Dallas Stars**	**NHL**	73	5	16	21	5	14	19	36	0	1	0	99	5.1	35	0	45	19	9	7	0	1	1	6	0	0	0
1997-98	**Dallas Stars**	**NHL**	77	7	17	24	8	17	25	40	0	1	1	81	8.6	38	1	54	20	3	16	3	1	4	6	0	0	0
1998-99♦	**Dallas Stars**	**NHL**	74	4	12	16	5	12	17	31	0	0	2	60	6.7	22	1	47	23	–3	17	2	4	6	6	0	0	1
99-2000	**Dallas Stars**	**NHL**	69	10	6	16	11	6	17	36	0	1	4	70	14.3	31	0	35	14	10	23	2	4	6	12	0	1	1
	NHL Totals		**1318**	**260**	**403**	**663**	**233**	**309**	**542**	**820**	**12**	**32**	**42**	**1923**	**13.5**	**952**	**54**	**1211**	**499**		**231**	**38**	**55**	**93**	**161**	**0**	**6**	**8**

QMJHL Second All-Star Team (1980) • Won Frank J. Selke Trophy (1988, 1989, 1992)

Traded to **St. Louis** by **Montreal** for Jim Montgomery, August 19, 1994. Traded to **Dallas** by **St. Louis** for Paul Broten, October 2, 1995. • Officially announced retirement, June 29, 2000.

• CARDIN, Claude

LW – L. 5'10", 178 lbs. b: Sorel, Que., 2/17/1941.

Season	Club	League	GP (Regular Season)	G	A	Pts	AG	AA	APts	PIM	PP	SH	GW	S	%	TGF	PGF	TGA	PGA	+/–	GP (Playoffs)	G	A	Pts	PIM	PP	SH	GW
1963-64	Sherbrooke Castors	QSHL	STATISTICS NOT AVAILABLE																									
	Quebec Aces	AHL	3	0	0	0	....	....	....	4	....	....	....	....	....	....	....	....	....	....	....	....	....	....	....	....	....	....
	Omaha Knights	CPHL	....	....	....	....	....	....	....	....	....	....	....	....	....	....	....	....	....	....	4	0	0	0	0	....	....	....
1964-65	Sherbrooke Castors	QSHL	STATISTICS NOT AVAILABLE																									
	Sherbrooke Castors	Al-Cup	13	10	9	19	....	....	....	50	....	....	....	....	....	....	....	....	....	....	....	....	....	....	....	....	....	....
1965-66	Sherbrooke Castors	QSHL	27	12	25	37	....	....	....	77	....	....	....	....	....	....	....	....	....	....	12	6	7	13	*38	....	....	....
	Sherbrooke Castors	Al-Cup	19	6	13	19	....	....	....	56	....	....	....	....	....	....	....	....	....	....	....	....	....	....	....	....	....	....
1966-67	Sherbrooke Castors	QSHL	31	13	34	47	....	....	....	92	....	....	....	....	....	....	....	....	....	....	10	0	7	7	28	....	....	....
1967-68	**St. Louis Blues**	**NHL**	1	0	0	0	0	0	0	0	0	0	0	1	0.0	0	0	1	0	–1	....	....	....	....	....	....	....	....
	Kansas City Blues	CPHL	63	17	35	52	....	....	....	193	....	....	....	....	....	....	....	....	....	....	6	3	5	8	23	....	....	....
1968-69	Portland Buckaroos	WHL	5	0	3	3	....	....	....	0	....	....	....	....	....	....	....	....	....	....	....	....	....	....	....	....	....	....
	Kansas City Blues	CHL	58	10	34	44	....	....	....	153	....	....	....	....	....	....	....	....	....	....	4	1	1	2	4	....	....	....

			REGULAR SEASON																		PLAYOFFS							
Season	Club	League	GP	G	A	Pts	AG	AA	APts	PIM	PP	SH	GW	S	%	TGF	PGF	TGA	PGA	+/-	GP	G	A	Pts	PIM	PP	SH	GW
1969-70	St-Hyacinthe Saints	QSHL	STATISTICS NOT AVAILABLE																									
	Kansas City Blues	CHL	3	1	2	3	....	....	....	5	....	....	....	....	....	....	....	....	....	....	....	....	....	....	....	....	....	....
1970-71	Syracuse Blazers	EHL	16	3	9	12	....	....	....	12	....	....	....	....	....	....	....	....	....	....	....	....	....	....	....	....	....	....
	Des Moines Oak Leafs	IHL	29	10	17	27	....	....	....	20	....	....	....	....	....	....	....	....	....	....	14	3	10	13	34	....	....	....
	NHL Totals		**1**	**0**	**0**	**0**	**0**	**0**	**0**	**0**	**0**	**0**	**0**	**1**	**0.0**	**0**	**0**	**1**	**0**		....	....	....	....	....	....	....	....

Traded to **St. Louis** by **Montreal** for cash, June 21, 1967.

• CARDWELL, Steve

Stephen Michael LW – L. 5'11", 190 lbs. b: Toronto, Ont., 8/13/1950. Pittsburgh's 5th, 63rd overall, in 1970.

Season	Club	League	GP	G	A	Pts	AG	AA	APts	PIM	PP	SH	GW	S	%	TGF	PGF	TGA	PGA	+/-	GP	G	A	Pts	PIM	PP	SH	GW
1968-69	Oshawa Generals	OHA-Jr.	50	11	11	22	....	....	....	54	....	....	....	....	....	....	....	....	....	....	....	....	....	....	....	....	....	....
1969-70	Oshawa Generals	OHA-Jr.	46	14	19	33	....	....	....	77	....	....	....	....	....	....	....	....	....	....	6	4	2	6	6	....	....	....
1970-71	**Pittsburgh Penguins**	**NHL**	**5**	**0**	**1**	**1**	**0**	**1**	**1**	**15**	**0**	**0**	**0**	**2**	**0.0**	**1**	**0**	**5**	**0**	**-4**	....	....	....	....	....	....	....	....
	Amarillo Wranglers	CHL	63	16	34	50	....	....	....	166	....	....	....	....	....	....	....	....	....	....	....	....	....	....	....	....	....	....
1971-72	**Pittsburgh Penguins**	**NHL**	**28**	**7**	**8**	**15**	**7**	**7**	**14**	**18**	**2**	**0**	**1**	**47**	**14.9**	**23**	**5**	**18**	**0**	**0**	**4**	**0**	**0**	**0**	**2**	**0**	**0**	**0**
	Hershey Bears	AHL	46	17	26	43	....	....	....	32	....	....	....	....	....	....	....	....	....	....	....	....	....	....	....	....	....	....
1972-73	**Pittsburgh Penguins**	**NHL**	**20**	**2**	**2**	**4**	**2**	**2**	**4**	**2**	**0**	**0**	**0**	**21**	**9.5**	**4**	**0**	**6**	**0**	**-2**	....	....	....	....	....	....	....	....
	Hershey Bears	AHL	30	16	23	39	....	....	....	20	....	....	....	....	....	....	....	....	....	....	7	5	2	7	22	....	....	....
1973-74	Minnesota Fighting Saints	WHA	77	23	23	46	....	....	....	100	....	....	....	....	....	....	....	....	....	....	10	0	0	0	20	....	....	....
1974-75	Cleveland Crusaders	WHA	75	9	13	22	....	....	....	127	....	....	....	....	....	....	....	....	....	....	5	0	1	1	14	....	....	....
1975-76	Hershey Bears	AHL	72	22	33	55	....	....	....	165	....	....	....	....	....	....	....	....	....	....	9	0	2	2	11	....	....	....
1976-77	Djurgardens IF Stockholm	Sweden-2	19	6	2	8	....	....	....	60	....	....	....	....	....	....	....	....	....	....	....	....	....	....	....	....	....	....
1977-78	Whitby Warriors	OHA-Sr.	15	12	8	20	....	....	....	62	....	....	....	....	....	....	....	....	....	....	....	....	....	....	....	....	....	....
	San Francisco Shamrocks	PHL	33	21	28	49	....	....	....	92	....	....	....	....	....	....	....	....	....	....	....	....	....	....	....	....	....	....
1978-79	Tucson Rustlers	PHL	22	3	10	13	....	....	....	51	....	....	....	....	....	....	....	....	....	....	....	....	....	....	....	....	....	....
	NHL Totals		**53**	**9**	**11**	**20**	**9**	**10**	**19**	**35**	**2**	**0**	**1**	**70**	**12.9**	**28**	**5**	**29**	**0**		**4**	**0**	**0**	**0**	**2**	**0**	**0**	**0**
	Other Major League Totals		152	32	36	68	....	....	....	227	....	....	....	....	....	....	....	....	....	....	15	0	1	1	34	....	....	....

Selected by **Ontario-Ottawa** (WHA) in 1972 WHA General Player Draft, February 12, 1972. WHA rights traded to **Minnesota** (WHA) by **Ottawa** (WHA) for cash, July, 1973. Selected by **Indianapolis** (WHA) from **Minnesota** (WHA) in 1974 WHA Expansion Draft, May, 1974. Traded to **Cleveland** (WHA) by **Indianapolis** (WHA) for future considerations, August, 1974.

• CARKNER, Terry

Terry Kenneth D – L. 6'3", 210 lbs. b: Smiths Falls, Ont., 3/7/1966. NY Rangers' 1st, 14th overall, in 1984.

Season	Club	League	GP	G	A	Pts	AG	AA	APts	PIM	PP	SH	GW	S	%	TGF	PGF	TGA	PGA	+/-	GP	G	A	Pts	PIM	PP	SH	GW
1980-81	Winchester Hawks	OHA-B	2	0	0	0	....	....	....	0	....	....	....	....	....	....	....	....	....	....	....	....	....	....	....	....	....	....
1981-82	Smiths Falls Settlers	OJHL-C	STATISTICS NOT AVAILABLE																									
1982-83	Brockville Braves	OJHL	47	8	32	40	....	....	....	94	....	....	....	....	....	....	....	....	....	....	....	....	....	....	....	....	....	....
1983-84	Peterborough Petes	OHL	66	4	21	25	....	....	....	91	....	....	....	....	....	....	....	....	....	....	8	0	6	6	13	....	....	....
1984-85	Peterborough Petes	OHL	64	14	47	61	....	....	....	125	....	....	....	....	....	....	....	....	....	....	17	2	10	12	11	....	....	....
1985-86	Peterborough Petes	OHL	54	12	32	44	....	....	....	106	....	....	....	....	....	....	....	....	....	....	16	1	7	8	17	....	....	....
	Canada	WJC-A	7	0	4	4	....	....	....	0	....	....	....	....	....	....	....	....	....	....	....	....	....	....	....	....	....	....
1986-87	**New York Rangers**	**NHL**	**52**	**2**	**13**	**15**	**2**	**9**	**11**	**118**	**0**	**0**	**0**	**33**	**6.1**	**52**	**8**	**51**	**6**	**-1**	**1**	**0**	**0**	**0**	**0**	**0**	**0**	**0**
	New Haven Nighthawks	AHL	12	2	6	8	....	....	....	56	....	....	....	....	....	....	....	....	....	....	3	1	0	1	0	....	....	....
1987-88	**Quebec Nordiques**	**NHL**	**63**	**3**	**24**	**27**	**3**	**17**	**20**	**159**	**2**	**0**	**1**	**54**	**5.6**	**58**	**36**	**47**	**17**	**-8**	....	....	....	....	....	....	....	....
1988-89	**Philadelphia Flyers**	**NHL**	**78**	**11**	**32**	**43**	**9**	**23**	**32**	**149**	**2**	**1**	**1**	**84**	**13.1**	**96**	**28**	**107**	**33**	**-6**	**19**	**1**	**5**	**6**	**28**	**0**	**1**	**0**
1989-90	**Philadelphia Flyers**	**NHL**	**63**	**4**	**18**	**22**	**3**	**13**	**16**	**169**	**1**	**0**	**1**	**60**	**6.7**	**62**	**11**	**90**	**31**	**-8**	....	....	....	....	....	....	....	....
1990-91	**Philadelphia Flyers**	**NHL**	**79**	**7**	**25**	**32**	**6**	**19**	**25**	**204**	**6**	**0**	**1**	**97**	**7.2**	**98**	**34**	**126**	**47**	**-15**	....	....	....	....	....	....	....	....
1991-92	**Philadelphia Flyers**	**NHL**	**73**	**4**	**12**	**16**	**4**	**9**	**13**	**195**	**0**	**1**	**0**	**70**	**5.7**	**60**	**7**	**102**	**35**	**-14**	....	....	....	....	....	....	....	....
1992-93	**Philadelphia Flyers**	**NHL**	**83**	**3**	**16**	**19**	**2**	**11**	**13**	**150**	**0**	**0**	**0**	**45**	**6.7**	**91**	**7**	**113**	**47**	**18**	....	....	....	....	....	....	....	....
	Canada	WC-A	8	0	0	0	....	....	....	0	....	....	....	....	....	....	....	....	....	....	....	....	....	....	....	....	....	....
1993-94	**Detroit Red Wings**	**NHL**	**68**	**1**	**6**	**7**	**1**	**5**	**6**	**130**	**0**	**0**	**0**	**32**	**3.1**	**60**	**2**	**65**	**20**	**13**	**7**	**0**	**0**	**0**	**4**	**0**	**0**	**0**
1994-95	**Detroit Red Wings**	**NHL**	**20**	**1**	**2**	**3**	**2**	**3**	**5**	**21**	**0**	**0**	**0**	**9**	**11.1**	**16**	**0**	**9**	**0**	**7**	....	....	....	....	....	....	....	....
1995-96	**Florida Panthers**	**NHL**	**73**	**3**	**10**	**13**	**3**	**8**	**11**	**80**	**1**	**0**	**0**	**42**	**7.1**	**67**	**3**	**83**	**29**	**10**	**22**	**0**	**4**	**4**	**10**	**0**	**0**	**0**
1996-97	**Florida Panthers**	**NHL**	**70**	**0**	**14**	**14**	**0**	**12**	**12**	**96**	**0**	**0**	**0**	**38**	**0.0**	**47**	**2**	**74**	**25**	**-4**	**5**	**0**	**0**	**0**	**6**	**0**	**0**	**0**
1997-98	**Florida Panthers**	**NHL**	**74**	**1**	**7**	**8**	**1**	**7**	**8**	**63**	**0**	**0**	**1**	**34**	**2.9**	**48**	**1**	**74**	**33**	**6**	....	....	....	....	....	....	....	....
1998-99	**Florida Panthers**	**NHL**	**62**	**2**	**9**	**11**	**2**	**9**	**11**	**54**	**0**	**0**	**0**	**25**	**8.0**	**37**	**0**	**57**	**20**	**0**	....	....	....	....	....	....	....	....
	NHL Totals		**858**	**42**	**188**	**230**	**38**	**145**	**183**	**1588**	**12**	**2**	**5**	**623**	**6.7**	**792**	**139**	**998**	**343**		**54**	**1**	**9**	**10**	**48**	**0**	**1**	**0**

OHL Second All-Star Team (1985) • OHL First All-Star Team (1986)

Traded to **Quebec** by **NY Rangers** with Jeff Jackson for John Ogrodnick and David Shaw, September 30, 1987. Traded to **Philadelphia** by **Quebec** for Greg Smyth and Philadelphia's 3rd round choice (John Tanner) in 1989 Entry Draft, July 25, 1988. Traded to **Detroit** by **Philadelphia** for Yves Racine and Detroit's 4th round choice (Sebastien Vallee) in 1994 Entry Draft, October 5, 1993. Signed as a free agent by **Florida**, August 8, 1995.

• CARLETON, Wayne

Kenneth Wayne "Swoop" LW – L. 6'3", 212 lbs. b: Sudbury, Ont., 8/4/1946.

Season	Club	League	GP	G	A	Pts	AG	AA	APts	PIM	PP	SH	GW	S	%	TGF	PGF	TGA	PGA	+/-	GP	G	A	Pts	PIM	PP	SH	GW
1961-62	Unionville Seaforths	MTJHL	15	9	3	12	....	....	....	....	....	....	....	....	....	....	....	....	....	....	....	....	....	....	....	....	....	....
	Toronto Marlboros	OHA-Jr.	16	5	8	13	....	....	....	5	....	....	....	....	....	....	....	....	....	....	12	2	4	6	4	....	....	....
1962-63	Toronto Marlboros	OHA-Jr.	38	27	24	51	....	....	....	11	....	....	....	....	....	....	....	....	....	....	11	6	4	10	21	....	....	....
1963-64	Toronto Marlboros	OHA-Jr.	54	42	22	64	....	....	....	26	....	....	....	....	....	....	....	....	....	....	5	3	2	5	0	....	....	....
	Toronto Marlboros	Mem-Cup	12	10	15	25	....	....	....	6	....	....	....	....	....	....	....	....	....	....	....	....	....	....	....	....	....	....
1964-65	Toronto Marlboros	OHA-Jr.	15	13	10	23	....	....	....	12	....	....	....	....	....	....	....	....	....	....	14	5	6	11	17	....	....	....
1965-66	Toronto Marlboros	OHA-Jr.	16	9	5	14	....	....	....	24	....	....	....	....	....	....	....	....	....	....	14	9	6	15	28	....	....	....
	Toronto Maple Leafs	**NHL**	**2**	**0**	**1**	**1**	**0**	**1**	**1**	**0**	....	....	....	....	....	....	....	....	....	....	....	....	....	....	....	....	....	....
	Tulsa Oilers	CPHL	....	....	....	....	....	....	....	....	....	....	....	....	....	....	....	....	....	....	6	3	4	7	0	....	....	....
1966-67	**Toronto Maple Leafs**	**NHL**	**5**	**1**	**0**	**1**	**1**	**0**	**1**	**14**	....	....	....	....	....	....	....	....	....	....	....	....	....	....	....	....	....	....
	Tulsa Oilers	CPHL	52	17	15	32	....	....	....	48	....	....	....	....	....	....	....	....	....	....	....	....	....	....	....	....	....	....
	Rochester Americans	AHL	13	5	5	10	....	....	....	8	....	....	....	....	....	....	....	....	....	....	13	5	2	7	*31	....	....	....
1967-68	**Toronto Maple Leafs**	**NHL**	**65**	**8**	**11**	**19**	**9**	**11**	**20**	**34**	**0**	**0**	**1**	**140**	**5.7**	**36**	**4**	**27**	**0**	**5**	....	....	....	....	....	....	....	....
1968-69	**Toronto Maple Leafs**	**NHL**	**12**	**1**	**3**	**4**	**1**	**3**	**4**	**6**	**0**	**0**	**0**	**24**	**4.2**	**5**	**1**	**12**	**0**	**-8**	....	....	....	....	....	....	....	....
	Rochester Americans	AHL	13	5	3	8	....	....	....	0	....	....	....	....	....	....	....	....	....	....	....	....	....	....	....	....	....	....
	Phoenix Roadrunners	WHL	32	16	13	29	....	....	....	18	....	....	....	....	....	....	....	....	....	....	....	....	....	....	....	....	....	....
1969-70	**Toronto Maple Leafs**	**NHL**	**7**	**0**	**1**	**1**	**0**	**1**	**1**	**6**	**0**	**0**	**0**	**6**	**0.0**	**3**	**0**	**2**	**0**	**1**	....	....	....	....	....	....	....	....
	Phoenix Roadrunners	WHL	6	1	3	4	....	....	....	0	....	....	....	....	....	....	....	....	....	....	....	....	....	....	....	....	....	....
♦	**Boston Bruins**	**NHL**	**42**	**6**	**19**	**25**	**6**	**18**	**24**	**23**	**0**	**0**	**1**	**80**	**7.5**	**35**	**6**	**23**	**0**	**6**	**14**	**2**	**4**	**6**	**14**	**0**	**0**	**0**
1970-71	**Boston Bruins**	**NHL**	**69**	**22**	**24**	**46**	**22**	**20**	**42**	**44**	**0**	**0**	**5**	**164**	**13.4**	**67**	**1**	**32**	**1**	**35**	**4**	**0**	**0**	**0**	**0**	**0**	**0**	**0**
1971-72	**California Golden Seals**	**NHL**	**76**	**17**	**14**	**31**	**17**	**12**	**29**	**45**	**4**	**0**	**0**	**188**	**9.0**	**57**	**11**	**81**	**12**	**-23**	....	....	....	....	....	....	....	....
1972-73	Ottawa Nationals	WHA	75	42	49	91	....	....	....	42	....	....	....	....	....	....	....	....	....	....	3	3	3	6	4	....	....	....
1973-74	Toronto Toros	WHA	78	37	55	92	....	....	....	31	....	....	....	....	....	....	....	....	....	....	12	2	12	14	4	....	....	....
1974-75	New England Whalers	WHA	73	35	39	74	....	....	....	50	....	....	....	....	....	....	....	....	....	....	6	2	5	7	14	....	....	....
1975-76	New England Whalers	WHA	35	12	21	33	....	....	....	6	....	....	....	....	....	....	....	....	....	....	....	....	....	....	....	....	....	....
	Edmonton Oilers	WHA	26	5	16	21	....	....	....	6	....	....	....	....	....	....	....	....	....	....	4	1	1	2	2	....	....	....
1976-77	Birmingham Bulls	WHA	3	1	0	1	....	....	....	0	....	....	....	....	....	....	....	....	....	....	....	....	....	....	....	....	....	....
	Barrie Flyers	OHA-Sr.	20	7	20	27	....	....	....	6	....	....	....	....	....	....	....	....	....	....	....	....	....	....	....	....	....	....
1977-78	Barrie Flyers	OHA-Sr.	35	21	23	44	....	....	....	27	....	....	....	....	....	....	....	....	....	....	....	....	....	....	....	....	....	....
	NHL Totals		**278**	**55**	**73**	**128**	**56**	**66**	**122**	**172**	....	....	....	....	....	....	....	....	....	....	**18**	**2**	**4**	**6**	**14**	....	....	....
	Other Major League Totals		290	132	180	312	....	....	....	135	....	....	....	....	....	....	....	....	....	....	25	8	21	29	24	....	....	....

WHA Second All-Star Team (1974) • Played in NHL All-Star Game (1968)

Traded to **Boston** by **Toronto** for Jim Harrison, December 10, 1969. Claimed by **California** from **Boston** in Intra-League Draft, June 8, 1971. Selected by **Ontario-Ottawa** (WHA) in 1972 WHA General Player Draft, February 12, 1972. Transferred to **Toronto** (WHA) after **Ottawa** (WHA) franchise relocated, May, 1973. Traded to **New England** (WHA) by **Toronto** (WHA) for future considerations (Jim Dorey, December, 1974), September, 1974. Traded to **Edmonton** (WHA) by **New England** (WHA) for Mike Rogers and future considerations, January, 1976. Signed as a free agent by **Birmingham** (WHA), January, 1977.

• CARLIN, Brian
Brian John LW – L. 5'10", 175 lbs. b: Calgary, Alta., 6/13/1950. Los Angeles' 5th, 86th overall, in 1970.

			REGULAR SEASON																		PLAYOFFS							
Season	Club	League	GP	G	A	Pts	AG	AA	APts	PIM	PP	SH	GW	S	%	TGF	PGF	TGA	PGA	+/–	GP	G	A	Pts	PIM	PP	SH	GW
1967-68	Calgary Centennials	WCJHL	57	11	16	27	....	....	....	47	....	....	....	....	....	....	....	....	....	....	....	....	....	....	....	....	....	....
1968-69	Calgary Centennials	WCJHL	56	15	14	29	....	....	....	40	....	....	....	....	....	....	....	....	....	....	11	3	1	4	....	....	....	....
1969-70	Calgary Centennials	WCJHL	48	16	24	40	....	....	....	33	....	....	....	....	....	....	....	....	....	....	....	....	....	....	....	....	....	....
1970-71	Medicine Hat Tigers	WCJHL	65	44	56	100	....	....	....	46	....	....	....	....	....	....	....	....	....	....	....	....	....	....	....	....	....	....
1971-72	**Los Angeles Kings**	**NHL**	**5**	**1**	**0**	**1**	**1**	**0**	**1**	**0**	**0**	**0**	**0**	**3**	**33.3**	**1**	**0**	**1**	**0**	**0**	....	....	....	....	....	....	....	....
	Springfield Kings	AHL	67	35	31	66	....	....	....	6	....	....	....	....	....	....	....	....	....	....	5	0	0	0	2	....	....	....
1972-73	Alberta Oilers	WHA	65	12	22	34	....	....	....	6	....	....	....	....	....	....	....	....	....	....	....	....	....	....	....	....	....	....
1973-74	Edmonton Oilers	WHA	5	1	0	1	....	....	....	0	....	....	....	....	....	....	....	....	....	....	....	....	....	....	....	....	....	....
	Winston-Salem Polar Bears	SHL	66	36	42	78	....	....	....	29	....	....	....	....	....	....	....	....	....	....	7	2	1	3	2	....	....	....
1974-75	Calgary Trojans	ASHL	STATISTICS NOT AVAILABLE																									
1975-76	Calgary Trojans	ASHL	STATISTICS NOT AVAILABLE																									
1976-77	Calgary Trojans	ASHL	20	18	20	38	....	....	....	10	....	....	....	....	....	....	....	....	....	....	....	....	....	....	....	....	....	....
	NHL Totals		**5**	**1**	**0**	**1**	**1**	**0**	**1**	**0**	**0**	**0**	**0**	**3**	**33.3**	**1**	**0**	**1**	**0**		....	....	....	....	....	....	....	....
	Other Major League Totals		70	13	22	35	....	....	....	6	....	....	....	....	....	....	....	....	....	....	....	....	....	....	....	....	....	....

SHL Second All-Star Team (1974) • Selected by **Alberta** (WHA) in 1972 WHA General Player Draft, February 12, 1972.

• CARLSON, Jack
Jack Anthony "The Big Bopper" LW – L. 6'3", 205 lbs. b: Virginia, MN, 8/23/1954. Detroit's 7th, 117th overall, in 1974.

Season	Club	League	GP	G	A	Pts	AG	AA	APts	PIM	PP	SH	GW	S	%	TGF	PGF	TGA	PGA	+/–	GP	G	A	Pts	PIM	PP	SH	GW
1972-73	Minnesota Rangers	USHL	35	15	18	33	....	....	....	49	....	....	....	....	....	....	....	....	....	....	....	....	....	....	....	....	....	....
1973-74	Marquette Iron Rangers	USHL	42	42	29	71	....	....	....	159	....	....	....	....	....	....	....	....	....	....	....	....	....	....	....	....	....	....
1974-75	Minnesota Fighting Saints	WHA	32	5	5	10	....	....	....	85	....	....	....	....	....	....	....	....	....	....	10	1	2	3	41	....	....	....
	Johnstown Jets	NAHL	50	27	22	49	....	....	....	248	....	....	....	....	....	....	....	....	....	....	....	....	....	....	....	....	....	....
1975-76	Minnesota Fighting Saints	WHA	58	8	10	18	....	....	....	189	....	....	....	....	....	....	....	....	....	....	....	....	....	....	....	....	....	....
	Edmonton Oilers	WHA	10	1	1	2	....	....	....	31	....	....	....	....	....	....	....	....	....	....	4	0	0	0	4	....	....	....
1976-77	Minnesota Fighting Saints	WHA	36	4	3	7	....	....	....	55	....	....	....	....	....	....	....	....	....	....	....	....	....	....	....	....	....	....
	New England Whalers	WHA	35	7	5	12	....	....	....	81	....	....	....	....	....	....	....	....	....	....	5	1	1	2	9	....	....	....
1977-78	New England Whalers	WHA	67	9	20	29	....	....	....	192	....	....	....	....	....	....	....	....	....	....	9	1	1	2	14	....	....	....
1978-79	New England Whalers	WHA	34	2	7	9	....	....	....	61	....	....	....	....	....	....	....	....	....	....	....	....	....	....	....	....	....	....
	Minnesota North Stars	**NHL**	**16**	**3**	**0**	**3**	**3**	**0**	**3**	**40**	**0**	**0**	**0**	**18**	**16.7**	**9**	**0**	**7**	**0**	**2**	....	....	....	....	....	....	....	....
1979-80	**Minnesota North Stars**	**NHL**	DID NOT PLAY – INJURED																									
1980-81	**Minnesota North Stars**	**NHL**	**43**	**7**	**2**	**9**	**5**	**1**	**6**	**108**	**0**	**0**	**0**	**24**	**29.2**	**18**	**0**	**23**	**0**	**–5**	**15**	**1**	**2**	**3**	**50**	**0**	**0**	**0**
1981-82	**Minnesota North Stars**	**NHL**	**57**	**8**	**4**	**12**	**6**	**3**	**9**	**103**	**1**	**0**	**1**	**39**	**20.5**	**15**	**1**	**19**	**0**	**–5**	**1**	**0**	**0**	**0**	**15**	**0**	**0**	**0**
1982-83	**St. Louis Blues**	**NHL**	**54**	**6**	**1**	**7**	**5**	**1**	**6**	**58**	**0**	**0**	**1**	**43**	**14.0**	**14**	**1**	**16**	**0**	**–3**	**4**	**0**	**0**	**0**	**5**	**0**	**0**	**0**
1983-84	**St. Louis Blues**	**NHL**	**58**	**6**	**8**	**14**	**5**	**5**	**10**	**95**	**0**	**0**	**0**	**35**	**17.1**	**21**	**1**	**14**	**3**	**9**	**5**	**0**	**0**	**0**	**2**	**0**	**0**	**0**
1984-85			OUT OF HOCKEY – RETIRED																									
1985-86			OUT OF HOCKEY – RETIRED																									
1986-87	**Minnesota North Stars**	**NHL**	**8**	**0**	**0**	**0**	**0**	**0**	**0**	**13**	**0**	**0**	**0**	**1**	**0.0**	**1**	**0**	**1**	**0**	**0**	....	....	....	....	....	....	....	....
	NHL Totals		**236**	**30**	**15**	**45**	**24**	**10**	**34**	**417**	**1**	**0**	**2**	**160**	**18.8**	**78**	**3**	**80**	**3**		**25**	**1**	**2**	**3**	**72**	**0**	**0**	**0**
	Other Major League Totals		272	36	51	87	....	....	....	694	....	....	....	....	....	....	....	....	....	....	28	3	4	7	68	....	....	....

• Brother of Steve

Selected by **Minnesota** (WHA) in 1974 WHA Amateur Draft, June, 1974. Signed as a free agent by **Edmonton** (WHA) after **Minnesota** (WHA) franchise folded, March 10, 1976. Claimed by **Calgary** (WHA) from **Edmonton** in 1976 WHA Intra-League Draft, June, 1976. Sold to **Edmonton** (WHA) by **Minnesota** (WHA) with Mike Antonovich, Bill Butters, Dave Keon, Jean-Louis Levasseur, Steve Carlson and John McKenzie fror cash, January, 1977. Traded to **New England** (WHA) by **Edmonton** (WHA) with Dave Keon, Steve Carlson, Dave Dryden and John McKenzie for future considerations (Dave Debol, June, 1977), Dan Arndt and cash, January, 1977. Rights traded to **Minnesota** by **Detroit** for future considerations, July 27, 1978. Traded to **Minnesota** by **New England** (WHA) for future considerations, February 1, 1979. • Missed entire 1979-80 season recovering from back surgery. Claimed by **St. Louis** from **Minnesota** in Waiver Draft, October 4, 1982. Signed as a free agent by **Minnesota**, November, 1986.

• CARLSON, Kent
D – L. 6'3", 200 lbs. b: Concord, NH, 1/11/1962. Montreal's 3rd, 32nd overall, in 1982.

Season	Club	League	GP	G	A	Pts	AG	AA	APts	PIM	PP	SH	GW	S	%	TGF	PGF	TGA	PGA	+/–	GP	G	A	Pts	PIM	PP	SH	GW
1981-82	St. Lawrence University	ECAC	28	8	14	22	....	....	....	24	....	....	....	....	....	....	....	....	....	....	....	....	....	....	....	....	....	....
1982-83	St. Lawrence University	ECAC	35	10	23	33	....	....	....	56	....	....	....	....	....	....	....	....	....	....	....	....	....	....	....	....	....	....
1983-84	**Montreal Canadiens**	**NHL**	**65**	**3**	**7**	**10**	**2**	**5**	**7**	**73**	**0**	**0**	**2**	**41**	**7.3**	**33**	**4**	**44**	**0**	**–15**	....	....	....	....	....	....	....	....
1984-85	**Montreal Canadiens**	**NHL**	**18**	**1**	**1**	**2**	**1**	**1**	**2**	**33**	**0**	**0**	**0**	**5**	**20.0**	**5**	**0**	**4**	**0**	**1**	....	....	....	....	....	....	....	....
	Sherbrooke Canadiens	AHL	13	1	4	5	....	....	....	7	....	....	....	....	....	....	....	....	....	....	2	1	1	2	0	....	....	....
1985-86	**Montreal Canadiens**	**NHL**	**2**	**0**	**0**	**0**	**0**	**0**	**0**	**0**	**0**	**0**	**0**	**0**	**0.0**	**0**	**0**	**0**	**0**	**0**	....	....	....	....	....	....	....	....
	Sherbrooke Canadiens	AHL	35	11	15	26	....	....	....	79	....	....	....	....	....	....	....	....	....	....	....	....	....	....	....	....	....	....
	St. Louis Blues	**NHL**	**26**	**2**	**3**	**5**	**2**	**2**	**4**	**42**	**0**	**0**	**0**	**14**	**14.3**	**6**	**0**	**4**	**0**	**2**	**5**	**0**	**0**	**0**	**11**	**0**	**0**	**0**
1986-87	**St. Louis Blues**	**NHL**	DID NOT PLAY – INJURED																									
1987-88	Peoria Rivermen	IHL	52	5	16	21	....	....	....	88	....	....	....	....	....	....	....	....	....	....	....	....	....	....	....	....	....	....
	St. Louis Blues	**NHL**	....	....	....	....	....	....	....	....	....	....	....	....	....	....	....	....	....	....	**3**	**0**	**0**	**0**	**2**	**0**	**0**	**0**
1988-89	**Washington Capitals**	**NHL**	**2**	**1**	**0**	**1**	**1**	**0**	**1**	**0**	**0**	**0**	**0**	**1**	**100.0**	**2**	**0**	**0**	**0**	**2**	....	....	....	....	....	....	....	....
	Baltimore Skipjacks	AHL	28	2	8	10	....	....	....	69	....	....	....	....	....	....	....	....	....	....	....	....	....	....	....	....	....	....
	NHL Totals		**113**	**7**	**11**	**18**	**6**	**8**	**14**	**148**	**0**	**0**	**2**	**61**	**11.5**	**46**	**4**	**52**	**0**		**8**	**0**	**0**	**0**	**13**	**0**	**0**	**0**

ECAC Second All-Star Team (1983)

• Missed majority of 1984-85 season recovering from hand injury suffered in game vs. NY Islanders, January 8, 1985. Traded to **St. Louis** by **Montreal** for Graham Herring and St. Louis' 5th round choice (Eric Aubertin) in 1986 Entry Draft, January 31, 1986. • Missed entire 1986-87 season recovering from spinal fusion surgery. Traded to **Winnipeg** by **St. Louis** with St. Louis' 12th round choice (Sergei Kharin) in 1989 Entry Draft and 4th round choice (Scott Levins) in 1990 Entry Draft for Peter Douris, September 29, 1988. Traded to **Washington** by **Winnipeg** for future considerations, October 19, 1988.

• CARLSON, Steve
Steve Edward C – L. 6'3", 180 lbs. b: Virginia, MN, 8/26/1955. Detroit's 10th, 131st overall, in 1975.

Season	Club	League	GP	G	A	Pts	AG	AA	APts	PIM	PP	SH	GW	S	%	TGF	PGF	TGA	PGA	+/–	GP	G	A	Pts	PIM	PP	SH	GW
1973-74	Marquette Iron Rangers	USHL	42	34	45	79	....	....	....	77	....	....	....	....	....	....	....	....	....	....	12	4	4	8	5	....	....	....
1974-75	Johnstown Jets	NAHL	70	30	58	88	....	....	....	84	....	....	....	....	....	....	....	....	....	....	12	6	4	10	....	....	....	....
1975-76	Johnstown Jets	NAHL	40	22	24	46	....	....	....	55	....	....	....	....	....	....	....	....	....	....	9	4	5	9	6	....	....	....
	Minnesota Fighting Saints	WHA	10	0	1	1	....	....	....	23	....	....	....	....	....	....	....	....	....	....	....	....	....	....	....	....	....	....
1976-77	Minnesota Fighting Saints	WHA	21	5	8	13	....	....	....	8	....	....	....	....	....	....	....	....	....	....	....	....	....	....	....	....	....	....
	New England Whalers	WHA	31	4	9	13	....	....	....	40	....	....	....	....	....	....	....	....	....	....	5	0	0	0	9	....	....	....
1977-78	Springfield Indians	AHL	37	21	15	36	....	....	....	48	....	....	....	....	....	....	....	....	....	....	....	....	....	....	....	....	....	....
	New England Whalers	WHA	38	6	7	13	....	....	....	11	....	....	....	....	....	....	....	....	....	....	13	2	7	9	2	....	....	....
1978-79	Edmonton Oilers	WHA	73	18	22	40	....	....	....	50	....	....	....	....	....	....	....	....	....	....	11	1	1	2	12	....	....	....
1979-80	**Los Angeles Kings**	**NHL**	**52**	**9**	**12**	**21**	**8**	**9**	**17**	**23**	**1**	**0**	**1**	**45**	**20.0**	**33**	**6**	**59**	**25**	**–7**	**4**	**1**	**1**	**2**	**7**	**0**	**0**	**0**
1980-81	Houston Apollos	CHL	27	13	21	34	....	....	....	29	....	....	....	....	....	....	....	....	....	....	....	....	....	....	....	....	....	....
	Springfield Indians	AHL	32	10	14	24	....	....	....	44	....	....	....	....	....	....	....	....	....	....	7	2	2	4	39	....	....	....
1981-82	Nashville South Stars	CHL	59	23	39	62	....	....	....	63	....	....	....	....	....	....	....	....	....	....	....	....	....	....	....	....	....	....
1982-83	Birmingham South Stars	CHL	69	25	42	67	....	....	....	73	....	....	....	....	....	....	....	....	....	....	9	1	4	5	4	....	....	....
1983-84	Baltimore Skipjacks	AHL	63	9	30	39	....	....	....	70	....	....	....	....	....	....	....	....	....	....	10	7	3	10	8	....	....	....
1984-85	Baltimore Skipjacks	AHL	76	18	29	47	....	....	....	69	....	....	....	....	....	....	....	....	....	....	15	2	6	8	4	....	....	....
1985-86	Baltimore Skipjacks	AHL	66	9	27	36	....	....	....	56	....	....	....	....	....	....	....	....	....	....	....	....	....	....	....	....	....	....
1986-87	Baltimore Skipjacks	AHL	67	12	13	25	....	....	....	32	....	....	....	....	....	....	....	....	....	....	....	....	....	....	....	....	....	....
	NHL Totals		**52**	**9**	**12**	**21**	**8**	**9**	**17**	**23**	**1**	**0**	**1**	**45**	**20.0**	**33**	**6**	**59**	**25**		**4**	**1**	**1**	**2**	**7**	**0**	**0**	**0**
	Other Major League Totals		173	33	47	80	....	....	....	132	....	....	....	....	....	....	....	....	....	....	29	3	8	11	23	....	....	....

• Brother of Jack • USHL First All-Star Team (1974)

Selected by **Minnesota** (WHA) in 1974 WHA Amateur Draft, June, 1974. Signed as a free agent by **New England** (WHA) after **Minnesota** (WHA) franchise folded, May, 1976: Claimed by **Florida-Minnesota** (WHA) from **New England** (WHA) in 1976 WHA Intra-League Draft, June, 1976. Traded to **Edmonton** (WHA) by **Minnesota** (WHA) with Mike Antonovich, Bill Butters, Dave Keon, Jack Carlson, Jean-Louis Levasseur and John McKenzie for cash, January, 1977. Traded to **New England** (WHA) by **Edmonton** (WHA) with Dave Keon, Jack Carlson, Dave Dryden and John McKenzie for future considerations (Dave Debol, June, 1977), Dan Arndt and cash, January, 1977. Claimed on waivers by **Edmonton** (WHA) from **New England** (WHA), May, 1978. NHL rights traded to **LA Kings** by **Detroit** for Steve Short, December 6, 1978. Reclaimed by **LA Kings** from **Edmonton** prior to Expansion Draft, June 9, 1979. Signed as a free agent by **Minnesota**, August 9, 1982. Signed as a free agent by **Pittsburgh**, August 15, 1983.

• CARLSSON, Anders "Masken" C – L. 5'11", 185 lbs. b: Gavle, Sweden, 11/25/1960. New Jersey's 5th, 66th overall, in 1986.

Season	Club	League	GP	G	A	Pts	AG	AA	APts	PIM	PP	SH	GW	S	%	TGF	PGF	TGA	PGA	+/-	GP	G	A	Pts	PIM	PP	SH	GW
			REGULAR SEASON																		PLAYOFFS							
1978-79	Brynas IF Gavle	Sweden	1	0	0	0				2																		
1979-80	Brynas IF Gavle	Sweden	17	0	1	1				6											1	0	0	0	0			
1980-81	Brynas IF Gavle	Sweden	36	8	8	16				36																		
1981-82	Brynas IF Gavle	Sweden	35	5	5	10				22																		
1982-83	Brynas IF Gavle	Sweden	35	18	13	31				26																		
1983-84	Brynas IF Gavle	Sweden	35	8	26	34				34																		
1984-85	Sodertalje SK	Sweden	36	20	14	34				18											8	0	3	3	18			
1985-86	Sodertalje SK	Sweden	36	12	26	38				20											7	2	4	6	0			
	Sweden	WEC-A	10	6	6	12				12																		
1986-87	**New Jersey Devils**	**NHL**	**48**	**2**	**18**	**20**	**2**	**13**	**15**	**14**	**0**	**0**	**0**	**35**	**5.7**	**32**	**6**	**38**	**1**	**–11**								
	Maine Mariners	AHL	6	0	6	6				2																		
	Sweden	WEC-A	10	4	3	7				6																		
1987-88	Sweden	Can-Cup	6	1	0	1				0																		
	New Jersey Devils	**NHL**	**9**	**1**	**0**	**1**	**1**	**0**	**1**	**0**	**0**	**0**	**0**	**6**	**16.7**	**2**	**0**	**8**	**1**	**–5**	**3**	**1**	**0**	**1**	**2**	**0**	**0**	**1**
	Utica Devils	AHL	33	12	22	34				16																		
1988-89	**New Jersey Devils**	**NHL**	**47**	**4**	**8**	**12**	**3**	**6**	**9**	**20**	**0**	**0**	**0**	**42**	**9.5**	**20**	**3**	**33**	**19**	**3**								
	Utica Devils	AHL	7	2	4	6				4																		
	Sweden	WEC-A	10	2	3	5				8																		
1989-90	Brynas IF Gavle	Sweden	40	12	*31	43				29											2	0	2	2	0			
	Sweden	WEC-A	8	1	0	1				2																		
1990-91	Brynas IF Gavle	Sweden	34	11	24	35				22											2	1	1	2	2			
	Sweden	WEC-A	6	1	1	2				6																		
1991-92	Boro HC	Sweden-2	29	33	23	56				32											9	3	3	6	4			
1992-93	Brynas IF Gavle	Sweden	40	13	18	31				28											10	3	2	5	6			
1993-94	Brynas IF Gavle	Sweden	36	6	11	17				47											7	2	2	4	4			
1994-95	Vasteras IK	Sweden	39	16	22	38				40											4	1	3	4	4			
1995-96	Leksands IF	Sweden	36	8	18	26				26											5	2	1	3	4			
1996-97	Leksands IF	Sweden	50	12	27	39				52											9	1	8	9	12			
	Sweden	WC-A	11	1	1	2				6																		
1997-98	Leksands IF	Sweden	41	11	20	31				28											2	0	0	0	0			
	Leksands IF	EuroHL	6	1	6	7				8																		
1998-99	Leksands IF	Sweden	48	23	34	57				38											4	1	1	2	2			
	Leksands IF	EuroHL	6	1	4	5				0											2	0	1	1	0			
99-2000	Leksands IF	Sweden	48	11	30	41				34																		
	NHL Totals		**104**	**7**	**26**	**33**	**6**	**19**	**25**	**34**	**0**	**0**	**0**	**83**	**8.4**	**54**	**9**	**79**	**21**		**3**	**1**	**0**	**1**	**2**	**0**	**0**	**1**

Swedish World All-Star Team (1986)

• CARLYLE, Randy Randolph Robert D – L. 5'10", 200 lbs. b: Sudbury, Ont., 4/19/1956. Toronto's 1st, 30th overall, in 1976.

Season	Club	League	GP	G	A	Pts	AG	AA	APts	PIM	PP	SH	GW	S	%	TGF	PGF	TGA	PGA	+/-	GP	G	A	Pts	PIM	PP	SH	GW
1973-74	Chelmsford Canadiens	NOJHA	STATISTICS NOT AVAILABLE																									
	Sudbury Wolves	OMJHL	12	0	8	8				21											4	0	0	0	6			
1974-75	Sudbury Wolves	OMJHL	67	17	47	64				118											15	3	6	9	21			
1975-76	Sudbury Wolves	OMJHL	60	15	64	79				126											17	6	13	19	70			
1976-77	**Toronto Maple Leafs**	**NHL**	**45**	**0**	**5**	**5**	**0**	**4**	**4**	**51**	**0**	**0**	**0**	**30**	**0.0**	**23**	**0**	**45**	**3**	**–19**	**9**	**0**	**1**	**1**	**20**	**0**	**0**	**0**
	Dallas Black Hawks	CHL	26	2	7	9				63																		
1977-78	**Toronto Maple Leafs**	**NHL**	**49**	**2**	**11**	**13**	**2**	**8**	**10**	**31**	**0**	**0**	**0**	**54**	**3.7**	**37**	**4**	**39**	**10**	**4**	**7**	**0**	**1**	**1**	**8**	**0**	**0**	**0**
	Dallas Black Hawks	CHL	21	3	14	17				31																		
1978-79	**Pittsburgh Penguins**	**NHL**	**70**	**13**	**34**	**47**	**11**	**25**	**36**	**78**	**3**	**1**	**3**	**208**	**6.3**	**116**	**32**	**99**	**19**	**4**	**7**	**0**	**0**	**0**	**12**	**0**	**0**	**0**
1979-80	**Pittsburgh Penguins**	**NHL**	**67**	**8**	**28**	**36**	**7**	**20**	**27**	**45**	**3**	**0**	**1**	**123**	**6.5**	**89**	**28**	**99**	**15**	**–23**	**5**	**1**	**0**	**1**	**4**	**0**	**0**	**0**
1980-81	**Pittsburgh Penguins**	**NHL**	**76**	**16**	**67**	**83**	**12**	**45**	**57**	**136**	**7**	**1**	**1**	**242**	**6.6**	**177**	**75**	**167**	**49**	**–16**	**5**	**4**	**5**	**9**	**9**	**0**	**1**	**0**
1981-82	**Pittsburgh Penguins**	**NHL**	**73**	**11**	**64**	**75**	**9**	**43**	**52**	**131**	**7**	**1**	**0**	**193**	**5.7**	**167**	**78**	**154**	**49**	**–16**	**5**	**1**	**3**	**4**	**16**	**0**	**0**	**0**
1982-83	**Pittsburgh Penguins**	**NHL**	**61**	**15**	**41**	**56**	**12**	**28**	**40**	**110**	**8**	**1**	**0**	**177**	**8.5**	**112**	**47**	**131**	**40**	**–26**								
1983-84	**Pittsburgh Penguins**	**NHL**	**50**	**3**	**23**	**26**	**2**	**16**	**18**	**82**	**0**	**0**	**1**	**107**	**2.8**	**68**	**30**	**91**	**28**	**–25**								
	Winnipeg Jets	**NHL**	**5**	**0**	**3**	**3**	**0**	**2**	**2**	**2**	**0**	**0**	**0**	**5**	**0.0**	**10**	**3**	**4**	**1**	**4**	**3**	**0**	**2**	**2**	**4**	**0**	**0**	**0**
1984-85	**Winnipeg Jets**	**NHL**	**71**	**13**	**38**	**51**	**11**	**26**	**37**	**98**	**6**	**0**	**2**	**135**	**9.6**	**155**	**45**	**128**	**41**	**23**	**8**	**1**	**5**	**6**	**13**	**1**	**0**	**0**
1985-86	**Winnipeg Jets**	**NHL**	**68**	**16**	**33**	**49**	**13**	**22**	**35**	**93**	**3**	**0**	**2**	**152**	**10.5**	**123**	**37**	**128**	**30**	**–12**								
1986-87	**Winnipeg Jets**	**NHL**	**71**	**16**	**26**	**42**	**14**	**19**	**33**	**93**	**5**	**0**	**4**	**172**	**9.3**	**106**	**27**	**100**	**15**	**–6**	**10**	**1**	**5**	**6**	**18**	**0**	**0**	**0**
1987-88	**Winnipeg Jets**	**NHL**	**78**	**15**	**44**	**59**	**13**	**32**	**45**	**210**	**8**	**0**	**1**	**165**	**9.1**	**134**	**75**	**103**	**24**	**–20**	**5**	**0**	**2**	**2**	**10**	**0**	**0**	**0**
1988-89	**Winnipeg Jets**	**NHL**	**78**	**6**	**38**	**44**	**5**	**27**	**32**	**78**	**2**	**0**	**2**	**124**	**4.8**	**108**	**38**	**108**	**19**	**–19**								
	Canada	WEC-A	9	1	4	5				4																		
1989-90	**Winnipeg Jets**	**NHL**	**53**	**3**	**15**	**18**	**3**	**11**	**14**	**50**	**2**	**0**	**0**	**92**	**3.3**	**71**	**11**	**63**	**11**	**8**								
1990-91	**Winnipeg Jets**	**NHL**	**52**	**9**	**19**	**28**	**8**	**14**	**22**	**44**	**2**	**0**	**1**	**89**	**10.1**	**66**	**14**	**59**	**13**	**6**								
1991-92	**Winnipeg Jets**	**NHL**	**66**	**1**	**9**	**10**	**1**	**7**	**8**	**54**	**0**	**0**	**0**	**84**	**1.2**	**49**	**4**	**68**	**27**	**4**	**5**	**1**	**0**	**1**	**6**	**0**	**0**	**0**
1992-93	**Winnipeg Jets**	**NHL**	**22**	**1**	**1**	**2**	**1**	**1**	**2**	**14**	**0**	**0**	**0**	**21**	**4.8**	**10**	**0**	**23**	**7**	**–6**								
1993-1995	**Winnipeg Jets**	**NHL**	DID NOT PLAY – FRONT OFFICE STAFF																									
1995-1996	**Winnipeg Jets**	**NHL**	DID NOT PLAY – ASSISTANT COACH																									
1996-1997	Manitoba Moose	IHL	DID NOT PLAY – ASSISTANT COACH																									
1997-2000	Manitoba Moose	IHL	DID NOT PLAY – COACHING																									
	NHL Totals		**1055**	**148**	**499**	**647**	**124**	**350**	**474**	**1400**	**56**	**4**	**18**	**2173**	**6.8**	**1621**	**548**	**1609**	**401**		**69**	**9**	**24**	**33**	**120**	**1**	**1**	**0**

OMJHL Second All-Star Team (1976) • NHL First All-Star Team (1981) • Won James Norris Trophy (1981 •)Played in NHL All-Star Game (1981, 1982, 1985, 1993)

Traded to **Pittsburgh** by **Toronto** with George Ferguson for Dave Burrows, June 14, 1978. Traded to **Winnipeg** by **Pittsburgh** for Winnipeg's 1st round choice (Doug Bodger) in 1984 Entry Draft and future considerations (Moe Mantha, May 1, 1984), March 5, 1984.

• CARNBACK, Patrik C – L. 6', 187 lbs. b: Goteborg, Sweden, 2/1/1968. Montreal's 7th, 125th overall, in 1988.

Season	Club	League	GP	G	A	Pts	AG	AA	APts	PIM	PP	SH	GW	S	%	TGF	PGF	TGA	PGA	+/-	GP	G	A	Pts	PIM	PP	SH	GW
1986-87	Vastra Frolunda	Sweden-2	10	3	1	4				15																		
1987-88	Vastra Frolunda	Sweden-2	33	16	19	35				24											11	4	5	9	8			
	Sweden	WJC-A	6	4	3	7				10																		
1988-89	Vastra Frolunda	Sweden-2	28	18	19	37				22											11	8	5	13	10			
1989-90	Vastra Frolunda	Sweden	40	26	27	53				34																		
1990-91	Vastra Frolunda	Sweden	22	10	9	19				46											28	15	24	39	24			
1991-92	Vastra Frolunda	Sweden	33	17	22	39				32											3	1	5	6	20			
	Sweden	Olympics	7	1	1	2				2																		
	Sweden	WC-A	8	2	2	4				16																		
1992-93	**Montreal Canadiens**	**NHL**	**6**	**0**	**0**	**0**	**0**	**0**	**0**	**2**	**0**	**0**	**0**	**4**	**0.0**	**0**	**0**	**4**	**0**	**–4**								
	Fredericton Canadiens	AHL	45	20	37	57				45											5	0	3	3	14			
1993-94	**Mighty Ducks of Anaheim**	**NHL**	**73**	**12**	**11**	**23**	**11**	**9**	**20**	**54**	**3**	**0**	**2**	**81**	**14.8**	**30**	**4**	**37**	**3**	**–8**								
	Sweden	WC-A	8	1	0	1				8																		
1994-95	Vastra Frolunda	Sweden	14	2	6	8				20																		
	Mighty Ducks of Anaheim	**NHL**	**41**	**6**	**15**	**21**	**11**	**22**	**33**	**32**	**0**	**0**	**0**	**58**	**10.3**	**24**	**2**	**32**	**2**	**–8**								
1995-96	**Mighty Ducks of Anaheim**	**NHL**	**34**	**6**	**12**	**18**	**6**	**10**	**16**	**34**	**1**	**0**	**0**	**54**	**11.1**	**30**	**10**	**17**	**0**	**3**								
	Kolner EC	Germany	5	1	6	7				2											14	8	8	16	33			
1996-97	Kolner EC	Germany	45	20	41	61				72											4	1	1	2	2			
	Kolner EC	EuroHL	6	1	3	4				6																		

Season	Club	League	GP	G	A	Pts	AG	AA	APts	PIM	PP	SH	GW	S	%	TGF	PGF	TGA	PGA	+/–	GP	G	A	Pts	PIM	PP	SH	GW
			REGULAR SEASON																		PLAYOFFS							
1997-98	Vasteras IK	Sweden	44	8	17	25	....	....	....	38	....	....	....	....	....	....	....	....	....	....	6	3	3	6	6	....	....	....
1998-99	Vasteras IK	Sweden	50	19	28	47	....	....	....	54	....	....	....	....	....	....	....	....	....	....	4	1	1	2	8	....	....	....
99-2000	Vasteras IK	Sweden	46	17	23	40	....	....	....	85	....	....	....	....	....	....	....	....	....	....	5	2	0	2	31	....	....	....
	NHL Totals		**154**	**24**	**38**	**62**	**28**	**41**	**69**	**122**	**4**	**0**	**2**	**197**	**12.2**	**84**	**16**	**90**	**5**		....	....	....	....	....	....	....	....

Swedish Rookie of the Year (1990)

Traded to **Anaheim** by **Montreal** with Todd Ewen for Anaheim's 3rd round choice (Chris Murray) in 1994 Entry Draft, August 10, 1993.

• CARNEY, Keith

Keith Edward D – L. 6'2", 205 lbs. b: Providence, RI, 2/3/1970. Buffalo's 3rd, 76th overall, in 1988.

Season	Club	League	GP	G	A	Pts	AG	AA	APts	PIM	PP	SH	GW	S	%	TGF	PGF	TGA	PGA	+/–	GP	G	A	Pts	PIM	PP	SH	GW
1987-88	Mount St. Charles Mounties	Hi-School	23	12	43	55	....	....	....	....	....	....	....	....	....	....	....	....	....	....	....	....	....	....	....	....	....	....
1988-89	University of Maine	H-East	40	4	22	26	....	....	....	24	....	....	....	....	....	....	....	....	....	....	....	....	....	....	....	....	....	....
1989-90	University of Maine	H-East	41	3	41	44	....	....	....	43	....	....	....	....	....	....	....	....	....	....	....	....	....	....	....	....	....	....
	United States	WJC-A	7	0	3	3	....	....	....	2	....	....	....	....	....	....	....	....	....	....	....	....	....	....	....	....	....	....
1990-91	University of Maine	H-East	40	7	49	56	....	....	....	38	....	....	....	....	....	....	....	....	....	....	....	....	....	....	....	....	....	....
1991-92	United States	Nat-Team	49	2	17	19	....	....	....	16	....	....	....	....	....	....	....	....	....	....	....	....	....	....	....	....	....	....
	Buffalo Sabres	**NHL**	**14**	**1**	**2**	**3**	**1**	**2**	**3**	**18**	**1**	**0**	**0**	**17**	**5.9**	**16**	**5**	**15**	**1**	**–3**	**7**	**0**	**3**	**3**	**0**	**0**	**0**	**0**
	Rochester Americans	AHL	24	1	10	11	....	....	....	2	....	....	....	....	....	....	....	....	....	....	2	0	2	2	0	....	....	....
1992-93	**Buffalo Sabres**	**NHL**	**30**	**2**	**4**	**6**	**2**	**3**	**5**	**55**	**0**	**0**	**1**	**26**	**7.7**	**26**	**5**	**24**	**6**	**3**	**8**	**0**	**3**	**3**	**6**	**0**	**0**	**0**
	Rochester Americans	AHL	41	5	21	26	....	....	....	32	....	....	....	....	....	....	....	....	....	....	....	....	....	....	....	....	....	....
1993-94	**Buffalo Sabres**	**NHL**	**7**	**1**	**3**	**4**	**1**	**2**	**3**	**4**	**0**	**0**	**0**	**6**	**16.7**	**7**	**2**	**7**	**1**	**–1**	....	....	....	....	....	....	....	....
	Chicago Blackhawks	**NHL**	**30**	**3**	**5**	**8**	**3**	**4**	**7**	**35**	**0**	**0**	**0**	**31**	**9.7**	**34**	**2**	**26**	**9**	**15**	**6**	**0**	**1**	**1**	**4**	**0**	**0**	**0**
	Indianapolis Ice	IHL	28	0	14	14	....	....	....	20	....	....	....	....	....	....	....	....	....	....	....	....	....	....	....	....	....	....
1994-95	**Chicago Blackhawks**	**NHL**	**18**	**1**	**0**	**1**	**2**	**0**	**2**	**11**	**0**	**0**	**1**	**14**	**7.1**	**8**	**1**	**9**	**1**	**–1**	**4**	**0**	**1**	**1**	**0**	**0**	**0**	**0**
1995-96	**Chicago Blackhawks**	**NHL**	**82**	**5**	**14**	**19**	**5**	**11**	**16**	**94**	**1**	**0**	**1**	**69**	**7.2**	**77**	**3**	**63**	**20**	**31**	**10**	**0**	**3**	**3**	**4**	**0**	**0**	**0**
1996-97	**Chicago Blackhawks**	**NHL**	**81**	**3**	**15**	**18**	**3**	**13**	**16**	**62**	**0**	**0**	**1**	**77**	**3.9**	**75**	**4**	**80**	**35**	**26**	**6**	**1**	**1**	**2**	**2**	**0**	**0**	**0**
1997-98	**Chicago Blackhawks**	**NHL**	**60**	**2**	**13**	**15**	**2**	**13**	**15**	**73**	**0**	**1**	**0**	**53**	**3.8**	**40**	**0**	**69**	**22**	**–7**	....	....	....	....	....	....	....	....
	United States	Olympics	4	0	0	0	....	....	....	2	....	....	....	....	....	....	....	....	....	....	....	....	....	....	....	....	....	....
	Phoenix Coyotes	**NHL**	**20**	**1**	**6**	**7**	**1**	**6**	**7**	**18**	**1**	**0**	**0**	**18**	**5.6**	**24**	**4**	**26**	**11**	**5**	**6**	**0**	**0**	**0**	**4**	**0**	**0**	**0**
1998-99	**Phoenix Coyotes**	**NHL**	**82**	**2**	**14**	**16**	**2**	**13**	**15**	**62**	**0**	**2**	**0**	**62**	**3.2**	**78**	**3**	**85**	**25**	**15**	**7**	**1**	**2**	**3**	**10**	**0**	**0**	**0**
99-2000	**Phoenix Coyotes**	**NHL**	**82**	**4**	**20**	**24**	**4**	**19**	**23**	**87**	**0**	**0**	**1**	**73**	**5.5**	....	....	....	....	**11**	**5**	**0**	**0**	**0**	**17**	**0**	**0**	**0**
	NHL Totals		**506**	**25**	**96**	**121**	**26**	**86**	**112**	**519**	**3**	**3**	**5**	**446**	**5.6**	**385**	**29**	**404**	**131**		**59**	**2**	**14**	**16**	**47**	**0**	**0**	**0**

Hockey East Second All-Star Team (1990) • NCAA East Second All-American Team (1990) • Hockey East First All-Star Team (1991) • NCAA East First All-American Team (1991)

Traded to **Chicago** by **Buffalo** with Buffalo's 6th round choice (Marc Magliarditi) in 1995 Entry Draft for Craig Muni and Chicago's 5th round choice (Daniel Bienvenue) in 1995 Entry Draft, October 26, 1993. Traded to **Phoenix** by **Chicago** with Jim Cummins for Chad Kilger and Jayson More, March 4, 1998.

• CARON, Alain

Alain Luc "Boom-Boom" RW – R. 5'9", 182 lbs. b: Dolbeau, Que., 4/27/1938 d: 12/18/1986.

Season	Club	League	GP	G	A	Pts	AG	AA	APts	PIM	PP	SH	GW	S	%	TGF	PGF	TGA	PGA	+/–	GP	G	A	Pts	PIM	PP	SH	GW
1956-57	Dolbeau Dragons	QJHL	45	69	48	117	....	....	....	118	....	....	....	....	....	....	....	....	....	....	....	....	....	....	....	....	....	....
1957-58	Chicoutimi Sagueneens	QHL	61	8	9	17	....	....	....	26	....	....	....	....	....	....	....	....	....	....	6	0	0	0	0	....	....	....
1958-59	Chicoutimi Sagueneens	QHL	56	15	18	33	....	....	....	67	....	....	....	....	....	....	....	....	....	....	....	....	....	....	....	....	....	....
1959-60	Sault Ste. Marie Thunderbirds	EPHL	25	10	4	14	....	....	....	4	....	....	....	....	....	....	....	....	....	....	....	....	....	....	....	....	....	....
	Quebec Aces	AHL	38	9	4	13	....	....	....	16	....	....	....	....	....	....	....	....	....	....	....	....	....	....	....	....	....	....
1960-61	Quebec Aces	AHL	9	5	1	6	....	....	....	2	....	....	....	....	....	....	....	....	....	....	....	....	....	....	....	....	....	....
	Sault Ste. Marie Thunderbirds	EPHL	35	11	6	17	....	....	....	16	....	....	....	....	....	....	....	....	....	....	....	....	....	....	....	....	....	....
1961-62	Amherst Ramblers	NSSHL	45	*76	46	*122	....	....	....	29	....	....	....	....	....	....	....	....	....	....	4	*7	7	14	4	....	....	....
	Quebec Aces	AHL	1	0	0	0	....	....	....	0	....	....	....	....	....	....	....	....	....	....	....	....	....	....	....	....	....	....
	Amherst Ramblers	Al-Cup	8	9	4	13	....	....	....	4	....	....	....	....	....	....	....	....	....	....	....	....	....	....	....	....	....	....
1962-63	St. Louis Braves	EPHL	54	*61	36	97	....	....	....	22	....	....	....	....	....	....	....	....	....	....	....	....	....	....	....	....	....	....
	Charlotte Checkers	EHL	13	10	5	15	....	....	....	7	....	....	....	....	....	....	....	....	....	....	....	....	....	....	....	....	....	....
1963-64	St. Louis Braves	CPHL	71	*77	48	*125	....	....	....	22	....	....	....	....	....	....	....	....	....	....	6	6	2	8	6	....	....	....
1964-65	St. Louis Braves	CPHL	60	46	19	65	....	....	....	31	....	....	....	....	....	....	....	....	....	....	....	....	....	....	....	....	....	....
	Buffalo Bisons	AHL	....	....	....	....	....	....	....	....	....	....	....	....	....	....	....	....	....	....	5	0	0	0	2	....	....	....
1965-66	Buffalo Bisons	AHL	72	*47	29	76	....	....	....	28	....	....	....	....	....	....	....	....	....	....	....	....	....	....	....	....	....	....
1966-67	Portland Buckaroos	WHL	71	35	25	60	....	....	....	24	....	....	....	....	....	....	....	....	....	....	4	0	0	0	2	....	....	....
1967-68	**Oakland Seals**	**NHL**	**58**	**9**	**13**	**22**	**10**	**13**	**23**	**18**	**3**	**0**	**0**	**121**	**7.4**	**34**	**18**	**38**	**0**	**–22**	....	....	....	....	....	....	....	....
	Buffalo Bisons	AHL	6	8	2	10	....	....	....	2	....	....	....	....	....	....	....	....	....	....	....	....	....	....	....	....	....	....
1968-69	**Montreal Canadiens**	**NHL**	**2**	**0**	**0**	**0**	**0**	**0**	**0**	**0**	**0**	**0**	**0**	**0**	**0.0**	**0**	**0**	**0**	**0**	**0**	....	....	....	....	....	....	....	....
	Houston Apollos	CHL	68	38	27	65	....	....	....	37	....	....	....	....	....	....	....	....	....	....	3	0	0	0	0	....	....	....
1969-70	Montreal Voyageurs	AHL	71	35	30	65	....	....	....	32	....	....	....	....	....	....	....	....	....	....	8	2	0	2	6	....	....	....
1970-71	San Diego Gulls	WHL	70	33	15	48	....	....	....	12	....	....	....	....	....	....	....	....	....	....	6	1	1	2	4	....	....	....
1971-72	Oklahoma City Blazers	CHL	67	22	20	42	....	....	....	28	....	....	....	....	....	....	....	....	....	....	6	1	0	1	0	....	....	....
1972-73	Quebec Nordiques	WHA	68	36	27	63	....	....	....	14	....	....	....	....	....	....	....	....	....	....	....	....	....	....	....	....	....	....
1973-74	Quebec Nordiques	WHA	59	31	15	46	....	....	....	10	....	....	....	....	....	....	....	....	....	....	....	....	....	....	....	....	....	....
1974-75	Quebec Nordiques	WHA	21	7	3	10	....	....	....	2	....	....	....	....	....	....	....	....	....	....	....	....	....	....	....	....	....	....
	Michigan–Baltimore Blades	WHA	47	8	5	13	....	....	....	4	....	....	....	....	....	....	....	....	....	....	....	....	....	....	....	....	....	....
	Syracuse Blazers	NAHL	1	1	0	1	....	....	....	0	....	....	....	....	....	....	....	....	....	....	....	....	....	....	....	....	....	....
1975-76	Beauce Jaros	NAHL	73	*78	59	137	....	....	....	26	....	....	....	....	....	....	....	....	....	....	14	*21	13	34	12	....	....	....
	NHL Totals		**60**	**9**	**13**	**22**	**10**	**13**	**23**	**18**	**3**	**0**	**0**	**121**	**7.4**	**34**	**18**	**38**	**0**		....	....	....	....	....	....	....	....
	Other Major League Totals		195	82	50	132	....	....	....	30	....	....	....	....	....	....	....	....	....	....	....	....	....	....	....	....	....	....

NSSHL First All-Star Team (1962) • EPHL First All-Star Team (1963) • CPHL First All-Star Team (1964) • NAHL Second All-Star Team (1976)

Traded to **Quebec** (AHL) by **Chicoutimi** (QHL) for cash, November, 1959. Claimed by **Oakland** from **Chicago** in Expansion Draft, June 6, 1967. Traded to **Montreal** by **Oakland** with Wally Boyer, Oakland's 1st round choices in 1968 (Jim Pritchard) and 1970 (Ray Martynuik) Amateur Drafts and future considerations (Lyle Bradley, June, 1968) for Norm Ferguson, Stan Fuller and future considerations (Francois Lacombe and Michel Jacques, June, 1968), May 21, 1968. Claimed by **Philadelphia** (San Diego-WHL) from **Montreal** in Reverse Draft, June 10, 1970. Claimed by **Providence** (AHL) from **San Diego** (WHL) for cash, June 7, 1971. Signed as a free agent by **Quebec** (WHA), August, 1972. Traded to **Michigan-Baltimore** (WHA) by **Quebec** (WHA) with Michel Rouleau and Pierre Guite for Marc Tardif and Steve Sutherland, December, 1974. Claimed by **Quebec** (WHA) from **Michigan-Baltimore** (WHA) in WHA Dispersal Draft, June 19, 1975.

• CARPENTER, Bob

Robert C – L. 6', 200 lbs. b: Beverly, MA, 7/13/1963. Washington's 1st, 3rd overall, in 1981.

Season	Club	League	GP	G	A	Pts	AG	AA	APts	PIM	PP	SH	GW	S	%	TGF	PGF	TGA	PGA	+/–	GP	G	A	Pts	PIM	PP	SH	GW
1979-80	St. John's Pioneers	Hi-School	33	28	37	65	....	....	....	....	....	....	....	....	....	....	....	....	....	....	....	....	....	....	....	....	....	....
1980-81	St. John's Pioneers	Hi-School	18	14	24	38	....	....	....	....	....	....	....	....	....	....	....	....	....	....	....	....	....	....	....	....	....	....
	United States	WJC-A	5	5	4	9	....	....	....	6	....	....	....	....	....	....	....	....	....	....	....	....	....	....	....	....	....	....
1981-82	Washington Capitals	DN-Cup	4	4	0	4	....	....	....	0	....	....	....	....	....	....	....	....	....	....	....	....	....	....	....	....	....	....
	Washington Capitals	**NHL**	**80**	**32**	**35**	**67**	**25**	**23**	**48**	**69**	**7**	**1**	**3**	**263**	**12.2**	**105**	**28**	**102**	**2**	**–23**	....	....	....	....	....	....	....	....
1982-83	**Washington Capitals**	**NHL**	**80**	**32**	**37**	**69**	**26**	**26**	**52**	**64**	**14**	**0**	**4**	**197**	**16.2**	**110**	**44**	**68**	**2**	**0**	**4**	**1**	**0**	**1**	**2**	**0**	**0**	**0**
1983-84	**Washington Capitals**	**NHL**	**80**	**28**	**40**	**68**	**22**	**27**	**49**	**51**	**8**	**0**	**5**	**228**	**12.3**	**93**	**31**	**63**	**1**	**0**	**8**	**2**	**1**	**3**	**25**	**1**	**0**	**0**
1984-85	United States	Can-Cup	6	1	4	5	....	....	....	4	....	....	....	....	....	....	....	....	....	....	....	....	....	....	....	....	....	....
	Washington Capitals	**NHL**	**80**	**53**	**42**	**95**	**43**	**29**	**72**	**87**	**12**	**0**	**7**	**260**	**20.4**	**139**	**51**	**76**	**8**	**20**	**5**	**1**	**4**	**5**	**8**	**0**	**0**	**0**
1985-86	**Washington Capitals**	**NHL**	**80**	**27**	**29**	**56**	**22**	**19**	**41**	**105**	**7**	**0**	**3**	**205**	**13.2**	**94**	**28**	**92**	**14**	**–12**	**9**	**5**	**4**	**9**	**12**	**2**	**0**	**1**
1986-87	**Washington Capitals**	**NHL**	**22**	**5**	**7**	**12**	**4**	**5**	**9**	**21**	**4**	**0**	**0**	**47**	**10.6**	**23**	**10**	**28**	**8**	**–7**	....	....	....	....	....	....	....	....
	New York Rangers	**NHL**	**28**	**2**	**8**	**10**	**2**	**6**	**8**	**20**	**1**	**0**	**0**	**41**	**4.9**	**16**	**4**	**26**	**2**	**–12**	....	....	....	....	....	....	....	....
	Los Angeles Kings	**NHL**	**10**	**2**	**3**	**5**	**2**	**2**	**4**	**6**	**0**	**0**	**0**	**23**	**8.7**	**11**	**0**	**24**	**5**	**–8**	**5**	**1**	**2**	**3**	**2**	**0**	**0**	**0**
	United States	WEC-A	10	2	2	4	....	....	....	8	....	....	....	....	....	....	....	....	....	....	....	....	....	....	....	....	....	....
1987-88	United States	Can-Cup	5	1	2	3	....	....	....	4	....	....	....	....	....	....	....	....	....	....	....	....	....	....	....	....	....	....
	Los Angeles Kings	**NHL**	**71**	**19**	**33**	**52**	**16**	**24**	**40**	**84**	**10**	**0**	**2**	**176**	**10.8**	**82**	**28**	**107**	**32**	**–21**	**5**	**1**	**1**	**2**	**0**	**0**	**0**	**0**
1988-89	**Los Angeles Kings**	**NHL**	**39**	**11**	**15**	**26**	**9**	**11**	**20**	**16**	**3**	**0**	**1**	**91**	**12.1**	**48**	**13**	**35**	**3**	**3**	....	....	....	....	....	....	....	....
	Boston Bruins	**NHL**	**18**	**5**	**9**	**14**	**4**	**6**	**10**	**10**	**1**	**0**	**2**	**46**	**10.9**	**16**	**3**	**9**	**0**	**4**	**8**	**1**	**1**	**2**	**4**	**1**	**0**	**1**
1989-90	**Boston Bruins**	**NHL**	**80**	**25**	**31**	**56**	**21**	**22**	**43**	**97**	**5**	**0**	**5**	**220**	**11.4**	**90**	**32**	**80**	**19**	**–3**	**21**	**4**	**6**	**10**	**39**	**2**	**0**	**1**
1990-91	**Boston Bruins**	**NHL**	**29**	**8**	**8**	**16**	**7**	**6**	**13**	**22**	**2**	**0**	**0**	**54**	**14.8**	**28**	**10**	**30**	**14**	**2**	**1**	**0**	**1**	**1**	**2**	**0**	**0**	**0**
1991-92	**Boston Bruins**	**NHL**	**60**	**25**	**23**	**48**	**23**	**17**	**40**	**46**	**6**	**1**	**6**	**171**	**14.6**	**72**	**21**	**69**	**15**	**–3**	**8**	**0**	**1**	**1**	**6**	**0**	**0**	**0**
1992-93	**Washington Capitals**	**NHL**	**68**	**11**	**17**	**28**	**9**	**12**	**21**	**65**	**2**	**0**	**0**	**141**	**7.8**	**51**	**10**	**66**	**9**	**–16**	**6**	**1**	**4**	**5**	**6**	**0**	**0**	**0**
1993-94	**New Jersey Devils**	**NHL**	**76**	**10**	**23**	**33**	**9**	**18**	**27**	**51**	**0**	**2**	**1**	**125**	**8.0**	**50**	**2**	**76**	**35**	**7**	**20**	**1**	**7**	**8**	**20**	**0**	**0**	**0**
1994-95♦	**New Jersey Devils**	**NHL**	**41**	**5**	**11**	**16**	**9**	**16**	**25**	**19**	**0**	**0**	**0**	**69**	**7.2**	**26**	**0**	**40**	**13**	**–1**	**17**	**1**	**4**	**5**	**6**	**1**	**0**	**0**

			REGULAR SEASON																		PLAYOFFS							
Season	Club	League	GP	G	A	Pts	AG	AA	APts	PIM	PP	SH	GW	S	%	TGF	PGF	TGA	PGA	+/–	GP	G	A	Pts	PIM	PP	SH	GW
1995-96	New Jersey Devils	NHL	52	5	5	10	5	4	9	14	0	1	0	63	7.9	21	0	45	14	–10	....	....	....	....	....	....	....	....
1996-97	New Jersey Devils	NHL	62	4	15	19	4	13	17	14	0	1	0	76	5.3	30	0	44	20	6	10	1	2	3	2	0	0	0
1997-98	New Jersey Devils	NHL	66	9	9	18	11	9	20	22	0	1	1	81	11.1	30	1	49	16	–4	6	1	0	1	0	0	0	0
1998-99	New Jersey Devils	NHL	56	2	8	10	2	8	10	36	0	0	0	69	2.9	25	1	46	19	–3	7	0	0	0	2	0	0	0
99-2000	Albany River Rats	AHL	DID NOT PLAY – ASSISTANT COACH																									
	New Jersey Devils	NHL	DID NOT PLAY – ASSISTANT COACH																									
	NHL Totals		1178	320	408	728	275	303	578	919	82	7	40	2646	12.1	1160	317	1175	251		140	21	38	59	136	7	0	3

Played in NHL All-Star Game (1985)

Traded to **NY Rangers** by **Washington** with Washington's 2nd round choice (Jason Prosofsky) in 1989 Entry Draft for Bob Crawford, Kelly Miller and Mike Ridley, January 1, 1987. Traded to **LA Kings** by **NY Rangers** with Tom Laidlaw for Jeff Crossman, Marcel Dionne and LA Kings' 3rd round choice (later traded to Minnesota — Minnesota selected Murray Garbutt) in 1989 Entry Draft, March 10, 1987. Traded to **Boston** by **LA Kings** for Steve Kasper to complete transaction that sent Jay Miller to LA Kings (January 22, 1989), January 23, 1989. • Missed majority of 1990-91 season recovering from kneecap injury suffered in game vs. Montreal, December 8, 1990. Signed as a free agent by **Washington**, June 30, 1992. Signed as a free agent by **New Jersey**, September 30, 1993. • Officially announced retirement, August 16, 1999. • Named Assistant Coach of **New Jersey**, March 23, 2000.

• CARR, Gene

Eugene William C – L. 5'11", 185 lbs. b: Nanaimo, B.C., 9/17/1951. St. Louis' 1st, 4th overall, in 1971.

Season	Club	League	GP	G	A	Pts	AG	AA	APts	PIM	PP	SH	GW	S	%	TGF	PGF	TGA	PGA	+/–	GP	G	A	Pts	PIM	PP	SH	GW
1967-68	Kelowna Buckaroos	BCJHL	STATISTICS NOT AVAILABLE																									
1968-69	Kelowna Buckaroos	BCJHL	STATISTICS NOT AVAILABLE																									
1969-70	Flin Flon Bombers	WCJHL	60	22	51	73	....	....	....	118	....	....	....	....	....	....	....	....	....	....	6	6	5	11	4	....	....	....
1970-71	Flin Flon Bombers	WCJHL	62	36	68	104	....	....	....	150	....	....	....	....	....	....	....	....	....	....	17	12	18	30	42	....	....	....
1971-72	St. Louis Blues	NHL	15	3	2	5	3	2	5	9	0	0	0	29	10.3	8	2	6	0	0	....	....	....	....	....	....	....	....
	New York Rangers	NHL	59	8	8	16	8	7	15	25	1	0	3	74	10.8	37	3	18	0	16	16	1	3	4	21	0	0	0
1972-73	New York Rangers	NHL	50	9	10	19	8	8	16	50	1	0	1	65	13.8	32	5	31	0	–4	1	0	1	1	0	0	0	0
1973-74	New York Rangers	NHL	29	1	5	6	1	4	5	15	1	0	0	23	4.3	10	2	16	0	–8	....	....	....	....	....	....	....	....
	Providence Reds	AHL	10	4	10	14	....	....	....	18	....	....	....	....	....	....	....	....	....	....	....	....	....	....	....	....	....	....
	Los Angeles Kings	NHL	21	6	11	17	6	9	15	36	0	1	1	37	16.2	19	4	14	1	2	5	2	1	3	14	1	0	0
1974-75	Los Angeles Kings	NHL	80	7	32	39	6	24	30	103	2	0	2	157	4.5	65	6	41	1	19	3	1	2	3	29	0	0	0
1975-76	Los Angeles Kings	NHL	38	8	11	19	7	8	15	16	0	0	1	61	13.1	27	5	23	0	–1	....	....	....	....	....	....	....	....
1976-77	Los Angeles Kings	NHL	68	15	12	27	13	9	22	25	0	1	2	99	15.2	34	3	36	10	5	9	1	1	2	2	0	0	0
1977-78	Los Angeles Kings	NHL	5	2	0	2	2	0	2	4	0	0	0	8	25.0	3	0	3	0	0	....	....	....	....	....	....	....	....
	Pittsburgh Penguins	NHL	70	17	37	54	15	29	44	76	4	0	2	145	11.7	81	37	61	2	–15	....	....	....	....	....	....	....	....
1978-79	Atlanta Flames	NHL	30	3	8	11	3	6	9	6	0	0	0	35	8.6	15	3	16	0	–4	1	0	0	0	0	0	0	0
	Tulsa Oilers	CHL	22	4	8	12	....	....	....	35	....	....	....	....	....	....	....	....	....	....	....	....	....	....	....	....	....	....
	NHL Totals		465	79	136	215	72	106	178	365	9	2	12	733	10.8	331	70	265	14		35	5	8	13	66	1	0	0

• Son of Red • WCJHL All-Star Team (1971)

Traded to **NY Rangers** by **St. Louis** with Jim Lorentz and Wayne Connelly for Jack Egers, Andre Dupont and Mike Murphy, November 15, 1971. Traded to **LA Kings** by **NY Rangers** for LA Kings' 1st round choice (Ron Duguay) in 1977 Amateur Draft, February 15, 1974. Traded to **Pittsburgh** by **LA Kings** with Dave Schultz and LA Kings' 4th round choice (Shane Pearsall) in 1978 Amateur Draft for Syl Apps Jr. and Hartland Monahan, November 2, 1977. Signed as a free agent by **Atlanta**, June 6, 1978. Claimed by **Winnipeg** from **Atlanta**, June 13, 1979.

• CARRIERE, Larry

Lawrence Robert D – L. 6'1", 190 lbs. b: Montreal, Que., 1/30/1952. Buffalo's 2nd, 25th overall, in 1972.

Season	Club	League	GP	G	A	Pts	AG	AA	APts	PIM	PP	SH	GW	S	%	TGF	PGF	TGA	PGA	+/–	GP	G	A	Pts	PIM	PP	SH	GW
1969-70	Loyola College	QUAA	32	10	34	44	....	....	....	....	....	....	....	....	....	....	....	....	....	....	....	....	....	....	....	....	....	....
1970-71	Loyola College	QUAA	27	8	24	32	....	....	....	72	....	....	....	....	....	....	....	....	....	....	....	....	....	....	....	....	....	....
1971-72	Loyola College	QUAA	32	20	29	49	....	....	....	69	....	....	....	....	....	....	....	....	....	....	....	....	....	....	....	....	....	....
1972-73	Buffalo Sabres	NHL	40	2	8	10	2	6	8	52	1	0	0	34	5.9	26	5	25	3	–1	6	0	1	1	8	0	0	0
	Cincinnati Swords	AHL	30	7	11	18	....	....	....	54	....	....	....	....	....	....	....	....	....	....	....	....	....	....	....	....	....	....
1973-74	Buffalo Sabres	NHL	78	6	24	30	6	20	26	103	3	0	0	113	5.3	108	20	101	16	3	....	....	....	....	....	....	....	....
1974-75	Buffalo Sabres	NHL	80	1	11	12	1	8	9	111	0	0	0	84	1.2	67	2	75	22	12	17	0	2	2	32	0	0	0
1975-76	Atlanta Flames	NHL	75	4	15	19	3	11	14	96	1	1	0	126	3.2	77	2	95	25	5	2	0	0	0	2	0	0	0
1976-77	Atlanta Flames	NHL	25	2	3	5	2	2	4	16	0	0	1	28	7.1	25	1	25	4	3	....	....	....	....	....	....	....	....
	Vancouver Canucks	NHL	49	1	9	10	1	7	8	55	0	1	0	65	1.5	43	1	63	10	–11	....	....	....	....	....	....	....	....
1977-78	Vancouver Canucks	NHL	7	0	3	3	0	2	2	11	0	0	0	10	0.0	5	0	7	2	0	....	....	....	....	....	....	....	....
	Tulsa Oilers	CHL	6	0	1	1	....	....	....	12	....	....	....	....	....	....	....	....	....	....	....	....	....	....	....	....	....	....
	Los Angeles Kings	NHL	2	0	0	0	0	0	0	0	0	0	0	0	0.0	0	0	0	0	0	....	....	....	....	....	....	....	....
	Springfield Indians	AHL	40	2	14	16	....	....	....	33	....	....	....	....	....	....	....	....	....	....	....	....	....	....	....	....	....	....
	Buffalo Sabres	NHL	9	0	0	0	0	0	0	18	0	0	0	4	0.0	2	1	2	0	–1	....	....	....	....	....	....	....	....
1978-79			OUT OF HOCKEY – RETIRED																									
1979-80	Toronto Maple Leafs	NHL	2	0	1	1	0	1	1	0	0	0	0	1	0.0	2	0	3	0	–1	2	0	0	0	0	0	0	0
	NHL Totals		367	16	74	90	15	57	72	462	5	2	1	465	3.4	355	32	396	82		27	0	3	3	42	0	0	0

Traded to **Atlanta** by **Buffalo** with Buffalo's 1st round choice (later traded to Washington — Washington selected Greg Carroll) in 1976 Amateur Draft and cash for Jacques Richard, October 1, 1975. Traded to **Vancouver** by **Atlanta** with Hilliard Graves for John Gould and LA Kings' 2nd round choice (previously acquired, Atlanta selected Brian Hill) in 1977 Amateur Draft, December 2, 1976. Traded to **LA Kings** by **Vancouver** for Sheldon Kannegiesser, November 21, 1977. Signed as a free agent by **Buffalo**, March 12, 1978. Signed as a free agent by **Toronto** to five-game tryout contract, April 5, 1980.

• CARROLL, Billy

William Allan C – L. 5'10", 190 lbs. b: Toronto, Ont., 1/19/1959. NY Islanders' 3rd, 38th overall, in 1979.

Season	Club	League	GP	G	A	Pts	AG	AA	APts	PIM	PP	SH	GW	S	%	TGF	PGF	TGA	PGA	+/–	GP	G	A	Pts	PIM	PP	SH	GW
1975-76	St. Michael's Buzzers	OHA-B	32	21	39	60	....	....	....	....	....	....	....	....	....	....	....	....	....	....	....	....	....	....	....	....	....	....
1976-77	London Knights	OMJHL	64	18	31	49	....	....	....	37	....	....	....	....	....	....	....	....	....	....	....	....	....	....	....	....	....	....
1977-78	London Knights	OMJHL	68	36	37	73	....	....	....	42	....	....	....	....	....	....	....	....	....	....	11	3	6	9	6	....	....	....
1978-79	London Knights	OMJHL	63	35	50	85	....	....	....	38	....	....	....	....	....	....	....	....	....	....	7	1	5	6	14	....	....	....
1979-80	Indianapolis Checkers	CHL	49	9	17	26	....	....	....	19	....	....	....	....	....	....	....	....	....	....	7	0	1	1	0	....	....	....
1980-81♦	New York Islanders	NHL	18	4	4	8	3	3	6	6	0	0	1	25	16.0	13	1	17	8	3	18	3	9	12	4	0	1	1
	Indianapolis Checkers	CHL	59	27	37	64	....	....	....	67	....	....	....	....	....	....	....	....	....	....	....	....	....	....	....	....	....	....
1981-82♦	New York Islanders	NHL	72	9	20	29	7	13	20	32	0	3	1	42	21.4	39	0	50	23	12	19	2	2	4	8	0	2	0
1982-83♦	New York Islanders	NHL	71	1	11	12	1	8	9	24	0	1	0	52	1.9	25	1	39	18	3	20	1	1	2	2	0	1	0
1983-84	New York Islanders	NHL	39	5	2	7	4	1	5	12	0	0	2	39	12.8	11	0	31	19	–1	5	0	0	0	0	0	0	0
1984-85♦	Edmonton Oilers	NHL	65	8	9	17	6	6	12	22	0	0	1	44	18.2	24	0	30	6	0	9	0	0	0	4	0	0	0
1985-86	Edmonton Oilers	NHL	5	0	2	2	0	1	1	0	0	0	0	0	0.0	2	0	2	2	2	....	....	....	....	....	....	....	....
	Nova Scotia Oilers	AHL	26	7	18	25	....	....	....	15	....	....	....	....	....	....	....	....	....	....	....	....	....	....	....	....	....	....
	Detroit Red Wings	NHL	21	2	4	6	2	3	5	11	0	0	0	13	15.4	6	0	27	13	–8	....	....	....	....	....	....	....	....
1986-87	Detroit Red Wings	NHL	31	1	2	3	1	1	2	6	0	0	1	12	8.3	6	0	24	9	–9	....	....	....	....	....	....	....	....
	NHL Totals		322	30	54	84	24	36	60	113	0	4	6	227	13.2	126	2	220	98		71	6	12	18	18	0	4	1

Named Metro OHA-B MVP (1976) • OMJHL Second All-Star Team (1979)

Claimed by **Edmonton** from **NY Islanders** in Waiver Draft, October 9, 1984. Traded to **Detroit** by **Edmonton** for Bruce Eakin, December 28, 1985.

• CARROLL, Greg

Gregory John C – L. 6', 185 lbs. b: Gimley, Man., 11/10/1956. Washington's 2nd, 15th overall, in 1976.

Season	Club	League	GP	G	A	Pts	AG	AA	APts	PIM	PP	SH	GW	S	%	TGF	PGF	TGA	PGA	+/–	GP	G	A	Pts	PIM	PP	SH	GW
1973-74	Edmonton Canadians	AJHL	STATISTICS NOT AVAILABLE																									
1974-75	Medicine Hat Tigers	WCJHL	70	22	37	59	....	....	....	77	....	....	....	....	....	....	....	....	....	....	3	3	2	5	0	....	....	....
1975-76	Medicine Hat Tigers	WCJHL	71	60	111	171	....	....	....	118	....	....	....	....	....	....	....	....	....	....	9	4	11	15	2	....	....	....
1976-77	Cincinnati Stingers	WHA	77	15	39	54	....	....	....	53	....	....	....	....	....	....	....	....	....	....	4	1	2	3	0	....	....	....
1977-78	New England Whalers	WHA	48	9	14	23	....	....	....	27	....	....	....	....	....	....	....	....	....	....	....	....	....	....	....	....	....	....
	Cincinnati Stingers	WHA	26	6	13	19	....	....	....	36	....	....	....	....	....	....	....	....	....	....	....	....	....	....	....	....	....	....

			REGULAR SEASON																		PLAYOFFS							
Season	Club	League	GP	G	A	Pts	AG	AA	APts	PIM	PP	SH	GW	S	%	TGF	PGF	TGA	PGA	+/–	GP	G	A	Pts	PIM	PP	SH	GW
1978-79	**Washington Capitals**	**NHL**	**24**	**5**	**6**	**11**	**4**	**4**	**8**	**12**	**0**	**0**	**0**	**29**	**17.2**	**16**	**0**	**25**	**7**	**–2**								
	Detroit Red Wings	**NHL**	**36**	**2**	**9**	**11**	**2**	**7**	**9**	**8**	**1**	**0**	**0**	**16**	**12.5**	**19**	**6**	**19**	**0**	**–6**								
1979-80	**Hartford Whalers**	**NHL**	**71**	**13**	**19**	**32**	**11**	**14**	**25**	**24**	**0**	**1**	**2**	**85**	**15.3**	**48**	**1**	**79**	**27**	**–5**								
	Springfield Indians	AHL	6	2	2	4				2																		
	NHL Totals		**131**	**20**	**34**	**54**	**17**	**25**	**42**	**44**	**1**	**1**	**2**	**130**	**15.4**	**83**	**7**	**123**	**34**									
	Other Major League Totals		151	30	66	96				116											4	1	2	3	0			

WCJHL Second All-Star Team (1976)

Selected by **Cincinnati** (WHA) in 1976 WHA Amateur Draft, June, 1976. Traded to **New England** (WHA) by **Cincinnati** (WHA) with Bryan Maxwell for the rights to Mike Liut, May, 1977. Traded to **Cincinnati** (WHA) by **New England** (WHA) for Ron Plumb, February, 1978. Signed as a free agent by **Washington** after being released by **Cincinnati** (WHA), September 21, 1978. Claimed on waivers by **Detroit** from **Washington**, January 6, 1979. Signed by **Hartford** as a free agent, October 30, 1979.

• CARRUTHERS, Dwight

Gordon Dwight D – R. 5'10", 186 lbs. b: Lashburn, Sask., 11/7/1944.

Season	Club	League	GP	G	A	Pts	AG	AA	APts	PIM	PP	SH	GW	S	%	TGF	PGF	TGA	PGA	+/–	GP	G	A	Pts	PIM	PP	SH	GW
1962-63	Weyburn Red Wings	SJHL	54	5	15	20				78											13	1	2	3	15			
1963-64	Weyburn Red Wings	SJHL	61	6	26	32				46											8	1	7	8	6			
1964-65	Weyburn Red Wings	SJHL	48	9	33	42				103											15	4	11	15	20			
1965-66	**Detroit Red Wings**	**NHL**	**1**	**0**	**0**	**0**	**0**	**0**	**0**	**0**																		
	Memphis Wings	CPHL	4	0	1	1				2																		
	Johnstown Jets	EHL	69	7	22	29				132											3	0	3	3	6			
1966-67	San Diego Gulls	WHL	29	2	3	5				10																		
1967-68	**Philadelphia Flyers**	**NHL**	**1**	**0**	**0**	**0**	**0**	**0**	**0**	**0**	**0**	**0**	**0**	**0**	**0.0**	**0**	**0**	**0**	**0**	**0**								
	Seattle Totems	WHL	70	9	16	25				34											9	2	4	6	8			
1968-69	Amarillo Wranglers	CHL	62	10	19	29				42																		
	Seattle Totems	WHL	1	0	1	1				0											4	0	0	0	2			
1969-70	Seattle–Phoenix Roadrunners	WHL	56	2	8	10				24																		
1970-71			REINSTATED AS AN AMATEUR																									
1971-1974	Spokane Flyers	WIHL	STATISTICS NOT AVAILABLE																									
1974-75	Spokane Flyers	WIHL	48	12	37	49				60																		
1975-76	Spokane Flyers	WIHL	33	4	20	24				46																		
	NHL Totals		**2**	**0**	**0**	**0**	**0**	**0**	**0**	**0**					**0.0**													

WIHL First All-Star Team (1972) • WIHL Second All-Star Team (1973, 1974)

Claimed by **Philadelphia** from **Detroit** in Expansion Draft, June 6, 1967. Traded to **Phoenix** (CHL) by **Seattle** (CHL) for cash, February 13, 1970.

• CARSON, Jimmy

James Charles C – R. 6'1", 200 lbs. b: Southfield, MI, 7/20/1968. Los Angeles' 1st, 2nd overall, in 1986.

Season	Club	League	GP	G	A	Pts	AG	AA	APts	PIM	PP	SH	GW	S	%	TGF	PGF	TGA	PGA	+/–	GP	G	A	Pts	PIM	PP	SH	GW
1983-84	Detroit Compuware	MNHL	STATISTICS NOT AVAILABLE																									
1984-85	Verdun Jr. Canadiens	QMJHL	68	44	72	116				12											14	9	17	26	12			
	Verdun Jr. Canadiens	Mem-Cup	3	0	1	1				4																		
1985-86	Verdun Jr. Canadiens	QMJHL	69	70	83	153				46											5	2	6	8	0			
	United States	WJC-A	7	4	1	5				0																		
1986-87	**Los Angeles Kings**	**NHL**	**80**	**37**	**42**	**79**	**32**	**31**	**63**	**22**	**18**	**0**	**2**	**215**	**17.2**	**105**	**48**	**64**	**2**	**–5**	**5**	**1**	**2**	**3**	**6**	**0**	**0**	**0**
	United States	WEC-A	10	2	3	5				4																		
1987-88	**Los Angeles Kings**	**NHL**	**80**	**55**	**52**	**107**	**47**	**37**	**84**	**45**	**22**	**0**	**7**	**264**	**20.8**	**141**	**68**	**94**	**2**	**–19**	**5**	**5**	**3**	**8**	**4**	**1**	**0**	**0**
1988-89	**Edmonton Oilers**	**NHL**	**80**	**49**	**51**	**100**	**42**	**36**	**78**	**36**	**19**	**0**	**5**	**240**	**20.4**	**128**	**49**	**77**	**1**	**3**	**7**	**2**	**1**	**3**	**6**	**1**	**0**	**1**
1989-90	**Edmonton Oilers**	**NHL**	**4**	**1**	**2**	**3**	**1**	**1**	**2**	**0**	**1**	**0**	**0**	**11**	**9.1**	**4**	**3**	**3**	**0**	**–2**								
	Detroit Red Wings	**NHL**	**44**	**20**	**16**	**36**	**17**	**11**	**28**	**8**	**10**	**0**	**1**	**127**	**15.7**	**55**	**24**	**37**	**0**	**–6**								
1990-91	**Detroit Red Wings**	**NHL**	**64**	**21**	**25**	**46**	**19**	**19**	**38**	**28**	**5**	**1**	**4**	**175**	**12.0**	**67**	**21**	**44**	**1**	**3**	**7**	**2**	**1**	**3**	**4**	**0**	**0**	**1**
1991-92	**Detroit Red Wings**	**NHL**	**80**	**34**	**35**	**69**	**31**	**26**	**57**	**30**	**11**	**0**	**3**	**150**	**22.7**	**93**	**26**	**50**	**0**	**17**	**11**	**2**	**3**	**5**	**0**	**0**	**0**	**0**
1992-93	**Detroit Red Wings**	**NHL**	**52**	**25**	**26**	**51**	**21**	**18**	**39**	**18**	**13**	**0**	**4**	**108**	**23.1**	**72**	**40**	**32**	**0**	**0**								
	Los Angeles Kings	**NHL**	**34**	**12**	**10**	**22**	**10**	**7**	**17**	**14**	**4**	**0**	**1**	**81**	**14.8**	**33**	**9**	**26**	**0**	**–2**	**18**	**5**	**4**	**9**	**2**	**2**	**0**	**0**
1993-94	**Los Angeles Kings**	**NHL**	**25**	**4**	**7**	**11**	**4**	**5**	**9**	**2**	**1**	**0**	**0**	**47**	**8.5**	**16**	**2**	**16**	**0**	**–2**								
	Vancouver Canucks	**NHL**	**34**	**7**	**10**	**17**	**6**	**8**	**14**	**22**	**2**	**0**	**1**	**82**	**8.5**	**27**	**11**	**30**	**1**	**–13**	**2**	**0**	**1**	**1**	**0**	**0**	**0**	**0**
1994-95	**Hartford Whalers**	**NHL**	**38**	**9**	**10**	**19**	**16**	**15**	**31**	**29**	**4**	**0**	**3**	**58**	**15.5**	**27**	**8**	**14**	**0**	**5**								
1995-96	**Hartford Whalers**	**NHL**	**11**	**1**	**0**	**1**	**1**	**0**	**1**	**0**	**0**	**0**	**0**	**9**	**11.1**	**2**	**0**	**1**	**0**	**1**								
	HC Lausanne	Switz.	13	3	4	7				14																		
1996-97	Detroit Vipers	IHL	18	7	16	23				4											13	4	6	10	12			
1997-98	Detroit Vipers	IHL	49	10	28	38				34											9	3	4	7	6			
	NHL Totals		**626**	**275**	**286**	**561**	**247**	**214**	**461**	**254**	**110**	**1**	**31**	**1567**	**17.5**	**770**	**309**	**488**	**7**		**55**	**17**	**15**	**32**	**22**	**4**	**0**	**2**

QMJHL Second All-Star Team (1986) • Named to NHL All-Rookie Team (1987) • Played in NHL All-Star Game (1989)

Traded to **Edmonton** by **LA Kings** with Martin Gelinas, LA Kings' 1st round choices in 1989 (later traded to New Jersey — New Jersey selected Jason Miller), 1991 (Martin Rucinsky) and 1993 (Nick Stajduhar) Entry Drafts and cash for Wayne Gretzky, Mike Krushelnyski and Marty McSorley, August 9, 1988. Traded to **Detroit** by **Edmonton** with Kevin McClelland and Edmonton's 5th round choice (later traded to Montreal — Montreal selected Brad Layzell) in 1991 Entry Draft for Petr Klima, Joe Murphy, Adam Graves and Jeff Sharples, November 2, 1989. Traded to **LA Kings** by **Detroit** with Marc Potvin and Gary Shuchuk for Paul Coffey, Sylvain Couturier and Jim Hiller, January 29, 1993. Traded to **Vancouver** by **LA Kings** for Dixon Ward, January 8, 1994. Signed as a free agent by **Hartford**, July 15, 1994.

• CARSON, Lindsay

Lindsay Warren C – L. 6'2", 195 lbs. b: Oxbow, Sask., 11/21/1960. Philadelphia's 4th, 56th overall, in 1979.

Season	Club	League	GP	G	A	Pts	AG	AA	APts	PIM	PP	SH	GW	S	%	TGF	PGF	TGA	PGA	+/–	GP	G	A	Pts	PIM	PP	SH	GW
1976-77	Battleford Barons	SJHL	59	31	39	70				111																		
1977-78	Saskatoon Blades	WCJHL	62	23	55	78				124																		
1978-79	Saskatoon Blades	WHL	37	21	29	50				55																		
	Billings Bighorns	WHL	30	13	22	35				50											8	4	7	11	2			
1979-80	Billings Bighorns	WHL	70	42	66	108				101											7	4	5	9	14			
1980-81	Saginaw Gears	IHL	79	11	25	36				84											20	4	12	16	45			
1981-82	**Philadelphia Flyers**	**NHL**	**18**	**0**	**1**	**1**	**0**	**1**	**1**	**32**	**0**	**0**	**0**	**24**	**0.0**	**1**	**0**	**18**	**2**	**–15**								
	Maine Mariners	AHL	54	20	31	51				92											4	0	0	0	12			
1982-83	**Philadelphia Flyers**	**NHL**	**78**	**18**	**19**	**37**	**15**	**13**	**28**	**67**	**0**	**0**	**2**	**150**	**12.0**	**54**	**1**	**34**	**1**	**20**	**1**	**0**	**0**	**0**	**0**	**0**	**0**	**0**
1983-84	**Philadelphia Flyers**	**NHL**	**16**	**1**	**3**	**4**	**1**	**2**	**3**	**10**	**0**	**0**	**1**	**16**	**6.3**	**6**	**0**	**13**	**0**	**–7**	**1**	**0**	**0**	**0**	**5**	**0**	**0**	**0**
	Springfield Indians	AHL	5	2	4	6				5																		
1984-85	**Philadelphia Flyers**	**NHL**	**77**	**20**	**19**	**39**	**16**	**13**	**29**	**123**	**1**	**0**	**1**	**120**	**16.7**	**52**	**2**	**55**	**5**	**0**	**17**	**0**	**3**	**3**	**24**	**0**	**0**	**0**
1985-86	**Philadelphia Flyers**	**NHL**	**50**	**9**	**12**	**21**	**7**	**8**	**15**	**84**	**0**	**0**	**0**	**59**	**15.3**	**27**	**0**	**17**	**0**	**10**	**1**	**0**	**0**	**0**	**5**	**0**	**0**	**0**
1986-87	**Philadelphia Flyers**	**NHL**	**71**	**11**	**15**	**26**	**9**	**11**	**20**	**141**	**0**	**1**	**2**	**100**	**11.0**	**45**	**2**	**50**	**5**	**–2**	**24**	**3**	**5**	**8**	**22**	**0**	**0**	**0**
1987-88	**Philadelphia Flyers**	**NHL**	**36**	**2**	**7**	**9**	**2**	**5**	**7**	**37**	**0**	**0**	**0**	**34**	**5.9**	**10**	**2**	**14**	**2**	**–4**								
	Hartford Whalers	**NHL**	**27**	**5**	**4**	**9**	**4**	**3**	**7**	**30**	**1**	**1**	**1**	**39**	**12.8**	**19**	**2**	**17**	**0**	**0**	**5**	**1**	**2**	**3**	**0**	**0**	**0**	**0**
1988-89	Binghamton Whalers	AHL	24	4	10	14				35																		
	NHL Totals		**373**	**66**	**80**	**146**	**54**	**56**	**110**	**524**	**2**	**2**	**7**	**542**	**12.2**	**214**	**9**	**218**	**15**		**49**	**4**	**10**	**14**	**56**	**0**	**0**	**0**

Traded to **Hartford** by **Philadelphia** for Paul Lawless, January 22, 1988.

• CARTER, Anson

C – R. 6'1", 185 lbs. b: Toronto, Ont., 6/6/1974. Quebec's 11th, 220th overall, in 1992.

Season	Club	League	GP	G	A	Pts	AG	AA	APts	PIM	PP	SH	GW	S	%	TGF	PGF	TGA	PGA	+/–	GP	G	A	Pts	PIM	PP	SH	GW
1989-90	Don Mills Bantam Flyers	MTHL	40	15	47	62				105																		
1990-91	Don Mills Flyers	MTHL	67	69	73	142				43																		
1991-92	Wexford Raiders	OJHL	42	18	22	40				24																		
1992-93	Michigan State Spartans	CCHA	34	15	7	22				20																		
1993-94	Michigan State Spartans	CCHA	39	30	24	54				36																		
	Canada	WJC-A	7	3	2	5				0																		
1994-95	Michigan State Spartans	CCHA	39	34	17	51				40																		
1995-96	Michigan State Spartans	CCHA	42	23	20	43				36																		
1996-97	**Washington Capitals**	**NHL**	**19**	**3**	**2**	**5**	**3**	**2**	**5**	**7**	**1**	**0**	**1**	**28**	**10.7**	**7**	**1**	**6**	**0**	**0**								
	Portland Pirates	AHL	27	19	19	38				11																		
	Boston Bruins	**NHL**	**19**	**8**	**5**	**13**	**8**	**4**	**12**	**2**	**1**	**1**	**1**	**51**	**15.7**	**17**	**5**	**24**	**5**	**–7**								
	Canada	WC-A	11	4	2	6				4																		
1997-98	**Boston Bruins**	**NHL**	**78**	**16**	**27**	**43**	**19**	**26**	**45**	**31**	**6**	**0**	**4**	**179**	**8.9**	**66**	**20**	**41**	**2**	**7**	**6**	**1**	**1**	**2**	**0**	**0**	**0**	**0**

			REGULAR SEASON																		PLAYOFFS							
Season	Club	League	GP	G	A	Pts	AG	AA	APts	PIM	PP	SH	GW	S	%	TGF	PGF	TGA	PGA	+/–	GP	G	A	Pts	PIM	PP	SH	GW
1998-99	**Boston Bruins**	**NHL**	**55**	**24**	**16**	**40**	**28**	**15**	**43**	**22**	**6**	**0**	**6**	**123**	**19.5**	**57**	**19**	**34**	**3**	**7**	**12**	**4**	**3**	**7**	**0**	**1**	**0**	**1**
	Utah Grizzlies	IHL	6	1	1	2	....	....	....	0	....	....	....	....	....	....	....	....	....	....	....	....	....	....	....	....	....	....
99-2000	**Boston Bruins**	**NHL**	**59**	**22**	**25**	**47**	**25**	**23**	**48**	**14**	**4**	**0**	**1**	**144**	**15.3**	**62**	**20**	**49**	**15**	**8**	....	....	....	....	....	....	....	....
	NHL Totals		**230**	**73**	**75**	**148**	**83**	**70**	**153**	**76**	**18**	**1**	**13**	**525**	**13.9**	**209**	**65**	**154**	**25**		**18**	**5**	**4**	**9**	**0**	**1**	**0**	**1**

CCHA First All-Star Team (1994, 1995) • NCAA West Second All-American Team (1995) • CCHA Second All-Star Team (1996)

Rights transferred to **Colorado** after **Quebec** franchise relocated, June 21, 1995. Traded to **Washington** by **Colorado** for Washington's 4th round choice (Ben Storey) in 1996 Entry Draft, April 3, 1996. Traded to **Boston** by **Washington** with Jim Carey, Jason Allison and Washington's 3rd round choice (Lee Goren) in 1997 Entry Draft for Bill Ranford, Adam Oates and Rick Tocchet, March 1, 1997.

• CARTER, John

John A. LW – L. 5'10", 181 lbs. b: Winchester, MA, 5/3/1963.

Season	Club	League	GP	G	A	Pts	AG	AA	APts	PIM	PP	SH	GW	S	%	TGF	PGF	TGA	PGA	+/–	GP	G	A	Pts	PIM	PP	SH	GW
1979-80	Middlesex Islanders	MBAHL	STATISTICS NOT AVAILABLE																									
1980-81	North Shore Raiders	MBAHL	STATISTICS NOT AVAILABLE																									
1981-82	Woburn High School	Hi-School	25	21	25	46	....	....	....	....	....	....	....	....	....	....	....	....	....	....	....	....	....	....	....	....	....	....
1982-83	RPI Engineers	ECAC	29	16	22	38	....	....	....	33	....	....	....	....	....	....	....	....	....	....	....	....	....	....	....	....	....	....
1983-84	RPI Engineers	ECAC	38	35	39	74	....	....	....	52	....	....	....	....	....	....	....	....	....	....	....	....	....	....	....	....	....	....
1984-85	RPI Engineers	ECAC	37	43	29	72	....	....	....	52	....	....	....	....	....	....	....	....	....	....	....	....	....	....	....	....	....	....
1985-86	RPI Engineers	ECAC	27	23	18	41	....	....	....	68	....	....	....	....	....	....	....	....	....	....	....	....	....	....	....	....	....	....
	United States	WEC-A	9	1	2	3	....	....	....	14	....	....	....	....	....	....	....	....	....	....	....	....	....	....	....	....	....	....
	Boston Bruins	**NHL**	**3**	**0**	**0**	**0**	**0**	**0**	**0**	**0**	**0**	**0**	**0**	**2**	**0.0**	**0**	**0**	**0**	**0**	**0**	....	....	....	....	....	....	....	....
1986-87	**Boston Bruins**	**NHL**	**8**	**0**	**1**	**1**	**0**	**1**	**1**	**0**	**0**	**0**	**0**	**12**	**0.0**	**4**	**0**	**1**	**0**	**3**	....	....	....	....	....	....	....	....
	Moncton Golden Flames	AHL	58	25	30	55	....	....	....	60	....	....	....	....	....	....	....	....	....	....	6	2	3	5	5	....	....	....
1987-88	**Boston Bruins**	**NHL**	**4**	**0**	**1**	**1**	**0**	**1**	**1**	**2**	**0**	**0**	**0**	**8**	**0.0**	**3**	**0**	**0**	**0**	**3**	....	....	....	....	....	....	....	....
	Maine Mariners	AHL	76	38	38	76	....	....	....	145	....	....	....	....	....	....	....	....	....	....	10	4	4	8	44	....	....	....
1988-89	**Boston Bruins**	**NHL**	**44**	**12**	**10**	**22**	**10**	**7**	**17**	**24**	**4**	**1**	**0**	**96**	**12.5**	**45**	**16**	**31**	**1**	**–1**	**10**	**1**	**2**	**3**	**6**	**0**	**0**	**0**
	Maine Mariners	AHL	24	13	6	19	....	....	....	12	....	....	....	....	....	....	....	....	....	....	....	....	....	....	....	....	....	....
1989-90	**Boston Bruins**	**NHL**	**76**	**17**	**22**	**39**	**15**	**16**	**31**	**26**	**2**	**1**	**1**	**142**	**12.0**	**58**	**7**	**50**	**16**	**17**	**21**	**6**	**3**	**9**	**45**	**0**	**1**	**0**
	Maine Mariners	AHL	2	2	2	4	....	....	....	2	....	....	....	....	....	....	....	....	....	....	....	....	....	....	....	....	....	....
1990-91	**Boston Bruins**	**NHL**	**50**	**4**	**7**	**11**	**4**	**5**	**9**	**68**	**1**	**1**	**2**	**61**	**6.6**	**27**	**1**	**45**	**6**	**–13**	....	....	....	....	....	....	....	....
	Maine Mariners	AHL	16	5	9	14	....	....	....	16	....	....	....	....	....	....	....	....	....	....	1	0	0	0	10	....	....	....
1991-92	**San Jose Sharks**	**NHL**	**4**	**0**	**0**	**0**	**0**	**0**	**0**	**0**	**0**	**0**	**0**	**5**	**0.0**	**0**	**0**	**6**	**4**	**–2**	....	....	....	....	....	....	....	....
	Kansas City Blades	IHL	42	11	15	26	....	....	....	116	....	....	....	....	....	....	....	....	....	....	15	6	9	15	18	....	....	....
1992-93	**San Jose Sharks**	**NHL**	**55**	**7**	**9**	**16**	**6**	**6**	**12**	**81**	**0**	**1**	**0**	**110**	**6.4**	**25**	**2**	**77**	**29**	**–25**	....	....	....	....	....	....	....	....
	Kansas City Blades	IHL	9	4	2	6	....	....	....	14	....	....	....	....	....	....	....	....	....	....	....	....	....	....	....	....	....	....
1993-94	Providence Bruins	AHL	47	11	5	16	....	....	....	82	....	....	....	....	....	....	....	....	....	....	....	....	....	....	....	....	....	....
1994-95	Worcester IceCats	AHL	64	18	9	27	....	....	....	96	....	....	....	....	....	....	....	....	....	....	....	....	....	....	....	....	....	....
	NHL Totals		**244**	**40**	**50**	**90**	**35**	**36**	**71**	**201**	**7**	**4**	**3**	**436**	**9.2**	**162**	**26**	**210**	**56**		**31**	**7**	**5**	**12**	**51**	**0**	**1**	**0**

ECAC Second All-Star Team (1984) • ECAC First All-Star Team (1985)

Signed as a free agent by **Boston**, March 27, 1986. Signed as a free agent by **San Jose**, August 22, 1991.

• CARTER, Ron

Ronald RW – L. 6'1", 205 lbs. b: Montreal, Que., 3/14/1958. Montreal's 4th, 36th overall, in 1978.

Season	Club	League	GP	G	A	Pts	AG	AA	APts	PIM	PP	SH	GW	S	%	TGF	PGF	TGA	PGA	+/–	GP	G	A	Pts	PIM	PP	SH	GW
1975-76	Sherbrooke Beavers	QMJHL	65	34	36	70	....	....	....	12	....	....	....	....	....	....	....	....	....	....	....	....	....	....	....	....	....	....
1976-77	Sherbrooke Beavers	QMJHL	72	77	50	127	....	....	....	18	....	....	....	....	....	....	....	....	....	....	....	....	....	....	....	....	....	....
	Sherbrooke Beavers	Mem-Cup	4	1	1	2	....	....	....	0	....	....	....	....	....	....	....	....	....	....	....	....	....	....	....	....	....	....
1977-78	Sherbrooke Beavers	QMJHL	71	*88	86	*174	....	....	....	28	....	....	....	....	....	....	....	....	....	....	....	....	....	....	....	....	....	....
1978-79	Springfield Indians	AHL	1	0	0	0	....	....	....	0	....	....	....	....	....	....	....	....	....	....	....	....	....	....	....	....	....	....
	Dallas Black Hawks	CHL	54	22	16	38	....	....	....	8	....	....	....	....	....	....	....	....	....	....	7	2	2	4	5	....	....	....
1979-80	**Edmonton Oilers**	**NHL**	**2**	**0**	**0**	**0**	**0**	**0**	**0**	**0**	**0**	**0**	**0**	**0**	**0.0**	**0**	**0**	**0**	**0**	**0**	....	....	....	....	....	....	....	....
	Houston Apollos	CHL	76	40	30	70	....	....	....	17	....	....	....	....	....	....	....	....	....	....	4	2	1	3	0	....	....	....
1980-81	Rochester Americans	AHL	38	31	19	50	....	....	....	8	....	....	....	....	....	....	....	....	....	....	....	....	....	....	....	....	....	....
	Erie Blades	EHL	38	23	21	44	....	....	....	6	....	....	....	....	....	....	....	....	....	....	....	....	....	....	....	....	....	....
1981-82	Rochester Americans	AHL	12	6	4	10	....	....	....	0	....	....	....	....	....	....	....	....	....	....	....	....	....	....	....	....	....	....
	Flint Generals	IHL	49	29	23	52	....	....	....	2	....	....	....	....	....	....	....	....	....	....	4	0	0	0	5	....	....	....
1982-83	Nashville South Stars	ACHL	58	47	49	96	....	....	....	21	....	....	....	....	....	....	....	....	....	....	....	....	....	....	....	....	....	....
1983-84	Virginia Lancers	ACHL	62	51	59	110	....	....	....	20	....	....	....	....	....	....	....	....	....	....	4	1	2	3	10	....	....	....
1984-85	Virginia Lancers	ACHL	57	56	48	104	....	....	....	10	....	....	....	....	....	....	....	....	....	....	4	1	2	3	2	....	....	....
1985-86	Virginia Lancers	ACHL	20	14	13	27	....	....	....	2	....	....	....	....	....	....	....	....	....	....	....	....	....	....	....	....	....	....
	Mohawk Valley Comets	ACHL	32	34	18	52	....	....	....	4	....	....	....	....	....	....	....	....	....	....	6	2	5	7	0	....	....	....
	NHL Totals		**2**	**0**	**0**	**0**	**0**	**0**	**0**	**0**	**0**	**0**	**0**	**0**	**0.0**	**0**	**0**	**0**	**0**		....	....	....	....	....	....	....	....

QMJHL First All-Star Team (1978) • ACHL Second All-Star Team (1983)

Signed as an underage free agent by **Edmonton** (WHA), July, 1978. NHL rights retained by **Edmonton** prior to Expansion Draft, June 9, 1979. Claimed on waivers by **Buffalo** from **Edmonton, July, 1980.**

• CASHMAN, Wayne

Wayne John LW – R. 6'1", 208 lbs. b: Kingston, Ont., 6/24/1945.

Season	Club	League	GP	G	A	Pts	AG	AA	APts	PIM	PP	SH	GW	S	%	TGF	PGF	TGA	PGA	+/–	GP	G	A	Pts	PIM	PP	SH	GW
1962-63	Kingston Frontenacs	OHA-B	STATISTICS NOT AVAILABLE																									
	Oshawa Generals	OHA-Jr.	1	0	1	1	....	....	....	0	....	....	....	....	....	....	....	....	....	....	....	....	....	....	....	....	....	....
1963-64	Oshawa Generals	OHA-Jr.	27	9	12	21	....	....	....	37	....	....	....	....	....	....	....	....	....	....	6	2	2	4	15	....	....	....
1964-65	Oshawa Generals	OHA-Jr.	55	27	46	73	....	....	....	104	....	....	....	....	....	....	....	....	....	....	6	3	2	5	11	....	....	....
	Boston Bruins	**NHL**	**1**	**0**	**0**	**0**	**0**	**0**	**0**	**0**	....	....	....	....	....	....	....	....	....	....	....	....	....	....	....	....	....	....
1965-66	Oshawa Generals	OHA-Jr.	48	26	44	70	....	....	....	98	....	....	....	....	....	....	....	....	....	....	17	*15	20	*35	21	....	....	....
	Oshawa Generals	Mem-Cup	14	10	27	37	....	....	....	51	....	....	....	....	....	....	....	....	....	....	....	....	....	....	....	....	....	....
1966-67	Oklahoma City Blazers	CPHL	70	20	36	56	....	....	....	98	....	....	....	....	....	....	....	....	....	....	11	3	4	7	4	....	....	....
1967-68	**Boston Bruins**	**NHL**	**12**	**0**	**4**	**4**	**0**	**4**	**4**	**2**	**0**	**0**	**0**	**12**	**0.0**	**4**	**1**	**8**	**0**	**–5**	**1**	**0**	**0**	**0**	**0**	**0**	**0**	**0**
	Oklahoma City Blazers	CPHL	42	21	30	51	....	....	....	66	....	....	....	....	....	....	....	....	....	....	....	....	....	....	....	....	....	....
1968-69	**Boston Bruins**	**NHL**	**51**	**8**	**23**	**31**	**8**	**20**	**28**	**49**	**1**	**0**	**1**	**66**	**12.1**	**49**	**7**	**23**	**0**	**19**	**6**	**0**	**1**	**1**	**0**	**0**	**0**	**0**
	Hershey Bears	AHL	21	6	9	15	....	....	....	30	....	....	....	....	....	....	....	....	....	....	....	....	....	....	....	....	....	....
1969-70♦	**Boston Bruins**	**NHL**	**70**	**9**	**26**	**35**	**10**	**24**	**34**	**79**	**0**	**0**	**1**	**104**	**8.7**	**56**	**7**	**34**	**7**	**22**	**14**	**5**	**4**	**9**	**50**	**0**	**2**	**0**
1970-71	**Boston Bruins**	**NHL**	**77**	**21**	**58**	**79**	**21**	**49**	**70**	**100**	**4**	**0**	**3**	**175**	**12.0**	**134**	**20**	**56**	**1**	**59**	**7**	**3**	**2**	**5**	**15**	**0**	**0**	**1**
1971-72♦	**Boston Bruins**	**NHL**	**74**	**23**	**29**	**52**	**23**	**25**	**48**	**103**	**1**	**0**	**3**	**150**	**15.3**	**98**	**7**	**51**	**2**	**42**	**15**	**4**	**7**	**11**	**42**	**1**	**0**	**0**
1972-73	Team Canada	Summit-72	2	0	2	2	....	....	....	14	....	....	....	....	....	....	....	....	....	....	....	....	....	....	....	....	....	....
	Boston Bruins	**NHL**	**76**	**29**	**39**	**68**	**27**	**31**	**58**	**100**	**6**	**0**	**3**	**169**	**17.2**	**98**	**16**	**77**	**0**	**5**	**5**	**1**	**1**	**2**	**4**	**0**	**0**	**0**
1973-74	**Boston Bruins**	**NHL**	**78**	**30**	**59**	**89**	**29**	**49**	**78**	**111**	**5**	**2**	**2**	**156**	**19.2**	**138**	**21**	**72**	**4**	**49**	**16**	**5**	**9**	**14**	**46**	**1**	**0**	**1**
1974-75	**Boston Bruins**	**NHL**	**42**	**11**	**22**	**33**	**10**	**16**	**26**	**24**	**2**	**0**	**3**	**75**	**14.7**	**57**	**16**	**34**	**0**	**7**	**1**	**0**	**2**	**2**	**0**	**0**	**0**	**0**
1975-76	**Boston Bruins**	**NHL**	**80**	**28**	**43**	**71**	**25**	**32**	**57**	**87**	**9**	**0**	**6**	**169**	**16.6**	**111**	**22**	**61**	**2**	**30**	**11**	**1**	**5**	**6**	**16**	**0**	**0**	**0**
1976-77	**Boston Bruins**	**NHL**	**65**	**15**	**37**	**52**	**13**	**29**	**42**	**76**	**3**	**0**	**3**	**105**	**14.3**	**77**	**21**	**52**	**0**	**4**	**14**	**1**	**8**	**9**	**18**	**0**	**0**	**0**
1977-78	**Boston Bruins**	**NHL**	**76**	**24**	**38**	**62**	**22**	**29**	**51**	**69**	**1**	**0**	**2**	**134**	**17.9**	**93**	**9**	**51**	**1**	**34**	**15**	**4**	**6**	**10**	**13**	**3**	**0**	**2**
1978-79	**Boston Bruins**	**NHL**	**75**	**27**	**40**	**67**	**23**	**29**	**52**	**63**	**10**	**0**	**4**	**133**	**20.3**	**110**	**39**	**55**	**0**	**16**	**10**	**4**	**5**	**9**	**8**	**1**	**0**	**1**
1979-80	**Boston Bruins**	**NHL**	**44**	**11**	**21**	**32**	**9**	**15**	**24**	**19**	**3**	**1**	**2**	**60**	**18.3**	**52**	**25**	**32**	**2**	**–3**	**10**	**3**	**3**	**6**	**32**	**1**	**0**	**0**
1980-81	**Boston Bruins**	**NHL**	**77**	**25**	**35**	**60**	**19**	**23**	**42**	**80**	**7**	**0**	**2**	**111**	**22.5**	**106**	**36**	**55**	**2**	**17**	**3**	**0**	**1**	**1**	**0**	**0**	**0**	**0**
1981-82	**Boston Bruins**	**NHL**	**64**	**12**	**31**	**43**	**9**	**21**	**30**	**59**	**3**	**0**	**1**	**90**	**13.3**	**64**	**18**	**63**	**0**	**–17**	**9**	**0**	**2**	**2**	**6**	**0**	**0**	**0**
1982-83	**Boston Bruins**	**NHL**	**65**	**4**	**11**	**15**	**3**	**8**	**11**	**20**	**1**	**0**	**1**	**36**	**11.1**	**38**	**12**	**24**	**0**	**2**	**8**	**0**	**1**	**1**	**0**	**0**	**0**	**0**
1983-1986			OUT OF HOCKEY – RETIRED																									
1986-1987	**New York Rangers**	**NHL**	DID NOT PLAY – SCOUTING																									
	New York Rangers	**NHL**	DID NOT PLAY – ASSISTANT COACH																									
1987-1992	**New York Rangers**	**NHL**	DID NOT PLAY – ASSISTANT COACH																									
1992-1996	**Tampa Bay Lightning**	**NHL**	DID NOT PLAY – ASSISTANT COACH																									
1996-1997	**Philadelphia Flyers**	**NHL**	DID NOT PLAY – ASSISTANT COACH																									

			REGULAR SEASON																		PLAYOFFS							
Season	Club	League	GP	G	A	Pts	AG	AA	APts	PIM	PP	SH	GW	S	%	TGF	PGF	TGA	PGA	+/–	GP	G	A	Pts	PIM	PP	SH	GW
1997-1998	Philadelphia Flyers	NHL	DID NOT PLAY – COACHING																									
	Philadelphia Flyers	NHL	DID NOT PLAY – ASSISTANT COACH																									
1998-2000	Philadelphia Flyers	NHL	DID NOT PLAY – ASSISTANT COACH																									
	NHL Totals		1027	277	516	793	251	404	655	1041	....	....	....	....	....	....	....	....	....	....	145	31	57	88	250	....	....	....

NHL Second All-Star Team (1974) • Played in NHL All-Star Game (1974)

• CASSELMAN, Mike

Michael S. C – L. 5'11", 190 lbs. b: Morrisburg, Ont., 8/23/1968. Detroit's 1st, 3rd overall, in 1990 Supplemental Draft.

Season	Club	League	GP	G	A	Pts	AG	AA	APts	PIM	PP	SH	GW	S	%	TGF	PGF	TGA	PGA	+/–	GP	G	A	Pts	PIM	PP	SH	GW
1983-84	Morrisburg Lions	OJHL-B	1	1	0	1	....	....	....	2	....	....	....	....	....	....	....	....	....	....	....	....	....	....	....	....	....	....
1984-1986			STATISTICS NOT AVAILABLE																									
1986-87	Morrisburg Lions	OJHL-B	30	14	5	19	....	....	....	....	....	....	....	....	....	....	....	....	....	....	....	....	....	....	....	....	....	....
1987-88	Clarkson University	ECAC	24	4	1	5	....	....	....	12	....	....	....	....	....	....	....	....	....	....	....	....	....	....	....	....	....	....
1988-89	Clarkson University	ECAC	31	3	14	17	....	....	....	36	....	....	....	....	....	....	....	....	....	....	....	....	....	....	....	....	....	....
1989-90	Clarkson University	ECAC	34	22	21	43	....	....	....	69	....	....	....	....	....	....	....	....	....	....	....	....	....	....	....	....	....	....
1990-91	Clarkson University	ECAC	40	19	35	54	....	....	....	44	....	....	....	....	....	....	....	....	....	....	....	....	....	....	....	....	....	....
1991-92	Toledo Storm	ECHL	61	39	60	99	....	....	....	83	....	....	....	....	....	....	....	....	....	....	5	0	1	1	6	....	....	....
	Adirondack Red Wings	AHL	1	0	0	0	....	....	....	0	....	....	....	....	....	....	....	....	....	....	....	....	....	....	....	....	....	....
1992-93	Adirondack Red Wings	AHL	60	12	19	31	....	....	....	27	....	....	....	....	....	....	....	....	....	....	8	3	3	6	0	....	....	....
	Toledo Storm	ECHL	3	0	1	1	....	....	....	2	....	....	....	....	....	....	....	....	....	....	....	....	....	....	....	....	....	....
1993-94	Adirondack Red Wings	AHL	77	17	38	55	....	....	....	34	....	....	....	....	....	....	....	....	....	....	12	2	4	6	10	....	....	....
1994-95	Adirondack Red Wings	AHL	60	17	43	60	....	....	....	42	....	....	....	....	....	....	....	....	....	....	4	0	0	0	2	....	....	....
1995-96	**Florida Panthers**	**NHL**	**3**	**0**	**0**	**0**	**0**	**0**	**0**	**0**	**0**	**0**	**0**	**2**	**0.0**	**0**	**0**	**1**	**0**	**–1**	....	....	....	....	....	....	....	....
	Carolina Monarchs	AHL	70	34	68	102	....	....	....	46	....	....	....	....	....	....	....	....	....	....	....	....	....	....	....	....	....	....
1996-97	Cincinnati Cyclones	IHL	68	30	34	64	....	....	....	54	....	....	....	....	....	....	....	....	....	....	3	1	0	1	2	....	....	....
1997-98	Cincinnati Cyclones	IHL	55	19	28	47	....	....	....	44	....	....	....	....	....	....	....	....	....	....	....	....	....	....	....	....	....	....
	Rochester Americans	AHL	25	8	7	15	....	....	....	14	....	....	....	....	....	....	....	....	....	....	4	1	1	2	2	....	....	....
1998-99	EV Landshut	Germany	49	20	29	49	....	....	....	64	....	....	....	....	....	....	....	....	....	....	3	0	1	1	0	....	....	....
99-2000	Munich Barons	Germany	54	14	29	43	....	....	....	44	....	....	....	....	....	....	....	....	....	....	12	4	*8	*12	4	....	....	....
	NHL Totals		**3**	**0**	**0**	**0**	**0**	**0**	**0**	**0**	**0**	**0**	**0**	**2**	**0.0**	**0**	**0**	**1**	**0**		....	....	....	....	....	....	....	....

ECHL Second All-Star Team (1992)

Signed as a free agent by **Florida**, October 31, 1995. Signed as a free agent by **San Jose**, September 24, 1997.

• CASSELS, Andrew

C – L. 6'1", 185 lbs. b: Bramalea, Ont., 7/23/1969. Montreal's 1st, 17th overall, in 1987.

Season	Club	League	GP	G	A	Pts	AG	AA	APts	PIM	PP	SH	GW	S	%	TGF	PGF	TGA	PGA	+/–	GP	G	A	Pts	PIM	PP	SH	GW
1984-85	Bramalea Blues	OJHL-B	4	2	0	2	....	....	....	0	....	....	....	....	....	....	....	....	....	....	....	....	....	....	....	....	....	....
1985-86	Bramalea Blues	OJHL-B	33	18	25	43	....	....	....	26	....	....	....	....	....	....	....	....	....	....	....	....	....	....	....	....	....	....
1986-87	Ottawa 67's	OHL	66	26	66	92	....	....	....	28	....	....	....	....	....	....	....	....	....	....	11	5	9	14	7	....	....	....
1987-88	Ottawa 67's	OHL	61	48	*103	*151	....	....	....	39	....	....	....	....	....	....	....	....	....	....	16	8	*24	*32	13	....	....	....
1988-89	Ottawa 67's	OHL	56	37	97	134	....	....	....	66	....	....	....	....	....	....	....	....	....	....	12	5	10	15	10	....	....	....
	Canada	WJC-A	7	2	5	7	....	....	....	2	....	....	....	....	....	....	....	....	....	....	....	....	....	....	....	....	....	....
1989-90	**Montreal Canadiens**	**NHL**	**6**	**2**	**0**	**2**	**2**	**0**	**2**	**2**	**0**	**0**	**1**	**5**	**40.0**	**3**	**0**	**2**	**0**	**1**	....	....	....	....	....	....	....	....
	Sherbrooke Canadiens	AHL	55	22	45	67	....	....	....	25	....	....	....	....	....	....	....	....	....	....	12	2	11	13	6	....	....	....
1990-91	Montreal Canadiens	Fr-Tour	1	0	1	1	....	....	....	0	....	....	....	....	....	....	....	....	....	....	....	....	....	....	....	....	....	....
	Montreal Canadiens	**NHL**	**54**	**6**	**19**	**25**	**5**	**14**	**19**	**20**	**1**	**0**	**3**	**55**	**10.9**	**39**	**10**	**28**	**1**	**2**	**8**	**0**	**2**	**2**	**2**	**0**	**0**	**0**
1991-92	**Hartford Whalers**	**NHL**	**67**	**11**	**30**	**41**	**10**	**23**	**33**	**18**	**2**	**2**	**3**	**99**	**11.1**	**58**	**18**	**56**	**19**	**3**	**7**	**2**	**4**	**6**	**6**	**1**	**0**	**0**
1992-93	**Hartford Whalers**	**NHL**	**84**	**21**	**64**	**85**	**17**	**44**	**61**	**62**	**8**	**3**	**1**	**134**	**15.7**	**117**	**53**	**128**	**53**	**–11**	....	....	....	....	....	....	....	....
1993-94	**Hartford Whalers**	**NHL**	**79**	**16**	**42**	**58**	**15**	**33**	**48**	**37**	**8**	**1**	**3**	**126**	**12.7**	**88**	**39**	**105**	**35**	**–21**	....	....	....	....	....	....	....	....
1994-95	**Hartford Whalers**	**NHL**	**46**	**7**	**30**	**37**	**12**	**44**	**56**	**18**	**1**	**0**	**1**	**74**	**9.5**	**51**	**16**	**52**	**14**	**–3**	....	....	....	....	....	....	....	....
1995-96	**Hartford Whalers**	**NHL**	**81**	**20**	**43**	**63**	**20**	**35**	**55**	**39**	**6**	**0**	**1**	**135**	**14.8**	**101**	**39**	**87**	**33**	**8**	....	....	....	....	....	....	....	....
	Canada	WC-A	6	1	0	1	....	....	....	0	....	....	....	....	....	....	....	....	....	....	....	....	....	....	....	....	....	....
1996-97	**Hartford Whalers**	**NHL**	**81**	**22**	**44**	**66**	**23**	**39**	**62**	**46**	**8**	**0**	**2**	**142**	**15.5**	**88**	**33**	**89**	**18**	**–16**	....	....	....	....	....	....	....	....
1997-98	**Calgary Flames**	**NHL**	**81**	**17**	**27**	**44**	**20**	**26**	**46**	**32**	**6**	**1**	**2**	**138**	**12.3**	**62**	**18**	**65**	**14**	**–7**	....	....	....	....	....	....	....	....
1998-99	**Calgary Flames**	**NHL**	**70**	**12**	**25**	**37**	**14**	**24**	**38**	**18**	**4**	**1**	**3**	**97**	**12.4**	**56**	**20**	**73**	**25**	**–12**	....	....	....	....	....	....	....	....
99-2000	**Vancouver Canucks**	**NHL**	**79**	**17**	**45**	**62**	**19**	**42**	**61**	**16**	**6**	**0**	**1**	**109**	**15.6**	**88**	**32**	**62**	**14**	**8**	....	....	....	....	....	....	....	....
	NHL Totals		**728**	**151**	**369**	**520**	**157**	**324**	**481**	**308**	**50**	**8**	**21**	**1114**	**13.6**	**751**	**278**	**747**	**226**		**15**	**2**	**6**	**8**	**8**	**1**	**0**	**0**

OHL First All-Star Team (1988,1989)

Traded to **Hartford** by **Montreal** for Hartford's 2nd round choice (Valeri Bure) in 1992 Entry Draft, September 17, 1991. Transferred to **Carolina** after **Hartford** franchise relocated, June 25, 1997. Traded to **Calgary** by **Carolina** with Jean-Sebastien Giguere for Gary Roberts and Trevor Kidd, August 25, 1997. Signed as a free agent by **Vancouver**, August 19, 1999.

• CASSIDY, Bruce

Bruce J. D – L. 5'11", 176 lbs. b: Ottawa, Ont., 5/20/1965. Chicago's 1st, 18th overall, in 1983.

Season	Club	League	GP	G	A	Pts	AG	AA	APts	PIM	PP	SH	GW	S	%	TGF	PGF	TGA	PGA	+/–	GP	G	A	Pts	PIM	PP	SH	GW
1981-82	Hawkesbury Hawks	OJHL	37	13	30	43	....	....	....	32	....	....	....	....	....	....	....	....	....	....	....	....	....	....	....	....	....	....
1982-83	Ottawa 67's	OHL	70	25	86	111	....	....	....	33	....	....	....	....	....	....	....	....	....	....	9	3	9	12	10	....	....	....
1983-84	Ottawa 67's	OHL	67	27	68	95	....	....	....	58	....	....	....	....	....	....	....	....	....	....	13	6	16	22	6	....	....	....
	Canada	WJC-A	7	0	0	0	....	....	....	6	....	....	....	....	....	....	....	....	....	....	....	....	....	....	....	....	....	....
	Chicago Black Hawks	**NHL**	**1**	**0**	**0**	**0**	**0**	**0**	**0**	**0**	**0**	**0**	**0**	**1**	**0.0**	**0**	**0**	**0**	**0**	**0**	....	....	....	....	....	....	....	....
	Ottawa 67's	Mem-Cup	5	*7	5	*12	....	....	....	2	....	....	....	....	....	....	....	....	....	....	....	....	....	....	....	....	....	....
1984-85	Ottawa 67's	OHL	28	13	27	40	....	....	....	15	....	....	....	....	....	....	....	....	....	....	....	....	....	....	....	....	....	....
1985-86	**Chicago Black Hawks**	**NHL**	**1**	**0**	**0**	**0**	**0**	**0**	**0**	**0**	**0**	**0**	**0**	**2**	**0.0**	**0**	**0**	**0**	**0**	**0**	....	....	....	....	....	....	....	....
	Nova Scotia Oilers	AHL	4	0	0	0	....	....	....	0	....	....	....	....	....	....	....	....	....	....	....	....	....	....	....	....	....	....
1986-87	**Chicago Blackhawks**	**NHL**	**2**	**0**	**0**	**0**	**0**	**0**	**0**	**0**	**0**	**0**	**0**	**0**	**0.0**	**2**	**1**	**2**	**0**	**–1**	....	....	....	....	....	....	....	....
	Nova Scotia Oilers	AHL	19	2	8	10	....	....	....	4	....	....	....	....	....	....	....	....	....	....	....	....	....	....	....	....	....	....
	Canada	Nat-Team	12	3	6	9	....	....	....	4	....	....	....	....	....	....	....	....	....	....	....	....	....	....	....	....	....	....
	Saginaw Generals	IHL	10	2	13	15	....	....	....	6	....	....	....	....	....	....	....	....	....	....	2	1	1	2	0	....	....	....
1987-88	**Chicago Blackhawks**	**NHL**	**21**	**3**	**10**	**13**	**3**	**7**	**10**	**6**	**2**	**0**	**0**	**46**	**6.5**	**28**	**14**	**18**	**1**	**–3**	....	....	....	....	....	....	....	....
	Saginaw Hawks	IHL	60	9	37	46	....	....	....	59	....	....	....	....	....	....	....	....	....	....	10	2	3	5	19	....	....	....
1988-89	**Chicago Blackhawks**	**NHL**	**9**	**0**	**2**	**2**	**0**	**1**	**1**	**4**	**0**	**0**	**0**	**12**	**0.0**	**3**	**2**	**7**	**1**	**–5**	**1**	**0**	**0**	**0**	**0**	**0**	**0**	**0**
	Saginaw Hawks	IHL	72	16	64	80	....	....	....	80	....	....	....	....	....	....	....	....	....	....	6	0	2	2	6	....	....	....
1989-90	**Chicago Blackhawks**	**NHL**	**2**	**1**	**1**	**2**	**1**	**1**	**2**	**0**	**1**	**0**	**0**	**3**	**33.3**	**3**	**1**	**3**	**0**	**–1**	....	....	....	....	....	....	....	....
	Indianapolis Ice	IHL	75	11	46	57	....	....	....	56	....	....	....	....	....	....	....	....	....	....	14	1	10	11	20	....	....	....
1990-91	HC Alleghe	Italy	36	23	52	75	....	....	....	20	....	....	....	....	....	....	....	....	....	....	10	7	8	15	2	....	....	....
1991-92	HC Alleghe	Alpenliga	18	13	28	41	....	....	....	16	....	....	....	....	....	....	....	....	....	....	....	....	....	....	....	....	....	....
	HC Alleghe	Italy	18	11	18	29	....	....	....	10	....	....	....	....	....	....	....	....	....	....	9	3	11	14	2	....	....	....
1992-93	HC Alleghe	Alpenliga	32	19	40	59	....	....	....	12	....	....	....	....	....	....	....	....	....	....	....	....	....	....	....	....	....	....
	HC Alleghe	Italy	16	6	22	28	....	....	....	4	....	....	....	....	....	....	....	....	....	....	9	6	8	14	6	....	....	....
1993-94	ESV Kaufbeuren	Germany	33	8	9	17	....	....	....	12	....	....	....	....	....	....	....	....	....	....	4	1	2	3	....	....	....	....
1994-95	Indianapolis Ice	IHL	29	2	13	15	....	....	....	16	....	....	....	....	....	....	....	....	....	....	....	....	....	....	....	....	....	....
1995-96	Indianapolis Ice	IHL	56	5	16	21	....	....	....	46	....	....	....	....	....	....	....	....	....	....	5	1	0	1	4	....	....	....
1996-97	Indianapolis Ice	IHL	10	0	4	4	....	....	....	11	....	....	....	....	....	....	....	....	....	....	....	....	....	....	....	....	....	....
	Jacksonville Lizard Kings	ECHL	DID NOT PLAY – COACHING																									
1997-2000	Jacksonville Lizard Kings	ECHL	DID NOT PLAY – COACHING																									
	NHL Totals		**36**	**4**	**13**	**17**	**4**	**9**	**13**	**10**	**3**	**0**	**0**	**64**	**6.3**	**36**	**18**	**30**	**2**		**1**	**0**	**0**	**0**	**0**	**0**	**0**	**0**

Named OHL Rookie-of-the-Year (1983) • OHL Second All-Star Team (1984) • Memorial Cup All-Star Team (1984) • IHL First All-Star Team (1989, 1990)

• Missed majority of 1984-85 season recovering from knee injury suffered during summer training, June, 1984. Signed as a free agent by **Chicago**, July 28, 1994.

• CASSIDY, Tom

Thomas John Ernest C – L. 5'11", 180 lbs. b: Blind River, Ont., 3/15/1952. California's 1st, 22nd overall, in 1972.

Season	Club	League	GP	G	A	Pts	AG	AA	APts	PIM	PP	SH	GW	S	%	TGF	PGF	TGA	PGA	+/–	GP	G	A	Pts	PIM	PP	SH	GW
1968-69	Sudbury Wolves	NOJHA	48	21	31	52	....	....	....	91	....	....	....	....	....	....	....	....	....	....	....	....	....	....	....	....	....	....
1969-70	Kitchener Rangers	OHA-Jr.	24	5	2	7	....	....	....	14	....	....	....	....	....	....	....	....	....	....	6	0	1	1	4	....	....	....
1970-71	Kitchener Rangers	OHA-Jr.	62	42	62	104	....	....	....	94	....	....	....	....	....	....	....	....	....	....	4	4	1	5	4	....	....	....
1971-72	Kitchener Rangers	OMJHL	55	32	44	76	....	....	....	109	....	....	....	....	....	....	....	....	....	....	3	0	2	2	9	....	....	....
1972-73	Baltimore Clippers	AHL	73	21	32	53	....	....	....	86	....	....	....	....	....	....	....	....	....	....	....	....	....	....	....	....	....	....

Season	Club	League	GP	G	A	Pts	AG	AA	APts	PIM	PP	SH	GW	S	%	TGF	PGF	TGA	PGA	+/–	GP	G	A	Pts	PIM	PP	SH	GW
			REGULAR SEASON																		PLAYOFFS							
1973-74	Springfield Kings	AHL	15	3	8	11	....	....	....	14	....	....	....	....	....	....	....	....	....	....	....	....	....	....	....	....	....	....
	Salt Lake Golden Eagles	WHL	31	12	11	23	....	....	....	4	....	....	....	....	....	....	....	....	....	....	....	....	....	....	....	....	....	....
1974-75	Springfield Indians	AHL	72	32	59	91	....	....	....	201	....	....	....	....	....	....	....	....	....	....	17	4	11	15	8	....	....	....
1975-76	Oklahoma City Blazers	CHL	76	35	50	85	....	....	....	124	....	....	....	....	....	....	....	....	....	....	4	1	2	3	4	....	....	....
1976-77	Columbus Owls	IHL	75	47	61	108	....	....	....	172	....	....	....	....	....	....	....	....	....	....	7	1	5	6	2	....	....	....
1977-78	**Pittsburgh Penguins**	**NHL**	**26**	**3**	**4**	**7**	**3**	**3**	**6**	**15**	**0**	**0**	**0**	**16**	**18.8**	**10**	**0**	**20**	**6**	**–4**	....	....	....	....	....	....	....	....
	Binghamton Dusters	AHL	40	7	7	14	....	....	....	19	....	....	....	....	....	....	....	....	....	....	....	....	....	....	....	....	....	....
1978-79	Rochester Americans	AHL	51	11	35	46	....	....	....	55	....	....	....	....	....	....	....	....	....	....	....	....	....	....	....	....	....	....
	Oklahoma City Stars	CHL	19	2	5	7	....	....	....	23	....	....	....	....	....	....	....	....	....	....	....	....	....	....	....	....	....	....
	NHL Totals		**26**	**3**	**4**	**7**	**3**	**3**	**6**	**15**	**0**	**0**	**0**	**16**	**18.8**	**10**	**0**	**20**	**6**		....	....	....	....	....	....	....	....

Traded to **LA Kings** by **California** for cash, March 12, 1974. Traded to **Toronto** by **LA Kings** for cash, September, 1975. Signed as a free agent by **Boston**, October 30, 1976. Signed as a free agent by **Pittsburgh**, October 11, 1977.

• CASSOLATO, Tony

Anthony Gerry RW – R. 5′11″, 180 lbs. b: Guelph, Ont., 5/7/1956.

Season	Club	League	GP	G	A	Pts	AG	AA	APts	PIM	PP	SH	GW	S	%	TGF	PGF	TGA	PGA	+/–	GP	G	A	Pts	PIM	PP	SH	GW
1972-73	Guelph Mad Hatters	OHA-B	STATISTICS NOT AVAILABLE																									
1973-74	Peterborough Petes	OMJHL	68	11	32	43	....	....	....	47	....	....	....	....	....	....	....	....	....	....	....	....	....	....	....	....	....	....
	Canada	WJC-A	3	0	0	0	....	....	....	0	....	....	....	....	....	....	....	....	....	....	....	....	....	....	....	....	....	....
1974-75	Peterborough Petes	OMJHL	70	43	41	84	....	....	....	52	....	....	....	....	....	....	....	....	....	....	11	3	5	8	15	....	....	....
1975-76	Peterborough Petes	OMJHL	60	26	39	65	....	....	....	59	....	....	....	....	....	....	....	....	....	....	....	....	....	....	....	....	....	....
1976-77	San Diego Mariners	WHA	43	13	12	25	....	....	....	26	....	....	....	....	....	....	....	....	....	....	3	0	0	0	4	....	....	....
	Charlotte Checkers	SHL	19	9	10	19	....	....	....	18	....	....	....	....	....	....	....	....	....	....	....	....	....	....	....	....	....	....
1977-78	Birmingham Bulls	WHA	77	18	25	43	....	....	....	59	....	....	....	....	....	....	....	....	....	....	4	0	0	0	4	....	....	....
1978-79	Birmingham Bulls	WHA	64	13	7	20	....	....	....	62	....	....	....	....	....	....	....	....	....	....	....	....	....	....	....	....	....	....
	Binghamton Dusters	AHL	6	1	1	2	....	....	....	0	....	....	....	....	....	....	....	....	....	....	....	....	....	....	....	....	....	....
1979-80	**Washington Capitals**	**NHL**	**9**	**0**	**2**	**2**	**0**	**1**	**1**	**0**	**0**	**0**	**0**	**6**	**0.0**	**3**	**0**	**1**	**0**	**2**	....	....	....	....	....	....	....	....
	Hershey Bears	AHL	73	21	33	54	....	....	....	45	....	....	....	....	....	....	....	....	....	....	16	6	*16	*22	6	....	....	....
1980-81	**Washington Capitals**	**NHL**	**2**	**0**	**0**	**0**	**0**	**0**	**0**	**0**	**0**	**0**	**0**	**1**	**0.0**	**0**	**0**	**0**	**0**	**0**	....	....	....	....	....	....	....	....
	Hershey Bears	AHL	74	*48	46	94	....	....	....	23	....	....	....	....	....	....	....	....	....	....	10	7	7	14	2	....	....	....
1981-82	**Washington Capitals**	**NHL**	**12**	**1**	**4**	**5**	**1**	**3**	**4**	**4**	**0**	**0**	**0**	**15**	**6.7**	**7**	**2**	**4**	**0**	**1**	....	....	....	....	....	....	....	....
	Hershey Bears	AHL	54	29	37	66	....	....	....	56	....	....	....	....	....	....	....	....	....	....	5	3	5	8	2	....	....	....
1982-83	Hershey Bears	AHL	75	53	38	91	....	....	....	22	....	....	....	....	....	....	....	....	....	....	5	0	3	3	0	....	....	....
1983-84	SC Riessersee	Germany	46	26	21	47	....	....	....	39	....	....	....	....	....	....	....	....	....	....	....	....	....	....	....	....	....	....
1984-85	SG Brunico	Italy	26	29	30	59	....	....	....	37	....	....	....	....	....	....	....	....	....	....	6	6	4	10	6	....	....	....
	NHL Totals		**23**	**1**	**6**	**7**	**1**	**4**	**5**	**4**	**0**	**0**	**0**	**22**	**4.5**	**10**	**2**	**5**	**0**		....	....	....	....	....	....	....	....
	Other Major League Totals		184	44	44	88	....	....	....	147	....	....	....	....	....	....	....	....	....	....	7	0	0	0	8	....	....	....

AHL Second All-Star Team (1981, 1983) • Won Fred T. Hunt Memorial Trophy (Sportsmanship - AHL) (1981)

Signed as a free agent by **San Diego** (WHA), October, 1976. Signed as a free agent by **Birmingham** (WHA) after **San Diego** (WHA) franchise folded, September, 1977. Signed as a free agent by **Washington**, August 12, 1979.

• CAUFIELD, Jay

John Jay RW – R. 6′4″, 237 lbs. b: Philadelphia, PA, 7/17/1960.

Season	Club	League	GP	G	A	Pts	AG	AA	APts	PIM	PP	SH	GW	S	%	TGF	PGF	TGA	PGA	+/–	GP	G	A	Pts	PIM	PP	SH	GW
1979-80	Milton Flyers	OHA-B	42	16	29	45	....	....	....	50	....	....	....	....	....	....	....	....	....	....	....	....	....	....	....	....	....	....
1980-1984	University of North Dakota	WCHA	DID NOT PLAY																									
1984-85	University of North Dakota	WCHA	1	0	0	0	....	....	....	0	....	....	....	....	....	....	....	....	....	....	....	....	....	....	....	....	....	....
1985-86	Toledo Goaldiggers	IHL	30	5	4	9	....	....	....	54	....	....	....	....	....	....	....	....	....	....	....	....	....	....	....	....	....	....
	New Haven Nighthawks	AHL	40	2	3	5	....	....	....	40	....	....	....	....	....	....	....	....	....	....	1	0	0	0	0	....	....	....
1986-87	**New York Rangers**	**NHL**	**13**	**2**	**1**	**3**	**2**	**1**	**3**	**45**	**0**	**0**	**0**	**8**	**25.0**	**5**	**0**	**7**	**0**	**–2**	**3**	**0**	**0**	**0**	**12**	**0**	**0**	**0**
	Flint Spirits	IHL	12	4	3	7	....	....	....	59	....	....	....	....	....	....	....	....	....	....	....	....	....	....	....	....	....	....
	New Haven Nighthawks	AHL	13	0	0	0	....	....	....	43	....	....	....	....	....	....	....	....	....	....	....	....	....	....	....	....	....	....
1987-88	**Minnesota North Stars**	**NHL**	**1**	**0**	**0**	**0**	**0**	**0**	**0**	**0**	**0**	**0**	**0**	**0**	**0.0**	**0**	**0**	**0**	**0**	**0**	....	....	....	....	....	....	....	....
	Kalamazoo Wings	IHL	65	5	10	15	....	....	....	273	....	....	....	....	....	....	....	....	....	....	6	0	1	1	47	....	....	....
1988-89	**Pittsburgh Penguins**	**NHL**	**58**	**1**	**4**	**5**	**1**	**3**	**4**	**285**	**0**	**0**	**0**	**10**	**10.0**	**12**	**0**	**17**	**1**	**–4**	**9**	**0**	**0**	**0**	**28**	**0**	**0**	**0**
1989-90	**Pittsburgh Penguins**	**NHL**	**37**	**1**	**2**	**3**	**1**	**1**	**2**	**123**	**0**	**0**	**0**	**6**	**16.7**	**4**	**0**	**4**	**0**	**0**	....	....	....	....	....	....	....	....
1990-91	**Pittsburgh Penguins**	**NHL**	**23**	**1**	**1**	**2**	**1**	**1**	**2**	**71**	**0**	**0**	**1**	**5**	**20.0**	**4**	**0**	**6**	**0**	**–2**	....	....	....	....	....	....	....	....
	Muskegon Lumberjacks	IHL	3	1	0	1	....	....	....	18	....	....	....	....	....	....	....	....	....	....	....	....	....	....	....	....	....	....
1991-92♦	**Pittsburgh Penguins**	**NHL**	**50**	**0**	**0**	**0**	**0**	**0**	**0**	**175**	**0**	**0**	**0**	**16**	**0.0**	**1**	**0**	**7**	**0**	**–6**	**5**	**0**	**0**	**0**	**2**	**0**	**0**	**0**
1992-93	**Pittsburgh Penguins**	**NHL**	**26**	**0**	**0**	**0**	**0**	**0**	**0**	**60**	**0**	**0**	**0**	**6**	**0.0**	**0**	**0**	**1**	**0**	**–1**	....	....	....	....	....	....	....	....
1993-94	Kalamazoo Wings	IHL	45	2	3	5	....	....	....	176	....	....	....	....	....	....	....	....	....	....	4	0	0	0	18	....	....	....
	NHL Totals		**208**	**5**	**8**	**13**	**5**	**6**	**11**	**759**	**0**	**0**	**1**	**51**	**9.8**	**26**	**0**	**42**	**1**		**17**	**0**	**0**	**0**	**42**	**0**	**0**	**0**

• Played football at University of North Dakota, 1980-1985. Signed as a free agent by **NY Rangers**, October 8, 1985. Traded to **Minnesota** by **NY Rangers** with Dave Gagner for Jari Gronstad and Paul Boutilier, October 8, 1987. Claimed by **Pittsburgh** from **Minnesota** in Waiver Draft, October 3, 1988.

• CAVALLINI, Gino

Gino J. LW – L. 6′1″, 215 lbs. b: Toronto, Ont., 11/24/1962.

Season	Club	League	GP	G	A	Pts	AG	AA	APts	PIM	PP	SH	GW	S	%	TGF	PGF	TGA	PGA	+/–	GP	G	A	Pts	PIM	PP	SH	GW
1979-80	Oak Ridges Dynes	OHA-B	42	23	24	47	....	....	....	102	....	....	....	....	....	....	....	....	....	....	....	....	....	....	....	....	....	....
1980-81	Oak Ridges Dynes	OHA-B	37	27	56	83	....	....	....	42	....	....	....	....	....	....	....	....	....	....	....	....	....	....	....	....	....	....
	Aurora Eagles	OJHL	2	0	0	0	....	....	....	0	....	....	....	....	....	....	....	....	....	....	....	....	....	....	....	....	....	....
1981-82	St. Michael's Buzzers	OJHL-B	33	22	33	55	....	....	....	50	....	....	....	....	....	....	....	....	....	....	....	....	....	....	....	....	....	....
1982-83	Bowling Green University	CCHA	40	8	16	24	....	....	....	52	....	....	....	....	....	....	....	....	....	....	....	....	....	....	....	....	....	....
1983-84	Bowling Green University	CCHA	43	25	23	48	....	....	....	16	....	....	....	....	....	....	....	....	....	....	....	....	....	....	....	....	....	....
1984-85	**Calgary Flames**	**NHL**	**27**	**6**	**10**	**16**	**5**	**7**	**12**	**14**	**1**	**0**	**0**	**44**	**13.6**	**29**	**6**	**12**	**0**	**11**	**3**	**0**	**0**	**0**	**4**	**0**	**0**	**0**
	Moncton Golden Flames	AHL	51	29	19	48	....	....	....	28	....	....	....	....	....	....	....	....	....	....	....	....	....	....	....	....	....	....
1985-86	**Calgary Flames**	**NHL**	**27**	**7**	**7**	**14**	**6**	**5**	**11**	**26**	**4**	**0**	**0**	**51**	**13.7**	**27**	**16**	**18**	**0**	**–7**	....	....	....	....	....	....	....	....
	Moncton Golden Flames	AHL	4	3	2	5	....	....	....	7	....	....	....	....	....	....	....	....	....	....	....	....	....	....	....	....	....	....
	St. Louis Blues	**NHL**	**30**	**6**	**5**	**11**	**5**	**3**	**8**	**36**	**1**	**0**	**0**	**44**	**13.6**	**16**	**2**	**16**	**0**	**–2**	**17**	**4**	**5**	**9**	**10**	**0**	**0**	**2**
1986-87	**St. Louis Blues**	**NHL**	**80**	**18**	**26**	**44**	**16**	**19**	**35**	**54**	**4**	**0**	**2**	**161**	**11.2**	**68**	**9**	**55**	**0**	**4**	**6**	**3**	**1**	**4**	**2**	**1**	**0**	**1**
1987-88	**St. Louis Blues**	**NHL**	**64**	**15**	**17**	**32**	**13**	**12**	**25**	**62**	**2**	**1**	**3**	**131**	**11.5**	**47**	**5**	**59**	**13**	**–4**	**10**	**5**	**5**	**10**	**19**	**2**	**0**	**0**
1988-89	**St. Louis Blues**	**NHL**	**74**	**20**	**23**	**43**	**17**	**16**	**33**	**79**	**1**	**0**	**4**	**153**	**13.1**	**65**	**9**	**56**	**2**	**2**	**9**	**0**	**2**	**2**	**17**	**0**	**0**	**0**
1989-90	**St. Louis Blues**	**NHL**	**80**	**15**	**15**	**30**	**13**	**11**	**24**	**77**	**1**	**0**	**4**	**134**	**11.2**	**46**	**5**	**49**	**0**	**–8**	**12**	**1**	**3**	**4**	**12**	**0**	**0**	**1**
1990-91	**St. Louis Blues**	**NHL**	**78**	**8**	**27**	**35**	**7**	**21**	**28**	**81**	**3**	**0**	**2**	**131**	**6.1**	**58**	**12**	**43**	**1**	**4**	**13**	**1**	**3**	**4**	**2**	**0**	**0**	**0**
1991-92	**St. Louis Blues**	**NHL**	**48**	**9**	**7**	**16**	**8**	**5**	**13**	**40**	**0**	**0**	**2**	**72**	**12.5**	**30**	**2**	**36**	**0**	**–8**	....	....	....	....	....	....	....	....
	Quebec Nordiques	**NHL**	**18**	**1**	**7**	**8**	**1**	**5**	**6**	**4**	**0**	**0**	**0**	**39**	**2.6**	**21**	**10**	**12**	**0**	**–1**	....	....	....	....	....	....	....	....
1992-93	**Quebec Nordiques**	**NHL**	**67**	**9**	**15**	**24**	**7**	**10**	**17**	**34**	**0**	**0**	**0**	**71**	**12.7**	**38**	**1**	**27**	**0**	**10**	**4**	**0**	**0**	**0**	**0**	**0**	**0**	**0**
1993-94	Milwaukee Admirals	IHL	78	43	35	78	....	....	....	64	....	....	....	....	....	....	....	....	....	....	4	3	4	7	6	....	....	....
1994-95	Milwaukee Admirals	IHL	80	53	35	88	....	....	....	54	....	....	....	....	....	....	....	....	....	....	15	7	2	9	10	....	....	....
1995-96	Milwaukee Admirals	IHL	82	43	39	82	....	....	....	20	....	....	....	....	....	....	....	....	....	....	5	3	1	4	2	....	....	....
1996-97	HC Bolzano	Italy	3	2	1	3	....	....	....	0	....	....	....	....	....	....	....	....	....	....	....	....	....	....	....	....	....	....
	EV Landshut	Germany	48	25	29	54	....	....	....	32	....	....	....	....	....	....	....	....	....	....	7	3	2	5	4	....	....	....
1997-98	EV Landshut	Germany	48	12	18	30	....	....	....	30	....	....	....	....	....	....	....	....	....	....	6	1	5	6	25	....	....	....
1998-99	VSV Villach	Alpenliga	33	28	31	59	....	....	....	32	....	....	....	....	....	....	....	....	....	....	....	....	....	....	....	....	....	....
	VSV Villach	Austria	17	9	19	28	....	....	....	10	....	....	....	....	....	....	....	....	....	....	6	5	1	6	0	....	....	....
99-2000	VSV Villach	IEL	32	25	38	63	....	....	....	6	....	....	....	....	....	....	....	....	....	....	....	....	....	....	....	....	....	....
	VSV Villach	EuroHL	6	4	5	9	....	....	....	4	....	....	....	....	....	....	....	....	....	....	....	....	....	....	....	....	....	....
	VSV Villach	Austria	15	13	16	29	....	....	....	8	....	....	....	....	....	....	....	....	....	....	....	....	....	....	....	....	....	....
	NHL Totals		**593**	**114**	**159**	**273**	**98**	**114**	**212**	**507**	**17**	**1**	**17**	**1031**	**11.1**	**445**	**77**	**383**	**16**		**74**	**14**	**19**	**33**	**66**	**3**	**0**	**4**

• Brother of Paul • IHL Second All-Star Team (1995)

Signed as a free agent by **Calgary**, May 16, 1984. Traded to **St. Louis** by **Calgary** with Eddy Beers and Charlie Bourgeois for Joe Mullen, Terry Johnson and Rik Wilson, February 1, 1986. Claimed on waivers by **Quebec** from **St Louis**, February 27, 1992.

• CAVALLINI, Paul "Wally" D – L. 6'1", 202 lbs. b: Toronto, Ont., 10/13/1965. Washington's 9th, 205th overall, in 1984.

			REGULAR SEASON																		PLAYOFFS							
Season	Club	League	GP	G	A	Pts	AG	AA	APts	PIM	PP	SH	GW	S	%	TGF	PGF	TGA	PGA	+/–	GP	G	A	Pts	PIM	PP	SH	GW
1982-83	Henry Carr Crusaders	OJHL-B	35	6	16	22	....	....	....	191	....	....	....	....	....	....	....	....	....	....	....	....	....	....	....	....	....	....
1983-84	Henry Carr Crusaders	OJHL-B	36	9	21	30	....	....	....	166	....	....	....	....	....	....	....	....	....	....	....	....	....	....	....	....	....	....
1984-85	Providence College	H-East	37	4	10	14	....	....	....	52	....	....	....	....	....	....	....	....	....	....	....	....	....	....	....	....	....	....
1985-86	Canada	Nat-Team	52	1	11	12	....	....	....	95	....	....	....	....	....	....	....	....	....	....	....	....	....	....	....	....	....	....
	Binghamton Whalers	AHL	15	3	4	7	....	....	....	20	....	....	....	....	....	....	....	....	....	....	6	0	2	2	56	....	....	....
1986-87	**Washington Capitals**	**NHL**	**6**	**0**	**2**	**2**	**0**	**1**	**1**	**8**	**0**	**0**	**0**	**6**	**0.0**	**4**	**1**	**7**	**0**	**–4**	....	....	....	....	....	....	....	....
	Binghamton Whalers	AHL	66	12	24	36	....	....	....	188	....	....	....	....	....	....	....	....	....	....	13	2	7	9	35	....	....	....
1987-88	**Washington Capitals**	**NHL**	**24**	**2**	**3**	**5**	**2**	**2**	**4**	**66**	**0**	**0**	**1**	**18**	**11.1**	**12**	**0**	**15**	**3**	**0**	....	....	....	....	....	....	....	....
	St. Louis Blues	**NHL**	**48**	**4**	**7**	**11**	**3**	**5**	**8**	**86**	**1**	**0**	**0**	**53**	**7.5**	**48**	**8**	**47**	**14**	**7**	**10**	**1**	**6**	**7**	**26**	**0**	**1**	**0**
1988-89	**St. Louis Blues**	**NHL**	**65**	**4**	**20**	**24**	**3**	**14**	**17**	**128**	**0**	**0**	**0**	**93**	**4.3**	**83**	**12**	**78**	**32**	**25**	**10**	**2**	**2**	**4**	**14**	**0**	**0**	**0**
1989-90	**St. Louis Blues**	**NHL**	**80**	**8**	**39**	**47**	**7**	**28**	**35**	**106**	**2**	**1**	**0**	**135**	**5.9**	**134**	**26**	**112**	**42**	**38**	**12**	**2**	**3**	**5**	**20**	**0**	**0**	**0**
1990-91	**St. Louis Blues**	**NHL**	**67**	**10**	**25**	**35**	**9**	**19**	**28**	**89**	**3**	**0**	**0**	**116**	**8.6**	**92**	**13**	**72**	**12**	**19**	**13**	**2**	**3**	**5**	**20**	**1**	**0**	**0**
1991-92	**St. Louis Blues**	**NHL**	**66**	**10**	**25**	**35**	**9**	**19**	**28**	**95**	**3**	**1**	**2**	**164**	**6.1**	**93**	**19**	**86**	**19**	**7**	**4**	**0**	**1**	**1**	**6**	**0**	**0**	**0**
1992-93	**St. Louis Blues**	**NHL**	**11**	**1**	**4**	**5**	**1**	**3**	**4**	**10**	**1**	**0**	**0**	**22**	**4.5**	**13**	**3**	**12**	**5**	**3**	....	....	....	....	....	....	....	....
	Washington Capitals	**NHL**	**71**	**5**	**8**	**13**	**4**	**5**	**9**	**46**	**0**	**0**	**0**	**77**	**6.5**	**53**	**1**	**57**	**8**	**3**	**6**	**0**	**2**	**2**	**18**	**0**	**0**	**0**
1993-94	**Dallas Stars**	**NHL**	**74**	**11**	**33**	**44**	**10**	**26**	**36**	**82**	**6**	**0**	**3**	**145**	**7.6**	**95**	**32**	**55**	**5**	**13**	**9**	**1**	**8**	**9**	**4**	**1**	**0**	**1**
1994-95	**Dallas Stars**	**NHL**	**44**	**1**	**11**	**12**	**2**	**16**	**18**	**28**	**0**	**0**	**0**	**69**	**1.4**	**43**	**14**	**27**	**6**	**8**	**5**	**0**	**2**	**2**	**6**	**0**	**0**	**0**
1995-96	**Dallas Stars**	**NHL**	**8**	**0**	**0**	**0**	**0**	**0**	**0**	**6**	**0**	**0**	**0**	**5**	**0.0**	**4**	**3**	**4**	**0**	**–3**	....	....	....	....	....	....	....	....
	NHL Totals		**564**	**56**	**177**	**233**	**50**	**138**	**188**	**750**	**16**	**2**	**6**	**903**	**6.2**	**674**	**132**	**572**	**146**		**69**	**8**	**27**	**35**	**114**	**2**	**1**	**1**

• Brother of Gino • Won Alka-Seltzer Plus Award (1990) • Played in NHL All-Star Game (1990)

Traded to **St. Louis** by **Washington** for Montreal's 2nd round choice (previously acquired, Washington selected Wade Bartley) in 1988 Entry Draft, December 11, 1987. Traded to **Washington** by **St. Louis** for Kevin Miller, November 2, 1992. Traded to **Dallas** by **Washington** for future considerations (Enrico Ciccone, June 25, 1993), June 20, 1993. • Officially announced retirement, November 7, 1995.

• CERNIK, Frantisek "Frank" W – R. 5'10", 189 lbs. b: Novy Jicin, Czech., 6/3/1953.

			REGULAR SEASON																		PLAYOFFS							
Season	Club	League	GP	G	A	Pts	AG	AA	APts	PIM	PP	SH	GW	S	%	TGF	PGF	TGA	PGA	+/–	GP	G	A	Pts	PIM	PP	SH	GW
1968-69	Bank Ostrava	Czech-Jr.	STATISTICS NOT AVAILABLE																									
1969-1973	TJ Vitkovice	Czech-Jr.	STATISTICS NOT AVAILABLE																									
1973-1975	TJ Vitkovice	Czech-2	STATISTICS NOT AVAILABLE																									
1975-76	Czechoslovakia	WEC-A	9	3	3	6	....	....	....	2	....	....	....	....	....	....	....	....	....	....	....	....	....	....	....	....	....	....
1976-77	Czechoslovakia	Can-Cup	7	0	1	1	....	....	....	4	....	....	....	....	....	....	....	....	....	....	....	....	....	....	....	....	....	....
	Dukla Jihlava	Czech.	45	30	13	43	....	....	....	30	....	....	....	....	....	....	....	....	....	....	....	....	....	....	....	....	....	....
1977-78	Dukla Jihlava	Czech-2	41	14	14	28	....	....	....	44	....	....	....	....	....	....	....	....	....	....	....	....	....	....	....	....	....	....
	Czechoslovakia	WEC-A	8	7	0	7	....	....	....	2	....	....	....	....	....	....	....	....	....	....	....	....	....	....	....	....	....	....
1978-79	TJ Vitkovice	Czech.	44	24	15	39	....	....	....	....	....	....	....	....	....	....	....	....	....	....	....	....	....	....	....	....	....	....
	Czechoslovakia	Nat-Team	13	4	0	4	....	....	....	0	....	....	....	....	....	....	....	....	....	....	....	....	....	....	....	....	....	....
1979-80	TJ Vitkovice	Czech.	42	16	12	28	....	....	....	....	....	....	....	....	....	....	....	....	....	....	....	....	....	....	....	....	....	....
1980-81	TJ Vitkovice	Czech.	43	25	26	51	....	....	....	....	....	....	....	....	....	....	....	....	....	....	....	....	....	....	....	....	....	....
	Czechoslovakia	WEC-A	8	2	0	2	....	....	....	4	....	....	....	....	....	....	....	....	....	....	....	....	....	....	....	....	....	....
1981-82	Czechoslovakia	Can-Cup	6	0	0	0	....	....	....	0	....	....	....	....	....	....	....	....	....	....	....	....	....	....	....	....	....	....
	TJ Vitkovice	Czech.	41	28	23	51	....	....	....	50	....	....	....	....	....	....	....	....	....	....	10	1	5	6	4	....	....	....
	Czechoslovakia	WEC-A	10	1	5	6	....	....	....	4	....	....	....	....	....	....	....	....	....	....	....	....	....	....	....	....	....	....
1982-83	TJ Vitkovice	Czech.	44	23	27	50	....	....	....	....	....	....	....	....	....	....	....	....	....	....	....	....	....	....	....	....	....	....
	Czechoslovakia	WEC-A	10	1	3	4	....	....	....	8	....	....	....	....	....	....	....	....	....	....	....	....	....	....	....	....	....	....
1983-84	TJ Vitkovice	Czech.	44	25	23	48	....	....	....	....	....	....	....	....	....	....	....	....	....	....	....	....	....	....	....	....	....	....
	Czechoslovakia	Olympics	7	3	0	3	....	....	....	4	....	....	....	....	....	....	....	....	....	....	....	....	....	....	....	....	....	....
1984-85	**Detroit Red Wings**	**NHL**	**49**	**5**	**4**	**9**	**4**	**3**	**7**	**13**	**0**	**0**	**0**	**50**	**10.0**	**15**	**1**	**21**	**0**	**–7**	....	....	....	....	....	....	....	....
1985-86	ESV Kaufbeuren	Germany	40	23	44	67	....	....	....	21	....	....	....	....	....	....	....	....	....	....	....	....	....	....	....	....	....	....
1986-87	VEU Feldkirch	Austria	39	23	37	60	....	....	....	23	....	....	....	....	....	....	....	....	....	....	....	....	....	....	....	....	....	....
1987-88	EC Graz	Austria-2	30	*64	40	*104	....	....	....	....	....	....	....	....	....	....	....	....	....	....	....	....	....	....	....	....	....	....
	NHL Totals		**49**	**5**	**4**	**9**	**4**	**3**	**7**	**13**	**0**	**0**	**0**	**50**	**10.0**	**15**	**1**	**21**	**0**		....	....	....	....	....	....	....	....

Signed as a free agent by **Quebec**, September 17, 1979. Signed as a free agent by **Detroit**, July 5, 1983.

• CHABOT, John John David C – L. 6'2", 200 lbs. b: Summerside, P.E.I., 5/18/1962. Montreal's 3rd, 40th overall, in 1980.

			REGULAR SEASON																		PLAYOFFS							
Season	Club	League	GP	G	A	Pts	AG	AA	APts	PIM	PP	SH	GW	S	%	TGF	PGF	TGA	PGA	+/–	GP	G	A	Pts	PIM	PP	SH	GW
1978-79	Gatineau Selectes	QAAA	STATISTICS NOT AVAILABLE																									
1979-80	Hull Olympiques	QMJHL	68	26	57	83	....	....	....	28	....	....	....	....	....	....	....	....	....	....	4	1	2	3	0	....	....	....
1980-81	Hull Olympiques	QMJHL	70	27	62	89	....	....	....	24	....	....	....	....	....	....	....	....	....	....	....	....	....	....	....	....	....	....
	Nova Scotia Voyageurs	AHL	1	0	0	0	....	....	....	0	....	....	....	....	....	....	....	....	....	....	2	0	0	0	0	....	....	....
1981-82	Sherbrooke Beavers	QMJHL	62	34	*109	143	....	....	....	42	....	....	....	....	....	....	....	....	....	....	19	6	26	32	6	....	....	....
	Sherbrooke Beavers	Mem-Cup	5	3	8	11	....	....	....	0	....	....	....	....	....	....	....	....	....	....	....	....	....	....	....	....	....	....
1982-83	Nova Scotia Voyageurs	AHL	76	16	73	89	....	....	....	19	....	....	....	....	....	....	....	....	....	....	7	1	3	4	0	....	....	....
1983-84	**Montreal Canadiens**	**NHL**	**56**	**18**	**25**	**43**	**14**	**17**	**31**	**13**	**4**	**1**	**2**	**69**	**26.1**	**53**	**12**	**52**	**9**	**–2**	**11**	**1**	**4**	**5**	**0**	**0**	**0**	**1**
1984-85	**Montreal Canadiens**	**NHL**	**10**	**1**	**6**	**7**	**1**	**4**	**5**	**2**	**0**	**0**	**0**	**8**	**12.5**	**11**	**5**	**3**	**0**	**3**	....	....	....	....	....	....	....	....
	Pittsburgh Penguins	**NHL**	**67**	**8**	**45**	**53**	**6**	**31**	**37**	**12**	**2**	**1**	**2**	**105**	**7.6**	**74**	**23**	**120**	**32**	**–37**	....	....	....	....	....	....	....	....
1985-86	**Pittsburgh Penguins**	**NHL**	**77**	**14**	**31**	**45**	**11**	**21**	**32**	**6**	**1**	**2**	**3**	**89**	**15.7**	**57**	**2**	**102**	**46**	**–1**	....	....	....	....	....	....	....	....
1986-87	**Pittsburgh Penguins**	**NHL**	**72**	**14**	**22**	**36**	**12**	**16**	**28**	**8**	**0**	**0**	**1**	**90**	**15.6**	**58**	**4**	**95**	**34**	**–7**	....	....	....	....	....	....	....	....
1987-88	**Detroit Red Wings**	**NHL**	**78**	**13**	**44**	**57**	**11**	**32**	**43**	**10**	**0**	**2**	**0**	**83**	**15.7**	**73**	**8**	**94**	**41**	**12**	**16**	**4**	**15**	**19**	**2**	**1**	**0**	**0**
1988-89	**Detroit Red Wings**	**NHL**	**52**	**2**	**10**	**12**	**2**	**7**	**9**	**6**	**0**	**2**	**0**	**49**	**4.1**	**16**	**1**	**61**	**28**	**–18**	**6**	**1**	**1**	**2**	**0**	**0**	**0**	**1**
	Adirondack Red Wings	AHL	8	3	12	15	....	....	....	0	....	....	....	....	....	....	....	....	....	....	....	....	....	....	....	....	....	....
1989-90	**Detroit Red Wings**	**NHL**	**69**	**9**	**40**	**49**	**8**	**29**	**37**	**24**	**0**	**2**	**0**	**91**	**9.9**	**64**	**17**	**88**	**46**	**5**	....	....	....	....	....	....	....	....
1990-91	**Detroit Red Wings**	**NHL**	**27**	**5**	**5**	**10**	**5**	**4**	**9**	**4**	**2**	**0**	**1**	**26**	**19.2**	**23**	**8**	**15**	**6**	**6**	....	....	....	....	....	....	....	....
	Adirondack Red Wings	AHL	27	11	30	41	....	....	....	4	....	....	....	....	....	....	....	....	....	....	2	0	1	1	0	....	....	....
1991-92	HC Milano Saima	Alpenliga	20	12	22	34	....	....	....	12	....	....	....	....	....	....	....	....	....	....	....	....	....	....	....	....	....	....
	HC Milano Saima	Italy	18	10	36	46	....	....	....	4	....	....	....	....	....	....	....	....	....	....	12	3	13	16	2	....	....	....
	Canada	Nat-Team	8	1	3	4	....	....	....	0	....	....	....	....	....	....	....	....	....	....	....	....	....	....	....	....	....	....
1992-93	HC Milano Devils	Alpenliga	13	6	17	23	....	....	....	0	....	....	....	....	....	....	....	....	....	....	....	....	....	....	....	....	....	....
	BSC Preussen Berlin	Germany	20	10	17	27	....	....	....	14	....	....	....	....	....	....	....	....	....	....	7	1	7	8	4	....	....	....
1993-94	BSC Preussen Berlin	Germany-2	32	9	29	38	....	....	....	27	....	....	....	....	....	....	....	....	....	....	10	5	6	11	8	....	....	....
1994-95	BSC Preussen Berlin	Germany	43	20	*48	*68	....	....	....	48	....	....	....	....	....	....	....	....	....	....	12	5	7	12	14	....	....	....
	Canada	Nat-Team	3	1	2	3	....	....	....	0	....	....	....	....	....	....	....	....	....	....	....	....	....	....	....	....	....	....
1995-96	Berlin Devils	Germany	50	16	*65	81	....	....	....	20	....	....	....	....	....	....	....	....	....	....	11	5	*14	19	14	....	....	....
1996-97	Berlin Capitals	Germany	45	12	34	46	....	....	....	43	....	....	....	....	....	....	....	....	....	....	4	2	1	3	0	....	....	....
	Berlin Capitals	EuroHL	6	3	3	6	....	....	....	10	....	....	....	....	....	....	....	....	....	....	....	....	....	....	....	....	....	....
	EV Zug	Switz.	....	....	....	....	....	....	....	....	....	....	....	....	....	....	....	....	....	....	2	0	1	1	0	....	....	....
1997-98	Frankfurt Lions	Germany	47	12	*46	58	....	....	....	72	....	....	....	....	....	....	....	....	....	....	7	0	5	5	2	....	....	....
1998-99	Frankfurt Lions	Germany	49	7	52	59	....	....	....	44	....	....	....	....	....	....	....	....	....	....	8	1	4	5	2	....	....	....
99-2000	Frankfurt Lions	Germany	38	10	33	43	....	....	....	16	....	....	....	....	....	....	....	....	....	....	5	1	3	4	10	....	....	....
	NHL Totals		**508**	**84**	**228**	**312**	**70**	**161**	**231**	**85**	**9**	**10**	**9**	**610**	**13.8**	**429**	**80**	**630**	**242**		**33**	**6**	**20**	**26**	**2**	**1**	**0**	**2**

Won Michel Briere Trophy (QMJHL MVP) (1982) • QMJHL First All-Star Team (1982) • Memorial Cup All-Star Team (1982)

Traded to **Pittsburgh** by **Montreal** for Ron Flockhart, November 9, 1984. Signed as a free agent by **Detroit**, June 25, 1987.

• CHALUPA, Milan D – R. 5'10", 183 lbs. b: Oudolen, Czech., 7/4/1953. Detroit's 3rd, 49th overall, in 1984.

			REGULAR SEASON																		PLAYOFFS							
Season	Club	League	GP	G	A	Pts	AG	AA	APts	PIM	PP	SH	GW	S	%	TGF	PGF	TGA	PGA	+/–	GP	G	A	Pts	PIM	PP	SH	GW
1966-1972	Jiskra Havlickuv Brod	Czech-Jr.	STATISTICS NOT AVAILABLE																									
1972-73	Dukla Liberec	Czech-Jr.	STATISTICS NOT AVAILABLE																									
1973-74	Dukla Jihlava	Czech.	....	6	8	14	....	....	....	....	....	....	....	....	....	....	....	....	....	....	....	....	....	....	....	....	....	....
1974-75	Dukla Jihlava	Czech.	....	4	7	11	....	....	....	....	....	....	....	....	....	....	....	....	....	....	....	....	....	....	....	....	....	....
1975-76	Czechoslovakia	Olympics	5	0	1	1	....	....	....	4	....	....	....	....	....	....	....	....	....	....	....	....	....	....	....	....	....	....
	Czechoslovakia	WEC-A	9	1	4	5	....	....	....	2	....	....	....	....	....	....	....	....	....	....	....	....	....	....	....	....	....	....

			REGULAR SEASON																		PLAYOFFS							
Season	Club	League	GP	G	A	Pts	AG	AA	APts	PIM	PP	SH	GW	S	%	TGF	PGF	TGA	PGA	+/-	GP	G	A	Pts	PIM	PP	SH	GW
1976-77	Czechoslovakia	Can-Cup	7	1	1	2				10																		
	Dukla Jihlava	Czech.		5	8	13																						
	Czechoslovakia	WEC-A	10	1	0	1				2																		
1977-78	Dukla Jihlava	Czech.	39	1	8	9				108																		
	Czechoslovakia	WEC-A	3	1	0	1				0																		
1978-79	Dukla Jihlava	Czech.	38	3	3	6				38																		
	Czechoslovakia	WEC-A	8	1	2	3				10																		
1979-80	Dukla Jihlava	Czech.	43	8	6	14				46											6	0	3	3	8			
	Czechoslovakia	Olympics	6	0	3	3				8																		
1980-81	Dukla Jihlava	Czech.	41	2	15	17				34											5	0	1	1	4			
	Czechoslovakia	WEC-A	5	0	1	1				5																		
1981-82	Czechoslovakia	Can-Cup	6	0	2	2				4																		
	Dukla Jihlava	Czech.	41	4	8	12				30																		
	Czechoslovakia	WEC-A	10	0	1	1				2																		
1982-83	Dukla Jihlava	Czech.	38	9	16	25				36																		
	Czechoslovakia	WEC-A	8	2	1	3				2																		
1983-84	Dukla Jihlava	Czech.	39	3	11	14				52																		
	Czechoslovakia	Olympics	7	2	1	3				6																		
1984-85	**Detroit Red Wings**	**NHL**	14	0	5	5	0	3	3	6	0	0	0	10	0.0	15	0	11	0	4								
	Adirondack Red Wings	AHL	1	0	0	0				2																		
	EHC Freiburg	Germany-2	STATISTICS NOT AVAILABLE																									
1985-86	EHC Freiburg	Germany-2	35	9	22	31				40											16	1	6	7	12			
1986-87	EHC Freiburg	Germany-2	53	17	38	55				66																		
1987-88	EHC Freiburg	Germany-2	31	9	31	40				36											18	2	22	24	16			
1988-89	EHC Freiburg	Germany	33	6	23	29				24											17	4	7	11	12			
1989-90	EHC Freiburg	Germany	31	0	14	14				24																		
	EHC Freiburg	Germany-Q	10	2	11	13				6																		
1990-91	EHC Freiburg	Germany	10	0	1	1				10																		
1991-92			OUT OF HOCKEY – RETIRED																									
1992-93	EHC Freiburg	Germany																			5	0	0	0	2			
1993-94	Dukla Jihlava	Czech-Rep	12	0	4	4				0																		
	NHL Totals		14	0	5	5	0	3	3	6	0	0	0	10	0.0	15	0	11	0									

• Career totals for Dukla Jihlava (Czech) are 440-49-104-153-476

• CHAMBERS, Shawn

Shawn Randall D – L. 6'2", 210 lbs. b: Sterling Hts., MI, 10/11/1966. Minnesota's 1st, 4th overall, in 1987 Supplemental Draft.

Season	Club	League	GP	G	A	Pts	AG	AA	APts	PIM	PP	SH	GW	S	%	TGF	PGF	TGA	PGA	+/-	GP	G	A	Pts	PIM	PP	SH	GW
1985-86	University of Alaska-Fairbanks	G-North	25	15	21	36				34																		
1986-87	University of Alaska-Fairbanks	G-North	17	11	19	30				84																		
	Seattle Thunderbirds	WHL	28	8	25	33				58																		
	Fort Wayne Komets	IHL	12	2	6	8				0											10	1	4	5	5			
1987-88	**Minnesota North Stars**	**NHL**	19	1	7	8	1	5	6	21	1	0	0	28	3.6	12	5	15	2	–6								
	Kalamazoo Wings	IHL	19	1	6	7				22																		
1988-89	**Minnesota North Stars**	**NHL**	72	5	19	24	4	13	17	80	1	2	0	131	3.8	82	23	89	26	–4	3	0	2	2	0	0	0	0
1989-90	**Minnesota North Stars**	**NHL**	78	8	18	26	7	13	20	81	0	1	2	116	6.9	83	15	114	44	–2	7	2	1	3	10	1	0	0
1990-91	Minnesota North Stars	Fr-Tour	1	0	1	1				4																		
	Minnesota North Stars	**NHL**	29	1	3	4	1	2	3	24	0	0	0	55	1.8	27	3	26	4	2	23	0	7	7	16	0	0	0
	Kalamazoo Wings	IHL	3	1	1	2				0																		
1991-92	**Washington Capitals**	**NHL**	2	0	0	0	0	0	0	2	0	0	0	1	0.0	1	0	4	0	–3								
	Baltimore Skipjacks	AHL	5	2	3	5				9																		
1992-93	**Tampa Bay Lightning**	**NHL**	55	10	29	39	8	20	28	36	5	0	1	152	6.6	76	35	90	28	–21								
	Atlanta Knights	IHL	6	0	2	2				18																		
1993-94	**Tampa Bay Lightning**	**NHL**	66	11	23	34	10	18	28	23	6	1	1	142	7.7	86	38	69	15	–6								
	United States	WC-A	8	0	3	3				4																		
1994-95	**Tampa Bay Lightning**	**NHL**	24	2	12	14	4	18	22	6	1	0	0	44	4.5	29	8	23	2	0								
♦	**New Jersey Devils**	**NHL**	21	2	5	7	4	7	11	6	1	0	0	23	8.7	16	4	13	3	2	20	4	5	9	2	2	0	0
1995-96	**New Jersey Devils**	**NHL**	64	2	21	23	2	17	19	18	2	0	1	112	1.8	59	22	58	22	1								
1996-97	United States	W-Cup	1	0	0	0				0																		
	New Jersey Devils	**NHL**	73	4	17	21	4	15	19	19	1	0	0	114	3.5	72	10	54	9	17	10	1	6	7	6	1	0	0
1997-98	**Dallas Stars**	**NHL**	57	2	22	24	2	22	24	26	1	1	0	73	2.7	60	19	36	6	11	14	0	3	3	20	0	0	0
1998-99♦	**Dallas Stars**	**NHL**	61	2	9	11	2	9	11	18	1	0	1	82	2.4	40	10	30	6	6	17	0	2	2	18	0	0	0
99-2000	**Dallas Stars**	**NHL**	4	0	0	0	0	0	0	4	0	0	0	2	0.0	2	1	3	0	–2								
	NHL Totals		625	50	185	235	49	159	208	364	20	5	6	1075	4.7	645	193	624	167		94	7	26	33	72	4	0	0

Traded to **Washington** by **Minnesota** for Steve Maltais and Trent Klatt, June 21, 1991. • Missed majority of 1990-91 and 1991-92 seasons recovering from knee injury originally suffered in game vs. Toronto, December 5, 1990. Claimed by **Tampa Bay** from **Washington** in Expansion Draft, June 18, 1992. Traded to **New Jersey** by **Tampa Bay** with Danton Cole for Alexander Semak and Ben Hankinson, March 14, 1995. Signed as a free agent by **Dallas**, July 17, 1997. • Missed remainder of 1999-2000 season recovering from knee injury suffered in game vs. Anaheim, October 8, 1999.

• CHAPDELAINE, Rene

Rene Ronald D – R. 6'1", 195 lbs. b: Weyburn, Sask., 9/27/1966. Los Angeles' 7th, 149th overall, in 1986.

Season	Club	League	GP	G	A	Pts	AG	AA	APts	PIM	PP	SH	GW	S	%	TGF	PGF	TGA	PGA	+/-	GP	G	A	Pts	PIM	PP	SH	GW
1983-84	Weyburn Red Wings	SJHL	STATISTICS NOT AVAILABLE																									
1984-85	Weyburn Red Wings	SJHL	61	3	17	20																						
1985-86	Lake Superior State	CCHA	32	1	4	5				47																		
1986-87	Lake Superior State	CCHA	28	1	5	6				51																		
1987-88	Lake Superior State	CCHA	35	1	9	10				44																		
1988-89	Lake Superior State	CCHA	46	4	9	13				62																		
1989-90	New Haven Nighthawks	AHL	41	0	1	1				35																		
1990-91	**Los Angeles Kings**	**NHL**	3	0	1	1	0	1	1	10	0	0	0	1	0.0	3	0	3	1	1								
	New Haven Nighthawks	AHL	65	3	11	14				49																		
	Phoenix Roadrunners	IHL	17	0	2	2				10											11	0	0	0	8			
1991-92	**Los Angeles Kings**	**NHL**	16	0	1	1	0	1	1	10	0	0	0	6	0.0	9	0	12	3	0								
	Phoenix Roadrunners	IHL	62	4	22	26				87																		
	New Haven Nighthawks	AHL																			4	0	2	2	0			
1992-93	**Los Angeles Kings**	**NHL**	13	0	0	0	0	0	0	12	0	0	0	5	0.0	4	0	12	2	–6								
	Phoenix Roadrunners	IHL	44	1	17	18				54																		
	San Diego Gulls	IHL	9	1	1	2				8											14	0	1	1	27			
1993-94	Peoria Rivermen	IHL	80	8	9	17				100											6	1	3	4	10			
1994-95	Peoria Rivermen	IHL	45	3	2	5				62											9	0	2	2	12			
1995-96	Peoria Rivermen	IHL	70	2	10	12				135											12	1	0	1	8			
1996-97	San Antonio Dragons	IHL	69	7	11	18				125											9	2	3	5	10			
1997-98	San Antonio Dragons	IHL	73	2	11	13				128																		
1998-99	Utah Grizzlies	IHL	19	2	2	4				16																		
	Long Beach Ice Dogs	IHL	29	1	1	2				28											8	0	2	2	18			
99-2000	Long Beach Ice Dogs	IHL	59	1	6	7				116											6	0	0	0	4			
	NHL Totals		32	0	2	2	0	2	2	32	0	0	0	12	0.0	16	0	27	6									

• CHAPMAN, Blair

Blair Douglas RW – R. 6'1", 190 lbs. b: Lloydminster, Sask., 6/13/1956. Pittsburgh's 1st, 2nd overall, in 1976.

Season	Club	League	GP	G	A	Pts	AG	AA	APts	PIM	PP	SH	GW	S	%	TGF	PGF	TGA	PGA	+/-	GP	G	A	Pts	PIM	PP	SH	GW
1972-73	Kelowna Buckaroos	BCJHL	52	31	49	80				80																		
1973-74	Saskatoon Blades	WCJHL	56	36	28	64				61											5	1	2	3	5			
1974-75	Saskatoon Blades	WCJHL	65	41	44	85				92											17	9	9	18	32			
1975-76	Saskatoon Blades	WCJHL	69	71	86	157				67											20	*24	19	43	21			
1976-77	**Pittsburgh Penguins**	**NHL**	80	14	23	37	13	18	31	16	1	0	3	152	9.2	65	12	66	1	–12	3	1	1	2	7	0	0	0
1977-78	**Pittsburgh Penguins**	**NHL**	75	24	20	44	22	15	37	37	4	0	2	180	13.3	68	12	78	11	–11								

			REGULAR SEASON																		PLAYOFFS							
Season	Club	League	GP	G	A	Pts	AG	AA	APts	PIM	PP	SH	GW	S	%	TGF	PGF	TGA	PGA	+/–	GP	G	A	Pts	PIM	PP	SH	GW
1978-79	**Pittsburgh Penguins**	**NHL**	**71**	**10**	**8**	**18**	**9**	**6**	**15**	**18**	**1**	**0**	**0**	**96**	**10.4**	**35**	**4**	**45**	**2**	**–12**	**7**	**1**	**0**	**1**	**2**	**0**	**0**	**0**
1979-80	**Pittsburgh Penguins**	**NHL**	**1**	**0**	**0**	**0**	**0**	**0**	**0**	**0**	**0**	**0**	**0**	**1**	**0.0**	**0**	**0**	**0**	**0**	**0**	....	....	....	....	....	....	....	....
	St. Louis Blues	**NHL**	**63**	**25**	**26**	**51**	**21**	**19**	**40**	**28**	**7**	**0**	**6**	**124**	**20.2**	**86**	**25**	**67**	**1**	**–5**	**3**	**0**	**0**	**0**	**0**	**0**	**0**	**0**
1980-81	**St. Louis Blues**	**NHL**	**55**	**20**	**26**	**46**	**16**	**17**	**33**	**41**	**5**	**0**	**3**	**114**	**17.5**	**67**	**24**	**40**	**0**	**3**	**9**	**2**	**5**	**7**	**6**	**0**	**0**	**0**
1981-82	**St. Louis Blues**	**NHL**	**18**	**6**	**11**	**17**	**5**	**7**	**12**	**8**	**2**	**0**	**0**	**28**	**21.4**	**25**	**10**	**15**	**1**	**1**	**3**	**0**	**0**	**0**	**0**	**0**	**0**	**0**
	Salt Lake Golden Eagles	CHL	1	1	0	1	....	....	....	0	....	....	....	....	....	....	....	....	....	....	....	....	....	....	....	....	....	....
1982-83	**St. Louis Blues**	**NHL**	**39**	**7**	**11**	**18**	**6**	**8**	**14**	**10**	**3**	**0**	**1**	**46**	**15.2**	**33**	**9**	**32**	**0**	**–8**	....	....	....	....	....	....	....	....
	Salt Lake Golden Eagles	CHL	22	17	6	23	....	....	....	20	....	....	....	....	....	....	....	....	....	....	6	4	3	7	0	....	....	....
	NHL Totals		**402**	**106**	**125**	**231**	**92**	**90**	**182**	**158**	**23**	**0**	**15**	**741**	**14.3**	**379**	**96**	**343**	**16**		**25**	**4**	**6**	**10**	**15**	**0**	**0**	**0**

• WCHL Second All-Star Team (1976) • Won WCHL Most Gentlemanly Player Award (1976)

Traded to **St. Louis** by **Pittsburgh** for Bob Stewart, November 13, 1979. • Missed majority of 1981-82 season recovering from back injury suffered in game vs. LA Kings, November 12, 1981.

• CHAPMAN, Brian

D – L. 6', 195 lbs. b: Brockville, Ont., 2/10/1968. Hartford's 3rd, 74th overall, in 1986.

Season	Club	League	GP	G	A	Pts	AG	AA	APts	PIM	PP	SH	GW	S	%	TGF	PGF	TGA	PGA	+/–	GP	G	A	Pts	PIM	PP	SH	GW
1984-85	Brockville Braves	OJHL	50	11	32	43	....	....	....	145	....	....	....	....	....	....	....	....	....	....	....	....	....	....	....	....	....	....
1985-86	Belleville Bulls	OHL	66	6	31	37	....	....	....	168	....	....	....	....	....	....	....	....	....	....	24	2	6	8	54	....	....	....
1986-87	Belleville Bulls	OHL	54	4	32	36	....	....	....	142	....	....	....	....	....	....	....	....	....	....	6	1	1	2	10	....	....	....
	Binghamton Whalers	AHL	....	....	....	....	....	....	....	....	....	....	....	....	....	....	....	....	....	....	1	0	0	0	0	....	....	....
1987-88	Belleville Bulls	OHL	63	11	57	68	....	....	....	180	....	....	....	....	....	....	....	....	....	....	6	1	4	5	13	....	....	....
1988-89	Binghamton Whalers	AHL	71	5	25	30	....	....	....	216	....	....	....	....	....	....	....	....	....	....	....	....	....	....	....	....	....	....
1989-90	Binghamton Whalers	AHL	68	2	15	17	....	....	....	180	....	....	....	....	....	....	....	....	....	....	....	....	....	....	....	....	....	....
1990-91	**Hartford Whalers**	**NHL**	**3**	**0**	**0**	**0**	**0**	**0**	**0**	**29**	**0**	**0**	**0**	**0**	**0.0**	**1**	**0**	**2**	**1**	**0**	....	....	....	....	....	....	....	....
	Springfield Indians	AHL	60	4	23	27	....	....	....	200	....	....	....	....	....	....	....	....	....	....	18	1	4	5	62	....	....	....
1991-92	Springfield Indians	AHL	73	3	26	29	....	....	....	245	....	....	....	....	....	....	....	....	....	....	10	2	2	4	25	....	....	....
1992-93	Springfield Indians	AHL	72	17	34	51	....	....	....	212	....	....	....	....	....	....	....	....	....	....	15	2	5	7	43	....	....	....
1993-94	Phoenix Roadrunners	IHL	78	6	35	41	....	....	....	280	....	....	....	....	....	....	....	....	....	....	....	....	....	....	....	....	....	....
1994-95	Phoenix Roadrunners	IHL	60	2	23	25	....	....	....	181	....	....	....	....	....	....	....	....	....	....	9	1	5	6	31	....	....	....
1995-96	Phoenix Roadrunners	IHL	66	8	11	19	....	....	....	187	....	....	....	....	....	....	....	....	....	....	4	0	1	1	14	....	....	....
1996-97	Phoenix Roadrunners	IHL	69	9	16	25	....	....	....	109	....	....	....	....	....	....	....	....	....	....	....	....	....	....	....	....	....	....
	Long Beach Ice Dogs	IHL	14	1	7	8	....	....	....	67	....	....	....	....	....	....	....	....	....	....	17	0	3	3	38	....	....	....
1997-98	Long Beach Ice Dogs	IHL	6	0	1	1	....	....	....	15	....	....	....	....	....	....	....	....	....	....	....	....	....	....	....	....	....	....
	Manitoba Moose	IHL	77	3	25	28	....	....	....	159	....	....	....	....	....	....	....	....	....	....	3	0	0	0	10	....	....	....
1998-99	Manitoba Moose	IHL	76	3	15	18	....	....	....	127	....	....	....	....	....	....	....	....	....	....	5	0	0	0	12	....	....	....
99-2000	Manitoba Moose	IHL	80	7	30	37	....	....	....	153	....	....	....	....	....	....	....	....	....	....	2	0	0	0	2	....	....	....
	NHL Totals		**3**	**0**	**0**	**0**	**0**	**0**	**0**	**29**	**0**	**0**	**0**	**0**	**0.0**	**1**	**0**	**2**	**1**		....	....	....	....	....	....	....	....

Signed as a free agent by **LA Kings**, July 15, 1993. Traded to **Manitoba** (IHL) by **Long Beach** (IHL) for Russ Romaniuk, October 16, 1997.

• CHARA, Zdeno

D – L. 6'9", 255 lbs. b: Trencin, Czech., 3/18/1977. NY Islanders' 3rd, 56th overall, in 1996.

Season	Club	League	GP	G	A	Pts	AG	AA	APts	PIM	PP	SH	GW	S	%	TGF	PGF	TGA	PGA	+/–	GP	G	A	Pts	PIM	PP	SH	GW
1994-95	Dukla Trencin	Slovak-Jr.	2	0	0	0	....	....	....	0	....	....	....	....	....	....	....	....	....	....	....	....	....	....	....	....	....	....
	Dukla Trencin-B	Slovak-Jr.	30	22	22	44	....	....	....	113	....	....	....	....	....	....	....	....	....	....	....	....	....	....	....	....	....	....
1995-96	Dukla Trencin	Slovak-Jr.	22	1	13	14	....	....	....	80	....	....	....	....	....	....	....	....	....	....	....	....	....	....	....	....	....	....
	Piestany	Slovakia-2	10	1	3	4	....	....	....	10	....	....	....	....	....	....	....	....	....	....	....	....	....	....	....	....	....	....
	HC Sparta Praha	Czech-Jr.	15	1	2	3	....	....	....	42	....	....	....	....	....	....	....	....	....	....	....	....	....	....	....	....	....	....
	HC Sparta Praha	Czech-Rep	1	0	0	0	....	....	....	0	....	....	....	....	....	....	....	....	....	....	....	....	....	....	....	....	....	....
1996-97	Prince George Cougars	WHL	49	3	19	22	....	....	....	120	....	....	....	....	....	....	....	....	....	....	15	1	7	8	45	....	....	....
1997-98	**New York Islanders**	**NHL**	**25**	**0**	**1**	**1**	**0**	**1**	**1**	**50**	**0**	**0**	**0**	**10**	**0.0**	**10**	**0**	**12**	**3**	**1**	....	....	....	....	....	....	....	....
	Kentucky Thoroughblades	AHL	48	4	9	13	....	....	....	125	....	....	....	....	....	....	....	....	....	....	1	0	0	0	4	....	....	....
1998-99	**New York Islanders**	**NHL**	**59**	**2**	**6**	**8**	**2**	**6**	**8**	**83**	**0**	**1**	**0**	**56**	**3.6**	**37**	**0**	**64**	**19**	**–8**	....	....	....	....	....	....	....	....
	Lowell Lock Monsters	AHL	23	2	2	4	....	....	....	47	....	....	....	....	....	....	....	....	....	....	....	....	....	....	....	....	....	....
	Slovakia	WC-A	6	1	0	1	....	....	....	6	....	....	....	....	....	....	....	....	....	....	....	....	....	....	....	....	....	....
99-2000	**New York Islanders**	**NHL**	**65**	**2**	**9**	**11**	**2**	**8**	**10**	**57**	**0**	**0**	**1**	**47**	**4.3**	**33**	**0**	**102**	**42**	**–27**	....	....	....	....	....	....	....	....
	Slovakia	WC-A	9	0	0	0	....	....	....	12	....	....	....	....	....	....	....	....	....	....	....	....	....	....	....	....	....	....
	NHL Totals		**149**	**4**	**16**	**20**	**4**	**15**	**19**	**190**	**0**	**1**	**1**	**113**	**3.5**	**80**	**0**	**178**	**64**		....	....	....	....	....	....	....	....

• CHARBONNEAU, Jose

RW – R. 6', 195 lbs. b: Ferme-Neuve, Que., 11/21/1966. Montreal's 1st, 12th overall, in 1985.

Season	Club	League	GP	G	A	Pts	AG	AA	APts	PIM	PP	SH	GW	S	%	TGF	PGF	TGA	PGA	+/–	GP	G	A	Pts	PIM	PP	SH	GW
1981-82	Laval Insulaires	QAAA	42	15	31	46	....	....	....	....	....	....	....	....	....	....	....	....	....	....	....	....	....	....	....	....	....	....
1982-83	Laval Insulaires	QAAA	48	40	50	90	....	....	....	....	....	....	....	....	....	....	....	....	....	....	....	....	....	....	....	....	....	....
1983-84	Drummondville Voltigeurs	QMJHL	65	31	59	90	....	....	....	110	....	....	....	....	....	....	....	....	....	....	....	....	....	....	....	....	....	....
1984-85	Drummondville Voltigeurs	QMJHL	46	34	40	74	....	....	....	91	....	....	....	....	....	....	....	....	....	....	12	5	10	15	20	....	....	....
1985-86	Drummondville Voltigeurs	QMJHL	57	44	45	89	....	....	....	158	....	....	....	....	....	....	....	....	....	....	23	16	20	36	40	....	....	....
1986-87	Sherbrooke Canadiens	AHL	72	14	27	41	....	....	....	94	....	....	....	....	....	....	....	....	....	....	16	5	12	17	17	....	....	....
1987-88	**Montreal Canadiens**	**NHL**	**16**	**0**	**2**	**2**	**0**	**1**	**1**	**6**	**0**	**0**	**0**	**22**	**0.0**	**6**	**0**	**5**	**0**	**1**	**8**	**0**	**0**	**0**	**4**	**0**	**0**	**0**
	Sherbrooke Canadiens	AHL	55	30	35	65	....	....	....	108	....	....	....	....	....	....	....	....	....	....	....	....	....	....	....	....	....	....
1988-89	**Montreal Canadiens**	**NHL**	**9**	**1**	**3**	**4**	**1**	**2**	**3**	**6**	**0**	**0**	**0**	**15**	**6.7**	**11**	**7**	**6**	**1**	**–1**	....	....	....	....	....	....	....	....
	Sherbrooke Canadiens	AHL	33	13	15	28	....	....	....	95	....	....	....	....	....	....	....	....	....	....	....	....	....	....	....	....	....	....
	Vancouver Canucks	**NHL**	**13**	**0**	**1**	**1**	**0**	**1**	**1**	**6**	**0**	**0**	**0**	**16**	**0.0**	**3**	**0**	**6**	**0**	**–3**	....	....	....	....	....	....	....	....
	Milwaukee Admirals	IHL	13	8	5	13	....	....	....	46	....	....	....	....	....	....	....	....	....	....	10	3	2	5	23	....	....	....
1989-90	Milwaukee Admirals	IHL	65	23	38	61	....	....	....	137	....	....	....	....	....	....	....	....	....	....	5	0	1	1	8	....	....	....
1990-91	Canada	Nat-Team	56	22	29	51	....	....	....	54	....	....	....	....	....	....	....	....	....	....	....	....	....	....	....	....	....	....
1991-92	SC Rapperswil-Jona	Switz-2	24	30	17	47	....	....	....	89	....	....	....	....	....	....	....	....	....	....	....	....	....	....	....	....	....	....
	EHC Eisbaren Berlin	Germany-2	11	3	6	9	....	....	....	16	....	....	....	....	....	....	....	....	....	....	....	....	....	....	....	....	....	....
1992-93	STIJ Galeen	Holland	7	7	13	*20	....	....	....	....	....	....	....	....	....	....	....	....	....	....	17	11	23	34	....	....	....	....
	Canada	Nat-Team	1	0	0	0	....	....	....	0	....	....	....	....	....	....	....	....	....	....	....	....	....	....	....	....	....	....
1993-94	**Vancouver Canucks**	**NHL**	**30**	**7**	**7**	**14**	**6**	**5**	**11**	**49**	**1**	**0**	**0**	**28**	**25.0**	**19**	**4**	**18**	**0**	**–3**	**3**	**1**	**0**	**1**	**4**	**0**	**0**	**0**
	Hamilton Canucks	AHL	7	3	2	5	....	....	....	8	....	....	....	....	....	....	....	....	....	....	....	....	....	....	....	....	....	....
1994-95	**Vancouver Canucks**	**NHL**	**3**	**1**	**0**	**1**	**2**	**0**	**2**	**0**	**0**	**0**	**0**	**2**	**50.0**	**3**	**0**	**3**	**0**	**0**	....	....	....	....	....	....	....	....
	Las Vegas Thunder	IHL	27	8	12	20	....	....	....	102	....	....	....	....	....	....	....	....	....	....	9	1	1	2	71	....	....	....
1995-96	EV Landshut	Germany	47	32	24	56	....	....	....	102	....	....	....	....	....	....	....	....	....	....	11	10	6	16	28	....	....	....
1996-97	EV Landshut	Germany	13	5	4	9	....	....	....	41	....	....	....	....	....	....	....	....	....	....	....	....	....	....	....	....	....	....
	Wedemark Scorpions	Germany-2	30	10	21	31	....	....	....	97	....	....	....	....	....	....	....	....	....	....	5	1	0	1	27	....	....	....
1997-98	Frankfurt Lions	Germany	40	13	16	29	....	....	....	156	....	....	....	....	....	....	....	....	....	....	7	4	1	5	18	....	....	....
1998-99	Frankfurt Lions	Germany	47	16	19	35	....	....	....	76	....	....	....	....	....	....	....	....	....	....	2	0	0	0	6	....	....	....
99-2000	Frankfurt Lions	Germany	55	18	30	48	....	....	....	98	....	....	....	....	....	....	....	....	....	....	5	0	1	1	12	....	....	....
	NHL Totals		**71**	**9**	**13**	**22**	**9**	**9**	**18**	**67**	**1**	**0**	**0**	**83**	**10.8**	**42**	**11**	**38**	**1**		**11**	**1**	**0**	**1**	**8**	**0**	**0**	**0**

Traded to **Vancouver** by **Montreal** for Dan Woodley, January 25, 1989. Signed as a free agent by **Vancouver**, October 3, 1993. • Played w/ RHI's Vancouver Voodoo in 1993 (14-25-43-68-10).

• CHARBONNEAU, Stephane

RW – R. 6'2", 195 lbs. b: Ste-Adele, Que., 6/27/1970.

Season	Club	League	GP	G	A	Pts	AG	AA	APts	PIM	PP	SH	GW	S	%	TGF	PGF	TGA	PGA	+/–	GP	G	A	Pts	PIM	PP	SH	GW
1986-87	Laval-Laurentides Regents	QAAA	42	17	26	43	....	....	....	....	....	....	....	....	....	....	....	....	....	....	....	....	....	....	....	....	....	....
1987-88	Hull Olympiques	QMJHL	51	10	20	30	....	....	....	70	....	....	....	....	....	....	....	....	....	....	11	5	8	13	12	....	....	....
1988-89	Hull Olympiques	QMJHL	64	23	29	52	....	....	....	142	....	....	....	....	....	....	....	....	....	....	9	2	2	4	22	....	....	....
1989-90	Shawinigan Cataractes	QMJHL	62	37	58	95	....	....	....	154	....	....	....	....	....	....	....	....	....	....	6	4	2	6	11	....	....	....
1990-91	Shawinigan Cataractes	QMJHL	6	4	3	7	....	....	....	2	....	....	....	....	....	....	....	....	....	....	....	....	....	....	....	....	....	....
	Chicoutimi Sagueneens	QMJHL	55	37	30	67	....	....	....	109	....	....	....	....	....	....	....	....	....	....	17	*13	9	22	43	....	....	....
	Chicoutimi Sagueneens	Mem-Cup	4	2	3	5	....	....	....	8	....	....	....	....	....	....	....	....	....	....	....	....	....	....	....	....	....	....
1991-92	**Quebec Nordiques**	**NHL**	**2**	**0**	**0**	**0**	**0**	**0**	**0**	**0**	**0**	**0**	**0**	**4**	**0.0**	**0**	**0**	**3**	**1**	**–2**	....	....	....	....	....	....	....	....
	Halifax Citadels	AHL	64	22	25	47	....	....	....	183	....	....	....	....	....	....	....	....	....	....	....	....	....	....	....	....	....	....
1992-93	Halifax Citadels	AHL	56	18	20	38	....	....	....	125	....	....	....	....	....	....	....	....	....	....	....	....	....	....	....	....	....	....
1993-94	Erie Panthers	ECHL	23	22	8	30	....	....	....	130	....	....	....	....	....	....	....	....	....	....	....	....	....	....	....	....	....	....
	Phoenix Roadrunners	IHL	32	7	6	13	....	....	....	43	....	....	....	....	....	....	....	....	....	....	....	....	....	....	....	....	....	....

Season	Club	League	REGULAR SEASON GP	G	A	Pts	AG	AA	APts	PIM	PP	SH	GW	S	%	TGF	PGF	TGA	PGA	+/–	PLAYOFFS GP	G	A	Pts	PIM	PP	SH	GW
1994-95	Cornwall Aces	AHL	1	0	1	1	....	....	....	0	....	....	....	....	....	....	....	....	....	....	....	....	....	....	....	....	....	....
	Fort Wayne Komets	IHL	4	0	0	0	....	....	....	8	....	....	....	....	....	....	....	....	....	....	....	....	....	....	....	....	....	....
	Portland Pirates	AHL	7	3	5	8	....	....	....	0	....	....	....	....	....	....	....	....	....	....	....	....	....	....	....	....	....	....
	Erie Panthers	ECHL	64	50	41	91	....	....	....	129	....	....	....	....	....	....	....	....	....	....	....	....	....	....	....	....	....	....
1995-96	Portland Pirates	AHL	23	5	3	8	....	....	....	23	....	....	....	....	....	....	....	....	....	....	1	0	0	0	0	....	....	....
	Flint Generals	ColHL	1	1	0	1	....	....	....	0	....	....	....	....	....	....	....	....	....	....	....	....	....	....	....	....	....	....
1996-97	Portland Pirates	AHL	9	1	0	1	....	....	....	2	....	....	....	....	....	....	....	....	....	....	....	....	....	....	....	....	....	....
	Baton Rouge Kingfish	ECHL	43	19	24	43	....	....	....	63	....	....	....	....	....	....	....	....	....	....	....	....	....	....	....	....	....	....
	Mississippi Sea Wolves	ECHL	13	8	6	14	....	....	....	14	....	....	....	....	....	....	....	....	....	....	3	2	0	2	18	....	....	....
	NHL Totals		**2**	**0**	**0**	**0**	**0**	**0**	**0**	**0**	**0**	**0**	**0**	**4**	**0.0**	**0**	**0**	**3**	**1**		....	....	....	....	....	....	....	....

ECHL Second All-Star Team (1995)

Signed as a free agent by **Quebec**, April 25, 1991. • Played w/ RHI's Montreal Roadrunners in 1994 (15-6-4-10-34), Philadelphia Bulldogs in 1995 (24-27-14-41-68) and 1996 (24-20-13-33-47) and MRHL's Philadelphia Sting in 1997 (4-6-4-10-4).

• CHARLEBOIS, Bob

Robert Richard LW – L. 6′, 175 lbs. b: Cornwall, Ont., 5/27/1944.

Season	Club	League	GP	G	A	Pts	AG	AA	APts	PIM	PP	SH	GW	S	%	TGF	PGF	TGA	PGA	+/–	GP	G	A	Pts	PIM	PP	SH	GW
1960-61	St-Jerome Alouettes	QJHL	35	41	46	87	....	....	....	....	....	....	....	....	....	....	....	....	....	....	....	....	....	....	....	....	....	....
1961-62	Montreal Jr. Canadiens	OHA-Jr.	46	9	9	18	....	....	....	28	....	....	....	....	....	....	....	....	....	....	6	2	1	3	6	....	....	....
1962-63	Montreal Jr. Canadiens	OHA-Jr.	50	23	15	38	....	....	....	78	....	....	....	....	....	....	....	....	....	....	10	5	5	10	20	....	....	....
1963-64	Montreal Jr. Canadiens	OHA-Jr.	53	35	43	78	....	....	....	50	....	....	....	....	....	....	....	....	....	....	17	10	12	22	14	....	....	....
1964-65	Omaha Knights	CPHL	70	24	34	58	....	....	....	43	....	....	....	....	....	....	....	....	....	....	6	4	3	7	2	....	....	....
1965-66	Houston Apollos	CPHL	70	23	26	49	....	....	....	32	....	....	....	....	....	....	....	....	....	....	....	....	....	....	....	....	....	....
1966-67	Houston Apollos	CPHL	67	27	34	61	....	....	....	38	....	....	....	....	....	....	....	....	....	....	6	0	1	1	2	....	....	....
1967-68	**Minnesota North Stars**	**NHL**	**7**	**1**	**0**	**1**	**1**	**0**	**1**	**0**	**1**	**0**	**0**	**8**	**12.5**	**1**	**1**	**4**	**1**	**–3**	....	....	....	....	....	....	....	....
	Memphis South Stars	CPHL	47	25	24	49	....	....	....	16	....	....	....	....	....	....	....	....	....	....	....	....	....	....	....	....	....	....
	Phoenix Roadrunners	WHL	15	2	8	10	....	....	....	4	....	....	....	....	....	....	....	....	....	....	4	1	2	3	0	....	....	....
1968-69	Phoenix Roadrunners	WHL	74	31	30	61	....	....	....	12	....	....	....	....	....	....	....	....	....	....	....	....	....	....	....	....	....	....
1969-70	Phoenix Roadrunners	WHL	73	24	34	58	....	....	....	12	....	....	....	....	....	....	....	....	....	....	....	....	....	....	....	....	....	....
1970-71	Phoenix Roadrunners	WHL	62	15	25	40	....	....	....	20	....	....	....	....	....	....	....	....	....	....	7	2	3	5	0	....	....	....
1971-72	Tulsa Oilers	CHL	6	0	0	0	....	....	....	4	....	....	....	....	....	....	....	....	....	....	....	....	....	....	....	....	....	....
1972-73	Ottawa Nationals	WHA	78	24	40	64	....	....	....	28	....	....	....	....	....	....	....	....	....	....	5	1	1	2	4	....	....	....
1973-74	New England Whalers	WHA	74	4	7	11	....	....	....	6	....	....	....	....	....	....	....	....	....	....	7	0	0	0	4	....	....	....
1974-75	New England Whalers	WHA	8	1	0	1	....	....	....	0	....	....	....	....	....	....	....	....	....	....	4	1	0	1	0	....	....	....
	Cape Cod Codders	NAHL	60	24	57	81	....	....	....	54	....	....	....	....	....	....	....	....	....	....	....	....	....	....	....	....	....	....
1975-76	New England Whalers	WHA	28	3	3	6	....	....	....	0	....	....	....	....	....	....	....	....	....	....	....	....	....	....	....	....	....	....
	Cape Cod Codders	NAHL	25	12	20	32	....	....	....	26	....	....	....	....	....	....	....	....	....	....	....	....	....	....	....	....	....	....
	Binghamton Dusters	NAHL	5	0	5	5	....	....	....	0	....	....	....	....	....	....	....	....	....	....	....	....	....	....	....	....	....	....
	NHL Totals		**7**	**1**	**0**	**1**	**1**	**0**	**1**	**0**	**1**	**0**	**0**	**8**	**12.5**	**1**	**1**	**4**	**1**		....	....	....	....	....	....	....	....
	Other Major League Totals		188	32	50	82	....	....	....	34	....	....	....	....	....	....	....	....	....	....	16	2	1	3	8	....	....	....

Traded to **Minnesota** by **Montreal** with Andre Boudrias and Bernard Cote for Minnesota's 1st round choice (Chuck Arnason) in 1971 Amateur Draft, June 6, 1967. Traded to **Phoenix** (WHL) by **Minnesota** with Leo Thiffault to complete earlier transaction that sent Walt McKechnie to Minnesota (February 17, 1968), June, 1968. Signed as a free agent by **Ottawa** (WHA), August, 1972. Traded to **New England** (WHA) by **Toronto** (WHA) for Brit Selby, September, 1973.

• CHARLESWORTH, Todd

D – L. 6′1″, 190 lbs. b: Calgary, Alta., 3/22/1965. Pittsburgh's 2nd, 22nd overall, in 1983.

Season	Club	League	GP	G	A	Pts	AG	AA	APts	PIM	PP	SH	GW	S	%	TGF	PGF	TGA	PGA	+/–	GP	G	A	Pts	PIM	PP	SH	GW
1981-82	Gloucester Rangers	OJHL	50	13	24	37	....	....	....	67	....	....	....	....	....	....	....	....	....	....	....	....	....	....	....	....	....	....
1982-83	Oshawa Generals	OHL	70	6	23	29	....	....	....	55	....	....	....	....	....	....	....	....	....	....	17	0	4	4	20	....	....	....
	Oshawa Generals	Mem-Cup	5	1	3	4	....	....	....	2	....	....	....	....	....	....	....	....	....	....	....	....	....	....	....	....	....	....
1983-84	Oshawa Generals	OHL	57	11	35	46	....	....	....	54	....	....	....	....	....	....	....	....	....	....	7	0	4	4	4	....	....	....
	Pittsburgh Penguins	**NHL**	**10**	**0**	**0**	**0**	**0**	**0**	**0**	**8**	**0**	**0**	**0**	**6**	**0.0**	**6**	**0**	**14**	**1**	**–7**	....	....	....	....	....	....	....	....
1984-85	**Pittsburgh Penguins**	**NHL**	**67**	**1**	**8**	**9**	**1**	**5**	**6**	**31**	**0**	**0**	**1**	**68**	**1.5**	**58**	**2**	**96**	**17**	**–23**	....	....	....	....	....	....	....	....
1985-86	**Pittsburgh Penguins**	**NHL**	**2**	**0**	**1**	**1**	**0**	**1**	**1**	**0**	**0**	**0**	**0**	**1**	**0.0**	**0**	**0**	**1**	**0**	**–1**	....	....	....	....	....	....	....	....
	Baltimore Skipjacks	AHL	19	1	3	4	....	....	....	10	....	....	....	....	....	....	....	....	....	....	....	....	....	....	....	....	....	....
	Muskegon Lumberjacks	IHL	51	9	27	36	....	....	....	78	....	....	....	....	....	....	....	....	....	....	14	3	8	11	14	....	....	....
1986-87	**Pittsburgh Penguins**	**NHL**	**1**	**0**	**0**	**0**	**0**	**0**	**0**	**0**	**0**	**0**	**0**	**0**	**0.0**	**1**	**0**	**1**	**0**	**0**	....	....	....	....	....	....	....	....
	Baltimore Skipjacks	AHL	75	5	21	26	....	....	....	64	....	....	....	....	....	....	....	....	....	....	....	....	....	....	....	....	....	....
1987-88	**Pittsburgh Penguins**	**NHL**	**6**	**2**	**0**	**2**	**2**	**0**	**2**	**2**	**0**	**0**	**0**	**4**	**50.0**	**3**	**0**	**3**	**0**	**0**	....	....	....	....	....	....	....	....
	Muskegon Lumberjacks	IHL	64	9	31	40	....	....	....	49	....	....	....	....	....	....	....	....	....	....	5	0	0	0	18	....	....	....
1988-89	Muskegon Lumberjacks	IHL	74	10	53	63	....	....	....	85	....	....	....	....	....	....	....	....	....	....	14	2	13	15	8	....	....	....
1989-90	**New York Rangers**	**NHL**	**7**	**0**	**0**	**0**	**0**	**0**	**0**	**6**	**0**	**0**	**0**	**4**	**0.0**	**1**	**0**	**6**	**2**	**–3**	....	....	....	....	....	....	....	....
	Flint Spirits	IHL	26	3	6	9	....	....	....	12	....	....	....	....	....	....	....	....	....	....	....	....	....	....	....	....	....	....
	Cape Breton Oilers	AHL	32	0	9	9	....	....	....	13	....	....	....	....	....	....	....	....	....	....	....	....	....	....	....	....	....	....
1990-91	Binghamton Rangers	AHL	11	0	3	3	....	....	....	2	....	....	....	....	....	....	....	....	....	....	....	....	....	....	....	....	....	....
	Muskegon Lumberjacks	IHL	62	5	32	37	....	....	....	46	....	....	....	....	....	....	....	....	....	....	5	1	3	4	2	....	....	....
1991-92	Muskegon Lumberjacks	IHL	DID NOT PLAY – INJURED																									
1992-93	Muskegon Fury	ColHL	45	9	37	46	....	....	....	22	....	....	....	....	....	....	....	....	....	....	7	1	3	4	4	....	....	....
1993-94	Muskegon Fury	ColHL	37	8	30	38	....	....	....	33	....	....	....	....	....	....	....	....	....	....	3	0	1	1	0	....	....	....
1994-95	Muskegon Fury	ColHL	62	21	49	70	....	....	....	60	....	....	....	....	....	....	....	....	....	....	17	1	14	15	12	....	....	....
	NHL Totals		**93**	**3**	**9**	**12**	**3**	**6**	**9**	**47**	**0**	**0**	**1**	**83**	**3.6**	**69**	**2**	**121**	**20**		....	....	....	....	....	....	....	....

IHL Second All-Star Team (1989) • ColHL First All-Star Team (1995)

Signed as a free agent by **Edmonton**, June 21, 1989. Traded to **NY Rangers** by **Edmonton** for future considerations, January 18, 1990. • Missed entire 1991-92 season recovering from thumb surgery, July, 1991.

• CHARRON, Eric

D – L. 6′3″, 200 lbs. b: Verdun, Que., 1/14/1970. Montreal's 1st, 20th overall, in 1988.

Season	Club	League	GP	G	A	Pts	AG	AA	APts	PIM	PP	SH	GW	S	%	TGF	PGF	TGA	PGA	+/–	GP	G	A	Pts	PIM	PP	SH	GW
1986-87	Lac St-Louis Lions	QAAA	41	1	8	9	....	....	....	92	....	....	....	....	....	....	....	....	....	....	....	....	....	....	....	....	....	....
1987-88	Trois-Rivieres Draveurs	QMJHL	67	3	13	16	....	....	....	135	....	....	....	....	....	....	....	....	....	....	....	....	....	....	....	....	....	....
1988-89	Trois-Rivieres Draveurs	QMJHL	38	2	16	18	....	....	....	111	....	....	....	....	....	....	....	....	....	....	....	....	....	....	....	....	....	....
	Verdun Jr. Canadiens	QMJHL	28	2	15	17	....	....	....	66	....	....	....	....	....	....	....	....	....	....	....	....	....	....	....	....	....	....
	Sherbrooke Canadiens	AHL	1	0	0	0	....	....	....	0	....	....	....	....	....	....	....	....	....	....	....	....	....	....	....	....	....	....
1989-90	St-Hyacinthe Lasers	QMJHL	68	13	38	51	....	....	....	152	....	....	....	....	....	....	....	....	....	....	11	3	4	7	67	....	....	....
	Sherbrooke Canadiens	AHL	....	....	....	....	....	....	....	....	....	....	....	....	....	....	....	....	....	....	2	0	0	0	0	....	....	....
1990-91	Fredericton Canadiens	AHL	71	1	11	12	....	....	....	108	....	....	....	....	....	....	....	....	....	....	2	1	0	1	29	....	....	....
1991-92	Fredericton Canadiens	AHL	59	2	11	13	....	....	....	98	....	....	....	....	....	....	....	....	....	....	6	1	0	1	4	....	....	....
1992-93	**Montreal Canadiens**	**NHL**	**3**	**0**	**0**	**0**	**0**	**0**	**0**	**2**	**0**	**0**	**0**	**0**	**0.0**	**0**	**0**	**0**	**0**	**0**	....	....	....	....	....	....	....	....
	Fredericton Canadiens	AHL	54	3	13	16	....	....	....	93	....	....	....	....	....	....	....	....	....	....	....	....	....	....	....	....	....	....
	Atlanta Knights	IHL	11	0	2	2	....	....	....	12	....	....	....	....	....	....	....	....	....	....	3	0	1	1	6	....	....	....
1993-94	**Tampa Bay Lightning**	**NHL**	**4**	**0**	**0**	**0**	**0**	**0**	**0**	**2**	**0**	**0**	**0**	**1**	**0.0**	**2**	**0**	**2**	**0**	**0**	....	....	....	....	....	....	....	....
	Atlanta Knights	IHL	66	5	18	23	....	....	....	144	....	....	....	....	....	....	....	....	....	....	14	1	4	5	28	....	....	....
1994-95	**Tampa Bay Lightning**	**NHL**	**45**	**1**	**4**	**5**	**2**	**6**	**8**	**26**	**0**	**0**	**0**	**33**	**3.0**	**26**	**1**	**33**	**9**	**1**	....	....	....	....	....	....	....	....
1995-96	**Tampa Bay Lightning**	**NHL**	**14**	**0**	**0**	**0**	**0**	**0**	**0**	**18**	**0**	**0**	**0**	**11**	**0.0**	**6**	**0**	**19**	**7**	**–6**	....	....	....	....	....	....	....	....
	Washington Capitals	**NHL**	**4**	**0**	**1**	**1**	**0**	**1**	**1**	**4**	**0**	**0**	**0**	**2**	**0.0**	**4**	**0**	**2**	**1**	**3**	**6**	**0**	**0**	**0**	**8**	**0**	**0**	**0**
	Portland Pirates	AHL	45	0	8	8	....	....	....	88	....	....	....	....	....	....	....	....	....	....	20	1	1	2	33	....	....	....
1996-97	**Washington Capitals**	**NHL**	**25**	**1**	**1**	**2**	**1**	**1**	**2**	**20**	**0**	**0**	**0**	**11**	**9.1**	**8**	**0**	**9**	**2**	**1**	....	....	....	....	....	....	....	....
	Portland Pirates	AHL	29	6	8	14	....	....	....	55	....	....	....	....	....	....	....	....	....	....	5	0	3	3	0	....	....	....
1997-98	**Calgary Flames**	**NHL**	**2**	**0**	**0**	**0**	**0**	**0**	**0**	**4**	**0**	**0**	**0**	**1**	**0.0**	**1**	**0**	**1**	**0**	**0**	....	....	....	....	....	....	....	....
	Saint John Flames	AHL	56	8	20	28	....	....	....	136	....	....	....	....	....	....	....	....	....	....	20	1	7	8	55	....	....	....

			REGULAR SEASON																		PLAYOFFS							
Season	**Club**	**League**	**GP**	**G**	**A**	**Pts**	**AG**	**AA**	**APts**	**PIM**	**PP**	**SH**	**GW**	**S**	**%**	**TGF**	**PGF**	**TGA**	**PGA**	**+/–**	**GP**	**G**	**A**	**Pts**	**PIM**	**PP**	**SH**	**GW**
1998-99	**Calgary Flames**	**NHL**	**12**	**0**	**1**	**1**	**0**	**1**	**1**	**14**	**0**	**0**	**0**	**9**	**0.0**	**3**	**0**	**12**	**3**	**–6**	....	....	....	....	....	....	....	....
	Saint John Flames	AHL	50	10	12	22	....	....	....	148	....	....	....	....	....	....	....	....	....	....	3	1	0	1	22	....	....	....
99-2000	**Calgary Flames**	**NHL**	**21**	**0**	**0**	**0**	**0**	**0**	**0**	**37**	**0**	**0**	**0**	**8**	**0.0**	**8**	**0**	**17**	**6**	**–3**	....	....	....	....	....	....	....	....
	Saint John Flames	AHL	37	2	15	17	....	....	....	82	....	....	....	....	....	....	....	....	....	....	....	....	....	....	....	....	....	....
	NHL Totals		**130**	**2**	**7**	**9**	**3**	**9**	**12**	**127**	**0**	**0**	**0**	**76**	**2.6**	**58**	**1**	**95**	**28**		**6**	**0**	**0**	**0**	**8**	**0**	**0**	**0**

Traded to **Tampa Bay** by **Montreal** with Alain Cote and future considerations (Donald Dufresne, June 18, 1993) for Rob Ramage, March 20, 1993. Traded to **Washington** by **Tampa Bay** for Washington's 7th round choice (Eero Somervuori) in 1997 Entry Draft, November 16, 1995. Traded to **Calgary** by **Washington** for Calgary's 7th round choice (Nathan Forster) in 1998 Entry Draft, September 4, 1997.

• CHARRON, Guy

Guy Joseph Jean C – L. 5'10", 170 lbs. b: Verdun, Que., 1/24/1949.

Season	Club	League	GP	G	A	Pts	AG	AA	APts	PIM	PP	SH	GW	S	%	TGF	PGF	TGA	PGA	+/–	GP	G	A	Pts	PIM	PP	SH	GW
1966-67	Verdun Jr. Maple Leafs	QJHL	STATISTICS NOT AVAILABLE																									
	Verdun Jr. Maple Leafs	Mem-Cup	4	0	1	1	....	....	....	4	....	....	....	....	....	....	....	....	....	....	....	....	....	....	....	....	....	....
1967-68	Verdun Jr. Maple Leafs	QJHL	42	29	36	65	....	....	....	....	....	....	....	....	....	....	....	....	....	....	....	....	....	....	....	....	....	....
	Verdun Jr. Maple Leafs	Mem-Cup	21	14	9	23	....	....	....	6	....	....	....	....	....	....	....	....	....	....	....	....	....	....	....	....	....	....
1968-69	Montreal Jr. Canadiens	OHA-Jr.	50	27	27	54	....	....	....	12	....	....	....	....	....	....	....	....	....	....	14	11	15	26	6	....	....	....
	Montreal Jr. Canadiens	Mem-Cup	8	*7	5	12	....	....	....	4	....	....	....	....	....	....	....	....	....	....	....	....	....	....	....	....	....	....
1969-70	**Montreal Canadiens**	**NHL**	**5**	**0**	**0**	**0**	**0**	**0**	**0**	**0**	**0**	**0**	**0**	**2**	**0.0**	**0**	**0**	**2**	**0**	**–2**	....	....	....	....	....	....	....	....
	Montreal Voyageurs	AHL	65	37	45	82	....	....	....	20	....	....	....	....	....	....	....	....	....	....	8	*8	4	12	2	....	....	....
1970-71	**Montreal Canadiens**	**NHL**	**15**	**2**	**2**	**4**	**2**	**2**	**4**	**2**	**0**	**0**	**0**	**13**	**15.4**	**6**	**0**	**8**	**0**	**–2**	....	....	....	....	....	....	....	....
	Montreal Voyageurs	AHL	23	5	13	18	....	....	....	6	....	....	....	....	....	....	....	....	....	....	....	....	....	....	....	....	....	....
	Detroit Red Wings	**NHL**	**24**	**8**	**4**	**12**	**8**	**3**	**11**	**4**	**2**	**0**	**1**	**55**	**14.5**	**17**	**2**	**15**	**0**	**0**	....	....	....	....	....	....	....	....
1971-72	**Detroit Red Wings**	**NHL**	**64**	**9**	**16**	**25**	**9**	**14**	**23**	**14**	**0**	**0**	**1**	**119**	**7.6**	**36**	**5**	**39**	**0**	**–8**	....	....	....	....	....	....	....	....
1972-73	**Detroit Red Wings**	**NHL**	**75**	**18**	**18**	**36**	**17**	**14**	**31**	**23**	**0**	**0**	**2**	**117**	**15.4**	**56**	**5**	**43**	**1**	**9**	....	....	....	....	....	....	....	....
1973-74	**Detroit Red Wings**	**NHL**	**76**	**25**	**30**	**55**	**24**	**25**	**49**	**10**	**6**	**0**	**2**	**205**	**12.2**	**80**	**25**	**88**	**2**	**–31**	....	....	....	....	....	....	....	....
1974-75	**Detroit Red Wings**	**NHL**	**26**	**1**	**10**	**11**	**1**	**7**	**8**	**6**	**0**	**0**	**1**	**27**	**3.7**	**16**	**11**	**14**	**0**	**–9**	....	....	....	....	....	....	....	....
	Kansas City Scouts	**NHL**	**51**	**13**	**29**	**42**	**11**	**22**	**33**	**21**	**4**	**0**	**0**	**157**	**8.3**	**53**	**27**	**73**	**6**	**–41**	....	....	....	....	....	....	....	....
1975-76	**Kansas City Scouts**	**NHL**	**78**	**27**	**44**	**71**	**24**	**33**	**57**	**12**	**9**	**0**	**4**	**226**	**11.9**	**89**	**30**	**134**	**24**	**–51**	....	....	....	....	....	....	....	....
1976-77	**Washington Capitals**	**NHL**	**80**	**36**	**46**	**82**	**33**	**35**	**68**	**10**	**6**	**1**	**4**	**261**	**13.8**	**105**	**34**	**106**	**7**	**–28**	....	....	....	....	....	....	....	....
	Canada	WEC-A	1	0	0	0	....	....	....	0	....	....	....	....	....	....	....	....	....	....	....	....	....	....	....	....	....	....
1977-78	**Washington Capitals**	**NHL**	**80**	**38**	**35**	**73**	**35**	**27**	**62**	**12**	**4**	**0**	**3**	**260**	**14.6**	**105**	**30**	**102**	**2**	**–25**	....	....	....	....	....	....	....	....
	Canada	WEC-A	9	0	1	1	....	....	....	0	....	....	....	....	....	....	....	....	....	....	....	....	....	....	....	....	....	....
1978-79	**Washington Capitals**	**NHL**	**80**	**28**	**42**	**70**	**24**	**30**	**54**	**24**	**9**	**0**	**4**	**225**	**12.4**	**104**	**32**	**92**	**6**	**–14**	....	....	....	....	....	....	....	....
	Canada	WEC-A	6	1	3	4	....	....	....	2	....	....	....	....	....	....	....	....	....	....	....	....	....	....	....	....	....	....
1979-80	**Washington Capitals**	**NHL**	**33**	**11**	**20**	**31**	**9**	**15**	**24**	**6**	**5**	**0**	**1**	**80**	**13.8**	**37**	**11**	**31**	**3**	**–2**	....	....	....	....	....	....	....	....
1980-81	**Washington Capitals**	**NHL**	**47**	**5**	**13**	**18**	**4**	**9**	**13**	**2**	**2**	**1**	**0**	**62**	**8.1**	**26**	**11**	**43**	**24**	**–4**	....	....	....	....	....	....	....	....
1981-82	EHC Arosa	Switz-2	PLAYER/COACH – STATISTICS UNAVAILABLE																									
1982-83	EHC Arosa	Switz-2	36	17	27	44	....	....	....	....	....	....	....	....	....	....	....	....	....	....	....	....	....	....	....	....	....	....
	New Haven Nighthawks	AHL	2	1	2	3	....	....	....	14	....	....	....	....	....	....	....	....	....	....	12	2	5	7	4	....	....	....
1983-1985	Quebec Remparts	QMJHL	DID NOT PLAY – COACHING																									
1985-1990	Canada	Nat-Team	DID NOT PLAY – COACHING																									
1990-1995	**Calgary Flames**	**NHL**	DID NOT PLAY – ASSISTANT COACH																									
1995-1997	**New York Islanders**	**NHL**	DID NOT PLAY – ASSISTANT COACH																									
1997-1998	EV Landshut	Germany	DID NOT PLAY – COACHING																									
1998-2000	Grand Rapids Griffins	IHL	DID NOT PLAY – COACHING																									
	NHL Totals		**734**	**221**	**309**	**530**	**201**	**236**	**437**	**146**	**47**	**2**	**23**	**1809**	**12.2**	**730**	**223**	**790**	**75**		....	....	....	....	....	....	....	....

Played in NHL All-Star Game (1977)

Traded to **Detroit** by **Montreal** with Mickey Redmond and Bill Collins for Frank Mahovlich, January 13, 1971. Traded to **Kansas City** by **Detroit** with Claude Houde for Bart Crashley, Ted Snell and Larry Giroux, December 14, 1974. Signed as a free agent by **Washington**, September 1, 1976.

• CHARTIER, Dave

C – R. 5'9", 170 lbs. b: St. Lazare, Man., 2/15/1961. Los Angeles' 9th, 174th overall, in 1982.

Season	Club	League	GP	G	A	Pts	AG	AA	APts	PIM	PP	SH	GW	S	%	TGF	PGF	TGA	PGA	+/–	GP	G	A	Pts	PIM	PP	SH	GW
1977-78	Brandon Travellers	MJHL	47	30	22	52	....	....	....	98	....	....	....	....	....	....	....	....	....	....	....	....	....	....	....	....	....	....
	Brandon Wheat Kings	WCJHL	2	1	0	1	....	....	....	0	....	....	....	....	....	....	....	....	....	....	....	....	....	....	....	....	....	....
1978-79	Brandon Wheat Kings	WHL	48	14	12	26	....	....	....	83	....	....	....	....	....	....	....	....	....	....	....	....	....	....	....	....	....	....
	Brandon Wheat Kings	Mem-Cup	5	0	0	0	....	....	....	2	....	....	....	....	....	....	....	....	....	....	....	....	....	....	....	....	....	....
1979-80	Brandon Wheat Kings	WHL	69	39	29	68	....	....	....	285	....	....	....	....	....	....	....	....	....	....	....	....	....	....	....	....	....	....
1980-81	Brandon Wheat Kings	WHL	69	64	60	124	....	....	....	295	....	....	....	....	....	....	....	....	....	....	....	....	....	....	....	....	....	....
	Winnipeg Jets	**NHL**	**1**	**0**	**0**	**0**	**0**	**0**	**0**	**0**	**0**	**0**	**0**	**0**	**0.0**	**0**	**0**	**0**	**0**	**0**	....	....	....	....	....	....	....	....
	Tulsa Oilers	CHL	1	1	0	1	....	....	....	4	....	....	....	....	....	....	....	....	....	....	8	1	2	3	9	....	....	....
1981-82	Tulsa Oilers	CHL	74	18	17	35	....	....	....	126	....	....	....	....	....	....	....	....	....	....	3	0	1	1	2	....	....	....
1982-83	Sherbrooke Jets	AHL	48	9	10	19	....	....	....	87	....	....	....	....	....	....	....	....	....	....	....	....	....	....	....	....	....	....
1983-84	Sherbrooke Jets	AHL	43	13	14	27	....	....	....	59	....	....	....	....	....	....	....	....	....	....	....	....	....	....	....	....	....	....
1984-85	Fort Wayne Komets	IHL	4	1	2	3	....	....	....	9	....	....	....	....	....	....	....	....	....	....	....	....	....	....	....	....	....	....
	NHL Totals		**1**	**0**	**0**	**0**	**0**	**0**	**0**	**0**	**0**	**0**	**0**	**0**	**0.0**	**0**	**0**	**0**	**0**		....	....	....	....	....	....	....	....

• CHARTRAND, Brad

RW – L. 5'11", 191 lbs. b: Winnipeg, Man., 12/14/1974.

Season	Club	League	GP	G	A	Pts	AG	AA	APts	PIM	PP	SH	GW	S	%	TGF	PGF	TGA	PGA	+/–	GP	G	A	Pts	PIM	PP	SH	GW
1988-89	Winnipeg Hawks	MAHA	24	30	50	80	....	....	....	40	....	....	....	....	....	....	....	....	....	....	....	....	....	....	....	....	....	....
1989-90	Winnipeg Hawks	MAHA	24	26	55	81	....	....	....	40	....	....	....	....	....	....	....	....	....	....	....	....	....	....	....	....	....	....
1990-91	Winnipeg Hawks	MAHA	34	26	45	71	....	....	....	40	....	....	....	....	....	....	....	....	....	....	....	....	....	....	....	....	....	....
1991-92	St. James Canadians	MJHL	STATISTICS NOT AVAILABLE																									
1992-93	Cornell University	ECAC	26	10	6	16	....	....	....	16	....	....	....	....	....	....	....	....	....	....	....	....	....	....	....	....	....	....
1993-94	Cornell University	ECAC	30	4	14	18	....	....	....	48	....	....	....	....	....	....	....	....	....	....	....	....	....	....	....	....	....	....
1994-95	Cornell University	ECAC	28	9	9	18	....	....	....	10	....	....	....	....	....	....	....	....	....	....	....	....	....	....	....	....	....	....
1995-96	Cornell University	ECAC	34	24	19	43	....	....	....	16	....	....	....	....	....	....	....	....	....	....	....	....	....	....	....	....	....	....
1996-97	Canada	Nat-Team	54	10	14	24	....	....	....	42	....	....	....	....	....	....	....	....	....	....	....	....	....	....	....	....	....	....
1997-98	Canada	Nat-Team	60	24	30	54	....	....	....	47	....	....	....	....	....	....	....	....	....	....	....	....	....	....	....	....	....	....
	HC Rapperswil-Jona	Switz.	8	2	3	5	....	....	....	4	....	....	....	....	....	....	....	....	....	....	....	....	....	....	....	....	....	....
1998-99	St. John's Maple Leafs	AHL	64	16	14	30	....	....	....	48	....	....	....	....	....	....	....	....	....	....	5	0	2	2	2	....	....	....
99-2000	**Los Angeles Kings**	**NHL**	**50**	**6**	**6**	**12**	**7**	**6**	**13**	**17**	**0**	**1**	**3**	**51**	**11.8**	**15**	**1**	**18**	**8**	**4**	**4**	**0**	**0**	**0**	**6**	**0**	**0**	**0**
	Lowell Lock Monsters	AHL	16	5	10	15	....	....	....	8	....	....	....	....	....	....	....	....	....	....	....	....	....	....	....	....	....	....
	Long Beach Ice Dogs	IHL	1	0	0	0	....	....	....	0	....	....	....	....	....	....	....	....	....	....	3	0	0	0	0	....	....	....
	NHL Totals		**50**	**6**	**6**	**12**	**7**	**6**	**13**	**17**	**0**	**1**	**3**	**51**	**11.8**	**15**	**1**	**18**	**8**		**4**	**0**	**0**	**0**	**6**	**0**	**0**	**0**

Signed as a free agent by **LA Kings**, July 15, 1999. Loaned to **Lowell** (AHL) by **LA Kings**, January 26, 2000.

• CHARTRAW, Rick

Raymond Richard D/RW – R. 6'2", 210 lbs. b: Caracas, Venezuela, 7/13/1954. Montreal's 3rd, 10th overall, in 1974.

Season	Club	League	GP	G	A	Pts	AG	AA	APts	PIM	PP	SH	GW	S	%	TGF	PGF	TGA	PGA	+/–	GP	G	A	Pts	PIM	PP	SH	GW
1972-73	Kitchener Rangers	OMJHL	59	10	22	32	....	....	....	101	....	....	....	....	....	....	....	....	....	....	....	....	....	....	....	....	....	....
1973-74	Kitchener Rangers	OMJHL	70	17	44	61	....	....	....	150	....	....	....	....	....	....	....	....	....	....	....	....	....	....	....	....	....	....
1974-75	**Montreal Canadiens**	**NHL**	**12**	**0**	**0**	**0**	**0**	**0**	**0**	**6**	**0**	**0**	**0**	**7**	**0.0**	**7**	**1**	**10**	**0**	**–4**	....	....	....	....	....	....	....	....
	Nova Scotia Voyageurs	AHL	58	7	20	27	....	....	....	148	....	....	....	....	....	....	....	....	....	....	6	1	2	3	4	....	....	....
1975-76♦	**Montreal Canadiens**	**NHL**	**16**	**1**	**3**	**4**	**1**	**2**	**3**	**25**	**0**	**0**	**0**	**22**	**4.5**	**17**	**0**	**5**	**0**	**12**	**2**	**0**	**0**	**0**	**0**	**0**	**0**	**0**
	Nova Scotia Voyageurs	AHL	33	12	24	36	....	....	....	49	....	....	....	....	....	....	....	....	....	....	....	....	....	....	....	....	....	....
1976-77	United States	Can-Cup	5	0	0	0	....	....	....	8	....	....	....	....	....	....	....	....	....	....	....	....	....	....	....	....	....	....
♦	**Montreal Canadiens**	**NHL**	**43**	**3**	**4**	**7**	**3**	**3**	**6**	**59**	**0**	**0**	**1**	**42**	**7.1**	**37**	**0**	**10**	**0**	**27**	**13**	**2**	**1**	**3**	**17**	**0**	**0**	**0**
1977-78♦	**Montreal Canadiens**	**NHL**	**68**	**4**	**12**	**16**	**4**	**9**	**13**	**64**	**0**	**0**	**1**	**75**	**5.3**	**43**	**0**	**28**	**1**	**16**	**10**	**1**	**0**	**1**	**10**	**0**	**0**	**1**
1978-79♦	**Montreal Canadiens**	**NHL**	**62**	**5**	**11**	**16**	**4**	**8**	**12**	**29**	**0**	**0**	**1**	**81**	**6.2**	**49**	**1**	**35**	**1**	**14**	**16**	**2**	**1**	**3**	**24**	**0**	**0**	**0**
1979-80	**Montreal Canadiens**	**NHL**	**66**	**5**	**7**	**12**	**4**	**5**	**9**	**35**	**0**	**0**	**0**	**65**	**7.7**	**33**	**0**	**27**	**0**	**6**	**10**	**2**	**2**	**4**	**0**	**0**	**0**	**0**
1980-81	**Montreal Canadiens**	**NHL**	**14**	**0**	**0**	**0**	**0**	**0**	**0**	**4**	**0**	**0**	**0**	**10**	**0.0**	**3**	**0**	**8**	**0**	**–5**	....	....	....	....	....	....	....	....
	Los Angeles Kings	**NHL**	**21**	**1**	**6**	**7**	**1**	**4**	**5**	**28**	**0**	**0**	**1**	**32**	**3.1**	**27**	**6**	**22**	**2**	**1**	**4**	**0**	**1**	**1**	**4**	**0**	**0**	**0**
1981-82	**Los Angeles Kings**	**NHL**	**33**	**2**	**8**	**10**	**2**	**5**	**7**	**56**	**1**	**0**	**0**	**32**	**6.3**	**33**	**2**	**61**	**19**	**–11**	**10**	**0**	**2**	**2**	**17**	**0**	**0**	**0**
	New Haven Nighthawks	AHL	33	3	9	12	....	....	....	39	....	....	....	....	....	....	....	....	....	....	....	....	....	....	....	....	....	....

			REGULAR SEASON																		PLAYOFFS							
Season	**Club**	**League**	**GP**	**G**	**A**	**Pts**	**AG**	**AA**	**APts**	**PIM**	**PP**	**SH**	**GW**	**S**	**%**	**TGF**	**PGF**	**TGA**	**PGA**	**+/–**	**GP**	**G**	**A**	**Pts**	**PIM**	**PP**	**SH**	**GW**
1982-83	**Los Angeles Kings**	**NHL**	**31**	**3**	**5**	**8**	**2**	**3**	**5**	**31**	**0**	**0**	**0**	**32**	**9.4**	**29**	**0**	**57**	**14**	**–14**	....	....	....	....	....	....	....	....
	New York Rangers	**NHL**	**26**	**2**	**2**	**4**	**2**	**1**	**3**	**37**	**0**	**0**	**0**	**21**	**9.5**	**14**	**0**	**22**	**10**	**2**	**9**	**0**	**2**	**2**	**6**	**0**	**0**	**0**
1983-84	**New York Rangers**	**NHL**	**4**	**0**	**0**	**0**	**0**	**0**	**0**	**4**	**0**	**0**	**0**	**0**	**0.0**	**0**	**0**	**3**	**0**	**–3**	....	....	....	....	....	....	....	....
	Tulsa Oilers	CHL	28	1	4	5	....	....	....	25	....	....	....	....	....	....	....	....	....	....	....	....	....	....	....	....	....	....
♦	**Edmonton Oilers**	**NHL**	**24**	**2**	**6**	**8**	**2**	**4**	**6**	**21**	**0**	**0**	**0**	**23**	**8.7**	**27**	**0**	**25**	**3**	**5**	**1**	**0**	**0**	**0**	**2**	**0**	**0**	**0**
1984-1992			OUT OF HOCKEY – RETIRED																									
1992-93	Los Angeles Jets	SCSHL	4	2	2	4	....	....	....	6	....	....	....	....	....	....	....	....	....	....	....	....	....	....	....	....	....	....
	NHL Totals		**420**	**28**	**64**	**92**	**25**	**44**	**69**	**399**	**1**	**0**	**4**	**442**	**6.3**	**319**	**10**	**313**	**50**		**75**	**7**	**9**	**16**	**80**	**0**	**0**	**1**

OMJHL First All-Star Team (1974) • AHL First All-Star Team (1975)

Traded to **LA Kings** by **Montreal** for LA Kings' 2nd round choice (Claude Lemieux) in 1983 Entry Draft, February 17, 1981. Claimed on waivers by **NY Rangers** from **LA Kings**, January 13, 1983. Traded to **Edmonton** by **NY Rangers** for Edmonton's 9th round choice (Heinz Ehlers) in 1984 Entry Draft, January 20, 1984.

• CHASE, Kelly

Kelly Wayne RW – R. 5'11", 201 lbs. b: Porcupine Plain, Sask., 10/25/1967.

Season	Club	League	GP	G	A	Pts	AG	AA	APts	PIM	PP	SH	GW	S	%	TGF	PGF	TGA	PGA	+/–	GP	G	A	Pts	PIM	PP	SH	GW
1984-85	Humboldt Broncos	SJHL	STATISTICS NOT AVAILABLE																									
1985-86	Saskatoon Blades	WHL	57	7	18	25	....	....	....	172	....	....	....	....	....	....	....	....	....	....	10	3	4	7	37	....	....	....
1986-87	Saskatoon Blades	WHL	68	17	29	46	....	....	....	285	....	....	....	....	....	....	....	....	....	....	11	2	8	10	37	....	....	....
1987-88	Saskatoon Blades	WHL	70	21	34	55	....	....	....	*343	....	....	....	....	....	....	....	....	....	....	9	3	5	8	32	....	....	....
1988-89	Peoria Rivermen	IHL	38	14	7	21	....	....	....	278	....	....	....	....	....	....	....	....	....	....	....	....	....	....	....	....	....	....
1989-90	**St. Louis Blues**	**NHL**	**43**	**1**	**3**	**4**	**1**	**2**	**3**	**244**	**0**	**0**	**0**	**9**	**11.1**	**7**	**0**	**8**	**0**	**–1**	**9**	**1**	**0**	**1**	**46**	**0**	**0**	**0**
	Peoria Rivermen	IHL	10	1	2	3	....	....	....	76	....	....	....	....	....	....	....	....	....	....	....	....	....	....	....	....	....	....
1990-91	**St. Louis Blues**	**NHL**	**2**	**1**	**0**	**1**	**1**	**0**	**1**	**15**	**0**	**0**	**1**	**1**	**100.0**	**1**	**0**	**0**	**0**	**1**	**6**	**0**	**0**	**0**	**18**	**0**	**0**	**0**
	Peoria Rivermen	IHL	61	20	34	54	....	....	....	406	....	....	....	....	....	....	....	....	....	....	10	4	3	7	61	....	....	....
1991-92	**St. Louis Blues**	**NHL**	**46**	**1**	**2**	**3**	**1**	**2**	**3**	**264**	**0**	**0**	**0**	**29**	**3.4**	**6**	**0**	**12**	**0**	**–6**	**1**	**0**	**0**	**0**	**7**	**0**	**0**	**0**
1992-93	**St. Louis Blues**	**NHL**	**49**	**2**	**5**	**7**	**2**	**3**	**5**	**204**	**0**	**0**	**0**	**28**	**7.1**	**9**	**0**	**18**	**0**	**–9**	....	....	....	....	....	....	....	....
1993-94	**St. Louis Blues**	**NHL**	**68**	**2**	**5**	**7**	**2**	**4**	**6**	**278**	**0**	**0**	**0**	**57**	**3.5**	**15**	**0**	**20**	**0**	**–5**	**4**	**0**	**1**	**1**	**6**	**0**	**0**	**0**
1994-95	**Hartford Whalers**	**NHL**	**28**	**0**	**4**	**4**	**0**	**6**	**6**	**141**	**0**	**0**	**0**	**15**	**0.0**	**6**	**0**	**5**	**0**	**1**	....	....	....	....	....	....	....	....
1995-96	**Hartford Whalers**	**NHL**	**55**	**2**	**4**	**6**	**2**	**3**	**5**	**230**	**0**	**0**	**1**	**19**	**10.5**	**6**	**0**	**10**	**0**	**–4**	....	....	....	....	....	....	....	....
1996-97	**Hartford Whalers**	**NHL**	**28**	**1**	**2**	**3**	**1**	**2**	**3**	**122**	**0**	**0**	**0**	**5**	**20.0**	**6**	**0**	**4**	**0**	**2**	....	....	....	....	....	....	....	....
	Toronto Maple Leafs	**NHL**	**2**	**0**	**0**	**0**	**0**	**0**	**0**	**27**	**0**	**0**	**0**	**1**	**0.0**	**0**	**0**	**0**	**0**	**0**	....	....	....	....	....	....	....	....
1997-98	**St. Louis Blues**	**NHL**	**67**	**4**	**3**	**7**	**5**	**3**	**8**	**231**	**0**	**0**	**1**	**29**	**13.8**	**16**	**0**	**6**	**0**	**10**	**7**	**0**	**0**	**0**	**23**	**0**	**0**	**0**
1998-99	**St. Louis Blues**	**NHL**	**45**	**3**	**7**	**10**	**4**	**7**	**11**	**143**	**0**	**0**	**1**	**25**	**12.0**	**15**	**2**	**11**	**0**	**2**	....	....	....	....	....	....	....	....
99-2000	**St. Louis Blues**	**NHL**	**25**	**0**	**1**	**1**	**0**	**1**	**1**	**118**	**0**	**0**	**0**	**14**	**0.0**	**1**	**0**	**6**	**0**	**–5**	....	....	....	....	....	....	....	....
	NHL Totals		**458**	**17**	**36**	**53**	**19**	**33**	**52**	**2017**	**0**	**0**	**4**	**232**	**7.3**	**88**	**2**	**100**	**0**		**27**	**1**	**1**	**2**	**100**	**0**	**0**	**0**

Won King Clancy Memorial Trophy (1998)

Signed as a free agent by **St. Louis**, February 23, 1988. Claimed by **Hartford** from **St. Louis** in NHL Waiver Draft, January 18, 1995. Traded to **Toronto** by **Hartford** for Toronto's 8th round choice (Hartford/Carolina selected Jaroslav Svoboda) in 1998 Entry Draft, March 18, 1997. Traded to **St. Louis** by **Toronto** for future considerations, September 30, 1997. • Missed majority of 1999-2000 season recovering from knee injury suffered in game vs. Dallas, November 8, 1999.

• CHASSE, Denis

RW – R. 6'2", 200 lbs. b: Montreal, Que., 2/7/1970.

Season	Club	League	GP	G	A	Pts	AG	AA	APts	PIM	PP	SH	GW	S	%	TGF	PGF	TGA	PGA	+/–	GP	G	A	Pts	PIM	PP	SH	GW
1985-86	Montreal-Bourassa	QAAA	32	5	3	8	....	....	....	....	....	....	....	....	....	....	....	....	....	....	....	....	....	....	....	....	....	....
1986-87	Montreal-Bourassa	QAAA	41	23	22	45	....	....	....	....	....	....	....	....	....	....	....	....	....	....	....	....	....	....	....	....	....	....
1987-88	St-Jean Lynx	QMJHL	13	0	1	1	....	....	....	2	....	....	....	....	....	....	....	....	....	....	1	0	0	0	0	....	....	....
1988-89	Verdun Jr. Canadiens	QMJHL	38	12	12	24	....	....	....	61	....	....	....	....	....	....	....	....	....	....	....	....	....	....	....	....	....	....
	Drummondville Voltigeurs	QMJHL	30	15	16	31	....	....	....	77	....	....	....	....	....	....	....	....	....	....	3	0	2	2	28	....	....	....
1989-90	Drummondville Voltigeurs	QMJHL	34	14	29	43	....	....	....	85	....	....	....	....	....	....	....	....	....	....	....	....	....	....	....	....	....	....
	Chicoutimi Sagueneens	QMJHL	33	19	27	46	....	....	....	105	....	....	....	....	....	....	....	....	....	....	7	7	4	11	50	....	....	....
1990-91	Drummondville Voltigeurs	QMJHL	62	47	54	101	....	....	....	246	....	....	....	....	....	....	....	....	....	....	13	9	11	20	56	....	....	....
	Drummondville Voltigeurs	Mem-Cup	4	3	0	3	....	....	....	10	....	....	....	....	....	....	....	....	....	....	....	....	....	....	....	....	....	....
1991-92	Halifax Citadels	AHL	73	26	35	61	....	....	....	254	....	....	....	....	....	....	....	....	....	....	....	....	....	....	....	....	....	....
1992-93	Halifax Citadels	AHL	75	35	41	76	....	....	....	242	....	....	....	....	....	....	....	....	....	....	....	....	....	....	....	....	....	....
1993-94	**St. Louis Blues**	**NHL**	**3**	**0**	**1**	**1**	**0**	**1**	**1**	**15**	**0**	**0**	**0**	**5**	**0.0**	**2**	**0**	**1**	**0**	**1**	....	....	....	....	....	....	....	....
	Cornwall Aces	AHL	48	27	39	66	....	....	....	194	....	....	....	....	....	....	....	....	....	....	....	....	....	....	....	....	....	....
1994-95	**St. Louis Blues**	**NHL**	**47**	**7**	**9**	**16**	**12**	**13**	**25**	**133**	**1**	**0**	**0**	**48**	**14.6**	**32**	**4**	**16**	**0**	**12**	**7**	**1**	**7**	**8**	**23**	**0**	**0**	**0**
1995-96	**St. Louis Blues**	**NHL**	**42**	**3**	**0**	**3**	**3**	**0**	**3**	**108**	**1**	**0**	**1**	**25**	**12.0**	**6**	**1**	**14**	**0**	**–9**	....	....	....	....	....	....	....	....
	Worcester IceCats	AHL	3	0	0	0	....	....	....	6	....	....	....	....	....	....	....	....	....	....	....	....	....	....	....	....	....	....
	Washington Capitals	**NHL**	**3**	**0**	**0**	**0**	**0**	**0**	**0**	**5**	**0**	**0**	**0**	**3**	**0.0**	**1**	**0**	**2**	**0**	**–1**	....	....	....	....	....	....	....	....
	Winnipeg Jets	**NHL**	**15**	**0**	**0**	**0**	**0**	**0**	**0**	**12**	**0**	**0**	**0**	**3**	**0.0**	**2**	**0**	**6**	**0**	**–4**	....	....	....	....	....	....	....	....
1996-97	**Ottawa Senators**	**NHL**	**22**	**1**	**4**	**5**	**1**	**4**	**5**	**19**	**0**	**0**	**0**	**12**	**8.3**	**6**	**0**	**3**	**0**	**3**	....	....	....	....	....	....	....	....
	Detroit Vipers	IHL	9	2	1	3	....	....	....	33	....	....	....	....	....	....	....	....	....	....	....	....	....	....	....	....	....	....
	Indianapolis Ice	IHL	3	0	0	0	....	....	....	10	....	....	....	....	....	....	....	....	....	....	4	1	1	2	23	....	....	....
1997-98	Mannheimer ERC	EuroHL	3	0	1	1	....	....	....	12	....	....	....	....	....	....	....	....	....	....	....	....	....	....	....	....	....	....
	Mannheimer ERC	Germany	15	2	5	7	....	....	....	72	....	....	....	....	....	....	....	....	....	....	....	....	....	....	....	....	....	....
	Augsburger EV Panther	Germany	30	6	6	12	....	....	....	97	....	....	....	....	....	....	....	....	....	....	....	....	....	....	....	....	....	....
1998-99	Bracknell Bees	Britain	33	13	22	35	....	....	....	108	....	....	....	....	....	....	....	....	....	....	6	2	1	3	24	....	....	....
99-2000	Bracknell Bees	BH-Cup	6	2	2	4	....	....	....	18	....	....	....	....	....	....	....	....	....	....	....	....	....	....	....	....	....	....
	Bracknell Bees	Britain	33	16	22	38	....	....	....	16	....	....	....	....	....	....	....	....	....	....	4	1	3	4	34	....	....	....
	NHL Totals		**132**	**11**	**14**	**25**	**16**	**18**	**34**	**292**	**2**	**0**	**1**	**96**	**11.5**	**49**	**5**	**42**	**0**		**7**	**1**	**7**	**8**	**23**	**0**	**0**	**0**

Signed as a free agent by **Quebec**, May 14, 1991. Traded to **St. Louis** by **Quebec** with Steve Duchesne for Garth Butcher, Ron Sutter and Bob Bassen, January 23, 1994. Traded to **Washington** by **St. Louis** for Rob Pearson, January 29, 1996. Traded to **Winnipeg** by **Washington** for Stewart Malgunas, February 15, 1996. Signed as a free agent by **Ottawa**, September 5, 1996. Traded to **Chicago** by **Ottawa** with the rights to Kevin Bolibruck and Ottawa's 6th round choice (traded back to Ottawa - Ottawa selected Christopher Neil) in 1998 Entry Draft for Mike Prokopec, March 18, 1997.

• CHEBATURKIN, Vladimir

D – L. 6'2", 213 lbs. b: Tyumen, USSR, 4/23/1975. NY Islanders' 3rd, 66th overall, in 1993.

Season	Club	League	GP	G	A	Pts	AG	AA	APts	PIM	PP	SH	GW	S	%	TGF	PGF	TGA	PGA	+/–	GP	G	A	Pts	PIM	PP	SH	GW
1992-93	Kristall Elektrostal	CIS-2	STATISTICS NOT AVAILABLE																									
	Russia	EJC-A	5	0	1	1	....	....	....	0	....	....	....	....	....	....	....	....	....	....	....	....	....	....	....	....	....	....
	Russia	WEC-A	6	0	1	1	....	....	....	0	....	....	....	....	....	....	....	....	....	....	....	....	....	....	....	....	....	....
1993-94	Kristall Elektrostal	CIS-2	42	4	4	8	....	....	....	38	....	....	....	....	....	....	....	....	....	....	....	....	....	....	....	....	....	....
1994-95	Kristall Elektrostal	CIS	52	2	6	8	....	....	....	90	....	....	....	....	....	....	....	....	....	....	....	....	....	....	....	....	....	....
	Russia	WJC-A	7	0	2	2	....	....	....	2	....	....	....	....	....	....	....	....	....	....	....	....	....	....	....	....	....	....
1995-96	Kristall Elektrostal	CIS	44	1	6	7	....	....	....	30	....	....	....	....	....	....	....	....	....	....	1	0	0	0	0	....	....	....
1996-97	Utah Grizzlies	IHL	68	0	4	4	....	....	....	34	....	....	....	....	....	....	....	....	....	....	....	....	....	....	....	....	....	....
1997-98	**New York Islanders**	**NHL**	**2**	**0**	**2**	**2**	**0**	**2**	**2**	**0**	**0**	**0**	**0**	**0**	**0.0**	**3**	**1**	**3**	**0**	**–1**	....	....	....	....	....	....	....	....
	Kentucky Thoroughblades	AHL	54	6	8	14	....	....	....	52	....	....	....	....	....	....	....	....	....	....	2	0	0	0	4	....	....	....
1998-99	**New York Islanders**	**NHL**	**8**	**0**	**0**	**0**	**0**	**0**	**0**	**12**	**0**	**0**	**0**	**4**	**0.0**	**8**	**0**	**3**	**1**	**6**	....	....	....	....	....	....	....	....
	Lowell Lock Monsters	AHL	69	2	12	14	....	....	....	85	....	....	....	....	....	....	....	....	....	....	3	0	0	0	0	....	....	....
99-2000	**New York Islanders**	**NHL**	**17**	**1**	**1**	**2**	**1**	**1**	**2**	**8**	**0**	**0**	**0**	**9**	**11.1**	**11**	**0**	**22**	**8**	**–3**	....	....	....	....	....	....	....	....
	Lowell Lock Monsters	AHL	63	1	8	9	....	....	....	118	....	....	....	....	....	....	....	....	....	....	7	0	4	4	11	....	....	....
	NHL Totals		**27**	**1**	**3**	**4**	**1**	**3**	**4**	**20**	**0**	**0**	**0**	**13**	**7.7**	**22**	**1**	**28**	**9**		....	....	....	....	....	....	....	....

Signed as a free agent by **St. Louis**, June 9, 2000.

• CHELIOS, Chris

D – R. 6'1", 190 lbs. b: Chicago, IL, 1/25/1962. Montreal's 5th, 40th overall, in 1981.

Season	Club	League	GP	G	A	Pts	AG	AA	APts	PIM	PP	SH	GW	S	%	TGF	PGF	TGA	PGA	+/–	GP	G	A	Pts	PIM	PP	SH	GW
1979-80	Moose Jaw Canucks	SJHL	53	12	31	43	....	....	....	118	....	....	....	....	....	....	....	....	....	....	....	....	....	....	....	....	....	....
1980-81	Moose Jaw Canucks	SJHL	54	23	64	87	....	....	....	175	....	....	....	....	....	....	....	....	....	....	....	....	....	....	....	....	....	....
1981-82	University of Wisconsin	WCHA	43	6	43	49	....	....	....	50	....	....	....	....	....	....	....	....	....	....	....	....	....	....	....	....	....	....
	United States	WJC-A	7	1	2	3	....	....	....	10	....	....	....	....	....	....	....	....	....	....	....	....	....	....	....	....	....	....
1982-83	University of Wisconsin	WCHA	26	9	17	26	....	....	....	50	....	....	....	....	....	....	....	....	....	....	....	....	....	....	....	....	....	....

			REGULAR SEASON																		PLAYOFFS							
Season	**Club**	**League**	**GP**	**G**	**A**	**Pts**	**AG**	**AA**	**APts**	**PIM**	**PP**	**SH**	**GW**	**S**	**%**	**TGF**	**PGF**	**TGA**	**PGA**	**+/–**	**GP**	**G**	**A**	**Pts**	**PIM**	**PP**	**SH**	**GW**
1983-84	United States	Nat-Team	60	14	35	49	....	....	....	58	....	....	....	....	....	....	....	....	....	....	....	....	....	....	....	....	....	....
	United States	Olympics	6	0	4	4	....	....	....	8	....	....	....	....	....	....	....	....	....	....	....	....	....	....	....	....	....	....
	Montreal Canadiens	**NHL**	**12**	**0**	**2**	**2**	**0**	**1**	**1**	**12**	**0**	**0**	**0**	**23**	**0.0**	**8**	**0**	**16**	**3**	**–5**	**15**	**1**	**9**	**10**	**17**	**1**	**0**	**0**
1984-85	United States	Can-Cup	6	0	2	2	....	....	....	2	....	....	....	....	....	....	....	....	....	....	....	....	....	....	....	....	....	....
	Montreal Canadiens	**NHL**	**74**	**9**	**55**	**64**	**7**	**37**	**44**	**87**	**2**	**1**	**0**	**199**	**4.5**	**139**	**43**	**106**	**21**	**11**	**9**	**2**	**8**	**10**	**17**	**2**	**0**	**0**
1985-86♦	**Montreal Canadiens**	**NHL**	**41**	**8**	**26**	**34**	**6**	**17**	**23**	**67**	**2**	**0**	**0**	**101**	**7.9**	**83**	**37**	**55**	**13**	**4**	**20**	**2**	**9**	**11**	**49**	**1**	**0**	**0**
1986-87	**Montreal Canadiens**	**NHL**	**71**	**11**	**33**	**44**	**9**	**24**	**33**	**124**	**6**	**0**	**2**	**141**	**7.8**	**102**	**35**	**97**	**25**	**–5**	**17**	**4**	**9**	**13**	**38**	**2**	**1**	**0**
	NHL All-Stars	RV-87	2	0	0	0	....	....	....	0	....	....	....	....	....	....	....	....	....	....	....	....	....	....	....	....	....	....
1987-88	United States	Can-Cup	5	0	2	2	....	....	....	2	....	....	....	....	....	....	....	....	....	....	....	....	....	....	....	....	....	....
	Montreal Canadiens	**NHL**	**71**	**20**	**41**	**61**	**17**	**29**	**46**	**172**	**10**	**1**	**5**	**199**	**10.1**	**125**	**38**	**105**	**32**	**14**	**11**	**3**	**1**	**4**	**29**	**1**	**0**	**0**
1988-89	**Montreal Canadiens**	**NHL**	**80**	**15**	**58**	**73**	**13**	**41**	**54**	**185**	**8**	**0**	**6**	**206**	**7.3**	**167**	**62**	**106**	**36**	**35**	**21**	**4**	**15**	**19**	**28**	**1**	**0**	**2**
1989-90	**Montreal Canadiens**	**NHL**	**53**	**9**	**22**	**31**	**8**	**16**	**24**	**136**	**1**	**2**	**1**	**123**	**7.3**	**82**	**19**	**74**	**31**	**20**	**5**	**0**	**1**	**1**	**8**	**0**	**0**	**0**
1990-91	**Chicago Blackhawks**	**NHL**	**77**	**12**	**52**	**64**	**11**	**40**	**51**	**192**	**5**	**2**	**2**	**187**	**6.4**	**143**	**63**	**97**	**40**	**23**	**6**	**1**	**7**	**8**	**46**	**1**	**0**	**0**
1991-92	United States	Can-Cup	8	1	3	4	....	....	....	4	....	....	....	....	....	....	....	....	....	....	....	....	....	....	....	....	....	....
	Chicago Blackhawks	**NHL**	**80**	**9**	**47**	**56**	**8**	**36**	**44**	**245**	**2**	**2**	**2**	**239**	**3.8**	**138**	**55**	**91**	**32**	**24**	**18**	**6**	**15**	**21**	**37**	**3**	**0**	**1**
1992-93	**Chicago Blackhawks**	**NHL**	**84**	**15**	**58**	**73**	**12**	**40**	**52**	**282**	**8**	**0**	**2**	**290**	**5.2**	**165**	**81**	**115**	**45**	**14**	**4**	**0**	**2**	**2**	**14**	**0**	**0**	**0**
1993-94	**Chicago Blackhawks**	**NHL**	**76**	**16**	**44**	**60**	**15**	**34**	**49**	**212**	**7**	**1**	**2**	**219**	**7.3**	**136**	**61**	**102**	**39**	**12**	**6**	**1**	**1**	**2**	**8**	**1**	**0**	**0**
	United States	WC-A	DID NOT PLAY																									
1994-95	EHC Biel-Bienne	Switz.	3	0	3	3	....	....	....	4	....	....	....	....	....	....	....	....	....	....	....	....	....	....	....	....	....	....
	Chicago Blackhawks	**NHL**	**48**	**5**	**33**	**38**	**9**	**49**	**58**	**72**	**3**	**1**	**0**	**166**	**3.0**	**94**	**40**	**59**	**22**	**17**	**16**	**4**	**7**	**11**	**12**	**0**	**1**	**3**
1995-96	**Chicago Blackhawks**	**NHL**	**81**	**14**	**58**	**72**	**14**	**48**	**62**	**140**	**7**	**0**	**3**	**219**	**6.4**	**151**	**54**	**115**	**43**	**25**	**9**	**0**	**3**	**3**	**8**	**0**	**0**	**0**
1996-97	United States	W-Cup	7	0	4	4	....	....	....	10	....	....	....	....	....	....	....	....	....	....	....	....	....	....	....	....	....	....
	Chicago Blackhawks	**NHL**	**72**	**10**	**38**	**48**	**11**	**34**	**45**	**112**	**2**	**0**	**2**	**194**	**5.2**	**111**	**34**	**93**	**32**	**16**	**6**	**0**	**1**	**1**	**8**	**0**	**0**	**0**
1997-98	**Chicago Blackhawks**	**NHL**	**81**	**3**	**39**	**42**	**4**	**38**	**42**	**151**	**1**	**0**	**0**	**205**	**1.5**	**105**	**38**	**112**	**38**	**–7**	....	....	....	....	....	....	....	....
	United States	Olympics	4	2	0	2	....	....	....	2	....	....	....	....	....	....	....	....	....	....	....	....	....	....	....	....	....	....
1998-99	**Chicago Blackhawks**	**NHL**	**65**	**8**	**26**	**34**	**9**	**25**	**34**	**89**	**2**	**1**	**0**	**172**	**4.7**	**79**	**26**	**97**	**40**	**–4**	....	....	....	....	....	....	....	....
	Detroit Red Wings	**NHL**	**10**	**1**	**1**	**2**	**1**	**1**	**2**	**4**	**1**	**0**	**1**	**15**	**6.7**	**10**	**2**	**4**	**1**	**5**	**10**	**0**	**4**	**4**	**14**	**0**	**0**	**0**
99-2000	**Detroit Red Wings**	**NHL**	**81**	**3**	**31**	**34**	**3**	**29**	**32**	**103**	**0**	**0**	**0**	**135**	**2.2**	**115**	**13**	**79**	**25**	**48**	**9**	**0**	**1**	**1**	**8**	**0**	**0**	**0**
	NHL Totals		**1157**	**168**	**664**	**832**	**157**	**539**	**696**	**2385**	**67**	**11**	**28**	**3033**	**5.5**	**1953**	**701**	**1523**	**518**		**182**	**28**	**93**	**121**	**341**	**13**	**2**	**6**

WCHA Second All-Star Team (1983) • NCAA Championship All-Tournament Team (1983) • NHL All-Rookie Team (1985) • NHL First All-Star Team (1989, 1993, 1995, 1996) • Won James Norris Memorial Trophy (1989, 1993, 1996) • NHL Second All-Star Team (1991, 1997) • Canada Cup All-Star Team (1991) • World Cup All-Star Team (1996) • Played in NHL All-Star Game (1985, 1990, 1991, 1992, 1993, 1994, 1996, 1997, 1998, 2000)

Traded to **Chicago** by **Montreal** with Montreal's 2nd round choice (Michael Pomichter) in 1991 Entry Draft for Denis Savard, June 29, 1990. Traded to **Detroit** by **Chicago** for Anders Eriksson and Detroit's 1st round choices in 1999 (Steve McCarthy) and 2001 Entry Drafts, March 23, 1999.

• CHERNOFF, Mike

Michael Terence LW – L. 5'10", 175 lbs. b: Yorkton, Sask., 5/13/1946.

Season	Club	League	GP	G	A	Pts	AG	AA	APts	PIM	PP	SH	GW	S	%	TGF	PGF	TGA	PGA	+/–	GP	G	A	Pts	PIM	PP	SH	GW
1963-64	Moose Jaw Canucks	SJHL	62	7	14	21	....	....	....	170	....	....	....	....	....	....	....	....	....	....	5	0	1	1	6	....	....	....
1964-65	Moose Jaw Canucks	SJHL	52	22	25	47	....	....	....	106	....	....	....	....	....	....	....	....	....	....	....	....	....	....	....	....	....	....
1965-66	Moose Jaw Canucks	SJHL	60	42	34	76	....	....	....	106	....	....	....	....	....	....	....	....	....	....	2	0	1	1	0	....	....	....
1966-67	St. Louis Braves	CPHL	70	14	16	30	....	....	....	55	....	....	....	....	....	....	....	....	....	....	....	....	....	....	....	....	....	....
1967-68	Dallas Black Hawks	CPHL	31	8	7	15	....	....	....	41	....	....	....	....	....	....	....	....	....	....	....	....	....	....	....	....	....	....
1968-69	**Minnesota North Stars**	**NHL**	**1**	**0**	**0**	**0**	**0**	**0**	**0**	**0**	**0**	**0**	**0**	**0**	**0.0**	**0**	**0**	**0**	**0**	**0**	....	....	....	....	....	....	....	....
	Memphis South Stars	CHL	68	20	31	51	....	....	....	48	....	....	....	....	....	....	....	....	....	....	....	....	....	....	....	....	....	....
1969-70	Iowa Stars	CHL	69	36	39	75	....	....	....	29	....	....	....	....	....	....	....	....	....	....	11	7	4	11	6	....	....	....
1970-71	Cleveland Barons	AHL	72	31	23	54	....	....	....	37	....	....	....	....	....	....	....	....	....	....	8	3	1	4	2	....	....	....
1971-72	Cleveland Barons	AHL	71	8	13	21	....	....	....	30	....	....	....	....	....	....	....	....	....	....	6	0	0	0	0	....	....	....
1972-73	Jacksonville Barons	AHL	76	35	33	68	....	....	....	37	....	....	....	....	....	....	....	....	....	....	....	....	....	....	....	....	....	....
1973-74	Vancouver Blazers	WHA	36	11	10	21	....	....	....	4	....	....	....	....	....	....	....	....	....	....	....	....	....	....	....	....	....	....
	Roanoke Valley Rebels	SHL	4	2	4	6	....	....	....	7	....	....	....	....	....	....	....	....	....	....	....	....	....	....	....	....	....	....
1974-75	Vancouver Blazers	WHA	3	0	0	0	....	....	....	0	....	....	....	....	....	....	....	....	....	....	....	....	....	....	....	....	....	....
	Tulsa Oilers	CHL	20	7	12	19	....	....	....	25	....	....	....	....	....	....	....	....	....	....	....	....	....	....	....	....	....	....
	Johnstown Jets	NAHL	41	9	19	28	....	....	....	32	....	....	....	....	....	....	....	....	....	....	14	8	6	14	0	....	....	....
	NHL Totals		**1**	**0**	**0**	**0**	**0**	**0**	**0**	**0**	**0**	**0**	**0**	**0**	**0.0**	**0**	**0**	**0**	**0**		....	....	....	....	....	....	....	....
	Other Major League Totals		39	11	10	21	....	....	....	4	....	....	....	....	....	....	....	....	....	....	....	....	....	....	....	....	....	....

Signed as a free agent by **Minnesota**, October, 1968. Selected by **Winnipeg** (WHA) in 1972 WHA General Player Draft, February 12, 1972. WHA rights traded to **Vancouver** (WHA) by **Winnipeg** (WHA) for cash, July, 1973.

• CHERNOMAZ, Rich

Richard M. RW – R. 5'8", 185 lbs. b: Selkirk, Man., 9/1/1963. Colorado's 2nd, 26th overall, in 1981.

Season	Club	League	GP	G	A	Pts	AG	AA	APts	PIM	PP	SH	GW	S	%	TGF	PGF	TGA	PGA	+/–	GP	G	A	Pts	PIM	PP	SH	GW
1979-80	Saskatoon Olympics	SJHL	51	33	37	70	....	....	....	75	....	....	....	....	....	....	....	....	....	....	....	....	....	....	....	....	....	....
	Saskatoon Blades	WHL	25	9	10	19	....	....	....	33	....	....	....	....	....	....	....	....	....	....	....	....	....	....	....	....	....	....
1980-81	Victoria Cougars	WHL	72	49	64	113	....	....	....	92	....	....	....	....	....	....	....	....	....	....	15	11	15	26	38	....	....	....
	Victoria Cougars	Mem-Cup	4	0	1	1	....	....	....	6	....	....	....	....	....	....	....	....	....	....	....	....	....	....	....	....	....	....
1981-82	Victoria Cougars	WHL	49	36	62	98	....	....	....	69	....	....	....	....	....	....	....	....	....	....	4	1	2	3	13	....	....	....
	Colorado Rockies	**NHL**	**2**	**0**	**0**	**0**	**0**	**0**	**0**	**0**	**0**	**0**	**0**	**2**	**0.0**	**0**	**0**	**2**	**0**	**–2**	....	....	....	....	....	....	....	....
1982-83	Victoria Cougars	WHL	64	71	53	124	....	....	....	113	....	....	....	....	....	....	....	....	....	....	12	10	5	15	18	....	....	....
1983-84	**New Jersey Devils**	**NHL**	**7**	**2**	**1**	**3**	**2**	**1**	**3**	**2**	**0**	**0**	**0**	**7**	**28.6**	**3**	**0**	**6**	**0**	**–3**	....	....	....	....	....	....	....	....
	Maine Mariners	AHL	69	17	29	46	....	....	....	39	....	....	....	....	....	....	....	....	....	....	2	0	1	1	0	....	....	....
1984-85	**New Jersey Devils**	**NHL**	**3**	**0**	**2**	**2**	**0**	**1**	**1**	**2**	**0**	**0**	**0**	**2**	**0.0**	**2**	**0**	**0**	**0**	**2**	....	....	....	....	....	....	....	....
	Maine Mariners	AHL	64	17	34	51	....	....	....	64	....	....	....	....	....	....	....	....	....	....	10	2	2	4	4	....	....	....
1985-86	Maine Mariners	AHL	78	21	28	49	....	....	....	82	....	....	....	....	....	....	....	....	....	....	5	0	0	0	2	....	....	....
1986-87	**New Jersey Devils**	**NHL**	**25**	**6**	**4**	**10**	**5**	**3**	**8**	**8**	**2**	**0**	**0**	**44**	**13.6**	**15**	**4**	**23**	**1**	**–11**	....	....	....	....	....	....	....	....
	Maine Mariners	AHL	58	35	27	62	....	....	....	65	....	....	....	....	....	....	....	....	....	....	....	....	....	....	....	....	....	....
1987-88	**Calgary Flames**	**NHL**	**2**	**1**	**0**	**1**	**1**	**0**	**1**	**0**	**0**	**0**	**0**	**5**	**20.0**	**3**	**0**	**2**	**0**	**1**	....	....	....	....	....	....	....	....
	Salt Lake Golden Eagles	IHL	73	48	47	95	....	....	....	122	....	....	....	....	....	....	....	....	....	....	18	4	14	18	30	....	....	....
1988-89	**Calgary Flames**	**NHL**	**1**	**0**	**0**	**0**	**0**	**0**	**0**	**0**	**0**	**0**	**0**	**2**	**0.0**	**0**	**0**	**1**	**0**	**–1**	....	....	....	....	....	....	....	....
	Salt Lake Golden Eagles	IHL	81	33	68	101	....	....	....	122	....	....	....	....	....	....	....	....	....	....	14	7	5	12	47	....	....	....
1989-90	Salt Lake Golden Eagles	IHL	65	39	35	74	....	....	....	170	....	....	....	....	....	....	....	....	....	....	11	6	6	12	32	....	....	....
1990-91	Salt Lake Golden Eagles	IHL	81	39	58	97	....	....	....	213	....	....	....	....	....	....	....	....	....	....	4	3	1	4	8	....	....	....
1991-92	**Calgary Flames**	**NHL**	**11**	**0**	**0**	**0**	**0**	**0**	**0**	**6**	**0**	**0**	**0**	**21**	**0.0**	**4**	**4**	**11**	**2**	**–9**	....	....	....	....	....	....	....	....
	Salt Lake Golden Eagles	IHL	66	20	40	60	....	....	....	201	....	....	....	....	....	....	....	....	....	....	5	1	2	3	10	....	....	....
1992-93	Salt Lake Golden Eagles	IHL	76	26	48	74	....	....	....	172	....	....	....	....	....	....	....	....	....	....	....	....	....	....	....	....	....	....
1993-94	St. John's Maple Leafs	AHL	78	45	65	110	....	....	....	199	....	....	....	....	....	....	....	....	....	....	11	5	11	16	18	....	....	....
1994-95	St. John's Maple Leafs	AHL	77	24	45	69	....	....	....	235	....	....	....	....	....	....	....	....	....	....	5	1	1	2	8	....	....	....
	Canada	WC-A	8	0	3	3	....	....	....	10	....	....	....	....	....	....	....	....	....	....	....	....	....	....	....	....	....	....
1995-96	Schwenningen Wild Wings	Germany	49	24	43	67	....	....	....	105	....	....	....	....	....	....	....	....	....	....	2	1	1	2	24	....	....	....
1996-97	Schwenningen Wild Wings	Germany	47	25	39	64	....	....	....	126	....	....	....	....	....	....	....	....	....	....	5	3	5	8	8	....	....	....
1997-98	Schwenningen Wild Wings	Germany	51	12	37	49	....	....	....	156	....	....	....	....	....	....	....	....	....	....	....	....	....	....	....	....	....	....
1998-99	Schwenningen Wild Wings	Germany	43	9	38	47	....	....	....	177	....	....	....	....	....	....	....	....	....	....	....	....	....	....	....	....	....	....
99-2000	Schwenningen Wild Wings	Germany	DID NOT PLAY – COACHING																									
	NHL Totals		**51**	**9**	**7**	**16**	**8**	**5**	**13**	**18**	**2**	**0**	**0**	**83**	**10.8**	**27**	**8**	**45**	**3**		....	....	....	....	....	....	....	....

WHL First All-Star Team (1983) • IHL Second All-Star Team (1988) • AHL First All-Star Team (1994) • Won Les Cunningham Award (MVP - AHL) (1994)

Transferred to **New Jersey** after **Colorado** franchise relocated, June 30, 1982. Signed as a free agent by **Calgary**, August 4, 1987. Signed as a free agent by **Toronto**, August 3, 1993. • Played w/ RHI's Utah Rollerblades in 1993 (13-9-24-33-43) and Las Vegas Fish in 1994 (17-24-30-54-63).

• CHERRY, Dick

Richard John D – L. 6', 195 lbs. b: Kingston, Ont., 3/28/1937.

Season	Club	League	GP	G	A	Pts	AG	AA	APts	PIM	PP	SH	GW	S	%	TGF	PGF	TGA	PGA	+/–	GP	G	A	Pts	PIM	PP	SH	GW
1955-56	Barrie Flyers	OHA-Jr.	48	18	32	50	....	....	....	69	....	....	....	....	....	....	....	....	....	....	18	1	3	4	19	....	....	....
1956-57	Barrie Flyers	OHA-Jr.	52	15	30	45	....	....	....	42	....	....	....	....	....	....	....	....	....	....	3	1	0	1	6	....	....	....
	Boston Bruins	**NHL**	**6**	**0**	**0**	**0**	**0**	**0**	**0**	**4**	....	....	....	....	....	....	....	....	....	....	....	....	....	....	....	....	....	....

			REGULAR SEASON																		PLAYOFFS							
Season	Club	League	GP	G	A	Pts	AG	AA	APts	PIM	PP	SH	GW	S	%	TGF	PGF	TGA	PGA	+/–	GP	G	A	Pts	PIM	PP	SH	GW
1957-58	Quebec Aces	QHL	47	3	15	18	....	....	....	27	....	....	....	....	....	....	....	....	....	....	....	....	....	....	....	....	....	....
	Springfield Indians	AHL	12	0	0	0	....	....	....	6	....	....	....	....	....	....	....	....	....	....	6	0	0	0	0	....	....	....
1958-59	Providence Reds	AHL	65	2	9	11	....	....	....	66	....	....	....	....	....	....	....	....	....	....	....	....	....	....	....	....	....	....
1959-60	Providence Reds	AHL	71	5	13	18	....	....	....	52	....	....	....	....	....	....	....	....	....	....	5	0	0	0	4	....	....	....
1960-61	Providence Reds	AHL	68	2	20	22	....	....	....	66	....	....	....	....	....	....	....	....	....	....	....	....	....	....	....	....	....	....
1961-62	Kingston Frontenacs	EPHL	43	11	24	35	....	....	....	29	....	....	....	....	....	....	....	....	....	....	10	4	3	7	9	....	....	....
1962-63	Kingston Frontenacs	EPHL	53	28	32	60	....	....	....	10	....	....	....	....	....	....	....	....	....	....	5	*6	3	9	0	....	....	....
1963-64			OUT OF HOCKEY – RETIRED																									
1964-65			OUT OF HOCKEY – RETIRED																									
1965-66	Kingston Aces	OHA-Sr.	25	20	27	47	....	....	....	27	....	....	....	....	....	....	....	....	....	....	....	....	....	....	....	....	....	....
	Guelph Regals	Al-Cup	5	0	2	2	....	....	....	2	....	....	....	....	....	....	....	....	....	....	....	....	....	....	....	....	....	....
1966-67	Oklahoma City Blazers	CPHL	69	8	25	33	....	....	....	86	....	....	....	....	....	....	....	....	....	....	11	1	4	5	13	....	....	....
1967-68			OUT OF HOCKEY – RETIRED																									
1968-69	**Philadelphia Flyers**	**NHL**	**71**	**9**	**6**	**15**	**9**	**5**	**14**	**18**	**1**	**1**	**2**	**91**	**9.9**	**23**	**2**	**51**	**19**	**–11**	**4**	**1**	**0**	**1**	**4**	**0**	**0**	**0**
1969-70	**Philadelphia Flyers**	**NHL**	**68**	**3**	**4**	**7**	**3**	**4**	**7**	**23**	**0**	**0**	**1**	**99**	**3.0**	**22**	**3**	**61**	**18**	**–24**	....	....	....	....	....	....	....	....
1970-71	Oklahoma City Blazers	CHL	64	14	50	64	....	....	....	44	....	....	....	....	....	....	....	....	....	....	5	0	6	6	4	....	....	....
1971-72	Kingston Aces	OHA-Sr.	21	3	14	17	....	....	....	27	....	....	....	....	....	....	....	....	....	....	....	....	....	....	....	....	....	....
1972-73	Kingston Aces	OHA-Sr.	41	10	33	43	....	....	....	14	....	....	....	....	....	....	....	....	....	....	....	....	....	....	....	....	....	....
1973-74			OUT OF HOCKEY – RETIRED																									
1974-75	Napanee Comets	OHA-Sr.	39	18	41	59	....	....	....	14	....	....	....	....	....	....	....	....	....	....	....	....	....	....	....	....	....	....
	NHL Totals		**145**	**12**	**10**	**22**	**12**	**9**	**21**	**45**	....	....	....	....	....	....	....	....	....	....	**4**	**1**	**0**	**1**	**4**	....	....	....

• Brother of Don (Grapes) • EPHL Second All-Star Team (1963) • OHA-Sr. Second All-Star Team (1966)

• Retired to teach high-school in Kingston, 1963-1965. Claimed by **Philadelphia** from **Boston** in Expansion Draft, June 6, 1967. Claimed by **Boston** from **Philadelphia** in Intra-League Draft, June 9, 1970.

• CHERVYAKOV, Denis

Denis V. D – L. 6', 185 lbs. b: Leningrad, USSR, 4/20/1970. Boston's 9th, 256th overall, in 1992.

Season	Club	League	GP	G	A	Pts	AG	AA	APts	PIM	PP	SH	GW	S	%	TGF	PGF	TGA	PGA	+/–	GP	G	A	Pts	PIM	PP	SH	GW
1990-91	Torpedo Yaroslavl	Fr-Tour	1	0	0	0	....	....	....	2	....	....	....	....	....	....	....	....	....	....	....	....	....	....	....	....	....	....
	SKA Leningrad	USSR	28	2	1	3	....	....	....	40	....	....	....	....	....	....	....	....	....	....	....	....	....	....	....	....	....	....
1991-92	Dynamo Riga	CIS	14	0	1	1	....	....	....	12	....	....	....	....	....	....	....	....	....	....	....	....	....	....	....	....	....	....
1992-93	**Boston Bruins**	**NHL**	**2**	**0**	**0**	**0**	**0**	**0**	**0**	**2**	**0**	**0**	**0**	**2**	**0.0**	**1**	**0**	**2**	**0**	**–1**	....	....	....	....	....	....	....	....
	Providence Bruins	AHL	48	4	12	16	....	....	....	99	....	....	....	....	....	....	....	....	....	....	....	....	....	....	....	....	....	....
	Atlanta Knights	IHL	1	0	0	0	....	....	....	0	....	....	....	....	....	....	....	....	....	....	....	....	....	....	....	....	....	....
1993-94	Providence Bruins	AHL	58	2	16	18	....	....	....	128	....	....	....	....	....	....	....	....	....	....	....	....	....	....	....	....	....	....
1994-95	Providence Bruins	AHL	65	1	18	19	....	....	....	130	....	....	....	....	....	....	....	....	....	....	10	0	2	2	14	....	....	....
1995-96	Providence Bruins	AHL	64	3	7	10	....	....	....	58	....	....	....	....	....	....	....	....	....	....	4	1	0	1	21	....	....	....
1996-97	Kentucky Thoroughblades	AHL	52	2	11	13	....	....	....	78	....	....	....	....	....	....	....	....	....	....	....	....	....	....	....	....	....	....
1997-98	HC Assat-Pori	Finland	2	0	0	0	....	....	....	2	....	....	....	....	....	....	....	....	....	....	....	....	....	....	....	....	....	....
	Lukko Rauma	Finland	24	0	0	0	....	....	....	14	....	....	....	....	....	....	....	....	....	....	....	....	....	....	....	....	....	....
	Tappara Tampere	Finland	14	0	2	2	....	....	....	14	....	....	....	....	....	....	....	....	....	....	4	0	0	0	0	....	....	....
1998-99	Portland Pirates	AHL	13	0	0	0	....	....	....	15	....	....	....	....	....	....	....	....	....	....	....	....	....	....	....	....	....	....
	Cincinnati Cyclones	IHL	32	3	3	6	....	....	....	62	....	....	....	....	....	....	....	....	....	....	....	....	....	....	....	....	....	....
	Baton Rouge Kingfish	ECHL	4	1	3	4	....	....	....	16	....	....	....	....	....	....	....	....	....	....	....	....	....	....	....	....	....	....
	Orlando Solar Bears	IHL	12	0	2	2	....	....	....	39	....	....	....	....	....	....	....	....	....	....	9	0	0	0	16	....	....	....
99-2000	Vasteras IK	Sweden	33	0	2	2	....	....	....	*136	....	....	....	....	....	....	....	....	....	....	....	....	....	....	....	....	....	....
	Hannover Scorpions	Germany	14	0	2	2	....	....	....	22	....	....	....	....	....	....	....	....	....	....	....	....	....	....	....	....	....	....
	NHL Totals		**2**	**0**	**0**	**0**	**0**	**0**	**0**	**2**	**0**	**0**	**0**	**2**	**0.0**	**1**	**0**	**2**	**0**		....	....	....	....	....	....	....	....

Signed as a free agent by **NY Islanders**, September 12, 1996.

• CHIASSON, Steve

D – L. 6'1", 205 lbs. b: Barrie, Ont., 4/14/1967 d: 5/3/1999. Detroit's 3rd, 50th overall, in 1985.

Season	Club	League	GP	G	A	Pts	AG	AA	APts	PIM	PP	SH	GW	S	%	TGF	PGF	TGA	PGA	+/–	GP	G	A	Pts	PIM	PP	SH	GW
1982-83	Peterborough Travellers	OMHA	40	25	35	60	....	....	....	120	....	....	....	....	....	....	....	....	....	....	....	....	....	....	....	....	....	....
1983-84	Guelph Platers	OHL	55	1	9	10	....	....	....	112	....	....	....	....	....	....	....	....	....	....	....	....	....	....	....	....	....	....
1984-85	Guelph Platers	OHL	61	8	22	30	....	....	....	139	....	....	....	....	....	....	....	....	....	....	....	....	....	....	....	....	....	....
1985-86	Guelph Platers	OHL	54	12	30	42	....	....	....	126	....	....	....	....	....	....	....	....	....	....	18	10	10	20	37	....	....	....
	Guelph Platers	Mem-Cup	4	1	4	5	....	....	....	4	....	....	....	....	....	....	....	....	....	....	....	....	....	....	....	....	....	....
1986-87	**Detroit Red Wings**	**NHL**	**45**	**1**	**4**	**5**	**1**	**3**	**4**	**73**	**0**	**0**	**0**	**44**	**2.3**	**31**	**10**	**32**	**4**	**–7**	**2**	**0**	**0**	**0**	**19**	**0**	**0**	**0**
	Canada	WJC-A	6	2	2	4	....	....	....	21	....	....	....	....	....	....	....	....	....	....	....	....	....	....	....	....	....	....
1987-88	**Detroit Red Wings**	**NHL**	**29**	**2**	**9**	**11**	**2**	**6**	**8**	**57**	**0**	**0**	**0**	**45**	**4.4**	**38**	**5**	**31**	**13**	**15**	**9**	**2**	**2**	**4**	**31**	**1**	**0**	**0**
	Adirondack Red Wings	AHL	23	6	11	17	....	....	....	58	....	....	....	....	....	....	....	....	....	....	....	....	....	....	....	....	....	....
1988-89	**Detroit Red Wings**	**NHL**	**65**	**12**	**35**	**47**	**10**	**25**	**35**	**149**	**5**	**2**	**0**	**187**	**6.4**	**115**	**36**	**112**	**27**	**–6**	**5**	**2**	**1**	**3**	**6**	**1**	**0**	**0**
1989-90	**Detroit Red Wings**	**NHL**	**67**	**14**	**28**	**42**	**12**	**20**	**32**	**114**	**4**	**0**	**2**	**190**	**7.4**	**106**	**33**	**112**	**23**	**–16**	....	....	....	....	....	....	....	....
1990-91	**Detroit Red Wings**	**NHL**	**42**	**3**	**17**	**20**	**3**	**13**	**16**	**80**	**1**	**0**	**1**	**101**	**3.0**	**55**	**16**	**50**	**11**	**0**	**5**	**3**	**1**	**4**	**19**	**1**	**0**	**0**
1991-92	**Detroit Red Wings**	**NHL**	**62**	**10**	**24**	**34**	**9**	**18**	**27**	**136**	**5**	**0**	**2**	**143**	**7.0**	**104**	**33**	**78**	**29**	**22**	**11**	**1**	**5**	**6**	**12**	**1**	**0**	**0**
1992-93	**Detroit Red Wings**	**NHL**	**79**	**12**	**50**	**62**	**10**	**34**	**44**	**155**	**6**	**0**	**1**	**227**	**5.3**	**159**	**61**	**130**	**46**	**14**	**7**	**2**	**2**	**4**	**19**	**1**	**0**	**1**
1993-94	**Detroit Red Wings**	**NHL**	**82**	**13**	**33**	**46**	**12**	**26**	**38**	**122**	**4**	**1**	**2**	**238**	**5.5**	**121**	**35**	**104**	**35**	**17**	**7**	**2**	**3**	**5**	**2**	**2**	**0**	**1**
1994-95	**Calgary Flames**	**NHL**	**45**	**2**	**23**	**25**	**4**	**34**	**38**	**39**	**1**	**0**	**0**	**110**	**1.8**	**69**	**23**	**48**	**12**	**10**	**7**	**1**	**2**	**3**	**9**	**1**	**0**	**0**
1995-96	**Calgary Flames**	**NHL**	**76**	**8**	**25**	**33**	**8**	**20**	**28**	**62**	**5**	**0**	**2**	**175**	**4.6**	**92**	**27**	**101**	**39**	**3**	**4**	**2**	**1**	**3**	**0**	**0**	**0**	**0**
1996-97	**Calgary Flames**	**NHL**	**47**	**5**	**11**	**16**	**5**	**10**	**15**	**32**	**1**	**2**	**1**	**112**	**4.5**	**50**	**19**	**49**	**7**	**–11**	....	....	....	....	....	....	....	....
	Hartford Whalers	**NHL**	**18**	**3**	**11**	**14**	**3**	**10**	**13**	**7**	**3**	**0**	**0**	**56**	**5.4**	**26**	**14**	**27**	**5**	**–10**	....	....	....	....	....	....	....	....
	Canada	WC-A	11	0	3	3	....	....	....	8	....	....	....	....	....	....	....	....	....	....	....	....	....	....	....	....	....	....
1997-98	**Carolina Hurricanes**	**NHL**	**66**	**7**	**27**	**34**	**8**	**26**	**34**	**65**	**6**	**0**	**0**	**173**	**4.0**	**75**	**29**	**65**	**17**	**–2**	....	....	....	....	....	....	....	....
1998-99	**Carolina Hurricanes**	**NHL**	**28**	**1**	**8**	**9**	**1**	**8**	**9**	**16**	**1**	**0**	**0**	**74**	**1.4**	**30**	**13**	**20**	**10**	**7**	**6**	**1**	**2**	**3**	**2**	**1**	**0**	**0**
	NHL Totals		**751**	**93**	**305**	**398**	**88**	**253**	**341**	**1107**	**42**	**5**	**11**	**1875**	**5.0**	**1071**	**354**	**959**	**278**		**63**	**16**	**19**	**35**	**119**	**9**	**0**	**2**

Won Stafford Smythe Memorial Trophy (Memorial Cup Tournament MVP) (1986) • Played in NHL All-Star Game (1993)

Traded to **Calgary** by **Detroit** for Mike Vernon, June 29, 1994. Traded to **Hartford** by **Calgary** with Colorado's 3rd round choice (previously acquired, Hartford/Carolina selected Francis Lessard) in 1997 Entry Draft for Hnat Domenichelli, Glen Featherstone, New Jersey's 2nd round choice (previously acquired, Calgary selected Dimitri Kokorev) in 1997 Entry Draft and Vancouver's 3rd round choice (previously acquired, Calgary selected Paul Manning) in 1998 Entry Draft, March 5, 1997. Transferred to **Carolina** after **Hartford** franchise relocated, June 25, 1997. • Died of injuries suffered in automobile accident, May 3, 1999.

• CHIBIREV, Igor

C – L. 6', 180 lbs. b: Kiev, USSR, 4/19/1968. Hartford's 8th, 266th overall, in 1993.

Season	Club	League	GP	G	A	Pts	AG	AA	APts	PIM	PP	SH	GW	S	%	TGF	PGF	TGA	PGA	+/–	GP	G	A	Pts	PIM	PP	SH	GW
1987-88	CSKA Moscow	USSR	29	5	1	6	....	....	....	8	....	....	....	....	....	....	....	....	....	....	....	....	....	....	....	....	....	....
	Soviet Union	WJC-A	7	4	3	7	....	....	....	0	....	....	....	....	....	....	....	....	....	....	....	....	....	....	....	....	....	....
1988-89	CSKA Moscow	USSR	34	7	9	16	....	....	....	16	....	....	....	....	....	....	....	....	....	....	....	....	....	....	....	....	....	....
	CSKA Moscow	Super-S	2	0	0	0	....	....	....	0	....	....	....	....	....	....	....	....	....	....	....	....	....	....	....	....	....	....
1989-90	CSKA Moscow	Fr-Tour	1	1	0	1	....	....	....	0	....	....	....	....	....	....	....	....	....	....	....	....	....	....	....	....	....	....
	CSKA Moscow	USSR	46	8	2	10	....	....	....	12	....	....	....	....	....	....	....	....	....	....	....	....	....	....	....	....	....	....
	CSKA Moscow	Super-S	5	1	1	2	....	....	....	0	....	....	....	....	....	....	....	....	....	....	....	....	....	....	....	....	....	....
1990-91	CSKA Moscow	Fr-Tour	1	0	1	1	....	....	....	0	....	....	....	....	....	....	....	....	....	....	....	....	....	....	....	....	....	....
	CSKA Moscow	USSR	40	10	9	19	....	....	....	4	....	....	....	....	....	....	....	....	....	....	....	....	....	....	....	....	....	....
	CSKA Moscow	Super-S	7	0	1	1	....	....	....	15	....	....	....	....	....	....	....	....	....	....	....	....	....	....	....	....	....	....
1991-92	CSKA Moscow	CIS	38	21	17	38	....	....	....	46	....	....	....	....	....	....	....	....	....	....	....	....	....	....	....	....	....	....
1992-93	Fort Wayne Komets	IHL	60	33	36	69	....	....	....	2	....	....	....	....	....	....	....	....	....	....	12	*7	13	20	2	....	....	....
1993-94	**Hartford Whalers**	**NHL**	**37**	**4**	**11**	**15**	**4**	**9**	**13**	**2**	**0**	**0**	**1**	**30**	**13.3**	**18**	**3**	**10**	**2**	**7**	....	....	....	....	....	....	....	....
	Springfield Indians	AHL	36	28	23	51	....	....	....	4	....	....	....	....	....	....	....	....	....	....	....	....	....	....	....	....	....	....
1994-95	**Hartford Whalers**	**NHL**	**8**	**3**	**1**	**4**	**5**	**1**	**6**	**0**	**0**	**0**	**0**	**9**	**33.3**	**5**	**1**	**3**	**0**	**1**	....	....	....	....	....	....	....	....
	Fort Wayne Komets	IHL	56	34	28	62	....	....	....	10	....	....	....	....	....	....	....	....	....	....	....	....	....	....	....	....	....	....
1995-96	HC Ambri-Piotta	Switz.	36	*37	33	*70	....	....	....	12	....	....	....	....	....	....	....	....	....	....	6	5	6	11	4	....	....	....
1996-97	HC Ambri-Piotta	Switz.	29	15	26	41	....	....	....	2	....	....	....	....	....	....	....	....	....	....	....	....	....	....	....	....	....	....
	KAC Klagenfurt	Austria	8	2	5	7	....	....	....	2	....	....	....	....	....	....	....	....	....	....	....	....	....	....	....	....	....	....
1997-98	HC Ambri-Piotta	Switz.	40	*35	41	76	....	....	....	24	....	....	....	....	....	....	....	....	....	....	13	9	14	23	8	....	....	....

			REGULAR SEASON																		PLAYOFFS							
Season	Club	League	GP	G	A	Pts	AG	AA	APts	PIM	PP	SH	GW	S	%	TGF	PGF	TGA	PGA	+/-	GP	G	A	Pts	PIM	PP	SH	GW
1998-99	HC Fribourg-Gotteron	Switz.	32	13	14	27	....	....	....	25	....	....	....	....	....	....	....	....	....	....	....	....	....	....	....	....	....	....
	HC Fribourg-Gotteron	EuroHL	4	1	3	4	....	....	....	0	....	....	....	....	....	....	....	....	....	....	....	....	....	....	....	....	....	....
99-2000	Hannover Scorpions	Germany	60	*36	33	69	....	....	....	24	....	....	....	....	....	....	....	....	....	....	....	....	....	....	....	....	....	....
	NHL Totals		**45**	**7**	**12**	**19**	**9**	**10**	**19**	**2**	**0**	**0**	**1**	**39**	**17.9**	**23**	**4**	**13**	**2**		....	....	....	....	....	....	....	....

• CHICOINE, Dan

Daniel RW – R. 5'11", 192 lbs. b: Sherbrooke, Que., 11/30/1957. Cleveland's 2nd, 23rd overall, in 1977.

Season	Club	League	GP	G	A	Pts	AG	AA	APts	PIM	PP	SH	GW	S	%	TGF	PGF	TGA	PGA	+/-	GP	G	A	Pts	PIM	PP	SH	GW
1973-74	Sherbrooke Castors	QMJHL	64	8	18	26	....	....	....	43	....	....	....	....	....	....	....	....	....	....	....	....	....	....	....	....	....	....
1974-75	Sherbrooke Castors	QMJHL	56	15	37	52	....	....	....	41	....	....	....	....	....	....	....	....	....	....	....	....	....	....	....	....	....	....
	Sherbrooke Castors	Mem-Cup	3	0	0	0	....	....	....	2	....	....	....	....	....	....	....	....	....	....	....	....	....	....	....	....	....	....
1975-76	Sherbrooke Castors	QMJHL	67	44	47	91	....	....	....	76	....	....	....	....	....	....	....	....	....	....	....	....	....	....	....	....	....	....
1976-77	Sherbrooke Castors	QMJHL	67	46	44	90	....	....	....	118	....	....	....	....	....	....	....	....	....	....	....	....	....	....	....	....	....	....
	Sherbrooke Castors	Mem-Cup	4	1	0	1	....	....	....	6	....	....	....	....	....	....	....	....	....	....	....	....	....	....	....	....	....	....
1977-78	**Cleveland Barons**	**NHL**	**6**	**0**	**0**	**0**	**0**	**0**	**0**	**0**	**0**	**0**	**0**	**5**	**0.0**	**2**	**0**	**4**	**0**	**–2**	....	....	....	....	....	....	....	....
	Phoenix Roadrunners	CHL	17	2	7	9	....	....	....	24	....	....	....	....	....	....	....	....	....	....	....	....	....	....	....	....	....	....
	New Haven Nighthawks	AHL	41	5	11	16	....	....	....	33	....	....	....	....	....	....	....	....	....	....	14	1	3	4	16	....	....	....
1978-79	**Minnesota North Stars**	**NHL**	**1**	**0**	**0**	**0**	**0**	**0**	**0**	**0**	**0**	**0**	**0**	**0**	**0.0**	**0**	**0**	**0**	**0**	**0**	....	....	....	....	....	....	....	....
	Oklahoma City Stars	CHL	60	26	22	48	....	....	....	53	....	....	....	....	....	....	....	....	....	....	....	....	....	....	....	....	....	....
1979-80	**Minnesota North Stars**	**NHL**	**24**	**1**	**2**	**3**	**1**	**1**	**2**	**12**	**0**	**0**	**0**	**25**	**4.0**	**8**	**0**	**18**	**0**	**–10**	**1**	**0**	**0**	**0**	**0**	**0**	**0**	**0**
	Oklahoma City Stars	CHL	26	2	12	14	....	....	....	21	....	....	....	....	....	....	....	....	....	....	....	....	....	....	....	....	....	....
1980-81	Oklahoma City Stars	CHL	31	5	12	17	....	....	....	31	....	....	....	....	....	....	....	....	....	....	3	1	0	1	4	....	....	....
1981-82			OUT OF HOCKEY – RETIRED																									
1982-83	Sherbrooke Jets	AHL	21	2	4	6	....	....	....	26	....	....	....	....	....	....	....	....	....	....	....	....	....	....	....	....	....	....
	NHL Totals		**31**	**1**	**2**	**3**	**1**	**1**	**2**	**12**	**0**	**0**	**0**	**30**	**3.3**	**10**	**0**	**22**	**0**		**1**	**0**	**0**	**0**	**0**	**0**	**0**	**0**

Placed on **Minnesota** Reserve List after **Cleveland-Minnesota** Dispersal Draft, June 15, 1978. Claimed by **Minnesota** as a fill-in during Expansion Draft, June 13, 1979. Traded to **Quebec** by **Minnesota** for Nelson Burton, June 9, 1981.

• CHINNICK, Rick

Richard Vaughn RW – L. 5'11", 180 lbs. b: Chatham, Ont., 8/15/1953. Minnesota's 3rd, 41st overall, in 1973.

Season	Club	League	GP	G	A	Pts	AG	AA	APts	PIM	PP	SH	GW	S	%	TGF	PGF	TGA	PGA	+/-	GP	G	A	Pts	PIM	PP	SH	GW
1971-72	Peterborough Petes	OMJHL	63	21	30	51	....	....	....	25	....	....	....	....	....	....	....	....	....	....	15	4	9	13	4	....	....	....
	Peterborough Petes	Mem-Cup	3	1	1	2	....	....	....	4	....	....	....	....	....	....	....	....	....	....	....	....	....	....	....	....	....	....
1972-73	Peterborough Petes	OMJHL	63	42	44	86	....	....	....	31	....	....	....	....	....	....	....	....	....	....	....	....	....	....	....	....	....	....
1973-74	**Minnesota North Stars**	**NHL**	**1**	**0**	**1**	**1**	**0**	**1**	**1**	**0**	**0**	**0**	**0**	**1**	**0.0**	**1**	**0**	**1**	**0**	**0**	....	....	....	....	....	....	....	....
	New Haven Nighthawks	AHL	76	18	15	33	....	....	....	12	....	....	....	....	....	....	....	....	....	....	10	2	3	5	2	....	....	....
1974-75	**Minnesota North Stars**	**NHL**	**3**	**0**	**1**	**1**	**0**	**1**	**1**	**0**	**0**	**0**	**0**	**6**	**0.0**	**1**	**0**	**1**	**0**	**0**	....	....	....	....	....	....	....	....
	New Haven Nighthawks	AHL	58	20	17	37	....	....	....	19	....	....	....	....	....	....	....	....	....	....	16	10	7	17	4	....	....	....
1975-76	New Haven Nighthawks	AHL	75	21	40	61	....	....	....	8	....	....	....	....	....	....	....	....	....	....	3	0	1	1	0	....	....	....
1976-77	Saginaw Gears	IHL	78	37	33	70	....	....	....	24	....	....	....	....	....	....	....	....	....	....	19	9	14	23	0	....	....	....
1977-78	Saginaw Gears	IHL	77	30	45	75	....	....	....	18	....	....	....	....	....	....	....	....	....	....	5	1	5	6	0	....	....	....
1978-79			OUT OF HOCKEY – RETIRED																									
1979-80			OUT OF HOCKEY – RETIRED																									
1980-81	Chatham Maroons	OHA-Sr.	34	25	32	57	....	....	....	....	....	....	....	....	....	....	....	....	....	....	....	....	....	....	....	....	....	....
	NHL Totals		**4**	**0**	**2**	**2**	**0**	**2**	**2**	**0**	**0**	**0**	**0**	**7**	**0.0**	**2**	**0**	**2**	**0**		....	....	....	....	....	....	....	....

Traded to **Detroit** by **Minnesota** for Bryan Hextall Jr., November 21, 1975.

• CHIPPERFIELD, Ron

Ronald James "The Magnificent 7" C – R. 5'11", 186 lbs. b: Brandon, Man., 3/28/1954. California's 2nd, 17th overall, in 1974.

Season	Club	League	GP	G	A	Pts	AG	AA	APts	PIM	PP	SH	GW	S	%	TGF	PGF	TGA	PGA	+/-	GP	G	A	Pts	PIM	PP	SH	GW
1969-70	Dauphin Kings	MJHL	34	*39	40	79	....	....	....	18	....	....	....	....	....	....	....	....	....	....	....	....	....	....	....	....	....	....
	Dauphin Kings	Mem-Cup	6	3	1	4	....	....	....	0	....	....	....	....	....	....	....	....	....	....	....	....	....	....	....	....	....	....
1970-71	Brandon Wheat Kings	WCJHL	64	40	43	83	....	....	....	62	....	....	....	....	....	....	....	....	....	....	....	....	....	....	....	....	....	....
1971-72	Brandon Wheat Kings	WCJHL	63	59	53	112	....	....	....	29	....	....	....	....	....	....	....	....	....	....	11	8	5	13	0	....	....	....
1972-73	Brandon Wheat Kings	WCJHL	59	72	41	113	....	....	....	63	....	....	....	....	....	....	....	....	....	....	6	1	3	4	2	....	....	....
1973-74	Brandon Wheat Kings	WCJHL	66	*90	72	*162	....	....	....	82	....	....	....	....	....	....	....	....	....	....	....	....	....	....	....	....	....	....
1974-75	Vancouver Blazers	WHA	78	19	20	39	....	....	....	30	....	....	....	....	....	....	....	....	....	....	....	....	....	....	....	....	....	....
1975-76	Calgary Cowboys	WHA	75	42	41	83	....	....	....	32	....	....	....	....	....	....	....	....	....	....	10	5	4	9	6	....	....	....
1976-77	Calgary Cowboys	WHA	81	27	27	54	....	....	....	32	....	....	....	....	....	....	....	....	....	....	....	....	....	....	....	....	....	....
1977-78	Edmonton Oilers	WHA	80	33	52	85	....	....	....	48	....	....	....	....	....	....	....	....	....	....	5	1	1	2	0	....	....	....
1978-79	Edmonton Oilers	WHA	55	32	37	69	....	....	....	47	....	....	....	....	....	....	....	....	....	....	13	9	10	19	8	....	....	....
1979-80	**Edmonton Oilers**	**NHL**	**67**	**18**	**19**	**37**	**15**	**14**	**29**	**24**	**2**	**1**	**1**	**129**	**14.0**	**51**	**9**	**65**	**8**	**–15**	....	....	....	....	....	....	....	....
	Quebec Nordiques	**NHL**	**12**	**4**	**4**	**8**	**3**	**3**	**6**	**8**	**0**	**0**	**1**	**26**	**15.4**	**14**	**4**	**20**	**1**	**–9**	....	....	....	....	....	....	....	....
1980-81	**Quebec Nordiques**	**NHL**	**4**	**0**	**1**	**1**	**0**	**1**	**1**	**2**	**0**	**0**	**0**	**0**	**0.0**	**1**	**0**	**2**	**0**	**–1**	....	....	....	....	....	....	....	....
	Rochester Americans	AHL	6	3	2	5	....	....	....	6	....	....	....	....	....	....	....	....	....	....	....	....	....	....	....	....	....	....
1981-82	HC Bolzano	Italy	30	*78	50	*128	....	....	....	40	....	....	....	....	....	....	....	....	....	....	6	*10	*8	*18	10	....	....	....
1982-83	HC Bolzano	Italy	32	78	58	136	....	....	....	54	....	....	....	....	....	....	....	....	....	....	....	....	....	....	....	....	....	....
1983-84	HC Bolzano	Italy	22	19	24	43	....	....	....	14	....	....	....	....	....	....	....	....	....	....	5	4	8	12	8	....	....	....
1984-85	HC Bolzano	Italy	DID NOT PLAY – COACHING																									
	NHL Totals		**83**	**22**	**24**	**46**	**18**	**18**	**36**	**34**	**2**	**1**	**2**	**155**	**14.2**	**66**	**13**	**87**	**9**		....	....	....	....	....	....	....	....
	Other Major League Totals		369	153	177	330	....	....	....	189	....	....	....	....	....	....	....	....	....	....	28	15	15	30	14	....	....	....

WCJHL First All-Star Team (1974)

Selected by **Vancouver** (WHA) in 1974 WHA Amateur Draft, June 1974. Rights traded to **Philadelphia** by **California** for George Pesut, December 11, 1974. Transferred to **Calgary** (WHA) after **Vancouver** (WHA) franchise relocated, May 7, 1975. Signed as a free agent by **Edmonton** (WHA) after **Calgary** (WHA) franchise folded, May 31, 1977. Rights retained by **Edmonton** prior to Expansion Draft, June 9,1979. Traded to **Quebec** by **Edmonton** for Ron Low, March 11, 1980

• CHISHOLM, Colin

D – R. 6'3", 200 lbs. b: Edmonton, Alta., 2/25/1963. Buffalo's 4th, 60th overall, in 1981.

Season	Club	League	GP	G	A	Pts	AG	AA	APts	PIM	PP	SH	GW	S	%	TGF	PGF	TGA	PGA	+/-	GP	G	A	Pts	PIM	PP	SH	GW
1979-80	Calgary Buffaloes	AAHA	STATISTICS NOT AVAILABLE																									
1980-81	Calgary Wranglers	WHL	70	0	18	18	....	....	....	156	....	....	....	....	....	....	....	....	....	....	22	2	3	5	34	....	....	....
1981-82	Calgary Wranglers	WHL	70	1	15	16	....	....	....	150	....	....	....	....	....	....	....	....	....	....	9	0	3	3	24	....	....	....
1982-83	University of Alberta	CWUAA	17	1	7	8	....	....	....	38	....	....	....	....	....	....	....	....	....	....	11	1	1	2	27	....	....	....
1983-84	University of Alberta	CWUAA	24	2	17	19	....	....	....	12	....	....	....	....	....	....	....	....	....	....	10	....	....	....	70	....	....	....
1984-85	University of Alberta	CWUAA	24	3	31	34	....	....	....	100	....	....	....	....	....	....	....	....	....	....	16	0	0	0	24	....	....	....
1985-86	University of Alberta	CWUAA	46	6	23	29	....	....	....	97	....	....	....	....	....	....	....	....	....	....	....	....	....	....	....	....	....	....
1986-87	**Minnesota North Stars**	**NHL**	**1**	**0**	**0**	**0**	**0**	**0**	**0**	**0**	**0**	**0**	**0**	**0**	**0.0**	**0**	**0**	**0**	**0**	**0**	....	....	....	....	....	....	....	....
	Springfield Indians	AHL	75	1	11	12	....	....	....	141	....	....	....	....	....	....	....	....	....	....	....	....	....	....	....	....	....	....
1987-88	Kalamazoo Wings	IHL	44	1	3	4	....	....	....	59	....	....	....	....	....	....	....	....	....	....	....	....	....	....	....	....	....	....
	NHL Totals		**1**	**0**	**0**	**0**	**0**	**0**	**0**	**0**	**0**	**0**	**0**	**0**	**0.0**	**0**	**0**	**0**	**0**		....	....	....	....	....	....	....	....

Signed as a free agent by **Minnesota**, June 11, 1986.

• CHORNEY, Marc

Marc P. D – L. 6', 200 lbs. b: Sudbury, Ont., 11/8/1959. Pittsburgh's 5th, 115th overall, in 1979.

Season	Club	League	GP	G	A	Pts	AG	AA	APts	PIM	PP	SH	GW	S	%	TGF	PGF	TGA	PGA	+/-	GP	G	A	Pts	PIM	PP	SH	GW
1977-78	University of North Dakota	WCHA	38	1	8	9	....	....	....	54	....	....	....	....	....	....	....	....	....	....	....	....	....	....	....	....	....	....
1978-79	University of North Dakota	WCHA	31	5	11	16	....	....	....	70	....	....	....	....	....	....	....	....	....	....	....	....	....	....	....	....	....	....
1979-80	University of North Dakota	WCHA	39	7	38	45	....	....	....	54	....	....	....	....	....	....	....	....	....	....	....	....	....	....	....	....	....	....
1980-81	University of North Dakota	WCHA	35	8	34	42	....	....	....	72	....	....	....	....	....	....	....	....	....	....	....	....	....	....	....	....	....	....
	Pittsburgh Penguins	**NHL**	**8**	**1**	**6**	**7**	**1**	**4**	**5**	**14**	**0**	**0**	**0**	**3**	**33.3**	**10**	**1**	**9**	**1**	**1**	**2**	**0**	**1**	**1**	**2**	**0**	**0**	**0**
1981-82	**Pittsburgh Penguins**	**NHL**	**60**	**1**	**6**	**7**	**1**	**4**	**5**	**63**	**0**	**0**	**1**	**37**	**2.7**	**36**	**1**	**62**	**16**	**–11**	**5**	**0**	**0**	**0**	**0**	**0**	**0**	**0**
	Erie Blades	AHL	6	1	3	4	....	....	....	4	....	....	....	....	....	....	....	....	....	....	....	....	....	....	....	....	....	....
1982-83	**Pittsburgh Penguins**	**NHL**	**67**	**3**	**5**	**8**	**2**	**3**	**5**	**66**	**0**	**0**	**0**	**66**	**4.5**	**42**	**2**	**116**	**46**	**–30**	....	....	....	....	....	....	....	....

Season	Club	League	REGULAR SEASON																		PLAYOFFS							
			GP	G	A	Pts	AG	AA	APts	PIM	PP	SH	GW	S	%	TGF	PGF	TGA	PGA	+/–	GP	G	A	Pts	PIM	PP	SH	GW
1983-84	Pittsburgh Penguins	NHL	4	0	1	1	0	1	1	8	0	0	0	5	0.0	3	1	10	4	–4	....	....	....	....	....	....	....	....
	Los Angeles Kings	NHL	71	3	9	12	2	6	8	58	0	0	0	57	5.3	52	2	86	12	–24	....	....	....	....	....	....	....	....
1984-85	Binghamton Whalers	AHL	48	4	25	29	....	....	....	38	....	....	....	....	....	....	....	....	....	....	7	0	4	4	9	....	....	....
1985-86	Thunder Bay Twins	CASH	STATISTICS NOT AVAILABLE																									
	NHL Totals		210	8	27	35	6	18	24	209	0	0	1	168	4.8	143	7	283	79		7	0	1	1	2	0	0	0

WCHA Second All-Star Team (1980) • NCAA Championship All-Tournament Team (1980) • WCHA First All-Star Team (1981) • NCAA West First All-American Team (1981)

Traded to **LA Kings** by **Pittsburgh** for LA Kings' 6th round choice (Stuart Marston) in 1985 Entry Draft, October 15, 1983. Signed as a free agent by **Washington**, July 11, 1984.

• CHORSKE, Tom

Thomas P. LW – R. 6'1", 212 lbs. b: Minneapolis, MN, 9/18/1966. Montreal's 2nd, 16th overall, in 1985.

Season	Club	League	GP	G	A	Pts	AG	AA	APts	PIM	PP	SH	GW	S	%	TGF	PGF	TGA	PGA	+/–	GP	G	A	Pts	PIM	PP	SH	GW
1984-85	Minneapolis Lakers	Hi-School	23	44	26	70	....	....	....	....	....	....	....	....	....	....	....	....	....	....	....	....	....	....	....	....	....	....
1985-86	University of Minnesota	WCHA	39	6	4	10	....	....	....	16	....	....	....	....	....	....	....	....	....	....	....	....	....	....	....	....	....	....
	United States	WJC-A	7	1	0	1	....	....	....	2	....	....	....	....	....	....	....	....	....	....	....	....	....	....	....	....	....	....
1986-87	University of Minnesota	WCHA	47	20	22	42	....	....	....	20	....	....	....	....	....	....	....	....	....	....	....	....	....	....	....	....	....	....
1987-88	United States	Nat-Team	36	9	16	25	....	....	....	24	....	....	....	....	....	....	....	....	....	....	....	....	....	....	....	....	....	....
1988-89	University of Minnesota	WCHA	37	25	24	49	....	....	....	28	....	....	....	....	....	....	....	....	....	....	....	....	....	....	....	....	....	....
	United States	WEC-A	9	2	1	3	....	....	....	6	....	....	....	....	....	....	....	....	....	....	....	....	....	....	....	....	....	....
1989-90	Montreal Canadiens	NHL	14	3	1	4	3	1	4	2	0	0	0	19	15.8	6	1	3	0	2	....	....	....	....	....	....	....	....
	Sherbrooke Canadiens	AHL	59	22	24	46	....	....	....	54	....	....	....	....	....	....	....	....	....	....	12	4	4	8	8	....	....	....
1990-91	Montreal Canadiens	Fr-Tour	2	0	1	1	....	....	....	0	....	....	....	....	....	....	....	....	....	....	....	....	....	....	....	....	....	....
	Montreal Canadiens	NHL	57	9	11	20	8	8	16	32	3	0	1	82	11.0	34	14	28	0	–8	....	....	....	....	....	....	....	....
1991-92	New Jersey Devils	NHL	76	19	17	36	17	13	30	32	0	3	2	143	13.3	53	0	70	25	8	7	0	3	3	4	0	0	0
1992-93	New Jersey Devils	NHL	50	7	12	19	6	8	14	25	0	0	1	63	11.1	30	0	41	10	–1	1	0	0	0	0	0	0	0
	Utica Devils	AHL	6	1	4	5	....	....	....	2	....	....	....	....	....	....	....	....	....	....	....	....	....	....	....	....	....	....
1993-94	New Jersey Devils	NHL	76	21	20	41	20	16	36	32	1	1	4	131	16.0	55	1	58	18	14	20	4	3	7	0	0	0	1
1994-95	HC Milano Devils	Italy	7	11	5	16	....	....	....	6	....	....	....	....	....	....	....	....	....	....	....	....	....	....	....	....	....	....
	HC Milano Devils	EuroHL	4	6	7	13	....	....	....	2	....	....	....	....	....	....	....	....	....	....	....	....	....	....	....	....	....	....
♦	New Jersey Devils	NHL	42	10	8	18	18	12	30	16	0	0	2	59	16.9	27	0	42	11	–4	17	1	5	6	4	0	0	0
1995-96	Ottawa Senators	NHL	72	15	14	29	15	11	26	21	0	2	1	118	12.7	44	3	87	37	–9	....	....	....	....	....	....	....	....
	United States	WC-A	8	1	2	3	....	....	....	16	....	....	....	....	....	....	....	....	....	....	....	....	....	....	....	....	....	....
1996-97	Ottawa Senators	NHL	68	18	8	26	19	7	26	16	1	1	1	116	15.5	39	3	47	10	–1	5	0	1	1	2	0	0	0
1997-98	New York Islanders	NHL	82	12	23	35	14	23	37	39	1	4	2	132	9.1	57	11	58	19	7	....	....	....	....	....	....	....	....
	United States	WC-A	6	1	1	2	....	....	....	0	....	....	....	....	....	....	....	....	....	....	....	....	....	....	....	....	....	....
1998-99	New York Islanders	NHL	2	0	1	1	0	1	1	2	0	0	0	9	0.0	1	0	2	2	1	....	....	....	....	....	....	....	....
	Washington Capitals	NHL	17	0	2	2	0	2	2	4	0	0	0	22	0.0	6	0	13	3	–4	....	....	....	....	....	....	....	....
	Calgary Flames	NHL	7	0	0	0	0	0	0	2	0	0	0	0	13.0	1	0	7	1	–5	....	....	....	....	....	....	....	....
	United States	WC-A	6	1	1	2	....	....	....	4	....	....	....	....	....	....	....	....	....	....	....	....	....	....	....	....	....	....
99-2000	Pittsburgh Penguins	NHL	33	1	5	6	1	5	6	2	0	0	0	14	7.1	8	0	17	7	–2	....	....	....	....	....	....	....	....
	NHL Totals		596	115	122	237	121	107	228	225	6	11	14	908	12.7	361	33	473	143		50	5	12	17	10	0	0	1

WCHA First All-Star Team (1989)

Traded to **New Jersey** by **Montreal** with Stephane Richer for Kirk Muller and Rollie Melanson, September 20, 1991. Claimed on waivers by **Ottawa** from **New Jersey**, October 5, 1995. Claimed by **NY Islanders** from **Ottawa** in NHL Waiver Draft, September 28, 1997. Traded to **Washington** by **NY Islanders** with NY Islanders' 8th round choice (Maxim Orlov) in 1999 Entry Draft for Washington's 6th round choice (Bjorn Melin) in 1999 Entry Draft, October 16, 1998. Traded to **Calgary** by **Washington** for Calgary's 7th round choice (later traded to LA Kings - LA Kings selected Tim Eriksson) in 2000 Entry Draft and Washington's 9th round choice (previously acquired, Washington selected Bjorn Nord) in 2000 Entry Draft, March 22, 1999. Signed as a free agent by **Pittsburgh**, September 2, 1999. • Missed remainder of 1999-2000 season recovering from thumb injury suffered in game vs. NY Islanders, February 3, 2000.

• CHOUINARD, Guy

Guy Camil "Gramps" C – R. 5'11", 182 lbs. b: Quebec City, Que., 10/20/1956. Atlanta's 1st, 28th overall, in 1974.

Season	Club	League	GP	G	A	Pts	AG	AA	APts	PIM	PP	SH	GW	S	%	TGF	PGF	TGA	PGA	+/–	GP	G	A	Pts	PIM	PP	SH	GW
1971-72	Quebec Remparts	QMJHL	58	29	41	70	....	....	....	6	....	....	....	....	....	....	....	....	....	....	....	....	....	....	....	....	....	....
1972-73	Quebec Remparts	QMJHL	59	43	*86	129	....	....	....	11	....	....	....	....	....	....	....	....	....	....	15	18	14	32	2	....	....	....
	Quebec Remparts	Mem-Cup	3	3	1	4	....	....	....	0	....	....	....	....	....	....	....	....	....	....	....	....	....	....	....	....	....	....
1973-74	Quebec Remparts	QMJHL	62	75	85	160	....	....	....	22	....	....	....	....	....	....	....	....	....	....	16	15	16	31	5	....	....	....
	Quebec Remparts	Mem-Cup	4	2	*6	*8	....	....	....	0	....	....	....	....	....	....	....	....	....	....	....	....	....	....	....	....	....	....
1974-75	Atlanta Flames	NHL	5	0	0	0	0	0	0	2	0	0	0	5	0.0	0	0	2	0	–2	....	....	....	....	....	....	....	....
	Omaha Knights	CHL	70	28	40	68	....	....	....	6	....	....	....	....	....	....	....	....	....	....	6	1	6	7	0	....	....	....
1975-76	Atlanta Flames	NHL	4	0	2	2	0	1	1	2	0	0	0	8	0.0	4	1	1	0	2	2	0	0	0	0	0	0	0
	Nova Scotia Voyageurs	AHL	70	40	40	80	....	....	....	14	....	....	....	....	....	....	....	....	....	....	9	6	*9	*15	0	....	....	....
1976-77	Atlanta Flames	NHL	80	17	33	50	15	25	40	8	3	0	0	167	10.2	65	27	50	0	–12	3	2	0	2	0	1	0	0
1977-78	Atlanta Flames	NHL	73	28	30	58	25	23	48	8	11	0	1	146	19.2	78	32	38	0	8	2	1	0	1	0	0	0	0
1978-79	Atlanta Flames	NHL	80	50	57	107	43	41	84	14	11	0	5	229	21.8	148	51	75	1	23	2	1	2	3	0	1	0	0
1979-80	Atlanta Flames	NHL	76	31	46	77	26	34	60	22	9	0	1	208	14.9	103	35	64	1	5	4	1	3	4	4	1	0	0
1980-81	Calgary Flames	NHL	52	31	52	83	24	35	59	24	10	0	1	141	22.0	109	50	41	0	18	16	3	14	17	4	0	0	0
1981-82	Calgary Flames	NHL	64	23	57	80	18	38	56	12	13	0	4	182	12.6	113	53	65	0	–5	3	0	1	1	0	0	0	0
1982-83	Calgary Flames	NHL	80	13	59	72	11	41	52	18	7	0	2	158	8.2	105	60	69	0	–24	9	1	6	7	4	0	0	0
1983-84	St. Louis Blues	NHL	64	12	34	46	10	23	33	10	4	0	2	117	10.3	69	34	50	0	–15	5	0	2	2	0	0	0	0
1984-85	Peoria Rivermen	IHL	9	2	5	7	....	....	....	0	....	....	....	....	....	....	....	....	....	....	....	....	....	....	....	....	....	....
	NHL Totals		578	205	370	575	172	261	433	120	68	0	16	1361	15.1	794	343	455	2		46	9	28	37	12	3	0	0

Won George Parsons Trophy (Memorial Cup Tournament Most Sportsmanlike Player) (1974) • Won Ken McKenzie Trophy (CHL's Rookie of the Year) (1975) • AHL Second All-Star Team (1976)

Transferred to **Calgary** after **Atlanta** franchise relocated, June 24, 1980. Traded to **St. Louis** by **Calgary** for future considerations, September 6, 1983

• CHRISTIAN, Dave

RW – R. 5'11", 175 lbs. b: Warroad, MN, 5/12/1959. Winnipeg's 2nd, 40th overall, in 1979.

Season	Club	League	GP	G	A	Pts	AG	AA	APts	PIM	PP	SH	GW	S	%	TGF	PGF	TGA	PGA	+/–	GP	G	A	Pts	PIM	PP	SH	GW
1976-77	Warroad Warriors	Hi-School	STATISTICS NOT AVAILABLE																									
1977-78	University of North Dakota	WCHA	38	8	16	24	....	....	....	14	....	....	....	....	....	....	....	....	....	....	....	....	....	....	....	....	....	....
1978-79	University of North Dakota	WCHA	40	22	24	46	....	....	....	22	....	....	....	....	....	....	....	....	....	....	....	....	....	....	....	....	....	....
	United States	WJC-A	5	2	1	3	....	....	....	0	....	....	....	....	....	....	....	....	....	....	....	....	....	....	....	....	....	....
1979-80	United States	Nat-Team	59	10	20	30	....	....	....	26	....	....	....	....	....	....	....	....	....	....	....	....	....	....	....	....	....	....
	United States	Olympics	7	0	8	8	....	....	....	6	....	....	....	....	....	....	....	....	....	....	....	....	....	....	....	....	....	....
	Winnipeg Jets	NHL	15	8	10	18	7	7	14	2	3	0	0	34	23.5	25	13	19	2	–5	....	....	....	....	....	....	....	....
1980-81	Winnipeg Jets	NHL	80	28	43	71	22	29	51	22	9	1	0	185	15.1	110	45	148	29	–54	....	....	....	....	....	....	....	....
	United States	WEC-A	8	8	3	11	....	....	....	6	....	....	....	....	....	....	....	....	....	....	....	....	....	....	....	....	....	....
1981-82	United States	Can-Cup	6	1	0	1	....	....	....	4	....	....	....	....	....	....	....	....	....	....	....	....	....	....	....	....	....	....
	Winnipeg Jets	NHL	80	25	51	76	20	34	54	28	6	1	3	218	11.5	133	63	131	20	–41	4	0	1	1	2	0	0	0
1982-83	Winnipeg Jets	NHL	55	18	26	44	15	18	33	23	4	0	2	131	13.7	84	37	63	11	–5	3	0	0	0	0	0	0	0
1983-84	Washington Capitals	NHL	80	29	52	81	23	35	58	28	9	0	6	164	17.7	121	38	58	1	26	8	5	4	9	5	1	0	0
1984-85	United States	Can-Cup	6	2	1	3	....	....	....	2	....	....	....	....	....	....	....	....	....	....	....	....	....	....	....	....	....	....
	Washington Capitals	NHL	80	26	43	69	21	29	50	14	5	0	2	152	17.1	99	24	63	8	20	5	1	1	2	0	0	0	0
1985-86	Washington Capitals	NHL	80	41	42	83	33	28	61	15	18	2	4	218	18.8	119	52	92	28	3	9	4	4	8	0	1	0	0
1986-87	Washington Capitals	NHL	76	23	27	50	20	20	40	8	5	0	2	152	15.1	88	26	79	12	–5	7	1	3	4	6	0	0	1
1987-88	Washington Capitals	NHL	80	37	21	58	32	15	47	26	14	0	5	187	19.8	90	40	73	9	–14	14	5	6	11	6	1	0	0
1988-89	Washington Capitals	NHL	80	34	31	65	29	22	51	12	16	1	1	177	19.2	107	47	78	20	2	6	1	1	2	0	1	0	0
	United States	WEC-A	6	4	3	7	....	....	....	2	....	....	....	....	....	....	....	....	....	....	....	....	....	....	....	....	....	....
1989-90	Washington Capitals	Fr-Tour	4	1	2	3	....	....	....	0	....	....	....	....	....	....	....	....	....	....	....	....	....	....	....	....	....	....
	Washington Capitals	NHL	28	3	8	11	3	6	9	4	0	0	1	54	5.6	24	7	37	8	–12	....	....	....	....	....	....	....	....
	Boston Bruins	NHL	50	12	17	29	10	12	22	8	2	0	3	99	12.1	51	12	36	1	4	21	4	1	5	4	1	0	0
1990-91	Boston Bruins	NHL	78	32	21	53	29	16	45	41	9	0	2	173	18.5	87	26	70	17	8	19	8	4	12	4	0	0	2
1991-92	United States	Can-Cup	7	1	1	2	....	....	....	0	....	....	....	....	....	....	....	....	....	....	....	....	....	....	....	....	....	....
	St. Louis Blues	NHL	78	20	24	44	18	18	36	41	1	3	3	142	14.1	73	17	66	12	2	4	3	0	3	0	0	0	0
1992-93	Chicago Blackhawks	NHL	60	4	14	18	3	10	13	12	1	0	1	75	5.3	31	10	20	5	6	1	0	0	0	0	0	0	0

			REGULAR SEASON																		PLAYOFFS							
Season	Club	League	GP	G	A	Pts	AG	AA	APts	PIM	PP	SH	GW	S	%	TGF	PGF	TGA	PGA	+/–	GP	G	A	Pts	PIM	PP	SH	GW
1993-94	Chicago Blackhawks	NHL	9	0	3	3	0	2	2	0	0	0	0	6	0.0	4	1	4	1	0	1	0	0	0	0	0	0	0
	Indianapolis Ice	IHL	40	8	18	26	....	....	....	6	....	....	....	....	....	....	....	....	....	....	....	....	....	....	....	....	....	....
1994-95	Minnesota Moose	IHL	81	38	42	80	....	....	....	16	....	....	....	....	....	....	....	....	....	....	3	0	1	1	0	....	....	....
1995-96	Minnesota Moose	IHL	69	21	25	46	....	....	....	8	....	....	....	....	....	....	....	....	....	....	....	....	....	....	....	....	....	....
	NHL Totals		1009	340	433	773	285	301	586	284	102	8	35	2167	15.7	1246	458	1037	184		102	32	25	57	27	5	0	3

Played in NHL All-Star Game (1991)

Traded to **Washington** by **Winnipeg** for Washington's 1st round choice (Bobby Dollas) in 1983 Entry Draft, June 8, 1983. Traded to **Boston** by **Washington** for Bob Joyce, December 13, 1989. Transferred to **St. Louis** by **Boston** with Boston's 3rd round choice (Vitali Prokhorov) and 7th round choice (Lance Burns) in 1992 Entry Draft as compensation for Boston's signing of free agents Glen Featherstone and Dave Thomlinson, July 30, 1991. Claimed by **Chicago** from **St. Louis** in Waiver Draft, October 4, 1992.

• CHRISTIAN, Jeff

Jeffrey LW – L. 6'2", 210 lbs. b: Burlington, Ont., 7/30/1970. New Jersey's 2nd, 23rd overall, in 1988.

Season	Club	League	GP	G	A	Pts	AG	AA	APts	PIM	PP	SH	GW	S	%	TGF	PGF	TGA	PGA	+/–	GP	G	A	Pts	PIM	PP	SH	GW
1986-87	Dundas Blues	OJHL-C	29	20	34	54	....	....	....	42	....	....	....	....	....	....	....	....	....	....	....	....	....	....	....	....	....	....
1987-88	London Knights	OHL	64	15	29	44	....	....	....	154	....	....	....	....	....	....	....	....	....	....	9	1	5	6	27	....	....	....
1988-89	London Knights	OHL	60	27	30	57	....	....	....	221	....	....	....	....	....	....	....	....	....	....	20	3	4	7	56	....	....	....
1989-90	London Knights	OHL	18	14	7	21	....	....	....	64	....	....	....	....	....	....	....	....	....	....	....	....	....	....	....	....	....	....
	Owen Sound Platers	OHL	37	19	26	45	....	....	....	145	....	....	....	....	....	....	....	....	....	....	10	6	7	13	43	....	....	....
1990-91	Utica Devils	AHL	80	24	42	66	....	....	....	165	....	....	....	....	....	....	....	....	....	....	....	....	....	....	....	....	....	....
1991-92	New Jersey Devils	NHL	2	0	0	0	0	0	0	2	0	0	0	1	0.0	0	0	0	0	0	....	....	....	....	....	....	....	....
	Utica Devils	AHL	76	27	24	51	....	....	....	198	....	....	....	....	....	....	....	....	....	....	4	0	0	0	16	....	....	....
1992-93	Utica Devils	AHL	22	4	6	10	....	....	....	39	....	....	....	....	....	....	....	....	....	....	....	....	....	....	....	....	....	....
	Hamilton Canucks	AHL	11	2	5	7	....	....	....	35	....	....	....	....	....	....	....	....	....	....	....	....	....	....	....	....	....	....
	Cincinnati Cyclones	IHL	36	5	12	17	....	....	....	113	....	....	....	....	....	....	....	....	....	....	....	....	....	....	....	....	....	....
1993-94	Albany River Rats	AHL	76	34	43	77	....	....	....	227	....	....	....	....	....	....	....	....	....	....	5	1	2	3	19	....	....	....
1994-95	Pittsburgh Penguins	NHL	1	0	0	0	0	0	0	0	0	0	0	2	0.0	0	0	0	0	0	....	....	....	....	....	....	....	....
	Cleveland Lumberjacks	IHL	56	13	24	37	....	....	....	126	....	....	....	....	....	....	....	....	....	....	2	0	1	1	8	....	....	....
1995-96	Pittsburgh Penguins	NHL	3	0	0	0	0	0	0	2	0	0	0	0	0.0	0	0	0	0	0	....	....	....	....	....	....	....	....
	Cleveland Lumberjacks	IHL	66	23	32	55	....	....	....	131	....	....	....	....	....	....	....	....	....	....	3	0	1	1	8	....	....	....
1996-97	Pittsburgh Penguins	NHL	11	2	2	4	2	2	4	13	0	0	0	18	11.1	5	0	8	0	–3	....	....	....	....	....	....	....	....
	Cleveland Lumberjacks	IHL	69	40	40	80	....	....	....	262	....	....	....	....	....	....	....	....	....	....	12	6	8	14	44	....	....	....
1997-98	Phoenix Coyotes	NHL	1	0	0	0	0	0	0	0	0	0	0	0	0.0	0	0	1	0	–1	....	....	....	....	....	....	....	....
	Las Vegas Thunder	IHL	30	12	15	27	....	....	....	90	....	....	....	....	....	....	....	....	....	....	4	2	2	4	20	....	....	....
1998-99	Houston Aeros	IHL	80	45	41	86	....	....	....	252	....	....	....	....	....	....	....	....	....	....	18	4	12	16	32	....	....	....
99-2000	Cleveland Lumberjacks	IHL	77	29	35	64	....	....	....	202	....	....	....	....	....	....	....	....	....	....	9	1	4	5	20	....	....	....
	NHL Totals		18	2	2	4	2	2	4	17	0	0	0	21	9.5	5	0	9	0		....	....	....	....	....	....	....	....

Signed as a free agent by **Pittsburgh**, August 2, 1994. Signed as a free agent by **Phoenix**, July 28, 1997. Signed as a free agent by **Chicago**, August 25, 1999.

• CHRISTIE, Mike

Michael Hunt D – L. 6', 190 lbs. b: Big Spring, TX, 12/20/1949.

Season	Club	League	GP	G	A	Pts	AG	AA	APts	PIM	PP	SH	GW	S	%	TGF	PGF	TGA	PGA	+/–	GP	G	A	Pts	PIM	PP	SH	GW
1968-69	University of Denver	WCHA	DID NOT PLAY – FRESHMAN																									
1969-70	University of Denver	WCHA	31	2	16	18	....	....	....	38	....	....	....	....	....	....	....	....	....	....	....	....	....	....	....	....	....	....
1970-71	University of Denver	WCHA	36	8	25	33	....	....	....	57	....	....	....	....	....	....	....	....	....	....	....	....	....	....	....	....	....	....
1971-72	University of Denver	WCHA	DID NOT PLAY – INJURED																									
1972-73	Dallas Black Hawks	CHL	32	5	11	16	....	....	....	51	....	....	....	....	....	....	....	....	....	....	....	....	....	....	....	....	....	....
1973-74	Dallas Black Hawks	CHL	71	5	37	42	....	....	....	110	....	....	....	....	....	....	....	....	....	....	10	1	2	3	23	....	....	....
1974-75	California Golden Seals	NHL	34	0	14	14	0	10	10	76	0	0	0	30	0.0	43	6	67	17	–13	....	....	....	....	....	....	....	....
1975-76	California Golden Seals	NHL	78	3	18	21	3	13	16	152	0	0	0	63	4.8	83	2	112	13	–18	....	....	....	....	....	....	....	....
1976-77	United States	Can-Cup	4	0	0	0	....	....	....	2	....	....	....	....	....	....	....	....	....	....	....	....	....	....	....	....	....	....
	Cleveland Barons	NHL	79	6	27	33	5	21	26	79	0	0	2	61	9.8	98	3	101	24	18	....	....	....	....	....	....	....	....
1977-78	Cleveland Barons	NHL	34	1	6	7	1	5	6	49	0	0	0	14	7.1	30	0	47	3	–14	....	....	....	....	....	....	....	....
	Colorado Rockies	NHL	35	2	8	10	2	6	8	28	0	0	0	36	5.6	44	5	55	10	–6	2	0	0	0	0	0	0	0
1978-79	Colorado Rockies	NHL	68	1	10	11	1	7	8	88	0	0	0	50	2.0	48	6	102	16	–44	....	....	....	....	....	....	....	....
1979-80	Colorado Rockies	NHL	74	1	17	18	1	12	13	78	0	0	0	50	2.0	62	2	120	30	–30	....	....	....	....	....	....	....	....
1980-81	Colorado Rockies	NHL	1	0	0	0	0	0	0	0	0	0	0	1	0.0	1	0	1	1	1	....	....	....	....	....	....	....	....
	Tulsa Oilers	CHL	20	1	0	1	....	....	....	27	....	....	....	....	....	....	....	....	....	....	....	....	....	....	....	....	....	....
	Vancouver Canucks	NHL	9	1	1	2	1	1	2	0	0	0	0	5	20.0	10	0	1	0	9	....	....	....	....	....	....	....	....
	Dallas Black Hawks	CHL	40	2	20	22	....	....	....	95	....	....	....	....	....	....	....	....	....	....	6	0	3	3	10	....	....	....
	NHL Totals		412	15	101	116	14	75	89	550	0	0	2	310	4.8	419	24	606	114		2	0	0	0	0	0	0	0

WCHA First All-Star Team (1971) • NCAA West First All-American Team (1971)

• Missed entire 1971-72 and majority of 1972-73 seasons recovering from knee injury suffered in training camp, September, 1971. Signed as a free agent by **Chicago**, September, 1972. Traded to **California** by **Chicago** with Len Frig for Ivan Boldirev, May 24, 1974. Transferred to **Cleveland** after **California** franchise relocated, August 26, 1976. Traded to **Colorado** by **Cleveland** for Dennis O'Brien, January 12, 1978. Traded to **Vancouver** by **Colorado** for cash, December 8, 1980

• CHRISTIE, Ryan

LW – L. 6'3", 200 lbs. b: Beamsville, Ont., 7/3/1978. Dallas' 4th, 112th overall, in 1996.

Season	Club	League	GP	G	A	Pts	AG	AA	APts	PIM	PP	SH	GW	S	%	TGF	PGF	TGA	PGA	+/–	GP	G	A	Pts	PIM	PP	SH	GW
1994-95	St. Catharines Falcons	OJHL-B	40	10	11	21	....	....	....	96	....	....	....	....	....	....	....	....	....	....	....	....	....	....	....	....	....	....
1995-96	Owen Sound Platers	OHL	66	29	17	46	....	....	....	93	....	....	....	....	....	....	....	....	....	....	6	1	1	2	0	....	....	....
1996-97	Owen Sound Platers	OHL	66	23	29	52	....	....	....	136	....	....	....	....	....	....	....	....	....	....	4	1	1	2	8	....	....	....
1997-98	Owen Sound Platers	OHL	66	39	41	80	....	....	....	208	....	....	....	....	....	....	....	....	....	....	11	3	5	8	13	....	....	....
1998-99	Michigan K-Wings	IHL	48	4	5	9	....	....	....	74	....	....	....	....	....	....	....	....	....	....	3	1	1	2	2	....	....	....
99-2000	Dallas Stars	NHL	5	0	0	0	0	0	0	0	0	0	0	1	0.0	1	0	2	0	–1	....	....	....	....	....	....	....	....
	Michigan K-Wings	IHL	76	24	25	49	....	....	....	140	....	....	....	....	....	....	....	....	....	....	....	....	....	....	....	....	....	....
	NHL Totals		5	0	0	0	0	0	0	0	0	0	0	1	0.0	1	0	2	0		....	....	....	....	....	....	....	....

• CHRISTOFF, Steve

Steven M. C – R. 6'1", 180 lbs. b: Richfield, MN, 1/23/1958. Minnesota's 3rd, 24th overall, in 1978.

Season	Club	League	GP	G	A	Pts	AG	AA	APts	PIM	PP	SH	GW	S	%	TGF	PGF	TGA	PGA	+/–	GP	G	A	Pts	PIM	PP	SH	GW
1975-76	Richfield Spartans	Hi-School	STATISTICS NOT AVAILABLE																									
1976-77	University of Minnesota	WCHA	38	7	9	16	....	....	....	20	....	....	....	....	....	....	....	....	....	....	....	....	....	....	....	....	....	....
1977-78	University of Minnesota	WCHA	38	32	34	66	....	....	....	18	....	....	....	....	....	....	....	....	....	....	....	....	....	....	....	....	....	....
1978-79	University of Minnesota	WCHA	43	38	39	77	....	....	....	50	....	....	....	....	....	....	....	....	....	....	....	....	....	....	....	....	....	....
	United States	WEC-A	8	3	2	5	....	....	....	4	....	....	....	....	....	....	....	....	....	....	....	....	....	....	....	....	....	....
1979-80	United States	Nat-Team	57	35	26	61	....	....	....	22	....	....	....	....	....	....	....	....	....	....	....	....	....	....	....	....	....	....
	United States	Olympics	7	2	1	3	....	....	....	6	....	....	....	....	....	....	....	....	....	....	....	....	....	....	....	....	....	....
	Minnesota North Stars	NHL	20	8	7	15	7	5	12	19	0	0	1	34	23.5	22	5	14	0	3	14	8	4	12	7	2	0	0
1980-81	Minnesota North Stars	DN-Cup	2	2	0	2	....	....	....	0	....	....	....	....	....	....	....	....	....	....	....	....	....	....	....	....	....	....
	Minnesota North Stars	NHL	56	26	13	39	20	9	29	58	9	0	2	132	19.7	63	20	56	4	–9	18	8	8	16	16	5	0	1
	Oklahoma City Stars	CHL	3	1	0	1	....	....	....	0	....	....	....	....	....	....	....	....	....	....	....	....	....	....	....	....	....	....
1981-82	United States	Can-Cup	6	1	5	6	....	....	....	4	....	....	....	....	....	....	....	....	....	....	....	....	....	....	....	....	....	....
	Minnesota North Stars	NHL	69	26	29	55	21	19	40	14	4	0	1	178	14.6	79	12	58	0	9	2	0	0	0	2	0	0	0
1982-83	Calgary Flames	NHL	45	9	8	17	7	6	13	4	0	0	2	52	17.3	31	1	33	0	–3	1	0	0	0	0	0	0	0
1983-84	Los Angeles Kings	NHL	58	8	7	15	6	5	11	13	0	0	1	74	10.8	24	3	40	0	–19	....	....	....	....	....	....	....	....
	NHL Totals		248	77	64	141	61	44	105	108	13	0	7	470	16.4	219	41	201	4		35	16	12	28	25	7	0	1

WCHA Second All-Star Team (1978) • NCAA Championship All-Tournament Team (1979)

Traded to **Calgary** by **Minnesota** with Bill Nyrop and St. Louis' 2nd round choice (previously acquired, Calgary selected Dave Reierson) in 1982 Entry Draft for Willi Plett and Calgary's 4th round choice (Dusan Pasek) in 1982 Entry Draft, June 7, 1982. Traded to **Minnesota** by **Calgary** with Calgary's 2nd round choice (Frantisek Musil) in 1983 Entry Draft for Mike Eaves and Keith Hanson, June 8, 1983. Traded to **LA Kings** by **Minnesota** with Fred Barrett for Dave Lewis, October 3, 1983.

• CHUBAROV, Artem

C – L. 6'1", 189 lbs. b: Gorky, USSR, 12/12/1979. Vancouver's 2nd, 31st overall, in 1998.

Season	Club	League	GP	G	A	Pts	AG	AA	APts	PIM	PP	SH	GW	S	%	TGF	PGF	TGA	PGA	+/-	GP	G	A	Pts	PIM	PP	SH	GW
			REGULAR SEASON																		PLAYOFFS							
1994-95	Torpedo Nizhny	CIS-Jr.	60	20	30	50	....	....	....	20	....	....	....	....	....	....	....	....	....	....	....	....	....	....	....	....	....	....
1995-96	Torpedo Nizhny	CIS-Jr.	60	22	25	47	....	....	....	20	....	....	....	....	....	....	....	....	....	....	....	....	....	....	....	....	....	....
1996-97	Torpedo Nizhny	Russia-3	40	24	5	29	....	....	....	16	....	....	....	....	....	....	....	....	....	....	....	....	....	....	....	....	....	....
	Torpedo Nizhny	Russia-2	15	1	1	2	....	....	....	8	....	....	....	....	....	....	....	....	....	....	....	....	....	....	....	....	....	....
1997-98	Dynamo Moscow	Russia	30	1	4	5	....	....	....	4	....	....	....	....	....	....	....	....	....	....	....	....	....	....	....	....	....	....
1998-99	Dynamo Moscow	Russia	34	8	2	10	....	....	....	10	....	....	....	....	....	....	....	....	....	....	12	0	0	0	4	....	....	....
	Russia	WJC-A	7	4	3	7	....	....	....	4	....	....	....	....	....	....	....	....	....	....	....	....	....	....	....	....	....	....
99-2000	**Vancouver Canucks**	**NHL**	**49**	**1**	**8**	**9**	**1**	**7**	**8**	**10**	**0**	**0**	**1**	**53**	**1.9**	**15**	**1**	**25**	**7**	**-4**	....	....	....	....	....	....	....	....
	Syracuse Crunch	AHL	14	7	6	13	....	....	....	4	....	....	....	....	....	....	....	....	....	....	1	0	0	0	0	....	....	....
	NHL Totals		**49**	**1**	**8**	**9**	**1**	**7**	**8**	**10**	**0**	**0**	**1**	**53**	**1.9**	**15**	**1**	**25**	**7**		....	....	....	....	....	....	....	....

• CHURCH, Brad

LW – L. 6'1", 210 lbs. b: Dauphin, Man., 11/14/1976. Washington's 1st, 17th overall, in 1995.

Season	Club	League	GP	G	A	Pts	AG	AA	APts	PIM	PP	SH	GW	S	%	TGF	PGF	TGA	PGA	+/-	GP	G	A	Pts	PIM	PP	SH	GW
1991-92	Parkland Rangers	MAHA	26	15	17	32	....	....	....	62	....	....	....	....	....	....	....	....	....	....	....	....	....	....	....	....	....	....
1992-93	Dauphin Kings	MJHL	45	15	23	38	....	....	....	80	....	....	....	....	....	....	....	....	....	....	....	....	....	....	....	....	....	....
1993-94	Prince Albert Raiders	WHL	71	33	20	53	....	....	....	197	....	....	....	....	....	....	....	....	....	....	....	....	....	....	....	....	....	....
1994-95	Prince Albert Raiders	WHL	62	26	24	50	....	....	....	184	....	....	....	....	....	....	....	....	....	....	15	6	9	15	32	....	....	....
1995-96	Prince Albert Raiders	WHL	69	42	46	88	....	....	....	123	....	....	....	....	....	....	....	....	....	....	18	15	*20	*35	74	....	....	....
1996-97	Portland Pirates	AHL	50	4	8	12	....	....	....	92	....	....	....	....	....	....	....	....	....	....	1	0	0	0	0	....	....	....
1997-98	**Washington Capitals**	**NHL**	**2**	**0**	**0**	**0**	**0**	**0**	**0**	**0**	**0**	**0**	**0**	**4**	**0.0**	**0**	**0**	**0**	**0**	**0**	....	....	....	....	....	....	....	....
	Portland Pirates	AHL	59	6	5	11	....	....	....	98	....	....	....	....	....	....	....	....	....	....	9	2	4	6	14	....	....	....
1998-99	Portland Pirates	AHL	10	1	3	4	....	....	....	18	....	....	....	....	....	....	....	....	....	....	....	....	....	....	....	....	....	....
	Hampton Roads Admirals	ECHL	24	10	9	19	....	....	....	129	....	....	....	....	....	....	....	....	....	....	....	....	....	....	....	....	....	....
	Hamilton Bulldogs	AHL	9	0	2	2	....	....	....	4	....	....	....	....	....	....	....	....	....	....	....	....	....	....	....	....	....	....
	New Orleans Brass	ECHL	5	3	4	7	....	....	....	4	....	....	....	....	....	....	....	....	....	....	11	1	1	2	22	....	....	....
99-2000	Hampton Roads Admirals	ECHL	11	4	3	7	....	....	....	31	....	....	....	....	....	....	....	....	....	....	....	....	....	....	....	....	....	....
	Portland Pirates	AHL	56	9	17	26	....	....	....	52	....	....	....	....	....	....	....	....	....	....	4	1	1	2	4	....	....	....
	NHL Totals		**2**	**0**	**0**	**0**	**0**	**0**	**0**	**0**	**0**	**0**	**0**	**4**	**0.0**	**0**	**0**	**0**	**0**		....	....	....	....	....	....	....	....

Traded to **Edmonton** by **Washington** for the rights to Barrie Moore, February 3, 1999.

• CHURLA, Shane

RW – R. 6'1", 200 lbs. b: Fernie, B.C., 6/24/1965. Hartford's 4th, 110th overall, in 1985.

Season	Club	League	GP	G	A	Pts	AG	AA	APts	PIM	PP	SH	GW	S	%	TGF	PGF	TGA	PGA	+/-	GP	G	A	Pts	PIM	PP	SH	GW
1983-84	Medicine Hat Tigers	WHL	48	3	7	10	....	....	....	115	....	....	....	....	....	....	....	....	....	....	14	1	5	6	41	....	....	....
1984-85	Medicine Hat Tigers	WHL	70	14	20	34	....	....	....	370	....	....	....	....	....	....	....	....	....	....	9	1	0	1	55	....	....	....
1985-86	Binghamton Whalers	AHL	52	4	10	14	....	....	....	306	....	....	....	....	....	....	....	....	....	....	3	0	0	0	22	....	....	....
1986-87	**Hartford Whalers**	**NHL**	**20**	**0**	**1**	**1**	**0**	**1**	**1**	**78**	**0**	**0**	**0**	**2**	**0.0**	**3**	**0**	**4**	**0**	**-1**	**2**	**0**	**0**	**0**	**42**	**0**	**0**	**0**
	Binghamton Whalers	AHL	24	1	5	6	....	....	....	249	....	....	....	....	....	....	....	....	....	....	....	....	....	....	....	....	....	....
1987-88	**Hartford Whalers**	**NHL**	**2**	**0**	**0**	**0**	**0**	**0**	**0**	**14**	**0**	**0**	**0**	**0**	**0.0**	**0**	**0**	**1**	**0**	**-1**	....	....	....	....	....	....	....	....
	Binghamton Whalers	AHL	25	5	8	13	....	....	....	168	....	....	....	....	....	....	....	....	....	....	....	....	....	....	....	....	....	....
	Calgary Flames	**NHL**	**29**	**1**	**5**	**6**	**1**	**4**	**5**	**132**	**0**	**0**	**0**	**15**	**6.7**	**16**	**0**	**14**	**0**	**2**	**7**	**0**	**1**	**1**	**17**	**0**	**0**	**0**
1988-89	**Calgary Flames**	**NHL**	**5**	**0**	**0**	**0**	**0**	**0**	**0**	**25**	**0**	**0**	**0**	**2**	**0.0**	**0**	**0**	**3**	**0**	**-3**	....	....	....	....	....	....	....	....
	Salt Lake Golden Eagles	IHL	32	3	13	16	....	....	....	278	....	....	....	....	....	....	....	....	....	....	....	....	....	....	....	....	....	....
	Minnesota North Stars	**NHL**	**13**	**1**	**0**	**1**	**1**	**0**	**1**	**54**	**0**	**0**	**0**	**6**	**16.7**	**1**	**0**	**1**	**0**	**0**	....	....	....	....	....	....	....	....
1989-90	**Minnesota North Stars**	**NHL**	**53**	**2**	**3**	**5**	**2**	**2**	**4**	**292**	**0**	**0**	**1**	**40**	**5.0**	**13**	**1**	**16**	**0**	**-4**	**7**	**0**	**0**	**0**	**44**	**0**	**0**	**0**
1990-91	Minnesota North Stars	Fr-Tour	3	0	0	0	....	....	....	4	....	....	....	....	....	....	....	....	....	....	....	....	....	....	....	....	....	....
	Minnesota North Stars	**NHL**	**40**	**2**	**2**	**4**	**2**	**2**	**4**	**286**	**0**	**0**	**0**	**32**	**6.3**	**12**	**0**	**11**	**0**	**1**	**22**	**2**	**1**	**3**	**90**	**0**	**0**	**1**
1991-92	**Minnesota North Stars**	**NHL**	**57**	**4**	**1**	**5**	**4**	**1**	**5**	**278**	**0**	**0**	**0**	**42**	**9.5**	**12**	**0**	**24**	**0**	**-12**	....	....	....	....	....	....	....	....
1992-93	**Minnesota North Stars**	**NHL**	**73**	**5**	**16**	**21**	**4**	**11**	**15**	**286**	**1**	**0**	**1**	**61**	**8.2**	**40**	**16**	**32**	**0**	**-8**	....	....	....	....	....	....	....	....
1993-94	**Dallas Stars**	**NHL**	**69**	**6**	**7**	**13**	**6**	**5**	**11**	**333**	**3**	**0**	**0**	**62**	**9.7**	**24**	**7**	**26**	**1**	**-8**	**9**	**1**	**3**	**4**	**35**	**1**	**0**	**0**
1994-95	**Dallas Stars**	**NHL**	**27**	**1**	**3**	**4**	**2**	**4**	**6**	**186**	**0**	**0**	**1**	**22**	**4.5**	**7**	**0**	**7**	**0**	**0**	**5**	**0**	**0**	**0**	**20**	**0**	**0**	**0**
1995-96	**Dallas Stars**	**NHL**	**34**	**3**	**4**	**7**	**3**	**3**	**6**	**168**	**0**	**0**	**0**	**18**	**16.7**	**15**	**3**	**8**	**0**	**4**	....	....	....	....	....	....	....	....
	Los Angeles Kings	**NHL**	**11**	**1**	**2**	**3**	**1**	**2**	**3**	**37**	**0**	**0**	**0**	**9**	**11.1**	**5**	**1**	**13**	**0**	**-9**	....	....	....	....	....	....	....	....
	New York Rangers	**NHL**	**10**	**0**	**0**	**0**	**0**	**0**	**0**	**26**	**0**	**0**	**0**	**5**	**0.0**	**0**	**0**	**3**	**0**	**-3**	**11**	**2**	**2**	**4**	**14**	**0**	**0**	**0**
1996-97	**New York Rangers**	**NHL**	**45**	**0**	**1**	**1**	**0**	**1**	**1**	**106**	**0**	**0**	**0**	**19**	**0.0**	**4**	**0**	**14**	**0**	**-10**	**15**	**0**	**0**	**0**	**20**	**0**	**0**	**0**
1997-98	**New York Rangers**	**NHL**	DID NOT PLAY – INJURED																									
	NHL Totals		**488**	**26**	**45**	**71**	**26**	**36**	**62**	**2301**	**4**	**0**	**3**	**335**	**7.8**	**152**	**28**	**177**	**1**		**78**	**5**	**7**	**12**	**282**	**1**	**0**	**1**

Traded to **Calgary** by **Hartford** with Dana Murzyn for Neil Sheehy, Carey Wilson, and the rights to Lane MacDonald, January 3, 1988. Traded to **Minnesota** by **Calgary** with Perry Berezan for Brian MacLellan and Minnesota's 4th round choice (Robert Reichel) in 1989 Entry Draft, March 4, 1989. Claimed by **San Jose** from **Minnesota** in Dispersal Draft, May 30, 1991. Traded to **Minnesota** by **San Jose** for Kelly Kisio, June 3, 1991. Transferred to **Dallas** after **Minnesota** franchise relocated, June 9, 1993. Traded to **LA Kings** by **Dallas** with Doug Zmolek for Darryl Sydor and LA Kings' 5th round choice (Ryan Christie) in 1996 Entry Draft, February 17, 1996. Traded to **NY Rangers** by **LA Kings** with Marty McSorley and Jari Kurri for Ray Ferraro, Ian Laperriere, Mattias Norstrom, Nathan Lafayette and NY Rangers' 4th round choice (Sean Blanchard) in 1997 Entry Draft, March 14, 1996. • Missed entire 1997-98 season recovering from knee surgery, July, 1997.

• CHYCHRUN, Jeff

D – R. 6'4", 215 lbs. b: LaSalle, Que., 5/3/1966. Philadelphia's 3rd, 37th overall, in 1984.

Season	Club	League	GP	G	A	Pts	AG	AA	APts	PIM	PP	SH	GW	S	%	TGF	PGF	TGA	PGA	+/-	GP	G	A	Pts	PIM	PP	SH	GW
1982-83	Nepean Raiders	OJHL	44	3	10	13	....	....	....	59	....	....	....	....	....	....	....	....	....	....	....	....	....	....	....	....	....	....
1983-84	Kingston Canadians	OHL	63	1	13	14	....	....	....	137	....	....	....	....	....	....	....	....	....	....	....	....	....	....	....	....	....	....
1984-85	Kingston Canadians	OHL	58	4	10	14	....	....	....	206	....	....	....	....	....	....	....	....	....	....	....	....	....	....	....	....	....	....
1985-86	Kingston Canadians	OHL	61	4	21	25	....	....	....	127	....	....	....	....	....	....	....	....	....	....	10	2	1	3	17	....	....	....
	Hershey Bears	AHL	....	....	....	....	....	....	....	....	....	....	....	....	....	....	....	....	....	....	4	0	1	1	9	....	....	....
	Kalamazoo Wings	IHL	....	....	....	....	....	....	....	....	....	....	....	....	....	....	....	....	....	....	3	1	0	1	0	....	....	....
1986-87	**Philadelphia Flyers**	**NHL**	**1**	**0**	**0**	**0**	**0**	**0**	**0**	**4**	**0**	**0**	**0**	**1**	**0.0**	**0**	**0**	**0**	**0**	**0**	....	....	....	....	....	....	....	....
	Hershey Bears	AHL	74	1	17	18	....	....	....	239	....	....	....	....	....	....	....	....	....	....	4	0	0	0	10	....	....	....
1987-88	**Philadelphia Flyers**	**NHL**	**3**	**0**	**0**	**0**	**0**	**0**	**0**	**4**	**0**	**0**	**0**	**1**	**0.0**	**0**	**0**	**3**	**2**	**-1**	....	....	....	....	....	....	....	....
	Hershey Bears	AHL	55	0	5	5	....	....	....	210	....	....	....	....	....	....	....	....	....	....	12	0	2	2	44	....	....	....
1988-89	**Philadelphia Flyers**	**NHL**	**80**	**1**	**4**	**5**	**1**	**3**	**4**	**245**	**0**	**0**	**1**	**53**	**1.9**	**58**	**2**	**70**	**25**	**11**	**19**	**0**	**2**	**2**	**65**	**0**	**0**	**0**
1989-90	**Philadelphia Flyers**	**NHL**	**79**	**2**	**7**	**9**	**2**	**5**	**7**	**250**	**0**	**0**	**1**	**52**	**3.8**	**51**	**1**	**76**	**14**	**-12**	....	....	....	....	....	....	....	....
1990-91	**Philadelphia Flyers**	**NHL**	**36**	**0**	**6**	**6**	**0**	**5**	**5**	**105**	**0**	**0**	**0**	**25**	**0.0**	**20**	**0**	**21**	**2**	**1**	....	....	....	....	....	....	....	....
1991-92	**Los Angeles Kings**	**NHL**	**26**	**0**	**3**	**3**	**0**	**2**	**2**	**76**	**0**	**0**	**0**	**22**	**0.0**	**17**	**0**	**25**	**4**	**-4**	....	....	....	....	....	....	....	....
	Phoenix Roadrunners	IHL	3	0	0	0	....	....	....	6	....	....	....	....	....	....	....	....	....	....	....	....	....	....	....	....	....	....
	Pittsburgh Penguins	**NHL**	**17**	**0**	**1**	**1**	**0**	**1**	**1**	**35**	**0**	**0**	**0**	**4**	**0.0**	**5**	**0**	**13**	**0**	**-8**	....	....	....	....	....	....	....	....
1992-93	**Pittsburgh Penguins**	**NHL**	**1**	**0**	**0**	**0**	**0**	**0**	**0**	**2**	**0**	**0**	**0**	**0**	**0.0**	**1**	**0**	**0**	**0**	**1**	....	....	....	....	....	....	....	....
	Los Angeles Kings	**NHL**	**17**	**0**	**1**	**1**	**0**	**1**	**1**	**23**	**0**	**0**	**0**	**3**	**0.0**	**3**	**0**	**6**	**0**	**-3**	....	....	....	....	....	....	....	....
	Phoenix Roadrunners	IHL	11	2	0	2	....	....	....	44	....	....	....	....	....	....	....	....	....	....	....	....	....	....	....	....	....	....
1993-94	**Edmonton Oilers**	**NHL**	**2**	**0**	**0**	**0**	**0**	**0**	**0**	**0**	**0**	**0**	**0**	**2**	**0.0**	**1**	**0**	**1**	**1**	**1**	....	....	....	....	....	....	....	....
	Cape Breton Oilers	AHL	41	2	16	18	....	....	....	111	....	....	....	....	....	....	....	....	....	....	....	....	....	....	....	....	....	....
	NHL Totals		**262**	**3**	**22**	**25**	**3**	**17**	**20**	**744**	**0**	**0**	**2**	**163**	**1.8**	**156**	**3**	**215**	**48**		**19**	**0**	**2**	**2**	**65**	**0**	**0**	**0**

• Missed majority of 1990-91 season recovering from wrist injury suffered in game vs. Toronto, November 23, 1990. Traded to **LA Kings** by **Philadelphia** with Jari Kurri for Steve Duchesne, Steve Kasper and LA Kings' 4th round choice (Aris Brimanis) in 1991 Entry Draft, May 30, 1991. Traded to **Pittsburgh** by **LA Kings** with Brian Benning and LA Kings' 1st round choice (later traded to Philadelphia — Philadelphia selected Jason Bowen) in 1992 Entry Draft for Paul Coffey, February 19, 1992. Traded to **LA Kings** by **Pittsburgh** for Peter Ahola, November 6, 1992. Traded to **Edmonton** by **LA Kings** for future considerations, November 2, 1993. Signed as a free agent by **Hartford**, May 27, 1994.

• CHYNOWETH, Dean

D – R. 6'1", 191 lbs. b: Calgary, Alta., 10/30/1968. NY Islanders' 1st, 13th overall, in 1987.

Season	Club	League	GP	G	A	Pts	AG	AA	APts	PIM	PP	SH	GW	S	%	TGF	PGF	TGA	PGA	+/-	GP	G	A	Pts	PIM	PP	SH	GW
1983-84	Calgary Rangers	AAHA	STATISTICS NOT AVAILABLE																									
1984-85	Calgary Buffaloes	AAHA	26	5	13	18	....	....	....	104	....	....	....	....	....	....	....	....	....	....	....	....	....	....	....	....	....	....
	Medicine Hat Tigers	WHL	2	0	0	0	....	....	....	0	....	....	....	....	....	....	....	....	....	....	....	....	....	....	....	....	....	....
1985-86	Medicine Hat Tigers	WHL	69	3	12	15	....	....	....	208	....	....	....	....	....	....	....	....	....	....	17	3	2	5	52	....	....	....
1986-87	Medicine Hat Tigers	WHL	67	3	19	22	....	....	....	285	....	....	....	....	....	....	....	....	....	....	13	4	2	6	28	....	....	....
	Medicine Hat Tigers	Mem-Cup	4	0	0	0	....	....	....	20	....	....	....	....	....	....	....	....	....	....	....	....	....	....	....	....	....	....

			REGULAR SEASON																		PLAYOFFS							
Season	Club	League	GP	G	A	Pts	AG	AA	APts	PIM	PP	SH	GW	S	%	TGF	PGF	TGA	PGA	+/–	GP	G	A	Pts	PIM	PP	SH	GW
1987-88	Medicine Hat Tigers	WHL	64	1	21	22	....	....	....	274	....	....	....	....	....	....	....	....	....	....	16	0	6	6	*87	....	....	....
	Medicine Hat Tigers	Mem-Cup	5	0	2	2	....	....	....	8	....	....	....	....	....	....	....	....	....	....	....	....	....	....	....	....	....	....
1988-89	**New York Islanders**	**NHL**	**6**	**0**	**0**	**0**	**0**	**0**	**0**	**48**	**0**	**0**	**0**	**0**	**0.0**	**0**	**0**	**7**	**3**	**–4**	....	....	....	....	....	....	....	....
1989-90	**New York Islanders**	**NHL**	**20**	**0**	**2**	**2**	**0**	**1**	**1**	**39**	**0**	**0**	**0**	**8**	**0.0**	**10**	**0**	**16**	**6**	**0**	....	....	....	....	....	....	....	....
	Springfield Indians	AHL	40	0	7	7	....	....	....	98	....	....	....	....	....	....	....	....	....	....	17	0	4	4	36	....	....	....
1990-91	**New York Islanders**	**NHL**	**25**	**1**	**1**	**2**	**1**	**1**	**2**	**59**	**0**	**0**	**0**	**14**	**7.1**	**12**	**0**	**19**	**1**	**–6**	....	....	....	....	....	....	....	....
	Capital District Islanders	AHL	44	1	5	6	....	....	....	176	....	....	....	....	....	....	....	....	....	....	....	....	....	....	....	....	....	....
1991-92	**New York Islanders**	**NHL**	**11**	**1**	**0**	**1**	**1**	**0**	**1**	**23**	**0**	**0**	**0**	**6**	**16.7**	**4**	**0**	**9**	**2**	**–3**	....	....	....	....	....	....	....	....
	Capital District Islanders	AHL	43	4	6	10	....	....	....	164	....	....	....	....	....	....	....	....	....	....	6	1	1	2	39	....	....	....
1992-93	Capital District Islanders	AHL	52	3	10	13	....	....	....	197	....	....	....	....	....	....	....	....	....	....	4	0	1	1	9	....	....	....
1993-94	**New York Islanders**	**NHL**	**39**	**0**	**4**	**4**	**0**	**3**	**3**	**122**	**0**	**0**	**0**	**26**	**0.0**	**26**	**0**	**37**	**14**	**3**	**2**	**0**	**0**	**0**	**2**	**0**	**0**	**0**
	Salt Lake Golden Eagles	IHL	5	0	1	1	....	....	....	33	....	....	....	....	....	....	....	....	....	....	....	....	....	....	....	....	....	....
1994-95	**New York Islanders**	**NHL**	**32**	**0**	**2**	**2**	**0**	**3**	**3**	**77**	**0**	**0**	**0**	**22**	**0.0**	**23**	**0**	**23**	**9**	**9**	....	....	....	....	....	....	....	....
1995-96	**New York Islanders**	**NHL**	**14**	**0**	**1**	**1**	**0**	**1**	**1**	**40**	**0**	**0**	**0**	**6**	**0.0**	**4**	**0**	**9**	**1**	**–4**	....	....	....	....	....	....	....	....
	Boston Bruins	**NHL**	**35**	**2**	**5**	**7**	**2**	**4**	**6**	**88**	**0**	**0**	**0**	**32**	**6.3**	**19**	**0**	**24**	**4**	**–1**	**4**	**0**	**0**	**0**	**24**	**0**	**0**	**0**
1996-97	**Boston Bruins**	**NHL**	**57**	**0**	**3**	**3**	**0**	**3**	**3**	**171**	**0**	**0**	**0**	**30**	**0.0**	**27**	**0**	**46**	**7**	**–12**	....	....	....	....	....	....	....	....
	Providence Bruins	AHL	2	0	0	0	....	....	....	13	....	....	....	....	....	....	....	....	....	....	....	....	....	....	....	....	....	....
1997-98	**Boston Bruins**	**NHL**	**2**	**0**	**0**	**0**	**0**	**0**	**0**	**0**	**0**	**0**	**0**	**1**	**0.0**	**0**	**0**	**4**	**0**	**–4**	....	....	....	....	....	....	....	....
	Providence Bruins	AHL	28	2	2	4	....	....	....	123	....	....	....	....	....	....	....	....	....	....	....	....	....	....	....	....	....	....
	Quebec Rafales	IHL	15	2	2	4	....	....	....	39	....	....	....	....	....	....	....	....	....	....	....	....	....	....	....	....	....	....
1998-2000	Utah Grizzlies	IHL	DID NOT PLAY – ASSISTANT COACH																									
	NHL Totals		**241**	**4**	**18**	**22**	**4**	**16**	**20**	**667**	**0**	**0**	**0**	**145**	**2.8**	**125**	**0**	**194**	**47**		**6**	**0**	**0**	**0**	**26**	**0**	**0**	**0**

Traded to **Boston** by **NY Islanders** for Boston's 5th round choice (Petr Sachl) in 1996 Entry Draft, December 9, 1995.

• CHYZOWSKI, Dave

David B. LW – L. 6'1", 190 lbs. b: Edmonton, Alta., 7/11/1971. NY Islanders' 1st, 2nd overall, in 1989.

Season	Club	League	GP	G	A	Pts	AG	AA	APts	PIM	PP	SH	GW	S	%	TGF	PGF	TGA	PGA	+/–	GP	G	A	Pts	PIM	PP	SH	GW
1985-86	Edmonton Carnwood Wireline	AAHA	STATISTICS NOT AVAILABLE																									
1986-87	St. Albert Saints	AJHL	49	22	30	52	....	....	....	114	....	....	....	....	....	....	....	....	....	....	....	....	....	....	....	....	....	....
1987-88	Kamloops Blazers	WHL	66	16	17	33	....	....	....	117	....	....	....	....	....	....	....	....	....	....	18	2	4	6	26	....	....	....
1988-89	Kamloops Blazers	WHL	68	56	48	104	....	....	....	139	....	....	....	....	....	....	....	....	....	....	16	15	13	28	32	....	....	....
1989-90	Kamloops Blazers	WHL	4	5	2	7	....	....	....	17	....	....	....	....	....	....	....	....	....	....	17	11	6	17	46	....	....	....
	Canada	WJC-A	7	9	4	13	....	....	....	2	....	....	....	....	....	....	....	....	....	....	....	....	....	....	....	....	....	....
	New York Islanders	**NHL**	**34**	**8**	**6**	**14**	**7**	**4**	**11**	**45**	**3**	**0**	**1**	**59**	**13.6**	**20**	**7**	**17**	**0**	**–4**	....	....	....	....	....	....	....	....
	Springfield Indians	AHL	4	0	0	0	....	....	....	7	....	....	....	....	....	....	....	....	....	....	....	....	....	....	....	....	....	....
	Kamloops Blazers	Mem-Cup	3	4	3	7	....	....	....	13	....	....	....	....	....	....	....	....	....	....	....	....	....	....	....	....	....	....
1990-91	**New York Islanders**	**NHL**	**56**	**5**	**9**	**14**	**5**	**7**	**12**	**61**	**0**	**0**	**0**	**66**	**7.6**	**22**	**2**	**39**	**0**	**–19**	....	....	....	....	....	....	....	....
	Capital District Islanders	AHL	7	3	6	9	....	....	....	22	....	....	....	....	....	....	....	....	....	....	....	....	....	....	....	....	....	....
1991-92	**New York Islanders**	**NHL**	**12**	**1**	**1**	**2**	**1**	**1**	**2**	**17**	**0**	**0**	**0**	**18**	**5.6**	**5**	**3**	**6**	**0**	**–4**	....	....	....	....	....	....	....	....
	Capital District Islanders	AHL	55	15	18	33	....	....	....	121	....	....	....	....	....	....	....	....	....	....	6	1	1	2	23	....	....	....
1992-93	Capital District Islanders	AHL	66	15	21	36	....	....	....	177	....	....	....	....	....	....	....	....	....	....	3	2	0	2	0	....	....	....
1993-94	**New York Islanders**	**NHL**	**3**	**1**	**0**	**1**	**1**	**0**	**1**	**4**	**0**	**0**	**0**	**4**	**25.0**	**1**	**0**	**2**	**0**	**–1**	**2**	**0**	**0**	**0**	**0**	**0**	**0**	**0**
	Salt Lake Golden Eagles	IHL	66	27	13	40	....	....	....	151	....	....	....	....	....	....	....	....	....	....	....	....	....	....	....	....	....	....
1994-95	**New York Islanders**	**NHL**	**13**	**0**	**0**	**0**	**0**	**0**	**0**	**11**	**0**	**0**	**0**	**11**	**0.0**	**2**	**0**	**4**	**0**	**–2**	....	....	....	....	....	....	....	....
	Kalamazoo Wings	IHL	4	0	4	4	....	....	....	8	....	....	....	....	....	....	....	....	....	....	16	9	5	14	27	....	....	....
1995-96	Adirondack Red Wings	AHL	80	44	39	83	....	....	....	160	....	....	....	....	....	....	....	....	....	....	3	0	0	0	6	....	....	....
1996-97	**Chicago Blackhawks**	**NHL**	**8**	**0**	**0**	**0**	**0**	**0**	**0**	**6**	**0**	**0**	**0**	**6**	**0.0**	**1**	**0**	**0**	**0**	**1**	....	....	....	....	....	....	....	....
	Indianapolis Ice	IHL	76	34	40	74	....	....	....	261	....	....	....	....	....	....	....	....	....	....	4	0	2	2	38	....	....	....
1997-98	Orlando Solar Bears	IHL	17	9	7	16	....	....	....	32	....	....	....	....	....	....	....	....	....	....	....	....	....	....	....	....	....	....
	San Antonio Dragons	IHL	10	1	5	6	....	....	....	39	....	....	....	....	....	....	....	....	....	....	....	....	....	....	....	....	....	....
	Kansas City Blades	IHL	38	19	14	33	....	....	....	88	....	....	....	....	....	....	....	....	....	....	11	5	4	9	11	....	....	....
1998-99	Kansas City Blades	IHL	67	24	15	39	....	....	....	147	....	....	....	....	....	....	....	....	....	....	....	....	....	....	....	....	....	....
99-2000	Kansas City Blades	IHL	81	37	33	70	....	....	....	138	....	....	....	....	....	....	....	....	....	....	....	....	....	....	....	....	....	....
	NHL Totals		**126**	**15**	**16**	**31**	**14**	**12**	**26**	**144**	**3**	**0**	**1**	**164**	**9.1**	**51**	**12**	**68**	**0**		**2**	**0**	**0**	**0**	**0**	**0**	**0**	**0**

WHL West All-Star Team (1989) • WJC-A All-Star Team (1990)

Signed as a free agent by **Detroit**, August 29, 1995. Signed as a free agent by **Chicago**, September 26, 1996.

• CIAVAGLIA, Peter

Peter A. C – L. 5'10", 173 lbs. b: Albany, NY, 7/15/1969. Calgary's 8th, 145th overall, in 1987.

Season	Club	League	GP	G	A	Pts	AG	AA	APts	PIM	PP	SH	GW	S	%	TGF	PGF	TGA	PGA	+/–	GP	G	A	Pts	PIM	PP	SH	GW
1985-86	The Nichols School	Hi-School	60	84	113	197	....	....	....	....	....	....	....	....	....	....	....	....	....	....	....	....	....	....	....	....	....	....
1986-87	The Nichols School	Hi-School	58	53	84	137	....	....	....	....	....	....	....	....	....	....	....	....	....	....	....	....	....	....	....	....	....	....
1987-88	Harvard University	ECAC	30	10	23	33	....	....	....	16	....	....	....	....	....	....	....	....	....	....	....	....	....	....	....	....	....	....
1988-89	Harvard University	ECAC	34	15	48	63	....	....	....	36	....	....	....	....	....	....	....	....	....	....	....	....	....	....	....	....	....	....
	United States	WJC-A	7	1	4	5	....	....	....	0	....	....	....	....	....	....	....	....	....	....	....	....	....	....	....	....	....	....
1989-90	Harvard University	ECAC	28	17	18	35	....	....	....	22	....	....	....	....	....	....	....	....	....	....	....	....	....	....	....	....	....	....
1990-91	Harvard University	ECAC	27	24	*38	*62	....	....	....	2	....	....	....	....	....	....	....	....	....	....	....	....	....	....	....	....	....	....
1991-92	**Buffalo Sabres**	**NHL**	**2**	**0**	**0**	**0**	**0**	**0**	**0**	**0**	**0**	**0**	**0**	**1**	**0.0**	**1**	**0**	**0**	**0**	**1**	....	....	....	....	....	....	....	....
	Rochester Americans	AHL	77	37	61	98	....	....	....	16	....	....	....	....	....	....	....	....	....	....	6	2	5	7	6	....	....	....
1992-93	**Buffalo Sabres**	**NHL**	**3**	**0**	**0**	**0**	**0**	**0**	**0**	**0**	**0**	**0**	**0**	**2**	**0.0**	**1**	**0**	**1**	**0**	**0**	....	....	....	....	....	....	....	....
	Rochester Americans	AHL	64	35	67	102	....	....	....	32	....	....	....	....	....	....	....	....	....	....	17	9	16	25	12	....	....	....
1993-94	United States	Nat-Team	18	2	9	11	....	....	....	6	....	....	....	....	....	....	....	....	....	....	....	....	....	....	....	....	....	....
	Leksands IF	Sweden	39	14	18	32	....	....	....	34	....	....	....	....	....	....	....	....	....	....	4	1	2	3	0	....	....	....
	United States	Olympics	8	2	4	6	....	....	....	0	....	....	....	....	....	....	....	....	....	....	....	....	....	....	....	....	....	....
	United States	WC-A	7	1	0	1	....	....	....	2	....	....	....	....	....	....	....	....	....	....	....	....	....	....	....	....	....	....
1994-95	Detroit Vipers	IHL	73	22	59	81	....	....	....	83	....	....	....	....	....	....	....	....	....	....	5	1	1	2	6	....	....	....
1995-96	Detroit Vipers	IHL	75	22	56	78	....	....	....	38	....	....	....	....	....	....	....	....	....	....	12	6	11	17	12	....	....	....
1996-97	Detroit Vipers	IHL	72	21	51	72	....	....	....	54	....	....	....	....	....	....	....	....	....	....	21	*14	19	*33	32	....	....	....
1997-98	Detroit Vipers	IHL	35	11	30	41	....	....	....	10	....	....	....	....	....	....	....	....	....	....	23	8	11	19	12	....	....	....
1998-99	Detroit Vipers	IHL	59	27	31	58	....	....	....	33	....	....	....	....	....	....	....	....	....	....	11	1	8	9	10	....	....	....
99-2000	Detroit Vipers	IHL	41	5	22	27	....	....	....	14	....	....	....	....	....	....	....	....	....	....	....	....	....	....	....	....	....	....
	NHL Totals		**5**	**0**	**0**	**0**	**0**	**0**	**0**	**0**	**0**	**0**	**0**	**3**	**0.0**	**2**	**0**	**1**	**0**		....	....	....	....	....	....	....	....

ECAC Second All-Star Team (1989) • ECAC First All-Star Team (1991) • NCAA East Second All-American Team (1991) • Won "Bud" Poile Trophy (Playoff MVP - IHL) (1997)

Signed as a free agent by **Buffalo**, August 30, 1991.

• CICCARELLI, Dino

RW – R. 5'10", 185 lbs. b: Sarnia, Ont., 2/8/1960.

Season	Club	League	GP	G	A	Pts	AG	AA	APts	PIM	PP	SH	GW	S	%	TGF	PGF	TGA	PGA	+/–	GP	G	A	Pts	PIM	PP	SH	GW
1974-75	Sarnia Army Vets	OMHA	STATISTICS NOT AVAILABLE																									
1975-76	Sarnia Bees	OHA-B	40	45	43	88	....	....	....	....	....	....	....	....	....	....	....	....	....	....	....	....	....	....	....	....	....	....
1976-77	London Knights	OMJHL	66	39	43	82	....	....	....	45	....	....	....	....	....	....	....	....	....	....	20	11	13	24	14	....	....	....
1977-78	London Knights	OMJHL	68	72	70	142	....	....	....	49	....	....	....	....	....	....	....	....	....	....	9	6	10	16	6	....	....	....
1978-79	London Knights	OMJHL	30	8	11	19	....	....	....	35	....	....	....	....	....	....	....	....	....	....	7	3	5	8	0	....	....	....
1979-80	London Knights	OMJHL	62	50	53	103	....	....	....	72	....	....	....	....	....	....	....	....	....	....	5	2	6	8	15	....	....	....
	Canada	WJC-A	5	5	1	6	....	....	....	2	....	....	....	....	....	....	....	....	....	....	....	....	....	....	....	....	....	....
	Oklahoma City	CHL	6	3	2	5	....	....	....	0	....	....	....	....	....	....	....	....	....	....	....	....	....	....	....	....	....	....
1980-81	**Minnesota North Stars**	**NHL**	**32**	**18**	**12**	**30**	**14**	**8**	**22**	**29**	**8**	**0**	**0**	**126**	**14.3**	**45**	**15**	**28**	**0**	**2**	**19**	**14**	**7**	**21**	**25**	**5**	**0**	**3**
	Oklahoma City Stars	CHL	48	32	25	57	....	....	....	45	....	....	....	....	....	....	....	....	....	....	....	....	....	....	....	....	....	....
1981-82	**Minnesota North Stars**	**NHL**	**76**	**55**	**51**	**106**	**44**	**34**	**78**	**138**	**20**	**0**	**4**	**289**	**19.0**	**145**	**54**	**77**	**0**	**14**	**4**	**3**	**1**	**4**	**2**	**2**	**0**	**1**
	Canada	WEC-A	9	2	1	3	....	....	....	0	....	....	....	....	....	....	....	....	....	....	....	....	....	....	....	....	....	....
1982-83	**Minnesota North Stars**	**NHL**	**77**	**37**	**38**	**75**	**30**	**26**	**56**	**94**	**14**	**0**	**4**	**210**	**17.6**	**111**	**38**	**57**	**0**	**16**	**9**	**4**	**6**	**10**	**11**	**1**	**0**	**2**
1983-84	**Minnesota North Stars**	**NHL**	**79**	**38**	**33**	**71**	**31**	**22**	**53**	**58**	**16**	**0**	**2**	**211**	**18.0**	**111**	**46**	**66**	**2**	**1**	**16**	**4**	**5**	**9**	**27**	**1**	**0**	**1**
1984-85	**Minnesota North Stars**	**NHL**	**51**	**15**	**17**	**32**	**12**	**12**	**24**	**41**	**5**	**0**	**0**	**133**	**11.3**	**51**	**14**	**48**	**1**	**–10**	**9**	**3**	**3**	**6**	**8**	**1**	**0**	**0**
1985-86	**Minnesota North Stars**	**NHL**	**75**	**44**	**45**	**89**	**35**	**30**	**65**	**51**	**19**	**0**	**5**	**262**	**16.8**	**122**	**46**	**64**	**0**	**12**	**5**	**0**	**1**	**1**	**6**	**0**	**0**	**0**

Season	Club	League	GP	G	A	Pts	AG	AA	APts	PIM	PP	SH	GW	S	%	TGF	PGF	TGA	PGA	+/-	GP	G	A	Pts	PIM	PP	SH	GW
			REGULAR SEASON																		PLAYOFFS							
1986-87	**Minnesota North Stars**	**NHL**	**80**	**52**	**51**	**103**	**45**	**37**	**82**	**88**	**22**	**0**	**5**	**255**	**20.4**	**143**	**55**	**78**	**0**	**10**	....	....	....	....	....	....	....	....
	Canada	WEC-A	10	4	2	6	....	....	....	2	....	....	....	....	....	....	....	....	....	....	....	....	....	....	....	....	....	....
1987-88	**Minnesota North Stars**	**NHL**	**67**	**41**	**45**	**86**	**35**	**32**	**67**	**79**	**13**	**1**	**2**	**262**	**15.6**	**107**	**48**	**109**	**21**	**–29**	....	....	....	....	....	....	....	....
1988-89	**Minnesota North Stars**	**NHL**	**65**	**32**	**27**	**59**	**27**	**19**	**46**	**64**	**13**	**0**	**5**	**208**	**15.4**	**82**	**34**	**64**	**0**	**–16**	....	....	....	....	....	....	....	....
	Washington Capitals	**NHL**	**11**	**12**	**3**	**15**	**10**	**2**	**12**	**12**	**3**	**0**	**3**	**39**	**30.8**	**20**	**8**	**2**	**0**	**10**	**6**	**3**	**3**	**6**	**12**	**3**	**0**	**0**
1989-90	Washington Capitals	Fr-Tour	3	3	0	3	....	....	....	2	....	....	....	....	....	....	....	....	....	....	....	....	....	....	....	....	....	....
	Washington Capitals	**NHL**	**80**	**41**	**38**	**79**	**35**	**27**	**62**	**122**	**10**	**0**	**6**	**267**	**15.4**	**120**	**38**	**88**	**1**	**–5**	**8**	**8**	**3**	**11**	**6**	**1**	**0**	**1**
1990-91	**Washington Capitals**	**NHL**	**54**	**21**	**18**	**39**	**19**	**14**	**33**	**66**	**2**	**0**	**2**	**186**	**11.3**	**60**	**15**	**62**	**0**	**–17**	**11**	**5**	**4**	**9**	**22**	**3**	**0**	**2**
1991-92	**Washington Capitals**	**NHL**	**78**	**38**	**38**	**76**	**35**	**29**	**64**	**78**	**13**	**0**	**7**	**279**	**13.6**	**109**	**37**	**82**	**0**	**–10**	**7**	**5**	**4**	**9**	**14**	**1**	**0**	**0**
1992-93	**Detroit Red Wings**	**NHL**	**82**	**41**	**56**	**97**	**34**	**39**	**73**	**81**	**21**	**0**	**8**	**200**	**20.5**	**143**	**67**	**64**	**0**	**12**	**7**	**4**	**2**	**6**	**16**	**3**	**0**	**0**
1993-94	**Detroit Red Wings**	**NHL**	**66**	**28**	**29**	**57**	**26**	**22**	**48**	**73**	**12**	**0**	**1**	**153**	**18.3**	**107**	**42**	**56**	**1**	**10**	**7**	**5**	**2**	**7**	**14**	**1**	**0**	**0**
1994-95	**Detroit Red Wings**	**NHL**	**42**	**16**	**27**	**43**	**28**	**40**	**68**	**39**	**6**	**0**	**3**	**106**	**15.1**	**63**	**26**	**25**	**0**	**12**	**16**	**9**	**2**	**11**	**22**	**6**	**0**	**2**
1995-96	**Detroit Red Wings**	**NHL**	**64**	**22**	**21**	**43**	**22**	**17**	**39**	**99**	**13**	**0**	**5**	**107**	**20.6**	**78**	**37**	**27**	**0**	**14**	**17**	**6**	**2**	**8**	**26**	**6**	**0**	**1**
1996-97	**Tampa Bay Lightning**	**NHL**	**77**	**35**	**25**	**60**	**37**	**22**	**59**	**116**	**12**	**0**	**6**	**229**	**15.3**	**92**	**32**	**72**	**1**	**–11**	....	....	....	....	....	....	....	....
1997-98	**Tampa Bay Lightning**	**NHL**	**34**	**11**	**6**	**17**	**13**	**6**	**19**	**42**	**3**	**0**	**3**	**104**	**10.6**	**22**	**9**	**27**	**0**	**–14**	....	....	....	....	....	....	....	....
	Florida Panthers	**NHL**	**28**	**5**	**11**	**16**	**6**	**11**	**17**	**28**	**2**	**0**	**1**	**57**	**8.8**	**29**	**13**	**18**	**0**	**–2**	....	....	....	....	....	....	....	....
1998-99	**Florida Panthers**	**NHL**	**14**	**6**	**1**	**7**	**7**	**1**	**8**	**27**	**5**	**0**	**1**	**23**	**26.1**	**10**	**7**	**4**	**0**	**–1**	....	....	....	....	....	....	....	....
	NHL Totals		**1232**	**608**	**592**	**1200**	**545**	**450**	**995**	**1425**	**232**	**1**	**73**	**3706**	**16.4**	**1770**	**681**	**1118**	**27**		**141**	**73**	**45**	**118**	**211**	**34**	**0**	**13**

OMJHL Second All-Star Team (1978) • Played in NHL All-Star Game (1982, 1983, 1989, 1997)

Signed as a free agent by **Minnesota**, September 28, 1979. Traded to **Washington** by **Minnesota** with Bob Rouse for Mike Gartner and Larry Murphy, March 7, 1989. Traded to **Detroit** by **Washington** for Kevin Miller, June 20, 1992. Traded to **Tampa Bay** by **Detroit** for Tampa Bay's 4th round choice (later traded to Toronto–Toronto selected Alexei Ponikarovsky) in 1998 Entry Draft, August 27, 1996. Traded to **Florida** by **Tampa Bay** with Jeff Norton for Mark Fitzpatrick and Jody Hull, January 15, 1998. • Missed majority of 1998-99 season with back injury suffered in game vs. Chicago, November 4, 1998. • Officially announced retirement, August 31, 1999.

• CICCONE, Enrico

D – L. 6'5", 220 lbs. b: Montreal, Que., 4/10/1970. Minnesota's 5th, 92nd overall, in 1990.

Season	Club	League	GP	G	A	Pts	AG	AA	APts	PIM	PP	SH	GW	S	%	TGF	PGF	TGA	PGA	+/-	GP	G	A	Pts	PIM	PP	SH	GW
1986-87	Lac St-Louis Lions	QAAA	38	10	20	30	....	....	....	172	....	....	....	....	....	....	....	....	....	....	....	....	....	....	....	....	....	....
1987-88	Shawinigan Cataractes	QMJHL	61	2	12	14	....	....	....	324	....	....	....	....	....	....	....	....	....	....	....	....	....	....	....	....	....	....
1988-89	Shawinigan Cataractes	QMJHL	34	7	11	18	....	....	....	132	....	....	....	....	....	....	....	....	....	....	....	....	....	....	....	....	....	....
	Trois-Rivieres Draveurs	QMJHL	24	0	7	7	....	....	....	153	....	....	....	....	....	....	....	....	....	....	....	....	....	....	....	....	....	....
1989-90	Trois-Rivieres Draveurs	QMJHL	40	4	24	28	....	....	....	227	....	....	....	....	....	....	....	....	....	....	3	0	0	0	15	....	....	....
1990-91	Kalamazoo Wings	IHL	57	4	9	13	....	....	....	384	....	....	....	....	....	....	....	....	....	....	4	0	1	1	32	....	....	....
1991-92	**Minnesota North Stars**	**NHL**	**11**	**0**	**0**	**0**	**0**	**0**	**0**	**48**	**0**	**0**	**0**	**2**	**0.0**	**2**	**0**	**4**	**0**	**–2**	....	....	....	....	....	....	....	....
	Kalamazoo Wings	IHL	53	4	16	20	....	....	....	406	....	....	....	....	....	....	....	....	....	....	10	0	1	1	58	....	....	....
1992-93	**Minnesota North Stars**	**NHL**	**31**	**0**	**1**	**1**	**0**	**1**	**1**	**115**	**0**	**0**	**0**	**13**	**0.0**	**10**	**0**	**11**	**3**	**2**	....	....	....	....	....	....	....	....
	Kalamazoo Wings	IHL	13	1	3	4	....	....	....	50	....	....	....	....	....	....	....	....	....	....	....	....	....	....	....	....	....	....
	Hamilton Canucks	AHL	6	1	3	4	....	....	....	44	....	....	....	....	....	....	....	....	....	....	....	....	....	....	....	....	....	....
1993-94	**Washington Capitals**	**NHL**	**46**	**1**	**1**	**2**	**1**	**1**	**2**	**174**	**0**	**0**	**0**	**23**	**4.3**	**10**	**0**	**13**	**1**	**–2**	....	....	....	....	....	....	....	....
	Portland Pirates	AHL	6	0	0	0	....	....	....	27	....	....	....	....	....	....	....	....	....	....	....	....	....	....	....	....	....	....
	Tampa Bay Lightning	**NHL**	**11**	**0**	**1**	**1**	**0**	**1**	**1**	**52**	**0**	**0**	**0**	**10**	**0.0**	**4**	**0**	**7**	**1**	**–2**	....	....	....	....	....	....	....	....
1994-95	**Tampa Bay Lightning**	**NHL**	**41**	**2**	**4**	**6**	**4**	**6**	**10**	***225**	**0**	**0**	**0**	**43**	**4.7**	**25**	**0**	**23**	**1**	**3**	....	....	....	....	....	....	....	....
1995-96	**Tampa Bay Lightning**	**NHL**	**55**	**2**	**3**	**5**	**2**	**2**	**4**	**258**	**0**	**0**	**0**	**48**	**4.2**	**27**	**1**	**47**	**17**	**–4**	....	....	....	....	....	....	....	....
	Chicago Blackhawks	**NHL**	**11**	**0**	**1**	**1**	**0**	**1**	**1**	**48**	**0**	**0**	**0**	**12**	**0.0**	**6**	**0**	**2**	**1**	**5**	**9**	**1**	**0**	**1**	**30**	**0**	**0**	**0**
1996-97	**Chicago Blackhawks**	**NHL**	**67**	**2**	**2**	**4**	**2**	**2**	**4**	**233**	**0**	**0**	**1**	**65**	**3.1**	**28**	**0**	**33**	**4**	**–1**	**4**	**0**	**0**	**0**	**18**	**0**	**0**	**0**
1997-98	**Carolina Hurricanes**	**NHL**	**14**	**0**	**3**	**3**	**0**	**3**	**3**	**83**	**0**	**0**	**0**	**8**	**0.0**	**5**	**0**	**3**	**1**	**3**	....	....	....	....	....	....	....	....
	Vancouver Canucks	**NHL**	**13**	**0**	**1**	**1**	**0**	**1**	**1**	**47**	**0**	**0**	**0**	**7**	**0.0**	**9**	**1**	**15**	**5**	**–2**	....	....	....	....	....	....	....	....
	Tampa Bay Lightning	**NHL**	**12**	**0**	**0**	**0**	**0**	**0**	**0**	**45**	**0**	**0**	**0**	**7**	**0.0**	**3**	**0**	**7**	**1**	**–3**	....	....	....	....	....	....	....	....
1998-99	**Tampa Bay Lightning**	**NHL**	**16**	**1**	**1**	**2**	**1**	**1**	**2**	**24**	**0**	**0**	**0**	**9**	**11.1**	**8**	**0**	**11**	**2**	**–1**	....	....	....	....	....	....	....	....
	Cleveland Lumberjacks	IHL	6	0	0	0	....	....	....	23	....	....	....	....	....	....	....	....	....	....	....	....	....	....	....	....	....	....
	Washington Capitals	**NHL**	**43**	**2**	**0**	**2**	**2**	**0**	**2**	**103**	**0**	**0**	**0**	**43**	**4.7**	**17**	**0**	**26**	**3**	**–6**	....	....	....	....	....	....	....	....
99-2000	Moskitos Essen	Germany	14	0	4	4	....	....	....	101	....	....	....	....	....	....	....	....	....	....	....	....	....	....	....	....	....	....
	NHL Totals		**371**	**10**	**18**	**28**	**12**	**19**	**31**	**1455**	**0**	**0**	**1**	**290**	**3.4**	**154**	**2**	**202**	**40**		**13**	**1**	**0**	**1**	**48**	**0**	**0**	**0**

Traded to **Washington** by **Dallas** to complete transaction that sent Paul Cavallini to Dallas (June 20, 1993), June 25, 1993. Traded to **Tampa Bay** by **Washington** with Washington's 3rd round choice (later traded to Anaheim — Anaheim selected Craig Reichert) in 1994 Entry Draft and the return of conditional draft choice transferred in the Pat Elynuik trade for Joe Reekie, March 21, 1994. Traded to **Chicago** by **Tampa Bay** with Tampa Bay's 2nd round choice (Jeff Paul) in 1996 Entry Draft for Patrick Poulin, Igor Ulanov and Chicago's 2nd round choice (later traded to New Jersey — New Jersey selected Pierre Dagenais) in 1996 Entry Draft, March 20, 1996. Traded to **Carolina** by **Chicago** for Ryan Risidore and Carolina's 5th round choice (later traded to Toronto–Toronto selected Morgan Warren) in 1998 Entry Draft, July 25, 1997. Traded to **Vancouver** by **Carolina** with Sean Burke and Geoff Sanderson for Kirk McLean and Martin Gelinas, January 3, 1998. Traded to **Tampa Bay** by **Vancouver** for Jamie Huscroft, March 14, 1998. Traded to **Washington** by **Tampa Bay** for cash, December 28, 1998. Signed as a free agent by **Montreal**, July 7, 2000.

• CICHOCKI, Chris

Christopher J. RW – R. 5'11", 185 lbs. b: Detroit, MI, 9/17/1963.

Season	Club	League	GP	G	A	Pts	AG	AA	APts	PIM	PP	SH	GW	S	%	TGF	PGF	TGA	PGA	+/-	GP	G	A	Pts	PIM	PP	SH	GW
1979-80	Grosse Point Majors	MNHL	70	50	70	120	....	....	....	....	....	....	....	....	....	....	....	....	....	....	....	....	....	....	....	....	....	....
1980-81	Paddock Pool Saints	GLJHL	STATISTICS NOT AVAILABLE																									
1981-82	Paddock Pool Saints	GLJHL	STATISTICS NOT AVAILABLE																									
1982-83	Michigan Tech Huskies	CCHA	36	12	10	22	....	....	....	10	....	....	....	....	....	....	....	....	....	....	....	....	....	....	....	....	....	....
1983-84	Michigan Tech Huskies	CCHA	40	25	20	45	....	....	....	36	....	....	....	....	....	....	....	....	....	....	....	....	....	....	....	....	....	....
1984-85	Michigan Tech Huskies	CCHA	40	30	24	54	....	....	....	14	....	....	....	....	....	....	....	....	....	....	....	....	....	....	....	....	....	....
1985-86	**Detroit Red Wings**	**NHL**	**59**	**10**	**11**	**21**	**8**	**7**	**15**	**21**	**1**	**1**	**0**	**76**	**13.2**	**32**	**4**	**43**	**7**	**–8**	....	....	....	....	....	....	....	....
	Adirondack Red Wings	AHL	9	4	4	8	....	....	....	6	....	....	....	....	....	....	....	....	....	....	....	....	....	....	....	....	....	....
1986-87	**Detroit Red Wings**	**NHL**	**2**	**0**	**0**	**0**	**0**	**0**	**0**	**2**	**0**	**0**	**0**	**0**	**0.0**	**1**	**0**	**3**	**0**	**–2**	....	....	....	....	....	....	....	....
	Adirondack Red Wings	AHL	55	31	34	65	....	....	....	27	....	....	....	....	....	....	....	....	....	....	....	....	....	....	....	....	....	....
	Maine Mariners	AHL	7	2	2	4	....	....	....	0	....	....	....	....	....	....	....	....	....	....	....	....	....	....	....	....	....	....
1987-88	**New Jersey Devils**	**NHL**	**5**	**1**	**0**	**1**	**1**	**0**	**1**	**2**	**0**	**0**	**0**	**2**	**50.0**	**3**	**0**	**2**	**0**	**1**	....	....	....	....	....	....	....	....
	Utica Devils	AHL	69	36	30	66	....	....	....	66	....	....	....	....	....	....	....	....	....	....	....	....	....	....	....	....	....	....
1988-89	**New Jersey Devils**	**NHL**	**2**	**0**	**1**	**1**	**0**	**1**	**1**	**2**	**0**	**0**	**0**	**2**	**0.0**	**1**	**0**	**1**	**0**	**0**	....	....	....	....	....	....	....	....
	Utica Devils	AHL	59	32	31	63	....	....	....	50	....	....	....	....	....	....	....	....	....	....	5	0	1	1	2	....	....	....
1989-90	Utica Devils	AHL	11	3	1	4	....	....	....	10	....	....	....	....	....	....	....	....	....	....	....	....	....	....	....	....	....	....
	Binghamton Whalers	AHL	60	21	26	47	....	....	....	22	....	....	....	....	....	....	....	....	....	....	....	....	....	....	....	....	....	....
1990-91	Binghamton Rangers	AHL	80	35	30	65	....	....	....	70	....	....	....	....	....	....	....	....	....	....	9	0	4	4	2	....	....	....
1991-92	Binghamton Rangers	AHL	75	28	29	57	....	....	....	132	....	....	....	....	....	....	....	....	....	....	6	5	4	9	4	....	....	....
1992-93	Binghamton Rangers	AHL	65	23	29	52	....	....	....	78	....	....	....	....	....	....	....	....	....	....	9	3	2	5	25	....	....	....
1993-94	Cincinnati Cyclones	IHL	69	22	20	42	....	....	....	101	....	....	....	....	....	....	....	....	....	....	11	2	2	4	12	....	....	....
1994-95	Cincinnati Cyclones	IHL	75	22	30	52	....	....	....	50	....	....	....	....	....	....	....	....	....	....	8	0	3	3	6	....	....	....
1995-96	Cincinnati Cyclones	IHL	57	4	7	11	....	....	....	30	....	....	....	....	....	....	....	....	....	....	14	0	1	1	10	....	....	....
1996-97	Cincinnati Cyclones	IHL	35	6	9	15	....	....	....	30	....	....	....	....	....	....	....	....	....	....	1	0	0	0	0	....	....	....
1997-98	Cincinnati Cyclones	IHL	6	0	0	0	....	....	....	0	....	....	....	....	....	....	....	....	....	....	....	....	....	....	....	....	....	....
	NHL Totals		**68**	**11**	**12**	**23**	**9**	**8**	**17**	**27**	**1**	**1**	**0**	**80**	**13.8**	**37**	**4**	**49**	**7**									

Signed as a free agent by **Detroit**, June 28, 1985. Traded to **New Jersey** by **Detroit** with Detroit's 3rd round choice (later traded to Buffalo — Buffalo selected Andrew McVicar) in 1987 Entry Draft for Mel Bridgman, March 9, 1987. Traded to **Hartford** by **New Jersey** for Jim Thompson, October 31, 1989. • Served as playing assistant coach with Cincinnati Cyclones (IHL), 1995-1999.

• CIERNIK, Ivan

LW – L. 6'1", 234 lbs. b: Levice, Czech., 10/30/1977. Ottawa's 6th, 216th overall, in 1996.

Season	Club	League	GP	G	A	Pts	AG	AA	APts	PIM	PP	SH	GW	S	%	TGF	PGF	TGA	PGA	+/-	GP	G	A	Pts	PIM	PP	SH	GW
1994-95	MHC Nitra	Slovak-Jr.	30	22	15	37	....	....	....	36	....	....	....	....	....	....	....	....	....	....	....	....	....	....	....	....	....	....
	MHC Nitra	Slovakia	7	1	0	1	....	....	....	2	....	....	....	....	....	....	....	....	....	....	....	....	....	....	....	....	....	....
1995-96	MHC Nitra	Slovakia	35	9	7	16	....	....	....	36	....	....	....	....	....	....	....	....	....	....	8	3	3	6	....	....	....	....
	Slovakia	WJC-A	6	2	0	2	....	....	....	2	....	....	....	....	....	....	....	....	....	....	....	....	....	....	....	....	....	....
1996-97	MHC Nitra	Slovakia	41	11	19	30	....	....	....	....	....	....	....	....	....	....	....	....	....	....	....	....	....	....	....	....	....	....
	Slovakia	WJC-A	6	1	2	3	....	....	....	18	....	....	....	....	....	....	....	....	....	....	....	....	....	....	....	....	....	....
1997-98	**Ottawa Senators**	**NHL**	**2**	**0**	**0**	**0**	**0**	**0**	**0**	**0**	**0**	**0**	**0**	**0**	**0.0**	**0**	**0**	**0**	**0**	**0**	....	....	....	....	....	....	....	....
	Worcester IceCats	AHL	53	9	12	21	....	....	....	38	....	....	....	....	....	....	....	....	....	....	1	0	0	0	2	....	....	....

			REGULAR SEASON																		PLAYOFFS							
Season	Club	League	GP	G	A	Pts	AG	AA	APts	PIM	PP	SH	GW	S	%	TGF	PGF	TGA	PGA	+/–	GP	G	A	Pts	PIM	PP	SH	GW
1998-99	Adirondack Red Wings	AHL	21	1	4	5	....	....	....	4	....	....	....	....	....	....	....	....	....	....	....	....	....	....	....	....	....	....
	Cincinnati Mighty Ducks	AHL	32	10	3	13	....	....	....	10	....	....	....	....	....	....	....	....	....	....	2	0	0	0	2	....	....	....
99-2000	Grand Rapids Griffins	IHL	66	13	12	25	....	....	....	64	....	....	....	....	....	....	....	....	....	....	6	0	6	6	2	....	....	....
	NHL Totals		**2**	**0**	**0**	**0**	**0**	**0**	**0**	**0**	**0**	**0**	**0**	**0**	**0.0**	**0**	**0**	**0**	**0**		....	....	....	....	....	....	....	....

Loaned to **Cincinnati** (AHL) by **Ottawa** with Ratislav Pavlikovsky and Erich Goldmann, January 12, 1999.

• CIERNY, Jozef

LW – L. 6'2", 185 lbs. b: Zvolen, Czech., 5/13/1974. Buffalo's 2nd, 35th overall, in 1992.

Season	Club	League	GP	G	A	Pts	AG	AA	APts	PIM	PP	SH	GW	S	%	TGF	PGF	TGA	PGA	+/–	GP	G	A	Pts	PIM	PP	SH	GW
1991-92	ZTK Zvolen	Czech-2	26	10	3	13	....	....	....	8	....	....	....	....	....	....	....	....	....	....	....	....	....	....	....	....	....	....
	Czechoslovakia	EJC-A	6	3	2	5	....	....	....	4	....	....	....	....	....	....	....	....	....	....	....	....	....	....	....	....	....	....
1992-93	Rochester Americans	AHL	54	27	27	54	....	....	....	36	....	....	....	....	....	....	....	....	....	....	....	....	....	....	....	....	....	....
1993-94	**Edmonton Oilers**	**NHL**	**1**	**0**	**0**	**0**	**0**	**0**	**0**	**0**	**0**	**0**	**0**	**0**	**0.0**	**0**	**0**	**1**	**0**	**–1**	....	....	....	....	....	....	....	....
	Cape Breton Oilers	AHL	73	30	27	57	....	....	....	88	....	....	....	....	....	....	....	....	....	....	4	1	1	2	4	....	....	....
1994-95	Cape Breton Oilers	AHL	73	28	24	52	....	....	....	58	....	....	....	....	....	....	....	....	....	....	....	....	....	....	....	....	....	....
1995-96	Detroit Vipers	IHL	20	2	5	7	....	....	....	16	....	....	....	....	....	....	....	....	....	....	....	....	....	....	....	....	....	....
	Los Angeles Ice Dogs	IHL	43	23	16	39	....	....	....	36	....	....	....	....	....	....	....	....	....	....	....	....	....	....	....	....	....	....
1996-97	Long Beach Ice Dogs	IHL	68	27	27	54	....	....	....	106	....	....	....	....	....	....	....	....	....	....	16	8	5	13	7	....	....	....
1997-98	Nurnberg Ice Tigers	Germany	45	20	22	42	....	....	....	61	....	....	....	....	....	....	....	....	....	....	....	....	....	....	....	....	....	....
1998-99	Nurnberg Ice Tigers	Germany	47	22	21	43	....	....	....	65	....	....	....	....	....	....	....	....	....	....	13	3	2	5	37	....	....	....
99-2000	Nurnberg Ice Tigers	Germany	67	19	15	34	....	....	....	68	....	....	....	....	....	....	....	....	....	....	....	....	....	....	....	....	....	....
	Nurnberg Ice Tigers	EuroHL	5	3	1	4	....	....	....	10	....	....	....	....	....	....	....	....	....	....	2	0	0	0	0	....	....	....
	NHL Totals		**1**	**0**	**0**	**0**	**0**	**0**	**0**	**0**	**0**	**0**	**0**	**0**	**0.0**	**0**	**0**	**1**	**0**		....	....	....	....	....	....	....	....

Traded to **Edmonton** by **Buffalo** with Buffalo's 4th round choice (Jussi Tarvainen) in 1994 Entry Draft for Craig Simpson, September 1, 1993.

• CIGER, Zdeno

LW – L. 6'1", 190 lbs. b: Martin, Czech., 10/19/1969. New Jersey's 3rd, 54th overall, in 1988.

Season	Club	League	GP	G	A	Pts	AG	AA	APts	PIM	PP	SH	GW	S	%	TGF	PGF	TGA	PGA	+/–	GP	G	A	Pts	PIM	PP	SH	GW
1986-87	Dukla Trencin	Czech-Jr.	STATISTICS NOT AVAILABLE																									
	Czechoslovakia	EJC-A	7	3	3	6	....	....	....	18	....	....	....	....	....	....	....	....	....	....	....	....	....	....	....	....	....	....
1987-88	Dukla Trencin	Czech.	8	3	4	7	....	....	....	2	....	....	....	....	....	....	....	....	....	....	....	....	....	....	....	....	....	....
	Czechoslovakia	WJC-A	7	5	0	5	....	....	....	0	....	....	....	....	....	....	....	....	....	....	....	....	....	....	....	....	....	....
1988-89	Dukla Trencin	Czech.	43	18	13	31	....	....	....	18	....	....	....	....	....	....	....	....	....	....	....	....	....	....	....	....	....	....
	Czechoslovakia	WEC-A	10	2	5	7	....	....	....	8	....	....	....	....	....	....	....	....	....	....	....	....	....	....	....	....	....	....
1989-90	Dukla Trencin	Czech.	44	17	24	41	....	....	....	8	....	....	....	....	....	....	....	....	....	....	9	1	4	5	....	....	....	....
	Czechoslovakia	WEC-A	10	5	1	6	....	....	....	4	....	....	....	....	....	....	....	....	....	....	....	....	....	....	....	....	....	....
1990-91	**New Jersey Devils**	**NHL**	**45**	**8**	**17**	**25**	**7**	**13**	**20**	**8**	**2**	**0**	**1**	**82**	**9.8**	**32**	**8**	**21**	**0**	**3**	**6**	**0**	**2**	**2**	**4**	**0**	**0**	**0**
	Utica Devils	AHL	8	5	4	9	....	....	....	2	....	....	....	....	....	....	....	....	....	....	....	....	....	....	....	....	....	....
1991-92	Czechoslovakia	Can-Cup	5	0	0	0	....	....	....	2	....	....	....	....	....	....	....	....	....	....	....	....	....	....	....	....	....	....
	New Jersey Devils	**NHL**	**20**	**6**	**5**	**11**	**5**	**4**	**9**	**10**	**1**	**0**	**0**	**33**	**18.2**	**18**	**5**	**15**	**0**	**–2**	**7**	**2**	**4**	**6**	**0**	**0**	**0**	**1**
1992-93	**New Jersey Devils**	**NHL**	**27**	**4**	**8**	**12**	**3**	**5**	**8**	**2**	**2**	**0**	**1**	**39**	**10.3**	**18**	**6**	**28**	**8**	**–8**	....	....	....	....	....	....	....	....
	Edmonton Oilers	**NHL**	**37**	**9**	**15**	**24**	**7**	**10**	**17**	**6**	**0**	**0**	**1**	**67**	**13.4**	**34**	**12**	**32**	**5**	**–5**	....	....	....	....	....	....	....	....
1993-94	**Edmonton Oilers**	**NHL**	**84**	**22**	**35**	**57**	**20**	**27**	**47**	**8**	**8**	**0**	**1**	**158**	**13.9**	**79**	**28**	**67**	**5**	**–11**	....	....	....	....	....	....	....	....
1994-95	Dukla Trencin	Slovakia	34	23	25	48	....	....	....	8	....	....	....	....	....	....	....	....	....	....	9	2	9	11	2	....	....	....
	Slovakia	WC-B	7	7	4	11	....	....	....	4	....	....	....	....	....	....	....	....	....	....	....	....	....	....	....	....	....	....
	Edmonton Oilers	**NHL**	**5**	**2**	**2**	**4**	**4**	**3**	**7**	**0**	**1**	**0**	**1**	**10**	**20.0**	**6**	**3**	**4**	**0**	**–1**	....	....	....	....	....	....	....	....
1995-96	**Edmonton Oilers**	**NHL**	**78**	**31**	**39**	**70**	**30**	**32**	**62**	**41**	**12**	**0**	**3**	**184**	**16.8**	**107**	**49**	**73**	**0**	**–15**	....	....	....	....	....	....	....	....
	Slovakia	WC-A	5	1	1	2	....	....	....	2	....	....	....	....	....	....	....	....	....	....	....	....	....	....	....	....	....	....
1996-97	Slovakia	W-Cup	3	1	0	1	....	....	....	2	....	....	....	....	....	....	....	....	....	....	....	....	....	....	....	....	....	....
	Slovan Bratislava	Slovakia	44	26	27	53	....	....	....	....	....	....	....	....	....	....	....	....	....	....	2	1	3	4	....	....	....	....
	Slovan Bratislava	EuroHL	6	4	5	9	....	....	....	2	....	....	....	....	....	....	....	....	....	....	2	1	1	2	2	....	....	....
	Slovakia	WC-A	8	4	1	5	....	....	....	12	....	....	....	....	....	....	....	....	....	....	....	....	....	....	....	....	....	....
1997-98	Slovan Bratislava	Slovakia	36	14	*31	45	....	....	....	2	....	....	....	....	....	....	....	....	....	....	11	6	*10	*16	4	....	....	....
	Slovan Bratislava	EuroHL	8	1	5	6	....	....	....	6	....	....	....	....	....	....	....	....	....	....	....	....	....	....	....	....	....	....
	Slovakia	Olympics	4	1	1	2	....	....	....	4	....	....	....	....	....	....	....	....	....	....	....	....	....	....	....	....	....	....
	Slovakia	WC-A	6	0	1	1	....	....	....	2	....	....	....	....	....	....	....	....	....	....	....	....	....	....	....	....	....	....
1998-99	Slovan Bratislava	Slovakia	40	26	32	*58	....	....	....	8	....	....	....	....	....	....	....	....	....	....	9	3	*10	13	2	....	....	....
	Slovan Bratislava	EuroHL	6	4	5	9	....	....	....	8	....	....	....	....	....	....	....	....	....	....	....	....	....	....	....	....	....	....
	Slovakia	WC-A	6	2	4	6	....	....	....	4	....	....	....	....	....	....	....	....	....	....	....	....	....	....	....	....	....	....
99-2000	Slovan Bratislava	Slovakia	51	23	39	62	....	....	....	48	....	....	....	....	....	....	....	....	....	....	8	1	*8	*9	0	....	....	....
	Slovan Bratislava	EuroHL	6	3	4	7	....	....	....	2	....	....	....	....	....	....	....	....	....	....	2	0	2	2	4	....	....	....
	NHL Totals		**296**	**82**	**121**	**203**	**76**	**94**	**170**	**75**	**26**	**0**	**8**	**573**	**14.3**	**294**	**111**	**240**	**18**		**13**	**2**	**6**	**8**	**4**	**0**	**0**	**1**

Czechoslovakian Rookie of the Year (1989)

Traded to **Edmonton** by **New Jersey** with Kevin Todd for Bernie Nicholls, January 13, 1993. Claimed by **Nashville** from **Edmonton** in NHL Waiver Draft, October 5, 1998.

• CIMELLARO, Tony

C – L. 5'11", 180 lbs. b: Kingston, Ont., 6/14/1971.

Season	Club	League	GP	G	A	Pts	AG	AA	APts	PIM	PP	SH	GW	S	%	TGF	PGF	TGA	PGA	+/–	GP	G	A	Pts	PIM	PP	SH	GW
1987-88	Kingston Legionaires	OMHA	35	23	27	50	....	....	....	23	....	....	....	....	....	....	....	....	....	....	....	....	....	....	....	....	....	....
1988-89	North Bay Centennials	OHL	11	2	1	3	....	....	....	7	....	....	....	....	....	....	....	....	....	....	....	....	....	....	....	....	....	....
	Kingston Raiders	OHL	47	6	7	13	....	....	....	12	....	....	....	....	....	....	....	....	....	....	....	....	....	....	....	....	....	....
1989-90	Kingston Frontenacs	OHL	62	8	31	39	....	....	....	26	....	....	....	....	....	....	....	....	....	....	7	1	4	5	2	....	....	....
1990-91	Kingston Frontenacs	OHL	64	26	25	51	....	....	....	42	....	....	....	....	....	....	....	....	....	....	....	....	....	....	....	....	....	....
1991-92	Belleville Bulls	OHL	48	39	44	83	....	....	....	51	....	....	....	....	....	....	....	....	....	....	5	6	4	10	10	....	....	....
1992-93	**Ottawa Senators**	**NHL**	**2**	**0**	**0**	**0**	**0**	**0**	**0**	**0**	**0**	**0**	**0**	**4**	**0.0**	**1**	**1**	**2**	**0**	**–2**	....	....	....	....	....	....	....	....
	New Haven Nighthawks	AHL	76	18	16	34	....	....	....	73	....	....	....	....	....	....	....	....	....	....	....	....	....	....	....	....	....	....
1993-94	P.E.I. Senators	AHL	19	1	0	1	....	....	....	30	....	....	....	....	....	....	....	....	....	....	....	....	....	....	....	....	....	....
	HC Asiago	Italy	16	16	11	27	....	....	....	13	....	....	....	....	....	....	....	....	....	....	....	....	....	....	....	....	....	....
1994-95	Blackburn Black Hawks	Britain-2	24	40	33	73	....	....	....	76	....	....	....	....	....	....	....	....	....	....	....	....	....	....	....	....	....	....
	Durham Wasps	Britain	4	2	5	7	....	....	....	10	....	....	....	....	....	....	....	....	....	....	....	....	....	....	....	....	....	....
1995-96	Vojens IK	Denmark	40	38	27	65	....	....	....	87	....	....	....	....	....	....	....	....	....	....	....	....	....	....	....	....	....	....
1996-97	Ratinger Lowen	Germany	46	4	9	13	....	....	....	42	....	....	....	....	....	....	....	....	....	....	7	1	1	2	22	....	....	....
1997-98	Adendorfer EC	Germany-2	50	25	39	64	....	....	....	131	....	....	....	....	....	....	....	....	....	....	2	1	2	3	14	....	....	....
1998-99	Waco Wizards	WPHL	61	28	54	82	....	....	....	110	....	....	....	....	....	....	....	....	....	....	4	2	1	3	4	....	....	....
99-2000	Waco Wizards	WPHL	27	14	15	29	....	....	....	52	....	....	....	....	....	....	....	....	....	....	....	....	....	....	....	....	....	....
	Adirondack IceHawks	UHL	46	11	24	35	....	....	....	46	....	....	....	....	....	....	....	....	....	....	2	0	0	0	0	....	....	....
	NHL Totals		**2**	**0**	**0**	**0**	**0**	**0**	**0**	**0**	**0**	**0**	**0**	**4**	**0.0**	**1**	**1**	**2**	**0**									

Signed as a free agent by **Ottawa**, July 30, 1992. • Signed as a free agent by **Adirondack** (UHL) after **Waco** (WPHL) franchise folded, December 21, 1999.

• CIMETTA, Robert

W – L. 6', 190 lbs. b: Toronto, Ont., 2/15/1970. Boston's 1st, 18th overall, in 1988.

Season	Club	League	GP	G	A	Pts	AG	AA	APts	PIM	PP	SH	GW	S	%	TGF	PGF	TGA	PGA	+/–	GP	G	A	Pts	PIM	PP	SH	GW
1985-86	Don Mills Flyers	MTHL	50	32	48	80	....	....	....	50	....	....	....	....	....	....	....	....	....	....	....	....	....	....	....	....	....	....
1986-87	Toronto Marlboros	OHL	66	21	35	56	....	....	....	65	....	....	....	....	....	....	....	....	....	....	....	....	....	....	....	....	....	....
1987-88	Toronto Marlboros	OHL	64	34	42	76	....	....	....	90	....	....	....	....	....	....	....	....	....	....	4	2	2	4	7	....	....	....
1988-89	Toronto Marlboros	OHL	58	*55	47	102	....	....	....	89	....	....	....	....	....	....	....	....	....	....	6	3	3	6	0	....	....	....
	Canada	WJC-A	7	7	4	11	....	....	....	4	....	....	....	....	....	....	....	....	....	....	....	....	....	....	....	....	....	....
	Boston Bruins	**NHL**	**7**	**2**	**0**	**2**	**2**	**0**	**2**	**0**	**0**	**0**	**1**	**4**	**50.0**	**2**	**0**	**6**	**0**	**–4**	**1**	**0**	**0**	**0**	**15**	**0**	**0**	**0**
1989-90	**Boston Bruins**	**NHL**	**47**	**8**	**9**	**17**	**7**	**6**	**13**	**33**	**0**	**0**	**0**	**28**	**28.6**	**28**	**5**	**19**	**0**	**4**	....	....	....	....	....	....	....	....
	Maine Mariners	AHL	9	3	2	5	....	....	....	13	....	....	....	....	....	....	....	....	....	....	....	....	....	....	....	....	....	....
1990-91	**Toronto Maple Leafs**	**NHL**	**25**	**2**	**4**	**6**	**2**	**3**	**5**	**21**	**2**	**0**	**1**	**18**	**11.1**	**11**	**2**	**14**	**0**	**–5**	....	....	....	....	....	....	....	....
	Newmarket Saints	AHL	29	16	18	34	....	....	....	24	....	....	....	....	....	....	....	....	....	....	....	....	....	....	....	....	....	....
1991-92	**Toronto Maple Leafs**	**NHL**	**24**	**4**	**3**	**7**	**4**	**2**	**6**	**12**	**0**	**0**	**0**	**31**	**12.9**	**14**	**3**	**8**	**2**	**5**	....	....	....	....	....	....	....	....
	St. John's Maple Leafs	AHL	19	4	13	17	....	....	....	23	....	....	....	....	....	....	....	....	....	....	10	3	7	10	24	....	....	....
1992-93	St. John's Maple Leafs	AHL	76	28	57	85	....	....	....	125	....	....	....	....	....	....	....	....	....	....	9	2	10	12	32	....	....	....
1993-94	Indianapolis Ice	IHL	79	26	54	80	....	....	....	178	....	....	....	....	....	....	....	....	....	....	....	....	....	....	....	....	....	....

			REGULAR SEASON																		PLAYOFFS							
Season	Club	League	GP	G	A	Pts	AG	AA	APts	PIM	PP	SH	GW	S	%	TGF	PGF	TGA	PGA	+/–	GP	G	A	Pts	PIM	PP	SH	GW
1994-95	Mannheim Eagles	Germany	39	29	31	60				*126											9	6	6	12	32			
1995-96	Mannheim Eagles	Germany	50	21	42	63				76											1	0	1	1	25			
1996-97	Berlin Capitals	Germany	8	4	5	9				16																		
	Alder Mannheim	Germany	36	18	21	39				40											9	5	9	14	10			
1997-98	Alder Mannheim	Germany	41	12	20	32				82											6	2	3	5	18			
1998-99	Berlin Capitals	Germany	34	11	13	24				94																		
99-2000	Berlin Capitals	Germany	49	6	16	22				123											3	0	0	0	10			
	NHL Totals		**103**	**16**	**16**	**32**	**15**	**11**	**26**	**66**	**2**	**0**	**2**	**81**	**19.8**	**55**	**10**	**47**	**2**		**1**	**0**	**0**	**0**	**15**	**0**	**0**	**0**

OHL First All-Star Team (1989)

Traded to **Toronto** by **Boston** for Steve Bancroft, November 9, 1990. Signed as a free agent by **Chicago**, September 8, 1993.

• CIRELLA, Joe

D – R. 6'3", 210 lbs. b: Hamilton, Ont., 5/9/1963. Colorado's 1st, 5th overall, in 1981.

Season	Club	League	GP	G	A	Pts	AG	AA	APts	PIM	PP	SH	GW	S	%	TGF	PGF	TGA	PGA	+/–	GP	G	A	Pts	PIM	PP	SH	GW
1979-80	Hamilton Tiger Cubs	OMHA	21	5	26	31																						
1980-81	Oshawa Generals	OMJHL	56	5	31	36				220											11	0	2	2	41			
1981-82	Oshawa Generals	OHL	3	0	1	1				0											11	7	10	17	32			
	Colorado Rockies	**NHL**	**65**	**7**	**12**	**19**	**6**	**8**	**14**	**52**	**2**	**0**	**1**	**71**	**9.9**	**57**	**10**	**90**	**7**	**–36**								
1982-83	Oshawa Generals	OHL	56	13	55	68				110											17	4	16	20	37			
	Canada	WJC-A	7	0	0	0				6																		
	New Jersey Devils	**NHL**	**2**	**0**	**1**	**1**	**0**	**1**	**1**	**4**	**0**	**0**	**0**	**3**	**0.0**	**2**	**2**	**2**	**0**	**–2**								
	Oshawa Generals	Mem-Cup	5	3	8	11				10																		
1983-84	**New Jersey Devils**	**NHL**	**79**	**11**	**33**	**44**	**9**	**22**	**31**	**137**	**6**	**0**	**0**	**156**	**7.1**	**101**	**37**	**125**	**18**	**–43**								
1984-85	**New Jersey Devils**	**NHL**	**66**	**6**	**18**	**24**	**5**	**12**	**17**	**141**	**2**	**0**	**0**	**97**	**6.2**	**72**	**23**	**111**	**17**	**–45**								
1985-86	**New Jersey Devils**	**NHL**	**66**	**6**	**23**	**29**	**5**	**15**	**20**	**147**	**2**	**0**	**0**	**89**	**6.7**	**97**	**25**	**116**	**32**	**–12**								
1986-87	**New Jersey Devils**	**NHL**	**65**	**9**	**22**	**31**	**8**	**16**	**24**	**111**	**6**	**0**	**0**	**115**	**7.8**	**102**	**36**	**122**	**36**	**–20**								
1987-88	**New Jersey Devils**	**NHL**	**80**	**8**	**31**	**39**	**7**	**22**	**29**	**191**	**2**	**0**	**2**	**135**	**5.9**	**111**	**32**	**124**	**60**	**15**	**19**	**0**	**7**	**7**	**49**	**0**	**0**	**0**
1988-89	**New Jersey Devils**	**NHL**	**80**	**3**	**19**	**22**	**3**	**13**	**16**	**155**	**0**	**1**	**1**	**84**	**3.6**	**61**	**5**	**142**	**72**	**–14**								
1989-90	**Quebec Nordiques**	**NHL**	**56**	**4**	**14**	**18**	**3**	**10**	**13**	**67**	**1**	**0**	**0**	**76**	**5.3**	**53**	**7**	**94**	**21**	**–27**								
1990-91	**Quebec Nordiques**	**NHL**	**39**	**2**	**10**	**12**	**2**	**8**	**10**	**59**	**0**	**0**	**0**	**60**	**3.3**	**41**	**13**	**80**	**24**	**–28**								
	New York Rangers	**NHL**	**19**	**1**	**0**	**1**	**1**	**0**	**1**	**52**	**0**	**0**	**0**	**22**	**4.5**	**14**	**2**	**15**	**4**	**1**	**6**	**0**	**2**	**2**	**26**	**0**	**0**	**0**
1991-92	**New York Rangers**	**NHL**	**67**	**3**	**12**	**15**	**3**	**9**	**12**	**121**	**1**	**0**	**0**	**58**	**5.2**	**57**	**6**	**61**	**21**	**11**	**13**	**0**	**4**	**4**	**23**	**0**	**0**	**0**
1992-93	**New York Rangers**	**NHL**	**55**	**3**	**6**	**9**	**2**	**4**	**6**	**85**	**0**	**1**	**0**	**37**	**8.1**	**46**	**2**	**57**	**14**	**1**								
1993-94	**Florida Panthers**	**NHL**	**63**	**1**	**9**	**10**	**1**	**7**	**8**	**99**	**0**	**0**	**0**	**63**	**1.6**	**54**	**3**	**76**	**33**	**8**								
1994-95	**Florida Panthers**	**NHL**	**20**	**0**	**1**	**1**	**0**	**1**	**1**	**21**	**0**	**0**	**0**	**13**	**0.0**	**9**	**2**	**20**	**6**	**–7**								
1995-96	**Ottawa Senators**	**NHL**	**6**	**0**	**0**	**0**	**0**	**0**	**0**	**4**	**0**	**0**	**0**	**3**	**0.0**	**2**	**0**	**7**	**2**	**–3**								
	Milwaukee Admirals	IHL	40	1	8	9				65											5	0	1	1	20			
1996-97	Kolner Haie	Germany	49	2	7	9				164											4	0	0	0	8			
	Kolner Haie	EuroHL	5	0	0	0				8																		
1997-1998	**Florida Panthers**	**NHL**	DID NOT PLAY – ASSISTANT COACH																									
1998-2000	Oshawa Generals	OHL	DID NOT PLAY – ASSISTANT COACH																									
	NHL Totals		**828**	**64**	**211**	**275**	**55**	**148**	**203**	**1446**	**22**	**2**	**4**	**1082**	**5.9**	**879**	**205**	**1242**	**367**		**38**	**0**	**13**	**13**	**98**	**0**	**0**	**0**

OHL First All-Star Team (1983) • Memorial Cup All-Star Team (1983) • Played in NHL All-Star Game (1984)

Transferred to **New Jersey** after **Colorado** franchise relocated, June 30, 1982. Traded to **Quebec** by **New Jersey** with Claude Loiselle and New Jersey's 8th round choice (Alexander Karpovtsev) in 1990 Entry Draft for Walt Poddubny and Quebec's 4th round choice (Mike Bodnarchuk) in 1990 Entry Draft, June 17, 1989. Traded to **NY Rangers** by **Quebec** for Aaron Miller and NY Rangers' 5th round choice (Bill Lindsay) in 1991 Entry Draft, January 17, 1991. Claimed by **Florida** from **NY Rangers** in Expansion Draft, June 24, 1993. Signed as a free agent by **Ottawa**, October 10, 1995. Signed as a free agent by **Milwaukee** (IHL) following release from Ottawa, December 1, 1995.

• CIRONE, Jason

Jason G. C – L. 5'9", 185 lbs. b: Toronto, Ont., 2/21/1971. Winnipeg's 3rd, 46th overall, in 1989.

Season	Club	League	GP	G	A	Pts	AG	AA	APts	PIM	PP	SH	GW	S	%	TGF	PGF	TGA	PGA	+/–	GP	G	A	Pts	PIM	PP	SH	GW
1986-87	Toronto Red Wings	MTHL	36	53	64	117				125																		
1987-88	Cornwall Royals	OHL	53	12	11	23				41											11	1	2	3	4			
1988-89	Cornwall Royals	OHL	64	39	44	83				67											17	19	8	27	14			
1989-90	Cornwall Royals	OHL	32	21	43	64				56											6	4	2	6	14			
1990-91	Cornwall Royals	OHL	40	31	29	60				66																		
	Windsor Spitfires	OHL	23	27	23	50				31											11	9	8	17	14			
1991-92	**Winnipeg Jets**	**NHL**	**3**	**0**	**0**	**0**	**0**	**0**	**0**	**2**	**0**	**0**	**0**	**1**	**0.0**	**1**	**0**	**1**	**0**	**0**								
	Moncton Hawks	AHL	64	32	27	59				124											10	1	1	2	8			
1992-93	HC Asiago	Alpenliga	25	24	14	38				36																		
	HC Asiago	Italy	16	6	5	11				18											2	1	5	6	18			
1993-94	Cincinnati Cyclones	IHL	26	4	2	6				61																		
	Birmingham Bulls	ECHL	11	3	3	6				45											10	8	8	16	*67			
1994-95	Cincinnati Cyclones	IHL	74	22	15	37				170											9	1	1	2	14			
1995-96	Rochester Americans	AHL	24	4	5	9				34																		
	San Diego Gulls	WCHL	3	2	1	3				20																		
	Los Angeles Ice Dogs	IHL	26	8	10	18				47																		
1996-97	Long Beach Ice Dogs	IHL	11	4	3	7				14																		
	Kansas City Blades	IHL	70	18	38	56				88											3	0	3	3	2			
1997-98	Kansas City Blades	IHL	82	22	30	52				166											11	3	3	6	20			
1998-99	Kansas City Blades	IHL	82	42	26	68				151											3	1	0	1	8			
99-2000	Kansas City Blades	IHL	71	19	24	43				133																		
	NHL Totals		**3**	**0**	**0**	**0**	**0**	**0**	**0**	**2**	**0**	**0**	**0**	**1**	**0.0**	**1**	**0**	**1**	**0**									

Traded to **Florida** by **Winnipeg** for Dave Tomlinson, August 3, 1993. • Played w/ RHI's Buffalo Stampede in 1994 (20-19-21-40-93) and 1995 (7-7-11-18-29).

• CISAR, Marian

RW – R. 6', 185 lbs. b: Bratislava, Czech., 2/25/1975. Los Angeles' 2nd, 37th overall, in 1996.

Season	Club	League	GP	G	A	Pts	AG	AA	APts	PIM	PP	SH	GW	S	%	TGF	PGF	TGA	PGA	+/–	GP	G	A	Pts	PIM	PP	SH	GW
1994-95	Sloven Bratislava	Slovakia-Jr.	38	42	28	70				16																		
	Slovakia	EJC-B	5	8	7	15				2																		
1995-96	Sloven Bratislava	Slovakia-Jr.	16	26	17	43				2																		
	Sloven Bratislava	Slovakia	13	3	3	6				0											6	3	0	3	0			
1996-97	Spokane Chiefs	WHL	70	31	35	66				52											9	6	2	8	4			
1997-98	Spokane Chiefs	WHL	52	33	40	73				34											18	8	5	13	8			
	Slovakia	WJC-A	6	4	1	5				29																		
1998-99	Milwaukee Admirals	IHL	51	11	17	28				31											2	0	0	0	12			
99-2000	**Nashville Predators**	**NHL**	**3**	**0**	**0**	**0**	**0**	**0**	**0**	**4**	**0**	**0**	**0**	**2**	**0.0**	**0**	**0**	**2**	**0**	**–2**								
	Milwaukee Admirals	IHL	78	20	32	52				82											1	0	0	0	0			
	NHL Totals		**3**	**0**	**0**	**0**	**0**	**0**	**0**	**4**	**0**	**0**	**0**	**2**	**0.0**	**0**	**0**	**2**	**0**									

Traded to **Nashville** by **LA Kings** for future considerations, May 29, 1998.

• CLACKSON, Kim

Kimbel Gerald D – R. 5'11", 195 lbs. b: Saskatoon, Sask., 2/13/1955. Pittsburgh's 5th, 85th overall, in 1975.

Season	Club	League	GP	G	A	Pts	AG	AA	APts	PIM	PP	SH	GW	S	%	TGF	PGF	TGA	PGA	+/–	GP	G	A	Pts	PIM	PP	SH	GW
1972-73	Victoria Cougars	WCJHL	64	1	1	2				235																		
1973-74	Victoria Cougars	WCJHL	1	0	0	0				0																		
	Flin Flon Bombers	WCJHL	47	2	6	8				263											7	1	1	2	39			
1974-75	Victoria Cougars	WCJHL	58	7	26	33				359											12	0	6	6	99			
1975-76	Indianapolis Racers	WHA	77	1	12	13				351											6	0	0	0	25			
1976-77	Indianapolis Racers	WHA	71	3	8	11				168											9	0	1	1	24			
1977-78	Winnipeg Jets	WHA	52	2	7	9				203											9	0	1	1	61			

			REGULAR SEASON																		PLAYOFFS							
Season	Club	League	GP	G	A	Pts	AG	AA	APts	PIM	PP	SH	GW	S	%	TGF	PGF	TGA	PGA	+/–	GP	G	A	Pts	PIM	PP	SH	GW
1978-79	Winnipeg Jets	WHA	71	0	12	12	....	....	....	210	....	....	....	....	....	....	....	....	....	....	9	0	5	5	28	....	....	....
1979-80	**Pittsburgh Penguins**	**NHL**	**45**	**0**	**3**	**3**	**0**	**2**	**2**	**166**	**0**	**0**	**0**	**12**	**0.0**	**13**	**1**	**20**	**0**	**–8**	**3**	**0**	**0**	**0**	**37**	**0**	**0**	**0**
1980-81	**Quebec Nordiques**	**NHL**	**61**	**0**	**5**	**5**	**0**	**3**	**3**	**204**	**0**	**0**	**0**	**20**	**0.0**	**28**	**0**	**32**	**1**	**–3**	**5**	**0**	**0**	**0**	**33**	**0**	**0**	**0**
	NHL Totals		**106**	**0**	**8**	**8**	**0**	**5**	**5**	**370**	**0**	**0**	**0**	**32**	**0.0**	**41**	**1**	**52**	**1**		**8**	**0**	**0**	**0**	**70**	**0**	**0**	**0**
	Other Major League Totals		271	6	39	45	....	....	....	932	....	....	....	....	....	....	....	....	....	....	33	0	7	7	138	....	....	....

Selected by **Minnesota** (WHA) in 1975 WHA Amateur Draft, June, 1975. Signed as a free agent by **Indianapolis** (WHA) after **Minnesota** (WHA) franchise folded, February 27, 1976. Traded to **Winnipeg** (WHA) by Indianapolis (WHA) for Winnipeg's 2nd and 3rd round choices in 1978 WHA Amateur Draft and Edmonton's 3rd round choice (previously acquired) in 1978 WHA Amateur Draft, September, 1977. Claimed by **Pittsburgh** as a fill-in during Expansion Draft, June 13, 1979. Transferred to **Quebec** by **Pittsburgh** as compensation for Pittsburgh's signing of free agent Paul Baxter, August 7, 1980.

• CLANCY, Terry

Terrance John RW – L. 5'11", 195 lbs. b: Ottawa, Ont., 4/2/1943.

Season	Club	League	GP	G	A	Pts	AG	AA	APts	PIM	PP	SH	GW	S	%	TGF	PGF	TGA	PGA	+/–	GP	G	A	Pts	PIM	PP	SH	GW
1960-61	St. Michael's Majors	OHA-Jr.	38	2	3	5	....	....	....	30	....	....	....	....	....	....	....	....	....	....	20	2	3	5	16	....	....	....
	St. Michael's Majors	Mem-Cup	7	4	2	6	....	....	....	6	....	....	....	....	....	....	....	....	....	....	....	....	....	....	....	....	....	....
1961-62	St. Michael's Majors	MTJHL	32	4	14	18	....	....	....	16	....	....	....	....	....	....	....	....	....	....	12	6	3	9	20	....	....	....
	St. Michael's Majors	Mem-Cup	5	1	1	2	....	....	....	14	....	....	....	....	....	....	....	....	....	....	....	....	....	....	....	....	....	....
1962-63	Montreal Jr. Canadiens	OHA-Jr.	27	6	7	13	....	....	....	29	....	....	....	....	....	....	....	....	....	....	10	1	6	7	10	....	....	....
1963-64	Canada	Nat-Team	STATISTICS NOT AVAILABLE																									
	Canada	Olympics	7	1	1	2	....	....	....	2	....	....	....	....	....	....	....	....	....	....	....	....	....	....	....	....	....	....
	Rochester Americans	AHL	3	0	0	0	....	....	....	0	....	....	....	....	....	....	....	....	....	....	....	....	....	....	....	....	....	....
1964-65	Rochester Americans	AHL	30	1	5	6	....	....	....	6	....	....	....	....	....	....	....	....	....	....	....	....	....	....	....	....	....	....
	Tulsa Oilers	CPHL	33	10	10	20	....	....	....	18	....	....	....	....	....	....	....	....	....	....	12	4	1	5	14	....	....	....
1965-66	Tulsa Oilers	CPHL	70	15	18	33	....	....	....	74	....	....	....	....	....	....	....	....	....	....	11	3	5	8	5	....	....	....
1966-67	Rochester Americans	AHL	72	14	24	38	....	....	....	51	....	....	....	....	....	....	....	....	....	....	10	0	2	2	4	....	....	....
1967-68	**Oakland Seals**	**NHL**	**7**	**0**	**0**	**0**	**0**	**0**	**0**	**2**	**0**	**0**	**0**	**4**	**0.0**	**2**	**0**	**6**	**0**	**–4**	....	....	....	....	....	....	....	....
	Vancouver Canucks	WHL	46	6	9	15	....	....	....	10	....	....	....	....	....	....	....	....	....	....	....	....	....	....	....	....	....	....
	Buffalo Bisons	AHL	14	4	1	5	....	....	....	4	....	....	....	....	....	....	....	....	....	....	....	....	....	....	....	....	....	....
1968-69	**Toronto Maple Leafs**	**NHL**	**2**	**0**	**0**	**0**	**0**	**0**	**0**	**0**	**0**	**0**	**0**	**3**	**0.0**	**0**	**0**	**1**	**0**	**–1**	....	....	....	....	....	....	....	....
	Tulsa Oilers	CHL	47	5	13	18	....	....	....	24	....	....	....	....	....	....	....	....	....	....	5	1	0	1	2	....	....	....
1969-70	**Toronto Maple Leafs**	**NHL**	**52**	**6**	**5**	**11**	**6**	**5**	**11**	**31**	**0**	**0**	**1**	**77**	**7.8**	**19**	**0**	**19**	**4**	**4**	....	....	....	....	....	....	....	....
1970-71	Phoenix Roadrunners	WHL	18	2	1	3	....	....	....	9	....	....	....	....	....	....	....	....	....	....	....	....	....	....	....	....	....	....
	Montreal Voyageurs	AHL	33	5	3	8	....	....	....	6	....	....	....	....	....	....	....	....	....	....	3	0	0	0	0	....	....	....
1971-72			DID NOT PLAY																									
1972-73	**Toronto Maple Leafs**	**NHL**	**32**	**0**	**1**	**1**	**0**	**1**	**1**	**6**	**0**	**0**	**0**	**12**	**0.0**	**8**	**0**	**29**	**11**	**–10**	....	....	....	....	....	....	....	....
1973-74	Albuquerque 6-Guns	CHL	19	4	0	4	....	....	....	21	....	....	....	....	....	....	....	....	....	....	....	....	....	....	....	....	....	....
	London Lions	Britain	35	6	13	19	....	....	....	22	....	....	....	....	....	....	....	....	....	....	....	....	....	....	....	....	....	....
1974-75	Virginia Wings	AHL	9	0	0	0	....	....	....	0	....	....	....	....	....	....	....	....	....	....	....	....	....	....	....	....	....	....
	NHL Totals		**93**	**6**	**6**	**12**	**6**	**6**	**12**	**39**	**0**	**0**	**1**	**96**	**6.3**	**29**	**0**	**55**	**15**		....	....	....	....	....	....	....	....

• Son of Francis (King)

Signed as a free agent by **Toronto**, October, 1964. Claimed by **Oakland** from **Toronto** in Expansion Draft, June 6, 1967. Traded to **Toronto** by **Oakland** for cash, May 14, 1968. Traded to **Montreal Canadiens** by **Toronto** for cash, December 23, 1970. Traded to **Toronto** by **Montreal Canadiens** for cash, August 30, 1971. Traded to **Detroit** by **Toronto** for cash, October 17, 1973.

• CLARK, Brett

D – L. 6'1", 185 lbs. b: Wapella, Sask., 12/23/1976. Montreal's 7th, 154th overall, in 1996.

Season	Club	League	GP	G	A	Pts	AG	AA	APts	PIM	PP	SH	GW	S	%	TGF	PGF	TGA	PGA	+/–	GP	G	A	Pts	PIM	PP	SH	GW
1994-95	Melville Millionaires	SJHL	62	19	32	51	....	....	....	77	....	....	....	....	....	....	....	....	....	....	....	....	....	....	....	....	....	....
1995-96	University of Maine	H-East	39	7	31	38	....	....	....	22	....	....	....	....	....	....	....	....	....	....	....	....	....	....	....	....	....	....
1996-97	Canada	Nat-Team	57	6	21	27	....	....	....	52	....	....	....	....	....	....	....	....	....	....	....	....	....	....	....	....	....	....
1997-98	**Montreal Canadiens**	**NHL**	**41**	**1**	**0**	**1**	**1**	**0**	**1**	**20**	**0**	**0**	**0**	**26**	**3.8**	**10**	**0**	**15**	**2**	**–3**	....	....	....	....	....	....	....	....
	Fredericton Canadiens	AHL	20	0	6	6	....	....	....	6	....	....	....	....	....	....	....	....	....	....	4	0	1	1	17	....	....	....
1998-99	**Montreal Canadiens**	**NHL**	**61**	**2**	**2**	**4**	**2**	**2**	**4**	**16**	**0**	**0**	**0**	**36**	**5.6**	**25**	**0**	**36**	**8**	**–3**	....	....	....	....	....	....	....	....
	Fredericton Canadiens	AHL	3	1	0	1	....	....	....	0	....	....	....	....	....	....	....	....	....	....	....	....	....	....	....	....	....	....
99-2000	**Atlanta Thrashers**	**NHL**	**14**	**0**	**1**	**1**	**0**	**1**	**1**	**4**	**0**	**0**	**0**	**13**	**0.0**	**3**	**0**	**18**	**3**	**–12**	....	....	....	....	....	....	....	....
	Orlando Solar Bears	IHL	63	9	17	26	....	....	....	31	....	....	....	....	....	....	....	....	....	....	6	0	1	1	0	....	....	....
	NHL Totals		**116**	**3**	**3**	**6**	**3**	**3**	**6**	**40**	**0**	**0**	**0**	**75**	**4.0**	**38**	**0**	**69**	**13**		....	....	....	....	....	....	....	....

Claimed by **Atlanta** from **Montreal** in Expansion Draft, June 25, 1999.

• CLARK, Chris

RW – R. 6', 202 lbs. b: Manchester, CT, 3/8/1976. Calgary's 3rd, 77th overall, in 1994.

Season	Club	League	GP	G	A	Pts	AG	AA	APts	PIM	PP	SH	GW	S	%	TGF	PGF	TGA	PGA	+/–	GP	G	A	Pts	PIM	PP	SH	GW
1990-91	South Windsor High School	Hi-School	23	16	15	31	....	....	....	24	....	....	....	....	....	....	....	....	....	....	....	....	....	....	....	....	....	....
1991-92	Springfield Olympics	EJHL-B	49	21	29	50	....	....	....	56	....	....	....	....	....	....	....	....	....	....	....	....	....	....	....	....	....	....
1992-93	Springfield Olympics	EJHL-B	43	17	60	77	....	....	....	120	....	....	....	....	....	....	....	....	....	....	....	....	....	....	....	....	....	....
1993-94	Springfield Jr. Blues	NAJHL	35	31	26	57	....	....	....	185	....	....	....	....	....	....	....	....	....	....	....	....	....	....	....	....	....	....
1994-95	Clarkson University	ECAC	32	12	11	23	....	....	....	92	....	....	....	....	....	....	....	....	....	....	....	....	....	....	....	....	....	....
1995-96	Clarkson University	ECAC	38	10	8	18	....	....	....	108	....	....	....	....	....	....	....	....	....	....	....	....	....	....	....	....	....	....
1996-97	Clarkson University	ECAC	37	23	25	48	....	....	....	*86	....	....	....	....	....	....	....	....	....	....	....	....	....	....	....	....	....	....
1997-98	Clarkson University	ECAC	35	18	21	39	....	....	....	*106	....	....	....	....	....	....	....	....	....	....	....	....	....	....	....	....	....	....
1998-99	Saint John Flames	AHL	73	13	27	40	....	....	....	123	....	....	....	....	....	....	....	....	....	....	7	2	4	6	15	....	....	....
99-2000	**Calgary Flames**	**NHL**	**22**	**0**	**1**	**1**	**0**	**1**	**1**	**14**	**0**	**0**	**0**	**17**	**0.0**	**3**	**1**	**5**	**0**	**–3**	....	....	....	....	....	....	....	....
	Saint John Flames	AHL	48	16	17	33	....	....	....	134	....	....	....	....	....	....	....	....	....	....	....	....	....	....	....	....	....	....
	NHL Totals		**22**	**0**	**1**	**1**	**0**	**1**	**1**	**14**	**0**	**0**	**0**	**17**	**0.0**	**3**	**1**	**5**	**0**		....	....	....	....	....	....	....	....

ECAC Second All-Star Team (1998)

• CLARK, Dan

D – L. 6'1", 195 lbs. b: Toronto, Ont., 11/3/1957. NY Rangers' 8th, 110th overall, in 1978.

Season	Club	League	GP	G	A	Pts	AG	AA	APts	PIM	PP	SH	GW	S	%	TGF	PGF	TGA	PGA	+/–	GP	G	A	Pts	PIM	PP	SH	GW
1974-75	Langley Lords	BCJHL	50	11	22	33	....	....	....	127	....	....	....	....	....	....	....	....	....	....	....	....	....	....	....	....	....	....
1975-76	Kamloops Chiefs	WCJHL	71	0	26	26	....	....	....	109	....	....	....	....	....	....	....	....	....	....	12	2	2	4	25	....	....	....
1976-77	Kamloops Chiefs	WCJHL	61	4	27	31	....	....	....	189	....	....	....	....	....	....	....	....	....	....	3	0	1	1	25	....	....	....
1977-78	Maine Mariners	AHL	6	0	1	1	....	....	....	6	....	....	....	....	....	....	....	....	....	....	....	....	....	....	....	....	....	....
	Milwaukee Admirals	IHL	67	7	18	25	....	....	....	245	....	....	....	....	....	....	....	....	....	....	5	0	0	0	4	....	....	....
1978-79	**New York Rangers**	**NHL**	**4**	**0**	**1**	**1**	**0**	**1**	**1**	**6**	**0**	**0**	**0**	**4**	**0.0**	**2**	**0**	**2**	**1**	**1**	....	....	....	....	....	....	....	....
	New Haven Nighthawks	AHL	71	8	20	28	....	....	....	167	....	....	....	....	....	....	....	....	....	....	10	0	3	3	27	....	....	....
1979-80	New Haven Nighthawks	AHL	75	0	24	24	....	....	....	247	....	....	....	....	....	....	....	....	....	....	10	1	4	5	21	....	....	....
1980-81	New Haven Nighthawks	AHL	54	2	16	18	....	....	....	163	....	....	....	....	....	....	....	....	....	....	4	0	0	0	8	....	....	....
1981-82	Hershey Bears	AHL	19	0	6	6	....	....	....	58	....	....	....	....	....	....	....	....	....	....	....	....	....	....	....	....	....	....
	Springfield Indians	AHL	10	0	3	3	....	....	....	26	....	....	....	....	....	....	....	....	....	....	....	....	....	....	....	....	....	....
1982-1985			DID NOT PLAY																									
1985-86	New Haven Nighthawks	AHL	10	1	2	3	....	....	....	35	....	....	....	....	....	....	....	....	....	....	....	....	....	....	....	....	....	....
	NHL Totals		**4**	**0**	**1**	**1**	**0**	**1**	**1**	**6**	**0**	**0**	**0**	**4**	**0.0**	**2**	**0**	**2**	**1**		....	....	....	....	....	....	....	....

• Re-entered NHL draft. Originally Philadelphia's 6th choice, 89th overall, in 1977 Amateur Draft.

• CLARK, Dean

D – L. 6'1", 180 lbs. b: Edmonton, Alta., 1/10/1964. Edmonton's 8th, 167th overall, in 1982.

Season	Club	League	GP	G	A	Pts	AG	AA	APts	PIM	PP	SH	GW	S	%	TGF	PGF	TGA	PGA	+/–	GP	G	A	Pts	PIM	PP	SH	GW
1981-82	St. Albert Saints	SAHA	59	21	32	53	....	....	....	146	....	....	....	....	....	....	....	....	....	....	....	....	....	....	....	....	....	....
1982-83	Kamloops Jr. Oilers	WHL	39	17	24	41	....	....	....	63	....	....	....	....	....	....	....	....	....	....	7	2	6	8	12	....	....	....
1983-84	Kamloops Jr. Oilers	WHL	54	18	28	46	....	....	....	64	....	....	....	....	....	....	....	....	....	....	13	0	3	3	12	....	....	....
	Edmonton Oilers	**NHL**	**1**	**0**	**0**	**0**	**0**	**0**	**0**	**0**	**0**	**0**	**0**	**0**	**0.0**	**0**	**0**	**0**	**0**	**0**	....	....	....	....	....	....	....	....
	Kamloops Jr. Oilers	Mem-Cup	4	0	2	2	....	....	....	14	....	....	....	....	....	....	....	....	....	....	....	....	....	....	....	....	....	....
1984-85	Kamloops Jr. Oilers	WHL	36	15	36	51	....	....	....	33	....	....	....	....	....	....	....	....	....	....	....	....	....	....	....	....	....	....
1985-86	Alberta Technical Institute	ACAC	17	3	14	17	....	....	....	43	....	....	....	....	....	....	....	....	....	....	....	....	....	....	....	....	....	....
1986-87	University of Alberta	CWUAA	40	10	23	33	....	....	....	55	....	....	....	....	....	....	....	....	....	....	....	....	....	....	....	....	....	....
	NHL Totals		**1**	**0**	**0**	**0**	**0**	**0**	**0**	**0**	**0**	**0**	**0**	**0**	**0.0**	**0**	**0**	**0**	**0**		....	....	....	....	....	....	....	....

• CLARK, Gordie

Gordon Corson RW – R. 5'10", 180 lbs. b: Glasgow, Scotland, 5/31/1952. Boston's 7th, 112th overall, in 1972.

Season	Club	League	GP	G	A	Pts	AG	AA	APts	PIM	PP	SH	GW	S	%	TGF	PGF	TGA	PGA	+/-	GP	G	A	Pts	PIM	PP	SH	GW
			REGULAR SEASON																		PLAYOFFS							
1968-69	Saint John Schooners	NBJHL	28	*38	31	69	....	....	....	57	....	....	....	....	....	....	....	....	....	....	17	*22	18	*40	9	....	....	....
1969-70	Fredericton Chevies	NBJHL	STATISTICS NOT AVAILABLE																									
1970-71	University of New Hampshire	ECAC	DID NOT PLAY – FRESHMAN																									
1971-72	University of New Hampshire	ECAC	30	27	30	57	....	....	....	28	....	....	....	....	....	....	....	....	....	....	....	....	....	....	....	....	....	....
1972-73	University of New Hampshire	ECAC	29	24	28	52	....	....	....	52	....	....	....	....	....	....	....	....	....	....	....	....	....	....	....	....	....	....
1973-74	University of New Hampshire	ECAC	31	25	28	53	....	....	....	20	....	....	....	....	....	....	....	....	....	....	....	....	....	....	....	....	....	....
1974-75	**Boston Bruins**	**NHL**	**1**	**0**	**0**	**0**	**0**	**0**	**0**	**0**	**0**	**0**	**0**	**1**	**0.0**	**0**	**0**	**0**	**0**	**0**	....	....	....	....	....	....	....	....
	Rochester Americans	AHL	65	22	42	64	....	....	....	34	....	....	....	....	....	....	....	....	....	....	12	7	5	12	6	....	....	....
1975-76	**Boston Bruins**	**NHL**	**7**	**0**	**1**	**1**	**0**	**1**	**1**	**0**	**0**	**0**	**0**	**3**	**0.0**	**2**	**0**	**7**	**0**	**–5**	**1**	**0**	**0**	**0**	**0**	**0**	**0**	**0**
	Rochester Americans	AHL	72	30	49	79	....	....	....	7	....	....	....	....	....	....	....	....	....	....	7	2	3	5	5	....	....	....
1976-77	Rochester Americans	AHL	58	34	38	72	....	....	....	50	....	....	....	....	....	....	....	....	....	....	12	7	9	16	4	....	....	....
1977-78	Rochester Americans	AHL	75	37	51	88	....	....	....	18	....	....	....	....	....	....	....	....	....	....	6	2	0	2	0	....	....	....
1978-79	Cincinnati Stingers	WHA	21	3	3	6	....	....	....	2	....	....	....	....	....	....	....	....	....	....	....	....	....	....	....	....	....	....
	Springfield Indians	AHL	33	12	15	27	....	....	....	8	....	....	....	....	....	....	....	....	....	....	....	....	....	....	....	....	....	....
	Maine Mariners	AHL	13	7	11	18	....	....	....	2	....	....	....	....	....	....	....	....	....	....	10	6	9	15	2	....	....	....
1979-80	Maine Mariners	AHL	79	*47	43	90	....	....	....	64	....	....	....	....	....	....	....	....	....	....	12	5	4	9	7	....	....	....
1980-81	Maine Mariners	AHL	59	25	29	54	....	....	....	32	....	....	....	....	....	....	....	....	....	....	15	6	9	15	4	....	....	....
1981-82	Maine Mariners	AHL	80	50	51	101	....	....	....	34	....	....	....	....	....	....	....	....	....	....	4	5	0	5	5	....	....	....
1982-83	SC Riessersee	Germany	35	40	19	59	....	....	....	46	....	....	....	....	....	....	....	....	....	....	6	4	2	6	5	....	....	....
	Maine Mariners	AHL	6	3	3	6	....	....	....	2	....	....	....	....	....	....	....	....	....	....	16	2	9	11	2	....	....	....
	NHL Totals		**8**	**0**	**1**	**1**	**0**	**1**	**1**	**0**	**0**	**0**	**0**	**4**	**0.0**	**2**	**0**	**7**	**0**		**1**	**0**	**0**	**0**	**0**	**0**	**0**	**0**
	Other Major League Totals		21	3	3	6	....	....	....	2	....	....	....	....	....	....	....	....	....	....	....	....	....	....	....	....	....	....

ECAC First All-Star Team (1972, 1973, 1974) • NCAA East First All-American Team (1973, 1974) • AHL Second All-Star Team (1976, 1977) • AHL First All-Star Team (1980, 1982)

Signed as a free agent by **Cincinnati** (WHA), August, 1978.

• CLARK, Wendel

Wendel L. LW/D – L. 5'11", 194 lbs. b: Kelvington, Sask., 10/25/1966. Toronto's 1st, 1st overall, in 1985.

Season	Club	League	GP	G	A	Pts	AG	AA	APts	PIM	PP	SH	GW	S	%	TGF	PGF	TGA	PGA	+/-	GP	G	A	Pts	PIM	PP	SH	GW
1982-83	Notre Dame Hounds	SAHA	27	21	28	49	....	....	....	83	....	....	....	....	....	....	....	....	....	....	....	....	....	....	....	....	....	....
1983-84	Saskatoon Blades	WHL	72	23	45	68	....	....	....	225	....	....	....	....	....	....	....	....	....	....	....	....	....	....	....	....	....	....
1984-85	Saskatoon Blades	WHL	64	32	55	87	....	....	....	253	....	....	....	....	....	....	....	....	....	....	3	3	3	6	7	....	....	....
	Canada	WJC-A	7	3	2	5	....	....	....	10	....	....	....	....	....	....	....	....	....	....	....	....	....	....	....	....	....	....
1985-86	**Toronto Maple Leafs**	**NHL**	**66**	**34**	**11**	**45**	**27**	**7**	**34**	**227**	**4**	**0**	**3**	**164**	**20.7**	**62**	**12**	**78**	**1**	**–27**	**10**	**5**	**1**	**6**	**47**	**1**	**0**	**1**
1986-87	**Toronto Maple Leafs**	**NHL**	**80**	**37**	**23**	**60**	**32**	**17**	**49**	**271**	**15**	**0**	**1**	**246**	**15.0**	**101**	**33**	**94**	**3**	**–23**	**13**	**6**	**5**	**11**	**38**	**3**	**0**	**1**
1987-88	**Toronto Maple Leafs**	**NHL**	**28**	**12**	**11**	**23**	**10**	**8**	**18**	**80**	**4**	**0**	**1**	**93**	**12.9**	**34**	**11**	**36**	**0**	**–13**	....	....	....	....	....	....	....	....
1988-89	**Toronto Maple Leafs**	**NHL**	**15**	**7**	**4**	**11**	**6**	**3**	**9**	**66**	**3**	**0**	**1**	**30**	**23.3**	**15**	**5**	**13**	**0**	**–3**	....	....	....	....	....	....	....	....
1989-90	**Toronto Maple Leafs**	**NHL**	**38**	**18**	**8**	**26**	**15**	**6**	**21**	**116**	**7**	**0**	**2**	**85**	**21.2**	**42**	**14**	**26**	**0**	**2**	**5**	**1**	**1**	**2**	**19**	**0**	**0**	**0**
1990-91	**Toronto Maple Leafs**	**NHL**	**63**	**18**	**16**	**34**	**16**	**12**	**28**	**152**	**4**	**0**	**2**	**181**	**9.9**	**68**	**18**	**58**	**3**	**–5**	....	....	....	....	....	....	....	....
1991-92	**Toronto Maple Leafs**	**NHL**	**43**	**19**	**21**	**40**	**17**	**16**	**33**	**123**	**7**	**0**	**4**	**158**	**12.0**	**57**	**24**	**48**	**1**	**–14**	....	....	....	....	....	....	....	....
1992-93	**Toronto Maple Leafs**	**NHL**	**66**	**17**	**22**	**39**	**14**	**15**	**29**	**193**	**2**	**0**	**5**	**146**	**11.6**	**60**	**14**	**44**	**0**	**2**	**21**	**10**	**10**	**20**	**51**	**2**	**0**	**1**
1993-94	**Toronto Maple Leafs**	**NHL**	**64**	**46**	**30**	**76**	**43**	**23**	**66**	**115**	**21**	**0**	**8**	**275**	**16.7**	**104**	**42**	**52**	**0**	**10**	**18**	**9**	**7**	**16**	**24**	**2**	**0**	**1**
1994-95	**Quebec Nordiques**	**NHL**	**37**	**12**	**18**	**30**	**21**	**27**	**48**	**45**	**5**	**0**	**0**	**95**	**12.6**	**42**	**15**	**29**	**1**	**–1**	**6**	**1**	**2**	**3**	**6**	**0**	**0**	**0**
1995-96	**New York Islanders**	**NHL**	**58**	**24**	**19**	**43**	**24**	**16**	**40**	**60**	**6**	**0**	**2**	**192**	**12.5**	**72**	**29**	**57**	**2**	**–12**	....	....	....	....	....	....	....	....
	Toronto Maple Leafs	**NHL**	**13**	**8**	**7**	**15**	**8**	**6**	**14**	**16**	**2**	**0**	**1**	**45**	**17.8**	**27**	**12**	**8**	**0**	**7**	**6**	**2**	**2**	**4**	**2**	**1**	**0**	**0**
1996-97	**Toronto Maple Leafs**	**NHL**	**65**	**30**	**19**	**49**	**32**	**17**	**49**	**75**	**6**	**0**	**6**	**212**	**14.2**	**66**	**16**	**52**	**0**	**–2**	....	....	....	....	....	....	....	....
1997-98	**Toronto Maple Leafs**	**NHL**	**47**	**12**	**7**	**19**	**14**	**7**	**21**	**80**	**4**	**0**	**3**	**140**	**8.6**	**31**	**13**	**39**	**0**	**–21**	....	....	....	....	....	....	....	....
1998-99	**Tampa Bay Lightning**	**NHL**	**65**	**28**	**14**	**42**	**33**	**13**	**46**	**35**	**11**	**0**	**2**	**171**	**16.4**	**54**	**22**	**57**	**0**	**–25**	....	....	....	....	....	....	....	....
	Detroit Red Wings	**NHL**	**12**	**4**	**2**	**6**	**5**	**2**	**7**	**2**	**0**	**0**	**1**	**44**	**9.1**	**12**	**4**	**7**	**0**	**1**	**10**	**2**	**3**	**5**	**10**	**1**	**0**	**0**
99-2000	**Chicago Blackhawks**	**NHL**	**13**	**2**	**0**	**2**	**2**	**0**	**2**	**13**	**0**	**0**	**0**	**27**	**7.4**	**3**	**0**	**5**	**0**	**–2**	....	....	....	....	....	....	....	....
	Toronto Maple Leafs	**NHL**	**20**	**2**	**2**	**4**	**2**	**2**	**4**	**21**	**0**	**0**	**1**	**36**	**5.6**	**6**	**0**	**9**	**0**	**–3**	**6**	**1**	**1**	**2**	**4**	**0**	**0**	**0**
	NHL Totals		**793**	**330**	**234**	**564**	**321**	**197**	**518**	**1690**	**101**	**0**	**43**	**2340**	**14.1**	**856**	**284**	**712**	**11**		**95**	**37**	**32**	**69**	**201**	**10**	**0**	**4**

WHL East First All-Star Team (1985) • NHL All-Rookie Team (1986) • Played in NHL All-Star Game (1986, 1999)

Traded to **Quebec** by **Toronto** with Sylvain Lefebvre, Landon Wilson and Toronto's 1st round choice (Jeffrey Kealty) in 1994 Entry Draft for Mats Sundin, Garth Butcher, Todd Warriner and Philadelphia's 1st round choice (previously acquired by Quebec — later traded to Washington — Washington selected Nolan Baumgartner) in 1994 Entry Draft, June 28, 1994. Transferred to **Colorado** after **Quebec** franchise relocated, June 21, 1995. Traded to **NY Islanders** by **Colorado** for Claude Lemieux, October 3, 1995. Traded to **Toronto** by **NY Islanders** with Mathieu Schneider and D.J. Smith for Darby Hendrickson, Sean Haggerty, Kenny Jonsson and Toronto's 1st round choice (Roberto Luongo) in 1997 Entry Draft, March 13, 1996. Signed as a free agent by **Tampa Bay**, July 31, 1998. Traded to **Detroit** by **Tampa Bay** with Detroit's 6th round choice (previously acquired, Detroit selected Kent McDonnell) in 1999 Entry Draft for Kevin Hodson and San Jose's 2nd round choice (previously acquired, Tampa Bay selected Sheldon Keefe) in 1999 Entry Draft, March 23, 1999. Signed as a free agent by **Chicago**, August 2, 1999. Signed as a free agent by **Toronto** following release by Chicago, January 14, 2000. • Officially announced retirement, June 29, 2000.

• CLARKE, Bobby

Robert Earle C – L. 5'10", 185 lbs. b: Flin Flon, Man., 8/13/1949. Philadelphia's 2nd, 17th overall, in 1969. **HHOF**

Season	Club	League	GP	G	A	Pts	AG	AA	APts	PIM	PP	SH	GW	S	%	TGF	PGF	TGA	PGA	+/-	GP	G	A	Pts	PIM	PP	SH	GW
1965-66	Flin Flon Midget Bombers	MAHA	STATISTICS NOT AVAILABLE																									
	Flin Flon Bombers	SJHL	4	4	3	7	....	....	....	0	....	....	....	....	....	....	....	....	....	....	....	....	....	....	....	....	....	....
1966-67	Flin Flon Bombers	MJHL	45	*71	*112	*183	....	....	....	123	....	....	....	....	....	....	....	....	....	....	14	10	*18	28	51	....	....	....
	Flin Flon Bombers	Mem-Cup	6	2	5	7	....	....	....	49	....	....	....	....	....	....	....	....	....	....	....	....	....	....	....	....	....	....
1967-68	Flin Flon Bombers	WCJHL	59	51	*117	*168	....	....	....	148	....	....	....	....	....	....	....	....	....	....	15	4	10	14	2	....	....	....
1968-69	Flin Flon Bombers	WCJHL	58	51	*86	*137	....	....	....	123	....	....	....	....	....	....	....	....	....	....	18	9	*16	*25	....	....	....	....
1969-70	**Philadelphia Flyers**	**NHL**	**76**	**15**	**31**	**46**	**16**	**29**	**45**	**68**	**5**	**1**	**0**	**214**	**7.0**	**69**	**24**	**68**	**24**	**1**	....	....	....	....	....	....	....	....
1970-71	**Philadelphia Flyers**	**NHL**	**77**	**27**	**36**	**63**	**27**	**30**	**57**	**78**	**10**	**1**	**5**	**185**	**14.6**	**78**	**20**	**70**	**21**	**9**	**4**	**0**	**0**	**0**	**2**	**0**	**0**	**0**
1971-72	**Philadelphia Flyers**	**NHL**	**78**	**35**	**46**	**81**	**35**	**40**	**75**	**87**	**11**	**1**	**3**	**225**	**15.6**	**105**	**32**	**69**	**18**	**22**	....	....	....	....	....	....	....	....
1972-73	Team Canada	Summit-72	8	2	4	6	....	....	....	18	....	....	....	....	....	....	....	....	....	....	....	....	....	....	....	....	....	....
	Philadelphia Flyers	**NHL**	**78**	**37**	**67**	**104**	**35**	**53**	**88**	**80**	**10**	**2**	**4**	**231**	**16.0**	**141**	**50**	**93**	**34**	**32**	**11**	**2**	**6**	**8**	**6**	**2**	**0**	**1**
1973-74♦	**Philadelphia Flyers**	**NHL**	**77**	**35**	**52**	**87**	**34**	**43**	**77**	**113**	**10**	**5**	**5**	**221**	**15.8**	**108**	**37**	**63**	**27**	**35**	**17**	**5**	**11**	**16**	**42**	**1**	**0**	**2**
1974-75♦	**Philadelphia Flyers**	**NHL**	**80**	**27**	***89**	**116**	**24**	**67**	**91**	**125**	**10**	**3**	**4**	**193**	**14.0**	**150**	**52**	**52**	**33**	**79**	**17**	**4**	***12**	**16**	**16**	**2**	**1**	**2**
1975-76	**Philadelphia Flyers**	**NHL**	**76**	**30**	***89**	**119**	**26**	**67**	**93**	**136**	**10**	**4**	**2**	**194**	**15.5**	**164**	**59**	**52**	**30**	**83**	**16**	**2**	***14**	**16**	**28**	**1**	**0**	**0**
1976-77	Canada	Can-Cup	6	1	2	3	....	....	....	0	....	....	....	....	....	....	....	....	....	....	....	....	....	....	....	....	....	....
	Philadelphia Flyers	**NHL**	**80**	**27**	**63**	**90**	**24**	**49**	**73**	**71**	**6**	**6**	**3**	**158**	**17.1**	**123**	**38**	**70**	**24**	**39**	**10**	**5**	**5**	**10**	**8**	**2**	**0**	**0**
1977-78	**Philadelphia Flyers**	**NHL**	**71**	**21**	**68**	**89**	**19**	**53**	**72**	**83**	**5**	**2**	**1**	**131**	**16.0**	**115**	**35**	**51**	**18**	**47**	**12**	**4**	**7**	**11**	**8**	**1**	**0**	**0**
1978-79	**Philadelphia Flyers**	**NHL**	**80**	**16**	**57**	**73**	**14**	**41**	**55**	**68**	**5**	**1**	**1**	**143**	**11.2**	**105**	**40**	**83**	**30**	**12**	**8**	**2**	**4**	**6**	**8**	**1**	**0**	**0**
	NHL All-Stars	Chal-Cup	3	0	1	1	....	....	....	0	....	....	....	....	....	....	....	....	....	....	....	....	....	....	....	....	....	....
1979-80	**Philadelphia Flyers**	**NHL**	**76**	**12**	**57**	**69**	**10**	**42**	**52**	**65**	**1**	**2**	**2**	**139**	**8.6**	**104**	**18**	**77**	**33**	**42**	**19**	**8**	**12**	**20**	**16**	**3**	**0**	**2**
1980-81	**Philadelphia Flyers**	**NHL**	**80**	**19**	**46**	**65**	**15**	**31**	**46**	**140**	**5**	**1**	**2**	**150**	**12.7**	**102**	**40**	**73**	**28**	**17**	**12**	**3**	**3**	**6**	**6**	**0**	**1**	**0**
1981-82	**Philadelphia Flyers**	**NHL**	**62**	**17**	**46**	**63**	**13**	**31**	**44**	**154**	**2**	**1**	**3**	**110**	**15.5**	**93**	**25**	**68**	**28**	**28**	**4**	**4**	**2**	**6**	**4**	**1**	**1**	**0**
	Canada	WEC-A	9	0	1	1	....	....	....	6	....	....	....	....	....	....	....	....	....	....	....	....	....	....	....	....	....	....
1982-83	**Philadelphia Flyers**	**NHL**	**80**	**23**	**62**	**85**	**19**	**43**	**62**	**115**	**6**	**1**	**2**	**164**	**14.0**	**108**	**25**	**64**	**18**	**37**	**3**	**1**	**0**	**1**	**2**	**0**	**0**	**0**
1983-84	**Philadelphia Flyers**	**NHL**	**73**	**17**	**43**	**60**	**14**	**29**	**43**	**70**	**3**	**1**	**1**	**129**	**13.2**	**83**	**18**	**68**	**26**	**23**	**3**	**2**	**1**	**3**	**6**	**0**	**0**	**0**
1984-1990	**Philadelphia Flyers**	**NHL**	DID NOT PLAY – GENERAL MANAGER																									
1990-1992	**Minnesota North Stars**	**NHL**	DID NOT PLAY – GENERAL MANAGER																									
1992-1993	**Philadelphia Flyers**	**NHL**	DID NOT PLAY – FRONT OFFICE STAFF																									
1993-1994	**Florida Panthers**	**NHL**	DID NOT PLAY – GENERAL MANAGER																									
1994-2000	**Philadelphia Flyers**	**NHL**	DID NOT PLAY – GENERAL MANAGER																									
	NHL Totals		**1144**	**358**	**852**	**1210**	**325**	**648**	**973**	**1453**	**99**	**32**	**38**	**2587**	**13.8**	**1648**	**513**	**1021**	**392**		**136**	**42**	**77**	**119**	**152**	**14**	**3**	**7**

WCJHL All-Star Team (1968, 1969) • Won Bill Masterton Trophy (1972) • NHL Second All-Star Team (1973, 1974) • Won Lester B. Pearson Award (1973) • Won Hart Trophy (1973, 1975, 1976) • NHL First All-Star Team (1975, 1976) • NHL Plus/Minus Leader (1976) • Won Lester Patrick Trophy (1980) • Won Frank J. Selke Trophy (1983) • Played in NHL All-Star Game (1970, 1971, 1972, 1973, 1974, 1975, 1977, 1978)

• CLEARY, Daniel

Daniel Michael Thomas LW – L. 6', 203 lbs. b: Carbonear, Nfld., 12/18/1978. Chicago's 1st, 13th overall, in 1997.

Season	Club	League	GP	G	A	Pts	AG	AA	APts	PIM	PP	SH	GW	S	%	TGF	PGF	TGA	PGA	+/-	GP	G	A	Pts	PIM	PP	SH	GW
1993-94	Kingston Voyageurs	OJHL	41	18	28	46	....	....	....	33	....	....	....	....	....	....	....	....	....	....	2	0	1	1	0	....	....	....
1994-95	Belleville Bulls	OHL	62	26	55	81	....	....	....	62	....	....	....	....	....	....	....	....	....	....	16	7	10	17	23	....	....	....
1995-96	Belleville Bulls	OHL	64	53	62	115	....	....	....	74	....	....	....	....	....	....	....	....	....	....	14	10	17	27	40	....	....	....

			REGULAR SEASON																		PLAYOFFS							
Season	Club	League	GP	G	A	Pts	AG	AA	APts	PIM	PP	SH	GW	S	%	TGF	PGF	TGA	PGA	+/–	GP	G	A	Pts	PIM	PP	SH	GW
1996-97	Belleville Bulls	OHL	64	32	48	80	....	....	....	88	....	....	....	....	....	....	....	....	....	....	6	3	4	7	6	....	....	....
1997-98	Belleville Bulls	OHL	30	16	31	47	....	....	....	14	....	....	....	....	....	....	....	....	....	....	10	6	*17	*23	10	....	....	....
	Chicago Blackhawks	**NHL**	**6**	**0**	**0**	**0**	**0**	**0**	**0**	**0**	**0**	**0**	**0**	**4**	**0.0**	**0**	**0**	**2**	**0**	**–2**	....	....	....	....	....	....	....	....
	Indianapolis Ice	IHL	4	2	1	3	....	....	....	6	....	....	....	....	....	....	....	....	....	....	....	....	....	....	....	....	....	....
1998-99	**Chicago Blackhawks**	**NHL**	**35**	**4**	**5**	**9**	**5**	**5**	**10**	**24**	**0**	**0**	**0**	**49**	**8.2**	**14**	**1**	**19**	**5**	**–1**	....	....	....	....	....	....	....	....
	Portland Pirates	AHL	30	9	17	26	....	....	....	74	....	....	....	....	....	....	....	....	....	....	....	....	....	....	....	....	....	....
	Hamilton Bulldogs	AHL	9	0	1	1	....	....	....	7	....	....	....	....	....	....	....	....	....	....	3	0	0	0	0	....	....	....
99-2000	**Edmonton Oilers**	**NHL**	**17**	**3**	**2**	**5**	**3**	**2**	**5**	**8**	**0**	**0**	**1**	**18**	**16.7**	**8**	**1**	**8**	**0**	**–1**	**4**	**0**	**1**	**1**	**2**	**0**	**0**	**0**
	Hamilton Bulldogs	AHL	58	22	52	74	....	....	....	108	....	....	....	....	....	....	....	....	....	....	5	2	3	5	18	....	....	....
	NHL Totals		**58**	**7**	**7**	**14**	**8**	**7**	**15**	**32**	**0**	**0**	**1**	**71**	**9.9**	**22**	**2**	**29**	**5**		**4**	**0**	**1**	**1**	**2**	**0**	**0**	**0**

OHL First All-Star Team (1996, 1997) • AHL Second All-Star Team (2000)

Traded to **Edmonton** by **Chicago** with Chad Kilger, Ethan Moreau and Christian Laflamme for Boris Mironov, Dean McAmmond and Jonas Elofsson, March 20, 1999.

• CLEMENT, Bill

William H. C – L. 6′1″, 194 lbs. b: Thurso, Que., 12/20/1950. Philadelphia's 1st, 18th overall, in 1970.

Season	Club	League	GP	G	A	Pts	AG	AA	APts	PIM	PP	SH	GW	S	%	TGF	PGF	TGA	PGA	+/–	GP	G	A	Pts	PIM	PP	SH	GW
1967-68	Ottawa 67's	OHA-Jr.	36	6	19	25	....	....	....	41	....	....	....	....	....	....	....	....	....	....	....	....	....	....	....	....	....	....
1968-69	Ottawa 67's	OHA-Jr.	53	18	28	46	....	....	....	101	....	....	....	....	....	....	....	....	....	....	7	1	4	5	6	....	....	....
1969-70	Ottawa 67's	OHA-Jr.	54	19	36	55	....	....	....	62	....	....	....	....	....	....	....	....	....	....	5	2	0	2	0	....	....	....
1970-71	Quebec Aces	AHL	69	19	39	58	....	....	....	88	....	....	....	....	....	....	....	....	....	....	1	0	0	0	0	....	....	....
1971-72	**Philadelphia Flyers**	**NHL**	**49**	**9**	**14**	**23**	**9**	**12**	**21**	**39**	**0**	**0**	**1**	**94**	**9.6**	**30**	**4**	**50**	**10**	**–14**	....	....	....	....	....	....	....	....
	Richmond Robins	AHL	26	8	9	17	....	....	....	20	....	....	....	....	....	....	....	....	....	....	....	....	....	....	....	....	....	....
1972-73	**Philadelphia Flyers**	**NHL**	**73**	**14**	**14**	**28**	**13**	**11**	**24**	**51**	**0**	**1**	**3**	**132**	**10.6**	**38**	**0**	**57**	**8**	**–11**	**2**	**0**	**0**	**0**	**0**	**0**	**0**	**0**
1973-74♦	**Philadelphia Flyers**	**NHL**	**39**	**9**	**8**	**17**	**9**	**7**	**16**	**34**	**0**	**2**	**2**	**54**	**16.7**	**24**	**1**	**12**	**4**	**15**	**4**	**1**	**0**	**1**	**4**	**0**	**0**	**0**
1974-75♦	**Philadelphia Flyers**	**NHL**	**68**	**21**	**16**	**37**	**18**	**12**	**30**	**42**	**1**	**0**	**2**	**140**	**15.0**	**44**	**4**	**31**	**12**	**21**	**12**	**1**	**0**	**1**	**8**	**0**	**0**	**0**
1975-76	**Washington Capitals**	**NHL**	**46**	**10**	**17**	**27**	**9**	**13**	**22**	**20**	**2**	**0**	**0**	**95**	**10.5**	**44**	**12**	**74**	**12**	**–30**	....	....	....	....	....	....	....	....
	Atlanta Flames	**NHL**	**31**	**13**	**14**	**27**	**11**	**10**	**21**	**29**	**2**	**1**	**3**	**71**	**18.3**	**39**	**5**	**36**	**5**	**3**	**2**	**0**	**1**	**1**	**0**	**0**	**0**	**0**
1976-77	**Atlanta Flames**	**NHL**	**67**	**17**	**26**	**43**	**15**	**20**	**35**	**27**	**2**	**5**	**1**	**114**	**14.9**	**61**	**9**	**77**	**21**	**–4**	**3**	**1**	**1**	**2**	**0**	**0**	**1**	**0**
1977-78	**Atlanta Flames**	**NHL**	**70**	**20**	**30**	**50**	**18**	**23**	**41**	**34**	**1**	**3**	**4**	**105**	**19.0**	**70**	**12**	**74**	**34**	**18**	**2**	**0**	**0**	**0**	**2**	**0**	**0**	**0**
1978-79	**Atlanta Flames**	**NHL**	**65**	**12**	**23**	**35**	**10**	**17**	**27**	**14**	**0**	**0**	**1**	**86**	**14.0**	**47**	**5**	**84**	**37**	**–5**	**2**	**0**	**0**	**0**	**0**	**0**	**0**	**0**
1979-80	**Atlanta Flames**	**NHL**	**64**	**7**	**14**	**21**	**6**	**10**	**16**	**32**	**0**	**2**	**2**	**51**	**13.7**	**28**	**1**	**53**	**29**	**3**	**4**	**0**	**0**	**0**	**4**	**0**	**0**	**0**
1980-81	**Calgary Flames**	**NHL**	**78**	**12**	**20**	**32**	**9**	**13**	**22**	**33**	**1**	**2**	**2**	**94**	**12.8**	**41**	**3**	**104**	**50**	**–16**	**16**	**2**	**1**	**3**	**6**	**0**	**0**	**0**
1981-82	**Calgary Flames**	**NHL**	**69**	**4**	**12**	**16**	**3**	**8**	**11**	**28**	**0**	**0**	**0**	**56**	**7.1**	**25**	**0**	**59**	**32**	**–2**	**3**	**0**	**0**	**0**	**2**	**0**	**0**	**0**
	NHL Totals		**719**	**148**	**208**	**356**	**130**	**156**	**286**	**383**	**9**	**16**	**21**	**1092**	**13.6**	**491**	**56**	**711**	**254**		**50**	**5**	**3**	**8**	**26**	**0**	**1**	**0**

Played in NHL All-Star Game (1976, 1978)

Traded to **Washington** by **Philadelphia** with Don McLean and Philadelphia's 1st round choice (Alex Forsyth) in 1975 Amateur Draft for Washington's 1st round choice (Mel Bridgman) in 1975 Amateur Draft, June 4, 1975. Traded to **Atlanta** by **Washington** for Gerry Meehan, Jean Lemieux and Buffalo's 1st round choice (previously acquired, Atlanta selected Greg Carroll) in 1976 Amateur Draft, January 22, 1976. Transferred to **Calgary** after **Atlanta** franchise relocated, June 24, 1980.

• CLIPPINGDALE, Steve

Steven J. LW – L. 6′2″, 195 lbs. b: Vancouver, B.C., 4/29/1956. Los Angeles' 1st, 21st overall, in 1976.

Season	Club	League	GP	G	A	Pts	AG	AA	APts	PIM	PP	SH	GW	S	%	TGF	PGF	TGA	PGA	+/–	GP	G	A	Pts	PIM	PP	SH	GW
1972-73	Nor-West Caps	KIJHL	STATISTICS NOT AVAILABLE																									
1973-74	University of Wisconsin	WCHA	4	1	3	4	....	....	....	0	....	....	....	....	....	....	....	....	....	....	....	....	....	....	....	....	....	....
1974-75	New Westminster Bruins	WCJHL	62	26	19	45	....	....	....	27	....	....	....	....	....	....	....	....	....	....	17	4	1	5	11	....	....	....
	New Westminster Bruins	Mem-Cup	3	2	1	3	....	....	....	0	....	....	....	....	....	....	....	....	....	....	....	....	....	....	....	....	....	....
1975-76	New Westminster Bruins	WCJHL	72	51	66	117	....	....	....	80	....	....	....	....	....	....	....	....	....	....	17	15	14	29	12	....	....	....
	New Westminster Bruins	Mem-Cup	4	1	5	6	....	....	....	2	....	....	....	....	....	....	....	....	....	....	....	....	....	....	....	....	....	....
1976-77	**Los Angeles Kings**	**NHL**	**16**	**1**	**2**	**3**	**1**	**2**	**3**	**9**	**0**	**0**	**0**	**11**	**9.1**	**5**	**0**	**2**	**0**	**3**	**1**	**0**	**0**	**0**	**0**	**0**	**0**	**0**
	Fort Worth Texans	CHL	54	24	17	41	....	....	....	49	....	....	....	....	....	....	....	....	....	....	....	....	....	....	....	....	....	....
1977-78	Springfield Indians	AHL	74	33	21	54	....	....	....	59	....	....	....	....	....	....	....	....	....	....	4	1	2	3	5	....	....	....
1978-79	Dallas Black Hawks	CHL	64	27	38	65	....	....	....	99	....	....	....	....	....	....	....	....	....	....	1	0	0	0	0	....	....	....
1979-80	**Washington Capitals**	**NHL**	**3**	**0**	**0**	**0**	**0**	**0**	**0**	**0**	**0**	**0**	**0**	**1**	**0.0**	**0**	**0**	**0**	**0**	**0**	....	....	....	....	....	....	....	....
	Hershey Bears	AHL	47	19	14	33	....	....	....	47	....	....	....	....	....	....	....	....	....	....	5	2	0	2	4	....	....	....
	NHL Totals		**19**	**1**	**2**	**3**	**1**	**2**	**3**	**9**	**0**	**0**	**0**	**12**	**8.3**	**5**	**0**	**2**	**0**		**1**	**0**	**0**	**0**	**0**	**0**	**0**	**0**

Traded to **Washington** by **LA Kings** for Mike Marson, June 11, 1979.

• CLOUTIER, Real

"Buddy" RW – L. 5′10″, 185 lbs. b: St. Emile, Que., 7/30/1956. Chicago's 1st, 9th overall, in 1976.

Season	Club	League	GP	G	A	Pts	AG	AA	APts	PIM	PP	SH	GW	S	%	TGF	PGF	TGA	PGA	+/–	GP	G	A	Pts	PIM	PP	SH	GW
1972-73	Quebec Remparts	QMJHL	57	39	60	99	....	....	....	15	....	....	....	....	....	....	....	....	....	....	15	8	13	21	14	....	....	....
	Quebec Remparts	Mem-Cup	3	0	1	1	....	....	....	2	....	....	....	....	....	....	....	....	....	....	....	....	....	....	....	....	....	....
1973-74	Quebec Remparts	QMJHL	69	93	123	216	....	....	....	40	....	....	....	....	....	....	....	....	....	....	16	26	24	50	28	....	....	....
	Quebec Remparts	Mem-Cup	4	*4	4	*8	....	....	....	4	....	....	....	....	....	....	....	....	....	....	....	....	....	....	....	....	....	....
1974-75	Quebec Nordiques	WHA	63	26	27	53	....	....	....	36	....	....	....	....	....	....	....	....	....	....	12	4	3	7	2	....	....	....
1975-76	Quebec Nordiques	WHA	80	60	54	114	....	....	....	27	....	....	....	....	....	....	....	....	....	....	5	4	5	9	0	....	....	....
1976-77	Quebec Nordiques	WHA	76	66	75	*141	....	....	....	39	....	....	....	....	....	....	....	....	....	....	17	*14	13	27	10	....	....	....
1977-78	Quebec Nordiques	WHA	73	56	73	129	....	....	....	19	....	....	....	....	....	....	....	....	....	....	10	9	7	16	15	....	....	....
1978-79	Quebec Nordiques	WHA	77	*75	54	*129	....	....	....	48	....	....	....	....	....	....	....	....	....	....	4	2	2	4	4	....	....	....
1979-80	**Quebec Nordiques**	**NHL**	**67**	**42**	**47**	**89**	**36**	**34**	**70**	**12**	**13**	**0**	**3**	**254**	**16.5**	**124**	**49**	**82**	**1**	**–6**	....	....	....	....	....	....	....	....
1980-81	**Quebec Nordiques**	**NHL**	**34**	**15**	**16**	**31**	**12**	**11**	**23**	**18**	**2**	**0**	**2**	**89**	**16.9**	**45**	**21**	**23**	**1**	**2**	**3**	**0**	**0**	**0**	**10**	**0**	**0**	**0**
1981-82	**Quebec Nordiques**	**NHL**	**67**	**37**	**60**	**97**	**29**	**40**	**69**	**34**	**8**	**0**	**5**	**214**	**17.3**	**130**	**50**	**55**	**1**	**26**	**16**	**7**	**5**	**12**	**10**	**1**	**0**	**1**
1982-83	**Quebec Nordiques**	**NHL**	**68**	**28**	**39**	**67**	**23**	**27**	**50**	**30**	**5**	**0**	**3**	**185**	**15.1**	**94**	**32**	**66**	**0**	**–4**	**4**	**0**	**0**	**0**	**0**	**0**	**0**	**0**
1983-84	**Buffalo Sabres**	**NHL**	**77**	**24**	**36**	**60**	**19**	**25**	**44**	**25**	**9**	**0**	**6**	**169**	**14.2**	**96**	**41**	**56**	**0**	**–1**	**2**	**0**	**0**	**0**	**0**	**0**	**0**	**0**
1984-85	**Buffalo Sabres**	**NHL**	**4**	**0**	**0**	**0**	**0**	**0**	**0**	**0**	**0**	**0**	**0**	**6**	**0.0**	**0**	**0**	**2**	**0**	**–2**	....	....	....	....	....	....	....	....
	Flint Generals	IHL	40	11	25	36	....	....	....	6	....	....	....	....	....	....	....	....	....	....	....	....	....	....	....	....	....	....
	Rochester Americans	AHL	12	4	3	7	....	....	....	0	....	....	....	....	....	....	....	....	....	....	....	....	....	....	....	....	....	....
	NHL Totals		**317**	**146**	**198**	**344**	**119**	**137**	**256**	**119**	**37**	**0**	**19**	**917**	**15.9**	**489**	**193**	**284**	**3**		**25**	**7**	**5**	**12**	**20**	**1**	**0**	**1**
	Other Major League Totals		369	283	283	566	....	....	....	169	....	....	....	....	....	....	....	....	....	....	48	33	30	63	31	....	....	....

QMJHL Second All-Star Team (1974) • WHA Second All-Star Team (1976, 1977, 1978) • Won W. D. (Bill) Hunter Trophy (WHA Scoring Leader) (1977, 1979) • WHA First All-Star Team (1979)

Played in NHL All-Star Game (1980)

Selected by **Quebec** (WHA) in 1974 WHA Amateur Draft, June, 1974. Rights retained by **Quebec** prior to Expansion Draft, June 9, 1979. • Quebec did not list Cloutier as a priority selection in the 1979 Expansion Draft as per their agreement with Chicago. They traded their 1st round choice (Denis Savard) in 1980 Entry Draft for Chicago agreeing not to reclaim Cloutier prior to Expansion Draft, June 9, 1979. Traded to **Buffalo** by **Quebec** with Quebec's 1st round choice (Adam Creighton) in 1983 Entry Draft for Tony McKegney, Andre Savard, Jean Sauve and Buffalo's 3rd round choice (Iiro Jarvi) in 1983 Entry Draft, June 8, 1983.

• CLOUTIER, Rejean

D – L. 6′, 185 lbs. b: Windsor, Que., 2/15/1960.

Season	Club	League	GP	G	A	Pts	AG	AA	APts	PIM	PP	SH	GW	S	%	TGF	PGF	TGA	PGA	+/–	GP	G	A	Pts	PIM	PP	SH	GW
1977-78	Sherbrooke Castors	QMJHL	23	8	11	19	....	....	....	59	....	....	....	....	....	....	....	....	....	....	....	....	....	....	....	....	....	....
1978-79	Sherbrooke Castors	QMJHL	70	6	31	37	....	....	....	93	....	....	....	....	....	....	....	....	....	....	12	2	11	13	13	....	....	....
1979-80	Sherbrooke Castors	QMJHL	65	11	57	68	....	....	....	163	....	....	....	....	....	....	....	....	....	....	15	3	11	14	44	....	....	....
	Detroit Red Wings	**NHL**	**3**	**0**	**1**	**1**	**0**	**1**	**1**	**0**	**0**	**0**	**0**	**1**	**0.0**	**3**	**0**	**1**	**0**	**2**	....	....	....	....	....	....	....	....
1980-81	Adirondack Red Wings	AHL	76	7	30	37	....	....	....	193	....	....	....	....	....	....	....	....	....	....	15	1	2	3	27	....	....	....
1981-82	**Detroit Red Wings**	**NHL**	**2**	**0**	**1**	**1**	**0**	**1**	**1**	**2**	....	....	....	....	....	....	....	....	....	....	....	....	....	....	....	....	....	....
	Adirondack Red Wings	AHL	64	11	27	38	....	....	....	140	....	....	....	....	....	....	....	....	....	....	5	0	2	2	6	....	....	....
1982-83	Adirondack Red Wings	AHL	80	13	44	57	....	....	....	137	....	....	....	....	....	....	....	....	....	....	6	2	3	5	15	....	....	....
1983-84	Adirondack Red Wings	AHL	77	9	30	39	....	....	....	208	....	....	....	....	....	....	....	....	....	....	7	2	4	6	9	....	....	....
1984-85	Adirondack Red Wings	AHL	3	0	0	0	....	....	....	2	....	....	....	....	....	....	....	....	....	....	....	....	....	....	....	....	....	....
	Nova Scotia Voyageurs	AHL	72	8	19	27	....	....	....	152	....	....	....	....	....	....	....	....	....	....	6	1	1	2	14	....	....	....
1985-86	Sherbrooke Canadiens	AHL	67	7	23	30	....	....	....	142	....	....	....	....	....	....	....	....	....	....	....	....	....	....	....	....	....	....
	Saginaw Generals	IHL	2	0	0	0	....	....	....	4	....	....	....	....	....	....	....	....	....	....	....	....	....	....	....	....	....	....
1986-87	Sherbrooke Canadiens	AHL	76	7	37	44	....	....	....	182	....	....	....	....	....	....	....	....	....	....	17	3	9	12	59	....	....	....
1987-88	SC Riessersee	Germany-2	STATISTICS NOT AVAILABLE																									

			REGULAR SEASON																		PLAYOFFS							
Season	Club	League	GP	G	A	Pts	AG	AA	APts	PIM	PP	SH	GW	S	%	TGF	PGF	TGA	PGA	+/–	GP	G	A	Pts	PIM	PP	SH	GW
1988-89	HC Grenoble	France	40	10	16	26				114																		
1989-1996			OUT OF HOCKEY – RETIRED																									
1996-97	Windsor Papetiers	QSPHL	12	1	4	5				58																		
	NHL Totals		**5**	**0**	**2**	**2**	**0**	**2**	**2**	**2**	**0**	**0**	**0**	**1**	**0.0**	**3**	**0**	**1**	**0**									

AHL Second All-Star Team (1983)

Signed as a free agent by **Detroit**, October 30, 1979. Traded to **Edmonton** by **Detroit** for Todd Bidner, October 17, 1984. Signed as a free agent by **Montreal**, August, 1985.

• CLOUTIER, Roland

C – L. 5'8", 157 lbs. b: Rouyn, Que., 10/6/1957. Detroit's 13th, 178th overall, in 1977.

Season	Club	League	GP	G	A	Pts	AG	AA	APts	PIM	PP	SH	GW	S	%	TGF	PGF	TGA	PGA	+/–	GP	G	A	Pts	PIM	PP	SH	GW
1975-76	Trois-Rivieres Draveurs	QMJHL	67	21	34	55				18																		
1976-77	Trois-Rivieres Draveurs	QMJHL	72	63	68	131				43																		
1977-78	**Detroit Red Wings**	**NHL**	**1**	**0**	**0**	**0**	**0**	**0**	**0**	**0**	**0**	**0**	**0**	**1**	**0.0**	**0**	**0**	**2**	**0**	**–2**								
	Kansas City Red Wings	CHL	70	18	38	56				13																		
1978-79	**Detroit Red Wings**	**NHL**	**19**	**6**	**6**	**12**	**5**	**4**	**9**	**2**	**1**	**0**	**1**	**40**	**15.0**	**16**	**5**	**11**	**0**	**0**								
	Kansas City Red Wings	CHL	59	32	29	61				21											4	0	0	0	12			
1979-80	**Quebec Nordiques**	**NHL**	**14**	**2**	**3**	**5**	**2**	**2**	**4**	**0**	**0**	**0**	**0**	**19**	**10.5**	**10**	**0**	**10**	**1**	**1**								
	Syracuse Firebirds	AHL	64	19	37	56				16											4	1	2	3	7			
1980-81	Nova Scotia Voyageurs	AHL	60	18	21	39				41											6	1	1	2	0			
1981-82	ASG Tours	France	30	27	*28	*55																						
1982-83	ASG Tours	France	32	32	28	60																						
1983-84	HC Gap	France	32	47	33	80																						
1984-85	HC Gap	France	31	37	31	68																						
1985-86	HC Gap	France	32	41	28	69																						
1986-87	HC Gap	France	33	57	30	87																						
1987-88	HC Gap	France	33	25	18	43				19																		
	NHL Totals		**34**	**8**	**9**	**17**	**7**	**6**	**13**	**2**	**1**	**0**	**1**	**60**	**13.3**	**26**	**5**	**23**	**1**									

Claimed by **Quebec** from **Detroit** in Expansion Draft, June 13, 1979.

• CLOUTIER, Sylvain

Sylvain Richard C – L. 6', 195 lbs. b: Mont-Laurier, Que., 2/13/1974. Detroit's 3rd, 70th overall, in 1992.

Season	Club	League	GP	G	A	Pts	AG	AA	APts	PIM	PP	SH	GW	S	%	TGF	PGF	TGA	PGA	+/–	GP	G	A	Pts	PIM	PP	SH	GW
1990-91	Sault Ste. Marie Legionaires	OMHA	34	51	40	91				92																		
1991-92	Guelph Storm	OHL	62	35	31	66				74																		
1992-93	Guelph Storm	OHL	44	26	29	55				78											5	0	5	5	14			
1993-94	Guelph Storm	OHL	66	45	71	116				127											9	7	9	16	32			
	Adirondack Red Wings	AHL	2	0	2	2				2																		
1994-95	Adirondack Red Wings	AHL	71	7	26	33				144																		
1995-96	Adirondack Red Wings	AHL	65	11	17	28				118											3	0	0	0	4			
	Toledo Storm	ECHL	6	4	2	6				4																		
1996-97	Adirondack Red Wings	AHL	77	13	36	49				190											4	0	2	2	4			
1997-98	Adirondack Red Wings	AHL	72	14	22	36				155																		
	Detroit Vipers	IHL	8	0	1	1				18											21	7	5	12	31			
1998-99	**Chicago Blackhawks**	**NHL**	**7**	**0**	**0**	**0**	**0**	**0**	**0**	**0**	**0**	**0**	**0**	**3**	**0.0**	**0**	**0**	**1**	**0**	**–1**								
	Indianapolis Ice	IHL	73	21	33	54				128											7	3	2	5	12			
99-2000	Albany River Rats	AHL	66	15	28	43				127											5	0	0	0	6			
	Orlando Solar Bears	IHL	9	1	1	2				25																		
	NHL Totals		**7**	**0**	**0**	**0**	**0**	**0**	**0**	**0**	**0**	**0**	**0**	**3**	**0.0**	**0**	**0**	**1**	**0**									

Signed as a free agent by **Chicago**, August 17, 1998. Claimed by **Atlanta** from **Chicago** in Expansion Draft, June 25, 1999. Traded to **New Jersey** by **Atlanta** with Jeff Williams and Atlanta's 7th round choice (Ken Magovan) in 2000 Entry Draft for Wes Mason and Eric Bertrand, November 1, 1999.

• CLYMER, Ben

D – L. 6'1", 195 lbs. b: Edina, MN, 4/11/1978. Boston's 3rd, 27th overall, in 1997.

Season	Club	League	GP	G	A	Pts	AG	AA	APts	PIM	PP	SH	GW	S	%	TGF	PGF	TGA	PGA	+/–	GP	G	A	Pts	PIM	PP	SH	GW
1993-94	Jefferson Jaguars	Hi-School	23	3	7	10				20																		
1994-95	Jefferson Jaguars	Hi-School	28	11	22	33				36																		
1995-96	Jefferson Jaguars	Hi-School	18	12	34	46				34											5	0	6	6	6			
	United States	WJC-A	6	0	4	4				14																		
1996-97	University of Minnesota	WCHA	29	7	13	20				64																		
	United States	WJC-A	6	0	2	2				2																		
1997-98	University of Minnesota	WCHA	1	0	0	0				2																		
1998-99	Seattle Thunderbirds	WHL	70	12	44	56				93											11	1	5	6	12			
99-2000	**Tampa Bay Lightning**	**NHL**	**60**	**2**	**6**	**8**	**2**	**6**	**8**	**87**	**2**	**0**	**0**	**98**	**2.0**	**43**	**8**	**71**	**10**	**–26**								
	Detroit Vipers	IHL	19	1	9	10				30																		
	United States	WC-A	7	0	0	0				4																		
	NHL Totals		**60**	**2**	**6**	**8**	**2**	**6**	**8**	**87**	**2**	**0**	**0**	**98**	**2.0**	**43**	**8**	**71**	**10**									

• Missed remainder of 1997-98 season recovering from shoulder injury suffered in game vs. Michigan, October 10, 1997.

• COALTER, Gary

Gary Merritt Charles RW – R. 5'10", 185 lbs. b: Toronto, Ont., 7/8/1950. NY Rangers' 5th, 67th overall, in 1970.

Season	Club	League	GP	G	A	Pts	AG	AA	APts	PIM	PP	SH	GW	S	%	TGF	PGF	TGA	PGA	+/–	GP	G	A	Pts	PIM	PP	SH	GW
1967-68	Hamilton Red Wings	OHA-Jr.	53	8	13	21				57											11	1	3	4	7			
1968-69	Hamilton Red Wings	OHA-Jr.	52	18	23	41				144											5	0	1	1	6			
1969-70	Hamilton Red Wings	OHA-Jr.	54	22	26	48				79																		
1970-71	Omaha Knights	CHL	68	15	24	39				88											11	4	3	7	29			
1971-72	Omaha Knights	CHL	72	15	31	46				105																		
1972-73	Providence Reds	AHL	45	10	13	23				67																		
	Omaha Knights	CHL	25	5	8	13				30											11	4	3	7	8			
1973-74	**California Golden Seals**	**NHL**	**4**	**0**	**0**	**0**	**0**	**0**	**0**	**0**	**0**	**0**	**0**	**6**	**0.0**	**0**	**0**	**4**	**0**	**–4**								
	Salt Lake Golden Eagles	WHL	71	38	31	69				45											5	0	0	0	11			
1974-75	**Kansas City Scouts**	**NHL**	**30**	**2**	**4**	**6**	**2**	**3**	**5**	**2**	**0**	**0**	**1**	**20**	**10.0**	**8**	**1**	**15**	**0**	**–8**								
	Baltimore Clippers	AHL	22	8	4	12				28																		
1975-76	Springfield Indians	AHL	55	15	17	32				47																		
1976-77	Maine Nordiques	NAHL	74	31	54	85				71											12	3	7	10	0			
1977-78	Philadelphia Firebirds	AHL	73	25	34	59				22											4	1	1	2	0			
1978-79	Philadelphia Firebirds	AHL	63	16	10	26				30																		
	NHL Totals		**34**	**2**	**4**	**6**	**2**	**3**	**5**	**2**	**0**	**0**	**1**	**26**	**7.7**	**8**	**1**	**19**	**0**									

Traded to **California** by **NY Rangers** with Dave Hrechkosy to complete transaction that sent Bert Marshall to NY Rangers (March 4, 1973), May 17, 1973. Claimed by **Kansas City** from **California** in Expansion Draft, June 12, 1974.

• COATES, Steve

Stephen John RW – R. 5'9", 172 lbs. b: Toronto, Ont., 7/2/1950.

Season	Club	League	GP	G	A	Pts	AG	AA	APts	PIM	PP	SH	GW	S	%	TGF	PGF	TGA	PGA	+/–	GP	G	A	Pts	PIM	PP	SH	GW
1969-70	Michigan Tech Huskies	WCHA	3	0	0	0				4																		
1970-71	Michigan Tech Huskies	WCHA	33	7	9	16				46																		
1971-72	Michigan Tech Huskies	WCHA	30	7	9	16				36																		
1972-73	Michigan Tech Huskies	WCHA	34	11	11	22				28																		
	Calumet Cooper Islanders	USHL	4	5	6	11				7																		
1973-74	Des Moines Capitols	IHL	72	31	39	70				167											10	6	3	9	35			
1974-75	Richmond Robins	AHL	50	7	7	14				168											7	3	0	3	7			
1975-76	Richmond Robins	AHL	69	25	19	44				141																		
1976-77	Springfield Indians	AHL	57	17	23	40				122																		
	Detroit Red Wings	**NHL**	**5**	**1**	**0**	**1**	**1**	**0**	**1**	**24**	**0**	**0**	**0**	**5**	**20.0**	**1**	**0**	**2**	**0**	**–1**								

			REGULAR SEASON																		PLAYOFFS							
Season	Club	League	GP	G	A	Pts	AG	AA	APts	PIM	PP	SH	GW	S	%	TGF	PGF	TGA	PGA	+/–	GP	G	A	Pts	PIM	PP	SH	GW
1977-78	Kansas City Red Wings	CHL	63	14	20	34				83																		
	Maine Mariners	AHL	15	3	2	5				11											6	0	2	2	8			
1978-79	Philadelphia Firebirds	AHL	74	15	25	40				107																		
1979-80	Syracuse Firebirds	AHL	67	10	23	33				95																		
	NHL Totals		5	1	0	1	1	0	1	24	0	0	0	5	20.0	1	0	2	0									

Signed as a free agent by **Philadelphia**, June, 1973. Traded to **Detroit** by **Philadelphia** with Terry Murray, Bob Ritchie and Dave Kelly for Rick Lapointe and Mike Korney, February 17, 1977.

• COCHRANE, Glen

Glen MacLeod D – L. 6'2", 205 lbs. b: Cranbrook, B.C., 1/29/1958. Philadelphia's 6th, 50th overall, in 1978.

Season	Club	League	GP	G	A	Pts	AG	AA	APts	PIM	PP	SH	GW	S	%	TGF	PGF	TGA	PGA	+/–	GP	G	A	Pts	PIM	PP	SH	GW
1974-75	The Pass Red Devils	MJHL	16	1	4	5				61																		
1975-76	The Pass Red Devils	MJHL	60	17	42	59				210																		
	Calgary Centennials	WCJHL	6	0	0	0				0																		
1976-77	Calgary Centennials	WCJHL	35	1	5	6				105																		
	Pincher Creek Panthers	AJHL	3	2	1	3				17																		
	Victoria Cougars	WCJHL	36	1	7	8				60											4	0	0	0	31			
1977-78	Victoria Cougars	WCJHL	72	7	40	47				311											13	1	5	6	51			
1978-79	**Philadelphia Flyers**	**NHL**	1	0	0	0	0	0	0	0	0	0	0	0	0.0	0	0	2	0	–2								
	Maine Mariners	AHL	76	1	22	23				320											10	3	4	7	24			
1979-80	Maine Mariners	AHL	77	1	11	12				269											8	2	0	2	83			
1980-81	**Philadelphia Flyers**	**NHL**	31	1	8	9	1	5	6	219	0	0	1	25	4.0	25	2	26	6	3	6	1	1	2	18	0	0	0
	Maine Mariners	AHL	38	4	13	17				201																		
1981-82	**Philadelphia Flyers**	**NHL**	63	6	12	18	5	8	13	329	0	1	0	67	9.0	68	1	63	15	19	2	0	0	0	2	0	0	0
1982-83	**Philadelphia Flyers**	**NHL**	77	2	22	24	2	15	17	237	0	0	1	94	2.1	99	1	63	7	42	3	0	0	0	4	0	0	0
1983-84	**Philadelphia Flyers**	**NHL**	67	7	16	23	6	11	17	225	0	0	3	69	10.1	65	1	58	10	16								
1984-85	**Philadelphia Flyers**	**NHL**	18	0	3	3	0	2	2	100	0	0	0	7	0.0	3	0	8	1	–4								
	Hershey Bears	AHL	9	0	8	8				35																		
1985-86	**Vancouver Canucks**	**NHL**	49	0	3	3	0	2	2	125	0	0	0	24	0.0	15	0	28	8	–5	2	0	0	0	5	0	0	0
1986-87	**Vancouver Canucks**	**NHL**	14	0	0	0	0	0	0	52	0	0	0	2	0.0	3	0	3	0	0								
1987-88	**Chicago Blackhawks**	**NHL**	73	1	8	9	1	6	7	204	0	0	0	21	4.8	20	0	29	2	–7	5	0	0	0	2	0	0	0
1988-89	**Chicago Blackhawks**	**NHL**	6	0	0	0	0	0	0	13	0	0	0	1	0.0	0	0	4	3	–1								
	Edmonton Oilers	**NHL**	12	0	0	0	0	0	0	52	0	0	0	3	0.0	2	1	3	0	–2								
	NHL Totals		411	17	72	89	15	49	64	1556	0	1	5	313	5.4	300	6	287	52		18	1	1	2	31	0	0	0

Traded to **Vancouver** by **Philadelphia** for Vancouver's 3rd round choice (later traded back to Vancouver–Vancouver selected Don Gibson) in 1986 Entry Draft, March 12, 1985. Claimed by **Chicago** from **Vancouver** in Waiver Draft, October 5, 1987. Claimed on waivers by **Edmonton** from **Chicago**, November 7, 1988.

• COFFEY, Paul

Paul Douglas D – L. 6', 195 lbs. b: Weston, Ont., 6/1/1961. Edmonton's 1st, 6th overall, in 1980.

Season	Club	League	GP	G	A	Pts	AG	AA	APts	PIM	PP	SH	GW	S	%	TGF	PGF	TGA	PGA	+/–	GP	G	A	Pts	PIM	PP	SH	GW
1977-78	North York Rangers	OJHL	50	14	33	47				64																		
	Kingston Canadians	OMJHL	8	2	2	4				11											5	0	0	0	0			
1978-79	Sault Ste. Marie Greyhounds	OMJHL	68	17	72	89				103																		
1979-80	Sault Ste. Marie Greyhounds	OMJHL	23	10	21	31				63																		
	Kitchener Rangers	OMJHL	52	19	52	71				130																		
1980-81	**Edmonton Oilers**	**NHL**	74	9	23	32	7	15	22	130	2	0	0	113	8.0	97	21	78	6	4	9	4	3	7	22	1	0	0
1981-82	**Edmonton Oilers**	**NHL**	80	29	60	89	23	40	63	106	13	0	1	234	12.4	203	64	120	16	35	5	1	1	2	6	1	0	0
1982-83	**Edmonton Oilers**	**NHL**	80	29	67	96	24	47	71	87	9	1	2	259	11.2	219	69	117	19	52	16	7	7	14	14	2	2	0
1983-84 ♦	**Edmonton Oilers**	**NHL**	80	40	86	126	32	59	91	104	14	1	4	258	15.5	230	71	128	21	52	19	8	14	22	21	2	0	1
1984-85	Canada	Can-Cup	8	3	8	11				4																		
♦	**Edmonton Oilers**	**NHL**	80	37	84	121	30	57	87	97	12	2	6	284	13.0	212	61	121	25	55	18	12	25	37	44	3	1	4
1985-86	**Edmonton Oilers**	**NHL**	79	48	90	138	38	61	99	120	9	9	3	307	15.6	247	68	162	44	61	10	1	9	10	30	1	0	0
1986-87 ♦	**Edmonton Oilers**	**NHL**	59	17	50	67	15	36	51	49	10	2	3	165	10.3	130	46	96	24	12	17	3	8	11	30	1	0	1
1987-88	Canada	Can-Cup	9	2	4	6				0																		
	Pittsburgh Penguins	**NHL**	46	15	52	67	13	37	50	93	6	2	2	193	7.8	125	67	84	25	–1								
1988-89	**Pittsburgh Penguins**	**NHL**	75	30	83	113	25	59	84	195	11	0	2	342	8.8	209	102	144	27	–10	11	2	13	15	31	2	0	1
1989-90	**Pittsburgh Penguins**	**NHL**	80	29	74	103	25	53	78	95	10	0	3	324	9.0	195	80	168	28	–25								
	Canada	WEC-A	10	1	6	7				10																		
1990-91 ♦	**Pittsburgh Penguins**	**NHL**	76	24	69	93	22	53	75	128	8	0	3	240	10.0	174	78	125	11	–18	12	2	9	11	6	0	0	0
1991-92	Canada	Can-Cup	8	1	6	7				8																		
	Pittsburgh Penguins	**NHL**	54	10	54	64	9	41	50	62	5	0	1	207	4.8	120	45	91	20	4								
	Los Angeles Kings	**NHL**	10	1	4	5	1	3	4	25	0	0	0	25	4.0	11	5	11	2	–3	6	4	3	7	2	3	0	0
1992-93	**Los Angeles Kings**	**NHL**	50	8	49	57	7	34	41	50	2	0	0	182	4.4	118	53	79	23	9								
	Detroit Red Wings	**NHL**	30	4	26	30	3	18	21	27	3	0	0	72	5.6	67	32	30	2	7	7	2	9	11	2	0	0	0
1993-94	**Detroit Red Wings**	**NHL**	80	14	63	77	13	49	62	106	5	0	3	278	5.0	169	57	105	21	28	7	1	6	7	8	0	0	0
1994-95	**Detroit Red Wings**	**NHL**	45	14	44	58	25	65	90	72	4	1	2	181	7.7	108	47	54	11	18	18	6	12	18	10	2	1	0
1995-96	**Detroit Red Wings**	**NHL**	76	14	60	74	14	49	63	90	3	1	3	234	6.0	133	58	68	12	19	17	5	9	14	30	3	2	1
1996-97	Canada	W-Cup	8	0	7	*7				12																		
	Hartford Whalers	**NHL**	20	3	5	8	3	4	7	18	1	0	1	39	7.7	23	7	20	4	0								
	Philadelphia Flyers	**NHL**	37	6	20	26	6	18	24	20	0	1	1	71	8.5	59	15	44	11	11	17	1	8	9	6	0	0	0
1997-98	**Philadelphia Flyers**	**NHL**	57	2	27	29	2	26	28	30	1	0	1	107	1.9	74	33	40	2	3								
1998-99	**Chicago Blackhawks**	**NHL**	10	0	4	4	0	4	4	0	0	0	0	8	0.0	8	6	8	0	–6								
	Carolina Hurricanes	**NHL**	44	2	8	10	2	8	10	28	1	0	0	79	2.5	44	14	33	2	–1	5	0	1	1	2	0	0	0
99-2000	**Carolina Hurricanes**	**NHL**	69	11	29	40	12	27	39	40	6	0	3	155	7.1	101	42	71	6	–6								
	NHL Totals		1391	396	1131	1527	351	863	1214	1772	135	20	44	4357	9.1	3076	1141	1997	362		194	59	137	196	264	21	6	8

OMJHL Second All-Star Team (1980) • NHL Second All-Star Team (1982, 1983, 1984, 1990) • Canada Cup All-Star Team (1984) • Won James Norris Memorial Trophy (1985, 1986, 1995) • NHL First All-Star Team (1985, 1986, 1989, 1995) • Played in NHL All-Star Game (1982, 1983, 1984, 1985, 1986, 1988, 1989, 1990, 1991, 1992, 1993, 1994, 1996, 1997)

Traded to **Pittsburgh** by **Edmonton** with Dave Hunter and Wayne Van Dorp for Craig Simpson, Dave Hannan, Moe Mantha and Chris Joseph, November 24, 1987. Traded to **LA Kings** by **Pittsburgh** for Brian Benning, Jeff Chychrun and LA Kings' 1st round choice (later traded to Philadelphia — Philadelphia selected Jason Bowen) in 1992 Entry Draft, February 19, 1992. Traded to **Detroit** by **LA Kings** with Sylvain Couturier and Jim Hiller for Jimmy Carson, Marc Potvin and Gary Shuchuk, January 29, 1993. Traded to **Hartford** by **Detroit** with Keith Primeau and Detroit's 1st round choice (Nikos Tselios) in 1997 Entry Draft for Brendan Shanahan and Brian Glynn, October 9, 1996. Traded to **Philadelphia** by **Hartford** with Hartford-Carolina's 3rd round choice (Kris Mallette) in 1997 Entry Draft for Kevin Haller, Philadelphia's 1st round choice (later traded to San Jose — San Jose selected Scott Hannan) in 1997 Entry Draft and Hartford's 7th round choice (previously acquired, Carolina selected Andrew Merrick) in 1997 Entry Draft, December 15, 1996. Traded to **Chicago** by **Philadelphia** for NY Islanders' 5th round choice (previously acquired, Philadelphia selected Francis Belanger) in 1998 Entry Draft, June 27, 1998. Traded to **Carolina** by **Chicago** for Nelson Emerson, December 29, 1998. Signed as a free agent by **Boston**, July 13, 2000.

• COLE, Danton

Danton E. C/RW – R. 5'11", 185 lbs. b: Pontiac, MI, 1/10/1967. Winnipeg's 6th, 123rd overall, in 1985.

Season	Club	League	GP	G	A	Pts	AG	AA	APts	PIM	PP	SH	GW	S	%	TGF	PGF	TGA	PGA	+/–	GP	G	A	Pts	PIM	PP	SH	GW
1983-84	Dunnville Terriers	OJHL-C	2	0	1	1				4																		
1984-85	Aurora Tigers	OJHL	41	51	44	95				91																		
	Aurora Tigers	Cen-Cup	STATISTICS NOT AVAILABLE																									
1985-86	Michigan State Spartans	CCHA	43	11	10	21				22																		
1986-87	Michigan State Spartans	CCHA	44	9	15	24				16																		
1987-88	Michigan State Spartans	CCHA	46	20	36	56				38																		
1988-89	Michigan State Spartans	CCHA	47	29	33	62				46																		
1989-90	**Winnipeg Jets**	**NHL**	2	1	1	2	1	1	2	0	0	0	0	2	50.0	2	0	4	1	–1								
	Moncton Hawks	AHL	80	31	42	73				18																		
	United States	WEC-A	10	2	1	3				6																		
1990-91	**Winnipeg Jets**	**NHL**	66	13	11	24	12	8	20	24	1	1	1	109	11.9	38	6	60	14	–14								
	Moncton Hawks	AHL	3	1	1	2				0																		
	United States	WEC-A	10	6	4	10				14																		
1991-92	**Winnipeg Jets**	**NHL**	52	7	5	12	6	4	10	32	1	2	0	65	10.8	19	2	46	14	–15								
1992-93	**Tampa Bay Lightning**	**NHL**	67	12	15	27	10	10	20	23	0	1	1	100	12.0	41	3	75	35	–2								
	Atlanta Knights	IHL	1	1	0	1				2																		
1993-94	**Tampa Bay Lightning**	**NHL**	81	20	23	43	19	18	37	32	8	1	4	149	13.4	65	21	64	27	7								
	United States	WC-A	5	1	1	2				2																		

			REGULAR SEASON																		PLAYOFFS							
Season	Club	League	GP	G	A	Pts	AG	AA	APts	PIM	PP	SH	GW	S	%	TGF	PGF	TGA	PGA	+/–	GP	G	A	Pts	PIM	PP	SH	GW
1994-95	**Tampa Bay Lightning**	**NHL**	26	3	3	6	5	4	9	6	1	0	0	56	5.4	17	3	21	6	–1	....	....	....	....	....	....	....	....
♦	**New Jersey Devils**	**NHL**	12	1	2	3	2	3	5	8	0	0	0	20	5.0	6	0	6	0	0	1	0	0	0	0	0	0	0
1995-96	**New York Islanders**	**NHL**	10	1	0	1	1	0	1	0	0	0	0	5	20.0	1	0	2	1	0	....	....	....	....	....	....	....	....
	Utah Grizzlies	IHL	34	28	15	43	....	....	....	22	....	....	....	....	....	....	....	....	....	....	....	....	....	....	....	....	....	....
	Chicago Blackhawks	**NHL**	2	0	0	0	0	0	0	0	0	0	0	1	0.0	0	0	0	0	0	....	....	....	....	....	....	....	....
	Indianapolis Ice	IHL	32	9	13	22	....	....	....	20	....	....	....	....	....	....	....	....	....	....	5	1	5	6	8	....	....	....
1996-97	Krefeld Pinguine	Germany	28	7	12	19	....	....	....	14	....	....	....	....	....	....	....	....	....	....	....	....	....	....	....	....	....	....
	Grand Rapids Griffins	IHL	35	8	18	26	....	....	....	24	....	....	....	....	....	....	....	....	....	....	5	3	1	4	2	....	....	....
1997-98	Grand Rapids Griffins	IHL	81	13	13	26	....	....	....	36	....	....	....	....	....	....	....	....	....	....	3	1	1	2	0	....	....	....
1998-99	Grand Rapids Griffins	IHL	72	14	11	25	....	....	....	50	....	....	....	....	....	....	....	....	....	....	....	....	....	....	....	....	....	....
1999-2000	Grand Rapids Griffins	IHL	2	0	0	0	....	....	....	0	....	....	....	....	....	....	....	....	....	....	....	....	....	....	....	....	....	....
	Grand Rapids Griffins	IHL	DID NOT PLAY – ASSISTANT COACH																									
	NHL Totals		318	58	60	118	56	48	104	125	11	5	6	507	11.4	189	35	278	98		1	0	0	0	0	0	0	0

Centennial Cup All-Star Team (1985)

Traded to **Tampa Bay** by **Winnipeg** for future considerations, June 19, 1992. Traded to **New Jersey** by **Tampa Bay** with Shawn Chambers for Alexander Semak and Ben Hankinson, March 14, 1995. Signed as a free agent by **NY Islanders**, August 26, 1995. Traded to **Chicago** by **NY Islanders** for Bob Halkidis, February 2, 1996. • Announced retirement, November 2, 1999.

• COLLEY, Tom

C – L. 5'9", 162 lbs. b: Toronto, Ont., 8/21/1953. Minnesota's 4th, 57th overall, in 1973.

Season	Club	League	GP	G	A	Pts	AG	AA	APts	PIM	PP	SH	GW	S	%	TGF	PGF	TGA	PGA	+/–	GP	G	A	Pts	PIM	PP	SH	GW
1971-72	Niagara Falls Flyers	OMJHL	63	23	22	45	....	....	....	53	....	....	....	....	....	....	....	....	....	....	6	3	1	4	14	....	....	....
1972-73	Sudbury Wolves	OMJHL	67	36	81	117	....	....	....	84	....	....	....	....	....	....	....	....	....	....	4	0	2	2	0	....	....	....
1973-74	New Haven Nighthawks	AHL	66	9	18	27	....	....	....	28	....	....	....	....	....	....	....	....	....	....	10	2	2	4	4	....	....	....
1974-75	**Minnesota North Stars**	**NHL**	1	0	0	0	0	0	0	2	0	0	0	0	0.0	0	0	3	0	–3	....	....	....	....	....	....	....	....
	New Haven Nighthawks	AHL	76	29	47	76	....	....	....	51	....	....	....	....	....	....	....	....	....	....	16	6	12	18	8	....	....	....
1975-76	New Haven Nighthawks	AHL	76	38	31	69	....	....	....	35	....	....	....	....	....	....	....	....	....	....	3	0	1	1	0	....	....	....
1976-77	New Haven Nighthawks	AHL	80	37	56	93	....	....	....	36	....	....	....	....	....	....	....	....	....	....	6	2	2	4	0	....	....	....
1977-78	New Haven Nighthawks	AHL	80	32	54	86	....	....	....	17	....	....	....	....	....	....	....	....	....	....	15	2	6	8	2	....	....	....
1978-79	New Haven Nighthawks	AHL	77	36	32	68	....	....	....	24	....	....	....	....	....	....	....	....	....	....	10	3	9	12	2	....	....	....
1979-80	New Haven Nighthawks	AHL	79	23	43	66	....	....	....	43	....	....	....	....	....	....	....	....	....	....	7	0	4	4	4	....	....	....
1980-81	Binghamton Whalers	AHL	74	17	33	50	....	....	....	31	....	....	....	....	....	....	....	....	....	....	6	4	3	7	2	....	....	....
1981-82	Collingwood Royals	OIHA	30	21	42	63	....	....	....	....	....	....	....	....	....	....	....	....	....	....	....	....	....	....	....	....	....	....
1982-83	Collingwood Royals	OHA-Sr.	30	22	36	58	....	....	....	....	....	....	....	....	....	....	....	....	....	....	....	....	....	....	....	....	....	....
1983-84	Collingwood Royals	OHA-Sr.	37	40	53	93	....	....	....	....	....	....	....	....	....	....	....	....	....	....	....	....	....	....	....	....	....	....
1984-85	Collingwood Royals	OHA-Sr.	STATISTICS NOT AVAILABLE																									
1985-86	Collingwood Royals	OHA-Sr.	36	21	34	55	....	....	....	....	....	....	....	....	....	....	....	....	....	....	....	....	....	....	....	....	....	....
	NHL Totals		1	0	0	0	0	0	0	2	0	0	0	0	0.0	0	0	3	0		....	....	....	....	....	....	....	....

• COLLINS, Bill

William Earl RW – R. 6'1", 178 lbs. b: Ottawa, Ont., 7/13/1943.

Season	Club	League	GP	G	A	Pts	AG	AA	APts	PIM	PP	SH	GW	S	%	TGF	PGF	TGA	PGA	+/–	GP	G	A	Pts	PIM	PP	SH	GW
1960-61	Toronto Marlboros	OHA-Jr.	37	4	9	13	....	....	....	46	....	....	....	....	....	....	....	....	....	....	....	....	....	....	....	....	....	....
1961-62	Whitby Mohawks	OHA-B	27	16	24	40	....	....	....	78	....	....	....	....	....	....	....	....	....	....	2	1	2	3	18	....	....	....
1962-63	Whitby Mohawks	OHA-B	22	22	22	44	....	....	....	32	....	....	....	....	....	....	....	....	....	....	4	7	4	11	18	....	....	....
	Sudbury Wolves	EPHL	....	....	....	....	....	....	....	....	....	....	....	....	....	....	....	....	....	....	6	1	1	2	2	....	....	....
1963-64	Denver Invaders	WHL	58	17	15	32	....	....	....	54	....	....	....	....	....	....	....	....	....	....	....	....	....	....	....	....	....	....
	Baltimore Clippers	AHL	11	0	1	1	....	....	....	0	....	....	....	....	....	....	....	....	....	....	....	....	....	....	....	....	....	....
1964-65	Baltimore Clippers	AHL	6	0	0	0	....	....	....	0	....	....	....	....	....	....	....	....	....	....	....	....	....	....	....	....	....	....
	St. Paul Rangers	CPHL	58	12	29	41	....	....	....	47	....	....	....	....	....	....	....	....	....	....	11	5	2	7	24	....	....	....
1965-66	Minnesota Rangers	CPHL	56	18	29	47	....	....	....	55	....	....	....	....	....	....	....	....	....	....	7	0	5	5	4	....	....	....
1966-67	Baltimore Clippers	AHL	69	20	18	38	....	....	....	50	....	....	....	....	....	....	....	....	....	....	6	1	1	2	12	....	....	....
1967-68	**Minnesota North Stars**	**NHL**	71	9	11	20	10	11	21	41	0	0	1	114	7.9	35	5	60	14	–16	10	2	4	6	4	0	0	1
1968-69	**Minnesota North Stars**	**NHL**	75	9	10	19	9	9	18	24	0	1	1	123	7.3	30	0	91	35	–26	....	....	....	....	....	....	....	....
1969-70	**Minnesota North Stars**	**NHL**	74	29	9	38	32	8	40	48	2	6	2	186	15.6	49	3	89	47	4	6	0	1	1	8	0	0	0
1970-71	**Montreal Canadiens**	**NHL**	40	6	2	8	6	2	8	39	0	0	1	57	10.5	15	0	36	22	1	....	....	....	....	....	....	....	....
	Detroit Red Wings	**NHL**	36	5	16	21	5	13	18	10	1	0	0	105	4.8	30	8	38	15	–1	....	....	....	....	....	....	....	....
1971-72	**Detroit Red Wings**	**NHL**	71	15	25	40	15	22	37	38	2	0	2	157	9.6	68	10	68	13	3	....	....	....	....	....	....	....	....
1972-73	**Detroit Red Wings**	**NHL**	78	21	21	42	20	17	37	44	1	1	6	186	11.3	61	2	83	23	–1	....	....	....	....	....	....	....	....
1973-74	**Detroit Red Wings**	**NHL**	54	13	15	28	12	12	24	37	2	3	0	134	9.7	46	5	72	11	–20	....	....	....	....	....	....	....	....
	St. Louis Blues	**NHL**	12	2	2	4	2	2	4	14	0	0	0	21	9.5	6	1	21	6	–10	....	....	....	....	....	....	....	....
1974-75	**St. Louis Blues**	**NHL**	70	22	15	37	19	11	30	34	2	2	2	142	15.5	56	7	82	37	4	2	1	0	1	0	0	0	0
1975-76	**New York Rangers**	**NHL**	50	4	4	8	3	3	6	38	0	1	0	47	8.5	14	1	39	7	–19	....	....	....	....	....	....	....	....
1976-77	**Philadelphia Flyers**	**NHL**	9	1	1	2	1	1	2	4	0	0	1	5	20.0	3	0	4	0	–1	....	....	....	....	....	....	....	....
	Washington Capitals	**NHL**	54	11	14	25	10	11	21	26	0	2	1	87	12.6	36	0	66	23	–7	....	....	....	....	....	....	....	....
1977-78	**Washington Capitals**	**NHL**	74	10	9	19	9	7	16	18	0	1	1	104	9.6	30	0	93	31	–32	....	....	....	....	....	....	....	....
	NHL Totals		768	157	154	311	153	129	282	415	10	17	18	1468	10.7	479	42	842	284		18	3	5	8	12	0	0	1

Traded to **NY Rangers** by **Toronto** with Dick Duff, Bob Nevin, Arnie Brown and Rod Seiling for Andy Bathgate and Don McKenney, February 22, 1964. Claimed by **Minnesota** from **NY Rangers** in Expansion Draft, June 6, 1967. Traded to **Montreal** by **Minnesota** to complete transaction that sent Jude Drouin to Minnesota (May 22, 1970), June 10, 1970. Traded to **Detroit** by **Montreal** with Mickey Redmond and Guy Charron for Frank Mahovlich, January 13, 1971. Traded to **St. Louis** by **Detroit** with Ted Harris and Garnet Bailey for Chris Evans, Bryan Watson and Jean Hamel, February 14, 1974. Traded to **NY Rangers** by **St. Louis** with John Davidson for Ted Irvine, Bert Wilson and Jerry Butler, June 18, 1975. Signed as a free agent by **Philadelphia**, October 20, 1976. Traded to **Washington** by **Philadelphia** for cash, December 4, 1976.

• COLLYARD, Bob

Robert Leander C – L. 5'9", 170 lbs. b: Hibbing, MN, 10/16/1949. St. Louis' 7th, 73rd overall, in 1969.

Season	Club	League	GP	G	A	Pts	AG	AA	APts	PIM	PP	SH	GW	S	%	TGF	PGF	TGA	PGA	+/–	GP	G	A	Pts	PIM	PP	SH	GW
1968-69	Colorado College	WCHA	25	31	17	48	....	....	....	46	....	....	....	....	....	....	....	....	....	....	....	....	....	....	....	....	....	....
1969-70	Colorado College	WCHA	30	18	39	57	....	....	....	36	....	....	....	....	....	....	....	....	....	....	....	....	....	....	....	....	....	....
1970-71	Colorado College	WCHA	30	20	37	57	....	....	....	6	....	....	....	....	....	....	....	....	....	....	....	....	....	....	....	....	....	....
	Kansas City Blues	CHL	2	0	0	0	....	....	....	0	....	....	....	....	....	....	....	....	....	....	....	....	....	....	....	....	....	....
1971-72	Kansas City Blues	CHL	59	13	22	35	....	....	....	14	....	....	....	....	....	....	....	....	....	....	....	....	....	....	....	....	....	....
1972-73	Fort Worth Wings	CHL	67	17	*50	67	....	....	....	53	....	....	....	....	....	....	....	....	....	....	4	2	3	5	2	....	....	....
1973-74	**St. Louis Blues**	**NHL**	10	1	3	4	1	2	3	4	0	0	0	12	8.3	5	0	4	0	1	....	....	....	....	....	....	....	....
	Denver Spurs	WHL	65	27	47	74	....	....	....	22	....	....	....	....	....	....	....	....	....	....	....	....	....	....	....	....	....	....
1974-75	Philadelphia Firebirds	NAHL	72	42	61	103	....	....	....	78	....	....	....	....	....	....	....	....	....	....	4	3	3	6	12	....	....	....
1975-76	Philadelphia Firebirds	NAHL	73	45	84	129	....	....	....	82	....	....	....	....	....	....	....	....	....	....	16	12	*25	*37	10	....	....	....
1976-77	Philadelphia Firebirds	NAHL	71	31	85	116	....	....	....	76	....	....	....	....	....	....	....	....	....	....	4	3	2	5	7	....	....	....
1977-78	Philadelphia Firebirds	AHL	79	28	62	90	....	....	....	42	....	....	....	....	....	....	....	....	....	....	4	0	1	1	0	....	....	....
	United States	WEC-A	10	1	5	6	....	....	....	2	....	....	....	....	....	....	....	....	....	....	....	....	....	....	....	....	....	....
1978-79	Philadelphia Firebirds	AHL	69	21	35	56	....	....	....	32	....	....	....	....	....	....	....	....	....	....	....	....	....	....	....	....	....	....
	United States	WEC-A	8	2	0	2	....	....	....	8	....	....	....	....	....	....	....	....	....	....	....	....	....	....	....	....	....	....
1979-80	VfL Bad Nauheim	Germany	37	19	34	53	....	....	....	58	....	....	....	....	....	....	....	....	....	....	....	....	....	....	....	....	....	....
1980-81	VfL Bad Nauheim	Germany	44	29	25	54	....	....	....	23	....	....	....	....	....	....	....	....	....	....	5	2	2	4	28	....	....	....
1981-82	Milwaukee Admirals	IHL	77	24	46	70	....	....	....	32	....	....	....	....	....	....	....	....	....	....	5	2	2	4	9	....	....	....
1982-83	Milwaukee Admirals	IHL	10	0	4	4	....	....	....	0	....	....	....	....	....	....	....	....	....	....	....	....	....	....	....	....	....	....
	Kalamazoo Wings	IHL	5	0	6	6	....	....	....	0	....	....	....	....	....	....	....	....	....	....	....	....	....	....	....	....	....	....
	NHL Totals		10	1	3	4	1	2	3	4	0	0	0	12	8.3	5	0	4	0		....	....	....	....	....	....	....	....

WCHA Second All-Star Team (1969) • NCAA West First All-American Team (1969, 1970) • WCHA First All-Star Team (1970, 1971) • CHL Second All-Star Team (1973) • NAHL Second All-Star Team (1975, 1976, 1977)

Claimed by **Washington** from **St. Louis** in Expansion Draft, June 12, 1974.

• COLMAN, Michael

D – R. 6'3", 225 lbs. b: Stoneham, MA, 8/4/1968 d: 4/5/1995.

Season	Club	League	GP	G	A	Pts	AG	AA	APts	PIM	PP	SH	GW	S	%	TGF	PGF	TGA	PGA	+/–	GP	G	A	Pts	PIM	PP	SH	GW
1987-88	Humboldt Broncos	SJHL	55	3	7	10	....	....	....	188	....	....	....	....	....	....	....	....	....	....	....	....	....	....	....	....	....	....
1988-89	Humboldt Broncos	SJHL	44	3	17	20	....	....	....	161	....	....	....	....	....	....	....	....	....	....	....	....	....	....	....	....	....	....
1989-90	Ferris State Bulldogs	CCHA	23	0	4	4	....	....	....	62	....	....	....	....	....	....	....	....	....	....	....	....	....	....	....	....	....	....

			REGULAR SEASON																		PLAYOFFS							
Season	Club	League	GP	G	A	Pts	AG	AA	APts	PIM	PP	SH	GW	S	%	TGF	PGF	TGA	PGA	+/–	GP	G	A	Pts	PIM	PP	SH	GW
1990-91	Kansas City Blades	IHL	66	1	6	7				115																		
1991-92	**San Jose Sharks**	**NHL**	**15**	**0**	**1**	**1**	**0**	**1**	**1**	**32**	**0**	**0**	**0**	**7**	**0.0**	**7**	**0**	**16**	**1**	**–8**								
	Kansas City Blades	IHL	59	0	4	4				130											3	0	0	0	4			
1992-93	Kansas City Blades	IHL	80	1	5	6				191											12	1	0	1	34			
1993-94	Kansas City Blades	IHL	77	4	7	11				215																		
	NHL Totals		**15**	**0**	**1**	**1**	**0**	**1**	**1**	**32**	**0**	**0**	**0**	**7**	**0.0**	**7**	**0**	**16**	**1**									

Signed as a free agent by **San Jose**, September 3, 1991. • Died of injuries suffered in automobile accident, April 5, 1994.

• COMEAU, Rey

Reynald Xavier C – L. 5'8", 190 lbs. b: Montreal, Que., 10/25/1948.

Season	Club	League	GP	G	A	Pts	AG	AA	APts	PIM	PP	SH	GW	S	%	TGF	PGF	TGA	PGA	+/–	GP	G	A	Pts	PIM	PP	SH	GW
1965-66	West Island Flyers	MMJHL	37	*40	32	72				37																		
1966-67	Verdun Maple Leafs	QJHL	STATISTICS NOT AVAILABLE																									
	Verdun Maple Leafs	Mem-Cup	4	3	1	4				2																		
1967-68	Verdun Maple Leafs	QJHL	36	29	50	79																						
	Verdun Maple Leafs	Mem-Cup	18	8	14	22				40																		
1968-69	Houston Apollos	CHL	1	0	0	0				0																		
	Cleveland Barons	AHL	71	17	23	40				26											4	1	0	1	0			
1969-70	Cleveland Barons	AHL	71	27	38	65				26																		
1970-71	Cleveland Barons	AHL	41	17	25	42				30																		
	Montreal Voyageurs	AHL	29	9	14	23				34											3	1	2	3	4			
1971-72	**Montreal Canadiens**	**NHL**	**4**	**0**	**0**	**0**	**0**	**0**	**0**	**0**	**0**	**0**	**0**	**2**	**0.0**	**0**	**0**	**0**	**0**	**0**								
	Nova Scotia Voyageurs	AHL	68	23	41	64				63											15	6	14	20	10			
1972-73	**Atlanta Flames**	**NHL**	**77**	**21**	**21**	**42**	**20**	**17**	**37**	**19**	**3**	**0**	**2**	**146**	**14.4**	**55**	**11**	**63**	**19**	**0**								
1973-74	**Atlanta Flames**	**NHL**	**78**	**11**	**23**	**34**	**11**	**19**	**30**	**16**	**0**	**1**	**4**	**130**	**8.5**	**44**	**3**	**94**	**38**	**–15**	**4**	**2**	**1**	**3**	**6**	**1**	**0**	**0**
1974-75	**Atlanta Flames**	**NHL**	**75**	**14**	**20**	**34**	**12**	**15**	**27**	**40**	**2**	**0**	**3**	**116**	**12.1**	**45**	**6**	**34**	**4**	**9**								
1975-76	**Atlanta Flames**	**NHL**	**79**	**17**	**22**	**39**	**15**	**16**	**31**	**42**	**1**	**0**	**2**	**124**	**13.7**	**46**	**3**	**39**	**5**	**9**								
1976-77	**Atlanta Flames**	**NHL**	**80**	**15**	**18**	**33**	**13**	**14**	**27**	**16**	**2**	**1**	**4**	**133**	**11.3**	**48**	**3**	**50**	**12**	**7**	**3**	**0**	**0**	**0**	**2**	**0**	**0**	**0**
1977-78	**Atlanta Flames**	**NHL**	**79**	**10**	**22**	**32**	**9**	**17**	**26**	**20**	**0**	**1**	**1**	**114**	**8.8**	**42**	**2**	**51**	**11**	**0**	**2**	**0**	**0**	**0**	**0**	**0**	**0**	**0**
1978-79	**Colorado Rockies**	**NHL**	**70**	**8**	**10**	**18**	**7**	**7**	**14**	**16**	**1**	**2**	**0**	**85**	**9.4**	**25**	**1**	**77**	**33**	**–20**								
1979-80	**Colorado Rockies**	**NHL**	**22**	**2**	**5**	**7**	**2**	**4**	**6**	**6**	**0**	**0**	**0**	**21**	**9.5**	**13**	**2**	**17**	**6**	**0**								
	Fort Worth Texans	CHL	57	14	35	49				16																		
1980-81	Fort Worth Texans	CHL	77	19	16	35				40											5	2	3	5	4			
	NHL Totals		**564**	**98**	**141**	**239**	**89**	**109**	**198**	**175**	**9**	**5**	**16**	**871**	**11.3**	**318**	**31**	**425**	**128**		**9**	**2**	**1**	**3**	**8**	**1**	**0**	**0**

QJHL Second All-Star Team (1966)

Traded to **Cleveland** (AHL) by **Montreal** for cash, July, 1969. Rights transferred to **Minnesota** when NHL club established working agreement with **Cleveland** (AHL), July, 1970. Traded to **Montreal** by **Minnesota** for Gord Labossiere, January 26, 1971. Claimed by **Vancouver** from **Montreal** in Intra-League Draft, June 8, 1971. Traded to **Montreal** by **Vancouver** for cash, September 14, 1971. Traded to **Atlanta** by **Montreal** for cash, June 16, 1972. Signed as a free agent by **Colorado**, June 23, 1978.

• COMRIE, Paul

C – L. 5'11", 192 lbs. b: Edmonton, Alta., 2/7/1977. Tampa Bay's 12th, 224th overall, in 1997.

Season	Club	League	GP	G	A	Pts	AG	AA	APts	PIM	PP	SH	GW	S	%	TGF	PGF	TGA	PGA	+/–	GP	G	A	Pts	PIM	PP	SH	GW
1993-94	Fort Saskatchewan Traders	AJHL	55	7	23	30				50											6	0	1	1	2			
1994-95	Fort Saskatchewan Traders	AJHL	51	30	37	67				121																		
1995-96	University of Denver	WCHA	38	13	10	23				61																		
1996-97	University of Denver	WCHA	40	21	28	49				72																		
1997-98	University of Denver	WCHA	33	17	23	40				72																		
1998-99	University of Denver	WCHA	40	18	31	49				84																		
	Hamilton Bulldogs	AHL	7	0	1	1				0											8	1	3	4	2			
99-2000	**Edmonton Oilers**	**NHL**	**15**	**1**	**2**	**3**	**1**	**2**	**3**	**4**	**0**	**0**	**0**	**11**	**9.1**	**5**	**0**	**7**	**0**	**–2**								
	Hamilton Bulldogs	AHL	12	3	3	6				6																		
	NHL Totals		**15**	**1**	**2**	**3**	**1**	**2**	**3**	**4**	**0**	**0**	**0**	**11**	**9.1**	**5**	**0**	**7**	**0**									

WCHA First All-Star Team (1999) • NCAA West Second All-American Team (1999)

Traded to **Edmonton** by **Tampa Bay** with Roman Hamrlik for Bryan Marchment, Steve Kelly and Jason Bonsignore, December 30, 1997.

• CONACHER, Brian

Brian Kennedy LW – L. 6'3", 197 lbs. b: Toronto, Ont., 8/31/1941.

Season	Club	League	GP	G	A	Pts	AG	AA	APts	PIM	PP	SH	GW	S	%	TGF	PGF	TGA	PGA	+/–	GP	G	A	Pts	PIM	PP	SH	GW
1958-59	Toronto Marlboros	OHA-Jr.	6	0	1	1				0											3	0	2	2	0			
1959-60	Toronto Marlboros	OHA-Jr.	42	17	17	34				2											3	0	0	0	2			
1960-61	Toronto Marlboros	OHA-Jr.	14	2	5	7				7																		
1961-62	Toronto Marlboros	OHA-Jr.	25	12	27	39				4											12	7	8	15	18			
	Rochester Americans	AHL	3	0	0	0				2																		
	Toronto Maple Leafs	**NHL**	**1**	**0**	**0**	**0**	**0**	**0**	**0**	**0**																		
1962-63	University of Western Ontario	OUAA	STATISTICS NOT AVAILABLE																									
1963-64	Canada	Nat-Team	STATISTICS NOT AVAILABLE																									
	Canada	Olympics	7	7	1	8				6																		
1964-65	Canada	Nat-Team	STATISTICS NOT AVAILABLE																									
	Canada	WEC-A	7	1	3	4				6																		
1965-66	**Toronto Maple Leafs**	**NHL**	**2**	**0**	**0**	**0**	**0**	**0**	**0**	**2**																		
	Rochester Americans	AHL	69	14	16	30				66											12	6	0	6	18			
1966-67♦	**Toronto Maple Leafs**	**NHL**	**66**	**14**	**13**	**27**	**16**	**13**	**29**	**47**											**12**	**3**	**2**	**5**	**21**	**0**	**0**	**2**
1967-68	**Toronto Maple Leafs**	**NHL**	**64**	**11**	**14**	**25**	**13**	**14**	**27**	**31**	**0**	**1**	**1**	**88**	**12.5**	**35**	**2**	**34**	**8**	**7**								
	Rochester Americans	AHL	5	2	2	4				6																		
1968-69	Canada	Nat-Team	STATISTICS NOT AVAILABLE																									
1969-70	Canada	Nat-Team	STATISTICS NOT AVAILABLE																									
1970-71	Canada	Nat-Team	STATISTICS NOT AVAILABLE																									
1971-72	**Detroit Red Wings**	**NHL**	**22**	**3**	**1**	**4**	**3**	**1**	**4**	**4**	**0**	**1**	**0**	**21**	**14.3**	**4**	**0**	**14**	**7**	**–3**								
	Fort Worth Wings	CHL	40	13	13	26				4											7	3	2	5	4			
1972-73	Ottawa Nationals	WHA	69	8	19	27				32											5	1	3	4	4			
1973-1975	Mohawk Valley Comets	NAHL	DID NOT PLAY – GENERAL MANAGER																									
1975-1976	Mohawk Valley Comets	NAHL	DID NOT PLAY – GENERAL MANAGER																									
	Mohawk Valley Comets	NAHL	3	2	1	3				2																		
	NHL Totals		**155**	**28**	**28**	**56**	**32**	**28**	**60**	**84**											**12**	**3**	**2**	**5**	**21**			
	Other Major League Totals		69	8	19	27				32											5	1	3	4	4			

• Son of Lionel • Played in NHL All-Star Game (1968)

Claimed by **Detroit** from **Toronto** in Intra-League Draft, June 12, 1968. Rights traded to **Minnesota** by **Detroit** with Danny Lawson for Wayne Connelly, February 15, 1969. Rights traded to **Toronto** by **Minnesota** with Terry O'Malley and cash for Murray Oliver, May 22, 1970. Rights traded to **Detroit** by **Toronto** for cash, August 20, 1971. Signed as a free agent by **Ottawa** (WHA), October, 1972.

• CONACHER, Pat

Patrick John LW – L. 5'8", 190 lbs. b: Edmonton, Alta., 5/1/1959. NY Rangers' 3rd, 76th overall, in 1979.

Season	Club	League	GP	G	A	Pts	AG	AA	APts	PIM	PP	SH	GW	S	%	TGF	PGF	TGA	PGA	+/–	GP	G	A	Pts	PIM	PP	SH	GW
1976-77	Battleford Barons	SJHL	57	22	35	57				65																		
1977-78	Billings Bighorns	WCJHL	72	31	44	75				105											20	15	14	29	22			
	Saskatoon Blades	Mem-Cup	11	1	7	8				4																		
1978-79	Billings Bighorns	WHL	39	25	37	62				50																		
	Saskatoon Blades	WHL	33	15	32	47				37																		
1979-80	**New York Rangers**	**NHL**	**17**	**0**	**5**	**5**	**0**	**4**	**4**	**4**	**0**	**0**	**0**	**15**	**0.0**	**6**	**0**	**16**	**0**	**–10**	**3**	**0**	**1**	**1**	**2**	**0**	**0**	**0**
	New Haven Nighthawks	AHL	53	11	14	25				43											7	1	1	2	4			
1980-81	**New York Rangers**	**NHL**	DID NOT PLAY – INJURED																									
1981-82	Springfield Indians	AHL	77	23	22	45				38																		
1982-83	**New York Rangers**	**NHL**	**5**	**0**	**1**	**1**	**0**	**1**	**1**	**4**	**0**	**0**	**0**	**5**	**0.0**	**1**	**0**	**1**	**0**	**0**								
	Tulsa Oilers	CHL	63	29	28	57				44																		
1983-84♦	**Edmonton Oilers**	**NHL**	**45**	**2**	**8**	**10**	**2**	**5**	**7**	**31**	**0**	**0**	**0**	**18**	**11.1**	**17**	**0**	**23**	**4**	**–2**	**3**	**1**	**0**	**1**	**2**	**0**	**0**	**0**
	Moncton Alpines	AHL	28	7	16	23				30																		

Season	Club	League	GP	G	A	Pts	AG	AA	APts	PIM	PP	SH	GW	S	%	TGF	PGF	TGA	PGA	+/-	GP	G	A	Pts	PIM	PP	SH	GW
			REGULAR SEASON																		PLAYOFFS							
1984-85	Nova Scotia Voyageurs	AHL	68	20	45	65	....	....	....	44	....	....	....	....	....	....	....	....	....	....	6	3	2	5	0	....	....	....
1985-86	New Jersey Devils	NHL	2	0	2	2	0	1	1	2	0	0	0	3	0.0	2	0	2	0	0	....	....	....	....	....	....	....	....
	Maine Mariners	AHL	69	15	30	45	....	....	....	83	....	....	....	....	....	....	....	....	....	....	5	1	1	2	11	....	....	....
1986-87	Maine Mariners	AHL	56	12	14	26	....	....	....	47	....	....	....	....	....	....	....	....	....	....	....	....	....	....	....	....	....	....
1987-88	New Jersey Devils	NHL	24	2	5	7	2	4	6	12	0	0	0	22	9.1	18	1	18	9	8	17	2	2	4	14	0	1	1
	Utica Devils	AHL	47	14	33	47	....	....	....	32	....	....	....	....	....	....	....	....	....	....	....	....	....	....	....	....	....	....
1988-89	New Jersey Devils	NHL	55	7	5	12	6	4	10	14	0	1	1	59	11.9	23	1	49	20	–7	....	....	....	....	....	....	....	....
1989-90	New Jersey Devils	NHL	19	3	3	6	3	2	5	4	0	0	0	18	16.7	11	0	14	5	2	5	1	0	1	10	0	0	0
	Utica Devils	AHL	57	13	36	49	....	....	....	53	....	....	....	....	....	....	....	....	....	....	....	....	....	....	....	....	....	....
1990-91	New Jersey Devils	NHL	49	5	11	16	5	8	13	27	0	0	0	45	11.1	28	0	37	18	9	7	0	2	2	2	0	0	0
	Utica Devils	AHL	4	0	1	1	....	....	....	6	....	....	....	....	....	....	....	....	....	....	....	....	....	....	....	....	....	....
1991-92	New Jersey Devils	NHL	44	7	3	10	6	2	8	16	0	1	1	38	18.4	15	0	35	20	0	7	1	1	2	4	0	1	0
1992-93	Los Angeles Kings	NHL	81	9	8	17	7	5	12	20	0	2	1	65	13.8	36	3	96	47	–16	24	6	4	10	6	0	0	0
1993-94	Los Angeles Kings	NHL	77	15	13	28	14	10	24	71	0	3	1	98	15.3	44	3	76	35	0	....	....	....	....	....	....	....	....
1994-95	Los Angeles Kings	NHL	48	7	9	16	12	13	25	12	0	1	0	64	10.9	27	0	56	20	–9	....	....	....	....	....	....	....	....
1995-96	Los Angeles Kings	NHL	35	5	2	7	5	2	7	18	0	1	2	35	14.3	12	0	27	7	–8	....	....	....	....	....	....	....	....
	Calgary Flames	NHL	7	0	0	0	0	0	0	0	0	0	0	1	0.0	2	0	5	2	–1	....	....	....	....	....	....	....	....
	New York Islanders	NHL	13	1	1	2	1	1	2	0	0	0	0	9	11.1	4	0	11	3	–4	....	....	....	....	....	....	....	....
1996-97	Canada	Nat-Team	DID NOT PLAY – ASSISTANT COACH																									
1997-98	Canada	Nat-Team	34	1	12	13	....	....	....	63	....	....	....	....	....	....	....	....	....	....	....	....	....	....	....	....	....	....
1998-99			OUT OF HOCKEY – RETIRED																									
99-2000	Kelowna Rockets	WHL	DID NOT PLAY – ASSISTANT COACH																									
	NHL Totals		521	63	76	139	63	62	125	235	0	9	6	495	12.7	246	8	466	190		66	11	10	21	40	0	2	1

• Missed entire 1980-81 season recovering from ankle injury suffered in pre-season rookie game, September, 1980. Signed as a free agent by **Edmonton**, October 4, 1983. Signed as a free agent by **New Jersey**, August 14, 1985. Traded to **LA Kings** by **New Jersey** for future considerations, September 3, 1992. Traded to **Calgary** by **LA Kings** for Craig Ferguson, February 10, 1996. Traded to **NY Islanders** by **Calgary** with Calgary's 6th round choice (later traded back to Calgary — Calgary selected Ilja Demidov) in 1997 Entry Draft for Bob Sweeney, March 20, 1996.

• CONN, Rob

Robert Phillip W – R. 6'2", 200 lbs. b: Calgary, Alta., 9/3/1968.

Season	Club	League	GP	G	A	Pts	AG	AA	APts	PIM	PP	SH	GW	S	%	TGF	PGF	TGA	PGA	+/-	GP	G	A	Pts	PIM	PP	SH	GW
1985-86	Calgary Royals	AAHA	41	16	28	44	....	....	....	70	....	....	....	....	....	....	....	....	....	....	....	....	....	....	....	....	....	....
1986-87	Calgary Canucks	AJHL	STATISTICS NOT AVAILABLE																									
1987-88	Calgary Canucks	AJHL	STATISTICS NOT AVAILABLE																									
1988-89	University of Alaska-Anchorage	G-North	33	21	17	38	....	....	....	46	....	....	....	....	....	....	....	....	....	....	....	....	....	....	....	....	....	....
1989-90	University of Alaska-Anchorage	G-North	34	27	21	48	....	....	....	46	....	....	....	....	....	....	....	....	....	....	....	....	....	....	....	....	....	....
1990-91	University of Alaska-Anchorage	G-North	43	28	32	60	....	....	....	53	....	....	....	....	....	....	....	....	....	....	....	....	....	....	....	....	....	....
1991-92	Chicago Blackhawks	NHL	2	0	0	0	0	0	0	2	0	0	0	3	0.0	1	0	0	0	1	....	....	....	....	....	....	....	....
	Indianapolis Ice	IHL	72	19	16	35	....	....	....	100	....	....	....	....	....	....	....	....	....	....	....	....	....	....	....	....	....	....
1992-93	Indianapolis Ice	IHL	75	13	14	27	....	....	....	81	....	....	....	....	....	....	....	....	....	....	5	0	1	1	6	....	....	....
1993-94	Indianapolis Ice	IHL	51	16	11	27	....	....	....	46	....	....	....	....	....	....	....	....	....	....	....	....	....	....	....	....	....	....
1994-95	Indianapolis Ice	IHL	10	4	4	8	....	....	....	11	....	....	....	....	....	....	....	....	....	....	....	....	....	....	....	....	....	....
	Albany River Rats	AHL	68	35	32	67	....	....	....	76	....	....	....	....	....	....	....	....	....	....	14	4	6	10	16	....	....	....
1995-96	Buffalo Sabres	NHL	28	2	5	7	2	4	6	18	0	0	0	36	5.6	8	0	17	0	–9	....	....	....	....	....	....	....	....
	Rochester Americans	AHL	36	22	15	37	....	....	....	40	....	....	....	....	....	....	....	....	....	....	19	7	6	13	10	....	....	....
1996-97	Indianapolis Ice	IHL	72	25	32	57	....	....	....	81	....	....	....	....	....	....	....	....	....	....	4	0	0	0	8	....	....	....
	NHL Totals		30	2	5	7	2	4	6	20	0	0	0	39	5.1	9	0	17	0		....	....	....	....	....	....	....	....

Signed as a free agent by **Chicago**, July 31, 1991. Traded to **New Jersey** by **Chicago** for Dean Malkoc, January 30, 1995. Claimed by **Buffalo** from **New Jersey** in NHL Waiver Draft, October 2, 1995. Signed as a free agent by **Chicago**, September 26, 1996.

• CONNELLY, Wayne

Wayne Francis C – R. 5'10", 170 lbs. b: Rouyn, Que., 12/16/1939.

Season	Club	League	GP	G	A	Pts	AG	AA	APts	PIM	PP	SH	GW	S	%	TGF	PGF	TGA	PGA	+/-	GP	G	A	Pts	PIM	PP	SH	GW
1955-56	New Hamburg Raiders	OHA-B	STATISTICS NOT AVAILABLE																									
	Kitchener Canucks	OHA-Jr.	9	0	1	1	....	....	....	2	....	....	....	....	....	....	....	....	....	....	8	0	0	0	0	....	....	....
1956-57	Peterborough Petes	OHA-Jr.	52	19	7	26	....	....	....	83	....	....	....	....	....	....	....	....	....	....	....	....	....	....	....	....	....	....
1957-58	Peterborough Petes	OHA-Jr.	52	18	19	37	....	....	....	32	....	....	....	....	....	....	....	....	....	....	5	0	1	1	6	....	....	....
1958-59	Peterborough Petes	OHA-Jr.	54	36	54	90	....	....	....	46	....	....	....	....	....	....	....	....	....	....	19	6	*13	*19	38	....	....	....
	Peterborough Petes	Mem-Cup	12	10	5	15	....	....	....	9	....	....	....	....	....	....	....	....	....	....	....	....	....	....	....	....	....	....
1959-60	Peterborough Petes	OHA-Jr.	47	*48	34	82	....	....	....	47	....	....	....	....	....	....	....	....	....	....	12	10	9	19	4	....	....	....
	Montreal Royals	EPHL	....	....	....	....	....	....	....	....	....	....	....	....	....	....	....	....	....	....	8	6	4	10	4	....	....	....
1960-61	Montreal Canadiens	NHL	3	0	0	0	0	0	0	0	....	....	....	....	....	....	....	....	....	....	....	....	....	....	....	....	....	....
	Montreal Royals	EPHL	64	28	21	49	....	....	....	36	....	....	....	....	....	....	....	....	....	....	....	....	....	....	....	....	....	....
1961-62	Hull-Ottawa Canadiens	EPHL	7	2	3	5	....	....	....	4	....	....	....	....	....	....	....	....	....	....	....	....	....	....	....	....	....	....
	Boston Bruins	NHL	61	8	12	20	9	11	20	34	....	....	....	....	....	....	....	....	....	....	....	....	....	....	....	....	....	....
1962-63	Boston Bruins	NHL	18	2	6	8	2	6	8	2	....	....	....	....	....	....	....	....	....	....	....	....	....	....	....	....	....	....
	Kingston Frontenacs	EPHL	34	10	24	34	....	....	....	19	....	....	....	....	....	....	....	....	....	....	5	1	4	5	2	....	....	....
1963-64	Boston Bruins	NHL	26	2	3	5	2	3	5	12	....	....	....	....	....	....	....	....	....	....	....	....	....	....	....	....	....	....
	San Francisco Seals	WHL	33	12	18	30	....	....	....	10	....	....	....	....	....	....	....	....	....	....	11	2	3	5	8	....	....	....
1964-65	San Francisco Seals	WHL	70	36	36	72	....	....	....	51	....	....	....	....	....	....	....	....	....	....	....	....	....	....	....	....	....	....
1965-66	San Francisco Seals	WHL	72	45	41	86	....	....	....	14	....	....	....	....	....	....	....	....	....	....	7	4	4	8	2	....	....	....
1966-67	Boston Bruins	NHL	64	13	17	30	15	17	32	12	....	....	....	....	....	....	....	....	....	....	....	....	....	....	....	....	....	....
1967-68	Minnesota North Stars	NHL	74	35	21	56	41	21	62	40	14	0	8	258	13.6	82	40	75	1	–32	14	*8	3	11	2	3	0	0
1968-69	Minnesota North Stars	NHL	55	14	16	30	15	14	29	11	4	0	1	193	7.3	55	22	58	0	–25	....	....	....	....	....	....	....	....
	Detroit Red Wings	NHL	19	4	9	13	4	8	12	0	1	0	0	58	6.9	22	10	20	1	–7	....	....	....	....	....	....	....	....
1969-70	Detroit Red Wings	NHL	76	23	36	59	25	34	59	10	5	0	5	242	9.5	114	42	56	11	27	4	1	3	4	2	1	0	0
1970-71	Detroit Red Wings	NHL	51	8	13	21	8	11	19	12	1	0	2	115	7.0	39	13	52	3	–23	....	....	....	....	....	....	....	....
	St. Louis Blues	NHL	28	5	16	21	5	13	18	9	3	0	0	102	4.9	35	19	22	0	–6	6	2	1	3	0	1	0	1
1971-72	St. Louis Blues	NHL	15	5	5	10	5	4	9	2	2	0	0	48	10.4	15	7	14	0	–6	....	....	....	....	....	....	....	....
	Vancouver Canucks	NHL	53	14	20	34	14	17	31	12	6	0	3	151	9.3	52	23	47	3	–15	....	....	....	....	....	....	....	....
1972-73	Minnesota Fighting Saints	WHA	78	40	30	70	....	....	....	16	....	....	....	....	....	....	....	....	....	....	5	1	3	4	0	....	....	....
1973-74	Minnesota Fighting Saints	WHA	78	42	53	95	....	....	....	16	....	....	....	....	....	....	....	....	....	....	11	6	7	13	4	....	....	....
1974-75	Minnesota Fighting Saints	WHA	76	38	33	71	....	....	....	16	....	....	....	....	....	....	....	....	....	....	12	8	4	12	10	....	....	....
1975-76	Minnesota Fighting Saints	WHA	59	24	23	47	....	....	....	19	....	....	....	....	....	....	....	....	....	....	....	....	....	....	....	....	....	....
	Cleveland Crusaders	WHA	12	5	2	7	....	....	....	4	....	....	....	....	....	....	....	....	....	....	3	1	0	1	2	....	....	....
1976-77	Calgary Cowboys	WHA	25	5	6	11	....	....	....	4	....	....	....	....	....	....	....	....	....	....	....	....	....	....	....	....	....	....
	Edmonton Oilers	WHA	38	13	15	28	....	....	....	18	....	....	....	....	....	....	....	....	....	....	5	0	1	1	0	....	....	....
	NHL Totals		543	133	174	307	145	159	304	156	....	....	....	....	....	....	....	....	....	....	24	11	7	18	4	....	....	....
	Other Major League Totals		366	167	162	329	....	....	....	93	....	....	....	....	....	....	....	....	....	....	36	16	15	31	16	....	....	....

OHA-Jr. First All-Star Team (1959) • WHL Second All-Star Team (1965, 1966)

Traded to **Boston** by **Montreal** (Hull-Ottawa-EPHL) for the loan of Bob Armstrong and Dallas Smith and cash, October 26, 1961. Traded to **San Francisco** (WHL) by **Boston** for cash, June 6, 1964. Traded to **Boston** by **San Francisco** (WHL) for cash, June 14, 1966. Claimed by **Minnesota** from **Boston** in Expansion Draft, June 6, 1967. Traded to **Detroit** by **Minnesota** for Danny Lawson and the rights to Brian Conacher, February 15, 1969. Traded to **St. Louis** by **Detroit** with Garry Unger for Red Berenson and Tim Ecclestone, February 6, 1971. Traded to **NY Rangers** by **St. Louis** with Gene Carr and Jim Lorentz for Andre Dupont, Jack Egers and Mike Murphy, November 15, 1971. Traded to **Vancouver** by **NY Rangers** with Dave Balon and Ron Stewart for Gary Doak and Jim Wiste, November 16, 1971. Selected by **Minnesota** (WHA) in 1972 WHA General Player Draft, February 12, 1972. Signed as a free agent by **Cleveland** (WHA) after **Minnesota** (WHA) franchise folded, March 10, 1976. Traded to **New England** (WHA) by **Cleveland** (WHA) for Fred O'Donnell and Bob McManama, June, 1976. Traded to **Calgary** (WHA) by **New England** (WHA) for cash, October, 1976. Traded to **Edmonton** (WHA) by **Calgary** (WHA) with Claude St. Sauveur for cash, January, 1977.

• CONNOLLY, Tim C – R. 6', 186 lbs. b: Baldwinsville, NY, 5/7/1981. NY Islanders' 1st, 5th overall, in 1999.

Season	Club	League	GP	G	A	Pts	AG	AA	APts	PIM	PP	SH	GW	S	%	TGF	PGF	TGA	PGA	+/-	GP	G	A	Pts	PIM	PP	SH	GW
			REGULAR SEASON																		PLAYOFFS							
1996-97	Syracuse Jr. Crunch	OJHL	50	42	62	104	....	....	....	34	....	....	....	....	....	....	....	....	....	....	....	....	....	....	....	....	....	....
1997-98	Erie Otters	OHL	59	30	32	62	....	....	....	32	....	....	....	....	....	....	....	....	....	....	7	1	6	7	6	....	....	....
1998-99	Erie Otters	OHL	46	34	34	68	....	....	....	50	....	....	....	....	....	....	....	....	....	....	....	....	....	....	....	....	....	....
	United States	WJC-A	6	1	0	1	....	....	....	8	....	....	....	....	....	....	....	....	....	....	....	....	....	....	....	....	....	....
99-2000	**New York Islanders**	**NHL**	**81**	**14**	**20**	**34**	**16**	**19**	**35**	**44**	**2**	**1**	**1**	**114**	**12.3**	**54**	**15**	**68**	**4**	**–25**	....	....	....	....	....	....	....	....
	NHL Totals		**81**	**14**	**20**	**34**	**16**	**19**	**35**	**44**	**2**	**1**	**1**	**114**	**12.3**	**54**	**15**	**68**	**4**		....	....	....	....	....	....	....	....

• CONNOR, Cam Cameron Duncan RW – L. 6'2", 200 lbs. b: Winnipeg, Man., 8/10/1954. Montreal's 1st, 5th overall, in 1974.

Season	Club	League	GP	G	A	Pts	AG	AA	APts	PIM	PP	SH	GW	S	%	TGF	PGF	TGA	PGA	+/-	GP	G	A	Pts	PIM	PP	SH	GW
1971-72	St. Boniface Saints	MJHL	32	4	10	14	....	....	....	97	....	....	....	....	....	....	....	....	....	....	....	....	....	....	....	....	....	....
	Winnipeg Jets	WCJHL	5	0	4	4	....	....	....	4	....	....	....	....	....	....	....	....	....	....	....	....	....	....	....	....	....	....
1972-73	St. Boniface Saints	MJHL	29	11	8	19	....	....	....	161	....	....	....	....	....	....	....	....	....	....	....	....	....	....	....	....	....	....
	Winnipeg Jets	WCJHL	14	3	1	4	....	....	....	35	....	....	....	....	....	....	....	....	....	....	....	....	....	....	....	....	....	....
1973-74	Flin Flon Bombers	WCJHL	65	47	44	91	....	....	....	376	....	....	....	....	....	....	....	....	....	....	7	4	9	13	28	....	....	....
1974-75	Phoenix Roadrunners	WHA	57	9	19	28	....	....	....	168	....	....	....	....	....	....	....	....	....	....	5	0	0	0	2	....	....	....
1975-76	Phoenix Roadrunners	WHA	73	18	21	39	....	....	....	295	....	....	....	....	....	....	....	....	....	....	5	1	0	1	21	....	....	....
1976-77	Houston Aeros	WHA	76	35	32	67	....	....	....	224	....	....	....	....	....	....	....	....	....	....	11	3	4	7	47	....	....	....
1977-78	Houston Aeros	WHA	68	21	16	37	....	....	....	217	....	....	....	....	....	....	....	....	....	....	2	1	0	1	22	....	....	....
1978-79♦	**Montreal Canadiens**	**NHL**	**23**	**1**	**3**	**4**	**1**	**2**	**3**	**39**	**0**	**0**	**0**	**12**	**8.3**	**7**	**0**	**5**	**0**	**2**	**8**	**1**	**0**	**1**	**0**	**0**	**0**	**1**
1979-80	**Edmonton Oilers**	**NHL**	**38**	**7**	**13**	**20**	**6**	**9**	**15**	**136**	**0**	**0**	**0**	**44**	**15.9**	**28**	**2**	**24**	**0**	**2**	....	....	....	....	....	....	....	....
	Houston Apollos	CHL	5	1	1	2	....	....	....	20	....	....	....	....	....	....	....	....	....	....	....	....	....	....	....	....	....	....
	New York Rangers	**NHL**	**12**	**0**	**3**	**3**	**0**	**2**	**2**	**37**	**0**	**0**	**0**	**10**	**0.0**	**8**	**0**	**5**	**0**	**3**	**2**	**0**	**0**	**0**	**2**	**0**	**0**	**0**
1980-81	**New York Rangers**	**NHL**	**15**	**1**	**3**	**4**	**1**	**2**	**3**	**44**	**0**	**0**	**0**	**16**	**6.3**	**11**	**0**	**5**	**0**	**6**	....	....	....	....	....	....	....	....
	New Haven Nighthawks	AHL	61	33	28	61	....	....	....	243	....	....	....	....	....	....	....	....	....	....	4	0	2	2	4	....	....	....
1981-82	Springfield Indians	AHL	78	17	34	51	....	....	....	195	....	....	....	....	....	....	....	....	....	....	....	....	....	....	....	....	....	....
	New York Rangers	**NHL**	....	....	....	....	....	....	....	....	**0**	**0**	**0**	**0**	**0.0**	**0**	**0**	**0**	**0**	**0**	**10**	**4**	**0**	**4**	**4**	**1**	**0**	**1**
1982-83	**New York Rangers**	**NHL**	**1**	**0**	**0**	**0**	**0**	**0**	**0**	**0**	**0**	**0**	**0**	**0**	**0.0**	**0**	**0**	**0**	**0**	**0**	....	....	....	....	....	....	....	....
	Tulsa Oilers	CHL	3	2	2	4	....	....	....	0	....	....	....	....	....	....	....	....	....	....	....	....	....	....	....	....	....	....
1983-84	Tulsa Oilers	CHL	64	18	32	50	....	....	....	218	....	....	....	....	....	....	....	....	....	....	6	1	1	2	34	....	....	....
	NHL Totals		**89**	**9**	**22**	**31**	**8**	**15**	**23**	**256**	**0**	**0**	**0**	**82**	**11.0**	**54**	**2**	**39**	**0**		**20**	**5**	**0**	**5**	**6**	**1**	**0**	**2**
	Other Major League Totals		274	83	88	171	....	....	....	904	....	....	....	....	....	....	....	....	....	....	23	5	4	9	92	....	....	....

Selected by **Phoenix** (WHA) in 1974 WHA Amateur Draft, June, 1974. Traded to **Houston** (WHA) by **Phoenix** (WHA) for Bob Liddington, October, 1976. Signed as a free agent by **Winnipeg** (WHA) after **Houston** (WHA) franchise folded, July, 1978. Claimed by **Edmonton** from **Montreal** in Expansion Draft, June 13, 1979. Traded to **NY Rangers** by **Edmonton** with Edmonton's 3rd round choice (Peter Sundstrom) in 1981 Entry Draft for Don Murdoch, March 11, 1980.

• CONROY, Al John Allan C – R. 5'8", 170 lbs. b: Calgary, Alta., 1/17/1966.

Season	Club	League	GP	G	A	Pts	AG	AA	APts	PIM	PP	SH	GW	S	%	TGF	PGF	TGA	PGA	+/-	GP	G	A	Pts	PIM	PP	SH	GW
1981-82	Hobema Hawks	AJHL	52	23	39	62	....	....	....	172	....	....	....	....	....	....	....	....	....	....	....	....	....	....	....	....	....	....
1982-83	Medicine Hat Tigers	WHL	68	38	57	95	....	....	....	203	....	....	....	....	....	....	....	....	....	....	5	4	3	7	16	....	....	....
1983-84	Medicine Hat Tigers	WHL	69	38	74	112	....	....	....	89	....	....	....	....	....	....	....	....	....	....	14	10	13	23	39	....	....	....
1984-85	Medicine Hat Tigers	WHL	68	41	97	138	....	....	....	150	....	....	....	....	....	....	....	....	....	....	10	1	9	10	20	....	....	....
1985-86	Medicine Hat Tigers	WHL	61	41	60	101	....	....	....	141	....	....	....	....	....	....	....	....	....	....	25	11	20	31	54	....	....	....
	Canada	WJC-A	7	4	4	8	....	....	....	6	....	....	....	....	....	....	....	....	....	....	....	....	....	....	....	....	....	....
1986-87	SC Rapperswil-Jona	Switz	36	30	32	62	....	....	....	0	....	....	....	....	....	....	....	....	....	....	....	....	....	....	....	....	....	....
	Rochester Americans	AHL	13	4	4	8	....	....	....	40	....	....	....	....	....	....	....	....	....	....	13	1	3	4	50	....	....	....
1987-88	HC Varese	Italy	36	25	39	64	....	....	....	71	....	....	....	....	....	....	....	....	....	....	10	6	4	10	20	....	....	....
	Adirondack Red Wings	AHL	13	5	8	13	....	....	....	20	....	....	....	....	....	....	....	....	....	....	11	1	3	4	41	....	....	....
1988-89	EHC Westfalen Dortmund	Germany-2	46	53	78	131	....	....	....	....	....	....	....	....	....	....	....	....	....	....	....	....	....	....	....	....	....	....
1989-90	Adirondack Red Wings	AHL	77	23	33	56	....	....	....	147	....	....	....	....	....	....	....	....	....	....	5	0	0	0	20	....	....	....
1990-91	Adirondack Red Wings	AHL	80	26	39	65	....	....	....	172	....	....	....	....	....	....	....	....	....	....	2	1	1	2	0	....	....	....
1991-92	**Philadelphia Flyers**	**NHL**	**31**	**2**	**9**	**11**	**2**	**7**	**9**	**74**	**0**	**0**	**0**	**25**	**8.0**	**19**	**1**	**17**	**0**	**1**	....	....	....	....	....	....	....	....
	Hershey Bears	AHL	47	17	28	45	....	....	....	90	....	....	....	....	....	....	....	....	....	....	6	4	2	6	12	....	....	....
1992-93	**Philadelphia Flyers**	**NHL**	**21**	**3**	**2**	**5**	**2**	**1**	**3**	**17**	**0**	**0**	**1**	**24**	**12.5**	**9**	**0**	**10**	**0**	**–1**	....	....	....	....	....	....	....	....
	Hershey Bears	AHL	60	28	32	60	....	....	....	130	....	....	....	....	....	....	....	....	....	....	....	....	....	....	....	....	....	....
1993-94	**Philadelphia Flyers**	**NHL**	**62**	**4**	**3**	**7**	**4**	**2**	**6**	**65**	**0**	**1**	**0**	**40**	**10.0**	**14**	**0**	**48**	**22**	**–12**	....	....	....	....	....	....	....	....
1994-95	Nippon Paper Kushiro	Japan	1	0	0	0	....	....	....	0	....	....	....	....	....	....	....	....	....	....	....	....	....	....	....	....	....	....
	Detroit Vipers	IHL	71	18	40	58	....	....	....	151	....	....	....	....	....	....	....	....	....	....	....	....	....	....	....	....	....	....
	Houston Aeros	IHL	9	3	4	7	....	....	....	17	....	....	....	....	....	....	....	....	....	....	4	1	2	3	8	....	....	....
1995-96	Houston Aeros	IHL	82	24	38	62	....	....	....	134	....	....	....	....	....	....	....	....	....	....	....	....	....	....	....	....	....	....
1996-97	Houston Aeros	IHL	70	15	32	47	....	....	....	171	....	....	....	....	....	....	....	....	....	....	13	4	10	14	26	....	....	....
1997-98	Nippon Paper Kushiro	Japan	40	21	41	62	....	....	....	66	....	....	....	....	....	....	....	....	....	....	....	....	....	....	....	....	....	....
1998-99	Nippon Paper Kushiro	Japan	37	18	36	54	....	....	....	89	....	....	....	....	....	....	....	....	....	....	2	0	2	2	0	....	....	....
99-2000	Nippon Paper Kushiro	Japan	30	18	24	42	....	....	....	....	....	....	....	....	....	....	....	....	....	....	5	0	4	4	4	....	....	....
	NHL Totals		**114**	**9**	**14**	**23**	**8**	**10**	**18**	**156**	**0**	**1**	**1**	**89**	**10.1**	**42**	**1**	**75**	**22**		....	....	....	....	....	....	....	....

WHL East First All-Star Team (1986)

Signed as a free agent by **Detroit**, August 16, 1989. Signed as a free agent by **Philadelphia**, August 21, 1991.

• CONROY, Craig Craig Michael "C.C." C – R. 6'2", 198 lbs. b: Potsdam, NY, 9/4/1971. Montreal's 7th, 123rd overall, in 1990.

Season	Club	League	GP	G	A	Pts	AG	AA	APts	PIM	PP	SH	GW	S	%	TGF	PGF	TGA	PGA	+/-	GP	G	A	Pts	PIM	PP	SH	GW
1989-90	Northwood Huskies	Hi-School	31	33	43	76	....	....	....	....	....	....	....	....	....	....	....	....	....	....	....	....	....	....	....	....	....	....
1990-91	Clarkson University	ECAC	40	8	21	29	....	....	....	24	....	....	....	....	....	....	....	....	....	....	....	....	....	....	....	....	....	....
1991-92	Clarkson University	ECAC	31	19	17	36	....	....	....	36	....	....	....	....	....	....	....	....	....	....	....	....	....	....	....	....	....	....
1992-93	Clarkson University	ECAC	35	10	23	33	....	....	....	26	....	....	....	....	....	....	....	....	....	....	....	....	....	....	....	....	....	....
1993-94	Clarkson University	ECAC	34	26	*40	*66	....	....	....	46	....	....	....	....	....	....	....	....	....	....	....	....	....	....	....	....	....	....
1994-95	**Montreal Canadiens**	**NHL**	**6**	**1**	**0**	**1**	**2**	**0**	**2**	**0**	**0**	**0**	**0**	**4**	**25.0**	**1**	**0**	**2**	**0**	**–1**	....	....	....	....	....	....	....	....
	Fredericton Canadiens	AHL	55	26	18	44	....	....	....	29	....	....	....	....	....	....	....	....	....	....	11	7	3	10	6	....	....	....
1995-96	**Montreal Canadiens**	**NHL**	**7**	**0**	**0**	**0**	**0**	**0**	**0**	**2**	**0**	**0**	**0**	**1**	**0.0**	**0**	**0**	**4**	**0**	**–4**	....	....	....	....	....	....	....	....
	Fredericton Canadiens	AHL	67	31	38	69	....	....	....	65	....	....	....	....	....	....	....	....	....	....	10	5	7	12	6	....	....	....
1996-97	Fredericton Canadiens	AHL	9	10	6	16	....	....	....	10	....	....	....	....	....	....	....	....	....	....	....	....	....	....	....	....	....	....
	St. Louis Blues	**NHL**	**61**	**6**	**11**	**17**	**6**	**10**	**16**	**43**	**0**	**0**	**1**	**74**	**8.1**	**23**	**1**	**39**	**17**	**0**	**6**	**0**	**0**	**0**	**8**	**0**	**0**	**0**
	Worcester IceCats	AHL	5	5	6	11	....	....	....	2	....	....	....	....	....	....	....	....	....	....	....	....	....	....	....	....	....	....
1997-98	**St. Louis Blues**	**NHL**	**81**	**14**	**29**	**43**	**16**	**28**	**44**	**46**	**0**	**3**	**1**	**118**	**11.9**	**54**	**1**	**56**	**23**	**20**	**10**	**1**	**2**	**3**	**8**	**0**	**0**	**1**
1998-99	**St. Louis Blues**	**NHL**	**69**	**14**	**25**	**39**	**16**	**24**	**40**	**38**	**0**	**1**	**1**	**134**	**10.4**	**51**	**2**	**57**	**22**	**14**	**13**	**2**	**1**	**3**	**6**	**0**	**0**	**0**
99-2000	**St. Louis Blues**	**NHL**	**79**	**12**	**15**	**27**	**13**	**14**	**27**	**36**	**1**	**2**	**3**	**98**	**12.2**	**35**	**2**	**53**	**25**	**5**	**7**	**0**	**2**	**2**	**2**	**0**	**0**	**0**
	NHL Totals		**303**	**47**	**80**	**127**	**53**	**76**	**129**	**165**	**1**	**6**	**6**	**429**	**11.0**	**164**	**6**	**211**	**87**		**36**	**3**	**5**	**8**	**24**	**0**	**0**	**1**

ECAC First All-Star Team (1994) • NCAA East First All-American Team (1994) • NCAA Final Four All-Tournament Team (1994)

Traded to **St. Louis** by **Montreal** with Pierre Turgeon and Rory Fitzpatrick for Murray Baron, Shayne Corson and St. Louis' 5th round choice (Gennady Razin) in 1997 Entry Draft, October 29, 1996.

• CONTINI, Joe Joseph Mario C – L. 5'10", 178 lbs. b: Galt, Ont., 1/29/1957. Colorado's 7th, 126th overall, in 1977.

Season	Club	League	GP	G	A	Pts	AG	AA	APts	PIM	PP	SH	GW	S	%	TGF	PGF	TGA	PGA	+/-	GP	G	A	Pts	PIM	PP	SH	GW
1973-74	Guelph Platers	OJHL	STATISTICS NOT AVAILABLE																									
1974-75	Hamilton Fincups	OMJHL	68	27	63	90	....	....	....	152	....	....	....	....	....	....	....	....	....	....	17	4	19	23	27	....	....	....
1975-76	Hamilton Fincups	OMJHL	54	28	52	80	....	....	....	105	....	....	....	....	....	....	....	....	....	....	14	9	20	29	50	....	....	....
	Hamilton Fincups	Mem-Cup	3	4	4	8	....	....	....	6	....	....	....	....	....	....	....	....	....	....	....	....	....	....	....	....	....	....
1976-77	St. Catharines Fincups	OMJHL	28	17	29	46	....	....	....	61	....	....	....	....	....	....	....	....	....	....	6	0	0	0	0	....	....	....
	Canada	WJC-A	7	4	5	9	....	....	....	32	....	....	....	....	....	....	....	....	....	....	....	....	....	....	....	....	....	....
1977-78	**Colorado Rockies**	**NHL**	**37**	**12**	**9**	**21**	**11**	**7**	**18**	**28**	**3**	**0**	**0**	**49**	**24.5**	**29**	**8**	**23**	**0**	**–2**	**2**	**0**	**0**	**0**	**0**	**0**	**0**	**0**
	Phoenix Roadrunners	CHL	2	0	0	0	....	....	....	2	....	....	....	....	....	....	....	....	....	....	....	....	....	....	....	....	....	....
	Flint Generals	IHL	31	17	28	45	....	....	....	25	....	....	....	....	....	....	....	....	....	....	....	....	....	....	....	....	....	....

			REGULAR SEASON																		PLAYOFFS							
Season	Club	League	GP	G	A	Pts	AG	AA	APts	PIM	PP	SH	GW	S	%	TGF	PGF	TGA	PGA	+/-	GP	G	A	Pts	PIM	PP	SH	GW
1978-79	**Colorado Rockies**	**NHL**	**30**	**5**	**12**	**17**	**4**	**9**	**13**	**6**	**2**	**0**	**1**	**26**	**19.2**	**27**	**14**	**32**	**0**	**−19**	....	....	....	....	....	....	....	....
	Philadelphia Firebirds	AHL	36	8	9	17	....	....	....	45	....	....	....	....	....	....	....	....	....	....	....	....	....	....	....	....	....	....
1979-80	Fort Worth Texans	CHL	8	1	2	3	....	....	....	13	....	....	....	....	....	....	....	....	....	....	....	....	....	....	....	....	....	....
	Oklahoma City Stars	CHL	58	19	43	62	....	....	....	56	....	....	....	....	....	....	....	....	....	....	....	....	....	....	....	....	....	....
1980-81	**Minnesota North Stars**	**NHL**	**1**	**0**	**0**	**0**	**0**	**0**	**0**	**0**	**0**	**0**	**0**	**0**	**0.0**	**0**	**0**	**0**	**0**	**0**	....	....	....	....	....	....	....	....
	Oklahoma City Stars	CHL	77	32	63	95	....	....	....	28	....	....	....	....	....	....	....	....	....	....	3	0	1	1	2	....	....	....
1981-82	Hershey Bears	AHL	56	20	37	57	....	....	....	68	....	....	....	....	....	....	....	....	....	....	5	1	5	6	6	....	....	....
	Muskegon Mohawks	IHL	17	9	7	16	....	....	....	4	....	....	....	....	....	....	....	....	....	....	....	....	....	....	....	....	....	....
	NHL Totals		**68**	**17**	**21**	**38**	**15**	**16**	**31**	**34**	**5**	**0**	**1**	**75**	**22.7**	**56**	**22**	**55**	**0**		**2**	**0**	**0**	**0**	**0**	**0**	**0**	**0**

Claimed by **Colorado** as a fill-in during Expansion Draft, June 13, 1979. Signed as a free agent by **Minnesota**, February 1, 1980.

• CONVERY, Brandon

Brandon William C – R. 6'1", 195 lbs. b: Kingston, Ont., 2/4/1974. Toronto's 1st, 8th overall, in 1992.

Season	Club	League	GP	G	A	Pts	AG	AA	APts	PIM	PP	SH	GW	S	%	TGF	PGF	TGA	PGA	+/-	GP	G	A	Pts	PIM	PP	SH	GW
1988-89	Kingston Voyageurs	OJHL-B	13	0	3	3	....	....	....	14	....	....	....	....	....	....	....	....	....	....	....	....	....	....	....	....	....	....
1989-90	Kingston Voyageurs	OJHL-B	42	13	25	38	....	....	....	4	....	....	....	....	....	....	....	....	....	....	....	....	....	....	....	....	....	....
1990-91	Sudbury Wolves	OHL	56	26	22	48	....	....	....	18	....	....	....	....	....	....	....	....	....	....	5	1	1	2	2	....	....	....
1991-92	Sudbury Wolves	OHL	44	40	26	66	....	....	....	44	....	....	....	....	....	....	....	....	....	....	5	3	2	5	4	....	....	....
1992-93	Sudbury Wolves	OHL	7	7	9	16	....	....	....	6	....	....	....	....	....	....	....	....	....	....	....	....	....	....	....	....	....	....
	Niagara Falls Thunder	OHL	51	38	39	77	....	....	....	24	....	....	....	....	....	....	....	....	....	....	4	1	3	4	4	....	....	....
	St. John's Maple Leafs	AHL	3	0	0	0	....	....	....	0	....	....	....	....	....	....	....	....	....	....	5	0	1	1	0	....	....	....
1993-94	Niagara Falls Thunder	OHL	29	24	29	53	....	....	....	30	....	....	....	....	....	....	....	....	....	....	....	....	....	....	....	....	....	....
	Canada	WJC-A	7	1	0	1	....	....	....	2	....	....	....	....	....	....	....	....	....	....	....	....	....	....	....	....	....	....
	Belleville Bulls	OHL	23	16	19	35	....	....	....	22	....	....	....	....	....	....	....	....	....	....	12	4	10	14	13	....	....	....
	St. John's Maple Leafs	AHL	....	....	....	....	....	....	....	....	....	....	....	....	....	....	....	....	....	....	1	0	0	0	0	....	....	....
1994-95	St. John's Maple Leafs	AHL	76	34	37	71	....	....	....	43	....	....	....	....	....	....	....	....	....	....	5	2	2	4	4	....	....	....
	Canada	WC-A	8	0	1	1	....	....	....	0	....	....	....	....	....	....	....	....	....	....	....	....	....	....	....	....	....	....
1995-96	**Toronto Maple Leafs**	**NHL**	**11**	**5**	**2**	**7**	**5**	**2**	**7**	**4**	**3**	**0**	**1**	**16**	**31.3**	**7**	**3**	**11**	**0**	**−7**	**5**	**0**	**0**	**0**	**2**	**0**	**0**	**0**
	St. John's Maple Leafs	AHL	57	22	23	45	....	....	....	28	....	....	....	....	....	....	....	....	....	....	....	....	....	....	....	....	....	....
1996-97	**Toronto Maple Leafs**	**NHL**	**39**	**2**	**8**	**10**	**2**	**7**	**9**	**20**	**0**	**0**	**0**	**41**	**4.9**	**13**	**3**	**25**	**6**	**−9**	....	....	....	....	....	....	....	....
	St. John's Maple Leafs	AHL	25	14	14	28	....	....	....	15	....	....	....	....	....	....	....	....	....	....	....	....	....	....	....	....	....	....
1997-98	St. John's Maple Leafs	AHL	49	27	36	63	....	....	....	35	....	....	....	....	....	....	....	....	....	....	....	....	....	....	....	....	....	....
	Vancouver Canucks	**NHL**	**7**	**0**	**2**	**2**	**0**	**2**	**2**	**0**	**0**	**0**	**0**	**2**	**0.0**	**4**	**3**	**1**	**0**	**0**	....	....	....	....	....	....	....	....
	Syracuse Crunch	AHL	2	1	2	3	....	....	....	5	....	....	....	....	....	....	....	....	....	....	....	....	....	....	....	....	....	....
1998-99	**Vancouver Canucks**	**NHL**	**12**	**2**	**7**	**9**	**2**	**7**	**9**	**8**	**0**	**0**	**1**	**12**	**16.7**	**12**	**3**	**5**	**1**	**5**	....	....	....	....	....	....	....	....
	Los Angeles Kings	**NHL**	**3**	**0**	**0**	**0**	**0**	**0**	**0**	**4**	**0**	**0**	**0**	**2**	**0.0**	**0**	**0**	**1**	**0**	**−1**	....	....	....	....	....	....	....	....
	Long Beach Ice Dogs	IHL	14	3	7	10	....	....	....	8	....	....	....	....	....	....	....	....	....	....	....	....	....	....	....	....	....	....
	Springfield Falcons	AHL	31	9	14	23	....	....	....	45	....	....	....	....	....	....	....	....	....	....	....	....	....	....	....	....	....	....
	NHL Totals		**72**	**9**	**19**	**28**	**9**	**18**	**27**	**36**	**3**	**0**	**2**	**73**	**12.3**	**36**	**12**	**43**	**7**		**5**	**0**	**0**	**0**	**2**	**0**	**0**	**0**

Traded to **Vancouver** by **Toronto** for Lonny Bohonos, March 7, 1998. Claimed on waivers by **Los Angeles** from **Vancouver**, November 21, 1998.

• COOK, Bob

Robert Arthur "Cookie" RW – R. 6', 190 lbs. b: Sudbury, Ont., 1/6/1946.

Season	Club	League	GP	G	A	Pts	AG	AA	APts	PIM	PP	SH	GW	S	%	TGF	PGF	TGA	PGA	+/-	GP	G	A	Pts	PIM	PP	SH	GW
1965-66	London Nationals	OHA-Jr.	14	2	10	12	....	....	....	14	....	....	....	....	....	....	....	....	....	....	....	....	....	....	....	....	....	....
	Kitchener Rangers	OHA-Jr.	31	10	7	17	....	....	....	72	....	....	....	....	....	....	....	....	....	....	19	9	5	14	51	....	....	....
1966-67	Vancouver Canucks	WHL	55	7	7	14	....	....	....	31	....	....	....	....	....	....	....	....	....	....	5	0	0	0	11	....	....	....
1967-68	Vancouver Canucks	WHL	1	0	0	0	....	....	....	0	....	....	....	....	....	....	....	....	....	....	....	....	....	....	....	....	....	....
	Rochester Americans	AHL	61	22	16	38	....	....	....	95	....	....	....	....	....	....	....	....	....	....	1	0	0	0	0	....	....	....
1968-69	Rochester Americans	AHL	59	4	6	10	....	....	....	24	....	....	....	....	....	....	....	....	....	....	....	....	....	....	....	....	....	....
	Tulsa Oilers	CHL	12	6	7	13	....	....	....	14	....	....	....	....	....	....	....	....	....	....	6	0	2	2	8	....	....	....
1969-70	Rochester Americans	AHL	71	26	18	44	....	....	....	78	....	....	....	....	....	....	....	....	....	....	....	....	....	....	....	....	....	....
1970-71	**Vancouver Canucks**	**NHL**	**2**	**0**	**0**	**0**	**0**	**0**	**0**	**0**	**0**	**0**	**0**	**2**	**0.0**	**0**	**0**	**0**	**0**	**0**	....	....	....	....	....	....	....	....
	Rochester Americans	AHL	68	22	19	41	....	....	....	66	....	....	....	....	....	....	....	....	....	....	....	....	....	....	....	....	....	....
1971-72	Fort Worth Wings	CHL	15	4	4	8	....	....	....	24	....	....	....	....	....	....	....	....	....	....	....	....	....	....	....	....	....	....
	Seattle Totems	WHL	15	3	3	6	....	....	....	27	....	....	....	....	....	....	....	....	....	....	....	....	....	....	....	....	....	....
	Tidewater Red Wings	AHL	35	9	8	17	....	....	....	40	....	....	....	....	....	....	....	....	....	....	....	....	....	....	....	....	....	....
1972-73	**Detroit Red Wings**	**NHL**	**13**	**3**	**1**	**4**	**3**	**1**	**4**	**4**	**1**	**0**	**0**	**23**	**13.0**	**4**	**1**	**14**	**0**	**−11**	....	....	....	....	....	....	....	....
	Virginia Wings	AHL	23	17	9	26	....	....	....	70	....	....	....	....	....	....	....	....	....	....	....	....	....	....	....	....	....	....
	New York Islanders	**NHL**	**33**	**8**	**6**	**14**	**7**	**5**	**12**	**14**	**1**	**0**	**0**	**83**	**9.6**	**22**	**2**	**29**	**0**	**−9**	....	....	....	....	....	....	....	....
1973-74	**New York Islanders**	**NHL**	**22**	**2**	**1**	**3**	**2**	**1**	**3**	**4**	**0**	**0**	**0**	**20**	**10.0**	**7**	**1**	**3**	**0**	**3**	....	....	....	....	....	....	....	....
	Baltimore Clippers	AHL	52	19	19	38	....	....	....	35	....	....	....	....	....	....	....	....	....	....	9	5	5	10	10	....	....	....
1974-75	**Minnesota North Stars**	**NHL**	**2**	**0**	**1**	**1**	**0**	**1**	**1**	**0**	**0**	**0**	**0**	**9**	**0.0**	**1**	**0**	**2**	**0**	**−1**	....	....	....	....	....	....	....	....
	Fort Worth Texans	CHL	22	3	6	9	....	....	....	37	....	....	....	....	....	....	....	....	....	....	....	....	....	....	....	....	....	....
	New Haven Nighthawks	AHL	50	15	26	41	....	....	....	43	....	....	....	....	....	....	....	....	....	....	16	7	5	12	14	....	....	....
	NHL Totals		**72**	**13**	**9**	**22**	**12**	**8**	**20**	**22**	**2**	**0**	**0**	**137**	**9.5**	**34**	**4**	**48**	**0**		....	....	....	....	....	....	....	....

Rights transferred to **Vancouver** (WHL) after WHL club purchased **Rochester** (AHL) franchise, August 13, 1968. NHL rights transferred to **Vancouver** after NHL club purchased **Vancouver** (WHL) franchise, December 19, 1969. Traded to **Detroit** by **Vancouver** for cash, November 21, 1971. Traded to **NY Islanders** by **Detroit** with Ralph Stewart for Ken Murray and Brian Lavender, January 17, 1973. Traded to **Minnesota** by **NY Islanders** for cash, January 5, 1975.

• COOKE, Matt

Matt David LW – L. 5'11", 200 lbs. b: Belleville, Ont., 9/7/1978. Vancouver's 8th, 144th overall, in 1997.

Season	Club	League	GP	G	A	Pts	AG	AA	APts	PIM	PP	SH	GW	S	%	TGF	PGF	TGA	PGA	+/-	GP	G	A	Pts	PIM	PP	SH	GW
1995-96	Windsor Spitfires	OHL	61	8	11	19	....	....	....	102	....	....	....	....	....	....	....	....	....	....	7	1	3	4	6	....	....	....
1996-97	Windsor Spitfires	OHL	65	45	50	95	....	....	....	146	....	....	....	....	....	....	....	....	....	....	5	5	5	10	10	....	....	....
1997-98	Windsor Spitfires	OHL	23	14	19	33	....	....	....	50	....	....	....	....	....	....	....	....	....	....	....	....	....	....	....	....	....	....
	Canada	WJC-A	6	1	1	2	....	....	....	6	....	....	....	....	....	....	....	....	....	....	....	....	....	....	....	....	....	....
	Kingston Frontenacs	OHL	25	8	13	21	....	....	....	49	....	....	....	....	....	....	....	....	....	....	12	8	8	16	20	....	....	....
1998-99	**Vancouver Canucks**	**NHL**	**30**	**0**	**2**	**2**	**0**	**2**	**2**	**27**	**0**	**0**	**0**	**22**	**0.0**	**3**	**1**	**17**	**3**	**−12**	....	....	....	....	....	....	....	....
	Syracuse Crunch	AHL	37	15	18	33	....	....	....	119	....	....	....	....	....	....	....	....	....	....	....	....	....	....	....	....	....	....
99-2000	**Vancouver Canucks**	**NHL**	**51**	**5**	**7**	**12**	**6**	**6**	**12**	**39**	**0**	**1**	**1**	**58**	**8.6**	**24**	**1**	**24**	**4**	**3**	....	....	....	....	....	....	....	....
	Syracuse Crunch	AHL	18	5	8	13	....	....	....	27	....	....	....	....	....	....	....	....	....	....	....	....	....	....	....	....	....	....
	NHL Totals		**81**	**5**	**9**	**14**	**6**	**8**	**14**	**66**	**0**	**1**	**1**	**80**	**6.3**	**27**	**2**	**41**	**7**		....	....	....	....	....	....	....	....

• COOPER, David

D – L. 6'2", 204 lbs. b: Ottawa, Ont., 11/2/1973. Buffalo's 1st, 11th overall, in 1992.

Season	Club	League	GP	G	A	Pts	AG	AA	APts	PIM	PP	SH	GW	S	%	TGF	PGF	TGA	PGA	+/-	GP	G	A	Pts	PIM	PP	SH	GW
1988-89	Edmonton Mets	AAHA	32	24	22	46	....	....	....	151	....	....	....	....	....	....	....	....	....	....	....	....	....	....	....	....	....	....
1989-90	Medicine Hat Tigers	WHL	61	4	11	15	....	....	....	65	....	....	....	....	....	....	....	....	....	....	3	0	2	2	2	....	....	....
1990-91	Medicine Hat Tigers	WHL	64	12	31	43	....	....	....	66	....	....	....	....	....	....	....	....	....	....	11	1	3	4	23	....	....	....
1991-92	Medicine Hat Tigers	WHL	72	17	47	64	....	....	....	176	....	....	....	....	....	....	....	....	....	....	4	1	4	5	8	....	....	....
1992-93	Medicine Hat Tigers	WHL	63	15	50	65	....	....	....	88	....	....	....	....	....	....	....	....	....	....	10	2	2	4	32	....	....	....
	Rochester Americans	AHL	....	....	....	....	....	....	....	....	....	....	....	....	....	....	....	....	....	....	2	0	0	0	2	....	....	....
1993-94	Rochester Americans	AHL	68	10	25	35	....	....	....	82	....	....	....	....	....	....	....	....	....	....	4	1	1	2	2	....	....	....
1994-95	Rochester Americans	AHL	21	2	4	6	....	....	....	48	....	....	....	....	....	....	....	....	....	....	....	....	....	....	....	....	....	....
	South Carolina Stingrays	ECHL	39	9	19	28	....	....	....	90	....	....	....	....	....	....	....	....	....	....	9	3	8	11	24	....	....	....
1995-96	Rochester Americans	AHL	67	9	18	27	....	....	....	79	....	....	....	....	....	....	....	....	....	....	8	0	1	1	12	....	....	....
1996-97	**Toronto Maple Leafs**	**NHL**	**19**	**3**	**3**	**6**	**3**	**3**	**6**	**16**	**2**	**0**	**0**	**23**	**13.0**	**14**	**6**	**12**	**1**	**−3**	....	....	....	....	....	....	....	....
	St. John's Maple Leafs	AHL	44	16	19	35	....	....	....	65	....	....	....	....	....	....	....	....	....	....	....	....	....	....	....	....	....	....

Season	Club	League	GP	G	A	Pts	AG	AA	APts	PIM	PP	SH	GW	S	%	TGF	PGF	TGA	PGA	+/–	GP	G	A	Pts	PIM	PP	SH	GW
			REGULAR SEASON																		PLAYOFFS							
1997-98	**Toronto Maple Leafs**	**NHL**	**9**	**0**	**4**	**4**	**0**	**4**	**4**	**8**	**0**	**0**	**0**	**13**	**0.0**	**5**	**1**	**2**	**0**	**2**	....	....	....	....	....	....	....	....
	St. John's Maple Leafs	AHL	60	19	23	42	....	....	....	117	....	....	....	....	....	....	....	....	....	....	4	0	1	1	6	....	....	....
1998-99	Saint John Flames	AHL	65	18	24	42	....	....	....	121	....	....	....	....	....	....	....	....	....	....	7	1	4	5	10	....	....	....
99-2000	Kassel Huskies	Germany	55	11	13	24	....	....	....	82	....	....	....	....	....	....	....	....	....	....	6	2	1	3	38	....	....	....
	NHL Totals		**28**	**3**	**7**	**10**	**3**	**7**	**10**	**24**	**2**	**0**	**0**	**36**	**8.3**	**19**	**7**	**14**	**1**		....	....	....	....	....	....	....	....

WHL East First All-Star Team (1992) • AHL Second All-Star Team (1998)

Signed as a free agent by **Toronto**, September 26, 1996. Traded to **Calgary** by **Toronto** for Ladislav Kohn, July 2, 1998.

• COOPER, Ed

Edward William LW – L. 5'10", 188 lbs. b: Loon Lake, Sask., 8/28/1960. Colorado's 4th, 85th overall, in 1980.

Season	Club	League	GP	G	A	Pts	AG	AA	APts	PIM	PP	SH	GW	S	%	TGF	PGF	TGA	PGA	+/–	GP	G	A	Pts	PIM	PP	SH	GW
1977-78	Estevan Bruins	SJHL	49	30	37	67	....	....	....	137	....	....	....	....	....	....	....	....	....	....	....	....	....	....	....	....	....	....
	New Westminster Bruins	WCJHL	1	0	0	0	....	....	....	0	....	....	....	....	....	....	....	....	....	....	....	....	....	....	....	....	....	....
1978-79	Portland Winter Hawks	WHL	66	8	17	25	....	....	....	61	....	....	....	....	....	....	....	....	....	....	25	6	4	10	15	....	....	....
1979-80	Portland Winter Hawks	WHL	44	35	43	78	....	....	....	76	....	....	....	....	....	....	....	....	....	....	8	5	2	7	21	....	....	....
1980-81	**Colorado Rockies**	**NHL**	**47**	**7**	**7**	**14**	**5**	**5**	**10**	**46**	**1**	**0**	**2**	**52**	**13.5**	**26**	**1**	**34**	**3**	**–6**	....	....	....	....	....	....	....	....
	Fort Worth Texans	CHL	26	6	9	15	....	....	....	21	....	....	....	....	....	....	....	....	....	....	....	....	....	....	....	....	....	....
1981-82	**Colorado Rockies**	**NHL**	**2**	**1**	**0**	**1**	**1**	**0**	**1**	**0**	**0**	**0**	**0**	**1**	**100.0**	**2**	**0**	**2**	**0**	**0**	....	....	....	....	....	....	....	....
	Fort Worth Texans	CHL	47	12	25	37	....	....	....	26	....	....	....	....	....	....	....	....	....	....	....	....	....	....	....	....	....	....
	Wichita Wind	CHL	4	1	4	5	....	....	....	0	....	....	....	....	....	....	....	....	....	....	6	1	1	2	0	....	....	....
1982-83			DID NOT PLAY																									
1983-84	Muskegon Mohawks	IHL	5	1	3	4	....	....	....	0	....	....	....	....	....	....	....	....	....	....	....	....	....	....	....	....	....	....
1984-85	Nelson Maple Leafs	WIHL	10	7	9	16	....	....	....	4	....	....	....	....	....	....	....	....	....	....	....	....	....	....	....	....	....	....
1985-86	Nelson Maple Leafs	WIHL	27	22	27	49	....	....	....	47	....	....	....	....	....	....	....	....	....	....	....	....	....	....	....	....	....	....
	NHL Totals		**49**	**8**	**7**	**15**	**6**	**5**	**11**	**46**	**1**	**0**	**2**	**53**	**15.1**	**28**	**1**	**36**	**3**		....	....	....	....	....	....	....	....

Traded to **Edmonton** by **Colorado** for Stan Weir, March 9, 1982. Traded to **Colorado** by **Edmonton** for Stan Weir, July 2, 1982.

• CORBET, Rene

LW – L. 6', 190 lbs. b: St-Hyacinthe, Que., 6/25/1973. Quebec's 2nd, 24th overall, in 1991.

Season	Club	League	GP	G	A	Pts	AG	AA	APts	PIM	PP	SH	GW	S	%	TGF	PGF	TGA	PGA	+/–	GP	G	A	Pts	PIM	PP	SH	GW
1989-90	Richelieu Riverains	QAAA	42	53	63	116	....	....	....	34	....	....	....	....	....	....	....	....	....	....	....	....	....	....	....	....	....	....
1990-91	Drummondville Voltigeurs	QMJHL	45	25	40	65	....	....	....	34	....	....	....	....	....	....	....	....	....	....	14	11	6	17	15	....	....	....
	Drummondville Voltigeurs	Mem-Cup	4	1	2	3	....	....	....	0	....	....	....	....	....	....	....	....	....	....	....	....	....	....	....	....	....	....
1991-92	Drummondville Voltigeurs	QMJHL	56	46	50	96	....	....	....	90	....	....	....	....	....	....	....	....	....	....	4	1	2	3	17	....	....	....
1992-93	Drummondville Voltigeurs	QMJHL	63	*79	69	*148	....	....	....	143	....	....	....	....	....	....	....	....	....	....	10	7	13	20	16	....	....	....
1993-94	**Quebec Nordiques**	**NHL**	**9**	**1**	**1**	**2**	**1**	**1**	**2**	**0**	**0**	**0**	**0**	**14**	**7.1**	**6**	**1**	**4**	**0**	**1**	....	....	....	....	....	....	....	....
	Cornwall Aces	AHL	68	37	40	77	....	....	....	56	....	....	....	....	....	....	....	....	....	....	13	7	2	9	18	....	....	....
1994-95	**Quebec Nordiques**	**NHL**	**8**	**0**	**3**	**3**	**0**	**4**	**4**	**2**	**0**	**0**	**0**	**4**	**0.0**	**4**	**0**	**1**	**0**	**3**	**2**	**0**	**1**	**1**	**0**	**0**	**0**	**0**
	Cornwall Aces	AHL	65	33	24	57	....	....	....	79	....	....	....	....	....	....	....	....	....	....	12	2	8	10	27	....	....	....
1995-96♦	**Colorado Avalanche**	**NHL**	**33**	**3**	**6**	**9**	**3**	**5**	**8**	**33**	**0**	**0**	**0**	**35**	**8.6**	**15**	**0**	**6**	**1**	**10**	**8**	**3**	**2**	**5**	**2**	**1**	**0**	**1**
	Cornwall Aces	AHL	9	5	6	11	....	....	....	10	....	....	....	....	....	....	....	....	....	....	....	....	....	....	....	....	....	....
1996-97	**Colorado Avalanche**	**NHL**	**76**	**12**	**15**	**27**	**13**	**13**	**26**	**67**	**1**	**0**	**3**	**128**	**9.4**	**41**	**6**	**27**	**6**	**14**	**17**	**2**	**2**	**4**	**27**	**0**	**0**	**0**
1997-98	**Colorado Avalanche**	**NHL**	**68**	**16**	**12**	**28**	**19**	**12**	**31**	**133**	**4**	**0**	**4**	**117**	**13.7**	**41**	**13**	**21**	**1**	**8**	**2**	**0**	**0**	**0**	**2**	**0**	**0**	**0**
1998-99	**Colorado Avalanche**	**NHL**	**53**	**8**	**14**	**22**	**9**	**13**	**22**	**58**	**2**	**0**	**1**	**82**	**9.8**	**29**	**11**	**20**	**5**	**3**	....	....	....	....	....	....	....	....
	Calgary Flames	**NHL**	**20**	**5**	**4**	**9**	**6**	**4**	**10**	**10**	**1**	**0**	**0**	**45**	**11.1**	**15**	**6**	**13**	**2**	**–2**	....	....	....	....	....	....	....	....
99-2000	**Calgary Flames**	**NHL**	**48**	**4**	**10**	**14**	**4**	**9**	**13**	**60**	**0**	**0**	**0**	**100**	**4.0**	**21**	**5**	**25**	**2**	**–7**	....	....	....	....	....	....	....	....
	Pittsburgh Penguins	**NHL**	**4**	**1**	**0**	**1**	**1**	**0**	**1**	**0**	**1**	**0**	**0**	**9**	**11.1**	**2**	**1**	**5**	**0**	**–4**	**7**	**1**	**1**	**2**	**9**	**0**	**0**	**0**
	NHL Totals		**319**	**50**	**65**	**115**	**56**	**61**	**117**	**363**	**9**	**0**	**8**	**534**	**9.4**	**174**	**43**	**122**	**17**		**36**	**6**	**6**	**12**	**40**	**1**	**0**	**1**

QMJHL First All-Star Team (1993) • Canadian Major Junior First All-Star Team (1993) • Won Dudley "Red" Garrett Memorial Trophy (Top Rookie - AHL) (1994)

Transferred to **Colorado** after **Quebec** franchise relocated, June 21, 1995. Traded to **Calgary** by **Colorado** with Wade Belak, Robyn Regehr and Colorado's 2nd round compensatory choice (Jarret Stoll) in 2000 Entry Draft for Theoren Fleury and Chris Dingman, February 28, 1999. Traded to **Pittsburgh** by **Calgary** with Tyler Moss for Brad Werenka, March 14, 2000.

• CORBETT, Mike

Michael Charles RW/D – L. 6'2", 195 lbs. b: Toronto, Ont., 10/4/1942.

Season	Club	League	GP	G	A	Pts	AG	AA	APts	PIM	PP	SH	GW	S	%	TGF	PGF	TGA	PGA	+/–	GP	G	A	Pts	PIM	PP	SH	GW
1959-60	St. Michael's Buzzers	OHA-B	STATISTICS NOT AVAILABLE																									
	St. Michael's Majors	OHA-Jr.	2	0	0	0	....	....	....	0	....	....	....	....	....	....	....	....	....	....	....	....	....	....	....	....	....	....
1960-61	St. Michael's Buzzers	OHA-B	STATISTICS NOT AVAILABLE																									
	St. Michael's Majors	OHA-Jr.	2	0	1	1	....	....	....	0	....	....	....	....	....	....	....	....	....	....	1	0	0	0	0	....	....	....
1961-62	St. Michael's Majors	MTJHL	31	19	33	52	....	....	....	44	....	....	....	....	....	....	....	....	....	....	11	7	6	13	37	....	....	....
	St. Michael's Majors	Mem-Cup	5	0	1	1	....	....	....	2	....	....	....	....	....	....	....	....	....	....	....	....	....	....	....	....	....	....
1962-63	Neil McNeil Maroons	MTJHL	37	*44	50	94	....	....	....	76	....	....	....	....	....	....	....	....	....	....	10	7	12	19	13	....	....	....
	Sudbury Wolves	EPHL	5	1	4	5	....	....	....	0	....	....	....	....	....	....	....	....	....	....	....	....	....	....	....	....	....	....
	Neil McNeil Maroons	Mem-Cup	6	3	2	5	....	....	....	27	....	....	....	....	....	....	....	....	....	....	....	....	....	....	....	....	....	....
1963-64	Rochester Americans	AHL	50	5	10	15	....	....	....	18	....	....	....	....	....	....	....	....	....	....	....	....	....	....	....	....	....	....
	Denver Invaders	WHL	6	1	0	1	....	....	....	29	....	....	....	....	....	....	....	....	....	....	5	0	3	3	8	....	....	....
1964-65	Tulsa Oilers	CPHL	55	4	18	22	....	....	....	63	....	....	....	....	....	....	....	....	....	....	9	0	1	1	10	....	....	....
1965-66	Minnesota Rangers	CPHL	4	0	2	2	....	....	....	2	....	....	....	....	....	....	....	....	....	....	....	....	....	....	....	....	....	....
	Baltimore Clippers	AHL	35	4	5	9	....	....	....	50	....	....	....	....	....	....	....	....	....	....	....	....	....	....	....	....	....	....
1966-67	Providence Reds	AHL	5	0	1	1	....	....	....	14	....	....	....	....	....	....	....	....	....	....	....	....	....	....	....	....	....	....
	Springfield Indians	AHL	5	0	0	0	....	....	....	12	....	....	....	....	....	....	....	....	....	....	....	....	....	....	....	....	....	....
1967-68	Vancouver Canucks	WHL	70	17	21	38	....	....	....	83	....	....	....	....	....	....	....	....	....	....	....	....	....	....	....	....	....	....
	Los Angeles Kings	**NHL**	....	....	....	....	....	....	....	....	....	....	....	....	....	....	....	....	....	....	**2**	**0**	**1**	**1**	**2**	**0**	**0**	**0**
1968-69	Springfield Kings	AHL	25	3	4	7	....	....	....	54	....	....	....	....	....	....	....	....	....	....	....	....	....	....	....	....	....	....
	Dayton Gems	IHL	34	3	13	16	....	....	....	61	....	....	....	....	....	....	....	....	....	....	9	2	6	8	4	....	....	....
1969-70	Galt Hornets	OHA-Sr.	28	3	17	20	....	....	....	69	....	....	....	....	....	....	....	....	....	....	....	....	....	....	....	....	....	....
1970-71	Orillia Terriers	OHA-Sr.	16	3	14	17	....	....	....	32	....	....	....	....	....	....	....	....	....	....	....	....	....	....	....	....	....	....
1971-72	Orillia Terriers	OHA-Sr.	16	3	14	17	....	....	....	32	....	....	....	....	....	....	....	....	....	....	....	....	....	....	....	....	....	....
	Oakville Oaks	OHA-Sr.	18	5	12	17	....	....	....	68	....	....	....	....	....	....	....	....	....	....	....	....	....	....	....	....	....	....
1972-73	Brantford Alexanders	OHA-Sr.	28	6	14	20	....	....	....	30	....	....	....	....	....	....	....	....	....	....	....	....	....	....	....	....	....	....
1973-74	Brantford Alexanders	OHA-Sr.	34	6	22	28	....	....	....	39	....	....	....	....	....	....	....	....	....	....	....	....	....	....	....	....	....	....
	NHL Totals		....	....	....	....	....	....	....	....	....	....	....	....	....	....	....	....	....	....	**2**	**0**	**1**	**1**	**2**	**0**	**0**	**0**

Claimed by **Baltimore** (AHL) from **Toronto** in Reverse Draft, June 9, 1965. Traded to **Providence** (AHL) by **Baltimore** (AHL) with Ed Lawson and Ken Stephanson for Aldo Guidolin, Willie Marshall, Jim Bartlett and Ian Anderson, June, 1966. Claimed on waivers by **Springfield** (AHL) from **Providence** (AHL), December 20, 1966. • Suspended by Springfield for remainder of 1966-67 season for refusing to play, January 12, 1967. NHL rights transferred to **LA Kings** after NHL club purchased **Springfield** (AHL) franchise, May, 1967. Loaned to **Vancouver** (WHL) by **LA Kings** (Springfield-AHL) with the loan of Larry Mavety and the trade of Bill Sweeney for cash, October, 1967.

• CORKUM, Bob

Robert Freeman C – R. 6', 222 lbs. b: Salisbury, MA, 12/18/1967. Buffalo's 3rd, 47th overall, in 1986.

Season	Club	League	GP	G	A	Pts	AG	AA	APts	PIM	PP	SH	GW	S	%	TGF	PGF	TGA	PGA	+/–	GP	G	A	Pts	PIM	PP	SH	GW
1984-85	Triton Regional High School	Hi-School	18	35	36	71	....	....	....	....	....	....	....	....	....	....	....	....	....	....	....	....	....	....	....	....	....	....
1985-86	University of Maine	H-East	39	7	26	33	....	....	....	53	....	....	....	....	....	....	....	....	....	....	....	....	....	....	....	....	....	....
1986-87	University of Maine	H-East	35	18	11	29	....	....	....	24	....	....	....	....	....	....	....	....	....	....	....	....	....	....	....	....	....	....
	United States	WJC-A	7	4	0	4	....	....	....	6	....	....	....	....	....	....	....	....	....	....	....	....	....	....	....	....	....	....
1987-88	University of Maine	H-East	40	14	18	32	....	....	....	64	....	....	....	....	....	....	....	....	....	....	....	....	....	....	....	....	....	....
1988-89	University of Maine	H-East	45	17	31	48	....	....	....	64	....	....	....	....	....	....	....	....	....	....	....	....	....	....	....	....	....	....
1989-90	**Buffalo Sabres**	**NHL**	**8**	**2**	**0**	**2**	**2**	**0**	**2**	**4**	**0**	**0**	**1**	**6**	**33.3**	**5**	**1**	**2**	**0**	**2**	**5**	**1**	**0**	**1**	**4**	**0**	**0**	**0**
	Rochester Americans	AHL	43	8	11	19	....	....	....	45	....	....	....	....	....	....	....	....	....	....	12	2	5	7	16	....	....	....
1990-91	Rochester Americans	AHL	69	13	21	34	....	....	....	77	....	....	....	....	....	....	....	....	....	....	15	4	4	8	4	....	....	....
1991-92	**Buffalo Sabres**	**NHL**	**20**	**2**	**4**	**6**	**2**	**3**	**5**	**21**	**0**	**0**	**0**	**23**	**8.7**	**9**	**0**	**24**	**6**	**–9**	**4**	**1**	**0**	**1**	**0**	**1**	**0**	**0**
	Rochester Americans	AHL	52	16	12	28	....	....	....	47	....	....	....	....	....	....	....	....	....	....	8	0	6	6	8	....	....	....
1992-93	**Buffalo Sabres**	**NHL**	**68**	**6**	**4**	**10**	**5**	**3**	**8**	**38**	**0**	**1**	**1**	**69**	**8.7**	**17**	**0**	**46**	**26**	**–3**	**5**	**0**	**0**	**0**	**2**	**0**	**0**	**0**
1993-94	**Mighty Ducks of Anaheim**	**NHL**	**76**	**23**	**28**	**51**	**21**	**22**	**43**	**18**	**3**	**3**	**0**	**180**	**12.8**	**68**	**12**	**87**	**35**	**4**	....	....	....	....	....	....	....	....
1994-95	**Mighty Ducks of Anaheim**	**NHL**	**44**	**10**	**9**	**19**	**18**	**13**	**31**	**25**	**0**	**0**	**1**	**100**	**10.0**	**28**	**4**	**48**	**17**	**–7**	....	....	....	....	....	....	....	....
1995-96	**Mighty Ducks of Anaheim**	**NHL**	**48**	**5**	**7**	**12**	**5**	**6**	**11**	**26**	**0**	**0**	**1**	**88**	**5.7**	**20**	**0**	**45**	**25**	**0**	....	....	....	....	....	....	....	....
	Philadelphia Flyers	**NHL**	**28**	**4**	**3**	**7**	**4**	**2**	**6**	**8**	**0**	**0**	**2**	**38**	**10.5**	**14**	**2**	**10**	**1**	**3**	**12**	**1**	**2**	**3**	**6**	**0**	**0**	**0**

			REGULAR SEASON																		PLAYOFFS							
Season	**Club**	**League**	**GP**	**G**	**A**	**Pts**	**AG**	**AA**	**APts**	**PIM**	**PP**	**SH**	**GW**	**S**	**%**	**TGF**	**PGF**	**TGA**	**PGA**	**+/–**	**GP**	**G**	**A**	**Pts**	**PIM**	**PP**	**SH**	**GW**
1996-97	**Phoenix Coyotes**	**NHL**	**80**	**9**	**11**	**20**	**10**	**10**	**20**	**40**	**0**	**1**	**3**	**119**	**7.6**	**38**	**2**	**61**	**18**	**–7**	**7**	**2**	**2**	**4**	**4**	**0**	**0**	**1**
1997-98	**Phoenix Coyotes**	**NHL**	**76**	**12**	**9**	**21**	**14**	**9**	**23**	**28**	**0**	**5**	**0**	**105**	**11.4**	**31**	**0**	**71**	**33**	**–7**	**6**	**1**	**0**	**1**	**4**	**0**	**0**	**0**
1998-99	**Phoenix Coyotes**	**NHL**	**77**	**9**	**10**	**19**	**11**	**10**	**21**	**17**	**0**	**0**	**0**	**146**	**6.2**	**29**	**0**	**58**	**20**	**–9**	**7**	**0**	**1**	**1**	**4**	**0**	**0**	**0**
99-2000	**Los Angeles Kings**	**NHL**	**45**	**5**	**6**	**11**	**6**	**6**	**12**	**14**	**0**	**0**	**0**	**45**	**11.1**	**18**	**0**	**38**	**20**	**0**	**4**	**0**	**0**	**0**	**0**	**0**	**0**	**0**
	NHL Totals		**570**	**87**	**91**	**178**	**98**	**84**	**182**	**239**	**3**	**10**	**9**	**919**	**9.5**	**277**	**21**	**490**	**201**		**50**	**6**	**5**	**11**	**24**	**1**	**0**	**1**

Claimed by **Anaheim** from **Buffalo** in Expansion Draft, June 24, 1993. Traded to **Philadelphia** by **Anaheim** for Chris Herperger and Winnipeg's 7th round choice (previously acquired, Anaheim selected Tony Monahan) in 1997 Entry Draft, February 6, 1996. Claimed by **Phoenix** from **Philadelphia** in Waiver Draft, September 30, 1996. Signed as a free agent by **LA Kings**, December 28, 1999.

• CORNFORTH, MarkMark

D – L. 6'1", 193 lbs. b: Montreal, Que., 11/13/1972.

Season	Club	League	GP	G	A	Pts	AG	AA	APts	PIM	PP	SH	GW	S	%	TGF	PGF	TGA	PGA	+/–	GP	G	A	Pts	PIM	PP	SH	GW
1989-90	Pembroke Lumber Kings	OJHL	56	17	25	42	....	....	....	104	....	....	....	....	....	....	....	....	....	....	....	....	....	....	....	....	....	....
1990-91	Pembroke Lumber Kings	OJHL	17	9	11	20	....	....	....	52	....	....	....	....	....	....	....	....	....	....	....	....	....	....	....	....	....	....
	Brockville Braves	OJHL	36	12	23	35	....	....	....	84	....	....	....	....	....	....	....	....	....	....	....	....	....	....	....	....	....	....
1991-92	Merrimack College	H-East	23	1	9	10	....	....	....	40	....	....	....	....	....	....	....	....	....	....	....	....	....	....	....	....	....	....
1992-93	Merrimack College	H-East	36	3	18	21	....	....	....	75	....	....	....	....	....	....	....	....	....	....	....	....	....	....	....	....	....	....
1993-94	Merrimack College	H-East	37	5	13	18	....	....	....	58	....	....	....	....	....	....	....	....	....	....	....	....	....	....	....	....	....	....
1994-95	Merrimack College	H-East	30	8	20	28	....	....	....	93	....	....	....	....	....	....	....	....	....	....	....	....	....	....	....	....	....	....
	Syracuse Crunch	AHL	2	0	1	1	....	....	....	2	....	....	....	....	....	....	....	....	....	....	....	....	....	....	....	....	....	....
1995-96	**Boston Bruins**	**NHL**	**6**	**0**	**0**	**0**	**0**	**0**	**0**	**4**	**0**	**0**	**0**	**1**	**0.0**	**7**	**0**	**4**	**1**	**4**	....	....	....	....	....	....	....	....
	Providence Bruins	AHL	65	5	10	15	....	....	....	117	....	....	....	....	....	....	....	....	....	....	4	0	0	0	4	....	....	....
1996-97	Providence Bruins	AHL	61	8	12	20	....	....	....	47	....	....	....	....	....	....	....	....	....	....	....	....	....	....	....	....	....	....
	Cleveland Lumberjacks	IHL	13	1	4	5	....	....	....	25	....	....	....	....	....	....	....	....	....	....	14	1	3	4	29	....	....	....
1997-98	Cleveland Lumberjacks	IHL	68	5	15	20	....	....	....	146	....	....	....	....	....	....	....	....	....	....	....	....	....	....	....	....	....	....
	Grand Rapids Griffins	IHL	8	1	2	3	....	....	....	20	....	....	....	....	....	....	....	....	....	....	3	0	0	0	17	....	....	....
1998-99	Providence Bruins	AHL	15	1	1	2	....	....	....	16	....	....	....	....	....	....	....	....	....	....	....	....	....	....	....	....	....	....
	Springfield Falcons	AHL	5	0	0	0	....	....	....	2	....	....	....	....	....	....	....	....	....	....	....	....	....	....	....	....	....	....
99-2000	Lowell Lock Monsters	AHL	1	0	0	0	....	....	....	2	....	....	....	....	....	....	....	....	....	....	....	....	....	....	....	....	....	....
	Springfield Falcons	AHL	1	0	0	0	....	....	....	2	....	....	....	....	....	....	....	....	....	....	....	....	....	....	....	....	....	....
	NHL Totals		**6**	**0**	**0**	**0**	**0**	**0**	**0**	**4**	**0**	**0**	**0**	**1**	**0.0**	**7**	**0**	**4**	**1**		....	....	....	....	....	....	....	....

Signed as a free agent by **Boston**, October 6, 1995. Signed as a free agent by **Springfield** (AHL), February 21, 1999.

• CORRIGAN, Mike

Michael Douglas LW – L. 5'10", 175 lbs. b: Ottawa, Ont., 1/11/1946.

Season	Club	League	GP	G	A	Pts	AG	AA	APts	PIM	PP	SH	GW	S	%	TGF	PGF	TGA	PGA	+/–	GP	G	A	Pts	PIM	PP	SH	GW
1961-62	St. Michael's Buzzers	OHA-B	STATISTICS NOT AVAILABLE																									
1962-63	Neil McNeil Maroons	MTJHL	31	15	15	30	....	....	....	22	....	....	....	....	....	....	....	....	....	....	10	1	2	3	13	....	....	....
	Neil McNeil Maroons	Mem-Cup	6	0	1	1	....	....	....	2	....	....	....	....	....	....	....	....	....	....	....	....	....	....	....	....	....	....
1963-64	London Nationals	OHA-B	STATISTICS NOT AVAILABLE																									
1964-65	Toronto Marlboros	OHA-Jr.	56	30	67	97	....	....	....	76	....	....	....	....	....	....	....	....	....	....	19	9	9	18	13	....	....	....
1965-66	Toronto Marlboros	OHA-Jr.	41	25	36	61	....	....	....	70	....	....	....	....	....	....	....	....	....	....	14	10	4	14	22	....	....	....
	Rochester Americans	AHL	3	1	0	1	....	....	....	4	....	....	....	....	....	....	....	....	....	....	....	....	....	....	....	....	....	....
	Victoria Maple Leafs	WHL	....	....	....	....	....	....	....	....	....	....	....	....	....	....	....	....	....	....	6	0	0	0	0	....	....	....
	Tulsa Oilers	CPHL	....	....	....	....	....	....	....	....	....	....	....	....	....	....	....	....	....	....	8	1	5	6	5	....	....	....
1966-67	Rochester Americans	AHL	49	11	21	32	....	....	....	34	....	....	....	....	....	....	....	....	....	....	....	....	....	....	....	....	....	....
	Tulsa Oilers	CPHL	15	4	3	7	....	....	....	6	....	....	....	....	....	....	....	....	....	....	....	....	....	....	....	....	....	....
1967-68	**Los Angeles Kings**	**NHL**	**5**	**0**	**0**	**0**	**0**	**0**	**0**	**2**	**0**	**0**	**0**	**5**	**0.0**	**1**	**0**	**7**	**4**	**–2**	....	....	....	....	....	....	....	....
	Springfield Kings	AHL	58	24	30	54	....	....	....	57	....	....	....	....	....	....	....	....	....	....	4	1	2	3	13	....	....	....
1968-69	Springfield Kings	AHL	66	17	16	33	....	....	....	85	....	....	....	....	....	....	....	....	....	....	....	....	....	....	....	....	....	....
1969-70	**Los Angeles Kings**	**NHL**	**36**	**6**	**4**	**10**	**6**	**4**	**10**	**30**	**2**	**0**	**1**	**67**	**9.0**	**17**	**4**	**35**	**5**	**–17**	....	....	....	....	....	....	....	....
	Springfield Kings	AHL	37	19	23	42	....	....	....	49	....	....	....	....	....	....	....	....	....	....	14	7	7	14	51	....	....	....
1970-71	**Vancouver Canucks**	**NHL**	**76**	**21**	**28**	**49**	**21**	**23**	**44**	**103**	**5**	**0**	**1**	**164**	**12.8**	**68**	**21**	**72**	**5**	**–20**	....	....	....	....	....	....	....	....
1971-72	**Vancouver Canucks**	**NHL**	**19**	**3**	**4**	**7**	**3**	**3**	**6**	**25**	**1**	**0**	**0**	**42**	**7.1**	**14**	**4**	**18**	**0**	**–8**	....	....	....	....	....	....	....	....
	Los Angeles Kings	**NHL**	**56**	**12**	**22**	**34**	**12**	**19**	**31**	**95**	**3**	**0**	**1**	**102**	**11.8**	**53**	**9**	**51**	**0**	**–7**	....	....	....	....	....	....	....	....
1972-73	**Los Angeles Kings**	**NHL**	**78**	**37**	**30**	**67**	**35**	**24**	**59**	**146**	**14**	**0**	**6**	**180**	**20.6**	**94**	**34**	**77**	**0**	**–17**	....	....	....	....	....	....	....	....
1973-74	**Los Angeles Kings**	**NHL**	**75**	**16**	**26**	**42**	**15**	**21**	**36**	**119**	**4**	**0**	**1**	**131**	**12.2**	**65**	**15**	**61**	**1**	**–10**	**3**	**0**	**1**	**1**	**4**	**0**	**0**	**0**
1974-75	**Los Angeles Kings**	**NHL**	**80**	**13**	**21**	**34**	**11**	**16**	**27**	**61**	**2**	**1**	**2**	**100**	**13.0**	**54**	**19**	**39**	**13**	**9**	**3**	**0**	**0**	**0**	**4**	**0**	**0**	**0**
1975-76	**Los Angeles Kings**	**NHL**	**71**	**22**	**21**	**43**	**19**	**16**	**35**	**71**	**9**	**0**	**4**	**135**	**16.3**	**70**	**25**	**53**	**6**	**–2**	**9**	**2**	**2**	**4**	**12**	**0**	**0**	**0**
1976-77	**Pittsburgh Penguins**	**NHL**	**73**	**14**	**27**	**41**	**13**	**21**	**34**	**36**	**2**	**0**	**1**	**124**	**11.3**	**66**	**16**	**64**	**1**	**–13**	**2**	**0**	**0**	**0**	**0**	**0**	**0**	**0**
	Fort Worth Texans	CHL	2	1	3	4	....	....	....	2	....	....	....	....	....	....	....	....	....	....	....	....	....	....	....	....	....	....
1977-78	**Pittsburgh Penguins**	**NHL**	**25**	**8**	**12**	**20**	**7**	**9**	**16**	**10**	**0**	**0**	**0**	**36**	**22.2**	**28**	**7**	**29**	**1**	**–7**	....	....	....	....	....	....	....	....
	NHL Totals		**594**	**152**	**195**	**347**	**142**	**156**	**298**	**698**	**42**	**1**	**17**	**1086**	**14.0**	**530**	**154**	**506**	**36**		**17**	**2**	**3**	**5**	**20**	**0**	**0**	**0**

Claimed by **LA Kings** from **Toronto** in Expansion Draft, June 6, 1967. Claimed by **Vancouver** from **LA Kings** in Expansion Draft, June 10, 1970. Claimed on waivers by **LA Kings** from **Vancouver**, November 22, 1971. Traded to **Pittsburgh** by **LA Kings** for Pittsburgh's 5th round choice (Julian Baretta) in 1977 Amateur Draft, October 18, 1976.

• CORRIVEAU, Yvon

LW – L. 6'1", 195 lbs. b: Welland, Ont., 2/8/1967. Washington's 1st, 19th overall, in 1985.

Season	Club	League	GP	G	A	Pts	AG	AA	APts	PIM	PP	SH	GW	S	%	TGF	PGF	TGA	PGA	+/–	GP	G	A	Pts	PIM	PP	SH	GW
1983-84	Welland Cougars	OJHL-B	36	16	21	37	....	....	....	51	....	....	....	....	....	....	....	....	....	....	....	....	....	....	....	....	....	....
1984-85	Toronto Marlboros	OHL	59	23	28	51	....	....	....	65	....	....	....	....	....	....	....	....	....	....	3	0	0	0	5	....	....	....
1985-86	Toronto Marlboros	OHL	59	54	36	90	....	....	....	75	....	....	....	....	....	....	....	....	....	....	4	1	1	2	0	....	....	....
	Washington Capitals	**NHL**	**2**	**0**	**0**	**0**	**0**	**0**	**0**	**0**	**0**	**0**	**0**	**3**	**0.0**	**1**	**0**	**2**	**0**	**–1**	**4**	**0**	**3**	**3**	**2**	**0**	**0**	**0**
1986-87	Toronto Marlboros	OHL	23	14	19	33	....	....	....	23	....	....	....	....	....	....	....	....	....	....	....	....	....	....	....	....	....	....
	Washington Capitals	**NHL**	**17**	**1**	**1**	**2**	**1**	**1**	**2**	**24**	**0**	**0**	**0**	**7**	**14.3**	**4**	**0**	**8**	**0**	**–4**	....	....	....	....	....	....	....	....
	Canada	WJC-A	6	2	1	3	....	....	....	4	....	....	....	....	....	....	....	....	....	....	....	....	....	....	....	....	....	....
	Binghamton Whalers	AHL	7	0	0	0	....	....	....	2	....	....	....	....	....	....	....	....	....	....	8	0	1	1	0	....	....	....
1987-88	**Washington Capitals**	**NHL**	**44**	**10**	**9**	**19**	**9**	**6**	**15**	**84**	**0**	**0**	**1**	**52**	**19.2**	**29**	**0**	**12**	**0**	**17**	**13**	**1**	**2**	**3**	**30**	**0**	**0**	**0**
	Binghamton Whalers	AHL	35	15	14	29	....	....	....	64	....	....	....	....	....	....	....	....	....	....	....	....	....	....	....	....	....	....
1988-89	**Washington Capitals**	**NHL**	**33**	**3**	**2**	**5**	**3**	**1**	**4**	**62**	**0**	**0**	**0**	**39**	**7.7**	**12**	**0**	**12**	**0**	**0**	**1**	**0**	**0**	**0**	**0**	**0**	**0**	**0**
	Baltimore Skipjacks	AHL	33	16	23	39	....	....	....	65	....	....	....	....	....	....	....	....	....	....	....	....	....	....	....	....	....	....
1989-90	Washington Capitals	Fr-Tour	3	1	2	3	....	....	....	4	....	....	....	....	....	....	....	....	....	....	....	....	....	....	....	....	....	....
	Washington Capitals	**NHL**	**50**	**9**	**6**	**15**	**8**	**4**	**12**	**50**	**1**	**0**	**1**	**76**	**11.8**	**25**	**3**	**23**	**0**	**–1**	....	....	....	....	....	....	....	....
	Hartford Whalers	**NHL**	**13**	**4**	**1**	**5**	**3**	**1**	**4**	**22**	**0**	**0**	**0**	**14**	**28.6**	**7**	**0**	**5**	**1**	**3**	**4**	**1**	**0**	**1**	**0**	**0**	**0**	**0**
1990-91	**Hartford Whalers**	**NHL**	**23**	**1**	**1**	**2**	**1**	**1**	**2**	**18**	**0**	**0**	**0**	**21**	**4.8**	**4**	**0**	**12**	**0**	**–8**	....	....	....	....	....	....	....	....
	Springfield Indians	AHL	44	17	25	42	....	....	....	10	....	....	....	....	....	....	....	....	....	....	18	*10	6	16	31	....	....	....
1991-92	**Hartford Whalers**	**NHL**	**38**	**12**	**8**	**20**	**11**	**6**	**17**	**36**	**3**	**0**	**0**	**69**	**17.4**	**33**	**7**	**26**	**5**	**5**	**7**	**3**	**2**	**5**	**18**	**2**	**0**	**1**
	Springfield Indians	AHL	39	26	15	41	....	....	....	40	....	....	....	....	....	....	....	....	....	....	....	....	....	....	....	....	....	....
1992-93	**San Jose Sharks**	**NHL**	**20**	**3**	**7**	**10**	**2**	**5**	**7**	**0**	**1**	**0**	**0**	**32**	**9.4**	**11**	**1**	**17**	**0**	**–7**	....	....	....	....	....	....	....	....
	Hartford Whalers	**NHL**	**37**	**5**	**5**	**10**	**4**	**3**	**7**	**14**	**1**	**0**	**1**	**45**	**11.1**	**17**	**3**	**28**	**1**	**–13**	....	....	....	....	....	....	....	....
1993-94	**Hartford Whalers**	**NHL**	**3**	**0**	**0**	**0**	**0**	**0**	**0**	**0**	**0**	**0**	**0**	**0**	**0.0**	**0**	**0**	**0**	**0**	**0**	....	....	....	....	....	....	....	....
	Springfield Indians	AHL	71	42	39	81	....	....	....	53	....	....	....	....	....	....	....	....	....	....	6	7	3	10	20	....	....	....
1994-95	Minnesota Moose	IHL	62	18	24	42	....	....	....	26	....	....	....	....	....	....	....	....	....	....	3	1	1	2	0	....	....	....
1995-96	Minnesota Moose	IHL	60	21	22	43	....	....	....	40	....	....	....	....	....	....	....	....	....	....	....	....	....	....	....	....	....	....
	Detroit Vipers	IHL	14	5	6	11	....	....	....	12	....	....	....	....	....	....	....	....	....	....	4	0	1	1	6	....	....	....
1996-97	Detroit Vipers	IHL	52	9	9	18	....	....	....	85	....	....	....	....	....	....	....	....	....	....	21	2	1	3	34	....	....	....
1997-98	Eisbaren Berlin	Germany	47	12	14	26	....	....	....	58	....	....	....	....	....	....	....	....	....	....	9	1	0	1	30	....	....	....
1998-99	Eisbaren Berlin	Germany	49	16	13	29	....	....	....	157	....	....	....	....	....	....	....	....	....	....	8	4	1	5	24	....	....	....
	Eisbaren Berlin	EuroHL	5	3	3	6	....	....	....	12	....	....	....	....	....	....	....	....	....	....	....	....	....	....	....	....	....	....
99-2000	Eisbaren Berlin	Germany	63	17	16	33	....	....	....	125	....	....	....	....	....	....	....	....	....	....	....	....	....	....	....	....	....	....
	NHL Totals		**280**	**48**	**40**	**88**	**42**	**28**	**70**	**310**	**6**	**0**	**3**	**358**	**13.4**	**143**	**14**	**145**	**7**		**29**	**5**	**7**	**12**	**50**	**2**	**0**	**1**

Traded to **Hartford** by **Washington** for Mike Liut, March 6, 1990. Traded to **Washington** by **Hartford** to complete June 15, 1992 deal in which Mark Hunter and future considerations were traded to Washington for Nick Kypreos, August 20, 1992. Claimed by **San Jose** from **Washington** in Waiver Draft, October 4, 1992. Traded to **Hartford** by **San Jose** to complete October 9, 1992 trade in which Michel Picard was traded to San Jose for future considerations, January 21, 1993.

• CORSON, Shayne

LW – L. 6'1", 202 lbs. b: Barrie, Ont., 8/13/1966. Montreal's 2nd, 8th overall, in 1984.

Season	Club	League	GP	G	A	Pts	AG	AA	APts	PIM	PP	SH	GW	S	%	TGF	PGF	TGA	PGA	+/–	GP	G	A	Pts	PIM	PP	SH	GW
			REGULAR SEASON																		PLAYOFFS							
1982-83	Barrie Flyers	OMHA	STATISTICS NOT AVAILABLE																									
	Barrie Colts	OJHL-B	23	13	29	42	....	....	....	87	....	....	....	....	....	....	....	....	....	....	....	....	....	....	....	....	....	....
1983-84	Brantford Alexanders	OHL	66	25	46	71	....	....	....	165	....	....	....	....	....	....	....	....	....	....	6	4	1	5	26	....	....	....
1984-85	Hamilton Steelhawks	OHL	54	27	63	90	....	....	....	154	....	....	....	....	....	....	....	....	....	....	11	3	7	10	19	....	....	....
	Canada	WJC-A	7	2	3	5	....	....	....	2	....	....	....	....	....	....	....	....	....	....	....	....	....	....	....	....	....	....
1985-86	Hamilton Steelhawks	OHL	47	41	57	98	....	....	....	153	....	....	....	....	....	....	....	....	....	....	....	....	....	....	....	....	....	....
	Canada	WJC-A	7	7	7	*14	....	....	....	6	....	....	....	....	....	....	....	....	....	....	....	....	....	....	....	....	....	....
	Montreal Canadiens	**NHL**	**3**	**0**	**0**	**0**	**0**	**0**	**0**	**2**	**0**	**0**	**0**	**1**	**0.0**	**0**	**0**	**4**	**1**	**–3**	....	....	....	....	....	....	....	....
1986-87	**Montreal Canadiens**	**NHL**	**55**	**12**	**11**	**23**	**10**	**8**	**18**	**144**	**0**	**1**	**3**	**69**	**17.4**	**42**	**3**	**41**	**12**	**10**	**17**	**6**	**5**	**11**	**30**	**1**	**1**	**1**
1987-88	**Montreal Canadiens**	**NHL**	**71**	**12**	**27**	**39**	**10**	**19**	**29**	**152**	**2**	**0**	**2**	**90**	**13.3**	**75**	**10**	**47**	**4**	**22**	**3**	**1**	**0**	**1**	**12**	**0**	**0**	**0**
1988-89	**Montreal Canadiens**	**NHL**	**80**	**26**	**24**	**50**	**22**	**17**	**39**	**193**	**10**	**0**	**3**	**133**	**19.5**	**84**	**35**	**56**	**6**	**–1**	**21**	**4**	**5**	**9**	**65**	**2**	**0**	**2**
1989-90	**Montreal Canadiens**	**NHL**	**76**	**31**	**44**	**75**	**27**	**32**	**59**	**144**	**7**	**0**	**6**	**192**	**16.1**	**124**	**39**	**54**	**2**	**33**	**11**	**2**	**8**	**10**	**20**	**0**	**0**	**0**
1990-91	Montreal Canadiens	Fr-Tour	4	2	2	4	....	....	....	31	....	....	....	....	....	....	....	....	....	....	....	....	....	....	....	....	....	....
	Montreal Canadiens	**NHL**	**71**	**23**	**24**	**47**	**21**	**18**	**39**	**138**	**7**	**0**	**2**	**164**	**14.0**	**78**	**21**	**54**	**6**	**9**	**13**	**9**	**6**	**15**	**36**	**4**	**1**	**3**
1991-92	Canada	Can-Cup	8	0	5	5	....	....	....	12	....	....	....	....	....	....	....	....	....	....	....	....	....	....	....	....	....	....
	Montreal Canadiens	**NHL**	**64**	**17**	**36**	**53**	**15**	**27**	**42**	**118**	**3**	**0**	**2**	**165**	**10.3**	**89**	**28**	**58**	**12**	**15**	**10**	**2**	**5**	**7**	**15**	**0**	**0**	**0**
1992-93	**Edmonton Oilers**	**NHL**	**80**	**16**	**31**	**47**	**13**	**21**	**34**	**209**	**9**	**2**	**1**	**164**	**9.8**	**84**	**40**	**91**	**28**	**–19**	....	....	....	....	....	....	....	....
	Canada	WC-A	8	3	7	10	....	....	....	6	....	....	....	....	....	....	....	....	....	....	....	....	....	....	....	....	....	....
1993-94	**Edmonton Oilers**	**NHL**	**64**	**25**	**29**	**54**	**23**	**22**	**45**	**118**	**11**	**0**	**3**	**171**	**14.6**	**88**	**35**	**86**	**25**	**–8**	....	....	....	....	....	....	....	....
	Canada	WC-A	7	3	0	3	....	....	....	4	....	....	....	....	....	....	....	....	....	....	....	....	....	....	....	....	....	....
1994-95	**Edmonton Oilers**	**NHL**	**48**	**12**	**24**	**36**	**21**	**35**	**56**	**86**	**2**	**0**	**1**	**131**	**9.2**	**59**	**26**	**59**	**9**	**–17**	....	....	....	....	....	....	....	....
1995-96	**St. Louis Blues**	**NHL**	**77**	**18**	**28**	**46**	**18**	**23**	**41**	**192**	**13**	**0**	**0**	**150**	**12.0**	**99**	**41**	**90**	**35**	**3**	**13**	**8**	**6**	**14**	**22**	**6**	**1**	**1**
1996-97	**St. Louis Blues**	**NHL**	**11**	**2**	**1**	**3**	**2**	**1**	**3**	**24**	**1**	**0**	**0**	**19**	**10.5**	**11**	**5**	**13**	**3**	**–4**	....	....	....	....	....	....	....	....
	Montreal Canadiens	**NHL**	**47**	**6**	**15**	**21**	**6**	**13**	**19**	**80**	**2**	**0**	**2**	**96**	**6.3**	**42**	**13**	**46**	**12**	**–5**	**5**	**1**	**0**	**1**	**4**	**0**	**1**	**0**
1997-98	**Montreal Canadiens**	**NHL**	**62**	**21**	**34**	**55**	**25**	**33**	**58**	**108**	**14**	**1**	**1**	**142**	**14.8**	**75**	**33**	**55**	**15**	**2**	**10**	**3**	**6**	**9**	**26**	**1**	**0**	**1**
	Canada	Olympics	6	1	1	2	....	....	....	2	....	....	....	....	....	....	....	....	....	....	....	....	....	....	....	....	....	....
1998-99	**Montreal Canadiens**	**NHL**	**63**	**12**	**20**	**32**	**14**	**19**	**33**	**147**	**7**	**0**	**4**	**142**	**8.5**	**52**	**24**	**48**	**10**	**–10**	....	....	....	....	....	....	....	....
99-2000	**Montreal Canadiens**	**NHL**	**70**	**8**	**20**	**28**	**9**	**19**	**28**	**115**	**2**	**0**	**1**	**121**	**6.6**	**62**	**23**	**56**	**15**	**–2**	....	....	....	....	....	....	....	....
	NHL Totals		**942**	**241**	**368**	**609**	**236**	**307**	**543**	**1970**	**90**	**4**	**31**	**1950**	**12.4**	**1064**	**376**	**858**	**195**		**103**	**36**	**41**	**77**	**230**	**14**	**4**	**8**

WJC-A All-Star Team (1986) • Played in NHL All-Star Game (1990, 1994, 1998)

Traded to **Edmonton** by **Montreal** with Brent Gilchrist and Vladimir Vujtek for Vincent Damphousse and Edmonton's 4th round choice (Adam Wiesel) in 1993 Entry Draft, August 27, 1992. Signed as a free agent by **St. Louis**, July 28, 1995. Traded to **Montreal** by **St. Louis** with Murray Baron and St. Louis' 5th round choice (Gennady Razin) in 1997 Entry Draft for Pierre Turgeon, Rory Fitzpatrick and Craig Conroy, October 29, 1996. Signed as a free agent by **Toronto**, July 4, 2000.

• CORY, Ross

Keith Ross D – L. 6'2", 195 lbs. b: Calgary, Alta., 2/4/1957.

Season	Club	League	GP	G	A	Pts	AG	AA	APts	PIM	PP	SH	GW	S	%	TGF	PGF	TGA	PGA	+/–	GP	G	A	Pts	PIM	PP	SH	GW
1976-77	University of British Columbia	CWUAA	33	7	20	27	....	....	....	54	....	....	....	....	....	....	....	....	....	....	....	....	....	....	....	....	....	....
1977-78	University of British Columbia	CWUAA	39	6	39	45	....	....	....	69	....	....	....	....	....	....	....	....	....	....	....	....	....	....	....	....	....	....
1978-79	University of British Columbia	CWUAA	29	4	20	24	....	....	....	83	....	....	....	....	....	....	....	....	....	....	....	....	....	....	....	....	....	....
1979-80	**Winnipeg Jets**	**NHL**	**46**	**2**	**9**	**11**	**2**	**7**	**9**	**32**	**1**	**0**	**0**	**47**	**4.3**	**35**	**12**	**46**	**7**	**–16**	....	....	....	....	....	....	....	....
	Tulsa Oilers	CHL	22	3	16	19	....	....	....	40	....	....	....	....	....	....	....	....	....	....	....	....	....	....	....	....	....	....
1980-81	**Winnipeg Jets**	**NHL**	**5**	**0**	**1**	**1**	**0**	**1**	**1**	**9**	**0**	**0**	**0**	**1**	**0.0**	**1**	**0**	**9**	**0**	**–8**	....	....	....	....	....	....	....	....
	Tulsa Oilers	CHL	71	10	46	56	....	....	....	94	....	....	....	....	....	....	....	....	....	....	8	1	6	7	6	....	....	....
1981-82	Tulsa Oilers	CHL	79	6	41	47	....	....	....	105	....	....	....	....	....	....	....	....	....	....	3	0	0	0	0	....	....	....
1982-83	Iserlohner EC	Germany	36	6	19	25	....	....	....	38	....	....	....	....	....	....	....	....	....	....	....	....	....	....	....	....	....	....
	NHL Totals		**51**	**2**	**10**	**12**	**2**	**8**	**10**	**41**	**1**	**0**	**0**	**48**	**4.2**	**36**	**12**	**55**	**7**									

CHL Second All-Star Team (1981, 1982)

Signed as a free agent by **Winnipeg**, October 1, 1979.

• COSSETTE, Jacques

RW – R. 5'9", 185 lbs. b: Rouyn, Que., 6/20/1954. Pittsburgh's 2nd, 27th overall, in 1974.

Season	Club	League	GP	G	A	Pts	AG	AA	APts	PIM	PP	SH	GW	S	%	TGF	PGF	TGA	PGA	+/–	GP	G	A	Pts	PIM	PP	SH	GW
1971-72	Montreal Jr. Canadiens	QMJHL	57	27	23	50	....	....	....	121	....	....	....	....	....	....	....	....	....	....	....	....	....	....	....	....	....	....
1972-73	Sorel Black Hawks	QMJHL	64	61	66	127	....	....	....	194	....	....	....	....	....	....	....	....	....	....	....	....	....	....	....	....	....	....
1973-74	Sorel Black Hawks	QMJHL	68	97	117	214	....	....	....	217	....	....	....	....	....	....	....	....	....	....	....	....	....	....	....	....	....	....
1974-75	Hershey Bears	AHL	62	15	17	32	....	....	....	92	....	....	....	....	....	....	....	....	....	....	5	1	1	2	0	....	....	....
1975-76	**Pittsburgh Penguins**	**NHL**	**7**	**0**	**2**	**2**	**0**	**1**	**1**	**9**	**0**	**0**	**0**	**6**	**0.0**	**4**	**0**	**6**	**0**	**–2**	....	....	....	....	....	....	....	....
	Hershey Bears	AHL	59	18	20	38	....	....	....	117	....	....	....	....	....	....	....	....	....	....	10	7	2	9	13	....	....	....
1976-77	Hershey Bears	AHL	71	38	29	67	....	....	....	49	....	....	....	....	....	....	....	....	....	....	6	3	2	5	4	....	....	....
1977-78	**Pittsburgh Penguins**	**NHL**	**19**	**1**	**2**	**3**	**1**	**2**	**3**	**4**	**1**	**0**	**0**	**17**	**5.9**	**6**	**2**	**9**	**0**	**–5**	....	....	....	....	....	....	....	....
	Binghamton Dusters	AHL	57	39	28	67	....	....	....	69	....	....	....	....	....	....	....	....	....	....	....	....	....	....	....	....	....	....
1978-79	**Pittsburgh Penguins**	**NHL**	**38**	**7**	**2**	**9**	**6**	**1**	**7**	**16**	**1**	**0**	**1**	**35**	**20.0**	**19**	**3**	**17**	**0**	**–1**	**3**	**0**	**1**	**1**	**4**	**0**	**0**	**0**
1979-80	Syracuse Firebirds	AHL	78	25	23	48	....	....	....	87	....	....	....	....	....	....	....	....	....	....	4	1	0	1	2	....	....	....
	NHL Totals		**64**	**8**	**6**	**14**	**7**	**4**	**11**	**29**	**2**	**0**	**1**	**58**	**13.8**	**29**	**5**	**32**	**0**		**3**	**0**	**1**	**1**	**4**	**0**	**0**	**0**

QMJHL First All-Star Team (1973, 1974)

• COSTELLO, Rich

Richard C – R. 6', 175 lbs. b: Farmington, MA, 6/27/1963. Philadelphia's 2nd, 37th overall, in 1981.

Season	Club	League	GP	G	A	Pts	AG	AA	APts	PIM	PP	SH	GW	S	%	TGF	PGF	TGA	PGA	+/–	GP	G	A	Pts	PIM	PP	SH	GW
1978-79	Natick Redmen	Hi-School	18	26	32	58	....	....	....	....	....	....	....	....	....	....	....	....	....	....	....	....	....	....	....	....	....	....
1979-80	Natick Redmen	Hi-School	18	30	36	66	....	....	....	....	....	....	....	....	....	....	....	....	....	....	....	....	....	....	....	....	....	....
1980-81	Pickering Pirates	OHA-B	40	18	24	42	....	....	....	35	....	....	....	....	....	....	....	....	....	....	....	....	....	....	....	....	....	....
1981-82	Providence College	ECAC	32	11	16	27	....	....	....	39	....	....	....	....	....	....	....	....	....	....	....	....	....	....	....	....	....	....
1982-83	Providence College	ECAC	43	19	26	45	....	....	....	60	....	....	....	....	....	....	....	....	....	....	....	....	....	....	....	....	....	....
1983-84	United States	Nat-Team	38	7	19	26	....	....	....	31	....	....	....	....	....	....	....	....	....	....	....	....	....	....	....	....	....	....
	Toronto Maple Leafs	**NHL**	**10**	**2**	**1**	**3**	**2**	**1**	**3**	**2**	**1**	**0**	**0**	**7**	**28.6**	**4**	**1**	**8**	**0**	**–5**	....	....	....	....	....	....	....	....
	St. Catharines Saints	AHL	20	0	0	0	....	....	....	12	....	....	....	....	....	....	....	....	....	....	4	1	0	1	0	....	....	....
1984-85	St. Catharines Saints	AHL	80	8	6	14	....	....	....	45	....	....	....	....	....	....	....	....	....	....	....	....	....	....	....	....	....	....
1985-86	**Toronto Maple Leafs**	**NHL**	**2**	**0**	**1**	**1**	**0**	**1**	**1**	**0**	**0**	**0**	**0**	**2**	**0.0**	**1**	**0**	**1**	**0**	**0**	....	....	....	....	....	....	....	....
	St. Catharines Saints	AHL	76	18	22	40	....	....	....	87	....	....	....	....	....	....	....	....	....	....	13	3	6	9	30	....	....	....
1986-87	Newmarket Saints	AHL	48	6	11	17	....	....	....	53	....	....	....	....	....	....	....	....	....	....	....	....	....	....	....	....	....	....
1987-88	SaiPa Lappeenranta	Finland-2	26	10	11	21	....	....	....	46	....	....	....	....	....	....	....	....	....	....	....	....	....	....	....	....	....	....
	Utica Devils	AHL	3	1	1	2	....	....	....	2	....	....	....	....	....	....	....	....	....	....	....	....	....	....	....	....	....	....
1988-89	Schwenninger ERC	Germany	11	6	8	14	....	....	....	14	....	....	....	....	....	....	....	....	....	....	....	....	....	....	....	....	....	....
1989-90	EC Ratingen	Germany-2	29	26	30	56	....	....	....	36	....	....	....	....	....	....	....	....	....	....	....	....	....	....	....	....	....	....
	HC Davos	Switz-2	12	4	11	15	....	....	....	....	....	....	....	....	....	....	....	....	....	....	12	4	10	14	....	....	....	....
1990-91	Albany Choppers	IHL	9	1	3	4	....	....	....	14	....	....	....	....	....	....	....	....	....	....	....	....	....	....	....	....	....	....
	NHL Totals		**12**	**2**	**2**	**4**	**2**	**2**	**4**	**2**	**1**	**0**	**0**	**9**	**22.2**	**5**	**1**	**9**	**0**		....	....	....	....	....	....	....	....

Rights traded to **Toronto** by **Philadelphia** with Hartford's 2nd round choice (previously acquired, Toronto selected Peter Ihnacak) in 1982 Entry Draft and future considerations (Ken Strong) for Darryl Sittler, January 20, 1982.

• COTE, Alain

Alain Gabriel D – R. 6', 207 lbs. b: Montmagny, Que., 4/14/1967. Boston's 1st, 31st overall, in 1985.

Season	Club	League	GP	G	A	Pts	AG	AA	APts	PIM	PP	SH	GW	S	%	TGF	PGF	TGA	PGA	+/–	GP	G	A	Pts	PIM	PP	SH	GW
1982-83	Ste-Foy Gouverneurs	QAAA	46	6	23	29	....	....	....	....	....	....	....	....	....	....	....	....	....	....	....	....	....	....	....	....	....	....
1983-84	Quebec Remparts	QMJHL	60	3	17	20	....	....	....	40	....	....	....	....	....	....	....	....	....	....	5	1	3	4	8	....	....	....
1984-85	Quebec Remparts	QMJHL	68	9	25	34	....	....	....	173	....	....	....	....	....	....	....	....	....	....	4	0	1	1	12	....	....	....
1985-86	Granby Bisons	QMJHL	22	4	12	16	....	....	....	48	....	....	....	....	....	....	....	....	....	....	....	....	....	....	....	....	....	....
	Canada	WJC-A	7	1	4	5	....	....	....	6	....	....	....	....	....	....	....	....	....	....	....	....	....	....	....	....	....	....
	Moncton Golden Flames	AHL	3	0	0	0	....	....	....	0	....	....	....	....	....	....	....	....	....	....	....	....	....	....	....	....	....	....
	Boston Bruins	**NHL**	**32**	**0**	**6**	**6**	**0**	**4**	**4**	**14**	**0**	**0**	**0**	**15**	**0.0**	**25**	**0**	**25**	**5**	**5**	....	....	....	....	....	....	....	....
1986-87	Granby Bisons	QMJHL	43	7	24	31	....	....	....	185	....	....	....	....	....	....	....	....	....	....	4	0	3	3	2	....	....	....
	Boston Bruins	**NHL**	**3**	**0**	**0**	**0**	**0**	**0**	**0**	**0**	**0**	**0**	**0**	**1**	**0.0**	**2**	**0**	**3**	**0**	**–1**	....	....	....	....	....	....	....	....

			REGULAR SEASON																		PLAYOFFS							
Season	Club	League	GP	G	A	Pts	AG	AA	APts	PIM	PP	SH	GW	S	%	TGF	PGF	TGA	PGA	+/-	GP	G	A	Pts	PIM	PP	SH	GW
1987-88	**Boston Bruins**	**NHL**	**2**	**0**	**0**	**0**	**0**	**0**	**0**	**0**	**0**	**0**	**0**	**1**	**0.0**	**0**	**0**	**1**	**0**	**–1**								
	Maine Mariners	AHL	69	9	34	43				108											9	2	4	6	19			
1988-89	**Boston Bruins**	**NHL**	**31**	**2**	**3**	**5**	**2**	**2**	**4**	**51**	**0**	**0**	**0**	**45**	**4.4**	**18**	**0**	**34**	**7**	**–9**								
	Maine Mariners	AHL	37	5	16	21				111																		
1989-90	**Washington Capitals**	**NHL**	**2**	**0**	**0**	**0**	**0**	**0**	**0**	**7**	**0**	**0**	**0**	**2**	**0.0**	**0**	**0**	**3**	**1**	**–2**								
	Baltimore Skipjacks	AHL	57	5	19	24				161											3	0	0	0	9			
1990-91	**Montreal Canadiens**	**NHL**	**28**	**0**	**6**	**6**	**0**	**5**	**5**	**26**	**0**	**0**	**0**	**24**	**0.0**	**35**	**1**	**35**	**9**	**8**	**11**	**0**	**2**	**2**	**26**	**0**	**0**	**0**
	Fredericton Canadiens	AHL	49	8	19	27				110																		
1991-92	**Montreal Canadiens**	**NHL**	**13**	**0**	**3**	**3**	**0**	**2**	**2**	**22**	**0**	**0**	**0**	**6**	**0.0**	**10**	**0**	**7**	**4**	**7**								
	Fredericton Canadiens	AHL	20	1	10	11				24											7	0	1	1	4			
1992-93	Fredericton Canadiens	AHL	61	10	17	27				83																		
	Tampa Bay Lightning	**NHL**	**2**	**0**	**0**	**0**	**0**	**0**	**0**	**0**	**0**	**0**	**0**	**1**	**0.0**	**0**	**0**	**1**	**0**	**–1**								
	Atlanta Knights	IHL	8	1	0	1				0											1	0	0	0	0			
1993-94	**Quebec Nordiques**	**NHL**	**6**	**0**	**0**	**0**	**0**	**0**	**0**	**4**	**0**	**0**	**0**	**4**	**0.0**	**3**	**0**	**5**	**0**	**–2**								
	Cornwall Aces	AHL	67	10	34	44				80											13	0	2	2	10			
1994-95	HK Olimpija Ljubljana	Slovenia	55	15	25	40																						
1995-96	San Francisco Spiders	IHL	80	5	26	31				133											4	0	0	0	10			
1996-97	Quebec Rafales	IHL	76	8	17	25				102											9	0	2	2	30			
1997-98	Yukijrushi-Sapporo	Japan	37	15	19	34				115																		
1998-99	Yukijrushi-Sapporo	Japan	38	5	20	25				49																		
99-2000	Nurnberg Ice Tigers	Germany	58	10	21	31				126																		
	Nurnberg Ice Tigers	EuroHL	6	0	2	2				12																		
	NHL Totals		**119**	**2**	**18**	**20**	**2**	**13**	**15**	**124**	**0**	**0**	**0**	**99**	**2.0**	**93**	**1**	**114**	**26**		**11**	**0**	**2**	**2**	**26**	**0**	**0**	**0**

WJC-A All-Star Team (1986)

Traded to **Washington** by **Boston** for Bobby Gould, September 28, 1989. Traded to **Montreal** by **Washington** for Marc Deschamps, June 22, 1990. Traded to **Tampa Bay** by **Montreal** with Eric Charron and future considerations (Donald Dufresne, June 18, 1993) for Rob Ramage, March 20, 1993. Signed as a free agent by **Quebec**, July 2, 1993.

• COTE, Alain

LW – L. 5'10", 203 lbs. b: Matau, Que., 5/3/1957. Montreal's 4th, 43rd overall, in 1977.

Season	Club	League	GP	G	A	Pts	AG	AA	APts	PIM	PP	SH	GW	S	%	TGF	PGF	TGA	PGA	+/-	GP	G	A	Pts	PIM	PP	SH	GW
1974-75	Chicoutimi Sagueneens	QMJHL	57	15	29	44				43																		
1975-76	Chicoutimi Sagueneens	QMJHL	72	35	49	84				93											5	3	3	6	2			
1976-77	Chicoutimi Sagueneens	QMJHL	56	42	45	87				86											8	1	5	6	14			
1977-78	Quebec Nordiques	WHA	27	3	5	8				8											11	1	2	3	0			
	Hampton Gulls	AHL	36	15	17	32				38																		
1978-79	Quebec Nordiques	WHA	79	14	13	27				23											4	0	0	0	2			
1979-80	**Quebec Nordiques**	**NHL**	**41**	**5**	**11**	**16**	**4**	**8**	**12**	**13**	**0**	**0**	**1**	**58**	**8.6**	**20**	**2**	**26**	**0**	**–8**								
	Syracuse Firebirds	AHL	6	0	5	5				9																		
1980-81	**Quebec Nordiques**	**NHL**	**51**	**8**	**18**	**26**	**6**	**12**	**18**	**64**	**1**	**2**	**2**	**65**	**12.3**	**36**	**2**	**39**	**14**	**9**	**4**	**0**	**0**	**0**	**6**	**0**	**0**	**0**
	Rochester Americans	AHL	23	1	6	7				14																		
1981-82	**Quebec Nordiques**	**NHL**	**79**	**15**	**16**	**31**	**12**	**11**	**23**	**82**	**0**	**0**	**1**	**95**	**15.8**	**50**	**1**	**86**	**26**	**–11**	**16**	**1**	**2**	**3**	**8**	**0**	**0**	**0**
1982-83	**Quebec Nordiques**	**NHL**	**79**	**12**	**28**	**40**	**10**	**19**	**29**	**45**	**0**	**0**	**0**	**88**	**13.6**	**50**	**0**	**79**	**28**	**–1**	**4**	**0**	**3**	**3**	**0**	**0**	**0**	**0**
1983-84	**Quebec Nordiques**	**NHL**	**77**	**19**	**24**	**43**	**15**	**16**	**31**	**41**	**0**	**1**	**1**	**116**	**16.4**	**65**	**0**	**69**	**25**	**21**	**9**	**0**	**2**	**2**	**17**	**0**	**0**	**0**
1984-85	**Quebec Nordiques**	**NHL**	**80**	**13**	**22**	**35**	**11**	**15**	**26**	**31**	**1**	**1**	**0**	**127**	**10.2**	**60**	**1**	**70**	**23**	**12**	**18**	**5**	**5**	**10**	**11**	**0**	**0**	**1**
1985-86	**Quebec Nordiques**	**NHL**	**78**	**13**	**21**	**34**	**10**	**14**	**24**	**29**	**0**	**3**	**2**	**119**	**10.9**	**60**	**1**	**90**	**28**	**–3**	**3**	**1**	**0**	**1**	**0**	**0**	**0**	**0**
1986-87	**Quebec Nordiques**	**NHL**	**80**	**12**	**24**	**36**	**10**	**17**	**27**	**38**	**0**	**2**	**1**	**137**	**8.8**	**64**	**0**	**93**	**25**	**–4**	**13**	**2**	**3**	**5**	**2**	**0**	**0**	**0**
1987-88	**Quebec Nordiques**	**NHL**	**76**	**4**	**18**	**22**	**3**	**13**	**16**	**26**	**0**	**0**	**0**	**84**	**4.8**	**36**	**2**	**60**	**29**	**3**								
1988-89	**Quebec Nordiques**	**NHL**	**55**	**2**	**8**	**10**	**2**	**6**	**8**	**14**	**0**	**1**	**0**	**31**	**6.5**	**20**	**0**	**34**	**13**	**–1**								
	NHL Totals		**696**	**103**	**190**	**293**	**83**	**131**	**214**	**383**	**2**	**10**	**8**	**920**	**11.2**	**461**	**9**	**646**	**211**		**67**	**9**	**15**	**24**	**44**	**0**	**0**	**1**
	Other Major League Totals		106	17	18	35				31											15	1	2	3	2			

Selected by **Quebec** (WHA) in 1977 WHA Amateur Draft, June, 1977. Reclaimed by **Montreal** from **Quebec** prior to Expansion Draft, June 9, 1979. Claimed by **Quebec** from **Montreal** in Expansion Draft, June 13, 1979.

• COTE, Patrick

LW – L. 6'3", 199 lbs. b: Lasalle, Que., 1/24/1975. Dallas' 2nd, 37th overall, in 1995.

Season	Club	League	GP	G	A	Pts	AG	AA	APts	PIM	PP	SH	GW	S	%	TGF	PGF	TGA	PGA	+/-	GP	G	A	Pts	PIM	PP	SH	GW
1992-93	Etoiles St-Laurent	QAAA	STATISTICS NOT AVAILABLE																									
1993-94	Beauport Harfangs	QMJHL	48	2	4	6				230											12	1	0	1	61			
1994-95	Beauport Harfangs	QMJHL	56	20	20	40				314											17	8	8	16	115			
1995-96	**Dallas Stars**	**NHL**	**2**	**0**	**0**	**0**	**0**	**0**	**0**	**5**	**0**	**0**	**0**	**0**	**0.0**	**0**	**0**	**2**	**0**	**–2**								
	Michigan K-Wings	IHL	57	4	6	10				239											3	0	0	0	2			
1996-97	**Dallas Stars**	**NHL**	**3**	**0**	**0**	**0**	**0**	**0**	**0**	**27**	**0**	**0**	**0**	**1**	**0.0**	**0**	**0**	**0**	**0**	**0**								
	Michigan K-Wings	IHL	58	14	10	24				237											4	2	0	2	6			
1997-98	**Dallas Stars**	**NHL**	**3**	**0**	**0**	**0**	**0**	**0**	**0**	**15**	**0**	**0**	**0**	**3**	**0.0**	**0**	**0**	**1**	**0**	**–1**								
	Michigan K-Wings	IHL	4	2	0	2				4																		
1998-99	**Nashville Predators**	**NHL**	**70**	**1**	**2**	**3**	**1**	**2**	**3**	**242**	**0**	**0**	**0**	**21**	**4.8**	**7**	**1**	**13**	**0**	**–7**								
99-2000	**Nashville Predators**	**NHL**	**21**	**0**	**0**	**0**	**0**	**0**	**0**	**70**				**8**	**0.0**					**–7**								
	NHL Totals		**99**	**1**	**2**	**3**	**1**	**2**	**3**	**359**	**0**	**0**	**0**	**33**	**3.0**	**7**	**1**	**16**	**0**									

Claimed by **Nashville** from **Dallas** in Expansion Draft, June 26, 1998. Traded to **Edmonton** by **Nashville** for Phoenix's 5th round choice (previously acquired, Nashville selected Matt Koalska) in 2000 Entry Draft, June 12, 2000.

• COTE, Ray

Raymond C.J. C – R. 5'11", 170 lbs. b: Pincher Creek, Alta., 5/31/1961.

Season	Club	League	GP	G	A	Pts	AG	AA	APts	PIM	PP	SH	GW	S	%	TGF	PGF	TGA	PGA	+/-	GP	G	A	Pts	PIM	PP	SH	GW
1977-78	Pincher Creek Panthers	AJHL	59	13	34	47				12																		
	Billings Bighorns	WCJHL	2	0	1	1				0																		
1978-79	Calgary Chinooks	AJHL	53	17	30	47				35																		
	Calgary Wranglers	WHL	7	2	1	3				0																		
1979-80	Calgary Wranglers	WHL	72	33	34	67				43																		
1980-81	Calgary Wranglers	WHL	70	36	52	88				73											22	10	13	23	11			
1981-82	Wichita Wind	CHL	80	20	34	54				83											7	3	2	5	2			
1982-83	Moncton Alpines	AHL	80	28	63	91				35																		
	Edmonton Oilers	**NHL**																			**14**	**3**	**2**	**5**	**0**	**0**	**0**	**0**
1983-84	**Edmonton Oilers**	**NHL**	**13**	**0**	**0**	**0**	**0**	**0**	**0**	**2**	**0**	**0**	**0**	**12**	**0.0**	**1**	**0**	**6**	**0**	**–5**								
	Moncton Alpines	AHL	66	26	36	62				99																		
1984-85	**Edmonton Oilers**	**NHL**	**2**	**0**	**0**	**0**	**0**	**0**	**0**	**2**	**0**	**0**	**0**	**1**	**0.0**	**0**	**0**	**0**	**0**	**0**								
	Nova Scotia Voyageurs	AHL	79	36	43	79				63											6	2	3	5	0			
1985-86	Schwenninger ERC	Germany	18	12	11	23				14																		
	Canada	Nat-Team	8	1	3	4				6																		
	Nova Scotia Oilers	AHL	20	7	3	10				17																		
1986-87	Canada	Nat-Team	68	20	30	50				34																		
	Adirondack Red Wings	AHL																			9	2	6	8	2			
1987-88	WEV Wien	Austria	21	12	9	21				10																		
1988-89	WEV Wien	Austria	40	18	31	49																						
	Canada	Nat-Team	8	2	2	4				4																		
1989-90	Boro HC	Sweden-2	31	19	23	42				38											3	1	0	1	4			
1990-91	Canada	Nat-Team	18	4	7	11				6																		
1991-92	Mannheimer ERC	Germany	11	3	8	11				0																		
	HC Davos	Switz-2	4	1	0	1																						
	NHL Totals		**15**	**0**	**0**	**0**	**0**	**0**	**0**	**4**	**0**	**0**	**0**	**13**	**0.0**	**1**	**0**	**6**	**0**		**14**	**3**	**2**	**5**	**0**	**0**	**0**	**0**

Signed as a free agent by **Edmonton**, October 6, 1981.

• COTE, Sylvain

D – R. 6', 190 lbs. b: Quebec City, Que., 1/19/1966. Hartford's 1st, 11th overall, in 1984.

			REGULAR SEASON																		PLAYOFFS							
Season	Club	League	GP	G	A	Pts	AG	AA	APts	PIM	PP	SH	GW	S	%	TGF	PGF	TGA	PGA	+/–	GP	G	A	Pts	PIM	PP	SH	GW
1981-82	Ste-Foy Gouverneurs	QAAA	37	1	6	7	....	....	....	....	....	....	....	....	....	....	....	....	....	....	....	....	....	....	....	....	....	....
1982-83	Quebec Remparts	QMJHL	66	10	24	34	....	....	....	50	....	....	....	....	....	....	....	....	....	....	....	....	....	....	....	....	....	....
1983-84	Quebec Remparts	QMJHL	66	15	50	65	....	....	....	89	....	....	....	....	....	....	....	....	....	....	5	1	1	2	0	....	....	....
	Canada	WJC-A	7	0	2	2	....	....	....	13	....	....	....	....	....	....	....	....	....	....	....	....	....	....	....	....	....	....
1984-85	**Hartford Whalers**	**NHL**	**67**	**3**	**9**	**12**	**2**	**6**	**8**	**17**	**1**	**0**	**1**	**90**	**3.3**	**44**	**11**	**64**	**1**	**–30**	....	....	....	....	....	....	....	....
1985-86	Hull Olympiques	QMJHL	26	10	33	43	....	....	....	14	....	....	....	....	....	....	....	....	....	....	13	6	*28	34	22	....	....	....
	Canada	WJC-A	7	1	4	5	....	....	....	4	....	....	....	....	....	....	....	....	....	....	....	....	....	....	....	....	....	....
	Hartford Whalers	**NHL**	**2**	**0**	**0**	**0**	**0**	**0**	**0**	**0**	**0**	**0**	**0**	**0**	**0.0**	**1**	**0**	**0**	**0**	**1**	....	....	....	....	....	....	....	....
	Binghamton Whalers	AHL	12	2	4	6	....	....	....	0	....	....	....	....	....	....	....	....	....	....	....	....	....	....	....	....	....	....
	Hull Olympiques	Mem-Cup	5	0	3	3	....	....	....	14	....	....	....	....	....	....	....	....	....	....	....	....	....	....	....	....	....	....
1986-87	**Hartford Whalers**	**NHL**	**67**	**2**	**8**	**10**	**2**	**6**	**8**	**20**	**0**	**0**	**0**	**100**	**2.0**	**52**	**0**	**56**	**15**	**11**	**2**	**0**	**2**	**2**	**2**	**0**	**0**	**0**
1987-88	**Hartford Whalers**	**NHL**	**67**	**7**	**21**	**28**	**6**	**15**	**21**	**30**	**0**	**1**	**0**	**142**	**4.9**	**65**	**11**	**77**	**15**	**–8**	**6**	**1**	**1**	**2**	**4**	**1**	**0**	**0**
1988-89	**Hartford Whalers**	**NHL**	**78**	**8**	**9**	**17**	**7**	**6**	**13**	**49**	**1**	**0**	**0**	**130**	**6.2**	**74**	**5**	**98**	**22**	**–7**	**3**	**0**	**1**	**1**	**4**	**0**	**0**	**0**
1989-90	**Hartford Whalers**	**NHL**	**28**	**4**	**2**	**6**	**3**	**1**	**4**	**14**	**1**	**0**	**1**	**50**	**8.0**	**24**	**1**	**32**	**11**	**2**	**5**	**0**	**0**	**0**	**2**	**0**	**0**	**0**
1990-91	**Hartford Whalers**	**NHL**	**73**	**7**	**12**	**19**	**6**	**9**	**15**	**17**	**1**	**0**	**0**	**154**	**4.5**	**69**	**14**	**111**	**39**	**–17**	**6**	**0**	**2**	**2**	**2**	**0**	**0**	**0**
1991-92	**Washington Capitals**	**NHL**	**78**	**11**	**29**	**40**	**10**	**22**	**32**	**31**	**6**	**0**	**2**	**151**	**7.3**	**110**	**38**	**74**	**9**	**7**	**7**	**1**	**2**	**3**	**4**	**0**	**0**	**0**
1992-93	**Washington Capitals**	**NHL**	**77**	**21**	**29**	**50**	**17**	**20**	**37**	**34**	**8**	**2**	**3**	**206**	**10.2**	**126**	**37**	**72**	**11**	**28**	**6**	**1**	**1**	**2**	**4**	**0**	**0**	**0**
1993-94	**Washington Capitals**	**NHL**	**84**	**16**	**35**	**51**	**15**	**27**	**42**	**66**	**3**	**2**	**2**	**212**	**7.5**	**139**	**35**	**100**	**26**	**30**	**9**	**1**	**8**	**9**	**6**	**0**	**0**	**0**
1994-95	**Washington Capitals**	**NHL**	**47**	**5**	**14**	**19**	**9**	**21**	**30**	**53**	**1**	**0**	**2**	**124**	**4.0**	**58**	**20**	**51**	**15**	**2**	**7**	**1**	**3**	**4**	**2**	**0**	**0**	**0**
1995-96	**Washington Capitals**	**NHL**	**81**	**5**	**33**	**38**	**5**	**27**	**32**	**40**	**3**	**0**	**2**	**212**	**2.4**	**94**	**32**	**81**	**24**	**5**	**6**	**2**	**0**	**2**	**12**	**1**	**0**	**0**
1996-97	Canada	W-Cup	2	0	1	1	....	....	....	0	....	....	....	....	....	....	....	....	....	....	....	....	....	....	....	....	....	....
	Washington Capitals	**NHL**	**57**	**6**	**18**	**24**	**6**	**16**	**22**	**28**	**2**	**0**	**0**	**131**	**4.6**	**71**	**19**	**56**	**15**	**11**	....	....	....	....	....	....	....	....
1997-98	**Washington Capitals**	**NHL**	**59**	**1**	**15**	**16**	**1**	**15**	**16**	**36**	**0**	**0**	**0**	**83**	**1.2**	**43**	**6**	**51**	**9**	**–5**	....	....	....	....	....	....	....	....
	Toronto Maple Leafs	**NHL**	**12**	**3**	**6**	**9**	**4**	**6**	**10**	**6**	**1**	**0**	**1**	**20**	**15.0**	**16**	**6**	**11**	**3**	**2**	....	....	....	....	....	....	....	....
1998-99	**Toronto Maple Leafs**	**NHL**	**79**	**5**	**24**	**29**	**6**	**23**	**29**	**28**	**0**	**0**	**1**	**119**	**4.2**	**93**	**16**	**76**	**21**	**22**	**17**	**2**	**1**	**3**	**10**	**0**	**0**	**0**
99-2000	**Toronto Maple Leafs**	**NHL**	**3**	**0**	**1**	**1**	**0**	**1**	**1**	**0**	**0**	**0**	**0**	**3**	**0.0**	**3**	**2**	**0**	**0**	**1**	....	....	....	....	....	....	....	....
	Chicago Blackhawks	**NHL**	**45**	**6**	**18**	**24**	**7**	**17**	**24**	**14**	**5**	**0**	**2**	**78**	**7.7**	**52**	**18**	**57**	**19**	**–4**	....	....	....	....	....	....	....	....
	Dallas Stars	**NHL**	**28**	**2**	**8**	**10**	**2**	**7**	**9**	**14**	**0**	**0**	**0**	**47**	**4.3**	**31**	**12**	**13**	**0**	**6**	**23**	**2**	**1**	**3**	**8**	**2**	**0**	**0**
	NHL Totals		**1032**	**112**	**291**	**403**	**108**	**245**	**353**	**497**	**33**	**5**	**17**	**2052**	**5.5**	**1165**	**283**	**1080**	**255**		**97**	**11**	**22**	**33**	**60**	**4**	**0**	**0**

QMJHL Second All-Star Team (1984) • QMJHL First All-Star Team (1986)

Traded to **Washington** by **Hartford** for Washington's 2nd round choice (Andrei Nikolishin) in 1992 Entry Draft, September 8, 1991. Traded to **Toronto** by **Washington** for Jeff Brown, March 24, 1998. Traded to **Chicago** by **Toronto** for Chicago's 2nd round choice in 2001 Entry Draft and a conditional choice in 2001 Entry Draft, October 8, 1999. Traded to **Dallas** by **Chicago** with Dave Manson for Kevin Dean, Derek Plante and Dallas' 2nd round choice in 2001 Entry Draft, February 8, 2000. Signed as a free agent by **Washington**, July 7, 2000.

• COULIS, Tim

Timothy W. LW – L. 6', 200 lbs. b: Kenora, Ont., 2/24/1958. Washington's 2nd, 18th overall, in 1978.

Season	Club	League	GP	G	A	Pts	AG	AA	APts	PIM	PP	SH	GW	S	%	TGF	PGF	TGA	PGA	+/–	GP	G	A	Pts	PIM	PP	SH	GW
1975-76	Sault Ste. Marie Greyhounds	OMJHL	37	15	18	33	....	....	....	226	....	....	....	....	....	....	....	....	....	....	4	1	1	2	16	....	....	....
1976-77	Sault Ste. Marie Greyhounds	OMJHL	27	13	20	33	....	....	....	114	....	....	....	....	....	....	....	....	....	....	....	....	....	....	....	....	....	....
	St. Catharines Fincups	OMJHL	28	10	22	32	....	....	....	136	....	....	....	....	....	....	....	....	....	....	14	4	5	9	20	....	....	....
1977-78	Hamilton Fincups	OMJHL	46	27	25	52	....	....	....	203	....	....	....	....	....	....	....	....	....	....	11	6	3	9	64	....	....	....
1978-79	**Washington Capitals**	**NHL**	DID NOT PLAY – INJURED																									
1979-80	**Washington Capitals**	**NHL**	**19**	**1**	**2**	**3**	**1**	**1**	**2**	**27**	**0**	**0**	**0**	**12**	**8.3**	**5**	**0**	**14**	**3**	**–6**	....	....	....	....	....	....	....	....
	Hershey Bears	AHL	47	6	12	18	....	....	....	138	....	....	....	....	....	....	....	....	....	....	....	....	....	....	....	....	....	....
1980-81	Dallas Black Hawks	CHL	63	16	15	31	....	....	....	149	....	....	....	....	....	....	....	....	....	....	6	2	1	3	24	....	....	....
1981-82	Dallas Black Hawks	CHL	68	20	32	52	....	....	....	209	....	....	....	....	....	....	....	....	....	....	9	5	1	6	92	....	....	....
1982-83	Dallas Black Hawks	CHL	DID NOT PLAY – SUSPENDED																									
1983-84	**Minnesota North Stars**	**NHL**	**2**	**0**	**0**	**0**	**0**	**0**	**0**	**4**	**0**	**0**	**0**	**0**	**0.0**	**0**	**0**	**1**	**0**	**–1**	....	....	....	....	....	....	....	....
	Salt Lake Golden Eagles	CHL	63	25	35	60	....	....	....	225	....	....	....	....	....	....	....	....	....	....	4	1	2	3	35	....	....	....
1984-85	**Minnesota North Stars**	**NHL**	**7**	**1**	**1**	**2**	**1**	**1**	**2**	**34**	**0**	**0**	**0**	**10**	**10.0**	**3**	**0**	**4**	**0**	**–1**	**3**	**1**	**0**	**1**	**2**	**0**	**0**	**1**
	Springfield Indians	AHL	52	13	17	30	....	....	....	86	....	....	....	....	....	....	....	....	....	....	....	....	....	....	....	....	....	....
1985-86	**Minnesota North Stars**	**NHL**	**19**	**2**	**2**	**4**	**2**	**1**	**3**	**73**	**0**	**0**	**0**	**13**	**15.4**	**6**	**0**	**11**	**0**	**–5**	....	....	....	....	....	....	....	....
	Springfield Indians	AHL	13	5	7	12	....	....	....	42	....	....	....	....	....	....	....	....	....	....	....	....	....	....	....	....	....	....
1986-87	Springfield Indians	AHL	38	12	19	31	....	....	....	212	....	....	....	....	....	....	....	....	....	....	....	....	....	....	....	....	....	....
1987-88	Kalamazoo Wings	IHL	18	2	6	8	....	....	....	23	....	....	....	....	....	....	....	....	....	....	....	....	....	....	....	....	....	....
	NHL Totals		**47**	**4**	**5**	**9**	**4**	**3**	**7**	**138**	**0**	**0**	**0**	**35**	**11.4**	**14**	**0**	**30**	**3**		**3**	**1**	**0**	**1**	**2**	**0**	**0**	**1**

• Missed entire 1978-79 season recovering from broken wrist, September, 1978. Traded to **Toronto** by **Washington** with Robert Picard and Washington's 2nd round choice (Bob McGill) in 1980 Entry Draft for Mike Palmateer and Toronto's 3rd round choice (Torrie Robertson), June 11, 1980. Signed as a free agent by **Vancouver**, October 13, 1981. • Suspended for entire 1982-83 season for attack on referee Bob Hall, April 24, 1982. Signed as a free agent by **Minnesota**, July 2, 1983.

• COULTER, Neal

Neal M. RW – R. 6'2", 190 lbs. b: London, Ont., 1/2/1963. NY Islanders' 4th, 63rd overall, in 1981.

Season	Club	League	GP	G	A	Pts	AG	AA	APts	PIM	PP	SH	GW	S	%	TGF	PGF	TGA	PGA	+/–	GP	G	A	Pts	PIM	PP	SH	GW
1979-80	Oakridge Selects	OMHA	60	35	30	65	....	....	....	150	....	....	....	....	....	....	....	....	....	....	....	....	....	....	....	....	....	....
1980-81	London Diamonds	OHA-B	17	13	7	20	....	....	....	38	....	....	....	....	....	....	....	....	....	....	....	....	....	....	....	....	....	....
	Toronto Marlboros	OMJHL	19	4	3	7	....	....	....	22	....	....	....	....	....	....	....	....	....	....	5	0	3	3	0	....	....	....
1981-82	Toronto Marlboros	OHL	62	14	16	30	....	....	....	79	....	....	....	....	....	....	....	....	....	....	....	....	....	....	....	....	....	....
1982-83	Toronto Marlboros	OHL	59	13	37	50	....	....	....	60	....	....	....	....	....	....	....	....	....	....	4	2	1	3	2	....	....	....
	Indianapolis Checkers	CHL	3	0	1	1	....	....	....	0	....	....	....	....	....	....	....	....	....	....	....	....	....	....	....	....	....	....
1983-84	Toledo Goaldiggers	IHL	5	1	3	4	....	....	....	0	....	....	....	....	....	....	....	....	....	....	....	....	....	....	....	....	....	....
	Indianapolis Checkers	CHL	58	7	10	17	....	....	....	25	....	....	....	....	....	....	....	....	....	....	4	2	0	2	0	....	....	....
1984-85	Springfield Indians	AHL	2	1	0	1	....	....	....	0	....	....	....	....	....	....	....	....	....	....	....	....	....	....	....	....	....	....
	Indianapolis Checkers	IHL	82	31	26	57	....	....	....	95	....	....	....	....	....	....	....	....	....	....	7	3	1	4	9	....	....	....
1985-86	**New York Islanders**	**NHL**	**16**	**3**	**4**	**7**	**2**	**3**	**5**	**4**	**0**	**0**	**0**	**17**	**17.6**	**9**	**0**	**13**	**3**	**–1**	....	....	....	....	....	....	....	....
	Springfield Indians	AHL	60	17	9	26	....	....	....	92	....	....	....	....	....	....	....	....	....	....	....	....	....	....	....	....	....	....
1986-87	**New York Islanders**	**NHL**	**9**	**2**	**1**	**3**	**2**	**1**	**3**	**7**	**0**	**0**	**0**	**5**	**40.0**	**4**	**0**	**9**	**3**	**–2**	....	....	....	....	....	....	....	....
	Springfield Indians	AHL	47	12	13	25	....	....	....	63	....	....	....	....	....	....	....	....	....	....	....	....	....	....	....	....	....	....
1987-88	**New York Islanders**	**NHL**	**1**	**0**	**0**	**0**	**0**	**0**	**0**	**0**	**0**	**0**	**0**	**0**	**0.0**	**0**	**0**	**1**	**0**	**–1**	....	....	....	....	....	....	....	....
	Springfield Indians	AHL	27	11	4	15	....	....	....	33	....	....	....	....	....	....	....	....	....	....	....	....	....	....	....	....	....	....
	NHL Totals		**26**	**5**	**5**	**10**	**4**	**4**	**8**	**11**	**0**	**0**	**0**	**22**	**22.7**	**13**	**0**	**23**	**6**		....	....	....	....	....	....	....	....

• COURNOYER, Yvan

Yvan Serge "The Roadrunner" RW – L. 5'7", 178 lbs. b: Drummondville, Que., 11/22/1943. **HHOF**

Season	Club	League	GP	G	A	Pts	AG	AA	APts	PIM	PP	SH	GW	S	%	TGF	PGF	TGA	PGA	+/–	GP	G	A	Pts	PIM	PP	SH	GW
1960-61	Lachine Maroons	MMJHL	42	37	31	68	....	....	....	....	....	....	....	....	....	....	....	....	....	....	....	....	....	....	....	....	....	....
1961-62	Montreal Jr. Canadiens	OHA-Jr.	35	15	16	31	....	....	....	8	....	....	....	....	....	....	....	....	....	....	6	4	4	8	0	....	....	....
1962-63	Montreal Jr. Canadiens	OHA-Jr.	36	37	27	64	....	....	....	24	....	....	....	....	....	....	....	....	....	....	10	3	4	7	6	....	....	....
1963-64	Montreal Jr. Canadiens	OHA-Jr.	53	*63	48	111	....	....	....	30	....	....	....	....	....	....	....	....	....	....	17	*19	8	27	15	....	....	....
	Montreal Canadiens	**NHL**	**5**	**4**	**0**	**4**	**5**	**0**	**5**	**0**	....	....	....	....	....	....	....	....	....	....	....	....	....	....	....	....	....	....
1964-65♦	**Montreal Canadiens**	**NHL**	**55**	**7**	**10**	**17**	**8**	**10**	**18**	**10**	....	....	....	....	....	....	....	....	....	....	**12**	**3**	**1**	**4**	**0**	**3**	**0**	**1**
	Quebec Aces	AHL	7	2	1	3	....	....	....	0	....	....	....	....	....	....	....	....	....	....	....	....	....	....	....	....	....	....
1965-66♦	**Montreal Canadiens**	**NHL**	**65**	**18**	**11**	**29**	**20**	**10**	**30**	**8**	....	....	....	....	....	....	....	....	....	....	**10**	**2**	**3**	**5**	**2**	**1**	**0**	**1**
1966-67	**Montreal Canadiens**	**NHL**	**69**	**25**	**15**	**40**	**29**	**15**	**44**	**14**	....	....	....	....	....	....	....	....	....	....	**10**	**2**	**3**	**5**	**6**	**2**	**0**	**1**
1967-68♦	**Montreal Canadiens**	**NHL**	**64**	**28**	**32**	**60**	**33**	**32**	**65**	**23**	**7**	**1**	**4**	**222**	**12.6**	**85**	**33**	**33**	**0**	**19**	**13**	**6**	**8**	**14**	**4**	**3**	**0**	**1**
1968-69♦	**Montreal Canadiens**	**NHL**	**76**	**43**	**44**	**87**	**46**	**39**	**85**	**31**	**14**	**0**	**8**	**245**	**17.6**	**120**	**37**	**64**	**0**	**19**	**14**	**4**	**7**	**11**	**5**	**0**	**2**	**2**
1969-70	**Montreal Canadiens**	**NHL**	**72**	**27**	**36**	**63**	**29**	**34**	**63**	**23**	**10**	**0**	**4**	**233**	**11.6**	**87**	**39**	**47**	**0**	**1**	....	....	....	....	....	....	....	....
1970-71♦	**Montreal Canadiens**	**NHL**	**65**	**37**	**36**	**73**	**37**	**30**	**67**	**21**	**18**	**0**	**5**	**197**	**18.8**	**110**	**47**	**43**	**0**	**20**	**20**	**10**	**12**	**22**	**6**	**2**	**0**	**1**
1971-72	**Montreal Canadiens**	**NHL**	**73**	**47**	**36**	**83**	**47**	**31**	**78**	**15**	**18**	**0**	**5**	**208**	**22.6**	**128**	**51**	**54**	**0**	**23**	**6**	**2**	**1**	**3**	**2**	**0**	**0**	**0**
1972-73	Team Canada	Summit-72	8	3	2	5	....	....	....	2	....	....	....	....	....	....	....	....	....	....	....	....	....	....	....	....	....	....
♦	**Montreal Canadiens**	**NHL**	**67**	**40**	**39**	**79**	**38**	**31**	**69**	**18**	**6**	**0**	**4**	**194**	**20.6**	**117**	**25**	**42**	**0**	**50**	**17**	***15**	**10**	***25**	**2**	**3**	**0**	**3**
1973-74	**Montreal Canadiens**	**NHL**	**67**	**40**	**33**	**73**	**39**	**27**	**66**	**18**	**10**	**0**	**9**	**187**	**21.4**	**107**	**31**	**60**	**0**	**16**	**6**	**5**	**2**	**7**	**2**	**0**	**0**	**2**
1974-75	**Montreal Canadiens**	**NHL**	**76**	**29**	**45**	**74**	**25**	**34**	**59**	**32**	**11**	**0**	**2**	**176**	**16.5**	**116**	**48**	**52**	**0**	**16**	**11**	**5**	**6**	**11**	**4**	**2**	**0**	**0**
1975-76♦	**Montreal Canadiens**	**NHL**	**71**	**32**	**36**	**68**	**28**	**27**	**55**	**20**	**8**	**0**	**12**	**163**	**19.6**	**103**	**38**	**28**	**0**	**37**	**13**	**3**	**6**	**9**	**4**	**2**	**0**	**1**

			REGULAR SEASON																		PLAYOFFS							
Season	**Club**	**League**	**GP**	**G**	**A**	**Pts**	**AG**	**AA**	**APts**	**PIM**	**PP**	**SH**	**GW**	**S**	**%**	**TGF**	**PGF**	**TGA**	**PGA**	**+/–**	**GP**	**G**	**A**	**Pts**	**PIM**	**PP**	**SH**	**GW**
1976-77♦	**Montreal Canadiens**	**NHL**	**60**	**25**	**28**	**53**	**23**	**22**	**45**	**8**	**6**	**0**	**2**	**122**	**20.5**	**70**	**14**	**29**	**0**	**27**	....	....	....	....	....	....	....	....
1977-78♦	**Montreal Canadiens**	**NHL**	**68**	**24**	**29**	**53**	**22**	**22**	**44**	**12**	**4**	**0**	**6**	**125**	**19.2**	**75**	**16**	**20**	**0**	**39**	**15**	**7**	**4**	**11**	**10**	**0**	**0**	**2**
1978-79♦	**Montreal Canadiens**	**NHL**	**15**	**2**	**5**	**7**	**2**	**4**	**6**	**2**	**0**	**0**	**0**	**23**	**8.7**	**11**	**3**	**3**	**0**	**5**	....	....	....	....	....	....	....	....
	NHL Totals		**968**	**428**	**435**	**863**	**431**	**368**	**799**	**255**	....	....	....	....	....	....	....	....	....	....	**147**	**64**	**63**	**127**	**47**	....	....	....

NHL Second All-Star Team (1969, 1971, 1972, 1973) • Won Conn Smythe Trophy (1973) • Played in NHL All-Star Game (1967, 1971, 1972, 1973, 1974, 1978)

• Missed remainder of 1978-79 season recovering from eventual career-ending back surgery, December, 1978.

• COURTEAU, Yves

RW – L. 6', 195 lbs. b: Montreal, Que., 4/25/1964. Detroit's 2nd, 23rd overall, in 1982.

Season	Club	League	GP	G	A	Pts	AG	AA	APts	PIM	PP	SH	GW	S	%	TGF	PGF	TGA	PGA	+/–	GP	G	A	Pts	PIM	PP	SH	GW
1979-80	Laval Insulaires	QAAA	42	51	44	95	....	....	....	....	....	....	....	....	....	....	....	....	....	....	....	....	....	....	....	....	....	....
1980-81	Laval Voisins	QMJHL	70	24	39	63	....	....	....	80	....	....	....	....	....	....	....	....	....	....	....	....	....	....	....	....	....	....
1981-82	Laval Voisins	QMJHL	64	30	38	68	....	....	....	15	....	....	....	....	....	....	....	....	....	....	18	14	13	27	28	....	....	....
1982-83	Laval Voisins	QMJHL	68	44	78	122	....	....	....	52	....	....	....	....	....	....	....	....	....	....	12	4	11	15	0	....	....	....
1983-84	Laval Voisins	QMJHL	62	45	75	120	....	....	....	52	....	....	....	....	....	....	....	....	....	....	14	11	16	27	6	....	....	....
	Canada	WJC-A	7	0	1	1	....	....	....	0	....	....	....	....	....	....	....	....	....	....	....	....	....	....	....	....	....	....
	Laval Voisins	Mem-Cup	3	2	3	5	....	....	....	0	....	....	....	....	....	....	....	....	....	....	....	....	....	....	....	....	....	....
1984-85	**Calgary Flames**	**NHL**	**14**	**1**	**4**	**5**	**1**	**3**	**4**	**4**	**0**	**0**	**1**	**18**	**5.6**	**9**	**0**	**7**	**0**	**2**	....	....	....	....	....	....	....	....
	Moncton Golden Flames	AHL	59	19	21	40	....	....	....	32	....	....	....	....	....	....	....	....	....	....	....	....	....	....	....	....	....	....
1985-86	**Calgary Flames**	**NHL**	**4**	**1**	**1**	**2**	**1**	**1**	**2**	**0**	**0**	**0**	**0**	**7**	**14.3**	**2**	**0**	**3**	**2**	**1**	**1**	**0**	**0**	**0**	**0**	**0**	**0**	**0**
	Moncton Golden Flames	AHL	70	26	22	48	....	....	....	19	....	....	....	....	....	....	....	....	....	....	10	4	2	6	5	....	....	....
1986-87	**Hartford Whalers**	**NHL**	**4**	**0**	**0**	**0**	**0**	**0**	**0**	**0**	**0**	**0**	**0**	**4**	**0.0**	**1**	**0**	**7**	**0**	**–6**	....	....	....	....	....	....	....	....
	Binghamton Whalers	AHL	57	15	28	43	....	....	....	8	....	....	....	....	....	....	....	....	....	....	7	1	4	5	12	....	....	....
1987-88	Binghamton Whalers	AHL	25	15	22	37	....	....	....	22	....	....	....	....	....	....	....	....	....	....	4	2	0	2	0	....	....	....
	NHL Totals		**22**	**2**	**5**	**7**	**2**	**4**	**6**	**4**	**0**	**0**	**1**	**29**	**6.9**	**12**	**0**	**17**	**2**		**1**	**0**	**0**	**0**	**0**	**0**	**0**	**0**

QMJHL Second All-Star Team (1984)

Rights traded to **Calgary** by **Detroit** for Bobby Francis, December 2, 1982. Traded to **Hartford** by **Calgary** for Mark Paterson, October 7, 1986. • Suffered eventual career-ending stomach injury in training camp, October, 1987.

• COURTENAY, Ed

Edward Emmett RW – R. 6'4", 215 lbs. b: Verdun, Que., 2/2/1968.

Season	Club	League	GP	G	A	Pts	AG	AA	APts	PIM	PP	SH	GW	S	%	TGF	PGF	TGA	PGA	+/–	GP	G	A	Pts	PIM	PP	SH	GW
1985-86	Lac St-Louis Lions	QAAA	37	37	30	67	....	....	....	....	....	....	....	....	....	....	....	....	....	....	....	....	....	....	....	....	....	....
	Laval Titan	QMJHL	2	0	0	0	....	....	....	0	....	....	....	....	....	....	....	....	....	....	8	2	4	6	2	....	....	....
1986-87	Laval Titan	QMJHL	48	15	20	35	....	....	....	12	....	....	....	....	....	....	....	....	....	....	1	0	0	0	0	....	....	....
1987-88	Granby Bisons	QMJHL	54	37	34	71	....	....	....	19	....	....	....	....	....	....	....	....	....	....	5	1	1	2	2	....	....	....
1988-89	Granby Bisons	QMJHL	68	59	55	114	....	....	....	68	....	....	....	....	....	....	....	....	....	....	4	1	1	2	22	....	....	....
	Kalamazoo Wings	IHL	1	0	0	0	....	....	....	0	....	....	....	....	....	....	....	....	....	....	1	0	0	0	2	....	....	....
1989-90	Kalamazoo Wings	IHL	57	25	28	53	....	....	....	16	....	....	....	....	....	....	....	....	....	....	3	0	0	0	0	....	....	....
1990-91	Kalamazoo Wings	IHL	76	35	36	71	....	....	....	37	....	....	....	....	....	....	....	....	....	....	8	2	3	5	12	....	....	....
1991-92	**San Jose Sharks**	**NHL**	**5**	**0**	**0**	**0**	**0**	**0**	**0**	**0**	**0**	**0**	**0**	**7**	**0.0**	**1**	**0**	**7**	**0**	**–6**	....	....	....	....	....	....	....	....
	Kansas City Blades	IHL	36	14	12	26	....	....	....	46	....	....	....	....	....	....	....	....	....	....	15	8	9	17	15	....	....	....
1992-93	**San Jose Sharks**	**NHL**	**39**	**7**	**13**	**20**	**6**	**9**	**15**	**10**	**2**	**0**	**1**	**56**	**12.5**	**26**	**16**	**25**	**0**	**–15**	....	....	....	....	....	....	....	....
	Kansas City Blades	IHL	32	15	12	27	....	....	....	25	....	....	....	....	....	....	....	....	....	....	....	....	....	....	....	....	....	....
1993-94	Kansas City Blades	IHL	62	27	21	48	....	....	....	60	....	....	....	....	....	....	....	....	....	....	....	....	....	....	....	....	....	....
1994-95	Chicago Wolves	IHL	47	14	16	30	....	....	....	20	....	....	....	....	....	....	....	....	....	....	....	....	....	....	....	....	....	....
	Peoria Rivermen	IHL	9	5	0	5	....	....	....	4	....	....	....	....	....	....	....	....	....	....	9	5	3	8	2	....	....	....
1995-96	San Francisco Spiders	IHL	20	6	3	9	....	....	....	8	....	....	....	....	....	....	....	....	....	....	....	....	....	....	....	....	....	....
	Reno Renegades	WCHL	7	3	7	10	....	....	....	8	....	....	....	....	....	....	....	....	....	....	....	....	....	....	....	....	....	....
	Jacksonville Lizard Kings	ECHL	3	0	2	2	....	....	....	4	....	....	....	....	....	....	....	....	....	....	18	5	12	17	23	....	....	....
1996-97	South Carolina Stingrays	ECHL	68	54	56	*110	....	....	....	70	....	....	....	....	....	....	....	....	....	....	....	....	....	....	....	....	....	....
1997-98	Sheffield Steelers	Britain	40	27	21	48	....	....	....	16	....	....	....	....	....	....	....	....	....	....	8	4	4	8	14	....	....	....
1998-99	Sheffield Steelers	BH-Cup	8	5	1	6	....	....	....	25	....	....	....	....	....	....	....	....	....	....	....	....	....	....	....	....	....	....
	Sheffield Steelers	Britain	42	26	26	52	....	....	....	12	....	....	....	....	....	....	....	....	....	....	6	5	3	8	0	....	....	....
99-2000	Sheffield Steelers	BH-Cup	9	5	7	12	....	....	....	2	....	....	....	....	....	....	....	....	....	....	....	....	....	....	....	....	....	....
	Sheffield Steelers	Britain	40	32	33	65	....	....	....	36	....	....	....	....	....	....	....	....	....	....	7	4	1	5	2	....	....	....
	NHL Totals		**44**	**7**	**13**	**20**	**6**	**9**	**15**	**10**	**2**	**0**	**1**	**63**	**11.1**	**27**	**16**	**32**	**0**		....	....	....	....	....	....	....	....

QMJHL Second All-Star Team (1989) • ECHL First All-Star Team (1997)

Signed as a free agent by **Minnesota**, October 1, 1989. Claimed by **San Jose** from **Minnesota** in Dispersal Draft, May 30, 1991.

• COURTNALL, Geoff

Geoff Lawton "7-11" LW – L. 6'1", 204 lbs. b: Duncan, B.C., 8/18/1962.

Season	Club	League	GP	G	A	Pts	AG	AA	APts	PIM	PP	SH	GW	S	%	TGF	PGF	TGA	PGA	+/–	GP	G	A	Pts	PIM	PP	SH	GW
1980-81	Cowichan Valley Capitals	BCJHL	STATISTICS NOT AVAILABLE																									
	Victoria Cougars	WHL	11	3	4	7	....	....	....	6	....	....	....	....	....	....	....	....	....	....	15	2	1	3	7	....	....	....
	Victoria Cougars	Mem-Cup	4	0	0	0	....	....	....	0	....	....	....	....	....	....	....	....	....	....	....	....	....	....	....	....	....	....
1981-82	Victoria Cougars	WHL	72	35	57	92	....	....	....	100	....	....	....	....	....	....	....	....	....	....	4	1	0	1	2	....	....	....
1982-83	Victoria Cougars	WHL	71	41	73	114	....	....	....	186	....	....	....	....	....	....	....	....	....	....	12	6	7	13	42	....	....	....
1983-84	**Boston Bruins**	**NHL**	**4**	**0**	**0**	**0**	**0**	**0**	**0**	**0**	**0**	**0**	**0**	**1**	**0.0**	**1**	**0**	**2**	**0**	**–1**	....	....	....	....	....	....	....	....
	Hershey Bears	AHL	74	14	12	26	....	....	....	51	....	....	....	....	....	....	....	....	....	....	....	....	....	....	....	....	....	....
1984-85	**Boston Bruins**	**NHL**	**64**	**12**	**16**	**28**	**10**	**11**	**21**	**82**	**0**	**0**	**1**	**91**	**13.2**	**35**	**0**	**38**	**0**	**–3**	**5**	**0**	**2**	**2**	**7**	**0**	**0**	**0**
	Hershey Bears	AHL	9	8	4	12	....	....	....	4	....	....	....	....	....	....	....	....	....	....	....	....	....	....	....	....	....	....
1985-86	**Boston Bruins**	**NHL**	**64**	**21**	**16**	**37**	**17**	**11**	**28**	**61**	**2**	**0**	**4**	**161**	**13.0**	**53**	**9**	**43**	**0**	**1**	**3**	**0**	**0**	**0**	**2**	**0**	**0**	**0**
	Moncton Golden Flames	AHL	12	8	8	16	....	....	....	6	....	....	....	....	....	....	....	....	....	....	....	....	....	....	....	....	....	....
1986-87	**Boston Bruins**	**NHL**	**65**	**13**	**23**	**36**	**11**	**17**	**28**	**117**	**2**	**0**	**1**	**178**	**7.3**	**48**	**11**	**41**	**0**	**–4**	**1**	**0**	**0**	**0**	**0**	**0**	**0**	**0**
1987-88	**Boston Bruins**	**NHL**	**62**	**32**	**26**	**58**	**27**	**19**	**46**	**108**	**8**	**0**	**4**	**220**	**14.5**	**86**	**25**	**37**	**0**	**24**	....	....	....	....	....	....	....	....
♦	**Edmonton Oilers**	**NHL**	**12**	**4**	**4**	**8**	**3**	**3**	**6**	**15**	**0**	**0**	**1**	**32**	**12.5**	**10**	**0**	**9**	**0**	**1**	**19**	**0**	**3**	**3**	**23**	**0**	**0**	**0**
1988-89	**Washington Capitals**	**NHL**	**79**	**42**	**38**	**80**	**36**	**27**	**63**	**112**	**16**	**0**	**6**	**239**	**17.6**	**114**	**52**	**52**	**1**	**11**	**6**	**2**	**5**	**7**	**12**	**1**	**0**	**0**
1989-90	Washington Capitals	Fr-Tour	4	4	1	5	....	....	....	4	....	....	....	....	....	....	....	....	....	....	....	....	....	....	....	....	....	....
	Washington Capitals	**NHL**	**80**	**35**	**39**	**74**	**30**	**28**	**58**	**104**	**9**	**0**	**2**	**307**	**11.4**	**114**	**35**	**52**	**0**	**27**	**15**	**4**	**9**	**13**	**32**	**1**	**0**	**2**
1990-91	**St. Louis Blues**	**NHL**	**66**	**27**	**30**	**57**	**25**	**23**	**48**	**56**	**9**	**0**	**6**	**216**	**12.5**	**85**	**23**	**43**	**0**	**19**	....	....	....	....	....	....	....	....
	Vancouver Canucks	**NHL**	**11**	**6**	**2**	**8**	**5**	**2**	**7**	**8**	**3**	**0**	**2**	**47**	**12.8**	**20**	**9**	**21**	**7**	**–3**	**6**	**3**	**5**	**8**	**4**	**0**	**0**	**0**
	Canada	WEC-A	10	5	1	6	....	....	....	16	....	....	....	....	....	....	....	....	....	....	....	....	....	....	....	....	....	....
1991-92	**Vancouver Canucks**	**NHL**	**70**	**23**	**34**	**57**	**21**	**26**	**47**	**116**	**12**	**0**	**3**	**281**	**8.2**	**81**	**38**	**50**	**1**	**–6**	**12**	**6**	**8**	**14**	**20**	**2**	**0**	**1**
1992-93	**Vancouver Canucks**	**NHL**	**84**	**31**	**46**	**77**	**26**	**32**	**58**	**167**	**9**	**0**	**11**	**214**	**14.5**	**109**	**27**	**56**	**1**	**27**	**12**	**4**	**10**	**14**	**12**	**1**	**0**	**1**
1993-94	**Vancouver Canucks**	**NHL**	**82**	**26**	**44**	**70**	**24**	**34**	**58**	**123**	**12**	**1**	**2**	**264**	**9.8**	**114**	**47**	**68**	**16**	**15**	**24**	**9**	**10**	**19**	**51**	**0**	**1**	**3**
1994-95	**Vancouver Canucks**	**NHL**	**45**	**16**	**18**	**34**	**28**	**27**	**55**	**81**	**7**	**0**	**1**	**144**	**11.1**	**51**	**24**	**30**	**5**	**2**	**11**	**4**	**2**	**6**	**34**	**3**	**1**	**1**
1995-96	**St. Louis Blues**	**NHL**	**69**	**24**	**16**	**40**	**24**	**13**	**37**	**101**	**7**	**1**	**1**	**228**	**10.5**	**60**	**26**	**57**	**14**	**–9**	**13**	**0**	**3**	**3**	**14**	**0**	**0**	**0**
1996-97	**St. Louis Blues**	**NHL**	**82**	**17**	**40**	**57**	**18**	**36**	**54**	**86**	**4**	**0**	**2**	**203**	**8.4**	**86**	**21**	**64**	**2**	**3**	**6**	**3**	**1**	**4**	**23**	**1**	**0**	**2**
1997-98	**St. Louis Blues**	**NHL**	**79**	**31**	**31**	**62**	**36**	**30**	**66**	**94**	**6**	**0**	**5**	**189**	**16.4**	**86**	**24**	**51**	**1**	**12**	**10**	**2**	**8**	**10**	**18**	**1**	**0**	**0**
1998-99	**St. Louis Blues**	**NHL**	**24**	**5**	**7**	**12**	**6**	**7**	**13**	**28**	**1**	**0**	**2**	**60**	**8.3**	**20**	**8**	**10**	**0**	**2**	**13**	**2**	**4**	**6**	**10**	**2**	**0**	**0**
99-2000	**St. Louis Blues**	**NHL**	**6**	**2**	**2**	**4**	**2**	**2**	**4**	**6**	**0**	**0**	**1**	**15**	**13.3**	**7**	**3**	**1**	**0**	**3**	....	....	....	....	....	....	....	....
	NHL Totals		**1048**	**367**	**432**	**799**	**349**	**348**	**697**	**1465**	**107**	**2**	**55**	**3090**	**11.9**	**1180**	**382**	**725**	**48**		**156**	**39**	**70**	**109**	**262**	**12**	**2**	**10**

• Brother of Russ

Signed as a free agent by **Boston**, July 6, 1983. Traded to **Edmonton** by **Boston** with Bill Ranford and Boston's 2nd round choice (Petro Koivunen) in 1988 Entry Draft for Andy Moog, March 8, 1988. Rights traded to **Washington** by **Edmonton** for Greg C. Adams, July 22, 1988. Traded to **St. Louis** by **Washington** for Peter Zezel and Mike Lalor, July 13, 1990. Traded to **Vancouver** by **St. Louis** with Robert Dirk, Sergio Momesso, Cliff Ronning and St. Louis' 5th round choice (Brian Loney) in 1992 Entry Draft for Dan Quinn and Garth Butcher, March 5, 1991. Signed as a free agent by **St. Louis**, July 14, 1995. • Suffered eventual career-ending head injury in game vs. San Jose, November 27, 1998. • Officially announced retirement, November 18, 1999.

• COURTNALL, Russ

RW – R. 5'11", 185 lbs. b: Duncan, B.C., 6/2/1965. Toronto's 1st, 7th overall, in 1983.

			REGULAR SEASON																		PLAYOFFS							
Season	Club	League	GP	G	A	Pts	AG	AA	APts	PIM	PP	SH	GW	S	%	TGF	PGF	TGA	PGA	+/-	GP	G	A	Pts	PIM	PP	SH	GW
1981-82	Notre Dame Midget Hounds	SAHA	STATISTICS NOT AVAILABLE																									
1982-83	Victoria Cougars	WHL	60	36	61	97	....	....	....	33	....	....	....	....	....	....	....	....	....	....	12	11	7	18	6	....	....	....
1983-84	Victoria Cougars	WHL	32	29	37	66	....	....	....	63	....	....	....	....	....	....	....	....	....	....	....	....	....	....	....	....	....	....
	Canada	WJC-A	7	7	6	13	....	....	....	0	....	....	....	....	....	....	....	....	....	....	....	....	....	....	....	....	....	....
	Canada	Nat-Team	16	4	7	11	....	....	....	10	....	....	....	....	....	....	....	....	....	....	....	....	....	....	....	....	....	....
	Canada	Olympics	7	1	3	4	....	....	....	2	....	....	....	....	....	....	....	....	....	....	....	....	....	....	....	....	....	....
	Toronto Maple Leafs	**NHL**	**14**	**3**	**9**	**12**	**2**	**6**	**8**	**6**	**1**	**0**	**0**	**29**	**10.3**	**17**	**3**	**15**	**1**	**0**	....	....	....	....	....	....	....	....
1984-85	**Toronto Maple Leafs**	**NHL**	**69**	**12**	**10**	**22**	**10**	**7**	**17**	**44**	**0**	**2**	**1**	**130**	**9.2**	**34**	**4**	**56**	**3**	**-23**	....	....	....	....	....	....	....	....
1985-86	**Toronto Maple Leafs**	**NHL**	**73**	**22**	**38**	**60**	**18**	**26**	**44**	**52**	**3**	**1**	**4**	**203**	**10.8**	**85**	**10**	**86**	**11**	**0**	**10**	**3**	**6**	**9**	**8**	**1**	**0**	**0**
1986-87	**Toronto Maple Leafs**	**NHL**	**79**	**29**	**44**	**73**	**25**	**32**	**57**	**90**	**3**	**6**	**3**	**282**	**10.3**	**104**	**30**	**110**	**16**	**-20**	**13**	**3**	**4**	**7**	**11**	**1**	**0**	**0**
1987-88	**Toronto Maple Leafs**	**NHL**	**65**	**23**	**26**	**49**	**20**	**19**	**39**	**47**	**6**	**3**	**1**	**212**	**10.8**	**80**	**28**	**78**	**10**	**-16**	**6**	**2**	**1**	**3**	**0**	**0**	**0**	**0**
1988-89	**Toronto Maple Leafs**	**NHL**	**9**	**1**	**1**	**2**	**1**	**1**	**2**	**4**	**0**	**1**	**0**	**11**	**9.1**	**4**	**0**	**7**	**1**	**-2**	....	....	....	....	....	....	....	....
	Montreal Canadiens	**NHL**	**64**	**22**	**17**	**39**	**19**	**12**	**31**	**15**	**7**	**0**	**3**	**136**	**16.2**	**57**	**12**	**35**	**1**	**11**	**21**	**8**	**5**	**13**	**18**	**1**	**0**	**2**
1989-90	**Montreal Canadiens**	**NHL**	**80**	**27**	**32**	**59**	**23**	**23**	**46**	**27**	**3**	**0**	**2**	**294**	**9.2**	**79**	**12**	**62**	**9**	**14**	**11**	**5**	**1**	**6**	**10**	**0**	**0**	**0**
1990-91	Montreal Canadiens	Fr-Tour	3	1	0	1	....	....	....	4	....	....	....	....	....	....	....	....	....	....	....	....	....	....	....	....	....	....
	Montreal Canadiens	**NHL**	**79**	**26**	**50**	**76**	**24**	**38**	**62**	**29**	**5**	**1**	**5**	**279**	**9.3**	**100**	**29**	**93**	**27**	**5**	**13**	**8**	**3**	**11**	**7**	**2**	**2**	**1**
	Canada	WEC-A	2	1	3	4	....	....	....	0	....	....	....	....	....	....	....	....	....	....	....	....	....	....	....	....	....	....
1991-92	Canada	Can-Cup	8	0	2	2	....	....	....	0	....	....	....	....	....	....	....	....	....	....	....	....	....	....	....	....	....	....
	Montreal Canadiens	**NHL**	**27**	**7**	**14**	**21**	**6**	**11**	**17**	**6**	**0**	**1**	**1**	**63**	**11.1**	**21**	**2**	**19**	**6**	**6**	**10**	**1**	**1**	**2**	**4**	**0**	**0**	**1**
1992-93	**Minnesota North Stars**	**NHL**	**84**	**36**	**43**	**79**	**30**	**30**	**60**	**49**	**14**	**2**	**3**	**294**	**12.2**	**102**	**41**	**71**	**11**	**1**	....	....	....	....	....	....	....	....
1993-94	**Dallas Stars**	**NHL**	**84**	**23**	**57**	**80**	**21**	**44**	**65**	**59**	**5**	**0**	**4**	**231**	**10.0**	**108**	**35**	**70**	**3**	**6**	**9**	**1**	**8**	**9**	**0**	**0**	**0**	**0**
1994-95	**Dallas Stars**	**NHL**	**32**	**7**	**10**	**17**	**12**	**15**	**27**	**13**	**2**	**0**	**1**	**90**	**7.8**	**27**	**10**	**25**	**0**	**-8**	....	....	....	....	....	....	....	....
	Vancouver Canucks	**NHL**	**13**	**4**	**14**	**18**	**7**	**21**	**28**	**4**	**0**	**2**	**1**	**42**	**9.5**	**22**	**6**	**8**	**2**	**10**	**11**	**4**	**8**	**12**	**21**	**0**	**2**	**1**
1995-96	**Vancouver Canucks**	**NHL**	**81**	**26**	**39**	**65**	**26**	**32**	**58**	**40**	**6**	**4**	**4**	**205**	**12.7**	**101**	**25**	**71**	**20**	**25**	**6**	**1**	**3**	**4**	**2**	**0**	**0**	**0**
1996-97	**Vancouver Canucks**	**NHL**	**47**	**9**	**19**	**28**	**10**	**17**	**27**	**24**	**1**	**0**	**1**	**101**	**8.9**	**37**	**9**	**39**	**15**	**4**	....	....	....	....	....	....	....	....
	New York Rangers	**NHL**	**14**	**2**	**5**	**7**	**2**	**4**	**6**	**2**	**1**	**1**	**1**	**24**	**8.3**	**12**	**3**	**13**	**1**	**-3**	**15**	**3**	**4**	**7**	**0**	**1**	**0**	**0**
1997-98	**Los Angeles Kings**	**NHL**	**58**	**12**	**6**	**18**	**14**	**6**	**20**	**27**	**1**	**4**	**4**	**97**	**12.4**	**28**	**4**	**41**	**15**	**-2**	**4**	**0**	**0**	**0**	**2**	**0**	**0**	**0**
1998-99	**Los Angeles Kings**	**NHL**	**57**	**6**	**13**	**19**	**7**	**13**	**20**	**19**	**0**	**1**	**1**	**77**	**7.8**	**25**	**1**	**43**	**10**	**-9**	....	....	....	....	....	....	....	....
	NHL Totals		**1029**	**297**	**447**	**744**	**277**	**357**	**634**	**557**	**58**	**29**	**40**	**2800**	**10.6**	**1043**	**264**	**942**	**162**		**129**	**39**	**44**	**83**	**83**	**6**	**4**	**5**

• Brother of Geoff • Played in NHL All-Star Game (1994)

Traded to **Montreal** by **Toronto** for John Kordic and Montreal's 6th round choice (Michael Doers) in 1989 Entry Draft, November 7, 1988. Traded to **Minnesota** by **Montreal** for Brian Bellows, August 31, 1992. Transferred to **Dallas** after **Minnesota** franchise relocated, June 9, 1993. Traded to **Vancouver** by **Dallas** for Greg Adams, Dan Kesa and Vancouver's 5th round choice (later traded to LA Kings — LA Kings selected Jason Morgan) in 1995 Entry Draft, April 7, 1995. Traded to **NY Rangers** by **Vancouver** with Esa Tikkanen for Sergei Nemchinov and Brian Noonan, March 8, 1997. Signed as a free agent by **LA Kings**, November 7, 1997.

• COURVILLE, Larry

LW – L. 6'1", 195 lbs. b: Timmins, Ont., 4/2/1975. Vancouver's 2nd, 61st overall, in 1995.

Season	Club	League	GP	G	A	Pts	AG	AA	APts	PIM	PP	SH	GW	S	%	TGF	PGF	TGA	PGA	+/-	GP	G	A	Pts	PIM	PP	SH	GW
1990-91	Waterloo Siskins	OJHL-B	47	20	18	38	....	....	....	144	....	....	....	....	....	....	....	....	....	....	....	....	....	....	....	....	....	....
1991-92	Cornwall Royals	OHL	60	8	12	20	....	....	....	80	....	....	....	....	....	....	....	....	....	....	6	0	0	0	8	....	....	....
1992-93	Newmarket Royals	OHL	64	21	18	39	....	....	....	181	....	....	....	....	....	....	....	....	....	....	7	0	6	6	14	....	....	....
1993-94	Newmarket Royals	OHL	39	20	19	39	....	....	....	134	....	....	....	....	....	....	....	....	....	....	....	....	....	....	....	....	....	....
	Moncton Hawks	AHL	8	2	0	2	....	....	....	37	....	....	....	....	....	....	....	....	....	....	10	2	2	4	27	....	....	....
1994-95	Sarnia Sting	OHL	16	9	9	18	....	....	....	58	....	....	....	....	....	....	....	....	....	....	....	....	....	....	....	....	....	....
	Canada	WJC-A	7	2	3	5	....	....	....	6	....	....	....	....	....	....	....	....	....	....	....	....	....	....	....	....	....	....
	Oshawa Generals	OHL	28	25	30	55	....	....	....	72	....	....	....	....	....	....	....	....	....	....	7	4	10	14	10	....	....	....
1995-96	**Vancouver Canucks**	**NHL**	**3**	**1**	**0**	**1**	**1**	**0**	**1**	**0**	**0**	**0**	**1**	**2**	**50.0**	**1**	**0**	**0**	**0**	**1**	....	....	....	....	....	....	....	....
	Syracuse Crunch	AHL	71	17	32	49	....	....	....	127	....	....	....	....	....	....	....	....	....	....	14	5	3	8	10	....	....	....
1996-97	**Vancouver Canucks**	**NHL**	**19**	**0**	**2**	**2**	**0**	**2**	**2**	**11**	**0**	**0**	**0**	**11**	**0.0**	**3**	**0**	**7**	**0**	**-4**	....	....	....	....	....	....	....	....
	Syracuse Crunch	AHL	54	20	24	44	....	....	....	103	....	....	....	....	....	....	....	....	....	....	3	0	1	1	20	....	....	....
1997-98	**Vancouver Canucks**	**NHL**	**11**	**0**	**0**	**0**	**0**	**0**	**0**	**5**	**0**	**0**	**0**	**3**	**0.0**	**0**	**0**	**7**	**0**	**-7**	....	....	....	....	....	....	....	....
	Syracuse Crunch	AHL	29	6	12	18	....	....	....	84	....	....	....	....	....	....	....	....	....	....	....	....	....	....	....	....	....	....
1998-99	Syracuse Crunch	AHL	71	13	28	41	....	....	....	155	....	....	....	....	....	....	....	....	....	....	....	....	....	....	....	....	....	....
99-2000	Kentucky Thoroughblades	AHL	61	11	12	23	....	....	....	107	....	....	....	....	....	....	....	....	....	....	9	1	5	6	16	....	....	....
	NHL Totals		**33**	**1**	**2**	**3**	**1**	**2**	**3**	**16**	**0**	**0**	**1**	**16**	**6.3**	**4**	**0**	**14**	**0**		....	....	....	....	....	....	....	....

OHL Second All-Star Team (1995) • Re-entered NHL Entry Draft. Originally Winnipeg's 6th choice, 119th overall in 1993 Entry Draft.

• COUTURIER, Sylvain

C – L. 6'2", 205 lbs. b: Greenfield Park, Que., 4/23/1968. Los Angeles' 3rd, 65th overall, in 1986.

Season	Club	League	GP	G	A	Pts	AG	AA	APts	PIM	PP	SH	GW	S	%	TGF	PGF	TGA	PGA	+/-	GP	G	A	Pts	PIM	PP	SH	GW
1983-84	Richelieu Regents	QAAA	42	11	29	40	....	....	....	....	....	....	....	....	....	....	....	....	....	....	....	....	....	....	....	....	....	....
1984-85	Richelieu Regents	QAAA	42	41	70	111	....	....	....	62	....	....	....	....	....	....	....	....	....	....	....	....	....	....	....	....	....	....
1985-86	Laval Titan	QMJHL	68	21	37	58	....	....	....	64	....	....	....	....	....	....	....	....	....	....	14	1	7	8	28	....	....	....
1986-87	Laval Titan	QMJHL	67	39	51	90	....	....	....	77	....	....	....	....	....	....	....	....	....	....	13	12	14	26	19	....	....	....
1987-88	Laval Titan	QMJHL	67	70	67	137	....	....	....	115	....	....	....	....	....	....	....	....	....	....	....	....	....	....	....	....	....	....
1988-89	**Los Angeles Kings**	**NHL**	**16**	**1**	**3**	**4**	**1**	**2**	**3**	**2**	**1**	**0**	**0**	**15**	**6.7**	**11**	**3**	**11**	**0**	**-3**	....	....	....	....	....	....	....	....
	New Haven Nighthawks	AHL	44	18	20	38	....	....	....	33	....	....	....	....	....	....	....	....	....	....	10	2	2	4	11	....	....	....
1989-90	New Haven Nighthawks	AHL	50	9	8	17	....	....	....	47	....	....	....	....	....	....	....	....	....	....	....	....	....	....	....	....	....	....
1990-91	**Los Angeles Kings**	**NHL**	**3**	**0**	**1**	**1**	**0**	**1**	**1**	**0**	**0**	**0**	**0**	**2**	**0.0**	**1**	**0**	**1**	**0**	**0**	....	....	....	....	....	....	....	....
	Phoenix Roadrunners	IHL	66	50	37	87	....	....	....	49	....	....	....	....	....	....	....	....	....	....	10	8	2	10	10	....	....	....
1991-92	**Los Angeles Kings**	**NHL**	**14**	**3**	**1**	**4**	**3**	**1**	**4**	**2**	**0**	**0**	**0**	**21**	**14.3**	**5**	**0**	**9**	**1**	**-3**	....	....	....	....	....	....	....	....
	Phoenix Roadrunners	IHL	39	19	20	39	....	....	....	68	....	....	....	....	....	....	....	....	....	....	....	....	....	....	....	....	....	....
1992-93	Phoenix Roadrunners	IHL	38	23	16	39	....	....	....	63	....	....	....	....	....	....	....	....	....	....	....	....	....	....	....	....	....	....
	Adirondack Red Wings	AHL	29	17	17	34	....	....	....	12	....	....	....	....	....	....	....	....	....	....	11	3	5	8	10	....	....	....
	Fort Wayne Komets	IHL	....	....	....	....	....	....	....	....	....	....	....	....	....	....	....	....	....	....	4	2	3	5	2	....	....	....
1993-94	Milwaukee Admirals	IHL	80	41	51	92	....	....	....	123	....	....	....	....	....	....	....	....	....	....	4	1	2	3	2	....	....	....
1994-95	Milwaukee Admirals	IHL	77	31	41	72	....	....	....	77	....	....	....	....	....	....	....	....	....	....	15	1	4	5	10	....	....	....
1995-96	Milwaukee Admirals	IHL	82	33	52	85	....	....	....	60	....	....	....	....	....	....	....	....	....	....	5	1	0	1	2	....	....	....
1996-97	Milwaukee Admirals	IHL	79	26	24	50	....	....	....	42	....	....	....	....	....	....	....	....	....	....	3	0	1	1	2	....	....	....
1997-98	Revier Lowen	Germany	42	12	13	25	....	....	....	56	....	....	....	....	....	....	....	....	....	....	....	....	....	....	....	....	....	....
1998-99	Berlin Capitals	Germany	50	19	12	31	....	....	....	62	....	....	....	....	....	....	....	....	....	....	....	....	....	....	....	....	....	....
99-2000	Berlin Capitals	Germany	51	11	14	25	....	....	....	52	....	....	....	....	....	....	....	....	....	....	7	0	3	3	16	....	....	....
	NHL Totals		**33**	**4**	**5**	**9**	**4**	**4**	**8**	**4**	**1**	**0**	**0**	**38**	**10.5**	**17**	**3**	**21**	**1**		....	....	....	....	....	....	....	....

Traded to **Detroit** by **LA Kings** with Paul Coffey and Jim Hiller for Jimmy Carson, Marc Potvin and Gary Shuchuk, January 29, 1993.

• COWAN, Jeff

LW – L. 6'2", 192 lbs. b: Scarborough, Ont., 9/27/1976.

Season	Club	League	GP	G	A	Pts	AG	AA	APts	PIM	PP	SH	GW	S	%	TGF	PGF	TGA	PGA	+/-	GP	G	A	Pts	PIM	PP	SH	GW
1992-93	Guelph Platers	OJHL-B	45	8	8	16	....	....	....	22	....	....	....	....	....	....	....	....	....	....	....	....	....	....	....	....	....	....
1993-94	Guelph Platers	OJHL-B	43	30	26	56	....	....	....	96	....	....	....	....	....	....	....	....	....	....	....	....	....	....	....	....	....	....
	Guelph Storm	OHL	17	1	0	1	....	....	....	5	....	....	....	....	....	....	....	....	....	....	....	....	....	....	....	....	....	....
1994-95	Guelph Storm	OHL	51	10	7	17	....	....	....	14	....	....	....	....	....	....	....	....	....	....	14	1	1	2	0	....	....	....
1995-96	Barrie Colts	OHL	66	38	14	52	....	....	....	29	....	....	....	....	....	....	....	....	....	....	5	1	2	3	6	....	....	....
1996-97	Saint John Flames	AHL	22	5	5	10	....	....	....	8	....	....	....	....	....	....	....	....	....	....	....	....	....	....	....	....	....	....
	Roanoke Express	ECHL	47	21	13	34	....	....	....	42	....	....	....	....	....	....	....	....	....	....	....	....	....	....	....	....	....	....
1997-98	Saint John Flames	AHL	69	15	13	28	....	....	....	23	....	....	....	....	....	....	....	....	....	....	13	4	1	5	14	....	....	....
1998-99	Saint John Flames	AHL	71	7	12	19	....	....	....	117	....	....	....	....	....	....	....	....	....	....	4	0	1	1	10	....	....	....
99-2000	**Calgary Flames**	**NHL**	**13**	**4**	**1**	**5**	**4**	**1**	**5**	**16**	**0**	**0**	**0**	**26**	**15.4**	**7**	**0**	**6**	**1**	**2**	....	....	....	....	....	....	....	....
	Saint John Flames	AHL	47	15	10	25	....	....	....	77	....	....	....	....	....	....	....	....	....	....	....	....	....	....	....	....	....	....
	NHL Totals		**13**	**4**	**1**	**5**	**4**	**1**	**5**	**16**	**0**	**0**	**0**	**26**	**15.4**	**7**	**0**	**6**	**1**		....	....	....	....	....	....	....	....

Signed as a free agent by **Calgary**, October 2, 1995.

• COWICK, Bruce

Robert Bruce LW – L. 6'1", 200 lbs. b: Victoria, B.C., 8/18/1951.

Season	Club	League	GP	G	A	Pts	AG	AA	APts	PIM	PP	SH	GW	S	%	TGF	PGF	TGA	PGA	+/–	GP	G	A	Pts	PIM	PP	SH	GW
			REGULAR SEASON																		PLAYOFFS							
1968-69	Victoria Cougars	BCJHL	STATISTICS NOT AVAILABLE																									
1969-70	Victoria Cougars	BCJHL	47	27	40	67				97																		
1970-71	Victoria Cougars	BCJHL	47	31	44	75				197																		
1971-72	San Diego Gulls	WHL	65	6	8	14				97											4	0	2	2	2			
1972-73	San Diego Gulls	WHL	61	17	13	30				165																		
1973-74	Richmond Robins	AHL	68	14	7	21				138											5	1	1	2	9			
	◆ **Philadelphia Flyers**	**NHL**																			**8**	**0**	**0**	**0**	**9**	**0**	**0**	**0**
1974-75	**Washington Capitals**	**NHL**	**65**	**5**	**6**	**11**	**4**	**4**	**8**	**41**	**0**	**0**	**0**	**73**	**6.8**	**20**	**3**	**59**	**0**	**–42**								
1975-76	**St. Louis Blues**	**NHL**	**5**	**0**	**0**	**0**	**0**	**0**	**0**	**2**	**0**	**0**	**0**	**3**	**0.0**	**1**	**0**	**0**	**0**	**1**								
	Providence Reds	AHL	38	3	6	9				38											1	0	0	0	0			
	NHL Totals		**70**	**5**	**6**	**11**	**4**	**4**	**8**	**43**	**0**	**0**	**0**	**76**	**6.6**	**21**	**3**	**59**	**0**		**8**	**0**	**0**	**0**	**9**	**0**	**0**	**0**

BCJHL Second All-Star Team (1970) • BCJHL First All-Star Team (1971)

Signed as a free agent by **San Diego** (WHL), October 2, 1971. Traded to **Philadelphia** by **San Diego** (WHL) for Jim Stanfield, Tom Trevelyan, Bob Currier and Bob Hurlburt, May 25, 1973. Claimed by **Washington** from **Philadelphia** in Expansion Draft, June 12, 1974. Claimed on waivers by **St. Louis** from **Washington**, May 21, 1975.

• COWIE, Rob

Robert D – L. 6', 195 lbs. b: Toronto, Ont., 11/3/1967.

Season	Club	League	GP	G	A	Pts	AG	AA	APts	PIM	PP	SH	GW	S	%	TGF	PGF	TGA	PGA	+/–	GP	G	A	Pts	PIM	PP	SH	GW
1985-86	St. Michael's Buzzers	OJHL-B	31	9	23	32				24																		
1986-87	St. Michael's Buzzers	OJHL-B	36	25	32	57				55																		
1987-88	Northeastern University	Hoc-East	36	7	8	15				38																		
1988-89	Northeastern University	Hoc-East	36	7	34	41				60																		
1989-90	Northeastern University	Hoc-East	34	14	31	45				54																		
1990-91	Northeastern University	Hoc-East	33	18	23	41				56																		
1991-92	Moncton Hawks	AHL	64	11	30	41				89											5	1	1	2	0			
1992-93	Moncton Hawks	AHL	67	12	20	32				91											5	3	5	8	2			
1993-94	Springfield Indians	AHL	78	17	57	74				124											6	3	6	9	4			
1994-95	**Los Angeles Kings**	**NHL**	**32**	**2**	**7**	**9**	**4**	**10**	**14**	**20**	**0**	**0**	**0**	**39**	**5.1**	**16**	**2**	**26**	**6**	**–6**								
	Phoenix Roadrunners	IHL	51	14	33	47				71																		
1995-96	**Los Angeles Kings**	**NHL**	**46**	**5**	**5**	**10**	**5**	**4**	**9**	**32**	**2**	**0**	**0**	**86**	**5.8**	**30**	**6**	**44**	**4**	**–16**								
	Phoenix Roadrunners	IHL	22	2	17	19				48											4	1	3	4	0			
1996-97	HC La Chaux-de-Fonds	Switz.	39	18	18	36				100																		
1997-98	Eisbaren Berlin	Germany	48	11	30	41				74											10	3	5	8	16			
1998-99	Eisbaren Berlin	Germany	49	14	29	43				72											8	3	3	6	30			
	Eisbaren Berlin	EuroHL	6	3	3	6				39											6	1	1	2	6			
99-2000	Eisbaren Berlin	Germany	58	15	24	39				103																		
	NHL Totals		**78**	**7**	**12**	**19**	**9**	**14**	**23**	**52**	**2**	**0**	**0**	**125**	**5.6**	**46**	**8**	**70**	**10**									

Hockey East Second All-Star Team (1989, 1991) • Hockey East First All-Star Team (1990)

Signed as a free agent by **Winnipeg**, July 4, 1991. Signed as a free agent by **Hartford**, August 9, 1993. Signed as a free agent by **LA Kings**, July 8, 1994.

• COXE, Craig

LW – L. 6'4", 210 lbs. b: Chula Vista, CA, 1/21/1964. Detroit's 4th, 66th overall, in 1982.

Season	Club	League	GP	G	A	Pts	AG	AA	APts	PIM	PP	SH	GW	S	%	TGF	PGF	TGA	PGA	+/–	GP	G	A	Pts	PIM	PP	SH	GW
1981-82	St. Albert Saints	AJHL	51	17	48	65				212																		
1982-83	Belleville Bulls	OHL	64	14	27	41				102											4	1	2	3	2			
1983-84	Belleville Bulls	OHL	45	17	28	45				90											3	2	0	2	4			
1984-85	**Vancouver Canucks**	**NHL**	**9**	**0**	**0**	**0**	**0**	**0**	**0**	**49**	**0**	**0**	**0**	**1**	**0.0**	**0**	**0**	**5**	**0**	**–5**								
	Fredericton Express	AHL	62	8	7	15				242											4	2	1	3	16			
1985-86	**Vancouver Canucks**	**NHL**	**57**	**3**	**5**	**8**	**2**	**3**	**5**	**176**	**1**	**0**	**0**	**48**	**6.3**	**15**	**2**	**26**	**0**	**–13**	**3**	**0**	**0**	**0**	**2**	**0**	**0**	**0**
1986-87	**Vancouver Canucks**	**NHL**	**15**	**1**	**0**	**1**	**1**	**0**	**1**	**31**	**1**	**0**	**0**	**7**	**14.3**	**1**	**1**	**3**	**0**	**–3**								
	Fredericton Express	AHL	46	1	12	13				168																		
1987-88	**Vancouver Canucks**	**NHL**	**64**	**5**	**12**	**17**	**4**	**9**	**13**	**186**	**1**	**0**	**1**	**43**	**11.6**	**26**	**3**	**24**	**0**	**–1**								
	Calgary Flames	**NHL**	**7**	**2**	**3**	**5**	**2**	**2**	**4**	**32**	**0**	**0**	**0**	**5**	**40.0**	**9**	**0**	**6**	**0**	**3**	**2**	**1**	**0**	**1**	**16**	**0**	**0**	**0**
1988-89	**St. Louis Blues**	**NHL**	**41**	**0**	**7**	**7**	**0**	**5**	**5**	**127**	**0**	**0**	**0**	**15**	**0.0**	**12**	**0**	**9**	**0**	**3**								
	Peoria Rivermen	IHL	8	2	7	9				38																		
1989-90	**Vancouver Canucks**	**NHL**	**25**	**1**	**4**	**5**	**1**	**3**	**4**	**66**	**0**	**0**	**1**	**11**	**9.1**	**8**	**0**	**12**	**0**	**–4**								
	Milwaukee Admirals	IHL	5	0	5	5				4																		
1990-91	**Vancouver Canucks**	**NHL**	**7**	**0**	**0**	**0**	**0**	**0**	**0**	**27**	**0**	**0**	**0**	**5**	**0.0**	**2**	**0**	**5**	**0**	**–3**								
	Milwaukee Admirals	IHL	36	9	21	30				116											6	3	2	5	22			
1991-92	**San Jose Sharks**	**NHL**	**10**	**2**	**0**	**2**	**2**	**0**	**2**	**19**	**0**	**0**	**0**	**11**	**18.2**	**5**	**0**	**9**	**0**	**–4**								
	Kansas City Blades	IHL	51	17	21	38				106																		
	Kalamazoo Wings	IHL	6	4	5	9				13											10	2	4	6	37			
1992-93	Cincinnati Cyclones	IHL	20	5	3	8				34																		
	Kalamazoo Wings	IHL	12	1	1	2				8																		
1993-94	Tulsa Oilers	CHL	64	26	57	83				236											11	4	9	13	38			
1994-95	Tulsa Oilers	CHL	12	7	7	14				28											7	0	1	1	30			
1995-96	Huntsville Channel Cats	SHL	20	7	13	20				56											10	8	13	21	33			
1996-97	Tulsa Oilers	CHL	64	29	59	88				95											5	2	2	4	8			
1997-98	Tulsa Oilers	CHL	25	11	22	33				34																		
	Wichita Thunder	CHL	31	9	29	38				75											15	1	10	11	62			
1998-99	Corpus Christi Icerays	WPHL	53	10	30	40				44											4	1	1	2	6			
99-2000	San Antonio Iguanas	CHL	20	1	5	6				33																		
	NHL Totals		**235**	**14**	**31**	**45**	**12**	**22**	**34**	**713**	**3**	**0**	**2**	**146**	**9.6**	**78**	**6**	**99**	**0**		**5**	**1**	**0**	**1**	**18**	**0**	**0**	**0**

Signed as a free agent by **Vancouver**, June 26, 1984. Traded to **Calgary** by **Vancouver** for Brian Bradley, Kevan Guy and Peter Bakovic, March 6, 1988. Traded to **St. Louis** by **Calgary** with Mike Bullard and Tim Corkery for Mark Hunter, Doug Gilmour, Steve Bozek and Michael Dark, September 6, 1988. Transferred to **Chicago** by **St. Louis** as compensation for St. Louis' signing of free agent Rik Wilson, September 27, 1989. Claimed by **Vancouver** in Waiver Draft, October 2, 1989. Claimed by **San Jose** from **Vancouver** in Expansion Draft, May 30, 1991. • Served as playier/assistant coach with **San Antonia** (CHL) during 1999-2000 season. • Played w/ RHI's Phoenix Cobras in 1994 (19-7-25-32-92) and Vancouver Voodoos in 1995 (15-9-13-22-44).

• CRAIG, Mike

RW – R. 6'1", 180 lbs. b: St. Mary's, Ont., 6/6/1971. Minnesota's 2nd, 28th overall, in 1989.

Season	Club	League	GP	G	A	Pts	AG	AA	APts	PIM	PP	SH	GW	S	%	TGF	PGF	TGA	PGA	+/–	GP	G	A	Pts	PIM	PP	SH	GW
1986-87	Woodstock Navy Vets	OJHL-C	32	29	19	48				64																		
1987-88	Oshawa Generals	OHL	61	6	10	16				39											7	7	0	1	11			
1988-89	Oshawa Generals	OHL	63	36	36	72				34											6	3	1	4	6			
1989-90	Oshawa Generals	OHL	43	36	40	76				85											17	10	16	26	46			
	Canada	WJC-A	7	3	0	3				8																		
	Oshawa Generals	Mem-Cup	3	*5	4	9				10																		
1990-91	**Minnesota North Stars**	**NHL**	**39**	**8**	**4**	**12**	**7**	**3**	**10**	**32**	**1**	**0**	**2**	**59**	**13.6**	**26**	**7**	**32**	**2**	**–11**	**10**	**1**	**1**	**2**	**20**	**1**	**0**	**1**
	Canada	WJC-A	7	6	5	11				8																		
1991-92	**Minnesota North Stars**	**NHL**	**67**	**15**	**16**	**31**	**14**	**12**	**26**	**155**	**4**	**0**	**4**	**136**	**11.0**	**47**	**17**	**44**	**2**	**–12**	**4**	**1**	**0**	**1**	**7**	**0**	**0**	**0**
1992-93	**Minnesota North Stars**	**NHL**	**70**	**15**	**23**	**38**	**12**	**16**	**28**	**106**	**7**	**0**	**0**	**131**	**11.5**	**70**	**31**	**50**	**0**	**–11**								
1993-94	**Dallas Stars**	**NHL**	**72**	**13**	**24**	**37**	**12**	**19**	**31**	**139**	**3**	**0**	**2**	**150**	**8.7**	**57**	**16**	**59**	**4**	**–14**	**4**	**0**	**0**	**0**	**2**	**0**	**0**	**0**
1994-95	**Toronto Maple Leafs**	**NHL**	**37**	**5**	**5**	**10**	**9**	**7**	**16**	**12**	**1**	**0**	**1**	**61**	**8.2**	**14**	**2**	**33**	**0**	**–21**	**2**	**0**	**1**	**1**	**2**	**0**	**0**	**0**
1995-96	**Toronto Maple Leafs**	**NHL**	**70**	**8**	**12**	**20**	**8**	**10**	**18**	**42**	**1**	**0**	**1**	**108**	**7.4**	**32**	**2**	**39**	**1**	**–8**	**6**	**0**	**0**	**0**	**18**	**0**	**0**	**0**
1996-97	**Toronto Maple Leafs**	**NHL**	**65**	**7**	**13**	**20**	**7**	**12**	**19**	**62**	**1**	**0**	**0**	**128**	**5.5**	**30**	**6**	**44**	**0**	**–20**								
1997-98	San Antonio Dragons	IHL	12	4	1	5				18																		
	Kansas City Blades	IHL	59	14	33	47				68											11	5	5	10	28			
1998-99	**San Jose Sharks**	**NHL**	**1**	**0**	**0**	**0**	**0**	**0**	**0**	**0**	**0**	**0**	**0**	**1**	**0.0**	**0**	**0**	**1**	**0**	**–1**								
	Kentucky Thoroughblades	AHL	52	27	17	44				72											12	5	4	9	18			
	NHL Totals		**421**	**71**	**97**	**168**	**69**	**79**	**148**	**548**	**18**	**0**	**10**	**774**	**9.2**	**276**	**81**	**302**	**9**		**26**	**2**	**2**	**4**	**49**	**1**	**0**	**1**

WJC-A All-Star Team (1991)

Transferred to **Dallas** after **Minnesota** franchise relocated, June 9, 1993. Signed as a free agent by **Toronto**, July 29, 1994. Signed as a free agent by **San Jose**, July 13, 1998.

• CRAIGHEAD, John RW – R. 6', 195 lbs. b: Vancouver, B.C., 11/23/1971.

Season	Club	League	REGULAR SEASON GP	G	A	Pts	AG	AA	APts	PIM	PP	SH	GW	S	%	TGF	PGF	TGA	PGA	+/–	PLAYOFFS GP	G	A	Pts	PIM	PP	SH	GW
1990-91	Burnaby Bluehawks	PCJHL	22	10	32	42				259																		
	New Westminster Royals	BCJHL	3	0	0	0				12																		
1991-92	West Palm Beach Blaze	SunHL	39	12	17	29				160																		
	Surrey Eagles	BCJHL	13	7	6	13				38																		
	Chilliwack Chiefs	BCJHL	25	12	16	28				116																		
1992-93	West Palm Beach Blaze	SunHL	36	12	9	21				158																		
	Louisville Icehawks	ECHL	5	1	0	1				33																		
1993-94	Huntington Blizzard	ECHL	9	4	2	6				44																		
	Richmond Renegades	ECHL	28	18	12	30				89																		
1994-95	Detroit Vipers	IHL	44	5	7	12				285												3	0	1	1	4			
1995-96	Detroit Vipers	IHL	63	7	9	16				368												10	2	3	5	28			
1996-97	**Toronto Maple Leafs**	**NHL**	**5**	**0**	**0**	**0**	**0**	**0**	**0**	**10**	**0**	**0**	**0**	**0**	**0.0**	**0**	**0**	**0**	**0**	**0**								
	St. John's Maple Leafs	AHL	53	9	10	19				318												7	1	1	2	22			
1997-98	Cleveland Lumberjacks	IHL	49	9	7	16				233																			
	Quebec Rafales	IHL	13	2	2	4				73																			
1998-99	Nurnberg Ice Tigers	Germany	34	4	6	10				144												13	1	4	5	*60			
99-2000	Nurnberg Ice Tigers	Germany	59	20	18	38				208																			
	Nurnberg Ice Tigers	EuroHL	6	1	3	4				12												2	0	1	1	2			
	NHL Totals		**5**	**0**	**0**	**0**	**0**	**0**	**0**	**10**	**0**	**0**	**0**	**0**	**0.0**	**0**	**0**	**0**	**0**										

Signed as a free agent by **Toronto**, July 22, 1996. • Played w/ RHI's Detroit Mustangs in 1995 (5-2-4-6-21).

• CRAIGWELL, Dale Dale A. C – L. 5'11", 180 lbs. b: Toronto, Ont., 4/24/1971. San Jose's 11th, 199th overall, in 1991.

Season	Club	League	GP	G	A	Pts	AG	AA	APts	PIM	PP	SH	GW	S	%	TGF	PGF	TGA	PGA	+/–	GP	G	A	Pts	PIM	PP	SH	GW
1987-88	Oshawa Major Midgets	OMHA	60	49	57	106				42																		
1988-89	Oshawa Generals	OHL	55	9	14	23				15																		
1989-90	Oshawa Generals	OHL	64	22	41	63				39											17	7	7	14	11			
	Oshawa Generals	Mem-Cup	4	1	5	6				0																		
1990-91	Oshawa Generals	OHL	56	27	68	95				34											16	7	16	23	9			
	Canada	WJC-A	7	1	2	3				0																		
1991-92	**San Jose Sharks**	**NHL**	**32**	**5**	**11**	**16**	**5**	**8**	**13**	**8**	**4**	**0**	**2**	**38**	**13.2**	**29**	**10**	**25**	**3**	**–3**								
	Kansas City Blades	IHL	48	6	19	25				29											12	4	7	11	4			
1992-93	**San Jose Sharks**	**NHL**	**8**	**3**	**1**	**4**	**2**	**1**	**3**	**4**	**0**	**0**	**0**	**7**	**42.9**	**5**	**0**	**9**	**0**	**–4**								
	Kansas City Blades	IHL	60	15	38	53				24											12	*7	5	12	2			
1993-94	**San Jose Sharks**	**NHL**	**58**	**3**	**6**	**9**	**3**	**5**	**8**	**16**	**0**	**1**	**0**	**35**	**8.6**	**21**	**2**	**51**	**19**	**–13**								
	Kansas City Blades	IHL	5	3	1	4				0																		
1994-95	Kansas City Blades	IHL	DID NOT PLAY – INJURED																									
1995-96	San Francisco Spiders	IHL	75	11	49	60				38											4	2	0	2	0			
1996-97	Kansas City Blades	IHL	82	17	51	68				34											3	1	0	1	0			
1997-98	Kansas City Blades	IHL	81	13	42	55				12											11	2	9	11	2			
1998-99	Augsburger EV Panther	Germany	16	1	4	5				4																		
	Kansas City Blades	IHL	61	11	28	39				14											3	0	2	2	2			
99-2000	Sheffield Steelers	Britain	24	7	17	24				0											7	0	6	6	8			
	NHL Totals		**98**	**11**	**18**	**29**	**10**	**14**	**24**	**28**	**4**	**1**	**2**	**80**	**13.8**	**55**	**12**	**85**	**22**									

• Missed entire 1994-95 season recovering from ankle injury suffered during training camp, September, 1994.

• CRASHLEY, Bart William Barton D – R. 6', 180 lbs. b: Toronto, Ont., 6/15/1946.

Season	Club	League	GP	G	A	Pts	AG	AA	APts	PIM	PP	SH	GW	S	%	TGF	PGF	TGA	PGA	+/–	GP	G	A	Pts	PIM	PP	SH	GW
1962-63	Hamilton Red Wings	OHA-Jr.	50	1	16	17				18											5	0	0	0	2			
1963-64	Hamilton Red Wings	OHA-Jr.	46	5	19	24				31																		
	Pittsburgh Hornets	AHL	1	0	0	0				0																		
1964-65	Hamilton Red Wings	OHA-Jr.	56	11	35	46				40																		
1965-66	Hamilton Red Wings	OHA-Jr.	46	8	31	39				55																		
	Detroit Red Wings	**NHL**	**1**	**0**	**0**	**0**	**0**	**0**	**0**	**0**																		
1966-67	**Detroit Red Wings**	**NHL**	**2**	**0**	**0**	**0**	**0**	**0**	**0**	**2**																		
	Pittsburgh Hornets	AHL	16	4	2	6				8																		
	Memphis Wings	CPHL	49	6	26	32				40											7	1	5	6	4			
1967-68	**Detroit Red Wings**	**NHL**	**57**	**2**	**14**	**16**	**2**	**14**	**16**	**18**	**0**	**0**	**0**	**86**	**2.3**	**68**	**3**	**66**	**7**	**6**								
	Fort Worth Wings	CPHL	13	0	4	4				16											13	3	9	12	12			
1968-69	**Detroit Red Wings**	**NHL**	**1**	**0**	**0**	**0**	**0**	**0**	**0**	**0**	**0**	**0**	**0**	**0**	**0.0**	**0**	**0**	**0**	**0**	**0**								
	Fort Worth Wings	CHL	37	6	14	20				40																		
1969-70	Montreal Voyageurs	AHL	45	4	9	13				4											7	0	0	0	0			
1970-71	Kansas City Blues	CHL	58	5	19	24				28																		
1971-72	Dallas Black Hawks	CHL	56	20	38	58				24											6	0	7	7	5			
1972-73	Los Angeles Sharks	WHA	70	18	27	45				10											6	0	2	2	2			
1973-74	Los Angeles Sharks	WHA	78	4	26	30				16																		
1974-75	**Kansas City Scouts**	**NHL**	**27**	**3**	**6**	**9**	**3**	**4**	**7**	**10**	**1**	**0**	**1**	**39**	**7.7**	**32**	**12**	**44**	**8**	**–16**								
	Detroit Red Wings	**NHL**	**48**	**2**	**15**	**17**	**2**	**11**	**13**	**14**	**0**	**0**	**0**	**43**	**4.7**	**50**	**6**	**62**	**8**	**–10**								
1975-76	**Los Angeles Kings**	**NHL**	**4**	**0**	**1**	**1**	**0**	**1**	**1**	**6**	**0**	**0**	**0**	**2**	**0.0**	**1**	**1**	**11**	**1**	**–10**								
	Fort Worth Texans	CHL	61	11	32	43				61																		
1976-77	Springfield Indians	AHL	18	2	3	5				10																		
	Fort Worth Texans	CHL	23	4	11	15				10																		
1977-78	Binghamton Dusters	AHL	60	4	17	21				18																		
1978-79			DID NOT PLAY																									
1979-80	VSV Villach	Austria	29	10	24	34				26																		
1980-81	IEV Innsbruck	Austria	STATISTICS NOT AVAILABLE																									
1981-82	IEV Innsbruck	Austria	STATISTICS NOT AVAILABLE																									
1982-1984			OUT OF HOCKEY – RETIRED																									
1984-85	IEV Innsbruck	Austria	36	1	18	19				14																		
	NHL Totals		**140**	**7**	**36**	**43**	**7**	**30**	**37**	**50**																		
	Other Major League Totals		148	22	53	75				26											6	0	2	2	2			

CHL First All-Star Team (1972) • Named CHL's Top Defenseman (1972)

Traded to **Montreal** by **Detroit** with Pete Mahovlich for Garry Monahan and Doug Piper, June 6, 1969. Selected by **LA Sharks** (WHA) in 1972 WHA General Player Draft, February 12, 1972. Claimed by **NY Islanders** from **Montreal** in Expansion Draft, June 6, 1972. Traded to **Kansas City** by **NY Islanders** to complete transaction that sent Bob Bourne to NY Islanders (September 10, 1974), September 16, 1974. Traded to **Detroit** by **Kansas City** with Ted Snell and Larry Giroux for Guy Charron and Claude Houde, December 14, 1974. Traded to **LA Kings** by **Detroit** with the rights to Marcel Dionne for Dan Maloney, Terry Harper and LA Kings' 2nd round choice (later traded to Minnesota — Minnesota selected Jim Roberts) in 1976 Amateur Draft, June 23, 1975. • Combined totals only for 1981-82 and 1984-85 seasons (129-25-86-111-14) available for IEV Innsbruck.

• CRAVEN, Murray Murray Dean LW – L. 6'3", 195 lbs. b: Medicine Hat, Alta., 7/20/1964. Detroit's 1st, 17th overall, in 1982.

Season	Club	League	GP	G	A	Pts	AG	AA	APts	PIM	PP	SH	GW	S	%	TGF	PGF	TGA	PGA	+/–	GP	G	A	Pts	PIM	PP	SH	GW
1979-80	Medicine Hat Midget Tigers	AAHA	STATISTICS NOT AVAILABLE																									
1980-81	Medicine Hat Tigers	WHL	69	5	10	15				18											5	0	0	0	2			
1981-82	Medicine Hat Tigers	WHL	72	35	46	81				49																		
1982-83	Medicine Hat Tigers	WHL	28	17	29	46				35																		
	Detroit Red Wings	**NHL**	**31**	**4**	**7**	**11**	**3**	**5**	**8**	**6**	**0**	**0**	**1**	**21**	**19.0**	**16**	**0**	**14**	**2**	**4**								
1983-84	Medicine Hat Tigers	WHL	48	38	56	94				53											4	5	3	8	4			
	Detroit Red Wings	**NHL**	**15**	**0**	**4**	**4**	**0**	**3**	**3**	**6**	**0**	**0**	**0**	**8**	**0.0**	**8**	**0**	**7**	**1**	**2**								
1984-85	**Philadelphia Flyers**	**NHL**	**80**	**26**	**35**	**61**	**21**	**24**	**45**	**30**	**2**	**2**	**5**	**142**	**18.3**	**99**	**12**	**57**	**15**	**45**	**19**	**4**	**6**	**10**	**11**	**1**	**1**	**1**
1985-86	**Philadelphia Flyers**	**NHL**	**78**	**21**	**33**	**54**	**17**	**22**	**39**	**34**	**2**	**0**	**6**	**182**	**11.5**	**82**	**17**	**61**	**20**	**24**	**5**	**0**	**3**	**3**	**4**	**0**	**0**	**0**
1986-87	**Philadelphia Flyers**	**NHL**	**77**	**19**	**30**	**49**	**16**	**22**	**38**	**38**	**5**	**3**	**2**	**98**	**19.4**	**72**	**23**	**64**	**16**	**1**	**12**	**3**	**1**	**4**	**9**	**2**	**0**	**0**
1987-88	**Philadelphia Flyers**	**NHL**	**72**	**30**	**46**	**76**	**26**	**33**	**59**	**58**	**6**	**2**	**2**	**184**	**16.3**	**112**	**39**	**68**	**20**	**25**	**7**	**2**	**5**	**7**	**4**	**0**	**0**	**1**
1988-89	**Philadelphia Flyers**	**NHL**	**51**	**9**	**28**	**37**	**8**	**20**	**28**	**52**	**0**	**0**	**2**	**89**	**10.1**	**49**	**14**	**44**	**13**	**4**	**1**	**0**	**0**	**0**	**0**	**0**	**0**	**0**

			REGULAR SEASON																		PLAYOFFS							
Season	**Club**	**League**	**GP**	**G**	**A**	**Pts**	**AG**	**AA**	**APts**	**PIM**	**PP**	**SH**	**GW**	**S**	**%**	**TGF**	**PGF**	**TGA**	**PGA**	**+/–**	**GP**	**G**	**A**	**Pts**	**PIM**	**PP**	**SH**	**GW**
1989-90	**Philadelphia Flyers**	**NHL**	**76**	**25**	**50**	**75**	**21**	**36**	**57**	**42**	**7**	**2**	**3**	**175**	**14.3**	**108**	**36**	**90**	**20**	**2**	....	....	....	....	....	....	....	....
	Canada	WEC-A	9	1	5	6	....	....	....	6	....	....	....	....	....	....	....	....	....	....	....	....	....	....	....	....	....	....
1990-91	**Philadelphia Flyers**	**NHL**	**77**	**19**	**47**	**66**	**17**	**36**	**53**	**53**	**6**	**0**	**0**	**170**	**11.2**	**87**	**30**	**82**	**23**	**–2**	....	....	....	....	....	....	....	....
	Canada	WEC-A	9	1	1	2	....	....	....	10	....	....	....	....	....	....	....	....	....	....	....	....	....	....	....	....	....	....
1991-92	**Philadelphia Flyers**	**NHL**	**12**	**3**	**3**	**6**	**3**	**2**	**5**	**8**	**1**	**0**	**0**	**19**	**15.8**	**11**	**2**	**8**	**1**	**2**	....	....	....	....	....	....	....	....
	Hartford Whalers	**NHL**	**61**	**24**	**30**	**54**	**22**	**23**	**45**	**38**	**8**	**4**	**1**	**133**	**18.0**	**72**	**21**	**84**	**29**	**–4**	**7**	**3**	**3**	**6**	**6**	**0**	**1**	**0**
1992-93	**Hartford Whalers**	**NHL**	**67**	**25**	**42**	**67**	**21**	**29**	**50**	**20**	**6**	**3**	**2**	**139**	**18.0**	**106**	**48**	**111**	**49**	**–4**	....	....	....	....	....	....	....	....
	Vancouver Canucks	**NHL**	**10**	**0**	**10**	**10**	**0**	**7**	**7**	**12**	**0**	**0**	**0**	**12**	**0.0**	**18**	**10**	**12**	**7**	**3**	**12**	**4**	**6**	**10**	**4**	**1**	**0**	**1**
1993-94	**Vancouver Canucks**	**NHL**	**78**	**15**	**40**	**55**	**14**	**31**	**45**	**30**	**2**	**1**	**3**	**115**	**13.0**	**99**	**36**	**77**	**19**	**5**	**22**	**4**	**9**	**13**	**18**	**0**	**0**	**1**
1994-95	**Chicago Blackhawks**	**NHL**	**16**	**4**	**3**	**7**	**7**	**4**	**11**	**2**	**1**	**0**	**2**	**29**	**13.8**	**10**	**4**	**7**	**3**	**2**	**16**	**5**	**5**	**10**	**4**	**0**	**0**	**1**
1995-96	**Chicago Blackhawks**	**NHL**	**66**	**18**	**29**	**47**	**18**	**24**	**42**	**36**	**5**	**1**	**7**	**86**	**20.9**	**71**	**16**	**53**	**18**	**20**	**9**	**1**	**4**	**5**	**2**	**1**	**0**	**0**
1996-97	**Chicago Blackhawks**	**NHL**	**75**	**8**	**27**	**35**	**8**	**24**	**32**	**12**	**2**	**0**	**1**	**122**	**6.6**	**53**	**13**	**63**	**23**	**0**	**2**	**0**	**0**	**0**	**2**	**0**	**0**	**0**
1997-98	**San Jose Sharks**	**NHL**	**67**	**12**	**17**	**29**	**14**	**17**	**31**	**25**	**2**	**3**	**3**	**107**	**11.2**	**51**	**12**	**51**	**16**	**4**	**6**	**1**	**1**	**2**	**0**	**0**	**0**	**0**
1998-99	**San Jose Sharks**	**NHL**	**43**	**4**	**10**	**14**	**5**	**10**	**15**	**18**	**0**	**1**	**1**	**55**	**7.3**	**23**	**6**	**37**	**17**	**–3**	....	....	....	....	....	....	....	....
99-2000	**San Jose Sharks**	**NHL**	**19**	**0**	**2**	**2**	**0**	**2**	**2**	**4**	**0**	**0**	**0**	**18**	**0.0**	**4**	**1**	**9**	**4**	**–2**	....	....	....	....	....	....	....	....
	NHL Totals		**1071**	**266**	**493**	**759**	**241**	**374**	**615**	**524**	**55**	**22**	**41**	**1904**	**14.0**	**1151**	**340**	**999**	**316**		**118**	**27**	**43**	**70**	**64**	**5**	**2**	**5**

Traded to **Philadelphia** by **Detroit** with Joe Paterson for Darryl Sittler, October 10, 1984. Traded to **Hartford** by **Philadelphia** with Philadelphia's 4th round choice (Kevin Smyth) in 1992 Entry Draft for Kevin Dineen, November 13, 1991. Traded to **Vancouver** by **Hartford** with Vancouver's 5th round choice (previously acquired, Vancouver selected Scott Walker) in 1993 Entry Draft for Robert Kron, Vancouver's 3rd round choice (Marek Malik) in 1993 Entry Draft and future considerations (Jim Sandlak, May 17, 1993), March 22, 1993. Traded to **Chicago** by **Vancouver** for Christian Ruutu, March 10, 1995. Traded to **San Jose** by **Chicago** for the rights to Petri Varis and San Jose's 6th round choice (Jari Viuhkola) in 1998 Entry Draft, July 25, 1997. • Missed remainder of 1999-2000 season recovering from abdominal injury suffered in game vs. New Jersey, November 18, 1999. • Officially released by **San Jose**, December 26, 1999.

• CRAWFORD, Bob

Robert Remi RW – R. 5'11", 180 lbs. b: Belleville, Ont., 4/6/1959. St. Louis' 2nd, 65th overall, in 1979.

Season	Club	League	GP	G	A	Pts	AG	AA	APts	PIM	PP	SH	GW	S	%	TGF	PGF	TGA	PGA	+/–	GP	G	A	Pts	PIM	PP	SH	GW
1976-77	Cornwall Royals	QMJHL	71	36	34	70	....	....	....	39	....	....	....	....	....	....	....	....	....	....	....	....	....	....	....	....	....	....
	United States	WJC-A	....	....	....	....	....	....	....	....	....	....	....	....	....	....	....	....	....	....	....	....	....	....	....	....	....	....
1977-78	Cornwall Royals	QMJHL	69	54	67	121	....	....	....	29	....	....	....	....	....	....	....	....	....	....	9	7	5	12	2	....	....	....
	United States	WJC-A	6	4	9	13	....	....	....	4	....	....	....	....	....	....	....	....	....	....	....	....	....	....	....	....	....	....
1978-79	Cornwall Royals	QMJHL	65	62	70	132	....	....	....	43	....	....	....	....	....	....	....	....	....	....	7	4	7	11	6	....	....	....
	United States	WJC-A	5	1	2	3	....	....	....	2	....	....	....	....	....	....	....	....	....	....	....	....	....	....	....	....	....	....
1979-80	**St. Louis Blues**	**NHL**	**8**	**1**	**0**	**1**	**1**	**0**	**1**	**2**	**0**	**0**	**0**	**12**	**8.3**	**1**	**0**	**7**	**0**	**–6**	....	....	....	....	....	....	....	....
	Salt Lake Golden Eagles	CHL	67	30	21	51	....	....	....	32	....	....	....	....	....	....	....	....	....	....	13	3	5	8	9	....	....	....
1980-81	Salt Lake Golden Eagles	CHL	79	35	26	61	....	....	....	27	....	....	....	....	....	....	....	....	....	....	17	7	8	15	2	....	....	....
1981-82	**St. Louis Blues**	**NHL**	**3**	**0**	**1**	**1**	**0**	**1**	**1**	**0**	**0**	**0**	**0**	**9**	**0.0**	**1**	**0**	**5**	**0**	**–4**	....	....	....	....	....	....	....	....
	Salt Lake Golden Eagles	CHL	74	54	45	99	....	....	....	43	....	....	....	....	....	....	....	....	....	....	10	4	2	6	2	....	....	....
1982-83	**St. Louis Blues**	**NHL**	**27**	**5**	**9**	**14**	**4**	**6**	**10**	**2**	**1**	**0**	**0**	**63**	**7.9**	**17**	**3**	**19**	**0**	**–5**	**4**	**0**	**0**	**0**	**0**	**0**	**0**	**0**
	Salt Lake Golden Eagles	CHL	25	15	23	38	....	....	....	2	....	....	....	....	....	....	....	....	....	....	....	....	....	....	....	....	....	....
1983-84	**Hartford Whalers**	**NHL**	**80**	**36**	**25**	**61**	**29**	**17**	**46**	**32**	**5**	**0**	**3**	**179**	**20.1**	**74**	**19**	**56**	**0**	**–1**	....	....	....	....	....	....	....	....
1984-85	**Hartford Whalers**	**NHL**	**45**	**14**	**14**	**28**	**11**	**10**	**21**	**8**	**2**	**0**	**0**	**90**	**15.6**	**36**	**6**	**33**	**0**	**–3**	....	....	....	....	....	....	....	....
1985-86	**Hartford Whalers**	**NHL**	**57**	**14**	**20**	**34**	**11**	**13**	**24**	**16**	**4**	**0**	**2**	**110**	**12.7**	**46**	**12**	**51**	**1**	**–16**	....	....	....	....	....	....	....	....
	New York Rangers	**NHL**	**11**	**1**	**2**	**3**	**1**	**1**	**2**	**10**	**0**	**0**	**0**	**15**	**6.7**	**7**	**0**	**6**	**1**	**2**	**7**	**0**	**1**	**1**	**8**	**0**	**0**	**0**
	New Haven Nighthawks	AHL	27	7	8	15	....	....	....	6	....	....	....	....	....	....	....	....	....	....	5	0	0	0	2	....	....	....
1986-87	**New York Rangers**	**NHL**	**3**	**0**	**0**	**0**	**0**	**0**	**0**	**2**	**0**	**0**	**0**	**1**	**0.0**	**0**	**0**	**1**	**0**	**–1**	....	....	....	....	....	....	....	....
	New Haven Nighthawks	AHL	4	3	0	3	....	....	....	7	....	....	....	....	....	....	....	....	....	....	....	....	....	....	....	....	....	....
	Washington Capitals	**NHL**	**12**	**0**	**0**	**0**	**0**	**0**	**0**	**0**	**0**	**0**	**0**	**14**	**0.0**	**2**	**0**	**2**	**0**	**0**	....	....	....	....	....	....	....	....
	Binghamton Whalers	AHL	5	0	2	2	....	....	....	0	....	....	....	....	....	....	....	....	....	....	....	....	....	....	....	....	....	....
	Salt Lake Golden Eagles	IHL	2	0	1	1	....	....	....	0	....	....	....	....	....	....	....	....	....	....	....	....	....	....	....	....	....	....
1987-88	Krefelder EV	Germany-2	28	36	28	64	....	....	....	....	....	....	....	....	....	....	....	....	....	....	18	*25	11	36	....	....	....	....
1988-89	Krefelder EV	Germany-3	33	53	27	80	....	....	....	39	....	....	....	....	....	....	....	....	....	....	18	21	14	35	....	....	....	....
	NHL Totals		**246**	**71**	**71**	**142**	**57**	**48**	**105**	**72**	**12**	**0**	**5**	**493**	**14.4**	**184**	**40**	**180**	**2**		**11**	**0**	**1**	**1**	**8**	**0**	**0**	**0**

• Brother of Marc and Lou • CHL First All-Star Team (1982)

Claimed by **Hartford** from **St. Louis** in Waiver Draft, October 3, 1983. Traded to **NY Rangers** by **Hartford** for Mike McEwen, March 11, 1986. Traded to **Washington** by **NY Rangers** with Kelly Miller and Mike Ridley for Bob Carpenter and Washington's 2nd round choice (Jason Prosofsky) in 1989 Entry Draft, January 1, 1987.

• CRAWFORD, Bobby

RW – L. 5'8", 180 lbs. b: Long Island, NY, 5/27/1960.

Season	Club	League	GP	G	A	Pts	AG	AA	APts	PIM	PP	SH	GW	S	%	TGF	PGF	TGA	PGA	+/–	GP	G	A	Pts	PIM	PP	SH	GW
1976-77	Austin Mavericks	MWJHL	44	26	34	60	....	....	....	16	....	....	....	....	....	....	....	....	....	....	....	....	....	....	....	....	....	....
1977-78	Austin Mavericks	USHL	10	11	6	17	....	....	....	0	....	....	....	....	....	....	....	....	....	....	....	....	....	....	....	....	....	....
	United States	WJC-A	6	4	9	13	....	....	....	4	....	....	....	....	....	....	....	....	....	....	....	....	....	....	....	....	....	....
	Oshawa Generals	OMJHL	38	21	16	37	....	....	....	2	....	....	....	....	....	....	....	....	....	....	6	1	4	5	2	....	....	....
1978-79	Oshawa Generals	OMJHL	68	41	58	99	....	....	....	68	....	....	....	....	....	....	....	....	....	....	5	3	3	6	13	....	....	....
1979-80	Oshawa Generals	OMJHL	68	61	68	129	....	....	....	48	....	....	....	....	....	....	....	....	....	....	7	4	4	8	8	....	....	....
1980-81	**Colorado Rockies**	**NHL**	**15**	**1**	**3**	**4**	**1**	**2**	**3**	**6**	**0**	**0**	**0**	**25**	**4.0**	**8**	**1**	**3**	**0**	**4**	....	....	....	....	....	....	....	....
	Fort Worth Texans	CHL	61	19	18	37	....	....	....	32	....	....	....	....	....	....	....	....	....	....	5	2	0	2	4	....	....	....
1981-82	Fort Worth Texans	CHL	80	23	31	54	....	....	....	45	....	....	....	....	....	....	....	....	....	....	....	....	....	....	....	....	....	....
1982-83	**Detroit Red Wings**	**NHL**	**1**	**0**	**0**	**0**	**0**	**0**	**0**	**0**	**0**	**0**	**0**	**1**	**0.0**	**0**	**0**	**0**	**0**	**0**	....	....	....	....	....	....	....	....
	Adirondack Red Wings	AHL	76	28	33	61	....	....	....	32	....	....	....	....	....	....	....	....	....	....	6	2	5	7	4	....	....	....
1983-84	HC La Chaux-de-Fonds	Switz-2	38	52	26	78	....	....	....	....	....	....	....	....	....	....	....	....	....	....	....	....	....	....	....	....	....	....
1984-85	EHC Olten	Switz-2	STATISTICS NOT AVAILABLE																									
1985-86	EHC Olten	Switz-2	STATISTICS NOT AVAILABLE																									
1986-87	EC Bad Tolz	Germany-2	36	43	53	96	....	....	....	14	....	....	....	....	....	....	....	....	....	....	14	24	17	41	....	....	....	....
1987-88	HC Merano	Italy	23	15	23	38	....	....	....	11	....	....	....	....	....	....	....	....	....	....	....	....	....	....	....	....	....	....
	SB Rosenheim	Germany	8	3	5	8	....	....	....	....	....	....	....	....	....	....	....	....	....	....	11	3	2	5	....	....	....	....
1988-89	SV Bayreuth	Germany-2	32	23	28	51	....	....	....	20	....	....	....	....	....	....	....	....	....	....	....	....	....	....	....	....	....	....
1989-90	EV Regensburg	Germany-3	23	34	35	69	....	....	....	24	....	....	....	....	....	....	....	....	....	....	12	*28	21	*49	16	....	....	....
1990-91	EV Regensburg	Germany-3	40	68	47	115	....	....	....	21	....	....	....	....	....	....	....	....	....	....	....	....	....	....	....	....	....	....
1991-92	EV Regensburg	Germany-3	30	*53	36	89	....	....	....	16	....	....	....	....	....	....	....	....	....	....	12	19	19	*38	8	....	....	....
	NHL Totals		**16**	**1**	**3**	**4**	**1**	**2**	**3**	**6**	**0**	**0**	**0**	**26**	**3.8**	**8**	**1**	**3**	**0**		....	....	....	....	....	....	....	....

OHA Second All-Star Team (1980)

Signed as a free agent by **NY Rangers**, November 16, 1979. Traded to **Colorado** by **NY Rangers** to complete transaction that sent Barry Beck to NY Rangers (November 2, 1979), January 15, 1980. Signed as a free agent by **Detroit**, June, 1982.

• CRAWFORD, Lou

Louis J. LW – L. 6', 185 lbs. b: Belleville, Ont., 11/5/1962.

Season	Club	League	GP	G	A	Pts	AG	AA	APts	PIM	PP	SH	GW	S	%	TGF	PGF	TGA	PGA	+/–	GP	G	A	Pts	PIM	PP	SH	GW
1978-79	Belleville Bobcats	OHA-B	45	25	30	55	....	....	....	107	....	....	....	....	....	....	....	....	....	....	....	....	....	....	....	....	....	....
1979-80	Belleville Bobcats	OHA-B	10	7	11	18	....	....	....	60	....	....	....	....	....	....	....	....	....	....	....	....	....	....	....	....	....	....
	Cornwall Royals	QMJHL	24	0	1	1	....	....	....	46	....	....	....	....	....	....	....	....	....	....	1	0	0	0	0	....	....	....
1980-81	Kitchener Rangers	OMJHL	53	2	7	9	....	....	....	134	....	....	....	....	....	....	....	....	....	....	....	....	....	....	....	....	....	....
1981-82	Kitchener Rangers	OHL	64	11	17	28	....	....	....	243	....	....	....	....	....	....	....	....	....	....	15	3	4	7	71	....	....	....
	Kitchener Rangers	Mem-Cup	5	0	1	1	....	....	....	20	....	....	....	....	....	....	....	....	....	....	....	....	....	....	....	....	....	....
1982-83	Rochester Americans	AHL	64	5	11	16	....	....	....	142	....	....	....	....	....	....	....	....	....	....	13	1	1	2	7	....	....	....
1983-84	Rochester Americans	AHL	76	7	6	13	....	....	....	234	....	....	....	....	....	....	....	....	....	....	17	2	4	6	87	....	....	....
1984-85	Rochester Americans	AHL	70	8	7	15	....	....	....	213	....	....	....	....	....	....	....	....	....	....	1	0	0	0	10	....	....	....
1985-86	Nova Scotia Oilers	AHL	78	8	11	19	....	....	....	214	....	....	....	....	....	....	....	....	....	....	....	....	....	....	....	....	....	....
1986-87	Nova Scotia Oilers	AHL	35	3	4	7	....	....	....	48	....	....	....	....	....	....	....	....	....	....	....	....	....	....	....	....	....	....
1987-88	Nova Scotia Oilers	AHL	65	15	15	30	....	....	....	170	....	....	....	....	....	....	....	....	....	....	4	1	2	3	9	....	....	....
1988-89	Adirondack Red Wings	AHL	74	23	23	46	....	....	....	179	....	....	....	....	....	....	....	....	....	....	9	0	6	6	32	....	....	....
1989-90	**Boston Bruins**	**NHL**	**7**	**0**	**0**	**0**	**0**	**0**	**0**	**20**	**0**	**0**	**0**	**6**	**0.0**	**2**	**0**	**1**	**0**	**1**	**1**	**0**	**0**	**0**	**0**	....	....	....
	Maine Mariners	AHL	62	15	13	28	....	....	....	162	....	....	....	....	....	....	....	....	....	....	....	....	....	....	....	....	....	....
1990-91	Maine Mariners	AHL	80	18	17	35	....	....	....	215	....	....	....	....	....	....	....	....	....	....	2	0	0	0	5	....	....	....
1991-92	**Boston Bruins**	**NHL**	**19**	**2**	**1**	**3**	**2**	**1**	**3**	**9**	**0**	**0**	**0**	**14**	**14.3**	**4**	**0**	**10**	**0**	**–6**	....	....	....	....	....	....	....	....
	Maine Mariners	AHL	54	17	15	32	....	....	....	171	....	....	....	....	....	....	....	....	....	....	....	....	....	....	....	....	....	....

			REGULAR SEASON																		PLAYOFFS							
Season	Club	League	GP	G	A	Pts	AG	AA	APts	PIM	PP	SH	GW	S	%	TGF	PGF	TGA	PGA	+/–	GP	G	A	Pts	PIM	PP	SH	GW
1992-93	Milwaukee Admirals	IHL	56	16	14	30	....	....	....	108	....	....	....	....	....	....	....	....	....	....	6	2	2	4	8	....	....	....
1993-94	St. John's Maple Leafs	AHL	3	0	0	0	....	....	....	0	....	....	....	....	....	....	....	....	....	....	....	....	....	....	....	....	....	....
	Brantford Smoke	ColHL	21	12	17	29	....	....	....	39	....	....	....	....	....	....	....	....	....	....	7	4	0	4	17	....	....	....
1994-1996	Belleville Bulls	OHL	DID NOT PLAY – ASSISTANT COACH																									
1996-2000	Belleville Bulls	OHL	DID NOT PLAY – COACHING																									
	NHL Totals		**26**	**2**	**1**	**3**	**2**	**1**	**3**	**29**	**0**	**0**	**0**	**20**	**10.0**	**6**	**0**	**11**	**0**		**1**	**0**	**0**	**0**	**0**	....	....	....

• Brother of Bob and Marc

Signed as a free agent by **Buffalo**, August 23, 1984. Signed as a free agent by **Detroit**, August 11, 1988. Signed as a free agent by **Boston**, July 6, 1989. • Named Head Coach of **St. John's** (AHL), June 15, 2000.

• CRAWFORD, Marc

Marc Joseph John LW – L. 5'11", 185 lbs. b: Belleville, Ont., 2/13/1961. Vancouver's 3rd, 70th overall, in 1980.

Season	Club	League	GP	G	A	Pts	AG	AA	APts	PIM	PP	SH	GW	S	%	TGF	PGF	TGA	PGA	+/–	GP	G	A	Pts	PIM	PP	SH	GW
1978-79	Cornwall Royals	QMJHL	70	28	41	69	....	....	....	206	....	....	....	....	....	....	....	....	....	....	....	....	....	....	....	....	....	....
1979-80	Cornwall Royals	QMJHL	54	27	36	63	....	....	....	127	....	....	....	....	....	....	....	....	....	....	18	8	20	28	48	....	....	....
	Cornwall Royals	Mem-Cup	5	2	0	2	....	....	....	6	....	....	....	....	....	....	....	....	....	....	....	....	....	....	....	....	....	....
1980-81	Cornwall Royals	QMJHL	63	42	57	99	....	....	....	242	....	....	....	....	....	....	....	....	....	....	19	*20	15	35	27	....	....	....
	Canada	WJC-A	5	1	3	4	....	....	....	4	....	....	....	....	....	....	....	....	....	....	....	....	....	....	....	....	....	....
	Cornwall Royals	Mem-Cup	5	1	*7	8	....	....	....	0	....	....	....	....	....	....	....	....	....	....	....	....	....	....	....	....	....	....
1981-82	**Vancouver Canucks**	**NHL**	**40**	**4**	**8**	**12**	**3**	**5**	**8**	**29**	**0**	**0**	**0**	**57**	**7.0**	**22**	**0**	**22**	**0**	**0**	**14**	**1**	**0**	**1**	**11**	**0**	**0**	**0**
	Dallas Black Hawks	CHL	34	13	21	34	....	....	....	71	....	....	....	....	....	....	....	....	....	....	....	....	....	....	....	....	....	....
1982-83	**Vancouver Canucks**	**NHL**	**41**	**4**	**5**	**9**	**3**	**3**	**6**	**28**	**0**	**0**	**1**	**34**	**11.8**	**19**	**0**	**22**	**0**	**–3**	**3**	**0**	**1**	**1**	**25**	**0**	**0**	**0**
	Fredericton Express	AHL	30	15	9	24	....	....	....	59	....	....	....	....	....	....	....	....	....	....	9	1	3	4	10	....	....	....
1983-84	**Vancouver Canucks**	**NHL**	**19**	**0**	**1**	**1**	**0**	**1**	**1**	**9**	**0**	**0**	**0**	**13**	**0.0**	**3**	**0**	**3**	**0**	**0**	....	....	....	....	....	....	....	....
	Fredericton Express	AHL	56	9	22	31	....	....	....	96	....	....	....	....	....	....	....	....	....	....	7	4	2	6	23	....	....	....
1984-85	**Vancouver Canucks**	**NHL**	**1**	**0**	**0**	**0**	**0**	**0**	**0**	**4**	**0**	**0**	**0**	**0**	**0.0**	**0**	**0**	**5**	**1**	**–4**	....	....	....	....	....	....	....	....
	Fredericton Express	AHL	65	12	29	41	....	....	....	177	....	....	....	....	....	....	....	....	....	....	5	0	1	1	10	....	....	....
1985-86	**Vancouver Canucks**	**NHL**	**54**	**11**	**14**	**25**	**9**	**9**	**18**	**92**	**0**	**0**	**0**	**80**	**13.8**	**35**	**1**	**41**	**0**	**–7**	**3**	**0**	**1**	**1**	**8**	**0**	**0**	**0**
	Fredericton Express	AHL	26	10	14	24	....	....	....	55	....	....	....	....	....	....	....	....	....	....	....	....	....	....	....	....	....	....
1986-87	**Vancouver Canucks**	**NHL**	**21**	**0**	**3**	**3**	**0**	**2**	**2**	**67**	**0**	**0**	**0**	**19**	**0.0**	**5**	**0**	**14**	**1**	**–8**	....	....	....	....	....	....	....	....
	Fredericton Express	AHL	25	8	11	19	....	....	....	21	....	....	....	....	....	....	....	....	....	....	....	....	....	....	....	....	....	....
1987-88	Fredericton Express	AHL	43	5	13	18	....	....	....	90	....	....	....	....	....	....	....	....	....	....	2	0	0	0	14	....	....	....
1988-89	Milwaukee Admirals	IHL	53	23	30	53	....	....	....	166	....	....	....	....	....	....	....	....	....	....	11	2	5	7	26	....	....	....
1989-1991	Cornwall Royals	OHL	DID NOT PLAY – COACHING																									
1991-1994	St. John's Maple Leafs	AHL	DID NOT PLAY – COACHING																									
1994-1995	**Quebec Nordiques**	**NHL**	DID NOT PLAY – COACHING																									
1995-1998	**Colorado Avalanche**	**NHL**	DID NOT PLAY – COACHING																									
1998-2000	**Vancouver Canucks**	**NHL**	DID NOT PLAY – COACHING																									
	NHL Totals		**176**	**19**	**31**	**50**	**15**	**20**	**35**	**229**	**0**	**0**	**1**	**203**	**9.4**	**84**	**1**	**107**	**2**		**20**	**1**	**2**	**3**	**44**	**0**	**0**	**0**

• Brother of Bob and Lou • Memorial Cup All-Star Team (1981) • Won Jack Adams Award (1995)

• Served as Player/Assistant Coach w/ **Milwaukee** (IHL) in 1987-88 and w/ **Fredericton** (AHL) in 1988-89.

• CREIGHTON, Adam

C – L. 6'5", 220 lbs. b: Burlington, Ont., 6/2/1965. Buffalo's 3rd, 11th overall, in 1983.

Season	Club	League	GP	G	A	Pts	AG	AA	APts	PIM	PP	SH	GW	S	%	TGF	PGF	TGA	PGA	+/–	GP	G	A	Pts	PIM	PP	SH	GW
1980-81	Welland Tigers	OMHA	48	37	29	66	....	....	....	55	....	....	....	....	....	....	....	....	....	....	....	....	....	....	....	....	....	....
	Welland Cougars	OHA-B	6	4	5	9	....	....	....	6	....	....	....	....	....	....	....	....	....	....	....	....	....	....	....	....	....	....
	Guelph Royals	OJHL	3	0	1	1	....	....	....	4	....	....	....	....	....	....	....	....	....	....	....	....	....	....	....	....	....	....
1981-82	Ottawa 67's	OHL	60	15	27	42	....	....	....	73	....	....	....	....	....	....	....	....	....	....	17	7	1	8	40	....	....	....
1982-83	Ottawa 67's	OHL	68	44	46	90	....	....	....	88	....	....	....	....	....	....	....	....	....	....	9	0	2	2	12	....	....	....
1983-84	Ottawa 67's	OHL	56	42	49	91	....	....	....	79	....	....	....	....	....	....	....	....	....	....	13	16	11	27	28	....	....	....
	Buffalo Sabres	**NHL**	**7**	**2**	**2**	**4**	**2**	**1**	**3**	**4**	**0**	**0**	**1**	**8**	**25.0**	**8**	**1**	**7**	**0**	**0**	....	....	....	....	....	....	....	....
	Ottawa 67's	Mem-Cup	5	5	*7	*12	....	....	....	15	....	....	....	....	....	....	....	....	....	....	....	....	....	....	....	....	....	....
1984-85	Ottawa 67's	OHL	10	4	14	18	....	....	....	23	....	....	....	....	....	....	....	....	....	....	5	6	2	8	11	....	....	....
	Canada	WJC-A	7	8	4	12	....	....	....	4	....	....	....	....	....	....	....	....	....	....	....	....	....	....	....	....	....	....
	Buffalo Sabres	**NHL**	**30**	**2**	**8**	**10**	**2**	**5**	**7**	**33**	**1**	**0**	**0**	**20**	**10.0**	**22**	**17**	**12**	**0**	**–7**	....	....	....	....	....	....	....	....
	Rochester Americans	AHL	6	5	3	8	....	....	....	2	....	....	....	....	....	....	....	....	....	....	5	2	1	3	20	....	....	....
1985-86	**Buffalo Sabres**	**NHL**	**19**	**1**	**1**	**2**	**1**	**1**	**2**	**2**	**0**	**0**	**1**	**9**	**11.1**	**5**	**2**	**5**	**0**	**–2**	....	....	....	....	....	....	....	....
	Rochester Americans	AHL	32	17	21	38	....	....	....	27	....	....	....	....	....	....	....	....	....	....	....	....	....	....	....	....	....	....
1986-87	**Buffalo Sabres**	**NHL**	**56**	**18**	**22**	**40**	**16**	**16**	**32**	**26**	**6**	**0**	**3**	**109**	**16.5**	**56**	**18**	**34**	**0**	**4**	....	....	....	....	....	....	....	....
1987-88	**Buffalo Sabres**	**NHL**	**36**	**10**	**17**	**27**	**9**	**12**	**21**	**87**	**4**	**0**	**1**	**61**	**16.4**	**40**	**13**	**23**	**3**	**7**	....	....	....	....	....	....	....	....
1988-89	**Buffalo Sabres**	**NHL**	**24**	**7**	**10**	**17**	**6**	**7**	**13**	**44**	**3**	**0**	**1**	**42**	**16.7**	**21**	**10**	**16**	**0**	**–5**	....	....	....	....	....	....	....	....
	Chicago Blackhawks	**NHL**	**43**	**15**	**14**	**29**	**13**	**10**	**23**	**92**	**8**	**0**	**3**	**113**	**13.3**	**48**	**19**	**34**	**1**	**–4**	**15**	**5**	**6**	**11**	**44**	**3**	**1**	**0**
1989-90	**Chicago Blackhawks**	**NHL**	**80**	**34**	**36**	**70**	**29**	**26**	**55**	**224**	**12**	**0**	**3**	**156**	**21.8**	**96**	**35**	**73**	**16**	**4**	**20**	**3**	**6**	**9**	**59**	**0**	**1**	**0**
1990-91	**Chicago Blackhawks**	**NHL**	**72**	**22**	**29**	**51**	**20**	**22**	**42**	**135**	**10**	**2**	**6**	**127**	**17.3**	**75**	**29**	**51**	**5**	**0**	**6**	**0**	**1**	**1**	**10**	**0**	**0**	**0**
1991-92	**Chicago Blackhawks**	**NHL**	**11**	**6**	**6**	**12**	**5**	**5**	**10**	**16**	**2**	**0**	**0**	**32**	**18.8**	**12**	**3**	**10**	**0**	**–1**	....	....	....	....	....	....	....	....
	New York Islanders	**NHL**	**66**	**15**	**9**	**24**	**14**	**7**	**21**	**102**	**2**	**0**	**2**	**108**	**13.9**	**44**	**8**	**41**	**1**	**–4**	....	....	....	....	....	....	....	....
1992-93	**Tampa Bay Lightning**	**NHL**	**83**	**19**	**20**	**39**	**16**	**14**	**30**	**110**	**7**	**1**	**0**	**168**	**11.3**	**70**	**26**	**76**	**13**	**–19**	....	....	....	....	....	....	....	....
1993-94	**Tampa Bay Lightning**	**NHL**	**53**	**10**	**10**	**20**	**9**	**8**	**17**	**37**	**2**	**0**	**1**	**77**	**13.0**	**37**	**8**	**36**	**0**	**–7**	....	....	....	....	....	....	....	....
1994-95	**St. Louis Blues**	**NHL**	**48**	**14**	**20**	**34**	**25**	**30**	**55**	**74**	**3**	**0**	**1**	**81**	**17.3**	**59**	**14**	**38**	**10**	**17**	**7**	**2**	**0**	**2**	**16**	**1**	**0**	**1**
1995-96	**St. Louis Blues**	**NHL**	**61**	**11**	**10**	**21**	**11**	**8**	**19**	**78**	**2**	**0**	**3**	**98**	**11.2**	**31**	**8**	**25**	**2**	**0**	**13**	**1**	**1**	**2**	**8**	**0**	**0**	**0**
1996-97	**Chicago Blackhawks**	**NHL**	**19**	**1**	**2**	**3**	**1**	**2**	**3**	**13**	**0**	**0**	**0**	**20**	**5.0**	**5**	**0**	**7**	**0**	**–2**	....	....	....	....	....	....	....	....
	Indianapolis Ice	IHL	6	1	7	8	....	....	....	11	....	....	....	....	....	....	....	....	....	....	....	....	....	....	....	....	....	....
1997-98	Augsburger Panther	Germany	22	10	9	19	....	....	....	45	....	....	....	....	....	....	....	....	....	....	....	....	....	....	....	....	....	....
1998-99	Augsburger Panther	Germany	9	0	2	2	....	....	....	30	....	....	....	....	....	....	....	....	....	....	....	....	....	....	....	....	....	....
	NHL Totals		**708**	**187**	**216**	**403**	**179**	**174**	**353**	**1077**	**62**	**3**	**26**	**1229**	**15.2**	**629**	**211**	**488**	**51**		**61**	**11**	**14**	**25**	**137**	**4**	**2**	**1**

• Son of Dave • Memorial Cup All-Star Team (1984) • Won Stafford Smythe Memorial Trophy (Memorial Cup Tournament MVP) (1984)

Traded to **Chicago** by **Buffalo** for Rick Vaive, December 26, 1988. Traded to **NY Islanders** by **Chicago** with Steve Thomas for Brent Sutter and Brad Lauer, October 25, 1991. Claimed by **Tampa Bay** from **NY Islanders** in NHL Waiver Draft, October 4, 1992. Traded to **St. Louis** by **Tampa Bay** for Tom Tilley, October 6, 1994. Signed as a free agent by **Chicago**, October 9, 1996.

• CRESSMAN, Dave

David Gregory LW – L. 6'1", 180 lbs. b: Kitchener, Ont., 1/2/1950. Minnesota's 4th, 48th overall, in 1970.

Season	Club	League	GP	G	A	Pts	AG	AA	APts	PIM	PP	SH	GW	S	%	TGF	PGF	TGA	PGA	+/–	GP	G	A	Pts	PIM	PP	SH	GW
1967-68	Kitchener Greenshirts	OHA-B	STATISTICS NOT AVAILABLE																									
	Kitchener Rangers	OHA-Jr.	1	0	3	3	....	....	....	0	....	....	....	....	....	....	....	....	....	....	19	0	1	1	2	....	....	....
1968-69	Kitchener Rangers	OHA-Jr.	54	29	26	55	....	....	....	33	....	....	....	....	....	....	....	....	....	....	....	....	....	....	....	....	....	....
1969-70	Kitchener Rangers	OHA-Jr.	50	18	39	57	....	....	....	69	....	....	....	....	....	....	....	....	....	....	6	3	7	10	4	....	....	....
1970-71	Galt Hornets	OHA-Sr.	STATISTICS NOT AVAILABLE																									
1971-72	Galt Hornets	OHA-Sr.	40	19	34	53	....	....	....	24	....	....	....	....	....	....	....	....	....	....	....	....	....	....	....	....	....	....
1972-73	Galt Hornets	OHA-Sr.	19	2	6	8	....	....	....	20	....	....	....	....	....	....	....	....	....	....	....	....	....	....	....	....	....	....
1973-74	Saginaw Gears	IHL	75	32	35	67	....	....	....	49	....	....	....	....	....	....	....	....	....	....	9	5	3	8	37	....	....	....
1974-75	**Minnesota North Stars**	**NHL**	**5**	**2**	**0**	**2**	**2**	**0**	**2**	**4**	**0**	**0**	**0**	**13**	**15.4**	**3**	**0**	**1**	**0**	**2**	....	....	....	....	....	....	....	....
	New Haven Nighthawks	AHL	66	11	15	26	....	....	....	41	....	....	....	....	....	....	....	....	....	....	16	7	*14	21	6	....	....	....
1975-76	**Minnesota North Stars**	**NHL**	**80**	**4**	**8**	**12**	**3**	**6**	**9**	**33**	**0**	**0**	**1**	**72**	**5.6**	**15**	**0**	**73**	**54**	**–4**	....	....	....	....	....	....	....	....
1976-77	New Haven Nighthawks	AHL	80	25	31	56	....	....	....	64	....	....	....	....	....	....	....	....	....	....	6	1	0	1	4	....	....	....
1977-78	Cambridge Hornets	OHA-Sr.	25	9	11	20	....	....	....	4	....	....	....	....	....	....	....	....	....	....	....	....	....	....	....	....	....	....
	NHL Totals		**85**	**6**	**8**	**14**	**5**	**6**	**11**	**37**	**0**	**0**	**1**	**85**	**7.1**	**18**	**0**	**74**	**54**		....	....	....	....	....	....	....	....

IHL Second All-Star Team (1974) • Sat out entire 1970-71 season to attend University of Guelph, September, 1970.

• CRISP, Terry

Terrance Arthur C – L. 5'10", 180 lbs. b: Parry Sound, Ont., 5/28/1943.

Season	Club	League	GP	G	A	Pts	AG	AA	APts	PIM	PP	SH	GW	S	%	TGF	PGF	TGA	PGA	+/–	GP	G	A	Pts	PIM	PP	SH	GW
1960-61	St. Mary's Lincolns	OHA-B	32	49	71	120	....	....	....	....	....	....	....	....	....	....	....	....	....	....	....	....	....	....	....	....	....	....
1961-62	Niagara Falls Flyers	OHA-Jr.	50	16	22	38	....	....	....	57	....	....	....	....	....	....	....	....	....	....	10	1	6	7	6	....	....	....
1962-63	Niagara Falls Flyers	OHA-Jr.	50	39	35	74	....	....	....	68	....	....	....	....	....	....	....	....	....	....	9	5	*12	*17	10	....	....	....
	Niagara Falls Flyers	Mem-Cup	16	11	12	23	....	....	....	22	....	....	....	....	....	....	....	....	....	....	....	....	....	....	....	....	....	....

			REGULAR SEASON																		PLAYOFFS							
Season	Club	League	GP	G	A	Pts	AG	AA	APts	PIM	PP	SH	GW	S	%	TGF	PGF	TGA	PGA	+/–	GP	G	A	Pts	PIM	PP	SH	GW
1963-64	Minneapolis Bruins	CPHL	42	15	20	35				22																		
1964-65	Minneapolis Bruins	CPHL	70	28	34	62				22											5	0	2	2	0			
1965-66	**Boston Bruins**	**NHL**	**3**	**0**	**0**	**0**	**0**	**0**	**0**	**0**																		
	Oklahoma City Blazers	CPHL	61	11	22	33				35											9	1	5	6	0			
1966-67	Oklahoma City Blazers	CPHL	69	31	42	73				37											11	3	7	10	0			
1967-68	**St. Louis Blues**	**NHL**	**73**	**9**	**20**	**29**	**10**	**20**	**30**	**10**	**0**	**1**	**1**	**135**	**6.7**	**47**	**2**	**46**	**10**	**9**	**18**	**1**	**5**	**6**	**6**	**0**	**0**	**0**
1968-69	**St. Louis Blues**	**NHL**	**57**	**6**	**9**	**15**	**6**	**8**	**14**	**14**	**1**	**1**	**0**	**40**	**15.0**	**19**	**1**	**18**	**8**	**8**	**12**	**3**	**4**	**7**	**20**	**0**	**2**	**0**
	Kansas City Blues	CHL	4	1	1	2				4																		
1969-70	**St. Louis Blues**	**NHL**	**26**	**5**	**6**	**11**	**5**	**6**	**11**	**2**	**0**	**0**	**1**	**44**	**11.4**	**19**	**7**	**19**	**7**	**0**	**16**	**2**	**3**	**5**	**2**	**1**	**0**	**0**
	Buffalo Bisons	AHL	51	15	34	49				14																		
1970-71	**St. Louis Blues**	**NHL**	**54**	**5**	**11**	**16**	**5**	**9**	**14**	**13**	**0**	**1**	**0**	**47**	**10.6**	**23**	**3**	**27**	**10**	**3**	**6**	**1**	**0**	**1**	**2**	**0**	**0**	**0**
1971-72	**St. Louis Blues**	**NHL**	**75**	**13**	**18**	**31**	**13**	**16**	**29**	**12**	**1**	**6**	**3**	**94**	**13.8**	**45**	**4**	**75**	**41**	**7**	**11**	**1**	**3**	**4**	**2**	**0**	**0**	**0**
1972-73	**New York Islanders**	**NHL**	**54**	**4**	**16**	**20**	**4**	**13**	**17**	**6**	**0**	**1**	**0**	**72**	**5.6**	**31**	**2**	**70**	**19**	**–22**								
	Philadelphia Flyers	**NHL**	**12**	**1**	**5**	**6**	**1**	**4**	**5**	**2**	**0**	**0**	**0**	**18**	**5.6**	**9**	**0**	**8**	**3**	**4**	**11**	**3**	**2**	**5**	**2**	**1**	**0**	**0**
1973-74♦	**Philadelphia Flyers**	**NHL**	**71**	**10**	**21**	**31**	**10**	**17**	**27**	**28**	**1**	**2**	**3**	**88**	**11.4**	**40**	**4**	**31**	**7**	**12**	**17**	**2**	**2**	**4**	**4**	**0**	**1**	**1**
1974-75♦	**Philadelphia Flyers**	**NHL**	**71**	**8**	**19**	**27**	**7**	**14**	**21**	**20**	**0**	**1**	**1**	**70**	**11.4**	**37**	**4**	**36**	**14**	**11**	**9**	**2**	**4**	**6**	**0**	**0**	**0**	**0**
1975-76	**Philadelphia Flyers**	**NHL**	**38**	**6**	**9**	**15**	**5**	**7**	**12**	**28**	**1**	**0**	**1**	**48**	**12.5**	**22**	**1**	**19**	**4**	**6**	**10**	**0**	**5**	**5**	**2**	**0**	**0**	**0**
1976-77	**Philadelphia Flyers**	**NHL**	**2**	**0**	**0**	**0**	**0**	**0**	**0**	**0**	**0**	**0**	**0**	**0**	**0.0**	**0**	**0**	**0**	**0**	**0**								
	NHL Totals		**536**	**67**	**134**	**201**	**66**	**114**	**180**	**135**											**110**	**15**	**28**	**43**	**40**			

Claimed by **St. Louis** from **Boston** in Expansion Draft, June 6, 1967. Claimed by **NY islanders** from **St. Louis** in Expansion Draft, June 6, 1972. Traded to **Philadelphia** by **NY Islanders** for Jean Potvin and future considerations (Glen Irwin, May 18, 1973), March 5, 1973. • Retired to become head coach of the **Springfield Indians** (AHL), October, 1984.

• CRISTOFOLI, Ed

RW – L. 6'2", 205 lbs. b: Trail, B.C., 5/14/1967. Montreal's 9th, 142nd overall, in 1985.

Season	Club	League	GP	G	A	Pts	AG	AA	APts	PIM	PP	SH	GW	S	%	TGF	PGF	TGA	PGA	+/–	GP	G	A	Pts	PIM	PP	SH	GW
1983-84	Penticton Knights	BCJHL	55	18	46	64				89																		
1984-85	Penticton Knights	BCJHL	48	36	34	70				58																		
	Penticton Knights	Cen-Cup	5	3	2	5				2																		
1985-86	University of Denver	WCHA	46	10	9	19				32																		
1986-87	University of Denver	WCHA	40	14	15	29				52																		
1987-88	University of Denver	WCHA	38	12	27	39				64																		
1988-89	University of Denver	WCHA	43	20	19	39				50																		
1989-90	**Montreal Canadiens**	**NHL**	**9**	**0**	**1**	**1**	**0**	**1**	**1**	**4**	**0**	**0**	**0**	**6**	**0.0**	**2**	**0**	**3**	**0**	**–1**								
	Sherbrooke Canadiens	AHL	57	16	19	35				31											12	2	4	6	14			
1990-91	Fredericton Canadiens	AHL	34	7	16	23				24																		
	Kansas City Blades	IHL	22	3	1	4				6																		
	NHL Totals		**9**	**0**	**1**	**1**	**0**	**1**	**1**	**4**	**0**	**0**	**0**	**6**	**0.0**	**2**	**0**	**3**	**0**									

• CROMBEEN, Mike

Michael Joseph RW – R. 5'11", 190 lbs. b: Sarnia, Ont., 4/16/1957. Cleveland's 1st, 5th overall, in 1977.

Season	Club	League	GP	G	A	Pts	AG	AA	APts	PIM	PP	SH	GW	S	%	TGF	PGF	TGA	PGA	+/–	GP	G	A	Pts	PIM	PP	SH	GW
1972-73	Sarnia Black Hawks	OMHA	STATISTICS NOT AVAILABLE																									
	Sarnia Bees	OHA-B	STATISTICS NOT AVAILABLE																									
1973-74	Kingston Canadians	OMJHL	69	19	29	48				59																		
1974-75	Kingston Canadians	OMJHL	69	56	58	114				50											2	0	0	0	0			
1975-76	Kingston Canadians	OMJHL	57	43	39	82				65											7	3	4	7	8			
1976-77	Kingston Canadians	OMJHL	49	42	36	78				16											10	5	9	14	23			
1977-78	**Cleveland Barons**	**NHL**	**48**	**3**	**4**	**7**	**3**	**3**	**6**	**13**	**2**	**0**	**0**	**65**	**4.6**	**12**	**3**	**35**	**0**	**–26**								
	Salt Lake Golden Eagles	CHL	12	4	4	8				4																		
	Binghamton Dusters	AHL	13	1	2	3				4																		
1978-79	**St. Louis Blues**	**NHL**	**37**	**3**	**8**	**11**	**3**	**6**	**9**	**34**	**0**	**0**	**0**	**51**	**5.9**	**20**	**0**	**38**	**5**	**–13**								
	Salt Lake Golden Eagles	CHL	30	6	9	15				48																		
1979-80	**St. Louis Blues**	**NHL**	**71**	**10**	**12**	**22**	**8**	**9**	**17**	**20**	**1**	**0**	**2**	**98**	**10.2**	**31**	**2**	**54**	**11**	**–14**	**2**	**0**	**0**	**0**	**0**	**0**	**0**	**0**
1980-81	**St. Louis Blues**	**NHL**	**66**	**9**	**14**	**23**	**7**	**9**	**16**	**58**	**0**	**1**	**1**	**91**	**9.9**	**46**	**0**	**65**	**20**	**1**	**11**	**3**	**0**	**3**	**8**	**0**	**0**	**2**
1981-82	**St. Louis Blues**	**NHL**	**71**	**19**	**8**	**27**	**15**	**5**	**20**	**32**	**0**	**1**	**1**	**99**	**19.2**	**44**	**2**	**87**	**35**	**–10**	**10**	**3**	**1**	**4**	**20**	**0**	**0**	**1**
1982-83	**St. Louis Blues**	**NHL**	**80**	**6**	**11**	**17**	**5**	**8**	**13**	**20**	**0**	**1**	**1**	**71**	**8.5**	**35**	**0**	**78**	**38**	**–5**	**4**	**0**	**1**	**1**	**4**	**0**	**0**	**0**
1983-84	**Hartford Whalers**	**NHL**	**56**	**1**	**4**	**5**	**1**	**3**	**4**	**25**	**0**	**0**	**0**	**46**	**2.2**	**10**	**0**	**51**	**28**	**–13**								
1984-85	**Hartford Whalers**	**NHL**	**46**	**4**	**7**	**11**	**3**	**5**	**8**	**16**	**0**	**1**	**1**	**31**	**12.9**	**17**	**0**	**26**	**9**	**0**								
	Binghamton Whalers	AHL	6	2	1	3				0																		
	NHL Totals		**475**	**55**	**68**	**123**	**45**	**48**	**93**	**218**	**3**	**4**	**6**	**552**	**10.0**	**215**	**7**	**434**	**146**		**27**	**6**	**2**	**8**	**32**	**0**	**0**	**3**

OMJHL Second All-Star Team (1976, 1977)

Claimed by **St. Louis** in **Cleveland-Minnesota** Dispersal Draft, June 13, 1978. Claimed by **Hartford** from **St. Louis** in Waiver Draft, October 3, 1983.

• CRONIN, Shawn

Shawn P. D – L. 6'2", 225 lbs. b: Joliet, IL, 8/20/1963.

Season	Club	League	GP	G	A	Pts	AG	AA	APts	PIM	PP	SH	GW	S	%	TGF	PGF	TGA	PGA	+/–	GP	G	A	Pts	PIM	PP	SH	GW
1982-83	University of Illinois-Chicago	CCHA	36	1	5	6				52																		
1983-84	University of Illinois-Chicago	CCHA	32	0	4	4				41																		
1984-85	University of Illinois-Chicago	CCHA	31	2	6	8				52																		
1985-86	University of Illinois-Chicago	CCHA	35	3	8	11				70																		
1986-87	Salt Lake Golden Eagles	IHL	53	8	16	24				118																		
	Binghamton Whalers	AHL	12	0	1	1				60											10	0	0	0	41			
1987-88	Binghamton Whalers	AHL	65	3	8	11				212											4	0	0	0	15			
1988-89	**Washington Capitals**	**NHL**	**1**	**0**	**0**	**0**	**0**	**0**	**0**	**0**	**0**	**0**	**0**	**0**	**0.0**	**0**	**0**	**0**	**0**	**0**								
	Baltimore Skipjacks	AHL	75	3	9	12				267																		
1989-90	**Winnipeg Jets**	**NHL**	**61**	**0**	**4**	**4**	**0**	**3**	**3**	**243**	**0**	**0**	**0**	**30**	**0.0**	**27**	**1**	**52**	**10**	**–16**	**5**	**0**	**0**	**0**	**7**	**0**	**0**	**0**
1990-91	**Winnipeg Jets**	**NHL**	**67**	**1**	**5**	**6**	**1**	**4**	**5**	**189**	**0**	**0**	**0**	**40**	**2.5**	**36**	**1**	**69**	**24**	**–10**								
1991-92	**Winnipeg Jets**	**NHL**	**65**	**0**	**4**	**4**	**0**	**3**	**3**	**271**	**0**	**0**	**0**	**25**	**0.0**	**29**	**0**	**51**	**11**	**–11**	**4**	**0**	**0**	**0**	**6**	**0**	**0**	**0**
1992-93	**Philadelphia Flyers**	**NHL**	**35**	**2**	**1**	**3**	**2**	**1**	**3**	**37**	**0**	**0**	**0**	**12**	**16.7**	**14**	**0**	**22**	**8**	**0**								
	Hershey Bears	AHL	7	0	1	1				12																		
1993-94	**San Jose Sharks**	**NHL**	**34**	**0**	**2**	**2**	**0**	**2**	**2**	**76**	**0**	**0**	**0**	**14**	**0.0**	**13**	**1**	**18**	**8**	**2**	**14**	**1**	**0**	**1**	**20**	**0**	**0**	**0**
1994-95	**San Jose Sharks**	**NHL**	**29**	**0**	**2**	**2**	**0**	**3**	**3**	**61**	**0**	**0**	**0**	**12**	**0.0**	**12**	**0**	**17**	**5**	**0**	**9**	**0**	**0**	**0**	**5**	**0**	**0**	**0**
1995-96	Fort Wayne Komets	IHL	48	0	1	1				120											5	0	0	0	8			
1996-97	Fort Wayne Komets	IHL	13	0	1	1				27																		
	NHL Totals		**292**	**3**	**18**	**21**	**3**	**16**	**19**	**877**	**0**	**0**	**0**	**133**	**2.3**	**131**	**3**	**229**	**66**		**32**	**1**	**0**	**1**	**38**	**0**	**0**	**0**

Signed as a free agent by **Hartford**, March, 1986. Signed as a free agent by **Washington**, June 6, 1988. Signed as a free agent by **Philadelphia**, June 12, 1989. Traded to **Winnipeg** by **Philadelphia** for future considerations (later cancelled as part of the trade that sent Keith Acton and Pete Peeters to Philadelphia by Winnipeg, October 3, 1989), July 21, 1989. Traded to **Quebec** by **Winnipeg** for Dan Lambert, August 25, 1992. Claimed by **Philadelphia** from **Quebec** in NHL Waiver Draft, October 4, 1992. Traded to **San Jose** by **Philadelphia** for cash, August 5, 1993.

• CROSS, Cory

D – L. 6'5", 219 lbs. b: Lloydminster, Alta., 1/3/1971. Tampa Bay's 1st, 1st overall, in 1992 Supplemental Draft.

Season	Club	League	GP	G	A	Pts	AG	AA	APts	PIM	PP	SH	GW	S	%	TGF	PGF	TGA	PGA	+/–	GP	G	A	Pts	PIM	PP	SH	GW
1990-91	University of Alberta	CWUAA	20	2	5	7				16																		
1991-92	University of Alberta	CWUAA	41	4	11	15				82																		
1992-93	University of Alberta	CWUAA	43	11	28	39				105																		
	Atlanta Knights	IHL	7	0	1	1				2											4	0	0	0	6			
1993-94	**Tampa Bay Lightning**	**NHL**	**5**	**0**	**0**	**0**	**0**	**0**	**0**	**6**	**0**	**0**	**0**	**5**	**0.0**	**0**	**0**	**3**	**0**	**–3**								
	Atlanta Knights	IHL	70	4	14	18				72											9	1	2	3	14			
1994-95	**Tampa Bay Lightning**	**NHL**	**43**	**1**	**5**	**6**	**2**	**7**	**9**	**41**	**0**	**0**	**1**	**35**	**2.9**	**29**	**4**	**37**	**6**	**–6**								
	Atlanta Knights	IHL	41	5	10	15				67																		
1995-96	**Tampa Bay Lightning**	**NHL**	**75**	**2**	**14**	**16**	**2**	**11**	**13**	**66**	**0**	**0**	**0**	**57**	**3.5**	**51**	**1**	**61**	**15**	**4**	**6**	**0**	**0**	**0**	**22**	**0**	**0**	**0**
1996-97	**Tampa Bay Lightning**	**NHL**	**72**	**4**	**5**	**9**	**4**	**4**	**8**	**95**	**0**	**0**	**2**	**75**	**5.3**	**54**	**0**	**71**	**23**	**6**								
	Canada	WC-A	11	0	2	2				49																		

			REGULAR SEASON																		PLAYOFFS							
Season	**Club**	**League**	**GP**	**G**	**A**	**Pts**	**AG**	**AA**	**APts**	**PIM**	**PP**	**SH**	**GW**	**S**	**%**	**TGF**	**PGF**	**TGA**	**PGA**	**+/–**	**GP**	**G**	**A**	**Pts**	**PIM**	**PP**	**SH**	**GW**
1997-98	**Tampa Bay Lightning**	**NHL**	**74**	**3**	**6**	**9**	**4**	**6**	**10**	**77**	**0**	**1**	**0**	**72**	**4.2**	**35**	**3**	**80**	**24**	**–24**	....	....	....	....	....	....	....	....
	Canada	WC-A	6	1	0	1	....	....	....	2	....	....	....	....	....	....	....	....	....	....	....	....	....	....	....	....	....	....
1998-99	**Tampa Bay Lighning**	**NHL**	**67**	**2**	**16**	**18**	**2**	**15**	**17**	**92**	**0**	**0**	**0**	**96**	**2.1**	**47**	**11**	**83**	**22**	**–25**	....	....	....	....	....	....	....	....
99-2000	**Toronto Maple Leafs**	**NHL**	**71**	**4**	**11**	**15**	**4**	**10**	**14**	**64**	**0**	**0**	**1**	**60**	**6.7**	**49**	**0**	**46**	**10**	**13**	**12**	**0**	**2**	**2**	**2**	**0**	**0**	**0**
	NHL Totals		**407**	**16**	**57**	**73**	**18**	**53**	**71**	**441**	**0**	**1**	**4**	**400**	**4.0**	**265**	**19**	**381**	**100**		**18**	**0**	**2**	**2**	**24**	**0**	**0**	**0**

Traded to **Toronto** by **Tampa Bay** with Tampa Bay's 7th round choice in 2001 Entry Draft for Fredrik Modin, October 1, 1999.

• CROSSMAN, Doug

Doug A. D – L. 6'2", 190 lbs. b: Peterborough, Ont., 6/13/1960. Chicago's 6th, 112th overall, in 1979.

Season	Club	League	GP	G	A	Pts	AG	AA	APts	PIM	PP	SH	GW	S	%	TGF	PGF	TGA	PGA	+/–	GP	G	A	Pts	PIM	PP	SH	GW
1976-77	Strathroy Blades	OHA-B	39	6	35	41	....	....	....	56	....	....	....	....	....	....	....	....	....	....	....	....	....	....	....	....	....	....
	London Knights	OMJHL	1	0	0	0	....	....	....	0	....	....	....	....	....	....	....	....	....	....	....	....	....	....	....	....	....	....
1977-78	Ottawa 67's	OMJHL	65	4	17	21	....	....	....	17	....	....	....	....	....	....	....	....	....	....	16	2	11	13	10	....	....	....
1978-79	Ottawa 67's	OMJHL	67	12	51	63	....	....	....	65	....	....	....	....	....	....	....	....	....	....	4	1	3	4	0	....	....	....
1979-80	Ottawa 67's	OMJHL	66	20	96	116	....	....	....	48	....	....	....	....	....	....	....	....	....	....	11	7	6	13	19	....	....	....
	Canada	WJC-A	5	0	2	2	....	....	....	2	....	....	....	....	....	....	....	....	....	....	....	....	....	....	....	....	....	....
1980-81	**Chicago Black Hawks**	**NHL**	**9**	**0**	**2**	**2**	**0**	**1**	**1**	**2**	**0**	**0**	**0**	**16**	**0.0**	**8**	**1**	**13**	**1**	**–5**	....	....	....	....	....	....	....	....
	New Brunswick Hawks	AHL	70	13	43	56	....	....	....	90	....	....	....	....	....	....	....	....	....	....	13	5	6	11	36	....	....	....
1981-82	**Chicago Black Hawks**	**NHL**	**70**	**12**	**28**	**40**	**9**	**19**	**28**	**24**	**7**	**0**	**1**	**127**	**9.4**	**100**	**40**	**87**	**8**	**–19**	**11**	**0**	**3**	**3**	**4**	**0**	**0**	**0**
1982-83	**Chicago Black Hawks**	**NHL**	**80**	**13**	**40**	**53**	**11**	**28**	**39**	**46**	**6**	**0**	**1**	**134**	**9.7**	**132**	**40**	**90**	**19**	**21**	**13**	**3**	**7**	**10**	**6**	**1**	**0**	**0**
1983-84	**Philadelphia Flyers**	**NHL**	**78**	**7**	**28**	**35**	**6**	**19**	**25**	**63**	**2**	**0**	**2**	**160**	**4.4**	**114**	**27**	**87**	**23**	**23**	**3**	**0**	**0**	**0**	**0**	**0**	**0**	**0**
1984-85	**Philadelphia Flyers**	**NHL**	**80**	**4**	**33**	**37**	**3**	**22**	**25**	**65**	**1**	**1**	**1**	**111**	**3.6**	**118**	**29**	**80**	**22**	**31**	**19**	**4**	**6**	**10**	**38**	**3**	**0**	**0**
1985-86	**Philadelphia Flyers**	**NHL**	**80**	**6**	**37**	**43**	**5**	**25**	**30**	**55**	**2**	**0**	**1**	**134**	**4.5**	**130**	**52**	**110**	**27**	**–5**	**5**	**0**	**1**	**1**	**4**	**0**	**0**	**0**
1986-87	**Philadelphia Flyers**	**NHL**	**78**	**9**	**31**	**40**	**8**	**23**	**31**	**29**	**7**	**0**	**1**	**122**	**7.4**	**122**	**33**	**115**	**44**	**18**	**26**	**4**	**14**	**18**	**31**	**2**	**0**	**0**
1987-88	Canada	Can-Cup	8	0	1	1	....	....	....	4	....	....	....	....	....	....	....	....	....	....	....	....	....	....	....	....	....	....
	Philadelphia Flyers	**NHL**	**76**	**9**	**29**	**38**	**8**	**21**	**29**	**43**	**6**	**0**	**0**	**153**	**5.9**	**113**	**28**	**129**	**43**	**–1**	**7**	**1**	**1**	**2**	**8**	**1**	**0**	**0**
1988-89	**Los Angeles Kings**	**NHL**	**74**	**10**	**15**	**25**	**8**	**11**	**19**	**53**	**2**	**0**	**0**	**137**	**7.3**	**106**	**29**	**102**	**14**	**–11**	**2**	**0**	**1**	**1**	**2**	**0**	**0**	**0**
	New Haven Nighthawks	AHL	3	0	0	0	....	....	....	0	....	....	....	....	....	....	....	....	....	....	....	....	....	....	....	....	....	....
1989-90	**New York Islanders**	**NHL**	**80**	**15**	**44**	**59**	**13**	**32**	**45**	**54**	**8**	**0**	**1**	**159**	**9.4**	**155**	**69**	**141**	**58**	**3**	**5**	**0**	**1**	**1**	**6**	**0**	**0**	**0**
1990-91	**New York Islanders**	**NHL**	**16**	**1**	**6**	**7**	**1**	**5**	**6**	**12**	**1**	**0**	**0**	**30**	**3.3**	**23**	**13**	**20**	**6**	**–4**	....	....	....	....	....	....	....	....
	Hartford Whalers	**NHL**	**41**	**4**	**19**	**23**	**4**	**14**	**18**	**19**	**2**	**0**	**0**	**62**	**6.5**	**57**	**30**	**44**	**4**	**–13**	....	....	....	....	....	....	....	....
	Detroit Red Wings	**NHL**	**17**	**3**	**4**	**7**	**3**	**3**	**6**	**17**	**1**	**0**	**0**	**16**	**18.8**	**24**	**8**	**23**	**1**	**–6**	**6**	**0**	**5**	**5**	**6**	**0**	**0**	**0**
1991-92	**Detroit Red Wings**	**NHL**	**26**	**0**	**8**	**8**	**0**	**6**	**6**	**14**	**0**	**0**	**0**	**21**	**0.0**	**22**	**6**	**9**	**1**	**8**	....	....	....	....	....	....	....	....
1992-93	**Tampa Bay Lightning**	**NHL**	**40**	**8**	**21**	**29**	**7**	**14**	**21**	**18**	**2**	**0**	**1**	**54**	**14.8**	**51**	**21**	**41**	**7**	**–4**	....	....	....	....	....	....	....	....
	St. Louis Blues	**NHL**	**19**	**2**	**7**	**9**	**2**	**5**	**7**	**10**	**2**	**0**	**0**	**24**	**8.3**	**21**	**10**	**15**	**1**	**–3**	....	....	....	....	....	....	....	....
1993-94	**St. Louis Blues**	**NHL**	**50**	**2**	**7**	**9**	**2**	**5**	**7**	**10**	**1**	**0**	**0**	**30**	**6.7**	**43**	**12**	**40**	**10**	**1**	....	....	....	....	....	....	....	....
	Peoria Rivermen	IHL	8	3	5	8	....	....	....	0	....	....	....	....	....	....	....	....	....	....	....	....	....	....	....	....	....	....
1994-95	Denver Grizzlies	IHL	77	6	43	49	....	....	....	31	....	....	....	....	....	....	....	....	....	....	17	3	6	9	7	....	....	....
1995-96	Baltimore Bandits	AHL	23	3	12	15	....	....	....	18	....	....	....	....	....	....	....	....	....	....	....	....	....	....	....	....	....	....
	Chicago Wolves	IHL	8	1	4	5	....	....	....	2	....	....	....	....	....	....	....	....	....	....	6	1	1	2	0	....	....	....
	NHL Totals		**914**	**105**	**359**	**464**	**90**	**253**	**343**	**534**	**50**	**1**	**9**	**1490**	**7.0**	**1339**	**448**	**1146**	**289**		**97**	**12**	**39**	**51**	**105**	**7**	**0**	**0**

OMJHL First All-Star Team (1980)

Traded to **Philadelphia** by **Chicago** with Chicago's 2nd round choice (Scott Mellanby) in 1984 Entry Draft for Behn Wilson, June 8, 1983. Traded to **LA Kings** by **Philadelphia** for Jay Wells, September 29, 1988. Traded to **NY Islanders** by **LA Kings** to complete transaction that sent Mark Fitzpatrick and Wayne McBean to NY Islanders (February 22, 1989), May 23, 1989. Traded to **Hartford** by **NY Islanders** for Ray Ferraro, November 13, 1990. Traded to **Detroit** by **Hartford** for Doug Houda, February 20, 1991. Traded to **Quebec** by **Detroit** with Dennis Vial for cash, June 15, 1992. Claimed by **Tampa Bay** from **Quebec** in Expansion Draft, June 18, 1992. Traded to **St. Louis** by **Tampa Bay** with Basil McRae and Tampa Bay's 4th round choice (Andrei Petrakov) in 1996 Entry Draft for Jason Ruff, January 28, 1993.

• CROTEAU, Gary

Gary Paul "Bull" LW – L. 6', 205 lbs. b: Sudbury, Ont., 6/20/1946.

Season	Club	League	GP	G	A	Pts	AG	AA	APts	PIM	PP	SH	GW	S	%	TGF	PGF	TGA	PGA	+/–	GP	G	A	Pts	PIM	PP	SH	GW
1964-65	St. Lawrence University	ECAC	14	18	13	31	....	....	....	....	....	....	....	....	....	....	....	....	....	....	....	....	....	....	....	....	....	....
1965-66	St. Lawrence University	ECAC	24	20	11	31	....	....	....	12	....	....	....	....	....	....	....	....	....	....	....	....	....	....	....	....	....	....
1966-67	St. Lawrence University	ECAC	27	21	17	38	....	....	....	....	....	....	....	....	....	....	....	....	....	....	....	....	....	....	....	....	....	....
1967-68	St. Lawrence University	ECAC	19	21	19	40	....	....	....	....	....	....	....	....	....	....	....	....	....	....	....	....	....	....	....	....	....	....
1968-69	**Los Angeles Kings**	**NHL**	**11**	**5**	**1**	**6**	**5**	**1**	**6**	**6**	**3**	**0**	**0**	**19**	**26.3**	**10**	**4**	**7**	**0**	**–1**	**11**	**3**	**2**	**5**	**8**	**1**	**0**	**0**
	Springfield Kings	AHL	53	24	20	44	....	....	....	27	....	....	....	....	....	....	....	....	....	....	....	....	....	....	....	....	....	....
1969-70	**Los Angeles Kings**	**NHL**	**3**	**0**	**0**	**0**	**0**	**0**	**0**	**0**	**0**	**0**	**0**	**1**	**0.0**	**0**	**0**	**0**	**0**	**0**	....	....	....	....	....	....	....	....
	Springfield Kings	AHL	52	23	21	44	....	....	....	22	....	....	....	....	....	....	....	....	....	....	....	....	....	....	....	....	....	....
	Detroit Red Wings	**NHL**	**10**	**0**	**2**	**2**	**0**	**2**	**2**	**2**	**0**	**0**	**0**	**5**	**0.0**	**2**	**0**	**3**	**0**	**–1**	....	....	....	....	....	....	....	....
1970-71	**California Golden Seals**	**NHL**	**74**	**15**	**28**	**43**	**15**	**23**	**38**	**12**	**2**	**0**	**1**	**182**	**8.2**	**67**	**9**	**81**	**1**	**–22**	....	....	....	....	....	....	....	....
1971-72	**California Golden Seals**	**NHL**	**73**	**12**	**12**	**24**	**12**	**10**	**22**	**11**	**1**	**0**	**1**	**107**	**11.2**	**35**	**1**	**52**	**0**	**–18**	....	....	....	....	....	....	....	....
1972-73	**California Golden Seals**	**NHL**	**47**	**6**	**15**	**21**	**6**	**12**	**18**	**8**	**1**	**0**	**0**	**77**	**7.8**	**27**	**2**	**38**	**0**	**–13**	....	....	....	....	....	....	....	....
1973-74	**California Golden Seals**	**NHL**	**76**	**14**	**21**	**35**	**13**	**17**	**30**	**16**	**1**	**0**	**2**	**149**	**9.4**	**58**	**9**	**98**	**2**	**–47**	....	....	....	....	....	....	....	....
1974-75	**Kansas City Scouts**	**NHL**	**77**	**8**	**11**	**19**	**7**	**8**	**15**	**16**	**0**	**1**	**1**	**137**	**5.8**	**31**	**6**	**80**	**19**	**–36**	....	....	....	....	....	....	....	....
1975-76	**Kansas City Scouts**	**NHL**	**79**	**19**	**14**	**33**	**17**	**10**	**27**	**12**	**4**	**0**	**1**	**139**	**13.7**	**44**	**12**	**89**	**33**	**–24**	....	....	....	....	....	....	....	....
1976-77	**Colorado Rockies**	**NHL**	**78**	**24**	**27**	**51**	**22**	**21**	**43**	**14**	**5**	**0**	**2**	**145**	**16.6**	**77**	**12**	**92**	**9**	**–18**	....	....	....	....	....	....	....	....
1977-78	**Colorado Rockies**	**NHL**	**62**	**17**	**22**	**39**	**15**	**17**	**32**	**24**	**8**	**0**	**0**	**104**	**16.3**	**68**	**24**	**64**	**5**	**–15**	....	....	....	....	....	....	....	....
1978-79	**Colorado Rockies**	**NHL**	**79**	**23**	**18**	**41**	**20**	**13**	**33**	**18**	**8**	**0**	**1**	**104**	**22.1**	**69**	**24**	**79**	**6**	**–28**	....	....	....	....	....	....	....	....
1979-80	**Colorado Rockies**	**NHL**	**15**	**1**	**4**	**5**	**1**	**3**	**4**	**4**	**1**	**0**	**0**	**6**	**16.7**	**12**	**1**	**15**	**0**	**–4**	....	....	....	....	....	....	....	....
1980-81	Fort Worth Texans	CHL	4	1	1	2	....	....	....	2	....	....	....	....	....	....	....	....	....	....	....	....	....	....	....	....	....	....
	NHL Totals		**684**	**144**	**175**	**319**	**133**	**137**	**270**	**143**	**34**	**1**	**9**	**1175**	**12.3**	**500**	**104**	**698**	**75**		**11**	**3**	**2**	**5**	**8**	**1**	**0**	**0**

ECAC First All-Star Team (1968)

Traded to **LA Kings** by **Toronto** with Brian Murphy and Wayne Thomas for Grant Moore and Lou Deveault, October 15, 1968. Traded to **Detroit** by **LA Kings** with Dale Rolfe and Larry Johnston for Garry Monahan, Matt Ravlich and Brian Gibbons, February 20, 1970. Claimed by **California** from **Detroit** in Intra-League Draft, June 9, 1970. Claimed by **Kansas City** from **California** in Expansion Draft, June 12, 1974. Transferred to **Colorado** after **Kansas City** franchise relocated, July 15, 1976.

• CROWDER, Bruce

Bruce James RW – R. 6', 180 lbs. b: Essex, Ont., 3/25/1957. Philadelphia's 14th, 153rd overall, in 1977.

Season	Club	League	GP	G	A	Pts	AG	AA	APts	PIM	PP	SH	GW	S	%	TGF	PGF	TGA	PGA	+/–	GP	G	A	Pts	PIM	PP	SH	GW
1974-75	Essex 73's	OHA-C	STATISTICS NOT AVAILABLE																									
1975-76	University of New Hampshire	ECAC	31	6	12	18	....	....	....	14	....	....	....	....	....	....	....	....	....	....	....	....	....	....	....	....	....	....
1976-77	University of New Hampshire	ECAC	39	9	9	18	....	....	....	28	....	....	....	....	....	....	....	....	....	....	....	....	....	....	....	....	....	....
1977-78	University of New Hampshire	ECAC	30	10	35	45	....	....	....	58	....	....	....	....	....	....	....	....	....	....	....	....	....	....	....	....	....	....
1978-79	University of New Hampshire	ECAC	35	22	30	52	....	....	....	34	....	....	....	....	....	....	....	....	....	....	....	....	....	....	....	....	....	....
1979-80	Maine Mariners	AHL	49	16	11	27	....	....	....	23	....	....	....	....	....	....	....	....	....	....	11	3	1	4	13	....	....	....
1980-81	Maine Mariners	AHL	68	25	19	44	....	....	....	94	....	....	....	....	....	....	....	....	....	....	20	*11	6	17	20	....	....	....
1981-82	**Boston Bruins**	**NHL**	**63**	**16**	**11**	**27**	**13**	**7**	**20**	**31**	**1**	**0**	**1**	**83**	**19.3**	**39**	**4**	**43**	**1**	**–7**	**11**	**5**	**3**	**8**	**9**	**1**	**0**	**0**
	Erie Blades	AHL	15	6	6	12	....	....	....	6	....	....	....	....	....	....	....	....	....	....	....	....	....	....	....	....	....	....
1982-83	**Boston Bruins**	**NHL**	**80**	**21**	**19**	**40**	**17**	**13**	**30**	**58**	**1**	**0**	**0**	**148**	**14.2**	**72**	**6**	**36**	**0**	**30**	**17**	**3**	**1**	**4**	**32**	**0**	**0**	**1**
1983-84	**Boston Bruins**	**NHL**	**74**	**6**	**14**	**20**	**5**	**10**	**15**	**44**	**0**	**0**	**0**	**65**	**9.2**	**37**	**2**	**34**	**0**	**1**	**3**	**0**	**0**	**0**	**0**	**0**	**0**	**0**
1984-85	**Pittsburgh Penguins**	**NHL**	**26**	**4**	**7**	**11**	**3**	**5**	**8**	**23**	**0**	**0**	**0**	**36**	**11.1**	**14**	**0**	**30**	**7**	**–9**	....	....	....	....	....	....	....	....
1985-86			OUT OF HOCKEY – RETIRED																									
1986-1990	University of Maine	H-East	DID NOT PLAY – ASSISTANT COACH																									
1990-1991	U. of Massachusetts-Lowell	H-East	DID NOT PLAY – ASSISTANT COACH																									
1991-1996	U. of Massachusetts-Lowell	H-East	DID NOT PLAY – COACHING																									
1996-2000	Northeastern University	H-East	DID NOT PLAY – COACHING																									
	NHL Totals		**243**	**47**	**51**	**98**	**38**	**35**	**73**	**156**	**2**	**0**	**1**	**332**	**14.2**	**162**	**12**	**143**	**8**		**31**	**8**	**4**	**12**	**41**	**1**	**0**	**1**

• Brother of Keith

Signed as a free agent by **Boston**, September 28, 1981. Claimed by **Pittsburgh** from **Boston** in Waiver Draft, October 9, 1984. • Officially announced retirement, February 1, 1985.

• CROWDER, Keith

Keith Scott RW – R. 6', 190 lbs. b: Windsor, Ont., 1/6/1959. Boston's 4th, 57th overall, in 1979.

			REGULAR SEASON																		PLAYOFFS							
Season	Club	League	GP	G	A	Pts	AG	AA	APts	PIM	PP	SH	GW	S	%	TGF	PGF	TGA	PGA	+/–	GP	G	A	Pts	PIM	PP	SH	GW
1975-76	Essex 73's	OHA-C	38	*56	42	*98	....	....	....	104	....	....	....	....	....	....	....	....	....	....	....	....	....	....	....	....	....	....
1976-77	Peterborough Petes	OMJHL	58	13	19	32	....	....	....	99	....	....	....	....	....	....	....	....	....	....	4	0	2	2	9	....	....	....
1977-78	Peterborough Petes	OMJHL	58	30	30	60	....	....	....	135	....	....	....	....	....	....	....	....	....	....	14	3	5	8	21	....	....	....
	Peterborough Petes	Mem-Cup	5	2	6	8	....	....	....	9	....	....	....	....	....	....	....	....	....	....	....	....	....	....	....	....	....	....
1978-79	Peterborough Petes	OMJHL	42	25	41	66	....	....	....	76	....	....	....	....	....	....	....	....	....	....	15	12	6	18	40	....	....	....
	Birmingham Bulls	WHA	5	1	0	1	....	....	....	17	....	....	....	....	....	....	....	....	....	....	....	....	....	....	....	....	....	....
	Peterborough Petes	Mem-Cup	5	0	4	4	....	....	....	*28	....	....	....	....	....	....	....	....	....	....	....	....	....	....	....	....	....	....
1979-80	Binghamton Dusters	AHL	13	4	0	4	....	....	....	15	....	....	....	....	....	....	....	....	....	....	....	....	....	....	....	....	....	....
	Grand Rapids Owls	IHL	20	10	13	23	....	....	....	22	....	....	....	....	....	....	....	....	....	....	....	....	....	....	....	....	....	....
1980-81	Boston Bruins	NHL	47	13	12	25	10	8	18	172	1	0	1	69	18.8	41	5	27	0	9	3	2	0	2	9	0	0	0
	Springfield Indians	AHL	26	12	18	30	....	....	....	34	....	....	....	....	....	....	....	....	....	....	....	....	....	....	....	....	....	....
1981-82	Boston Bruins	NHL	71	23	21	44	18	14	32	101	0	0	1	130	17.7	65	4	61	0	0	11	2	2	4	14	0	0	0
1982-83	Boston Bruins	NHL	74	35	39	74	29	27	56	105	10	0	5	156	22.4	109	40	48	1	22	17	1	6	7	54	1	0	0
1983-84	Boston Bruins	NHL	63	24	28	52	19	19	38	128	4	0	4	110	21.8	77	24	41	0	12	3	0	0	0	7	0	0	0
1984-85	Boston Bruins	NHL	79	32	38	70	26	26	52	152	14	0	1	173	18.5	107	35	41	0	31	4	3	2	5	19	0	0	1
1985-86	Boston Bruins	NHL	78	38	46	84	30	31	61	177	20	0	4	184	20.7	129	58	59	2	14	3	2	0	2	21	0	0	0
1986-87	Boston Bruins	NHL	58	22	30	52	19	22	41	106	4	0	5	114	19.3	76	15	41	0	20	4	0	1	1	4	0	0	0
1987-88	Boston Bruins	NHL	68	17	26	43	14	19	33	173	6	0	3	123	13.8	79	24	41	0	14	23	3	9	12	44	1	0	0
1988-89	Boston Bruins	NHL	69	15	18	33	13	13	26	147	5	0	2	121	12.4	70	27	37	0	6	10	0	2	2	37	0	0	0
1989-90	Los Angeles Kings	NHL	55	4	13	17	3	9	12	93	0	0	1	48	8.3	31	0	30	1	2	7	1	0	1	9	0	0	0
	NHL Totals		662	223	271	494	181	188	369	1354	64	0	27	1228	18.2	784	232	426	4		85	14	22	36	218	2	0	1
	Other Major League Totals		5	1	0	1	....	....	....	17	....	....	....	....	....	....	....	....	....	....	....	....	....	....	....	....	....	....

• Brother of Bruce

Signed as an underage free agent by **Birmingham** (WHA), July, 1978. Signed as a free agent by **LA Kings**, June 28, 1989.

• CROWDER, Troy

RW – R. 6'4", 220 lbs. b: Sudbury, Ont., 5/3/1968. New Jersey's 6th, 108th overall, in 1986.

Season	Club	League	GP	G	A	Pts	AG	AA	APts	PIM	PP	SH	GW	S	%	TGF	PGF	TGA	PGA	+/–	GP	G	A	Pts	PIM	PP	SH	GW
1984-85	Sudbury Walden Reps	NOHA	28	20	21	41	....	....	....	63	....	....	....	....	....	....	....	....	....	....	....	....	....	....	....	....	....	....
1985-86	Hamilton Steelhawks	OHL	56	4	4	8	....	....	....	178	....	....	....	....	....	....	....	....	....	....	....	....	....	....	....	....	....	....
1986-87	Belleville Bulls	OHL	21	5	5	10	....	....	....	52	....	....	....	....	....	....	....	....	....	....	....	....	....	....	....	....	....	....
	North Bay Centennials	OHL	35	6	11	17	....	....	....	90	....	....	....	....	....	....	....	....	....	....	23	3	9	12	99	....	....	....
1987-88	North Bay Centennials	OHL	9	1	2	3	....	....	....	44	....	....	....	....	....	....	....	....	....	....	....	....	....	....	....	....	....	....
	Belleville Bulls	OHL	46	12	27	39	....	....	....	103	....	....	....	....	....	....	....	....	....	....	6	2	3	5	24	....	....	....
	Utica Devils	AHL	3	0	0	0	....	....	....	36	....	....	....	....	....	....	....	....	....	....	....	....	....	....	....	....	....	....
	New Jersey Devils	NHL	....	....	....	....	....	....	....	....	....	....	....	....	....	....	....	....	....	....	1	0	0	0	12	0	0	0
1988-89	Utica Devils	AHL	62	6	4	10	....	....	....	152	....	....	....	....	....	....	....	....	....	....	2	0	0	0	25	....	....	....
1989-90	New Jersey Devils	NHL	10	0	0	0	0	0	0	23	0	0	0	4	0.0	0	0	0	0	0	2	0	0	0	10	0	0	0
	Nashville Knights	ECHL	3	0	0	0	....	....	....	15	....	....	....	....	....	....	....	....	....	....	....	....	....	....	....	....	....	....
1990-91	New Jersey Devils	NHL	59	6	3	9	5	2	7	182	0	0	0	46	13.0	15	0	25	0	-10	....	....	....	....	....	....	....	....
1991-92	Detroit Red Wings	NHL	7	0	0	0	0	0	0	35	0	0	0	2	0.0	1	0	2	1	0	1	0	0	0	0	0	0	0
1992-93	Detroit Red Wings	NHL	DID NOT PLAY – INJURED																									
1993-94			DID NOT PLAY – INJURED																									
1994-95	Los Angeles Kings	NHL	29	1	2	3	2	3	5	99	0	0	0	4	25.0	6	0	6	0	0	....	....	....	....	....	....	....	....
1995-96	Los Angeles Kings	NHL	15	1	0	1	1	0	1	42	0	0	0	11	9.1	2	0	5	0	–3	....	....	....	....	....	....	....	....
1996-97	Vancouver Canucks	NHL	30	1	2	3	1	2	3	52	0	0	0	11	9.1	3	0	9	0	–6	....	....	....	....	....	....	....	....
	Syracuse Crunch	AHL	2	0	0	0	....	....	....	0	....	....	....	....	....	....	....	....	....	....	....	....	....	....	....	....	....	....
1997-98	Hannover Scorpions	Germany	19	1	0	1	....	....	....	34	....	....	....	....	....	....	....	....	....	....	2	0	1	1	33	....	....	....
1998-99	Hershey Bears	AHL	25	0	1	1	....	....	....	44	....	....	....	....	....	....	....	....	....	....	....	....	....	....	....	....	....	....
	London Knights	Britain	22	3	4	7	....	....	....	75	....	....	....	....	....	....	....	....	....	....	6	1	1	2	4	....	....	....
	NHL Totals		150	9	7	16	9	7	16	433	0	0	0	78	11.5	27	0	47	1		4	0	0	0	22	0	0	0

• Missed majority of 1989-90 season in retirement. Signed as a free agent by **Detroit**, August 27, 1991. • Missed majority of 1991-92 season and all of 1992-93 and 1993-94 seasons recovering from back injury suffered in game vs. Montreal, October 10, 1991. Signed as a free agent by **LA Kings**, August 31, 1994. Signed as a free agent by **Vancouver**, October 4, 1996. • Played w/ RHI's LA Blades in 1995 (4-0-1-1-18). • Offically announced retirement, August 6, 1999.

• CROWE, Philip

Philip Ross LW – R. 6'2", 230 lbs. b: Nanton, Alta., 4/4/1970.

Season	Club	League	GP	G	A	Pts	AG	AA	APts	PIM	PP	SH	GW	S	%	TGF	PGF	TGA	PGA	+/–	GP	G	A	Pts	PIM	PP	SH	GW
1989-90	Olds Grizzlies	AJHL	47	8	21	29	....	....	....	248	....	....	....	....	....	....	....	....	....	....	....	....	....	....	....	....	....	....
1990-91	Olds Grizzlies	AJHL	50	16	24	40	....	....	....	290	....	....	....	....	....	....	....	....	....	....	....	....	....	....	....	....	....	....
1991-92	Adirondack Red Wings	AHL	6	1	0	1	....	....	....	29	....	....	....	....	....	....	....	....	....	....	....	....	....	....	....	....	....	....
	Columbus Chill	ECHL	32	4	7	11	....	....	....	145	....	....	....	....	....	....	....	....	....	....	....	....	....	....	....	....	....	....
	Toledo Storm	ECHL	2	0	0	0	....	....	....	0	....	....	....	....	....	....	....	....	....	....	5	0	0	0	58	....	....	....
1992-93	Phoenix Roadrunners	IHL	53	3	3	6	....	....	....	190	....	....	....	....	....	....	....	....	....	....	....	....	....	....	....	....	....	....
1993-94	Fort Wayne Komets	IHL	5	0	1	1	....	....	....	26	....	....	....	....	....	....	....	....	....	....	....	....	....	....	....	....	....	....
	Los Angeles Kings	NHL	31	0	2	2	0	2	2	77	0	0	0	5	0.0	7	0	3	0	4	....	....	....	....	....	....	....	....
	Phoenix Roadrunners	IHL	2	0	0	0	....	....	....	0	....	....	....	....	....	....	....	....	....	....	....	....	....	....	....	....	....	....
1994-95	Hershey Bears	AHL	46	11	6	17	....	....	....	132	....	....	....	....	....	....	....	....	....	....	6	0	1	1	19	....	....	....
1995-96	Philadelphia Flyers	NHL	16	1	1	2	1	1	2	28	0	0	0	6	16.7	3	0	3	0	0	....	....	....	....	....	....	....	....
	Hershey Bears	AHL	39	6	8	14	....	....	....	105	....	....	....	....	....	....	....	....	....	....	5	1	2	3	19	....	....	....
1996-97	Ottawa Senators	NHL	26	0	1	1	0	1	1	30	0	0	0	8	0.0	3	0	3	0	0	3	0	0	0	16	0	0	0
	Detroit Vipers	IHL	41	7	7	14	....	....	....	83	....	....	....	....	....	....	....	....	....	....	....	....	....	....	....	....	....	....
1997-98	Ottawa Senators	NHL	9	3	0	3	4	0	4	24	0	0	1	6	50.0	4	0	1	0	3	....	....	....	....	....	....	....	....
	Detroit Vipers	IHL	55	6	13	19	....	....	....	160	....	....	....	....	....	....	....	....	....	....	20	5	2	7	48	....	....	....
1998-99	Ottawa Senators	NHL	8	0	1	1	0	1	1	4	0	0	0	2	0.0	2	0	1	0	1	....	....	....	....	....	....	....	....
	Cincinnati Cyclones	IHL	39	2	6	8	....	....	....	62	....	....	....	....	....	....	....	....	....	....	....	....	....	....	....	....	....	....
	Detroit Vipers	IHL	2	0	0	0	....	....	....	9	....	....	....	....	....	....	....	....	....	....	....	....	....	....	....	....	....	....
	Las Vegas Thunder	IHL	14	1	3	4	....	....	....	18	....	....	....	....	....	....	....	....	....	....	....	....	....	....	....	....	....	....
99-2000	Nashville Predators	NHL	4	0	0	0	0	0	0	10	0	0	0	1	0.0	0	0	0	0	0	....	....	....	....	....	....	....	....
	Milwaukee Admirals	IHL	20	3	1	4	....	....	....	31	....	....	....	....	....	....	....	....	....	....	....	....	....	....	....	....	....	....
	NHL Totals		94	4	5	9	5	5	10	173	0	0	1	28	14.3	19	0	11	0		3	0	0	0	16	0	0	0

Signed as a free agent by **LA Kings**, November 8, 1993. Signed as a free agent by **Philadelphia**, July 19, 1994. Signed as a free agent by **Ottawa**, July 29, 1996. Claimed by **Atlanta** from **Ottawa** in Expansion Draft, June 25, 1999. Traded to **Nashville** by **Atlanta** for future considerations, June 26, 1999. • Missed majority of 1999-2000 season recovering from knee injury suffered in game vs. Milwaukee (IHL), January 2, 2000.

• CROWLEY, Mike

D – L. 5'11", 190 lbs. b: Bloomington, MN, 7/4/1975. Philadelphia's 5th, 140th overall, in 1993.

Season	Club	League	GP	G	A	Pts	AG	AA	APts	PIM	PP	SH	GW	S	%	TGF	PGF	TGA	PGA	+/–	GP	G	A	Pts	PIM	PP	SH	GW
1990-91	Jefferson Jaguars	Hi-School	20	3	9	12	....	....	....	2	....	....	....	....	....	....	....	....	....	....	....	....	....	....	....	....	....	....
1991-92	Jefferson Jaguars	Hi-School	28	5	18	23	....	....	....	8	....	....	....	....	....	....	....	....	....	....	....	....	....	....	....	....	....	....
1992-93	Jefferson Jaguars	Hi-School	22	10	32	42	....	....	....	18	....	....	....	....	....	....	....	....	....	....	....	....	....	....	....	....	....	....
1993-94	Jefferson Jaguars	Hi-School	28	23	54	77	....	....	....	26	....	....	....	....	....	....	....	....	....	....	....	....	....	....	....	....	....	....
1994-95	University of Minnesota	WCHA	41	11	27	38	....	....	....	60	....	....	....	....	....	....	....	....	....	....	....	....	....	....	....	....	....	....
	United States	WJC-A	7	0	3	3	....	....	....	8	....	....	....	....	....	....	....	....	....	....	....	....	....	....	....	....	....	....
1995-96	University of Minnesota	WCHA	42	17	46	63	....	....	....	28	....	....	....	....	....	....	....	....	....	....	....	....	....	....	....	....	....	....
	United States	WC-A	8	0	1	1	....	....	....	6	....	....	....	....	....	....	....	....	....	....	....	....	....	....	....	....	....	....
1996-97	University of Minnesota	WCHA	42	9	*47	*56	....	....	....	24	....	....	....	....	....	....	....	....	....	....	....	....	....	....	....	....	....	....
1997-98	Mighty Ducks of Anaheim	NHL	8	2	2	4	2	2	4	8	0	0	1	17	11.8	9	1	9	1	0	....	....	....	....	....	....	....	....
	Cincinnati Mighty Ducks	AHL	76	12	26	38	....	....	....	91	....	....	....	....	....	....	....	....	....	....	....	....	....	....	....	....	....	....
	United States	WC-A	6	1	0	1	....	....	....	0	....	....	....	....	....	....	....	....	....	....	....	....	....	....	....	....	....	....

Season	Club	League	REGULAR SEASON GP	G	A	Pts	AG	AA	APts	PIM	PP	SH	GW	S	%	TGF	PGF	TGA	PGA	+/–	PLAYOFFS GP	G	A	Pts	PIM	PP	SH	GW
1998-99	**Mighty Ducks of Anaheim**	**NHL**	**20**	**2**	**3**	**5**	**2**	**3**	**5**	**16**	**1**	**0**	**1**	**41**	**4.9**	**15**	**9**	**16**	**0**	**–10**	....	....	....	....	....	....	....	....
	Cincinnati Mighty Ducks	AHL	44	5	23	28	....	....	....	42	....	....	....	....	....	....	....	....	....	....	3	0	3	3	2	....	....	....
99-2000	Long Beach Ice Dogs	IHL	67	9	39	48	....	....	....	35	....	....	....	....	....	....	....	....	....	....	4	2	1	3	6	....	....	....
	NHL Totals		**28**	**4**	**5**	**9**	**4**	**5**	**9**	**24**	**1**	**0**	**2**	**58**	**6.9**	**24**	**10**	**25**	**1**		....	....	....	....	....	....	....	....

WCHA First All-Star Team (1996, 1997) • NCAA West First All-American Team (1996, 1997) • IHL First All-Star Team (2000)

Traded to **Anaheim** by **Philadelphia** with Anatoli Semenov for Brian Wesenberg, March 19, 1996. Signed as a free agent by **Long Beach** (IHL), August 24, 1999.

• CROWLEY, Ted

Edward J. D – R. 6'2", 188 lbs. b: Concord, MA, 5/3/1970. Toronto's 4th, 69th overall, in 1988.

Season	Club	League	GP	G	A	Pts	AG	AA	APts	PIM	PP	SH	GW	S	%	TGF	PGF	TGA	PGA	+/–	GP	G	A	Pts	PIM	PP	SH	GW
1987-88	Lawrence Academy	Hi-School	23	11	23	34	....	....	....	....	....	....	....	....	....	....	....	....	....	....	....	....	....	....	....	....	....	....
	United States	WJC-A	7	0	1	1	....	....	....	0	....	....	....	....	....	....	....	....	....	....	....	....	....	....	....	....	....	....
1988-89	Lawrence Academy	Hi-School	23	12	24	36	....	....	....	....	....	....	....	....	....	....	....	....	....	....	....	....	....	....	....	....	....	....
	United States	WJC-A	7	1	1	2	....	....	....	0	....	....	....	....	....	....	....	....	....	....	....	....	....	....	....	....	....	....
1989-90	Boston College	H-East	39	7	24	31	....	....	....	34	....	....	....	....	....	....	....	....	....	....	....	....	....	....	....	....	....	....
	United States	WJC-A	7	1	4	5	....	....	....	6	....	....	....	....	....	....	....	....	....	....	....	....	....	....	....	....	....	....
1990-91	Boston College	H-East	39	12	24	36	....	....	....	61	....	....	....	....	....	....	....	....	....	....	....	....	....	....	....	....	....	....
1991-92	United States	Nat-Team	42	6	7	13	....	....	....	65	....	....	....	....	....	....	....	....	....	....	....	....	....	....	....	....	....	....
	St. John's Maple Leafs	AHL	29	5	4	9	....	....	....	33	....	....	....	....	....	....	....	....	....	....	10	3	1	4	11	....	....	....
1992-93	St. John's Maple Leafs	AHL	79	19	38	57	....	....	....	41	....	....	....	....	....	....	....	....	....	....	9	2	2	4	4	....	....	....
1993-94	United States	Nat-Team	48	9	13	22	....	....	....	80	....	....	....	....	....	....	....	....	....	....	....	....	....	....	....	....	....	....
	United States	Olympics	8	0	2	2	....	....	....	8	....	....	....	....	....	....	....	....	....	....	....	....	....	....	....	....	....	....
	Hartford Whalers	**NHL**	**21**	**1**	**2**	**3**	**1**	**2**	**3**	**10**	**1**	**0**	**0**	**28**	**3.6**	**15**	**3**	**16**	**3**	**–1**	....	....	....	....	....	....	....	....
1994-95	Chicago Wolves	IHL	53	8	23	31	....	....	....	68	....	....	....	....	....	....	....	....	....	....	....	....	....	....	....	....	....	....
	Houston Aeros	IHL	23	4	9	13	....	....	....	35	....	....	....	....	....	....	....	....	....	....	3	0	1	1	0	....	....	....
1995-96	Providence Bruins	AHL	72	12	30	42	....	....	....	47	....	....	....	....	....	....	....	....	....	....	4	1	2	3	2	....	....	....
1996-97	Cincinnati Cyclones	IHL	39	9	9	18	....	....	....	24	....	....	....	....	....	....	....	....	....	....	....	....	....	....	....	....	....	....
	Phoenix Roadrunners	IHL	30	5	8	13	....	....	....	21	....	....	....	....	....	....	....	....	....	....	....	....	....	....	....	....	....	....
1997-98	Springfield Falcons	AHL	78	14	35	49	....	....	....	55	....	....	....	....	....	....	....	....	....	....	4	1	1	2	2	....	....	....
1998-99	**Colorado Avalanche**	**NHL**	**7**	**0**	**1**	**1**	**0**	**1**	**1**	**2**	**0**	**0**	**0**	**10**	**0.0**	**3**	**3**	**2**	**1**	**–1**	....	....	....	....	....	....	....	....
	Hershey Bears	AHL	18	1	5	6	....	....	....	27	....	....	....	....	....	....	....	....	....	....	....	....	....	....	....	....	....	....
	NY Islanders Islanders	**NHL**	**6**	**1**	**1**	**2**	**1**	**1**	**2**	**0**	**1**	**0**	**0**	**10**	**10.0**	**6**	**2**	**4**	**0**	**0**	....	....	....	....	....	....	....	....
	Lowell Lock Monsters	AHL	41	3	22	25	....	....	....	51	....	....	....	....	....	....	....	....	....	....	3	0	0	0	6	....	....	....
99-2000	Cleveland Lumberjacks	IHL	61	9	20	29	....	....	....	94	....	....	....	....	....	....	....	....	....	....	....	....	....	....	....	....	....	....
	Utah Grizzlies	IHL	16	3	2	5	....	....	....	16	....	....	....	....	....	....	....	....	....	....	5	1	1	2	12	....	....	....
	NHL Totals		**34**	**2**	**4**	**6**	**2**	**4**	**6**	**12**	**2**	**0**	**0**	**48**	**4.2**	**24**	**8**	**22**	**4**		....	....	....	....	....	....	....	....

Hockey East First All-Star Team (1991) • NCAA East Second All-American Team (1991)

Traded to **Hartford** by **Toronto** for Mark Greig and Hartford's 6th round choice (Doug Bonner) in 1995 Entry Draft, January 25, 1994. Signed as a free agent by **Boston**, August 9, 1995. Signed as a free agent by **Phoenix**, June 27, 1997. Signed as a free agent by **Colorado**, August 14, 1998. Traded to **NY Islanders** by **Colorado** for Michael Gaul, December 15, 1998. Signed as a free agent by **Chicago**, July 22, 1999. Traded to **Utah** (IHL) by **Cleveland** (IHL) for Ian Gordon, Joe Frederick and Sean Berans, March 16, 2000 with Chicago retaining NHL rights.

• CULHANE, Jim

D – L. 6', 190 lbs. b: Halleybury, Ont., 3/13/1965. Hartford's 6th, 214th overall, in 1984.

Season	Club	League	GP	G	A	Pts	AG	AA	APts	PIM	PP	SH	GW	S	%	TGF	PGF	TGA	PGA	+/–	GP	G	A	Pts	PIM	PP	SH	GW
1982-83	Hawkesbury Hawks	OJHL	30	4	18	22	....	....	....	89	....	....	....	....	....	....	....	....	....	....	....	....	....	....	....	....	....	....
1983-84	Western Michigan University	CCHA	42	1	14	15	....	....	....	88	....	....	....	....	....	....	....	....	....	....	....	....	....	....	....	....	....	....
1984-85	Western Michigan University	CCHA	37	2	8	10	....	....	....	84	....	....	....	....	....	....	....	....	....	....	....	....	....	....	....	....	....	....
1985-86	Western Michigan University	CCHA	40	1	21	22	....	....	....	61	....	....	....	....	....	....	....	....	....	....	....	....	....	....	....	....	....	....
1986-87	Western Michigan University	CCHA	43	9	24	33	....	....	....	163	....	....	....	....	....	....	....	....	....	....	....	....	....	....	....	....	....	....
1987-88	Binghamton Whalers	AHL	75	5	17	22	....	....	....	169	....	....	....	....	....	....	....	....	....	....	4	0	0	0	8	....	....	....
1988-89	Binghamton Whalers	AHL	72	6	11	17	....	....	....	200	....	....	....	....	....	....	....	....	....	....	....	....	....	....	....	....	....	....
1989-90	**Hartford Whalers**	**NHL**	**6**	**0**	**1**	**1**	**0**	**1**	**1**	**4**	**0**	**0**	**0**	**6**	**0.0**	**5**	**0**	**3**	**1**	**3**	....	....	....	....	....	....	....	....
	Binghamton Whalers	AHL	73	6	11	17	....	....	....	69	....	....	....	....	....	....	....	....	....	....	....	....	....	....	....	....	....	....
1990-91	Capital District Islanders	AHL	15	0	0	0	....	....	....	14	....	....	....	....	....	....	....	....	....	....	....	....	....	....	....	....	....	....
	Kansas City Blades	IHL	59	1	8	9	....	....	....	50	....	....	....	....	....	....	....	....	....	....	....	....	....	....	....	....	....	....
1991-92	Capital District Islanders	AHL	37	1	3	4	....	....	....	58	....	....	....	....	....	....	....	....	....	....	....	....	....	....	....	....	....	....
1992-2000	Western Michigan University	CCHA	DID NOT PLAY – ASSISTANT COACH																									
	NHL Totals		**6**	**0**	**1**	**1**	**0**	**1**	**1**	**4**	**0**	**0**	**0**	**6**	**0.0**	**5**	**0**	**3**	**1**		....	....	....	....	....	....	....	....

Signed as a free agent by **NY Islanders**, October, 1990.

• CULLEN, John

Barry John C – R. 5'10", 182 lbs. b: Puslinch, Ont., 8/2/1964. Buffalo's 2nd, 10th overall, in 1986 Supplemental Draft.

Season	Club	League	GP	G	A	Pts	AG	AA	APts	PIM	PP	SH	GW	S	%	TGF	PGF	TGA	PGA	+/–	GP	G	A	Pts	PIM	PP	SH	GW
1982-83	Cambridge Winterhawks	OJHL	45	42	56	98	....	....	....	52	....	....	....	....	....	....	....	....	....	....	....	....	....	....	....	....	....	....
	St. Thomas Pests	OJHL-B	8	6	1	7	....	....	....	2	....	....	....	....	....	....	....	....	....	....	....	....	....	....	....	....	....	....
1983-84	Boston University	ECAC	40	23	33	56	....	....	....	28	....	....	....	....	....	....	....	....	....	....	....	....	....	....	....	....	....	....
1984-85	Boston University	H-East	41	27	32	59	....	....	....	46	....	....	....	....	....	....	....	....	....	....	....	....	....	....	....	....	....	....
1985-86	Boston University	H-East	43	25	49	74	....	....	....	54	....	....	....	....	....	....	....	....	....	....	....	....	....	....	....	....	....	....
1986-87	Boston University	H-East	36	23	29	52	....	....	....	35	....	....	....	....	....	....	....	....	....	....	....	....	....	....	....	....	....	....
1987-88	Flint Spirits	IHL	81	48	*109	*157	....	....	....	113	....	....	....	....	....	....	....	....	....	....	16	11	*15	26	16	....	....	....
1988-89	**Pittsburgh Penguins**	**NHL**	**79**	**12**	**37**	**49**	**10**	**26**	**36**	**112**	**8**	**0**	**0**	**121**	**9.9**	**75**	**39**	**65**	**4**	**–25**	**11**	**3**	**6**	**9**	**28**	**0**	**0**	**0**
1989-90	**Pittsburgh Penguins**	**NHL**	**72**	**32**	**60**	**92**	**28**	**43**	**71**	**138**	**9**	**0**	**4**	**197**	**16.2**	**120**	**44**	**101**	**12**	**–13**	....	....	....	....	....	....	....	....
	Canada	WEC-A	10	1	3	4	....	....	....	0	....	....	....	....	....	....	....	....	....	....	....	....	....	....	....	....	....	....
1990-91	**Pittsburgh Penguins**	**NHL**	**65**	**31**	**63**	**94**	**28**	**48**	**76**	**83**	**10**	**0**	**2**	**171**	**18.1**	**123**	**49**	**76**	**2**	**0**	....	....	....	....	....	....	....	....
	Hartford Whalers	**NHL**	**13**	**8**	**8**	**16**	**7**	**6**	**13**	**18**	**4**	**0**	**1**	**34**	**23.5**	**21**	**13**	**15**	**1**	**–6**	**6**	**2**	**7**	**9**	**10**	**0**	**0**	**0**
1991-92	**Hartford Whalers**	**NHL**	**77**	**26**	**51**	**77**	**24**	**39**	**63**	**141**	**10**	**0**	**4**	**172**	**15.1**	**100**	**45**	**83**	**0**	**–28**	**7**	**2**	**1**	**3**	**12**	**1**	**0**	**1**
1992-93	**Hartford Whalers**	**NHL**	**19**	**5**	**4**	**9**	**4**	**3**	**7**	**58**	**3**	**0**	**0**	**38**	**13.2**	**12**	**4**	**23**	**0**	**–15**	....	....	....	....	....	....	....	....
	Toronto Maple Leafs	**NHL**	**47**	**13**	**28**	**41**	**11**	**19**	**30**	**53**	**10**	**0**	**1**	**86**	**15.1**	**58**	**38**	**30**	**2**	**–8**	**12**	**2**	**3**	**5**	**0**	**1**	**0**	**0**
1993-94	**Toronto Maple Leafs**	**NHL**	**53**	**13**	**17**	**30**	**12**	**13**	**25**	**67**	**2**	**0**	**4**	**80**	**16.3**	**40**	**10**	**32**	**0**	**–2**	**3**	**0**	**0**	**0**	**0**	**0**	**0**	**0**
1994-95	**Pittsburgh Penguins**	**NHL**	**46**	**13**	**24**	**37**	**23**	**35**	**58**	**66**	**2**	**0**	**1**	**88**	**14.8**	**52**	**13**	**43**	**0**	**–4**	**9**	**0**	**2**	**2**	**8**	**0**	**0**	**0**
1995-96	**Tampa Bay Lightning**	**NHL**	**76**	**16**	**34**	**50**	**16**	**28**	**44**	**65**	**8**	**0**	**3**	**152**	**10.5**	**75**	**26**	**52**	**4**	**1**	**5**	**3**	**3**	**6**	**0**	**0**	**1**	**0**
1996-97	**Tampa Bay Lightning**	**NHL**	**70**	**18**	**37**	**55**	**19**	**33**	**52**	**95**	**5**	**0**	**2**	**116**	**15.5**	**64**	**28**	**51**	**1**	**–14**	....	....	....	....	....	....	....	....
1997-98	**Tampa Bay Lightning**	**NHL**	DID NOT PLAY																									
1998-99	**Tampa Bay Lighning**	**NHL**	**4**	**0**	**0**	**0**	**0**	**0**	**0**	**2**	**0**	**0**	**0**	**3**	**0.0**	**1**	**1**	**2**	**0**	**–2**	....	....	....	....	....	....	....	....
	Cleveland Lumberjacks	IHL	6	2	7	9	....	....	....	0	....	....	....	....	....	....	....	....	....	....	....	....	....	....	....	....	....	....
99-2000	**Tampa Bay Lighning**	**NHL**	DID NOT PLAY – ASSISTANT COACH																									
	NHL Totals		**621**	**187**	**363**	**550**	**182**	**293**	**475**	**898**	**71**	**0**	**22**	**1258**	**14.9**	**741**	**310**	**573**	**26**		**53**	**12**	**22**	**34**	**58**	**2**	**1**	**1**

• Son of Barry • Hockey East First All-Star Team (1985, 1986) • NCAA East Second All-American Team (1986) • Hockey East Second All-Star Team (1987) • IHL First All-Star Team (1988) • Won James Gatschene Memorial Trophy (MVP - IHL) (1988) • Shared Garry F. Longman Memorial Trophy (Top Rookie - IHL) with Ed Belfour (1988) • Won Leo P. Lamoureux Memorial Trophy (Top Scorer - IHL) (1988) • Won Bill Masterton Memorial Trophy (1999) • Played in NHL All-Star Game (1991, 1992)

Signed as a free agent by **Pittsburgh**, June 21, 1988. Traded to **Hartford** by **Pittsburgh** with Jeff Parker and Zarley Zalapski for Ron Francis, Grant Jennings and Ulf Samuelsson, March 4, 1991. Traded to **Toronto** by **Hartford** for Toronto's 2nd round choice (later traded to San Jose - San Jose selected Vlastimil Kroupa), November 24, 1992. Signed as a free agent by **Pittsburgh**, August 3, 1994. Signed as a free agent by **Tampa Bay**, September 11, 1995. • Missed entire 1997-98 season recovering from treatment and surgery for non-Hodgkins Lymphoma. • Officially announced retirement and named Assistant Coach with **Tampa Bay**, November 27, 1998.

• CULLEN, Matt

C – L. 6'1", 195 lbs. b: Virginia, MN, 11/2/1976. Anaheim's 2nd, 35th overall, in 1996.

Season	Club	League	GP	G	A	Pts	AG	AA	APts	PIM	PP	SH	GW	S	%	TGF	PGF	TGA	PGA	+/–	GP	G	A	Pts	PIM	PP	SH	GW
1992-1994	Moorehead Spuds	Hi-School	STATISTICS NOT AVAILABLE																									
1994-95	Moorehead Spuds	Hi-School	28	44	45	89	....	....	....	78	....	....	....	....	....	....	....	....	....	....	....	....	....	....	....	....	....	....
1995-96	St. Cloud State Huskies	WCHA	39	12	29	41	....	....	....	28	....	....	....	....	....	....	....	....	....	....	....	....	....	....	....	....	....	....
	United States	WJC-A	6	3	1	4	....	....	....	0	....	....	....	....	....	....	....	....	....	....	....	....	....	....	....	....	....	....
1996-97	St. Cloud State Huskies	WCHA	36	15	30	45	....	....	....	70	....	....	....	....	....	....	....	....	....	....	....	....	....	....	....	....	....	....
	Baltimore Bandits	AHL	6	3	3	6	....	....	....	7	....	....	....	....	....	....	....	....	....	....	3	0	2	2	0	....	....	....

			REGULAR SEASON																		PLAYOFFS							
Season	Club	League	GP	G	A	Pts	AG	AA	APts	PIM	PP	SH	GW	S	%	TGF	PGF	TGA	PGA	+/-	GP	G	A	Pts	PIM	PP	SH	GW
1997-98	**Mighty Ducks of Anaheim**	**NHL**	**61**	**6**	**21**	**27**	**7**	**21**	**28**	**23**	**2**	**0**	**0**	**75**	**8.0**	**42**	**8**	**48**	**10**	**–4**	....	....	....	....	....	....	....	....
	Cincinnati Mighty Ducks	AHL	18	15	12	27	....	....	....	2	....	....	....	....	....	....	....	....	....	....	....	....	....	....	....	....	....	....
1998-99	**Mighty Ducks of Anaheim**	**NHL**	**75**	**11**	**14**	**25**	**13**	**13**	**26**	**47**	**5**	**1**	**1**	**112**	**9.8**	**40**	**11**	**51**	**10**	**–12**	**4**	**0**	**0**	**0**	**0**	**0**	**0**	**0**
	Cincinnati Mighty Ducks	AHL	3	1	2	3	....	....	....	8	....	....	....	....	....	....	....	....	....	....	....	....	....	....	....	....	....	....
	United States	WC-A	6	1	7	8	....	....	....	4	....	....	....	....	....	....	....	....	....	....	....	....	....	....	....	....	....	....
99-2000	**Mighty Ducks of Anaheim**	**NHL**	**80**	**13**	**26**	**39**	**15**	**24**	**39**	**24**	**1**	**0**	**1**	**137**	**9.5**	**58**	**13**	**59**	**19**	**5**	....	....	....	....	....	....	....	....
	NHL Totals		**216**	**30**	**61**	**91**	**35**	**58**	**93**	**94**	**8**	**1**	**2**	**324**	**9.3**	**140**	**32**	**158**	**39**		**4**	**0**	**0**	**0**	**0**	**0**	**0**	**0**

WCHA Second All-Star Team (1997)

• CULLEN, Ray

Raymond Murray C – R. 5'11", 180 lbs. b: Ottawa, Ont., 9/20/1941.

Season	Club	League	GP	G	A	Pts	AG	AA	APts	PIM	PP	SH	GW	S	%	TGF	PGF	TGA	PGA	+/-	GP	G	A	Pts	PIM	PP	SH	GW
1958-59	St. Catharines Teepees	OHA-Jr.	54	19	14	33	....	....	....	46	....	....	....	....	....	....	....	....	....	....	7	1	1	2	0	....	....	....
1959-60	St. Catharines Teepees	OHA-Jr.	48	*48	29	77	....	....	....	60	....	....	....	....	....	....	....	....	....	....	17	*15	17	*32	20	....	....	....
	St. Catharines Teepees	Mem-Cup	14	*13	11	24	....	....	....	24	....	....	....	....	....	....	....	....	....	....	....	....	....	....	....	....	....	....
1960-61	St. Catharines Teepees	OHA-Jr.	45	24	50	74	....	....	....	56	....	....	....	....	....	....	....	....	....	....	6	2	2	4	10	....	....	....
1961-62	St. Catharines Teepees	OHA-Jr.	50	36	42	78	....	....	....	63	....	....	....	....	....	....	....	....	....	....	6	4	2	6	0	....	....	....
1962-63	Knoxville Knights	EHL	67	66	43	109	....	....	....	32	....	....	....	....	....	....	....	....	....	....	5	4	1	5	0	....	....	....
1963-64	St. Louis Braves	CPHL	63	46	52	98	....	....	....	24	....	....	....	....	....	....	....	....	....	....	....	....	....	....	....	....	....	....
1964-65	Buffalo Bisons	AHL	70	28	36	64	....	....	....	18	....	....	....	....	....	....	....	....	....	....	9	3	6	9	17	....	....	....
1965-66	**New York Rangers**	**NHL**	**8**	**1**	**3**	**4**	**1**	**3**	**4**	**0**	....	....	....	....	....	....	....	....	....	....	....	....	....	....	....	....	....	....
	Baltimore Clippers	AHL	63	27	46	73	....	....	....	40	....	....	....	....	....	....	....	....	....	....	....	....	....	....	....	....	....	....
1966-67	**Detroit Red Wings**	**NHL**	**27**	**8**	**8**	**16**	**9**	**8**	**17**	**8**	....	....	....	....	....	....	....	....	....	....	....	....	....	....	....	....	....	....
	Pittsburgh Hornets	AHL	28	15	14	29	....	....	....	8	....	....	....	....	....	....	....	....	....	....	....	....	....	....	....	....	....	....
1967-68	**Minnesota North Stars**	**NHL**	**67**	**28**	**25**	**53**	**33**	**25**	**58**	**18**	**11**	**0**	**6**	**203**	**13.8**	**67**	**27**	**64**	**0**	**–24**	**14**	**2**	**6**	**8**	**2**	**1**	**0**	**0**
1968-69	**Minnesota North Stars**	**NHL**	**67**	**26**	**38**	**64**	**28**	**34**	**62**	**44**	**3**	**0**	**2**	**195**	**13.3**	**79**	**22**	**85**	**1**	**–27**	....	....	....	....	....	....	....	....
1969-70	**Minnesota North Stars**	**NHL**	**74**	**17**	**28**	**45**	**18**	**26**	**44**	**8**	**3**	**0**	**3**	**143**	**11.9**	**70**	**1**	**50**	**0**	**19**	**6**	**1**	**4**	**5**	**0**	**0**	**0**	**0**
1970-71	**Vancouver Canucks**	**NHL**	**70**	**12**	**21**	**33**	**12**	**18**	**30**	**42**	**4**	**0**	**3**	**114**	**10.5**	**49**	**24**	**49**	**0**	**–24**	....	....	....	....	....	....	....	....
	NHL Totals		**313**	**92**	**123**	**215**	**101**	**114**	**215**	**120**	....	....	....	....	....	....	....	....	....		**20**	**3**	**10**	**13**	**2**	....	....	....

• Brother of Brian and Barry • EHL First All-Star Team (1963) • EHL Rookie of the Year (1963) • CHL First All-Star Team (1964) • Won Dudley "Red" Garrett Memorial Award (Top Rookie - AHL) (1965)

Traded to **NY Rangers** by **Chicago** with John McKenzie for Dick Meissner, Dave Richardson, Tracy Pratt and Mel Pearson, June 4, 1965. Claimed by **Detroit** from **NY Rangers** in Intra-League Draft, June 15, 1966. Claimed by **Minnesota** from **Detroit** in Expansion Draft, June 6, 1967. Claimed by **Vancouver** from **Minnesota** in Expansion Draft, June 10, 1970.

• CULLIMORE, Jassen

Jassen A. D – L. 6'5", 225 lbs. b: Simcoe, Ont., 12/4/1972. Vancouver's 2nd, 29th overall, in 1991.

Season	Club	League	GP	G	A	Pts	AG	AA	APts	PIM	PP	SH	GW	S	%	TGF	PGF	TGA	PGA	+/-	GP	G	A	Pts	PIM	PP	SH	GW
1986-87	Caledonia Corvairs	OJHL-C	18	2	0	2	....	....	....	9	....	....	....	....	....	....	....	....	....	....	....	....	....	....	....	....	....	....
1987-88	Simcoe Rams	OJHL-C	35	11	14	25	....	....	....	92	....	....	....	....	....	....	....	....	....	....	....	....	....	....	....	....	....	....
1988-89	Peterborough Roadrunners	OJHL-B	29	11	17	28	....	....	....	88	....	....	....	....	....	....	....	....	....	....	....	....	....	....	....	....	....	....
	Peterborough Petes	OHL	20	2	1	3	....	....	....	6	....	....	....	....	....	....	....	....	....	....	....	....	....	....	....	....	....	....
1989-90	Peterborough Petes	OHL	59	2	6	8	....	....	....	61	....	....	....	....	....	....	....	....	....	....	11	0	2	2	8	....	....	....
1990-91	Peterborough Petes	OHL	62	8	16	24	....	....	....	74	....	....	....	....	....	....	....	....	....	....	4	1	0	1	7	....	....	....
1991-92	Peterborough Petes	OHL	54	9	37	46	....	....	....	65	....	....	....	....	....	....	....	....	....	....	10	3	6	9	8	....	....	....
	Canada	WJC-A	7	1	0	1	....	....	....	2	....	....	....	....	....	....	....	....	....	....	....	....	....	....	....	....	....	....
1992-93	Hamilton Canucks	AHL	56	5	7	12	....	....	....	60	....	....	....	....	....	....	....	....	....	....	....	....	....	....	....	....	....	....
1993-94	Hamilton Canucks	AHL	71	8	20	28	....	....	....	86	....	....	....	....	....	....	....	....	....	....	3	0	1	1	2	....	....	....
1994-95	**Vancouver Canucks**	**NHL**	**34**	**1**	**2**	**3**	**2**	**3**	**5**	**39**	**0**	**0**	**0**	**30**	**3.3**	**18**	**2**	**22**	**4**	**–2**	**11**	**0**	**0**	**0**	**12**	**0**	**0**	**0**
	Syracuse Crunch	AHL	33	2	7	9	....	....	....	66	....	....	....	....	....	....	....	....	....	....	....	....	....	....	....	....	....	....
1995-96	**Vancouver Canucks**	**NHL**	**27**	**1**	**1**	**2**	**1**	**1**	**2**	**21**	**0**	**0**	**1**	**12**	**8.3**	**21**	**0**	**23**	**6**	**4**	....	....	....	....	....	....	....	....
1996-97	**Vancouver Canucks**	**NHL**	**3**	**0**	**0**	**0**	**0**	**0**	**0**	**2**	**0**	**0**	**0**	**2**	**0.0**	**0**	**0**	**3**	**1**	**–2**	....	....	....	....	....	....	....	....
	Montreal Canadiens	**NHL**	**49**	**2**	**6**	**8**	**2**	**5**	**7**	**42**	**0**	**1**	**1**	**52**	**3.8**	**41**	**5**	**47**	**15**	**4**	**2**	**0**	**0**	**0**	**2**	**0**	**0**	**0**
1997-98	**Montreal Canadiens**	**NHL**	**3**	**0**	**0**	**0**	**0**	**0**	**0**	**4**	**0**	**0**	**0**	**1**	**0.0**	**0**	**0**	**0**	**0**	**0**	....	....	....	....	....	....	....	....
	Fredericton Canadiens	AHL	5	1	0	1	....	....	....	8	....	....	....	....	....	....	....	....	....	....	....	....	....	....	....	....	....	....
	Tampa Bay Lightning	**NHL**	**25**	**1**	**2**	**3**	**1**	**2**	**3**	**22**	**1**	**0**	**0**	**17**	**5.9**	**15**	**2**	**26**	**9**	**–4**	....	....	....	....	....	....	....	....
1998-99	**Tampa Bay Lighning**	**NHL**	**78**	**5**	**12**	**17**	**6**	**12**	**18**	**81**	**1**	**1**	**1**	**73**	**6.8**	**55**	**7**	**100**	**30**	**–22**	....	....	....	....	....	....	....	....
99-2000	**Tampa Bay Lightning**	**NHL**	**46**	**1**	**1**	**2**	**1**	**1**	**2**	**66**	**0**	**0**	**0**	**23**	**4.3**	**19**	**0**	**45**	**14**	**–12**	....	....	....	....	....	....	....	....
	Providence Bruins	AHL	16	5	10	15	....	....	....	31	....	....	....	....	....	....	....	....	....	....	....	....	....	....	....	....	....	....
	NHL Totals		**265**	**11**	**24**	**35**	**13**	**24**	**37**	**277**	**2**	**2**	**3**	**210**	**5.2**	**169**	**16**	**266**	**79**		**13**	**0**	**0**	**0**	**14**	**0**	**0**	**0**

OHL Second All-Star Team (1992)

Traded to **Montreal** by **Vancouver** for Donald Brashear, November 13, 1996. Claimed on waivers by **Tampa Bay** from **Montreal**, January 22, 1998. • Loaned to **Providence** (AHL) by **Tampa Bay**, October 1, 1999.

• CUMMINS, Barry

Barry Kenneth D – L. 5'9", 175 lbs. b: Regina, Sask., 1/25/1949.

Season	Club	League	GP	G	A	Pts	AG	AA	APts	PIM	PP	SH	GW	S	%	TGF	PGF	TGA	PGA	+/-	GP	G	A	Pts	PIM	PP	SH	GW
1966-67	Regina Pat Canadians	AAHA	17	0	3	3	....	....	....	33	....	....	....	....	....	....	....	....	....	....	....	....	....	....	....	....	....	....
	Regina Pats	CMJHL	....	....	....	....	....	....	....	....	....	....	....	....	....	....	....	....	....	....	16	0	4	4	28	....	....	....
1967-68	Regina Pats	SJHL	50	7	13	20	....	....	....	174	....	....	....	....	....	....	....	....	....	....	....	....	....	....	....	....	....	....
1968-69	Regina Pats	SJHL	STATISTICS NOT AVAILABLE																									
	Regina Pats	Mem-Cup	11	0	5	5	....	....	....	*38	....	....	....	....	....	....	....	....	....	....	....	....	....	....	....	....	....	....
1969-70	Saskatoon Blades	WCJHL	34	9	25	34	....	....	....	123	....	....	....	....	....	....	....	....	....	....	6	1	1	2	35	....	....	....
	Muskegon Mohawks	IHL	8	0	0	0	....	....	....	8	....	....	....	....	....	....	....	....	....	....	....	....	....	....	....	....	....	....
1970-71	Portland Buckaroos	WHL	58	0	1	1	....	....	....	38	....	....	....	....	....	....	....	....	....	....	10	0	0	0	0	....	....	....
1971-72	Portland Buckaroos	WHL	53	0	8	8	....	....	....	78	....	....	....	....	....	....	....	....	....	....	....	....	....	....	....	....	....	....
	Seattle Totems	WHL	17	1	2	3	....	....	....	23	....	....	....	....	....	....	....	....	....	....	....	....	....	....	....	....	....	....
1972-73	Salt Lake Golden Eagles	WHL	72	4	18	22	....	....	....	190	....	....	....	....	....	....	....	....	....	....	9	0	2	2	17	....	....	....
1973-74	**California Golden Seals**	**NHL**	**36**	**1**	**2**	**3**	**1**	**2**	**3**	**39**	**0**	**0**	**0**	**28**	**3.6**	**28**	**0**	**75**	**12**	**–35**	....	....	....	....	....	....	....	....
	Salt Lake Golden Eagles	WHL	37	2	12	14	....	....	....	100	....	....	....	....	....	....	....	....	....	....	5	0	1	1	8	....	....	....
1974-75	Springfield Indians	AHL	73	9	33	42	....	....	....	151	....	....	....	....	....	....	....	....	....	....	....	....	....	....	....	....	....	....
	NHL Totals		**36**	**1**	**2**	**3**	**1**	**2**	**3**	**39**	**0**	**0**	**0**	**28**	**3.6**	**28**	**0**	**75**	**12**		....	....	....	....	....	....	....	....

Claimed by **Portland** (WHL) from **Montreal** in Reverse Draft, June, 1970. Traded to **Seattle** (WHL) by **Portland** (WHL) for cash, June 10, 1970. Traded to **California** (Salt Lake-WHL) by **Seattle** (WHL) for $15,000, June, 1972.

• CUMMINS, Jim

RW – R. 6'2", 219 lbs. b: Dearborn, MI, 5/17/1970. NY Rangers' 5th, 67th overall, in 1989.

Season	Club	League	GP	G	A	Pts	AG	AA	APts	PIM	PP	SH	GW	S	%	TGF	PGF	TGA	PGA	+/-	GP	G	A	Pts	PIM	PP	SH	GW
1987-88	Detroit Compuware	NAJHL	31	11	15	26	....	....	....	146	....	....	....	....	....	....	....	....	....	....	....	....	....	....	....	....	....	....
1988-89	Michigan State Spartans	CCHA	30	3	8	11	....	....	....	98	....	....	....	....	....	....	....	....	....	....	....	....	....	....	....	....	....	....
1989-90	Michigan State Spartans	CCHA	41	8	7	15	....	....	....	94	....	....	....	....	....	....	....	....	....	....	....	....	....	....	....	....	....	....
1990-91	Michigan State Spartans	CCHA	34	9	6	15	....	....	....	110	....	....	....	....	....	....	....	....	....	....	....	....	....	....	....	....	....	....
1991-92	**Detroit Red Wings**	**NHL**	**1**	**0**	**0**	**0**	**0**	**0**	**0**	**7**	**0**	**0**	**0**	**0**	**0.0**	**0**	**0**	**0**	**0**	**0**	....	....	....	....	....	....	....	....
	Adirondack Red Wings	AHL	65	7	13	20	....	....	....	338	....	....	....	....	....	....	....	....	....	....	5	0	0	0	19	....	....	....
1992-93	**Detroit Red Wings**	**NHL**	**7**	**1**	**1**	**2**	**1**	**1**	**2**	**58**	**0**	**0**	**0**	**5**	**20.0**	**2**	**0**	**2**	**0**	**0**	....	....	....	....	....	....	....	....
	Adirondack Red Wings	AHL	43	16	4	20	....	....	....	179	....	....	....	....	....	....	....	....	....	....	9	3	1	4	4	....	....	....
1993-94	**Philadelphia Flyers**	**NHL**	**22**	**1**	**2**	**3**	**1**	**2**	**3**	**71**	**0**	**0**	**0**	**17**	**5.9**	**3**	**0**	**3**	**0**	**0**	....	....	....	....	....	....	....	....
	Hershey Bears	AHL	17	6	6	12	....	....	....	70	....	....	....	....	....	....	....	....	....	....	....	....	....	....	....	....	....	....
	Tampa Bay Lightning	**NHL**	**4**	**0**	**0**	**0**	**0**	**0**	**0**	**13**	**0**	**0**	**0**	**3**	**0.0**	**1**	**0**	**2**	**0**	**–1**	....	....	....	....	....	....	....	....
	Atlanta Knights	IHL	7	4	5	9	....	....	....	14	....	....	....	....	....	....	....	....	....	....	13	1	2	3	90	....	....	....
1994-95	**Tampa Bay Lightning**	**NHL**	**10**	**1**	**0**	**1**	**2**	**0**	**2**	**41**	**0**	**0**	**1**	**3**	**33.3**	**2**	**0**	**5**	**0**	**–3**	....	....	....	....	....	....	....	....
	Chicago Blackhawks	**NHL**	**27**	**3**	**1**	**4**	**5**	**1**	**6**	**117**	**0**	**0**	**0**	**20**	**15.0**	**7**	**0**	**10**	**0**	**–3**	**14**	**1**	**1**	**2**	**4**	**0**	**0**	**1**
1995-96	**Chicago Blackhawks**	**NHL**	**52**	**2**	**4**	**6**	**2**	**3**	**5**	**180**	**0**	**0**	**2**	**34**	**5.9**	**11**	**0**	**12**	**0**	**–1**	**10**	**0**	**0**	**0**	**2**	**0**	**0**	**0**
1996-97	**Chicago Blackhawks**	**NHL**	**65**	**6**	**6**	**12**	**6**	**5**	**11**	**199**	**0**	**0**	**0**	**61**	**9.8**	**20**	**0**	**16**	**0**	**4**	**6**	**0**	**0**	**0**	**24**	**0**	**0**	**0**

			REGULAR SEASON																		PLAYOFFS							
Season	Club	League	GP	G	A	Pts	AG	AA	APts	PIM	PP	SH	GW	S	%	TGF	PGF	TGA	PGA	+/–	GP	G	A	Pts	PIM	PP	SH	GW
1997-98	**Chicago Blackhawks**	**NHL**	**55**	**0**	**2**	**2**	**0**	**2**	**2**	**178**	**0**	**0**	**0**	**33**	**0.0**	**5**	**0**	**14**	**0**	**–9**	....	....	....	....	....	....	....	....
	Phoenix Coyotes	**NHL**	**20**	**0**	**0**	**0**	**0**	**0**	**0**	**47**	**0**	**0**	**0**	**10**	**0.0**	**2**	**0**	**9**	**0**	**–7**	**3**	**0**	**0**	**0**	**4**	**0**	**0**	**0**
1998-99	**Phoenix Coyotes**	**NHL**	**55**	**1**	**7**	**8**	**1**	**7**	**8**	**190**	**0**	**0**	**0**	**26**	**3.8**	**13**	**0**	**11**	**1**	**3**	**3**	**0**	**1**	**1**	**0**	**0**	**0**	**0**
99-2000	**Montreal Canadiens**	**NHL**	**47**	**3**	**5**	**8**	**3**	**5**	**8**	**92**	**0**	**0**	**0**	**33**	**9.1**	**10**	**1**	**14**	**0**	**–5**	....	....	....	....	....	....	....	....
	NHL Totals		**365**	**18**	**28**	**46**	**21**	**26**	**47**	**1193**	**0**	**0**	**3**	**245**	**7.3**	**76**	**1**	**98**	**1**		**36**	**1**	**2**	**3**	**34**	**0**	**0**	**1**

Traded to **Detroit** by **NY Rangers** with Kevin Miller and Dennis Vial for Joey Kocur and Per Djoos, March 5, 1991. Traded to **Philadelphia** by **Detroit** with Philadelphia's 4th round choice (previously acquired by Detroit — later traded to Boston — Boston selected Charles Paquette) in 1993 Entry Draft for Greg Johnson and Philadelphia's 5th round choice (Frederic Deschenes) in 1994 Entry Draft, June 20, 1993. Traded to **Tampa Bay** by **Philadelphia** with Philadelphia's 4th round choice (later traded back to Philadelphia — Philadelphia selected Radovan Somik) in 1995 Entry Draft for Rob DiMaio, March 18, 1994. Traded to **Chicago** by **Tampa Bay** with Tom Tilley and Jeff Buchanan for Paul Ysebaert and Rich Sutter, February 22, 1995. Traded to **Phoenix** by **Chicago** with Keith Carney for Chad Kilger and Jayson More, March 4, 1998. Traded to **Montreal** by **Phoenix** for NY Rangers' 6th round choice (previously acquired, Phoenix selected Erik Leverstrom) in 1999 Entry Draft, June 26, 1999. Signed as a free agent by **Anaheim**, July 5, 2000.

• CUNNEYWORTH, Randy

Randy William LW – L. 6', 198 lbs. b: Etobicoke, Ont., 5/10/1961. Buffalo's 9th, 167th overall, in 1980.

Season	Club	League	GP	G	A	Pts	AG	AA	APts	PIM	PP	SH	GW	S	%	TGF	PGF	TGA	PGA	+/–	GP	G	A	Pts	PIM	PP	SH	GW
1978-79	Dixie Beehives	OHA-B	44	17	14	31	....	....	....	127	....	....	....	....	....	....	....	....	....	....	....	....	....	....	....	....	....	....
1979-80	Ottawa 67's	OMJHL	63	16	25	41	....	....	....	145	....	....	....	....	....	....	....	....	....	....	11	0	1	1	13	....	....	....
1980-81	Ottawa 67's	OMJHL	67	54	74	128	....	....	....	240	....	....	....	....	....	....	....	....	....	....	15	5	8	13	35	....	....	....
	Buffalo Sabres	**NHL**	**1**	**0**	**0**	**0**	**0**	**0**	**0**	**2**	**0**	**0**	**0**	**1**	**0.0**	**1**	**0**	**1**	**0**	**0**	....	....	....	....	....	....	....	....
	Rochester Americans	AHL	1	0	1	1	....	....	....	2	....	....	....	....	....	....	....	....	....	....	....	....	....	....	....	....	....	....
1981-82	**Buffalo Sabres**	**NHL**	**20**	**2**	**4**	**6**	**2**	**3**	**5**	**47**	**0**	**0**	**0**	**33**	**6.1**	**10**	**0**	**13**	**0**	**–3**	....	....	....	....	....	....	....	....
	Rochester Americans	AHL	57	12	15	27	....	....	....	86	....	....	....	....	....	....	....	....	....	....	9	4	0	4	30	....	....	....
1982-83	Rochester Americans	AHL	78	23	33	56	....	....	....	111	....	....	....	....	....	....	....	....	....	....	16	4	4	8	35	....	....	....
1983-84	Rochester Americans	AHL	54	18	17	35	....	....	....	85	....	....	....	....	....	....	....	....	....	....	17	5	5	10	55	....	....	....
1984-85	Rochester Americans	AHL	72	30	38	68	....	....	....	148	....	....	....	....	....	....	....	....	....	....	5	2	1	3	16	....	....	....
1985-86	**Pittsburgh Penguins**	**NHL**	**75**	**15**	**30**	**45**	**12**	**20**	**32**	**74**	**2**	**2**	**2**	**134**	**11.2**	**68**	**9**	**68**	**21**	**12**	....	....	....	....	....	....	....	....
1986-87	**Pittsburgh Penguins**	**NHL**	**79**	**26**	**27**	**53**	**22**	**20**	**42**	**142**	**3**	**2**	**5**	**169**	**15.4**	**79**	**12**	**86**	**33**	**14**	....	....	....	....	....	....	....	....
1987-88	**Pittsburgh Penguins**	**NHL**	**71**	**35**	**39**	**74**	**30**	**28**	**58**	**141**	**14**	**0**	**6**	**229**	**15.3**	**112**	**45**	**69**	**15**	**13**	....	....	....	....	....	....	....	....
1988-89	**Pittsburgh Penguins**	**NHL**	**70**	**25**	**19**	**44**	**21**	**13**	**34**	**156**	**10**	**0**	**1**	**163**	**15.3**	**76**	**32**	**69**	**3**	**–22**	**11**	**3**	**5**	**8**	**26**	**1**	**0**	**1**
1989-90	**Winnipeg Jets**	**NHL**	**28**	**5**	**6**	**11**	**4**	**4**	**8**	**34**	**2**	**0**	**1**	**51**	**9.8**	**18**	**6**	**19**	**0**	**–7**	....	....	....	....	....	....	....	....
	Hartford Whalers	**NHL**	**43**	**9**	**9**	**18**	**8**	**6**	**14**	**41**	**2**	**0**	**1**	**70**	**12.9**	**29**	**4**	**31**	**2**	**–4**	**4**	**0**	**0**	**0**	**2**	**0**	**0**	**0**
1990-91	**Hartford Whalers**	**NHL**	**32**	**9**	**5**	**14**	**8**	**4**	**12**	**49**	**0**	**0**	**1**	**56**	**16.1**	**18**	**1**	**26**	**3**	**–6**	**1**	**0**	**0**	**0**	**0**	**0**	**0**	**0**
	Springfield Indians	AHL	2	0	0	0	....	....	....	5	....	....	....	....	....	....	....	....	....	....	....	....	....	....	....	....	....	....
1991-92	**Hartford Whalers**	**NHL**	**39**	**7**	**10**	**17**	**6**	**8**	**14**	**71**	**0**	**0**	**1**	**63**	**11.1**	**27**	**6**	**32**	**6**	**–5**	**7**	**3**	**0**	**3**	**9**	**1**	**1**	**1**
1992-93	**Hartford Whalers**	**NHL**	**39**	**5**	**4**	**9**	**4**	**3**	**7**	**63**	**0**	**0**	**1**	**47**	**10.6**	**16**	**0**	**20**	**3**	**–1**	....	....	....	....	....	....	....	....
1993-94	**Hartford Whalers**	**NHL**	**63**	**9**	**8**	**17**	**8**	**6**	**14**	**87**	**0**	**1**	**1**	**121**	**7.4**	**26**	**0**	**38**	**10**	**–2**	....	....	....	....	....	....	....	....
	Chicago Blackhawks	**NHL**	**16**	**4**	**3**	**7**	**4**	**2**	**6**	**13**	**0**	**0**	**1**	**33**	**12.1**	**8**	**1**	**8**	**2**	**1**	**6**	**0**	**0**	**0**	**8**	**0**	**0**	**0**
1994-95	**Ottawa Senators**	**NHL**	**48**	**5**	**5**	**10**	**9**	**7**	**16**	**68**	**2**	**0**	**0**	**71**	**7.0**	**21**	**2**	**48**	**10**	**–19**	....	....	....	....	....	....	....	....
1995-96	**Ottawa Senators**	**NHL**	**81**	**17**	**19**	**36**	**17**	**16**	**33**	**130**	**4**	**0**	**2**	**142**	**12.0**	**56**	**12**	**92**	**17**	**–31**	....	....	....	....	....	....	....	....
1996-97	**Ottawa Senators**	**NHL**	**76**	**12**	**24**	**36**	**13**	**21**	**34**	**99**	**6**	**0**	**3**	**115**	**10.4**	**57**	**15**	**57**	**8**	**–7**	**7**	**1**	**1**	**2**	**10**	**0**	**0**	**0**
1997-98	**Ottawa Senators**	**NHL**	**71**	**2**	**11**	**13**	**2**	**11**	**13**	**63**	**1**	**0**	**0**	**81**	**2.5**	**24**	**5**	**48**	**15**	**–14**	**6**	**0**	**1**	**1**	**6**	**0**	**0**	**0**
1998-99	**Buffalo Sabres**	**NHL**	**14**	**2**	**2**	**4**	**2**	**2**	**4**	**0**	**0**	**0**	**1**	**12**	**16.7**	**5**	**0**	**4**	**0**	**1**	**3**	**0**	**0**	**0**	**0**	**0**	**0**	**0**
	Rochester Americans	AHL	52	10	18	28	....	....	....	55	....	....	....	....	....	....	....	....	....	....	20	3	14	17	58	....	....	....
99-2000	Rochester Americans	AHL	52	8	16	24	....	....	....	81	....	....	....	....	....	....	....	....	....	....	....	....	....	....	....	....	....	....
	NHL Totals		**866**	**189**	**225**	**414**	**172**	**174**	**346**	**1280**	**46**	**5**	**27**	**1591**	**11.9**	**651**	**150**	**729**	**148**		**45**	**7**	**7**	**14**	**61**	**2**	**1**	**2**

Traded to **Pittsburgh** by **Buffalo** with Mike Moller for Pat Hughes, October 4, 1985. Traded to **Winnipeg** by **Pittsburgh** with Rick Tabaracci and Dave McLlwain for Jim Kyte, Andrew McBain and Randy Gilhen, June 17, 1989. Traded to **Hartford** by **Winnipeg** for Paul MacDermid, December 13, 1989. Traded to **Chicago** by **Hartford** with Gary Suter and Hartford's 3rd round choice (later traded to Vancouver — Vancouver selected Larry Courville) in 1995 Entry Draft for Frantisek Kucera and Jocelyn Lemieux, March 11, 1994. Signed as a free agent by **Ottawa**, July 15, 1994. Signed as a free agent by **Buffalo**, August 27, 1998. • Suffered season-ending knee injury in game vs. Quebec (AHL), February 18, 2000.

• CUNNINGHAM, Jim

James Joseph LW – L. 5'11", 185 lbs. b: St. Paul, MN, 8/15/1956.

Season	Club	League	GP	G	A	Pts	AG	AA	APts	PIM	PP	SH	GW	S	%	TGF	PGF	TGA	PGA	+/–	GP	G	A	Pts	PIM	PP	SH	GW
1974-75	St. Paul Vulcans	MWJHL	57	21	31	52	....	....	....	183	....	....	....	....	....	....	....	....	....	....	....	....	....	....	....	....	....	....
1975-76	St. Paul Vulcans	MWJHL	47	16	58	74	....	....	....	148	....	....	....	....	....	....	....	....	....	....	....	....	....	....	....	....	....	....
1976-77	Michigan State Spartans	WCHA	34	11	25	36	....	....	....	59	....	....	....	....	....	....	....	....	....	....	....	....	....	....	....	....	....	....
1977-78	**Philadelphia Flyers**	**NHL**	**1**	**0**	**0**	**0**	**0**	**0**	**0**	**4**	**0**	**0**	**0**	**0**	**0.0**	**1**	**0**	**0**	**0**	**1**	....	....	....	....	....	....	....	....
	Maine Mariners	AHL	48	1	6	7	....	....	....	106	....	....	....	....	....	....	....	....	....	....	8	0	1	1	20	....	....	....
1978-79	Maine Mariners	AHL	78	8	16	24	....	....	....	223	....	....	....	....	....	....	....	....	....	....	10	2	4	6	10	....	....	....
1979-80	Cincinnati Stingers	CHL	5	0	1	1	....	....	....	5	....	....	....	....	....	....	....	....	....	....	....	....	....	....	....	....	....	....
	Maine Mariners	AHL	51	7	19	26	....	....	....	179	....	....	....	....	....	....	....	....	....	....	....	....	....	....	....	....	....	....
	Adirondack Red Wings	AHL	13	2	3	5	....	....	....	78	....	....	....	....	....	....	....	....	....	....	5	1	0	1	16	....	....	....
1980-81	Maine Mariners	AHL	44	3	5	8	....	....	....	141	....	....	....	....	....	....	....	....	....	....	....	....	....	....	....	....	....	....
1981-1983			OUT OF HOCKEY – RETIRED																									
1983-84	Toledo Goaldiggers	IHL	3	0	0	0	....	....	....	4	....	....	....	....	....	....	....	....	....	....	....	....	....	....	....	....	....	....
	NHL Totals		**1**	**0**	**0**	**0**	**0**	**0**	**0**	**4**	**0**	**0**	**0**	**0**	**0.0**	**1**	**0**	**0**	**0**		....	....	....	....	....	....	....	....

Signed as a free agent by **Philadelphia**, September, 1977. Claimed by **Winnipeg** from **Philadelphia** in Expansion Draft, June 13, 1979.

• CURRAN, Brian

Brian Phillip "Biff" D – L. 6'5", 220 lbs. b: Toronto, Ont., 11/5/1963. Boston's 2nd, 22nd overall, in 1982.

Season	Club	League	GP	G	A	Pts	AG	AA	APts	PIM	PP	SH	GW	S	%	TGF	PGF	TGA	PGA	+/–	GP	G	A	Pts	PIM	PP	SH	GW
1979-80	Notre Dame Midget Hounds	SAHA	STATISTICS NOT AVAILABLE																									
1980-81	Portland Winter Hawks	WHL	59	2	28	30	....	....	....	275	....	....	....	....	....	....	....	....	....	....	7	0	1	1	13	....	....	....
	Portland Winter Hawks	Mem-Cup	4	0	2	2	....	....	....	6	....	....	....	....	....	....	....	....	....	....	....	....	....	....	....	....	....	....
1981-82	Portland Winter Hawks	WHL	51	2	16	18	....	....	....	132	....	....	....	....	....	....	....	....	....	....	14	1	7	8	63	....	....	....
1982-83	Portland Winter Hawks	WHL	56	1	30	31	....	....	....	187	....	....	....	....	....	....	....	....	....	....	14	1	3	4	57	....	....	....
	Portland Winter Hawks	Mem-Cup	4	0	2	2	....	....	....	26	....	....	....	....	....	....	....	....	....	....	....	....	....	....	....	....	....	....
1983-84	**Boston Bruins**	**NHL**	**16**	**1**	**1**	**2**	**1**	**1**	**2**	**57**	**0**	**0**	**0**	**6**	**16.7**	**9**	**0**	**11**	**2**	**0**	**3**	**0**	**0**	**0**	**7**	**0**	**0**	**0**
	Hershey Bears	AHL	23	0	2	2	....	....	....	94	....	....	....	....	....	....	....	....	....	....	....	....	....	....	....	....	....	....
1984-85	**Boston Bruins**	**NHL**	**56**	**0**	**1**	**1**	**0**	**1**	**1**	**158**	**0**	**0**	**0**	**17**	**0.0**	**23**	**0**	**34**	**3**	**–8**	....	....	....	....	....	....	....	....
	Hershey Bears	AHL	4	0	0	0	....	....	....	19	....	....	....	....	....	....	....	....	....	....	....	....	....	....	....	....	....	....
1985-86	**Boston Bruins**	**NHL**	**43**	**2**	**5**	**7**	**2**	**3**	**5**	**192**	**0**	**0**	**0**	**23**	**8.7**	**33**	**0**	**38**	**11**	**6**	**2**	**0**	**0**	**0**	**4**	**0**	**0**	**0**
1986-87	**New York Islanders**	**NHL**	**68**	**0**	**10**	**10**	**0**	**7**	**7**	**356**	**0**	**0**	**0**	**34**	**0.0**	**47**	**1**	**64**	**21**	**3**	**8**	**0**	**0**	**0**	**51**	**0**	**0**	**0**
1987-88	**New York Islanders**	**NHL**	**22**	**0**	**1**	**1**	**0**	**1**	**1**	**68**	**0**	**0**	**0**	**12**	**0.0**	**8**	**0**	**21**	**4**	**–9**	....	....	....	....	....	....	....	....
	Springfield Indians	AHL	8	1	0	1	....	....	....	43	....	....	....	....	....	....	....	....	....	....	....	....	....	....	....	....	....	....
	Toronto Maple Leafs	**NHL**	**7**	**0**	**1**	**1**	**0**	**1**	**1**	**19**	**0**	**0**	**0**	**1**	**0.0**	**6**	**0**	**3**	**0**	**3**	**6**	**0**	**0**	**0**	**41**	**0**	**0**	**0**
1988-89	**Toronto Maple Leafs**	**NHL**	**47**	**1**	**4**	**5**	**1**	**3**	**4**	**185**	**0**	**0**	**0**	**18**	**5.6**	**24**	**0**	**30**	**6**	**0**	....	....	....	....	....	....	....	....
1989-90	**Toronto Maple Leafs**	**NHL**	**72**	**2**	**9**	**11**	**2**	**6**	**8**	**301**	**0**	**0**	**0**	**21**	**9.5**	**49**	**0**	**70**	**19**	**–2**	**5**	**0**	**1**	**1**	**19**	**0**	**0**	**0**
1990-91	**Toronto Maple Leafs**	**NHL**	**4**	**0**	**0**	**0**	**0**	**0**	**0**	**7**	**0**	**0**	**0**	**0**	**0.0**	**0**	**0**	**2**	**0**	**–2**	....	....	....	....	....	....	....	....
	Newmarket Saints	AHL	6	0	1	1	....	....	....	32	....	....	....	....	....	....	....	....	....	....	....	....	....	....	....	....	....	....
	Buffalo Sabres	**NHL**	**17**	**0**	**1**	**1**	**0**	**1**	**1**	**43**	**0**	**0**	**0**	**7**	**0.0**	**8**	**0**	**11**	**0**	**–3**	....	....	....	....	....	....	....	....
	Rochester Americans	AHL	10	0	0	0	....	....	....	36	....	....	....	....	....	....	....	....	....	....	....	....	....	....	....	....	....	....
1991-92	**Buffalo Sabres**	**NHL**	**3**	**0**	**0**	**0**	**0**	**0**	**0**	**14**	**0**	**0**	**0**	**1**	**0.0**	**1**	**0**	**1**	**0**	**0**	....	....	....	....	....	....	....	....
	Rochester Americans	AHL	36	0	3	3	....	....	....	122	....	....	....	....	....	....	....	....	....	....	....	....	....	....	....	....	....	....
1992-93	Cape Breton Oilers	AHL	61	2	24	26	....	....	....	223	....	....	....	....	....	....	....	....	....	....	12	0	3	3	12	....	....	....
1993-94	**Washington Capitals**	**NHL**	**26**	**1**	**0**	**1**	**1**	**0**	**1**	**61**	**0**	**0**	**0**	**11**	**9.1**	**11**	**0**	**14**	**1**	**–2**	....	....	....	....	....	....	....	....
	Portland Pirates	AHL	46	1	6	7	....	....	....	247	....	....	....	....	....	....	....	....	....	....	15	0	1	1	59	....	....	....
1994-95	Portland Pirates	AHL	59	2	10	12	....	....	....	328	....	....	....	....	....	....	....	....	....	....	7	0	0	0	24	....	....	....
1995-96	Portland Pirates	AHL	34	1	2	3	....	....	....	122	....	....	....	....	....	....	....	....	....	....	....	....	....	....	....	....	....	....
	Michigan K-Wings	IHL	18	0	5	5	....	....	....	55	....	....	....	....	....	....	....	....	....	....	10	0	4	4	38	....	....	....
1996-97	Philadelphia Phantoms	AHL	3	0	0	0	....	....	....	8	....	....	....	....	....	....	....	....	....	....	....	....	....	....	....	....	....	....

			REGULAR SEASON																		PLAYOFFS							
Season	Club	League	GP	G	A	Pts	AG	AA	APts	PIM	PP	SH	GW	S	%	TGF	PGF	TGA	PGA	+/–	GP	G	A	Pts	PIM	PP	SH	GW
1997-98	Monroe Moccasins	WPHL	68	7	17	24	....	....	....	239	....	....	....	....	....	....	....	....	....	....	....	....	....	....	....	....	....	....
	Utah Grizzlies	IHL	1	0	0	0	....	....	....	2	....	....	....	....	....	....	....	....	....	....	....	....	....	....	....	....	....	....
	Las Vegas Thunder	IHL	9	0	2	2	....	....	....	49	....	....	....	....	....	....	....	....	....	....	2	0	0	0	20	....	....	....
1998-99	Jacksonville Lizard Kings	WPHL	DID NOT PLAY – COACHING																									
99-2000	Monroe Moccasins	WPHL	DID NOT PLAY – COACHING																									
	NHL Totals		**381**	**7**	**33**	**40**	**7**	**24**	**31**	**1461**	**0**	**0**	**0**	**151**	**4.6**	**219**	**1**	**299**	**67**		**24**	**0**	**1**	**1**	**122**	**0**	**0**	**0**

Signed as a free agent by **NY Islanders**, August 29, 1986. Traded to **Toronto** by **NY Islanders** for Toronto's 6th round choice (Pavel Gross) in 1988 Entry Draft, March 8, 1988. Traded to **Buffalo** by **Toronto** with Lou Franceschetti for Mike Foligno and Buffalo's 8th round choice (Thomas Kucharcik) in 1991 Entry Draft, December 17, 1990. Signed as a free agent by **Edmonton**, October 27, 1992. Signed as a free agent by **Washington**, October 21, 1993.

• CURRIE, Dan

"Curdog" LW – L. 6'2", 195 lbs. b: Burlington, Ont., 3/15/1968. Edmonton's 4th, 84th overall, in 1986.

Season	Club	League	GP	G	A	Pts	AG	AA	APts	PIM	PP	SH	GW	S	%	TGF	PGF	TGA	PGA	+/–	GP	G	A	Pts	PIM	PP	SH	GW
1984-85	Burlington Midget Cougars	OMHA	29	28	27	55	....	....	....	35	....	....	....	....	....	....	....	....	....	....	....	....	....	....	....	....	....	....
	Burlington Cougars	OJHL-B	2	0	0	0	....	....	....	0	....	....	....	....	....	....	....	....	....	....	....	....	....	....	....	....	....	....
1985-86	Sault Ste. Marie Greyhounds	OHL	66	21	24	45	....	....	....	37	....	....	....	....	....	....	....	....	....	....	....	....	....	....	....	....	....	....
1986-87	Sault Ste. Marie Greyhounds	OHL	66	31	52	83	....	....	....	53	....	....	....	....	....	....	....	....	....	....	4	2	1	3	2	....	....	....
1987-88	Sault Ste. Marie Greyhounds	OHL	57	50	59	109	....	....	....	53	....	....	....	....	....	....	....	....	....	....	6	3	9	12	4	....	....	....
	Canada	WJC-A	7	4	3	7	....	....	....	2	....	....	....	....	....	....	....	....	....	....	....	....	....	....	....	....	....	....
	Nova Scotia Oilers	AHL	3	4	2	6	....	....	....	0	....	....	....	....	....	....	....	....	....	....	5	4	3	7	0	....	....	....
1988-89	Cape Breton Oilers	AHL	77	29	36	65	....	....	....	29	....	....	....	....	....	....	....	....	....	....	....	....	....	....	....	....	....	....
1989-90	Cape Breton Oilers	AHL	77	36	40	76	....	....	....	28	....	....	....	....	....	....	....	....	....	....	6	4	4	8	0	....	....	....
1990-91	**Edmonton Oilers**	**NHL**	**5**	**0**	**0**	**0**	**0**	**0**	**0**	**0**	**0**	**0**	**0**	**5**	**0.0**	**0**	**0**	**0**	**0**	**0**	....	....	....	....	....	....	....	....
	Cape Breton Oilers	AHL	71	47	45	92	....	....	....	51	....	....	....	....	....	....	....	....	....	....	4	3	1	4	8	....	....	....
1991-92	**Edmonton Oilers**	**NHL**	**7**	**1**	**0**	**1**	**1**	**0**	**1**	**0**	**0**	**0**	**0**	**3**	**33.3**	**2**	**0**	**3**	**0**	**–1**	....	....	....	....	....	....	....	....
	Cape Breton Oilers	AHL	66	*50	42	92	....	....	....	39	....	....	....	....	....	....	....	....	....	....	5	4	5	9	4	....	....	....
	Canada	Nat-Team	13	5	6	11	....	....	....	8	....	....	....	....	....	....	....	....	....	....	....	....	....	....	....	....	....	....
1992-93	**Edmonton Oilers**	**NHL**	**5**	**0**	**0**	**0**	**0**	**0**	**0**	**4**	**0**	**0**	**0**	**11**	**0.0**	**0**	**0**	**4**	**0**	**–4**	....	....	....	....	....	....	....	....
	Cape Breton Oilers	AHL	75	57	41	98	....	....	....	73	....	....	....	....	....	....	....	....	....	....	16	7	4	11	29	....	....	....
1993-94	**Los Angeles Kings**	**NHL**	**5**	**1**	**1**	**2**	**1**	**1**	**2**	**0**	**0**	**0**	**0**	**12**	**8.3**	**3**	**0**	**4**	**0**	**–1**	....	....	....	....	....	....	....	....
	Phoenix Roadrunners	IHL	74	37	49	86	....	....	....	96	....	....	....	....	....	....	....	....	....	....	....	....	....	....	....	....	....	....
1994-95	Phoenix Roadrunners	IHL	16	2	6	8	....	....	....	8	....	....	....	....	....	....	....	....	....	....	....	....	....	....	....	....	....	....
	Minnesota Moose	IHL	54	18	35	53	....	....	....	34	....	....	....	....	....	....	....	....	....	....	3	0	0	0	2	....	....	....
1995-96	Chicago Wolves	IHL	79	39	34	73	....	....	....	53	....	....	....	....	....	....	....	....	....	....	9	5	4	9	12	....	....	....
1996-97	Chicago Wolves	IHL	55	18	10	28	....	....	....	18	....	....	....	....	....	....	....	....	....	....	....	....	....	....	....	....	....	....
	Fort Wayne Komets	IHL	24	10	12	22	....	....	....	6	....	....	....	....	....	....	....	....	....	....	....	....	....	....	....	....	....	....
1997-98	Fort Wayne Komets	IHL	77	29	22	51	....	....	....	17	....	....	....	....	....	....	....	....	....	....	4	0	2	2	2	....	....	....
1998-99	Hannover Scorpions	Germany	44	6	12	18	....	....	....	50	....	....	....	....	....	....	....	....	....	....	....	....	....	....	....	....	....	....
99-2000	Bakersfield Condors	WCHL	70	42	41	83	....	....	....	34	....	....	....	....	....	....	....	....	....	....	4	2	1	3	2	....	....	....
	NHL Totals		**22**	**2**	**1**	**3**	**2**	**1**	**3**	**4**	**0**	**0**	**0**	**31**	**6.5**	**5**	**0**	**11**	**0**		....	....	....	....	....	....	....	....

OHL First All-Star Team (1988) • AHL Second All-Star Team (1992) • AHL First All-Star Team (1993)

Signed as a free agent by **LA Kings**, July 16, 1993.

• CURRIE, Glen

Glen Allen C – L. 6'2", 180 lbs. b: Montreal, Que., 7/18/1958. Washington's 5th, 38th overall, in 1978.

Season	Club	League	GP	G	A	Pts	AG	AA	APts	PIM	PP	SH	GW	S	%	TGF	PGF	TGA	PGA	+/–	GP	G	A	Pts	PIM	PP	SH	GW
1975-76	Laval National	QMJHL	72	15	54	69	....	....	....	20	....	....	....	....	....	....	....	....	....	....	....	....	....	....	....	....	....	....
1976-77	Laval National	QMJHL	72	28	51	79	....	....	....	42	....	....	....	....	....	....	....	....	....	....	7	1	4	5	15	....	....	....
1977-78	Laval National	QMJHL	72	63	82	145	....	....	....	29	....	....	....	....	....	....	....	....	....	....	5	3	1	4	0	....	....	....
1978-79	Port Huron Flags	IHL	69	27	36	63	....	....	....	43	....	....	....	....	....	....	....	....	....	....	7	5	4	9	2	....	....	....
1979-80	**Washington Capitals**	**NHL**	**32**	**2**	**0**	**2**	**2**	**0**	**2**	**2**	**0**	**0**	**0**	**25**	**8.0**	**5**	**0**	**15**	**8**	**–2**	....	....	....	....	....	....	....	....
	Hershey Bears	AHL	45	17	26	43	....	....	....	16	....	....	....	....	....	....	....	....	....	....	....	....	....	....	....	....	....	....
1980-81	**Washington Capitals**	**NHL**	**40**	**5**	**13**	**18**	**4**	**9**	**13**	**16**	**2**	**1**	**0**	**52**	**9.6**	**26**	**7**	**43**	**19**	**–5**	....	....	....	....	....	....	....	....
	Hershey Bears	AHL	35	18	21	39	....	....	....	10	....	....	....	....	....	....	....	....	....	....	....	....	....	....	....	....	....	....
1981-82	**Washington Capitals**	**NHL**	**43**	**7**	**7**	**14**	**6**	**5**	**11**	**14**	**0**	**1**	**0**	**45**	**15.6**	**24**	**1**	**47**	**22**	**–2**	....	....	....	....	....	....	....	....
	Hershey Bears	AHL	31	12	12	24	....	....	....	6	....	....	....	....	....	....	....	....	....	....	....	....	....	....	....	....	....	....
1982-83	**Washington Capitals**	**NHL**	**68**	**11**	**28**	**39**	**9**	**19**	**28**	**20**	**0**	**0**	**2**	**54**	**20.4**	**50**	**0**	**50**	**18**	**18**	**4**	**0**	**3**	**3**	**4**	**0**	**0**	**0**
	Hershey Bears	AHL	12	5	11	16	....	....	....	6	....	....	....	....	....	....	....	....	....	....	....	....	....	....	....	....	....	....
1983-84	**Washington Capitals**	**NHL**	**80**	**12**	**24**	**36**	**10**	**16**	**26**	**20**	**0**	**2**	**2**	**71**	**16.9**	**53**	**3**	**56**	**15**	**9**	**8**	**1**	**0**	**1**	**0**	**0**	**0**	**0**
1984-85	**Washington Capitals**	**NHL**	**44**	**1**	**5**	**6**	**1**	**3**	**4**	**19**	**0**	**0**	**0**	**27**	**3.7**	**14**	**0**	**24**	**12**	**2**	....	....	....	....	....	....	....	....
	Binghamton Whalers	AHL	17	1	5	6	....	....	....	6	....	....	....	....	....	....	....	....	....	....	8	2	5	7	2	....	....	....
1985-86	**Los Angeles Kings**	**NHL**	**12**	**1**	**2**	**3**	**1**	**1**	**2**	**9**	**1**	**0**	**0**	**11**	**9.1**	**5**	**1**	**9**	**5**	**0**	....	....	....	....	....	....	....	....
	New Haven Nighthawks	AHL	8	0	4	4	....	....	....	2	....	....	....	....	....	....	....	....	....	....	2	0	0	0	10	....	....	....
1986-87	New Haven Nighthawks	AHL	54	12	16	28	....	....	....	16	....	....	....	....	....	....	....	....	....	....	6	2	1	3	0	....	....	....
1987-88	**Los Angeles Kings**	**NHL**	**7**	**0**	**0**	**0**	**0**	**0**	**0**	**0**	**0**	**0**	**0**	**3**	**0.0**	**1**	**0**	**3**	**0**	**–2**	....	....	....	....	....	....	....	....
	New Haven Nighthawks	AHL	55	15	19	34	....	....	....	14	....	....	....	....	....	....	....	....	....	....	....	....	....	....	....	....	....	....
	NHL Totals		**326**	**39**	**79**	**118**	**33**	**53**	**86**	**100**	**3**	**4**	**4**	**288**	**13.5**	**178**	**12**	**247**	**99**		**12**	**1**	**3**	**4**	**4**	**0**	**0**	**0**

QMJHL Second All-Star Team (1978)

Traded to **LA Kings** by **Washington** for Daryl Evans, September 9, 1985. • Missed majority of 1985-86 season recovering from back injury suffered in training camp, September, 1985.

• CURRIE, Tony

RW – R. 5'11", 166 lbs. b: Sydney Mines, N.S., 11/12/1957. St. Louis' 4th, 63rd overall, in 1977.

Season	Club	League	GP	G	A	Pts	AG	AA	APts	PIM	PP	SH	GW	S	%	TGF	PGF	TGA	PGA	+/–	GP	G	A	Pts	PIM	PP	SH	GW
1972-73	Penticton Panthers	BCJHL	STATISTICS NOT AVAILABLE																									
1973-74	Spruce Grove Mets	AJHL	29	20	16	36	....	....	....	35	....	....	....	....	....	....	....	....	....	....	....	....	....	....	....	....	....	....
	Edmonton Oil Kings	WCJHL	22	0	1	1	....	....	....	2	....	....	....	....	....	....	....	....	....	....	....	....	....	....	....	....	....	....
1974-75	Spruce Grove Mets	AJHL	35	36	44	80	....	....	....	73	....	....	....	....	....	....	....	....	....	....	....	....	....	....	....	....	....	....
	Edmonton Oil Kings	WCJHL	39	28	17	45	....	....	....	12	....	....	....	....	....	....	....	....	....	....	....	....	....	....	....	....	....	....
	Spruce Grove Mets	Cen-Cup	....	....	....	....	....	....	....	....	....	....	....	....	....	....	....	....	....	....	....	....	....	....	....	....	....	....
1975-76	Edmonton Oil Kings	WCJHL	71	41	40	81	....	....	....	56	....	....	....	....	....	....	....	....	....	....	5	0	1	1	5	....	....	....
1976-77	Portland Winter Hawks	WCJHL	72	73	52	125	....	....	....	50	....	....	....	....	....	....	....	....	....	....	10	4	7	11	14	....	....	....
1977-78	**St. Louis Blues**	**NHL**	**22**	**4**	**5**	**9**	**4**	**4**	**8**	**4**	**1**	**0**	**0**	**35**	**11.4**	**19**	**8**	**21**	**0**	**–10**	....	....	....	....	....	....	....	....
	Salt Lake Golden Eagles	CHL	53	33	17	50	....	....	....	17	....	....	....	....	....	....	....	....	....	....	....	....	....	....	....	....	....	....
1978-79	**St. Louis Blues**	**NHL**	**36**	**4**	**15**	**19**	**3**	**11**	**14**	**0**	**1**	**0**	**2**	**57**	**7.0**	**30**	**3**	**36**	**0**	**–9**	....	....	....	....	....	....	....	....
	Salt Lake Golden Eagles	CHL	28	22	12	34	....	....	....	6	....	....	....	....	....	....	....	....	....	....	....	....	....	....	....	....	....	....
1979-80	**St. Louis Blues**	**NHL**	**40**	**19**	**14**	**33**	**16**	**10**	**26**	**4**	**2**	**0**	**3**	**70**	**27.1**	**42**	**9**	**24**	**0**	**9**	**2**	**0**	**0**	**0**	**0**	**0**	**0**	**0**
	Salt Lake Golden Eagles	CHL	33	24	23	47	....	....	....	17	....	....	....	....	....	....	....	....	....	....	....	....	....	....	....	....	....	....
1980-81	**St. Louis Blues**	**NHL**	**61**	**23**	**32**	**55**	**18**	**21**	**39**	**38**	**2**	**0**	**4**	**112**	**20.5**	**78**	**17**	**30**	**1**	**32**	**11**	**4**	**12**	**16**	**4**	**1**	**0**	**0**
1981-82	**St. Louis Blues**	**NHL**	**48**	**18**	**22**	**40**	**14**	**15**	**29**	**17**	**4**	**0**	**2**	**103**	**17.5**	**57**	**15**	**49**	**0**	**–7**	....	....	....	....	....	....	....	....
	Vancouver Canucks	**NHL**	**12**	**5**	**3**	**8**	**4**	**2**	**6**	**2**	**2**	**0**	**0**	**29**	**17.2**	**12**	**2**	**9**	**0**	**1**	**3**	**0**	**0**	**0**	**10**	**0**	**0**	**0**
1982-83	**Vancouver Canucks**	**NHL**	**8**	**1**	**1**	**2**	**1**	**1**	**2**	**0**	**0**	**0**	**0**	**6**	**16.7**	**3**	**0**	**6**	**0**	**–3**	....	....	....	....	....	....	....	....
	Fredericton Express	AHL	68	47	48	95	....	....	....	16	....	....	....	....	....	....	....	....	....	....	12	5	12	17	6	....	....	....
1983-84	**Vancouver Canucks**	**NHL**	**18**	**3**	**3**	**6**	**2**	**2**	**4**	**2**	**1**	**0**	**0**	**22**	**13.6**	**13**	**4**	**10**	**0**	**–1**	....	....	....	....	....	....	....	....
	Fredericton Express	AHL	12	6	11	17	....	....	....	16	....	....	....	....	....	....	....	....	....	....	....	....	....	....	....	....	....	....
	Hartford Whalers	**NHL**	**32**	**12**	**16**	**28**	**10**	**11**	**21**	**4**	**6**	**0**	**2**	**54**	**22.2**	**40**	**17**	**26**	**0**	**–3**	....	....	....	....	....	....	....	....
1984-85	**Hartford Whalers**	**NHL**	**13**	**3**	**8**	**11**	**2**	**5**	**7**	**12**	**1**	**0**	**0**	**20**	**15.0**	**16**	**7**	**13**	**0**	**–4**	....	....	....	....	....	....	....	....
	Nova Scotia Voyageurs	AHL	53	16	31	47	....	....	....	8	....	....	....	....	....	....	....	....	....	....	6	1	3	4	0	....	....	....
1985-86	Fredericton Express	AHL	75	35	40	75	....	....	....	23	....	....	....	....	....	....	....	....	....	....	6	5	2	7	4	....	....	....
1986-87	Schwenninger ERC	Germany	34	28	30	58	....	....	....	82	....	....	....	....	....	....	....	....	....	....	3	0	2	2	4	....	....	....
	EHC Kloten	Switz.	8	4	3	7	....	....	....	....	....	....	....	....	....	....	....	....	....	....	9	5	2	7	....	....	....	....

Season	Club	League	GP	G	A	Pts	AG	AA	APts	PIM	PP	SH	GW	S	%	TGF	PGF	TGA	PGA	+/–	GP	G	A	Pts	PIM	PP	SH	GW
			REGULAR SEASON																		PLAYOFFS							
1987-88	Schwenninger ERC	Germany	36	17	43	60	....	....	....	57	....	....	....	....	....	....	....	....	....	....	5	2	1	3	8	....	....	....
1988-89	HC Varese	Italy	49	39	44	83	....	....	....	36	....	....	....	....	....	....	....	....	....	....	....	....	....	....	....	....	....	....
1989-90	HC Varese	Italy	33	24	31	55	....	....	....	17	....	....	....	....	....	....	....	....	....	....	6	1	6	7	4	....	....	....
	NHL Totals		290	92	119	211	74	82	156	83	20	0	13	508	18.1	310	82	224	1		16	4	12	16	14	1	0	0

CHL First All-Star Team (1978) • AHL First All-Star Team (1983)

Traded to **Vancouver** by **St. Louis** with Jim Nill, Rick Heinz and St. Louis' 4th round choice (Shawn Kilroy) in 1982 Entry Draft for Glen Hanlon, March 9, 1982. Signed as a free agent by **Hartford**, January 21, 1984. Claimed on waivers by **Edmonton** from **Hartford**, December 5, 1984. Signed as a free agent by **Quebec**, August 25, 1985.

• CURTALE, Tony

Anthony Glenn D – L. 6', 185 lbs. b: Detroit, MI, 1/29/1962. Calgary's 2nd, 31st overall, in 1980.

Season	Club	League	GP	G	A	Pts	AG	AA	APts	PIM	PP	SH	GW	S	%	TGF	PGF	TGA	PGA	+/–	GP	G	A	Pts	PIM	PP	SH	GW
1978-79	St. Clair Shores Falcons	MNHL	63	42	63	105	....	....	....	150	....	....	....	....	....	....	....	....	....	....	....	....	....	....	....	....	....	....
1979-80	Brantford Alexanders	OMJHL	59	10	35	45	....	....	....	227	....	....	....	....	....	....	....	....	....	....	5	0	4	4	4	....	....	....
1980-81	Brantford Alexanders	OMJHL	59	14	71	85	....	....	....	141	....	....	....	....	....	....	....	....	....	....	6	1	4	5	26	....	....	....
	Calgary Flames	NHL	2	0	0	0	0	0	0	0	0	0	0	4	0.0	0	0	1	0	–1	....	....	....	....	....	....	....	....
1981-82	Brantford Alexanders	OHL	36	17	32	49	....	....	....	118	....	....	....	....	....	....	....	....	....	....	8	1	2	3	35	....	....	....
	Oklahoma City Stars	CHL	....	....	....	....	....	....	....	....	....	....	....	....	....	....	....	....	....	....	4	0	2	2	8	....	....	....
1982-83	Colorado Flames	CHL	74	7	22	29	....	....	....	61	....	....	....	....	....	....	....	....	....	....	5	1	0	1	6	....	....	....
1983-84	Peoria Prancers	IHL	2	0	0	0	....	....	....	2	....	....	....	....	....	....	....	....	....	....	....	....	....	....	....	....	....	....
	Colorado Flames	CHL	54	3	20	23	....	....	....	80	....	....	....	....	....	....	....	....	....	....	6	0	4	4	2	....	....	....
1984-85	Peoria Rivermen	IHL	50	5	31	36	....	....	....	81	....	....	....	....	....	....	....	....	....	....	17	1	7	8	43	....	....	....
1985-86	Peoria Rivermen	IHL	70	7	51	58	....	....	....	116	....	....	....	....	....	....	....	....	....	....	11	1	3	4	57	....	....	....
1986-87	Peoria Rivermen	IHL	72	8	21	29	....	....	....	126	....	....	....	....	....	....	....	....	....	....	....	....	....	....	....	....	....	....
	NHL Totals		2	0	0	0	0	0	0	0	0	0	0	4	0.0	0	0	1	0		....	....	....	....	....	....	....	....

• CURTIS, Paul

Paul Edwin D – L. 6', 185 lbs. b: Peterborough, Ont., 9/29/1947.

Season	Club	League	GP	G	A	Pts	AG	AA	APts	PIM	PP	SH	GW	S	%	TGF	PGF	TGA	PGA	+/–	GP	G	A	Pts	PIM	PP	SH	GW
1963-64	Peterborough Petes	OHA-Jr.	2	0	1	1	....	....	....	7	....	....	....	....	....	....	....	....	....	....	1	0	0	0	4	....	....	....
1964-65	Peterborough Petes	OHA-Jr.	56	0	7	7	....	....	....	90	....	....	....	....	....	....	....	....	....	....	12	0	2	2	19	....	....	....
1965-66	Peterborough Petes	OHA-Jr.	48	3	17	20	....	....	....	116	....	....	....	....	....	....	....	....	....	....	6	1	1	2	9	....	....	....
1966-67	Peterborough Petes	OHA-Jr.	44	2	8	10	....	....	....	91	....	....	....	....	....	....	....	....	....	....	6	1	2	3	2	....	....	....
1967-68	Houston Apollos	CPHL	62	1	8	9	....	....	....	150	....	....	....	....	....	....	....	....	....	....	....	....	....	....	....	....	....	....
1968-69	Houston Apollos	CHL	70	3	27	30	....	....	....	72	....	....	....	....	....	....	....	....	....	....	3	0	0	0	0	....	....	....
1969-70	Montreal Canadiens	NHL	1	0	0	0	0	0	0	0	0	0	0	1	0.0	0	0	1	0	–1	....	....	....	....	....	....	....	....
	Montreal Voyageurs	AHL	69	3	27	30	....	....	....	52	....	....	....	....	....	....	....	....	....	....	8	0	5	5	4	....	....	....
1970-71	Los Angeles Kings	NHL	64	1	13	14	1	11	12	82	0	0	0	66	1.5	46	2	71	9	–18	....	....	....	....	....	....	....	....
1971-72	Los Angeles Kings	NHL	64	1	12	13	1	10	11	57	0	0	0	66	1.5	65	1	109	13	–32	....	....	....	....	....	....	....	....
1972-73	Los Angeles Kings	NHL	27	0	5	5	0	4	4	16	0	0	0	16	0.0	17	0	20	1	–2	....	....	....	....	....	....	....	....
	St. Louis Blues	NHL	29	1	4	5	1	3	4	6	0	0	0	37	2.7	23	1	22	2	2	5	0	0	0	2	0	0	0
1973-74	Cincinnati Swords	AHL	42	1	7	8	....	....	....	33	....	....	....	....	....	....	....	....	....	....	....	....	....	....	....	....	....	....
	Providence Reds	AHL	24	2	14	16	....	....	....	4	....	....	....	....	....	....	....	....	....	....	15	5	8	13	22	....	....	....
1974-75	Michigan-Baltimore Stags	WHA	76	4	15	19	....	....	....	32	....	....	....	....	....	....	....	....	....	....	....	....	....	....	....	....	....	....
1975-76	Baltimore Clippers	AHL	54	2	8	10	....	....	....	33	....	....	....	....	....	....	....	....	....	....	....	....	....	....	....	....	....	....
	NHL Totals		185	3	34	37	3	28	31	161	0	0	0	186	1.6	151	4	223	25		5	0	0	0	2	0	0	0
	Other Major League Totals		76	4	15	19	....	....	....	32	....	....	....	....	....	....	....	....	....	....	....	....	....	....	....	....	....	....

AHL Second All-Star Team (1970)

Claimed by **LA Kings** from **Montreal** in Intra-League Draft, June 9, 1970. Traded to **St. Louis** by **LA Kings** for Frank St. Marsaille, January 22, 1973. Traded to **Buffalo** by **St. Louis** for Jake Rathwell, June 14, 1973. Traded to **NY Rangers** by **Buffalo** for Real Lemieux, January 21, 1974. Signed as a free agent by **Michigan** (WHA), August, 1974. Signed as a free agent by **Baltimore** (AHL), November, 1975.

• CUSSON, Jean

LW – L. 5'10", 170 lbs. b: Verdun, Que., 10/5/1942.

Season	Club	League	GP	G	A	Pts	AG	AA	APts	PIM	PP	SH	GW	S	%	TGF	PGF	TGA	PGA	+/–	GP	G	A	Pts	PIM	PP	SH	GW
1964-65	University of Montreal	OQAA	15	19	16	35	....	....	....	....	....	....	....	....	....	....	....	....	....	....	....	....	....	....	....	....	....	....
1965-66	Canada	Nat-Team	STATISTICS NOT AVAILABLE																									
1966-67	New Haven Blades	EHL	70	14	11	25	....	....	....	41	....	....	....	....	....	....	....	....	....	....	....	....	....	....	....	....	....	....
	Canada	WEC-A	7	3	0	3	....	....	....	0	....	....	....	....	....	....	....	....	....	....	....	....	....	....	....	....	....	....
1967-68	Canada	Nat-Team	20	15	7	22	....	....	....	6	....	....	....	....	....	....	....	....	....	....	....	....	....	....	....	....	....	....
	Ottawa Nationals	OHA-Sr.	8	6	6	12	....	....	....	0	....	....	....	....	....	....	....	....	....	....	....	....	....	....	....	....	....	....
	Oakland Seals	NHL	2	0	0	0	0	0	0	0	0	0	0	1	0.0	0	0	1	0	–1	....	....	....	....	....	....	....	....
1969-1971	Sherbrooke Beavers	QSHL	STATISTICS NOT AVAILABLE																									
1971-1974	HC Davos	Switz-2	PLAYER/COACH – STATISTICS UNAVAILABLE																									
	NHL Totals		2	0	0	0	0	0	0	0	0	0	0	1	0.0	0	0	1	0									

Signed as a free agent by **Oakland** to three-game amateur tryout contract, March, 1968. Signed as a free agent by **Sherbrooke** (QSHL), July 15, 1968.

• CYR, Denis

RW – L. 5'10", 180 lbs. b: Verdun, Que., 2/4/1961. Calgary's 1st, 13th overall, in 1980.

Season	Club	League	GP	G	A	Pts	AG	AA	APts	PIM	PP	SH	GW	S	%	TGF	PGF	TGA	PGA	+/–	GP	G	A	Pts	PIM	PP	SH	GW
1977-78	Montreal Juniors	QMJHL	72	46	55	101	....	....	....	25	....	....	....	....	....	....	....	....	....	....	....	....	....	....	....	....	....	....
1978-79	Montreal Juniors	QMJHL	70	70	56	126	....	....	....	88	....	....	....	....	....	....	....	....	....	....	11	7	5	12	26	....	....	....
1979-80	Montreal Juniors	QMJHL	70	70	76	146	....	....	....	61	....	....	....	....	....	....	....	....	....	....	10	10	13	23	6	....	....	....
1980-81	Montreal Juniors	QMJHL	57	50	40	90	....	....	....	53	....	....	....	....	....	....	....	....	....	....	7	6	6	12	37	....	....	....
	Canada	WJC-A	5	2	1	3	....	....	....	0	....	....	....	....	....	....	....	....	....	....	....	....	....	....	....	....	....	....
	Calgary Flames	NHL	10	1	4	5	1	3	4	0	0	0	0	10	10.0	9	1	6	0	2	....	....	....	....	....	....	....	....
1981-82	Calgary Flames	NHL	45	12	10	22	9	7	16	13	2	0	2	71	16.9	43	9	29	0	5	....	....	....	....	....	....	....	....
	Oklahoma City Stars	CHL	14	10	4	14	....	....	....	16	....	....	....	....	....	....	....	....	....	....	....	....	....	....	....	....	....	....
1982-83	Calgary Flames	NHL	11	1	1	2	1	1	2	0	0	0	0	15	6.7	7	0	6	0	1	....	....	....	....	....	....	....	....
	Chicago Black Hawks	NHL	41	7	8	15	6	6	12	2	0	0	0	36	19.4	19	2	11	0	6	1	0	0	0	0	0	0	0
1983-84	Chicago Black Hawks	NHL	46	12	13	25	10	9	19	19	6	0	1	72	16.7	46	14	33	1	0	....	....	....	....	....	....	....	....
	Springfield Indians	AHL	17	4	13	17	....	....	....	11	....	....	....	....	....	....	....	....	....	....	3	0	0	0	0	....	....	....
1984-85	St. Louis Blues	NHL	9	5	3	8	4	2	6	0	0	0	1	12	41.7	10	1	11	3	1	3	0	0	0	0	0	0	0
	Peoria Rivermen	IHL	62	26	51	77	....	....	....	28	....	....	....	....	....	....	....	....	....	....	20	*18	14	*32	14	....	....	....
1985-86	St. Louis Blues	NHL	31	3	4	7	2	3	5	2	0	0	0	21	14.3	9	0	22	2	–11	....	....	....	....	....	....	....	....
	Peoria Rivermen	IHL	34	15	26	41	....	....	....	15	....	....	....	....	....	....	....	....	....	....	11	5	4	9	2	....	....	....
1986-87	Peoria Rivermen	IHL	81	29	41	70	....	....	....	10	....	....	....	....	....	....	....	....	....	....	....	....	....	....	....	....	....	....
	NHL Totals		193	41	43	84	33	31	64	36	8	0	4	237	17.3	143	27	118	6		4	0	0	0	0	0	0	0

QMJHL Second All-Star Team (1979) • QMJHL First All-Star Team (1980)

Traded to **Chicago** by **Calgary** for the rights to Carey Wilson, November 8, 1982. Signed as a free agent by **St. Louis**, September 14, 1984.

• CYR, Paul

Paul A. LW – L. 5'10", 180 lbs. b: Port Alberni, B.C., 10/31/1963. Buffalo's 2nd, 9th overall, in 1982.

Season	Club	League	GP	G	A	Pts	AG	AA	APts	PIM	PP	SH	GW	S	%	TGF	PGF	TGA	PGA	+/–	GP	G	A	Pts	PIM	PP	SH	GW
1979-80	Nanaimo Clippers	BCJHL	60	28	52	80	....	....	....	202	....	....	....	....	....	....	....	....	....	....	....	....	....	....	....	....	....	....
	Victoria Cougars	WHL	....	....	....	....	....	....	....	....	....	....	....	....	....	....	....	....	....	....	7	0	0	0	4	....	....	....
1980-81	Victoria Cougars	WHL	64	36	22	58	....	....	....	85	....	....	....	....	....	....	....	....	....	....	14	6	5	11	46	....	....	....
	Victoria Cougars	Mem-Cup	4	2	3	5	....	....	....	6	....	....	....	....	....	....	....	....	....	....	....	....	....	....	....	....	....	....
1981-82	Victoria Cougars	WHL	58	52	56	108	....	....	....	167	....	....	....	....	....	....	....	....	....	....	4	3	2	5	12	....	....	....
	Canada	WJC-A	7	4	6	10	....	....	....	12	....	....	....	....	....	....	....	....	....	....	....	....	....	....	....	....	....	....
1982-83	Victoria Cougars	WHL	20	21	22	43	....	....	....	61	....	....	....	....	....	....	....	....	....	....	....	....	....	....	....	....	....	....
	Canada	WJC-A	7	1	3	4	....	....	....	19	....	....	....	....	....	....	....	....	....	....	....	....	....	....	....	....	....	....
	Buffalo Sabres	NHL	36	15	12	27	12	8	20	59	5	0	2	65	23.1	46	16	36	0	–6	10	1	3	4	6	1	0	0
1983-84	Buffalo Sabres	NHL	71	16	27	43	13	18	31	52	5	0	1	142	11.3	73	30	46	0	–3	3	0	1	1	0	0	0	0
1984-85	Buffalo Sabres	NHL	71	22	24	46	18	16	34	63	5	0	1	169	13.0	73	21	60	1	–7	5	2	2	4	15	0	0	0
1985-86	Buffalo Sabres	NHL	71	20	31	51	16	21	37	120	4	1	2	151	13.2	87	31	61	9	4	....	....	....	....	....	....	....	....
1986-87	Buffalo Sabres	NHL	73	11	16	27	9	12	21	122	0	0	1	131	8.4	45	0	99	38	–16	....	....	....	....	....	....	....	....

Season	Club	League	GP	G	A	Pts	AG	AA	APts	PIM	PP	SH	GW	S	%	TGF	PGF	TGA	PGA	+/–	GP	G	A	Pts	PIM	PP	SH	GW
			REGULAR SEASON																		PLAYOFFS							
1987-88	**Buffalo Sabres**	**NHL**	**20**	**1**	**1**	**2**	**1**	**1**	**2**	**38**	**0**	**1**	**1**	**20**	**5.0**	**10**	**2**	**18**	**8**	**–2**	....	....	....	....	....	....	....	....
	New York Rangers	**NHL**	**40**	**4**	**13**	**17**	**3**	**9**	**12**	**41**	**1**	**1**	**0**	**72**	**5.6**	**23**	**3**	**35**	**10**	**–5**	....	....	....	....	....	....	....	....
1988-89	**New York Rangers**	**NHL**	**1**	**0**	**0**	**0**	**0**	**0**	**0**	**2**	**0**	**0**	**0**	**0**	**0.0**	**0**	**0**	**0**	**0**	**0**	....	....	....	....	....	....	....	....
1989-90	**New York Rangers**	**NHL**	DID NOT PLAY – INJURED																									
1990-91	**Hartford Whalers**	**NHL**	**70**	**12**	**13**	**25**	**11**	**10**	**21**	**107**	**0**	**1**	**2**	**128**	**9.4**	**37**	**2**	**65**	**22**	**–8**	**6**	**1**	**0**	**1**	**10**	**0**	**0**	**0**
1991-92	**Hartford Whalers**	**NHL**	**17**	**0**	**3**	**3**	**0**	**2**	**2**	**19**	**0**	**0**	**0**	**20**	**0.0**	**4**	**0**	**15**	**7**	**–4**	....	....	....	....	....	....	....	....
	Springfield Indians	AHL	43	11	18	29	....	....	....	30	....	....	....	....	....	....	....	....	....	....	11	0	3	3	12	....	....	....
1992-93	Springfield Indians	AHL	41	7	14	21	....	....	....	44	....	....	....	....	....	....	....	....	....	....	15	3	2	5	12	....	....	....
	NHL Totals		**470**	**101**	**140**	**241**	**83**	**97**	**180**	**623**	**20**	**4**	**10**	**898**	**11.2**	**398**	**105**	**435**	**95**		**24**	**4**	**6**	**10**	**31**	**1**	**0**	**0**

WHL Second All-Star Team (1982)

Traded to **NY Rangers** by **Buffalo** with Buffalo's 10th round choice (Eric Fenton) in 1988 Entry Draft for Mike Donnelly and NY Rangers' 5th round choice (Alexander Mogilny) in 1988 Entry Draft, December 31, 1987. • Missed entire 1988-89 season recovering from knee surgery. Signed as a free agent by **Hartford**, September 30, 1990.

• CZERKAWSKI, Mariusz

RW – L. 6', 195 lbs. b: Radomsko, Poland, 4/13/1972. Boston's 5th, 106th overall, in 1991.

Season	Club	League	GP	G	A	Pts	AG	AA	APts	PIM	PP	SH	GW	S	%	TGF	PGF	TGA	PGA	+/–	GP	G	A	Pts	PIM	PP	SH	GW
1988-89	GKS Tychy	Poland-Jr.	STATISTICS NOT AVAILABLE																									
	Poland	EJC-B	5	5	6	11	....	....	....	6	....	....	....	....	....	....	....	....	....	....	....	....	....	....	....	....	....	....
1989-90	GKS Tychy	Poland-Jr.	STATISTICS NOT AVAILABLE																									
	Poland	EJC-A	6	9	3	12	....	....	....	14	....	....	....	....	....	....	....	....	....	....	....	....	....	....	....	....	....	....
	Poland	WJC-A	7	1	0	1	....	....	....	4	....	....	....	....	....	....	....	....	....	....	....	....	....	....	....	....	....	....
1990-91	GKS Tychy	Poland	24	25	15	40	....	....	....	....	....	....	....	....	....	....	....	....	....	....	....	....	....	....	....	....	....	....
	Poland	WJC-B	7	12	3	15	....	....	....	2	....	....	....	....	....	....	....	....	....	....	....	....	....	....	....	....	....	....
	Poland	WEC-B	7	6	2	8	....	....	....	4	....	....	....	....	....	....	....	....	....	....	....	....	....	....	....	....	....	....
1991-92	Djurgardens IF Stockholm	Sweden	39	8	5	13	....	....	....	4	....	....	....	....	....	....	....	....	....	....	3	0	0	0	2	....	....	....
	Poland	Olympics	5	0	1	1	....	....	....	4	....	....	....	....	....	....	....	....	....	....	....	....	....	....	....	....	....	....
	Poland	WC-A	6	0	0	0	....	....	....	4	....	....	....	....	....	....	....	....	....	....	....	....	....	....	....	....	....	....
1992-93	SC Hammarby	Sweden-2	32	*39	30	*69	....	....	....	74	....	....	....	....	....	....	....	....	....	....	13	*16	7	*23	34	....	....	....
1993-94	Djurgardens IF Stockholm	Sweden	39	13	21	34	....	....	....	20	....	....	....	....	....	....	....	....	....	....	6	3	1	4	2	....	....	....
	Boston Bruins	**NHL**	**4**	**2**	**1**	**3**	**2**	**1**	**3**	**0**	**1**	**0**	**0**	**11**	**18.2**	**4**	**1**	**5**	**0**	**–2**	**13**	**3**	**3**	**6**	**4**	**1**	**0**	**0**
1994-95	Kiekko-Espoo	Finland	7	9	3	12	....	....	....	10	....	....	....	....	....	....	....	....	....	....	....	....	....	....	....	....	....	....
	Boston Bruins	**NHL**	**47**	**12**	**14**	**26**	**21**	**21**	**42**	**31**	**1**	**0**	**2**	**126**	**9.5**	**42**	**15**	**23**	**0**	**4**	**5**	**1**	**0**	**1**	**0**	**0**	**0**	**0**
1995-96	**Boston Bruins**	**NHL**	**33**	**5**	**6**	**11**	**5**	**5**	**10**	**10**	**1**	**0**	**0**	**63**	**7.9**	**16**	**1**	**26**	**0**	**–11**	....	....	....	....	....	....	....	....
	Edmonton Oilers	**NHL**	**37**	**12**	**17**	**29**	**12**	**14**	**26**	**8**	**2**	**0**	**1**	**79**	**15.2**	**41**	**10**	**24**	**0**	**7**	....	....	....	....	....	....	....	....
1996-97	**Edmonton Oilers**	**NHL**	**76**	**26**	**21**	**47**	**28**	**19**	**47**	**16**	**4**	**0**	**3**	**182**	**14.3**	**61**	**18**	**43**	**0**	**0**	**12**	**2**	**1**	**3**	**10**	**0**	**0**	**0**
1997-98	**New York Islanders**	**NHL**	**68**	**12**	**13**	**25**	**14**	**13**	**27**	**23**	**2**	**0**	**1**	**136**	**8.8**	**37**	**6**	**20**	**0**	**11**	....	....	....	....	....	....	....	....
	Poland	WC-B	3	2	1	3	....	....	....	0	....	....	....	....	....	....	....	....	....	....	....	....	....	....	....	....	....	....
1998-99	**New York Islanders**	**NHL**	**78**	**21**	**17**	**38**	**25**	**16**	**41**	**14**	**4**	**0**	**1**	**205**	**10.2**	**53**	**14**	**49**	**0**	**–10**	....	....	....	....	....	....	....	....
99-2000	**New York Islanders**	**NHL**	**79**	**35**	**35**	**70**	**39**	**32**	**71**	**34**	**16**	**0**	**4**	**276**	**12.7**	**85**	**35**	**67**	**1**	**–16**	....	....	....	....	....	....	....	....
	NHL Totals		**422**	**125**	**124**	**249**	**146**	**121**	**267**	**136**	**31**	**0**	**12**	**1078**	**11.6**	**339**	**100**	**257**	**1**		**30**	**6**	**4**	**10**	**14**	**1**	**0**	**0**

Named Best Player at WJC-B (1990) • Played in NHL All-Star Game (2000)

Traded to **Edmonton** by **Boston** with Sean Brown and Boston's 1st round choice (Matthieu Descoteaux) in 1996 Entry Draft for Bill Ranford, January 11, 1996. Traded to **NY Islanders** by **Edmonton** for Dan Lacouture, August 25, 1997.

• DACKELL, Andreas

Andreas L. RW – R. 5'11", 195 lbs. b: Gavle, Sweden, 12/29/1972. Ottawa's 3rd, 136th overall, in 1996.

Season	Club	League	GP	G	A	Pts	AG	AA	APts	PIM	PP	SH	GW	S	%	TGF	PGF	TGA	PGA	+/–	GP	G	A	Pts	PIM	PP	SH	GW
1990-91	Stromsbro-Gavle HC	Sweden-2	29	21	9	30	....	....	....	12	....	....	....	....	....	....	....	....	....	....	....	....	....	....	....	....	....	....
	Brynas IF Gavle	Sweden	3	0	1	1	....	....	....	2	....	....	....	....	....	....	....	....	....	....	....	....	....	....	....	....	....	....
1991-92	Brynas IF Gavle	Sweden-2	26	17	24	41	....	....	....	42	....	....	....	....	....	....	....	....	....	....	2	3	1	4	2	....	....	....
	Brynas IF Gavle	Sweden	4	0	0	0	....	....	....	2	....	....	....	....	....	....	....	....	....	....	2	0	1	1	4	....	....	....
1992-93	Brynas IF Gavle	Sweden	40	12	15	27	....	....	....	12	....	....	....	....	....	....	....	....	....	....	10	4	5	9	2	....	....	....
1993-94	Brynas IF Gavle	Sweden	38	12	17	29	....	....	....	47	....	....	....	....	....	....	....	....	....	....	7	2	2	4	8	....	....	....
	Sweden	Olympics	4	0	0	0	....	....	....	0	....	....	....	....	....	....	....	....	....	....	....	....	....	....	....	....	....	....
	Sweden	WC-A	7	2	2	4	....	....	....	25	....	....	....	....	....	....	....	....	....	....	....	....	....	....	....	....	....	....
1994-95	Brynas IF Gavle	Sweden	39	17	16	33	....	....	....	34	....	....	....	....	....	....	....	....	....	....	14	3	3	6	14	....	....	....
	Sweden	WC-A	8	3	4	7	....	....	....	4	....	....	....	....	....	....	....	....	....	....	....	....	....	....	....	....	....	....
1995-96	Brynas IF Gavle	Sweden	22	6	6	12	....	....	....	8	....	....	....	....	....	....	....	....	....	....	....	....	....	....	....	....	....	....
	Sweden	WC-A	6	0	1	1	....	....	....	0	....	....	....	....	....	....	....	....	....	....	....	....	....	....	....	....	....	....
1996-97	**Ottawa Senators**	**NHL**	**79**	**12**	**19**	**31**	**13**	**17**	**30**	**8**	**2**	**0**	**3**	**79**	**15.2**	**53**	**14**	**47**	**2**	**–6**	**7**	**1**	**0**	**1**	**0**	**0**	**0**	**0**
1997-98	**Ottawa Senators**	**NHL**	**82**	**15**	**18**	**33**	**18**	**18**	**36**	**24**	**3**	**2**	**2**	**130**	**11.5**	**58**	**13**	**70**	**14**	**–11**	**11**	**1**	**1**	**2**	**2**	**1**	**0**	**0**
1998-99	**Ottawa Senators**	**NHL**	**77**	**15**	**35**	**50**	**18**	**34**	**52**	**30**	**6**	**0**	**3**	**107**	**14.0**	**82**	**30**	**50**	**7**	**9**	**4**	**0**	**1**	**1**	**0**	**0**	**0**	**0**
99-2000	**Ottawa Senators**	**NHL**	**82**	**10**	**25**	**35**	**11**	**23**	**34**	**18**	**0**	**0**	**1**	**99**	**10.1**	**58**	**11**	**51**	**9**	**5**	**6**	**2**	**1**	**3**	**2**	**0**	**0**	**1**
	NHL Totals		**320**	**52**	**97**	**149**	**60**	**92**	**152**	**80**	**11**	**2**	**9**	**415**	**12.5**	**251**	**68**	**218**	**32**		**28**	**4**	**3**	**7**	**4**	**1**	**0**	**1**

• DAHL, Kevin

"Buck" D – R. 5'11", 190 lbs. b: Regina, Sask., 12/30/1968. Montreal's 12th, 230th overall, in 1988.

Season	Club	League	GP	G	A	Pts	AG	AA	APts	PIM	PP	SH	GW	S	%	TGF	PGF	TGA	PGA	+/–	GP	G	A	Pts	PIM	PP	SH	GW
1985-86	Stratford Cullitons	OJHL-B	29	8	15	23	....	....	....	99	....	....	....	....	....	....	....	....	....	....	....	....	....	....	....	....	....	....
1986-87	Bowling Green University	CCHA	32	2	6	8	....	....	....	54	....	....	....	....	....	....	....	....	....	....	....	....	....	....	....	....	....	....
1987-88	Bowling Green University	CCHA	44	2	23	25	....	....	....	78	....	....	....	....	....	....	....	....	....	....	....	....	....	....	....	....	....	....
1988-89	Bowling Green University	CCHA	46	9	26	35	....	....	....	51	....	....	....	....	....	....	....	....	....	....	....	....	....	....	....	....	....	....
1989-90	Bowling Green University	CCHA	43	8	22	30	....	....	....	74	....	....	....	....	....	....	....	....	....	....	....	....	....	....	....	....	....	....
1990-91	Fredericton Canadiens	AHL	32	1	15	16	....	....	....	45	....	....	....	....	....	....	....	....	....	....	9	0	1	1	11	....	....	....
	Winston-Salem Thunderbirds	ECHL	36	7	17	24	....	....	....	58	....	....	....	....	....	....	....	....	....	....	....	....	....	....	....	....	....	....
1991-92	Canada	Nat-Team	45	2	15	17	....	....	....	44	....	....	....	....	....	....	....	....	....	....	....	....	....	....	....	....	....	....
	Canada	Olympics	8	2	0	2	....	....	....	6	....	....	....	....	....	....	....	....	....	....	....	....	....	....	....	....	....	....
	Salt Lake Golden Eagles	IHL	13	0	2	2	....	....	....	12	....	....	....	....	....	....	....	....	....	....	5	0	0	0	13	....	....	....
1992-93	**Calgary Flames**	**NHL**	**61**	**2**	**9**	**11**	**2**	**6**	**8**	**56**	**1**	**0**	**0**	**40**	**5.0**	**57**	**3**	**75**	**30**	**9**	**6**	**0**	**2**	**2**	**8**	**0**	**0**	**0**
1993-94	**Calgary Flames**	**NHL**	**33**	**0**	**3**	**3**	**0**	**2**	**2**	**23**	**0**	**0**	**0**	**20**	**0.0**	**18**	**1**	**34**	**15**	**–2**	**6**	**0**	**0**	**0**	**4**	**0**	**0**	**0**
	Saint John Flames	AHL	2	0	0	0	....	....	....	0	....	....	....	....	....	....	....	....	....	....	....	....	....	....	....	....	....	....
1994-95	**Calgary Flames**	**NHL**	**34**	**4**	**8**	**12**	**7**	**12**	**19**	**38**	**0**	**0**	**0**	**30**	**13.3**	**24**	**0**	**31**	**15**	**8**	**3**	**0**	**0**	**0**	**0**	**0**	**0**	**0**
1995-96	**Calgary Flames**	**NHL**	**32**	**1**	**1**	**2**	**1**	**1**	**2**	**26**	**0**	**0**	**1**	**17**	**5.9**	**15**	**1**	**23**	**7**	**–2**	**1**	**0**	**0**	**0**	**0**	**0**	**0**	**0**
	Saint John Flames	AHL	23	4	11	15	....	....	....	37	....	....	....	....	....	....	....	....	....	....	....	....	....	....	....	....	....	....
1996-97	**Phoenix Coyotes**	**NHL**	**2**	**0**	**0**	**0**	**0**	**0**	**0**	**0**	**0**	**0**	**0**	**2**	**0.0**	**0**	**0**	**0**	**0**	**0**	....	....	....	....	....	....	....	....
	Las Vegas Thunder	IHL	73	10	21	31	....	....	....	101	....	....	....	....	....	....	....	....	....	....	3	0	0	0	2	....	....	....
1997-98	**Calgary Flames**	**NHL**	**19**	**0**	**1**	**1**	**0**	**1**	**1**	**6**	**0**	**0**	**0**	**17**	**0.0**	**10**	**1**	**19**	**7**	**–3**	....	....	....	....	....	....	....	....
	Chicago Wolves	IHL	45	8	9	17	....	....	....	61	....	....	....	....	....	....	....	....	....	....	20	1	8	9	32	....	....	....
1998-99	**Toronto Maple Leafs**	**NHL**	**3**	**0**	**0**	**0**	**0**	**0**	**0**	**2**	**0**	**0**	**0**	**0**	**0.0**	**1**	**0**	**1**	**0**	**0**	....	....	....	....	....	....	....	....
	Chicago Wolves	IHL	34	3	6	9	....	....	....	61	....	....	....	....	....	....	....	....	....	....	10	2	3	5	8	....	....	....
99-2000	Chicago Wolves	IHL	27	1	2	3	....	....	....	44	....	....	....	....	....	....	....	....	....	....	3	0	1	1	2	....	....	....
	NHL Totals		**184**	**7**	**22**	**29**	**10**	**22**	**32**	**151**	**1**	**0**	**1**	**126**	**5.6**	**125**	**6**	**183**	**74**		**16**	**0**	**2**	**2**	**12**	**0**	**0**	**0**

Signed as a free agent by **Calgary**, July 27, 1991. Signed as a free agent by **Phoenix**, September 4, 1996. Signed as a free agent by **Calgary**, September 8, 1997. Signed as a free agent by **St. Louis**, September 4, 1998. Claimed by **Toronto** from **St. Louis** in NHL Waiver Draft, October 5, 1998. Signed as a free agent by **NY Islanders**, August 12, 1999.

• DAHLEN, Ulf

Ulf R. RW – L. 6'3", 195 lbs. b: Ostersund, Sweden, 1/12/1967. NY Rangers' 1st, 7th overall, in 1985.

Season	Club	League	GP	G	A	Pts	AG	AA	APts	PIM	PP	SH	GW	S	%	TGF	PGF	TGA	PGA	+/–	GP	G	A	Pts	PIM	PP	SH	GW
1983-84	Ostersunds IK	Sweden-2	36	15	11	26	....	....	....	10	....	....	....	....	....	....	....	....	....	....	....	....	....	....	....	....	....	....
1984-85	Ostersunds IK	Sweden-2	31	27	*26	*53	....	....	....	20	....	....	....	....	....	....	....	....	....	....	5	6	0	6	4	....	....	....
	Sweden	EJC-A	5	7	4	11	....	....	....	0	....	....	....	....	....	....	....	....	....	....	....	....	....	....	....	....	....	....
1985-86	IF Bjorkloven Umea	Sweden	22	4	3	7	....	....	....	8	....	....	....	....	....	....	....	....	....	....	....	....	....	....	....	....	....	....
	Sweden	WJC-A	7	3	4	7	....	....	....	4	....	....	....	....	....	....	....	....	....	....	....	....	....	....	....	....	....	....
1986-87	IF Bjorkloven Umea	Sweden	31	9	12	21	....	....	....	20	....	....	....	....	....	....	....	....	....	....	6	6	2	8	4	....	....	....
	Sweden	WJC-A	7	7	8	*15	....	....	....	2	....	....	....	....	....	....	....	....	....	....	....	....	....	....	....	....	....	....

			REGULAR SEASON																		PLAYOFFS							
Season	Club	League	GP	G	A	Pts	AG	AA	APts	PIM	PP	SH	GW	S	%	TGF	PGF	TGA	PGA	+/–	GP	G	A	Pts	PIM	PP	SH	GW
1987-88	**New York Rangers**	**NHL**	**70**	**29**	**23**	**52**	**25**	**16**	**41**	**26**	**11**	**0**	**4**	**159**	**18.2**	**73**	**27**	**41**	**0**	**5**	....	....	....	....	....	....	....	....
	Colorado Rangers	IHL	2	2	2	4	....	....	....	0	....	....	....	....	....	....	....	....	....	....	....	....	....	....	....	....	....	....
1988-89	**New York Rangers**	**NHL**	**56**	**24**	**19**	**43**	**20**	**13**	**33**	**50**	**8**	**0**	**1**	**147**	**16.3**	**64**	**26**	**44**	**0**	**–6**	**4**	**0**	**0**	**0**	**0**	**0**	**0**	**0**
	Sweden	WEC-A	10	2	2	4	....	....	....	4	....	....	....	....	....	....	....	....	....	....	....	....	....	....	....	....	....	....
1989-90	**New York Rangers**	**NHL**	**63**	**18**	**18**	**36**	**15**	**13**	**28**	**30**	**13**	**0**	**4**	**111**	**16.2**	**66**	**38**	**32**	**0**	**–4**	....	....	....	....	....	....	....	....
	Minnesota North Stars	**NHL**	**13**	**2**	**4**	**6**	**2**	**3**	**5**	**0**	**0**	**0**	**0**	**24**	**8.3**	**14**	**4**	**9**	**0**	**1**	**7**	**1**	**4**	**5**	**2**	**0**	**0**	**0**
1990-91	Minnesota North Stars	Fr-Tour	4	0	0	0	....	....	....	0	....	....	....	....	....	....	....	....	....	....	....	....	....	....	....	....	....	....
	Minnesota North Stars	**NHL**	**66**	**21**	**18**	**39**	**19**	**14**	**33**	**6**	**4**	**0**	**3**	**133**	**15.8**	**55**	**12**	**36**	**0**	**7**	**15**	**2**	**6**	**8**	**4**	**0**	**0**	**0**
1991-92	Sweden	Can-Cup	6	2	1	3	....	....	....	5	....	....	....	....	....	....	....	....	....	....	....	....	....	....	....	....	....	....
	Minnesota North Stars	**NHL**	**79**	**36**	**30**	**66**	**33**	**23**	**56**	**10**	**16**	**1**	**5**	**216**	**16.7**	**90**	**39**	**58**	**2**	**–5**	**7**	**0**	**3**	**3**	**2**	**0**	**0**	**0**
1992-93	**Minnesota North Stars**	**NHL**	**83**	**35**	**39**	**74**	**29**	**27**	**56**	**6**	**13**	**0**	**6**	**223**	**15.7**	**100**	**51**	**69**	**0**	**–20**	....	....	....	....	....	....	....	....
	Sweden	WC-A	6	5	2	7	....	....	....	0	....	....	....	....	....	....	....	....	....	....	....	....	....	....	....	....	....	....
1993-94	**Dallas Stars**	**NHL**	**65**	**19**	**38**	**57**	**18**	**30**	**48**	**10**	**12**	**0**	**3**	**147**	**12.9**	**82**	**43**	**40**	**0**	**–1**	....	....	....	....	....	....	....	....
	San Jose Sharks	**NHL**	**13**	**6**	**6**	**12**	**6**	**5**	**11**	**0**	**3**	**0**	**2**	**43**	**14.0**	**21**	**9**	**12**	**0**	**0**	**14**	**6**	**2**	**8**	**0**	**3**	**0**	**1**
1994-95	**San Jose Sharks**	**NHL**	**46**	**11**	**23**	**34**	**19**	**34**	**53**	**11**	**4**	**1**	**4**	**85**	**12.9**	**48**	**16**	**34**	**0**	**–2**	**11**	**5**	**4**	**9**	**0**	**3**	**0**	**1**
1995-96	**San Jose Sharks**	**NHL**	**59**	**16**	**12**	**28**	**16**	**10**	**26**	**27**	**5**	**0**	**2**	**103**	**15.5**	**45**	**20**	**46**	**0**	**–21**	....	....	....	....	....	....	....	....
1996-97	Sweden	W-Cup	4	1	1	2	....	....	....	0	....	....	....	....	....	....	....	....	....	....	....	....	....	....	....	....	....	....
	San Jose Sharks	**NHL**	**43**	**8**	**11**	**19**	**8**	**10**	**18**	**8**	**3**	**0**	**1**	**78**	**10.3**	**33**	**13**	**31**	**0**	**–11**	....	....	....	....	....	....	....	....
	Chicago Blackhawks	**NHL**	**30**	**6**	**8**	**14**	**6**	**7**	**13**	**10**	**1**	**0**	**3**	**53**	**11.3**	**20**	**3**	**8**	**0**	**9**	**5**	**0**	**1**	**1**	**0**	**0**	**0**	**0**
1997-98	HV-71 Jonkoping	Sweden	29	9	22	31	....	....	....	16	....	....	....	....	....	....	....	....	....	....	5	1	3	4	12	....	....	....
	Sweden	Olympics	4	1	0	1	....	....	....	2	....	....	....	....	....	....	....	....	....	....	....	....	....	....	....	....	....	....
	Sweden	WC-A	10	3	3	6	....	....	....	0	....	....	....	....	....	....	....	....	....	....	....	....	....	....	....	....	....	....
1998-99	HV-71 Jonkoping	Sweden	25	14	15	29	....	....	....	4	....	....	....	....	....	....	....	....	....	....	....	....	....	....	....	....	....	....
99-2000	**Washington Capitals**	**NHL**	**75**	**15**	**23**	**38**	**17**	**21**	**38**	**8**	**5**	**0**	**4**	**106**	**14.2**	**50**	**11**	**28**	**0**	**11**	**5**	**0**	**1**	**1**	**2**	**0**	**0**	**0**
	NHL Totals		**761**	**246**	**272**	**518**	**233**	**226**	**459**	**202**	**98**	**2**	**42**	**1628**	**15.1**	**761**	**312**	**488**	**2**		**68**	**14**	**21**	**35**	**10**	**6**	**0**	**2**

Swedish Junior Player-of-the-Year (1985) • EJC-A All-Star Team (1985) • Named Best Forward at EJC-A (1985) • WJC-A All-Star Team (1987) • Swedish World All-Star Team (1993) • WC-A All-Star Team (1993)

Traded to **Minnesota** by **NY Rangers** with LA Kings' 4th round choice (previously acquired, Minnesota selected Cal McGowan) in 1990 Entry Draft and future considerations for Mike Gartner, March 6, 1990. Transferred to **Dallas** after **Minnesota** franchise relocated, June 9, 1993. Traded to **San Jose** by **Dallas** with Dallas' 7th round choice (Brad Mehalko) in 1995 Entry Draft for Doug Zmolek and Mike Lalor, March 19, 1994. Traded to **Chicago** by **San Jose** with Chris Terreri and Michal Sykora for Ed Belfour, January 25, 1997. Signed as a free agent by **Washington**, August 16, 1999.

• DAHLIN, Kjell

RW – L. 6', 175 lbs. b: Timra, Sweden, 2/2/1963. Montreal's 7th, 82nd overall, in 1981.

Season	Club	League	GP	G	A	Pts	AG	AA	APts	PIM	PP	SH	GW	S	%	TGF	PGF	TGA	PGA	+/–	GP	G	A	Pts	PIM	PP	SH	GW
1978-79	Timra IF	Sweden-2	2	0	0	0	....	....	....	0	....	....	....	....	....	....	....	....	....	....	....	....	....	....	....	....	....	....
1979-80	Timra IF	Sweden-2	14	4	1	5	....	....	....	0	....	....	....	....	....	....	....	....	....	....	1	0	0	0	0	....	....	....
	Sweden	EJC-A	5	1	0	1	....	....	....	0	....	....	....	....	....	....	....	....	....	....	....	....	....	....	....	....	....	....
1980-81	Timra IF	Sweden-2	36	15	14	29	....	....	....	24	....	....	....	....	....	....	....	....	....	....	....	....	....	....	....	....	....	....
	Sweden	EJC-A	5	4	5	9	....	....	....	4	....	....	....	....	....	....	....	....	....	....	....	....	....	....	....	....	....	....
1981-82	Timra IF	Sweden	36	16	7	23	....	....	....	14	....	....	....	....	....	....	....	....	....	....	....	....	....	....	....	....	....	....
	Sweden	WJC-A	7	5	1	6	....	....	....	4	....	....	....	....	....	....	....	....	....	....	....	....	....	....	....	....	....	....
1982-83	Farjestads BK Karlstad	Sweden	32	10	8	18	....	....	....	2	....	....	....	....	....	....	....	....	....	....	7	0	0	0	2	....	....	....
	Sweden	WJC-A	7	3	4	7	....	....	....	....	....	....	....	....	....	....	....	....	....	....	....	....	....	....	....	....	....	....
1983-84	Farjestads BK Karlstad	Sweden	36	19	9	28	....	....	....	16	....	....	....	....	....	....	....	....	....	....	....	....	....	....	....	....	....	....
1984-85	Farjestads BK Karlstad	Sweden	35	21	25	46	....	....	....	10	....	....	....	....	....	....	....	....	....	....	....	....	....	....	....	....	....	....
1985-86♦	**Montreal Canadiens**	**NHL**	**77**	**32**	**39**	**71**	**26**	**26**	**52**	**4**	**14**	**0**	**3**	**172**	**18.6**	**116**	**52**	**54**	**0**	**10**	**16**	**2**	**3**	**5**	**4**	**0**	**0**	**0**
1986-87	**Montreal Canadiens**	**NHL**	**41**	**12**	**8**	**20**	**10**	**6**	**16**	**0**	**3**	**1**	**0**	**53**	**22.6**	**26**	**6**	**23**	**0**	**–3**	**8**	**2**	**4**	**6**	**0**	**0**	**0**	**0**
1987-88	**Montreal Canadiens**	**NHL**	**48**	**13**	**12**	**25**	**11**	**9**	**20**	**6**	**2**	**0**	**2**	**51**	**25.5**	**35**	**8**	**23**	**1**	**5**	**11**	**2**	**4**	**6**	**2**	**0**	**0**	**0**
1988-89	Farjestads BK Karlstad	Sweden	37	23	20	43	....	....	....	24	....	....	....	....	....	....	....	....	....	....	2	1	0	1	0	....	....	....
1989-90	Farjestads BK Karlstad	Sweden	30	26	12	38	....	....	....	12	....	....	....	....	....	....	....	....	....	....	10	4	5	9	6	....	....	....
1990-91	Farjestads BK Karlstad	Sweden	31	9	8	17	....	....	....	14	....	....	....	....	....	....	....	....	....	....	8	4	3	7	2	....	....	....
1991-92	Farjestads BK Karlstad	Sweden	25	6	10	16	....	....	....	10	....	....	....	....	....	....	....	....	....	....	6	4	1	5	4	....	....	....
1992-93	Farjestads BK Karlstad	Sweden	36	4	8	12	....	....	....	4	....	....	....	....	....	....	....	....	....	....	3	2	0	2	4	....	....	....
1993-94	Farjestads BK Karlstad	Sweden	16	0	1	1	....	....	....	0	....	....	....	....	....	....	....	....	....	....	8	1	0	1	0	....	....	....
	Grums IK	Sweden-2	4	0	5	5	....	....	....	0	....	....	....	....	....	....	....	....	....	....	....	....	....	....	....	....	....	....
	NHL Totals		**166**	**57**	**59**	**116**	**47**	**41**	**88**	**10**	**19**	**1**	**5**	**276**	**20.7**	**177**	**66**	**100**	**1**		**35**	**6**	**11**	**17**	**6**	**0**	**0**	**0**

Swedish Junior Player-of-the-Year (1981) • NHL All-Rookie Team (1986)

• Missed majority of 1986-87 season recovering from knee injury suffered in game vs. Vancouver, January 7, 1987.

• DAHLQUIST, Chris

Christopher Charles D – L. 6'1", 195 lbs. b: Fridley, MN, 12/14/1962.

Season	Club	League	GP	G	A	Pts	AG	AA	APts	PIM	PP	SH	GW	S	%	TGF	PGF	TGA	PGA	+/–	GP	G	A	Pts	PIM	PP	SH	GW
1981-82	Lake Superior State	CCHA	39	4	10	14	....	....	....	62	....	....	....	....	....	....	....	....	....	....	....	....	....	....	....	....	....	....
1982-83	Lake Superior State	CCHA	35	0	12	12	....	....	....	63	....	....	....	....	....	....	....	....	....	....	....	....	....	....	....	....	....	....
1983-84	Lake Superior State	CCHA	40	4	19	23	....	....	....	76	....	....	....	....	....	....	....	....	....	....	....	....	....	....	....	....	....	....
1984-85	Lake Superior State	CCHA	32	4	10	14	....	....	....	18	....	....	....	....	....	....	....	....	....	....	....	....	....	....	....	....	....	....
1985-86	**Pittsburgh Penguins**	**NHL**	**5**	**1**	**2**	**3**	**1**	**1**	**2**	**2**	**0**	**0**	**0**	**5**	**20.0**	**7**	**1**	**6**	**1**	**1**	....	....	....	....	....	....	....	....
	Baltimore Skipjacks	AHL	65	4	21	25	....	....	....	64	....	....	....	....	....	....	....	....	....	....	....	....	....	....	....	....	....	....
1986-87	**Pittsburgh Penguins**	**NHL**	**19**	**0**	**1**	**1**	**0**	**1**	**1**	**20**	**0**	**0**	**0**	**15**	**0.0**	**13**	**1**	**15**	**1**	**–2**	....	....	....	....	....	....	....	....
	Baltimore Skipjacks	AHL	51	1	16	17	....	....	....	50	....	....	....	....	....	....	....	....	....	....	....	....	....	....	....	....	....	....
1987-88	**Pittsburgh Penguins**	**NHL**	**44**	**3**	**6**	**9**	**3**	**4**	**7**	**69**	**0**	**0**	**0**	**35**	**8.6**	**28**	**1**	**39**	**15**	**3**	....	....	....	....	....	....	....	....
1988-89	**Pittsburgh Penguins**	**NHL**	**43**	**1**	**5**	**6**	**1**	**4**	**5**	**42**	**0**	**0**	**0**	**27**	**3.7**	**23**	**2**	**45**	**16**	**–8**	**2**	**0**	**0**	**0**	**0**	**0**	**0**	**0**
	Muskegon Lumberjacks	IHL	10	3	6	9	....	....	....	14	....	....	....	....	....	....	....	....	....	....	....	....	....	....	....	....	....	....
1989-90	**Pittsburgh Penguins**	**NHL**	**62**	**4**	**10**	**14**	**3**	**7**	**10**	**56**	**0**	**0**	**0**	**57**	**7.0**	**43**	**0**	**66**	**21**	**–2**	....	....	....	....	....	....	....	....
	Muskegon Lumberjacks	IHL	6	1	1	2	....	....	....	8	....	....	....	....	....	....	....	....	....	....	....	....	....	....	....	....	....	....
	United States	WEC-A	10	1	0	1	....	....	....	18	....	....	....	....	....	....	....	....	....	....	....	....	....	....	....	....	....	....
1990-91	**Pittsburgh Penguins**	**NHL**	**22**	**1**	**2**	**3**	**1**	**2**	**3**	**30**	**0**	**0**	**0**	**15**	**6.7**	**15**	**0**	**20**	**5**	**0**	....	....	....	....	....	....	....	....
	Minnesota North Stars	**NHL**	**42**	**2**	**6**	**8**	**2**	**5**	**7**	**33**	**0**	**0**	**0**	**37**	**5.4**	**32**	**0**	**48**	**15**	**–1**	**23**	**1**	**6**	**7**	**20**	**0**	**0**	**0**
1991-92	**Minnesota North Stars**	**NHL**	**74**	**1**	**13**	**14**	**1**	**10**	**11**	**68**	**0**	**0**	**0**	**63**	**1.6**	**53**	**2**	**91**	**30**	**–10**	**7**	**0**	**0**	**0**	**6**	**0**	**0**	**0**
1992-93	**Calgary Flames**	**NHL**	**74**	**3**	**7**	**10**	**2**	**5**	**7**	**66**	**0**	**0**	**1**	**64**	**4.7**	**54**	**2**	**76**	**24**	**0**	**6**	**3**	**1**	**4**	**4**	**0**	**0**	**0**
1993-94	**Calgary Flames**	**NHL**	**77**	**1**	**11**	**12**	**1**	**9**	**10**	**52**	**0**	**0**	**0**	**57**	**1.8**	**54**	**0**	**83**	**34**	**5**	**1**	**0**	**0**	**0**	**0**	**0**	**0**	**0**
1994-95	**Ottawa Senators**	**NHL**	**46**	**1**	**7**	**8**	**2**	**10**	**12**	**36**	**1**	**0**	**0**	**45**	**2.2**	**20**	**1**	**65**	**16**	**–30**	....	....	....	....	....	....	....	....
1995-96	**Ottawa Senators**	**NHL**	**24**	**1**	**1**	**2**	**1**	**1**	**2**	**14**	**0**	**0**	**0**	**13**	**7.7**	**11**	**0**	**23**	**5**	**–7**	....	....	....	....	....	....	....	....
	Cincinnati Cyclones	IHL	38	4	8	12	....	....	....	50	....	....	....	....	....	....	....	....	....	....	2	1	3	4	0	....	....	....
1996-97	Las Vegas Thunder	IHL	18	1	4	5	....	....	....	26	....	....	....	....	....	....	....	....	....	....	....	....	....	....	....	....	....	....
	NHL Totals		**532**	**19**	**71**	**90**	**18**	**59**	**77**	**488**	**1**	**0**	**1**	**433**	**4.4**	**353**	**10**	**577**	**183**		**39**	**4**	**7**	**11**	**30**	**0**	**0**	**0**

Signed as a free agent by **Pittsburgh**, May 7, 1985. Traded to **Minnesota** by **Pittsburgh** with Jim Johnson for Larry Murphy and Peter Taglianetti, December 11, 1990. Claimed by **Calgary** from **Minnesota** in NHL Waiver Draft, October 4, 1992. Signed as a free agent by **Ottawa**, July 4, 1994.

• DAIGLE, Alain

Roland Alain RW – R. 5'10", 180 lbs. b: Trois-Rivieres, Que., 8/24/1954. Chicago's 2nd, 34th overall, in 1974.

Season	Club	League	GP	G	A	Pts	AG	AA	APts	PIM	PP	SH	GW	S	%	TGF	PGF	TGA	PGA	+/–	GP	G	A	Pts	PIM	PP	SH	GW
1969-70	Trois-Rivieres Ducs	QJHL	26	5	3	8	....	....	....	13	....	....	....	....	....	....	....	....	....	....	....	....	....	....	....	....	....	....
1970-71	Trois-Rivieres Draveurs	QJHL	62	28	34	62	....	....	....	66	....	....	....	....	....	....	....	....	....	....	11	2	5	7	10	....	....	....
1971-72	Trois-Rivieres Draveurs	QMJHL	60	30	31	61	....	....	....	161	....	....	....	....	....	....	....	....	....	....	2	1	0	1	20	....	....	....
1972-73	Trois-Rivieres Draveurs	QMJHL	61	42	32	74	....	....	....	97	....	....	....	....	....	....	....	....	....	....	....	....	....	....	....	....	....	....
1973-74	Trois-Rivieres Draveurs	QMJHL	67	80	68	148	....	....	....	72	....	....	....	....	....	....	....	....	....	....	....	....	....	....	....	....	....	....
1974-75	**Chicago Black Hawks**	**NHL**	**52**	**5**	**4**	**9**	**4**	**3**	**7**	**6**	**0**	**0**	**0**	**47**	**10.6**	**13**	**0**	**22**	**3**	**–6**	**2**	**0**	**0**	**0**	**0**	**0**	**0**	**0**
1975-76	**Chicago Black Hawks**	**NHL**	**71**	**15**	**9**	**24**	**13**	**7**	**20**	**15**	**8**	**0**	**2**	**85**	**17.6**	**38**	**15**	**41**	**0**	**–18**	**4**	**0**	**0**	**0**	**0**	**0**	**0**	**0**
1976-77	**Chicago Black Hawks**	**NHL**	**73**	**12**	**8**	**20**	**11**	**6**	**17**	**11**	**2**	**0**	**1**	**89**	**13.5**	**38**	**6**	**33**	**0**	**–1**	**1**	**0**	**0**	**0**	**0**	**0**	**0**	**0**
1977-78	**Chicago Black Hawks**	**NHL**	**53**	**6**	**6**	**12**	**5**	**5**	**10**	**13**	**1**	**0**	**0**	**84**	**7.1**	**17**	**2**	**27**	**0**	**–12**	**4**	**0**	**1**	**1**	**0**	**0**	**0**	**0**
1978-79	**Chicago Black Hawks**	**NHL**	**74**	**11**	**14**	**25**	**9**	**10**	**19**	**55**	**0**	**0**	**0**	**80**	**13.8**	**47**	**1**	**59**	**15**	**2**	**4**	**0**	**0**	**0**	**0**	**0**	**0**	**0**
	New Brunswick Hawks	AHL	5	2	1	3	....	....	....	4	....	....	....	....	....	....	....	....	....	....	....	....	....	....	....	....	....	....
1979-80	**Chicago Black Hawks**	**NHL**	**66**	**7**	**9**	**16**	**6**	**7**	**13**	**22**	**0**	**1**	**0**	**56**	**12.5**	**30**	**2**	**40**	**6**	**–6**	**2**	**0**	**0**	**0**	**0**	**0**	**0**	**0**

Season	Club	League	GP	G	A	Pts	AG	AA	APts	PIM	PP	SH	GW	S	%	TGF	PGF	TGA	PGA	+/-	GP	G	A	Pts	PIM	PP	SH	GW
			REGULAR SEASON																		PLAYOFFS							
1980-81	HC Gap	France	28	22	13	35																						
	New Brunswick Hawks	AHL	15	5	5	10				14											7	1	1	2	7			
1981-82	IEV Innsbruck	Austria	24	32	19	51				62																		
1982-83	Sherbrooke Jets	AHL	43	11	22	33				18																		
1983-84	Sherbrooke Jets	AHL	79	22	26	48				24																		
	NHL Totals		**389**	**56**	**50**	**106**	**48**	**38**	**86**	**122**	**11**	**1**	**3**	**441**	**12.7**	**183**	**26**	**222**	**24**		**17**	**0**	**1**	**1**	**0**	**0**	**0**	**0**

• DAIGLE, Alexandre

C – L. 6', 195 lbs. b: Montreal, Que., 2/7/1975. Ottawa's 1st, 1st overall, in 1993.

Season	Club	League	GP	G	A	Pts	AG	AA	APts	PIM	PP	SH	GW	S	%	TGF	PGF	TGA	PGA	+/-	GP	G	A	Pts	PIM	PP	SH	GW
1990-91	Laval-Laurentides Regents	QAAA	42	50	60	110				98																		
1991-92	Victoriaville Tigres	QMJHL	66	35	75	110				63																		
1992-93	Victoriaville Tigres	QMJHL	53	45	92	137				85											6	5	6	11	4			
	Canada	WJC-A	7	0	6	6				27																		
1993-94	**Ottawa Senators**	**NHL**	84	20	31	51	19	24	43	40	4	0	2	168	11.9	69	28	98	12	–45								
1994-95	Victoriaville Tigres	QMJHL	18	14	20	34				16																		
	Canada	WJC-A	7	2	8	10				4																		
	Ottawa Senators	**NHL**	47	16	21	37	28	31	59	14	4	1	2	105	15.2	52	18	62	6	–22								
1995-96	**Ottawa Senators**	**NHL**	50	5	12	17	5	10	15	24	1	0	0	77	6.5	29	14	50	5	–30								
1996-97	**Ottawa Senators**	**NHL**	82	26	25	51	28	22	50	33	4	0	5	203	12.8	71	30	74	0	–33	7	0	0	0	2	0	0	0
1997-98	**Ottawa Senators**	**NHL**	38	7	9	16	8	9	17	8	4	0	2	68	10.3	24	11	21	1	–7								
	Philadelphia Flyers	**NHL**	37	9	17	26	11	17	28	6	4	0	3	78	11.5	32	9	24	0	–1	5	0	2	2	0	0	0	0
1998-99	**Philadelphia Flyers**	**NHL**	31	3	2	5	4	2	6	2	1	0	1	26	11.5	6	1	6	0	–1								
	Tampa Bay Lightning	**NHL**	32	6	6	12	7	6	13	2	3	0	0	56	10.7	21	10	23	0	–12								
99-2000	**New York Rangers**	**NHL**	58	8	18	26	9	17	26	23	1	0	1	52	15.4	34	9	30	0	–5								
	Hartford Wolf Pack	AHL	16	6	13	19				4																		
	NHL Totals		**459**	**100**	**141**	**241**	**119**	**138**	**257**	**152**	**26**	**1**	**16**	**833**	**12.0**	**338**	**130**	**388**	**24**		**12**	**0**	**2**	**2**	**2**	**0**	**0**	**0**

QMJHL Second All-Star Team (1992) • Canadian Major Junior Rookie of the Year (1992) • QMJHL First All-Star Team (1993)

Traded to **Philadelphia** by **Ottawa** for Vaclav Prospal, Pat Falloon and Dallas' 2nd round choice (previously acquired, Ottawa selected Chris Bala) in 1998 Entry Draft, January 17, 1998. Traded to **Edmonton** by **Philadelphia** for Andrei Kovalenko, January 29, 1999. Traded to **Tampa Bay** by **Edmonton** for Alexander Selivanov, January 29, 1999. Traded to **NY Rangers** by **Tampa Bay** for cash, October 3, 1999.

• DAIGNEAULT, J.J.

Jean-Jacques D – L. 5'10", 192 lbs. b: Montreal, Que., 10/12/1965. Vancouver's 1st, 10th overall, in 1984.

Season	Club	League	GP	G	A	Pts	AG	AA	APts	PIM	PP	SH	GW	S	%	TGF	PGF	TGA	PGA	+/-	GP	G	A	Pts	PIM	PP	SH	GW
1979-80	Montreal Hurricanes	QAAA	STATISTICS NOT AVAILABLE																									
1980-81	Montreal Concordia	QAAA	48	7	48	55																						
1981-82	Laval Voisins	QMJHL	64	4	25	29				41											18	1	3	4	2			
1982-83	Longueuil Chevaliers	QMJHL	70	26	58	84				58											15	4	11	15	35			
1983-84	Longueuil Chevaliers	QMJHL	10	2	11	13				6											14	3	13	16	30			
	Canada	WJC-A	7	0	2	2				2																		
	Canada	Nat-Team	55	5	14	19				40																		
	Canada	Olympics	7	1	1	2				0																		
1984-85	**Vancouver Canucks**	**NHL**	67	4	23	27	3	16	19	69	2	0	0	93	4.3	67	17	67	3	–14								
1985-86	**Vancouver Canucks**	**NHL**	64	5	23	28	4	15	19	45	4	0	0	114	4.4	68	36	54	2	–20	3	0	2	2	0	0	0	0
1986-87	**Philadelphia Flyers**	**NHL**	77	6	16	22	5	12	17	56	0	0	1	82	7.3	72	13	48	1	12	9	1	0	1	0	0	0	1
1987-88	**Philadelphia Flyers**	**NHL**	28	2	2	4	2	1	3	12	2	0	0	20	10.0	13	6	15	0	–8								
	Hershey Bears	AHL	10	1	5	6				8																		
1988-89	Hershey Bears	AHL	12	0	10	10				13																		
	Sherbrooke Canadiens	AHL	63	10	33	43				48											6	1	3	4	2			
1989-90	**Montreal Canadiens**	**NHL**	36	2	10	12	2	7	9	14	0	0	1	40	5.0	40	5	27	3	11	9	0	0	0	2	0	0	0
	Sherbrooke Canadiens	AHL	28	8	19	27				18																		
1990-91	Montreal Canadiens	Fr-Tour	1	0	0	0				0																		
	Montreal Canadiens	**NHL**	51	3	16	19	3	12	15	31	2	0	0	68	4.4	59	14	58	11	–2	5	0	1	1	0	0	0	0
1991-92	**Montreal Canadiens**	**NHL**	79	4	14	18	4	11	15	36	2	0	0	108	3.7	78	16	75	29	16	11	0	3	3	4	0	0	0
1992-93♦	**Montreal Canadiens**	**NHL**	66	8	10	18	7	7	14	57	0	0	1	68	11.8	76	5	76	30	25	20	1	3	4	22	0	0	0
1993-94	**Montreal Canadiens**	**NHL**	68	2	12	14	2	9	11	73	0	0	1	61	3.3	61	1	61	17	16	7	0	1	1	12	0	0	0
1994-95	**Montreal Canadiens**	**NHL**	45	3	5	8	5	7	12	40	0	0	0	36	8.3	34	0	43	11	2								
1995-96	**Montreal Canadiens**	**NHL**	7	0	1	1	0	1	1	6	0	0	0	3	0.0	6	0	8	2	0								
	St. Louis Blues	**NHL**	37	1	3	4	1	2	3	24	0	0	0	45	2.2	14	6	18	4	–6								
	Worcester IceCats	AHL	9	1	10	11				10																		
	Pittsburgh Penguins	**NHL**	13	3	3	6	3	2	5	23	2	0	0	13	23.1	25	11	16	2	0	17	1	9	10	36	1	0	1
1996-97	**Pittsburgh Penguins**	**NHL**	53	3	14	17	3	12	15	36	0	0	1	49	6.1	44	11	44	6	–5								
	Mighty Ducks of Anaheim	**NHL**	13	2	9	11	2	8	10	22	0	0	0	13	15.4	22	11	9	3	5	11	2	7	9	16	1	0	1
1997-98	**Mighty Ducks of Anaheim**	**NHL**	53	2	15	17	2	15	17	28	1	0	1	74	2.7	47	14	59	16	–10								
	New York Islanders	**NHL**	18	0	6	6	0	6	6	21	0	0	0	18	0.0	15	3	17	6	1								
1998-99	**Nashville Predators**	**NHL**	35	2	2	4	2	2	4	38	1	0	1	38	5.3	25	4	42	17	–4								
	Phoenix Coyotes	**NHL**	35	0	7	7	0	7	7	32	0	0	0	27	0.0	24	4	31	3	–8	6	0	0	0	8	0	0	0
99-2000	**Phoenix Coyotes**	**NHL**	53	1	6	7	1	6	7	22	0	0	0	44	2.3	23	2	40	3	–16	1	0	0	0	0	0	0	0
	NHL Totals		**898**	**53**	**197**	**250**	**51**	**158**	**209**	**685**	**16**	**0**	**7**	**1014**	**5.2**	**813**	**179**	**808**	**169**		**99**	**5**	**26**	**31**	**100**	**2**	**0**	**3**

QMJHL First All-Star Team (1983)

Traded to **Philadelphia** by **Vancouver** with Vancouver's 2nd round choice (Kent Hawley) in 1986 Entry Draft and 5th round choice (later traded back to Vancouver–Vancouver selected Sean Fabian) in 1987 Entry Draft for Dave Richter, Rich Sutter and Vancouver's 3rd round choice (previously acquired, Vancouver selected Don Gibson) in 1986 Entry Draft, June 6, 1986. Traded to **Montreal** by **Philadelphia** for Scott Sandelin, November 7, 1988. Traded to **St. Louis** by **Montreal** for Pat Jablonski, November 7, 1995. Traded to **Pittsburgh** by **St. Louis** for Pittsburgh's 6th round choice (Stephen Wagner) in 1996 Entry Draft, March 20, 1996. Traded to **Anaheim** by **Pittsburgh** for Garry Valk, February 21, 1997. Traded to **NY Islanders** by **Anaheim** with Joe Sacco and Mark Janssens for Travis Green, Doug Houda and Tony Tuzzolino, February 6, 1998. Claimed by **Nashville** from **NY Islanders** in Expansion Draft, June 26, 1998. Traded to **Phoenix** by **Nashville** for future considerations, January 13, 1999.

• DAILEY, Bob

Robert Scott D – R. 6'5", 220 lbs. b: Kingston, Ont., 5/3/1953. Vancouver's 2nd, 9th overall, in 1973.

Season	Club	League	GP	G	A	Pts	AG	AA	APts	PIM	PP	SH	GW	S	%	TGF	PGF	TGA	PGA	+/-	GP	G	A	Pts	PIM	PP	SH	GW
1969-70	Trenton Travellers	OMHA	STATISTICS NOT AVAILABLE																									
1970-71	Markham Waxers	OHA-B	STATISTICS NOT AVAILABLE																									
	Toronto Marlboros	OHA-Jr.	36	2	3	5				36																		
1971-72	Toronto Marlboros	OMJHL	62	11	39	50				135											10	3	7	10	18			
1972-73	Toronto Marlboros	OMJHL	60	9	55	64				200											16	9	11	20	22			
	Toronto Marlboros	Mem-Cup	3	0	1	1				*19																		
1973-74	**Vancouver Canucks**	**NHL**	76	7	17	24	7	14	21	143	0	0	0	124	5.6	82	8	133	27	–32								
1974-75	**Vancouver Canucks**	**NHL**	70	12	36	48	10	27	37	103	7	0	1	170	7.1	113	40	98	16	–9	5	1	3	4	14	0	0	0
1975-76	**Vancouver Canucks**	**NHL**	67	15	24	39	13	18	31	119	9	0	3	187	8.0	105	38	94	22	–5	2	1	1	2	0	1	0	0
1976-77	**Vancouver Canucks**	**NHL**	44	4	16	20	4	12	16	52	2	0	1	100	4.0	56	14	75	17	–16								
	Philadelphia Flyers	**NHL**	32	5	14	19	4	11	15	38	2	0	0	77	6.5	55	12	33	6	16	10	4	9	13	15	2	0	0
1977-78	**Philadelphia Flyers**	**NHL**	76	21	36	57	19	28	47	62	5	2	2	211	10.0	136	40	77	26	45	12	1	5	6	22	0	0	0
1978-79	**Philadelphia Flyers**	**NHL**	70	9	30	39	8	22	30	63	1	0	1	164	5.5	109	25	87	24	21	8	1	2	3	14	0	0	0
1979-80	**Philadelphia Flyers**	**NHL**	61	13	26	39	11	19	30	71	2	1	4	185	7.0	100	18	74	22	30	19	4	13	17	22	1	1	2
1980-81	**Philadelphia Flyers**	**NHL**	53	7	27	34	5	18	23	141	1	0	0	141	5.0	66	20	57	19	8	7	0	1	1	18	0	0	0
1981-82	**Philadelphia Flyers**	**NHL**	12	1	5	6	1	3	4	22	0	0	0	22	4.5	16	1	16	5	4								
1982-1985			OUT OF HOCKEY – RETIRED																									
1985-86	Hershey Bears	AHL	5	0	0	0				8																		
	NHL Totals		**561**	**94**	**231**	**325**	**82**	**172**	**254**	**814**	**29**	**3**	**12**	**1381**	**6.8**	**838**	**216**	**744**	**184**		**63**	**12**	**34**	**46**	**105**	**4**	**1**	**2**

OMJHL Second All-Star Team (1973) • Played in NHL All-Star Game (1978, 1981)

Traded to **Philadelphia** by **Vancouver** for Larry Goodenough and Jack McIlhargey, January 20, 1977. • Missed remainder of 1981-82 recovering from ankle injury suffered in game with Buffalo, November 1, 1981. • Officially announced retirement, July, 1982. • Attempted comeback with **Hershey** (AHL), March, 1986.

• DALEY, Pat Patrick Lloyd LW – L. 6'1", 176 lbs. b: Maryville, France, 3/27/1959. Winnipeg's 4th, 82nd overall, in 1979.

			REGULAR SEASON																		PLAYOFFS							
Season	Club	League	GP	G	A	Pts	AG	AA	APts	PIM	PP	SH	GW	S	%	TGF	PGF	TGA	PGA	+/–	GP	G	A	Pts	PIM	PP	SH	GW
1974-75	James M. Hill High	Hi-School	STATISTICS NOT AVAILABLE																									
1975-76	Laval National	QMJHL	70	8	11	19	....	....	....	47	....	....	....	....	....	....	....	....	....	....	....	....	....	....	....	....	....	....
1976-77	Laval National	QMJHL	63	23	36	59	....	....	....	135	....	....	....	....	....	....	....	....	....	....	....	....	....	....	....	....	....	....
1977-78	Laval National	QMJHL	69	44	76	120	....	....	....	174	....	....	....	....	....	....	....	....	....	....	....	....	....	....	....	....	....	....
	Canada	WJC-A	6	3	2	5	....	....	....	2	....	....	....	....	....	....	....	....	....	....	....	....	....	....	....	....	....	....
1978-79	Montreal Juniors	QMJHL	67	25	50	75	....	....	....	139	....	....	....	....	....	....	....	....	....	....	....	....	....	....	....	....	....	....
1979-80	**Winnipeg Jets**	**NHL**	**5**	**1**	**0**	**1**	**1**	**0**	**1**	**4**	**0**	**0**	**0**	**6**	**16.7**	**2**	**0**	**4**	**0**	**–2**	....	....	....	....	....	....	....	....
	Tulsa Oilers	CHL	65	9	16	25	....	....	....	141	....	....	....	....	....	....	....	....	....	....	3	1	0	1	13	....	....	....
1980-81	**Winnipeg Jets**	**NHL**	**7**	**0**	**0**	**0**	**0**	**0**	**0**	**9**	**0**	**0**	**0**	**4**	**0.0**	**1**	**0**	**4**	**0**	**–3**	....	....	....	....	....	....	....	....
	Tulsa Oilers	CHL	68	18	22	40	....	....	....	189	....	....	....	....	....	....	....	....	....	....	8	3	5	8	24	....	....	....
1981-82	Fredericton Express	AHL	71	14	13	27	....	....	....	120	....	....	....	....	....	....	....	....	....	....	....	....	....	....	....	....	....	....
1982-83	ASG Tours	France	STATISTICS NOT AVAILABLE																									
1983-84	ASG Tours	France	STATISTICS NOT AVAILABLE																									
1984-85	ASG Tours	France	32	27	15	42	....	....	....		....	....	....	....	....	....	....	....	....	....	....	....	....	....	....	....	....	....
1985-86	Paris Francais Volant	France	STATISTICS NOT AVAILABLE																									
	France	WC-B	7	4	3	7	....	....	....	4	....	....	....	....	....	....	....	....	....	....	....	....	....	....	....	....	....	....
1986-87	Paris Francais Volant	France	STATISTICS NOT AVAILABLE																									
	France	WC-B	6	1	3	4	....	....	....	8	....	....	....	....	....	....	....	....	....	....	....	....	....	....	....	....	....	....
1987-88	HC Gap	France	30	10	8	18	....	....	....	34	....	....	....	....	....	....	....	....	....	....	....	....	....	....	....	....	....	....
1988-89	HC Rouen	France	35	10	22	32	....	....	....	62	....	....	....	....	....	....	....	....	....	....	5	2	1	3	0	....	....	....
1989-90	HC Rouen	France	26	9	13	22	....	....	....	32	....	....	....	....	....	....	....	....	....	....	4	0	0	0	2	....	....	....
1990-91	HC Rouen	France	27	6	4	10	....	....	....	18	....	....	....	....	....	....	....	....	....	....	9	1	1	2	6	....	....	....
1991-1993			OUT OF HOCKEY – RETIRED																									
1993-94	HC Brest	France	25	5	4	9	....	....	....	51	....	....	....	....	....	....	....	....	....	....	....	....	....	....	....	....	....	....
	NHL Totals		**12**	**1**	**0**	**1**	**1**	**0**	**1**	**13**	**0**	**0**	**0**	**10**	**10.0**	**3**	**0**	**8**	**0**		....	....	....	....	....	....	....	....

QMJHL First All-Star Team (1978)

Signed as a free agent by **Quebec**, July, 1981.

• DALGARNO, Brad Brad W. RW – R. 6'3", 215 lbs. b: Vancouver, B.C., 8/11/1967. NY Islanders' 1st, 6th overall, in 1985.

Season	Club	League	GP	G	A	Pts	AG	AA	APts	PIM	PP	SH	GW	S	%	TGF	PGF	TGA	PGA	+/–	GP	G	A	Pts	PIM	PP	SH	GW
1983-84	Markham Waxers	OJHL-B	40	17	11	28	....	....	....	59	....	....	....	....	....	....	....	....	....	....	....	....	....	....	....	....	....	....
	Orillia Travelways	OJHL	4	1	1	2	....	....	....	6	....	....	....	....	....	....	....	....	....	....	....	....	....	....	....	....	....	....
1984-85	Hamilton Steelhawks	OHL	66	23	30	53	....	....	....	86	....	....	....	....	....	....	....	....	....	....	....	....	....	....	....	....	....	....
1985-86	Hamilton Steelhawks	OHL	54	22	43	65	....	....	....	79	....	....	....	....	....	....	....	....	....	....	....	....	....	....	....	....	....	....
	New York Islanders	**NHL**	**2**	**1**	**0**	**1**	**1**	**0**	**1**	**0**	**0**	**0**	**0**	**3**	**33.3**	**2**	**0**	**1**	**0**	**1**	....	....	....	....	....	....	....	....
1986-87	Hamilton Steelhawks	OHL	60	27	32	59	....	....	....	100	....	....	....	....	....	....	....	....	....	....	....	....	....	....	....	....	....	....
	New York Islanders	**NHL**	....	....	....	....	....	....	....	....	....	....	....	....	....	....	....	....	....	....	**1**	**0**	**1**	**1**	**0**	**0**	**0**	**0**
1987-88	**New York Islanders**	**NHL**	**38**	**2**	**8**	**10**	**2**	**6**	**8**	**58**	**0**	**0**	**1**	**39**	**5.1**	**19**	**5**	**10**	**0**	**4**	**4**	**0**	**0**	**0**	**19**	**0**	**0**	**0**
	Springfield Indians	AHL	39	13	11	24	....	....	....	76	....	....	....	....	....	....	....	....	....	....	....	....	....	....	....	....	....	....
1988-89	**New York Islanders**	**NHL**	**55**	**11**	**10**	**21**	**9**	**7**	**16**	**86**	**2**	**0**	**1**	**83**	**13.3**	**42**	**14**	**36**	**0**	**–8**	....	....	....	....	....	....	....	....
1989-90	**New York Islanders**	**NHL**	DID NOT PLAY – INJURED																									
1990-91	**New York Islanders**	**NHL**	**41**	**3**	**12**	**15**	**3**	**9**	**12**	**24**	**0**	**0**	**1**	**34**	**8.8**	**19**	**1**	**28**	**0**	**–10**	....	....	....	....	....	....	....	....
	Capital District Islanders	AHL	27	6	14	20	....	....	....	26	....	....	....	....	....	....	....	....	....	....	....	....	....	....	....	....	....	....
1991-92	**New York Islanders**	**NHL**	**15**	**2**	**1**	**3**	**2**	**1**	**3**	**12**	**1**	**0**	**0**	**17**	**11.8**	**5**	**2**	**11**	**0**	**–8**	....	....	....	....	....	....	....	....
	Capital District Islanders	AHL	14	7	8	15	....	....	....	34	....	....	....	....	....	....	....	....	....	....	....	....	....	....	....	....	....	....
1992-93	**New York Islanders**	**NHL**	**57**	**15**	**17**	**32**	**12**	**12**	**24**	**62**	**2**	**0**	**2**	**62**	**24.2**	**50**	**3**	**30**	**0**	**17**	**18**	**2**	**2**	**4**	**14**	**0**	**0**	**0**
	Capital District Islanders	AHL	19	10	4	14	....	....	....	16	....	....	....	....	....	....	....	....	....	....	....	....	....	....	....	....	....	....
1993-94	**New York Islanders**	**NHL**	**73**	**11**	**19**	**30**	**10**	**15**	**25**	**62**	**3**	**0**	**1**	**97**	**11.3**	**49**	**6**	**38**	**9**	**14**	**4**	**0**	**1**	**1**	**4**	**0**	**0**	**0**
1994-95	**New York Islanders**	**NHL**	**22**	**3**	**2**	**5**	**5**	**3**	**8**	**14**	**1**	**1**	**0**	**18**	**16.7**	**7**	**1**	**17**	**3**	**–8**	....	....	....	....	....	....	....	....
1995-96	**New York Islanders**	**NHL**	**18**	**1**	**2**	**3**	**1**	**2**	**3**	**14**	**0**	**0**	**0**	**11**	**9.1**	**4**	**1**	**5**	**0**	**–2**	....	....	....	....	....	....	....	....
	NHL Totals		**321**	**49**	**71**	**120**	**45**	**55**	**100**	**332**	**9**	**1**	**6**	**364**	**13.5**	**197**	**33**	**176**	**12**		**27**	**2**	**4**	**6**	**37**	**0**	**0**	**0**

• Missed remainder of 1988-89 and entire 1989-90 seasons recovering from eye injury suffered in game vs. Detroit, February 21, 1989.

• DALLMAN, Marty C – R. 5'10", 180 lbs. b: Niagara Falls, Ont., 2/15/1963. Los Angeles' 3rd, 81st overall, in 1981.

Season	Club	League	GP	G	A	Pts	AG	AA	APts	PIM	PP	SH	GW	S	%	TGF	PGF	TGA	PGA	+/–	GP	G	A	Pts	PIM	PP	SH	GW
1979-80	Niagara Falls Canucks	OJHL-B	44	32	38	70	....	....	....	37	....	....	....	....	....	....	....	....	....	....	4	7	5	12	10	....	....	....
	Niagara Falls Flyers	OHA-Jr.	2	0	0	0	....	....	....	0	....	....	....	....	....	....	....	....	....	....	....	....	....	....	....	....	....	....
1980-81	RPI Engineers	ECAC	22	9	10	19	....	....	....	8	....	....	....	....	....	....	....	....	....	....	....	....	....	....	....	....	....	....
1981-82	RPI Engineers	ECAC	28	22	18	40	....	....	....	27	....	....	....	....	....	....	....	....	....	....	....	....	....	....	....	....	....	....
1982-83	RPI Engineers	ECAC	27	21	29	50	....	....	....	28	....	....	....	....	....	....	....	....	....	....	....	....	....	....	....	....	....	....
1983-84	RPI Engineers	ECAC	38	30	24	54	....	....	....	32	....	....	....	....	....	....	....	....	....	....	....	....	....	....	....	....	....	....
1984-85	New Haven Nighthawks	AHL	78	18	39	57	....	....	....	26	....	....	....	....	....	....	....	....	....	....	....	....	....	....	....	....	....	....
1985-86	New Haven Nighthawks	AHL	69	23	33	56	....	....	....	92	....	....	....	....	....	....	....	....	....	....	5	0	4	4	4	....	....	....
1986-87	Baltimore Skipjacks	AHL	6	0	1	1	....	....	....	0	....	....	....	....	....	....	....	....	....	....	....	....	....	....	....	....	....	....
	Newmarket Saints	AHL	42	24	24	48	....	....	....	44	....	....	....	....	....	....	....	....	....	....	....	....	....	....	....	....	....	....
1987-88	**Toronto Maple Leafs**	**NHL**	**2**	**0**	**1**	**1**	**0**	**1**	**1**	**0**	**0**	**0**	**0**	**1**	**0.0**	**1**	**0**	**0**	**0**	**1**	....	....	....	....	....	....	....	....
	Newmarket Saints	AHL	76	50	39	89	....	....	....	52	....	....	....	....	....	....	....	....	....	....	....	....	....	....	....	....	....	....
1988-89	**Toronto Maple Leafs**	**NHL**	**4**	**0**	**0**	**0**	**0**	**0**	**0**	**0**	**0**	**0**	**0**	**2**	**0.0**	**1**	**1**	**0**	**0**	**0**	....	....	....	....	....	....	....	....
	Newmarket Saints	AHL	37	26	20	46	....	....	....	24	....	....	....	....	....	....	....	....	....	....	....	....	....	....	....	....	....	....
1989-90	WEV Wien	Austria	34	36	33	69	....	....	....	89	....	....	....	....	....	....	....	....	....	....	....	....	....	....	....	....	....	....
1990-91	WEV Wien	Austria	39	39	18	57	....	....	....	70	....	....	....	....	....	....	....	....	....	....	....	....	....	....	....	....	....	....
1991-92	WEV Wien	Austria	39	46	23	69	....	....	....	....	....	....	....	....	....	....	....	....	....	....	....	....	....	....	....	....	....	....
1992-93	EK Zell-am-Zee	Austria	43	30	17	47	....	....	....	....	....	....	....	....	....	....	....	....	....	....	....	....	....	....	....	....	....	....
	Austria	WC-A	6	0	1	1	....	....	....	10	....	....	....	....	....	....	....	....	....	....	....	....	....	....	....	....	....	....
1993-94	EC Graz	Austria	57	35	43	78	....	....	....	....	....	....	....	....	....	....	....	....	....	....	....	....	....	....	....	....	....	....
	Austria	Olympics	7	4	4	8	....	....	....	8	....	....	....	....	....	....	....	....	....	....	....	....	....	....	....	....	....	....
1994-95	HC Fribourg-Gotteron	Switz.	4	1	1	2	....	....	....	4	....	....	....	....	....	....	....	....	....	....	....	....	....	....	....	....	....	....
	South Carolina Stingrays	ECHL	22	11	16	27	....	....	....	22	....	....	....	....	....	....	....	....	....	....	6	5	9	14	4	....	....	....
1995-96	WEV Wien	Austria	33	22	29	51	....	....	....	67	....	....	....	....	....	....	....	....	....	....	....	....	....	....	....	....	....	....
1996-97	Nottingham Panthers	BH-Cup	11	4	9	13	....	....	....	0	....	....	....	....	....	....	....	....	....	....	....	....	....	....	....	....	....	....
	Nottingham Panthers	Britain	40	24	32	56	....	....	....	28	....	....	....	....	....	....	....	....	....	....	8	5	3	8	10	....	....	....
1997-98	Nottingham Panthers	BH-Cup	12	9	8	17	....	....	....	10	....	....	....	....	....	....	....	....	....	....	....	....	....	....	....	....	....	....
	Nottingham Panthers	Britain	33	13	20	33	....	....	....	12	....	....	....	....	....	....	....	....	....	....	6	3	2	5	0	....	....	....
1998-99	Abilene Aviators	WPHL	59	30	37	67	....	....	....	48	....	....	....	....	....	....	....	....	....	....	3	2	2	4	0	....	....	....
99-2000	Abilene Aviators	WPHL	DID NOT PLAY – COACHING																									
	NHL Totals		**6**	**0**	**1**	**1**	**0**	**1**	**1**	**0**	**0**	**0**	**0**	**3**	**0.0**	**2**	**1**	**0**	**0**		....	....	....	....	....	....	....	....

ECAC Second All-Star Team (1984) • AHL Second All-Star Team (1988)

Signed as a free agent by **Toronto**, November, 1986.

• DALLMAN, Rod LW – L. 5'11", 185 lbs. b: Prince Albert, Sask., 1/26/1967. NY Islanders' 8th, 118th overall, in 1985.

Season	Club	League	GP	G	A	Pts	AG	AA	APts	PIM	PP	SH	GW	S	%	TGF	PGF	TGA	PGA	+/–	GP	G	A	Pts	PIM	PP	SH	GW
1983-84	Prince Albert Midget Raiders	AAHA	21	14	6	20	....	....	....	69	....	....	....	....	....	....	....	....	....	....	....	....	....	....	....	....	....	....
1984-85	Prince Albert Raiders	WHL	40	8	11	19	....	....	....	133	....	....	....	....	....	....	....	....	....	....	12	3	4	7	51	....	....	....
	Prince Albert Raiders	Mem-Cup	4	0	0	0	....	....	....	32	....	....	....	....	....	....	....	....	....	....	....	....	....	....	....	....	....	....
1985-86	Prince Albert Raiders	WHL	59	20	21	41	....	....	....	198	....	....	....	....	....	....	....	....	....	....	....	....	....	....	....	....	....	....
1986-87	Prince Albert Raiders	WHL	47	13	21	34	....	....	....	240	....	....	....	....	....	....	....	....	....	....	5	0	1	1	32	....	....	....
1987-88	**New York Islanders**	**NHL**	**3**	**1**	**0**	**1**	**1**	**0**	**1**	**6**	**0**	**0**	**0**	**2**	**50.0**	**1**	**0**	**0**	**0**	**1**	....	....	....	....	....	....	....	....
	Springfield Indians	AHL	59	9	17	26	....	....	....	355	....	....	....	....	....	....	....	....	....	....	....	....	....	....	....	....	....	....
	Peoria Rivermen	IHL	8	3	4	7	....	....	....	18	....	....	....	....	....	....	....	....	....	....	7	0	2	2	65	....	....	....
1988-89	**New York Islanders**	**NHL**	**1**	**0**	**0**	**0**	**0**	**0**	**0**	**15**	**0**	**0**	**0**	**1**	**0.0**	**0**	**0**	**1**	**0**	**–1**	....	....	....	....	....	....	....	....
	Springfield Indians	AHL	67	12	12	24	....	....	....	360	....	....	....	....	....	....	....	....	....	....	....	....	....	....	....	....	....	....

			REGULAR SEASON																		PLAYOFFS							
Season	Club	League	GP	G	A	Pts	AG	AA	APts	PIM	PP	SH	GW	S	%	TGF	PGF	TGA	PGA	+/–	GP	G	A	Pts	PIM	PP	SH	GW
1989-90	Springfield Indians	AHL	43	10	20	30	....	....	....	129	....	....	....	....	....	....	....	....	....	....	15	5	5	10	59	....	....	....
	New York Islanders	**NHL**	....	....	....	....	....	....	....	....	....	....	....	....	....	....	....	....	....	....	1	0	1	1	0	0	0	0
1990-91	Hershey Bears	AHL	2	0	0	0	....	....	....	0	....	....	....	....	....	....	....	....	....	....	....	....	....	....	....	....	....	....
	San Diego Gulls	IHL	15	3	5	8	....	....	....	85	....	....	....	....	....	....	....	....	....	....	....	....	....	....	....	....	....	....
1991-92	**Philadelphia Flyers**	**NHL**	2	0	0	0	0	0	0	5	0	0	0	2	0.0	0	0	0	0	0	....	....	....	....	....	....	....	....
	Hershey Bears	AHL	31	4	13	17	....	....	....	114	....	....	....	....	....	....	....	....	....	....	....	....	....	....	....	....	....	....
	NHL Totals		6	1	0	1	1	0	1	26	0	0	0	5	20.0	1	0	1	0		1	0	1	1	0	0	0	0

Signed as a free agent by **Philadelphia**, July 31, 1990.

• DAMPHOUSSE, Vincent

Vincent Francois C – L. 6'1", 191 lbs. b: Montreal, Que., 12/17/1967. Toronto's 1st, 6th overall, in 1986.

Season	Club	League	GP	G	A	Pts	AG	AA	APts	PIM	PP	SH	GW	S	%	TGF	PGF	TGA	PGA	+/–	GP	G	A	Pts	PIM	PP	SH	GW
1982-83	Bourassa Angevins	QAAA	48	33	45	78	....	....	....	....	....	....	....	....	....	....	....	....	....	....	....	....	....	....	....	....	....	....
1983-84	Laval Voisins	QMJHL	66	29	36	65	....	....	....	25	....	....	....	....	....	....	....	....	....	....	....	....	....	....	....	....	....	....
	Laval Voisins	Mem-Cup	3	0	0	0	....	....	....	4	....	....	....	....	....	....	....	....	....	....	....	....	....	....	....	....	....	....
1984-85	Laval Vosins	QMJHL	68	35	68	103	....	....	....	62	....	....	....	....	....	....	....	....	....	....	....	....	....	....	....	....	....	....
1985-86	Laval Voisins	QMJHL	69	45	110	155	....	....	....	70	....	....	....	....	....	....	....	....	....	....	14	9	27	36	12	....	....	....
1986-87	**Toronto Maple Leafs**	**NHL**	80	21	25	46	18	18	36	26	4	0	1	142	14.8	73	10	69	0	–6	12	1	5	6	8	1	0	0
1987-88	**Toronto Maple Leafs**	**NHL**	75	12	36	48	10	26	36	40	1	0	2	111	10.8	66	9	57	2	2	6	0	1	1	10	0	0	0
1988-89	**Toronto Maple Leafs**	**NHL**	80	26	42	68	22	30	52	75	6	0	4	190	13.7	84	22	73	3	–8	....	....	....	....	....	....	....	....
1989-90	**Toronto Maple Leafs**	**NHL**	80	33	61	94	28	44	72	56	9	0	5	229	14.4	127	40	87	2	2	5	0	2	2	2	0	0	0
1990-91	**Toronto Maple Leafs**	**NHL**	79	26	47	73	24	36	60	65	10	1	4	247	10.5	93	35	99	10	–31	....	....	....	....	....	....	....	....
1991-92	**Edmonton Oilers**	**NHL**	80	38	51	89	35	39	74	53	12	1	8	247	15.4	123	47	88	22	10	16	6	8	14	8	1	0	0
1992-93♦	**Montreal Canadiens**	**NHL**	84	39	58	97	32	40	72	98	9	3	8	287	13.6	134	50	92	13	5	20	11	12	23	16	5	0	3
1993-94	**Montreal Canadiens**	**NHL**	84	40	51	91	37	40	77	75	13	0	10	274	14.6	117	51	70	4	0	7	1	2	3	8	0	0	0
1994-95	EC Ratinger-Lowen	Germany	11	5	7	12	....	....	....	24	....	....	....	....	....	....	....	....	....	....	....	....	....	....	....	....	....	....
	Montreal Canadiens	**NHL**	48	10	30	40	18	44	62	42	4	0	4	123	8.1	67	23	32	3	15	....	....	....	....	....	....	....	....
1995-96	**Montreal Canadiens**	**NHL**	80	38	56	94	37	46	83	158	11	4	3	254	15.0	127	51	97	26	5	6	4	4	8	0	0	1	2
1996-97	Canada	W-Cup	8	2	0	2	....	....	....	8	....	....	....	....	....	....	....	....	....	....	....	....	....	....	....	....	....	....
	Montreal Canadiens	**NHL**	82	27	54	81	29	48	77	82	7	2	3	244	11.1	101	30	102	25	–6	5	0	0	0	2	0	0	0
1997-98	**Montreal Canadiens**	**NHL**	76	18	41	59	21	40	61	58	2	1	5	164	11.0	87	27	59	13	14	10	3	6	9	22	1	0	0
1998-99	**Montreal Canadiens**	**NHL**	65	12	24	36	14	23	37	46	3	2	2	147	8.2	55	20	54	12	–7	....	....	....	....	....	....	....	....
	San Jose Sharks	**NHL**	12	7	6	13	8	6	14	4	3	0	1	43	16.3	19	9	10	3	3	6	3	2	5	6	0	2	0
99-2000	**San Jose Sharks**	**NHL**	82	21	49	70	24	45	69	58	3	1	1	204	10.3	101	45	71	19	4	12	1	7	8	16	1	0	0
	NHL Totals		1087	368	631	999	357	525	882	936	97	15	61	2906	12.7	1374	469	1060	157		105	30	49	79	98	9	3	5

QMJHL Second All-Star Team (1986) • Played in NHL All-Star Game (1991, 1992)

Traded to **Edmonton** by **Toronto** with Peter Ing, Scott Thornton, Luke Richardson, future considerations and cash for Grant Fuhr, Glenn Anderson and Craig Berube, September 19, 1991. Traded to **Montreal** by **Edmonton** with Edmonton's 4th round choice (Adam Wiesel) in 1993 Entry Draft for Shayne Corson, Brent Gilchrist and Vladimir Vujtek, August 27, 1992. Traded to **San Jose** by **Montreal** for Phoenix's 5th round choice (previously acquired, Montreal selected Marc-Andre Thinel) in 1999 Entry Draft, San Jose's 1st round choice (Marcel Hossa) in 2000 Entry Draft and 2nd round choice in 2001 Entry Draft, March 23, 1999.

• DANDENAULT, Mathieu

RW/D – R. 6', 174 lbs. b: Sherbrooke, Que., 2/3/1976. Detroit's 2nd, 49th overall, in 1994.

Season	Club	League	GP	G	A	Pts	AG	AA	APts	PIM	PP	SH	GW	S	%	TGF	PGF	TGA	PGA	+/–	GP	G	A	Pts	PIM	PP	SH	GW
1990-91	Gloucester Bantam Rangers	OMHA	44	52	50	102	....	....	....	30	....	....	....	....	....	....	....	....	....	....	....	....	....	....	....	....	....	....
1991-92	Vanier Voyageurs	OJHL	33	27	31	58	....	....	....	20	....	....	....	....	....	....	....	....	....	....	....	....	....	....	....	....	....	....
	Gloucester Rangers	OJHL	6	3	4	7	....	....	....	0	....	....	....	....	....	....	....	....	....	....	....	....	....	....	....	....	....	....
1992-93	Gloucester Rangers	OJHL	55	11	26	37	....	....	....	64	....	....	....	....	....	....	....	....	....	....	....	....	....	....	....	....	....	....
1993-94	Sherbrooke Faucons	QMJHL	67	17	36	53	....	....	....	67	....	....	....	....	....	....	....	....	....	....	12	4	10	14	12	....	....	....
1994-95	Sherbrooke Faucons	QMJHL	67	37	70	107	....	....	....	76	....	....	....	....	....	....	....	....	....	....	7	1	7	8	10	....	....	....
1995-96	**Detroit Red Wings**	**NHL**	34	5	7	12	5	6	11	6	1	0	0	32	15.6	18	1	11	0	6	....	....	....	....	....	....	....	....
	Adirondack Red Wings	AHL	4	0	0	0	....	....	....	0	....	....	....	....	....	....	....	....	....	....	....	....	....	....	....	....	....	....
1996-97♦	**Detroit Red Wings**	**NHL**	65	3	9	12	3	8	11	28	0	0	0	81	3.7	31	2	41	2	–10	....	....	....	....	....	....	....	....
1997-98♦	**Detroit Red Wings**	**NHL**	68	5	12	17	6	12	18	43	0	0	0	75	6.7	30	0	27	2	5	3	1	0	1	0	1	0	0
1998-99	**Detroit Red Wings**	**NHL**	75	4	10	14	5	10	15	59	0	0	0	94	4.3	44	3	29	5	17	10	0	1	1	0	0	0	0
99-2000	**Detroit Red Wings**	**NHL**	81	6	12	18	7	11	18	20	0	0	0	98	6.1	38	0	54	4	–12	6	0	0	0	2	0	0	0
	NHL Totals		323	23	50	73	26	47	73	156	1	0	0	380	6.1	161	6	162	13		19	1	1	2	2	1	0	0

• DANEYKO, Ken

Kenneth Stephen D – L. 6'1", 215 lbs. b: Windsor, Ont., 4/17/1964. New Jersey's 2nd, 18th overall, in 1982.

Season	Club	League	GP	G	A	Pts	AG	AA	APts	PIM	PP	SH	GW	S	%	TGF	PGF	TGA	PGA	+/–	GP	G	A	Pts	PIM	PP	SH	GW
1980-81	St. Albert Saints	AJHL	1	0	0	0	....	....	....	4	....	....	....	....	....	....	....	....	....	....	....	....	....	....	....	....	....	....
	Spokane Flyers	WHL	62	6	13	19	....	....	....	140	....	....	....	....	....	....	....	....	....	....	4	0	0	0	6	....	....	....
1981-82	Spokane Flyers	WHL	26	1	11	12	....	....	....	147	....	....	....	....	....	....	....	....	....	....	....	....	....	....	....	....	....	....
	Seattle Breakers	WHL	38	1	22	23	....	....	....	151	....	....	....	....	....	....	....	....	....	....	14	1	9	10	49	....	....	....
1982-83	Seattle Breakers	WHL	69	17	43	60	....	....	....	150	....	....	....	....	....	....	....	....	....	....	4	1	3	4	14	....	....	....
1983-84	Kamloops Jr. Oilers	WHL	19	6	28	34	....	....	....	52	....	....	....	....	....	....	....	....	....	....	17	4	9	13	28	....	....	....
	New Jersey Devils	**NHL**	11	1	4	5	1	3	4	17	0	0	0	17	5.9	11	0	15	3	–1	....	....	....	....	....	....	....	....
	Kamloops Jr. Oilers	Mem-Cup	4	2	2	4	....	....	....	10	....	....	....	....	....	....	....	....	....	....	....	....	....	....	....	....	....	....
1984-85	**New Jersey Devils**	**NHL**	1	0	0	0	0	0	0	10	0	0	0	1	0.0	0	0	1	0	–1	....	....	....	....	....	....	....	....
	Maine Mariners	AHL	80	4	9	13	....	....	....	206	....	....	....	....	....	....	....	....	....	....	11	1	3	4	36	....	....	....
1985-86	**New Jersey Devils**	**NHL**	44	0	10	10	0	7	7	100	0	0	0	48	0.0	42	1	56	15	0	....	....	....	....	....	....	....	....
	Maine Mariners	AHL	21	3	2	5	....	....	....	75	....	....	....	....	....	....	....	....	....	....	....	....	....	....	....	....	....	....
	Canada	WEC-A	7	0	0	0	....	....	....	0	....	....	....	....	....	....	....	....	....	....	....	....	....	....	....	....	....	....
1986-87	**New Jersey Devils**	**NHL**	79	2	12	14	2	9	11	183	0	0	0	113	1.8	92	21	129	45	–13	....	....	....	....	....	....	....	....
1987-88	**New Jersey Devils**	**NHL**	80	5	7	12	4	5	9	239	1	0	0	82	6.1	67	5	94	29	–3	20	1	6	7	83	0	0	1
1988-89	**New Jersey Devils**	**NHL**	80	5	5	10	4	4	8	283	1	0	0	108	4.6	56	4	106	32	–22	....	....	....	....	....	....	....	....
	Canada	WEC-A	8	0	0	0	....	....	....	4	....	....	....	....	....	....	....	....	....	....	....	....	....	....	....	....	....	....
1989-90	**New Jersey Devils**	**NHL**	74	6	15	21	5	11	16	219	0	1	1	64	9.4	68	1	66	14	15	6	2	0	2	21	0	0	0
1990-91	**New Jersey Devils**	**NHL**	80	4	16	20	4	12	16	249	1	2	1	106	3.8	71	10	101	30	–10	7	0	1	1	10	0	0	0
1991-92	**New Jersey Devils**	**NHL**	80	1	7	8	1	5	6	170	0	0	0	57	1.8	61	1	87	34	7	7	0	3	3	16	0	0	0
1992-93	**New Jersey Devils**	**NHL**	84	2	11	13	2	8	10	236	0	0	0	71	2.8	67	1	104	42	4	5	0	0	0	8	0	0	0
1993-94	**New Jersey Devils**	**NHL**	78	1	9	10	1	7	8	176	0	0	0	60	1.7	72	0	74	29	27	20	0	1	1	45	0	0	0
1994-95♦	**New Jersey Devils**	**NHL**	25	1	2	3	2	3	5	54	0	0	0	27	3.7	19	0	19	4	4	20	1	0	1	22	0	0	0
1995-96	**New Jersey Devils**	**NHL**	80	2	4	6	2	3	5	115	0	0	0	67	3.0	39	1	62	14	–10	....	....	....	....	....	....	....	....
1996-97	**New Jersey Devils**	**NHL**	77	2	7	9	2	6	8	70	0	0	0	63	3.2	62	0	56	18	24	10	0	0	0	28	0	0	0
1997-98	**New Jersey Devils**	**NHL**	37	0	1	1	0	1	1	57	0	0	0	18	0.0	22	0	25	6	3	6	0	1	1	10	0	0	0
1998-99	**New Jersey Devils**	**NHL**	82	2	9	11	2	9	11	63	0	0	0	63	3.2	71	1	70	27	27	7	0	0	0	8	0	0	0
99-2000♦	**New Jersey Devils**	**NHL**	78	0	6	6	0	6	6	98	0	0	0	74	0.0	52	0	58	19	13	23	1	2	3	14	0	0	0
	NHL Totals		1070	34	125	159	32	99	131	2339	3	3	3	1039	3.3	872	46	1123	361		131	5	14	19	265	0	0	1

• Missed majority of 1997-98 season after voluntarily entering NHL/NHLPA substance abuse program, November 6, 1998. • Won Bill Masterton Memorial Trophy (2000)

• DANIELS, Jeff

Jeff D. LW – L. 6'1", 200 lbs. b: Oshawa, Ont., 6/24/1968. Pittsburgh's 6th, 109th overall, in 1986.

Season	Club	League	GP	G	A	Pts	AG	AA	APts	PIM	PP	SH	GW	S	%	TGF	PGF	TGA	PGA	+/–	GP	G	A	Pts	PIM	PP	SH	GW
1983-84	Oshawa Legionaires	OMHA	57	59	72	131	....	....	....	22	....	....	....	....	....	....	....	....	....	....	....	....	....	....	....	....	....	....
1984-85	Oshawa Generals	OHL	59	7	11	18	....	....	....	16	....	....	....	....	....	....	....	....	....	....	....	....	....	....	....	....	....	....
	Oshawa Legionaires	OJHL-B	7	7	2	9	....	....	....	11	....	....	....	....	....	....	....	....	....	....	....	....	....	....	....	....	....	....
1985-86	Oshawa Generals	OHL	62	13	19	32	....	....	....	23	....	....	....	....	....	....	....	....	....	....	6	0	1	1	0	....	....	....
1986-87	Oshawa Generals	OHL	54	14	9	23	....	....	....	22	....	....	....	....	....	....	....	....	....	....	15	3	2	5	5	....	....	....
	Oshawa Generals	Mem-Cup	3	1	1	2	....	....	....	0	....	....	....	....	....	....	....	....	....	....	....	....	....	....	....	....	....	....
1987-88	Oshawa Generals	OHL	64	29	39	68	....	....	....	59	....	....	....	....	....	....	....	....	....	....	4	2	3	5	0	....	....	....
1988-89	Muskegon Lumberjacks	IHL	58	21	21	42	....	....	....	58	....	....	....	....	....	....	....	....	....	....	11	3	5	8	11	....	....	....
1989-90	Muskegon Lumberjacks	IHL	80	30	47	77	....	....	....	39	....	....	....	....	....	....	....	....	....	....	6	1	1	2	7	....	....	....
1990-91	**Pittsburgh Penguins**	**NHL**	11	0	2	2	0	2	2	2	0	0	0	6	0.0	4	0	5	1	0	....	....	....	....	....	....	....	....
	Muskegon Lumberjacks	IHL	62	23	29	52	....	....	....	18	....	....	....	....	....	....	....	....	....	....	5	1	3	4	2	....	....	....

			REGULAR SEASON																		PLAYOFFS							
Season	**Club**	**League**	**GP**	**G**	**A**	**Pts**	**AG**	**AA**	**APts**	**PIM**	**PP**	**SH**	**GW**	**S**	**%**	**TGF**	**PGF**	**TGA**	**PGA**	**+/–**	**GP**	**G**	**A**	**Pts**	**PIM**	**PP**	**SH**	**GW**
1991-92	**Pittsburgh Penguins**	**NHL**	**2**	**0**	**0**	**0**	**0**	**0**	**0**	**0**	**0**	**0**	**0**	**0**	**0.0**	**0**	**0**	**0**	**0**	**0**								
	Muskegon Lumberjacks	IHL	44	19	16	35				38											10	5	4	9	9			
1992-93	**Pittsburgh Penguins**	**NHL**	**58**	**5**	**4**	**9**	**4**	**3**	**7**	**14**	**0**	**0**	**1**	**30**	**16.7**	**18**	**1**	**25**	**3**	**–5**	**12**	**3**	**2**	**5**	**0**	**0**	**0**	**1**
	Cleveland Lumberjacks	IHL	3	2	1	3				0																		
1993-94	**Pittsburgh Penguins**	**NHL**	**63**	**3**	**5**	**8**	**3**	**4**	**7**	**20**	**0**	**0**	**1**	**46**	**6.5**	**13**	**0**	**16**	**2**	**–1**								
	Florida Panthers	**NHL**	**7**	**0**	**0**	**0**	**0**	**0**	**0**	**0**	**0**	**0**	**0**	**6**	**0.0**	**2**	**0**	**2**	**0**	**0**								
1994-95	**Florida Panthers**	**NHL**	**3**	**0**	**0**	**0**	**0**	**0**	**0**	**0**	**0**	**0**	**0**	**0**	**0.0**	**0**	**0**	**0**	**0**	**0**								
	Detroit Vipers	IHL	25	8	12	20				6											5	1	0	1	0			
1995-96	Springfield Falcons	AHL	72	22	20	42				32											10	3	0	3	2			
1996-97	**Hartford Whalers**	**NHL**	**10**	**0**	**2**	**2**	**0**	**2**	**2**	**0**	**0**	**0**	**0**	**6**	**0.0**	**3**	**0**	**1**	**0**	**2**								
	Springfield Falcons	AHL	38	18	14	32				19											16	7	3	10	4			
1997-98	**Carolina Hurricanes**	**NHL**	**2**	**0**	**0**	**0**	**0**	**0**	**0**	**0**	**0**	**0**	**0**	**1**	**0.0**	**0**	**0**	**0**	**0**	**0**								
	Beast of New Haven	AHL	71	24	27	51				34											3	0	1	1	0			
1998-99	**Nashville Predators**	**NHL**	**9**	**1**	**3**	**4**	**1**	**3**	**4**	**2**	**0**	**0**	**0**	**8**	**12.5**	**4**	**0**	**5**	**0**	**–1**								
	Milwaukee Admirals	IHL	62	12	31	43				19											2	1	1	2	0			
99-2000	**Carolina Hurricanes**	**NHL**	**69**	**3**	**4**	**7**	**3**	**4**	**7**	**10**	**0**	**0**	**0**	**28**	**10.7**	**10**	**0**	**31**	**13**	**–8**								
	NHL Totals		**234**	**12**	**20**	**32**	**11**	**18**	**29**	**48**	**0**	**0**	**2**	**131**	**9.2**	**54**	**1**	**85**	**19**		**12**	**3**	**2**	**5**	**0**	**0**	**0**	**1**

Traded to **Florida** by **Pittsburgh** for Greg Hawgood, March 19, 1994. Signed as a free agent by **Hartford**, August 18, 1995. Transferred to **Carolina** after **Hartford** franchise relocated, June 25, 1997. Claimed by **Nashville** from **Carolina** in Expansion Draft, June 26, 1998. Signed as a free agent by **Carolina**, August 31, 1999.

• DANIELS, Kimbi

C – R. 5'10", 175 lbs. b: Brandon, Man., 1/19/1972. Philadelphia's 5th, 44th overall, in 1990.

Season	Club	League	GP	G	A	Pts	AG	AA	APts	PIM	PP	SH	GW	S	%	TGF	PGF	TGA	PGA	+/–	GP	G	A	Pts	PIM	PP	SH	GW
1987-88	West Kildonan North Stars	MJHL	18	5	11	16				28																		
1988-89	Swift Current Broncos	WHL	68	30	31	61				48											12	6	6	12	12			
	Swift Current Broncos	Mem-Cup	5	*5	1	6				8																		
1989-90	Swift Current Broncos	WHL	69	43	51	94				84											4	1	3	4	10			
1990-91	Swift Current Broncos	WHL	69	54	64	118				68											3	4	2	6	6			
	Philadelphia Flyers	**NHL**	**2**	**0**	**1**	**1**	**0**	**1**	**1**	**0**	**0**	**0**	**0**	**2**	**0.0**	**1**	**0**	**3**	**0**	**–2**								
1991-92	**Philadelphia Flyers**	**NHL**	**25**	**1**	**1**	**2**	**1**	**1**	**2**	**4**	**0**	**0**	**1**	**16**	**6.3**	**10**	**1**	**13**	**0**	**–4**								
	Canada	WJC-A	7	3	4	7				16																		
	Seattle Thunderbirds	WHL	19	7	14	21				133											15	5	10	15	27			
1992-93	Tri-City Americans	WHL	9	9	12	21				12											3	0	1	1	8			
1993-94	Salt Lake Golden Eagles	IHL	25	6	9	15				8																		
	Detroit Falcons	ColHL	23	11	28	39				42																		
1994-95	HK Olimpija Ljubljana	Alpenliga	STATISTICS NOT AVAILABLE																									
	Minnesota Moose	IHL	10	1	4	5				2																		
1995-96	Baltimore Bandits	AHL	7	2	1	3				2																		
	Jacksonville Lizard Kings	ECHL	26	12	22	34				129																		
	Charlotte Checkers	ECHL	18	16	14	30				6											16	8	6	14	24			
1996-97	Charlotte Checkers	ECHL	32	12	24	36				116																		
	Wheeling Nailers	ECHL	17	5	24	29				10											3	1	4	5	6			
	Rochester Americans	AHL	6	1	3	4				2																		
	Hamilton Bulldogs	AHL	3	0	0	0				0											16	5	8	13	4			
1997-98	Providence Bruins	AHL	32	2	5	7				30																		
	San Antonio Dragons	IHL	13	2	12	14				20																		
	Quebec Rafales	IHL	28	7	9	16				69																		
1998-99	HK Olimpija Ljubljana	Alpenliga	26	10	26	36				28																		
	New Orleans Brass	ECHL	29	11	28	39				61																		
99-2000	Quebec Citadelles	AHL	25	6	4	10				4																		
	Tallahassee Tiger Sharks	ECHL	34	11	12	23				38																		
	NHL Totals		**27**	**1**	**2**	**3**	**1**	**2**	**3**	**4**	**0**	**0**	**1**	**18**	**5.6**	**11**	**1**	**16**	**0**									

• Returned to **Seattle** (WHL) by **Philadelphia**, January 24, 1992.

• DANIELS, Scott

LW – L. 6'3", 215 lbs. b: Prince Albert, Sask., 9/19/1969. Hartford's 6th, 136th overall, in 1989.

Season	Club	League	GP	G	A	Pts	AG	AA	APts	PIM	PP	SH	GW	S	%	TGF	PGF	TGA	PGA	+/–	GP	G	A	Pts	PIM	PP	SH	GW
1985-86	Notre Dame Hounds	SJHL	25	13	17	30				51																		
1986-87	Kamloops Blazers	WHL	43	6	4	10				68																		
	New Westminster Bruins	WHL	19	4	7	11				30																		
1987-88	New Westminster Bruins	WHL	37	6	11	17				157																		
	Regina Pats	WHL	19	2	3	5				83																		
1988-89	Regina Pats	WHL	64	21	26	47				241																		
1989-90	Regina Pats	WHL	52	28	31	59				171																		
1990-91	Springfield Indians	AHL	40	2	6	8				121																		
	Louisville IceHawks	ECHL	9	5	3	8				34											1	0	2	2	0			
1991-92	Springfield Indians	AHL	54	7	15	22				213											10	0	0	0	32			
1992-93	**Hartford Whalers**	**NHL**	**1**	**0**	**0**	**0**	**0**	**0**	**0**	**19**	**0**	**0**	**0**	**0**	**0.0**	**0**	**0**	**0**	**0**	**0**								
	Springfield Indians	AHL	60	11	12	23				181											12	2	7	9	12			
1993-94	Springfield Indians	AHL	52	9	11	20				185											6	0	1	1	53			
1994-95	**Hartford Whalers**	**NHL**	**12**	**0**	**2**	**2**	**0**	**3**	**3**	**55**	**0**	**0**	**0**	**7**	**0.0**	**4**	**0**	**3**	**0**	**1**								
	Springfield Falcons	AHL	48	9	5	14				277																		
1995-96	**Hartford Whalers**	**NHL**	**53**	**3**	**4**	**7**	**3**	**3**	**6**	**254**	**0**	**0**	**0**	**43**	**7.0**	**11**	**1**	**14**	**0**	**–4**								
	Springfield Falcons	AHL	6	4	1	5				17																		
1996-97	**Philadelphia Flyers**	**NHL**	**56**	**5**	**3**	**8**	**5**	**3**	**8**	**237**	**0**	**0**	**2**	**48**	**10.4**	**15**	**0**	**14**	**1**	**2**								
1997-98	**New Jersey Devils**	**NHL**	**26**	**0**	**3**	**3**	**0**	**3**	**3**	**102**	**0**	**0**	**0**	**17**	**0.0**	**4**	**0**	**3**	**0**	**1**	**1**	**0**	**0**	**0**	**0**	**0**	**0**	**0**
1998-99	**New Jersey Devils**	**NHL**	**1**	**0**	**0**	**0**	**0**	**0**	**0**	**0**	**0**	**0**	**0**	**0**	**0.0**	**0**	**0**	**0**	**0**	**0**								
	Albany River Rats	AHL	13	1	5	6				97																		
	NHL Totals		**149**	**8**	**12**	**20**	**8**	**12**	**20**	**667**	**0**	**0**	**2**	**115**	**7.0**	**34**	**1**	**34**	**1**		**1**	**0**	**0**	**0**	**0**	**0**	**0**	**0**

Signed as a free agent by **Philadelphia**, June 27, 1996. Claimed by **New Jersey** from **Philadelphia** in NHL Waiver Draft, September 28, 1997. • Played w/ RHI's Edmonton Sled Dogs (5-4-6-10-2) and Las Vegas Flash (9-5-7-12-34) in 1994.

• DAOUST, Dan

Daniel Armand "Dangerous Danny" C – L. 5'10", 160 lbs. b: Montreal, Que., 2/29/1960.

Season	Club	League	GP	G	A	Pts	AG	AA	APts	PIM	PP	SH	GW	S	%	TGF	PGF	TGA	PGA	+/–	GP	G	A	Pts	PIM	PP	SH	GW
1977-78	Cornwall Royals	QMJHL	68	24	44	68				74																		
1978-79	Cornwall Royals	QMJHL	72	42	55	97				85																		
1979-80	Cornwall Royals	QMJHL	70	40	62	102				82																		
	Cornwall Royals	Mem-Cup	5	1	4	5				8																		
1980-81	Nova Scotia Voyageurs	AHL	80	38	60	98				106											6	1	3	4	10			
1981-82	Nova Scotia Voyageurs	AHL	61	25	40	65				75											9	5	2	7	11			
1982-83	**Montreal Canadiens**	**NHL**	**4**	**0**	**1**	**1**	**0**	**1**	**1**	**4**	**0**	**0**	**0**	**6**	**0.0**	**1**	**0**	**3**	**0**	**–2**								
	Toronto Maple Leafs	**NHL**	**48**	**18**	**33**	**51**	**15**	**23**	**38**	**31**	**9**	**0**	**0**	**119**	**15.1**	**81**	**37**	**53**	**8**	**–1**								
1983-84	**Toronto Maple Leafs**	**NHL**	**78**	**18**	**56**	**74**	**14**	**38**	**52**	**88**	**8**	**0**	**1**	**154**	**11.7**	**116**	**54**	**79**	**1**	**–16**								
1984-85	**Toronto Maple Leafs**	**NHL**	**79**	**17**	**37**	**54**	**14**	**25**	**39**	**98**	**1**	**3**	**2**	**141**	**12.1**	**80**	**20**	**120**	**33**	**–27**								
1985-86	**Toronto Maple Leafs**	**NHL**	**80**	**7**	**13**	**20**	**6**	**9**	**15**	**88**	**1**	**0**	**0**	**92**	**7.6**	**35**	**5**	**101**	**50**	**–21**	**10**	**2**	**2**	**4**	**19**	**0**	**0**	**0**
1986-87	**Toronto Maple Leafs**	**NHL**	**33**	**4**	**3**	**7**	**3**	**2**	**5**	**35**	**0**	**0**	**1**	**25**	**16.0**	**11**	**1**	**16**	**6**	**0**	**13**	**5**	**2**	**7**	**42**	**0**	**0**	**2**
	Newmarket Saints	AHL	1	0	0	0				4																		
1987-88	**Toronto Maple Leafs**	**NHL**	**67**	**9**	**8**	**17**	**8**	**6**	**14**	**57**	**0**	**0**	**1**	**57**	**15.8**	**21**	**0**	**52**	**24**	**–7**	**4**	**0**	**0**	**0**	**2**	**0**	**0**	**0**
1988-89	**Toronto Maple Leafs**	**NHL**	**68**	**7**	**5**	**12**	**6**	**4**	**10**	**54**	**0**	**2**	**1**	**66**	**10.6**	**20**	**2**	**86**	**48**	**–20**								
1989-90	**Toronto Maple Leafs**	**NHL**	**65**	**7**	**11**	**18**	**6**	**8**	**14**	**89**	**0**	**4**	**0**	**53**	**13.2**	**28**	**2**	**59**	**34**	**1**	**5**	**0**	**1**	**1**	**20**	**0**	**0**	**0**
1990-91	HC Ajoie	Switz-2	27	21	32	53				106											10	6	8	14	17			
1991-92	EHC Biel-Bienne	Switz.	5	5	9	14				8																		
	HC Lyss	Switz-2	25	24	16	40				58											9	3	6	9	44			
	ESV Kaufberen	Germany	7	2	0	2				14																		
1992-93	HC Thurgau	Switz-2	36	23	31	54				123											5	4	5	9	8			

			REGULAR SEASON																		PLAYOFFS							
Season	Club	League	GP	G	A	Pts	AG	AA	APts	PIM	PP	SH	GW	S	%	TGF	PGF	TGA	PGA	+/–	GP	G	A	Pts	PIM	PP	SH	GW
1993-94	HC Thurgau	Switz-2	36	21	26	47	....	....	....	97	....	....	....	....	....	....	....	....	....	....	2	0	1	1	2	....	....	....
1994-95	HC Thurgau	Switz-2	36	23	42	65	....	....	....	105	....	....	....	....	....	....	....	....	....	....	6	7	5	12	41	....	....	....
1995-96	HC Thurgau	Switz-2	36	25	40	65	....	....	....	50	....	....	....	....	....	....	....	....	....	....	5	3	6	9	10	....	....	....
1996-97	HC Thurgau	Switz-2	19	10	24	34	....	....	....	20	....	....	....	....	....	....	....	....	....	....	3	1	1	2	8	....	....	....
	NHL Totals		**522**	**87**	**167**	**254**	**72**	**116**	**188**	**544**	**19**	**9**	**6**	**713**	**12.2**	**393**	**121**	**569**	**204**		**32**	**7**	**5**	**12**	**83**	**0**	**0**	**2**

AHL First All-Star Team (1981) • NHL All-Rookie Team (1983)

Signed as a free agent by **Montreal**, March 9, 1981. Traded to **Toronto** by **Montreal** for Toronto's 3rd round choice (later traded to Minnesota — Minnesota selected Ken Hodge Jr.) in 1984 Entry Draft, December 17, 1982. • Played w/ RHI's Toronto Planets in 1993 (6-9-10-19-20).

• DARBY, Craig

C – R. 6'3", 200 lbs. b: Oneida, NY, 9/26/1972. Montreal's 3rd, 43rd overall, in 1991.

Season	Club	League	GP	G	A	Pts	AG	AA	APts	PIM	PP	SH	GW	S	%	TGF	PGF	TGA	PGA	+/–	GP	G	A	Pts	PIM	PP	SH	GW
1989-90	Albany Academy	Hi-School	29	32	53	85	....	....	....	....	....	....	....	....	....	....	....	....	....	....	....	....	....	....	....	....	....	....
1990-91	Albany Academy	Hi-School	29	33	61	94	....	....	....	....	....	....	....	....	....	....	....	....	....	....	....	....	....	....	....	....	....	....
1991-92	Providence College	H-East	35	17	24	41	....	....	....	47	....	....	....	....	....	....	....	....	....	....	....	....	....	....	....	....	....	....
1992-93	Providence College	H-East	35	11	21	32	....	....	....	62	....	....	....	....	....	....	....	....	....	....	....	....	....	....	....	....	....	....
1993-94	Fredericton Canadiens	AHL	66	23	33	56	....	....	....	51	....	....	....	....	....	....	....	....	....	....	....	....	....	....	....	....	....	....
1994-95	**Montreal Canadiens**	**NHL**	**10**	**0**	**2**	**2**	**0**	**3**	**3**	**0**	**0**	**0**	**0**	**4**	**0.0**	**3**	**0**	**8**	**0**	**–5**	....	....	....	....	....	....	....	....
	Fredericton Canadiens	AHL	64	21	47	68	....	....	....	82	....	....	....	....	....	....	....	....	....	....	....	....	....	....	....	....	....	....
	New York Islanders	**NHL**	**3**	**0**	**0**	**0**	**0**	**0**	**0**	**0**	**0**	**0**	**0**	**1**	**0.0**	**0**	**0**	**1**	**0**	**–1**	....	....	....	....	....	....	....	....
1995-96	**New York Islanders**	**NHL**	**10**	**0**	**2**	**2**	**0**	**2**	**2**	**0**	**0**	**0**	**0**	**1**	**0.0**	**2**	**0**	**3**	**0**	**–1**	....	....	....	....	....	....	....	....
	Worcester IceCats	AHL	68	22	28	50	....	....	....	47	....	....	....	....	....	....	....	....	....	....	4	1	1	2	2	....	....	....
1996-97	**Philadelphia Flyers**	**NHL**	**9**	**1**	**4**	**5**	**1**	**4**	**5**	**2**	**0**	**1**	**0**	**13**	**7.7**	**5**	**0**	**4**	**1**	**2**	....	....	....	....	....	....	....	....
	Philadelphia Phantoms	AHL	59	26	33	59	....	....	....	24	....	....	....	....	....	....	....	....	....	....	10	3	6	9	0	....	....	....
1997-98	**Philadelphia Flyers**	**NHL**	**3**	**1**	**0**	**1**	**1**	**0**	**1**	**0**	**0**	**0**	**0**	**3**	**33.3**	**1**	**0**	**1**	**0**	**0**	....	....	....	....	....	....	....	....
	Philadelphia Phantoms	AHL	77	*42	45	87	....	....	....	34	....	....	....	....	....	....	....	....	....	....	20	5	9	14	4	....	....	....
1998-99	Milwaukee Admirals	IHL	81	32	22	54	....	....	....	33	....	....	....	....	....	....	....	....	....	....	2	3	0	3	0	....	....	....
99-2000	**Montreal Canadiens**	**NHL**	**76**	**7**	**10**	**17**	**8**	**9**	**17**	**14**	**0**	**1**	**2**	**90**	**7.8**	**23**	**0**	**50**	**13**	**–14**	....	....	....	....	....	....	....	....
	NHL Totals		**111**	**9**	**18**	**27**	**10**	**18**	**28**	**16**	**0**	**2**	**2**	**112**	**8.0**	**34**	**0**	**67**	**14**		....	....	....	....	....	....	....	....

AHL First All-Star Team (1998)

Traded to **NY Islanders** by **Montreal** with Kirk Muller and Mathieu Schneider for Pierre Turgeon and Vladimir Malakhov, April 5, 1995. Claimed on waivers by **Philadelphia** from **NY Islanders**, June 4, 1996. Claimed by **Nashville** from **Philadelphia** in Expansion Draft, June 26, 1998. Signed as a free agent by **Montreal**, August 4, 1999.

• DARK, Michael

D – R. 6'3", 210 lbs. b: Sarnia, Ont., 9/17/1963. Montreal's 10th, 124th overall, in 1982.

Season	Club	League	GP	G	A	Pts	AG	AA	APts	PIM	PP	SH	GW	S	%	TGF	PGF	TGA	PGA	+/–	GP	G	A	Pts	PIM	PP	SH	GW
1979-80	Sarnia Selects	OMHA	50	18	32	50	....	....	....	....	....	....	....	....	....	....	....	....	....	....	....	....	....	....	....	....	....	....
1980-81	Sarnia Bees	OHA-B	41	20	40	60	....	....	....	....	....	....	....	....	....	....	....	....	....	....	....	....	....	....	....	....	....	....
1981-82	Sarnia Bees	OJHL-B	41	13	30	43	....	....	....	86	....	....	....	....	....	....	....	....	....	....	....	....	....	....	....	....	....	....
1982-83	RPI Engineers	ECAC	29	3	16	19	....	....	....	54	....	....	....	....	....	....	....	....	....	....	....	....	....	....	....	....	....	....
1983-84	RPI Engineers	ECAC	38	2	12	14	....	....	....	60	....	....	....	....	....	....	....	....	....	....	....	....	....	....	....	....	....	....
1984-85	RPI Engineers	ECAC	36	7	26	33	....	....	....	76	....	....	....	....	....	....	....	....	....	....	....	....	....	....	....	....	....	....
1985-86	RPI Engineers	ECAC	32	7	29	36	....	....	....	58	....	....	....	....	....	....	....	....	....	....	....	....	....	....	....	....	....	....
1986-87	**St. Louis Blues**	**NHL**	**13**	**2**	**0**	**2**	**2**	**0**	**2**	**2**	**0**	**0**	**0**	**4**	**50.0**	**7**	**0**	**7**	**0**	**0**	....	....	....	....	....	....	....	....
	Peoria Rivermen	IHL	42	4	11	15	....	....	....	93	....	....	....	....	....	....	....	....	....	....	....	....	....	....	....	....	....	....
1987-88	**St. Louis Blues**	**NHL**	**30**	**3**	**6**	**9**	**3**	**4**	**7**	**12**	**0**	**0**	**1**	**27**	**11.1**	**11**	**0**	**6**	**1**	**6**	....	....	....	....	....	....	....	....
	Peoria Rivermen	IHL	37	21	12	33	....	....	....	97	....	....	....	....	....	....	....	....	....	....	2	0	0	0	4	....	....	....
1988-89	Salt Lake Golden Eagles	IHL	36	3	12	15	....	....	....	57	....	....	....	....	....	....	....	....	....	....	....	....	....	....	....	....	....	....
	New Haven Nighthawks	AHL	7	0	4	4	....	....	....	4	....	....	....	....	....	....	....	....	....	....	....	....	....	....	....	....	....	....
1989-90	Peterborough Pirates	Aut-Cup	8	6	10	16	....	....	....	26	....	....	....	....	....	....	....	....	....	....	....	....	....	....	....	....	....	....
	Peterborough Pirates	Britain	30	36	24	60	....	....	....	*136	....	....	....	....	....	....	....	....	....	....	....	....	....	....	....	....	....	....
1990-91			DID NOT PLAY																									
1991-92	St. Thomas Wildcats	ColHL	2	0	0	0	....	....	....	0	....	....	....	....	....	....	....	....	....	....	....	....	....	....	....	....	....	....
	Flint Bulldogs	ColHL	1	0	0	0	....	....	....	15	....	....	....	....	....	....	....	....	....	....	....	....	....	....	....	....	....	....
1992-1995			OUT OF HOCKEY – RETIRED																									
1995-96	Brantford Smoke	ColHL	11	3	12	15	....	....	....	18	....	....	....	....	....	....	....	....	....	....	3	1	0	1	2	....	....	....
1996-97	Port Huron Border Cats	ColHL	17	0	2	2	....	....	....	10	....	....	....	....	....	....	....	....	....	....	5	1	3	4	0	....	....	....
1997-98	Port Huron Border Cats	UHL	12	1	6	7	....	....	....	6	....	....	....	....	....	....	....	....	....	....	4	0	0	0	4	....	....	....
1998-99	Port Huron Border Cats	UHL	2	0	0	0	....	....	....	0	....	....	....	....	....	....	....	....	....	....	....	....	....	....	....	....	....	....
	NHL Totals		**43**	**5**	**6**	**11**	**5**	**4**	**9**	**14**	**0**	**0**	**1**	**31**	**16.1**	**18**	**0**	**13**	**1**		....	....	....	....	....	....	....	....

ECAC First All-Star Team (1986) • NCAA East All-American Team (1986)

Traded to **St. Louis** by **Montreal** with Mark Hunter and Montreal's 2nd (Herb Raglan), 3rd (Nelson Emerson), 5th (Dan Brooks) and 6th (Rick Burchill) round choices in 1985 Entry Draft for St. Louis' 1st (Jose Charbonneau), 2nd (Todd Richard), 4th (Martin Desjardins), 5th (Tom Sagissor) and 6th (Donald Dufresne) round choices in 1985 Entry Draft, June 15, 1985. Traded to **Calgary** by **St. Louis** with Doug Gilmour, Steve Bozek and Mark Hunter for Mike Bullard, Craig Coxe and Tim Corkery, September 6, 1988.

• DAVID, Richard

LW – L. 6', 195 lbs. b: Notre Dame de la Salette, Que., 4/8/1958. Montreal's 5th, 42nd overall, in 1978.

Season	Club	League	GP	G	A	Pts	AG	AA	APts	PIM	PP	SH	GW	S	%	TGF	PGF	TGA	PGA	+/–	GP	G	A	Pts	PIM	PP	SH	GW
1973-74	Hull Festivals	QMJHL	65	24	22	46	....	....	....	16	....	....	....	....	....	....	....	....	....	....	....	....	....	....	....	....	....	....
1974-75	Sorel Black Hawks	QMJHL	34	13	15	28	....	....	....	64	....	....	....	....	....	....	....	....	....	....	....	....	....	....	....	....	....	....
1975-76	Trois-Rivieres Draveurs	QMJHL	73	53	68	121	....	....	....	79	....	....	....	....	....	....	....	....	....	....	....	....	....	....	....	....	....	....
1976-77	Trois-Rivieres Draveurs	QMJHL	66	52	58	110	....	....	....	103	....	....	....	....	....	....	....	....	....	....	....	....	....	....	....	....	....	....
1977-78	Trois-Rivieres Draveurs	QMJHL	69	50	61	111	....	....	....	81	....	....	....	....	....	....	....	....	....	....	13	17	16	33	7	....	....	....
	Trois-Rivieres Draveurs	Mem-Cup	4	3	2	5	....	....	....	0	....	....	....	....	....	....	....	....	....	....	....	....	....	....	....	....	....	....
1978-79	Quebec Nordiques	WHA	14	0	4	4	....	....	....	4	....	....	....	....	....	....	....	....	....	....	....	....	....	....	....	....	....	....
	Binghamton Dusters	AHL	10	5	2	7	....	....	....	2	....	....	....	....	....	....	....	....	....	....	....	....	....	....	....	....	....	....
1979-80	**Quebec Nordiques**	**NHL**	**10**	**0**	**0**	**0**	**0**	**0**	**0**	**2**	**0**	**0**	**0**	**10**	**0.0**	**1**	**0**	**3**	**0**	**–2**	....	....	....	....	....	....	....	....
	Syracuse Firebirds	AHL	66	29	32	61	....	....	....	36	....	....	....	....	....	....	....	....	....	....	4	0	1	1	0	....	....	....
1980-81	HC Lausanne	Switz.	STATISTICS NOT AVAILABLE																									
	Rochester Americans	AHL	1	0	0	0	....	....	....	0	....	....	....	....	....	....	....	....	....	....	....	....	....	....	....	....	....	....
	Erie Blades	EHL	32	10	32	42	....	....	....	47	....	....	....	....	....	....	....	....	....	....	8	5	5	10	6	....	....	....
1981-82	**Quebec Nordiques**	**NHL**	**5**	**1**	**1**	**2**	**1**	**1**	**2**	**4**	**0**	**0**	**0**	**6**	**16.7**	**3**	**1**	**5**	**0**	**–3**	**1**	**0**	**0**	**0**	**0**	**0**	**0**	**0**
	Fredericton Express	AHL	74	*51	32	83	....	....	....	18	....	....	....	....	....	....	....	....	....	....	....	....	....	....	....	....	....	....
1982-83	**Quebec Nordiques**	**NHL**	**16**	**3**	**3**	**6**	**2**	**2**	**4**	**4**	**2**	**0**	**1**	**13**	**23.1**	**9**	**3**	**8**	**0**	**–2**	....	....	....	....	....	....	....	....
	Fredericton Express	AHL	48	20	36	56	....	....	....	17	....	....	....	....	....	....	....	....	....	....	12	9	3	12	6	....	....	....
1983-84			OUT OF HOCKEY – RETIRED																									
1984-85	HC Sierre	Switz-2	STATISTICS NOT AVAILABLE																									
	NHL Totals		**31**	**4**	**4**	**8**	**3**	**3**	**6**	**10**	**2**	**0**	**1**	**29**	**13.8**	**13**	**4**	**16**	**0**		**1**	**0**	**0**	**0**	**0**	**0**	**0**	**0**
	Other Major League Totals		14	0	4	4	....	....	....	4	....	....	....	....	....	....	....	....	....	....	....	....	....	....	....	....	....	....

QMJHL East First All-Star Team (1976) • AHL Second All-Star Team (1982)

Signed as an underage free agent by **Quebec** (WHA), June, 1978. Rights retained by **Quebec** prior to Expansion Draft, June 9, 1979.

• DAVIDSSON, Johan

C – R. 6'1", 190 lbs. b: Jonkoping, Sweden, 1/6/1976. Anaheim's 2nd, 28th overall, in 1994.

Season	Club	League	GP	G	A	Pts	AG	AA	APts	PIM	PP	SH	GW	S	%	TGF	PGF	TGA	PGA	+/–	GP	G	A	Pts	PIM	PP	SH	GW
1992-93	HV-71 Jonkoping	Sweden	8	1	0	1	....	....	....	0	....	....	....	....	....	....	....	....	....	....	....	....	....	....	....	....	....	....
	Sweden	EJC-A	6	1	3	4	....	....	....	4	....	....	....	....	....	....	....	....	....	....	....	....	....	....	....	....	....	....
1993-94	HV-71 Jonkoping	Sweden-Jr.	5	2	3	5	....	....	....	0	....	....	....	....	....	....	....	....	....	....	....	....	....	....	....	....	....	....
	HV-71 Jonkoping	Sweden	38	2	5	7	....	....	....	4	....	....	....	....	....	....	....	....	....	....	....	....	....	....	....	....	....	....
	Sweden	EJC-A	5	5	7	12	....	....	....	0	....	....	....	....	....	....	....	....	....	....	....	....	....	....	....	....	....	....
	Sweden	WJC-A	6	1	4	5	....	....	....	6	....	....	....	....	....	....	....	....	....	....	....	....	....	....	....	....	....	....
1994-95	HV-71 Jonkoping	Sweden-Jr.	3	4	1	5	....	....	....	0	....	....	....	....	....	....	....	....	....	....	....	....	....	....	....	....	....	....
	HV-71 Jonkoping	Sweden	37	4	7	11	....	....	....	20	....	....	....	....	....	....	....	....	....	....	13	3	2	5	0	....	....	....
	Sweden	WJC-A	7	4	2	6	....	....	....	2	....	....	....	....	....	....	....	....	....	....	....	....	....	....	....	....	....	....

			REGULAR SEASON																		PLAYOFFS							
Season	Club	League	GP	G	A	Pts	AG	AA	APts	PIM	PP	SH	GW	S	%	TGF	PGF	TGA	PGA	+/-	GP	G	A	Pts	PIM	PP	SH	GW
1995-96	HV-71 Jonkoping	Sweden	39	7	11	18				20											4	0	2	2	0			
	Sweden	WJC-A	7	3	6	9				4																		
1996-97	HV-71 Jonkoping	Sweden	50	18	21	39				18											5	0	3	3	2			
1997-98	HIFK Helsinki	Finland	43	10	30	40				8											9	3	10	13	0			
1998-99	**Mighty Ducks of Anaheim**	**NHL**	**64**	**3**	**5**	**8**	**4**	**5**	**9**	**14**	**1**	**0**	**1**	**48**	**6.3**	**16**	**6**	**21**	**2**	**–9**	**1**	**0**	**0**	**0**	**0**	**0**	**0**	**0**
	Cincinnati Mighty Ducks	IHL	9	1	6	7				2																		
99-2000	**Mighty Ducks of Anaheim**	**NHL**	**5**	**1**	**0**	**1**	**1**	**0**	**1**	**2**	**0**	**0**	**1**	**8**	**12.5**	**2**	**0**	**2**	**0**	**0**								
	Cincinnati Mighty Ducks	AHL	56	9	31	40				24																		
	New York Islanders	**NHL**	**14**	**2**	**4**	**6**	**2**	**4**	**6**	**0**	**0**	**0**	**0**	**21**	**9.5**	**8**	**1**	**7**	**0**	**0**								
	NHL Totals		**83**	**6**	**9**	**15**	**7**	**9**	**16**	**16**	**1**	**0**	**2**	**77**	**7.8**	**26**	**7**	**30**	**2**		**1**	**0**	**0**	**0**	**0**	**0**	**0**	**0**

Traded to **NY Islanders** by **Anaheim** with future considerations for Jorgen Jonsson, March 11, 2000.

• DAVIS, Kim

C – L. 5'11", 170 lbs. b: Flin Flon, Man., 10/31/1957. Pittsburgh's 2nd, 48th overall, in 1977.

Season	Club	League	GP	G	A	Pts	AG	AA	APts	PIM	PP	SH	GW	S	%	TGF	PGF	TGA	PGA	+/-	GP	G	A	Pts	PIM	PP	SH	GW
1974-75	Flin Flon Bombers	WCJHL	64	8	7	15				169																		
1975-76	Flin Flon Bombers	WCJHL	71	32	45	77				163																		
1976-77	Flin Flon Bombers	WCJHL	69	56	55	111				250																		
1977-78	**Pittsburgh Penguins**	**NHL**	**1**	**0**	**0**	**0**	**0**	**0**	**0**	**0**	**0**	**0**	**0**	**0**	**0.0**	**0**	**0**	**0**	**0**	**0**								
	Grand Rapids Owls	IHL	63	28	43	71				191																		
1978-79	**Pittsburgh Penguins**	**NHL**	**1**	**1**	**0**	**1**	**1**	**0**	**1**	**0**	**0**	**0**	**1**	**1**	**100.0**	**1**	**0**	**1**	**0**	**0**								
	Grand Rapids Owls	IHL	80	44	59	103				235											22	12	15	*27	77			
1979-80	**Pittsburgh Penguins**	**NHL**	**24**	**3**	**7**	**10**	**3**	**5**	**8**	**43**	**0**	**0**	**1**	**25**	**12.0**	**12**	**2**	**17**	**0**	**–7**	**4**	**0**	**0**	**0**	**0**	**0**	**0**	**0**
	Syracuse Firebirds	AHL	44	13	13	26				62																		
1980-81	**Pittsburgh Penguins**	**NHL**	**8**	**1**	**0**	**1**	**1**	**0**	**1**	**4**	**0**	**0**	**0**	**2**	**50.0**	**2**	**0**	**5**	**0**	**–3**								
	Binghamton Whalers	AHL	8	1	1	2				26																		
	Toronto Maple Leafs	**NHL**	**2**	**0**	**0**	**0**	**0**	**0**	**0**	**4**	**0**	**0**	**0**	**2**	**0.0**	**1**	**0**	**2**	**1**	**0**								
	Springfield Indians	AHL	26	5	4	9				56																		
	New Brunswick Hawks	AHL	32	8	13	21				165											2	0	0	0	21			
1981-82	New Brunswick Hawks	AHL	79	11	24	35				47											14	1	2	3	8			
	NHL Totals		**36**	**5**	**7**	**12**	**5**	**5**	**10**	**51**	**0**	**0**	**2**	**30**	**16.7**	**16**	**2**	**25**	**1**		**4**	**0**	**0**	**0**	**0**	**0**	**0**	**0**

Traded to **Toronto** by **Pittsburgh** with Paul Marshall for Dave Burrows and Paul Gardner, November 18, 1980.

• DAVIS, Mal

Malcolm Sterling LW – L. 5'11", 180 lbs. b: Lockport, N.S., 10/10/1956.

Season	Club	League	GP	G	A	Pts	AG	AA	APts	PIM	PP	SH	GW	S	%	TGF	PGF	TGA	PGA	+/-	GP	G	A	Pts	PIM	PP	SH	GW
1974-75	Amherst Ramblers	NYJHL	STATISTICS NOT AVAILABLE																									
1975-76	St. Mary's University	AUAA	20	11	7	18				21																		
1976-77	St. Mary's University	AUAA	20	16	5	21				2																		
1977-78	St. Mary's University	AUAA	20	*23	13	36				8																		
1978-79	**Detroit Red Wings**	**NHL**	**6**	**0**	**0**	**0**	**0**	**0**	**0**	**0**	**0**	**0**	**0**	**1**	**0.0**	**1**	**0**	**3**	**0**	**–2**								
	Kansas City Red Wings	CHL	71	42	24	66				29											4	2	0	2	4			
1979-80	Adirondack Red Wings	AHL	79	34	31	65				45											5	2	2	4	19			
1980-81	**Detroit Red Wings**	**NHL**	**5**	**2**	**0**	**2**	**2**	**0**	**2**	**0**	**0**	**0**	**0**	**12**	**16.7**	**5**	**0**	**0**	**0**	**5**								
	Adirondack Red Wings	AHL	58	23	12	35				48											17	6	4	10	9			
1981-82	Rochester Americans	AHL	75	32	33	65				14											9	2	3	5	2			
1982-83	**Buffalo Sabres**	**NHL**	**24**	**8**	**12**	**20**	**7**	**8**	**15**	**0**	**3**	**0**	**3**	**32**	**25.0**	**32**	**15**	**23**	**0**	**–6**	**6**	**1**	**0**	**1**	**0**	**0**	**0**	**0**
	Rochester Americans	AHL	57	43	32	75				15																		
1983-84	**Buffalo Sabres**	**NHL**	**11**	**2**	**1**	**3**	**2**	**1**	**3**	**4**	**1**	**0**	**0**	**12**	**16.7**	**11**	**5**	**7**	**0**	**–1**	**1**	**0**	**0**	**0**	**0**	**0**	**0**	**0**
	Rochester Americans	AHL	71	55	48	103				53											15	6	9	15	33			
1984-85	**Buffalo Sabres**	**NHL**	**47**	**17**	**9**	**26**	**14**	**6**	**20**	**26**	**5**	**0**	**5**	**62**	**27.4**	**47**	**20**	**26**	**0**	**1**								
	Rochester Americans	AHL	6	4	4	8				14																		
1985-86	**Buffalo Sabres**	**NHL**	**7**	**2**	**0**	**2**	**2**	**0**	**2**	**4**	**2**	**0**	**0**	**5**	**40.0**	**5**	**3**	**3**	**0**	**–1**								
	Rochester Americans	AHL	38	21	15	36				23																		
1986-87	TPS Turku	Finland	39	24	15	39				93											5	3	0	3	13			
	Canada	Nat-Team	3	1	3	4				2																		
1987-88	TPS Turku	Finland	44	32	12	44				68																		
1988-89	TPS Turku	Finland	34	21	15	36				31											10	*9	3	12	4			
	Canada	Nat-Team	3	1	3	4				2																		
1989-90	TPS Turku	Finland	38	27	11	38				44											8	7	0	7	4			
1990-91	TPS Turku	Finland	29	11	6	17				32																		
1991-92	EHC Essen-West	Germany-2	18	19	7	26				43											4	6	3	9	4			
	NHL Totals		**100**	**31**	**22**	**53**	**27**	**15**	**42**	**34**	**11**	**0**	**8**	**124**	**25.0**	**101**	**43**	**62**	**0**		**7**	**1**	**0**	**1**	**0**	**0**	**0**	**0**

CHL First All-Star Team (1979) • AHL First All-Star Team (1984) • Shared Les Cunningham Award (MVP - AHL) with Garry Lariviere (1984)

Signed as a free agent by **Detroit**, October 12, 1978. Signed as a free agent by **Buffalo**, September 2, 1981. Claimed by **LA Kings** from **Buffalo** in Waiver Draft, October 6, 1986.

• DAVYDOV, Evgeny

LW – R. 6', 200 lbs. b: Chelyabinsk, USSR, 5/27/1967. Winnipeg's 14th, 235th overall, in 1989.

Season	Club	League	GP	G	A	Pts	AG	AA	APts	PIM	PP	SH	GW	S	%	TGF	PGF	TGA	PGA	+/-	GP	G	A	Pts	PIM	PP	SH	GW
1984-85	Traktor Chelyabinsk	USSR	5	1	0	1				2																		
	Soviet Union	EJC-A	5	4	0	4				6																		
1985-86	Traktor Chelyabinsk	USSR	39	11	5	16				22																		
	Soviet Union	WJC-A	7	3	1	4				2																		
1986-87	CSKA Moscow	USSR	32	11	2	13				8																		
1987-88	CSKA Moscow	USSR	44	16	7	23				18																		
1988-89	CSKA Moscow	USSR	35	9	7	16				4																		
1989-90	CSKA Moscow	USSR	44	17	6	23				16																		
1990-91	CSKA Moscow	USSR	44	10	10	20				26																		
1991-92	CSKA Moscow	CIS	27	13	12	25				14																		
	Russia	Olympics	8	3	3	6				2																		
	Winnipeg Jets	**NHL**	**12**	**4**	**3**	**7**	**4**	**2**	**6**	**8**	**2**	**0**	**0**	**32**	**12.5**	**15**	**5**	**3**	**0**	**7**	**7**	**2**	**2**	**4**	**2**	**1**	**0**	**0**
1992-93	**Winnipeg Jets**	**NHL**	**79**	**28**	**21**	**49**	**23**	**14**	**37**	**66**	**7**	**0**	**2**	**176**	**15.9**	**72**	**23**	**51**	**0**	**–2**	**4**	**0**	**0**	**0**	**0**	**0**	**0**	**0**
1993-94	**Florida Panthers**	**NHL**	**21**	**2**	**6**	**8**	**2**	**5**	**7**	**8**	**0**	**0**	**0**	**22**	**9.1**	**14**	**6**	**11**	**0**	**–3**								
	Ottawa Senators	**NHL**	**40**	**5**	**7**	**12**	**5**	**5**	**10**	**38**	**1**	**0**	**0**	**44**	**11.4**	**19**	**2**	**23**	**0**	**–6**								
1994-95	**Ottawa Senators**	**NHL**	**3**	**1**	**2**	**3**	**2**	**3**	**5**	**0**	**0**	**0**	**0**	**2**	**50.0**	**3**	**0**	**1**	**0**	**2**								
	San Diego Gulls	IHL	11	2	1	3				14																		
	Chicago Wolves	IHL	18	10	12	22				26											3	1	0	1	0			
1995-96	EHC Olten	Switz-2	STATISTICS NOT AVAILABLE																									
	HC Amiens	France	3	3	0	3				4											13	15	9	*24	*54			
1996-97	Brynas IF Gavle	Sweden	46	*30	18	48				103																		
1997-98	Brynas IF Gavle	Sweden	40	17	16	33				32											3	1	0	1	0			
1998-99	AK Bars Kazan	Russia	14	2	2	4				45																		
	AK Bars Kazan	EuroHL	4	0	4	4				0																		
	EV Zug	Switz.	11	4	3	7				4											4	0	1	1	4			
	EV Zug	EuroHL	1	0	0	0				0											2	1	0	1	0			
99-2000	EHC Olten	Switz-2	36	26	30	56				70																		
	NHL Totals		**155**	**40**	**39**	**79**	**36**	**29**	**65**	**120**	**10**	**0**	**2**	**276**	**14.5**	**123**	**36**	**89**	**0**		**11**	**2**	**2**	**4**	**2**	**1**	**0**	**0**

Traded to **Florida** by **Winnipeg** for Florida's 4th round draft choice (later traded to Edmonton — Edmonton selected Adam Copeland) in 1984 Entry Draft. September 30, 1993. Traded to **Ottawa** by **Florida** with Scott Levins, Florida's 6th round choice (Mike Gaffney) in 1994 Entry Draft and Dallas' 4th round choice (previously acquired, Ottawa selected Kevin Bolibruck) in 1995 Entry Draft for Bob Kudelski, January 6, 1994.

• DAWE, Jason RW – L. 5'10", 189 lbs. b: North York, Ont., 5/29/1973. Buffalo's 2nd, 35th overall, in 1991.

			REGULAR SEASON																		PLAYOFFS							
Season	Club	League	GP	G	A	Pts	AG	AA	APts	PIM	PP	SH	GW	S	%	TGF	PGF	TGA	PGA	+/–	GP	G	A	Pts	PIM	PP	SH	GW
1988-89	Don Mills Bantam Flyers	MTHL	44	35	28	63	....	....	....	103	....	....	....	....	....	....	....	....	....	....	....	....	....	....	....	....	....	....
1989-90	Peterborough Petes	OHL	50	15	18	33	....	....	....	19	....	....	....	....	....	....	....	....	....	....	12	4	7	11	4	....	....	....
1990-91	Peterborough Petes	OHL	66	43	27	70	....	....	....	43	....	....	....	....	....	....	....	....	....	....	4	3	1	4	0	....	....	....
1991-92	Peterborough Petes	OHL	66	53	55	108	....	....	....	55	....	....	....	....	....	....	....	....	....	....	4	5	0	5	0	....	....	....
1992-93	Peterborough Petes	OHL	59	58	68	126	....	....	....	80	....	....	....	....	....	....	....	....	....	....	21	18	33	51	18	....	....	....
	Canada	WJC-A	7	3	3	6	....	....	....	8	....	....	....	....	....	....	....	....	....	....	....	....	....	....	....	....	....	....
	Rochester Americans	AHL	....	....	....	....	....	....	....	....	....	....	....	....	....	....	....	....	....	....	3	1	0	1	0	....	....	....
	Peterborough Petes	Mem-Cup	5	3	6	9	....	....	....	4	....	....	....	....	....	....	....	....	....	....	....	....	....	....	....	....	....	....
1993-94	**Buffalo Sabres**	**NHL**	**32**	**6**	**7**	**13**	**6**	**5**	**11**	**12**	**3**	**0**	**1**	**35**	**17.1**	**18**	**5**	**12**	**0**	**1**	**6**	**0**	**1**	**1**	**6**	**0**	**0**	**0**
	Rochester Americans	AHL	48	22	14	36	....	....	....	44	....	....	....	....	....	....	....	....	....	....	....	....	....	....	....	....	....	....
1994-95	Rochester Americans	AHL	44	27	19	46	....	....	....	24	....	....	....	....	....	....	....	....	....	....	....	....	....	....	....	....	....	....
	Buffalo Sabres	**NHL**	**42**	**7**	**4**	**11**	**12**	**6**	**18**	**19**	**0**	**1**	**2**	**51**	**13.7**	**15**	**4**	**17**	**0**	**–6**	**5**	**2**	**1**	**3**	**6**	**0**	**0**	**0**
1995-96	**Buffalo Sabres**	**NHL**	**67**	**25**	**25**	**50**	**25**	**20**	**45**	**33**	**8**	**1**	**0**	**130**	**19.2**	**61**	**19**	**58**	**8**	**–8**	....	....	....	....	....	....	....	....
	Rochester Americans	AHL	7	5	4	9	....	....	....	2	....	....	....	....	....	....	....	....	....	....	....	....	....	....	....	....	....	....
	Canada	WC-A	8	3	0	3	....	....	....	2	....	....	....	....	....	....	....	....	....	....	....	....	....	....	....	....	....	....
1996-97	**Buffalo Sabres**	**NHL**	**81**	**22**	**26**	**48**	**23**	**23**	**46**	**32**	**4**	**1**	**3**	**136**	**16.2**	**73**	**19**	**52**	**12**	**14**	**11**	**2**	**1**	**3**	**6**	**0**	**0**	**0**
1997-98	**Buffalo Sabres**	**NHL**	**68**	**19**	**17**	**36**	**22**	**17**	**39**	**36**	**4**	**1**	**3**	**115**	**16.5**	**51**	**16**	**44**	**19**	**10**	....	....	....	....	....	....	....	....
	New York Islanders	**NHL**	**13**	**1**	**2**	**3**	**1**	**2**	**3**	**6**	**0**	**0**	**0**	**19**	**5.3**	**5**	**0**	**7**	**0**	**–2**	....	....	....	....	....	....	....	....
1998-99	**New York Islanders**	**NHL**	**22**	**2**	**3**	**5**	**2**	**3**	**5**	**8**	**0**	**0**	**0**	**29**	**6.9**	**8**	**2**	**8**	**2**	**0**	....	....	....	....	....	....	....	....
	Montreal Canadiens	**NHL**	**37**	**4**	**5**	**9**	**5**	**5**	**10**	**14**	**1**	**0**	**1**	**52**	**7.7**	**15**	**3**	**14**	**2**	**0**	....	....	....	....	....	....	....	....
99-2000	**New York Rangers**	**NHL**	**3**	**0**	**1**	**1**	**0**	**1**	**1**	**2**	**0**	**0**	**0**	**8**	**0.0**	**2**	**1**	**1**	**0**	**0**	....	....	....	....	....	....	....	....
	Hartford Wolf Pack	AHL	27	9	9	18	....	....	....	24	....	....	....	....	....	....	....	....	....	....	21	10	7	17	37	....	....	....
	Milwaukee Admirals	IHL	41	11	13	24	....	....	....	24	....	....	....	....	....	....	....	....	....	....	....	....	....	....	....	....	....	....
	NHL Totals		**365**	**86**	**90**	**176**	**96**	**82**	**178**	**162**	**20**	**4**	**10**	**575**	**15.0**	**248**	**69**	**213**	**43**		**22**	**4**	**3**	**7**	**18**	**0**	**0**	**0**

OHL First All-Star Team (1993) • Canadian Major Junior Second All-Star Team (1993) • Won George Parsons Trophy (Memorial Cup Tournament Most Sportsmanlike Player) (1993)

Traded to **NY Islanders** by **Buffalo** for Jason Holland and Paul Kruse, March 24, 1998. Claimed on waivers by **Montreal** from **NY Islanders**, December 15, 1998. Signed as a free agent by **Nashville**, October 2, 1999. Traded to **NY Rangers** by **Nashville** for John Namestnikov, February 3, 2000.

• DAY, Joe Joseph Christopher C – L. 5'11", 180 lbs. b: Chicago, IL, 5/11/1968. Hartford's 8th, 186th overall, in 1987.

			REGULAR SEASON																		PLAYOFFS							
Season	Club	League	GP	G	A	Pts	AG	AA	APts	PIM	PP	SH	GW	S	%	TGF	PGF	TGA	PGA	+/–	GP	G	A	Pts	PIM	PP	SH	GW
1984-85	Chicago Young Americans	MNHL	STATISTICS NOT AVAILABLE																									
	Chicago Jr. Hawks	MWJHL	STATISTICS NOT AVAILABLE																									
1985-86	St. Michael's Buzzers	OJHL-B	30	23	18	41	....	....	....	69	....	....	....	....	....	....	....	....	....	....	....	....	....	....	....	....	....	....
1986-87	St. Lawrence University	ECAC	33	9	11	20	....	....	....	25	....	....	....	....	....	....	....	....	....	....	....	....	....	....	....	....	....	....
1987-88	St. Lawrence University	ECAC	30	21	16	37	....	....	....	36	....	....	....	....	....	....	....	....	....	....	....	....	....	....	....	....	....	....
	United States	WJC-A	7	2	1	3	....	....	....	14	....	....	....	....	....	....	....	....	....	....	....	....	....	....	....	....	....	....
1988-89	St. Lawrence University	ECAC	36	21	27	48	....	....	....	44	....	....	....	....	....	....	....	....	....	....	....	....	....	....	....	....	....	....
1989-90	St. Lawrence University	ECAC	32	19	26	45	....	....	....	30	....	....	....	....	....	....	....	....	....	....	....	....	....	....	....	....	....	....
1990-91	Springfield Indians	AHL	75	24	29	53	....	....	....	82	....	....	....	....	....	....	....	....	....	....	18	5	5	10	27	....	....	....
1991-92	**Hartford Whalers**	**NHL**	**24**	**0**	**3**	**3**	**0**	**2**	**2**	**10**	**0**	**0**	**0**	**13**	**0.0**	**3**	**0**	**15**	**10**	**–2**	....	....	....	....	....	....	....	....
	Springfield Indians	AHL	50	33	25	58	....	....	....	92	....	....	....	....	....	....	....	....	....	....	....	....	....	....	....	....	....	....
1992-93	**Hartford Whalers**	**NHL**	**24**	**1**	**7**	**8**	**1**	**5**	**6**	**47**	**0**	**0**	**0**	**10**	**10.0**	**13**	**0**	**27**	**6**	**–8**	....	....	....	....	....	....	....	....
	Springfield Indians	AHL	33	15	20	35	....	....	....	118	....	....	....	....	....	....	....	....	....	....	15	0	8	8	40	....	....	....
1993-94	**New York Islanders**	**NHL**	**24**	**0**	**0**	**0**	**0**	**0**	**0**	**30**	**0**	**0**	**0**	**16**	**0.0**	**4**	**0**	**11**	**0**	**–7**	....	....	....	....	....	....	....	....
	Salt Lake Golden Eagles	IHL	33	16	10	26	....	....	....	153	....	....	....	....	....	....	....	....	....	....	....	....	....	....	....	....	....	....
1994-95	Detroit Vipers	IHL	32	16	10	26	....	....	....	126	....	....	....	....	....	....	....	....	....	....	5	0	2	2	21	....	....	....
1995-96	Detroit Vipers	IHL	53	19	19	38	....	....	....	105	....	....	....	....	....	....	....	....	....	....	....	....	....	....	....	....	....	....
	Las Vegas Thunder	IHL	29	11	17	28	....	....	....	70	....	....	....	....	....	....	....	....	....	....	15	7	3	10	46	....	....	....
1996-97	Baltimore Bandits	AHL	11	3	0	3	....	....	....	22	....	....	....	....	....	....	....	....	....	....	....	....	....	....	....	....	....	....
	Las Vegas Thunder	IHL	30	9	14	23	....	....	....	41	....	....	....	....	....	....	....	....	....	....	3	0	0	0	6	....	....	....
1997-98	Las Vegas Thunder	IHL	82	30	25	55	....	....	....	183	....	....	....	....	....	....	....	....	....	....	4	0	3	3	14	....	....	....
1998-99	Las Vegas Thunder	IHL	DID NOT PLAY – SUSPENDED																									
	NHL Totals		**72**	**1**	**10**	**11**	**1**	**7**	**8**	**87**	**0**	**0**	**0**	**39**	**2.6**	**20**	**0**	**53**	**16**		....	....	....	....	....	....	....	....

ECAC Second All-Star Team (1990)

Signed as a free agent by **NY Islanders**, August 24, 1993. Signed as a free agent by **Las Vegas** (IHL), January, 25, 1997. • Suspended for entire 1998-99 season by **Las Vegas** (IHL) for refusing to report to training camp, September 22, 1998.

• DAZE, Eric LW – L. 6'6", 234 lbs. b: Montreal, Que., 7/2/1975. Chicago's 5th, 90th overall, in 1993.

			REGULAR SEASON																		PLAYOFFS							
Season	Club	League	GP	G	A	Pts	AG	AA	APts	PIM	PP	SH	GW	S	%	TGF	PGF	TGA	PGA	+/–	GP	G	A	Pts	PIM	PP	SH	GW
1990-91	Laval Bantam Regents	QAAA	30	25	20	45	....	....	....	30	....	....	....	....	....	....	....	....	....	....	....	....	....	....	....	....	....	....
1991-92	Laval-Laurentides Regents	QAAA	35	30	29	59	....	....	....	40	....	....	....	....	....	....	....	....	....	....	....	....	....	....	....	....	....	....
1992-93	Beauport Harfangs	QMJHL	68	19	36	55	....	....	....	24	....	....	....	....	....	....	....	....	....	....	....	....	....	....	....	....	....	....
1993-94	Beauport Harfangs	QMJHL	66	59	48	107	....	....	....	31	....	....	....	....	....	....	....	....	....	....	15	16	8	24	2	....	....	....
1994-95	Beauport Harfangs	QMJHL	57	54	45	99	....	....	....	20	....	....	....	....	....	....	....	....	....	....	16	9	12	21	23	....	....	....
	Canada	WJC-A	7	8	2	10	....	....	....	0	....	....	....	....	....	....	....	....	....	....	....	....	....	....	....	....	....	....
	Chicago Blackhawks	**NHL**	**4**	**1**	**1**	**2**	**2**	**1**	**3**	**2**	**0**	**0**	**0**	**1**	**100.0**	**2**	**0**	**0**	**0**	**2**	**16**	**0**	**1**	**1**	**4**	**0**	**0**	**0**
1995-96	**Chicago Blackhawks**	**NHL**	**80**	**30**	**23**	**53**	**30**	**19**	**49**	**18**	**2**	**0**	**2**	**167**	**18.0**	**76**	**12**	**48**	**0**	**16**	**10**	**3**	**5**	**8**	**0**	**0**	**0**	**1**
1996-97	**Chicago Blackhawks**	**NHL**	**71**	**22**	**19**	**41**	**23**	**17**	**40**	**16**	**11**	**0**	**4**	**176**	**12.5**	**67**	**26**	**46**	**1**	**–4**	**6**	**2**	**1**	**3**	**2**	**0**	**0**	**0**
1997-98	**Chicago Blackhawks**	**NHL**	**80**	**31**	**11**	**42**	**36**	**11**	**47**	**22**	**10**	**0**	**7**	**216**	**14.4**	**64**	**25**	**39**	**4**	**4**	....	....	....	....	....	....	....	....
	Canada	WC-A	3	1	4	5	....	....	....	0	....	....	....	....	....	....	....	....	....	....	....	....	....	....	....	....	....	....
1998-99	**Chicago Blackhawks**	**NHL**	**72**	**22**	**20**	**42**	**26**	**19**	**45**	**22**	**8**	**0**	**2**	**189**	**11.6**	**63**	**23**	**57**	**4**	**–13**	....	....	....	....	....	....	....	....
	Canada	WC-A	2	0	1	1	....	....	....	0	....	....	....	....	....	....	....	....	....	....	....	....	....	....	....	....	....	....
99-2000	**Chicago Blackhawks**	**NHL**	**59**	**23**	**13**	**36**	**26**	**12**	**38**	**28**	**6**	**0**	**1**	**143**	**16.1**	**51**	**18**	**63**	**14**	**–16**	....	....	....	....	....	....	....	....
	NHL Totals		**366**	**129**	**87**	**216**	**143**	**79**	**222**	**108**	**37**	**0**	**16**	**892**	**14.5**	**323**	**104**	**253**	**23**		**32**	**5**	**7**	**12**	**6**	**0**	**0**	**1**

QMJHL First All-Star Team (1994, 1995) • WJC-A All-Star Team (1995) • Canadian Major Junior Most Sportsmanlike Player of the Year (1995) • NHL All-Rookie Team (1996)

• DEA, Billy William Fraser "Hard Rock" LW – L. 5'8", 175 lbs. b: Edmonton, Alta., 4/3/1933.

			REGULAR SEASON																		PLAYOFFS							
Season	Club	League	GP	G	A	Pts	AG	AA	APts	PIM	PP	SH	GW	S	%	TGF	PGF	TGA	PGA	+/–	GP	G	A	Pts	PIM	PP	SH	GW
1949-50	Lethbridge Native Sons	WCJHL	29	20	13	33	....	....	....	4	....	....	....	....	....	....	....	....	....	....	10	4	0	4	0	....	....	....
1950-51	Lethbridge Native Sons	WCJHL	38	25	22	47	....	....	....	6	....	....	....	....	....	....	....	....	....	....	7	3	1	4	0	....	....	....
1951-52	Lethbridge Native Sons	WCJHL	41	44	28	72	....	....	....	10	....	....	....	....	....	....	....	....	....	....	4	2	3	5	0	....	....	....
1952-53	Lethbridge Native Sons	WCJHL	34	34	21	55	....	....	....	53	....	....	....	....	....	....	....	....	....	....	14	*12	9	*21	12	....	....	....
	Saskatoon Quakers	WHL	3	2	1	3	....	....	....	0	....	....	....	....	....	....	....	....	....	....	....	....	....	....	....	....	....	....
	Lethbridge Native Sons	Mem-Cup	11	11	4	15	....	....	....	6	....	....	....	....	....	....	....	....	....	....	....	....	....	....	....	....	....	....
1953-54	**New York Rangers**	**NHL**	**14**	**1**	**1**	**2**	**1**	**1**	**2**	**2**																		
	Vancouver Canucks	WHL	53	21	13	34	....	....	....	8	....	....	....	....	....	....	....	....	....	....	12	6	5	11	4	....	....	....
1954-55	Vancouver Canucks	WHL	59	18	13	31	....	....	....	13	....	....	....	....	....	....	....	....	....	....	4	0	1	1	0	....	....	....
1955-56	Edmonton Flyers	WHL	70	29	42	71	....	....	....	14	....	....	....	....	....	....	....	....	....	....	3	2	1	3	4	....	....	....
1956-57	**Detroit Red Wings**	**NHL**	**69**	**15**	**15**	**30**	**19**	**16**	**35**	**14**											**5**	**2**	**0**	**2**	**2**	**1**	**0**	**0**
1957-58	**Detroit Red Wings**	**NHL**	**29**	**4**	**4**	**8**	**5**	**4**	**9**	**6**																		
	Chicago Black Hawks	**NHL**	**34**	**5**	**8**	**13**	**6**	**8**	**14**	**4**																		
1958-59	Buffalo Bisons	AHL	70	25	45	70	....	....	....	19	....	....	....	....	....	....	....	....	....	....	11	5	4	9	4	....	....	....
1959-60	Buffalo Bisons	AHL	72	28	26	54	....	....	....	20	....	....	....	....	....	....	....	....	....	....	....	....	....	....	....	....	....	....
1960-61	Buffalo Bisons	AHL	72	35	39	74	....	....	....	10	....	....	....	....	....	....	....	....	....	....	4	1	2	3	0	....	....	....
1961-62	Buffalo Bisons	AHL	70	30	22	52	....	....	....	17	....	....	....	....	....	....	....	....	....	....	11	0	2	2	2	....	....	....
1962-63	Buffalo Bisons	AHL	72	20	12	32	....	....	....	25	....	....	....	....	....	....	....	....	....	....	13	2	8	10	0	....	....	....
1963-64	Buffalo Bisons	AHL	72	25	16	41	....	....	....	4	....	....	....	....	....	....	....	....	....	....	....	....	....	....	....	....	....	....
1964-65	Buffalo Bisons	AHL	72	21	19	40	....	....	....	15	....	....	....	....	....	....	....	....	....	....	9	3	0	3	0	....	....	....
1965-66	Buffalo Bisons	AHL	70	32	23	55	....	....	....	17	....	....	....	....	....	....	....	....	....	....	....	....	....	....	....	....	....	....
1966-67	Buffalo Bisons	AHL	71	25	39	64	....	....	....	5	....	....	....	....	....	....	....	....	....	....	....	....	....	....	....	....	....	....
	Chicago Black Hawks	**NHL**	....	....	....	....	....	....	....	....											**2**	**0**	**0**	**0**	**2**	**0**	**0**	**0**

			REGULAR SEASON																		PLAYOFFS							
Season	Club	League	GP	G	A	Pts	AG	AA	APts	PIM	PP	SH	GW	S	%	TGF	PGF	TGA	PGA	+/–	GP	G	A	Pts	PIM	PP	SH	GW
1967-68	**Pittsburgh Penguins**	**NHL**	**73**	**16**	**12**	**28**	**19**	**12**	**31**	**6**	**1**	**0**	**3**	**137**	**11.7**	**47**	**7**	**64**	**9**	**–15**	....	....	....	....	....	....	....	....
1968-69	**Pittsburgh Penguins**	**NHL**	**66**	**10**	**8**	**18**	**11**	**7**	**18**	**4**	**2**	**0**	**1**	**111**	**9.0**	**29**	**5**	**61**	**5**	**–32**	....	....	....	....	....	....	....	....
1969-70	Baltimore Clippers	AHL	7	0	1	1	....	....	....	42	....	....	....	....	....	....	....	....	....	....	....	....	....	....	....	....	....	....
	Detroit Red Wings	**NHL**	**70**	**10**	**3**	**13**	**11**	**3**	**14**	**6**	**0**	**0**	**3**	**63**	**15.9**	**25**	**0**	**30**	**8**	**3**	**4**	**0**	**1**	**1**	**2**	**0**	**0**	**0**
1970-71	**Detroit Red Wings**	**NHL**	**42**	**6**	**3**	**9**	**6**	**2**	**8**	**2**	**1**	**0**	**0**	**30**	**20.0**	**13**	**1**	**26**	**9**	**–5**	....	....	....	....	....	....	....	....
	Fort Worth Wings	CHL	26	8	15	23	....	....	....	10	....	....	....	....	....	....	....	....	....	....	4	0	4	4	0	....	....	....
1971-72	Tidewater Red Wings	AHL	72	7	7	14	....	....	....	8	....	....	....	....	....	....	....	....	....	....	....	....	....	....	....	....	....	....
	NHL Totals		**397**	**67**	**54**	**121**	**78**	**53**	**131**	**44**	....	....	....	....	....	....	....	....	....	....	**11**	**2**	**1**	**3**	**6**	....	....	....

WCJHL First All-Star Team (1952)

Traded to **Detroit** by **NY Rangers** with Aggie Kukulowicz and cash for Dave Creighton and Bronco Horvath, August 18, 1955. Traded to **Chicago** by **Detroit** with Bill Dineen, Lorne Ferguson and Earl Reibel for Nick Mickoski, Bob Bailey, Hec Lalande and John McIntyre, December 17, 1957. Claimed by **Pittsburgh** from **Chicago** in Expansion Draft, June 6, 1967. Traded to **Detroit** by **Pittsburgh** for Mike McMahon, October 28, 1969.

• DEADMARSH, Adam

LW/C – R. 6', 205 lbs. b: Trail, B.C., 5/10/1975. Quebec's 2nd, 14th overall, in 1993.

Season	Club	League	GP	G	A	Pts	AG	AA	APts	PIM	PP	SH	GW	S	%	TGF	PGF	TGA	PGA	+/–	GP	G	A	Pts	PIM	PP	SH	GW
1990-91	Beaver Valley Nite Hawks	KIJHL	35	28	44	72	....	....	....	95	....	....	....	....	....	....	....	....	....	....	....	....	....	....	....	....	....	....
1991-92	Portland Winter Hawks	WHL	68	30	30	60	....	....	....	81	....	....	....	....	....	....	....	....	....	....	6	3	3	6	13	....	....	....
1992-93	Portland Winter Hawks	WHL	58	33	36	69	....	....	....	126	....	....	....	....	....	....	....	....	....	....	16	7	8	15	29	....	....	....
	United States	WJC-A	7	0	0	0	....	....	....	10	....	....	....	....	....	....	....	....	....	....	....	....	....	....	....	....	....	....
1993-94	Portland Winter Hawks	WHL	65	43	56	99	....	....	....	212	....	....	....	....	....	....	....	....	....	....	10	9	8	17	33	....	....	....
	United States	WJC-A	7	0	0	0	....	....	....	8	....	....	....	....	....	....	....	....	....	....	....	....	....	....	....	....	....	....
1994-95	Portland Winter Hawks	WHL	29	28	20	48	....	....	....	129	....	....	....	....	....	....	....	....	....	....	....	....	....	....	....	....	....	....
	United States	WJC-A	7	6	4	10	....	....	....	10	....	....	....	....	....	....	....	....	....	....	....	....	....	....	....	....	....	....
	Quebec Nordiques	**NHL**	**48**	**9**	**8**	**17**	**16**	**12**	**28**	**56**	**0**	**0**	**0**	**48**	**18.8**	**27**	**0**	**12**	**1**	**16**	**6**	**0**	**1**	**1**	**0**	**0**	**0**	**0**
1995-96♦	**Colorado Avalanche**	**NHL**	**78**	**21**	**27**	**48**	**21**	**22**	**43**	**142**	**3**	**0**	**2**	**151**	**13.9**	**75**	**18**	**42**	**5**	**20**	**22**	**5**	**12**	**17**	**25**	**1**	**0**	**0**
1996-97	United States	W-Cup	7	2	2	4	....	....	....	8	....	....	....	....	....	....	....	....	....	....	....	....	....	....	....	....	....	....
	Colorado Avalanche	**NHL**	**78**	**33**	**27**	**60**	**35**	**24**	**59**	**136**	**10**	**3**	**4**	**198**	**16.7**	**94**	**39**	**52**	**5**	**8**	**17**	**3**	**6**	**9**	**24**	**1**	**0**	**1**
1997-98	**Colorado Avalanche**	**NHL**	**73**	**22**	**21**	**43**	**26**	**21**	**47**	**125**	**10**	**0**	**6**	**187**	**11.8**	**70**	**28**	**51**	**9**	**0**	**7**	**2**	**0**	**2**	**4**	**1**	**0**	**0**
	United States	Olympics	4	1	0	1	....	....	....	2	....	....	....	....	....	....	....	....	....	....	....	....	....	....	....	....	....	....
1998-99	**Colorado Avalanche**	**NHL**	**66**	**22**	**27**	**49**	**26**	**26**	**52**	**99**	**10**	**0**	**3**	**152**	**14.5**	**74**	**33**	**52**	**9**	**–2**	**19**	**8**	**4**	**12**	**20**	**3**	**0**	**0**
99-2000	**Colorado Avalanche**	**NHL**	**71**	**18**	**27**	**45**	**20**	**25**	**45**	**106**	**5**	**0**	**4**	**153**	**11.8**	**80**	**36**	**65**	**11**	**–10**	**17**	**4**	**11**	**15**	**21**	**1**	**0**	**1**
	NHL Totals		**414**	**125**	**137**	**262**	**144**	**130**	**274**	**664**	**38**	**3**	**19**	**889**	**14.1**	**420**	**154**	**274**	**40**		**88**	**22**	**34**	**56**	**94**	**7**	**0**	**2**

Transferred to **Colorado** after **Quebec** franchise relocated, June 21, 1995.

• DEADMARSH, Butch

Ernest Charles LW – L. 5'11", 186 lbs. b: Trail, B.C., 4/5/1950. Buffalo's 2nd, 15th overall, in 1970.

Season	Club	League	GP	G	A	Pts	AG	AA	APts	PIM	PP	SH	GW	S	%	TGF	PGF	TGA	PGA	+/–	GP	G	A	Pts	PIM	PP	SH	GW
1966-1968	Kelowna Buckaroos	BCJHL	STATISTICS NOT AVAILABLE																									
1968-69	Brandon Wheat Kings	WCJHL	47	19	23	42	....	....	....	130	....	....	....	....	....	....	....	....	....	....	5	2	2	4	....	....	....	....
1969-70	Brandon Wheat Kings	WCJHL	54	37	33	70	....	....	....	*301	....	....	....	....	....	....	....	....	....	....	4	3	5	8	20	....	....	....
1970-71	**Buffalo Sabres**	**NHL**	**10**	**0**	**0**	**0**	**0**	**0**	**0**	**9**	**0**	**0**	**0**	**7**	**0.0**	**1**	**1**	**3**	**0**	**–3**	....	....	....	....	....	....	....	....
	Salt Lake Golden Eagles	WHL	59	11	9	20	....	....	....	128	....	....	....	....	....	....	....	....	....	....	....	....	....	....	....	....	....	....
1971-72	**Buffalo Sabres**	**NHL**	**12**	**1**	**1**	**2**	**1**	**1**	**2**	**4**	**0**	**0**	**0**	**10**	**10.0**	**3**	**0**	**13**	**0**	**–10**	....	....	....	....	....	....	....	....
	Cincinnati Swords	AHL	64	34	27	61	....	....	....	145	....	....	....	....	....	....	....	....	....	....	10	6	8	14	33	....	....	....
1972-73	**Buffalo Sabres**	**NHL**	**34**	**1**	**1**	**2**	**1**	**1**	**2**	**26**	**1**	**0**	**0**	**15**	**6.7**	**6**	**2**	**7**	**0**	**–3**	....	....	....	....	....	....	....	....
	Cincinnati Swords	AHL	12	7	4	11	....	....	....	20	....	....	....	....	....	....	....	....	....	....	....	....	....	....	....	....	....	....
	Atlanta Flames	**NHL**	**19**	**1**	**0**	**1**	**1**	**0**	**1**	**8**	**0**	**0**	**0**	**19**	**5.3**	**5**	**1**	**8**	**0**	**–4**	....	....	....	....	....	....	....	....
1973-74	**Atlanta Flames**	**NHL**	**42**	**6**	**1**	**7**	**6**	**1**	**7**	**89**	**0**	**0**	**1**	**49**	**12.2**	**15**	**0**	**14**	**0**	**1**	**4**	**0**	**0**	**0**	**17**	**0**	**0**	**0**
1974-75	**Kansas City Scouts**	**NHL**	**20**	**3**	**2**	**5**	**3**	**1**	**4**	**19**	**1**	**0**	**1**	**32**	**9.4**	**9**	**2**	**20**	**8**	**–5**	....	....	....	....	....	....	....	....
	Vancouver Blazers	WHA	38	7	8	15	....	....	....	128	....	....	....	....	....	....	....	....	....	....	....	....	....	....	....	....	....	....
1975-76	Calgary Cowboys	WHA	79	26	28	54	....	....	....	196	....	....	....	....	....	....	....	....	....	....	8	0	1	1	14	....	....	....
1976-77	Minnesota Fighting Saints	WHA	35	9	4	13	....	....	....	51	....	....	....	....	....	....	....	....	....	....	....	....	....	....	....	....	....	....
	Calgary Cowboys	WHA	38	13	17	30	....	....	....	77	....	....	....	....	....	....	....	....	....	....	....	....	....	....	....	....	....	....
1977-78	Edmonton Oilers	WHA	20	1	3	4	....	....	....	32	....	....	....	....	....	....	....	....	....	....	....	....	....	....	....	....	....	....
	Cincinnati Stingers	WHA	45	7	6	13	....	....	....	86	....	....	....	....	....	....	....	....	....	....	....	....	....	....	....	....	....	....
	NHL Totals		**137**	**12**	**5**	**17**	**12**	**4**	**16**	**155**	**2**	**0**	**2**	**132**	**9.1**	**39**	**6**	**65**	**8**		**4**	**0**	**0**	**0**	**17**	**0**	**0**	**0**
	Other Major League Totals		255	63	66	129	....	....	....	570	....	....	....	....	....	....	....	....	....	....	8	0	1	1	14	....	....	....

Traded to **Atlanta** by **Buffalo** for Norm Gratton, February 14, 1973. Selected by **Cincinnati** (WHA), in 1973 WHA Professional Player Draft, June, 1973. Claimed by **Kansas City** from **Atlanta** in Expansion Draft, June 12, 1974. Traded to **Vancouver** (WHA) by **Kansas City** for cash, December, 1974. Transferred to **Calgary** (WHA) after **Vancouver** (WHA) franchise relocated, May 7, 1975. Traded to **Minnesota** (WHA) by **Calgary** (WHA) with Jack Carlson and Dave Antonovich for Jim Harrison, September, 1976. Traded to **Calgary** (WHA) by **Minnesota** (WHA) for Rich Lemieux, January, 1977. • Lemieux refused to report and transaction was cancelled. Traded to **Calgary** (WHA) by **Minnesota** (WHA) with John Arbour and Danny Gruen for cash, January, 1977. Signed as a free agent by **Edmonton** (WHA) after **Calgary** (WHA) franchise folded, May 31, 1977. Traded to **Cincinnati** (WHA) by **Edmonton** (WHA) for Del Hall, December, 1977.

• DEAN, Barry

Barry James LW – L. 6'1", 195 lbs. b: Maple Creek, Sask., 2/26/1955. Kansas City's 1st, 2nd overall, in 1975.

Season	Club	League	GP	G	A	Pts	AG	AA	APts	PIM	PP	SH	GW	S	%	TGF	PGF	TGA	PGA	+/–	GP	G	A	Pts	PIM	PP	SH	GW
1971-72	Saskatoon Olympics	SJHL	STATISTICS NOT AVAILABLE																									
	Medicine Hat Tigers	WCJHL	26	2	5	7	....	....	....	46	....	....	....	....	....	....	....	....	....	....	7	0	0	0	2	....	....	....
1972-73	Medicine Hat Tigers	WCJHL	58	23	30	53	....	....	....	208	....	....	....	....	....	....	....	....	....	....	17	6	10	16	35	....	....	....
	Medicine Hat Tigers	Mem-Cup	2	0	2	2	....	....	....	12	....	....	....	....	....	....	....	....	....	....	....	....	....	....	....	....	....	....
1973-74	Medicine Hat Tigers	WCJHL	66	23	73	96	....	....	....	213	....	....	....	....	....	....	....	....	....	....	6	4	8	12	13	....	....	....
1974-75	Medicine Hat Tigers	WCJHL	64	40	75	115	....	....	....	159	....	....	....	....	....	....	....	....	....	....	5	4	6	10	28	....	....	....
1975-76	Phoenix Roadrunners	WHA	71	9	25	34	....	....	....	110	....	....	....	....	....	....	....	....	....	....	....	....	....	....	....	....	....	....
1976-77	**Colorado Rockies**	**NHL**	**79**	**14**	**25**	**39**	**13**	**19**	**32**	**92**	**2**	**0**	**0**	**130**	**10.8**	**61**	**15**	**77**	**5**	**–26**	....	....	....	....	....	....	....	....
1977-78	**Philadelphia Flyers**	**NHL**	**56**	**7**	**18**	**25**	**6**	**14**	**20**	**34**	**0**	**0**	**2**	**76**	**9.2**	**36**	**3**	**22**	**1**	**12**	....	....	....	....	....	....	....	....
1978-79	**Philadelphia Flyers**	**NHL**	**30**	**4**	**13**	**17**	**3**	**9**	**12**	**20**	**0**	**0**	**1**	**52**	**7.7**	**22**	**5**	**22**	**4**	**–1**	....	....	....	....	....	....	....	....
	Maine Mariners	AHL	36	18	17	35	....	....	....	94	....	....	....	....	....	....	....	....	....	....	5	2	1	3	0	....	....	....
1979-80	Maine Mariners	AHL	77	23	26	49	....	....	....	106	....	....	....	....	....	....	....	....	....	....	12	8	9	17	21	....	....	....
1980-81	Wichita Wind	CHL	30	14	14	28	....	....	....	54	....	....	....	....	....	....	....	....	....	....	....	....	....	....	....	....	....	....
1981-82	Fredericton Express	AHL	25	3	16	19	....	....	....	6	....	....	....	....	....	....	....	....	....	....	....	....	....	....	....	....	....	....
	NHL Totals		**165**	**25**	**56**	**81**	**22**	**42**	**64**	**146**	**2**	**0**	**3**	**258**	**9.7**	**119**	**23**	**121**	**10**		....	....	....	....	....	....	....	....
	Other Major League Totals		71	9	25	34	....	....	....	110	....	....	....	....	....	....	....	....	....	....	....	....	....	....	....	....	....	....

WCJHL First All-Star Team (1975)

Selected by **Edmonton** (WHA) in 1975 WHA Amateur Draft, May, 1975. Traded to **Phoenix** (WHA) by **Edmonton** (WHA) for Phoenix's 1st round choice (Blair Chapman) and 3rd round choice (Harold Philipoff) in 1976 WHA Amateur Draft, June, 1975. Rights transferred to **Colorado** after **Kansas City** franchise relocated, June, 1976. Traded to **Philadelphia** by **Colorado** for Mark Suzor, August 5, 1977. Claimed by **Philadelphia** as a fill-in during Expansion Draft, June 13, 1979. Traded to **Edmonton** by **Philadelphia** for Ron Areshenkoff and Edmonton's 10th round choice (Bob O'Brien) in 1980 Entry Draft, June 11, 1980.

• DEAN, Kevin

Kevin Charles D – L. 6'3", 205 lbs. b: Madison, WI, 4/1/1969. New Jersey's 4th, 86th overall, in 1987.

Season	Club	League	GP	G	A	Pts	AG	AA	APts	PIM	PP	SH	GW	S	%	TGF	PGF	TGA	PGA	+/–	GP	G	A	Pts	PIM	PP	SH	GW
1985-86	Culver Academy Eagles	Hi-School	35	28	44	72	....	....	....	48	....	....	....	....	....	....	....	....	....	....	....	....	....	....	....	....	....	....
1986-87	Culver Academy Eagles	Hi-School	25	19	25	44	....	....	....	30	....	....	....	....	....	....	....	....	....	....	....	....	....	....	....	....	....	....
1987-88	Univeristy of New Hampshire	H-East	27	1	6	7	....	....	....	34	....	....	....	....	....	....	....	....	....	....	....	....	....	....	....	....	....	....
	United States	WJC-A	7	0	0	0	....	....	....	0	....	....	....	....	....	....	....	....	....	....	....	....	....	....	....	....	....	....
1988-89	University of New Hampshire	H-East	34	1	12	13	....	....	....	28	....	....	....	....	....	....	....	....	....	....	....	....	....	....	....	....	....	....
1989-90	University of New Hampshire	H-East	39	2	6	8	....	....	....	42	....	....	....	....	....	....	....	....	....	....	....	....	....	....	....	....	....	....
1990-91	University of New Hampshire	H-East	31	10	12	22	....	....	....	22	....	....	....	....	....	....	....	....	....	....	....	....	....	....	....	....	....	....
	Utica Devils	AHL	7	0	1	1	....	....	....	2	....	....	....	....	....	....	....	....	....	....	....	....	....	....	....	....	....	....
1991-92	Utica Devils	AHL	23	0	3	3	....	....	....	6	....	....	....	....	....	....	....	....	....	....	....	....	....	....	....	....	....	....
	Cincinnati Cyclones	ECHL	30	3	22	25	....	....	....	43	....	....	....	....	....	....	....	....	....	....	9	1	6	7	8	....	....	....
1992-93	Cincinnati Cyclones	IHL	13	2	1	3	....	....	....	15	....	....	....	....	....	....	....	....	....	....	....	....	....	....	....	....	....	....
	Utica Devils	AHL	57	2	16	18	....	....	....	76	....	....	....	....	....	....	....	....	....	....	5	1	0	1	8	....	....	....
1993-94	Albany River Rats	AHL	70	9	33	42	....	....	....	92	....	....	....	....	....	....	....	....	....	....	5	0	2	2	7	....	....	....

			REGULAR SEASON																		PLAYOFFS							
Season	Club	League	GP	G	A	Pts	AG	AA	APts	PIM	PP	SH	GW	S	%	TGF	PGF	TGA	PGA	+/–	GP	G	A	Pts	PIM	PP	SH	GW
1994-95♦	**New Jersey Devils**	**NHL**	**17**	**0**	**1**	**1**	**0**	**1**	**1**	**4**	**0**	**0**	**0**	**11**	**0.0**	**11**	**0**	**5**	**0**	**6**	**3**	**0**	**2**	**2**	**0**	**0**	**0**	**0**
	Albany River Rats	AHL	68	5	37	42	....	....	....	66	....	....	....	....	....	....	....	....	....	....	8	0	4	4	4	....	....	....
1995-96	**New Jersey Devils**	**NHL**	**41**	**0**	**6**	**6**	**0**	**5**	**5**	**28**	**0**	**0**	**0**	**29**	**0.0**	**27**	**5**	**22**	**4**	**4**	....	....	....	....	....	....	....	....
	Albany River Rats	AHL	1	1	0	1	....	....	....	2	....	....	....	....	....	....	....	....	....	....	....	....	....	....	....	....	....	....
1996-97	**New Jersey Devils**	**NHL**	**28**	**2**	**4**	**6**	**2**	**4**	**6**	**6**	**0**	**0**	**0**	**21**	**9.5**	**17**	**1**	**14**	**0**	**2**	**1**	**1**	**0**	**1**	**0**	**0**	**0**	**1**
	Albany River Rats	AHL	2	0	1	1	....	....	....	4	....	....	....	....	....	....	....	....	....	....	....	....	....	....	....	....	....	....
1997-98	**New Jersey Devils**	**NHL**	**50**	**1**	**8**	**9**	**1**	**8**	**9**	**12**	**1**	**0**	**0**	**28**	**3.6**	**32**	**3**	**26**	**9**	**12**	**5**	**1**	**0**	**1**	**2**	**0**	**0**	**0**
	Albany River Rats	AHL	2	0	1	1	....	....	....	2	....	....	....	....	....	....	....	....	....	....	....	....	....	....	....	....	....	....
	United States	WC-A	3	0	0	0	....	....	....	0	....	....	....	....	....	....	....	....	....	....	....	....	....	....	....	....	....	....
1998-99	**New Jersey Devils**	**NHL**	**62**	**1**	**10**	**11**	**1**	**10**	**11**	**22**	**1**	**0**	**0**	**51**	**2.0**	**41**	**4**	**43**	**10**	**4**	**7**	**0**	**0**	**0**	**0**	**0**	**0**	**0**
99-2000	**Atlanta Thrashers**	**NHL**	**23**	**1**	**0**	**1**	**1**	**0**	**1**	**14**	**0**	**1**	**0**	**9**	**11.1**	**13**	**0**	**33**	**15**	**–5**	....	....	....	....	....	....	....	....
	Dallas Stars	**NHL**	**14**	**0**	**0**	**0**	**0**	**0**	**0**	**10**	**0**	**0**	**0**	**6**	**0.0**	**4**	**0**	**5**	**0**	**–1**	....	....	....	....	....	....	....	....
	Chicago Blackhawks	**NHL**	**27**	**2**	**8**	**10**	**2**	**7**	**9**	**12**	**0**	**0**	**0**	**32**	**6.3**	**25**	**1**	**23**	**8**	**9**	....	....	....	....	....	....	....	....
	NHL Totals		**262**	**7**	**37**	**44**	**7**	**35**	**42**	**108**	**2**	**1**	**0**	**187**	**3.7**	**170**	**14**	**171**	**46**		**16**	**2**	**2**	**4**	**2**	**0**	**0**	**1**

AHL First All-Star Team (1995)

Claimed by **Atlanta** from **New Jersey** in Expansion Draft, June 25, 1999. Traded to **Dallas** by **Atlanta** for Dallas' 9th round choice (Mark McRae) in 2000 Entry Draft, December 15, 1999. Traded to **Chicago** by **Dallas** with Derek Plante and Dallas' 2nd round choice in 2001 Entry Draft for Sylvain Cote and Dave Manson, February 8, 2000.

• DEBENEDET, Nelson

Nelson Flavio LW – L. 6'1", 195 lbs. b: Cordeno, Italy, 12/31/1947.

Season	Club	League	GP	G	A	Pts	AG	AA	APts	PIM	PP	SH	GW	S	%	TGF	PGF	TGA	PGA	+/–	GP	G	A	Pts	PIM	PP	SH	GW
1966-67	Michigan State Spartans	WCHA	27	0	7	7	....	....	....	14	....	....	....	....	....	....	....	....	....	....	....	....	....	....	....	....	....	....
1967-68	Michigan State Spartans	WCHA	29	4	3	7	....	....	....	25	....	....	....	....	....	....	....	....	....	....	....	....	....	....	....	....	....	....
1968-69	Michigan State Spartans	WCHA	28	10	7	17	....	....	....	40	....	....	....	....	....	....	....	....	....	....	....	....	....	....	....	....	....	....
1969-70	University of Toronto	OUAA	STATISTICS NOT AVAILABLE																									
	Fort Wayne Komets	IHL	8	0	3	3	....	....	....	6	....	....	....	....	....	....	....	....	....	....	....	....	....	....	....	....	....	....
1970-71	University of Toronto	OUAA	15	3	9	12	....	....	....	29	....	....	....	....	....	....	....	....	....	....	11	2	10	12	0	....	....	....
1971-72	Fort Worth Wings	CHL	14	2	4	6	....	....	....	15	....	....	....	....	....	....	....	....	....	....	....	....	....	....	....	....	....	....
	Tidewater Red Wings	AHL	22	4	3	7	....	....	....	12	....	....	....	....	....	....	....	....	....	....	....	....	....	....	....	....	....	....
	Port Huron Wings	IHL	30	7	5	12	....	....	....	19	....	....	....	....	....	....	....	....	....	....	....	....	....	....	....	....	....	....
1972-73	Virginia Wings	AHL	76	29	27	56	....	....	....	64	....	....	....	....	....	....	....	....	....	....	13	2	5	7	6	....	....	....
1973-74	**Detroit Red Wings**	**NHL**	**15**	**4**	**1**	**5**	**4**	**1**	**5**	**2**	**0**	**0**	**0**	**13**	**30.8**	**9**	**1**	**7**	**0**	**1**	....	....	....	....	....	....	....	....
	Virginia Wings	AHL	39	8	15	23	....	....	....	40	....	....	....	....	....	....	....	....	....	....	....	....	....	....	....	....	....	....
1974-75	**Pittsburgh Penguins**	**NHL**	**31**	**6**	**3**	**9**	**5**	**2**	**7**	**11**	**1**	**0**	**0**	**28**	**21.4**	**12**	**2**	**17**	**4**	**–3**	....	....	....	....	....	....	....	....
	Hershey Bears	AHL	25	6	6	12	....	....	....	13	....	....	....	....	....	....	....	....	....	....	12	2	4	6	2	....	....	....
1975-76	Hershey Bears	AHL	69	14	19	33	....	....	....	12	....	....	....	....	....	....	....	....	....	....	9	4	5	9	6	....	....	....
	NHL Totals		**46**	**10**	**4**	**14**	**9**	**3**	**12**	**13**	**1**	**0**	**0**	**41**	**24.4**	**21**	**3**	**24**	**4**		....	....	....	....	....	....	....	....

Signed as a free agent by **Detroit**, September, 1971. Traded to **Pittsburgh** by **Detroit** for Hank Nowak and Pittsburgh's 3rd round choice (Dan Mandryk) in 1974 Amateur Draft, May 27, 1974.

• DeBLOIS, Lucien

C – R. 5'11", 200 lbs. b: Joliette, Que., 6/21/1957. NY Rangers' 1st, 8th overall, in 1977.

Season	Club	League	GP	G	A	Pts	AG	AA	APts	PIM	PP	SH	GW	S	%	TGF	PGF	TGA	PGA	+/–	GP	G	A	Pts	PIM	PP	SH	GW
1973-74	Sorel Black Hawks	QMJHL	56	30	35	65	....	....	....	53	....	....	....	....	....	....	....	....	....	....	....	....	....	....	....	....	....	....
1974-75	Sorel Black Hawks	QMJHL	72	46	53	99	....	....	....	62	....	....	....	....	....	....	....	....	....	....	....	....	....	....	....	....	....	....
1975-76	Sorel Black Hawks	QMJHL	70	56	55	111	....	....	....	112	....	....	....	....	....	....	....	....	....	....	5	1	1	2	32	....	....	....
1976-77	Sorel Black Hawks	QMJHL	72	56	78	134	....	....	....	131	....	....	....	....	....	....	....	....	....	....	....	....	....	....	....	....	....	....
1977-78	**New York Rangers**	**NHL**	**71**	**22**	**8**	**30**	**20**	**6**	**26**	**27**	**1**	**0**	**3**	**111**	**19.8**	**61**	**7**	**66**	**1**	**–11**	**3**	**0**	**0**	**0**	**2**	**0**	**0**	**0**
1978-79	**New York Rangers**	**NHL**	**62**	**11**	**17**	**28**	**9**	**12**	**21**	**26**	**0**	**0**	**1**	**106**	**10.4**	**53**	**17**	**47**	**1**	**–10**	**9**	**2**	**0**	**2**	**4**	**1**	**0**	**0**
	New Haven Nighthawks	AHL	7	4	6	10	....	....	....	6	....	....	....	....	....	....	....	....	....	....	....	....	....	....	....	....	....	....
1979-80	**New York Rangers**	**NHL**	**6**	**3**	**1**	**4**	**3**	**1**	**4**	**7**	**0**	**0**	**0**	**16**	**18.8**	**5**	**0**	**7**	**1**	**–1**	....	....	....	....	....	....	....	....
	Colorado Rockies	**NHL**	**70**	**24**	**19**	**43**	**20**	**14**	**34**	**36**	**4**	**0**	**1**	**151**	**15.9**	**57**	**10**	**66**	**1**	**–18**	....	....	....	....	....	....	....	....
1980-81	**Colorado Rockies**	**NHL**	**74**	**26**	**16**	**42**	**20**	**11**	**31**	**78**	**9**	**1**	**2**	**183**	**14.2**	**61**	**22**	**81**	**0**	**–42**	....	....	....	....	....	....	....	....
	Canada	WEC-A	8	3	0	3	....	....	....	4	....	....	....	....	....	....	....	....	....	....	....	....	....	....	....	....	....	....
1981-82	**Winnipeg Jets**	**NHL**	**65**	**25**	**27**	**52**	**20**	**18**	**38**	**87**	**1**	**1**	**2**	**149**	**16.8**	**75**	**7**	**92**	**14**	**–10**	**4**	**2**	**1**	**3**	**4**	**0**	**0**	**0**
1982-83	**Winnipeg Jets**	**NHL**	**79**	**27**	**27**	**54**	**22**	**19**	**41**	**69**	**1**	**3**	**7**	**183**	**14.8**	**74**	**7**	**125**	**33**	**–25**	**3**	**0**	**0**	**0**	**5**	**0**	**0**	**0**
1983-84	**Winnipeg Jets**	**NHL**	**80**	**34**	**45**	**79**	**27**	**31**	**58**	**50**	**8**	**1**	**2**	**195**	**17.4**	**129**	**42**	**119**	**17**	**–15**	**3**	**0**	**1**	**1**	**4**	**0**	**0**	**0**
1984-85	**Montreal Canadiens**	**NHL**	**51**	**12**	**11**	**23**	**10**	**7**	**17**	**20**	**4**	**1**	**2**	**85**	**14.1**	**52**	**18**	**27**	**2**	**9**	**8**	**2**	**4**	**6**	**4**	**1**	**0**	**0**
1985-86♦	**Montreal Canadiens**	**NHL**	**61**	**14**	**17**	**31**	**11**	**11**	**22**	**48**	**2**	**0**	**1**	**102**	**13.7**	**51**	**7**	**49**	**8**	**3**	**11**	**0**	**0**	**0**	**7**	**0**	**0**	**0**
1986-87	**New York Rangers**	**NHL**	**40**	**3**	**8**	**11**	**3**	**6**	**9**	**27**	**1**	**0**	**0**	**45**	**6.7**	**20**	**3**	**27**	**3**	**–7**	**2**	**0**	**0**	**0**	**2**	**0**	**0**	**0**
1987-88	**New York Rangers**	**NHL**	**74**	**9**	**21**	**30**	**8**	**15**	**23**	**103**	**2**	**0**	**0**	**99**	**9.1**	**52**	**15**	**66**	**26**	**–3**	....	....	....	....	....	....	....	....
1988-89	**New York Rangers**	**NHL**	**73**	**9**	**24**	**33**	**8**	**17**	**25**	**107**	**0**	**0**	**2**	**117**	**7.7**	**44**	**0**	**87**	**37**	**–6**	**4**	**0**	**0**	**0**	**4**	**0**	**0**	**0**
1989-90	**Quebec Nordiques**	**NHL**	**70**	**9**	**8**	**17**	**8**	**6**	**14**	**45**	**1**	**0**	**1**	**83**	**10.8**	**28**	**2**	**96**	**41**	**–29**	....	....	....	....	....	....	....	....
1990-91	**Quebec Nordiques**	**NHL**	**14**	**2**	**2**	**4**	**2**	**2**	**4**	**13**	**0**	**0**	**1**	**8**	**25.0**	**6**	**0**	**9**	**4**	**1**	....	....	....	....	....	....	....	....
	Toronto Maple Leafs	**NHL**	**38**	**10**	**12**	**22**	**9**	**9**	**18**	**30**	**0**	**1**	**0**	**57**	**17.5**	**23**	**0**	**46**	**19**	**–4**	....	....	....	....	....	....	....	....
1991-92	**Toronto Maple Leafs**	**NHL**	**54**	**8**	**11**	**19**	**7**	**8**	**15**	**39**	**0**	**1**	**1**	**75**	**10.7**	**25**	**0**	**51**	**23**	**–3**	....	....	....	....	....	....	....	....
	Winnipeg Jets	**NHL**	**11**	**1**	**2**	**3**	**1**	**2**	**3**	**2**	**0**	**0**	**1**	**15**	**6.7**	**5**	**0**	**5**	**1**	**1**	**5**	**1**	**0**	**1**	**2**	**0**	**0**	**1**
	NHL Totals		**993**	**249**	**276**	**525**	**208**	**195**	**403**	**814**	**34**	**9**	**27**	**1780**	**14.0**	**821**	**157**	**1066**	**232**		**52**	**7**	**6**	**13**	**38**	**2**	**0**	**1**

QMJHL East First All-Star Team (1976) • QMJHL First All-Star Team (1977)

Traded to **Colorado** by **NY Rangers** with Pat Hickey, Mike McEwen, Dean Turner and future considerations (Bobby Crawford, January 15, 1980) for Barry Beck, November 2, 1979. Traded to **Winnipeg** by **Colorado** for Brent Ashton and Winnipeg's 3rd round choice (Dave Kasper) in 1982 Entry Draft, July 15, 1981. Traded to **Montreal** by **Winnipeg** for Perry Turnbull, June 13, 1984. Signed as a free agent by **NY Rangers**, September 8, 1986. Signed as a free agent by **Quebec**, August 2, 1989. Traded to **Toronto** by **Quebec** with Aaron Broten and Michel Petit for Scott Pearson and Toronto's 2nd round choices in 1991 (later traded to Washington — Washington selected Eric Lavigne) and 1992 (Toumos Gronman) Entry Drafts, November 17, 1990. Traded to **Winnipeg** by **Toronto** for Mark Osborne, March 10, 1992.

• DEBOL, Dave

C – R. 5'11", 175 lbs. b: St. Claire Shores, MI, 3/27/1956. Chicago's 4th, 63rd overall, in 1976.

Season	Club	League	GP	G	A	Pts	AG	AA	APts	PIM	PP	SH	GW	S	%	TGF	PGF	TGA	PGA	+/–	GP	G	A	Pts	PIM	PP	SH	GW
1973-74	St. Clair Shores Falcons	NAJHL	STATISTICS NOT AVAILABLE																									
1974-75	University of Michigan	WCHA	33	13	18	31	....	....	....	0	....	....	....	....	....	....	....	....	....	....	....	....	....	....	....	....	....	....
1975-76	University of Michigan	WCHA	42	39	22	61	....	....	....	22	....	....	....	....	....	....	....	....	....	....	....	....	....	....	....	....	....	....
1976-77	University of Michigan	WCHA	45	*43	56	*99	....	....	....	40	....	....	....	....	....	....	....	....	....	....	....	....	....	....	....	....	....	....
	United States	WEC-A	8	3	3	6	....	....	....	2	....	....	....	....	....	....	....	....	....	....	....	....	....	....	....	....	....	....
1977-78	University of Michigan	WCHA	46	20	38	58	....	....	....	16	....	....	....	....	....	....	....	....	....	....	....	....	....	....	....	....	....	....
	United States	WEC-A	10	4	4	8	....	....	....	0	....	....	....	....	....	....	....	....	....	....	....	....	....	....	....	....	....	....
	Cincinnati Stingers	WHA	9	3	2	5	....	....	....	2	....	....	....	....	....	....	....	....	....	....	....	....	....	....	....	....	....	....
1978-79	Cincinnati Stingers	WHA	59	10	27	37	....	....	....	9	....	....	....	....	....	....	....	....	....	....	....	....	....	....	....	....	....	....
1979-80	**Hartford Whalers**	**NHL**	**48**	**12**	**14**	**26**	**10**	**10**	**20**	**4**	**0**	**0**	**1**	**96**	**12.5**	**35**	**0**	**41**	**1**	**–5**	**3**	**0**	**0**	**0**	**0**	**0**	**0**	**0**
	Springfield Indians	AHL	16	4	12	16	....	....	....	2	....	....	....	....	....	....	....	....	....	....	....	....	....	....	....	....	....	....
	Cincinnati Stingers	CHL	10	8	8	16	....	....	....	2	....	....	....	....	....	....	....	....	....	....	....	....	....	....	....	....	....	....
1980-81	**Hartford Whalers**	**NHL**	**44**	**14**	**12**	**26**	**11**	**8**	**19**	**0**	**2**	**0**	**0**	**70**	**20.0**	**38**	**6**	**44**	**0**	**–12**	....	....	....	....	....	....	....	....
	Binghamton Whalers	AHL	18	4	11	15	....	....	....	0	....	....	....	....	....	....	....	....	....	....	....	....	....	....	....	....	....	....
	United States	WEC-A	8	5	4	9	....	....	....	14	....	....	....	....	....	....	....	....	....	....	....	....	....	....	....	....	....	....
1981-82	Cincinnati Tigers	CHL	50	16	24	40	....	....	....	6	....	....	....	....	....	....	....	....	....	....	....	....	....	....	....	....	....	....
	Oklahoma City Stars	CHL	21	13	15	28	....	....	....	2	....	....	....	....	....	....	....	....	....	....	4	0	3	3	2	....	....	....
1982-83	Birmingham South Stars	CHL	55	25	28	53	....	....	....	8	....	....	....	....	....	....	....	....	....	....	13	5	5	10	2	....	....	....
1983-84	EHC Wetzikon	Switz-2	38	56	41	97	....	....	....	....	....	....	....	....	....	....	....	....	....	....	....	....	....	....	....	....	....	....
	NHL Totals		**92**	**26**	**26**	**52**	**21**	**18**	**39**	**4**	**2**	**0**	**1**	**166**	**15.7**	**73**	**6**	**85**	**1**		**3**	**0**	**0**	**0**	**0**	**0**	**0**	**0**
	Other Major League Totals		68	13	29	42				11																		

WCHA Second All-Star Team (1976) • WCHA First All-Star Team (1977) • NCAA West First All-American Team (1977) • NCAA Championship All-Tournament Team (1977)

Selected by **New England** (WHA) in 1976 WHA Amateur Draft, June, 1976. WHA rights traded to **Edmonton** (WHA) by **New England** (WHA) to complete transaction that sent Jack Carlson, Steve Carlson, Dave Keon, Dave Dryden and John McKenzie to New England, June, 1977. WHA rights traded to **Cincinnati** (WHA) by **Edmonton** (WHA) with draft choices (later voided) for Dennis Sobchuk, December, 1977. Claimed by **Hartford** from **Cincinnati** (WHA) in WHA Dispersal Draft, June, 1979.

• DeBRUSK, Louie

Louie Dennis LW – L. 6'2", 230 lbs. b: Cambridge, Ont., 3/19/1971. NY Rangers' 4th, 49th overall, in 1989.

			REGULAR SEASON																		PLAYOFFS							
Season	Club	League	GP	G	A	Pts	AG	AA	APts	PIM	PP	SH	GW	S	%	TGF	PGF	TGA	PGA	+/-	GP	G	A	Pts	PIM	PP	SH	GW
1986-87	Port Elgin Huskies	OJHL-C	10	2	1	3	....	....	....	4	....	....	....	....	....	....	....	....	....	....	....	....	....	....	....	....	....	....
1987-88	Stratford Cullitons	OJHL-B	45	13	14	27	....	....	....	205	....	....	....	....	....	....	....	....	....	....	....	....	....	....	....	....	....	....
1988-89	London Knights	OHL	59	11	11	22	....	....	....	149	....	....	....	....	....	....	....	....	....	....	19	1	1	2	43	....	....	....
1989-90	London Knights	OHL	61	21	19	40	....	....	....	198	....	....	....	....	....	....	....	....	....	....	6	2	2	4	24	....	....	....
1990-91	London Knights	OHL	61	31	33	64	....	....	....	*223	....	....	....	....	....	....	....	....	....	....	7	2	2	4	14	....	....	....
	Binghamton Rangers	AHL	2	0	0	0	....	....	....	7	....	....	....	....	....	....	....	....	....	....	2	0	0	0	9	....	....	....
1991-92	**Edmonton Oilers**	**NHL**	**25**	**2**	**1**	**3**	**2**	**1**	**3**	**124**	**0**	**0**	**1**	**7**	**28.6**	**8**	**0**	**4**	**0**	**4**	....	....	....	....	....	....	....	....
	Cape Breton Oilers	AHL	28	2	2	4	....	....	....	73	....	....	....	....	....	....	....	....	....	....	....	....	....	....	....	....	....	....
1992-93	**Edmonton Oilers**	**NHL**	**51**	**8**	**2**	**10**	**7**	**1**	**8**	**205**	**0**	**0**	**1**	**33**	**24.2**	**17**	**3**	**30**	**0**	**–16**	....	....	....	....	....	....	....	....
1993-94	**Edmonton Oilers**	**NHL**	**48**	**4**	**6**	**10**	**4**	**5**	**9**	**185**	**0**	**0**	**0**	**27**	**14.8**	**14**	**1**	**22**	**0**	**–9**	....	....	....	....	....	....	....	....
	Cape Breton Oilers	AHL	5	3	1	4	....	....	....	58	....	....	....	....	....	....	....	....	....	....	....	....	....	....	....	....	....	....
1994-95	**Edmonton Oilers**	**NHL**	**34**	**2**	**0**	**2**	**4**	**0**	**4**	**93**	**0**	**0**	**0**	**14**	**14.3**	**3**	**0**	**7**	**0**	**–4**	....	....	....	....	....	....	....	....
1995-96	**Edmonton Oilers**	**NHL**	**38**	**1**	**3**	**4**	**1**	**2**	**3**	**96**	**0**	**0**	**0**	**17**	**5.9**	**4**	**0**	**11**	**0**	**–7**	....	....	....	....	....	....	....	....
1996-97	**Edmonton Oilers**	**NHL**	**32**	**2**	**0**	**2**	**2**	**0**	**2**	**94**	**0**	**0**	**0**	**10**	**20.0**	**2**	**0**	**8**	**0**	**–6**	**6**	**0**	**0**	**0**	**4**	**0**	**0**	**0**
1997-98	**Tampa Bay Lightning**	**NHL**	**54**	**1**	**2**	**3**	**1**	**2**	**3**	**166**	**0**	**0**	**0**	**14**	**7.1**	**5**	**0**	**7**	**0**	**–2**	....	....	....	....	....	....	....	....
	San Antonio Dragons	IHL	17	7	4	11	....	....	....	130	....	....	....	....	....	....	....	....	....	....	....	....	....	....	....	....	....	....
1998-99	**Phoenix Coyotes**	**NHL**	**15**	**0**	**0**	**0**	**0**	**0**	**0**	**34**	**0**	**0**	**0**	**6**	**0.0**	**0**	**0**	**2**	**0**	**–2**	**6**	**2**	**0**	**2**	**6**	**0**	**0**	**0**
	Las Vegas Thunder	IHL	26	3	6	9	....	....	....	160	....	....	....	....	....	....	....	....	....	....	....	....	....	....	....	....	....	....
	Springfield Falcons	AHL	3	1	0	1	....	....	....	0	....	....	....	....	....	....	....	....	....	....	....	....	....	....	....	....	....	....
	Long Beach Ice Dogs	IHL	24	5	5	10	....	....	....	134	....	....	....	....	....	....	....	....	....	....	....	....	....	....	....	....	....	....
99-2000	**Phoenix Coyotes**	**NHL**	**61**	**4**	**3**	**7**	**4**	**3**	**7**	**78**	**0**	**0**	**0**	**24**	**16.7**	**10**	**0**	**9**	**0**	**1**	**3**	**0**	**0**	**0**	**0**	**0**	**0**	**0**
	NHL Totals		**358**	**24**	**17**	**41**	**25**	**14**	**39**	**1075**	**0**	**0**	**2**	**152**	**15.8**	**63**	**4**	**100**	**0**		**15**	**2**	**0**	**2**	**10**	**0**	**0**	**0**

Traded to **Edmonton** by **NY Rangers** with Bernie Nicholls and Steven Rice for Mark Messier and future considerations (Jeff Beukeboom for David Shaw, November 12, 1991), October 4, 1991. Signed as a free agent by **Tampa Bay**, September 23, 1997. Traded to **Phoenix** by **Tampa Bay** with Tampa Bay's 5th round choice (Jay Leach) in 1998 Entry Draft for Craig Janney, June 11, 1998.

• DEFAZIO, Dean

LW – L. 5'11", 185 lbs. b: Ottawa, Ont., 4/16/1963. Pittsburgh's 8th, 175th overall, in 1981.

Season	Club	League	GP	G	A	Pts	AG	AA	APts	PIM	PP	SH	GW	S	%	TGF	PGF	TGA	PGA	+/-	GP	G	A	Pts	PIM	PP	SH	GW
1979-80	Ottawa Jr. Senators	OJHL	47	27	25	52	....	....	....	80	....	....	....	....	....	....	....	....	....	....	....	....	....	....	....	....	....	....
1980-81	Brantford Alexanders	OMJHL	60	6	13	19	....	....	....	104	....	....	....	....	....	....	....	....	....	....	6	1	0	1	19	....	....	....
1981-82	Brantford Alexanders	OHL	10	2	6	8	....	....	....	30	....	....	....	....	....	....	....	....	....	....	....	....	....	....	....	....	....	....
	Sudbury Wolves	OHL	50	21	32	53	....	....	....	81	....	....	....	....	....	....	....	....	....	....	....	....	....	....	....	....	....	....
1982-83	Oshawa Generals	OHL	52	22	23	45	....	....	....	108	....	....	....	....	....	....	....	....	....	....	17	8	9	17	16	....	....	....
	Oshawa Generals	Mem-Cup	5	1	1	2	....	....	....	*36	....	....	....	....	....	....	....	....	....	....	....	....	....	....	....	....	....	....
1983-84	**Pittsburgh Penguins**	**NHL**	**22**	**0**	**2**	**2**	**0**	**1**	**1**	**28**	**0**	**0**	**0**	**12**	**0.0**	**4**	**0**	**15**	**0**	**–11**	....	....	....	....	....	....	....	....
	Baltimore Skipjacks	AHL	46	18	13	31	....	....	....	114	....	....	....	....	....	....	....	....	....	....	10	2	2	4	19	....	....	....
1984-85	Baltimore Skipjacks	AHL	78	10	17	27	....	....	....	88	....	....	....	....	....	....	....	....	....	....	10	2	1	3	64	....	....	....
1985-86	Baltimore Skipjacks	AHL	75	14	24	38	....	....	....	171	....	....	....	....	....	....	....	....	....	....	....	....	....	....	....	....	....	....
1986-87	Newmarket Saints	AHL	76	7	13	20	....	....	....	116	....	....	....	....	....	....	....	....	....	....	....	....	....	....	....	....	....	....
1987-88	Baltimore Skipjacks	AHL	22	1	2	3	....	....	....	75	....	....	....	....	....	....	....	....	....	....	....	....	....	....	....	....	....	....
	New Haven Nighthawks	AHL	26	5	12	17	....	....	....	21	....	....	....	....	....	....	....	....	....	....	....	....	....	....	....	....	....	....
	Flint Spirits	IHL	30	8	6	14	....	....	....	39	....	....	....	....	....	....	....	....	....	....	....	....	....	....	....	....	....	....
1988-89	EHC Straubing	Germany-3	7	5	3	8	....	....	....	18	....	....	....	....	....	....	....	....	....	....	9	5	12	17	8	....	....	....
	NHL Totals		**22**	**0**	**2**	**2**	**0**	**1**	**1**	**28**	**0**	**0**	**0**	**12**	**0.0**	**4**	**0**	**15**	**0**		....	....	....	....	....	....	....	....

• DEGRAY, Dale

Dale Edward "Digger" D – R. 6', 200 lbs. b: Oshawa, Ont., 9/1/1963. Calgary's 7th, 162nd overall, in 1981.

Season	Club	League	GP	G	A	Pts	AG	AA	APts	PIM	PP	SH	GW	S	%	TGF	PGF	TGA	PGA	+/-	GP	G	A	Pts	PIM	PP	SH	GW
1979-80	Oshawa Legionaires	OJHL	43	14	14	28	....	....	....	34	....	....	....	....	....	....	....	....	....	....	....	....	....	....	....	....	....	....
	Oshawa Generals	OMJHL	1	0	0	0	....	....	....	2	....	....	....	....	....	....	....	....	....	....	....	....	....	....	....	....	....	....
1980-81	Oshawa Generals	OMJHL	61	11	10	21	....	....	....	93	....	....	....	....	....	....	....	....	....	....	8	1	1	2	19	....	....	....
1981-82	Oshawa Generals	OHL	66	11	23	34	....	....	....	162	....	....	....	....	....	....	....	....	....	....	12	3	4	7	49	....	....	....
1982-83	Oshawa Generals	OHL	69	20	30	50	....	....	....	149	....	....	....	....	....	....	....	....	....	....	17	7	7	14	36	....	....	....
	Oshawa Generals	Mem-Cup	5	2	3	5	....	....	....	14	....	....	....	....	....	....	....	....	....	....	....	....	....	....	....	....	....	....
1983-84	Colorado Flames	CHL	67	16	14	30	....	....	....	67	....	....	....	....	....	....	....	....	....	....	6	1	1	2	2	....	....	....
1984-85	Moncton Golden Flames	AHL	77	24	37	61	....	....	....	63	....	....	....	....	....	....	....	....	....	....	....	....	....	....	....	....	....	....
1985-86	**Calgary Flames**	**NHL**	**1**	**0**	**0**	**0**	**0**	**0**	**0**	**0**	**0**	**0**	**0**	**1**	**0.0**	**1**	**0**	**2**	**0**	**–1**	....	....	....	....	....	....	....	....
	Moncton Golden Flames	AHL	76	10	31	41	....	....	....	128	....	....	....	....	....	....	....	....	....	....	6	0	1	1	0	....	....	....
1986-87	**Calgary Flames**	**NHL**	**27**	**6**	**7**	**13**	**5**	**5**	**10**	**29**	**0**	**0**	**1**	**57**	**10.5**	**20**	**1**	**26**	**4**	**–3**	....	....	....	....	....	....	....	....
	Moncton Golden Flames	AHL	45	10	22	32	....	....	....	57	....	....	....	....	....	....	....	....	....	....	5	2	1	3	19	....	....	....
1987-88	**Toronto Maple Leafs**	**NHL**	**56**	**6**	**18**	**24**	**5**	**13**	**18**	**63**	**1**	**0**	**1**	**122**	**4.9**	**62**	**19**	**50**	**11**	**4**	**5**	**0**	**1**	**1**	**16**	**0**	**0**	**0**
	Newmarket Saints	AHL	8	2	10	12	....	....	....	8	....	....	....	....	....	....	....	....	....	....	....	....	....	....	....	....	....	....
1988-89	**Los Angeles Kings**	**NHL**	**63**	**6**	**22**	**28**	**5**	**16**	**21**	**97**	**0**	**0**	**1**	**87**	**6.9**	**77**	**18**	**64**	**8**	**3**	**8**	**1**	**2**	**3**	**12**	**1**	**0**	**0**
1989-90	New Haven Nighthawks	AHL	16	2	10	12	....	....	....	38	....	....	....	....	....	....	....	....	....	....	....	....	....	....	....	....	....	....
	Buffalo Sabres	**NHL**	**6**	**0**	**0**	**0**	**0**	**0**	**0**	**6**	**0**	**0**	**0**	**5**	**0.0**	**2**	**0**	**6**	**0**	**–4**	....	....	....	....	....	....	....	....
	Rochester Americans	AHL	50	6	25	31	....	....	....	118	....	....	....	....	....	....	....	....	....	....	17	5	6	11	59	....	....	....
1990-91	Rochester Americans	AHL	64	9	25	34	....	....	....	121	....	....	....	....	....	....	....	....	....	....	15	3	4	7	*76	....	....	....
1991-92	HC Alleghe	Alpenliga	18	10	12	22	....	....	....	74	....	....	....	....	....	....	....	....	....	....	....	....	....	....	....	....	....	....
	HC Alleghe	Italy	18	6	16	22	....	....	....	36	....	....	....	....	....	....	....	....	....	....	9	0	6	6	10	....	....	....
1992-93	San Diego Gulls	IHL	79	18	64	82	....	....	....	181	....	....	....	....	....	....	....	....	....	....	14	3	11	14	77	....	....	....
1993-94	San Diego Gulls	IHL	80	20	50	70	....	....	....	163	....	....	....	....	....	....	....	....	....	....	9	2	1	3	8	....	....	....
1994-95	Detroit Vipers	IHL	14	1	8	9	....	....	....	18	....	....	....	....	....	....	....	....	....	....	....	....	....	....	....	....	....	....
	Cleveland Lumberjacks	IHL	64	19	49	68	....	....	....	134	....	....	....	....	....	....	....	....	....	....	4	0	4	4	10	....	....	....
	Canada	WC-A	6	1	1	2	....	....	....	6	....	....	....	....	....	....	....	....	....	....	....	....	....	....	....	....	....	....
1995-96	Cincinnati Cyclones	IHL	79	13	46	59	....	....	....	96	....	....	....	....	....	....	....	....	....	....	16	1	6	7	35	....	....	....
1996-97	Manitoba Moose	IHL	44	9	15	24	....	....	....	42	....	....	....	....	....	....	....	....	....	....	....	....	....	....	....	....	....	....
	Cincinnati Cyclones	IHL	30	5	16	21	....	....	....	55	....	....	....	....	....	....	....	....	....	....	....	....	....	....	....	....	....	....
1997-98	Manitoba Moose	IHL	15	0	7	7	....	....	....	16	....	....	....	....	....	....	....	....	....	....	....	....	....	....	....	....	....	....
	Quebec Rafales	IHL	31	4	9	13	....	....	....	27	....	....	....	....	....	....	....	....	....	....	....	....	....	....	....	....	....	....
	Cleveland Lumberjacks	IHL	11	1	9	10	....	....	....	4	....	....	....	....	....	....	....	....	....	....	9	3	7	10	8	....	....	....
1998-99	Indianapolis Ice	IHL	27	3	11	14	....	....	....	18	....	....	....	....	....	....	....	....	....	....	....	....	....	....	....	....	....	....
99-2000	Rockford IceHogs	UHL	DID NOT PLAY – COACHING																									
	NHL Totals		**153**	**18**	**47**	**65**	**15**	**34**	**49**	**195**	**1**	**0**	**3**	**272**	**6.6**	**162**	**38**	**148**	**23**		**13**	**1**	**3**	**4**	**28**	**1**	**0**	**0**

AHL Second All-Star Team (1985) • IHL Second All-Star Team (1993, 1995)

Traded to **Toronto** by **Calgary** for Toronto's 5th round choice (Scott Matusovich) in 1988 Entry Draft, September 17, 1987. Claimed by **LA Kings** from **Toronto** in Waiver Draft, October 3, 1988. Traded to **Buffalo** by **LA Kings** for Bob Halkidis, November 24, 1989. • Suffered career-ending shoulder injury in game vs. Orlando (IHL), December 10, 1998.

• DELISLE, Jonathan

RW – R. 5'10", 180 lbs. b: Ste-Anne-des-Plaines, Que., 6/30/1977. Montreal's 4th, 86th overall, in 1995.

Season	Club	League	GP	G	A	Pts	AG	AA	APts	PIM	PP	SH	GW	S	%	TGF	PGF	TGA	PGA	+/-	GP	G	A	Pts	PIM	PP	SH	GW
1992-93	Laval Regents	QAAA	14	3	3	6	....	....	....	12	....	....	....	....	....	....	....	....	....	....	13	2	5	7	24	....	....	....
1993-94	Verdun College-Francais	QMJHL	61	16	17	33	....	....	....	130	....	....	....	....	....	....	....	....	....	....	4	0	1	1	14	....	....	....
1994-95	Hull Olympiques	QMJHL	60	21	38	59	....	....	....	218	....	....	....	....	....	....	....	....	....	....	19	11	8	19	43	....	....	....
	Hull Olympiques	Mem-Cup	3	2	0	2	....	....	....	12	....	....	....	....	....	....	....	....	....	....	....	....	....	....	....	....	....	....
1995-96	Hull Olympiques	QMJHL	62	31	57	88	....	....	....	193	....	....	....	....	....	....	....	....	....	....	18	6	13	19	64	....	....	....
1996-97	Hull Olympiques	QMJHL	61	35	54	89	....	....	....	228	....	....	....	....	....	....	....	....	....	....	14	11	13	24	46	....	....	....
	Hull Olympiques	Mem-Cup	4	1	6	7	....	....	....	12	....	....	....	....	....	....	....	....	....	....	....	....	....	....	....	....	....	....
1997-98	Fredericton Canadiens	AHL	78	15	21	36	....	....	....	138	....	....	....	....	....	....	....	....	....	....	4	0	1	1	7	....	....	....
1998-99	**Montreal Canadiens**	**NHL**	**1**	**0**	**0**	**0**	**0**	**0**	**0**	**0**	**0**	**0**	**0**	**0**	**0.0**	**0**	**0**	**0**	**0**	**0**	....	....	....	....	....	....	....	....
	Fredericton Canadiens	AHL	78	7	29	36	....	....	....	118	....	....	....	....	....	....	....	....	....	....	15	3	6	9	39	....	....	....
99-2000	Quebec Citadelles	AHL	62	7	19	26	....	....	....	142	....	....	....	....	....	....	....	....	....	....	3	0	0	0	4	....	....	....
	NHL Totals		**1**	**0**	**0**	**0**	**0**	**0**	**0**	**0**	**0**	**0**	**0**	**0**	**0.0**	**0**	**0**	**0**	**0**		....	....	....	....	....	....	....	....

			REGULAR SEASON																		PLAYOFFS							
Season	Club	League	GP	G	A	Pts	AG	AA	APts	PIM	PP	SH	GW	S	%	TGF	PGF	TGA	PGA	+/–	GP	G	A	Pts	PIM	PP	SH	GW

• DELISLE, Xavier

C – R. 5'11", 182 lbs. b: Quebec City, Que., 5/24/1977. Tampa Bay's 5th, 157th overall, in 1996.

Season	Club	League	GP	G	A	Pts	AG	AA	APts	PIM	PP	SH	GW	S	%	TGF	PGF	TGA	PGA	+/–	GP	G	A	Pts	PIM	PP	SH	GW
1992-93	Ste-Foy Gouverneurs	QAAA	41	20	23	43	....	....	....	....	....	....	....	....	....	....	....	....	....	....	....	....	....	....	....	....	....	....
1993-94	Granby Bisons	QMJHL	46	11	22	33	....	....	....	25	....	....	....	....	....	....	....	....	....	....	7	2	0	2	0	....	....	....
1994-95	Granby Bisons	QMJHL	72	18	36	54	....	....	....	48	....	....	....	....	....	....	....	....	....	....	13	2	6	8	4	....	....	....
1995-96	Granby Bisons	QMJHL	67	45	75	120	....	....	....	45	....	....	....	....	....	....	....	....	....	....	20	13	*27	*40	12	....	....	....
	Granby Bisons	Mem-Cup	4	2	2	4	....	....	....	5	....	....	....	....	....	....	....	....	....	....	....	....	....	....	....	....	....	....
1996-97	Granby Bisons	QMJHL	59	36	56	92	....	....	....	20	....	....	....	....	....	....	....	....	....	....	5	1	4	5	6	....	....	....
1997-98	Adirondack Red Wings	AHL	76	10	19	29	....	....	....	47	....	....	....	....	....	....	....	....	....	....	3	0	0	0	0	....	....	....
1998-99	**Tampa Bay Lightning**	**NHL**	2	0	0	0	0	0	0	0	0	0	0	1	0.0	0	0	0	0	0	....	....	....	....	....	....	....	....
	Cleveland Lumberjacks	IHL	77	15	29	44	....	....	....	36	....	....	....	....	....	....	....	....	....	....	....	....	....	....	....	....	....	....
99-2000	Detroit Vipers	IHL	20	2	6	8	....	....	....	18	....	....	....	....	....	....	....	....	....	....	....	....	....	....	....	....	....	....
	Toledo Storm	ECHL	2	0	1	1	....	....	....	0	....	....	....	....	....	....	....	....	....	....	....	....	....	....	....	....	....	....
	Quebec Citadelles	AHL	42	17	28	45	....	....	....	8	....	....	....	....	....	....	....	....	....	....	3	1	2	3	0	....	....	....
	NHL Totals		**2**	**0**	**0**	**0**	**0**	**0**	**0**	**0**	**0**	**0**	**0**	**1**	**0.0**	**0**	**0**	**0**	**0**		....	....	....	....	....	....	....	....

QMJHL Second All-Star Team (1996) • Memorial Cup All-Star Team (1996)

• DELMORE, Andy

D – R. 6'1", 192 lbs. b: LaSalle, Ont., 12/26/1976.

Season	Club	League	GP	G	A	Pts	AG	AA	APts	PIM	PP	SH	GW	S	%	TGF	PGF	TGA	PGA	+/–	GP	G	A	Pts	PIM	PP	SH	GW
1992-93	Chatham Maroons	OJHL-B	47	4	21	25	....	....	....	38	....	....	....	....	....	....	....	....	....	....	....	....	....	....	....	....	....	....
1993-94	North Bay Centennials	OHL	45	2	7	9	....	....	....	33	....	....	....	....	....	....	....	....	....	....	17	0	0	0	2	....	....	....
	North Bay Centennials	Mem-Cup	3	0	0	0	....	....	....	0	....	....	....	....	....	....	....	....	....	....	....	....	....	....	....	....	....	....
1994-95	North Bay Centennials	OHL	40	2	14	16	....	....	....	21	....	....	....	....	....	....	....	....	....	....	....	....	....	....	....	....	....	....
	Sarnia Sting	OHL	27	5	13	18	....	....	....	27	....	....	....	....	....	....	....	....	....	....	3	0	0	0	2	....	....	....
1995-96	Sarnia Sting	OHL	64	21	38	59	....	....	....	45	....	....	....	....	....	....	....	....	....	....	10	3	7	10	2	....	....	....
1996-97	Sarnia Sting	OHL	64	18	60	78	....	....	....	39	....	....	....	....	....	....	....	....	....	....	12	2	10	12	10	....	....	....
	Fredericton Canadiens	AHL	4	0	1	1	....	....	....	0	....	....	....	....	....	....	....	....	....	....	....	....	....	....	....	....	....	....
1997-98	Philadelphia Phantoms	AHL	73	9	30	39	....	....	....	46	....	....	....	....	....	....	....	....	....	....	18	4	4	8	21	....	....	....
1998-99	**Philadelphia Flyers**	**NHL**	2	0	1	1	0	1	1	0	0	0	0	2	0.0	2	1	4	2	–1	....	....	....	....	....	....	....	....
	Philadelphia Phantoms	AHL	70	5	18	23	....	....	....	51	....	....	....	....	....	....	....	....	....	....	15	1	4	5	6	....	....	....
99-2000	**Philadelphia Flyers**	**NHL**	27	2	5	7	2	5	7	8	0	0	1	55	3.6	18	6	16	3	–1	18	5	2	7	14	1	0	1
	Philadelphia Phantoms	AHL	39	12	14	26	....	....	....	31	....	....	....	....	....	....	....	....	....	....	....	....	....	....	....	....	....	....
	NHL Totals		**29**	**2**	**6**	**8**	**2**	**6**	**8**	**8**	**0**	**0**	**1**	**57**	**3.5**	**20**	**7**	**20**	**5**		**18**	**5**	**2**	**7**	**14**	**1**	**0**	**1**

OHL First All-Star Team (1997)

Signed as a free agent by **Philadelphia**, June 9, 1997.

• DELORME, Gilbert

D – R. 6'1", 199 lbs. b: Boucherville, Que., 11/25/1962. Montreal's 2nd, 18th overall, in 1981.

Season	Club	League	GP	G	A	Pts	AG	AA	APts	PIM	PP	SH	GW	S	%	TGF	PGF	TGA	PGA	+/–	GP	G	A	Pts	PIM	PP	SH	GW
1977-78	Richelieu Cantonniers	QAAA	40	7	25	32	....	....	....	32	....	....	....	....	....	....	....	....	....	....	....	....	....	....	....	....	....	....
1978-79	Chicoutimi Sagueneens	QMJHL	72	13	47	60	....	....	....	53	....	....	....	....	....	....	....	....	....	....	....	....	....	....	....	....	....	....
1979-80	Chicoutimi Sagueneens	QMJHL	71	25	86	111	....	....	....	68	....	....	....	....	....	....	....	....	....	....	12	2	10	12	26	....	....	....
1980-81	Chicoutimi Sagueneens	QMJHL	70	27	79	106	....	....	....	77	....	....	....	....	....	....	....	....	....	....	12	10	12	22	16	....	....	....
	Canada	WJC-A	5	1	0	1	....	....	....	0	....	....	....	....	....	....	....	....	....	....	....	....	....	....	....	....	....	....
1981-82	**Montreal Canadiens**	**NHL**	60	3	8	11	2	5	7	55	0	0	0	80	3.8	55	2	43	9	19	....	....	....	....	....	....	....	....
1982-83	**Montreal Canadiens**	**NHL**	78	12	21	33	10	15	25	89	3	0	2	166	7.2	116	16	83	10	27	3	0	0	0	2	0	0	0
1983-84	**Montreal Canadiens**	**NHL**	27	2	7	9	2	5	7	8	0	0	0	37	5.4	24	2	28	2	–4	....	....	....	....	....	....	....	....
	St. Louis Blues	**NHL**	44	0	5	5	0	3	3	41	0	0	0	68	0.0	30	6	37	6	–7	11	1	3	4	11	0	0	0
1984-85	**St. Louis Blues**	**NHL**	74	2	12	14	2	8	10	53	1	0	0	85	2.4	76	4	97	32	7	3	0	0	0	0	0	0	0
1985-86	**Quebec Nordiques**	**NHL**	64	2	18	20	2	12	14	51	1	0	0	102	2.0	86	26	73	12	–1	2	0	0	0	5	0	0	0
1986-87	**Quebec Nordiques**	**NHL**	19	2	0	2	2	0	2	14	0	0	0	22	9.1	13	0	17	3	–1	....	....	....	....	....	....	....	....
	Detroit Red Wings	**NHL**	24	2	3	5	2	2	4	33	0	0	0	24	8.3	17	0	28	10	–1	16	0	2	2	14	0	0	0
1987-88	**Detroit Red Wings**	**NHL**	55	2	8	10	2	6	8	81	0	0	0	46	4.3	45	0	52	16	9	15	0	3	3	22	0	0	0
1988-89	**Detroit Red Wings**	**NHL**	42	1	3	4	1	2	3	51	0	0	0	23	4.3	27	1	46	9	–11	6	0	1	1	2	0	0	0
1989-90	**Pittsburgh Penguins**	**NHL**	54	3	7	10	3	5	8	44	0	0	0	37	8.1	46	1	57	15	3	....	....	....	....	....	....	....	....
1990-91	**Pittsburgh Penguins**	**NHL**	DID NOT PLAY – INJURED																		....	....	....	....	....	....	....	....
1991-92	Muskegon Lumberjacks	IHL	60	6	6	12	....	....	....	89	....	....	....	....	....	....	....	....	....	....	7	2	2	4	12	....	....	....
	NHL Totals		**541**	**31**	**92**	**123**	**28**	**63**	**91**	**520**	**5**	**0**	**2**	**690**	**4.5**	**535**	**58**	**561**	**124**		**56**	**1**	**9**	**10**	**56**	**0**	**0**	**0**

QMJHL Second All-Star Team (1981)

Traded to **St. Louis** by **Montreal** with Greg Paslawski and Doug Wickenheiser for Perry Turnbull, December 21, 1983. Traded to **Quebec** by **St. Louis** for Bruce Bell, October 2, 1985. Traded to **Detroit** by **Quebec** with Brent Ashton and Mark Kumpel for Basil McRae, John Ogrodnick and Doug Shedden, January 17, 1987. Signed as a free agent by **Pittsburgh**, June 28, 1989. • Missed entire 1990-91 season recovering from broken leg suffered during dryland training, July, 1990. • Played w/ RHI's Montreal Roadrunner in 1996 (1-0-0-0-1).

• DELORME, Ron

Ronald Elmer "Chief" C – R. 6'2", 185 lbs. b: North Battleford, Sask., 9/3/1955. Kansas City's 4th, 56th overall, in 1975.

Season	Club	League	GP	G	A	Pts	AG	AA	APts	PIM	PP	SH	GW	S	%	TGF	PGF	TGA	PGA	+/–	GP	G	A	Pts	PIM	PP	SH	GW
1972-73	Prince Albert Mintos	SJHL	45	14	22	36	....	....	....	....	....	....	....	....	....	....	....	....	....	....	....	....	....	....	....	....	....	....
1973-74	Swift Current Broncos	WCJHL	59	19	15	34	....	....	....	96	....	....	....	....	....	....	....	....	....	....	13	1	2	3	17	....	....	....
1974-75	Lethbridge Broncos	WCJHL	69	30	57	87	....	....	....	144	....	....	....	....	....	....	....	....	....	....	6	1	7	8	20	....	....	....
1975-76	Lethbridge Broncos	WCJHL	26	8	12	20	....	....	....	87	....	....	....	....	....	....	....	....	....	....	7	3	6	9	24	....	....	....
	Denver-Ottawa Civics	WHA	22	1	3	4	....	....	....	28	....	....	....	....	....	....	....	....	....	....	....	....	....	....	....	....	....	....
	Tucson Mavericks	CHL	18	2	5	7	....	....	....	18	....	....	....	....	....	....	....	....	....	....	....	....	....	....	....	....	....	....
1976-77	Baltimore Clippers	SHL	25	4	6	10	....	....	....	4	....	....	....	....	....	....	....	....	....	....	....	....	....	....	....	....	....	....
	Colorado Rockies	**NHL**	29	6	4	10	5	3	8	23	0	0	2	31	19.4	16	2	27	2	–11	....	....	....	....	....	....	....	....
	Tulsa Oilers	CHL	6	1	2	3	....	....	....	0	....	....	....	....	....	....	....	....	....	....	....	....	....	....	....	....	....	....
1977-78	**Colorado Rockies**	**NHL**	68	10	11	21	9	8	17	47	0	0	0	76	13.2	35	3	53	1	–20	2	0	0	0	10	0	0	0
1978-79	**Colorado Rockies**	**NHL**	77	20	8	28	17	6	23	68	2	0	3	85	23.5	40	4	67	1	–30	....	....	....	....	....	....	....	....
1979-80	**Colorado Rockies**	**NHL**	75	19	24	43	16	17	33	76	5	0	4	98	19.4	75	26	73	0	–24	....	....	....	....	....	....	....	....
1980-81	**Colorado Rockies**	**NHL**	65	11	16	27	9	11	20	70	3	0	0	65	16.9	58	13	56	0	–11	....	....	....	....	....	....	....	....
1981-82	**Vancouver Canucks**	**NHL**	59	9	8	17	7	5	12	177	0	0	0	47	19.1	29	0	38	1	–8	15	0	2	2	31	0	0	0
1982-83	**Vancouver Canucks**	**NHL**	56	5	8	13	4	6	10	87	0	0	0	38	13.2	21	0	27	0	–6	4	0	0	0	10	0	0	0
1983-84	**Vancouver Canucks**	**NHL**	64	2	2	4	2	1	3	68	0	0	0	18	11.1	13	0	15	0	–2	4	1	0	1	8	0	0	0
1984-85	**Vancouver Canucks**	**NHL**	31	1	2	3	1	1	2	51	0	0	0	13	7.7	4	0	13	1	–8	....	....	....	....	....	....	....	....
	NHL Totals		**524**	**83**	**83**	**166**	**70**	**58**	**128**	**667**	**10**	**0**	**9**	**471**	**17.6**	**291**	**48**	**369**	**6**		**25**	**1**	**2**	**3**	**59**	**0**	**0**	**0**
	Other Major League Totals		22	1	3	4	....	....	....	28	....	....	....	....	....	....	....	....	....	....	....	....	....	....	....	....	....	....

Selected by **Denver** (WHA) in 1975 WHA Amateur Draft, June, 1975. Rights transferred to **Colorado** after **Kansas City** franchise relocated, July 15, 1976. Claimed by **Vancouver** from **Colorado** in Waiver Draft, October 5, 1981.

• DELPARTE, Guy

Guy Phillipe LW – L. 5'10", 175 lbs. b: Sault Ste. Marie, Ont., 8/30/1949. Montreal's 6th, 63rd overall, in 1969.

Season	Club	League	GP	G	A	Pts	AG	AA	APts	PIM	PP	SH	GW	S	%	TGF	PGF	TGA	PGA	+/–	GP	G	A	Pts	PIM	PP	SH	GW
1966-67	Garson Native Sons	NOJHA	STATISTICS NOT AVAILABLE																									
1967-68	Sudbury Wolves	NOJHA	STATISTICS NOT AVAILABLE																									
1968-69	St. Catharines Black Hawks	OHA-Jr.	24	4	11	15	....	....	....	34	....	....	....	....	....	....	....	....	....	....	....	....	....	....	....	....	....	....
	London Knights	OHA-Jr.	32	6	17	23	....	....	....	62	....	....	....	....	....	....	....	....	....	....	6	1	2	3	20	....	....	....
1969-70	Johnstown Jets	EHL	68	31	39	70	....	....	....	28	....	....	....	....	....	....	....	....	....	....	9	1	5	6	0	....	....	....
1970-71	Johnstown Jets	EHL	67	11	27	38	....	....	....	66	....	....	....	....	....	....	....	....	....	....	10	5	3	8	30	....	....	....
1971-72	Johnstown Jets	EHL	75	25	41	66	....	....	....	66	....	....	....	....	....	....	....	....	....	....	11	5	8	13	8	....	....	....
1972-73	Nova Scotia Voyageurs	AHL	64	8	12	20	....	....	....	42	....	....	....	....	....	....	....	....	....	....	8	0	0	0	2	....	....	....
1973-74	Nova Scotia Voyageurs	AHL	69	8	24	32	....	....	....	107	....	....	....	....	....	....	....	....	....	....	6	0	2	2	17	....	....	....
1974-75	Nova Scotia Voyageurs	AHL	53	10	11	21	....	....	....	127	....	....	....	....	....	....	....	....	....	....	6	1	2	3	14	....	....	....
1975-76	Oklahoma City Blazers	CHL	72	10	14	24	....	....	....	74	....	....	....	....	....	....	....	....	....	....	4	0	3	3	0	....	....	....
1976-77	**Colorado Rockies**	**NHL**	48	1	8	9	1	6	7	18	0	0	0	37	2.7	19	1	35	7	–10	....	....	....	....	....	....	....	....
	Rhode Island Reds	AHL	11	0	3	3	....	....	....	8	....	....	....	....	....	....	....	....	....	....	....	....	....	....	....	....	....	....
	Oklahoma City Blazers	CHL	16	4	5	9	....	....	....	10	....	....	....	....	....	....	....	....	....	....	....	....	....	....	....	....	....	....

			REGULAR SEASON																		PLAYOFFS							
Season	Club	League	GP	G	A	Pts	AG	AA	APts	PIM	PP	SH	GW	S	%	TGF	PGF	TGA	PGA	+/–	GP	G	A	Pts	PIM	PP	SH	GW
1977-78	Maine Mariners	AHL	78	16	21	37	....	....	....	82	....	....	....	....	....	....	....	....	....	....	12	3	1	4	11	....	....	....
1978-79	Maine Mariners	AHL	67	10	26	36	....	....	....	63	....	....	....	....	....	....	....	....	....	....	....	....	....	....	....	....	....	....
1979-80	Maine Mariners	AHL	78	10	20	30	....	....	....	111	....	....	....	....	....	....	....	....	....	....	9	0	3	3	0	....	....	....
1980-81	Springfield Indians	AHL	73	3	7	10	....	....	....	81	....	....	....	....	....	....	....	....	....	....	7	1	3	4	24	....	....	....
	NHL Totals		**48**	**1**	**8**	**9**	**1**	**6**	**7**	**18**	**0**	**0**	**0**	**37**	**2.7**	**19**	**1**	**35**	**7**		....	....	....	....	....	....	....	....

Signed as a free agent by **Colorado**, October 4, 1976. Signed as a free agent by **Philadelphia**, September, 1977.

• DELVECCHIO, Alex

Alex Peter "Fats" C/LW – L. 6′, 195 lbs. b: Fort William, Ont., 12/4/1932. **HHOF**

Season	Club	League	GP	G	A	Pts	AG	AA	APts	PIM	PP	SH	GW	S	%	TGF	PGF	TGA	PGA	+/–	GP	G	A	Pts	PIM	PP	SH	GW
1947-48	Fort William Rangers	TBJHL	1	0	0	0	....	....	....	0	....	....	....	....	....	....	....	....	....	....	....	....	....	....	....	....	....	....
1948-49	Fort William Rangers	TBJHL	12	16	8	24	....	....	....	*53	....	....	....	....	....	....	....	....	....	....	1	2	0	2	0	....	....	....
	Port Arthur Bruins	Mem-Cup	5	2	2	4	....	....	....	1	....	....	....	....	....	....	....	....	....	....	....	....	....	....	....	....	....	....
1949-50	Fort William Rangers	TBJHL	18	16	*20	36	....	....	....	36	....	....	....	....	....	....	....	....	....	....	5	4	4	8	15	....	....	....
1950-51	Oshawa Generals	OHA-Jr.	54	49	*72	121	....	....	....	36	....	....	....	....	....	....	....	....	....	....	....	....	....	....	....	....	....	....
	Detroit Red Wings	**NHL**	**1**	**0**	**0**	**0**	**0**	**0**	**0**	**0**	....	....	....	....	....	....	....	....	....	....	....	....	....	....	....	....	....	....
1951-52♦	**Detroit Red Wings**	**NHL**	**65**	**15**	**22**	**37**	**20**	**27**	**47**	**22**	....	....	....	....	....	....	....	....	....	....	**8**	**0**	**3**	**3**	**4**	....	....	....
	Indianapolis Capitols	AHL	6	3	6	9	....	....	....	4	....	....	....	....	....	....	....	....	....	....	....	....	....	....	....	....	....	....
1952-53	**Detroit Red Wings**	**NHL**	**70**	**16**	**43**	**59**	**21**	**53**	**74**	**28**	....	....	....	....	....	....	....	....	....	....	**6**	**2**	**4**	**6**	**2**	....	....	....
1953-54♦	**Detroit Red Wings**	**NHL**	**69**	**11**	**18**	**29**	**15**	**22**	**37**	**34**	....	....	....	....	....	....	....	....	....	....	**12**	**2**	**7**	**9**	**7**	....	....	....
1954-55♦	**Detroit Red Wings**	**NHL**	**69**	**17**	**31**	**48**	**22**	**36**	**58**	**37**	....	....	....	....	....	....	....	....	....	....	**11**	**7**	**8**	**15**	**2**	....	....	....
1955-56	**Detroit Red Wings**	**NHL**	**70**	**25**	**26**	**51**	**34**	**31**	**65**	**24**	....	....	....	....	....	....	....	....	....	....	**10**	**7**	**3**	**10**	**2**	....	....	....
1956-57	**Detroit Red Wings**	**NHL**	**48**	**16**	**25**	**41**	**21**	**28**	**49**	**8**	....	....	....	....	....	....	....	....	....	....	**5**	**3**	**2**	**5**	**2**	....	....	....
1957-58	**Detroit Red Wings**	**NHL**	**70**	**21**	**38**	**59**	**26**	**40**	**66**	**22**	....	....	....	....	....	....	....	....	....	....	**4**	**0**	**1**	**1**	**0**	....	....	....
1958-59	**Detroit Red Wings**	**NHL**	**70**	**19**	**35**	**54**	**23**	**36**	**59**	**6**	....	....	....	....	....	....	....	....	....	....	....	....	....	....	....	....	....	....
1959-60	**Detroit Red Wings**	**NHL**	**70**	**19**	**28**	**47**	**22**	**27**	**49**	**8**	....	....	....	....	....	....	....	....	....	....	**6**	**2**	**6**	**8**	**0**	....	....	....
1960-61	**Detroit Red Wings**	**NHL**	**70**	**27**	**35**	**62**	**31**	**34**	**65**	**26**	....	....	....	....	....	....	....	....	....	....	**11**	**4**	**5**	**9**	**0**	....	....	....
1961-62	**Detroit Red Wings**	**NHL**	**70**	**26**	**43**	**69**	**30**	**42**	**72**	**18**	....	....	....	....	....	....	....	....	....	....	....	....	....	....	....	....	....	....
1962-63	**Detroit Red Wings**	**NHL**	**70**	**20**	**44**	**64**	**23**	**44**	**67**	**8**	....	....	....	....	....	....	....	....	....	....	**11**	**3**	**6**	**9**	**2**	....	....	....
1963-64	**Detroit Red Wings**	**NHL**	**70**	**23**	**30**	**53**	**29**	**32**	**61**	**11**	....	....	....	....	....	....	....	....	....	....	**14**	**3**	**8**	**11**	**0**	....	....	....
1964-65	**Detroit Red Wings**	**NHL**	**68**	**25**	**42**	**67**	**30**	**44**	**74**	**16**	....	....	....	....	....	....	....	....	....	....	**7**	**2**	**3**	**5**	**4**	....	....	....
1965-66	**Detroit Red Wings**	**NHL**	**70**	**31**	**38**	**69**	**36**	**36**	**72**	**16**	....	....	....	....	....	....	....	....	....	....	**12**	**0**	***11**	**11**	**4**	....	....	....
1966-67	**Detroit Red Wings**	**NHL**	**70**	**17**	**38**	**55**	**20**	**37**	**57**	**10**	....	....	....	....	....	....	....	....	....	....	....	....	....	....	....	....	....	....
1967-68	**Detroit Red Wings**	**NHL**	**74**	**22**	**48**	**70**	**26**	**48**	**74**	**14**	**3**	**0**	**2**	**212**	**10.4**	**106**	**28**	**90**	**20**	**8**	....	....	....	....	....	....	....	....
1968-69	**Detroit Red Wings**	**NHL**	**72**	**25**	**58**	**83**	**27**	**52**	**79**	**8**	**7**	**0**	**2**	**221**	**11.3**	**123**	**28**	**63**	**11**	**43**	....	....	....	....	....	....	....	....
1969-70	**Detroit Red Wings**	**NHL**	**73**	**21**	**47**	**68**	**23**	**44**	**67**	**24**	**4**	**0**	**3**	**218**	**9.6**	**100**	**36**	**57**	**19**	**26**	**4**	**0**	**2**	**2**	**0**	**0**	**0**	**0**
1970-71	**Detroit Red Wings**	**NHL**	**77**	**21**	**34**	**55**	**21**	**28**	**49**	**6**	**6**	**0**	**2**	**171**	**12.3**	**87**	**36**	**91**	**22**	**–18**	....	....	....	....	....	....	....	....
1971-72	**Detroit Red Wings**	**NHL**	**75**	**20**	**45**	**65**	**20**	**39**	**59**	**22**	**9**	**0**	**5**	**123**	**16.3**	**90**	**29**	**80**	**0**	**–19**	....	....	....	....	....	....	....	....
1972-73	**Detroit Red Wings**	**NHL**	**77**	**18**	**53**	**71**	**17**	**42**	**59**	**13**	**8**	**0**	**3**	**130**	**13.8**	**109**	**39**	**64**	**0**	**6**	....	....	....	....	....	....	....	....
1973-1974	**Detroit Red Wings**	**NHL**	**11**	**1**	**4**	**5**	**1**	**3**	**4**	**2**	**1**	**0**	**0**	**9**	**11.1**	**8**	**7**	**15**	**1**	**–13**	....	....	....	....	....	....	....	....
	Detroit Red Wings	**NHL**	DID NOT PLAY – COACHING																									
1974-1977	**Detroit Red Wings**	**NHL**	DID NOT PLAY – COACHING																									
	NHL Totals		**1549**	**456**	**825**	**1281**	**538**	**825**	**1363**	**383**	....	....	....	....	....	....	....	....	....	....	**121**	**35**	**69**	**104**	**29**	....	....	....

NHL Second All-Star Team (1953, 1959) • Won Lady Byng Trophy (1959, 1966, 1969) • Won Lester Patrick Trophy (1974) • Played in NHL All-Star Game (1953, 1954, 1955, 1956, 1957, 1958, 1959, 1961, 1962, 1963, 1964, 1965, 1967) • Named Head Coach of **Detroit**, November 7, 1973.

• DEMARCO, Ab Jr.

Albert Thomas D – R. 6′, 170 lbs. b: Cleveland, OH, 2/27/1949.

Season	Club	League	GP	G	A	Pts	AG	AA	APts	PIM	PP	SH	GW	S	%	TGF	PGF	TGA	PGA	+/–	GP	G	A	Pts	PIM	PP	SH	GW
1965-66	Scollard Golden Bears	NOHA	STATISTICS NOT AVAILABLE																									
1966-67	North Bay Trappers	NOJHA	STATISTICS NOT AVAILABLE																									
1967-68	Kitchener Rangers	OHA-Jr.	49	9	30	39	....	....	....	24	....	....	....	....	....	....	....	....	....	....	19	13	11	24	21	....	....	....
1968-69	Ottawa Nationals	OHA-Sr.	8	4	8	12	....	....	....	7	....	....	....	....	....	....	....	....	....	....	....	....	....	....	....	....	....	....
	Canada	WEC-A	9	1	0	1	....	....	....	6	....	....	....	....	....	....	....	....	....	....	....	....	....	....	....	....	....	....
1969-70	**New York Rangers**	**NHL**	**3**	**0**	**0**	**0**	**0**	**0**	**0**	**0**	**0**	**0**	**0**	**6**	**0.0**	**0**	**0**	**1**	**0**	**–1**	**5**	**0**	**0**	**0**	**2**	**0**	**0**	**0**
	Omaha Knights	CHL	60	6	30	36	....	....	....	19	....	....	....	....	....	....	....	....	....	....	....	....	....	....	....	....	....	....
1970-71	**New York Rangers**	**NHL**	**2**	**0**	**1**	**1**	**0**	**1**	**1**	**0**	**0**	**0**	**0**	**2**	**0.0**	**2**	**0**	**1**	**0**	**1**	....	....	....	....	....	....	....	....
	Omaha Knights	CHL	54	17	25	42	....	....	....	18	....	....	....	....	....	....	....	....	....	....	....	....	....	....	....	....	....	....
1971-72	**New York Rangers**	**NHL**	**48**	**4**	**7**	**11**	**4**	**6**	**10**	**4**	**1**	**0**	**0**	**95**	**4.2**	**37**	**1**	**22**	**4**	**18**	**4**	**0**	**1**	**1**	**0**	**0**	**0**	**0**
1972-73	**New York Rangers**	**NHL**	**51**	**4**	**13**	**17**	**4**	**10**	**14**	**15**	**1**	**0**	**2**	**104**	**3.8**	**68**	**5**	**51**	**4**	**16**	....	....	....	....	....	....	....	....
	St. Louis Blues	**NHL**	**14**	**4**	**9**	**13**	**4**	**7**	**11**	**2**	**2**	**1**	**1**	**51**	**7.8**	**25**	**9**	**17**	**5**	**4**	**4**	**1**	**1**	**2**	**2**	**1**	**0**	**0**
1973-74	**St. Louis Blues**	**NHL**	**23**	**3**	**9**	**12**	**3**	**7**	**10**	**11**	**1**	**0**	**0**	**71**	**4.2**	**29**	**9**	**15**	**1**	**6**	....	....	....	....	....	....	....	....
	Pittsburgh Penguins	**NHL**	**34**	**7**	**12**	**19**	**7**	**10**	**17**	**4**	**3**	**0**	**1**	**101**	**6.9**	**54**	**18**	**32**	**1**	**5**	....	....	....	....	....	....	....	....
1974-75	**Pittsburgh Penguins**	**NHL**	**8**	**2**	**1**	**3**	**2**	**1**	**3**	**4**	**1**	**0**	**0**	**25**	**8.0**	**11**	**2**	**16**	**3**	**–4**	....	....	....	....	....	....	....	....
	Vancouver Canucks	**NHL**	**61**	**10**	**14**	**24**	**9**	**10**	**19**	**21**	**8**	**0**	**1**	**117**	**8.5**	**64**	**38**	**31**	**3**	**–2**	**2**	**0**	**0**	**0**	**0**	**0**	**0**	**0**
1975-76	**Vancouver Canucks**	**NHL**	**34**	**3**	**8**	**11**	**3**	**6**	**9**	**2**	**2**	**0**	**0**	**33**	**9.1**	**22**	**12**	**15**	**2**	**–3**	....	....	....	....	....	....	....	....
	Los Angeles Kings	**NHL**	**30**	**4**	**3**	**7**	**3**	**2**	**5**	**6**	**2**	**0**	**1**	**70**	**5.7**	**27**	**6**	**26**	**2**	**–3**	**9**	**0**	**0**	**0**	**11**	**0**	**0**	**0**
1976-77	**Los Angeles Kings**	**NHL**	**33**	**3**	**3**	**6**	**3**	**2**	**5**	**6**	**0**	**0**	**0**	**82**	**3.7**	**23**	**2**	**33**	**4**	**–8**	**1**	**0**	**0**	**0**	**2**	**0**	**0**	**0**
	Fort Worth Texans	CHL	31	4	15	19	....	....	....	20	....	....	....	....	....	....	....	....	....	....	....	....	....	....	....	....	....	....
1977-78	Edmonton Oilers	WHA	47	6	8	14	....	....	....	20	....	....	....	....	....	....	....	....	....	....	1	0	0	0	0	....	....	....
1978-79	**Boston Bruins**	**NHL**	**3**	**0**	**0**	**0**	**0**	**0**	**0**	**0**	**0**	**0**	**0**	**5**	**0.0**	**1**	**0**	**1**	**0**	**0**	....	....	....	....	....	....	....	....
1979-80	HC Ambri-Piotta	Switz-2	STATISTICS NOT AVAILABLE																									
	NHL Totals		**344**	**44**	**80**	**124**	**42**	**62**	**104**	**75**	**21**	**1**	**6**	**762**	**5.8**	**363**	**102**	**261**	**29**		**25**	**1**	**2**	**3**	**17**	**1**	**0**	**0**
	Other Major League Totals		47	6	8	14	....	....	....	20	....	....	....	....	....	....	....	....	....	....	1	0	0	0	0	....	....	....

• Son of Ab Sr.

Signed as a free agent by **NY Rangers**, June 10, 1969. Selected by **Chicago** (WHA) in 1972 WHA General Player Draft, February 12, 1972. Traded to **St. Louis** by **NY Rangers** for Mike Murphy, March 2, 1973. Traded to **Pittsburgh** by **St. Louis** with Steve Durbano and Bob Kelly for Bryan Watson, Greg Polis and Pittsburgh's 2nd round choice (Bob Hess) in 1974 Amateur Draft, January 17, 1974. Traded to **Vancouver** by **Pittsburgh** for Barry Wilkins, November 4, 1974. Traded to **LA Kings** by **Vancouver** for LA Kings' 2nd choice (later traded to Atlanta — Atlanta selected Brian Hill) in 1977 Amateur Draft, January 14, 1976. Traded to **Atlanta** by **LA Kings** for Randy Manery, May 23, 1977. WHA rights transferred to **Edmonton** (WHA) after **Chicago** (WHA) franchise folded, May, 1975. Signed as a free agent by **Boston**, October 23, 1978.

• DEMITRA, Pavol

LW – L. 6′, 196 lbs. b: Dubnica, Czech., 11/29/1974. Ottawa's 9th, 227th overall, in 1993.

Season	Club	League	GP	G	A	Pts	AG	AA	APts	PIM	PP	SH	GW	S	%	TGF	PGF	TGA	PGA	+/–	GP	G	A	Pts	PIM	PP	SH	GW
1991-92	Spartak Dubnica	Czech-2	28	13	10	23	....	....	....	12	....	....	....	....	....	....	....	....	....	....	....	....	....	....	....	....	....	....
	Czechoslovakia	EJC-A	6	4	8	12	....	....	....	2	....	....	....	....	....	....	....	....	....	....	....	....	....	....	....	....	....	....
1992-93	Spartak Dubnica	Czech-2	4	3	0	3	....	....	....	....	....	....	....	....	....	....	....	....	....	....	....	....	....	....	....	....	....	....
	Czech-Republic	WJC-A	7	4	4	8	....	....	....	8	....	....	....	....	....	....	....	....	....	....	....	....	....	....	....	....	....	....
	Dukla Trencin	Czech.	46	11	17	28	....	....	....	0	....	....	....	....	....	....	....	....	....	....	....	....	....	....	....	....	....	....
1993-94	**Ottawa Senators**	**NHL**	**12**	**1**	**1**	**2**	**1**	**1**	**2**	**4**	**1**	**0**	**0**	**10**	**10.0**	**3**	**2**	**8**	**0**	**–7**	....	....	....	....	....	....	....	....
	P.E.I. Senators	AHL	41	18	23	41	....	....	....	8	....	....	....	....	....	....	....	....	....	....	....	....	....	....	....	....	....	....
1994-95	P.E.I. Senators	AHL	61	26	48	74	....	....	....	23	....	....	....	....	....	....	....	....	....	....	5	0	7	7	0	....	....	....
	Ottawa Senators	**NHL**	**16**	**4**	**3**	**7**	**7**	**4**	**11**	**0**	**1**	**0**	**0**	**21**	**19.0**	**11**	**5**	**10**	**0**	**–4**	....	....	....	....	....	....	....	....
1995-96	**Ottawa Senators**	**NHL**	**31**	**7**	**10**	**17**	**7**	**8**	**15**	**6**	**2**	**0**	**1**	**66**	**10.6**	**24**	**9**	**18**	**0**	**–3**	....	....	....	....	....	....	....	....
	P.E.I. Senators	AHL	48	28	53	81	....	....	....	44	....	....	....	....	....	....	....	....	....	....	....	....	....	....	....	....	....	....
	Slovakia	WC-A	5	1	2	3	....	....	....	2	....	....	....	....	....	....	....	....	....	....	....	....	....	....	....	....	....	....
1996-97	Slovakia	W-Cup	3	0	0	0	....	....	....	4	....	....	....	....	....	....	....	....	....	....	....	....	....	....	....	....	....	....
	Dukla Trencin	Slovakia	1	1	1	2	....	....	....	....	....	....	....	....	....	....	....	....	....	....	....	....	....	....	....	....	....	....
	Las Vegas Thunder	IHL	22	8	13	21	....	....	....	10	....	....	....	....	....	....	....	....	....	....	....	....	....	....	....	....	....	....
	St. Louis Blues	**NHL**	**8**	**3**	**0**	**3**	**3**	**0**	**3**	**2**	**2**	**0**	**1**	**15**	**20.0**	**5**	**2**	**3**	**0**	**0**	**6**	**1**	**3**	**4**	**6**	**0**	**0**	**0**
	Grand Rapids Griffins	IHL	42	20	30	50	....	....	....	24	....	....	....	....	....	....	....	....	....	....	....	....	....	....	....	....	....	....

Season	Club	League	REGULAR SEASON GP	G	A	Pts	AG	AA	APts	PIM	PP	SH	GW	S	%	TGF	PGF	TGA	PGA	+/–	PLAYOFFS GP	G	A	Pts	PIM	PP	SH	GW
1997-98	**St. Louis Blues**	**NHL**	**61**	**22**	**30**	**52**	**26**	**29**	**55**	**22**	**4**	**4**	**6**	**147**	**15.0**	**72**	**22**	**43**	**4**	**11**	**10**	**3**	**3**	**6**	**2**	**0**	**0**	**0**
1998-99	**St. Louis Blues**	**NHL**	**82**	**37**	**52**	**89**	**44**	**50**	**94**	**16**	**14**	**0**	**10**	**259**	**14.3**	**113**	**44**	**60**	**4**	**13**	**13**	**5**	**4**	**9**	**4**	**3**	**0**	**1**
99-2000	**St. Louis Blues**	**NHL**	**71**	**28**	**47**	**75**	**32**	**44**	**76**	**8**	**8**	**0**	**4**	**241**	**11.6**	**102**	**34**	**34**	**0**	**34**	....	....	....	....	....	....	....	....
	NHL Totals		**281**	**102**	**143**	**245**	**120**	**136**	**256**	**58**	**32**	**4**	**22**	**759**	**13.4**	**330**	**118**	**176**	**8**		**29**	**9**	**10**	**19**	**12**	**3**	**0**	**1**

Won Lady Byng Trophy (2000) • Played in NHL All-Star Game (1999, 2000)

Traded to **St. Louis** by **Ottawa** for Christer Olsson, November 27, 1996.

• DEMPSEY, Nathan

D – R. 6', 170 lbs. b: Spruce Grove, Alta., 7/14/1974. Toronto's 12th, 245th overall, in 1992.

Season	Club	League	GP	G	A	Pts	AG	AA	APts	PIM	PP	SH	GW	S	%	TGF	PGF	TGA	PGA	+/–	GP	G	A	Pts	PIM	PP	SH	GW
1989-90	Edmonton Southside	AAHA	STATISTICS NOT AVAILABLE																									
1990-91	St. Albert Saints	AJHL	34	11	20	31	....	....	....	73	....	....	....	....	....	....	....	....	....	....	....	....	....	....	....	....	....	....
1991-92	Regina Pats	WHL	70	4	22	26	....	....	....	72	....	....	....	....	....	....	....	....	....	....	....	....	....	....	....	....	....	....
1992-93	Regina Pats	WHL	72	12	29	41	....	....	....	95	....	....	....	....	....	....	....	....	....	....	13	3	8	11	14	....	....	....
	St. John's Maple Leafs	AHL	....	....	....	....	....	....	....	....	....	....	....	....	....	....	....	....	....	....	2	0	0	0	0	....	....	....
1993-94	Regina Pats	WHL	56	14	36	50	....	....	....	100	....	....	....	....	....	....	....	....	....	....	4	0	0	0	4	....	....	....
1994-95	St. John's Maple Leafs	AHL	74	7	30	37	....	....	....	91	....	....	....	....	....	....	....	....	....	....	5	1	0	1	11	....	....	....
1995-96	St. John's Maple Leafs	AHL	73	5	15	20	....	....	....	103	....	....	....	....	....	....	....	....	....	....	4	1	0	1	9	....	....	....
1996-97	**Toronto Maple Leafs**	**NHL**	**14**	**1**	**1**	**2**	**1**	**1**	**2**	**2**	**0**	**0**	**0**	**11**	**9.1**	**2**	**0**	**5**	**1**	**–2**	....	....	....	....	....	....	....	....
	St. John's Maple Leafs	AHL	52	8	18	26	....	....	....	108	....	....	....	....	....	....	....	....	....	....	6	1	0	1	4	....	....	....
1997-98	St. John's Maple Leafs	AHL	68	12	16	28	....	....	....	85	....	....	....	....	....	....	....	....	....	....	4	0	0	0	0	....	....	....
1998-99	St. John's Maple Leafs	AHL	67	2	29	31	....	....	....	70	....	....	....	....	....	....	....	....	....	....	5	0	1	1	2	....	....	....
99-2000	**Toronto Maple Leafs**	**NHL**	**6**	**0**	**2**	**2**	**0**	**2**	**2**	**2**	**0**	**0**	**0**	**3**	**0.0**	**5**	**0**	**4**	**1**	**2**	....	....	....	....	....	....	....	....
	St. John's Maple Leafs	AHL	44	15	12	27	....	....	....	40	....	....	....	....	....	....	....	....	....	....	....	....	....	....	....	....	....	....
	NHL Totals		**20**	**1**	**3**	**4**	**1**	**3**	**4**	**4**	**0**	**0**	**0**	**14**	**7.1**	**7**	**0**	**9**	**2**		....	....	....	....	....	....	....	....

WHL East Second All-Star Team (1994)

• DENNIS, Norm

Norman Marshall C – L. 5'10", 175 lbs. b: Aurora, Ont., 12/10/1942.

Season	Club	League	GP	G	A	Pts	AG	AA	APts	PIM	PP	SH	GW	S	%	TGF	PGF	TGA	PGA	+/–	GP	G	A	Pts	PIM	PP	SH	GW
1959-60	Brockville Jr. Canadiens	OVJHL	STATISTICS NOT AVAILABLE																									
	Brockville Jr. Canadiens	Mem-Cup	13	0	4	4	....	....	....	4	....	....	....	....	....	....	....	....	....	....	....	....	....	....	....	....	....	....
1960-61	Hull Canadiens	IPSHL	STATISTICS NOT AVAILABLE																									
1961-62	Montreal Jr. Canadiens	OHA-Jr.	50	28	44	72	....	....	....	56	....	....	....	....	....	....	....	....	....	....	6	2	3	5	14	....	....	....
1962-63	Montreal Jr. Canadiens	OHA-Jr.	37	23	32	55	....	....	....	59	....	....	....	....	....	....	....	....	....	....	8	1	7	8	6	....	....	....
	Hull-Ottawa Canadiens	EPHL	1	0	0	0	....	....	....	0	....	....	....	....	....	....	....	....	....	....	....	....	....	....	....	....	....	....
1963-64	Omaha Knights	CPHL	72	30	22	52	....	....	....	43	....	....	....	....	....	....	....	....	....	....	10	3	2	5	6	....	....	....
1964-65	Cleveland–Hershey Bears	AHL	7	1	1	2	....	....	....	4	....	....	....	....	....	....	....	....	....	....	....	....	....	....	....	....	....	....
	Omaha Knights	CPHL	66	30	40	70	....	....	....	59	....	....	....	....	....	....	....	....	....	....	6	2	5	7	11	....	....	....
1965-66	Houston Apollos	CPHL	70	23	36	59	....	....	....	82	....	....	....	....	....	....	....	....	....	....	....	....	....	....	....	....	....	....
1966-67	Houston Apollos	CPHL	54	13	33	46	....	....	....	25	....	....	....	....	....	....	....	....	....	....	4	0	2	2	0	....	....	....
1967-68	Cleveland Barons	AHL	72	11	25	36	....	....	....	42	....	....	....	....	....	....	....	....	....	....	....	....	....	....	....	....	....	....
1968-69	**St. Louis Blues**	**NHL**	**2**	**0**	**0**	**0**	**0**	**0**	**0**	**2**	**0**	**0**	**0**	**4**	**0.0**	**1**	**0**	**0**	**0**	**1**	....	....	....	....	....	....	....	....
	Kansas City Blues	CHL	70	23	38	61	....	....	....	65	....	....	....	....	....	....	....	....	....	....	4	0	0	0	11	....	....	....
1969-70	**St. Louis Blues**	**NHL**	**5**	**3**	**0**	**3**	**3**	**0**	**3**	**5**	**0**	**0**	**0**	**8**	**37.5**	**3**	**1**	**2**	**0**	**0**	**2**	**0**	**0**	**0**	**2**	**0**	**0**	**0**
	Kansas City Blues	CHL	62	16	47	63	....	....	....	68	....	....	....	....	....	....	....	....	....	....	....	....	....	....	....	....	....	....
1970-71	**St. Louis Blues**	**NHL**	**4**	**0**	**0**	**0**	**0**	**0**	**0**	**0**	**0**	**0**	**0**	**0**	**0.0**	**0**	**0**	**4**	**0**	**–4**	**3**	**0**	**0**	**0**	**0**	**0**	**0**	**0**
	Kansas City Blues	CHL	70	25	43	68	....	....	....	52	....	....	....	....	....	....	....	....	....	....	....	....	....	....	....	....	....	....
1971-72	**St. Louis Blues**	**NHL**	**1**	**0**	**0**	**0**	**0**	**0**	**0**	**4**	**0**	**0**	**0**	**1**	**0.0**	**0**	**0**	**1**	**0**	**–1**	....	....	....	....	....	....	....	....
	Kansas City Blues	CHL	72	31	47	78	....	....	....	67	....	....	....	....	....	....	....	....	....	....	....	....	....	....	....	....	....	....
1972-73	Denver Spurs	WHL	72	27	50	77	....	....	....	35	....	....	....	....	....	....	....	....	....	....	5	4	1	5	0	....	....	....
1973-74	Providence Reds	AHL	75	23	50	73	....	....	....	43	....	....	....	....	....	....	....	....	....	....	15	2	12	14	19	....	....	....
1974-75	Providence Reds	AHL	36	2	11	13	....	....	....	22	....	....	....	....	....	....	....	....	....	....	3	0	0	0	0	....	....	....
1975-76	Trail Smoke Eaters	WIHL	24	3	8	11	....	....	....	24	....	....	....	....	....	....	....	....	....	....	....	....	....	....	....	....	....	....
1976-77	Trail Smoke Eaters	WIHL	24	0	5	5	....	....	....	4	....	....	....	....	....	....	....	....	....	....	....	....	....	....	....	....	....	....
1977-78	Trail Smoke Eaters	WIHL	24	2	6	8	....	....	....	4	....	....	....	....	....	....	....	....	....	....	....	....	....	....	....	....	....	....
	NHL Totals		**12**	**3**	**0**	**3**	**3**	**0**	**3**	**11**	**0**	**0**	**0**	**13**	**23.1**	**4**	**1**	**7**	**0**		**5**	**0**	**0**	**0**	**2**	**0**	**0**	**0**

CHL First All-Star Team (1971)

Traded to **St. Louis** by **Montreal** for cash, October 28, 1968. Traded to **Buffalo** (AHL) by **St. Louis** with Norm Beaudin for cash, May 13, 1969. Traded to **NY Rangers** by **St. Louis** with Don Borgeson for Bob Kelly, September 8, 1973.

• DePALMA, Larry

Lawrence Edward LW – L. 6', 195 lbs. b: Trenton, MI, 10/27/1965.

Season	Club	League	GP	G	A	Pts	AG	AA	APts	PIM	PP	SH	GW	S	%	TGF	PGF	TGA	PGA	+/–	GP	G	A	Pts	PIM	PP	SH	GW
1983-84	Redford Royals	GLJHL	STATISTICS NOT AVAILABLE																									
1984-85	New Westminster Bruins	WHL	65	14	16	30	....	....	....	87	....	....	....	....	....	....	....	....	....	....	10	1	1	2	25	....	....	....
1985-86	Saskatoon Blades	WHL	65	61	51	112	....	....	....	232	....	....	....	....	....	....	....	....	....	....	13	7	9	16	58	....	....	....
	Minnesota North Stars	**NHL**	**1**	**0**	**0**	**0**	**0**	**0**	**0**	**0**	**0**	**0**	**0**	**0**	**0.0**	**0**	**0**	**0**	**0**	**0**	....	....	....	....	....	....	....	....
1986-87	**Minnesota North Stars**	**NHL**	**56**	**9**	**6**	**15**	**8**	**4**	**12**	**219**	**2**	**0**	**0**	**56**	**16.1**	**20**	**2**	**26**	**1**	**–7**	....	....	....	....	....	....	....	....
	Springfield Indians	AHL	9	2	2	4	....	....	....	82	....	....	....	....	....	....	....	....	....	....	....	....	....	....	....	....	....	....
1987-88	**Minnesota North Stars**	**NHL**	**7**	**1**	**1**	**2**	**1**	**1**	**2**	**15**	**0**	**0**	**0**	**8**	**12.5**	**2**	**0**	**4**	**0**	**–2**	....	....	....	....	....	....	....	....
	Baltimore Skipjacks	AHL	16	8	10	18	....	....	....	121	....	....	....	....	....	....	....	....	....	....	....	....	....	....	....	....	....	....
	Kalamazoo Wings	IHL	22	6	11	17	....	....	....	215	....	....	....	....	....	....	....	....	....	....	....	....	....	....	....	....	....	....
1988-89	**Minnesota North Stars**	**NHL**	**43**	**5**	**7**	**12**	**4**	**5**	**9**	**102**	**1**	**0**	**1**	**42**	**11.9**	**16**	**2**	**28**	**0**	**–14**	**2**	**0**	**0**	**0**	**6**	**0**	**0**	**0**
1989-90	Kalamazoo Wings	IHL	36	7	14	21	....	....	....	218	....	....	....	....	....	....	....	....	....	....	4	1	1	2	32	....	....	....
1990-91	**Minnesota North Stars**	**NHL**	**14**	**3**	**0**	**3**	**3**	**0**	**3**	**26**	**1**	**0**	**1**	**18**	**16.7**	**7**	**3**	**9**	**0**	**–5**	....	....	....	....	....	....	....	....
	Kalamazoo Wings	IHL	55	27	32	59	....	....	....	160	....	....	....	....	....	....	....	....	....	....	11	5	4	9	25	....	....	....
1991-92	Kansas City Blades	IHL	62	28	29	57	....	....	....	188	....	....	....	....	....	....	....	....	....	....	15	7	13	20	34	....	....	....
1992-93	**San Jose Sharks**	**NHL**	**20**	**2**	**6**	**8**	**2**	**4**	**6**	**41**	**1**	**0**	**0**	**29**	**6.9**	**16**	**10**	**20**	**0**	**–14**	....	....	....	....	....	....	....	....
	Kansas City Blades	IHL	30	11	11	22	....	....	....	83	....	....	....	....	....	....	....	....	....	....	10	1	4	5	20	....	....	....
1993-94	Atlanta Knights	IHL	21	10	10	20	....	....	....	109	....	....	....	....	....	....	....	....	....	....	....	....	....	....	....	....	....	....
	Salt Lake Golden Eagles	IHL	34	4	12	16	....	....	....	125	....	....	....	....	....	....	....	....	....	....	....	....	....	....	....	....	....	....
	Las Vegas Thunder	IHL	1	0	0	0	....	....	....	17	....	....	....	....	....	....	....	....	....	....	....	....	....	....	....	....	....	....
	Pittsburgh Penguins	**NHL**	**7**	**1**	**0**	**1**	**1**	**0**	**1**	**5**	**0**	**0**	**0**	**2**	**50.0**	**1**	**0**	**0**	**0**	**1**	**1**	**0**	**0**	**0**	**0**	**0**	**0**	**0**
	Cleveland Lumberjacks	IHL	9	4	1	5	....	....	....	49	....	....	....	....	....	....	....	....	....	....	....	....	....	....	....	....	....	....
1994-95	Cleveland Lumberjacks	IHL	25	6	6	12	....	....	....	113	....	....	....	....	....	....	....	....	....	....	....	....	....	....	....	....	....	....
	San Diego Gulls	IHL	38	14	8	22	....	....	....	86	....	....	....	....	....	....	....	....	....	....	2	0	0	0	20	....	....	....
1995-96	Minnesota Moose	IHL	55	9	17	26	....	....	....	173	....	....	....	....	....	....	....	....	....	....	....	....	....	....	....	....	....	....
1996-97	Milwaukee Admirals	IHL	68	13	13	26	....	....	....	131	....	....	....	....	....	....	....	....	....	....	3	0	1	1	4	....	....	....
	NHL Totals		**148**	**21**	**20**	**41**	**19**	**14**	**33**	**408**	**5**	**0**	**2**	**155**	**13.5**	**62**	**17**	**87**	**1**		**3**	**0**	**0**	**0**	**6**	**0**	**0**	**0**

WHL East Second All-Star Team (1986)

Signed to an amateur try-out contract by **Minnesota**, February 17, 1986. Signed as a free agent by **Minnesota**, May 12, 1986. Signed as a free agent by **San Jose**, August 30, 1991. Signed as a free agent by **NY Islanders**, November 29, 1993. Claimed on waivers by **Pittsburgh** from **NY Islanders**, March 9, 1994.

• DERLAGO, Bill

William Anthony "Billy D." C – L. 5'10", 194 lbs. b: Birtle, Man., 8/25/1958. Vancouver's 1st, 4th overall, in 1978.

Season	Club	League	GP	G	A	Pts	AG	AA	APts	PIM	PP	SH	GW	S	%	TGF	PGF	TGA	PGA	+/–	GP	G	A	Pts	PIM	PP	SH	GW
1973-74	McCauley Selects	MAHA	30	26	26	52	....	....	....	32	....	....	....	....	....	....	....	....	....	....	....	....	....	....	....	....	....	....
1974-75	Brandon Travellers	MJHL	STATISTICS NOT AVAILABLE																									
	Brandon Wheat Kings	WCJHL	17	0	4	4	....	....	....	2	....	....	....	....	....	....	....	....	....	....	5	1	1	2	0	....	....	....
1975-76	Brandon Wheat Kings	WCJHL	68	49	54	103	....	....	....	43	....	....	....	....	....	....	....	....	....	....	5	3	3	6	0	....	....	....
1976-77	Brandon Wheat Kings	WCJHL	72	*96	82	*178	....	....	....	63	....	....	....	....	....	....	....	....	....	....	16	*14	*16	*30	31	....	....	....
1977-78	Brandon Wheat Kings	WCJHL	52	*89	63	152	....	....	....	105	....	....	....	....	....	....	....	....	....	....	8	9	13	22	10	....	....	....
1978-79	**Vancouver Canucks**	**NHL**	**9**	**4**	**4**	**8**	**3**	**3**	**6**	**2**	**1**	**0**	**0**	**28**	**14.3**	**11**	**6**	**7**	**0**	**–2**	....	....	....	....	....	....	....	....
	Dallas Black Hawks	CHL	11	5	8	13	....	....	....	9	....	....	....	....	....	....	....	....	....	....	....	....	....	....	....	....	....	....

Season	Club	League	REGULAR SEASON																		PLAYOFFS							
			GP	G	A	Pts	AG	AA	APts	PIM	PP	SH	GW	S	%	TGF	PGF	TGA	PGA	+/–	GP	G	A	Pts	PIM	PP	SH	GW
1979-80	**Vancouver Canucks**	**NHL**	**54**	**11**	**15**	**26**	**9**	**11**	**20**	**27**	**4**	**0**	**1**	**75**	**14.7**	**37**	**10**	**44**	**0**	**–17**	....	....	....	....	....	....	....	....
	Toronto Maple Leafs	**NHL**	**23**	**5**	**12**	**17**	**4**	**9**	**13**	**13**	**1**	**0**	**0**	**45**	**11.1**	**24**	**8**	**22**	**0**	**–6**	**3**	**0**	**0**	**0**	**4**	**0**	**0**	**0**
1980-81	**Toronto Maple Leafs**	**NHL**	**80**	**35**	**39**	**74**	**27**	**26**	**53**	**26**	**6**	**0**	**3**	**208**	**16.8**	**98**	**24**	**94**	**9**	**–11**	**3**	**1**	**0**	**1**	**2**	**1**	**0**	**0**
1981-82	**Toronto Maple Leafs**	**NHL**	**75**	**34**	**50**	**84**	**27**	**33**	**60**	**42**	**6**	**0**	**2**	**198**	**17.2**	**118**	**29**	**109**	**25**	**5**	....	....	....	....	....	....	....	....
1982-83	**Toronto Maple Leafs**	**NHL**	**58**	**13**	**24**	**37**	**11**	**17**	**28**	**27**	**5**	**0**	**1**	**135**	**9.6**	**53**	**25**	**66**	**19**	**–19**	**4**	**3**	**0**	**3**	**2**	**2**	**0**	**0**
1983-84	**Toronto Maple Leafs**	**NHL**	**79**	**40**	**20**	**60**	**32**	**14**	**46**	**50**	**8**	**2**	**3**	**210**	**19.0**	**93**	**23**	**105**	**27**	**–8**	....	....	....	....	....	....	....	....
1984-85	**Toronto Maple Leafs**	**NHL**	**62**	**31**	**31**	**62**	**25**	**21**	**46**	**21**	**7**	**5**	**4**	**147**	**21.1**	**86**	**29**	**100**	**28**	**–15**	....	....	....	....	....	....	....	....
1985-86	**Toronto Maple Leafs**	**NHL**	**1**	**0**	**0**	**0**	**0**	**0**	**0**	**0**	**0**	**0**	**0**	**2**	**0.0**	**0**	**0**	**2**	**2**	**0**	....	....	....	....	....	....	....	....
	Boston Bruins	**NHL**	**39**	**5**	**16**	**21**	**4**	**11**	**15**	**15**	**1**	**1**	**1**	**40**	**12.5**	**30**	**7**	**30**	**11**	**4**	....	....	....	....	....	....	....	....
	Winnipeg Jets	**NHL**	**27**	**5**	**5**	**10**	**4**	**3**	**7**	**6**	**1**	**0**	**0**	**35**	**14.3**	**14**	**4**	**31**	**8**	**–13**	**3**	**1**	**0**	**1**	**0**	**0**	**0**	**0**
1986-87	**Winnipeg Jets**	**NHL**	**30**	**3**	**6**	**9**	**3**	**4**	**7**	**12**	**1**	**0**	**1**	**26**	**11.5**	**17**	**4**	**17**	**1**	**–3**	....	....	....	....	....	....	....	....
	Quebec Nordiques	**NHL**	**18**	**3**	**5**	**8**	**3**	**4**	**7**	**6**	**0**	**0**	**0**	**20**	**15.0**	**8**	**1**	**11**	**0**	**–4**	....	....	....	....	....	....	....	....
	Fredericton Express	AHL	16	7	8	15	....	....	....	2	....	....	....	....	....	....	....	....	....	....	....	....	....	....	....	....	....	....
1987-88	HC Ambri-Piotta	Switz.	28	10	18	28	....	....	....	....	....	....	....	....	....	....	....	....	....	....	4	2	5	7	....	....	....	....
	NHL Totals		**555**	**189**	**227**	**416**	**152**	**156**	**308**	**247**	**41**	**8**	**16**	**1169**	**16.2**	**589**	**170**	**638**	**130**		**13**	**5**	**0**	**5**	**8**	**3**	**0**	**0**

WCJHL All-Star Team (1977) • WCJHL Second All-Star Team (1978)

• Missed majorty of 1978-79 season recovering from knee injury suffered in practice, December, 1978. Traded to **Toronto** by **Vancouver** with Rick Vaive for Tiger Williams and Jerry Butler, February 18, 1980. Traded to **Boston** by **Toronto** for Tom Fergus, October 11, 1985. Traded to **Winnipeg** by **Boston** for Wade Campbell, January 31, 1986. Traded to **Quebec** by **Winnipeg** for Quebec's 4th round choice (Mark Brownschilde) in 1989 Entry Draft, January 5, 1987.

• DESJARDINS, Eric

D – R. 6'1", 200 lbs. b: Rouyn, Que., 6/14/1969. Montreal's 3rd, 38th overall, in 1987.

Season	Club	League	GP	G	A	Pts	AG	AA	APts	PIM	PP	SH	GW	S	%	TGF	PGF	TGA	PGA	+/–	GP	G	A	Pts	PIM	PP	SH	GW
1985-86	Laval Laurentide	QAAA	42	6	30	36	....	....	....	54	....	....	....	....	....	....	....	....	....	....	....	....	....	....	....	....	....	....
1986-87	Granby Bisons	QMJHL	66	14	24	38	....	....	....	178	....	....	....	....	....	....	....	....	....	....	8	3	2	5	10	....	....	....
1987-88	Granby Bisons	QMJHL	62	18	49	67	....	....	....	138	....	....	....	....	....	....	....	....	....	....	5	0	3	3	10	....	....	....
	Canada	WJC-A	7	0	0	0	....	....	....	6	....	....	....	....	....	....	....	....	....	....	....	....	....	....	....	....	....	....
	Sherbrooke Canadiens	AHL	3	0	0	0	....	....	....	6	....	....	....	....	....	....	....	....	....	....	4	0	2	2	2	....	....	....
1988-89	**Montreal Canadiens**	**NHL**	**36**	**2**	**12**	**14**	**2**	**8**	**10**	**26**	**1**	**0**	**0**	**39**	**5.1**	**44**	**12**	**26**	**3**	**9**	**14**	**1**	**1**	**2**	**6**	**1**	**0**	**0**
	Canada	WJC-A	7	1	4	5	....	....	....	6	....	....	....	....	....	....	....	....	....	....	....	....	....	....	....	....	....	....
1989-90	**Montreal Canadiens**	**NHL**	**55**	**3**	**13**	**16**	**3**	**9**	**12**	**51**	**1**	**0**	**0**	**48**	**6.3**	**55**	**4**	**60**	**10**	**1**	**6**	**0**	**0**	**0**	**10**	**0**	**0**	**0**
1990-91	Montreal Canadiens	Fr-Tour	2	0	0	0	....	....	....	0	....	....	....	....	....	....	....	....	....	....	....	....	....	....	....	....	....	....
	Montreal Canadiens	**NHL**	**62**	**7**	**18**	**25**	**6**	**14**	**20**	**27**	**0**	**0**	**1**	**114**	**6.1**	**79**	**24**	**65**	**17**	**7**	**13**	**1**	**4**	**5**	**8**	**1**	**0**	**0**
1991-92	Canada	Can-Cup	8	1	2	3	....	....	....	6	....	....	....	....	....	....	....	....	....	....	....	....	....	....	....	....	....	....
	Montreal Canadiens	**NHL**	**77**	**6**	**32**	**38**	**5**	**24**	**29**	**50**	**4**	**0**	**2**	**141**	**4.3**	**108**	**37**	**83**	**29**	**17**	**11**	**3**	**3**	**6**	**4**	**1**	**0**	**0**
1992-93♦	**Montreal Canadiens**	**NHL**	**82**	**13**	**32**	**45**	**11**	**22**	**33**	**98**	**7**	**0**	**1**	**163**	**8.0**	**147**	**41**	**131**	**45**	**20**	**20**	**4**	**10**	**14**	**23**	**1**	**0**	**1**
1993-94	**Montreal Canadiens**	**NHL**	**84**	**12**	**23**	**35**	**11**	**18**	**29**	**97**	**6**	**1**	**3**	**193**	**6.2**	**99**	**28**	**104**	**32**	**–1**	**7**	**0**	**2**	**2**	**4**	**0**	**0**	**0**
1994-95	**Montreal Canadiens**	**NHL**	**9**	**0**	**6**	**6**	**0**	**9**	**9**	**2**	**0**	**0**	**0**	**14**	**0.0**	**11**	**4**	**11**	**6**	**2**	....	....	....	....	....	....	....	....
	Philadelphia Flyers	**NHL**	**34**	**5**	**18**	**23**	**9**	**27**	**36**	**12**	**1**	**0**	**1**	**79**	**6.3**	**53**	**15**	**42**	**14**	**10**	**15**	**4**	**4**	**8**	**10**	**1**	**0**	**2**
1995-96	**Philadelphia Flyers**	**NHL**	**80**	**7**	**40**	**47**	**7**	**33**	**40**	**45**	**5**	**0**	**2**	**184**	**3.8**	**130**	**55**	**95**	**39**	**19**	**12**	**0**	**6**	**6**	**2**	**0**	**0**	**0**
1996-97	Canada	W-Cup	8	1	2	3	....	....	....	4	....	....	....	....	....	....	....	....	....	....	....	....	....	....	....	....	....	....
	Philadelphia Flyers	**NHL**	**82**	**12**	**34**	**46**	**13**	**30**	**43**	**50**	**5**	**1**	**1**	**183**	**6.6**	**121**	**31**	**83**	**18**	**25**	**19**	**2**	**8**	**10**	**12**	**0**	**0**	**0**
1997-98	**Philadelphia Flyers**	**NHL**	**77**	**6**	**27**	**33**	**7**	**26**	**33**	**36**	**2**	**1**	**0**	**150**	**4.0**	**95**	**30**	**74**	**20**	**11**	**5**	**0**	**1**	**1**	**0**	**0**	**0**	**0**
	Canada	Olympics	6	0	0	0	....	....	....	2	....	....	....	....	....	....	....	....	....	....	....	....	....	....	....	....	....	....
1998-99	**Philadelphia Flyers**	**NHL**	**68**	**15**	**36**	**51**	**18**	**35**	**53**	**38**	**6**	**0**	**2**	**190**	**7.9**	**108**	**40**	**65**	**15**	**18**	**6**	**2**	**2**	**4**	**4**	**1**	**0**	**1**
99-2000	**Philadelphia Flyers**	**NHL**	**81**	**14**	**41**	**55**	**16**	**38**	**54**	**32**	**8**	**0**	**4**	**207**	**6.8**	**135**	**52**	**82**	**19**	**20**	**18**	**2**	**10**	**12**	**2**	**1**	**0**	**1**
	NHL Totals		**827**	**102**	**332**	**434**	**108**	**293**	**401**	**564**	**46**	**3**	**17**	**1705**	**6.0**	**1185**	**373**	**921**	**267**		**146**	**19**	**51**	**70**	**85**	**7**	**0**	**5**

QMJHL Second All-Star Team (1987) • QMJHL First All-Star Team (1988) • NHL Second All-Star Team (1999, 2000) • Played in NHL All-Star Game (1992, 1996, 2000)

Traded to **Philadelphia** by **Montreal** with Gilbert Dionne and John LeClair for Mark Recchi and Philadelphia's 3rd round choice (Martin Hohenberger) in 1995 Entry Draft, February 9, 1995.

• DESJARDINS, Martin

Martin R. C – L. 6', 180 lbs. b: Ste-Rose, Que., 1/28/1967. Montreal's 5th, 75th overall, in 1985.

Season	Club	League	GP	G	A	Pts	AG	AA	APts	PIM	PP	SH	GW	S	%	TGF	PGF	TGA	PGA	+/–	GP	G	A	Pts	PIM	PP	SH	GW
1982-83	Laurentides Pionniers	QAAA	45	25	29	54	....	....	....	....	....	....	....	....	....	....	....	....	....	....	....	....	....	....	....	....	....	....
1983-84	Laurentides Pionniers	QAAA	38	38	43	81	....	....	....	....	....	....	....	....	....	....	....	....	....	....	....	....	....	....	....	....	....	....
1984-85	Trois-Rivieres Draveurs	QMJHL	66	29	34	63	....	....	....	76	....	....	....	....	....	....	....	....	....	....	7	4	6	10	6	....	....	....
1985-86	Trois-Rivieres Draveurs	QMJHL	71	49	69	118	....	....	....	103	....	....	....	....	....	....	....	....	....	....	4	2	4	6	4	....	....	....
1986-87	Trois-Rivieres Draveurs	QMJHL	52	32	52	84	....	....	....	77	....	....	....	....	....	....	....	....	....	....	....	....	....	....	....	....	....	....
	Longueuil Chevaliers	QMJHL	17	7	10	17	....	....	....	12	....	....	....	....	....	....	....	....	....	....	19	8	10	18	18	....	....	....
	Longueuil Chevaliers	Mem-Cup	5	0	1	1	....	....	....	4	....	....	....	....	....	....	....	....	....	....	....	....	....	....	....	....	....	....
1987-88	Sherbrooke Canadiens	AHL	75	34	36	70	....	....	....	117	....	....	....	....	....	....	....	....	....	....	5	1	1	2	8	....	....	....
1988-89	Sherbrooke Canadiens	AHL	70	17	27	44	....	....	....	104	....	....	....	....	....	....	....	....	....	....	6	2	7	9	21	....	....	....
1989-90	**Montreal Canadiens**	**NHL**	**8**	**0**	**2**	**2**	**0**	**1**	**1**	**2**	**0**	**0**	**0**	**7**	**0.0**	**3**	**0**	**9**	**2**	**–4**	....	....	....	....	....	....	....	....
	Sherbrooke Canadiens	AHL	65	21	26	47	....	....	....	72	....	....	....	....	....	....	....	....	....	....	12	4	*13	17	28	....	....	....
1990-91	Montreal Canadiens	Fr-Tour	1	0	0	0	....	....	....	2	....	....	....	....	....	....	....	....	....	....	....	....	....	....	....	....	....	....
	Fredericton Canadiens	AHL	2	0	1	1	....	....	....	6	....	....	....	....	....	....	....	....	....	....	....	....	....	....	....	....	....	....
	Indianapolis Ice	IHL	71	15	42	57	....	....	....	110	....	....	....	....	....	....	....	....	....	....	7	2	1	3	8	....	....	....
1991-92	Indianapolis Ice	IHL	36	4	7	11	....	....	....	52	....	....	....	....	....	....	....	....	....	....	....	....	....	....	....	....	....	....
1992-93	HC Lausanne	Switz-2	29	22	14	36	....	....	....	56	....	....	....	....	....	....	....	....	....	....	4	1	4	5	8	....	....	....
1993-94	HC Lausanne	Switz-2	25	23	15	38	....	....	....	38	....	....	....	....	....	....	....	....	....	....	13	8	5	13	30	....	....	....
1994-95	HC Lausanne	Switz-2	36	19	30	49	....	....	....	52	....	....	....	....	....	....	....	....	....	....	11	4	9	13	14	....	....	....
1995-96	HC Lausanne	Switz	33	5	11	16	....	....	....	68	....	....	....	....	....	....	....	....	....	....	....	....	....	....	....	....	....	....
1996-97	HC Geneve-Servette	Switz-2	41	23	22	45	....	....	....	114	....	....	....	....	....	....	....	....	....	....	5	2	3	5	6	....	....	....
1997-98	Berlin Capitals	Germany	44	8	13	21	....	....	....	24	....	....	....	....	....	....	....	....	....	....	....	....	....	....	....	....	....	....
	NHL Totals		**8**	**0**	**2**	**2**	**0**	**1**	**1**	**2**	**0**	**0**	**0**	**7**	**0.0**	**3**	**0**	**9**	**2**		....	....	....	....	....	....	....	....

Traded to **Chicago** by **Montreal** for cash, October 10, 1990.

• DEULING, Jarrett

Jarrett Rufus LW – L. 6', 205 lbs. b: Vernon, B.C., 3/4/1974. NY Islanders' 2nd, 56th overall, in 1992.

Season	Club	League	GP	G	A	Pts	AG	AA	APts	PIM	PP	SH	GW	S	%	TGF	PGF	TGA	PGA	+/–	GP	G	A	Pts	PIM	PP	SH	GW
1989-90	Whitehorse Bears	Yukon	28	34	48	72	....	....	....	84	....	....	....	....	....	....	....	....	....	....	....	....	....	....	....	....	....	....
1990-91	Kamloops Blazers	WHL	48	4	12	16	....	....	....	43	....	....	....	....	....	....	....	....	....	....	12	5	2	7	7	....	....	....
1991-92	Kamloops Blazers	WHL	68	28	26	54	....	....	....	79	....	....	....	....	....	....	....	....	....	....	17	10	6	16	18	....	....	....
	Kamloops Blazers	Mem-Cup	5	0	2	2	....	....	....	10	....	....	....	....	....	....	....	....	....	....	....	....	....	....	....	....	....	....
1992-93	Kamloops Blazers	WHL	68	31	32	63	....	....	....	93	....	....	....	....	....	....	....	....	....	....	13	6	7	13	14	....	....	....
1993-94	Kamloops Blazers	WHL	70	44	59	103	....	....	....	171	....	....	....	....	....	....	....	....	....	....	18	*13	8	21	43	....	....	....
	Kamloops Blazers	Mem-Cup	4	1	1	2	....	....	....	6	....	....	....	....	....	....	....	....	....	....	....	....	....	....	....	....	....	....
1994-95	Worcester IceCats	AHL	63	11	8	19	....	....	....	37	....	....	....	....	....	....	....	....	....	....	....	....	....	....	....	....	....	....
1995-96	**New York Islanders**	**NHL**	**14**	**0**	**1**	**1**	**0**	**1**	**1**	**11**	**0**	**0**	**0**	**11**	**0.0**	**3**	**1**	**3**	**0**	**–1**	....	....	....	....	....	....	....	....
	Worcester IceCats	AHL	57	16	7	23	....	....	....	57	....	....	....	....	....	....	....	....	....	....	4	1	2	3	2	....	....	....
1996-97	**New York Islanders**	**NHL**	**1**	**0**	**0**	**0**	**0**	**0**	**0**	**0**	**0**	**0**	**0**	**0**	**0.0**	**0**	**0**	**0**	**0**	**0**	....	....	....	....	....	....	....	....
	Kentucky Thoroughblades	AHL	58	15	31	46	....	....	....	57	....	....	....	....	....	....	....	....	....	....	4	3	0	3	8	....	....	....
1997-98	Milwaukee Admirals	IHL	64	18	18	36	....	....	....	84	....	....	....	....	....	....	....	....	....	....	10	4	3	7	36	....	....	....
1998-99	Kentucky Thoroughblades	AHL	60	22	31	53	....	....	....	68	....	....	....	....	....	....	....	....	....	....	12	3	6	9	8	....	....	....
99-2000	Kentucky Thoroughblades	AHL	75	17	25	42	....	....	....	83	....	....	....	....	....	....	....	....	....	....	8	1	1	2	6	....	....	....
	NHL Totals		**15**	**0**	**1**	**1**	**0**	**1**	**1**	**11**	**0**	**0**	**0**	**11**	**0.0**	**3**	**1**	**3**	**0**		....	....	....	....	....	....	....	....

Signed as a free agent by **San Jose**, August 27, 1998.

• DEVEREAUX, Boyd

Boyd Fletcher C – L. 6'2", 195 lbs. b: Seaforth, Ont., 4/16/1978. Edmonton's 1st, 6th overall, in 1996.

Season	Club	League	GP	G	A	Pts	AG	AA	APts	PIM	PP	SH	GW	S	%	TGF	PGF	TGA	PGA	+/–	GP	G	A	Pts	PIM	PP	SH	GW
1992-93	Seaforth Sailors	OJHL-D	34	7	20	27	....	....	....	13	....	....	....	....	....	....	....	....	....	....	....	....	....	....	....	....	....	....
1993-94	Stratford Cullitons	OJHL-B	46	12	27	39	....	....	....	8	....	....	....	....	....	....	....	....	....	....	....	....	....	....	....	....	....	....
1994-95	Stratford Cullitons	OJHL-B	45	31	74	105	....	....	....	21	....	....	....	....	....	....	....	....	....	....	....	....	....	....	....	....	....	....
1995-96	Kitchener Rangers	OHL	66	20	38	58	....	....	....	35	....	....	....	....	....	....	....	....	....	....	12	3	7	10	4	....	....	....

			REGULAR SEASON																		PLAYOFFS							
Season	Club	League	GP	G	A	Pts	AG	AA	APts	PIM	PP	SH	GW	S	%	TGF	PGF	TGA	PGA	+/–	GP	G	A	Pts	PIM	PP	SH	GW
1996-97	Kitchener Rangers	OHL	54	28	41	69				37											13	4	11	15	8			
	Canada	WJC-A	7	4	0	4				0																		
	Hamilton Bulldogs	AHL																			1	0	1	1	0			
1997-98	**Edmonton Oilers**	**NHL**	**38**	**1**	**4**	**5**	**1**	**4**	**5**	**6**	**0**	**0**	**0**	**27**	**3.7**	**9**	**0**	**20**	**6**	**–5**								
	Hamilton Bulldogs	AHL	14	5	6	11				6											9	1	1	2	8			
1998-99	**Edmonton Oilers**	**NHL**	**61**	**6**	**8**	**14**	**7**	**8**	**15**	**23**	**0**	**1**	**4**	**39**	**15.4**	**18**	**0**	**31**	**15**	**2**	**1**	**0**	**0**	**0**	**0**	**0**	**0**	**0**
	Hamilton Bulldogs	AHL	7	4	6	10				2											8	0	3	3	4			
99-2000	**Edmonton Oilers**	**NHL**	**76**	**8**	**19**	**27**	**9**	**18**	**27**	**20**	**0**	**1**	**2**	**108**	**7.4**	**32**	**0**	**36**	**11**	**7**								
	NHL Totals		**175**	**15**	**31**	**46**	**17**	**30**	**47**	**49**	**0**	**2**	**6**	**174**	**8.6**	**59**	**0**	**87**	**32**		**1**	**0**	**0**	**0**	**0**	**0**	**0**	**0**

Canadian Major Junior Scholastic Player of the Year (1996)

• DEVINE, Kevin

LW – L. 5'8", 165 lbs. b: Toronto, Ont., 12/9/1954. Toronto's 7th, 121st overall, in 1974.

Season	Club	League	GP	G	A	Pts	AG	AA	APts	PIM	PP	SH	GW	S	%	TGF	PGF	TGA	PGA	+/–	GP	G	A	Pts	PIM	PP	SH	GW
1970-71	Charlottetown Islanders	MJrHL	40	11	22	33				90											7	3	1	4	2			
	Charlottetown Islanders	Cen-Cup	21	8	10	18				55																		
1971-72	Toronto Marlboros	OMJHL	55	5	12	17				86																		
1972-73	Toronto Marlboros	OMJHL	58	30	40	70				150																		
	Toronto Marlboros	Mem-Cup	3	0	2	2				4																		
1973-74	Toronto Marlboros	OMJHL	67	40	29	69				218																		
1974-75	San Diego Mariners	WHA	46	4	10	14				48											10	1	0	1	14			
	Syracuse Blazers	NAHL	27	11	12	23				23																		
1975-76	San Diego Mariners	WHA	80	21	28	49				102											11	3	1	4	36			
1976-77	San Diego Mariners	WHA	81	30	20	50				114											7	1	3	4	14			
1977-78	Indianapolis Racers	WHA	76	19	23	42				141																		
1978-79	Quebec Nordiques	WHA	5	0	0	0				6																		
	San Diego Hawks	PHL	58	36	36	72				119																		
1979-80	Indianapolis Checkers	CHL	79	27	26	53				171											7	1	1	2	26			
1980-81	Indianapolis Checkers	CHL	80	28	26	54				153											5	3	0	3	10			
1981-82	Indianapolis Checkers	CHL	80	24	27	51				199											13	8	1	9	32			
1982-83	**New York Islanders**	**NHL**	**2**	**0**	**1**	**1**	**0**	**1**	**1**	**8**	**0**	**0**	**0**	**3**	**0.0**	**1**	**0**	**0**	**0**	**1**								
	Indianapolis Checkers	CHL	78	21	27	48				245											13	4	7	11	14			
1983-84	Indianapolis Checkers	CHL	71	23	30	53				201											10	4	3	7	8			
1984-85	Indianapolis Checkers	IHL	78	16	35	51				139											7	0	4	4	38			
	NHL Totals		**2**	**0**	**1**	**1**	**0**	**1**	**1**	**8**	**0**	**0**	**0**	**3**	**0.0**	**1**	**0**	**0**	**0**									
	Other Major League Totals		288	74	81	155				411											28	5	4	9	64			

MJrHL Second All-Star Team (1971)

Selected by **San Diego** (WHA) in 1974 WHA Amateur Draft, June, 1974. Signed as a free agent by **Edmonton** (WHA) after **San Diego** (WHA) franchise folded, August, 1977. Traded to **Indianapolis** (WHA) by **Edmonton** (WHA) with Barry Wilkins, Rusty Patenaude and Claude St. Sauveur for Blair MacDonald, Dave Inkpen and Mike Zuke, September, 1977. Traded to **Quebec** (WHA) by **Indianapolis** (WHA) for cash, September, 1978. Signed as a free agent by **NY Islanders**, October 9, 1979.

• de VRIES, Greg

D – L. 6'3", 215 lbs. b: Sundridge, Ont., 1/4/1973.

Season	Club	League	GP	G	A	Pts	AG	AA	APts	PIM	PP	SH	GW	S	%	TGF	PGF	TGA	PGA	+/–	GP	G	A	Pts	PIM	PP	SH	GW
1988-89	Cortina Astros	OMHA	35	28	40	68																						
1989-90	Aurora Eagles	OJHL-B	42	1	16	17				32																		
1990-91	Stratford Cullitons	OJHL-B	40	8	32	40				120											3	2	1	3	20			
1991-92	Bowling Green University	CCHA	24	0	3	3				20																		
1992-93	Niagara Falls Thunder	OHL	62	3	23	26				86											4	0	1	1	6			
1993-94	Niagara Falls Thunder	OHL	64	5	40	45				135																		
	Cape Breton Oilers	AHL	9	0	0	0				11											1	0	0	0	0			
1994-95	Cape Breton Oilers	AHL	77	5	19	24				68																		
1995-96	**Edmonton Oilers**	**NHL**	**13**	**1**	**1**	**2**	**1**	**1**	**2**	**12**	**0**	**0**	**0**	**8**	**12.5**	**12**	**0**	**14**	**0**	**–2**								
	Cape Breton Oilers	AHL	58	9	30	39				174																		
1996-97	**Edmonton Oilers**	**NHL**	**37**	**0**	**4**	**4**	**0**	**4**	**4**	**52**	**0**	**0**	**0**	**31**	**0.0**	**23**	**1**	**36**	**12**	**–2**	**12**	**0**	**1**	**1**	**8**	**0**	**0**	**0**
	Hamilton Bulldogs	AHL	34	4	14	18				26																		
1997-98	**Edmonton Oilers**	**NHL**	**65**	**7**	**4**	**11**	**8**	**4**	**12**	**80**	**1**	**0**	**0**	**53**	**13.2**	**30**	**1**	**65**	**19**	**–17**	**7**	**0**	**0**	**0**	**21**	**0**	**0**	**0**
1998-99	**Nashville Predators**	**NHL**	**6**	**0**	**0**	**0**	**0**	**0**	**0**	**4**	**0**	**0**	**0**	**1**	**1.0**	**2**	**0**	**8**	**2**	**–4**								
	Colorado Avalanche	**NHL**	**67**	**1**	**3**	**4**	**1**	**3**	**4**	**60**	**0**	**0**	**0**	**56**	**56.0**	**33**	**2**	**44**	**10**	**–3**	**19**	**0**	**2**	**2**	**22**	**0**	**0**	**0**
99-2000	**Colorado Avalanche**	**NHL**	**69**	**2**	**7**	**9**	**2**	**6**	**8**	**73**	**0**	**0**	**0**	**40**	**5.0**	**32**	**0**	**51**	**12**	**–7**	**5**	**0**	**0**	**0**	**4**	**0**	**0**	**0**
	NHL Totals		**257**	**11**	**19**	**30**	**12**	**18**	**30**	**281**	**1**	**0**	**0**	**189**	**5.8**	**132**	**4**	**218**	**55**		**43**	**0**	**3**	**3**	**55**	**0**	**0**	**0**

Signed as a free agent by **Edmonton**, March 20, 1994. Traded to **Nashville** by **Edmonton** with Eric Fichaud and Drake Berehowsky for Mikhail Shtalenkov and Jim Dowd, October 1, 1998. Traded to **Colorado** by **Nashville** for Colorado's 2nd round choice (Ed Hill) in 1999 Entry Draft, October 24, 1998.

• DEZIEL, Michel

LW – L. 5'11", 180 lbs. b: Sorel, Que., 1/31/1954. Buffalo's 3rd, 47th overall, in 1974.

Season	Club	League	GP	G	A	Pts	AG	AA	APts	PIM	PP	SH	GW	S	%	TGF	PGF	TGA	PGA	+/–	GP	G	A	Pts	PIM	PP	SH	GW
1970-71	Sorel Black Hawks	QJHL	60	25	22	47				44											7	2	5	7	0			
1971-72	Sorel Black Hawks	QMJHL	48	29	32	61				30											4	0	2	2	2			
1972-73	Sorel Black Hawks	QMJHL	64	50	72	122				49																		
1973-74	Sorel Black Hawks	QMJHL	69	92	135	227				69																		
1974-75	Hershey Bears	AHL	69	27	24	51				10											8	0	3	3	16			
	Buffalo Sabres	**NHL**																			**1**	**0**	**0**	**0**	**0**	**0**	**0**	**0**
1975-76	Hershey Bears	AHL	71	25	30	55				42											4	0	0	0	2			
1976-77	Rhode Island Reds	AHL	70	15	28	43				10																		
1977-78	Binghamton Dusters	AHL	8	2	0	2				2																		
1978-79			DID NOT PLAY																									
1979-80	Milwaukee Admirals	IHL	9	1	0	1				2																		
	NHL Totals																				**1**	**0**	**0**	**0**	**0**	**0**	**0**	**0**

QMJHL First All-Star Team (1974)

• Di PIETRO, Paul

C – R. 5'9", 181 lbs. b: Sault Ste. Marie, Ont., 9/8/1970. Montreal's 6th, 102nd overall, in 1990.

Season	Club	League	GP	G	A	Pts	AG	AA	APts	PIM	PP	SH	GW	S	%	TGF	PGF	TGA	PGA	+/–	GP	G	A	Pts	PIM	PP	SH	GW
1985-86	Sault Ste. Marie Legionnaires	NOHA	38	33	25	58				87																		
1986-87	Sudbury Wolves	OHL	49	5	11	16				13																		
1987-88	Sudbury Wolves	OHL	63	25	42	67				27																		
1988-89	Sudbury Wolves	OHL	57	31	48	79				27																		
1989-90	Sudbury Wolves	OHL	66	56	63	119				57											7	3	6	9	7			
1990-91	Fredericton Canadiens	AHL	78	39	31	70				38											9	5	6	11	2			
1991-92	**Montreal Canadiens**	**NHL**	**33**	**4**	**6**	**10**	**4**	**5**	**9**	**25**	**0**	**0**	**0**	**27**	**14.8**	**13**	**0**	**8**	**0**	**5**								
	Fredericton Canadiens	AHL	43	26	31	57				52											7	3	4	7	8			
1992-93♦	**Montreal Canadiens**	**NHL**	**29**	**4**	**13**	**17**	**3**	**9**	**12**	**14**	**0**	**0**	**0**	**43**	**9.3**	**24**	**3**	**11**	**1**	**11**	**17**	**8**	**5**	**13**	**8**	**0**	**0**	**1**
	Fredericton Canadiens	AHL	26	8	16	24				16																		
1993-94	**Montreal Canadiens**	**NHL**	**70**	**13**	**20**	**33**	**12**	**16**	**28**	**37**	**2**	**0**	**0**	**115**	**11.3**	**52**	**10**	**44**	**0**	**–2**	**7**	**2**	**4**	**6**	**2**	**2**	**0**	**1**
1994-95	**Montreal Canadiens**	**NHL**	**22**	**4**	**5**	**9**	**7**	**7**	**14**	**4**	**0**	**0**	**1**	**41**	**9.8**	**15**	**3**	**16**	**1**	**–3**								
	Toronto Maple Leafs	**NHL**	**12**	**1**	**1**	**2**	**2**	**1**	**3**	**6**	**0**	**0**	**0**	**19**	**5.3**	**2**	**0**	**9**	**1**	**–6**	**7**	**1**	**1**	**2**	**0**	**0**	**0**	**0**
1995-96	**Toronto Maple Leafs**	**NHL**	**20**	**4**	**4**	**8**	**4**	**3**	**7**	**4**	**1**	**0**	**0**	**23**	**17.4**	**8**	**2**	**11**	**2**	**–3**								
	St. John's Maple Leafs	AHL	2	2	2	4				0																		
	Houston Aeros	IHL	36	18	23	41				44																		
	Las Vegas Thunder	IHL	13	5	6	11				10											13	4	8	12	16			
1996-97	**Los Angeles Kings**	**NHL**	**6**	**1**	**0**	**1**	**1**	**0**	**1**	**6**	**0**	**0**	**0**	**10**	**10.0**	**1**	**0**	**3**	**0**	**–2**								
	Phoenix Roadrunners	IHL	33	9	20	29				32																		
	Cincinnati Cyclones	IHL	32	15	14	29				28											3	1	1	2	2			
1997-98	Kassel Huskies	Germany	48	20	32	52				16																		

			REGULAR SEASON																		PLAYOFFS							
Season	Club	League	GP	G	A	Pts	AG	AA	APts	PIM	PP	SH	GW	S	%	TGF	PGF	TGA	PGA	+/-	GP	G	A	Pts	PIM	PP	SH	GW
1998-99	HC Ambri-Piotta	Switz.	45	*38	44	82				22											15	6	12	18	22			
99-2000	EV Zug	Switz.	45	20	34	54				58											10	3	5	8	10			
	Canada	Nat-Team	4	0	3	3				0																		
	NHL Totals		**192**	**31**	**49**	**80**	**33**	**41**	**74**	**96**	**3**	**0**	**1**	**278**	**11.2**	**115**	**18**	**102**	**5**		**31**	**11**	**10**	**21**	**10**	**2**	**0**	**2**

Traded to **Toronto** by **Montreal** for Phoenix's 4th round choice (previously acquired, Montreal selected Kim Staal) in 1996 Entry Draft, April 6, 1995. Signed as a free agent by **LA Kings**, July 23, 1996.

• DIDUCK, Gerald

D – R. 6'2", 217 lbs. b: Edmonton, Alta., 4/6/1965. NY Islanders' 2nd, 16th overall, in 1983.

Season	Club	League	GP	G	A	Pts	AG	AA	APts	PIM	PP	SH	GW	S	%	TGF	PGF	TGA	PGA	+/-	GP	G	A	Pts	PIM	PP	SH	GW
1980-81	Sherwood Park Kings	AAHA	STATISTICS NOT AVAILABLE																									
1981-82	Lethbridge Broncos	WHL	71	1	15	16				81											12	0	3	3	27			
1982-83	Lethbridge Broncos	WHL	67	8	16	24				151											20	3	12	15	49			
	Lethbridge Broncos	Mem-Cup	3	0	1	1				2																		
1983-84	Lethbridge Broncos	WHL	65	10	24	34				133											5	1	4	5	27			
	Canada	WJC-A	7	0	0	0				4																		
	Indianapolis Checkers	CHL																			10	1	6	7	19			
1984-85	**New York Islanders**	**NHL**	65	2	8	10	2	5	7	80	0	0	0	52	3.8	58	2	62	8	2								
1985-86	**New York Islanders**	**NHL**	10	1	2	3	1	1	2	2	0	0	0	6	16.7	11	0	8	2	5								
	Springfield Indians	AHL	61	6	14	20				173																		
1986-87	**New York Islanders**	**NHL**	30	2	3	5	2	2	4	67	0	0	0	54	3.7	28	8	33	10	–3	14	0	1	1	35	0	0	0
	Springfield Indians	AHL	45	6	8	14				120																		
1987-88	**New York Islanders**	**NHL**	68	7	12	19	6	9	15	113	4	0	1	128	5.5	82	21	59	20	22	6	1	0	1	42	1	0	0
1988-89	**New York Islanders**	**NHL**	65	11	21	32	9	15	24	155	6	0	0	132	8.3	98	33	88	32	9								
1989-90	**New York Islanders**	**NHL**	76	3	17	20	3	12	15	163	1	0	0	102	2.9	82	9	101	30	2	5	0	0	0	12	0	0	0
1990-91	Montreal Canadiens	Fr-Tour	4	0	1	1				31																		
	Montreal Canadiens	**NHL**	32	1	2	3	1	2	3	39	0	0	0	34	2.9	33	1	35	6	3								
	Vancouver Canucks	**NHL**	31	3	7	10	3	5	8	66	0	0	1	66	4.5	24	6	35	9	–8	6	1	0	1	11	1	0	0
1991-92	**Vancouver Canucks**	**NHL**	77	6	21	27	5	16	21	229	2	0	1	128	4.7	78	26	75	20	–3	5	0	0	0	10	0	0	0
1992-93	**Vancouver Canucks**	**NHL**	80	6	14	20	5	10	15	171	0	1	0	92	6.5	100	17	82	31	32	12	4	2	6	12	0	0	0
1993-94	**Vancouver Canucks**	**NHL**	55	1	10	11	1	8	9	72	0	0	0	50	2.0	44	6	58	22	2	24	1	7	8	22	0	0	0
1994-95	**Vancouver Canucks**	**NHL**	22	1	3	4	2	4	6	15	1	0	0	25	4.0	12	3	25	8	–8								
	Chicago Blackhawks	**NHL**	13	1	0	1	2	0	2	48	1	0	0	42	2.4	8	1	5	1	3	16	1	3	4	22	0	0	0
1995-96	**Hartford Whalers**	**NHL**	79	1	9	10	1	7	8	88	0	0	0	93	1.1	62	1	88	34	7								
1996-97	**Hartford Whalers**	**NHL**	56	1	10	11	1	9	10	40	0	0	1	59	1.7	40	4	55	10	–9								
	Phoenix Coyotes	**NHL**	11	1	2	3	1	2	3	23	1	0	0	21	4.8	12	3	9	2	2	7	0	0	0	10	0	0	0
1997-98	**Phoenix Coyotes**	**NHL**	78	8	10	18	9	10	19	118	1	0	4	104	7.7	62	2	79	33	14	6	0	2	2	20	0	0	0
1998-99	**Phoenix Coyotes**	**NHL**	44	0	2	2	0	2	2	72	0	0	0	39	0.0	25	0	24	8	9	3	0	0	0	2	0	0	0
99-2000	Canada	Nat-Team	12	3	0	3				6																		
	Toronto Maple Leafs	**NHL**	26	0	3	3	0	3	3	33	0	0	0	18	0.0	18	0	20	4	2	10	0	1	1	14	0	0	0
	NHL Totals		**918**	**56**	**156**	**212**	**54**	**122**	**176**	**1594**	**17**	**1**	**8**	**1245**	**4.5**	**877**	**143**	**941**	**290**		**114**	**8**	**16**	**24**	**212**	**2**	**0**	**0**

Traded to **Montreal** by **NY Islanders** for Craig Ludwig, September 4, 1990. Traded to **Vancouver** by **Montreal** for Vancouver's 4th round choice (Vladimir Vujtek) in 1991 Entry Draft, January 12, 1991. Traded to **Chicago** by **Vancouver** for Bogdan Savenko and Hartford's 3rd round choice (previously acquired, Vancouver selected Larry Courville) in 1995 Entry Draft, April 7, 1995. Signed as a free agent by **Hartford**, August 24, 1995. Traded to **Phoenix** by **Hartford** for Chris Murray, March 18, 1997. Signed as a free agent by **Toronto**, February 3, 2000.

• DIETRICH, Don

Don Armond D – L. 6'1", 195 lbs. b: Deloraine, Man., 4/5/1961. Chicago's 14th, 183rd overall, in 1980.

Season	Club	League	GP	G	A	Pts	AG	AA	APts	PIM	PP	SH	GW	S	%	TGF	PGF	TGA	PGA	+/-	GP	G	A	Pts	PIM	PP	SH	GW
1978-79	Brandon Wheat Kings	WHL	69	6	37	43				29											21	3	2	5	10			
	Brandon Wheat Kings	Mem-Cup	5	0	1	1				2																		
1979-80	Brandon Wheat Kings	WHL	63	15	45	60				56											11	4	5	9	15			
1980-81	Brandon Wheat Kings	WHL	72	16	64	80				84											5	2	6	8	0			
1981-82	New Brunswick Hawks	AHL	62	1	5	6				14											2	0	0	0	0			
1982-83	Springfield Indians	AHL	76	6	26	32				26																		
1983-84	**Chicago Black Hawks**	**NHL**	17	0	5	5	0	3	3	0	0	0	0	22	0.0	11	0	16	4	–1								
	Springfield Indians	AHL	50	14	21	35				14																		
1984-85	Maine Mariners	AHL	75	6	21	27				36											11	3	4	7	4			
1985-86	**New Jersey Devils**	**NHL**	11	0	2	2	0	1	1	10	0	0	0	14	0.0	10	3	15	0	–8								
	Maine Mariners	AHL	68	9	11	20				33											3	0	0	0	0			
1986-87	Schwenninger ERC	Germany	35	14	29	43				34											3	1	1	2	0			
	EHC Kloten	Switz.	2	0	1	1															8	0	1	1				
1987-88	Schwenninger ERC	Germany	22	5	18	23				8											5	0	1	1	2			
	Hershey Bears	AHL	3	0	0	0				0																		
1988-89	Schwenninger ERC	Germany	35	12	23	35				24											3	1	0	1	2			
1989-90	ETC Timmendorfer	Germany-2	36	24	22	46				14											20	8	22	30	10			
	Canada	Nat-Team	3	0	2	2				2																		
1990-91	Moncton Hawks	AHL	3	0	2	2				0																		
	New Haven Nighthawks	AHL	13	0	2	2				0																		
	Roanoke Valley Rebels	ECHL	2	0	1	1				8																		
	NHL Totals		**28**	**0**	**7**	**7**	**0**	**4**	**4**	**10**	**0**	**0**	**0**	**36**	**0.0**	**21**	**3**	**31**	**4**									

Traded to **New Jersey** by **Chicago** with Rich Preston and Chicago's 2nd round choice (Eric Weinrich) for Bob MacMillan and New Jersey's 5th round choice (Rick Herbert) in 1985 Entry Draft, June 19, 1984.

• DILLABOUGH, Bob

Robert Wellington C – L. 5'10", 180 lbs. b: Belleville, Ont., 4/27/1941.

Season	Club	League	GP	G	A	Pts	AG	AA	APts	PIM	PP	SH	GW	S	%	TGF	PGF	TGA	PGA	+/-	GP	G	A	Pts	PIM	PP	SH	GW
1957-58	Hamilton Tiger Cubs	OHA-Jr.	2	0	2	2				0											5	0	0	0	0			
1958-59	Hamilton Tiger Cubs	OHA-Jr.	54	11	20	31				58																		
1959-60	Hamilton Tiger Cubs	OHA-Jr.	48	14	20	34				22																		
1960-61	Hamilton Red Wings	OHA-Jr.	48	27	20	47				28											12	8	8	16	2			
1961-62	**Detroit Red Wings**	**NHL**	5	0	0	0	0	0	0	2																		
	Hershey Bears	AHL	5	2	1	3				2																		
	Sudbury Wolves	EPHL	34	17	16	33				12											5	0	1	1	14			
1962-63	Edmonton Flyers	WHL	10	2	0	2				4																		
	Pittsburgh Hornets	AHL	52	15	19	34				32																		
	Detroit Red Wings	**NHL**																			1	0	0	0	0	0	0	0
1963-64	Pittsburgh Hornets	AHL	72	9	19	28				18											5	2	2	4	6			
	Detroit Red Wings	**NHL**																			1	0	0	0	0	0	0	0
1964-65	**Detroit Red Wings**	**NHL**	4	0	0	0	0	0	0	2											4	0	0	0	0	0	0	0
	Pittsburgh Hornets	AHL	52	13	25	38				18											4	0	3	3	2			
1965-66	**Boston Bruins**	**NHL**	53	7	13	20	8	12	20	18																		
1966-67	**Boston Bruins**	**NHL**	60	6	12	18	7	12	19	14																		
1967-68	**Pittsburgh Penguins**	**NHL**	47	7	12	19	8	12	20	18	1	0	0	70	10.0	26	2	35	4	–7								
	Baltimore Clippers	AHL	6	1	0	1				2																		
1968-69	**Pittsburgh Penguins**	**NHL**	14	0	0	0	0	0	0	2	0	0	0	2	0.0	0	0	7	1	–6								
	Oakland Seals	**NHL**	48	7	12	19	7	11	18	4	0	0	3	51	13.7	28	0	40	8	–4	7	3	0	3	0	0	1	0
1969-70	**Oakland Seals**	**NHL**	52	5	5	10	5	5	10	16	1	1	0	45	11.1	18	5	49	18	–18	4	0	0	0	0	0	0	0
1970-71	Rochester Americans	AHL	1	0	0	0				2																		
	Phoenix Roadrunners	WHL	45	3	12	15				14											7	1	1	2	0			

			REGULAR SEASON																		PLAYOFFS							
Season	Club	League	GP	G	A	Pts	AG	AA	APts	PIM	PP	SH	GW	S	%	TGF	PGF	TGA	PGA	+/–	GP	G	A	Pts	PIM	PP	SH	GW
1971-72	Tidewater Red Wings	AHL	15	0	0	0	....	....	....	4	....	....	....	....	....	....	....	....	....	....	....	....	....	....	....	....	....	....
1972-73	Cleveland Crusaders	WHA	72	8	8	16	....	....	....	8	....	....	....	....	....	....	....	....	....	....	9	1	0	1	0	....	....	....
1973-74	Toledo Hornets	IHL	51	14	23	37	....	....	....	20	....	....	....	....	....	....	....	....	....	....	2	0	0	0	0	....	....	....
	NHL Totals		**283**	**32**	**54**	**86**	**35**	**52**	**87**	**76**	....	....	....	....	....	....	....	....	....		**17**	**3**	**0**	**3**	**0**	....	....	....
	Other Major League Totals		72	8	8	16	....	....	....	8	....	....	....	....	....	....	....	....	....	....	9	1	0	1	0	....	....	....

Traded to **Boston** by **Detroit** with Albert Langlois, Ron Harris and Parker MacDonald for Ab McDonald, Bob McCord and Ken Stephanson, May 31, 1965. Claimed by **Pittsburgh** from **Boston** in Expansion Draft, June 6, 1967. Traded to **Oakland** by **Pittsburgh** for Billy Harris, November 29, 1968. Claimed by **Vancouver** from **Oakland** in Expansion Draft, June 10, 1970. Loaned to **Phoenix** (WHL) by **Vancouver** (Rochester-AHL) for cash, November 11, 1970. Traded to **Detroit** by **Vancouver** with Irv Spencer for John Cunniff and Gary Bredin, June 8, 1971. Signed as a free agent by **Cleveland** (WHA), August, 1972.

• DILLON, Gary

Gary Kevin C – L. 5'10", 173 lbs. b: Toronto, Ont., 2/28/1959. Colorado's 3rd, 85th overall, in 1979.

Season	Club	League	GP	G	A	Pts	AG	AA	APts	PIM	PP	SH	GW	S	%	TGF	PGF	TGA	PGA	+/–	GP	G	A	Pts	PIM	PP	SH	GW
1974-75	Markham Waxers	OHA-B	31	26	29	55	....	....	....	46	....	....	....	....	....	....	....	....	....	....	....	....	....	....	....	....	....	....
1975-76	Toronto Marlboros	OMJHL	60	23	46	69	....	....	....	68	....	....	....	....	....	....	....	....	....	....	10	2	9	11	45	....	....	....
1976-77	Toronto Marlboros	OMJHL	64	40	62	102	....	....	....	77	....	....	....	....	....	....	....	....	....	....	6	2	3	5	6	....	....	....
1977-78	Toronto Marlboros	OMJHL	64	39	45	84	....	....	....	112	....	....	....	....	....	....	....	....	....	....	5	2	1	3	38	....	....	....
1978-79	Toronto Marlboros	OMJHL	59	57	63	120	....	....	....	40	....	....	....	....	....	....	....	....	....	....	3	0	0	0	2	....	....	....
1979-80	Fort Worth Texans	CHL	77	30	26	56	....	....	....	34	....	....	....	....	....	....	....	....	....	....	15	8	9	17	2	....	....	....
1980-81	**Colorado Rockies**	**NHL**	**13**	**1**	**1**	**2**	**1**	**1**	**2**	**29**	**0**	**0**	**0**	**15**	**6.7**	**4**	**0**	**10**	**0**	**–6**	....	....	....	....	....	....	....	....
	Fort Worth Texans	CHL	54	9	16	25	....	....	....	28	....	....	....	....	....	....	....	....	....	....	5	2	1	3	2	....	....	....
1981-82	Fredericton Express	AHL	54	18	21	39	....	....	....	68	....	....	....	....	....	....	....	....	....	....	....	....	....	....	....	....	....	....
	NHL Totals		**13**	**1**	**1**	**2**	**1**	**1**	**2**	**29**	**0**	**0**	**0**	**15**	**6.7**	**4**	**0**	**10**	**0**		....	....	....	....	....	....	....	....

• Brother of Wayne • OHA First All-Star Team (1979)

Signed as a free agent by **Quebec**, October 7, 1981.

• DILLON, Wayne

Gerald Wayne "Tommy" C – L. 6', 185 lbs. b: Toronto, Ont., 5/25/1955. NY Rangers' 1st, 12th overall, in 1975.

Season	Club	League	GP	G	A	Pts	AG	AA	APts	PIM	PP	SH	GW	S	%	TGF	PGF	TGA	PGA	+/–	GP	G	A	Pts	PIM	PP	SH	GW
1970-71	Markham Waxers	OHA-B	STATISTICS NOT AVAILABLE																									
1971-72	Toronto Marlboros	OMJHL	56	14	14	28	....	....	....	8	....	....	....	....	....	....	....	....	....	....	10	0	1	1	0	....	....	....
1972-73	Toronto Marlboros	OMJHL	59	47	60	107	....	....	....	25	....	....	....	....	....	....	....	....	....	....	10	2	10	12	10	....	....	....
	Toronto Marlboros	Mem-Cup	3	1	3	4	....	....	....	0	....	....	....	....	....	....	....	....	....	....	....	....	....	....	....	....	....	....
1973-74	Toronto Toros	WHA	71	30	35	65	....	....	....	13	....	....	....	....	....	....	....	....	....	....	12	5	6	11	9	....	....	....
1974-75	Toronto Toros	WHA	77	29	66	95	....	....	....	22	....	....	....	....	....	....	....	....	....	....	6	4	4	8	4	....	....	....
1975-76	**New York Rangers**	**NHL**	**79**	**21**	**24**	**45**	**18**	**18**	**36**	**10**	**3**	**0**	**1**	**138**	**15.2**	**67**	**8**	**70**	**0**	**–11**	....	....	....	....	....	....	....	....
1976-77	**New York Rangers**	**NHL**	**78**	**17**	**29**	**46**	**15**	**22**	**37**	**33**	**1**	**0**	**1**	**158**	**10.8**	**58**	**7**	**65**	**0**	**–14**	....	....	....	....	....	....	....	....
1977-78	**New York Rangers**	**NHL**	**59**	**5**	**13**	**18**	**5**	**10**	**15**	**15**	**1**	**0**	**1**	**50**	**10.0**	**25**	**5**	**30**	**2**	**–8**	**3**	**0**	**1**	**1**	**0**	**0**	**0**	**0**
	New Haven Nighthawks	AHL	3	2	0	2	....	....	....	0	....	....	....	....	....	....	....	....	....	....	....	....	....	....	....	....	....	....
1978-79	Birmingham Bulls	WHA	64	12	27	39	....	....	....	43	....	....	....	....	....	....	....	....	....	....	....	....	....	....	....	....	....	....
1979-80	**Winnipeg Jets**	**NHL**	**13**	**0**	**0**	**0**	**0**	**0**	**0**	**2**	**0**	**0**	**0**	**5**	**0.0**	**0**	**0**	**6**	**0**	**–6**	....	....	....	....	....	....	....	....
	Canada	Nat-Team	4	1	0	1	....	....	....	4	....	....	....	....	....	....	....	....	....	....	....	....	....	....	....	....	....	....
1980-81	SC Rapperswil-Jona	Switz-2	STATISTICS NOT AVAILABLE																									
1981-82	Fredericton Express	AHL	37	7	13	20	....	....	....	25	....	....	....	....	....	....	....	....	....	....	....	....	....	....	....	....	....	....
	NHL Totals		**229**	**43**	**66**	**109**	**38**	**50**	**88**	**60**	**5**	**0**	**3**	**351**	**12.3**	**150**	**20**	**171**	**2**		**3**	**0**	**1**	**1**	**0**	**0**	**0**	**0**
	Other Major League Totals		212	71	128	199	....	....	....	78	....	....	....	....	....	....	....	....	....	....	18	9	10	19	13	....	....	....

• Brother of Gary

Signed as an underage free agent by **Toronto** (WHA), August, 1973. Transferred to **Birmingham** (WHA) after **Toronto** (WHA) franchise relocated, June 30, 1976. Traded to **Winnipeg** by **NY Rangers** for future considerations, July, 25, 1979.

• DiMAIO, Rob

Robert C – R. 5'10", 190 lbs. b: Calgary, Alta., 2/19/1968. NY Islanders' 6th, 118th overall, in 1987.

Season	Club	League	GP	G	A	Pts	AG	AA	APts	PIM	PP	SH	GW	S	%	TGF	PGF	TGA	PGA	+/–	GP	G	A	Pts	PIM	PP	SH	GW
1983-84	Calgary Royals	AAHA	STATISTICS NOT AVAILABLE																									
1984-85	Kamloops Blazers	WHL	55	9	18	27	....	....	....	29	....	....	....	....	....	....	....	....	....	....	7	1	3	4	2	....	....	....
1985-86	Kamloops Blazers	WHL	6	1	0	1	....	....	....	0	....	....	....	....	....	....	....	....	....	....	....	....	....	....	....	....	....	....
	Medicine Hat Tigers	WHL	55	20	30	50	....	....	....	82	....	....	....	....	....	....	....	....	....	....	22	6	6	12	39	....	....	....
1986-87	Medicine Hat Tigers	WHL	70	27	43	70	....	....	....	130	....	....	....	....	....	....	....	....	....	....	20	7	11	18	46	....	....	....
	Medicine Hat Tigers	Mem-Cup	5	*4	1	5	....	....	....	17	....	....	....	....	....	....	....	....	....	....	....	....	....	....	....	....	....	....
1987-88	Medicine Hat Tigers	WHL	54	47	43	90	....	....	....	120	....	....	....	....	....	....	....	....	....	....	14	12	19	*31	59	....	....	....
	Canada	WJC-A	7	1	0	1	....	....	....	10	....	....	....	....	....	....	....	....	....	....	....	....	....	....	....	....	....	....
	Medicine Hat Tigers	Mem-Cup	5	4	5	9	....	....	....	21	....	....	....	....	....	....	....	....	....	....	....	....	....	....	....	....	....	....
1988-89	**New York Islanders**	**NHL**	**16**	**1**	**0**	**1**	**1**	**0**	**1**	**30**	**0**	**0**	**1**	**16**	**6.3**	**3**	**0**	**17**	**8**	**–6**	....	....	....	....	....	....	....	....
	Springfield Indians	AHL	40	13	18	31	....	....	....	67	....	....	....	....	....	....	....	....	....	....	....	....	....	....	....	....	....	....
1989-90	**New York Islanders**	**NHL**	**7**	**0**	**0**	**0**	**0**	**0**	**0**	**2**	**0**	**0**	**0**	**2**	**0.0**	**0**	**0**	**0**	**0**	**0**	**1**	**1**	**0**	**1**	**4**	**0**	**0**	**0**
	Springfield Indians	AHL	54	25	27	52	....	....	....	69	....	....	....	....	....	....	....	....	....	....	16	4	7	11	45	....	....	....
1990-91	**New York Islanders**	**NHL**	**1**	**0**	**0**	**0**	**0**	**0**	**0**	**0**	**0**	**0**	**0**	**0**	**0.0**	**0**	**0**	**0**	**0**	**0**	....	....	....	....	....	....	....	....
	Capital District Islanders	AHL	12	3	4	7	....	....	....	22	....	....	....	....	....	....	....	....	....	....	....	....	....	....	....	....	....	....
1991-92	**New York Islanders**	**NHL**	**50**	**5**	**2**	**7**	**5**	**2**	**7**	**43**	**0**	**2**	**0**	**43**	**11.6**	**10**	**0**	**57**	**24**	**–23**	....	....	....	....	....	....	....	....
1992-93	**Tampa Bay Lightning**	**NHL**	**54**	**9**	**15**	**24**	**7**	**10**	**17**	**62**	**2**	**0**	**0**	**75**	**12.0**	**32**	**3**	**34**	**5**	**0**	....	....	....	....	....	....	....	....
1993-94	**Tampa Bay Lightning**	**NHL**	**39**	**8**	**7**	**15**	**7**	**5**	**12**	**40**	**2**	**0**	**1**	**51**	**15.7**	**18**	**7**	**17**	**1**	**–5**	....	....	....	....	....	....	....	....
	Philadelphia Flyers	**NHL**	**14**	**3**	**5**	**8**	**3**	**4**	**7**	**6**	**0**	**0**	**1**	**30**	**10.0**	**12**	**1**	**10**	**0**	**1**	....	....	....	....	....	....	....	....
1994-95	**Philadelphia Flyers**	**NHL**	**36**	**3**	**1**	**4**	**5**	**1**	**6**	**53**	**0**	**0**	**0**	**34**	**8.8**	**12**	**0**	**13**	**9**	**8**	**15**	**2**	**4**	**6**	**4**	**0**	**1**	**1**
1995-96	**Philadelphia Flyers**	**NHL**	**59**	**6**	**15**	**21**	**6**	**12**	**18**	**58**	**1**	**1**	**0**	**49**	**12.2**	**29**	**5**	**38**	**14**	**0**	**3**	**0**	**0**	**0**	**0**	**0**	**0**	**0**
1996-97	**Boston Bruins**	**NHL**	**72**	**13**	**15**	**28**	**14**	**13**	**27**	**82**	**0**	**3**	**2**	**152**	**8.6**	**45**	**4**	**80**	**18**	**–21**	....	....	....	....	....	....	....	....
1997-98	**Boston Bruins**	**NHL**	**79**	**10**	**17**	**27**	**12**	**17**	**29**	**82**	**0**	**0**	**4**	**112**	**8.9**	**42**	**7**	**64**	**16**	**–13**	**6**	**1**	**0**	**1**	**8**	**0**	**0**	**0**
1998-99	**Boston Bruins**	**NHL**	**71**	**7**	**14**	**21**	**8**	**13**	**21**	**95**	**1**	**0**	**0**	**121**	**5.8**	**31**	**5**	**52**	**12**	**–14**	**12**	**2**	**0**	**2**	**8**	**0**	**0**	**1**
99-2000	**Boston Bruins**	**NHL**	**50**	**5**	**16**	**21**	**6**	**15**	**21**	**42**	**0**	**0**	**0**	**93**	**5.4**	**25**	**0**	**42**	**16**	**–1**	....	....	....	....	....	....	....	....
	New York Rangers	**NHL**	**12**	**1**	**3**	**4**	**1**	**3**	**4**	**8**	**0**	**0**	**0**	**18**	**5.6**	**4**	**1**	**13**	**2**	**–8**	....	....	....	....	....	....	....	....
	NHL Totals		**560**	**71**	**110**	**181**	**75**	**95**	**170**	**603**	**6**	**6**	**9**	**796**	**8.9**	**263**	**33**	**437**	**125**		**37**	**6**	**4**	**10**	**24**	**0**	**1**	**2**

Won Stafford Smythe Memorial Trophy (Memorial Cup Tournament MVP) (1988)

Claimed by **Tampa Bay** from **NY Islanders** in Expansion Draft, June 18, 1992. Traded to **Philadelphia** by **Tampa Bay** for Jim Cummins and Philadelphia's 4th round choice (later traded back to Philadelphia — Philadelphia selected Radovan Somik) in 1995 Entry Draft, March 18, 1994. Claimed by **San Jose** from **Philadelphia** in NHL Waiver Draft, September 30, 1996. Traded to **Boston** by **San Jose** for Boston's 5th round choice (Adam Nittel) in 1997 Entry Draft, September 30, 1996. Traded to **NY Rangers** by **Boston** for Mike Knuble, March 10, 2000.

• DINEEN, Gary

Gary Daniel Patrick C – L. 5'10", 175 lbs. b: Montreal, Que., 12/24/1943.

Season	Club	League	GP	G	A	Pts	AG	AA	APts	PIM	PP	SH	GW	S	%	TGF	PGF	TGA	PGA	+/–	GP	G	A	Pts	PIM	PP	SH	GW
1960-61	St. Michael's Majors	OHA-Jr.	12	0	0	0	....	....	....	0	....	....	....	....	....	....	....	....	....	....	6	0	0	0	0	....	....	....
	St. Michael's Majors	Mem-Cup	1	0	0	0	....	....	....	0	....	....	....	....	....	....	....	....	....	....	....	....	....	....	....	....	....	....
1961-62	St. Michael's Majors	MTJHL	33	26	*35	*61	....	....	....	19	....	....	....	....	....	....	....	....	....	....	11	7	11	18	0	....	....	....
	St. Michael's Majors	Mem-Cup	5	2	4	6	....	....	....	2	....	....	....	....	....	....	....	....	....	....	....	....	....	....	....	....	....	....
1962-63	Neil McNeil Maroons	MTJHL	38	32	*63	*95	....	....	....	33	....	....	....	....	....	....	....	....	....	....	10	*12	*18	*30	0	....	....	....
	Neil McNeil Maroons	Mem-Cup	6	1	5	6	....	....	....	2	....	....	....	....	....	....	....	....	....	....	....	....	....	....	....	....	....	....
1963-64	Canada	Nat-Team	PLAYED EXHIBITION SEASON ONLY																									
	Canada	Olympics	7	3	6	9	....	....	....	10	....	....	....	....	....	....	....	....	....	....	....	....	....	....	....	....	....	....
	Toronto Marlboros	OHA-Jr.	2	1	5	6	....	....	....	4	....	....	....	....	....	....	....	....	....	....	9	5	12	17	8	....	....	....
	Toronto Marlboros	Mem-Cup	10	10	10	20	....	....	....	0	....	....	....	....	....	....	....	....	....	....	....	....	....	....	....	....	....	....
1964-65	University of British Columbia	WCIAA	STATISTICS NOT AVAILABLE																									
	Canada	WEC-A	7	6	5	11	....	....	....	4	....	....	....	....	....	....	....	....	....	....	....	....	....	....	....	....	....	....
1965-66	Canada	Nat-Team	PLAYED EXHIBITION SEASON ONLY																									
1966-67	Canada	Nat-Team	PLAYED EXHIBITION SEASON ONLY																									
	Canada	WEC-A	7	1	4	5	....	....	....	6	....	....	....	....	....	....	....	....	....	....	....	....	....	....	....	....	....	....
1967-68	Ottawa Nationals	OHA-Sr.	20	7	20	27	....	....	....	4	....	....	....	....	....	....	....	....	....	....	....	....	....	....	....	....	....	....
	Canada	Olympics	7	1	2	3	....	....	....	6	....	....	....	....	....	....	....	....	....	....	....	....	....	....	....	....	....	....

			REGULAR SEASON																		PLAYOFFS							
Season	Club	League	GP	G	A	Pts	AG	AA	APts	PIM	PP	SH	GW	S	%	TGF	PGF	TGA	PGA	+/-	GP	G	A	Pts	PIM	PP	SH	GW
1968-69	**Minnesota North Stars**	**NHL**	**4**	**0**	**1**	**1**	**0**	**1**	**1**	**0**	**0**	**0**	**0**	**2**	**0.0**	**2**	**2**	**2**	**0**	**–2**								
	Memphis South Stars	CHL	63	11	38	49				0																		
1969-70	Iowa Stars	CHL	15	3	2	5				2																		
	Salt Lake Golden Eagles	WHL	10	1	2	3				0																		
	Springfield Kings	AHL	8	1	2	3				0																		
1970-71	Springfield Kings	AHL	56	12	22	34				28											12	4	7	11	6			
1971-72	Springfield Kings	AHL	DID NOT PLAY – COACHING																									
	NHL Totals		**4**	**0**	**1**	**1**	**0**	**1**	**1**	**0**	**0**	**0**	**0**	**2**	**0.0**	**2**	**2**	**2**	**0**									

Rights traded to **Minnesota** by **Toronto** for cash, June, 1967. Claimed by **LA Kings** (Springfield-AHL) by **Minnesota** in Reverse Draft, June 10, 1970.

• DINEEN, Gord

Gordon M. D – R. 6', 195 lbs. b: Quebec City, Que., 9/21/1962. NY Islanders' 2nd, 42nd overall, in 1981.

Season	Club	League	GP	G	A	Pts	AG	AA	APts	PIM	PP	SH	GW	S	%	TGF	PGF	TGA	PGA	+/-	GP	G	A	Pts	PIM	PP	SH	GW
1979-80	St. Michael's Buzzers	OHA-B	42	11	24	35				103																		
1980-81	Sault Ste. Marie Greyhounds	OMJHL	68	4	26	30				158											19	1	7	8	58			
1981-82	Sault Ste. Marie Greyhounds	OHL	68	9	45	54				185											13	1	2	3	52			
1982-83	**New York Islanders**	**NHL**	**2**	**0**	**0**	**0**	**0**	**0**	**0**	**4**	**0**	**0**	**0**	**3**	**0.0**	**1**	**1**	**2**	**0**	**–2**								
	Indianapolis Checkers	CHL	73	10	47	57				78											13	2	10	12	29			
1983-84	**New York Islanders**	**NHL**	**43**	**1**	**11**	**12**	**1**	**7**	**8**	**32**	**0**	**0**	**0**	**37**	**2.7**	**49**	**2**	**39**	**2**	**10**	**9**	**1**	**1**	**2**	**28**	**0**	**0**	**0**
	Indianapolis Checkers	CHL	26	4	13	17				63																		
1984-85	**New York Islanders**	**NHL**	**48**	**1**	**12**	**13**	**1**	**8**	**9**	**89**	**0**	**0**	**0**	**45**	**2.2**	**48**	**2**	**45**	**9**	**10**	**10**	**0**	**0**	**0**	**26**	**0**	**0**	**0**
	Springfield Indians	AHL	25	1	8	9				46																		
1985-86	**New York Islanders**	**NHL**	**57**	**1**	**8**	**9**	**1**	**5**	**6**	**81**	**0**	**0**	**0**	**52**	**1.9**	**58**	**1**	**59**	**17**	**15**	**3**	**0**	**0**	**0**	**2**	**0**	**0**	**0**
	Springfield Indians	AHL	11	2	3	5				20																		
1986-87	**New York Islanders**	**NHL**	**71**	**4**	**10**	**14**	**3**	**7**	**10**	**110**	**0**	**0**	**0**	**59**	**6.8**	**47**	**0**	**76**	**21**	**–8**	**7**	**0**	**4**	**4**	**4**	**0**	**0**	**0**
1987-88	**New York Islanders**	**NHL**	**57**	**4**	**12**	**16**	**3**	**9**	**12**	**62**	**1**	**0**	**0**	**50**	**8.0**	**63**	**7**	**78**	**31**	**9**								
	Minnesota North Stars	**NHL**	**13**	**1**	**1**	**2**	**1**	**1**	**2**	**21**	**0**	**0**	**0**	**6**	**16.7**	**9**	**0**	**23**	**9**	**–5**								
1988-89	**Minnesota North Stars**	**NHL**	**2**	**0**	**1**	**1**	**0**	**1**	**1**	**2**	**0**	**0**	**0**	**7**	**0.0**	**1**	**1**	**5**	**1**	**–4**								
	Kalamazoo Wings	IHL	25	2	6	8				49																		
	Pittsburgh Penguins	**NHL**	**38**	**1**	**2**	**3**	**1**	**1**	**2**	**42**	**0**	**0**	**0**	**25**	**4.0**	**29**	**2**	**43**	**11**	**–5**	**11**	**0**	**2**	**2**	**8**	**0**	**0**	**0**
1989-90	**Pittsburgh Penguins**	**NHL**	**69**	**1**	**8**	**9**	**1**	**6**	**7**	**125**	**0**	**0**	**0**	**38**	**2.6**	**58**	**0**	**83**	**31**	**6**								
1990-91	**Pittsburgh Penguins**	**NHL**	**9**	**0**	**0**	**0**	**0**	**0**	**0**	**6**	**0**	**0**	**0**	**6**	**0.0**	**4**	**0**	**9**	**1**	**–4**								
	Muskegon Lumberjacks	IHL	40	1	14	15				57											5	0	2	2	0			
1991-92	**Pittsburgh Penguins**	**NHL**	**1**	**0**	**0**	**0**	**0**	**0**	**0**	**0**	**0**	**0**	**0**	**0**	**0.0**	**1**	**0**	**3**	**0**	**–2**								
	Muskegon Lumberjacks	IHL	79	8	37	45				83											14	2	4	6	33			
1992-93	**Ottawa Senators**	**NHL**	**32**	**2**	**4**	**6**	**2**	**3**	**5**	**30**	**1**	**0**	**0**	**36**	**5.6**	**25**	**5**	**54**	**15**	**–19**								
	San Diego Gulls	IHL	41	6	23	29				36																		
1993-94	**Ottawa Senators**	**NHL**	**77**	**0**	**21**	**21**	**0**	**16**	**16**	**89**	**0**	**0**	**0**	**62**	**0.0**	**59**	**9**	**160**	**58**	**–52**								
	San Diego Gulls	IHL	3	0	0	0				2																		
1994-95	**New York Islanders**	**NHL**	**9**	**0**	**0**	**0**	**0**	**0**	**0**	**2**	**0**	**0**	**0**	**4**	**0.0**	**2**	**0**	**8**	**1**	**–5**								
	Denver Grizzlies	IHL	68	5	27	32				75											17	1	6	7	8			
1995-96	Utah Grizzlies	IHL	82	1	17	18				89											22	0	3	3	14			
1996-97	Utah Grizzlies	IHL	81	5	29	34				62											7	0	3	3	4			
1997-98	Utah Grizzlies	IHL	82	3	34	37				63											4	0	2	2	2			
1998-99	Utah Grizzlies	IHL	77	5	22	27				78																		
99-2000	Utah Grizzlies	IHL	50	0	18	18				26																		
	Chicago Wolves	IHL	17	1	2	3				14											16	0	5	5	12			
	NHL Totals		**528**	**16**	**90**	**106**	**14**	**64**	**78**	**695**	**2**	**0**	**0**	**430**	**3.7**	**454**	**30**	**687**	**207**		**40**	**1**	**7**	**8**	**68**	**0**	**0**	**0**

• Son of Bill • Brother of Peter and Kevin • CHL First All-Star Team (1983) • Won Bob Gassoff Trophy (CHL's Most Improved Defenseman) (1983) • Won Bobby Orr Trophy (CHL's Top Defenseman) (1983) • IHL First All-Star Team (1992) • IHL Second All-Star Team (1998)

Traded to **Minnesota** by **NY Islanders** for Chris Pryor and Minnesota's 7th round choice (Brett Harkins) in 1989 Entry Draft, March 8, 1988. Traded to **Pittsburgh** by **Minnesota** with Scott Bjugstad for Ville Siren and Steve Gotaas, December 17, 1988. Signed as a free agent by **Ottawa**, August 31, 1992. Signed as a free agent by **NY Islanders**, July 26, 1994. • Traded to **Chicago** (IHL) by **Utah** (IHL) for Brendan Buckley and Sean Berens, March 16, 2000.

• DINEEN, Kevin

Kevin William RW – R. 5'11", 189 lbs. b: Quebec City, Que., 10/28/1963. Hartford's 3rd, 56th overall, in 1982.

Season	Club	League	GP	G	A	Pts	AG	AA	APts	PIM	PP	SH	GW	S	%	TGF	PGF	TGA	PGA	+/-	GP	G	A	Pts	PIM	PP	SH	GW
1980-81	St. Michael's Buzzers	OHA-B	40	15	28	43				167																		
1981-82	University of Denver	WCHA	26	10	10	20				70																		
1982-83	University of Denver	WCHA	36	16	13	29				108																		
1983-84	Canada	Nat-Team	52	5	11	16				2																		
	Canada	Olympics	7	0	0	0				8																		
1984-85	**Hartford Whalers**	**NHL**	**57**	**25**	**16**	**41**	**20**	**11**	**31**	**120**	**8**	**4**	**2**	**141**	**17.7**	**53**	**14**	**54**	**9**	**–6**								
	Binghamton Whalers	AHL	25	15	8	23				41																		
	Canada	WEC-A	10	3	2	5				10																		
1985-86	**Hartford Whalers**	**NHL**	**57**	**33**	**35**	**68**	**26**	**24**	**50**	**124**	**6**	**0**	**8**	**167**	**19.8**	**93**	**25**	**57**	**5**	**16**	**10**	**6**	**7**	**13**	**18**	**1**	**0**	**2**
1986-87	**Hartford Whalers**	**NHL**	**78**	**40**	**39**	**79**	**35**	**28**	**63**	**110**	**11**	**0**	**7**	**234**	**17.1**	**128**	**50**	**71**	**0**	**7**	**6**	**2**	**1**	**3**	**31**	**1**	**0**	**0**
	NHL All-Stars	RV-87	2	1	0	1				0																		
	Canada	WEC-A	9	4	2	6				20																		
1987-88	Canada	Can-Cup	3	1	2	3				0																		
	Hartford Whalers	**NHL**	**74**	**25**	**25**	**50**	**21**	**18**	**39**	**217**	**5**	**0**	**4**	**223**	**11.2**	**86**	**40**	**63**	**3**	**–14**	**6**	**4**	**4**	**8**	**8**	**1**	**0**	**1**
1988-89	**Hartford Whalers**	**NHL**	**79**	**45**	**44**	**89**	**38**	**31**	**69**	**167**	**20**	**1**	**4**	**294**	**15.3**	**122**	**53**	**79**	**4**	**–6**	**4**	**1**	**0**	**1**	**10**	**0**	**0**	**0**
	Canada	WEC-A	10	3	7	10				12																		
1989-90	**Hartford Whalers**	**NHL**	**67**	**25**	**41**	**66**	**21**	**29**	**50**	**164**	**8**	**2**	**2**	**214**	**11.7**	**90**	**40**	**55**	**12**	**7**	**6**	**3**	**2**	**5**	**18**	**0**	**0**	**1**
1990-91	**Hartford Whalers**	**NHL**	**61**	**17**	**30**	**47**	**16**	**23**	**39**	**104**	**4**	**0**	**2**	**161**	**10.6**	**59**	**23**	**56**	**5**	**–15**	**6**	**1**	**0**	**1**	**16**	**0**	**0**	**0**
1991-92	**Hartford Whalers**	**NHL**	**16**	**4**	**2**	**6**	**4**	**2**	**6**	**23**	**1**	**0**	**1**	**28**	**14.3**	**7**	**2**	**15**	**4**	**–6**								
	Philadelphia Flyers	**NHL**	**64**	**26**	**30**	**56**	**24**	**23**	**47**	**130**	**5**	**3**	**4**	**197**	**13.2**	**82**	**25**	**77**	**21**	**1**								
1992-93	**Philadelphia Flyers**	**NHL**	**83**	**35**	**28**	**63**	**29**	**19**	**48**	**201**	**6**	**3**	**7**	**241**	**14.5**	**117**	**27**	**97**	**21**	**14**								
	Canada	WC-A	8	1	2	3				8																		
1993-94	**Philadelphia Flyers**	**NHL**	**71**	**19**	**23**	**42**	**18**	**18**	**36**	**113**	**5**	**1**	**2**	**156**	**12.2**	**77**	**21**	**83**	**18**	**–9**								
1994-95	**Philadelphia Flyers**	**NHL**	**40**	**8**	**5**	**13**	**14**	**7**	**21**	**39**	**4**	**0**	**2**	**55**	**14.5**	**22**	**4**	**22**	**3**	**–1**	**15**	**6**	**4**	**10**	**18**	**1**	**0**	**1**
	Houston Aeros	IHL	17	6	4	10				42																		
1995-96	**Philadelphia Flyers**	**NHL**	**26**	**0**	**2**	**2**	**0**	**2**	**2**	**50**	**0**	**0**	**0**	**31**	**0.0**	**4**	**2**	**12**	**2**	**–8**								
	Hartford Whalers	**NHL**	**20**	**2**	**7**	**9**	**2**	**6**	**8**	**67**	**0**	**0**	**0**	**35**	**5.7**	**18**	**2**	**12**	**3**	**7**								
1996-97	**Hartford Whalers**	**NHL**	**78**	**19**	**29**	**48**	**20**	**26**	**46**	**141**	**8**	**0**	**5**	**185**	**10.3**	**79**	**31**	**65**	**11**	**–6**								
1997-98	**Carolina Hurricanes**	**NHL**	**54**	**7**	**16**	**23**	**8**	**16**	**24**	**105**	**0**	**0**	**1**	**96**	**7.3**	**31**	**6**	**37**	**5**	**–7**								
1998-99	**Carolina Hurricanes**	**NHL**	**67**	**8**	**10**	**18**	**9**	**10**	**19**	**97**	**0**	**0**	**1**	**86**	**9.3**	**29**	**3**	**21**	**0**	**5**	**6**	**0**	**0**	**0**	**8**	**0**	**0**	**0**
99-2000	**Ottawa Senators**	**NHL**	**67**	**4**	**8**	**12**	**4**	**7**	**11**	**57**	**0**	**0**	**1**	**71**	**5.6**	**22**	**0**	**21**	**1**	**2**								
	NHL Totals		**1059**	**342**	**390**	**732**	**309**	**300**	**609**	**2029**	**91**	**14**	**53**	**2615**	**13.1**	**1119**	**368**	**897**	**127**		**59**	**23**	**18**	**41**	**127**	**4**	**0**	**5**

• Son of Bill • Brother of Peter and Gord • Won Bud Light/NHL Man of the Year Award (1991) • Played in NHL All-Star Game (1988, 1989)

Traded to **Philadelphia** by **Hartford** for Murray Craven and Philadelphia's 4th round choice (Kevin Smyth) in 1992 Entry Draft, November 13, 1991. Traded to **Hartford** by **Philadelphia** for Hartford/Carolina's 3rd (Kris Mallette) and 7th (later traded back to Hartford/Carolina - Carolina selected Andrew Merrick) round choices in 1997 Entry Draft, December 28, 1995. Transferred to **Carolina** after **Hartford** franchise relocated, June 25, 1997. Signed as a free agent by **Ottawa**, September 1, 1999. Selected by **Columbus** from **Ottawa** in Expansion Draft, June 23, 2000.

• DINEEN, Peter

Peter Kevin D – R. 5'11", 181 lbs. b: Kingston, Ont., 11/19/1960. Philadelphia's 9th, 189th overall, in 1980.

Season	Club	League	GP	G	A	Pts	AG	AA	APts	PIM	PP	SH	GW	S	%	TGF	PGF	TGA	PGA	+/-	GP	G	A	Pts	PIM	PP	SH	GW
1977-78	Kamloops Chiefs	BCJHL	56	13	31	44				160																		
	Seattle Breakers	WCJHL	2	0	0	0				0																		
1978-79	Kingston Canadians	OMJHL	60	7	14	21				70											11	2	6	8	29			
1979-80	Kingston Canadians	OMJHL	32	4	10	14				54											3	0	0	0	13			
1980-81	Maine Mariners	AHL	41	6	7	13				100											16	1	2	3	82			
1981-82	Maine Mariners	AHL	71	6	14	20				156											3	0	0	0	2			
1982-83	Maine Mariners	AHL	2	0	0	0				0																		
	Moncton Alpines	AHL	59	0	10	10				76																		

Season	Club	League	GP	G	A	Pts	AG	AA	APts	PIM	PP	SH	GW	S	%	TGF	PGF	TGA	PGA	+/-	GP	G	A	Pts	PIM	PP	SH	GW
			REGULAR SEASON																		PLAYOFFS							
1983-84	Moncton Alpines	AHL	63	0	10	10	....	....	....	120	....	....	....	....	....	....	....	....	....	....	....	....	....	....	....	....	....	....
	Hershey Bears	AHL	12	0	1	1	....	....	....	32	....	....	....	....	....	....	....	....	....	....	....	....	....	....	....	....	....	....
1984-85	Hershey Bears	AHL	79	4	19	23	....	....	....	144	....	....	....	....	....	....	....	....	....	....	....	....	....	....	....	....	....	....
1985-86	Binghamton Whalers	AHL	11	0	1	1	....	....	....	35	....	....	....	....	....	....	....	....	....	....	....	....	....	....	....	....	....	....
	Moncton Golden Flames	AHL	55	5	13	18	....	....	....	136	....	....	....	....	....	....	....	....	....	....	9	1	0	1	9	....	....	....
1986-87	**Los Angeles Kings**	**NHL**	**11**	**0**	**2**	**2**	**0**	**1**	**1**	**8**	**0**	**0**	**0**	**5**	**0.0**	**4**	**0**	**15**	**2**	**–9**	....	....	....	....	....	....	....	....
	New Haven Nighthawks	AHL	59	2	17	19	....	....	....	140	....	....	....	....	....	....	....	....	....	....	7	0	1	1	27	....	....	....
1987-88	Adirondack Red Wings	AHL	76	8	26	34	....	....	....	137	....	....	....	....	....	....	....	....	....	....	11	0	2	2	20	....	....	....
1988-89	Adirondack Red Wings	AHL	32	2	12	14	....	....	....	61	....	....	....	....	....	....	....	....	....	....	17	2	5	7	22	....	....	....
1989-90	**Detroit Red Wings**	**NHL**	**2**	**0**	**0**	**0**	**0**	**0**	**0**	**5**	**0**	**0**	**0**	**0**	**0.0**	**1**	**0**	**1**	**0**	**0**	....	....	....	....	....	....	....	....
	Adirondack Red Wings	AHL	27	3	6	9	....	....	....	28	....	....	....	....	....	....	....	....	....	....	6	0	1	1	10	....	....	....
1990-91	San Diego Gulls	IHL	24	0	1	1	....	....	....	17	....	....	....	....	....	....	....	....	....	....	....	....	....	....	....	....	....	....
	NHL Totals		**13**	**0**	**2**	**2**	**0**	**1**	**1**	**13**	**0**	**0**	**0**	**5**	**0.0**	**5**	**0**	**16**	**2**		....	....	....	....	....	....	....	....

• Son of Bill • Brother of Gord and Kevin

Traded to **Edmonton** by **Philadelphia** for Bob Hoffmeyer, October 22, 1982. Signed as a free agent by **Boston**, July 16, 1984. Signed as a free agent by **LA Kings**, July 30, 1986. Signed as a free agent by **Detroit**, September 16, 1987. Missed majority of 1989-90 season due to shoulder injury suffered in game vs. St. Louis, December 5, 1989.

• DINGMAN, Chris

Christopher LW – L. 6'4", 235 lbs. b: Edmonton, Alta., 7/6/1976. Calgary's 1st, 19th overall, in 1994.

Season	Club	League	GP	G	A	Pts	AG	AA	APts	PIM	PP	SH	GW	S	%	TGF	PGF	TGA	PGA	+/-	GP	G	A	Pts	PIM	PP	SH	GW
1991-92	Edmonton Mercurys	AAHA	36	23	18	41	....	....	....	72	....	....	....	....	....	....	....	....	....	....	....	....	....	....	....	....	....	....
1992-93	Brandon Wheat Kings	WHL	50	10	17	27	....	....	....	64	....	....	....	....	....	....	....	....	....	....	4	0	0	0	0	....	....	....
1993-94	Brandon Wheat Kings	WHL	45	21	20	41	....	....	....	77	....	....	....	....	....	....	....	....	....	....	13	1	7	8	39	....	....	....
1994-95	Brandon Wheat Kings	WHL	66	40	43	83	....	....	....	201	....	....	....	....	....	....	....	....	....	....	3	1	0	1	9	....	....	....
	Brandon Wheat Kings	Mem-Cup	2	0	0	0	....	....	....	0	....	....	....	....	....	....	....	....	....	....	....	....	....	....	....	....	....	....
1995-96	Brandon Wheat Kings	WHL	40	16	29	45	....	....	....	109	....	....	....	....	....	....	....	....	....	....	19	12	11	23	60	....	....	....
	Saint John Flames	AHL	....	....	....	....	....	....	....	....	....	....	....	....	....	....	....	....	....	....	1	0	0	0	0	....	....	....
	Brandon Wheat Kings	Mem-Cup	4	1	1	2	....	....	....	8	....	....	....	....	....	....	....	....	....	....	....	....	....	....	....	....	....	....
1996-97	Saint John Flames	AHL	71	5	6	11	....	....	....	195	....	....	....	....	....	....	....	....	....	....	....	....	....	....	....	....	....	....
1997-98	**Calgary Flames**	**NHL**	**70**	**3**	**3**	**6**	**4**	**3**	**7**	**149**	**1**	**0**	**0**	**47**	**6.4**	**13**	**1**	**24**	**1**	**–11**	....	....	....	....	....	....	....	....
1998-99	**Calgary Flames**	**NHL**	**2**	**0**	**0**	**0**	**0**	**0**	**0**	**17**	**0**	**0**	**0**	**1**	**0.0**	**0**	**0**	**2**	**0**	**–2**	....	....	....	....	....	....	....	....
	Saint John Flames	AHL	50	5	7	12	....	....	....	140	....	....	....	....	....	....	....	....	....	....	....	....	....	....	....	....	....	....
	Colorado Avalanche	**NHL**	**1**	**0**	**0**	**0**	**0**	**0**	**0**	**7**	**0**	**0**	**0**	**0**	**0.0**	**0**	**0**	**0**	**0**	**0**	....	....	....	....	....	....	....	....
	Hershey Bears	AHL	17	1	3	4	....	....	....	102	....	....	....	....	....	....	....	....	....	....	5	0	2	2	6	....	....	....
99-2000	**Colorado Avalanche**	**NHL**	**68**	**8**	**3**	**11**	**9**	**3**	**12**	**132**	**2**	**0**	**1**	**54**	**14.8**	**15**	**4**	**13**	**0**	**–2**	....	....	....	....	....	....	....	....
	NHL Totals		**141**	**11**	**6**	**17**	**13**	**6**	**19**	**305**	**3**	**0**	**1**	**102**	**10.8**	**28**	**5**	**39**	**1**		....	....	....	....	....	....	....	....

Traded to **Colorado** by **Calgary** with Theoren Fleury for Rene Corbet, Wade Belak, Robyn Regehr and Colorado's 2nd round compensatory choice (Jarret Stoll) in 2000 Entry Draft, February 28, 1999.

• DIONNE, Gilbert

LW – L. 6', 194 lbs. b: Drummondville, Que., 9/19/1970. Montreal's 5th, 81st overall, in 1990.

Season	Club	League	GP	G	A	Pts	AG	AA	APts	PIM	PP	SH	GW	S	%	TGF	PGF	TGA	PGA	+/-	GP	G	A	Pts	PIM	PP	SH	GW
1986-87	Niagara Falls Canucks	OJHL-B	17	9	6	15	....	....	....	16	....	....	....	....	....	....	....	....	....	....	....	....	....	....	....	....	....	....
1987-88	Niagara Falls Canucks	OJHL-B	36	36	48	84	....	....	....	60	....	....	....	....	....	....	....	....	....	....	....	....	....	....	....	....	....	....
1988-89	Kitchener Rangers	OHL	66	11	33	44	....	....	....	13	....	....	....	....	....	....	....	....	....	....	5	1	1	2	4	....	....	....
1989-90	Kitchener Rangers	OHL	64	48	57	105	....	....	....	85	....	....	....	....	....	....	....	....	....	....	17	13	10	23	22	....	....	....
	Kitchener Rangers	Mem-Cup	5	4	6	10	....	....	....	8	....	....	....	....	....	....	....	....	....	....	....	....	....	....	....	....	....	....
1990-91	**Montreal Canadiens**	**NHL**	**2**	**0**	**0**	**0**	**0**	**0**	**0**	**0**	**0**	**0**	**0**	**0**	**0.0**	**0**	**0**	**2**	**0**	**–2**	....	....	....	....	....	....	....	....
	Fredericton Canadiens	AHL	77	40	47	87	....	....	....	62	....	....	....	....	....	....	....	....	....	....	9	6	5	11	8	....	....	....
1991-92	**Montreal Canadiens**	**NHL**	**39**	**21**	**13**	**34**	**19**	**10**	**29**	**10**	**7**	**0**	**2**	**90**	**23.3**	**48**	**18**	**23**	**0**	**7**	**11**	**3**	**4**	**7**	**10**	**1**	**0**	**1**
	Fredericton Canadiens	AHL	29	19	27	46	....	....	....	20	....	....	....	....	....	....	....	....	....	....	....	....	....	....	....	....	....	....
1992-93♦	**Montreal Canadiens**	**NHL**	**75**	**20**	**28**	**48**	**17**	**19**	**36**	**63**	**6**	**1**	**2**	**145**	**13.8**	**67**	**22**	**45**	**5**	**5**	**20**	**6**	**6**	**12**	**20**	**1·**	**0**	**1**
	Fredericton Canadiens	AHL	3	4	3	7	....	....	....	0	....	....	....	....	....	....	....	....	....	....	....	....	....	....	....	....	....	....
1993-94	**Montreal Canadiens**	**NHL**	**74**	**19**	**26**	**45**	**18**	**20**	**38**	**31**	**3**	**0**	**5**	**162**	**11.7**	**71**	**24**	**59**	**3**	**–9**	**5**	**1**	**2**	**3**	**0**	**0**	**0**	**0**
1994-95	**Montreal Canadiens**	**NHL**	**6**	**0**	**3**	**3**	**0**	**4**	**4**	**2**	**0**	**0**	**0**	**4**	**0.0**	**3**	**1**	**5**	**0**	**–3**	....	....	....	....	....	....	....	....
	Philadelphia Flyers	**NHL**	**20**	**0**	**6**	**6**	**0**	**9**	**9**	**2**	**0**	**0**	**0**	**29**	**0.0**	**9**	**3**	**7**	**0**	**–1**	**3**	**0**	**0**	**0**	**4**	**0**	**0**	**0**
1995-96	**Philadelphia Flyers**	**NHL**	**2**	**0**	**1**	**1**	**0**	**1**	**1**	**0**	**0**	**0**	**0**	**0**	**0.0**	**1**	**0**	**1**	**0**	**0**	....	....	....	....	....	....	....	....
	Florida Panthers	**NHL**	**5**	**1**	**2**	**3**	**1**	**2**	**3**	**0**	**0**	**0**	**0**	**12**	**8.3**	**4**	**1**	**3**	**0**	**0**	....	....	....	....	....	....	....	....
	Carolina Monarchs	AHL	55	43	58	101	....	....	....	29	....	....	....	....	....	....	....	....	....	....	....	....	....	....	....	....	....	....
1996-97	Carolina Monarchs	AHL	72	41	47	88	....	....	....	69	....	....	....	....	....	....	....	....	....	....	....	....	....	....	....	....	....	....
1997-98	Cincinnati Cyclones	IHL	76	42	57	99	....	....	....	54	....	....	....	....	....	....	....	....	....	....	9	3	4	7	28	....	....	....
1998-99	Cincinnati Cyclones	IHL	76	35	53	88	....	....	....	123	....	....	....	....	....	....	....	....	....	....	3	0	2	2	6	....	....	....
99-2000	Cincinnati Cyclones	IHL	81	34	49	83	....	....	....	88	....	....	....	....	....	....	....	....	....	....	11	4	3	7	8	....	....	....
	NHL Totals		**223**	**61**	**79**	**140**	**55**	**65**	**120**	**108**	**16**	**1**	**9**	**442**	**13.8**	**203**	**69**	**145**	**8**		**39**	**10**	**12**	**22**	**34**	**2**	**0**	**2**

• Brother of Marcel • NHL All-Rookie Team (1992) • AHL Second All-Star Team (1996) • IHL First All-Star Team (1998) • IHL Second All-Star Team (2000)

Traded to **Philadelphia** by **Montreal** with Eric Desjardins and John LeClair for Mark Recchi and Philadelphia's 3rd round choice (Martin Hohenberger) in 1995 Entry Draft, February 9, 1995. Signed as a free agent by **Florida**, January 29, 1996. Signed as a free agent by **Cincinnati** (IHL), July 23, 1997. Signed as a free agent by **Carolina**, August 31, 1999.

• DIONNE, Marcel

Marcel Elphege "Little Beaver" C – R. 5'9", 190 lbs. b: Drummondville, Que., 8/3/1951. Detroit's 1st, 2nd overall, in 1971. **HHOF**

Season	Club	League	GP	G	A	Pts	AG	AA	APts	PIM	PP	SH	GW	S	%	TGF	PGF	TGA	PGA	+/-	GP	G	A	Pts	PIM	PP	SH	GW
1966-67	Montreal Laurentides	QAAA	24	32	39	71	....	....	....	....	....	....	....	....	....	....	....	....	....	....	....	....	....	....	....	....	....	....
1967-68	Drummondville Rangers	QJHL	48	34	35	69	....	....	....	45	....	....	....	....	....	....	....	....	....	....	10	14	7	21	4	....	....	....
	Drummondville Rangers	Mem-Cup	4	9	4	13	....	....	....	5	....	....	....	....	....	....	....	....	....	....	....	....	....	....	....	....	....	....
1968-69	St. Catharines Black Hawks	OHA-Jr.	48	37	63	100	....	....	....	38	....	....	....	....	....	....	....	....	....	....	18	15	20	35	8	....	....	....
1969-70	St. Catharines Black Hawks	OHA-Jr.	54	*55	*77	*132	....	....	....	46	....	....	....	....	....	....	....	....	....	....	10	12	20	32	10	....	....	....
1970-71	St. Catharines Black Hawks	OHA-Jr.	46	62	81	*143	....	....	....	20	....	....	....	....	....	....	....	....	....	....	15	*29	*26	*55	11	....	....	....
1971-72	**Detroit Red Wings**	**NHL**	**78**	**28**	**49**	**77**	**28**	**43**	**71**	**14**	**7**	**0**	**2**	**268**	**10.4**	**107**	**44**	**64**	**1**	**0**	....	....	....	....	....	....	....	....
1972-73	Team Canada	Summit-72	DID NOT PLAY																									
	Detroit Red Wings	**NHL**	**77**	**40**	**50**	**90**	**38**	**40**	**78**	**21**	**10**	**0**	**6**	**282**	**14.2**	**116**	**46**	**77**	**3**	**–4**								
1973-74	**Detroit Red Wings**	**NHL**	**74**	**24**	**54**	**78**	**23**	**45**	**68**	**10**	**3**	**0**	**1**	**280**	**8.6**	**106**	**42**	**96**	**1**	**–31**	....	....	....	....	....	....	....	....
1974-75	**Detroit Red Wings**	**NHL**	**80**	**47**	**74**	**121**	**41**	**56**	**97**	**14**	**15**	**10**	**2**	**378**	**12.4**	**167**	**72**	**140**	**30**	**–15**	....	....	....	....	....	....	....	....
1975-76	**Los Angeles Kings**	**NHL**	**80**	**40**	**54**	**94**	**35**	**40**	**75**	**38**	**7**	**1**	**6**	**329**	**12.2**	**116**	**35**	**92**	**13**	**2**	**9**	**6**	**1**	**7**	**0**	**3**	**0**	**0**
1976-77	Canada	Can-Cup	7	1	5	6	....	....	....	4	....	....	....	....	....	....	....	....	....	....	....	....	....	....	....	....	....	....
	Los Angeles Kings	**NHL**	**80**	**53**	**69**	**122**	**48**	**53**	**101**	**12**	**14**	**1**	**5**	**378**	**14.0**	**151**	**64**	**91**	**14**	**10**	**9**	**5**	**9**	**14**	**2**	**1**	**0**	**1**
1977-78	**Los Angeles Kings**	**NHL**	**70**	**36**	**43**	**79**	**33**	**33**	**66**	**37**	**9**	**0**	**4**	**294**	**12.2**	**107**	**43**	**75**	**3**	**–8**	**2**	**0**	**0**	**0**	**0**	**0**	**0**	**0**
	Canada	WEC-A	10	9	3	12	....	....	....	2	....	....	....	....	....	....	....	....	....	....	....	....	....	....	....	....	....	....
1978-79	**Los Angeles Kings**	**NHL**	**80**	**59**	**71**	**130**	**51**	**52**	**103**	**30**	**19**	**0**	**7**	**362**	**16.3**	**169**	**67**	**87**	**8**	**23**	**2**	**0**	**1**	**1**	**0**	**0**	**0**	**0**
	NHL All-Stars	Chal-Cup	2	0	1	1	....	....	....	0	....	....	....	....	....	....	....	....	....	....	....	....	....	....	....	....	....	....
	Canada	WEC-A	7	2	1	3	....	....	....	4	....	....	....	....	....	....	....	....	....	....	....	....	....	....	....	....	....	....
1979-80	**Los Angeles Kings**	**NHL**	**80**	**53**	**84**	***137**	**45**	**62**	**107**	**32**	**17**	**0**	**6**	**348**	**15.2**	**184**	**74**	**80**	**5**	**35**	**4**	**0**	**3**	**3**	**4**	**0**	**0**	**0**
1980-81	**Los Angeles Kings**	**NHL**	**80**	**58**	**77**	**135**	**45**	**51**	**96**	**70**	**23**	**4**	**9**	**342**	**17.0**	**203**	**76**	**79**	**7**	**55**	**4**	**1**	**3**	**4**	**7**	**1**	**0**	**0**
1981-82	Canada	Can-Cup	6	4	1	5	....	....	....	4	....	....	....	....	....	....	....	....	....	....	....	....	....	....	....	....	....	....
	Los Angeles Kings	**NHL**	**78**	**50**	**67**	**117**	**40**	**45**	**85**	**50**	**17**	**1**	**5**	**351**	**14.2**	**149**	**58**	**115**	**14**	**–10**	**10**	**7**	**4**	**11**	**0**	**4**	**0**	**0**
1982-83	**Los Angeles Kings**	**NHL**	**80**	**56**	**51**	**107**	**46**	**35**	**81**	**22**	**17**	**1**	**7**	**345**	**16.2**	**145**	**53**	**86**	**4**	**10**	....	....	....	....	....	....	....	....
	Canada	WEC-A	10	6	3	9	....	....	....	2	....	....	....	....	....	....	....	....	....	....	....	....	....	....	....	....	....	....
1983-84	**Los Angeles Kings**	**NHL**	**66**	**39**	**53**	**92**	**31**	**36**	**67**	**28**	**13**	**0**	**2**	**278**	**14.0**	**125**	**51**	**72**	**6**	**8**	....	....	....	....	....	....	....	....
1984-85	**Los Angeles Kings**	**NHL**	**80**	**46**	**80**	**126**	**38**	**55**	**93**	**46**	**16**	**1**	**2**	**316**	**14.6**	**151**	**62**	**90**	**12**	**11**	**3**	**1**	**2**	**3**	**2**	**1**	**0**	**0**
1985-86	**Los Angeles Kings**	**NHL**	**80**	**36**	**58**	**94**	**29**	**39**	**68**	**42**	**11**	**0**	**4**	**284**	**12.7**	**118**	**42**	**128**	**30**	**–22**	....	....	....	....	....	....	....	....
	Canada	WEC-A	10	4	4	8	....	....	....	8	....	....	....	....	....	....	....	....	....	....	....	....	....	....	....	....	....	....
1986-87	**Los Angeles Kings**	**NHL**	**67**	**24**	**50**	**74**	**21**	**36**	**57**	**54**	**9**	**0**	**2**	**224**	**10.7**	**104**	**44**	**72**	**4**	**–8**	....	....	....	....	....	....	....	....
	New York Rangers	**NHL**	**14**	**4**	**6**	**10**	**3**	**4**	**7**	**6**	**1**	**0**	**0**	**49**	**8.2**	**12**	**5**	**15**	**0**	**–8**	**6**	**1**	**1**	**2**	**2**	**1**	**0**	**0**

			REGULAR SEASON																		PLAYOFFS							
Season	**Club**	**League**	**GP**	**G**	**A**	**Pts**	**AG**	**AA**	**APts**	**PIM**	**PP**	**SH**	**GW**	**S**	**%**	**TGF**	**PGF**	**TGA**	**PGA**	**+/–**	**GP**	**G**	**A**	**Pts**	**PIM**	**PP**	**SH**	**GW**
1987-88	**New York Rangers**	**NHL**	**67**	**31**	**34**	**65**	**26**	**24**	**50**	**54**	**22**	**0**	**4**	**184**	**16.8**	**90**	**63**	**43**	**2**	**–14**	....	....	....	....	....	....	....	....
1988-89	**New York Rangers**	**NHL**	**37**	**7**	**16**	**23**	**6**	**11**	**17**	**20**	**4**	**0**	**0**	**74**	**9.5**	**37**	**20**	**23**	**0**	**–6**	....	....	....	....	....	....	....	....
	Denver Rangers	IHL	9	0	13	13	....	....	....	6	....	....	....	....	....	....	....	....	....	....	....	....	....	....	....	....	....	....
	NHL Totals		**1348**	**731**	**1040**	**1771**	**627**	**760**	**1387**	**600**	**234**	**19**	**74**	**5366**	**13.6**	**2357**	**961**	**1525**	**157**		**49**	**21**	**24**	**45**	**17**	**11**	**0**	**1**

• Brother of Gilbert • OHA-Jr. Second All-Star Team (1970) • OHA-Jr. First All-Star Team (1971) • Won Lady Byng Trophy (1975, 1977) • NHL First All-Star Team (1977, 1980) • Named Best Forward at WEC-A (1978) • NHL Second All-Star Team (1979, 1981) • Won Lester B. Pearson Award (1979, 1980) • Won Art Ross Trophy (1980) • Played in NHL All-Star Game (1975, 1976, 1977, 1978, 1980, 1981, 1983, 1985)

• Signed as a free agent by **LA Kings**, June 17, 1975. • NHL orchestrated trade to **LA Kings** by **Detroit** with Bart Crashley for Terry Harper, Dan Maloney and LA Kings 2nd round choice (later traded to Minnesota — Minnesota selected Jim Roberts) in 1976 Amateur Draft, June 23, 1975. Traded to **NY Rangers** by **LA Kings** with Jeff Crossman and LA Kings' 3rd round choice (later traded to Minnesota — Minnesota selected Murray Garbutt) in 1989 Entry Draft for Bob Carpenter and Tom Laidlaw, March 10, 1987.

• DIRK, Robert

D – L. 6'4", 210 lbs. b: Regina, Sask., 8/20/1966. St. Louis' 4th, 53rd overall, in 1984.

Season	Club	League	GP	G	A	Pts	AG	AA	APts	PIM	PP	SH	GW	S	%	TGF	PGF	TGA	PGA	+/–	GP	G	A	Pts	PIM	PP	SH	GW
1982-83	Notre Dame Midget Hounds	SAHA	23	1	6	7	....	....	....	8	....	....	....	....	....	....	....	....	....	....	....	....	....	....	....	....	....	....
	Kelowna Blazers	BCJHL	27	3	7	10	....	....	....	43	....	....	....	....	....	....	....	....	....	....	13	5	16	21	34	....	....	....
	Regina Pats	WHL	1	0	0	0	....	....	....	0	....	....	....	....	....	....	....	....	....	....	....	....	....	....	....	....	....	....
1983-84	Regina Pats	WHL	62	2	10	12	....	....	....	64	....	....	....	....	....	....	....	....	....	....	23	1	12	13	24	....	....	....
1984-85	Regina Pats	WHL	69	10	34	44	....	....	....	97	....	....	....	....	....	....	....	....	....	....	8	0	0	0	4	....	....	....
1985-86	Regina Pats	WHL	72	19	60	79	....	....	....	140	....	....	....	....	....	....	....	....	....	....	10	3	5	8	8	....	....	....
1986-87	Peoria Rivermen	IHL	76	5	17	22	....	....	....	155	....	....	....	....	....	....	....	....	....	....	....	....	....	....	....	....	....	....
1987-88	**St. Louis Blues**	**NHL**	**7**	**0**	**1**	**1**	**0**	**1**	**1**	**16**	**0**	**0**	**0**	**2**	**0.0**	**2**	**0**	**4**	**2**	**0**	**6**	**0**	**1**	**1**	**2**	**0**	**0**	**0**
	Peoria Rivermen	IHL	54	4	21	25	....	....	....	126	....	....	....	....	....	....	....	....	....	....	....	....	....	....	....	....	....	....
1988-89	**St. Louis Blues**	**NHL**	**9**	**0**	**1**	**1**	**0**	**1**	**1**	**11**	**0**	**0**	**0**	**7**	**0.0**	**5**	**0**	**12**	**4**	**–3**	....	....	....	....	....	....	....	....
	Peoria Rivermen	IHL	22	0	2	2	....	....	....	54	....	....	....	....	....	....	....	....	....	....	....	....	....	....	....	....	....	....
1989-90	**St. Louis Blues**	**NHL**	**37**	**1**	**1**	**2**	**1**	**1**	**2**	**128**	**0**	**0**	**0**	**14**	**7.1**	**28**	**0**	**22**	**3**	**9**	**3**	**0**	**0**	**0**	**0**	**0**	**0**	**0**
	Peoria Rivermen	IHL	24	1	2	3	....	....	....	79	....	....	....	....	....	....	....	....	....	....	....	....	....	....	....	....	....	....
1990-91	**St. Louis Blues**	**NHL**	**41**	**1**	**3**	**4**	**1**	**2**	**3**	**100**	**0**	**0**	**0**	**20**	**5.0**	**31**	**0**	**29**	**0**	**2**	....	....	....	....	....	....	....	....
	Peoria Rivermen	IHL	3	0	0	0	....	....	....	2	....	....	....	....	....	....	....	....	....	....	....	....	....	....	....	....	....	....
	Vancouver Canucks	**NHL**	**11**	**1**	**0**	**1**	**1**	**0**	**1**	**20**	**0**	**0**	**0**	**9**	**11.1**	**7**	**0**	**16**	**2**	**–7**	**6**	**0**	**0**	**0**	**13**	**0**	**0**	**0**
1991-92	**Vancouver Canucks**	**NHL**	**72**	**2**	**7**	**9**	**2**	**5**	**7**	**126**	**0**	**0**	**0**	**44**	**4.5**	**51**	**0**	**67**	**22**	**6**	**13**	**0**	**0**	**0**	**20**	**0**	**0**	**0**
1992-93	**Vancouver Canucks**	**NHL**	**69**	**4**	**8**	**12**	**3**	**5**	**8**	**150**	**0**	**0**	**2**	**41**	**9.8**	**66**	**0**	**68**	**27**	**25**	**9**	**0**	**0**	**0**	**6**	**0**	**0**	**0**
1993-94	**Vancouver Canucks**	**NHL**	**65**	**2**	**3**	**5**	**2**	**2**	**4**	**105**	**0**	**0**	**0**	**38**	**5.3**	**51**	**0**	**58**	**25**	**18**	....	....	....	....	....	....	....	....
	Chicago Blackhawks	**NHL**	**6**	**0**	**0**	**0**	**0**	**0**	**0**	**26**	**0**	**0**	**0**	**4**	**0.0**	**1**	**0**	**2**	**1**	**0**	**2**	**0**	**0**	**0**	**15**	**0**	**0**	**0**
1994-95	**Mighty Ducks of Anaheim**	**NHL**	**38**	**1**	**3**	**4**	**2**	**4**	**6**	**56**	**0**	**0**	**0**	**15**	**6.7**	**27**	**0**	**46**	**16**	**–3**	....	....	....	....	....	....	....	....
1995-96	**Mighty Ducks of Anaheim**	**NHL**	**44**	**1**	**2**	**3**	**1**	**2**	**3**	**42**	**0**	**0**	**0**	**20**	**5.0**	**34**	**0**	**46**	**20**	**8**	....	....	....	....	....	....	....	....
	Montreal Canadiens	**NHL**	**3**	**0**	**0**	**0**	**0**	**0**	**0**	**6**	**0**	**0**	**0**	**0**	**0.0**	**1**	**0**	**1**	**0**	**0**	....	....	....	....	....	....	....	....
1996-97	Detroit Vipers	IHL	48	2	8	10	....	....	....	36	....	....	....	....	....	....	....	....	....	....	....	....	....	....	....	....	....	....
	Chicago Wolves	IHL	31	1	5	6	....	....	....	26	....	....	....	....	....	....	....	....	....	....	3	0	0	0	0	....	....	....
1997-98	Adirondack IceHawks	UHL	DID NOT PLAY – COACHING																									
1998-2000	Saginaw Gears	UHL	DID NOT PLAY – COACHING																									
	NHL Totals		**402**	**13**	**29**	**42**	**13**	**23**	**36**	**786**	**0**	**0**	**2**	**214**	**6.1**	**304**	**0**	**371**	**122**		**39**	**0**	**1**	**1**	**56**	**0**	**0**	**0**

WHL East Second All-Star Team (1986)

Traded to **Vancouver** by **St. Louis** with Geoff Courtnall, Sergio Momesso, Cliff Ronning and St. Louis' 5th round choice (Brian Loney) in 1992 Entry Draft for Dan Quinn and Garth Butcher, March 5, 1991. Traded to **Chicago** by **Vancouver** for Chicago's 4th round choice (Mike Dubinsky) in 1994 Entry Draft, March 21, 1994. Traded to **Anaheim** by **Chicago** for Tampa Bay's 4th round choice (previously acquired, Chicago selected Chris Van Dyk) in 1995 Entry Draft, July 12, 1994. Traded to **Montreal** by **Anaheim** for Jim Campbell, January 21, 1996.

• DJOOS, Per

D – R. 5'11", 176 lbs. b: Mora, Sweden, 5/11/1968. Detroit's 7th, 127th overall, in 1986.

Season	Club	League	GP	G	A	Pts	AG	AA	APts	PIM	PP	SH	GW	S	%	TGF	PGF	TGA	PGA	+/–	GP	G	A	Pts	PIM	PP	SH	GW
1984-85	Mora IF	Sweden-2	20	2	3	5	....	....	....	2	....	....	....	....	....	....	....	....	....	....	....	....	....	....	....	....	....	....
1985-86	Mora IF	Sweden-2	32	9	5	14	....	....	....	16	....	....	....	....	....	....	....	....	....	....	....	....	....	....	....	....	....	....
	Sweden	EJC-A	5	2	4	6	....	....	....	2	....	....	....	....	....	....	....	....	....	....	....	....	....	....	....	....	....	....
1986-87	Brynas IF Gavle	Sweden	23	1	2	3	....	....	....	16	....	....	....	....	....	....	....	....	....	....	....	....	....	....	....	....	....	....
1987-88	Brynas IF Gavle	Sweden	34	4	11	15	....	....	....	18	....	....	....	....	....	....	....	....	....	....	....	....	....	....	....	....	....	....
	Sweden	WJC-A	7	0	2	2	....	....	....	4	....	....	....	....	....	....	....	....	....	....	....	....	....	....	....	....	....	....
1988-89	Brynas IF Gavle	Sweden	40	1	17	18	....	....	....	44	....	....	....	....	....	....	....	....	....	....	....	....	....	....	....	....	....	....
1989-90	Brynas IF Gavle	Sweden	37	5	13	18	....	....	....	34	....	....	....	....	....	....	....	....	....	....	5	1	3	4	6	....	....	....
	Sweden	WEC-A	7	1	0	1	....	....	....	10	....	....	....	....	....	....	....	....	....	....	....	....	....	....	....	....	....	....
1990-91	**Detroit Red Wings**	**NHL**	**26**	**0**	**12**	**12**	**0**	**9**	**9**	**16**	**0**	**0**	**0**	**23**	**0.0**	**31**	**7**	**26**	**0**	**–2**	....	....	....	....	....	....	....	....
	Adirondack Red Wings	AHL	20	2	9	11	....	....	....	6	....	....	....	....	....	....	....	....	....	....	....	....	....	....	....	....	....	....
	Binghamton Rangers	AHL	14	1	8	9	....	....	....	10	....	....	....	....	....	....	....	....	....	....	9	2	2	4	4	....	....	....
1991-92	**New York Rangers**	**NHL**	**50**	**1**	**18**	**19**	**1**	**14**	**15**	**40**	**1**	**0**	**1**	**39**	**2.6**	**48**	**15**	**27**	**1**	**7**	....	....	....	....	....	....	....	....
1992-93	**New York Rangers**	**NHL**	**6**	**1**	**1**	**2**	**1**	**1**	**2**	**2**	**0**	**0**	**0**	**4**	**25.0**	**4**	**1**	**3**	**0**	**0**	....	....	....	....	....	....	....	....
	Binghamton Rangers	AHL	70	16	53	69	....	....	....	75	....	....	....	....	....	....	....	....	....	....	14	2	8	10	8	....	....	....
1993-94	HC Lugano	Switz.	36	10	25	35	....	....	....	36	....	....	....	....	....	....	....	....	....	....	9	0	7	7	4	....	....	....
1994-95	Vastra Frolunda	Sweden	22	5	4	9	....	....	....	12	....	....	....	....	....	....	....	....	....	....	....	....	....	....	....	....	....	....
1995-96	Vastra Frolunda	Sweden	9	0	2	2	....	....	....	2	....	....	....	....	....	....	....	....	....	....	....	....	....	....	....	....	....	....
1996-97	Brynas IF Gavle	Sweden	50	3	15	18	....	....	....	76	....	....	....	....	....	....	....	....	....	....	....	....	....	....	....	....	....	....
1997-98	Brynas IF Gavle	Sweden	44	9	23	32	....	....	....	40	....	....	....	....	....	....	....	....	....	....	3	0	1	1	2	....	....	....
1998-99	Brynas IF Gavle	Sweden	50	5	*43	48	....	....	....	56	....	....	....	....	....	....	....	....	....	....	14	1	*12	13	6	....	....	....
	Sweden	WC-A	10	2	3	5	....	....	....	0	....	....	....	....	....	....	....	....	....	....	....	....	....	....	....	....	....	....
99-2000	Brynas IF Gavle	Sweden	48	5	23	28	....	....	....	40	....	....	....	....	....	....	....	....	....	....	11	3	4	7	14	....	....	....
	Brynas IF Gavle	EuroHL	6	2	4	6	....	....	....	4	....	....	....	....	....	....	....	....	....	....	....	....	....	....	....	....	....	....
	NHL Totals		**82**	**2**	**31**	**33**	**2**	**24**	**26**	**58**	**1**	**0**	**1**	**66**	**3.0**	**83**	**23**	**56**	**1**		....	....	....	....	....	....	....	....

EJC-A All-Star Team (1986) • AHL Second All-Star Team (1993)

Traded to **NY Rangers** by **Detroit** with Joey Kocur for Kevin Miller, Jim Cummins and Dennis Vial, March 5, 1991.

• DOAK, Gary

Gary Walter D – R. 5'11", 175 lbs. b: Goderich, Ont., 2/26/1946.

Season	Club	League	GP	G	A	Pts	AG	AA	APts	PIM	PP	SH	GW	S	%	TGF	PGF	TGA	PGA	+/–	GP	G	A	Pts	PIM	PP	SH	GW
1962-63	Hamilton Red Wings	OHA-Jr.	50	3	10	13	....	....	....	83	....	....	....	....	....	....	....	....	....	....	5	0	0	0	17	....	....	....
1963-64	Hamilton Red Wings	OHA-Jr.	55	2	31	33	....	....	....	162	....	....	....	....	....	....	....	....	....	....	....	....	....	....	....	....	....	....
	Pittsburgh Hornets	AHL	1	0	0	0	....	....	....	0	....	....	....	....	....	....	....	....	....	....	....	....	....	....	....	....	....	....
1964-65	Hamilton Red Wings	OHA-Jr.	56	8	26	34	....	....	....	216	....	....	....	....	....	....	....	....	....	....	....	....	....	....	....	....	....	....
	Pittsburgh Hornets	AHL	2	1	0	1	....	....	....	4	....	....	....	....	....	....	....	....	....	....	3	0	0	0	4	....	....	....
1965-66	**Detroit Red Wings**	**NHL**	**4**	**0**	**0**	**0**	**0**	**0**	**0**	**12**	....	....	....	....	....	....	....	....	....	....	....	....	....	....	....	....	....	....
	Pittsburgh Hornets	AHL	48	0	6	6	....	....	....	88	....	....	....	....	....	....	....	....	....	....	....	....	....	....	....	....	....	....
	Boston Bruins	**NHL**	**20**	**0**	**8**	**8**	**0**	**8**	**8**	**28**	....	....	....	....	....	....	....	....	....	....	....	....	....	....	....	....	....	....
1966-67	**Boston Bruins**	**NHL**	**29**	**0**	**1**	**1**	**0**	**1**	**1**	**50**	....	....	....	....	....	....	....	....	....	....	....	....	....	....	....	....	....	....
	Oklahoma City Blazers	CPHL	17	4	3	7	....	....	....	96	....	....	....	....	....	....	....	....	....	....	....	....	....	....	....	....	....	....
1967-68	**Boston Bruins**	**NHL**	**59**	**2**	**10**	**12**	**2**	**10**	**12**	**100**	**0**	**0**	**1**	**53**	**3.8**	**57**	**0**	**51**	**7**	**13**	**4**	**0**	**0**	**0**	**4**	**0**	**0**	**0**
1968-69	**Boston Bruins**	**NHL**	**22**	**3**	**3**	**6**	**3**	**3**	**6**	**37**	**0**	**0**	**0**	**22**	**13.6**	**22**	**2**	**13**	**4**	**11**	....	....	....	....	....	....	....	....
1969-70♦	**Boston Bruins**	**NHL**	**44**	**1**	**7**	**8**	**1**	**7**	**8**	**63**	**0**	**0**	**1**	**36**	**2.8**	**30**	**1**	**31**	**9**	**7**	**8**	**0**	**0**	**0**	**9**	**0**	**0**	**0**
	Oklahoma City Blazers	CHL	13	1	5	6	....	....	....	53	....	....	....	....	....	....	....	....	....	....	....	....	....	....	....	....	....	....
1970-71	**Vancouver Canucks**	**NHL**	**77**	**2**	**10**	**12**	**2**	**8**	**10**	**112**	**0**	**0**	**0**	**60**	**3.3**	**69**	**2**	**119**	**47**	**–5**	....	....	....	....	....	....	....	....
1971-72	**Vancouver Canucks**	**NHL**	**6**	**0**	**1**	**1**	**0**	**1**	**1**	**23**	**0**	**0**	**0**	**4**	**0.0**	**3**	**0**	**5**	**1**	**–1**	....	....	....	....	....	....	....	....
	New York Rangers	**NHL**	**49**	**1**	**10**	**11**	**1**	**9**	**10**	**54**	**0**	**0**	**0**	**33**	**3.0**	**40**	**0**	**32**	**8**	**16**	**12**	**0**	**0**	**0**	**46**	**0**	**0**	**0**
1972-73	**Detroit Red Wings**	**NHL**	**44**	**0**	**5**	**5**	**0**	**4**	**4**	**51**	**0**	**0**	**0**	**28**	**0.0**	**31**	**0**	**30**	**4**	**5**	....	....	....	....	....	....	....	....
	Boston Bruins	**NHL**	**5**	**0**	**0**	**0**	**0**	**0**	**0**	**2**	**0**	**0**	**0**	**1**	**0.0**	**0**	**0**	**1**	**0**	**–1**	**2**	**0**	**0**	**0**	**2**	**0**	**0**	**0**
1973-74	**Boston Bruins**	**NHL**	**69**	**0**	**4**	**4**	**0**	**3**	**3**	**44**	**0**	**0**	**0**	**30**	**0.0**	**20**	**0**	**27**	**5**	**–2**	....	....	....	....	....	....	....	....
1974-75	**Boston Bruins**	**NHL**	**40**	**0**	**0**	**0**	**0**	**0**	**0**	**30**	**0**	**0**	**0**	**27**	**0.0**	**11**	**0**	**15**	**1**	**–3**	**3**	**0**	**0**	**0**	**4**	**0**	**0**	**0**
1975-76	**Boston Bruins**	**NHL**	**58**	**1**	**6**	**7**	**1**	**4**	**5**	**60**	**0**	**0**	**1**	**70**	**1.4**	**71**	**1**	**58**	**13**	**25**	**12**	**1**	**0**	**1**	**22**	**0**	**0**	**0**
1976-77	**Boston Bruins**	**NHL**	**76**	**3**	**13**	**16**	**3**	**10**	**13**	**107**	**0**	**0**	**0**	**70**	**4.3**	**91**	**1**	**85**	**10**	**15**	**14**	**0**	**2**	**2**	**26**	**0**	**0**	**0**
1977-78	**Boston Bruins**	**NHL**	**61**	**4**	**13**	**17**	**4**	**10**	**14**	**50**	**1**	**0**	**2**	**66**	**6.1**	**83**	**3**	**53**	**10**	**37**	**12**	**1**	**0**	**1**	**4**	**0**	**0**	**1**

			REGULAR SEASON																		PLAYOFFS							
Season	Club	League	GP	G	A	Pts	AG	AA	APts	PIM	PP	SH	GW	S	%	TGF	PGF	TGA	PGA	+/–	GP	G	A	Pts	PIM	PP	SH	GW
1978-79	**Boston Bruins**	**NHL**	**63**	**6**	**11**	**17**	**5**	**8**	**13**	**28**	**1**	**0**	**0**	**64**	**9.4**	**76**	**4**	**71**	**11**	**12**	**7**	**0**	**2**	**2**	**4**	**0**	**0**	**0**
1979-80	**Boston Bruins**	**NHL**	**52**	**0**	**5**	**5**	**0**	**4**	**4**	**45**	**0**	**0**	**0**	**29**	**0.0**	**41**	**0**	**30**	**3**	**14**	**4**	**0**	**0**	**0**	**0**	**0**	**0**	**0**
1980-81	**Boston Bruins**	**NHL**	**11**	**0**	**0**	**0**	**0**	**0**	**0**	**12**	**0**	**0**	**0**	**4**	**0.0**	**6**	**0**	**9**	**0**	**–3**	....	....	....	....	....	....	....	....
	NHL Totals		**789**	**23**	**107**	**130**	**22**	**90**	**112**	**908**	....	....	....	....	....	....	....	....	....		**78**	**2**	**4**	**6**	**121**	....	....	....

Traded to **Boston** by **Detroit** with Bill Lesuk, Ron Murphy and future considerations (Steve Atkinson, June 6, 1966) for Dean Prentice and Leo Boivin, February 16, 1966. • Missed majority of 1968-69 season recovering from mononucleosis. Claimed by **Vancouver** from **Boston** in Expansion Draft, June 10, 1970. Traded to **NY Rangers** by **Vancouver** with Jim Wiste for Dave Balon, Wayne Connelly and Ron Stewart, November 16, 1971. Traded to **Detroit** by **NY Rangers** with Rick Newell for Joe Zanussi and Detroit's 1st round choice (Albert Blanchard) in 1972 Amateur Draft, May 24, 1972. Traded to **Boston** by **Detroit** for Garnet Bailey and future considerations (Murray Wing, June 4, 1973), March 1, 1973.

• DOAN, Shane

Shane Albert RW – R. 6'2", 217 lbs. b: Halkirk, Alta., 10/10/1976. Winnipeg's 1st, 7th overall, in 1995.

Season	Club	League	GP	G	A	Pts	AG	AA	APts	PIM	PP	SH	GW	S	%	TGF	PGF	TGA	PGA	+/–	GP	G	A	Pts	PIM	PP	SH	GW
1991-92	Killam Selects	AAHA	56	80	84	164	....	....	....	74	....	....	....	....	....	....	....	....	....	....	....	....	....	....	....	....	....	....
1992-93	Kamloops Blazers	WHL	51	7	12	19	....	....	....	65	....	....	....	....	....	....	....	....	....	....	13	0	1	1	8	....	....	....
1993-94	Kamloops Blazers	WHL	52	24	24	48	....	....	....	88	....	....	....	....	....	....	....	....	....	....	....	....	....	....	....	....	....	....
1994-95	Kamloops Blazers	WHL	71	37	57	94	....	....	....	106	....	....	....	....	....	....	....	....	....	....	21	6	10	16	16	....	....	....
	Kamloops Blazers	Mem-Cup	4	4	5	*9	....	....	....	6	....	....	....	....	....	....	....	....	....	....	....	....	....	....	....	....	....	....
1995-96	**Winnipeg Jets**	**NHL**	**74**	**7**	**10**	**17**	**7**	**8**	**15**	**101**	**1**	**0**	**3**	**106**	**6.6**	**30**	**8**	**32**	**1**	**–9**	**6**	**0**	**0**	**0**	**6**	**0**	**0**	**0**
1996-97	**Phoenix Coyotes**	**NHL**	**63**	**4**	**8**	**12**	**4**	**7**	**11**	**49**	**0**	**0**	**0**	**100**	**4.0**	**29**	**3**	**29**	**0**	**–3**	**4**	**0**	**0**	**0**	**2**	**0**	**0**	**0**
1997-98	**Phoenix Coyotes**	**NHL**	**33**	**5**	**6**	**11**	**6**	**6**	**12**	**35**	**0**	**0**	**3**	**42**	**11.9**	**18**	**1**	**20**	**0**	**–3**	**6**	**1**	**0**	**1**	**6**	**0**	**0**	**0**
	Springfield Falcons	AHL	39	21	21	42	....	....	....	64	....	....	....	....	....	....	....	....	....	....	....	....	....	....	....	....	....	....
1998-99	**Phoenix Coyotes**	**NHL**	**79**	**6**	**16**	**22**	**7**	**15**	**22**	**54**	**0**	**0**	**0**	**156**	**3.8**	**37**	**1**	**42**	**1**	**–5**	**7**	**2**	**2**	**4**	**6**	**0**	**0**	**2**
	Canada	WC-A	4	0	0	0	....	....	....	0	....	....	....	....	....	....	....	....	....	....	....	....	....	....	....	....	....	....
99-2000	**Phoenix Coyotes**	**NHL**	**81**	**26**	**25**	**51**	**29**	**23**	**52**	**66**	**1**	**1**	**4**	**221**	**11.8**	**63**	**4**	**55**	**2**	**6**	**4**	**1**	**2**	**3**	**8**	**1**	**0**	**0**
	NHL Totals		**330**	**48**	**65**	**113**	**53**	**59**	**112**	**305**	**2**	**1**	**10**	**625**	**7.7**	**177**	**17**	**178**	**4**		**27**	**4**	**4**	**8**	**28**	**1**	**0**	**2**

Memorial Cup All-Star Team (1995) • Won Stafford Smythe Memorial Trophy (Memorial Cup Tournament MVP) (1995)

Transferred to **Phoenix** after **Winnipeg** franchise relocated, July 1, 1996.

• DOBBIN, Brian

RW – R. 5'11", 205 lbs. b: Petrolia, Ont., 8/18/1966. Philadelphia's 7th, 100th overall, in 1984.

Season	Club	League	GP	G	A	Pts	AG	AA	APts	PIM	PP	SH	GW	S	%	TGF	PGF	TGA	PGA	+/–	GP	G	A	Pts	PIM	PP	SH	GW
1980-81	Mooretown Flags	OHA-C	38	21	17	38	....	....	....	14	....	....	....	....	....	....	....	....	....	....	....	....	....	....	....	....	....	....
1981-82	Mooretown Flags	OJHL-C	38	31	24	55	....	....	....	50	....	....	....	....	....	....	....	....	....	....	....	....	....	....	....	....	....	....
1982-83	Kingston Canadians	OHL	69	16	39	55	....	....	....	35	....	....	....	....	....	....	....	....	....	....	....	....	....	....	....	....	....	....
1983-84	London Knights	OHL	70	30	40	70	....	....	....	70	....	....	....	....	....	....	....	....	....	....	....	....	....	....	....	....	....	....
1984-85	London Knights	OHL	53	42	57	99	....	....	....	63	....	....	....	....	....	....	....	....	....	....	8	7	4	11	2	....	....	....
1985-86	London Knights	OHL	59	38	55	93	....	....	....	113	....	....	....	....	....	....	....	....	....	....	5	2	1	3	9	....	....	....
	Hershey Bears	AHL	2	1	0	1	....	....	....	0	....	....	....	....	....	....	....	....	....	....	18	5	5	10	21	....	....	....
1986-87	**Philadelphia Flyers**	**NHL**	**12**	**2**	**1**	**3**	**2**	**1**	**3**	**14**	**0**	**0**	**0**	**13**	**15.4**	**4**	**1**	**1**	**0**	**2**	....	....	....	....	....	....	....	....
	Hershey Bears	AHL	52	26	35	61	....	....	....	66	....	....	....	....	....	....	....	....	....	....	5	4	2	6	15	....	....	....
1987-88	**Philadelphia Flyers**	**NHL**	**21**	**3**	**5**	**8**	**3**	**4**	**7**	**6**	**0**	**0**	**1**	**15**	**20.0**	**11**	**4**	**8**	**0**	**–1**	....	....	....	....	....	....	....	....
	Hershey Bears	AHL	54	36	47	83	....	....	....	58	....	....	....	....	....	....	....	....	....	....	12	7	8	15	15	....	....	....
1988-89	**Philadelphia Flyers**	**NHL**	**14**	**0**	**1**	**1**	**0**	**1**	**1**	**8**	**0**	**0**	**0**	**13**	**0.0**	**2**	**0**	**8**	**0**	**–6**	**2**	**0**	**0**	**0**	**17**	**0**	**0**	**0**
	Hershey Bears	AHL	59	43	48	91	....	....	....	61	....	....	....	....	....	....	....	....	....	....	11	7	6	13	12	....	....	....
1989-90	**Philadelphia Flyers**	**NHL**	**9**	**1**	**1**	**2**	**1**	**1**	**2**	**11**	**1**	**0**	**0**	**11**	**9.1**	**4**	**2**	**1**	**0**	**1**	....	....	....	....	....	....	....	....
	Hershey Bears	AHL	68	38	47	85	....	....	....	58	....	....	....	....	....	....	....	....	....	....	....	....	....	....	....	....	....	....
1990-91	Hershey Bears	AHL	80	35	43	78	....	....	....	82	....	....	....	....	....	....	....	....	....	....	7	1	2	3	7	....	....	....
1991-92	New Haven Nighthawks	AHL	33	16	21	37	....	....	....	20	....	....	....	....	....	....	....	....	....	....	....	....	....	....	....	....	....	....
	Boston Bruins	**NHL**	**7**	**1**	**0**	**1**	**1**	**0**	**1**	**22**	**0**	**0**	**0**	**4**	**25.0**	**1**	**0**	**1**	**0**	**0**	....	....	....	....	....	....	....	....
	Maine Mariners	AHL	33	21	15	36	....	....	....	14	....	....	....	....	....	....	....	....	....	....	....	....	....	....	....	....	....	....
1992-93	Milwaukee Admirals	IHL	80	39	45	84	....	....	....	50	....	....	....	....	....	....	....	....	....	....	6	4	3	7	6	....	....	....
1993-94	Milwaukee Admirals	IHL	81	48	53	101	....	....	....	73	....	....	....	....	....	....	....	....	....	....	4	1	0	1	4	....	....	....
1994-95	Milwaukee Admirals	IHL	76	21	40	61	....	....	....	62	....	....	....	....	....	....	....	....	....	....	9	0	4	4	2	....	....	....
1995-96	Cincinnati Cyclones	IHL	82	28	37	65	....	....	....	97	....	....	....	....	....	....	....	....	....	....	17	2	2	4	14	....	....	....
1996-97	Austin Ice Bats	WPHL	23	14	18	32	....	....	....	25	....	....	....	....	....	....	....	....	....	....	6	2	5	7	11	....	....	....
	Muskegon Fury	ColHL	2	0	0	0	....	....	....	2	....	....	....	....	....	....	....	....	....	....	....	....	....	....	....	....	....	....
	Grand Rapids Griffins	IHL	29	4	5	9	....	....	....	39	....	....	....	....	....	....	....	....	....	....	....	....	....	....	....	....	....	....
1997-98	Port Huron Border Cats	UHL	71	38	46	84	....	....	....	54	....	....	....	....	....	....	....	....	....	....	4	2	1	3	2	....	....	....
1998-99	Port Huron Border Cats	UHL	21	10	13	23	....	....	....	16	....	....	....	....	....	....	....	....	....	....	7	0	0	0	0	....	....	....
99-2000	Saginaw Gears	UHL	DID NOT PLAY – GENERAL MANAGER																									
	NHL Totals		**63**	**7**	**8**	**15**	**7**	**7**	**14**	**61**	**1**	**0**	**1**	**56**	**12.5**	**22**	**7**	**19**	**0**		**2**	**0**	**0**	**0**	**17**	**0**	**0**	**0**

AHL First All-Star Team (1989) • AHL Second All-Star Team (1990) • IHL Second All-Star Team (1994)

Traded to **Boston** by **Philadelphia** with Gord Murphy, Philadelphia's 3rd round choice (Sergei Zholtok) in 1992 Entry Draft and 4th round choice (Charles Paquette) in 1993 Entry Draft for Garry Galley, Wes Walz and Boston's 3rd round choice (Milos Holan) in 1993 Entry Draft, January 2, 1992.

• DOBSON, Jim

James Herold RW – R. 6'1", 195 lbs. b: Winnipeg, Man., 2/29/1960. Minnesota's 5th, 90th overall, in 1979.

Season	Club	League	GP	G	A	Pts	AG	AA	APts	PIM	PP	SH	GW	S	%	TGF	PGF	TGA	PGA	+/–	GP	G	A	Pts	PIM	PP	SH	GW
1977-78	Langley Thunder	BCJHL	STATISTICS NOT AVAILABLE																									
	New Westminster Bruins	WCJHL	12	4	2	6	....	....	....	121	....	....	....	....	....	....	....	....	....	....	11	5	3	8	2	....	....	....
	New Westminster Bruins	Mem-Cup	5	0	1	1	....	....	....	4	....	....	....	....	....	....	....	....	....	....	....	....	....	....	....	....	....	....
1978-79	Portland Winter Hawks	WHL	71	38	39	77	....	....	....	143	....	....	....	....	....	....	....	....	....	....	....	....	....	....	....	....	....	....
1979-80	Portland Winter Hawks	WHL	72	66	68	134	....	....	....	181	....	....	....	....	....	....	....	....	....	....	....	....	....	....	....	....	....	....
	Minnesota North Stars	**NHL**	**1**	**0**	**0**	**0**	**0**	**0**	**0**	**0**	**0**	**0**	**0**	**0**	**0.0**	**0**	**0**	**0**	**0**	**0**	....	....	....	....	....	....	....	....
1980-81	**Minnesota North Stars**	**NHL**	**1**	**0**	**0**	**0**	**0**	**0**	**0**	**0**	**0**	**0**	**0**	**0**	**0.0**	**0**	**0**	**0**	**0**	**0**	....	....	....	....	....	....	....	....
	Oklahoma City Stars	CHL	35	23	16	39	....	....	....	46	....	....	....	....	....	....	....	....	....	....	....	....	....	....	....	....	....	....
1981-82	**Minnesota North Stars**	**NHL**	**6**	**0**	**0**	**0**	**0**	**0**	**0**	**4**	**0**	**0**	**0**	**5**	**0.0**	**1**	**0**	**1**	**0**	**0**	....	....	....	....	....	....	....	....
	Nashville South Stars	CHL	29	19	13	32	....	....	....	29	....	....	....	....	....	....	....	....	....	....	....	....	....	....	....	....	....	....
	Colorado Rockies	**NHL**	**3**	**0**	**0**	**0**	**0**	**0**	**0**	**2**	**0**	**0**	**0**	**5**	**0.0**	**0**	**0**	**1**	**0**	**–1**	....	....	....	....	....	....	....	....
	Fort Worth Texans	CHL	34	15	12	27	....	....	....	65	....	....	....	....	....	....	....	....	....	....	....	....	....	....	....	....	....	....
1982-83	Birmingham South Stars	CHL	80	36	37	73	....	....	....	100	....	....	....	....	....	....	....	....	....	....	13	8	4	12	4	....	....	....
1983-84	**Quebec Nordiques**	**NHL**	**1**	**0**	**0**	**0**	**0**	**0**	**0**	**0**	**0**	**0**	**0**	**1**	**0.0**	**0**	**0**	**1**	**0**	**–1**	....	....	....	....	....	....	....	....
	Fredericton Express	AHL	75	33	44	77	....	....	....	74	....	....	....	....	....	....	....	....	....	....	7	3	2	5	2	....	....	....
1984-85	Fredericton Express	AHL	21	8	10	18	....	....	....	52	....	....	....	....	....	....	....	....	....	....	5	3	0	3	5	....	....	....
1985-86	New Haven Nighthawks	AHL	29	5	6	11	....	....	....	12	....	....	....	....	....	....	....	....	....	....	1	0	0	0	0	....	....	....
	NHL Totals		**12**	**0**	**0**	**0**	**0**	**0**	**0**	**6**	**0**	**0**	**0**	**11**	**0.0**	**1**	**0**	**3**	**0**		....	....	....	....	....	....	....	....

WHL All-Star Team (1980)

Rights traded to **Colorado** by **Minnesota** with Kevin Maxwell for cash, December 31, 1981. Signed as a free agent by **Minnesota**, September 20, 1982. Traded to **Quebec** by **Minnesota** for Jay Miller, June 29, 1983. • Missed majority of 1984-85 season recovering from knee injury suffered in training camp, October, 1984. Signed as a free agent by **NY Rangers**, December 13, 1985.

• DOIG, Jason

D – R. 6'3", 220 lbs. b: Montreal, Que., 1/29/1977. Winnipeg's 3rd, 34th overall, in 1995.

Season	Club	League	GP	G	A	Pts	AG	AA	APts	PIM	PP	SH	GW	S	%	TGF	PGF	TGA	PGA	+/–	GP	G	A	Pts	PIM	PP	SH	GW
1990-91	North Shore Selects	QAAA	31	30	33	63	....	....	....	53	....	....	....	....	....	....	....	....	....	....	....	....	....	....	....	....	....	....
1991-92	North Shore Selects	QAAA	29	11	11	22	....	....	....	20	....	....	....	....	....	....	....	....	....	....	....	....	....	....	....	....	....	....
1992-93	Lac St-Louis Lions	QAAA	35	11	16	27	....	....	....	40	....	....	....	....	....	....	....	....	....	....	7	5	5	10	16	....	....	....
1993-94	St-Jean Lynx	QMJHL	63	8	17	25	....	....	....	65	....	....	....	....	....	....	....	....	....	....	5	0	2	2	2	....	....	....
1994-95	Laval Titan	QMJHL	55	13	42	55	....	....	....	259	....	....	....	....	....	....	....	....	....	....	20	4	13	17	39	....	....	....
1995-96	Laval Titan	QMJHL	5	3	6	9	....	....	....	20	....	....	....	....	....	....	....	....	....	....	....	....	....	....	....	....	....	....
	Granby Predateurs	QMJHL	24	4	30	34	....	....	....	91	....	....	....	....	....	....	....	....	....	....	20	10	22	32	*110	....	....	....
	Winnipeg Jets	**NHL**	**15**	**1**	**1**	**2**	**1**	**1**	**2**	**28**	**0**	**0**	**0**	**7**	**14.3**	**7**	**0**	**9**	**0**	**–2**	....	....	....	....	....	....	....	....
	Springfield Falcons	AHL	5	0	0	0	....	....	....	28	....	....	....	....	....	....	....	....	....	....	....	....	....	....	....	....	....	....
	Granby Predateurs	Mem-Cup	4	3	2	5	....	....	....	10	....	....	....	....	....	....	....	....	....	....	....	....	....	....	....	....	....	....

			REGULAR SEASON																		PLAYOFFS							
Season	Club	League	GP	G	A	Pts	AG	AA	APts	PIM	PP	SH	GW	S	%	TGF	PGF	TGA	PGA	+/–	GP	G	A	Pts	PIM	PP	SH	GW
1996-97	Granby Predateurs	QMJHL	39	14	33	47				211											5	0	4	4	27			
	Canada	WJC-A	7	0	2	2				37																		
	Las Vegas Thunder	IHL	6	0	1	1				19																		
	Springfield Falcons	AHL	5	0	3	3				2											17	1	4	5	37			
1997-98	**Phoenix Coyotes**	**NHL**	**4**	**0**	**1**	**1**	**0**	**1**	**1**	**12**	**0**	**0**	**0**	**1**	**0.0**	**1**	**0**	**5**	**0**	**–4**								
	Springfield Falcons	AHL	46	2	25	27				153											3	0	0	0	2			
1998-99	**Phoenix Coyotes**	**NHL**	**9**	**0**	**1**	**1**	**0**	**1**	**1**	**10**	**0**	**0**	**0**	**0**	**0.0**	**3**	**0**	**1**	**0**	**2**								
	Springfield Falcons	AHL	32	3	5	8				67																		
	Hartford Wolf Pack	AHL	8	1	4	5				40											7	1	1	2	39			
99-2000	**New York Rangers**	**NHL**	**7**	**0**	**1**	**1**	**0**	**1**	**1**	**22**	**0**	**0**	**0**	**3**	**0.0**	**3**	**0**	**5**	**0**	**–2**								
	Hartford Wolf Pack	AHL	27	3	11	14				70											21	1	5	6	20			
	NHL Totals		**35**	**1**	**4**	**5**	**1**	**4**	**5**	**72**	**0**	**0**	**0**	**11**	**9.1**	**14**	**0**	**20**	**0**									

Memorial Cup All-Star Team (1996)

Transferred to **Phoenix** after **Winnipeg** franchise relocated, July 1, 1996. Traded to **NY Rangers** by **Phoenix** with Phoenix's 6th round choice (Jay Dardis) in 1999 Entry Draft for Stan Neckar, March 23, 1999.

• DOLLAS, Bobby

D – L. 6'2", 212 lbs. b: Montreal, Que., 1/31/1965. Winnipeg's 2nd, 14th overall, in 1983.

Season	Club	League	GP	G	A	Pts	AG	AA	APts	PIM	PP	SH	GW	S	%	TGF	PGF	TGA	PGA	+/–	GP	G	A	Pts	PIM	PP	SH	GW
1980-81	Lac St-Louis Lions	QAAA	46	9	14	23																						
1981-82	Lac St-Louis Lions	QAAA	44	9	31	40				138																		
1982-83	Laval Voisins	QMJHL	63	16	45	61				144											11	5	5	10	23			
1983-84	Laval Voisins	QMJHL	54	12	33	45				80											14	1	8	9	23			
	Winnipeg Jets	**NHL**	**1**	**0**	**0**	**0**	**0**	**0**	**0**	**0**	**0**	**0**	**0**	**0**	**0.0**	**0**	**0**	**2**	**0**	**–2**								
	Laval Voisins	Mem-Cup	3	0	1	1				7																		
1984-85	**Winnipeg Jets**	**NHL**	**9**	**0**	**0**	**0**	**0**	**0**	**0**	**0**	**0**	**0**	**0**	**2**	**0.0**	**8**	**0**	**4**	**0**	**4**								
	Canada	WJC-A	7	0	2	2				12																		
	Sherbrooke Canadiens	AHL	8	1	3	4				4											17	3	6	9	17			
1985-86	**Winnipeg Jets**	**NHL**	**46**	**0**	**5**	**5**	**0**	**3**	**3**	**66**	**0**	**0**	**0**	**50**	**0.0**	**39**	**1**	**50**	**9**	**–3**	**3**	**0**	**0**	**0**	**2**	**0**	**0**	**0**
	Sherbrooke Canadiens	AHL	25	4	7	11				29																		
1986-87	Sherbrooke Canadiens	AHL	75	6	18	24				87											16	2	4	6	13			
1987-88	**Quebec Nordiques**	**NHL**	**9**	**0**	**0**	**0**	**0**	**0**	**0**	**2**	**0**	**0**	**0**	**5**	**0.0**	**1**	**0**	**6**	**1**	**–4**								
	Moncton Hawks	AHL	26	4	10	14				20																		
	Fredericton Express	AHL	33	4	8	12				27											15	2	2	4	24			
1988-89	**Quebec Nordiques**	**NHL**	**16**	**0**	**3**	**3**	**0**	**2**	**2**	**16**	**0**	**0**	**0**	**11**	**0.0**	**12**	**0**	**29**	**6**	**–11**								
	Halifax Citadels	AHL	57	5	19	24				65											4	1	0	1	14			
1989-90	Canada	Nat-Team	68	8	29	37				60																		
1990-91	**Detroit Red Wings**	**NHL**	**56**	**3**	**5**	**8**	**3**	**4**	**7**	**20**	**0**	**0**	**1**	**59**	**5.1**	**44**	**3**	**52**	**17**	**6**	**7**	**1**	**0**	**1**	**13**	**0**	**0**	**0**
1991-92	**Detroit Red Wings**	**NHL**	**27**	**3**	**1**	**4**	**3**	**1**	**4**	**20**	**0**	**1**	**0**	**26**	**11.5**	**20**	**0**	**19**	**3**	**4**	**2**	**0**	**1**	**1**	**0**	**0**	**0**	**0**
	Adirondack Red Wings	AHL	19	1	6	7				33											18	7	4	11	22			
1992-93	**Detroit Red Wings**	**NHL**	**6**	**0**	**0**	**0**	**0**	**0**	**0**	**2**	**0**	**0**	**0**	**5**	**0.0**	**3**	**0**	**4**	**0**	**–1**								
	Adirondack Red Wings	AHL	64	7	36	43				54											11	3	8	11	8			
1993-94	**Mighty Ducks of Anaheim**	**NHL**	**77**	**9**	**11**	**20**	**8**	**9**	**17**	**55**	**1**	**0**	**1**	**121**	**7.4**	**74**	**10**	**74**	**30**	**20**								
	Canada	WC-A	8	0	1	1				4																		
1994-95	**Mighty Ducks of Anaheim**	**NHL**	**45**	**7**	**13**	**20**	**12**	**19**	**31**	**12**	**3**	**1**	**1**	**70**	**10.0**	**53**	**15**	**64**	**23**	**–3**								
1995-96	**Mighty Ducks of Anaheim**	**NHL**	**82**	**8**	**22**	**30**	**8**	**18**	**26**	**64**	**0**	**1**	**1**	**117**	**6.8**	**87**	**17**	**102**	**41**	**9**								
1996-97	**Mighty Ducks of Anaheim**	**NHL**	**79**	**4**	**14**	**18**	**4**	**12**	**16**	**55**	**1**	**0**	**1**	**96**	**4.2**	**88**	**8**	**100**	**37**	**17**	**11**	**0**	**0**	**0**	**4**	**0**	**0**	**0**
1997-98	**Mighty Ducks of Anaheim**	**NHL**	**22**	**0**	**1**	**1**	**0**	**1**	**1**	**27**	**0**	**0**	**0**	**11**	**0.0**	**7**	**1**	**25**	**7**	**–12**								
	Edmonton Oilers	**NHL**	**30**	**2**	**5**	**7**	**2**	**5**	**7**	**22**	**0**	**0**	**0**	**27**	**7.4**	**25**	**7**	**16**	**4**	**6**	**11**	**0**	**0**	**0**	**16**	**0**	**0**	**0**
1998-99	**Pittsburgh Penguins**	**NHL**	**70**	**2**	**8**	**10**	**2**	**8**	**10**	**60**	**0**	**0**	**0**	**34**	**5.9**	**33**	**0**	**48**	**12**	**–3**	**13**	**1**	**0**	**1**	**6**	**0**	**0**	**0**
99-2000	**Ottawa Senators**	**NHL**	**1**	**0**	**0**	**0**	**0**	**0**	**0**	**0**	**0**	**0**	**0**	**0**	**0.0**	**2**	**0**	**0**	**0**	**2**								
	Long Beach Ice Dogs	IHL	13	2	4	6				8																		
	Calgary Flames	**NHL**	**49**	**3**	**7**	**10**	**3**	**6**	**9**	**28**	**1**	**0**	**0**	**36**	**8.3**	**36**	**1**	**54**	**23**	**4**								
	NHL Totals		**625**	**41**	**95**	**136**	**45**	**88**	**133**	**449**	**6**	**3**	**5**	**670**	**6.1**	**532**	**63**	**649**	**213**		**47**	**2**	**1**	**3**	**41**	**0**	**0**	**0**

QMJHL Second All-Star Team (1983) • WJC-A All-Star Team (1985) • AHL First All-Star Team (1993) • Won Eddie Shore Award (AHL's Outstanding Defenseman) (1993)

Traded to **Quebec** by **Winnipeg** for Stu Kulak, December 17, 1987. Signed as a free agent by **Detroit**, October 18, 1990. Claimed by **Anaheim** from **Detroit** in Expansion Draft, June 24, 1993. Traded to **Edmonton** by **Anaheim** for Drew Bannister, January 9, 1998. Traded to **Pittsburgh** by **Edmonton** with Tony Hrkac for Josef Beranek, June 16, 1998. Signed as a free agent by **Long Beach**, October 12, 1999. Signed as a free agent by **Ottawa**, November 9, 1999. Claimed on waivers by **Calgary** from **Ottawa**, November 11, 1999.

• DOME, Robert

RW – L. 6', 215 lbs. b: Skalica, Czech., 1/29/1979. Pittsburgh's 1st, 17th overall, in 1997.

Season	Club	League	GP	G	A	Pts	AG	AA	APts	PIM	PP	SH	GW	S	%	TGF	PGF	TGA	PGA	+/–	GP	G	A	Pts	PIM	PP	SH	GW
1994-95	HC Dukla	Slovak-Jr.	36	36	43	79				39																		
	Slovakia	EJC-B	5	7	10	17				2																		
1995-96	Utah Grizzlies	IHL	56	10	9	19				28																		
1996-97	Long Beach Ice Dogs	IHL	13	4	6	10				14																		
	Las Vegas Thunder	IHL	43	10	7	17				22																		
1997-98	**Pittsburgh Penguins**	**NHL**	**30**	**5**	**2**	**7**	**6**	**2**	**8**	**12**	**1**	**0**	**0**	**29**	**17.2**	**8**	**1**	**8**	**0**	**–1**								
	Syracuse Crunch	AHL	36	21	25	46				77																		
1998-99	Syracuse Crunch	AHL	48	18	17	35				70																		
	Houston Aeros	IHL	20	2	4	6				24																		
99-2000	**Pittsburgh Penguins**	**NHL**	**22**	**2**	**5**	**7**	**2**	**5**	**7**	**0**	**0**	**0**	**0**	**27**	**7.4**	**13**	**1**	**11**	**0**	**1**								
	Wilkes-Barre Penguins	AHL	51	12	26	38				83																		
	NHL Totals		**52**	**7**	**7**	**14**	**8**	**7**	**15**	**12**	**1**	**0**	**0**	**56**	**12.5**	**21**	**2**	**19**	**0**									

• DOMENICHELLI, Hnat

Hnat A. C – L. 6', 194 lbs. b: Edmonton, Alta., 2/17/1976. Hartford's 2nd, 83rd overall, in 1994.

Season	Club	League	GP	G	A	Pts	AG	AA	APts	PIM	PP	SH	GW	S	%	TGF	PGF	TGA	PGA	+/–	GP	G	A	Pts	PIM	PP	SH	GW
1991-92	Edmonton Freeze	AAHA	34	34	49	83				101																		
1992-93	Kamloops Blazers	WHL	45	12	8	20				15											11	1	1	2	2			
1993-94	Kamloops Blazers	WHL	69	27	40	67				31											19	10	12	22	0			
	Kamloops Blazers	Mem-Cup	4	2	2	4				4																		
1994-95	Kamloops Blazers	WHL	72	52	62	114				34											19	9	9	18	9			
	Kamloops Blazers	Mem-Cup	4	2	1	3				2																		
1995-96	Kamloops Blazers	WHL	62	59	89	148				37											16	7	9	16	29			
	Canada	WJC-A	6	2	3	5				6																		
1996-97	**Hartford Whalers**	**NHL**	**13**	**2**	**1**	**3**	**2**	**1**	**3**	**7**	**1**	**0**	**0**	**14**	**14.3**	**4**	**1**	**7**	**0**	**–4**								
	Springfield Falcons	AHL	39	24	24	48				12																		
	Calgary Flames	**NHL**	**10**	**1**	**2**	**3**	**1**	**2**	**3**	**2**	**1**	**0**	**0**	**16**	**6.3**	**4**	**1**	**2**	**0**	**1**								
	Saint John Flames	AHL	1	1	1	2				0											5	5	0	5	2			
1997-98	**Calgary Flames**	**NHL**	**31**	**9**	**7**	**16**	**11**	**7**	**18**	**6**	**1**	**0**	**1**	**70**	**12.9**	**25**	**6**	**15**	**0**	**4**								
	Saint John Flames	AHL	48	33	13	46				24											19	7	8	15	14			
1998-99	**Calgary Flames**	**NHL**	**23**	**5**	**5**	**10**	**6**	**5**	**11**	**11**	**3**	**0**	**0**	**45**	**11.1**	**15**	**7**	**12**	**0**	**–4**								
	Saint John Flames	AHL	51	25	21	46				26											7	4	4	8	2			
99-2000	**Calgary Flames**	**NHL**	**32**	**5**	**9**	**14**	**6**	**8**	**14**	**12**	**1**	**0**	**1**	**57**	**8.8**	**20**	**5**	**19**	**4**	**0**								
	Saint John Flames	AHL	12	6	7	13				8																		
	Atlanta Thrashers	**NHL**	**27**	**6**	**9**	**15**	**7**	**8**	**15**	**4**	**0**	**0**	**0**	**68**	**8.8**	**23**	**8**	**39**	**3**	**–21**								
	NHL Totals		**136**	**28**	**33**	**61**	**33**	**31**	**64**	**42**	**7**	**0**	**2**	**270**	**10.4**	**91**	**28**	**94**	**7**									

WHL West Second All-Star Team (1995) • WHL West First All-Star Team (1996) • Canadian Major Junior First All-Star Team (1996) • Canadian Major Junior Most Sportsmanlike Player of the Year (1996)

Traded to **Calgary** by **Hartford** with Glen Featherstone, New Jersey's 2nd round choice (previously acquired, Calgary selected Dimitri Kokorev) in 1997 Entry Draft and Vancouver's 3rd round choice (previously acquired, Calgary selected Paul Manning) in 1998 Entry Draft for Steve Chiasson and Colorado's 3rd round choice (previously acquired, Carolina selected Francis Lessard) in 1997 Entry Draft, March 5, 1997. Traded to **Atlanta** by **Calgary** with Dmitri Vlasenkov for Darryl Shannon and Jason Botterill, February 11, 2000.

			REGULAR SEASON																		PLAYOFFS							
Season	Club	League	GP	G	A	Pts	AG	AA	APts	PIM	PP	SH	GW	S	%	TGF	PGF	TGA	PGA	+/–	GP	G	A	Pts	PIM	PP	SH	GW

• DOMI, Tie

Tie Tahir "The Albanian Assasin" RW – R. 5'10", 200 lbs. b: Windsor, Ont., 11/1/1969. Toronto's 2nd, 27th overall, in 1988.

Season	Club	League	GP	G	A	Pts	AG	AA	APts	PIM	PP	SH	GW	S	%	TGF	PGF	TGA	PGA	+/–	GP	G	A	Pts	PIM	PP	SH	GW
1984-85	Belle River Canadiens	OJHL-C	28	7	5	12	....	....	....	98	....	....	....	....	....	....	....	....	....	....	....	....	....	....	....	....	....	....
1985-86	Windsor Bulldogs	OJHL-B	42	8	17	25	....	....	....	*346	....	....	....	....	....	....	....	....	....	....	....	....	....	....	....	....	....	....
1986-87	Peterborough Roadrunners	OJHL-B	2	0	0	0	....	....	....	10	....	....	....	....	....	....	....	....	....	....	....	....	....	....	....	....	....	....
	Peterborough Petes	OHL	18	1	1	2	....	....	....	79	....	....	....	....	....	....	....	....	....	....	....	....	....	....	....	....	....	....
1987-88	Peterborough Petes	OHL	60	22	21	43	....	....	....	*292	....	....	....	....	....	....	....	....	....	....	12	3	9	12	24	....	....	....
1988-89	Peterborough Petes	OHL	43	14	16	30	....	....	....	175	....	....	....	....	....	....	....	....	....	....	17	10	9	19	*70	....	....	....
	Peterborough Petes	Mem-Cup	5	2	0	2	....	....	....	*26	....	....	....	....	....	....	....	....	....	....	....	....	....	....	....	....	....	....
1989-90	**Toronto Maple Leafs**	**NHL**	**2**	**0**	**0**	**0**	**0**	**0**	**0**	**42**	**0**	**0**	**0**	**0**	**0.0**	**0**	**0**	**0**	**0**	**0**	....	....	....	....	....	....	....	....
	Newmarket Saints	AHL	57	14	11	25	....	....	....	285	....	....	....	....	....	....	....	....	....	....	....	....	....	....	....	....	....	....
1990-91	**New York Rangers**	**NHL**	**28**	**1**	**0**	**1**	**1**	**0**	**1**	**185**	**0**	**0**	**0**	**5**	**20.0**	**2**	**0**	**7**	**0**	**–5**	....	....	....	....	....	....	....	....
	Binghamton Rangers	AHL	25	11	6	17	....	....	....	219	....	....	....	....	....	....	....	....	....	....	7	3	2	5	16	....	....	....
1991-92	**New York Rangers**	**NHL**	**42**	**2**	**4**	**6**	**2**	**3**	**5**	**246**	**0**	**0**	**1**	**20**	**10.0**	**8**	**1**	**11**	**0**	**–4**	**6**	**1**	**1**	**2**	**32**	**0**	**0**	**0**
1992-93	**New York Rangers**	**NHL**	**12**	**2**	**0**	**2**	**2**	**0**	**2**	**95**	**0**	**0**	**0**	**11**	**18.2**	**3**	**0**	**4**	**0**	**–1**	....	....	....	....	....	....	....	....
	Winnipeg Jets	**NHL**	**49**	**3**	**10**	**13**	**2**	**7**	**9**	**249**	**0**	**0**	**0**	**29**	**10.3**	**23**	**0**	**22**	**1**	**2**	**6**	**1**	**0**	**1**	**23**	**0**	**0**	**0**
1993-94	**Winnipeg Jets**	**NHL**	**81**	**8**	**11**	**19**	**7**	**9**	**16**	***347**	**0**	**0**	**1**	**98**	**8.2**	**30**	**3**	**36**	**1**	**–8**	....	....	....	....	....	....	....	....
1994-95	**Winnipeg Jets**	**NHL**	**31**	**4**	**4**	**8**	**7**	**6**	**13**	**128**	**0**	**0**	**0**	**34**	**11.8**	**11**	**0**	**17**	**0**	**–6**	....	....	....	....	....	....	....	....
	Toronto Maple Leafs	**NHL**	**9**	**0**	**1**	**1**	**0**	**1**	**1**	**31**	**0**	**0**	**0**	**12**	**0.0**	**3**	**0**	**2**	**0**	**1**	**7**	**1**	**0**	**1**	**0**	**0**	**0**	**0**
1995-96	**Toronto Maple Leafs**	**NHL**	**72**	**7**	**6**	**13**	**7**	**5**	**12**	**297**	**0**	**0**	**1**	**61**	**11.5**	**23**	**1**	**26**	**1**	**–3**	**6**	**0**	**2**	**2**	**4**	**0**	**0**	**0**
1996-97	**Toronto Maple Leafs**	**NHL**	**80**	**11**	**17**	**28**	**12**	**15**	**27**	**275**	**2**	**0**	**1**	**98**	**11.2**	**38**	**4**	**52**	**1**	**–17**	....	....	....	....	....	....	....	....
1997-98	**Toronto Maple Leafs**	**NHL**	**80**	**4**	**10**	**14**	**5**	**10**	**15**	**365**	**0**	**0**	**0**	**72**	**5.6**	**24**	**1**	**28**	**0**	**–5**	....	....	....	....	....	....	....	....
1998-99	**Toronto Maple Leafs**	**NHL**	**72**	**8**	**14**	**22**	**9**	**13**	**22**	**198**	**0**	**0**	**1**	**65**	**12.3**	**30**	**0**	**25**	**0**	**5**	**14**	**0**	**2**	**2**	**24**	**0**	**0**	**0**
99-2000	**Toronto Maple Leafs**	**NHL**	**70**	**5**	**9**	**14**	**6**	**8**	**14**	**198**	**0**	**0**	**2**	**64**	**7.8**	**22**	**2**	**25**	**0**	**–5**	**12**	**0**	**1**	**1**	**20**	**0**	**0**	**0**
	NHL Totals		**628**	**55**	**86**	**141**	**60**	**77**	**137**	**2656**	**2**	**0**	**7**	**569**	**9.7**	**217**	**12**	**255**	**4**		**51**	**3**	**6**	**9**	**103**	**0**	**0**	**0**

Traded to **NY Rangers** by **Toronto** with Mark LaForest for Greg Johnston, June 28, 1990. Traded to **Winnipeg** by **NY Rangers** with Kris King for Ed Olczyk, December 28, 1992. Traded to **Toronto** by **Winnipeg** for Mike Eastwood and Toronto's 3rd round choice (Brad Isbister) in 1995 Entry Draft, April 7, 1995.

• DONALDSON, Gary

Robert Gary RW – R. 5'9", 155 lbs. b: Trail, B.C., 7/15/1952. Chicago's 9th, 141st overall, in 1972.

Season	Club	League	GP	G	A	Pts	AG	AA	APts	PIM	PP	SH	GW	S	%	TGF	PGF	TGA	PGA	+/–	GP	G	A	Pts	PIM	PP	SH	GW
1970-71	Penticton Broncos	BCJHL	60	37	53	90	....	....	....	61	....	....	....	....	....	....	....	....	....	....	....	....	....	....	....	....	....	....
1971-72	Victoria Cougars	WCJHL	62	31	44	75	....	....	....	53	....	....	....	....	....	....	....	....	....	....	....	....	....	....	....	....	....	....
1972-73	Dallas Black Hawks	CHL	71	15	24	39	....	....	....	46	....	....	....	....	....	....	....	....	....	....	7	2	1	3	14	....	....	....
1973-74	**Chicago Black Hawks**	**NHL**	**1**	**0**	**0**	**0**	**0**	**0**	**0**	**0**	**0**	**0**	**0**	**3**	**0.0**	**1**	**0**	**0**	**0**	**1**	....	....	....	....	....	....	....	....
	Dallas Black Hawks	CHL	71	21	21	42	....	....	....	66	....	....	....	....	....	....	....	....	....	....	10	3	3	6	24	....	....	....
1974-75	Dallas Black Hawks	CHL	77	24	28	52	....	....	....	46	....	....	....	....	....	....	....	....	....	....	8	3	1	4	7	....	....	....
1975-76	Dallas Black Hawks	CHL	68	33	39	72	....	....	....	26	....	....	....	....	....	....	....	....	....	....	6	2	0	2	0	....	....	....
1976-77	Houston Aeros	WHA	5	0	0	0	....	....	....	6	....	....	....	....	....	....	....	....	....	....	....	....	....	....	....	....	....	....
	Oklahoma City Blazers	CHL	74	23	34	57	....	....	....	37	....	....	....	....	....	....	....	....	....	....	....	....	....	....	....	....	....	....
	NHL Totals		**1**	**0**	**0**	**0**	**0**	**0**	**0**	**0**	**0**	**0**	**0**	**3**	**0.0**	**1**	**0**	**0**	**0**		....	....	....	....	....	....	....	....
	Other Major League Totals		5	0	0	0	....	....	....	6	....	....	....	....	....	....	....	....	....	....	....	....	....	....	....	....	....	....

Signed as a free agent by **Houston** (WHA), August, 1976.

• DONATELLI, Clark

John Clark LW – L. 5'10", 180 lbs. b: Providence, RI, 11/22/1967. NY Rangers' 4th, 98th overall, in 1984.

Season	Club	League	GP	G	A	Pts	AG	AA	APts	PIM	PP	SH	GW	S	%	TGF	PGF	TGA	PGA	+/–	GP	G	A	Pts	PIM	PP	SH	GW
1983-84	Stratford Cullitons	OJHL-B	38	41	49	90	....	....	....	46	....	....	....	....	....	....	....	....	....	....	....	....	....	....	....	....	....	....
	United States	WJC-A	7	1	2	3	....	....	....	6	....	....	....	....	....	....	....	....	....	....	....	....	....	....	....	....	....	....
1984-85	Boston University	H-East	40	17	18	35	....	....	....	46	....	....	....	....	....	....	....	....	....	....	....	....	....	....	....	....	....	....
	United States	WJC-A	7	2	3	5	....	....	....	12	....	....	....	....	....	....	....	....	....	....	....	....	....	....	....	....	....	....
	United States	WEC-A	10	3	1	4	....	....	....	14	....	....	....	....	....	....	....	....	....	....	....	....	....	....	....	....	....	....
1985-86	Boston University	H-East	43	28	34	62	....	....	....	30	....	....	....	....	....	....	....	....	....	....	....	....	....	....	....	....	....	....
	United States	WEC-A	10	3	3	6	....	....	....	8	....	....	....	....	....	....	....	....	....	....	....	....	....	....	....	....	....	....
1986-87	Boston University	H-East	37	15	23	38	....	....	....	46	....	....	....	....	....	....	....	....	....	....	....	....	....	....	....	....	....	....
	United States	WEC-A	9	1	2	3	....	....	....	6	....	....	....	....	....	....	....	....	....	....	....	....	....	....	....	....	....	....
1987-88	United States	Nat-Team	50	11	27	38	....	....	....	26	....	....	....	....	....	....	....	....	....	....	....	....	....	....	....	....	....	....
	United States	Olympics	6	2	1	3	....	....	....	6	....	....	....	....	....	....	....	....	....	....	....	....	....	....	....	....	....	....
1988-89			DID NOT PLAY																									
1989-90	**Minnesota North Stars**	**NHL**	**25**	**3**	**3**	**6**	**3**	**2**	**5**	**17**	**0**	**0**	**1**	**25**	**12.0**	**13**	**2**	**23**	**1**	**–11**	....	....	....	....	....	....	....	....
	Kalamazoo Wings	IHL	27	8	9	17	....	....	....	47	....	....	....	....	....	....	....	....	....	....	4	0	2	2	12	....	....	....
1990-91	San Diego Gulls	IHL	46	17	10	27	....	....	....	45	....	....	....	....	....	....	....	....	....	....	....	....	....	....	....	....	....	....
1991-92	United States	Nat-Team	42	13	25	38	....	....	....	50	....	....	....	....	....	....	....	....	....	....	....	....	....	....	....	....	....	....
	United States	Olympics	8	2	1	3	....	....	....	6	....	....	....	....	....	....	....	....	....	....	....	....	....	....	....	....	....	....
	Boston Bruins	**NHL**	**10**	**0**	**1**	**1**	**0**	**1**	**1**	**22**	**0**	**0**	**0**	**7**	**0.0**	**1**	**0**	**13**	**4**	**–8**	**2**	**0**	**0**	**0**	**0**	**0**	**0**	**0**
1992-93	Providence Bruins	AHL	57	12	14	26	....	....	....	40	....	....	....	....	....	....	....	....	....	....	4	2	1	3	2	....	....	....
1993-94	San Diego Gulls	IHL	50	11	32	43	....	....	....	54	....	....	....	....	....	....	....	....	....	....	9	0	1	1	23	....	....	....
1994-95	San Diego Gulls	IHL	70	22	25	47	....	....	....	48	....	....	....	....	....	....	....	....	....	....	5	0	1	1	6	....	....	....
1995-96	Los Angeles Ice Dogs	IHL	22	1	3	4	....	....	....	12	....	....	....	....	....	....	....	....	....	....	....	....	....	....	....	....	....	....
	Detroit Vipers	IHL	36	0	12	12	....	....	....	40	....	....	....	....	....	....	....	....	....	....	11	0	2	2	2	....	....	....
	NHL Totals		**35**	**3**	**4**	**7**	**3**	**3**	**6**	**39**	**0**	**0**	**1**	**32**	**9.4**	**14**	**2**	**36**	**5**		**2**	**0**	**0**	**0**	**0**	**0**	**0**	**0**

Hockey East Second All-Star Team (1986)

Traded to **Edmonton** by **NY Rangers** with Ville Kentala, Reijo Ruotsalainen and Jim Wiemer for Mike Golden, Don Jackson, Miroslav Horava and future considerations (Stu Kulak, March 10, 1987), October 23, 1986. Signed as a free agent by **Minnesota**, June 20, 1989. Signed as a free agent by **Boston**, March 10, 1992. • Played w/ RHI's San Diego Barracudas in 1994 (18-5-18-23-28).

• DONATO, Ted

Edward Paul LW – L. 5'10", 181 lbs. b: Boston, MA, 4/28/1969. Boston's 6th, 98th overall, in 1987.

Season	Club	League	GP	G	A	Pts	AG	AA	APts	PIM	PP	SH	GW	S	%	TGF	PGF	TGA	PGA	+/–	GP	G	A	Pts	PIM	PP	SH	GW
1986-87	Catholic Memorial Knights	Hi-School	22	29	34	63	....	....	....	30	....	....	....	....	....	....	....	....	....	....	....	....	....	....	....	....	....	....
1987-88	Harvard University	ECAC	28	12	14	26	....	....	....	24	....	....	....	....	....	....	....	....	....	....	....	....	....	....	....	....	....	....
	United States	WJC-A	7	3	2	5	....	....	....	18	....	....	....	....	....	....	....	....	....	....	....	....	....	....	....	....	....	....
1988-89	Harvard University	ECAC	34	14	37	51	....	....	....	30	....	....	....	....	....	....	....	....	....	....	....	....	....	....	....	....	....	....
1989-90	Harvard University	ECAC	16	5	6	11	....	....	....	34	....	....	....	....	....	....	....	....	....	....	....	....	....	....	....	....	....	....
1990-91	Harvard University	ECAC	27	19	*37	56	....	....	....	26	....	....	....	....	....	....	....	....	....	....	....	....	....	....	....	....	....	....
1991-92	United States	Nat-Team	52	11	22	33	....	....	....	24	....	....	....	....	....	....	....	....	....	....	....	....	....	....	....	....	....	....
	United States	Olympics	8	4	3	7	....	....	....	8	....	....	....	....	....	....	....	....	....	....	....	....	....	....	....	....	....	....
	Boston Bruins	**NHL**	**10**	**1**	**2**	**3**	**1**	**2**	**3**	**8**	**0**	**0**	**0**	**13**	**7.7**	**4**	**0**	**5**	**0**	**–1**	**15**	**3**	**4**	**7**	**4**	**0**	**0**	**1**
1992-93	**Boston Bruins**	**NHL**	**82**	**15**	**20**	**35**	**12**	**14**	**26**	**61**	**3**	**2**	**5**	**118**	**12.7**	**65**	**27**	**60**	**24**	**2**	**4**	**0**	**1**	**1**	**0**	**0**	**0**	**0**
1993-94	**Boston Bruins**	**NHL**	**84**	**22**	**32**	**54**	**20**	**25**	**45**	**59**	**9**	**2**	**1**	**158**	**13.9**	**76**	**22**	**72**	**18**	**0**	**13**	**4**	**2**	**6**	**10**	**2**	**0**	**1**
1994-95	TuTo Turku	Finland	14	5	5	10	....	....	....	47	....	....	....	....	....	....	....	....	....	....	....	....	....	....	....	....	....	....
	Boston Bruins	**NHL**	**47**	**10**	**10**	**20**	**18**	**15**	**33**	**10**	**1**	**0**	**1**	**71**	**14.1**	**33**	**8**	**30**	**8**	**3**	**5**	**0**	**0**	**0**	**4**	**0**	**0**	**0**
1995-96	**Boston Bruins**	**NHL**	**82**	**23**	**26**	**49**	**23**	**21**	**44**	**46**	**7**	**0**	**1**	**152**	**15.1**	**75**	**30**	**60**	**21**	**6**	**5**	**1**	**2**	**3**	**2**	**1**	**0**	**0**
1996-97	**Boston Bruins**	**NHL**	**67**	**25**	**26**	**51**	**26**	**23**	**49**	**37**	**6**	**2**	**2**	**172**	**14.5**	**76**	**22**	**82**	**19**	**–9**	....	....	....	....	....	....	....	....
	United States	WC-A	8	4	2	6	....	....	....	8	....	....	....	....	....	....	....	....	....	....	....	....	....	....	....	....	....	....
1997-98	**Boston Bruins**	**NHL**	**79**	**16**	**23**	**39**	**19**	**23**	**42**	**54**	**3**	**0**	**5**	**129**	**12.4**	**64**	**20**	**41**	**3**	**6**	**5**	**0**	**0**	**0**	**2**	**0**	**0**	**0**

			REGULAR SEASON																		PLAYOFFS							
Season	Club	League	GP	G	A	Pts	AG	AA	APts	PIM	PP	SH	GW	S	%	TGF	PGF	TGA	PGA	+/–	GP	G	A	Pts	PIM	PP	SH	GW
1998-99	**Boston Bruins**	NHL	14	1	3	4	1	3	4	4	0	0	0	22	4.5	7	4	4	1	0	....	....	....	....	....	....	....	....
	New York Islanders	NHL	55	7	11	18	8	11	19	27	2	0	0	68	10.3	26	11	29	4	–10	....	....	....	....	....	....	....	....
	Ottawa Senators	NHL	13	3	2	5	4	2	6	10	1	0	0	16	18.8	8	1	5	0	2	1	0	0	0	0	0	0	0
	United States	WC-A	6	2	6	8	....	....	....	6	....	....	....	....	....	....	....	....	....	....	....	....	....	....	....	....	....	....
99-2000	**Mighty Ducks of Anaheim**	NHL	81	11	19	30	12	18	30	26	2	0	3	138	8.0	43	9	47	10	–3	....	....	....	....	....	....	....	....
	NHL Totals		614	134	174	308	144	157	301	342	34	6	18	1057	12.7	477	154	435	108		48	8	9	17	22	3	0	2

NCAA Championship All-Tournament Team (1989) • NCAA Championship Tournament MVP (1989) • ECAC First All-Star Team (1991)

Traded to **NY Islanders** by **Boston** for Ken Belanger, November 7, 1998. Traded to **Ottawa** by **NY Islanders** for Ottawa's 4th round choice (later traded to Phoenix - Phoenix selected Preston Mizzi) in 1999 Entry Draft, March 20, 1999. Traded to **Anaheim** by **Ottawa** with the rights to Antti-Jussi Niemi for Patrick Lalime, June 18, 1999.

• DONNELLY, Dave

David C – L. 5'11", 185 lbs. b: Edmonton, Alta., 2/2/1962. Minnesota's 2nd, 27th overall, in 1981.

Season	Club	League	GP	G	A	Pts	AG	AA	APts	PIM	PP	SH	GW	S	%	TGF	PGF	TGA	PGA	+/–	GP	G	A	Pts	PIM	PP	SH	GW
1979-80	St. Albert Saints	AJHL	59	27	33	60	....	....	....	146	....	....	....	....	....	....	....	....	....	....	....	....	....	....	....	....	....	....
1980-81	St. Albert Saints	AJHL	54	39	55	*94	....	....	....	243	....	....	....	....	....	....	....	....	....	....	17	*20	*14	*34	87	....	....	....
1981-82	University of North Dakota	WCHA	38	10	15	25	....	....	....	38	....	....	....	....	....	....	....	....	....	....	....	....	....	....	....	....	....	....
1982-83	University of North Dakota	WCHA	34	18	16	34	....	....	....	106	....	....	....	....	....	....	....	....	....	....	....	....	....	....	....	....	....	....
1983-84	Canada	Nat-Team	64	17	13	30	....	....	....	52	....	....	....	....	....	....	....	....	....	....	....	....	....	....	....	....	....	....
	Canada	Olympics	7	1	1	2	....	....	....	12	....	....	....	....	....	....	....	....	....	....	....	....	....	....	....	....	....	....
	Boston Bruins	NHL	16	3	4	7	2	3	5	2	0	0	0	22	13.6	15	0	2	0	13	3	0	0	0	0	0	0	0
1984-85	**Boston Bruins**	NHL	38	6	8	14	5	5	10	46	0	1	1	33	18.2	18	0	27	8	–1	1	0	0	0	0	0	0	0
	Hershey Bears	AHL	26	11	6	17	....	....	....	28	....	....	....	....	....	....	....	....	....	....	....	....	....	....	....	....	....	....
1985-86	**Boston Bruins**	NHL	8	0	0	0	0	0	0	17	0	0	0	8	0.0	5	0	5	3	3	....	....	....	....	....	....	....	....
1986-87	**Chicago Blackhawks**	NHL	71	6	12	18	5	9	14	81	0	0	0	64	9.4	30	0	59	22	–7	1	0	0	0	0	0	0	0
1987-88	**Edmonton Oilers**	NHL	4	0	0	0	0	0	0	4	0	0	0	3	0.0	0	0	0	0	0	....	....	....	....	....	....	....	....
1988-89	KalPa Kuopio	Finland	43	20	22	42	....	....	....	*98	....	....	....	....	....	....	....	....	....	....	2	0	2	2	14	....	....	....
1989-90	EV Landshut	Germany	33	12	21	33	....	....	....	*87	....	....	....	....	....	....	....	....	....	....	....	....	....	....	....	....	....	....
1990-91	Maine Mariners	AHL	67	21	30	51	....	....	....	135	....	....	....	....	....	....	....	....	....	....	2	1	2	3	10	....	....	....
1991-92	Canada	Nat-Team	12	5	9	14	....	....	....	10	....	....	....	....	....	....	....	....	....	....	....	....	....	....	....	....	....	....
	NHL Totals		137	15	24	39	12	17	29	150	0	1	1	130	11.5	68	0	93	33		5	0	0	0	0	0	0	0

Rights traded to **Boston** by **Minnesota** with Brad Palmer for Boston agreeing not to select Brian Bellows in 1982 Entry Draft, June 9, 1982. Traded to **Detroit** by **Boston** for Dwight Foster, March 11, 1986. Signed as a free agent by **Chicago**, September, 1986. Traded to **Edmonton** by **Chicago** for cash, October 19, 1987.

• DONNELLY, Gord

D – R. 6'1", 202 lbs. b: Montreal, Que., 4/5/1962. St. Louis' 3rd, 62nd overall, in 1981.

Season	Club	League	GP	G	A	Pts	AG	AA	APts	PIM	PP	SH	GW	S	%	TGF	PGF	TGA	PGA	+/–	GP	G	A	Pts	PIM	PP	SH	GW
1977-78	Notre Dame Monarchs	QAAA	STATISTICS NOT AVAILABLE																									
1978-79	Laval National	QMJHL	71	1	14	15	....	....	....	79	....	....	....	....	....	....	....	....	....	....	....	....	....	....	....	....	....	....
1979-80	Laval National	QMJHL	44	5	10	15	....	....	....	47	....	....	....	....	....	....	....	....	....	....	....	....	....	....	....	....	....	....
	Chicoutimi Sagueneens	QMJHL	24	1	5	6	....	....	....	64	....	....	....	....	....	....	....	....	....	....	....	....	....	....	....	....	....	....
1980-81	Sherbrooke Castors	QMJHL	67	15	23	38	....	....	....	252	....	....	....	....	....	....	....	....	....	....	14	1	2	3	*35	....	....	....
1981-82	Sherbrooke Castors	QMJHL	60	8	41	49	....	....	....	250	....	....	....	....	....	....	....	....	....	....	22	2	7	9	*106	....	....	....
	Sherbrooke Castors	Mem-Cup	5	0	1	1	....	....	....	14	....	....	....	....	....	....	....	....	....	....	....	....	....	....	....	....	....	....
1982-83	Salt Lake Golden Eagles	CHL	67	3	12	15	....	....	....	222	....	....	....	....	....	....	....	....	....	....	6	1	1	2	8	....	....	....
1983-84	**Quebec Nordiques**	NHL	38	0	5	5	0	3	3	60	0	0	0	14	0.0	17	1	19	2	–1	....	....	....	....	....	....	....	....
	Fredericton Express	AHL	30	2	3	5	....	....	....	146	....	....	....	....	....	....	....	....	....	....	7	1	1	2	43	....	....	....
1984-85	**Quebec Nordiques**	NHL	22	0	0	0	0	0	0	33	0	0	0	9	0.0	4	0	3	0	1	....	....	....	....	....	....	....	....
	Fredericton Express	AHL	42	1	5	6	....	....	....	134	....	....	....	....	....	....	....	....	....	....	6	0	1	1	25	....	....	....
1985-86	**Quebec Nordiques**	NHL	36	2	2	4	2	1	3	85	0	0	0	30	6.7	11	0	13	2	0	1	0	0	0	0	0	0	0
	Fredericton Express	AHL	38	3	5	8	....	....	....	103	....	....	....	....	....	....	....	....	....	....	5	0	0	0	33	....	....	....
1986-87	**Quebec Nordiques**	NHL	38	0	2	2	0	1	1	143	0	0	0	14	0.0	6	0	9	0	–3	13	0	0	0	53	0	0	0
1987-88	**Quebec Nordiques**	NHL	63	4	3	7	3	2	5	301	1	0	0	46	8.7	10	2	24	0	–16	....	....	....	....	....	....	....	....
1988-89	**Quebec Nordiques**	NHL	16	4	0	4	3	0	3	46	1	0	0	14	28.6	5	1	12	0	–8	....	....	....	....	....	....	....	....
	Winnipeg Jets	NHL	57	6	10	16	5	7	12	228	0	0	0	53	11.3	25	1	36	0	–12	....	....	....	....	....	....	....	....
1989-90	**Winnipeg Jets**	NHL	55	3	3	6	3	2	5	222	0	0	0	43	7.0	17	0	15	1	3	6	0	1	1	8	0	0	0
1990-91	**Winnipeg Jets**	NHL	57	3	4	7	3	3	6	265	0	0	0	35	8.6	25	0	40	2	–13	....	....	....	....	....	....	....	....
1991-92	**Winnipeg Jets**	NHL	4	0	0	0	0	0	0	11	0	0	0	5	0.0	1	0	6	0	–5	....	....	....	....	....	....	....	....
	Buffalo Sabres	NHL	67	2	3	5	2	2	4	305	0	0	1	25	8.0	10	0	17	0	–7	6	0	1	1	0	0	0	0
1992-93	**Buffalo Sabres**	NHL	60	3	8	11	2	5	7	221	0	0	0	38	7.9	22	0	17	0	5	....	....	....	....	....	....	....	....
1993-94	**Buffalo Sabres**	NHL	7	0	0	0	0	0	0	31	0	0	0	2	0.0	3	0	3	1	1	....	....	....	....	....	....	....	....
	Dallas Stars	NHL	18	0	1	1	0	1	1	66	0	0	0	5	0.0	2	0	6	0	–4	....	....	....	....	....	....	....	....
1994-95	Kalamazoo Wings	IHL	7	2	2	4	....	....	....	18	....	....	....	....	....	....	....	....	....	....	....	....	....	....	....	....	....	....
	Dallas Stars	NHL	16	1	0	1	2	0	2	52	0	0	0	9	11.1	4	0	3	0	1	....	....	....	....	....	....	....	....
1995-96	Houston Aeros	IHL	73	3	4	7	....	....	....	333	....	....	....	....	....	....	....	....	....	....	....	....	....	....	....	....	....	....
1996-97	Houston Aeros	IHL	5	0	0	0	....	....	....	25	....	....	....	....	....	....	....	....	....	....	....	....	....	....	....	....	....	....
	Chicago Wolves	IHL	59	3	5	8	....	....	....	144	....	....	....	....	....	....	....	....	....	....	4	0	2	2	28	....	....	....
1997-98	VSV Villach	Alpenliga	12	0	5	5	....	....	....	28	....	....	....	....	....	....	....	....	....	....	....	....	....	....	....	....	....	....
	VSV Villach	Austria	19	6	8	14	....	....	....	61	....	....	....	....	....	....	....	....	....	....	5	0	0	0	42	....	....	....
1998-99	VSV Villach	Alpenliga	31	2	8	10	....	....	....	148	....	....	....	....	....	....	....	....	....	....	....	....	....	....	....	....	....	....
	VSV Villach	Austria	23	1	1	2	....	....	....	44	....	....	....	....	....	....	....	....	....	....	....	....	....	....	....	....	....	....
99-2000	VSV Villach	IEL	32	3	6	9	....	....	....	106	....	....	....	....	....	....	....	....	....	....	....	....	....	....	....	....	....	....
	VSV Villach	EuroHL	5	1	1	2	....	....	....	58	....	....	....	....	....	....	....	....	....	....	....	....	....	....	....	....	....	....
	VSV Villach	Austria	15	0	1	1	....	....	....	63	....	....	....	....	....	....	....	....	....	....	....	....	....	....	....	....	....	....
	NHL Totals		554	28	41	69	25	27	52	2069	2	0	1	342	8.2	162	5	223	8		26	0	2	2	61	0	0	0

Rights transferred to **Quebec** by **St. Louis** with the rights to Claude Julien as compensation for St. Louis' signing of Jacques Demers as coach, August 19, 1983. Traded to **Winnipeg** by **Quebec** for Mario Marois, December 6, 1988. Traded to **Buffalo** by **Winnipeg** with Dave McLlwain, Winnipeg's 5th round choice (Yuri Khmylev) in 1992 Entry Draft and future considerations for Darrin Shannon, Mike Hartman and Dean Kennedy, October 11, 1991. Traded to **Dallas** by **Buffalo** for James Black and Dallas' 7th round choice (Steve Webb) in 1994 Entry Draft, December 15, 1993.

• DONNELLY, Mike

LW – L. 5'11", 185 lbs. b: Detroit, MI, 10/10/1963.

Season	Club	League	GP	G	A	Pts	AG	AA	APts	PIM	PP	SH	GW	S	%	TGF	PGF	TGA	PGA	+/–	GP	G	A	Pts	PIM	PP	SH	GW
1978-79	Markham Waxers	OJHL	STATISTICS NOT AVAILABLE																									
1979-80	Richmond Hill Rams	OJHL	29	17	17	34	....	....	....	37	....	....	....	....	....	....	....	....	....	....	....	....	....	....	....	....	....	....
	Belleville Bulls	OJHL	13	9	5	14	....	....	....	6	....	....	....	....	....	....	....	....	....	....	....	....	....	....	....	....	....	....
1980-81	Belleville Bulls	OJHL	5	1	2	3	....	....	....	4	....	....	....	....	....	....	....	....	....	....	....	....	....	....	....	....	....	....
	Richmond Hill Rams	OJHL	20	9	16	25	....	....	....	22	....	....	....	....	....	....	....	....	....	....	....	....	....	....	....	....	....	....
1981-82	Waterford Lakers	GLJHL	46	48	64	112	....	....	....	....	....	....	....	....	....	....	....	....	....	....	....	....	....	....	....	....	....	....
1982-83	Michigan State Spartans	CCHA	24	7	13	20	....	....	....	8	....	....	....	....	....	....	....	....	....	....	....	....	....	....	....	....	....	....
1983-84	Michigan State Spartans	CCHA	44	18	14	32	....	....	....	40	....	....	....	....	....	....	....	....	....	....	....	....	....	....	....	....	....	....
1984-85	Michigan State Spartans	CCHA	44	26	21	47	....	....	....	48	....	....	....	....	....	....	....	....	....	....	....	....	....	....	....	....	....	....
1985-86	Michigan State Spartans	CCHA	44	*59	38	97	....	....	....	65	....	....	....	....	....	....	....	....	....	....	....	....	....	....	....	....	....	....
1986-87	**New York Rangers**	NHL	5	1	1	2	1	1	2	0	0	0	0	5	20.0	3	1	2	0	0	....	....	....	....	....	....	....	....
	New Haven Nighthawks	AHL	58	27	34	61	....	....	....	52	....	....	....	....	....	....	....	....	....	....	7	2	0	2	9	....	....	....
1987-88	**New York Rangers**	NHL	17	2	2	4	2	1	3	8	0	0	0	30	6.7	5	0	11	1	–5	....	....	....	....	....	....	....	....
	Colorado Rangers	IHL	8	7	11	18	....	....	....	15	....	....	....	....	....	....	....	....	....	....	....	....	....	....	....	....	....	....
	Buffalo Sabres	NHL	40	6	8	14	5	6	11	44	0	0	0	69	8.7	24	4	25	4	–1	....	....	....	....	....	....	....	....
1988-89	**Buffalo Sabres**	NHL	22	4	6	10	3	4	7	10	0	0	0	25	16.0	14	3	13	1	–1	....	....	....	....	....	....	....	....
	Rochester Americans	AHL	53	32	37	69	....	....	....	53	....	....	....	....	....	....	....	....	....	....	....	....	....	....	....	....	....	....
1989-90	**Buffalo Sabres**	NHL	12	1	2	3	1	1	2	8	0	0	0	20	5.0	5	0	10	1	–4	....	....	....	....	....	....	....	....
	Rochester Americans	AHL	68	43	55	98	....	....	....	71	....	....	....	....	....	....	....	....	....	....	16	*12	7	19	9	....	....	....
1990-91	**Los Angeles Kings**	NHL	53	7	5	12	6	4	10	41	0	0	2	76	9.2	22	0	29	10	3	12	5	4	9	6	0	0	0
	New Haven Nighthawks	AHL	18	10	6	16	....	....	....	2	....	....	....	....	....	....	....	....	....	....	....	....	....	....	....	....	....	....
1991-92	**Los Angeles Kings**	NHL	80	29	16	45	26	12	38	20	0	1	4	197	14.7	54	1	74	26	5	6	1	0	1	4	0	0	0
1992-93	**Los Angeles Kings**	NHL	84	29	40	69	24	28	52	45	8	1	2	244	11.9	102	33	83	31	17	24	6	7	13	14	0	0	0
1993-94	**Los Angeles Kings**	NHL	81	21	21	42	20	16	36	34	4	2	3	177	11.9	62	15	59	14	2	....	....	....	....	....	....	....	....

Season	Club	League	REGULAR SEASON																		PLAYOFFS							
			GP	G	A	Pts	AG	AA	APts	PIM	PP	SH	GW	S	%	TGF	PGF	TGA	PGA	+/-	GP	G	A	Pts	PIM	PP	SH	GW
1994-95	**Los Angeles Kings**	**NHL**	9	1	1	2	2	1	3	4	0	0	0	22	4.5	3	2	9	1	-7	....	....	....	....	....	....	....	....
	Dallas Stars	**NHL**	35	11	14	25	19	21	40	29	3	0	3	94	11.7	30	8	23	4	3	5	0	1	1	6	0	0	0
1995-96	**Dallas Stars**	**NHL**	24	2	5	7	2	4	6	10	0	0	0	21	9.5	9	2	9	0	-2	....	....	....	....	....	....	....	....
	Michigan K-Wings	IHL	21	8	15	23	....	....	....	20	....	....	....	....	....	....	....	....	....	....	8	3	0	3	10	....	....	....
1996-97	**New York Islanders**	**NHL**	3	0	0	0	0	0	0	2	0	0	0	5	0.0	0	0	0	0	0	....	....	....	....	....	....	....	....
	Utah Grizzlies	IHL	14	7	2	9	....	....	....	33	....	....	....	....	....	....	....	....	....	....	....	....	....	....	....	....	....	....
	Detroit Vipers	IHL	19	4	4	8	....	....	....	12	....	....	....	....	....	....	....	....	....	....	....	....	....	....	....	....	....	....
1997-98	Detroit Vipers	IHL	6	0	2	2	....	....	....	2	....	....	....	....	....	....	....	....	....	....	....	....	....	....	....	....	....	....
	SC Bern	Switz.	5	3	1	4	....	....	....	0	....	....	....	....	....	....	....	....	....	....	1	0	1	1	27	....	....	....
	NHL Totals		465	114	121	235	111	99	210	255	15	4	14	985	11.6	333	69	347	93		47	12	12	24	30	0	0	0

CCHA First All-Star Team (1986) • NCAA West First All-American Team (1986) • NCAA Championship All-Tournament Team (1986) • NCAA Championship Tournament MVP (1986)

Signed as a free agent by **NY Rangers**, August 15, 1986. Traded to **Buffalo** by **NY Rangers** with NY Rangers' 5th round choice (Alexander Mogilny) in 1988 Entry Draft for Paul Cyr and Buffalo's 10th round choice (Eric Fenton) in 1988 Entry Draft, December 31, 1987. Traded to **LA Kings** by **Buffalo** for Mikko Makela, September 30, 1990. Traded to **Dallas** by **LA Kings** with LA Kings' 7th round choice (Eoin McInerney) in 1996 Entry Draft for Dallas' 4th round choice (later traded to Washington — Washington selected Justin Davis) in 1996 Entry Draft, February 17, 1995. Signed as a free agent by **NY Islanders**, August 19, 1996.

• DONOVAN, Shean

RW – R. 6'3", 210 lbs. b: Timmins, Ont., 1/22/1975. San Jose's 2nd, 28th overall, in 1993.

Season	Club	League	GP	G	A	Pts	AG	AA	APts	PIM	PP	SH	GW	S	%	TGF	PGF	TGA	PGA	+/-	GP	G	A	Pts	PIM	PP	SH	GW
1990-91	Kanata Valley Lasers	OJHL	44	8	5	13	....	....	....	8	....	....	....	....	....	....	....	....	....	....	....	....	....	....	....	....	....	....
1991-92	Ottawa 67's	OHL	58	11	8	19	....	....	....	14	....	....	....	....	....	....	....	....	....	....	11	1	0	1	5	....	....	....
1992-93	Ottawa 67's	OHL	66	29	23	52	....	....	....	33	....	....	....	....	....	....	....	....	....	....	....	....	....	....	....	....	....	....
1993-94	Ottawa 67's	OHL	62	35	49	84	....	....	....	63	....	....	....	....	....	....	....	....	....	....	17	10	11	21	14	....	....	....
1994-95	Ottawa 67's	OHL	29	22	19	41	....	....	....	41	....	....	....	....	....	....	....	....	....	....	....	....	....	....	....	....	....	....
	Canada	WJC-A	7	0	0	0	....	....	....	6	....	....	....	....	....	....	....	....	....	....	....	....	....	....	....	....	....	....
	San Jose Sharks	**NHL**	14	0	0	0	0	0	0	6	0	0	0	13	0.0	2	0	11	3	-6	7	0	1	1	6	0	0	0
	Kansas City Blades	IHL	5	0	2	2	....	....	....	7	....	....	....	....	....	....	....	....	....	....	14	5	3	8	23	....	....	....
1995-96	**San Jose Sharks**	**NHL**	74	13	8	21	13	7	20	39	0	1	2	73	17.8	31	2	62	16	-17	....	....	....	....	....	....	....	....
	Kansas City Blades	IHL	4	0	0	0	....	....	....	8	....	....	....	....	....	....	....	....	....	....	5	0	0	0	8	....	....	....
1996-97	**San Jose Sharks**	**NHL**	73	9	6	15	10	5	15	42	0	1	0	115	7.8	24	0	56	14	-18	....	....	....	....	....	....	....	....
	Kentucky Thoroughblades	AHL	3	1	3	4	....	....	....	18	....	....	....	....	....	....	....	....	....	....	....	....	....	....	....	....	....	....
	Canada	WC-A	10	0	1	1	....	....	....	31	....	....	....	....	....	....	....	....	....	....	....	....	....	....	....	....	....	....
1997-98	**San Jose Sharks**	**NHL**	20	3	3	6	4	3	7	22	0	0	0	24	12.5	10	0	8	1	3	....	....	....	....	....	....	....	....
	Colorado Avalanche	**NHL**	47	5	7	12	6	7	13	48	0	0	0	57	8.8	16	0	13	0	3	....	....	....	....	....	....	....	....
1998-99	**Colorado Avalanche**	**NHL**	68	7	12	19	8	12	20	37	1	0	1	81	8.6	25	3	19	1	4	5	0	0	0	2	0	0	0
99-2000	**Colorado Avalanche**	**NHL**	18	1	0	1	1	0	1	8	0	0	0	13	7.7	2	0	6	0	-4	....	....	....	....	....	....	....	....
	Atlanta Thrashers	**NHL**	33	4	7	11	4	6	10	18	1	0	1	53	7.5	13	3	30	7	-13	....	....	....	....	....	....	....	....
	NHL Totals		347	42	43	85	46	40	86	220	2	2	4	429	9.8	123	8	205	42		12	0	1	1	8	0	0	0

Traded to **Colorado** by **San Jose** with San Jose's 1st round choice (Alex Tanguay) in 1998 Entry Draft for Mike Ricci and Colorado's 2nd round choice (later traded to Buffalo — Buffalo selected Jaroslav Kristek), in 1998 Entry Draft, November 21, 1997. Traded to **Atlanta** by **Colorado** for Rick Tabaracci, December 8, 1999.

• DORE, Andre

Andre Hector "Trap" D – R. 6'2", 200 lbs. b: Montreal, Que., 2/11/1958. NY Rangers' 5th, 60th overall, in 1978.

Season	Club	League	GP	G	A	Pts	AG	AA	APts	PIM	PP	SH	GW	S	%	TGF	PGF	TGA	PGA	+/-	GP	G	A	Pts	PIM	PP	SH	GW
1975-76	Hull Festivals	QMJHL	59	4	11	15	....	....	....	67	....	....	....	....	....	....	....	....	....	....	....	....	....	....	....	....	....	....
1976-77	Hull Olympiques	QMJHL	72	9	42	51	....	....	....	178	....	....	....	....	....	....	....	....	....	....	3	0	3	3	29	....	....	....
1977-78	Hull Olympiques	QMJHL	15	3	9	12	....	....	....	22	....	....	....	....	....	....	....	....	....	....	....	....	....	....	....	....	....	....
	Trois-Rivieres Draveurs	QMJHL	27	2	14	16	....	....	....	61	....	....	....	....	....	....	....	....	....	....	....	....	....	....	....	....	....	....
	Quebec Remparts	QMJHL	32	6	17	23	....	....	....	51	....	....	....	....	....	....	....	....	....	....	4	0	0	0	2	....	....	....
1978-79	**New York Rangers**	**NHL**	2	0	0	0	0	0	0	0	0	0	0	0	0.0	1	0	1	0	0	....	....	....	....	....	....	....	....
	New Haven Nighthawks	AHL	71	6	23	29	....	....	....	134	....	....	....	....	....	....	....	....	....	....	10	0	3	3	12	....	....	....
1979-80	**New York Rangers**	**NHL**	2	0	0	0	0	0	0	0	0	0	0	0	0.0	0	0	1	0	-1	....	....	....	....	....	....	....	....
	New Haven Nighthawks	AHL	63	9	21	30	....	....	....	99	....	....	....	....	....	....	....	....	....	....	9	1	1	2	20	....	....	....
1980-81	**New York Rangers**	**NHL**	15	1	3	4	1	2	3	15	0	0	0	15	6.7	9	0	12	2	-1	....	....	....	....	....	....	....	....
	New Haven Nighthawks	AHL	58	8	41	49	....	....	....	105	....	....	....	....	....	....	....	....	....	....	....	....	....	....	....	....	....	....
1981-82	**New York Rangers**	**NHL**	56	4	16	20	3	11	14	64	0	0	0	40	10.0	56	1	57	12	10	10	1	1	2	16	0	0	0
	Springfield Indians	AHL	23	3	8	11	....	....	....	20	....	....	....	....	....	....	....	....	....	....	....	....	....	....	....	....	....	....
1982-83	**New York Rangers**	**NHL**	39	3	12	15	2	8	10	39	0	0	1	33	9.1	49	1	39	8	17	....	....	....	....	....	....	....	....
	St. Louis Blues	**NHL**	38	2	15	17	2	10	12	25	0	0	0	41	4.9	53	2	53	11	9	4	0	1	1	8	0	0	0
1983-84	**St. Louis Blues**	**NHL**	55	3	12	15	2	8	10	58	0	0	1	51	5.9	54	4	73	26	3	....	....	....	....	....	....	....	....
	Quebec Nordiques	**NHL**	25	1	16	17	1	11	12	25	0	0	0	30	3.3	32	3	34	6	1	9	0	0	0	8	0	0	0
1984-85	**New York Rangers**	**NHL**	25	0	7	7	0	5	5	35	0	0	0	14	0.0	24	2	27	3	-2	....	....	....	....	....	....	....	....
	New Haven Nighthawks	AHL	39	3	22	25	....	....	....	48	....	....	....	....	....	....	....	....	....	....	....	....	....	....	....	....	....	....
1985-86	Hershey Bears	AHL	65	10	18	28	....	....	....	128	....	....	....	....	....	....	....	....	....	....	18	0	6	6	35	....	....	....
	NHL Totals		257	14	81	95	11	55	66	261	0	0	2	224	6.3	278	13	297	68		23	1	2	3	32	0	0	0

Traded to **St. Louis** by **NY Rangers** for Vaclav Nedomansky and Glen Hanlon, January 4, 1983. Traded to **Quebec** by **St. Louis** for Dave Pichette, February 10, 1984. Claimed by **NY Rangers** from **Quebec** in Waiver Draft, October 9, 1984.

• DORE, Daniel

RW – R. 6'3", 202 lbs. b: Ferme-Neuve, Que., 4/9/1970. Quebec's 2nd, 5th overall, in 1988.

Season	Club	League	GP	G	A	Pts	AG	AA	APts	PIM	PP	SH	GW	S	%	TGF	PGF	TGA	PGA	+/-	GP	G	A	Pts	PIM	PP	SH	GW
1985-86	L'Outaouais Frontaliers	QAAA	41	8	12	20	....	....	....	....	....	....	....	....	....	....	....	....	....	....	....	....	....	....	....	....	....	....
1986-87	Drummondville Voltigeurs	QMJHL	68	23	41	64	....	....	....	229	....	....	....	....	....	....	....	....	....	....	8	0	1	1	18	....	....	....
1987-88	Drummondville Voltigeurs	QMJHL	64	24	39	63	....	....	....	218	....	....	....	....	....	....	....	....	....	....	17	7	11	18	42	....	....	....
	Drummondville Voltigeurs	Mem-Cup	3	0	0	0	....	....	....	4	....	....	....	....	....	....	....	....	....	....	....	....	....	....	....	....	....	....
1988-89	Drummondville Voltigeurs	QMJHL	62	33	58	91	....	....	....	236	....	....	....	....	....	....	....	....	....	....	4	2	3	5	14	....	....	....
1989-90	Chicoutimi Sagueneens	QMJHL	24	6	23	29	....	....	....	112	....	....	....	....	....	....	....	....	....	....	6	0	3	3	27	....	....	....
	Quebec Nordiques	**NHL**	16	2	3	5	2	2	4	59	1	0	0	5	40.0	7	4	11	0	-8	....	....	....	....	....	....	....	....
1990-91	**Quebec Nordiques**	**NHL**	1	0	0	0	0	0	0	0	0	0	0	0	0.0	1	0	0	0	1	....	....	....	....	....	....	....	....
	Halifax Citadels	AHL	50	7	10	17	....	....	....	139	....	....	....	....	....	....	....	....	....	....	....	....	....	....	....	....	....	....
1991-92	Halifax Citadels	AHL	29	4	1	5	....	....	....	45	....	....	....	....	....	....	....	....	....	....	....	....	....	....	....	....	....	....
	Greensboro Monarchs	ECHL	6	1	0	1	....	....	....	34	....	....	....	....	....	....	....	....	....	....	....	....	....	....	....	....	....	....
1992-93	Hershey Bears	AHL	65	12	10	22	....	....	....	192	....	....	....	....	....	....	....	....	....	....	....	....	....	....	....	....	....	....
1993-94	Chatham Wheels	ColHL	4	1	2	3	....	....	....	13	....	....	....	....	....	....	....	....	....	....	....	....	....	....	....	....	....	....
	NHL Totals		17	2	3	5	2	2	4	59	1	0	0	5	40.0	8	4	11	0		....	....	....	....	....	....	....	....

Signed as a free agent by **Philadelphia**, December 14, 1992. • Played w/ RHI's Montreal Roadrunners in 1994 (20-5-12-17-26) and 1995 (23-5-10-15-120); Empire State Cobras in 1996 (7-0-2-2-13).

• DOREY, Jim

Robert James "Flipper" D – L. 6'1", 190 lbs. b: Kingston, Ont., 8/17/1947. Toronto's 4th, 23rd overall, in 1964.

Season	Club	League	GP	G	A	Pts	AG	AA	APts	PIM	PP	SH	GW	S	%	TGF	PGF	TGA	PGA	+/-	GP	G	A	Pts	PIM	PP	SH	GW
1963-64	Stamford Jr. Bees	OHA-B	STATISTICS NOT AVAILABLE																									
	Niagara Falls Flyers	OHA-Jr.	21	1	0	1	....	....	....	4	....	....	....	....	....	....	....	....	....	....	....	....	....	....	....	....	....	....
1964-65	Stamford Jr. Bees	OHA-B	STATISTICS NOT AVAILABLE																									
1965-66	London Nationals	OHA-Jr.	47	5	20	25	....	....	....	168	....	....	....	....	....	....	....	....	....	....	....	....	....	....	....	....	....	....
1966-67	London Nationals	OHA-Jr.	48	8	41	49	....	....	....	*196	....	....	....	....	....	....	....	....	....	....	6	2	7	9	24	....	....	....
1967-68	Rochester Americans	AHL	20	0	3	3	....	....	....	16	....	....	....	....	....	....	....	....	....	....	....	....	....	....	....	....	....	....
	Phoenix Roadrunners	WHL	4	0	0	0	....	....	....	2	....	....	....	....	....	....	....	....	....	....	....	....	....	....	....	....	....	....
	Tulsa Oilers	CPHL	35	4	24	28	....	....	....	81	....	....	....	....	....	....	....	....	....	....	11	3	5	8	16	....	....	....
1968-69	**Toronto Maple Leafs**	**NHL**	61	8	22	30	8	20	28	200	0	1	0	133	6.0	80	9	78	16	9	4	0	1	1	21	0	0	0
1969-70	**Toronto Maple Leafs**	**NHL**	46	6	11	17	6	10	16	99	0	0	0	122	4.9	48	4	44	9	9	....	....	....	....	....	....	....	....
1970-71	**Toronto Maple Leafs**	**NHL**	74	7	22	29	7	18	25	198	0	1	1	171	4.1	89	19	78	14	6	6	0	1	1	19	0	0	0
1971-72	**Toronto Maple Leafs**	**NHL**	50	4	19	23	4	16	20	56	1	0	2	104	3.8	53	7	47	11	10	....	....	....	....	....	....	....	....
	New York Rangers	**NHL**	1	0	0	0	0	0	0	0	0	0	0	0	0.0	0	0	0	0	0	1	0	0	0	0	0	0	0
1972-73	New England Whalers	WHA	75	7	56	63	....	....	....	95	....	....	....	....	....	....	....	....	....	....	15	3	*16	19	*41	....	....	....
1973-74	New England Whalers	WHA	77	6	40	46	....	....	....	134	....	....	....	....	....	....	....	....	....	....	6	0	6	6	26	....	....	....

			REGULAR SEASON																		PLAYOFFS							
Season	Club	League	GP	G	A	Pts	AG	AA	APts	PIM	PP	SH	GW	S	%	TGF	PGF	TGA	PGA	+/–	GP	G	A	Pts	PIM	PP	SH	GW
1974-75	New England Whalers	WHA	31	5	17	22	....	....	....	43	....	....	....	....	....	....	....	....	....	....	....	....	....	....	....	....	....	....
	Toronto Toros	WHA	43	11	23	34	....	....	....	69	....	....	....	....	....	....	....	....	....	....	6	2	6	8	2	....	....	....
1975-76	Toronto Toros	WHA	74	9	51	60	....	....	....	134	....	....	....	....	....	....	....	....	....	....	....	....	....	....	....	....	....	....
1976-77	Quebec Nordiques	WHA	73	13	34	47	....	....	....	102	....	....	....	....	....	....	....	....	....	....	10	0	2	2	28	....	....	....
1977-78	Quebec Nordiques	WHA	26	1	9	10	....	....	....	23	....	....	....	....	....	....	....	....	....	....	11	0	3	3	34	....	....	....
1978-79	Quebec Nordiques	WHA	32	0	2	2	....	....	....	17	....	....	....	....	....	....	....	....	....	....	3	0	0	0	0	....	....	....
	Philadelphia Firebirds	AHL	5	0	1	1	....	....	....	6	....	....	....	....	....	....	....	....	....	....	....	....	....	....	....	....	....	....
1979-80			OUT OF HOCKEY – RETIRED																									
1980-81	New Haven Nighthawks	AHL	21	0	7	7	....	....	....	30	....	....	....	....	....	....	....	....	....	....	....	....	....	....	....	....	....	....
	NHL Totals		**232**	**25**	**74**	**99**	**25**	**64**	**89**	**553**	**1**	**2**	**3**	**530**	**4.7**	**270**	**39**	**247**	**50**		**11**	**0**	**2**	**2**	**40**	**0**	**0**	**0**
	Other Major League Totals		431	52	232	284	....	....	....	617	....	....	....	....	....	....	....	....	....	....	51	5	33	38	131	....	....	....

WHA Second All-Star Team (1973)

Selected by **Ontario-Ottawa** (WHA) in 1972 WHA General Player Draft, February 12, 1972. Traded to **NY Rangers** by **Toronto** for Pierre Jarry, February 20, 1972. WHA rights traded to **New England** (WHA) by **Ottawa** (WHA) for cash, July 5, 1972. Traded to **Toronto** (WHA) by **New England** (WHA) to complete transaction that sent Wayne Carleton to New England (September, 1974), December, 1974. Transferred to **Birmingham** (WHA) after **Toronto** (WHA) franchise relocated, June 30, 1976. Traded to **Quebec** (WHA) by **Birmingham** (WHA) to complete transaction that sent Dale Hoganson to Birmingham (June 30, 1976), October, 1976.

• DORION, Dan

C – R. 5'9", 180 lbs. b: Astoria, NY, 3/2/1963. New Jersey's 12th, 232nd overall, in 1982.

Season	Club	League	GP	G	A	Pts	AG	AA	APts	PIM	PP	SH	GW	S	%	TGF	PGF	TGA	PGA	+/–	GP	G	A	Pts	PIM	PP	SH	GW
1980-81	New Hyde Park Arrows	NYJHL	40	41	41	82	....	....	....	....	....	....	....	....	....	....	....	....	....	....	....	....	....	....	....	....	....	....
1981-82	Austin Mavericks	USHL	50	52	44	96	....	....	....	20	....	....	....	....	....	....	....	....	....	....	....	....	....	....	....	....	....	....
1982-83	University of Western Michigan	CCHA	34	11	20	31	....	....	....	23	....	....	....	....	....	....	....	....	....	....	....	....	....	....	....	....	....	....
1983-84	University of Western Michigan	CCHA	42	41	50	91	....	....	....	42	....	....	....	....	....	....	....	....	....	....	....	....	....	....	....	....	....	....
1984-85	University of Western Michigan	CCHA	39	21	46	67	....	....	....	28	....	....	....	....	....	....	....	....	....	....	....	....	....	....	....	....	....	....
	United States	WEC-A	5	2	3	5	....	....	....	2	....	....	....	....	....	....	....	....	....	....	....	....	....	....	....	....	....	....
1985-86	University of Western Michigan	CCHA	42	42	62	104	....	....	....	48	....	....	....	....	....	....	....	....	....	....	....	....	....	....	....	....	....	....
	New Jersey Devils	**NHL**	**3**	**1**	**1**	**2**	**1**	**1**	**2**	**0**	**0**	**0**	**0**	**6**	**16.7**	**3**	**0**	**4**	**0**	**–1**	....	....	....	....	....	....	....	....
	Maine Mariners	AHL	....	....	....	....	....	....	....	....	....	....	....	....	....	....	....	....	....	....	5	2	2	4	0	....	....	....
1986-87	Maine Mariners	AHL	70	16	22	38	....	....	....	47	....	....	....	....	....	....	....	....	....	....	....	....	....	....	....	....	....	....
1987-88	**New Jersey Devils**	**NHL**	**1**	**0**	**0**	**0**	**0**	**0**	**0**	**2**	**0**	**0**	**0**	**0**	**0.0**	**0**	**0**	**0**	**0**	**0**	....	....	....	....	....	....	....	....
	Utica Devils	AHL	65	30	35	65	....	....	....	98	....	....	....	....	....	....	....	....	....	....	....	....	....	....	....	....	....	....
1988-89	Utica Devils	AHL	15	7	4	11	....	....	....	19	....	....	....	....	....	....	....	....	....	....	....	....	....	....	....	....	....	....
	Maine Mariners	AHL	16	2	3	5	....	....	....	13	....	....	....	....	....	....	....	....	....	....	....	....	....	....	....	....	....	....
1989-90	HC Fassa	Italy	29	37	32	69	....	....	....	66	....	....	....	....	....	....	....	....	....	....	1	1	0	1	0	....	....	....
1990-91			OUT OF HOCKEY – RETIRED																									
1991-92	Solihull Barons	Aut-Cup	6	13	6	19	....	....	....	4	....	....	....	....	....	....	....	....	....	....	....	....	....	....	....	....	....	....
	Nottingham Panthers	Aut-Cup	15	14	10	24	....	....	....	6	....	....	....	....	....	....	....	....	....	....	....	....	....	....	....	....	....	....
	Nottingham Panthers	Britain	31	63	66	129	....	....	....	48	....	....	....	....	....	....	....	....	....	....	8	17	9	26	37	....	....	....
1992-93	Nottingham Panthers	BH-Cup	10	24	7	31	....	....	....	14	....	....	....	....	....	....	....	....	....	....	....	....	....	....	....	....	....	....
	Nottingham Panthers	Britain	13	26	12	38	....	....	....	16	....	....	....	....	....	....	....	....	....	....	....	....	....	....	....	....	....	....
	Humberside Seahawks	Britain	19	37	28	65	....	....	....	22	....	....	....	....	....	....	....	....	....	....	8	9	12	21	18	....	....	....
1993-94	Humberside Seahawks	Britain	28	46	39	85	....	....	....	46	....	....	....	....	....	....	....	....	....	....	6	8	5	13	6	....	....	....
	Roanoke Valley Rebels	ECHL	8	3	3	6	....	....	....	4	....	....	....	....	....	....	....	....	....	....	....	....	....	....	....	....	....	....
1994-95	Romford Raiders	BH-Cup	8	6	13	19	....	....	....	10	....	....	....	....	....	....	....	....	....	....	....	....	....	....	....	....	....	....
	NHL Totals		**4**	**1**	**1**	**2**	**1**	**1**	**2**	**2**	**0**	**0**	**0**	**6**	**16.7**	**3**	**0**	**4**	**0**		....	....	....	....	....	....	....	....

CCHA First All-Star Team (1984, 1986) • NCAA West Second All-American Team (1984) • NCAA West First All-American Team (1986) • British League's First All-Star Team (1992) • British League's MVP (1992)

Traded to **Boston** by **New Jersey** for Jean-Marc Lanthier, December 9, 1988. • Romford Raiders (Britain) franchise folded operations on December 5, 1994.

• DORNHOEFER, Gary

Gerhardt Otto RW – R. 6'1", 190 lbs. b: Kitchener, Ont., 2/2/1943.

Season	Club	League	GP	G	A	Pts	AG	AA	APts	PIM	PP	SH	GW	S	%	TGF	PGF	TGA	PGA	+/–	GP	G	A	Pts	PIM	PP	SH	GW
1961-62	Niagara Falls Flyers	OHA-Jr.	50	8	31	39	....	....	....	121	....	....	....	....	....	....	....	....	....	....	6	2	3	5	15	....	....	....
1962-63	Niagara Falls Flyers	OHA-Jr.	38	16	34	50	....	....	....	58	....	....	....	....	....	....	....	....	....	....	16	11	13	24	*56	....	....	....
	Niagara Falls Flyers	Mem-Cup	9	2	3	5	....	....	....	33	....	....	....	....	....	....	....	....	....	....	....	....	....	....	....	....	....	....
1963-64	**Boston Bruins**	**NHL**	**32**	**12**	**10**	**22**	**15**	**10**	**25**	**20**	....	....	....	....	....	....	....	....	....	....	....	....	....	....	....	....	....	....
	Minneapolis Bruins	CPHL	39	21	30	51	....	....	....	67	....	....	....	....	....	....	....	....	....	....	....	....	....	....	....	....	....	....
1964-65	**Boston Bruins**	**NHL**	**20**	**0**	**1**	**1**	**0**	**1**	**1**	**13**	....	....	....	....	....	....	....	....	....	....	....	....	....	....	....	....	....	....
	San Francisco Seals	WHL	37	10	25	35	....	....	....	59	....	....	....	....	....	....	....	....	....	....	....	....	....	....	....	....	....	....
1965-66	**Boston Bruins**	**NHL**	**10**	**0**	**1**	**1**	**0**	**1**	**1**	**2**	....	....	....	....	....	....	....	....	....	....	....	....	....	....	....	....	....	....
	Hershey Bears	AHL	54	16	20	36	....	....	....	56	....	....	....	....	....	....	....	....	....	....	3	1	1	2	14	....	....	....
1966-67	Hershey Bears	AHL	71	19	22	41	....	....	....	110	....	....	....	....	....	....	....	....	....	....	5	0	1	1	7	....	....	....
1967-68	**Philadelphia Flyers**	**NHL**	**65**	**13**	**30**	**43**	**15**	**30**	**45**	**134**	**2**	**0**	**4**	**96**	**13.5**	**59**	**18**	**44**	**9**	**6**	**3**	**0**	**0**	**0**	**15**	**0**	**0**	**0**
1968-69	**Philadelphia Flyers**	**NHL**	**60**	**8**	**16**	**24**	**8**	**14**	**22**	**80**	**2**	**0**	**0**	**111**	**7.2**	**41**	**10**	**51**	**0**	**–20**	**4**	**0**	**1**	**1**	**20**	**0**	**0**	**0**
1969-70	**Philadelphia Flyers**	**NHL**	**65**	**26**	**29**	**55**	**28**	**27**	**55**	**96**	**4**	**2**	**1**	**146**	**17.8**	**71**	**13**	**59**	**3**	**2**	....	....	....	....	....	....	....	....
1970-71	**Philadelphia Flyers**	**NHL**	**57**	**20**	**20**	**40**	**20**	**17**	**37**	**93**	**5**	**0**	**2**	**96**	**20.8**	**51**	**15**	**35**	**2**	**3**	**2**	**0**	**0**	**0**	**4**	**0**	**0**	**0**
1971-72	**Philadelphia Flyers**	**NHL**	**75**	**17**	**32**	**49**	**17**	**28**	**45**	**183**	**2**	**3**	**2**	**167**	**10.2**	**68**	**20**	**77**	**14**	**–15**	....	....	....	....	....	....	....	....
1972-73	**Philadelphia Flyers**	**NHL**	**77**	**30**	**49**	**79**	**28**	**39**	**67**	**168**	**3**	**0**	**4**	**187**	**16.0**	**109**	**30**	**78**	**16**	**17**	**11**	**3**	**3**	**6**	**16**	**1**	**0**	**1**
1973-74♦	**Philadelphia Flyers**	**NHL**	**57**	**11**	**39**	**50**	**11**	**32**	**43**	**125**	**3**	**0**	**4**	**109**	**10.1**	**63**	**23**	**33**	**6**	**13**	**14**	**5**	**6**	**11**	**43**	**2**	**1**	**1**
1974-75♦	**Philadelphia Flyers**	**NHL**	**69**	**17**	**27**	**44**	**15**	**20**	**35**	**102**	**3**	**2**	**4**	**115**	**14.8**	**71**	**20**	**35**	**7**	**23**	**17**	**5**	**5**	**10**	**33**	**0**	**0**	**2**
1975-76	**Philadelphia Flyers**	**NHL**	**74**	**28**	**35**	**63**	**25**	**26**	**51**	**128**	**13**	**0**	**3**	**152**	**18.4**	**86**	**33**	**49**	**10**	**14**	**16**	**3**	**4**	**7**	**43**	**1**	**0**	**0**
1976-77	**Philadelphia Flyers**	**NHL**	**79**	**25**	**34**	**59**	**23**	**26**	**49**	**85**	**5**	**0**	**3**	**115**	**21.7**	**110**	**20**	**46**	**3**	**47**	**9**	**1**	**0**	**1**	**22**	**0**	**0**	**0**
1977-78	**Philadelphia Flyers**	**NHL**	**47**	**7**	**5**	**12**	**6**	**4**	**10**	**62**	**2**	**0**	**0**	**61**	**11.5**	**24**	**6**	**22**	**1**	**–3**	**4**	**0**	**0**	**0**	**7**	**0**	**0**	**0**
	NHL Totals		**787**	**214**	**328**	**542**	**211**	**275**	**486**	**1291**	....	....	....	....	....	....	....	....	....		**80**	**17**	**19**	**36**	**203**	....	....	....

Played in NHL All-Star Game (1973, 1977)

Claimed by **Philadelphia** from **Boston** in Expansion Draft, June 6, 1967.

• DOUGLAS, Jordy

Jordy Paul LW – L. 6', 200 lbs. b: Winnipeg, Man., 1/20/1958. Toronto's 4th, 81st overall, in 1978.

Season	Club	League	GP	G	A	Pts	AG	AA	APts	PIM	PP	SH	GW	S	%	TGF	PGF	TGA	PGA	+/–	GP	G	A	Pts	PIM	PP	SH	GW
1974-75	Kern-Hill Nationals	AJBHL	48	26	25	51	....	....	....	77	....	....	....	....	....	....	....	....	....	....	....	....	....	....	....	....	....	....
1975-76	Flin Flon Bombers	WCJHL	72	12	22	34	....	....	....	48	....	....	....	....	....	....	....	....	....	....	....	....	....	....	....	....	....	....
1976-77	Flin Flon Bombers	WCJHL	59	40	23	63	....	....	....	71	....	....	....	....	....	....	....	....	....	....	....	....	....	....	....	....	....	....
1977-78	Flin Flon Bombers	WCJHL	71	60	56	116	....	....	....	131	....	....	....	....	....	....	....	....	....	....	17	14	22	36	20	....	....	....
1978-79	Springfield Indians	AHL	26	7	9	16	....	....	....	21	....	....	....	....	....	....	....	....	....	....	....	....	....	....	....	....	....	....
	New England Whalers	WHA	51	6	10	16	....	....	....	15	....	....	....	....	....	....	....	....	....	....	10	4	0	4	23	....	....	....
1979-80	**Hartford Whalers**	**NHL**	**77**	**33**	**24**	**57**	**28**	**17**	**45**	**39**	**5**	**0**	**5**	**188**	**17.6**	**79**	**11**	**84**	**5**	**–11**	....	....	....	....	....	....	....	....
1980-81	**Hartford Whalers**	**NHL**	**55**	**13**	**9**	**22**	**10**	**6**	**16**	**29**	**3**	**0**	**1**	**98**	**13.3**	**40**	**7**	**56**	**0**	**–23**	....	....	....	....	....	....	....	....
1981-82	**Hartford Whalers**	**NHL**	**30**	**10**	**7**	**17**	**8**	**5**	**13**	**44**	**4**	**0**	**2**	**74**	**13.5**	**25**	**7**	**30**	**1**	**–11**	....	....	....	....	....	....	....	....
	Binghamton Whalers	AHL	2	0	0	0	....	....	....	0	....	....	....	....	....	....	....	....	....	....	....	....	....	....	....	....	....	....
1982-83	**Minnesota North Stars**	**NHL**	**68**	**13**	**14**	**27**	**11**	**10**	**21**	**30**	**1**	**0**	**2**	**89**	**14.6**	**39**	**6**	**45**	**5**	**–7**	**5**	**0**	**0**	**0**	**2**	**0**	**0**	**0**
1983-84	**Minnesota North Stars**	**NHL**	**14**	**3**	**4**	**7**	**2**	**3**	**5**	**10**	**0**	**0**	**1**	**21**	**14.3**	**10**	**0**	**14**	**2**	**–2**	....	....	....	....	....	....	....	....
	Winnipeg Jets	**NHL**	**17**	**4**	**2**	**6**	**3**	**1**	**4**	**8**	**1**	**0**	**1**	**14**	**28.6**	**10**	**2**	**17**	**0**	**–9**	**1**	**0**	**0**	**0**	**2**	**0**	**0**	**0**
1984-85	**Winnipeg Jets**	**NHL**	**7**	**0**	**2**	**2**	**0**	**1**	**1**	**0**	**0**	**0**	**0**	**6**	**0.0**	**5**	**2**	**9**	**0**	**–6**	....	....	....	....	....	....	....	....
	Sherbrooke Canadiens	AHL	53	23	21	44	....	....	....	16	....	....	....	....	....	....	....	....	....	....	....	....	....	....	....	....	....	....
1985-86	Ilves Tampere	Finland	36	36	13	49	....	....	....	51	....	....	....	....	....	....	....	....	....	....	....	....	....	....	....	....	....	....
1986-87	Ilves Tampere	Finland	31	7	5	12	....	....	....	42	....	....	....	....	....	....	....	....	....	....	....	....	....	....	....	....	....	....
	NHL Totals		**268**	**76**	**62**	**138**	**62**	**43**	**105**	**160**	**14**	**0**	**12**	**490**	**15.5**	**208**	**35**	**255**	**13**		**6**	**0**	**0**	**0**	**4**	**0**	**0**	**0**
	Other Major League Totals		51	6	10	16	....	....	....	15	....	....	....	....	....	....	....	....	....	....	10	4	0	4	23	....	....	....

Signed as an underage free agent by **New England** (WHA), June, 1978. Reclaimed by **Toronto** from **Hartford** prior to Expansion Draft, June 9, 1979. Claimed as a priority selection by **Hartford**, June 9, 1979. Traded to **Minnesota** by **Hartford** with Hartford's 5th round draft choice (Jiri Poner) in 1984 Entry Draft for Mark Johnson and Kent-Erik Andersson, October 1, 1982. Traded to **Winnipeg** by **Minnesota** for Tim Trimper, January 12, 1984.

• DOUGLAS, Kent

Kent Gemmell D – L. 5'10", 180 lbs. b: Cobalt, Ont., 2/6/1936.

			REGULAR SEASON																		PLAYOFFS							
Season	Club	League	GP	G	A	Pts	AG	AA	APts	PIM	PP	SH	GW	S	%	TGF	PGF	TGA	PGA	+/–	GP	G	A	Pts	PIM	PP	SH	GW
1954-55	Kitchener Canucks	OHA-Jr.	21	2	5	7	....	....	....	104	....	....	....	....	....	....	....	....	....	....	....	....	....	....	....	....	....	....
1955-56	Kitchener Canucks	OHA-Jr.	48	16	22	38	....	....	....	193	....	....	....	....	....	....	....	....	....	....	8	3	1	4	40	....	....	....
	Springfield Indians	AHL	3	1	0	1	....	....	....	4	....	....	....	....	....	....	....	....	....	....	....	....	....	....	....	....	....	....
1956-57	Owen Sound Mercurys	OHA-Sr.	52	9	4	13	....	....	....	*205	....	....	....	....	....	....	....	....	....	....	....	....	....	....	....	....	....	....
1957-58	Winnipeg Warriors	WHL	68	10	24	34	....	....	....	135	....	....	....	....	....	....	....	....	....	....	7	0	1	1	25	....	....	....
1958-59	Vancouver Canucks	WHL	48	14	12	26	....	....	....	144	....	....	....	....	....	....	....	....	....	....	....	....	....	....	....	....	....	....
	Springfield Indians	AHL	9	2	4	6	....	....	....	28	....	....	....	....	....	....	....	....	....	....	....	....	....	....	....	....	....	....
1959-60	Springfield Indians	AHL	67	12	18	30	....	....	....	157	....	....	....	....	....	....	....	....	....	....	10	1	4	5	*45	....	....	....
1960-61	Springfield Indians	AHL	65	8	28	36	....	....	....	138	....	....	....	....	....	....	....	....	....	....	8	1	1	2	14	....	....	....
1961-62	Springfield Indians	AHL	59	18	41	59	....	....	....	151	....	....	....	....	....	....	....	....	....	....	11	2	*8	*10	10	....	....	....
1962-63♦	**Toronto Maple Leafs**	**NHL**	**70**	**7**	**15**	**22**	**8**	**15**	**23**	**105**	....	....	....	....	....	....	....	....	....	....	**10**	**1**	**1**	**2**	**2**	**0**	**0**	**0**
1963-64♦	**Toronto Maple Leafs**	**NHL**	**43**	**0**	**1**	**1**	**0**	**1**	**1**	**29**	....	....	....	....	....	....	....	....	....	....	....	....	....	....	....	....	....	....
	Rochester Americans	AHL	27	6	13	19	....	....	....	38	....	....	....	....	....	....	....	....	....	....	2	0	1	1	2	....	....	....
1964-65	**Toronto Maple Leafs**	**NHL**	**67**	**5**	**23**	**28**	**6**	**24**	**30**	**129**	....	....	....	....	....	....	....	....	....	....	**5**	**0**	**1**	**1**	**19**	**0**	**0**	**0**
1965-66	**Toronto Maple Leafs**	**NHL**	**64**	**6**	**14**	**20**	**7**	**13**	**20**	**97**	....	....	....	....	....	....	....	....	....	....	**4**	**0**	**1**	**1**	**12**	**0**	**0**	**0**
1966-67♦	**Toronto Maple Leafs**	**NHL**	**39**	**2**	**12**	**14**	**2**	**12**	**14**	**48**	....	....	....	....	....	....	....	....	....	....	....	....	....	....	....	....	....	....
	Tulsa Oilers	CPHL	13	1	2	3	....	....	....	21	....	....	....	....	....	....	....	....	....	....	....	....	....	....	....	....	....	....
	Rochester Americans	AHL	11	7	9	16	....	....	....	6	....	....	....	....	....	....	....	....	....	....	10	3	3	6	6	....	....	....
1967-68	**Oakland Seals**	**NHL**	**40**	**4**	**11**	**15**	**5**	**11**	**16**	**80**	**1**	**0**	**0**	**103**	**3.9**	**48**	**20**	**57**	**11**	**–18**	....	....	....	....	....	....	....	....
	Detroit Red Wings	**NHL**	**36**	**7**	**10**	**17**	**8**	**10**	**18**	**46**	**0**	**0**	**0**	**62**	**11.3**	**53**	**3**	**61**	**17**	**6**	....	....	....	....	....	....	....	....
1968-69	**Detroit Red Wings**	**NHL**	**69**	**2**	**29**	**31**	**2**	**26**	**28**	**97**	**1**	**0**	**0**	**114**	**1.8**	**92**	**28**	**94**	**34**	**4**	....	....	....	....	....	....	....	....
1969-70	Rochester Americans	AHL	64	9	31	40	....	....	....	145	....	....	....	....	....	....	....	....	....	....	....	....	....	....	....	....	....	....
1970-71	Baltimore Clippers	AHL	71	9	36	45	....	....	....	72	....	....	....	....	....	....	....	....	....	....	6	1	3	4	16	....	....	....
1971-72	Baltimore Clippers	AHL	75	6	31	37	....	....	....	180	....	....	....	....	....	....	....	....	....	....	18	0	4	4	26	....	....	....
1972-73	New York Raiders	WHA	60	3	15	18	....	....	....	74	....	....	....	....	....	....	....	....	....	....	....	....	....	....	....	....	....	....
	Long Island Ducks	EHL	1	0	0	0	....	....	....	0	....	....	....	....	....	....	....	....	....	....	....	....	....	....	....	....	....	....
1973-74	Baltimore Clippers	AHL	71	7	46	53	....	....	....	176	....	....	....	....	....	....	....	....	....	....	9	2	4	6	34	....	....	....
1974-75	Baltimore Clippers	AHL	37	5	19	24	....	....	....	67	....	....	....	....	....	....	....	....	....	....	....	....	....	....	....	....	....	....
	Toledo Goaldiggers	IHL	22	2	9	11	....	....	....	10	....	....	....	....	....	....	....	....	....	....	19	2	7	9	6	....	....	....
1975-76	Baltimore Clippers	AHL	66	5	33	38	....	....	....	140	....	....	....	....	....	....	....	....	....	....	....	....	....	....	....	....	....	....
	NHL Totals		**428**	**33**	**115**	**148**	**38**	**112**	**150**	**631**	....	....	....	....	....	....	....	....	....	....	**19**	**1**	**3**	**4**	**33**	....	....	....
	Other Major League Totals		60	3	15	18	....	....	....	74	....	....	....	....	....	....	....	....	....	....	....	....	....	....	....	....	....	....

AHL First All-Star Team (1962) • Won Eddie Shore Award (Outstanding Defenseman - AHL) (1962) • Won Calder Memorial Trophy (1963) • AHL Second All-Star Team (1971) • Played in NHL All-Star Game (1962, 1963, 1964)

Traded to **Toronto** by **Springfield** (AHL) for Jim Wilcox, Roger Cote, Wally Boyer, Bill White and Dick Mattiussi, June 7, 1962. Claimed by **Oakland** from **Toronto** in Expansion Draft, June 6, 1967. Traded to **Detroit** by **Oakland** for John Brenneman, Ted Hampson and Bert Marshall, January 9, 1968. Traded to **Vancouver** (WHL) by **Detroit** for cash, June 20, 1969. • NHL rights transferred to **Vancouver** after NHL club purchased **Vancouver** (WHL) franchise, December 13, 1969. Traded to **Baltimore** (AHL) by **Vancouver** for cash, October 25, 1970. Selected by **NY Raiders** (WHA) in 1972 WHA General Player Draft, February 12, 1972.

• DOURIS, Peter

Peter W. RW – R. 6'1", 195 lbs. b: Toronto, Ont., 2/19/1966. Winnipeg's 1st, 30th overall, in 1984.

Season	Club	League	GP	G	A	Pts	AG	AA	APts	PIM	PP	SH	GW	S	%	TGF	PGF	TGA	PGA	+/–	GP	G	A	Pts	PIM	PP	SH	GW
1982-83	Don Mills Flyers	MTHL	STATISTICS NOT AVAILABLE																									
1983-84	University of New Hampshire	ECAC	37	19	15	34	....	....	....	14	....	....	....	....	....	....	....	....	....	....	....	....	....	....	....	....	....	....
1984-85	University of New Hampshire	H-East	42	27	24	51	....	....	....	34	....	....	....	....	....	....	....	....	....	....	....	....	....	....	....	....	....	....
1985-86	Canada	Nat-Team	33	16	7	23	....	....	....	18	....	....	....	....	....	....	....	....	....	....	....	....	....	....	....	....	....	....
	Canada	WJC-A	7	4	2	6	....	....	....	6	....	....	....	....	....	....	....	....	....	....	....	....	....	....	....	....	....	....
	Winnipeg Jets	**NHL**	**11**	**0**	**0**	**0**	**0**	**0**	**0**	**0**	**0**	**0**	**0**	**0**	**0.0**	**3**	**0**	**5**	**1**	**–1**	....	....	....	....	....	....	....	....
1986-87	**Winnipeg Jets**	**NHL**	**6**	**0**	**0**	**0**	**0**	**0**	**0**	**0**	**0**	**0**	**0**	**3**	**0.0**	**0**	**0**	**1**	**0**	**–1**	....	....	....	....	....	....	....	....
	Sherbrooke Canadiens	AHL	62	14	28	42	....	....	....	24	....	....	....	....	....	....	....	....	....	....	17	7	*15	*22	16	....	....	....
1987-88	**Winnipeg Jets**	**NHL**	**4**	**0**	**2**	**2**	**0**	**1**	**1**	**0**	**0**	**0**	**0**	**2**	**0.0**	**2**	**0**	**3**	**0**	**–1**	**1**	**0**	**0**	**0**	**0**	**0**	**0**	**0**
	Moncton Hawks	AHL	73	42	37	79	....	....	....	53	....	....	....	....	....	....	....	....	....	....	....	....	....	....	....	....	....	....
1988-89	Peoria Rivermen	IHL	81	28	41	69	....	....	....	32	....	....	....	....	....	....	....	....	....	....	4	1	2	3	0	....	....	....
1989-90	**Boston Bruins**	**NHL**	**36**	**5**	**6**	**11**	**4**	**4**	**8**	**15**	**1**	**0**	**0**	**63**	**7.9**	**19**	**1**	**10**	**0**	**8**	**8**	**0**	**1**	**1**	**8**	**0**	**0**	**0**
	Maine Mariners	AHL	38	17	20	37	....	....	....	14	....	....	....	....	....	....	....	....	....	....	....	....	....	....	....	....	....	....
1990-91	**Boston Bruins**	**NHL**	**39**	**5**	**2**	**7**	**5**	**2**	**7**	**9**	**1**	**0**	**1**	**46**	**10.9**	**12**	**1**	**23**	**0**	**–12**	**7**	**0**	**1**	**1**	**6**	**0**	**0**	**0**
	Maine Mariners	AHL	35	16	15	31	....	....	....	9	....	....	....	....	....	....	....	....	....	....	2	3	0	3	2	....	....	....
1991-92	**Boston Bruins**	**NHL**	**54**	**10**	**13**	**23**	**9**	**10**	**19**	**10**	**0**	**0**	**1**	**107**	**9.3**	**38**	**0**	**36**	**7**	**9**	**7**	**2**	**3**	**5**	**0**	**0**	**0**	**1**
	Maine Mariners	AHL	12	4	3	7	....	....	....	2	....	....	....	....	....	....	....	....	....	....	....	....	....	....	....	....	....	....
1992-93	**Boston Bruins**	**NHL**	**19**	**4**	**4**	**8**	**3**	**3**	**6**	**4**	**0**	**1**	**0**	**33**	**12.1**	**11**	**0**	**7**	**1**	**5**	**4**	**1**	**0**	**1**	**0**	**0**	**0**	**0**
	Providence Bruins	AHL	50	29	26	55	....	....	....	12	....	....	....	....	....	....	....	....	....	....	....	....	....	....	....	....	....	....
1993-94	**Mighty Ducks of Anaheim**	**NHL**	**74**	**12**	**22**	**34**	**11**	**17**	**28**	**21**	**1**	**0**	**1**	**142**	**8.5**	**59**	**14**	**55**	**5**	**–5**	....	....	....	....	....	....	....	....
1994-95	**Mighty Ducks of Anaheim**	**NHL**	**46**	**10**	**11**	**21**	**18**	**16**	**34**	**12**	**0**	**0**	**4**	**69**	**14.5**	**30**	**0**	**35**	**9**	**4**	....	....	....	....	....	....	....	....
1995-96	**Mighty Ducks of Anaheim**	**NHL**	**31**	**8**	**7**	**15**	**8**	**6**	**14**	**9**	**2**	**0**	**3**	**45**	**17.8**	**17**	**4**	**28**	**12**	**–3**	....	....	....	....	....	....	....	....
1996-97	Milwaukee Admirals	IHL	80	36	36	72	....	....	....	14	....	....	....	....	....	....	....	....	....	....	3	2	2	4	2	....	....	....
1997-98	**Dallas Stars**	**NHL**	**1**	**0**	**0**	**0**	**0**	**0**	**0**	**0**	**0**	**0**	**0**	**3**	**0.0**	**1**	**0**	**2**	**0**	**–1**	....	....	....	....	....	....	....	....
	Michigan K-Wings	IHL	78	26	31	57	....	....	....	29	....	....	....	....	....	....	....	....	....	....	4	0	5	5	2	....	....	....
1998-99	EV Landshut	Germany	51	17	26	43	....	....	....	59	....	....	....	....	....	....	....	....	....	....	3	1	0	1	0	....	....	....
99-2000	Munich Barons	Germany	56	18	34	52	....	....	....	24	....	....	....	....	....	....	....	....	....	....	12	3	6	9	2	....	....	....
	NHL Totals		**321**	**54**	**67**	**121**	**58**	**59**	**117**	**80**	**5**	**1**	**10**	**513**	**10.5**	**192**	**20**	**205**	**35**		**27**	**3**	**5**	**8**	**14**	**0**	**0**	**1**

Traded to **St. Louis** by **Winnipeg** for Kent Carlson, St. Louis' 12th round choice (Sergei Kharin) in 1989 Entry Draft and 4th round choice (Scott Levins) in 1990 Entry Draft, September 29, 1988. Signed as a free agent by **Boston**, June 27, 1989. Signed as a free agent by **Anaheim**, July 22, 1993. Signed as a free agent by **Dallas**, July 16, 1997.

• DOWD, Jim

James Thomas C – R. 6'1", 190 lbs. b: Brick, NJ, 12/25/1968. New Jersey's 7th, 149th overall, in 1987.

Season	Club	League	GP	G	A	Pts	AG	AA	APts	PIM	PP	SH	GW	S	%	TGF	PGF	TGA	PGA	+/–	GP	G	A	Pts	PIM	PP	SH	GW
1983-84	Brick Green Dragons	Hi-School	20	19	30	49	....	....	....	....	....	....	....	....	....	....	....	....	....	....	....	....	....	....	....	....	....	....
1984-85	Brick Green Dragons	Hi-School	24	58	55	113	....	....	....	....	....	....	....	....	....	....	....	....	....	....	....	....	....	....	....	....	....	....
1985-86	Brick Green Dragons	Hi-School	24	47	51	98	....	....	....	....	....	....	....	....	....	....	....	....	....	....	....	....	....	....	....	....	....	....
1986-87	Brick Green Dragons	Hi-School	24	22	33	55	....	....	....	....	....	....	....	....	....	....	....	....	....	....	....	....	....	....	....	....	....	....
1987-88	Lake Superior State	CCHA	45	18	27	45	....	....	....	16	....	....	....	....	....	....	....	....	....	....	....	....	....	....	....	....	....	....
1988-89	Lake Superior State	CCHA	46	24	35	59	....	....	....	40	....	....	....	....	....	....	....	....	....	....	....	....	....	....	....	....	....	....
1989-90	Lake Superior State	CCHA	46	25	*67	92	....	....	....	30	....	....	....	....	....	....	....	....	....	....	....	....	....	....	....	....	....	....
1990-91	Lake Superior State	CCHA	44	24	*54	*78	....	....	....	53	....	....	....	....	....	....	....	....	....	....	....	....	....	....	....	....	....	....
1991-92	**New Jersey Devils**	**NHL**	**1**	**0**	**0**	**0**	**0**	**0**	**0**	**0**	**0**	**0**	**0**	**0**	**0.0**	**0**	**0**	**0**	**0**	**0**	....	....	....	....	....	....	....	....
	Utica Devils	AHL	78	17	42	59	....	....	....	47	....	....	....	....	....	....	....	....	....	....	4	2	2	4	4	....	....	....
1992-93	**New Jersey Devils**	**NHL**	**1**	**0**	**0**	**0**	**0**	**0**	**0**	**0**	**0**	**0**	**0**	**1**	**0.0**	**0**	**0**	**1**	**0**	**–1**	....	....	....	....	....	....	....	....
	Utica Devils	AHL	78	27	45	72	....	....	....	62	....	....	....	....	....	....	....	....	....	....	5	1	7	8	10	....	....	....
1993-94	**New Jersey Devils**	**NHL**	**15**	**5**	**10**	**15**	**5**	**8**	**13**	**0**	**2**	**0**	**0**	**26**	**19.2**	**20**	**9**	**3**	**0**	**8**	**19**	**2**	**6**	**8**	**8**	**0**	**0**	**0**
	Albany River Rats	AHL	58	26	37	63	....	....	....	76	....	....	....	....	....	....	....	....	....	....	....	....	....	....	....	....	....	....
1994-95♦	**New Jersey Devils**	**NHL**	**10**	**1**	**4**	**5**	**2**	**6**	**8**	**0**	**1**	**0**	**0**	**14**	**7.1**	**7**	**3**	**9**	**0**	**–5**	**11**	**2**	**1**	**3**	**8**	**0**	**0**	**1**
1995-96	**New Jersey Devils**	**NHL**	**28**	**4**	**9**	**13**	**4**	**7**	**11**	**17**	**0**	**0**	**0**	**41**	**9.8**	**16**	**0**	**20**	**3**	**–1**	....	....	....	....	....	....	....	....
	Vancouver Canucks	**NHL**	**38**	**1**	**6**	**7**	**1**	**5**	**6**	**6**	**0**	**0**	**0**	**35**	**2.9**	**11**	**0**	**27**	**8**	**–8**	**1**	**0**	**0**	**0**	**0**	**0**	**0**	**0**
1996-97	**New York Islanders**	**NHL**	**3**	**0**	**0**	**0**	**0**	**0**	**0**	**0**	**0**	**0**	**0**	**0**	**0.0**	**1**	**1**	**1**	**0**	**–1**	....	....	....	....	....	....	....	....
	Utah Grizzlies	IHL	48	10	21	31	....	....	....	27	....	....	....	....	....	....	....	....	....	....	....	....	....	....	....	....	....	....
	Saint John Flames	AHL	24	5	11	16	....	....	....	18	....	....	....	....	....	....	....	....	....	....	5	1	2	3	0	....	....	....
1997-98	**Calgary Flames**	**NHL**	**48**	**6**	**8**	**14**	**7**	**8**	**15**	**12**	**0**	**1**	**0**	**58**	**10.3**	**24**	**2**	**27**	**15**	**10**	....	....	....	....	....	....	....	....
	Saint John Flames	AHL	35	8	30	38	....	....	....	20	....	....	....	....	....	....	....	....	....	....	19	3	13	16	10	....	....	....

			REGULAR SEASON																		PLAYOFFS							
Season	**Club**	**League**	**GP**	**G**	**A**	**Pts**	**AG**	**AA**	**APts**	**PIM**	**PP**	**SH**	**GW**	**S**	**%**	**TGF**	**PGF**	**TGA**	**PGA**	**+/–**	**GP**	**G**	**A**	**Pts**	**PIM**	**PP**	**SH**	**GW**
1998-99	**Edmonton Oilers**	**NHL**	**1**	**0**	**0**	**0**	**0**	**0**	**0**	**0**	**0**	**0**	**0**	**1**	**0.0**	**0**	**0**	**0**	**0**	**0**	....	....	....	....	....	....	....	....
	Hamilton Bulldogs	AHL	51	15	29	44	....	....	....	82	....	....	....	....	....	....	....	....	....	....	11	3	6	9	8	....	....	....
99-2000	**Edmonton Oilers**	**NHL**	**69**	**5**	**18**	**23**	**6**	**17**	**23**	**45**	**2**	**0**	**1**	**103**	**4.9**	**43**	**14**	**34**	**15**	**10**	**5**	**2**	**1**	**3**	**4**	**0**	**0**	**0**
	NHL Totals		**214**	**22**	**55**	**77**	**25**	**51**	**76**	**80**	**5**	**1**	**1**	**279**	**7.9**	**122**	**29**	**122**	**41**		**36**	**6**	**8**	**14**	**20**	**0**	**0**	**1**

CCHA Second All-Star Team (1990) • NCAA West Second All-American Team (1990) • CCHA First All-Star Team (1991) • NCAA West First All-American Team (1991)

Traded to **Hartford** by **New Jersey** with New Jersey's 2nd round choice (later traded to Calgary – Calgary selected Dmitri Kokorev) in 1997 Entry Draft for Jocelyn Lemieux and Hartford's 2nd round choice in 1998 Entry Draft, December 19, 1995. Traded to **Vancouver** by **Hartford** with Frantisek Kucera and Hartford's 2nd round choice (Ryan Bonni) in 1997 Entry Draft for Jeff Brown and Vancouver's 3rd round choice in 1998 Entry Draft, December 19, 1995. Claimed by **NY Islanders** from **Vancouver** in NHL Waiver Draft, September 30, 1996. Signed as a free agent by **Calgary**, August, 1997. Traded to **Nashville** by **Calgary** for future considerations, June 26, 1998. Traded to **Edmonton** by **Nashville** with Mikhail Shtalenkov for Eric Fichaud, Drake Berehowsky and Greg de Vries, October 1, 1998. Selected by **Minnesota** from **Edmonton** in Expansion Draft, June 23, 2000.

• DOWNEY, Aaron

Aaron Douglas "Diesel" RW – R. 6', 210 lbs. b: Shelburne, Ont., 8/27/1974.

Season	Club	League	GP	G	A	Pts	AG	AA	APts	PIM	PP	SH	GW	S	%	TGF	PGF	TGA	PGA	+/–	GP	G	A	Pts	PIM	PP	SH	GW
1990-91	Grand Valley Harvesters	OJHL-C	27	6	8	14	....	....	....	57	....	....	....	....	....	....	....	....	....	....	....	....	....	....	....	....	....	....
1991-92	Collingwood Blues	OJHL-B	40	9	8	17	....	....	....	111	....	....	....	....	....	....	....	....	....	....	....	....	....	....	....	....	....	....
1992-93	Guelph Storm	OHL	53	3	3	6	....	....	....	88	....	....	....	....	....	....	....	....	....	....	5	1	0	1	0	....	....	....
1993-94	Cole Harbour Red Wings	MJrHL	35	8	20	28	....	....	....	210	....	....	....	....	....	....	....	....	....	....	....	....	....	....	....	....	....	....
1994-95	Cole Harbour Red Wings	MJrHL	40	10	31	41	....	....	....	320	....	....	....	....	....	....	....	....	....	....	....	....	....	....	....	....	....	....
1995-96	Hampton Roads Admirals	ECHL	65	12	11	23	....	....	....	354	....	....	....	....	....	....	....	....	....	....	....	....	....	....	....	....	....	....
1996-97	Manitoba Moose	IHL	2	0	0	0	....	....	....	17	....	....	....	....	....	....	....	....	....	....	....	....	....	....	....	....	....	....
	Portland Pirates	AHL	3	0	0	0	....	....	....	19	....	....	....	....	....	....	....	....	....	....	....	....	....	....	....	....	....	....
	Hampton Roads Admirals	ECHL	64	8	8	16	....	....	....	338	....	....	....	....	....	....	....	....	....	....	9	0	3	3	26	....	....	....
1997-98	Providence Bruins	AHL	78	5	10	15	....	....	....	*407	....	....	....	....	....	....	....	....	....	....	....	....	....	....	....	....	....	....
1998-99	Providence Bruins	AHL	75	10	12	22	....	....	....	*401	....	....	....	....	....	....	....	....	....	....	19	1	1	2	46	....	....	....
99-2000	**Boston Bruins**	**NHL**	**1**	**0**	**0**	**0**	**0**	**0**	**0**	**0**	**0**	**0**	**0**	**0**	**0.0**	**0**	**0**	**0**	**0**	**0**	....	....	....	....	....	....	....	....
	Providence Bruins	AHL	47	6	4	10	....	....	....	221	....	....	....	....	....	....	....	....	....	....	14	1	0	1	24	....	....	....
	NHL Totals		**1**	**0**	**0**	**0**	**0**	**0**	**0**	**0**	**0**	**0**	**0**	**0**	**0.0**	**0**	**0**	**0**	**0**		....	....	....	....	....	....	....	....

Signed as a free agent by **Boston**, January 20, 1998.

• DOYON, Mario

D – R. 6', 174 lbs. b: Quebec City, Que., 8/27/1968. Chicago's 5th, 119th overall, in 1986.

Season	Club	League	GP	G	A	Pts	AG	AA	APts	PIM	PP	SH	GW	S	%	TGF	PGF	TGA	PGA	+/–	GP	G	A	Pts	PIM	PP	SH	GW
1984-85	Ste-Foy Gouverneurs	QAAA	42	14	17	31	....	....	....	82	....	....	....	....	....	....	....	....	....	....	....	....	....	....	....	....	....	....
1985-86	Drummondville Voltigeurs	QMJHL	71	5	14	19	....	....	....	129	....	....	....	....	....	....	....	....	....	....	23	5	4	9	32	....	....	....
1986-87	Drummondville Voltigeurs	QMJHL	65	18	47	65	....	....	....	150	....	....	....	....	....	....	....	....	....	....	8	1	3	4	30	....	....	....
1987-88	Drummondville Voltigeurs	QMJHL	68	23	54	77	....	....	....	233	....	....	....	....	....	....	....	....	....	....	17	3	14	17	46	....	....	....
	Drummondville	Mem-Cup	3	0	1	1	....	....	....	2	....	....	....	....	....	....	....	....	....	....	....	....	....	....	....	....	....	....
1988-89	**Chicago Blackhawks**	**NHL**	**7**	**1**	**1**	**2**	**1**	**1**	**2**	**6**	**1**	**0**	**0**	**7**	**14.3**	**4**	**2**	**0**	**0**	**2**	....	....	....	....	....	....	....	....
	Saginaw Hawks	IHL	71	16	32	48	....	....	....	69	....	....	....	....	....	....	....	....	....	....	6	0	0	0	8	....	....	....
1989-90	Indianapolis Ice	IHL	66	9	25	34	....	....	....	50	....	....	....	....	....	....	....	....	....	....	....	....	....	....	....	....	....	....
	Quebec Nordiques	**NHL**	**9**	**2**	**3**	**5**	**2**	**2**	**4**	**6**	**1**	**0**	**0**	**19**	**10.5**	**11**	**3**	**10**	**1**	**–1**	....	....	....	....	....	....	....	....
	Halifax Citadels	AHL	5	1	2	3	....	....	....	0	....	....	....	....	....	....	....	....	....	....	6	1	3	4	2	....	....	....
1990-91	**Quebec Nordiques**	**NHL**	**12**	**0**	**0**	**0**	**0**	**0**	**0**	**4**	**0**	**0**	**0**	**12**	**0.0**	**8**	**2**	**9**	**0**	**–3**	....	....	....	....	....	....	....	....
	Halifax Citadels	AHL	59	14	23	37	....	....	....	58	....	....	....	....	....	....	....	....	....	....	....	....	....	....	....	....	....	....
1991-92	Halifax Citadels	AHL	9	0	0	0	....	....	....	22	....	....	....	....	....	....	....	....	....	....	....	....	....	....	....	....	....	....
	New Haven Nighthawks	AHL	64	11	29	40	....	....	....	44	....	....	....	....	....	....	....	....	....	....	5	1	1	2	2	....	....	....
1992-93	Halifax Citadels	AHL	79	5	31	36	....	....	....	73	....	....	....	....	....	....	....	....	....	....	....	....	....	....	....	....	....	....
1993-94	Fredericton Canadiens	AHL	56	12	21	33	....	....	....	44	....	....	....	....	....	....	....	....	....	....	....	....	....	....	....	....	....	....
	Kansas City Blades	IHL	5	0	3	3	....	....	....	0	....	....	....	....	....	....	....	....	....	....	....	....	....	....	....	....	....	....
1994-95	HC Bolzano	Italy	34	5	23	28	....	....	....	65	....	....	....	....	....	....	....	....	....	....	11	8	7	15	26	....	....	....
	HC Bolzano	EuroHL	19	1	6	7	....	....	....	22	....	....	....	....	....	....	....	....	....	....	....	....	....	....	....	....	....	....
1995-96	San Francisco Spiders	IHL	74	13	23	36	....	....	....	61	....	....	....	....	....	....	....	....	....	....	4	1	3	4	0	....	....	....
1996-97	SC Langnau	Switz-2	42	20	28	48	....	....	....	88	....	....	....	....	....	....	....	....	....	....	8	4	1	5	12	....	....	....
1997-98	SC Langnau	Switz-2	27	11	20	31	....	....	....	79	....	....	....	....	....	....	....	....	....	....	....	....	....	....	....	....	....	....
1998-99	SC Langnau	Switz.	44	14	26	40	....	....	....	74	....	....	....	....	....	....	....	....	....	....	....	....	....	....	....	....	....	....
99-2000	Kolner Haie	Germany	45	9	18	27	....	....	....	30	....	....	....	....	....	....	....	....	....	....	10	0	6	6	8	....	....	....
	NHL Totals		**28**	**3**	**4**	**7**	**3**	**3**	**6**	**16**	**2**	**0**	**0**	**38**	**7.9**	**23**	**7**	**19**	**1**		....	....	....	....	....	....	....	....

Traded to **Quebec** by **Chicago** with Everett Sanipass and Dan Vincelette for Greg Millen, Michel Goulet and Quebec's 6th round choice (Kevin St. Jacques) in 1991 Entry Draft, March 5, 1990.
• Played w/ RHI's Montreal Roadrunners in 1995 (22-9-26-35-46).

• DRAKE, Dallas

Dallas James RW – L. 6'1", 185 lbs. b: Trail, B.C., 2/4/1969. Detroit's 6th, 116th overall, in 1989.

Season	Club	League	GP	G	A	Pts	AG	AA	APts	PIM	PP	SH	GW	S	%	TGF	PGF	TGA	PGA	+/–	GP	G	A	Pts	PIM	PP	SH	GW
1984-85	Rossland Jr. Warriors	KIJHL	30	13	37	50	....	....	....	....	....	....	....	....	....	....	....	....	....	....	....	....	....	....	....	....	....	....
1985-86	Rossland Jr. Warriors	KIJHL	41	53	73	126	....	....	....	....	....	....	....	....	....	....	....	....	....	....	....	....	....	....	....	....	....	....
1986-87	Rossland Jr. Warriors	KIJHL	40	55	80	135	....	....	....	....	....	....	....	....	....	....	....	....	....	....	....	....	....	....	....	....	....	....
1987-88	Vernon Lakers	BCJHL	47	39	85	124	....	....	....	50	....	....	....	....	....	....	....	....	....	....	11	9	17	26	30	....	....	....
1988-89	Northern Michigan University	WCHA	38	17	22	39	....	....	....	22	....	....	....	....	....	....	....	....	....	....	7	1	2	3	4	....	....	....
1989-90	Northern Michigan University	WCHA	36	13	24	37	....	....	....	42	....	....	....	....	....	....	....	....	....	....	....	....	....	....	....	....	....	....
1990-91	Northern Michigan University	WCHA	44	22	36	58	....	....	....	89	....	....	....	....	....	....	....	....	....	....	....	....	....	....	....	....	....	....
1991-92	Northern Michigan University	WCHA	38	*39	41	*80	....	....	....	46	....	....	....	....	....	....	....	....	....	....	....	....	....	....	....	....	....	....
1992-93	**Detroit Red Wings**	**NHL**	**72**	**18**	**26**	**44**	**15**	**18**	**33**	**93**	**3**	**2**	**5**	**89**	**20.2**	**62**	**11**	**54**	**18**	**15**	**7**	**3**	**3**	**6**	**6**	**1**	**0**	**0**
1993-94	**Detroit Red Wings**	**NHL**	**47**	**10**	**22**	**32**	**9**	**17**	**26**	**37**	**0**	**1**	**2**	**78**	**12.8**	**48**	**10**	**47**	**14**	**5**	....	....	....	....	....	....	....	....
	Adirondack Red Wings	AHL	1	2	0	2	....	....	....	0	....	....	....	....	....	....	....	....	....	....	....	....	....	....	....	....	....	....
	Winnipeg Jets	**NHL**	**15**	**3**	**5**	**8**	**3**	**4**	**7**	**12**	**1**	**1**	**1**	**34**	**8.8**	**9**	**2**	**17**	**4**	**–6**	....	....	....	....	....	....	....	....
1994-95	**Winnipeg Jets**	**NHL**	**43**	**8**	**18**	**26**	**14**	**27**	**41**	**30**	**0**	**0**	**1**	**66**	**12.1**	**38**	**7**	**48**	**11**	**–6**	....	....	....	....	....	....	....	....
1995-96	**Winnipeg Jets**	**NHL**	**69**	**19**	**20**	**39**	**19**	**16**	**35**	**36**	**4**	**4**	**2**	**121**	**15.7**	**63**	**16**	**79**	**25**	**–7**	**3**	**0**	**0**	**0**	**0**	**0**	**0**	**0**
1996-97	**Phoenix Coyotes**	**NHL**	**63**	**17**	**19**	**36**	**18**	**17**	**35**	**52**	**5**	**1**	**1**	**113**	**15.0**	**50**	**13**	**53**	**5**	**–11**	**7**	**0**	**1**	**1**	**2**	**0**	**0**	**0**
1997-98	**Phoenix Coyotes**	**NHL**	**60**	**11**	**29**	**40**	**13**	**28**	**41**	**71**	**3**	**0**	**2**	**112**	**9.8**	**59**	**13**	**36**	**7**	**17**	**4**	**0**	**1**	**1**	**2**	**0**	**0**	**0**
1998-99	**Phoenix Coyotes**	**NHL**	**53**	**9**	**22**	**31**	**11**	**21**	**32**	**65**	**0**	**0**	**3**	**105**	**8.6**	**46**	**5**	**25**	**1**	**17**	**7**	**4**	**3**	**7**	**4**	**2**	**0**	**1**
99-2000	**Phoenix Coyotes**	**NHL**	**79**	**15**	**30**	**45**	**17**	**28**	**45**	**62**	**0**	**2**	**5**	**127**	**11.8**	**61**	**3**	**64**	**17**	**11**	**5**	**0**	**1**	**1**	**4**	**0**	**0**	**0**
	NHL Totals		**501**	**110**	**191**	**301**	**119**	**176**	**295**	**458**	**16**	**11**	**22**	**845**	**13.0**	**436**	**80**	**423**	**102**		**33**	**7**	**9**	**16**	**18**	**3**	**0**	**1**

WCHA First All-Star Team (1992) • NCAA West First All-American Team (1992)

Traded to **Winnipeg** by **Detroit** with Tim Cheveldae for Bob Essensa and Sergei Bautin, March 8, 1994. Transferred to **Phoenix** after **Winnipeg** franchise relocated, July 1, 1996. Selected by **Minnesota** from **Phoenix** in Expansion Draft, June 23, 2000. Signed as a free agent by **St. Louis**, July 1, 2000.

• DRAPER, Kris

C – L. 5'11", 185 lbs. b: Toronto, Ont., 5/24/1971. Winnipeg's 4th, 62nd overall, in 1989.

Season	Club	League	GP	G	A	Pts	AG	AA	APts	PIM	PP	SH	GW	S	%	TGF	PGF	TGA	PGA	+/–	GP	G	A	Pts	PIM	PP	SH	GW
1987-88	Don Mills Flyers	MTHL	40	35	32	67	....	....	....	46	....	....	....	....	....	....	....	....	....	....	....	....	....	....	....	....	....	....
1988-89	Canada	Nat-Team	60	11	15	26	....	....	....	16	....	....	....	....	....	....	....	....	....	....	....	....	....	....	....	....	....	....
1989-90	Canada	Nat-Team	61	12	22	34	....	....	....	44	....	....	....	....	....	....	....	....	....	....	....	....	....	....	....	....	....	....
	Canada	WJC-A	7	0	2	2	....	....	....	4	....	....	....	....	....	....	....	....	....	....	....	....	....	....	....	....	....	....
1990-91	Ottawa 67's	OHL	39	19	42	61	....	....	....	35	....	....	....	....	....	....	....	....	....	....	17	8	11	19	20	....	....	....
	Canada	WJC-A	7	1	3	4	....	....	....	0	....	....	....	....	....	....	....	....	....	....	....	....	....	....	....	....	....	....
	Winnipeg Jets	**NHL**	**3**	**1**	**0**	**1**	**1**	**0**	**1**	**5**	**0**	**0**	**0**	**1**	**100.0**	**1**	**0**	**1**	**0**	**0**	....	....	....	....	....	....	....	....
	Moncton Hawks	AHL	7	2	1	3	....	....	....	2	....	....	....	....	....	....	....	....	....	....	....	....	....	....	....	....	....	....
1991-92	**Winnipeg Jets**	**NHL**	**10**	**2**	**0**	**2**	**2**	**0**	**2**	**2**	**0**	**0**	**0**	**19**	**10.5**	**4**	**0**	**6**	**2**	**0**	**2**	**0**	**0**	**0**	**0**	**0**	**0**	**0**
	Moncton Hawks	AHL	61	11	18	29	....	....	....	113	....	....	....	....	....	....	....	....	....	....	4	0	1	1	6	....	....	....
1992-93	**Winnipeg Jets**	**NHL**	**7**	**0**	**0**	**0**	**0**	**0**	**0**	**2**	**0**	**0**	**0**	**5**	**0.0**	**0**	**0**	**8**	**2**	**–6**	....	....	....	....	....	....	....	....
	Moncton Hawks	AHL	67	12	23	35	....	....	....	40	....	....	....	....	....	....	....	....	....	....	5	2	2	4	18	....	....	....
1993-94	**Detroit Red Wings**	**NHL**	**39**	**5**	**8**	**13**	**5**	**6**	**11**	**31**	**0**	**1**	**0**	**55**	**9.1**	**21**	**1**	**19**	**10**	**11**	**7**	**2**	**2**	**4**	**4**	**0**	**1**	**0**
	Adirondack Red Wings	AHL	46	20	23	43	....	....	....	49	....	....	....	....	....	....	....	....	....	....	....	....	....	....	....	....	....	....
1994-95	**Detroit Red Wings**	**NHL**	**36**	**2**	**6**	**8**	**4**	**9**	**13**	**22**	**0**	**0**	**0**	**44**	**4.5**	**13**	**0**	**23**	**11**	**1**	**18**	**4**	**1**	**5**	**12**	**0**	**1**	**1**
1995-96	**Detroit Red Wings**	**NHL**	**52**	**7**	**9**	**16**	**7**	**7**	**14**	**32**	**0**	**1**	**0**	**51**	**13.7**	**20**	**0**	**23**	**5**	**2**	**18**	**4**	**2**	**6**	**18**	**0**	**1**	**0**

			REGULAR SEASON																		PLAYOFFS							
Season	Club	League	GP	G	A	Pts	AG	AA	APts	PIM	PP	SH	GW	S	%	TGF	PGF	TGA	PGA	+/-	GP	G	A	Pts	PIM	PP	SH	GW
1996-97♦	**Detroit Red Wings**	**NHL**	**76**	**8**	**5**	**13**	**8**	**4**	**12**	**73**	**1**	**0**	**1**	**85**	**9.4**	**17**	**1**	**38**	**11**	**-11**	**20**	**2**	**4**	**6**	**12**	**0**	**1**	**0**
1997-98♦	**Detroit Red Wings**	**NHL**	**64**	**13**	**10**	**23**	**15**	**10**	**25**	**45**	**1**	**0**	**4**	**96**	**13.5**	**35**	**3**	**43**	**16**	**5**	**19**	**1**	**3**	**4**	**12**	**0**	**0**	**1**
1998-99	**Detroit Red Wings**	**NHL**	**80**	**4**	**14**	**18**	**5**	**13**	**18**	**79**	**0**	**1**	**1**	**78**	**5.1**	**30**	**0**	**40**	**12**	**2**	**10**	**0**	**1**	**1**	**6**	**0**	**0**	**0**
99-2000	**Detroit Red Wings**	**NHL**	**51**	**5**	**7**	**12**	**6**	**6**	**12**	**28**	**0**	**0**	**3**	**76**	**6.6**	**21**	**0**	**24**	**6**	**3**	**9**	**2**	**0**	**2**	**6**	**0**	**0**	**0**
	Canada	WC-A	3	1	0	1	....	....	....	0	....	....	....	....	....	....	....	....	....	....	....	....	....	....	....	....	....	....
	NHL Totals		**418**	**47**	**59**	**106**	**53**	**55**	**108**	**319**	**2**	**3**	**9**	**510**	**9.2**	**162**	**5**	**225**	**75**		**103**	**15**	**13**	**28**	**70**	**0**	**4**	**2**

Traded to **Detroit** by **Winnipeg** for future considerations, June 30, 1993.

• DRISCOLL, Peter

Peter John "Grenade" LW – L. 6', 190 lbs. b: Kingston, Ont., 10/27/1954. Toronto's 4th, 67th overall, in 1974.

Season	Club	League	GP	G	A	Pts	AG	AA	APts	PIM	PP	SH	GW	S	%	TGF	PGF	TGA	PGA	+/-	GP	G	A	Pts	PIM	PP	SH	GW
1972-73	North Bay Trappers	NOJHA	STATISTICS NOT AVAILABLE																									
1973-74	Kingston Canadians	OMJHL	54	13	21	34	....	....	....	216	....	....	....	....	....	....	....	....	....	....	....	....	....	....	....	....	....	....
1974-75	Vancouver Blazers	WHA	21	3	2	5	....	....	....	40	....	....	....	....	....	....	....	....	....	....	....	....	....	....	....	....	....	....
	Tulsa Oilers	CHL	56	9	10	19	....	....	....	183	....	....	....	....	....	....	....	....	....	....	....	....	....	....	....	....	....	....
1975-76	Calgary Cowboys	WHA	75	16	18	34	....	....	....	127	....	....	....	....	....	....	....	....	....	....	10	2	5	7	41	....	....	....
1976-77	Calgary Cowboys	WHA	76	23	29	52	....	....	....	120	....	....	....	....	....	....	....	....	....	....	....	....	....	....	....	....	....	....
1977-78	Quebec Nordiques	WHA	21	3	7	10	....	....	....	28	....	....	....	....	....	....	....	....	....	....	....	....	....	....	....	....	....	....
	Indianapolis Racers	WHA	56	25	21	46	....	....	....	130	....	....	....	....	....	....	....	....	....	....	....	....	....	....	....	....	....	....
1978-79	Indianapolis Racers	WHA	8	3	1	4	....	....	....	17	....	....	....	....	....	....	....	....	....	....	....	....	....	....	....	....	....	....
	Edmonton Oilers	WHA	69	17	23	40	....	....	....	115	....	....	....	....	....	....	....	....	....	....	13	1	6	7	8	....	....	....
1979-80	**Edmonton Oilers**	**NHL**	**39**	**1**	**5**	**6**	**1**	**4**	**5**	**54**	**0**	**0**	**0**	**23**	**4.3**	**10**	**3**	**18**	**0**	**-11**	**3**	**0**	**0**	**0**	**0**	**0**	**0**	**0**
	Houston Apollos	CHL	8	7	4	11	....	....	....	16	....	....	....	....	....	....	....	....	....	....	....	....	....	....	....	....	....	....
1980-81	**Edmonton Oilers**	**NHL**	**21**	**2**	**3**	**5**	**2**	**2**	**4**	**43**	**1**	**0**	**0**	**17**	**11.8**	**11**	**1**	**9**	**0**	**1**	....	....	....	....	....	....	....	....
	Wichita Wind	CHL	34	11	14	25	....	....	....	75	....	....	....	....	....	....	....	....	....	....	....	....	....	....	....	....	....	....
1981-82	Wichita Wind	CHL	75	25	29	54	....	....	....	229	....	....	....	....	....	....	....	....	....	....	....	....	....	....	....	....	....	....
	NHL Totals		**60**	**3**	**8**	**11**	**3**	**6**	**9**	**97**	**1**	**0**	**0**	**40**	**7.5**	**21**	**4**	**27**	**0**		**3**	**0**	**0**	**0**	**0**	**0**	**0**	**0**
	Other Major League Totals		326	90	101	191	....	....	....	577	....	....	....	....	....	....	....	....	....	....	23	3	11	14	49	....	....	....

Selected by **Vancouver** (WHA) in 1974 WHA Amateur Draft, June, 1974. Transferred to **Calgary** (WHA) after **Vancouver** (WHA) franchise relocated, May 7, 1975. Signed as a free agent by **Quebec** (WHA) after **Calgary** (WHA) franchise folded, May 31, 1977. Traded to **Indianapolis** (WHA) by **Quebec** (WHA) for cash, December, 1977. Traded to **Edmonton** (WHA) by **Indianapolis** (WHA) with Wayne Gretzky and Eddie Mio for $700,000 and future considerations, November 2, 1978. Rights retained by **Edmonton** prior to Expansion Draft, June 9, 1979.

• DRIVER, Bruce

D – L. 6', 185 lbs. b: Toronto, Ont., 4/29/1962. Colorado's 6th, 108th overall, in 1981.

Season	Club	League	GP	G	A	Pts	AG	AA	APts	PIM	PP	SH	GW	S	%	TGF	PGF	TGA	PGA	+/-	GP	G	A	Pts	PIM	PP	SH	GW
1978-79	Royal York Royals	OJHL	49	10	32	42	....	....	....	....	....	....	....	....	....	....	....	....	....	....	....	....	....	....	....	....	....	....
1979-80	Royal York Royals	OJHL	43	13	57	70	....	....	....	102	....	....	....	....	....	....	....	....	....	....	....	....	....	....	....	....	....	....
1980-81	University of Wisconsin	WCHA	42	5	15	20	....	....	....	42	....	....	....	....	....	....	....	....	....	....	....	....	....	....	....	....	....	....
1981-82	University of Wisconsin	WCHA	46	7	37	44	....	....	....	84	....	....	....	....	....	....	....	....	....	....	....	....	....	....	....	....	....	....
1982-83	University of Wisconsin	WCHA	49	19	42	61	....	....	....	100	....	....	....	....	....	....	....	....	....	....	....	....	....	....	....	....	....	....
1983-84	Canada	Nat-Team	61	11	17	28	....	....	....	44	....	....	....	....	....	....	....	....	....	....	....	....	....	....	....	....	....	....
	Canada	Olympics	7	3	1	4	....	....	....	10	....	....	....	....	....	....	....	....	....	....	....	....	....	....	....	....	....	....
	New Jersey Devils	**NHL**	**4**	**0**	**2**	**2**	**0**	**1**	**1**	**0**	**0**	**0**	**0**	**5**	**0.0**	**4**	**2**	**4**	**0**	**-2**	....	....	....	....	....	....	....	....
	Maine Mariners	AHL	12	2	6	8	....	....	....	15	....	....	....	....	....	....	....	....	....	....	16	0	10	10	8	....	....	....
1984-85	**New Jersey Devils**	**NHL**	**67**	**9**	**23**	**32**	**7**	**16**	**23**	**36**	**3**	**1**	**0**	**143**	**6.3**	**87**	**34**	**98**	**23**	**-22**	....	....	....	....	....	....	....	....
1985-86	**New Jersey Devils**	**NHL**	**40**	**3**	**15**	**18**	**2**	**10**	**12**	**32**	**1**	**0**	**1**	**64**	**4.7**	**63**	**14**	**58**	**18**	**9**	....	....	....	....	....	....	....	....
	Maine Mariners	AHL	15	4	7	11	....	....	....	16	....	....	....	....	....	....	....	....	....	....	....	....	....	....	....	....	....	....
1986-87	**New Jersey Devils**	**NHL**	**74**	**6**	**28**	**34**	**5**	**20**	**25**	**36**	**0**	**0**	**0**	**132**	**4.5**	**94**	**28**	**122**	**30**	**-26**	....	....	....	....	....	....	....	....
	Canada	WEC-A	8	0	0	0	....	....	....	4	....	....	....	....	....	....	....	....	....	....	....	....	....	....	....	....	....	....
1987-88	**New Jersey Devils**	**NHL**	**74**	**15**	**40**	**55**	**13**	**29**	**42**	**68**	**7**	**0**	**0**	**190**	**7.9**	**131**	**57**	**112**	**45**	**7**	**20**	**3**	**7**	**10**	**14**	**3**	**0**	**0**
1988-89	**New Jersey Devils**	**NHL**	**27**	**1**	**15**	**16**	**1**	**11**	**12**	**24**	**1**	**0**	**0**	**69**	**1.4**	**39**	**18**	**33**	**12**	**0**	....	....	....	....	....	....	....	....
1989-90	**New Jersey Devils**	**NHL**	**75**	**7**	**46**	**53**	**6**	**33**	**39**	**63**	**1**	**0**	**0**	**185**	**3.8**	**131**	**39**	**119**	**33**	**6**	**6**	**1**	**5**	**6**	**6**	**0**	**0**	**0**
1990-91	**New Jersey Devils**	**NHL**	**73**	**9**	**36**	**45**	**8**	**27**	**35**	**62**	**7**	**0**	**2**	**195**	**4.6**	**113**	**40**	**96**	**34**	**11**	**7**	**1**	**2**	**3**	**12**	**1**	**0**	**0**
1991-92	**New Jersey Devils**	**NHL**	**78**	**7**	**35**	**42**	**6**	**26**	**32**	**66**	**3**	**1**	**1**	**205**	**3.4**	**106**	**36**	**101**	**36**	**5**	**7**	**0**	**4**	**4**	**2**	**0**	**0**	**0**
1992-93	**New Jersey Devils**	**NHL**	**83**	**14**	**40**	**54**	**12**	**28**	**40**	**66**	**6**	**0**	**0**	**177**	**7.9**	**115**	**47**	**94**	**16**	**-10**	**5**	**1**	**3**	**4**	**4**	**0**	**1**	**0**
1993-94	**New Jersey Devils**	**NHL**	**66**	**8**	**24**	**32**	**7**	**19**	**26**	**63**	**3**	**1**	**0**	**109**	**7.3**	**86**	**24**	**51**	**18**	**29**	**20**	**3**	**5**	**8**	**12**	**2**	**0**	**0**
1994-95♦	**New Jersey Devils**	**NHL**	**41**	**4**	**12**	**16**	**7**	**18**	**25**	**18**	**1**	**0**	**1**	**62**	**6.5**	**35**	**13**	**31**	**8**	**-1**	**17**	**1**	**6**	**7**	**8**	**1**	**0**	**0**
1995-96	**New York Rangers**	**NHL**	**66**	**3**	**34**	**37**	**3**	**28**	**31**	**42**	**3**	**0**	**0**	**140**	**2.1**	**89**	**45**	**53**	**11**	**2**	**11**	**0**	**7**	**7**	**4**	**0**	**0**	**0**
1996-97	**New York Rangers**	**NHL**	**79**	**5**	**25**	**30**	**5**	**22**	**27**	**48**	**2**	**0**	**2**	**154**	**3.2**	**85**	**31**	**63**	**17**	**8**	**15**	**0**	**1**	**1**	**2**	**0**	**0**	**0**
1997-98	**New York Rangers**	**NHL**	**75**	**5**	**15**	**20**	**6**	**15**	**21**	**46**	**1**	**0**	**0**	**116**	**4.3**	**66**	**21**	**65**	**17**	**-3**	....	....	....	....	....	....	....	....
	NHL Totals		**922**	**96**	**390**	**486**	**88**	**303**	**391**	**670**	**39**	**3**	**7**	**1946**	**4.9**	**1244**	**449**	**1100**	**318**		**108**	**10**	**40**	**50**	**64**	**7**	**1**	**0**

WCHA First All-Star Team (1982) • NCAA West First All-American Team (1982) • NCAA Championship All-Tournament Team (1982) • WCHA Second All-Star Team (1983)

Rights transferred to **New Jersey** after **Colorado** franchise relocated, June 30, 1982. Signed as a free agent by **NY Rangers**, September 28, 1995.

• DROLET, Rene

Rene Georges RW – R. 5'8", 160 lbs. b: Quebec City, Que., 11/13/1944.

Season	Club	League	GP	G	A	Pts	AG	AA	APts	PIM	PP	SH	GW	S	%	TGF	PGF	TGA	PGA	+/-	GP	G	A	Pts	PIM	PP	SH	GW
1960-61	Quebec Citadelle	QJHL	6	3	1	4	....	....	....	0	....	....	....	....	....	....	....	....	....	....	....	....	....	....	....	....	....	....
1961-62	Quebec Citadelle	QJHL	50	49	47	96	....	....	....	....	....	....	....	....	....	....	....	....	....	....	10	6	5	11	2	....	....	....
	Quebec Citadelle	Mem-Cup	9	6	6	12	....	....	....	8	....	....	....	....	....	....	....	....	....	....	....	....	....	....	....	....	....	....
1962-63	Quebec Citadelle	QJHL	45	*52	*54	106	....	....	....	....	....	....	....	....	....	....	....	....	....	....	12	9	12	21	7	....	....	....
	Quebec Aces	AHL	1	0	0	0	....	....	....	0	....	....	....	....	....	....	....	....	....	....	....	....	....	....	....	....	....	....
1963-64	Montreal Jr. Canadiens	OHA-Jr.	34	13	19	32	....	....	....	9	....	....	....	....	....	....	....	....	....	....	5	2	6	8	4	....	....	....
1964-65	Montreal Jr. Canadiens	OHA-Jr.	56	35	39	74	....	....	....	16	....	....	....	....	....	....	....	....	....	....	7	1	4	5	6	....	....	....
	Quebec Aces	AHL	3	0	1	1	....	....	....	6	....	....	....	....	....	....	....	....	....	....	....	....	....	....	....	....	....	....
1965-66	Muskegon Zephyrs	IHL	68	42	53	95	....	....	....	24	....	....	....	....	....	....	....	....	....	....	4	2	1	3	2	....	....	....
	Quebec Aces	AHL	1	0	0	0	....	....	....	0	....	....	....	....	....	....	....	....	....	....	....	....	....	....	....	....	....	....
1966-67	Quebec Aces	AHL	48	6	7	13	....	....	....	0	....	....	....	....	....	....	....	....	....	....	5	0	0	0	2	....	....	....
1967-68	Quebec Aces	AHL	61	18	22	40	....	....	....	6	....	....	....	....	....	....	....	....	....	....	15	6	8	14	2	....	....	....
1968-69	Quebec Aces	AHL	61	30	42	72	....	....	....	14	....	....	....	....	....	....	....	....	....	....	15	4	*10	14	28	....	....	....
1969-70	Quebec Aces	AHL	71	32	48	80	....	....	....	42	....	....	....	....	....	....	....	....	....	....	6	2	1	3	2	....	....	....
1970-71	Quebec Aces	AHL	72	20	37	57	....	....	....	26	....	....	....	....	....	....	....	....	....	....	1	1	1	2	0	....	....	....
1971-72	**Philadelphia Flyers**	**NHL**	**1**	**0**	**0**	**0**	**0**	**0**	**0**	**0**	**0**	**0**	**0**	**3**	**0.0**	**0**	**0**	**0**	**0**	**0**	....	....	....	....	....	....	....	....
	Richmond Robins	AHL	74	31	30	61	....	....	....	18	....	....	....	....	....	....	....	....	....	....	....	....	....	....	....	....	....	....
1972-73	Richmond Robins	AHL	76	34	53	87	....	....	....	30	....	....	....	....	....	....	....	....	....	....	4	2	1	3	0	....	....	....
1973-74	Richmond Robins	AHL	76	26	47	73	....	....	....	18	....	....	....	....	....	....	....	....	....	....	5	5	2	7	2	....	....	....
1974-75	**Detroit Red Wings**	**NHL**	**1**	**0**	**0**	**0**	**0**	**0**	**0**	**0**	**0**	**0**	**0**	**0**	**0.0**	**0**	**0**	**0**	**0**	**0**	....	....	....	....	....	....	....	....
	Virginia Wings	AHL	72	26	52	78	....	....	....	36	....	....	....	....	....	....	....	....	....	....	5	1	3	4	2	....	....	....
1975-76	Rochester Americans	AHL	74	23	40	63	....	....	....	42	....	....	....	....	....	....	....	....	....	....	7	0	1	1	0	....	....	....
1976-77	Rochester Americans	AHL	80	28	37	65	....	....	....	42	....	....	....	....	....	....	....	....	....	....	12	5	4	9	4	....	....	....
1977-78	Rochester Americans	AHL	70	24	27	51	....	....	....	20	....	....	....	....	....	....	....	....	....	....	6	5	1	6	2	....	....	....
	NHL Totals		**2**	**0**	**0**	**0**	**0**	**0**	**0**	**0**	**0**	**0**	**0**	**3**	**0.0**	**0**	**0**	**0**	**0**		....	....	....	....	....	....	....	....

QJHL First All-Star Team • IHL Second All-Star Team (1966)

• 1960-61 statistics for Quebec (QJHL) are playoff totals only. Regular season totals unavailable. NHL rights transferred to **Philadelphia** after NHL club purchased **Quebec** (AHL) franchise, May 8, 1967. Claimed by **Quebec** (AHL) from **Philadelphia** in Reverse Draft, June 12, 1969. • NHL rights retained by Philadelphia. Claimed by **Detroit** (Tidewater-AHL) from **Philadelphia** in Reverse Draft, June 13, 1974.

• DROPPA, Ivan

D – L. 6'2", 209 lbs. b: Liptovsky Mikulas, Czech., 2/1/1972. Chicago's 2nd, 37th overall, in 1990.

Season	Club	League	GP	G	A	Pts	AG	AA	APts	PIM	PP	SH	GW	S	%	TGF	PGF	TGA	PGA	+/-	GP	G	A	Pts	PIM	PP	SH	GW
1989-90	VSZ Kosice	Czech-Jr.	STATISTICS NOT AVAILABLE																									
	Czechoslovakia	EJC-A	6	4	2	6	....	....	....	2	....	....	....	....	....	....	....	....	....	....	....	....	....	....	....	....	....	....
1990-91	VSZ Kosice	Czech.	54	1	7	8	....	....	....	12	....	....	....	....	....	....	....	....	....	....	....	....	....	....	....	....	....	....
	Czechoslovakia	WJC-A	5	0	1	1	....	....	....	4	....	....	....	....	....	....	....	....	....	....	....	....	....	....	....	....	....	....
1991-92	VSZ Kosice	Czech.	43	4	9	13	....	....	....	24	....	....	....	....	....	....	....	....	....	....	....	....	....	....	....	....	....	....
	Czechoslovakia	WJC-A	6	0	3	3	....	....	....	6	....	....	....	....	....	....	....	....	....	....	....	....	....	....	....	....	....	....

			REGULAR SEASON																		PLAYOFFS							
Season	Club	League	GP	G	A	Pts	AG	AA	APts	PIM	PP	SH	GW	S	%	TGF	PGF	TGA	PGA	+/–	GP	G	A	Pts	PIM	PP	SH	GW
1992-93	Indianapolis Ice	IHL	77	14	29	43	....	....	....	92	....	....	....	....	....	....	....	....	....	....	5	0	1	1	2	....	....	....
1993-94	**Chicago Blackhawks**	**NHL**	**12**	**0**	**1**	**1**	**0**	**1**	**1**	**12**	**0**	**0**	**0**	**13**	**0.0**	**8**	**0**	**7**	**1**	**2**	....	....	....	....	....	....	....	....
	Indianapolis Ice	IHL	55	9	10	19	....	....	....	71	....	....	....	....	....	....	....	....	....	....	....	....	....	....	....	....	....	....
1994-95	Indianapolis Ice	IHL	67	5	28	33	....	....	....	91	....	....	....	....	....	....	....	....	....	....	....	....	....	....	....	....	....	....
1995-96	**Chicago Blackhawks**	**NHL**	**7**	**0**	**0**	**0**	**0**	**0**	**0**	**2**	**0**	**0**	**0**	**1**	**0.0**	**3**	**0**	**1**	**0**	**2**	....	....	....	....	....	....	....	....
	Indianapolis Ice	IHL	72	6	30	36	....	....	....	71	....	....	....	....	....	....	....	....	....	....	3	0	1	1	2	....	....	....
1996-97	Slovakia	W-Cup	3	0	1	1	....	....	....	2	....	....	....	....	....	....	....	....	....	....	....	....	....	....	....	....	....	....
	Indianapolis Ice	IHL	26	1	13	14	....	....	....	44	....	....	....	....	....	....	....	....	....	....	....	....	....	....	....	....	....	....
	Carolina Monarchs	AHL	47	4	22	26	....	....	....	48	....	....	....	....	....	....	....	....	....	....	....	....	....	....	....	....	....	....
	Slovakia	WC-A	8	0	2	2	....	....	....	6	....	....	....	....	....	....	....	....	....	....	....	....	....	....	....	....	....	....
1997-98	HC Kosice	Slovakia	23	4	14	18	....	....	....	14	....	....	....	....	....	....	....	....	....	....	11	2	4	6	29	....	....	....
	Slovakia	Olympics	4	0	0	0	....	....	....	0	....	....	....	....	....	....	....	....	....	....	....	....	....	....	....	....	....	....
	Slovakia	WC-A	6	0	0	0	....	....	....	8	....	....	....	....	....	....	....	....	....	....	....	....	....	....	....	....	....	....
1998-99	Nurnberg Ice Tigers	Germany	42	10	14	24	....	....	....	97	....	....	....	....	....	....	....	....	....	....	13	1	7	8	50	....	....	....
	Slovakia	WC-A	4	1	1	2	....	....	....	4	....	....	....	....	....	....	....	....	....	....	....	....	....	....	....	....	....	....
99-2000	Kassel Huskies	Germany	26	2	11	13	....	....	....	24	....	....	....	....	....	....	....	....	....	....	8	1	0	1	16	....	....	....
	Slovakia	WC-A	9	0	1	1	....	....	....	0	....	....	....	....	....	....	....	....	....	....	....	....	....	....	....	....	....	....
	NHL Totals		**19**	**0**	**1**	**1**	**0**	**1**	**1**	**14**	**0**	**0**	**0**	**14**	**0.0**	**11**	**0**	**8**	**1**		....	....	....	....	....	....	....	....

Traded to **Florida** by **Chicago** for Alain Nasreddine and a conditional choice in 1999 Entry Draft, December 18, 1996.

• DROUIN, Jude

C – R. 5'10", 160 lbs. b: Mont Louis, Que., 10/28/1948. Montreal's 3rd, 17th overall, in 1966.

Season	Club	League	GP	G	A	Pts	AG	AA	APts	PIM	PP	SH	GW	S	%	TGF	PGF	TGA	PGA	+/–	GP	G	A	Pts	PIM	PP	SH	GW
1965-66	Verdun Maple Leafs	QJHL	38	33	32	65	....	....	....	103	....	....	....	....	....	....	....	....	....	....	....	....	....	....	....	....	....	....
1966-67	Montreal Jr. Canadiens	OHA-Jr.	47	32	36	68	....	....	....	64	....	....	....	....	....	....	....	....	....	....	3	0	3	3	9	....	....	....
1967-68	Houston Apollos	CPHL	68	22	38	60	....	....	....	59	....	....	....	....	....	....	....	....	....	....	....	....	....	....	....	....	....	....
1968-69	**Montreal Canadiens**	**NHL**	**9**	**0**	**1**	**1**	**0**	**1**	**1**	**0**	**0**	**0**	**0**	**3**	**0.0**	**2**	**0**	**1**	**0**	**1**	....	....	....	....	....	....	....	....
	Houston Apollos	CHL	53	23	31	54	....	....	....	117	....	....	....	....	....	....	....	....	....	....	3	1	1	2	23	....	....	....
1969-70	**Montreal Canadiens**	**NHL**	**3**	**0**	**0**	**0**	**0**	**0**	**0**	**2**	**0**	**0**	**0**	**8**	**0.0**	**0**	**0**	**2**	**0**	**–2**	....	....	....	....	....	....	....	....
	Montreal Voyageurs	AHL	65	37	*69	*106	....	....	....	88	....	....	....	....	....	....	....	....	....	....	8	0	6	6	2	....	....	....
1970-71	**Minnesota North Stars**	**NHL**	**75**	**16**	**52**	**68**	**16**	**44**	**60**	**49**	**4**	**0**	**2**	**208**	**7.7**	**88**	**31**	**53**	**1**	**5**	**12**	**5**	**7**	**12**	**10**	**1**	**0**	**0**
1971-72	**Minnesota North Stars**	**NHL**	**63**	**13**	**43**	**56**	**13**	**37**	**50**	**31**	**3**	**0**	**5**	**213**	**6.1**	**78**	**28**	**46**	**0**	**4**	**7**	**4**	**4**	**8**	**6**	**1**	**0**	**1**
1972-73	**Minnesota North Stars**	**NHL**	**78**	**27**	**46**	**73**	**25**	**37**	**62**	**61**	**3**	**0**	**5**	**279**	**9.7**	**95**	**21**	**63**	**1**	**12**	**6**	**1**	**3**	**4**	**0**	**0**	**0**	**0**
1973-74	**Minnesota North Stars**	**NHL**	**65**	**19**	**24**	**43**	**18**	**20**	**38**	**30**	**4**	**0**	**2**	**200**	**9.5**	**55**	**14**	**53**	**1**	**–11**	....	....	....	....	....	....	....	....
1974-75	**Minnesota North Stars**	**NHL**	**38**	**4**	**18**	**22**	**3**	**13**	**16**	**16**	**1**	**0**	**1**	**72**	**5.6**	**30**	**5**	**46**	**2**	**–19**	....	....	....	....	....	....	....	....
	New York Islanders	**NHL**	**40**	**14**	**18**	**32**	**12**	**13**	**25**	**6**	**2**	**0**	**2**	**93**	**15.1**	**47**	**11**	**28**	**0**	**8**	**17**	**6**	***12**	**18**	**6**	**1**	**0**	**1**
1975-76	**New York Islanders**	**NHL**	**76**	**21**	**41**	**62**	**18**	**31**	**49**	**58**	**10**	**0**	**2**	**153**	**13.7**	**87**	**34**	**35**	**0**	**18**	**13**	**6**	**9**	**15**	**0**	**1**	**0**	**1**
1976-77	**New York Islanders**	**NHL**	**78**	**24**	**29**	**53**	**22**	**22**	**44**	**27**	**4**	**0**	**2**	**135**	**17.8**	**82**	**20**	**44**	**0**	**18**	**12**	**5**	**6**	**11**	**6**	**1**	**0**	**0**
1977-78	**New York Islanders**	**NHL**	**56**	**5**	**17**	**22**	**5**	**13**	**18**	**12**	**0**	**0**	**0**	**78**	**6.4**	**40**	**4**	**22**	**0**	**14**	**5**	**0**	**0**	**0**	**5**	**0**	**0**	**0**
1978-79			DID NOT PLAY																									
1979-80	**Winnipeg Jets**	**NHL**	**78**	**8**	**16**	**24**	**7**	**12**	**19**	**50**	**1**	**2**	**1**	**84**	**9.5**	**38**	**6**	**103**	**33**	**–38**	....	....	....	....	....	....	....	....
1980-81	**Winnipeg Jets**	**NHL**	**7**	**0**	**0**	**0**	**0**	**0**	**0**	**4**	**0**	**0**	**0**	**1**	**0.0**	**0**	**0**	**5**	**3**	**–2**	....	....	....	....	....	....	....	....
	NHL Totals		**666**	**151**	**305**	**456**	**139**	**243**	**382**	**346**	**32**	**2**	**22**	**1527**	**9.9**	**642**	**174**	**501**	**41**		**72**	**27**	**41**	**68**	**33**	**5**	**0**	**3**

AHL First All-Star Team (1970) • Won Dudley "Red" Garrett Memorial Award (Top Rookie - AHL) (1970) • Won John B. Sollenberger Trophy (Top Scorer - AHL) (1970)

Traded to **Minnesota** by **Montreal** for future considerations (Bill Collins, June 10, 1970), May 22, 1970. Traded to **NY Islanders** by **Minnesota** for Craig Cameron, January 7, 1975. • Sat out entire 1978-79 season to become a free agent. Signed as a free agent by **Winnipeg**, October 5, 1979.

• DROUIN, P.C.

Pierre Claude LW – L. 6'2", 208 lbs. b: St. Lambert, Que., 4/22/1974.

Season	Club	League	GP	G	A	Pts	AG	AA	APts	PIM	PP	SH	GW	S	%	TGF	PGF	TGA	PGA	+/–	GP	G	A	Pts	PIM	PP	SH	GW
1991-92	Gloucester Rangers	OJHL	49	23	51	74	....	....	....	59	....	....	....	....	....	....	....	....	....	....	....	....	....	....	....	....	....	....
1992-93	Cornell University	ECAC	23	3	6	9	....	....	....	30	....	....	....	....	....	....	....	....	....	....	....	....	....	....	....	....	....	....
1993-94	Cornell University	ECAC	21	6	13	19	....	....	....	32	....	....	....	....	....	....	....	....	....	....	....	....	....	....	....	....	....	....
1994-95	Cornell University	ECAC	26	4	16	20	....	....	....	48	....	....	....	....	....	....	....	....	....	....	....	....	....	....	....	....	....	....
1995-96	Cornell University	ECAC	31	18	14	32	....	....	....	60	....	....	....	....	....	....	....	....	....	....	....	....	....	....	....	....	....	....
1996-97	**Boston Bruins**	**NHL**	**3**	**0**	**0**	**0**	**0**	**0**	**0**	**0**	**0**	**0**	**0**	**1**	**0.0**	**1**	**0**	**0**	**0**	**1**	....	....	....	....	....	....	....	....
	Providence Bruins	AHL	42	12	11	23	....	....	....	10	....	....	....	....	....	....	....	....	....	....	....	....	....	....	....	....	....	....
1997-98	Providence Bruins	AHL	7	0	2	2	....	....	....	4	....	....	....	....	....	....	....	....	....	....	....	....	....	....	....	....	....	....
	Charlotte Checkers	ECHL	62	21	46	67	....	....	....	57	....	....	....	....	....	....	....	....	....	....	7	2	4	6	4	....	....	....
1998-99	Bracknell Bees	BH-Cup	10	6	3	9	....	....	....	14	....	....	....	....	....	....	....	....	....	....	....	....	....	....	....	....	....	....
	Bracknell Bees	Britain	42	12	21	33	....	....	....	12	....	....	....	....	....	....	....	....	....	....	7	4	1	5	0	....	....	....
99-2000	Bracknell Bees	BH-Cup	10	2	6	8	....	....	....	12	....	....	....	....	....	....	....	....	....	....	....	....	....	....	....	....	....	....
	Bracknell Bees	Britain	35	10	28	38	....	....	....	42	....	....	....	....	....	....	....	....	....	....	6	2	3	5	4	....	....	....
	NHL Totals		**3**	**0**	**0**	**0**	**0**	**0**	**0**	**0**	**0**	**0**	**0**	**1**	**0.0**	**1**	**0**	**0**	**0**		....	....	....	....	....	....	....	....

Signed as a free agent by **Boston**, October 14, 1996.

• DRUCE, John

John W. RW – R. 6'2", 195 lbs. b: Peterborough, Ont., 2/23/1966. Washington's 2nd, 40th overall, in 1985.

Season	Club	League	GP	G	A	Pts	AG	AA	APts	PIM	PP	SH	GW	S	%	TGF	PGF	TGA	PGA	+/–	GP	G	A	Pts	PIM	PP	SH	GW
1983-84	Peterborough Lumber	OJHL-B	40	15	18	33	....	....	....	69	....	....	....	....	....	....	....	....	....	....	....	....	....	....	....	....	....	....
	Peterborough Petes	OHL	1	0	0	0	....	....	....	0	....	....	....	....	....	....	....	....	....	....	....	....	....	....	....	....	....	....
1984-85	Peterborough Petes	OHL	54	12	14	26	....	....	....	90	....	....	....	....	....	....	....	....	....	....	17	6	2	8	21	....	....	....
1985-86	Peterborough Petes	OHL	49	22	24	46	....	....	....	84	....	....	....	....	....	....	....	....	....	....	16	0	5	5	34	....	....	....
1986-87	Binghamton Whalers	AHL	77	13	9	22	....	....	....	131	....	....	....	....	....	....	....	....	....	....	12	0	3	3	28	....	....	....
1987-88	Binghamton Whalers	AHL	68	32	29	61	....	....	....	82	....	....	....	....	....	....	....	....	....	....	1	0	0	0	0	....	....	....
1988-89	**Washington Capitals**	**NHL**	**48**	**8**	**7**	**15**	**7**	**5**	**12**	**62**	**0**	**0**	**1**	**59**	**13.6**	**22**	**0**	**15**	**0**	**7**	**1**	**0**	**0**	**0**	**0**	**0**	**0**	**0**
	Baltimore Skipjacks	AHL	16	2	11	13	....	....	....	10	....	....	....	....	....	....	....	....	....	....	....	....	....	....	....	....	....	....
1989-90	Washington Capitals	Fr-Tour	2	0	0	0	....	....	....	2	....	....	....	....	....	....	....	....	....	....	....	....	....	....	....	....	....	....
	Washington Capitals	**NHL**	**45**	**8**	**3**	**11**	**7**	**2**	**9**	**52**	**1**	**0**	**1**	**66**	**12.1**	**15**	**1**	**23**	**6**	**–3**	**15**	**14**	**3**	**17**	**23**	**8**	**1**	**4**
	Baltimore Skipjacks	AHL	26	15	16	31	....	....	....	38	....	....	....	....	....	....	....	....	....	....	....	....	....	....	....	....	....	....
1990-91	**Washington Capitals**	**NHL**	**80**	**22**	**36**	**58**	**20**	**27**	**47**	**46**	**7**	**1**	**4**	**209**	**10.5**	**94**	**38**	**64**	**12**	**4**	**11**	**1**	**1**	**2**	**7**	**1**	**0**	**0**
1991-92	**Washington Capitals**	**NHL**	**67**	**19**	**18**	**37**	**17**	**14**	**31**	**39**	**1**	**0**	**3**	**129**	**14.7**	**50**	**4**	**35**	**3**	**14**	**7**	**1**	**0**	**1**	**2**	**0**	**0**	**1**
1992-93	**Winnipeg Jets**	**NHL**	**50**	**6**	**14**	**20**	**5**	**10**	**15**	**37**	**0**	**0**	**0**	**60**	**10.0**	**31**	**2**	**41**	**8**	**–4**	**2**	**0**	**0**	**0**	**0**	**0**	**0**	**0**
1993-94	**Los Angeles Kings**	**NHL**	**55**	**14**	**17**	**31**	**13**	**13**	**26**	**50**	**1**	**1**	**0**	**104**	**13.5**	**50**	**5**	**30**	**1**	**16**	....	....	....	....	....	....	....	....
	Phoenix Roadrunners	IHL	8	5	6	11	....	....	....	9	....	....	....	....	....	....	....	....	....	....	....	....	....	....	....	....	....	....
1994-95	**Los Angeles Kings**	**NHL**	**43**	**15**	**5**	**20**	**27**	**7**	**34**	**20**	**3**	**0**	**1**	**75**	**20.0**	**30**	**6**	**31**	**4**	**–3**	....	....	....	....	....	....	....	....
1995-96	**Los Angeles Kings**	**NHL**	**64**	**9**	**12**	**21**	**9**	**10**	**19**	**14**	**0**	**0**	**0**	**103**	**8.7**	**23**	**3**	**68**	**22**	**–26**	....	....	....	....	....	....	....	....
	Philadelphia Flyers	**NHL**	**13**	**4**	**4**	**8**	**4**	**3**	**7**	**13**	**0**	**0**	**0**	**25**	**16.0**	**10**	**1**	**3**	**0**	**6**	**2**	**0**	**2**	**2**	**2**	**0**	**0**	**0**
1996-97	**Philadelphia Flyers**	**NHL**	**43**	**7**	**8**	**15**	**7**	**7**	**14**	**12**	**1**	**0**	**0**	**73**	**9.6**	**16**	**1**	**25**	**5**	**–5**	**13**	**1**	**0**	**1**	**2**	**0**	**1**	**0**
1997-98	**Philadelphia Flyers**	**NHL**	**23**	**1**	**2**	**3**	**1**	**2**	**3**	**2**	**0**	**0**	**0**	**18**	**5.6**	**4**	**0**	**5**	**1**	**0**	**2**	**0**	**0**	**0**	**2**	**0**	**0**	**0**
	Philadelphia Phantoms	AHL	39	21	28	49	....	....	....	45	....	....	....	....	....	....	....	....	....	....	....	....	....	....	....	....	....	....
1998-99	Hannover Scorpions	Germnay	36	15	7	22	....	....	....	34	....	....	....	....	....	....	....	....	....	....	....	....	....	....	....	....	....	....
99-2000	Augsburger Panther	Germany	12	2	0	2	....	....	....	47	....	....	....	....	....	....	....	....	....	....	3	0	0	0	4	....	....	....
	NHL Totals		**531**	**113**	**126**	**239**	**117**	**100**	**217**	**347**	**14**	**2**	**10**	**921**	**12.3**	**345**	**61**	**340**	**62**		**53**	**17**	**6**	**23**	**38**	**9**	**2**	**5**

Traded to **Winnipeg** by **Washington** with Toronto's 4th round choice (previously acquired by Washington — later traded to Detroit — Detroit selected John Jakopin) in 1993 Entry Draft for Pat Elynuik, October 1, 1992. Signed as a free agent by **LA Kings**, August 2, 1993. Traded to **Philadelphia** by **LA Kings** with LA Kings' 7th round choice (Todd Fedoruk) in 1997 Entry Draft for LA Kings' 4th round choice (previously acquired, LA Kings selected Mikael Simons) in 1996 Entry Draft, March 19, 1996.

• DRUKEN, Harold

C – L. 6', 205 lbs. b: St. John's, Nfld., 1/26/1979. Vancouver's 3rd, 36th overall, in 1997.

Season	Club	League	GP	G	A	Pts	AG	AA	APts	PIM	PP	SH	GW	S	%	TGF	PGF	TGA	PGA	+/–	PO GP	PO G	PO A	PO Pts	PO PIM	PO PP	PO SH	PO GW
1995-96	Noble Knights	Hi-School	30	37	28	65	....	....	....	28	....	....	....	....	....	....	....	....	....	....	....	....	....	....	....	....	....	....
1996-97	Detroit Whalers	OHL	63	27	31	58	....	....	....	14	....	....	....	....	....	....	....	....	....	....	5	3	2	5	0	....	....	....
1997-98	Plymouth Whalers	OHL	64	38	44	82	....	....	....	12	....	....	....	....	....	....	....	....	....	....	15	9	11	20	4	....	....	....
1998-99	Plymouth Whalers	OHL	60	*58	45	103	....	....	....	34	....	....	....	....	....	....	....	....	....	....	11	9	12	21	14	....	....	....
	Canada	WJC-A	7	1	1	2	....	....	....	2	....	....	....	....	....	....	....	....	....	....	....	....	....	....	....	....	....	....
99-2000	**Vancouver Canucks**	**NHL**	**33**	**7**	**9**	**16**	**8**	**8**	**16**	**10**	**2**	**0**	**0**	**69**	**10.1**	**25**	**3**	**8**	**0**	**14**	....	....	....	....	....	....	....	....
	Syracuse Crunch	AHL	47	20	25	45	....	....	....	32	....	....	....	....	....	....	....	....	....	....	4	1	2	3	6	....	....	....
	NHL Totals		**33**	**7**	**9**	**16**	**8**	**8**	**16**	**10**	**2**	**0**	**0**	**69**	**10.1**	**25**	**3**	**8**	**0**		....	....	....	....	....	....	....	....

OHL Second All-Star Team (1999)

• DRULIA, Stan

Stanley W. RW – R. 5'11", 190 lbs. b: Elmira, NY, 1/5/1968. Pittsburgh's 11th, 214th overall, in 1986.

Season	Club	League	GP	G	A	Pts	AG	AA	APts	PIM	PP	SH	GW	S	%	TGF	PGF	TGA	PGA	+/–	PO GP	PO G	PO A	PO Pts	PO PIM	PO PP	PO SH	PO GW
1983-84	Fort Erie Meteors	OJHL-B	39	29	36	65	....	....	....	104	....	....	....	....	....	....	....	....	....	....	....	....	....	....	....	....	....	....
1984-85	Belleville Bulls	OHL	63	24	31	55	....	....	....	33	....	....	....	....	....	....	....	....	....	....	....	....	....	....	....	....	....	....
1985-86	Belleville Bulls	OHL	66	43	36	79	....	....	....	73	....	....	....	....	....	....	....	....	....	....	24	4	11	15	15	....	....	....
1986-87	Hamilton Steelhawks	OHL	55	27	51	78	....	....	....	26	....	....	....	....	....	....	....	....	....	....	9	4	4	8	2	....	....	....
1987-88	Hamilton Steelhawks	OHL	65	52	69	121	....	....	....	44	....	....	....	....	....	....	....	....	....	....	14	8	16	24	12	....	....	....
1988-89	Niagara Falls Thunder	OHL	47	52	93	145	....	....	....	59	....	....	....	....	....	....	....	....	....	....	17	11	*26	37	18	....	....	....
	Maine Mariners	AHL	3	1	1	2	....	....	....	0	....	....	....	....	....	....	....	....	....	....	....	....	....	....	....	....	....	....
1989-90	Phoenix Roadrunners	IHL	16	6	3	9	....	....	....	2	....	....	....	....	....	....	....	....	....	....	....	....	....	....	....	....	....	....
	Cape Breton Oilers	AHL	31	5	7	12	....	....	....	2	....	....	....	....	....	....	....	....	....	....	....	....	....	....	....	....	....	....
1990-91	Knoxville Cherokees	ECHL	64	*63	77	*140	....	....	....	39	....	....	....	....	....	....	....	....	....	....	3	3	2	5	4	....	....	....
1991-92	New Haven Nighthawks	AHL	77	49	53	102	....	....	....	46	....	....	....	....	....	....	....	....	....	....	5	2	4	6	4	....	....	....
1992-93	**Tampa Bay Lightning**	**NHL**	**24**	**2**	**1**	**3**	**2**	**1**	**3**	**10**	**0**	**0**	**1**	**22**	**9.1**	**10**	**1**	**10**	**2**	**1**	....	....	....	....	....	....	....	....
	Atlanta Knights	IHL	47	28	26	54	....	....	....	38	....	....	....	....	....	....	....	....	....	....	3	2	3	5	4	....	....	....
1993-94	Atlanta Knights	IHL	79	54	60	114	....	....	....	70	....	....	....	....	....	....	....	....	....	....	14	13	12	25	8	....	....	....
1994-95	Atlanta Knights	IHL	66	41	49	90	....	....	....	60	....	....	....	....	....	....	....	....	....	....	5	1	5	6	2	....	....	....
1995-96	Atlanta Knights	IHL	75	38	56	94	....	....	....	80	....	....	....	....	....	....	....	....	....	....	3	0	2	2	18	....	....	....
1996-97	Detroit Vipers	IHL	73	33	38	71	....	....	....	42	....	....	....	....	....	....	....	....	....	....	21	5	*21	26	14	....	....	....
1997-98	Detroit Vipers	IHL	58	25	35	60	....	....	....	50	....	....	....	....	....	....	....	....	....	....	15	2	4	6	16	....	....	....
1998-99	Detroit Vipers	IHL	82	23	52	75	....	....	....	64	....	....	....	....	....	....	....	....	....	....	11	5	4	9	10	....	....	....
99-2000	**Tampa Bay Lightning**	**NHL**	**68**	**11**	**22**	**33**	**12**	**20**	**32**	**24**	**1**	**2**	**1**	**94**	**11.7**	**47**	**10**	**78**	**23**	**–18**	....	....	....	....	....	....	....	....
	NHL Totals		**92**	**13**	**23**	**36**	**14**	**21**	**35**	**34**	**1**	**2**	**2**	**116**	**11.2**	**57**	**11**	**88**	**25**		....	....	....	....	....	....	....	....

OHL First All-Star Team (1989) • ECHL First All-Star Team (1991) • MVP - ECHL (1991) • AHL Second All-Star Team (1992) • IHL First All-Star Team (1994, 1995) • Won "Bud" Poile Trophy (Playoff MVP - IHL) (1994)

Signed as a free agent by **Edmonton**, February 24, 1989. Signed as a free agent by **Tampa Bay**, September 1, 1992. Signed as a free agent by **Tampa Bay**, September 29, 1999.

• DRURY, Chris

C – R. 5'10", 188 lbs. b: Trumbull, CT, 8/20/1976. Quebec's 5th, 72nd overall, in 1994.

Season	Club	League	GP	G	A	Pts	AG	AA	APts	PIM	PP	SH	GW	S	%	TGF	PGF	TGA	PGA	+/–	PO GP	PO G	PO A	PO Pts	PO PIM	PO PP	PO SH	PO GW
1991-92	Fairfield Prep Jesuits	Hi-School	25	22	27	49	....	....	....	....	....	....	....	....	....	....	....	....	....	....	....	....	....	....	....	....	....	....
1992-93	Fairfield Prep Jesuits	Hi-School	24	25	32	57	....	....	....	15	....	....	....	....	....	....	....	....	....	....	....	....	....	....	....	....	....	....
1993-94	Fairfield Prep Jesuits	Hi-School	24	37	18	55	....	....	....	....	....	....	....	....	....	....	....	....	....	....	....	....	....	....	....	....	....	....
1994-95	Boston University	H-East	39	12	15	27	....	....	....	38	....	....	....	....	....	....	....	....	....	....	....	....	....	....	....	....	....	....
1995-96	Boston University	H-East	37	35	33	*68	....	....	....	46	....	....	....	....	....	....	....	....	....	....	....	....	....	....	....	....	....	....
	United States	WJC-A	6	2	2	4	....	....	....	2	....	....	....	....	....	....	....	....	....	....	....	....	....	....	....	....	....	....
1996-97	Boston University	H-East	41	*38	24	62	....	....	....	64	....	....	....	....	....	....	....	....	....	....	....	....	....	....	....	....	....	....
	United States	WC-A	8	0	1	1	....	....	....	2	....	....	....	....	....	....	....	....	....	....	....	....	....	....	....	....	....	....
1997-98	Boston University	H-East	38	28	29	57	....	....	....	88	....	....	....	....	....	....	....	....	....	....	....	....	....	....	....	....	....	....
	United States	WC-A	6	1	2	3	....	....	....	12	....	....	....	....	....	....	....	....	....	....	....	....	....	....	....	....	....	....
1998-99	**Colorado Avalanche**	**NHL**	**79**	**20**	**24**	**44**	**23**	**23**	**46**	**62**	**6**	**0**	**3**	**138**	**14.5**	**56**	**18**	**29**	**0**	**9**	**19**	**6**	**2**	**8**	**4**	**0**	**0**	**4**
99-2000	**Colorado Avalanche**	**NHL**	**82**	**20**	**47**	**67**	**22**	**44**	**66**	**42**	**7**	**0**	**2**	**213**	**9.4**	**82**	**32**	**46**	**4**	**8**	**17**	**4**	**10**	**14**	**4**	**1**	**0**	**2**
	NHL Totals		**161**	**40**	**71**	**111**	**45**	**67**	**112**	**104**	**13**	**0**	**5**	**351**	**11.4**	**138**	**50**	**75**	**4**		**36**	**10**	**12**	**22**	**8**	**1**	**0**	**6**

• Brother of Ted • Hockey East Second All-Star Team (1996, 1997) • NCAA East Second All-American Team (1996) • NCAA East First All-American Team (1997, 1998) • NCAA Championship All-Tournament Team (1997) • Hockey East First All-Star Team (1998) • Won Hobey Baker Memorial Award (Top U.S. Collegiate Player) (1998) • NHL All-Rookie Team (1999) • Won Calder Memorial Trophy (1999)

Rights transferred to **Colorado** after **Quebec** franchise relocated, June 21, 1995.

• DRURY, Ted

Theodore Evans C – L. 6', 208 lbs. b: Boston, MA, 9/13/1971. Calgary's 2nd, 42nd overall, in 1989.

Season	Club	League	GP	G	A	Pts	AG	AA	APts	PIM	PP	SH	GW	S	%	TGF	PGF	TGA	PGA	+/–	PO GP	PO G	PO A	PO Pts	PO PIM	PO PP	PO SH	PO GW
1987-88	Fairfield Prep Jesuits	Hi-School	24	21	28	49	....	....	....	....	....	....	....	....	....	....	....	....	....	....	....	....	....	....	....	....	....	....
1988-89	Fairfield Prep Jesuits	Hi-School	25	35	31	66	....	....	....	....	....	....	....	....	....	....	....	....	....	....	....	....	....	....	....	....	....	....
1989-90	Fairfield Prep Jesuits	ECAC	17	9	13	22	....	....	....	10	....	....	....	....	....	....	....	....	....	....	....	....	....	....	....	....	....	....
	United States	WJC-A	7	2	1	3	....	....	....	2	....	....	....	....	....	....	....	....	....	....	....	....	....	....	....	....	....	....
1990-91	Harvard University	ECAC	25	18	18	36	....	....	....	22	....	....	....	....	....	....	....	....	....	....	....	....	....	....	....	....	....	....
	United States	WJC-A	8	5	7	12	....	....	....	2	....	....	....	....	....	....	....	....	....	....	....	....	....	....	....	....	....	....
1991-92	United States	Nat-Team	53	11	23	34	....	....	....	30	....	....	....	....	....	....	....	....	....	....	....	....	....	....	....	....	....	....
	United States	Olympics	7	1	1	2	....	....	....	0	....	....	....	....	....	....	....	....	....	....	....	....	....	....	....	....	....	....
1992-93	Harvard University	ECAC	31	22	*41	*63	....	....	....	28	....	....	....	....	....	....	....	....	....	....	....	....	....	....	....	....	....	....
	United States	WC-A	6	0	0	0	....	....	....	0	....	....	....	....	....	....	....	....	....	....	....	....	....	....	....	....	....	....
1993-94	**Calgary Flames**	**NHL**	**34**	**5**	**7**	**12**	**5**	**5**	**10**	**26**	**0**	**1**	**1**	**43**	**11.6**	**19**	**2**	**28**	**6**	**–5**	....	....	....	....	....	....	....	....
	United States	Nat-Team	11	1	4	5	....	....	....	11	....	....	....	....	....	....	....	....	....	....	....	....	....	....	....	....	....	....
	United States	Olympics	7	1	2	3	....	....	....	2	....	....	....	....	....	....	....	....	....	....	....	....	....	....	....	....	....	....
	Hartford Whalers	**NHL**	**16**	**1**	**5**	**6**	**1**	**4**	**5**	**10**	**0**	**0**	**0**	**37**	**2.7**	**7**	**0**	**20**	**3**	**–10**	....	....	....	....	....	....	....	....
1994-95	**Hartford Whalers**	**NHL**	**34**	**3**	**6**	**9**	**5**	**9**	**14**	**21**	**0**	**0**	**0**	**31**	**9.7**	**13**	**0**	**18**	**2**	**–3**	....	....	....	....	....	....	....	....
	Springfield Falcons	AHL	2	0	1	1	....	....	....	0	....	....	....	....	....	....	....	....	....	....	....	....	....	....	....	....	....	....
1995-96	**Ottawa Senators**	**NHL**	**42**	**9**	**7**	**16**	**9**	**6**	**15**	**54**	**1**	**0**	**1**	**80**	**11.3**	**20**	**5**	**54**	**20**	**–19**	....	....	....	....	....	....	....	....
1996-97	**Mighty Ducks of Anaheim**	**NHL**	**73**	**9**	**9**	**18**	**10**	**8**	**18**	**54**	**1**	**0**	**2**	**114**	**7.9**	**25**	**1**	**39**	**6**	**–9**	**10**	**1**	**0**	**1**	**4**	**0**	**0**	**0**
1997-98	**Mighty Ducks of Anaheim**	**NHL**	**73**	**6**	**10**	**16**	**7**	**10**	**17**	**82**	**0**	**1**	**0**	**110**	**5.5**	**25**	**0**	**56**	**21**	**–10**	....	....	....	....	....	....	....	....
	United States	WC-A	6	0	1	1	....	....	....	4	....	....	....	....	....	....	....	....	....	....	....	....	....	....	....	....	....	....
1998-99	**Mighty Ducks of Anaheim**	**NHL**	**75**	**5**	**6**	**11**	**6**	**6**	**12**	**83**	**0**	**0**	**0**	**79**	**6.3**	**18**	**0**	**24**	**8**	**2**	**4**	**0**	**0**	**0**	**0**	**0**	**0**	**0**
99-2000	**Mighty Ducks of Anaheim**	**NHL**	**11**	**1**	**1**	**2**	**1**	**1**	**2**	**6**	**0**	**0**	**0**	**9**	**11.1**	**2**	**0**	**3**	**0**	**–1**	....	....	....	....	....	....	....	....
	New York Islanders	**NHL**	**55**	**2**	**1**	**3**	**2**	**1**	**3**	**31**	**1**	**0**	**0**	**48**	**4.2**	**9**	**1**	**23**	**7**	**–8**	....	....	....	....	....	....	....	....
	NHL Totals		**413**	**41**	**52**	**93**	**46**	**50**	**96**	**367**	**3**	**2**	**4**	**551**	**7.4**	**138**	**9**	**265**	**73**		**14**	**1**	**0**	**1**	**4**	**0**	**0**	**0**

• Brother of Chris • ECAC First All-Star Team (1993) • NCAA East First All-America Team (1993)

Traded to **Hartford** by **Calgary** with Gary Suter and Paul Ranheim for James Patrick, Zarley Zalapski and Michael Nylander, March 10, 1994. Claimed by **Ottawa** from **Hartford** in NHL Waiver Draft, October 2, 1995. Traded to **Anaheim** by **Ottawa** with the rights to Marc Moro for Jason York and Shaun Van Allen, October 1, 1996. Traded to **NY Islanders** by **Anaheim** for Tony Hrkac and Dean Malkoc, October 29, 1999. Selected by **Columbus** from **NY Islanders** in Expansion Draft, June 23, 2000.

• DUBE, Christian

C – R. 5'11", 170 lbs. b: Sherbrooke, Que., 4/25/1977. NY Rangers' 1st, 39th overall, in 1995.

Season	Club	League	GP	G	A	Pts	AG	AA	APts	PIM	PP	SH	GW	S	%	TGF	PGF	TGA	PGA	+/–	PO GP	PO G	PO A	PO Pts	PO PIM	PO PP	PO SH	PO GW
1992-93	HC Martigny	Switz-2	27	36	40	76	....	....	....	34	....	....	....	....	....	....	....	....	....	....	....	....	....	....	....	....	....	....
1993-94	Sherbrooke Faucons	QMJHL	72	31	41	72	....	....	....	22	....	....	....	....	....	....	....	....	....	....	11	3	2	5	8	....	....	....
1994-95	Sherbrooke Faucons	QMJHL	71	36	65	101	....	....	....	43	....	....	....	....	....	....	....	....	....	....	7	1	7	8	8	....	....	....
1995-96	Sherbrooke Faucons	QMJHL	62	52	93	145	....	....	....	105	....	....	....	....	....	....	....	....	....	....	7	5	5	10	6	....	....	....
	Canada	WJC-A	6	4	2	6	....	....	....	0	....	....	....	....	....	....	....	....	....	....	....	....	....	....	....	....	....	....
1996-97	Hull Olympiques	QMJHL	19	15	22	37	....	....	....	37	....	....	....	....	....	....	....	....	....	....	14	7	16	23	14	....	....	....
	Canada	WJC-A	7	4	3	7	....	....	....	0	....	....	....	....	....	....	....	....	....	....	....	....	....	....	....	....	....	....
	New York Rangers	**NHL**	**27**	**1**	**1**	**2**	**1**	**1**	**2**	**4**	**1**	**0**	**0**	**14**	**7.1**	**5**	**4**	**5**	**0**	**–4**	**3**	**0**	**0**	**0**	**0**	**0**	**0**	**0**
	Hull Olympiques	Mem-Cup	4	6	*7	*13	....	....	....	2	....	....	....	....	....	....	....	....	....	....	....	....	....	....	....	....	....	....
1997-98	Hartford Wolf Pack	AHL	79	11	46	57	....	....	....	46	....	....	....	....	....	....	....	....	....	....	9	0	4	4	6	....	....	....

Season	Club	League	GP	G	A	Pts	AG	AA	APts	PIM	PP	SH	GW	S	%	TGF	PGF	TGA	PGA	+/–	GP	G	A	Pts	PIM	PP	SH	GW
			REGULAR SEASON																		PLAYOFFS							
1998-99	**New York Rangers**	**NHL**	**6**	**0**	**0**	**0**	**0**	**0**	**0**	**0**	**0**	**0**	**0**	**0**	**0.0**	**0**	**0**	**0**	**0**	**0**	....	....	....	....	....	....	....	....
	Hartford Wolf Pack	AHL	58	21	30	51	....	....	....	20	....	....	....	....	....	....	....	....	....	....	6	0	3	3	4	....	....	....
99-2000	HC Lugano	Switz.	45	*25	26	51	....	....	....	52	....	....	....	....	....	....	....	....	....	....	14	8	*12	*20	14	....	....	....
	HC Lugano	EuroHL	6	2	2	4	....	....	....	2	....	....	....	....	....	....	....	....	....	....	4	2	2	4	2	....	....	....
	NHL Totals		**33**	**1**	**1**	**2**	**1**	**1**	**2**	**4**	**1**	**0**	**0**	**14**	**7.1**	**5**	**4**	**5**	**0**		**3**	**0**	**0**	**0**	**0**	**0**	**0**	**0**

• Son of Norm • QMJHL First All-Star Team (1996) • Canadian Major Junior First All-Star Team (1996) • Canadian Major Junior Player of the Year (1996) • WJC-A All-Star Team (1997) • Won Stafford Smythe Memorial Trophy (Memorial Cup Tournament MVP) (1997)

• DUBE, Norm

Normand G. LW – L. 5'11", 185 lbs. b: Sherbrooke, Que., 9/12/1951. Los Angeles' 6th, 90th overall, in 1971.

Season	Club	League	GP	G	A	Pts	AG	AA	APts	PIM	PP	SH	GW	S	%	TGF	PGF	TGA	PGA	+/–	GP	G	A	Pts	PIM	PP	SH	GW
1969-70	Sherbrooke Castors	QJHL	52	19	34	53	....	....	....	27	....	....	....	....	....	....	....	....	....	....	....	....	....	....	....	....	....	....
1970-71	Sherbrooke Castors	QJHL	62	72	66	138	....	....	....	17	....	....	....	....	....	....	....	....	....	....	8	4	7	11	10	....	....	....
1971-72	University of Sherbrooke	QCHA	21	25	30	55	....	....	....	67	....	....	....	....	....	....	....	....	....	....	....	....	....	....	....	....	....	....
1972-73	Springfield Kings	AHL	66	30	30	60	....	....	....	21	....	....	....	....	....	....	....	....	....	....	....	....	....	....	....	....	....	....
1973-74	Springfield Kings	AHL	48	32	21	53	....	....	....	10	....	....	....	....	....	....	....	....	....	....	....	....	....	....	....	....	....	....
1974-75	**Kansas City Scouts**	**NHL**	**56**	**8**	**10**	**18**	**7**	**7**	**14**	**54**	**2**	**0**	**1**	**77**	**10.4**	**28**	**4**	**36**	**0**	**–12**	....	....	....	....	....	....	....	....
	Providence Reds	AHL	14	5	0	5	....	....	....	4	....	....	....	....	....	....	....	....	....	....	....	....	....	....	....	....	....	....
1975-76	**Kansas City Scouts**	**NHL**	**1**	**0**	**0**	**0**	**0**	**0**	**0**	**0**	**0**	**0**	**0**	**0**	**0.0**	**0**	**0**	**0**	**0**	**0**	....	....	....	....	....	....	....	....
	Springfield Indians	AHL	67	31	38	69	....	....	....	28	....	....	....	....	....	....	....	....	....	....	....	....	....	....	....	....	....	....
1976-77	Beauce Jaros	NAHL	29	20	32	52	....	....	....	12	....	....	....	....	....	....	....	....	....	....	....	....	....	....	....	....	....	....
	Quebec Nordiques	WHA	39	15	18	33	....	....	....	8	....	....	....	....	....	....	....	....	....	....	14	3	12	15	11	....	....	....
1977-78	Quebec Nordiques	WHA	73	16	31	47	....	....	....	17	....	....	....	....	....	....	....	....	....	....	10	2	2	4	6	....	....	....
1978-79	Quebec Nordiques	WHA	36	2	13	15	....	....	....	4	....	....	....	....	....	....	....	....	....	....	....	....	....	....	....	....	....	....
	Binghamton Dusters	AHL	36	9	24	33	....	....	....	18	....	....	....	....	....	....	....	....	....	....	8	4	5	9	14	....	....	....
1979-80	Nova Scotia Voyageurs	AHL	79	40	*61	*101	....	....	....	49	....	....	....	....	....	....	....	....	....	....	6	4	2	6	2	....	....	....
1980-81	HC Sierre	Switz-2	STATISTICS NOT AVAILABLE																									
1981-82	HC Sierre	Switz-2	STATISTICS NOT AVAILABLE																									
1982-83	HC Sierre	Switz-2	32	36	28	64	....	....	....	....	....	....	....	....	....	....	....	....	....	....	....	....	....	....	....	....	....	....
1983-84	HC Sierre	Switz-2	32	38	35	73	....	....	....	....	....	....	....	....	....	....	....	....	....	....	....	....	....	....	....	....	....	....
1984-85	HC Sierre	Switz-2	STATISTICS NOT AVAILABLE																									
	NHL Totals		**57**	**8**	**10**	**18**	**7**	**7**	**14**	**54**	**2**	**0**	**1**	**77**	**10.4**	**28**	**4**	**36**	**0**		....	....	....	....	....	....	....	....
	Other Major League Totals		148	33	62	95	....	....	....	29	....	....	....	....	....	....	....	....	....	....	24	5	14	19	17	....	....	....

• Father of Christian • QJHL Second All-Star Team (1971) • QCHA First All-Star Team (1972) • AHL First All-Star Team (1980) • Won Fred T. Hunt Memorial Trophy (Sportsmanship-AHL) (1980) • Won John B. Sollenberger Trophy (Top Scorer - AHL) (1980) • Won Les Cunningham Award (MVP - AHL) (1980)

Selected by **Ontario-Ottawa** (WHA) in 1972 WHA General Player Draft, February 12, 1972. Claimed by **Kansas City** from **LA Kings** in Expansion Draft, June 12, 1974. WHA rights traded to **Quebec** (WHA) by **Birmingham** (WHA) for future considerations, June 30, 1976.

• DUBERMAN, Justin

RW – R. 6'1", 185 lbs. b: New Haven, CT, 3/23/1970. Montreal's 12th, 230th overall, in 1989.

Season	Club	League	GP	G	A	Pts	AG	AA	APts	PIM	PP	SH	GW	S	%	TGF	PGF	TGA	PGA	+/–	GP	G	A	Pts	PIM	PP	SH	GW
1986-87	Art Van Major Midgets	USAHA	65	54	80	134	....	....	....	....	....	....	....	....	....	....	....	....	....	....	....	....	....	....	....	....	....	....
1987-88	Detroit Compuware	NAJHL	56	61	43	104	....	....	....	....	....	....	....	....	....	....	....	....	....	....	....	....	....	....	....	....	....	....
1988-89	University of North Dakota	WCHA	33	3	1	4	....	....	....	30	....	....	....	....	....	....	....	....	....	....	....	....	....	....	....	....	....	....
1989-90	University of North Dakota	WCHA	42	10	9	19	....	....	....	50	....	....	....	....	....	....	....	....	....	....	....	....	....	....	....	....	....	....
1990-91	University of North Dakota	WCHA	42	19	18	37	....	....	....	68	....	....	....	....	....	....	....	....	....	....	....	....	....	....	....	....	....	....
1991-92	University of North Dakota	WCHA	39	17	27	44	....	....	....	90	....	....	....	....	....	....	....	....	....	....	....	....	....	....	....	....	....	....
1992-93	Cleveland Lumberjacks	IHL	77	29	42	71	....	....	....	69	....	....	....	....	....	....	....	....	....	....	4	0	0	0	12	....	....	....
1993-94	**Pittsburgh Penguins**	**NHL**	**4**	**0**	**0**	**0**	**0**	**0**	**0**	**0**	**0**	**0**	**0**	**2**	**0.0**	**1**	**0**	**1**	**0**	**0**	....	....	....	....	....	....	....	....
	Cleveland Lumberjacks	IHL	59	9	13	22	....	....	....	63	....	....	....	....	....	....	....	....	....	....	....	....	....	....	....	....	....	....
1994-95	JyP-HT Jyvaskyla	Finland	2	0	0	0	....	....	....	4	....	....	....	....	....	....	....	....	....	....	....	....	....	....	....	....	....	....
	Johnstown Chiefs	ECHL	24	13	14	27	....	....	....	30	....	....	....	....	....	....	....	....	....	....	5	0	7	7	20	....	....	....
	Chicago Wolves	IHL	13	1	3	4	....	....	....	39	....	....	....	....	....	....	....	....	....	....	....	....	....	....	....	....	....	....
1995-96	Cornwall Aces	AHL	1	0	0	0	....	....	....	0	....	....	....	....	....	....	....	....	....	....	....	....	....	....	....	....	....	....
	South Carolina Stingrays	ECHL	47	24	24	48	....	....	....	119	....	....	....	....	....	....	....	....	....	....	....	....	....	....	....	....	....	....
	Portland Pirates	AHL	15	6	5	11	....	....	....	23	....	....	....	....	....	....	....	....	....	....	10	1	2	3	8	....	....	....
1996-97	Newcastle Cobras	Britain	30	20	18	38	....	....	....	106	....	....	....	....	....	....	....	....	....	....	6	2	1	3	16	....	....	....
1997-98	Newcastle Cobras	BH-Cup	14	6	7	13	....	....	....	12	....	....	....	....	....	....	....	....	....	....	....	....	....	....	....	....	....	....
	Newcastle Cobras	Britain	37	8	10	18	....	....	....	28	....	....	....	....	....	....	....	....	....	....	6	0	2	2	6	....	....	....
	NHL Totals		**4**	**0**	**0**	**0**	**0**	**0**	**0**	**0**	**0**	**0**	**0**	**2**	**0.0**	**1**	**0**	**1**	**0**		....	....	....	....	....	....	....	....

Signed as a free agent by **Pittsburgh**, November 2, 1992. • Played w/ RHI's Oakland Skates in 1995 (21-21-19-40-43) and 1996 (19-10-17-27-32).

• DUBINSKY, Steve

C – L. 6', 190 lbs. b: Montreal, Que., 7/9/1970. Chicago's 9th, 226th overall, in 1990.

Season	Club	League	GP	G	A	Pts	AG	AA	APts	PIM	PP	SH	GW	S	%	TGF	PGF	TGA	PGA	+/–	GP	G	A	Pts	PIM	PP	SH	GW
1989-90	Clarkson University	ECAC	35	7	10	17	....	....	....	24	....	....	....	....	....	....	....	....	....	....	....	....	....	....	....	....	....	....
1990-91	Clarkson University	ECAC	39	13	23	36	....	....	....	26	....	....	....	....	....	....	....	....	....	....	....	....	....	....	....	....	....	....
1991-92	Clarkson University	ECAC	32	20	31	51	....	....	....	40	....	....	....	....	....	....	....	....	....	....	....	....	....	....	....	....	....	....
1992-93	Clarkson University	ECAC	35	18	26	44	....	....	....	58	....	....	....	....	....	....	....	....	....	....	....	....	....	....	....	....	....	....
1993-94	**Chicago Blackhawks**	**NHL**	**27**	**2**	**6**	**8**	**2**	**5**	**7**	**16**	**0**	**0**	**0**	**20**	**10.0**	**8**	**1**	**7**	**1**	**1**	**6**	**0**	**0**	**0**	**10**	**0**	**0**	**0**
	Indianapolis Ice	IHL	54	15	25	40	....	....	....	63	....	....	....	....	....	....	....	....	....	....	....	....	....	....	....	....	....	....
1994-95	**Chicago Blackhawks**	**NHL**	**16**	**0**	**0**	**0**	**0**	**0**	**0**	**8**	**0**	**0**	**0**	**16**	**0.0**	**2**	**1**	**6**	**0**	**–5**	....	....	....	....	....	....	....	....
	Indianapolis Ice	IHL	62	16	11	27	....	....	....	29	....	....	....	....	....	....	....	....	....	....	....	....	....	....	....	....	....	....
1995-96	**Chicago Blackhawks**	**NHL**	**43**	**2**	**3**	**5**	**2**	**2**	**4**	**14**	**0**	**0**	**0**	**33**	**6.1**	**11**	**0**	**12**	**4**	**3**	....	....	....	....	....	....	....	....
	Indianapolis Ice	IHL	16	8	8	16	....	....	....	10	....	....	....	....	....	....	....	....	....	....	....	....	....	....	....	....	....	....
1996-97	**Chicago Blackhawks**	**NHL**	**5**	**0**	**0**	**0**	**0**	**0**	**0**	**0**	**0**	**0**	**0**	**4**	**0.0**	**2**	**0**	**1**	**1**	**2**	**4**	**1**	**0**	**1**	**4**	**0**	**0**	**0**
	Indianapolis Ice	IHL	77	32	40	72	....	....	....	53	....	....	....	....	....	....	....	....	....	....	1	3	1	4	0	....	....	....
1997-98	**Chicago Blackhawks**	**NHL**	**82**	**5**	**13**	**18**	**6**	**13**	**19**	**57**	**0**	**1**	**0**	**112**	**4.5**	**22**	**0**	**42**	**14**	**–6**	....	....	....	....	....	....	....	....
1998-99	**Chicago Blackhawks**	**NHL**	**1**	**0**	**0**	**0**	**0**	**0**	**0**	**0**	**0**	**0**	**0**	**1**	**0.0**	**0**	**0**	**0**	**0**	**0**	....	....	....	....	....	....	....	....
	Calgary Flames	**NHL**	**61**	**4**	**10**	**14**	**5**	**10**	**15**	**14**	**0**	**2**	**0**	**69**	**5.8**	**20**	**0**	**50**	**23**	**–7**	....	....	....	....	....	....	....	....
99-2000	**Calgary Flames**	**NHL**	**23**	**0**	**1**	**1**	**0**	**1**	**1**	**4**	**0**	**0**	**0**	**29**	**0.0**	**4**	**0**	**27**	**11**	**–12**	....	....	....	....	....	....	....	....
	NHL Totals		**258**	**13**	**33**	**46**	**15**	**31**	**46**	**113**	**0**	**3**	**0**	**284**	**4.6**	**69**	**2**	**145**	**54**		**10**	**1**	**0**	**1**	**14**	**0**	**0**	**0**

Traded to **Calgary** by **Chicago** with Jeff Shantz for Marty McInnis, Jamie Allison and Eric Andersson, October 27, 1998. • Suffered season-ending knee injury in game vs. Chicago, December 12, 1999.

• DUCHESNE, Gaetan

LW – L. 5'11", 200 lbs. b: Les Saulles, Que., 7/11/1962. Washington's 8th, 152nd overall, in 1981.

Season	Club	League	GP	G	A	Pts	AG	AA	APts	PIM	PP	SH	GW	S	%	TGF	PGF	TGA	PGA	+/–	GP	G	A	Pts	PIM	PP	SH	GW
1978-79	Ste-Foy Couillard	QAAA	25	3	12	15	....	....	....	....	....	....	....	....	....	....	....	....	....	....	....	....	....	....	....	....	....	....
1979-80	Quebec Remparts	QMJHL	46	9	28	37	....	....	....	22	....	....	....	....	....	....	....	....	....	....	5	0	2	2	9	....	....	....
1980-81	Quebec Remparts	QMJHL	72	27	45	72	....	....	....	63	....	....	....	....	....	....	....	....	....	....	7	1	4	5	6	....	....	....
1981-82	Quebec Remparts	QMJHL	2	0	0	0	....	....	....	0	....	....	....	....	....	....	....	....	....	....	....	....	....	....	....	....	....	....
	Washington Capitals	**NHL**	**74**	**9**	**14**	**23**	**7**	**9**	**16**	**46**	**0**	**0**	**1**	**78**	**11.5**	**37**	**0**	**65**	**22**	**–6**	....	....	....	....	....	....	....	....
1982-83	**Washington Capitals**	**NHL**	**77**	**18**	**19**	**37**	**15**	**13**	**28**	**52**	**0**	**1**	**6**	**126**	**14.3**	**54**	**0**	**54**	**15**	**15**	**4**	**1**	**1**	**2**	**4**	**0**	**0**	**0**
	Hershey Bears	AHL	1	1	0	1	....	....	....	0	....	....	....	....	....	....	....	....	....	....	....	....	....	....	....	....	....	....
1983-84	**Washington Capitals**	**NHL**	**79**	**17**	**19**	**36**	**14**	**13**	**27**	**29**	**3**	**2**	**1**	**116**	**14.7**	**64**	**6**	**61**	**18**	**15**	**8**	**2**	**1**	**3**	**2**	**0**	**0**	**1**
1984-85	**Washington Capitals**	**NHL**	**67**	**15**	**23**	**38**	**12**	**16**	**28**	**32**	**0**	**1**	**1**	**84**	**17.9**	**53**	**0**	**56**	**19**	**16**	**5**	**0**	**1**	**1**	**7**	**0**	**0**	**0**
1985-86	**Washington Capitals**	**NHL**	**80**	**11**	**28**	**39**	**9**	**19**	**28**	**39**	**0**	**1**	**3**	**119**	**9.2**	**57**	**1**	**63**	**17**	**10**	**9**	**4**	**3**	**7**	**12**	**0**	**1**	**0**
1986-87	**Washington Capitals**	**NHL**	**74**	**17**	**35**	**52**	**15**	**25**	**40**	**53**	**0**	**1**	**4**	**108**	**15.7**	**69**	**1**	**73**	**23**	**18**	**7**	**3**	**0**	**3**	**14**	**0**	**0**	**0**
1987-88	**Quebec Nordiques**	**NHL**	**80**	**24**	**23**	**47**	**20**	**16**	**36**	**83**	**4**	**1**	**2**	**138**	**17.4**	**61**	**12**	**80**	**39**	**8**	....	....	....	....	....	....	....	....
1988-89	**Quebec Nordiques**	**NHL**	**70**	**8**	**21**	**29**	**7**	**15**	**22**	**56**	**2**	**1**	**1**	**110**	**7.3**	**49**	**7**	**73**	**31**	**0**	....	....	....	....	....	....	....	....
1989-90	**Minnesota North Stars**	**NHL**	**72**	**12**	**8**	**20**	**10**	**6**	**16**	**33**	**0**	**1**	**1**	**93**	**12.9**	**31**	**0**	**46**	**20**	**5**	**7**	**0**	**0**	**0**	**6**	**0**	**0**	**0**
1990-91	Minnesota North Stars	Fr-Tour	3	1	0	1	....	....	....	2	....	....	....	....	....	....	....	....	....	....	....	....	....	....	....	....	....	....
	Minnesota North Stars	**NHL**	**68**	**9**	**9**	**18**	**8**	**7**	**15**	**18**	**0**	**0**	**1**	**100**	**9.0**	**31**	**1**	**44**	**18**	**4**	**23**	**2**	**3**	**5**	**34**	**0**	**0**	**0**
1991-92	**Minnesota North Stars**	**NHL**	**73**	**8**	**15**	**23**	**7**	**11**	**18**	**102**	**0**	**2**	**1**	**106**	**7.5**	**37**	**0**	**56**	**25**	**6**	**7**	**1**	**0**	**1**	**6**	**0**	**0**	**0**
1992-93	**Minnesota North Stars**	**NHL**	**84**	**16**	**13**	**29**	**13**	**9**	**22**	**30**	**0**	**2**	**3**	**134**	**11.9**	**40**	**0**	**71**	**37**	**6**	....	....	....	....	....	....	....	....

Season	Club	League	GP	G	A	Pts	AG	AA	APts	PIM	PP	SH	GW	S	%	TGF	PGF	TGA	PGA	+/-	GP	G	A	Pts	PIM	PP	SH	GW
			REGULAR SEASON																		PLAYOFFS							
1993-94	**San Jose Sharks**	**NHL**	**84**	**12**	**18**	**30**	**11**	**14**	**25**	**28**	**0**	**1**	**3**	**121**	**9.9**	**54**	**2**	**78**	**34**	**8**	**14**	**1**	**4**	**5**	**12**	**0**	**0**	**0**
1994-95	**San Jose Sharks**	**NHL**	**33**	**2**	**7**	**9**	**4**	**10**	**14**	**16**	**0**	**0**	**0**	**48**	**4.2**	**11**	**0**	**32**	**15**	**–6**	....	....	....	....	....	....	....	....
	Florida Panthers	**NHL**	**13**	**1**	**2**	**3**	**2**	**3**	**5**	**0**	**0**	**0**	**0**	**14**	**7.1**	**6**	**0**	**3**	**0**	**3**	....	....	....	....	....	....	....	....
1995-96			OUT OF HOCKEY – RETIRED																									
1996-97	Quebec Rafales	IHL	66	10	18	28	....	....	....	54	....	....	....	....	....	....	....	....	....	....	9	5	0	5	4	....	....	....
1997-98	Quebec Rafales	IHL	3	0	0	0	....	....	....	2	....	....	....	....	....	....	....	....	....	....	....	....	....	....	....	....	....	....
	NHL Totals		**1028**	**179**	**254**	**433**	**154**	**186**	**340**	**617**	**9**	**14**	**28**	**1495**	**12.0**	**654**	**30**	**855**	**333**		**84**	**14**	**13**	**27**	**97**	**0**	**1**	**1**

Traded to **Quebec** by **Washington** with Alan Haworth and Washington's 1st round choice (Joe Sakic) in 1987 Entry Draft for Clint Malarchuk and Dale Hunter, June 13, 1987. Traded to **Minnesota** by **Quebec** for Kevin Kaminski, June 19, 1989. Transferred to **Dallas** after **Minnesota** franchise relocated, June 9, 1993. Traded to **San Jose** by **Dallas** for San Jose's 6th round choice (later traded back to San Jose — San Jose selected Petri Varis) in 1993 Entry Draft, June 20, 1993. Traded to **Florida** by **San Jose** for Florida's 6th round choice (Timo Hakanen) in 1995 Entry Draft, April 7, 1995.

• DUCHESNE, Steve

D – L. 5'11", 195 lbs. b: Sept-Iles, Que., 6/30/1965.

Season	Club	League	GP	G	A	Pts	AG	AA	APts	PIM	PP	SH	GW	S	%	TGF	PGF	TGA	PGA	+/-	GP	G	A	Pts	PIM	PP	SH	GW
1983-84	Wawa Travellers	NOJHA	10	9	23	32	....	....	....	9	....	....	....	....	....	....	....	....	....	....	....	....	....	....	....	....	....	....
	Drummondville Voltigeurs	QMJHL	67	1	34	35	....	....	....	79	....	....	....	....	....	....	....	....	....	....	....	....	....	....	....	....	....	....
1984-85	Drummondville Voltigeurs	QMJHL	65	22	54	76	....	....	....	94	....	....	....	....	....	....	....	....	....	....	5	4	7	11	8	....	....	....
1985-86	New Haven Nighthawks	AHL	75	14	35	49	....	....	....	76	....	....	....	....	....	....	....	....	....	....	5	0	2	2	9	....	....	....
1986-87	**Los Angeles Kings**	**NHL**	**75**	**13**	**25**	**38**	**11**	**18**	**29**	**74**	**5**	**0**	**2**	**113**	**11.5**	**109**	**27**	**100**	**26**	**8**	**5**	**2**	**2**	**4**	**4**	**1**	**0**	**0**
1987-88	**Los Angeles Kings**	**NHL**	**71**	**16**	**39**	**55**	**14**	**28**	**42**	**109**	**5**	**0**	**4**	**190**	**8.4**	**126**	**40**	**118**	**32**	**0**	**5**	**1**	**3**	**4**	**14**	**1**	**0**	**0**
1988-89	**Los Angeles Kings**	**NHL**	**79**	**25**	**50**	**75**	**21**	**35**	**56**	**92**	**8**	**5**	**2**	**215**	**11.6**	**169**	**50**	**123**	**35**	**31**	**11**	**4**	**4**	**8**	**12**	**2**	**0**	**0**
1989-90	**Los Angeles Kings**	**NHL**	**79**	**20**	**42**	**62**	**17**	**30**	**47**	**36**	**6**	**0**	**1**	**224**	**8.9**	**141**	**56**	**115**	**27**	**–3**	**10**	**2**	**9**	**11**	**6**	**1**	**0**	**0**
1990-91	**Los Angeles Kings**	**NHL**	**78**	**21**	**41**	**62**	**19**	**31**	**50**	**66**	**8**	**0**	**3**	**171**	**12.3**	**152**	**58**	**88**	**13**	**19**	**12**	**4**	**8**	**12**	**8**	**1**	**0**	**0**
1991-92	**Philadelphia Flyers**	**NHL**	**78**	**18**	**38**	**56**	**16**	**29**	**45**	**86**	**7**	**2**	**3**	**229**	**7.9**	**119**	**47**	**104**	**25**	**–7**	....	....	....	....	....	....	....	....
1992-93	**Quebec Nordiques**	**NHL**	**82**	**20**	**62**	**82**	**17**	**43**	**60**	**57**	**8**	**0**	**2**	**227**	**8.8**	**173**	**76**	**98**	**16**	**15**	**6**	**0**	**5**	**5**	**6**	**0**	**0**	**0**
1993-94	**St. Louis Blues**	**NHL**	**36**	**12**	**19**	**31**	**11**	**15**	**26**	**14**	**8**	**0**	**1**	**115**	**10.4**	**60**	**28**	**45**	**14**	**1**	**4**	**0**	**2**	**2**	**2**	**0**	**0**	**0**
	Canada	WC-A	6	0	1	1	....	....	....	0	....	....	....	....	....	....	....	....	....	....	....	....	....	....	....	....	....	....
1994-95	**St. Louis Blues**	**NHL**	**47**	**12**	**26**	**38**	**21**	**38**	**59**	**36**	**1**	**0**	**1**	**116**	**10.3**	**83**	**29**	**44**	**19**	**29**	**7**	**0**	**4**	**4**	**2**	**0**	**0**	**0**
1995-96	**Ottawa Senators**	**NHL**	**62**	**12**	**24**	**36**	**12**	**20**	**32**	**42**	**7**	**0**	**2**	**163**	**7.4**	**82**	**40**	**87**	**22**	**–23**	....	....	....	....	....	....	....	....
	Canada	WC-A	8	1	3	4	....	....	....	4	....	....	....	....	....	....	....	....	....	....	....	....	....	....	....	....	....	....
1996-97	**Ottawa Senators**	**NHL**	**78**	**19**	**28**	**47**	**20**	**25**	**45**	**38**	**10**	**2**	**3**	**208**	**9.1**	**101**	**36**	**94**	**20**	**–9**	**7**	**1**	**4**	**5**	**0**	**1**	**0**	**1**
1997-98	**St. Louis Blues**	**NHL**	**80**	**14**	**42**	**56**	**16**	**41**	**57**	**32**	**5**	**1**	**1**	**153**	**9.2**	**119**	**46**	**82**	**18**	**9**	**10**	**0**	**4**	**4**	**6**	**0**	**0**	**0**
1998-99	**Los Angeles Kings**	**NHL**	**60**	**4**	**19**	**23**	**5**	**18**	**23**	**22**	**1**	**0**	**1**	**99**	**4.0**	**59**	**19**	**58**	**12**	**–6**	....	....	....	....	....	....	....	....
	Philadelphia Flyers	**NHL**	**11**	**2**	**5**	**7**	**2**	**5**	**7**	**2**	**1**	**0**	**1**	**19**	**10.5**	**13**	**8**	**7**	**2**	**0**	**6**	**0**	**2**	**2**	**2**	**0**	**0**	**0**
99-2000	**Detroit Red Wings**	**NHL**	**79**	**10**	**31**	**41**	**11**	**29**	**40**	**42**	**1**	**0**	**1**	**154**	**6.5**	**89**	**23**	**64**	**10**	**12**	**9**	**0**	**4**	**4**	**10**	**0**	**0**	**0**
	NHL Totals		**995**	**218**	**491**	**709**	**213**	**405**	**618**	**748**	**81**	**10**	**28**	**2396**	**9.1**	**1595**	**583**	**1227**	**291**		**92**	**14**	**51**	**65**	**72**	**7**	**0**	**1**

QMJHL First All-Star Team (1985) • NHL All-Rookie Team (1987) • Played in NHL All-Star Game (1989, 1990, 1993)

Signed as a free agent by **LA Kings,** October 1, 1984. Traded to **Philadelphia** by **LA Kings** with Steve Kasper and LA Kings' 4th round choice (Aris Brimanis) in 1991 Entry Draft for Jari Kurri and Jeff Chychrun, May 30, 1991. Traded to **Quebec** by **Philadelphia** with Peter Forsberg, Kerry Huffman, Mike Ricci, Ron Hextall, Philadelphia's 1st round choice (Jocelyn Thibault) in 1993 Entry Draft, $15,000,000 and future considerations (Chris Simon and Philadelphia's 1st round choice (later traded to Toronto — later traded to Washington — Washington selected Nolan Baumgartner) in 1994 Entry Draft, July 21, 1992) for Eric Lindros, June 30, 1992. Traded to **St. Louis** by **Quebec** with Denis Chasse for Garth Butcher, Ron Sutter and Bob Bassen, January 23, 1994. Traded to **Ottawa** by **St. Louis** for Ottawa's 2nd round choice (later traded to Buffalo — Buffalo selected Cory Sarich) in 1996 Entry Draft, August 4, 1995. Traded to **St. Louis** by **Ottawa** for Igor Kravchuk, August 25, 1997. Signed as a free agent by **LA Kings**, July 2, 1998. Traded to **Philadelphia** by **Los Angeles** for Dave Babych and Philadelphia's 5th round choice (Nathan Marsters) in 2000 Entry Draft, March 23, 1999. Signed as a free agent by **Detroit**, September 3, 1999.

• DUDLEY, Rick

Richard Clarence LW – L. 6', 190 lbs. b: Toronto, Ont., 1/31/1949.

Season	Club	League	GP	G	A	Pts	AG	AA	APts	PIM	PP	SH	GW	S	%	TGF	PGF	TGA	PGA	+/-	GP	G	A	Pts	PIM	PP	SH	GW
1968-69	Dixie Beehives	OHA-B	STATISTICS NOT AVAILABLE																									
	St. Catharines Black Hawks	OHA-Jr.	26	8	7	15	....	....	....	43	....	....	....	....	....	....	....	....	....	....	16	2	1	3	46	....	....	....
1969-70	Iowa Stars	CHL	26	3	3	6	....	....	....	36	....	....	....	....	....	....	....	....	....	....	11	0	3	3	4	....	....	....
1970-71	Cleveland Barons	AHL	16	1	0	1	....	....	....	2	....	....	....	....	....	....	....	....	....	....	....	....	....	....	....	....	....	....
	Flint Generals	IHL	15	1	5	6	....	....	....	30	....	....	....	....	....	....	....	....	....	....	....	....	....	....	....	....	....	....
1971-72	Cincinnati Swords	AHL	51	6	23	29	....	....	....	272	....	....	....	....	....	....	....	....	....	....	9	0	4	4	58	....	....	....
1972-73	**Buffalo Sabres**	**NHL**	**6**	**0**	**1**	**1**	**0**	**1**	**1**	**7**	**0**	**0**	**0**	**6**	**0.0**	**1**	**0**	**3**	**0**	**–2**	....	....	....	....	....	....	....	....
	Cincinnati Swords	AHL	64	40	44	84	....	....	....	159	....	....	....	....	....	....	....	....	....	....	15	7	15	22	*56	....	....	....
1973-74	**Buffalo Sabres**	**NHL**	**67**	**13**	**13**	**26**	**12**	**11**	**23**	**71**	**0**	**0**	**2**	**100**	**13.0**	**38**	**2**	**37**	**1**	**0**	....	....	....	....	....	....	....	....
1974-75	**Buffalo Sabres**	**NHL**	**78**	**31**	**39**	**70**	**27**	**29**	**56**	**116**	**4**	**0**	**6**	**226**	**13.7**	**93**	**10**	**54**	**0**	**29**	**10**	**3**	**1**	**4**	**26**	**1**	**0**	**1**
1975-76	Cincinnati Stingers	WHA	74	43	38	81	....	....	....	156	....	....	....	....	....	....	....	....	....	....	....	....	....	....	....	....	....	....
1976-77	Cincinnati Stingers	WHA	77	41	47	88	....	....	....	102	....	....	....	....	....	....	....	....	....	....	4	0	1	1	7	....	....	....
1977-78	Cincinnati Stingers	WHA	72	30	41	71	....	....	....	156	....	....	....	....	....	....	....	....	....	....	....	....	....	....	....	....	....	....
1978-79	Cincinnati Stingers	WHA	47	17	20	37	....	....	....	102	....	....	....	....	....	....	....	....	....	....	....	....	....	....	....	....	....	....
	Buffalo Sabres	**NHL**	**24**	**5**	**6**	**11**	**4**	**4**	**8**	**2**	**0**	**0**	**1**	**36**	**13.9**	**22**	**0**	**11**	**0**	**11**	**3**	**1**	**1**	**2**	**2**	**0**	**0**	**0**
1979-80	**Buffalo Sabres**	**NHL**	**66**	**11**	**22**	**33**	**9**	**16**	**25**	**58**	**0**	**0**	**2**	**109**	**10.1**	**51**	**15**	**26**	**1**	**11**	**12**	**3**	**0**	**3**	**41**	**1**	**0**	**1**
1980-81	**Buffalo Sabres**	**NHL**	**38**	**10**	**13**	**23**	**8**	**9**	**17**	**10**	**2**	**0**	**0**	**49**	**20.4**	**30**	**5**	**18**	**0**	**7**	....	....	....	....	....	....	....	....
	Winnipeg Jets	**NHL**	**30**	**5**	**5**	**10**	**4**	**3**	**7**	**28**	**0**	**0**	**0**	**53**	**9.4**	**14**	**1**	**35**	**10**	**–12**	....	....	....	....	....	....	....	....
1981-82	Fredericton Express	AHL	7	1	3	4	....	....	....	30	....	....	....	....	....	....	....	....	....	....	....	....	....	....	....	....	....	....
	NHL Totals		**309**	**75**	**99**	**174**	**64**	**73**	**137**	**292**	**6**	**0**	**11**	**579**	**13.0**	**249**	**33**	**184**	**12**		**25**	**7**	**2**	**9**	**69**	**2**	**0**	**2**
	Other Major League Totals		270	131	146	277	....	....	....	516	....	....	....	....	....	....	....	....	....	....	4	0	1	1	7	....	....	....

WHA Second All-Star Team (1977)

Signed as a free agent by **Buffalo**, September, 1971. Selected by **Miami-Philadelphia** (WHA) in 1972 WHA General Player Draft, February 12, 1972. Selected by **LA Sharks** in 1973 WHA Professional Player Draft, June,1973. WHA rights transferred to **Michigan** (WHA) after **LA Sharks** (WHA) franchise relocated, April 11, 1974. Signed as a free agent by **Cincinnati** (WHA) after **Michigan-Baltimore** (WHA) franchise folded, May, 1975. Rights transferred to **Buffalo** by **Cincinnati** (WHA) for NHL club agreeing to buy out remainder of contract, February, 1979. Claimed on waivers by **Winnipeg** from **Buffalo**, January 12, 1981.

• DUERDEN, Dave

LW – L. 6'2", 201 lbs. b: Oshawa, Ont., 4/11/1977. Florida's 4th, 80th overall, in 1995.

Season	Club	League	GP	G	A	Pts	AG	AA	APts	PIM	PP	SH	GW	S	%	TGF	PGF	TGA	PGA	+/-	GP	G	A	Pts	PIM	PP	SH	GW
1991-92	Ajax Bantam Knights	OMHA	60	47	48	95	....	....	....	100	....	....	....	....	....	....	....	....	....	....	....	....	....	....	....	....	....	....
1992-93	Ajax Knights	OMHA	60	21	48	69	....	....	....	45	....	....	....	....	....	....	....	....	....	....	....	....	....	....	....	....	....	....
1993-94	Wexford Raiders	OJHL	47	17	27	44	....	....	....	26	....	....	....	....	....	....	....	....	....	....	....	....	....	....	....	....	....	....
1994-95	Peterborough Petes	OHL	66	20	33	53	....	....	....	21	....	....	....	....	....	....	....	....	....	....	11	6	2	8	6	....	....	....
1995-96	Peterborough Petes	OHL	66	35	35	70	....	....	....	47	....	....	....	....	....	....	....	....	....	....	24	14	13	27	16	....	....	....
1996-97	Peterborough Petes	OHL	66	36	48	84	....	....	....	34	....	....	....	....	....	....	....	....	....	....	4	2	4	6	0	....	....	....
1997-98	Port Huron Border Cats	UHL	7	0	4	4	....	....	....	10	....	....	....	....	....	....	....	....	....	....	....	....	....	....	....	....	....	....
	Beast of New Haven	AHL	36	6	7	13	....	....	....	10	....	....	....	....	....	....	....	....	....	....	....	....	....	....	....	....	....	....
	Fort Wayne Komets	IHL	7	0	1	1	....	....	....	0	....	....	....	....	....	....	....	....	....	....	....	....	....	....	....	....	....	....
1998-99	Miami Matadors	ECHL	13	10	7	17	....	....	....	0	....	....	....	....	....	....	....	....	....	....	....	....	....	....	....	....	....	....
	Kentucky Thoroughblades	AHL	36	8	9	17	....	....	....	9	....	....	....	....	....	....	....	....	....	....	6	0	2	2	0	....	....	....
99-2000	**Florida Panthers**	**NHL**	**2**	**0**	**0**	**0**	**0**	**0**	**0**	**0**	**0**	**0**	**0**	**1**	**0.0**	**0**	**0**	**0**	**0**	**0**	....	....	....	....	....	....	....	....
	Louisville Panthers	AHL	74	25	38	63	....	....	....	6	....	....	....	....	....	....	....	....	....	....	4	0	1	1	0	....	....	....
	NHL Totals		**2**	**0**	**0**	**0**	**0**	**0**	**0**	**0**	**0**	**0**	**0**	**1**	**0.0**	**0**	**0**	**0**	**0**		....	....	....	....	....	....	....	....

OHL Second All-Star Team (1997)

• DUFF, Dick

Terrance Richard LW – L. 5'9", 166 lbs. b: Kirkland Lake, Ont., 2/18/1936.

Season	Club	League	GP	G	A	Pts	AG	AA	APts	PIM	PP	SH	GW	S	%	TGF	PGF	TGA	PGA	+/-	GP	G	A	Pts	PIM	PP	SH	GW
1952-53	St. Michael's Buzzers	OHA-B	STATISTICS NOT AVAILABLE																									
	St. Michael's Majors	OHA-Jr.	16	3	2	5	....	....	....	2	....	....	....	....	....	....	....	....	....	....	16	6	9	15	15	....	....	....
1953-54	St. Michael's Majors	OHA-Jr.	59	35	40	75	....	....	....	120	....	....	....	....	....	....	....	....	....	....	8	2	3	5	23	....	....	....
1954-55	St. Michael's Majors	OHA-Jr.	47	33	20	53	....	....	....	113	....	....	....	....	....	....	....	....	....	....	5	5	2	7	22	....	....	....
	Toronto Maple Leafs	**NHL**	**3**	**0**	**0**	**0**	**0**	**0**	**0**	**2**	....	....	....	....	....	....	....	....	....	....	....	....	....	....	....	....	....	....
1955-56	**Toronto Maple Leafs**	**NHL**	**69**	**18**	**19**	**37**	**25**	**23**	**48**	**74**	....	....	....	....	....	....	....	....	....	....	**5**	**1**	**4**	**5**	**2**	....	....	....
1956-57	**Toronto Maple Leafs**	**NHL**	**70**	**26**	**14**	**40**	**34**	**15**	**49**	**50**	....	....	....	....	....	....	....	....	....	....	....	....	....	....	....	....	....	....
1957-58	**Toronto Maple Leafs**	**NHL**	**65**	**26**	**23**	**49**	**32**	**24**	**56**	**79**	....	....	....	....	....	....	....	....	....	....	....	....	....	....	....	....	....	....

			REGULAR SEASON																		PLAYOFFS							
Season	Club	League	GP	G	A	Pts	AG	AA	APts	PIM	PP	SH	GW	S	%	TGF	PGF	TGA	PGA	+/–	GP	G	A	Pts	PIM	PP	SH	GW
1958-59	**Toronto Maple Leafs**	**NHL**	**69**	**29**	**24**	**53**	**35**	**24**	**59**	**73**	....	....	....	....	....	....	....	....	....	....	**12**	**4**	**3**	**7**	**8**	....	....	....
1959-60	**Toronto Maple Leafs**	**NHL**	**67**	**19**	**22**	**41**	**22**	**21**	**43**	**51**	....	....	....	....	....	....	....	....	....	....	**10**	**2**	**4**	**6**	**6**	....	....	....
1960-61	**Toronto Maple Leafs**	**NHL**	**67**	**16**	**17**	**33**	**18**	**16**	**34**	**54**	....	....	....	....	....	....	....	....	....	....	**5**	**0**	**1**	**1**	**2**	....	....	....
1961-62◆	**Toronto Maple Leafs**	**NHL**	**51**	**17**	**20**	**37**	**19**	**19**	**38**	**37**	....	....	....	....	....	....	....	....	....	....	**12**	**3**	**10**	**13**	**20**	....	....	....
1962-63◆	**Toronto Maple Leafs**	**NHL**	**69**	**16**	**19**	**35**	**19**	**19**	**38**	**56**	....	....	....	....	....	....	....	....	....	....	**10**	**4**	**1**	**5**	**2**	....	....	....
1963-64	**Toronto Maple Leafs**	**NHL**	**52**	**7**	**10**	**17**	**9**	**10**	**19**	**59**	....	....	....	....	....	....	....	....	....	....	....	....	....	....	....	....	....	....
	New York Rangers	**NHL**	**14**	**4**	**4**	**8**	**5**	**4**	**9**	**2**	....	....	....	....	....	....	....	....	....	....	....	....	....	....	....	....	....	....
1964-65	**New York Rangers**	**NHL**	**29**	**3**	**9**	**12**	**4**	**9**	**13**	**20**	....	....	....	....	....	....	....	....	....	....	....	....	....	....	....	....	....	....
◆	**Montreal Canadiens**	**NHL**	**40**	**9**	**7**	**16**	**11**	**7**	**18**	**16**	....	....	....	....	....	....	....	....	....	....	**13**	**3**	**6**	**9**	**17**	....	....	....
1965-66◆	**Montreal Canadiens**	**NHL**	**63**	**21**	**24**	**45**	**24**	**23**	**47**	**78**	....	....	....	....	....	....	....	....	....	....	**10**	**2**	**5**	**7**	**2**	....	....	....
1966-67	**Montreal Canadiens**	**NHL**	**51**	**12**	**11**	**23**	**14**	**11**	**25**	**23**	....	....	....	....	....	....	....	....	....	....	**10**	**2**	**3**	**5**	**4**	....	....	....
1967-68◆	**Montreal Canadiens**	**NHL**	**66**	**25**	**21**	**46**	**29**	**21**	**50**	**21**	**6**	**0**	**8**	**111**	**22.5**	**66**	**18**	**42**	**0**	**6**	**13**	**3**	**4**	**7**	**4**	**0**	**0**	**1**
1968-69◆	**Montreal Canadiens**	**NHL**	**68**	**19**	**21**	**40**	**20**	**19**	**39**	**24**	**5**	**0**	**2**	**138**	**13.8**	**64**	**17**	**60**	**0**	**–13**	**14**	**6**	**8**	**14**	**11**	**3**	**1**	**0**
1969-70	**Montreal Canadiens**	**NHL**	**17**	**1**	**1**	**2**	**1**	**1**	**2**	**4**	**0**	**0**	**0**	**21**	**4.8**	**7**	**2**	**10**	**0**	**–5**	....	....	....	....	....	....	....	....
	Los Angeles Kings	**NHL**	**32**	**5**	**8**	**13**	**5**	**7**	**12**	**8**	**0**	**0**	**0**	**37**	**13.5**	**22**	**5**	**33**	**1**	**–15**	....	....	....	....	....	....	....	....
1970-71	**Los Angeles Kings**	**NHL**	**7**	**1**	**0**	**1**	**1**	**0**	**1**	**0**	**0**	**0**	**0**	**4**	**25.0**	**1**	**0**	**3**	**0**	**–2**	....	....	....	....	....	....	....	....
	Buffalo Sabres	**NHL**	**53**	**7**	**13**	**20**	**7**	**11**	**18**	**12**	**0**	**0**	**1**	**67**	**10.4**	**36**	**2**	**50**	**0**	**–16**	....	....	....	....	....	....	....	....
1971-72	**Buffalo Sabres**	**NHL**	**8**	**2**	**2**	**4**	**2**	**2**	**4**	**0**	**0**	**0**	**0**	**5**	**40.0**	**6**	**1**	**7**	**0**	**–2**	....	....	....	....	....	....	....	....
	NHL Totals		**1030**	**283**	**289**	**572**	**336**	**286**	**622**	**743**	....	....	....	....	....	....	....	....	....	....	**114**	**30**	**49**	**79**	**78**	....	....	....

Played in NHL All-Star Game (1956, 1957, 1958, 1962, 1963, 1965, 1967)

Traded to **NY Rangers** by **Toronto** with Arnie Brown, Bob Nevin, Bill Collins and Rod Seiling for Andy Bathgate and Don McKenney, February 22, 1964. Traded to **Montreal** by **NY Rangers** with Dave McComb for Bill Hicke and the loan of Jean-Guy Morissette for remainder of 1964-65 season, December 22, 1964. Traded to **LA Kings** by **Montreal** for Dennis Hextall, January 23, 1970. Traded to **Buffalo** by **LA Kings** with Eddie Shack for Mike McMahon Jr. and future considerations, November 24, 1970.

• DUFOUR, Luc

LW – L. 5'11", 180 lbs. b: Chicoutimi, Que., 2/13/1963. Boston's 2nd, 35th overall, in 1981.

Season	Club	League	GP	G	A	Pts	AG	AA	APts	PIM	PP	SH	GW	S	%	TGF	PGF	TGA	PGA	+/–	GP	G	A	Pts	PIM	PP	SH	GW
1978-79	Laurentides Boisbriand	QAAA	38	30	28	58	....	....	....	....	....	....	....	....	....	....	....	....	....	....	....	....	....	....	....	....	....	....
1979-80	Laurentides Boisbriand	QAAA	42	33	33	66	....	....	....	56	....	....	....	....	....	....	....	....	....	....	....	....	....	....	....	....	....	....
1980-81	Chicoutimi Sagueneens	QMJHL	69	43	53	96	....	....	....	89	....	....	....	....	....	....	....	....	....	....	4	1	2	3	8	....	....	....
1981-82	Chicoutimi Sagueneens	QMJHL	62	55	60	115	....	....	....	94	....	....	....	....	....	....	....	....	....	....	20	12	19	31	26	....	....	....
1982-83	**Boston Bruins**	**NHL**	**73**	**14**	**11**	**25**	**11**	**8**	**19**	**107**	**0**	**0**	**1**	**121**	**11.6**	**47**	**2**	**26**	**0**	**19**	**17**	**1**	**0**	**1**	**30**	**0**	**0**	**1**
1983-84	**Boston Bruins**	**NHL**	**41**	**6**	**4**	**10**	**5**	**3**	**8**	**47**	**0**	**0**	**1**	**39**	**15.4**	**19**	**1**	**16**	**0**	**2**	....	....	....	....	....	....	....	....
	Hershey Bears	AHL	37	9	19	28	....	....	....	51	....	....	....	....	....	....	....	....	....	....	....	....	....	....	....	....	....	....
1984-85	Hershey Bears	AHL	6	1	1	2	....	....	....	10	....	....	....	....	....	....	....	....	....	....	....	....	....	....	....	....	....	....
	Quebec Nordiques	**NHL**	**30**	**2**	**3**	**5**	**2**	**2**	**4**	**27**	**0**	**0**	**0**	**18**	**11.1**	**7**	**0**	**12**	**0**	**–5**	....	....	....	....	....	....	....	....
	Fredericton Express	AHL	12	2	0	2	....	....	....	13	....	....	....	....	....	....	....	....	....	....	....	....	....	....	....	....	....	....
	St. Louis Blues	**NHL**	**23**	**1**	**3**	**4**	**1**	**2**	**3**	**18**	**0**	**0**	**0**	**38**	**2.6**	**5**	**0**	**13**	**0**	**–8**	**1**	**0**	**0**	**0**	**2**	**0**	**0**	**0**
1985-86	Maine Mariners	AHL	75	15	20	35	....	....	....	57	....	....	....	....	....	....	....	....	....	....	5	0	0	0	8	....	....	....
1986-87	HC Auronzo	Italy	34	35	40	75	....	....	....	52	....	....	....	....	....	....	....	....	....	....	....	....	....	....	....	....	....	....
	NHL Totals		**167**	**23**	**21**	**44**	**19**	**15**	**34**	**199**	**0**	**0**	**2**	**216**	**10.6**	**78**	**3**	**67**	**0**		**18**	**1**	**0**	**1**	**32**	**0**	**0**	**1**

QMJHL First All-Star Team (1982)

Traded to **Quebec** by **Boston** with Boston's 4th round choice (Peter Massey) in 1985 Entry Draft for Louis Sleigher, October 25, 1984. Traded to **St. Louis** by **Quebec** for Alain Lemieux, January 29, 1985.

• DUFOUR, Marc

Marc Carol RW – R. 6', 175 lbs. b: Trois Rivieres, Que., 9/11/1941.

Season	Club	League	GP	G	A	Pts	AG	AA	APts	PIM	PP	SH	GW	S	%	TGF	PGF	TGA	PGA	+/–	GP	G	A	Pts	PIM	PP	SH	GW
1959-60	Guelph Biltmores	OHA-Jr.	38	7	13	20	....	....	....	12	....	....	....	....	....	....	....	....	....	....	5	0	1	1	2	....	....	....
1960-61	Trois-Rivieres Reds	QJHL	....	....	....	....	....	....	....	....	....	....	....	....	....	....	....	....	....	....	10	8	10	18	6	....	....	....
	Guelph Royals	OHA-Jr.	4	0	0	0	....	....	....	0	....	....	....	....	....	....	....	....	....	....	....	....	....	....	....	....	....	....
	Trois-Rivieres Reds	Mem-Cup	9	10	8	18	....	....	....	30	....	....	....	....	....	....	....	....	....	....	....	....	....	....	....	....	....	....
1961-62	Brandon Wheat Kings	MJHL	33	*37	20	57	....	....	....	48	....	....	....	....	....	....	....	....	....	....	9	*9	8	*17	12	....	....	....
	Brandon Wheat Kings	Mem-Cup	11	*10	6	*16	....	....	....	20	....	....	....	....	....	....	....	....	....	....	....	....	....	....	....	....	....	....
	Edmonton Oil Kings	Mem-Cup	3	2	2	4	....	....	....	10	....	....	....	....	....	....	....	....	....	....	....	....	....	....	....	....	....	....
1962-63	Sudbury Wolves	EPHL	71	50	49	99	....	....	....	27	....	....	....	....	....	....	....	....	....	....	8	2	7	9	4	....	....	....
1963-64	**New York Rangers**	**NHL**	**10**	**1**	**0**	**1**	**1**	**0**	**1**	**2**	....	....	....	....	....	....	....	....	....	....	....	....	....	....	....	....	....	....
	Baltimore Clippers	AHL	38	7	16	23	....	....	....	28	....	....	....	....	....	....	....	....	....	....	....	....	....	....	....	....	....	....
	Los Angeles Blades	WHL	12	2	3	5	....	....	....	0	....	....	....	....	....	....	....	....	....	....	6	1	0	1	0	....	....	....
1964-65	**New York Rangers**	**NHL**	**2**	**0**	**0**	**0**	**0**	**0**	**0**	**0**	....	....	....	....	....	....	....	....	....	....	....	....	....	....	....	....	....	....
	St. Paul Rangers	CPHL	69	43	50	93	....	....	....	33	....	....	....	....	....	....	....	....	....	....	11	4	*14	*18	21	....	....	....
1965-66	Baltimore Clippers	AHL	65	14	23	37	....	....	....	8	....	....	....	....	....	....	....	....	....	....	....	....	....	....	....	....	....	....
1966-67	Vancouver Canucks	WHL	70	19	17	36	....	....	....	18	....	....	....	....	....	....	....	....	....	....	8	1	1	2	2	....	....	....
1967-68	Springfield Kings	AHL	65	20	25	45	....	....	....	12	....	....	....	....	....	....	....	....	....	....	4	3	1	4	0	....	....	....
1968-69	**Los Angeles Kings**	**NHL**	**2**	**0**	**0**	**0**	**0**	**0**	**0**	**0**	**0**	**0**	**0**	**2**	**0.0**	**0**	**0**	**1**	**0**	**–1**	....	....	....	....	....	....	....	....
	Springfield Kings	AHL	70	34	36	70	....	....	....	20	....	....	....	....	....	....	....	....	....	....	....	....	....	....	....	....	....	....
1969-70	Springfield Kings	AHL	71	32	53	85	....	....	....	22	....	....	....	....	....	....	....	....	....	....	14	2	6	8	4	....	....	....
1970-71	Baltimore Clippers	AHL	69	31	51	82	....	....	....	15	....	....	....	....	....	....	....	....	....	....	6	0	5	5	0	....	....	....
1971-72	Baltimore Clippers	AHL	59	15	36	51	....	....	....	12	....	....	....	....	....	....	....	....	....	....	18	7	6	13	8	....	....	....
1972-73	Baltimore Clippers	AHL	67	30	32	62	....	....	....	16	....	....	....	....	....	....	....	....	....	....	....	....	....	....	....	....	....	....
1973-74	Baltimore Clippers	AHL	74	42	62	104	....	....	....	21	....	....	....	....	....	....	....	....	....	....	9	4	3	7	2	....	....	....
1974-75	Baltimore Clippers	AHL	29	8	7	15	....	....	....	12	....	....	....	....	....	....	....	....	....	....	....	....	....	....	....	....	....	....
	NHL Totals		**14**	**1**	**0**	**1**	**1**	**0**	**1**	**2**	....	....	....	....	....	....	....	....	....	....	....	....	....	....	....	....	....	....

EPHL Second All-Star Team (1963) • CPHL First All-Star Team (1965) • AHL First All-Star Team (1971) • AHL Second All-Star Team (1974)

• Regular season totals for Trois-Rivieres (QJHL) during 1960-61 season unavailable. Loaned to **Edmonton** by **Brandon** for Memorial Cup playoffs, April, 1962. Claimed by **LA Kings** from **NY Rangers** in Expansion Draft, June 6, 1967. Claimed by **Baltimore** from **LA Kings** (Springfield-AHL) in Reverse Draft, June 10, 1970. Selected by **Winnipeg** (WHA) in 1972 WHA General Player Draft, February 12, 1972. Rights traded to **NY Raiders** (WHA) by **Winnipeg** (WHA) for the rights to Danny Johnson, June, 1972. Signed as a free agent by **Baltimore** (AHL) after securing release from **NY Raiders** (WHA), October, 1972.

• DUFRESNE, Donald

D – R. 6'1", 206 lbs. b: Quebec City, Que., 4/10/1967. Montreal's 8th, 117th overall, in 1985.

Season	Club	League	GP	G	A	Pts	AG	AA	APts	PIM	PP	SH	GW	S	%	TGF	PGF	TGA	PGA	+/–	GP	G	A	Pts	PIM	PP	SH	GW
1982-83	Montreal L'est Cantonniers	QAAA	44	3	17	20	....	....	....	....	....	....	....	....	....	....	....	....	....	....	....	....	....	....	....	....	....	....
1983-84	Trois-Rivieres Draveurs	QMJHL	67	7	12	19	....	....	....	97	....	....	....	....	....	....	....	....	....	....	....	....	....	....	....	....	....	....
1984-85	Trois-Rivieres Draveurs	QMJHL	65	5	30	35	....	....	....	112	....	....	....	....	....	....	....	....	....	....	7	1	3	4	12	....	....	....
1985-86	Trois-Rivieres Draveurs	QMJHL	63	8	32	40	....	....	....	160	....	....	....	....	....	....	....	....	....	....	1	0	0	0	0	....	....	....
1986-87	Trois-Rivieres Draveurs	QMJHL	51	5	21	26	....	....	....	79	....	....	....	....	....	....	....	....	....	....	....	....	....	....	....	....	....	....
	Longueuil Chevaliers	QMJHL	16	0	8	8	....	....	....	18	....	....	....	....	....	....	....	....	....	....	20	1	8	9	38	....	....	....
	Longueuil Chevaliers	Mem-Cup	5	0	0	0	....	....	....	0	....	....	....	....	....	....	....	....	....	....	....	....	....	....	....	....	....	....
1987-88	Sherbrooke Canadiens	AHL	47	1	8	9	....	....	....	107	....	....	....	....	....	....	....	....	....	....	6	1	0	1	34	....	....	....
1988-89	**Montreal Canadiens**	**NHL**	**13**	**0**	**1**	**1**	**0**	**1**	**1**	**43**	**0**	**0**	**0**	**5**	**0.0**	**5**	**0**	**4**	**2**	**3**	**6**	**1**	**1**	**2**	**4**	**0**	**0**	**0**
	Sherbrooke Canadiens	AHL	47	0	12	12	....	....	....	170	....	....	....	....	....	....	....	....	....	....	....	....	....	....	....	....	....	....
1989-90	**Montreal Canadiens**	**NHL**	**18**	**0**	**4**	**4**	**0**	**3**	**3**	**23**	**0**	**0**	**0**	**6**	**0.0**	**14**	**0**	**14**	**1**	**1**	**10**	**0**	**1**	**1**	**18**	**0**	**0**	**0**
	Sherbrooke Canadiens	AHL	38	2	11	13	....	....	....	104	....	....	....	....	....	....	....	....	....	....	....	....	....	....	....	....	....	....
1990-91	Montreal Canadiens	Fr-Tour	3	0	0	0	....	....	....	29	....	....	....	....	....	....	....	....	....	....	....	....	....	....	....	....	....	....
	Montreal Canadiens	**NHL**	**53**	**2**	**13**	**15**	**2**	**10**	**12**	**55**	**0**	**0**	**0**	**32**	**6.3**	**43**	**1**	**46**	**9**	**5**	**10**	**0**	**1**	**1**	**21**	**0**	**0**	**0**
	Fredericton Canadiens	AHL	10	1	4	5	....	....	....	35	....	....	....	....	....	....	....	....	....	....	1	0	0	0	0	....	....	....
1991-92	**Montreal Canadiens**	**NHL**	**3**	**0**	**0**	**0**	**0**	**0**	**0**	**2**	**0**	**0**	**0**	**2**	**0.0**	**2**	**0**	**0**	**0**	**2**	....	....	....	....	....	....	....	....
	Fredericton Canadiens	AHL	31	8	12	20	....	....	....	60	....	....	....	....	....	....	....	....	....	....	7	0	0	0	10	....	....	....
1992-93◆	**Montreal Canadiens**	**NHL**	**32**	**1**	**2**	**3**	**1**	**1**	**2**	**32**	**0**	**0**	**0**	**13**	**7.7**	**18**	**0**	**19**	**1**	**0**	**2**	**0**	**0**	**0**	**0**	**0**	**0**	**0**
1993-94	**Tampa Bay Lightning**	**NHL**	**51**	**2**	**6**	**8**	**2**	**5**	**7**	**48**	**0**	**0**	**0**	**49**	**4.1**	**29**	**1**	**40**	**10**	**–2**	....	....	....	....	....	....	....	....
	Los Angeles Kings	**NHL**	**9**	**0**	**0**	**0**	**0**	**0**	**0**	**10**	**0**	**0**	**0**	**7**	**0.0**	**3**	**0**	**10**	**2**	**–5**	....	....	....	....	....	....	....	....
1994-95	**St. Louis Blues**	**NHL**	**22**	**0**	**3**	**3**	**0**	**4**	**4**	**10**	**0**	**0**	**0**	**11**	**0.0**	**15**	**1**	**16**	**4**	**2**	**3**	**0**	**0**	**0**	**4**	**0**	**0**	**0**

Season	Club	League	GP	G	A	Pts	AG	AA	APts	PIM	PP	SH	GW	S	%	TGF	PGF	TGA	PGA	+/–	GP	G	A	Pts	PIM	PP	SH	GW
			REGULAR SEASON																		PLAYOFFS							
1995-96	**St. Louis Blues**	**NHL**	3	0	0	0	0	0	0	4	0	0	0	1	0.0	0	0	2	0	–2	....	....	....	....	....	....	....	....
	Worcester IceCats	AHL	13	1	1	2	....	....	....	14	....	....	....	....	....	....	....	....	....	....	....	....	....	....	....	....	....	....
	Edmonton Oilers	**NHL**	42	1	6	7	1	5	6	16	0	0	0	20	5.0	19	1	27	7	–2	....	....	....	....	....	....	....	....
1996-97	**Edmonton Oilers**	**NHL**	22	0	1	1	0	1	1	15	0	0	0	10	0.0	12	1	15	3	–1	3	0	0	0	0	0	0	0
1997-98	Quebec Rafales	IHL	15	0	4	4	....	....	....	20	....	....	....	....	....	....	....	....	....	....	....	....	....	....	....	....	....	....
	NHL Totals		268	6	36	42	6	30	36	258	0	0	0	156	3.8	160	5	193	39		34	1	3	4	47	0	0	0

QMJHL Second All-Star Team (1986, 1987)

Traded to **Tampa Bay** by **Montreal** to complete transaction that sent Rob Ramage to Montreal (March 20, 1993), June 18, 1993. Traded to **LA Kings** by **Tampa Bay** for LA Kings' 6th round choice (Daniel Juden) in 1994 Entry Draft, March 19, 1994. Claimed by **St. Louis** from **LA Kings** in NHL Waiver Draft, January 18, 1995. Traded to **Edmonton** by **St. Louis** with Jeff Norton for Igor Kravchuk and Ken Sutton, January 4, 1996.

• DUGGAN, Ken

Kenneth B. D – L. 6'3", 210 lbs. b: Toronto, Ont., 2/21/1963.

Season	Club	League	GP	G	A	Pts	AG	AA	APts	PIM	PP	SH	GW	S	%	TGF	PGF	TGA	PGA	+/–	GP	G	A	Pts	PIM	PP	SH	GW
1980-81	Bramalea Blues	OJHL	42	3	19	22	....	....	....	58	....	....	....	....	....	....	....	....	....	....	....	....	....	....	....	....	....	....
1981-82	Bramalea Blues	OJHL	STATISTICS NOT AVAILABLE																									
1982-83	University of Toronto	OUAA	35	0	5	5	....	....	....	32	....	....	....	....	....	....	....	....	....	....	....	....	....	....	....	....	....	....
1983-84	University of Toronto	OUAA	47	11	17	28	....	....	....	54	....	....	....	....	....	....	....	....	....	....	....	....	....	....	....	....	....	....
1984-85	University of Toronto	OUAA	45	6	19	25	....	....	....	105	....	....	....	....	....	....	....	....	....	....	....	....	....	....	....	....	....	....
1985-86	University of Toronto	OUAA	44	13	41	54	....	....	....	111	....	....	....	....	....	....	....	....	....	....	....	....	....	....	....	....	....	....
1986-87	New Haven Nighthawks	AHL	13	0	1	1	....	....	....	4	....	....	....	....	....	....	....	....	....	....	....	....	....	....	....	....	....	....
	Flint Spirits	IHL	66	2	23	25	....	....	....	51	....	....	....	....	....	....	....	....	....	....	6	0	2	2	2	....	....	....
1987-88	**Minnesota North Stars**	**NHL**	1	0	0	0	0	0	0	0	0	0	0	0	0.0	0	0	0	0	0	....	....	....	....	....	....	....	....
	Flint Spirits	IHL	1	0	0	0	....	....	....	0	....	....	....	....	....	....	....	....	....	....	....	....	....	....	....	....	....	....
1988-89	Canada	Nat-Team	3	0	1	1	....	....	....	2	....	....	....	....	....	....	....	....	....	....	....	....	....	....	....	....	....	....
	NHL Totals		1	0	0	0	0	0	0	0	0	0	0	0	0.0	0	0	0	0		....	....	....	....	....	....	....	....

Signed as a free agent by **NY Rangers**, May 22, 1986. Signed as a free agent by **Minnesota**, January, 1988.

• DUGUAY, Ron

Ronald "Doogie" C/RW – R. 6'2", 200 lbs. b: Sudbury, Ont., 7/6/1957. NY Rangers' 2nd, 13th overall, in 1977.

Season	Club	League	GP	G	A	Pts	AG	AA	APts	PIM	PP	SH	GW	S	%	TGF	PGF	TGA	PGA	+/–	GP	G	A	Pts	PIM	PP	SH	GW
1973-74	Sudbury Wolves	OMJHL	59	20	20	40	....	....	....	73	....	....	....	....	....	....	....	....	....	....	4	0	3	3	4	....	....	....
1974-75	Sudbury Wolves	OMJHL	64	26	52	78	....	....	....	43	....	....	....	....	....	....	....	....	....	....	15	11	6	17	19	....	....	....
1975-76	Sudbury Wolves	OMJHL	61	42	92	134	....	....	....	101	....	....	....	....	....	....	....	....	....	....	17	11	9	20	37	....	....	....
1976-77	Sudbury Wolves	OMJHL	61	43	66	109	....	....	....	109	....	....	....	....	....	....	....	....	....	....	6	4	3	7	5	....	....	....
	Canada	WJC-A	5	1	4	5	....	....	....	11	....	....	....	....	....	....	....	....	....	....	....	....	....	....	....	....	....	....
1977-78	**New York Rangers**	**NHL**	71	20	20	40	18	15	33	43	3	0	1	129	15.5	65	12	74	4	–17	3	1	1	2	2	1	0	0
1978-79	**New York Rangers**	**NHL**	79	27	36	63	23	26	49	35	1	2	3	178	15.2	85	17	84	26	10	18	5	4	9	11	0	1	0
1979-80	**New York Rangers**	**NHL**	73	28	22	50	24	16	40	37	3	3	2	154	18.2	65	8	81	18	–6	9	5	2	7	11	2	0	0
1980-81	**New York Rangers**	**NHL**	50	17	21	38	13	14	27	83	5	1	0	103	16.5	54	10	62	20	2	14	8	9	17	16	0	1	1
1981-82	Canada	Can-Cup	7	0	2	2	....	....	....	6	....	....	....	....	....	....	....	....	....	....	....	....	....	....	....	....	....	....
	New York Rangers	**NHL**	72	40	36	76	32	24	56	82	10	1	3	202	19.8	114	35	89	28	18	10	5	1	6	31	1	0	0
1982-83	**New York Rangers**	**NHL**	72	19	25	44	16	17	33	58	5	0	2	160	11.9	71	16	89	21	–13	9	2	2	4	28	0	0	0
1983-84	**Detroit Red Wings**	**NHL**	80	33	47	80	27	32	59	34	13	1	1	215	15.3	128	61	117	24	–26	4	2	3	5	2	1	0	0
1984-85	**Detroit Red Wings**	**NHL**	80	38	51	89	31	35	66	51	11	3	4	201	18.9	141	49	128	20	–16	3	1	0	1	7	1	0	0
1985-86	**Detroit Red Wings**	**NHL**	67	19	29	48	15	19	34	26	8	0	2	153	12.4	81	32	107	28	–30	....	....	....	....	....	....	....	....
	Pittsburgh Penguins	**NHL**	13	6	7	13	5	5	10	6	3	0	0	33	18.2	15	8	23	2	–14	....	....	....	....	....	....	....	....
1986-87	**Pittsburgh Penguins**	**NHL**	40	5	13	18	4	9	13	30	0	0	0	55	9.1	23	7	28	4	–8	....	....	....	....	....	....	....	....
	New York Rangers	**NHL**	34	9	12	21	8	9	17	9	2	1	0	66	13.6	33	15	44	18	–8	6	2	0	2	4	1	0	0
1987-88	**New York Rangers**	**NHL**	48	4	4	8	3	3	6	23	0	2	0	59	6.8	21	3	54	27	–9	....	....	....	....	....	....	....	....
	Colorado Rangers	IHL	2	0	0	0	....	....	....	0	....	....	....	....	....	....	....	....	....	....	....	....	....	....	....	....	....	....
	Los Angeles Kings	**NHL**	15	2	6	8	2	4	6	17	0	0	1	21	9.5	13	3	17	2	–5	2	0	0	0	0	0	0	0
1988-89	**Los Angeles Kings**	**NHL**	70	7	17	24	6	12	18	48	0	0	0	80	8.8	53	0	49	19	23	11	0	0	0	6	0	0	0
1989-90	Mannheimer ERC	Germany	22	11	7	18	....	....	....	38	....	....	....	....	....	....	....	....	....	....	3	0	1	1	20	....	....	....
1990-91	San Diego Gulls	IHL	51	15	24	39	....	....	....	87	....	....	....	....	....	....	....	....	....	....	....	....	....	....	....	....	....	....
1991-92	San Diego Gulls	IHL	60	18	18	36	....	....	....	32	....	....	....	....	....	....	....	....	....	....	4	0	1	1	0	....	....	....
1992-1996			OUT OF HOCKEY – RETIRED																									
1996-97	San Diego Gulls	WCHL	2	1	1	2	....	....	....	0	....	....	....	....	....	....	....	....	....	....	....	....	....	....	....	....	....	....
1997-98	San Diego Gulls	WCHL	3	0	3	3	....	....	....	2	....	....	....	....	....	....	....	....	....	....	....	....	....	....	....	....	....	....
1998-99	Jacksonville Lizard Kings	ECHL	1	0	0	0	....	....	....	0	....	....	....	....	....	....	....	....	....	....	....	....	....	....	....	....	....	....
	NHL Totals		864	274	346	620	227	240	467	582	64	14	19	1809	15.1	962	276	1046	261		89	31	22	53	118	7	2	1

Played in NHL All-Star Game (1982)

Traded to **Detroit** by **NY Rangers** with Eddie Mio and Eddie Johnstone for Willie Huber, Mark Osborne and Mike Blaisdell, June 13, 1983. Traded to **Pittsburgh** by **Detroit** for Doug Shedden, March 11, 1986. Traded to **NY Rangers** by **Pittsburgh** for Chris Kontos, January 21, 1987. Traded to **LA Kings** by **NY Rangers**, February 23, 1988.

• DUMONT, Jean-Pierre

RW – L. 6'2", 200 lbs. b: Montreal, Que., 4/1/1978. NY Islanders' 1st, 3rd overall, in 1996.

Season	Club	League	GP	G	A	Pts	AG	AA	APts	PIM	PP	SH	GW	S	%	TGF	PGF	TGA	PGA	+/–	GP	G	A	Pts	PIM	PP	SH	GW
1993-94	Val d'Or Foreurs	QMJHL	25	9	11	20	....	....	....	10	....	....	....	....	....	....	....	....	....	....	....	....	....	....	....	....	....	....
1994-95	Val d'Or Foreurs	QMJHL	48	5	14	19	....	....	....	24	....	....	....	....	....	....	....	....	....	....	....	....	....	....	....	....	....	....
1995-96	Val d'Or Foreurs	QMJHL	66	48	57	105	....	....	....	109	....	....	....	....	....	....	....	....	....	....	13	12	8	20	22	....	....	....
1996-97	Val d'Or Foreurs	QMJHL	62	44	64	108	....	....	....	86	....	....	....	....	....	....	....	....	....	....	13	9	7	16	12	....	....	....
1997-98	Val d'Or Foreurs	QMJHL	55	57	42	99	....	....	....	63	....	....	....	....	....	....	....	....	....	....	19	31	15	46	18	....	....	....
	Canada	WJC-A	7	0	0	0	....	....	....	0	....	....	....	....	....	....	....	....	....	....	....	....	....	....	....	....	....	....
	Val d'Or Foreurs	Mem-Cup	3	3	2	5	....	....	....	4	....	....	....	....	....	....	....	....	....	....	....	....	....	....	....	....	....	....
1998-99	**Chicago Blackhawks**	**NHL**	25	9	6	15	11	6	17	10	0	0	2	42	21.4	21	2	14	2	7	....	....	....	....	....	....	....	....
	Portland Pirates	AHL	50	32	14	46	....	....	....	39	....	....	....	....	....	....	....	....	....	....	....	....	....	....	....	....	....	....
	Chicago Wolves	IHL	....	....	....	....	....	....	....	....	....	....	....	....	....	....	....	....	....	....	10	4	1	5	6	....	....	....
99-2000	**Chicago Blackhawks**	**NHL**	47	10	8	18	11	7	18	18	0	0	1	86	11.6	28	5	30	1	–6	....	....	....	....	....	....	....	....
	Cleveland Lumberjacks	IHL	7	5	2	7	....	....	....	8	....	....	....	....	....	....	....	....	....	....	....	....	....	....	....	....	....	....
	Rochester Americans	AHL	13	7	10	17	....	....	....	18	....	....	....	....	....	....	....	....	....	....	21	14	7	21	32	....	....	....
	NHL Totals		72	19	14	33	22	13	35	28	0	0	3	128	14.8	49	7	44	3		....	....	....	....	....	....	....	....

QMJHL Second All-Star Team (1997)

Rights traded to **Chicago** by **NY Islanders** with Chicago's 5th round choice (later traded to Philadelphia - Philadelphia selected Francis Belanger) in 1998 Entry Draft for Dmitri Nabokov, May 30, 1998. Traded to **Buffalo** by **Chicago** with Doug Gilmour and future considerations for Michal Grosek, March 10, 2000.

• DUNBAR, Dale

D – L. 6', 200 lbs. b: Winthrop, MA, 10/14/1961.

Season	Club	League	GP	G	A	Pts	AG	AA	APts	PIM	PP	SH	GW	S	%	TGF	PGF	TGA	PGA	+/–	GP	G	A	Pts	PIM	PP	SH	GW
1979-80	Winthrop High School	Hi-School	STATISTICS NOT AVAILABLE																									
1980-81	Boston University	ECAC	6	0	0	0	....	....	....	4	....	....	....	....	....	....	....	....	....	....	....	....	....	....	....	....	....	....
1981-82	Boston University	ECAC	DID NOT PLAY – ACADEMICALLY INELIGIBLE																									
1982-83	Boston University	ECAC	23	1	7	8	....	....	....	36	....	....	....	....	....	....	....	....	....	....	....	....	....	....	....	....	....	....
1983-84	Boston University	ECAC	34	0	15	15	....	....	....	49	....	....	....	....	....	....	....	....	....	....	....	....	....	....	....	....	....	....
1984-85	Boston University	H-East	39	2	19	21	....	....	....	62	....	....	....	....	....	....	....	....	....	....	....	....	....	....	....	....	....	....
1985-86	**Vancouver Canucks**	**NHL**	1	0	0	0	0	0	0	2	0	0	0	0	0.0	0	0	0	0	0	....	....	....	....	....	....	....	....
	Fredericton Express	AHL	32	2	10	12	....	....	....	26	....	....	....	....	....	....	....	....	....	....	....	....	....	....	....	....	....	....
1986-87	Peoria Rivermen	IHL	46	2	8	10	....	....	....	32	....	....	....	....	....	....	....	....	....	....	....	....	....	....	....	....	....	....
1987-88	Maine Mariners	AHL	66	1	7	8	....	....	....	120	....	....	....	....	....	....	....	....	....	....	9	1	1	2	33	....	....	....

			REGULAR SEASON																		PLAYOFFS							
Season	Club	League	GP	G	A	Pts	AG	AA	APts	PIM	PP	SH	GW	S	%	TGF	PGF	TGA	PGA	+/–	GP	G	A	Pts	PIM	PP	SH	GW
1988-89	**Boston Bruins**	**NHL**	**1**	**0**	**0**	**0**	**0**	**0**	**0**	**0**	**0**	**0**	**0**	**2**	**0.0**	**0**	**0**	**0**	**0**	**0**	....	....	....	....	....	....	....	....
	Maine Mariners	AHL	65	1	9	10	....	....	....	49	....	....	....	....	....	....	....	....	....	....	....	....	....	....	....	....	....	....
1989-90	HC Vaasa	Finland-2	25	2	17	19	....	....	....	34	....	....	....	....	....	....	....	....	....	....	....	....	....	....	....	....	....	....
1990-91	Solihull Barons	Un-Cup	1	0	0	0	....	....	....	2	....	....	....	....	....	....	....	....	....	....	....	....	....	....	....	....	....	....
	NHL Totals		**2**	**0**	**0**	**0**	**0**	**0**	**0**	**2**	**0**	**0**	**0**	**2**	**0.0**	**0**	**0**	**0**	**0**		....	....	....	....	....	....	....	....

Signed as a free agent by **Vancouver**, May 10, 1985. Signed as a free agent by **Boston**, August 25, 1987. • Suffered career-ending knee injury in Norwich Union Cup game vs. Cardiff, October, 1990.

• DUNCAN, Iain

Iain C. LW – L. 6'1", 200 lbs. b: Weston, Ont., 8/4/1963. Winnipeg's 8th, 134th overall, in 1983.

Season	Club	League	GP	G	A	Pts	AG	AA	APts	PIM	PP	SH	GW	S	%	TGF	PGF	TGA	PGA	+/–	GP	G	A	Pts	PIM	PP	SH	GW
1980-81	North York Raiders	OHA-B	13	3	11	14	....	....	....	30	....	....	....	....	....	....	....	....	....	....	....	....	....	....	....	....	....	....
	Wexford Warriors	OHA-B	2	1	0	1	....	....	....	0	....	....	....	....	....	....	....	....	....	....	....	....	....	....	....	....	....	....
1981-82	North York Rangers	OJHL	STATISTICS NOT AVAILABLE																									
1982-83	North York Flames	OJHL-B	15	10	14	24	....	....	....	89	....	....	....	....	....	....	....	....	....	....	....	....	....	....	....	....	....	....
	Orillia Travelways	OJHL	3	1	0	1	....	....	....	6	....	....	....	....	....	....	....	....	....	....	....	....	....	....	....	....	....	....
1983-84	Bowling Green University	CCHA	44	9	11	20	....	....	....	65	....	....	....	....	....	....	....	....	....	....	....	....	....	....	....	....	....	....
1984-85	Bowling Green University	CCHA	37	9	21	30	....	....	....	105	....	....	....	....	....	....	....	....	....	....	....	....	....	....	....	....	....	....
1985-86	Bowling Green University	CCHA	41	26	26	52	....	....	....	124	....	....	....	....	....	....	....	....	....	....	....	....	....	....	....	....	....	....
1986-87	Bowling Green University	CCHA	39	28	40	68	....	....	....	141	....	....	....	....	....	....	....	....	....	....	....	....	....	....	....	....	....	....
	Winnipeg Jets	**NHL**	**6**	**1**	**2**	**3**	**1**	**1**	**2**	**0**	**0**	**0**	**0**	**7**	**14.3**	**3**	**1**	**1**	**0**	**1**	**7**	**0**	**2**	**2**	**6**	**0**	**0**	**0**
1987-88	**Winnipeg Jets**	**NHL**	**62**	**19**	**23**	**42**	**16**	**16**	**32**	**73**	**4**	**0**	**4**	**104**	**18.3**	**56**	**13**	**46**	**1**	**–2**	**4**	**0**	**1**	**1**	**0**	**0**	**0**	**0**
	Moncton Hawks	AHL	8	1	3	4	....	....	....	26	....	....	....	....	....	....	....	....	....	....	....	....	....	....	....	....	....	....
1988-89	**Winnipeg Jets**	**NHL**	**57**	**14**	**30**	**44**	**12**	**21**	**33**	**74**	**1**	**0**	**0**	**91**	**15.4**	**65**	**25**	**57**	**0**	**–17**	....	....	....	....	....	....	....	....
1989-90	Moncton Hawks	AHL	49	16	25	41	....	....	....	81	....	....	....	....	....	....	....	....	....	....	....	....	....	....	....	....	....	....
1990-91	**Winnipeg Jets**	**NHL**	**2**	**0**	**0**	**0**	**0**	**0**	**0**	**2**	**0**	**0**	**0**	**2**	**0.0**	**0**	**0**	**1**	**0**	**–1**	....	....	....	....	....	....	....	....
	Moncton Hawks	AHL	66	19	45	64	....	....	....	105	....	....	....	....	....	....	....	....	....	....	8	3	4	7	40	....	....	....
1991-92	Phoenix Roadrunners	IHL	46	12	24	36	....	....	....	103	....	....	....	....	....	....	....	....	....	....	....	....	....	....	....	....	....	....
1992-93	Adirondack Red Wings	AHL	1	0	0	0	....	....	....	2	....	....	....	....	....	....	....	....	....	....	....	....	....	....	....	....	....	....
	Toledo Storm	ECHL	50	40	50	90	....	....	....	190	....	....	....	....	....	....	....	....	....	....	16	9	*19	28	55	....	....	....
1993-94	Toledo Storm	ECHL	8	6	8	14	....	....	....	23	....	....	....	....	....	....	....	....	....	....	14	6	11	17	32	....	....	....
1994-95	Toledo Storm	ECHL	37	9	34	43	....	....	....	133	....	....	....	....	....	....	....	....	....	....	4	1	2	3	10	....	....	....
1995-96			DID NOT PLAY																									
1996-97	Nashville Nighthawks	CHL	12	7	11	18	....	....	....	68	....	....	....	....	....	....	....	....	....	....	....	....	....	....	....	....	....	....
1997-98	Nashville Ice Flyers	CHL	35	4	22	26	....	....	....	77	....	....	....	....	....	....	....	....	....	....	....	....	....	....	....	....	....	....
	NHL Totals		**127**	**34**	**55**	**89**	**29**	**38**	**67**	**149**	**5**	**0**	**4**	**204**	**16.7**	**124**	**39**	**105**	**1**		**11**	**0**	**3**	**3**	**6**	**0**	**0**	**0**

CCHA First All-Star Team (1987) • NHL All-Rookie Team (1988) • ECHL Second All-Star Team (1993)

• Played w/ RHI's New Jersey R@R in 1994 (16-9-28-37-55) and 1995 (17-16-16-33-62).

• DUNCANSON, Craig

LW – L. 6', 190 lbs. b: Sudbury, Ont., 3/17/1967. Los Angeles' 1st, 9th overall, in 1985.

Season	Club	League	GP	G	A	Pts	AG	AA	APts	PIM	PP	SH	GW	S	%	TGF	PGF	TGA	PGA	+/–	GP	G	A	Pts	PIM	PP	SH	GW
1982-83	St. Michael's Buzzers	OJHL-B	32	14	19	33	....	....	....	68	....	....	....	....	....	....	....	....	....	....	....	....	....	....	....	....	....	....
1983-84	Sudbury Wolves	OHL	62	38	38	76	....	....	....	178	....	....	....	....	....	....	....	....	....	....	....	....	....	....	....	....	....	....
1984-85	Sudbury Wolves	OHL	53	35	28	63	....	....	....	129	....	....	....	....	....	....	....	....	....	....	....	....	....	....	....	....	....	....
1985-86	Sudbury Wolves	OHL	21	12	17	29	....	....	....	55	....	....	....	....	....	....	....	....	....	....	....	....	....	....	....	....	....	....
	Cornwall Royals	OHL	40	31	50	81	....	....	....	135	....	....	....	....	....	....	....	....	....	....	6	4	7	11	2	....	....	....
	Los Angeles Kings	**NHL**	**2**	**0**	**1**	**1**	**0**	**1**	**1**	**0**	**0**	**0**	**0**	**0**	**0.0**	**1**	**0**	**2**	**0**	**–1**	....	....	....	....	....	....	....	....
	New Haven Nighthawks	AHL	....	....	....	....	....	....	....	....	....	....	....	....	....	....	....	....	....	....	2	0	0	0	5	....	....	....
1986-87	Cornwall Royals	OHL	52	22	45	67	....	....	....	88	....	....	....	....	....	....	....	....	....	....	5	4	3	7	20	....	....	....
	Los Angeles Kings	**NHL**	**2**	**0**	**0**	**0**	**0**	**0**	**0**	**24**	**0**	**0**	**0**	**1**	**0.0**	**2**	**2**	**0**	**0**	**0**	....	....	....	....	....	....	....	....
1987-88	**Los Angeles Kings**	**NHL**	**9**	**0**	**0**	**0**	**0**	**0**	**0**	**12**	**0**	**0**	**0**	**8**	**0.0**	**2**	**1**	**6**	**0**	**–5**	....	....	....	....	....	....	....	....
	New Haven Nighthawks	AHL	57	15	25	40	....	....	....	170	....	....	....	....	....	....	....	....	....	....	....	....	....	....	....	....	....	....
1988-89	**Los Angeles Kings**	**NHL**	**5**	**0**	**0**	**0**	**0**	**0**	**0**	**0**	**0**	**0**	**0**	**1**	**0.0**	**0**	**0**	**1**	**0**	**–1**	....	....	....	....	....	....	....	....
	New Haven Nighthawks	AHL	69	25	39	64	....	....	....	200	....	....	....	....	....	....	....	....	....	....	17	4	8	12	60	....	....	....
1989-90	**Los Angeles Kings**	**NHL**	**10**	**3**	**2**	**5**	**3**	**1**	**4**	**9**	**0**	**0**	**0**	**12**	**25.0**	**6**	**0**	**5**	**0**	**1**	....	....	....	....	....	....	....	....
	New Haven Nighthawks	AHL	51	17	30	47	....	....	....	152	....	....	....	....	....	....	....	....	....	....	....	....	....	....	....	....	....	....
1990-91	**Winnipeg Jets**	**NHL**	**7**	**2**	**0**	**2**	**2**	**0**	**2**	**16**	**0**	**0**	**0**	**6**	**33.3**	**2**	**0**	**7**	**0**	**–5**	....	....	....	....	....	....	....	....
	Moncton Hawks	AHL	58	16	34	50	....	....	....	107	....	....	....	....	....	....	....	....	....	....	9	3	11	14	31	....	....	....
1991-92	Baltimore Skipjacks	AHL	46	20	26	46	....	....	....	98	....	....	....	....	....	....	....	....	....	....	....	....	....	....	....	....	....	....
	Moncton Hawks	AHL	19	12	9	21	....	....	....	6	....	....	....	....	....	....	....	....	....	....	11	6	4	10	10	....	....	....
1992-93	**New York Rangers**	**NHL**	**3**	**0**	**1**	**1**	**0**	**1**	**1**	**0**	**0**	**0**	**0**	**1**	**0.0**	**1**	**0**	**1**	**0**	**0**	....	....	....	....	....	....	....	....
	Binghamton Rangers	AHL	69	35	59	94	....	....	....	126	....	....	....	....	....	....	....	....	....	....	14	7	5	12	9	....	....	....
1993-94	Binghamton Rangers	AHL	70	25	44	69	....	....	....	83	....	....	....	....	....	....	....	....	....	....	....	....	....	....	....	....	....	....
1994-95	Binghamton Rangers	AHL	62	21	43	64	....	....	....	105	....	....	....	....	....	....	....	....	....	....	11	4	4	8	16	....	....	....
1995-96	Orlando Solar Bears	IHL	79	19	24	43	....	....	....	123	....	....	....	....	....	....	....	....	....	....	22	3	10	13	16	....	....	....
1996-97	Fort Wayne Komets	IHL	61	14	24	38	....	....	....	64	....	....	....	....	....	....	....	....	....	....	....	....	....	....	....	....	....	....
	Cincinnati Cyclones	IHL	21	3	11	14	....	....	....	19	....	....	....	....	....	....	....	....	....	....	3	1	1	2	0	....	....	....
1997-2000	Laurentian University	OUAA	DID NOT PLAY – COACHING																									
	NHL Totals		**38**	**5**	**4**	**9**	**5**	**3**	**8**	**61**	**0**	**0**	**0**	**29**	**17.2**	**14**	**3**	**22**	**0**		....	....	....	....	....	....	....	....

Traded to **Minnesota** by **LA Kings** for Daniel Berthiaume, September 6, 1990. Traded to **Winnipeg** by **Minnesota** for Brian Hunt, September 6, 1990. Traded to **Washington** by **Winnipeg** with Brent Hughes and Simon Wheeldon for Bob Joyce, Tyler Larter and Kent Paynter, May 21, 1991. Signed as a free agent by **NY Rangers**, September 4, 1992.

• DUNDAS, Rocky

RW – R. 6', 195 lbs. b: Regina, Sask., 1/30/1967. Montreal's 4th, 47th overall, in 1985.

Season	Club	League	GP	G	A	Pts	AG	AA	APts	PIM	PP	SH	GW	S	%	TGF	PGF	TGA	PGA	+/–	GP	G	A	Pts	PIM	PP	SH	GW
1982-83	Edmonton Maple Leafs	AAHA	38	52	46	98	....	....	....	122	....	....	....	....	....	....	....	....	....	....	....	....	....	....	....	....	....	....
	Edmonton Mets	AJHL	38	52	46	98	....	....	....	122	....	....	....	....	....	....	....	....	....	....	....	....	....	....	....	....	....	....
	Regina Pats	WHL	1	0	0	0	....	....	....	0	....	....	....	....	....	....	....	....	....	....	....	....	....	....	....	....	....	....
1983-84	Kelowna Wings	WHL	72	15	24	39	....	....	....	57	....	....	....	....	....	....	....	....	....	....	....	....	....	....	....	....	....	....
1984-85	Kelowna Wings	WHL	71	32	44	76	....	....	....	117	....	....	....	....	....	....	....	....	....	....	6	1	1	2	14	....	....	....
1985-86	Spokane Chiefs	WHL	71	31	70	101	....	....	....	160	....	....	....	....	....	....	....	....	....	....	9	2	5	7	28	....	....	....
1986-87	Spokane Chiefs	WHL	19	13	17	30	....	....	....	69	....	....	....	....	....	....	....	....	....	....	....	....	....	....	....	....	....	....
	Medicine Hat Tigers	WHL	29	22	24	46	....	....	....	63	....	....	....	....	....	....	....	....	....	....	20	4	8	12	44	....	....	....
	Medicine Hat Tigers	Mem-Cup	5	0	2	2	....	....	....	11	....	....	....	....	....	....	....	....	....	....	....	....	....	....	....	....	....	....
1987-88	Baltimore Skipjacks	AHL	9	0	1	1	....	....	....	46	....	....	....	....	....	....	....	....	....	....	....	....	....	....	....	....	....	....
	Sherbrooke Canadiens	AHL	38	9	6	15	....	....	....	104	....	....	....	....	....	....	....	....	....	....	3	0	0	0	7	....	....	....
1988-89	Sherbrooke Canadiens	AHL	63	12	29	41	....	....	....	212	....	....	....	....	....	....	....	....	....	....	2	2	0	2	8	....	....	....
1989-90	**Toronto Maple Leafs**	**NHL**	**5**	**0**	**0**	**0**	**0**	**0**	**0**	**14**	**0**	**0**	**0**	**1**	**0.0**	**1**	**0**	**2**	**0**	**–1**	....	....	....	....	....	....	....	....
	Newmarket Saints	AHL	62	18	15	33	....	....	....	158	....	....	....	....	....	....	....	....	....	....	....	....	....	....	....	....	....	....
	NHL Totals		**5**	**0**	**0**	**0**	**0**	**0**	**0**	**14**	**0**	**0**	**0**	**1**	**0.0**	**1**	**0**	**2**	**0**		....	....	....	....	....	....	....	....

Signed as a free agent by **Toronto**, October 4, 1989.

• DUNLOP, Blake

Blake Robert C – R. 5'10", 170 lbs. b: Hamilton, Ont., 4/4/1953. Minnesota's 1st, 18th overall, in 1973.

Season	Club	League	GP	G	A	Pts	AG	AA	APts	PIM	PP	SH	GW	S	%	TGF	PGF	TGA	PGA	+/–	GP	G	A	Pts	PIM	PP	SH	GW
1969-70	Ottawa Jr. Montagnards	OJHL	STATISTICS NOT AVAILABLE																									
	Ottawa 67's	OMJHL	45	17	15	32	....	....	....	10	....	....	....	....	....	....	....	....	....	....	11	3	5	8	6	....	....	....
1970-71	Ottawa 67's	OMJHL	62	44	46	90	....	....	....	39	....	....	....	....	....	....	....	....	....	....	11	3	6	9	9	....	....	....
1971-72	Ottawa 67's	OMJHL	62	32	52	84	....	....	....	41	....	....	....	....	....	....	....	....	....	....	18	9	12	21	2	....	....	....
1972-73	Ottawa 67's	OMJHL	62	60	*99	*159	....	....	....	50	....	....	....	....	....	....	....	....	....	....	9	10	16	26	6	....	....	....
1973-74	**Minnesota North Stars**	**NHL**	**12**	**0**	**0**	**0**	**0**	**0**	**0**	**2**	**0**	**0**	**0**	**11**	**0.0**	**1**	**0**	**4**	**0**	**–3**	....	....	....	....	....	....	....	....
	New Haven Nighthawks	AHL	59	37	41	78	....	....	....	25	....	....	....	....	....	....	....	....	....	....	10	7	7	14	4	....	....	....
1974-75	**Minnesota North Stars**	**NHL**	**52**	**9**	**18**	**27**	**8**	**13**	**21**	**8**	**2**	**0**	**3**	**82**	**11.0**	**42**	**11**	**38**	**0**	**–7**	....	....	....	....	....	....	....	....
1975-76	**Minnesota North Stars**	**NHL**	**33**	**9**	**11**	**20**	**8**	**8**	**16**	**8**	**1**	**0**	**1**	**55**	**16.4**	**25**	**5**	**29**	**0**	**–9**	....	....	....	....	....	....	....	....
	New Haven Nighthawks	AHL	10	2	10	12	....	....	....	8	....	....	....	....	....	....	....	....	....	....	....	....	....	....	....	....	....	....

Season	Club	League	GP	G	A	Pts	AG	AA	APts	PIM	PP	SH	GW	S	%	TGF	PGF	TGA	PGA	+/–	GP	G	A	Pts	PIM	PP	SH	GW
			REGULAR SEASON																		PLAYOFFS							
1976-77	**Minnesota North Stars**	**NHL**	**3**	**0**	**1**	**1**	**0**	**1**	**1**	**0**	**0**	**0**	**0**	**8**	**0.0**	**1**	**0**	**3**	**0**	**–2**	....	....	....	....	....	....	....	....
	New Haven Nighthawks	AHL	76	33	60	93	....	....	....	16	....	....	....	....	....	....	....	....	....	....	6	2	4	6	14	....	....	....
1977-78	Fort Worth Texans	CHL	6	4	2	6	....	....	....	11	....	....	....	....	....	....	....	....	....	....	....	....	....	....	....	....	....	....
	Philadelphia Flyers	**NHL**	**3**	**0**	**1**	**1**	**0**	**1**	**1**	**0**	**0**	**0**	**0**	**1**	**0.0**	**2**	**0**	**1**	**0**	**1**	....	....	....	....	....	....	....	....
	Maine Mariners	AHL	62	29	53	82	....	....	....	24	....	....	....	....	....	....	....	....	....	....	10	5	4	9	12	....	....	....
1978-79	**Philadelphia Flyers**	**NHL**	**66**	**20**	**28**	**48**	**17**	**20**	**37**	**16**	**5**	**0**	**5**	**122**	**16.4**	**65**	**14**	**36**	**12**	**27**	**8**	**1**	**1**	**2**	**4**	**0**	**0**	**0**
	Maine Mariners	AHL	12	9	5	14	....	....	....	6	....	....	....	....	....	....	....	....	....	....	....	....	....	....	....	....	....	....
1979-80	**St. Louis Blues**	**NHL**	**72**	**18**	**27**	**45**	**15**	**20**	**35**	**28**	**8**	**0**	**2**	**101**	**17.8**	**62**	**21**	**49**	**2**	**–6**	**3**	**0**	**2**	**2**	**2**	**0**	**0**	**0**
1980-81	**St. Louis Blues**	**NHL**	**80**	**20**	**67**	**87**	**16**	**45**	**61**	**40**	**6**	**0**	**2**	**134**	**14.9**	**123**	**43**	**67**	**3**	**16**	**11**	**0**	**3**	**3**	**4**	**0**	**0**	**0**
1981-82	**St. Louis Blues**	**NHL**	**77**	**25**	**53**	**78**	**20**	**35**	**55**	**32**	**10**	**1**	**1**	**129**	**19.4**	**105**	**38**	**86**	**10**	**–9**	**10**	**2**	**2**	**4**	**4**	**0**	**0**	**0**
1982-83	**St. Louis Blues**	**NHL**	**78**	**22**	**44**	**66**	**18**	**31**	**49**	**14**	**8**	**0**	**2**	**135**	**16.3**	**90**	**25**	**86**	**15**	**–6**	**4**	**1**	**1**	**2**	**0**	**1**	**0**	**0**
1983-84	**St. Louis Blues**	**NHL**	**17**	**1**	**10**	**11**	**1**	**7**	**8**	**4**	**0**	**0**	**0**	**18**	**5.6**	**17**	**4**	**25**	**11**	**–1**	....	....	....	....	....	....	....	....
	Detroit Red Wings	**NHL**	**57**	**6**	**14**	**20**	**5**	**10**	**15**	**20**	**1**	**1**	**0**	**67**	**9.0**	**32**	**1**	**63**	**19**	**–13**	**4**	**0**	**1**	**1**	**4**	**0**	**0**	**0**
	NHL Totals		**550**	**130**	**274**	**404**	**108**	**191**	**299**	**172**	**41**	**2**	**16**	**863**	**15.1**	**565**	**162**	**487**	**72**		**40**	**4**	**10**	**14**	**18**	**1**	**0**	**0**

OMJHL Second All-Star Team (1973) • AHL First All-Star Team (1978) • Won Fred T. Hunt Memorial Trophy (Sportsmanship - AHL) (1978) • Won Les Cunningham Award (MVP - AHL) (1978) • Won Bill Masterton Trophy (1981)

Traded to **Philadelphia** by **Minnesota** with Minnesota's 3rd round choice (Gord Salt) in 1978 Amateur Draft for Harvey Bennett Jr., October 28, 1977. Traded to **St. Louis** by **Philadelphia** with Rick Lapointe for Phil Myre, June 7, 1979. Signed as a free agent by **Detroit**, December 2, 1983.

• DUNN, Dave

David George "Red"   D – L. 6'2", 200 lbs.   b: Moosomin, Sask., 8/19/1948.

Season	Club	League	GP	G	A	Pts	AG	AA	APts	PIM	PP	SH	GW	S	%	TGF	PGF	TGA	PGA	+/–	GP	G	A	Pts	PIM	PP	SH	GW
1965-66	Wapella Hawks	SIHA	STATISTICS NOT AVAILABLE																									
1966-67	University of Saskatchewan	WCIAA	14	3	7	10	....	....	....	12	....	....	....	....	....	....	....	....	....	....	....	....	....	....	....	....	....	....
1967-68	University of Saskatchewan	WCIAA	16	2	5	7	....	....	....	21	....	....	....	....	....	....	....	....	....	....	....	....	....	....	....	....	....	....
1968-69	University of Saskatchewan	WCIAA	20	4	10	14	....	....	....	50	....	....	....	....	....	....	....	....	....	....	....	....	....	....	....	....	....	....
1969-70	University of Saskatchewan	WCIAA	14	14	8	22	....	....	....	22	....	....	....	....	....	....	....	....	....	....	....	....	....	....	....	....	....	....
1970-71	Rochester Americans	AHL	56	2	13	15	....	....	....	74	....	....	....	....	....	....	....	....	....	....	....	....	....	....	....	....	....	....
1971-72	Rochester Americans	AHL	8	1	0	1	....	....	....	18	....	....	....	....	....	....	....	....	....	....	....	....	....	....	....	....	....	....
	Seattle Totems	WHL	46	10	12	22	....	....	....	104	....	....	....	....	....	....	....	....	....	....	....	....	....	....	....	....	....	....
1972-73	Seattle Totems	WHL	63	19	56	75	....	....	....	147	....	....	....	....	....	....	....	....	....	....	....	....	....	....	....	....	....	....
1973-74	**Vancouver Canucks**	**NHL**	**68**	**11**	**22**	**33**	**11**	**18**	**29**	**76**	**0**	**0**	**1**	**97**	**11.3**	**56**	**10**	**59**	**0**	**–13**	....	....	....	....	....	....	....	....
1974-75	**Vancouver Canucks**	**NHL**	**1**	**0**	**0**	**0**	**0**	**0**	**0**	**11**	**0**	**0**	**0**	**1**	**0.0**	**0**	**0**	**0**	**0**	**0**	....	....	....	....	....	....	....	....
	Toronto Maple Leafs	**NHL**	**72**	**3**	**11**	**14**	**3**	**8**	**11**	**142**	**0**	**0**	**2**	**76**	**3.9**	**58**	**3**	**86**	**21**	**–10**	**7**	**1**	**1**	**2**	**24**	**0**	**0**	**0**
1975-76	**Toronto Maple Leafs**	**NHL**	**43**	**0**	**8**	**8**	**0**	**6**	**6**	**84**	**0**	**0**	**0**	**43**	**0.0**	**36**	**3**	**51**	**13**	**–5**	**3**	**0**	**0**	**0**	**17**	**0**	**0**	**0**
	Oklahoma City Blazers	CHL	9	1	7	8	....	....	....	10	....	....	....	....	....	....	....	....	....	....	....	....	....	....	....	....	....	....
1976-77	Winnipeg Jets	WHA	40	3	11	14	....	....	....	129	....	....	....	....	....	....	....	....	....	....	20	4	4	8	23	....	....	....
1977-78	Winnipeg Jets	WHA	66	6	20	26	....	....	....	79	....	....	....	....	....	....	....	....	....	....	9	1	2	3	0	....	....	....
	NHL Totals		**184**	**14**	**41**	**55**	**14**	**32**	**46**	**313**	**0**	**0**	**3**	**217**	**6.5**	**150**	**16**	**196**	**34**		**10**	**1**	**1**	**2**	**41**	**0**	**0**	**0**
	Other Major League Totals		106	9	31	40	....	....	....	208	....	....	....	....	....	....	....	....	....	....	29	5	6	11	23	....	....	....

WHL First All-Star Team (1973) • Won Hal Laycoe Cup (WHL Top Defenseman) (1973)

Signed as a free agent by **Vancouver** September 20, 1970. Traded to **Toronto** by **Vancouver** for Garry Monahan and John Grisdale, October 16, 1974. Signed as a free agent by **Winnipeg** (WHA), September, 1976.

• DUNN, Richie

Richard L.   D – L. 6', 200 lbs.   b: Boston, MA, 5/12/1957.

Season	Club	League	GP	G	A	Pts	AG	AA	APts	PIM	PP	SH	GW	S	%	TGF	PGF	TGA	PGA	+/–	GP	G	A	Pts	PIM	PP	SH	GW
1974-75	Stoughton Vikings	Hi-School	STATISTICS NOT AVAILABLE																									
	Kingston Canadians	OMJHL	....	....	....	....	....	....	....	....	....	....	....	....	....	....	....	....	....	....	8	1	1	2	4	....	....	....
1975-76	Kingston Canadians	OMJHL	61	7	18	25	....	....	....	62	....	....	....	....	....	....	....	....	....	....	4	0	0	0	4	....	....	....
1976-77	Windsor Spitfires	OMJHL	66	5	21	26	....	....	....	98	....	....	....	....	....	....	....	....	....	....	9	0	5	5	4	....	....	....
	United States	WJC-A	....	....	....	....	....	....	....	....	....	....	....	....	....	....	....	....	....	....	....	....	....	....	....	....	....	....
1977-78	**Buffalo Sabres**	**NHL**	**25**	**0**	**3**	**3**	**0**	**2**	**2**	**16**	**0**	**0**	**0**	**23**	**0.0**	**10**	**0**	**13**	**0**	**–3**	**1**	**0**	**0**	**0**	**2**	**0**	**0**	**0**
	Hershey Bears	AHL	54	7	22	29	....	....	....	17	....	....	....	....	....	....	....	....	....	....	....	....	....	....	....	....	....	....
1978-79	**Buffalo Sabres**	**NHL**	**24**	**0**	**3**	**3**	**0**	**2**	**2**	**14**	**0**	**0**	**0**	**18**	**0.0**	**11**	**1**	**12**	**0**	**–2**	....	....	....	....	....	....	....	....
	Hershey Bears	AHL	34	5	18	23	....	....	....	10	....	....	....	....	....	....	....	....	....	....	4	0	1	1	4	....	....	....
1979-80	**Buffalo Sabres**	**NHL**	**80**	**7**	**31**	**38**	**6**	**23**	**29**	**61**	**4**	**0**	**2**	**147**	**4.8**	**100**	**26**	**62**	**13**	**25**	**14**	**2**	**8**	**10**	**8**	**2**	**0**	**0**
1980-81	**Buffalo Sabres**	**NHL**	**79**	**7**	**42**	**49**	**5**	**28**	**33**	**34**	**4**	**0**	**1**	**175**	**4.0**	**137**	**46**	**90**	**20**	**21**	**8**	**0**	**5**	**5**	**6**	**0**	**0**	**0**
1981-82	United States	Can-Cup	6	1	3	4	....	....	....	4	....	....	....	....	....	....	....	....	....	....	....	....	....	....	....	....	....	....
	Buffalo Sabres	**NHL**	**72**	**7**	**19**	**26**	**6**	**13**	**19**	**73**	**0**	**0**	**1**	**122**	**5.7**	**96**	**17**	**103**	**30**	**6**	**4**	**0**	**1**	**1**	**0**	**0**	**0**	**0**
1982-83	**Calgary Flames**	**NHL**	**80**	**3**	**11**	**14**	**2**	**8**	**10**	**47**	**0**	**0**	**1**	**88**	**3.4**	**75**	**5**	**84**	**10**	**–4**	**9**	**1**	**1**	**2**	**8**	**0**	**0**	**0**
1983-84	**Hartford Whalers**	**NHL**	**63**	**5**	**20**	**25**	**4**	**14**	**18**	**30**	**0**	**0**	**0**	**82**	**6.1**	**76**	**18**	**96**	**18**	**–20**	....	....	....	....	....	....	....	....
1984-85	**Hartford Whalers**	**NHL**	**13**	**1**	**4**	**5**	**1**	**3**	**4**	**2**	**0**	**0**	**0**	**17**	**5.9**	**14**	**1**	**21**	**5**	**–3**	....	....	....	....	....	....	....	....
	Binghamton Whalers	AHL	64	9	39	48	....	....	....	43	....	....	....	....	....	....	....	....	....	....	8	2	2	4	8	....	....	....
1985-86	**Buffalo Sabres**	**NHL**	**29**	**4**	**5**	**9**	**3**	**3**	**6**	**25**	**4**	**0**	**0**	**55**	**7.3**	**33**	**14**	**33**	**9**	**–5**	....	....	....	....	....	....	....	....
	Rochester Americans	AHL	34	6	17	23	....	....	....	12	....	....	....	....	....	....	....	....	....	....	....	....	....	....	....	....	....	....
	United States	WEC-A	10	1	1	2	....	....	....	2	....	....	....	....	....	....	....	....	....	....	....	....	....	....	....	....	....	....
1986-87	**Buffalo Sabres**	**NHL**	**2**	**0**	**1**	**1**	**0**	**1**	**1**	**2**	**0**	**0**	**0**	**1**	**0.0**	**5**	**0**	**2**	**0**	**2**	....	....	....	....	....	....	....	....
	Rochester Americans	AHL	64	6	26	32	....	....	....	47	....	....	....	....	....	....	....	....	....	....	18	1	6	7	6	....	....	....
1987-88	**Buffalo Sabres**	**NHL**	**12**	**2**	**0**	**2**	**2**	**0**	**2**	**8**	**0**	**0**	**0**	**19**	**10.5**	**7**	**2**	**14**	**2**	**–7**	....	....	....	....	....	....	....	....
	Rochester Americans	AHL	68	12	35	47	....	....	....	52	....	....	....	....	....	....	....	....	....	....	7	3	3	6	2	....	....	....
1988-89	**Buffalo Sabres**	**NHL**	**4**	**0**	**1**	**1**	**0**	**1**	**1**	**2**	**0**	**0**	**0**	**2**	**0.0**	**2**	**1**	**4**	**2**	**–1**	....	....	....	....	....	....	....	....
	Rochester Americans	AHL	69	9	35	44	....	....	....	81	....	....	....	....	....	....	....	....	....	....	....	....	....	....	....	....	....	....
1989-90	Rochester Americans	AHL	41	7	7	14	....	....	....	34	....	....	....	....	....	....	....	....	....	....	7	0	4	4	4	....	....	....
	NHL Totals		**483**	**36**	**140**	**176**	**29**	**98**	**127**	**314**	**12**	**0**	**5**	**749**	**4.8**	**566**	**131**	**534**	**109**		**36**	**3**	**15**	**18**	**24**	**2**	**0**	**0**

AHL First All-Star Team (1985, 1987) • Won Eddie Shore Award (Outstanding Defenseman - AHL) (1985) • AHL Second All-Star Team (1988)

Signed as a free agent by **Buffalo**, October 3, 1977. Traded to **Calgary** by **Buffalo** with Don Edwards and Buffalo's 2nd round choice (Rich Kromm) in 1982 Entry Draft for Calgary's 1st (Paul Cyr) and 2nd (Jens Johansson) round choices in the 1982 Entry Draft and 3rd round choice (John Tucker) in 1983 Entry Draft, June 9, 1982. Traded to **Hartford** by **Calgary** with Joel Quenneville for Mickey Volcan, July 5, 1983. Signed as a free agent by **Buffalo**, July 10, 1986.

• DUPERE, Denis

Denis Gilles   LW – L. 6'1", 200 lbs.   b: Jonquiere, Que., 6/21/1948.

Season	Club	League	GP	G	A	Pts	AG	AA	APts	PIM	PP	SH	GW	S	%	TGF	PGF	TGA	PGA	+/–	GP	G	A	Pts	PIM	PP	SH	GW
1964-65	Jonquiere Marquis	QJHL	STATISTICS NOT AVAILABLE																									
1965-66	Jonquiere Marquis	QJHL	STATISTICS NOT AVAILABLE																									
	Jonquiere Marquis	Mem-Cup	3	1	1	2	....	....	....	0	....	....	....	....	....	....	....	....	....	....	....	....	....	....	....	....	....	....
1966-67	Jonquiere Marquis	QJHL	STATISTICS NOT AVAILABLE																									
	Kitchener Rangers	OHA-Jr.	4	1	1	2	....	....	....	0	....	....	....	....	....	....	....	....	....	....	....	....	....	....	....	....	....	....
1967-68	Kitchener Rangers	OHA-Jr.	54	35	24	59	....	....	....	22	....	....	....	....	....	....	....	....	....	....	19	2	7	9	20	....	....	....
1968-69	Ottawa Nationals	OHA-Sr.	5	4	4	8	....	....	....	7	....	....	....	....	....	....	....	....	....	....	....	....	....	....	....	....	....	....
	Canada	Nat-Team	STATISTICS NOT AVAILABLE																									
1969-70	Omaha Knights	CHL	72	33	19	52	....	....	....	35	....	....	....	....	....	....	....	....	....	....	12	5	7	12	11	....	....	....
1970-71	**Toronto Maple Leafs**	**NHL**	**20**	**1**	**2**	**3**	**1**	**2**	**3**	**4**	**1**	**0**	**0**	**18**	**5.6**	**4**	**1**	**8**	**4**	**–1**	**6**	**0**	**0**	**0**	**0**	**0**	**0**	**0**
	Tulsa Oilers	CHL	48	20	34	54	....	....	....	40	....	....	....	....	....	....	....	....	....	....	....	....	....	....	....	....	....	....
1971-72	**Toronto Maple Leafs**	**NHL**	**77**	**7**	**10**	**17**	**7**	**9**	**16**	**4**	**1**	**0**	**0**	**55**	**12.7**	**23**	**6**	**40**	**28**	**5**	**5**	**0**	**0**	**0**	**0**	**0**	**0**	**0**
1972-73	**Toronto Maple Leafs**	**NHL**	**61**	**13**	**23**	**36**	**12**	**18**	**30**	**10**	**4**	**0**	**0**	**129**	**10.1**	**56**	**12**	**66**	**18**	**–4**	....	....	....	....	....	....	....	....
1973-74	**Toronto Maple Leafs**	**NHL**	**34**	**8**	**9**	**17**	**8**	**7**	**15**	**8**	**2**	**0**	**0**	**53**	**15.1**	**28**	**9**	**18**	**2**	**3**	**3**	**0**	**0**	**0**	**0**	**0**	**0**	**0**
1974-75	**Washington Capitals**	**NHL**	**53**	**20**	**15**	**35**	**17**	**11**	**28**	**8**	**8**	**0**	**0**	**133**	**15.0**	**44**	**18**	**70**	**3**	**–41**	....	....	....	....	....	....	....	....
	St. Louis Blues	**NHL**	**22**	**3**	**6**	**9**	**3**	**4**	**7**	**8**	**1**	**0**	**0**	**35**	**8.6**	**13**	**1**	**8**	**0**	**4**	....	....	....	....	....	....	....	....
1975-76	**Kansas City Scouts**	**NHL**	**43**	**6**	**8**	**14**	**5**	**6**	**11**	**16**	**2**	**0**	**0**	**37**	**16.2**	**19**	**2**	**26**	**1**	**–8**	....	....	....	....	....	....	....	....
1976-77	**Colorado Rockies**	**NHL**	**57**	**7**	**11**	**18**	**6**	**8**	**14**	**4**	**1**	**3**	**2**	**60**	**11.7**	**30**	**3**	**41**	**17**	**3**	....	....	....	....	....	....	....	....
	Rhode Island Reds	AHL	4	3	3	6	....	....	....	0	....	....	....	....	....	....	....	....	....	....	....	....	....	....	....	....	....	....
1977-78	**Colorado Rockies**	**NHL**	**54**	**15**	**15**	**30**	**14**	**12**	**26**	**4**	**2**	**2**	**4**	**67**	**22.4**	**41**	**7**	**40**	**15**	**9**	**2**	**1**	**0**	**1**	**0**	**1**	**0**	**0**
	Hampton Gulls	AHL	1	2	0	2	....	....	....	0	....	....	....	....	....	....	....	....	....	....	....	....	....	....	....	....	....	....
	Philadelphia Firebirds	AHL	12	3	2	5	....	....	....	10	....	....	....	....	....	....	....	....	....	....	....	....	....	....	....	....	....	....

Season	Club	League	REGULAR SEASON																		PLAYOFFS							
Season	Club	League	GP	G	A	Pts	AG	AA	APts	PIM	PP	SH	GW	S	%	TGF	PGF	TGA	PGA	+/–	GP	G	A	Pts	PIM	PP	SH	GW
1978-79			DID NOT PLAY																									
1979-80	Nelson Maple Leafs	WIHL	10	2	5	7	....	....	....	....	....	....	....	....	....	....	....	....	....	....	....	....	....	....	....	....	....	....
1980-81	HC Lyon	France	18	16	11	27	....	....	....	....	....	....	....	....	....	....	....	....	....	....	....	....	....	....	....	....	....	....
	NHL Totals		**421**	**80**	**99**	**179**	**73**	**77**	**150**	**66**	**22**	**5**	**6**	**587**	**13.6**	**258**	**59**	**317**	**88**		**16**	**1**	**0**	**1**	**0**	**1**	**0**	**0**

Played in NHL All-Star Game (1975)

Traded to **Toronto** by **NY Rangers** to complete transaction that sent Tim Horton to NY Rangers, (March 3, 1970), May 14, 1970. Claimed by **Washington** from **Toronto** in Expansion Draft, June 12, 1974. Traded to **St. Louis** by **Washington** for Garnet Bailey and Stan Gilbertson, February 10, 1975. Traded to **Kansas City** by **St. Louis** with Craig Patrick and cash for Lynn Powis and Kansas City's 2nd round choice (Brian Sutter) in 1976 Amateur Draft, June 18, 1975. Transferred to **Colorado** when **Kansas City** franchise relocated, July 15, 1976.

• DUPONT, Andre

"Moose" D – L. 6', 200 lbs. b: Trois Rivieres, Que., 7/27/1949. NY Rangers' 1st, 8th overall, in 1969.

Season	Club	League	GP	G	A	Pts	AG	AA	APts	PIM	PP	SH	GW	S	%	TGF	PGF	TGA	PGA	+/–	GP	G	A	Pts	PIM	PP	SH	GW
1965-66	Trois-Rivieres Reds	QJHL	5	2	0	2	....	....	....	11	....	....	....	....	....	....	....	....	....	....	....	....	....	....	....	....	....	....
1966-67	Trois-Rivieres Leafs	QJHL	45	5	24	29	....	....	....	*310	....	....	....	....	....	....	....	....	....	....	14	2	7	9	52	....	....	....
	Thetford Mines Jr. Canadiens	Mem-Cup	1	0	0	0	....	....	....	4	....	....	....	....	....	....	....	....	....	....	....	....	....	....	....	....	....	....
1967-68	Trois-Rivieres Leafs	QJHL	....	....	....	....	....	....	....	....	....	....	....	....	....	....	....	....	....	....	4	0	7	7	10	....	....	....
	Verdun Maple Leafs	Mem-Cup	5	0	1	1	....	....	....	10	....	....	....	....	....	....	....	....	....	....	....	....	....	....	....	....	....	....
1968-69	Montreal Jr. Canadiens	OHA-Jr.	38	2	14	16	....	....	....	212	....	....	....	....	....	....	....	....	....	....	14	2	8	10	*76	....	....	....
	Montreal Jr. Canadiens	Mem-Cup	8	2	3	5	....	....	....	*39	....	....	....	....	....	....	....	....	....	....	....	....	....	....	....	....	....	....
1969-70	Omaha Knights	CHL	64	11	26	37	....	....	....	258	....	....	....	....	....	....	....	....	....	....	12	1	8	9	*75	....	....	....
1970-71	**New York Rangers**	**NHL**	**7**	**1**	**2**	**3**	**1**	**2**	**3**	**21**	**0**	**0**	**0**	**17**	**5.9**	**5**	**1**	**3**	**0**	**1**	....	....	....	....	....	....	....	....
	Omaha Knights	CHL	54	15	31	46	....	....	....	*308	....	....	....	....	....	....	....	....	....	....	11	0	7	7	*45	....	....	....
1971-72	**St. Louis Blues**	**NHL**	**60**	**3**	**10**	**13**	**3**	**9**	**12**	**147**	**0**	**0**	**0**	**133**	**2.3**	**63**	**1**	**66**	**15**	**11**	**11**	**1**	**0**	**1**	**20**	**0**	**0**	**0**
	Providence Reds	AHL	18	1	8	9	....	....	....	95	....	....	....	....	....	....	....	....	....	....	....	....	....	....	....	....	....	....
1972-73	**St. Louis Blues**	**NHL**	**25**	**1**	**6**	**7**	**1**	**5**	**6**	**51**	**0**	**0**	**0**	**38**	**2.6**	**24**	**2**	**30**	**6**	**–2**	....	....	....	....	....	....	....	....
	Philadelphia Flyers	**NHL**	**46**	**3**	**20**	**23**	**3**	**16**	**19**	**164**	**1**	**0**	**1**	**103**	**2.9**	**71**	**16**	**63**	**16**	**8**	**11**	**1**	**2**	**3**	**29**	**0**	**0**	**0**
1973-74♦	**Philadelphia Flyers**	**NHL**	**75**	**3**	**20**	**23**	**3**	**16**	**19**	**216**	**2**	**0**	**1**	**165**	**1.8**	**88**	**20**	**49**	**15**	**34**	**16**	**4**	**3**	**7**	**67**	**0**	**0**	**0**
1974-75♦	**Philadelphia Flyers**	**NHL**	**80**	**11**	**21**	**32**	**10**	**16**	**26**	**276**	**2**	**0**	**4**	**164**	**6.7**	**97**	**13**	**70**	**27**	**41**	**17**	**3**	**2**	**5**	**49**	**1**	**0**	**2**
1975-76	**Philadelphia Flyers**	**NHL**	**75**	**9**	**27**	**36**	**8**	**20**	**28**	**214**	**3**	**0**	**2**	**139**	**6.5**	**105**	**23**	**72**	**30**	**40**	**15**	**2**	**2**	**4**	**46**	**2**	**0**	**0**
1976-77	**Philadelphia Flyers**	**NHL**	**59**	**10**	**19**	**29**	**9**	**15**	**24**	**168**	**1**	**0**	**0**	**110**	**9.1**	**110**	**8**	**61**	**16**	**57**	**10**	**1**	**1**	**2**	**35**	**0**	**0**	**0**
1977-78	**Philadelphia Flyers**	**NHL**	**69**	**2**	**12**	**14**	**2**	**9**	**11**	**225**	**0**	**0**	**0**	**108**	**1.9**	**72**	**1**	**66**	**26**	**31**	**12**	**2**	**1**	**3**	**13**	**0**	**0**	**0**
1978-79	**Philadelphia Flyers**	**NHL**	**77**	**3**	**9**	**12**	**3**	**7**	**10**	**135**	**0**	**0**	**0**	**128**	**2.3**	**89**	**2**	**95**	**29**	**21**	**8**	**0**	**0**	**0**	**17**	**0**	**0**	**0**
1979-80	**Philadelphia Flyers**	**NHL**	**58**	**1**	**7**	**8**	**1**	**5**	**6**	**107**	**0**	**0**	**0**	**67**	**1.5**	**75**	**0**	**49**	**11**	**37**	**19**	**0**	**4**	**4**	**50**	**0**	**0**	**0**
1980-81	**Quebec Nordiques**	**NHL**	**63**	**5**	**8**	**13**	**4**	**5**	**9**	**93**	**1**	**1**	**0**	**72**	**6.9**	**89**	**8**	**116**	**41**	**6**	**1**	**0**	**0**	**0**	**0**	**0**	**0**	**0**
1981-82	**Quebec Nordiques**	**NHL**	**60**	**4**	**12**	**16**	**3**	**8**	**11**	**100**	**0**	**0**	**2**	**62**	**6.5**	**78**	**1**	**103**	**29**	**3**	**16**	**0**	**3**	**3**	**18**	**0**	**0**	**0**
1982-83	**Quebec Nordiques**	**NHL**	**46**	**3**	**12**	**15**	**2**	**8**	**10**	**69**	**0**	**0**	**0**	**42**	**7.1**	**53**	**0**	**64**	**22**	**11**	**4**	**0**	**0**	**0**	**8**	**0**	**0**	**0**
	NHL Totals		**800**	**59**	**185**	**244**	**53**	**141**	**194**	**1986**	**10**	**1**	**10**	**1348**	**4.4**	**1019**	**96**	**907**	**283**		**140**	**14**	**18**	**32**	**352**	**3**	**0**	**2**

QJHL Second All-Star Team (1968) • CHL Second All-Star Team (1970) • Won Ken McKenzie Trophy (CHL's Rookie of the Year) (1970) • CHL First All-Star Team (1971) • Named CHL's Top Defenseman (1971) • Shared Tommy Ivan Trophy (MVP - CHL) with Gerry Ouellette, Peter McDuffe & Joe Zanussi (1971) • Played in NHL All-Star Game (1976)

• Regular season totals for Trois-Rivieres (QJHL) in 1967-68 unavailable. Loaned to **Verdun** (MMJHL) by **Trois-Rivieres** (QJHL) for Memorial Cup playoffs, March, 1968. Traded to **St. Louis** by **NY Rangers** with Jack Egers and Mike Murphy for Gene Carr, Jim Lorentz and Wayne Connelly, November 15, 1971. Traded to **Philadelphia** by **St. Louis** with St. Louis' 3rd round choice (Bob Stumpf) in 1973 Amateur Draft for Brent Hughes and Pierre Plante, December 14, 1972. Traded to **Quebec** by **Philadelphia** for cash and Quebec's 7th round choice (Vladimir Svitek) in 1981 Entry Draft, September 15, 1980.

• DUPONT, Jerome

Jerome Robert "Jerry" D – L. 6'3", 190 lbs. b: Ottawa, Ont., 2/21/1962. Chicago's 2nd, 15th overall, in 1980.

Season	Club	League	GP	G	A	Pts	AG	AA	APts	PIM	PP	SH	GW	S	%	TGF	PGF	TGA	PGA	+/–	GP	G	A	Pts	PIM	PP	SH	GW
1977-78	Gloucester Rangers	OMHA	63	29	42	71	....	....	....	143	....	....	....	....	....	....	....	....	....	....	....	....	....	....	....	....	....	....
1978-79	Toronto Marlboros	OMJHL	68	5	21	26	....	....	....	49	....	....	....	....	....	....	....	....	....	....	3	0	0	0	0	....	....	....
1979-80	Toronto Marlboros	OMJHL	67	7	37	44	....	....	....	88	....	....	....	....	....	....	....	....	....	....	4	1	1	2	5	....	....	....
	Markham Waxers	OJHL	1	0	1	1	....	....	....	0	....	....	....	....	....	....	....	....	....	....	....	....	....	....	....	....	....	....
1980-81	Toronto Marlboros	OMJHL	67	6	38	44	....	....	....	116	....	....	....	....	....	....	....	....	....	....	5	2	2	4	9	....	....	....
1981-82	Toronto Marlboros	OHL	7	0	8	8	....	....	....	18	....	....	....	....	....	....	....	....	....	....	10	3	9	12	24	....	....	....
	Chicago Black Hawks	**NHL**	**34**	**0**	**4**	**4**	**0**	**3**	**3**	**51**	**0**	**0**	**0**	**22**	**0.0**	**21**	**1**	**22**	**0**	**–2**	....	....	....	....	....	....	....	....
1982-83	**Chicago Black Hawks**	**NHL**	**1**	**0**	**0**	**0**	**0**	**0**	**0**	**0**	**0**	**0**	**0**	**0**	**0.0**	**0**	**0**	**0**	**0**	**0**	....	....	....	....	....	....	....	....
	Springfield Indians	AHL	78	12	22	34	....	....	....	114	....	....	....	....	....	....	....	....	....	....	....	....	....	....	....	....	....	....
1983-84	**Chicago Black Hawks**	**NHL**	**36**	**2**	**2**	**4**	**2**	**1**	**3**	**116**	**0**	**0**	**0**	**28**	**7.1**	**13**	**1**	**25**	**2**	**–11**	**4**	**0**	**0**	**0**	**15**	**0**	**0**	**0**
	Springfield Indians	AHL	12	2	3	5	....	....	....	65	....	....	....	....	....	....	....	....	....	....	....	....	....	....	....	....	....	....
1984-85	**Chicago Black Hawks**	**NHL**	**55**	**3**	**10**	**13**	**2**	**7**	**9**	**105**	**0**	**0**	**1**	**54**	**5.6**	**44**	**1**	**47**	**9**	**5**	**15**	**0**	**2**	**2**	**41**	**0**	**0**	**0**
1985-86	**Chicago Black Hawks**	**NHL**	**75**	**2**	**13**	**15**	**2**	**9**	**11**	**173**	**0**	**0**	**0**	**69**	**2.9**	**62**	**1**	**108**	**30**	**–17**	**1**	**0**	**0**	**0**	**0**	**0**	**0**	**0**
1986-87	**Toronto Maple Leafs**	**NHL**	**13**	**0**	**0**	**0**	**0**	**0**	**0**	**23**	**0**	**0**	**0**	**5**	**0.0**	**3**	**0**	**8**	**0**	**–5**	....	....	....	....	....	....	....	....
	Newmarket Saints	AHL	29	1	8	9	....	....	....	47	....	....	....	....	....	....	....	....	....	....	....	....	....	....	....	....	....	....
	NHL Totals		**214**	**7**	**29**	**36**	**6**	**20**	**26**	**468**	**0**	**0**	**1**	**178**	**3.9**	**143**	**4**	**210**	**41**		**20**	**0**	**2**	**2**	**56**	**0**	**0**	**0**

Transferred to **Toronto** by **Chicago** with Ken Yaremchuk and Chicago's 4th round choice (Joe Sacco) in 1987 Entry Draft as compensation for Chicago's signing of free agent Gary Nylund, September 6, 1986.

• DUPONT, Norm

Normand LW – L. 5'10", 185 lbs. b: Montreal, Que., 2/5/1957. Montreal's 2nd, 18th overall, in 1977.

Season	Club	League	GP	G	A	Pts	AG	AA	APts	PIM	PP	SH	GW	S	%	TGF	PGF	TGA	PGA	+/–	GP	G	A	Pts	PIM	PP	SH	GW
1973-74	Montreal Red-White-Blue	QMJHL	70	55	70	125	....	....	....	4	....	....	....	....	....	....	....	....	....	....	....	....	....	....	....	....	....	....
1974-75	Montreal Red-White-Blue	QMJHL	72	*84	74	*158	....	....	....	13	....	....	....	....	....	....	....	....	....	....	....	....	....	....	....	....	....	....
1975-76	Montreal Jr. Canadiens	QMJHL	70	69	63	132	....	....	....	8	....	....	....	....	....	....	....	....	....	....	6	7	3	10	0	....	....	....
1976-77	Montreal Juniors	QMJHL	71	70	83	153	....	....	....	52	....	....	....	....	....	....	....	....	....	....	13	9	10	19	9	....	....	....
1977-78	Nova Scotia Voyageurs	AHL	81	31	29	60	....	....	....	21	....	....	....	....	....	....	....	....	....	....	....	....	....	....	....	....	....	....
1978-79	Nova Scotia Voyageurs	AHL	48	27	31	58	....	....	....	10	....	....	....	....	....	....	....	....	....	....	10	*7	4	11	2	....	....	....
1979-80	**Montreal Canadiens**	**NHL**	**35**	**1**	**3**	**4**	**1**	**2**	**3**	**4**	**0**	**0**	**0**	**18**	**5.6**	**9**	**0**	**7**	**0**	**2**	**8**	**1**	**1**	**2**	**0**	**0**	**0**	**1**
1980-81	**Winnipeg Jets**	**NHL**	**80**	**27**	**26**	**53**	**21**	**17**	**38**	**8**	**8**	**0**	**1**	**215**	**12.6**	**71**	**23**	**106**	**1**	**–57**	....	....	....	....	....	....	....	....
1981-82	**Winnipeg Jets**	**NHL**	**62**	**13**	**25**	**38**	**10**	**17**	**27**	**22**	**4**	**0**	**2**	**148**	**8.8**	**61**	**28**	**59**	**2**	**–24**	**4**	**2**	**0**	**2**	**0**	**2**	**0**	**0**
1982-83	**Winnipeg Jets**	**NHL**	**39**	**7**	**16**	**23**	**6**	**11**	**17**	**6**	**6**	**0**	**1**	**71**	**9.9**	**37**	**23**	**30**	**0**	**–16**	**1**	**1**	**1**	**2**	**0**	**1**	**0**	**0**
	Sherbrooke Jets	AHL	3	2	1	3	....	....	....	2	....	....	....	....	....	....	....	....	....	....	....	....	....	....	....	....	....	....
1983-84	**Hartford Whalers**	**NHL**	**40**	**7**	**15**	**22**	**6**	**10**	**16**	**12**	**2**	**0**	**0**	**85**	**8.2**	**38**	**9**	**45**	**0**	**–16**	....	....	....	....	....	....	....	....
	Binghamton Whalers	AHL	27	14	24	38	....	....	....	6	....	....	....	....	....	....	....	....	....	....	....	....	....	....	....	....	....	....
1984-85	EHC Biel-Bienne	Switz.	38	41	33	74	....	....	....	....	....	....	....	....	....	....	....	....	....	....	3	3	0	3	....	....	....	....
1985-86	EHC Biel-Bienne	Switz.	36	44	*45	*89	....	....	....	....	....	....	....	....	....	....	....	....	....	....	....	....	....	....	....	....	....	....
1986-87	EHC Biel-Bienne	Switz.	35	30	42	72	....	....	....	....	....	....	....	....	....	....	....	....	....	....	3	....	....	....	....	....	....	....
1987-88	EHC Biel-Bienne	Switz.	37	*50	35	*85	....	....	....	....	....	....	....	....	....	....	....	....	....	....	....	....	....	....	....	....	....	....
1988-89	EHC Biel-Bienne	Switz.	36	*38	*37	*75	....	....	....	....	....	....	....	....	....	....	....	....	....	....	7	3	4	7	0	....	....	....
1990-91	EHC Biel-Bienne	Switz.	36	*38	*37	*75	....	....	....	....	....	....	....	....	....	....	....	....	....	....	3	3	4	7	....	....	....	....
1991-92	HC Ajoie	Switz-2	25	43	48	91	....	....	....	....	....	....	....	....	....	....	....	....	....	....	....	....	....	....	....	....	....	....
1992-93	HC Ajoie	Switz-2	25	15	17	32	....	....	....	20	....	....	....	....	....	....	....	....	....	....	....	....	....	....	....	....	....	....
	NHL Totals		**256**	**55**	**85**	**140**	**44**	**57**	**101**	**52**	**20**	**0**	**4**	**537**	**10.2**	**216**	**83**	**247**	**3**		**13**	**4**	**2**	**6**	**0**	**3**	**0**	**1**

QMJHL First All-Star Team (1975) • QMJHL West First All-Star Team (1976) • QMJHL Second All-Star Team (1977) • Won Dudley "Red" Garrett Memorial Award (Top Rookie - AHL) (1978)

Traded to **Winnipeg** by **Montreal** for Winnipeg's 2nd round choice (David Maley) in 1982 Entry Draft, September 26, 1980. Traded to **Hartford** by **Winnipeg** for Hartford's 4th round choice (Chris Mills) in 1984 Entry Draft, July 4, 1983.

• DUPRE, Yanick

LW – L. 6', 189 lbs. b: Montreal, Que., 11/20/1972 d: 8/19/1997. Philadelphia's 2nd, 50th overall, in 1991.

Season	Club	League	GP	G	A	Pts	AG	AA	APts	PIM	PP	SH	GW	S	%	TGF	PGF	TGA	PGA	+/–	GP	G	A	Pts	PIM	PP	SH	GW
1988-89	Laval Laurentide	QAAA	37	13	21	34	....	....	....	39	....	....	....	....	....	....	....	....	....	....	....	....	....	....	....	....	....	....
1989-90	Chicoutimi Sagueneens	QMJHL	24	5	9	14	....	....	....	27	....	....	....	....	....	....	....	....	....	....	....	....	....	....	....	....	....	....
	Drummondville Voltigeurs	QMJHL	29	10	10	20	....	....	....	42	....	....	....	....	....	....	....	....	....	....	....	....	....	....	....	....	....	....
1990-91	Drummondville Voltigeurs	QMJHL	58	29	38	67	....	....	....	87	....	....	....	....	....	....	....	....	....	....	11	8	5	13	33	....	....	....
	Drummondville Voltigeurs	Mem-Cup	5	0	3	3	....	....	....	4	....	....	....	....	....	....	....	....	....	....	....	....	....	....	....	....	....	....

Season	Club	League	GP	G	A	Pts	AG	AA	APts	PIM	PP	SH	GW	S	%	TGF	PGF	TGA	PGA	+/–	GP	G	A	Pts	PIM	PP	SH	GW
			REGULAR SEASON																		PLAYOFFS							
1991-92	Drummondville Voltigeurs	QMJHL	28	19	17	36	....	....	....	48	....	....	....	....	....	....	....	....	....	....	....	....	....	....	....	....	....	....
	Verdun College-Francais	QMJHL	12	7	14	21	....	....	....	21	....	....	....	....	....	....	....	....	....	....	19	9	9	18	20	....	....	....
	Verdun College-Francais	Mem-Cup	2	0	1	1	....	....	....	2	....	....	....	....	....	....	....	....	....	....	....	....	....	....	....	....	....	....
	Philadelphia Flyers	**NHL**	**1**	**0**	**0**	**0**	**0**	**0**	**0**	**0**	**0**	**0**	**0**	**0**	**0.0**	**0**	**0**	**0**	**0**	**0**	....	....	....	....	....	....	....	....
1992-93	Hershey Bears	AHL	63	13	24	37	....	....	....	22	....	....	....	....	....	....	....	....	....	....	....	....	....	....	....	....	....	....
1993-94	Hershey Bears	AHL	51	22	20	42	....	....	....	42	....	....	....	....	....	....	....	....	....	....	8	1	3	4	2	....	....	....
1994-95	**Philadelphia Flyers**	**NHL**	**22**	**0**	**0**	**0**	**0**	**0**	**0**	**8**	**0**	**0**	**0**	**21**	**0.0**	**4**	**1**	**11**	**1**	**–7**	....	....	....	....	....	....	....	....
	Hershey Bears	AHL	41	15	19	34	....	....	....	35	....	....	....	....	....	....	....	....	....	....	....	....	....	....	....	....	....	....
1995-96	**Philadelphia Flyers**	**NHL**	**12**	**2**	**0**	**2**	**2**	**0**	**2**	**8**	**0**	**0**	**1**	**10**	**20.0**	**2**	**0**	**2**	**0**	**0**	....	....	....	....	....	....	....	....
	Hershey Bears	AHL	52	20	36	56	....	....	....	81	....	....	....	....	....	....	....	....	....	....	....	....	....	....	....	....	....	....
	NHL Totals		**35**	**2**	**0**	**2**	**2**	**0**	**2**	**16**	**0**	**0**	**1**	**31**	**6.5**	**6**	**1**	**13**	**1**		....	....	....	....	....	....	....	....

• DURBANO, Steve

Steven Harry D – L. 6'1", 210 lbs. b: Toronto, Ont., 12/12/1951. NY Rangers' 2nd, 13th overall, in 1971.

Season	Club	League	GP	G	A	Pts	AG	AA	APts	PIM	PP	SH	GW	S	%	TGF	PGF	TGA	PGA	+/–	GP	G	A	Pts	PIM	PP	SH	GW
1967-68	York Steel	OHA-B	21	1	9	10	....	....	....	....	....	....	....	....	....	....	....	....	....	....	....	....	....	....	....	....	....	....
1968-69	Toronto Marlboros	OHA-Jr.	45	5	6	11	....	....	....	158	....	....	....	....	....	....	....	....	....	....	4	0	1	1	17	....	....	....
1969-70	Toronto Marlboros	OHA-Jr.	53	7	25	32	....	....	....	*371	....	....	....	....	....	....	....	....	....	....	16	2	3	5	49	....	....	....
1970-71	Toronto Marlboros	OHA-Jr.	49	7	32	39	....	....	....	*324	....	....	....	....	....	....	....	....	....	....	12	2	2	4	*75	....	....	....
1971-72	Omaha Knights	CHL	70	7	34	41	....	....	....	*402	....	....	....	....	....	....	....	....	....	....	....	....	....	....	....	....	....	....
1972-73	**St. Louis Blues**	**NHL**	**49**	**3**	**18**	**21**	**3**	**14**	**17**	**231**	**0**	**0**	**0**	**83**	**3.6**	**63**	**18**	**51**	**3**	**–3**	**5**	**0**	**2**	**2**	**8**	**0**	**0**	**0**
1973-74	**St. Louis Blues**	**NHL**	**36**	**4**	**5**	**9**	**4**	**4**	**8**	**146**	**2**	**0**	**0**	**40**	**10.0**	**33**	**13**	**21**	**0**	**–1**	....	....	....	....	....	....	....	....
	Pittsburgh Penguins	**NHL**	**33**	**4**	**14**	**18**	**4**	**12**	**16**	**138**	**2**	**0**	**0**	**68**	**5.9**	**51**	**8**	**31**	**5**	**17**	....	....	....	....	....	....	....	....
1974-75	**Pittsburgh Penguins**	**NHL**	**1**	**0**	**1**	**1**	**0**	**1**	**1**	**10**	**0**	**0**	**0**	**1**	**0.0**	**1**	**1**	**0**	**0**	**0**	....	....	....	....	....	....	....	....
1975-76	**Pittsburgh Penguins**	**NHL**	**32**	**0**	**8**	**8**	**0**	**6**	**6**	***161**	**0**	**0**	**0**	**41**	**0.0**	**31**	**2**	**23**	**3**	**9**	....	....	....	....	....	....	....	....
	Kansas City Scouts	**NHL**	**37**	**1**	**11**	**12**	**1**	**8**	**9**	***209**	**0**	**0**	**0**	**65**	**1.5**	**29**	**7**	**71**	**19**	**–30**	....	....	....	....	....	....	....	....
1976-77	**Colorado Rockies**	**NHL**	**19**	**0**	**2**	**2**	**0**	**2**	**2**	**129**	**0**	**0**	**0**	**17**	**0.0**	**8**	**0**	**18**	**4**	**–6**	....	....	....	....	....	....	....	....
	Rhode Island Reds	AHL	9	1	2	3	....	....	....	55	....	....	....	....	....	....	....	....	....	....	....	....	....	....	....	....	....	....
1977-78	Birmingham Bulls	WHA	45	6	4	10	....	....	....	*284	....	....	....	....	....	....	....	....	....	....	4	0	2	2	16	....	....	....
1978-79	**St. Louis Blues**	**NHL**	**13**	**1**	**1**	**2**	**1**	**1**	**2**	**103**	**0**	**0**	**0**	**18**	**5.6**	**5**	**0**	**12**	**0**	**–7**	....	....	....	....	....	....	....	....
	Salt Lake Golden Eagles	CHL	10	1	4	5	....	....	....	41	....	....	....	....	....	....	....	....	....	....	....	....	....	....	....	....	....	....
	NHL Totals		**220**	**13**	**60**	**73**	**13**	**48**	**61**	**1127**	**4**	**0**	**0**	**333**	**3.9**	**221**	**49**	**227**	**34**		**5**	**0**	**2**	**2**	**8**	**0**	**0**	**0**
	Other Major League Totals		45	6	4	10	....	....	....	284	....	....	....	....	....	....	....	....	....	....	4	0	2	2	16	....	....	....

OHA-Jr. Second All-Star Team (1971)

Selected by **Quebec** (WHA) in 1972 WHA General Player Draft, February 12, 1972. Traded to **St. Louis** by **NY Rangers** for future considerations (Peter McDuffe and Curt Bennett, June 7, 1972), May 24, 1972. • Missed remainder of 1974-75 season recovering from wrist injury suffered in game vs. Philadelphia, October 18, 1974. Traded to **Pittsburgh** by **St. Louis** with Ab DeMarco Jr. and Bob Kelly for Bryan Watson, Greg Polis and Pittsburgh's 2nd round choice (Bob Hess) in 1974 Amateur Draft, January 17, 1974. Traded to **Kansas City** by **Pittsburgh** with Chuck Arnason and Pittsburgh's 1st round choice (Paul Gardner) in 1976 Amateur Draft for Simon Nolet, Ed Gilbert and Kansas City's 1st round choice (Blair Chapman) in 1976 Amateur Draft, January 9, 1976. Transferred to **Colorado** after **Kansas City** franchise relocated, July 15, 1976. WHA rights traded to **Birmingham** (WHA) by **Quebec** (WHA) for cash, June, 1977. Signed as a free agent by **Detroit**, July 14, 1977. Loaned to **Birmingham** (WHA) by **Detroit** with the loan of Dave Hanson and future considerations for Vaclav Nedomansky and Tim Sheehy, November 18, 1977. Signed as a free agent by **St. Louis**, August 11, 1978.

• DURIS, Vitezslav

"Slava" D – L. 6'1", 185 lbs. b: Plzen, Czech., 1/5/1954.

Season	Club	League	GP	G	A	Pts	AG	AA	APts	PIM	PP	SH	GW	S	%	TGF	PGF	TGA	PGA	+/–	GP	G	A	Pts	PIM	PP	SH	GW
1977-78	Dukla Jihlava	Czech.	44	3	6	9	....	....	....	47	....	....	....	....	....	....	....	....	....	....	....	....	....	....	....	....	....	....
1978-79	Dukla Jihlava	Czech.	38	3	9	12	....	....	....	24	....	....	....	....	....	....	....	....	....	....	....	....	....	....	....	....	....	....
	Czechoslovakia	WEC-A	8	1	1	2	....	....	....	8	....	....	....	....	....	....	....	....	....	....	....	....	....	....	....	....	....	....
1979-80	Dukla Jihlava	Czech-2	STATISTICS NOT AVAILABLE																									
	Czechoslovakia	Nat-Team	8	1	1	2	....	....	....	8	....	....	....	....	....	....	....	....	....	....	....	....	....	....	....	....	....	....
	Czechoslovakia	Olympics	6	0	1	1	....	....	....	2	....	....	....	....	....	....	....	....	....	....	....	....	....	....	....	....	....	....
1980-81	**Toronto Maple Leafs**	**NHL**	**57**	**1**	**12**	**13**	**1**	**8**	**9**	**50**	**0**	**0**	**0**	**70**	**1.4**	**64**	**1**	**79**	**29**	**13**	**3**	**0**	**1**	**1**	**2**	**0**	**0**	**0**
1981-82	Cincinnati Tigers	CHL	66	14	41	55	....	....	....	57	....	....	....	....	....	....	....	....	....	....	....	....	....	....	....	....	....	....
1982-83	**Toronto Maple Leafs**	**NHL**	**32**	**2**	**8**	**10**	**2**	**6**	**8**	**12**	**0**	**1**	**0**	**48**	**4.2**	**50**	**15**	**54**	**22**	**3**	....	....	....	....	....	....	....	....
1983-84	ECD Iserlohn	Germany-2	STATISTICS NOT AVAILABLE																									
1984-85	ECD Iserlohn	Germany	36	12	19	31	....	....	....	52	....	....	....	....	....	....	....	....	....	....	3	1	1	2	2	....	....	....
1985-86	EHC Freiberg	Germany	44	5	21	26	....	....	....	....	....	....	....	....	....	....	....	....	....	....	....	....	....	....	....	....	....	....
1986-87	ECD Iserlohn	Germany	36	12	25	37	....	....	....	33	....	....	....	....	....	....	....	....	....	....	3	3	2	5	4	....	....	....
1987-88	EV Landshut	Germany	33	3	17	20	....	....	....	33	....	....	....	....	....	....	....	....	....	....	4	1	1	2	4	....	....	....
1988-89	EV Landshut	Germany	22	0	2	2	....	....	....	12	....	....	....	....	....	....	....	....	....	....	....	....	....	....	....	....	....	....
	EHC Freiburg	Germany	10	2	4	6	....	....	....	23	....	....	....	....	....	....	....	....	....	....	18	4	20	24	27	....	....	....
1989-90	EHC Freiburg	Germany	28	4	8	12	....	....	....	17	....	....	....	....	....	....	....	....	....	....	....	....	....	....	....	....	....	....
1990-91	EHC Freiburg	Germany	....	....	....	....	....	....	....	....	....	....	....	....	....	....	....	....	....	....	4	1	0	1	4	....	....	....
	NHL Totals		**89**	**3**	**20**	**23**	**3**	**14**	**17**	**62**	**0**	**1**	**0**	**118**	**2.5**	**114**	**16**	**133**	**51**		**3**	**0**	**1**	**1**	**2**	**0**	**0**	**0**

Signed as a free agent by **Toronto**, September 25, 1980.

• DVORAK, Miroslav

D – R. 5'10", 195 lbs. b: Hluboka-nad-Vltavou, Czech., 10/11/1951. Philadelphia's 2nd, 46th overall, in 1982.

Season	Club	League	GP	G	A	Pts	AG	AA	APts	PIM	PP	SH	GW	S	%	TGF	PGF	TGA	PGA	+/–	GP	G	A	Pts	PIM	PP	SH	GW
1965-1972	Motor Ceske Budjovice	Czech.	STATISTICS NOT AVAILABLE																									
1972-73	Dukla Jihlava	Czech.	....	4	7	11	....	....	....	....	....	....	....	....	....	....	....	....	....	....	....	....	....	....	....	....	....	....
1973-74	Dukla Jihlava	Czech.	....	14	7	21	....	....	....	....	....	....	....	....	....	....	....	....	....	....	....	....	....	....	....	....	....	....
	Czechoslovakia	WEC-A	4	0	3	3	....	....	....	4	....	....	....	....	....	....	....	....	....	....	....	....	....	....	....	....	....	....
1974-75	Motor Ceske Budejovice	Czech.	....	10	18	28	....	....	....	....	....	....	....	....	....	....	....	....	....	....	....	....	....	....	....	....	....	....
	Czechoslovakia	WEC-A	10	2	4	6	....	....	....	2	....	....	....	....	....	....	....	....	....	....	....	....	....	....	....	....	....	....
1975-76	Motor Ceske Budejovice	Czech.	31	9	2	11	....	....	....	18	....	....	....	....	....	....	....	....	....	....	....	....	....	....	....	....	....	....
	Czechoslovakia	Olympics	5	0	2	2	....	....	....	2	....	....	....	....	....	....	....	....	....	....	....	....	....	....	....	....	....	....
	Czechoslovakia	WEC-A	8	0	0	0	....	....	....	4	....	....	....	....	....	....	....	....	....	....	....	....	....	....	....	....	....	....
1976-77	Czechoslovakia	Can-Cup	7	0	1	1	....	....	....	4	....	....	....	....	....	....	....	....	....	....	....	....	....	....	....	....	....	....
	Motor Ceske Budejovice	Czech.	....	4	14	18	....	....	....	....	....	....	....	....	....	....	....	....	....	....	....	....	....	....	....	....	....	....
	Czechoslovakia	WEC-A	9	0	1	1	....	....	....	8	....	....	....	....	....	....	....	....	....	....	....	....	....	....	....	....	....	....
1977-78	Motor Ceske Budejovice	Czech.	43	10	16	26	....	....	....	48	....	....	....	....	....	....	....	....	....	....	....	....	....	....	....	....	....	....
	Czechoslovakia	Nat-Team	16	1	3	4	....	....	....	....	....	....	....	....	....	....	....	....	....	....	....	....	....	....	....	....	....	....
	Czechoslovakia	WEC-A	10	0	3	3	....	....	....	4	....	....	....	....	....	....	....	....	....	....	....	....	....	....	....	....	....	....
1978-79	Motor Ceske Budejovice	Czech.	42	3	19	22	....	....	....	14	....	....	....	....	....	....	....	....	....	....	....	....	....	....	....	....	....	....
	Czechoslovakia	Nat-Team	24	0	3	3	....	....	....	....	....	....	....	....	....	....	....	....	....	....	....	....	....	....	....	....	....	....
	Czechoslovakia	WEC-A	8	0	0	0	....	....	....	0	....	....	....	....	....	....	....	....	....	....	....	....	....	....	....	....	....	....
1979-80	Motor Ceske Budejovice	Czech.	44	7	17	24	....	....	....	27	....	....	....	....	....	....	....	....	....	....	6	1	1	2	0	....	....	....
	Czechoslovakia	Nat-Team	24	4	5	9	....	....	....	4	....	....	....	....	....	....	....	....	....	....	....	....	....	....	....	....	....	....
	Czechoslovakia	Olympics	6	1	1	2	....	....	....	0	....	....	....	....	....	....	....	....	....	....	....	....	....	....	....	....	....	....
1980-81	Motor Ceske Budejovice	Czech.	44	8	27	35	....	....	....	....	....	....	....	....	....	....	....	....	....	....	....	....	....	....	....	....	....	....
	Czechoslovakia	Nat-Team	28	5	3	8	....	....	....	....	....	....	....	....	....	....	....	....	....	....	....	....	....	....	....	....	....	....
	Czechoslovakia	WEC-A	8	1	2	3	....	....	....	4	....	....	....	....	....	....	....	....	....	....	....	....	....	....	....	....	....	....
1981-82	Czechoslovakia	Can-Cup	6	0	3	3	....	....	....	2	....	....	....	....	....	....	....	....	....	....	....	....	....	....	....	....	....	....
	Motor Ceske Budejovice	Czech	38	6	20	26	....	....	....	24	....	....	....	....	....	....	....	....	....	....	....	....	....	....	....	....	....	....
	Czechoslovakia	Nat-Team	35	0	15	15	....	....	....	6	....	....	....	....	....	....	....	....	....	....	10	0	5	5	4	....	....	....
	Czechoslovakia	WEC-A	10	0	5	5	....	....	....	4	....	....	....	....	....	....	....	....	....	....	....	....	....	....	....	....	....	....
1982-83	**Philadelphia Flyers**	**NHL**	**80**	**4**	**33**	**37**	**3**	**23**	**26**	**20**	**2**	**1**	**0**	**112**	**3.6**	**113**	**29**	**83**	**26**	**27**	**3**	**0**	**1**	**1**	**0**	**0**	**0**	**0**
	Czechoslovakia	WEC-A	10	0	3	3	....	....	....	14	....	....	....	....	....	....	....	....	....	....	....	....	....	....	....	....	....	....
1983-84	**Philadelphia Flyers**	**NHL**	**66**	**4**	**27**	**31**	**3**	**18**	**21**	**27**	**0**	**1**	**0**	**85**	**4.7**	**93**	**18**	**86**	**30**	**19**	**2**	**0**	**0**	**0**	**2**	**0**	**0**	**0**
1984-85	**Philadelphia Flyers**	**NHL**	**47**	**3**	**14**	**17**	**2**	**10**	**12**	**4**	**0**	**1**	**1**	**51**	**5.9**	**47**	**9**	**32**	**6**	**12**	**13**	**0**	**1**	**1**	**4**	**0**	**0**	**0**
1985-86	EC Kassel	Germany-2	43	13	46	59	....	....	....	46	....	....	....	....	....	....	....	....	....	....	17	8	23	31	20	....	....	....

Season	Club	League	GP	G	A	Pts	AG	AA	APts	PIM	PP	SH	GW	S	%	TGF	PGF	TGA	PGA	+/–	GP	G	A	Pts	PIM	PP	SH	GW
			REGULAR SEASON																		PLAYOFFS							
1986-87	EC Kassel	Germany-2	52	8	54	62	....	....	....	44	....	....	....	....	....	....	....	....	....	....	....	....	....	....	....	....	....	....
1987-88	EHC Essen-West	Germany-2	36	10	36	46	....	....	....	16	....	....	....	....	....	....	....	....	....	....	18	4	5	9	8	....	....	....
1988-89	Motor Ceske Budejovice	Czech.	27	0	7	7	....	....	....	16	....	....	....	....	....	....	....	....	....	....	12	0	3	3	0	....	....	....
	NHL Totals		193	11	74	85	8	51	59	51	2	3	1	248	4.4	253	56	201	62		18	0	2	2	6	0	0	0

WEC-A Second All-Star Team (1982)

• DVORAK, Radek

RW – R. 6'1", 194 lbs. b: Tabor, Czech., 3/9/1977. Florida's 1st, 10th overall, in 1995.

Season	Club	League	GP	G	A	Pts	AG	AA	APts	PIM	PP	SH	GW	S	%	TGF	PGF	TGA	PGA	+/–	GP	G	A	Pts	PIM	PP	SH	GW
1992-93	Motor Ceske Budejovice	Czech-Jr.	35	44	46	90	....	....	....	....	....	....	....	....	....	....	....	....	....	....	....	....	....	....	....	....	....	....
1993-94	Motor Ceske Budejovice	Czech-Jr.	20	17	18	35	....	....	....	....	....	....	....	....	....	....	....	....	....	....	....	....	....	....	....	....	....	....
	Motor Ceske Budejovice	Czech-Rep	8	0	0	0	....	....	....	0	....	....	....	....	....	....	....	....	....	....	....	....	....	....	....	....	....	....
	Czech-Republic	EJC-A	5	2	3	5	....	....	....	6	....	....	....	....	....	....	....	....	....	....	....	....	....	....	....	....	....	....
1994-95	Motor Ceske Budejovice	Czech-Rep	10	3	5	8	....	....	....	2	....	....	....	....	....	....	....	....	....	....	9	5	1	6	....	....	....	....
	Czech-Republic	EJC-A	5	4	3	7	....	....	....	6	....	....	....	....	....	....	....	....	....	....	....	....	....	....	....	....	....	....
1995-96	Florida Panthers	NHL	77	13	14	27	13	11	24	20	0	0	4	126	10.3	44	2	38	1	5	16	1	3	4	0	0	0	0
1996-97	Florida Panthers	NHL	78	18	21	39	19	19	38	30	2	0	1	139	12.9	56	12	47	1	–2	3	0	0	0	0	0	0	0
1997-98	Florida Panthers	NHL	64	12	24	36	14	24	38	33	2	3	0	112	10.7	45	5	55	14	–1	....	....	....	....	....	....	....	....
1998-99	Florida Panthers	NHL	82	19	24	43	22	23	45	29	0	4	0	182	10.4	60	9	72	28	7	....	....	....	....	....	....	....	....
	Czech-Republic	WC-A	12	4	4	8	....	....	....	6	....	....	....	....	....	....	....	....	....	....	....	....	....	....	....	....	....	....
99-2000	Florida Panthers	NHL	35	7	10	17	8	9	17	6	0	0	1	67	10.4	23	1	28	11	5	....	....	....	....	....	....	....	....
	New York Rangers	NHL	46	11	22	33	12	20	32	10	2	1	0	90	12.2	51	13	46	8	0	....	....	....	....	....	....	....	....
	NHL Totals		382	80	115	195	88	106	194	128	6	8	6	716	11.2	279	42	286	63		19	1	3	4	0	0	0	0

Traded to **San Jose** by **Florida** for Mike Vernon, San Jose's 3rd round choice (Sean O'Connor) in 2000 Entry Draft and future considerations, December 30, 1999. Traded to **NY Rangers** by **San Jose** for Todd Harvey and NY Rangers' 4th round choice in 2001 Entry Draft, December 30, 1999.

• DWYER, Gordie

LW – L. 6'2", 216 lbs. b: Dalhousie, NB, 1/25/1978. Montreal's 5th, 152nd overall, in 1998.

Season	Club	League	GP	G	A	Pts	AG	AA	APts	PIM	PP	SH	GW	S	%	TGF	PGF	TGA	PGA	+/–	GP	G	A	Pts	PIM	PP	SH	GW
1994-95	Hull Olympiques	QMJHL	57	3	7	10	....	....	....	204	....	....	....	....	....	....	....	....	....	....	17	1	3	4	54	....	....	....
1995-96	Hull Olympiques	QMJHL	25	5	9	14	....	....	....	199	....	....	....	....	....	....	....	....	....	....	....	....	....	....	....	....	....	....
	Laval Titan	QMJHL	22	5	17	22	....	....	....	72	....	....	....	....	....	....	....	....	....	....	....	....	....	....	....	....	....	....
	Beauport Harfangs	QMJHL	22	4	9	13	....	....	....	87	....	....	....	....	....	....	....	....	....	....	20	3	5	8	104	....	....	....
1996-97	Drummondville Voltigeurs	QMJHL	66	21	48	69	....	....	....	393	....	....	....	....	....	....	....	....	....	....	8	6	1	7	39	....	....	....
1997-98	Quebec Remparts	QMJHL	59	18	27	45	....	....	....	365	....	....	....	....	....	....	....	....	....	....	14	4	9	13	67	....	....	....
1998-99	Fredericton Canadiens	AHL	14	0	0	0	....	....	....	46	....	....	....	....	....	....	....	....	....	....	....	....	....	....	....	....	....	....
	New Orleans Brass	ECHL	36	1	3	4	....	....	....	163	....	....	....	....	....	....	....	....	....	....	11	0	0	0	27	....	....	....
99-2000	Quebec Citadelles	AHL	7	0	0	0	....	....	....	37	....	....	....	....	....	....	....	....	....	....	....	....	....	....	....	....	....	....
	Tampa Bay Lightning	NHL	24	0	1	1	0	1	1	135	0	0	0	7	0.0	4	0	10	0	–6	....	....	....	....	....	....	....	....
	Detroit Vipers	IHL	27	0	2	2	....	....	....	147	....	....	....	....	....	....	....	....	....	....	....	....	....	....	....	....	....	....
	NHL Totals		24	0	1	1	0	1	1	135	0	0	0	7	0.0	4	0	10	0		....	....	....	....	....	....	....	....

• Re-entered NHL draft. Originally St. Louis' 2nd choice, 67th overall, in 1996 Entry Draft.

Traded to **Tampa Bay** by **Montreal** for Mike McBain, November 26, 1999.

• DWYER, Mike

Michael LW – L. 5'11", 172 lbs. b: Brampton, Ont., 9/16/1957. Colorado's 4th, 74th overall, in 1977.

Season	Club	League	GP	G	A	Pts	AG	AA	APts	PIM	PP	SH	GW	S	%	TGF	PGF	TGA	PGA	+/–	GP	G	A	Pts	PIM	PP	SH	GW
1975-76	Windsor Spitfires	OMJHL	42	20	28	48	....	....	....	24	....	....	....	....	....	....	....	....	....	....	....	....	....	....	....	....	....	....
1976-77	Niagara Falls Flyers	OMJHL	59	30	38	68	....	....	....	127	....	....	....	....	....	....	....	....	....	....	....	....	....	....	....	....	....	....
	Windsor Spitfires	OMJHL	5	5	1	6	....	....	....	11	....	....	....	....	....	....	....	....	....	....	....	....	....	....	....	....	....	....
1977-78	Phoenix Roadrunners	CHL	25	12	8	20	....	....	....	16	....	....	....	....	....	....	....	....	....	....	....	....	....	....	....	....	....	....
	Hampton Gulls	AHL	9	2	1	3	....	....	....	4	....	....	....	....	....	....	....	....	....	....	....	....	....	....	....	....	....	....
1978-79	Colorado Rockies	NHL	12	2	3	5	2	2	4	2	0	0	0	10	20.0	9	1	12	0	–4	....	....	....	....	....	....	....	....
	Philadelphia Firebirds	AHL	60	20	27	47	....	....	....	52	....	....	....	....	....	....	....	....	....	....	....	....	....	....	....	....	....	....
1979-80	Colorado Rockies	NHL	10	0	0	0	0	0	0	19	0	0	0	12	0.0	0	0	6	1	–5	....	....	....	....	....	....	....	....
	Fort Worth Texans	CHL	13	3	4	7	....	....	....	22	....	....	....	....	....	....	....	....	....	....	....	....	....	....	....	....	....	....
	Birmingham Bulls	CHL	40	16	18	34	....	....	....	90	....	....	....	....	....	....	....	....	....	....	....	....	....	....	....	....	....	....
1980-81	Calgary Flames	NHL	4	0	1	1	0	1	1	4	0	0	0	6	0.0	1	0	2	0	–1	1	1	0	1	0	0	0	0
	Birmingham Bulls	CHL	49	16	34	50	....	....	....	135	....	....	....	....	....	....	....	....	....	....	....	....	....	....	....	....	....	....
	Wichita Wind	CHL	12	8	8	16	....	....	....	28	....	....	....	....	....	....	....	....	....	....	15	6	11	17	36	....	....	....
1981-82	Calgary Flames	NHL	5	0	2	2	0	1	1	0	0	0	0	5	0.0	3	0	3	0	0	....	....	....	....	....	....	....	....
	Oklahoma City Stars	CHL	28	9	21	30	....	....	....	35	....	....	....	....	....	....	....	....	....	....	....	....	....	....	....	....	....	....
1982-83	Colorado Flames	CHL	51	15	33	48	....	....	....	61	....	....	....	....	....	....	....	....	....	....	6	4	4	8	2	....	....	....
	NHL Totals		31	2	6	8	2	4	6	25	0	0	0	33	6.1	13	1	23	1		1	1	0	1	0	0	0	0

Signed as a free agent by **Calgary**, October 17, 1980.

• DYKHUIS, Karl

D – L. 6'3", 214 lbs. b: Sept-Iles, Que., 7/8/1972. Chicago's 1st, 16th overall, in 1990.

Season	Club	League	GP	G	A	Pts	AG	AA	APts	PIM	PP	SH	GW	S	%	TGF	PGF	TGA	PGA	+/–	GP	G	A	Pts	PIM	PP	SH	GW
1987-88	Lac St-Jean Cascades	QAAA	37	2	12	14	....	....	....	....	....	....	....	....	....	....	....	....	....	....	....	....	....	....	....	....	....	....
1988-89	Hull Olympiques	QMJHL	63	2	29	31	....	....	....	59	....	....	....	....	....	....	....	....	....	....	9	1	9	10	6	....	....	....
1989-90	Hull Olympiques	QMJHL	69	10	46	56	....	....	....	119	....	....	....	....	....	....	....	....	....	....	11	2	5	7	2	....	....	....
1990-91	Longueuil College-Francais	QMJHL	3	1	4	5	....	....	....	6	....	....	....	....	....	....	....	....	....	....	8	2	5	7	6	....	....	....
	Canada	Nat-Team	37	2	9	11	....	....	....	16	....	....	....	....	....	....	....	....	....	....	....	....	....	....	....	....	....	....
	Canada	WJC-A	7	0	3	3	....	....	....	2	....	....	....	....	....	....	....	....	....	....	....	....	....	....	....	....	....	....
1991-92	Verdun College-Francais	QMJHL	29	5	19	24	....	....	....	55	....	....	....	....	....	....	....	....	....	....	17	0	12	12	14	....	....	....
	Canada	Nat-Team	19	1	2	3	....	....	....	16	....	....	....	....	....	....	....	....	....	....	....	....	....	....	....	....	....	....
	Canada	WJC-A	7	0	0	0	....	....	....	8	....	....	....	....	....	....	....	....	....	....	....	....	....	....	....	....	....	....
	Chicago Blackhawks	NHL	6	1	3	4	1	2	3	4	1	0	0	12	8.3	6	3	6	2	–1	....	....	....	....	....	....	....	....
	Verdun College-Francais	Mem-Cup	3	0	0	0	....	....	....	0	....	....	....	....	....	....	....	....	....	....	....	....	....	....	....	....	....	....
1992-93	Chicago Blackhawks	NHL	12	0	5	5	0	3	3	0	0	0	0	10	0.0	10	3	9	4	2	....	....	....	....	....	....	....	....
	Indianapolis Ice	IHL	59	5	18	23	....	....	....	76	....	....	....	....	....	....	....	....	....	....	5	1	1	2	8	....	....	....
1993-94	Indianapolis Ice	IHL	73	7	25	32	....	....	....	132	....	....	....	....	....	....	....	....	....	....	....	....	....	....	....	....	....	....
1994-95	Indianapolis Ice	IHL	52	2	21	23	....	....	....	63	....	....	....	....	....	....	....	....	....	....	....	....	....	....	....	....	....	....
	Philadelphia Flyers	NHL	33	2	6	8	4	9	13	37	1	0	1	46	4.3	28	4	19	2	7	15	4	4	8	14	2	0	2
	Hershey Bears	AHL	1	0	0	0	....	....	....	0	....	....	....	....	....	....	....	....	....	....	....	....	....	....	....	....	....	....
1995-96	Philadelphia Flyers	NHL	82	5	15	20	5	12	17	101	1	0	0	104	4.8	82	24	54	8	12	12	2	2	4	22	1	0	0
1996-97	Philadelphia Flyers	NHL	62	4	15	19	4	13	17	35	2	0	1	101	4.0	59	10	59	16	6	18	0	3	3	2	0	0	0
1997-98	Tampa Bay Lightning	NHL	78	5	9	14	6	9	15	110	0	1	0	91	5.5	51	4	80	25	–8	....	....	....	....	....	....	....	....
1998-99	Tampa Bay Lightning	NHL	33	2	1	3	2	1	3	18	0	0	0	27	7.4	16	0	50	13	–21	....	....	....	....	....	....	....	....
	Philadelphia Flyers	NHL	45	2	4	6	2	4	6	32	1	0	0	61	3.3	32	9	38	13	–2	5	1	0	1	4	0	0	0
99-2000	Philadelphia Flyers	NHL	5	0	1	1	0	1	1	6	0	0	0	5	0.0	1	0	3	0	–2	....	....	....	....	....	....	....	....
	Montreal Canadiens	NHL	67	7	12	19	8	11	19	40	3	1	0	64	10.9	48	11	52	12	–3	....	....	....	....	....	....	....	....
	NHL Totals		423	28	71	99	32	65	97	383	9	2	2	521	5.4	333	68	370	95		50	7	9	16	42	3	0	2

QMJHL First All-Star Team (1990)

Traded to **Philadelphia** by **Chicago** for Bob Wilkie and Philadelphia's 5th round choice (Kyle Calder) in 1995 Entry Draft, February 16, 1995. Traded to **Tampa Bay** by **Philadelphia** with Mikael Renberg for Philadelphia's 1st round choices (previously acquired by Tampa Bay) in 1998 (Simon Gagne), 1999 (Maxime Ouellet), 2000, and 2001 Entry Drafts, August 20, 1997. Traded to **Philadelphia** by **Tampa Bay** for Petr Svoboda, December 28, 1998. Traded to **Montreal** by **Philadelphia** for cash, October 20, 1999.

• DYKSTRA, Steve

D – L. 6'2", 190 lbs. b: Edmonton, Alta., 12/1/1962.

			REGULAR SEASON																		PLAYOFFS							
Season	Club	League	GP	G	A	Pts	AG	AA	APts	PIM	PP	SH	GW	S	%	TGF	PGF	TGA	PGA	+/-	GP	G	A	Pts	PIM	PP	SH	GW
1980-81	Sherwood Park Crusaders	AJHL	STATISTICS NOT AVAILABLE																									
1981-82	Seattle Breakers	WHL	57	8	26	34	....	....	....	139	....	....	....	....	....	....	....	....	....	....	10	3	1	4	42	....	....	....
1982-83	Rochester Americans	AHL	70	2	16	18	....	....	....	100	....	....	....	....	....	....	....	....	....	....	15	0	5	5	27	....	....	....
1983-84	Rochester Americans	AHL	63	3	19	22	....	....	....	141	....	....	....	....	....	....	....	....	....	....	6	0	0	0	46	....	....	....
1984-85	Flint Generals	IHL	15	1	7	8	....	....	....	36	....	....	....	....	....	....	....	....	....	....	....	....	....	....	....	....	....	....
	Rochester Americans	AHL	51	9	23	32	....	....	....	113	....	....	....	....	....	....	....	....	....	....	2	0	1	1	10	....	....	....
1985-86	**Buffalo Sabres**	**NHL**	**64**	**4**	**21**	**25**	**3**	**14**	**17**	**108**	**1**	**1**	**0**	**70**	**5.7**	**59**	**9**	**56**	**7**	**1**	....	....	....	....	....	....	....	....
1986-87	**Buffalo Sabres**	**NHL**	**37**	**0**	**1**	**1**	**0**	**1**	**1**	**179**	**0**	**0**	**0**	**21**	**0.0**	**13**	**0**	**25**	**5**	**-7**	....	....	....	....	....	....	....	....
	Rochester Americans	AHL	18	0	0	0	....	....	....	77	....	....	....	....	....	....	....	....	....	....	....	....	....	....	....	....	....	....
1987-88	**Buffalo Sabres**	**NHL**	**27**	**1**	**1**	**2**	**1**	**1**	**2**	**91**	**0**	**0**	**0**	**11**	**9.1**	**16**	**0**	**18**	**2**	**0**	....	....	....	....	....	....	....	....
	Rochester Americans	AHL	7	0	1	1	....	....	....	33	....	....	....	....	....	....	....	....	....	....	....	....	....	....	....	....	....	....
	Edmonton Oilers	**NHL**	**15**	**2**	**3**	**5**	**2**	**2**	**4**	**39**	**0**	**0**	**0**	**15**	**13.3**	**14**	**0**	**15**	**2**	**1**	....	....	....	....	....	....	....	....
1988-89	**Pittsburgh Penguins**	**NHL**	**65**	**1**	**6**	**7**	**1**	**4**	**5**	**126**	**0**	**0**	**0**	**38**	**2.6**	**36**	**2**	**83**	**37**	**-12**	**1**	**0**	**0**	**0**	**2**	**0**	**0**	**0**
1989-90	**Hartford Whalers**	**NHL**	**9**	**0**	**0**	**0**	**0**	**0**	**0**	**2**	**0**	**0**	**0**	**10**	**0.0**	**5**	**0**	**3**	**0**	**2**	....	....	....	....	....	....	....	....
	Binghamton Whalers	AHL	53	5	17	22	....	....	....	55	....	....	....	....	....	....	....	....	....	....	....	....	....	....	....	....	....	....
	Maine Mariners	AHL	16	0	4	4	....	....	....	20	....	....	....	....	....	....	....	....	....	....	....	....	....	....	....	....	....	....
1990-91	San Diego Gulls	IHL	72	6	18	24	....	....	....	141	....	....	....	....	....	....	....	....	....	....	....	....	....	....	....	....	....	....
1991-92			DID NOT PLAY																									
1992-93			DID NOT PLAY																									
1993-94	Toledo Storm	ECHL	11	3	5	8	....	....	....	37	....	....	....	....	....	....	....	....	....	....	12	0	2	2	23	....	....	....
1994-95	Toledo Storm	ECHL	10	1	5	6	....	....	....	19	....	....	....	....	....	....	....	....	....	....	....	....	....	....	....	....	....	....
	Fort Worth Fire	CHL	10	0	2	2	....	....	....	12	....	....	....	....	....	....	....	....	....	....	....	....	....	....	....	....	....	....
1995-96	Fort Worth Fire	CHL	57	4	12	16	....	....	....	84	....	....	....	....	....	....	....	....	....	....	....	....	....	....	....	....	....	....
1996-97			OUT OF HOCKEY – RETIRED																									
1997-98	Fort Worth Fire	CHL	23	2	12	14	....	....	....	32	....	....	....	....	....	....	....	....	....	....	....	....	....	....	....	....	....	....
	NHL Totals		**217**	**8**	**32**	**40**	**7**	**22**	**29**	**545**	**1**	**1**	**0**	**165**	**4.8**	**143**	**11**	**200**	**53**		**1**	**0**	**0**	**0**	**2**	**0**	**0**	**0**

Signed as a free agent by **Buffalo**, December 10, 1982. Traded to **Edmonton** by **Buffalo** with Buffalo's 7th round choice (David Payne) in 1989 Entry Draft for Scott Metcalfe and Edmonton's 9th round choice (Donald Audette) in 1989 Entry Draft, February 11, 1988. Claimed by **Pittsburgh** from **Edmonton** in Waiver Draft, October 3, 1988. Signed as a free agent by **Hartford**, October 9, 1989. Traded to **Boston** by **Hartford** for Jeff Sirkka, March 3, 1990. • Played w/ RHI's LA Blades in 1993 (3-1-0-1-4).

• DZIEDZIC, Joe

LW – L. 6'3", 227 lbs. b: Minneapolis, MN, 12/18/1971. Pittsburgh's 2nd, 61st overall, in 1990.

Season	Club	League	GP	G	A	Pts	AG	AA	APts	PIM	PP	SH	GW	S	%	TGF	PGF	TGA	PGA	+/-	GP	G	A	Pts	PIM	PP	SH	GW
1988-89	Edison Tommies	Hi-School	22	46	27	73	....	....	....	34	....	....	....	....	....	....	....	....	....	....	....	....	....	....	....	....	....	....
1989-90	Edison Tommies	Hi-School	17	29	19	48	....	....	....	10	....	....	....	....	....	....	....	....	....	....	....	....	....	....	....	....	....	....
	St. Paul Vulcans	USHL	STATISTICS NOT AVAILABLE																									
1990-91	University of Minnesota	WCHA	20	6	4	10	....	....	....	26	....	....	....	....	....	....	....	....	....	....	....	....	....	....	....	....	....	....
1991-92	University of Minnesota	WCHA	34	8	9	17	....	....	....	68	....	....	....	....	....	....	....	....	....	....	....	....	....	....	....	....	....	....
1992-93	University of Minnesota	WCHA	41	11	14	25	....	....	....	62	....	....	....	....	....	....	....	....	....	....	....	....	....	....	....	....	....	....
1993-94	University of Minnesota	WCHA	18	7	10	17	....	....	....	48	....	....	....	....	....	....	....	....	....	....	....	....	....	....	....	....	....	....
1994-95	Cleveland Lumberjacks	IHL	68	15	15	30	....	....	....	74	....	....	....	....	....	....	....	....	....	....	4	1	0	1	10	....	....	....
1995-96	**Pittsburgh Penguins**	**NHL**	**69**	**5**	**5**	**10**	**5**	**4**	**9**	**68**	**0**	**0**	**3**	**44**	**11.4**	**15**	**0**	**21**	**1**	**-5**	**16**	**1**	**2**	**3**	**19**	**0**	**0**	**0**
1996-97	**Pittsburgh Penguins**	**NHL**	**59**	**9**	**9**	**18**	**10**	**8**	**18**	**63**	**0**	**0**	**1**	**85**	**10.6**	**23**	**0**	**27**	**0**	**-4**	**5**	**0**	**1**	**1**	**4**	**0**	**0**	**0**
1997-98	Cleveland Lumberjacks	IHL	65	21	20	41	....	....	....	176	....	....	....	....	....	....	....	....	....	....	10	3	4	7	28	....	....	....
1998-99	**Phoenix Coyotes**	**NHL**	**2**	**0**	**0**	**0**	**0**	**0**	**0**	**0**	**0**	**0**	**0**	**1**	**0.0**	**0**	**0**	**2**	**0**	**-2**	....	....	....	....	....	....	....	....
	Springfield Falcons	AHL	61	18	27	45	....	....	....	128	....	....	....	....	....	....	....	....	....	....	3	1	1	2	20	....	....	....
	NHL Totals		**130**	**14**	**14**	**28**	**15**	**12**	**27**	**131**	**0**	**0**	**4**	**130**	**10.8**	**38**	**0**	**50**	**1**		**21**	**1**	**3**	**4**	**23**	**0**	**0**	**0**

Signed as a free agent by **Phoenix**, August 27, 1998.

• EAGLES, Mike

Michael Bryant C/LW – L. 5'10", 195 lbs. b: Sussex, N.B., 3/7/1963. Quebec's 5th, 116th overall, in 1981.

Season	Club	League	GP	G	A	Pts	AG	AA	APts	PIM	PP	SH	GW	S	%	TGF	PGF	TGA	PGA	+/-	GP	G	A	Pts	PIM	PP	SH	GW
1979-80	Melville Millionaires	SJHL	55	46	30	76	....	....	....	77	....	....	....	....	....	....	....	....	....	....	....	....	....	....	....	....	....	....
	Billings Bighorns	WHL	5	0	1	1	....	....	....	0	....	....	....	....	....	....	....	....	....	....	....	....	....	....	....	....	....	....
1980-81	Kitchener Rangers	OMJHL	56	11	27	38	....	....	....	64	....	....	....	....	....	....	....	....	....	....	18	4	2	6	36	....	....	....
	Kitchener Rangers	Mem-Cup	5	1	1	2	....	....	....	4	....	....	....	....	....	....	....	....	....	....	....	....	....	....	....	....	....	....
1981-82	Kitchener Rangers	OHL	62	26	40	66	....	....	....	148	....	....	....	....	....	....	....	....	....	....	15	3	11	14	27	....	....	....
	Kitchener Rangers	Mem-Cup	5	3	3	6	....	....	....	0	....	....	....	....	....	....	....	....	....	....	....	....	....	....	....	....	....	....
1982-83	Kitchener Rangers	OHL	58	26	36	62	....	....	....	133	....	....	....	....	....	....	....	....	....	....	12	5	7	12	27	....	....	....
	Canada	WJC-A	7	2	4	6	....	....	....	2	....	....	....	....	....	....	....	....	....	....	....	....	....	....	....	....	....	....
	Quebec Nordiques	**NHL**	**2**	**0**	**0**	**0**	**0**	**0**	**0**	**2**	**0**	**0**	**0**	**1**	**0.0**	**0**	**0**	**1**	**0**	**-1**	....	....	....	....	....	....	....	....
1983-84	Fredericton Express	AHL	68	13	29	42	....	....	....	85	....	....	....	....	....	....	....	....	....	....	4	0	0	0	5	....	....	....
1984-85	Fredericton Express	AHL	36	4	20	24	....	....	....	80	....	....	....	....	....	....	....	....	....	....	3	0	0	0	2	....	....	....
1985-86	**Quebec Nordiques**	**NHL**	**73**	**11**	**12**	**23**	**9**	**8**	**17**	**49**	**1**	**0**	**1**	**68**	**16.2**	**32**	**2**	**50**	**23**	**3**	**3**	**0**	**0**	**0**	**2**	**0**	**0**	**0**
1986-87	**Quebec Nordiques**	**NHL**	**73**	**13**	**19**	**32**	**11**	**14**	**25**	**55**	**0**	**2**	**2**	**95**	**13.7**	**44**	**0**	**83**	**24**	**-15**	**4**	**1**	**0**	**1**	**10**	**0**	**0**	**0**
1987-88	**Quebec Nordiques**	**NHL**	**76**	**10**	**10**	**20**	**9**	**7**	**16**	**74**	**1**	**2**	**2**	**89**	**11.2**	**30**	**1**	**82**	**35**	**-18**	....	....	....	....	....	....	....	....
1988-89	**Chicago Blackhawks**	**NHL**	**47**	**5**	**11**	**16**	**4**	**8**	**12**	**44**	**0**	**0**	**0**	**39**	**12.8**	**24**	**0**	**46**	**14**	**-8**	....	....	....	....	....	....	....	....
1989-90	**Chicago Blackhawks**	**NHL**	**23**	**1**	**2**	**3**	**1**	**1**	**2**	**34**	**0**	**0**	**0**	**23**	**4.3**	**6**	**0**	**11**	**1**	**-4**	....	....	....	....	....	....	....	....
	Indianapolis Ice	IHL	24	11	13	24	....	....	....	47	....	....	....	....	....	....	....	....	....	....	13	*10	10	20	34	....	....	....
1990-91	**Winnipeg Jets**	**NHL**	**44**	**0**	**9**	**9**	**0**	**7**	**7**	**79**	**0**	**0**	**0**	**51**	**0.0**	**18**	**0**	**33**	**5**	**-10**	....	....	....	....	....	....	....	....
	Indianapolis Ice	IHL	25	15	14	29	....	....	....	47	....	....	....	....	....	....	....	....	....	....	....	....	....	....	....	....	....	....
1991-92	**Winnipeg Jets**	**NHL**	**65**	**7**	**10**	**17**	**6**	**8**	**14**	**118**	**0**	**1**	**0**	**60**	**11.7**	**21**	**0**	**63**	**25**	**-17**	**7**	**0**	**0**	**0**	**8**	**0**	**0**	**0**
1992-93	**Winnipeg Jets**	**NHL**	**84**	**8**	**18**	**26**	**7**	**12**	**19**	**131**	**1**	**0**	**1**	**67**	**11.9**	**43**	**1**	**91**	**48**	**-1**	**5**	**0**	**1**	**1**	**6**	**0**	**0**	**0**
1993-94	**Winnipeg Jets**	**NHL**	**73**	**4**	**8**	**12**	**4**	**6**	**10**	**96**	**0**	**1**	**0**	**53**	**7.5**	**13**	**1**	**67**	**35**	**-20**	....	....	....	....	....	....	....	....
1994-95	**Winnipeg Jets**	**NHL**	**27**	**2**	**1**	**3**	**4**	**1**	**5**	**40**	**0**	**0**	**0**	**13**	**15.4**	**4**	**0**	**26**	**9**	**-13**	....	....	....	....	....	....	....	....
	Washington Capitals	**NHL**	**13**	**1**	**3**	**4**	**2**	**4**	**6**	**8**	**0**	**0**	**0**	**15**	**6.7**	**8**	**2**	**8**	**4**	**2**	**7**	**0**	**2**	**2**	**4**	**0**	**0**	**0**
1995-96	**Washington Capitals**	**NHL**	**70**	**4**	**7**	**11**	**4**	**6**	**10**	**75**	**0**	**0**	**0**	**70**	**5.7**	**25**	**0**	**44**	**18**	**-1**	**6**	**1**	**1**	**2**	**2**	**0**	**0**	**0**
1996-97	**Washington Capitals**	**NHL**	**70**	**1**	**7**	**8**	**1**	**6**	**7**	**42**	**0**	**0**	**0**	**38**	**2.6**	**15**	**0**	**31**	**12**	**-4**	....	....	....	....	....	....	....	....
1997-98	**Washington Capitals**	**NHL**	**36**	**1**	**3**	**4**	**1**	**3**	**4**	**16**	**0**	**0**	**0**	**25**	**4.0**	**9**	**0**	**13**	**2**	**-2**	**12**	**0**	**2**	**2**	**2**	**0**	**0**	**0**
1998-99	**Washington Capitals**	**NHL**	**52**	**4**	**2**	**6**	**5**	**2**	**7**	**50**	**0**	**0**	**0**	**41**	**9.8**	**11**	**0**	**23**	**7**	**-5**	....	....	....	....	....	....	....	....
99-2000	**Washington Capitals**	**NHL**	**25**	**2**	**0**	**2**	**2**	**0**	**2**	**15**	**0**	**0**	**1**	**13**	**15.4**	**4**	**0**	**13**	**2**	**-7**	....	....	....	....	....	....	....	....
	NHL Totals		**853**	**74**	**122**	**196**	**70**	**93**	**163**	**928**	**3**	**6**	**7**	**761**	**9.7**	**307**	**7**	**685**	**264**		**44**	**2**	**6**	**8**	**34**	**0**	**0**	**0**

• Missed majority of 1984-85 season recovering from hand injury suffered in practice, October, 1984. Traded to **Chicago** by **Quebec** for Bob Mason, July 5, 1988. Traded to **Winnipeg** by **Chicago** for Winnipeg's 4th round choice (Igor Kravchuk) in 1991 Entry Draft, December 14, 1990. Traded to **Washington** by **Winnipeg** with Igor Ulanov for Washington's 3rd (later traded to Dallas — Dallas selected Sergei Gusev) and 5th (Brian Elder) round choices in 1995 Entry Draft, April 7, 1995.

• EAKIN, Bruce

Bruce Glen C – L. 5'11", 190 lbs. b: Winnipeg, Man., 9/28/1962. Calgary's 9th, 204th overall, in 1981.

Season	Club	League	GP	G	A	Pts	AG	AA	APts	PIM	PP	SH	GW	S	%	TGF	PGF	TGA	PGA	+/-	GP	G	A	Pts	PIM	PP	SH	GW
1979-80	St. James Canadians	MJHL	48	42	62	104	....	....	....	76	....	....	....	....	....	....	....	....	....	....	....	....	....	....	....	....	....	....
1980-81	Saskatoon Blades	WHL	52	18	46	64	....	....	....	54	....	....	....	....	....	....	....	....	....	....	....	....	....	....	....	....	....	....
1981-82	Saskatoon Blades	WHL	66	42	*125	167	....	....	....	120	....	....	....	....	....	....	....	....	....	....	5	4	6	10	0	....	....	....
	Canada	WJC-A	7	4	7	11	....	....	....	4	....	....	....	....	....	....	....	....	....	....	....	....	....	....	....	....	....	....
	Calgary Flames	**NHL**	**1**	**0**	**0**	**0**	**0**	**0**	**0**	**0**	**0**	**0**	**0**	**0**	**0.0**	**0**	**0**	**2**	**0**	**-2**	....	....	....	....	....	....	....	....
	Oklahoma City Stars	CHL	3	0	3	3	....	....	....	0	....	....	....	....	....	....	....	....	....	....	4	2	0	2	2	....	....	....
1982-83	Colorado Flames	CHL	73	24	46	70	....	....	....	45	....	....	....	....	....	....	....	....	....	....	6	1	6	7	2	....	....	....
1983-84	**Calgary Flames**	**NHL**	**7**	**2**	**1**	**3**	**2**	**1**	**3**	**4**	**0**	**0**	**0**	**8**	**25.0**	**4**	**1**	**4**	**0**	**-1**	....	....	....	....	....	....	....	....
	Colorado Flames	CHL	67	33	69	102	....	....	....	18	....	....	....	....	....	....	....	....	....	....	6	4	2	6	0	....	....	....
1984-85	**Calgary Flames**	**NHL**	**1**	**0**	**0**	**0**	**0**	**0**	**0**	**0**	**0**	**0**	**0**	**0**	**0.0**	**0**	**0**	**0**	**0**	**0**	....	....	....	....	....	....	....	....
	Moncton Golden Flames	AHL	78	35	48	83	....	....	....	60	....	....	....	....	....	....	....	....	....	....	....	....	....	....	....	....	....	....
1985-86	**Detroit Red Wings**	**NHL**	**4**	**0**	**1**	**1**	**0**	**1**	**1**	**0**	**0**	**0**	**0**	**1**	**0.0**	**1**	**0**	**8**	**3**	**-4**	....	....	....	....	....	....	....	....
	Adirondack Red Wings	AHL	25	8	10	18	....	....	....	23	....	....	....	....	....	....	....	....	....	....	....	....	....	....	....	....	....	....
	Nova Scotia Oilers	AHL	14	6	12	18	....	....	....	12	....	....	....	....	....	....	....	....	....	....	....	....	....	....	....	....	....	....

			REGULAR SEASON																		PLAYOFFS							
Season	Club	League	GP	G	A	Pts	AG	AA	APts	PIM	PP	SH	GW	S	%	TGF	PGF	TGA	PGA	+/–	GP	G	A	Pts	PIM	PP	SH	GW
1986-87	New Haven Nighthawks	AHL	4	1	2	3	....	....	....	4	....	....	....	....	....	....	....	....	....	....	....	....	....	....	....	....	....	....
	EHC Olten	Switz.	32	12	25	37	....	....	....	....	....	....	....	....	....	....	....	....	....	....	....	....	....	....	....	....	....	....
	Springfield Indians	AHL	11	0	5	5	....	....	....	6	....	....	....	....	....	....	....	....	....	....	....	....	....	....	....	....	....	....
1987-88	KalPa Kuopio	Finland	36	6	17	23	....	....	....	50	....	....	....	....	....	....	....	....	....	....	....	....	....	....	....	....	....	....
1988-89	EHC Neuss	Germany-3	23	18	23	41	....	....	....	52	....	....	....	....	....	....	....	....	....	....	....	....	....	....	....	....	....	....
1989-90	EHC Essen-West	Germany-2	32	40	69	109	....	....	....	47	....	....	....	....	....	....	....	....	....	....	18	18	26	44	33	....	....	....
	SC Herisau	Switz.	1	0	0	0	....	....	....	0	....	....	....	....	....	....	....	....	....	....	....	....	....	....	....	....	....	....
1990-91	EHC Essen-West	Germany-2	49	42	69	111	....	....	....	72	....	....	....	....	....	....	....	....	....	....	....	....	....	....	....	....	....	....
1991-92	EHC Nurnberg	Germany-2	29	17	38	55	....	....	....	38	....	....	....	....	....	....	....	....	....	....	5	0	1	1	6	....	....	....
1992-93	Krefelder EV	Germany	42	28	34	62	....	....	....	84	....	....	....	....	....	....	....	....	....	....	4	1	2	3	6	....	....	....
1993-94	Krefelder EV	Germany	44	19	28	47	....	....	....	80	....	....	....	....	....	....	....	....	....	....	6	1	4	5	8	....	....	....
1994-95	Dusseldorfer EG	Germany	19	5	5	10	....	....	....	4	....	....	....	....	....	....	....	....	....	....	10	2	10	12	12	....	....	....
1995-96	Dusseldorfer EG	Germany	10	0	0	0	....	....	....	8	....	....	....	....	....	....	....	....	....	....	....	....	....	....	....	....	....	....
	Kassel Huskies	Germany	38	15	21	36	....	....	....	44	....	....	....	....	....	....	....	....	....	....	8	3	5	8	4	....	....	....
1996-97	Kassel Huskies	Germany	49	13	34	47	....	....	....	38	....	....	....	....	....	....	....	....	....	....	10	2	7	9	24	....	....	....
1997-98	Kassel Huskies	Germany	48	11	22	33	....	....	....	71	....	....	....	....	....	....	....	....	....	....	....	....	....	....	....	....	....	....
	Kassel Huskies	EuroHL	6	3	1	4	....	....	....	24	....	....	....	....	....	....	....	....	....	....	....	....	....	....	....	....	....	....
1998-99	London Knights	BH-Cup	11	3	3	6	....	....	....	6	....	....	....	....	....	....	....	....	....	....	....	....	....	....	....	....	....	....
	London Knights	Britain	11	3	12	15	....	....	....	22	....	....	....	....	....	....	....	....	....	....	....	....	....	....	....	....	....	....
	NHL Totals		**13**	**2**	**2**	**4**	**2**	**2**	**4**	**4**	**0**	**0**	**0**	**9**	**22.2**	**5**	**1**	**14**	**3**		....	....	....	....	....	....	....	....

WHL First All-Star Team (1982) • CHL Second All-Star Team (1984)

Signed as a free agent by **Detroit**, July 18, 1985. Traded to **Edmonton** by **Detroit** for Billy Carroll, December 28, 1985. • Signed as a free agent by **Springfield** (AHL), March 10, 1987.

• EAKINS, Dallas

Dallas F. D – L. 6'2", 200 lbs. b: Dade City, FL, 2/27/1967. Washington's 11th, 208th overall, in 1985.

Season	Club	League	GP	G	A	Pts	AG	AA	APts	PIM	PP	SH	GW	S	%	TGF	PGF	TGA	PGA	+/–	GP	G	A	Pts	PIM	PP	SH	GW
1983-84	Peterborough Travelways	OMHA	29	7	20	27	....	....	....	67	....	....	....	....	....	....	....	....	....	....	....	....	....	....	....	....	....	....
	Peterborough Lumber	OJHL-B	5	0	3	3	....	....	....	4	....	....	....	....	....	....	....	....	....	....	....	....	....	....	....	....	....	....
1984-85	Peterborough Petes	OHL	48	0	8	8	....	....	....	96	....	....	....	....	....	....	....	....	....	....	7	0	0	0	18	....	....	....
1985-86	Peterborough Petes	OHL	60	6	16	22	....	....	....	134	....	....	....	....	....	....	....	....	....	....	16	0	1	1	30	....	....	....
1986-87	Peterborough Petes	OHL	54	3	11	14	....	....	....	145	....	....	....	....	....	....	....	....	....	....	12	1	4	5	37	....	....	....
1987-88	Peterborough Petes	OHL	64	11	27	38	....	....	....	129	....	....	....	....	....	....	....	....	....	....	12	3	12	15	16	....	....	....
1988-89	Baltimore Skipjacks	AHL	62	0	10	10	....	....	....	139	....	....	....	....	....	....	....	....	....	....	....	....	....	....	....	....	....	....
1989-90	Moncton Hawks	AHL	75	2	11	13	....	....	....	189	....	....	....	....	....	....	....	....	....	....	....	....	....	....	....	....	....	....
1990-91	Moncton Hawks	AHL	75	1	12	13	....	....	....	132	....	....	....	....	....	....	....	....	....	....	9	0	1	1	44	....	....	....
1991-92	Moncton Hawks	AHL	67	3	13	16	....	....	....	136	....	....	....	....	....	....	....	....	....	....	11	2	1	3	16	....	....	....
1992-93	**Winnipeg Jets**	**NHL**	**14**	**0**	**2**	**2**	**0**	**1**	**1**	**38**	**0**	**0**	**0**	**9**	**0.0**	**10**	**0**	**13**	**5**	**2**	....	....	....	....	....	....	....	....
	Moncton Hawks	AHL	55	4	6	10	....	....	....	132	....	....	....	....	....	....	....	....	....	....	....	....	....	....	....	....	....	....
1993-94	**Florida Panthers**	**NHL**	**1**	**0**	**0**	**0**	**0**	**0**	**0**	**0**	**0**	**0**	**0**	**2**	**0.0**	**0**	**0**	**1**	**1**	**0**	....	....	....	....	....	....	....	....
	Cincinnati Cyclones	IHL	80	1	18	19	....	....	....	143	....	....	....	....	....	....	....	....	....	....	8	0	1	1	41	....	....	....
1994-95	**Florida Panthers**	**NHL**	**17**	**0**	**1**	**1**	**0**	**1**	**1**	**35**	**0**	**0**	**0**	**3**	**0.0**	**12**	**0**	**12**	**2**	**2**	....	....	....	....	....	....	....	....
	Cincinnati Cyclones	IHL	59	6	12	18	....	....	....	69	....	....	....	....	....	....	....	....	....	....	....	....	....	....	....	....	....	....
1995-96	**St. Louis Blues**	**NHL**	**16**	**0**	**1**	**1**	**0**	**1**	**1**	**34**	**0**	**0**	**0**	**6**	**0.0**	**4**	**0**	**10**	**4**	**–2**	....	....	....	....	....	....	....	....
	Worcester IceCats	AHL	4	0	0	0	....	....	....	12	....	....	....	....	....	....	....	....	....	....	....	....	....	....	....	....	....	....
	Winnipeg Jets	**NHL**	**2**	**0**	**0**	**0**	**0**	**0**	**0**	**0**	**0**	**0**	**0**	**0**	**0.0**	**1**	**0**	**0**	**0**	**1**	....	....	....	....	....	....	....	....
1996-97	**Phoenix Coyotes**	**NHL**	**4**	**0**	**0**	**0**	**0**	**0**	**0**	**10**	**0**	**0**	**0**	**2**	**0.0**	**1**	**0**	**4**	**0**	**–3**	....	....	....	....	....	....	....	....
	Springfield Falcons	AHL	38	6	7	13	....	....	....	63	....	....	....	....	....	....	....	....	....	....	....	....	....	....	....	....	....	....
	New York Rangers	**NHL**	**3**	**0**	**0**	**0**	**0**	**0**	**0**	**6**	**0**	**0**	**0**	**2**	**0.0**	**1**	**0**	**2**	**0**	**–1**	**4**	**0**	**0**	**0**	**4**	**0**	**0**	**0**
	Binghamton Rangers	AHL	19	1	7	8	....	....	....	15	....	....	....	....	....	....	....	....	....	....	....	....	....	....	....	....	....	....
1997-98	**Florida Panthers**	**NHL**	**23**	**0**	**1**	**1**	**0**	**1**	**1**	**44**	**0**	**0**	**0**	**16**	**0.0**	**10**	**0**	**9**	**0**	**1**	....	....	....	....	....	....	....	....
	Beast of New Haven	AHL	4	0	1	1	....	....	....	7	....	....	....	....	....	....	....	....	....	....	....	....	....	....	....	....	....	....
1998-99	**Toronto Maple Leafs**	**NHL**	**18**	**0**	**2**	**2**	**0**	**2**	**2**	**24**	**0**	**0**	**0**	**11**	**0.0**	**15**	**0**	**18**	**6**	**3**	**1**	**0**	**0**	**0**	**0**	**0**	**0**	**0**
	Chicago Wolves	IHL	2	0	0	0	....	....	....	0	....	....	....	....	....	....	....	....	....	....	....	....	....	....	....	....	....	....
	St. John's Maple Leafs	AHL	20	3	7	10	....	....	....	16	....	....	....	....	....	....	....	....	....	....	5	0	1	1	6	....	....	....
99-2000	**New York Islanders**	**NHL**	**2**	**0**	**1**	**1**	**0**	**1**	**1**	**2**	**0**	**0**	**0**	**4**	**0.0**	**4**	**0**	**2**	**1**	**3**	....	....	....	....	....	....	....	....
	Chicago Wolves	IHL	68	5	26	31	....	....	....	99	....	....	....	....	....	....	....	....	....	....	16	1	4	5	16	....	....	....
	NHL Totals		**100**	**0**	**8**	**8**	**0**	**7**	**7**	**193**	**0**	**0**	**0**	**55**	**0.0**	**58**	**0**	**71**	**19**		**5**	**0**	**0**	**0**	**4**	**0**	**0**	**0**

IHL Second All-Star Team (2000)

Signed as a free agent by **Winnipeg**, October 17, 1989. Signed as a free agent by **Florida**, July 8, 1993. Traded to **St. Louis** by **Florida** for St. Louis' 4th round choice (Ivan Novoseltsev) in 1997 Entry Draft, September 28, 1995. Claimed on waivers by **Winnipeg** from **St. Louis**, March 20, 1996. Transferred to **Phoenix** after **Winnipeg** franchise relocated, July 1, 1996. Traded to **NY Rangers** by **Phoenix** with Mike Eastwood for Jayson More, February 6, 1997. Signed as a free agent by **Florida**, July 30, 1997. Signed as a free agent by **Toronto**, July 28, 1998. Signed as a free agent by **NY Islanders**, August 12, 1999. Traded to **Chicago** by **NY Islanders** for future considerations, March 3, 2000.

• EASTWOOD, Mike

Michael Barry C – R. 6'3", 209 lbs. b: Ottawa, Ont., 7/1/1967. Toronto's 5th, 91st overall, in 1987.

Season	Club	League	GP	G	A	Pts	AG	AA	APts	PIM	PP	SH	GW	S	%	TGF	PGF	TGA	PGA	+/–	GP	G	A	Pts	PIM	PP	SH	GW
1984-85	Nepean Raiders	OJHL	46	10	13	23	....	....	....	18	....	....	....	....	....	....	....	....	....	....	....	....	....	....	....	....	....	....
1985-86	Nepean Raiders	OJHL	7	4	2	6	....	....	....	6	....	....	....	....	....	....	....	....	....	....	....	....	....	....	....	....	....	....
1986-87	Pembroke Lumber Kings	OJHL	54	58	45	103	....	....	....	62	....	....	....	....	....	....	....	....	....	....	23	36	11	47	32	....	....	....
	Pembroke Lumber Kings	Cen-Cup	4	3	3	6	....	....	....	10	....	....	....	....	....	....	....	....	....	....	....	....	....	....	....	....	....	....
1987-88	Western Michigan University	CCHA	42	5	8	13	....	....	....	14	....	....	....	....	....	....	....	....	....	....	....	....	....	....	....	....	....	....
1988-89	Western Michigan University	CCHA	40	10	13	23	....	....	....	87	....	....	....	....	....	....	....	....	....	....	....	....	....	....	....	....	....	....
1989-90	Western Michigan University	CCHA	40	25	27	52	....	....	....	36	....	....	....	....	....	....	....	....	....	....	....	....	....	....	....	....	....	....
1990-91	Western Michigan University	CCHA	42	29	32	61	....	....	....	84	....	....	....	....	....	....	....	....	....	....	....	....	....	....	....	....	....	....
1991-92	**Toronto Maple Leafs**	**NHL**	**9**	**0**	**2**	**2**	**0**	**2**	**2**	**4**	**0**	**0**	**0**	**6**	**0.0**	**3**	**2**	**5**	**0**	**–4**	....	....	....	....	....	....	....	....
	St. John's Maple Leafs	AHL	61	18	25	43	....	....	....	28	....	....	....	....	....	....	....	....	....	....	16	9	10	19	16	....	....	....
1992-93	**Toronto Maple Leafs**	**NHL**	**12**	**1**	**6**	**7**	**1**	**4**	**5**	**21**	**0**	**0**	**0**	**11**	**9.1**	**9**	**1**	**10**	**0**	**–2**	**10**	**1**	**2**	**3**	**8**	**0**	**0**	**0**
	St. John's Maple Leafs	AHL	60	24	35	59	....	....	....	32	....	....	....	....	....	....	....	....	....	....	....	....	....	....	....	....	....	....
1993-94	**Toronto Maple Leafs**	**NHL**	**54**	**8**	**10**	**18**	**7**	**8**	**15**	**28**	**1**	**0**	**2**	**41**	**19.5**	**24**	**6**	**19**	**3**	**2**	**18**	**3**	**2**	**5**	**12**	**1**	**0**	**1**
1994-95	**Toronto Maple Leafs**	**NHL**	**36**	**5**	**5**	**10**	**9**	**7**	**16**	**32**	**0**	**0**	**0**	**38**	**13.2**	**13**	**2**	**27**	**4**	**–12**	....	....	....	....	....	....	....	....
	Winnipeg Jets	**NHL**	**13**	**3**	**6**	**9**	**5**	**9**	**14**	**4**	**0**	**0**	**0**	**17**	**17.6**	**12**	**1**	**9**	**1**	**3**	....	....	....	....	....	....	....	....
1995-96	**Winnipeg Jets**	**NHL**	**80**	**14**	**14**	**28**	**14**	**11**	**25**	**20**	**2**	**0**	**3**	**94**	**14.9**	**45**	**3**	**77**	**21**	**–14**	**6**	**0**	**1**	**1**	**2**	**0**	**0**	**0**
1996-97	**Phoenix Coyotes**	**NHL**	**33**	**1**	**3**	**4**	**1**	**3**	**4**	**4**	**0**	**0**	**0**	**22**	**4.5**	**10**	**0**	**20**	**7**	**–3**	....	....	....	....	....	....	....	....
	New York Rangers	**NHL**	**27**	**1**	**7**	**8**	**1**	**6**	**7**	**10**	**0**	**0**	**0**	**22**	**4.5**	**10**	**0**	**10**	**2**	**2**	**15**	**1**	**2**	**3**	**22**	**0**	**0**	**0**
1997-98	**New York Rangers**	**NHL**	**48**	**5**	**5**	**10**	**6**	**5**	**11**	**16**	**0**	**0**	**0**	**34**	**14.7**	**12**	**0**	**23**	**9**	**–2**	....	....	....	....	....	....	....	....
	St. Louis Blues	**NHL**	**10**	**1**	**0**	**1**	**1**	**0**	**1**	**6**	**0**	**0**	**1**	**4**	**25.0**	**1**	**0**	**1**	**0**	**0**	**3**	**1**	**0**	**1**	**0**	**0**	**0**	**1**
1998-99	**St. Louis Blues**	**NHL**	**82**	**9**	**21**	**30**	**11**	**20**	**31**	**36**	**0**	**0**	**0**	**76**	**11.8**	**36**	**0**	**49**	**19**	**6**	**13**	**1**	**1**	**2**	**6**	**0**	**0**	**0**
99-2000	**St. Louis Blues**	**NHL**	**79**	**19**	**15**	**34**	**21**	**14**	**35**	**32**	**1**	**3**	**3**	**83**	**22.9**	**44**	**3**	**50**	**14**	**5**	**7**	**1**	**1**	**2**	**6**	**0**	**0**	**0**
	NHL Totals		**483**	**67**	**94**	**161**	**77**	**89**	**166**	**213**	**4**	**3**	**9**	**448**	**15.0**	**219**	**18**	**300**	**80**		**72**	**8**	**9**	**17**	**56**	**1**	**0**	**2**

CCHA Second All-Star Team (1991)

Traded to **Winnipeg** by **Toronto** with Toronto's 3rd round choice (Brad Isbister) in 1995 Entry Draft for Tie Domi, April 7, 1995. Transferred to **Phoenix** after **Winnipeg** franchise relocated, July 1, 1996. Traded to **NY Rangers** by **Phoenix** with Dallas Eakins for Jayson More, February 6, 1997. Traded to **St. Louis** by **NY Rangers** for Harry York, March 24, 1998.

• EATON, Mark

D – L. 6'2", 205 lbs. b: Wilmington, DE, 5/6/1977.

Season	Club	League	GP	G	A	Pts	AG	AA	APts	PIM	PP	SH	GW	S	%	TGF	PGF	TGA	PGA	+/–	GP	G	A	Pts	PIM	PP	SH	GW
1995-96	Waterloo Black Hawks	USHL	50	4	21	25	....	....	....	....	....	....	....	....	....	....	....	....	....	....	....	....	....	....	....	....	....	....
1996-97	Waterloo Black Hawks	USHL	50	6	32	38	....	....	....	62	....	....	....	....	....	....	....	....	....	....	....	....	....	....	....	....	....	....
1997-98	Notre Dame University	CCHA	41	12	17	29	....	....	....	32	....	....	....	....	....	....	....	....	....	....	....	....	....	....	....	....	....	....
1998-99	Philadelphia Phantoms	AHL	74	9	27	36	....	....	....	38	....	....	....	....	....	....	....	....	....	....	16	4	8	12	0	....	....	....
99-2000	**Philadelphia Flyers**	**NHL**	**27**	**1**	**1**	**2**	**1**	**1**	**2**	**8**	**0**	**0**	**1**	**25**	**4.0**	**18**	**3**	**18**	**4**	**1**	**7**	**0**	**0**	**0**	**0**	**0**	**0**	**0**
	Philadelphia Phantoms	AHL	47	9	17	26	....	....	....	6	....	....	....	....	....	....	....	....	....	....	....	....	....	....	....	....	....	....
	NHL Totals		**27**	**1**	**1**	**2**	**1**	**1**	**2**	**8**	**0**	**0**	**1**	**25**	**4.0**	**18**	**3**	**18**	**4**		**7**	**0**	**0**	**0**	**0**	**0**	**0**	**0**

Signed as a free agent by **Philadelphia**, August 4, 1998.

• EATOUGH, Jeff

RW – R. 5'9", 168 lbs. b: Toronto, Ont., 6/2/1963. Buffalo's 5th, 80th overall, in 1981.

			REGULAR SEASON																		PLAYOFFS							
Season	Club	League	GP	G	A	Pts	AG	AA	APts	PIM	PP	SH	GW	S	%	TGF	PGF	TGA	PGA	+/–	GP	G	A	Pts	PIM	PP	SH	GW
1979-80	Aurora Eagles	OJHL	40	16	25	41	....	....	....	186	....	....	....	....	....	....	....	....	....	....	....	....	....	....	....	....	....	....
	Niagara Falls Flyers	OMJHL	6	0	1	1	....	....	....	4	....	....	....	....	....	....	....	....	....	....	....	....	....	....	....	....	....	....
1980-81	Cornwall Royals	OMJHL	68	30	42	72	....	....	....	142	....	....	....	....	....	....	....	....	....	....	18	5	7	12	52	....	....	....
	Canada	WJC-A	5	1	2	3	....	....	....	4	....	....	....	....	....	....	....	....	....	....	....	....	....	....	....	....	....	....
	Cornwall Royals	Mem-Cup	5	0	3	3	....	....	....	12	....	....	....	....	....	....	....	....	....	....	....	....	....	....	....	....	....	....
1981-82	Cornwall Royals	OHL	66	53	37	90	....	....	....	180	....	....	....	....	....	....	....	....	....	....	5	0	5	5	21	....	....	....
	Buffalo Sabres	**NHL**	**1**	**0**	**0**	**0**	**0**	**0**	**0**	**0**	**0**	**0**	**0**	**0**	**0.0**	**0**	**0**	**1**	**0**	**–1**	....	....	....	....	....	....	....	....
1982-83	Cornwall Royals	OHL	9	5	3	8	....	....	....	18	....	....	....	....	....	....	....	....	....	....	....	....	....	....	....	....	....	....
	North Bay Centennials	OHL	50	25	24	49	....	....	....	73	....	....	....	....	....	....	....	....	....	....	8	2	5	7	12	....	....	....
1983-84	Rochester Americans	AHL	24	1	5	6	....	....	....	5	....	....	....	....	....	....	....	....	....	....	....	....	....	....	....	....	....	....
	Flint Generals	IHL	5	4	1	5	....	....	....	6	....	....	....	....	....	....	....	....	....	....	....	....	....	....	....	....	....	....
1984-85	Flint Generals	IHL	4	0	1	1	....	....	....	0	....	....	....	....	....	....	....	....	....	....	....	....	....	....	....	....	....	....
	Pinebridge Bucks	ACHL	12	4	8	12	....	....	....	31	....	....	....	....	....	....	....	....	....	....	....	....	....	....	....	....	....	....
	Mohawk Valley Stars	ACHL	42	27	33	60	....	....	....	37	....	....	....	....	....	....	....	....	....	....	....	....	....	....	....	....	....	....
1985-86	Mohawk Valley Comets	ACHL	27	18	19	37	....	....	....	43	....	....	....	....	....	....	....	....	....	....	6	5	8	13	4	....	....	....
	Flint Spirits	IHL	4	1	0	1	....	....	....	2	....	....	....	....	....	....	....	....	....	....	....	....	....	....	....	....	....	....
1986-87	Mohawk Valley Comets	ACHL	53	43	42	85	....	....	....	93	....	....	....	....	....	....	....	....	....	....	13	5	7	12	46	....	....	....
1987-88	Carolina Thunderbirds	AAHL	9	3	8	11	....	....	....	16	....	....	....	....	....	....	....	....	....	....	....	....	....	....	....	....	....	....
	NHL Totals		**1**	**0**	**0**	**0**	**0**	**0**	**0**	**0**	**0**	**0**	**0**	**0**	**0.0**	**0**	**0**	**1**	**0**		....	....	....	....	....	....	....	....

ACHL First All-Star Team (1987)

• EAVES, Mike

Michael Gordon C – R. 5'10", 180 lbs. b: Denver, CO, 6/10/1956. St. Louis' 8th, 113th overall, in 1976.

			REGULAR SEASON																		PLAYOFFS							
Season	Club	League	GP	G	A	Pts	AG	AA	APts	PIM	PP	SH	GW	S	%	TGF	PGF	TGA	PGA	+/–	GP	G	A	Pts	PIM	PP	SH	GW
1973-74	Nepean Raiders	OJHL	54	54	48	*102	....	....	....	....	....	....	....	....	....	....	....	....	....	....	....	....	....	....	....	....	....	....
1974-75	University of Wisconsin	WCHA	38	17	37	54	....	....	....	12	....	....	....	....	....	....	....	....	....	....	....	....	....	....	....	....	....	....
1975-76	University of Wisconsin	WCHA	34	18	25	43	....	....	....	22	....	....	....	....	....	....	....	....	....	....	....	....	....	....	....	....	....	....
	United States	WEC-A	10	2	1	3	....	....	....	0	....	....	....	....	....	....	....	....	....	....	....	....	....	....	....	....	....	....
1976-77	University of Wisconsin	WCHA	45	28	53	81	....	....	....	18	....	....	....	....	....	....	....	....	....	....	....	....	....	....	....	....	....	....
1977-78	University of Wisconsin	WCHA	43	31	*58	*89	....	....	....	16	....	....	....	....	....	....	....	....	....	....	....	....	....	....	....	....	....	....
	United States	WEC-A	10	4	3	7	....	....	....	2	....	....	....	....	....	....	....	....	....	....	....	....	....	....	....	....	....	....
1978-79	**Minnesota North Stars**	**NHL**	**3**	**0**	**0**	**0**	**0**	**0**	**0**	**0**	**0**	**0**	**0**	**5**	**0.0**	**0**	**0**	**3**	**2**	**–1**	....	....	....	....	....	....	....	....
	Oklahoma City Stars	CHL	68	26	61	87	....	....	....	21	....	....	....	....	....	....	....	....	....	....	....	....	....	....	....	....	....	....
1979-80	**Minnesota North Stars**	**NHL**	**56**	**18**	**28**	**46**	**15**	**20**	**35**	**11**	**9**	**0**	**3**	**80**	**22.5**	**62**	**26**	**36**	**3**	**3**	**15**	**2**	**5**	**7**	**4**	**0**	**0**	**0**
	Oklahoma City Stars	CHL	12	9	8	17	....	....	....	2	....	....	....	....	....	....	....	....	....	....	....	....	....	....	....	....	....	....
1980-81	Minnesota North Stars	DN-Cup	2	0	1	1	....	....	....	0	....	....	....	....	....	....	....	....	....	....	....	....	....	....	....	....	....	....
	Minnesota North Stars	**NHL**	**48**	**10**	**24**	**34**	**8**	**16**	**24**	**18**	**1**	**1**	**1**	**104**	**9.6**	**53**	**13**	**42**	**3**	**1**	....	....	....	....	....	....	....	....
1981-82	United States	Can-Cup	6	3	3	6	....	....	....	4	....	....	....	....	....	....	....	....	....	....	....	....	....	....	....	....	....	....
	Minnesota North Stars	**NHL**	**25**	**11**	**10**	**21**	**9**	**7**	**16**	**0**	**2**	**0**	**1**	**62**	**17.7**	**31**	**10**	**21**	**2**	**2**	....	....	....	....	....	....	....	....
1982-83	**Minnesota North Stars**	**NHL**	**75**	**16**	**16**	**32**	**13**	**11**	**24**	**21**	**1**	**5**	**2**	**143**	**11.2**	**42**	**2**	**68**	**25**	**–3**	**9**	**0**	**0**	**0**	**0**	**0**	**0**	**0**
1983-84	**Calgary Flames**	**NHL**	**61**	**14**	**36**	**50**	**11**	**25**	**36**	**20**	**3**	**0**	**3**	**118**	**11.9**	**81**	**22**	**68**	**18**	**9**	**11**	**4**	**4**	**8**	**2**	**1**	**1**	**1**
1984-85	**Calgary Flames**	**NHL**	**56**	**14**	**29**	**43**	**11**	**20**	**31**	**10**	**1**	**2**	**1**	**96**	**14.6**	**63**	**10**	**66**	**27**	**14**	....	....	....	....	....	....	....	....
1985-86	**Calgary Flames**	**NHL**	DID NOT PLAY – ASSISTANT COACH																									
	Calgary Flames	**NHL**	....	....	....	....	....	....	....	....	....	....	....	....	....	....	....	....	....	....	**8**	**1**	**1**	**2**	**8**	**0**	**0**	**0**
1986-87	U. of Wisconsin-Eau Claire	NCHA	DID NOT PLAY – COACHING																									
1987-88	St. Cloud State	WCHA	DID NOT PLAY – ASSISTANT COACH																									
1988-1990	**Philadelphia Flyers**	**NHL**	DID NOT PLAY – ASSISTANT COACH																									
1990-1993	Hershey Bears	AHL	DID NOT PLAY – COACHING																									
1993-1994	**Philadelphia Flyers**	**NHL**	DID NOT PLAY – ASSISTANT COACH																									
1994-1997	HIFK Helsinki	Finland	DID NOT PLAY – COACHING																									
1997-2000	**Pittsburgh Penguins**	**NHL**	DID NOT PLAY – ASSISTANT COACH																									
	NHL Totals		**324**	**83**	**143**	**226**	**67**	**99**	**166**	**80**	**17**	**8**	**11**	**608**	**13.7**	**332**	**83**	**304**	**80**		**43**	**7**	**10**	**17**	**14**	**1**	**1**	**1**

• Brother of Murray • WCHA Second All-Star Team (1977) • NCAA West First All-American Team (1977, 1978) • WCHA First All-Star Team (1978) • CHL Second All-Star Team (1979) • Won Ken McKenzie Trophy (CHL's Rookie of the Year) (1979)

Rights traded to **Cleveland** by **St. Louis** for Len Frig, August 17, 1977. Rights transferred to **Minnesota** Reserve List after **Cleveland-Minnesota** Dispersal Draft, June 15, 1978. Traded to **Calgary** by **Minnesota** with Keith Hanson for Steve Christoff and Calgary's 2nd round choice (Frantisek Musil) in 1983 Entry Draft, June 8, 1983. • Suffered eventual career-ending head injury in exhibition game vs. Quebec, September 21, 1985. • Officially announced retirement and named Assistant Coach of **Calgary**, October 21, 1985. • Came out of retirement as an emergency injury replacement for Carey Wilson, May 4, 1986.

• EAVES, Murray

Murray James C – R. 5'10", 185 lbs. b: Calgary, Alta., 5/10/1960. Winnipeg's 3rd, 44th overall, in 1980.

			REGULAR SEASON																		PLAYOFFS							
Season	Club	League	GP	G	A	Pts	AG	AA	APts	PIM	PP	SH	GW	S	%	TGF	PGF	TGA	PGA	+/–	GP	G	A	Pts	PIM	PP	SH	GW
1977-78	Windsor Jr. Spitfires	OHA-B	STATISTICS NOT AVAILABLE																									
	Windsor Spitfires	OMJHL	3	0	0	0	....	....	....	0	....	....	....	....	....	....	....	....	....	....	....	....	....	....	....	....	....	....
1978-79	University of Michigan	CCHA	23	12	22	34	....	....	....	14	....	....	....	....	....	....	....	....	....	....	....	....	....	....	....	....	....	....
1979-80	University of Michigan	CCHA	33	36	49	85	....	....	....	34	....	....	....	....	....	....	....	....	....	....	....	....	....	....	....	....	....	....
1980-81	**Winnipeg Jets**	**NHL**	**12**	**1**	**2**	**3**	**1**	**1**	**2**	**5**	**1**	**0**	**0**	**12**	**8.3**	**7**	**2**	**14**	**2**	**–7**	....	....	....	....	....	....	....	....
	Tulsa Oilers	CHL	59	24	34	58	....	....	....	59	....	....	....	....	....	....	....	....	....	....	8	5	5	10	13	....	....	....
1981-82	**Winnipeg Jets**	**NHL**	**2**	**0**	**0**	**0**	**0**	**0**	**0**	**0**	**0**	**0**	**0**	**0**	**0.0**	**0**	**0**	**0**	**0**	**0**	....	....	....	....	....	....	....	....
	Tulsa Oilers	CHL	68	30	49	79	....	....	....	33	....	....	....	....	....	....	....	....	....	....	3	0	2	2	0	....	....	....
1982-83	**Winnipeg Jets**	**NHL**	**26**	**2**	**7**	**9**	**2**	**5**	**7**	**2**	**0**	**0**	**0**	**17**	**11.8**	**9**	**0**	**15**	**1**	**–5**	....	....	....	....	....	....	....	....
	Sherbrooke Jets	AHL	40	25	34	59	....	....	....	16	....	....	....	....	....	....	....	....	....	....	....	....	....	....	....	....	....	....
1983-84	**Winnipeg Jets**	**NHL**	**2**	**0**	**0**	**0**	**0**	**0**	**0**	**0**	**0**	**0**	**0**	**1**	**0.0**	**0**	**0**	**1**	**1**	**0**	**2**	**0**	**0**	**0**	**2**	**0**	**0**	**0**
	Sherbrooke Jets	AHL	78	47	68	115	....	....	....	40	....	....	....	....	....	....	....	....	....	....	....	....	....	....	....	....	....	....
1984-85	**Winnipeg Jets**	**NHL**	**3**	**0**	**3**	**3**	**0**	**2**	**2**	**0**	**0**	**0**	**0**	**2**	**0.0**	**3**	**0**	**0**	**0**	**3**	**2**	**0**	**1**	**1**	**0**	**0**	**0**	**0**
	Sherbrooke Canadiens	AHL	47	26	42	68	....	....	....	28	....	....	....	....	....	....	....	....	....	....	15	5	13	18	35	....	....	....
1985-86	**Winnipeg Jets**	**NHL**	**4**	**1**	**0**	**1**	**1**	**0**	**1**	**0**	**0**	**0**	**0**	**6**	**16.7**	**1**	**0**	**3**	**0**	**–2**	....	....	....	....	....	....	....	....
	Sherbrooke Canadiens	AHL	68	22	51	73	....	....	....	26	....	....	....	....	....	....	....	....	....	....	....	....	....	....	....	....	....	....
1986-87	Nova Scotia Oilers	AHL	76	26	38	64	....	....	....	46	....	....	....	....	....	....	....	....	....	....	4	1	1	2	2	....	....	....
1987-88	**Detroit Red Wings**	**NHL**	**7**	**0**	**1**	**1**	**0**	**1**	**1**	**2**	**0**	**0**	**0**	**4**	**0.0**	**1**	**0**	**2**	**0**	**–1**	....	....	....	....	....	....	....	....
	Adirondack Red Wings	AHL	65	39	54	93	....	....	....	65	....	....	....	....	....	....	....	....	....	....	11	3	*11	14	8	....	....	....
1988-89	Adirondack Red Wings	AHL	80	46	72	118	....	....	....	11	....	....	....	....	....	....	....	....	....	....	16	*13	12	25	10	....	....	....
1989-90	**Detroit Red Wings**	**NHL**	**1**	**0**	**0**	**0**	**0**	**0**	**0**	**0**	**0**	**0**	**0**	**2**	**0.0**	**0**	**0**	**2**	**0**	**–2**	....	....	....	....	....	....	....	....
	Adirondack Red Wings	AHL	78	40	49	89	....	....	....	35	....	....	....	....	....	....	....	....	....	....	6	2	3	5	2	....	....	....
1990-91	HC Varese	Italy	32	22	37	59	....	....	....	23	....	....	....	....	....	....	....	....	....	....	10	9	9	18	4	....	....	....
1991-92	HC Varese	Alpenliga	15	9	10	19	....	....	....	4	....	....	....	....	....	....	....	....	....	....	....	....	....	....	....	....	....	....
	EHC Kloten	Switz.	4	2	3	5	....	....	....	2	....	....	....	....	....	....	....	....	....	....	....	....	....	....	....	....	....	....
	HC Varese	Italy	18	12	32	44	....	....	....	9	....	....	....	....	....	....	....	....	....	....	8	5	11	16	36	....	....	....
	Canada	Nat-Team	4	0	2	2	....	....	....	0	....	....	....	....	....	....	....	....	....	....	....	....	....	....	....	....	....	....
1992-93	HC Milano Devils	Alpenliga	4	1	2	3	....	....	....	0	....	....	....	....	....	....	....	....	....	....	....	....	....	....	....	....	....	....
	HC Milano Devils	Italy	16	12	31	43	....	....	....	6	....	....	....	....	....	....	....	....	....	....	11	5	8	13	2	....	....	....
1993-94	Canada	Nat-Team	13	4	7	11	....	....	....	8	....	....	....	....	....	....	....	....	....	....	....	....	....	....	....	....	....	....
1994-95	Houston Aeros	IHL	31	3	9	12	....	....	....	18	....	....	....	....	....	....	....	....	....	....	....	....	....	....	....	....	....	....
	Adirondack Red Wings	AHL	4	0	1	1	....	....	....	0	....	....	....	....	....	....	....	....	....	....	....	....	....	....	....	....	....	....
1995-1998	Adirondack Red Wings	AHL	DID NOT PLAY – ASSISTANT COACH																									
1998-1999	Toledo Storm	ECHL	DID NOT PLAY – COACHING																									
1999-2000	Wheeling Nailers	ECHL	DID NOT PLAY – COACHING																									
	NHL Totals		**57**	**4**	**13**	**17**	**4**	**9**	**13**	**9**	**1**	**0**	**0**	**44**	**9.1**	**21**	**2**	**37**	**4**		**4**	**0**	**1**	**1**	**2**	**0**	**0**	**0**

• Brother of Mike • WCHA Second All-Star Team (1980) • NCAA West First All-American Team (1980) • AHL First All-Star Team (1984) • AHL Second All-Star Team (1989) • Won Fred T. Hunt Memorial Trophy (Sportsmanship - AHL) (1989, 1990)

Traded to **Edmonton** by **Winnipeg** for future considerations, July 3, 1986. Signed as a free agent by **Detroit**, July 1, 1987.

• ECCLESTONE, Tim

Timothy James LW – R. 5'10", 195 lbs. b: Toronto, Ont., 9/24/1947. NY Rangers' 2nd, 9th overall, in 1964.

			REGULAR SEASON																		PLAYOFFS							
Season	Club	League	GP	G	A	Pts	AG	AA	APts	PIM	PP	SH	GW	S	%	TGF	PGF	TGA	PGA	+/–	GP	G	A	Pts	PIM	PP	SH	GW
1965-66	Etobicoke Indians	OHA-B	STATISTICS NOT AVAILABLE																									
1966-67	Kitchener Rangers	OHA-Jr.	48	27	37	64	....	....	....	35	....	....	....	....	....	....	....	....	....	....	13	3	12	15	14	....	....	....
1967-68	**St. Louis Blues**	**NHL**	**50**	**6**	**8**	**14**	**7**	**8**	**15**	**16**	**3**	**0**	**0**	**97**	**6.2**	**22**	**4**	**18**	**1**	**1**	**12**	**1**	**2**	**3**	**2**	**0**	**0**	**0**
	Kansas City Blues	CPHL	13	4	4	8	....	....	....	9	....	....	....	....	....	....	....	....	....	....	....	....	....	....	....	....	....	....
1968-69	**St. Louis Blues**	**NHL**	**68**	**11**	**23**	**34**	**12**	**20**	**32**	**31**	**1**	**0**	**4**	**151**	**7.3**	**52**	**8**	**25**	**1**	**20**	**12**	**2**	**2**	**4**	**20**	**0**	**0**	**0**
1969-70	**St. Louis Blues**	**NHL**	**65**	**16**	**21**	**37**	**17**	**20**	**37**	**59**	**5**	**0**	**2**	**166**	**9.6**	**56**	**17**	**36**	**4**	**7**	**16**	**3**	**4**	**7**	**48**	**1**	**0**	**1**
1970-71	**St. Louis Blues**	**NHL**	**47**	**15**	**24**	**39**	**15**	**20**	**35**	**34**	**6**	**0**	**4**	**143**	**10.5**	**48**	**22**	**41**	**8**	**–7**	....	....	....	....	....	....	....	....
	Detroit Red Wings	**NHL**	**27**	**4**	**10**	**14**	**4**	**8**	**12**	**13**	**1**	**0**	**0**	**62**	**6.5**	**25**	**8**	**34**	**2**	**–15**	....	....	....	....	....	....	....	....
1971-72	**Detroit Red Wings**	**NHL**	**72**	**18**	**35**	**53**	**18**	**30**	**48**	**33**	**10**	**0**	**1**	**189**	**9.5**	**80**	**30**	**73**	**2**	**–21**	....	....	....	....	....	....	....	....
1972-73	**Detroit Red Wings**	**NHL**	**78**	**18**	**30**	**48**	**17**	**24**	**41**	**28**	**3**	**1**	**2**	**175**	**10.3**	**73**	**17**	**57**	**7**	**6**	....	....	....	....	....	....	....	....
1973-74	**Detroit Red Wings**	**NHL**	**14**	**0**	**5**	**5**	**0**	**4**	**4**	**6**	**0**	**0**	**0**	**22**	**0.0**	**7**	**3**	**12**	**2**	**–6**	....	....	....	....	....	....	....	....
	Toronto Maple Leafs	**NHL**	**46**	**9**	**14**	**23**	**9**	**12**	**21**	**32**	**1**	**2**	**1**	**79**	**11.4**	**33**	**3**	**30**	**8**	**8**	**4**	**0**	**1**	**1**	**0**	**0**	**0**	**0**
1974-75	**Toronto Maple Leafs**	**NHL**	**5**	**1**	**1**	**2**	**1**	**1**	**2**	**0**	**0**	**0**	**0**	**3**	**33.3**	**3**	**0**	**3**	**1**	**1**	....	....	....	....	....	....	....	....
	Atlanta Flames	**NHL**	**62**	**13**	**21**	**34**	**11**	**16**	**27**	**34**	**0**	**1**	**4**	**103**	**12.6**	**47**	**5**	**51**	**16**	**7**	....	....	....	....	....	....	....	....
1975-76	**Atlanta Flames**	**NHL**	**69**	**6**	**21**	**27**	**5**	**16**	**21**	**30**	**1**	**1**	**0**	**117**	**5.1**	**53**	**7**	**57**	**18**	**7**	....	....	....	....	....	....	....	....
1976-77	**Atlanta Flames**	**NHL**	**78**	**9**	**18**	**27**	**8**	**14**	**22**	**26**	**0**	**1**	**0**	**116**	**7.8**	**44**	**1**	**65**	**32**	**10**	**3**	**0**	**2**	**2**	**6**	**0**	**0**	**0**
1977-78	**Atlanta Flames**	**NHL**	**11**	**0**	**2**	**2**	**0**	**2**	**2**	**2**	**0**	**0**	**0**	**11**	**0.0**	**4**	**0**	**4**	**1**	**1**	**1**	**0**	**0**	**0**	**0**	**0**	**0**	**0**
	Tulsa Oilers	CHL	6	1	3	4	....	....	....	0	....	....	....	....	....	....	....	....	....	....	....	....	....	....	....	....	....	....
	NHL Totals		**692**	**126**	**233**	**359**	**124**	**195**	**319**	**344**	**31**	**6**	**18**	**1434**	**8.8**	**547**	**125**	**506**	**103**		**48**	**6**	**11**	**17**	**76**	**1**	**0**	**1**

OHA-Jr. Second All-Star Team (1967) • Played in NHL All-Star Game (1971)

Traded to **St. Louis** by **NY Rangers** with Gary Sabourin, Bob Plager and Gord Kannegiesser for Rod Seiling, June 6, 1967. Traded to **Detroit** by **St. Louis** with Red Berenson for Garry Unger and Wayne Connelly, February 6, 1971. Traded to **Toronto** by **Detroit** for Pierre Jarry, November 29, 1973. Traded to **Washington** by **Toronto** with Willie Brossart for Rod Seiling, November 2, 1974. Traded to **Atlanta** by **Washington** for cash, November 2, 1974.

• EDBERG, Rolf

Rolf Arne "Rattan" C – L. 5'10", 174 lbs. b: Stockholm, Sweden, 9/29/1950.

Season	Club	League	GP	G	A	Pts	AG	AA	APts	PIM	PP	SH	GW	S	%	TGF	PGF	TGA	PGA	+/–	GP	G	A	Pts	PIM	PP	SH	GW
1966-67	Hammarby IF	Sweden-2	22	10	6	16	....	....	....	....	....	....	....	....	....	....	....	....	....	....	....	....	....	....	....	....	....	....
1967-68	Hammarby IF	Sweden-2	STATISTICS NOT AVAILABLE																									
	Sweden	EJC-A	5	4	1	5	....	....	....	2	....	....	....	....	....	....	....	....	....	....	....	....	....	....	....	....	....	....
1968-69	Hammarby IF	Sweden	20	7	5	12	....	....	....	....	....	....	....	....	....	....	....	....	....	....	....	....	....	....	....	....	....	....
1969-70	Hammarby IF	Sweden-2	STATISTICS NOT AVAILABLE																									
1970-71	AIK Solna Stockholm	Sweden	14	9	9	18	....	....	....	10	....	....	....	....	....	....	....	....	....	....	14	8	4	12	14	....	....	....
1971-72	AIK Solna Stockholm	Sweden	14	6	9	15	....	....	....	8	....	....	....	....	....	....	....	....	....	....	14	3	4	7	14	....	....	....
1972-73	AIK Solna Stockholm	Sweden	12	5	2	7	....	....	....	8	....	....	....	....	....	....	....	....	....	....	13	5	3	8	10	....	....	....
1973-74	AIK Solna Stockholm	Sweden	14	8	6	14	....	....	....	4	....	....	....	....	....	....	....	....	....	....	20	11	10	21	18	....	....	....
1974-75	AIK Solna Stockholm	Sweden	30	17	15	32	....	....	....	18	....	....	....	....	....	....	....	....	....	....	....	....	....	....	....	....	....	....
1975-76	AIK Solna Stockholm	Sweden	36	14	13	27	....	....	....	31	....	....	....	....	....	....	....	....	....	....	....	....	....	....	....	....	....	....
1976-77	AIK Solna Stockholm	Sweden	35	11	14	25	....	....	....	30	....	....	....	....	....	....	....	....	....	....	....	....	....	....	....	....	....	....
	Sweden	WEC-A	10	5	1	6	....	....	....	2	....	....	....	....	....	....	....	....	....	....	....	....	....	....	....	....	....	....
1977-78	AIK Solna Stockholm	Sweden	23	5	9	14	....	....	....	14	....	....	....	....	....	....	....	....	....	....	5	2	3	5	4	....	....	....
	Sweden	WEC-A	10	7	5	12	....	....	....	4	....	....	....	....	....	....	....	....	....	....	....	....	....	....	....	....	....	....
1978-79	**Washington Capitals**	**NHL**	**76**	**14**	**27**	**41**	**12**	**20**	**32**	**6**	**1**	**0**	**2**	**133**	**10.5**	**59**	**4**	**46**	**2**	**11**	....	....	....	....	....	....	....	....
	Sweden	WEC-A	6	4	3	7	....	....	....	2	....	....	....	....	....	....	....	....	....	....	....	....	....	....	....	....	....	....
1979-80	**Washington Capitals**	**NHL**	**63**	**23**	**23**	**46**	**20**	**17**	**37**	**12**	**4**	**1**	**7**	**136**	**16.9**	**62**	**15**	**60**	**8**	**–5**	....	....	....	....	....	....	....	....
1980-81	**Washington Capitals**	**NHL**	**45**	**8**	**8**	**16**	**6**	**5**	**11**	**6**	**0**	**0**	**0**	**48**	**16.7**	**19**	**1**	**30**	**13**	**1**	....	....	....	....	....	....	....	....
1981-82	AIK Solna Stockholm	DN-Cup	4	2	2	4	....	....	....	4	....	....	....	....	....	....	....	....	....	....	....	....	....	....	....	....	....	....
	AIK Solna Stockholm	Sweden	29	16	11	27	....	....	....	34	....	....	....	....	....	....	....	....	....	....	7	2	0	2	2	....	....	....
1982-83	AIK Solna Stockholm	Sweden	29	9	15	24	....	....	....	6	....	....	....	....	....	....	....	....	....	....	3	1	1	2	2	....	....	....
1983-84	Hammarby IF	Sweden-2	29	14	18	32	....	....	....	12	....	....	....	....	....	....	....	....	....	....	12	5	10	15	....	....	....	....
1984-85	Hammarby IF	Sweden	20	8	4	12	....	....	....	14	....	....	....	....	....	....	....	....	....	....	....	....	....	....	....	....	....	....
	NHL Totals		**184**	**45**	**58**	**103**	**38**	**42**	**80**	**24**	**5**	**1**	**9**	**317**	**14.2**	**140**	**20**	**136**	**23**		....	....	....	....	....	....	....	....

Won Golden Puck Award as Swedish Player of the Year (1978)

Signed as a free agent by **Washington**, June 10, 1978.

• EDESTRAND, Darryl

D – L. 5'11", 180 lbs. b: Strathroy, Ont., 11/6/1945.

Season	Club	League	GP	G	A	Pts	AG	AA	APts	PIM	PP	SH	GW	S	%	TGF	PGF	TGA	PGA	+/–	GP	G	A	Pts	PIM	PP	SH	GW
1962-63	London Nationals	OHA-B	STATISTICS NOT AVAILABLE																									
	Toronto Marlboros	MTJHL	2	0	1	1	....	....	....	2	....	....	....	....	....	....	....	....	....	....	1	0	0	0	0	....	....	....
1963-64	London Nationals	OHA-B	STATISTICS NOT AVAILABLE																									
1964-65	Toronto Marlboros	OHA-Jr.	5	0	0	0	....	....	....	5	....	....	....	....	....	....	....	....	....	....	....	....	....	....	....	....	....	....
1965-66	London Nationals	OHA-Jr.	45	4	20	24	....	....	....	132	....	....	....	....	....	....	....	....	....	....	....	....	....	....	....	....	....	....
	Rochester Americans	AHL	17	1	2	3	....	....	....	10	....	....	....	....	....	....	....	....	....	....	4	1	0	1	2	....	....	....
1966-67	Rochester Americans	AHL	7	0	1	1	....	....	....	4	....	....	....	....	....	....	....	....	....	....	....	....	....	....	....	....	....	....
1967-68	**St. Louis Blues**	**NHL**	**12**	**0**	**0**	**0**	**0**	**0**	**0**	**2**	**0**	**0**	**0**	**12**	**0.0**	**5**	**1**	**7**	**1**	**–2**	....	....	....	....	....	....	....	....
	Kansas City Blues	CPHL	53	2	32	34	....	....	....	84	....	....	....	....	....	....	....	....	....	....	7	0	3	3	4	....	....	....
1968-69	Quebec Aces	AHL	74	7	23	30	....	....	....	108	....	....	....	....	....	....	....	....	....	....	15	1	5	6	23	....	....	....
1969-70	**Philadelphia Flyers**	**NHL**	**2**	**0**	**0**	**0**	**0**	**0**	**0**	**6**	**0**	**0**	**0**	**3**	**0.0**	**1**	**0**	**2**	**0**	**–1**	....	....	....	....	....	....	....	....
	Quebec Aces	AHL	71	10	30	40	....	....	....	106	....	....	....	....	....	....	....	....	....	....	6	0	1	1	8	....	....	....
1970-71	Hershey Bears	AHL	72	6	30	36	....	....	....	109	....	....	....	....	....	....	....	....	....	....	4	0	0	0	2	....	....	....
1971-72	**Pittsburgh Penguins**	**NHL**	**77**	**10**	**23**	**33**	**10**	**20**	**30**	**52**	**2**	**1**	**3**	**156**	**6.4**	**75**	**18**	**84**	**15**	**–12**	**4**	**0**	**2**	**2**	**0**	**0**	**0**	**0**
1972-73	**Pittsburgh Penguins**	**NHL**	**78**	**15**	**24**	**39**	**14**	**19**	**33**	**88**	**4**	**1**	**2**	**155**	**9.7**	**112**	**16**	**110**	**17**	**3**	....	....	....	....	....	....	....	....
1973-74	**Pittsburgh Penguins**	**NHL**	**3**	**0**	**0**	**0**	**0**	**0**	**0**	**0**	**0**	**0**	**0**	**0**	**0.0**	**3**	**3**	**2**	**0**	**–2**	....	....	....	....	....	....	....	....
	Boston Bruins	**NHL**	**52**	**3**	**8**	**11**	**3**	**7**	**10**	**20**	**1**	**0**	**2**	**66**	**4.5**	**53**	**2**	**37**	**5**	**19**	**16**	**1**	**2**	**3**	**15**	**0**	**0**	**0**
1974-75	**Boston Bruins**	**NHL**	**68**	**1**	**9**	**10**	**1**	**7**	**8**	**56**	**0**	**0**	**0**	**86**	**1.2**	**41**	**2**	**34**	**3**	**8**	**3**	**0**	**1**	**1**	**7**	**0**	**0**	**0**
1975-76	**Boston Bruins**	**NHL**	**77**	**4**	**17**	**21**	**3**	**13**	**16**	**103**	**1**	**0**	**1**	**131**	**3.1**	**85**	**9**	**79**	**10**	**7**	**12**	**1**	**3**	**4**	**23**	**0**	**0**	**0**
1976-77	**Boston Bruins**	**NHL**	**17**	**0**	**3**	**3**	**0**	**2**	**2**	**16**	**0**	**0**	**0**	**28**	**0.0**	**19**	**1**	**16**	**2**	**4**	**3**	**0**	**0**	**0**	**2**	**0**	**0**	**0**
	Rochester Americans	AHL	42	4	13	17	....	....	....	62	....	....	....	....	....	....	....	....	....	....	12	1	3	4	8	....	....	....
1977-78	**Boston Bruins**	**NHL**	**1**	**0**	**0**	**0**	**0**	**0**	**0**	**0**	**0**	**0**	**0**	**0**	**0.0**	**0**	**0**	**1**	**0**	**–1**	....	....	....	....	....	....	....	....
	Rochester Americans	AHL	64	6	27	33	....	....	....	28	....	....	....	....	....	....	....	....	....	....	....	....	....	....	....	....	....	....
	Los Angeles Kings	**NHL**	**13**	**0**	**2**	**2**	**0**	**2**	**2**	**15**	**0**	**0**	**0**	**29**	**0.0**	**11**	**1**	**21**	**3**	**–8**	**2**	**1**	**1**	**2**	**4**	**0**	**0**	**0**
1978-79	**Los Angeles Kings**	**NHL**	**55**	**1**	**4**	**5**	**1**	**3**	**4**	**46**	**0**	**0**	**0**	**62**	**1.6**	**45**	**0**	**61**	**8**	**–8**	**2**	**0**	**0**	**0**	**6**	**0**	**0**	**0**
1979-80	Binghamton Dusters	AHL	57	3	17	20	....	....	....	34	....	....	....	....	....	....	....	....	....	....	....	....	....	....	....	....	....	....
	NHL Totals		**455**	**34**	**90**	**124**	**32**	**73**	**105**	**404**	**8**	**2**	**8**	**728**	**4.7**	**450**	**53**	**454**	**64**		**42**	**3**	**9**	**12**	**57**	**0**	**0**	**0**

Claimed by **St. Louis** from **Toronto** in Expansion Draft; June 6, 1967. Traded to **Philadelphia** by **St. Louis** with Gerry Melynk for Lou Angotti and Ian Campbell, June 11, 1968. Traded to **Pittsburgh** (Hershey-AHL) by **Philadelphia** with Larry McKillop for Barry Ashbee, May 22, 1970. Traded to **Boston** by **Pittsburgh** for Nick Beverley, October 25, 1973. Traded to **LA Kings** by **Boston** for cash, March 13, 1978. Claimed by **LA Kings** as a fill-in during Expansion Draft, June 13, 1979.

• EDUR, Tom

Thomas "Bomber" D – R. 6'1", 185 lbs. b: Toronto, Ont., 11/18/1954. Boston's 4th, 54th overall, in 1974.

			REGULAR SEASON																		PLAYOFFS							
Season	**Club**	**League**	**GP**	**G**	**A**	**Pts**	**AG**	**AA**	**APts**	**PIM**	**PP**	**SH**	**GW**	**S**	**%**	**TGF**	**PGF**	**TGA**	**PGA**	**+/-**	**GP**	**G**	**A**	**Pts**	**PIM**	**PP**	**SH**	**GW**
1971-72	Markham Waxers	OHA-B	STATISTICS NOT AVAILABLE																									
1972-73	Toronto Marlboros	OMJHL	57	14	48	62	....	....	....	32	....	....	....	....	....	....	....	....	....	....	10	1	14	15	10	....	....	....
	Toronto Marlboros	Mem-Cup	3	0	1	1	....	....	....	0	....	....	....	....	....	....	....	....	....	....	....	....	....	....	....	....	....	....
1973-74	Cleveland Crusaders	WHA	76	7	31	38	....	....	....	26	....	....	....	....	....	....	....	....	....	....	5	1	2	3	0	....	....	....
1974-75	Cleveland Crusaders	WHA	61	3	20	23	....	....	....	28	....	....	....	....	....	....	....	....	....	....	5	2	0	2	0	....	....	....
1975-76	Cleveland Crusaders	WHA	80	7	28	35	....	....	....	62	....	....	....	....	....	....	....	....	....	....	3	0	2	2	0	....	....	....
1976-77	**Colorado Rockies**	**NHL**	**80**	**7**	**25**	**32**	**6**	**19**	**25**	**39**	**3**	**0**	**1**	**150**	**4.7**	**113**	**18**	**108**	**27**	**14**	....	....	....	....	....	....	....	....
1977-78	**Colorado Rockies**	**NHL**	**20**	**5**	**7**	**12**	**5**	**5**	**10**	**10**	**1**	**0**	**0**	**38**	**13.2**	**37**	**7**	**27**	**7**	**10**	....	....	....	....	....	....	....	....
	Pittsburgh Penguins	**NHL**	**58**	**5**	**38**	**43**	**5**	**29**	**34**	**18**	**2**	**0**	**1**	**135**	**3.7**	**104**	**29**	**106**	**22**	**–9**	....	....	....	....	....	....	....	....
	NHL Totals		**158**	**17**	**70**	**87**	**16**	**53**	**69**	**67**	**6**	**0**	**2**	**323**	**5.3**	**254**	**54**	**241**	**56**		....	....	....	....	....	....	....	....
	Other Major League Totals		217	17	79	96	....	....	....	116	....	....	....	....	....	....	....	....	....	....	13	3	4	7	0	....	....	....

Signed as an underage free agent by **Cleveland** (WHA), August, 1973. Rights traded to **Colorado** by **Boston** for cash, September 7, 1977. Traded to **Pittsburgh** by **Colorado** for Dennis Owchar, December 2, 1977. • Retired following 1977-78 season to study Christianity, July, 1978. Selected by **Edmonton** from **Pittsburgh** in 1979 Expansion Draft, June 13, 1979.

• EGELAND, Allan

C – L. 6', 175 lbs. b: Lethbridge, Alta., 1/31/1973. Tampa Bay's 3rd, 55th overall, in 1993.

Season	Club	League	GP	G	A	Pts	AG	AA	APts	PIM	PP	SH	GW	S	%	TGF	PGF	TGA	PGA	+/-	GP	G	A	Pts	PIM	PP	SH	GW
1989-90	Lethbridge YMCA	AAHA	36	21	30	51	....	....	....	52	....	....	....	....	....	....	....	....	....	....	....	....	....	....	....	....	....	....
1990-91	Lethbridge Hurricanes	WHL	67	2	16	18	....	....	....	57	....	....	....	....	....	....	....	....	....	....	9	0	0	0	0	....	....	....
1991-92	Tacoma Rockets	WHL	72	35	39	74	....	....	....	135	....	....	....	....	....	....	....	....	....	....	4	0	1	1	18	....	....	....
1992-93	Tacoma Rockets	WHL	71	56	57	113	....	....	....	119	....	....	....	....	....	....	....	....	....	....	7	9	7	16	18	....	....	....
1993-94	Tacoma Rockets	WHL	70	47	76	123	....	....	....	204	....	....	....	....	....	....	....	....	....	....	8	5	3	8	26	....	....	....
1994-95	Atlanta Knights	IHL	60	8	16	24	....	....	....	112	....	....	....	....	....	....	....	....	....	....	5	0	1	1	16	....	....	....
1995-96	**Tampa Bay Lightning**	**NHL**	**5**	**0**	**0**	**0**	**0**	**0**	**0**	**2**	**0**	**0**	**0**	**1**	**0.0**	**0**	**0**	**0**	**0**	**0**	....	....	....	....	....	....	....	....
	Atlanta Knights	IHL	68	22	22	44	....	....	....	182	....	....	....	....	....	....	....	....	....	....	3	0	1	1	0	....	....	....
1996-97	**Tampa Bay Lightning**	**NHL**	**4**	**0**	**0**	**0**	**0**	**0**	**0**	**5**	**0**	**0**	**0**	**1**	**0.0**	**0**	**0**	**3**	**0**	**–3**	....	....	....	....	....	....	....	....
	Adirondack Red Wings	AHL	52	18	32	50	....	....	....	184	....	....	....	....	....	....	....	....	....	....	2	0	1	1	4	....	....	....
1997-98	**Tampa Bay Lightning**	**NHL**	**8**	**0**	**0**	**0**	**0**	**0**	**0**	**9**	**0**	**0**	**0**	**4**	**0.0**	**0**	**0**	**1**	**1**	**0**	....	....	....	....	....	....	....	....
	Adirondack Red Wings	AHL	35	11	22	33	....	....	....	78	....	....	....	....	....	....	....	....	....	....	3	0	2	2	10	....	....	....
1998-99	Orlando Solar Bears	IHL	62	7	23	30	....	....	....	182	....	....	....	....	....	....	....	....	....	....	....	....	....	....	....	....	....	....
	Saint John Flames	AHL	14	5	5	10	....	....	....	49	....	....	....	....	....	....	....	....	....	....	7	1	4	5	21	....	....	....
99-2000	Saint John Flames	AHL	11	1	5	6	....	....	....	42	....	....	....	....	....	....	....	....	....	....	....	....	....	....	....	....	....	....
	Long Beach Ice Dogs	IHL	47	4	12	16	....	....	....	104	....	....	....	....	....	....	....	....	....	....	6	0	0	0	19	....	....	....
	NHL Totals		**17**	**0**	**0**	**0**	**0**	**0**	**0**	**16**	**0**	**0**	**0**	**6**	**0.0**	**0**	**0**	**4**	**1**		....	....	....	....	....	....	....	....

WHL West First All-Star Team (1993) • WHL West Second All-Star Team (1994)

Signed as a free agent by **Calgary**, July 20, 1999. Traded to **Los Angeles** by **Calgary** for future considerations, February 18, 2000.

• EGERS, Jack

John Richard RW – L. 6'1", 175 lbs. b: Sudbury, Ont., 1/28/1949. NY Rangers' 4th, 20th overall, in 1966.

Season	Club	League	GP	G	A	Pts	AG	AA	APts	PIM	PP	SH	GW	S	%	TGF	PGF	TGA	PGA	+/-	GP	G	A	Pts	PIM	PP	SH	GW
1964-65	Kitchener Greenshirts	OHA-B	STATISTICS NOT AVAILABLE																									
1965-66	Kitchener Greenshirts	OHA-B	STATISTICS NOT AVAILABLE																									
	Kitchener Rangers	OHA-Jr.	5	1	1	2	....	....	....	2	....	....	....	....	....	....	....	....	....	....	....	....	....	....	....	....	....	....
1966-67	Kitchener Rangers	OHA-Jr.	40	18	9	27	....	....	....	48	....	....	....	....	....	....	....	....	....	....	9	0	0	0	6	....	....	....
1967-68	Kitchener Rangers	OHA-Jr.	54	*53	37	90	....	....	....	78	....	....	....	....	....	....	....	....	....	....	13	5	6	11	21	....	....	....
1968-69	Omaha Knights	CHL	59	28	30	58	....	....	....	47	....	....	....	....	....	....	....	....	....	....	7	3	4	7	7	....	....	....
1969-70	**New York Rangers**	**NHL**	**6**	**3**	**0**	**3**	**3**	**0**	**3**	**2**	**2**	**0**	**0**	**18**	**16.7**	**8**	**4**	**4**	**0**	**0**	**5**	**3**	**1**	**4**	**10**	**1**	**0**	**0**
	Omaha Knights	CHL	70	42	*48	*90	....	....	....	83	....	....	....	....	....	....	....	....	....	....	3	3	3	6	2	....	....	....
1970-71	**New York Rangers**	**NHL**	**60**	**7**	**10**	**17**	**7**	**8**	**15**	**50**	**3**	**0**	**3**	**88**	**8.0**	**32**	**9**	**16**	**1**	**8**	**3**	**0**	**0**	**0**	**2**	**0**	**0**	**0**
1971-72	**New York Rangers**	**NHL**	**17**	**2**	**1**	**3**	**2**	**1**	**3**	**14**	**1**	**0**	**0**	**13**	**15.4**	**5**	**2**	**1**	**0**	**2**	....	....	....	....	....	....	....	....
	St. Louis Blues	**NHL**	**63**	**21**	**25**	**46**	**21**	**22**	**43**	**34**	**5**	**0**	**2**	**210**	**10.0**	**70**	**21**	**45**	**1**	**5**	**11**	**1**	**4**	**5**	**14**	**0**	**0**	**0**
1972-73	**St. Louis Blues**	**NHL**	**78**	**24**	**24**	**48**	**23**	**19**	**42**	**26**	**4**	**0**	**4**	**240**	**10.0**	**84**	**22**	**61**	**0**	**1**	**5**	**0**	**1**	**1**	**2**	**0**	**0**	**0**
1973-74	**St. Louis Blues**	**NHL**	**6**	**0**	**1**	**1**	**0**	**1**	**1**	**6**	**0**	**0**	**0**	**15**	**0.0**	**4**	**1**	**2**	**0**	**1**	....	....	....	....	....	....	....	....
	New York Rangers	**NHL**	**28**	**1**	**3**	**4**	**1**	**2**	**3**	**6**	**0**	**0**	**0**	**9**	**11.1**	**10**	**1**	**8**	**0**	**1**	**8**	**1**	**0**	**1**	**4**	**0**	**0**	**0**
1974-75	**Washington Capitals**	**NHL**	**14**	**3**	**2**	**5**	**3**	**1**	**4**	**8**	**1**	**0**	**1**	**21**	**14.3**	**7**	**4**	**17**	**0**	**–14**	....	....	....	....	....	....	....	....
1975-76	**Washington Capitals**	**NHL**	**12**	**3**	**3**	**6**	**3**	**2**	**5**	**8**	**2**	**0**	**0**	**18**	**16.7**	**9**	**7**	**4**	**0**	**–2**	....	....	....	....	....	....	....	....
	Baltimore Clippers	AHL	15	4	4	8	....	....	....	19	....	....	....	....	....	....	....	....	....	....	....	....	....	....	....	....	....	....
1976-77	Brantford Alexanders	OHA-Sr.	30	20	19	39	....	....	....	55	....	....	....	....	....	....	....	....	....	....	....	....	....	....	....	....	....	....
	NHL Totals		**284**	**64**	**69**	**133**	**63**	**56**	**119**	**154**	**18**	**0**	**10**	**632**	**10.1**	**229**	**71**	**158**	**2**		**32**	**5**	**6**	**11**	**32**	**1**	**0**	**0**

OHA-Jr. First All-Star Team (1968) • CHL First All-Star Team (1970)

Traded to **St. Louis** by **NY Rangers** with Andre Dupont and Mike Murphy for Gene Carr, Jim Lorentz and Wayne Connelly, November 15, 1971. Traded to **NY Rangers** by **St. Louis** for Glen Sather and Rene Villemure, October 28, 1973. Claimed by **Washington** from **NY Rangers** in Expansion Draft, June 12, 1974.

• EHMAN, Gerry

Gerald Joseph RW – R. 6', 190 lbs. b: Cudworth, Sask., 11/3/1932.

Season	Club	League	GP	G	A	Pts	AG	AA	APts	PIM	PP	SH	GW	S	%	TGF	PGF	TGA	PGA	+/-	GP	G	A	Pts	PIM	PP	SH	GW
1951-52	Flin Flon Bombers	SJHL	50	40	*42	82	....	....	....	18	....	....	....	....	....	....	....	....	....	....	14	5	11	16	0	....	....	....
1952-53	Edmonton Flyers	WHL	22	3	3	6	....	....	....	0	....	....	....	....	....	....	....	....	....	....	....	....	....	....	....	....	....	....
	St. Louis Flyers	AHL	39	3	1	4	....	....	....	8	....	....	....	....	....	....	....	....	....	....	....	....	....	....	....	....	....	....
1953-54	Sherbrooke Saints	QHL	65	13	21	34	....	....	....	29	....	....	....	....	....	....	....	....	....	....	5	0	2	2	0	....	....	....
1954-55	Quebec Aces	QHL	59	14	25	39	....	....	....	58	....	....	....	....	....	....	....	....	....	....	8	2	3	5	12	....	....	....
1955-56	Vancouver Canucks	WHL	15	5	7	12	....	....	....	6	....	....	....	....	....	....	....	....	....	....	15	9	2	11	14	....	....	....
1956-57	Springfield Indians	AHL	64	23	35	58	....	....	....	18	....	....	....	....	....	....	....	....	....	....	....	....	....	....	....	....	....	....
1957-58	**Boston Bruins**	**NHL**	**1**	**1**	**0**	**1**	**1**	**0**	**1**	**0**	....	....	....	....	....	....	....	....	....	....	....	....	....	....	....	....	....	....
	Springfield Indians	AHL	68	40	39	79	....	....	....	32	....	....	....	....	....	....	....	....	....	....	13	*10	6	16	8	....	....	....
1958-59	**Detroit Red Wings**	**NHL**	**6**	**0**	**1**	**1**	**0**	**1**	**1**	**4**	....	....	....	....	....	....	....	....	....	....	....	....	....	....	....	....	....	....
	Hershey Bears	AHL	23	8	7	15	....	....	....	4	....	....	....	....	....	....	....	....	....	....	....	....	....	....	....	....	....	....
	Toronto Maple Leafs	**NHL**	**38**	**12**	**13**	**25**	**14**	**13**	**27**	**12**	....	....	....	....	....	....	....	....	....	....	**12**	**6**	**7**	**13**	**8**	**2**	**0**	**2**
1959-60	**Toronto Maple Leafs**	**NHL**	**69**	**12**	**16**	**28**	**14**	**16**	**30**	**26**	....	....	....	....	....	....	....	....	....	....	**9**	**0**	**0**	**0**	**0**	**0**	**0**	**0**
1960-61	**Toronto Maple Leafs**	**NHL**	**14**	**1**	**1**	**2**	**1**	**1**	**2**	**2**	....	....	....	....	....	....	....	....	....	....	....	....	....	....	....	....	....	....
	Rochester Americans	AHL	53	32	23	55	....	....	....	14	....	....	....	....	....	....	....	....	....	....	....	....	....	....	....	....	....	....
1961-62	Rochester Americans	AHL	66	29	37	66	....	....	....	26	....	....	....	....	....	....	....	....	....	....	2	1	1	2	0	....	....	....
1962-63	Rochester Americans	AHL	72	30	40	70	....	....	....	32	....	....	....	....	....	....	....	....	....	....	1	0	0	0	0	....	....	....
1963-64♦	**Toronto Maple Leafs**	**NHL**	**4**	**1**	**1**	**2**	**1**	**1**	**2**	**0**	....	....	....	....	....	....	....	....	....	....	**9**	**1**	**0**	**1**	**4**	**0**	**0**	**0**
	Rochester Americans	AHL	66	36	49	*85	....	....	....	26	....	....	....	....	....	....	....	....	....	....	2	0	1	1	0	....	....	....
1964-65	Rochester Americans	AHL	70	38	49	87	....	....	....	20	....	....	....	....	....	....	....	....	....	....	10	2	5	7	10	....	....	....
1965-66	Rochester Americans	AHL	70	39	49	88	....	....	....	28	....	....	....	....	....	....	....	....	....	....	12	5	4	9	8	....	....	....
1966-67	Rochester Americans	AHL	68	33	36	69	....	....	....	27	....	....	....	....	....	....	....	....	....	....	13	2	7	9	6	....	....	....
1967-68	**Oakland Seals**	**NHL**	**73**	**19**	**25**	**44**	**22**	**25**	**47**	**20**	**6**	**0**	**3**	**189**	**10.1**	**64**	**24**	**49**	**4**	**–5**	....	....	....	....	....	....	....	....
1968-69	**Oakland Seals**	**NHL**	**70**	**21**	**24**	**45**	**22**	**21**	**43**	**12**	**4**	**0**	**3**	**160**	**13.1**	**70**	**18**	**68**	**3**	**–13**	**7**	**2**	**2**	**4**	**0**	**0**	**0**	**0**
1969-70	**Oakland Seals**	**NHL**	**76**	**11**	**19**	**30**	**12**	**18**	**30**	**8**	**3**	**0**	**1**	**156**	**7.1**	**52**	**11**	**73**	**7**	**–25**	**4**	**1**	**1**	**2**	**0**	**1**	**0**	**0**
1970-71	**California Golden Seals**	**NHL**	**78**	**18**	**18**	**36**	**18**	**15**	**33**	**16**	**1**	**0**	**3**	**154**	**11.7**	**54**	**10**	**88**	**4**	**–40**	....	....	....	....	....	....	....	....
	NHL Totals		**429**	**96**	**118**	**214**	**105**	**111**	**216**	**100**	....	....	....	....	....	....	....	....	....	....	**41**	**10**	**10**	**20**	**12**	....	....	....

SJHL First All-Star Team (1952) • AHL First All-Star Team (1958, 1964, 1966) • AHL Second All-Star Team (1961) • Won John B. Sollenberger Trophy (Top Scorer - AHL) (1964) • Played in NHL All-Star Game (1964)

Claimed by **Boston** (Springfield-AHL) from **Detroit** (Edmonton-WHL) in Inter-League Draft, June 1, 1953. Traded to **Detroit** by **Springfield** (AHL) for Hank Bassen, Dennis Olson and Bill McCreary, May 1, 1958. Traded to **Toronto** by **Detroit** (Hershey-AHL) for cash and the loan of Willie Marshall, December 23, 1958. Traded to **Oakland** by **Toronto** (Rochester-AHL) for Bryan Hextall Jr. and J.P. Parise, October 12, 1967.

• EISENHUT, Neil

C – L. 6'1", 190 lbs. b: Osoyoos, B.C., 2/9/1967. Vancouver's 11th, 233rd overall, in 1987.

			REGULAR SEASON																		PLAYOFFS							
Season	Club	League	GP	G	A	Pts	AG	AA	APts	PIM	PP	SH	GW	S	%	TGF	PGF	TGA	PGA	+/–	GP	G	A	Pts	PIM	PP	SH	GW
1985-86	Penticton Knights	BCJHL	13	2	6	8	....	....	....	10	....	....	....	....	....	....	....	....	....	....	....	....	....	....	....	....	....	....
1986-87	Langley Eagles	BCJHL	43	41	34	75	....	....	....	28	....	....	....	....	....	....	....	....	....	....	....	....	....	....	....	....	....	....
1987-88	University of North Dakota	WCHA	42	12	20	32	....	....	....	14	....	....	....	....	....	....	....	....	....	....	....	....	....	....	....	....	....	....
1988-89	University of North Dakota	WCHA	41	22	16	38	....	....	....	26	....	....	....	....	....	....	....	....	....	....	....	....	....	....	....	....	....	....
1989-90	University of North Dakota	WCHA	45	22	32	54	....	....	....	46	....	....	....	....	....	....	....	....	....	....	....	....	....	....	....	....	....	....
1990-91	University of North Dakota	WCHA	20	9	15	24	....	....	....	10	....	....	....	....	....	....	....	....	....	....	....	....	....	....	....	....	....	....
1991-92	Milwaukee Admirals	IHL	76	13	23	36	....	....	....	26	....	....	....	....	....	....	....	....	....	....	2	1	2	3	0	....	....	....
1992-93	Hamilton Canucks	AHL	72	22	40	62	....	....	....	41	....	....	....	....	....	....	....	....	....	....	....	....	....	....	....	....	....	....
1993-94	**Vancouver Canucks**	**NHL**	**13**	**1**	**3**	**4**	**1**	**2**	**3**	**21**	**0**	**0**	**0**	**13**	**7.7**	**4**	**0**	**7**	**3**	**0**	....	....	....	....	....	....	....	....
	Hamilton Canucks	AHL	60	17	36	53	....	....	....	30	....	....	....	....	....	....	....	....	....	....	4	1	4	5	0	....	....	....
1994-95	**Calgary Flames**	**NHL**	**3**	**0**	**0**	**0**	**0**	**0**	**0**	**0**	**0**	**0**	**0**	**2**	**0.0**	**0**	**0**	**0**	**0**	**0**	....	....	....	....	....	....	....	....
	Saint John Flames	AHL	75	16	39	55	....	....	....	30	....	....	....	....	....	....	....	....	....	....	5	1	1	2	6	....	....	....
1995-96	Orlando Solar Bears	IHL	59	10	18	28	....	....	....	30	....	....	....	....	....	....	....	....	....	....	....	....	....	....	....	....	....	....
	Binghamton Rangers	AHL	10	3	3	6	....	....	....	2	....	....	....	....	....	....	....	....	....	....	4	3	2	5	0	....	....	....
1996-97	Flint Generals	ColHL	21	10	33	43	....	....	....	20	....	....	....	....	....	....	....	....	....	....	5	1	4	5	8	....	....	....
	Binghamton Rangers	AHL	55	25	26	51	....	....	....	16	....	....	....	....	....	....	....	....	....	....	4	1	2	3	0	....	....	....
1997-98	Krefeld Pinguine	Germany	42	9	13	22	....	....	....	16	....	....	....	....	....	....	....	....	....	....	3	1	2	3	2	....	....	....
1998-99	Krefeld Pinguine	Germany	46	18	25	43	....	....	....	69	....	....	....	....	....	....	....	....	....	....	4	1	1	2	8	....	....	....
99-2000	Krefeld Pinguine	Germany	52	10	27	37	....	....	....	46	....	....	....	....	....	....	....	....	....	....	4	0	2	2	10	....	....	....
	NHL Totals		**16**	**1**	**3**	**4**	**1**	**2**	**3**	**21**	**0**	**0**	**0**	**15**	**6.7**	**4**	**0**	**7**	**3**		....	....	....	....	....	....	....	....

Signed as a free agent by **Calgary**, June 16, 1994.

• EKLUND, Per-Erik

"Pelle" C – L. 5'10", 175 lbs. b: Stockholm, Sweden, 3/22/1963. Philadelphia's 7th, 167th overall, in 1983.

			REGULAR SEASON																		PLAYOFFS							
Season	Club	League	GP	G	A	Pts	AG	AA	APts	PIM	PP	SH	GW	S	%	TGF	PGF	TGA	PGA	+/–	GP	G	A	Pts	PIM	PP	SH	GW
1978-79	Stocksunds IF	Sweden-3	1	2	0	2	....	....	....	0	....	....	....	....	....	....	....	....	....	....	....	....	....	....	....	....	....	....
1979-80	Stocksunds IF	Sweden-3	17	8	2	10	....	....	....	....	....	....	....	....	....	....	....	....	....	....	....	....	....	....	....	....	....	....
1980-81	Stocksunds IF	Sweden-3	19	13	20	33	....	....	....	....	....	....	....	....	....	....	....	....	....	....	....	....	....	....	....	....	....	....
	Sweden	EJC-A	4	0	0	0	....	....	....	4	....	....	....	....	....	....	....	....	....	....	....	....	....	....	....	....	....	....
1981-82	AIK Solna Stockholm	DN-Cup	4	1	0	1	....	....	....	0	....	....	....	....	....	....	....	....	....	....	....	....	....	....	....	....	....	....
	AIK Solna Stockholm	Sweden	23	2	3	5	....	....	....	2	....	....	....	....	....	....	....	....	....	....	....	....	....	....	....	....	....	....
	Sweden	WJC-A	6	1	3	4	....	....	....	2	....	....	....	....	....	....	....	....	....	....	....	....	....	....	....	....	....	....
1982-83	AIK Solna Stockholm	Sweden	34	13	17	30	....	....	....	14	....	....	....	....	....	....	....	....	....	....	3	1	4	5	2	....	....	....
	Sweden	WJC-A	7	5	1	6	....	....	....	....	....	....	....	....	....	....	....	....	....	....	....	....	....	....	....	....	....	....
1983-84	AIK Solna Stockholm	Sweden	35	9	18	27	....	....	....	24	....	....	....	....	....	....	....	....	....	....	6	*6	6	12	2	....	....	....
	Sweden	Olympics	7	2	6	8	....	....	....	0	....	....	....	....	....	....	....	....	....	....	....	....	....	....	....	....	....	....
1984-85	AIK Solna Stockholm	Sweden	35	16	33	49	....	....	....	10	....	....	....	....	....	....	....	....	....	....	....	....	....	....	....	....	....	....
	Sweden	Can-Cup	8	1	1	2	....	....	....	0	....	....	....	....	....	....	....	....	....	....	....	....	....	....	....	....	....	....
	Sweden	WEC-A	10	2	4	6	....	....	....	2	....	....	....	....	....	....	....	....	....	....	....	....	....	....	....	....	....	....
1985-86	**Philadelphia Flyers**	**NHL**	**70**	**15**	**51**	**66**	**12**	**34**	**46**	**12**	**8**	**0**	**5**	**141**	**10.6**	**88**	**61**	**33**	**2**	**–4**	**5**	**0**	**2**	**2**	**0**	**0**	**0**	**0**
	Sweden	WEC-A	4	2	1	3	....	....	....	4	....	....	....	....	....	....	....	....	....	....	....	....	....	....	....	....	....	....
1986-87	**Philadelphia Flyers**	**NHL**	**72**	**14**	**41**	**55**	**12**	**30**	**42**	**2**	**5**	**0**	**0**	**127**	**11.0**	**79**	**37**	**47**	**3**	**–2**	**26**	**7**	**20**	**27**	**2**	**2**	**0**	**0**
1987-88	**Philadelphia Flyers**	**NHL**	**71**	**10**	**32**	**42**	**9**	**23**	**32**	**12**	**2**	**0**	**2**	**101**	**9.9**	**71**	**31**	**46**	**0**	**–6**	**7**	**0**	**3**	**3**	**0**	**0**	**0**	**0**
1988-89	**Philadelphia Flyers**	**NHL**	**79**	**18**	**51**	**69**	**15**	**36**	**51**	**23**	**8**	**1**	**2**	**121**	**14.9**	**111**	**60**	**60**	**14**	**5**	**19**	**3**	**8**	**11**	**2**	**3**	**0**	**1**
1989-90	**Philadelphia Flyers**	**NHL**	**70**	**23**	**39**	**62**	**20**	**28**	**48**	**16**	**5**	**3**	**2**	**126**	**18.3**	**87**	**26**	**65**	**11**	**7**	....	....	....	....	....	....	....	....
	Sweden	WEC-A	10	1	7	8	....	....	....	4	....	....	....	....	....	....	....	....	....	....	....	....	....	....	....	....	....	....
1990-91	**Philadelphia Flyers**	**NHL**	**73**	**19**	**50**	**69**	**17**	**38**	**55**	**14**	**8**	**0**	**4**	**131**	**14.5**	**98**	**43**	**70**	**13**	**–2**	....	....	....	....	....	....	....	....
	Sweden	WEC-A	10	1	3	4	....	....	....	2	....	....	....	....	....	....	....	....	....	....	....	....	....	....	....	....	....	....
1991-92	**Philadelphia Flyers**	**NHL**	**51**	**7**	**16**	**23**	**6**	**12**	**18**	**4**	**1**	**2**	**1**	**74**	**9.5**	**45**	**18**	**34**	**7**	**0**	....	....	....	....	....	....	....	....
1992-93	**Philadelphia Flyers**	**NHL**	**55**	**11**	**38**	**49**	**9**	**26**	**35**	**16**	**4**	**0**	**0**	**82**	**13.4**	**71**	**21**	**52**	**14**	**12**	....	....	....	....	....	....	....	....
1993-94	**Philadelphia Flyers**	**NHL**	**48**	**1**	**16**	**17**	**1**	**12**	**13**	**8**	**0**	**0**	**0**	**49**	**2.0**	**31**	**7**	**35**	**10**	**–1**	....	....	....	....	....	....	....	....
	Dallas Stars	**NHL**	**5**	**2**	**1**	**3**	**2**	**1**	**3**	**2**	**0**	**0**	**0**	**4**	**50.0**	**4**	**1**	**4**	**0**	**–1**	**9**	**0**	**3**	**3**	**4**	**0**	**0**	**0**
1994-95	Leksands IF	Sweden	32	13	*36	*49	....	....	....	12	....	....	....	....	....	....	....	....	....	....	2	0	1	1	4	....	....	....
	Sweden	WC-A	8	1	2	3	....	....	....	0	....	....	....	....	....	....	....	....	....	....	....	....	....	....	....	....	....	....
1995-96	Leksands IF	Sweden	29	3	16	19	....	....	....	6	....	....	....	....	....	....	....	....	....	....	4	1	0	1	2	....	....	....
	Sweden	WC-A	6	0	3	3	....	....	....	4	....	....	....	....	....	....	....	....	....	....	....	....	....	....	....	....	....	....
1996-97	Leksands IF	Sweden	36	6	15	21	....	....	....	10	....	....	....	....	....	....	....	....	....	....	9	2	5	7	4	....	....	....
1997-98	Leksands IF	Sweden	38	8	18	26	....	....	....	18	....	....	....	....	....	....	....	....	....	....	4	1	0	1	2	....	....	....
1998-99	Leksands IF	Sweden	37	8	17	25	....	....	....	10	....	....	....	....	....	....	....	....	....	....	4	1	2	3	4	....	....	....
	Leksands IF	EuroHL	4	0	1	1	....	....	....	0	....	....	....	....	....	....	....	....	....	....	2	0	0	0	2	....	....	....
	NHL Totals		**594**	**120**	**335**	**455**	**103**	**240**	**343**	**109**	**41**	**6**	**16**	**956**	**12.6**	**685**	**305**	**446**	**74**		**66**	**10**	**36**	**46**	**8**	**5**	**0**	**1**

Won Golden Puck Award as Swedish Player of the Year (1984) • Swedish Elite League All-Star Team (1984)

Traded to **Dallas** by **Philadelphia** for Dallas' 8th round choice (Raymond Giroux) in 1994 Entry Draft, March 21, 1994.

• EKMAN, Nils

LW – L. 5'11", 175 lbs. b: Stockholm, Sweden, 3/11/1976. Calgary's 6th, 107th overall, in 1994.

			REGULAR SEASON																		PLAYOFFS							
Season	Club	League	GP	G	A	Pts	AG	AA	APts	PIM	PP	SH	GW	S	%	TGF	PGF	TGA	PGA	+/–	GP	G	A	Pts	PIM	PP	SH	GW
1993-94	Hammarby IF	Sweden-Jr.	11	4	5	9	....	....	....	14	....	....	....	....	....	....	....	....	....	....	....	....	....	....	....	....	....	....
	Hammarby IF	Sweden-2	18	7	2	9	....	....	....	4	....	....	....	....	....	....	....	....	....	....	....	....	....	....	....	....	....	....
	Sweden	EJC-A	4	1	1	2	....	....	....	4	....	....	....	....	....	....	....	....	....	....	....	....	....	....	....	....	....	....
1994-95	Hammarby IF	Sweden-Jr.	2	2	1	3	....	....	....	0	....	....	....	....	....	....	....	....	....	....	....	....	....	....	....	....	....	....
	Hammarby IF	Sweden-2	29	10	7	17	....	....	....	18	....	....	....	....	....	....	....	....	....	....	....	....	....	....	....	....	....	....
1995-96	Hammarby IF	Sweden-2	26	9	7	16	....	....	....	53	....	....	....	....	....	....	....	....	....	....	1	0	0	0	0	....	....	....
	Sweden	WJC-A	7	2	1	3	....	....	....	4	....	....	....	....	....	....	....	....	....	....	....	....	....	....	....	....	....	....
1996-97	Kiekko-Espoo	Finland	50	24	19	43	....	....	....	60	....	....	....	....	....	....	....	....	....	....	4	2	0	2	4	....	....	....
1997-98	Kiekko-Espoo	Finland	43	14	14	28	....	....	....	86	....	....	....	....	....	....	....	....	....	....	7	2	2	4	27	....	....	....
	Saint John Flames	AHL	....	....	....	....	....	....	....	....	....	....	....	....	....	....	....	....	....	....	1	0	0	0	2	....	....	....
1998-99	Kiekko-Espoo	Finland	52	20	14	34	....	....	....	96	....	....	....	....	....	....	....	....	....	....	3	1	1	2	6	....	....	....
99-2000	Detroit Vipers	IHL	10	7	2	9	....	....	....	8	....	....	....	....	....	....	....	....	....	....	....	....	....	....	....	....	....	....
	Tampa Bay Lightning	**NHL**	**28**	**2**	**2**	**4**	**2**	**2**	**4**	**36**	**1**	**0**	**0**	**42**	**4.8**	**13**	**5**	**16**	**0**	**–8**	....	....	....	....	....	....	....	....
	Long Beach Ice Dogs	IHL	27	11	12	23	....	....	....	26	....	....	....	....	....	....	....	....	....	....	5	3	3	6	4	....	....	....
	NHL Totals		**28**	**2**	**2**	**4**	**2**	**2**	**4**	**36**	**1**	**0**	**0**	**42**	**4.8**	**13**	**5**	**16**	**0**		....	....	....	....	....	....	....	....

• Won Garry F. Longman Memorial Trophy (Top Rookie - IHL) (2000)

Traded to **Tampa Bay** by **Calgary** with Calgary's 4th round choice (later traded to NY Islanders - NY Islanders selected Vladimir Gorbunov) in 2000 Entry Draft for Andreas Johansson, November 20, 1999.

• ELDEBRINK, Anders

D – R. 5'11", 190 lbs. b: Kalix, Sweden, 12/11/1960.

			REGULAR SEASON																		PLAYOFFS							
Season	Club	League	GP	G	A	Pts	AG	AA	APts	PIM	PP	SH	GW	S	%	TGF	PGF	TGA	PGA	+/–	GP	G	A	Pts	PIM	PP	SH	GW
1976-77	Sodertalje SK	Sweden	2	0	0	0	....	....	....	2	....	....	....	....	....	....	....	....	....	....	....	....	....	....	....	....	....	....
1977-78	Sodertalje SK	Sweden	27	4	2	6	....	....	....	14	....	....	....	....	....	....	....	....	....	....	....	....	....	....	....	....	....	....
1978-79	Sodertalje SK	Sweden-2	36	8	10	18	....	....	....	40	....	....	....	....	....	....	....	....	....	....	9	3	5	8	8	....	....	....
1979-80	Sodertalje SK	Sweden-2	35	15	11	26	....	....	....	16	....	....	....	....	....	....	....	....	....	....	....	....	....	....	....	....	....	....
1980-81	Sodertalje SK	Sweden	36	5	18	23	....	....	....	37	....	....	....	....	....	....	....	....	....	....	....	....	....	....	....	....	....	....
	Sweden	WEC-A	8	0	0	0	....	....	....	2	....	....	....	....	....	....	....	....	....	....	....	....	....	....	....	....	....	....
1981-82	**Vancouver Canucks**	**NHL**	**38**	**1**	**8**	**9**	**1**	**5**	**6**	**21**	**0**	**0**	**0**	**47**	**2.1**	**38**	**8**	**32**	**0**	**–2**	**13**	**0**	**0**	**0**	**10**	**0**	**0**	**0**
1982-83	**Vancouver Canucks**	**NHL**	**5**	**1**	**1**	**2**	**1**	**1**	**2**	**0**	**0**	**0**	**0**	**5**	**20.0**	**5**	**2**	**4**	**0**	**–1**	....	....	....	....	....	....	....	....
	Fredericton Express	AHL	47	7	26	33	....	....	....	14	....	....	....	....	....	....	....	....	....	....	12	2	11	13	0	....	....	....
	Quebec Nordiques	**NHL**	**12**	**1**	**2**	**3**	**1**	**1**	**2**	**8**	**0**	**0**	**0**	**14**	**7.1**	**11**	**2**	**12**	**2**	**–1**	**1**	**0**	**0**	**0**	**0**	**0**	**0**	**0**
1983-84	Sodertalje SK	Sweden	36	10	17	27	....	....	....	40	....	....	....	....	....	....	....	....	....	....	3	3	0	3	2	....	....	....
1984-85	Sweden	Can-Cup	8	0	4	4	....	....	....	6	....	....	....	....	....	....	....	....	....	....	....	....	....	....	....	....	....	....
	Sodertalje SK	Sweden	34	10	12	22	....	....	....	20	....	....	....	....	....	....	....	....	....	....	8	2	6	8	*14	....	....	....
	Sweden	WEC-A	8	2	1	3	....	....	....	18	....	....	....	....	....	....	....	....	....	....	....	....	....	....	....	....	....	....

			REGULAR SEASON																		PLAYOFFS							
Season	Club	League	GP	G	A	Pts	AG	AA	APts	PIM	PP	SH	GW	S	%	TGF	PGF	TGA	PGA	+/-	GP	G	A	Pts	PIM	PP	SH	GW
1985-86	Sodertalje SK	Sweden	34	13	16	29	....	....	....	30	....	....	....	....	....	....	....	....	....	....	7	4	2	6	8	....	....	....
	Sweden	WEC-A	7	1	0	1	....	....	....	6	....	....	....	....	....	....	....	....	....	....	....	....	....	....	....	....	....	....
1986-87	Sodertalje SK	Sweden	31	11	15	26	....	....	....	40	....	....	....	....	....	....	....	....	....	....	....	....	....	....	....	....	....	....
	Sweden	WEC-A	10	3	2	5	....	....	....	4	....	....	....	....	....	....	....	....	....	....	....	....	....	....	....	....	....	....
1987-88	Sweden	Can-Cup	6	1	2	3	....	....	....	4	....	....	....	....	....	....	....	....	....	....	....	....	....	....	....	....	....	....
	Sodertalje SK	Sweden	40	12	18	30	....	....	....	54	....	....	....	....	....	....	....	....	....	....	2	0	0	0	0	....	....	....
	Sweden	Olympics	8	4	6	10	....	....	....	4	....	....	....	....	....	....	....	....	....	....	....	....	....	....	....	....	....	....
1988-89	Sodertalje SK	Sweden	38	13	22	35	....	....	....	42	....	....	....	....	....	....	....	....	....	....	5	5	3	8	10	....	....	....
	Sweden	WEC-A	9	5	3	8	....	....	....	2	....	....	....	....	....	....	....	....	....	....	....	....	....	....	....	....	....	....
1989-90	Sodertalje SK	Sweden	39	10	20	30	....	....	....	32	....	....	....	....	....	....	....	....	....	....	2	0	1	1	8	....	....	....
	Sweden	WEC-A	10	2	5	7	....	....	....	10	....	....	....	....	....	....	....	....	....	....	....	....	....	....	....	....	....	....
1990-91	EHC Kloten	Switz.	34	15	23	38	....	....	....	....	....	....	....	....	....	....	....	....	....	....	10	1	6	7	....	....	....	....
1991-92	EHC Kloten	Switz.	38	16	17	33	....	....	....	22	....	....	....	....	....	....	....	....	....	....	....	....	....	....	....	....	....	....
1992-93	EHC Kloten	Switz.	36	14	26	40	....	....	....	65	....	....	....	....	....	....	....	....	....	....	11	3	8	11	2	....	....	....
1993-94	EHC Kloten	Switz.	36	14	29	43	....	....	....	18	....	....	....	....	....	....	....	....	....	....	12	4	8	12	14	....	....	....
1994-95	EHC Kloten	Switz.	25	8	16	24	....	....	....	16	....	....	....	....	....	....	....	....	....	....	12	1	10	11	10	....	....	....
1995-96	Sodertalje SK	Sweden	32	9	11	20	....	....	....	28	....	....	....	....	....	....	....	....	....	....	4	2	3	5	4	....	....	....
1996-97	EHC Kloten	Switz.	39	10	13	23	....	....	....	22	....	....	....	....	....	....	....	....	....	....	....	....	....	....	....	....	....	....
1997-98	Sodertalje SK	Sweden	42	8	11	19	....	....	....	28	....	....	....	....	....	....	....	....	....	....	....	....	....	....	....	....	....	....
	NHL Totals		**55**	**3**	**11**	**14**	**3**	**7**	**10**	**29**	**0**	**0**	**0**	**66**	**4.5**	**54**	**12**	**48**	**2**		**14**	**0**	**0**	**0**	**10**	**0**	**0**	**0**

Swedish World All-Star Team (1984, 1985, 1987, 1988, 1989) • Won Golden Puck Award as Swedish Player of the Year (1985) • Won Golden Helmet Award (Player's Choice MVP) in Swedish Elite League (1988, 1989) • WEC-A All-Star Team (1989)

Signed as a free agent by **Vancouver**, May 18, 1981. Traded to **Quebec** by **Vancouver** for John Garrett, February 4, 1983.

• ELIAS, Patrik

LW – L. 6'1", 200 lbs. b: Trebic, Czech., 4/13/1976. New Jersey's 2nd, 51st overall, in 1994.

Season	Club	League	GP	G	A	Pts	AG	AA	APts	PIM	PP	SH	GW	S	%	TGF	PGF	TGA	PGA	+/-	GP	G	A	Pts	PIM	PP	SH	GW
1992-93	Poldi Kladno	Czech.	2	0	0	0	....	....	....	....	....	....	....	....	....	....	....	....	....	....	....	....	....	....	....	....	....	....
1993-94	Poldi Kladno	Czech-Rep	15	1	2	3	....	....	....	....	....	....	....	....	....	....	....	....	....	....	11	2	2	4	....	....	....	....
	Czech-Republic	EJC-A	5	2	5	7	....	....	....	2	....	....	....	....	....	....	....	....	....	....	....	....	....	....	....	....	....	....
1994-95	Poldi Kladno	Czech-Rep	28	4	3	7	....	....	....	37	....	....	....	....	....	....	....	....	....	....	7	1	2	3	12	....	....	....
1995-96	**New Jersey Devils**	**NHL**	**1**	**0**	**0**	**0**	**0**	**0**	**0**	**0**	**0**	**0**	**0**	**2**	**0.0**	**1**	**0**	**2**	**0**	**–1**	....	....	....	....	....	....	....	....
	Albany River Rats	AHL	74	27	36	63	....	....	....	83	....	....	....	....	....	....	....	....	....	....	4	1	1	2	2	....	....	....
1996-97	**New Jersey Devils**	**NHL**	**17**	**2**	**3**	**5**	**2**	**3**	**5**	**2**	**0**	**0**	**0**	**23**	**8.7**	**11**	**3**	**12**	**0**	**–4**	**8**	**2**	**3**	**5**	**4**	**1**	**0**	**0**
	Albany River Rats	AHL	57	24	43	67	....	....	....	76	....	....	....	....	....	....	....	....	....	....	6	1	2	3	8	....	....	....
1997-98	**New Jersey Devils**	**NHL**	**74**	**18**	**19**	**37**	**21**	**19**	**40**	**28**	**5**	**0**	**6**	**147**	**12.2**	**60**	**21**	**23**	**2**	**18**	**4**	**0**	**1**	**1**	**0**	**0**	**0**	**0**
	Albany River Rats	AHL	3	3	0	3	....	....	....	2	....	....	....	....	....	....	....	....	....	....	....	....	....	....	....	....	....	....
	Czech-Republic	WC-A	3	1	0	1	....	....	....	0	....	....	....	....	....	....	....	....	....	....	....	....	....	....	....	....	....	....
1998-99	**New Jersey Devils**	**NHL**	**74**	**17**	**33**	**50**	**20**	**32**	**52**	**34**	**3**	**0**	**2**	**157**	**10.8**	**72**	**24**	**33**	**4**	**19**	**7**	**0**	**5**	**5**	**6**	**0**	**0**	**0**
99-2000	SK Slavia Trebic-2	Czech-Rep	2	2	1	3	....	....	....	2	....	....	....	....	....	....	....	....	....	....	....	....	....	....	....	....	....	....
	HC Pardubice	Czech-Rep	5	1	4	5	....	....	....	31	....	....	....	....	....	....	....	....	....	....	....	....	....	....	....	....	....	....
♦	**New Jersey Devils**	**NHL**	**72**	**35**	**37**	**72**	**39**	**34**	**73**	**58**	**9**	**0**	**9**	**183**	**19.1**	**87**	**28**	**49**	**6**	**16**	**23**	**7**	***13**	**20**	**9**	**2**	**1**	**1**
	NHL Totals		**238**	**72**	**92**	**164**	**82**	**88**	**170**	**122**	**17**	**0**	**17**	**512**	**14.1**	**231**	**76**	**119**	**12**		**42**	**9**	**22**	**31**	**19**	**3**	**1**	**1**

EJC-A All-Star Team (1994) • NHL All-Rookie Team (1998) • Played in NHL All-Star Game (2000)

• ELICH, Matt

RW – R. 6'3", 187 lbs. b: Detroit, MI, 9/22/1979. Tampa Bay's 3rd, 61st overall, in 1997.

Season	Club	League	GP	G	A	Pts	AG	AA	APts	PIM	PP	SH	GW	S	%	TGF	PGF	TGA	PGA	+/-	GP	G	A	Pts	PIM	PP	SH	GW
1993-94	Detroit Little Caesars	MNHL	40	20	20	40	....	....	....	110	....	....	....	....	....	....	....	....	....	....	....	....	....	....	....	....	....	....
1994-95	Detroit Little Caesars	MNHL	45	31	22	53	....	....	....	170	....	....	....	....	....	....	....	....	....	....	....	....	....	....	....	....	....	....
1995-96	Windsor Spitfires	OHL	52	10	2	12	....	....	....	17	....	....	....	....	....	....	....	....	....	....	5	1	0	1	2	....	....	....
1996-97	Windsor Spitfires	OHL	58	15	13	28	....	....	....	19	....	....	....	....	....	....	....	....	....	....	5	0	1	1	6	....	....	....
1997-98	Windsor Spitfires	OHL	20	9	12	21	....	....	....	8	....	....	....	....	....	....	....	....	....	....	....	....	....	....	....	....	....	....
	Kingston Frontenacs	OHL	34	14	4	18	....	....	....	2	....	....	....	....	....	....	....	....	....	....	12	2	4	6	2	....	....	....
1998-99	Kingston Frontenacs	OHL	67	44	30	74	....	....	....	32	....	....	....	....	....	....	....	....	....	....	5	3	5	8	0	....	....	....
99-2000	**Tampa Bay Lightning**	**NHL**	**8**	**1**	**1**	**2**	**1**	**1**	**2**	**0**	**0**	**0**	**0**	**5**	**20.0**	**2**	**0**	**3**	**0**	**–1**	....	....	....	....	....	....	....	....
	Detroit Vipers	IHL	48	12	4	16	....	....	....	12	....	....	....	....	....	....	....	....	....	....	....	....	....	....	....	....	....	....
	NHL Totals		**8**	**1**	**1**	**2**	**1**	**1**	**2**	**0**	**0**	**0**	**0**	**5**	**20.0**	**2**	**0**	**3**	**0**		....	....	....	....	....	....	....	....

• ELIK, Todd

Todd Sloan C – L. 6'2", 195 lbs. b: Brampton, Ont., 4/15/1966.

Season	Club	League	GP	G	A	Pts	AG	AA	APts	PIM	PP	SH	GW	S	%	TGF	PGF	TGA	PGA	+/-	GP	G	A	Pts	PIM	PP	SH	GW
1982-83	St. Michael's Buzzers	OJHL-B	35	25	26	51	....	....	....	55	....	....	....	....	....	....	....	....	....	....	....	....	....	....	....	....	....	....
1983-84	Kingston Canadians	OHL	64	5	16	21	....	....	....	17	....	....	....	....	....	....	....	....	....	....	....	....	....	....	....	....	....	....
1984-85	Kingston Canadians	OHL	34	14	11	25	....	....	....	6	....	....	....	....	....	....	....	....	....	....	....	....	....	....	....	....	....	....
	North Bay Centennials	OHL	23	4	6	10	....	....	....	2	....	....	....	....	....	....	....	....	....	....	4	2	0	2	0	....	....	....
1985-86	North Bay Centennials	OHL	40	12	34	46	....	....	....	20	....	....	....	....	....	....	....	....	....	....	10	7	6	13	0	....	....	....
1986-87	University of Regina	CWUAA	27	26	34	60	....	....	....	137	....	....	....	....	....	....	....	....	....	....	....	....	....	....	....	....	....	....
	Canada	Nat-Team	1	0	0	0	....	....	....	0	....	....	....	....	....	....	....	....	....	....	....	....	....	....	....	....	....	....
1987-88	Colorado Rangers	IHL	81	44	56	100	....	....	....	83	....	....	....	....	....	....	....	....	....	....	12	8	12	20	9	....	....	....
1988-89	Denver Rangers	IHL	28	20	15	35	....	....	....	22	....	....	....	....	....	....	....	....	....	....	....	....	....	....	....	....	....	....
	New Haven Nighthawks	AHL	43	11	25	36	....	....	....	31	....	....	....	....	....	....	....	....	....	....	17	10	12	22	44	....	....	....
1989-90	**Los Angeles Kings**	**NHL**	**48**	**10**	**23**	**33**	**9**	**16**	**25**	**41**	**1**	**0**	**0**	**86**	**11.6**	**40**	**3**	**37**	**4**	**4**	**10**	**3**	**9**	**12**	**10**	**1**	**0**	**0**
	New Haven Nighthawks	AHL	32	20	23	43	....	....	....	42	....	....	....	....	....	....	....	....	....	....	....	....	....	....	....	....	....	....
1990-91	**Los Angeles Kings**	**NHL**	**74**	**21**	**37**	**58**	**19**	**28**	**47**	**58**	**2**	**0**	**4**	**153**	**13.7**	**78**	**14**	**44**	**0**	**20**	**12**	**2**	**7**	**9**	**6**	**0**	**0**	**0**
1991-92	**Minnesota North Stars**	**NHL**	**62**	**14**	**32**	**46**	**13**	**24**	**37**	**125**	**4**	**3**	**1**	**118**	**11.9**	**59**	**13**	**63**	**17**	**0**	**5**	**1**	**1**	**2**	**2**	**0**	**0**	**1**
1992-93	**Minnesota North Stars**	**NHL**	**46**	**13**	**18**	**31**	**11**	**12**	**23**	**48**	**4**	**0**	**1**	**76**	**17.1**	**46**	**10**	**45**	**4**	**–5**	....	....	....	....	....	....	....	....
	Edmonton Oilers	**NHL**	**14**	**1**	**9**	**10**	**1**	**6**	**7**	**8**	**0**	**0**	**0**	**28**	**3.6**	**12**	**2**	**9**	**0**	**1**	....	....	....	....	....	....	....	....
1993-94	**Edmonton Oilers**	**NHL**	**4**	**0**	**0**	**0**	**0**	**0**	**0**	**6**	**0**	**0**	**0**	**5**	**0.0**	**1**	**1**	**0**	**0**	**0**	....	....	....	....	....	....	....	....
	San Jose Sharks	**NHL**	**75**	**25**	**41**	**66**	**23**	**32**	**55**	**89**	**9**	**0**	**4**	**180**	**13.9**	**83**	**34**	**52**	**0**	**–3**	**14**	**5**	**5**	**10**	**12**	**1**	**0**	**0**
1994-95	**San Jose Sharks**	**NHL**	**22**	**7**	**10**	**17**	**12**	**15**	**27**	**18**	**4**	**0**	**0**	**50**	**14.0**	**24**	**6**	**19**	**4**	**3**	....	....	....	....	....	....	....	....
	St. Louis Blues	**NHL**	**13**	**2**	**4**	**6**	**4**	**6**	**10**	**4**	**0**	**0**	**0**	**26**	**7.7**	**8**	**1**	**3**	**1**	**5**	**7**	**4**	**3**	**7**	**2**	**1**	**1**	**0**
1995-96	**Boston Bruins**	**NHL**	**59**	**13**	**33**	**46**	**13**	**27**	**40**	**40**	**6**	**0**	**2**	**108**	**12.0**	**62**	**24**	**36**	**0**	**2**	**4**	**0**	**2**	**2**	**16**	**0**	**0**	**0**
	Providence Bruins	AHL	7	2	7	9	....	....	....	10	....	....	....	....	....	....	....	....	....	....	....	....	....	....	....	....	....	....
1996-97	**Boston Bruins**	**NHL**	**31**	**4**	**12**	**16**	**4**	**11**	**15**	**16**	**1**	**0**	**0**	**72**	**5.6**	**20**	**3**	**29**	**0**	**–12**	....	....	....	....	....	....	....	....
	Providence Bruins	AHL	37	16	29	45	....	....	....	63	....	....	....	....	....	....	....	....	....	....	10	1	6	7	33	....	....	....
1997-98	HC Lugano	Switz.	39	30	36	66	....	....	....	*222	....	....	....	....	....	....	....	....	....	....	7	6	5	11	12	....	....	....
1998-99	SC Langnau	Switz.	36	14	46	60	....	....	....	169	....	....	....	....	....	....	....	....	....	....	8	6	21	27	44	....	....	....
99-2000	SC Langnau	Switz.	41	19	35	54	....	....	....	*176	....	....	....	....	....	....	....	....	....	....	4	0	9	9	33	....	....	....
	Canada	Nat-Team	4	4	0	4	....	....	....	0	....	....	....	....	....	....	....	....	....	....	....	....	....	....	....	....	....	....
	NHL Totals		**448**	**110**	**219**	**329**	**109**	**177**	**286**	**453**	**31**	**3**	**12**	**902**	**12.2**	**433**	**111**	**337**	**30**		**52**	**15**	**27**	**42**	**48**	**3**	**1**	**1**

Signed as a free agent by **NY Rangers**, February 26, 1988. Traded to **LA Kings** by **NY Rangers** with Igor Liba, Michael Boyce and future considerations for Dean Kennedy and Denis Larocque, December 12, 1988. Traded to **Minnesota** by **LA Kings** for Randy Gilhen, Charlie Huddy, Jim Thomson and NY Rangers' 4th round choice (previously acquired, LA Kings selected Alexei Zhitnik) in 1991 Entry Draft, June 22, 1991. Traded to **Edmonton** by **Minnesota** for Brent Gilchrist, March 5, 1993. Claimed on waivers by **San Jose** from **Edmonton**, October 26, 1993. Traded to **St. Louis** by **San Jose** for Kevin Miller, March 23, 1995. Signed as a free agent by **Boston**, August 8, 1995.

• ELLETT, Dave

David George John D – L. 6'2", 205 lbs. b: Cleveland, OH, 3/30/1964. Winnipeg's 3rd, 75th overall, in 1982.

Season	Club	League	GP	G	A	Pts	AG	AA	APts	PIM	PP	SH	GW	S	%	TGF	PGF	TGA	PGA	+/-	GP	G	A	Pts	PIM	PP	SH	GW
1981-82	Ottawa Jr. Senators	OJHL	50	9	35	44	....	....	....	....	....	....	....	....	....	....	....	....	....	....	....	....	....	....	....	....	....	....
1982-83	Bowling Green University	CCHA	40	4	13	17	....	....	....	34	....	....	....	....	....	....	....	....	....	....	....	....	....	....	....	....	....	....
1983-84	Bowling Green University	CCHA	43	15	39	54	....	....	....	96	....	....	....	....	....	....	....	....	....	....	....	....	....	....	....	....	....	....
1984-85	**Winnipeg Jets**	**NHL**	**80**	**11**	**27**	**38**	**9**	**18**	**27**	**85**	**3**	**0**	**0**	**146**	**7.5**	**120**	**16**	**99**	**15**	**20**	**8**	**1**	**5**	**6**	**4**	**1**	**0**	**0**
1985-86	**Winnipeg Jets**	**NHL**	**80**	**15**	**31**	**46**	**12**	**21**	**33**	**96**	**2**	**0**	**1**	**168**	**8.9**	**127**	**39**	**171**	**45**	**–38**	**3**	**0**	**1**	**1**	**0**	**0**	**0**	**0**
1986-87	**Winnipeg Jets**	**NHL**	**78**	**13**	**31**	**44**	**11**	**23**	**34**	**53**	**5**	**0**	**2**	**159**	**8.2**	**111**	**23**	**83**	**14**	**19**	**10**	**0**	**8**	**8**	**2**	**0**	**0**	**0**
1987-88	United States	Can-Cup	DID NOT PLAY																									
	Winnipeg Jets	**NHL**	**68**	**13**	**45**	**58**	**11**	**32**	**43**	**106**	**5**	**0**	**1**	**198**	**6.6**	**135**	**74**	**93**	**24**	**–8**	**5**	**1**	**2**	**3**	**10**	**1**	**0**	**0**

			REGULAR SEASON																		PLAYOFFS							
Season	**Club**	**League**	**GP**	**G**	**A**	**Pts**	**AG**	**AA**	**APts**	**PIM**	**PP**	**SH**	**GW**	**S**	**%**	**TGF**	**PGF**	**TGA**	**PGA**	**+/–**	**GP**	**G**	**A**	**Pts**	**PIM**	**PP**	**SH**	**GW**
1988-89	**Winnipeg Jets**	**NHL**	**75**	**22**	**34**	**56**	19	24	43	62	9	2	5	209	10.5	145	58	137	32	–18	....	....	....	....	....	....	....	....
	Canada	WEC-A	10	4	2	6	....	....	....	14	....	....	....	....	....	....	....	....	....	....	....	....	....	....	....	....	....	....
1989-90	**Winnipeg Jets**	**NHL**	**77**	**17**	**29**	**46**	15	21	36	96	8	0	1	205	8.3	130	43	125	23	–15	7	2	0	2	6	2	0	1
1990-91	**Winnipeg Jets**	**NHL**	**17**	**4**	**7**	**11**	4	5	9	6	1	1	0	41	9.8	28	15	19	2	–4	....	....	....	....	....	....	....	....
	Toronto Maple Leafs	**NHL**	**60**	**8**	**30**	**38**	7	23	30	69	5	0	1	154	5.2	98	38	92	28	–4	....	....	....	....	....	....	....	....
1991-92	**Toronto Maple Leafs**	**NHL**	**79**	**18**	**33**	**51**	16	25	41	95	9	1	4	225	8.0	115	52	105	29	–13	....	....	....	....	....	....	....	....
1992-93	**Toronto Maple Leafs**	**NHL**	**70**	**6**	**34**	**40**	5	23	28	46	4	0	1	186	3.2	127	59	68	19	19	**21**	**4**	**8**	**12**	**8**	**2**	**0**	**0**
1993-94	**Toronto Maple Leafs**	**NHL**	**68**	**7**	**36**	**43**	6	28	34	42	5	0	1	146	4.8	114	52	74	18	6	**18**	**3**	**15**	**18**	**31**	**3**	**0**	**0**
1994-95	**Toronto Maple Leafs**	**NHL**	**33**	**5**	**10**	**15**	9	15	24	26	3	0	1	84	6.0	39	16	42	13	–6	**7**	**0**	**2**	**2**	**0**	**0**	**0**	**0**
1995-96	**Toronto Maple Leafs**	**NHL**	**80**	**3**	**19**	**22**	3	16	19	59	1	1	0	153	2.0	76	18	95	27	–10	**6**	**0**	**0**	**0**	**4**	**0**	**0**	**0**
1996-97	**Toronto Maple Leafs**	**NHL**	**56**	**4**	**10**	**14**	4	9	13	34	0	0	1	83	4.8	48	4	67	15	–8	....	....	....	....	....	....	....	....
	New Jersey Devils	**NHL**	**20**	**2**	**5**	**7**	2	4	6	6	1	0	1	22	9.1	20	8	10	0	2	**10**	**0**	**3**	**3**	**10**	**0**	**0**	**0**
1997-98	**Boston Bruins**	**NHL**	**82**	**3**	**20**	**23**	4	20	24	67	2	0	1	129	2.3	85	24	75	17	3	**6**	**0**	**1**	**1**	**6**	**0**	**0**	**0**
1998-99	**Boston Bruins**	**NHL**	**54**	**0**	**6**	**6**	0	6	6	25	0	0	0	45	0.0	40	7	24	2	11	**8**	**0**	**0**	**0**	**4**	**0**	**0**	**0**
99-2000	**St. Louis Blues**	**NHL**	**52**	**2**	**8**	**10**	2	7	9	12	0	0	1	41	4.9	29	8	27	2	–4	**7**	**0**	**1**	**1**	**2**	**0**	**0**	**0**
	NHL Totals		**1129**	**153**	**415**	**568**	**139**	**320**	**459**	**985**	**63**	**5**	**22**	**2394**	**6.4**	**1587**	**554**	**1406**	**325**		**116**	**11**	**46**	**57**	**87**	**9**	**0**	**1**

CCHA Second All-Star Team (1984) • NCAA Championship All-Tournament Team (1984) • Played in NHL All-Star Game (1989, 1992)

Traded to **Toronto** by **Winnipeg** with Paul Fenton for Ed Olczyk and Mark Osborne, November 10, 1990. Traded to **New Jersey** by **Toronto** with Doug Gilmour and New Jersey's 3rd round choice (previously acquired, New Jersey selected Andre Lakos) in 1999 Entry Draft for Jason Smith, Steve Sullivan and the rights to Alyn McCauley, February 25, 1997. Signed as a free agent by **Boston**, July 29, 1997. Signed as a free agent by **St. Louis**, October 22, 1999.

• ELLIS, Ron

Ronald John Edward RW – R. 5'9", 195 lbs. b: Lindsay, Ont., 1/8/1945.

Season	Club	League	GP	G	A	Pts	AG	AA	APts	PIM	PP	SH	GW	S	%	TGF	PGF	TGA	PGA	+/–	GP	G	A	Pts	PIM	PP	SH	GW
1960-61	Toronto Midget Marlboros	OMHA	STATISTICS NOT AVAILABLE																									
	Toronto Marlboros	OHA-Jr.	3	2	1	3	....	....	....	2	....	....	....	....	....	....	....	....	....	....	....	....	....	....	....	....	....	....
1961-62	Toronto Marlboros	OHA-Jr.	33	17	12	29	....	....	....	16	....	....	....	....	....	....	....	....	....	....	12	6	5	11	4	....	....	....
1962-63	Toronto Marlboros	OHA-Jr.	36	21	22	43	....	....	....	8	....	....	....	....	....	....	....	....	....	....	10	9	9	18	2	....	....	....
1963-64	Toronto Marlboros	OHA-Jr.	54	46	38	84	....	....	....	20	....	....	....	....	....	....	....	....	....	....	9	4	10	14	10	....	....	....
	Toronto Maple Leafs	**NHL**	**1**	**0**	**0**	**0**	0	0	0	0	....	....	....	....	....	....	....	....	....	....	....	....	....	....	....	....	....	....
	Toronto Marlboros	Mem-Cup	8	5	9	14	....	....	....	6	....	....	....	....	....	....	....	....	....	....	....	....	....	....	....	....	....	....
1964-65	**Toronto Maple Leafs**	**NHL**	**62**	**23**	**16**	**39**	28	16	44	14	....	....	....	....	....	....	....	....	....	....	**6**	**3**	**0**	**3**	**2**	**0**	**0**	**0**
1965-66	**Toronto Maple Leafs**	**NHL**	**70**	**19**	**23**	**42**	22	22	44	24	....	....	....	....	....	....	....	....	....	....	**4**	**0**	**0**	**0**	**2**	**0**	**0**	**0**
1966-67♦	**Toronto Maple Leafs**	**NHL**	**67**	**22**	**23**	**45**	26	22	48	14	....	....	....	....	....	....	....	....	....	....	**12**	**2**	**1**	**3**	**4**	**0**	**0**	**0**
1967-68	**Toronto Maple Leafs**	**NHL**	**74**	**28**	**20**	**48**	33	20	53	8	1	1	5	215	13.0	67	9	57	5	6	....	....	....	....	....	....	....	....
1968-69	**Toronto Maple Leafs**	**NHL**	**72**	**25**	**21**	**46**	27	19	46	12	4	0	5	180	13.9	73	11	59	2	5	**4**	**2**	**1**	**3**	**2**	**1**	**0**	**0**
1969-70	**Toronto Maple Leafs**	**NHL**	**76**	**35**	**19**	**54**	38	18	56	14	6	1	3	227	15.4	86	18	65	8	11	....	....	....	....	....	....	....	....
1970-71	**Toronto Maple Leafs**	**NHL**	**78**	**24**	**29**	**53**	24	24	48	10	2	0	2	234	10.3	85	17	58	7	17	**6**	**1**	**1**	**2**	**2**	**1**	**0**	**0**
1971-72	**Toronto Maple Leafs**	**NHL**	**78**	**23**	**24**	**47**	23	21	44	17	4	0	7	191	12.0	83	25	54	3	7	**5**	**1**	**1**	**2**	**4**	**1**	**0**	**0**
1972-73	Team Canada	Summit-72	8	0	3	3	....	....	....	8	....	....	....	....	....	....	....	....	....	....	....	....	....	....	....	....	....	....
	Toronto Maple Leafs	**NHL**	**78**	**22**	**29**	**51**	21	23	44	22	4	1	2	228	9.6	89	24	83	17	–1	....	....	....	....	....	....	....	....
1973-74	**Toronto Maple Leafs**	**NHL**	**70**	**23**	**25**	**48**	22	21	43	12	3	0	3	158	14.6	75	14	57	4	8	**4**	**2**	**1**	**3**	**0**	**0**	**0**	**0**
1974-75	**Toronto Maple Leafs**	**NHL**	**79**	**32**	**29**	**61**	28	22	50	25	11	0	5	177	18.1	101	26	80	14	9	**7**	**3**	**0**	**3**	**2**	**1**	**0**	**0**
1975-76			OUT OF HOCKEY – RETIRED																									
1976-77	Canada	WEC-A	10	5	4	9	....	....	....	2	....	....	....	....	....	....	....	....	....	....	....	....	....	....	....	....	....	....
1977-78	**Toronto Maple Leafs**	**NHL**	**80**	**26**	**24**	**50**	24	19	43	17	3	0	5	128	20.3	75	10	73	16	8	**13**	**3**	**2**	**5**	**0**	**0**	**0**	**2**
1978-79	**Toronto Maple Leafs**	**NHL**	**63**	**16**	**12**	**28**	14	9	23	10	4	0	1	97	16.5	44	6	34	3	7	**6**	**1**	**1**	**2**	**2**	**0**	**0**	**0**
1979-80	**Toronto Maple Leafs**	**NHL**	**59**	**12**	**11**	**23**	10	8	18	6	0	1	2	55	21.8	34	1	66	24	–9	**3**	**0**	**0**	**0**	**0**	**0**	**0**	**0**
1980-81	**Toronto Maple Leafs**	**NHL**	**27**	**2**	**3**	**5**	2	2	4	2	0	0	0	19	10.5	5	0	18	12	–1	....	....	....	....	....	....	....	....
	NHL Totals		**1034**	**332**	**308**	**640**	**342**	**266**	**608**	**207**	....	....	....	....	....	....	....	....	....	....	**70**	**18**	**8**	**26**	**20**	....	....	....

OHA-Jr. Second All-Star Team (1964) • Played in NHL All-Star Game (1964, 1965, 1968, 1970) • Came out of retirement to play for **Team Canada** in the 1977 World Hockey Championships, April 21, 1977.

• ELOMO, Miika

LW – L. 6', 200 lbs. b: Turku, Finland, 4/21/1977. Washington's 2nd, 23rd overall, in 1995.

Season	Club	League	GP	G	A	Pts	AG	AA	APts	PIM	PP	SH	GW	S	%	TGF	PGF	TGA	PGA	+/–	GP	G	A	Pts	PIM	PP	SH	GW
1993-94	TPS Turku	Finland-Jr.	30	8	5	13	....	....	....	24	....	....	....	....	....	....	....	....	....	....	5	1	1	2	2	....	....	....
1994-95	TPS Turku	Finland-Jr.	14	3	8	11	....	....	....	24	....	....	....	....	....	....	....	....	....	....	....	....	....	....	....	....	....	....
	Finland	WJC-A	7	0	1	1	....	....	....	6	....	....	....	....	....	....	....	....	....	....	....	....	....	....	....	....	....	....
	Kiekko-67 Turku	Finland-2	14	9	2	11	....	....	....	39	....	....	....	....	....	....	....	....	....	....	....	....	....	....	....	....	....	....
1995-96	TPS Turku	Finland-Jr.	6	0	2	2	....	....	....	18	....	....	....	....	....	....	....	....	....	....	....	....	....	....	....	....	....	....
	Finland	WJC-A	6	4	5	9	....	....	....	10	....	....	....	....	....	....	....	....	....	....	....	....	....	....	....	....	....	....
	Kiekko-67 Turku	Finland-2	21	9	6	15	....	....	....	100	....	....	....	....	....	....	....	....	....	....	....	....	....	....	....	....	....	....
	TPS Turku	Finland	10	1	1	2	....	....	....	8	....	....	....	....	....	....	....	....	....	....	3	0	0	0	2	....	....	....
1996-97	Portland Pirates	AHL	52	8	9	17	....	....	....	37	....	....	....	....	....	....	....	....	....	....	....	....	....	....	....	....	....	....
1997-98	Portland Pirates	AHL	33	1	1	2	....	....	....	54	....	....	....	....	....	....	....	....	....	....	....	....	....	....	....	....	....	....
	HIFK Helsinki	Finland	16	4	1	5	....	....	....	6	....	....	....	....	....	....	....	....	....	....	9	4	3	7	6	....	....	....
1998-99	TPS Turku	Finland	36	5	10	15	....	....	....	76	....	....	....	....	....	....	....	....	....	....	10	3	5	8	6	....	....	....
99-2000	**Washington Capitals**	**NHL**	**2**	**0**	**1**	**1**	0	1	1	2	0	0	0	3	0.0	1	0	0	0	1	....	....	....	....	....	....	....	....
	Portland Pirates	AHL	59	21	14	35	....	....	....	50	....	....	....	....	....	....	....	....	....	....	....	....	....	....	....	....	....	....
	NHL Totals		**2**	**0**	**1**	**1**	**0**	**1**	**1**	**2**	**0**	**0**	**0**	**3**	**0.0**	**1**	**0**	**0**	**0**		....	....	....	....	....	....	....	....

Traded to **Calgary** by **Washington** with Buffalo's compensatory 4th round choice (previously acquired, Calgary selected Levente Szuper) in 2000 Entry Draft for Anaheim's 2nd round choice (previously acquired, Washington selected Matt Pettinger) in 2000 Entry Draft, June 24, 2000.

• ELORANTA, Kari

D – L. 6'2", 200 lbs. b: Lahti, Finland, 2/29/1956.

Season	Club	League	GP	G	A	Pts	AG	AA	APts	PIM	PP	SH	GW	S	%	TGF	PGF	TGA	PGA	+/–	GP	G	A	Pts	PIM	PP	SH	GW
1974-75	H-Reipas Lahti	Finland-3	19	10	12	22	....	....	....	24	....	....	....	....	....	....	....	....	....	....	....	....	....	....	....	....	....	....
	Finland	WJC-A	5	0	0	0	....	....	....	4	....	....	....	....	....	....	....	....	....	....	....	....	....	....	....	....	....	....
	Finland	EJC-A	5	0	1	1	....	....	....	0	....	....	....	....	....	....	....	....	....	....	....	....	....	....	....	....	....	....
1975-76	H-Reipas Lahti	Finland-Jr.	STATISTICS NOT AVAILABLE																									
	Finland	WJC-A	4	0	1	1	....	....	....	2	....	....	....	....	....	....	....	....	....	....	....	....	....	....	....	....	....	....
1976-77	H-Reipas Lahti	Finland	36	4	6	10	....	....	....	34	....	....	....	....	....	....	....	....	....	....	....	....	....	....	....	....	....	....
1977-78	H-Reipas Lahti	Finland	36	6	6	12	....	....	....	14	....	....	....	....	....	....	....	....	....	....	....	....	....	....	....	....	....	....
1978-79	Leksands IF	Sweden	36	7	10	17	....	....	....	47	....	....	....	....	....	....	....	....	....	....	3	0	0	0	2	....	....	....
	Finland	WEC-A	6	0	0	0	....	....	....	4	....	....	....	....	....	....	....	....	....	....	....	....	....	....	....	....	....	....
1979-80	Leksands IF	Sweden	33	4	5	9	....	....	....	26	....	....	....	....	....	....	....	....	....	....	2	0	0	0	4	....	....	....
	Finland	Nat-Team	20	1	3	4	....	....	....	22	....	....	....	....	....	....	....	....	....	....	....	....	....	....	....	....	....	....
	Finland	Olympics	7	0	4	4	....	....	....	0	....	....	....	....	....	....	....	....	....	....	....	....	....	....	....	....	....	....
1980-81	Leksands IF	Sweden	36	2	14	16	....	....	....	35	....	....	....	....	....	....	....	....	....	....	....	....	....	....	....	....	....	....
	Finland	WEC-A	8	1	2	3	....	....	....	6	....	....	....	....	....	....	....	....	....	....	....	....	....	....	....	....	....	....
1981-82	**Calgary Flames**	**NHL**	**19**	**0**	**5**	**5**	0	3	3	14	0	0	0	11	0.0	10	3	21	0	–14	....	....	....	....	....	....	....	....
	Oklahoma City Stars	CHL	39	3	27	30	....	....	....	31	....	....	....	....	....	....	....	....	....	....	....	....	....	....	....	....	....	....
	St. Louis Blues	**NHL**	**12**	**1**	**7**	**8**	1	5	6	6	1	0	1	22	4.5	27	13	17	8	5	**5**	**0**	**0**	**0**	**0**	**0**	**0**	**0**
1982-83	**Calgary Flames**	**NHL**	**80**	**4**	**40**	**44**	3	28	31	43	0	0	0	68	5.9	122	13	109	13	13	**9**	**1**	**3**	**4**	**17**	**0**	**0**	**0**
1983-84	**Calgary Flames**	**NHL**	**78**	**5**	**34**	**39**	4	23	27	44	2	0	0	59	8.5	117	29	98	22	12	**6**	**0**	**2**	**2**	**2**	**0**	**0**	**0**
1984-85	**Calgary Flames**	**NHL**	**65**	**2**	**11**	**13**	2	7	9	39	0	0	0	43	4.7	61	7	60	7	1	....	....	....	....	....	....	....	....
1985-86	HV-71 Jonkoping	Sweden	36	4	16	20	....	....	....	46	....	....	....	....	....	....	....	....	....	....	2	0	0	0	0	....	....	....
	Finland	Nat-Team	12	1	0	1	....	....	....	8	....	....	....	....	....	....	....	....	....	....	....	....	....	....	....	....	....	....
	Finland	WEC-A	10	3	1	4	....	....	....	2	....	....	....	....	....	....	....	....	....	....	....	....	....	....	....	....	....	....
1986-87	HV-71 Jonkoping	Sweden	35	3	18	21	....	....	....	34	....	....	....	....	....	....	....	....	....	....	....	....	....	....	....	....	....	....
	Finland	Nat-Team	1	0	0	0	....	....	....	0	....	....	....	....	....	....	....	....	....	....	....	....	....	....	....	....	....	....
	Calgary Flames	**NHL**	**13**	**1**	**6**	**7**	1	4	5	9	0	0	0	11	9.1	21	6	16	4	3	**6**	**0**	**2**	**2**	**0**	**0**	**0**	**0**
1987-88	HC Lugano	Switz.	36	5	26	31	....	....	....	28	....	....	....	....	....	....	....	....	....	....	7	2	4	6	8	....	....	....
	Finland	Nat-Team	5	1	0	1	....	....	....	2	....	....	....	....	....	....	....	....	....	....	....	....	....	....	....	....	....	....
	Finland	Olympics	8	0	6	6	....	....	....	2	....	....	....	....	....	....	....	....	....	....	....	....	....	....	....	....	....	....

			REGULAR SEASON																		PLAYOFFS							
Season	Club	League	GP	G	A	Pts	AG	AA	APts	PIM	PP	SH	GW	S	%	TGF	PGF	TGA	PGA	+/-	GP	G	A	Pts	PIM	PP	SH	GW
1988-89	HC Lugano	Switz.	36	11	21	32															10	2	6	8	8			
	Finland	Nat-Team	7	1	0	1				2																		
	Finland	WEC-A	10	1	3	4				12																		
1989-90	HC Lugano	Switz.	36	7	25	32				32											9	2	4	6	6			
1990-91	H-Reipas Lahti	Finland	44	7	18	25				18																		
1991-92	Finland	Can-Cup	6	0	1	1				4																		
	Rogle BK Angelholm	Sweden-2	35	5	17	22				22											5	0	0	0	22			
	Finland	Nat-Team	11	0	3	3				2																		
	Finland	Olympics	8	0	2	2				4																		
1992-93	Rogle BK Angelholm	Sweden	38	9	8	17				44																		
1993-94	Rogle BK Angelholm	Sweden	40	2	13	15				14											3	0	0	0	0			
1994-95	Rogle BK Angelholm	Sweden	17	1	3	4				8											28	2	11	13	6			
1995-96	H-Reipas Lahti	Finland-2	44	5	25	30				34																		
1996-97	H-Reipas Lahti	Finland-2	1	0	0	0				0																		
	NHL Totals		**267**	**13**	**103**	**116**	**11**	**70**	**81**	**155**	**3**	**0**	**1**	**214**	**6.1**	**358**	**71**	**321**	**54**		**26**	**1**	**7**	**8**	**19**	**0**	**0**	**0**

Signed as a free agent by **Calgary**, September 15, 1981. Traded to **St. Louis** by **Calgary** for future considerations, March 8, 1982. Traded to **Calgary** by **St. Louis** for cash, June 3, 1982.

• ELORANTA, Mikko

LW – L. 6', 185 lbs. b: Aura, Finland, 8/24/1972. Boston's 9th, 247th overall, in 1999.

Season	Club	League	GP	G	A	Pts	AG	AA	APts	PIM	PP	SH	GW	S	%	TGF	PGF	TGA	PGA	+/-	GP	G	A	Pts	PIM	PP	SH	GW
1989-90	TPS Turku	Finland-Jr.	2	0	0	0				0																		
1990-91	TPS Turku	Finland-Jr.	35	8	8	16				18																		
1991-92	TPS Turku	Finland-Jr.	19	3	1	4				8											8	0	0	0	0			
1992-93	TPS Turku	Finland-Jr.	31	11	6	17				20											6	0	4	4	6			
1993-94	Kiekko-67 Turku	Finland-2	45	3	4	7				24																		
1994-95	Kiekko-67 Turku	Finland-2	40	14	13	27				32											7	4	1	5	20			
1995-96	Kiekko-67 Turku	Finland-2	8	6	7	13				2																		
	Ilves Tampere	Finland	43	18	15	33				86											3	0	2	2	2			
1996-97	TPS Turku	EuroHL	6	3	1	4				6											1	0	0	0	0			
	TPS Turku	Finland	31	6	15	21				52											10	5	2	7	6			
1997-98	TPS Turku	EuroHL	3	1	0	1				12																		
	TPS Turku	Finland	46	23	14	37				82											2	0	0	0	8			
1998-99	TPS Turku	Finland	52	19	21	40				103											10	1	6	7	26			
	Finland	WC-A	12	1	2	3				6																		
99-2000	**Boston Bruins**	**NHL**	**50**	**6**	**12**	**18**	**7**	**11**	**18**	**36**	**1**	**0**	**0**	**59**	**10.2**	**23**	**2**	**36**	**5**	**–10**								
	NHL Totals		**50**	**6**	**12**	**18**	**7**	**11**	**18**	**36**	**1**	**0**	**0**	**59**	**10.2**	**23**	**2**	**36**	**5**									

• ELYNUIK, Pat

RW – R. 6', 185 lbs. b: Foam Lake, Sask., 10/30/1967. Winnipeg's 1st, 8th overall, in 1986.

Season	Club	League	GP	G	A	Pts	AG	AA	APts	PIM	PP	SH	GW	S	%	TGF	PGF	TGA	PGA	+/-	GP	G	A	Pts	PIM	PP	SH	GW
1983-84	Prince Albert Midget Raiders	SAHA	26	33	30	63				64																		
	Prince Albert Raiders	WHL	2	1	0	1				0																		
1984-85	Prince Albert Raiders	WHL	70	23	20	43				54											13	9	3	12	7			
	Prince Albert Raiders	Mem-Cup	5	1	0	1				12																		
1985-86	Prince Albert Raiders	WHL	68	53	53	106				62											20	7	9	16	17			
1986-87	Prince Albert Raiders	WHL	64	51	62	113				40											8	5	5	10	12			
	Canada	WJC-A	6	6	5	11				2																		
1987-88	**Winnipeg Jets**	**NHL**	**13**	**1**	**3**	**4**	**1**	**2**	**3**	**12**	**0**	**0**	**0**	**12**	**8.3**	**7**	**1**	**7**	**3**	**2**								
	Moncton Hawks	AHL	30	11	18	29				35																		
1988-89	**Winnipeg Jets**	**NHL**	**56**	**26**	**25**	**51**	**22**	**18**	**40**	**29**	**5**	**0**	**6**	**100**	**26.0**	**73**	**17**	**53**	**2**	**5**								
	Moncton Hawks	AHL	7	8	2	10				2																		
1989-90	**Winnipeg Jets**	**NHL**	**80**	**32**	**42**	**74**	**28**	**30**	**58**	**83**	**14**	**0**	**3**	**132**	**24.2**	**111**	**37**	**73**	**1**	**2**	**7**	**2**	**4**	**6**	**2**	**0**	**0**	**0**
1990-91	**Winnipeg Jets**	**NHL**	**80**	**31**	**34**	**65**	**28**	**26**	**54**	**73**	**16**	**0**	**4**	**150**	**20.7**	**108**	**53**	**68**	**0**	**–13**								
1991-92	**Winnipeg Jets**	**NHL**	**60**	**25**	**25**	**50**	**23**	**19**	**42**	**65**	**9**	**0**	**1**	**127**	**19.7**	**79**	**35**	**46**	**0**	**–2**	**7**	**2**	**2**	**4**	**4**	**2**	**0**	**0**
1992-93	**Washington Capitals**	**NHL**	**80**	**22**	**35**	**57**	**18**	**24**	**42**	**66**	**8**	**0**	**1**	**121**	**18.2**	**94**	**42**	**49**	**0**	**3**	**6**	**2**	**3**	**5**	**19**	**0**	**0**	**0**
1993-94	**Washington Capitals**	**NHL**	**4**	**1**	**1**	**2**	**1**	**1**	**2**	**0**	**1**	**0**	**0**	**8**	**12.5**	**3**	**1**	**5**	**0**	**–3**								
	Tampa Bay Lightning	**NHL**	**63**	**12**	**14**	**26**	**11**	**11**	**22**	**64**	**3**	**1**	**1**	**103**	**11.7**	**44**	**11**	**53**	**2**	**–18**								
1994-95	**Ottawa Senators**	**NHL**	**41**	**3**	**7**	**10**	**5**	**10**	**15**	**51**	**0**	**0**	**0**	**58**	**5.2**	**21**	**9**	**25**	**2**	**–11**								
1995-96	**Ottawa Senators**	**NHL**	**29**	**1**	**2**	**3**	**1**	**2**	**3**	**16**	**0**	**0**	**0**	**27**	**3.7**	**7**	**0**	**5**	**0**	**2**								
	Fort Wayne Komets	IHL	42	22	28	50				43																		
1996-97	Michigan K-Wings	IHL	81	24	34	58				62											4	1	0	1	0			
	NHL Totals		**506**	**154**	**188**	**342**	**138**	**143**	**281**	**459**	**56**	**1**	**16**	**838**	**18.4**	**547**	**206**	**384**	**10**		**20**	**6**	**9**	**15**	**25**	**2**	**0**	**0**

WHL East First All-Star Team (1986, 1987)

Traded to **Washington** by **Winnipeg** for John Druce and Toronto's 4th round choice (previously acquired by Washington — later traded to Detroit — Detroit selected John Jakopin) in 1993 Entry Draft, October 1, 1992. Traded to **Tampa Bay** by **Washington** for future considerations, October 22, 1993. Signed as a free agent by **Ottawa**, June 21, 1994. Signed as a free agent by **Dallas**, September 6, 1996.

• EMERSON, Nelson

Nelson D. RW – R. 5'11", 180 lbs. b: Hamilton, Ont., 8/17/1967. St. Louis's 2nd, 44th overall, in 1985.

Season	Club	League	GP	G	A	Pts	AG	AA	APts	PIM	PP	SH	GW	S	%	TGF	PGF	TGA	PGA	+/-	GP	G	A	Pts	PIM	PP	SH	GW
1984-85	Stratford Cullitons	OJHL-B	40	23	38	61				70																		
1985-86	Stratford Cullitons	OJHL-B	39	*54	58	*112				91																		
1986-87	Bowling Green University	CCHA	45	26	35	61				28																		
1987-88	Bowling Green University	CCHA	45	34	49	83				54																		
1988-89	Bowling Green University	CCHA	44	22	46	68				46																		
1989-90	Bowling Green University	CCHA	44	30	52	82				42																		
	Peoria Rivermen	IHL	3	1	1	2				0																		
1990-91	**St. Louis Blues**	**NHL**	**4**	**0**	**3**	**3**	**0**	**2**	**2**	**2**	**0**	**0**	**0**	**3**	**0.0**	**3**	**0**	**5**	**0**	**–2**								
	Peoria Rivermen	IHL	73	36	79	115				91											17	9	12	21	16			
1991-92	**St. Louis Blues**	**NHL**	**79**	**23**	**36**	**59**	**21**	**27**	**48**	**66**	**3**	**0**	**2**	**143**	**16.1**	**80**	**31**	**54**	**0**	**–5**	**6**	**3**	**3**	**6**	**21**	**2**	**0**	**0**
	Canada	WC-A	3	0	1	1				2																		
1992-93	**St. Louis Blues**	**NHL**	**82**	**22**	**51**	**73**	**18**	**35**	**53**	**62**	**5**	**2**	**4**	**196**	**11.2**	**115**	**62**	**66**	**15**	**2**	**11**	**1**	**6**	**7**	**6**	**0**	**0**	**0**
1993-94	**Winnipeg Jets**	**NHL**	**83**	**33**	**41**	**74**	**31**	**32**	**63**	**80**	**4**	**5**	**6**	**282**	**11.7**	**112**	**60**	**109**	**19**	**–38**								
	Canada	WC-A	8	2	2	4				4																		
1994-95	**Winnipeg Jets**	**NHL**	**48**	**14**	**23**	**37**	**25**	**34**	**59**	**26**	**4**	**1**	**1**	**122**	**11.5**	**49**	**19**	**54**	**12**	**–12**								
1995-96	**Hartford Whalers**	**NHL**	**81**	**29**	**29**	**58**	**29**	**24**	**53**	**78**	**12**	**2**	**5**	**247**	**11.7**	**98**	**46**	**78**	**19**	**–7**								
1996-97	**Hartford Whalers**	**NHL**	**66**	**9**	**29**	**38**	**10**	**26**	**36**	**34**	**2**	**1**	**2**	**194**	**4.6**	**61**	**27**	**63**	**8**	**–21**								
1997-98	**Carolina Hurricanes**	**NHL**	**81**	**21**	**24**	**45**	**25**	**24**	**49**	**50**	**6**	**0**	**4**	**203**	**10.3**	**67**	**34**	**53**	**3**	**–17**								
	Canada	WC-A	6	2	1	3				2																		
1998-99	**Carolina Hurricanes**	**NHL**	**35**	**8**	**13**	**21**	**9**	**13**	**22**	**36**	**3**	**0**	**0**	**84**	**9.5**	**27**	**14**	**15**	**3**	**1**								
	Chicago Blackhawks	**NHL**	**27**	**4**	**10**	**14**	**5**	**10**	**15**	**13**	**0**	**0**	**1**	**94**	**4.3**	**25**	**6**	**20**	**9**	**8**								
	Ottawa Senators	**NHL**	**3**	**1**	**1**	**2**	**1**	**1**	**2**	**2**	**0**	**0**	**0**	**10**	**10.0**	**3**	**2**	**2**	**0**	**–1**	**4**	**1**	**3**	**4**	**0**	**0**	**0**	**0**
99-2000	**Atlanta Thrashers**	**NHL**	**58**	**14**	**19**	**33**	**16**	**18**	**34**	**47**	**4**	**0**	**0**	**183**	**7.7**	**48**	**15**	**74**	**17**	**–24**								
	Los Angeles Kings	**NHL**	**5**	**1**	**1**	**2**	**1**	**1**	**2**	**0**	**0**	**0**	**0**	**13**	**7.7**	**3**	**0**	**2**	**0**	**1**	**1**	**0**	**0**	**0**	**0**	**0**	**0**	**0**
	NHL Totals		**652**	**179**	**280**	**459**	**191**	**247**	**438**	**496**	**43**	**11**	**25**	**1774**	**10.1**	**691**	**316**	**595**	**105**		**22**	**5**	**12**	**17**	**27**	**2**	**0**	**0**

NCAA West Second All-American Team (1988) • CCHA First All-Star Team (1988, 1990) • CCHA Second All-Star Team (1989) • NCAA West First All-American Team (1990) • IHL First All-Star Team (1991) • Won Garry F. Longman Memorial Trophy (Top Rookie - IHL) (1991)

Traded to **Winnipeg** by **St. Louis** with Stephane Quintal for Phil Housley, September 24, 1993. Traded to **Hartford** by **Winnipeg** for Darren Turcotte, October 6, 1995. Transferred to **Carolina** after **Hartford** franchise relocated, June 25, 1997. Traded to **Chicago** by **Carolina** for Paul Coffey, December 29, 1998. Traded to **Ottawa** by **Chicago** for Chris Murray, March 23, 1999. Signed as a free agent by **Atlanta**, August 3, 1999. Traded to **Los Angeles** by **Atlanta** with Kelly Buchberger for Donald Audette and Frantisek Kaberle, March 13, 2000.

Season	Club	League	GP	G	A	Pts	AG	AA	APts	PIM	PP	SH	GW	S	%	TGF	PGF	TGA	PGA	+/–	GP	G	A	Pts	PIM	PP	SH	GW
			REGULAR SEASON																		PLAYOFFS							

• EMMA, David

David A. C – L. 5'11", 180 lbs. b: Cranston, RI, 1/14/1969. New Jersey's 6th, 110th overall, in 1989.

Season	Club	League	GP	G	A	Pts	AG	AA	APts	PIM	PP	SH	GW	S	%	TGF	PGF	TGA	PGA	+/–	GP	G	A	Pts	PIM	PP	SH	GW
1986-87	Bishop Hendrickson Hawks	Hi-School	STATISTICS NOT AVAILABLE																									
1987-88	Boston College	Hoc-East	30	19	16	35	....	....	....	30	....	....	....	....	....	....	....	....	....	....	....	....	....	....	....	....	....	....
	United States	WJC-A	7	0	0	0	....	....	....	2	....	....	....	....	....	....	....	....	....	....	....	....	....	....	....	....	....	....
1988-89	Boston College	Hoc-East	36	20	31	51	....	....	....	36	....	....	....	....	....	....	....	....	....	....	....	....	....	....	....	....	....	....
	United States	WJC-A	7	6	2	8	....	....	....	6	....	....	....	....	....	....	....	....	....	....	....	....	....	....	....	....	....	....
1989-90	Boston College	Hoc-East	42	38	34	*72	....	....	....	46	....	....	....	....	....	....	....	....	....	....	....	....	....	....	....	....	....	....
1990-91	Boston College	Hoc-East	39	*35	46	*81	....	....	....	44	....	....	....	....	....	....	....	....	....	....	....	....	....	....	....	....	....	....
	United States	WEC-A	10	1	0	1	....	....	....	8	....	....	....	....	....	....	....	....	....	....	....	....	....	....	....	....	....	....
1991-92	United States	Nat-Team	55	15	16	31	....	....	....	32	....	....	....	....	....	....	....	....	....	....	....	....	....	....	....	....	....	....
	United States	Olympics	6	0	1	1	....	....	....	6	....	....	....	....	....	....	....	....	....	....	....	....	....	....	....	....	....	....
	Utica Devils	AHL	15	4	7	11	....	....	....	12	....	....	....	....	....	....	....	....	....	....	4	1	1	2	2	....	....	....
1992-93	**New Jersey Devils**	**NHL**	**2**	**0**	**0**	**0**	**0**	**0**	**0**	**0**	**0**	**0**	**0**	**2**	**0.0**	**0**	**0**	**0**	**0**	**0**	....	....	....	....	....	....	....	....
	Utica Devils	AHL	61	21	40	61	....	....	....	47	....	....	....	....	....	....	....	....	....	....	5	2	1	3	6	....	....	....
1993-94	**New Jersey Devils**	**NHL**	**15**	**5**	**5**	**10**	**5**	**4**	**9**	**2**	**1**	**0**	**2**	**24**	**20.8**	**18**	**7**	**12**	**1**	**0**	....	....	....	....	....	....	....	....
	Albany River Rats	AHL	56	26	29	55	....	....	....	53	....	....	....	....	....	....	....	....	....	....	5	1	2	3	8	....	....	....
1994-95	**New Jersey Devils**	**NHL**	**6**	**0**	**1**	**1**	**0**	**1**	**1**	**0**	**0**	**0**	**0**	**4**	**0.0**	**1**	**0**	**4**	**1**	**–2**	....	....	....	....	....	....	....	....
	Albany River Rats	AHL	1	0	0	0	....	....	....	0	....	....	....	....	....	....	....	....	....	....	....	....	....	....	....	....	....	....
1995-96	Detroit Vipers	IHL	79	30	32	62	....	....	....	75	....	....	....	....	....	....	....	....	....	....	11	5	2	7	2	....	....	....
1996-97	**Boston Bruins**	**NHL**	**5**	**0**	**0**	**0**	**0**	**0**	**0**	**0**	**0**	**0**	**0**	**3**	**0.0**	**0**	**0**	**2**	**1**	**–1**	....	....	....	....	....	....	....	....
	Providence Bruins	AHL	53	10	18	28	....	....	....	24	....	....	....	....	....	....	....	....	....	....	....	....	....	....	....	....	....	....
	Phoenix Roadrunners	IHL	8	0	4	4	....	....	....	4	....	....	....	....	....	....	....	....	....	....	....	....	....	....	....	....	....	....
1997-98	KAC Klagenfurt	Alpenliga	16	6	17	23	....	....	....	....	....	....	....	....	....	....	....	....	....	....	....	....	....	....	....	....	....	....
	KAC Klagenfurt	Austria	33	22	22	44	....	....	....	48	....	....	....	....	....	....	....	....	....	....	....	....	....	....	....	....	....	....
1998-99	KAC Klagenfurt	Alpenliga	26	15	32	47	....	....	....	49	....	....	....	....	....	....	....	....	....	....	....	....	....	....	....	....	....	....
	KAC Klagenfurt	Austria	15	8	7	15	....	....	....	16	....	....	....	....	....	....	....	....	....	....	....	....	....	....	....	....	....	....
	United States	WC-Q	3	1	1	2	....	....	....	0	....	....	....	....	....	....	....	....	....	....	....	....	....	....	....	....	....	....
	United States	WC-A	6	1	3	4	....	....	....	0	....	....	....	....	....	....	....	....	....	....	....	....	....	....	....	....	....	....
99-2000	KAC Klagenfurt	IEL	32	26	28	54	....	....	....	28	....	....	....	....	....	....	....	....	....	....	....	....	....	....	....	....	....	....
	KAC Klagenfurt	Austria	15	9	6	15	....	....	....	18	....	....	....	....	....	....	....	....	....	....	....	....	....	....	....	....	....	....
	NHL Totals		**28**	**5**	**6**	**11**	**5**	**5**	**10**	**2**	**1**	**0**	**2**	**33**	**15.2**	**19**	**7**	**18**	**3**		....	....	....	....	....	....	....	....

Hockey East Second All-Star Team (1989) • Hockey East First All-Star Team (1990, 1991) • NCAA East First All-American Team (1990, 1991) • Won Hobey Baker Memorial Award (Top U.S. Collegiate Player) (1991)

Signed as a free agent by **Boston**, August 27, 1996.

• EMMONS, Gary

C – R. 6', 185 lbs. b: Winnipeg, Man., 12/30/1963. NY Rangers' 1st, 14th overall, in 1986 Supplemental Draft.

Season	Club	League	GP	G	A	Pts	AG	AA	APts	PIM	PP	SH	GW	S	%	TGF	PGF	TGA	PGA	+/–	GP	G	A	Pts	PIM	PP	SH	GW
1981-82	Swift Current Broncos	SJHL	STATISTICS NOT AVAILABLE																									
1982-83	Prince Albert Raiders	SJHL	STATISTICS NOT AVAILABLE																									
1983-84	Northern Michigan University	CCHA	40	28	21	49	....	....	....	42	....	....	....	....	....	....	....	....	....	....	....	....	....	....	....	....	....	....
1984-85	Northern Michigan University	CCHA	40	25	28	53	....	....	....	22	....	....	....	....	....	....	....	....	....	....	....	....	....	....	....	....	....	....
1985-86	Northern Michigan University	CCHA	36	45	30	75	....	....	....	34	....	....	....	....	....	....	....	....	....	....	....	....	....	....	....	....	....	....
1986-87	Northern Michigan University	CCHA	35	32	34	66	....	....	....	59	....	....	....	....	....	....	....	....	....	....	....	....	....	....	....	....	....	....
1987-88	Milwaukee Admirals	IHL	13	3	4	7	....	....	....	4	....	....	....	....	....	....	....	....	....	....	....	....	....	....	....	....	....	....
	Nova Scotia Oilers	AHL	59	18	27	45	....	....	....	22	....	....	....	....	....	....	....	....	....	....	....	....	....	....	....	....	....	....
1988-89	Canada	Nat-Team	49	16	26	42	....	....	....	42	....	....	....	....	....	....	....	....	....	....	....	....	....	....	....	....	....	....
1989-90	Kalamazoo Wings	IHL	81	41	59	100	....	....	....	38	....	....	....	....	....	....	....	....	....	....	8	2	7	9	2	....	....	....
1990-91	KAC Klagenfurt	Austria	8	2	2	4	....	....	....	....	....	....	....	....	....	....	....	....	....	....	....	....	....	....	....	....	....	....
	Kalamazoo Wings	IHL	62	25	33	58	....	....	....	26	....	....	....	....	....	....	....	....	....	....	11	5	8	13	6	....	....	....
1991-92	Kansas City Blades	IHL	80	29	54	83	....	....	....	60	....	....	....	....	....	....	....	....	....	....	15	6	13	19	8	....	....	....
1992-93	Kansas City Blades	IHL	80	37	44	81	....	....	....	80	....	....	....	....	....	....	....	....	....	....	12	*7	6	13	8	....	....	....
1993-94	**San Jose Sharks**	**NHL**	**3**	**1**	**0**	**1**	**1**	**0**	**1**	**0**	**1**	**0**	**0**	**6**	**16.7**	**1**	**1**	**4**	**0**	**–4**	....	....	....	....	....	....	....	....
	Kansas City Blades	IHL	63	20	49	69	....	....	....	28	....	....	....	....	....	....	....	....	....	....	....	....	....	....	....	....	....	....
1994-95	Kansas City Blades	IHL	81	22	38	60	....	....	....	42	....	....	....	....	....	....	....	....	....	....	21	9	19	28	24	....	....	....
1995-96	Kansas City Blades	IHL	73	24	39	63	....	....	....	72	....	....	....	....	....	....	....	....	....	....	1	0	0	0	4	....	....	....
1996-97	Kansas City Blades	IHL	67	15	30	45	....	....	....	36	....	....	....	....	....	....	....	....	....	....	3	0	1	1	4	....	....	....
1997-1998	Kansas City Blades	IHL	DID NOT PLAY – FRONT OFFICE STAFF																									
1998-2000	Kansas City Blades	IHL	DID NOT PLAY – ASSISTANT COACH																									
	NHL Totals		**3**	**1**	**0**	**1**	**1**	**0**	**1**	**0**	**1**	**0**	**0**	**6**	**16.7**	**1**	**1**	**4**	**0**		....	....	....	....	....	....	....	....

WCHA First All-Star Team (1986, 1987) • NCAA West Second All-American Team (1987)

Signed as a free agent by **Edmonton**, July 27, 1987. Signed as a free agent by **Minnesota**, July 11, 1989. Signed as a free agent by **San Jose**, October 19, 1993.

• EMMONS, John

C – L. 6'1", 203 lbs. b: San Jose, CA, 8/17/1974. Calgary's 7th, 122nd overall, in 1993.

Season	Club	League	GP	G	A	Pts	AG	AA	APts	PIM	PP	SH	GW	S	%	TGF	PGF	TGA	PGA	+/–	GP	G	A	Pts	PIM	PP	SH	GW
1990-91	New Canaan Rams	Hi-School	20	19	37	56	....	....	....	20	....	....	....	....	....	....	....	....	....	....	....	....	....	....	....	....	....	....
1991-92	New Canaan Rams	Hi-School	22	24	49	73	....	....	....	24	....	....	....	....	....	....	....	....	....	....	....	....	....	....	....	....	....	....
1992-93	Yale University	ECAC	28	3	5	8	....	....	....	66	....	....	....	....	....	....	....	....	....	....	....	....	....	....	....	....	....	....
	United States	WJC-A	7	0	0	0	....	....	....	6	....	....	....	....	....	....	....	....	....	....	....	....	....	....	....	....	....	....
1993-94	Yale University	ECAC	25	5	12	17	....	....	....	66	....	....	....	....	....	....	....	....	....	....	....	....	....	....	....	....	....	....
1994-95	Yale University	ECAC	28	4	16	20	....	....	....	57	....	....	....	....	....	....	....	....	....	....	....	....	....	....	....	....	....	....
1995-96	Yale University	ECAC	31	8	20	28	....	....	....	124	....	....	....	....	....	....	....	....	....	....	....	....	....	....	....	....	....	....
1996-97	Dayton Bombers	ECHL	69	20	37	57	....	....	....	62	....	....	....	....	....	....	....	....	....	....	....	....	....	....	....	....	....	....
	Fort Wayne Komets	IHL	1	0	0	0	....	....	....	0	....	....	....	....	....	....	....	....	....	....	....	....	....	....	....	....	....	....
1997-98	Michigan K-Wings	IHL	81	9	25	34	....	....	....	85	....	....	....	....	....	....	....	....	....	....	4	1	1	2	10	....	....	....
1998-99	Detroit Vipers	IHL	75	13	22	35	....	....	....	172	....	....	....	....	....	....	....	....	....	....	11	4	5	9	22	....	....	....
99-2000	**Ottawa Senators**	**NHL**	**10**	**0**	**0**	**0**	**0**	**0**	**0**	**6**	**0**	**0**	**0**	**3**	**0.0**	**0**	**0**	**2**	**0**	**–2**	....	....	....	....	....	....	....	....
	Grand Rapids Griffins	IHL	64	10	16	26	....	....	....	78	....	....	....	....	....	....	....	....	....	....	16	1	4	5	28	....	....	....
	NHL Totals		**10**	**0**	**0**	**0**	**0**	**0**	**0**	**6**	**0**	**0**	**0**	**3**	**0.0**	**0**	**0**	**2**	**0**		....	....	....	....	....	....	....	....

Signed as a free agent by **Ottawa**, August 7, 1998.

• ENDEAN, Craig

LW – L. 5'11", 170 lbs. b: Kamloops, B.C., 4/13/1968. Winnipeg's 5th, 92nd overall, in 1986.

Season	Club	League	GP	G	A	Pts	AG	AA	APts	PIM	PP	SH	GW	S	%	TGF	PGF	TGA	PGA	+/–	GP	G	A	Pts	PIM	PP	SH	GW
1982-83	Prince George Chieftans	BCAHA	STATISTICS NOT AVAILABLE																									
1983-84	Seattle Breakers	WHL	67	16	6	22	....	....	....	14	....	....	....	....	....	....	....	....	....	....	5	2	2	4	2	....	....	....
1984-85	Seattle Breakers	WHL	69	37	60	97	....	....	....	28	....	....	....	....	....	....	....	....	....	....	....	....	....	....	....	....	....	....
1985-86	Seattle Thunderbirds	WHL	70	58	70	128	....	....	....	34	....	....	....	....	....	....	....	....	....	....	5	5	1	6	0	....	....	....
1986-87	Seattle Thunderbirds	WHL	17	20	20	40	....	....	....	18	....	....	....	....	....	....	....	....	....	....	....	....	....	....	....	....	....	....
	Regina Pats	WHL	59	49	57	106	....	....	....	16	....	....	....	....	....	....	....	....	....	....	3	5	0	5	4	....	....	....
	Winnipeg Jets	**NHL**	**2**	**0**	**1**	**1**	**0**	**1**	**1**	**0**	**0**	**0**	**0**	**0**	**0.0**	**2**	**0**	**1**	**0**	**1**	....	....	....	....	....	....	....	....
1987-88	Regina Pats	WHL	69	50	86	136	....	....	....	50	....	....	....	....	....	....	....	....	....	....	4	4	9	13	8	....	....	....
1988-89	Moncton Hawks	AHL	18	3	9	12	....	....	....	16	....	....	....	....	....	....	....	....	....	....	....	....	....	....	....	....	....	....
	Fort Wayne Komets	IHL	34	10	18	28	....	....	....	0	....	....	....	....	....	....	....	....	....	....	10	4	7	11	6	....	....	....
1989-90	Fort Wayne Komets	IHL	20	2	11	13	....	....	....	8	....	....	....	....	....	....	....	....	....	....	....	....	....	....	....	....	....	....
	Adirondack Red Wings	AHL	7	3	3	6	....	....	....	4	....	....	....	....	....	....	....	....	....	....	....	....	....	....	....	....	....	....
1990-91	Canada	Nat-Team	3	2	0	2	....	....	....	2	....	....	....	....	....	....	....	....	....	....	....	....	....	....	....	....	....	....
1991-92	Winston-Salem Thunderbirds	ECHL	54	25	46	71	....	....	....	27	....	....	....	....	....	....	....	....	....	....	4	1	6	7	2	....	....	....
1992-93	Roanoke Valley Rampage	ECHL	37	15	36	51	....	....	....	51	....	....	....	....	....	....	....	....	....	....	....	....	....	....	....	....	....	....
	NHL Totals		**2**	**0**	**1**	**1**	**0**	**1**	**1**	**0**	**0**	**0**	**0**	**0**	**0.0**	**2**	**0**	**1**	**0**		....	....	....	....	....	....	....	....

WHL East Second All-Star Team (1987) • WHL East First All-Star Team (1988)

			REGULAR SEASON																		PLAYOFFS							
Season	Club	League	GP	G	A	Pts	AG	AA	APts	PIM	PP	SH	GW	S	%	TGF	PGF	TGA	PGA	+/–	GP	G	A	Pts	PIM	PP	SH	GW

• ENGBLOM, Brian

Brian Paul D – L. 6'2", 200 lbs. b: Winnipeg, Man., 1/27/1957. Montreal's 3rd, 22nd overall, in 1975.

Season	Club	League	GP	G	A	Pts	AG	AA	APts	PIM	PP	SH	GW	S	%	TGF	PGF	TGA	PGA	+/–	GP	G	A	Pts	PIM	PP	SH	GW
1972-73	Winnipeg Monarchs	MJHL	48	17	46	63	....	....	....	....	....	....	....	....	....	....	....	....	....	....	....	....	....	....	....	....	....	....
1973-74	University of Wisconsin	WCHA	36	10	21	31	....	....	....	54	....	....	....	....	....	....	....	....	....	....	....	....	....	....	....	....	....	....
1974-75	University of Wisconsin	WCHA	38	13	23	36	....	....	....	58	....	....	....	....	....	....	....	....	....	....	....	....	....	....	....	....	....	....
1975-76	Nova Scotia Voyageurs	AHL	73	4	34	38	....	....	....	79	....	....	....	....	....	....	....	....	....	....	9	1	7	8	26	....	....	....
1976-77	Nova Scotia Voyageurs	AHL	80	8	42	50	....	....	....	89	....	....	....	....	....	....	....	....	....	....	11	3	10	13	10	....	....	....
♦	**Montreal Canadiens**	**NHL**	....	....	....	....	....	....	....	....	....	....	....	....	....	....	....	....	....	....	**2**	**0**	**0**	**0**	**2**	**0**	**0**	**0**
1977-78♦	**Montreal Canadiens**	**NHL**	**28**	**1**	**2**	**3**	**1**	**2**	**3**	**23**	**0**	**0**	**0**	**28**	**3.6**	**24**	**0**	**16**	**1**	**9**	**5**	**0**	**0**	**0**	**2**	**0**	**0**	**0**
	Nova Scotia Voyageurs	AHL	7	1	5	6	....	....	....	4	....	....	....	....	....	....	....	....	....	....	....	....	....	....	....	....	....	....
1978-79♦	**Montreal Canadiens**	**NHL**	**62**	**3**	**11**	**14**	**3**	**8**	**11**	**60**	**0**	**0**	**0**	**60**	**5.0**	**58**	**3**	**38**	**4**	**21**	**16**	**0**	**1**	**1**	**11**	**0**	**0**	**0**
1979-80	**Montreal Canadiens**	**NHL**	**70**	**3**	**20**	**23**	**3**	**15**	**18**	**43**	**0**	**0**	**0**	**86**	**3.5**	**102**	**4**	**92**	**16**	**22**	**10**	**2**	**4**	**6**	**6**	**1**	**0**	**1**
1980-81	**Montreal Canadiens**	**NHL**	**80**	**3**	**25**	**28**	**2**	**17**	**19**	**96**	**1**	**0**	**0**	**120**	**2.5**	**138**	**11**	**80**	**16**	**63**	**3**	**1**	**0**	**1**	**4**	**0**	**0**	**0**
1981-82	Canada	Can-Cup	5	1	0	1	....	....	....	4	....	....	....	....	....	....	....	....	....	....	....	....	....	....	....	....	....	....
	Montreal Canadiens	**NHL**	**76**	**4**	**29**	**33**	**3**	**19**	**22**	**76**	**1**	**0**	**0**	**109**	**3.7**	**167**	**23**	**91**	**25**	**78**	**5**	**0**	**2**	**2**	**14**	**0**	**0**	**0**
1982-83	**Washington Capitals**	**NHL**	**73**	**5**	**22**	**27**	**4**	**15**	**19**	**59**	**4**	**0**	**0**	**103**	**4.9**	**119**	**22**	**133**	**32**	**–4**	**4**	**0**	**2**	**2**	**2**	**0**	**0**	**0**
	Canada	WEC-A	10	1	2	3	....	....	....	0	....	....	....	....	....	....	....	....	....	....	....	....	....	....	....	....	....	....
1983-84	**Washington Capitals**	**NHL**	**6**	**0**	**1**	**1**	**0**	**1**	**1**	**8**	**0**	**0**	**0**	**15**	**0.0**	**6**	**0**	**13**	**3**	**–4**	....	....	....	....	....	....	....	....
	Los Angeles Kings	**NHL**	**74**	**2**	**27**	**29**	**2**	**18**	**20**	**59**	**2**	**0**	**0**	**127**	**1.6**	**120**	**22**	**147**	**40**	**–9**	....	....	....	....	....	....	....	....
1984-85	**Los Angeles Kings**	**NHL**	**79**	**4**	**19**	**23**	**3**	**13**	**16**	**70**	**3**	**0**	**0**	**100**	**4.0**	**99**	**12**	**109**	**20**	**–2**	**3**	**0**	**0**	**0**	**2**	**0**	**0**	**0**
1985-86	**Los Angeles Kings**	**NHL**	**49**	**3**	**13**	**16**	**2**	**9**	**11**	**61**	**0**	**0**	**0**	**53**	**5.7**	**56**	**3**	**98**	**32**	**–13**	....	....	....	....	....	....	....	....
	Buffalo Sabres	**NHL**	**30**	**1**	**4**	**5**	**1**	**3**	**4**	**16**	**0**	**0**	**0**	**24**	**4.2**	**37**	**1**	**43**	**10**	**3**	....	....	....	....	....	....	....	....
1986-87	**Calgary Flames**	**NHL**	**32**	**0**	**4**	**4**	**0**	**3**	**3**	**28**	**0**	**0**	**0**	**31**	**0.0**	**26**	**0**	**36**	**3**	**–7**	....	....	....	....	....	....	....	....
	NHL Totals		**659**	**29**	**177**	**206**	**24**	**123**	**147**	**599**	**11**	**0**	**0**	**856**	**3.4**	**952**	**101**	**896**	**202**		**48**	**3**	**9**	**12**	**43**	**1**	**0**	**1**

WCHA First All-Star Team (1975) • NCAA West First All-American Team (1975) • AHL First All-Star Team (1977) • Won Eddie Shore Award (Outstanding Defenseman - AHL) (1977) • NHL Plus/Minus Leader (1981) • NHL Second All-Star Team (1982)

Traded to **Washington** by **Montreal** with Rod Langway, Doug Jarvis and Craig Laughlin for Ryan Walter and Rick Green, September 9, 1982. Traded to **LA Kings** by **Washington** with Ken Houston for Larry Murphy, October 18, 1983. Traded to **Buffalo** by **LA Kings** with Doug Smith for Larry Playfair, Sean McKenna and Ken Baumgartner, January 30, 1986. Traded to **Calgary** by **Buffalo** for Jim Korn, October 3, 1986. • Suffered eventual career-ending neck injury in game vs. Quebec, December 12, 1986.

• ENGELE, Jerry

Jerome Wilfred D – L. 6', 197 lbs. b: Humboldt, Sask., 11/26/1950.

Season	Club	League	GP	G	A	Pts	AG	AA	APts	PIM	PP	SH	GW	S	%	TGF	PGF	TGA	PGA	+/–	GP	G	A	Pts	PIM	PP	SH	GW
1966-67	Saskatoon Blades	CMJHL	54	1	9	10	....	....	....	162	....	....	....	....	....	....	....	....	....	....	7	0	0	0	0	....	....	....
1967-68	Saskatoon Blades	WCJHL	58	0	11	11	....	....	....	153	....	....	....	....	....	....	....	....	....	....	7	1	1	2	15	....	....	....
1968-69	Saskatoon Blades	WCJHL	52	0	9	9	....	....	....	155	....	....	....	....	....	....	....	....	....	....	4	0	0	0	0	....	....	....
1969-70	Saskatoon Blades	WCJHL	36	0	7	7	....	....	....	164	....	....	....	....	....	....	....	....	....	....	5	0	2	2	29	....	....	....
1970-71	Saskatoon Blades	WCJHL	63	2	21	23	....	....	....	181	....	....	....	....	....	....	....	....	....	....	....	....	....	....	....	....	....	....
1971-72	St. Petersburg Suns	EHL	72	6	16	22	....	....	....	110	....	....	....	....	....	....	....	....	....	....	6	1	1	2	19	....	....	....
1972-73	Sun Coast Suns	EHL	72	7	33	40	....	....	....	171	....	....	....	....	....	....	....	....	....	....	5	1	0	1	8	....	....	....
1973-74	Saginaw Gears	IHL	71	1	27	28	....	....	....	150	....	....	....	....	....	....	....	....	....	....	13	2	5	7	10	....	....	....
1974-75	New Haven Nighthawks	AHL	75	1	21	22	....	....	....	182	....	....	....	....	....	....	....	....	....	....	9	0	3	3	44	....	....	....
1975-76	**Minnesota North Stars**	**NHL**	**17**	**0**	**1**	**1**	**0**	**1**	**1**	**16**	**0**	**0**	**0**	**16**	**0.0**	**3**	**1**	**18**	**4**	**–12**	....	....	....	....	....	....	....	....
	New Haven Nighthawks	AHL	58	1	20	21	....	....	....	232	....	....	....	....	....	....	....	....	....	....	3	1	0	1	6	....	....	....
1976-77	**Minnesota North Stars**	**NHL**	**31**	**1**	**7**	**8**	**1**	**5**	**6**	**41**	**0**	**0**	**1**	**36**	**2.8**	**29**	**0**	**29**	**3**	**3**	**2**	**0**	**1**	**1**	**0**	**0**	**0**	**0**
	New Haven Nighthawks	AHL	52	2	10	12	....	....	....	84	....	....	....	....	....	....	....	....	....	....	....	....	....	....	....	....	....	....
1977-78	**Minnesota North Stars**	**NHL**	**52**	**1**	**5**	**6**	**1**	**4**	**5**	**105**	**0**	**1**	**0**	**44**	**2.3**	**37**	**1**	**51**	**5**	**–10**	....	....	....	....	....	....	....	....
	Fort Worth Texans	CHL	3	0	0	0	....	....	....	2	....	....	....	....	....	....	....	....	....	....	....	....	....	....	....	....	....	....
1978-79	Nova Scotia Voyageurs	AHL	75	4	24	28	....	....	....	186	....	....	....	....	....	....	....	....	....	....	9	0	2	2	13	....	....	....
1979-80	Saskatoon Blades	WHL	DID NOT PLAY – COACHING																									
	NHL Totals		**100**	**2**	**13**	**15**	**2**	**10**	**12**	**162**	**0**	**1**	**1**	**96**	**2.1**	**69**	**2**	**98**	**12**		**2**	**0**	**1**	**1**	**0**	**0**	**0**	**0**

Signed as a free agent by **Minnesota**, June, 1975. Transferred to **Montreal** by **Minnesota** as compensation for Minnesota's signing of free agent Mike Polich, September 6, 1978.

• ENGLISH, John

D – R. 6'2", 190 lbs. b: Toronto, Ont., 5/13/1966. Los Angeles' 3rd, 48th overall, in 1984.

Season	Club	League	GP	G	A	Pts	AG	AA	APts	PIM	PP	SH	GW	S	%	TGF	PGF	TGA	PGA	+/–	GP	G	A	Pts	PIM	PP	SH	GW
1982-83	St. Michael's Buzzers	OJHL-B	34	2	10	12	....	....	....	92	....	....	....	....	....	....	....	....	....	....	....	....	....	....	....	....	....	....
1983-84	Sault Ste. Marie Greyhounds	OHL	64	6	11	17	....	....	....	144	....	....	....	....	....	....	....	....	....	....	16	0	6	6	45	....	....	....
1984-85	Sault Ste. Marie Greyhounds	OHL	15	0	3	3	....	....	....	61	....	....	....	....	....	....	....	....	....	....	....	....	....	....	....	....	....	....
	Hamilton Steelhawks	OHL	41	2	22	24	....	....	....	105	....	....	....	....	....	....	....	....	....	....	17	3	3	6	43	....	....	....
1985-86	Hamilton Steelhawks	OHL	12	2	10	12	....	....	....	57	....	....	....	....	....	....	....	....	....	....	....	....	....	....	....	....	....	....
	Ottawa 67's	OHL	43	8	28	36	....	....	....	120	....	....	....	....	....	....	....	....	....	....	....	....	....	....	....	....	....	....
1986-87	New Haven Nighthawks	AHL	3	0	0	0	....	....	....	6	....	....	....	....	....	....	....	....	....	....	....	....	....	....	....	....	....	....
	Flint Spirits	IHL	18	1	2	3	....	....	....	83	....	....	....	....	....	....	....	....	....	....	6	1	2	3	12	....	....	....
1987-88	**Los Angeles Kings**	**NHL**	**3**	**1**	**3**	**4**	**1**	**2**	**3**	**4**	**1**	**0**	**0**	**5**	**20.0**	**6**	**2**	**4**	**2**	**2**	**1**	**0**	**0**	**0**	**0**	**0**	**0**	**0**
	New Haven Nighthawks	AHL	65	4	22	26	....	....	....	236	....	....	....	....	....	....	....	....	....	....	....	....	....	....	....	....	....	....
1988-89	Cape Breton Oilers	AHL	13	0	3	3	....	....	....	80	....	....	....	....	....	....	....	....	....	....	....	....	....	....	....	....	....	....
	New Haven Nighthawks	AHL	49	5	19	24	....	....	....	197	....	....	....	....	....	....	....	....	....	....	....	....	....	....	....	....	....	....
	NHL Totals		**3**	**1**	**3**	**4**	**1**	**2**	**3**	**4**	**1**	**0**	**0**	**5**	**20.0**	**6**	**2**	**4**	**2**		**1**	**0**	**0**	**0**	**0**	**0**	**0**	**0**

Traded to **Edmonton** by **LA Kings** with Brian Wilks for Jim Wiemer and Alan May, March 7, 1989.

• ENNIS, Jim

D – L. 6', 200 lbs. b: Edmonton, Alta., 7/10/1967. Edmonton's 6th, 126th overall, in 1986.

Season	Club	League	GP	G	A	Pts	AG	AA	APts	PIM	PP	SH	GW	S	%	TGF	PGF	TGA	PGA	+/–	GP	G	A	Pts	PIM	PP	SH	GW
1984-85	Sherwood Park Crusaders	AJHL	STATISTICS NOT AVAILABLE																									
1985-86	Boston University	H-East	40	1	4	5	....	....	....	22	....	....	....	....	....	....	....	....	....	....	....	....	....	....	....	....	....	....
1986-87	Boston University	H-East	26	3	4	7	....	....	....	27	....	....	....	....	....	....	....	....	....	....	....	....	....	....	....	....	....	....
1987-88	**Edmonton Oilers**	**NHL**	**5**	**1**	**0**	**1**	**1**	**0**	**1**	**10**	**1**	**0**	**0**	**9**	**11.1**	**4**	**2**	**2**	**0**	**0**	....	....	....	....	....	....	....	....
	Nova Scotia Oilers	AHL	59	8	12	20	....	....	....	102	....	....	....	....	....	....	....	....	....	....	5	0	1	1	16	....	....	....
1988-89	Cape Breton Oilers	AHL	67	3	15	18	....	....	....	94	....	....	....	....	....	....	....	....	....	....	....	....	....	....	....	....	....	....
1989-90	Binghamton Whalers	AHL	69	3	12	15	....	....	....	61	....	....	....	....	....	....	....	....	....	....	....	....	....	....	....	....	....	....
	NHL Totals		**5**	**1**	**0**	**1**	**1**	**0**	**1**	**10**	**1**	**0**	**0**	**9**	**11.1**	**4**	**2**	**2**	**0**		....	....	....	....	....	....	....	....

Traded to **Hartford** by **Edmonton** for Norm MacIver, October 10, 1989.

• ERICKSON, Aut

Autry Raymond D – L. 6'1", 188 lbs. b: Lethbridge, Alta., 1/25/1938.

Season	Club	League	GP	G	A	Pts	AG	AA	APts	PIM	PP	SH	GW	S	%	TGF	PGF	TGA	PGA	+/–	GP	G	A	Pts	PIM	PP	SH	GW
1954-55	Lethbridge Native Sons	WCJHL	39	3	2	5	....	....	....	54	....	....	....	....	....	....	....	....	....	....	11	0	2	2	2	....	....	....
1955-56	Lethbridge Native Sons	WCJHL	47	6	14	20	....	....	....	75	....	....	....	....	....	....	....	....	....	....	11	6	2	8	14	....	....	....
	Saskatoon Quakers	WHL	1	0	0	0	....	....	....	0	....	....	....	....	....	....	....	....	....	....	....	....	....	....	....	....	....	....
1956-57	Prince Albert Mintos	SJHL	49	12	15	27	....	....	....	*159	....	....	....	....	....	....	....	....	....	....	13	4	5	9	4	....	....	....
1957-58	Prince Albert Mintos	SJHL	47	14	32	46	....	....	....	108	....	....	....	....	....	....	....	....	....	....	6	0	4	4	7	....	....	....
	Saskatoon-St. Paul Regals	WHL	2	0	0	0	....	....	....	0	....	....	....	....	....	....	....	....	....	....	....	....	....	....	....	....	....	....
	Regina Pats	SJHL	....	....	....	....	....	....	....	....	....	....	....	....	....	....	....	....	....	....	16	6	8	14	16	....	....	....
	Regina Pats	Mem-Cup	16	6	5	11	....	....	....	16	....	....	....	....	....	....	....	....	....	....	....	....	....	....	....	....	....	....
1958-59	Calgary Stampeders	WHL	62	4	15	19	....	....	....	93	....	....	....	....	....	....	....	....	....	....	8	0	1	1	4	....	....	....
1959-60	**Boston Bruins**	**NHL**	**58**	**1**	**6**	**7**	**1**	**6**	**7**	**29**	....	....	....	....	....	....	....	....	....	....	....	....	....	....	....	....	....	....
1960-61	**Boston Bruins**	**NHL**	**68**	**2**	**6**	**8**	**2**	**6**	**8**	**65**	....	....	....	....	....	....	....	....	....	....	....	....	....	....	....	....	....	....
1961-62	Buffalo Bisons	AHL	64	7	23	30	....	....	....	88	....	....	....	....	....	....	....	....	....	....	11	1	1	2	6	....	....	....
1962-63	**Chicago Black Hawks**	**NHL**	**3**	**0**	**0**	**0**	**0**	**0**	**0**	**8**	....	....	....	....	....	....	....	....	....	....	....	....	....	....	....	....	....	....
	Buffalo Bisons	AHL	68	3	19	22	....	....	....	97	....	....	....	....	....	....	....	....	....	....	12	0	4	4	25	....	....	....
1963-64	**Chicago Black Hawks**	**NHL**	**31**	**0**	**1**	**1**	**0**	**1**	**1**	**34**	....	....	....	....	....	....	....	....	....	....	**6**	**0**	**0**	**0**	**0**	**0**	**0**	**0**
	Buffalo Bisons	AHL	34	3	13	16	....	....	....	36	....	....	....	....	....	....	....	....	....	....	....	....	....	....	....	....	....	....
1964-65	Pittsburgh Hornets	AHL	64	3	19	22	....	....	....	94	....	....	....	....	....	....	....	....	....	....	4	0	0	0	6	....	....	....
1965-66	Victoria Maple Leafs	WHL	65	7	14	21	....	....	....	109	....	....	....	....	....	....	....	....	....	....	14	1	5	6	10	....	....	....
1966-67	Victoria Maple Leafs	WHL	70	8	28	36	....	....	....	76	....	....	....	....	....	....	....	....	....	....	....	....	....	....	....	....	....	....
♦	**Toronto Maple Leafs**	**NHL**	....	....	....	....	....	....	....	....	....	....	....	....	....	....	....	....	....	....	**1**	**0**	**0**	**0**	**2**	**0**	**0**	**0**

			REGULAR SEASON																		PLAYOFFS							
Season	Club	League	GP	G	A	Pts	AG	AA	APts	PIM	PP	SH	GW	S	%	TGF	PGF	TGA	PGA	+/-	GP	G	A	Pts	PIM	PP	SH	GW
1967-68	**Oakland Seals**	**NHL**	**65**	**4**	**11**	**15**	**5**	**11**	**16**	**46**	**0**	**0**	**0**	**66**	**6.1**	**46**	**4**	**74**	**15**	**–17**	....	....	....	....	....	....	....	....
1968-69	Phoenix Roadrunners	WHL	68	8	29	37	....	....	....	83	....	....	....	....	....	....	....	....	....	....	....	....	....	....	....	....	....	....
1969-70	**Oakland Seals**	**NHL**	**1**	**0**	**0**	**0**	**0**	**0**	**0**	**0**	**0**	**0**	**0**	**1**	**0.0**	**0**	**0**	**2**	**1**	**–1**	....	....	....	....	....	....	....	....
	Phoenix Roadrunners	WHL	18	0	4	4	....	....	....	8	....	....	....	....	....	....	....	....	....	....	....	....	....	....	....	....	....	....
1970-71	Phoenix Roadrunners	WHL	DID NOT PLAY – COACHING																									
	NHL Totals		**226**	**7**	**24**	**31**	**8**	**24**	**32**	**182**	....	....	....	....	....	....	....	....	....		**7**	**0**	**0**	**0**	**2**	....	....	....

WCJHL First All-Star Team (1956) • SJHL First All-Star Team (1957, 1958) • WHL Second All-Star Team (1967)

Claimed by **Chicago** from **Saskatoon-St. Paul** (WHL) in Inter-League Draft, June 3, 1958. Claimed by **Boston** from **Chicago** in Intra-League Draft, June 10, 1959. Claimed by **Chicago** from **Boston** in Intra-League Draft, June 13, 1961. Traded to **Detroit** by **Chicago** with Ron Murphy for John Miszuk, Art Stratton and Ian Cushenan, June 9, 1964. Traded to **Toronto** by **Detroit** with Marcel Pronovost, Larry Jeffrey, Ed Joyal and Lowell MacDonald for Billy Harris, Gary Jarrett and Andy Bathgate, May 20, 1965. Claimed by **Oakland** from **Toronto** in Expansion Draft, June 6, 1967. • Underwent career-ending spinal fusion surgery, January, 1970. • Named Head Coach of **Phoenix** (WHL), September 1, 1970.

• ERICKSON, Bryan

Bryan Lee RW – R. 5'9", 175 lbs. b: Roseau, MN, 3/7/1960.

1978-79	Roseau Rams	Hi-School	STATISTICS NOT AVAILABLE																									
	United States	WJC-A	5	2	1	3	....	....	....	6	....	....	....	....	....	....	....	....	....	....	....	....	....	....	....	....	....	....
1979-80	University of Minnesota	WCHA	23	10	15	25	....	....	....	14	....	....	....	....	....	....	....	....	....	....	....	....	....	....	....	....	....	....
	United States	WJC-A	4	2	2	4	....	....	....	2	....	....	....	....	....	....	....	....	....	....	....	....	....	....	....	....	....	....
1980-81	University of Minnesota	WCHA	44	39	47	86	....	....	....	30	....	....	....	....	....	....	....	....	....	....	....	....	....	....	....	....	....	....
1981-82	University of Minnesota	WCHA	35	25	20	45	....	....	....	20	....	....	....	....	....	....	....	....	....	....	....	....	....	....	....	....	....	....
	United States	WEC-A	7	1	1	2	....	....	....	6	....	....	....	....	....	....	....	....	....	....	....	....	....	....	....	....	....	....
1982-83	University of Minnesota	WCHA	42	35	47	82	....	....	....	34	....	....	....	....	....	....	....	....	....	....	....	....	....	....	....	....	....	....
	Hershey Bears	AHL	1	0	1	1	....	....	....	0	....	....	....	....	....	....	....	....	....	....	3	3	0	3	0	....	....	....
1983-84	**Washington Capitals**	**NHL**	**45**	**12**	**17**	**29**	**10**	**12**	**22**	**16**	**4**	**0**	**2**	**66**	**18.2**	**37**	**7**	**20**	**0**	**10**	**8**	**2**	**3**	**5**	**7**	**1**	**0**	**0**
	Hershey Bears	AHL	31	16	12	28	....	....	....	11	....	....	....	....	....	....	....	....	....	....	....	....	....	....	....	....	....	....
1984-85	United States	Can-Cup	6	2	2	4	....	....	....	4	....	....	....	....	....	....	....	....	....	....	....	....	....	....	....	....	....	....
	Washington Capitals	**NHL**	**57**	**15**	**13**	**28**	**12**	**9**	**21**	**23**	**1**	**0**	**1**	**79**	**19.0**	**41**	**8**	**25**	**3**	**11**	....	....	....	....	....	....	....	....
	Binghamton Whalers	AHL	13	6	11	17	....	....	....	8	....	....	....	....	....	....	....	....	....	....	....	....	....	....	....	....	....	....
1985-86	Binghamton Whalers	AHL	7	5	3	8	....	....	....	2	....	....	....	....	....	....	....	....	....	....	....	....	....	....	....	....	....	....
	Los Angeles Kings	**NHL**	**55**	**20**	**23**	**43**	**16**	**15**	**31**	**36**	**6**	**0**	**4**	**108**	**18.5**	**63**	**18**	**58**	**14**	**1**	....	....	....	....	....	....	....	....
	United States	WEC-A	10	8	1	9	....	....	....	10	....	....	....	....	....	....	....	....	....	....	....	....	....	....	....	....	....	....
	New Haven Nighthawks	AHL	14	8	3	11	....	....	....	11	....	....	....	....	....	....	....	....	....	....	....	....	....	....	....	....	....	....
1986-87	**Los Angeles Kings**	**NHL**	**68**	**20**	**30**	**50**	**17**	**22**	**39**	**26**	**6**	**2**	**4**	**142**	**14.1**	**79**	**34**	**73**	**16**	**–12**	**3**	**1**	**1**	**2**	**0**	**0**	**0**	**0**
	United States	WEC-A	10	4	4	8	....	....	....	8	....	....	....	....	....	....	....	....	....	....	....	....	....	....	....	....	....	....
1987-88	**Los Angeles Kings**	**NHL**	**42**	**6**	**15**	**21**	**5**	**11**	**16**	**20**	**2**	**0**	**0**	**68**	**8.8**	**36**	**15**	**35**	**0**	**–14**	....	....	....	....	....	....	....	....
	New Haven Nighthawks	AHL	3	0	0	0	....	....	....	0	....	....	....	....	....	....	....	....	....	....	....	....	....	....	....	....	....	....
	Pittsburgh Penguins	**NHL**	**11**	**1**	**4**	**5**	**1**	**3**	**4**	**0**	**0**	**0**	**0**	**13**	**7.7**	**8**	**0**	**6**	**0**	**2**	....	....	....	....	....	....	....	....
1988-89	HC Merano	Italy	38	38	56	94	....	....	....	29	....	....	....	....	....	....	....	....	....	....	....	....	....	....	....	....	....	....
1989-90	Moncton Hawks	AHL	13	4	7	11	....	....	....	4	....	....	....	....	....	....	....	....	....	....	....	....	....	....	....	....	....	....
1990-91	**Winnipeg Jets**	**NHL**	**6**	**0**	**7**	**7**	**0**	**5**	**5**	**0**	**0**	**0**	**0**	**16**	**0.0**	**7**	**4**	**3**	**1**	**1**	....	....	....	....	....	....	....	....
	Moncton Hawks	AHL	36	18	14	32	....	....	....	16	....	....	....	....	....	....	....	....	....	....	9	9	2	11	6	....	....	....
1991-92	**Winnipeg Jets**	**NHL**	**10**	**2**	**4**	**6**	**2**	**3**	**5**	**0**	**0**	**0**	**1**	**16**	**12.5**	**11**	**1**	**2**	**1**	**9**	....	....	....	....	....	....	....	....
1992-93	**Winnipeg Jets**	**NHL**	**41**	**4**	**12**	**16**	**3**	**8**	**11**	**14**	**2**	**0**	**1**	**45**	**8.9**	**21**	**5**	**21**	**7**	**2**	**3**	**0**	**0**	**0**	**0**	**0**	**0**	**0**
	Moncton Hawks	AHL	2	1	1	2	....	....	....	4	....	....	....	....	....	....	....	....	....	....	....	....	....	....	....	....	....	....
1993-94	**Winnipeg Jets**	**NHL**	**16**	**0**	**0**	**0**	**0**	**0**	**0**	**6**	**0**	**0**	**0**	**8**	**0.0**	**0**	**0**	**11**	**4**	**–7**	....	....	....	....	....	....	....	....
	Moncton Hawks	AHL	3	0	1	1	....	....	....	2	....	....	....	....	....	....	....	....	....	....	....	....	....	....	....	....	....	....
	NHL Totals		**351**	**80**	**125**	**205**	**66**	**88**	**154**	**141**	**21**	**2**	**13**	**561**	**14.3**	**303**	**92**	**254**	**46**		**14**	**3**	**4**	**7**	**7**	**1**	**0**	**0**

WCHA Second All-Star Team (1982) • WCHA First All-Star Team (1983)

Signed as a free agent by **Washington**, April 5, 1983. Traded to **LA Kings** by **Washington** for Bruce Shoebottom, October 31, 1985. Traded to **Pittsburgh** by **LA Kings** for Chris Kontos and Pittsburgh's 6th round choice (Micah Aivazoff) in 1988 Entry Draft, February 5, 1988. Signed as a free agent by **Winnipeg**, March 2, 1990. • Missed majority of 1991-92 season recovering from abdominal injury suffered in game vs. LA Kings, October 12, 1991. • Missed majority of 1993-94 season recovering from groin injury suffered in game vs. Quebec, December 23, 1993.

• ERICKSON, Grant

Grant Charles LW – . 5'9", 165 lbs. b: Pierceland, Sask., 4/28/1947.

1965-66	Estevan Bruins	SJHL	57	30	20	50	....	....	....	22	....	....	....	....	....	....	....	....	....	....	25	2	13	15	12	....	....	....
1966-67	Estevan Bruins	CMJHL	55	35	49	84	....	....	....	49	....	....	....	....	....	....	....	....	....	....	13	6	8	14	8	....	....	....
1967-68	Oklahoma City Blazers	CPHL	70	27	34	61	....	....	....	65	....	....	....	....	....	....	....	....	....	....	1	0	1	1	0	....	....	....
1968-69	**Boston Bruins**	**NHL**	**2**	**1**	**0**	**1**	**1**	**0**	**1**	**0**	**0**	**0**	**0**	**2**	**50.0**	**2**	**0**	**0**	**0**	**2**	....	....	....	....	....	....	....	....
	Oklahoma City Blazers	CHL	64	28	37	65	....	....	....	66	....	....	....	....	....	....	....	....	....	....	4	3	2	5	0	....	....	....
1969-70	**Minnesota North Stars**	**NHL**	**4**	**0**	**0**	**0**	**0**	**0**	**0**	**0**	**0**	**0**	**0**	**4**	**0.0**	**1**	**0**	**4**	**0**	**–3**	....	....	....	....	....	....	....	....
	Iowa Stars	CHL	68	31	38	69	....	....	....	67	....	....	....	....	....	....	....	....	....	....	11	6	3	9	16	....	....	....
1970-71	Cleveland Barons	AHL	57	18	25	43	....	....	....	41	....	....	....	....	....	....	....	....	....	....	8	3	0	3	4	....	....	....
1971-72	Cleveland Barons	AHL	76	26	24	50	....	....	....	45	....	....	....	....	....	....	....	....	....	....	5	0	0	0	4	....	....	....
1972-73	Cleveland Crusaders	WHA	77	15	29	44	....	....	....	23	....	....	....	....	....	....	....	....	....	....	9	2	1	3	2	....	....	....
1973-74	Cleveland Crusaders	WHA	78	23	27	50	....	....	....	26	....	....	....	....	....	....	....	....	....	....	....	....	....	....	....	....	....	....
1974-75	Cleveland Crusaders	WHA	78	12	15	27	....	....	....	24	....	....	....	....	....	....	....	....	....	....	5	0	0	0	0	....	....	....
1975-76	Syracuse Blazers	NAHL	9	5	2	7	....	....	....	6	....	....	....	....	....	....	....	....	....	....	....	....	....	....	....	....	....	....
	Phoenix Roadrunners	WHA	33	4	7	11	....	....	....	6	....	....	....	....	....	....	....	....	....	....	5	0	2	2	0	....	....	....
	Tucson Mavericks	CHL	29	12	10	22	....	....	....	16	....	....	....	....	....	....	....	....	....	....	....	....	....	....	....	....	....	....
1976-77	Rhode Island Reds	AHL	27	3	9	12	....	....	....	11	....	....	....	....	....	....	....	....	....	....	....	....	....	....	....	....	....	....
	Oklahoma City Blazers	CHL	22	6	10	16	....	....	....	2	....	....	....	....	....	....	....	....	....	....	....	....	....	....	....	....	....	....
	NHL Totals		**6**	**1**	**0**	**1**	**1**	**0**	**1**	**0**	**0**	**0**	**0**	**6**	**16.7**	**3**	**0**	**4**	**0**		....	....	....	....	....	....	....	....
	Other Major League Totals		266	54	78	132	....	....	....	79	....	....	....	....	....	....	....	....	....	....	19	2	3	5	2	....	....	....

SJHL Rookie-of-the-Year (1966)

Claimed by **Minnesota** from **Boston** in Intra-League Draft, June 11, 1969. Selected by **Calgary-Cleveland** (WHA) in 1972 WHA General Player Draft, February 12, 1972. Traded to **Phoenix** (WHA) by **Cleveland** (WHA) for Rick Newell and Rob Watt, November, 1975. Traded to **Birmingham** (WHA) by **Phoenix** (WHA) for future considerations, August, 1976.

• ERIKSSON, Anders

"Butsy" D – L. 6'2", 220 lbs. b: Bollnas, Sweden, 1/9/1975. Detroit's 1st, 22nd overall, in 1993.

1989-1991	Bollnas IS	Sweden-4	STATISTICS NOT AVAILABLE																									
1991-92	MoDo AIK	Sweden-Jr.	STATISTICS NOT AVAILABLE																									
1992-93	MoDo AIK	Sweden-Jr.	10	5	3	8	....	....	....	14	....	....	....	....	....	....	....	....	....	....	....	....	....	....	....	....	....	....
	MoDo AIK	Sweden	20	0	2	2	....	....	....	2	....	....	....	....	....	....	....	....	....	....	1	0	0	0	0	....	....	....
	Sweden	EJC-A	6	2	1	3	....	....	....	14	....	....	....	....	....	....	....	....	....	....	....	....	....	....	....	....	....	....
1993-94	MoDo AIK	Sweden-Jr.	3	1	2	3	....	....	....	34	....	....	....	....	....	....	....	....	....	....	....	....	....	....	....	....	....	....
	MoDo AIK	Sweden	38	2	8	10	....	....	....	42	....	....	....	....	....	....	....	....	....	....	11	0	0	0	8	....	....	....
	Sweden	WJC-A	7	1	3	4	....	....	....	10	....	....	....	....	....	....	....	....	....	....	....	....	....	....	....	....	....	....
1994-95	MoDo AIK	Sweden	39	3	6	9	....	....	....	54	....	....	....	....	....	....	....	....	....	....	....	....	....	....	....	....	....	....
	Sweden	WJC-A	7	3	7	10	....	....	....	10	....	....	....	....	....	....	....	....	....	....	....	....	....	....	....	....	....	....
1995-96	**Detroit Red Wings**	**NHL**	**1**	**0**	**0**	**0**	**0**	**0**	**0**	**2**	**0**	**0**	**0**	**0**	**0.0**	**1**	**0**	**0**	**0**	**1**	**3**	**0**	**0**	**0**	**0**	**0**	**0**	**0**
	Adirondack Red Wings	AHL	75	6	36	42	....	....	....	64	....	....	....	....	....	....	....	....	....	....	3	0	0	0	0	....	....	....
1996-97	**Detroit Red Wings**	**NHL**	**23**	**0**	**6**	**6**	**0**	**5**	**5**	**10**	**0**	**0**	**0**	**27**	**0.0**	**17**	**0**	**13**	**1**	**5**	....	....	....	....	....	....	....	....
	Adirondack Red Wings	AHL	44	3	25	28	....	....	....	36	....	....	....	....	....	....	....	....	....	....	4	0	1	1	4	....	....	....
1997-98♦	**Detroit Red Wings**	**NHL**	**66**	**7**	**14**	**21**	**8**	**14**	**22**	**32**	**1**	**0**	**2**	**91**	**7.7**	**58**	**6**	**41**	**10**	**21**	**18**	**0**	**5**	**5**	**16**	**0**	**0**	**0**

			REGULAR SEASON																		PLAYOFFS							
Season	Club	League	GP	G	A	Pts	AG	AA	APts	PIM	PP	SH	GW	S	%	TGF	PGF	TGA	PGA	+/–	GP	G	A	Pts	PIM	PP	SH	GW
1998-99	**Detroit Red Wings**	**NHL**	**61**	**2**	**10**	**12**	**2**	**10**	**12**	**34**	**0**	**0**	**1**	**67**	**3.0**	**37**	**2**	**35**	**5**	**5**								
	Chicago Blackhawks	**NHL**	**11**	**0**	**8**	**8**	**0**	**8**	**8**	**0**	**0**	**0**	**0**	**12**	**0.0**	**17**	**6**	**8**	**3**	**6**								
	Sweden	WC-A	10	0	3	3				14																		
99-2000	**Chicago Blackhawks**	**NHL**	**73**	**3**	**25**	**28**	**3**	**23**	**26**	**20**	**0**	**0**	**1**	**86**	**3.5**	**67**	**15**	**65**	**17**	**4**								
	NHL Totals		**235**	**12**	**63**	**75**	**13**	**60**	**73**	**98**	**1**	**0**	**4**	**283**	**4.2**	**197**	**29**	**162**	**36**		**21**	**0**	**5**	**5**	**16**	**0**	**0**	**0**

WJC-A All-Star Team (1995)

Traded to **Chicago** by **Detroit** with Detroit's 1st round choices in 1999 (Steve McCarthy) and 2001 Entry Drafts for Chris Chelios, March 23, 1999.

• ERIKSSON, Peter

Peter Kessler LW – R. 6'4", 218 lbs. b: Kramfors, Sweden, 7/12/1965. Edmonton's 4th, 64th overall, in 1987.

Season	Club	League	GP	G	A	Pts	AG	AA	APts	PIM	PP	SH	GW	S	%	TGF	PGF	TGA	PGA	+/–	GP	G	A	Pts	PIM	PP	SH	GW
1984-85	HV-71 Jonkoping	Sweden-2	3	3	0	3				0																		
1985-86	HV-71 Jonkoping	Sweden	30	7	8	15				18											1	0	0	0	0			
1986-87	HV-71 Jonkoping	Sweden	36	14	5	19				16																		
1987-88	Sweden	Can-Cup	3	0	0	0				0																		
	HV-71 Jonkoping	Sweden	37	14	9	23				20											2	1	0	1	0			
	Sweden	Olympics	3	0	1	1				0																		
1988-89	HV-71 Jonkoping	Sweden	40	10	27	37				48											3	1	2	3	0			
	Sweden	WEC-A	7	0	1	1				8																		
1989-90	**Edmonton Oilers**	**NHL**	**20**	**3**	**3**	**6**	**3**	**2**	**5**	**24**	**1**	**0**	**0**	**23**	**13.0**	**15**	**5**	**11**	**0**	**–1**								
	Cape Breton Oilers	AHL	21	5	12	17				36											5	2	2	4	2			
1990-91	HV-71 Jonkoping	Sweden	35	15	7	22				58											2	1	0	1	2			
1991-92	HV-71 Jonkoping	Sweden	34	10	12	22				28											3	1	0	1	0			
1992-93	HV-71 Jonkoping	Sweden	40	13	15	28				40																		
1993-94	HV-71 Jonkoping	Sweden	38	6	7	13				34																		
1994-95	IF Troja-Ljungby	Sweden-2	36	16	10	26				34											8	3	2	5	10			
1995-96	IF Troja-Ljungby	Sweden-2	31	20	10	30				20											9	2	2	4	12			
1996-97	IF Troja-Ljungby	Sweden-2	29	11	20	31				56											9	4	2	6	6			
	NHL Totals		**20**	**3**	**3**	**6**	**3**	**2**	**5**	**24**	**1**	**0**	**0**	**23**	**13.0**	**15**	**5**	**11**	**0**									

• ERIKSSON, Roland

Bengt Roland C – L. 6'3", 190 lbs. b: Storatuna, Sweden, 3/1/1954. Minnesota's 8th, 131st overall, in 1974.

Season	Club	League	GP	G	A	Pts	AG	AA	APts	PIM	PP	SH	GW	S	%	TGF	PGF	TGA	PGA	+/–	GP	G	A	Pts	PIM	PP	SH	GW
1969-1971	IF Tunabro Borlange	Sweden-Jr.	STATISTICS NOT AVAILABLE																									
1970-71	Sweden	EJC-A	3	3	1	4				0																		
1971-72	HC Tunabro	Sweden	14	5	3	8				6											6	2	4	6	2			
	Sweden	EJC-A	5	4	2	6				0																		
1972-73	HC Tunabro	Sweden	14	10	2	12				0											6	5	5	10	0			
	Sweden	EJC-A	5	3	5	8				0																		
1973-74	HC Tunabro	Sweden-2	14	7	5	12				2											14	9	4	13	4			
	Sweden	WJC-A	5	5	4	9				0																		
1974-75	Leksands IF	Sweden	28	11	16	27				14											5	3	1	4	0			
1975-76	Leksands IF	Sweden	36	21	14	35				16											10	*9	3	*12	0			
	Sweden	WEC-A	10	8	7	15				0																		
1976-77	Sweden	Can-Cup	5	2	2	4				2																		
	Minnesota North Stars	**NHL**	**80**	**25**	**44**	**69**	**23**	**34**	**57**	**10**	**10**	**0**	**1**	**249**	**10.0**	**101**	**46**	**85**	**1**	**–29**	**2**	**1**	**0**	**1**	**0**	**0**	**0**	**0**
	Sweden	WEC-A	10	7	6	13				0																		
1977-78	**Minnesota North Stars**	**NHL**	**78**	**21**	**39**	**60**	**19**	**30**	**49**	**12**	**3**	**0**	**1**	**257**	**8.2**	**85**	**30**	**91**	**7**	**–29**								
	Sweden	WEC-A	10	1	2	3				2																		
1978-79	**Vancouver Canucks**	**NHL**	**35**	**2**	**12**	**14**	**2**	**9**	**11**	**4**	**0**	**0**	**0**	**69**	**2.9**	**28**	**12**	**28**	**0**	**–12**								
	Winnipeg Jets	WHA	33	5	10	15				2											10	1	4	5	0			
1979-80	Leksands IF	Sweden	35	18	21	39				12											2	3	1	4	0			
1980-81	Dusseldorfer EG	Germany	40	31	*55	86				24											11	6	15	21	0			
	Sweden	WEC-A	8	2	1	3				2																		
1981-82	Dusseldorfer EG	Germany	37	30	38	68				14																		
1982-83	Leksands IF	Sweden	36	20	27	47				16																		
	Sweden	WEC-A	10	2	2	4				2																		
1983-84	Leksands IF	Sweden	36	20	20	40				20																		
1984-85	HV-71 Jonkoping	Sweden-2	32	31	42	73				4																		
1985-86	HV-71 Jonkoping	Sweden	35	11	15	26				10											2	0	0	0	2			
1986-87	Vasteras IK	Sweden-2	31	23	26	49				8											12	4	9	13	4			
1987-88	Vasteras IK	Sweden	31	19	23	42				4																		
	Vasteras IK	Sweden-2	14	9	*15	*24				0																		
1988-89	Vasteras IK	Sweden	18	5	18	23				0											5	3	2	5	0			
	Vasteras IK	Sweden-Q	21	8	7	15				8																		
	NHL Totals		**193**	**48**	**95**	**143**	**44**	**73**	**117**	**26**	**13**	**0**	**2**	**575**	**8.3**	**214**	**88**	**204**	**8**		**2**	**1**	**0**	**1**	**0**	**0**	**0**	**0**
	Other Major League Totals		33	5	10	15				2											10	1	4	5	0			

Named Swedish Junior Player-of-the-Year (1973) • WJC-A All-Star Team (1974) • Played in NHL All-Star Game (1978)

Signed as a free agent by **Vancouver**, June 7, 1978. Signed as a free agent by **Winnipeg** (WHA) after being released by **Vancouver**, January, 1979.

• ERIKSSON, Thomas

Thomas B. D – L. 6'2", 182 lbs. b: Stockholm, Sweden, 10/16/1959. Philadelphia's 6th, 98th overall, in 1979.

Season	Club	League	GP	G	A	Pts	AG	AA	APts	PIM	PP	SH	GW	S	%	TGF	PGF	TGA	PGA	+/–	GP	G	A	Pts	PIM	PP	SH	GW
1976-77	Djurgardens IF Stockholm	Sweden-2	20	0	4	4																						
1977-78	Djurgardens IF Stockholm	Sweden	25	6	4	10				30																		
1978-79	Djurgardens IF Stockholm	Sweden	35	6	11	17				70											6	1	0	1	4			
	Sweden	WJC-A	6	2	0	2				13																		
	Sweden	WEC-A	6	1	1	2				6																		
1979-80	Djurgardens IF Stockholm	Sweden	36	12	10	22				64																		
	Sweden	Olympics	7	2	0	2				10																		
1980-81	**Philadelphia Flyers**	**NHL**	**24**	**1**	**10**	**11**	**1**	**7**	**8**	**14**	**1**	**0**	**0**	**49**	**2.0**	**37**	**15**	**23**	**5**	**4**	**7**	**0**	**2**	**2**	**6**	**0**	**0**	**0**
	Maine Mariners	AHL	54	11	20	31				75																		
1981-82	Sweden	Can-Cup	3	0	0	0				0																		
	Philadelphia Flyers	**NHL**	**1**	**0**	**0**	**0**	**0**	**0**	**0**	**4**	**0**	**0**	**0**	**0**	**0.0**	**0**	**0**	**1**	**0**	**–1**								
	Djurgardens IF Stockholm	Sweden	27	7	5	12				48																		
	Sweden	WEC-A	10	0	0	0				14																		
1982-83	Djurgardens IF Stockholm	Sweden	32	12	9	21				51											8	1	0	1	*26			
	Sweden	WEC-A	10	0	1	1				12																		
1983-84	**Philadelphia Flyers**	**NHL**	**68**	**11**	**33**	**44**	**9**	**22**	**31**	**37**	**2**	**0**	**1**	**110**	**10.0**	**111**	**22**	**80**	**19**	**28**	**3**	**0**	**1**	**1**	**0**	**0**	**0**	**0**
1984-85	Sweden	Can-Cup	7	0	3	3				2																		
	Philadelphia Flyers	**NHL**	**72**	**10**	**29**	**39**	**8**	**20**	**28**	**36**	**4**	**1**	**1**	**125**	**8.0**	**107**	**31**	**67**	**15**	**24**	**9**	**0**	**0**	**0**	**6**	**0**	**0**	**0**
1985-86	**Philadelphia Flyers**	**NHL**	**43**	**0**	**4**	**4**	**0**	**3**	**3**	**16**	**0**	**0**	**0**	**32**	**0.0**	**15**	**9**	**20**	**2**	**–12**								
1986-87	Djurgardens IF Stockholm	Sweden	34	8	11	19				64																		
1987-88	Djurgardens IF Stockholm	Sweden	39	13	17	30				36											3	0	0	0	2			
	Sweden	Olympics	7	0	3	3				6																		
1988-89	Djurgardens IF Stockholm	Sweden	38	6	13	19				50											8	3	3	6	*20			
	Sweden	WEC-A	8	1	1	2				8																		
1989-90	Djurgardens IF Stockholm	Sweden	39	11	12	23				*106											8	2	2	4	*22			
	Sweden	WEC-A	9	4	1	5				14																		
1990-91	Djurgardens IF Stockholm	Sweden	39	16	11	27				62											7	3	2	5	12			
1991-92	Djurgardens IF Stockholm	Sweden	31	7	7	14				46											10	1	0	1	2			

			REGULAR SEASON																		PLAYOFFS							
Season	Club	League	GP	G	A	Pts	AG	AA	APts	PIM	PP	SH	GW	S	%	TGF	PGF	TGA	PGA	+/-	GP	G	A	Pts	PIM	PP	SH	GW
1992-93	Djurgardens IF Stockholm	Sweden	37	7	10	17	....	....	....	48	....	....	....	....	....	....	....	....	....	....	6	1	2	3	4	....	....	....
1993-94	Djurgardens IF Stockholm	Sweden	38	5	13	18	....	....	....	46	....	....	....	....	....	....	....	....	....	....	6	1	4	5	....	....	....	....
1994-95	Vasteras IK	Sweden	40	8	7	15	....	....	....	46	....	....	....	....	....	....	....	....	....	....	4	0	1	1	0	....	....	....
	NHL Totals		**208**	**22**	**76**	**98**	**18**	**52**	**70**	**107**	**7**	**1**	**2**	**316**	**7.0**	**270**	**77**	**191**	**41**		**19**	**0**	**3**	**3**	**12**	**0**	**0**	**0**

Swedish World All-Star Team (1980, 1983, 1990, 1991) • NHL All-Rookie Team (1984)

• ERIXON, Jan

Jan Erik "Exit" LW – L. 6', 196 lbs. b: Skelleftea, Sweden, 7/8/1962. NY Rangers' 2nd, 30th overall, in 1981.

Season	Club	League	GP	G	A	Pts	AG	AA	APts	PIM	PP	SH	GW	S	%	TGF	PGF	TGA	PGA	+/-	GP	G	A	Pts	PIM	PP	SH	GW
1979-80	Skelleftea AIK	Sweden	15	1	0	1	....	....	....	2	....	....	....	....	....	....	....	....	....	....	....	....	....	....	....	....	....	....
1980-81	Skelleftea AIK	Sweden	32	6	6	12	....	....	....	4	....	....	....	....	....	....	....	....	....	....	3	1	0	1	0	....	....	....
	Sweden	WJC-A	5	1	6	7	....	....	....	2	....	....	....	....	....	....	....	....	....	....	....	....	....	....	....	....	....	....
1981-82	Sweden	Can-Cup	2	0	0	0	....	....	....	0	....	....	....	....	....	....	....	....	....	....	....	....	....	....	....	....	....	....
	Skelleftea AIK	Sweden	30	7	7	14	....	....	....	26	....	....	....	....	....	....	....	....	....	....	....	....	....	....	....	....	....	....
	Sweden	WEC-A	10	1	4	5	....	....	....	4	....	....	....	....	....	....	....	....	....	....	....	....	....	....	....	....	....	....
1982-83	Skelleftea AIK	Sweden	36	10	19	29	....	....	....	32	....	....	....	....	....	....	....	....	....	....	....	....	....	....	....	....	....	....
	Sweden	WEC-A	7	4	0	4	....	....	....	8	....	....	....	....	....	....	....	....	....	....	....	....	....	....	....	....	....	....
1983-84	**New York Rangers**	**NHL**	**75**	**5**	**25**	**30**	**4**	**17**	**21**	**16**	**1**	**0**	**0**	**94**	**5.3**	**64**	**5**	**56**	**11**	**14**	**5**	**2**	**0**	**2**	**4**	**0**	**0**	**1**
1984-85	**New York Rangers**	**NHL**	**66**	**7**	**22**	**29**	**6**	**15**	**21**	**33**	**0**	**1**	**0**	**72**	**9.7**	**53**	**0**	**87**	**23**	**–11**	**2**	**0**	**0**	**0**	**2**	**0**	**0**	**0**
1985-86	**New York Rangers**	**NHL**	**31**	**2**	**17**	**19**	**2**	**11**	**13**	**4**	**0**	**0**	**0**	**33**	**6.1**	**27**	**0**	**29**	**14**	**12**	**12**	**0**	**1**	**1**	**4**	**0**	**0**	**0**
1986-87	**New York Rangers**	**NHL**	**68**	**8**	**18**	**26**	**7**	**13**	**20**	**24**	**0**	**1**	**1**	**73**	**11.0**	**58**	**5**	**72**	**22**	**3**	**6**	**1**	**0**	**1**	**0**	**0**	**0**	**0**
1987-88	**New York Rangers**	**NHL**	**70**	**7**	**19**	**26**	**6**	**14**	**20**	**33**	**0**	**1**	**0**	**99**	**7.1**	**42**	**0**	**67**	**28**	**3**	....	....	....	....	....	....	....	....
1988-89	**New York Rangers**	**NHL**	**44**	**4**	**11**	**15**	**3**	**8**	**11**	**27**	**0**	**0**	**2**	**41**	**9.8**	**27**	**0**	**51**	**21**	**–3**	**4**	**0**	**1**	**1**	**2**	**0**	**0**	**0**
1989-90	**New York Rangers**	**NHL**	**58**	**4**	**9**	**13**	**3**	**6**	**9**	**8**	**0**	**0**	**1**	**61**	**6.6**	**24**	**1**	**59**	**19**	**–17**	**10**	**1**	**0**	**1**	**2**	**0**	**1**	**0**
1990-91	**New York Rangers**	**NHL**	**53**	**7**	**18**	**25**	**6**	**14**	**20**	**8**	**0**	**3**	**0**	**40**	**17.5**	**43**	**0**	**59**	**29**	**13**	**6**	**1**	**2**	**3**	**0**	**0**	**0**	**0**
1991-92	**New York Rangers**	**NHL**	**46**	**8**	**9**	**17**	**7**	**7**	**14**	**4**	**0**	**1**	**0**	**51**	**15.7**	**32**	**0**	**32**	**13**	**13**	**13**	**2**	**3**	**5**	**2**	**0**	**1**	**1**
1992-93	**New York Rangers**	**NHL**	**45**	**5**	**11**	**16**	**4**	**8**	**12**	**10**	**0**	**1**	**1**	**36**	**13.9**	**26**	**0**	**29**	**14**	**11**	....	....	....	....	....	....	....	....
1993-94	Skelleftea AIK	Sweden-2	13	2	10	12	....	....	....	10	....	....	....	....	....	....	....	....	....	....	7	2	3	5	20	....	....	....
	NHL Totals		**556**	**57**	**159**	**216**	**48**	**113**	**161**	**167**	**1**	**8**	**5**	**600**	**9.5**	**396**	**11**	**541**	**194**		**58**	**7**	**7**	**14**	**16**	**0**	**2**	**2**

WJC-A All-Star Team (1981) • Missed majority of 1985-86 season recovering from leg injury suffered in game vs. St. Louis, January 12, 1986.

• ERREY, Bob

Robert LW – L. 5'10", 185 lbs. b: Montreal, Que., 9/21/1964. Pittsburgh's 1st, 15th overall, in 1983.

Season	Club	League	GP	G	A	Pts	AG	AA	APts	PIM	PP	SH	GW	S	%	TGF	PGF	TGA	PGA	+/-	GP	G	A	Pts	PIM	PP	SH	GW
1979-80	Peterborough Oilers	OHA-B	29	13	11	24	....	....	....	12	....	....	....	....	....	....	....	....	....	....	....	....	....	....	....	....	....	....
1980-81	Peterborough Oilers	OHA-B	42	28	42	70	....	....	....	93	....	....	....	....	....	....	....	....	....	....	....	....	....	....	....	....	....	....
	Peterborough Petes	OMJHL	6	0	0	0	....	....	....	0	....	....	....	....	....	....	....	....	....	....	....	....	....	....	....	....	....	....
1981-82	Peterborough Petes	OHL	68	29	31	60	....	....	....	39	....	....	....	....	....	....	....	....	....	....	9	3	1	4	9	....	....	....
1982-83	Peterborough Petes	OHL	67	53	47	100	....	....	....	74	....	....	....	....	....	....	....	....	....	....	4	1	3	4	7	....	....	....
1983-84	**Pittsburgh Penguins**	**NHL**	**65**	**9**	**13**	**22**	**7**	**9**	**16**	**29**	**1**	**0**	**0**	**84**	**10.7**	**38**	**5**	**53**	**0**	**–20**	....	....	....	....	....	....	....	....
1984-85	**Pittsburgh Penguins**	**NHL**	**16**	**0**	**2**	**2**	**0**	**1**	**1**	**7**	**0**	**0**	**0**	**12**	**0.0**	**6**	**0**	**14**	**0**	**–8**	....	....	....	....	....	....	....	....
	Baltimore Skipjacks	AHL	59	17	24	41	....	....	....	14	....	....	....	....	....	....	....	....	....	....	8	3	4	7	11	....	....	....
1985-86	**Pittsburgh Penguins**	**NHL**	**37**	**11**	**6**	**17**	**9**	**4**	**13**	**8**	**1**	**0**	**2**	**57**	**19.3**	**26**	**4**	**23**	**2**	**1**	....	....	....	....	....	....	....	....
	Baltimore Skipjacks	AHL	18	8	7	15	....	....	....	28	....	....	....	....	....	....	....	....	....	....	....	....	....	....	....	....	....	....
1986-87	**Pittsburgh Penguins**	**NHL**	**72**	**16**	**18**	**34**	**14**	**13**	**27**	**46**	**2**	**1**	**1**	**138**	**11.6**	**48**	**6**	**73**	**26**	**–5**	....	....	....	....	....	....	....	....
1987-88	**Pittsburgh Penguins**	**NHL**	**17**	**3**	**6**	**9**	**3**	**4**	**7**	**18**	**0**	**0**	**0**	**18**	**16.7**	**16**	**0**	**12**	**2**	**6**	....	....	....	....	....	....	....	....
1988-89	**Pittsburgh Penguins**	**NHL**	**76**	**26**	**32**	**58**	**22**	**23**	**45**	**124**	**0**	**3**	**5**	**130**	**20.0**	**104**	**3**	**92**	**31**	**40**	**11**	**1**	**2**	**3**	**12**	**0**	**0**	**0**
1989-90	**Pittsburgh Penguins**	**NHL**	**78**	**20**	**19**	**39**	**17**	**14**	**31**	**109**	**0**	**1**	**1**	**127**	**15.7**	**70**	**3**	**90**	**26**	**3**	....	....	....	....	....	....	....	....
1990-91♦	**Pittsburgh Penguins**	**NHL**	**79**	**20**	**22**	**42**	**18**	**17**	**35**	**115**	**0**	**1**	**2**	**131**	**15.3**	**63**	**1**	**72**	**21**	**11**	**24**	**5**	**2**	**7**	**29**	**0**	**1**	**0**
1991-92♦	**Pittsburgh Penguins**	**NHL**	**78**	**19**	**16**	**35**	**17**	**12**	**29**	**119**	**0**	**3**	**1**	**122**	**15.6**	**56**	**3**	**72**	**20**	**1**	**14**	**3**	**0**	**3**	**10**	**0**	**1**	**0**
1992-93	**Pittsburgh Penguins**	**NHL**	**54**	**8**	**6**	**14**	**7**	**4**	**11**	**76**	**0**	**0**	**2**	**79**	**10.1**	**20**	**0**	**33**	**11**	**–2**	....	....	....	....	....	....	....	....
	Buffalo Sabres	**NHL**	**8**	**1**	**3**	**4**	**1**	**2**	**3**	**4**	**0**	**0**	**0**	**9**	**11.1**	**6**	**0**	**4**	**0**	**2**	**4**	**0**	**1**	**1**	**10**	**0**	**0**	**0**
1993-94	**San Jose Sharks**	**NHL**	**64**	**12**	**18**	**30**	**11**	**14**	**25**	**126**	**5**	**0**	**2**	**89**	**13.5**	**41**	**16**	**54**	**18**	**–11**	**14**	**3**	**2**	**5**	**10**	**1**	**0**	**0**
1994-95	**San Jose Sharks**	**NHL**	**13**	**2**	**2**	**4**	**4**	**3**	**7**	**27**	**0**	**0**	**0**	**19**	**10.5**	**9**	**1**	**5**	**1**	**4**	....	....	....	....	....	....	....	....
	Detroit Red Wings	**NHL**	**30**	**6**	**11**	**17**	**11**	**16**	**27**	**31**	**0**	**0**	**1**	**53**	**11.3**	**27**	**7**	**16**	**5**	**9**	**18**	**1**	**5**	**6**	**30**	**1**	**0**	**0**
1995-96	**Detroit Red Wings**	**NHL**	**71**	**11**	**21**	**32**	**11**	**17**	**28**	**66**	**2**	**2**	**2**	**85**	**12.9**	**59**	**4**	**41**	**16**	**30**	**14**	**0**	**4**	**4**	**8**	**0**	**0**	**0**
1996-97	**Detroit Red Wings**	**NHL**	**36**	**1**	**2**	**3**	**1**	**2**	**3**	**27**	**0**	**0**	**0**	**34**	**2.9**	**9**	**0**	**20**	**8**	**–3**	....	....	....	....	....	....	....	....
	San Jose Sharks	**NHL**	**30**	**3**	**6**	**9**	**3**	**5**	**8**	**20**	**0**	**0**	**0**	**38**	**7.9**	**14**	**0**	**24**	**8**	**–2**	....	....	....	....	....	....	....	....
	Canada	WC-A	11	2	1	3	....	....	....	6	....	....	....	....	....	....	....	....	....	....	....	....	....	....	....	....	....	....
1997-98	**Dallas Stars**	**NHL**	**59**	**2**	**9**	**11**	**2**	**9**	**11**	**46**	**0**	**0**	**0**	**34**	**5.9**	**19**	**0**	**20**	**8**	**7**	....	....	....	....	....	....	....	....
	New York Rangers	**NHL**	**12**	**0**	**0**	**0**	**0**	**0**	**0**	**7**	**0**	**0**	**0**	**11**	**0.0**	**2**	**1**	**8**	**2**	**–5**	....	....	....	....	....	....	....	....
1998-99	Hartford Wolf Pack	AHL	69	18	27	45	....	....	....	59	....	....	....	....	....	....	....	....	....	....	7	0	3	3	8	....	....	....
	NHL Totals		**895**	**170**	**212**	**382**	**158**	**169**	**327**	**1005**	**11**	**11**	**19**	**1270**	**13.4**	**633**	**54**	**726**	**205**		**99**	**13**	**16**	**29**	**109**	**2**	**2**	**0**

OHL First All-Star Team (1983)

Traded to **Buffalo** by **Pittsburgh** for Mike Ramsey, March 22, 1993. Signed as a free agent by **San Jose**, August 17, 1993. Traded to **Detroit** by **San Jose** for Detroit's 5th round choice (Michal Bros) in 1995 Entry Draft, February 27, 1995. Claimed on waivers by **San Jose** from **Detroit**, February 8, 1997. Signed as a free agent by **Dallas**, July 28, 1997. Traded to **NY Rangers** by **Dallas** with Todd Harvey and Dallas' 4th round choice (Boyd Kane) in 1998 Entry Draft for Brian Skrudland, Mike Keane and NY Rangers' 6th round choice (Pavel Patera) in 1998 Entry Draft, March 24, 1998. • Officially announced retirement to join Pittsburgh Penguins' radio broadcast team, September 27, 1999..

• ESAU, Len

Len Leonard D – R. 6'3", 190 lbs. b: Meadow Lake, Sask., 6/3/1968. Toronto's 5th, 86th overall, in 1988.

Season	Club	League	GP	G	A	Pts	AG	AA	APts	PIM	PP	SH	GW	S	%	TGF	PGF	TGA	PGA	+/-	GP	G	A	Pts	PIM	PP	SH	GW
1986-87	Humboldt Broncos	SJHL	57	4	26	30	....	....	....	278	....	....	....	....	....	....	....	....	....	....	....	....	....	....	....	....	....	....
	Humboldt Broncos	Cen-Cup	2	0	0	0	....	....	....	2	....	....	....	....	....	....	....	....	....	....	....	....	....	....	....	....	....	....
1987-88	Humboldt Broncos	SJHL	57	16	37	53	....	....	....	229	....	....	....	....	....	....	....	....	....	....	....	....	....	....	....	....	....	....
1988-89	St. Cloud State Huskies	NCAA-2	35	12	27	39	....	....	....	69	....	....	....	....	....	....	....	....	....	....	....	....	....	....	....	....	....	....
1989-90	St. Cloud State Huskies	NCAA-2	29	8	11	19	....	....	....	83	....	....	....	....	....	....	....	....	....	....	....	....	....	....	....	....	....	....
1990-91	Newmarket Saints	AHL	76	4	14	18	....	....	....	28	....	....	....	....	....	....	....	....	....	....	....	....	....	....	....	....	....	....
1991-92	**Toronto Maple Leafs**	**NHL**	**2**	**0**	**0**	**0**	**0**	**0**	**0**	**0**	**0**	**0**	**0**	**0**	**0.0**	**0**	**0**	**1**	**1**	**0**	....	....	....	....	....	....	....	....
	St. John's Maple Leafs	AHL	78	9	29	38	....	....	....	68	....	....	....	....	....	....	....	....	....	....	13	0	2	2	14	....	....	....
1992-93	**Quebec Nordiques**	**NHL**	**4**	**0**	**1**	**1**	**0**	**1**	**1**	**2**	**0**	**0**	**0**	**1**	**0.0**	**2**	**0**	**1**	**0**	**1**	....	....	....	....	....	....	....	....
	Halifax Citadels	AHL	75	11	31	42	....	....	....	79	....	....	....	....	....	....	....	....	....	....	....	....	....	....	....	....	....	....
1993-94	**Calgary Flames**	**NHL**	**6**	**0**	**3**	**3**	**0**	**2**	**2**	**7**	**0**	**0**	**0**	**4**	**0.0**	**6**	**0**	**7**	**0**	**–1**	....	....	....	....	....	....	....	....
	Saint John Flames	AHL	75	12	36	48	....	....	....	129	....	....	....	....	....	....	....	....	....	....	7	2	2	4	6	....	....	....
1994-95	Saint John Flames	AHL	54	13	27	40	....	....	....	73	....	....	....	....	....	....	....	....	....	....	5	0	2	2	0	....	....	....
	Edmonton Oilers	**NHL**	**14**	**0**	**6**	**6**	**0**	**9**	**9**	**15**	**0**	**0**	**0**	**17**	**0.0**	**11**	**4**	**15**	**0**	**–8**	....	....	....	....	....	....	....	....
	Calgary Flames	**NHL**	**1**	**0**	**0**	**0**	**0**	**0**	**0**	**0**	**0**	**0**	**0**	**4**	**0.0**	**0**	**0**	**2**	**0**	**–2**	....	....	....	....	....	....	....	....
	Canada	WC-A	7	0	1	1	....	....	....	2	....	....	....	....	....	....	....	....	....	....	....	....	....	....	....	....	....	....
1995-96	Cincinnati Cyclones	IHL	82	15	21	36	....	....	....	150	....	....	....	....	....	....	....	....	....	....	17	5	6	11	26	....	....	....
1996-97	Milwaukee Admirals	IHL	49	6	16	22	....	....	....	70	....	....	....	....	....	....	....	....	....	....	....	....	....	....	....	....	....	....
	Detroit Vipers	IHL	30	6	8	14	....	....	....	36	....	....	....	....	....	....	....	....	....	....	13	1	4	5	38	....	....	....
1997-98	Milwaukee Admirals	IHL	26	3	9	12	....	....	....	32	....	....	....	....	....	....	....	....	....	....	....	....	....	....	....	....	....	....
	Indianapolis Ice	IHL	55	6	33	39	....	....	....	28	....	....	....	....	....	....	....	....	....	....	5	0	0	0	4	....	....	....
1998-99	Seibu-Tetsudo Tokyo	Japan	21	6	11	17	....	....	....	....	....	....	....	....	....	....	....	....	....	....	3	0	1	1	....	....	....	....
99-2000	Cincinnati Cyclones	IHL	78	8	17	25	....	....	....	64	....	....	....	....	....	....	....	....	....	....	10	0	2	2	14	....	....	....
	NHL Totals		**27**	**0**	**10**	**10**	**0**	**12**	**12**	**24**	**0**	**0**	**0**	**26**	**0.0**	**19**	**4**	**26**	**1**		....	....	....	....	....	....	....	....

Traded to **Quebec** by **Toronto** for Ken McRae, July 21, 1992. Signed as a free agent by **Calgary**, September 6, 1993. Claimed by **Edmonton** from **Calgary** in NHL Waiver Draft, January 18, 1995. Claimed on waivers by **Calgary** from **Edmonton**, March 7, 1995. Signed as a free agent by **Florida**, August 31, 1995. Signed as a free agent by **Cincinnati** (IHL), August 30, 1999.

• ESPOSITO, Phil

Philip Anthony C – L. 6'1", 205 lbs. b: Sault Ste. Marie, Ont., 2/20/1942. **HHOF**

Season	Club	League	GP	G	A	Pts	AG	AA	APts	PIM	PP	SH	GW	S	%	TGF	PGF	TGA	PGA	+/-	GP	G	A	Pts	PIM	PP	SH	GW
1959-60	S.S. Marie Algona Contractors	NOJHA	STATISTICS NOT AVAILABLE																									
1960-61	Sarnia Legionaires	OHA-B	32	47	61	108	....	....	....	....	....	....	....	....	....	....	....	....	....	....	....	....	....	....	....	....	....	....
1961-62	St. Catharines Teepees	OHA-Jr.	49	32	39	71	....	....	....	54	....	....	....	....	....	....	....	....	....	....	6	1	4	5	9	....	....	....
	Sault Ste. Marie Thunderbirds	EPHL	6	0	3	3	....	....	....	2	....	....	....	....	....	....	....	....	....	....	....	....	....	....	....	....	....	....

			REGULAR SEASON																		PLAYOFFS							
Season	Club	League	GP	G	A	Pts	AG	AA	APts	PIM	PP	SH	GW	S	%	TGF	PGF	TGA	PGA	+/-	GP	G	A	Pts	PIM	PP	SH	GW
1962-63	St. Louis Braves	EPHL	71	36	54	90	....	....	....	51	....	....	....	....	....	....	....	....	....	....	....	....	....	....	....	....	....	....
1963-64	**Chicago Black Hawks**	**NHL**	**27**	**3**	**2**	**5**	**4**	**2**	**6**	**2**	....	....	....	....	....	....	....	....	....	....	**4**	**0**	**0**	**0**	**0**	**0**	**0**	**0**
	St. Louis Braves	CPHL	43	26	54	80	....	....	....	65	....	....	....	....	....	....	....	....	....	....	....	....	....	....	....	....	....	....
1964-65	**Chicago Black Hawks**	**NHL**	**70**	**23**	**32**	**55**	**28**	**33**	**61**	**44**	....	....	....	....	....	....	....	....	....	....	**13**	**3**	**3**	**6**	**15**	**0**	**0**	**0**
1965-66	**Chicago Black Hawks**	**NHL**	**69**	**27**	**26**	**53**	**31**	**25**	**56**	**49**	....	....	....	....	....	....	....	....	....	....	**6**	**1**	**1**	**2**	**2**	**1**	**0**	**0**
1966-67	**Chicago Black Hawks**	**NHL**	**69**	**21**	**40**	**61**	**24**	**39**	**63**	**40**	....	....	....	....	....	....	....	....	....	....	**6**	**0**	**0**	**0**	**7**	**0**	**0**	**0**
1967-68	**Boston Bruins**	**NHL**	**74**	**35**	***49**	**84**	**41**	**49**	**90**	**21**	**9**	**1**	**3**	**284**	**12.3**	**113**	**37**	**69**	**12**	**19**	**4**	**0**	**3**	**3**	**0**	**0**	**0**	**0**
1968-69	**Boston Bruins**	**NHL**	**74**	**49**	***77**	**126**	**52**	**69**	**121**	**79**	**10**	**2**	**9**	**351**	**14.0**	**164**	**50**	**69**	**11**	**56**	**10**	***8**	***10**	***18**	**8**	**5**	**2**	**0**
1969-70♦	**Boston Bruins**	**NHL**	**76**	***43**	**56**	**99**	**47**	**53**	**100**	**50**	**18**	**1**	**5**	**405**	**10.6**	**157**	**80**	**69**	**20**	**28**	**14**	***13**	***14**	***27**	**16**	**4**	**2**	**0**
1970-71	**Boston Bruins**	**NHL**	**78**	***76**	**76**	***152**	**76**	**64**	**140**	**71**	**25**	**1**	**16**	**550**	**13.8**	**214**	**78**	**72**	**7**	**71**	**7**	**3**	**7**	**10**	**6**	**2**	**0**	**0**
1971-72♦	**Boston Bruins**	**NHL**	**76**	***66**	**67**	***133**	**67**	**58**	**125**	**76**	**28**	**2**	**16**	**426**	**15.5**	**186**	**71**	**67**	**7**	**55**	**15**	**9**	**15**	***24**	**24**	**2**	**0**	**3**
1972-73	Team Canada	Summit-72	8	*7	*6	*13	....	....	....	15	....	....	....	....	....	....	....	....	....	....	....	....	....	....	....	....	....	....
	Boston Bruins	**NHL**	**78**	***55**	***75**	***130**	**52**	**60**	**112**	**87**	**19**	**5**	**11**	**411**	**13.4**	**174**	**67**	**117**	**26**	**16**	**2**	**0**	**1**	**1**	**2**	**0**	**0**	**0**
1973-74	**Boston Bruins**	**NHL**	**78**	***68**	**77**	***145**	**66**	**64**	**130**	**58**	**14**	**4**	**9**	**393**	**17.3**	**201**	**65**	**109**	**24**	**51**	**16**	**9**	**5**	**14**	**25**	**4**	**0**	**2**
1974-75	**Boston Bruins**	**NHL**	**79**	***61**	**66**	**127**	**54**	**50**	**104**	**62**	**27**	**4**	**8**	**347**	**17.6**	**174**	**79**	**110**	**33**	**18**	**3**	**4**	**1**	**5**	**0**	**1**	**0**	**0**
1975-76	**Boston Bruins**	**NHL**	**12**	**6**	**10**	**16**	**5**	**7**	**12**	**8**	**3**	**0**	**0**	**57**	**10.5**	**20**	**10**	**16**	**5**	**–1**	....	....	....	....	....	....	....	....
	New York Rangers	**NHL**	**62**	**29**	**38**	**67**	**25**	**28**	**53**	**28**	**16**	**1**	**2**	**217**	**13.4**	**96**	**45**	**104**	**14**	**–39**	....	....	....	....	....	....	....	....
1976-77	Canada	Can-Cup	7	4	3	7	....	....	....	0	....	....	....	....	....	....	....	....	....	....	....	....	....	....	....	....	....	....
	New York Rangers	**NHL**	**80**	**34**	**46**	**80**	**31**	**35**	**66**	**52**	**15**	**0**	**4**	**344**	**9.9**	**119**	**48**	**114**	**15**	**–28**	....	....	....	....	....	....	....	....
	Canada	WEC-A	10	7	3	10	....	....	....	14	....	....	....	....	....	....	....	....	....	....	....	....	....	....	....	....	....	....
1977-78	**New York Rangers**	**NHL**	**79**	**38**	**43**	**81**	**35**	**33**	**68**	**53**	**21**	**0**	**5**	**259**	**14.7**	**117**	**56**	**98**	**15**	**–22**	**3**	**0**	**1**	**1**	**5**	**0**	**0**	**0**
1978-79	**New York Rangers**	**NHL**	**80**	**42**	**36**	**78**	**36**	**26**	**62**	**37**	**14**	**0**	**7**	**215**	**19.5**	**113**	**35**	**82**	**3**	**–1**	**18**	**8**	**12**	**20**	**20**	**2**	**0**	**2**
1979-80	**New York Rangers**	**NHL**	**80**	**34**	**44**	**78**	**29**	**32**	**61**	**73**	**13**	**0**	**5**	**245**	**13.9**	**118**	**42**	**89**	**0**	**–13**	**9**	**3**	**3**	**6**	**8**	**1**	**0**	**1**
1980-81	**New York Rangers**	**NHL**	**41**	**7**	**13**	**20**	**5**	**9**	**14**	**20**	**3**	**0**	**0**	**91**	**7.7**	**47**	**13**	**54**	**7**	**–13**	....	....	....	....	....	....	....	....
	NHL Totals		**1282**	**717**	**873**	**1590**	**708**	**736**	**1444**	**910**	....	....	....	....	....	....	....	....	....	....	**130**	**61**	**76**	**137**	**138**	....	....	....

• Brother of Tony • OHA-Jr. Second All-Star Team (1962) • NHL Second All-Star Team (1968, 1975) • NHL First All-Star Team (1969, 1970, 1971, 1972, 1973, 1974) • Won Art Ross Trophy (1969, 1971, 1972, 1973, 1974) • Won Hart Trophy (1969, 1974) • Won Lester B. Pearson Award (1971, 1974) • Won Lester Patrick Trophy (1978)

Played in NHL All-Star Game (1969, 1970, 1971, 1972, 1973, 1974, 1975, 1977, 1978, 1980)

Traded to **Boston** by **Chicago** with Ken Hodge and Fred Stanfield for Pit Martin, Jack Norris, and Gilles Marotte, May 15, 1967. Traded to **NY Rangers** by **Boston** with Carol Vadnais for Brad Park, Jean Ratelle and Joe Zanussi, November 7, 1975.

• EVANS, Chris

Christopher Bruce D – L. 5'9", 180 lbs. b: Toronto, Ont., 9/14/1946.

Season	Club	League	GP	G	A	Pts	AG	AA	APts	PIM	PP	SH	GW	S	%	TGF	PGF	TGA	PGA	+/-	GP	G	A	Pts	PIM	PP	SH	GW
1965-66	Markham Waxers	OHA-B	30	12	24	36	....	....	....	....	....	....	....	....	....	....	....	....	....	....	....	....	....	....	....	....	....	....
1966-67	Toronto Marlboros	OHA-Jr.	48	7	21	28	....	....	....	84	....	....	....	....	....	....	....	....	....	....	17	2	3	5	34	....	....	....
	Toronto Marlboros	Mem-Cup	9	1	0	1	....	....	....	16	....	....	....	....	....	....	....	....	....	....	....	....	....	....	....	....	....	....
1967-68	Toronto Marlboros	OHA-Jr.	39	5	14	19	....	....	....	42	....	....	....	....	....	....	....	....	....	....	....	....	....	....	....	....	....	....
	Tulsa Oilers	CPHL	2	0	0	0	....	....	....	0	....	....	....	....	....	....	....	....	....	....	....	....	....	....	....	....	....	....
1968-69	Tulsa Oilers	CHL	70	9	35	44	....	....	....	88	....	....	....	....	....	....	....	....	....	....	7	0	3	3	6	....	....	....
1969-70	**Toronto Maple Leafs**	**NHL**	**2**	**0**	**0**	**0**	**0**	**0**	**0**	**0**	**0**	**0**	**0**	**0**	**0.0**	**0**	**0**	**6**	**1**	**–5**	....	....	....	....	....	....	....	....
	Phoenix Roadrunners	WHL	70	7	16	23	....	....	....	60	....	....	....	....	....	....	....	....	....	....	....	....	....	....	....	....	....	....
1970-71	Kansas City Blues	CHL	71	10	32	42	....	....	....	111	....	....	....	....	....	....	....	....	....	....	....	....	....	....	....	....	....	....
1971-72	**Buffalo Sabres**	**NHL**	**61**	**6**	**18**	**24**	**6**	**16**	**22**	**98**	**2**	**0**	**0**	**99**	**6.1**	**82**	**26**	**91**	**15**	**–20**	....	....	....	....	....	....	....	....
	Cincinnati Swords	AHL	5	0	5	5	....	....	....	2	....	....	....	....	....	....	....	....	....	....	....	....	....	....	....	....	....	....
	St. Louis Blues	**NHL**	**2**	**0**	**0**	**0**	**0**	**0**	**0**	**0**	**0**	**0**	**0**	**0**	**0.0**	**1**	**0**	**1**	**0**	**0**	**7**	**1**	**0**	**1**	**4**	**0**	**0**	**0**
1972-73	**St. Louis Blues**	**NHL**	**77**	**9**	**12**	**21**	**8**	**9**	**17**	**31**	**0**	**2**	**3**	**138**	**6.5**	**44**	**4**	**68**	**26**	**–2**	**5**	**0**	**1**	**1**	**4**	**0**	**0**	**0**
1973-74	**St. Louis Blues**	**NHL**	**54**	**4**	**7**	**11**	**4**	**6**	**10**	**8**	**0**	**1**	**0**	**48**	**8.3**	**14**	**1**	**38**	**30**	**5**	....	....	....	....	....	....	....	....
	Detroit Red Wings	**NHL**	**23**	**0**	**2**	**2**	**0**	**2**	**2**	**2**	**0**	**0**	**0**	**19**	**0.0**	**5**	**0**	**22**	**13**	**–4**	....	....	....	....	....	....	....	....
1974-75	**Kansas City Scouts**	**NHL**	**2**	**0**	**2**	**2**	**0**	**1**	**1**	**2**	**0**	**0**	**0**	**4**	**0.0**	**3**	**2**	**3**	**1**	**–1**	....	....	....	....	....	....	....	....
	St. Louis Blues	**NHL**	**20**	**0**	**1**	**1**	**0**	**1**	**1**	**2**	**0**	**0**	**0**	**7**	**0.0**	**2**	**0**	**16**	**13**	**–1**	....	....	....	....	....	....	....	....
	Denver Spurs	CHL	31	3	13	16	....	....	....	47	....	....	....	....	....	....	....	....	....	....	2	1	1	2	2	....	....	....
1975-76	Calgary Cowboys	WHA	75	3	20	23	....	....	....	50	....	....	....	....	....	....	....	....	....	....	10	5	5	10	4	....	....	....
1976-77	Calgary Cowboys	WHA	81	7	27	34	....	....	....	60	....	....	....	....	....	....	....	....	....	....	....	....	....	....	....	....	....	....
1977-78	Birmingham Bulls	WHA	12	1	2	3	....	....	....	4	....	....	....	....	....	....	....	....	....	....	....	....	....	....	....	....	....	....
	Quebec Nordiques	WHA	36	0	2	2	....	....	....	22	....	....	....	....	....	....	....	....	....	....	....	....	....	....	....	....	....	....
1978-79	Phoenix Roadrunners	PHL	57	9	41	50	....	....	....	46	....	....	....	....	....	....	....	....	....	....	....	....	....	....	....	....	....	....
1979-80	ECD Sauerland	Germany-2	STATISTICS NOT AVAILABLE																									
1980-81	ECD Sauerland	Germany-2	STATISTICS NOT AVAILABLE																									
	Wichita Wind	CHL	6	1	2	3	....	....	....	14	....	....	....	....	....	....	....	....	....	....	....	....	....	....	....	....	....	....
	NHL Totals		**241**	**19**	**42**	**61**	**18**	**35**	**53**	**143**	**2**	**3**	**3**	**315**	**6.0**	**151**	**33**	**245**	**99**		**12**	**1**	**1**	**2**	**8**	**0**	**0**	**0**
	Other Major League Totals		204	11	51	62	....	....	....	136	....	....	....	....	....	....	....	....	....	....	10	5	5	10	4	....	....	....

PHL First All-Star Team (1979)

Claimed by **St. Louis** from **Phoenix** (WHL) in Intra-League Draft, June 9, 1970. Claimed by **Buffalo** from **St. Louis** in Expansion Draft, June 10, 1970. Selected by **New England** (WHA) in 1972 WHA General Player Draft, February 12, 1972. Traded to **St. Louis** by **Buffalo** for George Morrison and St. Louis' 2nd round choice (Larry Carriere) in 1972 Amateur Draft, March 5, 1972. Traded to **Detroit** by **St. Louis** with Bryan Watson and Jean Hamel for Ted Harris, Bill Collins and Garnet Bailey, February 14, 1974. Claimed by **Kansas City** from **Detroit** in Expansion Draft, June 12, 1974. Traded to **St. Louis** by **Kansas City** with Kansas City's 4th round choice (Mike Liut) in 1976 Amateur Draft for Larry Giroux, October 29, 1974. WHA rights traded to **Calgary** (WHA) by **New England** (WHA) for cash, August, 1975. Signed as a free agent by **Edmonton** (WHA) after **Calgary** (WHA) franchise folded, May 31, 1977. Traded to **Birmingham** (WHA) by **Edmonton** (WHA) with Pete Laframboise and Dan Arndt for Lou Nistico and Jeff Jacques, September, 1977. Claimed on waivers by **Quebec** (WHA) from **Birmingham** (WHA), November, 1977.

• EVANS, Daryl

Daryl Thomas "Reggie" LW – L. 5'9", 185 lbs. b: Toronto, Ont., 1/12/1961. Los Angeles' 11th, 178th overall, in 1980.

Season	Club	League	GP	G	A	Pts	AG	AA	APts	PIM	PP	SH	GW	S	%	TGF	PGF	TGA	PGA	+/-	GP	G	A	Pts	PIM	PP	SH	GW
1977-78	Toronto Young Nationals	OHA-B	40	25	35	60	....	....	....	50	....	....	....	....	....	....	....	....	....	....	....	....	....	....	....	....	....	....
1978-79	Niagara Falls Flyers	OMJHL	65	38	26	64	....	....	....	110	....	....	....	....	....	....	....	....	....	....	20	5	5	10	32	....	....	....
1979-80	Niagara Falls Flyers	OMJHL	63	43	52	95	....	....	....	47	....	....	....	....	....	....	....	....	....	....	10	5	13	18	6	....	....	....
1980-81	Niagara Falls Flyers	OMJHL	5	3	4	7	....	....	....	11	....	....	....	....	....	....	....	....	....	....	....	....	....	....	....	....	....	....
	Brantford Alexanders	OMJHL	58	58	54	112	....	....	....	50	....	....	....	....	....	....	....	....	....	....	6	4	5	9	6	....	....	....
	Saginaw Gears	IHL	3	3	2	5	....	....	....	0	....	....	....	....	....	....	....	....	....	....	....	....	....	....	....	....	....	....
1981-82	**Los Angeles Kings**	**NHL**	**14**	**2**	**6**	**8**	**2**	**4**	**6**	**2**	**0**	**0**	**0**	**25**	**8.0**	**13**	**3**	**8**	**0**	**2**	**10**	**5**	**8**	**13**	**12**	**1**	**0**	**1**
	New Haven Nighthawks	AHL	41	14	14	28	....	....	....	10	....	....	....	....	....	....	....	....	....	....	....	....	....	....	....	....	....	....
1982-83	**Los Angeles Kings**	**NHL**	**80**	**18**	**22**	**40**	**15**	**15**	**30**	**21**	**1**	**1**	**0**	**242**	**7.4**	**79**	**28**	**96**	**27**	**–18**	....	....	....	....	....	....	....	....
1983-84	**Los Angeles Kings**	**NHL**	**4**	**0**	**1**	**1**	**0**	**1**	**1**	**0**	**0**	**0**	**0**	**6**	**0.0**	**2**	**1**	**0**	**0**	**1**	....	....	....	....	....	....	....	....
	New Haven Nighthawks	AHL	69	51	34	85	....	....	....	14	....	....	....	....	....	....	....	....	....	....	....	....	....	....	....	....	....	....
1984-85	**Los Angeles Kings**	**NHL**	**7**	**1**	**0**	**1**	**1**	**0**	**1**	**2**	**0**	**0**	**0**	**12**	**8.3**	**3**	**0**	**1**	**0**	**2**	....	....	....	....	....	....	....	....
	New Haven Nighthawks	AHL	59	22	24	46	....	....	....	12	....	....	....	....	....	....	....	....	....	....	....	....	....	....	....	....	....	....
1985-86	**Washington Capitals**	**NHL**	**6**	**0**	**1**	**1**	**0**	**1**	**1**	**0**	**0**	**0**	**0**	**14**	**0.0**	**1**	**1**	**1**	**0**	**–1**	....	....	....	....	....	....	....	....
	Binghamton Whalers	AHL	69	40	52	92	....	....	....	50	....	....	....	....	....	....	....	....	....	....	5	6	2	8	0	....	....	....
1986-87	**Toronto Maple Leafs**	**NHL**	**2**	**1**	**0**	**1**	**1**	**0**	**1**	**0**	**1**	**0**	**0**	**2**	**50.0**	**1**	**1**	**2**	**0**	**–2**	**1**	**0**	**0**	**0**	**0**	**0**	**0**	**0**
	Newmarket Saints	AHL	74	27	46	73	....	....	....	17	....	....	....	....	....	....	....	....	....	....	....	....	....	....	....	....	....	....
1987-88	Newmarket Saints	AHL	57	29	36	65	....	....	....	10	....	....	....	....	....	....	....	....	....	....	....	....	....	....	....	....	....	....
1988-89	Newmarket Saints	AHL	64	29	30	59	....	....	....	16	....	....	....	....	....	....	....	....	....	....	5	1	1	2	0	....	....	....
1989-90	HC Gardena-Groden	Italy-2	32	32	65	97	....	....	....	28	....	....	....	....	....	....	....	....	....	....	....	....	....	....	....	....	....	....
1990-91	Whitley Warriors	Britain	6	10	9	19	....	....	....	6	....	....	....	....	....	....	....	....	....	....	8	18	22	40	6	....	....	....
	NHL Totals		**113**	**22**	**30**	**52**	**19**	**21**	**40**	**25**	**2**	**1**	**0**	**301**	**7.3**	**99**	**34**	**108**	**27**		**11**	**5**	**8**	**13**	**12**	**1**	**0**	**1**

OMJHL First All-Star Team (1981) • AHL Second All-Star Team (1984)

Traded to **Washington** by **LA Kings** for Glen Currie, September 9, 1985. Signed as a free agent by **Toronto**, August, 1986.

• EVANS, Doug

Douglas Thomas LW – L. 5'9", 185 lbs. b: Peterborough, Ont., 6/2/1963.

Season	Club	League	GP	G	A	Pts	AG	AA	APts	PIM	PP	SH	GW	S	%	TGF	PGF	TGA	PGA	+/-	GP	G	A	Pts	PIM	PP	SH	GW
1980-81	Peterborough Petes	OMJHL	51	9	24	33	....	....	....	139	....	....	....	....	....	....	....	....	....	....	....	....	....	....	....	....	....	....
1981-82	Peterborough Petes	OHL	56	17	49	66	....	....	....	176	....	....	....	....	....	....	....	....	....	....	9	0	2	2	41	....	....	....
1982-83	Peterborough Petes	OHL	65	31	55	86	....	....	....	165	....	....	....	....	....	....	....	....	....	....	4	0	3	3	23	....	....	....
1983-84	Peterborough Petes	OHL	61	45	79	124	....	....	....	98	....	....	....	....	....	....	....	....	....	....	8	4	12	16	26	....	....	....

			REGULAR SEASON																		PLAYOFFS							
Season	**Club**	**League**	**GP**	**G**	**A**	**Pts**	**AG**	**AA**	**APts**	**PIM**	**PP**	**SH**	**GW**	**S**	**%**	**TGF**	**PGF**	**TGA**	**PGA**	**+/–**	**GP**	**G**	**A**	**Pts**	**PIM**	**PP**	**SH**	**GW**
1984-85	Peoria Rivermen	IHL	81	36	61	97	....	....	....	189	....	....	....	....	....	....	....	....	....	....	20	8	11	19	*88	....	....	....
1985-86	**St. Louis Blues**	**NHL**	**13**	**1**	**0**	**1**	**1**	**0**	**1**	**2**	**0**	**0**	**0**	**12**	**8.3**	**1**	**0**	**1**	**0**	**0**	....	....	....	....	....	....	....	....
	Peoria Rivermen	IHL	60	46	51	97	....	....	....	179	....	....	....	....	....	....	....	....	....	....	10	4	6	10	32	....	....	....
1986-87	**St. Louis Blues**	**NHL**	**53**	**3**	**13**	**16**	**3**	**9**	**12**	**91**	**0**	**0**	**0**	**51**	**5.9**	**30**	**0**	**30**	**2**	**2**	**5**	**0**	**0**	**0**	**10**	**0**	**0**	**0**
	Peoria Rivermen	IHL	18	10	15	25	....	....	....	39	....	....	....	....	....	....	....	....	....	....	....	....	....	....	....	....	....	....
1987-88	**St. Louis Blues**	**NHL**	**41**	**5**	**7**	**12**	**4**	**5**	**9**	**49**	**0**	**0**	**1**	**32**	**15.6**	**15**	**0**	**26**	**4**	**–7**	**2**	**0**	**0**	**0**	**0**	**0**	**0**	**0**
	Peoria Rivermen	IHL	11	4	16	20	....	....	....	64	....	....	....	....	....	....	....	....	....	....	....	....	....	....	....	....	....	....
1988-89	**St. Louis Blues**	**NHL**	**53**	**7**	**12**	**19**	**6**	**8**	**14**	**81**	**0**	**1**	**0**	**48**	**14.6**	**26**	**0**	**38**	**15**	**3**	**7**	**1**	**2**	**3**	**16**	**0**	**0**	**0**
1989-90	**St. Louis Blues**	**NHL**	**3**	**0**	**0**	**0**	**0**	**0**	**0**	**0**	**0**	**0**	**0**	**1**	**0.0**	**0**	**0**	**0**	**0**	**0**	....	....	....	....	....	....	....	....
	Peoria Rivermen	IHL	42	19	28	47	....	....	....	128	....	....	....	....	....	....	....	....	....	....	....	....	....	....	....	....	....	....
	Winnipeg Jets	**NHL**	**27**	**10**	**8**	**18**	**9**	**6**	**15**	**33**	**2**	**1**	**1**	**36**	**27.8**	**25**	**4**	**17**	**3**	**7**	**7**	**2**	**2**	**4**	**10**	**0**	**0**	**0**
1990-91	**Winnipeg Jets**	**NHL**	**70**	**7**	**27**	**34**	**6**	**21**	**27**	**108**	**1**	**0**	**0**	**70**	**10.0**	**52**	**8**	**52**	**7**	**–1**	....	....	....	....	....	....	....	....
1991-92	**Winnipeg Jets**	**NHL**	**30**	**7**	**7**	**14**	**6**	**5**	**11**	**68**	**1**	**0**	**0**	**39**	**17.9**	**35**	**16**	**18**	**1**	**2**	**1**	**0**	**0**	**0**	**2**	**0**	**0**	**0**
	Moncton Hawks	AHL	10	7	8	15	....	....	....	10	....	....	....	....	....	....	....	....	....	....	....	....	....	....	....	....	....	....
	Peoria Rivermen	IHL	16	5	14	19	....	....	....	38	....	....	....	....	....	....	....	....	....	....	....	....	....	....	....	....	....	....
1992-93	**Philadelphia Flyers**	**NHL**	**65**	**8**	**13**	**21**	**7**	**9**	**16**	**70**	**0**	**0**	**1**	**60**	**13.3**	**33**	**1**	**52**	**11**	**–9**	....	....	....	....	....	....	....	....
1993-94	Peoria Rivermen	IHL	76	27	63	90	....	....	....	108	....	....	....	....	....	....	....	....	....	....	6	2	6	8	10	....	....	....
1994-95	Peoria Rivermen	IHL	74	13	39	52	....	....	....	103	....	....	....	....	....	....	....	....	....	....	9	2	9	11	10	....	....	....
1995-96	Peoria Rivermen	IHL	74	19	48	67	....	....	....	81	....	....	....	....	....	....	....	....	....	....	1	0	0	0	0	....	....	....
1996-97	Peoria Rivermen	ECHL	67	23	59	82	....	....	....	128	....	....	....	....	....	....	....	....	....	....	10	10	12	22	20	....	....	....
1997-98	Peoria Rivermen	ECHL	52	27	37	64	....	....	....	98	....	....	....	....	....	....	....	....	....	....	3	0	1	1	4	....	....	....
1998-99	Peoria Riverman	ECHL	57	14	46	60	....	....	....	112	....	....	....	....	....	....	....	....	....	....	4	0	5	5	10	....	....	....
	NHL Totals		**355**	**48**	**87**	**135**	**42**	**63**	**105**	**502**	**4**	**2**	**3**	**349**	**13.8**	**217**	**29**	**234**	**43**		**22**	**3**	**4**	**7**	**38**	**0**	**0**	**0**

• Brother of Paul and Kevin • IHL First All-Star Team (1986)

Signed as a free agent by **St. Louis**, June 10, 1985. Traded to **Winnipeg** by **St. Louis** for Ron Wilson, January 22, 1990. Traded to **Boston** by **Winnipeg** for Daniel Berthiaume, June 10, 1992. Claimed by **Philadelphia** from **Boston** in Waiver Draft, October 4, 1992. • Played w/ RHI's St. Louis Vipers in 1996 (4-2-7-9-3) and San Jose Rhinos in 1997 (23-3-4-7-151).

• EVANS, John Paul

C – L. 5'9", 185 lbs. b: Toronto, Ont., 5/2/1954. Los Angeles' 3rd, 84th overall, in 1974.

Season	Club	League	GP	G	A	Pts	AG	AA	APts	PIM	PP	SH	GW	S	%	TGF	PGF	TGA	PGA	+/–	GP	G	A	Pts	PIM	PP	SH	GW
1970-71	North York Rangers	OHA-B	STATISTICS NOT AVAILABLE																									
1971-72	Kitchener Rangers	OMJHL	57	30	38	68	....	....	....	10	....	....	....	....	....	....	....	....	....	....	5	2	2	4	0	....	....	....
1972-73	Kitchener Rangers	OMJHL	63	29	47	76	....	....	....	22	....	....	....	....	....	....	....	....	....	....	....	....	....	....	....	....	....	....
1973-74	Kitchener Rangers	OMJHL	69	52	60	112	....	....	....	45	....	....	....	....	....	....	....	....	....	....	....	....	....	....	....	....	....	....
1974-75	Saginaw Gears	IHL	60	21	35	56	....	....	....	42	....	....	....	....	....	....	....	....	....	....	....	....	....	....	....	....	....	....
1975-76	Saginaw Gears	IHL	78	32	53	85	....	....	....	65	....	....	....	....	....	....	....	....	....	....	12	3	10	13	6	....	....	....
1976-77	Saginaw Gears	IHL	78	50	62	112	....	....	....	53	....	....	....	....	....	....	....	....	....	....	19	10	*15	25	2	....	....	....
1977-78	Springfield Indians	AHL	8	4	6	10	....	....	....	6	....	....	....	....	....	....	....	....	....	....	....	....	....	....	....	....	....	....
	Maine Mariners	AHL	66	26	35	61	....	....	....	28	....	....	....	....	....	....	....	....	....	....	12	3	6	9	14	....	....	....
1978-79	**Philadelphia Flyers**	**NHL**	**44**	**6**	**5**	**11**	**5**	**4**	**9**	**12**	**0**	**0**	**1**	**39**	**15.4**	**14**	**0**	**28**	**11**	**–3**	....	....	....	....	....	....	....	....
	Maine Mariners	AHL	32	16	24	40	....	....	....	36	....	....	....	....	....	....	....	....	....	....	10	4	*13	*17	10	....	....	....
1979-80	Maine Mariners	AHL	80	21	56	77	....	....	....	66	....	....	....	....	....	....	....	....	....	....	12	3	7	10	18	....	....	....
1980-81	**Philadelphia Flyers**	**NHL**	**1**	**0**	**0**	**0**	**0**	**0**	**0**	**2**	**0**	**0**	**0**	**0**	**0.0**	**0**	**0**	**0**	**0**	**0**	....	....	....	....	....	....	....	....
	Maine Mariners	AHL	78	28	52	80	....	....	....	49	....	....	....	....	....	....	....	....	....	....	20	4	7	11	36	....	....	....
1981-82	Maine Mariners	AHL	79	33	57	90	....	....	....	42	....	....	....	....	....	....	....	....	....	....	4	2	3	5	2	....	....	....
1982-83	**Philadelphia Flyers**	**NHL**	**58**	**8**	**20**	**28**	**7**	**14**	**21**	**20**	**0**	**1**	**1**	**51**	**15.7**	**45**	**2**	**41**	**14**	**16**	**1**	**0**	**0**	**0**	**0**	**0**	**0**	**0**
1983-84	Birmingham Bulls	ACHL	1	0	0	0	....	....	....	0	....	....	....	....	....	....	....	....	....	....	....	....	....	....	....	....	....	....
	Maine Mariners	AHL	76	23	36	59	....	....	....	65	....	....	....	....	....	....	....	....	....	....	17	3	7	10	4	....	....	....
1984-85	Maine Mariners	AHL	78	17	36	53	....	....	....	26	....	....	....	....	....	....	....	....	....	....	11	3	2	5	0	....	....	....
	NHL Totals		**103**	**14**	**25**	**39**	**12**	**18**	**30**	**34**	**0**	**1**	**2**	**90**	**15.6**	**59**	**2**	**69**	**25**		**1**	**0**	**0**	**0**	**0**	**0**	**0**	**0**

IHL First All-Star Team (1977) • AHL Second All-Star Team (1981)

Traded to **Philadelphia** by **LA Kings** to complete transaction that sent Steve Short to LA Kings (June 17, 1977), November 3, 1977.

• EVANS, Kevin

Kevin Robert LW – L. 5'9", 185 lbs. b: Peterborough, Ont., 7/10/1965.

Season	Club	League	GP	G	A	Pts	AG	AA	APts	PIM	PP	SH	GW	S	%	TGF	PGF	TGA	PGA	+/–	GP	G	A	Pts	PIM	PP	SH	GW
1980-81	Peterborough Jr. Petes	OHA-B	18	10	29	39	....	....	....	51	....	....	....	....	....	....	....	....	....	....	....	....	....	....	....	....	....	....
1981-82	Lakefield Chiefs	OJHL-B	STATISTICS NOT AVAILABLE																									
1982-83	Lakefield Chiefs	OJHL-C	33	18	47	65	....	....	....	181	....	....	....	....	....	....	....	....	....	....	....	....	....	....	....	....	....	....
1983-84	Peterborough Jr. Petes	OJHL-B	39	17	34	51	....	....	....	210	....	....	....	....	....	....	....	....	....	....	....	....	....	....	....	....	....	....
	Peterborough Petes	OHL	2	0	0	0	....	....	....	0	....	....	....	....	....	....	....	....	....	....	....	....	....	....	....	....	....	....
1984-85	London Knights	OHL	52	3	7	10	....	....	....	148	....	....	....	....	....	....	....	....	....	....	6	0	0	0	8	....	....	....
1985-86	Victoria Cougars	WHL	66	16	39	55	....	....	....	*441	....	....	....	....	....	....	....	....	....	....	....	....	....	....	....	....	....	....
	Kalamazoo Wings	IHL	11	3	5	8	....	....	....	97	....	....	....	....	....	....	....	....	....	....	6	3	0	3	56	....	....	....
1986-87	Kalamazoo Wings	IHL	73	19	31	50	....	....	....	*648	....	....	....	....	....	....	....	....	....	....	3	1	0	1	24	....	....	....
1987-88	Kalamazoo Wings	IHL	54	9	28	37	....	....	....	404	....	....	....	....	....	....	....	....	....	....	5	1	1	2	46	....	....	....
1988-89	Kalamazoo Wings	IHL	50	22	34	56	....	....	....	326	....	....	....	....	....	....	....	....	....	....	....	....	....	....	....	....	....	....
1989-90	Kalamazoo Wings	IHL	76	30	54	84	....	....	....	346	....	....	....	....	....	....	....	....	....	....	10	8	4	12	86	....	....	....
1990-91	**Minnesota North Stars**	**NHL**	**4**	**0**	**0**	**0**	**0**	**0**	**0**	**19**	**0**	**0**	**0**	**2**	**0.0**	**0**	**0**	**3**	**0**	**–3**	....	....	....	....	....	....	....	....
	Kalamazoo Wings	IHL	16	10	12	22	....	....	....	70	....	....	....	....	....	....	....	....	....	....	....	....	....	....	....	....	....	....
1991-92	**San Jose Sharks**	**NHL**	**5**	**0**	**1**	**1**	**0**	**1**	**1**	**25**	**0**	**0**	**0**	**4**	**0.0**	**1**	**0**	**1**	**0**	**0**	....	....	....	....	....	....	....	....
	Kansas City Blades	IHL	66	10	39	49	....	....	....	342	....	....	....	....	....	....	....	....	....	....	14	2	*13	15	70	....	....	....
1992-93	Kalamazoo Wings	IHL	49	7	24	31	....	....	....	283	....	....	....	....	....	....	....	....	....	....	....	....	....	....	....	....	....	....
1993-94	Peoria Rivermen	IHL	67	10	29	39	....	....	....	254	....	....	....	....	....	....	....	....	....	....	4	0	0	0	6	....	....	....
1994-95	Peoria Rivermen	IHL	29	5	9	14	....	....	....	121	....	....	....	....	....	....	....	....	....	....	....	....	....	....	....	....	....	....
	Kansas City Blades	IHL	26	3	6	9	....	....	....	192	....	....	....	....	....	....	....	....	....	....	19	2	4	6	*111	....	....	....
1995-96	Memphis RiverKings	CHL	38	11	32	43	....	....	....	356	....	....	....	....	....	....	....	....	....	....	6	2	9	11	48	....	....	....
1996-97	Mississippi Sea Wolves	ECHL	63	19	27	46	....	....	....	505	....	....	....	....	....	....	....	....	....	....	3	1	1	2	21	....	....	....
1997-98	Mississippi Sea Wolves	ECHL	38	8	18	26	....	....	....	234	....	....	....	....	....	....	....	....	....	....	....	....	....	....	....	....	....	....
	Memphis Riverkings	CHL	DID NOT PLAY – COACHING																									
1998-99	Memphis Riverkings	CHL	DID NOT PLAY – COACHING																									
99-2000	Memphis RiverKings	CHL	7	0	5	5	....	....	....	64	....	....	....	....	....	....	....	....	....	....	....	....	....	....	....	....	....	....
	Tupelo T-Rex	WPHL	25	0	2	2	....	....	....	131	....	....	....	....	....	....	....	....	....	....	2	0	1	1	4	....	....	....
	NHL Totals		**9**	**0**	**1**	**1**	**0**	**1**	**1**	**44**	**0**	**0**	**0**	**6**	**0.0**	**1**	**0**	**4**	**0**		....	....	....	....	....	....	....	....

• Brother of Paul and Doug

Signed as a free agent by **Minnesota**, August 8, 1988. Claimed by **San Jose** from **Minnesota** in Dispersal Draft, May 30, 1991. Signed as a free agent by **Minnesota**, July 20, 1992. • Released as coach of **Memphis** (CHL) after U.S. Immigration officials revoked work visa, September 8, 1999.

• EVANS, Paul

Paul Edward Vincent C/LW – L. 5'11", 175 lbs. b: Peterborough, Ont., 2/24/1955. Toronto's 8th, 149th overall, in 1975.

Season	Club	League	GP	G	A	Pts	AG	AA	APts	PIM	PP	SH	GW	S	%	TGF	PGF	TGA	PGA	+/–	GP	G	A	Pts	PIM	PP	SH	GW
1973-74	Peterborough Petes	OMJHL	67	15	30	45	....	....	....	181	....	....	....	....	....	....	....	....	....	....	....	....	....	....	....	....	....	....
	Canada	WJC-A	5	1	0	1	....	....	....	8	....	....	....	....	....	....	....	....	....	....	....	....	....	....	....	....	....	....
1974-75	Peterborough Petes	OMJHL	70	25	70	95	....	....	....	192	....	....	....	....	....	....	....	....	....	....	10	5	7	12	39	....	....	....
1975-76	Oklahoma City Blazers	CHL	67	7	23	30	....	....	....	179	....	....	....	....	....	....	....	....	....	....	4	0	1	1	24	....	....	....
1976-77	**Toronto Maple Leafs**	**NHL**	**7**	**1**	**1**	**2**	**1**	**1**	**2**	**19**	**0**	**0**	**0**	**10**	**10.0**	**5**	**1**	**1**	**0**	**3**	**2**	**0**	**0**	**0**	**0**	**0**	**0**	**0**
	Dallas Black Hawks	CHL	71	18	46	64	....	....	....	163	....	....	....	....	....	....	....	....	....	....	5	0	2	2	15	....	....	....
1977-78	**Toronto Maple Leafs**	**NHL**	**4**	**0**	**0**	**0**	**0**	**0**	**0**	**2**	**0**	**0**	**0**	**0**	**0.0**	**0**	**0**	**1**	**0**	**–1**	....	....	....	....	....	....	....	....
	Dallas Black Hawks	CHL	74	16	39	55	....	....	....	116	....	....	....	....	....	....	....	....	....	....	13	1	11	12	20	....	....	....
1978-79	Saginaw Gears	IHL	11	0	11	11	....	....	....	24	....	....	....	....	....	....	....	....	....	....	....	....	....	....	....	....	....	....
	Flint Generals	IHL	38	7	27	34	....	....	....	93	....	....	....	....	....	....	....	....	....	....	....	....	....	....	....	....	....	....
	NHL Totals		**11**	**1**	**1**	**2**	**1**	**1**	**2**	**21**	**0**	**0**	**0**	**10**	**10.0**	**5**	**1**	**2**	**0**		**2**	**0**	**0**	**0**	**0**	**0**	**0**	**0**

• Brother of Doug and Kevin

			REGULAR SEASON																			PLAYOFFS							
Season	Club	League	GP	G	A	Pts	AG	AA	APts	PIM	PP	SH	GW	S	%	TGF	PGF	TGA	PGA	+/–	GP	G	A	Pts	PIM	PP	SH	GW

• EVANS, Shawn

D – L. 6'3", 195 lbs. b: Kingston, Ont., 9/7/1965. New Jersey's 2nd, 24th overall, in 1983.

Season	Club	League	GP	G	A	Pts	AG	AA	APts	PIM	PP	SH	GW	S	%	TGF	PGF	TGA	PGA	+/–	GP	G	A	Pts	PIM	PP	SH	GW
1981-82	Kitchener Jr. Rangers	OJHL-B	21	9	13	22	....	....	....	55	....	....	....	....	....	....	....	....	....	....	....	....	....	....	....	....	....	....
1982-83	Peterborough Petes	OHL	58	7	41	48	....	....	....	116	....	....	....	....	....	....	....	....	....	....	4	2	0	2	12	....	....	....
1983-84	Peterborough Petes	OHL	67	21	88	109	....	....	....	116	....	....	....	....	....	....	....	....	....	....	8	1	16	17	8	....	....	....
1984-85	Peterborough Petes	OHL	66	16	83	99	....	....	....	78	....	....	....	....	....	....	....	....	....	....	16	6	18	24	6	....	....	....
1985-86	**St. Louis Blues**	**NHL**	**7**	**0**	**0**	**0**	**0**	**0**	**0**	**2**	**0**	**0**	**0**	**1**	**0.0**	**2**	**0**	**3**	**0**	**–1**	....	....	....	....	....	....	....	....
	Peoria Rivermen	IHL	55	8	26	34	....	....	....	36	....	....	....	....	....	....	....	....	....	....	....	....	....	....	....	....	....	....
1986-87	Nova Scotia Oilers	AHL	55	7	28	35	....	....	....	29	....	....	....	....	....	....	....	....	....	....	5	0	4	4	6	....	....	....
1987-88	Nova Scotia Oilers	AHL	79	8	62	70	....	....	....	109	....	....	....	....	....	....	....	....	....	....	5	1	1	2	40	....	....	....
1988-89	Springfield Indians	AHL	68	9	50	59	....	....	....	125	....	....	....	....	....	....	....	....	....	....	....	....	....	....	....	....	....	....
1989-90	**New York Islanders**	**NHL**	**2**	**1**	**0**	**1**	**1**	**0**	**1**	**0**	**1**	**0**	**0**	**4**	**25.0**	**3**	**2**	**3**	**1**	**–1**	....	....	....	....	....	....	....	....
	Springfield Indians	AHL	63	6	35	41	....	....	....	102	....	....	....	....	....	....	....	....	....	....	18	6	11	17	35	....	....	....
1990-91	Maine Mariners	AHL	51	9	37	46	....	....	....	44	....	....	....	....	....	....	....	....	....	....	2	0	1	1	0	....	....	....
1991-92	Springfield Indians	AHL	80	11	67	78	....	....	....	81	....	....	....	....	....	....	....	....	....	....	11	0	8	8	16	....	....	....
1992-93	Milwaukee Admirals	IHL	79	13	65	78	....	....	....	83	....	....	....	....	....	....	....	....	....	....	6	0	3	3	6	....	....	....
1993-94	HC Milano Devils	Italy	13	2	10	12	....	....	....	6	....	....	....	....	....	....	....	....	....	....	8	0	2	2	20	....	....	....
1994-95	Milwaukee Admirals	IHL	58	6	34	40	....	....	....	20	....	....	....	....	....	....	....	....	....	....	....	....	....	....	....	....	....	....
	Fort Wayne Komets	IHL	11	2	8	10	....	....	....	6	....	....	....	....	....	....	....	....	....	....	4	1	3	4	2	....	....	....
1995-96	Fort Wayne Komets	IHL	81	5	61	66	....	....	....	78	....	....	....	....	....	....	....	....	....	....	5	3	3	6	2	....	....	....
1996-97	Fort Wayne Komets	IHL	41	7	13	20	....	....	....	34	....	....	....	....	....	....	....	....	....	....	....	....	....	....	....	....	....	....
	Manitoba Moose	IHL	17	2	3	5	....	....	....	4	....	....	....	....	....	....	....	....	....	....	....	....	....	....	....	....	....	....
	Cincinnati Cyclones	IHL	21	3	9	12	....	....	....	24	....	....	....	....	....	....	....	....	....	....	3	0	0	0	14	....	....	....
1997-98	Baton Rouge Kingfish	ECHL	49	5	17	22	....	....	....	40	....	....	....	....	....	....	....	....	....	....	....	....	....	....	....	....	....	....
	Cincinnati Cyclones	IHL	3	0	0	0	....	....	....	2	....	....	....	....	....	....	....	....	....	....	....	....	....	....	....	....	....	....
1998-99	Mohawk Valley Prowlers	UHL	11	0	5	5	....	....	....	20	....	....	....	....	....	....	....	....	....	....	....	....	....	....	....	....	....	....
	Mohawk Valley Prowlers	UHL	DID NOT PLAY – ASSISTANT COACH																									
99-2000	Mohawk Valley Prowlers	UHL	DID NOT PLAY – COACHING																									
	NHL Totals		**9**	**1**	**0**	**1**	**1**	**0**	**1**	**2**	**1**	**0**	**0**	**5**	**20.0**	**5**	**2**	**6**	**1**		....	....	....	....	....	....	....	....

OHL Second All-Star Team (1984) • AHL First All-Star Team (1992) • IHL First All-Star Team (1993)

Traded to **St. Louis** by **New Jersey** with New Jersey's 5th round choice (Michael Wolak) in 1986 Entry Draft for Mark Johnson, September 19, 1985. Traded to **Edmonton** by **St. Louis** for Todd Ewen, October 15, 1986. Signed as a free agent by **NY Islanders**, June 20, 1988. Signed as a free agent by **Boston**, December 17, 1990. Signed as a free agent by **Hartford**, August 15, 1991. • Officially announced retirement and named Assistant Coach of **Mohawk Valley** (UHL), November 7, 1998.

• EVASON, Dean

Dean C. C – R. 5'10", 180 lbs. b: Flin Flon, Man., 8/22/1964. Washington's 3rd, 89th overall, in 1982.

Season	Club	League	GP	G	A	Pts	AG	AA	APts	PIM	PP	SH	GW	S	%	TGF	PGF	TGA	PGA	+/–	GP	G	A	Pts	PIM	PP	SH	GW
1980-81	Cowichan Valley Capitals	BCJHL	STATISTICS NOT AVAILABLE																									
	Spokane Flyers	WHL	3	1	1	2	....	....	....	0	....	....	....	....	....	....	....	....	....	....	....	....	....	....	....	....	....	....
1981-82	Spokane Flyers	WHL	26	8	14	22	....	....	....	65	....	....	....	....	....	....	....	....	....	....	....	....	....	....	....	....	....	....
	Kamloops Jr. Oilers	WHL	44	21	55	76	....	....	....	47	....	....	....	....	....	....	....	....	....	....	4	2	1	3	0	....	....	....
1982-83	Kamloops Jr. Oilers	WHL	70	71	93	164	....	....	....	102	....	....	....	....	....	....	....	....	....	....	7	5	7	12	18	....	....	....
1983-84	Kamloops Jr. Oilers	WHL	57	49	88	137	....	....	....	89	....	....	....	....	....	....	....	....	....	....	17	*21	20	41	33	....	....	....
	Canada	WJC-A	7	6	3	9	....	....	....	0	....	....	....	....	....	....	....	....	....	....	....	....	....	....	....	....	....	....
	Washington Capitals	**NHL**	**2**	**0**	**0**	**0**	**0**	**0**	**0**	**2**	**0**	**0**	**0**	**0**	**0.0**	**0**	**0**	**0**	**0**	**0**	....	....	....	....	....	....	....	....
	Kamloops Jr. Oilers	Mem-Cup	4	2	2	4	....	....	....	0	....	....	....	....	....	....	....	....	....	....	....	....	....	....	....	....	....	....
1984-85	**Washington Capitals**	**NHL**	**15**	**3**	**4**	**7**	**2**	**3**	**5**	**2**	**0**	**0**	**1**	**18**	**16.7**	**11**	**0**	**2**	**0**	**9**	....	....	....	....	....	....	....	....
	Hartford Whalers	**NHL**	**2**	**0**	**0**	**0**	**0**	**0**	**0**	**0**	**0**	**0**	**1**	**13**	**0.0**	**6**	**0**	**0**	**0**	**6**	....	....	....	....	....	....	....	....
	Binghamton Whalers	AHL	65	27	49	76	....	....	....	38	....	....	....	....	....	....	....	....	....	....	8	3	5	8	9	....	....	....
1985-86	**Hartford Whalers**	**NHL**	**55**	**20**	**28**	**48**	**16**	**19**	**35**	**65**	**5**	**2**	**4**	**101**	**19.8**	**69**	**21**	**51**	**6**	**3**	**10**	**1**	**4**	**5**	**10**	**0**	**0**	**0**
	Binghamton Whalers	AHL	26	9	17	26	....	....	....	29	....	....	....	....	....	....	....	....	....	....	....	....	....	....	....	....	....	....
1986-87	**Hartford Whalers**	**NHL**	**80**	**22**	**37**	**59**	**19**	**27**	**46**	**67**	**7**	**2**	**2**	**124**	**17.7**	**83**	**19**	**89**	**30**	**5**	**5**	**3**	**2**	**5**	**35**	**0**	**0**	**0**
1987-88	**Hartford Whalers**	**NHL**	**77**	**10**	**18**	**28**	**9**	**13**	**22**	**115**	**6**	**0**	**0**	**126**	**7.9**	**44**	**15**	**80**	**22**	**–29**	**6**	**1**	**1**	**2**	**2**	**0**	**0**	**0**
1988-89	**Hartford Whalers**	**NHL**	**67**	**11**	**17**	**28**	**9**	**12**	**21**	**60**	**0**	**0**	**0**	**95**	**11.6**	**38**	**1**	**58**	**12**	**–9**	**4**	**1**	**2**	**3**	**10**	**0**	**1**	**0**
1989-90	**Hartford Whalers**	**NHL**	**78**	**18**	**25**	**43**	**15**	**18**	**33**	**138**	**2**	**2**	**2**	**150**	**12.0**	**61**	**4**	**76**	**26**	**7**	**7**	**2**	**2**	**4**	**22**	**0**	**0**	**0**
1990-91	**Hartford Whalers**	**NHL**	**75**	**6**	**23**	**29**	**5**	**17**	**22**	**170**	**1**	**0**	**0**	**85**	**7.1**	**39**	**3**	**70**	**28**	**–6**	**6**	**0**	**4**	**4**	**29**	**0**	**0**	**0**
1991-92	**San Jose Sharks**	**NHL**	**74**	**11**	**15**	**26**	**10**	**11**	**21**	**99**	**1**	**0**	**1**	**88**	**12.5**	**39**	**9**	**67**	**15**	**–22**	....	....	....	....	....	....	....	....
1992-93	**San Jose Sharks**	**NHL**	**84**	**12**	**19**	**31**	**10**	**13**	**23**	**132**	**3**	**0**	**1**	**107**	**11.2**	**47**	**13**	**111**	**42**	**–35**	....	....	....	....	....	....	....	....
1993-94	**Dallas Stars**	**NHL**	**80**	**11**	**33**	**44**	**10**	**26**	**36**	**66**	**3**	**2**	**2**	**118**	**9.3**	**66**	**22**	**82**	**26**	**–12**	**9**	**0**	**2**	**2**	**12**	**0**	**0**	**0**
1994-95	**Dallas Stars**	**NHL**	**47**	**8**	**7**	**15**	**14**	**10**	**24**	**48**	**1**	**0**	**0**	**53**	**15.1**	**28**	**2**	**40**	**17**	**3**	**5**	**1**	**2**	**3**	**12**	**0**	**1**	**0**
1995-96	**Calgary Flames**	**NHL**	**67**	**7**	**7**	**14**	**7**	**6**	**13**	**38**	**1**	**0**	**1**	**68**	**10.3**	**21**	**4**	**50**	**27**	**–6**	**3**	**0**	**1**	**1**	**0**	**0**	**0**	**0**
1996-97	Canada	Nat-Team	56	25	46	71	....	....	....	106	....	....	....	....	....	....	....	....	....	....	....	....	....	....	....	....	....	....
	EV Zug	Switz.	3	0	1	1	....	....	....	2	....	....	....	....	....	....	....	....	....	....	4	0	2	2	4	....	....	....
	Canada	WC-A	11	2	3	5	....	....	....	20	....	....	....	....	....	....	....	....	....	....	....	....	....	....	....	....	....	....
1997-98	EV Landshut	Germany	47	7	23	30	....	....	....	52	....	....	....	....	....	....	....	....	....	....	6	0	3	3	18	....	....	....
1998-99	EV Landshut	Germany	45	13	25	38	....	....	....	76	....	....	....	....	....	....	....	....	....	....	3	0	1	1	2	....	....	....
	Calgary Hitmen	WHL	DID NOT PLAY – ASSISTANT COACH																									
99-2000	Kamloops Blazers	WHL	DID NOT PLAY – COACHING																									
	NHL Totals		**803**	**139**	**233**	**372**	**126**	**175**	**301**	**1002**	**30**	**8**	**15**	**1146**	**12.1**	**552**	**113**	**776**	**251**		**55**	**9**	**20**	**29**	**132**	**0**	**2**	**0**

WHL West First All-Star Team (1984)

Traded to **Hartford** by **Washington** with Peter Sidorkiewicz for David Jensen, March 12, 1985. Traded to **San Jose** by **Hartford** for Dan Keczmer, October 2, 1991. Traded to **Dallas** by **San Jose** for San Jose's 6th round choice (previously acquired, San Jose selected Petri Varis) in 1993 Entry Draft, June 26, 1993. Signed as a free agent by **Calgary**, August 1, 1995.

• EWEN, Todd

Todd Gordon RW – R. 6'2", 230 lbs. b: Saskatoon, Sask., 3/22/1966. Edmonton's 9th, 168th overall, in 1984.

Season	Club	League	GP	G	A	Pts	AG	AA	APts	PIM	PP	SH	GW	S	%	TGF	PGF	TGA	PGA	+/–	GP	G	A	Pts	PIM	PP	SH	GW
1981-82	St. Alberts Sabres	AAHA	STATISTICS NOT AVAILABLE																									
1982-83	Vernon Lakers	BCJHL	42	14	10	24	....	....	....	178	....	....	....	....	....	....	....	....	....	....	....	....	....	....	....	....	....	....
	Kamloops Jr. Oilers	WHL	3	0	0	0	....	....	....	2	....	....	....	....	....	....	....	....	....	....	2	0	0	0	0	....	....	....
1983-84	New Westminster Bruins	WHL	68	11	13	24	....	....	....	176	....	....	....	....	....	....	....	....	....	....	7	2	1	3	15	....	....	....
1984-85	New Westminster Bruins	WHL	56	11	20	31	....	....	....	304	....	....	....	....	....	....	....	....	....	....	10	1	8	9	60	....	....	....
1985-86	New Westminster Bruins	WHL	60	28	24	52	....	....	....	289	....	....	....	....	....	....	....	....	....	....	....	....	....	....	....	....	....	....
	Maine Mariners	AHL	....	....	....	....	....	....	....	....	....	....	....	....	....	....	....	....	....	....	3	0	0	0	7	....	....	....
1986-87	**St. Louis Blues**	**NHL**	**23**	**2**	**0**	**2**	**2**	**0**	**2**	**84**	**0**	**0**	**0**	**11**	**18.2**	**4**	**0**	**5**	**0**	**–1**	**4**	**0**	**0**	**0**	**23**	**0**	**0**	**0**
	Peoria Rivermen	IHL	16	3	3	6	....	....	....	110	....	....	....	....	....	....	....	....	....	....	....	....	....	....	....	....	....	....
1987-88	**St. Louis Blues**	**NHL**	**64**	**4**	**2**	**6**	**3**	**1**	**4**	**227**	**0**	**0**	**0**	**38**	**10.5**	**8**	**0**	**13**	**0**	**–5**	**6**	**0**	**0**	**0**	**21**	**0**	**0**	**0**
1988-89	**St. Louis Blues**	**NHL**	**34**	**4**	**5**	**9**	**3**	**4**	**7**	**171**	**0**	**0**	**0**	**22**	**18.2**	**14**	**0**	**10**	**0**	**4**	**2**	**0**	**0**	**0**	**21**	**0**	**0**	**0**
1989-90	**St. Louis Blues**	**NHL**	**3**	**0**	**0**	**0**	**0**	**0**	**0**	**11**	**0**	**0**	**0**	**3**	**0.0**	**0**	**0**	**2**	**0**	**–2**	....	....	....	....	....	....	....	....
	Peoria Rivermen	IHL	2	0	0	0	....	....	....	12	....	....	....	....	....	....	....	....	....	....	....	....	....	....	....	....	....	....
	Montreal Canadiens	**NHL**	**41**	**4**	**6**	**10**	**3**	**4**	**7**	**158**	**0**	**0**	**2**	**26**	**15.4**	**14**	**0**	**13**	**0**	**1**	**10**	**0**	**0**	**0**	**4**	**0**	**0**	**0**
1990-91	Montreal Canadiens	Fr-Tour	2	0	0	0	....	....	....	20	....	....	....	....	....	....	....	....	....	....	....	....	....	....	....	....	....	....
	Montreal Canadiens	**NHL**	**28**	**3**	**2**	**5**	**3**	**2**	**5**	**128**	**0**	**0**	**0**	**13**	**23.1**	**11**	**1**	**6**	**0**	**4**	....	....	....	....	....	....	....	....
1991-92	**Montreal Canadiens**	**NHL**	**46**	**1**	**2**	**3**	**1**	**2**	**3**	**130**	**0**	**0**	**0**	**19**	**5.3**	**6**	**0**	**4**	**1**	**3**	**3**	**0**	**0**	**0**	**18**	**0**	**0**	**0**
1992-93♦	**Montreal Canadiens**	**NHL**	**75**	**5**	**9**	**14**	**4**	**6**	**10**	**193**	**0**	**0**	**1**	**59**	**8.5**	**27**	**0**	**22**	**1**	**6**	**1**	**0**	**0**	**0**	**0**	**0**	**0**	**0**
1993-94	**Mighty Ducks of Anaheim**	**NHL**	**76**	**9**	**9**	**18**	**8**	**7**	**15**	**272**	**0**	**0**	**2**	**59**	**15.3**	**31**	**3**	**35**	**0**	**–7**	....	....	....	....	....	....	....	....
1994-95	**Mighty Ducks of Anaheim**	**NHL**	**24**	**0**	**0**	**0**	**0**	**0**	**0**	**90**	**0**	**0**	**0**	**14**	**0.0**	**6**	**0**	**8**	**0**	**–2**	....	....	....	....	....	....	....	....

			REGULAR SEASON																		PLAYOFFS							
Season	Club	League	GP	G	A	Pts	AG	AA	APts	PIM	PP	SH	GW	S	%	TGF	PGF	TGA	PGA	+/–	GP	G	A	Pts	PIM	PP	SH	GW
1995-96	**Mighty Ducks of Anaheim...**	**NHL**	**53**	**4**	**3**	**7**	**4**	**2**	**6**	**285**	**0**	**0**	**1**	**52**	**7.7**	**11**	**0**	**16**	**0**	**–5**	....	....	....	....	....	....	....	....
1996-97	**San Jose Sharks...**	**NHL**	**51**	**0**	**2**	**2**	**0**	**2**	**2**	**162**	**0**	**0**	**0**	**22**	**0.0**	**4**	**0**	**9**	**0**	**–5**	....	....	....	....	....	....	....	....
1997-98	**San Jose Sharks**	**NHL**	DID NOT PLAY – INJURED																									
	NHL Totals		**518**	**36**	**40**	**76**	**31**	**30**	**61**	**1911**	**0**	**0**	**6**	**338**	**10.7**	**136**	**4**	**143**	**2**		**26**	**0**	**0**	**0**	**87**	**0**	**0**	**0**

Traded to **St. Louis** by **Edmonton** for Shawn Evans, October 15, 1986. Traded to **Montreal** by **St. Louis** for St. Louis' 3rd round choice (previously acquired, St. Louis selected Nathan Lafayette) in 1991 Entry Draft, December 12, 1989. Traded to **Anaheim** by **Montreal** with Patrik Carnback for Anaheim's 3rd round choice (Chris Murray) in 1994 Entry Draft, August 10, 1993. Signed as a free agent by **San Jose**, September 4, 1996. • Missed entire 1997-98 season recovering from knee surgery, September, 1997.

• FAIRBAIRN, Bill

William John "Magnet" RW – R. 5'10", 170 lbs. b: Brandon, Man., 1/7/1947.

Season	Club	League	GP	G	A	Pts	AG	AA	APts	PIM	PP	SH	GW	S	%	TGF	PGF	TGA	PGA	+/–	GP	G	A	Pts	PIM	PP	SH	GW
1963-64	Brandon Bobcats	MAHA	STATISTICS NOT AVAILABLE																									
	Brandon Wheat Kings	MJHL	4	1	1	2	....	....	....	2	....	....	....	....	....	....	....	....	....	....	....	....	....	....	....	....	....	....
	Brandon Wheat Kings	Mem-Cup	2	1	0	1	....	....	....	0	....	....	....	....	....	....	....	....	....	....	....	....	....	....	....	....	....	....
1964-65	Brandon Wheat Kings	SJHL	55	28	31	59	....	....	....	26	....	....	....	....	....	....	....	....	....	....	9	6	5	11	11	....	....	....
1965-66	Brandon Wheat Kings	SJHL	60	36	76	112	....	....	....	94	....	....	....	....	....	....	....	....	....	....	11	5	12	17	6	....	....	....
1966-67	Brandon Wheat Kings	CMJHL	55	60	82	142	....	....	....	75	....	....	....	....	....	....	....	....	....	....	13	12	18	30	33	....	....	....
	Omaha Knights	CPHL	3	0	0	0	....	....	....	2	....	....	....	....	....	....	....	....	....	....	....	....	....	....	....	....	....	....
	Port Arthur Marrs	Mem-Cup	5	3	4	7	....	....	....	4	....	....	....	....	....	....	....	....	....	....	....	....	....	....	....	....	....	....
1967-68	Omaha Knights	CPHL	70	23	33	56	....	....	....	46	....	....	....	....	....	....	....	....	....	....	....	....	....	....	....	....	....	....
1968-69	**New York Rangers**	**NHL**	**1**	**0**	**0**	**0**	**0**	**0**	**0**	**0**	**0**	**0**	**0**	**1**	**0.0**	**0**	**0**	**1**	**0**	**–1**	....	....	....	....	....	....	....	....
	Omaha Knights	CHL	68	28	47	75	....	....	....	62	....	....	....	....	....	....	....	....	....	....	7	3	6	9	9	....	....	....
1969-70	**New York Rangers**	**NHL**	**76**	**23**	**33**	**56**	**25**	**31**	**56**	**23**	**3**	**0**	**5**	**153**	**15.0**	**88**	**17**	**47**	**0**	**24**	**6**	**0**	**1**	**1**	**10**	**0**	**0**	**0**
1970-71	**New York Rangers**	**NHL**	**56**	**7**	**23**	**30**	**7**	**19**	**26**	**32**	**2**	**0**	**1**	**88**	**8.0**	**47**	**13**	**38**	**0**	**–4**	**4**	**0**	**0**	**0**	**0**	**0**	**0**	**0**
1971-72	**New York Rangers**	**NHL**	**78**	**22**	**37**	**59**	**22**	**32**	**54**	**53**	**2**	**4**	**6**	**139**	**15.8**	**87**	**12**	**55**	**16**	**36**	**16**	**5**	**7**	**12**	**11**	**2**	**0**	**1**
1972-73	**New York Rangers**	**NHL**	**78**	**30**	**33**	**63**	**28**	**26**	**54**	**23**	**5**	**2**	**5**	**174**	**17.2**	**102**	**15**	**73**	**22**	**36**	**10**	**1**	**8**	**9**	**2**	**0**	**0**	**0**
1973-74	**New York Rangers**	**NHL**	**78**	**18**	**44**	**62**	**17**	**36**	**53**	**12**	**4**	**3**	**3**	**185**	**9.7**	**94**	**21**	**88**	**26**	**11**	**13**	**3**	**5**	**8**	**6**	**0**	**0**	**0**
1974-75	**New York Rangers**	**NHL**	**80**	**24**	**37**	**61**	**21**	**28**	**49**	**10**	**7**	**2**	**3**	**191**	**12.6**	**96**	**24**	**84**	**25**	**13**	**3**	**4**	**0**	**4**	**13**	**2**	**1**	**0**
1975-76	**New York Rangers**	**NHL**	**80**	**13**	**15**	**28**	**11**	**11**	**22**	**8**	**2**	**1**	**2**	**160**	**8.1**	**54**	**4**	**94**	**30**	**–14**	....	....	....	....	....	....	....	....
1976-77	**New York Rangers**	**NHL**	**9**	**1**	**2**	**3**	**1**	**2**	**3**	**0**	**0**	**0**	**0**	**10**	**10.0**	**6**	**0**	**10**	**5**	**1**	....	....	....	....	....	....	....	....
	Minnesota North Stars	**NHL**	**51**	**9**	**20**	**29**	**8**	**15**	**23**	**2**	**0**	**2**	**2**	**83**	**10.8**	**55**	**6**	**66**	**16**	**–1**	**2**	**0**	**1**	**1**	**0**	**0**	**0**	**0**
1977-78	**Minnesota North Stars**	**NHL**	**6**	**0**	**1**	**1**	**0**	**1**	**1**	**0**	**0**	**0**	**0**	**7**	**0.0**	**4**	**0**	**7**	**2**	**–1**	....	....	....	....	....	....	....	....
	St. Louis Blues	**NHL**	**60**	**14**	**16**	**30**	**13**	**12**	**25**	**10**	**2**	**1**	**1**	**82**	**17.1**	**44**	**4**	**72**	**9**	**–23**	....	....	....	....	....	....	....	....
1978-79	**St. Louis Blues**	**NHL**	**5**	**1**	**0**	**1**	**1**	**0**	**1**	**0**	**0**	**0**	**0**	**8**	**12.5**	**1**	**0**	**7**	**4**	**–2**	....	....	....	....	....	....	....	....
	NHL Totals		**658**	**162**	**261**	**423**	**154**	**213**	**367**	**173**	**27**	**15**	**28**	**1281**	**12.6**	**678**	**116**	**642**	**155**		**54**	**13**	**22**	**35**	**42**	**4**	**1**	**1**

CHL Second All-Star Team (1969)

• Loaned to **Port Arthur** (TBJHL) by **Brandon** (MJHL) for Memorial Cup playoffs, March, 1967. Traded to **Minnesota** by **NY Rangers** with Nick Beverley for Bill Goldsworthy, November 11, 1976. Claimed on waivers by **St. Louis** from **Minnesota**, October 24, 1977.

• FAIRCHILD, Kelly

C – L. 5'11", 195 lbs. b: Hibbing, MN, 4/9/1973. Los Angeles' 6th, 152nd overall, in 1991.

Season	Club	League	GP	G	A	Pts	AG	AA	APts	PIM	PP	SH	GW	S	%	TGF	PGF	TGA	PGA	+/–	GP	G	A	Pts	PIM	PP	SH	GW
1988-89	Hibbing Blue Jackets	Hi-School	22	9	8	17	....	....	....	24	....	....	....	....	....	....	....	....	....	....	....	....	....	....	....	....	....	....
1989-90	Grand Rapids Thunderhawks	Hi-School	28	12	17	29	....	....	....	73	....	....	....	....	....	....	....	....	....	....	....	....	....	....	....	....	....	....
1990-91	Grand Rapids Thunderhawks	Hi-School	28	28	45	73	....	....	....	25	....	....	....	....	....	....	....	....	....	....	....	....	....	....	....	....	....	....
1991-92	University of Wisconsin	WCHA	37	11	10	21	....	....	....	45	....	....	....	....	....	....	....	....	....	....	....	....	....	....	....	....	....	....
1992-93	University of Wisconsin	WCHA	42	25	29	54	....	....	....	54	....	....	....	....	....	....	....	....	....	....	....	....	....	....	....	....	....	....
1993-94	University of Wisconsin	WCHA	42	20	44	*64	....	....	....	81	....	....	....	....	....	....	....	....	....	....	....	....	....	....	....	....	....	....
1994-95	St. John's Maple Leafs	AHL	53	27	23	50	....	....	....	51	....	....	....	....	....	....	....	....	....	....	4	0	2	2	4	....	....	....
1995-96	**Toronto Maple Leafs**	**NHL**	**1**	**0**	**1**	**1**	**0**	**1**	**1**	**2**	**0**	**0**	**0**	**1**	**0.0**	**1**	**0**	**0**	**0**	**1**	....	....	....	....	....	....	....	....
	St. John's Maple Leafs	AHL	78	29	49	78	....	....	....	85	....	....	....	....	....	....	....	....	....	....	2	0	1	1	4	....	....	....
1996-97	**Toronto Maple Leafs**	**NHL**	**22**	**0**	**2**	**2**	**0**	**2**	**2**	**2**	**0**	**0**	**0**	**14**	**0.0**	**6**	**1**	**11**	**1**	**–5**	....	....	....	....	....	....	....	....
	St. John's Maple Leafs	AHL	29	9	22	31	....	....	....	36	....	....	....	....	....	....	....	....	....	....	....	....	....	....	....	....	....	....
	Orlando Solar Bears	IHL	25	9	6	15	....	....	....	20	....	....	....	....	....	....	....	....	....	....	9	6	5	11	16	....	....	....
1997-98	St. John's Maple Leafs	AHL	17	5	2	7	....	....	....	24	....	....	....	....	....	....	....	....	....	....	....	....	....	....	....	....	....	....
	Orlando Solar Bears	IHL	22	2	6	8	....	....	....	20	....	....	....	....	....	....	....	....	....	....	....	....	....	....	....	....	....	....
	Milwaukee Admirals	IHL	40	20	24	44	....	....	....	32	....	....	....	....	....	....	....	....	....	....	10	5	2	7	4	....	....	....
1998-99	**Dallas Stars**	**NHL**	**1**	**0**	**0**	**0**	**0**	**0**	**0**	**0**	**0**	**0**	**0**	**4**	**0.0**	**0**	**0**	**0**	**0**	**0**	....	....	....	....	....	....	....	....
	Michigan K-Wings	IHL	74	17	33	50	....	....	....	88	....	....	....	....	....	....	....	....	....	....	5	2	2	4	16	....	....	....
99-2000	Michigan K-Wings	IHL	78	21	41	62	....	....	....	89	....	....	....	....	....	....	....	....	....	....	....	....	....	....	....	....	....	....
	NHL Totals		**24**	**0**	**3**	**3**	**0**	**3**	**3**	**4**	**0**	**0**	**0**	**19**	**0.0**	**7**	**1**	**11**	**1**		....	....	....	....	....	....	....	....

WCHA First All-Star Team (1994)

Traded to **Toronto** by **LA Kings** with Dixon Ward, Guy Leveque and Shayne Toporowski for Eric Lacroix, Chris Snell and Toronto's 4th round choice (Eric Belanger) in 1996 Entry Draft, October 3, 1994. Traded to **Milwaukee** (IHL) by **Orlando** (IHL) with Dave McIntyre for Sean McCann and Dave Mackey, January 11, 1998. Signed as a free agent by **Dallas**, July 2, 1998.

• FALKENBERG, Bob

Robert Arthur "Steady" D – R. 6', 185 lbs. b: Stettler, Alta., 1/1/1946.

Season	Club	League	GP	G	A	Pts	AG	AA	APts	PIM	PP	SH	GW	S	%	TGF	PGF	TGA	PGA	+/–	GP	G	A	Pts	PIM	PP	SH	GW
1962-63	Edmonton Oil Kings	CAHL	STATISTICS NOT AVAILABLE																									
	Edmonton Oil Kings	Mem-Cup	20	6	10	16	....	....	....	4	....	....	....	....	....	....	....	....	....	....	....	....	....	....	....	....	....	....
1963-64	Edmonton Oil Kings	CAHL	14	3	12	15	....	....	....	0	....	....	....	....	....	....	....	....	....	....	5	1	3	4	0	....	....	....
	Edmonton Oil Kings	Mem-Cup	19	1	5	6	....	....	....	2	....	....	....	....	....	....	....	....	....	....	....	....	....	....	....	....	....	....
1964-65	Edmonton Oil Kings	CAHL	....	....	....	....	....	....	....	....	....	....	....	....	....	....	....	....	....	....	5	1	2	3	2	....	....	....
	Edmonton Oil Kings	Mem-Cup	20	6	11	17	....	....	....	31	....	....	....	....	....	....	....	....	....	....	....	....	....	....	....	....	....	....
1965-66	Edmonton Oil Kings	ASHL	27	6	9	15	....	....	....	34	....	....	....	....	....	....	....	....	....	....	11	3	4	7	11	....	....	....
	Memphis Wings	CPHL	3	0	1	1	....	....	....	0	....	....	....	....	....	....	....	....	....	....	....	....	....	....	....	....	....	....
	Edmonton Oil Kings	Mem-Cup	19	11	18	29	....	....	....	30	....	....	....	....	....	....	....	....	....	....	....	....	....	....	....	....	....	....
1966-67	**Detroit Red Wings**	**NHL**	**16**	**1**	**1**	**2**	**1**	**1**	**2**	**10**	....	....	....	....	....	....	....	....	....	....	....	....	....	....	....	....	....	....
	Pittsburgh Hornets	AHL	53	2	15	17	....	....	....	28	....	....	....	....	....	....	....	....	....	....	....	....	....	....	....	....	....	....
1967-68	**Detroit Red Wings**	**NHL**	**20**	**0**	**3**	**3**	**0**	**3**	**3**	**10**	**0**	**0**	**0**	**14**	**0.0**	**11**	**0**	**13**	**0**	**–2**	....	....	....	....	....	....	....	....
	Fort Worth Wings	CPHL	48	2	13	15	....	....	....	57	....	....	....	....	....	....	....	....	....	....	....	....	....	....	....	....	....	....
1968-69	**Detroit Red Wings**	**NHL**	**5**	**0**	**0**	**0**	**0**	**0**	**0**	**0**	**0**	**0**	**0**	**0**	**0.0**	**0**	**0**	**3**	**0**	**–3**	....	....	....	....	....	....	....	....
	Baltimore Clippers	AHL	4	0	1	1	....	....	....	0	....	....	....	....	....	....	....	....	....	....	....	....	....	....	....	....	....	....
	Fort Worth Wings	CHL	51	2	8	10	....	....	....	26	....	....	....	....	....	....	....	....	....	....	....	....	....	....	....	....	....	....
1969-70	Cleveland Barons	AHL	58	1	17	18	....	....	....	57	....	....	....	....	....	....	....	....	....	....	....	....	....	....	....	....	....	....
1970-71	**Detroit Red Wings**	**NHL**	**9**	**0**	**1**	**1**	**0**	**1**	**1**	**6**	**0**	**0**	**0**	**4**	**0.0**	**2**	**0**	**6**	**1**	**–3**	....	....	....	....	....	....	....	....
	Fort Worth Wings	CHL	61	2	31	33	....	....	....	118	....	....	....	....	....	....	....	....	....	....	4	0	2	2	2	....	....	....
1971-72	**Detroit Red Wings**	**NHL**	**4**	**0**	**0**	**0**	**0**	**0**	**0**	**0**	**0**	**0**	**0**	**3**	**0.0**	**3**	**0**	**1**	**0**	**2**	....	....	....	....	....	....	....	....
	Tidewater Red Wings	AHL	74	4	21	25	....	....	....	57	....	....	....	....	....	....	....	....	....	....	....	....	....	....	....	....	....	....
1972-73	Alberta Oilers	WHA	76	6	23	29	....	....	....	44	....	....	....	....	....	....	....	....	....	....	....	....	....	....	....	....	....	....
1973-74	Edmonton Oilers	WHA	78	3	14	17	....	....	....	32	....	....	....	....	....	....	....	....	....	....	5	0	2	2	14	....	....	....
1974-75	San Diego Mariners	WHA	78	2	18	20	....	....	....	42	....	....	....	....	....	....	....	....	....	....	10	0	1	1	4	....	....	....
1975-76	San Diego Mariners	WHA	79	3	13	16	....	....	....	31	....	....	....	....	....	....	....	....	....	....	11	1	2	3	6	....	....	....
1976-77	San Diego Mariners	WHA	64	0	6	6	....	....	....	34	....	....	....	....	....	....	....	....	....	....	2	0	0	0	0	....	....	....
1977-78	Edmonton Oilers	WHA	2	0	0	0	....	....	....	0	....	....	....	....	....	....	....	....	....	....	....	....	....	....	....	....	....	....
	NHL Totals		**54**	**1**	**5**	**6**	**1**	**5**	**6**	**26**	....	....	....	....	....	....	....	....	....	....	....	....	....	....	....	....	....	....
	Other Major League Totals		377	14	74	88	....	....	....	183	....	....	....	....	....	....	....	....	....	....	28	1	5	6	24	....	....	....

• Regular season totals for **Edmonton** (CAHL) in 1964-65 unavailable. • Selected by **Alberta** (WHA) in the 1972 WHA General Player Draft, February 12, 1972. Traded to **San Diego** (WHA) by **Edmonton** (WHA) to complete transaction that sent Bobby Sheehan to Edmonton (March, 1974), May, 1974. Signed as a free agent by **Edmonton** (WHA) after **San Diego** (WHA) franchise folded, October, 1977.

• FALLOON, Pat

Pat J. RW – R. 5'11", 190 lbs. b: Foxwarren, Man., 9/22/1972. San Jose's 1st, 2nd overall, in 1991.

Season	Club	League	GP	G	A	Pts	AG	AA	APts	PIM	PP	SH	GW	S	%	TGF	PGF	TGA	PGA	+/-	GP	G	A	Pts	PIM	PP	SH	GW
			REGULAR SEASON																		PLAYOFFS							
1987-88	Yellowhead Pass Selects	AAHA	52	74	69	143	....	....	....	50	....	....	....	....	....	....	....	....	....	....	....	....	....	....	....	....	....	....
1988-89	Spokane Chiefs	WHL	72	22	56	78	....	....	....	41	....	....	....	....	....	....	....	....	....	....	....	....	....	....	....	....	....	....
1989-90	Spokane Chiefs	WHL	71	60	64	124	....	....	....	48	....	....	....	....	....	....	....	....	....	....	6	5	8	13	4	....	....	....
1990-91	Spokane Chiefs	WHL	61	64	74	138	....	....	....	33	....	....	....	....	....	....	....	....	....	....	15	10	14	24	10	....	....	....
	Canada	WJC-A	7	3	3	6	....	....	....	2	....	....	....	....	....	....	....	....	....	....	....	....	....	....	....	....	....	....
	Spokane Chiefs	Mem-Cup	4	*8	4	*12	....	....	....	2	....	....	....	....	....	....	....	....	....	....	....	....	....	....	....	....	....	....
1991-92	**San Jose Sharks**	**NHL**	**79**	**25**	**34**	**59**	**23**	**26**	**49**	**16**	**5**	**0**	**1**	**181**	**13.8**	**85**	**29**	**92**	**4**	**-32**	....	....	....	....	....	....	....	....
	Canada	WC-A	6	2	1	3	....	....	....	2	....	....	....	....	....	....	....	....	....	....	....	....	....	....	....	....	....	....
1992-93	**San Jose Sharks**	**NHL**	**41**	**14**	**14**	**28**	**12**	**10**	**22**	**12**	**5**	**1**	**1**	**131**	**10.7**	**38**	**13**	**53**	**3**	**-25**	....	....	....	....	....	....	....	....
1993-94	**San Jose Sharks**	**NHL**	**83**	**22**	**31**	**53**	**20**	**24**	**44**	**18**	**6**	**0**	**1**	**193**	**11.4**	**82**	**26**	**61**	**2**	**-3**	**14**	**1**	**2**	**3**	**6**	**0**	**0**	**0**
1994-95	**San Jose Sharks**	**NHL**	**46**	**12**	**7**	**19**	**21**	**10**	**31**	**25**	**0**	**0**	**3**	**91**	**13.2**	**28**	**3**	**29**	**0**	**-4**	**11**	**3**	**1**	**4**	**0**	**0**	**0**	**0**
1995-96	**San Jose Sharks**	**NHL**	**9**	**3**	**0**	**3**	**3**	**0**	**3**	**4**	**0**	**0**	**0**	**18**	**16.7**	**7**	**1**	**7**	**0**	**-1**	....	....	....	....	....	....	....	....
	Philadelphia Flyers	**NHL**	**62**	**22**	**26**	**48**	**22**	**21**	**43**	**6**	**9**	**0**	**2**	**152**	**14.5**	**64**	**27**	**22**	**0**	**15**	**12**	**3**	**2**	**5**	**2**	**2**	**0**	**0**
1996-97	**Philadelphia Flyers**	**NHL**	**52**	**11**	**12**	**23**	**12**	**11**	**23**	**10**	**2**	**0**	**4**	**124**	**8.9**	**32**	**10**	**30**	**0**	**-8**	**14**	**3**	**1**	**4**	**2**	**1**	**0**	**0**
1997-98	**Philadelphia Flyers**	**NHL**	**30**	**5**	**7**	**12**	**6**	**7**	**13**	**8**	**1**	**0**	**0**	**63**	**7.9**	**22**	**8**	**11**	**0**	**3**	....	....	....	....	....	....	....	....
	Ottawa Senators	**NHL**	**28**	**3**	**3**	**6**	**4**	**3**	**7**	**8**	**2**	**0**	**0**	**73**	**4.1**	**10**	**5**	**16**	**0**	**-11**	**1**	**0**	**0**	**0**	**0**	**0**	**0**	**0**
1998-99	**Edmonton Oilers**	**NHL**	**82**	**17**	**23**	**40**	**20**	**22**	**42**	**20**	**8**	**0**	**2**	**152**	**11.2**	**62**	**23**	**43**	**0**	**-4**	**4**	**0**	**1**	**1**	**4**	**0**	**0**	**0**
99-2000	**Edmonton Oilers**	**NHL**	**33**	**5**	**13**	**18**	**6**	**12**	**18**	**4**	**1**	**0**	**0**	**51**	**9.8**	**28**	**6**	**16**	**0**	**6**	....	....	....	....	....	....	....	....
	Pittsburgh Penguins	**NHL**	**30**	**4**	**9**	**13**	**4**	**8**	**12**	**10**	**0**	**0**	**0**	**41**	**9.8**	**16**	**3**	**15**	**0**	**-2**	**10**	**1**	**0**	**1**	**2**	**0**	**0**	**0**
	NHL Totals		**575**	**143**	**179**	**322**	**153**	**154**	**307**	**141**	**39**	**1**	**14**	**1270**	**11.3**	**474**	**154**	**395**	**9**		**66**	**11**	**7**	**18**	**16**	**3**	**0**	**0**

WHL West Second All-Star Team (1989) • WHL West First All-Star Team (1991) • Canadian Major Junior Most Sportsmanlike Player of the Year (1991) • Memorial Cup All-Star Team (1991) • Won Stafford Smythe Memorial Trophy (Memorial Cup Tournament MVP) (1991)

Traded to **Philadelphia** by **San Jose** for Martin Spanhel, Philadelphia's 1st round choice (later traded to Phoenix — Phoenix selected Daniel Briere) in 1996 Entry Draft and Philadelphia's 4th round choice (later traded to Buffalo — Buffalo selected Mike Martone), in 1996 Entry Draft, November 16, 1995. Traded to **Ottawa** by **Philadelphia** with Vaclav Prospal and Dallas' 2nd round choice (previously acquired, Ottawa selected Chris Bala) in 1998 Entry Draft for Alexandre Daigle, January 17, 1998. Signed as a free agent by **Edmonton**, August 21, 1998. Claimed on waivers by **Pittsburgh** from **Edmonton**, February 4, 2000.

• FARKAS, Jeff

Jeffrey Thomas C – L. 6'1", 175 lbs. b: Amherst, MA, 1/24/1978. Toronto's 1st, 57th overall, in 1997.

Season	Club	League	GP	G	A	Pts	AG	AA	APts	PIM	PP	SH	GW	S	%	TGF	PGF	TGA	PGA	+/-	GP	G	A	Pts	PIM	PP	SH	GW
1993-94	The Nichols School	Hi-School	28	27	57	99	....	....	....	25	....	....	....	....	....	....	....	....	....	....	....	....	....	....	....	....	....	....
1994-95	Niagara Scenics	EJHL-B	47	54	55	99	....	....	....	70	....	....	....	....	....	....	....	....	....	....	....	....	....	....	....	....	....	....
1995-96	Niagara Scenics	OJHL	47	42	70	112	....	....	....	75	....	....	....	....	....	....	....	....	....	....	....	....	....	....	....	....	....	....
	United States	WJC-A	6	1	1	2	....	....	....	6	....	....	....	....	....	....	....	....	....	....	....	....	....	....	....	....	....	....
1996-97	Boston College	H-East	35	13	23	36	....	....	....	34	....	....	....	....	....	....	....	....	....	....	....	....	....	....	....	....	....	....
	United States	WJC-A	6	1	1	2	....	....	....	4	....	....	....	....	....	....	....	....	....	....	....	....	....	....	....	....	....	....
1997-98	Boston College	H-East	40	11	28	39	....	....	....	42	....	....	....	....	....	....	....	....	....	....	....	....	....	....	....	....	....	....
	United States	WJC-A	7	*6	4	*10	....	....	....	6	....	....	....	....	....	....	....	....	....	....	....	....	....	....	....	....	....	....
1998-99	Boston College	H-East	43	32	25	57	....	....	....	56	....	....	....	....	....	....	....	....	....	....	....	....	....	....	....	....	....	....
99-2000	Boston College	H-East	41	32	26	*58	....	....	....	61	....	....	....	....	....	....	....	....	....	....	....	....	....	....	....	....	....	....
	Toronto Maple Leafs	**NHL**	....	....	....	....	....	....	....	....	....	....	....	....	....	....	....	....	....	....	**3**	**1**	**0**	**1**	**0**	**0**	**0**	**0**
	NHL Totals		....	....	....	....	....	....	....	....	....	....	....	....	....	....	....	....	....	....	**3**	**1**	**0**	**1**	**0**	**0**	**0**	**0**

Hockey East First All-Star Team (2000) • NCAA East First All-American Team (2000) • NCAA Championship All-Tournament Team (2000)

• FARRISH, Dave

David Allan D – L. 6'1", 195 lbs. b: Wingham, Ont., 8/1/1956. NY Rangers' 2nd, 24th overall, in 1976.

Season	Club	League	GP	G	A	Pts	AG	AA	APts	PIM	PP	SH	GW	S	%	TGF	PGF	TGA	PGA	+/-	GP	G	A	Pts	PIM	PP	SH	GW
1973-74	Sudbury Wolves	OMJHL	58	11	20	31	....	....	....	205	....	....	....	....	....	....	....	....	....	....	4	0	0	0	14	....	....	....
1974-75	Sudbury Wolves	OMJHL	60	20	44	64	....	....	....	258	....	....	....	....	....	....	....	....	....	....	14	3	4	7	32	....	....	....
1975-76	Sudbury Wolves	OMJHL	66	26	49	75	....	....	....	155	....	....	....	....	....	....	....	....	....	....	17	3	12	15	22	....	....	....
1976-77	**New York Rangers**	**NHL**	**80**	**2**	**17**	**19**	**2**	**13**	**15**	**102**	**0**	**0**	**0**	**116**	**1.7**	**74**	**0**	**99**	**9**	**-16**	....	....	....	....	....	....	....	....
1977-78	**New York Rangers**	**NHL**	**66**	**3**	**5**	**8**	**3**	**4**	**7**	**62**	**0**	**1**	**0**	**100**	**3.0**	**66**	**1**	**89**	**11**	**-13**	**3**	**0**	**0**	**0**	**0**	**0**	**0**	**0**
	New Haven Nighthawks	AHL	10	0	3	3	....	....	....	4	....	....	....	....	....	....	....	....	....	....	....	....	....	....	....	....	....	....
1978-79	**New York Rangers**	**NHL**	**71**	**1**	**19**	**20**	**1**	**14**	**15**	**61**	**0**	**0**	**1**	**96**	**1.0**	**80**	**2**	**105**	**24**	**-3**	**7**	**0**	**2**	**2**	**14**	**0**	**0**	**0**
1979-80	**Quebec Nordiques**	**NHL**	**4**	**0**	**0**	**0**	**0**	**0**	**0**	**0**	**0**	**0**	**0**	**2**	**0.0**	**0**	**0**	**1**	**1**	**0**	....	....	....	....	....	....	....	....
	Syracuse Firebirds	AHL	14	4	10	14	....	....	....	17	....	....	....	....	....	....	....	....	....	....	....	....	....	....	....	....	....	....
	Toronto Maple Leafs	**NHL**	**20**	**1**	**8**	**9**	**1**	**6**	**7**	**30**	**0**	**0**	**0**	**32**	**3.1**	**29**	**2**	**28**	**6**	**5**	**3**	**0**	**0**	**0**	**10**	**0**	**0**	**0**
	New Brunswick Hawks	AHL	20	3	1	4	....	....	....	22	....	....	....	....	....	....	....	....	....	....	....	....	....	....	....	....	....	....
1980-81	**Toronto Maple Leafs**	**NHL**	**74**	**2**	**18**	**20**	**2**	**12**	**14**	**90**	**1**	**0**	**0**	**110**	**1.8**	**83**	**15**	**85**	**10**	**-7**	**1**	**0**	**0**	**0**	**0**	**0**	**0**	**0**
1981-82	New Brunswick Hawks	AHL	67	13	24	37	....	....	....	80	....	....	....	....	....	....	....	....	....	....	15	4	5	9	20	....	....	....
1982-83	**Toronto Maple Leafs**	**NHL**	**56**	**4**	**24**	**28**	**3**	**17**	**20**	**38**	**3**	**0**	**0**	**91**	**4.4**	**77**	**33**	**59**	**16**	**1**	....	....	....	....	....	....	....	....
	St. Catharines Saints	AHL	14	2	12	14	....	....	....	18	....	....	....	....	....	....	....	....	....	....	....	....	....	....	....	....	....	....
1983-84	**Toronto Maple Leafs**	**NHL**	**59**	**4**	**19**	**23**	**3**	**13**	**16**	**57**	**1**	**0**	**0**	**77**	**5.2**	**63**	**27**	**59**	**10**	**-13**	....	....	....	....	....	....	....	....
	St. Catharines Saints	AHL	4	0	2	2	....	....	....	6	....	....	....	....	....	....	....	....	....	....	7	0	1	1	4	....	....	....
1984-85	St. Catharines Saints	AHL	68	4	12	16	....	....	....	56	....	....	....	....	....	....	....	....	....	....	....	....	....	....	....	....	....	....
1985-86	Hershey Bears	AHL	74	5	17	22	....	....	....	78	....	....	....	....	....	....	....	....	....	....	18	0	4	4	24	....	....	....
1986-87	SC Riessersee	Germany	26	7	10	17	....	....	....	74	....	....	....	....	....	....	....	....	....	....	....	....	....	....	....	....	....	....
	HC Davos	Switz.	10	8	9	17	....	....	....	....	....	....	....	....	....	....	....	....	....	....	7	2	*8	10	....	....	....	....
1987-88	VSV Villach	Austria	33	8	43	51	....	....	....	33	....	....	....	....	....	....	....	....	....	....	....	....	....	....	....	....	....	....
	HC Davos	Switz.	....	....	....	....	....	....	....	....	....	....	....	....	....	....	....	....	....	....	7	1	6	7	....	....	....	....
	New Haven Nighthawks	AHL	30	4	14	18	....	....	....	26	....	....	....	....	....	....	....	....	....	....	....	....	....	....	....	....	....	....
1988-89	Baltimore Skipjacks	AHL	60	2	13	15	....	....	....	62	....	....	....	....	....	....	....	....	....	....	....	....	....	....	....	....	....	....
1989-90	Moncton Hawks	AHL	1	0	0	0	....	....	....	0	....	....	....	....	....	....	....	....	....	....	....	....	....	....	....	....	....	....
1990-1992	Moncton Hawks	AHL	DID NOT PLAY – COACHING																									
1992-1993	**New Jersey Devils**	**NHL**	DID NOT PLAY – ASSISTANT COACH																									
1993-1995	Salt Lake Golden Eagles	IHL	DID NOT PLAY – COACHING																									
1995-1996	Fort Wayne Komets	IHL	DID NOT PLAY – COACHING																									
1997-2000	Springfield Falcons	AHL	DID NOT PLAY – COACHING																									
	NHL Totals		**430**	**17**	**110**	**127**	**15**	**79**	**94**	**440**	**5**	**1**	**1**	**624**	**2.7**	**472**	**80**	**525**	**87**		**14**	**0**	**2**	**2**	**24**	**0**	**0**	**0**

OMJHL First All-Star Team (1976) • AHL First All-Star Team (1982) • Won Eddie Shore Award (Outstanding Defenseman - AHL) (1982)

Claimed by **Quebec** from **NY Rangers** in Expansion Draft, June 13, 1979. Traded to **Toronto** by **Quebec** with Terry Martin for Reg Thomas, December 13, 1979. Signed as a free agent by **Philadelphia**, October 7, 1985.

• FATA, Rico

C – L. 5'11", 197 lbs. b: Sault Ste. Marie, Ont., 2/12/1980. Calgary's 1st, 6th overall, in 1998.

Season	Club	League	GP	G	A	Pts	AG	AA	APts	PIM	PP	SH	GW	S	%	TGF	PGF	TGA	PGA	+/-	GP	G	A	Pts	PIM	PP	SH	GW
1994-95	Sault Ste. Marie Legion	NOHA	STATISTICS NOT AVAILABLE																									
1995-96	Sault Ste. Marie Greyhounds	OHL	62	11	15	26	....	....	....	52	....	....	....	....	....	....	....	....	....	....	4	0	0	0	0	....	....	....
1996-97	London Knights	OHL	59	19	34	53	....	....	....	76	....	....	....	....	....	....	....	....	....	....	....	....	....	....	....	....	....	....
1997-98	London Knights	OHL	64	43	33	76	....	....	....	110	....	....	....	....	....	....	....	....	....	....	16	9	5	14	*49	....	....	....
1998-99	**Calgary Flames**	**NHL**	**20**	**0**	**1**	**1**	**0**	**1**	**1**	**4**	**0**	**0**	**0**	**13**	**0.0**	**3**	**0**	**3**	**0**	**0**	....	....	....	....	....	....	....	....
	London Knights	OHL	23	15	18	33	....	....	....	41	....	....	....	....	....	....	....	....	....	....	25	10	12	22	42	....	....	....
	Canada	WC-A	7	1	3	4	....	....	....	8	....	....	....	....	....	....	....	....	....	....	....	....	....	....	....	....	....	....
99-2000	**Calgary Flames**	**NHL**	**2**	**0**	**0**	**0**	**0**	**0**	**0**	**0**	**0**	**0**	**0**	**0**	**0.0**	**0**	**0**	**1**	**0**	**-1**	....	....	....	....	....	....	....	....
	Saint John Flames	AHL	76	29	29	58	....	....	....	65	....	....	....	....	....	....	....	....	....	....	3	0	0	0	4	....	....	....
	NHL Totals		**22**	**0**	**1**	**1**	**0**	**1**	**1**	**4**	**0**	**0**	**0**	**13**	**0.0**	**3**	**0**	**4**	**0**		....	....	....	....	....	....	....	....

• FAUBERT, Mario

D – R. 6'1", 175 lbs. b: Valleyfield, Que., 12/2/1954. Pittsburgh's 3rd, 62nd overall, in 1974.

Season	Club	League	GP	G	A	Pts	AG	AA	APts	PIM	PP	SH	GW	S	%	TGF	PGF	TGA	PGA	+/-	GP	G	A	Pts	PIM	PP	SH	GW
1971-72	Valleyfield Braves	QJHL	STATISTICS NOT AVAILABLE																									
1972-73	St. Louis University	CCHA	38	3	36	39	....	....	....	68	....	....	....	....	....	....	....	....	....	....	....	....	....	....	....	....	....	....
1973-74	St. Louis University	CCHA	40	8	35	43	....	....	....	62	....	....	....	....	....	....	....	....	....	....	....	....	....	....	....	....	....	....
1974-75	**Pittsburgh Penguins**	**NHL**	**10**	**1**	**0**	**1**	**1**	**0**	**1**	**6**	**1**	**0**	**0**	**13**	**7.7**	**4**	**1**	**5**	**0**	**-2**	....	....	....	....	....	....	....	....
	Hershey Bears	AHL	54	13	21	34	....	....	....	76	....	....	....	....	....	....	....	....	....	....	11	2	7	9	4	....	....	....

Season	Club	League	GP	G	A	Pts	AG	AA	APts	PIM	PP	SH	GW	S	%	TGF	PGF	TGA	PGA	+/–	GP	G	A	Pts	PIM	PP	SH	GW
			REGULAR SEASON																		PLAYOFFS							
1975-76	Pittsburgh Penguins	NHL	21	1	8	9	1	6	7	10	1	0	0	22	4.5	26	5	19	4	6	....	....	....	....	....	....	....	....
	Hershey Bears	AHL	39	7	16	23	....	....	....	37	....	....	....	....	....	....	....	....	....	....	10	4	6	10	14	....	....	....
1976-77	Pittsburgh Penguins	NHL	47	2	11	13	2	8	10	32	0	0	0	67	3.0	35	13	29	3	–4	3	1	0	1	2	1	0	0
	Hershey Bears	AHL	32	8	19	27	....	....	....	42	....	....	....	....	....	....	....	....	....	....	....	....	....	....	....	....	....	....
1977-78	Pittsburgh Penguins	NHL	18	0	6	6	0	5	5	11	0	0	0	26	0.0	24	7	17	2	2	....	....	....	....	....	....	....	....
	Binghamton Dusters	AHL	7	0	3	3	....	....	....	12	....	....	....	....	....	....	....	....	....	....	....	....	....	....	....	....	....	....
1978-79	Binghamton Dusters	AHL	73	7	33	40	....	....	....	50	....	....	....	....	....	....	....	....	....	....	10	3	7	10	6	....	....	....
1979-80	Pittsburgh Penguins	NHL	49	5	13	18	4	9	13	31	4	0	0	83	6.0	49	17	55	4	–19	2	0	1	1	0	0	0	0
1980-81	Pittsburgh Penguins	NHL	72	8	44	52	6	29	35	188	3	0	1	142	5.6	123	50	124	33	–18	5	1	1	2	4	1	0	0
1981-82	Pittsburgh Penguins	NHL	14	4	8	12	3	5	8	14	4	0	2	40	10.0	22	15	11	2	–2	....	....	....	....	....	....	....	....
	NHL Totals		231	21	90	111	17	62	79	292	13	0	3	393	5.3	283	108	260	48		10	2	2	4	6	2	0	0

CCHA Second All-Star Team (1974) • Suffered career-ending leg injury in game vs. St. Louis, November 18, 1981.

• FAUSS, Ted

Theodore William D – L. 6'2", 205 lbs. b: Clark Mills, NY, 6/30/1961.

Season	Club	League	GP	G	A	Pts	AG	AA	APts	PIM	PP	SH	GW	S	%	TGF	PGF	TGA	PGA	+/–	GP	G	A	Pts	PIM	PP	SH	GW
1979-80	Clarkson College	ECAC	34	2	4	6	....	....	....	36	....	....	....	....	....	....	....	....	....	....	....	....	....	....	....	....	....	....
	Ottawa 67's	OHL	....	....	....	....	....	....	....	....	....	....	....	....	....	....	....	....	....	....	1	0	0	0	0	....	....	....
1980-81	Clarkson College	ECAC	37	0	5	5	....	....	....	56	....	....	....	....	....	....	....	....	....	....	....	....	....	....	....	....	....	....
1981-82	Clarkson College	ECAC	35	3	6	9	....	....	....	79	....	....	....	....	....	....	....	....	....	....	....	....	....	....	....	....	....	....
1982-83	Clarkson College	ECAC	25	4	6	10	....	....	....	60	....	....	....	....	....	....	....	....	....	....	....	....	....	....	....	....	....	....
	Nova Scotia Voyageurs	AHL	5	0	1	1	....	....	....	11	....	....	....	....	....	....	....	....	....	....	7	0	1	1	6	....	....	....
1983-84	Nova Scotia Voyageurs	AHL	71	4	11	15	....	....	....	123	....	....	....	....	....	....	....	....	....	....	7	0	2	2	28	....	....	....
1984-85	Sherbrooke Canadiens	AHL	77	1	9	10	....	....	....	62	....	....	....	....	....	....	....	....	....	....	17	2	2	4	27	....	....	....
1985-86			DID NOT PLAY																									
1986-87	Toronto Maple Leafs	NHL	15	0	1	1	0	1	1	11	0	0	0	4	0.0	17	0	13	0	4	....	....	....	....	....	....	....	....
	Newmarket Saints	AHL	59	0	5	5	....	....	....	81	....	....	....	....	....	....	....	....	....	....	....	....	....	....	....	....	....	....
1987-88	Toronto Maple Leafs	NHL	13	0	1	1	0	1	1	4	0	0	0	2	0.0	10	0	7	3	6	....	....	....	....	....	....	....	....
	Newmarket Saints	AHL	49	0	11	11	....	....	....	86	....	....	....	....	....	....	....	....	....	....	....	....	....	....	....	....	....	....
1988-89	Binghamton Whalers	AHL	53	4	11	15	....	....	....	66	....	....	....	....	....	....	....	....	....	....	....	....	....	....	....	....	....	....
1989-1993			DID NOT PLAY																									
1993-94	Utica Bulldogs	ColHL	20	3	4	7	....	....	....	48	....	....	....	....	....	....	....	....	....	....	....	....	....	....	....	....	....	....
1994-95	Utica Bulldogs	ColHL	5	1	1	2	....	....	....	8	....	....	....	....	....	....	....	....	....	....	....	....	....	....	....	....	....	....
	NHL Totals		28	0	2	2	0	2	2	15	0	0	0	6	0.0	27	0	20	3		....	....	....	....	....	....	....	....

Signed as a free agent by **Montreal**, March, 1983. • Sat out entire 1985-86 season and returned to university. Signed as a free agent by **Toronto**, July 21, 1986.

• FAUST, Andre

C – L. 5'11", 191 lbs. b: Joliette, Que., 10/7/1969. New Jersey's 8th, 173rd overall, in 1989.

Season	Club	League	GP	G	A	Pts	AG	AA	APts	PIM	PP	SH	GW	S	%	TGF	PGF	TGA	PGA	+/–	GP	G	A	Pts	PIM	PP	SH	GW
1984-85	Anjou Majors	QAAA	36	34	34	68	....	....	....	14	....	....	....	....	....	....	....	....	....	....	....	....	....	....	....	....	....	....
1985-86	Anjou Majors	QAAA	39	39	41	80	....	....	....	26	....	....	....	....	....	....	....	....	....	....	....	....	....	....	....	....	....	....
1986-87	Upper Canada College	Hi-School	32	40	38	78	....	....	....	20	....	....	....	....	....	....	....	....	....	....	....	....	....	....	....	....	....	....
1987-88	Upper Canada College	Hi-School	45	66	59	125	....	....	....	30	....	....	....	....	....	....	....	....	....	....	....	....	....	....	....	....	....	....
1988-89	Princeton University	ECAC	27	15	24	39	....	....	....	28	....	....	....	....	....	....	....	....	....	....	....	....	....	....	....	....	....	....
1989-90	Princeton University	ECAC	22	9	28	37	....	....	....	20	....	....	....	....	....	....	....	....	....	....	....	....	....	....	....	....	....	....
1990-91	Princeton University	ECAC	26	15	22	37	....	....	....	51	....	....	....	....	....	....	....	....	....	....	....	....	....	....	....	....	....	....
1991-92	Princeton University	ECAC	27	14	21	35	....	....	....	38	....	....	....	....	....	....	....	....	....	....	....	....	....	....	....	....	....	....
1992-93	Philadelphia Flyers	NHL	10	2	2	4	2	1	3	4	0	0	0	11	18.2	5	0	0	0	5	....	....	....	....	....	....	....	....
	Hershey Bears	AHL	62	26	25	51	....	....	....	71	....	....	....	....	....	....	....	....	....	....	....	....	....	....	....	....	....	....
1993-94	Philadelphia Flyers	NHL	37	8	5	13	7	4	11	10	0	0	1	33	24.2	16	1	16	0	–1	....	....	....	....	....	....	....	....
	Hershey Bears	AHL	13	6	7	13	....	....	....	10	....	....	....	....	....	....	....	....	....	....	10	4	3	7	26	....	....	....
1994-95	Hershey Bears	AHL	55	12	28	40	....	....	....	72	....	....	....	....	....	....	....	....	....	....	6	1	5	6	12	....	....	....
1995-96	Springfield Falcons	AHL	50	19	19	38	....	....	....	40	....	....	....	....	....	....	....	....	....	....	10	5	2	7	6	....	....	....
1996-97	Augsburger Panther	Germany	46	21	19	40	....	....	....	84	....	....	....	....	....	....	....	....	....	....	4	3	1	4	2	....	....	....
1997-98	Augsburger Panther	Germany	41	13	20	33	....	....	....	87	....	....	....	....	....	....	....	....	....	....	....	....	....	....	....	....	....	....
1998-99	Augsburger Panther	Germany	47	19	18	37	....	....	....	92	....	....	....	....	....	....	....	....	....	....	5	1	2	3	6	....	....	....
99-2000	Augsburger Panther	Germany	50	11	20	31	....	....	....	50	....	....	....	....	....	....	....	....	....	....	3	0	0	0	16	....	....	....
	NHL Totals		47	10	7	17	9	5	14	14	0	0	1	44	22.7	21	1	16	0		....	....	....	....	....	....	....	....

ECAC Second All-Star Team (1990, 1992)

Signed as a free agent by **Philadelphia**, October 5, 1992. Traded to **Winnipeg** by **Philadelphia** for Winnipeg's 7th round choice (later traded to Carolina — Carolina selected Andrew Merrick) in 1997 Entry Draft, September 20, 1995.

• FEAMSTER, Dave

David Allan D – L. 5'11", 180 lbs. b: Detroit, MI, 9/10/1958. Chicago's 6th, 96th overall, in 1978.

Season	Club	League	GP	G	A	Pts	AG	AA	APts	PIM	PP	SH	GW	S	%	TGF	PGF	TGA	PGA	+/–	GP	G	A	Pts	PIM	PP	SH	GW
1975-76	Detroit Jr. Wings	GLJHL	41	19	22	41	....	....	....	....	....	....	....	....	....	....	....	....	....	....	....	....	....	....	....	....	....	....
1976-77	Colorado College	CCHA	37	9	28	37	....	....	....	96	....	....	....	....	....	....	....	....	....	....	....	....	....	....	....	....	....	....
1977-78	Colorado College	CCHA	39	8	33	41	....	....	....	90	....	....	....	....	....	....	....	....	....	....	....	....	....	....	....	....	....	....
	United States	WJC-A	6	0	5	5	....	....	....	8	....	....	....	....	....	....	....	....	....	....	....	....	....	....	....	....	....	....
1978-79	Colorado College	CCHA	37	11	45	56	....	....	....	98	....	....	....	....	....	....	....	....	....	....	....	....	....	....	....	....	....	....
1979-80	Colorado College	CCHA	37	17	33	50	....	....	....	135	....	....	....	....	....	....	....	....	....	....	....	....	....	....	....	....	....	....
1980-81	Dallas Black Hawks	CHL	77	12	33	45	....	....	....	117	....	....	....	....	....	....	....	....	....	....	6	2	3	5	23	....	....	....
1981-82	Chicago Black Hawks	NHL	29	0	2	2	0	1	1	29	0	0	0	24	0.0	25	0	41	10	–6	15	2	4	6	53	0	0	1
	New Brunswick Hawks	AHL	42	6	30	36	....	....	....	69	....	....	....	....	....	....	....	....	....	....	....	....	....	....	....	....	....	....
1982-83	Chicago Black Hawks	NHL	78	6	12	18	5	8	13	69	0	0	0	68	8.8	66	1	61	11	15	13	1	0	1	4	0	0	0
1983-84	Chicago Black Hawks	NHL	46	6	7	13	5	5	10	42	0	0	0	44	13.6	33	0	48	7	–8	5	0	1	1	4	0	0	0
1984-85	Chicago Black Hawks	NHL	16	1	3	4	1	2	3	14	0	0	0	10	10.0	14	0	10	1	5	....	....	....	....	....	....	....	....
	NHL Totals		169	13	24	37	11	16	27	154	0	0	0	146	8.9	138	1	160	29		33	3	5	8	61	0	0	1

WCHA First All-Star Team (1980) • NCAA West First All-American Team (1980)

• FEATHERSTONE, Glen

D – L. 6'4", 209 lbs. b: Toronto, Ont., 7/8/1968. St. Louis' 4th, 73rd overall, in 1986.

Season	Club	League	GP	G	A	Pts	AG	AA	APts	PIM	PP	SH	GW	S	%	TGF	PGF	TGA	PGA	+/–	GP	G	A	Pts	PIM	PP	SH	GW
1984-85	Toronto Young Nationals	MTHL	45	7	24	31	....	....	....	94	....	....	....	....	....	....	....	....	....	....	....	....	....	....	....	....	....	....
	North York Red Wings	OJHL	2	0	0	0	....	....	....	4	....	....	....	....	....	....	....	....	....	....	....	....	....	....	....	....	....	....
1985-86	Windsor Spitfires	OHL	49	0	6	6	....	....	....	135	....	....	....	....	....	....	....	....	....	....	14	1	1	2	23	....	....	....
1986-87	Windsor Spitfires	OHL	47	6	11	17	....	....	....	154	....	....	....	....	....	....	....	....	....	....	14	2	6	8	19	....	....	....
1987-88	Windsor Spitfires	OHL	53	7	27	34	....	....	....	201	....	....	....	....	....	....	....	....	....	....	12	6	9	15	47	....	....	....
	Windsor Spitfires	Mem-Cup	4	0	0	0	....	....	....	18	....	....	....	....	....	....	....	....	....	....	....	....	....	....	....	....	....	....
1988-89	St. Louis Blues	NHL	18	0	2	2	0	1	1	22	0	0	0	9	0.0	13	0	21	5	–3	6	0	0	0	25	0	0	0
	Peoria Rivermen	IHL	37	5	19	24	....	....	....	97	....	....	....	....	....	....	....	....	....	....	....	....	....	....	....	....	....	....
1989-90	St. Louis Blues	NHL	58	0	12	12	0	9	9	145	0	0	0	34	0.0	46	4	54	11	–1	12	0	2	2	47	0	0	0
	Peoria Rivermen	IHL	15	1	4	5	....	....	....	43	....	....	....	....	....	....	....	....	....	....	....	....	....	....	....	....	....	....
1990-91	St. Louis Blues	NHL	68	5	15	20	5	11	16	204	1	0	1	59	8.5	61	4	41	3	19	9	0	0	0	31	0	0	0
1991-92	Boston Bruins	NHL	7	1	0	1	1	0	1	20	0	0	0	8	12.5	5	1	8	2	–2	....	....	....	....	....	....	....	....
1992-93	Boston Bruins	NHL	34	5	5	10	4	3	7	102	1	0	0	33	15.2	32	2	27	3	6	....	....	....	....	....	....	....	....
	Providence Bruins	AHL	8	3	4	7	....	....	....	60	....	....	....	....	....	....	....	....	....	....	....	....	....	....	....	....	....	....
1993-94	Boston Bruins	NHL	58	1	8	9	1	6	7	152	0	0	1	55	1.8	31	1	41	6	–5	1	0	0	0	0	0	0	0
1994-95	New York Rangers	NHL	6	1	0	1	2	0	2	18	0	0	0	6	16.7	4	0	4	0	0	....	....	....	....	....	....	....	....
	Hartford Whalers	NHL	13	1	1	2	2	1	3	32	0	0	0	16	6.3	4	0	11	0	–7	....	....	....	....	....	....	....	....
1995-96	Hartford Whalers	NHL	68	2	10	12	2	8	10	138	0	0	1	62	3.2	54	2	63	21	10	....	....	....	....	....	....	....	....
1996-97	Hartford Whalers	NHL	41	2	5	7	2	4	6	87	0	0	0	40	5.0	38	6	42	10	0	....	....	....	....	....	....	....	....
	Calgary Flames	NHL	13	1	3	4	1	3	4	19	0	0	0	27	3.7	14	4	11	0	–1	....	....	....	....	....	....	....	....

Season	Club	League	GP	G	A	Pts	AG	AA	APts	PIM	PP	SH	GW	S	%	TGF	PGF	TGA	PGA	+/–	GP	G	A	Pts	PIM	PP	SH	GW
			REGULAR SEASON																		PLAYOFFS							
1997-98	Indianapolis Ice	IHL	73	10	28	38				187											5	0	3	3	16			
1998-99	Chicago Wolves	IHL	62	5	21	26				191											10	0	3	3	26			
99-2000	Chicago Wolves	IHL	62	7	12	19				109											16	3	5	8	38			
	NHL Totals		**384**	**19**	**61**	**80**	**20**	**46**	**66**	**939**	**2**	**0**	**3**	**349**	**5.4**	**302**	**24**	**323**	**61**		**28**	**0**	**2**	**2**	**103**	**0**	**0**	**0**

Signed as a free agent by **Boston**, July 25, 1991. Traded to **NY Rangers** by **Boston** for Daniel Lacroix, August 19, 1994. Traded to **Hartford** by **NY Rangers** with Michael Stewart, NY Rangers' 1st round choice (Jean-Sebastien Giguere) in 1995 Entry Draft and 4th round choice (Steve Wasylko) in 1996 Entry Draft for Pat Verbeek, March 23, 1995. Traded to **Calgary** by **Hartford** with Hnat Domenichelli, New Jersey's 2nd round choice (previously acquired, Calgary selected Dimitri Kokorev) in 1997 Entry Draft and Vancouver's 3rd round choice (previously acquired, Calgary selected Paul Manning) in 1998 Entry Draft for Steve Chiasson and Colorado's 3rd round choice (previously acquired, Carolina selected Francis Lessard) in 1997 Entry Draft, March 5, 1997. Signed as a free agent by **Chicago** (IHL), September 8, 1998.

• FEATHERSTONE, Tony

Anthony James RW – R. 5'11", 187 lbs. b: Toronto, Ont., 7/31/1949. Oakland's 1st, 7th overall, in 1969.

Season	Club	League	GP	G	A	Pts	AG	AA	APts	PIM	PP	SH	GW	S	%	TGF	PGF	TGA	PGA	+/–	GP	G	A	Pts	PIM	PP	SH	GW
1967-68	Peterborough Petes	OHA-Jr.	43	11	11	22				109											5	3	0	3	28			
1968-69	Peterborough Petes	OHA-Jr.	54	29	38	67				167											10	3	5	8	56			
1969-70	**Oakland Seals**	**NHL**	**9**	**0**	**1**	**1**	**0**	**1**	**1**	**17**	**0**	**0**	**0**	**13**	**0.0**	**1**	**0**	**8**	**0**	**–7**	**2**	**0**	**0**	**0**	**0**	**0**	**0**	**0**
	Providence Reds	AHL	55	15	25	40				78																		
1970-71	**California Golden Seals**	**NHL**	**67**	**8**	**8**	**16**	**8**	**7**	**15**	**44**	**1**	**0**	**1**	**90**	**8.9**	**38**	**4**	**39**	**1**	**–4**								
1971-72	Nova Scotia Voyageurs	AHL	56	5	10	15				50											15	5	4	9	36			
1972-73	Nova Scotia Voyageurs	AHL	74	49	54	103				78											13	*10	13	23	34			
1973-74	**Minnesota North Stars**	**NHL**	**54**	**9**	**12**	**21**	**9**	**10**	**19**	**4**	**0**	**2**	**0**	**92**	**9.8**	**30**	**2**	**53**	**16**	**–9**								
1974-75	Toronto Toros	WHA	76	25	38	63				26											6	2	1	3	25			
1975-76	Toronto Toros	WHA	32	4	7	11				5																		
	NHL Totals		**130**	**17**	**21**	**38**	**17**	**18**	**35**	**65**	**1**	**2**	**1**	**195**	**8.7**	**69**	**6**	**100**	**17**		**2**	**0**	**0**	**0**	**0**	**0**	**0**	**0**
	Other Major League Totals		108	29	45	74				31											6	2	1	3	25			

AHL First All-Star Team (1973)

Traded to **Montreal** by **California** for Ray Martyniuk, October 6, 1971. Traded to **Minnesota** by **Montreal** with Murray Anderson for future considerations, May 29, 1973. Selected by **Toronto** (WHA) in WHA Professional Player Draft, June, 1973.

• FEDERKO, Bernie

Bernard Allan C – L. 6', 178 lbs. b: Foam Lake, Sask., 5/12/1956. St. Louis' 1st, 7th overall, in 1976.

Season	Club	League	GP	G	A	Pts	AG	AA	APts	PIM	PP	SH	GW	S	%	TGF	PGF	TGA	PGA	+/–	GP	G	A	Pts	PIM	PP	SH	GW
1972-73	Foam Lake Flyers	SAHA	STATISTICS NOT AVAILABLE																									
1973-74	Saskatoon Blades	WHL	68	22	28	50				19											6	0	0	0	2			
1974-75	Saskatoon Blades	WHL	66	39	68	107				30											17	*15	7	22	8			
1975-76	Saskatoon Blades	WHL	72	72	*115	*187				108											20	18	*27	*45	8			
1976-77	**St. Louis Blues**	**NHL**	**31**	**14**	**9**	**23**	**13**	**7**	**20**	**15**	**6**	**0**	**3**	**67**	**20.9**	**30**	**11**	**25**	**0**	**–6**	**4**	**1**	**1**	**2**	**2**	**0**	**0**	**0**
	Kansas City Blues	CHL	42	30	39	69				41																		
1977-78	**St. Louis Blues**	**NHL**	**72**	**17**	**24**	**41**	**15**	**19**	**34**	**27**	**4**	**0**	**1**	**128**	**13.3**	**56**	**20**	**71**	**0**	**–35**								
1978-79	**St. Louis Blues**	**NHL**	**74**	**31**	**64**	**95**	**27**	**47**	**74**	**14**	**7**	**0**	**1**	**156**	**19.9**	**118**	**40**	**94**	**1**	**–15**								
1979-80	**St. Louis Blues**	**NHL**	**79**	**38**	**56**	**94**	**32**	**41**	**73**	**24**	**7**	**0**	**4**	**184**	**20.7**	**127**	**45**	**79**	**0**	**3**	**3**	**1**	**0**	**1**	**2**	**0**	**0**	**0**
1980-81	**St. Louis Blues**	**NHL**	**78**	**31**	**73**	**104**	**24**	**49**	**73**	**47**	**9**	**2**	**4**	**170**	**18.2**	**129**	**52**	**69**	**1**	**9**	**11**	**8**	**10**	**18**	**2**	**4**	**0**	**1**
1981-82	**St. Louis Blues**	**NHL**	**74**	**30**	**62**	**92**	**24**	**41**	**65**	**70**	**11**	**0**	**6**	**177**	**16.9**	**119**	**44**	**87**	**2**	**–10**	**10**	**3**	**15**	**18**	**10**	**1**	**0**	**1**
1982-83	**St. Louis Blues**	**NHL**	**75**	**24**	**60**	**84**	**20**	**42**	**62**	**24**	**9**	**0**	**1**	**184**	**13.0**	**113**	**45**	**78**	**0**	**–10**	**4**	**2**	**3**	**5**	**0**	**1**	**0**	**0**
1983-84	**St. Louis Blues**	**NHL**	**79**	**41**	**66**	**107**	**33**	**45**	**78**	**43**	**14**	**0**	**4**	**197**	**20.8**	**138**	**58**	**83**	**0**	**–3**	**11**	**4**	**4**	**8**	**10**	**1**	**0**	**1**
1984-85	**St. Louis Blues**	**NHL**	**76**	**30**	**73**	**103**	**24**	**50**	**74**	**27**	**6**	**0**	**3**	**174**	**17.2**	**124**	**45**	**90**	**1**	**–10**	**3**	**0**	**2**	**2**	**4**	**0**	**0**	**0**
1985-86	**St. Louis Blues**	**NHL**	**80**	**34**	**68**	**102**	**27**	**46**	**73**	**34**	**16**	**0**	**2**	**167**	**20.4**	**139**	**56**	**74**	**1**	**10**	**19**	**7**	**14**	***21**	**17**	**1**	**0**	**1**
1986-87	**St. Louis Blues**	**NHL**	**64**	**20**	**52**	**72**	**17**	**38**	**55**	**32**	**9**	**0**	**3**	**130**	**15.4**	**97**	**48**	**74**	**0**	**–25**	**6**	**3**	**3**	**6**	**18**	**1**	**0**	**0**
1987-88	**St. Louis Blues**	**NHL**	**79**	**20**	**69**	**89**	**17**	**50**	**67**	**52**	**9**	**0**	**2**	**119**	**16.8**	**123**	**55**	**82**	**2**	**–12**	**10**	**2**	**6**	**8**	**18**	**2**	**0**	**0**
1988-89	**St. Louis Blues**	**NHL**	**66**	**22**	**45**	**67**	**19**	**32**	**51**	**54**	**9**	**0**	**6**	**115**	**19.1**	**96**	**46**	**70**	**0**	**–20**	**10**	**4**	**8**	**12**	**0**	**2**	**0**	**0**
1989-90	**Detroit Red Wings**	**NHL**	**73**	**17**	**40**	**57**	**15**	**29**	**44**	**24**	**3**	**0**	**0**	**108**	**15.7**	**77**	**34**	**54**	**3**	**–8**								
	NHL Totals		**1000**	**369**	**761**	**1130**	**307**	**536**	**843**	**487**	**119**	**2**	**40**	**2076**	**17.8**	**1486**	**599**	**1030**	**11**		**91**	**35**	**66**	**101**	**83**	**13**	**0**	**4**

WHL All-Star Team (1976) • CHL Second All-Star Team (1977) • Won Ken McKenzie Trophy (CHL's Rookie of the Year) (1977) • Played in NHL All-Star Game (1980, 1981)

Traded to **Detroit** by **St. Louis** with Tony McKegney for Adam Oates and Paul MacLean, June 15, 1989. • First player in NHL history to record at least 50 assists in 10 consecutive seasons (1979–1988)

• FEDOROV, Sergei

Sergei V. "FedEx" C – L. 6'1", 200 lbs. b: Pskov, USSR, 12/13/1969. Detroit's 4th, 74th overall, in 1989.

Season	Club	League	GP	G	A	Pts	AG	AA	APts	PIM	PP	SH	GW	S	%	TGF	PGF	TGA	PGA	+/–	GP	G	A	Pts	PIM	PP	SH	GW
1985-86	Dynamo Minsk	USSR	15	6	1	7				10																		
1986-87	CSKA Moscow	USSR	29	6	6	12				12																		
1987-88	CSKA Moscow	USSR	48	7	9	16				20																		
	Soviet Union	WJC-A	7	5	7	12				0																		
1988-89	CSKA Moscow	USSR	44	9	8	17				35																		
	Soviet Union	WJC-A	7	4	8	12				4																		
	Soviet Union	WEC-A	10	6	3	9				10																		
1989-90	CSKA Moscow	Fr-Tour	1	0	0	0				2																		
	CSKA Moscow	USSR	48	19	10	29				22																		
	CSKA Moscow	Super-S	5	2	2	4				11																		
	Soviet Union	WEC-A	10	4	2	6				10																		
1990-91	**Detroit Red Wings**	**NHL**	**77**	**31**	**48**	**79**	**28**	**37**	**65**	**66**	**11**	**3**	**5**	**259**	**12.0**	**100**	**35**	**73**	**19**	**11**	**7**	**1**	**5**	**6**	**4**	**0**	**0**	**1**
1991-92	Soviet Union	Can-Cup	5	2	2	4				6																		
	Detroit Red Wings	**NHL**	**80**	**32**	**54**	**86**	**29**	**41**	**70**	**72**	**7**	**2**	**5**	**249**	**12.9**	**123**	**42**	**75**	**20**	**26**	**11**	**5**	**5**	**10**	**8**	**1**	**2**	**1**
1992-93	**Detroit Red Wings**	**NHL**	**73**	**34**	**53**	**87**	**28**	**37**	**65**	**72**	**13**	**4**	**3**	**217**	**15.7**	**124**	**52**	**62**	**23**	**33**	**7**	**3**	**6**	**9**	**23**	**1**	**1**	**0**
1993-94	**Detroit Red Wings**	**NHL**	**82**	**56**	**64**	**120**	**52**	**50**	**102**	**34**	**13**	**4**	**10**	**337**	**16.6**	**170**	**51**	**99**	**28**	**48**	**7**	**1**	**7**	**8**	**6**	**0**	**0**	**0**
1994-95	**Detroit Red Wings**	**NHL**	**42**	**20**	**30**	**50**	**35**	**44**	**79**	**24**	**7**	**3**	**5**	**147**	**13.6**	**60**	**24**	**33**	**3**	**6**	**17**	**7**	***17**	***24**	**6**	**3**	**0**	**0**
1995-96	**Detroit Red Wings**	**NHL**	**78**	**39**	**68**	**107**	**38**	**56**	**94**	**48**	**11**	**3**	**11**	**306**	**12.7**	**143**	**56**	**56**	**18**	**49**	**19**	**2**	***18**	**20**	**10**	**0**	**0**	**2**
1996-97	Russia	W-Cup	5	3	3	6				2																		
♦	**Detroit Red Wings**	**NHL**	**74**	**30**	**33**	**63**	**32**	**29**	**61**	**30**	**9**	**2**	**4**	**273**	**11.0**	**94**	**26**	**51**	**12**	**29**	**20**	**8**	**12**	**20**	**12**	**3**	**0**	**4**
1997-98♦	**Detroit Red Wings**	**NHL**	**21**	**6**	**11**	**17**	**7**	**11**	**18**	**25**	**2**	**0**	**2**	**68**	**8.8**	**30**	**12**	**14**	**6**	**10**	**22**	***10**	**10**	**20**	**12**	**2**	**1**	**1**
	Russia	Olympics	6	1	5	6				8																		
1998-99	**Detroit Red Wings**	**NHL**	**77**	**26**	**37**	**63**	**31**	**36**	**67**	**66**	**6**	**2**	**3**	**224**	**11.6**	**84**	**34**	**56**	**15**	**9**	**10**	**1**	**8**	**9**	**8**	**0**	**0**	**0**
99-2000	**Detroit Red Wings**	**NHL**	**68**	**27**	**35**	**62**	**30**	**32**	**62**	**22**	**4**	**4**	**7**	**263**	**10.3**	**90**	**33**	**60**	**11**	**8**	**9**	**4**	**4**	**8**	**4**	**2**	**0**	**1**
	NHL Totals		**672**	**301**	**433**	**734**	**310**	**373**	**683**	**459**	**83**	**27**	**55**	**2343**	**12.8**	**1018**	**365**	**579**	**155**		**129**	**42**	**92**	**134**	**93**	**12**	**4**	**10**

NHL All-Rookie Team (1991) • NHL First All-Star Team (1994) • Won Frank J. Selke Trophy (1994, 1996) • Won Lester B. Pearson Award (1994) • Won Hart Trophy (1994) • Played in NHL All-Star Game (1992, 1994, 1996)

• FEDOTOV, Anatoli

D – L. 5'11", 178 lbs. b: Saratov, USSR, 5/11/1966. Anaheim's 10th, 238th overall, in 1993.

Season	Club	League	GP	G	A	Pts	AG	AA	APts	PIM	PP	SH	GW	S	%	TGF	PGF	TGA	PGA	+/–	GP	G	A	Pts	PIM	PP	SH	GW
1982-83	Kristall Saratov	USSR-Jr.	STATISTICS NOT AVAILABLE																									
	Soviet Union	EJC-A	5	1	0	1				16																		
1983-84	Kristall Saratov	USSR-Jr.	STATISTICS NOT AVAILABLE																									
	Soviet Union	EJC-A	5	0	0	0				6																		
1984-85	Kristall Saratov	USSR-2	STATISTICS NOT AVAILABLE																									
	Soviet Union	WJC-A	6	0	2	2				2																		
1985-86	Dynamo Moscow	USSR	35	0	2	2				10																		
	Soviet Union	WJC-A	7	1	5	6				0																		
1986-87	Dynamo Moscow	USSR	18	3	2	5				12																		
1987-88	Soviet Union	Can-Cup	8	0	1	1				4																		
	Dynamo Moscow	USSR	48	2	3	5				38																		
1988-89	Dynamo Moscow	USSR	40	2	1	3				24																		
1989-90	Dynamo Moscow	Fr-Tour	1	0	0	0				4																		
	Dynamo Moscow	USSR	41	2	4	6				22																		
	Dynamo Moscow	Super-S	3	0	1	1				4																		
1990-91			DID NOT PLAY																									

Season	Club	League	GP	G	A	Pts	AG	AA	APts	PIM	PP	SH	GW	S	%	TGF	PGF	TGA	PGA	+/–	GP	G	A	Pts	PIM	PP	SH	GW
			REGULAR SEASON																		PLAYOFFS							
1991-92	Dynamo Moscow	CIS	5	0	0	0	....	....	....	4	....	....	....	....	....	....	....	....	....	....	6	1	0	1	4	....	....	....
1992-93	**Winnipeg Jets**	**NHL**	**1**	**0**	**2**	**2**	**0**	**1**	**1**	**0**	**0**	**0**	**0**	**1**	**0.0**	**4**	**2**	**1**	**0**	**1**	....	....	....	....	....	....	....	....
	Moncton Hawks	AHL	76	10	37	47	....	....	....	99	....	....	....	....	....	....	....	....	....	....	2	0	0	0	0	....	....	....
1993-94	**Mighty Ducks of Anaheim**	**NHL**	**3**	**0**	**0**	**0**	**0**	**0**	**0**	**0**	**0**	**0**	**0**	**1**	**0.0**	**1**	**1**	**1**	**0**	**–1**	....	....	....	....	....	....	....	....
	San Diego Gulls	IHL	66	14	12	26	....	....	....	42	....	....	....	....	....	....	....	....	....	....	8	0	1	1	6	....	....	....
1994-95	San Diego Gulls	IHL	53	5	12	17	....	....	....	16	....	....	....	....	....	....	....	....	....	....	....	....	....	....	....	....	....	....
1995-96	Oiji Seishi-Tokyo	Japan	32	20	17	37	....	....	....	....	....	....	....	....	....	....	....	....	....	....	....	....	....	....	....	....	....	....
1996-97	Tappara Tampere	Finland	44	9	9	18	....	....	....	62	....	....	....	....	....	....	....	....	....	....	3	0	0	0	4	....	....	....
	Russia	WC-A	9	2	2	4	....	....	....	10	....	....	....	....	....	....	....	....	....	....	....	....	....	....	....	....	....	....
1997-98	HV-71 Jonkoping	Sweden	24	0	1	1	....	....	....	44	....	....	....	....	....	....	....	....	....	....	4	0	0	0	4	....	....	....
1998-99	Oiji Seishi-Tokyo	Japan	38	7	23	30	....	....	....	76	....	....	....	....	....	....	....	....	....	....	6	0	6	6	....	....	....	....
99-2000	Oiji Seishi-Tokyo	Japan	17	2	6	8	....	....	....	....	....	....	....	....	....	....	....	....	....	....	3	0	0	0	2	....	....	....
	NHL Totals		**4**	**0**	**2**	**2**	**0**	**1**	**1**	**0**	**0**	**0**	**0**	**2**	**0.0**	**5**	**3**	**2**	**0**		....	....	....	....	....	....	....	....

Signed as a free agent by **Winnipeg** to AHL contract, July 4, 1991. • NHL ruled that **Winnipeg** had promoted Fedotov illegally and had no claim to his NHL rights. Fedotov entered NHL Entry Draft and was selected by Anaheim, June 26, 1993.

• FEDYK, Brent

LW – R. 6', 194 lbs. b: Yorkton, Sask., 3/8/1967. Detroit's 1st, 8th overall, in 1985.

Season	Club	League	GP	G	A	Pts	AG	AA	APts	PIM	PP	SH	GW	S	%	TGF	PGF	TGA	PGA	+/–	GP	G	A	Pts	PIM	PP	SH	GW
1982-83	Regina Pat Canadians	SAHA	70	78	65	143	....	....	....	20	....	....	....	....	....	....	....	....	....	....	....	....	....	....	....	....	....	....
	Regina Pats	WHL	1	0	0	0	....	....	....	0	....	....	....	....	....	....	....	....	....	....	....	....	....	....	....	....	....	....
1983-84	Regina Pats	WHL	63	15	28	43	....	....	....	30	....	....	....	....	....	....	....	....	....	....	23	8	7	15	6	....	....	....
1984-85	Regina Pats	WHL	66	35	35	70	....	....	....	48	....	....	....	....	....	....	....	....	....	....	8	5	4	9	0	....	....	....
1985-86	Regina Pats	WHL	50	43	34	77	....	....	....	47	....	....	....	....	....	....	....	....	....	....	5	0	1	1	0	....	....	....
1986-87	Regina Pats	WHL	12	9	6	15	....	....	....	9	....	....	....	....	....	....	....	....	....	....	....	....	....	....	....	....	....	....
	Seattle Thunderbirds	WHL	13	5	11	16	....	....	....	9	....	....	....	....	....	....	....	....	....	....	....	....	....	....	....	....	....	....
	Portland Winter Hawks	WHL	11	5	4	9	....	....	....	6	....	....	....	....	....	....	....	....	....	....	14	5	6	11	0	....	....	....
1987-88	**Detroit Red Wings**	**NHL**	**2**	**0**	**1**	**1**	**0**	**1**	**1**	**2**	**0**	**0**	**0**	**2**	**0.0**	**1**	**0**	**2**	**0**	**–1**	....	....	....	....	....	....	....	....
	Adirondack Red Wings	AHL	34	9	11	20	....	....	....	22	....	....	....	....	....	....	....	....	....	....	5	0	2	2	6	....	....	....
1988-89	**Detroit Red Wings**	**NHL**	**5**	**2**	**0**	**2**	**2**	**0**	**2**	**0**	**1**	**0**	**0**	**6**	**33.3**	**3**	**1**	**3**	**0**	**–1**	....	....	....	....	....	....	....	....
	Adirondack Red Wings	AHL	66	40	28	68	....	....	....	33	....	....	....	....	....	....	....	....	....	....	15	7	8	15	23	....	....	....
1989-90	**Detroit Red Wings**	**NHL**	**27**	**1**	**4**	**5**	**1**	**3**	**4**	**6**	**0**	**0**	**0**	**28**	**3.6**	**11**	**1**	**13**	**2**	**–1**	....	....	....	....	....	....	....	....
	Adirondack Red Wings	AHL	33	14	15	29	....	....	....	24	....	....	....	....	....	....	....	....	....	....	6	2	1	3	4	....	....	....
1990-91	**Detroit Red Wings**	**NHL**	**67**	**16**	**19**	**35**	**15**	**14**	**29**	**38**	**0**	**0**	**1**	**74**	**21.6**	**45**	**0**	**40**	**15**	**20**	**6**	**1**	**0**	**1**	**2**	**0**	**0**	**1**
1991-92	**Detroit Red Wings**	**NHL**	**61**	**5**	**8**	**13**	**5**	**6**	**11**	**42**	**0**	**0**	**1**	**60**	**8.3**	**20**	**0**	**35**	**10**	**–5**	**1**	**0**	**0**	**0**	**2**	**0**	**0**	**0**
	Adirondack Red Wings	AHL	1	0	2	2	....	....	....	0	....	....	....	....	....	....	....	....	....	....	....	....	....	....	....	....	....	....
1992-93	**Philadelphia Flyers**	**NHL**	**74**	**21**	**38**	**59**	**17**	**26**	**43**	**48**	**4**	**1**	**2**	**167**	**12.6**	**95**	**24**	**73**	**16**	**14**	....	....	....	....	....	....	....	....
1993-94	**Philadelphia Flyers**	**NHL**	**72**	**20**	**18**	**38**	**19**	**14**	**33**	**74**	**5**	**0**	**1**	**104**	**19.2**	**52**	**11**	**65**	**10**	**–14**	....	....	....	....	....	....	....	....
1994-95	**Philadelphia Flyers**	**NHL**	**30**	**8**	**4**	**12**	**14**	**6**	**20**	**14**	**3**	**0**	**2**	**41**	**19.5**	**23**	**12**	**16**	**3**	**–2**	**9**	**2**	**2**	**4**	**8**	**0**	**0**	**0**
1995-96	**Philadelphia Flyers**	**NHL**	**24**	**10**	**5**	**15**	**10**	**4**	**14**	**24**	**4**	**0**	**0**	**42**	**23.8**	**19**	**4**	**15**	**1**	**1**	....	....	....	....	....	....	....	....
	Dallas Stars	**NHL**	**41**	**10**	**9**	**19**	**10**	**7**	**17**	**30**	**4**	**0**	**0**	**71**	**14.1**	**28**	**12**	**41**	**8**	**–17**	....	....	....	....	....	....	....	....
1996-97	Michigan K-Wings	IHL	9	1	2	3	....	....	....	4	....	....	....	....	....	....	....	....	....	....	....	....	....	....	....	....	....	....
1997-98	Detroit Vipers	IHL	40	18	23	41	....	....	....	24	....	....	....	....	....	....	....	....	....	....	....	....	....	....	....	....	....	....
	Cincinnati Cyclones	IHL	26	21	13	34	....	....	....	14	....	....	....	....	....	....	....	....	....	....	9	5	5	10	2	....	....	....
1998-99	**New York Rangers**	**NHL**	**67**	**4**	**6**	**10**	**5**	**6**	**11**	**30**	**0**	**1**	**0**	**47**	**8.5**	**13**	**1**	**38**	**15**	**–11**	....	....	....	....	....	....	....	....
99-2000	Kassel Huskies	Germany	24	5	6	11	....	....	....	8	....	....	....	....	....	....	....	....	....	....	....	....	....	....	....	....	....	....
	NHL Totals		**470**	**97**	**112**	**209**	**98**	**87**	**185**	**308**	**21**	**2**	**7**	**642**	**15.1**	**310**	**66**	**341**	**80**		**16**	**3**	**2**	**5**	**12**	**0**	**0**	**1**

WHL East Second All-Star Team (1986)

Traded to **Philadelphia** by **Detroit** for Philadelphia's 4th round choice (later traded to Boston — Boston selected Charles Paquette) in 1993 Entry Draft, October 1, 1992. Traded to **Dallas** by **Philadelphia** for Trent Klatt, December 13, 1995. Signed as a free agent by **NY Rangers**, August 13, 1998.

• FELIX, Chris

Christopher Robin D – R. 5'11", 190 lbs. b: Bramalea, Ont., 5/27/1964.

Season	Club	League	GP	G	A	Pts	AG	AA	APts	PIM	PP	SH	GW	S	%	TGF	PGF	TGA	PGA	+/–	GP	G	A	Pts	PIM	PP	SH	GW
1979-80	Chinguacosy York Data	OMHA	STATISTICS NOT AVAILABLE																									
1980-81	Bramalea Midget Blues	OMHA	50	26	28	54	....	....	....	....	....	....	....	....	....	....	....	....	....	....	....	....	....	....	....	....	....	....
1981-82	Sault Ste. Marie Greyhounds	OHL	66	3	18	21	....	....	....	37	....	....	....	....	....	....	....	....	....	....	....	....	....	....	....	....	....	....
1982-83	Sault Ste. Marie Greyhounds	OHL	68	16	57	73	....	....	....	39	....	....	....	....	....	....	....	....	....	....	16	2	12	14	10	....	....	....
1983-84	Sault Ste. Marie Greyhounds	OHL	70	32	61	93	....	....	....	77	....	....	....	....	....	....	....	....	....	....	16	3	20	23	16	....	....	....
1984-85	Sault Ste. Marie Greyhounds	OHL	63	29	72	101	....	....	....	85	....	....	....	....	....	....	....	....	....	....	16	7	*21	28	25	....	....	....
	Sault Ste. Marie Greyhounds	Mem-Cup	3	2	6	8	....	....	....	10	....	....	....	....	....	....	....	....	....	....	....	....	....	....	....	....	....	....
1985-86	Canada	Nat-Team	73	7	33	40	....	....	....	33	....	....	....	....	....	....	....	....	....	....	....	....	....	....	....	....	....	....
1986-87	Canada	Nat-Team	78	14	38	52	....	....	....	36	....	....	....	....	....	....	....	....	....	....	....	....	....	....	....	....	....	....
1987-88	Canada	Nat-Team	62	6	25	31	....	....	....	66	....	....	....	....	....	....	....	....	....	....	....	....	....	....	....	....	....	....
	Canada	Olympics	6	1	2	3	....	....	....	2	....	....	....	....	....	....	....	....	....	....	....	....	....	....	....	....	....	....
	Fort Wayne Komets	IHL	19	5	17	22	....	....	....	24	....	....	....	....	....	....	....	....	....	....	6	4	4	8	0	....	....	....
	Washington Capitals	**NHL**	....	....	....	....	....	....	....	....	....	....	....	....	....	....	....	....	....	....	**1**	**0**	**0**	**0**	**0**	**0**	**0**	**0**
1988-89	**Washington Capitals**	**NHL**	**21**	**0**	**8**	**8**	**0**	**6**	**6**	**8**	**0**	**0**	**0**	**18**	**0.0**	**30**	**13**	**10**	**0**	**7**	**1**	**0**	**1**	**1**	**0**	**0**	**0**	**0**
	Baltimore Skipjacks	AHL	50	8	29	37	....	....	....	44	....	....	....	....	....	....	....	....	....	....	....	....	....	....	....	....	....	....
1989-90	**Washington Capitals**	**NHL**	**6**	**1**	**0**	**1**	**1**	**0**	**1**	**2**	**1**	**0**	**0**	**3**	**33.3**	**5**	**4**	**7**	**0**	**–6**	....	....	....	....	....	....	....	....
	Washington Capitals	Fr-Tour	4	0	1	1	....	....	....	0	....	....	....	....	....	....	....	....	....	....	....	....	....	....	....	....	....	....
	Baltimore Skipjacks	AHL	73	19	42	61	....	....	....	115	....	....	....	....	....	....	....	....	....	....	12	0	11	11	18	....	....	....
1990-91	**Washington Capitals**	**NHL**	**8**	**0**	**4**	**4**	**0**	**3**	**3**	**0**	**0**	**0**	**0**	**7**	**0.0**	**4**	**3**	**1**	**0**	**0**	....	....	....	....	....	....	....	....
	Baltimore Skipjacks	AHL	27	4	24	28	....	....	....	26	....	....	....	....	....	....	....	....	....	....	6	1	4	5	6	....	....	....
1991-92	IEV Innsbruck	Austria	44	13	41	54	....	....	....	37	....	....	....	....	....	....	....	....	....	....	....	....	....	....	....	....	....	....
1992-93	IEV Innsbruck	Austria	30	8	28	36	....	....	....	18	....	....	....	....	....	....	....	....	....	....	....	....	....	....	....	....	....	....
1993-94	IEV Innsbruck	Austria	45	18	28	46	....	....	....	34	....	....	....	....	....	....	....	....	....	....	....	....	....	....	....	....	....	....
1994-95	KAC Klagenfurt	Austria	26	11	21	32	....	....	....	93	....	....	....	....	....	....	....	....	....	....	7	1	4	5	10	....	....	....
1995-96	HC Geneve-Servette	Switz-2	36	20	23	43	....	....	....	91	....	....	....	....	....	....	....	....	....	....	3	0	1	1	0	....	....	....
1996-97	Ilves Tampere	Finland	49	2	12	14	....	....	....	50	....	....	....	....	....	....	....	....	....	....	8	0	1	1	22	....	....	....
1997-98	ESV Kaufbeuren	Germany	15	0	4	4	....	....	....	20	....	....	....	....	....	....	....	....	....	....	....	....	....	....	....	....	....	....
	Adler Mannheim	Germany	25	0	1	1	....	....	....	6	....	....	....	....	....	....	....	....	....	....	3	1	0	1	0	....	....	....
	Adler Mannheim	EuroHL	1	0	0	0	....	....	....	2	....	....	....	....	....	....	....	....	....	....	....	....	....	....	....	....	....	....
1998-99	South Carolina Stingrays	ECHL	70	5	15	20	....	....	....	70	....	....	....	....	....	....	....	....	....	....	3	0	2	2	8	....	....	....
99-2000	New Mexico Scorpions	WPHL	65	10	40	50	....	....	....	78	....	....	....	....	....	....	....	....	....	....	15	0	8	8	30	....	....	....
	NHL Totals		**35**	**1**	**12**	**13**	**1**	**9**	**10**	**10**	**1**	**0**	**0**	**28**	**3.6**	**39**	**20**	**18**	**0**		**2**	**0**	**1**	**1**	**0**	**0**	**0**	**0**

Signed as a free agent by **Washington**, March 1, 1988.

• FELSNER, Brian

LW – L. 5'11", 189 lbs. b: Mt. Clemens, MI, 11/11/1972.

Season	Club	League	GP	G	A	Pts	AG	AA	APts	PIM	PP	SH	GW	S	%	TGF	PGF	TGA	PGA	+/–	GP	G	A	Pts	PIM	PP	SH	GW
1992-93	Detroit Ambassadors	NAJHL	50	25	35	60	....	....	....	....	....	....	....	....	....	....	....	....	....	....	....	....	....	....	....	....	....	....
1993-94	Lake Superior State	CCHA	6	1	1	2	....	....	....	6	....	....	....	....	....	....	....	....	....	....	....	....	....	....	....	....	....	....
1994-95	Lake Superior State	CCHA	41	24	28	52	....	....	....	51	....	....	....	....	....	....	....	....	....	....	....	....	....	....	....	....	....	....
1995-96	Lake Superior State	CCHA	38	16	36	52	....	....	....	40	....	....	....	....	....	....	....	....	....	....	....	....	....	....	....	....	....	....
1996-97	Orlando Solar Bears	IHL	75	29	41	70	....	....	....	38	....	....	....	....	....	....	....	....	....	....	7	2	3	5	6	....	....	....
1997-98	**Chicago Blackhawks**	**NHL**	**12**	**1**	**3**	**4**	**1**	**3**	**4**	**12**	....	....	....	....	....	....	....	....	....	....	....	....	....	....	....	....	....	....
	Indianapolis Ice	IHL	53	17	36	53	....	....	....	36	....	....	....	....	....	....	....	....	....	....	....	....	....	....	....	....	....	....
	Milwaukee Admirals	IHL	15	7	8	15	....	....	....	20	....	....	....	....	....	....	....	....	....	....	10	3	9	12	12	....	....	....

			REGULAR SEASON																		PLAYOFFS							
Season	Club	League	GP	G	A	Pts	AG	AA	APts	PIM	PP	SH	GW	S	%	TGF	PGF	TGA	PGA	+/–	GP	G	A	Pts	PIM	PP	SH	GW
1998-99	Detroit Vipers	IHL	72	20	35	55	....	....	....	49	....	....	....	....	....	....	....	....	....	....	11	4	6	10	12	....	....	....
99-2000	Houston Aeros	IHL	28	7	16	23	....	....	....	20	....	....	....	....	....	....	....	....	....	....	....	....	....	....	....	....	....	....
	Cincinnati Cyclones	IHL	38	15	17	32	....	....	....	18	....	....	....	....	....	....	....	....	....	....	11	4	5	9	20	....	....	....
	NHL Totals		**12**	**1**	**3**	**4**	**1**	**3**	**4**	**12**	....	....	....	....	....	....	....	....	....	....	....	....	....	....	....	....	....	....

Brother of Denny

• Played football at Lanse Creuse High School, 1987-1992. • Ruled academically ineligable by NCAA for remainder of 1993-94 season. Signed as a free agent by **Chicago**, September 5, 1997. Traded to **Ottawa** by **Chicago** for Justin Hocking, August 21, 1998. Signed as a free agent by **Houston** (IHL) , October 9, 1999. Traded to **Cincinnati** (IHL) by **Houston** (IHL) for Steve Bancroft with Ottawa retaining NHL rights, January 19, 2000.

• FELSNER, Denny

LW – L. 6′, 195 lbs. b: Warren, MI, 4/29/1970. St. Louis' 3rd, 55th overall, in 1989.

Season	Club	League	GP	G	A	Pts	AG	AA	APts	PIM	PP	SH	GW	S	%	TGF	PGF	TGA	PGA	+/–	GP	G	A	Pts	PIM	PP	SH	GW
1986-87	Detroit Falcons	NAJHL	37	22	33	55	....	....	....	18	....	....	....	....	....	....	....	....	....	....	....	....	....	....	....	....	....	....
1987-88	Detroit Jr. Red Wings	NAJHL	39	35	43	78	....	....	....	46	....	....	....	....	....	....	....	....	....	....	....	....	....	....	....	....	....	....
1988-89	University of Michigan	CCHA	39	30	19	49	....	....	....	22	....	....	....	....	....	....	....	....	....	....	....	....	....	....	....	....	....	....
1989-90	University of Michigan	CCHA	33	27	16	43	....	....	....	24	....	....	....	....	....	....	....	....	....	....	....	....	....	....	....	....	....	....
1990-91	University of Michigan	CCHA	46	*40	35	75	....	....	....	58	....	....	....	....	....	....	....	....	....	....	....	....	....	....	....	....	....	....
1991-92	University of Michigan	CCHA	44	42	52	94	....	....	....	46	....	....	....	....	....	....	....	....	....	....	....	....	....	....	....	....	....	....
	St. Louis Blues	**NHL**	**3**	**0**	**1**	**1**	**0**	**1**	**1**	**0**	**0**	**0**	**0**	**2**	**0.0**	**1**	**0**	**1**	**0**	**0**	**1**	**0**	**0**	**0**	**0**	**0**	**0**	**0**
1992-93	**St. Louis Blues**	**NHL**	**6**	**0**	**3**	**3**	**0**	**2**	**2**	**2**	**0**	**0**	**0**	**4**	**0.0**	**6**	**0**	**2**	**0**	**4**	**9**	**2**	**3**	**5**	**2**	**1**	**0**	**0**
	Peoria Rivermen	IHL	29	14	21	35	....	....	....	8	....	....	....	....	....	....	....	....	....	....	....	....	....	....	....	....	....	....
1993-94	**St. Louis Blues**	**NHL**	**6**	**1**	**0**	**1**	**1**	**0**	**1**	**2**	**0**	**0**	**0**	**6**	**16.7**	**3**	**1**	**3**	**0**	**–1**	....	....	....	....	....	....	....	....
	Peoria Rivermen	IHL	6	8	3	11	....	....	....	14	....	....	....	....	....	....	....	....	....	....	....	....	....	....	....	....	....	....
1994-95	**St. Louis Blues**	**NHL**	**3**	**0**	**0**	**0**	**0**	**0**	**0**	**2**	**0**	**0**	**0**	**2**	**0.0**	**0**	**0**	**1**	**0**	**–1**	....	....	....	....	....	....	....	....
	Peoria Rivermen	IHL	25	10	12	22	....	....	....	14	....	....	....	....	....	....	....	....	....	....	8	2	3	5	0	....	....	....
1995-96	Syracuse Crunch	AHL	66	23	34	57	....	....	....	22	....	....	....	....	....	....	....	....	....	....	14	5	12	17	0	....	....	....
1996-97	Chicago Wolves	IHL	39	10	12	22	....	....	....	4	....	....	....	....	....	....	....	....	....	....	....	....	....	....	....	....	....	....
	Milwaukee Admirals	IHL	14	1	3	4	....	....	....	2	....	....	....	....	....	....	....	....	....	....	....	....	....	....	....	....	....	....
1997-98	Chesapeake Icebreakers	ECHL	50	30	37	67	....	....	....	6	....	....	....	....	....	....	....	....	....	....	....	....	....	....	....	....	....	....
	Detroit Vipers	IHL	3	0	0	0	....	....	....	0	....	....	....	....	....	....	....	....	....	....	....	....	....	....	....	....	....	....
1998-99	Chesapeake Icebreakers	ECHL	50	29	45	74	....	....	....	32	....	....	....	....	....	....	....	....	....	....	8	4	1	5	2	....	....	....
99-2000	Jackson Bandits	ECHL	28	10	10	20	....	....	....	6	....	....	....	....	....	....	....	....	....	....	....	....	....	....	....	....	....	....
	NHL Totals		**18**	**1**	**4**	**5**	**1**	**3**	**4**	**6**	**0**	**0**	**0**	**14**	**7.1**	**10**	**1**	**7**	**0**		**10**	**2**	**3**	**5**	**2**	**1**	**0**	**0**

Brother of Brian • CCHA First All-Star Team (1991, 1992) • NCAA West Second All-American Team (1991) • NCAA West First All-American Team (1992) • ECHL First All-Star Team (1999)

Signed as a free agent by **Vancouver**, August 31, 1995. • Missed majority of 1999-2000 season recovering from shoulder surgery, August, 1999.

• FELTRIN, Tony

Anthony Louis D – L. 6′1″, 184 lbs. b: Ladysmith, B.C., 12/6/1961. Pittsburgh's 3rd, 72nd overall, in 1980.

Season	Club	League	GP	G	A	Pts	AG	AA	APts	PIM	PP	SH	GW	S	%	TGF	PGF	TGA	PGA	+/–	GP	G	A	Pts	PIM	PP	SH	GW
1977-78	Nanaimo Clippers	BCJHL	63	2	13	15	....	....	....	65	....	....	....	....	....	....	....	....	....	....	....	....	....	....	....	....	....	....
1978-79	Victoria Cougars	WHL	47	2	11	13	....	....	....	119	....	....	....	....	....	....	....	....	....	....	7	0	1	1	4	....	....	....
1979-80	Victoria Cougars	WHL	71	6	25	31	....	....	....	138	....	....	....	....	....	....	....	....	....	....	17	0	8	8	21	....	....	....
1980-81	Victoria Cougars	WHL	43	4	25	29	....	....	....	81	....	....	....	....	....	....	....	....	....	....	....	....	....	....	....	....	....	....
	Pittsburgh Penguins	**NHL**	**2**	**0**	**0**	**0**	**0**	**0**	**0**	**0**	**0**	**0**	**0**	**0**	**0.0**	**1**	**0**	**4**	**0**	**–3**	....	....	....	....	....	....	....	....
	Victoria Cougars	Mem-Cup	5	1	4	5	....	....	....	0	....	....	....	....	....	....	....	....	....	....	....	....	....	....	....	....	....	....
1981-82	**Pittsburgh Penguins**	**NHL**	**4**	**0**	**0**	**0**	**0**	**0**	**0**	**4**	**0**	**0**	**0**	**3**	**0.0**	**1**	**0**	**4**	**0**	**–3**	....	....	....	....	....	....	....	....
	Erie Blades	AHL	72	4	15	19	....	....	....	117	....	....	....	....	....	....	....	....	....	....	....	....	....	....	....	....	....	....
1982-83	**Pittsburgh Penguins**	**NHL**	**32**	**3**	**3**	**6**	**2**	**2**	**4**	**40**	**0**	**0**	**0**	**36**	**8.3**	**14**	**0**	**30**	**5**	**–11**	....	....	....	....	....	....	....	....
	Baltimore Skipjacks	AHL	31	2	3	5	....	....	....	34	....	....	....	....	....	....	....	....	....	....	....	....	....	....	....	....	....	....
	Muskegon Mohawks	IHL	2	0	0	0	....	....	....	0	....	....	....	....	....	....	....	....	....	....	....	....	....	....	....	....	....	....
1983-84	Baltimore Skipjacks	AHL	4	0	0	0	....	....	....	2	....	....	....	....	....	....	....	....	....	....	....	....	....	....	....	....	....	....
	Salt Lake Golden Eagles	CHL	65	8	22	30	....	....	....	94	....	....	....	....	....	....	....	....	....	....	5	2	0	2	5	....	....	....
1984-85	Salt Lake Golden Eagles	IHL	81	8	19	27	....	....	....	125	....	....	....	....	....	....	....	....	....	....	7	2	1	3	14	....	....	....
1985-86	**New York Rangers**	**NHL**	**10**	**0**	**0**	**0**	**0**	**0**	**0**	**21**	**0**	**0**	**0**	**8**	**0.0**	**3**	**0**	**6**	**0**	**–3**	....	....	....	....	....	....	....	....
	New Haven Nighthawks	AHL	22	0	2	2	....	....	....	38	....	....	....	....	....	....	....	....	....	....	....	....	....	....	....	....	....	....
1986-1996	**New York Rangers**	**NHL**	DID NOT PLAY – SCOUTING																									
1996-2000	**New York Islanders**	**NHL**	DID NOT PLAY – SCOUTING																									
	NHL Totals		**48**	**3**	**3**	**6**	**2**	**2**	**4**	**65**	**0**	**0**	**0**	**47**	**6.4**	**19**	**0**	**44**	**5**		....	....	....	....	....	....	....	....

Signed as a free agent by **NY Rangers**, October 8, 1985. • Suffered career-ending eye injury in game vs. Nova Scotia (AHL), December 31, 1985.

• FENTON, Paul

Paul John LW – L. 5′11″, 180 lbs. b: Springfield, MA, 12/22/1959.

Season	Club	League	GP	G	A	Pts	AG	AA	APts	PIM	PP	SH	GW	S	%	TGF	PGF	TGA	PGA	+/–	GP	G	A	Pts	PIM	PP	SH	GW
1979-80	Boston University	ECAC	24	8	17	25	....	....	....	14	....	....	....	....	....	....	....	....	....	....	....	....	....	....	....	....	....	....
1980-81	Boston University	ECAC	5	3	2	5	....	....	....	0	....	....	....	....	....	....	....	....	....	....	....	....	....	....	....	....	....	....
1981-82	Boston University	ECAC	28	20	13	33	....	....	....	20	....	....	....	....	....	....	....	....	....	....	....	....	....	....	....	....	....	....
1982-83	Peoria Prancers	IHL	82	60	51	111	....	....	....	53	....	....	....	....	....	....	....	....	....	....	....	....	....	....	....	....	....	....
	Colorado Flames	CHL	1	0	1	1	....	....	....	0	....	....	....	....	....	....	....	....	....	....	3	2	0	2	2	....	....	....
1983-84	Binghamton Whalers	AHL	78	41	24	65	....	....	....	67	....	....	....	....	....	....	....	....	....	....	....	....	....	....	....	....	....	....
1984-85	**Hartford Whalers**	**NHL**	**33**	**7**	**5**	**12**	**6**	**3**	**9**	**10**	**0**	**0**	**2**	**53**	**13.2**	**17**	**1**	**11**	**1**	**6**	....	....	....	....	....	....	....	....
	Binghamton Whalers	AHL	45	26	21	47	....	....	....	18	....	....	....	....	....	....	....	....	....	....	....	....	....	....	....	....	....	....
	United States	WEC-A	9	2	1	3	....	....	....	8	....	....	....	....	....	....	....	....	....	....	....	....	....	....	....	....	....	....
1985-86	**Hartford Whalers**	**NHL**	**1**	**0**	**0**	**0**	**0**	**0**	**0**	**0**	**0**	**0**	**0**	**3**	**0.0**	**1**	**0**	**0**	**0**	**1**	....	....	....	....	....	....	....	....
	Binghamton Whalers	AHL	75	53	35	88	....	....	....	87	....	....	....	....	....	....	....	....	....	....	6	2	0	2	2	....	....	....
1986-87	**New York Rangers**	**NHL**	**8**	**0**	**0**	**0**	**0**	**0**	**0**	**2**	**0**	**0**	**0**	**11**	**0.0**	**1**	**0**	**6**	**0**	**–5**	....	....	....	....	....	....	....	....
	New Haven Nighthawks	AHL	70	37	38	75	....	....	....	45	....	....	....	....	....	....	....	....	....	....	7	6	4	10	6	....	....	....
1987-88	**Los Angeles Kings**	**NHL**	**71**	**20**	**23**	**43**	**17**	**16**	**33**	**46**	**8**	**1**	**1**	**166**	**12.0**	**70**	**24**	**72**	**12**	**–14**	**5**	**2**	**1**	**3**	**2**	**1**	**0**	**0**
	New Haven Nighthawks	AHL	5	11	5	16	....	....	....	9	....	....	....	....	....	....	....	....	....	....	....	....	....	....	....	....	....	....
1988-89	**Los Angeles Kings**	**NHL**	**21**	**2**	**3**	**5**	**2**	**2**	**4**	**6**	**0**	**0**	**0**	**26**	**7.7**	**6**	**1**	**6**	**0**	**–1**	....	....	....	....	....	....	....	....
	Winnipeg Jets	**NHL**	**59**	**14**	**9**	**23**	**12**	**6**	**18**	**33**	**1**	**0**	**0**	**109**	**12.8**	**31**	**3**	**44**	**1**	**–15**	....	....	....	....	....	....	....	....
	United States	WEC-A	10	1	3	4	....	....	....	14	....	....	....	....	....	....	....	....	....	....	....	....	....	....	....	....	....	....
1989-90	**Winnipeg Jets**	**NHL**	**80**	**32**	**18**	**50**	**28**	**13**	**41**	**40**	**4**	**1**	**1**	**152**	**21.1**	**74**	**11**	**74**	**13**	**2**	**7**	**2**	**0**	**2**	**23**	**2**	**0**	**0**
1990-91	**Winnipeg Jets**	**NHL**	**17**	**4**	**4**	**8**	**4**	**3**	**7**	**18**	**1**	**0**	**1**	**28**	**14.3**	**11**	**5**	**11**	**1**	**–4**	....	....	....	....	....	....	....	....
	Toronto Maple Leafs	**NHL**	**30**	**5**	**10**	**15**	**5**	**8**	**13**	**0**	**1**	**1**	**0**	**46**	**10.9**	**20**	**3**	**25**	**5**	**–3**	....	....	....	....	....	....	....	....
	Calgary Flames	**NHL**	**31**	**5**	**7**	**12**	**5**	**5**	**10**	**10**	**0**	**1**	**1**	**59**	**8.5**	**20**	**0**	**21**	**3**	**2**	**5**	**0**	**0**	**0**	**2**	**0**	**0**	**0**
1991-92	**San Jose Sharks**	**NHL**	**60**	**11**	**4**	**15**	**10**	**3**	**13**	**33**	**3**	**2**	**1**	**96**	**11.5**	**21**	**4**	**67**	**11**	**–39**	....	....	....	....	....	....	....	....
	NHL Totals		**411**	**100**	**83**	**183**	**89**	**59**	**148**	**198**	**18**	**6**	**7**	**749**	**13.4**	**272**	**52**	**337**	**47**		**17**	**4**	**1**	**5**	**27**	**3**	**0**	**0**

IHL Second All-Star Team (1983) • AHL First All-Star Team (1986) • AHL Second All-Star Team (1987)

Signed as a free agent by **Hartford**, October 6, 1983. Signed as a free agent by **NY Rangers**, September 11, 1986. Claimed by **LA Kings** from **NY Rangers** in Waiver Draft, October 5, 1987. Traded to **Winnipeg** by **LA Kings** for Gilles Hamel, November 25, 1988. Traded to **Toronto** by **Winnipeg** with Dave Ellett for Ed Olczyk and Mark Osborne, November 10, 1989. Traded to **Washington** by **Toronto** with John Kordic for Washington's 5th round choice (Alexei Kudashov) in 1991 Entry Draft, January 24, 1991. Traded to **Calgary** by **Washington** for Ken Sabourin, January 24, 1991. Traded to **Hartford** by **Calgary** for future cash, August 26, 1991. Traded to **San Jose** by **Hartford** for Mike McHugh, October 18, 1991.

• FENYVES, David

David Alan D – L. 6′, 192 lbs. b: Dunnville, Ont., 4/29/1960.

Season	Club	League	GP	G	A	Pts	AG	AA	APts	PIM	PP	SH	GW	S	%	TGF	PGF	TGA	PGA	+/–	GP	G	A	Pts	PIM	PP	SH	GW
1976-77	Dunnville Mudcats	OHA-B	46	10	21	31	....	....	....	52	....	....	....	....	....	....	....	....	....	....	....	....	....	....	....	....	....	....
1977-78	Peterborough Petes	OMJHL	59	3	12	15	....	....	....	36	....	....	....	....	....	....	....	....	....	....	21	1	1	2	19	....	....	....
	Peterborough Petes	Mem-Cup	5	0	1	1	....	....	....	0	....	....	....	....	....	....	....	....	....	....	....	....	....	....	....	....	....	....
1978-79	Peterborough Petes	OMJHL	66	2	23	25	....	....	....	122	....	....	....	....	....	....	....	....	....	....	19	0	5	5	18	....	....	....
	Peterborough Petes	Mem-Cup	5	0	0	0	....	....	....	0	....	....	....	....	....	....	....	....	....	....	....	....	....	....	....	....	....	....
1979-80	Peterborough Petes	OMJHL	66	9	36	45	....	....	....	92	....	....	....	....	....	....	....	....	....	....	14	0	3	3	14	....	....	....
	Canada	WJC-A	5	0	0	0	....	....	....	8	....	....	....	....	....	....	....	....	....	....	....	....	....	....	....	....	....	....
1980-81	Rochester Americans	AHL	77	6	16	22	....	....	....	146	....	....	....	....	....	....	....	....	....	....	....	....	....	....	....	....	....	....
1981-82	Rochester Americans	AHL	73	3	14	17	....	....	....	68	....	....	....	....	....	....	....	....	....	....	5	0	1	1	4	....	....	....

			REGULAR SEASON																		PLAYOFFS							
Season	Club	League	GP	G	A	Pts	AG	AA	APts	PIM	PP	SH	GW	S	%	TGF	PGF	TGA	PGA	+/–	GP	G	A	Pts	PIM	PP	SH	GW
1982-83	**Buffalo Sabres**	**NHL**	**24**	**0**	**8**	**8**	**0**	**6**	**6**	**14**	**0**	**0**	**0**	**20**	**0.0**	**23**	**0**	**39**	**6**	**–10**	**4**	**0**	**0**	**0**	**0**	**0**	**0**	**0**
	Rochester Americans	AHL	51	2	19	21	....	....	....	45	....	....	....	....	....	....	....	....	....	....	....	....	....	....	....	....	....	....
1983-84	**Buffalo Sabres**	**NHL**	**10**	**0**	**4**	**4**	**0**	**3**	**3**	**9**	**0**	**0**	**0**	**4**	**0.0**	**9**	**0**	**4**	**2**	**7**	**2**	**0**	**0**	**0**	**7**	**0**	**0**	**0**
	Rochester Americans	AHL	70	3	16	19	....	....	....	55	....	....	....	....	....	....	....	....	....	....	16	1	4	5	22	....	....	....
1984-85	**Buffalo Sabres**	**NHL**	**60**	**1**	**8**	**9**	**1**	**5**	**6**	**27**	**0**	**0**	**0**	**50**	**2.0**	**35**	**0**	**52**	**17**	**0**	**5**	**0**	**0**	**0**	**2**	**0**	**0**	**0**
	Rochester Americans	AHL	9	0	3	3	....	....	....	8	....	....	....	....	....	....	....	....	....	....	....	....	....	....	....	....	....	....
1985-86	**Buffalo Sabres**	**NHL**	**47**	**0**	**7**	**7**	**0**	**5**	**5**	**37**	**0**	**0**	**0**	**31**	**0.0**	**42**	**2**	**42**	**14**	**12**	....	....	....	....	....	....	....	....
1986-87	**Buffalo Sabres**	**NHL**	**7**	**1**	**0**	**1**	**1**	**0**	**1**	**0**	**0**	**0**	**0**	**3**	**33.3**	**3**	**0**	**6**	**0**	**–3**	....	....	....	....	....	....	....	....
	Rochester Americans	AHL	71	6	16	22	....	....	....	57	....	....	....	....	....	....	....	....	....	....	18	3	12	15	10	....	....	....
1987-88	**Philadelphia Flyers**	**NHL**	**5**	**0**	**0**	**0**	**0**	**0**	**0**	**0**	**0**	**0**	**0**	**3**	**0.0**	**3**	**1**	**3**	**0**	**–1**	....	....	....	....	....	....	....	....
	Hershey Bears	AHL	75	11	40	51	....	....	....	47	....	....	....	....	....	....	....	....	....	....	12	1	8	9	10	....	....	....
1988-89	**Philadelphia Flyers**	**NHL**	**1**	**0**	**1**	**1**	**0**	**1**	**1**	**0**	**0**	**0**	**0**	**0**	**0.0**	**1**	**0**	**2**	**1**	**0**	....	....	....	....	....	....	....	....
	Hershey Bears	AHL	79	15	51	66	....	....	....	41	....	....	....	....	....	....	....	....	....	....	12	2	6	8	6	....	....	....
1989-90	**Philadelphia Flyers**	**NHL**	**12**	**0**	**0**	**0**	**0**	**0**	**0**	**4**	**0**	**0**	**0**	**10**	**0.0**	**6**	**0**	**12**	**0**	**–6**	....	....	....	....	....	....	....	....
	Hershey Bears	AHL	66	6	37	43	....	....	....	57	....	....	....	....	....	....	....	....	....	....	....	....	....	....	....	....	....	....
1990-91	**Philadelphia Flyers**	**NHL**	**40**	**1**	**4**	**5**	**1**	**3**	**4**	**28**	**0**	**0**	**0**	**32**	**3.1**	**27**	**0**	**26**	**0**	**1**	....	....	....	....	....	....	....	....
	Hershey Bears	AHL	29	4	11	15	....	....	....	13	....	....	....	....	....	....	....	....	....	....	7	0	3	3	6	....	....	....
1991-92	Hershey Bears	AHL	68	4	24	28	....	....	....	29	....	....	....	....	....	....	....	....	....	....	6	1	1	2	10	....	....	....
1992-93	Hershey Bears	AHL	42	3	11	14	....	....	....	14	....	....	....	....	....	....	....	....	....	....	....	....	....	....	....	....	....	....
	NHL Totals		**206**	**3**	**32**	**35**	**3**	**23**	**26**	**119**	**0**	**0**	**0**	**153**	**2.0**	**149**	**3**	**186**	**40**		**11**	**0**	**0**	**0**	**9**	**0**	**0**	**0**

OMJHL Second All-Star Team (1980) • AHL Second All-Star Team (1987) • Won Jack A. Butterfield Trophy (Playoff MVP - AHL) (1987) • AHL First All-Star Team (1988, 1989) • Won Eddie Shore Award (Outstanding Defenseman - AHL) (1988, 1989)

Signed as a free agent by **Buffalo**, October 31, 1979. Claimed by **Philadelphia** from **Buffalo** in Waiver Draft, October 5, 1987.

• FERENCE, Andrew

D – L. 5'10", 190 lbs. b: Edmonton, Alta., 3/17/1979. Pittsburgh's 8th, 208th overall, in 1997.

Season	Club	League	GP	G	A	Pts	AG	AA	APts	PIM	PP	SH	GW	S	%	TGF	PGF	TGA	PGA	+/–	GP	G	A	Pts	PIM	PP	SH	GW
1995-96	Portland Winter Hawks	WHL	72	9	31	40	....	....	....	159	....	....	....	....	....	....	....	....	....	....	7	1	3	4	12	....	....	....
1996-97	Portland Winter Hawks	WHL	72	12	32	44	....	....	....	163	....	....	....	....	....	....	....	....	....	....	6	1	2	3	12	....	....	....
1997-98	Portland Winter Hawks	WHL	72	11	57	68	....	....	....	142	....	....	....	....	....	....	....	....	....	....	16	2	18	20	28	....	....	....
1998-99	Portland Winter Hawks	WHL	40	11	21	32	....	....	....	104	....	....	....	....	....	....	....	....	....	....	4	1	4	5	10	....	....	....
	Kansas City Blades	IHL	5	1	2	3	....	....	....	4	....	....	....	....	....	....	....	....	....	....	3	0	0	0	9	....	....	....
	Canada	WJC-A	7	1	2	3	....	....	....	6	....	....	....	....	....	....	....	....	....	....	....	....	....	....	....	....	....	....
99-2000	**Pittsburgh Penguins**	**NHL**	**30**	**2**	**4**	**6**	**2**	**4**	**6**	**20**	**0**	**0**	**1**	**26**	**7.7**	**25**	**1**	**24**	**3**	**3**	....	....	....	....	....	....	....	....
	Wilkes-Barre Penguins	AHL	44	8	20	28	....	....	....	58	....	....	....	....	....	....	....	....	....	....	....	....	....	....	....	....	....	....
	NHL Totals		**30**	**2**	**4**	**6**	**2**	**4**	**6**	**20**	**0**	**0**	**1**	**26**	**7.7**	**25**	**1**	**24**	**3**		....	....	....	....	....	....	....	....

WHL West First All-Star Team (1998) • WHL West Second All-Star Team (1999)

• FERENCE, Brad

D – R. 6'3", 196 lbs. b: Calgary, Alta., 4/2/1979. Vancouver's 1st, 10th overall, in 1997.

Season	Club	League	GP	G	A	Pts	AG	AA	APts	PIM	PP	SH	GW	S	%	TGF	PGF	TGA	PGA	+/–	GP	G	A	Pts	PIM	PP	SH	GW
1994-95	Calgary Bantam Royals	AAHA	60	19	47	66	....	....	....	220	....	....	....	....	....	....	....	....	....	....	....	....	....	....	....	....	....	....
1995-96	Calgary Bantam Royals	AAHA	22	7	21	28	....	....	....	140	....	....	....	....	....	....	....	....	....	....	....	....	....	....	....	....	....	....
	Spokane Chiefs	WHL	5	0	2	2	....	....	....	18	....	....	....	....	....	....	....	....	....	....	....	....	....	....	....	....	....	....
1996-97	Spokane Chiefs	WHL	67	6	20	26	....	....	....	324	....	....	....	....	....	....	....	....	....	....	9	0	4	4	21	....	....	....
1997-98	Spokane Chiefs	WHL	54	9	30	39	....	....	....	213	....	....	....	....	....	....	....	....	....	....	18	0	7	7	59	....	....	....
	Canada	WJC-A	7	0	1	1	....	....	....	6	....	....	....	....	....	....	....	....	....	....	....	....	....	....	....	....	....	....
	Spokane Chiefs	Mem-Cup	4	1	2	3	....	....	....	12	....	....	....	....	....	....	....	....	....	....	....	....	....	....	....	....	....	....
1998-99	Spokane Chiefs	WHL	31	3	22	25	....	....	....	125	....	....	....	....	....	....	....	....	....	....	....	....	....	....	....	....	....	....
	Tri-City Americans	WHL	20	6	15	21	....	....	....	116	....	....	....	....	....	....	....	....	....	....	12	1	9	10	63	....	....	....
	Canada	WJC-A	7	0	2	2	....	....	....	25	....	....	....	....	....	....	....	....	....	....	....	....	....	....	....	....	....	....
99-2000	**Florida Panthers**	**NHL**	**13**	**0**	**2**	**2**	**0**	**2**	**2**	**46**	**0**	**0**	**0**	**10**	**0.0**	**6**	**0**	**4**	**0**	**2**	....	....	....	....	....	....	....	....
	Louisville Panthers	AHL	58	2	7	9	....	....	....	231	....	....	....	....	....	....	....	....	....	....	2	0	0	0	2	....	....	....
	NHL Totals		**13**	**0**	**2**	**2**	**0**	**2**	**2**	**46**	**0**	**0**	**0**	**10**	**0.0**	**6**	**0**	**4**	**0**		....	....	....	....	....	....	....	....

Memorial Cup All-Star Team (1998)

Traded to **Florida** by **Vancouver** with Pavel Bure, Bret Hedican and Vancouver's 3rd round choice (Robert Fried) in 2000 Entry Draft for Ed Jovanovski, Dave Gagner, Mike Brown, Kevin Weekes and Florida's 1st round choice (Nathan Smith) in 2000 Entry Draft, January 17, 1999.

• FERGUS, Tom

Thomas Joseph C – L. 6'3", 210 lbs. b: Chicago, IL, 6/16/1962. Boston's 2nd, 60th overall, in 1980.

Season	Club	League	GP	G	A	Pts	AG	AA	APts	PIM	PP	SH	GW	S	%	TGF	PGF	TGA	PGA	+/–	GP	G	A	Pts	PIM	PP	SH	GW
1978-79	St. George Lions	OHA-B	22	21	20	41	....	....	....	....	....	....	....	....	....	....	....	....	....	....	....	....	....	....	....	....	....	....
1979-80	Peterborough Petes	OMJHL	63	8	6	14	....	....	....	14	....	....	....	....	....	....	....	....	....	....	14	1	5	6	6	....	....	....
	Peterborough Petes	Mem-Cup	5	1	0	1	....	....	....	4	....	....	....	....	....	....	....	....	....	....	....	....	....	....	....	....	....	....
1980-81	Peterborough Petes	OMJHL	63	43	45	88	....	....	....	33	....	....	....	....	....	....	....	....	....	....	5	1	4	5	2	....	....	....
1981-82	**Boston Bruins**	**NHL**	**61**	**15**	**24**	**39**	**12**	**16**	**28**	**12**	**2**	**0**	**2**	**116**	**12.9**	**58**	**5**	**38**	**0**	**15**	**6**	**3**	**0**	**3**	**0**	**2**	**0**	**0**
1982-83	**Boston Bruins**	**NHL**	**80**	**28**	**35**	**63**	**23**	**24**	**47**	**39**	**4**	**0**	**6**	**169**	**16.6**	**89**	**16**	**50**	**3**	**26**	**15**	**2**	**2**	**4**	**15**	**0**	**0**	**0**
1983-84	**Boston Bruins**	**NHL**	**69**	**25**	**36**	**61**	**20**	**25**	**45**	**12**	**6**	**0**	**3**	**123**	**20.3**	**82**	**15**	**63**	**4**	**8**	**3**	**2**	**0**	**2**	**9**	**1**	**0**	**0**
1984-85	**Boston Bruins**	**NHL**	**79**	**30**	**43**	**73**	**24**	**29**	**53**	**75**	**4**	**0**	**2**	**183**	**16.4**	**108**	**28**	**69**	**3**	**14**	**5**	**0**	**0**	**0**	**4**	**0**	**0**	**0**
	United States	WEC-A	8	4	2	6	....	....	....	14	....	....	....	....	....	....	....	....	....	....	....	....	....	....	....	....	....	....
1985-86	**Toronto Maple Leafs**	**NHL**	**78**	**31**	**42**	**73**	**25**	**28**	**53**	**64**	**3**	**2**	**3**	**168**	**18.5**	**113**	**30**	**144**	**37**	**–24**	**10**	**5**	**7**	**12**	**6**	**3**	**0**	**1**
1986-87	**Toronto Maple Leafs**	**NHL**	**57**	**21**	**28**	**49**	**18**	**20**	**38**	**57**	**2**	**1**	**2**	**119**	**17.6**	**71**	**14**	**73**	**17**	**1**	**2**	**0**	**1**	**1**	**2**	**0**	**0**	**0**
	Newmarket Saints	AHL	1	0	1	1	....	....	....	0	....	....	....	....	....	....	....	....	....	....	....	....	....	....	....	....	....	....
1987-88	**Toronto Maple Leafs**	**NHL**	**63**	**19**	**31**	**50**	**16**	**22**	**38**	**81**	**5**	**0**	**0**	**124**	**15.3**	**63**	**7**	**69**	**18**	**5**	**6**	**2**	**3**	**5**	**2**	**0**	**1**	**0**
1988-89	**Toronto Maple Leafs**	**NHL**	**80**	**22**	**45**	**67**	**19**	**32**	**51**	**48**	**10**	**1**	**3**	**151**	**14.6**	**92**	**37**	**121**	**28**	**–38**	....	....	....	....	....	....	....	....
1989-90	**Toronto Maple Leafs**	**NHL**	**54**	**19**	**26**	**45**	**16**	**19**	**35**	**62**	**4**	**0**	**2**	**120**	**15.8**	**72**	**16**	**77**	**3**	**–18**	**5**	**2**	**1**	**3**	**4**	**0**	**0**	**0**
1990-91	**Toronto Maple Leafs**	**NHL**	**14**	**5**	**4**	**9**	**5**	**3**	**8**	**8**	**2**	**0**	**0**	**17**	**29.4**	**13**	**7**	**11**	**0**	**–5**	....	....	....	....	....	....	....	....
1991-92	**Toronto Maple Leafs**	**NHL**	**11**	**1**	**3**	**4**	**1**	**2**	**3**	**4**	**0**	**0**	**0**	**24**	**4.2**	**5**	**3**	**13**	**0**	**–11**	....	....	....	....	....	....	....	....
	Vancouver Canucks	**NHL**	**44**	**14**	**20**	**34**	**13**	**15**	**28**	**17**	**6**	**0**	**3**	**79**	**17.7**	**48**	**20**	**42**	**15**	**1**	**13**	**5**	**3**	**8**	**6**	**0**	**0**	**1**
1992-93	**Vancouver Canucks**	**NHL**	**36**	**5**	**9**	**14**	**4**	**6**	**10**	**20**	**1**	**1**	**0**	**29**	**17.2**	**18**	**3**	**26**	**12**	**1**	....	....	....	....	....	....	....	....
1993-94	EV Zug	Switz.	32	21	29	50	....	....	....	104	....	....	....	....	....	....	....	....	....	....	....	....	....	....	....	....	....	....
1994-95	EV Zug	Switz.	22	12	12	24	....	....	....	56	....	....	....	....	....	....	....	....	....	....	12	3	10	13	16	....	....	....
	NHL Totals		**726**	**235**	**346**	**581**	**196**	**241**	**437**	**499**	**49**	**5**	**26**	**1422**	**16.5**	**832**	**201**	**796**	**140**		**65**	**21**	**17**	**38**	**48**	**6**	**1**	**2**

Traded to **Toronto** by **Boston** for Bill Derlago, October 11, 1985. • Missed majority of 1990-91 season recovering from abdominal muscle injury originally suffered in game vs. St. Louis, February 6, 1990. Traded to **Vancouver** by **Toronto** for cash, December 18, 1991.

• FERGUSON, Craig

C – L. 5'11", 190 lbs. b: Castro Valley, CA, 4/8/1970. Montreal's 7th, 146th overall, in 1989.

Season	Club	League	GP	G	A	Pts	AG	AA	APts	PIM	PP	SH	GW	S	%	TGF	PGF	TGA	PGA	+/–	GP	G	A	Pts	PIM	PP	SH	GW
1986-87	Sydney Flyers	NSAHA	STATISTICS NOT AVAILABLE																									
1987-88	Sydney Riverview Rural	Hi-School	STATISTICS NOT AVAILABLE																									
1988-89	Yale University	ECAC	24	11	6	17	....	....	....	20	....	....	....	....	....	....	....	....	....	....	....	....	....	....	....	....	....	....
1989-90	Yale University	ECAC	28	6	13	19	....	....	....	36	....	....	....	....	....	....	....	....	....	....	....	....	....	....	....	....	....	....
1990-91	Yale University	ECAC	29	11	10	21	....	....	....	34	....	....	....	....	....	....	....	....	....	....	....	....	....	....	....	....	....	....
1991-92	Yale University	ECAC	27	9	16	25	....	....	....	26	....	....	....	....	....	....	....	....	....	....	....	....	....	....	....	....	....	....
1992-93	Fredericton Canadiens	AHL	55	15	13	28	....	....	....	20	....	....	....	....	....	....	....	....	....	....	5	0	1	1	2	....	....	....
	Wheeling Thunderbirds	ECHL	9	6	5	11	....	....	....	24	....	....	....	....	....	....	....	....	....	....	....	....	....	....	....	....	....	....
1993-94	**Montreal Canadiens**	**NHL**	**2**	**0**	**1**	**1**	**0**	**1**	**1**	**0**	**0**	**0**	**0**	**0**	**0.0**	**1**	**0**	**0**	**0**	**1**	....	....	....	....	....	....	....	....
	Fredericton Canadiens	AHL	57	29	32	61	....	....	....	60	....	....	....	....	....	....	....	....	....	....	....	....	....	....	....	....	....	....
1994-95	Fredericton Canadiens	AHL	80	27	35	62	....	....	....	62	....	....	....	....	....	....	....	....	....	....	17	6	2	8	6	....	....	....
	Montreal Canadiens	**NHL**	**1**	**0**	**0**	**0**	**0**	**0**	**0**	**0**	**0**	**0**	**0**	**3**	**0.0**	**0**	**0**	**1**	**1**	**0**	....	....	....	....	....	....	....	....
1995-96	**Montreal Canadiens**	**NHL**	**10**	**1**	**0**	**1**	**1**	**0**	**1**	**2**	**0**	**0**	**0**	**9**	**11.1**	**2**	**1**	**7**	**1**	**–5**	....	....	....	....	....	....	....	....
	Calgary Flames	**NHL**	**8**	**0**	**0**	**0**	**0**	**0**	**0**	**4**	**0**	**0**	**0**	**11**	**0.0**	**0**	**0**	**4**	**0**	**–4**	....	....	....	....	....	....	....	....
	Saint John Flames	AHL	18	5	13	18	....	....	....	8	....	....	....	....	....	....	....	....	....	....	....	....	....	....	....	....	....	....
	Phoenix Roadrunners	IHL	31	6	9	15	....	....	....	25	....	....	....	....	....	....	....	....	....	....	4	0	2	2	6	....	....	....

			REGULAR SEASON																		PLAYOFFS							
Season	Club	League	GP	G	A	Pts	AG	AA	APts	PIM	PP	SH	GW	S	%	TGF	PGF	TGA	PGA	+/-	GP	G	A	Pts	PIM	PP	SH	GW
1996-97	**Florida Panthers**	**NHL**	**3**	**0**	**0**	**0**	**0**	**0**	**0**	**0**	**0**	**0**	**0**	**5**	**0.0**	**0**	**0**	**1**	**0**	**–1**	....	....	....	....	....	....	....	....
	Carolina Monarchs	AHL	74	29	41	70	....	....	....	57	....	....	....	....	....	....	....	....	....	....	....	....	....	....	....	....	....	....
1997-98	Beast of New Haven	AHL	64	24	28	52	....	....	....	41	....	....	....	....	....	....	....	....	....	....	3	2	1	3	2	....	....	....
1998-99	Beast of New Haven	AHL	61	18	27	45	....	....	....	76	....	....	....	....	....	....	....	....	....	....	....	....	....	....	....	....	....	....
99-2000	**Florida Panthers**	**NHL**	**3**	**0**	**0**	**0**	**0**	**0**	**0**	**0**	**0**	**0**	**0**	**2**	**0.0**	**1**	**0**	**3**	**0**	**–2**	....	....	....	....	....	....	....	....
	Louisville Panthers	AHL	61	29	27	56	....	....	....	28	....	....	....	....	....	....	....	....	....	....	4	1	3	4	2	....	....	....
	NHL Totals		**27**	**1**	**1**	**2**	**1**	**1**	**2**	**6**	**0**	**0**	**0**	**30**	**3.3**	**4**	**1**	**16**	**2**		....	....	....	....	....	....	....	....

• Son of Norm

Traded to **Calgary** by **Montreal** with Yves Sarault for Calgary's 8th round choice (Petr Kubos) in 1997 Entry Draft, November 26, 1995. Traded to **LA Kings** by **Calgary** for Pat Conacher, February 10, 1996. Signed as a free agent by **Florida**, July 24, 1996.

• FERGUSON, George

George Stephen C – R. 6′, 195 lbs. b: Trenton, Ont., 8/22/1952. Toronto's 1st, 11th overall, in 1972.

Season	Club	League	GP	G	A	Pts	AG	AA	APts	PIM	PP	SH	GW	S	%	TGF	PGF	TGA	PGA	+/-	GP	G	A	Pts	PIM	PP	SH	GW
1968-69	Trenton Titans	OMHA	STATISTICS NOT AVAILABLE																									
1969-70	Oshawa Generals	OHA-Jr.	49	19	21	40	....	....	....	20	....	....	....	....	....	....	....	....	....	....	6	2	2	4	2	....	....	....
1970-71	Oshawa Generals	OHA-Jr.	8	2	0	2	....	....	....	19	....	....	....	....	....	....	....	....	....	....	....	....	....	....	....	....	....	....
	Toronto Marlboros	OMJHL	43	12	15	27	....	....	....	83	....	....	....	....	....	....	....	....	....	....	13	1	3	4	26	....	....	....
1971-72	Toronto Marlboros	OMJHL	62	36	56	92	....	....	....	104	....	....	....	....	....	....	....	....	....	....	10	3	8	11	22	....	....	....
1972-73	**Toronto Maple Leafs**	**NHL**	**72**	**10**	**13**	**23**	**9**	**10**	**19**	**34**	**3**	**0**	**1**	**92**	**10.9**	**39**	**7**	**49**	**0**	**–17**	....	....	....	....	....	....	....	....
1973-74	**Toronto Maple Leafs**	**NHL**	**16**	**0**	**4**	**4**	**0**	**3**	**3**	**4**	**0**	**0**	**0**	**19**	**0.0**	**7**	**2**	**5**	**1**	**1**	**3**	**0**	**1**	**1**	**2**	**0**	**0**	**0**
	Oklahoma City Blazers	CHL	35	16	33	49	....	....	....	21	....	....	....	....	....	....	....	....	....	....	....	....	....	....	....	....	....	....
1974-75	**Toronto Maple Leafs**	**NHL**	**69**	**19**	**30**	**49**	**17**	**22**	**39**	**61**	**3**	**1**	**5**	**134**	**14.2**	**68**	**11**	**57**	**5**	**5**	**7**	**1**	**0**	**1**	**7**	**0**	**0**	**0**
1975-76	**Toronto Maple Leafs**	**NHL**	**79**	**12**	**32**	**44**	**11**	**24**	**35**	**76**	**3**	**2**	**2**	**140**	**8.6**	**57**	**13**	**65**	**32**	**11**	**10**	**2**	**4**	**6**	**2**	**0**	**0**	**1**
1976-77	**Toronto Maple Leafs**	**NHL**	**50**	**9**	**15**	**24**	**8**	**12**	**20**	**24**	**0**	**2**	**0**	**73**	**12.3**	**35**	**7**	**48**	**20**	**0**	**9**	**0**	**3**	**3**	**7**	**0**	**0**	**0**
1977-78	**Toronto Maple Leafs**	**NHL**	**73**	**7**	**16**	**23**	**6**	**12**	**18**	**37**	**0**	**0**	**0**	**119**	**5.9**	**35**	**1**	**54**	**11**	**–9**	**13**	**5**	**1**	**6**	**7**	**0**	**0**	**0**
1978-79	**Pittsburgh Penguins**	**NHL**	**80**	**21**	**29**	**50**	**18**	**21**	**39**	**37**	**0**	**3**	**2**	**201**	**10.4**	**74**	**1**	**94**	**31**	**10**	**7**	**2**	**1**	**3**	**0**	**0**	**0**	**1**
1979-80	**Pittsburgh Penguins**	**NHL**	**73**	**21**	**28**	**49**	**18**	**20**	**38**	**36**	**1**	**3**	**3**	**176**	**11.9**	**62**	**6**	**93**	**37**	**0**	**5**	**0**	**3**	**3**	**4**	**0**	**0**	**0**
1980-81	**Pittsburgh Penguins**	**NHL**	**79**	**25**	**18**	**43**	**19**	**12**	**31**	**42**	**7**	**3**	**1**	**181**	**13.8**	**73**	**24**	**120**	**41**	**–30**	**5**	**2**	**6**	**8**	**9**	**0**	**0**	**0**
1981-82	**Pittsburgh Penguins**	**NHL**	**71**	**22**	**31**	**53**	**17**	**21**	**38**	**45**	**4**	**3**	**0**	**168**	**13.1**	**76**	**16**	**116**	**50**	**–6**	**5**	**0**	**1**	**1**	**0**	**0**	**0**	**0**
1982-83	**Pittsburgh Penguins**	**NHL**	**7**	**0**	**0**	**0**	**0**	**0**	**0**	**2**	**0**	**0**	**0**	**10**	**0.0**	**0**	**0**	**14**	**7**	**–7**	....	....	....	....	....	....	....	....
	Minnesota North Stars	**NHL**	**65**	**8**	**12**	**20**	**7**	**8**	**15**	**14**	**0**	**1**	**2**	**82**	**9.8**	**33**	**3**	**52**	**21**	**–1**	**9**	**0**	**3**	**3**	**4**	**0**	**0**	**0**
1983-84	**Minnesota North Stars**	**NHL**	**63**	**6**	**10**	**16**	**5**	**7**	**12**	**19**	**0**	**0**	**0**	**57**	**10.5**	**28**	**1**	**62**	**29**	**–6**	**13**	**2**	**0**	**2**	**2**	**0**	**0**	**1**
	NHL Totals		**797**	**160**	**238**	**398**	**135**	**172**	**307**	**431**	**21**	**18**	**16**	**1452**	**11.0**	**587**	**92**	**829**	**285**		**86**	**14**	**23**	**37**	**44**	**0**	**0**	**3**

Traded to **Pittsburgh** by **Toronto** with Randy Carlyle for Dave Burrows, June 14, 1978. Traded to **Minnesota** by **Pittsburgh** with Pittsburgh's 1st round choice (Brian Lawton) in 1983 Entry Draft for Ron Meighan, Anders Hakansson and Minnesota's 1st round choice (Bob Errey) in 1983 Entry Draft, October 28, 1982.

• FERGUSON, John

John Bowie LW – L. 5′11″, 190 lbs. b: Vancouver, B.C., 9/5/1938.

Season	Club	League	GP	G	A	Pts	AG	AA	APts	PIM	PP	SH	GW	S	%	TGF	PGF	TGA	PGA	+/-	GP	G	A	Pts	PIM	PP	SH	GW
1956-57	Melville Millionaires	SJHL	51	11	17	28	....	....	....	49	....	....	....	....	....	....	....	....	....	....	....	....	....	....	....	....	....	....
1957-58	Melville Millionaires	SJHL	50	14	30	44	....	....	....	100	....	....	....	....	....	....	....	....	....	....	....	....	....	....	....	....	....	....
1958-59	Melville Millionaires	SJHL	44	32	34	66	....	....	....	83	....	....	....	....	....	....	....	....	....	....	....	....	....	....	....	....	....	....
1959-60	Fort Wayne Komets	IHL	68	32	33	65	....	....	....	126	....	....	....	....	....	....	....	....	....	....	13	1	1	2	17	....	....	....
1960-61	Cleveland Barons	AHL	62	13	21	34	....	....	....	126	....	....	....	....	....	....	....	....	....	....	....	....	....	....	....	....	....	....
1961-62	Cleveland Barons	AHL	70	20	21	41	....	....	....	146	....	....	....	....	....	....	....	....	....	....	6	2	2	4	6	....	....	....
1962-63	Cleveland Barons	AHL	72	38	40	78	....	....	....	179	....	....	....	....	....	....	....	....	....	....	7	3	3	6	17	....	....	....
1963-64	**Montreal Canadiens**	**NHL**	**59**	**18**	**27**	**45**	**22**	**28**	**50**	**125**	....	....	....	....	....	....	....	....	....	....	**7**	**0**	**1**	**1**	**25**	**0**	**0**	**0**
1964-65♦	**Montreal Canadiens**	**NHL**	**69**	**17**	**27**	**44**	**20**	**28**	**48**	**156**	....	....	....	....	....	....	....	....	....	....	**13**	**3**	**1**	**4**	**28**	**0**	**0**	**0**
1965-66♦	**Montreal Canadiens**	**NHL**	**65**	**11**	**14**	**25**	**12**	**13**	**25**	**153**	....	....	....	....	....	....	....	....	....	....	**10**	**2**	**0**	**2**	***44**	**0**	**0**	**0**
1966-67	**Montreal Canadiens**	**NHL**	**67**	**20**	**22**	**42**	**23**	**21**	**44**	***177**	....	....	....	....	....	....	....	....	....	....	**10**	**4**	**2**	**6**	**22**	**1**	**0**	**2**
1967-68♦	**Montreal Canadiens**	**NHL**	**61**	**15**	**18**	**33**	**17**	**18**	**35**	**117**	**0**	**0**	**3**	**153**	**9.8**	**61**	**12**	**31**	**0**	**18**	**13**	**3**	**5**	**8**	**25**	**0**	**0**	**1**
1968-69♦	**Montreal Canadiens**	**NHL**	**71**	**29**	**23**	**52**	**31**	**20**	**51**	**185**	**2**	**0**	**7**	**185**	**15.7**	**73**	**6**	**37**	**0**	**30**	**14**	**4**	**3**	**7**	***80**	**2**	**2**	**0**
1969-70	**Montreal Canadiens**	**NHL**	**48**	**19**	**13**	**32**	**21**	**12**	**33**	**139**	**6**	**0**	**7**	**116**	**16.4**	**51**	**14**	**27**	**1**	**11**	....	....	....	....	....	....	....	....
1970-71♦	**Montreal Canadiens**	**NHL**	**60**	**16**	**14**	**30**	**16**	**12**	**28**	**162**	**3**	**0**	**4**	**117**	**13.7**	**48**	**9**	**37**	**0**	**2**	**18**	**4**	**6**	**10**	**36**	**1**	**0**	**1**
	NHL Totals		**500**	**145**	**158**	**303**	**162**	**152**	**314**	**1214**	....	....	....	....	....	....	....	....	....		**85**	**20**	**18**	**38**	**260**	....	....	....

AHL First All-Star Team (1963) • Played in NHL All-Star Game (1965, 1967)

Traded to **Montreal** by **Cleveland** (AHL) for cash, June, 1963.

• FERGUSON, Norm

Norman Gerard RW – R. 5′9″, 165 lbs. b: Sydney, N.S., 10/16/1945.

Season	Club	League	GP	G	A	Pts	AG	AA	APts	PIM	PP	SH	GW	S	%	TGF	PGF	TGA	PGA	+/-	GP	G	A	Pts	PIM	PP	SH	GW
1963-64	Lachine Maroons	QJHL	42	32	60	92	....	....	....	12	....	....	....	....	....	....	....	....	....	....	....	....	....	....	....	....	....	....
	Montreal NDG Monarchs	Mem-Cup	4	2	1	3	....	....	....	2	....	....	....	....	....	....	....	....	....	....	....	....	....	....	....	....	....	....
1964-65	Montreal Jr. Canadiens	OHA-Jr.	51	17	16	33	....	....	....	17	....	....	....	....	....	....	....	....	....	....	6	2	0	2	0	....	....	....
1965-66	Montreal Jr. Canadiens	OHA-Jr.	43	16	29	45	....	....	....	27	....	....	....	....	....	....	....	....	....	....	10	4	3	7	2	....	....	....
1966-67	Houston Apollos	CPHL	55	8	6	14	....	....	....	20	....	....	....	....	....	....	....	....	....	....	1	0	0	0	0	....	....	....
1967-68	Cleveland Barons	AHL	72	42	33	75	....	....	....	24	....	....	....	....	....	....	....	....	....	....	....	....	....	....	....	....	....	....
1968-69	**Oakland Seals**	**NHL**	**76**	**34**	**20**	**54**	**36**	**18**	**54**	**31**	**7**	**0**	**3**	**217**	**15.7**	**73**	**14**	**68**	**0**	**–9**	**7**	**1**	**4**	**5**	**7**	**0**	**0**	**0**
1969-70	**Oakland Seals**	**NHL**	**72**	**11**	**9**	**20**	**12**	**8**	**20**	**19**	**2**	**0**	**2**	**125**	**8.8**	**31**	**6**	**40**	**0**	**–15**	**3**	**0**	**0**	**0**	**0**	**0**	**0**	**0**
1970-71	**California Golden Seals**	**NHL**	**54**	**14**	**17**	**31**	**14**	**14**	**28**	**9**	**2**	**0**	**2**	**90**	**15.6**	**41**	**9**	**53**	**0**	**–21**	....	....	....	....	....	....	....	....
1971-72	**California Golden Seals**	**NHL**	**77**	**14**	**20**	**34**	**14**	**17**	**31**	**13**	**4**	**0**	**3**	**94**	**14.9**	**51**	**8**	**48**	**0**	**–5**	....	....	....	....	....	....	....	....
1972-73	New York Raiders	WHA	56	28	40	68	....	....	....	8	....	....	....	....	....	....	....	....	....	....	....	....	....	....	....	....	....	....
1973-74	New York-Jersey Knights	WHA	75	15	21	36	....	....	....	12	....	....	....	....	....	....	....	....	....	....	....	....	....	....	....	....	....	....
1974-75	San Diego Mariners	WHA	78	36	33	69	....	....	....	6	....	....	....	....	....	....	....	....	....	....	10	6	5	11	0	....	....	....
1975-76	San Diego Mariners	WHA	79	37	37	74	....	....	....	12	....	....	....	....	....	....	....	....	....	....	4	2	0	2	9	....	....	....
1976-77	San Diego Mariners	WHA	77	39	32	71	....	....	....	5	....	....	....	....	....	....	....	....	....	....	7	2	4	6	0	....	....	....
1977-78	Edmonton Oilers	WHA	71	26	21	47	....	....	....	2	....	....	....	....	....	....	....	....	....	....	5	0	0	0	0	....	....	....
	NHL Totals		**279**	**73**	**66**	**139**	**76**	**57**	**133**	**72**	**15**	**0**	**10**	**526**	**13.9**	**196**	**37**	**209**	**0**		**10**	**1**	**4**	**5**	**7**	**0**	**0**	**0**
	Other Major League Totals		436	181	184	365	....	....	....	45	....	....	....	....	....	....	....	....	....	....	26	10	9	19	9	....	....	....

• Father of Craig

Traded to **Oakland** by **Montreal** with Stan Fuller and future considerations (Francois Lacombe and Michel Jacques, June, 1968) for Wally Boyer, Alain Caron, Oakland's 1st round choices in 1968 (Jim Pritchard) and 1970 (Ray Martyniuk) Amateur Drafts and future considerations (Lyle Bradley, June, 1968), May 21, 1968. Selected by **NY Raiders** (WHA) in 1972 WHA General Player Draft, February 12, 1972. Claimed by **NY Islanders** from **Oakland** in Expansion Draft, June 6, 1972. Transferred to **San Diego** (WHA) after **New York-Jersey** franchise relocated, April 30, 1974. Signed as a free agent by **Edmonton** (WHA) after **San Diego** franchise folded, May, 1977.

• FERGUSON, Scott

D – L. 6′1″, 195 lbs. b: Camrose, Alta., 1/6/1973.

Season	Club	League	GP	G	A	Pts	AG	AA	APts	PIM	PP	SH	GW	S	%	TGF	PGF	TGA	PGA	+/-	GP	G	A	Pts	PIM	PP	SH	GW
1990-91	Sherwood Park Crusaders	AJHL	32	2	9	11	....	....	....	91	....	....	....	....	....	....	....	....	....	....	....	....	....	....	....	....	....	....
	Kamloops Blazers	WHL	4	0	0	0	....	....	....	0	....	....	....	....	....	....	....	....	....	....	....	....	....	....	....	....	....	....
1991-92	Kamloops Blazers	WHL	62	4	10	14	....	....	....	138	....	....	....	....	....	....	....	....	....	....	12	0	2	2	21	....	....	....
	Kamloops Blazers	Mem-Cup	2	0	0	0	....	....	....	2	....	....	....	....	....	....	....	....	....	....	....	....	....	....	....	....	....	....
1992-93	Kamloops Blazers	WHL	71	4	19	23	....	....	....	206	....	....	....	....	....	....	....	....	....	....	13	0	2	2	24	....	....	....
1993-94	Kamloops Blazers	WHL	68	5	49	54	....	....	....	180	....	....	....	....	....	....	....	....	....	....	19	5	11	16	48	....	....	....
	Kamloops Blazers	Mem-Cup	3	0	3	3	....	....	....	10	....	....	....	....	....	....	....	....	....	....	....	....	....	....	....	....	....	....
1994-95	Cape Breton Oilers	AHL	58	4	6	10	....	....	....	103	....	....	....	....	....	....	....	....	....	....	....	....	....	....	....	....	....	....
	Wheeling Thunderbirds	ECHL	5	1	5	6	....	....	....	16	....	....	....	....	....	....	....	....	....	....	....	....	....	....	....	....	....	....
1995-96	Cape Breton Oilers	AHL	80	5	16	21	....	....	....	196	....	....	....	....	....	....	....	....	....	....	....	....	....	....	....	....	....	....
1996-97	Hamilton Bulldogs	AHL	74	6	14	20	....	....	....	115	....	....	....	....	....	....	....	....	....	....	21	5	7	12	59	....	....	....
1997-98	**Edmonton Oilers**	**NHL**	**1**	**0**	**0**	**0**	**0**	**0**	**0**	**0**	**0**	**0**	**0**	**0**	**0.0**	**2**	**1**	**0**	**0**	**1**	....	....	....	....	....	....	....	....
	Hamilton Bulldogs	AHL	77	7	17	24	....	....	....	150	....	....	....	....	....	....	....	....	....	....	9	0	3	3	16	....	....	....

Season	Club	League	REGULAR SEASON GP	G	A	Pts	AG	AA	APts	PIM	PP	SH	GW	S	%	TGF	PGF	TGA	PGA	+/–	PLAYOFFS GP	G	A	Pts	PIM	PP	SH	GW
1998-99	**Mighty Ducks of Anaheim**	**NHL**	**2**	**0**	**1**	**1**	**0**	**1**	**1**	**0**	**0**	**0**	**0**	**1**	**0.0**	**1**	**0**	**1**	**0**	**0**	....	....	....	....	....	....	....	....
	Cincinnati Mighty Ducks	AHL	78	4	31	35	....	....	....	59	....	....	....	....	....	....	....	....	....	....	3	0	0	0	4	....	....	....
99-2000	Cincinnati Mighty Ducks	AHL	77	7	25	32	....	....	....	166	....	....	....	....	....	....	....	....	....	....	....	....	....	....	....	....	....	....
	NHL Totals		**3**	**0**	**1**	**1**	**0**	**1**	**1**	**0**	**0**	**0**	**0**	**1**	**0.0**	**3**	**1**	**1**	**0**		....	....	....	....	....	....	....	....

WHL West Second All-Star Team (1994)

Signed as a free agent by **Edmonton**, June 2, 1994. Traded to **Ottawa** by **Edmonton** for Frantisek Musil, March 9, 1998. Signed as a free agent by **Anaheim**, July 27, 1998. Signed as a free agent by **Edmonton**, July 5, 2000.

• FERNER, Mark

Mark E. D – L. 6', 193 lbs. b: Regina, Sask., 9/5/1965. Buffalo's 12th, 202nd overall, in 1983.

Season	Club	League	GP	G	A	Pts	AG	AA	APts	PIM	PP	SH	GW	S	%	TGF	PGF	TGA	PGA	+/–	GP	G	A	Pts	PIM	PP	SH	GW
1981-82	Regina Loggers	AAHA	STATISTICS NOT AVAILABLE																									
1982-83	Kamloops Jr. Oilers	WHL	69	6	15	21	....	....	....	81	....	....	....	....	....	....	....	....	....	....	7	0	0	0	7	....	....	....
1983-84	Kamloops Jr. Oilers	WHL	72	9	30	39	....	....	....	169	....	....	....	....	....	....	....	....	....	....	14	1	8	9	20	....	....	....
	Kamloops Jr. Oilers	Mem-Cup	4	0	1	1	....	....	....	20	....	....	....	....	....	....	....	....	....	....	....	....	....	....	....	....	....	....
1984-85	Kamloops Blazers	WHL	69	15	39	54	....	....	....	91	....	....	....	....	....	....	....	....	....	....	15	4	9	13	21	....	....	....
1985-86	Rochester Americans	AHL	63	3	14	17	....	....	....	87	....	....	....	....	....	....	....	....	....	....	....	....	....	....	....	....	....	....
1986-87	**Buffalo Sabres**	**NHL**	**13**	**0**	**3**	**3**	**0**	**2**	**2**	**9**	**0**	**0**	**0**	**5**	**0.0**	**7**	**0**	**6**	**1**	**2**	....	....	....	....	....	....	....	....
	Rochester Americans	AHL	54	0	12	12	....	....	....	157	....	....	....	....	....	....	....	....	....	....	....	....	....	....	....	....	....	....
1987-88	Rochester Americans	AHL	69	1	25	26	....	....	....	165	....	....	....	....	....	....	....	....	....	....	7	1	4	5	31	....	....	....
1988-89	**Buffalo Sabres**	**NHL**	**2**	**0**	**0**	**0**	**0**	**0**	**0**	**2**	**0**	**0**	**0**	**0**	**0.0**	**1**	**0**	**3**	**0**	**–2**	....	....	....	....	....	....	....	....
	Rochester Americans	AHL	55	0	18	18	....	....	....	97	....	....	....	....	....	....	....	....	....	....	....	....	....	....	....	....	....	....
1989-90	**Washington Capitals**	**NHL**	**2**	**0**	**0**	**0**	**0**	**0**	**0**	**0**	**0**	**0**	**0**	**2**	**0.0**	**0**	**0**	**1**	**0**	**–1**	....	....	....	....	....	....	....	....
	Baltimore Skipjacks	AHL	74	7	28	35	....	....	....	76	....	....	....	....	....	....	....	....	....	....	11	1	2	3	21	....	....	....
1990-91	**Washington Capitals**	**NHL**	**7**	**0**	**1**	**1**	**0**	**1**	**1**	**4**	**0**	**0**	**0**	**3**	**0.0**	**2**	**0**	**4**	**0**	**–2**	....	....	....	....	....	....	....	....
	Baltimore Skipjacks	AHL	61	14	40	54	....	....	....	38	....	....	....	....	....	....	....	....	....	....	6	1	4	5	24	....	....	....
1991-92	Baltimore Skipjacks	AHL	57	7	38	45	....	....	....	67	....	....	....	....	....	....	....	....	....	....	....	....	....	....	....	....	....	....
	St. John's Maple Leafs	AHL	15	1	8	9	....	....	....	6	....	....	....	....	....	....	....	....	....	....	14	2	14	16	38	....	....	....
1992-93	New Haven Senators	AHL	34	5	7	12	....	....	....	69	....	....	....	....	....	....	....	....	....	....	....	....	....	....	....	....	....	....
	San Diego Gulls	IHL	26	0	15	15	....	....	....	34	....	....	....	....	....	....	....	....	....	....	11	1	2	3	8	....	....	....
1993-94	**Mighty Ducks of Anaheim**	**NHL**	**50**	**3**	**5**	**8**	**3**	**4**	**7**	**30**	**0**	**0**	**0**	**44**	**6.8**	**32**	**4**	**57**	**13**	**–16**	....	....	....	....	....	....	....	....
1994-95	**Mighty Ducks of Anaheim**	**NHL**	**14**	**0**	**1**	**1**	**0**	**1**	**1**	**6**	**0**	**0**	**0**	**15**	**0.0**	**10**	**2**	**18**	**6**	**–4**	....	....	....	....	....	....	....	....
	San Diego Gulls	IHL	46	3	12	15	....	....	....	51	....	....	....	....	....	....	....	....	....	....	....	....	....	....	....	....	....	....
	Detroit Red Wings	**NHL**	**3**	**0**	**0**	**0**	**0**	**0**	**0**	**0**	**0**	**0**	**0**	**1**	**0.0**	**2**	**0**	**2**	**0**	**0**	....	....	....	....	....	....	....	....
	Adirondack Red Wings	AHL	3	0	0	0	....	....	....	2	....	....	....	....	....	....	....	....	....	....	1	0	0	0	0	....	....	....
1995-96	Orlando Solar Bears	IHL	43	4	18	22	....	....	....	37	....	....	....	....	....	....	....	....	....	....	23	4	10	14	8	....	....	....
1996-97	Orlando Solar Bears	IHL	61	12	18	30	....	....	....	55	....	....	....	....	....	....	....	....	....	....	....	....	....	....	....	....	....	....
	Long Beach Ice Dogs	IHL	17	2	6	8	....	....	....	31	....	....	....	....	....	....	....	....	....	....	18	3	4	7	6	....	....	....
1997-98	Kassel Huskies	Germany	9	1	1	2	....	....	....	12	....	....	....	....	....	....	....	....	....	....	....	....	....	....	....	....	....	....
	Kassel Huskies	EuroHL	3	0	0	0	....	....	....	0	....	....	....	....	....	....	....	....	....	....	....	....	....	....	....	....	....	....
	Long Beach Ice Dogs	IHL	65	1	30	31	....	....	....	66	....	....	....	....	....	....	....	....	....	....	16	2	11	13	10	....	....	....
1998-99	Long Beach Ice Dogs	IHL	59	2	24	26	....	....	....	78	....	....	....	....	....	....	....	....	....	....	8	1	3	4	14	....	....	....
99-2000	Houston Aeros	IHL	25	2	6	8	....	....	....	20	....	....	....	....	....	....	....	....	....	....	....	....	....	....	....	....	....	....
	Schwenningen Wild Wings	Germany	21	2	3	5	....	....	....	30	....	....	....	....	....	....	....	....	....	....	....	....	....	....	....	....	....	....
	NHL Totals		**91**	**3**	**10**	**13**	**3**	**8**	**11**	**51**	**0**	**0**	**0**	**70**	**4.3**	**54**	**6**	**91**	**20**		....	....	....	....	....	....	....	....

WHL West First All-Star Team (1985)

Traded to **Washington** by **Buffalo** for Scott McCrory, June 1, 1989. Traded to **Toronto** by **Washington** for cash, February 27, 1992. Signed as a free agent by **Ottawa**, August 6, 1992. Claimed by **Anaheim** from **Ottawa** in Expansion Draft, June, 24, 1993. Traded to **Detroit** by **Anaheim** with Stu Grimson and Anaheim's 6th round choice (Magnus Nilsson) in 1996 Entry Draft for Mike Sillinger and Jason York, April 4, 1994. Signed as a free agent by **Schwenningen** (Germany) following release by **Houston** (IHL), December 10, 1999.

• FERRARO, Chris

C/RW – R. 5'10", 180 lbs. b: Port Jefferson, NY, 1/24/1973. NY Rangers' 4th, 85th overall, in 1992.

Season	Club	League	GP	G	A	Pts	AG	AA	APts	PIM	PP	SH	GW	S	%	TGF	PGF	TGA	PGA	+/–	GP	G	A	Pts	PIM	PP	SH	GW
1990-91	Dubuque Fighting Saints	USHL	45	53	44	97	....	....	....	84	....	....	....	....	....	....	....	....	....	....	8	3	9	12	12	....	....	....
1991-92	Dubuque Fighting Saints	USHL	20	30	19	49	....	....	....	52	....	....	....	....	....	....	....	....	....	....	....	....	....	....	....	....	....	....
	Waterloo Black Hawks	USHL	18	19	31	50	....	....	....	54	....	....	....	....	....	....	....	....	....	....	4	5	6	11	14	....	....	....
	United States	WJC-A	7	4	3	7	....	....	....	2	....	....	....	....	....	....	....	....	....	....	....	....	....	....	....	....	....	....
1992-93	University of Maine	H-East	39	25	26	51	....	....	....	46	....	....	....	....	....	....	....	....	....	....	....	....	....	....	....	....	....	....
	United States	WJC-A	7	4	7	11	....	....	....	8	....	....	....	....	....	....	....	....	....	....	....	....	....	....	....	....	....	....
1993-94	University of Maine	H-East	4	0	1	1	....	....	....	8	....	....	....	....	....	....	....	....	....	....	....	....	....	....	....	....	....	....
	United States	Nat-Team	48	8	34	42	....	....	....	58	....	....	....	....	....	....	....	....	....	....	....	....	....	....	....	....	....	....
1994-95	Atlanta Knights	IHL	54	13	14	27	....	....	....	72	....	....	....	....	....	....	....	....	....	....	....	....	....	....	....	....	....	....
	Binghamton Rangers	AHL	13	6	4	10	....	....	....	38	....	....	....	....	....	....	....	....	....	....	10	2	3	5	16	....	....	....
1995-96	**New York Rangers**	**NHL**	**2**	**1**	**0**	**1**	**1**	**0**	**1**	**0**	**1**	**0**	**0**	**4**	**25.0**	**1**	**1**	**3**	**0**	**–3**	....	....	....	....	....	....	....	....
	Binghamton Rangers	AHL	77	32	67	99	....	....	....	208	....	....	....	....	....	....	....	....	....	....	4	4	2	6	13	....	....	....
1996-97	**New York Rangers**	**NHL**	**12**	**1**	**1**	**2**	**1**	**1**	**2**	**6**	**0**	**0**	**0**	**23**	**4.3**	**3**	**2**	**0**	**0**	**1**	....	....	....	....	....	....	....	....
	Binghamton Rangers	AHL	53	29	34	63	....	....	....	94	....	....	....	....	....	....	....	....	....	....	....	....	....	....	....	....	....	....
1997-98	**Pittsburgh Penguins**	**NHL**	**46**	**3**	**4**	**7**	**4**	**4**	**8**	**43**	**0**	**0**	**0**	**42**	**7.1**	**10**	**1**	**11**	**0**	**–2**	....	....	....	....	....	....	....	....
1998-99	**Edmonton Oilers**	**NHL**	**2**	**1**	**0**	**1**	**1**	**0**	**1**	**0**	**0**	**0**	**0**	**1**	**100.0**	**1**	**0**	**0**	**0**	**1**	....	....	....	....	....	....	....	....
	Hamilton Bulldogs	AHL	72	35	41	76	....	....	....	104	....	....	....	....	....	....	....	....	....	....	11	8	5	13	20	....	....	....
99-2000	**New York Islanders**	**NHL**	**11**	**1**	**3**	**4**	**1**	**3**	**4**	**8**	**0**	**0**	**0**	**15**	**6.7**	**7**	**2**	**4**	**0**	**1**	....	....	....	....	....	....	....	....
	Providence Bruins	AHL	21	9	9	18	....	....	....	32	....	....	....	....	....	....	....	....	....	....	....	....	....	....	....	....	....	....
	Chicago Wolves	IHL	25	7	18	25	....	....	....	40	....	....	....	....	....	....	....	....	....	....	16	5	8	13	14	....	....	....
	NHL Totals		**73**	**7**	**8**	**15**	**8**	**8**	**16**	**57**	**1**	**0**	**0**	**85**	**8.2**	**22**	**6**	**18**	**0**		....	....	....	....	....	....	....	....

• Brother of Peter

Claimed on waivers by **Pittsburgh** from **NY Rangers**, October 1, 1997. Signed as a free agent by **Edmonton**, August 13, 1998. Signed as a free agent by **NY Islanders**, July 22, 1999.

• FERRARO, Peter

Peter Joseph C – R. 5'10", 180 lbs. b: Port Jefferson, NY, 1/24/1973. NY Rangers' 1st, 24th overall, in 1992.

Season	Club	League	GP	G	A	Pts	AG	AA	APts	PIM	PP	SH	GW	S	%	TGF	PGF	TGA	PGA	+/–	GP	G	A	Pts	PIM	PP	SH	GW
1990-91	Dubuque Fighting Saints	USHL	29	21	31	52	....	....	....	83	....	....	....	....	....	....	....	....	....	....	8	7	5	12	10	....	....	....
1991-92	Dubuque Fighting Saints	USHL	21	25	25	50	....	....	....	92	....	....	....	....	....	....	....	....	....	....	....	....	....	....	....	....	....	....
	Waterloo Black Hawks	USHL	21	23	28	51	....	....	....	76	....	....	....	....	....	....	....	....	....	....	4	8	5	13	16	....	....	....
	United States	WJC-A	7	3	5	8	....	....	....	12	....	....	....	....	....	....	....	....	....	....	....	....	....	....	....	....	....	....
1992-93	University of Maine	H-East	36	18	32	50	....	....	....	106	....	....	....	....	....	....	....	....	....	....	....	....	....	....	....	....	....	....
	United States	WJC-A	7	7	4	11	....	....	....	8	....	....	....	....	....	....	....	....	....	....	....	....	....	....	....	....	....	....
1993-94	University of Maine	H-East	4	3	6	9	....	....	....	16	....	....	....	....	....	....	....	....	....	....	....	....	....	....	....	....	....	....
	United States	Nat-Team	60	30	34	64	....	....	....	87	....	....	....	....	....	....	....	....	....	....	....	....	....	....	....	....	....	....
	United States	Olympics	8	6	0	6	....	....	....	6	....	....	....	....	....	....	....	....	....	....	....	....	....	....	....	....	....	....
1994-95	Atlanta Knights	IHL	61	15	24	39	....	....	....	118	....	....	....	....	....	....	....	....	....	....	....	....	....	....	....	....	....	....
	Binghamton Rangers	AHL	12	2	6	8	....	....	....	67	....	....	....	....	....	....	....	....	....	....	11	4	3	7	51	....	....	....
1995-96	**New York Rangers**	**NHL**	**5**	**0**	**1**	**1**	**0**	**1**	**1**	**0**	**0**	**0**	**0**	**6**	**0.0**	**1**	**1**	**6**	**1**	**–5**	....	....	....	....	....	....	....	....
	Binghamton Rangers	AHL	68	48	53	101	....	....	....	157	....	....	....	....	....	....	....	....	....	....	4	1	6	7	22	....	....	....
1996-97	**New York Rangers**	**NHL**	**2**	**0**	**0**	**0**	**0**	**0**	**0**	**0**	**0**	**0**	**0**	**3**	**0.0**	**1**	**0**	**1**	**0**	**0**	**2**	**0**	**0**	**0**	**0**	**0**	**0**	**0**
	Binghamton Rangers	AHL	75	38	39	77	....	....	....	171	....	....	....	....	....	....	....	....	....	....	4	3	1	4	18	....	....	....
1997-98	**Pittsburgh Penguins**	**NHL**	**29**	**3**	**4**	**7**	**4**	**4**	**8**	**12**	**0**	**0**	**0**	**34**	**8.8**	**9**	**0**	**11**	**0**	**–2**	....	....	....	....	....	....	....	....
	New York Rangers	**NHL**	**1**	**0**	**0**	**0**	**0**	**0**	**0**	**2**	**0**	**0**	**0**	**3**	**0.0**	**1**	**1**	**2**	**0**	**–2**	....	....	....	....	....	....	....	....
	Hartford Wolf Pack	AHL	36	17	23	40	....	....	....	54	....	....	....	....	....	....	....	....	....	....	15	8	6	14	59	....	....	....

			REGULAR SEASON																		PLAYOFFS							
Season	Club	League	GP	G	A	Pts	AG	AA	APts	PIM	PP	SH	GW	S	%	TGF	PGF	TGA	PGA	+/–	GP	G	A	Pts	PIM	PP	SH	GW
1998-99	**Boston Bruins**	**NHL**	**46**	**6**	**8**	**14**	**7**	**8**	**15**	**44**	**1**	**0**	**1**	**61**	**9.8**	**18**	**2**	**8**	**2**	**10**	....	....	....	....	....	....	....	....
	Providence Bruins	AHL	16	15	10	25	....	....	....	14	....	....	....	....	....	....	....	....	....	....	19	9	12	21	38	....	....	....
99-2000	**Boston Bruins**	**NHL**	**5**	**0**	**1**	**1**	**0**	**1**	**1**	**0**	**0**	**0**	**0**	**3**	**0.0**	**1**	**0**	**2**	**0**	**–1**	....	....	....	....	....	....	....	....
	Providence Bruins	AHL	48	21	25	46	....	....	....	98	....	....	....	....	....	....	....	....	....	....	13	5	7	12	14	....	....	....
	NHL Totals		**88**	**9**	**14**	**23**	**11**	**14**	**25**	**58**	**1**	**0**	**1**	**110**	**8.2**	**31**	**4**	**30**	**3**		**2**	**0**	**0**	**0**	**0**	**0**	**0**	**0**

• Brother of Chris • WJC-A All-Star Team (1992) • AHL First All-Star Team (1996) • Won Jack A. Butterfield Trophy (Playoff MVP - AHL) (1999)

Claimed on waivers by **Pittsburgh** from **NY Rangers**, October 1, 1997. Claimed on waivers by **NY Rangers** from **Pittsburgh**, January 9, 1998. Signed as a free agent by **Boston**, August 5, 1998. Claimed by **Atlanta** from **Boston** in Expansion Draft, June 25, 1999. Traded to **Boston** by **Atlanta** for Randy Robitaille, June 25, 1999.

• FERRARO, Ray

C – L. 5'9", 200 lbs. b: Trail, B.C., 8/23/1964. Hartford's 5th, 88th overall, in 1982.

Season	Club	League	GP	G	A	Pts	AG	AA	APts	PIM	PP	SH	GW	S	%	TGF	PGF	TGA	PGA	+/–	GP	G	A	Pts	PIM	PP	SH	GW
1981-82	Penticton Knights	BCJHL	40	65	67	132	....	....	....	90	....	....	....	....	....	....	....	....	....	....	....	....	....	....	....	....	....	....
1982-83	Portland Winter Hawks	WHL	50	41	49	90	....	....	....	39	....	....	....	....	....	....	....	....	....	....	14	14	10	24	13	....	....	....
	Portland Winter Hawks	Mem-Cup	4	1	2	3	....	....	....	4	....	....	....	....	....	....	....	....	....	....	....	....	....	....	....	....	....	....
1983-84	Brandon Wheat Kings	WHL	72	*108	84	*192	....	....	....	84	....	....	....	....	....	....	....	....	....	....	11	13	15	28	20	....	....	....
1984-85	**Hartford Whalers**	**NHL**	**44**	**11**	**17**	**28**	**9**	**12**	**21**	**40**	**6**	**0**	**2**	**59**	**18.6**	**35**	**15**	**21**	**0**	**–1**	....	....	....	....	....	....	....	....
	Binghamton Whalers	AHL	37	20	13	33	....	....	....	29	....	....	....	....	....	....	....	....	....	....	....	....	....	....	....	....	....	....
1985-86	**Hartford Whalers**	**NHL**	**76**	**30**	**47**	**77**	**24**	**32**	**56**	**57**	**14**	**0**	**0**	**132**	**22.7**	**110**	**41**	**59**	**0**	**10**	**10**	**3**	**6**	**9**	**4**	**3**	**0**	**0**
1986-87	**Hartford Whalers**	**NHL**	**80**	**27**	**32**	**59**	**23**	**23**	**46**	**42**	**14**	**0**	**2**	**96**	**28.1**	**82**	**44**	**48**	**1**	**–9**	**6**	**1**	**1**	**2**	**8**	**0**	**0**	**0**
1987-88	**Hartford Whalers**	**NHL**	**68**	**21**	**29**	**50**	**18**	**21**	**39**	**81**	**6**	**0**	**2**	**105**	**20.0**	**70**	**29**	**40**	**0**	**1**	**6**	**1**	**1**	**2**	**6**	**1**	**0**	**0**
1988-89	**Hartford Whalers**	**NHL**	**80**	**41**	**35**	**76**	**35**	**25**	**60**	**86**	**11**	**0**	**7**	**169**	**24.3**	**100**	**29**	**70**	**0**	**1**	**4**	**2**	**0**	**2**	**4**	**0**	**0**	**0**
	Canada	WEC-A	9	1	5	6	....	....	....	8	....	....	....	....	....	....	....	....	....	....	....	....	....	....	....	....	....	....
1989-90	**Hartford Whalers**	**NHL**	**79**	**25**	**29**	**54**	**21**	**21**	**42**	**109**	**7**	**0**	**4**	**138**	**18.1**	**75**	**31**	**59**	**0**	**–15**	**7**	**0**	**3**	**3**	**2**	**0**	**0**	**0**
1990-91	**Hartford Whalers**	**NHL**	**15**	**2**	**5**	**7**	**2**	**4**	**6**	**18**	**1**	**0**	**0**	**18**	**11.1**	**13**	**6**	**8**	**0**	**–1**	....	....	....	....	....	....	....	....
	New York Islanders	**NHL**	**61**	**19**	**16**	**35**	**17**	**12**	**29**	**52**	**5**	**0**	**1**	**91**	**20.9**	**48**	**14**	**45**	**0**	**–11**	....	....	....	....	....	....	....	....
1991-92	**New York Islanders**	**NHL**	**80**	**40**	**40**	**80**	**36**	**30**	**66**	**92**	**7**	**0**	**4**	**154**	**26.0**	**103**	**23**	**55**	**0**	**25**	....	....	....	....	....	....	....	....
	Canada	WC-A	6	2	1	3	....	....	....	6	....	....	....	....	....	....	....	....	....	....	....	....	....	....	....	....	....	....
1992-93	**New York Islanders**	**NHL**	**46**	**14**	**13**	**27**	**12**	**9**	**21**	**40**	**3**	**0**	**1**	**72**	**19.4**	**43**	**7**	**36**	**0**	**0**	**18**	**13**	**7**	**20**	**18**	**0**	**0**	**0**
	Capital District Islanders	AHL	1	0	2	2	....	....	....	2	....	....	....	....	....	....	....	....	....	....	....	....	....	....	....	....	....	....
1993-94	**New York Islanders**	**NHL**	**82**	**21**	**32**	**53**	**20**	**25**	**45**	**83**	**5**	**0**	**3**	**136**	**15.4**	**75**	**18**	**58**	**2**	**1**	**4**	**1**	**0**	**1**	**6**	**0**	**0**	**0**
1994-95	**New York Islanders**	**NHL**	**47**	**22**	**21**	**43**	**39**	**31**	**70**	**30**	**2**	**0**	**1**	**94**	**23.4**	**50**	**9**	**41**	**1**	**1**	....	....	....	....	....	....	....	....
1995-96	**New York Rangers**	**NHL**	**65**	**25**	**29**	**54**	**25**	**24**	**49**	**82**	**8**	**0**	**4**	**160**	**15.6**	**76**	**27**	**36**	**0**	**13**	....	....	....	....	....	....	....	....
	Los Angeles Kings	**NHL**	**11**	**4**	**2**	**6**	**4**	**2**	**6**	**10**	**1**	**0**	**0**	**18**	**22.2**	**7**	**3**	**18**	**1**	**–13**	....	....	....	....	....	....	....	....
	Canada	WC-A	8	0	4	4	....	....	....	2	....	....	....	....	....	....	....	....	....	....	....	....	....	....	....	....	....	....
1996-97	**Los Angeles Kings**	**NHL**	**81**	**25**	**21**	**46**	**26**	**19**	**45**	**112**	**11**	**0**	**2**	**152**	**16.4**	**77**	**26**	**73**	**0**	**–22**	....	....	....	....	....	....	....	....
1997-98	**Los Angeles Kings**	**NHL**	**40**	**6**	**9**	**15**	**7**	**9**	**16**	**42**	**0**	**0**	**2**	**45**	**13.3**	**20**	**6**	**24**	**0**	**–10**	**3**	**0**	**1**	**1**	**2**	**0**	**0**	**0**
1998-99	**Los Angeles Kings**	**NHL**	**65**	**13**	**18**	**31**	**15**	**17**	**32**	**59**	**4**	**0**	**4**	**84**	**15.5**	**47**	**11**	**36**	**0**	**0**	....	....	....	....	....	....	....	....
99-2000	**Atlanta Thrashers**	**NHL**	**81**	**19**	**25**	**44**	**21**	**23**	**44**	**88**	**10**	**0**	**3**	**170**	**11.2**	**66**	**29**	**73**	**3**	**–33**	....	....	....	....	....	....	....	....
	NHL Totals		**1101**	**365**	**420**	**785**	**354**	**339**	**693**	**1123**	**115**	**0**	**42**	**1893**	**19.3**	**1097**	**368**	**800**	**8**		**58**	**21**	**19**	**40**	**50**	**4**	**0**	**0**

WHL First All-Star Team (1984) • Played in NHL All-Star Game (1992)

Traded to **NY Islanders** by **Hartford** for Doug Crossman, November 13, 1990. Signed as a free agent by **NY Rangers**, August 9, 1995. Traded to **LA Kings** by **NY Rangers** with Ian Laperriere, Mattias Norstrom, Nathan Lafayette and NY Rangers' 4th round choice (Sean Blanchard) in 1997 Entry Draft for Marty McSorley, Jari Kurri and Shane Churla, March 14, 1996. Signed as a free agent by **Atlanta**, August 9, 1999.

• FETISOV, Viacheslav

D – L. 6'1", 220 lbs. b: Moscow, USSR, 4/20/1958. New Jersey's 6th, 150th overall, in 1983.

Season	Club	League	GP	G	A	Pts	AG	AA	APts	PIM	PP	SH	GW	S	%	TGF	PGF	TGA	PGA	+/–	GP	G	A	Pts	PIM	PP	SH	GW
1974-75	CSKA Moscow	USSR-Jr.	1	0	0	0	....	....	....	0	....	....	....	....	....	....	....	....	....	....	....	....	....	....	....	....	....	....
	Soviet Union	EJC-A	5	1	0	1	....	....	....	0	....	....	....	....	....	....	....	....	....	....	....	....	....	....	....	....	....	....
1975-76	CSKA Moscow	USSR-Jr.	STATISTICS NOT AVAILABLE																									
	Soviet Union	WJC-A	4	0	0	0	....	....	....	11	....	....	....	....	....	....	....	....	....	....	....	....	....	....	....	....	....	....
	CSKA Moscow	USSR	1	0	0	0	....	....	....	0	....	....	....	....	....	....	....	....	....	....	....	....	....	....	....	....	....	....
	Soviet Union	EJC-A	4	2	0	2	....	....	....	0	....	....	....	....	....	....	....	....	....	....	....	....	....	....	....	....	....	....
1976-77	CSKA Moscow	USSR	28	3	4	7	....	....	....	14	....	....	....	....	....	....	....	....	....	....	....	....	....	....	....	....	....	....
	Soviet Union	WJC-A	7	3	2	5	....	....	....	4	....	....	....	....	....	....	....	....	....	....	....	....	....	....	....	....	....	....
	Soviet Union	WEC-A	5	3	3	6	....	....	....	2	....	....	....	....	....	....	....	....	....	....	....	....	....	....	....	....	....	....
1977-78	CSKA Moscow	USSR	35	9	18	27	....	....	....	46	....	....	....	....	....	....	....	....	....	....	....	....	....	....	....	....	....	....
	Soviet Union	WJC-A	7	3	5	8	....	....	....	6	....	....	....	....	....	....	....	....	....	....	....	....	....	....	....	....	....	....
	Soviet Union	WEC-A	10	4	6	10	....	....	....	11	....	....	....	....	....	....	....	....	....	....	....	....	....	....	....	....	....	....
1978-79	CSKA Moscow	USSR	29	10	19	29	....	....	....	40	....	....	....	....	....	....	....	....	....	....	....	....	....	....	....	....	....	....
1979-80	CSKA Moscow	USSR	37	10	14	24	....	....	....	46	....	....	....	....	....	....	....	....	....	....	....	....	....	....	....	....	....	....
	CSKA Moscow	Super-S	4	0	1	1	....	....	....	0	....	....	....	....	....	....	....	....	....	....	....	....	....	....	....	....	....	....
	Soviet Union	Olympics	7	5	4	9	....	....	....	10	....	....	....	....	....	....	....	....	....	....	....	....	....	....	....	....	....	....
1980-81	CSKA Moscow	USSR	48	13	16	29	....	....	....	44	....	....	....	....	....	....	....	....	....	....	....	....	....	....	....	....	....	....
	Soviet Union	WEC-A	8	1	4	5	....	....	....	6	....	....	....	....	....	....	....	....	....	....	....	....	....	....	....	....	....	....
1981-82	Soviet Union	Can-Cup	7	1	7	8	....	....	....	10	....	....	....	....	....	....	....	....	....	....	....	....	....	....	....	....	....	....
	CSKA Moscow	USSR	46	15	26	41	....	....	....	20	....	....	....	....	....	....	....	....	....	....	....	....	....	....	....	....	....	....
	Soviet Union	WEC-A	10	4	3	7	....	....	....	6	....	....	....	....	....	....	....	....	....	....	....	....	....	....	....	....	....	....
1982-83	CSKA Moscow	USSR	43	6	17	23	....	....	....	46	....	....	....	....	....	....	....	....	....	....	....	....	....	....	....	....	....	....
	USSR	Super-S	6	1	4	5	....	....	....	10	....	....	....	....	....	....	....	....	....	....	....	....	....	....	....	....	....	....
	Soviet Union	WEC-A	10	3	7	10	....	....	....	8	....	....	....	....	....	....	....	....	....	....	....	....	....	....	....	....	....	....
1983-84	CSKA Moscow	USSR	44	19	30	49	....	....	....	38	....	....	....	....	....	....	....	....	....	....	....	....	....	....	....	....	....	....
	Soviet Union	Olympics	7	3	8	11	....	....	....	8	....	....	....	....	....	....	....	....	....	....	....	....	....	....	....	....	....	....
1984-85	CSKA Moscow	USSR	20	13	12	25	....	....	....	6	....	....	....	....	....	....	....	....	....	....	....	....	....	....	....	....	....	....
	Soviet Union	WEC-A	10	6	7	13	....	....	....	15	....	....	....	....	....	....	....	....	....	....	....	....	....	....	....	....	....	....
1985-86	CSKA Moscow	USSR	40	15	19	34	....	....	....	12	....	....	....	....	....	....	....	....	....	....	....	....	....	....	....	....	....	....
	CSKA Moscow	Super-S	6	3	3	6	....	....	....	6	....	....	....	....	....	....	....	....	....	....	....	....	....	....	....	....	....	....
	Soviet Union	WEC-A	10	6	9	15	....	....	....	10	....	....	....	....	....	....	....	....	....	....	....	....	....	....	....	....	....	....
1986-87	CSKA Moscow	USSR	39	13	20	33	....	....	....	18	....	....	....	....	....	....	....	....	....	....	....	....	....	....	....	....	....	....
	USSR	RV-87	2	0	1	1	....	....	....	2	....	....	....	....	....	....	....	....	....	....	....	....	....	....	....	....	....	....
	Soviet Union	WEC-A	10	2	8	10	....	....	....	2	....	....	....	....	....	....	....	....	....	....	....	....	....	....	....	....	....	....
1987-88	Soviet Union	Can-Cup	9	2	5	7	....	....	....	9	....	....	....	....	....	....	....	....	....	....	....	....	....	....	....	....	....	....
	CSKA Moscow	USSR	46	18	17	35	....	....	....	26	....	....	....	....	....	....	....	....	....	....	....	....	....	....	....	....	....	....
	Soviet Union	Olympics	8	4	*9	13	....	....	....	6	....	....	....	....	....	....	....	....	....	....	....	....	....	....	....	....	....	....
1988-89	CSKA Moscow	USSR	23	9	8	17	....	....	....	18	....	....	....	....	....	....	....	....	....	....	....	....	....	....	....	....	....	....
	CSKA Moscow	Super-S	7	2	3	5	....	....	....	7	....	....	....	....	....	....	....	....	....	....	....	....	....	....	....	....	....	....
	Soviet Union	WEC-A	10	2	4	6	....	....	....	17	....	....	....	....	....	....	....	....	....	....	....	....	....	....	....	....	....	....
1989-90	**New Jersey Devils**	**NHL**	**72**	**8**	**34**	**42**	**7**	**24**	**31**	**52**	**2**	**0**	**0**	**108**	**7.4**	**107**	**24**	**108**	**34**	**9**	**6**	**0**	**2**	**2**	**10**	**0**	**0**	**0**
	Soviet Union	WEC-A	8	2	8	10	....	....	....	8	....	....	....	....	....	....	....	....	....	....	....	....	....	....	....	....	....	....
1990-91	**New Jersey Devils**	**NHL**	**67**	**3**	**16**	**19**	**3**	**12**	**15**	**62**	**1**	**0**	**0**	**71**	**4.2**	**64**	**12**	**78**	**31**	**5**	**7**	**0**	**0**	**0**	**17**	**0**	**0**	**0**
	Utica Devils	AHL	1	1	1	2	....	....	....	0	....	....	....	....	....	....	....	....	....	....	....	....	....	....	....	....	....	....
	Soviet Union	WEC-A	10	3	1	4	....	....	....	4	....	....	....	....	....	....	....	....	....	....	....	....	....	....	....	....	....	....
1991-92	**New Jersey Devils**	**NHL**	**70**	**3**	**23**	**26**	**3**	**17**	**20**	**108**	**0**	**0**	**1**	**70**	**4.3**	**80**	**18**	**66**	**15**	**11**	**6**	**0**	**3**	**3**	**8**	**0**	**0**	**0**
1992-93	**New Jersey Devils**	**NHL**	**76**	**4**	**23**	**27**	**3**	**16**	**19**	**158**	**1**	**1**	**0**	**63**	**6.3**	**81**	**13**	**80**	**19**	**7**	**5**	**0**	**2**	**2**	**4**	**0**	**0**	**0**
1993-94	**New Jersey Devils**	**NHL**	**52**	**1**	**14**	**15**	**1**	**11**	**12**	**30**	**0**	**0**	**0**	**36**	**2.8**	**45**	**8**	**37**	**14**	**14**	**14**	**1**	**0**	**1**	**8**	**0**	**0**	**0**
1994-95	CSKA Moscow	CIS	1	0	1	1	....	....	....	4	....	....	....	....	....	....	....	....	....	....	....	....	....	....	....	....	....	....
	New Jersey Devils	**NHL**	**4**	**0**	**1**	**1**	**0**	**1**	**1**	**0**	**0**	**0**	**0**	**1**	**0.0**	**2**	**0**	**4**	**0**	**–2**	....	....	....	....	....	....	....	....
	Detroit Red Wings	**NHL**	**14**	**3**	**11**	**14**	**5**	**16**	**21**	**2**	**3**	**0**	**0**	**36**	**8.3**	**23**	**7**	**15**	**2**	**3**	**18**	**0**	**8**	**8**	**14**	**0**	**0**	**0**
1995-96	**Detroit Red Wings**	**NHL**	**69**	**7**	**35**	**42**	**7**	**29**	**36**	**96**	**1**	**1**	**1**	**127**	**5.5**	**94**	**27**	**33**	**3**	**37**	**19**	**1**	**4**	**5**	**34**	**0**	**0**	**1**

			REGULAR SEASON																		PLAYOFFS							
Season	Club	League	GP	G	A	Pts	AG	AA	APts	PIM	PP	SH	GW	S	%	TGF	PGF	TGA	PGA	+/–	GP	G	A	Pts	PIM	PP	SH	GW
1996-97	Russia	W-Cup	4	0	2	2	....	....	....	12	....	....	....	....	....	....	....	....	....	....	....	....	....	....	....	....	....	....
♦	Detroit Red Wings	NHL	64	5	23	28	5	20	25	76	0	0	1	95	5.3	71	11	37	3	26	20	0	4	4	42	0	0	0
1997-98♦	Detroit Red Wings	NHL	58	2	12	14	2	12	14	72	0	0	1	55	3.6	41	7	34	4	4	21	0	3	3	10	0	0	0
1998-2000	New Jersey Devils	NHL	DID NOT PLAY – ASSISTANT COACH																									
	NHL Totals		546	36	192	228	36	158	194	656	8	2	4	662	5.4	608	127	492	125		116	2	26	28	147	0	0	1

Named Best Defenseman at EJC-A (1976) • WJC-A All-Star Team (1978) • Named Best Defenseman at WJC-A (1978) • WEC-A All-Star Team (1978, 1982, 1983, 1985, 1986, 1987, 1989, 1990, 1991) • Named Best Defenseman at WEC-A (1978, 1982, 1985, 1986, 1989) • USSR First All-Star Team (1979, 1980, 1982, 1983, 1984, 1985, 1986, 1987, 1988) • USSR Player of the Year (1982, 1986) • Leningradskaya-Pravda Trophy (Top Scoring Defenseman) (1984, 1986, 1987, 1988) • Canada Cup All-Star Team (1987) • Played in NHL All-Star Game (1997, 1998)

• Re-entered NHL draft. Originally Montreal's 14th choice, 201st overall, in 1978 Amateur Draft. • Traded to **Detroit** by **New Jersey** for Detroit's 3rd round choice (David Gosselin) in 1995 Entry Draft, April 3, 1995.

• FIDLER, Mike

Michael Edward LW – L. 5'11", 195 lbs. b: Everett, MA, 8/19/1956. California's 3rd, 41st overall, in 1976.

Season	Club	League	GP	G	A	Pts	AG	AA	APts	PIM	PP	SH	GW	S	%	TGF	PGF	TGA	PGA	+/–	GP	G	A	Pts	PIM	PP	SH	GW
1973-74	Malden Catholic High School	Hi-School	20	*45	34	79	....	....	....	....	....	....	....	....	....	....	....	....	....	....	....	....	....	....	....	....	....	....
1974-75	Boston University	ECAC	31	24	24	48	....	....	....	12	....	....	....	....	....	....	....	....	....	....	....	....	....	....	....	....	....	....
1975-76	Boston University	ECAC	29	22	24	46	....	....	....	78	....	....	....	....	....	....	....	....	....	....	....	....	....	....	....	....	....	....
1976-77	Cleveland Barons	NHL	46	17	16	33	15	12	27	17	7	0	3	112	15.2	50	18	37	0	–5	....	....	....	....	....	....	....	....
	Salt Lake Golden Eagles	CHL	10	12	6	18	....	....	....	0	....	....	....	....	....	....	....	....	....	....	....	....	....	....	....	....	....	....
1977-78	Cleveland Barons	NHL	78	23	28	51	21	22	43	38	4	0	3	181	12.7	79	21	71	0	–13	....	....	....	....	....	....	....	....
	United States	WEC-A	10	8	2	10	....	....	....	18	....	....	....	....	....	....	....	....	....	....	....	....	....	....	....	....	....	....
1978-79	Minnesota North Stars	NHL	59	23	26	49	20	19	39	42	4	0	3	158	14.6	56	15	66	0	–25	....	....	....	....	....	....	....	....
	Oklahoma City Stars	CHL	8	6	4	10	....	....	....	7	....	....	....	....	....	....	....	....	....	....	....	....	....	....	....	....	....	....
1979-80	Minnesota North Stars	NHL	24	5	4	9	4	3	7	13	1	0	0	38	13.2	18	4	12	1	3	....	....	....	....	....	....	....	....
1980-81	Minnesota North Stars	DN-Cup	3	1	1	2	....	....	....	2	....	....	....	....	....	....	....	....	....	....	....	....	....	....	....	....	....	....
	Minnesota North Stars	NHL	20	5	12	17	4	8	12	6	0	0	0	42	11.9	25	10	11	1	5	....	....	....	....	....	....	....	....
	Hartford Whalers	NHL	38	9	9	18	7	6	13	4	2	0	0	59	15.3	29	7	38	1	–15	....	....	....	....	....	....	....	....
1981-82	Hartford Whalers	NHL	2	0	1	1	0	1	1	0	0	0	0	2	0.0	2	1	1	0	0	....	....	....	....	....	....	....	....
	Oklahoma City Stars	CHL	6	3	5	8	....	....	....	0	....	....	....	....	....	....	....	....	....	....	....	....	....	....	....	....	....	....
	Erie Blades	AHL	5	1	2	3	....	....	....	0	....	....	....	....	....	....	....	....	....	....	....	....	....	....	....	....	....	....
1982-83	Chicago Black Hawks	NHL	4	2	1	3	2	1	3	4	0	0	0	6	33.3	3	0	4	0	–1	....	....	....	....	....	....	....	....
	Springfield Indians	AHL	30	10	17	27	....	....	....	38	....	....	....	....	....	....	....	....	....	....	....	....	....	....	....	....	....	....
	United States	WC-B	7	6	7	13	....	....	....	4	....	....	....	....	....	....	....	....	....	....	....	....	....	....	....	....	....	....
1983-84	New Haven Nighthawks	AHL	16	6	7	13	....	....	....	6	....	....	....	....	....	....	....	....	....	....	....	....	....	....	....	....	....	....
	WEV Wein	Austria	10	11	13	24	....	....	....	18	....	....	....	....	....	....	....	....	....	....	....	....	....	....	....	....	....	....
	NHL Totals		271	84	97	181	73	72	145	124	18	0	9	598	14.0	262	76	240	3		....	....	....	....	....	....	....	....

Transferred to **Cleveland** after **California** franchise relocated, August 26, 1976. Protected by **Minnesota** prior to **Cleveland-Minnesota** Dispersal Draft, June 15, 1978. • Missed majority of 1979-80 season recovering from shoulder surgery, June, 1979. Traded to **Hartford** by **Minnesota** for Gordie Roberts, December 16, 1980. Signed as a free agent by **Boston**, December 1, 1981. Signed as a free agent by **Chicago**, November 28, 1982.

• FILIMONOV, Dmitri

D – R. 6'4", 220 lbs. b: Perm, USSR, 10/14/1971. Winnipeg's 2nd, 49th overall, in 1991.

Season	Club	League	GP	G	A	Pts	AG	AA	APts	PIM	PP	SH	GW	S	%	TGF	PGF	TGA	PGA	+/–	GP	G	A	Pts	PIM	PP	SH	GW
1988-89	Dynamo Moscow	USSR-Jr.	STATISTICS NOT AVAILABLE																									
	Soviet Union	EJC-A	6	3	0	3	....	....	....	0	....	....	....	....	....	....	....	....	....	....	....	....	....	....	....	....	....	....
1989-90	Dynamo Moscow	USSR-Jr.	STATISTICS NOT AVAILABLE																									
1990-91	Dynamo Moscow	Fr-Tour	1	0	0	0	....	....	....	0	....	....	....	....	....	....	....	....	....	....	....	....	....	....	....	....	....	....
	Dynamo Moscow	USSR	45	4	6	10	....	....	....	12	....	....	....	....	....	....	....	....	....	....	....	....	....	....	....	....	....	....
	Dynamo Moscow	Super-S	7	2	1	3	....	....	....	2	....	....	....	....	....	....	....	....	....	....	....	....	....	....	....	....	....	....
1991-92	Soviet Union	Can-Cup	5	0	0	0	....	....	....	0	....	....	....	....	....	....	....	....	....	....	....	....	....	....	....	....	....	....
	Dynamo Moscow	CIS	38	3	2	5	....	....	....	12	....	....	....	....	....	....	....	....	....	....	....	....	....	....	....	....	....	....
1992-93	Dynamo Moscow	CIS	42	2	3	5	....	....	....	30	....	....	....	....	....	....	....	....	....	....	10	1	2	3	2	....	....	....
1993-94	Ottawa Senators	NHL	30	1	4	5	1	3	4	18	0	0	0	15	6.7	17	3	26	2	–10	....	....	....	....	....	....	....	....
	P.E.I. Senators	AHL	48	10	16	26	....	....	....	14	....	....	....	....	....	....	....	....	....	....	....	....	....	....	....	....	....	....
1994-95	P.E.I. Senators	AHL	32	6	19	25	....	....	....	14	....	....	....	....	....	....	....	....	....	....	9	0	1	1	2	....	....	....
1995-96	Indianapolis Ice	IHL	10	0	1	1	....	....	....	12	....	....	....	....	....	....	....	....	....	....	....	....	....	....	....	....	....	....
1996-97	KalPa Kuopio	Finland	27	2	1	3	....	....	....	12	....	....	....	....	....	....	....	....	....	....	....	....	....	....	....	....	....	....
1997-98	Molot Perm	Russia	45	9	10	19	....	....	....	30	....	....	....	....	....	....	....	....	....	....	....	....	....	....	....	....	....	....
1998-99	Molot Perm	Russia	42	4	10	14	....	....	....	20	....	....	....	....	....	....	....	....	....	....	6	1	0	1	0	....	....	....
99-2000	Molot-Perm	Russia	37	8	6	14	....	....	....	26	....	....	....	....	....	....	....	....	....	....	....	....	....	....	....	....	....	....
	NHL Totals		30	1	4	5	1	3	4	18	0	0	0	15	6.7	17	3	26	2		....	....	....	....	....	....	....	....

EJC-A All-Star Team (1989)

Rights traded to **Ottawa** by **Winnipeg** for Ottawa's 4th round choice (Ruslan Batyrshin) in 1993 Entry Draft, March 4, 1993.

• FINLEY, Jeff

John Jeffrey D – L. 6'2", 205 lbs. b: Edmonton, Alta., 4/14/1967. NY Islanders' 4th, 55th overall, in 1985.

Season	Club	League	GP	G	A	Pts	AG	AA	APts	PIM	PP	SH	GW	S	%	TGF	PGF	TGA	PGA	+/–	GP	G	A	Pts	PIM	PP	SH	GW
1983-84	Summerland Buckaroos	BCJHL	49	0	21	21	....	....	....	14	....	....	....	....	....	....	....	....	....	....	....	....	....	....	....	....	....	....
	Portland Winter Hawks	WHL	5	0	0	0	....	....	....	5	....	....	....	....	....	....	....	....	....	....	5	0	1	1	4	....	....	....
1984-85	Portland Winter Hawks	WHL	69	6	44	50	....	....	....	57	....	....	....	....	....	....	....	....	....	....	6	1	2	3	2	....	....	....
1985-86	Portland Winter Hawks	WHL	70	11	59	70	....	....	....	83	....	....	....	....	....	....	....	....	....	....	15	1	7	8	16	....	....	....
	Portland Winter Hawks	Mem-Cup	4	0	2	2	....	....	....	2	....	....	....	....	....	....	....	....	....	....	....	....	....	....	....	....	....	....
1986-87	Portland Winter Hawks	WHL	72	13	53	66	....	....	....	113	....	....	....	....	....	....	....	....	....	....	20	1	*21	22	27	....	....	....
1987-88	New York Islanders	NHL	10	0	5	5	0	4	4	15	0	0	0	9	0.0	15	2	8	0	5	1	0	0	0	2	0	0	0
	Springfield Indians	AHL	52	5	18	23	....	....	....	50	....	....	....	....	....	....	....	....	....	....	....	....	....	....	....	....	....	....
1988-89	New York Islanders	NHL	4	0	0	0	0	0	0	6	0	0	0	1	0.0	2	0	1	0	1	....	....	....	....	....	....	....	....
	Springfield Indians	AHL	65	3	16	19	....	....	....	55	....	....	....	....	....	....	....	....	....	....	....	....	....	....	....	....	....	....
1989-90	New York Islanders	NHL	11	0	1	1	0	1	1	0	0	0	0	7	0.0	7	0	11	4	0	5	0	2	2	2	0	0	0
	Springfield Indians	AHL	57	1	15	16	....	....	....	41	....	....	....	....	....	....	....	....	....	....	13	1	4	5	23	....	....	....
1990-91	New York Islanders	NHL	11	0	0	0	0	0	0	4	0	0	0	0	0.0	5	0	11	5	–1	....	....	....	....	....	....	....	....
	Capital District Islanders	AHL	67	10	34	44	....	....	....	34	....	....	....	....	....	....	....	....	....	....	....	....	....	....	....	....	....	....
1991-92	New York Islanders	NHL	51	1	10	11	1	8	9	26	0	0	0	25	4.0	49	11	69	25	–6	....	....	....	....	....	....	....	....
	Capital District Islanders	AHL	20	1	9	10	....	....	....	6	....	....	....	....	....	....	....	....	....	....	....	....	....	....	....	....	....	....
1992-93	Capital District Islanders	AHL	61	6	29	35	....	....	....	34	....	....	....	....	....	....	....	....	....	....	4	0	1	1	0	....	....	....
1993-94	Philadelphia Flyers	NHL	55	1	8	9	1	6	7	24	0	0	0	43	2.3	45	3	46	20	16	....	....	....	....	....	....	....	....
1994-95	Hershey Bears	AHL	36	2	9	11	....	....	....	33	....	....	....	....	....	....	....	....	....	....	6	0	1	1	8	....	....	....
1995-96	Winnipeg Jets	NHL	65	1	5	6	1	4	5	81	0	0	0	27	3.7	44	3	70	27	–2	6	0	0	0	4	0	0	0
	Springfield Falcons	AHL	14	3	12	15	....	....	....	22	....	....	....	....	....	....	....	....	....	....	....	....	....	....	....	....	....	....
1996-97	Phoenix Coyotes	NHL	65	3	7	10	3	6	9	40	1	0	1	38	7.9	40	2	59	13	–8	1	0	0	0	2	0	0	0
1997-98	New York Rangers	NHL	63	1	6	7	1	6	7	55	0	0	0	32	3.1	33	2	43	9	–3	....	....	....	....	....	....	....	....
1998-99	New York Rangers	NHL	2	0	0	0	0	0	0	0	0	0	0	0	0.0	0	0	1	0	–1	....	....	....	....	....	....	....	....
	Hartford Wolf Pack	AHL	42	2	10	12	....	....	....	28	....	....	....	....	....	....	....	....	....	....	....	....	....	....	....	....	....	....
	St. Louis Blues	NHL	30	1	2	3	1	2	3	20	0	0	0	16	6.3	27	0	17	2	12	13	1	2	3	8	0	0	1
99-2000	St. Louis Blues	NHL	74	2	8	10	2	7	9	38	0	0	2	31	6.5	60	2	43	11	26	7	0	2	2	4	0	0	0
	Canada	WC-A	7	1	1	2	....	....	....	0	....	....	....	....	....	....	....	....	....	....	....	....	....	....	....	....	....	....
	NHL Totals		441	10	52	62	10	44	54	309	1	0	3	229	4.4	327	25	379	116		33	1	6	7	22	0	0	1

Rights traded to **Ottawa** by **NY Islanders** for Chris Luongo, June 30, 1993. Signed as a free agent by **Philadelphia**, July 30, 1993. Traded to **Winnipeg** by **Philadelphia** for Russ Romaniuk, June 27, 1995. Transferred to **Phoenix** after **Winnipeg** franchise relocated, July 1, 1996. Signed as a free agent by **NY Rangers**, August 18, 1997. Traded to **St. Louis** by **NY Rangers** with Geoff Smith for future considerations (Chris Kenady, February 22, 1999), February 13, 1999.

• FINN, Steven

D – L. 6', 191 lbs. b: Laval, Que., 8/20/1966. Quebec's 3rd, 57th overall, in 1984.

Season	Club	League	GP	G	A	Pts	AG	AA	APts	PIM	PP	SH	GW	S	%	TGF	PGF	TGA	PGA	+/-	PO GP	PO G	PO A	PO Pts	PO PIM	PO PP	PO SH	PO GW
1981-82	Laval Insulaires	QAAA	42	18	33	51	....	....	....	....	....	....	....	....	....	....	....	....	....	....	....	....	....	....	....	....	....	....
1982-83	Laval Voisins	QMJHL	69	7	30	37	....	....	....	108	....	....	....	....	....	....	....	....	....	....	6	0	2	2	6	....	....	....
1983-84	Laval Voisins	QMJHL	68	7	39	46	....	....	....	159	....	....	....	....	....	....	....	....	....	....	14	1	6	7	27	....	....	....
	Laval Voisins	Mem-Cup	3	0	0	0	....	....	....	16	....	....	....	....	....	....	....	....	....	....	....	....	....	....	....	....	....	....
1984-85	Laval Voisins	QMJHL	61	20	33	53	....	....	....	169	....	....	....	....	....	....	....	....	....	....	....	....	....	....	....	....	....	....
	Fredericton Express	AHL	4	0	0	0	....	....	....	14	....	....	....	....	....	....	....	....	....	....	6	1	1	2	4	....	....	....
1985-86	Laval Voisins	QMJHL	29	4	15	19	....	....	....	111	....	....	....	....	....	....	....	....	....	....	14	6	16	22	57	....	....	....
	Quebec Nordiques	**NHL**	**17**	**0**	**1**	**1**	**0**	**1**	**1**	**28**	**0**	**0**	**0**	**8**	**0.0**	**7**	**0**	**8**	**1**	**0**	....	....	....	....	....	....	....	....
1986-87	**Quebec Nordiques**	**NHL**	**36**	**2**	**5**	**7**	**2**	**4**	**6**	**40**	**0**	**0**	**0**	**36**	**5.6**	**27**	**6**	**31**	**2**	**–8**	**13**	**0**	**2**	**2**	**29**	**0**	**0**	**0**
	Fredericton Express	AHL	38	7	19	26	....	....	....	73	....	....	....	....	....	....	....	....	....	....	....	....	....	....	....	....	....	....
1987-88	**Quebec Nordiques**	**NHL**	**75**	**3**	**7**	**10**	**3**	**5**	**8**	**198**	**1**	**0**	**0**	**70**	**4.3**	**57**	**3**	**86**	**28**	**–4**	....	....	....	....	....	....	....	....
1988-89	**Quebec Nordiques**	**NHL**	**77**	**2**	**6**	**8**	**2**	**4**	**6**	**235**	**0**	**1**	**0**	**86**	**2.3**	**50**	**2**	**97**	**28**	**–21**	....	....	....	....	....	....	....	....
1989-90	**Quebec Nordiques**	**NHL**	**64**	**3**	**9**	**12**	**3**	**6**	**9**	**208**	**1**	**0**	**0**	**74**	**4.1**	**40**	**2**	**94**	**23**	**–33**	....	....	....	....	....	....	....	....
1990-91	**Quebec Nordiques**	**NHL**	**71**	**6**	**13**	**19**	**5**	**10**	**15**	**228**	**0**	**0**	**0**	**91**	**6.6**	**66**	**0**	**116**	**24**	**–26**	....	....	....	....	....	....	....	....
1991-92	**Quebec Nordiques**	**NHL**	**65**	**4**	**7**	**11**	**4**	**5**	**9**	**194**	**0**	**0**	**0**	**63**	**6.3**	**56**	**5**	**81**	**21**	**–9**	....	....	....	....	....	....	....	....
1992-93	**Quebec Nordiques**	**NHL**	**80**	**5**	**9**	**14**	**4**	**6**	**10**	**160**	**0**	**0**	**0**	**61**	**8.2**	**54**	**0**	**71**	**14**	**–3**	**6**	**0**	**1**	**1**	**8**	**0**	**0**	**0**
1993-94	**Quebec Nordiques**	**NHL**	**80**	**4**	**13**	**17**	**4**	**10**	**14**	**159**	**0**	**0**	**1**	**74**	**5.4**	**40**	**2**	**58**	**11**	**–9**	....	....	....	....	....	....	....	....
1994-95	**Quebec Nordiques**	**NHL**	**40**	**0**	**3**	**3**	**0**	**4**	**4**	**64**	**0**	**0**	**0**	**28**	**0.0**	**25**	**0**	**28**	**4**	**1**	**4**	**0**	**1**	**1**	**2**	**0**	**0**	**0**
1995-96	**Tampa Bay Lightning**	**NHL**	**16**	**0**	**0**	**0**	**0**	**0**	**0**	**24**	**0**	**0**	**0**	**12**	**0.0**	**5**	**0**	**13**	**2**	**–6**	....	....	....	....	....	....	....	....
	Los Angeles Kings	**NHL**	**50**	**3**	**2**	**5**	**3**	**2**	**5**	**102**	**0**	**0**	**0**	**42**	**7.1**	**38**	**1**	**60**	**17**	**–6**	....	....	....	....	....	....	....	....
1996-97	**Los Angeles Kings**	**NHL**	**54**	**2**	**3**	**5**	**2**	**3**	**5**	**84**	**0**	**0**	**1**	**35**	**5.7**	**30**	**0**	**50**	**12**	**–8**	....	....	....	....	....	....	....	....
1997-98	Long Beach Ice Dogs	IHL	75	6	14	20	....	....	....	134	....	....	....	....	....	....	....	....	....	....	17	1	4	5	48	....	....	....
	NHL Totals		**725**	**34**	**78**	**112**	**32**	**60**	**92**	**1724**	**2**	**1**	**2**	**680**	**5.0**	**495**	**21**	**793**	**187**		**23**	**0**	**4**	**4**	**39**	**0**	**0**	**0**

QMJHL First All-Star Team (1984) • QMJHL Second All-Star Team (1985)

Transferred to **Colorado** after **Quebec** franchise relocated, June 21, 1995. Traded to **Tampa Bay** by **Colorado** for Tampa Bay's 4th round choice (Brad Larsen) in 1997 Entry Draft, October 5, 1995. Traded to **LA Kings** by **Tampa Bay** for Michel Petit, November 13, 1995.

• FIORENTINO, Peter

Peter N. D – R. 6'1", 205 lbs. b: Niagara Falls, Ont., 12/22/1968. NY Rangers' 10th, 215th overall, in 1988.

Season	Club	League	GP	G	A	Pts	AG	AA	APts	PIM	PP	SH	GW	S	%	TGF	PGF	TGA	PGA	+/-	PO GP	PO G	PO A	PO Pts	PO PIM	PO PP	PO SH	PO GW
1984-85	Niagara Falls Canucks	OJHL-B	38	7	10	17	....	....	....	149	....	....	....	....	....	....	....	....	....	....	....	....	....	....	....	....	....	....
1985-86	Sault Ste. Marie Greyhounds	OHL	58	1	6	7	....	....	....	87	....	....	....	....	....	....	....	....	....	....	....	....	....	....	....	....	....	....
1986-87	Sault Ste. Marie Greyhounds	OHL	64	1	12	13	....	....	....	187	....	....	....	....	....	....	....	....	....	....	....	....	....	....	....	....	....	....
1987-88	Sault Ste. Marie Greyhounds	OHL	65	5	27	32	....	....	....	252	....	....	....	....	....	....	....	....	....	....	6	2	2	4	21	....	....	....
1988-89	Sault Ste. Marie Greyhounds	OHL	55	5	24	29	....	....	....	220	....	....	....	....	....	....	....	....	....	....	....	....	....	....	....	....	....	....
	Denver Rangers	IHL	10	0	0	0	....	....	....	39	....	....	....	....	....	....	....	....	....	....	4	0	0	0	24	....	....	....
1989-90	Flint Spirits	IHL	64	2	7	9	....	....	....	302	....	....	....	....	....	....	....	....	....	....	....	....	....	....	....	....	....	....
1990-91	Binghamton Rangers	AHL	55	2	11	13	....	....	....	361	....	....	....	....	....	....	....	....	....	....	1	0	0	0	0	....	....	....
1991-92	**New York Rangers**	**NHL**	**1**	**0**	**0**	**0**	**0**	**0**	**0**	**0**	**0**	**0**	**0**	**2**	**0.0**	**0**	**0**	**0**	**0**	**0**	....	....	....	....	....	....	....	....
	Binghamton Rangers	AHL	70	2	11	13	....	....	....	340	....	....	....	....	....	....	....	....	....	....	5	0	1	1	24	....	....	....
1992-93	Binghamton Rangers	AHL	64	9	5	14	....	....	....	286	....	....	....	....	....	....	....	....	....	....	13	0	3	3	22	....	....	....
1993-94	Binghamton Rangers	AHL	68	7	15	22	....	....	....	220	....	....	....	....	....	....	....	....	....	....	....	....	....	....	....	....	....	....
1994-95	Binghamton Rangers	AHL	66	9	16	25	....	....	....	183	....	....	....	....	....	....	....	....	....	....	2	0	1	1	11	....	....	....
1995-96	Las Vegas Thunder	IHL	54	5	7	12	....	....	....	192	....	....	....	....	....	....	....	....	....	....	....	....	....	....	....	....	....	....
	Indianapolis Ice	IHL	10	0	0	0	....	....	....	27	....	....	....	....	....	....	....	....	....	....	5	0	0	0	2	....	....	....
1996-97	Binghamton Rangers	AHL	63	1	10	11	....	....	....	191	....	....	....	....	....	....	....	....	....	....	4	0	2	2	0	....	....	....
1997-98	Quebec Rafales	IHL	12	0	2	2	....	....	....	46	....	....	....	....	....	....	....	....	....	....	....	....	....	....	....	....	....	....
	Hartford Wolf Pack	AHL	1	0	0	0	....	....	....	0	....	....	....	....	....	....	....	....	....	....	....	....	....	....	....	....	....	....
	Binghamton Icemen	UHL	35	2	9	11	....	....	....	78	....	....	....	....	....	....	....	....	....	....	5	1	1	2	2	....	....	....
	NHL Totals		**1**	**0**	**0**	**0**	**0**	**0**	**0**	**0**	**0**	**0**	**0**	**2**	**0.0**	**0**	**0**	**0**	**0**		....	....	....	....	....	....	....	....

• FISCHER, Jiri

D – L. 6'5", 210 lbs. b: Horovice, Czech., 7/31/1980. Detroit's 1st, 25th overall, in 1998.

Season	Club	League	GP	G	A	Pts	AG	AA	APts	PIM	PP	SH	GW	S	%	TGF	PGF	TGA	PGA	+/-	PO GP	PO G	PO A	PO Pts	PO PIM	PO PP	PO SH	PO GW
1995-96	Poldi Kladno	Czech-Jr.	39	6	10	16	....	....	....	....	....	....	....	....	....	....	....	....	....	....	....	....	....	....	....	....	....	....
1996-97	Poldi Kladno	Czech-Jr.	38	7	21	28	....	....	....	....	....	....	....	....	....	....	....	....	....	....	....	....	....	....	....	....	....	....
1997-98	Hull Olympiques	QMJHL	70	3	19	22	....	....	....	112	....	....	....	....	....	....	....	....	....	....	11	1	4	5	16	....	....	....
1998-99	Hull Olympiques	QMJHL	65	22	56	78	....	....	....	141	....	....	....	....	....	....	....	....	....	....	23	6	17	23	44	....	....	....
99-2000	**Detroit Red Wings**	**NHL**	**52**	**0**	**8**	**8**	**0**	**7**	**7**	**45**	**0**	**0**	**0**	**41**	**0.0**	**25**	**0**	**25**	**1**	**1**	....	....	....	....	....	....	....	....
	Cincinnati Mighty Ducks	AHL	7	0	2	2	....	....	....	10	....	....	....	....	....	....	....	....	....	....	....	....	....	....	....	....	....	....
	NHL Totals		**52**	**0**	**8**	**8**	**0**	**7**	**7**	**45**	**0**	**0**	**0**	**41**	**0.0**	**25**	**0**	**25**	**1**		....	....	....	....	....	....	....	....

QMJHL First All-Star Team (1999)

• FISCHER, Ron

Ronald Alexander D – R. 6'2", 195 lbs. b: Merritt, B.C., 4/12/1959.

Season	Club	League	GP	G	A	Pts	AG	AA	APts	PIM	PP	SH	GW	S	%	TGF	PGF	TGA	PGA	+/-	PO GP	PO G	PO A	PO Pts	PO PIM	PO PP	PO SH	PO GW
1978-79	Sherwood Park Crusaders	AJHL	STATISTICS NOT AVAILABLE																									
1979-80	University of Calgary	CWUAA	33	4	12	16	....	....	....	54	....	....	....	....	....	....	....	....	....	....	....	....	....	....	....	....	....	....
1980-81	University of Calgary	CWUAA	29	7	24	31	....	....	....	63	....	....	....	....	....	....	....	....	....	....	....	....	....	....	....	....	....	....
	Rochester Americans	AHL	4	0	0	0	....	....	....	0	....	....	....	....	....	....	....	....	....	....	....	....	....	....	....	....	....	....
1981-82	**Buffalo Sabres**	**NHL**	**15**	**0**	**7**	**7**	**0**	**5**	**5**	**6**	**0**	**0**	**0**	**16**	**0.0**	**18**	**1**	**22**	**2**	**–3**	....	....	....	....	....	....	....	....
	Rochester Americans	AHL	61	6	20	26	....	....	....	122	....	....	....	....	....	....	....	....	....	....	9	1	2	3	22	....	....	....
1982-83	**Buffalo Sabres**	**NHL**	**3**	**0**	**0**	**0**	**0**	**0**	**0**	**0**	**0**	**0**	**0**	**1**	**0.0**	**1**	**0**	**1**	**0**	**0**	....	....	....	....	....	....	....	....
	Rochester Americans	AHL	40	2	19	21	....	....	....	56	....	....	....	....	....	....	....	....	....	....	....	....	....	....	....	....	....	....
1983-84	Rochester Americans	AHL	80	10	32	42	....	....	....	94	....	....	....	....	....	....	....	....	....	....	15	4	3	7	19	....	....	....
1984-85	SC Riessersee	Germany	34	9	15	24	....	....	....	53	....	....	....	....	....	....	....	....	....	....	18	11	25	36	36	....	....	....
1985-86	SC Riessersee	Germany	36	15	35	50	....	....	....	74	....	....	....	....	....	....	....	....	....	....	18	10	25	35	16	....	....	....
1986-87	SB Rosenheim	Germany	35	4	38	42	....	....	....	56	....	....	....	....	....	....	....	....	....	....	7	1	7	8	....	....	....	....
1987-88	SB Rosenheim	Germany	33	12	16	28	....	....	....	72	....	....	....	....	....	....	....	....	....	....	14	7	9	16	17	....	....	....
	West Germany	Olympics	8	1	1	2	....	....	....	6	....	....	....	....	....	....	....	....	....	....	....	....	....	....	....	....	....	....
1988-89	SB Rosenheim	Germany	33	11	32	43	....	....	....	28	....	....	....	....	....	....	....	....	....	....	11	5	12	17	13	....	....	....
	West Germany	WEC-A	10	2	1	3	....	....	....	6	....	....	....	....	....	....	....	....	....	....	....	....	....	....	....	....	....	....
1989-90	SB Rosenheim	Germany	36	16	20	36	....	....	....	20	....	....	....	....	....	....	....	....	....	....	11	3	4	7	14	....	....	....
1990-91	SB Rosenheim	Germany	31	5	16	21	....	....	....	31	....	....	....	....	....	....	....	....	....	....	11	1	8	9	8	....	....	....
1991-92	SB Rosenheim	Germany	41	4	30	34	....	....	....	52	....	....	....	....	....	....	....	....	....	....	....	....	....	....	....	....	....	....
	Germany	Olympics	8	1	3	4	....	....	....	4	....	....	....	....	....	....	....	....	....	....	....	....	....	....	....	....	....	....
	Germany	WC-A	6	1	2	3	....	....	....	4	....	....	....	....	....	....	....	....	....	....	....	....	....	....	....	....	....	....
1992-93	SB Rosenheim	Germany-2	50	9	51	60	....	....	....	53	....	....	....	....	....	....	....	....	....	....	....	....	....	....	....	....	....	....
1993-94	SB Rosenheim	Germany	43	10	25	35	....	....	....	26	....	....	....	....	....	....	....	....	....	....	....	....	....	....	....	....	....	....
1994-95	SB Rosenheim	Germany	29	1	13	14	....	....	....	20	....	....	....	....	....	....	....	....	....	....	7	3	6	9	16	....	....	....
1995-96	SB Rosenheim	Germany	50	5	38	43	....	....	....	46	....	....	....	....	....	....	....	....	....	....	4	0	1	1	7	....	....	....
	NHL Totals		**18**	**0**	**7**	**7**	**0**	**5**	**5**	**6**	**0**	**0**	**0**	**17**	**0.0**	**19**	**1**	**23**	**2**		....	....	....	....	....	....	....	....

Signed as a free agent by **Buffalo**, March 19, 1981.

• FISHER, Craig

C – L. 6'3", 180 lbs. b: Oshawa, Ont., 6/30/1970. Philadelphia's 3rd, 56th overall, in 1988.

Season	Club	League	GP	G	A	Pts	AG	AA	APts	PIM	PP	SH	GW	S	%	TGF	PGF	TGA	PGA	+/-	PO GP	PO G	PO A	PO Pts	PO PIM	PO PP	PO SH	PO GW
1986-87	Oshawa Legionaires	OJHL-B	34	22	26	48	....	....	....	18	....	....	....	....	....	....	....	....	....	....	....	....	....	....	....	....	....	....
1987-88	Oshawa Legionaires	OJHL-B	36	42	34	76	....	....	....	48	....	....	....	....	....	....	....	....	....	....	....	....	....	....	....	....	....	....
1988-89	University of Miami-Ohio	CCHA	37	22	20	42	....	....	....	37	....	....	....	....	....	....	....	....	....	....	....	....	....	....	....	....	....	....
1989-90	University of Miami-Ohio	CCHA	39	37	29	66	....	....	....	38	....	....	....	....	....	....	....	....	....	....	....	....	....	....	....	....	....	....
	Philadelphia Flyers	**NHL**	**2**	**0**	**0**	**0**	**0**	**0**	**0**	**0**	**0**	**0**	**0**	**5**	**0.0**	**1**	**0**	**1**	**0**	**0**	....	....	....	....	....	....	....	....
1990-91	**Philadelphia Flyers**	**NHL**	**2**	**0**	**0**	**0**	**0**	**0**	**0**	**0**	**0**	**0**	**0**	**2**	**0.0**	**0**	**0**	**0**	**0**	**0**	....	....	....	....	....	....	....	....
	Hershey Bears	AHL	77	43	36	79	....	....	....	46	....	....	....	....	....	....	....	....	....	....	7	5	3	8	2	....	....	....
1991-92	Cape Breton Oilers	AHL	60	20	25	45	....	....	....	28	....	....	....	....	....	....	....	....	....	....	1	0	0	0	0	....	....	....

			REGULAR SEASON																		PLAYOFFS							
Season	**Club**	**League**	**GP**	**G**	**A**	**Pts**	**AG**	**AA**	**APts**	**PIM**	**PP**	**SH**	**GW**	**S**	**%**	**TGF**	**PGF**	**TGA**	**PGA**	**+/–**	**GP**	**G**	**A**	**Pts**	**PIM**	**PP**	**SH**	**GW**
1992-93	Cape Breton Oilers	AHL	75	32	29	61	....	....	....	74	....	....	....	....	....	....	....	....	....	....	1	0	0	0	2	....	....	....
1993-94	Cape Breton Oilers	AHL	16	5	5	10	....	....	....	11	....	....	....	....	....	....	....	....	....	....	....	....	....	....	....	....	....	....
	Winnipeg Jets	**NHL**	**4**	**0**	**0**	**0**	**0**	**0**	**0**	**2**	**0**	**0**	**0**	**5**	**0.0**	**1**	**0**	**2**	**0**	**–1**	....	....	....	....	....	....	....	....
	Moncton Hawks	AHL	46	26	35	61	....	....	....	36	....	....	....	....	....	....	....	....	....	....	21	11	11	22	28	....	....	....
1994-95	Indianapolis Ice	IHL	77	53	40	93	....	....	....	65	....	....	....	....	....	....	....	....	....	....	....	....	....	....	....	....	....	....
1995-96	Orlando Solar Bears	IHL	82	*74	56	130	....	....	....	81	....	....	....	....	....	....	....	....	....	....	14	10	7	17	6	....	....	....
1996-97	Utah Grizzlies	IHL	15	6	7	13	....	....	....	4	....	....	....	....	....	....	....	....	....	....	....	....	....	....	....	....	....	....
	Florida Panthers	**NHL**	**4**	**0**	**0**	**0**	**0**	**0**	**0**	**0**	**0**	**0**	**0**	**2**	**0.0**	**2**	**0**	**4**	**0**	**–2**	....	....	....	....	....	....	....	....
	Carolina Monarchs	AHL	42	33	29	62	....	....	....	16	....	....	....	....	....	....	....	....	....	....	....	....	....	....	....	....	....	....
1997-98	Kolner Haie	Germany	34	9	8	17	....	....	....	34	....	....	....	....	....	....	....	....	....	....	....	....	....	....	....	....	....	....
	Kolner Haie	EuroHL•	4	0	0	0	....	....	....	4	....	....	....	....	....	....	....	....	....	....	....	....	....	....	....	....	....	....
1998-99	Rochester Americans	AHL	70	29	52	81	....	....	....	28	....	....	....	....	....	....	....	....	....	....	20	9	11	20	10	....	....	....
99-2000	Rochester Americans	AHL	17	15	8	23	....	....	....	8	....	....	....	....	....	....	....	....	....	....	....	....	....	....	....	....	....	....
	NHL Totals		**12**	**0**	**0**	**0**	**0**	**0**	**0**	**2**	**0**	**0**	**0**	**14**	**0.0**	**4**	**0**	**7**	**0**		....	....	....	....	....	....	....	....

CCHA First All-Star Team (1990) • IHL First All-Star Team (1996)

Traded to **Edmonton** by **Philadelphia** with Scott Mellanby and Craig Berube for Dave Brown, Corey Foster and Jari Kurri, May 30, 1991. Traded to **Winnipeg** by **Edmonton** for cash, December 9, 1993. Signed as a free agent by **Chicago**, June 9, 1994. Signed as a free agent by **NY Islanders**, July 29, 1996. Traded to **Florida** by **NY Islanders** for cash, December 7, 1996. Signed as a free agent by **Buffalo**, August 31, 1998. • Missed remainder of 1999-2000 season recovering from head injury suffered in game vs. Wilkes-Barre (AHL), November 12, 1999.

• FISHER, Mike

C – R. 6'1", 193 lbs. b: Peterborough, Ont., 6/5/1980. Ottawa's 2nd, 44th overall, in 1998.

Season	Club	League	GP	G	A	Pts	AG	AA	APts	PIM	PP	SH	GW	S	%	TGF	PGF	TGA	PGA	+/–	GP	G	A	Pts	PIM	PP	SH	GW
1996-97	Peterborough Jr. Petes	OJHL	51	26	30	56	....	....	....	35	....	....	....	....	....	....	....	....	....	....	....	....	....	....	....	....	....	....
1997-98	Sudbury Wolves	OHL	66	24	25	49	....	....	....	65	....	....	....	....	....	....	....	....	....	....	9	2	2	4	13	....	....	....
1998-99	Sudbury Wolves	OHL	68	41	65	106	....	....	....	55	....	....	....	....	....	....	....	....	....	....	4	2	1	3	4	....	....	....
99-2000	**Ottawa Senators**	**NHL**	**32**	**4**	**5**	**9**	**4**	**5**	**9**	**15**	**0**	**0**	**1**	**49**	**8.2**	**13**	**0**	**20**	**1**	**–6**	....	....	....	....	....	....	....	....
	NHL Totals		**32**	**4**	**5**	**9**	**4**	**5**	**9**	**15**	**0**	**0**	**1**	**49**	**8.2**	**13**	**0**	**20**	**1**		....	....	....	....	....	....	....	....

• Missed remainder of 1999-2000 season recovering from knee injury suffered in game vs. Boston, December 30, 1999.

• FITCHNER, Bob

Robert Douglas C – L. 6', 190 lbs. b: Sudbury, Ont., 12/22/1950. Pittsburgh's 6th, 77th overall, in 1970.

Season	Club	League	GP	G	A	Pts	AG	AA	APts	PIM	PP	SH	GW	S	%	TGF	PGF	TGA	PGA	+/–	GP	G	A	Pts	PIM	PP	SH	GW
1968-69	Brandon Wheat Kings	WCJHL	60	21	24	45	....	....	....	83	....	....	....	....	....	....	....	....	....	....	....	....	....	....	....	....	....	....
1969-70	Brandon Wheat Kings	WCJHL	60	20	44	64	....	....	....	119	....	....	....	....	....	....	....	....	....	....	....	....	....	....	....	....	....	....
1970-71	Amarillo Wranglers	CHL	70	9	10	19	....	....	....	49	....	....	....	....	....	....	....	....	....	....	....	....	....	....	....	....	....	....
1971-72	Hershey Bears	AHL	3	0	0	0	....	....	....	0	....	....	....	....	....	....	....	....	....	....	....	....	....	....	....	....	....	....
	Fort Wayne Komets	IHL	52	11	17	28	....	....	....	106	....	....	....	....	....	....	....	....	....	....	8	0	4	4	31	....	....	....
1972-73	Fort Wayne Komets	IHL	73	26	37	63	....	....	....	157	....	....	....	....	....	....	....	....	....	....	9	4	*10	*14	22	....	....	....
1973-74	Edmonton Oilers	WHA	31	1	2	3	....	....	....	21	....	....	....	....	....	....	....	....	....	....	....	....	....	....	....	....	....	....
	Winston-Salem Polar Bears	SHL	31	16	16	32	....	....	....	107	....	....	....	....	....	....	....	....	....	....	7	3	5	8	6	....	....	....
1974-75	Indianapolis Racers	WHA	78	11	19	30	....	....	....	96	....	....	....	....	....	....	....	....	....	....	....	....	....	....	....	....	....	....
1975-76	Indianapolis Racers	WHA	52	15	16	31	....	....	....	112	....	....	....	....	....	....	....	....	....	....	....	....	....	....	....	....	....	....
	Quebec Nordiques	WHA	21	7	9	16	....	....	....	22	....	....	....	....	....	....	....	....	....	....	5	1	0	1	8	....	....	....
1976-77	Quebec Nordiques	WHA	81	9	30	39	....	....	....	105	....	....	....	....	....	....	....	....	....	....	17	3	3	6	16	....	....	....
1977-78	Quebec Nordiques	WHA	72	15	28	43	....	....	....	76	....	....	....	....	....	....	....	....	....	....	11	1	6	7	10	....	....	....
1978-79	Quebec Nordiques	WHA	72	10	35	45	....	....	....	69	....	....	....	....	....	....	....	....	....	....	4	1	3	4	0	....	....	....
1979-80	**Quebec Nordiques**	**NHL**	**70**	**11**	**20**	**31**	**9**	**15**	**24**	**59**	**5**	**1**	**0**	**88**	**12.5**	**42**	**10**	**90**	**34**	**–24**	....	....	....	....	....	....	....	....
1980-81	**Quebec Nordiques**	**NHL**	**8**	**1**	**0**	**1**	**1**	**0**	**1**	**0**	**0**	**0**	**0**	**1**	**100.0**	**1**	**0**	**4**	**2**	**–1**	**3**	**0**	**0**	**0**	**10**	**0**	**0**	**0**
	Rochester Americans	AHL	34	5	10	15	....	....	....	60	....	....	....	....	....	....	....	....	....	....	....	....	....	....	....	....	....	....
	NHL Totals		**78**	**12**	**20**	**32**	**10**	**15**	**25**	**59**	**5**	**1**	**0**	**89**	**13.5**	**43**	**10**	**94**	**36**		**3**	**0**	**0**	**0**	**10**	**0**	**0**	**0**
	Other Major League Totals		407	68	139	207	....	....	....	501	....	....	....	....	....	....	....	....	....	....	37	6	12	18	34	....	....	....

Signed as a free agent by **Edmonton** (WHA), August, 1973. Claimed by **Indianapolis** (WHA) from **Edmonton** (WHA) in WHA Expansion Draft, May 30, 1974. Traded to **Quebec** (WHA) by **Indianapolis** (WHA) with Bill Prentice and Michel Dubois for Michel Parizeau, February, 1976. Rights retained by **Quebec** prior to Expansion Draft, June 9, 1979.

• FITZGERALD, Rusty

C – L. 6'1", 210 lbs. b: Minneapolis, MN, 10/4/1972. Pittsburgh's 2nd, 38th overall, in 1991.

Season	Club	League	GP	G	A	Pts	AG	AA	APts	PIM	PP	SH	GW	S	%	TGF	PGF	TGA	PGA	+/–	GP	G	A	Pts	PIM	PP	SH	GW
1987-88	William M. Kelly High	Hi-School	20	19	26	45	....	....	....	18	....	....	....	....	....	....	....	....	....	....	....	....	....	....	....	....	....	....
1988-89	William M. Kelly High	Hi-School	22	24	25	49	....	....	....	26	....	....	....	....	....	....	....	....	....	....	....	....	....	....	....	....	....	....
1989-90	William M. Kelly High	Hi-School	21	25	26	51	....	....	....	24	....	....	....	....	....	....	....	....	....	....	....	....	....	....	....	....	....	....
1990-91	Duluth East Hounds	Hi-School	15	14	11	25	....	....	....	24	....	....	....	....	....	....	....	....	....	....	....	....	....	....	....	....	....	....
1991-92	University of Minnesota-Duluth	WCHA	37	9	11	20	....	....	....	40	....	....	....	....	....	....	....	....	....	....	....	....	....	....	....	....	....	....
1992-93	University of Minnesota-Duluth	WCHA	39	24	23	47	....	....	....	48	....	....	....	....	....	....	....	....	....	....	....	....	....	....	....	....	....	....
1993-94	University of Minnesota-Duluth	WCHA	37	11	25	36	....	....	....	59	....	....	....	....	....	....	....	....	....	....	....	....	....	....	....	....	....	....
1994-95	University of Minnesota-Duluth	WCHA	34	16	22	38	....	....	....	50	....	....	....	....	....	....	....	....	....	....	....	....	....	....	....	....	....	....
	Pittsburgh Penguins	**NHL**	**4**	**1**	**0**	**1**	**2**	**0**	**2**	**0**	**0**	**0**	**0**	**5**	**20.0**	**2**	**0**	**0**	**0**	**2**	**5**	**0**	**0**	**0**	**4**	**0**	**0**	**0**
	Cleveland Lumberjacks	IHL	2	0	1	1	....	....	....	0	....	....	....	....	....	....	....	....	....	....	3	3	0	3	6	....	....	....
1995-96	**Pittsburgh Penguins**	**NHL**	**21**	**1**	**2**	**3**	**1**	**2**	**3**	**12**	**0**	**0**	**0**	**15**	**6.7**	**9**	**0**	**3**	**1**	**7**	....	....	....	....	....	....	....	....
	Cleveland Lumberjacks	IHL	46	17	19	36	....	....	....	90	....	....	....	....	....	....	....	....	....	....	1	0	0	0	2	....	....	....
1996-97	Cleveland Lumberjacks	IHL	DID NOT PLAY – INJURED																									
1997-98	Cleveland Lumberjacks	IHL	34	3	5	8	....	....	....	36	....	....	....	....	....	....	....	....	....	....	1	0	0	0	0	....	....	....
1998-99	Quad City Mallards	UHL	53	29	25	54	....	....	....	40	....	....	....	....	....	....	....	....	....	....	12	4	4	8	9	....	....	....
99-2000	Quad City Mallards	UHL	18	8	9	17	....	....	....	13	....	....	....	....	....	....	....	....	....	....	....	....	....	....	....	....	....	....
	Manitoba Moose	IHL	53	18	15	33	....	....	....	31	....	....	....	....	....	....	....	....	....	....	1	0	0	0	2	....	....	....
	NHL Totals		**25**	**2**	**2**	**4**	**3**	**2**	**5**	**12**	**0**	**0**	**0**	**20**	**10.0**	**11**	**0**	**3**	**1**		**5**	**0**	**0**	**0**	**4**	**0**	**0**	**0**

• Missed entire 1996-97 and majority of 1997-98 seasons recovering from knee injury suffered in training camp, October 1, 1996.

• FITZGERALD, Tom

Thomas J. RW/C – R. 6', 190 lbs. b: Billerica, MA, 8/28/1968. NY Islanders' 1st, 17th overall, in 1986.

Season	Club	League	GP	G	A	Pts	AG	AA	APts	PIM	PP	SH	GW	S	%	TGF	PGF	TGA	PGA	+/–	GP	G	A	Pts	PIM	PP	SH	GW
1984-85	Austin Mustangs	Hi-School	18	20	21	41	....	....	....	....	....	....	....	....	....	....	....	....	....	....	....	....	....	....	....	....	....	....
1985-86	Austin Mustangs	Hi-School	24	35	38	73	....	....	....	....	....	....	....	....	....	....	....	....	....	....	....	....	....	....	....	....	....	....
1986-87	Providence College	H-East	27	8	14	22	....	....	....	22	....	....	....	....	....	....	....	....	....	....	....	....	....	....	....	....	....	....
	United States	WJC-A	7	3	0	3	....	....	....	2	....	....	....	....	....	....	....	....	....	....	....	....	....	....	....	....	....	....
1987-88	Providence College	H-East	36	19	15	34	....	....	....	50	....	....	....	....	....	....	....	....	....	....	....	....	....	....	....	....	....	....
1988-89	**New York Islanders**	**NHL**	**23**	**3**	**5**	**8**	**3**	**4**	**7**	**10**	**0**	**0**	**1**	**24**	**12.5**	**11**	**0**	**16**	**6**	**1**	....	....	....	....	....	....	....	....
	Springfield Indians	AHL	61	24	18	42	....	....	....	43	....	....	....	....	....	....	....	....	....	....	....	....	....	....	....	....	....	....
	United States	WEC-A	10	0	2	2	....	....	....	12	....	....	....	....	....	....	....	....	....	....	....	....	....	....	....	....	....	....
1989-90	**New York Islanders**	**NHL**	**19**	**2**	**5**	**7**	**2**	**4**	**6**	**4**	**0**	**0**	**1**	**24**	**8.3**	**8**	**0**	**17**	**6**	**–3**	**4**	**1**	**0**	**1**	**4**	**0**	**0**	**0**
	Springfield Indians	AHL	53	30	23	53	....	....	....	32	....	....	....	....	....	....	....	....	....	....	14	2	9	11	13	....	....	....
1990-91	**New York Islanders**	**NHL**	**41**	**5**	**5**	**10**	**5**	**4**	**9**	**24**	**0**	**0**	**2**	**60**	**8.3**	**15**	**0**	**31**	**7**	**–9**	....	....	....	....	....	....	....	....
	Capital District Islanders	AHL	27	7	7	14	....	....	....	50	....	....	....	....	....	....	....	....	....	....	....	....	....	....	....	....	....	....
	United States	WEC-A	10	1	0	1	....	....	....	6	....	....	....	....	....	....	....	....	....	....	....	....	....	....	....	....	....	....
1991-92	**New York Islanders**	**NHL**	**45**	**6**	**11**	**17**	**5**	**8**	**13**	**28**	**0**	**2**	**2**	**71**	**8.5**	**23**	**0**	**37**	**11**	**–3**	....	....	....	....	....	....	....	....
	Capital District Islanders	AHL	4	1	1	2	....	....	....	4	....	....	....	....	....	....	....	....	....	....	....	....	....	....	....	....	....	....
1992-93	**New York Islanders**	**NHL**	**77**	**9**	**18**	**27**	**7**	**12**	**19**	**34**	**0**	**3**	**1**	**83**	**10.8**	**32**	**0**	**62**	**28**	**–2**	**18**	**2**	**5**	**7**	**18**	**0**	**0**	**0**
1993-94	**Florida Panthers**	**NHL**	**83**	**18**	**14**	**32**	**17**	**11**	**28**	**54**	**0**	**3**	**1**	**144**	**12.5**	**38**	**4**	**62**	**25**	**–3**	....	....	....	....	....	....	....	....
1994-95	**Florida Panthers**	**NHL**	**48**	**3**	**13**	**16**	**5**	**19**	**24**	**31**	**0**	**0**	**0**	**78**	**3.8**	**22**	**2**	**37**	**14**	**–3**	....	....	....	....	....	....	....	....
1995-96	**Florida Panthers**	**NHL**	**82**	**13**	**21**	**34**	**13**	**17**	**30**	**75**	**1**	**6**	**2**	**141**	**9.2**	**43**	**2**	**69**	**25**	**–3**	**22**	**4**	**4**	**8**	**34**	**0**	**0**	**2**
1996-97	**Florida Panthers**	**NHL**	**71**	**10**	**14**	**24**	**11**	**12**	**23**	**64**	**0**	**2**	**1**	**135**	**7.4**	**34**	**0**	**47**	**20**	**7**	**5**	**0**	**1**	**1**	**0**	**0**	**0**	**0**

			REGULAR SEASON																		PLAYOFFS							
Season	**Club**	**League**	**GP**	**G**	**A**	**Pts**	**AG**	**AA**	**APts**	**PIM**	**PP**	**SH**	**GW**	**S**	**%**	**TGF**	**PGF**	**TGA**	**PGA**	**+/-**	**GP**	**G**	**A**	**Pts**	**PIM**	**PP**	**SH**	**GW**
1997-98	**Florida Panthers**	**NHL**	69	10	5	15	12	5	17	57	0	1	1	105	9.5	22	0	59	33	–4	....	....	....	....	....	....	....	....
	Colorado Avalanche	**NHL**	11	2	1	3	2	1	3	22	0	1	0	14	14.3	5	0	9	4	0	7	0	1	1	20	0	0	0
1998-99	**Nashville Predators**	**NHL**	80	13	19	32	15	18	33	48	0	0	1	180	7.2	51	4	96	31	–18	....	....	....	....	....	....	....	....
99-2000	**Nashville Predators**	**NHL**	82	13	9	22	15	8	23	66	0	3	1	119	10.9	34	0	77	25	–18	....	....	....	....	....	....	....	....
	NHL Totals		731	107	140	247	112	123	235	517	1	21	14	1178	9.1	338	12	619	235		56	7	11	18	76	0	0	2

Claimed by **Florida** from **NY Islanders** in Expansion Draft, June 24, 1993. Traded to **Colorado** by **Florida** for the rights to Mark Parrish and Anaheim's 3rd round choice (previously acquired, Florida selected Lance Ward) in 1998 Entry Draft, March 24, 1998. Signed as a free agent by **Nashville**, July 6, 1998.

• FITZPATRICK, Rory

Rory B. D – R. 6'2", 208 lbs. b: Rochester, NY, 1/11/1975. Montreal's 2nd, 47th overall, in 1993.

Season	Club	League	GP	G	A	Pts	AG	AA	APts	PIM	PP	SH	GW	S	%	TGF	PGF	TGA	PGA	+/-	GP	G	A	Pts	PIM	PP	SH	GW
1990-91	Rochester Monarchs	USHL-B	40	0	5	5	....	....	....	....	....	....	....	....	....	....	....	....	....	....	....	....	....	....	....	....	....	....
1991-92	Rochester Mustangs	USHL	28	8	28	36	....	....	....	141	....	....	....	....	....	....	....	....	....	....	....	....	....	....	....	....	....	....
1992-93	Sudbury Wolves	OHL	58	4	20	24	....	....	....	68	....	....	....	....	....	....	....	....	....	....	14	0	0	0	17	....	....	....
1993-94	Sudbury Wolves	OHL	65	12	34	46	....	....	....	112	....	....	....	....	....	....	....	....	....	....	10	2	5	7	10	....	....	....
1994-95	Sudbury Wolves	OHL	56	12	36	48	....	....	....	72	....	....	....	....	....	....	....	....	....	....	18	3	15	18	21	....	....	....
	United States	WJC-A	7	0	2	2	....	....	....	8	....	....	....	....	....	....	....	....	....	....	....	....	....	....	....	....	....	....
	Fredericton Canadiens	AHL	....	....	....	....	....	....	....	....	....	....	....	....	....	....	....	....	....	....	10	1	2	3	5	....	....	....
1995-96	**Montreal Canadiens**	**NHL**	42	0	2	2	0	2	2	18	0	0	0	31	0.0	15	1	27	6	–7	6	1	1	2	0	0	0	0
	Fredericton Canadiens	AHL	18	4	6	10	....	....	....	36	....	....	....	....	....	....	....	....	....	....	....	....	....	....	....	....	....	....
1996-97	**Montreal Canadiens**	**NHL**	6	0	1	1	0	1	1	6	0	0	0	5	0.0	4	0	6	0	–2	....	....	....	....	....	....	....	....
	St. Louis Blues	**NHL**	2	0	0	0	0	0	0	2	0	0	0	1	0.0	0	0	2	0	–2	....	....	....	....	....	....	....	....
	Worcester IceCats	AHL	49	4	13	17	....	....	....	78	....	....	....	....	....	....	....	....	....	....	5	1	2	3	0	....	....	....
1997-98	Worcester IceCats	AHL	62	8	22	30	....	....	....	111	....	....	....	....	....	....	....	....	....	....	11	0	3	3	26	....	....	....
1998-99	**St. Louis Blues**	**NHL**	1	0	0	0	0	0	0	2	0	0	0	0	0.0	0	0	3	0	–3	....	....	....	....	....	....	....	....
	Worcester IceCats	AHL	53	5	16	21	....	....	....	82	....	....	....	....	....	....	....	....	....	....	4	0	1	1	17	....	....	....
99-2000	Worcester IceCats	AHL	28	0	5	5	....	....	....	48	....	....	....	....	....	....	....	....	....	....	....	....	....	....	....	....	....	....
	Milwaukee Admirals	IHL	27	2	1	3	....	....	....	27	....	....	....	....	....	....	....	....	....	....	3	0	2	2	2	....	....	....
	NHL Totals		51	0	3	3	0	3	3	28	0	0	0	37	0.0	19	1	38	6		6	1	1	2	0	0	0	0

Traded to **St. Louis** by **Montreal** with Pierre Turgeon and Craig Conroy for Murray Baron, Shayne Corson and St. Louis' 5th round choice (Gennady Razin) in 1997 Entry Draft, October 29, 1996. Claimed by **Boston** from **St. Louis** in NHL Waiver Draft, October 5, 1998. Claimed on waivers by **St. Louis** from **Boston**, October 7, 1998. Traded to **Nashville** by **St. Louis** for Dan Keczmer, February 9, 2000.

• FITZPATRICK, Ross

C – L. 6', 195 lbs. b: Penticton, B.C., 10/7/1960. Philadelphia's 7th, 147th overall, in 1980.

Season	Club	League	GP	G	A	Pts	AG	AA	APts	PIM	PP	SH	GW	S	%	TGF	PGF	TGA	PGA	+/-	GP	G	A	Pts	PIM	PP	SH	GW
1977-78	Penticton Vees	BCJHL	66	68	64	132	....	....	....	76	....	....	....	....	....	....	....	....	....	....	....	....	....	....	....	....	....	....
1978-79	University of Western Michigan	CCHA	35	16	21	37	....	....	....	31	....	....	....	....	....	....	....	....	....	....	....	....	....	....	....	....	....	....
1979-80	University of Western Michigan	CCHA	34	26	33	59	....	....	....	22	....	....	....	....	....	....	....	....	....	....	....	....	....	....	....	....	....	....
1980-81	University of Western Michigan	CCHA	36	28	43	71	....	....	....	22	....	....	....	....	....	....	....	....	....	....	....	....	....	....	....	....	....	....
1981-82	University of Western Michigan	CCHA	33	30	28	58	....	....	....	34	....	....	....	....	....	....	....	....	....	....	....	....	....	....	....	....	....	....
1982-83	**Philadelphia Flyers**	**NHL**	1	0	0	0	0	0	0	0	0	0	0	3	0.0	0	0	1	0	–1	....	....	....	....	....	....	....	....
	Maine Mariners	AHL	66	29	28	57	....	....	....	32	....	....	....	....	....	....	....	....	....	....	15	5	1	6	12	....	....	....
1983-84	**Philadelphia Flyers**	**NHL**	12	4	2	6	3	1	4	0	0	0	1	21	19.0	8	0	4	0	4	....	....	....	....	....	....	....	....
	Springfield Indians	AHL	45	33	30	63	....	....	....	28	....	....	....	....	....	....	....	....	....	....	4	3	2	5	2	....	....	....
1984-85	**Philadelphia Flyers**	**NHL**	5	1	0	1	1	0	1	0	1	0	0	10	10.0	3	2	4	0	–3	....	....	....	....	....	....	....	....
	Hershey Bears	AHL	35	26	15	41	....	....	....	8	....	....	....	....	....	....	....	....	....	....	....	....	....	....	....	....	....	....
1985-86	**Philadelphia Flyers**	**NHL**	2	0	0	0	0	0	0	0	0	0	0	0	0.0	0	0	1	0	–1	....	....	....	....	....	....	....	....
	Hershey Bears	AHL	77	50	47	97	....	....	....	28	....	....	....	....	....	....	....	....	....	....	17	9	7	16	10	....	....	....
1986-87	Hershey Bears	AHL	66	45	40	85	....	....	....	34	....	....	....	....	....	....	....	....	....	....	5	1	4	5	10	....	....	....
1987-88	Hershey Bears	AHL	35	14	17	31	....	....	....	12	....	....	....	....	....	....	....	....	....	....	12	*11	4	15	8	....	....	....
1988-89	WEV Wien	Austria	38	26	23	49	....	....	....	....	....	....	....	....	....	....	....	....	....	....	....	....	....	....	....	....	....	....
	Hershey Bears	AHL	11	6	9	15	....	....	....	4	....	....	....	....	....	....	....	....	....	....	9	2	2	4	4	....	....	....
1989-90	Hershey Bears	AHL	74	45	*58	103	....	....	....	26	....	....	....	....	....	....	....	....	....	....	....	....	....	....	....	....	....	....
1990-91	Binghamton Rangers	AHL	69	26	29	55	....	....	....	26	....	....	....	....	....	....	....	....	....	....	10	3	1	4	4	....	....	....
1991-92	Binghamton Rangers	AHL	76	34	38	72	....	....	....	32	....	....	....	....	....	....	....	....	....	....	10	1	3	4	2	....	....	....
	NHL Totals		20	5	2	7	4	1	5	0	1	0	1	34	14.7	11	2	10	0		....	....	....	....	....	....	....	....

CCHA First All-Star Team (1981) • AHL Second All-Star Team (1986, 1990)

• Missed majority of 1984-85 season recovering from shoulder injury suffered in game vs. Sherbrooke (AHL), January 10, 1985. Signed as a free agent by **NY Rangers**, July 24, 1990.

• FITZPATRICK, Sandy

Alexander Stewart C – L. 6'1", 195 lbs. b: Paisley, Scotland, 12/22/1944.

Season	Club	League	GP	G	A	Pts	AG	AA	APts	PIM	PP	SH	GW	S	%	TGF	PGF	TGA	PGA	+/-	GP	G	A	Pts	PIM	PP	SH	GW
1961-62	Guelph Royals	OHA-Jr.	48	5	7	12	....	....	....	21	....	....	....	....	....	....	....	....	....	....	....	....	....	....	....	....	....	....
1962-63	Guelph Royals	OHA-Jr.	50	9	25	34	....	....	....	52	....	....	....	....	....	....	....	....	....	....	....	....	....	....	....	....	....	....
1963-64	Kitchener Rangers	OHA-Jr.	56	23	28	51	....	....	....	61	....	....	....	....	....	....	....	....	....	....	....	....	....	....	....	....	....	....
1964-65	Kitchener Rangers	OHA-Jr.	56	51	55	106	....	....	....	140	....	....	....	....	....	....	....	....	....	....	....	....	....	....	....	....	....	....
	New York Rangers	**NHL**	4	0	0	0	0	0	0	2	....	....	....	....	....	....	....	....	....	....	....	....	....	....	....	....	....	....
	St. Paul Rangers	CPHL	....	....	....	....	....	....	....	....	....	....	....	....	....	....	....	....	....	....	3	0	0	0	0	....	....	....
1965-66	Minnesota Rangers	CPHL	68	15	30	45	....	....	....	74	....	....	....	....	....	....	....	....	....	....	7	5	3	8	4	....	....	....
1966-67	Omaha Knights	CPHL	49	7	19	26	....	....	....	57	....	....	....	....	....	....	....	....	....	....	11	0	0	0	9	....	....	....
1967-68	**Minnesota North Stars**	**NHL**	18	3	6	9	3	6	9	6	0	0	0	26	11.5	10	2	8	0	0	12	0	0	0	0	0	0	0
	Memphis South Stars	CPHL	56	15	29	44	....	....	....	56	....	....	....	....	....	....	....	....	....	....	....	....	....	....	....	....	....	....
1968-69	Memphis South Stars	CHL	66	14	26	40	....	....	....	32	....	....	....	....	....	....	....	....	....	....	....	....	....	....	....	....	....	....
1969-70	San Diego Gulls	WHL	67	17	29	46	....	....	....	16	....	....	....	....	....	....	....	....	....	....	3	0	0	0	4	....	....	....
1970-71	San Diego Gulls	WHL	70	13	21	34	....	....	....	41	....	....	....	....	....	....	....	....	....	....	6	0	2	2	2	....	....	....
1971-72	San Diego Gulls	WHL	24	2	5	7	....	....	....	19	....	....	....	....	....	....	....	....	....	....	....	....	....	....	....	....	....	....
	NHL Totals		22	3	6	9	3	6	9	8	....	....	....	....	....	....	....	....	....		12	0	0	0	0	....	....	....

Claimed by **Minnesota** from **NY Rangers** in Expansion Draft, June 6, 1967. Traded to **San Diego** (WHL) by **Minnesota** for cash, July 15, 1969.

• FLATLEY, Pat

RW – R. 6'2", 197 lbs. b: Toronto, Ont., 10/3/1963. NY Islanders' 1st, 21st overall, in 1982.

Season	Club	League	GP	G	A	Pts	AG	AA	APts	PIM	PP	SH	GW	S	%	TGF	PGF	TGA	PGA	+/-	GP	G	A	Pts	PIM	PP	SH	GW
1980-81	Henry Carr Crusaders	OHA-B	42	30	*61	91	....	....	....	122	....	....	....	....	....	....	....	....	....	....	....	....	....	....	....	....	....	....
1981-82	University of Wisconsin	WCHA	17	10	9	19	....	....	....	40	....	....	....	....	....	....	....	....	....	....	....	....	....	....	....	....	....	....
1982-83	University of Wisconsin	WCHA	26	17	24	41	....	....	....	48	....	....	....	....	....	....	....	....	....	....	....	....	....	....	....	....	....	....
	Canada	WJC-A	7	4	0	4	....	....	....	6	....	....	....	....	....	....	....	....	....	....	....	....	....	....	....	....	....	....
	Canada	WEC-A	6	0	0	0	....	....	....	2	....	....	....	....	....	....	....	....	....	....	....	....	....	....	....	....	....	....
1983-84	Canada	Nat-Team	57	31	17	48	....	....	....	136	....	....	....	....	....	....	....	....	....	....	....	....	....	....	....	....	....	....
	Canada	Olympics	7	3	3	6	....	....	....	20	....	....	....	....	....	....	....	....	....	....	....	....	....	....	....	....	....	....
	New York Islanders	**NHL**	16	2	7	9	2	5	7	6	1	0	0	17	11.8	12	2	7	0	3	21	9	6	15	14	1	0	1
1984-85	**New York Islanders**	**NHL**	78	20	31	51	16	21	37	106	2	0	4	135	14.8	70	10	72	4	–8	4	1	0	1	6	0	0	0
1985-86	**New York Islanders**	**NHL**	73	18	34	52	14	23	37	66	6	0	2	120	15.0	75	12	50	7	20	3	0	0	0	21	0	0	0
1986-87	**New York Islanders**	**NHL**	63	16	35	51	14	25	39	81	6	0	4	113	14.2	69	21	45	14	17	11	3	2	5	6	0	0	0
1987-88	**New York Islanders**	**NHL**	40	9	15	24	8	11	19	28	5	1	0	83	10.8	37	16	19	5	7	....	....	....	....	....	....	....	....
1988-89	**New York Islanders**	**NHL**	41	10	15	25	8	11	19	31	2	1	1	72	13.9	39	14	38	8	–5	....	....	....	....	....	....	....	....
	Springfield Indians	AHL	2	1	1	2	....	....	....	2	....	....	....	....	....	....	....	....	....	....	....	....	....	....	....	....	....	....
1989-90	**New York Islanders**	**NHL**	62	17	32	49	15	23	38	101	4	0	2	136	12.5	74	24	52	12	10	5	3	0	3	2	2	0	0
1990-91	**New York Islanders**	**NHL**	56	20	25	45	18	19	37	74	8	0	4	137	14.6	62	21	56	13	–2	....	....	....	....	....	....	....	....
1991-92	**New York Islanders**	**NHL**	38	8	28	36	7	21	28	31	4	1	0	76	10.5	50	9	41	14	14	....	....	....	....	....	....	....	....
1992-93	**New York Islanders**	**NHL**	80	13	47	60	11	32	43	63	1	2	1	139	9.4	89	19	94	29	5	15	2	7	9	12	0	0	0
1993-94	**New York Islanders**	**NHL**	64	12	30	42	11	23	34	40	2	1	2	112	10.7	64	9	63	20	12	....	....	....	....	....	....	....	....

Season	Club	League	REGULAR SEASON GP	G	A	Pts	AG	AA	APts	PIM	PP	SH	GW	S	%	TGF	PGF	TGA	PGA	+/–	PLAYOFFS GP	G	A	Pts	PIM	PP	SH	GW
1994-95	**New York Islanders**	**NHL**	**45**	**7**	**20**	**27**	**12**	**30**	**42**	**12**	**1**	**0**	**1**	**81**	**8.6**	**45**	**7**	**43**	**14**	**9**								
1995-96	**New York Islanders**	**NHL**	**56**	**8**	**9**	**17**	**8**	**7**	**15**	**21**	**0**	**0**	**0**	**89**	**9.0**	**25**	**4**	**52**	**7**	**–24**								
1996-97	**New York Rangers**	**NHL**	**68**	**10**	**12**	**22**	**11**	**11**	**22**	**26**	**0**	**0**	**2**	**96**	**10.4**	**32**	**2**	**25**	**1**	**6**	**11**	**0**	**0**	**0**	**14**	**0**	**0**	**0**
	NHL Totals		**780**	**170**	**340**	**510**	**155**	**262**	**417**	**686**	**42**	**6**	**23**	**1406**	**12.1**	**743**	**170**	**657**	**148**		**70**	**18**	**15**	**33**	**75**	**3**	**0**	**1**

WCHA First All-Star Team (1983) • NCAA West First All-American Team (1983) • NCAA Championship All-Tournament Team (1983)

Signed as a free agent by **NY Rangers**, September 26, 1996.

• FLEMING, Gerry

Gerry Alexander LW – L. 6'5", 253 lbs. b: Montreal, Que., 10/16/1967.

Season	Club	League	GP	G	A	Pts	AG	AA	APts	PIM	PP	SH	GW	S	%	TGF	PGF	TGA	PGA	+/–	GP	G	A	Pts	PIM	PP	SH	GW
1983-84	Verdun Juniors	QMJHL	52	4	11	15				270											3	0	4	4	2			
1984-85	Verdun Jr. Canadiens	QMJHL	44	15	23	38				160											14	5	6	11	*96			
	Verdun Jr. Canadiens	Mem-Cup	3	0	0	0				18																		
1985-86	Verdun Jr. Canadiens	QMJHL	47	15	21	36				339											4	0	1	1	18			
1986-87	University of P.E.I.	AUAA	20	19	11	30				73																		
1987-88	University of P.E.I.	AUAA	23	11	15	26				61																		
1988-89	University of P.E.I.	AUAA	17	11	23	34				61																		
1989-90	Fredericton Alpines	NBSHL	24	12	18	30				83											5	3	6	9				
1990-91	University of P.E.I.	AUAA	9	2	6	8				41																		
	Charlottetown Islanders	PEI-Sr.	STATISTICS NOT AVAILABLE																									
1991-92	Fredericton Canadiens	AHL	37	4	6	10				133											1	0	0	0	7			
1992-93	Fredericton Canadiens	AHL	64	9	17	26				262											5	1	2	3	14			
1993-94	**Montreal Canadiens**	**NHL**	**5**	**0**	**0**	**0**	**0**	**0**	**0**	**25**	**0**	**0**	**0**	**4**	**0.0**	**0**	**0**	**4**	**0**	**–4**								
	Fredericton Canadiens	AHL	46	6	16	22				188																		
1994-95	**Montreal Canadiens**	**NHL**	**6**	**0**	**0**	**0**	**0**	**0**	**0**	**17**	**0**	**0**	**0**	**1**	**0.0**	**0**	**0**	**1**	**0**	**–1**								
	Fredericton Canadiens	AHL	16	3	3	6				60											10	2	0	2	67			
1995-96	Fredericton Canadiens	AHL	40	8	9	17				127											10	3	1	4	19			
1996-97	Fredericton Canadiens	AHL	40	5	11	16				164																		
1997-98	Fredericton Canadiens	AHL	28	3	3	6				101											1	0	0	0	0			
1998-1999	Fredericton Canadiens	AHL	DID NOT PLAY – ASSISTANT COACH																									
1999-2000	Quebec Citadelles	AHL	DID NOT PLAY – ASSISTANT COACH																									
	NHL Totals		**11**	**0**	**0**	**0**	**0**	**0**	**0**	**42**	**0**	**0**	**0**	**5**	**0.0**	**0**	**0**	**5**	**0**									

Signed as a free agent by **Montreal**, February 17, 1992. • Named Head Caoch of **Tallahassee** (ECHL), July 12, 2000.

• FLEMING, Reggie

Reginald Stephen D/LW – L. 5'8", 170 lbs. b: Montreal, Que., 4/21/1936.

Season	Club	League	GP	G	A	Pts	AG	AA	APts	PIM	PP	SH	GW	S	%	TGF	PGF	TGA	PGA	+/–	GP	G	A	Pts	PIM	PP	SH	GW
1953-54	Montreal Jr. Canadiens	QJHL	48	7	7	14				47											8	0	0	0	14			
1954-55	Montreal Jr. Canadiens	QJHL	44	3	11	14				*139											5	0	0	0	11			
1955-56	St. Michael's Majors	OHA-Jr.	42	1	8	9				93											8	0	2	2	18			
1956-57	Shawinigan Cataracts	QHL	61	2	9	11				109																		
1957-58	Shawinigan Cataracts	QHL	51	6	15	21				*227											8	3	2	5	16			
1958-59	Rochester Americans	AHL	70	6	16	22				112											5	0	1	1	13			
1959-60	**Montreal Canadiens**	**NHL**	**3**	**0**	**0**	**0**	**0**	**0**	**0**	**2**																		
	Kingston Frontenacs	EPHL	52	19	49	68				91																		
	Rochester Americans	AHL	9	1	5	6				4																		
1960-61♦	**Chicago Black Hawks**	**NHL**	**66**	**4**	**4**	**8**	**5**	**4**	**9**	**145**											**12**	**1**	**0**	**1**	**12**	**0**	**1**	**0**
1961-62	**Chicago Black Hawks**	**NHL**	**70**	**7**	**9**	**16**	**8**	**9**	**17**	**71**											**12**	**2**	**2**	**4**	**27**	**0**	**0**	**1**
1962-63	**Chicago Black Hawks**	**NHL**	**64**	**7**	**7**	**14**	**8**	**7**	**15**	**99**											**6**	**0**	**0**	**0**	**27**	**0**	**0**	**0**
1963-64	**Chicago Black Hawks**	**NHL**	**61**	**3**	**6**	**9**	**4**	**6**	**10**	**140**											**7**	**0**	**0**	**0**	**18**	**0**	**0**	**0**
1964-65	**Boston Bruins**	**NHL**	**67**	**18**	**23**	**41**	**22**	**24**	**46**	**136**																		
1965-66	**Boston Bruins**	**NHL**	**34**	**4**	**6**	**10**	**4**	**6**	**10**	***42**																		
	New York Rangers	**NHL**	**35**	**10**	**14**	**24**	**11**	**13**	**24**	***124**																		
1966-67	**New York Rangers**	**NHL**	**61**	**15**	**16**	**31**	**17**	**16**	**33**	**146**											**4**	**0**	**2**	**2**	**11**	**0**	**0**	**0**
1967-68	**New York Rangers**	**NHL**	**73**	**17**	**7**	**24**	**20**	**7**	**27**	**132**	**0**	**1**	**0**	**143**	**11.9**	**34**	**0**	**38**	**5**	**1**	**6**	**0**	**2**	**2**	**4**	**0**	**0**	**0**
1968-69	**New York Rangers**	**NHL**	**72**	**8**	**12**	**20**	**8**	**11**	**19**	**138**	**2**	**0**	**1**	**117**	**6.8**	**36**	**5**	**46**	**2**	**–13**	**3**	**0**	**0**	**0**	**7**	**0**	**0**	**0**
1969-70	**Philadelphia Flyers**	**NHL**	**65**	**9**	**18**	**27**	**10**	**17**	**27**	**134**	**2**	**0**	**1**	**129**	**7.0**	**44**	**11**	**42**	**5**	**–4**								
1970-71	**Buffalo Sabres**	**NHL**	**78**	**6**	**10**	**16**	**6**	**8**	**14**	**159**	**0**	**0**	**0**	**54**	**11.1**	**21**	**3**	**50**	**24**	**–8**								
1971-72	Cincinnati Swords	AHL	11	3	5	8				62																		
	Salt Lake Golden Eagles	WHL	56	20	28	48				134																		
1972-73	Chicago Cougars	WHA	74	23	45	68				95																		
1973-74	Chicago Cougars	WHA	45	2	12	14				49											12	0	4	4	12			
1974-75	Kenosha Flyers	ContHL	21	18	27	45																						
	Saginaw Gears	IHL	9	1	6	7				14											17	8	13	21	45			
1975-76	Lake County Flyers	ContHL	STATISTICS NOT AVAILABLE																									
	Milwaukee Admirals	USHL	1	0	0	0				0																		
1976-77	Milwaukee Admirals	USHL	23	5	21	26				81																		
1977-78	Hammond Cardinals	ContHL	STATISTICS NOT AVAILABLE																									
	NHL Totals		**749**	**108**	**132**	**240**	**123**	**128**	**251**	**1468**											**50**	**3**	**6**	**9**	**106**			
	Other Major League Totals		119	25	57	82				144											12	0	4	4	12			

Played in NHL All-Star Game (1961)

Traded to **Chicago** by **Montreal** with Cec Hoekstra, Ab McDonald and Bob Courcy for Terry Gray, Glen Skov and the rights to Danny Lewicki, Lorne Ferguson and Bob Bailey, June 7, 1960. Traded to **Boston** by **Chicago** with Ab McDonald for Doug Mohns, June 8, 1964. Traded to **NY Rangers** by **Boston** for John McKenzie, January 10, 1966. Traded to **Philadelphia** by **NY Rangers** for Leon Rochefort and Don Blackburn, June 6, 1969. Claimed by **Buffalo** from **Philadelphia** in Expansion Draft, June 10, 1970. Selected by **LA Sharks** (WHA) in 1972 WHA General Player Draft, February 12, 1972. WHA rights traded to **Chicago** (WHA) by **LA Sharks** (WHA) for cash, August, 1972.

• FLESCH, John

John Patrick LW – L. 6'2", 200 lbs. b: Sudbury, Ont., 7/15/1953. Atlanta's 5th, 69th overall, in 1973.

Season	Club	League	GP	G	A	Pts	AG	AA	APts	PIM	PP	SH	GW	S	%	TGF	PGF	TGA	PGA	+/–	GP	G	A	Pts	PIM	PP	SH	GW
1971-72	Sudbury Wolves	NOJHA	48	17	24	41				182																		
1972-73	Lake Superior State	CCHA	29	28	32	60				108																		
1973-74	Omaha Knights	CHL	69	27	27	54				98											5	1	2	3	4			
1974-75	**Minnesota North Stars**	**NHL**	**57**	**8**	**15**	**23**	**7**	**11**	**18**	**47**	**2**	**0**	**1**	**77**	**10.4**	**32**	**5**	**47**	**1**	**–19**								
1975-76	**Minnesota North Stars**	**NHL**	**33**	**3**	**2**	**5**	**3**	**1**	**4**	**47**	**1**	**0**	**0**	**26**	**11.5**	**7**	**2**	**13**	**0**	**–8**								
	New Haven Nighthawks	AHL	31	11	10	21				95											3	1	0	1	2			
1976-77	Columbus Owls	IHL	74	34	39	73				210											7	1	5	6	15			
1977-78	**Pittsburgh Penguins**	**NHL**	**29**	**7**	**5**	**12**	**6**	**4**	**10**	**19**	**0**	**0**	**2**	**34**	**20.6**	**18**	**0**	**25**	**0**	**–7**								
1978-79	Grand Rapids Owls	IHL	67	26	56	82				149											22	10	15	25	36			
1979-80	**Colorado Rockies**	**NHL**	**5**	**0**	**1**	**1**	**0**	**1**	**1**	**4**	**0**	**0**	**0**	**3**	**0.0**	**3**	**1**	**4**	**1**	**–1**								
	Grand Rapids Owls	IHL	76	39	54	93				66																		
1980-81	Milwaukee Admirals	IHL	70	27	44	71				70											7	1	3	4	6			
1981-82	Milwaukee Admirals	IHL	82	39	54	93				45											5	2	2	4	4			
1982-83	Milwaukee Admirals	IHL	51	24	31	55				56											11	5	7	12	10			
1983-84	Milwaukee Admirals	IHL	81	43	44	87				27											4	0	2	2	0			
1984-85	Kalamazoo Wings	IHL	82	38	40	78				72											11	9	4	13	2			
1985-86	Kalamazoo Wings	IHL	48	15	15	30				33											6	0	3	3	2			
	NHL Totals		**124**	**18**	**23**	**41**	**16**	**17**	**33**	**117**	**3**	**0**	**3**	**140**	**12.9**	**60**	**8**	**89**	**2**									

IHL Second All-Star Team (1979) • IHL First All-Star Team (1982)

Traded to **Minnesota** by **Atlanta** with Don Martineau for Buster Harvey and Jerry Byers, May 27, 1974. Signed as a free agent by **Pittsburgh**, February 4, 1978. Signed as a free agent by **Colorado**, January 13, 1980. Traded to **Kalamazoo** (IHL) by **Milwaukee** (IHL) for Kevin Schamehorn, October, 1984.

			REGULAR SEASON																		PLAYOFFS							
Season	**Club**	**League**	**GP**	**G**	**A**	**Pts**	**AG**	**AA**	**APts**	**PIM**	**PP**	**SH**	**GW**	**S**	**%**	**TGF**	**PGF**	**TGA**	**PGA**	**+/-**	**GP**	**G**	**A**	**Pts**	**PIM**	**PP**	**SH**	**GW**

• FLETCHER, Steven

LW/D – L. 6'2", 180 lbs. b: Montreal, Que., 3/31/1962. Calgary's 11th, 202nd overall, in 1980.

Season	Club	League	GP	G	A	Pts	AG	AA	APts	PIM	PP	SH	GW	S	%	TGF	PGF	TGA	PGA	+/-	GP	G	A	Pts	PIM	PP	SH	GW
1979-80	Hull Olympiques	QMJHL	61	2	14	16	....	....	....	183	....	....	....	....	....	....	....	....	....	....	....	....	....	....	....	....	....	....
1980-81	Hull Olympiques	QMJHL	66	4	13	17	....	....	....	231	....	....	....	....	....	....	....	....	....	....	....	....	....	....	....	....	....	....
1981-82	Hull Olympiques	QMJHL	60	4	20	24	....	....	....	230	....	....	....	....	....	....	....	....	....	....	....	....	....	....	....	....	....	....
1982-83	Sherbrooke Jets	AHL	36	0	1	1	....	....	....	119	....	....	....	....	....	....	....	....	....	....	....	....	....	....	....	....	....	....
	Fort Wayne Komets	IHL	34	1	9	10	....	....	....	115	....	....	....	....	....	....	....	....	....	....	10	1	6	7	45	....	....	....
1983-84	Sherbrooke Jets	AHL	77	3	7	10	....	....	....	208	....	....	....	....	....	....	....	....	....	....	....	....	....	....	....	....	....	....
1984-85	Sherbrooke Canadiens	AHL	50	2	4	6	....	....	....	192	....	....	....	....	....	....	....	....	....	....	13	0	0	0	48	....	....	....
1985-86	Sherbrooke Canadiens	AHL	64	2	12	14	....	....	....	293	....	....	....	....	....	....	....	....	....	....	....	....	....	....	....	....	....	....
1986-87	Sherbrooke Canadiens	AHL	70	15	11	26	....	....	....	261	....	....	....	....	....	....	....	....	....	....	17	5	5	10	*82	....	....	....
1987-88	Sherbrooke Canadiens	AHL	76	8	21	29	....	....	....	338	....	....	....	....	....	....	....	....	....	....	6	2	1	3	28	....	....	....
	Montreal Canadiens	**NHL**	....	....	....	....	....	....	....	....	....	....	....	....	....	....	....	....	....	....	**1**	**0**	**0**	**0**	**5**	**0**	**0**	**0**
1988-89	**Winnipeg Jets**	**NHL**	**3**	**0**	**0**	**0**	**0**	**0**	**0**	**5**	**0**	**0**	**0**	**1**	**0.0**	**0**	**0**	**1**	**0**	**–1**	....	....	....	....	....	....	....	....
	Moncton Hawks	AHL	23	1	1	2	....	....	....	89	....	....	....	....	....	....	....	....	....	....	....	....	....	....	....	....	....	....
	Halifax Citadels	AHL	29	5	8	13	....	....	....	91	....	....	....	....	....	....	....	....	....	....	....	....	....	....	....	....	....	....
1989-90	Hershey Bears	AHL	28	1	1	2	....	....	....	132	....	....	....	....	....	....	....	....	....	....	....	....	....	....	....	....	....	....
1990-91	Fort Wayne Komets	IHL	66	7	9	16	....	....	....	289	....	....	....	....	....	....	....	....	....	....	15	2	0	2	70	....	....	....
1991-92	Fort Wayne Komets	IHL	60	8	3	11	....	....	....	320	....	....	....	....	....	....	....	....	....	....	5	0	0	0	14	....	....	....
1992-93	Fort Wayne Komets	IHL	52	5	6	11	....	....	....	337	....	....	....	....	....	....	....	....	....	....	3	0	0	0	2	....	....	....
1993-94	Fort Wayne Komets	IHL	47	4	6	10	....	....	....	277	....	....	....	....	....	....	....	....	....	....	5	0	0	0	33	....	....	....
1994-95	Fort Wayne Komets	IHL	43	0	2	2	....	....	....	204	....	....	....	....	....	....	....	....	....	....	1	0	0	0	0	....	....	....
1995-96	Fort Wayne Komets	IHL	2	2	0	2	....	....	....	39	....	....	....	....	....	....	....	....	....	....	....	....	....	....	....	....	....	....
	Atlanta Knights	IHL	23	0	1	1	....	....	....	110	....	....	....	....	....	....	....	....	....	....	....	....	....	....	....	....	....	....
	NHL Totals		**3**	**0**	**0**	**0**	**0**	**0**	**0**	**5**	**0**	**0**	**0**	**1**	**0.0**	**0**	**0**	**1**	**0**		**1**	**0**	**0**	**0**	**5**	**0**	**0**	**0**

Signed as a free agent by **Montreal**, August 21, 1984. Signed as a free agent by **Winnipeg**, July 15, 1988. Traded to **Philadelphia** by **Winnipeg** for future considerations, December 12, 1988.

• FLETT, Bill

William Myer "Cowboy" RW – R. 6'1", 205 lbs. b: Vermillion, Alta., 7/21/1943 d: 7/12/1999.

Season	Club	League	GP	G	A	Pts	AG	AA	APts	PIM	PP	SH	GW	S	%	TGF	PGF	TGA	PGA	+/-	GP	G	A	Pts	PIM	PP	SH	GW
1960-61	Melville Millionaires	SJHL	27	16	2	18	....	....	....	14	....	....	....	....	....	....	....	....	....	....	7	3	1	4	10	....	....	....
1961-62	Melville Millionaires	SJHL	24	8	14	22	....	....	....	44	....	....	....	....	....	....	....	....	....	....	....	....	....	....	....	....	....	....
1962-63	Melville Millionaires	SJHL	53	31	54	85	....	....	....	80	....	....	....	....	....	....	....	....	....	....	18	7	11	18	40	....	....	....
	Estevan Bruins	Mem-Cup	6	1	1	2	....	....	....	2	....	....	....	....	....	....	....	....	....	....	....	....	....	....	....	....	....	....
1963-64	Rochester Americans	AHL	1	0	0	0	....	....	....	0	....	....	....	....	....	....	....	....	....	....	....	....	....	....	....	....	....	....
	Charlotte Checkers	EHL	41	26	21	47	....	....	....	48	....	....	....	....	....	....	....	....	....	....	3	0	1	1	6	....	....	....
	Denver Invaders	WHL	....	....	....	....	....	....	....	....	....	....	....	....	....	....	....	....	....	....	1	0	0	0	0	....	....	....
1964-65	Tulsa Oilers	CPHL	39	8	22	30	....	....	....	58	....	....	....	....	....	....	....	....	....	....	12	1	2	3	6	....	....	....
	Victoria Maple Leafs	WHL	23	1	7	8	....	....	....	14	....	....	....	....	....	....	....	....	....	....	....	....	....	....	....	....	....	....
1965-66	Tulsa Oilers	CPHL	55	23	23	46	....	....	....	0	....	....	....	....	....	....	....	....	....	....	....	....	....	....	....	....	....	....
1966-67	Tulsa Oilers	CPHL	62	16	28	44	....	....	....	108	....	....	....	....	....	....	....	....	....	....	....	....	....	....	....	....	....	....
1967-68	**Los Angeles Kings**	**NHL**	**73**	**26**	**20**	**46**	**30**	**20**	**50**	**97**	**3**	**0**	**6**	**205**	**12.7**	**74**	**19**	**60**	**9**	**4**	**7**	**1**	**2**	**3**	**8**	**0**	**0**	**0**
1968-69	**Los Angeles Kings**	**NHL**	**72**	**24**	**25**	**49**	**25**	**22**	**47**	**53**	**4**	**0**	**6**	**198**	**12.1**	**65**	**14**	**77**	**2**	**–24**	**10**	**3**	**4**	**7**	**11**	**1**	**1**	**0**
1969-70	**Los Angeles Kings**	**NHL**	**69**	**14**	**18**	**32**	**15**	**17**	**32**	**70**	**2**	**0**	**0**	**198**	**7.1**	**53**	**15**	**75**	**10**	**–27**	....	....	....	....	....	....	....	....
	Springfield Kings	AHL	5	2	6	8	....	....	....	6	....	....	....	....	....	....	....	....	....	....	....	....	....	....	....	....	....	....
1970-71	**Los Angeles Kings**	**NHL**	**64**	**13**	**24**	**37**	**13**	**20**	**33**	**57**	**5**	**0**	**0**	**182**	**7.1**	**56**	**14**	**82**	**10**	**–30**	....	....	....	....	....	....	....	....
1971-72	**Los Angeles Kings**	**NHL**	**45**	**7**	**12**	**19**	**7**	**10**	**17**	**18**	**1**	**0**	**0**	**113**	**6.2**	**30**	**5**	**55**	**0**	**–30**	....	....	....	....	....	....	....	....
	Philadelphia Flyers	**NHL**	**31**	**11**	**10**	**21**	**11**	**9**	**20**	**26**	**3**	**0**	**1**	**116**	**9.5**	**38**	**11**	**24**	**2**	**5**	....	....	....	....	....	....	....	....
1972-73	**Philadelphia Flyers**	**NHL**	**69**	**43**	**31**	**74**	**41**	**25**	**66**	**53**	**11**	**3**	**6**	**283**	**15.2**	**119**	**41**	**70**	**23**	**31**	**11**	**3**	**4**	**7**	**0**	**0**	**1**	**1**
1973-74♦	**Philadelphia Flyers**	**NHL**	**67**	**17**	**27**	**44**	**16**	**22**	**38**	**51**	**1**	**1**	**5**	**222**	**7.7**	**76**	**24**	**35**	**3**	**20**	**17**	**0**	**6**	**6**	**21**	**0**	**0**	**0**
1974-75	**Toronto Maple Leafs**	**NHL**	**77**	**15**	**25**	**40**	**13**	**19**	**32**	**38**	**4**	**3**	**2**	**186**	**8.1**	**59**	**17**	**74**	**32**	**0**	**5**	**0**	**0**	**0**	**2**	**0**	**0**	**0**
1975-76	**Atlanta Flames**	**NHL**	**78**	**23**	**17**	**40**	**20**	**13**	**33**	**30**	**1**	**2**	**3**	**171**	**13.5**	**63**	**3**	**69**	**18**	**9**	**2**	**0**	**0**	**0**	**0**	**0**	**0**	**0**
1976-77	**Atlanta Flames**	**NHL**	**24**	**4**	**4**	**8**	**4**	**3**	**7**	**6**	**1**	**0**	**1**	**35**	**11.4**	**13**	**3**	**14**	**5**	**1**	....	....	....	....	....	....	....	....
	Edmonton Oilers	WHA	48	34	20	54	....	....	....	20	....	....	....	....	....	....	....	....	....	....	5	0	2	2	2	....	....	....
1977-78	Edmonton Oilers	WHA	74	41	28	69	....	....	....	34	....	....	....	....	....	....	....	....	....	....	....	....	....	....	....	....	....	....
1978-79	Edmonton Oilers	WHA	73	28	36	64	....	....	....	14	....	....	....	....	....	....	....	....	....	....	10	5	2	7	2	....	....	....
1979-80	**Edmonton Oilers**	**NHL**	**20**	**5**	**2**	**7**	**4**	**1**	**5**	**2**	**1**	**0**	**0**	**26**	**19.2**	**12**	**3**	**27**	**1**	**–17**	....	....	....	....	....	....	....	....
	NHL Totals		**689**	**202**	**215**	**417**	**199**	**181**	**380**	**501**	**37**	**9**	**30**	**1935**	**10.4**	**658**	**169**	**662**	**115**		**52**	**7**	**16**	**23**	**42**	**1**	**2**	**1**
	Other Major League Totals		195	103	84	187	....	....	....	68	....	....	....	....	....	....	....	....	....	....	15	5	4	9	4	....	....	....

Played in NHL All-Star Game (1971)

Claimed by **LA Kings** from **Toronto** in Expansion Draft, June 6, 1967. Traded to **Philadelphia** by **LA Kings** with Eddie Joyal, Jean Potvin and Ross Lonsberry for Bill Lesuk, Jim Johnson and Serge Bernier, January 28, 1972. Traded to **Toronto** by **Philadelphia** for Dave Fortier and Randy Osburn, May 27, 1974. Claimed on waivers by **Atlanta** from **Toronto**, May 20, 1975. Traded to **Edmonton** (WHA) by **Atlanta** for cash, December, 1976. Rights retained by **Edmonton** prior to Expansion Draft, June 9, 1979.

• FLEURY, Theoren

Theoren W. RW – R. 5'6", 180 lbs. b: Oxbow, Sask., 6/29/1968. Calgary's 9th, 166th overall, in 1987.

Season	Club	League	GP	G	A	Pts	AG	AA	APts	PIM	PP	SH	GW	S	%	TGF	PGF	TGA	PGA	+/-	GP	G	A	Pts	PIM	PP	SH	GW
1983-84	St. James Canadians	MAHA	22	33	31	64	....	....	....	88	....	....	....	....	....	....	....	....	....	....	....	....	....	....	....	....	....	....
1984-85	Moose Jaw Warriors	WHL	71	29	46	75	....	....	....	82	....	....	....	....	....	....	....	....	....	....	....	....	....	....	....	....	....	....
1985-86	Moose Jaw Warriors	WHL	72	43	65	108	....	....	....	124	....	....	....	....	....	....	....	....	....	....	13	7	13	20	16	....	....	....
1986-87	Moose Jaw Warriors	WHL	66	61	68	129	....	....	....	110	....	....	....	....	....	....	....	....	....	....	9	7	9	16	34	....	....	....
	Canada	WJC-A	6	2	3	5	....	....	....	2	....	....	....	....	....	....	....	....	....	....	....	....	....	....	....	....	....	....
1987-88	Moose Jaw Warriors	WHL	65	68	92	*160	....	....	....	235	....	....	....	....	....	....	....	....	....	....	....	....	....	....	....	....	....	....
	Canada	WJC-A	7	6	2	8	....	....	....	4	....	....	....	....	....	....	....	....	....	....	....	....	....	....	....	....	....	....
	Salt Lake Golden Eagles	IHL	2	3	4	7	....	....	....	7	....	....	....	....	....	....	....	....	....	....	8	11	5	16	16	....	....	....
1988-89♦	**Calgary Flames**	**NHL**	**36**	**14**	**20**	**34**	**12**	**14**	**26**	**46**	**5**	**0**	**3**	**89**	**15.7**	**50**	**25**	**21**	**1**	**5**	**22**	**5**	**6**	**11**	**24**	**3**	**0**	**3**
	Salt Lake Golden Eagles	IHL	40	37	37	74	....	....	....	81	....	....	....	....	....	....	....	....	....	....	....	....	....	....	....	....	....	....
1989-90	Calgary Flames	Fr-Tour	4	1	0	1	....	....	....	6	....	....	....	....	....	....	....	....	....	....	....	....	....	....	....	....	....	....
	Calgary Flames	**NHL**	**80**	**31**	**35**	**66**	**27**	**25**	**52**	**157**	**9**	**3**	**6**	**200**	**15.5**	**95**	**32**	**48**	**7**	**22**	**6**	**2**	**3**	**5**	**10**	**0**	**0**	**0**
	Canada	WEC-A	9	4	7	11	....	....	....	10	....	....	....	....	....	....	....	....	....	....	....	....	....	....	....	....	....	....
1990-91	**Calgary Flames**	**NHL**	**79**	**51**	**53**	**104**	**47**	**40**	**87**	**136**	**9**	**7**	**9**	**249**	**20.5**	**155**	**57**	**63**	**13**	**48**	**7**	**2**	**5**	**7**	**14**	**0**	**0**	**1**
	Canada	WEC-A	8	5	5	10	....	....	....	8	....	....	....	....	....	....	....	....	....	....	....	....	....	....	....	....	....	....
1991-92	Canada	Can-Cup	7	1	4	5	....	....	....	12	....	....	....	....	....	....	....	....	....	....	....	....	....	....	....	....	....	....
	Calgary Flames	**NHL**	**80**	**33**	**40**	**73**	**30**	**30**	**60**	**133**	**11**	**1**	**6**	**225**	**14.7**	**121**	**53**	**82**	**14**	**0**	....	....	....	....	....	....	....	....
1992-93	**Calgary Flames**	**NHL**	**83**	**34**	**66**	**100**	**28**	**46**	**74**	**88**	**12**	**2**	**4**	**250**	**13.6**	**145**	**61**	**83**	**13**	**14**	**6**	**5**	**7**	**12**	**27**	**3**	**1**	**0**
1993-94	**Calgary Flames**	**NHL**	**83**	**40**	**45**	**85**	**37**	**35**	**72**	**186**	**16**	**1**	**6**	**278**	**14.4**	**134**	**55**	**81**	**32**	**30**	**7**	**6**	**4**	**10**	**5**	**1**	**0**	**2**
1994-95	Tappara Tampere	Finland	10	8	9	17	....	....	....	22	....	....	....	....	....	....	....	....	....	....	....	....	....	....	....	....	....	....
	Calgary Flames	**NHL**	**47**	**29**	**29**	**58**	**51**	**43**	**94**	**112**	**9**	**2**	**5**	**173**	**16.8**	**81**	**30**	**60**	**15**	**6**	**7**	**7**	**7**	**14**	**2**	**2**	**1**	**0**
1995-96	**Calgary Flames**	**NHL**	**80**	**46**	**50**	**96**	**45**	**41**	**86**	**112**	**17**	**5**	**4**	**353**	**13.0**	**126**	**45**	**90**	**26**	**17**	**4**	**2**	**1**	**3**	**14**	**0**	**0**	**0**
1996-97	Canada	W-Cup	8	4	2	6	....	....	....	8	....	....	....	....	....	....	....	....	....	....	....	....	....	....	....	....	....	....
	Calgary Flames	**NHL**	**81**	**29**	**38**	**67**	**31**	**34**	**65**	**104**	**9**	**2**	**3**	**336**	**8.6**	**103**	**40**	**84**	**9**	**–12**	....	....	....	....	....	....	....	....
1997-98	**Calgary Flames**	**NHL**	**82**	**27**	**51**	**78**	**32**	**50**	**82**	**197**	**3**	**2**	**4**	**282**	**9.6**	**113**	**32**	**109**	**28**	**0**	....	....	....	....	....	....	....	....
	Canada	Olympics	6	1	3	4	....	....	....	2	....	....	....	....	....	....	....	....	....	....	....	....	....	....	....	....	....	....
1998-99	**Calgary Flames**	**NHL**	**60**	**30**	**39**	**69**	**35**	**38**	**73**	**68**	**7**	**3**	**3**	**250**	**12.0**	**87**	**28**	**61**	**20**	**18**	....	....	....	....	....	....	....	....
	Colorado Avalanche	**NHL**	**15**	**10**	**14**	**24**	**12**	**13**	**25**	**18**	**1**	**0**	**2**	**51**	**19.6**	**31**	**9**	**14**	**0**	**8**	**18**	**5**	**12**	**17**	**20**	**2**	**0**	**0**
99-2000	**New York Rangers**	**NHL**	**80**	**15**	**49**	**64**	**17**	**45**	**62**	**68**	**1**	**0**	**1**	**246**	**6.1**	**82**	**27**	**73**	**14**	**–4**	....	....	....	....	....	....	....	....
	NHL Totals		**886**	**389**	**529**	**918**	**404**	**454**	**858**	**1425**	**109**	**28**	**56**	**2982**	**13.0**	**1323**	**494**	**869**	**192**		**77**	**34**	**45**	**79**	**116**	**11**	**2**	**6**

WJC-A All-Star Team (1988) • WHL East Second All-Star Team (1988) • Co-winner of Alka-Seltzer Plus Award with Marty McSorley (1991) • NHL Second All-Star Team (1995) • Played in NHL All-Star Game (1991, 1992, 1996, 1997, 1998, 1999)

Traded to **Colorado** by **Calgary** with Chris Dingman for Rene Corbet, Wade Belak, Robyn Regehr and Colorado's 2nd round compensatory choice (Jarret Stoll) in 2000 Entry Draft, February 28, 1999. Signed as a free agent by **NY Rangers**, July 8, 1999.

• FLICHEL, Todd

Todd A. D – R. 6'3", 195 lbs. b: Osgoode, Ont., 9/14/1964. Winnipeg's 10th, 176th overall, in 1983.

Season	Club	League	GP	G	A	Pts	AG	AA	APts	PIM	PP	SH	GW	S	%	TGF	PGF	TGA	PGA	+/–	GP	G	A	Pts	PIM	PP	SH	GW
			REGULAR SEASON																		PLAYOFFS							
1982-83	Gloucester Rangers	OJHL	44	2	21	23	....	....	....	118	....	....	....	....	....	....	....	....	....	....	....	....	....	....	....	....	....	....
1983-84	Bowling Green University	CCHA	44	1	3	4	....	....	....	12	....	....	....	....	....	....	....	....	....	....	....	....	....	....	....	....	....	....
1984-85	Bowling Green University	CCHA	42	5	7	12	....	....	....	62	....	....	....	....	....	....	....	....	....	....	....	....	....	....	....	....	....	....
1985-86	Bowling Green University	CCHA	42	3	10	13	....	....	....	84	....	....	....	....	....	....	....	....	....	....	....	....	....	....	....	....	....	....
1986-87	Bowling Green University	CCHA	42	4	15	19	....	....	....	77	....	....	....	....	....	....	....	....	....	....	....	....	....	....	....	....	....	....
1987-88	**Winnipeg Jets**	**NHL**	**2**	**0**	**0**	**0**	**0**	**0**	**0**	**2**	**0**	**0**	**0**	**1**	**0.0**	**0**	**0**	**4**	**0**	**–4**	....	....	....	....	....	....	....	....
	Moncton Hawks	AHL	65	5	12	17	....	....	....	102	....	....	....	....	....	....	....	....	....	....	....	....	....	....	....	....	....	....
1988-89	**Winnipeg Jets**	**NHL**	**1**	**0**	**0**	**0**	**0**	**0**	**0**	**0**	**0**	**0**	**0**	**1**	**0.0**	**0**	**0**	**1**	**0**	**–1**	....	....	....	....	....	....	....	....
	Moncton Hawks	AHL	74	2	29	31	....	....	....	81	....	....	....	....	....	....	....	....	....	....	10	1	4	5	25	....	....	....
1989-90	**Winnipeg Jets**	**NHL**	**3**	**0**	**1**	**1**	**0**	**1**	**1**	**2**	**0**	**0**	**0**	**1**	**0.0**	**1**	**0**	**2**	**1**	**0**	....	....	....	....	....	....	....	....
	Moncton Hawks	AHL	65	7	14	21	....	....	....	74	....	....	....	....	....	....	....	....	....	....	....	....	....	....	....	....	....	....
1990-91	Moncton Hawks	AHL	75	8	21	29	....	....	....	44	....	....	....	....	....	....	....	....	....	....	9	0	0	0	8	....	....	....
1991-92	Fort Wayne Komets	IHL	64	3	10	13	....	....	....	79	....	....	....	....	....	....	....	....	....	....	7	0	0	0	2	....	....	....
1992-93	Cincinnati Cyclones	IHL	52	5	10	15	....	....	....	46	....	....	....	....	....	....	....	....	....	....	....	....	....	....	....	....	....	....
	Rochester Americans	AHL	15	1	3	4	....	....	....	4	....	....	....	....	....	....	....	....	....	....	16	2	4	6	22	....	....	....
1993-94	Rochester Americans	AHL	2	0	0	0	....	....	....	0	....	....	....	....	....	....	....	....	....	....	....	....	....	....	....	....	....	....
	NHL Totals		**6**	**0**	**1**	**1**	**0**	**1**	**1**	**4**	**0**	**0**	**0**	**3**	**0.0**	**1**	**0**	**7**	**1**		....	....	....	....	....	....	....	....

• FLOCKHART, Rob

Robert Walter LW – L. 6', 185 lbs. b: Sicamous, B.C., 2/6/1956. Vancouver's 2nd, 44th overall, in 1976.

Season	Club	League	GP	G	A	Pts	AG	AA	APts	PIM	PP	SH	GW	S	%	TGF	PGF	TGA	PGA	+/–	GP	G	A	Pts	PIM	PP	SH	GW
1971-72	Revelstoke Bruins	KIJHL	44	41	47	88	....	....	....	54	....	....	....	....	....	....	....	....	....	....	....	....	....	....	....	....	....	....
1972-73	The Pas Blue Devils	AJHL	44	35	45	80	....	....	....	92	....	....	....	....	....	....	....	....	....	....	....	....	....	....	....	....	....	....
1973-74	Kamloops Chiefs	WCJHL	67	13	16	29	....	....	....	49	....	....	....	....	....	....	....	....	....	....	....	....	....	....	....	....	....	....
1974-75	Kamloops Chiefs	WCJHL	36	19	20	39	....	....	....	52	....	....	....	....	....	....	....	....	....	....	....	....	....	....	....	....	....	....
	Canada	WJC-A	4	1	0	1	....	....	....	6	....	....	....	....	....	....	....	....	....	....	....	....	....	....	....	....	....	....
1975-76	Kamloops Chiefs	WCJHL	72	51	47	98	....	....	....	91	....	....	....	....	....	....	....	....	....	....	11	3	9	12	32	....	....	....
1976-77	**Vancouver Canucks**	**NHL**	**5**	**0**	**0**	**0**	**0**	**0**	**0**	**0**	**0**	**0**	**0**	**1**	**0.0**	**1**	**0**	**0**	**0**	**1**	....	....	....	....	....	....	....	....
	Tulsa Oilers	CHL	65	22	32	54	....	....	....	70	....	....	....	....	....	....	....	....	....	....	9	2	6	8	12	....	....	....
1977-78	**Vancouver Canucks**	**NHL**	**24**	**0**	**1**	**1**	**0**	**1**	**1**	**12**	**0**	**0**	**0**	**15**	**0.0**	**5**	**0**	**19**	**0**	**–14**	....	....	....	....	....	....	....	....
	Tulsa Oilers	CHL	43	17	11	28	....	....	....	55	....	....	....	....	....	....	....	....	....	....	7	2	3	5	14	....	....	....
1978-79	**Vancouver Canucks**	**NHL**	**14**	**1**	**1**	**2**	**1**	**1**	**2**	**0**	**0**	**0**	**0**	**10**	**10.0**	**2**	**0**	**8**	**3**	**–3**	....	....	....	....	....	....	....	....
	Dallas Black Hawks	CHL	44	18	27	45	....	....	....	46	....	....	....	....	....	....	....	....	....	....	9	3	3	6	*34	....	....	....
1979-80	**Minnesota North Stars**	**NHL**	**10**	**1**	**3**	**4**	**1**	**2**	**3**	**2**	**0**	**0**	**1**	**10**	**10.0**	**7**	**2**	**9**	**0**	**–4**	**1**	**1**	**0**	**1**	**2**	**0**	**0**	**0**
	Oklahoma City Stars	CHL	67	31	40	71	....	....	....	51	....	....	....	....	....	....	....	....	....	....	....	....	....	....	....	....	....	....
1980-81	**Minnesota North Stars**	**NHL**	**2**	**0**	**0**	**0**	**0**	**0**	**0**	**0**	**0**	**0**	**0**	**1**	**0.0**	**0**	**0**	**2**	**0**	**–2**	....	....	....	....	....	....	....	....
	Oklahoma City Stars	CHL	75	33	42	75	....	....	....	89	....	....	....	....	....	....	....	....	....	....	3	0	1	1	6	....	....	....
1981-82	Nashville South Stars	CHL	79	27	30	57	....	....	....	98	....	....	....	....	....	....	....	....	....	....	3	0	0	0	2	....	....	....
1982-83	Springfield Indians	AHL	74	22	34	56	....	....	....	55	....	....	....	....	....	....	....	....	....	....	....	....	....	....	....	....	....	....
1983-84	Toledo Goaldiggers	IHL	54	33	20	53	....	....	....	33	....	....	....	....	....	....	....	....	....	....	....	....	....	....	....	....	....	....
1984-85	New Haven Nighthawks	AHL	2	0	2	2	....	....	....	0	....	....	....	....	....	....	....	....	....	....	....	....	....	....	....	....	....	....
	Springfield Indians	AHL	14	5	8	13	....	....	....	22	....	....	....	....	....	....	....	....	....	....	....	....	....	....	....	....	....	....
	NHL Totals		**55**	**2**	**5**	**7**	**2**	**4**	**6**	**14**	**0**	**0**	**1**	**37**	**5.4**	**15**	**2**	**38**	**3**		**1**	**1**	**0**	**1**	**2**	**0**	**0**	**0**

• Brother of Ron • CHL First All-Star Team (1980)

Signed as a free agent by **Minnesota**, October 12, 1979. Signed as a free agent by **Chicago**, December 1, 1982.

• FLOCKHART, Ron

Ronald E. "Flockey Hockey" C – L. 5'11", 190 lbs. b: Smithers, B.C., 10/10/1960.

Season	Club	League	GP	G	A	Pts	AG	AA	APts	PIM	PP	SH	GW	S	%	TGF	PGF	TGA	PGA	+/–	GP	G	A	Pts	PIM	PP	SH	GW
1977-78	Revelstoke Bruins	BCJHL	43	21	19	40	....	....	....	37	....	....	....	....	....	....	....	....	....	....	....	....	....	....	....	....	....	....
	Medicine Hat Tigers	WCJHL	5	1	0	1	....	....	....	2	....	....	....	....	....	....	....	....	....	....	....	....	....	....	....	....	....	....
1978-79	Revelstoke Bruins	BCJHL	61	47	41	88	....	....	....	54	....	....	....	....	....	....	....	....	....	....	....	....	....	....	....	....	....	....
1979-80	Regina Pats	WHL	65	54	76	130	....	....	....	63	....	....	....	....	....	....	....	....	....	....	17	11	23	34	18	....	....	....
	Regina Pats	Mem-Cup	4	3	*6	*9	....	....	....	4	....	....	....	....	....	....	....	....	....	....	....	....	....	....	....	....	....	....
1980-81	**Philadelphia Flyers**	**NHL**	**14**	**3**	**7**	**10**	**2**	**5**	**7**	**11**	**0**	**0**	**0**	**24**	**12.5**	**15**	**1**	**8**	**0**	**6**	**3**	**1**	**0**	**1**	**2**	**0**	**0**	**0**
	Maine Mariners	AHL	59	33	33	66	....	....	....	26	....	....	....	....	....	....	....	....	....	....	....	....	....	....	....	....	....	....
1981-82	**Philadelphia Flyers**	**NHL**	**72**	**33**	**39**	**72**	**26**	**26**	**52**	**44**	**10**	**0**	**2**	**240**	**13.8**	**94**	**32**	**45**	**1**	**18**	**4**	**0**	**1**	**1**	**2**	**0**	**0**	**0**
1982-83	**Philadelphia Flyers**	**NHL**	**73**	**29**	**31**	**60**	**24**	**21**	**45**	**49**	**3**	**2**	**6**	**241**	**12.0**	**84**	**25**	**62**	**6**	**3**	**2**	**1**	**1**	**2**	**2**	**1**	**0**	**0**
1983-84	**Philadelphia Flyers**	**NHL**	**8**	**0**	**3**	**3**	**0**	**2**	**2**	**4**	**0**	**0**	**0**	**12**	**0.0**	**6**	**0**	**5**	**0**	**1**	....	....	....	....	....	....	....	....
	Pittsburgh Penguins	**NHL**	**68**	**27**	**18**	**45**	**22**	**12**	**34**	**40**	**5**	**0**	**1**	**202**	**13.4**	**64**	**16**	**67**	**0**	**–19**	....	....	....	....	....	....	....	....
1984-85	**Pittsburgh Penguins**	**NHL**	**12**	**0**	**5**	**5**	**0**	**3**	**3**	**4**	**0**	**0**	**0**	**20**	**0.0**	**7**	**1**	**6**	**4**	**4**	....	....	....	....	....	....	....	....
	Montreal Canadiens	**NHL**	**42**	**10**	**12**	**22**	**8**	**8**	**16**	**14**	**1**	**0**	**2**	**58**	**17.2**	**32**	**7**	**23**	**1**	**3**	**2**	**1**	**1**	**2**	**2**	**0**	**0**	**1**
1985-86	**St. Louis Blues**	**NHL**	**79**	**22**	**45**	**67**	**18**	**30**	**48**	**26**	**5**	**2**	**3**	**199**	**11.1**	**89**	**29**	**52**	**0**	**8**	**8**	**1**	**3**	**4**	**6**	**0**	**0**	**0**
1986-87	**St. Louis Blues**	**NHL**	**60**	**16**	**19**	**35**	**14**	**14**	**28**	**12**	**2**	**0**	**2**	**101**	**15.8**	**48**	**5**	**52**	**0**	**–9**	....	....	....	....	....	....	....	....
1987-88	**St. Louis Blues**	**NHL**	**21**	**5**	**4**	**9**	**4**	**3**	**7**	**4**	**0**	**0**	**1**	**27**	**18.5**	**16**	**0**	**11**	**0**	**5**	....	....	....	....	....	....	....	....
1988-89	Peoria Rivermen	IHL	2	0	2	2	....	....	....	0	....	....	....	....	....	....	....	....	....	....	....	....	....	....	....	....	....	....
	Boston Bruins	**NHL**	**4**	**0**	**0**	**0**	**0**	**0**	**0**	**0**	**0**	**0**	**0**	**3**	**0.0**	**0**	**0**	**4**	**1**	**–3**	....	....	....	....	....	....	....	....
	Maine Mariners	AHL	9	5	6	11	....	....	....	0	....	....	....	....	....	....	....	....	....	....	....	....	....	....	....	....	....	....
	SG Cortina	Italy	31	31	34	65	....	....	....	25	....	....	....	....	....	....	....	....	....	....	....	....	....	....	....	....	....	....
1989-90	HC Bolzano	Italy	36	48	85	133	....	....	....	15	....	....	....	....	....	....	....	....	....	....	9	5	9	14	0	....	....	....
1990-91	HC Bolzano	Italy	33	35	44	79	....	....	....	32	....	....	....	....	....	....	....	....	....	....	10	7	12	19	2	....	....	....
1991-92	HC Bolzano	Alpenliga	12	6	7	13	....	....	....	2	....	....	....	....	....	....	....	....	....	....	....	....	....	....	....	....	....	....
	HC Bolzano	Italy	DID NOT PLAY – INJURED																									
1992-93	Dallas Freeze	CHL	DID NOT PLAY – COACHING																									
	NHL Totals		**453**	**145**	**183**	**328**	**118**	**124**	**242**	**208**	**26**	**4**	**17**	**1127**	**12.9**	**455**	**116**	**335**	**13**		**19**	**4**	**6**	**10**	**14**	**1**	**0**	**1**

• Brother of Rob

Signed as a free agent by **Philadelphia**, July 2, 1980. Traded to **Pittsburgh** by **Philadelphia** with Andy Brickley, Mark Taylor and Philadelphia's 1st (Roger Belanger) and 3rd (later traded to Vancouver — Vancouver selected Mike Stevens) round choices in 1984 Entry Draft for Rich Sutter and Pittsburgh's 2nd (Greg Smyth) and 3rd (David McLay) round choices in 1984 Entry Draft, October 23, 1983. Traded to **Montreal** by **Pittsburgh** for John Chabot, November 9, 1984. Traded to **St. Louis** by **Montreal** for Perry Ganchar, August 26, 1985. Traded to **Boston** by **St. Louis** for future considerations, February 13, 1989. • Missed majority of 1991-92 season recovering from knee injury suffered in Alpenliga, October, 1991.

• FLOYD, Larry

Larry David C – L. 5'8", 180 lbs. b: Peterborough, Ont., 5/1/1961.

Season	Club	League	GP	G	A	Pts	AG	AA	APts	PIM	PP	SH	GW	S	%	TGF	PGF	TGA	PGA	+/–	GP	G	A	Pts	PIM	PP	SH	GW
1978-79	Peterborough Jr. Petes	OHA-B	43	54	64	118	....	....	....	63	....	....	....	....	....	....	....	....	....	....	....	....	....	....	....	....	....	....
	Peterborough Petes	OMJHL	8	4	5	9	....	....	....	2	....	....	....	....	....	....	....	....	....	....	14	5	4	9	10	....	....	....
	Peterborough Petes	Mem-Cup	5	1	2	3	....	....	....	2	....	....	....	....	....	....	....	....	....	....	....	....	....	....	....	....	....	....
1979-80	Peterborough Petes	OMJHL	66	21	37	58	....	....	....	54	....	....	....	....	....	....	....	....	....	....	14	6	9	15	10	....	....	....
	Peterborough Petes	Mem-Cup	5	*5	1	6	....	....	....	5	....	....	....	....	....	....	....	....	....	....	....	....	....	....	....	....	....	....
1980-81	Peterborough Petes	OMJHL	44	26	37	63	....	....	....	43	....	....	....	....	....	....	....	....	....	....	5	2	2	4	0	....	....	....
	Wexford Raiders	OJHL	3	1	2	3	....	....	....	6	....	....	....	....	....	....	....	....	....	....	....	....	....	....	....	....	....	....
1981-82	Peterborough Petes	OHL	39	32	37	69	....	....	....	26	....	....	....	....	....	....	....	....	....	....	9	9	6	15	20	....	....	....
	Rochester Americans	AHL	1	0	2	2	....	....	....	0	....	....	....	....	....	....	....	....	....	....	7	1	1	2	0	....	....	....
1982-83	**New Jersey Devils**	**NHL**	**5**	**1**	**0**	**1**	**1**	**0**	**1**	**2**	**0**	**0**	**0**	**9**	**11.1**	**1**	**0**	**5**	**0**	**–4**	....	....	....	....	....	....	....	....
	Wichita Wind	CHL	75	40	43	83	....	....	....	16	....	....	....	....	....	....	....	....	....	....	....	....	....	....	....	....	....	....
1983-84	**New Jersey Devils**	**NHL**	**7**	**1**	**3**	**4**	**1**	**2**	**3**	**7**	**0**	**0**	**0**	**15**	**6.7**	**4**	**0**	**11**	**3**	**–4**	....	....	....	....	....	....	....	....
	Maine Mariners	AHL	74	37	49	86	....	....	....	40	....	....	....	....	....	....	....	....	....	....	16	9	8	17	4	....	....	....
1984-85	Maine Mariners	AHL	72	30	51	81	....	....	....	24	....	....	....	....	....	....	....	....	....	....	3	0	1	1	2	....	....	....
1985-86	Maine Mariners	AHL	80	29	58	87	....	....	....	25	....	....	....	....	....	....	....	....	....	....	5	3	3	6	0	....	....	....
1986-87	Maine Mariners	AHL	77	30	44	74	....	....	....	50	....	....	....	....	....	....	....	....	....	....	....	....	....	....	....	....	....	....
1987-88	IEV Innsbruck	Austria	33	10	22	32	....	....	....	18	....	....	....	....	....	....	....	....	....	....	....	....	....	....	....	....	....	....
	Utica Devils	AHL	28	21	21	42	....	....	....	14	....	....	....	....	....	....	....	....	....	....	....	....	....	....	....	....	....	....
1988-89	Cape Breton Oilers	AHL	70	16	33	49	....	....	....	40	....	....	....	....	....	....	....	....	....	....	....	....	....	....	....	....	....	....
1989-90	Phoenix Roadrunners	IHL	76	39	40	79	....	....	....	50	....	....	....	....	....	....	....	....	....	....	....	....	....	....	....	....	....	....

			REGULAR SEASON																		PLAYOFFS							
Season	Club	League	GP	G	A	Pts	AG	AA	APts	PIM	PP	SH	GW	S	%	TGF	PGF	TGA	PGA	+/–	GP	G	A	Pts	PIM	PP	SH	GW
1990-91	San Diego Gulls	IHL	73	24	54	78	....	....	....	34	....	....	....	....	....	....	....	....	....	....	....	....	....	....	....	....	....	....
1991-92	San Diego Gulls	IHL	71	18	45	63	....	....	....	58	....	....	....	....	....	....	....	....	....	....	4	0	2	2	0	....	....	....
1992-93	San Diego Gulls	IHL	80	27	31	58	....	....	....	28	....	....	....	....	....	....	....	....	....	....	14	3	1	4	4	....	....	....
1993-94	San Diego Gulls	IHL	52	10	20	30	....	....	....	45	....	....	....	....	....	....	....	....	....	....	8	1	0	1	5	....	....	....
	NHL Totals		**12**	**2**	**3**	**5**	**2**	**2**	**4**	**9**	**0**	**0**	**0**	**24**	**8.3**	**5**	**0**	**16**	**3**		....	....	....	....	....	....	....	....

Won Ken McKenzie Trophy (Rookie of the Year - CHL) (1983)

Signed as a free agent by **New Jersey**, September 16, 1982. • Played w/ RHI's San Diego Barracudas in 1993 (13-7-18-35-8) and 1994 (11-6-10-16-4).

• FOGARTY, Bryan

D – L. 6'2", 206 lbs. b: Brantford, Ont., 6/11/1969. Quebec's 1st, 9th overall, in 1987.

Season	Club	League	GP	G	A	Pts	AG	AA	APts	PIM	PP	SH	GW	S	%	TGF	PGF	TGA	PGA	+/–	GP	G	A	Pts	PIM	PP	SH	GW
1983-84	Brantford Alexanders	OJHL-B	1	0	1	1	....	....	....	0	....	....	....	....	....	....	....	....	....	....	....	....	....	....	....	....	....	....
1984-85	Aurora Tigers	OJHL	42	9	12	21	....	....	....	57	....	....	....	....	....	....	....	....	....	....	....	....	....	....	....	....	....	....
	Aurora Tigers	Cen-Cup	4	2	2	4	....	....	....	8	....	....	....	....	....	....	....	....	....	....	....	....	....	....	....	....	....	....
1985-86	Kingston Canadians	OHL	47	2	19	21	....	....	....	14	....	....	....	....	....	....	....	....	....	....	10	1	3	4	4	....	....	....
1986-87	Kingston Canadians	OHL	56	20	50	70	....	....	....	46	....	....	....	....	....	....	....	....	....	....	12	2	3	5	5	....	....	....
1987-88	Kingston Canadians	OHL	48	11	36	47	....	....	....	50	....	....	....	....	....	....	....	....	....	....	....	....	....	....	....	....	....	....
1988-89	Niagara Falls Thunder	OHL	60	47	*108	*155	....	....	....	88	....	....	....	....	....	....	....	....	....	....	17	10	22	32	36	....	....	....
1989-90	**Quebec Nordiques**	**NHL**	**45**	**4**	**10**	**14**	**3**	**7**	**10**	**31**	**2**	**0**	**0**	**93**	**4.3**	**39**	**13**	**74**	**1**	**–47**	....	....	....	....	....	....	....	....
	Halifax Citadels	AHL	22	5	14	19	....	....	....	6	....	....	....	....	....	....	....	....	....	....	6	2	4	6	0	....	....	....
1990-91	**Quebec Nordiques**	**NHL**	**45**	**9**	**22**	**31**	**8**	**17**	**25**	**24**	**3**	**0**	**2**	**107**	**8.4**	**59**	**25**	**46**	**1**	**–11**	....	....	....	....	....	....	....	....
	Halifax Citadels	AHL	5	0	2	2	....	....	....	0	....	....	....	....	....	....	....	....	....	....	....	....	....	....	....	....	....	....
1991-92	**Quebec Nordiques**	**NHL**	**20**	**3**	**12**	**15**	**3**	**9**	**12**	**16**	**0**	**0**	**0**	**30**	**10.0**	**27**	**10**	**32**	**0**	**–15**	....	....	....	....	....	....	....	....
	Halifax Citadels	AHL	2	0	0	0	....	....	....	2	....	....	....	....	....	....	....	....	....	....	....	....	....	....	....	....	....	....
	New Haven Nighthawks	AHL	4	0	1	1	....	....	....	6	....	....	....	....	....	....	....	....	....	....	....	....	....	....	....	....	....	....
	Muskegon Lumberjacks	IHL	8	2	4	6	....	....	....	30	....	....	....	....	....	....	....	....	....	....	....	....	....	....	....	....	....	....
1992-93	**Pittsburgh Penguins**	**NHL**	**12**	**0**	**4**	**4**	**0**	**3**	**3**	**4**	**0**	**0**	**0**	**11**	**0.0**	**11**	**7**	**7**	**0**	**–3**	....	....	....	....	....	....	....	....
	Cleveland Lumberjacks	IHL	15	2	5	7	....	....	....	8	....	....	....	....	....	....	....	....	....	....	3	0	1	1	17	....	....	....
1993-94	Atlanta Knights	IHL	8	1	5	6	....	....	....	4	....	....	....	....	....	....	....	....	....	....	....	....	....	....	....	....	....	....
	Las Vegas Thunder	IHL	33	3	16	19	....	....	....	38	....	....	....	....	....	....	....	....	....	....	....	....	....	....	....	....	....	....
	Kansas City Blades	IHL	3	2	1	3	....	....	....	2	....	....	....	....	....	....	....	....	....	....	....	....	....	....	....	....	....	....
	Montreal Canadiens	**NHL**	**13**	**1**	**2**	**3**	**1**	**2**	**3**	**10**	**0**	**0**	**0**	**22**	**4.5**	**11**	**3**	**13**	**1**	**–4**	....	....	....	....	....	....	....	....
1994-95	**Montreal Canadiens**	**NHL**	**21**	**5**	**2**	**7**	**9**	**3**	**12**	**34**	**3**	**0**	**0**	**41**	**12.2**	**15**	**6**	**13**	**1**	**–3**	....	....	....	....	....	....	....	....
1995-96	Minnesota Moose	IHL	17	3	12	15	....	....	....	24	....	....	....	....	....	....	....	....	....	....	....	....	....	....	....	....	....	....
	Detroit Vipers	IHL	18	1	5	6	....	....	....	14	....	....	....	....	....	....	....	....	....	....	....	....	....	....	....	....	....	....
	HC Davos	Switz.	2	0	0	0	....	....	....	0	....	....	....	....	....	....	....	....	....	....	3	1	1	2	0	....	....	....
1996-97	HC Milano Devils	Alpenliga	7	3	7	10	....	....	....	10	....	....	....	....	....	....	....	....	....	....	....	....	....	....	....	....	....	....
	HC Milano Devils	Italy	10	4	11	15	....	....	....	18	....	....	....	....	....	....	....	....	....	....	6	4	9	13	26	....	....	....
	Kansas City Blades	IHL	22	3	9	12	....	....	....	10	....	....	....	....	....	....	....	....	....	....	....	....	....	....	....	....	....	....
1997-98	Hannover Scorpions	Germany	39	8	17	25	....	....	....	75	....	....	....	....	....	....	....	....	....	....	4	1	0	1	2	....	....	....
1998-99	Indianapolis Ice	IHL	36	7	15	22	....	....	....	28	....	....	....	....	....	....	....	....	....	....	....	....	....	....	....	....	....	....
	Baton Rouge Kingfish	ECHL	5	4	3	7	....	....	....	24	....	....	....	....	....	....	....	....	....	....	4	1	3	4	8	....	....	....
99-2000	St. John's Maple Leafs	AHL	3	0	0	0	....	....	....	0	....	....	....	....	....	....	....	....	....	....	....	....	....	....	....	....	....	....
	Knoxville Speed	UHL	16	5	12	17	....	....	....	29	....	....	....	....	....	....	....	....	....	....	....	....	....	....	....	....	....	....
	Hannover Scorpions	Germany	30	7	17	24	....	....	....	40	....	....	....	....	....	....	....	....	....	....	....	....	....	....	....	....	....	....
	NHL Totals		**156**	**22**	**52**	**74**	**24**	**41**	**65**	**119**	**8**	**0**	**2**	**304**	**7.2**	**162**	**64**	**185**	**4**		....	....	....	....	....	....	....	....

OHL First All-Star Team (1987, 1989) • Canadian Major Junior Defenseman of the Year (1989) • Canadian Major Junior Player of the Year (1989)

Traded to **Pittsburgh** by **Quebec** for Scott Young, March 10, 1992. Signed as a free agent by **Tampa Bay**, September 28, 1993. Signed as a free agent by **Montreal**, February 25, 1994. Signed as a free agent by **Buffalo**, September 8, 1995. Signed as a free agent by **Chicago**, September 2, 1998. Signed as a free agent by **Toronto**, September 14, 1999. Signed as a free agent by **Knoxville** (UHL) following release by **Toronto**, October 20, 1999.

• FOGOLIN, Lee Jr.

Lee Jr. Joseph "Foggie" D – R. 6', 200 lbs. b: Chicago, IL, 2/7/1955. Buffalo's 1st, 11th overall, in 1974.

Season	Club	League	GP	G	A	Pts	AG	AA	APts	PIM	PP	SH	GW	S	%	TGF	PGF	TGA	PGA	+/–	GP	G	A	Pts	PIM	PP	SH	GW
1970-71	Thunder Bay Marrs	TBJHL	STATISTICS NOT AVAILABLE																									
	Thunder Bay Marrs	Cen-Cup	5	0	2	2	....	....	....	6	....	....	....	....	....	....	....	....	....	....	....	....	....	....	....	....	....	....
1971-72	Thunder Bay Marrs	TBJHL	STATISTICS NOT AVAILABLE																									
1972-73	Oshawa Generals	OMJHL	55	5	21	26	....	....	....	132	....	....	....	....	....	....	....	....	....	....	....	....	....	....	....	....	....	....
1973-74	Oshawa Generals	OMJHL	47	7	19	26	....	....	....	108	....	....	....	....	....	....	....	....	....	....	....	....	....	....	....	....	....	....
1974-75	**Buffalo Sabres**	**NHL**	**50**	**2**	**2**	**4**	**2**	**1**	**3**	**59**	**2**	**0**	**0**	**14**	**14.3**	**20**	**4**	**18**	**2**	**0**	**8**	**0**	**0**	**0**	**6**	**0**	**0**	**0**
1975-76	**Buffalo Sabres**	**NHL**	**58**	**0**	**9**	**9**	**0**	**7**	**7**	**64**	**0**	**0**	**0**	**61**	**0.0**	**62**	**1**	**52**	**6**	**15**	**9**	**0**	**4**	**4**	**23**	**0**	**0**	**0**
	Hershey Bears	AHL	20	1	8	9	....	....	....	61	....	....	....	....	....	....	....	....	....	....	....	....	....	....	....	....	....	....
1976-77	United States	Can-Cup	2	0	0	0	....	....	....	6	....	....	....	....	....	....	....	....	....	....	....	....	....	....	....	....	....	....
	Buffalo Sabres	**NHL**	**71**	**3**	**15**	**18**	**3**	**12**	**15**	**100**	**1**	**0**	**2**	**76**	**3.9**	**71**	**7**	**58**	**3**	**9**	**4**	**0**	**0**	**0**	**2**	**0**	**0**	**0**
1977-78	**Buffalo Sabres**	**NHL**	**76**	**0**	**23**	**23**	**0**	**18**	**18**	**98**	**0**	**0**	**0**	**77**	**0.0**	**78**	**2**	**75**	**6**	**7**	**6**	**0**	**2**	**2**	**23**	**0**	**0**	**0**
1978-79	**Buffalo Sabres**	**NHL**	**74**	**3**	**19**	**22**	**3**	**14**	**17**	**103**	**0**	**0**	**0**	**70**	**4.3**	**80**	**0**	**103**	**19**	**–4**	**3**	**0**	**0**	**0**	**4**	**0**	**0**	**0**
1979-80	**Edmonton Oilers**	**NHL**	**80**	**5**	**10**	**15**	**4**	**7**	**11**	**104**	**0**	**0**	**0**	**90**	**5.6**	**74**	**2**	**115**	**35**	**–8**	**3**	**0**	**0**	**0**	**4**	**0**	**0**	**0**
1980-81	**Edmonton Oilers**	**NHL**	**80**	**13**	**17**	**30**	**10**	**11**	**21**	**139**	**0**	**4**	**1**	**89**	**14.6**	**97**	**2**	**136**	**43**	**2**	**9**	**0**	**0**	**0**	**12**	**0**	**0**	**0**
1981-82	**Edmonton Oilers**	**NHL**	**80**	**4**	**25**	**29**	**3**	**17**	**20**	**154**	**0**	**0**	**0**	**98**	**4.1**	**111**	**1**	**107**	**37**	**40**	**5**	**1**	**1**	**2**	**14**	**0**	**1**	**0**
1982-83	**Edmonton Oilers**	**NHL**	**72**	**0**	**18**	**18**	**0**	**12**	**12**	**92**	**0**	**0**	**0**	**66**	**0.0**	**93**	**2**	**99**	**32**	**24**	**16**	**0**	**5**	**5**	**36**	**0**	**0**	**0**
1983-84♦	**Edmonton Oilers**	**NHL**	**80**	**5**	**16**	**21**	**4**	**11**	**15**	**125**	**0**	**0**	**0**	**73**	**6.8**	**104**	**2**	**99**	**30**	**33**	**19**	**1**	**4**	**5**	**23**	**0**	**0**	**0**
1984-85♦	**Edmonton Oilers**	**NHL**	**79**	**4**	**14**	**18**	**3**	**10**	**13**	**126**	**0**	**1**	**1**	**63**	**6.3**	**82**	**2**	**95**	**31**	**16**	**18**	**3**	**1**	**4**	**16**	**0**	**0**	**1**
1985-86	**Edmonton Oilers**	**NHL**	**80**	**4**	**22**	**26**	**3**	**15**	**18**	**129**	**0**	**0**	**0**	**71**	**5.6**	**102**	**1**	**78**	**24**	**47**	**8**	**0**	**2**	**2**	**10**	**0**	**0**	**0**
1986-87	**Edmonton Oilers**	**NHL**	**35**	**1**	**3**	**4**	**1**	**2**	**3**	**17**	**0**	**0**	**0**	**37**	**2.7**	**31**	**2**	**40**	**9**	**–2**	....	....	....	....	....	....	....	....
	Buffalo Sabres	**NHL**	**9**	**0**	**2**	**2**	**0**	**1**	**1**	**8**	**0**	**0**	**0**	**5**	**0.0**	**4**	**0**	**14**	**8**	**–2**	....	....	....	....	....	....	....	....
	NHL Totals		**924**	**44**	**195**	**239**	**36**	**138**	**174**	**1318**	**3**	**5**	**4**	**890**	**4.9**	**1009**	**28**	**1089**	**285**		**108**	**5**	**19**	**24**	**173**	**0**	**1**	**1**

• Son of Lee Sr. • Played in NHL All-Star Game (1986)

Claimed by **Edmonton** from **Buffalo** in Expansion Draft, June 13, 1979. Traded to **Buffalo** by **Edmonton** with Mark Napier and Edmonton's 4th round choice (John Bradley) in 1987 Entry Draft for Normand Lacombe, Wayne Van Dorp and Buffalo's 4th round choice (Peter Ericksson) in 1987 Entry Draft, March 6, 1987.

• FOLCO, Peter

D – L. 6', 185 lbs. b: Montreal, Que., 8/13/1953. Vancouver's 10th, 131st overall, in 1973.

Season	Club	League	GP	G	A	Pts	AG	AA	APts	PIM	PP	SH	GW	S	%	TGF	PGF	TGA	PGA	+/–	GP	G	A	Pts	PIM	PP	SH	GW
1969-70	Verdun Maple Leafs	QJHL	43	1	7	8	....	....	....	24	....	....	....	....	....	....	....	....	....	....	11	0	0	0	2	....	....	....
1970-71	Verdun Maple Leafs	QJHL	54	8	20	28	....	....	....	22	....	....	....	....	....	....	....	....	....	....	5	0	1	1	0	....	....	....
1971-72	Verdun Maple Leafs	QMJHL	40	7	16	23	....	....	....	59	....	....	....	....	....	....	....	....	....	....	4	0	0	0	7	....	....	....
1972-73	Quebec Remparts	QMJHL	55	8	47	55	....	....	....	26	....	....	....	....	....	....	....	....	....	....	....	....	....	....	....	....	....	....
	Quebec Remparts	Mem-Cup	2	0	0	0	....	....	....	2	....	....	....	....	....	....	....	....	....	....	....	....	....	....	....	....	....	....
1973-74	**Vancouver Canucks**	**NHL**	**2**	**0**	**0**	**0**	**0**	**0**	**0**	**0**	**0**	**0**	**0**	**0**	**0.0**	**0**	**0**	**1**	**0**	**–1**	....	....	....	....	....	....	....	....
	Seattle Totems	WHL	69	3	26	29	....	....	....	57	....	....	....	....	....	....	....	....	....	....	....	....	....	....	....	....	....	....
1974-75	Seattle Totems	CHL	59	4	19	23	....	....	....	101	....	....	....	....	....	....	....	....	....	....	....	....	....	....	....	....	....	....
1975-76	Toronto Toros	WHA	19	1	8	9	....	....	....	15	....	....	....	....	....	....	....	....	....	....	....	....	....	....	....	....	....	....
	Beauce Jaros	NAHL	51	8	51	59	....	....	....	84	....	....	....	....	....	....	....	....	....	....	6	0	4	4	4	....	....	....
1976-77	Birmingham Bulls	WHA	2	0	0	0	....	....	....	0	....	....	....	....	....	....	....	....	....	....	....	....	....	....	....	....	....	....
	Beauce Jaros	NAHL	19	5	12	17	....	....	....	28	....	....	....	....	....	....	....	....	....	....	....	....	....	....	....	....	....	....
	Philadelphia Firebirds	NAHL	41	0	25	25	....	....	....	28	....	....	....	....	....	....	....	....	....	....	4	1	1	2	2	....	....	....
	NHL Totals		**2**	**0**	**0**	**0**	**0**	**0**	**0**	**0**	**0**	**0**	**0**	**0**	**0.0**	**0**	**0**	**1**	**0**		....	....	....	....	....	....	....	....
	Other Major League Totals		21	1	8	9	....	....	....	15	....	....	....	....	....	....	....	....	....	....	....	....	....	....	....	....	....	....

Signed as a free agent by **Toronto** (WHA), September, 1975. Transferred to **Birmingham** (WHA) after **Toronto** (WHA) franchise relocated, June 30, 1976. Traded to **Philadelphia** (NAHL) by **Birmingham** for cash, December, 1976.

Season	Club	League	REGULAR SEASON GP	G	A	Pts	AG	AA	APts	PIM	PP	SH	GW	S	%	TGF	PGF	TGA	PGA	+/–	PLAYOFFS GP	G	A	Pts	PIM	PP	SH	GW
• FOLEY, Gerry Gerald James RW – R. 5'11", 165 lbs. b: Ware, MA, 9/22/1932.																												
1950-51	North Bay Trappers	NOJHA	STATISTICS NOT AVAILABLE																									
1951-52	St. Catharines Teepees	OHA-Jr.	53	13	23	36	....	....	....	41	....	....	....	....	....	....	....	....	....	....	14	5	6	11	20	....	....	....
1952-53	Seattle Bombers	WHL	70	29	30	59	....	....	....	46	....	....	....	....	....	....	....	....	....	....	5	1	2	3	0	....	....	....
1953-54	Ottawa Senators	QHL	43	9	6	15	....	....	....	57	....	....	....	....	....	....	....	....	....	....	22	7	4	11	14	....	....	....
	Pittsburgh Hornets	AHL	16	1	3	4	....	....	....	13	....	....	....	....	....	....	....	....	....	....	....	....	....	....	....	....	....	....
1954-55	**Toronto Maple Leafs**	**NHL**	**4**	**0**	**0**	**0**	**0**	**0**	**0**	**8**	....	....	....	....	....	....	....	....	....	....	....	....	....	....	....	....	....	....
	Pittsburgh Hornets	AHL	61	16	21	37	....	....	....	61	....	....	....	....	....	....	....	....	....	....	10	5	3	8	8	....	....	....
1955-56	Pittsburgh Hornets	AHL	59	29	29	58	....	....	....	109	....	....	....	....	....	....	....	....	....	....	3	2	0	2	2	....	....	....
1956-57	**New York Rangers**	**NHL**	**69**	**7**	**9**	**16**	**9**	**10**	**19**	**48**	....	....	....	....	....	....	....	....	....	....	**3**	**0**	**0**	**0**	**0**	**0**	**0**	**0**
1957-58	**New York Rangers**	**NHL**	**68**	**2**	**5**	**7**	**2**	**5**	**7**	**43**	....	....	....	....	....	....	....	....	....	....	**6**	**0**	**1**	**1**	**2**	**0**	**0**	**0**
1958-59	Buffalo Bisons	AHL	68	9	22	31	....	....	....	36	....	....	....	....	....	....	....	....	....	....	11	*5	2	7	15	....	....	....
1959-60	Springfield Indians	AHL	31	5	13	18	....	....	....	7	....	....	....	....	....	....	....	....	....	....	10	1	6	7	4	....	....	....
1960-61	Springfield Indians	AHL	53	15	29	44	....	....	....	27	....	....	....	....	....	....	....	....	....	....	3	1	4	5	0	....	....	....
1961-62	Sudbury Wolves	EPHL	58	18	34	52	....	....	....	36	....	....	....	....	....	....	....	....	....	....	5	2	5	7	0	....	....	....
1962-63	Springfield Indians	AHL	51	11	13	24	....	....	....	18	....	....	....	....	....	....	....	....	....	....	....	....	....	....	....	....	....	....
1963-64	Springfield Indians	AHL	62	8	18	26	....	....	....	26	....	....	....	....	....	....	....	....	....	....	....	....	....	....	....	....	....	....
1964-65	Springfield Indians	AHL	71	21	34	55	....	....	....	36	....	....	....	....	....	....	....	....	....	....	....	....	....	....	....	....	....	....
1965-66	Springfield Indians	AHL	49	12	14	26	....	....	....	26	....	....	....	....	....	....	....	....	....	....	6	3	1	4	6	....	....	....
1966-67	Springfield Indians	AHL	66	26	35	61	....	....	....	31	....	....	....	....	....	....	....	....	....	....	....	....	....	....	....	....	....	....
1967-68	Springfield Kings	AHL	71	25	33	58	....	....	....	39	....	....	....	....	....	....	....	....	....	....	4	1	0	1	0	....	....	....
1968-69	**Los Angeles Kings**	**NHL**	**1**	**0**	**0**	**0**	**0**	**0**	**0**	**0**	**0**	**0**	**0**	**4**	**0.0**	**0**	**0**	**1**	**0**	**–1**	....	....	....	....	....	....	....	....
	Denver Spurs	WHL	51	10	24	34	....	....	....	16	....	....	....	....	....	....	....	....	....	....	....	....	....	....	....	....	....	....
	NHL Totals		**142**	**9**	**14**	**23**	**11**	**15**	**26**	**99**	....	....	....	....	....	....	....	....	....		**9**	**0**	**1**	**1**	**2**	....	....	....

Won WHL Rookie of the Year Award (1953)

Traded to **Toronto** by **Cleveland** (AHL) with Bob Bailey for Chuck Blair and $30,000, May 30, 1953. Claimed by **NY Rangers** from **Toronto** in Intra-League Draft, June 5, 1956. NHL rights transferred to **LA Kings** after NHL club purchased **Springfield** (AHL) franchise, May, 1967.

Season	Club	League	GP	G	A	Pts	AG	AA	APts	PIM	PP	SH	GW	S	%	TGF	PGF	TGA	PGA	+/–	GP	G	A	Pts	PIM	PP	SH	GW
• FOLEY, Rick Gilbert Anthony D – L. 6'4", 223 lbs. b: Niagara Falls, Ont., 9/22/1945.																												
1962-63	Toronto Marlboros	MTJHL	30	6	24	30	....	....	....	64	....	....	....	....	....	....	....	....	....	....	9	3	5	8	23	....	....	....
1963-64	Toronto Marlboros	OHA-Jr.	8	0	0	0	....	....	....	17	....	....	....	....	....	....	....	....	....	....	....	....	....	....	....	....	....	....
	Oshawa Generals	OHA-Jr.	8	0	3	3	....	....	....	42	....	....	....	....	....	....	....	....	....	....	....	....	....	....	....	....	....	....
1964-65	St. Thomas Barons	OHA-B	STATISTICS NOT AVAILABLE																									
1965-66	St. Thomas Barons	OHA-B	STATISTICS NOT AVAILABLE																									
1966-67	Charlotte Checkers	EHL	68	5	42	47	....	....	....	222	....	....	....	....	....	....	....	....	....	....	8	1	4	5	29	....	....	....
1967-68	Jersey-Charlotte Checkers	EHL	71	17	78	95	....	....	....	192	....	....	....	....	....	....	....	....	....	....	14	5	7	12	*69	....	....	....
1968-69	Dallas Black Hawks	CHL	2	0	0	0	....	....	....	4	....	....	....	....	....	....	....	....	....	....	....	....	....	....	....	....	....	....
	Portland Buckaroos	WHL	5	0	0	0	....	....	....	10	....	....	....	....	....	....	....	....	....	....	....	....	....	....	....	....	....	....
	Charlotte Checkers	EHL	66	22	58	80	....	....	....	216	....	....	....	....	....	....	....	....	....	....	3	2	0	2	6	....	....	....
1969-70	Portland Buckaroos	WHL	71	7	38	45	....	....	....	227	....	....	....	....	....	....	....	....	....	....	8	0	4	4	65	....	....	....
1970-71	**Chicago Black Hawks**	**NHL**	**2**	**0**	**1**	**1**	**0**	**1**	**1**	**8**	**0**	**0**	**0**	**4**	**0.0**	**1**	**0**	**0**	**0**	**1**	**4**	**0**	**1**	**1**	**4**	**0**	**0**	**0**
	Portland Buckaroos	WHL	66	17	54	71	....	....	....	*306	....	....	....	....	....	....	....	....	....	....	9	2	9	11	*44	....	....	....
1971-72	**Philadelphia Flyers**	**NHL**	**58**	**11**	**25**	**36**	**11**	**22**	**33**	**168**	**5**	**0**	**0**	**124**	**8.9**	**65**	**33**	**51**	**3**	**–16**	....	....	....	....	....	....	....	....
1972-73	Richmond Robins	AHL	26	6	15	21	....	....	....	69	....	....	....	....	....	....	....	....	....	....	....	....	....	....	....	....	....	....
	San Diego Gulls	WHL	31	5	14	19	....	....	....	110	....	....	....	....	....	....	....	....	....	....	6	2	6	8	*32	....	....	....
1973-74	**Detroit Red Wings**	**NHL**	**7**	**0**	**0**	**0**	**0**	**0**	**0**	**4**	**0**	**0**	**0**	**5**	**0.0**	**3**	**1**	**11**	**2**	**–7**	....	....	....	....	....	....	....	....
	Baltimore Clippers	AHL	65	14	56	70	....	....	....	164	....	....	....	....	....	....	....	....	....	....	9	2	6	8	28	....	....	....
1974-75	Syracuse Eagles	AHL	69	13	40	53	....	....	....	306	....	....	....	....	....	....	....	....	....	....	1	0	2	2	0	....	....	....
1975-76	Toronto Toros	WHA	11	1	2	3	....	....	....	6	....	....	....	....	....	....	....	....	....	....	....	....	....	....	....	....	....	....
	Baltimore Clippers	AHL	4	2	2	4	....	....	....	14	....	....	....	....	....	....	....	....	....	....	....	....	....	....	....	....	....	....
1976-77	Brantford Alexanders	OHA-Sr.	17	2	14	16	....	....	....	76	....	....	....	....	....	....	....	....	....	....	....	....	....	....	....	....	....	....
1977-78	Brantford Alexanders	OHA-Sr.	6	1	3	4	....	....	....	20	....	....	....	....	....	....	....	....	....	....	....	....	....	....	....	....	....	....
	NHL Totals		**67**	**11**	**26**	**37**	**11**	**23**	**34**	**180**	**5**	**0**	**0**	**133**	**8.3**	**69**	**34**	**62**	**5**		**4**	**0**	**1**	**1**	**4**	**0**	**0**	**0**
	Other Major League Totals		11	1	2	3	....	....	....	6	....	....	....	....	....	....	....	....	....	....	....	....	....	....	....	....	....	....

EHL South First All-Star Team (1968, 1969) • WHL First All-Star Team (1971)

Claimed by **Portland** (WHL) from **Toronto** in Reverse Draft, June 13, 1968. Traded to **Philadelphia** by **Chicago** for Andre Lacroix, October 15, 1971. Selected by **Miami-Philadelphia** (WHA) in 1972 WHA General Player Draft, February 12, 1972. Traded to **Detroit** by **Philadelphia** for Serge Lajeunesse, May 15, 1973. Signed as a free agent by **Toronto** (WHA), June, 1975.

Season	Club	League	GP	G	A	Pts	AG	AA	APts	PIM	PP	SH	GW	S	%	TGF	PGF	TGA	PGA	+/–	GP	G	A	Pts	PIM	PP	SH	GW
• FOLIGNO, Mike Michael Anthony RW – R. 6'2", 195 lbs. b: Sudbury, Ont., 1/29/1959. Detroit's 1st, 3rd overall, in 1979.																												
1974-75	Copper Cliff Cubs	NOJHA	STATISTICS NOT AVAILABLE																									
1975-76	Sudbury Wolves	OMJHL	57	22	14	36	....	....	....	45	....	....	....	....	....	....	....	....	....	....	16	4	3	7	6	....	....	....
1976-77	Sudbury Wolves	OMJHL	66	31	44	75	....	....	....	62	....	....	....	....	....	....	....	....	....	....	6	3	1	4	7	....	....	....
1977-78	Sudbury Wolves	OMJHL	67	47	39	86	....	....	....	112	....	....	....	....	....	....	....	....	....	....	....	....	....	....	....	....	....	....
1978-79	Sudbury Wolves	OMJHL	68	65	85	*150	....	....	....	98	....	....	....	....	....	....	....	....	....	....	10	5	5	10	14	....	....	....
1979-80	**Detroit Red Wings**	**NHL**	**80**	**36**	**35**	**71**	**31**	**26**	**57**	**109**	**9**	**0**	**0**	**196**	**18.4**	**106**	**33**	**76**	**1**	**–2**	....	....	....	....	....	....	....	....
1980-81	**Detroit Red Wings**	**NHL**	**80**	**28**	**35**	**63**	**22**	**23**	**45**	**210**	**3**	**0**	**5**	**181**	**15.5**	**116**	**38**	**91**	**0**	**–13**	....	....	....	....	....	....	....	....
	Canada	WEC-A	7	2	0	2	....	....	....	8	....	....	....	....	....	....	....	....	....	....	....	....	....	....	....	....	....	....
1981-82	**Detroit Red Wings**	**NHL**	**26**	**13**	**13**	**26**	**10**	**9**	**19**	**28**	**3**	**0**	**0**	**70**	**18.6**	**33**	**6**	**30**	**1**	**–2**	....	....	....	....	....	....	....	....
	Buffalo Sabres	**NHL**	**56**	**20**	**31**	**51**	**16**	**21**	**37**	**149**	**4**	**0**	**6**	**124**	**16.1**	**78**	**17**	**40**	**0**	**21**	**4**	**2**	**0**	**2**	**9**	**2**	**0**	**0**
1982-83	**Buffalo Sabres**	**NHL**	**66**	**22**	**25**	**47**	**18**	**17**	**35**	**135**	**4**	**0**	**4**	**130**	**16.9**	**76**	**14**	**56**	**3**	**9**	**10**	**2**	**3**	**5**	**39**	**0**	**0**	**0**
1983-84	**Buffalo Sabres**	**NHL**	**70**	**32**	**31**	**63**	**26**	**21**	**47**	**151**	**6**	**0**	**5**	**183**	**17.5**	**105**	**27**	**46**	**0**	**32**	**3**	**2**	**1**	**3**	**19**	**0**	**0**	**0**
1984-85	**Buffalo Sabres**	**NHL**	**77**	**27**	**29**	**56**	**22**	**20**	**42**	**154**	**6**	**0**	**6**	**167**	**16.2**	**93**	**27**	**50**	**0**	**16**	**5**	**1**	**3**	**4**	**12**	**0**	**0**	**0**
1985-86	**Buffalo Sabres**	**NHL**	**79**	**41**	**39**	**80**	**33**	**26**	**59**	**168**	**7**	**1**	**4**	**223**	**18.4**	**121**	**36**	**68**	**8**	**25**	....	....	....	....	....	....	....	....
	Canada	WEC-A	10	0	5	5	....	....	....	16	....	....	....	....	....	....	....	....	....	....	....	....	....	....	....	....	....	....
1986-87	**Buffalo Sabres**	**NHL**	**75**	**30**	**29**	**59**	**26**	**21**	**47**	**176**	**11**	**1**	**5**	**185**	**16.2**	**96**	**34**	**62**	**13**	**13**	....	....	....	....	....	....	....	....
	Canada	WEC-A	10	0	4	4	....	....	....	34	....	....	....	....	....	....	....	....	....	....	....	....	....	....	....	....	....	....
1987-88	**Buffalo Sabres**	**NHL**	**74**	**29**	**28**	**57**	**25**	**20**	**45**	**220**	**10**	**0**	**7**	**159**	**18.2**	**92**	**41**	**69**	**7**	**–11**	**6**	**3**	**2**	**5**	**31**	**0**	**0**	**0**
1988-89	**Buffalo Sabres**	**NHL**	**75**	**27**	**22**	**49**	**23**	**16**	**39**	**156**	**11**	**0**	**5**	**144**	**18.8**	**82**	**28**	**65**	**4**	**–7**	**5**	**3**	**1**	**4**	**21**	**1**	**1**	**1**
1989-90	**Buffalo Sabres**	**NHL**	**61**	**15**	**25**	**40**	**13**	**18**	**31**	**99**	**3**	**0**	**1**	**107**	**14.0**	**59**	**11**	**35**	**0**	**13**	**6**	**0**	**1**	**1**	**12**	**0**	**0**	**0**
1990-91	**Buffalo Sabres**	**NHL**	**31**	**4**	**5**	**9**	**4**	**4**	**8**	**42**	**0**	**0**	**0**	**27**	**14.8**	**17**	**2**	**11**	**0**	**4**	....	....	....	....	....	....	....	....
	Toronto Maple Leafs	**NHL**	**37**	**8**	**7**	**15**	**7**	**5**	**12**	**65**	**1**	**0**	**0**	**56**	**14.3**	**24**	**4**	**23**	**0**	**–3**	....	....	....	....	....	....	....	....
1991-92	**Toronto Maple Leafs**	**NHL**	**33**	**6**	**8**	**14**	**5**	**6**	**11**	**50**	**2**	**0**	**1**	**41**	**14.6**	**20**	**6**	**21**	**4**	**–3**	....	....	....	....	....	....	....	....
1992-93	**Toronto Maple Leafs**	**NHL**	**55**	**13**	**5**	**18**	**11**	**3**	**14**	**84**	**5**	**0**	**2**	**95**	**13.7**	**29**	**11**	**16**	**0**	**2**	**18**	**2**	**6**	**8**	**42**	**1**	**0**	**2**
1993-94	**Toronto Maple Leafs**	**NHL**	**4**	**0**	**0**	**0**	**0**	**0**	**0**	**4**	**0**	**0**	**0**	**3**	**0.0**	**1**	**0**	**1**	**0**	**0**	....	....	....	....	....	....	....	....
	Florida Panthers	**NHL**	**39**	**4**	**5**	**9**	**4**	**4**	**8**	**49**	**0**	**0**	**0**	**32**	**12.5**	**17**	**1**	**9**	**0**	**7**	....	....	....	....	....	....	....	....
1994-95			OUT OF HOCKEY – RETIRED																									
1995-1996	St. John's Maple Leafs	AHL	DID NOT PLAY – ASSISTANT COACH																									
1996-1998	**Toronto Maple Leafs**	**NHL**	DID NOT PLAY – SCOUTING																									
1998-2000	Hershey Bears	AHL	DID NOT PLAY – COACHING																									
	NHL Totals		**1018**	**355**	**372**	**727**	**296**	**260**	**556**	**2049**	**85**	**2**	**51**	**2123**	**16.7**	**1165**	**336**	**769**	**41**		**57**	**15**	**17**	**32**	**185**	**4**	**1**	**3**

OMJHL First All-Star Team (1979)

Traded to **Buffalo** by **Detroit** with Dale McCourt and Brent Peterson for Danny Gare, Jim Schoenfeld and Derek Smith, December 2, 1981. Traded to **Toronto** by **Buffalo** with Buffalo's 8th round choice (Thomas Kucharcik) in 1991 Entry Draft for Brian Curran and Lou Franceschetti, December 17, 1990. • Missed majority of 1991-92 season recovering from broken leg suffered in game vs. Buffalo, December 21, 1991. Traded to **Florida** by **Toronto** for cash, November 5, 1993.

• FONTAINE, Len
Leonard Joseph RW – R. 5'7", 165 lbs. b: Quebec City, Que., 2/25/1948.

			REGULAR SEASON																		PLAYOFFS							
Season	Club	League	GP	G	A	Pts	AG	AA	APts	PIM	PP	SH	GW	S	%	TGF	PGF	TGA	PGA	+/-	GP	G	A	Pts	PIM	PP	SH	GW
1967-68	Sarnia Legionaires	OHA-B	STATISTICS NOT AVAILABLE																									
1968-69	Port Huron Flags	IHL	53	15	22	37	....	....	....	10	....	....	....	....	....	....	....	....	....	....	3	0	1	1	2	....	....	....
1969-70	Port Huron Flags	IHL	69	20	29	49	....	....	....	16	....	....	....	....	....	....	....	....	....	....	15	3	6	9	4	....	....	....
1970-71	Port Huron Flags	IHL	71	29	40	69	....	....	....	37	....	....	....	....	....	....	....	....	....	....	14	6	6	12	2	....	....	....
1971-72	Port Huron Wings	IHL	70	41	45	86	....	....	....	54	....	....	....	....	....	....	....	....	....	....	15	7	5	12	13	....	....	....
1972-73	**Detroit Red Wings**	**NHL**	**39**	**8**	**10**	**18**	**7**	**8**	**15**	**6**	**1**	**0**	**0**	**37**	**21.6**	**22**	**3**	**21**	**0**	**–2**	....	....	....	....	....	....	....	....
	Virginia Wings	AHL	17	7	10	17	....	....	....	2	....	....	....	....	....	....	....	....	....	....	13	3	11	14	16	....	....	....
1973-74	**Detroit Red Wings**	**NHL**	**7**	**0**	**1**	**1**	**0**	**1**	**1**	**4**	**0**	**0**	**0**	**6**	**0.0**	**2**	**0**	**4**	**0**	**–2**	....	....	....	....	....	....	....	....
	Virginia Wings	AHL	59	24	39	63	....	....	....	33	....	....	....	....	....	....	....	....	....	....	....	....	....	....	....	....	....	....
1974-75	Michigan-Baltimore Stags	WHA	21	1	8	9	....	....	....	6	....	....	....	....	....	....	....	....	....	....	....	....	....	....	....	....	....	....
	Port Huron Flags	IHL	20	19	9	28	....	....	....	12	....	....	....	....	....	....	....	....	....	....	5	1	1	2	0	....	....	....
1975-76	Port Huron Flags	IHL	74	*53	59	*112	....	....	....	57	....	....	....	....	....	....	....	....	....	....	15	10	9	19	20	....	....	....
1976-77	Toledo Goaldiggers	IHL	61	42	37	79	....	....	....	51	....	....	....	....	....	....	....	....	....	....	....	....	....	....	....	....	....	....
1977-78	Toledo Goaldiggers	IHL	74	34	54	88	....	....	....	16	....	....	....	....	....	....	....	....	....	....	17	11	13	24	12	....	....	....
1978-79	Toledo Goaldiggers	IHL	78	29	60	89	....	....	....	30	....	....	....	....	....	....	....	....	....	....	6	3	3	6	0	....	....	....
1979-80	Toledo Goaldiggers	IHL	70	35	43	78	....	....	....	10	....	....	....	....	....	....	....	....	....	....	4	2	1	3	0	....	....	....
1980-81	Toledo Goaldiggers	IHL	16	4	6	10	....	....	....	0	....	....	....	....	....	....	....	....	....	....	....	....	....	....	....	....	....	....
1981-82	Flint Generals	IHL	62	34	47	81	....	....	....	12	....	....	....	....	....	....	....	....	....	....	4	0	0	0	11	....	....	....
1982-83	Flint Generals	IHL	71	21	37	58	....	....	....	10	....	....	....	....	....	....	....	....	....	....	5	0	3	3	0	....	....	....
	NHL Totals		**46**	**8**	**11**	**19**	**7**	**9**	**16**	**10**	**1**	**0**	**0**	**43**	**18.6**	**24**	**3**	**25**	**0**		....	....	....	....	....	....	....	....
	Other Major League Totals		21	1	8	9	....	....	....	6	....	....	....	....	....	....	....	....	....	....	....	....	....	....	....	....	....	....

IHL Second All-Star Team (1971) • IHL First All-Star Team (1972, 1976) • Won James Gatschene Memorial Trophy (MVP - IHL) (1972, 1976) • Won Leo P. Lamoureux Memorial Trophy (Top Scorer - IHL) (1976)

Selected by **LA Sharks** in 1972 WHA General Player Draft, February 12, 1972. Signed as a free agent by **Detroit**, May 1, 1972. Transferred to **Michigan** (WHA) after **LA Sharks** (WHA) franchise relocated, April 11, 1974. Traded to **Toledo** (IHL) by **Port Huron** (IHL) for Larry Gould and Don O'Driscoll, October 7, 1976.

• FONTAS, Jon
C – R. 5'10", 185 lbs. b: Arlington, MA, 4/16/1958.

Season	Club	League	GP	G	A	Pts	AG	AA	APts	PIM	PP	SH	GW	S	%	TGF	PGF	TGA	PGA	+/-	GP	G	A	Pts	PIM	PP	SH	GW
1973-74	Choate-Rosemary Wild Boars	Hi-School	STATISTICS NOT AVAILABLE																									
1975-76	University of New Hampshire	ECAC	31	10	23	33	....	....	....	41	....	....	....	....	....	....	....	....	....	....	....	....	....	....	....	....	....	....
1976-77	University of New Hampshire	ECAC	36	27	37	64	....	....	....	16	....	....	....	....	....	....	....	....	....	....	....	....	....	....	....	....	....	....
1977-78	University of New Hampshire	ECAC	30	31	33	64	....	....	....	12	....	....	....	....	....	....	....	....	....	....	....	....	....	....	....	....	....	....
1978-79	Saginaw Gears	IHL	79	36	45	81	....	....	....	32	....	....	....	....	....	....	....	....	....	....	4	2	2	4	0	....	....	....
1979-80	**Minnesota North Stars**	**NHL**	**1**	**0**	**0**	**0**	**0**	**0**	**0**	**0**	**0**	**0**	**0**	**0**	**0.0**	**0**	**0**	**1**	**0**	**–1**	....	....	....	....	....	....	....	....
	Oklahoma City Stars	CHL	68	22	26	48	....	....	....	16	....	....	....	....	....	....	....	....	....	....	....	....	....	....	....	....	....	....
1980-81	**Minnesota North Stars**	**NHL**	**1**	**0**	**0**	**0**	**0**	**0**	**0**	**0**	**0**	**0**	**0**	**0**	**0.0**	**0**	**0**	**0**	**0**	**0**	....	....	....	....	....	....	....	....
	Oklahoma City Stars	CHL	5	1	1	2	....	....	....	0	....	....	....	....	....	....	....	....	....	....	....	....	....	....	....	....	....	....
	Baltimore Clippers	EHL	63	25	47	72	....	....	....	44	....	....	....	....	....	....	....	....	....	....	4	0	2	2	0	....	....	....
1981-82	Jokerit Helsinki	Finland	36	20	23	43	....	....	....	51	....	....	....	....	....	....	....	....	....	....	....	....	....	....	....	....	....	....
1982-83	JoKP Joensuu	Finland-2	36	25	34	59	....	....	....	57	....	....	....	....	....	....	....	....	....	....	5	4	1	5	29	....	....	....
1983-84	JoKP Joensuu	Finland-2	36	27	36	63	....	....	....	24	....	....	....	....	....	....	....	....	....	....	3	1	4	5	12	....	....	....
1984-85	SaiPa Lappeenranta	Finland-2	36	12	15	27	....	....	....	44	....	....	....	....	....	....	....	....	....	....	....	....	....	....	....	....	....	....
	NHL Totals		**2**	**0**	**0**	**0**	**0**	**0**	**0**	**0**	**0**	**0**	**0**	**0**	**0.0**	**0**	**0**	**1**	**0**		....	....	....	....	....	....	....	....

Signed as a free agent by **Minnesota**, September, 1979.

• FONTEYNE, Val
Valere Ronald LW – L. 5'10", 160 lbs. b: Wetaskiwin, Alta., 12/2/1933.

Season	Club	League	GP	G	A	Pts	AG	AA	APts	PIM	PP	SH	GW	S	%	TGF	PGF	TGA	PGA	+/-	GP	G	A	Pts	PIM	PP	SH	GW
1951-52	Medicine Hat Tigers	WCJHL	41	9	9	18	....	....	....	5	....	....	....	....	....	....	....	....	....	....	....	....	....	....	....	....	....	....
1952-53	Medicine Hat Tigers	WCJHL	31	7	14	21	....	....	....	4	....	....	....	....	....	....	....	....	....	....	4	4	2	6	0	....	....	....
1953-54	Medicine Hat Tigers	WCJHL	36	14	14	28	....	....	....	18	....	....	....	....	....	....	....	....	....	....	10	1	5	6	12	....	....	....
1954-55	New Westminster Royals	WHL	7	0	1	1	....	....	....	0	....	....	....	....	....	....	....	....	....	....	....	....	....	....	....	....	....	....
	Kelowna Packers	OSHL	41	9	10	19	....	....	....	2	....	....	....	....	....	....	....	....	....	....	4	0	0	0	0	....	....	....
1955-56	Seattle Americans	WHL	70	18	18	36	....	....	....	0	....	....	....	....	....	....	....	....	....	....	....	....	....	....	....	....	....	....
1956-57	Seattle Americans	WHL	70	24	40	64	....	....	....	6	....	....	....	....	....	....	....	....	....	....	6	5	1	6	2	....	....	....
1957-58	Seattle Totems	WHL	70	34	41	75	....	....	....	11	....	....	....	....	....	....	....	....	....	....	9	4	4	8	0	....	....	....
1958-59	Seattle Totems	WHL	64	32	49	81	....	....	....	2	....	....	....	....	....	....	....	....	....	....	12	6	5	11	0	....	....	....
1959-60	**Detroit Red Wings**	**NHL**	**69**	**4**	**7**	**11**	**5**	**7**	**12**	**2**	....	....	....	....	....	....	....	....	....	....	**6**	**0**	**4**	**4**	**0**	**0**	**0**	**0**
1960-61	**Detroit Red Wings**	**NHL**	**66**	**6**	**11**	**17**	**7**	**11**	**18**	**4**	....	....	....	....	....	....	....	....	....	....	**11**	**2**	**3**	**5**	**0**	**0**	**0**	**0**
1961-62	**Detroit Red Wings**	**NHL**	**70**	**5**	**5**	**10**	**6**	**5**	**11**	**4**	....	....	....	....	....	....	....	....	....	....	....	....	....	....	....	....	....	....
1962-63	**Detroit Red Wings**	**NHL**	**67**	**6**	**14**	**20**	**7**	**14**	**21**	**2**	....	....	....	....	....	....	....	....	....	....	**11**	**0**	**0**	**0**	**2**	**0**	**0**	**0**
1963-64	**New York Rangers**	**NHL**	**69**	**7**	**18**	**25**	**9**	**19**	**28**	**4**	....	....	....	....	....	....	....	....	....	....	....	....	....	....	....	....	....	....
1964-65	**New York Rangers**	**NHL**	**27**	**0**	**1**	**1**	**0**	**1**	**1**	**2**	....	....	....	....	....	....	....	....	....	....	....	....	....	....	....	....	....	....
	Detroit Red Wings	**NHL**	**16**	**2**	**5**	**7**	**2**	**5**	**7**	**4**	....	....	....	....	....	....	....	....	....	....	**5**	**0**	**1**	**1**	**0**	**0**	**0**	**0**
1965-66	**Detroit Red Wings**	**NHL**	**59**	**5**	**10**	**15**	**6**	**9**	**15**	**0**	....	....	....	....	....	....	....	....	....	....	**12**	**1**	**0**	**1**	**4**	**0**	**1**	**0**
	Pittsburgh Hornets	AHL	12	5	7	12	....	....	....	6	....	....	....	....	....	....	....	....	....	....	....	....	....	....	....	....	....	....
1966-67	**Detroit Red Wings**	**NHL**	**28**	**1**	**1**	**2**	**1**	**1**	**2**	**0**	....	....	....	....	....	....	....	....	....	....	....	....	....	....	....	....	....	....
	Pittsburgh Hornets	AHL	17	5	11	16	....	....	....	0	....	....	....	....	....	....	....	....	....	....	9	3	5	8	4	....	....	....
1967-68	**Pittsburgh Penguins**	**NHL**	**69**	**6**	**28**	**34**	**7**	**28**	**35**	**0**	**0**	**0**	**2**	**114**	**5.3**	**45**	**5**	**71**	**8**	**–23**	....	....	....	....	....	....	....	....
1968-69	**Pittsburgh Penguins**	**NHL**	**74**	**12**	**17**	**29**	**13**	**15**	**28**	**2**	**0**	**1**	**2**	**109**	**11.0**	**44**	**7**	**84**	**22**	**–25**	....	....	....	....	....	....	....	....
1969-70	**Pittsburgh Penguins**	**NHL**	**68**	**11**	**15**	**26**	**12**	**14**	**26**	**2**	**3**	**0**	**1**	**73**	**15.1**	**37**	**11**	**47**	**17**	**–4**	**10**	**0**	**2**	**2**	**0**	**0**	**0**	**0**
1970-71	**Pittsburgh Penguins**	**NHL**	**70**	**4**	**9**	**13**	**4**	**7**	**11**	**0**	**1**	**1**	**0**	**59**	**6.8**	**21**	**2**	**48**	**21**	**–8**	....	....	....	....	....	....	....	....
1971-72	**Pittsburgh Penguins**	**NHL**	**68**	**6**	**13**	**19**	**6**	**11**	**17**	**0**	**1**	**0**	**0**	**35**	**17.1**	**35**	**5**	**50**	**19**	**–1**	**4**	**0**	**0**	**0**	**2**	**0**	**0**	**0**
1972-73	Alberta Oilers	WHA	77	7	32	39	....	....	....	2	....	....	....	....	....	....	....	....	....	....	....	....	....	....	....	....	....	....
1973-74	Edmonton Oilers	WHA	72	9	13	22	....	....	....	2	....	....	....	....	....	....	....	....	....	....	5	1	0	1	0	....	....	....
	NHL Totals		**820**	**75**	**154**	**229**	**85**	**147**	**232**	**26**	....	....	....	....	....	....	....	....	....	....	**59**	**3**	**10**	**13**	**8**	....	....	....
	Other Major League Totals		149	16	45	61	....	....	....	4	....	....	....	....	....	....	....	....	....	....	5	1	0	1	0	....	....	....

WHL Coast Division First All-Star Team (1958, 1959)

Claimed by **NY Rangers** from **Detroit** in Intra-League Draft, June 4, 1963. Claimed on waivers by **Detroit** from **NY Rangers**, February 8, 1965. Claimed by **Pittsburgh** from **Detroit** in Expansion Draft, June 6, 1967. Selected by **Alberta** (WHA) in WHA General Player Draft, February 12, 1972.

• FOOTE, Adam
D – R. 6'1", 212 lbs. b: Toronto, Ont., 7/10/1971. Quebec's 2nd, 22nd overall, in 1989.

Season	Club	League	GP	G	A	Pts	AG	AA	APts	PIM	PP	SH	GW	S	%	TGF	PGF	TGA	PGA	+/-	GP	G	A	Pts	PIM	PP	SH	GW
1987-88	Brooklin Whitby Midgets	OMHA	65	25	43	68	....	....	....	108	....	....	....	....	....	....	....	....	....	....	....	....	....	....	....	....	....	....
1988-89	Sault Ste. Marie Greyhounds	OHL	66	7	32	39	....	....	....	120	....	....	....	....	....	....	....	....	....	....	....	....	....	....	....	....	....	....
1989-90	Sault Ste. Marie Greyhounds	OHL	61	12	43	55	....	....	....	199	....	....	....	....	....	....	....	....	....	....	....	....	....	....	....	....	....	....
	Canada	Nat-Team	3	1	0	1	....	....	....	0	....	....	....	....	....	....	....	....	....	....	....	....	....	....	....	....	....	....
1990-91	Sault Ste. Marie Greyhounds	OHL	59	18	51	69	....	....	....	93	....	....	....	....	....	....	....	....	....	....	14	5	12	17	28	....	....	....
	Sault Ste. Marie Greyhounds	Mem-Cup	3	0	1	1	....	....	....	6	....	....	....	....	....	....	....	....	....	....	....	....	....	....	....	....	....	....
1991-92	**Quebec Nordiques**	**NHL**	**46**	**2**	**5**	**7**	**2**	**4**	**6**	**44**	**0**	**0**	**0**	**55**	**3.6**	**42**	**5**	**66**	**25**	**–4**	....	....	....	....	....	....	....	....
	Halifax Citadels	AHL	6	0	1	1	....	....	....	2	....	....	....	....	....	....	....	....	....	....	....	....	....	....	....	....	....	....
1992-93	**Quebec Nordiques**	**NHL**	**81**	**4**	**12**	**16**	**3**	**8**	**11**	**168**	**0**	**1**	**0**	**54**	**7.4**	**74**	**0**	**101**	**33**	**6**	**6**	**0**	**1**	**1**	**2**	**0**	**0**	**0**
1993-94	**Quebec Nordiques**	**NHL**	**45**	**2**	**6**	**8**	**2**	**5**	**7**	**67**	**0**	**0**	**0**	**42**	**4.8**	**42**	**3**	**64**	**28**	**3**	....	....	....	....	....	....	....	....
1994-95	**Quebec Nordiques**	**NHL**	**35**	**0**	**7**	**7**	**0**	**10**	**10**	**52**	**0**	**0**	**0**	**24**	**0.0**	**35**	**1**	**25**	**8**	**17**	**6**	**0**	**1**	**1**	**14**	**0**	**0**	**0**
1995-96♦	**Colorado Avalanche**	**NHL**	**73**	**5**	**11**	**16**	**5**	**9**	**14**	**88**	**1**	**0**	**1**	**49**	**10.2**	**68**	**5**	**64**	**28**	**27**	**22**	**1**	**3**	**4**	**36**	**0**	**0**	**0**
1996-97	Canada	W-Cup	8	1	0	1	....	....	....	16	....	....	....	....	....	....	....	....	....	....	....	....	....	....	....	....	....	....
	Colorado Avalanche	**NHL**	**78**	**2**	**19**	**21**	**2**	**17**	**19**	**135**	**0**	**0**	**0**	**60**	**3.3**	**72**	**5**	**69**	**18**	**16**	**17**	**0**	**4**	**4**	**62**	**0**	**0**	**0**

			REGULAR SEASON																		PLAYOFFS							
Season	Club	League	GP	G	A	Pts	AG	AA	APts	PIM	PP	SH	GW	S	%	TGF	PGF	TGA	PGA	+/–	GP	G	A	Pts	PIM	PP	SH	GW
1997-98	**Colorado Avalanche**	**NHL**	77	3	14	17	4	14	18	124	0	0	1	64	4.7	57	1	84	25	–3	7	0	0	0	23	0	0	0
	Canada	Olympics	6	0	1	1	....	....	....	4	....	....	....	....	....	....	....	....	....	....	....	....	....	....	....	....	....	....
1998-99	**Colorado Avalanche**	**NHL**	64	5	16	21	6	15	21	92	3	0	0	83	6.0	82	22	69	29	20	19	2	3	5	24	1	0	0
99-2000	**Colorado Avalanche**	**NHL**	59	5	13	18	6	12	18	98	1	0	2	63	7.9	58	9	67	23	5	16	0	7	7	28	0	0	0
	NHL Totals		558	28	103	131	30	94	124	868	5	1	4	494	5.7	530	51	609	217		93	3	19	22	189	1	0	0

OHL First All-Star Team (1991)

Transferred to **Colorado** after **Quebec** franchise relocated, June 21, 1995.

• FORBES, Colin

LW – L. 6'3", 205 lbs. b: New Westminster, B.C., 2/16/1976. Philadelphia's 5th, 166th overall, in 1994.

Season	Club	League	GP	G	A	Pts	AG	AA	APts	PIM	PP	SH	GW	S	%	TGF	PGF	TGA	PGA	+/–	GP	G	A	Pts	PIM	PP	SH	GW
1993-94	Sherwood Park Crusaders	AJHL	47	18	22	40	....	....	....	76	....	....	....	....	....	....	....	....	....	....	....	....	....	....	....	....	....	....
1994-95	Portland Winter Hawks	WHL	72	24	31	55	....	....	....	108	....	....	....	....	....	....	....	....	....	....	9	1	3	4	10	....	....	....
1995-96	Portland Winter Hawks	WHL	72	33	44	77	....	....	....	137	....	....	....	....	....	....	....	....	....	....	7	2	5	7	14	....	....	....
	Hershey Bears	AHL	2	1	0	1	....	....	....	2	....	....	....	....	....	....	....	....	....	....	4	0	2	2	2	....	....	....
1996-97	**Philadelphia Flyers**	**NHL**	3	1	0	1	1	0	1	0	0	0	0	3	33.3	1	0	1	0	0	3	0	0	0	0	0	0	0
	Philadelphia Phantoms	AHL	74	21	28	49	....	....	....	108	....	....	....	....	....	....	....	....	....	....	10	5	5	10	33	....	....	....
1997-98	**Philadelphia Flyers**	**NHL**	63	12	7	19	14	7	21	59	2	0	2	93	12.9	28	2	31	7	2	5	0	0	0	2	0	0	0
	Philadelphia Phantoms	AHL	13	7	4	11	....	....	....	22	....	....	....	....	....	....	....	....	....	....	....	....	....	....	....	....	....	....
1998-99	**Philadelphia Flyers**	**NHL**	66	9	7	16	11	7	18	51	0	0	4	92	9.8	22	0	38	16	0	....	....	....	....	....	....	....	....
	Tampa Bay Lightning	**NHL**	14	3	1	4	4	1	5	10	0	1	0	25	12.0	8	0	15	2	–5	....	....	....	....	....	....	....	....
99-2000	**Tampa Bay Lightning**	**NHL**	8	0	0	0	0	0	0	18	0	0	0	3	0.0	0	0	5	1	–4	....	....	....	....	....	....	....	....
	Ottawa Senators	**NHL**	45	2	5	7	2	5	7	12	0	0	0	54	3.7	16	0	17	0	–1	5	1	0	1	14	0	0	0
	NHL Totals		199	27	20	47	32	20	52	150	2	1	6	270	10.0	75	2	107	26		13	1	0	1	16	0	0	0

Traded to **Tampa Bay** by **Philadelphia** with Philadelphia's 4th round choice (Michal Lanisak) in 1999 Entry Draft for Mikael Andersson and Sandy McCarthy, March 20, 1999. Traded to **Ottawa** by **Tampa Bay** for Bruce Gardiner, November 11, 1999.

• FORBES, Dave

David Stephen LW – L. 5'10", 180 lbs. b: Montreal, Que., 11/16/1948.

Season	Club	League	GP	G	A	Pts	AG	AA	APts	PIM	PP	SH	GW	S	%	TGF	PGF	TGA	PGA	+/–	GP	G	A	Pts	PIM	PP	SH	GW
1966-67	Lachine Maroons	QJHL	STATISTICS NOT AVAILABLE																									
1967-68	American International U.	NCAA	5	13	10	23	....	....	....	....	....	....	....	....	....	....	....	....	....	....	....	....	....	....	....	....	....	....
1968-69	American International U.	NCAA	21	32	25	57	....	....	....	....	....	....	....	....	....	....	....	....	....	....	....	....	....	....	....	....	....	....
1969-70	American International U.	NCAA	17	27	15	42	....	....	....	....	....	....	....	....	....	....	....	....	....	....	....	....	....	....	....	....	....	....
1970-71	American International U.	NCAA	21	30	22	52	....	....	....	....	....	....	....	....	....	....	....	....	....	....	....	....	....	....	....	....	....	....
1971-72	Oklahoma City Blazers	CHL	42	8	11	19	....	....	....	83	....	....	....	....	....	....	....	....	....	....	....	....	....	....	....	....	....	....
	Boston Braves	AHL	3	0	0	0	....	....	....	2	....	....	....	....	....	....	....	....	....	....	7	1	0	1	0	....	....	....
	Dayton Gems	IHL	10	5	2	7	....	....	....	29	....	....	....	....	....	....	....	....	....	....	....	....	....	....	....	....	....	....
1972-73	Boston Braves	AHL	27	10	11	21	....	....	....	32	....	....	....	....	....	....	....	....	....	....	10	3	5	8	27	....	....	....
	Dayton Gems	IHL	49	20	29	49	....	....	....	194	....	....	....	....	....	....	....	....	....	....	....	....	....	....	....	....	....	....
1973-74	**Boston Bruins**	**NHL**	63	10	16	26	10	13	23	41	0	0	1	64	15.6	34	0	25	0	9	16	0	2	2	6	0	0	0
	Boston Braves	AHL	11	2	6	8	....	....	....	35	....	....	....	....	....	....	....	....	....	....	....	....	....	....	....	....	....	....
1974-75	**Boston Bruins**	**NHL**	69	18	12	30	16	9	25	80	0	0	2	89	20.2	51	1	31	3	22	3	0	0	0	0	0	0	0
1975-76	**Boston Bruins**	**NHL**	79	16	13	29	14	10	24	52	0	4	1	165	9.7	48	1	49	17	15	12	1	1	2	5	0	1	0
1976-77	**Boston Bruins**	**NHL**	73	9	11	20	8	8	16	47	0	2	1	56	16.1	30	0	48	31	13	14	0	1	1	2	0	0	0
1977-78	**Washington Capitals**	**NHL**	77	11	11	22	10	8	18	119	0	0	0	143	7.7	40	1	97	24	–34	....	....	....	....	....	....	....	....
1978-79	**Washington Capitals**	**NHL**	2	0	1	1	0	1	1	2	0	0	0	2	0.0	1	0	1	0	0	....	....	....	....	....	....	....	....
	Cincinnati Stingers	WHA	73	6	5	11	....	....	....	83	....	....	....	....	....	....	....	....	....	....	3	0	1	1	7	....	....	....
1979-80	Binghamton Dusters	AHL	38	15	15	30	....	....	....	47	....	....	....	....	....	....	....	....	....	....	....	....	....	....	....	....	....	....
	NHL Totals		363	64	64	128	58	49	107	341	0	6	5	519	12.3	204	3	251	75		45	1	4	5	13	0	1	0
	Other Major League Totals		73	6	5	11				83											3	0	1	1	7			

Signed as a free agent by **Boston**, September, 1973. Claimed by **Washington** from **Boston** in Waiver Draft, October 10, 1977. Signed as a free agent by **Cincinnati** (WHA) after clearing NHL waivers, October 25, 1978.

• FORBES, Mike

Michael D. D – R. 6'2", 200 lbs. b: Brampton, Ont., 9/20/1957. Boston's 3rd, 52nd overall, in 1977.

Season	Club	League	GP	G	A	Pts	AG	AA	APts	PIM	PP	SH	GW	S	%	TGF	PGF	TGA	PGA	+/–	GP	G	A	Pts	PIM	PP	SH	GW
1973-74	Georgetown Bees	OHA-B	STATISTICS NOT AVAILABLE																									
1974-75	Kingston Canadians	OMJHL	64	0	10	10	....	....	....	98	....	....	....	....	....	....	....	....	....	....	8	1	1	2	14	....	....	....
1975-76	Kingston Canadians	OMJHL	48	4	13	17	....	....	....	117	....	....	....	....	....	....	....	....	....	....	5	0	0	0	5	....	....	....
1976-77	St. Catharines Fincups	OMJHL	61	12	41	53	....	....	....	134	....	....	....	....	....	....	....	....	....	....	14	1	5	6	41	....	....	....
1977-78	**Boston Bruins**	**NHL**	32	0	4	4	0	3	3	15	0	0	0	22	0.0	14	3	19	3	–5	....	....	....	....	....	....	....	....
	Rochester Americans	AHL	32	3	12	15	....	....	....	65	....	....	....	....	....	....	....	....	....	....	6	0	1	1	22	....	....	....
1978-79	Rochester Americans	AHL	75	4	20	24	....	....	....	97	....	....	....	....	....	....	....	....	....	....	....	....	....	....	....	....	....	....
1979-80	**Edmonton Oilers**	**NHL**	2	0	0	0	0	0	0	0	0	0	0	3	0.0	1	0	6	1	–4	....	....	....	....	....	....	....	....
	Houston Apollos	CHL	55	5	30	35	....	....	....	63	....	....	....	....	....	....	....	....	....	....	....	....	....	....	....	....	....	....
1980-81	Wichita Wind	CHL	79	4	44	48	....	....	....	129	....	....	....	....	....	....	....	....	....	....	15	1	16	17	46	....	....	....
1981-82	**Edmonton Oilers**	**NHL**	16	1	7	8	1	5	6	26	0	0	0	14	7.1	31	2	16	1	14	....	....	....	....	....	....	....	....
	Wichita Wind	CHL	49	4	28	32	....	....	....	94	....	....	....	....	....	....	....	....	....	....	6	0	2	2	4	....	....	....
1982-83	Wichita Wind	CHL	75	15	46	61	....	....	....	73	....	....	....	....	....	....	....	....	....	....	....	....	....	....	....	....	....	....
1983-84	Montana Magic	CHL	76	13	38	51	....	....	....	83	....	....	....	....	....	....	....	....	....	....	....	....	....	....	....	....	....	....
1984-85			DID NOT PLAY																									
1985-86	Muskegon Lumberjacks	IHL	14	1	7	8	....	....	....	13	....	....	....	....	....	....	....	....	....	....	13	0	2	2	19	....	....	....
1986-87	Muskegon Lumberjacks	IHL	67	3	22	25	....	....	....	113	....	....	....	....	....	....	....	....	....	....	15	1	10	11	4	....	....	....
	NHL Totals		50	1	11	12	1	8	9	41	0	0	0	39	2.6	46	5	41	5		....	....	....	....	....	....	....	....

CHL Second All-Star Team (1983)

Claimed by **Edmonton** from **Boston** in Expansion Draft, June 13, 1979.

• FOREY, Connie

Conley Michael LW – L. 6'2", 185 lbs. b: Montreal, Que., 10/18/1950. Pittsburgh's 4th, 49th overall, in 1970.

Season	Club	League	GP	G	A	Pts	AG	AA	APts	PIM	PP	SH	GW	S	%	TGF	PGF	TGA	PGA	+/–	GP	G	A	Pts	PIM	PP	SH	GW
1968-69	Ottawa 67's	OHA-Jr.	53	9	10	19	....	....	....	22	....	....	....	....	....	....	....	....	....	....	7	2	1	3	6	....	....	....
1969-70	Ottawa 67's	OHA-Jr.	54	24	28	52	....	....	....	39	....	....	....	....	....	....	....	....	....	....	....	....	....	....	....	....	....	....
1970-71	Amarillo Wranglers	CHL	67	17	22	39	....	....	....	55	....	....	....	....	....	....	....	....	....	....	....	....	....	....	....	....	....	....
1971-72	Hershey Bears	AHL	39	11	5	16	....	....	....	20	....	....	....	....	....	....	....	....	....	....	4	0	0	0	0	....	....	....
	Fort Wayne Komets	IHL	2	0	0	0	....	....	....	0	....	....	....	....	....	....	....	....	....	....	....	....	....	....	....	....	....	....
1972-73	New Haven Nighthawks	AHL	71	21	18	39	....	....	....	40	....	....	....	....	....	....	....	....	....	....	....	....	....	....	....	....	....	....
1973-74	**St. Louis Blues**	**NHL**	4	0	0	0	0	0	0	2	0	0	0	2	0.0	0	0	2	1	–1	....	....	....	....	....	....	....	....
	Denver Spurs	WHL	49	14	12	26	....	....	....	57	....	....	....	....	....	....	....	....	....	....	....	....	....	....	....	....	....	....
1974-75	Mohawk Valley Comets	NAHL	6	1	1	2	....	....	....	10	....	....	....	....	....	....	....	....	....	....	....	....	....	....	....	....	....	....
	NHL Totals		4	0	0	0	0	0	0	2	0	0	0	2	0.0	0	0	2	1		....	....	....	....	....	....	....	....

Claimed by **NY Islanders** from **Hershey** (AHL) in Inter-League Draft, June 6, 1972. Claimed by **St. Louis** (Denver-WHL) from **NY Islanders** in Reverse Draft, June 6, 1973. • Suspended by WHL for remainder of 1973-74 season and all of 1974-75 season for assaulting referee Malcolm Ashford, February 21, 1974.

• FORSBERG, Peter

C – L. 6', 205 lbs. b: Ornskoldsvik, Sweden, 7/20/1973. Philadelphia's 1st, 6th overall, in 1991.

Season	Club	League	GP	G	A	Pts	AG	AA	APts	PIM	PP	SH	GW	S	%	TGF	PGF	TGA	PGA	+/–	GP	G	A	Pts	PIM	PP	SH	GW
1989-90	MoDo AIK	Sweden-Jr.	30	15	12	27	....	....	....	42	....	....	....	....	....	....	....	....	....	....	....	....	....	....	....	....	....	....
	MoDo AIK	Sweden	1	0	1	1	....	....	....	4	....	....	....	....	....	....	....	....	....	....	....	....	....	....	....	....	....	....
1990-91	MoDo AIK	Sweden-Jr.	39	38	64	102	....	....	....	56	....	....	....	....	....	....	....	....	....	....	....	....	....	....	....	....	....	....
	MoDo AIK	Sweden	23	7	10	17	....	....	....	22	....	....	....	....	....	....	....	....	....	....	....	....	....	....	....	....	....	....
	Sweden	EJC-A	6	5	12	17	....	....	....	16	....	....	....	....	....	....	....	....	....	....	....	....	....	....	....	....	....	....
1991-92	MoDo AIK	Sweden	39	9	18	27	....	....	....	78	....	....	....	....	....	....	....	....	....	....	....	....	....	....	....	....	....	....
	Sweden	WJC-A	7	3	8	11	....	....	....	30	....	....	....	....	....	....	....	....	....	....	....	....	....	....	....	....	....	....
	Sweden	WC-A	8	4	2	6	....	....	....	6	....	....	....	....	....	....	....	....	....	....	....	....	....	....	....	....	....	....

			REGULAR SEASON																		PLAYOFFS							
Season	**Club**	**League**	**GP**	**G**	**A**	**Pts**	**AG**	**AA**	**APts**	**PIM**	**PP**	**SH**	**GW**	**S**	**%**	**TGF**	**PGF**	**TGA**	**PGA**	**+/–**	**GP**	**G**	**A**	**Pts**	**PIM**	**PP**	**SH**	**GW**
1992-93	MoDo AIK	Sweden-Jr.	2	0	3	3	....	....	....	4	....	....	....	....	....	....	....	....	....	....	....	....	....	....	....	....	....	....
	MoDo AIK	Sweden	39	23	24	47	....	....	....	92	....	....	....	....	....	....	....	....	....	....	3	4	1	5	0	....	....	....
	Sweden	WJC-A	7	7	24	*31	....	....	....	8	....	....	....	....	....	....	....	....	....	....	....	....	....	....	....	....	....	....
	Sweden	WC-A	8	1	1	2	....	....	....	12	....	....	....	....	....	....	....	....	....	....	....	....	....	....	....	....	....	....
1993-94	MoDo AIK	Sweden	39	18	26	44	....	....	....	82	....	....	....	....	....	....	....	....	....	....	11	9	7	16	14	....	....	....
	Sweden	Olympics	8	2	6	8	....	....	....	6	....	....	....	....	....	....	....	....	....	....	....	....	....	....	....	....	....	....
1994-95	MoDo Hockey	Sweden	11	5	9	14	....	....	....	20	....	....	....	....	....	....	....	....	....	....	....	....	....	....	....	....	....	....
	Quebec Nordiques	**NHL**	**47**	**15**	**35**	**50**	**27**	**52**	**79**	**16**	**3**	**0**	**3**	**86**	**17.4**	**65**	**22**	**40**	**14**	**17**	**6**	**2**	**4**	**6**	**4**	**1**	**0**	**0**
1995-96♦	**Colorado Avalanche**	**NHL**	**82**	**30**	**86**	**116**	**30**	**71**	**101**	**47**	**7**	**3**	**3**	**217**	**13.8**	**147**	**55**	**96**	**30**	**26**	**22**	**10**	**11**	**21**	**18**	**3**	**0**	**1**
1996-97	Sweden	W-Cup	4	1	4	5	....	....	....	6	....	....	....	....	....	....	....	....	....	....	....	....	....	....	....	....	....	....
	Colorado Avalanche	**NHL**	**65**	**28**	**58**	**86**	**30**	**52**	**82**	**73**	**5**	**4**	**4**	**188**	**14.9**	**118**	**42**	**54**	**9**	**31**	**14**	**5**	**12**	**17**	**10**	**3**	**0**	**0**
1997-98	**Colorado Avalanche**	**NHL**	**72**	**25**	**66**	**91**	**29**	**65**	**94**	**94**	**7**	**3**	**7**	**202**	**12.4**	**121**	**52**	**74**	**11**	**6**	**7**	**6**	**5**	**11**	**12**	**2**	**0**	**0**
	Sweden	Olympics	4	1	4	5	....	....	....	6	....	....	....	....	....	....	....	....	....	....	....	....	....	....	....	....	....	....
	Sweden	WC-A	7	6	5	11	....	....	....	0	....	....	....	....	....	....	....	....	....	....	....	....	....	....	....	....	....	....
1998-99	**Colorado Avalanche**	**NHL**	**78**	**30**	**67**	**97**	**35**	**65**	**100**	**108**	**9**	**2**	**7**	**217**	**13.8**	**123**	**50**	**70**	**24**	**27**	**19**	**8**	**16**	***24**	**31**	**1**	**1**	**0**
99-2000	**Colorado Avalanche**	**NHL**	**49**	**14**	**37**	**51**	**16**	**34**	**50**	**52**	**3**	**0**	**2**	**105**	**13.3**	**68**	**28**	**35**	**4**	**9**	**16**	**7**	**8**	**15**	**12**	**2**	**1**	**4**
	NHL Totals		**393**	**142**	**349**	**491**	**167**	**339**	**506**	**390**	**34**	**12**	**26**	**1015**	**14.0**	**642**	**249**	**369**	**92**		**84**	**38**	**56**	**94**	**87**	**12**	**2**	**5**

WJC-A All-Star Team (1993) • Named Best Forward at WJC-A (1993) • WC-A All-Star Team (1998) • Named Best Forward at WC-A (1998) NHL All-Rookie Team (1995) • Won Calder Memorial Trophy (1995) • NHL First All-Star Team (1998, 1999) • Played in NHL All-Star Game (1996, 1998, 1999)

Traded to **Quebec** by **Philadelphia** with Steve Duchesne, Kerry Huffman, Mike Ricci, Ron Hextall, Philadelphia's 1st round choice (Jocelyn Thibault) in 1993 Entry Draft, $15,000,000 and future considerations (Chris Simon and Philadelphia's 1st round choice (later traded to Toronto — later traded to Washington — Washington selected Nolan Baumgartner) in 1994 Entry Draft, July 21, 1992) for Eric Lindros, June 30, 1992. Transferred to **Colorado** after **Quebec** franchise relocated, June 21, 1995.

• FORSLUND, Tomas

RW – L. 5'11", 200 lbs. b: Falun, Sweden, 11/24/1968. Calgary's 4th, 85th overall, in 1988.

Season	Club	League	GP	G	A	Pts	AG	AA	APts	PIM	PP	SH	GW	S	%	TGF	PGF	TGA	PGA	+/–	GP	G	A	Pts	PIM	PP	SH	GW
1984-85	HC Dobel	Sweden-2	5	2	1	3	....	....	....	6	....	....	....	....	....	....	....	....	....	....	....	....	....	....	....	....	....	....
1985-86	Leksands IF	Sweden-Jr.	STATISTICS NOT AVAILABLE																									
	Sweden	EJC-A	5	0	1	1	....	....	....	2	....	....	....	....	....	....	....	....	....	....	....	....	....	....	....	....	....	....
1986-87	Leksands IF	Sweden	23	3	5	8	....	....	....	4	....	....	....	....	....	....	....	....	....	....	....	....	....	....	....	....	....	....
1987-88	Leksands IF	Sweden	36	9	10	19	....	....	....	22	....	....	....	....	....	....	....	....	....	....	3	1	1	2	2	....	....	....
	Sweden	WJC-A	7	0	0	0	....	....	....	10	....	....	....	....	....	....	....	....	....	....	....	....	....	....	....	....	....	....
1988-89	Leksands IF	Sweden	39	14	16	30	....	....	....	58	....	....	....	....	....	....	....	....	....	....	10	2	4	6	6	....	....	....
1989-90	Leksands IF	Sweden	38	14	21	35	....	....	....	48	....	....	....	....	....	....	....	....	....	....	3	0	1	1	2	....	....	....
1990-91	Leksands IF	Sweden	22	5	10	15	....	....	....	10	....	....	....	....	....	....	....	....	....	....	21	6	9	15	26	....	....	....
1991-92	Sweden	Can-Cup	6	1	0	1	....	....	....	2	....	....	....	....	....	....	....	....	....	....	....	....	....	....	....	....	....	....
	Calgary Flames	**NHL**	**38**	**5**	**9**	**14**	**5**	**7**	**12**	**12**	**0**	**0**	**1**	**48**	**10.4**	**16**	**0**	**32**	**10**	**–6**	....	....	....	....	....	....	....	....
	Salt Lake Golden Eagles	IHL	22	10	6	16	....	....	....	25	....	....	....	....	....	....	....	....	....	....	5	2	2	4	2	....	....	....
1992-93	**Calgary Flames**	**NHL**	**6**	**0**	**2**	**2**	**0**	**1**	**1**	**0**	**0**	**0**	**0**	**3**	**0.0**	**2**	**0**	**2**	**0**	**0**	....	....	....	....	....	....	....	....
	Salt Lake Golden Eagles	IHL	63	31	23	54	....	....	....	68	....	....	....	....	....	....	....	....	....	....	....	....	....	....	....	....	....	....
1993-94	Leksands IF	Sweden	38	16	17	33	....	....	....	66	....	....	....	....	....	....	....	....	....	....	....	....	....	....	....	....	....	....
	Sweden	WC-A	5	2	2	4	....	....	....	4	....	....	....	....	....	....	....	....	....	....	....	....	....	....	....	....	....	....
1994-95	Leksands IF	Sweden	34	24	10	34	....	....	....	46	....	....	....	....	....	....	....	....	....	....	3	1	0	1	25	....	....	....
	Sweden	WC-A	8	2	0	2	....	....	....	10	....	....	....	....	....	....	....	....	....	....	....	....	....	....	....	....	....	....
1995-96	Leksands IF	Sweden	35	13	13	26	....	....	....	65	....	....	....	....	....	....	....	....	....	....	5	1	2	3	4	....	....	....
	Sweden	WC-A	6	0	1	1	....	....	....	2	....	....	....	....	....	....	....	....	....	....	....	....	....	....	....	....	....	....
1996-97	Kolner Haie	Germany	48	16	22	38	....	....	....	42	....	....	....	....	....	....	....	....	....	....	4	0	1	1	2	....	....	....
	Kolner Haie	EuroHL	6	1	3	4	....	....	....	8	....	....	....	....	....	....	....	....	....	....	....	....	....	....	....	....	....	....
1997-98	Kolner Haie	Germany	46	15	29	44	....	....	....	66	....	....	....	....	....	....	....	....	....	....	3	2	1	3	2	....	....	....
1998-99	Kolner Haie	Germany	51	19	34	53	....	....	....	44	....	....	....	....	....	....	....	....	....	....	5	3	3	6	8	....	....	....
99-2000	Kolner Haie	Germany	51	14	24	38	....	....	....	49	....	....	....	....	....	....	....	....	....	....	9	2	1	3	4	....	....	....
	NHL Totals		**44**	**5**	**11**	**16**	**5**	**8**	**13**	**12**	**0**	**0**	**1**	**51**	**9.8**	**18**	**0**	**34**	**10**		....	....	....	....	....	....	....	....

• FORSYTH, Alex

C – L. 6'2", 195 lbs. b: Galt, Ont., 1/6/1955. Washington's 1st, 18th overall, in 1975.

Season	Club	League	GP	G	A	Pts	AG	AA	APts	PIM	PP	SH	GW	S	%	TGF	PGF	TGA	PGA	+/–	GP	G	A	Pts	PIM	PP	SH	GW
1973-74	Kingston Canadians	OMJHL	58	11	11	22	....	....	....	17	....	....	....	....	....	....	....	....	....	....	....	....	....	....	....	....	....	....
1974-75	Kingston Canadians	OMJHL	64	27	31	58	....	....	....	72	....	....	....	....	....	....	....	....	....	....	8	6	4	10	2	....	....	....
1975-76	Richmond Robins	AHL	71	7	16	23	....	....	....	24	....	....	....	....	....	....	....	....	....	....	8	2	5	7	0	....	....	....
1976-77	**Washington Capitals**	**NHL**	**1**	**0**	**0**	**0**	**0**	**0**	**0**	**0**	**0**	**0**	**0**	**0**	**0.0**	**0**	**0**	**0**	**0**	**0**	....	....	....	....	....	....	....	....
	Springfield Indians	AHL	74	14	33	47	....	....	....	47	....	....	....	....	....	....	....	....	....	....	....	....	....	....	....	....	....	....
1977-78	Tulsa Oilers	CHL	69	15	16	31	....	....	....	29	....	....	....	....	....	....	....	....	....	....	7	0	0	0	0	....	....	....
	NHL Totals		**1**	**0**	**0**	**0**	**0**	**0**	**0**	**0**	**0**	**0**	**0**	**0**	**0.0**	**0**	**0**	**0**	**0**		....	....	....	....	....	....	....	....

• FORTIER, Dave

David Edward D – L. 5'11", 190 lbs. b: Sudbury, Ont., 6/17/1951. Toronto's 2nd, 23rd overall, in 1971.

Season	Club	League	GP	G	A	Pts	AG	AA	APts	PIM	PP	SH	GW	S	%	TGF	PGF	TGA	PGA	+/–	GP	G	A	Pts	PIM	PP	SH	GW
1969-70	Garson Falcons	NOJHA	STATISTICS NOT AVAILABLE																									
1970-71	St. Catharines Black Hawks	OHA-Jr.	60	8	16	24	....	....	....	196	....	....	....	....	....	....	....	....	....	....	15	0	6	6	74	....	....	....
1971-72	Tulsa Oilers	CHL	71	7	20	27	....	....	....	217	....	....	....	....	....	....	....	....	....	....	13	0	8	8	39	....	....	....
1972-73	**Toronto Maple Leafs**	**NHL**	**23**	**1**	**4**	**5**	**1**	**3**	**4**	**63**	**0**	**0**	**0**	**29**	**3.4**	**32**	**0**	**46**	**4**	**–10**	....	....	....	....	....	....	....	....
	Tulsa Oilers	CHL	50	2	20	22	....	....	....	148	....	....	....	....	....	....	....	....	....	....	....	....	....	....	....	....	....	....
1973-74	Oklahoma City Blazers	CHL	72	10	38	48	....	....	....	200	....	....	....	....	....	....	....	....	....	....	10	0	1	1	35	....	....	....
1974-75	**New York Islanders**	**NHL**	**65**	**6**	**12**	**18**	**5**	**9**	**14**	**79**	**1**	**0**	**0**	**74**	**8.1**	**61**	**5**	**48**	**6**	**14**	**14**	**0**	**2**	**2**	**33**	**0**	**0**	**0**
1975-76	**New York Islanders**	**NHL**	**59**	**0**	**2**	**2**	**0**	**1**	**1**	**68**	**0**	**0**	**0**	**58**	**0.0**	**28**	**2**	**19**	**2**	**9**	**6**	**0**	**0**	**0**	**0**	**0**	**0**	**0**
1976-77	**Vancouver Canucks**	**NHL**	**58**	**1**	**3**	**4**	**1**	**2**	**3**	**125**	**0**	**0**	**0**	**46**	**2.2**	**28**	**0**	**58**	**15**	**–15**	....	....	....	....	....	....	....	....
1977-78	Indianapolis Racers	WHA	54	1	15	16	....	....	....	86	....	....	....	....	....	....	....	....	....	....	....	....	....	....	....	....	....	....
1978-79	Erie Blades	NEHL	44	1	22	23	....	....	....	145	....	....	....	....	....	....	....	....	....	....	....	....	....	....	....	....	....	....
	NHL Totals		**205**	**8**	**21**	**29**	**7**	**15**	**22**	**335**	**1**	**0**	**0**	**207**	**3.9**	**149**	**7**	**171**	**27**		**20**	**0**	**2**	**2**	**33**	**0**	**0**	**0**
	Other Major League Totals		54	1	15	16	....	....	....	86	....	....	....	....	....	....	....	....	....	....	....	....	....	....	....	....	....	....

NOJHA First All-Star Team (1970)

Selected by **Quebec** (WHA) in 1972 WHA General Player Draft, February 13, 1972. Traded to **Philadelphia** by **Toronto** with Randy Osburn for Bill Flett, May 27, 1974. Claimed by **NY Islanders** from **Philadelphia** in Intra-League Draft, June 10, 1974. Traded to **Vancouver** by **NY Islanders** with Ralph Stewart for cash, October 6, 1976. Signed as a free agent by **Indianapolis** (WHA), September, 1977.

• FORTIER, Marc

C – R. 6', 192 lbs. b: Windsor, Que., 2/26/1966.

Season	Club	League	GP	G	A	Pts	AG	AA	APts	PIM	PP	SH	GW	S	%	TGF	PGF	TGA	PGA	+/–	GP	G	A	Pts	PIM	PP	SH	GW
1982-83	Montreal East Cantonniers	QAAA	48	35	36	71	....	....	....	....	....	....	....	....	....	....	....	....	....	....	....	....	....	....	....	....	....	....
1983-84	Chicoutimi Sagueneens	QMJHL	67	16	30	46	....	....	....	51	....	....	....	....	....	....	....	....	....	....	....	....	....	....	....	....	....	....
1984-85	Chicoutimi Sagueneens	QMJHL	68	35	63	98	....	....	....	114	....	....	....	....	....	....	....	....	....	....	14	8	4	12	16	....	....	....
1985-86	Chicoutimi Sagueneens	QMJHL	71	47	86	133	....	....	....	49	....	....	....	....	....	....	....	....	....	....	9	2	14	16	12	....	....	....
1986-87	Chicoutimi Sagueneens	QMJHL	65	66	*135	*201	....	....	....	39	....	....	....	....	....	....	....	....	....	....	19	11	*40	*51	20	....	....	....
1987-88	**Quebec Nordiques**	**NHL**	**27**	**4**	**10**	**14**	**3**	**7**	**10**	**12**	**3**	**0**	**1**	**40**	**10.0**	**19**	**11**	**26**	**1**	**–17**	....	....	....	....	....	....	....	....
	Fredericton Express	AHL	50	26	36	62	....	....	....	48	....	....	....	....	....	....	....	....	....	....	....	....	....	....	....	....	....	....
1988-89	**Quebec Nordiques**	**NHL**	**57**	**20**	**19**	**39**	**17**	**13**	**30**	**45**	**2**	**2**	**2**	**90**	**22.2**	**51**	**13**	**79**	**23**	**–18**	....	....	....	....	....	....	....	....
	Halifax Citadels	AHL	16	11	11	22	....	....	....	14	....	....	....	....	....	....	....	....	....	....	....	....	....	....	....	....	....	....
1989-90	**Quebec Nordiques**	**NHL**	**59**	**13**	**17**	**30**	**11**	**12**	**23**	**28**	**3**	**1**	**1**	**89**	**14.6**	**48**	**13**	**58**	**7**	**–16**	....	....	....	....	....	....	....	....
	Halifax Citadels	AHL	15	5	6	11	....	....	....	6	....	....	....	....	....	....	....	....	....	....	....	....	....	....	....	....	....	....
1990-91	**Quebec Nordiques**	**NHL**	**14**	**0**	**4**	**4**	**0**	**3**	**3**	**6**	**0**	**0**	**0**	**13**	**0.0**	**8**	**3**	**8**	**0**	**–3**	....	....	....	....	....	....	....	....
	Halifax Citadels	AHL	58	24	32	56	....	....	....	85	....	....	....	....	....	....	....	....	....	....	....	....	....	....	....	....	....	....
1991-92	**Quebec Nordiques**	**NHL**	**39**	**5**	**9**	**14**	**5**	**7**	**12**	**33**	**2**	**0**	**1**	**42**	**11.9**	**27**	**4**	**30**	**0**	**–7**	....	....	....	....	....	....	....	....
	Halifax Citadels	AHL	16	9	16	25	....	....	....	44	....	....	....	....	....	....	....	....	....	....	....	....	....	....	....	....	....	....
1992-93	**Ottawa Senators**	**NHL**	**10**	**0**	**1**	**1**	**0**	**1**	**1**	**6**	**0**	**0**	**0**	**12**	**0.0**	**2**	**0**	**10**	**1**	**–7**	....	....	....	....	....	....	....	....
	New Haven Senators	AHL	16	9	15	24	....	....	....	42	....	....	....	....	....	....	....	....	....	....	....	....	....	....	....	....	....	....
	Los Angeles Kings	**NHL**	**6**	**0**	**0**	**0**	**0**	**0**	**0**	**5**	**0**	**0**	**0**	**2**	**0.0**	**0**	**0**	**3**	**1**	**–2**	....	....	....	....	....	....	....	....
	Phoenix Roadrunners	IHL	17	4	9	13	....	....	....	34	....	....	....	....	....	....	....	....	....	....	....	....	....	....	....	....	....	....

			REGULAR SEASON																		PLAYOFFS							
Season	Club	League	GP	G	A	Pts	AG	AA	APts	PIM	PP	SH	GW	S	%	TGF	PGF	TGA	PGA	+/–	GP	G	A	Pts	PIM	PP	SH	GW
1993-94	Phoenix Roadrunners	IHL	81	39	61	100	....	....	....	96	....	....	....	....	....	....	....	....	....	....	....	....	....	....	....	....	....	....
1994-95	Canada	Nat-Team	4	1	3	4	....	....	....	0	....	....	....	....	....	....	....	....	....	....	....	....	....	....	....	....	....	....
	ZSC Lions Zurich	Switz.	35	11	40	51	....	....	....	*104	....	....	....	....	....	....	....	....	....	....	5	2	6	8	2	....	....	....
1995-96	ZSC Lions Zurich	Switz.	36	17	*38	55	....	....	....	30	....	....	....	....	....	....	....	....	....	....	4	1	2	3	4	....	....	....
1996-97	ZSC Lions Zurich	Switz.	24	8	19	27	....	....	....	39	....	....	....	....	....	....	....	....	....	....	....	....	....	....	....	....	....	....
	Eisbaren Berlin	Germany	18	3	8	11	....	....	....	10	....	....	....	....	....	....	....	....	....	....	8	5	4	9	2	....	....	....
1997-98	Eisbaren Berlin	Germany	43	8	36	44	....	....	....	38	....	....	....	....	....	....	....	....	....	....	10	2	5	7	6	....	....	....
1998-99	Eisbaren Berlin	Germany	49	8	40	48	....	....	....	86	....	....	....	....	....	....	....	....	....	....	8	3	2	5	12	....	....	....
	Eisbaren Berlin	EuroHL	5	1	0	1	....	....	....	2	....	....	....	....	....	....	....	....	....	....	6	3	5	8	6	....	....	....
99-2000	Eisbaren Berlin	Germany	64	11	49	60	....	....	....	72	....	....	....	....	....	....	....	....	....	....	....	....	....	....	....	....	....	....
	NHL Totals		**212**	**42**	**60**	**102**	**36**	**43**	**79**	**135**	**10**	**3**	**5**	**288**	**14.6**	**155**	**44**	**214**	**33**		....	....	....	....	....	....	....	....

QMJHL First All-Star Team (1987)

Signed as a free agent by **Quebec**, February 3, 1987. Signed as a free agent by **Ottawa**, October 1, 1992. Traded to **LA Kings** by **Ottawa** with Jim Thomson for Bob Kudelski and Shawn McCosh, December 19, 1992.

• FORTIN, Ray

Raymond Henri D – L. 5'8", 180 lbs. b: Drummondville, Que., 3/11/1941.

Season	Club	League	GP	G	A	Pts	AG	AA	APts	PIM	PP	SH	GW	S	%	TGF	PGF	TGA	PGA	+/–	GP	G	A	Pts	PIM	PP	SH	GW
1961-62	Drummondville Rockets	ETSHL	....	....	....	....	....	....	....	....	....	....	....	....	....	....	....	....	....	....	10	1	1	2	4	....	....	....
1962-1964	Drummondville Rockets	ETSHL	STATISTICS NOT AVAILABLE																									
1965-66	Drummondville Aigles	QSHL	42	5	12	17	....	....	....	54	....	....	....	....	....	....	....	....	....	....	5	0	0	0	13	....	....	....
	Sherbrooke Castors	Al-Cup	19	0	4	4	....	....	....	16	....	....	....	....	....	....	....	....	....	....	....	....	....	....	....	....	....	....
1966-67	Drummondville Aigles	QSHL	42	9	17	26	....	....	....	54	....	....	....	....	....	....	....	....	....	....	9	1	4	5	6	....	....	....
	Drummondville Aigles	Al-Cup	9	1	1	2	....	....	....	14	....	....	....	....	....	....	....	....	....	....	....	....	....	....	....	....	....	....
1967-68	**St. Louis Blues**	**NHL**	**24**	**0**	**2**	**2**	**0**	**2**	**2**	**8**	**0**	**0**	**0**	**25**	**0.0**	**10**	**0**	**16**	**3**	**–3**	**3**	**0**	**0**	**0**	**2**	**0**	**0**	**0**
	Kansas City Blues	CHL	22	1	2	3	....	....	....	22	....	....	....	....	....	....	....	....	....	....	....	....	....	....	....	....	....	....
1968-69	**St. Louis Blues**	**NHL**	**11**	**1**	**0**	**1**	**1**	**0**	**1**	**6**	**0**	**0**	**0**	**10**	**10.0**	**7**	**0**	**3**	**0**	**4**	....	....	....	....	....	....	....	....
	Kansas City Blues	CHL	50	6	18	24	....	....	....	59	....	....	....	....	....	....	....	....	....	....	....	....	....	....	....	....	....	....
1969-70	**St. Louis Blues**	**NHL**	**57**	**1**	**4**	**5**	**1**	**4**	**5**	**19**	**0**	**0**	**0**	**66**	**1.5**	**39**	**4**	**33**	**1**	**3**	**3**	**0**	**0**	**0**	**6**	**0**	**0**	**0**
1970-71	Springfield Kings	AHL	25	2	14	16	....	....	....	18	....	....	....	....	....	....	....	....	....	....	....	....	....	....	....	....	....	....
	Montreal Voyageurs	AHL	29	4	11	15	....	....	....	20	....	....	....	....	....	....	....	....	....	....	3	0	2	2	4	....	....	....
1971-72	Boston Braves	AHL	76	3	24	27	....	....	....	64	....	....	....	....	....	....	....	....	....	....	8	0	0	0	6	....	....	....
1972-73	Boston Braves	AHL	74	1	20	21	....	....	....	28	....	....	....	....	....	....	....	....	....	....	1	0	0	0	0	....	....	....
1973-74	San Diego Gulls	WHL	69	1	15	16	....	....	....	36	....	....	....	....	....	....	....	....	....	....	4	0	1	1	4	....	....	....
	NHL Totals		**92**	**2**	**6**	**8**	**2**	**6**	**8**	**33**	**0**	**0**	**0**	**101**	**2.0**	**56**	**4**	**52**	**4**		**6**	**0**	**0**	**0**	**8**	**0**	**0**	**0**

CHL Second All-Star Team (1969) • AHL Second All-Star Team (1971)

• 1961-62 regular season statistics for Drummondville (ETSHL) unavailable. Signed as a free agent by **St. Louis**, June, 1967. Traded to **LA Kings** by **St. Louis** for Bob Wall, May 11, 1970. Traded to **Montreal** by **LA Kings** with Gord Labossiere for Ralph Backstrom, January 26, 1971. Claimed by **Hershey** (AHL) from **Montreal** in Reverse Draft, June, 1971. Traded to **Boston** by **Hershey** (AHL) for cash, August, 1971.

• FOSTER, Corey

Corey J. D – L. 6'3", 204 lbs. b: Ottawa, Ont., 10/27/1969. New Jersey's 1st, 12th overall, in 1988.

Season	Club	League	GP	G	A	Pts	AG	AA	APts	PIM	PP	SH	GW	S	%	TGF	PGF	TGA	PGA	+/–	GP	G	A	Pts	PIM	PP	SH	GW
1985-86	Ottawa West Canadians	OMHA	37	15	35	50	....	....	....	30	....	....	....	....	....	....	....	....	....	....	....	....	....	....	....	....	....	....
1986-87	Peterborough Jr. Petes	OJHL-B	23	7	16	23	....	....	....	46	....	....	....	....	....	....	....	....	....	....	....	....	....	....	....	....	....	....
	Peterborough Petes	OHL	30	3	4	7	....	....	....	4	....	....	....	....	....	....	....	....	....	....	1	0	0	0	0	....	....	....
1987-88	Peterborough Petes	OHL	66	13	31	44	....	....	....	58	....	....	....	....	....	....	....	....	....	....	11	5	9	14	13	....	....	....
1988-89	Peterborough Petes	OHL	55	14	42	56	....	....	....	42	....	....	....	....	....	....	....	....	....	....	17	1	17	18	12	....	....	....
	Canada	WJC-A	7	1	3	4	....	....	....	4	....	....	....	....	....	....	....	....	....	....	....	....	....	....	....	....	....	....
	New Jersey Devils	**NHL**	**2**	**0**	**0**	**0**	**0**	**0**	**0**	**0**	**0**	**0**	**0**	**2**	**0.0**	**0**	**0**	**2**	**0**	**–2**	....	....	....	....	....	....	....	....
	Peterborough Petes	Mem-Cup	5	0	4	4	....	....	....	0	....	....	....	....	....	....	....	....	....	....	....	....	....	....	....	....	....	....
1989-90	Cape Breton Oilers	AHL	54	7	17	24	....	....	....	32	....	....	....	....	....	....	....	....	....	....	1	0	0	0	0	....	....	....
1990-91	Cape Breton Oilers	AHL	67	14	11	25	....	....	....	51	....	....	....	....	....	....	....	....	....	....	4	2	4	6	4	....	....	....
1991-92	**Philadelphia Flyers**	**NHL**	**25**	**3**	**4**	**7**	**3**	**3**	**6**	**20**	**1**	**0**	**0**	**67**	**4.5**	**17**	**6**	**25**	**0**	**–14**	....	....	....	....	....	....	....	....
	Hershey Bears	AHL	19	5	9	14	....	....	....	26	....	....	....	....	....	....	....	....	....	....	6	1	1	2	5	....	....	....
1992-93	Hershey Bears	AHL	80	9	25	34	....	....	....	102	....	....	....	....	....	....	....	....	....	....	....	....	....	....	....	....	....	....
1993-94	Hershey Bears	AHL	66	21	37	58	....	....	....	96	....	....	....	....	....	....	....	....	....	....	9	2	5	7	10	....	....	....
1994-95	P.E.I. Senators	AHL	78	13	34	47	....	....	....	61	....	....	....	....	....	....	....	....	....	....	11	2	5	7	12	....	....	....
1995-96	**Pittsburgh Penguins**	**NHL**	**11**	**2**	**2**	**4**	**2**	**2**	**4**	**2**	**1**	**0**	**0**	**8**	**25.0**	**7**	**3**	**6**	**0**	**–2**	**3**	**0**	**0**	**0**	**4**	**0**	**0**	**0**
	Cleveland Lumberjacks	IHL	61	10	36	46	....	....	....	93	....	....	....	....	....	....	....	....	....	....	....	....	....	....	....	....	....	....
1996-97	**New York Islanders**	**NHL**	**7**	**0**	**0**	**0**	**0**	**0**	**0**	**2**	**0**	**0**	**0**	**1**	**0.0**	**1**	**0**	**4**	**1**	**–2**	....	....	....	....	....	....	....	....
	Cleveland Lumberjacks	IHL	51	5	29	34	....	....	....	71	....	....	....	....	....	....	....	....	....	....	14	0	9	9	22	....	....	....
1997-98	Kokudo Toyko	Japan	37	18	13	31	....	....	....	101	....	....	....	....	....	....	....	....	....	....	....	....	....	....	....	....	....	....
1998-99	Kokudo Toyko	Japan	36	6	21	27	....	....	....	155	....	....	....	....	....	....	....	....	....	....	9	0	2	2	16	....	....	....
99-2000	Kokudo Toyko	Japan	28	11	15	26	....	....	....	....	....	....	....	....	....	....	....	....	....	....	7	1	6	7	8	....	....	....
	NHL Totals		**45**	**5**	**6**	**11**	**5**	**5**	**10**	**24**	**2**	**0**	**0**	**78**	**6.4**	**25**	**9**	**37**	**1**		**3**	**0**	**0**	**0**	**4**	**0**	**0**	**0**

Traded to **Edmonton** by **New Jersey** for Edmonton's 1st round choice (Jason Miller) in 1989 Entry Draft, June 17, 1989. Traded to **Philadelphia** by **Edmonton** with Dave Brown and Jari Kurri for Craig Fisher, Scott Mellanby and Craig Berube, May 30, 1991. Signed as a free agent by **Ottawa**, June 20, 1994. Signed as a free agent by **Pittsburgh**, August 7, 1995. Claimed by **NY Islanders** from **Pittsburgh** in Waiver Draft, September 30, 1996.

• FOSTER, Dwight

Dwight Alexander "Dewey" RW – R. 5'10", 190 lbs. b: Toronto, Ont., 4/2/1957. Boston's 1st, 16th overall, in 1977.

Season	Club	League	GP	G	A	Pts	AG	AA	APts	PIM	PP	SH	GW	S	%	TGF	PGF	TGA	PGA	+/–	GP	G	A	Pts	PIM	PP	SH	GW
1973-74	Kitchener Rangers	OMJHL	67	23	32	55	....	....	....	61	....	....	....	....	....	....	....	....	....	....	....	....	....	....	....	....	....	....
1974-75	Kitchener Rangers	OMJHL	70	39	51	90	....	....	....	88	....	....	....	....	....	....	....	....	....	....	....	....	....	....	....	....	....	....
1975-76	Kitchener Rangers	OMJHL	61	36	58	94	....	....	....	110	....	....	....	....	....	....	....	....	....	....	8	4	6	10	28	....	....	....
1976-77	Kitchener Rangers	OMJHL	64	60	*83	*143	....	....	....	88	....	....	....	....	....	....	....	....	....	....	3	2	4	6	2	....	....	....
	Canada	WJC-A	7	2	5	7	....	....	....	4	....	....	....	....	....	....	....	....	....	....	....	....	....	....	....	....	....	....
1977-78	Kitchener Rangers	OMJHL	61	36	58	94	....	....	....	110	....	....	....	....	....	....	....	....	....	....	8	4	6	10	28	....	....	....
	Boston Bruins	**NHL**	**14**	**2**	**1**	**3**	**2**	**1**	**3**	**6**	**0**	**0**	**0**	**24**	**8.3**	**3**	**0**	**2**	**0**	**1**	....	....	....	....	....	....	....	....
	Rochester Americans	AHL	3	0	3	3	....	....	....	2	....	....	....	....	....	....	....	....	....	....	....	....	....	....	....	....	....	....
1978-79	**Boston Bruins**	**NHL**	**44**	**11**	**13**	**24**	**9**	**9**	**18**	**14**	**2**	**0**	**0**	**57**	**19.3**	**33**	**7**	**34**	**7**	**–1**	**11**	**1**	**3**	**4**	**0**	**0**	**0**	**0**
	Rochester Americans	AHL	21	11	18	29	....	....	....	8	....	....	....	....	....	....	....	....	....	....	....	....	....	....	....	....	....	....
1979-80	**Boston Bruins**	**NHL**	**57**	**10**	**28**	**38**	**8**	**20**	**28**	**42**	**1**	**1**	**2**	**68**	**14.7**	**53**	**7**	**30**	**7**	**23**	**9**	**3**	**5**	**8**	**2**	**0**	**1**	**1**
	Binghamton Dusters	AHL	7	1	3	4	....	....	....	2	....	....	....	....	....	....	....	....	....	....	....	....	....	....	....	....	....	....
1980-81	**Boston Bruins**	**NHL**	**77**	**24**	**28**	**52**	**19**	**19**	**38**	**62**	**3**	**3**	**5**	**107**	**22.4**	**76**	**12**	**91**	**31**	**4**	**3**	**1**	**1**	**2**	**0**	**0**	**0**	**0**
1981-82	**Colorado Rockies**	**NHL**	**70**	**12**	**19**	**31**	**9**	**13**	**22**	**41**	**1**	**1**	**0**	**97**	**12.4**	**52**	**10**	**109**	**14**	**–53**	....	....	....	....	....	....	....	....
1982-83	**New Jersey Devils**	**NHL**	**4**	**0**	**0**	**0**	**0**	**0**	**0**	**2**	**0**	**0**	**0**	**2**	**0.0**	**0**	**0**	**1**	**0**	**–1**	....	....	....	....	....	....	....	....
	Wichita Wind	CHL	2	0	1	1	....	....	....	2	....	....	....	....	....	....	....	....	....	....	....	....	....	....	....	....	....	....
	Detroit Red Wings	**NHL**	**58**	**17**	**22**	**39**	**14**	**15**	**29**	**58**	**3**	**1**	**1**	**83**	**20.5**	**65**	**16**	**72**	**15**	**–8**	....	....	....	....	....	....	....	....
1983-84	**Detroit Red Wings**	**NHL**	**52**	**9**	**12**	**21**	**7**	**8**	**15**	**50**	**0**	**2**	**1**	**75**	**12.0**	**36**	**1**	**56**	**17**	**–4**	**3**	**0**	**1**	**1**	**0**	**0**	**0**	**0**
1984-85	**Detroit Red Wings**	**NHL**	**50**	**16**	**16**	**32**	**13**	**11**	**24**	**56**	**0**	**3**	**0**	**69**	**23.2**	**44**	**0**	**69**	**37**	**12**	**3**	**0**	**0**	**0**	**0**	**0**	**0**	**0**
1985-86	**Detroit Red Wings**	**NHL**	**55**	**6**	**12**	**18**	**5**	**8**	**13**	**48**	**1**	**1**	**0**	**41**	**14.6**	**25**	**2**	**70**	**34**	**–13**	....	....	....	....	....	....	....	....
	Boston Bruins	**NHL**	**13**	**0**	**0**	**0**	**0**	**0**	**0**	**4**	**0**	**0**	**0**	**8**	**0.0**	**2**	**1**	**11**	**5**	**–5**	**3**	**0**	**2**	**2**	**2**	**0**	**0**	**0**
1986-87	**Boston Bruins**	**NHL**	**47**	**4**	**12**	**16**	**3**	**9**	**12**	**37**	**0**	**1**	**0**	**23**	**17.4**	**24**	**0**	**39**	**16**	**1**	**3**	**0**	**0**	**0**	**0**	**0**	**0**	**0**
	NHL Totals		**541**	**111**	**163**	**274**	**89**	**113**	**202**	**420**	**11**	**13**	**9**	**654**	**17.0**	**413**	**56**	**584**	**183**		**35**	**5**	**12**	**17**	**4**	**0**	**1**	**1**

Signed as a free agent by **Colorado**, July 21, 1981. Transferred to **New Jersey** when **Colorado** franchise relocated, June 30, 1982. Rights traded to **Detroit** by **New Jersey** for cash, October 29, 1982. Traded to **Boston** by **Detroit** for Dave Donnelly, March 11, 1986.

• FOTIU, Nick

Nicholas Evlampios "Nicky Boy" LW – L. 6'2", 210 lbs. b: Staten Island, NY, 5/25/1952.

Season	Club	League	GP	G	A	Pts	AG	AA	APts	PIM	PP	SH	GW	S	%	TGF	PGF	TGA	PGA	+/–	GP	G	A	Pts	PIM	PP	SH	GW
1971-72	New Hyde Park Arrows	NYJHL	32	6	17	23	....	....	....	135	....	....	....	....	....	....	....	....	....	....	5	4	4	8	14	....	....	....
1972-73	New Hyde Park Arrows	NYJHL	DID NOT PLAY – INJURED																									
1973-74	Cape Cod Cubs	NAHL	72	12	24	36	....	....	....	*371	....	....	....	....	....	....	....	....	....	....	13	4	7	11	*80	....	....	....

Season	Club	League	GP	G	A	Pts	AG	AA	APts	PIM	PP	SH	GW	S	%	TGF	PGF	TGA	PGA	+/-	GP	G	A	Pts	PIM	PP	SH	GW
			REGULAR SEASON																		PLAYOFFS							
1974-75	New England Whalers	WHA	61	2	2	4	....	....	....	144	....	....	....	....	....	....	....	....	....	....	4	2	0	2	27	....	....	....
	Cape Cod Codders	NAHL	5	2	1	3	....	....	....	13	....	....	....	....	....	....	....	....	....	....	....	....	....	....	....	....	....	....
1975-76	New England Whalers	WHA	49	3	2	5	....	....	....	94	....	....	....	....	....	....	....	....	....	....	16	3	2	5	57	....	....	....
	Cape Cod Codders	NAHL	6	2	1	3	....	....	....	15	....	....	....	....	....	....	....	....	....	....	....	....	....	....	....	....	....	....
1976-77	**New York Rangers**	**NHL**	**70**	**4**	**8**	**12**	**4**	**6**	**10**	**174**	**0**	**0**	**0**	**48**	**8.3**	**16**	**0**	**39**	**0**	**–23**	....	....	....	....	....	....	....	....
1977-78	**New York Rangers**	**NHL**	**59**	**2**	**7**	**9**	**2**	**5**	**7**	**105**	**0**	**0**	**0**	**32**	**6.3**	**13**	**0**	**27**	**0**	**–14**	**3**	**0**	**0**	**0**	**5**	**0**	**0**	**0**
	New Haven Nighthawks	AHL	5	1	1	2	....	....	....	9	....	....	....	....	....	....	....	....	....	....	....	....	....	....	....	....	....	....
1978-79	**New York Rangers**	**NHL**	**71**	**3**	**5**	**8**	**3**	**4**	**7**	**190**	**0**	**0**	**1**	**51**	**5.9**	**22**	**1**	**18**	**0**	**3**	**4**	**0**	**0**	**0**	**6**	**0**	**0**	**0**
1979-80	**Hartford Whalers**	**NHL**	**74**	**10**	**8**	**18**	**8**	**6**	**14**	**107**	**0**	**0**	**0**	**54**	**18.5**	**28**	**0**	**26**	**0**	**2**	**3**	**0**	**0**	**0**	**6**	**0**	**0**	**0**
1980-81	**Hartford Whalers**	**NHL**	**42**	**4**	**3**	**7**	**3**	**2**	**5**	**79**	**0**	**0**	**0**	**36**	**11.1**	**17**	**1**	**23**	**0**	**–7**	....	....	....	....	....	....	....	....
	New York Rangers	**NHL**	**27**	**5**	**6**	**11**	**4**	**4**	**8**	**91**	**1**	**0**	**0**	**28**	**17.9**	**16**	**1**	**21**	**0**	**–6**	**2**	**0**	**0**	**0**	**4**	**0**	**0**	**0**
1981-82	New York Rangers	DN-Cup	4	1	0	1	....	....	....	....	....	....	....	....	....	....	....	....	....	....	....	....	....	....	....	....	....	....
	New York Rangers	**NHL**	**70**	**8**	**10**	**18**	**6**	**7**	**13**	**151**	**0**	**0**	**1**	**76**	**10.5**	**22**	**0**	**30**	**1**	**–7**	**10**	**0**	**2**	**2**	**6**	**0**	**0**	**0**
1982-83	**New York Rangers**	**NHL**	**72**	**8**	**13**	**21**	**7**	**9**	**16**	**90**	**1**	**0**	**1**	**61**	**13.1**	**35**	**2**	**27**	**0**	**6**	**5**	**0**	**1**	**1**	**6**	**0**	**0**	**0**
1983-84	**New York Rangers**	**NHL**	**40**	**7**	**6**	**13**	**6**	**4**	**10**	**115**	**0**	**0**	**2**	**40**	**17.5**	**21**	**0**	**13**	**0**	**8**	....	....	....	....	....	....	....	....
1984-85	**New York Rangers**	**NHL**	**46**	**4**	**7**	**11**	**3**	**5**	**8**	**54**	**0**	**0**	**1**	**44**	**9.1**	**15**	**0**	**22**	**0**	**–7**	....	....	....	....	....	....	....	....
1985-86	New Haven Nighthawks	AHL	9	4	2	6	....	....	....	21	....	....	....	....	....	....	....	....	....	....	....	....	....	....	....	....	....	....
	Calgary Flames	**NHL**	**9**	**0**	**1**	**1**	**0**	**1**	**1**	**21**	**0**	**0**	**0**	**7**	**0.0**	**1**	**0**	**4**	**0**	**–3**	**11**	**0**	**1**	**1**	**34**	**0**	**0**	**0**
1986-87	**Calgary Flames**	**NHL**	**42**	**5**	**3**	**8**	**4**	**2**	**6**	**145**	**0**	**0**	**1**	**31**	**16.1**	**12**	**0**	**15**	**0**	**–3**	....	....	....	....	....	....	....	....
1987-88	**Philadelphia Flyers**	**NHL**	**23**	**0**	**0**	**0**	**0**	**0**	**0**	**40**	**0**	**0**	**0**	**9**	**0.0**	**0**	**0**	**9**	**0**	**–9**	....	....	....	....	....	....	....	....
1988-89	**Edmonton Oilers**	**NHL**	**1**	**0**	**0**	**0**	**0**	**0**	**0**	**0**	**0**	**0**	**0**	**0**	**0.0**	**1**	**0**	**0**	**0**	**1**	....	....	....	....	....	....	....	....
1989-90	New Haven Nighthawks	AHL	31	0	3	3	....	....	....	40	....	....	....	....	....	....	....	....	....	....	....	....	....	....	....	....	....	....
1990-1992			OUT OF HOCKEY – RETIRED																									
1992-1994	Nashville Knights	ECHL	DID NOT PLAY – COACHING																									
1995-1998	Johnstown Chiefs	ECHL	DID NOT PLAY – COACHING																									
1998-1999	**San Jose Sharks**	**NHL**	DID NOT PLAY – SCOUTING																									
1999-2000	Kentucky Thoroughblades	AHL	DID NOT PLAY – ASSISTANT COACH																									
	NHL Totals		**646**	**60**	**77**	**137**	**50**	**55**	**105**	**1362**	**2**	**0**	**7**	**517**	**11.6**	**219**	**5**	**274**	**1**		**38**	**0**	**4**	**4**	**67**	**0**	**0**	**0**
	Other Major League Totals		110	5	4	9	....	....	....	238	....	....	....	....	....	....	....	....	....	....	20	5	2	7	84	....	....	....

• Missed entire 1972-73 season recovering from knee surgery, June, 1972. Signed as a free agent by **New England** (WHA), June, 1974. Signed as a free agent by **NY Rangers**, July 23, 1976. Claimed by **Hartford** from **NY Rangers** in Expansion Draft, June 13, 1979. Traded to **NY Rangers** by **Hartford** for NY Rangers' 5th round choice (Bill Maguire) in 1981 Entry Draft, January 15, 1981. Traded to **Calgary** by **NY Rangers** for future considerations, March 11, 1986. Signed as a free agent by **Philadelphia**, October 30, 1987. Signed as a free agent by **Edmonton**, March, 1989. Signed as a freee agent by **New Haven** (AHL), October 30, 1989. • Player/coach w/ RHI's New Jersey R&R in 1994 (2-0-0-0-6).

• FOX, Greg

Gregory Brent D – L. 6'2", 190 lbs. b: Port McNeil, B.C., 8/12/1953. Atlanta's 12th, 162nd overall, in 1973.

Season	Club	League	GP	G	A	Pts	AG	AA	APts	PIM	PP	SH	GW	S	%	TGF	PGF	TGA	PGA	+/-	GP	G	A	Pts	PIM	PP	SH	GW
1971-72	Kelowna Buckaroos	BCJHL	53	9	35	44	....	....	....	161	....	....	....	....	....	....	....	....	....	....	....	....	....	....	....	....	....	....
1972-73	University of Michigan	CCHA	30	2	15	17	....	....	....	68	....	....	....	....	....	....	....	....	....	....	....	....	....	....	....	....	....	....
1973-74	University of Michigan	CCHA	32	0	11	11	....	....	....	64	....	....	....	....	....	....	....	....	....	....	....	....	....	....	....	....	....	....
1974-75	University of Michigan	CCHA	36	0	19	19	....	....	....	80	....	....	....	....	....	....	....	....	....	....	....	....	....	....	....	....	....	....
1975-76	University of Michigan	CCHA	39	1	21	22	....	....	....	99	....	....	....	....	....	....	....	....	....	....	....	....	....	....	....	....	....	....
1976-77	Tulsa Oilers	CHL	10	1	7	8	....	....	....	6	....	....	....	....	....	....	....	....	....	....	....	....	....	....	....	....	....	....
	Nova Scotia Voyageurs	AHL	56	2	14	16	....	....	....	110	....	....	....	....	....	....	....	....	....	....	12	0	4	4	8	....	....	....
1977-78	**Atlanta Flames**	**NHL**	**16**	**1**	**2**	**3**	**1**	**2**	**3**	**25**	**1**	**0**	**0**	**15**	**6.7**	**14**	**1**	**14**	**6**	**5**	**2**	**0**	**1**	**1**	**8**	**0**	**0**	**0**
	Nova Scotia Voyageurs	AHL	51	2	10	12	....	....	....	124	....	....	....	....	....	....	....	....	....	....	9	2	3	5	38	....	....	....
1978-79	**Atlanta Flames**	**NHL**	**64**	**0**	**12**	**12**	**0**	**9**	**9**	**70**	**0**	**0**	**0**	**39**	**0.0**	**71**	**0**	**58**	**12**	**25**	....	....	....	....	....	....	....	....
	Chicago Black Hawks	**NHL**	**14**	**0**	**5**	**5**	**0**	**4**	**4**	**16**	**0**	**0**	**0**	**18**	**0.0**	**19**	**0**	**13**	**3**	**9**	**4**	**0**	**1**	**1**	**0**	**0**	**0**	**0**
1979-80	**Chicago Black Hawks**	**NHL**	**71**	**4**	**11**	**15**	**3**	**8**	**11**	**73**	**0**	**0**	**1**	**58**	**6.9**	**53**	**0**	**88**	**22**	**–13**	**7**	**0**	**0**	**0**	**8**	**0**	**0**	**0**
1980-81	**Chicago Black Hawks**	**NHL**	**75**	**3**	**16**	**19**	**2**	**11**	**13**	**112**	**0**	**0**	**0**	**69**	**4.3**	**68**	**3**	**111**	**36**	**–10**	**3**	**0**	**1**	**1**	**2**	**0**	**0**	**0**
1981-82	**Chicago Black Hawks**	**NHL**	**79**	**2**	**19**	**21**	**2**	**13**	**15**	**137**	**0**	**0**	**0**	**89**	**2.2**	**94**	**2**	**158**	**53**	**–13**	**15**	**1**	**3**	**4**	**27**	**0**	**0**	**1**
1982-83	**Chicago Black Hawks**	**NHL**	**76**	**0**	**12**	**12**	**0**	**8**	**8**	**81**	**0**	**0**	**0**	**55**	**0.0**	**69**	**2**	**79**	**23**	**11**	**13**	**0**	**3**	**3**	**22**	**0**	**0**	**0**
1983-84	**Chicago Black Hawks**	**NHL**	**24**	**0**	**5**	**5**	**0**	**3**	**3**	**31**	**0**	**0**	**0**	**15**	**0.0**	**18**	**0**	**22**	**4**	**0**	....	....	....	....	....	....	....	....
	Pittsburgh Penguins	**NHL**	**49**	**2**	**5**	**7**	**2**	**3**	**5**	**66**	**0**	**0**	**0**	**27**	**7.4**	**38**	**1**	**101**	**22**	**–42**	....	....	....	....	....	....	....	....
1984-85	**Pittsburgh Penguins**	**NHL**	**26**	**2**	**5**	**7**	**2**	**3**	**5**	**26**	**0**	**0**	**0**	**14**	**14.3**	**28**	**1**	**38**	**5**	**–6**	....	....	....	....	....	....	....	....
	Baltimore Skipjacks	AHL	36	3	14	17	....	....	....	38	....	....	....	....	....	....	....	....	....	....	15	1	4	5	14	....	....	....
	NHL Totals		**494**	**14**	**92**	**106**	**12**	**64**	**76**	**637**	**1**	**0**	**1**	**399**	**3.5**	**472**	**10**	**682**	**186**		**44**	**1**	**9**	**10**	**67**	**0**	**0**	**1**

Traded to **Chicago** by **Atlanta** with Tom Lysiak, Harold Phillipoff, Pat Ribble and Miles Zaharko for Ivan Boldirev, Darcy Rota and Phil Russell, March 13, 1979. Traded to **Pittsburgh** by **Chicago** for Randy Boyd, December 6, 1983.

• FOX, Jim

James Charles RW – R. 5'8", 185 lbs. b: Coniston, Ont., 5/18/1960. Los Angeles' 2nd, 10th overall, in 1980.

Season	Club	League	GP	G	A	Pts	AG	AA	APts	PIM	PP	SH	GW	S	%	TGF	PGF	TGA	PGA	+/-	GP	G	A	Pts	PIM	PP	SH	GW
1975-76	North Bay Trappers	NOJHA	44	30	45	75	....	....	....	16	....	....	....	....	....	....	....	....	....	....	....	....	....	....	....	....	....	....
	Sudbury Wolves	OHL	....	....	....	....	....	....	....	....	....	....	....	....	....	....	....	....	....	....	4	3	3	6	0	....	....	....
1976-77	North Bay Trappers	NOJHA	38	44	64	*108	....	....	....	4	....	....	....	....	....	....	....	....	....	....	19	*13	*25	*38	....	....	....	....
1977-78	Ottawa 67's	OMJHL	59	44	83	127	....	....	....	12	....	....	....	....	....	....	....	....	....	....	13	7	14	21	0	....	....	....
1978-79	Ottawa 67's	OMJHL	53	37	66	103	....	....	....	4	....	....	....	....	....	....	....	....	....	....	4	2	1	3	2	....	....	....
1979-80	Ottawa 67's	OMJHL	52	65	*101	*166	....	....	....	30	....	....	....	....	....	....	....	....	....	....	11	6	14	20	2	....	....	....
	Canada	WJC-A	5	3	2	5	....	....	....	0	....	....	....	....	....	....	....	....	....	....	....	....	....	....	....	....	....	....
1980-81	**Los Angeles Kings**	**NHL**	**71**	**18**	**25**	**43**	**14**	**17**	**31**	**8**	**2**	**0**	**2**	**92**	**19.6**	**59**	**13**	**47**	**1**	**0**	**4**	**0**	**1**	**1**	**0**	**0**	**0**	**0**
1981-82	**Los Angeles Kings**	**NHL**	**77**	**30**	**38**	**68**	**24**	**25**	**49**	**23**	**5**	**1**	**0**	**157**	**19.1**	**91**	**16**	**93**	**3**	**–15**	**9**	**1**	**4**	**5**	**0**	**0**	**0**	**0**
1982-83	**Los Angeles Kings**	**NHL**	**77**	**28**	**40**	**68**	**23**	**28**	**51**	**8**	**7**	**0**	**1**	**137**	**20.4**	**92**	**29**	**74**	**0**	**–11**	....	....	....	....	....	....	....	....
1983-84	**Los Angeles Kings**	**NHL**	**80**	**30**	**42**	**72**	**24**	**29**	**53**	**26**	**10**	**0**	**5**	**153**	**19.6**	**102**	**30**	**85**	**1**	**–12**	....	....	....	....	....	....	....	....
1984-85	**Los Angeles Kings**	**NHL**	**79**	**30**	**53**	**83**	**24**	**36**	**60**	**10**	**6**	**0**	**2**	**174**	**17.2**	**111**	**26**	**82**	**1**	**4**	**3**	**0**	**1**	**1**	**0**	**0**	**0**	**0**
1985-86	**Los Angeles Kings**	**NHL**	**39**	**14**	**17**	**31**	**11**	**11**	**22**	**2**	**2**	**0**	**0**	**81**	**17.3**	**44**	**12**	**45**	**4**	**–9**	....	....	....	....	....	....	....	....
	Canada	WEC-A	10	3	2	5	....	....	....	4	....	....	....	....	....	....	....	....	....	....	....	....	....	....	....	....	....	....
1986-87	**Los Angeles Kings**	**NHL**	**76**	**19**	**42**	**61**	**16**	**31**	**47**	**48**	**4**	**0**	**2**	**162**	**11.7**	**82**	**23**	**70**	**1**	**–10**	**5**	**3**	**2**	**5**	**0**	**1**	**0**	**0**
1987-88	**Los Angeles Kings**	**NHL**	**68**	**16**	**35**	**51**	**14**	**25**	**39**	**18**	**2**	**0**	**1**	**120**	**13.3**	**78**	**24**	**62**	**1**	**–7**	**1**	**0**	**0**	**0**	**0**	**0**	**0**	**0**
1988-89	**Los Angeles Kings**	**NHL**	DID NOT PLAY – INJURED																									
1989-90	**Los Angeles Kings**	**NHL**	**11**	**1**	**1**	**2**	**1**	**1**	**2**	**0**	**0**	**0**	**1**	**7**	**14.3**	**3**	**0**	**5**	**1**	**–1**	....	....	....	....	....	....	....	....
1990-91	EC Weisswasser	Germany-2	26	7	15	22	....	....	....	25	....	....	....	....	....	....	....	....	....	....	5	1	2	3	0	....	....	....
	NHL Totals		**578**	**186**	**293**	**479**	**151**	**203**	**354**	**143**	**38**	**1**	**14**	**1083**	**17.2**	**662**	**173**	**563**	**13**		**22**	**4**	**8**	**12**	**0**	**1**	**0**	**0**

OMJHL First All-Star Team (1980)

• Missed entire 1988-89 season recovering from knee injury originally suffered in game vs. Boston, March 10, 1988.

• FRANCESCHETTI, Lou

Lou C. RW – L. 6', 200 lbs. b: Toronto, Ont., 3/28/1958. Washington's 8th, 71st overall, in 1978.

Season	Club	League	GP	G	A	Pts	AG	AA	APts	PIM	PP	SH	GW	S	%	TGF	PGF	TGA	PGA	+/-	GP	G	A	Pts	PIM	PP	SH	GW
1975-76	Toronto Young Nationals	OJHL	17	12	11	23	....	....	....	27	....	....	....	....	....	....	....	....	....	....	....	....	....	....	....	....	....	....
	St.Catharines Black Hawks	OMJHL	1	0	0	0	....	....	....	0	....	....	....	....	....	....	....	....	....	....	....	....	....	....	....	....	....	....
1976-77	Niagara Falls Flyers	OMJHL	61	23	30	53	....	....	....	80	....	....	....	....	....	....	....	....	....	....	....	....	....	....	....	....	....	....
1977-78	Niagara Falls Flyers	OMJHL	62	40	50	90	....	....	....	46	....	....	....	....	....	....	....	....	....	....	....	....	....	....	....	....	....	....
1978-79	Saginaw Gears	IHL	2	1	1	2	....	....	....	0	....	....	....	....	....	....	....	....	....	....	....	....	....	....	....	....	....	....
	Port Huron Flags	IHL	76	45	58	103	....	....	....	131	....	....	....	....	....	....	....	....	....	....	....	....	....	....	....	....	....	....
1979-80	Port Huron Flags	IHL	15	3	8	11	....	....	....	31	....	....	....	....	....	....	....	....	....	....	....	....	....	....	....	....	....	....
	Hershey Bears	AHL	65	27	29	56	....	....	....	58	....	....	....	....	....	....	....	....	....	....	14	6	9	15	32	....	....	....
1980-81	Hershey Bears	AHL	79	32	36	68	....	....	....	173	....	....	....	....	....	....	....	....	....	....	10	3	7	10	30	....	....	....
1981-82	**Washington Capitals**	**NHL**	**30**	**2**	**10**	**12**	**2**	**7**	**9**	**23**	**0**	**0**	**1**	**25**	**8.0**	**24**	**6**	**22**	**0**	**–4**	....	....	....	....	....	....	....	....
	Hershey Bears	AHL	50	22	33	55	....	....	....	89	....	....	....	....	....	....	....	....	....	....	....	....	....	....	....	....	....	....
1982-83	Hershey Bears	AHL	80	31	44	75	....	....	....	176	....	....	....	....	....	....	....	....	....	....	5	1	2	3	16	....	....	....
1983-84	**Washington Capitals**	**NHL**	**2**	**0**	**0**	**0**	**0**	**0**	**0**	**0**	**0**	**0**	**0**	**2**	**0.0**	**0**	**0**	**2**	**0**	**–2**	**3**	**0**	**0**	**0**	**8**	**0**	**0**	**0**
	Hershey Bears	AHL	73	26	34	60	....	....	....	130	....	....	....	....	....	....	....	....	....	....	....	....	....	....	....	....	....	....
1984-85	**Washington Capitals**	**NHL**	**22**	**4**	**7**	**11**	**3**	**5**	**8**	**45**	**0**	**0**	**1**	**19**	**21.1**	**14**	**0**	**13**	**0**	**1**	**5**	**1**	**1**	**2**	**15**	**0**	**0**	**0**
	Binghamton Whalers	AHL	52	29	43	72	....	....	....	75	....	....	....	....	....	....	....	....	....	....	....	....	....	....	....	....	....	....
1985-86	**Washington Capitals**	**NHL**	**76**	**7**	**14**	**21**	**6**	**9**	**15**	**131**	**0**	**0**	**2**	**57**	**12.3**	**41**	**1**	**44**	**0**	**–4**	**8**	**0**	**0**	**0**	**15**	**0**	**0**	**0**

			REGULAR SEASON																		PLAYOFFS							
Season	Club	League	GP	G	A	Pts	AG	AA	APts	PIM	PP	SH	GW	S	%	TGF	PGF	TGA	PGA	+/–	GP	G	A	Pts	PIM	PP	SH	GW
1986-87	**Washington Capitals**	**NHL**	**75**	**12**	**9**	**21**	**10**	**7**	**17**	**127**	**0**	**0**	**1**	**77**	**15.6**	**47**	**2**	**62**	**8**	**–9**	**7**	**0**	**0**	**0**	**23**	**0**	**0**	**0**
1987-88	**Washington Capitals**	**NHL**	**59**	**4**	**8**	**12**	**3**	**6**	**9**	**113**	**1**	**0**	**1**	**53**	**7.5**	**24**	**1**	**22**	**1**	**2**	**4**	**0**	**0**	**0**	**14**	**0**	**0**	**0**
	Binghamton Whalers	AHL	6	2	4	6	....	....	....	4	....	....	....	....	....	....	....	....	....	....	....	....	....	....	....	....	....	....
1988-89	**Washington Capitals**	**NHL**	**63**	**7**	**10**	**17**	**6**	**7**	**13**	**123**	**0**	**0**	**0**	**55**	**12.7**	**28**	**1**	**34**	**3**	**–4**	**6**	**1**	**0**	**1**	**8**	**0**	**0**	**1**
	Baltimore Skipjacks	AHL	10	8	7	15	....	....	....	30	....	....	....	....	....	....	....	....	....	....	....	....	....	....	....	....	....	....
1989-90	**Toronto Maple Leafs**	**NHL**	**80**	**21**	**15**	**36**	**18**	**11**	**29**	**127**	**0**	**2**	**4**	**76**	**27.6**	**57**	**4**	**93**	**28**	**–12**	**5**	**0**	**1**	**1**	**26**	**0**	**0**	**0**
1990-91	**Toronto Maple Leafs**	**NHL**	**16**	**1**	**1**	**2**	**1**	**1**	**2**	**30**	**0**	**0**	**0**	**7**	**14.3**	**4**	**0**	**13**	**7**	**–2**	....	....	....	....	....	....	....	....
	Buffalo Sabres	**NHL**	**35**	**1**	**7**	**8**	**1**	**5**	**6**	**28**	**0**	**0**	**1**	**20**	**5.0**	**22**	**1**	**22**	**3**	**2**	**6**	**1**	**0**	**1**	**2**	**0**	**0**	**0**
1991-92	**Buffalo Sabres**	**NHL**	**1**	**0**	**0**	**0**	**0**	**0**	**0**	**0**	**0**	**0**	**0**	**0**	**0.0**	**0**	**0**	**0**	**0**	**0**	....	....	....	....	....	....	....	....
	New Haven Nighthawks	AHL	25	6	7	13	....	....	....	59	....	....	....	....	....	....	....	....	....	....	....	....	....	....	....	....	....	....
	Rochester Americans	AHL	49	15	25	40	....	....	....	64	....	....	....	....	....	....	....	....	....	....	15	3	5	8	31	....	....	....
1992-93	Jacksonville Bullets	SHL	4	0	0	0	....	....	....	0	....	....	....	....	....	....	....	....	....	....	....	....	....	....	....	....	....	....
1993-94	Detroit Falcons	ColHL	2	1	1	2	....	....	....	6	....	....	....	....	....	....	....	....	....	....	....	....	....	....	....	....	....	....
1994-95	HC Selva	Italy-2	STATISTICS NOT AVAILABLE																									
	Minnesota Moose	IHL	4	1	0	1	....	....	....	12	....	....	....	....	....	....	....	....	....	....	3	0	0	0	0	....	....	....
	London Blues	ColHL	37	14	41	55	....	....	....	64	....	....	....	....	....	....	....	....	....	....	5	0	5	5	16	....	....	....
1995-96	Nashville Knights	ECHL	18	5	13	18	....	....	....	39	....	....	....	....	....	....	....	....	....	....	3	0	0	0	2	....	....	....
	NHL Totals		**459**	**59**	**81**	**140**	**50**	**58**	**108**	**747**	**1**	**2**	**11**	**391**	**15.1**	**261**	**16**	**327**	**50**		**44**	**3**	**2**	**5**	**111**	**0**	**0**	**1**

Traded to **Toronto** by **Washington** for Toronto's 5th round choice (Mark Ouimet) in 1990 Entry Draft, June 29, 1989. Traded to **Buffalo** by **Toronto** with Brian Curran for Mike Foligno and Buffalo's 8th round choice (Thomas Kucharcik) in 1991 Entry Draft, December 17, 1990. • Played w/ RHI's Toronto Planets in 1993 (5-2-4-6-16), Buffalo Stampede in 1995 (10-2-9-11-9) and Buffalo Wings in 1998 (1-0-0-0-0).

• FRANCIS, Bobby

Robert Emile C – R. 5'9", 175 lbs. b: North Battleford, Sask., 12/5/1958.

Season	Club	League	GP	G	A	Pts	AG	AA	APts	PIM	PP	SH	GW	S	%	TGF	PGF	TGA	PGA	+/–	GP	G	A	Pts	PIM	PP	SH	GW
1972-73	Brooklyn Stars	NYJHL	38	36	34	70	....	....	....	44	....	....	....	....	....	....	....	....	....	....	....	....	....	....	....	....	....	....
1973-74	Brooklyn Stars	NYJHL	41	41	53	94	....	....	....	63	....	....	....	....	....	....	....	....	....	....	12	*17	11	*28	24	....	....	....
1974-75	Bronx Shamrocks	NYJHL	40	53	59	112	....	....	....	71	....	....	....	....	....	....	....	....	....	....	....	....	....	....	....	....	....	....
1975-76	Berwick Vikings	NEJHL	40	62	*74	136	....	....	....	61	....	....	....	....	....	....	....	....	....	....	....	....	....	....	....	....	....	....
1976-77	University of New Hampshire	ECAC	13	2	7	9	....	....	....	12	....	....	....	....	....	....	....	....	....	....	....	....	....	....	....	....	....	....
1977-78	University of New Hampshire	ECAC	27	7	14	21	....	....	....	6	....	....	....	....	....	....	....	....	....	....	....	....	....	....	....	....	....	....
1978-79	University of New Hampshire	ECAC	35	20	46	66	....	....	....	44	....	....	....	....	....	....	....	....	....	....	....	....	....	....	....	....	....	....
1979-80	University of New Hampshire	ECAC	30	19	23	42	....	....	....	30	....	....	....	....	....	....	....	....	....	....	....	....	....	....	....	....	....	....
1980-81	Birmingham Bulls	CHL	18	6	21	27	....	....	....	20	....	....	....	....	....	....	....	....	....	....	....	....	....	....	....	....	....	....
	Muskegon Mohawks	IHL	27	16	17	33	....	....	....	33	....	....	....	....	....	....	....	....	....	....	....	....	....	....	....	....	....	....
1981-82	Oklahoma City Stars	CHL	80	48	66	*114	....	....	....	76	....	....	....	....	....	....	....	....	....	....	4	1	2	3	11	....	....	....
1982-83	Colorado Flames	CHL	26	20	16	36	....	....	....	24	....	....	....	....	....	....	....	....	....	....	....	....	....	....	....	....	....	....
	Detroit Red Wings	**NHL**	**14**	**2**	**0**	**2**	**2**	**0**	**2**	**0**	**0**	**0**	**0**	**4**	**50.0**	**2**	**0**	**3**	**0**	**–1**	....	....	....	....	....	....	....	....
	Adirondack Red Wings	AHL	17	3	8	11	....	....	....	0	....	....	....	....	....	....	....	....	....	....	....	....	....	....	....	....	....	....
1983-84	Colorado Flames	CHL	68	32	50	82	....	....	....	53	....	....	....	....	....	....	....	....	....	....	1	0	1	1	0	....	....	....
1984-85	Salt Lake Golden Eagles	IHL	53	24	16	40	....	....	....	36	....	....	....	....	....	....	....	....	....	....	6	1	1	2	0	....	....	....
1985-86	Salt Lake Golden Eagles	IHL	82	32	44	76	....	....	....	163	....	....	....	....	....	....	....	....	....	....	5	0	4	4	10	....	....	....
1986-87	Salt Lake Golden Eagles	IHL	82	29	69	98	....	....	....	86	....	....	....	....	....	....	....	....	....	....	17	9	8	17	13	....	....	....
1987-1989	Salt Lake Golden Eagles	IHL	DID NOT PLAY – ASSISTANT COACH																									
1989-1993	Salt Lake Golden Eagles	IHL	DID NOT PLAY – COACHING																									
1993-1995	Saint John Flames	AHL	DID NOT PLAY – COACHING																									
1995-1997	Providence Bruins	AHL	DID NOT PLAY – COACHING																									
1997-1999	**Boston Bruins**	**NHL**	DID NOT PLAY – ASSISTANT COACH																									
1999-2000	**Phoenix Coyotes**	**NHL**	DID NOT PLAY – COACHING																									
	NHL Totals		**14**	**2**	**0**	**2**	**2**	**0**	**2**	**0**	**0**	**0**	**0**	**4**	**50.0**	**2**	**0**	**3**	**0**		....	....	....	....	....	....	....	....

• Son of Emile • CHL First All-Star Team (1982) • Won Ken McKenzie Trophy (Rookie of the Year - CHL) (1982) • Won Tommy Ivan Trophy (MVP - CHL) (1982)

Signed as a free agent by **Calgary**, October 27, 1980. Traded to **Detroit** by **Calgary** for the rights to Yves Courteau, December 2, 1982.

• FRANCIS, Ron

Ronald Michael C – L. 6'3", 200 lbs. b: Sault Ste. Marie, Ont., 3/1/1963. Hartford's 1st, 4th overall, in 1981.

Season	Club	League	GP	G	A	Pts	AG	AA	APts	PIM	PP	SH	GW	S	%	TGF	PGF	TGA	PGA	+/–	GP	G	A	Pts	PIM	PP	SH	GW
1979-80	Sault Ste. Marie Legion	NOHA	45	57	92	149	....	....	....	....	....	....	....	....	....	....	....	....	....	....	....	....	....	....	....	....	....	....
1980-81	Sault Ste. Marie Greyhounds	OMJHL	64	26	43	69	....	....	....	33	....	....	....	....	....	....	....	....	....	....	19	7	8	15	34	....	....	....
1981-82	Sault Ste. Marie Greyhounds	OHL	25	18	30	48	....	....	....	46	....	....	....	....	....	....	....	....	....	....	....	....	....	....	....	....	....	....
	Hartford Whalers	**NHL**	**59**	**25**	**43**	**68**	**20**	**29**	**49**	**51**	**12**	**0**	**1**	**163**	**15.3**	**91**	**38**	**93**	**27**	**–13**	....	....	....	....	....	....	....	....
1982-83	**Hartford Whalers**	**NHL**	**79**	**31**	**59**	**90**	**25**	**41**	**66**	**60**	**4**	**2**	**4**	**212**	**14.6**	**114**	**33**	**129**	**23**	**–25**	....	....	....	....	....	....	....	....
1983-84	**Hartford Whalers**	**NHL**	**72**	**23**	**60**	**83**	**18**	**41**	**59**	**45**	**5**	**0**	**5**	**202**	**11.4**	**119**	**59**	**78**	**8**	**–10**	....	....	....	....	....	....	....	....
1984-85	**Hartford Whalers**	**NHL**	**80**	**24**	**57**	**81**	**20**	**39**	**59**	**66**	**4**	**0**	**1**	**195**	**12.3**	**129**	**63**	**95**	**6**	**–23**	....	....	....	....	....	....	....	....
	Canada	WEC-A	10	2	5	7	....	....	....	2	....	....	....	....	....	....	....	....	....	....	....	....	....	....	....	....	....	....
1985-86	**Hartford Whalers**	**NHL**	**53**	**24**	**53**	**77**	**19**	**36**	**55**	**24**	**7**	**1**	**4**	**120**	**20.0**	**113**	**48**	**64**	**7**	**8**	**10**	**1**	**2**	**3**	**4**	**0**	**0**	**0**
1986-87	**Hartford Whalers**	**NHL**	**75**	**30**	**63**	**93**	**26**	**46**	**72**	**45**	**7**	**0**	**7**	**189**	**15.9**	**140**	**61**	**70**	**1**	**10**	**6**	**2**	**2**	**4**	**6**	**1**	**0**	**0**
1987-88	**Hartford Whalers**	**NHL**	**80**	**25**	**50**	**75**	**21**	**36**	**57**	**87**	**11**	**1**	**3**	**172**	**14.5**	**104**	**51**	**71**	**10**	**–8**	**6**	**2**	**5**	**7**	**2**	**1**	**0**	**0**
1988-89	**Hartford Whalers**	**NHL**	**69**	**29**	**48**	**77**	**25**	**34**	**59**	**36**	**8**	**0**	**4**	**156**	**18.6**	**116**	**49**	**83**	**20**	**4**	**4**	**0**	**2**	**2**	**0**	**0**	**0**	**0**
1989-90	**Hartford Whalers**	**NHL**	**80**	**32**	**69**	**101**	**28**	**50**	**78**	**73**	**15**	**1**	**5**	**170**	**18.8**	**137**	**61**	**77**	**14**	**13**	**7**	**3**	**3**	**6**	**8**	**1**	**0**	**0**
1990-91	**Hartford Whalers**	**NHL**	**67**	**21**	**55**	**76**	**19**	**42**	**61**	**51**	**10**	**1**	**6**	**149**	**14.1**	**97**	**40**	**70**	**11**	**–2**	....	....	....	....	....	....	....	....
♦	**Pittsburgh Penguins**	**NHL**	**14**	**2**	**9**	**11**	**2**	**7**	**9**	**21**	**0**	**0**	**1**	**25**	**8.0**	**22**	**6**	**17**	**1**	**0**	**24**	**7**	**10**	**17**	**24**	**0**	**0**	**4**
1991-92♦	**Pittsburgh Penguins**	**NHL**	**70**	**21**	**33**	**54**	**19**	**25**	**44**	**30**	**5**	**1**	**2**	**121**	**17.4**	**107**	**44**	**89**	**19**	**–7**	**21**	**8**	***19**	**27**	**6**	**2**	**0**	**2**
1992-93	**Pittsburgh Penguins**	**NHL**	**84**	**24**	**76**	**100**	**20**	**52**	**72**	**68**	**9**	**2**	**4**	**215**	**11.2**	**156**	**84**	**96**	**30**	**6**	**12**	**6**	**11**	**17**	**19**	**1**	**0**	**1**
1993-94	**Pittsburgh Penguins**	**NHL**	**82**	**27**	**66**	**93**	**25**	**51**	**76**	**62**	**8**	**0**	**2**	**216**	**12.5**	**134**	**60**	**111**	**34**	**–3**	**6**	**0**	**2**	**2**	**6**	**0**	**0**	**0**
1994-95	**Pittsburgh Penguins**	**NHL**	**44**	**11**	***48**	**59**	**19**	**71**	**90**	**18**	**3**	**0**	**1**	**94**	**11.7**	**77**	**25**	**43**	**21**	**30**	**12**	**6**	**13**	**19**	**4**	**2**	**0**	**0**
1995-96	**Pittsburgh Penguins**	**NHL**	**77**	**27**	***92**	**119**	**27**	**76**	**103**	**56**	**12**	**1**	**4**	**158**	**17.1**	**189**	**92**	**101**	**29**	**25**	**11**	**3**	**6**	**9**	**4**	**2**	**0**	**1**
1996-97	**Pittsburgh Penguins**	**NHL**	**81**	**27**	**63**	**90**	**29**	**56**	**85**	**20**	**10**	**1**	**2**	**183**	**14.8**	**141**	**50**	**110**	**26**	**7**	**5**	**1**	**2**	**3**	**2**	**1**	**0**	**0**
1997-98	**Pittsburgh Penguins**	**NHL**	**81**	**25**	**62**	**87**	**29**	**61**	**90**	**20**	**7**	**0**	**5**	**189**	**13.2**	**126**	**50**	**73**	**9**	**12**	**6**	**1**	**5**	**6**	**2**	**0**	**0**	**0**
1998-99	**Carolina Hurricanes**	**NHL**	**82**	**21**	**31**	**52**	**25**	**30**	**55**	**34**	**8**	**0**	**2**	**133**	**15.8**	**78**	**29**	**67**	**16**	**–2**	**3**	**0**	**1**	**1**	**0**	**0**	**0**	**0**
99-2000	**Carolina Hurricanes**	**NHL**	**78**	**23**	**50**	**73**	**26**	**46**	**72**	**18**	**7**	**0**	**4**	**150**	**15.3**	**104**	**43**	**59**	**8**	**10**	....	....	....	....	....	....	....	....
	NHL Totals		**1407**	**472**	**1087**	**1559**	**442**	**869**	**1311**	**885**	**152**	**11**	**67**	**3212**	**14.7**	**2294**	**986**	**1596**	**320**		**133**	**40**	**83**	**123**	**87**	**11**	**0**	**8**

Won Alka-Seltzer Plus Award (1995) • Won Frank J. Selke Trophy (1995) • Won Lady Byng Trophy (1995, 1998) • Played in NHL All-Star Game (1983, 1985, 1990, 1996)

Traded to **Pittsburgh** by **Hartford** with Grant Jennings and Ulf Samuelsson for John Cullen, Jeff Parker and Zarley Zalapski, March 4, 1991. Signed as a free agent by **Carolina**, July 13, 1998.

• FRASER, Curt

Curtis Martin "Frazz" LW – L. 6'1", 200 lbs. b: Cincinnati, OH, 1/12/1958. Vancouver's 2nd, 22nd overall, in 1978.

Season	Club	League	GP	G	A	Pts	AG	AA	APts	PIM	PP	SH	GW	S	%	TGF	PGF	TGA	PGA	+/–	GP	G	A	Pts	PIM	PP	SH	GW
1972-73	North Shore Winter Club	BCAHA	STATISTICS NOT AVAILABLE																									
1973-74	Kelowna Buckeroos	BCJHL	52	32	32	64	....	....	....	85	....	....	....	....	....	....	....	....	....	....	....	....	....	....	....	....	....	....
1974-75	Victoria Cougars	WCJHL	68	17	32	49	....	....	....	105	....	....	....	....	....	....	....	....	....	....	12	2	3	5	22	....	....	....
1975-76	Victoria Cougars	WCJHL	71	43	64	107	....	....	....	167	....	....	....	....	....	....	....	....	....	....	18	3	8	11	38	....	....	....
1976-77	Victoria Cougars	WCJHL	60	34	41	75	....	....	....	82	....	....	....	....	....	....	....	....	....	....	4	4	2	6	4	....	....	....
1977-78	Victoria Cougars	WCJHL	66	48	44	92	....	....	....	256	....	....	....	....	....	....	....	....	....	....	13	10	7	17	28	....	....	....
	Canada	WJC-A	5	0	2	2	....	....	....	0	....	....	....	....	....	....	....	....	....	....	....	....	....	....	....	....	....	....
1978-79	**Vancouver Canucks**	**NHL**	**78**	**16**	**19**	**35**	**14**	**14**	**28**	**116**	**2**	**0**	**2**	**184**	**8.7**	**51**	**7**	**52**	**1**	**–7**	**3**	**0**	**2**	**2**	**6**	**0**	**0**	**0**
1979-80	**Vancouver Canucks**	**NHL**	**78**	**17**	**25**	**42**	**14**	**18**	**32**	**143**	**0**	**0**	**3**	**148**	**11.5**	**58**	**0**	**51**	**0**	**7**	**4**	**0**	**0**	**0**	**2**	**0**	**0**	**0**
1980-81	**Vancouver Canucks**	**NHL**	**77**	**25**	**24**	**49**	**19**	**16**	**35**	**118**	**7**	**0**	**2**	**188**	**13.3**	**68**	**22**	**65**	**0**	**–19**	**3**	**1**	**0**	**1**	**2**	**0**	**0**	**0**
1981-82	**Vancouver Canucks**	**NHL**	**79**	**28**	**39**	**67**	**22**	**26**	**48**	**175**	**11**	**0**	**5**	**233**	**12.0**	**95**	**28**	**65**	**0**	**2**	**17**	**3**	**7**	**10**	**98**	**0**	**0**	**0**
1982-83	**Vancouver Canucks**	**NHL**	**36**	**6**	**7**	**13**	**5**	**5**	**10**	**99**	**2**	**0**	**0**	**67**	**9.0**	**25**	**7**	**25**	**0**	**–7**	....	....	....	....	....	....	....	....
	Chicago Black Hawks	**NHL**	**38**	**6**	**13**	**19**	**5**	**9**	**14**	**77**	**0**	**0**	**2**	**42**	**14.3**	**29**	**2**	**25**	**0**	**2**	**13**	**4**	**4**	**8**	**18**	**1**	**0**	**1**
1983-84	**Chicago Black Hawks**	**NHL**	**29**	**5**	**12**	**17**	**4**	**8**	**12**	**28**	**1**	**0**	**0**	**45**	**11.1**	**25**	**3**	**13**	**0**	**9**	**5**	**0**	**0**	**0**	**14**	**0**	**0**	**0**
1984-85	**Chicago Black Hawks**	**NHL**	**73**	**25**	**25**	**50**	**20**	**17**	**37**	**109**	**4**	**0**	**5**	**136**	**18.4**	**77**	**8**	**66**	**0**	**3**	**15**	**6**	**3**	**9**	**36**	**0**	**0**	**1**
1985-86	**Chicago Black Hawks**	**NHL**	**61**	**29**	**39**	**68**	**23**	**26**	**49**	**84**	**7**	**0**	**1**	**144**	**20.1**	**90**	**26**	**53**	**0**	**11**	**3**	**0**	**1**	**1**	**12**	**0**	**0**	**0**
1986-87	**Chicago Blackhawks**	**NHL**	**75**	**25**	**25**	**50**	**22**	**18**	**40**	**182**	**3**	**0**	**2**	**183**	**13.7**	**69**	**10**	**54**	**0**	**5**	**2**	**1**	**1**	**2**	**10**	**0**	**0**	**0**

			REGULAR SEASON																		PLAYOFFS							
Season	Club	League	GP	G	A	Pts	AG	AA	APts	PIM	PP	SH	GW	S	%	TGF	PGF	TGA	PGA	+/–	GP	G	A	Pts	PIM	PP	SH	GW
1987-88	United States	Can-Cup	5	0	1	1	....	....	....	4	....	....	....	....	....	....	....	....	....	....	....	....	....	....	....	....	....	....
	Chicago Blackhawks	**NHL**	**27**	**4**	**6**	**10**	**3**	**4**	**7**	**57**	**1**	**0**	**1**	**51**	**7.8**	**16**	**4**	**26**	**1**	**–13**	....	....	....	....	....	....	....	....
	Minnesota North Stars	**NHL**	**10**	**1**	**1**	**2**	**1**	**1**	**2**	**20**	**0**	**0**	**0**	**21**	**4.8**	**5**	**2**	**10**	**0**	**–7**	....	....	....	....	....	....	....	....
1988-89	**Minnesota North Stars**	**NHL**	**35**	**5**	**5**	**10**	**4**	**4**	**8**	**76**	**1**	**0**	**0**	**58**	**8.6**	**16**	**4**	**27**	**0**	**–15**	....	....	....	....	....	....	....	....
1989-90	**Minnesota North Stars**	**NHL**	**8**	**1**	**0**	**1**	**1**	**0**	**1**	**22**	**0**	**0**	**0**	**7**	**14.3**	**1**	**0**	**6**	**0**	**–5**	....	....	....	....	....	....	....	....
1990-1992	Milwaukee Admirals	IHL	DID NOT PLAY – ASSISTANT COACH																									
1992-1994	Milwaukee Admirals	IHL	DID NOT PLAY – COACHING																									
1995-1999	Orlando Solar Bears	IHL	DID NOT PLAY – COACHING																									
1999-2000	**Atlanta Thrashers**	**NHL**	DID NOT PLAY – COACHING																									
	NHL Totals		**704**	**193**	**240**	**433**	**157**	**166**	**323**	**1306**	**39**	**0**	**23**	**1507**	**12.8**	**625**	**123**	**538**	**2**		**65**	**15**	**18**	**33**	**198**	**1**	**0**	**2**

Traded to **Chicago** by **Vancouver** for Tony Tanti, January 6, 1983. • Missed majority of 1983-84 season recovering from kneee injury suffered in game vs. Minnesota, November 5, 1983. Traded to **Minnesota** by **Chicago** for Dirk Graham, January 4, 1988.

• FRASER, Iain

Iain James C – L. 5'10", 175 lbs. b: Scarborough, Ont., 8/10/1969. NY Islanders' 14th, 233rd overall, in 1989.

Season	Club	League	GP	G	A	Pts	AG	AA	APts	PIM	PP	SH	GW	S	%	TGF	PGF	TGA	PGA	+/–	GP	G	A	Pts	PIM	PP	SH	GW
1986-87	Oshawa Legionaires	OJHL-B	31	18	22	40	....	....	....	119	....	....	....	....	....	....	....	....	....	....	....	....	....	....	....	....	....	....
	Oshawa Generals	OHL	5	2	1	3	....	....	....	0	....	....	....	....	....	....	....	....	....	....	....	....	....	....	....	....	....	....
	Oshawa Generals	Mem-Cup	1	0	0	0	....	....	....	2	....	....	....	....	....	....	....	....	....	....	....	....	....	....	....	....	....	....
1987-88	Oshawa Generals	OHL	16	4	4	8	....	....	....	22	....	....	....	....	....	....	....	....	....	....	6	2	3	5	2	....	....	....
1988-89	Oshawa Generals	OHL	62	33	57	90	....	....	....	87	....	....	....	....	....	....	....	....	....	....	6	2	8	10	12	....	....	....
1989-90	Oshawa Generals	OHL	56	40	65	105	....	....	....	75	....	....	....	....	....	....	....	....	....	....	17	10	*22	32	8	....	....	....
	Oshawa Generals	Mem-Cup	4	3	7	10	....	....	....	2	....	....	....	....	....	....	....	....	....	....	....	....	....	....	....	....	....	....
1990-91	Capital District Islanders	AHL	32	5	13	18	....	....	....	16	....	....	....	....	....	....	....	....	....	....	....	....	....	....	....	....	....	....
	Richmond Renegades	ECHL	3	1	1	2	....	....	....	0	....	....	....	....	....	....	....	....	....	....	....	....	....	....	....	....	....	....
1991-92	Capital District Islanders	AHL	45	9	11	20	....	....	....	24	....	....	....	....	....	....	....	....	....	....	....	....	....	....	....	....	....	....
1992-93	**New York Islanders**	**NHL**	**7**	**2**	**2**	**4**	**2**	**1**	**3**	**2**	**1**	**0**	**0**	**7**	**28.6**	**5**	**2**	**4**	**0**	**–1**	....	....	....	....	....	....	....	....
	Capital District Islanders	AHL	74	41	69	110	....	....	....	16	....	....	....	....	....	....	....	....	....	....	4	0	1	1	0	....	....	....
1993-94	**Quebec Nordiques**	**NHL**	**60**	**17**	**20**	**37**	**16**	**16**	**32**	**23**	**2**	**0**	**2**	**109**	**15.6**	**47**	**8**	**52**	**8**	**–5**	....	....	....	....	....	....	....	....
1994-95	**Dallas Stars**	**NHL**	**4**	**0**	**0**	**0**	**0**	**0**	**0**	**0**	**0**	**0**	**0**	**2**	**0.0**	**1**	**0**	**4**	**0**	**–3**	....	....	....	....	....	....	....	....
	Edmonton Oilers	**NHL**	**9**	**3**	**0**	**3**	**5**	**0**	**5**	**0**	**0**	**0**	**0**	**5**	**60.0**	**4**	**0**	**1**	**0**	**3**	....	....	....	....	....	....	....	....
	Denver Grizzlies	IHL	1	0	0	0	....	....	....	0	....	....	....	....	....	....	....	....	....	....	....	....	....	....	....	....	....	....
	Canada	WC-A	8	2	7	9	....	....	....	8	....	....	....	....	....	....	....	....	....	....	....	....	....	....	....	....	....	....
1995-96	**Winnipeg Jets**	**NHL**	**12**	**1**	**1**	**2**	**1**	**1**	**2**	**4**	**0**	**0**	**0**	**12**	**8.3**	**4**	**0**	**3**	**0**	**1**	**4**	**0**	**0**	**0**	**0**	**0**	**0**	**0**
	Springfield Falcons	AHL	53	24	47	71	....	....	....	27	....	....	....	....	....	....	....	....	....	....	6	0	6	6	2	....	....	....
1996-97	**San Jose Sharks**	**NHL**	**2**	**0**	**0**	**0**	**0**	**0**	**0**	**2**	**0**	**0**	**0**	**0**	**0.0**	**0**	**0**	**1**	**0**	**–1**	....	....	....	....	....	....	....	....
	Kentucky Thoroughblades	AHL	57	27	33	60	....	....	....	24	....	....	....	....	....	....	....	....	....	....	....	....	....	....	....	....	....	....
1997-98	Kansas City Blades	IHL	77	16	44	60	....	....	....	45	....	....	....	....	....	....	....	....	....	....	11	2	6	8	6	....	....	....
1998-99	EHC Herisau	Switz-2	STATISTICS NOT AVAILABLE																									
	Schwenningen Wild Wings	Germany	15	4	5	9	....	....	....	2	....	....	....	....	....	....	....	....	....	....	....	....	....	....	....	....	....	....
99-2000	Schwenningen Wild Wings	Germany	68	20	33	53	....	....	....	30	....	....	....	....	....	....	....	....	....	....	....	....	....	....	....	....	....	....
	NHL Totals		**94**	**23**	**23**	**46**	**24**	**18**	**42**	**31**	**3**	**0**	**2**	**135**	**17.0**	**61**	**10**	**65**	**8**		**4**	**0**	**0**	**0**	**0**	**0**	**0**	**0**

Memorial Cup All-Star Team (1990) • Won Stafford Smythe Memorial Trophy (Memorial Cup Tournament MVP) (1990) • AHL Second All-Star Team (1993)

Signed as a free agent by **Quebec**, August 3, 1993. Traded to **Dallas** by **Quebec** for Dallas' 7th round choice (Dan Hinote) in 1996 Entry Draft, January 31, 1995. Claimed on waivers by **Edmonton** from **Dallas**, March 3, 1995. Signed as a free agent by **Winnipeg**, October 11, 1995. Signed as a free agent by **San Jose**, September 1, 1996.

• FRASER, Scott

C – R. 6'1", 178 lbs. b: Moncton, N.B., 5/3/1972. Montreal's 12th, 193rd overall, in 1991.

Season	Club	League	GP	G	A	Pts	AG	AA	APts	PIM	PP	SH	GW	S	%	TGF	PGF	TGA	PGA	+/–	GP	G	A	Pts	PIM	PP	SH	GW
1987-88	Moncton Flyers	NBAHA	STATISTICS NOT AVAILABLE																									
1988-89	Wexford Raiders	OJHL-B	42	3	13	16	....	....	....	54	....	....	....	....	....	....	....	....	....	....	....	....	....	....	....	....	....	....
1990-91	Dartmouth College	ECAC	24	10	10	20	....	....	....	30	....	....	....	....	....	....	....	....	....	....	....	....	....	....	....	....	....	....
1991-92	Dartmouth College	ECAC	24	11	7	18	....	....	....	60	....	....	....	....	....	....	....	....	....	....	....	....	....	....	....	....	....	....
1992-93	Dartmouth College	ECAC	26	21	23	44	....	....	....	13	....	....	....	....	....	....	....	....	....	....	....	....	....	....	....	....	....	....
	Canada	Nat-Team	5	1	0	1	....	....	....	0	....	....	....	....	....	....	....	....	....	....	....	....	....	....	....	....	....	....
1993-94	Dartmouth College	ECAC	24	17	13	30	....	....	....	34	....	....	....	....	....	....	....	....	....	....	....	....	....	....	....	....	....	....
	Canada	Nat-Team	4	0	1	1	....	....	....	4	....	....	....	....	....	....	....	....	....	....	....	....	....	....	....	....	....	....
1994-95	Fredericton Canadiens	AHL	65	23	25	48	....	....	....	36	....	....	....	....	....	....	....	....	....	....	16	3	5	8	14	....	....	....
	Wheeling Thunderbirds	ECHL	8	4	2	6	....	....	....	8	....	....	....	....	....	....	....	....	....	....	....	....	....	....	....	....	....	....
1995-96	**Montreal Canadiens**	**NHL**	**15**	**2**	**0**	**2**	**2**	**0**	**2**	**4**	**0**	**0**	**0**	**9**	**22.2**	**3**	**0**	**4**	**0**	**–1**	....	....	....	....	....	....	....	....
	Fredericton Canadiens	AHL	58	37	37	74	....	....	....	43	....	....	....	....	....	....	....	....	....	....	10	9	7	16	2	....	....	....
1996-97	Fredericton Canadiens	AHL	7	3	8	11	....	....	....	0	....	....	....	....	....	....	....	....	....	....	....	....	....	....	....	....	....	....
	Saint John Flames	AHL	37	22	10	32	....	....	....	24	....	....	....	....	....	....	....	....	....	....	....	....	....	....	....	....	....	....
	San Antonio Dragons	IHL	8	0	1	1	....	....	....	2	....	....	....	....	....	....	....	....	....	....	....	....	....	....	....	....	....	....
	Carolina Monarchs	AHL	18	9	19	28	....	....	....	12	....	....	....	....	....	....	....	....	....	....	....	....	....	....	....	....	....	....
1997-98	**Edmonton Oilers**	**NHL**	**29**	**12**	**11**	**23**	**14**	**11**	**25**	**6**	**6**	**0**	**2**	**61**	**19.7**	**30**	**16**	**8**	**0**	**6**	**11**	**1**	**1**	**2**	**0**	**0**	**0**	**0**
	Hamilton Bulldogs	AHL	50	29	32	61	....	....	....	26	....	....	....	....	....	....	....	....	....	....	....	....	....	....	....	....	....	....
1998-99	**New York Rangers**	**NHL**	**28**	**2**	**4**	**6**	**2**	**4**	**6**	**14**	**1**	**0**	**0**	**35**	**5.7**	**7**	**3**	**16**	**0**	**–12**	....	....	....	....	....	....	....	....
	Hartford Wolf Pack	AHL	36	13	24	37	....	....	....	20	....	....	....	....	....	....	....	....	....	....	6	4	3	7	4	....	....	....
	NHL Totals		**72**	**16**	**15**	**31**	**18**	**15**	**33**	**24**	**7**	**0**	**2**	**105**	**15.2**	**40**	**19**	**28**	**0**		**11**	**1**	**1**	**2**	**0**	**0**	**0**	**0**

ECAC Second All-Star Team (1993)

Traded to **Calgary** by **Montreal** for David Ling and Calgary's 6th round choice in 1998 Entry Draft, October 24, 1996. Traded to **San Antonio** (IHL) by **Calgary** for Brent Bilodeau, February, 1997. Signed as a free agent by **Edmonton**, July 28, 1997. Signed as a free agent by **NY Rangers**, August 29, 1998.

• FRAWLEY, Dan

William Daniel RW – R. 6'1", 195 lbs. b: Sturgeon Falls, Ont., 6/2/1962. Chicago's 15th, 204th overall, in 1980.

Season	Club	League	GP	G	A	Pts	AG	AA	APts	PIM	PP	SH	GW	S	%	TGF	PGF	TGA	PGA	+/–	GP	G	A	Pts	PIM	PP	SH	GW
1978-79	Valley East Eagles	OMHA	23	42	43	85	....	....	....	....	....	....	....	....	....	....	....	....	....	....	....	....	....	....	....	....	....	....
1979-80	Sudbury Wolves	OMJHL	63	21	26	47	....	....	....	67	....	....	....	....	....	....	....	....	....	....	8	0	1	1	2	....	....	....
1980-81	Cornwall Royals	OMJHL	28	10	14	24	....	....	....	76	....	....	....	....	....	....	....	....	....	....	18	5	12	17	37	....	....	....
	Cornwall Royals	Mem-Cup	5	1	4	5	....	....	....	21	....	....	....	....	....	....	....	....	....	....	....	....	....	....	....	....	....	....
1981-82	Cornwall Royals	OHL	64	27	50	77	....	....	....	239	....	....	....	....	....	....	....	....	....	....	5	3	8	11	19	....	....	....
1982-83	Springfield Indians	AHL	80	30	27	57	....	....	....	107	....	....	....	....	....	....	....	....	....	....	....	....	....	....	....	....	....	....
1983-84	**Chicago Black Hawks**	**NHL**	**3**	**0**	**0**	**0**	**0**	**0**	**0**	**0**	**0**	**0**	**0**	**2**	**0.0**	**0**	**0**	**1**	**0**	**–1**	....	....	....	....	....	....	....	....
	Springfield Indians	AHL	69	22	34	56	....	....	....	137	....	....	....	....	....	....	....	....	....	....	4	0	1	1	12	....	....	....
1984-85	**Chicago Black Hawks**	**NHL**	**30**	**4**	**3**	**7**	**3**	**2**	**5**	**64**	**0**	**0**	**1**	**24**	**16.7**	**12**	**0**	**15**	**1**	**–2**	**1**	**0**	**0**	**0**	**0**	**0**	**0**	**0**
	Milwaukee Admirals	IHL	26	11	12	23	....	....	....	125	....	....	....	....	....	....	....	....	....	....	....	....	....	....	....	....	....	....
1985-86	**Pittsburgh Penguins**	**NHL**	**69**	**10**	**11**	**21**	**8**	**7**	**15**	**174**	**4**	**0**	**1**	**79**	**12.7**	**33**	**11**	**42**	**1**	**–19**	....	....	....	....	....	....	....	....
1986-87	**Pittsburgh Penguins**	**NHL**	**78**	**14**	**14**	**28**	**12**	**10**	**22**	**218**	**0**	**0**	**1**	**109**	**12.8**	**41**	**2**	**49**	**0**	**–10**	....	....	....	....	....	....	....	....
1987-88	**Pittsburgh Penguins**	**NHL**	**47**	**6**	**8**	**14**	**5**	**6**	**11**	**152**	**1**	**2**	**1**	**66**	**9.1**	**23**	**2**	**34**	**13**	**0**	....	....	....	....	....	....	....	....
1988-89	**Pittsburgh Penguins**	**NHL**	**46**	**3**	**4**	**7**	**3**	**3**	**6**	**66**	**0**	**0**	**1**	**37**	**8.1**	**15**	**1**	**15**	**0**	**–1**	....	....	....	....	....	....	....	....
	Muskegon Lumberjacks	IHL	24	12	16	28	....	....	....	35	....	....	....	....	....	....	....	....	....	....	14	6	4	10	31	....	....	....
1989-90	Muskegon Lumberjacks	IHL	82	31	47	78	....	....	....	165	....	....	....	....	....	....	....	....	....	....	15	9	12	21	51	....	....	....
1990-91	Rochester Americans	AHL	74	15	31	46	....	....	....	152	....	....	....	....	....	....	....	....	....	....	14	4	7	11	34	....	....	....
1991-92	Rochester Americans	AHL	78	28	23	51	....	....	....	208	....	....	....	....	....	....	....	....	....	....	16	7	5	12	35	....	....	....
1992-93	Rochester Americans	AHL	75	17	27	44	....	....	....	216	....	....	....	....	....	....	....	....	....	....	17	1	7	8	70	....	....	....
1993-94			OUT OF HOCKEY – RETIRED																									
1994-95			OUT OF HOCKEY – RETIRED																									
1995-96	Rochester Americans	AHL	77	12	15	27	....	....	....	194	....	....	....	....	....	....	....	....	....	....	19	5	6	11	8	....	....	....
1996-97	Rochester Americans	AHL	77	11	22	33	....	....	....	115	....	....	....	....	....	....	....	....	....	....	10	2	2	4	8	....	....	....
1997-98	Rochester Americans	AHL	75	12	20	32	....	....	....	175	....	....	....	....	....	....	....	....	....	....	4	0	0	0	2	....	....	....
	NHL Totals		**273**	**37**	**40**	**77**	**31**	**28**	**59**	**674**	**5**	**2**	**5**	**317**	**11.7**	**124**	**16**	**156**	**15**		**1**	**0**	**0**	**0**	**0**	**0**	**0**	**0**

Claimed by **Pittsburgh** from **Chicago** in Waiver Draft, October 7, 1985.

• FREADRICH, Kyle

LW – L. 6'6", 225 lbs. b: Edmonton, Alta., 12/28/1978. Vancouver's 4th, 64th overall, in 1997.

Season	Club	League	GP	G	A	Pts	AG	AA	APts	PIM	PP	SH	GW	S	%	TGF	PGF	TGA	PGA	+/–	PO GP	PO G	PO A	PO Pts	PO PIM	PO PP	PO SH	PO GW
1995-96	Killam Selects	AAHA	37	11	22	33	....	....	....	176	....	....	....	....	....	....	....	....	....	....	....	....	....	....	....	....	....	....
1996-97	Prince George Cougars	WHL	12	0	0	0	....	....	....	12	....	....	....	....	....	....	....	....	....	....	....	....	....	....	....	....	....	....
	Regina Pats	WHL	50	1	3	4	....	....	....	152	....	....	....	....	....	....	....	....	....	....	4	0	0	0	8	....	....	....
1997-98	Regina Pats	WHL	62	6	5	11	....	....	....	259	....	....	....	....	....	....	....	....	....	....	9	0	1	1	25	....	....	....
1998-99	Regina Pats	WHL	52	2	2	4	....	....	....	215	....	....	....	....	....	....	....	....	....	....	....	....	....	....	....	....	....	....
	Syracuse Crunch	AHL	5	0	0	0	....	....	....	20	....	....	....	....	....	....	....	....	....	....	....	....	....	....	....	....	....	....
	Louisiana IceGators	ECHL	5	0	0	0	....	....	....	17	....	....	....	....	....	....	....	....	....	....	4	0	0	0	2	....	....	....
99-2000	**Tampa Bay Lightning**	**NHL**	**10**	**0**	**0**	**0**	**0**	**0**	**0**	**39**	**0**	**0**	**0**	**0**	**0.0**	**0**	**0**	**1**	**0**	**–1**	....	....	....	....	....	....	....	....
	Louisiana IceGators	ECHL	3	0	0	0	....	....	....	17	....	....	....	....	....	....	....	....	....	....	....	....	....	....	....	....	....	....
	Detroit Vipers	IHL	45	0	1	1	....	....	....	203	....	....	....	....	....	....	....	....	....	....	....	....	....	....	....	....	....	....
	NHL Totals		**10**	**0**	**0**	**0**	**0**	**0**	**0**	**39**	**0**	**0**	**0**	**0**	**0.0**	**0**	**0**	**1**	**0**		....	....	....	....	....	....	....	....

Signed as a free agent by **Tampa Bay**, July 16, 1999.

• FREER, Mark

Mark Paul C – L. 5'10", 180 lbs. b: Peterborough, Ont., 7/14/1968.

Season	Club	League	GP	G	A	Pts	AG	AA	APts	PIM	PP	SH	GW	S	%	TGF	PGF	TGA	PGA	+/–	PO GP	PO G	PO A	PO Pts	PO PIM	PO PP	PO SH	PO GW
1984-85	Peterborough Midget Petes	OMHA	49	53	68	121	....	....	....	63	....	....	....	....	....	....	....	....	....	....	....	....	....	....	....	....	....	....
1985-86	Peterborough Petes	OHL	65	16	28	44	....	....	....	24	....	....	....	....	....	....	....	....	....	....	14	3	4	7	13	....	....	....
1986-87	Peterborough Petes	OHL	65	39	43	82	....	....	....	44	....	....	....	....	....	....	....	....	....	....	12	2	6	8	5	....	....	....
	Philadelphia Flyers	**NHL**	**1**	**0**	**1**	**1**	**0**	**1**	**1**	**0**	**0**	**0**	**0**	**0**	**0.0**	**1**	**0**	**0**	**0**	**1**	....	....	....	....	....	....	....	....
1987-88	Peterborough Petes	OHL	63	38	70	108	....	....	....	63	....	....	....	....	....	....	....	....	....	....	12	5	12	17	4	....	....	....
	Philadelphia Flyers	**NHL**	**1**	**0**	**0**	**0**	**0**	**0**	**0**	**0**	**0**	**0**	**0**	**0**	**0.0**	**0**	**0**	**2**	**0**	**–2**	....	....	....	....	....	....	....	....
1988-89	**Philadelphia Flyers**	**NHL**	**5**	**0**	**1**	**1**	**0**	**1**	**1**	**0**	**0**	**0**	**0**	**1**	**0.0**	**1**	**0**	**1**	**0**	**0**	....	....	....	....	....	....	....	....
	Hershey Bears	AHL	75	30	49	79	....	....	....	77	....	....	....	....	....	....	....	....	....	....	12	4	6	10	2	....	....	....
1989-90	**Philadelphia Flyers**	**NHL**	**2**	**0**	**0**	**0**	**0**	**0**	**0**	**0**	**0**	**0**	**0**	**2**	**0.0**	**0**	**0**	**0**	**0**	**0**	....	....	....	....	....	....	....	....
	Hershey Bears	AHL	65	28	36	64	....	....	....	31	....	....	....	....	....	....	....	....	....	....	....	....	....	....	....	....	....	....
1990-91	Hershey Bears	AHL	77	18	44	62	....	....	....	45	....	....	....	....	....	....	....	....	....	....	7	1	3	4	17	....	....	....
1991-92	**Philadelphia Flyers**	**NHL**	**50**	**6**	**7**	**13**	**5**	**5**	**10**	**18**	**0**	**0**	**2**	**41**	**14.6**	**16**	**1**	**17**	**1**	**–1**	....	....	....	....	....	....	....	....
	Hershey Bears	AHL	31	13	11	24	....	....	....	38	....	....	....	....	....	....	....	....	....	....	6	0	3	3	2	....	....	....
1992-93	**Ottawa Senators**	**NHL**	**63**	**10**	**14**	**24**	**8**	**10**	**18**	**39**	**3**	**3**	**0**	**80**	**12.5**	**42**	**15**	**86**	**24**	**–35**	....	....	....	....	....	....	....	....
1993-94	**Calgary Flames**	**NHL**	**2**	**0**	**0**	**0**	**0**	**0**	**0**	**4**	**0**	**0**	**0**	**0**	**0.0**	**0**	**0**	**0**	**0**	**0**	....	....	....	....	....	....	....	....
	Saint John Flames	AHL	77	33	53	86	....	....	....	45	....	....	....	....	....	....	....	....	....	....	7	2	4	6	16	....	....	....
1994-95	Houston Aeros	IHL	80	38	42	80	....	....	....	54	....	....	....	....	....	....	....	....	....	....	4	0	1	1	4	....	....	....
	Canada	WC-A	6	1	0	1	....	....	....	2	....	....	....	....	....	....	....	....	....	....	....	....	....	....	....	....	....	....
1995-96	Houston Aeros	IHL	80	22	31	53	....	....	....	67	....	....	....	....	....	....	....	....	....	....	....	....	....	....	....	....	....	....
1996-97	Houston Aeros	IHL	81	21	36	57	....	....	....	43	....	....	....	....	....	....	....	....	....	....	12	2	3	5	4	....	....	....
1997-98	Houston Aeros	IHL	74	14	38	52	....	....	....	41	....	....	....	....	....	....	....	....	....	....	4	2	2	4	4	....	....	....
1998-99	Houston Aeros	IHL	79	17	28	45	....	....	....	66	....	....	....	....	....	....	....	....	....	....	19	*11	11	*22	12	....	....	....
99-2000	Houston Aeros	IHL	75	20	35	55	....	....	....	55	....	....	....	....	....	....	....	....	....	....	11	0	4	4	4	....	....	....
	NHL Totals		**124**	**16**	**23**	**39**	**13**	**17**	**30**	**61**	**3**	**3**	**2**	**124**	**12.9**	**60**	**16**	**106**	**25**		....	....	....	....	....	....	....	....

Won "Bud" Poile Trophy (Playoff MVP - IHL) (1999)

Signed as a free agent by **Philadelphia**, October 7, 1986. Claimed by **Ottawa** from **Philadelphia** in Expansion Draft, June 18, 1992. Signed as a free agent by **Calgary**, August 10, 1993. Signed as a free agent by **Houston** (IHL), July 27, 1994.

• FRIDAY, Tim

D – R. 6', 190 lbs. b: Burbank, CA, 3/5/1961.

Season	Club	League	GP	G	A	Pts	AG	AA	APts	PIM	PP	SH	GW	S	%	TGF	PGF	TGA	PGA	+/–	PO GP	PO G	PO A	PO Pts	PO PIM	PO PP	PO SH	PO GW
1980-81	Marion Hill High School	Hi-School	STATISTICS NOT AVAILABLE																									
1981-82	RPI Engineers	ECAC	25	2	12	14	....	....	....	10	....	....	....	....	....	....	....	....	....	....	....	....	....	....	....	....	....	....
1982-83	RPI Engineers	ECAC	28	3	16	19	....	....	....	10	....	....	....	....	....	....	....	....	....	....	....	....	....	....	....	....	....	....
1983-84	RPI Engineers	ECAC	32	4	14	18	....	....	....	22	....	....	....	....	....	....	....	....	....	....	....	....	....	....	....	....	....	....
1984-85	RPI Engineers	ECAC	36	5	29	34	....	....	....	26	....	....	....	....	....	....	....	....	....	....	....	....	....	....	....	....	....	....
1985-86	**Detroit Red Wings**	**NHL**	**23**	**0**	**3**	**3**	**0**	**2**	**2**	**6**	**0**	**0**	**0**	**13**	**0.0**	**16**	**3**	**23**	**1**	**–9**	....	....	....	....	....	....	....	....
	Adirondack Red Wings	AHL	43	2	31	33	....	....	....	23	....	....	....	....	....	....	....	....	....	....	16	0	6	6	6	....	....	....
	NHL Totals		**23**	**0**	**3**	**3**	**0**	**2**	**2**	**6**	**0**	**0**	**0**	**13**	**0.0**	**16**	**3**	**23**	**1**		....	....	....	....	....	....	....	....

Signed as a free agent by **Detroit**, May 27, 1985. • Suffered eventual career-ending shoulder injury in game vs. Philadelphia, December 3, 1985.

• FRIDGEN, Dan

LW – L. 5'11", 175 lbs. b: Arnprior, Ont., 5/18/1959.

Season	Club	League	GP	G	A	Pts	AG	AA	APts	PIM	PP	SH	GW	S	%	TGF	PGF	TGA	PGA	+/–	PO GP	PO G	PO A	PO Pts	PO PIM	PO PP	PO SH	PO GW
1977-78	Pembroke Lumber Kings	OJHL	STATISTICS NOT AVAILABLE																									
1978-79	Colgate University	ECAC	26	20	12	32	....	....	....	54	....	....	....	....	....	....	....	....	....	....	....	....	....	....	....	....	....	....
1979-80	Colgate University	ECAC	25	19	18	37	....	....	....	74	....	....	....	....	....	....	....	....	....	....	....	....	....	....	....	....	....	....
1980-81	Colgate University	ECAC	33	*37	31	68	....	....	....	*164	....	....	....	....	....	....	....	....	....	....	....	....	....	....	....	....	....	....
1981-82	Colgate University	ECAC	29	*38	17	55	....	....	....	95	....	....	....	....	....	....	....	....	....	....	....	....	....	....	....	....	....	....
	Hartford Whalers	**NHL**	**2**	**0**	**1**	**1**	**0**	**1**	**1**	**0**	**0**	**0**	**0**	**5**	**0.0**	**1**	**1**	**2**	**0**	**–2**	....	....	....	....	....	....	....	....
1982-83	**Hartford Whalers**	**NHL**	**11**	**2**	**2**	**4**	**2**	**1**	**3**	**2**	**0**	**0**	**0**	**12**	**16.7**	**8**	**0**	**6**	**0**	**2**	....	....	....	....	....	....	....	....
	Binghamton Whalers	AHL	48	22	16	38	....	....	....	24	....	....	....	....	....	....	....	....	....	....	4	1	0	1	12	....	....	....
1983-84	Binghamton Whalers	AHL	77	23	27	50	....	....	....	61	....	....	....	....	....	....	....	....	....	....	....	....	....	....	....	....	....	....
1984-85			OUT OF HOCKEY – RETIRED																									
1985-1989	Union College	ECHA	DID NOT PLAY – ASSISTANT COACH																									
1989-1994	RPI Engineers	ECHA	DID NOT PLAY – ASSISTANT COACH																									
1994-2000	RPI Engineers	ECHA	DID NOT PLAY – COACHING																									
	NHL Totals		**13**	**2**	**3**	**5**	**2**	**2**	**4**	**2**	**0**	**0**	**0**	**17**	**11.8**	**9**	**1**	**8**	**0**		....	....	....	....	....	....	....	....

ECAC Second All-Star Team (1981)

Signed as a free agent by **Hartford**, April 5, 1982.

• FRIEDMAN, Doug

Fredrick Douglas LW – L. 6'1", 205 lbs. b: Cape Elizabeth, ME, 9/1/1971. Quebec's 13th, 222nd overall, in 1991.

Season	Club	League	GP	G	A	Pts	AG	AA	APts	PIM	PP	SH	GW	S	%	TGF	PGF	TGA	PGA	+/–	PO GP	PO G	PO A	PO Pts	PO PIM	PO PP	PO SH	PO GW
1989-90	Lawrence Academy	Hi-School	20	9	26	35	....	....	....	....	....	....	....	....	....	....	....	....	....	....	....	....	....	....	....	....	....	....
1990-91	Boston University	H-East	36	6	6	12	....	....	....	37	....	....	....	....	....	....	....	....	....	....	....	....	....	....	....	....	....	....
1991-92	Boston University	H-East	34	11	8	19	....	....	....	42	....	....	....	....	....	....	....	....	....	....	....	....	....	....	....	....	....	....
1992-93	Boston University	H-East	38	17	24	41	....	....	....	62	....	....	....	....	....	....	....	....	....	....	....	....	....	....	....	....	....	....
1993-94	Boston University	H-East	41	9	23	32	....	....	....	110	....	....	....	....	....	....	....	....	....	....	....	....	....	....	....	....	....	....
1994-95	Cornwall Aces	AHL	55	6	9	15	....	....	....	56	....	....	....	....	....	....	....	....	....	....	3	0	0	0	0	....	....	....
1995-96	Cornwall Aces	AHL	80	12	22	34	....	....	....	178	....	....	....	....	....	....	....	....	....	....	8	1	1	2	17	....	....	....
1996-97	Hershey Bears	AHL	61	12	21	33	....	....	....	245	....	....	....	....	....	....	....	....	....	....	23	6	9	15	49	....	....	....
1997-98	**Edmonton Oilers**	**NHL**	**16**	**0**	**0**	**0**	**0**	**0**	**0**	**20**	**0**	**0**	**0**	**8**	**0.0**	**3**	**0**	**5**	**2**	**0**	....	....	....	....	....	....	....	....
	Hamilton Bulldogs	AHL	55	19	27	46	....	....	....	235	....	....	....	....	....	....	....	....	....	....	9	4	4	8	40	....	....	....
1998-99	**Nashville Predators**	**NHL**	**2**	**0**	**1**	**1**	**0**	**1**	**1**	**14**	**0**	**0**	**0**	**3**	**0.0**	**1**	**0**	**1**	**0**	**0**	....	....	....	....	....	....	....	....
	Milwaukee Admirals	IHL	69	26	25	51	....	....	....	251	....	....	....	....	....	....	....	....	....	....	2	1	2	3	8	....	....	....
99-2000	Kentucky Thoroughblades	AHL	73	13	23	36	....	....	....	237	....	....	....	....	....	....	....	....	....	....	9	1	3	4	45	....	....	....
	NHL Totals		**18**	**0**	**1**	**1**	**0**	**1**	**1**	**34**	**0**	**0**	**0**	**11**	**0.0**	**4**	**0**	**6**	**2**		....	....	....	....	....	....	....	....

Rights transferred to **Colorado** after **Quebec** franchise relocated, June 21, 1995. Signed as a free agent by **Edmonton**, July 14, 1997. Claimed by **Nashville** from **Edmonton** in Expansion Draft, June 26, 1998. Signed as a free agent by **San Jose**, August 26, 1999.

• FRIESEN, Jeff

Jeff Daryl C – L. 6'1", 200 lbs. b: Meadow Lake, Sask., 8/5/1976. San Jose's 1st, 11th overall, in 1994.

Season	Club	League	GP	G	A	Pts	AG	AA	APts	PIM	PP	SH	GW	S	%	TGF	PGF	TGA	PGA	+/–	PO GP	PO G	PO A	PO Pts	PO PIM	PO PP	PO SH	PO GW
1991-92	Saskatoon Contacts	SAHA	35	37	51	88	....	....	....	75	....	....	....	....	....	....	....	....	....	....	....	....	....	....	....	....	....	....
	Regina Pats	WHL	4	3	1	4	....	....	....	2	....	....	....	....	....	....	....	....	....	....	....	....	....	....	....	....	....	....
1992-93	Regina Pats	WHL	70	45	38	83	....	....	....	23	....	....	....	....	....	....	....	....	....	....	13	7	10	17	8	....	....	....
1993-94	Regina Pats	WHL	66	51	67	118	....	....	....	48	....	....	....	....	....	....	....	....	....	....	4	3	2	5	2	....	....	....
	Canada	WJC-A	5	0	2	2	....	....	....	0	....	....	....	....	....	....	....	....	....	....	....	....	....	....	....	....	....	....

Season	Club	League	GP	G	A	Pts	AG	AA	APts	PIM	PP	SH	GW	S	%	TGF	PGF	TGA	PGA	+/–	GP	G	A	Pts	PIM	PP	SH	GW
			REGULAR SEASON																		PLAYOFFS							
1994-95	Regina Pats	WHL	25	21	23	44	....	....	....	22	....	....	....	....	....	....	....	....	....	....	....	....	....	....	....	....	....	....
	Canada	WJC-A	7	5	2	7	....	....	....	4	....	....	....	....	....	....	....	....	....	....	....	....	....	....	....	....	....	....
	San Jose Sharks	**NHL**	**48**	**15**	**10**	**25**	**27**	**15**	**42**	**14**	**5**	**1**	**2**	**86**	**17.4**	**40**	**11**	**58**	**21**	**–8**	**11**	**1**	**5**	**6**	**4**	**0**	**0**	**0**
1995-96	**San Jose Sharks**	**NHL**	**79**	**15**	**31**	**46**	**15**	**25**	**40**	**42**	**2**	**0**	**0**	**123**	**12.2**	**73**	**19**	**102**	**29**	**–19**	....	....	....	....	....	....	....	....
	Canada	WC-A	8	2	0	2	....	....	....	6	....	....	....	....	....	....	....	....	....	....	....	....	....	....	....	....	....	....
1996-97	**San Jose Sharks**	**NHL**	**82**	**28**	**34**	**62**	**30**	**30**	**60**	**75**	**6**	**2**	**5**	**200**	**14.0**	**86**	**21**	**96**	**23**	**–8**	....	....	....	....	....	....	....	....
	Canada	WC-A	11	3	4	7	....	....	....	16	....	....	....	....	....	....	....	....	....	....	....	....	....	....	....	....	....	....
1997-98	**San Jose Sharks**	**NHL**	**79**	**31**	**32**	**63**	**36**	**31**	**67**	**40**	**7**	**6**	**7**	**186**	**16.7**	**86**	**30**	**64**	**16**	**8**	**6**	**0**	**1**	**1**	**2**	**0**	**0**	**0**
1998-99	**San Jose Sharks**	**NHL**	**78**	**22**	**35**	**57**	**26**	**34**	**60**	**42**	**10**	**1**	**3**	**215**	**10.2**	**73**	**33**	**52**	**15**	**3**	**6**	**2**	**2**	**4**	**14**	**1**	**0**	**0**
	Canada	WC-A	7	2	2	4	....	....	....	0	....	....	....	....	....	....	....	....	....	....	....	....	....	....	....	....	....	....
99-2000	**San Jose Sharks**	**NHL**	**82**	**26**	**35**	**61**	**29**	**32**	**61**	**47**	**11**	**3**	**7**	**191**	**13.6**	**95**	**41**	**81**	**25**	**–2**	**11**	**2**	**2**	**4**	**10**	**0**	**0**	**0**
	NHL Totals		**448**	**137**	**177**	**314**	**163**	**167**	**330**	**260**	**41**	**13**	**24**	**1001**	**13.7**	**453**	**155**	**453**	**129**		**34**	**5**	**10**	**15**	**30**	**1**	**0**	**0**

Canadian Major Junior Rookie of the Year (1993) • NHL All-Rookie Team (1995)

• FRIEST, Ron Ronald LW – L. 5′11″, 185 lbs. b: Windsor, Ont., 11/4/1958.

Season	Club	League	GP	G	A	Pts	AG	AA	APts	PIM	PP	SH	GW	S	%	TGF	PGF	TGA	PGA	+/–	GP	G	A	Pts	PIM	PP	SH	GW
1976-77	Niagara Falls Flyers	OMJHL	5	1	0	1	....	....	....	2	....	....	....	....	....	....	....	....	....	....	....	....	....	....	....	....	....	....
	Windsor Spitfires	OMJHL	57	19	18	37	....	....	....	52	....	....	....	....	....	....	....	....	....	....	9	4	3	7	11	....	....	....
1977-78	Windsor Spitfires	OMJHL	67	11	20	31	....	....	....	197	....	....	....	....	....	....	....	....	....	....	6	1	1	2	9	....	....	....
1978-79	Oklahoma City Stars	CHL	2	0	4	4	....	....	....	0	....	....	....	....	....	....	....	....	....	....	....	....	....	....	....	....	....	....
	Flint Generals	IHL	54	21	18	39	....	....	....	141	....	....	....	....	....	....	....	....	....	....	11	4	3	7	19	....	....	....
1979-80	Oklahoma City Stars	CHL	11	3	3	6	....	....	....	39	....	....	....	....	....	....	....	....	....	....	....	....	....	....	....	....	....	....
	Baltimore Clippers	EHL	48	35	40	75	....	....	....	162	....	....	....	....	....	....	....	....	....	....	10	8	1	9	49	....	....	....
1980-81	**Minnesota North Stars**	**NHL**	**4**	**1**	**0**	**1**	**1**	**0**	**1**	**10**	**0**	**0**	**0**	**6**	**16.7**	**1**	**0**	**3**	**0**	**–2**	....	....	....	....	....	....	....	....
	Oklahoma City Stars	CHL	71	25	20	45	....	....	....	170	....	....	....	....	....	....	....	....	....	....	3	2	1	3	7	....	....	....
1981-82	**Minnesota North Stars**	**NHL**	**10**	**0**	**0**	**0**	**0**	**0**	**0**	**31**	**0**	**0**	**0**	**5**	**0.0**	**1**	**0**	**5**	**0**	**–4**	**2**	**0**	**0**	**0**	**5**	**0**	**0**	**0**
	Nashville South Stars	CHL	68	32	31	63	....	....	....	199	....	....	....	....	....	....	....	....	....	....	....	....	....	....	....	....	....	....
1982-83	**Minnesota North Stars**	**NHL**	**50**	**6**	**7**	**13**	**5**	**5**	**10**	**150**	**0**	**0**	**0**	**44**	**13.6**	**18**	**0**	**22**	**0**	**–4**	**4**	**1**	**0**	**1**	**2**	**0**	**0**	**0**
	NHL Totals		**64**	**7**	**7**	**14**	**6**	**5**	**11**	**191**	**0**	**0**	**0**	**55**	**12.7**	**20**	**0**	**30**	**0**		**6**	**1**	**0**	**1**	**7**	**0**	**0**	**0**

Signed as a free agent by **Minnesota**, June 26, 1980.

• FRIG, Len Leonard Elroy D – R. 5′11″, 190 lbs. b: Lethbridge, Alta., 10/30/1950. Chicago's 3rd, 42nd overall, in 1970.

Season	Club	League	GP	G	A	Pts	AG	AA	APts	PIM	PP	SH	GW	S	%	TGF	PGF	TGA	PGA	+/–	GP	G	A	Pts	PIM	PP	SH	GW
1967-1969	Lethbridge Sugar Kings	AJHL	STATISTICS NOT AVAILABLE																									
1969-70	Calgary Centennials	WCJHL	59	9	15	24	....	....	....	119	....	....	....	....	....	....	....	....	....	....	16	6	8	14	32	....	....	....
1970-71	Calgary Centennials	WCJHL	51	13	32	45	....	....	....	175	....	....	....	....	....	....	....	....	....	....	....	....	....	....	....	....	....	....
1971-72	Dallas Black Hawks	CHL	66	4	30	34	....	....	....	224	....	....	....	....	....	....	....	....	....	....	12	1	8	9	22	....	....	....
1972-73	Dallas Black Hawks	CHL	72	10	22	32	....	....	....	105	....	....	....	....	....	....	....	....	....	....	7	1	2	3	14	....	....	....
	Chicago Black Hawks	**NHL**	....	....	....	....	....	....	....	....	**0**	**0**	**0**	**0**	**0.0**	**0**	**0**	**0**	**0**	**0**	**4**	**1**	**1**	**2**	**0**	**1**	**0**	**0**
1973-74	**Chicago Black Hawks**	**NHL**	**66**	**4**	**10**	**14**	**4**	**8**	**12**	**35**	**0**	**0**	**0**	**71**	**5.6**	**46**	**7**	**28**	**5**	**16**	**7**	**1**	**0**	**1**	**0**	**1**	**0**	**0**
1974-75	**California Golden Seals**	**NHL**	**80**	**3**	**17**	**20**	**3**	**13**	**16**	**127**	**3**	**0**	**0**	**149**	**2.0**	**91**	**17**	**137**	**35**	**–28**	....	....	....	....	....	....	....	....
1975-76	**California Golden Seals**	**NHL**	**62**	**3**	**12**	**15**	**3**	**9**	**12**	**55**	**1**	**0**	**0**	**108**	**2.8**	**69**	**15**	**82**	**23**	**–5**	....	....	....	....	....	....	....	....
1976-77	**Cleveland Barons**	**NHL**	**66**	**2**	**7**	**9**	**2**	**5**	**7**	**213**	**0**	**0**	**0**	**81**	**2.5**	**47**	**1**	**97**	**20**	**–31**	....	....	....	....	....	....	....	....
1977-78	**St. Louis Blues**	**NHL**	**30**	**1**	**3**	**4**	**1**	**2**	**3**	**45**	**0**	**0**	**1**	**32**	**3.1**	**14**	**1**	**32**	**6**	**–13**	....	....	....	....	....	....	....	....
	Salt Lake Golden Eagles	CHL	29	3	7	10	....	....	....	104	....	....	....	....	....	....	....	....	....	....	6	1	0	1	33	....	....	....
1978-79	Salt Lake Golden Eagles	CHL	76	12	32	44	....	....	....	137	....	....	....	....	....	....	....	....	....	....	10	2	3	5	15	....	....	....
1979-80	**St. Louis Blues**	**NHL**	**7**	**0**	**2**	**2**	**0**	**1**	**1**	**4**	**0**	**0**	**0**	**12**	**0.0**	**5**	**0**	**12**	**2**	**–5**	**3**	**0**	**0**	**0**	**0**	**0**	**0**	**0**
	Salt Lake Golden Eagles	CHL	71	7	33	40	....	....	....	89	....	....	....	....	....	....	....	....	....	....	11	1	6	7	4	....	....	....
1980-81	Salt Lake Golden Eagles	CHL	74	9	48	57	....	....	....	194	....	....	....	....	....	....	....	....	....	....	13	1	2	3	29	....	....	....
1981-82			DID NOT PLAY																									
1982-83			DID NOT PLAY																									
1983-84	Salt Lake Golden Eagles	CHL	2	0	0	0	....	....	....	4	....	....	....	....	....	....	....	....	....	....	....	....	....	....	....	....	....	....
1984-85	Salt Lake Golden Eagles	IHL	78	3	16	19	....	....	....	110	....	....	....	....	....	....	....	....	....	....	5	0	2	2	11	....	....	....
1985-86	Salt Lake Golden Eagles	IHL	18	0	5	5	....	....	....	24	....	....	....	....	....	....	....	....	....	....	....	....	....	....	....	....	....	....
	NHL Totals		**311**	**13**	**51**	**64**	**13**	**38**	**51**	**479**	**4**	**0**	**1**	**453**	**2.9**	**272**	**41**	**388**	**91**		**14**	**2**	**1**	**3**	**0**	**2**	**0**	**0**

WCJHL All-Star Team (1971) • CHL First All-Star Team (1973, 1979, 1980) • Named CHL's Top Defenseman (1973)

Traded to **California** by **Chicago** with Mike Christie for Ivan Boldirev, May 24, 1974. Transferred to **Cleveland** after **California** franchise relocated, August 26, 1976. Traded to **St. Louis** by **Cleveland** for the rights to Mike Eaves, August 17, 1977. • Played w/ RHI's Utah Rollerbees in 1994 (1-0-0-0-12).

• FRYCER, Miroslav Miroslav Opava "Mirko" RW – L. 6′, 200 lbs. b: Ostrava, Czech., 9/27/1959.

Season	Club	League	GP	G	A	Pts	AG	AA	APts	PIM	PP	SH	GW	S	%	TGF	PGF	TGA	PGA	+/–	GP	G	A	Pts	PIM	PP	SH	GW
1976-77	TJ Vitkovice	Czech-Jr.	STATISTICS NOT AVAILABLE																									
	Czechoslovakia	EJC-A	6	2	5	7	....	....	....	12	....	....	....	....	....	....	....	....	....	....	....	....	....	....	....	....	....	....
1977-78	TJ Vitkovice	Czech.	34	12	10	22	....	....	....	24	....	....	....	....	....	....	....	....	....	....	....	....	....	....	....	....	....	....
	Czechoslovakia	WJC-A	6	2	1	3	....	....	....	2	....	....	....	....	....	....	....	....	....	....	....	....	....	....	....	....	....	....
1978-79	TJ Vitkovice	Czech.	44	22	12	34	....	....	....	....	....	....	....	....	....	....	....	....	....	....	....	....	....	....	....	....	....	....
	Czechoslovakia	WJC-A	6	1	0	1	....	....	....	8	....	....	....	....	....	....	....	....	....	....	....	....	....	....	....	....	....	....
	Czechoslovakia	WEC-A	1	0	0	0	....	....	....	2	....	....	....	....	....	....	....	....	....	....	....	....	....	....	....	....	....	....
1979-80	TJ Vitkovice	Czech.	44	31	15	46	....	....	....	....	....	....	....	....	....	....	....	....	....	....	....	....	....	....	....	....	....	....
	Czechoslovakia	Olympics	6	1	2	3	....	....	....	7	....	....	....	....	....	....	....	....	....	....	....	....	....	....	....	....	....	....
1980-81	TJ Vitkovice	Czech.	34	33	24	57	....	....	....	....	....	....	....	....	....	....	....	....	....	....	....	....	....	....	....	....	....	....
	Czechoslovakia	WEC-A	8	1	2	3	....	....	....	0	....	....	....	....	....	....	....	....	....	....	....	....	....	....	....	....	....	....
1981-82	**Quebec Nordiques**	**NHL**	**49**	**20**	**17**	**37**	**16**	**11**	**27**	**47**	**5**	**0**	**2**	**89**	**22.5**	**49**	**10**	**51**	**0**	**–12**	....	....	....	....	....	....	....	....
	Fredericton Express	AHL	11	9	5	14	....	....	....	16	....	....	....	....	....	....	....	....	....	....	....	....	....	....	....	....	....	....
	Toronto Maple Leafs	**NHL**	**10**	**4**	**6**	**10**	**3**	**4**	**7**	**31**	**1**	**0**	**2**	**23**	**17.4**	**11**	**2**	**16**	**0**	**–7**	....	....	....	....	....	....	....	....
1982-83	**Toronto Maple Leafs**	**NHL**	**67**	**25**	**30**	**55**	**20**	**21**	**41**	**90**	**5**	**0**	**4**	**133**	**18.8**	**81**	**23**	**56**	**0**	**2**	**4**	**2**	**5**	**7**	**0**	**0**	**0**	**0**
1983-84	**Toronto Maple Leafs**	**NHL**	**47**	**10**	**16**	**26**	**8**	**11**	**19**	**55**	**1**	**0**	**2**	**78**	**12.8**	**39**	**14**	**49**	**0**	**–24**	....	....	....	....	....	....	....	....
1984-85	**Toronto Maple Leafs**	**NHL**	**65**	**25**	**30**	**55**	**20**	**20**	**40**	**55**	**5**	**0**	**1**	**182**	**13.7**	**76**	**22**	**64**	**3**	**–7**	....	....	....	....	....	....	....	....
1985-86	**Toronto Maple Leafs**	**NHL**	**73**	**32**	**43**	**75**	**26**	**29**	**55**	**74**	**7**	**0**	**3**	**201**	**15.9**	**96**	**29**	**94**	**3**	**–24**	**10**	**1**	**3**	**4**	**10**	**0**	**0**	**0**
1986-87	**Toronto Maple Leafs**	**NHL**	**29**	**7**	**8**	**15**	**6**	**6**	**12**	**28**	**3**	**0**	**0**	**52**	**13.5**	**21**	**7**	**30**	**1**	**–15**	....	....	....	....	....	....	....	....
1987-88	**Toronto Maple Leafs**	**NHL**	**38**	**12**	**20**	**32**	**10**	**14**	**24**	**41**	**1**	**0**	**2**	**76**	**15.8**	**45**	**3**	**34**	**0**	**8**	**3**	**0**	**0**	**0**	**6**	**0**	**0**	**0**
1988-89	**Detroit Red Wings**	**NHL**	**23**	**7**	**8**	**15**	**6**	**6**	**12**	**47**	**2**	**0**	**1**	**40**	**17.5**	**23**	**6**	**23**	**2**	**–4**	....	....	....	....	....	....	....	....
	Edmonton Oilers	**NHL**	**14**	**5**	**5**	**10**	**4**	**4**	**8**	**18**	**2**	**0**	**0**	**33**	**15.2**	**15**	**5**	**8**	**0**	**2**	....	....	....	....	....	....	....	....
1989-90	EHC Freiburg	Germany	36	16	14	30	....	....	....	18	....	....	....	....	....	....	....	....	....	....	11	4	13	17	18	....	....	....
1990-91	EHC Freiburg	Germany	21	11	24	35	....	....	....	28	....	....	....	....	....	....	....	....	....	....	10	7	11	18	11	....	....	....
1991-92	SG Brunico	Alpenliga	18	9	24	33	....	....	....	21	....	....	....	....	....	....	....	....	....	....	....	....	....	....	....	....	....	....
	SG Brunico	Italy	17	19	15	34	....	....	....	16	....	....	....	....	....	....	....	....	....	....	3	1	3	4	4	....	....	....
1992-93	ESV Konigsbrunn	Germany-3	STATISTICS NOT AVAILABLE																									
	NHL Totals		**415**	**147**	**183**	**330**	**119**	**126**	**245**	**486**	**32**	**0**	**17**	**907**	**16.2**	**456**	**121**	**425**	**9**		**17**	**3**	**8**	**11**	**16**	**0**	**0**	**0**

Played in NHL All-Star Game (1985)

Signed as a free agent by **Quebec**, April 2, 1980. Traded to **Toronto** by **Quebec** with Quebec's 7th round choice (Jeff Triano) in 1982 Entry Draft for Wilf Paiement, March 9, 1982. Traded to **Detroit** by **Toronto** for Darren Veitch, June 10, 1988. Traded to **Edmonton** by **Detroit** for Edmonton's 10th round choice (Rick Judson) in 1989 Entry Draft, January 3, 1989.

• FTOREK, Robbie Robert Brian "Britz" C/LW – L. 5′10″, 155 lbs. b: Needham, MA, 1/2/1952. USHOF

Season	Club	League	GP	G	A	Pts	AG	AA	APts	PIM	PP	SH	GW	S	%	TGF	PGF	TGA	PGA	+/–	GP	G	A	Pts	PIM	PP	SH	GW
1968-69	Needham Hilltoppers	Hi-School	18	38	36	74	....	....	....	....	....	....	....	....	....	....	....	....	....	....	....	....	....	....	....	....	....	....
1969-70	Needham Hilltoppers	Hi-School	23	54	64	118	....	....	....	....	....	....	....	....	....	....	....	....	....	....	....	....	....	....	....	....	....	....
1970-71	Halifax Atlantics	MJrHL	28	23	37	60	....	....	....	34	....	....	....	....	....	....	....	....	....	....	12	*15	9	24	18	....	....	....
1971-72	United States	Nat-Team	STATISTICS NOT AVAILABLE																									
	United States	Olympics	6	0	2	2	....	....	....	0	....	....	....	....	....	....	....	....	....	....	....	....	....	....	....	....	....	....
	United States	WEC-B	6	7	3	10	....	....	....	....	....	....	....	....	....	....	....	....	....	....	....	....	....	....	....	....	....	....

			REGULAR SEASON																		PLAYOFFS							
Season	Club	League	GP	G	A	Pts	AG	AA	APts	PIM	PP	SH	GW	S	%	TGF	PGF	TGA	PGA	+/–	GP	G	A	Pts	PIM	PP	SH	GW
1972-73	**Detroit Red Wings**	**NHL**	**3**	**0**	**0**	**0**	**0**	**0**	**0**	**0**	**0**	**0**	**0**	**0**	**0.0**	**0**	**0**	**0**	**0**	**0**	....	....	....	....	....	....	....	....
	Virginia Wings	AHL	55	17	42	59	....	....	....	36	....	....	....	....	....	....	....	....	....	....	5	2	2	4	4	....	....	....
1973-74	**Detroit Red Wings**	**NHL**	**12**	**2**	**5**	**7**	**2**	**4**	**6**	**4**	**1**	**0**	**0**	**10**	**20.0**	**9**	**3**	**5**	**0**	**1**	....	....	....	....	....	....	....	....
	Virginia Wings	AHL	65	24	42	66	....	....	....	37	....	....	....	....	....	....	....	....	....	....	....	....	....	....	....	....	....	....
1974-75	Tulsa Oilers	CHL	11	6	10	16	....	....	....	14	....	....	....	....	....	....	....	....	....	....	....	....	....	....	....	....	....	....
	Phoenix Roadrunners	WHA	53	31	37	68	....	....	....	29	....	....	....	....	....	....	....	....	....	....	5	2	5	7	2	....	....	....
1975-76	Phoenix Roadrunners	WHA	80	41	72	113	....	....	....	109	....	....	....	....	....	....	....	....	....	....	5	1	3	4	2	....	....	....
1976-77	United States	Can-Cup	5	3	2	5	....	....	....	16	....	....	....	....	....	....	....	....	....	....	....	....	....	....	....	....	....	....
	Phoenix Roadrunners	WHA	80	46	71	117	....	....	....	86	....	....	....	....	....	....	....	....	....	....	....	....	....	....	....	....	....	....
1977-78	Cincinnati Stingers	WHA	80	59	50	109	....	....	....	54	....	....	....	....	....	....	....	....	....	....	....	....	....	....	....	....	....	....
1978-79	Cincinnati Stingers	WHA	80	39	*77	116	....	....	....	87	....	....	....	....	....	....	....	....	....	....	3	3	2	5	6	....	....	....
1979-80	**Quebec Nordiques**	**NHL**	**52**	**18**	**33**	**51**	**15**	**24**	**39**	**28**	**7**	**0**	**3**	**112**	**16.1**	**76**	**30**	**47**	**7**	**6**	....	....	....	....	....	....	....	....
1980-81	**Quebec Nordiques**	**NHL**	**78**	**24**	**49**	**73**	**19**	**33**	**52**	**104**	**8**	**0**	**3**	**148**	**16.2**	**98**	**41**	**108**	**32**	**–19**	**5**	**1**	**2**	**3**	**17**	**1**	**0**	**0**
1981-82	United States	Can-Cup	4	0	0	0	....	....	....	0	....	....	....	....	....	....	....	....	....	....	....	....	....	....	....	....	....	....
	Quebec Nordiques	**NHL**	**19**	**1**	**8**	**9**	**1**	**5**	**6**	**4**	**0**	**0**	**0**	**20**	**5.0**	**11**	**3**	**15**	**5**	**–2**	....	....	....	....	....	....	....	....
	New York Rangers	**NHL**	**30**	**8**	**24**	**32**	**6**	**16**	**22**	**24**	**2**	**0**	**2**	**49**	**16.3**	**46**	**7**	**37**	**6**	**8**	**10**	**7**	**4**	**11**	**11**	**4**	**0**	**1**
1982-83	**New York Rangers**	**NHL**	**61**	**12**	**19**	**31**	**10**	**13**	**23**	**41**	**1**	**0**	**0**	**56**	**21.4**	**45**	**2**	**47**	**15**	**11**	**4**	**1**	**0**	**1**	**0**	**0**	**0**	**0**
1983-84	**New York Rangers**	**NHL**	**31**	**3**	**2**	**5**	**2**	**1**	**3**	**22**	**0**	**0**	**1**	**7**	**42.9**	**9**	**0**	**7**	**0**	**2**	....	....	....	....	....	....	....	....
	Tulsa Oilers	CHL	25	11	11	22	....	....	....	10	....	....	....	....	....	....	....	....	....	....	9	4	5	9	2	....	....	....
1984-85	**New York Rangers**	**NHL**	**48**	**9**	**10**	**19**	**7**	**7**	**14**	**35**	**0**	**1**	**1**	**61**	**14.8**	**23**	**0**	**43**	**13**	**–7**	....	....	....	....	....	....	....	....
	New Haven Nighthawks	AHL	17	9	7	16	....	....	....	30	....	....	....	....	....	....	....	....	....	....	....	....	....	....	....	....	....	....
1985-86	New Haven Nighthawks	AHL	1	0	0	0	....	....	....	0	....	....	....	....	....	....	....	....	....	....	....	....	....	....	....	....	....	....
1986-1987	New Haven Nighthawks	AHL	DID NOT PLAY – COACHING																									
1987-1989	**Los Angeles Kings**	**NHL**	DID NOT PLAY – COACHING																									
1989-1990	Halifax Citadels	AHL	DID NOT PLAY – COACHING																									
1990-1991	**Quebec Nordiques**	**NHL**	DID NOT PLAY – ASSISTANT COACH																									
1991-1992	**New Jersey Devils**	**NHL**	DID NOT PLAY – ASSISTANT COACH																									
1992-1993	Utica Devils	AHL	DID NOT PLAY – COACHING																									
1993-1996	Albany River Rats	AHL	DID NOT PLAY – COACHING																									
1996-1998	**New Jersey Devils**	**NHL**	DID NOT PLAY – ASSISTANT COACH																									
1998-2000	**New Jersey Devils**	**NHL**	DID NOT PLAY – COACHING																									
	NHL Totals		**334**	**77**	**150**	**227**	**62**	**103**	**165**	**262**	**19**	**1**	**10**	**463**	**16.6**	**317**	**86**	**309**	**78**		**19**	**9**	**6**	**15**	**28**	**5**	**0**	**1**
	Other Major League Totals		373	216	307	523	....	....	....	365	....	....	....	....	....	....	....	....	....	....	13	6	10	16	10	....	....	....

WEC-B All-Star Team (1972) • WHA Second All-Star Team (1976, 1978) • WHA First All-Star Team (1977, 1979) • Won Gary Davidson Trophy (WHA MVP) (1977)

Selected by **New England** (WHA) in 1972 WHA General Player Draft, February 13, 1972. Signed as a free agent by **Detroit**, August 15, 1972. WHA rights traded to **Phoenix** (WHA) by **New England** (WHA) for cash, June, 1974. Signed as a free agent by **Cincinnati** (WHA) after **Phoenix** (WHA) franchise folded, May 30, 1977. Signed as a free agent by **Quebec**, August 13, 1979. Traded to **NY Rangers** by **Quebec** with Quebec's 8th round choice (Brian Glynn) in 1982 Entry Draft for Jere Gillis and Dean Talafous (later changed to Pat Hickey when Talafous decided to retire), December 30, 1981.

• FULLAN, Larry

Lawrence James LW – L. 5'11", 185 lbs. b: Toronto, Ont., 8/11/1949.

Season	Club	League	GP	G	A	Pts	AG	AA	APts	PIM	PP	SH	GW	S	%	TGF	PGF	TGA	PGA	+/–	GP	G	A	Pts	PIM	PP	SH	GW
1967-68	St. Michael's Buzzers	OHA-B	STATISTICS NOT AVAILABLE																									
1968-69	Colgate University	ECAC	DID NOT PLAY – FRESHMAN																									
1969-70	Cornell University	ECAC	12	28	19	47	....	....	....		....	....	....	....	....	....	....	....	....	....	....	....	....	....	....	....	....	....
1970-71	Cornell University	ECAC	27	20	32	52	....	....	....	12	....	....	....	....	....	....	....	....	....	....	....	....	....	....	....	....	....	....
1971-72	Cornell University	ECAC	29	20	43	63	....	....	....	28	....	....	....	....	....	....	....	....	....	....	....	....	....	....	....	....	....	....
1972-73	Nova Scotia Voyageurs	AHL	50	4	10	14	....	....	....	4	....	....	....	....	....	....	....	....	....	....	13	2	0	2	4	....	....	....
1973-74	Nova Scotia Voyageurs	AHL	76	37	47	84	....	....	....	19	....	....	....	....	....	....	....	....	....	....	6	2	5	7	10	....	....	....
1974-75	**Washington Capitals**	**NHL**	**4**	**1**	**0**	**1**	**1**	**0**	**1**	**0**	**1**	**0**	**0**	**5**	**20.0**	**1**	**1**	**2**	**0**	**–2**	....	....	....	....	....	....	....	....
	Richmond Robins	AHL	71	23	42	65	....	....	....	38	....	....	....	....	....	....	....	....	....	....	7	2	1	3	24	....	....	....
1975-76	Richmond Robins	AHL	76	18	57	75	....	....	....	26	....	....	....	....	....	....	....	....	....	....	8	2	6	8	2	....	....	....
	NHL Totals		**4**	**1**	**0**	**1**	**1**	**0**	**1**	**0**	**1**	**0**	**0**	**5**	**20.0**	**1**	**1**	**2**	**0**		....	....	....	....	....	....	....	....

• OHA-B First All-Star Team (1968) • ECAC First All-Star Team (1972) • NCAA East First All-American Team (1972)

Signed as a free agent by **Montreal**, June, 1972. Claimed by **Washington** from **Montreal** in Expansion Draft, June 12, 1974.

• FUSCO, Mark

D – R. 5'9", 175 lbs. b: Burlington, MA, 3/12/1961.

Season	Club	League	GP	G	A	Pts	AG	AA	APts	PIM	PP	SH	GW	S	%	TGF	PGF	TGA	PGA	+/–	GP	G	A	Pts	PIM	PP	SH	GW
1977-1979	Belmont Hill Hillies	Hi-School	STATISTICS NOT AVAILABLE																									
1979-80	Harvard University	ECAC	26	13	16	29	....	....	....	20	....	....	....	....	....	....	....	....	....	....	....	....	....	....	....	....	....	....
1980-81	Harvard University	ECAC	23	7	13	20	....	....	....	28	....	....	....	....	....	....	....	....	....	....	....	....	....	....	....	....	....	....
	United States	WJC-A	3	0	0	0	....	....	....	2	....	....	....	....	....	....	....	....	....	....	....	....	....	....	....	....	....	....
1981-82	Harvard University	ECAC	30	11	29	40	....	....	....	46	....	....	....	....	....	....	....	....	....	....	....	....	....	....	....	....	....	....
1982-83	Harvard University	ECAC	33	13	33	46	....	....	....	30	....	....	....	....	....	....	....	....	....	....	....	....	....	....	....	....	....	....
1983-84	United States	Nat-Team	50	4	24	28	....	....	....	20	....	....	....	....	....	....	....	....	....	....	....	....	....	....	....	....	....	....
	United States	Olympics	6	0	0	0	....	....	....	6	....	....	....	....	....	....	....	....	....	....	....	....	....	....	....	....	....	....
	Hartford Whalers	**NHL**	**17**	**0**	**4**	**4**	**0**	**3**	**3**	**2**	**0**	**0**	**0**	**17**	**0.0**	**13**	**2**	**20**	**3**	**–6**	....	....	....	....	....	....	....	....
1984-85	United States	Can-Cup	1	0	0	0	....	....	....	2	....	....	....	....	....	....	....	....	....	....	....	....	....	....	....	....	....	....
	Hartford Whalers	**NHL**	**63**	**3**	**8**	**11**	**2**	**5**	**7**	**40**	**0**	**0**	**0**	**70**	**4.3**	**53**	**2**	**83**	**17**	**–15**	....	....	....	....	....	....	....	....
	United States	WEC-A	10	0	1	1	....	....	....	4	....	....	....	....	....	....	....	....	....	....	....	....	....	....	....	....	....	....
	NHL Totals		**80**	**3**	**12**	**15**	**2**	**8**	**10**	**42**	**0**	**0**	**0**	**87**	**3.4**	**66**	**4**	**103**	**20**		....	....	....	....	....	....	....	....

ECAC First All-Star Team (1981, 1983) • NCAA East First All-American Team (1981, 1982, 1983) • ECAC Second All-Star Team (1982) • NCAA Championship All-Tournament Team (1983) • Won Hobey Baker Memorial Award (Top U.S. Collegiate Player) (1983)

Signed as a free agent by **Hartford**, February 25, 1984.

• GAETZ, Link

"Missing Link" D – L. 6'3", 215 lbs. b: Vancouver, B.C., 10/2/1968. Minnesota's 2nd, 40th overall, in 1988.

Season	Club	League	GP	G	A	Pts	AG	AA	APts	PIM	PP	SH	GW	S	%	TGF	PGF	TGA	PGA	+/–	GP	G	A	Pts	PIM	PP	SH	GW
1985-86	Quesnel Millionaires	PCJHL	15	0	7	7	....	....	....	4	....	....	....	....	....	....	....	....	....	....	....	....	....	....	....	....	....	....
	Abbotsford Falcons	BCJHL	2	0	0	0	....	....	....	2	....	....	....	....	....	....	....	....	....	....	....	....	....	....	....	....	....	....
1986-87	New Westminster Bruins	WHL	44	2	7	9	....	....	....	52	....	....	....	....	....	....	....	....	....	....	....	....	....	....	....	....	....	....
	Merritt Centennials	BCJHL	7	4	2	6	....	....	....	27	....	....	....	....	....	....	....	....	....	....	....	....	....	....	....	....	....	....
	Delta Flyers	BCJHL	16	5	10	15	....	....	....	26	....	....	....	....	....	....	....	....	....	....	....	....	....	....	....	....	....	....
1987-88	Spokane Chiefs	WHL	59	9	20	29	....	....	....	313	....	....	....	....	....	....	....	....	....	....	10	2	2	4	70	....	....	....
1988-89	**Minnesota North Stars**	**NHL**	**12**	**0**	**2**	**2**	**0**	**1**	**1**	**53**	**0**	**0**	**0**	**8**	**0.0**	**6**	**1**	**13**	**5**	**–3**	....	....	....	....	....	....	....	....
	Kalamazoo Wings	IHL	37	3	4	7	....	....	....	192	....	....	....	....	....	....	....	....	....	....	5	0	0	0	56	....	....	....
1989-90	**Minnesota North Stars**	**NHL**	**5**	**0**	**0**	**0**	**0**	**0**	**0**	**33**	**0**	**0**	**0**	**4**	**0.0**	**1**	**1**	**5**	**0**	**–5**	....	....	....	....	....	....	....	....
	Kalamazoo Wings	IHL	61	5	16	21	....	....	....	318	....	....	....	....	....	....	....	....	....	....	9	2	2	4	59	....	....	....
1990-91	Minnesota North Stars	Fr-Tour	3	0	0	0	....	....	....	32	....	....	....	....	....	....	....	....	....	....	....	....	....	....	....	....	....	....
	Kansas City Blades	IHL	18	1	10	11	....	....	....	178	....	....	....	....	....	....	....	....	....	....	....	....	....	....	....	....	....	....
	Kalamazoo Wings	IHL	9	0	1	1	....	....	....	44	....	....	....	....	....	....	....	....	....	....	....	....	....	....	....	....	....	....
1991-92	**San Jose Sharks**	**NHL**	**48**	**6**	**6**	**12**	**5**	**5**	**10**	**326**	**3**	**0**	**0**	**73**	**8.2**	**34**	**14**	**52**	**5**	**–27**	....	....	....	....	....	....	....	....
1992-93	Nashville Knights	ECHL	3	1	0	1	....	....	....	10	....	....	....	....	....	....	....	....	....	....	....	....	....	....	....	....	....	....
	Kansas City Blades	IHL	2	0	0	0	....	....	....	14	....	....	....	....	....	....	....	....	....	....	....	....	....	....	....	....	....	....
1993-94	Cape Breton Oilers	AHL	21	0	1	1	....	....	....	140	....	....	....	....	....	....	....	....	....	....	....	....	....	....	....	....	....	....
	Nashville Knights	ECHL	24	1	1	2	....	....	....	261	....	....	....	....	....	....	....	....	....	....	....	....	....	....	....	....	....	....
	West Palm Beach Blaze	SunHL	6	0	3	3	....	....	....	15	....	....	....	....	....	....	....	....	....	....	3	0	1	1	8	....	....	....
1994-95	San Antonio Iguanas	CHL	13	0	3	3	....	....	....	156	....	....	....	....	....	....	....	....	....	....	....	....	....	....	....	....	....	....
1995-96	Mexico City Toreros	NAAHL	STATISTICS NOT AVAILABLE																									
	San Francisco Spiders	IHL	3	0	0	0	....	....	....	32	....	....	....	....	....	....	....	....	....	....	....	....	....	....	....	....	....	....
1996-97	Madison Monsters	ColHL	26	2	4	6	....	....	....	178	....	....	....	....	....	....	....	....	....	....	....	....	....	....	....	....	....	....

			REGULAR SEASON																		PLAYOFFS							
Season	Club	League	GP	G	A	Pts	AG	AA	APts	PIM	PP	SH	GW	S	%	TGF	PGF	TGA	PGA	+/-	GP	G	A	Pts	PIM	PP	SH	GW
1997-98	Anchorage Aces	WCHL	11	0	1	1				130																		
	Miramichi Leafs	NMSHL	STATISTICS NOT AVAILABLE																									
	Miramichi Leafs	Al-Cup	2	0	0	0				4																		
1998-99	Toledo Storm	ECHL	1	0	0	0				2																		
99-2000	Easton Ramblers	WGHL	11	0	0	0				112																		
	NHL Totals		**65**	**6**	**8**	**14**	**5**	**6**	**11**	**412**	**3**	**0**	**0**	**85**	**7.1**	**41**	**16**	**70**	**10**									

Claimed by **San Jose** from **Minnesota** in Dispersal Draft, May 30, 1991. • Missed majority of 1992-93 season recovering from injuries suffered in automobile accident, April 2, 1992. Traded to **Edmonton** by **San Jose** for Edmonton's 10th round choice (Tomas Pisa) in 1994 Entry Draft, September 10, 1993. • Played w/ RHI's Sacramento River Rats in 1994 (8-1-3-4-46).

• GAGE, Jody

Joseph William RW – R. 6', 190 lbs. b: Toronto, Ont., 11/29/1959. Detroit's 2nd, 45th overall, in 1979.

Season	Club	League	GP	G	A	Pts	AG	AA	APts	PIM	PP	SH	GW	S	%	TGF	PGF	TGA	PGA	+/-	GP	G	A	Pts	PIM	PP	SH	GW
1975-76	Toronto Young Nationals	OJHL	53	28	52	80				145																		
1976-77	St. Catharines Fincups	OMJHL	47	13	20	33				2											2	0	0	0	0			
1977-78	Hamilton Fincups	OMJHL	32	15	18	33				19																		
	Kitchener Rangers	OMJHL	36	17	27	44				21											9	4	3	7	4			
1978-79	Kitchener Rangers	OMJHL	58	46	43	89				40											10	1	2	3	6			
1979-80	Adirondack Red Wings	AHL	63	25	21	46				15											5	2	1	3	0			
1980-81	**Detroit Red Wings**	**NHL**	**16**	**2**	**2**	**4**	**2**	**1**	**3**	**22**	**0**	**0**	**0**	**26**	**7.7**	**7**	**1**	**18**	**2**	**–10**								
	Adirondack Red Wings	AHL	59	17	31	48				44											17	9	6	15	12			
1981-82	**Detroit Red Wings**	**NHL**	**31**	**9**	**10**	**19**	**7**	**7**	**14**	**2**	**0**	**0**	**1**	**47**	**19.1**	**35**	**4**	**32**	**0**	**–1**								
	Adirondack Red Wings	AHL	47	21	20	41				21																		
1982-83	Adirondack Red Wings	AHL	65	23	30	53				33											6	1	5	6	8			
1983-84	**Detroit Red Wings**	**NHL**	**3**	**0**	**0**	**0**	**0**	**0**	**0**	**0**	**0**	**0**	**0**	**1**	**0.0**	**0**	**0**	**0**	**0**	**0**								
	Adirondack Red Wings	AHL	73	40	32	72				32											6	3	4	7	2			
1984-85	Adirondack Red Wings	AHL	78	27	33	60				55																		
1985-86	**Buffalo Sabres**	**NHL**	**7**	**3**	**2**	**5**	**2**	**1**	**3**	**0**	**3**	**0**	**0**	**18**	**16.7**	**8**	**3**	**8**	**0**	**–3**								
	Rochester Americans	AHL	73	42	57	99				56																		
1986-87	Rochester Americans	AHL	70	26	39	65				60											17	*14	5	19	24			
1987-88	**Buffalo Sabres**	**NHL**	**2**	**0**	**0**	**0**	**0**	**0**	**0**	**0**	**0**	**0**	**0**	**1**	**0.0**	**0**	**0**	**2**	**0**	**–2**								
	Rochester Americans	AHL	76	*60	44	104				46											5	2	5	7	10			
1988-89	Rochester Americans	AHL	65	31	38	69				60																		
1989-90	Rochester Americans	AHL	75	45	38	83				42											17	4	6	10	12			
1990-91	Rochester Americans	AHL	73	42	43	85				34											15	6	10	16	14			
1991-92	**Buffalo Sabres**	**NHL**	**9**	**0**	**1**	**1**	**0**	**1**	**1**	**2**	**0**	**0**	**0**	**9**	**0.0**	**3**	**2**	**2**	**0**	**–1**								
	Rochester Americans	AHL	67	40	40	80				54											16	5	9	14	10			
1992-93	Rochester Americans	AHL	71	40	40	80				76											9	5	8	13	2			
1993-94	Rochester Americans	AHL	44	18	21	39				57																		
1994-95	Rochester Americans	AHL	23	4	5	9				20											2	0	0	0	0			
1995-96	Rochester Americans	AHL	16	3	12	15				20																		
	NHL Totals		**68**	**14**	**15**	**29**	**11**	**10**	**21**	**26**	**3**	**0**	**1**	**102**	**13.7**	**53**	**10**	**62**	**2**									

AHL First All-Star Team (1986, 1988, 1991) • Won Les Cunningham Award (MVP - AHL) (1988)

Signed as a free agent by **Buffalo**, July 31, 1985.

• GAGNE, Paul

Paul I. LW – L. 5'10", 180 lbs. b: Iroquois Falls, Ont., 2/6/1962. Colorado's 1st, 19th overall, in 1980.

Season	Club	League	GP	G	A	Pts	AG	AA	APts	PIM	PP	SH	GW	S	%	TGF	PGF	TGA	PGA	+/-	GP	G	A	Pts	PIM	PP	SH	GW
1977-78	Iroquois Falls Abitibi	NOJHA	43	45	40	85																						
1978-79	Windsor Spitfires	OMJHL	67	24	18	42				64											7	1	1	2	2			
1979-80	Windsor Spitfires	OMJHL	65	48	53	101				87											13	7	8	15	19			
1980-81	**Colorado Rockies**	**NHL**	**61**	**25**	**16**	**41**	**19**	**11**	**30**	**12**	**9**	**0**	**2**	**99**	**25.3**	**61**	**26**	**59**	**0**	**–24**								
1981-82	**Colorado Rockies**	**NHL**	**59**	**10**	**12**	**22**	**8**	**8**	**16**	**17**	**2**	**0**	**0**	**104**	**9.6**	**39**	**4**	**65**	**3**	**–27**								
1982-83	**New Jersey Devils**	**NHL**	**53**	**14**	**15**	**29**	**11**	**10**	**21**	**13**	**4**	**0**	**3**	**76**	**18.4**	**40**	**10**	**32**	**0**	**–2**								
	Wichita Wind	CHL	16	1	9	10				9																		
1983-84	**New Jersey Devils**	**NHL**	**66**	**14**	**18**	**32**	**11**	**12**	**23**	**33**	**3**	**0**	**1**	**109**	**12.8**	**49**	**5**	**68**	**2**	**–22**								
1984-85	**New Jersey Devils**	**NHL**	**79**	**24**	**19**	**43**	**20**	**13**	**33**	**28**	**3**	**0**	**1**	**152**	**15.8**	**62**	**12**	**61**	**0**	**–11**								
1985-86	**New Jersey Devils**	**NHL**	**47**	**19**	**19**	**38**	**15**	**13**	**28**	**14**	**4**	**0**	**3**	**91**	**20.9**	**55**	**15**	**57**	**2**	**–15**								
1986-87	**New Jersey Devils**	**NHL**	DID NOT PLAY – INJURED																									
1987-88	**New Jersey Devils**	**NHL**	DID NOT PLAY – INJURED																									
1988-89	**Toronto Maple Leafs**	**NHL**	**16**	**3**	**2**	**5**	**3**	**1**	**4**	**6**	**1**	**0**	**1**	**14**	**21.4**	**8**	**1**	**18**	**3**	**–8**								
	Newmarket Saints	AHL	56	33	41	74				29											5	4	4	8	5			
1989-90	Newmarket Saints	AHL	28	13	14	27				11																		
	New York Islanders	**NHL**	**9**	**1**	**0**	**1**	**1**	**0**	**1**	**4**	**0**	**0**	**0**	**10**	**10.0**	**3**	**0**	**4**	**0**	**–1**								
	Springfield Indians	AHL	36	18	29	47				6											13	10	6	16	2			
1990-91	EV Landshut	Germany	44	37	30	67				35											5	7	*7	14	7			
1991-92	EV Landshut	Germany	44	30	23	53				49											8	6	8	14	18			
1992-93	EHC Olten	Switz-2	36	39	28	67				47											7	7	7	14	18			
1993-94	EHC Olten	Switz	30	16	16	32				52											6	4	3	7	35			
1994-95	EHC Olten	Switz-2	32	37	30	67				98											3	1	1	2	35			
1995-96	EHC Olten	Switz-2	28	22	19	41				62																		
	ZSC Zurich	Switz.	8	5	2	7				6											4	0	1	1	8			
1996-97	EHC Biel-Bienne	Switz-2	41	33	33	66				73											4	1	3	4	2			
1997-98	EHC Biel-Bienne	Switz-2	45	34	36	70				75																		
1998-99	EHC Biel-Bienne	Switz-2	40	29	29	58																						
99-2000	EHC Biel-Bienne	Switz-2	DID NOT PLAY – COACHING																									
	NHL Totals		**390**	**110**	**101**	**211**	**88**	**68**	**156**	**127**	**26**	**0**	**11**	**655**	**16.8**	**317**	**73**	**364**	**10**									

OMJHL Second All-Star Team (1980)

Transferred to **New Jersey** after **Colorado** franchise relocated, June 30, 1982. • Missed remainder of 1985-86 and entire 1986-87 and 1987-88 seasons recovering from back injury suffered in game vs. Winnipeg, March 25, 1986. Signed as a free agent by **Toronto**, July 28, 1988. Traded to **NY Islanders** by **Toronto** with Derek Laxdal and Jack Capuano for Gilles Thibaudeau and Mike Stevens, December 20, 1989.

• GAGNE, Simon

C – L. 6', 185 lbs. b: Ste. Foy, Que., 2/29/1980. Philadelphia's 1st, 22nd overall, in 1998.

Season	Club	League	GP	G	A	Pts	AG	AA	APts	PIM	PP	SH	GW	S	%	TGF	PGF	TGA	PGA	+/-	GP	G	A	Pts	PIM	PP	SH	GW
1995-96	Ste-Foy Gouverneurs	QAAA	27	13	9	22				18																		
1996-97	Beauport Harfangs	QMJHL	51	9	22	31				49																		
1997-98	Quebec Remparts	QMJHL	53	30	39	69				26											12	11	5	16	23			
1998-99	Quebec Remparts	QMJHL	61	50	70	120				42											13	9	8	17	4			
	Canada	WJC-A	7	7	1	8				2																		
99-2000	**Philadelphia Flyers**	**NHL**	**80**	**20**	**28**	**48**	**22**	**26**	**48**	**22**	**8**	**1**	**4**	**159**	**12.6**													
	NHL Totals		**80**	**20**	**28**	**48**	**22**	**26**	**48**	**22**	**8**	**1**	**4**	**159**	**12.6**													

QMJHL Second All-Star Team (1999) • NHL All-Rookie Team (2000)

• GAGNER, Dave

David R. C – L. 5'10", 188 lbs. b: Chatham, Ont., 12/11/1964. NY Rangers' 1st, 12th overall, in 1983.

Season	Club	League	GP	G	A	Pts	AG	AA	APts	PIM	PP	SH	GW	S	%	TGF	PGF	TGA	PGA	+/-	GP	G	A	Pts	PIM	PP	SH	GW
1979-80	Chatham Maroons	OHA-B	6	1	0	1				0																		
1980-81	Newmarket Royals	OJHL	41	33	55	88				42																		
1981-82	Brantford Alexanders	OHL	68	30	46	76				31											11	3	6	9	6			
1982-83	Brantford Alexanders	OHL	70	55	66	121				57											8	5	5	10	4			
1983-84	Brantford Alexanders	OHL	12	7	13	20				4											6	0	4	4	6			
	Canada	Nat-Team	50	19	18	37				26																		
	Canada	WJC-A	7	4	2	6				4																		
	Canada	Olympics	7	5	2	7				6																		
1984-85	**New York Rangers**	**NHL**	**38**	**6**	**6**	**12**	**5**	**4**	**9**	**16**	**0**	**1**	**0**	**52**	**11.5**	**20**	**0**	**39**	**3**	**–16**								
	New Haven Nighthawks	AHL	38	13	20	33				23																		

Season	Club	League	GP	G	A	Pts	AG	AA	APts	PIM	PP	SH	GW	S	%	TGF	PGF	TGA	PGA	+/–	GP	G	A	Pts	PIM	PP	SH	GW
			REGULAR SEASON																		PLAYOFFS							
1985-86	**New York Rangers**	**NHL**	**32**	**4**	**6**	**10**	**3**	**4**	**7**	**19**	**0**	**0**	**0**	**41**	**9.8**	**17**	**0**	**17**	**1**	**1**	....	....	....	....	....	....	....	....
	New Haven Nighthawks	AHL	16	10	11	21	....	....	....	11	....	....	....	....	....	....	....	....	....	....	4	1	2	3	2	....	....	....
1986-87	**New York Rangers**	**NHL**	**10**	**1**	**4**	**5**	**1**	**3**	**4**	**12**	**0**	**0**	**0**	**16**	**6.3**	**5**	**0**	**7**	**1**	**–1**	....	....	....	....	....	....	....	....
	New Haven Nighthawks	AHL	56	22	41	63	....	....	....	50	....	....	....	....	....	....	....	....	....	....	7	1	5	6	18	....	....	....
1987-88	**Minnesota North Stars**	**NHL**	**51**	**8**	**11**	**19**	**7**	**8**	**15**	**55**	**0**	**2**	**0**	**87**	**9.2**	**27**	**3**	**64**	**26**	**–14**	....	....	....	....	....	....	....	....
	Kalamazoo Wings	IHL	14	16	10	26	....	....	....	26	....	....	....	....	....	....	....	....	....	....	....	....	....	....	....	....	....	....
1988-89	**Minnesota North Stars**	**NHL**	**75**	**35**	**43**	**78**	**30**	**30**	**60**	**104**	**11**	**3**	**3**	**183**	**19.1**	**110**	**40**	**85**	**28**	**13**	....	....	....	....	....	....	....	....
	Kalamazoo Wings	IHL	1	0	1	1	....	....	....	4	....	....	....	....	....	....	....	....	....	....	....	....	....	....	....	....	....	....
1989-90	**Minnesota North Stars**	**NHL**	**79**	**40**	**38**	**78**	**34**	**27**	**61**	**54**	**10**	**0**	**3**	**238**	**16.8**	**94**	**34**	**67**	**6**	**–1**	**7**	**2**	**3**	**5**	**16**	**1**	**0**	**0**
1990-91	Minnesota North Stars	Fr-Tour	2	0	0	0	....	....	....	2	....	....	....	....	....	....	....	....	....	....	....	....	....	....	....	....	....	....
	Minnesota North Stars	**NHL**	**73**	**40**	**42**	**82**	**37**	**32**	**69**	**114**	**20**	**0**	**5**	**223**	**17.9**	**108**	**46**	**62**	**9**	**9**	**23**	**12**	**15**	**27**	**28**	**6**	**1**	**1**
1991-92	**Minnesota North Stars**	**NHL**	**78**	**31**	**40**	**71**	**28**	**30**	**58**	**107**	**17**	**0**	**3**	**229**	**13.5**	**99**	**45**	**58**	**0**	**–4**	**7**	**2**	**4**	**6**	**8**	**2**	**0**	**0**
1992-93	**Minnesota North Stars**	**NHL**	**84**	**33**	**43**	**76**	**27**	**30**	**57**	**143**	**17**	**0**	**5**	**230**	**14.3**	**103**	**53**	**63**	**0**	**–13**	....	....	....	....	....	....	....	....
	Canada	WC-A	8	3	1	4	....	....	....	6	....	....	....	....	....	....	....	....	....	....	....	....	....	....	....	....	....	....
1993-94	**Dallas Stars**	**NHL**	**76**	**32**	**29**	**61**	**30**	**22**	**52**	**83**	**10**	**0**	**6**	**213**	**15.0**	**90**	**39**	**38**	**0**	**13**	**9**	**5**	**1**	**6**	**2**	**3**	**0**	**0**
1994-95	HC Courmaosta	Italy	3	0	0	0	....	....	....	0	....	....	....	....	....	....	....	....	....	....	....	....	....	....	....	....	....	....
	HC Courmaosta	EuroHL	1	0	4	4	....	....	....	0	....	....	....	....	....	....	....	....	....	....	....	....	....	....	....	....	....	....
	Dallas Stars	**NHL**	**48**	**14**	**28**	**42**	**25**	**41**	**66**	**42**	**7**	**0**	**2**	**138**	**10.1**	**55**	**25**	**30**	**2**	**2**	**5**	**1**	**1**	**2**	**4**	**1**	**0**	**0**
1995-96	**Dallas Stars**	**NHL**	**45**	**14**	**13**	**27**	**14**	**11**	**25**	**44**	**6**	**0**	**2**	**145**	**9.7**	**41**	**23**	**37**	**2**	**–17**	....	....	....	....	....	....	....	....
	Toronto Maple Leafs	**NHL**	**28**	**7**	**15**	**22**	**7**	**12**	**19**	**59**	**1**	**0**	**1**	**70**	**10.0**	**28**	**6**	**35**	**11**	**–2**	**6**	**0**	**2**	**2**	**6**	**0**	**0**	**0**
1996-97	**Calgary Flames**	**NHL**	**82**	**27**	**33**	**60**	**29**	**29**	**58**	**48**	**9**	**0**	**4**	**228**	**11.8**	**87**	**31**	**69**	**15**	**2**	....	....	....	....	....	....	....	....
1997-98	**Florida Panthers**	**NHL**	**78**	**20**	**28**	**48**	**23**	**27**	**50**	**55**	**5**	**1**	**1**	**165**	**12.1**	**63**	**26**	**63**	**5**	**–21**	....	....	....	....	....	....	....	....
1998-99	**Florida Panthers**	**NHL**	**36**	**4**	**10**	**14**	**5**	**10**	**15**	**39**	**2**	**0**	**0**	**50**	**8.0**	**21**	**13**	**15**	**0**	**–7**	....	....	....	....	....	....	....	....
	Vancouver Canucks	**NHL**	**33**	**2**	**12**	**14**	**2**	**12**	**14**	**24**	**0**	**0**	**1**	**50**	**4.0**	**17**	**6**	**20**	**0**	**–9**	....	....	....	....	....	....	....	....
	NHL Totals		**946**	**318**	**401**	**719**	**307**	**332**	**639**	**1018**	**115**	**7**	**36**	**2358**	**13.5**	**985**	**390**	**769**	**109**		**57**	**22**	**26**	**48**	**64**	**13**	**1**	**1**

OHL Second All-Star Team (1983) • Played in NHL All-Star Game (1991)

Traded to **Minnesota** by **NY Rangers** with Jay Caufield for Jari Gronstrand and Paul Boutilier, October 8, 1987. Transferred to **Dallas** after **Minnesota** franchise relocated, June 9, 1993. Traded to **Toronto** by **Dallas** with Dallas' 6th round choice (Dmitriy Yakushin) in 1996 Entry Draft for Benoit Hogue and Randy Wood, January 29, 1996. Traded to **Calgary** by **Toronto** for Calgary's 3rd round choice (Mike Lankshear) in 1996 Entry Draft, June 22, 1996. Signed as a free agent by **Florida**, July 12, 1997. Traded to **Vancouver** by **Florida** with Ed Jovanovski, Mike Brown, Kevin Weekes and Florida's 1st round choice (Nathan Smith) in 2000 Entry Draft for Pavel Bure, Bret Hedican, Brad Ference and Vancouver's 3rd round choice (Robert Fried) in 2000 Entry Draft, January 17, 1999.

• GAGNON, Germaine

LW – L. 6', 175 lbs. b: Chicoutimi, Que., 12/9/1942.

Season	Club	League	GP	G	A	Pts	AG	AA	APts	PIM	PP	SH	GW	S	%	TGF	PGF	TGA	PGA	+/–	GP	G	A	Pts	PIM	PP	SH	GW
1960-61	Lachine Maroons	MMJHL	STATISTICS NOT AVAILABLE																									
	Hull Canadiens	Al-Cup	3	0	0	0	....	....	....	0	....	....	....	....	....	....	....	....	....	....	....	....	....	....	....	....	....	....
1961-62	Montreal Jr. Canadiens	OHA-Jr.	48	20	37	57	....	....	....	63	....	....	....	....	....	....	....	....	....	....	6	3	4	7	4	....	....	....
1962-63	Montreal Jr. Canadiens	OHA-Jr.	50	19	38	57	....	....	....	72	....	....	....	....	....	....	....	....	....	....	10	3	4	7	16	....	....	....
	Hull-Ottawa Canadiens	EPHL	1	0	0	0	....	....	....	0	....	....	....	....	....	....	....	....	....	....	....	....	....	....	....	....	....	....
1963-64	Omaha Knights	CPHL	59	10	25	35	....	....	....	32	....	....	....	....	....	....	....	....	....	....	10	7	4	11	6	....	....	....
1964-65	Quebec Aces	AHL	14	2	7	9	....	....	....	10	....	....	....	....	....	....	....	....	....	....	....	....	....	....	....	....	....	....
	Omaha Knights	CPHL	55	13	25	38	....	....	....	73	....	....	....	....	....	....	....	....	....	....	6	0	1	1	11	....	....	....
1965-66	Houston Apollos	CPHL	64	14	30	44	....	....	....	58	....	....	....	....	....	....	....	....	....	....	....	....	....	....	....	....	....	....
1966-67	Quebec Aces	AHL	7	0	1	1	....	....	....	0	....	....	....	....	....	....	....	....	....	....	....	....	....	....	....	....	....	....
	Providence Reds	AHL	5	0	0	0	....	....	....	0	....	....	....	....	....	....	....	....	....	....	....	....	....	....	....	....	....	....
	Houston Apollos	CPHL	30	6	10	16	....	....	....	43	....	....	....	....	....	....	....	....	....	....	5	2	2	4	0	....	....	....
1967-68	Memphis South Stars	CPHL	65	26	34	60	....	....	....	23	....	....	....	....	....	....	....	....	....	....	3	0	0	0	0	....	....	....
1968-69	Vancouver Canucks	WHL	61	8	21	29	....	....	....	16	....	....	....	....	....	....	....	....	....	....	8	1	2	3	0	....	....	....
1969-70	Vancouver Canucks	WHL	72	16	27	43	....	....	....	23	....	....	....	....	....	....	....	....	....	....	11	2	3	5	4	....	....	....
1970-71	Montreal Voyageurs	AHL	61	20	28	48	....	....	....	36	....	....	....	....	....	....	....	....	....	....	3	3	1	4	0	....	....	....
1971-72	**Montreal Canadiens**	**NHL**	**4**	**0**	**0**	**0**	**0**	**0**	**0**	**0**	**0**	**0**	**0**	**3**	**0.0**	**1**	**0**	**1**	**0**	**0**	....	....	....	....	....	....	....	....
	Nova Scotia Voyageurs	AHL	70	25	56	81	....	....	....	34	....	....	....	....	....	....	....	....	....	....	15	5	*15	20	8	....	....	....
1972-73	**New York Islanders**	**NHL**	**63**	**12**	**29**	**41**	**11**	**23**	**34**	**31**	**3**	**1**	**1**	**126**	**9.5**	**62**	**14**	**86**	**14**	**–24**	....	....	....	....	....	....	....	....
1973-74	**New York Islanders**	**NHL**	**62**	**8**	**14**	**22**	**8**	**12**	**20**	**8**	**0**	**0**	**0**	**68**	**11.8**	**35**	**7**	**49**	**27**	**6**	....	....	....	....	....	....	....	....
	Chicago Black Hawks	**NHL**	**14**	**3**	**14**	**17**	**3**	**12**	**15**	**4**	**0**	**0**	**1**	**19**	**15.8**	**23**	**2**	**15**	**0**	**6**	**11**	**2**	**2**	**4**	**2**	**1**	**0**	**1**
1974-75	**Chicago Black Hawks**	**NHL**	**80**	**16**	**35**	**51**	**14**	**26**	**40**	**21**	**8**	**0**	**2**	**97**	**16.5**	**85**	**39**	**53**	**12**	**5**	**8**	**0**	**1**	**1**	**0**	**0**	**0**	**0**
1975-76	**Chicago Black Hawks**	**NHL**	**5**	**0**	**0**	**0**	**0**	**0**	**0**	**2**	**0**	**0**	**0**	**10**	**0.0**	**1**	**1**	**1**	**0**	**–1**	....	....	....	....	....	....	....	....
	Springfield Indians	AHL	4	0	1	1	....	....	....	2	....	....	....	....	....	....	....	....	....	....	....	....	....	....	....	....	....	....
	Kansas City Scouts	**NHL**	**31**	**1**	**9**	**10**	**1**	**7**	**8**	**6**	**1**	**0**	**0**	**30**	**3.3**	**17**	**5**	**28**	**2**	**–14**	....	....	....	....	....	....	....	....
	New Haven Nighthawks	AHL	26	12	16	28	....	....	....	14	....	....	....	....	....	....	....	....	....	....	3	1	0	1	0	....	....	....
	NHL Totals		**259**	**40**	**101**	**141**	**37**	**80**	**117**	**72**	**12**	**1**	**4**	**353**	**11.3**	**224**	**68**	**233**	**55**		**19**	**2**	**3**	**5**	**2**	**1**	**0**	**1**

Loaned to **Vancouver** (WHL) by **Montreal** for cash, October 10, 1968. Claimed by **Salt Lake** (WHL) from **Montreal** in Reverse Draft, June 12, 1969. Traded to **Vancouver** (WHL) by **Salt Lake** (WHL) with cash for Billy McNeill, August 19, 1969. • Rights transferred to **Vancouver** when NHL club purchased **Vancouver** (WHL) franchise, December 19, 1969. Traded to **Montreal** by **Vancouver** for cash, November 3, 1970. Traded to **NY Islanders** by **Montreal** to complete transaction that sent Denis DeJordy, Tony Featherstone, Murray Anderson, Chico Resch and Alec Campbell to NY Islanders (June 6, 1972), June 26, 1972. Traded to **Chicago** by **NY Islanders** for cash and future considerations (Walt Ledingham, May 24, 1974), March 7, 1974. Claimed on waivers by **Kansas City** from **Chicago**, October 28, 1975.

• GAGNON, Sean

D – L. 6'2", 219 lbs. b: Sault Ste. Marie, Ont., 9/11/1973.

Season	Club	League	GP	G	A	Pts	AG	AA	APts	PIM	PP	SH	GW	S	%	TGF	PGF	TGA	PGA	+/–	GP	G	A	Pts	PIM	PP	SH	GW
1989-90	Sault Ste. Marie Elks	NOHA	46	21	26	47	....	....	....	218	....	....	....	....	....	....	....	....	....	....	....	....	....	....	....	....	....	....
1990-91			STATISTICS NOT AVAILABLE																									
	Sudbury Wolves	OHL	4	3	4	7	....	....	....	60	....	....	....	....	....	....	....	....	....	....	....	....	....	....	....	....	....	....
1991-92	Sudbury Wolves	OHL	44	3	4	7	....	....	....	60	....	....	....	....	....	....	....	....	....	....	5	0	1	1	0	....	....	....
1992-93	Sudbury Wolves	OHL	6	1	1	2	....	....	....	16	....	....	....	....	....	....	....	....	....	....	....	....	....	....	....	....	....	....
	Ottawa 67's	OHL	33	2	10	12	....	....	....	68	....	....	....	....	....	....	....	....	....	....	....	....	....	....	....	....	....	....
	Sault Ste. Marie Greyhounds	OHL	24	1	5	6	....	....	....	65	....	....	....	....	....	....	....	....	....	....	15	2	2	4	25	....	....	....
	Sault Ste. Marie Greyhounds	Mem-Cup	4	0	1	1	....	....	....	8	....	....	....	....	....	....	....	....	....	....	....	....	....	....	....	....	....	....
1993-94	Sault Ste. Marie Greyhounds	OHL	42	4	12	16	....	....	....	147	....	....	....	....	....	....	....	....	....	....	14	1	1	2	52	....	....	....
1994-95	Dayton Bombers	ECHL	68	9	23	32	....	....	....	339	....	....	....	....	....	....	....	....	....	....	8	0	3	3	69	....	....	....
1995-96	Dayton Bombers	ECHL	68	7	22	29	....	....	....	326	....	....	....	....	....	....	....	....	....	....	3	0	1	1	33	....	....	....
1996-97	Fort Wayne Komets	IHL	72	7	7	14	....	....	....	*457	....	....	....	....	....	....	....	....	....	....	....	....	....	....	....	....	....	....
1997-98	**Phoenix Coyotes**	**NHL**	**5**	**0**	**1**	**1**	**0**	**1**	**1**	**14**	**0**	**0**	**0**	**3**	**0.0**	**2**	**0**	**1**	**0**	**1**	....	....	....	....	....	....	....	....
	Springfield Falcons	AHL	54	4	13	17	....	....	....	330	....	....	....	....	....	....	....	....	....	....	2	0	1	1	17	....	....	....
1998-99	**Phoenix Coyotes**	**NHL**	**2**	**0**	**0**	**0**	**0**	**0**	**0**	**7**	**0**	**0**	**0**	**1**	**0.0**	**0**	**0**	**2**	**0**	**–2**	....	....	....	....	....	....	....	....
	Springfield Falcons	AHL	68	8	14	22	....	....	....	331	....	....	....	....	....	....	....	....	....	....	3	0	0	0	14	....	....	....
99-2000	Jokerit Helsinki	Finland	42	3	5	8	....	....	....	183	....	....	....	....	....	....	....	....	....	....	11	4	1	5	22	....	....	....
	NHL Totals		**7**	**0**	**1**	**1**	**0**	**1**	**1**	**21**	**0**	**0**	**0**	**4**	**0.0**	**2**	**0**	**3**	**0**		....	....	....	....	....	....	....	....

Signed as a free agent by **Phoenix**, May 14, 1997. Signed as a free agent by **Ottawa**, July 7, 2000.

• GAINEY, Bob

Robert Michael LW – L. 6'2", 200 lbs. b: Peterborough, Ont., 12/13/1953. Montreal's 1st, 8th overall, in 1973. **HHOF**

Season	Club	League	GP	G	A	Pts	AG	AA	APts	PIM	PP	SH	GW	S	%	TGF	PGF	TGA	PGA	+/–	GP	G	A	Pts	PIM	PP	SH	GW
1970-71	Peterborough Jr. Petes	OHA-B	STATISTICS NOT AVAILABLE																									
	Peterborough Petes	OHA-Jr.	....	....	....	....	....	....	....	....	....	....	....	....	....	....	....	....	....	....	4	0	0	0	4	....	....	....
1971-72	Peterborough Jr. Petes	OHA-B	STATISTICS NOT AVAILABLE																									
	Peterborough Petes	OMJHL	4	2	1	3	....	....	....	33	....	....	....	....	....	....	....	....	....	....	....	....	....	....	....	....	....	....
1972-73	Peterborough Petes	OMJHL	52	22	21	43	....	....	....	99	....	....	....	....	....	....	....	....	....	....	....	....	....	....	....	....	....	....
1973-74	**Montreal Canadiens**	**NHL**	**66**	**3**	**7**	**10**	**3**	**6**	**9**	**34**	**0**	**0**	**0**	**55**	**5.5**	**19**	**0**	**28**	**0**	**–9**	**6**	**0**	**0**	**0**	**6**	**0**	**0**	**0**
	Nova Scotia Voyageurs	AHL	6	2	5	7	....	....	....	4	....	....	....	....	....	....	....	....	....	....	....	....	....	....	....	....	....	....
1974-75	**Montreal Canadiens**	**NHL**	**80**	**17**	**20**	**37**	**15**	**15**	**30**	**49**	**1**	**0**	**2**	**132**	**12.9**	**66**	**4**	**42**	**3**	**23**	**11**	**2**	**4**	**6**	**4**	**0**	**0**	**1**
1975-76♦	**Montreal Canadiens**	**NHL**	**78**	**15**	**13**	**28**	**13**	**10**	**23**	**57**	**1**	**2**	**1**	**155**	**9.7**	**49**	**2**	**46**	**19**	**20**	**13**	**1**	**3**	**4**	**20**	**0**	**0**	**0**
1976-77	Canada	Can-Cup	5	2	0	2	....	....	....	2	....	....	....	....	....	....	....	....	....	....	....	....	....	....	....	....	....	....
♦	**Montreal Canadiens**	**NHL**	**80**	**14**	**19**	**33**	**13**	**15**	**28**	**41**	**0**	**1**	**3**	**143**	**9.8**	**61**	**0**	**41**	**11**	**31**	**14**	**4**	**1**	**5**	**25**	**0**	**1**	**1**
1977-78♦	**Montreal Canadiens**	**NHL**	**66**	**15**	**16**	**31**	**14**	**12**	**26**	**57**	**0**	**2**	**1**	**140**	**10.7**	**50**	**8**	**49**	**18**	**11**	**15**	**2**	**7**	**9**	**14**	**0**	**1**	**0**

Season	Club	League	GP	G	A	Pts	AG	AA	APts	PIM	PP	SH	GW	S	%	TGF	PGF	TGA	PGA	+/–	GP	G	A	Pts	PIM	PP	SH	GW
			REGULAR SEASON																		PLAYOFFS							
1978-79♦	**Montreal Canadiens**	**NHL**	**79**	**20**	**18**	**38**	**17**	**13**	**30**	**44**	**1**	**1**	**1**	**153**	**13.1**	**68**	**1**	**71**	**15**	**11**	**16**	**6**	**10**	**16**	**10**	**0**	**0**	**1**
1979-80	**Montreal Canadiens**	**NHL**	**64**	**14**	**19**	**33**	**12**	**14**	**26**	**32**	**4**	**1**	**3**	**153**	**9.2**	**65**	**16**	**72**	**21**	**–2**	**10**	**1**	**1**	**2**	**4**	**0**	**0**	**1**
1980-81	**Montreal Canadiens**	**NHL**	**78**	**23**	**24**	**47**	**18**	**16**	**34**	**36**	**5**	**3**	**3**	**181**	**12.7**	**86**	**15**	**87**	**29**	**13**	**3**	**0**	**0**	**0**	**2**	**0**	**0**	**0**
1981-82	Canada	Can-Cup	7	1	3	4	....	....	....	2	....	....	....	....	....	....	....	....	....	....	....	....	....	....	....	....	....	....
	Montreal Canadiens	**NHL**	**79**	**21**	**24**	**45**	**17**	**16**	**33**	**24**	**1**	**3**	**1**	**172**	**12.2**	**76**	**4**	**67**	**32**	**37**	**5**	**0**	**1**	**1**	**8**	**0**	**0**	**0**
	Canada	WEC-A	10	2	1	3	....	....	....	0	....	....	....	....	....	....	....	....	....	....	....	....	....	....	....	....	....	....
1982-83	**Montreal Canadiens**	**NHL**	**80**	**12**	**18**	**30**	**10**	**12**	**22**	**43**	**0**	**1**	**3**	**150**	**8.0**	**63**	**0**	**92**	**36**	**7**	**3**	**0**	**0**	**0**	**4**	**0**	**0**	**0**
	Canada	WEC-A	10	0	6	6	....	....	....	2	....	....	....	....	....	....	....	....	....	....	....	....	....	....	....	....	....	....
1983-84	**Montreal Canadiens**	**NHL**	**77**	**17**	**22**	**39**	**14**	**15**	**29**	**41**	**0**	**0**	**3**	**125**	**13.6**	**65**	**1**	**76**	**22**	**10**	**15**	**1**	**5**	**6**	**9**	**0**	**0**	**0**
1984-85	**Montreal Canadiens**	**NHL**	**79**	**19**	**13**	**32**	**15**	**9**	**24**	**40**	**0**	**3**	**3**	**166**	**11.4**	**67**	**1**	**83**	**30**	**13**	**12**	**1**	**3**	**4**	**13**	**0**	**0**	**0**
1985-86♦	**Montreal Canadiens**	**NHL**	**80**	**20**	**23**	**43**	**16**	**15**	**31**	**20**	**0**	**2**	**4**	**135**	**14.8**	**66**	**0**	**94**	**38**	**10**	**20**	**5**	**5**	**10**	**12**	**0**	**1**	**3**
1986-87	**Montreal Canadiens**	**NHL**	**47**	**8**	**8**	**16**	**7**	**6**	**13**	**19**	**0**	**1**	**3**	**73**	**11.0**	**27**	**0**	**45**	**18**	**0**	**17**	**1**	**3**	**4**	**6**	**0**	**0**	**0**
1987-88	**Montreal Canadiens**	**NHL**	**78**	**11**	**11**	**22**	**9**	**8**	**17**	**14**	**0**	**0**	**1**	**101**	**10.9**	**34**	**0**	**60**	**34**	**8**	**6**	**0**	**1**	**1**	**6**	**0**	**0**	**0**
1988-89	**Montreal Canadiens**	**NHL**	**49**	**10**	**7**	**17**	**8**	**5**	**13**	**34**	**1**	**0**	**2**	**65**	**15.4**	**35**	**1**	**39**	**18**	**13**	**16**	**1**	**4**	**5**	**8**	**0**	**0**	**0**
1989-90	Epinal Squirrels	France-2	18	14	12	26	....	....	....	16	....	....	....	....	....	....	....	....	....	....	10	6	7	13	14	....	....	....
1990-1993	**Minnesota North Stars**	**NHL**	DID NOT PLAY – COACHING																									
1993-1996	**Dallas Stars**	**NHL**	DID NOT PLAY – COACHING																									
1996-2000	**Dallas Stars**	**NHL**	DID NOT PLAY – GENERAL MANAGER																									
	NHL Totals		**1160**	**239**	**262**	**501**	**201**	**187**	**388**	**585**	**14**	**20**	**34**	**2099**	**11.4**	**897**	**53**	**992**	**344**		**182**	**25**	**48**	**73**	**151**	**0**	**3**	**7**

Won Frank J. Selke Trophy (1978, 1979, 1980, 1981) • Won Conn Smythe Trophy (1979) • Played in NHL All-Star Game (1977, 1978, 1980, 1981)

• GALANOV, Maxim

D – L. 6'1", 205 lbs. b: Krasnoyarsk, USSR, 3/13/1974. NY Rangers' 3rd, 61st overall, in 1993.

Season	Club	League	GP	G	A	Pts	AG	AA	APts	PIM	PP	SH	GW	S	%	TGF	PGF	TGA	PGA	+/–	GP	G	A	Pts	PIM	PP	SH	GW
1992-93	Lada Togliatti	CIS	41	4	2	6	....	....	....	12	....	....	....	....	....	....	....	....	....	....	10	1	1	2	12	....	....	....
	Russia	WJC-A	7	1	0	1	....	....	....	4	....	....	....	....	....	....	....	....	....	....	....	....	....	....	....	....	....	....
1993-94	Lada Togliatti	CIS	7	1	0	1	....	....	....	4	....	....	....	....	....	....	....	....	....	....	12	1	0	1	8	....	....	....
1994-95	Lada Togliatti	CIS	45	5	6	11	....	....	....	54	....	....	....	....	....	....	....	....	....	....	9	0	1	1	12	....	....	....
1995-96	Binghamton Rangers	AHL	72	17	36	53	....	....	....	24	....	....	....	....	....	....	....	....	....	....	4	1	1	2	0	....	....	....
1996-97	Binghamton Rangers	AHL	73	13	30	43	....	....	....	30	....	....	....	....	....	....	....	....	....	....	3	0	0	0	2	....	....	....
1997-98	**New York Rangers**	**NHL**	**6**	**0**	**1**	**1**	**0**	**1**	**1**	**2**	**0**	**0**	**0**	**5**	**0.0**	**7**	**2**	**4**	**0**	**1**	....	....	....	....	....	....	....	....
	Hartford Wolf Pack	AHL	61	6	24	30	....	....	....	22	....	....	....	....	....	....	....	....	....	....	13	3	6	9	2	....	....	....
1998-99	**Pittsburgh Penguins**	**NHL**	**51**	**4**	**3**	**7**	**5**	**3**	**8**	**14**	**2**	**0**	**0**	**44**	**9.1**	**32**	**9**	**35**	**4**	**–8**	**1**	**0**	**0**	**0**	**0**	**0**	**0**	**0**
99-2000	**Atlanta Thrashers**	**NHL**	**40**	**4**	**3**	**7**	**4**	**3**	**7**	**20**	**0**	**0**	**0**	**47**	**8.5**	**25**	**4**	**53**	**20**	**–12**	....	....	....	....	....	....	....	....
	Russia	WC-A	6	0	0	0	....	....	....	0	....	....	....	....	....	....	....	....	....	....	....	....	....	....	....	....	....	....
	NHL Totals		**97**	**8**	**7**	**15**	**9**	**7**	**16**	**36**	**2**	**0**	**0**	**96**	**8.3**	**64**	**15**	**92**	**24**		**1**	**0**	**0**	**0**	**0**	**0**	**0**	**0**

Claimed by **Pittsburgh** from **NY Rangers** in NHL Waiver Draft, October 5, 1998. Claimed by **Atlanta** from **Pittsburgh** in Expansion Draft, June 25, 1999. • Missed majority of 1999-2000 season recovering from hand injury suffered in game vs. NY Rangers, October 17, 1999.

• GALARNEAU, Michel

C – R. 6'2", 180 lbs. b: Montreal, Que., 3/1/1961. Hartford's 2nd, 29th overall, in 1980.

Season	Club	League	GP	G	A	Pts	AG	AA	APts	PIM	PP	SH	GW	S	%	TGF	PGF	TGA	PGA	+/–	GP	G	A	Pts	PIM	PP	SH	GW
1976-77	Rosemont Selectes	QAAA	STATISTICS NOT AVAILABLE																									
1977-78	Hull Olympiques	QMJHL	3	1	0	1	....	....	....	0	....	....	....	....	....	....	....	....	....	....	....	....	....	....	....	....	....	....
1978-79	Hull Olympiques	QMJHL	67	22	37	59	....	....	....	70	....	....	....	....	....	....	....	....	....	....	....	....	....	....	....	....	....	....
1979-80	Hull Olympiques	QMJHL	72	39	64	103	....	....	....	49	....	....	....	....	....	....	....	....	....	....	4	3	1	4	12	....	....	....
1980-81	Hull Olympiques	QMJHL	30	9	21	30	....	....	....	48	....	....	....	....	....	....	....	....	....	....	....	....	....	....	....	....	....	....
	Hartford Whalers	**NHL**	**30**	**2**	**6**	**8**	**2**	**4**	**6**	**9**	**0**	**0**	**1**	**19**	**10.5**	**12**	**1**	**23**	**0**	**–12**	....	....	....	....	....	....	....	....
	Binghamton Whalers	AHL	9	1	0	1	....	....	....	4	....	....	....	....	....	....	....	....	....	....	5	0	1	1	0	....	....	....
1981-82	**Hartford Whalers**	**NHL**	**10**	**0**	**0**	**0**	**0**	**0**	**0**	**4**	**0**	**0**	**0**	**10**	**0.0**	**1**	**0**	**8**	**0**	**–7**	....	....	....	....	....	....	....	....
	Binghamton Whalers	AHL	64	15	17	32	....	....	....	52	....	....	....	....	....	....	....	....	....	....	14	2	0	2	2	....	....	....
1982-83	**Hartford Whalers**	**NHL**	**38**	**5**	**4**	**9**	**4**	**3**	**7**	**21**	**0**	**0**	**0**	**29**	**17.2**	**14**	**0**	**22**	**0**	**–8**	....	....	....	....	....	....	....	....
	Binghamton Whalers	AHL	25	4	6	10	....	....	....	20	....	....	....	....	....	....	....	....	....	....	....	....	....	....	....	....	....	....
1983-84	Fredericton Express	AHL	2	0	0	0	....	....	....	0	....	....	....	....	....	....	....	....	....	....	....	....	....	....	....	....	....	....
	Binghamton Whalers	AHL	4	1	0	1	....	....	....	0	....	....	....	....	....	....	....	....	....	....	....	....	....	....	....	....	....	....
	Montana Magic	CHL	66	18	22	40	....	....	....	44	....	....	....	....	....	....	....	....	....	....	....	....	....	....	....	....	....	....
1984-85	SC Eindhoven	Holland	STATISTICS NOT AVAILABLE																									
1985-86	HC Amiens	France	STATISTICS NOT AVAILABLE																									
1986-87	HC Amiens	France	30	51	33	84	....	....	....	....	....	....	....	....	....	....	....	....	....	....	....	....	....	....	....	....	....	....
1987-88	HC Amiens	France	30	28	22	50	....	....	....	36	....	....	....	....	....	....	....	....	....	....	....	....	....	....	....	....	....	....
1988-89	HC Amiens	France	3	2	1	3	....	....	....	2	....	....	....	....	....	....	....	....	....	....	....	....	....	....	....	....	....	....
1989-90	HC Amiens	France	12	11	8	19	....	....	....	13	....	....	....	....	....	....	....	....	....	....	3	2	0	2	2	....	....	....
1990-91	HC Amiens	France	28	13	15	28	....	....	....	34	....	....	....	....	....	....	....	....	....	....	4	4	1	5	14	....	....	....
1991-92	HC Briacon	France	32	25	24	49	....	....	....	50	....	....	....	....	....	....	....	....	....	....	....	....	....	....	....	....	....	....
1992-93	HC Anglet	France-2	26	22	23	45	....	....	....	26	....	....	....	....	....	....	....	....	....	....	....	....	....	....	....	....	....	....
1993-94	HC Brest	France-2	26	21	20	41	....	....	....	51	....	....	....	....	....	....	....	....	....	....	....	....	....	....	....	....	....	....
1994-95	HC Brest	France	27	14	19	33	....	....	....	54	....	....	....	....	....	....	....	....	....	....	9	4	2	6	2	....	....	....
	France	WC-A	6	1	1	2	....	....	....	2	....	....	....	....	....	....	....	....	....	....	....	....	....	....	....	....	....	....
1995-96	HC Brest	France	27	9	12	21	....	....	....	38	....	....	....	....	....	....	....	....	....	....	10	0	5	5	37	....	....	....
1996-97	HC Brest	France	30	5	11	16	....	....	....	55	....	....	....	....	....	....	....	....	....	....	10	2	5	7	14	....	....	....
1997-98	HC Brest	France-3	STATISTICS NOT AVAILABLE																									
1998-99	HC Brest	France-2	28	31	27	58	....	....	....	....	....	....	....	....	....	....	....	....	....	....	....	....	....	....	....	....	....	....
99-2000	HC Brest	France-2	29	13	16	29	....	....	....	....	....	....	....	....	....	....	....	....	....	....	....	....	....	....	....	....	....	....
	NHL Totals		**78**	**7**	**10**	**17**	**6**	**7**	**13**	**34**	**0**	**0**	**1**	**58**	**12.1**	**27**	**1**	**53**	**0**		....	....	....	....	....	....	....	....

• GALLANT, Gerard

Gerard A. LW – L. 5'10", 190 lbs. b: Summerside, P.E.I., 9/2/1963. Detroit's 4th, 107th overall, in 1981.

Season	Club	League	GP	G	A	Pts	AG	AA	APts	PIM	PP	SH	GW	S	%	TGF	PGF	TGA	PGA	+/–	GP	G	A	Pts	PIM	PP	SH	GW
1979-80	Summerside Crystals	MJrHL	45	60	55	115	....	....	....	90	....	....	....	....	....	....	....	....	....	....	....	....	....	....	....	....	....	....
1980-81	Sherbrooke Beavers	QMJHL	68	41	59	100	....	....	....	265	....	....	....	....	....	....	....	....	....	....	14	6	13	19	46	....	....	....
1981-82	Sherbrooke Beavers	QMJHL	58	34	58	92	....	....	....	260	....	....	....	....	....	....	....	....	....	....	22	14	24	38	84	....	....	....
	Sherbrooke Beavers	Mem-Cup	5	5	3	8	....	....	....	28	....	....	....	....	....	....	....	....	....	....	....	....	....	....	....	....	....	....
1982-83	St-Jean Beavers	QMJHL	33	28	25	53	....	....	....	139	....	....	....	....	....	....	....	....	....	....	....	....	....	....	....	....	....	....
	Verdun Juniors	QMJHL	29	26	49	75	....	....	....	105	....	....	....	....	....	....	....	....	....	....	15	*14	19	*33	84	....	....	....
	Verdun Juniors	Mem-Cup	4	3	1	4	....	....	....	23	....	....	....	....	....	....	....	....	....	....	....	....	....	....	....	....	....	....
1983-84	Adirondack Red Wings	AHL	77	31	33	64	....	....	....	195	....	....	....	....	....	....	....	....	....	....	7	1	3	4	34	....	....	....
1984-85	**Detroit Red Wings**	**NHL**	**32**	**6**	**12**	**18**	**5**	**8**	**13**	**66**	**0**	**0**	**2**	**44**	**13.6**	**26**	**0**	**17**	**0**	**9**	**3**	**0**	**0**	**0**	**11**	**0**	**0**	**0**
	Adirondack Red Wings	AHL	46	18	29	47	....	....	....	131	....	....	....	....	....	....	....	....	....	....	....	....	....	....	....	....	....	....
1985-86	**Detroit Red Wings**	**NHL**	**52**	**20**	**19**	**39**	**16**	**13**	**29**	**106**	**3**	**1**	**2**	**116**	**17.2**	**58**	**10**	**66**	**8**	**–10**	....	....	....	....	....	....	....	....
1986-87	**Detroit Red Wings**	**NHL**	**80**	**38**	**34**	**72**	**33**	**25**	**58**	**216**	**17**	**0**	**4**	**191**	**19.9**	**106**	**43**	**71**	**3**	**–5**	**16**	**8**	**6**	**14**	**43**	**2**	**0**	**0**
1987-88	**Detroit Red Wings**	**NHL**	**73**	**34**	**39**	**73**	**29**	**28**	**57**	**242**	**10**	**0**	**3**	**197**	**17.3**	**118**	**41**	**58**	**5**	**24**	**16**	**6**	**9**	**15**	**55**	**1**	**0**	**1**
1988-89	**Detroit Red Wings**	**NHL**	**76**	**39**	**54**	**93**	**33**	**38**	**71**	**230**	**13**	**0**	**7**	**221**	**17.6**	**140**	**52**	**84**	**3**	**7**	**6**	**1**	**2**	**3**	**40**	**0**	**0**	**0**
	Canada	WEC-A	8	2	3	5	....	....	....	10	....	....	....	....	....	....	....	....	....	....	....	....	....	....	....	....	....	....
1989-90	**Detroit Red Wings**	**NHL**	**69**	**36**	**44**	**80**	**31**	**32**	**63**	**254**	**12**	**3**	**5**	**219**	**16.4**	**120**	**41**	**96**	**11**	**–6**	....	....	....	....	....	....	....	....
1990-91	**Detroit Red Wings**	**NHL**	**45**	**10**	**16**	**26**	**9**	**12**	**21**	**111**	**3**	**0**	**1**	**82**	**12.2**	**57**	**15**	**36**	**0**	**6**	....	....	....	....	....	....	....	....
1991-92	**Detroit Red Wings**	**NHL**	**69**	**14**	**22**	**36**	**13**	**17**	**30**	**187**	**4**	**0**	**1**	**116**	**12.1**	**61**	**11**	**35**	**1**	**16**	**11**	**2**	**2**	**4**	**25**	**0**	**0**	**1**
1992-93	**Detroit Red Wings**	**NHL**	**67**	**10**	**20**	**30**	**8**	**14**	**22**	**188**	**0**	**0**	**0**	**81**	**12.3**	**53**	**3**	**30**	**0**	**20**	**6**	**1**	**2**	**3**	**4**	**0**	**0**	**0**
1993-94	**Tampa Bay Lightning**	**NHL**	**51**	**4**	**9**	**13**	**4**	**7**	**11**	**74**	**1**	**0**	**2**	**45**	**8.9**	**17**	**2**	**22**	**1**	**–6**	....	....	....	....	....	....	....	....
1994-95	**Tampa Bay Lightning**	**NHL**	**1**	**0**	**0**	**0**	**0**	**0**	**0**	**0**	**0**	**0**	**0**	**1**	**0.0**	**0**	**0**	**0**	**0**	**0**	....	....	....	....	....	....	....	....
	Atlanta Knights	IHL	16	3	3	6	....	....	....	31	....	....	....	....	....	....	....	....	....	....	....	....	....	....	....	....	....	....
1995-96	Detroit Vipers	IHL	3	2	1	3	....	....	....	6	....	....	....	....	....	....	....	....	....	....	....	....	....	....	....	....	....	....
	Summerside Capitals	MJrHL	DID NOT PLAY – COACHING																									

Season	Club	League	GP	G	A	Pts	AG	AA	APts	PIM	PP	SH	GW	S	%	TGF	PGF	TGA	PGA	+/–	GP	G	A	Pts	PIM	PP	SH	GW
			REGULAR SEASON																		PLAYOFFS							
1996-1998	Summerside Capitals	MJrHL	DID NOT PLAY – COACHING																									
1998-1999	Fort Wayne Komets	IHL	DID NOT PLAY – ASSISTANT COACH																									
1999-2000	Louisville Panthers	AHL	DID NOT PLAY – ASSISTANT COACH																									
	NHL Totals		**615**	**211**	**269**	**480**	**181**	**194**	**375**	**1674**	**63**	**4**	**27**	**1313**	**16.1**	**756**	**218**	**515**	**32**		**58**	**18**	**21**	**39**	**178**	**3**	**0**	**2**

NHL Second All-Star Team (1989)

Signed as a free agent by **Tampa Bay**, July 21, 1993. Signed as a free agent by **Detroit Vipers** (IHL), October 23, 1995. • Suffered career-ending back injury in practice, November 4, 1995. • Named Assistant Coach of **Columbus**, July 18, 2000.

• GALLEY, Garry

Garry Michael "Ga-Ga" D – L. 6', 202 lbs. b: Montreal, Que., 4/16/1963. Los Angeles' 4th, 103rd overall, in 1983.

Season	Club	League	GP	G	A	Pts	AG	AA	APts	PIM	PP	SH	GW	S	%	TGF	PGF	TGA	PGA	+/–	GP	G	A	Pts	PIM	PP	SH	GW
1979-80	Ottawa 79's	OMHA	STATISTICS NOT AVAILABLE																									
	Ottawa Jr. Senators	OJHL	2	1	0	1	....	....	....	4	....	....	....	....	....	....	....	....	....	....	....	....	....	....	....	....	....	....
1980-81	Gloucester Rangers	OJHL	49	18	26	44	....	....	....	103	....	....	....	....	....	....	....	....	....	....	....	....	....	....	....	....	....	....
1981-82	Bowling Green University	CCHA	42	3	36	39	....	....	....	48	....	....	....	....	....	....	....	....	....	....	....	....	....	....	....	....	....	....
1982-83	Bowling Green University	CCHA	40	17	29	46	....	....	....	40	....	....	....	....	....	....	....	....	....	....	....	....	....	....	....	....	....	....
1983-84	Bowling Green University	CCHA	44	15	52	67	....	....	....	61	....	....	....	....	....	....	....	....	....	....	....	....	....	....	....	....	....	....
1984-85	**Los Angeles Kings**	**NHL**	**78**	**8**	**30**	**38**	**6**	**20**	**26**	**82**	**1**	**1**	**2**	**131**	**6.1**	**101**	**15**	**94**	**11**	**3**	**3**	**1**	**0**	**1**	**2**	**0**	**0**	**0**
1985-86	**Los Angeles Kings**	**NHL**	**49**	**9**	**13**	**22**	**7**	**9**	**16**	**46**	**1**	**0**	**1**	**57**	**15.8**	**58**	**7**	**75**	**15**	**–9**	....	....	....	....	....	....	....	....
	New Haven Nighthawks	AHL	4	2	6	8	....	....	....	6	....	....	....	....	....	....	....	....	....	....	....	....	....	....	....	....	....	....
1986-87	**Los Angeles Kings**	**NHL**	**30**	**5**	**11**	**16**	**4**	**8**	**12**	**57**	**2**	**0**	**1**	**43**	**11.6**	**28**	**6**	**37**	**6**	**–9**	....	....	....	....	....	....	....	....
	Washington Capitals	**NHL**	**18**	**1**	**10**	**11**	**1**	**7**	**8**	**10**	**1**	**0**	**0**	**27**	**3.7**	**20**	**12**	**5**	**0**	**3**	**2**	**0**	**0**	**0**	**0**	**0**	**0**	**0**
1987-88	**Washington Capitals**	**NHL**	**58**	**7**	**23**	**30**	**6**	**16**	**22**	**44**	**3**	**0**	**0**	**100**	**7.0**	**63**	**31**	**24**	**3**	**11**	**13**	**2**	**4**	**6**	**13**	**0**	**0**	**0**
1988-89	**Boston Bruins**	**NHL**	**78**	**8**	**22**	**30**	**7**	**16**	**23**	**80**	**2**	**1**	**0**	**145**	**5.5**	**71**	**24**	**65**	**11**	**–7**	**9**	**0**	**1**	**1**	**33**	**0**	**0**	**0**
1989-90	**Boston Bruins**	**NHL**	**71**	**8**	**27**	**35**	**7**	**19**	**26**	**75**	**1**	**0**	**0**	**142**	**5.6**	**79**	**8**	**85**	**16**	**2**	**21**	**3**	**3**	**6**	**34**	**1**	**0**	**2**
1990-91	**Boston Bruins**	**NHL**	**70**	**6**	**21**	**27**	**5**	**16**	**21**	**84**	**1**	**0**	**0**	**128**	**4.7**	**79**	**17**	**83**	**21**	**0**	**16**	**1**	**5**	**6**	**17**	**0**	**0**	**0**
1991-92	**Boston Bruins**	**NHL**	**38**	**2**	**12**	**14**	**2**	**9**	**11**	**83**	**1**	**0**	**0**	**51**	**3.9**	**42**	**6**	**50**	**11**	**–3**	....	....	....	....	....	....	....	....
	Philadelphia Flyers	**NHL**	**39**	**3**	**15**	**18**	**3**	**11**	**14**	**34**	**2**	**0**	**1**	**74**	**4.1**	**42**	**11**	**43**	**13**	**1**	....	....	....	....	....	....	....	....
1992-93	**Philadelphia Flyers**	**NHL**	**83**	**13**	**49**	**62**	**11**	**34**	**45**	**115**	**4**	**1**	**3**	**231**	**5.6**	**146**	**42**	**142**	**56**	**18**	....	....	....	....	....	....	....	....
	Canada	WC-A	8	1	2	3	....	....	....	0	....	....	....	....	....	....	....	....	....	....	....	....	....	....	....	....	....	....
1993-94	**Philadelphia Flyers**	**NHL**	**81**	**10**	**60**	**70**	**9**	**47**	**56**	**91**	**5**	**1**	**0**	**186**	**5.4**	**145**	**63**	**133**	**40**	**–11**	....	....	....	....	....	....	....	....
1994-95	**Philadelphia Flyers**	**NHL**	**33**	**2**	**20**	**22**	**4**	**30**	**34**	**20**	**1**	**0**	**0**	**66**	**3.0**	**49**	**25**	**34**	**10**	**0**	....	....	....	....	....	....	....	....
	Buffalo Sabres	**NHL**	**14**	**1**	**9**	**10**	**2**	**13**	**15**	**10**	**2**	**0**	**0**	**31**	**3.2**	**29**	**13**	**13**	**1**	**4**	**5**	**0**	**3**	**3**	**4**	**0**	**0**	**0**
1995-96	**Buffalo Sabres**	**NHL**	**78**	**10**	**44**	**54**	**10**	**36**	**46**	**81**	**7**	**1**	**2**	**175**	**5.7**	**116**	**53**	**94**	**29**	**–2**	....	....	....	....	....	....	....	....
	Canada	WC-A	8	0	2	2	....	....	....	6	....	....	....	....	....	....	....	....	....	....	....	....	....	....	....	....	....	....
1996-97	**Buffalo Sabres**	**NHL**	**71**	**4**	**34**	**38**	**4**	**30**	**34**	**102**	**1**	**1**	**1**	**84**	**4.8**	**83**	**26**	**61**	**14**	**10**	**12**	**0**	**6**	**6**	**14**	**0**	**0**	**0**
1997-98	**Los Angeles Kings**	**NHL**	**74**	**9**	**28**	**37**	**11**	**27**	**38**	**63**	**7**	**0**	**0**	**128**	**7.0**	**81**	**29**	**66**	**9**	**–5**	**4**	**0**	**1**	**1**	**2**	**0**	**0**	**0**
1998-99	**Los Angeles Kings**	**NHL**	**60**	**4**	**12**	**16**	**5**	**12**	**17**	**30**	**3**	**0**	**0**	**77**	**5.2**	**40**	**8**	**45**	**4**	**–9**	....	....	....	....	....	....	....	....
99-2000	**Los Angeles Kings**	**NHL**	**70**	**9**	**21**	**30**	**10**	**19**	**29**	**52**	**2**	**0**	**1**	**96**	**9.4**	**77**	**23**	**58**	**13**	**9**	**4**	**0**	**0**	**0**	**0**	**0**	**0**	**0**
	NHL Totals		**1093**	**119**	**461**	**580**	**114**	**379**	**493**	**1159**	**47**	**6**	**12**	**1972**	**6.0**	**1349**	**419**	**1207**	**283**		**89**	**7**	**23**	**30**	**119**	**1**	**0**	**2**

CCHA First All-Star Team (1983, 1984) • NCAA East First All-American Team (1984) • NCAA Championship All-Tournament Team (1984) • Played in NHL All-Star Game (1991, 1994)

Traded to **Washington** by **LA Kings** for Al Jensen, February 14, 1987. Signed as a free agent by **Boston**, July 8, 1988. Traded to **Philadelphia** by **Boston** with Wes Walz and Boston's 3rd round choice (Milos Holan) in 1993 Entry Draft for Gord Murphy, Brian Dobbin, Philadelphia's 3rd round choice (Sergei Zholtok) in 1992 Entry Draft and 4th round choice (Charles Paquette) in 1993 Entry Draft, January 2, 1992. Traded to **Buffalo** by **Philadelphia** for Petr Svoboda, April 7, 1995. Signed as a free agent by **LA Kings**, July 15, 1997.

• GALLIMORE, Jamie

James Wilfred RW – R. 6', 180 lbs. b: Edmonton, Alta., 11/28/1957. Minnesota's 5th, 97th overall, in 1977.

Season	Club	League	GP	G	A	Pts	AG	AA	APts	PIM	PP	SH	GW	S	%	TGF	PGF	TGA	PGA	+/–	GP	G	A	Pts	PIM	PP	SH	GW
1973-74	Edmonton Mets	AAHA	STATISTICS NOT AVAILABLE																									
1974-75	Kamloops Chiefs	WCJHL	56	3	5	8	....	....	....	50	....	....	....	....	....	....	....	....	....	....	3	0	1	1	27	....	....	....
1975-76	Kamloops Chiefs	WCJHL	28	5	7	12	....	....	....	57	....	....	....	....	....	....	....	....	....	....	1	0	0	0	0	....	....	....
1976-77	Kamloops Chiefs	WCJHL	72	24	22	46	....	....	....	121	....	....	....	....	....	....	....	....	....	....	6	1	1	2	2	....	....	....
1977-78	**Minnesota North Stars**	**NHL**	**2**	**0**	**0**	**0**	**0**	**0**	**0**	**0**	**0**	**0**	**0**	**0**	**0.0**	**0**	**0**	**0**	**0**	**0**	....	....	....	....	....	....	....	....
	Fort Wayne Komets	IHL	23	6	6	12	....	....	....	21	....	....	....	....	....	....	....	....	....	....	....	....	....	....	....	....	....	....
	Fort Worth Texans	CHL	47	8	2	10	....	....	....	24	....	....	....	....	....	....	....	....	....	....	9	0	0	0	29	....	....	....
1978-79	Oklahoma City Stars	CHL	38	8	6	14	....	....	....	26	....	....	....	....	....	....	....	....	....	....	....	....	....	....	....	....	....	....
1979-80	Oklahoma City Stars	CHL	67	5	8	13	....	....	....	35	....	....	....	....	....	....	....	....	....	....	....	....	....	....	....	....	....	....
1980-81			DID NOT PLAY																									
1981-82	Wichita Wind	CHL	3	0	1	1	....	....	....	11	....	....	....	....	....	....	....	....	....	....	....	....	....	....	....	....	....	....
	NHL Totals		**2**	**0**	**0**	**0**	**0**	**0**	**0**	**0**	**0**	**0**	**0**	**0**	**0.0**	**0**	**0**	**0**	**0**		....	....	....	....	....	....	....	....

• GAMBUCCI, Gary

Gary Allan C – L. 5'9", 175 lbs. b: Hibbing, MN, 9/27/1946.

Season	Club	League	GP	G	A	Pts	AG	AA	APts	PIM	PP	SH	GW	S	%	TGF	PGF	TGA	PGA	+/–	GP	G	A	Pts	PIM	PP	SH	GW
1965-66	University of Minnesota	WCHA	28	23	17	40	....	....	....	18	....	....	....	....	....	....	....	....	....	....	....	....	....	....	....	....	....	....
1966-67	University of Minnesota	WCHA	29	17	10	27	....	....	....	23	....	....	....	....	....	....	....	....	....	....	....	....	....	....	....	....	....	....
1967-68	University of Minnesota	WCHA	31	12	29	41	....	....	....	31	....	....	....	....	....	....	....	....	....	....	....	....	....	....	....	....	....	....
1968-69	United States	Nat-Team	STATISTICS NOT AVAILABLE																									
	United States	WEC-A	10	1	1	2	....	....	....	6	....	....	....	....	....	....	....	....	....	....	....	....	....	....	....	....	....	....
1969-70	Rochester Mustangs	USHL	STATISTICS NOT AVAILABLE																									
	United States	Nat-Team	6	3	1	4	....	....	....	4	....	....	....	....	....	....	....	....	....	....	....	....	....	....	....	....	....	....
	United States	WEC-B	7	*11	7	18	....	....	....	4	....	....	....	....	....	....	....	....	....	....	....	....	....	....	....	....	....	....
	Muskegon Mohawks	IHL	4	2	1	3	....	....	....	5	....	....	....	....	....	....	....	....	....	....	....	....	....	....	....	....	....	....
1970-71	United States	Nat-Team	....	51	47	98	....	....	....	....	....	....	....	....	....	....	....	....	....	....	....	....	....	....	....	....	....	....
	United States	WEC-A	10	7	3	10	....	....	....	4	....	....	....	....	....	....	....	....	....	....	....	....	....	....	....	....	....	....
1971-72	**Minnesota North Stars**	**NHL**	**9**	**1**	**0**	**1**	**1**	**0**	**1**	**0**	**0**	**0**	**0**	**3**	**33.3**	**3**	**1**	**0**	**0**	**2**	....	....	....	....	....	....	....	....
	Cleveland Barons	AHL	56	10	11	21	....	....	....	37	....	....	....	....	....	....	....	....	....	....	6	0	0	0	10	....	....	....
1972-73	Cleveland-Jacksonville Barons	AHL	75	26	50	76	....	....	....	47	....	....	....	....	....	....	....	....	....	....	....	....	....	....	....	....	....	....
1973-74	**Minnesota North Stars**	**NHL**	**42**	**1**	**7**	**8**	**1**	**6**	**7**	**9**	**0**	**0**	**0**	**26**	**3.8**	**15**	**2**	**12**	**4**	**5**	....	....	....	....	....	....	....	....
	New Haven Nighthawks	AHL	2	1	2	3	....	....	....	2	....	....	....	....	....	....	....	....	....	....	....	....	....	....	....	....	....	....
	Portland Buckaroos	WHL	21	11	15	26	....	....	....	20	....	....	....	....	....	....	....	....	....	....	....	....	....	....	....	....	....	....
1974-75	Minnesota Fighting Saints	WHA	67	19	18	37	....	....	....	19	....	....	....	....	....	....	....	....	....	....	12	4	0	4	6	....	....	....
1975-76	Minnesota Fighting Saints	WHA	45	10	6	16	....	....	....	14	....	....	....	....	....	....	....	....	....	....	....	....	....	....	....	....	....	....
	United States	WEC-A	10	1	4	5	....	....	....	17	....	....	....	....	....	....	....	....	....	....	....	....	....	....	....	....	....	....
	NHL Totals		**51**	**2**	**7**	**9**	**2**	**6**	**8**	**9**	**0**	**0**	**0**	**29**	**6.9**	**18**	**3**	**12**	**4**		....	....	....	....	....	....	....	....
	Other Major League Totals		112	29	24	53	....	....	....	33	....	....	....	....	....	....	....	....	....	....	12	4	0	4	6	....	....	....

WCHA Second All-Star Team (1966) • WCHA First All-Star Team (1968) • NCAA West First All-American Team (1968) • WEC-B All-Star Team (1970)

Signed as a free agent by **Montreal**, May, 1971. Rights traded to **Minnesota** by **Montreal** with Bob Paradise for cash and future considerations, May, 1971. Selected by **Miami-Philadelphia** (WHA) in 1972 WHA General Player Draft, February 12, 1972. WHA rights transferred to **Vancouver** after **Philadelphia** franchise relocated, May, 1973. WHA rights traded to **Minnesota** (WHA) by **Vancouver** (WHA) for cash, June, 1974.

• GANCHAR, Perry

RW – R. 5'9", 180 lbs. b: Saskatoon, Sask., 10/28/1963. St. Louis' 3rd, 113th overall, in 1982.

Season	Club	League	GP	G	A	Pts	AG	AA	APts	PIM	PP	SH	GW	S	%	TGF	PGF	TGA	PGA	+/–	GP	G	A	Pts	PIM	PP	SH	GW
1978-79	Saskatoon Olympics	SJHL	50	21	33	54	....	....	....	72	....	....	....	....	....	....	....	....	....	....	....	....	....	....	....	....	....	....
1979-80	Saskatoon Blades	WHL	27	9	14	23	....	....	....	60	....	....	....	....	....	....	....	....	....	....	....	....	....	....	....	....	....	....
1980-81	Saskatoon Blades	WHL	72	26	53	79	....	....	....	117	....	....	....	....	....	....	....	....	....	....	....	....	....	....	....	....	....	....
1981-82	Saskatoon Blades	WHL	53	38	52	90	....	....	....	82	....	....	....	....	....	....	....	....	....	....	5	3	3	6	17	....	....	....
1982-83	Saskatoon Blades	WHL	68	68	48	116	....	....	....	105	....	....	....	....	....	....	....	....	....	....	6	1	4	5	24	....	....	....
	Salt Lake Golden Eagles	CHL	....	....	....	....	....	....	....	....	....	....	....	....	....	....	....	....	....	....	1	0	1	1	0	....	....	....
1983-84	**St. Louis Blues**	**NHL**	**1**	**0**	**0**	**0**	**0**	**0**	**0**	**0**	**0**	**0**	**0**	**0**	**0.0**	**1**	**0**	**0**	**0**	**1**	**7**	**3**	**1**	**4**	**0**	**2**	**0**	**0**
	Montana Magic	CHL	59	23	22	45	....	....	....	77	....	....	....	....	....	....	....	....	....	....	....	....	....	....	....	....	....	....
1984-85	**St. Louis Blues**	**NHL**	**7**	**0**	**2**	**2**	**0**	**1**	**1**	**0**	**0**	**0**	**0**	**4**	**0.0**	**3**	**0**	**3**	**0**	**0**	....	....	....	....	....	....	....	....
	Peoria Rivermen	IHL	63	41	29	70	....	....	....	114	....	....	....	....	....	....	....	....	....	....	20	4	11	15	49	....	....	....
1985-86	Sherbrooke Canadiens	AHL	75	25	29	54	....	....	....	42	....	....	....	....	....	....	....	....	....	....	....	....	....	....	....	....	....	....
1986-87	Sherbrooke Canadiens	AHL	68	22	29	51	....	....	....	64	....	....	....	....	....	....	....	....	....	....	17	9	8	17	37	....	....	....

			REGULAR SEASON																		PLAYOFFS							
Season	**Club**	**League**	**GP**	**G**	**A**	**Pts**	**AG**	**AA**	**APts**	**PIM**	**PP**	**SH**	**GW**	**S**	**%**	**TGF**	**PGF**	**TGA**	**PGA**	**+/–**	**GP**	**G**	**A**	**Pts**	**PIM**	**PP**	**SH**	**GW**
1987-88	**Montreal Canadiens**	**NHL**	**1**	**1**	**0**	**1**	**1**	**0**	**1**	**0**	**0**	**0**	**0**	**1**	**100.0**	**1**	**0**	**2**	**0**	**–1**	....	....	....	....	....	....	....	....
	Sherbrooke Canadiens	AHL	28	12	18	30	....	....	....	61	....	....	....	....	....	....	....	....	....	....	....	....	....	....	....	....	....	....
	Pittsburgh Penguins	**NHL**	**30**	**2**	**5**	**7**	**2**	**4**	**6**	**36**	**0**	**0**	**0**	**34**	**5.9**	**12**	**2**	**10**	**0**	**0**	....	....	....	....	....	....	....	....
1988-89	**Pittsburgh Penguins**	**NHL**	**3**	**0**	**0**	**0**	**0**	**0**	**0**	**0**	**0**	**0**	**0**	**3**	**0.0**	**0**	**0**	**3**	**0**	**–3**	....	....	....	....	....	....	....	....
	Muskegon Lumberjacks	IHL	70	39	34	73	....	....	....	114	....	....	....	....	....	....	....	....	....	....	14	7	8	15	6	....	....	....
1989-90	Muskegon Lumberjacks	IHL	79	40	45	85	....	....	....	111	....	....	....	....	....	....	....	....	....	....	14	3	5	8	27	....	....	....
1990-91	Muskegon Lumberjacks	IHL	80	37	38	75	....	....	....	87	....	....	....	....	....	....	....	....	....	....	5	2	1	3	0	....	....	....
1991-92	Muskegon Lumberjacks	IHL	65	29	20	49	....	....	....	65	....	....	....	....	....	....	....	....	....	....	14	9	9	18	18	....	....	....
1992-93	Cleveland Lumberjacks	IHL	79	37	37	74	....	....	....	156	....	....	....	....	....	....	....	....	....	....	3	0	0	0	4	....	....	....
1993-94	Cleveland Lumberjacks	IHL	63	14	17	31	....	....	....	48	....	....	....	....	....	....	....	....	....	....	....	....	....	....	....	....	....	....
1994-95	Cleveland Lumberjacks	IHL	60	11	17	28	....	....	....	56	....	....	....	....	....	....	....	....	....	....	....	....	....	....	....	....	....	....
1995-96	Cleveland Lumberjacks	IHL	1	0	0	0	....	....	....	0	....	....	....	....	....	....	....	....	....	....	....	....	....	....	....	....	....	....
1996-1997	Cleveland Lumberjacks	IHL	DID NOT PLAY – ASSISTANT COACH																									
1997-2000	Cleveland Lumberjacks	IHL	DID NOT PLAY – COACHING																									
	NHL Totals		**42**	**3**	**7**	**10**	**3**	**5**	**8**	**36**	**0**	**0**	**0**	**42**	**7.1**	**17**	**2**	**18**	**0**		**7**	**3**	**1**	**4**	**0**	**2**	**0**	**0**

IHL Second All-Star Team (1985)

Traded to **Montreal** by **St. Louis** for Ron Flockhart, August 26, 1985. Traded to **Pittsburgh** by **Montreal** for future considerations, December 17, 1987. • Retired to become Assistant Coach of Cleveland Lumberjacks, October 15, 1995.

• GANS, Dave

David C – R. 5'10", 180 lbs. b: Brantford, Ont., 6/6/1964. Los Angeles' 3rd, 64th overall, in 1982.

Season	Club	League	GP	G	A	Pts	AG	AA	APts	PIM	PP	SH	GW	S	%	TGF	PGF	TGA	PGA	+/–	GP	G	A	Pts	PIM	PP	SH	GW
1980-81	Brantford Penguins	OHA-B	36	46	45	91	....	....	....	146	....	....	....	....	....	....	....	....	....	....	....	....	....	....	....	....	....	....
1981-82	Oshawa Generals	OHL	66	23	51	74	....	....	....	112	....	....	....	....	....	....	....	....	....	....	12	3	6	9	45	....	....	....
1982-83	Oshawa Generals	OHL	64	41	64	105	....	....	....	90	....	....	....	....	....	....	....	....	....	....	17	14	*24	*38	27	....	....	....
	Los Angeles Kings	**NHL**	**3**	**0**	**0**	**0**	**0**	**0**	**0**	**0**	**0**	**0**	**0**	**0**	**0.0**	**0**	**0**	**1**	**0**	**–1**	....	....	....	....	....	....	....	....
	Oshawa Generals	Mem-Cup	5	4	6	10	....	....	....	2	....	....	....	....	....	....	....	....	....	....	....	....	....	....	....	....	....	....
1983-84	Oshawa Generals	OHL	62	56	76	132	....	....	....	89	....	....	....	....	....	....	....	....	....	....	6	3	4	7	9	....	....	....
1984-85	Toledo Goaldiggers	IHL	81	52	53	105	....	....	....	65	....	....	....	....	....	....	....	....	....	....	6	4	3	7	26	....	....	....
1985-86	**Los Angeles Kings**	**NHL**	**3**	**0**	**0**	**0**	**0**	**0**	**0**	**2**	**0**	**0**	**0**	**3**	**0.0**	**1**	**0**	**1**	**0**	**0**	....	....	....	....	....	....	....	....
	New Haven Nighthawks	AHL	17	11	12	23	....	....	....	14	....	....	....	....	....	....	....	....	....	....	....	....	....	....	....	....	....	....
	Hershey Bears	AHL	56	24	32	56	....	....	....	88	....	....	....	....	....	....	....	....	....	....	18	10	5	15	60	....	....	....
1986-87	New Haven Nighthawks	AHL	29	10	11	21	....	....	....	20	....	....	....	....	....	....	....	....	....	....	....	....	....	....	....	....	....	....
	Hershey Bears	AHL	20	7	8	15	....	....	....	28	....	....	....	....	....	....	....	....	....	....	5	0	0	0	21	....	....	....
1987-88	Newmarket Saints	AHL	16	2	7	9	....	....	....	11	....	....	....	....	....	....	....	....	....	....	....	....	....	....	....	....	....	....
	NHL Totals		**6**	**0**	**0**	**0**	**0**	**0**	**0**	**2**	**0**	**0**	**0**	**3**	**0.0**	**1**	**0**	**2**	**0**		....	....	....	....	....	....	....	....

Won George Parsons Trophy (Memorial Cup Tournament Most Sportsmanlike Player) (1983)

• GARDINER, Bruce

C – R. 6'1", 193 lbs. b: Barrie, Ont., 2/11/1972. St. Louis' 6th, 131st overall, in 1991.

Season	Club	League	GP	G	A	Pts	AG	AA	APts	PIM	PP	SH	GW	S	%	TGF	PGF	TGA	PGA	+/–	GP	G	A	Pts	PIM	PP	SH	GW
1988-89	Barrie Colts	OJHL-B	41	17	28	45	....	....	....	29	....	....	....	....	....	....	....	....	....	....	....	....	....	....	....	....	....	....
1989-90	Barrie Colts	OJHL-B	40	19	26	45	....	....	....	89	....	....	....	....	....	....	....	....	....	....	13	10	11	21	32	....	....	....
1990-91	Colgate University	ECAC	27	4	9	13	....	....	....	72	....	....	....	....	....	....	....	....	....	....	....	....	....	....	....	....	....	....
1991-92	Colgate University	ECAC	23	7	8	15	....	....	....	77	....	....	....	....	....	....	....	....	....	....	....	....	....	....	....	....	....	....
1992-93	Colgate University	ECAC	33	17	12	29	....	....	....	64	....	....	....	....	....	....	....	....	....	....	....	....	....	....	....	....	....	....
1993-94	Colgate University	ECAC	33	23	23	46	....	....	....	68	....	....	....	....	....	....	....	....	....	....	....	....	....	....	....	....	....	....
	Peoria Rivermen	IHL	3	0	0	0	....	....	....	0	....	....	....	....	....	....	....	....	....	....	....	....	....	....	....	....	....	....
1994-95	P.E.I. Senators	AHL	72	17	20	37	....	....	....	132	....	....	....	....	....	....	....	....	....	....	7	4	1	5	4	....	....	....
1995-96	P.E.I. Senators	AHL	38	11	13	24	....	....	....	87	....	....	....	....	....	....	....	....	....	....	5	2	4	6	4	....	....	....
1996-97	**Ottawa Senators**	**NHL**	**67**	**11**	**10**	**21**	**12**	**9**	**21**	**49**	**0**	**1**	**2**	**94**	**11.7**	**29**	**1**	**35**	**11**	**4**	**7**	**0**	**1**	**1**	**2**	**0**	**0**	**0**
1997-98	**Ottawa Senators**	**NHL**	**55**	**7**	**11**	**18**	**8**	**11**	**19**	**50**	**0**	**0**	**0**	**64**	**10.9**	**25**	**0**	**29**	**6**	**2**	**11**	**1**	**3**	**4**	**2**	**0**	**0**	**1**
1998-99	**Ottawa Senators**	**NHL**	**59**	**4**	**8**	**12**	**5**	**8**	**13**	**43**	**0**	**0**	**1**	**70**	**5.7**	**19**	**0**	**21**	**8**	**6**	**3**	**0**	**0**	**0**	**4**	**0**	**0**	**0**
99-2000	**Ottawa Senators**	**NHL**	**10**	**0**	**3**	**3**	**0**	**3**	**3**	**4**	**0**	**0**	**0**	**18**	**0.0**	**4**	**0**	**4**	**1**	**1**	....	....	....	....	....	....	....	....
	Tampa Bay Lightning	**NHL**	**41**	**3**	**6**	**9**	**3**	**6**	**9**	**37**	**0**	**0**	**0**	**30**	**10.0**	**9**	**0**	**43**	**13**	**–21**	....	....	....	....	....	....	....	....
	NHL Totals		**232**	**25**	**38**	**63**	**28**	**37**	**65**	**183**	**0**	**1**	**3**	**276**	**9.1**	**86**	**1**	**132**	**39**		**21**	**1**	**4**	**5**	**8**	**0**	**0**	**1**

ECAC Second All-Star Team (1994)

Signed as a free agent by **Ottawa**, June 14, 1994. Traded to **Tampa Bay** by **Ottawa** for Colin Forbes, November 11, 1999. Selected by **Columbus** from **Tampa Bay** in Expansion Draft, June 23, 2000.

• GARDNER, Bill

William Scott C – L. 5'10", 180 lbs. b: Toronto, Ont., 3/18/1960. Chicago's 3rd, 49th overall, in 1979.

Season	Club	League	GP	G	A	Pts	AG	AA	APts	PIM	PP	SH	GW	S	%	TGF	PGF	TGA	PGA	+/–	GP	G	A	Pts	PIM	PP	SH	GW
1976-77	Seneca Eagles	OHA-B	68	30	72	102	....	....	....	80	....	....	....	....	....	....	....	....	....	....	....	....	....	....	....	....	....	....
	Peterborough Petes	OMJHL	1	0	0	0	....	....	....	0	....	....	....	....	....	....	....	....	....	....	....	....	....	....	....	....	....	....
1977-78	Peterborough Petes	OMJHL	65	23	32	55	....	....	....	10	....	....	....	....	....	....	....	....	....	....	21	7	10	17	4	....	....	....
	Peterborough Petes	Mem-Cup	5	4	1	5	....	....	....	0	....	....	....	....	....	....	....	....	....	....	....	....	....	....	....	....	....	....
1978-79	Peterborough Petes	OMJHL	68	33	71	104	....	....	....	19	....	....	....	....	....	....	....	....	....	....	18	4	20	24	6	....	....	....
	Peterborough Petes	Mem-Cup	5	0	6	6	....	....	....	0	....	....	....	....	....	....	....	....	....	....	....	....	....	....	....	....	....	....
1979-80	Peterborough Petes	OMJHL	59	43	63	106	....	....	....	17	....	....	....	....	....	....	....	....	....	....	14	13	14	27	8	....	....	....
	Canada	WJC-A	5	0	4	4	....	....	....	14	....	....	....	....	....	....	....	....	....	....	....	....	....	....	....	....	....	....
	Peterborough Petes	Mem-Cup	5	3	5	8	....	....	....	0	....	....	....	....	....	....	....	....	....	....	....	....	....	....	....	....	....	....
1980-81	**Chicago Black Hawks**	**NHL**	**1**	**0**	**0**	**0**	**0**	**0**	**0**	**0**	**0**	**0**	**0**	**0**	**0.0**	**0**	**0**	**0**	**0**	**0**	....	....	....	....	....	....	....	....
	New Brunswick Hawks	AHL	48	19	29	48	....	....	....	12	....	....	....	....	....	....	....	....	....	....	13	5	10	15	0	....	....	....
1981-82	**Chicago Black Hawks**	**NHL**	**69**	**8**	**15**	**23**	**6**	**10**	**16**	**20**	**1**	**4**	**0**	**66**	**12.1**	**31**	**6**	**84**	**50**	**–9**	**15**	**1**	**4**	**5**	**6**	**0**	**0**	**0**
1982-83	**Chicago Black Hawks**	**NHL**	**77**	**15**	**25**	**40**	**12**	**17**	**29**	**12**	**2**	**0**	**2**	**105**	**14.3**	**54**	**6**	**74**	**36**	**10**	**13**	**1**	**0**	**1**	**9**	**1**	**0**	**0**
1983-84	**Chicago Black Hawks**	**NHL**	**79**	**27**	**21**	**48**	**22**	**14**	**36**	**12**	**3**	**3**	**3**	**114**	**23.7**	**76**	**17**	**97**	**39**	**1**	**5**	**0**	**1**	**1**	**0**	**0**	**0**	**0**
1984-85	**Chicago Black Hawks**	**NHL**	**74**	**17**	**34**	**51**	**14**	**23**	**37**	**12**	**5**	**1**	**1**	**120**	**14.2**	**68**	**11**	**88**	**38**	**7**	**12**	**1**	**3**	**4**	**2**	**0**	**0**	**0**
1985-86	**Chicago Black Hawks**	**NHL**	**46**	**3**	**10**	**13**	**2**	**7**	**9**	**6**	**0**	**0**	**0**	**29**	**10.3**	**20**	**1**	**48**	**21**	**–8**	....	....	....	....	....	....	....	....
	Hartford Whalers	**NHL**	**18**	**1**	**8**	**9**	**1**	**5**	**6**	**4**	**0**	**0**	**0**	**12**	**8.3**	**10**	**0**	**18**	**2**	**–6**	....	....	....	....	....	....	....	....
1986-87	**Hartford Whalers**	**NHL**	**8**	**0**	**1**	**1**	**0**	**1**	**1**	**0**	**0**	**0**	**0**	**7**	**0.0**	**1**	**0**	**5**	**2**	**–2**	....	....	....	....	....	....	....	....
	Binghamton Whalers	AHL	50	17	44	61	....	....	....	18	....	....	....	....	....	....	....	....	....	....	13	4	8	12	14	....	....	....
1987-88	**Chicago Blackhawks**	**NHL**	**2**	**1**	**0**	**1**	**1**	**0**	**1**	**2**	**1**	**0**	**0**	**1**	**100.0**	**1**	**1**	**1**	**0**	**–1**	....	....	....	....	....	....	....	....
	Saginaw Hawks	IHL	54	18	49	67	....	....	....	46	....	....	....	....	....	....	....	....	....	....	10	4	4	8	14	....	....	....
1988-89	**Chicago Blackhawks**	**NHL**	**6**	**1**	**1**	**2**	**1**	**1**	**2**	**0**	**1**	**0**	**1**	**4**	**25.0**	**3**	**1**	**0**	**0**	**2**	....	....	....	....	....	....	....	....
	Saginaw Hawks	IHL	74	27	45	72	....	....	....	10	....	....	....	....	....	....	....	....	....	....	6	3	1	4	0	....	....	....
1989-90	Kapfenberger SV	Austria	35	34	47	81	....	....	....	32	....	....	....	....	....	....	....	....	....	....	....	....	....	....	....	....	....	....
1990-91	EC Graz	Austria	38	35	*48	*83	....	....	....	20	....	....	....	....	....	....	....	....	....	....	....	....	....	....	....	....	....	....
1991-92	EC Graz	Austria	44	23	*74	*97	....	....	....	....	....	....	....	....	....	....	....	....	....	....	....	....	....	....	....	....	....	....
1992-93	IEV Innsbruck	Austria	25	17	32	49	....	....	....	....	....	....	....	....	....	....	....	....	....	....	....	....	....	....	....	....	....	....
	EV Landshut	Germany	15	4	6	10	....	....	....	34	....	....	....	....	....	....	....	....	....	....	5	1	3	4	2	....	....	....
	NHL Totals		**380**	**73**	**115**	**188**	**59**	**78**	**137**	**68**	**13**	**8**	**7**	**458**	**15.9**	**264**	**43**	**415**	**188**		**45**	**3**	**8**	**11**	**17**	**1**	**0**	**0**

Memorial Cup All-Star Team (1980)

Traded to **Hartford** by **Chicago** for Hartford's 3rd round choice (Mike Dagenais) in 1987 Entry Draft, February 3, 1986. Signed as a free agent by **Chicago**, September 25, 1987.

• GARDNER, Dave

David Calvin C – R. 6', 185 lbs. b: Toronto, Ont., 8/23/1952. Montreal's 3rd, 8th overall, in 1972.

Season	Club	League	GP	G	A	Pts	AG	AA	APts	PIM	PP	SH	GW	S	%	TGF	PGF	TGA	PGA	+/–	GP	G	A	Pts	PIM	PP	SH	GW
1969-70	St. Michael's Buzzers	OHA-B	36	54	42	96	....	....	....	....	....	....	....	....	....	....	....	....	....	....	....	....	....	....	....	....	....	....
1970-71	Toronto Marlboros	OMJHL	62	56	*81	137	....	....	....	7	....	....	....	....	....	....	....	....	....	....	13	7	10	17	2	....	....	....
1971-72	Toronto Marlboros	OMJHL	57	53	*76	*129	....	....	....	16	....	....	....	....	....	....	....	....	....	....	10	7	*17	*24	4	....	....	....
1972-73	**Montreal Canadiens**	**NHL**	**5**	**1**	**1**	**2**	**1**	**1**	**2**	**0**	**1**	**0**	**0**	**6**	**16.7**	**3**	**3**	**0**	**0**	**0**	....	....	....	....	....	....	....	....
	Nova Scotia Voyageurs	AHL	66	28	44	72	....	....	....	15	....	....	....	....	....	....	....	....	....	....	13	5	6	11	4	....	....	....
1973-74	**Montreal Canadiens**	**NHL**	**31**	**1**	**10**	**11**	**1**	**8**	**9**	**2**	**0**	**0**	**0**	**26**	**3.8**	**14**	**4**	**6**	**0**	**4**	....	....	....	....	....	....	....	....
	St. Louis Blues	**NHL**	**15**	**5**	**2**	**7**	**5**	**2**	**7**	**6**	**1**	**0**	**0**	**29**	**17.2**	**9**	**3**	**12**	**0**	**–6**	....	....	....	....	....	....	....	....

Season	Club	League	GP	G	A	Pts	AG	AA	APts	PIM	PP	SH	GW	S	%	TGF	PGF	TGA	PGA	+/–	GP	G	A	Pts	PIM	PP	SH	GW
			REGULAR SEASON																		PLAYOFFS							
1974-75	**St. Louis Blues**	**NHL**	**8**	**0**	**2**	**2**	**0**	**1**	**1**	**0**	**0**	**0**	**0**	**8**	**0.0**	**2**	**2**	**3**	**0**	**–3**	....	....	....	....	....	....	....	....
	California Golden Seals	**NHL**	**64**	**16**	**20**	**36**	**14**	**15**	**29**	**6**	**6**	**1**	**0**	**133**	**12.0**	**48**	**18**	**50**	**1**	**–19**	....	....	....	....	....	....	....	....
1975-76	**California Golden Seals**	**NHL**	**74**	**16**	**32**	**48**	**14**	**24**	**38**	**8**	**2**	**0**	**1**	**157**	**10.2**	**74**	**33**	**45**	**0**	**–4**	....	....	....	....	....	....	....	....
1976-77	**Cleveland Barons**	**NHL**	**76**	**16**	**22**	**38**	**14**	**17**	**31**	**9**	**5**	**0**	**3**	**141**	**11.3**	**66**	**39**	**47**	**0**	**–20**	....	....	....	....	....	....	....	....
1977-78	**Cleveland Barons**	**NHL**	**75**	**19**	**25**	**44**	**17**	**19**	**36**	**10**	**3**	**0**	**3**	**106**	**17.9**	**69**	**21**	**65**	**1**	**–16**	....	....	....	....	....	....	....	....
1978-79	Springfield Indians	AHL	10	1	3	4	....	....	....	0	....	....	....	....	....	....	....	....	....	....	....	....	....	....	....	....	....	....
	Tulsa Oilers	CHL	20	4	10	14	....	....	....	2	....	....	....	....	....	....	....	....	....	....	....	....	....	....	....	....	....	....
	Dallas Black Hawks	CHL	39	6	27	33	....	....	....	6	....	....	....	....	....	....	....	....	....	....	9	5	7	12	4	....	....	....
1979-80	Binghamton Dusters	AHL	18	3	9	12	....	....	....	2	....	....	....	....	....	....	....	....	....	....	....	....	....	....	....	....	....	....
	Philadelphia Flyers	**NHL**	**2**	**1**	**1**	**2**	**1**	**1**	**2**	**0**	**0**	**0**	**0**	**1**	**100.0**	**3**	**0**	**2**	**0**	**1**	....	....	....	....	....	....	....	....
	Maine Mariners	AHL	37	20	35	55	....	....	....	16	....	....	....	....	....	....	....	....	....	....	12	2	5	7	4	....	....	....
1980-81	HC Ambri-Piotta	Switz-2	STATISTICS NOT AVAILABLE																									
1981-82	HC Ambri-Piotta	Switz-2	STATISTICS NOT AVAILABLE																									
1982-83	HC Ambri-Piotta	Switz-2	36	36	22	58	....	....	....	....	....	....	....	....	....	....	....	....	....	....	....	....	....	....	....	....	....	....
1983-84	EHC Visp	Switz-2	38	41	33	74	....	....	....	....	....	....	....	....	....	....	....	....	....	....	....	....	....	....	....	....	....	....
1984-85	EHC Visp	Switz-2	38	47	47	94	....	....	....	....	....	....	....	....	....	....	....	....	....	....	....	....	....	....	....	....	....	....
	NHL Totals		**350**	**75**	**115**	**190**	**67**	**88**	**155**	**41**	**18**	**1**	**7**	**607**	**12.4**	**288**	**123**	**230**	**2**		....	....	....	....	....	....	....	....

• Son of Cal • Brother of Paul • OMJHL Second All-Star Team (1971, 1972)

Traded to **St. Louis** by **Montreal** for St. Louis' 1st round choice (Doug Risebrough) in 1974 Amateur Draft, March 9, 1974. Traded to **California** by **St. Louis** with Butch Williams for Craig Patrick and Stan Gilbertson, November 11, 1974. Transferred to **Cleveland** after **California** franchise relocated, August 26, 1976. Placed on **Minnesota** Reserve List after **Minnesota-Cleveland** Dispersal Draft, June 15, 1978. Transferred to **LA Kings** by **Minnesota** with Rick Hampton and Steve Jensen as compensation for Minnesota's signing of free agent Gary Sargent, July 15, 1978. Signed as a free agent by **Philadelphia**, January 21, 1980.

• GARDNER, Paul

Paul Malone C – L. 6', 195 lbs. b: Toronto, Ont., 3/5/1956. Kansas City's 1st, 11th overall, in 1976.

Season	Club	League	GP	G	A	Pts	AG	AA	APts	PIM	PP	SH	GW	S	%	TGF	PGF	TGA	PGA	+/–	GP	G	A	Pts	PIM	PP	SH	GW
1973-74	St. Michael's Buzzers	OHA-B	44	87	44	131	....	....	....	....	....	....	....	....	....	....	....	....	....	....	....	....	....	....	....	....	....	....
1974-75	Oshawa Generals	OMJHL	64	27	36	63	....	....	....	54	....	....	....	....	....	....	....	....	....	....	5	0	0	0	9	....	....	....
1975-76	Oshawa Generals	OMJHL	65	69	75	144	....	....	....	75	....	....	....	....	....	....	....	....	....	....	4	2	3	5	2	....	....	....
1976-77	**Colorado Rockies**	**NHL**	**60**	**30**	**29**	**59**	**27**	**22**	**49**	**25**	**11**	**0**	**0**	**191**	**15.7**	**71**	**25**	**74**	**0**	**–28**	....	....	....	....	....	....	....	....
	Rhode Island Reds	AHL	14	10	4	14	....	....	....	12	....	....	....	....	....	....	....	....	....	....	....	....	....	....	....	....	....	....
1977-78	**Colorado Rockies**	**NHL**	**46**	**30**	**22**	**52**	**27**	**17**	**44**	**29**	**13**	**0**	**3**	**133**	**22.6**	**73**	**34**	**56**	**0**	**–17**	....	....	....	....	....	....	....	....
1978-79	**Colorado Rockies**	**NHL**	**64**	**23**	**26**	**49**	**20**	**19**	**39**	**32**	**14**	**0**	**0**	**170**	**13.5**	**67**	**36**	**56**	**0**	**–25**	....	....	....	....	....	....	....	....
	Toronto Maple Leafs	**NHL**	**11**	**7**	**2**	**9**	**6**	**1**	**7**	**0**	**2**	**0**	**1**	**20**	**35.0**	**11**	**5**	**6**	**0**	**0**	**6**	**0**	**1**	**1**	**4**	**0**	**0**	**0**
1979-80	**Toronto Maple Leafs**	**NHL**	**45**	**11**	**13**	**24**	**9**	**9**	**18**	**10**	**4**	**0**	**1**	**74**	**14.9**	**36**	**15**	**29**	**0**	**–8**	....	....	....	....	....	....	....	....
	New Brunswick Hawks	AHL	20	11	16	27	....	....	....	14	....	....	....	....	....	....	....	....	....	....	15	10	5	15	12	....	....	....
1980-81	Springfield Indians	AHL	14	9	12	21	....	....	....	6	....	....	....	....	....	....	....	....	....	....	....	....	....	....	....	....	....	....
	Pittsburgh Penguins	**NHL**	**62**	**34**	**40**	**74**	**26**	**27**	**53**	**59**	**18**	**0**	**1**	**183**	**18.6**	**92**	**45**	**52**	**0**	**–5**	**5**	**1**	**0**	**1**	**8**	**1**	**0**	**0**
1981-82	**Pittsburgh Penguins**	**NHL**	**59**	**36**	**33**	**69**	**28**	**22**	**50**	**28**	**21**	**0**	**2**	**157**	**22.9**	**99**	**62**	**45**	**1**	**–7**	**5**	**1**	**5**	**6**	**2**	**1**	**0**	**0**
1982-83	**Pittsburgh Penguins**	**NHL**	**70**	**28**	**27**	**55**	**23**	**19**	**42**	**12**	**20**	**0**	**1**	**155**	**18.1**	**82**	**53**	**52**	**0**	**–23**	....	....	....	....	....	....	....	....
1983-84	**Pittsburgh Penguins**	**NHL**	**16**	**0**	**5**	**5**	**0**	**3**	**3**	**6**	**0**	**0**	**0**	**21**	**0.0**	**8**	**6**	**6**	**0**	**–4**	....	....	....	....	....	....	....	....
	Baltimore Skipjacks	AHL	54	32	48	80	....	....	....	14	....	....	....	....	....	....	....	....	....	....	10	12	10	22	0	....	....	....
1984-85	**Washington Capitals**	**NHL**	**12**	**2**	**4**	**6**	**2**	**3**	**5**	**6**	**2**	**0**	**0**	**17**	**11.8**	**11**	**6**	**6**	**0**	**–1**	....	....	....	....	....	....	....	....
	Binghamton Whalers	AHL	64	*51	79	*130	....	....	....	10	....	....	....	....	....	....	....	....	....	....	5	3	9	12	0	....	....	....
1985-86	**Buffalo Sabres**	**NHL**	**2**	**0**	**0**	**0**	**0**	**0**	**0**	**0**	**0**	**0**	**0**	**4**	**0.0**	**1**	**1**	**3**	**0**	**–3**	....	....	....	....	....	....	....	....
	Rochester Americans	AHL	71	*61	51	*112	....	....	....	16	....	....	....	....	....	....	....	....	....	....	....	....	....	....	....	....	....	....
1986-1990	Newmarket Saints	AHL	DID NOT PLAY – COACHING																									
1990-1992	**Washington Capitals**	**NHL**	DID NOT PLAY – SCOUTING																									
1992-1993	Baltimore Skipjacks	AHL	DID NOT PLAY – ASSISTANT COACH																									
1993-1996	Maine Pirates	AHL	DID NOT PLAY – ASSISTANT COACH																									
1996-1997	Maine Pirates	AHL	DID NOT PLAY – ASSISTANT COACH																									
	Portland Pirates	AHL	1	0	1	1	....	....	....	2	....	....	....	....	....	....	....	....	....	....	....	....	....	....	....	....	....	....
1997-1998	**Nashville Predators**	**NHL**	DID NOT PLAY – SCOUTING																									
1998-2000	**Nashville Predators**	**NHL**	DID NOT PLAY – ASSISTANT COACH																									
	NHL Totals		**447**	**201**	**201**	**402**	**168**	**142**	**310**	**207**	**105**	**0**	**9**	**1125**	**17.9**	**551**	**288**	**385**	**1**		**16**	**2**	**6**	**8**	**14**	**2**	**0**	**0**

• Son of Cal • Brother of Dave • Named Metro OHA-B MVP (1974) • AHL First All-Star Team (1985, 1986) • Won Fred T. Hunt Memorial Trophy (Sportsmanship - AHL) (1985) • Won John B. Sollenberger Trophy (Top Scorer - AHL) (1985, 1986) • Won Les Cunningham Award (MVP - AHL) (1985, 1986)

Rights transferred to **Colorado** after **Kansas City** relocated, July 15, 1976. Traded to **Toronto** by **Colorado** for Don Ashby and Trevor Johansen, March 13, 1979. Traded to **Pittsburgh** by **Toronto** with Dave Burrows for Kim Davis and Paul Marshall, November 18, 1980. Signed as a free agent by **Washington**, July 17, 1984. Signed as a free agent by **Buffalo**, July 31, 1985.
• Played w/ RHI's New England Stingers in 1994 (5-4-3-7-0).

• GARE, Danny

Daniel Mirl RW – R. 5'9", 175 lbs. b: Nelson, B.C., 5/14/1954. Buffalo's 2nd, 29th overall, in 1974.

Season	Club	League	GP	G	A	Pts	AG	AA	APts	PIM	PP	SH	GW	S	%	TGF	PGF	TGA	PGA	+/–	GP	G	A	Pts	PIM	PP	SH	GW
1971-72	Calgary Centennials	WCJHL	56	10	17	27	....	....	....	15	....	....	....	....	....	....	....	....	....	....	13	1	1	2	2	....	....	....
1972-73	Calgary Centennials	WCJHL	65	45	43	88	....	....	....	107	....	....	....	....	....	....	....	....	....	....	6	5	5	10	18	....	....	....
1973-74	Calgary Centennials	WCJHL	65	68	59	127	....	....	....	238	....	....	....	....	....	....	....	....	....	....	14	10	12	22	53	....	....	....
1974-75	**Buffalo Sabres**	**NHL**	**78**	**31**	**31**	**62**	**27**	**23**	**50**	**75**	**5**	**0**	**2**	**274**	**11.3**	**85**	**12**	**33**	**0**	**40**	**17**	**7**	**6**	**13**	**19**	**0**	**0**	**1**
1975-76	**Buffalo Sabres**	**NHL**	**79**	**50**	**23**	**73**	**44**	**17**	**61**	**129**	**8**	**1**	**9**	**303**	**16.5**	**113**	**29**	**61**	**9**	**32**	**9**	**5**	**2**	**7**	**21**	**0**	**0**	**2**
1976-77	Canada	Can-Cup	1	0	0	0	....	....	....	0	....	....	....	....	....	....	....	....	....	....	....	....	....	....	....	....	....	....
	Buffalo Sabres	**NHL**	**35**	**11**	**15**	**26**	**10**	**12**	**22**	**73**	**3**	**0**	**0**	**92**	**12.0**	**40**	**10**	**25**	**2**	**7**	**4**	**0**	**0**	**0**	**18**	**0**	**0**	**0**
1977-78	**Buffalo Sabres**	**NHL**	**69**	**39**	**38**	**77**	**36**	**29**	**65**	**95**	**9**	**0**	**2**	**265**	**14.7**	**105**	**28**	**46**	**1**	**32**	**8**	**4**	**6**	**10**	**37**	**2**	**0**	**0**
1978-79	**Buffalo Sabres**	**NHL**	**71**	**27**	**40**	**67**	**23**	**29**	**52**	**90**	**7**	**0**	**3**	**260**	**10.4**	**99**	**31**	**53**	**3**	**18**	**3**	**0**	**0**	**0**	**9**	**0**	**0**	**0**
1979-80	**Buffalo Sabres**	**NHL**	**76**	***56**	**33**	**89**	**48**	**24**	**72**	**90**	**17**	**0**	**11**	**270**	**20.7**	**144**	**48**	**48**	**1**	**49**	**14**	**4**	**7**	**11**	**35**	**4**	**0**	**1**
1980-81	**Buffalo Sabres**	**NHL**	**73**	**46**	**39**	**85**	**36**	**26**	**62**	**109**	**15**	**0**	**7**	**248**	**18.5**	**130**	**52**	**67**	**1**	**12**	**3**	**3**	**0**	**3**	**8**	**2**	**0**	**1**
1981-82	Canada	Can-Cup	7	1	5	6	....	....	....	2	....	....	....	....	....	....	....	....	....	....	....	....	....	....	....	....	....	....
	Buffalo Sabres	**NHL**	**22**	**7**	**14**	**21**	**6**	**9**	**15**	**25**	**2**	**0**	**1**	**71**	**9.9**	**30**	**10**	**21**	**1**	**0**	....	....	....	....	....	....	....	....
	Detroit Red Wings	**NHL**	**36**	**13**	**9**	**22**	**10**	**6**	**16**	**74**	**2**	**1**	**0**	**100**	**13.0**	**34**	**6**	**35**	**3**	**–4**	....	....	....	....	....	....	....	....
1982-83	**Detroit Red Wings**	**NHL**	**79**	**26**	**35**	**61**	**21**	**24**	**45**	**107**	**6**	**0**	**3**	**224**	**11.6**	**85**	**20**	**93**	**12**	**–16**	....	....	....	....	....	....	....	....
1983-84	**Detroit Red Wings**	**NHL**	**63**	**13**	**13**	**26**	**10**	**9**	**19**	**147**	**1**	**0**	**2**	**148**	**8.8**	**43**	**2**	**45**	**7**	**3**	**4**	**2**	**0**	**2**	**38**	**0**	**0**	**0**
1984-85	**Detroit Red Wings**	**NHL**	**71**	**27**	**29**	**56**	**22**	**20**	**42**	**163**	**3**	**0**	**3**	**167**	**16.2**	**83**	**19**	**70**	**11**	**5**	**2**	**0**	**0**	**0**	**10**	**0**	**0**	**0**
1985-86	**Detroit Red Wings**	**NHL**	**57**	**7**	**9**	**16**	**6**	**6**	**12**	**102**	**1**	**0**	**0**	**108**	**6.5**	**29**	**4**	**69**	**25**	**–19**	....	....	....	....	....	....	....	....
1986-87	**Edmonton Oilers**	**NHL**	**18**	**1**	**3**	**4**	**1**	**2**	**3**	**6**	**0**	**0**	**0**	**22**	**4.5**	**8**	**1**	**5**	**0**	**2**	....	....	....	....	....	....	....	....
	NHL Totals		**827**	**354**	**331**	**685**	**300**	**236**	**536**	**1285**	**79**	**2**	**43**	**2552**	**13.9**	**1028**	**272**	**671**	**76**		**64**	**25**	**21**	**46**	**195**	**8**	**0**	**5**

WCJHL First All-Star Team (1974) • NHL Second All-Star Team (1980) • Played in NHL All-Star Game (1980, 1981)

Traded to **Detroit** by **Buffalo** with Jim Schoenfeld and Derek Smith for Mike Foligno, Dale McCourt and Brent Peterson, December 2, 1981. Signed as a free agent by **Edmonton**, September, 1986.

• GARLAND, Scott

Stephen Scott C – R. 6'1", 185 lbs. b: Regina, Sask., 5/16/1952 d: 6/9/1979.

Season	Club	League	GP	G	A	Pts	AG	AA	APts	PIM	PP	SH	GW	S	%	TGF	PGF	TGA	PGA	+/–	GP	G	A	Pts	PIM	PP	SH	GW
1970-71	Montreal Jr. Canadiens	OHA-Jr.	29	4	8	12	....	....	....	94	....	....	....	....	....	....	....	....	....	....	....	....	....	....	....	....	....	....
1971-72	Sarnia Bees	OHA-B	34	9	14	23	....	....	....	159	....	....	....	....	....	....	....	....	....	....	....	....	....	....	....	....	....	....
	Peterborough Petes	OMJHL	5	1	0	1	....	....	....	7	....	....	....	....	....	....	....	....	....	....	....	....	....	....	....	....	....	....
1972-73	Tulsa Oilers	CHL	62	15	20	35	....	....	....	192	....	....	....	....	....	....	....	....	....	....	....	....	....	....	....	....	....	....
1973-74	Oklahoma City Blazers	CHL	51	11	10	21	....	....	....	106	....	....	....	....	....	....	....	....	....	....	9	0	1	1	14	....	....	....
1974-75	Oklahoma City Blazers	CHL	61	18	27	45	....	....	....	132	....	....	....	....	....	....	....	....	....	....	5	0	2	2	42	....	....	....
1975-76	**Toronto Maple Leafs**	**NHL**	**16**	**4**	**3**	**7**	**3**	**2**	**5**	**8**	**1**	**0**	**0**	**17**	**23.5**	**12**	**3**	**9**	**0**	**0**	**7**	**1**	**2**	**3**	**35**	**1**	**0**	**0**
	Oklahoma City Blazers	CHL	58	19	40	59	....	....	....	53	....	....	....	....	....	....	....	....	....	....	....	....	....	....	....	....	....	....
1976-77	**Toronto Maple Leafs**	**NHL**	**69**	**9**	**20**	**29**	**8**	**15**	**23**	**83**	**3**	**0**	**1**	**84**	**10.7**	**53**	**12**	**59**	**0**	**–18**	....	....	....	....	....	....	....	....

			REGULAR SEASON																		PLAYOFFS							
Season	**Club**	**League**	**GP**	**G**	**A**	**Pts**	**AG**	**AA**	**APts**	**PIM**	**PP**	**SH**	**GW**	**S**	**%**	**TGF**	**PGF**	**TGA**	**PGA**	**+/–**	**GP**	**G**	**A**	**Pts**	**PIM**	**PP**	**SH**	**GW**
1977-78	Tulsa Oilers	CHL	20	6	7	13	....	....	....	19	....	....	....	....	....	....	....	....	....	....	7	2	0	2	31	....	....	....
1978-79	**Los Angeles Kings**	**NHL**	**6**	**0**	**1**	**1**	**0**	**1**	**1**	**24**	**0**	**0**	**0**	**1**	**0.0**	**1**	**0**	**5**	**0**	**–4**	....	....	....	....	....	....	....	....
	Springfield Indians	AHL	45	11	20	31	....	....	....	114	....	....	....	....	....	....	....	....	....	....	....	....	....	....	....	....	....	....
	NHL Totals		**91**	**13**	**24**	**37**	**11**	**18**	**29**	**115**	**4**	**0**	**1**	**102**	**12.7**	**66**	**15**	**73**	**0**		**7**	**1**	**2**	**3**	**35**	**1**	**0**	**0**

Signed as a free agent by **Toronto**, September 30, 1973. Traded to **LA Kings** by **Toronto** with Brian Glennie, Kurt Walker and Toronto's 2nd round choice (Mark Hardy) in 1979 Entry Draft for Dave Hutchison and Lorne Stamler, June 14, 1978. • Died of injuries suffered in automobile accident, June 9, 1979.

• GARNER, Rob

Robert William C – L. 5'11", 180 lbs. b: Weston, Ont., 8/17/1958. Pittsburgh's 3rd, 75th overall, in 1978.

Season	Club	League	GP	G	A	Pts	AG	AA	APts	PIM	PP	SH	GW	S	%	TGF	PGF	TGA	PGA	+/–	GP	G	A	Pts	PIM	PP	SH	GW
1974-75	Barrie Co-Op	OMHA	STATISTICS NOT AVAILABLE																									
1975-76	Markham Waxers	OHA-B	26	18	8	26	....	....	....	34	....	....	....	....	....	....	....	....	....	....	....	....	....	....	....	....	....	....
	Toronto Marlboros	OMJHL	37	6	8	14	....	....	....	28	....	....	....	....	....	....	....	....	....	....	10	4	3	7	20	....	....	....
1976-77	Toronto Marlboros	OMJHL	62	31	35	66	....	....	....	58	....	....	....	....	....	....	....	....	....	....	6	2	2	4	13	....	....	....
1977-78	Toronto Marlboros	OMJHL	48	38	35	73	....	....	....	111	....	....	....	....	....	....	....	....	....	....	5	2	1	3	24	....	....	....
1978-79	Binghamton Dusters	AHL	77	15	19	34	....	....	....	97	....	....	....	....	....	....	....	....	....	....	10	5	3	8	19	....	....	....
1979-80	Cincinnati Stingers	CHL	27	5	8	13	....	....	....	36	....	....	....	....	....	....	....	....	....	....	....	....	....	....	....	....	....	....
	Syracuse Firebirds	AHL	46	12	13	25	....	....	....	21	....	....	....	....	....	....	....	....	....	....	4	0	0	0	21	....	....	....
1980-81	Binghamton Whalers	AHL	62	18	20	38	....	....	....	77	....	....	....	....	....	....	....	....	....	....	6	1	6	7	13	....	....	....
1981-82	Erie Blades	AHL	75	25	27	52	....	....	....	60	....	....	....	....	....	....	....	....	....	....	....	....	....	....	....	....	....	....
1982-83	**Pittsburgh Penguins**	**NHL**	**1**	**0**	**0**	**0**	**0**	**0**	**0**	**0**	**0**	**0**	**0**	**1**	**0.0**	**0**	**0**	**0**	**0**	**0**	....	....	....	....	....	....	....	....
	Baltimore Skipjacks	AHL	70	21	32	53	....	....	....	48	....	....	....	....	....	....	....	....	....	....	....	....	....	....	....	....	....	....
	NHL Totals		**1**	**0**	**0**	**0**	**0**	**0**	**0**	**0**	**0**	**0**	**0**	**1**	**0.0**	**0**	**0**	**0**	**0**		....	....	....	....	....	....	....	....

• GARPENLOV, Johan

LW – L. 6', 185 lbs. b: Stockholm, Sweden, 3/21/1968. Detroit's 5th, 85th overall, in 1986.

Season	Club	League	GP	G	A	Pts	AG	AA	APts	PIM	PP	SH	GW	S	%	TGF	PGF	TGA	PGA	+/–	GP	G	A	Pts	PIM	PP	SH	GW
1984-85	Nacka HK	Sweden-2	4	1	2	3	....	....	....	2	....	....	....	....	....	....	....	....	....	....	....	....	....	....	....	....	....	....
	Sweden	EJC-A	5	1	0	1	....	....	....	0	....	....	....	....	....	....	....	....	....	....	....	....	....	....	....	....	....	....
1985-86	Nacka HK	Sweden-2	20	8	12	20	....	....	....	22	....	....	....	....	....	....	....	....	....	....	....	....	....	....	....	....	....	....
	Sweden	EJC-A	5	5	2	7	....	....	....	12	....	....	....	....	....	....	....	....	....	....	....	....	....	....	....	....	....	....
1986-87	Djurgardens IF Stockholm	Sweden	29	5	8	13	....	....	....	22	....	....	....	....	....	....	....	....	....	....	2	0	0	0	0	....	....	....
	Sweden	WJC-A	7	2	3	5	....	....	....	6	....	....	....	....	....	....	....	....	....	....	....	....	....	....	....	....	....	....
1987-88	Djurgardens IF Stockholm	Sweden	30	7	10	17	....	....	....	12	....	....	....	....	....	....	....	....	....	....	3	1	3	4	4	....	....	....
	Sweden	WJC-A	7	5	1	6	....	....	....	12	....	....	....	....	....	....	....	....	....	....	....	....	....	....	....	....	....	....
1988-89	Djurgardens IF Stockholm	Sweden	36	12	19	31	....	....	....	20	....	....	....	....	....	....	....	....	....	....	8	3	4	7	10	....	....	....
1989-90	Djurgardens IF Stockholm	Sweden	39	20	13	33	....	....	....	35	....	....	....	....	....	....	....	....	....	....	8	2	4	6	4	....	....	....
	Sweden	WEC-A	10	4	4	8	....	....	....	4	....	....	....	....	....	....	....	....	....	....	....	....	....	....	....	....	....	....
1990-91	**Detroit Red Wings**	**NHL**	**71**	**18**	**22**	**40**	**16**	**17**	**33**	**18**	**2**	**0**	**3**	**91**	**19.8**	**62**	**14**	**61**	**9**	**–4**	**6**	**0**	**1**	**1**	**4**	**0**	**0**	**0**
	Sweden	WEC-A	10	4	0	4	....	....	....	6	....	....	....	....	....	....	....	....	....	....	....	....	....	....	....	....	....	....
1991-92	Sweden	Can-Cup	6	0	1	1	....	....	....	10	....	....	....	....	....	....	....	....	....	....	....	....	....	....	....	....	....	....
	Detroit Red Wings	**NHL**	**16**	**1**	**1**	**2**	**1**	**1**	**2**	**4**	**0**	**0**	**0**	**13**	**7.7**	**8**	**0**	**8**	**2**	**2**	....	....	....	....	....	....	....	....
	Adirondack Red Wings	AHL	9	3	3	6	....	....	....	6	....	....	....	....	....	....	....	....	....	....	....	....	....	....	....	....	....	....
	San Jose Sharks	**NHL**	**12**	**5**	**6**	**11**	**5**	**5**	**10**	**4**	**1**	**0**	**1**	**21**	**23.8**	**21**	**8**	**16**	**1**	**–2**	....	....	....	....	....	....	....	....
	Sweden	WC-A	8	1	1	2	....	....	....	10	....	....	....	....	....	....	....	....	....	....	....	....	....	....	....	....	....	....
1992-93	**San Jose Sharks**	**NHL**	**79**	**22**	**44**	**66**	**18**	**30**	**48**	**56**	**14**	**0**	**1**	**171**	**12.9**	**95**	**39**	**84**	**2**	**–26**	....	....	....	....	....	....	....	....
1993-94	**San Jose Sharks**	**NHL**	**80**	**18**	**35**	**53**	**17**	**27**	**44**	**28**	**7**	**0**	**3**	**125**	**14.4**	**78**	**20**	**49**	**0**	**9**	**14**	**4**	**6**	**10**	**6**	**0**	**0**	**2**
1994-95	**San Jose Sharks**	**NHL**	**13**	**1**	**1**	**2**	**2**	**1**	**3**	**2**	**0**	**0**	**0**	**16**	**6.3**	**9**	**1**	**11**	**0**	**–3**	....	....	....	....	....	....	....	....
	Florida Panthers	**NHL**	**27**	**3**	**9**	**12**	**5**	**13**	**18**	**0**	**0**	**0**	**0**	**28**	**10.7**	**22**	**8**	**10**	**0**	**4**	....	....	....	....	....	....	....	....
1995-96	**Florida Panthers**	**NHL**	**82**	**23**	**28**	**51**	**23**	**23**	**46**	**36**	**8**	**0**	**7**	**130**	**17.7**	**70**	**34**	**47**	**1**	**–10**	**20**	**4**	**2**	**6**	**8**	**0**	**0**	**0**
1996-97	Sweden	W-Cup	4	1	1	2	....	....	....	2	....	....	....	....	....	....	....	....	....	....	....	....	....	....	....	....	....	....
	Florida Panthers	**NHL**	**53**	**11**	**25**	**36**	**12**	**22**	**34**	**47**	**1**	**0**	**1**	**83**	**13.3**	**51**	**13**	**29**	**1**	**10**	**4**	**2**	**0**	**2**	**4**	**2**	**0**	**1**
1997-98	**Florida Panthers**	**NHL**	**39**	**2**	**3**	**5**	**2**	**3**	**5**	**8**	**0**	**0**	**0**	**43**	**4.7**	**18**	**1**	**27**	**4**	**–6**	....	....	....	....	....	....	....	....
1998-99	**Florida Panthers**	**NHL**	**64**	**8**	**9**	**17**	**9**	**9**	**18**	**42**	**0**	**1**	**0**	**71**	**11.3**	**20**	**1**	**38**	**10**	**–9**	....	....	....	....	....	....	....	....
99-2000	**Atlanta Thrashers**	**NHL**	**73**	**2**	**14**	**16**	**2**	**13**	**15**	**31**	**0**	**0**	**0**	**79**	**2.5**	**25**	**3**	**66**	**14**	**–30**	....	....	....	....	....	....	....	....
	NHL Totals		**609**	**114**	**197**	**311**	**112**	**164**	**276**	**276**	**33**	**1**	**16**	**871**	**13.1**	**479**	**142**	**446**	**44**		**44**	**10**	**9**	**19**	**22**	**2**	**0**	**3**

Traded to **San Jose** by **Detroit** for Bob McGill and Vancouver's 8th round choice (previously acquired, Detroit selected C.J. Denomme) in 1992 Entry Draft, March 9, 1992. Traded to **Florida** by **San Jose** for future considerations, March 3, 1995. Claimed by **Atlanta** from **Florida** in Expansion Draft, June 25, 1999.

• GARTNER, Mike

Michael Alfred RW – R. 6', 187 lbs. b: Ottawa, Ont., 10/29/1959. Washington's 1st, 4th overall, in 1979.

Season	Club	League	GP	G	A	Pts	AG	AA	APts	PIM	PP	SH	GW	S	%	TGF	PGF	TGA	PGA	+/–	GP	G	A	Pts	PIM	PP	SH	GW
1974-75	Barrie Co-Ops	OMHA	STATISTICS NOT AVAILABLE																									
	Mississagua Reps	MTHL	STATISTICS NOT AVAILABLE																									
1975-76	Toronto Young Nationals	MTHL	26	18	18	36	....	....	....	46	....	....	....	....	....	....	....	....	....	....	....	....	....	....	....	....	....	....
	St. Catharines Black Hawks	OMJHL	3	1	3	4	....	....	....	0	....	....	....	....	....	....	....	....	....	....	4	1	0	1	2	....	....	....
1976-77	Niagara Falls Flyers	OMJHL	62	33	42	75	....	....	....	125	....	....	....	....	....	....	....	....	....	....	....	....	....	....	....	....	....	....
1977-78	Niagara Falls Flyers	OMJHL	64	41	49	90	....	....	....	56	....	....	....	....	....	....	....	....	....	....	....	....	....	....	....	....	....	....
	Canada	WJC-A	6	3	3	6	....	....	....	4	....	....	....	....	....	....	....	....	....	....	....	....	....	....	....	....	....	....
1978-79	Cincinnati Stingers	WHA	78	27	25	52	....	....	....	123	....	....	....	....	....	....	....	....	....	....	3	0	2	2	2	....	....	....
1979-80	**Washington Capitals**	**NHL**	**77**	**36**	**32**	**68**	**31**	**23**	**54**	**66**	**4**	**0**	**3**	**228**	**15.8**	**97**	**23**	**61**	**2**	**15**	....	....	....	....	....	....	....	....
1980-81	**Washington Capitals**	**NHL**	**80**	**48**	**46**	**94**	**37**	**31**	**68**	**100**	**13**	**0**	**3**	**326**	**14.7**	**123**	**36**	**97**	**5**	**–5**	....	....	....	....	....	....	....	....
	Canada	WEC-A	8	4	0	4	....	....	....	8	....	....	....	....	....	....	....	....	....	....	....	....	....	....	....	....	....	....
1981-82	Washington Capitals	DN-Cup	4	0	2	2	....	....	....	....	....	....	....	....	....	....	....	....	....	....	....	....	....	....	....	....	....	....
	Washington Capitals	**NHL**	**80**	**35**	**45**	**80**	**28**	**30**	**58**	**121**	**5**	**2**	**5**	**300**	**11.7**	**122**	**29**	**113**	**9**	**–11**	....	....	....	....	....	....	....	....
	Canada	WEC-A	10	3	2	5	....	....	....	6	....	....	....	....	....	....	....	....	....	....	....	....	....	....	....	....	....	....
1982-83	**Washington Capitals**	**NHL**	**73**	**38**	**38**	**76**	**31**	**26**	**57**	**54**	**10**	**1**	**3**	**269**	**14.1**	**101**	**33**	**76**	**6**	**–2**	**4**	**0**	**0**	**0**	**4**	**0**	**0**	**0**
	Canada	WEC-A	10	4	1	5	....	....	....	12	....	....	....	....	....	....	....	....	....	....	....	....	....	....	....	....	....	....
1983-84	**Washington Capitals**	**NHL**	**80**	**40**	**45**	**85**	**32**	**31**	**63**	**90**	**8**	**0**	**7**	**286**	**14.0**	**119**	**39**	**60**	**2**	**22**	**8**	**3**	**7**	**10**	**16**	**2**	**0**	**0**
1984-85	Canada	Can-Cup	8	3	2	5	....	....	....	10	....	....	....	....	....	....	....	....	....	....	....	....	....	....	....	....	....	....
	Washington Capitals	**NHL**	**80**	**50**	**52**	**102**	**41**	**35**	**76**	**71**	**17**	**0**	**11**	**330**	**15.2**	**143**	**54**	**74**	**2**	**17**	**5**	**4**	**3**	**7**	**9**	**1**	**0**	**1**
1985-86	**Washington Capitals**	**NHL**	**74**	**35**	**40**	**75**	**28**	**27**	**55**	**63**	**11**	**2**	**4**	**279**	**12.5**	**112**	**48**	**79**	**10**	**–5**	**9**	**2**	**10**	**12**	**4**	**0**	**0**	**0**
1986-87	**Washington Capitals**	**NHL**	**78**	**41**	**32**	**73**	**35**	**23**	**58**	**61**	**5**	**6**	**10**	**317**	**12.9**	**118**	**33**	**98**	**14**	**1**	**7**	**4**	**3**	**7**	**14**	**0**	**0**	**0**
1987-88	Canada	Can-Cup	9	2	2	4	....	....	....	6	....	....	....	....	....	....	....	....	....	....	....	....	....	....	....	....	....	....
	Washington Capitals	**NHL**	**80**	**48**	**33**	**81**	**41**	**24**	**65**	**73**	**19**	**0**	**7**	**316**	**15.2**	**135**	**54**	**78**	**17**	**20**	**14**	**3**	**4**	**7**	**14**	**1**	**0**	**0**
1988-89	**Washington Capitals**	**NHL**	**56**	**26**	**29**	**55**	**22**	**21**	**43**	**71**	**6**	**0**	**1**	**190**	**13.7**	**91**	**30**	**57**	**4**	**8**	....	....	....	....	....	....	....	....
	Minnesota North Stars	**NHL**	**13**	**7**	**7**	**14**	**6**	**5**	**11**	**2**	**3**	**0**	**0**	**33**	**21.2**	**21**	**9**	**11**	**2**	**3**	**5**	**0**	**0**	**0**	**6**	**0**	**0**	**0**
1989-90	**Minnesota North Stars**	**NHL**	**67**	**34**	**36**	**70**	**29**	**26**	**55**	**32**	**15**	**4**	**2**	**240**	**14.2**	**115**	**47**	**83**	**7**	**–8**	....	....	....	....	....	....	....	....
	New York Rangers	**NHL**	**12**	**11**	**5**	**16**	**9**	**4**	**13**	**6**	**6**	**0**	**3**	**48**	**22.9**	**22**	**10**	**8**	**0**	**4**	**10**	**5**	**3**	**8**	**12**	**4**	**0**	**1**
1990-91	**New York Rangers**	**NHL**	**79**	**49**	**20**	**69**	**45**	**15**	**60**	**53**	**22**	**1**	**4**	**262**	**18.7**	**120**	**57**	**75**	**3**	**–9**	**6**	**1**	**1**	**2**	**0**	**1**	**0**	**0**
1991-92	**New York Rangers**	**NHL**	**76**	**40**	**41**	**81**	**36**	**31**	**67**	**55**	**15**	**0**	**6**	**286**	**14.0**	**115**	**46**	**61**	**3**	**11**	**13**	**8**	**8**	**16**	**4**	**3**	**0**	**1**
1992-93	**New York Rangers**	**NHL**	**84**	**45**	**23**	**68**	**37**	**16**	**53**	**59**	**13**	**0**	**3**	**323**	**13.9**	**113**	**44**	**77**	**4**	**–4**	....	....	....	....	....	....	....	....
	Canada	WC-A	7	3	4	7	....	....	....	12	....	....	....	....	....	....	....	....	....	....	....	....	....	....	....	....	....	....
1993-94	**New York Rangers**	**NHL**	**71**	**28**	**24**	**52**	**26**	**19**	**45**	**58**	**10**	**5**	**4**	**245**	**11.4**	**82**	**30**	**52**	**11**	**11**	....	....	....	....	....	....	....	....
	Toronto Maple Leafs	**NHL**	**10**	**6**	**6**	**12**	**6**	**5**	**11**	**4**	**1**	**0**	**0**	**30**	**20.0**	**18**	**4**	**6**	**1**	**9**	**18**	**5**	**6**	**11**	**14**	**1**	**0**	**3**
1994-95	**Toronto Maple Leafs**	**NHL**	**38**	**12**	**8**	**20**	**21**	**12**	**33**	**6**	**2**	**1**	**1**	**91**	**13.2**	**32**	**9**	**25**	**2**	**0**	**5**	**2**	**2**	**4**	**2**	**0**	**0**	**0**

Season	Club	League	GP	G	A	Pts	AG	AA	APts	PIM	PP	SH	GW	S	%	TGF	PGF	TGA	PGA	+/–	GP	G	A	Pts	PIM	PP	SH	GW
			REGULAR SEASON																		PLAYOFFS							
1995-96	**Toronto Maple Leafs**	**NHL**	**82**	**35**	**19**	**54**	**34**	**16**	**50**	**52**	**15**	**0**	**4**	**275**	**12.7**	**96**	**40**	**51**	**0**	**5**	**6**	**4**	**1**	**5**	**4**	**2**	**0**	**1**
1996-97	**Phoenix Coyotes**	**NHL**	**82**	**32**	**31**	**63**	**34**	**28**	**62**	**38**	**13**	**1**	**7**	**271**	**11.8**	**93**	**39**	**71**	**6**	**–11**	**7**	**1**	**2**	**3**	**4**	**0**	**0**	**0**
1997-98	**Phoenix Coyotes**	**NHL**	**60**	**12**	**15**	**27**	**14**	**15**	**29**	**24**	**4**	**0**	**2**	**145**	**8.3**	**41**	**12**	**37**	**4**	**–4**	**5**	**1**	**0**	**1**	**18**	**1**	**0**	**0**
	NHL Totals		**1432**	**708**	**627**	**1335**	**623**	**463**	**1086**	**1159**	**217**	**23**	**90**	**5090**	**13.9**	**2029**	**726**	**1350**	**114**		**122**	**43**	**50**	**93**	**125**	**16**	**0**	**7**
	Other Major League Totals		78	27	25	52	....	....	....	123	....	....	....	....	....	....	....	....	....	....	3	0	2	2	2	....	....	....

OMJHL First All-Star Team (1978) • Played in NHL All-Star Game (1981, 1985, 1986, 1988, 1990, 1993, 1996)

Signed as a underage free agent by **Birmingham** (WHA), May, 1978. Traded to **Minnesota** by **Washington** with Larry Murphy for Dino Ciccarelli and Bob Rouse, March 7, 1989. Traded to **NY Rangers** by **Minnesota** for Ulf Dahlen, LA Kings' 4th round choice (previously acquired, Minnesota selected Cal McGowan) in 1990 Entry Draft and future considerations, March 6, 1990. Traded to **Toronto** by **NY Rangers** for Glenn Anderson, the rights to Scott Malone and Toronto's 4th round choice (Alexander Korobolin) in 1994 Entry Draft, March 21, 1994. Traded to **Phoenix** by **Toronto** for Chicago's 4th round choice (previously acquired, Toronto selected Vladimir Antipov) in 1996 Entry Draft, June 22, 1996.

• GASSOFF, Bob

Robert Allen D – L. 5'10", 195 lbs. b: Quesnel, B.C., 4/17/1953 d: 5/27/1977. St. Louis' 3rd, 48th overall, in 1973.

Season	Club	League	GP	G	A	Pts	AG	AA	APts	PIM	PP	SH	GW	S	%	TGF	PGF	TGA	PGA	+/–	GP	G	A	Pts	PIM	PP	SH	GW
1970-71	Vernon Lakers	BCJHL	STATISTICS NOT AVAILABLE																									
1971-72	Medicine Hat Tigers	WCJHL	64	1	16	17	....	....	....	314	....	....	....	....	....	....	....	....	....	....	7	0	2	2	29	....	....	....
1972-73	Medicine Hat Tigers	WCJHL	68	11	51	62	....	....	....	*388	....	....	....	....	....	....	....	....	....	....	17	2	10	12	*152	....	....	....
1973-74	**St. Louis Blues**	**NHL**	**28**	**0**	**3**	**3**	**0**	**2**	**2**	**84**	**0**	**0**	**0**	**20**	**0.0**	**12**	**0**	**31**	**3**	**–16**	....	....	....	....	....	....	....	....
	Denver Spurs	WHL	45	4	10	14	....	....	....	*301	....	....	....	....	....	....	....	....	....	....	....	....	....	....	....	....	....	....
1974-75	**St. Louis Blues**	**NHL**	**60**	**4**	**14**	**18**	**3**	**10**	**13**	**222**	**1**	**0**	**1**	**77**	**5.2**	**64**	**4**	**57**	**8**	**11**	**2**	**0**	**0**	**0**	**0**	**0**	**0**	**0**
	Denver Spurs	CHL	19	2	11	13	....	....	....	114	....	....	....	....	....	....	....	....	....	....	....	....	....	....	....	....	....	....
1975-76	**St. Louis Blues**	**NHL**	**80**	**1**	**12**	**13**	**1**	**9**	**10**	**306**	**0**	**0**	**0**	**100**	**1.0**	**73**	**2**	**106**	**27**	**–8**	**3**	**0**	**0**	**0**	**6**	**0**	**0**	**0**
1976-77	**St. Louis Blues**	**NHL**	**77**	**6**	**18**	**24**	**5**	**14**	**19**	**254**	**0**	**0**	**3**	**110**	**5.5**	**81**	**0**	**98**	**15**	**–2**	**4**	**0**	**1**	**1**	**10**	**0**	**0**	**0**
	NHL Totals		**245**	**11**	**47**	**58**	**9**	**35**	**44**	**866**	**1**	**0**	**4**	**307**	**3.6**	**230**	**6**	**292**	**53**		**9**	**0**	**1**	**1**	**16**	**0**	**0**	**0**

• Brother of Brad. • Died of injuries suffered in motorbike accident, May 27, 1977.

• GASSOFF, Brad

Howard Bradley LW – L. 5'11", 195 lbs. b: Quesnel, B.C., 11/13/1955. Vancouver's 2nd, 28th overall, in 1975.

Season	Club	League	GP	G	A	Pts	AG	AA	APts	PIM	PP	SH	GW	S	%	TGF	PGF	TGA	PGA	+/–	GP	G	A	Pts	PIM	PP	SH	GW
1971-72	Drumheller Miners	AJHL	STATISTICS NOT AVAILABLE																									
1972-73	Medicine Hat Tigers	WCJHL	67	13	22	35	....	....	....	122	....	....	....	....	....	....	....	....	....	....	17	3	3	6	67	....	....	....
	Medicine Hat	Mem-Cup	2	1	1	2	....	....	....	10	....	....	....	....	....	....	....	....	....	....	....	....	....	....	....	....	....	....
1973-74	Medicine Hat Tigers	WCJHL	61	16	25	41	....	....	....	245	....	....	....	....	....	....	....	....	....	....	6	1	0	1	22	....	....	....
1974-75	Kamloops Chiefs	WCJHL	69	50	59	109	....	....	....	251	....	....	....	....	....	....	....	....	....	....	6	4	1	5	24	....	....	....
1975-76	**Vancouver Canucks**	**NHL**	**4**	**0**	**0**	**0**	**0**	**0**	**0**	**5**	**0**	**0**	**0**	**3**	**0.0**	**0**	**0**	**2**	**0**	**–2**	....	....	....	....	....	....	....	....
	Tulsa Oilers	CHL	68	36	28	64	....	....	....	295	....	....	....	....	....	....	....	....	....	....	9	*5	6	*11	32	....	....	....
1976-77	**Vancouver Canucks**	**NHL**	**37**	**6**	**4**	**10**	**5**	**3**	**8**	**35**	**1**	**0**	**0**	**53**	**11.3**	**16**	**5**	**35**	**0**	**–24**	....	....	....	....	....	....	....	....
	Tulsa Oilers	CHL	31	12	16	28	....	....	....	58	....	....	....	....	....	....	....	....	....	....	....	....	....	....	....	....	....	....
1977-78	**Vancouver Canucks**	**NHL**	**47**	**9**	**6**	**15**	**8**	**5**	**13**	**70**	**0**	**0**	**1**	**40**	**22.5**	**28**	**3**	**31**	**0**	**–6**	....	....	....	....	....	....	....	....
	Tulsa Oilers	CHL	18	11	9	20	....	....	....	29	....	....	....	....	....	....	....	....	....	....	....	....	....	....	....	....	....	....
1978-79	**Vancouver Canucks**	**NHL**	**34**	**4**	**7**	**11**	**3**	**5**	**8**	**53**	**0**	**0**	**0**	**44**	**9.1**	**13**	**0**	**24**	**0**	**–11**	**3**	**0**	**0**	**0**	**0**	**0**	**0**	**0**
	Dallas Black Hawks	CHL	36	11	20	31	....	....	....	164	....	....	....	....	....	....	....	....	....	....	....	....	....	....	....	....	....	....
1979-80	Dallas Black Hawks	CHL	68	14	48	62	....	....	....	*353	....	....	....	....	....	....	....	....	....	....	....	....	....	....	....	....	....	....
1980-81	Quesnel Kangaroos	BCHA-I	STATISTICS NOT AVAILABLE																									
	NHL Totals		**122**	**19**	**17**	**36**	**16**	**13**	**29**	**163**	**1**	**0**	**1**	**140**	**13.6**	**57**	**8**	**92**	**0**		**3**	**0**	**0**	**0**	**0**	**0**	**0**	**0**

• Brother of Bob • CHL Second All-Star Team (1976) • Won Ken McKenzie Trophy (CHL's Rookie of the Year) (1976)

• GATZOS, Steve

RW – R. 5'11", 185 lbs. b: Toronto, Ont., 6/22/1961. Pittsburgh's 1st, 28th overall, in 1981.

Season	Club	League	GP	G	A	Pts	AG	AA	APts	PIM	PP	SH	GW	S	%	TGF	PGF	TGA	PGA	+/–	GP	G	A	Pts	PIM	PP	SH	GW
1978-79	Sault Ste. Marie Greyhounds	OMJHL	36	3	9	12	....	....	....	26	....	....	....	....	....	....	....	....	....	....	....	....	....	....	....	....	....	....
1979-80	Sault Ste. Marie Greyhounds	OMJHL	64	36	38	74	....	....	....	64	....	....	....	....	....	....	....	....	....	....	....	....	....	....	....	....	....	....
1980-81	Sault Ste. Marie Greyhounds	OMJHL	68	78	50	128	....	....	....	114	....	....	....	....	....	....	....	....	....	....	19	16	9	25	23	....	....	....
1981-82	**Pittsburgh Penguins**	**NHL**	**16**	**6**	**8**	**14**	**5**	**5**	**10**	**14**	**1**	**0**	**0**	**36**	**16.7**	**21**	**5**	**16**	**0**	**0**	**1**	**0**	**0**	**0**	**0**	**0**	**0**	**0**
	Erie Blades	AHL	54	18	19	37	....	....	....	67	....	....	....	....	....	....	....	....	....	....	....	....	....	....	....	....	....	....
1982-83	**Pittsburgh Penguins**	**NHL**	**44**	**6**	**7**	**13**	**5**	**5**	**10**	**52**	**2**	**0**	**1**	**70**	**8.6**	**20**	**4**	**33**	**1**	**–16**	....	....	....	....	....	....	....	....
	Baltimore Skipjacks	AHL	12	5	4	9	....	....	....	22	....	....	....	....	....	....	....	....	....	....	....	....	....	....	....	....	....	....
1983-84	**Pittsburgh Penguins**	**NHL**	**23**	**3**	**3**	**6**	**2**	**2**	**4**	**15**	**0**	**0**	**1**	**29**	**10.3**	**10**	**2**	**17**	**0**	**–9**	....	....	....	....	....	....	....	....
	Baltimore Skipjacks	AHL	48	14	19	33	....	....	....	43	....	....	....	....	....	....	....	....	....	....	....	....	....	....	....	....	....	....
1984-85	**Pittsburgh Penguins**	**NHL**	**6**	**0**	**2**	**2**	**0**	**1**	**1**	**2**	**0**	**0**	**0**	**6**	**0.0**	**4**	**1**	**9**	**0**	**–6**	....	....	....	....	....	....	....	....
	Muskegon Mohawks	IHL	24	18	10	28	....	....	....	24	....	....	....	....	....	....	....	....	....	....	....	....	....	....	....	....	....	....
1985-86	Baltimore Skipjacks	AHL	53	25	8	33	....	....	....	34	....	....	....	....	....	....	....	....	....	....	....	....	....	....	....	....	....	....
1986-87			STATISTICS NOT AVAILABLE																									
1987-88	Tilburg Trappers	Holland	36	53	59	112	....	....	....	....	....	....	....	....	....	....	....	....	....	....	....	....	....	....	....	....	....	....
1988-89	SaiPa Lappeenranta	Finland	41	27	18	45	....	....	....	62	....	....	....	....	....	....	....	....	....	....	....	....	....	....	....	....	....	....
1989-90	HK Medvescak	Slovenia	28	43	16	59	....	....	....	....	....	....	....	....	....	....	....	....	....	....	....	....	....	....	....	....	....	....
1990-91	Fife Flyers	Britain	17	29	24	53	....	....	....	43	....	....	....	....	....	....	....	....	....	....	....	....	....	....	....	....	....	....
	Roanoke Valley Rebels	ECHL	16	14	13	27	....	....	....	2	....	....	....	....	....	....	....	....	....	....	....	....	....	....	....	....	....	....
1991-92	Roanoke Valley Rebels	ECHL	DID NOT PLAY – ASSISTANT COACH																									
1992-93	Roanoke Valley Rampage	ECHL	1	1	1	2	....	....	....	0	....	....	....	....	....	....	....	....	....	....	....	....	....	....	....	....	....	....
	Tallahasse Tiger Sharks	ECHL	DID NOT PLAY – COACHING																									
1993-94	Tallahasse Tiger Sharks	ECHL	DID NOT PLAY – COACHING																									
1994-95	SIJ Geleen	Holland	DID NOT PLAY – COACHING																									
	NHL Totals		**89**	**15**	**20**	**35**	**12**	**13**	**25**	**83**	**3**	**0**	**2**	**141**	**10.6**	**55**	**12**	**75**	**1**		**1**	**0**	**0**	**0**	**0**	**0**	**0**	**0**

• GAUDREAU, Rob

Robert R. RW – R. 5'11", 185 lbs. b: Lincoln, RI, 1/20/1970. Pittsburgh's 8th, 172nd overall, in 1988.

Season	Club	League	GP	G	A	Pts	AG	AA	APts	PIM	PP	SH	GW	S	%	TGF	PGF	TGA	PGA	+/–	GP	G	A	Pts	PIM	PP	SH	GW
1986-87	Bishop Hendrickson Hawks	Hi-School	33	41	39	80	....	....	....	....	....	....	....	....	....	....	....	....	....	....	....	....	....	....	....	....	....	....
1987-88	Bishop Hendrickson Hawks	Hi-School	32	52	60	112	....	....	....	....	....	....	....	....	....	....	....	....	....	....	....	....	....	....	....	....	....	....
1988-89	Providence College	H-East	42	28	29	57	....	....	....	32	....	....	....	....	....	....	....	....	....	....	....	....	....	....	....	....	....	....
1989-90	Providence College	H-East	32	20	18	38	....	....	....	12	....	....	....	....	....	....	....	....	....	....	....	....	....	....	....	....	....	....
	United States	WJC-A	7	3	1	4	....	....	....	6	....	....	....	....	....	....	....	....	....	....	....	....	....	....	....	....	....	....
1990-91	Providence College	H-East	36	34	27	61	....	....	....	20	....	....	....	....	....	....	....	....	....	....	....	....	....	....	....	....	....	....
1991-92	Providence College	H-East	36	21	34	55	....	....	....	22	....	....	....	....	....	....	....	....	....	....	....	....	....	....	....	....	....	....
1992-93	**San Jose Sharks**	**NHL**	**59**	**23**	**20**	**43**	**19**	**14**	**33**	**18**	**5**	**2**	**1**	**191**	**12.0**	**76**	**33**	**76**	**15**	**–18**	....	....	....	....	....	....	....	....
	Kansas City Blades	IHL	19	8	6	14	....	....	....	6	....	....	....	....	....	....	....	....	....	....	....	....	....	....	....	....	....	....
	United States	WC-A	5	3	3	6	....	....	....	2	....	....	....	....	....	....	....	....	....	....	....	....	....	....	....	....	....	....
1993-94	**San Jose Sharks**	**NHL**	**84**	**15**	**20**	**35**	**14**	**16**	**30**	**28**	**6**	**0**	**4**	**151**	**9.9**	**61**	**32**	**60**	**21**	**–10**	**14**	**2**	**0**	**2**	**0**	**1**	**1**	**0**
1994-95	**Ottawa Senators**	**NHL**	**36**	**5**	**9**	**14**	**9**	**13**	**22**	**8**	**0**	**0**	**0**	**65**	**7.7**	**26**	**8**	**37**	**3**	**–16**	....	....	....	....	....	....	....	....
1995-96	**Ottawa Senators**	**NHL**	**52**	**8**	**5**	**13**	**8**	**4**	**12**	**15**	**1**	**1**	**0**	**76**	**10.5**	**25**	**9**	**41**	**6**	**–19**	....	....	....	....	....	....	....	....
	P.E.I. Senators	AHL	3	2	0	2	....	....	....	4	....	....	....	....	....	....	....	....	....	....	....	....	....	....	....	....	....	....
1996-97	HC Bolzano	Alpenliga	2	0	1	1	....	....	....	0	....	....	....	....	....	....	....	....	....	....	....	....	....	....	....	....	....	....
	HC La Chaux-de-Fonds	Switz.	37	19	23	42	....	....	....	62	....	....	....	....	....	....	....	....	....	....	....	....	....	....	....	....	....	....
	NHL Totals		**231**	**51**	**54**	**105**	**50**	**47**	**97**	**69**	**12**	**3**	**5**	**483**	**10.6**	**188**	**82**	**214**	**45**		**14**	**2**	**0**	**2**	**0**	**1**	**1**	**0**

Hockey East Second All-Star Team (1991) • Hockey East First All-Star Team (1992) • NCAA East Second All-American Team (1992)

Rights traded to **Minnesota** by **Pittsburgh** for Richard Zemlak, November 1, 1988. Claimed by **San Jose** from **Minnesota** in Dispersal Draft, May 30, 1991. Claimed by **Ottawa** from **San Jose** in Waiver Draft, January 18, 1995.

• GAUL, Michael

D – R. 6'1", 200 lbs. b: Lachine, Que., 4/22/1973. Los Angeles' 10th, 262nd overall, in 1991.

Season	Club	League	GP	G	A	Pts	AG	AA	APts	PIM	PP	SH	GW	S	%	TGF	PGF	TGA	PGA	+/–	GP	G	A	Pts	PIM	PP	SH	GW
1989-90	Lac St-Louis Lions	QAAA	39	5	9	14	....	....	....	....	....	....	....	....	....	....	....	....	....	....	....	....	....	....	....	....	....	....
1990-91	St. Lawrence University	ECAC	31	1	3	4	....	....	....	46	....	....	....	....	....	....	....	....	....	....	....	....	....	....	....	....	....	....
1991-92	Laval Titan	QMJHL	50	6	38	44	....	....	....	44	....	....	....	....	....	....	....	....	....	....	10	0	2	2	20	....	....	....
1992-93	Laval Titan	QMJHL	57	16	57	73	....	....	....	66	....	....	....	....	....	....	....	....	....	....	13	3	10	13	10	....	....	....
1993-94	Laval Titan	QMJHL	22	10	17	27	....	....	....	24	....	....	....	....	....	....	....	....	....	....	21	5	15	20	14	....	....	....

			REGULAR SEASON																		PLAYOFFS							
Season	Club	League	GP	G	A	Pts	AG	AA	APts	PIM	PP	SH	GW	S	%	TGF	PGF	TGA	PGA	+/–	GP	G	A	Pts	PIM	PP	SH	GW
1994-95	Phoenix Roadrunners	IHL	4	0	1	1	....	....	....	2	....	....	....	....	....	....	....	....	....	....	....	....	....	....	....	....	....	....
	Knoxville Cherokees	ECHL	68	13	41	54	....	....	....	51	....	....	....	....	....	....	....	....	....	....	4	2	1	3	2	....	....	....
1995-96	Knoxville Cherokees	ECHL	54	13	48	61	....	....	....	44	....	....	....	....	....	....	....	....	....	....	....	....	....	....	....	....	....	....
1996-97	ETC Timmendorfer	Germany-2	51	40	52	92	....	....	....	100	....	....	....	....	....	....	....	....	....	....	....	....	....	....	....	....	....	....
1997-98	Hershey Bears	AHL	60	12	47	59	....	....	....	69	....	....	....	....	....	....	....	....	....	....	7	0	7	7	6	....	....	....
	Mobile Mysticks	ECHL	5	0	7	7	....	....	....	0	....	....	....	....	....	....	....	....	....	....	....	....	....	....	....	....	....	....
1998-99	Lowell Lock Monsters	AHL	18	3	5	8	....	....	....	14	....	....	....	....	....	....	....	....	....	....	....	....	....	....	....	....	....	....
	Colorado Avalanche	**NHL**	**1**	**0**	**0**	**0**	**0**	**0**	**0**	**0**	**0**	**0**	**0**	**1**	**0.0**	**0**	**0**	**0**	**0**	**0**	....	....	....	....	....	....	....	....
	Hershey Bears	AHL	43	9	31	40	....	....	....	22	....	....	....	....	....	....	....	....	....	....	5	1	1	2	6	....	....	....
99-2000	Hershey Bears	AHL	65	12	57	69	....	....	....	52	....	....	....	....	....	....	....	....	....	....	12	0	8	8	....	....	....	....
	NHL Totals		**1**	**0**	**0**	**0**	**0**	**0**	**0**	**0**	**0**	**0**	**0**	**1**	**0.0**	**0**	**0**	**0**	**0**		....	....	....	....	....	....	....	....

• AHL Second All-Star Team (2000)

Signed as a free agent by **NY Islanders**, July 16, 1998. Traded to **Colorado** by **NY Islanders** for Ted Crowley, December 15, 1998.

• GAULIN, Jean-Marc

RW – R. 5'10", 180 lbs. b: Balve, Germany, 3/3/1962. Quebec's 2nd, 53rd overall, in 1981.

Season	Club	League	GP	G	A	Pts	AG	AA	APts	PIM	PP	SH	GW	S	%	TGF	PGF	TGA	PGA	+/–	GP	G	A	Pts	PIM	PP	SH	GW
1978-79	Sherbrooke Beavers	QMJHL	71	26	41	67	....	....	....	89	....	....	....	....	....	....	....	....	....	....	....	....	....	....	....	....	....	....
1979-80	Sherbrooke Beavers	QMJHL	16	6	15	21	....	....	....	14	....	....	....	....	....	....	....	....	....	....	....	....	....	....	....	....	....	....
	Sorel Black Hawks	QMJHL	43	15	25	40	....	....	....	105	....	....	....	....	....	....	....	....	....	....	....	....	....	....	....	....	....	....
1980-81	Sorel Black Hawks	QMJHL	70	50	40	90	....	....	....	157	....	....	....	....	....	....	....	....	....	....	7	0	3	3	6	....	....	....
	Canada	WJC-A	5	2	0	2	....	....	....	4	....	....	....	....	....	....	....	....	....	....	....	....	....	....	....	....	....	....
1981-82	Hull Olympiques	QMJHL	56	50	50	100	....	....	....	93	....	....	....	....	....	....	....	....	....	....	11	2	15	17	9	....	....	....
1982-83	**Quebec Nordiques**	**NHL**	**1**	**0**	**0**	**0**	**0**	**0**	**0**	**0**	**0**	**0**	**0**	**0**	**0.0**	**0**	**0**	**0**	**0**	**0**	....	....	....	....	....	....	....	....
	Fredericton Express	AHL	67	11	17	28	....	....	....	58	....	....	....	....	....	....	....	....	....	....	9	0	0	0	21	....	....	....
1983-84	**Quebec Nordiques**	**NHL**	**2**	**0**	**0**	**0**	**0**	**0**	**0**	**0**	**0**	**0**	**0**	**0**	**0.0**	**0**	**0**	**1**	**0**	**–1**	....	....	....	....	....	....	....	....
	Fredericton Express	AHL	62	14	28	42	....	....	....	80	....	....	....	....	....	....	....	....	....	....	7	2	5	7	0	....	....	....
1984-85	**Quebec Nordiques**	**NHL**	**22**	**3**	**3**	**6**	**2**	**2**	**4**	**8**	**0**	**0**	**0**	**24**	**12.5**	**10**	**0**	**8**	**0**	**2**	**1**	**0**	**0**	**0**	**0**	**0**	**0**	**0**
	Fredericton Express	AHL	27	10	9	19	....	....	....	32	....	....	....	....	....	....	....	....	....	....	5	1	3	4	2	....	....	....
1985-86	**Quebec Nordiques**	**NHL**	**1**	**1**	**0**	**1**	**1**	**0**	**1**	**0**	**0**	**0**	**0**	**2**	**50.0**	**1**	**0**	**1**	**0**	**0**	....	....	....	....	....	....	....	....
	Fredericton Express	AHL	58	16	26	42	....	....	....	66	....	....	....	....	....	....	....	....	....	....	6	2	3	5	31	....	....	....
1986-87	Fredericton Express	AHL	17	1	1	2	....	....	....	15	....	....	....	....	....	....	....	....	....	....	....	....	....	....	....	....	....	....
	Muskegon Lumberjacks	IHL	5	1	3	4	....	....	....	6	....	....	....	....	....	....	....	....	....	....	....	....	....	....	....	....	....	....
1987-88	HC Mont-Blanc	France-2	23	19	17	36	....	....	....	26	....	....	....	....	....	....	....	....	....	....	....	....	....	....	....	....	....	....
1988-89	Paris Francais Volants	France	37	35	29	64	....	....	....	20	....	....	....	....	....	....	....	....	....	....	6	9	3	12	0	....	....	....
1989-90	Paris Francais Volants	France	36	40	29	69	....	....	....	18	....	....	....	....	....	....	....	....	....	....	3	1	0	1	4	....	....	....
1990-91	Paris Francais Volants	France	28	21	18	39	....	....	....	16	....	....	....	....	....	....	....	....	....	....	4	4	1	5	6	....	....	....
1991-92	Paris Francais Volants	France	33	38	28	66	....	....	....	32	....	....	....	....	....	....	....	....	....	....	....	....	....	....	....	....	....	....
1992-93	HC Lausanne	Switz-2	STATISTICS NOT AVAILABLE																									
1993-94	HC Lyon	France-2	20	29	24	53	....	....	....	32	....	....	....	....	....	....	....	....	....	....	6	11	4	15	10	....	....	....
1994-95	HC Lyon	France-2	28	27	19	46	....	....	....	30	....	....	....	....	....	....	....	....	....	....	....	....	....	....	....	....	....	....
1995-96	HC Lyon	France-2	27	22	19	41	....	....	....	34	....	....	....	....	....	....	....	....	....	....	....	....	....	....	....	....	....	....
	NHL Totals		**26**	**4**	**3**	**7**	**3**	**2**	**5**	**8**	**0**	**0**	**0**	**26**	**15.4**	**11**	**0**	**10**	**0**		**1**	**0**	**0**	**0**	**0**	**0**	**0**	**0**

QMJHL Second All-Star Team (1981)

• GAUME, Dallas

C – L. 5'10", 185 lbs. b: Innisfal, Alta., 8/27/1963.

Season	Club	League	GP	G	A	Pts	AG	AA	APts	PIM	PP	SH	GW	S	%	TGF	PGF	TGA	PGA	+/–	GP	G	A	Pts	PIM	PP	SH	GW
1982-83	University of Denver	WCHA	37	19	47	66	....	....	....	12	....	....	....	....	....	....	....	....	....	....	....	....	....	....	....	....	....	....
1983-84	University of Denver	WCHA	32	12	25	37	....	....	....	22	....	....	....	....	....	....	....	....	....	....	....	....	....	....	....	....	....	....
1984-85	University of Denver	WCHA	39	15	48	63	....	....	....	28	....	....	....	....	....	....	....	....	....	....	....	....	....	....	....	....	....	....
1985-86	University of Denver	WCHA	47	32	*67	*99	....	....	....	18	....	....	....	....	....	....	....	....	....	....	....	....	....	....	....	....	....	....
1986-87	Binghamton Whalers	AHL	77	18	39	57	....	....	....	31	....	....	....	....	....	....	....	....	....	....	12	1	1	2	7	....	....	....
1987-88	Binghamton Whalers	AHL	63	24	49	73	....	....	....	39	....	....	....	....	....	....	....	....	....	....	4	1	2	3	0	....	....	....
1988-89	**Hartford Whalers**	**NHL**	**4**	**1**	**1**	**2**	**1**	**1**	**2**	**0**	**0**	**0**	**0**	**5**	**20.0**	**2**	**0**	**1**	**0**	**1**	....	....	....	....	....	....	....	....
	Binghamton Whalers	AHL	57	23	43	66	....	....	....	16	....	....	....	....	....	....	....	....	....	....	....	....	....	....	....	....	....	....
1989-90	Binghamton Whalers	AHL	76	26	39	65	....	....	....	43	....	....	....	....	....	....	....	....	....	....	....	....	....	....	....	....	....	....
1990-91	Trondheim IHK	Norway	8	5	6	11	....	....	....	6	....	....	....	....	....	....	....	....	....	....	....	....	....	....	....	....	....	....
1991-92	Trondheim IHK	Norway	32	30	*41	*71	....	....	....	....	....	....	....	....	....	....	....	....	....	....	4	4	2	6	....	....	....	....
1992-93	Trondheim IHK	Norway	DID NOT PLAY – INJURED																									
1993-94	Trondheim IHK	Norway	32	25	*36	61	....	....	....	....	....	....	....	....	....	....	....	....	....	....	2	0	2	2	2	....	....	....
	Canada	Nat-Team	4	0	1	1	....	....	....	0	....	....	....	....	....	....	....	....	....	....	....	....	....	....	....	....	....	....
1994-95	Trondheim IHK	Norway	16	9	14	23	....	....	....	14	....	....	....	....	....	....	....	....	....	....	....	....	....	....	....	....	....	....
1995-96	Trondheim IHK	Norway	28	11	28	39	....	....	....	10	....	....	....	....	....	....	....	....	....	....	4	6	1	7	0	....	....	....
	Canada	Nat-Team	3	0	4	4	....	....	....	4	....	....	....	....	....	....	....	....	....	....	....	....	....	....	....	....	....	....
1996-97	Trondheim IHK	Norway	38	20	32	52	....	....	....	....	....	....	....	....	....	....	....	....	....	....	4	2	4	6	....	....	....	....
1997-98	Trondheim IHK	Norway	24	10	16	26	....	....	....	14	....	....	....	....	....	....	....	....	....	....	....	....	....	....	....	....	....	....
1998-99	Trondheim IHK	Norway	44	19	41	60	....	....	....	22	....	....	....	....	....	....	....	....	....	....	....	....	....	....	....	....	....	....
	NHL Totals		**4**	**1**	**1**	**2**	**1**	**1**	**2**	**0**	**0**	**0**	**0**	**5**	**20.0**	**2**	**0**	**1**	**0**		....	....	....	....	....	....	....	....

WCHA First All-Star Team (1986) • NCAA West First All-American Team (1986)

Signed as a free agent by **Hartford**, July 10, 1986. • Missed entire 1992-93 season recovering from knee injury suffered in training camp, September 2, 1992.

• GAUTHIER, Daniel

LW – L. 6'1", 190 lbs. b: Charlemagne, Que., 5/17/1970. Pittsburgh's 3rd, 62nd overall, in 1988.

Season	Club	League	GP	G	A	Pts	AG	AA	APts	PIM	PP	SH	GW	S	%	TGF	PGF	TGA	PGA	+/–	GP	G	A	Pts	PIM	PP	SH	GW
1985-86	Val d'Or Miners	NOHA	31	2	12	14	....	....	....	31	....	....	....	....	....	....	....	....	....	....	....	....	....	....	....	....	....	....
1986-87	Longueuil Chevaliers	QMJHL	64	23	22	45	....	....	....	23	....	....	....	....	....	....	....	....	....	....	18	4	5	9	15	....	....	....
	Longueuil Chevaliers	Mem-Cup	3	0	0	0	....	....	....	2	....	....	....	....	....	....	....	....	....	....	....	....	....	....	....	....	....	....
1987-88	Victoriaville Tigres	QMJHL	66	43	47	90	....	....	....	53	....	....	....	....	....	....	....	....	....	....	5	2	1	3	0	....	....	....
1988-89	Victoriaville Tigres	QMJHL	64	41	75	116	....	....	....	84	....	....	....	....	....	....	....	....	....	....	16	12	17	29	30	....	....	....
1989-90	Victoriaville Tigres	QMJHL	62	45	69	114	....	....	....	32	....	....	....	....	....	....	....	....	....	....	16	8	*19	27	16	....	....	....
1990-91	Albany Choppers	IHL	1	1	0	1	....	....	....	0	....	....	....	....	....	....	....	....	....	....	....	....	....	....	....	....	....	....
	Knoxville Cherokees	ECHL	61	41	*93	134	....	....	....	40	....	....	....	....	....	....	....	....	....	....	2	0	4	4	4	....	....	....
1991-92	Muskegon Lumberjacks	IHL	68	19	18	37	....	....	....	28	....	....	....	....	....	....	....	....	....	....	9	3	6	9	8	....	....	....
1992-93	Cleveland Lumberjacks	IHL	80	40	66	106	....	....	....	88	....	....	....	....	....	....	....	....	....	....	4	2	2	4	14	....	....	....
1993-94	Cincinnati Cyclones	IHL	74	30	34	64	....	....	....	101	....	....	....	....	....	....	....	....	....	....	10	2	3	5	14	....	....	....
1994-95	**Chicago Blackhawks**	**NHL**	**5**	**0**	**0**	**0**	**0**	**0**	**0**	**0**	**0**	**0**	**0**	**4**	**0.0**	**1**	**0**	**1**	**0**	**0**	....	....	....	....	....	....	....	....
	Indianapolis Ice	IHL	66	22	50	72	....	....	....	53	....	....	....	....	....	....	....	....	....	....	....	....	....	....	....	....	....	....
1995-96	Indianapolis Ice	IHL	70	28	39	67	....	....	....	44	....	....	....	....	....	....	....	....	....	....	....	....	....	....	....	....	....	....
	Peoria Rivermen	IHL	10	3	5	8	....	....	....	10	....	....	....	....	....	....	....	....	....	....	11	4	6	10	6	....	....	....
1996-97	VEU Feldkirch	Austria	29	12	18	30	....	....	....	22	....	....	....	....	....	....	....	....	....	....	....	....	....	....	....	....	....	....
	Frankfurt Lions	Germany	8	1	0	1	....	....	....	6	....	....	....	....	....	....	....	....	....	....	....	....	....	....	....	....	....	....
	EHC Hannover	Germany	2	1	0	1	....	....	....	0	....	....	....	....	....	....	....	....	....	....	....	....	....	....	....	....	....	....
1997-98	VEU Feldkirch	Alpenliga	21	8	20	28	....	....	....	12	....	....	....	....	....	....	....	....	....	....	....	....	....	....	....	....	....	....
	VEU Feldkirch	Austria	27	5	17	22	....	....	....	30	....	....	....	....	....	....	....	....	....	....	....	....	....	....	....	....	....	....
	VEU Feldkirch	EuroHL	6	2	5	7	....	....	....	2	....	....	....	....	....	....	....	....	....	....	4	2	2	4	4	....	....	....
1998-99	VEU Feldkirch	Alpenliga	34	24	32	56	....	....	....	18	....	....	....	....	....	....	....	....	....	....	....	....	....	....	....	....	....	....
	VEU Feldkirch	Austria	11	4	3	7	....	....	....	4	....	....	....	....	....	....	....	....	....	....	....	....	....	....	....	....	....	....
	VEU Feldkirch	EuroHL	6	4	2	6	....	....	....	16	....	....	....	....	....	....	....	....	....	....	....	....	....	....	....	....	....	....
99-2000	SC Langnau	Switz.	45	13	22	35	....	....	....	32	....	....	....	....	....	....	....	....	....	....	6	7	5	12	2	....	....	....
	NHL Totals		**5**	**0**	**0**	**0**	**0**	**0**	**0**	**0**	**0**	**0**	**0**	**4**	**0.0**	**1**	**0**	**1**	**0**		....	....	....	....	....	....	....	....

ECHL First-All-Star Team (1991) • Rookie of the Year - ECHL (1991)

Signed as a free agent by **Florida**, July 14, 1993. Signed as a free agent by **Chicago**, June 14, 1994. • Played w/ RHI's Montreal Roadrunners (8-12-9-21-20) and 1997 (12-12-21-33-16) and w/ Ottawa Loggers in 1996 (11-8-17-25-6)

			REGULAR SEASON																		PLAYOFFS							
Season	Club	League	GP	G	A	Pts	AG	AA	APts	PIM	PP	SH	GW	S	%	TGF	PGF	TGA	PGA	+/–	GP	G	A	Pts	PIM	PP	SH	GW

• GAUTHIER, Denis

Denis Jr. D – L. 6'2", 210 lbs. b: Montreal, Que., 10/1/1976. Calgary's 1st, 20th overall, in 1995.

Season	Club	League	GP	G	A	Pts	AG	AA	APts	PIM	PP	SH	GW	S	%	TGF	PGF	TGA	PGA	+/–	GP	G	A	Pts	PIM	PP	SH	GW
1991-92	St-Jean-de-Richelieu	QAAA	STATISTICS NOT AVAILABLE																									
1992-93	Drummondville Voltigeurs	QMJHL	60	1	7	8				136											10	0	5	5	40			
1993-94	Drummondville Voltigeurs	QMJHL	60	0	7	7				176											9	2	0	2	41			
1994-95	Drummondville Voltigeurs	QMJHL	64	9	31	40				190											4	0	5	5	12			
1995-96	Drummondville Voltigeurs	QMJHL	53	25	49	74				140											6	4	4	8	32			
	Canada	WJC-A	6	1	1	2				6																		
	Saint John Flames	AHL	5	2	0	2				8											16	1	6	7	20			
1996-97	Saint John Flames	AHL	73	3	28	31				74											5	0	0	0	6			
1997-98	**Calgary Flames**	**NHL**	**10**	**0**	**0**	**0**	**0**	**0**	**0**	**16**	**0**	**0**	**0**	**3**	**0.0**	**2**	**0**	**7**	**0**	**–5**								
	Saint John Flames	AHL	68	4	20	24				154											21	0	4	4	83			
1998-99	**Calgary Flames**	**NHL**	**55**	**3**	**4**	**7**	**4**	**4**	**8**	**68**	**0**	**0**	**0**	**40**	**7.5**	**25**	**0**	**35**	**13**	**3**								
	Saint John Flames	AHL	16	0	3	3				31																		
99-2000	**Calgary Flames**	**NHL**	**39**	**1**	**1**	**2**	**1**	**1**	**2**	**50**	**0**	**0**	**0**	**29**	**3.4**	**21**	**2**	**45**	**22**	**–4**								
	NHL Totals		**104**	**4**	**5**	**9**	**5**	**5**	**10**	**134**	**0**	**0**	**0**	**72**	**5.6**	**48**	**2**	**87**	**35**									

QMJHL First All-Star Team (1996) • Canadian Major Junior First All-Star Team (1996) • Missed remainder of 1999-2000 season recovering from hip injury suffered in game vs. St. Louis, February 1, 2000.

• GAUTHIER, Jean

Jean Philippe D – R. 6'1", 190 lbs. b: Montreal, Que., 4/29/1937.

Season	Club	League	GP	G	A	Pts	AG	AA	APts	PIM	PP	SH	GW	S	%	TGF	PGF	TGA	PGA	+/–	GP	G	A	Pts	PIM	PP	SH	GW
1955-56	St. Boniface Canadiens	MJHL	23	1	9	10				*99											4	2	1	3	*27			
	St. Boniface Canadiens	Mem-Cup	6	0	2	2				10																		
1956-57	St. Boniface Canadiens	TBJHL	....	9	16	25				*133																		
	St. Boniface Canadiens	Mem-Cup	12	1	5	6				28																		
	Flin Flon Bombers	Mem-Cup	7	0	4	4				14																		
1957-58	Kingston CKLC's	EOHL	46	8	20	28				118											7	0	3	3	12			
1958-59	Hull-Ottawa Canadiens	EOHL	52	5	5	10				110											8	2	3	5	29			
1959-60	Hull-Ottawa Canadiens	EPHL	68	2	23	25				152											7	0	1	1	8			
1960-61	**Montreal Canadiens**	**NHL**	**4**	**0**	**1**	**1**	**0**	**1**	**1**	**8**																		
	Hull-Ottawa Canadiens	EPHL	64	8	13	21				*138											14	0	5	5	*42			
1961-62	**Montreal Canadiens**	**NHL**	**12**	**0**	**1**	**1**	**0**	**1**	**1**	**10**																		
	Hull-Ottawa Canadiens	EPHL	47	11	20	31				85											13	5	4	9	*38			
1962-63	**Montreal Canadiens**	**NHL**	**65**	**1**	**17**	**18**	**1**	**17**	**18**	**46**											**5**	**0**	**0**	**0**	**12**	**0**	**0**	**0**
1963-64	**Montreal Canadiens**	**NHL**	**1**	**0**	**0**	**0**	**0**	**0**	**0**	**2**																		
	Quebec Aces	AHL	29	3	7	10				58											9	1	2	3	4			
1964-65	Omaha Knights	CPHL	70	14	37	51				182											6	4	1	5	10			
♦	**Montreal Canadiens**	**NHL**																			**2**	**0**	**0**	**0**	**4**	**0**	**0**	**0**
1965-66	**Montreal Canadiens**	**NHL**	**2**	**0**	**0**	**0**	**0**	**0**	**0**	**0**																		
	Quebec Aces	AHL	3	0	0	0				2											6	0	3	3	4			
	Houston Apollos	CPHL	66	13	9	22				4																		
1966-67	**Montreal Canadiens**	**NHL**	**2**	**0**	**0**	**0**	**0**	**0**	**0**	**2**																		
	Seattle Totems	WHL	69	9	22	31				68											10	1	3	4	12			
1967-68	**Philadelphia Flyers**	**NHL**	**65**	**5**	**7**	**12**	**6**	**7**	**13**	**74**	**1**	**1**	**0**	**104**	**4.8**	**54**	**10**	**55**	**11**	**0**	**7**	**1**	**3**	**4**	**6**	**1**	**0**	**0**
1968-69	**Boston Bruins**	**NHL**	**11**	**0**	**2**	**2**	**0**	**2**	**2**	**8**	**0**	**0**	**0**	**10**	**0.0**	**6**	**1**	**9**	**2**	**–2**								
	Providence Reds	AHL	39	5	14	19				58																		
1969-70	**Montreal Canadiens**	**NHL**	**4**	**0**	**1**	**1**	**0**	**1**	**1**	**0**	**0**	**0**	**0**	**2**	**0.0**	**1**	**0**	**1**	**0**	**0**								
	Montreal Voyageurs	AHL	54	6	22	28				70											8	3	2	5	18			
1970-71	Montreal Voyageurs	AHL	52	3	19	22				80											3	0	1	1	2			
1971-72	Baltimore Clippers	AHL	64	3	37	40				104											18	5	7	12	38			
1972-73	New York Raiders	WHA	31	2	1	3				21																		
	Long Island Ducks	EHL	4	1	1	2				10																		
1973-74	Rochester Americans	AHL	41	3	9	12				63											5	0	2	2	6			
	NHL Totals		**166**	**6**	**29**	**35**	**7**	**29**	**36**	**150**											**14**	**1**	**3**	**4**	**22**			
	Other Major League Totals		31	2	1	3				21																		

CPHL First All-Star Team (1965) • CPHL Second All-Star Team (1966)

• Loaned to **Flin Flon** (SJHL) by **Fort William** (TBJHL) for Memorial Cup playoffs, March, 1957. Claimed by **Philadelphia** from **Montreal** in Expansion Draft, June 6, 1967. Claimed by **Boston** from **Philadelphia** in Intra-League Draft, June 12, 1968. Claimed by **Cleveland** (AHL) from **Oklahoma City** (CHL) in Reverse Draft, June 12, 1969. Traded to **Montreal** by **Cleveland** (AHL) for cash, October, 1969. Selected by **Dayton-Houston** (WHA) in 1972 WHA General Player Draft, February 13, 1972. WHA rights traded to **NY Raiders** (WHA) by **Houston** (WHA) for cash and future considerations, August, 1972.

• GAUTHIER, Luc

D – R. 5'9", 195 lbs. b: Longueuil, Que., 4/19/1964.

Season	Club	League	GP	G	A	Pts	AG	AA	APts	PIM	PP	SH	GW	S	%	TGF	PGF	TGA	PGA	+/–	GP	G	A	Pts	PIM	PP	SH	GW
1982-83	Longueuil Chevaliers	QMJHL	67	3	18	21				132											15	0	4	4	35			
1983-84	Longueuil Chevaliers	QMJHL	70	8	54	62				207											17	4	9	13	24			
1984-85	Longueuil Chevaliers	QMJHL	60	13	47	60				111																		
	Flint Generals	IHL	21	1	0	1				20																		
1985-86	Saginaw Generals	IHL	66	9	29	38				160																		
1986-87	Sherbrooke Canadiens	AHL	78	5	17	22				8											17	2	4	6	31			
1987-88	Sherbrooke Canadiens	AHL	61	4	10	14				105											6	0	0	0	18			
1988-89	Sherbrooke Canadiens	AHL	77	8	20	28				178											6	0	0	0	10			
1989-90	Sherbrooke Canadiens	AHL	79	3	23	26				139											12	0	4	4	35			
1990-91	**Montreal Canadiens**	**NHL**	**3**	**0**	**0**	**0**	**0**	**0**	**0**	**2**	**0**	**0**	**0**	**0**	**0.0**	**3**	**0**	**2**	**0**	**1**								
	Fredericton Canadiens	AHL	69	7	20	27				238											9	1	1	2	10			
1991-92	Fredericton Canadiens	AHL	80	4	14	18				252											7	1	1	2	26			
1992-93	Fredericton Canadiens	AHL	78	9	33	42				167											5	2	1	3	20			
1993-1996	Fredericton Canadiens	AHL	DID NOT PLAY – ASSISTANT COACH																									
1996-1997	Fredericton Canadiens	AHL	DID NOT PLAY – ASSISTANT COACH																									
	Fredericton Canadiens	AHL	2	0	0	0				0																		
1997-2000	**Nashville Predators**	**NHL**	DID NOT PLAY – SCOUTING																									
	NHL Totals		**3**	**0**	**0**	**0**	**0**	**0**	**0**	**2**	**0**	**0**	**0**	**0**	**0.0**	**3**	**0**	**2**	**0**									

Signed as a free agent by **Montreal**, October 7, 1986.

• GAUVREAU, Jocelyn

D – L. 5'11", 180 lbs. b: Masham, Que., 3/4/1964. Montreal's 2nd, 31st overall, in 1982.

Season	Club	League	GP	G	A	Pts	AG	AA	APts	PIM	PP	SH	GW	S	%	TGF	PGF	TGA	PGA	+/–	GP	G	A	Pts	PIM	PP	SH	GW
1980-81	Hull Olympiques	QMJHL	54	12	12	24				55																		
1981-82	Hull Olympiques	QMJHL	19	5	8	13				8																		
	Granby Bisons	QMJHL	33	12	21	33				66											14	3	10	13	16			
1982-83	Granby Bisons	QMJHL	68	33	63	96				42																		
	Nova Scotia Voyageurs	AHL	1	0	0	0				0											5	0	1	1	0			
1983-84	Granby Bisons	QMJHL	58	19	39	58				55											4	2	3	5	0			
	Montreal Canadiens	**NHL**	**2**	**0**	**0**	**0**	**0**	**0**	**0**	**0**	**0**	**0**	**0**	**0**	**0.0**	**0**	**0**	**2**	**0**	**–2**								
	Nova Scotia Voyageurs	AHL	1	0	2	2				0											3	1	1	2	0			
1984-85	Sherbrooke Canadiens	AHL	10	1	2	3				4																		
	NHL Totals		**2**	**0**	**0**	**0**	**0**	**0**	**0**	**0**	**0**	**0**	**0**	**0**	**0.0**	**0**	**0**	**2**	**0**									

QMJHL Second All-Star Team (1983)

• GAVEY, Aaron

C – L. 6'2", 200 lbs. b: Sudbury, Ont., 2/22/1974. Tampa Bay's 4th, 74th overall, in 1992.

Season	Club	League	GP	G	A	Pts	AG	AA	APts	PIM	PP	SH	GW	S	%	TGF	PGF	TGA	PGA	+/–	GP	G	A	Pts	PIM	PP	SH	GW
1990-91	Peterborough Jr. Petes	OJHL-B	42	26	30	56				68																		
1991-92	Sault Ste. Marie Greyhounds	OHL	48	7	11	18				27											19	5	1	6	10			
	Sault Ste. Marie Greyhounds	Mem-Cup	4	0	2	2				4																		

Season	Club	League	GP	G	A	Pts	AG	AA	APts	PIM	PP	SH	GW	S	%	TGF	PGF	TGA	PGA	+/–	GP	G	A	Pts	PIM	PP	SH	GW
			REGULAR SEASON																		PLAYOFFS							
1992-93	Sault Ste. Marie Greyhounds	OHL	62	45	39	84	....	....	....	116	....	....	....	....	....	....	....	....	....	....	18	5	9	14	36	....	....	....
	Sault Ste. Marie Greyhounds	Mem-Cup	4	1	4	5	....	....	....	8	....	....	....	....	....	....	....	....	....	....	....	....	....	....	....	....	....	....
1993-94	Sault Ste. Marie Greyhounds	OHL	60	42	60	102	....	....	....	116	....	....	....	....	....	....	....	....	....	....	14	11	10	21	22	....	....	....
	Canada	WJC-A	7	4	2	6	....	....	....	26	....	....	....	....	....	....	....	....	....	....	....	....	....	....	....	....	....	....
1994-95	Atlanta Knights	IHL	66	18	17	35	....	....	....	85	....	....	....	....	....	....	....	....	....	....	5	0	1	1	9	....	....	....
1995-96	**Tampa Bay Lightning**	**NHL**	**73**	**8**	**4**	**12**	**8**	**3**	**11**	**56**	**1**	**1**	**2**	**65**	**12.3**	**20**	**6**	**35**	**15**	**–6**	**6**	**0**	**0**	**0**	**4**	**0**	**0**	**0**
1996-97	**Tampa Bay Lightning**	**NHL**	**16**	**1**	**2**	**3**	**1**	**2**	**3**	**12**	**0**	**0**	**0**	**8**	**12.5**	**5**	**0**	**9**	**3**	**–1**	....	....	....	....	....	....	....	....
	Calgary Flames	**NHL**	**41**	**7**	**9**	**16**	**7**	**8**	**15**	**34**	**3**	**0**	**1**	**54**	**13.0**	**27**	**11**	**33**	**6**	**–11**	....	....	....	....	....	....	....	....
1997-98	**Calgary Flames**	**NHL**	**26**	**2**	**3**	**5**	**2**	**3**	**5**	**24**	**0**	**0**	**1**	**27**	**7.4**	**5**	**0**	**15**	**5**	**–5**	....	....	....	....	....	....	....	....
	Saint John Flames	AHL	8	4	3	7	....	....	....	28	....	....	....	....	....	....	....	....	....	....	....	....	....	....	....	....	....	....
1998-99	**Dallas Stars**	**NHL**	**7**	**0**	**0**	**0**	**0**	**0**	**0**	**10**	**0**	**0**	**0**	**4**	**0.0**	**1**	**0**	**2**	**0**	**–1**	....	....	....	....	....	....	....	....
	Michigan K-Wings	IHL	67	24	33	57	....	....	....	128	....	....	....	....	....	....	....	....	....	....	5	2	3	5	4	....	....	....
99-2000	**Dallas Stars**	**NHL**	**41**	**7**	**6**	**13**	**8**	**6**	**14**	**44**	**1**	**0**	**2**	**39**	**17.9**	**17**	**2**	**17**	**2**	**0**	**13**	**1**	**2**	**3**	**10**	**0**	**0**	**1**
	Michigan K-Wings	IHL	28	14	15	29	....	....	....	73	....	....	....	....	....	....	....	....	....	....	....	....	....	....	....	....	....	....
	NHL Totals		**204**	**25**	**24**	**49**	**26**	**22**	**48**	**180**	**5**	**1**	**6**	**197**	**12.7**	**75**	**19**	**111**	**31**		**19**	**1**	**2**	**3**	**14**	**0**	**0**	**1**

Traded to **Calgary** by **Tampa Bay** for Rick Tabaracci, November 19, 1996. Traded to **Dallas** by **Calgary** for Bob Bassen, July 14, 1998. Traded to **Minnesota** by **Dallas** with Pavel Patera, Dallas' 8th round choice (Eric Johansson) in 2000 Entry Draft and Minnesota's 4th round choice (previously acquired) in 2002 Entry Draft for Brad Lukowich and Minnesota's 3rd and 9th round choices in 2001 Entry Draft, June 25, 2000.

• GAVIN, Stew

Robert Stewart LW – L. 6', 190 lbs. b: Ottawa, Ont., 3/15/1960. Toronto's 4th, 74th overall, in 1980.

Season	Club	League	GP	G	A	Pts	AG	AA	APts	PIM	PP	SH	GW	S	%	TGF	PGF	TGA	PGA	+/–	GP	G	A	Pts	PIM	PP	SH	GW
1976-77	Nepean Raiders	OJHL	49	28	22	50	....	....	....	38	....	....	....	....	....	....	....	....	....	....	....	....	....	....	....	....	....	....
	Ottawa 67's	OMJHL	1	0	0	0	....	....	....	0	....	....	....	....	....	....	....	....	....	....	12	1	0	1	0	....	....	....
	Ottawa 67's	Mem-Cup	5	0	0	0	....	....	....	4	....	....	....	....	....	....	....	....	....	....	....	....	....	....	....	....	....	....
1977-78	Toronto Marlboros	OMJHL	67	16	24	40	....	....	....	19	....	....	....	....	....	....	....	....	....	....	5	0	5	5	17	....	....	....
1978-79	Toronto Marlboros	OMJHL	61	24	25	49	....	....	....	83	....	....	....	....	....	....	....	....	....	....	3	1	0	1	0	....	....	....
1979-80	Toronto Marlboros	OMJHL	68	27	30	57	....	....	....	52	....	....	....	....	....	....	....	....	....	....	4	1	1	2	2	....	....	....
1980-81	**Toronto Maple Leafs**	**NHL**	**14**	**1**	**2**	**3**	**1**	**1**	**2**	**13**	**0**	**0**	**0**	**13**	**7.7**	**8**	**0**	**10**	**2**	**0**	....	....	....	....	....	....	....	....
	New Brunswick Hawks	AHL	46	7	12	19	....	....	....	42	....	....	....	....	....	....	....	....	....	....	13	1	0	1	2	....	....	....
1981-82	**Toronto Maple Leafs**	**NHL**	**38**	**5**	**6**	**11**	**4**	**4**	**8**	**29**	**1**	**0**	**0**	**66**	**7.6**	**32**	**7**	**44**	**13**	**–6**	....	....	....	....	....	....	....	....
1982-83	**Toronto Maple Leafs**	**NHL**	**63**	**6**	**5**	**11**	**5**	**3**	**8**	**44**	**0**	**0**	**0**	**77**	**7.8**	**23**	**1**	**41**	**12**	**–7**	**4**	**0**	**0**	**0**	**0**	**0**	**0**	**0**
	St. Catharines Saints	AHL	6	2	4	6	....	....	....	17	....	....	....	....	....	....	....	....	....	....	....	....	....	....	....	....	....	....
1983-84	**Toronto Maple Leafs**	**NHL**	**80**	**10**	**22**	**32**	**8**	**15**	**23**	**90**	**0**	**1**	**3**	**96**	**10.4**	**59**	**2**	**93**	**30**	**–6**	....	....	....	....	....	....	....	....
1984-85	**Toronto Maple Leafs**	**NHL**	**73**	**12**	**13**	**25**	**10**	**9**	**19**	**38**	**0**	**0**	**0**	**148**	**8.1**	**34**	**0**	**76**	**20**	**–22**	....	....	....	....	....	....	....	....
1985-86	**Hartford Whalers**	**NHL**	**76**	**26**	**29**	**55**	**21**	**19**	**40**	**51**	**3**	**3**	**4**	**161**	**16.1**	**86**	**18**	**74**	**18**	**12**	**10**	**4**	**1**	**5**	**13**	**0**	**0**	**0**
1986-87	**Hartford Whalers**	**NHL**	**79**	**20**	**21**	**41**	**17**	**15**	**32**	**28**	**3**	**2**	**4**	**162**	**12.3**	**83**	**17**	**85**	**29**	**10**	**6**	**2**	**4**	**6**	**10**	**0**	**0**	**0**
1987-88	**Hartford Whalers**	**NHL**	**56**	**11**	**10**	**21**	**9**	**7**	**16**	**59**	**2**	**3**	**1**	**125**	**8.8**	**38**	**10**	**59**	**14**	**–17**	**6**	**2**	**2**	**4**	**4**	**0**	**0**	**0**
1988-89	**Minnesota North Stars**	**NHL**	**73**	**8**	**18**	**26**	**7**	**13**	**20**	**34**	**0**	**1**	**0**	**129**	**6.2**	**42**	**1**	**69**	**31**	**3**	**5**	**3**	**1**	**4**	**10**	**0**	**0**	**0**
1989-90	**Minnesota North Stars**	**NHL**	**80**	**12**	**13**	**25**	**10**	**9**	**19**	**76**	**0**	**3**	**1**	**146**	**8.2**	**45**	**0**	**79**	**43**	**9**	**7**	**0**	**2**	**2**	**12**	**0**	**0**	**0**
1990-91	Minnesota North Stars	Fr-Tour	2	1	0	1	....	....	....	0	....	....	....	....	....	....	....	....	....	....	....	....	....	....	....	....	....	....
	Minnesota North Stars	**NHL**	**38**	**4**	**4**	**8**	**4**	**3**	**7**	**36**	**0**	**1**	**0**	**56**	**7.1**	**19**	**0**	**42**	**20**	**–3**	**21**	**3**	**10**	**13**	**20**	**0**	**1**	**1**
1991-92	**Minnesota North Stars**	**NHL**	**35**	**5**	**4**	**9**	**5**	**3**	**8**	**27**	**0**	**1**	**1**	**49**	**10.2**	**13**	**0**	**29**	**16**	**0**	**7**	**0**	**0**	**0**	**6**	**0**	**0**	**0**
1992-93	**Minnesota North Stars**	**NHL**	**63**	**10**	**8**	**18**	**8**	**5**	**13**	**59**	**0**	**0**	**0**	**114**	**8.8**	**30**	**0**	**46**	**12**	**–4**	....	....	....	....	....	....	....	....
1993-94	**Dallas Stars**	**NHL**	DID NOT PLAY – SCOUTING																									
1994-95	Kansas City Blades	IHL	18	2	2	4	....	....	....	32	....	....	....	....	....	....	....	....	....	....	....	....	....	....	....	....	....	....
1995-96	Minnesota Moose	IHL	22	4	7	11	....	....	....	21	....	....	....	....	....	....	....	....	....	....	....	....	....	....	....	....	....	....
	NHL Totals		**768**	**130**	**155**	**285**	**109**	**106**	**215**	**584**	**9**	**15**	**14**	**1342**	**9.7**	**512**	**56**	**747**	**260**		**66**	**14**	**20**	**34**	**75**	**0**	**1**	**1**

Traded to **Hartford** by **Toronto** for Chris Kotsopoulos, October 7, 1985. Claimed by **Minnesota** from **Hartford** in Waiver Draft, October 3, 1988.

• GEALE, Bob

Robert Charles C – R. 5'11", 175 lbs. b: Edmonton, Alta., 4/17/1962. Pittsburgh's 6th, 156th overall, in 1980.

Season	Club	League	GP	G	A	Pts	AG	AA	APts	PIM	PP	SH	GW	S	%	TGF	PGF	TGA	PGA	+/–	GP	G	A	Pts	PIM	PP	SH	GW
1978-79	Sherwood Park Crusaders	AJHL	60	11	33	44	....	....	....	44	....	....	....	....	....	....	....	....	....	....	....	....	....	....	....	....	....	....
1979-80	Portland Winter Hawks	WHL	72	17	29	46	....	....	....	32	....	....	....	....	....	....	....	....	....	....	8	0	3	3	9	....	....	....
1980-81	Portland Winter Hawks	WHL	54	30	32	62	....	....	....	54	....	....	....	....	....	....	....	....	....	....	....	....	....	....	....	....	....	....
1981-82	Portland Winter Hawks	WHL	72	31	54	85	....	....	....	89	....	....	....	....	....	....	....	....	....	....	15	8	10	18	26	....	....	....
	Portland Winter Hawks	Mem-Cup	4	1	2	3	....	....	....	5	....	....	....	....	....	....	....	....	....	....	....	....	....	....	....	....	....	....
1982-83	Baltimore Skipjacks	AHL	56	4	10	14	....	....	....	6	....	....	....	....	....	....	....	....	....	....	....	....	....	....	....	....	....	....
1983-84	Baltimore Skipjacks	AHL	74	17	23	40	....	....	....	50	....	....	....	....	....	....	....	....	....	....	7	1	0	1	2	....	....	....
1984-85	**Pittsburgh Penguins**	**NHL**	**1**	**0**	**0**	**0**	**0**	**0**	**0**	**2**	**0**	**0**	**0**	**1**	**0.0**	**0**	**0**	**1**	**0**	**–1**	....	....	....	....	....	....	....	....
	Baltimore Skipjacks	AHL	77	26	23	49	....	....	....	42	....	....	....	....	....	....	....	....	....	....	15	3	8	11	11	....	....	....
1985-86	Baltimore Skipjacks	AHL	21	5	7	12	....	....	....	9	....	....	....	....	....	....	....	....	....	....	....	....	....	....	....	....	....	....
1986-87	Heilbronner EC	Germany-3	40	76	102	178	....	....	....	67	....	....	....	....	....	....	....	....	....	....	3	3	3	6	6	....	....	....
1987-88	Heilbronner EC	Germany-2	37	33	40	73	....	....	....	42	....	....	....	....	....	....	....	....	....	....	12	13	16	29	....	....	....	....
1988-89	Heilbronner EC	Germany-2	36	32	35	67	....	....	....	....	....	....	....	....	....	....	....	....	....	....	11	6	9	15	....	....	....	....
1989-90			STATISTICS NOT AVAILABLE																									
1990-91	Heilbronner EC	Germany-3	41	33	44	77	....	....	....	37	....	....	....	....	....	....	....	....	....	....	....	....	....	....	....	....	....	....
	NHL Totals		**1**	**0**	**0**	**0**	**0**	**0**	**0**	**2**	**0**	**0**	**0**	**1**	**0.0**	**0**	**0**	**1**	**0**		....	....	....	....	....	....	....	....

• GELDART, Gary

Gary Daniel D – L. 5'8", 160 lbs. b: Moncton, N.B., 6/14/1950. Minnesota's 7th, 89th overall, in 1970.

Season	Club	League	GP	G	A	Pts	AG	AA	APts	PIM	PP	SH	GW	S	%	TGF	PGF	TGA	PGA	+/–	GP	G	A	Pts	PIM	PP	SH	GW
1965-66	Moncton Red Wings	NBAHA	....	9	*15	24	....	....	....	*35	....	....	....	....	....	....	....	....	....	....	....	....	....	....	....	....	....	....
1966-67	Halifax Canadians	MJrHL	30	4	15	19	....	....	....	58	....	....	....	....	....	....	....	....	....	....	16	0	4	4	26	....	....	....
1967-68	Fredericton Jr. Red Wings	NBJHL	4	1	3	4	....	....	....	8	....	....	....	....	....	....	....	....	....	....	12	1	10	11	25	....	....	....
	Fredericton Red Wings	NBSHL	29	3	21	24	....	....	....	72	....	....	....	....	....	....	....	....	....	....	5	2	2	4	7	....	....	....
1968-69	Hamilton Red Wings	OHA-Jr.	52	3	30	33	....	....	....	103	....	....	....	....	....	....	....	....	....	....	5	0	3	3	12	....	....	....
1969-70	Hamilton Red Wings	OHA-Jr.	18	1	13	14	....	....	....	29	....	....	....	....	....	....	....	....	....	....	....	....	....	....	....	....	....	....
	London Knights	OHA-Jr.	30	5	28	33	....	....	....	48	....	....	....	....	....	....	....	....	....	....	12	2	8	10	29	....	....	....
1970-71	**Minnesota North Stars**	**NHL**	**4**	**0**	**0**	**0**	**0**	**0**	**0**	**5**	**0**	**0**	**0**	**3**	**0.0**	**1**	**0**	**0**	**0**	**1**	....	....	....	....	....	....	....	....
	Cleveland Barons	AHL	67	5	19	24	....	....	....	84	....	....	....	....	....	....	....	....	....	....	....	....	....	....	....	....	....	....
1971-72	Cleveland Barons	AHL	71	3	19	22	....	....	....	44	....	....	....	....	....	....	....	....	....	....	6	0	3	3	8	....	....	....
1972-73	Cleveland-Jacksonville Barons	AHL	74	6	32	38	....	....	....	81	....	....	....	....	....	....	....	....	....	....	....	....	....	....	....	....	....	....
1973-74	Nova Scotia Voyageurs	AHL	49	1	21	22	....	....	....	59	....	....	....	....	....	....	....	....	....	....	6	0	2	2	2	....	....	....
1974-75	Nova Scotia Voyageurs	AHL	65	2	17	19	....	....	....	111	....	....	....	....	....	....	....	....	....	....	6	0	0	0	9	....	....	....
1975-76	Nova Scotia Voyageurs	AHL	....	....	....	....	....	....	....	....	....	....	....	....	....	....	....	....	....	....	9	0	2	2	0	....	....	....
1976-77	New Haven Nighthawks	AHL	79	6	34	40	....	....	....	110	....	....	....	....	....	....	....	....	....	....	6	0	0	0	2	....	....	....
1977-78	New Haven Nighthawks	AHL	9	0	0	0	....	....	....	12	....	....	....	....	....	....	....	....	....	....	14	0	1	1	32	....	....	....
	NHL Totals		**4**	**0**	**0**	**0**	**0**	**0**	**0**	**5**	**0**	**0**	**0**	**3**	**0.0**	**1**	**0**	**0**	**0**		....	....	....	....	....	....	....	....

AHL Second All-Star Team (1977)

Traded to **Montreal** by **Minnesota** for cash, September, 1973. • Missed entire 1975-76 regular season recovering from knee surgery, September, 1975.

• GELINAS, Martin

LW – L. 5'11", 195 lbs. b: Shawinigan, Que., 6/5/1970. Los Angeles' 1st, 7th overall, in 1988.

Season	Club	League	GP	G	A	Pts	AG	AA	APts	PIM	PP	SH	GW	S	%	TGF	PGF	TGA	PGA	+/–	GP	G	A	Pts	PIM	PP	SH	GW
1985-86	Noranda Aces	NOHA	5	1	1	2	....	....	....	0	....	....	....	....	....	....	....	....	....	....	....	....	....	....	....	....	....	....
1986-87	Montreal L'est Cantonniers	QAAA	41	36	42	78	....	....	....	36	....	....	....	....	....	....	....	....	....	....	....	....	....	....	....	....	....	....
1987-88	Hull Olympiques	QMJHL	65	63	68	131	....	....	....	74	....	....	....	....	....	....	....	....	....	....	17	15	18	33	32	....	....	....
	Hull Olympiques	Mem-Cup	4	2	2	4	....	....	....	8	....	....	....	....	....	....	....	....	....	....	....	....	....	....	....	....	....	....
1988-89	Hull Olympiques	QMJHL	41	38	39	77	....	....	....	31	....	....	....	....	....	....	....	....	....	....	9	5	4	9	14	....	....	....
	Canada	WJC-A	7	0	2	2	....	....	....	8	....	....	....	....	....	....	....	....	....	....	....	....	....	....	....	....	....	....
	Edmonton Oilers	**NHL**	**6**	**1**	**2**	**3**	**1**	**1**	**2**	**0**	**0**	**0**	**0**	**14**	**7.1**	**4**	**0**	**5**	**0**	**–1**	....	....	....	....	....	....	....	....
1989-90♦	**Edmonton Oilers**	**NHL**	**46**	**17**	**8**	**25**	**15**	**6**	**21**	**30**	**5**	**0**	**2**	**71**	**23.9**	**33**	**7**	**26**	**0**	**0**	**20**	**2**	**3**	**5**	**6**	**0**	**0**	**0**
1990-91	**Edmonton Oilers**	**NHL**	**73**	**20**	**20**	**40**	**18**	**15**	**33**	**34**	**4**	**0**	**2**	**124**	**16.1**	**56**	**11**	**52**	**0**	**–7**	**18**	**3**	**6**	**9**	**25**	**0**	**0**	**1**
1991-92	**Edmonton Oilers**	**NHL**	**68**	**11**	**18**	**29**	**10**	**14**	**24**	**62**	**1**	**0**	**0**	**94**	**11.7**	**47**	**6**	**28**	**1**	**14**	**15**	**1**	**3**	**4**	**10**	**0**	**0**	**0**
1992-93	**Edmonton Oilers**	**NHL**	**65**	**11**	**12**	**23**	**9**	**8**	**17**	**30**	**0**	**0**	**1**	**93**	**11.8**	**39**	**1**	**36**	**1**	**3**	....	....	....	....	....	....	....	....

			REGULAR SEASON																		PLAYOFFS							
Season	Club	League	GP	G	A	Pts	AG	AA	APts	PIM	PP	SH	GW	S	%	TGF	PGF	TGA	PGA	+/-	GP	G	A	Pts	PIM	PP	SH	GW
1993-94	**Quebec Nordiques**	NHL	31	6	6	12	6	5	11	8	0	0	0	53	11.3	17	1	18	0	–2	....	....	....	....	....	....	....	....
	Vancouver Canucks	NHL	33	8	8	16	7	6	13	26	3	0	1	54	14.8	26	8	25	1	–6	24	5	4	9	14	2	0	1
1994-95	**Vancouver Canucks**	NHL	46	13	10	23	23	15	38	36	1	0	4	75	17.3	27	2	30	13	8	3	0	1	1	0	0	0	0
1995-96	**Vancouver Canucks**	NHL	81	30	26	56	30	21	51	59	3	4	5	181	16.6	75	9	78	20	8	6	1	1	2	12	1	0	0
1996-97	**Vancouver Canucks**	NHL	74	35	33	68	37	29	66	42	6	1	3	177	19.8	89	19	85	21	6	....	....	....	....	....	....	....	....
1997-98	**Vancouver Canucks**	NHL	24	4	4	8	5	4	9	10	1	1	1	49	8.2	16	2	26	6	–6	....	....	....	....	....	....	....	....
	Carolina Hurricanes	NHL	40	12	14	26	14	14	28	30	2	1	4	98	12.2	35	8	29	3	1	....	....	....	....	....	....	....	....
	Canada	WC-A	6	1	0	1	....	....	....	6	....	....	....	....	....	....	....	....	....	....	....	....	....	....	....	....	....	....
1998-99	**Carolina Hurricanes**	NHL	76	13	15	28	15	14	29	67	0	0	2	111	11.7	39	0	38	2	3	6	0	3	3	2	0	0	0
99-2000	**Carolina Hurricanes**	NHL	81	14	16	30	16	15	31	40	3	0	0	139	10.1	48	7	51	0	–10	....	....	....	....	....	....	....	....
	NHL Totals		744	195	192	387	206	167	373	474	29	7	25	1333	14.6	551	81	527	68		92	12	21	33	69	3	0	2

QMJHL First All-Star Team (1988) • Canadian Major Junior Rookie of the Year (1988) • Won George Parsons Trophy (Memorial Cup Tournament Most Sportsmanlike Player) (1988)

Traded to **Edmonton** by **LA Kings** with Jimmy Carson and LA Kings' 1st round choices in 1989 (later traded to New Jersey — New Jersey selected Jason Miller), 1991 (Martin Rucinsky) and 1993 (Nick Stajduhar) Entry Drafts and cash for Wayne Gretzky, Mike Krushelnyski and Marty McSorley, August 9, 1988. Traded to **Quebec** by **Edmonton** with Edmonton's 6th round choice (Nicholas Checco) in 1993 Entry Draft for Scott Pearson, June 20, 1993. Claimed on waivers by **Vancouver** from **Quebec**, January 15, 1994. Traded to **Carolina** by **Vancouver** with Kirk McLean for Sean Burke, Geoff Sanderson and Enrico Ciccone, January 3, 1998.

• GENDRON, Jean-Guy

LW – L. 5'9", 165 lbs. b: Montreal, Que., 8/30/1934.

Season	Club	League	GP	G	A	Pts	AG	AA	APts	PIM	PP	SH	GW	S	%	TGF	PGF	TGA	PGA	+/-	GP	G	A	Pts	PIM	PP	SH	GW
1951-52	Trois-Rivieres Reds	QJHL	41	9	28	37	....	....	....	77	....	....	....	....	....	....	....	....	....	....	5	0	1	1	16	....	....	....
1952-53	Trois-Rivieres Reds	QJHL	47	19	10	29	....	....	....	98	....	....	....	....	....	....	....	....	....	....	6	2	3	5	12	....	....	....
	Quebec Aces	QMHL	....	....	....	....	....	....	....	....	....	....	....	....	....	....	....	....	....	....	3	0	0	0	0	....	....	....
1953-54	Trois-Rivieres Reds	QJHL	54	42	45	87	....	....	....	*179	....	....	....	....	....	....	....	....	....	....	4	0	1	1	8	....	....	....
1954-55	Providence Reds	AHL	47	24	15	39	....	....	....	38	....	....	....	....	....	....	....	....	....	....	....	....	....	....	....	....	....	....
1955-56	**New York Rangers**	NHL	63	5	7	12	7	8	15	38	....	....	....	....	....	....	....	....	....	....	5	2	1	3	2	1	0	0
1956-57	**New York Rangers**	NHL	70	9	6	15	11	7	18	40	....	....	....	....	....	....	....	....	....	....	5	0	1	1	6	0	0	0
1957-58	**New York Rangers**	NHL	70	10	17	27	12	17	29	68	....	....	....	....	....	....	....	....	....	....	6	1	0	1	11	0	0	1
1958-59	**Boston Bruins**	NHL	60	15	9	24	18	9	27	57	....	....	....	....	....	....	....	....	....	....	7	1	0	1	18	0	0	1
1959-60	**Boston Bruins**	NHL	67	24	11	35	28	11	39	64	....	....	....	....	....	....	....	....	....	....	....	....	....	....	....	....	....	....
1960-61	**Boston Bruins**	NHL	13	1	7	8	1	7	8	24	....	....	....	....	....	....	....	....	....	....	....	....	....	....	....	....	....	....
	Montreal Canadiens	NHL	53	9	12	21	10	12	22	51	....	....	....	....	....	....	....	....	....	....	5	0	0	0	2	0	0	0
1961-62	**New York Rangers**	NHL	69	14	11	25	16	10	26	71	....	....	....	....	....	....	....	....	....	....	6	3	1	4	2	0	0	0
1962-63	**Boston Bruins**	NHL	66	21	22	43	24	22	46	42	....	....	....	....	....	....	....	....	....	....	....	....	....	....	....	....	....	....
1963-64	**Boston Bruins**	NHL	54	5	13	18	6	14	20	43	....	....	....	....	....	....	....	....	....	....	....	....	....	....	....	....	....	....
	Providence Reds	AHL	6	1	1	2	....	....	....	0	....	....	....	....	....	....	....	....	....	....	....	....	....	....	....	....	....	....
1964-65	Quebec Aces	AHL	53	20	14	34	....	....	....	61	....	....	....	....	....	....	....	....	....	....	5	1	1	2	8	....	....	....
1965-66	Quebec Aces	AHL	58	26	35	61	....	....	....	70	....	....	....	....	....	....	....	....	....	....	6	1	0	1	6	....	....	....
1966-67	Quebec Aces	AHL	68	28	45	73	....	....	....	72	....	....	....	....	....	....	....	....	....	....	5	2	1	3	4	....	....	....
1967-68	**Philadelphia Flyers**	NHL	1	0	1	1	0	1	1	2	0	0	0	2	0.0	1	0	0	0	1	....	....	....	....	....	....	....	....
	Quebec Aces	AHL	72	29	58	87	....	....	....	72	....	....	....	....	....	....	....	....	....	....	15	7	*14	*21	24	....	....	....
1968-69	**Philadelphia Flyers**	NHL	74	20	35	55	21	31	52	65	5	1	2	198	10.1	80	31	57	0	–8	4	0	0	0	6	0	0	0
1969-70	**Philadelphia Flyers**	NHL	71	23	21	44	25	20	45	54	5	0	1	155	14.8	68	20	41	1	8	....	....	....	....	....	....	....	....
1970-71	**Philadelphia Flyers**	NHL	76	20	16	36	20	13	33	46	5	0	1	145	13.8	53	24	38	0	–9	4	0	1	1	0	0	0	0
1971-72	**Philadelphia Flyers**	NHL	56	6	13	19	6	11	17	36	2	0	0	95	6.3	32	9	26	1	–2	....	....	....	....	....	....	....	....
1972-73	Quebec Nordiques	WHA	63	17	33	50	....	....	....	113	....	....	....	....	....	....	....	....	....	....	....	....	....	....	....	....	....	....
1973-74	Quebec Nordiques	WHA	64	11	8	19	....	....	....	42	....	....	....	....	....	....	....	....	....	....	....	....	....	....	....	....	....	....
	NHL Totals		863	182	201	383	205	193	398	701	....	....	....	....	....	....	....	....	....		42	7	4	11	47	....	....	....
	Other Major League Totals		127	28	41	69	....	....	....	155	....	....	....	....	....	....	....	....	....	....	....	....	....	....	....	....	....	....

Traded to **NY Rangers** by **Providence** (AHL) for Bill Ezinicki and cash, May 8, 1955. Claimed by **Boston** from **NY Rangers** in Intra-League Draft, June 3, 1958. Traded to **Montreal** by **Boston** for Andre Pronovost, November 27, 1960. Claimed by **NY Rangers** from **Montreal** in Intra-League Draft, June 13, 1961. Claimed by **Boston** from **NY Rangers** in Intra-League Draft, June 4, 1962. NHL rights transferred to **Philadelphia** after NHL club purchased **Quebec** (AHL) franchise, May 8, 1967. Claimed by **Montreal** from **Philadelphia** in Intra-League Draft, June 11, 1969. Traded to **Philadelphia** by **Montreal** for cash, June 12, 1969. Selected by **LA Sharks** (WHA) in 1972 WHA General Player Draft, February 12, 1972. Signed as a free agent by **Quebec** (WHA) after **LA Sharks** (WHA) dropped Gendron from their negotiating list, June, 1972.

• GENDRON, Martin

RW – R. 5'9", 190 lbs. b: Valleyfield, Que., 2/15/1974. Washington's 4th, 71st overall, in 1992.

Season	Club	League	GP	G	A	Pts	AG	AA	APts	PIM	PP	SH	GW	S	%	TGF	PGF	TGA	PGA	+/-	GP	G	A	Pts	PIM	PP	SH	GW
1989-90	Lac St-Louis Lions	QAAA	42	42	32	74	....	....	....	26	....	....	....	....	....	....	....	....	....	....	2	3	1	4	0	....	....	....
1990-91	St-Hyacinthe Laser	QMJHL	55	34	23	57	....	....	....	33	....	....	....	....	....	....	....	....	....	....	4	1	2	3	0	....	....	....
1991-92	St-Hyacinthe Laser	QMJHL	69	*71	66	137	....	....	....	45	....	....	....	....	....	....	....	....	....	....	6	7	4	11	14	....	....	....
1992-93	St-Hyacinthe Laser	QMJHL	63	73	61	134	....	....	....	44	....	....	....	....	....	....	....	....	....	....	....	....	....	....	....	....	....	....
	Canada	WJC-A	7	5	2	7	....	....	....	2	....	....	....	....	....	....	....	....	....	....	....	....	....	....	....	....	....	....
	Baltimore Skipjacks	AHL	10	1	2	3	....	....	....	2	....	....	....	....	....	....	....	....	....	....	3	0	0	0	0	....	....	....
1993-94	Hull Olympiques	QMJHL	37	39	36	75	....	....	....	18	....	....	....	....	....	....	....	....	....	....	20	*21	17	38	8	....	....	....
	Canada	Nat-Team	19	4	5	9	....	....	....	2	....	....	....	....	....	....	....	....	....	....	....	....	....	....	....	....	....	....
	Canada	WJC-A	7	6	4	10	....	....	....	6	....	....	....	....	....	....	....	....	....	....	....	....	....	....	....	....	....	....
1994-95	**Washington Capitals**	NHL	8	2	1	3	4	1	5	2	0	0	0	11	18.2	5	0	2	0	3	....	....	....	....	....	....	....	....
	Portland Pirates	AHL	72	36	32	68	....	....	....	54	....	....	....	....	....	....	....	....	....	....	4	5	1	6	2	....	....	....
1995-96	**Washington Capitals**	NHL	20	2	1	3	2	1	3	8	0	0	0	22	9.1	3	1	7	0	–5	....	....	....	....	....	....	....	....
	Portland Pirates	AHL	48	38	29	67	....	....	....	39	....	....	....	....	....	....	....	....	....	....	22	*15	18	33	8	....	....	....
1996-97	Las Vegas Thunder	IHL	81	51	39	90	....	....	....	20	....	....	....	....	....	....	....	....	....	....	3	2	1	3	0	....	....	....
1997-98	**Chicago Blackhawks**	NHL	2	0	0	0	0	0	0	0	0	0	0	3	0.0	0	0	1	0	–1	....	....	....	....	....	....	....	....
	Indianapolis Ice	IHL	17	8	6	14	....	....	....	16	....	....	....	....	....	....	....	....	....	....	....	....	....	....	....	....	....	....
	Milwaukee Admirals	IHL	40	20	19	39	....	....	....	14	....	....	....	....	....	....	....	....	....	....	....	....	....	....	....	....	....	....
	Fredericton Canadiens	AHL	10	5	10	15	....	....	....	4	....	....	....	....	....	....	....	....	....	....	2	0	0	0	4	....	....	....
1998-99	Fredericton Canadiens	AHL	65	33	34	67	....	....	....	26	....	....	....	....	....	....	....	....	....	....	15	*12	5	17	2	....	....	....
99-2000	Syracuse Crunch	AHL	64	19	17	36	....	....	....	16	....	....	....	....	....	....	....	....	....	....	....	....	....	....	....	....	....	....
	Springfield Falcons	AHL	14	6	10	16	....	....	....	6	....	....	....	....	....	....	....	....	....	....	4	0	2	2	4	....	....	....
	NHL Totals		30	4	2	6	6	2	8	10	0	0	0	36	11.1	8	1	10	0		....	....	....	....	....	....	....	....

QMJHL First All-Star Team (1992) • Canadian Major Junior Most Sportsmanlike Player of the Year (1992) • QMJHL Second All-Star Team (1993) • Canadian Major Junior First All-Star Team (1993)

Traded to **Chicago** by **Washington** with Washington's 6th round choice (Jonathan Pelletier) in 1998 Entry Draft for Chicago's 5th round choice (Erik Wendell) in 1998 Entry Draft, October 10, 1997. Traded to **Montreal** by **Chicago** for David Ling, March 14, 1998. Signed as a free agent **Vancouver**, August 25, 1999. Loaned to **Springfield** (AHL) by **Syracuse** (AHL) for loan of Sean McCann, March 15, 2000.

• GEOFFRION, Bernie

Bernard Andre Joseph "Boom-Boom" RW – R. 5'9", 166 lbs. b: Montreal, Que., 2/16/1931. **HHOF**

Season	Club	League	GP	G	A	Pts	AG	AA	APts	PIM	PP	SH	GW	S	%	TGF	PGF	TGA	PGA	+/-	GP	G	A	Pts	PIM	PP	SH	GW
1945-46	Mount St-Louis College	Hi-School	STATISTICS NOT AVAILABLE																									
1946-47	Montreal Concordia Civics	QJHL	26	7	8	15	....	....	....	6	....	....	....	....	....	....	....	....	....	....	....	....	....	....	....	....	....	....
1947-48	Laval Nationale	QJHL	29	20	15	35	....	....	....	49	....	....	....	....	....	....	....	....	....	....	11	7	5	12	11	....	....	....
	Laval Nationale	Mem-Cup	8	3	2	5	....	....	....	11	....	....	....	....	....	....	....	....	....	....	....	....	....	....	....	....	....	....
1948-49	Laval Nationale	QJHL	42	41	35	76	....	....	....	49	....	....	....	....	....	....	....	....	....	....	9	3	6	9	22	....	....	....
1949-50	Laval Nationale	QJHL	34	*52	34	*86	....	....	....	77	....	....	....	....	....	....	....	....	....	....	3	6	0	6	8	....	....	....
	Montreal Royals	QSHL	1	0	0	0	....	....	....	0	....	....	....	....	....	....	....	....	....	....	....	....	....	....	....	....	....	....
1950-51	Montreal Nationale	QJHL	36	54	44	98	....	....	....	80	....	....	....	....	....	....	....	....	....	....	....	....	....	....	....	....	....	....
	Montreal Canadiens	NHL	18	8	6	14	10	7	17	9	....	....	....	....	....	....	....	....	....	....	11	1	1	2	6	....	....	....
1951-52	**Montreal Canadiens**	NHL	67	30	24	54	40	30	70	66	....	....	....	....	....	....	....	....	....	....	11	3	1	4	6	....	....	....
1952-53♦	**Montreal Canadiens**	NHL	65	22	17	39	29	21	50	37	....	....	....	....	....	....	....	....	....	....	12	*6	4	10	12	....	....	....
1953-54	**Montreal Canadiens**	NHL	54	29	25	54	40	30	70	87	....	....	....	....	....	....	....	....	....	....	11	6	5	11	18	....	....	....
1954-55	**Montreal Canadiens**	NHL	70	*38	37	*75	50	43	93	57	....	....	....	....	....	....	....	....	....	....	12	8	5	13	8	....	....	....
1955-56♦	**Montreal Canadiens**	NHL	59	29	33	62	40	39	79	66	....	....	....	....	....	....	....	....	....	....	10	5	9	14	6	....	....	....
1956-57♦	**Montreal Canadiens**	NHL	41	19	21	40	24	23	47	18	....	....	....	....	....	....	....	....	....	....	10	*11	7	*18	2	....	....	....
1957-58♦	**Montreal Canadiens**	NHL	42	27	23	50	34	24	58	51	....	....	....	....	....	....	....	....	....	....	10	6	5	11	2	....	....	....

			REGULAR SEASON																		PLAYOFFS							
Season	Club	League	GP	G	A	Pts	AG	AA	APts	PIM	PP	SH	GW	S	%	TGF	PGF	TGA	PGA	+/–	GP	G	A	Pts	PIM	PP	SH	GW
1958-59♦	**Montreal Canadiens**	**NHL**	**59**	**22**	**44**	**66**	**26**	**45**	**71**	**30**											**11**	**5**	**8**	**13**	**10**			
1959-60♦	**Montreal Canadiens**	**NHL**	**59**	**30**	**41**	**71**	**36**	**40**	**76**	**36**											**8**	**2**	***10**	***12**	**4**			
1960-61	**Montreal Canadiens**	**NHL**	**64**	***50**	**45**	***95**	**59**	**44**	**103**	**29**											**4**	**2**	**1**	**3**	**0**			
1961-62	**Montreal Canadiens**	**NHL**	**62**	**23**	**36**	**59**	**26**	**35**	**61**	**36**											**5**	**0**	**1**	**1**	**6**			
1962-63	**Montreal Canadiens**	**NHL**	**51**	**23**	**18**	**41**	**27**	**18**	**45**	**73**											**5**	**0**	**1**	**1**	**4**			
1963-64	**Montreal Canadiens**	**NHL**	**55**	**21**	**18**	**39**	**26**	**19**	**45**	**41**											**7**	**1**	**1**	**2**	**4**			
1964-65	Quebec Aces	AHL	DID NOT PLAY – COACHING																									
1965-66	Quebec Aces	AHL	DID NOT PLAY – COACHING																									
1966-67	**New York Rangers**	**NHL**	**58**	**17**	**25**	**42**	**20**	**24**	**44**	**42**											**4**	**2**	**0**	**2**	**0**			
1967-68	**New York Rangers**	**NHL**	**59**	**5**	**16**	**21**	**6**	**16**	**22**	**11**	**4**	**0**	**0**	**84**	**6.0**	**42**	**30**	**11**	**0**	**1**	**1**	**0**	**1**	**1**	**0**	**0**	**0**	**0**
	NHL Totals		**883**	**393**	**429**	**822**	**493**	**458**	**951**	**689**											**132**	**58**	**60**	**118**	**88**			

• Father of Danny • QJHL First All-Star Team (1949, 1950, 1951) • Won Calder Memorial Trophy (1952) • NHL Second All-Star Team (1955, 1960) • Won Art Ross Trophy (1955, 1961) • NHL First All-Star Team (1961) • Won Hart Trophy (1961) • Played in NHL All-Star Game (1952, 1953, 1954, 1955, 1956, 1958, 1959, 1960, 1961, 1962, 1963)

Signed as a free agent by **Montreal**, February 14, 1951. Claimed on waivers by **NY Rangers** from **Montreal**, June 9, 1966.

• GEOFFRION, Danny

Daniel RW – R. 5'10", 185 lbs. b: Montreal, Que., 1/24/1958. Montreal's 1st, 8th overall, in 1978.

Season	Club	League	GP	G	A	Pts	AG	AA	APts	PIM	PP	SH	GW	S	%	TGF	PGF	TGA	PGA	+/–	GP	G	A	Pts	PIM	PP	SH	GW
1973-74	Cornwall Royals	QMJHL	28	6	5	11				5																		
1974-75	Cornwall Royals	QMJHL	71	33	53	86				70																		
1975-76	Cornwall Royals	QMJHL	53	42	58	100				123																		
1976-77	Cornwall Royals	QMJHL	65	39	57	96				148																		
1977-78	Cornwall Royals	QMJHL	71	68	75	143				183											9	4	12	16	37			
1978-79	Quebec Nordiques	WHA	77	12	14	26				74											4	1	2	3	2			
1979-80	**Montreal Canadiens**	**NHL**	**32**	**0**	**6**	**6**	**0**	**4**	**4**	**12**	**0**	**0**	**0**	**19**	**0.0**	**9**	**2**	**6**	**0**	**1**	**2**	**0**	**0**	**0**	**7**	**0**	**0**	**0**
1980-81	**Winnipeg Jets**	**NHL**	**78**	**20**	**26**	**46**	**16**	**17**	**33**	**82**	**3**	**0**	**0**	**142**	**14.1**	**64**	**13**	**84**	**1**	**–32**								
1981-82	**Winnipeg Jets**	**NHL**	**1**	**0**	**0**	**0**	**0**	**0**	**0**	**5**	**0**	**0**	**0**	**2**	**0.0**	**0**	**0**	**0**	**0**	**0**								
	Tulsa Oilers	CHL	63	24	25	49				76											3	1	0	1	6			
1982-83	Sherbrooke Jets	AHL	80	37	39	76				46																		
1983-84	Yukijirushi Sopporo	Japan	30	17	25	42																						
	NHL Totals		**111**	**20**	**32**	**52**	**16**	**21**	**37**	**99**	**3**	**0**	**0**	**163**	**12.3**	**73**	**15**	**90**	**1**		**2**	**0**	**0**	**0**	**7**	**0**	**0**	**0**
	Other Major League Totals		77	12	14	26				74											4	1	2	3	2			

• Son of Bernie • QMJHL West Division Second All-Star Team (1976)

Signed as an underage free agent by **New England** (WHA), May, 1978. Reclaimed by **Montreal** from **Quebec** prior to Expansion Draft, June 9, 1979. Claimed by **Quebec** from **Montreal** in Waiver Draft, October 8, 1980. Traded to **Winnipeg** by **Quebec** for cash, October 8, 1980.

• GERMAIN, Eric

D – L. 6'1", 195 lbs. b: Quebec City, Que., 6/26/1966.

Season	Club	League	GP	G	A	Pts	AG	AA	APts	PIM	PP	SH	GW	S	%	TGF	PGF	TGA	PGA	+/–	GP	G	A	Pts	PIM	PP	SH	GW
1981-82	Ste-Foy Gouverneurs	QAAA	45	0	1	1																						
1982-83	Ste-Foy Gouverneurs	QAAA	45	3	9	12																						
1983-84	St-Jean Beavers	QMJHL	57	2	15	17				60											4	1	0	1	6			
1984-85	St-Jean Beavers	QMJHL	66	10	31	41				243											5	4	0	4	14			
1985-86	St-Jean Castors	QMJHL	66	5	38	43				183											10	0	6	6	56			
1986-87	Flint Spirits	IHL	21	0	2	2				23																		
	Fredericton Express	AHL	44	2	8	10				28																		
1987-88	**Los Angeles Kings**	**NHL**	**4**	**0**	**1**	**1**	**0**	**1**	**1**	**13**	**0**	**0**	**0**	**2**	**0.0**	**6**	**0**	**9**	**1**	**–2**	**1**	**0**	**0**	**0**	**4**	**0**	**0**	**0**
	New Haven Nighthawks	AHL	69	0	10	10				0																		
1988-89	New Haven Nighthawks	AHL	55	0	9	9				93											17	0	3	3	23			
1989-90	New Haven Nighthawks	AHL	59	3	12	15				112																		
1990-91	Binghamton Rangers	AHL	60	4	10	14				144											10	0	1	1	14			
1991-92	Moncton Hawks	AHL	3	0	2	2				4																		
	Binghamton Rangers	AHL	47	3	6	9				86											3	0	0	0	0			
1992-93			DID NOT PLAY																									
1993-94	Binghamton Rangers	AHL	3	0	0	0				6																		
	Richmond Renegades	ECHL	56	3	16	19				192																		
1994-95	Richmond Renegades	ECHL	10	0	2	2				55																		
	Rochester Americans	AHL	18	1	7	8				13											5	0	2	2	18			
1995-96	Erie Panthers	ECHL	67	4	13	17				245																		
1996-97	Columbus Cottonmouths	CHL	66	7	15	22				176											3	0	0	0	2			
1997-98	Columbus Cottonmouths	CHL	57	0	5	5				113											13	0	1	1	10			
	NHL Totals		**4**	**0**	**1**	**1**	**0**	**1**	**1**	**13**	**0**	**0**	**0**	**2**	**0.0**	**6**	**0**	**9**	**1**		**1**	**0**	**0**	**0**	**4**	**0**	**0**	**0**

Signed as a free agent by **LA Kings**, July 1, 1986. Signed as a free agent by **NY Rangers**, July 11, 1990. • Played w/ RHI's New England Stingers in 1994 (18-3-7-10-24) and New Jersey R&R in 1996 (8-0-0-0-6).

• GERNANDER, Ken

C – L. 5'10", 180 lbs. b: Coleraine, MN, 6/30/1969. Winnipeg's 4th, 96th overall, in 1987.

Season	Club	League	GP	G	A	Pts	AG	AA	APts	PIM	PP	SH	GW	S	%	TGF	PGF	TGA	PGA	+/–	GP	G	A	Pts	PIM	PP	SH	GW
1985-86	Greenway Raiders	Hi-School	23	14	23	37																						
1986-87	Greenway Raiders	Hi-School	26	35	34	69																						
	Des Moines Buccaneers	USHL	STATISTICS NOT AVAILABLE																									
1987-88	University of Minnesota	WCHA	44	14	14	28				14																		
1988-89	University of Minnesota	WCHA	44	9	11	20				2																		
1989-90	University of Minnesota	WCHA	44	32	17	49				24																		
1990-91	University of Minnesota	WCHA	44	23	20	43				24																		
1991-92	Fort Wayne Komets	IHL	13	7	6	13				2																		
	Moncton Hawks	AHL	43	8	18	26				9											8	1	1	2	2			
1992-93	Moncton Hawks	AHL	71	18	29	47				20											5	1	4	5	0			
1993-94	Moncton Hawks	AHL	71	22	25	47				12											19	6	1	7	0			
1994-95	Binghamton Rangers	AHL	80	28	25	53				24											11	2	2	4	6			
1995-96	**New York Rangers**	**NHL**	**10**	**2**	**3**	**5**	**2**	**2**	**4**	**4**	**2**	**0**	**0**	**10**	**20.0**	**6**	**4**	**5**	**0**	**–3**	**6**	**0**	**0**	**0**	**0**	**0**	**0**	**0**
	Binghamton Rangers	AHL	63	44	29	73				38																		
1996-97	Binghamton Rangers	AHL	46	13	18	31				30											2	0	1	1	0			
	New York Rangers	**NHL**																			**9**	**0**	**0**	**0**	**0**	**0**	**0**	**0**
1997-98	Hartford Wolf Pack	AHL	80	35	28	63				26											12	5	6	11	4			
1998-99	Hartford Wolf Pack	AHL	70	23	26	49				32											7	1	2	3	2			
	United States	WC-Q	3	0	1	1				0																		
99-2000	Hartford Wolf Pack	AHL	79	28	29	57				24											23	5	5	10	0			
	NHL Totals		**10**	**2**	**3**	**5**	**2**	**2**	**4**	**4**	**2**	**0**	**0**	**10**	**20.0**	**6**	**4**	**5**	**0**		**15**	**0**	**0**	**0**	**0**	**0**	**0**	**0**

Won Fred Hunt Memorial Trophy (Sportsmanship - AHL) (1996)

Signed as a free agent by **NY Rangers**, July 4, 1994.

• GIALLONARDO, Mario

D – L. 5'11", 201 lbs. b: Toronto, Ont., 9/23/1957.

Season	Club	League	GP	G	A	Pts	AG	AA	APts	PIM	PP	SH	GW	S	%	TGF	PGF	TGA	PGA	+/–	GP	G	A	Pts	PIM	PP	SH	GW
1974-75	Markham Waxers	OHA-B	STATISTICS NOT AVAILABLE																									
1975-76	Union College Dutchmen	ECAC-3	DID NOT PLAY – FRESHMAN																									
1976-77	Union College Dutchmen	ECAC-3	25	5	26	31																						
	Windsor Spitfires	OMJHL	5	0	1	1				7											9	1	1	2	25			
1977-78	Union College Dutchmen	ECAC-3	DID NOT PLAY – SUSPENDED																									
	Toledo Goaldiggers	IHL	25	1	6	7				34											17	0	9	9	28			
1978-79	Philadelphia Firebirds	AHL	70	1	18	19				100																		
1979-80	**Colorado Rockies**	**NHL**	**8**	**0**	**1**	**1**	**0**	**1**	**1**	**2**	**0**	**0**	**0**	**4**	**0.0**	**3**	**0**	**7**	**1**	**–3**								
	Fort Worth Texans	CHL	70	8	25	33				105											15	2	4	6	47			

			REGULAR SEASON																		PLAYOFFS							
Season	Club	League	GP	G	A	Pts	AG	AA	APts	PIM	PP	SH	GW	S	%	TGF	PGF	TGA	PGA	+/-	GP	G	A	Pts	PIM	PP	SH	GW
1980-81	**Colorado Rockies**	**NHL**	**15**	**0**	**2**	**2**	**0**	**1**	**1**	**4**	**0**	**0**	**0**	**8**	**0.0**	**13**	**0**	**14**	**2**	**1**	....	....	....	....	....	....	....	....
	Fort Worth Texans	CHL	57	4	18	22	....	....	....	113	....	....	....	....	....	....	....	....	....	....	....	....	....	....	....	....	....	....
1981-82	Fort Worth Texans	CHL	13	0	4	4	....	....	....	20	....	....	....	....	....	....	....	....	....	....	....	....	....	....	....	....	....	....
	NHL Totals		**23**	**0**	**3**	**3**	**0**	**2**	**2**	**6**	**0**	**0**	**0**	**12**	**0.0**	**16**	**0**	**21**	**3**		....	....	....	....	....	....	....	....

Named Metro OHA-B MVP (1975) • Suspended for 1977-78 season by NCAA after entire Union College team quit to protest firing of coach Ned Harkness, December, 1977. Signed as a free agent by **Colorado**, December 21, 1978.

• GIBBS, Barry

Barry Paul D – R. 5'11", 195 lbs. b: Lloydminster, Sask., 9/28/1948. Boston's 1st, 1st overall, in 1966.

Season	Club	League	GP	G	A	Pts	AG	AA	APts	PIM	PP	SH	GW	S	%	TGF	PGF	TGA	PGA	+/-	GP	G	A	Pts	PIM	PP	SH	GW
1964-65	Estevan Bruins	SJHL	51	3	4	7	....	....	....	56	....	....	....	....	....	....	....	....	....	....	6	0	1	1	6	....	....	....
1965-66	Estevan Bruins	SJHL	59	3	23	26	....	....	....	45	....	....	....	....	....	....	....	....	....	....	12	0	2	2	14	....	....	....
	Estevan Bruins	Mem-Cup	13	1	0	1	....	....	....	14	....	....	....	....	....	....	....	....	....	....	....	....	....	....	....	....	....	....
1966-67	Estevan Bruins	CMJHL	56	10	32	42	....	....	....	81	....	....	....	....	....	....	....	....	....	....	13	2	2	4	21	....	....	....
1967-68	**Boston Bruins**	**NHL**	**16**	**0**	**0**	**0**	**0**	**0**	**0**	**2**	**0**	**0**	**0**	**3**	**0.0**	**4**	**0**	**6**	**1**	**–1**	....	....	....	....	....	....	....	....
	Oklahoma City Blazers	CPHL	41	7	16	23	....	....	....	154	....	....	....	....	....	....	....	....	....	....	7	1	2	3	24	....	....	....
1968-69	**Boston Bruins**	**NHL**	**8**	**0**	**0**	**0**	**0**	**0**	**0**	**2**	**0**	**0**	**0**	**3**	**0.0**	**2**	**0**	**5**	**0**	**–3**	....	....	....	....	....	....	....	....
	Oklahoma City Blazers	CHL	55	3	25	28	....	....	....	*194	....	....	....	....	....	....	....	....	....	....	12	0	4	4	*53	....	....	....
1969-70	**Minnesota North Stars**	**NHL**	**56**	**3**	**13**	**16**	**3**	**12**	**15**	**182**	**1**	**0**	**1**	**100**	**3.0**	**75**	**7**	**101**	**21**	**–12**	**6**	**1**	**0**	**1**	**7**	**1**	**0**	**0**
1970-71	**Minnesota North Stars**	**NHL**	**68**	**5**	**15**	**20**	**5**	**13**	**18**	**132**	**3**	**0**	**2**	**116**	**4.3**	**62**	**11**	**80**	**19**	**–10**	**12**	**0**	**1**	**1**	**47**	**0**	**0**	**0**
1971-72	**Minnesota North Stars**	**NHL**	**75**	**4**	**20**	**24**	**4**	**17**	**21**	**128**	**1**	**1**	**0**	**160**	**2.5**	**87**	**14**	**94**	**25**	**4**	**7**	**1**	**1**	**2**	**9**	**0**	**0**	**0**
1972-73	**Minnesota North Stars**	**NHL**	**63**	**10**	**24**	**34**	**9**	**19**	**28**	**54**	**2**	**0**	**0**	**163**	**6.1**	**91**	**15**	**87**	**25**	**14**	**5**	**1**	**0**	**1**	**0**	**1**	**0**	**0**
1973-74	**Minnesota North Stars**	**NHL**	**76**	**9**	**29**	**38**	**9**	**24**	**33**	**82**	**3**	**0**	**0**	**151**	**6.0**	**109**	**17**	**144**	**35**	**–17**	....	....	....	....	....	....	....	....
1974-75	**Minnesota North Stars**	**NHL**	**37**	**4**	**20**	**24**	**3**	**15**	**18**	**22**	**2**	**0**	**1**	**101**	**4.0**	**64**	**22**	**76**	**21**	**–13**	....	....	....	....	....	....	....	....
	Atlanta Flames	**NHL**	**39**	**3**	**13**	**16**	**3**	**10**	**13**	**39**	**1**	**0**	**2**	**60**	**5.0**	**43**	**11**	**50**	**12**	**–6**	....	....	....	....	....	....	....	....
1975-76	**Atlanta Flames**	**NHL**	**76**	**8**	**21**	**29**	**7**	**16**	**23**	**92**	**1**	**0**	**0**	**125**	**6.4**	**101**	**14**	**110**	**24**	**1**	**2**	**1**	**0**	**1**	**2**	**0**	**0**	**0**
1976-77	**Atlanta Flames**	**NHL**	**66**	**1**	**16**	**17**	**1**	**12**	**13**	**63**	**0**	**0**	**0**	**81**	**1.2**	**80**	**5**	**103**	**23**	**–5**	**3**	**0**	**0**	**0**	**2**	**0**	**0**	**0**
1977-78	**Atlanta Flames**	**NHL**	**27**	**1**	**5**	**6**	**1**	**4**	**5**	**24**	**0**	**0**	**0**	**42**	**2.4**	**32**	**1**	**40**	**7**	**–2**	....	....	....	....	....	....	....	....
	St. Louis Blues	**NHL**	**51**	**6**	**12**	**18**	**5**	**9**	**14**	**45**	**4**	**0**	**0**	**103**	**5.8**	**82**	**22**	**93**	**22**	**–11**	....	....	....	....	....	....	....	....
1978-79	**St. Louis Blues**	**NHL**	**76**	**2**	**27**	**29**	**2**	**20**	**22**	**46**	**0**	**0**	**0**	**86**	**2.3**	**88**	**5**	**159**	**34**	**–42**	....	....	....	....	....	....	....	....
1979-80	**Los Angeles Kings**	**NHL**	**63**	**2**	**9**	**11**	**2**	**7**	**9**	**32**	**0**	**0**	**0**	**55**	**3.6**	**55**	**2**	**90**	**24**	**–13**	**1**	**0**	**0**	**0**	**0**	**0**	**0**	**0**
1980-81	Houston Apollos	CHL	33	1	6	7	....	....	....	43	....	....	....	....	....	....	....	....	....	....	....	....	....	....	....	....	....	....
	Oklahoma City Stars	CHL	17	0	3	3	....	....	....	16	....	....	....	....	....	....	....	....	....	....	3	0	1	1	9	....	....	....
	NHL Totals		**797**	**58**	**224**	**282**	**54**	**178**	**232**	**945**	**18**	**1**	**6**	**1349**	**4.3**	**975**	**146**	**1238**	**293**		**36**	**4**	**2**	**6**	**67**	**2**	**0**	**0**

CHL First All-Star Team (1969) • Named Top Defenseman - CHL (1969) • Played in NHL All-Star Game (1973)

Traded to **Minnesota** by **Boston** with Tommy Williams for Minnesota's 1st round choice (Don Tannahill) in 1969 Amateur Draft and future considerations (Fred O'Donnell, May 7, 1971), May 7, 1969. Traded to **Atlanta** by **Minnesota** for Dean Talafous and Dwight Bialowas, January 3, 1975. Traded to **St. Louis** by **Atlanta** with Phil Myre and Curt Bennett for Yves Belanger, Dick Redmond, Bob MacMillan and St. Louis' 2nd round choice (Mike Perovich) in 1979 Entry Draft, December 12, 1977. Traded to **NY Islanders** by **St. Louis** with Terry Richardson for future considerations, June 9, 1979. Traded to **LA Kings** by **NY Islanders** for future considerations (Tom Williams, August 16, 1979), June 9, 1979.

• GIBSON, Don

D – R. 6'1", 210 lbs. b: Deloraine, Man., 12/29/1967. Vancouver's 2nd, 49th overall, in 1986.

Season	Club	League	GP	G	A	Pts	AG	AA	APts	PIM	PP	SH	GW	S	%	TGF	PGF	TGA	PGA	+/-	GP	G	A	Pts	PIM	PP	SH	GW
1985-86	Winkler Flyers	MJHL	34	24	29	53	....	....	....	210	....	....	....	....	....	....	....	....	....	....	....	....	....	....	....	....	....	....
1986-87	Michigan State Spartans	CCHA	43	3	3	6	....	....	....	74	....	....	....	....	....	....	....	....	....	....	....	....	....	....	....	....	....	....
1987-88	Michigan State Spartans	CCHA	43	7	12	19	....	....	....	118	....	....	....	....	....	....	....	....	....	....	....	....	....	....	....	....	....	....
1988-89	Michigan State Spartans	CCHA	39	7	10	17	....	....	....	107	....	....	....	....	....	....	....	....	....	....	....	....	....	....	....	....	....	....
1989-90	Michigan State Spartans	CCHA	44	5	22	27	....	....	....	167	....	....	....	....	....	....	....	....	....	....	....	....	....	....	....	....	....	....
	Milwaukee Admirals	IHL	1	0	0	0	....	....	....	4	....	....	....	....	....	....	....	....	....	....	5	0	1	1	41	....	....	....
1990-91	**Vancouver Canucks**	**NHL**	**14**	**0**	**3**	**3**	**0**	**2**	**2**	**20**	**0**	**0**	**0**	**9**	**0.0**	**11**	**1**	**11**	**0**	**–1**	....	....	....	....	....	....	....	....
	Milwaukee Admirals	IHL	21	4	3	7	....	....	....	76	....	....	....	....	....	....	....	....	....	....	....	....	....	....	....	....	....	....
1991-92	Milwaukee Admirals	IHL	35	6	9	15	....	....	....	105	....	....	....	....	....	....	....	....	....	....	4	1	0	1	7	....	....	....
1992-93	Milwaukee Admirals	IHL	68	3	14	17	....	....	....	381	....	....	....	....	....	....	....	....	....	....	6	0	1	1	11	....	....	....
1993-94	Milwaukee Admirals	IHL	43	4	6	10	....	....	....	233	....	....	....	....	....	....	....	....	....	....	3	0	0	0	10	....	....	....
	NHL Totals		**14**	**0**	**3**	**3**	**0**	**2**	**2**	**20**	**0**	**0**	**0**	**9**	**0.0**	**11**	**1**	**11**	**0**		....	....	....	....	....	....	....	....

CCHA Second All-Star Team (1990)

• GIBSON, Doug

Douglas John C – L. 5'10", 175 lbs. b: Peterborough, Ont., 9/28/1953. Boston's 3rd, 36th overall, in 1973.

Season	Club	League	GP	G	A	Pts	AG	AA	APts	PIM	PP	SH	GW	S	%	TGF	PGF	TGA	PGA	+/-	GP	G	A	Pts	PIM	PP	SH	GW
1970-71	Peterborough Petes	OMJHL	60	27	43	70	....	....	....	13	....	....	....	....	....	....	....	....	....	....	5	2	3	5	0	....	....	....
1971-72	Peterborough Petes	OMJHL	63	51	48	99	....	....	....	15	....	....	....	....	....	....	....	....	....	....	15	16	13	29	14	....	....	....
	Peterborough Petes	Mem-Cup	3	*3	*3	*6	....	....	....	2	....	....	....	....	....	....	....	....	....	....	....	....	....	....	....	....	....	....
1972-73	Peterborough Petes	OMJHL	63	52	62	114	....	....	....	10	....	....	....	....	....	....	....	....	....	....	14	9	13	22	6	....	....	....
1973-74	**Boston Bruins**	**NHL**	**2**	**0**	**0**	**0**	**0**	**0**	**0**	**0**	**0**	**0**	**0**	**0**	**0.0**	**0**	**0**	**1**	**0**	**–1**	**1**	**0**	**0**	**0**	**0**	**0**	**0**	**0**
	Boston Braves	AHL	76	31	51	82	....	....	....	16	....	....	....	....	....	....	....	....	....	....	....	....	....	....	....	....	....	....
1974-75	Rochester Americans	AHL	75	*44	*72	*116	....	....	....	31	....	....	....	....	....	....	....	....	....	....	12	5	7	12	15	....	....	....
1975-76	**Boston Bruins**	**NHL**	**50**	**7**	**18**	**25**	**6**	**13**	**19**	**0**	**1**	**0**	**1**	**41**	**17.1**	**30**	**5**	**18**	**1**	**8**	....	....	....	....	....	....	....	....
	Rochester Americans	AHL	17	11	20	31	....	....	....	11	....	....	....	....	....	....	....	....	....	....	....	....	....	....	....	....	....	....
1976-77	Rochester Americans	AHL	78	41	56	97	....	....	....	11	....	....	....	....	....	....	....	....	....	....	12	5	10	15	2	....	....	....
1977-78	**Washington Capitals**	**NHL**	**11**	**2**	**1**	**3**	**2**	**1**	**3**	**0**	**0**	**0**	**0**	**10**	**20.0**	**7**	**1**	**9**	**0**	**–3**	....	....	....	....	....	....	....	....
	Hershey Bears	AHL	71	24	35	59	....	....	....	8	....	....	....	....	....	....	....	....	....	....	....	....	....	....	....	....	....	....
1978-79	Hershey Bears	AHL	22	8	13	21	....	....	....	10	....	....	....	....	....	....	....	....	....	....	....	....	....	....	....	....	....	....
1979-80	Hershey Bears	AHL	72	20	24	44	....	....	....	17	....	....	....	....	....	....	....	....	....	....	16	*12	9	21	0	....	....	....
1980-81	SC Riessersee	Germany	54	31	42	73	....	....	....	8	....	....	....	....	....	....	....	....	....	....	10	6	10	16	2	....	....	....
1981-82	SC Riessersee	Germany	44	20	17	37	....	....	....	12	....	....	....	....	....	....	....	....	....	....	....	....	....	....	....	....	....	....
1982-83	SC Riessersee	Germany	36	14	37	51	....	....	....	7	....	....	....	....	....	....	....	....	....	....	....	....	....	....	....	....	....	....
1983-84	VEU Feldkirch	Austria	20	27	12	39	....	....	....	*137	....	....	....	....	....	....	....	....	....	....	....	....	....	....	....	....	....	....
	NHL Totals		**63**	**9**	**19**	**28**	**8**	**14**	**22**	**0**	**1**	**0**	**1**	**51**	**17.6**	**37**	**6**	**28**	**1**		**1**	**0**	**0**	**0**	**0**	**0**	**0**	**0**

AHL First All-Star Team (1975, 1977) • Won John B. Sollenberger Trophy (Top Scorer - AHL) (1975) • Won Les Cunningham Award (MVP - AHL) (1975, 1977)

Claimed on waivers by **Washington** from **Boston**, May 29, 1977.

• GIBSON, John

John William D – L. 6'3", 210 lbs. b: St. Catharines, Ont., 6/2/1959. Los Angeles' 5th, 71st overall, in 1979.

Season	Club	League	GP	G	A	Pts	AG	AA	APts	PIM	PP	SH	GW	S	%	TGF	PGF	TGA	PGA	+/-	GP	G	A	Pts	PIM	PP	SH	GW
1976-77	Niagara Falls Flyers	OMJHL	59	2	13	15	....	....	....	178	....	....	....	....	....	....	....	....	....	....	....	....	....	....	....	....	....	....
1977-78	Niagara Falls Flyers	OMJHL	60	8	20	28	....	....	....	133	....	....	....	....	....	....	....	....	....	....	....	....	....	....	....	....	....	....
1978-79	Niagara Falls Flyers	OMJHL	46	15	26	41	....	....	....	218	....	....	....	....	....	....	....	....	....	....	20	3	3	6	67	....	....	....
	Winnipeg Jets	WHA	9	0	1	1	....	....	....	5	....	....	....	....	....	....	....	....	....	....	....	....	....	....	....	....	....	....
1979-80	Niagara Falls Flyers	OMJHL	6	2	2	4	....	....	....	20	....	....	....	....	....	....	....	....	....	....	....	....	....	....	....	....	....	....
	Binghamton Whalers	AHL	1	0	0	0	....	....	....	0	....	....	....	....	....	....	....	....	....	....	....	....	....	....	....	....	....	....
	Saginaw Gears	IHL	67	13	36	49	....	....	....	293	....	....	....	....	....	....	....	....	....	....	5	1	2	3	38	....	....	....
1980-81	**Los Angeles Kings**	**NHL**	**4**	**0**	**0**	**0**	**0**	**0**	**0**	**21**	**0**	**0**	**0**	**5**	**0.0**	**2**	**1**	**6**	**0**	**–5**	....	....	....	....	....	....	....	....
	Houston Apollos	CHL	33	5	5	10	....	....	....	94	....	....	....	....	....	....	....	....	....	....	....	....	....	....	....	....	....	....
	Birmingham Bulls	CHL	16	6	3	9	....	....	....	42	....	....	....	....	....	....	....	....	....	....	....	....	....	....	....	....	....	....
	Saginaw Gears	IHL	12	0	7	7	....	....	....	82	....	....	....	....	....	....	....	....	....	....	10	0	1	1	55	....	....	....
1981-82	**Los Angeles Kings**	**NHL**	**6**	**0**	**0**	**0**	**0**	**0**	**0**	**18**	**0**	**0**	**0**	**6**	**0.0**	**6**	**0**	**3**	**1**	**4**	....	....	....	....	....	....	....	....
	New Haven Nighthawks	AHL	7	1	0	1	....	....	....	24	....	....	....	....	....	....	....	....	....	....	....	....	....	....	....	....	....	....
	Toronto Maple Leafs	**NHL**	**27**	**0**	**2**	**2**	**0**	**1**	**1**	**67**	**0**	**0**	**0**	**31**	**0.0**	**18**	**0**	**44**	**13**	**–13**	....	....	....	....	....	....	....	....
	Cincinnati Tigers	CHL	6	1	2	3	....	....	....	30	....	....	....	....	....	....	....	....	....	....	....	....	....	....	....	....	....	....
	New Brunswick Hawks	AHL	12	0	2	2	....	....	....	6	....	....	....	....	....	....	....	....	....	....	15	0	1	1	39	....	....	....
1982-83	St. Catharines Saints	AHL	21	1	4	5	....	....	....	38	....	....	....	....	....	....	....	....	....	....	....	....	....	....	....	....	....	....
1983-84	**Winnipeg Jets**	**NHL**	**11**	**0**	**0**	**0**	**0**	**0**	**0**	**14**	**0**	**0**	**0**	**4**	**0.0**	**11**	**0**	**10**	**1**	**2**	....	....	....	....	....	....	....	....
	Sherbrooke Jets	AHL	49	4	11	15	....	....	....	174	....	....	....	....	....	....	....	....	....	....	....	....	....	....	....	....	....	....
1984-85			DID NOT PLAY																									

Season	Club	League	REGULAR SEASON																		PLAYOFFS							
			GP	G	A	Pts	AG	AA	APts	PIM	PP	SH	GW	S	%	TGF	PGF	TGA	PGA	+/–	GP	G	A	Pts	PIM	PP	SH	GW
1985-86			DID NOT PLAY																									
1986-87	Flint Spirits	IHL	4	0	1	1	....	....	....	0	....	....	....	....	....	....	....	....	....	....	....	....	....	....	....	....	....	....
	Brantford Mott's Clamatos	OHA-Sr.	26	4	11	15	....	....	....	45	....	....	....	....	....	....	....	....	....	....	....	....	....	....	....	....	....	....
	NHL Totals		**48**	**0**	**2**	**2**	**0**	**1**	**1**	**120**	**0**	**0**	**0**	**46**	**0.0**	**37**	**1**	**63**	**15**		....	....	....	....	....	....	....	....
	Other Major League Totals		9	0	1	1	....	....	....	5	....	....	....	....	....	....	....	....	....	....	....	....	....	....	....	....	....	....

IHL First All-Star Team (1980) • Won Governors' Trophy (Top Defenseman - IHL) (1980)

Signed as a free agent by **Winnipeg** (WHA), March, 1979. Traded to **Toronto** by **LA Kings** with Billy Harris for Ian Turnbull, November 11, 1981. Signed as a free agent by **Winnipeg**, September 19, 1983.

• GIFFIN, Lee

RW – R. 6', 188 lbs. b: Chatham, Ont., 4/1/1967. Pittsburgh's 2nd, 23rd overall, in 1985.

Season	Club	League	GP	G	A	Pts	AG	AA	APts	PIM	PP	SH	GW	S	%	TGF	PGF	TGA	PGA	+/–	GP	G	A	Pts	PIM	PP	SH	GW
1982-83	Newmarket Flyers	OJHL-B	47	10	21	31	....	....	....	123	....	....	....	....	....	....	....	....	....	....	....	....	....	....	....	....	....	....
1983-84	Oshawa Generals	OHL	70	23	27	50	....	....	....	88	....	....	....	....	....	....	....	....	....	....	7	1	4	5	12	....	....	....
1984-85	Oshawa Generals	OHL	62	36	42	78	....	....	....	78	....	....	....	....	....	....	....	....	....	....	5	1	2	3	2	....	....	....
1985-86	Oshawa Generals	OHL	54	29	37	66	....	....	....	28	....	....	....	....	....	....	....	....	....	....	6	0	5	5	8	....	....	....
1986-87	Oshawa Generals	OHL	48	31	69	100	....	....	....	46	....	....	....	....	....	....	....	....	....	....	23	*17	19	36	14	....	....	....
	Pittsburgh Penguins	**NHL**	**8**	**1**	**1**	**2**	**1**	**1**	**2**	**0**	**0**	**0**	**0**	**8**	**12.5**	**4**	**0**	**2**	**0**	**2**	....	....	....	....	....	....	....	....
	Oshawa Generals	Mem-Cup	4	3	1	4	....	....	....	0	....	....	....	....	....	....	....	....	....	....	....	....	....	....	....	....	....	....
1987-88	**Pittsburgh Penguins**	**NHL**	**19**	**0**	**2**	**2**	**0**	**1**	**1**	**9**	**0**	**0**	**0**	**8**	**0.0**	**5**	**1**	**6**	**0**	**–2**	....	....	....	....	....	....	....	....
	Muskegon Lumberjacks	IHL	48	26	37	63	....	....	....	61	....	....	....	....	....	....	....	....	....	....	6	1	3	4	2	....	....	....
1988-89	Muskegon Lumberjacks	IHL	63	30	44	74	....	....	....	93	....	....	....	....	....	....	....	....	....	....	12	5	7	12	8	....	....	....
1989-90	Flint Spirits	IHL	73	30	44	74	....	....	....	68	....	....	....	....	....	....	....	....	....	....	4	1	2	3	0	....	....	....
1990-91	Kansas City Blades	IHL	60	25	43	68	....	....	....	48	....	....	....	....	....	....	....	....	....	....	....	....	....	....	....	....	....	....
	Canada	Nat-Team	5	0	2	2	....	....	....	2	....	....	....	....	....	....	....	....	....	....	....	....	....	....	....	....	....	....
1991-92	Capital District Islanders	AHL	77	19	26	45	....	....	....	58	....	....	....	....	....	....	....	....	....	....	7	3	3	6	18	....	....	....
1992-93	Chatham Wheels	ColHL	29	14	26	40	....	....	....	65	....	....	....	....	....	....	....	....	....	....	5	6	3	9	0	....	....	....
	Muskegon Fury	ColHL	....	....	....	....	....	....	....	....	....	....	....	....	....	....	....	....	....	....	5	6	3	9	0	....	....	....
1993-94			DID NOT PLAY																									
1994-95	Saginaw Wheels	ColHL	13	5	7	12	....	....	....	13	....	....	....	....	....	....	....	....	....	....	10	2	13	15	24	....	....	....
1995-96	Saginaw Wheels	ColHL	58	20	47	67	....	....	....	94	....	....	....	....	....	....	....	....	....	....	5	1	2	3	8	....	....	....
1996-97	Kansas City Blades	IHL	2	0	0	0	....	....	....	0	....	....	....	....	....	....	....	....	....	....	....	....	....	....	....	....	....	....
	Mobile Mysticks	ECHL	20	7	9	16	....	....	....	4	....	....	....	....	....	....	....	....	....	....	3	1	0	1	0	....	....	....
1997-98	Mobile Mysticks	ECHL	45	16	29	45	....	....	....	46	....	....	....	....	....	....	....	....	....	....	3	2	0	2	0	....	....	....
1998-99	Mobile Mysticks	ECHL	54	16	21	37	....	....	....	44	....	....	....	....	....	....	....	....	....	....	2	0	1	1	24	....	....	....
	NHL Totals		**27**	**1**	**3**	**4**	**1**	**2**	**3**	**9**	**0**	**0**	**0**	**16**	**6.3**	**9**	**1**	**8**	**0**		....	....	....	....	....	....	....	....

OHL First All-Star Team (1987)

Traded to **NY Rangers** by **Pittsburgh** for future considerations, September 14, 1989.

• GILBERT, Ed

Edward Ferguson C – L. 6', 185 lbs. b: Hamilton, Ont., 3/12/1952. Montreal's 5th, 46th overall, in 1972.

Season	Club	League	GP	G	A	Pts	AG	AA	APts	PIM	PP	SH	GW	S	%	TGF	PGF	TGA	PGA	+/–	GP	G	A	Pts	PIM	PP	SH	GW
1969-70	Hamilton Kilty B's	OHA-B	25	13	9	22	....	....	....	15	....	....	....	....	....	....	....	....	....	....	....	....	....	....	....	....	....	....
	Hamilton Red Wings	OHA-Jr.	43	8	17	25	....	....	....	10	....	....	....	....	....	....	....	....	....	....	....	....	....	....	....	....	....	....
1970-71	Hamilton Red Wings	OHA-Jr.	57	20	35	55	....	....	....	28	....	....	....	....	....	....	....	....	....	....	7	2	1	3	0	....	....	....
1971-72	Hamilton Red Wings	OMJHL	62	33	41	74	....	....	....	40	....	....	....	....	....	....	....	....	....	....	....	....	....	....	....	....	....	....
1972-73	Nova Scotia Voyageurs	AHL	72	21	18	39	....	....	....	20	....	....	....	....	....	....	....	....	....	....	13	4	8	12	2	....	....	....
1973-74	Nova Scotia Voyageurs	AHL	75	30	44	74	....	....	....	40	....	....	....	....	....	....	....	....	....	....	6	0	2	2	0	....	....	....
1974-75	**Kansas City Scouts**	**NHL**	**80**	**16**	**22**	**38**	**14**	**16**	**30**	**14**	**9**	**2**	**0**	**190**	**8.4**	**50**	**19**	**97**	**21**	**–45**	....	....	....	....	....	....	....	....
1975-76	**Kansas City Scouts**	**NHL**	**41**	**4**	**8**	**12**	**3**	**6**	**9**	**8**	**1**	**0**	**0**	**74**	**5.4**	**17**	**5**	**49**	**8**	**–29**	....	....	....	....	....	....	....	....
	Pittsburgh Penguins	**NHL**	**38**	**1**	**1**	**2**	**1**	**1**	**2**	**0**	**0**	**0**	**0**	**18**	**5.6**	**3**	**1**	**20**	**17**	**–1**	....	....	....	....	....	....	....	....
1976-77	**Pittsburgh Penguins**	**NHL**	**7**	**0**	**0**	**0**	**0**	**0**	**0**	**0**	**0**	**0**	**0**	**4**	**0.0**	**0**	**0**	**5**	**2**	**–3**	....	....	....	....	....	....	....	....
	Hershey Bears	AHL	68	20	29	49	....	....	....	12	....	....	....	....	....	....	....	....	....	....	6	1	0	1	0	....	....	....
1977-78			DID NOT PLAY																									
1978-79	Cincinnati Stingers	WHA	29	3	3	6	....	....	....	6	....	....	....	....	....	....	....	....	....	....	....	....	....	....	....	....	....	....
	NHL Totals		**166**	**21**	**31**	**52**	**18**	**23**	**41**	**22**	**10**	**2**	**0**	**286**	**7.3**	**70**	**25**	**171**	**48**		....	....	....	....	....	....	....	....
	Other Major League Totals		29	3	3	6	....	....	....	6	....	....	....	....	....	....	....	....	....	....	....	....	....	....	....	....	....	....

Selected by **Quebec** (WHA) in 1972 WHA General Player Draft, February 12, 1972. Claimed by **Kansas City** from **Montreal** in Expansion Draft, June 12, 1974. Traded to **Pittsburgh** by **Kansas City** with Simon Nolet and Kansas City's 1st round choice (Blair Chapman) in 1976 Amateur Draft for Steve Durbano, Chuck Arnason and Pittsburgh's 1st round choice (Greg Carroll) in 1976 Amateur Draft, January 9, 1976. Signed as a free agent by **Cincinnati** (WHA), October, 1978.

• GILBERT, Greg

Gregory Scott LW – L. 6'1", 191 lbs. b: Mississauga, Ont., 1/22/1962. NY Islanders' 5th, 80th overall, in 1980.

Season	Club	League	GP	G	A	Pts	AG	AA	APts	PIM	PP	SH	GW	S	%	TGF	PGF	TGA	PGA	+/–	GP	G	A	Pts	PIM	PP	SH	GW
1978-79	Mississagua Reps	MTHL	34	31	20	51	....	....	....	....	....	....	....	....	....	....	....	....	....	....	....	....	....	....	....	....	....	....
1979-80	Toronto Marlboros	OMJHL	68	10	11	21	....	....	....	35	....	....	....	....	....	....	....	....	....	....	4	0	0	0	0	....	....	....
1980-81	Toronto Marlboros	OMJHL	64	30	37	67	....	....	....	73	....	....	....	....	....	....	....	....	....	....	5	2	6	8	16	....	....	....
1981-82	Toronto Marlboros	OHL	65	41	67	108	....	....	....	119	....	....	....	....	....	....	....	....	....	....	10	4	12	16	23	....	....	....
♦	**New York Islanders**	**NHL**	**1**	**1**	**0**	**1**	**1**	**0**	**1**	**0**	**0**	**0**	**0**	**2**	**50.0**	**2**	**0**	**2**	**0**	**0**	**4**	**1**	**1**	**2**	**2**	**0**	**0**	**0**
1982-83♦	**New York Islanders**	**NHL**	**45**	**8**	**11**	**19**	**7**	**8**	**15**	**30**	**0**	**0**	**0**	**37**	**21.6**	**24**	**1**	**22**	**0**	**1**	**10**	**1**	**0**	**1**	**14**	**0**	**0**	**0**
	Indianapolis Checkers	CHL	24	11	16	27	....	....	....	23	....	....	....	....	....	....	....	....	....	....	....	....	....	....	....	....	....	....
1983-84	**New York Islanders**	**NHL**	**79**	**31**	**35**	**66**	**25**	**24**	**49**	**59**	**6**	**0**	**2**	**118**	**26.3**	**113**	**23**	**49**	**10**	**51**	**21**	**5**	**7**	**12**	**39**	**2**	**0**	**1**
1984-85	**New York Islanders**	**NHL**	**58**	**13**	**25**	**38**	**11**	**17**	**28**	**36**	**2**	**0**	**2**	**82**	**15.9**	**54**	**8**	**65**	**15**	**–4**	....	....	....	....	....	....	....	....
1985-86	**New York Islanders**	**NHL**	**60**	**9**	**19**	**28**	**7**	**13**	**20**	**82**	**1**	**0**	**2**	**58**	**15.5**	**50**	**8**	**45**	**8**	**5**	**2**	**0**	**0**	**0**	**9**	**0**	**0**	**0**
	Springfield Indians	AHL	2	0	0	0	....	....	....	2	....	....	....	....	....	....	....	....	....	....	....	....	....	....	....	....	....	....
1986-87	**New York Islanders**	**NHL**	**51**	**6**	**7**	**13**	**5**	**5**	**10**	**26**	**0**	**0**	**0**	**50**	**12.0**	**24**	**3**	**49**	**16**	**–12**	**10**	**2**	**2**	**4**	**6**	**0**	**0**	**1**
1987-88	**New York Islanders**	**NHL**	**76**	**17**	**28**	**45**	**14**	**20**	**34**	**46**	**1**	**1**	**0**	**77**	**22.1**	**62**	**4**	**71**	**27**	**14**	**4**	**0**	**0**	**0**	**6**	**0**	**0**	**0**
1988-89	**New York Islanders**	**NHL**	**55**	**8**	**13**	**21**	**7**	**9**	**16**	**45**	**0**	**0**	**1**	**73**	**11.0**	**31**	**0**	**47**	**17**	**1**	....	....	....	....	....	....	....	....
	Chicago Blackhawks	**NHL**	**4**	**0**	**0**	**0**	**0**	**0**	**0**	**0**	**0**	**0**	**0**	**2**	**0.0**	**2**	**0**	**1**	**0**	**1**	**15**	**1**	**5**	**6**	**20**	**0**	**0**	**0**
1989-90	**Chicago Blackhawks**	**NHL**	**70**	**12**	**25**	**37**	**10**	**18**	**28**	**54**	**0**	**0**	**3**	**108**	**11.1**	**62**	**2**	**39**	**6**	**27**	**19**	**5**	**8**	**13**	**34**	**0**	**0**	**0**
1990-91	**Chicago Blackhawks**	**NHL**	**72**	**10**	**15**	**25**	**9**	**11**	**20**	**58**	**1**	**0**	**0**	**98**	**10.2**	**44**	**7**	**42**	**11**	**6**	**5**	**0**	**1**	**1**	**2**	**0**	**0**	**0**
1991-92	**Chicago Blackhawks**	**NHL**	**50**	**7**	**5**	**12**	**6**	**4**	**10**	**35**	**0**	**0**	**1**	**45**	**15.6**	**24**	**3**	**31**	**6**	**–4**	**10**	**1**	**3**	**4**	**16**	**0**	**0**	**1**
1992-93	**Chicago Blackhawks**	**NHL**	**77**	**13**	**19**	**32**	**11**	**13**	**24**	**57**	**0**	**1**	**2**	**72**	**18.1**	**45**	**2**	**54**	**16**	**5**	**3**	**0**	**0**	**0**	**0**	**0**	**0**	**0**
1993-94♦	**New York Rangers**	**NHL**	**76**	**4**	**11**	**15**	**4**	**9**	**13**	**29**	**1**	**0**	**0**	**64**	**6.3**	**27**	**2**	**30**	**2**	**–3**	**23**	**1**	**3**	**4**	**8**	**0**	**0**	**0**
1994-95	**St. Louis Blues**	**NHL**	**46**	**11**	**14**	**25**	**19**	**21**	**40**	**11**	**0**	**0**	**3**	**57**	**19.3**	**38**	**0**	**21**	**5**	**22**	**7**	**0**	**3**	**3**	**6**	**0**	**0**	**0**
1995-96	**St. Louis Blues**	**NHL**	**17**	**0**	**1**	**1**	**0**	**1**	**1**	**8**	**0**	**0**	**0**	**9**	**0.0**	**1**	**0**	**3**	**1**	**–1**	....	....	....	....	....	....	....	....
1996-2000	Worcester IceCats	AHL	DID NOT PLAY – COACHING																									
	NHL Totals		**837**	**150**	**228**	**378**	**136**	**173**	**309**	**576**	**12**	**2**	**16**	**952**	**15.8**	**603**	**63**	**571**	**140**		**133**	**17**	**33**	**50**	**162**	**2**	**0**	**3**

Traded to **Chicago** by **NY Islanders** for Chicago's 5th round choice (Steve Young) in 1989 Entry Draft, March 7, 1989. Signed as a free agent by **NY Rangers**, July 29, 1993. Claimed by **St. Louis** from **NY Rangers** in Waiver Draft, January 19, 1995.

• GILBERT, Rod

Rodrigue Gabriel RW – R. 5'9", 180 lbs. b: Montreal, Que., 7/1/1941. **HHOF**

Season	Club	League	GP	G	A	Pts	AG	AA	APts	PIM	PP	SH	GW	S	%	TGF	PGF	TGA	PGA	+/–	GP	G	A	Pts	PIM	PP	SH	GW
1957-58	Guelph Biltmores	OHA-Jr.	32	14	16	30	....	....	....	14	....	....	....	....	....	....	....	....	....	....	....	....	....	....	....	....	....	....
1958-59	Guelph Biltmores	OHA-Jr.	54	27	34	61	....	....	....	40	....	....	....	....	....	....	....	....	....	....	10	5	4	9	14	....	....	....
1959-60	Guelph Biltmores	OHA-Jr.	47	39	52	91	....	....	....	40	....	....	....	....	....	....	....	....	....	....	5	3	3	6	4	....	....	....
	Trois-Rivieres Lions	EPHL	3	4	6	10	....	....	....	0	....	....	....	....	....	....	....	....	....	....	5	2	2	4	2	....	....	....
1960-61	Guelph Royals	OHA-Jr.	47	*54	49	*103	....	....	....	47	....	....	....	....	....	....	....	....	....	....	6	4	4	8	6	....	....	....
	New York Rangers	**NHL**	**1**	**0**	**1**	**1**	**0**	**1**	**1**	**2**	....	....	....	....	....	....	....	....	....	....	....	....	....	....	....	....	....	....
1961-62	**New York Rangers**	**NHL**	**1**	**0**	**0**	**0**	**0**	**0**	**0**	**0**	....	....	....	....	....	....	....	....	....	....	**4**	**2**	**3**	**5**	**4**	**0**	**0**	**0**
	Kitchener-Waterloo Beavers	EPHL	21	12	11	23	....	....	....	22	....	....	....	....	....	....	....	....	....	....	4	0	0	0	4	....	....	....
1962-63	**New York Rangers**	**NHL**	**70**	**11**	**20**	**31**	**13**	**20**	**33**	**20**	....	....	....	....	....	....	....	....	....	....	....	....	....	....	....	....	....	....
1963-64	**New York Rangers**	**NHL**	**70**	**24**	**40**	**64**	**30**	**42**	**72**	**62**	....	....	....	....	....	....	....	....	....	....	....	....	....	....	....	....	....	....
1964-65	**New York Rangers**	**NHL**	**70**	**25**	**36**	**61**	**30**	**37**	**67**	**52**	....	....	....	....	....	....	....	....	....	....	....	....	....	....	....	....	....	....
1965-66	**New York Rangers**	**NHL**	**34**	**10**	**15**	**25**	**11**	**14**	**25**	**20**	....	....	....	....	....	....	....	....	....	....	....	....	....	....	....	....	....	....

			REGULAR SEASON																		PLAYOFFS							
Season	Club	League	GP	G	A	Pts	AG	AA	APts	PIM	PP	SH	GW	S	%	TGF	PGF	TGA	PGA	+/–	GP	G	A	Pts	PIM	PP	SH	GW
1966-67	**New York Rangers**	**NHL**	64	28	18	46	33	18	51	12	....	....	....	....	....	....	....	....	....	....	4	2	2	4	6	1	0	0
1967-68	**New York Rangers**	**NHL**	73	29	48	77	34	48	82	12	8	0	6	281	10.3	102	32	57	0	13	6	5	0	5	4	0	0	0
1968-69	**New York Rangers**	**NHL**	66	28	49	77	30	44	74	22	8	0	5	301	9.3	103	39	52	0	12	4	1	0	1	2	0	0	0
1969-70	**New York Rangers**	**NHL**	72	16	37	53	17	35	52	22	3	0	1	230	7.0	78	30	47	1	2	6	4	5	9	0	3	0	0
1970-71	**New York Rangers**	**NHL**	78	30	31	61	30	26	56	65	8	0	5	226	13.3	86	25	39	0	22	13	4	6	10	8	1	0	1
1971-72	**New York Rangers**	**NHL**	73	43	54	97	43	47	90	64	6	0	4	238	18.1	147	42	54	0	51	16	7	8	15	11	4	0	2
1972-73	Team Canada	Summit-72	6	1	3	4	....	....	....	9	....	....	....	....	....	....	....	....	....	....	....	....	....	....	....	....	....	....
	New York Rangers	**NHL**	76	25	59	84	23	47	70	25	6	0	4	183	13.7	106	32	62	0	12	10	5	1	6	2	0	0	1
1973-74	**New York Rangers**	**NHL**	75	36	41	77	35	34	69	20	16	0	8	168	21.4	104	39	54	0	11	13	3	5	8	4	1	0	1
1974-75	**New York Rangers**	**NHL**	76	36	61	97	32	46	78	22	11	0	1	239	15.1	133	64	69	1	1	3	1	3	4	2	0	0	0
1975-76	**New York Rangers**	**NHL**	70	36	50	86	32	37	69	32	9	0	4	211	17.1	112	39	81	0	–8	....	....	....	....	....	....	....	....
1976-77	**New York Rangers**	**NHL**	77	27	48	75	24	37	61	50	7	0	2	187	14.4	95	38	74	0	–17	....	....	....	....	....	....	....	....
	Canada	WEC-A	9	2	2	4	....	....	....	12	....	....	....	....	....	....	....	....	....	....	....	....	....	....	....	....	....	....
1977-78	**New York Rangers**	**NHL**	19	2	7	9	2	5	7	6	1	0	0	27	7.4	17	8	19	0	–10	....	....	....	....	....	....	....	....
	NHL Totals		1065	406	615	1021	419	538	957	508	....	....	....	....	....	....	....	....	....		79	34	33	67	43	....	....	....

OHA-Jr. First All-Star Team (1961) • NHL Second All-Star Team (1968) • NHL First All-Star Team (1972) • Won Bill Masterton Trophy (1976) • Won Lester Patrick Trophy (1991) • Played in NHL All-Star Game (1964, 1965, 1967, 1969, 1970, 1972, 1975, 1977)

• Missed majority of 1961-62 season recovering from back injury originally suffered in game vs. Toronto (OHA-Jr.), March 3, 1961.

• GILBERTSON, Stan

Stanley Frank LW – L. 6', 175 lbs. b: Duluth, MN, 10/29/1944.

Season	Club	League	GP	G	A	Pts	AG	AA	APts	PIM	PP	SH	GW	S	%	TGF	PGF	TGA	PGA	+/–	GP	G	A	Pts	PIM	PP	SH	GW
1962-63	Estevan Bruins	SJHL	53	15	9	24	....	....	....	41	....	....	....	....	....	....	....	....	....	....	11	3	2	5	4	....	....	....
	Estevan Bruins	Mem-Cup	4	1	0	1	....	....	....	2	....	....	....	....	....	....	....	....	....	....	....	....	....	....	....	....	....	....
1963-64	Estevan Bruins	SJHL	15	4	1	5	....	....	....	6	....	....	....	....	....	....	....	....	....	....	....	....	....	....	....	....	....	....
	Regina Pats	SJHL	46	34	32	66	....	....	....	79	....	....	....	....	....	....	....	....	....	....	19	17	16	33	70	....	....	....
	Estevan Bruins	Mem-Cup	5	0	0	0	....	....	....	6	....	....	....	....	....	....	....	....	....	....	....	....	....	....	....	....	....	....
1964-65	Regina Pats	SJHL	53	41	42	83	....	....	....	148	....	....	....	....	....	....	....	....	....	....	12	9	9	18	46	....	....	....
	Minneapolis Bruins	CPHL	4	0	1	1	....	....	....	0	....	....	....	....	....	....	....	....	....	....	....	....	....	....	....	....	....	....
	Regina Pats	Mem-Cup	10	4	4	8	....	....	....	25	....	....	....	....	....	....	....	....	....	....	....	....	....	....	....	....	....	....
1965-66	Clinton Comets	EHL	34	7	12	19	....	....	....	64	....	....	....	....	....	....	....	....	....	....	....	....	....	....	....	....	....	....
	San Francisco Seals	WHL	43	1	8	9	....	....	....	32	....	....	....	....	....	....	....	....	....	....	7	1	1	2	6	....	....	....
1966-67	California Seals	WHL	59	6	11	17	....	....	....	25	....	....	....	....	....	....	....	....	....	....	6	1	3	4	0	....	....	....
1967-68	Vancouver Canucks	WHL	69	18	24	42	....	....	....	35	....	....	....	....	....	....	....	....	....	....	....	....	....	....	....	....	....	....
1968-69	Hershey Bears	AHL	72	27	19	46	....	....	....	28	....	....	....	....	....	....	....	....	....	....	11	7	6	13	6	....	....	....
1969-70	Hershey Bears	AHL	64	24	20	44	....	....	....	18	....	....	....	....	....	....	....	....	....	....	7	3	1	4	6	....	....	....
1970-71	Hershey Bears	AHL	68	31	18	49	....	....	....	50	....	....	....	....	....	....	....	....	....	....	4	2	0	2	0	....	....	....
1971-72	**California Golden Seals**	**NHL**	78	16	16	32	16	14	30	47	3	0	2	141	11.3	61	11	62	6	–6	....	....	....	....	....	....	....	....
1972-73	**California Golden Seals**	**NHL**	66	6	15	21	6	12	18	19	3	0	0	110	5.5	39	9	64	0	–34	....	....	....	....	....	....	....	....
1973-74	**California Golden Seals**	**NHL**	76	18	12	30	17	10	27	39	4	0	2	136	13.2	40	7	76	2	–41	....	....	....	....	....	....	....	....
1974-75	**California Golden Seals**	**NHL**	15	1	4	5	1	3	4	2	1	0	0	26	3.8	11	3	22	6	–8	....	....	....	....	....	....	....	....
	St. Louis Blues	**NHL**	22	1	4	5	1	3	4	4	0	0	0	32	3.1	10	2	16	3	–5	....	....	....	....	....	....	....	....
	Denver Spurs	CHL	10	11	4	15	....	....	....	7	....	....	....	....	....	....	....	....	....	....	....	....	....	....	....	....	....	....
	Washington Capitals	**NHL**	25	11	7	18	10	5	15	12	2	0	1	67	16.4	26	8	61	6	–37	....	....	....	....	....	....	....	....
1975-76	**Washington Capitals**	**NHL**	31	13	14	27	11	10	21	6	5	0	0	62	21.0	39	16	50	2	–25	....	....	....	....	....	....	....	....
	Pittsburgh Penguins	**NHL**	48	13	8	21	11	6	17	6	3	0	1	86	15.1	38	9	32	0	–3	3	1	1	2	2	0	0	0
1976-77	**Pittsburgh Penguins**	**NHL**	67	6	9	15	5	7	12	13	0	0	0	62	9.7	26	0	36	1	–9	....	....	....	....	....	....	....	....
	NHL Totals		428	85	89	174	78	70	148	148	21	0	6	722	11.8	290	65	419	26		3	1	1	2	2	0	0	0

AHL Second All-Star Team (1971)

Loaned to **Estevan** by **Regina** for Memorial Cup playoffs, April, 1964. Signed as a free agent by **Boston** (San Francisco-WHL), January 13, 1966. Traded to **Vancouver** (WHL) by **Boston** for cash, October, 1967. Traded to **Boston** by **Vancouver** (WHL) for cash, June, 1968. Loaned to **Hershey** (AHL) by **Boston**, October, 1968. Claimed by **California** from **Boston** in Intra-League Draft, June 8, 1971. Traded to **St. Louis** by **California** with Craig Patrick for Dave Gardner and Butch Williams, November 11, 1974. Traded to **Washington** by **St. Louis** with Garnet Bailey for Denis Dupere, February 10, 1975. Traded to **Pittsburgh** by **Washington** for Harvey Bennett Jr., December 16, 1975. • Suffered career-ending leg injury in automobile accident, September 30, 1977.

• GILCHRIST, Brent

LW – L. 5'11", 180 lbs. b: Moose Jaw, Sask., 4/3/1967. Montreal's 6th, 79th overall, in 1985.

Season	Club	League	GP	G	A	Pts	AG	AA	APts	PIM	PP	SH	GW	S	%	TGF	PGF	TGA	PGA	+/–	GP	G	A	Pts	PIM	PP	SH	GW
1982-83	Vernon Vipers	BCAHA	STATISTICS NOT AVAILABLE																									
1983-84	Kelowna Wings	WHL	69	16	11	27	....	....	....	16	....	....	....	....	....	....	....	....	....	....	....	....	....	....	....	....	....	....
1984-85	Kelowna Wings	WHL	51	35	38	73	....	....	....	58	....	....	....	....	....	....	....	....	....	....	6	5	2	7	8	....	....	....
1985-86	Spokane Chiefs	WHL	52	45	45	90	....	....	....	57	....	....	....	....	....	....	....	....	....	....	9	6	7	13	19	....	....	....
1986-87	Spokane Chiefs	WHL	46	45	55	100	....	....	....	71	....	....	....	....	....	....	....	....	....	....	5	2	7	9	6	....	....	....
	Sherbrooke Canadiens	AHL	....	....	....	....	....	....	....	....	....	....	....	....	....	....	....	....	....	....	10	2	7	9	2	....	....	....
1987-88	Sherbrooke Canadiens	AHL	77	26	48	74	....	....	....	83	....	....	....	....	....	....	....	....	....	....	6	1	3	4	6	....	....	....
1988-89	**Montreal Canadiens**	**NHL**	49	8	16	24	7	11	18	16	0	0	2	68	11.8	37	7	23	2	9	9	1	1	2	10	0	0	0
	Sherbrooke Canadiens	AHL	7	6	5	11	....	....	....	7	....	....	....	....	....	....	....	....	....	....	....	....	....	....	....	....	....	....
1989-90	**Montreal Canadiens**	**NHL**	57	9	15	24	8	11	19	28	1	0	0	80	11.3	36	3	38	8	3	8	2	0	2	2	0	0	0
1990-91	Montreal Canadiens	Fr-Tour	2	0	0	0	....	....	....	12	....	....	....	....	....	....	....	....	....	....	....	....	....	....	....	....	....	....
	Montreal Canadiens	**NHL**	51	6	9	15	5	7	12	10	1	0	1	81	7.4	25	1	31	4	–3	13	5	3	8	6	0	0	1
1991-92	**Montreal Canadiens**	**NHL**	79	23	27	50	21	20	41	57	2	0	3	146	15.8	75	11	55	20	29	11	2	4	6	6	1	0	0
1992-93	**Edmonton Oilers**	**NHL**	60	10	10	20	8	7	15	47	2	0	0	94	10.6	25	5	45	15	–10	....	....	....	....	....	....	....	....
	Minnesota North Stars	**NHL**	8	0	1	1	0	1	1	2	0	0	0	12	0.0	2	1	5	2	–2	....	....	....	....	....	....	....	....
1993-94	**Dallas Stars**	**NHL**	76	17	14	31	16	11	27	31	3	1	5	103	16.5	50	8	66	24	0	9	3	1	4	2	1	0	0
1994-95	**Dallas Stars**	**NHL**	32	9	4	13	16	6	22	16	1	3	1	70	12.9	18	1	28	8	–3	5	0	1	1	2	0	0	0
1995-96	**Dallas Stars**	**NHL**	77	20	22	42	20	18	38	36	6	1	2	164	12.2	56	13	93	39	–11	....	....	....	....	....	....	....	....
1996-97	**Dallas Stars**	**NHL**	67	10	20	30	11	18	29	24	2	0	2	116	8.6	47	9	41	9	6	6	2	2	4	2	0	0	0
1997-98♦	**Detroit Red Wings**	**NHL**	61	13	14	27	15	14	29	40	5	0	3	124	10.5	45	11	43	13	4	15	2	1	3	12	0	0	0
1998-99	**Detroit Red Wings**	**NHL**	5	1	0	1	1	0	1	0	0	0	1	4	25.0	2	0	3	0	–1	3	0	0	0	0	0	0	0
99-2000	**Detroit Red Wings**	**NHL**	24	4	2	6	4	2	6	24	0	0	0	33	12.1	8	0	9	2	1	6	0	0	0	6	0	0	0
	NHL Totals		646	130	154	284	132	126	258	331	23	5	20	1095	11.9	426	70	480	146		85	17	13	30	48	2	0	1

Traded to **Edmonton** by **Montreal** with Shayne Corson and Vladimir Vujtek for Vincent Damphousse and Edmonton's 4th round choice (Adam Wiesel) in 1993 Entry Draft, August 27, 1992. Traded to **Minnesota** by **Edmonton** for Todd Elik, March 5, 1993. Transferred to **Dallas** after **Minnesota** franchise relocated, June 9, 1993. Signed as a free agent by **Detroit**, August 1, 1997. Claimed by **Tampa Bay** from **Detroit** in NHL Waiver Draft, October 5, 1998. Traded to **Detroit** by **Tampa Bay** for future considerations, October 5, 1998. • Missed majority of 1998-99 and 1999-2000 seasons recovering from hernia surgery, September 22, 1998.

• GILES, Curt

Curtis Jon "Pengy" D – L. 5'8", 175 lbs. b: The Pas, Man., 11/30/1958. Minnesota's 4th, 54th overall, in 1978.

Season	Club	League	GP	G	A	Pts	AG	AA	APts	PIM	PP	SH	GW	S	%	TGF	PGF	TGA	PGA	+/–	GP	G	A	Pts	PIM	PP	SH	GW
1973-1975	Humboldt Broncos	SJHL	STATISTICS NOT AVAILABLE																									
1975-76	University of Minnesota-Duluth	WCHA	34	5	17	22	....	....	....	76	....	....	....	....	....	....	....	....	....	....	....	....	....	....	....	....	....	....
1976-77	University of Minnesota-Duluth	WCHA	37	12	37	49	....	....	....	64	....	....	....	....	....	....	....	....	....	....	....	....	....	....	....	....	....	....
1977-78	University of Minnesota-Duluth	WCHA	34	11	36	47	....	....	....	62	....	....	....	....	....	....	....	....	....	....	....	....	....	....	....	....	....	....
1978-79	University of Minnesota-Duluth	WCHA	30	3	38	41	....	....	....	38	....	....	....	....	....	....	....	....	....	....	....	....	....	....	....	....	....	....
1979-80	**Minnesota North Stars**	**NHL**	37	2	7	9	2	5	7	31	1	0	1	48	4.2	35	11	37	4	–9	12	2	4	6	10	2	0	0
	Oklahoma City Stars	CHL	42	4	24	28	....	....	....	35	....	....	....	....	....	....	....	....	....	....	....	....	....	....	....	....	....	....
1980-81	Minnesota North Stars	DN-Cup	3	1	1	2	....	....	....	*8	....	....	....	....	....	....	....	....	....	....	....	....	....	....	....	....	....	....
	Minnesota North Stars	**NHL**	67	5	22	27	4	15	19	56	1	0	1	82	6.1	79	20	67	17	9	19	1	4	5	14	0	0	0
1981-82	**Minnesota North Stars**	**NHL**	74	3	12	15	2	8	10	87	0	0	1	65	4.6	92	11	79	13	15	4	0	0	0	2	0	0	0
	Canada	WEC-A	10	0	1	1	....	....	....	12	....	....	....	....	....	....	....	....	....	....	....	....	....	....	....	....	....	....
1982-83	**Minnesota North Stars**	**NHL**	76	2	21	23	2	15	17	70	0	0	0	78	2.6	87	6	94	24	11	5	0	2	2	6	0	0	0
1983-84	**Minnesota North Stars**	**NHL**	70	6	22	28	5	15	20	59	2	0	0	78	7.7	90	24	102	38	2	16	1	3	4	25	1	0	0
1984-85	**Minnesota North Stars**	**NHL**	77	5	25	30	4	17	21	49	3	0	0	98	5.1	99	20	96	20	3	9	0	0	0	17	0	0	0
1985-86	**Minnesota North Stars**	**NHL**	69	6	21	27	5	14	19	30	0	0	1	59	10.2	92	11	101	39	19	5	0	1	1	10	0	0	0

			REGULAR SEASON																		PLAYOFFS							
Season	Club	League	GP	G	A	Pts	AG	AA	APts	PIM	PP	SH	GW	S	%	TGF	PGF	TGA	PGA	+/–	GP	G	A	Pts	PIM	PP	SH	GW
1986-87	Minnesota North Stars	NHL	11	0	3	3	0	2	2	4	0	0	0	5	0.0	9	0	13	6	2	....	....	....	....	....	....	....	....
	New York Rangers	NHL	61	2	17	19	2	12	14	50	0	0	0	52	3.8	70	5	65	3	3	5	0	0	0	6	0	0	0
1987-88	New York Rangers	NHL	13	0	0	0	0	0	0	10	0	0	0	12	0.0	7	0	16	4	–5	....	....	....	....	....	....	....	....
	Minnesota North Stars	NHL	59	1	12	13	1	9	10	66	0	0	0	60	1.7	44	10	84	22	–28	....	....	....	....	....	....	....	....
1988-89	Minnesota North Stars	NHL	76	5	10	15	4	7	11	77	0	1	0	64	7.8	61	2	94	37	2	5	0	0	0	4	0	0	0
1989-90	Minnesota North Stars	NHL	74	1	12	13	1	9	10	48	0	0	0	55	1.8	61	0	88	30	3	7	0	1	1	6	0	0	0
1990-91	Minnesota North Stars	Fr-Tour	3	0	0	0	....	....	....	4	....	....	....	....	....	....	....	....	....	....	....	....	....	....	....	....	....	....
	Minnesota North Stars	NHL	70	4	10	14	4	8	12	48	0	0	0	53	7.5	55	2	81	31	3	10	1	0	1	16	0	0	0
1991-92	Canada	Nat-Team	31	3	6	9	....	....	....	37	....	....	....	....	....	....	....	....	....	....	....	....	....	....	....	....	....	....
	Canada	Olympics	8	1	0	1	....	....	....	6	....	....	....	....	....	....	....	....	....	....	....	....	....	....	....	....	....	....
	St. Louis Blues	NHL	13	1	1	2	1	1	2	8	0	0	0	4	25.0	7	1	11	2	–3	3	1	1	2	0	1	0	0
1992-93	St. Louis Blues	NHL	48	0	4	4	0	3	3	40	0	0	0	23	0.0	26	2	43	17	–2	3	0	0	0	2	0	0	0
	NHL Totals		895	43	199	242	37	140	177	733	7	1	4	836	5.1	914	125	1071	307		103	6	16	22	118	4	0	0

WCHA First All-Star Team (1978, 1979) • NCAA West First All-American Team (1978, 1979)

Traded to **NY Rangers** by **Minnesota** with Tony McKegney and Minnesota's 2nd round choice (Troy Mallette) in 1988 Entry Draft for Bob Brooke and Minnesota's 4th round choice (previously acquired, Minnesota selected Jeffrey Stolp) in 1988 Entry Draft, November 13, 1986. Traded to **Minnesota** by **NY Rangers** for Byron Lomow and future considerations, November 20, 1987. Signed as a free agent by **St. Louis**, February 29, 1992.

• GILHEN, Randy

Randy Alan C – L. 6′, 190 lbs. b: Zweibrucken, W. Germany, 6/13/1963. Hartford's 6th, 109th overall, in 1982.

Season	Club	League	GP	G	A	Pts	AG	AA	APts	PIM	PP	SH	GW	S	%	TGF	PGF	TGA	PGA	+/–	GP	G	A	Pts	PIM	PP	SH	GW
1979-80	Saskatoon Olympics	SJHL	55	18	34	52	....	....	....	112	....	....	....	....	....	....	....	....	....	....	....	....	....	....	....	....	....	....
	Saskatoon Blades	WHL	9	2	4	6	....	....	....	20	....	....	....	....	....	....	....	....	....	....	....	....	....	....	....	....	....	....
1980-81	Saskatoon Blades	WHL	68	10	5	15	....	....	....	154	....	....	....	....	....	....	....	....	....	....	....	....	....	....	....	....	....	....
1981-82	Saskatoon Blades	WHL	25	15	9	24	....	....	....	45	....	....	....	....	....	....	....	....	....	....	....	....	....	....	....	....	....	....
	Winnipeg Warriors	WHL	36	26	28	54	....	....	....	42	....	....	....	....	....	....	....	....	....	....	....	....	....	....	....	....	....	....
1982-83	Winnipeg Warriors	WHL	71	57	44	101	....	....	....	84	....	....	....	....	....	....	....	....	....	....	3	2	2	4	0	....	....	....
	Hartford Whalers	NHL	2	0	1	1	0	1	1	0	0	0	0	4	0.0	2	1	1	0	0	....	....	....	....	....	....	....	....
1983-84	Binghamton Whalers	AHL	73	8	12	20	....	....	....	72	....	....	....	....	....	....	....	....	....	....	....	....	....	....	....	....	....	....
1984-85	Salt Lake Golden Eagles	IHL	57	20	20	40	....	....	....	28	....	....	....	....	....	....	....	....	....	....	....	....	....	....	....	....	....	....
	Binghamton Whalers	AHL	18	3	3	6	....	....	....	9	....	....	....	....	....	....	....	....	....	....	8	4	1	5	16	....	....	....
1985-86	Fort Wayne Komets	IHL	82	44	40	84	....	....	....	48	....	....	....	....	....	....	....	....	....	....	15	10	8	18	6	....	....	....
1986-87	Winnipeg Jets	NHL	2	0	0	0	0	0	0	0	0	0	0	3	0.0	0	0	2	0	–2	....	....	....	....	....	....	....	....
	Sherbrooke Canadiens	AHL	75	36	29	65	....	....	....	44	....	....	....	....	....	....	....	....	....	....	17	7	13	20	10	....	....	....
1987-88	Winnipeg Jets	NHL	13	3	2	5	3	1	4	15	0	0	0	21	14.3	10	0	6	1	5	4	1	0	1	10	0	1	1
	Moncton Hawks	AHL	68	40	47	87	....	....	....	51	....	....	....	....	....	....	....	....	....	....	....	....	....	....	....	....	....	....
1988-89	Winnipeg Jets	NHL	64	5	3	8	4	2	6	38	0	1	1	76	6.6	19	1	67	25	–24	....	....	....	....	....	....	....	....
1989-90	Pittsburgh Penguins	NHL	61	5	11	16	4	8	12	54	0	0	1	67	7.5	23	1	52	22	–8	....	....	....	....	....	....	....	....
1990-91 ♦	Pittsburgh Penguins	NHL	72	15	10	25	14	8	22	51	1	2	1	112	13.4	37	1	60	27	3	16	1	0	1	14	0	0	0
1991-92	Los Angeles Kings	NHL	33	3	6	9	3	5	8	14	0	1	0	32	9.4	12	0	29	14	–3	....	....	....	....	....	....	....	....
	New York Rangers	NHL	40	7	7	14	6	5	11	14	0	0	0	67	10.4	25	0	25	5	5	13	1	2	3	2	0	0	0
1992-93	New York Rangers	NHL	33	3	2	5	2	1	3	8	0	1	1	34	8.8	10	0	35	17	–8	....	....	....	....	....	....	....	....
	Tampa Bay Lightning	NHL	11	0	2	2	0	1	1	6	0	0	0	11	0.0	5	0	13	2	–6	....	....	....	....	....	....	....	....
1993-94	Florida Panthers	NHL	20	4	4	8	4	3	7	16	0	0	0	52	7.7	14	3	22	12	1	....	....	....	....	....	....	....	....
	Winnipeg Jets	NHL	40	3	3	6	3	2	5	34	0	0	0	43	7.0	9	1	45	24	–13	....	....	....	....	....	....	....	....
1994-95	Winnipeg Jets	NHL	44	5	6	11	9	9	18	52	0	1	1	47	10.6	15	0	48	16	–17	....	....	....	....	....	....	....	....
1995-96	Winnipeg Jets	NHL	22	2	3	5	2	2	4	12	0	0	0	26	7.7	9	1	14	7	1	....	....	....	....	....	....	....	....
1996-97	Manitoba Moose	IHL	79	21	24	45	....	....	....	101	....	....	....	....	....	....	....	....	....	....	....	....	....	....	....	....	....	....
1997-98	Manitoba Moose	IHL	22	4	2	6	....	....	....	14	....	....	....	....	....	....	....	....	....	....	....	....	....	....	....	....	....	....
	NHL Totals		457	55	60	115	54	48	102	314	1	6	5	595	9.2	190	9	419	172		33	3	2	5	26	0	1	1

Signed as a free agent by **Winnipeg**, November 8, 1985. Traded to **Pittsburgh** by **Winnipeg** with Jim Kyte and Andrew McBain for Randy Cunneyworth, Rick Tabaracci and Dave McLlwain, June 17, 1989. Claimed by **Minnesota** from **Pittsburgh** in Expansion Draft, May 30, 1991. Traded to **LA Kings** by **Minnesota** with Charlie Huddy, Jim Thomson and NY Rangers' 4th round choice (previously acquired, LA Kings selected Alexei Zhitnik) in 1991 Entry Draft for Todd Elik, June 22, 1991. Traded to **NY Rangers** by **LA Kings** for Corey Millen, December 23, 1991. Traded to **Tampa Bay** by **NY Rangers** for Mike Hartman, March 22, 1993. Claimed by **Florida** from **Tampa Bay** in Expansion Draft, June 24, 1993. Traded to **Winnipeg** by **Florida** for Stu Barnes and St. Louis' 6th round choice (previously acquired, later traded to Edmonton — later returned to Winnipeg — Winnipeg selected Chris Kibermanis) in 1994 Entry Draft, November 25, 1993.

• GILL, Hal

Harold Priestley D – L. 6′7″, 240 lbs. b: Concord, MA, 4/6/1975. Boston's 8th, 207th overall, in 1993.

Season	Club	League	GP	G	A	Pts	AG	AA	APts	PIM	PP	SH	GW	S	%	TGF	PGF	TGA	PGA	+/–	GP	G	A	Pts	PIM	PP	SH	GW
1992-93	Nashoba High School	Hi-School	20	25	25	50	....	....	....	....	....	....	....	....	....	....	....	....	....	....	....	....	....	....	....	....	....	....
1993-94	Providence College	H-East	31	1	2	3	....	....	....	26	....	....	....	....	....	....	....	....	....	....	....	....	....	....	....	....	....	....
1994-95	Providence College	H-East	26	1	3	4	....	....	....	22	....	....	....	....	....	....	....	....	....	....	....	....	....	....	....	....	....	....
1995-96	Providence College	H-East	39	5	12	17	....	....	....	54	....	....	....	....	....	....	....	....	....	....	....	....	....	....	....	....	....	....
1996-97	Providence College	H-East	35	5	16	21	....	....	....	52	....	....	....	....	....	....	....	....	....	....	....	....	....	....	....	....	....	....
1997-98	Boston Bruins	NHL	68	2	4	6	2	4	6	47	0	0	0	56	3.6	35	0	48	17	4	6	0	0	0	4	0	0	0
	Providence Bruins	AHL	4	1	0	1	....	....	....	23	....	....	....	....	....	....	....	....	....	....	....	....	....	....	....	....	....	....
1998-99	Boston Bruins	NHL	80	3	7	10	4	7	11	63	0	0	2	102	2.9	48	0	79	21	–10	12	0	0	0	14	0	0	0
99-2000	Boston Bruins	NHL	81	3	9	12	3	8	11	51	0	0	0	120	2.5	58	0	82	24	0	....	....	....	....	....	....	....	....
	United States	WC-A	7	0	0	0	....	....	....	14	....	....	....	....	....	....	....	....	....	....	....	....	....	....	....	....	....	....
	NHL Totals		229	8	20	28	9	19	28	161	0	0	2	278	2.9	141	0	209	62		18	0	0	0	18	0	0	0

• GILL, Todd

Todd Sheldon D – L. 6′, 185 lbs. b: Cardinal, Ont., 11/9/1965. Toronto's 2nd, 25th overall, in 1984.

Season	Club	League	GP	G	A	Pts	AG	AA	APts	PIM	PP	SH	GW	S	%	TGF	PGF	TGA	PGA	+/–	GP	G	A	Pts	PIM	PP	SH	GW
1980-81	Cardinal Broncos	OHA-B	35	10	14	24	....	....	....	65	....	....	....	....	....	....	....	....	....	....	....	....	....	....	....	....	....	....
1981-82	Brockville Braves	OJHL	48	5	16	21	....	....	....	169	....	....	....	....	....	....	....	....	....	....	....	....	....	....	....	....	....	....
1982-83	Windsor Spitfires	OHL	70	12	24	36	....	....	....	108	....	....	....	....	....	....	....	....	....	....	3	0	0	0	11	....	....	....
1983-84	Windsor Spitfires	OHL	68	9	48	57	....	....	....	184	....	....	....	....	....	....	....	....	....	....	3	1	1	2	10	....	....	....
1984-85	Windsor Spitfires	OHL	53	17	40	57	....	....	....	148	....	....	....	....	....	....	....	....	....	....	4	0	1	1	14	....	....	....
	Toronto Maple Leafs	NHL	10	1	0	1	1	0	1	13	0	0	0	9	11.1	4	0	5	0	–1	....	....	....	....	....	....	....	....
1985-86	Toronto Maple Leafs	NHL	15	1	2	3	1	1	2	28	0	0	0	9	11.1	13	2	12	1	0	1	0	0	0	0	0	0	0
	St. Catharines Saints	AHL	58	8	25	33	....	....	....	90	....	....	....	....	....	....	....	....	....	....	10	1	6	7	17	....	....	....
1986-87	Toronto Maple Leafs	NHL	61	4	27	31	3	20	23	92	1	0	0	51	7.8	76	11	82	14	–3	13	2	2	4	42	0	0	0
	Newmarket Saints	AHL	11	1	8	9	....	....	....	33	....	....	....	....	....	....	....	....	....	....	....	....	....	....	....	....	....	....
1987-88	Toronto Maple Leafs	NHL	65	8	17	25	7	12	19	131	1	0	3	109	7.3	74	11	108	25	–20	6	1	3	4	20	1	0	0
	Newmarket Saints	AHL	2	0	1	1	....	....	....	2	....	....	....	....	....	....	....	....	....	....	....	....	....	....	....	....	....	....
1988-89	Toronto Maple Leafs	NHL	59	11	14	25	9	10	19	72	0	0	1	92	12.0	55	7	57	6	–3	....	....	....	....	....	....	....	....
1989-90	Toronto Maple Leafs	NHL	48	1	14	15	1	10	11	92	0	0	0	44	2.3	43	6	49	4	–8	5	0	3	3	16	0	0	0
1990-91	Toronto Maple Leafs	NHL	72	2	22	24	2	17	19	113	0	0	0	90	2.2	66	7	79	16	–4	....	....	....	....	....	....	....	....
1991-92	Toronto Maple Leafs	NHL	74	2	15	17	2	11	13	91	1	0	0	82	2.4	49	6	85	20	–22	....	....	....	....	....	....	....	....
	Canada	WC-A	6	0	3	3	....	....	....	6	....	....	....	....	....	....	....	....	....	....	....	....	....	....	....	....	....	....
1992-93	Toronto Maple Leafs	NHL	69	11	32	43	9	22	31	66	5	0	2	113	9.7	94	40	61	11	4	21	1	10	11	26	0	0	0
1993-94	Toronto Maple Leafs	NHL	45	4	24	28	4	19	23	44	2	0	1	74	5.4	80	34	45	7	8	18	1	5	6	37	0	0	1
1994-95	Toronto Maple Leafs	NHL	47	7	25	32	12	37	49	64	3	1	2	82	8.5	58	22	57	13	–8	7	0	3	3	6	0	0	0
1995-96	Toronto Maple Leafs	NHL	74	7	18	25	7	15	22	116	1	0	2	109	6.4	71	15	89	18	–15	6	0	0	0	24	0	0	0
1996-97	San Jose Sharks	NHL	79	0	21	21	0	19	19	101	0	0	0	101	0.0	75	9	123	37	–20	....	....	....	....	....	....	....	....
1997-98	San Jose Sharks	NHL	64	8	13	21	9	13	22	31	4	0	1	100	8.0	57	18	71	19	–13	....	....	....	....	....	....	....	....
	St. Louis Blues	NHL	11	5	4	9	6	4	10	10	3	0	1	22	22.7	17	7	9	1	2	10	2	2	4	10	1	1	0
1998-99	St. Louis Blues	NHL	28	2	3	5	2	3	5	16	1	0	0	36	5.6	18	4	26	6	–6	....	....	....	....	....	....	....	....
	Detroit Red Wings	NHL	23	2	2	4	2	2	4	11	0	0	1	25	8.0	13	1	22	6	–4	2	0	1	1	0	0	0	0
99-2000	Phoenix Coyotes	NHL	41	1	6	7	1	6	7	30	0	0	1	41	2.4	21	0	36	5	–10	....	....	....	....	....	....	....	....
	Detroit Red Wings	NHL	13	2	0	2	2	0	2	15	0	0	1	20	10.0	8	0	7	1	2	9	0	1	1	4	0	0	0
	NHL Totals		898	79	259	338	80	221	301	1136	22	1	16	1209	6.5	892	200	1023	210		98	7	30	37	185	2	1	1

Traded to **San Jose** by **Toronto** for Jamie Baker and San Jose's 5th round choice (Peter Cava) in 1996 Entry Draft, June 14, 1996. Traded to **St. Louis** by **San Jose** for Joe Murphy, March 24, 1998. Claimed on waivers by **Detroit** from **St. Louis**, December 30, 1998. Signed as a free agent by **Phoenix**, July 21, 1999. Traded to **Detroit** by **Phoenix** for Philippe Audet, March 13, 2000.

• GILLEN, Don

Donald RW – R. 6'3", 210 lbs. b: Dodsland, Sask., 12/24/1960. Philadelphia's 5th, 77th overall, in 1979.

			REGULAR SEASON																		PLAYOFFS							
Season	Club	League	GP	G	A	Pts	AG	AA	APts	PIM	PP	SH	GW	S	%	TGF	PGF	TGA	PGA	+/–	GP	G	A	Pts	PIM	PP	SH	GW
1976-77	Weyburn Red Wings	SJHL	58	13	24	37	....	....	....	170	....	....	....	....	....	....	....	....	....	....	....	....	....	....	....	....	....	....
1977-78	Brandon Wheat Kings	WHL	60	18	18	36	....	....	....	128	....	....	....	....	....	....	....	....	....	....	8	0	1	1	11	....	....	....
1978-79	Brandon Wheat Kings	WHL	64	21	30	51	....	....	....	212	....	....	....	....	....	....	....	....	....	....	22	10	10	20	34	....	....	....
	Brandon Wheat Kings	Mem-Cup	5	0	1	1	....	....	....	24	....	....	....	....	....	....	....	....	....	....	....	....	....	....	....	....	....	....
1979-80	Brandon Wheat Kings	WHL	69	31	56	87	....	....	....	372	....	....	....	....	....	....	....	....	....	....	10	5	3	8	43	....	....	....
	Philadelphia Flyers	NHL	1	1	0	1	1	0	1	0	0	0	0	2	50.0	1	0	0	0	1	....	....	....	....	....	....	....	....
	Maine Mariners	AHL	....	....	....	....	....	....	....	....	....	....	....	....	....	....	....	....	....	....	7	1	2	3	19	....	....	....
1980-81	Maine Mariners	AHL	79	30	29	59	....	....	....	255	....	....	....	....	....	....	....	....	....	....	20	4	4	8	49	....	....	....
1981-82	Hartford Whalers	NHL	34	1	4	5	1	3	4	22	0	0	0	25	4.0	7	0	18	0	–11	....	....	....	....	....	....	....	....
	Binghamton Whalers	AHL	42	20	10	30	....	....	....	100	....	....	....	....	....	....	....	....	....	....	15	6	5	11	23	....	....	....
1982-83	Binghamton Whalers	AHL	80	38	39	77	....	....	....	245	....	....	....	....	....	....	....	....	....	....	1	0	1	1	0	....	....	....
1983-84	Binghamton Whalers	AHL	73	27	37	64	....	....	....	140	....	....	....	....	....	....	....	....	....	....	....	....	....	....	....	....	....	....
	NHL Totals		**35**	**2**	**4**	**6**	**2**	**3**	**5**	**22**	**0**	**0**	**0**	**27**	**7.4**	**8**	**0**	**18**	**0**		....	....	....	....	....	....	....	....

Traded to **Hartford** by **Philadelphia** with Rick MacLeish, Blake Wesley and Philadelphia's 1st (Paul Lawless), 2nd (Mark Paterson) and 3rd (Kevin Dineen) round choices in 1982 Entry Draft for Ray Allison, Fred Arthur and Hartford's 1st (Ron Sutter) and 3rd (Miroslav Dvorak) round choices in 1982 Entry Draft, July 3, 1981.

• GILLIES, Clark

"Jethro" LW – L. 6'3", 215 lbs. b: Moose Jaw, Sask., 4/7/1954. NY Islanders' 1st, 4th overall, in 1974.

Season	Club	League	GP	G	A	Pts	AG	AA	APts	PIM	PP	SH	GW	S	%	TGF	PGF	TGA	PGA	+/–	GP	G	A	Pts	PIM	PP	SH	GW
1971-72	Regina Pats	WCJHL	68	31	48	79	....	....	....	199	....	....	....	....	....	....	....	....	....	....	15	5	10	15	49	....	....	....
1972-73	Regina Pats	WCJHL	68	40	52	92	....	....	....	192	....	....	....	....	....	....	....	....	....	....	4	0	3	3	34	....	....	....
1973-74	Regina Pats	WCJHL	65	46	66	112	....	....	....	179	....	....	....	....	....	....	....	....	....	....	16	9	8	17	32	....	....	....
	Regina Pats	Mem-Cup	3	1	3	4	....	....	....	19	....	....	....	....	....	....	....	....	....	....	....	....	....	....	....	....	....	....
1974-75	New York Islanders	NHL	80	25	22	47	22	16	38	66	8	0	4	165	15.2	71	21	55	1	–4	17	4	2	6	36	0	0	2
1975-76	New York Islanders	NHL	80	34	27	61	30	20	50	96	15	0	6	210	16.2	113	57	36	0	20	13	2	4	6	16	0	0	1
1976-77	New York Islanders	NHL	70	33	22	55	30	17	47	93	12	0	5	215	15.3	81	25	39	1	18	12	4	4	8	15	0	0	4
1977-78	New York Islanders	NHL	80	35	50	85	32	39	71	76	9	0	2	277	12.6	146	54	43	0	49	7	2	0	2	15	1	0	0
1978-79	New York Islanders	NHL	75	35	56	91	30	41	71	68	11	0	5	210	16.7	148	57	34	0	57	10	1	2	3	11	0	0	0
	NHL All-Stars	Chal-Cup	3	1	2	3	....	....	....	2	....	....	....	....	....	....	....	....	....	....	....	....	....	....	....	....	....	....
1979-80 ♦	New York Islanders	NHL	73	19	35	54	16	26	42	49	7	0	5	175	10.9	101	33	39	0	29	21	6	10	16	63	1	0	2
1980-81 ♦	New York Islanders	NHL	80	33	45	78	26	30	56	99	9	0	3	188	17.6	129	47	56	0	26	18	6	9	15	28	3	0	0
1981-82	Canada	Can-Cup	7	2	5	7	....	....	....	8	....	....	....	....	....	....	....	....	....	....	....	....	....	....	....	....	....	....
♦	New York Islanders	NHL	79	38	39	77	30	26	56	75	8	0	5	200	19.0	123	33	51	0	39	19	8	6	14	34	4	0	3
1982-83 ♦	New York Islanders	NHL	70	21	20	41	17	14	31	76	4	0	2	145	14.5	70	22	39	0	9	8	0	2	2	10	0	0	0
1983-84	New York Islanders	NHL	76	12	16	28	10	11	21	65	3	0	2	138	8.7	71	14	52	0	5	21	12	7	19	19	3	0	0
1984-85	New York Islanders	NHL	54	15	17	32	12	12	24	73	5	0	2	125	12.0	54	14	40	0	0	10	1	0	1	9	0	0	0
1985-86	New York Islanders	NHL	55	4	10	14	3	7	10	55	1	0	0	74	5.4	26	3	31	0	–8	3	1	0	1	6	0	0	0
1986-87	Buffalo Sabres	NHL	61	10	17	27	9	12	21	81	1	0	2	106	9.4	42	5	37	0	0	....	....	....	....	....	....	....	....
1987-88	Buffalo Sabres	NHL	25	5	2	7	4	1	5	51	0	0	1	23	21.7	12	0	11	0	1	5	0	1	1	25	0	0	0
	NHL Totals		**958**	**319**	**378**	**697**	**271**	**272**	**543**	**1023**	**93**	**0**	**44**	**2251**	**14.2**	**1187**	**385**	**563**	**2**		**164**	**47**	**47**	**94**	**287**	**12**	**0**	**12**

WCJHL First All-Star Team (1974) • NHL First All-Star Team (1978, 1979) • Played in NHL All-Star Game (1978)

Claimed by **Buffalo** from **NY Islanders** in Waiver Draft, October 6, 1986. • Suffered eventual career-ending knee injury in game vs. Edmonton, November 7, 1987.

• GILLIS, Jere

Jere Alan LW – L. 6', 194 lbs. b: Bend, OR, 1/18/1957. Vancouver's 1st, 4th overall, in 1977.

Season	Club	League	GP	G	A	Pts	AG	AA	APts	PIM	PP	SH	GW	S	%	TGF	PGF	TGA	PGA	+/–	GP	G	A	Pts	PIM	PP	SH	GW
1973-74	Sherbrooke Beavers	QMJHL	69	21	19	40	....	....	....	96	....	....	....	....	....	....	....	....	....	....	....	....	....	....	....	....	....	....
1974-75	Sherbrooke Beavers	QMJHL	54	38	57	95	....	....	....	89	....	....	....	....	....	....	....	....	....	....	....	....	....	....	....	....	....	....
1975-76	Sherbrooke Beavers	QMJHL	60	47	55	102	....	....	....	38	....	....	....	....	....	....	....	....	....	....	17	8	14	22	27	....	....	....
1976-77	Sherbrooke Beavers	QMJHL	72	55	85	140	....	....	....	80	....	....	....	....	....	....	....	....	....	....	18	11	12	23	40	....	....	....
	Sherbrooke Beavers	Mem-Cup	4	4	1	5	....	....	....	0	....	....	....	....	....	....	....	....	....	....	....	....	....	....	....	....	....	....
1977-78	Vancouver Canucks	NHL	79	23	18	41	21	14	35	35	2	0	2	154	14.9	59	15	68	0	–24	....	....	....	....	....	....	....	....
1978-79	Vancouver Canucks	NHL	78	13	12	25	11	9	20	33	4	0	3	143	9.1	51	12	76	6	–31	1	0	1	1	0	0	0	0
1979-80	Vancouver Canucks	NHL	67	13	17	30	11	12	23	108	5	1	5	130	10.0	57	19	69	31	0	....	....	....	....	....	....	....	....
1980-81	Vancouver Canucks	NHL	11	0	4	4	0	3	3	4	0	0	0	11	0.0	6	0	10	4	0	....	....	....	....	....	....	....	....
	New York Rangers	NHL	35	10	10	20	8	7	15	4	1	0	1	63	15.9	33	4	24	1	6	14	2	5	7	9	0	0	0
1981-82	New York Rangers	DN-Cup	4	0	1	1	....	....	....	....	....	....	....	....	....	....	....	....	....	....	....	....	....	....	....	....	....	....
	New York Rangers	NHL	26	3	9	12	2	6	8	16	0	0	1	41	7.3	18	0	20	0	–2	....	....	....	....	....	....	....	....
	Quebec Nordiques	NHL	12	2	1	3	2	1	3	0	0	0	1	16	12.5	7	0	5	0	2	....	....	....	....	....	....	....	....
	Fredericton Express	AHL	28	2	17	19	....	....	....	10	....	....	....	....	....	....	....	....	....	....	....	....	....	....	....	....	....	....
1982-83	Buffalo Sabres	NHL	3	0	0	0	0	0	0	0	0	0	0	3	0.0	0	0	6	0	–6	....	....	....	....	....	....	....	....
	Rochester Americans	AHL	53	18	24	42	....	....	....	69	....	....	....	....	....	....	....	....	....	....	16	1	7	8	11	....	....	....
1983-84	Vancouver Canucks	NHL	37	9	13	22	7	9	16	7	0	1	0	55	16.4	29	3	27	3	2	4	2	1	3	0	0	0	0
	Fredericton Express	AHL	36	22	28	50	....	....	....	35	....	....	....	....	....	....	....	....	....	....	....	....	....	....	....	....	....	....
1984-85	Vancouver Canucks	NHL	37	5	11	16	4	7	11	23	0	0	1	56	8.9	25	1	34	3	–7	....	....	....	....	....	....	....	....
	Fredericton Express	AHL	7	2	1	3	....	....	....	2	....	....	....	....	....	....	....	....	....	....	....	....	....	....	....	....	....	....
1985-86	Fredericton Express	AHL	29	4	14	18	....	....	....	21	....	....	....	....	....	....	....	....	....	....	....	....	....	....	....	....	....	....
1986-87	Philadelphia Flyers	NHL	1	0	0	0	0	0	0	0	0	0	0	0	0.0	0	0	0	0	0	....	....	....	....	....	....	....	....
	Hershey Bears	AHL	47	13	22	35	....	....	....	32	....	....	....	....	....	....	....	....	....	....	5	0	0	0	9	....	....	....
1987-88	SC Brunico	Italy	24	20	16	36	....	....	....	10	....	....	....	....	....	....	....	....	....	....	....	....	....	....	....	....	....	....
1988-89	Solihull Barons	Britain	18	46	47	93	....	....	....	12	....	....	....	....	....	....	....	....	....	....	....	....	....	....	....	....	....	....
1989-90	Solihull Barons	Aut-Cup	8	8	21	29	....	....	....	12	....	....	....	....	....	....	....	....	....	....	....	....	....	....	....	....	....	....
	Solihull Barons	Britain	30	50	35	85	....	....	....	16	....	....	....	....	....	....	....	....	....	....	4	2	4	6	6	....	....	....
1990-91	Telford Tigers	Un-Cup	4	3	1	4	....	....	....	0	....	....	....	....	....	....	....	....	....	....	....	....	....	....	....	....	....	....
	Peterborough Pirates	Britain	6	13	4	17	....	....	....	22	....	....	....	....	....	....	....	....	....	....	....	....	....	....	....	....	....	....
1991-92	Telford Tigers	Britain	DID NOT PLAY – COACHING																									
1992-1996			OUT OF HOCKEY – RETIRED																									
1996-97	Acton Vale Nova	QSPHL	5	0	3	3	....	....	....	2	....	....	....	....	....	....	....	....	....	....	....	....	....	....	....	....	....	....
	NHL Totals		**386**	**78**	**95**	**173**	**66**	**68**	**134**	**230**	**12**	**2**	**14**	**672**	**11.6**	**285**	**54**	**339**	**48**		**19**	**4**	**7**	**11**	**9**	**0**	**0**	**0**

QMJHL First All-Star Team (1977) • Memorial Cup All-Star Team (1977)

Traded to **NY Rangers** by **Vancouver** with Jeff Bandura for Mario Marois and Jim Mayer, November 11, 1980. Traded to **Quebec** by **NY Rangers** with Dean Talafous (later changed to Pat Hickey (March 8, 1982) when Talafous decided to retire) for Robbie Ftorek and Quebec's 8th round choice (Brian Glynn) in 1982 Entry Draft, December 30, 1981. Signed as a free agent by **Buffalo**, September 11, 1982. Signed as a free agent by **Vancouver**, September 26, 1983. Signed as a free agent by **Philadelphia**, October, 1986.

• GILLIS, Mike

Michael David LW – L. 6'1", 195 lbs. b: Sudbury, Ont., 12/1/1958. Colorado's 1st, 5th overall, in 1978.

Season	Club	League	GP	G	A	Pts	AG	AA	APts	PIM	PP	SH	GW	S	%	TGF	PGF	TGA	PGA	+/–	GP	G	A	Pts	PIM	PP	SH	GW
1975-76	Kingston Canadians	OMJHL	64	16	45	61	....	....	....	34	....	....	....	....	....	....	....	....	....	....	7	1	2	3	11	....	....	....
1976-77	Kingston Canadians	OMJHL	4	2	2	4	....	....	....	4	....	....	....	....	....	....	....	....	....	....	....	....	....	....	....	....	....	....
1977-78	Kingston Canadians	OMJHL	43	21	46	67	....	....	....	86	....	....	....	....	....	....	....	....	....	....	5	3	12	15	0	....	....	....
1978-79	Colorado Rockies	NHL	30	1	7	8	1	5	6	6	0	0	0	54	1.9	14	5	27	0	–18	....	....	....	....	....	....	....	....
	Philadelphia Firebirds	AHL	2	0	0	0	....	....	....	0	....	....	....	....	....	....	....	....	....	....	....	....	....	....	....	....	....	....
1979-80	Colorado Rockies	NHL	40	4	5	9	3	4	7	22	1	0	0	56	7.1	13	1	30	0	–18	....	....	....	....	....	....	....	....
	Fort Worth Texans	CHL	29	9	13	22	....	....	....	43	....	....	....	....	....	....	....	....	....	....	....	....	....	....	....	....	....	....
1980-81	Colorado Rockies	NHL	51	11	7	18	9	5	14	54	1	0	2	78	14.1	28	3	46	0	–21	....	....	....	....	....	....	....	....
	Boston Bruins	NHL	17	2	4	6	2	3	5	15	0	0	0	26	7.7	12	0	14	0	–2	1	0	0	0	0	0	0	0
1981-82	Boston Bruins	NHL	53	9	8	17	7	5	12	54	0	0	0	66	13.6	39	1	29	1	10	11	1	2	3	6	0	0	0

Season	Club	League	GP	G	A	Pts	AG	AA	APts	PIM	PP	SH	GW	S	%	TGF	PGF	TGA	PGA	+/-	GP	G	A	Pts	PIM	PP	SH	GW
			REGULAR SEASON																		PLAYOFFS							
1982-83	**Boston Bruins**	**NHL**	5	0	1	1	0	1	1	0	0	0	0	2	0.0	1	0	0	0	1	12	1	3	4	2	0	0	0
	Baltimore Skipjacks	AHL	74	32	81	113	....	....	....	33	....	....	....	....	....	....	....	....	....	....	....	....	....	....	....	....	....	....
1983-84	**Boston Bruins**	**NHL**	50	6	11	17	5	7	12	35	0	0	1	59	10.2	25	3	29	0	–7	3	0	0	0	2	0	0	0
	Hershey Bears	AHL	26	8	21	29	....	....	....	13	....	....	....	....	....	....	....	....	....	....	....	....	....	....	....	....	....	....
	NHL Totals		246	33	43	76	27	30	57	186	2	0	3	341	9.7	132	13	175	1		27	2	5	7	10	0	0	0

• Brother of Paul

• Missed majority of 1976-77 recovering from leg injury suffered in game vs. Sudbury (OMJHL), October 1, 1976. Claimed by **Colorado** as a fill-in during Expansion Draft, June 13, 1979. Traded to **Boston** by **Colorado** for Bob Miller, February 18, 1981.

• GILLIS, Paul

Paul Christopher C – L. 5′11″, 198 lbs. b: Toronto, Ont., 12/31/1963. Quebec's 2nd, 34th overall, in 1982.

Season	Club	League	GP	G	A	Pts	AG	AA	APts	PIM	PP	SH	GW	S	%	TGF	PGF	TGA	PGA	+/-	GP	G	A	Pts	PIM	PP	SH	GW
1979-80	St. Michael's Buzzers	OHA-B	44	20	36	56	....	....	....	114	....	....	....	....	....	....	....	....	....	....	....	....	....	....	....	....	....	....
1980-81	Niagara Falls Flyers	OMJHL	59	14	19	33	....	....	....	165	....	....	....	....	....	....	....	....	....	....	....	....	....	....	....	....	....	....
1981-82	Niagara Falls Flyers	OHL	65	27	62	89	....	....	....	247	....	....	....	....	....	....	....	....	....	....	5	1	5	6	26	....	....	....
1982-83	North Bay Centennials	OHL	61	34	52	86	....	....	....	151	....	....	....	....	....	....	....	....	....	....	6	1	3	4	26	....	....	....
	Quebec Nordiques	**NHL**	7	0	2	2	0	1	1	2	0	0	0	1	0.0	2	0	3	0	–1	....	....	....	....	....	....	....	....
1983-84	**Quebec Nordiques**	**NHL**	57	8	9	17	6	6	12	59	0	0	1	58	13.8	32	0	37	15	10	1	0	0	0	2	0	0	0
	Fredericton Express	AHL	18	7	8	15	....	....	....	47	....	....	....	....	....	....	....	....	....	....	....	....	....	....	....	....	....	....
1984-85	**Quebec Nordiques**	**NHL**	77	14	28	42	11	19	30	168	0	0	3	104	13.5	59	1	72	26	12	18	1	7	8	73	0	0	0
1985-86	**Quebec Nordiques**	**NHL**	80	19	24	43	15	16	31	203	0	2	2	136	14.0	53	0	95	40	–2	3	0	2	2	14	0	0	0
1986-87	**Quebec Nordiques**	**NHL**	76	13	26	39	11	19	30	267	0	0	3	118	11.0	48	0	75	22	–5	13	2	4	6	65	0	0	0
1987-88	**Quebec Nordiques**	**NHL**	80	7	10	17	6	7	13	164	1	0	0	82	8.5	30	4	96	41	–29	....	....	....	....	....	....	....	....
1988-89	**Quebec Nordiques**	**NHL**	79	15	25	40	13	18	31	163	5	0	1	97	15.5	63	17	95	35	–14	....	....	....	....	....	....	....	....
1989-90	**Quebec Nordiques**	**NHL**	71	8	14	22	7	10	17	234	0	1	0	68	11.8	28	1	80	29	–24	....	....	....	....	....	....	....	....
1990-91	**Quebec Nordiques**	**NHL**	49	3	8	11	3	6	9	91	0	1	0	57	5.3	20	0	49	10	–19	....	....	....	....	....	....	....	....
	Chicago Blackhawks	**NHL**	13	0	5	5	0	4	4	53	0	0	0	9	0.0	6	0	5	0	1	2	0	0	0	2	0	0	0
1991-92	**Chicago Blackhawks**	**NHL**	2	0	0	0	0	0	0	6	0	0	0	1	0.0	0	0	3	0	–3	....	....	....	....	....	....	....	....
	Indianapolis Ice	IHL	42	10	15	25	....	....	....	170	....	....	....	....	....	....	....	....	....	....	....	....	....	....	....	....	....	....
	Hartford Whalers	**NHL**	12	0	2	2	0	2	2	48	0	0	0	6	0.0	2	0	4	2	0	5	0	1	1	0	0	0	0
1992-93	**Hartford Whalers**	**NHL**	21	1	1	2	1	1	2	40	0	0	0	8	12.5	2	0	6	2	–2	....	....	....	....	....	....	....	....
1993-1994	**Hartford Whalers**	**NHL**	DID NOT PLAY – ASSISTANT COACH																									
1994-1995	Springfield Falcons	AHL	DID NOT PLAY – COACHING																									
1995-1997	Windsor Spitfires	OHL	DID NOT PLAY – COACHING																									
1997-1999	Quad City Mallards	UHL	DID NOT PLAY – COACHING																									
1999-2000	Guelph Storm	OHL	DID NOT PLAY – COACHING																									
	NHL Totals		624	88	154	242	73	109	182	1498	6	4	10	745	11.8	345	23	620	222		42	3	14	17	156	0	0	0

• Brother of Mike

Traded to **Chicago** by **Quebec** with Dan Vincelette for Ryan McGill and Mike McNeill, March 5, 1991. Traded to **Hartford** by **Chicago** for future considerations, January 27, 1992.

• GILMOUR, Doug

Douglas Robert "Killer" C – L. 5′11″, 175 lbs. b: Kingston, Ont., 6/25/1963. St. Louis' 4th, 134th overall, in 1982.

Season	Club	League	GP	G	A	Pts	AG	AA	APts	PIM	PP	SH	GW	S	%	TGF	PGF	TGA	PGA	+/-	GP	G	A	Pts	PIM	PP	SH	GW
1978-79	Kingston Legionaires	OMHA	STATISTICS NOT AVAILABLE																									
1979-80	Kingston Voyageurs	OJHL-B	15	2	5	7	....	....	....	26	....	....	....	....	....	....	....	....	....	....	....	....	....	....	....	....	....	....
	Belleville Bulls	OJHL	25	9	14	23	....	....	....	18	....	....	....	....	....	....	....	....	....	....	....	....	....	....	....	....	....	....
1980-81	Cornwall Royals	QMJHL	51	12	23	35	....	....	....	35	....	....	....	....	....	....	....	....	....	....	....	....	....	....	....	....	....	....
	Canada	WJC-A	5	0	0	0	....	....	....	0	....	....	....	....	....	....	....	....	....	....	....	....	....	....	....	....	....	....
	Cornwall Royals	Mem-Cup	5	2	5	7	....	....	....	8	....	....	....	....	....	....	....	....	....	....	....	....	....	....	....	....	....	....
1981-82	Cornwall Royals	OHL	67	46	73	119	....	....	....	42	....	....	....	....	....	....	....	....	....	....	5	6	9	15	2	....	....	....
1982-83	Cornwall Royals	OHL	68	70	*107	*177	....	....	....	62	....	....	....	....	....	....	....	....	....	....	8	8	10	18	16	....	....	....
1983-84	**St. Louis Blues**	**NHL**	80	25	28	53	20	19	39	57	3	1	1	157	15.9	74	12	75	19	6	11	2	9	11	10	1	0	1
1984-85	**St. Louis Blues**	**NHL**	78	21	36	57	17	24	41	49	3	1	3	162	13.0	75	15	85	28	3	3	1	1	2	2	0	0	0
1985-86	**St. Louis Blues**	**NHL**	74	25	28	53	20	19	39	41	2	1	5	183	13.7	80	17	93	27	–3	19	9	12	*21	25	1	2	2
1986-87	**St. Louis Blues**	**NHL**	80	42	63	105	36	46	82	58	17	1	2	207	20.3	134	57	104	25	–2	6	2	2	4	16	1	0	1
1987-88	Canada	Can-Cup	8	2	0	2	....	....	....	4	....	....	....	....	....	....	....	....	....	....	....	....	....	....	....	....	....	....
	St. Louis Blues	**NHL**	72	36	50	86	31	36	67	59	19	2	4	163	22.1	110	58	91	26	–13	10	3	14	17	18	1	0	0
1988-89♦	**Calgary Flames**	**NHL**	72	26	59	85	22	42	64	44	11	0	5	161	16.1	132	50	53	16	45	22	11	11	22	20	3	0	3
1989-90	Calgary Flames	Fr-Tour	4	1	3	4	....	....	....	4	....	....	....	....	....	....	....	....	....	....	....	....	....	....	....	....	....	....
	Calgary Flames	**NHL**	78	24	67	91	21	48	69	54	12	1	3	152	15.8	129	48	98	37	20	6	3	1	4	8	0	0	1
	Canada	WEC-A	9	1	4	5	....	....	....	18	....	....	....	....	....	....	....	....	....	....	....	....	....	....	....	....	....	....
1990-91	**Calgary Flames**	**NHL**	78	20	61	81	18	47	65	144	2	2	5	135	14.8	115	26	98	36	27	7	1	1	2	0	0	0	1
1991-92	**Calgary Flames**	**NHL**	38	11	27	38	10	20	30	46	4	1	1	64	17.2	54	20	37	15	12	....	....	....	....	....	....	....	....
	Toronto Maple Leafs	**NHL**	40	15	34	49	14	26	40	32	6	0	3	104	14.4	69	21	51	16	13	....	....	....	....	....	....	....	....
1992-93	**Toronto Maple Leafs**	**NHL**	83	32	95	127	27	66	93	100	15	3	2	211	15.2	170	83	85	30	32	21	10	*25	35	30	4	0	1
1993-94	**Toronto Maple Leafs**	**NHL**	83	27	84	111	25	65	90	105	10	1	3	167	16.2	157	64	100	32	25	18	6	22	28	42	5	0	1
1994-95	HC Rapperswil-Jona	Switz	9	2	13	15	....	....	....	16	....	....	....	....	....	....	....	....	....	....	....	....	....	....	....	....	....	....
	Toronto Maple Leafs	**NHL**	44	10	23	33	18	34	52	26	3	0	1	73	13.7	55	23	49	12	–5	7	0	6	6	6	0	0	0
1995-96	**Toronto Maple Leafs**	**NHL**	81	32	40	72	31	33	64	77	10	2	3	180	17.8	112	54	91	28	–5	6	1	7	8	12	1	0	0
1996-97	**Toronto Maple Leafs**	**NHL**	61	15	45	60	16	40	56	46	2	1	1	103	14.6	92	27	88	18	–5	....	....	....	....	....	....	....	....
	New Jersey Devils	**NHL**	20	7	15	22	7	13	20	22	2	0	0	40	17.5	29	9	14	1	7	10	0	4	4	14	0	0	0
1997-98	**New Jersey Devils**	**NHL**	63	13	40	53	15	39	54	68	3	0	5	94	13.8	81	35	51	15	10	6	5	2	7	4	1	0	1
1998-99	**Chicago Blackhawks**	**NHL**	72	16	40	56	19	39	58	56	7	1	4	110	14.5	83	36	97	34	–16	....	....	....	....	....	....	....	....
99-2000	**Chicago Blackhawks**	**NHL**	63	22	34	56	25	32	57	51	8	0	3	100	22.0	79	32	60	1	–12	....	....	....	....	....	....	....	....
	Buffalo Sabres	**NHL**	11	3	14	17	3	13	16	12	2	0	0	13	23.1	18	4	14	3	3	5	0	1	1	0	0	0	0
	NHL Totals		1271	422	883	1305	395	701	1096	1147	141	18	54	2579	16.4	1848	691	1434	419		157	54	118	172	207	18	2	12

OHL First All-Star Team (1983) • Won Frank J. Selke Trophy (1993) • Played in NHL All-Star Game (1993, 1994)

Traded to **Calgary** by **St. Louis** with Mark Hunter, Steve Bozek and Michael Dark for Mike Bullard, Craig Coxe and Tim Corkery, September 6, 1988. Traded to **Toronto** by **Calgary** with Jamie Macoun, Ric Nattress, Kent Manderville and Rick Wamsley for Gary Leeman, Alexander Godynyuk, Jeff Reese, Michel Petit and Craig Berube, January 2, 1992. Traded to **New Jersey** by **Toronto** with Dave Ellett and New Jersey's 3rd round choice (previously acquired, New Jersey selected Andre Lakos) in 1999 Entry Draft for Jason Smith, Steve Sullivan and the rights to Alyn McCauley, February 25, 1997. Signed as a free agent by **Chicago**, July 28, 1998. Traded to **Buffalo** by **Chicago** with J.P. Dumont and future considerations for Michal Grosek, March 10, 2000.

• GINGRAS, Gaston

Gaston Reginald D – L. 6′1″, 200 lbs. b: Temiscamingue, Que., 2/13/1959. Montreal's 1st, 27th overall, in 1979.

Season	Club	League	GP	G	A	Pts	AG	AA	APts	PIM	PP	SH	GW	S	%	TGF	PGF	TGA	PGA	+/-	GP	G	A	Pts	PIM	PP	SH	GW
1974-75	North Bay Trappers	NOJHA	41	11	27	38	....	....	....	74	....	....	....	....	....	....	....	....	....	....	....	....	....	....	....	....	....	....
1975-76	Kitchener Rangers	OMJHL	66	13	31	44	....	....	....	94	....	....	....	....	....	....	....	....	....	....	8	3	3	6	7	....	....	....
1976-77	Kitchener Rangers	OMJHL	59	13	62	75	....	....	....	134	....	....	....	....	....	....	....	....	....	....	3	0	1	1	6	....	....	....
1977-78	Kitchener Rangers	OMJHL	32	13	24	37	....	....	....	31	....	....	....	....	....	....	....	....	....	....	....	....	....	....	....	....	....	....
	Hamilton Fincups	OMJHL	29	11	19	30	....	....	....	37	....	....	....	....	....	....	....	....	....	....	15	3	11	14	13	....	....	....
1978-79	Birmingham Bulls	WHA	60	13	21	34	....	....	....	35	....	....	....	....	....	....	....	....	....	....	....	....	....	....	....	....	....	....
1979-80	**Montreal Canadiens**	**NHL**	34	3	7	10	3	5	8	18	2	0	1	60	5.0	45	14	21	1	11	10	1	6	7	8	0	0	0
	Nova Scotia Voyageurs	AHL	30	11	27	38	....	....	....	17	....	....	....	....	....	....	....	....	....	....	....	....	....	....	....	....	....	....
1980-81	**Montreal Canadiens**	**NHL**	55	5	16	21	4	11	15	22	3	0	1	133	3.8	65	28	35	3	5	1	1	0	1	0	1	0	0
1981-82	**Montreal Canadiens**	**NHL**	34	6	18	24	5	12	17	28	3	0	3	89	6.7	57	21	30	4	10	5	0	1	1	0	0	0	0
1982-83	**Montreal Canadiens**	**NHL**	22	1	8	9	1	6	7	8	1	0	1	60	1.7	40	11	21	2	10	....	....	....	....	....	....	....	....
	Toronto Maple Leafs	**NHL**	45	10	18	28	8	12	20	10	4	0	1	95	10.5	57	22	39	11	7	3	1	2	3	2	0	0	0
1983-84	**Toronto Maple Leafs**	**NHL**	59	7	20	27	6	14	20	16	4	0	0	125	5.6	53	18	77	12	–30	....	....	....	....	....	....	....	....
1984-85	**Toronto Maple Leafs**	**NHL**	5	0	2	2	0	1	1	0	0	0	0	17	0.0	4	3	10	2	–7	....	....	....	....	....	....	....	....
	St. Catharines Saints	AHL	36	7	12	19	....	....	....	13	....	....	....	....	....	....	....	....	....	....	....	....	....	....	....	....	....	....
	Sherbrooke Canadiens	AHL	21	3	14	17	....	....	....	6	....	....	....	....	....	....	....	....	....	....	17	5	4	9	4	....	....	....
1985-86♦	**Montreal Canadiens**	**NHL**	34	8	18	26	6	12	18	12	7	0	0	77	10.4	39	16	33	0	–10	11	2	3	5	4	1	0	0
	Sherbrooke Canadiens	AHL	42	11	20	31	....	....	....	14	....	....	....	....	....	....	....	....	....	....	....	....	....	....	....	....	....	....
1986-87	**Montreal Canadiens**	**NHL**	66	11	34	45	9	25	34	21	7	0	2	173	6.4	91	37	56	0	–2	5	0	2	2	0	0	0	0

			REGULAR SEASON																		PLAYOFFS							
Season	Club	League	GP	G	A	Pts	AG	AA	APts	PIM	PP	SH	GW	S	%	TGF	PGF	TGA	PGA	+/–	GP	G	A	Pts	PIM	PP	SH	GW
1987-88	**Montreal Canadiens**	**NHL**	**2**	**0**	**1**	**1**	**0**	**1**	**1**	**2**	**0**	**0**	**0**	**2**	**0.0**	**1**	**0**	**0**	**0**	**1**	....	....	....	....	....	....	....	....
	St. Louis Blues	**NHL**	**68**	**7**	**22**	**29**	**6**	**16**	**22**	**18**	**3**	**0**	**0**	**131**	**5.3**	**84**	**34**	**52**	**2**	**0**	**10**	**1**	**3**	**4**	**4**	**0**	**0**	**0**
1988-89	**St. Louis Blues**	**NHL**	**52**	**3**	**10**	**13**	**3**	**7**	**10**	**6**	**2**	**0**	**0**	**98**	**3.1**	**58**	**19**	**44**	**6**	**1**	**7**	**0**	**1**	**1**	**2**	**0**	**0**	**0**
1989-90	EHC Biel-Bienne	Switz.	36	17	20	37	....	....	....	....	....	....	....	....	....	....	....	....	....	....	6	3	3	6	....	....	....	....
1990-91	EHC Biel-Bienne	Switz.	13	1	7	8	....	....	....	....	....	....	....	....	....	....	....	....	....	....	....	....	....	....	....	....	....	....
1991-92	HC Lugano	Switz.	38	10	19	29	....	....	....	24	....	....	....	....	....	....	....	....	....	....	....	....	....	....	....	....	....	....
1992-93	HC Gardena-Groden	Alpenliga	30	10	19	29	....	....	....	28	....	....	....	....	....	....	....	....	....	....	....	....	....	....	....	....	....	....
	HC Gardena-Groden	Italy	16	2	21	23	....	....	....	12	....	....	....	....	....	....	....	....	....	....	3	1	3	4	4	....	....	....
1993-94	HC Gardena-Groden	Alpenliga	27	5	15	20	....	....	....	6	....	....	....	....	....	....	....	....	....	....	....	....	....	....	....	....	....	....
	HC Gardena-Groden	Italy	19	3	14	17	....	....	....	14	....	....	....	....	....	....	....	....	....	....	2	0	0	0	0	....	....	....
1994-95	Fredericton Canadiens	AHL	19	3	6	9	....	....	....	4	....	....	....	....	....	....	....	....	....	....	17	2	12	14	8	....	....	....
1995-96	Fredericton Canadiens	AHL	39	2	21	23	....	....	....	18	....	....	....	....	....	....	....	....	....	....	....	....	....	....	....	....	....	....
1996-1998			OUT OF HOCKEY – RETIRED																									
1998-99	Chesapeake Icebreakers	ECHL	5	0	4	4	....	....	....	6	....	....	....	....	....	....	....	....	....	....	....	....	....	....	....	....	....	....
	NHL Totals		**476**	**61**	**174**	**235**	**51**	**122**	**173**	**161**	**36**	**0**	**9**	**1060**	**5.8**	**594**	**223**	**418**	**43**		**52**	**6**	**18**	**24**	**20**	**2**	**0**	**0**
	Other Major League Totals		60	13	21	34	....	....	....	35	....	....	....	....	....	....	....	....	....	....	....	....	....	....	....	....	....	....

Signed as an underage free agent by **Birmingham** (WHA), June, 1978. Traded to **Toronto** by **Montreal** for Toronto's 2nd round choice (Benoit Brunet) in 1986 Entry Draft, December 17, 1982. Traded to **Montreal** by **Toronto** for Larry Landon, February 14, 1985. Traded to **St. Louis** by **Montreal** with Montreal's 3rd round choice (later traded to Winnipeg — Winnipeg selected Kris Draper) in 1989 Entry Draft for Larry Trader and St. Louis' 3rd round choice (Pierre Sevigny) in 1989 Entry Draft, October 13, 1987. Signed as a free agent by **Chesapeake** (ECHL), February 9, 1999.

• GIRARD, Bob

Robert LW – L. 6', 180 lbs. b: Montreal, Que., 4/12/1949.

Season	Club	League	GP	G	A	Pts	AG	AA	APts	PIM	PP	SH	GW	S	%	TGF	PGF	TGA	PGA	+/–	GP	G	A	Pts	PIM	PP	SH	GW
1972-73	Amqui Aces	QSHL	45	18	33	51	....	....	....	....	....	....	....	....	....	....	....	....	....	....	....	....	....	....	....	....	....	....
1973-74	Charlotte Checkers	SHL	23	5	17	22	....	....	....	12	....	....	....	....	....	....	....	....	....	....	....	....	....	....	....	....	....	....
	Salt Lake Golden Eagles	WHL	50	2	19	21	....	....	....	37	....	....	....	....	....	....	....	....	....	....	1	0	0	0	2	....	....	....
1974-75	Salt Lake Golden Eagles	CHL	74	13	32	45	....	....	....	60	....	....	....	....	....	....	....	....	....	....	11	0	2	2	10	....	....	....
1975-76	**California Golden Seals**	**NHL**	**80**	**16**	**26**	**42**	**14**	**19**	**33**	**54**	**3**	**0**	**1**	**137**	**11.7**	**70**	**18**	**74**	**19**	**–3**	....	....	....	....	....	....	....	....
1976-77	**Cleveland Barons**	**NHL**	**68**	**11**	**10**	**21**	**10**	**8**	**18**	**33**	**1**	**1**	**1**	**101**	**10.9**	**37**	**5**	**70**	**14**	**–24**	....	....	....	....	....	....	....	....
	Salt Lake Golden Eagles	CHL	4	2	6	8	....	....	....	0	....	....	....	....	....	....	....	....	....	....	....	....	....	....	....	....	....	....
1977-78	**Cleveland Barons**	**NHL**	**25**	**0**	**4**	**4**	**0**	**3**	**3**	**11**	**0**	**0**	**0**	**24**	**0.0**	**5**	**0**	**22**	**9**	**–8**	....	....	....	....	....	....	....	....
	Washington Capitals	**NHL**	**52**	**9**	**14**	**23**	**8**	**11**	**19**	**6**	**1**	**0**	**2**	**42**	**21.4**	**47**	**4**	**47**	**1**	**–3**	....	....	....	....	....	....	....	....
1978-79	**Washington Capitals**	**NHL**	**79**	**9**	**15**	**24**	**8**	**11**	**19**	**36**	**0**	**0**	**0**	**59**	**15.3**	**42**	**0**	**79**	**22**	**–15**	....	....	....	....	....	....	....	....
1979-80	**Washington Capitals**	**NHL**	**1**	**0**	**0**	**0**	**0**	**0**	**0**	**0**	**0**	**0**	**0**	**0**	**0.0**	**0**	**0**	**1**	**1**	**0**	....	....	....	....	....	....	....	....
	Hershey Bears	AHL	74	15	26	41	....	....	....	63	....	....	....	....	....	....	....	....	....	....	16	5	5	10	6	....	....	....
	NHL Totals		**305**	**45**	**69**	**114**	**40**	**52**	**92**	**140**	**5**	**1**	**4**	**363**	**12.4**	**201**	**27**	**293**	**66**		....	....	....	....	....	....	....	....

Signed as a free agent by **California**, September, 1973. Transferred to **Cleveland** after **California** franchise relocated, August 26, 1976. Traded to **Washington** by **Cleveland** with Cleveland's 2nd round choice (Paul McKinnon) in 1978 Amateur Draft for Walt McKechnie, December 9, 1977. Claimed by **Washington** as a fill-in during Expansion Draft, June 13, 1979.

• GIRARD, Jonathan

D – R. 5'11", 192 lbs. b: Joliette, Que., 5/27/1980. Boston's 1st, 48th overall, in 1998.

Season	Club	League	GP	G	A	Pts	AG	AA	APts	PIM	PP	SH	GW	S	%	TGF	PGF	TGA	PGA	+/–	GP	G	A	Pts	PIM	PP	SH	GW
1995-96	Laval Laurentide	QAAA	39	11	22	33	....	....	....	44	....	....	....	....	....	....	....	....	....	....	....	....	....	....	....	....	....	....
1996-97	Laval Titan	QMJHL	39	11	23	34	....	....	....	13	....	....	....	....	....	....	....	....	....	....	3	0	3	3	0	....	....	....
1997-98	Laval Titan	QMJHL	64	20	47	67	....	....	....	44	....	....	....	....	....	....	....	....	....	....	16	2	16	18	13	....	....	....
1998-99	Acadie Bathurst Titan	QMJHL	50	9	58	67	....	....	....	60	....	....	....	....	....	....	....	....	....	....	23	13	18	31	22	....	....	....
	Boston Bruins	**NHL**	**3**	**0**	**0**	**0**	**0**	**0**	**0**	**0**	**0**	**0**	**0**	**3**	**0.0**	**2**	**1**	**0**	**0**	**1**	....	....	....	....	....	....	....	....
99-2000	Moncton Wildcats	QMJHL	26	10	25	35	....	....	....	36	....	....	....	....	....	....	....	....	....	....	16	3	15	18	36	....	....	....
	Boston Bruins	**NHL**	**23**	**1**	**2**	**3**	**1**	**2**	**3**	**2**	**0**	**0**	**0**	**17**	**5.9**	**9**	**2**	**8**	**0**	**–1**	....	....	....	....	....	....	....	....
	Providence Bruins	AHL	5	0	1	1	....	....	....	0	....	....	....	....	....	....	....	....	....	....	....	....	....	....	....	....	....	....
	NHL Totals		**26**	**1**	**2**	**3**	**1**	**2**	**3**	**2**	**0**	**0**	**0**	**20**	**5.0**	**11**	**3**	**8**	**0**		....	....	....	....	....	....	....	....

QMJHL Second All-Star Team (1998) • QMJHL First All-Star Team (1999, 2000)

• GIROUX, Larry

Larry Douglas "Buffalo Head" D – R. 6', 190 lbs. b: Weyburn, Sask., 8/28/1951.

Season	Club	League	GP	G	A	Pts	AG	AA	APts	PIM	PP	SH	GW	S	%	TGF	PGF	TGA	PGA	+/–	GP	G	A	Pts	PIM	PP	SH	GW
1967-68	Weyburn Red Wings	WCJHL	2	0	0	0	....	....	....	0	....	....	....	....	....	....	....	....	....	....	....	....	....	....	....	....	....	....
1968-69	Weyburn Red Wings	SJHL	STATISTICS NOT AVAILABLE																									
1969-70	Weyburn Red Wings	SJHL	36	14	33	47	....	....	....	96	....	....	....	....	....	....	....	....	....	....	....	....	....	....	....	....	....	....
	Weyburn Red Wings	Mem-Cup	22	5	16	21	....	....	....	31	....	....	....	....	....	....	....	....	....	....	....	....	....	....	....	....	....	....
1970-71	Swift Current Broncos	WCJHL	62	14	28	42	....	....	....	173	....	....	....	....	....	....	....	....	....	....	....	....	....	....	....	....	....	....
1971-72	Kimberley Dynamiters	WIHL	STATISTICS NOT AVAILABLE																									
	Des Moines Oak Leafs	IHL	5	0	1	1	....	....	....	6	....	....	....	....	....	....	....	....	....	....	....	....	....	....	....	....	....	....
1972-73	Denver Spurs	WHL	2	0	1	1	....	....	....	2	....	....	....	....	....	....	....	....	....	....	....	....	....	....	....	....	....	....
	Fort Worth Wings	CHL	72	5	42	47	....	....	....	130	....	....	....	....	....	....	....	....	....	....	4	0	0	0	24	....	....	....
1973-74	**St. Louis Blues**	**NHL**	**74**	**5**	**17**	**22**	**5**	**14**	**19**	**59**	**2**	**0**	**1**	**131**	**3.8**	**63**	**18**	**65**	**6**	**–14**	....	....	....	....	....	....	....	....
1974-75	**Kansas City Scouts**	**NHL**	**21**	**0**	**6**	**6**	**0**	**4**	**4**	**24**	**0**	**0**	**0**	**27**	**0.0**	**21**	**7**	**38**	**4**	**–20**	....	....	....	....	....	....	....	....
	Denver Spurs	CHL	10	1	6	7	....	....	....	37	....	....	....	....	....	....	....	....	....	....	....	....	....	....	....	....	....	....
	Detroit Red Wings	**NHL**	**39**	**2**	**20**	**22**	**2**	**15**	**17**	**60**	**1**	**0**	**1**	**56**	**3.6**	**56**	**24**	**57**	**15**	**–10**	....	....	....	....	....	....	....	....
	Virginia Wings	AHL	14	3	10	13	....	....	....	31	....	....	....	....	....	....	....	....	....	....	....	....	....	....	....	....	....	....
1975-76	**Detroit Red Wings**	**NHL**	**10**	**1**	**1**	**2**	**1**	**1**	**2**	**25**	**0**	**0**	**0**	**9**	**11.1**	**7**	**1**	**21**	**5**	**–10**	....	....	....	....	....	....	....	....
	New Haven Nighthawks	AHL	67	1	24	25	....	....	....	121	....	....	....	....	....	....	....	....	....	....	3	0	0	0	6	....	....	....
1976-77	**Detroit Red Wings**	**NHL**	**2**	**0**	**0**	**0**	**0**	**0**	**0**	**2**	**0**	**0**	**0**	**7**	**0.0**	**1**	**0**	**1**	**0**	**0**	....	....	....	....	....	....	....	....
	Kansas City Blues	CHL	75	11	34	45	....	....	....	194	....	....	....	....	....	....	....	....	....	....	10	0	*8	8	25	....	....	....
1977-78	**Detroit Red Wings**	**NHL**	**5**	**0**	**3**	**3**	**0**	**2**	**2**	**4**	**0**	**0**	**0**	**10**	**0.0**	**5**	**2**	**8**	**0**	**–5**	**2**	**0**	**0**	**0**	**2**	**0**	**0**	**0**
	Kansas City Red Wings	CHL	73	11	49	60	....	....	....	256	....	....	....	....	....	....	....	....	....	....	....	....	....	....	....	....	....	....
1978-79	**St. Louis Blues**	**NHL**	**73**	**5**	**22**	**27**	**4**	**16**	**20**	**111**	**0**	**0**	**1**	**107**	**4.7**	**72**	**5**	**111**	**19**	**–25**	....	....	....	....	....	....	....	....
1979-80	**St. Louis Blues**	**NHL**	**3**	**0**	**0**	**0**	**0**	**0**	**0**	**4**	**0**	**0**	**0**	**6**	**0.0**	**0**	**0**	**4**	**1**	**–3**	....	....	....	....	....	....	....	....
	Salt Lake Golden Eagles	CHL	5	0	1	1	....	....	....	2	....	....	....	....	....	....	....	....	....	....	....	....	....	....	....	....	....	....
	Hartford Whalers	**NHL**	**47**	**2**	**5**	**7**	**2**	**4**	**6**	**44**	**0**	**0**	**0**	**63**	**3.2**	**49**	**1**	**56**	**9**	**1**	**3**	**0**	**0**	**0**	**2**	**0**	**0**	**0**
	Springfield Indians	AHL	5	0	1	1	....	....	....	14	....	....	....	....	....	....	....	....	....	....	....	....	....	....	....	....	....	....
	NHL Totals		**274**	**15**	**74**	**89**	**14**	**56**	**70**	**333**	**3**	**0**	**3**	**416**	**3.6**	**274**	**58**	**361**	**59**		**5**	**0**	**0**	**0**	**4**	**0**	**0**	**0**

CHL First All-Star Team (1973, 1978) • Named CHL's Top Defenseman (1978)

Signed as a free agent by **St. Louis**, October, 1972. Traded to **Kansas City** by **St. Louis** for Chris Evans and Kansas City's 4th round choice (Mike Liut) in 1976 Amateur Draft, October 29, 1974. Traded to **Detroit** by **Kansas City** with Bart Crashley and Ted Snell for Guy Charron and Claude Houde, December 14, 1974. Claimed by **St. Louis** from **Detroit** in Waiver Draft, October 9, 1978. Signed as a free agent by **Hartford**, December 13, 1979.

• GIROUX, Pierre

Yves Pierre Richard C – R. 5'11", 185 lbs. b: Brownsburg, Que., 11/17/1955. Chicago's 4th, 61st overall, in 1975.

Season	Club	League	GP	G	A	Pts	AG	AA	APts	PIM	PP	SH	GW	S	%	TGF	PGF	TGA	PGA	+/–	GP	G	A	Pts	PIM	PP	SH	GW
1972-73	Sorel Black Hawks	QMJHL	48	4	13	17	....	....	....	25	....	....	....	....	....	....	....	....	....	....	....	....	....	....	....	....	....	....
1973-74	Sorel Black Hawks	QMJHL	41	4	11	15	....	....	....	23	....	....	....	....	....	....	....	....	....	....	....	....	....	....	....	....	....	....
1974-75	Hull Festivals	QMJHL	72	57	61	118	....	....	....	118	....	....	....	....	....	....	....	....	....	....	4	1	3	4	0	....	....	....
1975-76	Dallas Black Hawks	CHL	62	8	14	22	....	....	....	69	....	....	....	....	....	....	....	....	....	....	10	0	1	1	0	....	....	....
1976-77	Flint Generals	IHL	73	21	36	57	....	....	....	87	....	....	....	....	....	....	....	....	....	....	5	2	0	2	0	....	....	....
1977-78	Dallas Black Hawks	CHL	16	2	5	7	....	....	....	2	....	....	....	....	....	....	....	....	....	....	....	....	....	....	....	....	....	....
	Flint Generals	IHL	40	25	23	48	....	....	....	121	....	....	....	....	....	....	....	....	....	....	5	0	0	0	56	....	....	....
1978-79	New Brunswick Hawks	AHL	8	0	2	2	....	....	....	20	....	....	....	....	....	....	....	....	....	....	....	....	....	....	....	....	....	....
	Flint Generals	IHL	70	41	42	83	....	....	....	146	....	....	....	....	....	....	....	....	....	....	11	4	9	13	9	....	....	....
1979-80	Flint Generals	IHL	80	33	38	71	....	....	....	197	....	....	....	....	....	....	....	....	....	....	5	2	1	3	16	....	....	....
1980-81	Flint Generals	IHL	81	55	47	102	....	....	....	303	....	....	....	....	....	....	....	....	....	....	7	5	5	10	0	....	....	....
1981-82	New Haven Nighthawks	AHL	38	6	11	17	....	....	....	114	....	....	....	....	....	....	....	....	....	....	....	....	....	....	....	....	....	....

Season	Club	League	REGULAR SEASON																		PLAYOFFS							
			GP	G	A	Pts	AG	AA	APts	PIM	PP	SH	GW	S	%	TGF	PGF	TGA	PGA	+/–	GP	G	A	Pts	PIM	PP	SH	GW
1982-83	**Los Angeles Kings**	**NHL**	**6**	**1**	**0**	**1**	**1**	**0**	**1**	**17**	**0**	**0**	**0**	**1**	**100.0**	**2**	**1**	**4**	**2**	**–1**	....	....	....	....	....	....	....	....
	New Haven Nighthawks	AHL	62	16	31	47	....	....	....	337	....	....	....	....	....	....	....	....	....	....	9	1	3	4	26	....	....	....
1983-84	Flint Generals	IHL	56	24	37	61	....	....	....	274	....	....	....	....	....	....	....	....	....	....	....	....	....	....	....	....	....	....
	NHL Totals		**6**	**1**	**0**	**1**	**1**	**0**	**1**	**17**	**0**	**0**	**0**	**1**	**100.0**	**2**	**1**	**4**	**2**		....	....	....	....	....	....	....	....

IHL First All-Star Team (1981)

Signed as a free agent by **LA Kings**, August 5, 1982.

• GIROUX, Ray

D – L. 6', 180 lbs. b: North Bay, Ont., 7/20/1976. Philadelphia's 7th, 202nd overall, in 1994.

Season	Club	League	GP	G	A	Pts	AG	AA	APts	PIM	PP	SH	GW	S	%	TGF	PGF	TGA	PGA	+/–	GP	G	A	Pts	PIM	PP	SH	GW
1992-93	Powasson Hawks	NOJHA	45	8	18	26	....	....	....	117	....	....	....	....	....	....	....	....	....	....	....	....	....	....	....	....	....	....
1993-94	Powasson Hawks	NOJHA	36	10	40	50	....	....	....	42	....	....	....	....	....	....	....	....	....	....	....	....	....	....	....	....	....	....
1994-95	Yale University	ECAC	27	1	3	4	....	....	....	8	....	....	....	....	....	....	....	....	....	....	....	....	....	....	....	....	....	....
1995-96	Yale University	ECAC	30	3	16	19	....	....	....	36	....	....	....	....	....	....	....	....	....	....	....	....	....	....	....	....	....	....
1996-97	Yale University	ECAC	32	9	12	21	....	....	....	38	....	....	....	....	....	....	....	....	....	....	....	....	....	....	....	....	....	....
1997-98	Yale University	ECAC	35	9	*30	39	....	....	....	62	....	....	....	....	....	....	....	....	....	....	....	....	....	....	....	....	....	....
1998-99	Lowell Lock Monsters	AHL	59	13	19	32	....	....	....	92	....	....	....	....	....	....	....	....	....	....	3	1	1	2	0	....	....	....
99-2000	**New York Islanders**	**NHL**	**14**	**0**	**9**	**9**	**0**	**8**	**8**	**10**	**0**	**0**	**0**	**24**	**0.0**	**13**	**9**	**8**	**4**	**0**	....	....	....	....	....	....	....	....
	Lowell Lock Monsters	AHL	49	12	21	33	....	....	....	34	....	....	....	....	....	....	....	....	....	....	7	0	0	0	2	....	....	....
	NHL Totals		**14**	**0**	**9**	**9**	**0**	**8**	**8**	**10**	**0**	**0**	**0**	**24**	**0.0**	**13**	**9**	**8**	**4**		....	....	....	....	....	....	....	....

ECAC First All-Star Team (1998) • NCAA East First All-American Team (1998)

Rights traded to **NY Islanders** by **Philadelphia** for NY Islanders' 6th round choice (later traded to Montreal - Montreal selected Scott Selig) in 2000 Entry Draft, August 25, 1998.

• GLADNEY, Bob

Robert Lawrence D – L. 5'11", 185 lbs. b: Come-by-Chance, Nfld., 8/27/1957. Toronto's 3rd, 24th overall, in 1977.

Season	Club	League	GP	G	A	Pts	AG	AA	APts	PIM	PP	SH	GW	S	%	TGF	PGF	TGA	PGA	+/–	GP	G	A	Pts	PIM	PP	SH	GW
1973-74	Clarenville Midget Caribous	NFAHA	STATISTICS NOT AVAILABLE																									
	Clarenville Caribous	Nfld-Sr.	2	4	2	6	....	....	....	0	....	....	....	....	....	....	....	....	....	....	....	....	....	....	....	....	....	....
1974-75	Oshawa Generals	OMJHL	68	12	50	62	....	....	....	84	....	....	....	....	....	....	....	....	....	....	5	2	3	5	2	....	....	....
1975-76	Oshawa Generals	OMJHL	66	26	52	78	....	....	....	47	....	....	....	....	....	....	....	....	....	....	5	1	4	5	2	....	....	....
1976-77	Oshawa Generals	OMJHL	54	20	42	62	....	....	....	56	....	....	....	....	....	....	....	....	....	....	....	....	....	....	....	....	....	....
1977-78	Saginaw Gears	IHL	69	15	50	65	....	....	....	35	....	....	....	....	....	....	....	....	....	....	5	1	4	5	2	....	....	....
1978-79	Saginaw Gears	IHL	67	16	42	58	....	....	....	51	....	....	....	....	....	....	....	....	....	....	4	2	3	5	2	....	....	....
1979-80	New Brunswick Hawks	AHL	26	0	6	6	....	....	....	18	....	....	....	....	....	....	....	....	....	....	10	0	2	2	4	....	....	....
1980-81	Saginaw Gears	IHL	78	12	71	83	....	....	....	54	....	....	....	....	....	....	....	....	....	....	13	3	9	12	12	....	....	....
1981-82	Saginaw Gears	IHL	17	4	9	13	....	....	....	10	....	....	....	....	....	....	....	....	....	....	....	....	....	....	....	....	....	....
	New Haven Nighthawks	AHL	63	7	26	33	....	....	....	12	....	....	....	....	....	....	....	....	....	....	4	1	2	3	0	....	....	....
1982-83	**Los Angeles Kings**	**NHL**	**1**	**0**	**0**	**0**	**0**	**0**	**0**	**2**	**0**	**0**	**0**	**2**	**0.0**	**0**	**0**	**2**	**0**	**–2**	....	....	....	....	....	....	....	....
	New Haven Nighthawks	AHL	80	19	47	66	....	....	....	22	....	....	....	....	....	....	....	....	....	....	12	0	7	7	8	....	....	....
1983-84	**Pittsburgh Penguins**	**NHL**	**13**	**1**	**5**	**6**	**1**	**3**	**4**	**2**	**0**	**0**	**0**	**15**	**6.7**	**13**	**3**	**12**	**1**	**–1**	....	....	....	....	....	....	....	....
	Baltimore Skipjacks	AHL	9	4	7	11	....	....	....	10	....	....	....	....	....	....	....	....	....	....	....	....	....	....	....	....	....	....
	NHL Totals		**14**	**1**	**5**	**6**	**1**	**3**	**4**	**4**	**0**	**0**	**0**	**17**	**5.9**	**13**	**3**	**14**	**1**		....	....	....	....	....	....	....	....

IHL Second All-Star Team (1981) • AHL First All-Star Team (1983)

Traded to **LA Kings** by **Toronto** with Toronto's 6th round choice (Kevin Stevens) in 1983 Entry Draft for Don Luce, August 10, 1981. Signed as a free agent by **Pittsburgh**, September 12, 1983. • Suffered career-ending eye injury in game vs. Rochester (AHL), December 9, 1983.

• GLENNIE, Brian

Brian Alexander "Blunt" D – L. 6'1", 197 lbs. b: Toronto, Ont., 8/29/1946.

Season	Club	League	GP	G	A	Pts	AG	AA	APts	PIM	PP	SH	GW	S	%	TGF	PGF	TGA	PGA	+/–	GP	G	A	Pts	PIM	PP	SH	GW
1964-65	Toronto Marlboros	OHA-Jr.	56	2	18	20	....	....	....	84	....	....	....	....	....	....	....	....	....	....	19	0	9	9	22	....	....	....
1965-66	Toronto Marlboros	OHA-Jr.	48	5	18	23	....	....	....	134	....	....	....	....	....	....	....	....	....	....	14	0	4	4	57	....	....	....
1966-67	Toronto Marlboros	OHA-Jr.	43	5	39	44	....	....	....	113	....	....	....	....	....	....	....	....	....	....	17	2	12	14	44	....	....	....
	Toronto Marlboros	Mem-Cup	9	2	9	11	....	....	....	18	....	....	....	....	....	....	....	....	....	....	....	....	....	....	....	....	....	....
1967-68	Ottawa Nationals	OHA-Sr.	30	2	10	12	....	....	....	20	....	....	....	....	....	....	....	....	....	....	....	....	....	....	....	....	....	....
	Canada	Nat-Team	10	2	10	12	....	....	....	20	....	....	....	....	....	....	....	....	....	....	....	....	....	....	....	....	....	....
	Canada	Olympics	7	0	1	1	....	....	....	10	....	....	....	....	....	....	....	....	....	....	....	....	....	....	....	....	....	....
1968-69	Rochester Americans	AHL	15	1	1	2	....	....	....	16	....	....	....	....	....	....	....	....	....	....	....	....	....	....	....	....	....	....
	Tulsa Oilers	CHL	25	4	7	11	....	....	....	40	....	....	....	....	....	....	....	....	....	....	7	1	3	4	12	....	....	....
1969-70	**Toronto Maple Leafs**	**NHL**	**52**	**1**	**14**	**15**	**1**	**13**	**14**	**50**	**0**	**0**	**0**	**44**	**2.3**	**44**	**1**	**65**	**18**	**–4**	....	....	....	....	....	....	....	....
1970-71	**Toronto Maple Leafs**	**NHL**	**54**	**0**	**8**	**8**	**0**	**7**	**7**	**31**	**0**	**0**	**0**	**42**	**0.0**	**25**	**1**	**36**	**11**	**–1**	**3**	**0**	**0**	**0**	**0**	**0**	**0**	**0**
1971-72	**Toronto Maple Leafs**	**NHL**	**61**	**2**	**8**	**10**	**2**	**7**	**9**	**44**	**0**	**0**	**1**	**80**	**2.5**	**45**	**0**	**46**	**12**	**11**	**5**	**0**	**0**	**0**	**25**	**0**	**0**	**0**
1972-73	Team Canada	Summit-72	DID NOT PLAY																									
	Toronto Maple Leafs	**NHL**	**44**	**1**	**10**	**11**	**1**	**8**	**9**	**54**	**0**	**0**	**0**	**74**	**1.4**	**50**	**2**	**61**	**15**	**2**	....	....	....	....	....	....	....	....
1973-74	**Toronto Maple Leafs**	**NHL**	**65**	**4**	**18**	**22**	**4**	**15**	**19**	**100**	**1**	**1**	**0**	**65**	**6.2**	**76**	**2**	**68**	**21**	**27**	**3**	**0**	**0**	**0**	**10**	**0**	**0**	**0**
1974-75	**Toronto Maple Leafs**	**NHL**	**63**	**1**	**7**	**8**	**1**	**5**	**6**	**110**	**0**	**0**	**0**	**55**	**1.8**	**54**	**2**	**75**	**18**	**–5**	....	....	....	....	....	....	....	....
1975-76	**Toronto Maple Leafs**	**NHL**	**69**	**0**	**8**	**8**	**0**	**6**	**6**	**75**	**0**	**0**	**0**	**65**	**0.0**	**49**	**0**	**51**	**12**	**10**	**6**	**0**	**1**	**1**	**15**	**0**	**0**	**0**
1976-77	**Toronto Maple Leafs**	**NHL**	**69**	**1**	**10**	**11**	**1**	**8**	**9**	**73**	**0**	**0**	**0**	**63**	**1.6**	**64**	**1**	**87**	**23**	**–1**	**2**	**0**	**0**	**0**	**0**	**0**	**0**	**0**
1977-78	**Toronto Maple Leafs**	**NHL**	**77**	**2**	**15**	**17**	**2**	**12**	**14**	**62**	**0**	**0**	**0**	**64**	**3.1**	**69**	**5**	**63**	**23**	**24**	**13**	**0**	**0**	**0**	**16**	**0**	**0**	**0**
1978-79	**Los Angeles Kings**	**NHL**	**18**	**2**	**2**	**4**	**2**	**1**	**3**	**22**	**0**	**0**	**1**	**11**	**18.2**	**18**	**0**	**21**	**5**	**2**	....	....	....	....	....	....	....	....
	NHL Totals		**572**	**14**	**100**	**114**	**14**	**82**	**96**	**621**	**1**	**1**	**2**	**563**	**2.5**	**494**	**14**	**573**	**158**		**32**	**0**	**1**	**1**	**66**	**0**	**0**	**0**

Traded to **LA Kings** by **Toronto** with Kurt Walker, Scott Garland, Toronto's 2nd round choice (Mark Hardy) in 1979 Entry Draft and future considerations for Dave Hutchison and Lorne Stamler, June 14, 1978.

• GLENNON, Matt

Matthew Joseph LW – L. 6', 185 lbs. b: Hull, MA, 9/20/1968. Boston's 7th, 119th overall, in 1987.

Season	Club	League	GP	G	A	Pts	AG	AA	APts	PIM	PP	SH	GW	S	%	TGF	PGF	TGA	PGA	+/–	GP	G	A	Pts	PIM	PP	SH	GW
1985-86	Archbishop Williams High	Hi-School	18	18	22	40	....	....	....	6	....	....	....	....	....	....	....	....	....	....	....	....	....	....	....	....	....	....
1986-87	Archbishop Williams High	Hi-School	18	22	36	58	....	....	....	20	....	....	....	....	....	....	....	....	....	....	....	....	....	....	....	....	....	....
1987-88	Boston College	H-East	16	3	3	6	....	....	....	16	....	....	....	....	....	....	....	....	....	....	....	....	....	....	....	....	....	....
1988-89	Boston College	H-East	16	1	6	7	....	....	....	4	....	....	....	....	....	....	....	....	....	....	....	....	....	....	....	....	....	....
1989-90	Boston College	H-East	31	7	11	18	....	....	....	16	....	....	....	....	....	....	....	....	....	....	....	....	....	....	....	....	....	....
1990-91	Boston College	H-East	33	6	9	15	....	....	....	36	....	....	....	....	....	....	....	....	....	....	....	....	....	....	....	....	....	....
1991-92	**Boston Bruins**	**NHL**	**3**	**0**	**0**	**0**	**0**	**0**	**0**	**2**	**0**	**0**	**0**	**2**	**0.0**	**0**	**0**	**0**	**0**	**0**	....	....	....	....	....	....	....	....
	Maine Mariners	AHL	32	6	12	18	....	....	....	13	....	....	....	....	....	....	....	....	....	....	....	....	....	....	....	....	....	....
	Johnstown Chiefs	ECHL	30	9	46	55	....	....	....	77	....	....	....	....	....	....	....	....	....	....	6	2	4	6	25	....	....	....
1992-93	Providence Bruins	AHL	6	1	3	4	....	....	....	4	....	....	....	....	....	....	....	....	....	....	....	....	....	....	....	....	....	....
	NHL Totals		**3**	**0**	**0**	**0**	**0**	**0**	**0**	**2**	**0**	**0**	**0**	**2**	**0.0**	**0**	**0**	**0**	**0**		....	....	....	....	....	....	....	....

• GLOECKNER, Lorry

D – L. 6'2", 210 lbs. b: Kindersley, Sask., 1/25/1956. Boston's 2nd, 34th overall, in 1976.

Season	Club	League	GP	G	A	Pts	AG	AA	APts	PIM	PP	SH	GW	S	%	TGF	PGF	TGA	PGA	+/–	GP	G	A	Pts	PIM	PP	SH	GW
1972-73	Nanaimo Clippers	BCJHL	STATISTICS NOT AVAILABLE																									
	Victoria Cougars	WCJHL	4	0	0	0	....	....	....	4	....	....	....	....	....	....	....	....	....	....	....	....	....	....	....	....	....	....
1973-74	Nanaimo Clippers	BCJHL	35	3	15	18	....	....	....	45	....	....	....	....	....	....	....	....	....	....	....	....	....	....	....	....	....	....
	Victoria Cougars	WCJHL	33	1	7	8	....	....	....	45	....	....	....	....	....	....	....	....	....	....	....	....	....	....	....	....	....	....
1974-75	Victoria Cougars	WCJHL	65	2	12	14	....	....	....	79	....	....	....	....	....	....	....	....	....	....	12	0	4	4	20	....	....	....
1975-76	Victoria Cougars	WCJHL	71	7	48	55	....	....	....	123	....	....	....	....	....	....	....	....	....	....	15	0	8	8	38	....	....	....
1976-77	Victoria Cougars	WCJHL	58	5	22	27	....	....	....	52	....	....	....	....	....	....	....	....	....	....	4	0	2	2	0	....	....	....
1977-78			DID NOT PLAY																									
1978-79	**Detroit Red Wings**	**NHL**	**13**	**0**	**2**	**2**	**0**	**1**	**1**	**6**	**0**	**0**	**0**	**13**	**0.0**	**10**	**0**	**17**	**0**	**–7**	....	....	....	....	....	....	....	....
	Kansas City Red Wings	CHL	51	0	17	17	....	....	....	44	....	....	....	....	....	....	....	....	....	....	4	0	1	1	9	....	....	....
1979-80	Johnstown Red Wings	EHL	63	6	29	35	....	....	....	83	....	....	....	....	....	....	....	....	....	....	....	....	....	....	....	....	....	....
	NHL Totals		**13**	**0**	**2**	**2**	**0**	**1**	**1**	**6**	**0**	**0**	**0**	**13**	**0.0**	**10**	**0**	**17**	**0**		....	....	....	....	....	....	....	....

• Sat out entire 1977-78 season after failing to come to contract terms with Boston. Signed as a free agent by **Detroit**, October 12, 1978.

• GLOOR, Dan Dan Harold C – L. 5'9", 170 lbs. b: Stratford, Ont., 12/4/1952. Vancouver's 7th, 99th overall, in 1972.

			REGULAR SEASON																	PLAYOFFS							
Season	Club	League	GP	G	A	Pts	AG	AA	APts	PIM	PP	SH	GW	S	%	TGF	PGF	TGA	PGA	+/-	GP	G	A	Pts	PIM	PP	SH	GW
1969-70	Peterborough Petes	OHA-Jr.	54	38	37	75	....	....	....	17	....	....	....	....	....	....	....	....	....	....	6	3	5	8	4	....	....	....
1970-71	Peterborough Petes	OMJHL	48	21	48	69	....	....	....	15	....	....	....	....	....	....	....	....	....	....	5	1	1	2	0	....	....	....
1971-72	Peterborough Petes	OMJHL	63	24	37	61	....	....	....	37	....	....	....	....	....	....	....	....	....	....	15	4	6	10	6	....	....	....
	Peterborough Petes	Mem-Cup	3	0	1	1	....	....	....	4	....	....	....	....	....	....	....	....	....	....	....	....	....	....	....	....	....	....
1972-73	Des Moines Capitols	IHL	73	42	51	93	....	....	....	45	....	....	....	....	....	....	....	....	....	....	3	0	1	1	0	....	....	....
1973-74	**Vancouver Canucks**	**NHL**	**2**	**0**	**0**	**0**	**0**	**0**	**0**	**0**	**0**	**0**	**0**	**0**	**0.0**	**0**	**0**	**2**	**0**	**-2**	....	....	....	....	....	....	....	....
	Seattle Totems	WHL	76	36	48	84	....	....	....	26	....	....	....	....	....	....	....	....	....	....	....	....	....	....	....	....	....	....
1974-75	Seattle Totems	CHL	73	21	36	57	....	....	....	28	....	....	....	....	....	....	....	....	....	....	....	....	....	....	....	....	....	....
1975-76	Tulsa Oilers	CHL	65	23	48	71	....	....	....	16	....	....	....	....	....	....	....	....	....	....	9	4	3	7	0	....	....	....
1976-77	Tulsa Oilers	CHL	76	33	43	76	....	....	....	18	....	....	....	....	....	....	....	....	....	....	9	4	5	9	4	....	....	....
1977-78	IEV Innsbruck	Austria	28	21	18	39	....	....	....	....	....	....	....	....	....	....	....	....	....	....	5	2	7	9	....	....	....	....
1978-79	Phoenix Roadrunners	PHL	40	11	21	32	....	....	....	30	....	....	....	....	....	....	....	....	....	....	....	....	....	....	....	....	....	....
	NHL Totals		**2**	**0**	**0**	**0**	**0**	**0**	**0**	**0**	**0**	**0**	**0**	**0**	**0.0**	**0**	**0**	**2**	**0**		....	....	....	....	....	....	....	....

Won Garry F. Longman Memorial Trophy (Top Rookie - IHL) (1973)

• GLOVER, Howie Howard Edward RW – R. 5'11", 180 lbs. b: Toronto, Ont., 2/14/1935.

Season	Club	League	GP	G	A	Pts	AG	AA	APts	PIM	PP	SH	GW	S	%	TGF	PGF	TGA	PGA	+/-	GP	G	A	Pts	PIM	PP	SH	GW
1952-53	Weston Dukes	OHA-B	STATISTICS NOT AVAILABLE																									
	Toronto Marlboros	OHA-Jr.	19	1	4	5	....	....	....	9	....	....	....	....	....	....	....	....	....	....	6	0	1	1	6	....	....	....
1953-54	Toronto Marlboros	OHA-Jr.	19	5	3	8	....	....	....	17	....	....	....	....	....	....	....	....	....	....	....	....	....	....	....	....	....	....
	Kitchener Greenshirts	OHA-Jr.	42	17	9	26	....	....	....	53	....	....	....	....	....	....	....	....	....	....	4	0	0	0	7	....	....	....
1954-55	Kitchener–Barrie	OHA-Jr.	48	10	9	19	....	....	....	72	....	....	....	....	....	....	....	....	....	....	....	....	....	....	....	....	....	....
1955-56	Toledo-Marion Mercurys	IHL	60	23	23	46	....	....	....	108	....	....	....	....	....	....	....	....	....	....	9	1	3	4	4	....	....	....
	Cleveland Barons	AHL	2	0	1	1	....	....	....	0	....	....	....	....	....	....	....	....	....	....	....	....	....	....	....	....	....	....
1956-57	North Bay Trappers	NOHA	DID NOT PLAY – SUSPENDED																									
1957-58	Winnipeg Warriors	WHL	67	38	34	72	....	....	....	72	....	....	....	....	....	....	....	....	....	....	7	4	1	5	8	....	....	....
1958-59	**Chicago Black Hawks**	**NHL**	**13**	**0**	**1**	**1**	**0**	**1**	**1**	**2**	....	....	....	....	....	....	....	....	....	....	....	....	....	....	....	....	....	....
	Calgary Stampeders	WHL	42	12	22	34	....	....	....	63	....	....	....	....	....	....	....	....	....	....	8	4	3	7	8	....	....	....
1959-60	Buffalo Bisons	AHL	68	31	25	56	....	....	....	95	....	....	....	....	....	....	....	....	....	....	....	....	....	....	....	....	....	....
1960-61	**Detroit Red Wings**	**NHL**	**66**	**21**	**8**	**29**	**24**	**8**	**32**	**46**	....	....	....	....	....	....	....	....	....	....	**11**	**1**	**2**	**3**	**2**	**1**	**0**	**0**
1961-62	**Detroit Red Wings**	**NHL**	**39**	**7**	**8**	**15**	**8**	**8**	**16**	**44**	....	....	....	....	....	....	....	....	....	....	....	....	....	....	....	....	....	....
1962-63	Pittsburgh Hornets	AHL	71	22	30	52	....	....	....	94	....	....	....	....	....	....	....	....	....	....	....	....	....	....	....	....	....	....
1963-64	**New York Rangers**	**NHL**	**25**	**1**	**0**	**1**	**1**	**0**	**1**	**9**	....	....	....	....	....	....	....	....	....	....	....	....	....	....	....	....	....	....
1964-65	Cleveland Barons	AHL	26	21	7	28	....	....	....	49	....	....	....	....	....	....	....	....	....	....	....	....	....	....	....	....	....	....
1965-66	Cleveland Barons	AHL	56	9	14	23	....	....	....	96	....	....	....	....	....	....	....	....	....	....	12	5	0	5	21	....	....	....
1966-67	Cleveland Barons	AHL	48	18	16	34	....	....	....	66	....	....	....	....	....	....	....	....	....	....	5	2	0	2	0	....	....	....
1967-68	Cleveland Barons	AHL	69	41	22	63	....	....	....	121	....	....	....	....	....	....	....	....	....	....	....	....	....	....	....	....	....	....
1968-69	**Montreal Canadiens**	**NHL**	**1**	**0**	**0**	**0**	**0**	**0**	**0**	**0**	**0**	**0**	**0**	**0**	**0.0**	**0**	**0**	**0**	**0**	**0**	....	....	....	....	....	....	....	....
	Cleveland Barons	AHL	73	24	35	59	....	....	....	44	....	....	....	....	....	....	....	....	....	....	5	2	1	3	4	....	....	....
1969-70	Cleveland Barons	AHL	32	12	14	26	....	....	....	49	....	....	....	....	....	....	....	....	....	....	....	....	....	....	....	....	....	....
	NHL Totals		**144**	**29**	**17**	**46**	**33**	**17**	**50**	**101**	....	....	....	....	**0.0**	....	....	....	....	....	**11**	**1**	**2**	**3**	**2**	....	....	....

• Brother of Fred

• Suspended for entire 1956-57 season by NOHA for assaulting referee Bud McDonald in pre-season game vs. Sudbury (NOHA), October, 1956. Claimed by **Chicago** from **Winnipeg** (WHL) in Inter-League Draft, June 3, 1958. Traded to **Detroit** by **Chicago** for Jim Morrison, June 5, 1960. Traded to **Portland** (WHL) by **Detroit** for cash, May 27, 1963. Traded to **NY Rangers** by **Portland** (WHL) for Pat Hannigan, September 19, 1963. • Suspended by **NY Rangers** for refusing demotion to **Baltimore** (AHL), January, 1964. Traded to **Montreal** by **NY Rangers** for Ray Brunel and Bev Bell, April 19, 1964. Traded to **Cleveland** (AHL) by **Montreal** for cash, April 19, 1964. Traded to **Montreal** by **Cleveland** (AHL) for Jim Mikol and Bill Staub, August, 1968.

• GLYNN, Brian D – L. 6'4", 218 lbs. b: Iserlohn, West Germany, 11/23/1967. Calgary's 2nd, 37th overall, in 1986.

Season	Club	League	GP	G	A	Pts	AG	AA	APts	PIM	PP	SH	GW	S	%	TGF	PGF	TGA	PGA	+/-	GP	G	A	Pts	PIM	PP	SH	GW
1983-84	Melville Millionaires	SJHL	19	1	2	3	....	....	....	12	....	....	....	....	....	....	....	....	....	....	....	....	....	....	....	....	....	....
1984-85	Melville Millionaires	SJHL	49	13	16	29	....	....	....	154	....	....	....	....	....	....	....	....	....	....	....	....	....	....	....	....	....	....
	Saskatoon Blades	WHL	12	1	0	1	....	....	....	2	....	....	....	....	....	....	....	....	....	....	3	0	0	0	0	....	....	....
1985-86	Saskatoon Blades	WHL	66	7	25	32	....	....	....	131	....	....	....	....	....	....	....	....	....	....	13	0	3	3	30	....	....	....
1986-87	Saskatoon Blades	WHL	44	2	26	28	....	....	....	163	....	....	....	....	....	....	....	....	....	....	11	1	3	4	19	....	....	....
1987-88	**Calgary Flames**	**NHL**	**67**	**5**	**14**	**19**	**4**	**10**	**14**	**87**	**4**	**0**	**1**	**84**	**6.0**	**71**	**14**	**82**	**23**	**-2**	**1**	**0**	**0**	**0**	**0**	**0**	**0**	**0**
1988-89	**Calgary Flames**	**NHL**	**9**	**0**	**1**	**1**	**0**	**1**	**1**	**19**	**0**	**0**	**0**	**4**	**0.0**	**6**	**1**	**5**	**1**	**1**	....	....	....	....	....	....	....	....
	Salt Lake Golden Eagles	IHL	31	3	10	13	....	....	....	105	....	....	....	....	....	....	....	....	....	....	14	3	7	10	31	....	....	....
1989-90	**Calgary Flames**	**NHL**	**1**	**0**	**0**	**0**	**0**	**0**	**0**	**0**	**0**	**0**	**0**	**0**	**0.0**	**0**	**0**	**1**	**0**	**-1**	....	....	....	....	....	....	....	....
	Salt Lake Golden Eagles	IHL	80	17	44	61	....	....	....	164	....	....	....	....	....	....	....	....	....	....	....	....	....	....	....	....	....	....
1990-91	Salt Lake Golden Eagles	IHL	8	1	3	4	....	....	....	18	....	....	....	....	....	....	....	....	....	....	....	....	....	....	....	....	....	....
	Minnesota North Stars	**NHL**	**66**	**8**	**11**	**19**	**7**	**8**	**15**	**83**	**3**	**0**	**0**	**111**	**7.2**	**66**	**19**	**52**	**0**	**-5**	**23**	**2**	**6**	**8**	**18**	**2**	**0**	**0**
1991-92	**Minnesota North Stars**	**NHL**	**37**	**2**	**12**	**14**	**2**	**9**	**11**	**24**	**0**	**0**	**0**	**53**	**3.8**	**39**	**13**	**50**	**8**	**-16**	....	....	....	....	....	....	....	....
	Edmonton Oilers	**NHL**	**25**	**2**	**6**	**8**	**2**	**5**	**7**	**6**	**0**	**1**	**0**	**29**	**6.9**	**33**	**7**	**31**	**16**	**11**	**16**	**4**	**1**	**5**	**12**	**1**	**0**	**1**
1992-93	**Edmonton Oilers**	**NHL**	**64**	**4**	**12**	**16**	**3**	**8**	**11**	**60**	**2**	**0**	**0**	**80**	**5.0**	**49**	**12**	**82**	**32**	**-13**	....	....	....	....	....	....	....	....
1993-94	**Ottawa Senators**	**NHL**	**48**	**2**	**13**	**15**	**2**	**10**	**12**	**41**	**1**	**0**	**0**	**66**	**3.0**	**45**	**17**	**62**	**19**	**-15**	....	....	....	....	....	....	....	....
	Vancouver Canucks	**NHL**	**16**	**0**	**0**	**0**	**0**	**0**	**0**	**12**	**0**	**0**	**0**	**5**	**0.0**	**8**	**2**	**14**	**4**	**-4**	**17**	**0**	**3**	**3**	**10**	**0**	**0**	**0**
1994-95	**Hartford Whalers**	**NHL**	**43**	**1**	**6**	**7**	**2**	**9**	**11**	**32**	**0**	**0**	**0**	**35**	**2.9**	**28**	**2**	**38**	**10**	**-2**	....	....	....	....	....	....	....	....
1995-96	**Hartford Whalers**	**NHL**	**54**	**0**	**4**	**4**	**0**	**3**	**3**	**44**	**0**	**0**	**0**	**46**	**0.0**	**29**	**7**	**44**	**7**	**-15**	....	....	....	....	....	....	....	....
1996-97	**Hartford Whalers**	**NHL**	**1**	**1**	**0**	**1**	**1**	**0**	**1**	**2**	**0**	**0**	**0**	**2**	**50.0**	**3**	**1**	**0**	**0**	**2**	....	....	....	....	....	....	....	....
	San Antonio Dragons	IHL	62	13	11	24	....	....	....	46	....	....	....	....	....	....	....	....	....	....	9	2	6	8	4	....	....	....
1997-98	Kolner Haie	Germany	48	10	12	22	....	....	....	59	....	....	....	....	....	....	....	....	....	....	3	0	0	0	16	....	....	....
	Kolner Haie	EuroHL	6	3	2	5	....	....	....	10	....	....	....	....	....	....	....	....	....	....	....	....	....	....	....	....	....	....
	NHL Totals		**431**	**25**	**79**	**104**	**23**	**63**	**86**	**410**	**10**	**1**	**1**	**515**	**4.9**	**377**	**95**	**461**	**120**		**57**	**6**	**10**	**16**	**40**	**3**	**0**	**1**

IHL First All-Star Team (1990) • Won Governors' Trophy (Outstanding Defenseman - IHL) (1990)

Traded to **Minnesota** by **Calgary** for Frantisek Musil, October 26, 1990. Traded to **Edmonton** by **Minnesota** for David Shaw, January 21, 1992. Traded to **Ottawa** by **Edmonton** for Ottawa's 8th round choice (Rob Quinn) in 1994 Entry Draft, September 15, 1993. Claimed on waivers by **Vancouver** from **Ottawa**, February 5, 1994. Claimed by **Hartford** from **Vancouver** in Waiver Draft, January 18, 1995. Traded to **Detroit** by **Hartford** with Brendan Shanahan for Paul Coffey, Keith Primeau and Detroit's 1st round choice (Nikos Tselios) in 1997 Entry Draft, October 9, 1996.

• GODDEN, Ernie Ernie Alfred C – L. 5'8", 160 lbs. b: Keswick, Ont., 3/13/1961. Toronto's 3rd, 55th overall, in 1981.

Season	Club	League	GP	G	A	Pts	AG	AA	APts	PIM	PP	SH	GW	S	%	TGF	PGF	TGA	PGA	+/-	GP	G	A	Pts	PIM	PP	SH	GW
1976-77	Newmarket Saints	OHA-B	44	19	24	43	....	....	....	89	....	....	....	....	....	....	....	....	....	....	....	....	....	....	....	....	....	....
1977-78	Newmarket Saints	OHA-B	40	20	24	44	....	....	....	67	....	....	....	....	....	....	....	....	....	....	....	....	....	....	....	....	....	....
1978-79	Windsor Spitfires	OMJHL	64	25	31	56	....	....	....	165	....	....	....	....	....	....	....	....	....	....	7	2	1	3	18	....	....	....
1979-80	Windsor Spitfires	OMJHL	62	40	41	81	....	....	....	158	....	....	....	....	....	....	....	....	....	....	16	9	7	16	36	....	....	....
1980-81	Windsor Spitfires	OMJHL	68	87	66	153	....	....	....	185	....	....	....	....	....	....	....	....	....	....	11	13	16	29	44	....	....	....
1981-82	**Toronto Maple Leafs**	**NHL**	**5**	**1**	**1**	**2**	**1**	**1**	**2**	**6**	**0**	**0**	**0**	**5**	**20.0**	**3**	**0**	**2**	**0**	**1**	....	....	....	....	....	....	....	....
	Cincinnati Tigers	CHL	67	32	37	69	....	....	....	178	....	....	....	....	....	....	....	....	....	....	3	1	0	1	38	....	....	....
1982-83	St. Catharines Saints	AHL	64	27	23	50	....	....	....	106	....	....	....	....	....	....	....	....	....	....	....	....	....	....	....	....	....	....
1983-84	St. Catharines Saints	AHL	78	31	36	67	....	....	....	69	....	....	....	....	....	....	....	....	....	....	7	4	1	5	28	....	....	....
1984-85	KAC Klagenfurter	Austria	39	34	23	57	....	....	....	68	....	....	....	....	....	....	....	....	....	....	....	....	....	....	....	....	....	....
	NHL Totals		**5**	**1**	**1**	**2**	**1**	**1**	**2**	**6**	**0**	**0**	**0**	**5**	**20.0**	**3**	**0**	**2**	**0**		....	....	....	....	....	....	....	....

OMJHL First All-Star Team (1981)

• GODFREY, Warren Warren Edward "Rocky" D – L. 6'1", 190 lbs. b: Toronto, Ont., 3/23/1931 d: 2/12/1998.

Season	Club	League	GP	G	A	Pts	AG	AA	APts	PIM	PP	SH	GW	S	%	TGF	PGF	TGA	PGA	+/-	GP	G	A	Pts	PIM	PP	SH	GW
1949-50	Galt Black Hawks	OHA-Jr.	17	4	2	6	....	....	....	8	....	....	....	....	....	....	....	....	....	....	....	....	....	....	....	....	....	....
1950-51	Waterloo Hurricanes	OHA-Jr.	51	11	14	25	....	....	....	131	....	....	....	....	....	....	....	....	....	....	....	....	....	....	....	....	....	....
	Kitchener Dutchmen	OHA-Sr.	3	0	1	1	....	....	....	0	....	....	....	....	....	....	....	....	....	....	....	....	....	....	....	....	....	....
1951-52	Tacoma Rockets	PCHL	61	8	17	25	....	....	....	66	....	....	....	....	....	....	....	....	....	....	7	1	0	1	2	....	....	....
1952-53	**Boston Bruins**	**NHL**	**60**	**1**	**13**	**14**	**1**	**16**	**17**	**40**	....	....	....	....	....	....	....	....	....	....	**11**	**0**	**1**	**1**	**2**	**0**	**0**	**0**

			REGULAR SEASON																		PLAYOFFS							
Season	Club	League	GP	G	A	Pts	AG	AA	APts	PIM	PP	SH	GW	S	%	TGF	PGF	TGA	PGA	+/–	GP	G	A	Pts	PIM	PP	SH	GW
1953-54	**Boston Bruins**	NHL	70	5	9	14	7	11	18	71	....	....	....	....	....	....	....	....	....	....	4	0	0	0	4	0	0	0
1954-55	**Boston Bruins**	NHL	62	1	17	18	1	19	20	58	....	....	....	....	....	....	....	....	....	....	3	0	0	0	0	0	0	0
1955-56	**Detroit Red Wings**	NHL	67	2	6	8	3	7	10	86	....	....	....	....	....	....	....	....	....	....	....	....	....	....	....	....	....	....
1956-57	**Detroit Red Wings**	NHL	69	1	8	9	1	9	10	103	....	....	....	....	....	....	....	....	....	....	5	0	0	0	6	0	0	0
1957-58	**Detroit Red Wings**	NHL	67	2	16	18	2	16	18	56	....	....	....	....	....	....	....	....	....	....	4	0	0	0	0	0	0	0
1958-59	**Detroit Red Wings**	NHL	69	6	4	10	7	4	11	44	....	....	....	....	....	....	....	....	....	....	....	....	....	....	....	....	....	....
1959-60	**Detroit Red Wings**	NHL	69	5	9	14	6	9	15	60	....	....	....	....	....	....	....	....	....	....	6	1	0	1	10	0	0	0
1960-61	**Detroit Red Wings**	NHL	63	3	16	19	3	15	18	62	....	....	....	....	....	....	....	....	....	....	11	0	2	2	18	0	0	0
1961-62	**Detroit Red Wings**	NHL	69	4	13	17	5	12	17	84	....	....	....	....	....	....	....	....	....	....	....	....	....	....	....	....	....	....
1962-63	**Boston Bruins**	NHL	66	2	9	11	2	9	11	56	....	....	....	....	....	....	....	....	....	....	....	....	....	....	....	....	....	....
1963-64	**Detroit Red Wings**	NHL	4	0	0	0	0	0	0	2	....	....	....	....	....	....	....	....	....	....	....	....	....	....	....	....	....	....
	Pittsburgh Hornets	AHL	57	6	21	27	....	....	....	53	....	....	....	....	....	....	....	....	....	....	5	1	1	2	0	....	....	....
1964-65	Pittsburgh Hornets	AHL	56	7	25	32	....	....	....	44	....	....	....	....	....	....	....	....	....	....	4	1	2	3	6	....	....	....
	Detroit Red Wings	NHL	11	0	0	0	0	0	0	8	....	....	....	....	....	....	....	....	....	....	4	0	1	1	2	0	0	0
1965-66	Memphis Wings	CPHL	11	0	5	5	....	....	....	10	....	....	....	....	....	....	....	....	....	....	....	....	....	....	....	....	....	....
	Detroit Red Wings	NHL	26	0	4	4	0	4	4	22	....	....	....	....	....	....	....	....	....	....	4	0	0	0	0	0	0	0
1966-67	Memphis Wings	CPHL	2	0	0	0	....	....	....	0	....	....	....	....	....	....	....	....	....	....	....	....	....	....	....	....	....	....
	Detroit Red Wings	NHL	2	0	0	0	0	0	0	0	....	....	....	....	....	....	....	....	....	....	....	....	....	....	....	....	....	....
	Pittsburgh Hornets	AHL	59	2	12	14	....	....	....	54	....	....	....	....	....	....	....	....	....	....	9	2	1	3	14	....	....	....
1967-68	**Detroit Red Wings**	NHL	12	0	1	1	0	1	1	0	0	0	0	9	0.0	16	0	6	1	11	....	....	....	....	....	....	....	....
	Fort Worth Wings	CPHL	41	2	13	15	....	....	....	52	....	....	....	....	....	....	....	....	....	....	13	0	3	3	12	....	....	....
1968-69	Rochester Americans	AHL	67	3	17	20	....	....	....	70	....	....	....	....	....	....	....	....	....	....	....	....	....	....	....	....	....	....
	NHL Totals		786	32	125	157	38	132	170	752	....	....	....	....	....	....	....	....	....	....	52	1	4	5	42	....	....	....

Played in NHL All-Star Game (1955)

Traded to **Detroit** by **Boston** with Gilles Boisvert, Rene Chevrefils, Norm Corcoran and Ed Sandford for Marcel Bonin, Lorne Davis, Terry Sawchuk and Vic Stasiuk, June 3, 1955. Claimed by **Boston** from **Detroit** in Intra-League Draft, June 4, 1962. Traded to **Detroit** by **Boston** for Gerry Odrowski, October 10, 1963. Traded to **Vancouver** (WHL) by **Detroit** for cash, August 19, 1968.

• GODIN, Eddy

Joseph Eddy Alain RW – L. 5'10", 190 lbs. b: Donnacona, Que., 3/29/1957. Washington's 3rd, 39th overall, in 1977.

Season	Club	League	GP	G	A	Pts	AG	AA	APts	PIM	PP	SH	GW	S	%	TGF	PGF	TGA	PGA	+/–	GP	G	A	Pts	PIM	PP	SH	GW
1974-75	Quebec Remparts	QMJHL	72	24	33	57	....	....	....	79	....	....	....	....	....	....	....	....	....	....	....	....	....	....	....	....	....	....
1975-76	Quebec Remparts	QMJHL	72	38	62	100	....	....	....	89	....	....	....	....	....	....	....	....	....	....	15	6	14	20	56	....	....	....
	Quebec Remparts	Mem-Cup	3	1	0	1	....	....	....	2	....	....	....	....	....	....	....	....	....	....	....	....	....	....	....	....	....	....
1976-77	Quebec Remparts	QMJHL	71	62	83	145	....	....	....	83	....	....	....	....	....	....	....	....	....	....	14	11	11	22	4	....	....	....
1977-78	**Washington Capitals**	NHL	18	3	3	6	3	2	5	6	0	0	0	23	13.0	7	1	20	0	–14	....	....	....	....	....	....	....	....
	Hershey Bears	AHL	50	22	20	42	....	....	....	26	....	....	....	....	....	....	....	....	....	....	....	....	....	....	....	....	....	....
1978-79	**Washington Capitals**	NHL	9	0	3	3	0	2	2	6	0	0	0	10	0.0	5	1	6	0	–2	....	....	....	....	....	....	....	....
	Hershey Bears	AHL	56	16	15	31	....	....	....	21	....	....	....	....	....	....	....	....	....	....	4	1	1	2	2	....	....	....
1979-80	Hershey Bears	AHL	71	34	27	61	....	....	....	39	....	....	....	....	....	....	....	....	....	....	16	5	9	14	13	....	....	....
1980-81	Hershey Bears	AHL	71	23	24	47	....	....	....	16	....	....	....	....	....	....	....	....	....	....	8	0	3	3	0	....	....	....
1981-82	Hershey Bears	AHL	74	16	23	39	....	....	....	23	....	....	....	....	....	....	....	....	....	....	5	4	1	5	0	....	....	....
1982-83	Hershey Bears	AHL	21	4	2	6	....	....	....	4	....	....	....	....	....	....	....	....	....	....	....	....	....	....	....	....	....	....
	NHL Totals		27	3	6	9	3	4	7	12	0	0	0	33	9.1	12	2	26	0		....	....	....	....	....	....	....	....

QMJHL East Division Second All-Star Team (1976) • Claimed by **Washington** as a fill-in during Expansion Draft, June 13, 1979.

• GODYNYUK, Alexander

D – L. 6', 207 lbs. b: Kiev, Ukraine, 1/27/1970. Toronto's 5th, 115th overall, in 1990.

Season	Club	League	GP	G	A	Pts	AG	AA	APts	PIM	PP	SH	GW	S	%	TGF	PGF	TGA	PGA	+/–	GP	G	A	Pts	PIM	PP	SH	GW
1986-87	Sokol Kiev	USSR	9	0	1	1	....	....	....	2	....	....	....	....	....	....	....	....	....	....	....	....	....	....	....	....	....	....
	Soviet Union	EJC-A	7	0	3	3	....	....	....	6	....	....	....	....	....	....	....	....	....	....	....	....	....	....	....	....	....	....
1987-88	Sokol Kiev	USSR	2	0	0	0	....	....	....	2	....	....	....	....	....	....	....	....	....	....	....	....	....	....	....	....	....	....
	Soviet Union	EJC-A	6	0	0	0	....	....	....	4	....	....	....	....	....	....	....	....	....	....	....	....	....	....	....	....	....	....
1988-89	Sokol Kiev	USSR	30	3	3	6	....	....	....	12	....	....	....	....	....	....	....	....	....	....	....	....	....	....	....	....	....	....
	Soviet Union	WJC-A	7	0	1	1	....	....	....	2	....	....	....	....	....	....	....	....	....	....	....	....	....	....	....	....	....	....
1989-90	Sokol Kiev	Fr-Tour	1	0	0	0	....	....	....	2	....	....	....	....	....	....	....	....	....	....	....	....	....	....	....	....	....	....
	Sokol Kiev	USSR	37	3	2	5	....	....	....	31	....	....	....	....	....	....	....	....	....	....	....	....	....	....	....	....	....	....
	Soviet Union	WJC-A	7	3	2	5	....	....	....	4	....	....	....	....	....	....	....	....	....	....	....	....	....	....	....	....	....	....
1990-91	Sokol Kiev	Fr-Tour	1	0	0	0	....	....	....	4	....	....	....	....	....	....	....	....	....	....	....	....	....	....	....	....	....	....
	Sokol Kiev	USSR	19	3	1	4	....	....	....	20	....	....	....	....	....	....	....	....	....	....	....	....	....	....	....	....	....	....
	Toronto Maple Leafs	NHL	18	0	3	3	0	2	2	16	0	0	0	15	0.0	7	0	10	0	–3	....	....	....	....	....	....	....	....
	Newmarket Saints	AHL	11	0	1	1	....	....	....	29	....	....	....	....	....	....	....	....	....	....	....	....	....	....	....	....	....	....
1991-92	**Toronto Maple Leafs**	NHL	31	3	6	9	3	5	8	59	1	0	1	30	10.0	23	3	36	4	–12	....	....	....	....	....	....	....	....
	Calgary Flames	NHL	6	0	1	1	0	1	1	4	0	0	0	12	0.0	3	0	6	1	–2	....	....	....	....	....	....	....	....
	Salt Lake Golden Eagles	IHL	17	2	1	3	....	....	....	24	....	....	....	....	....	....	....	....	....	....	....	....	....	....	....	....	....	....
1992-93	**Calgary Flames**	NHL	27	3	4	7	2	3	5	19	0	0	0	35	8.6	31	6	22	3	6	....	....	....	....	....	....	....	....
1993-94	**Florida Panthers**	NHL	26	0	10	10	0	8	8	35	0	0	0	43	0.0	26	8	18	5	5	....	....	....	....	....	....	....	....
	Hartford Whalers	NHL	43	3	9	12	3	7	10	40	0	0	1	67	4.5	42	4	46	16	8	....	....	....	....	....	....	....	....
1994-95	**Hartford Whalers**	NHL	14	0	0	0	0	0	0	8	0	0	0	16	0.0	11	0	12	2	1	....	....	....	....	....	....	....	....
1995-96	**Hartford Whalers**	NHL	3	0	0	0	0	0	0	2	0	0	0	1	0.0	1	0	3	1	–1	....	....	....	....	....	....	....	....
	Springfield Falcons	AHL	14	1	3	4	....	....	....	19	....	....	....	....	....	....	....	....	....	....	....	....	....	....	....	....	....	....
	Detroit Vipers	IHL	7	0	3	3	....	....	....	12	....	....	....	....	....	....	....	....	....	....	....	....	....	....	....	....	....	....
	Minnesota Moose	IHL	45	9	17	26	....	....	....	81	....	....	....	....	....	....	....	....	....	....	....	....	....	....	....	....	....	....
1996-97	**Hartford Whalers**	NHL	55	1	6	7	1	5	6	41	0	0	1	34	2.9	29	1	46	8	–10	....	....	....	....	....	....	....	....
1997-98	Chicago Wolves	IHL	50	5	11	16	....	....	....	85	....	....	....	....	....	....	....	....	....	....	1	0	0	0	0	....	....	....
1998-99	SC Bern	Switz.	43	9	16	25	....	....	....	20	....	....	....	....	....	....	....	....	....	....	5	1	0	1	2	....	....	....
	Ukraine	WC-A	3	0	0	0	....	....	....	0	....	....	....	....	....	....	....	....	....	....	....	....	....	....	....	....	....	....
99-2000	Eisbaren Berlin	Germany	48	6	19	25	....	....	....	42	....	....	....	....	....	....	....	....	....	....	....	....	....	....	....	....	....	....
	NHL Totals		223	10	39	49	9	31	40	224	1	0	3	253	4.0	173	22	199	40		....	....	....	....	....	....	....	....

Named Best Defenseman at EJC-A (1987) • WJC-A All-Star Team (1990) • Named Best Defenseman at WJC-A (1990)

Traded to **Calgary** by **Toronto** with Craig Berube, Gary Leeman, Michel Petit and Jeff Reese for Doug Gilmour, Jamie Macoun, Ric Nattress, Rick Wamsley and Kent Manderville, January 2, 1992. Claimed by **Florida** from **Calgary** in Expansion Draft, June 24, 1993. Traded to **Hartford** by **Florida** for Jim McKenzie, December 16, 1993. Transferred to **Carolina** after **Hartford** franchise relocated, June 25, 1997. Traded to **St. Louis** by **Carolina** with Carolina's 6th round choice (Brad Vott) in 1998 Entry Draft for Stephen Leach, June 27, 1997.

• GOEGAN, Pete

Peter John D – L. 6'1", 195 lbs. b: Fort William, Ont., 3/6/1934.

Season	Club	League	GP	G	A	Pts	AG	AA	APts	PIM	PP	SH	GW	S	%	TGF	PGF	TGA	PGA	+/–	GP	G	A	Pts	PIM	PP	SH	GW
1951-52	Fort William Canadiens	TBJHL	29	2	6	8	....	....	....	84	....	....	....	....	....	....	....	....	....	....	....	....	....	....	....	....	....	....
1952-53	Fort William Canadiens	TBJHL	21	12	11	23	....	....	....	108	....	....	....	....	....	....	....	....	....	....	6	2	1	3	14	....	....	....
	Fort William Canadiens	Mem-Cup	5	1	1	2	....	....	....	26	....	....	....	....	....	....	....	....	....	....	....	....	....	....	....	....	....	....
1953-54	Fort William Canadiens	TBJHL	23	4	11	15	....	....	....	147	....	....	....	....	....	....	....	....	....	....	4	1	3	4	8	....	....	....
	Fort William Canadiens	Mem-Cup	13	1	0	1	....	....	....	33	....	....	....	....	....	....	....	....	....	....	....	....	....	....	....	....	....	....
1954-55	Fort William Beavers	NOHA	STATISTICS NOT AVAILABLE																									
	Fort William Beavers	Al-Cup	13	4	1	5	....	....	....	33	....	....	....	....	....	....	....	....	....	....	....	....	....	....	....	....	....	....
1955-56	Sault Ste. Marie Indians	NOHA	59	6	15	21	....	....	....	104	....	....	....	....	....	....	....	....	....	....	7	2	1	3	6	....	....	....
1956-57	Cleveland Barons	AHL	51	3	17	20	....	....	....	121	....	....	....	....	....	....	....	....	....	....	11	0	0	0	30	....	....	....
1957-58	Cleveland Barons	AHL	55	6	17	23	....	....	....	94	....	....	....	....	....	....	....	....	....	....	....	....	....	....	....	....	....	....
	Detroit Red Wings	NHL	14	0	2	2	0	2	2	28	....	....	....	....	....	....	....	....	....	....	4	0	0	0	18	0	0	0
1958-59	**Detroit Red Wings**	NHL	67	1	11	12	1	11	12	109	....	....	....	....	....	....	....	....	....	....	....	....	....	....	....	....	....	....
1959-60	**Detroit Red Wings**	NHL	21	3	0	3	3	0	3	6	....	....	....	....	....	....	....	....	....	....	6	1	0	1	13	0	0	0
	Edmonton Flyers	WHL	40	11	16	27	....	....	....	107	....	....	....	....	....	....	....	....	....	....	....	....	....	....	....	....	....	....
1960-61	**Detroit Red Wings**	NHL	67	5	29	34	6	28	34	78	....	....	....	....	....	....	....	....	....	....	11	0	1	1	18	0	0	0
1961-62	**Detroit Red Wings**	NHL	39	5	5	10	6	5	11	24	....	....	....	....	....	....	....	....	....	....	....	....	....	....	....	....	....	....
	New York Rangers	NHL	7	0	2	2	0	2	2	6	....	....	....	....	....	....	....	....	....	....	....	....	....	....	....	....	....	....
	Springfield Indians	AHL	7	0	1	1	....	....	....	12	....	....	....	....	....	....	....	....	....	....	11	3	3	6	20	....	....	....

Season	Club	League	GP	G	A	Pts	AG	AA	APts	PIM	PP	SH	GW	S	%	TGF	PGF	TGA	PGA	+/–	GP	G	A	Pts	PIM	PP	SH	GW
			REGULAR SEASON																		PLAYOFFS							
1962-63	**Detroit Red Wings**	**NHL**	**62**	**1**	**8**	**9**	**1**	**8**	**9**	**48**	....	....	....	....	....	....	....	....	....	....	**11**	**0**	**2**	**2**	**12**	**0**	**0**	**0**
1963-64	**Detroit Red Wings**	**NHL**	**12**	**0**	**0**	**0**	**0**	**0**	**0**	**8**	....	....	....	....	....	....	....	....	....	....	....	....	....	....	....	....	....	....
	Pittsburgh Hornets	AHL	55	6	17	23	....	....	....	127	....	....	....	....	....	....	....	....	....	....	5	0	0	0	6	....	....	....
1964-65	**Detroit Red Wings**	**NHL**	**4**	**1**	**0**	**1**	**1**	**0**	**1**	**2**	....	....	....	....	....	....	....	....	....	....	....	....	....	....	....	....	....	....
	Pittsburgh Hornets	AHL	68	9	14	23	....	....	....	163	....	....	....	....	....	....	....	....	....	....	2	0	0	0	2	....	....	....
1965-66	**Detroit Red Wings**	**NHL**	**13**	**0**	**2**	**2**	**0**	**2**	**2**	**14**	....	....	....	....	....	....	....	....	....	....	**1**	**0**	**0**	**0**	**0**	**0**	**0**	**0**
	Pittsburgh Hornets	AHL	52	4	17	21	....	....	....	85	....	....	....	....	....	....	....	....	....	....	....	....	....	....	....	....	....	....
1966-67	**Detroit Red Wings**	**NHL**	**31**	**2**	**6**	**8**	**2**	**6**	**8**	**12**	....	....	....	....	....	....	....	....	....	....	....	....	....	....	....	....	....	....
	Pittsburgh Hornets	AHL	34	4	16	20	....	....	....	60	....	....	....	....	....	....	....	....	....	....	9	1	5	6	17	....	....	....
1967-68	**Minnesota North Stars**	**NHL**	**46**	**1**	**2**	**3**	**1**	**2**	**3**	**30**	**0**	**0**	**0**	**35**	**2.9**	**21**	**1**	**45**	**9**	**–16**	....	....	....	....	....	....	....	....
	Phoenix Roadrunners	WHL	15	2	5	7	....	....	....	18	....	....	....	....	....	....	....	....	....	....	4	0	0	0	0	....	....	....
1968-69	Denver Spurs	WHL	34	1	10	11	....	....	....	40	....	....	....	....	....	....	....	....	....	....	....	....	....	....	....	....	....	....
	Baltimore Clippers	AHL	25	0	4	4	....	....	....	30	....	....	....	....	....	....	....	....	....	....	4	0	1	1	0	....	....	....
	NHL Totals		**383**	**19**	**67**	**86**	**21**	**66**	**87**	**365**	....	....	....	....	....	....	....	....	....	....	**33**	**1**	**3**	**4**	**61**	....	....	....

Traded to **Detroit** by **Cleveland** (AHL) for Gord Hollingworth and cash, February 20, 1958. Traded to **NY Rangers** by **Detroit** for Noel Price, February 16, 1962. Traded to **Detroit** by **NY Rangers** for Noel Price, October 8, 1962. Claimed by **Minnesota** from **Detroit** in Expansion Draft, June 6, 1967.

• GOERTZ, Dave

D – R. 5'11", 210 lbs. b: Edmonton, Alta., 3/28/1965. Pittsburgh's 10th, 232nd overall, in 1983.

Season	Club	League	GP	G	A	Pts	AG	AA	APts	PIM	PP	SH	GW	S	%	TGF	PGF	TGA	PGA	+/–	GP	G	A	Pts	PIM	PP	SH	GW
1980-81	Sherwood Park Crusaders	AJHL	35	12	19	31	....	....	....	110	....	....	....	....	....	....	....	....	....	....	....	....	....	....	....	....	....	....
1981-82	Regina Pats	WHL	67	5	19	24	....	....	....	181	....	....	....	....	....	....	....	....	....	....	19	1	2	3	61	....	....	....
1982-83	Regina Pats	WHL	69	4	22	26	....	....	....	132	....	....	....	....	....	....	....	....	....	....	5	0	2	2	9	....	....	....
1983-84	Prince Albert Raiders	WHL	60	13	47	60	....	....	....	111	....	....	....	....	....	....	....	....	....	....	5	2	3	5	0	....	....	....
	Baltimore Skipjacks	AHL	1	0	0	0	....	....	....	2	....	....	....	....	....	....	....	....	....	....	6	0	0	0	0	....	....	....
1984-85	Prince Albert Raiders	WHL	48	3	48	51	....	....	....	62	....	....	....	....	....	....	....	....	....	....	13	4	14	18	29	....	....	....
	Baltimore Skipjacks	AHL	....	....	....	....	....	....	....	....	....	....	....	....	....	....	....	....	....	....	2	0	2	2	0	....	....	....
	Prince Albert Raiders	Mem-Cup	5	3	6	9	....	....	....	23	....	....	....	....	....	....	....	....	....	....	....	....	....	....	....	....	....	....
1985-86	Baltimore Skipjacks	AHL	74	1	15	16	....	....	....	76	....	....	....	....	....	....	....	....	....	....	....	....	....	....	....	....	....	....
1986-87	Baltimore Skipjacks	AHL	16	0	3	3	....	....	....	8	....	....	....	....	....	....	....	....	....	....	....	....	....	....	....	....	....	....
	Muskegon Lumberjacks	IHL	44	3	17	20	....	....	....	44	....	....	....	....	....	....	....	....	....	....	15	0	4	4	14	....	....	....
1987-88	**Pittsburgh Penguins**	**NHL**	**2**	**0**	**0**	**0**	**0**	**0**	**0**	**2**	**0**	**0**	**0**	**2**	**0.0**	**2**	**0**	**3**	**0**	**–1**	....	....	....	....	....	....	....	....
	Muskegon Lumberjacks	IHL	73	8	36	44	....	....	....	87	....	....	....	....	....	....	....	....	....	....	6	0	4	4	14	....	....	....
1988-89	Muskegon Lumberjacks	IHL	74	1	32	33	....	....	....	102	....	....	....	....	....	....	....	....	....	....	14	0	4	4	10	....	....	....
1989-90	Muskegon Lumberjacks	IHL	51	3	18	21	....	....	....	64	....	....	....	....	....	....	....	....	....	....	....	....	....	....	....	....	....	....
1990-91	Muskegon Lumberjacks	IHL	30	6	10	16	....	....	....	46	....	....	....	....	....	....	....	....	....	....	2	0	0	0	0	....	....	....
	NHL Totals		**2**	**0**	**0**	**0**	**0**	**0**	**0**	**2**	**0**	**0**	**0**	**2**	**0.0**	**2**	**0**	**3**	**0**		....	....	....	....	....	....	....	....

Memorial Cup All-Star Team (1985)

• GOLDMANN, Erich

D – L. 6'3", 212 lbs. b: Dingolfing, West Germany, 4/7/1976. Ottawa's 5th, 212th overall, in 1996.

Season	Club	League	GP	G	A	Pts	AG	AA	APts	PIM	PP	SH	GW	S	%	TGF	PGF	TGA	PGA	+/–	GP	G	A	Pts	PIM	PP	SH	GW
1993-94	EV Landshut	Germany	33	0	0	0	....	....	....	4	....	....	....	....	....	....	....	....	....	....	7	0	0	0	0	....	....	....
	Germany	WJC-A	7	0	0	0	....	....	....	6	....	....	....	....	....	....	....	....	....	....	....	....	....	....	....	....	....	....
1994-95	Adler Mannheim	Germany	31	0	0	0	....	....	....	22	....	....	....	....	....	....	....	....	....	....	10	1	0	1	2	....	....	....
	Germany	WJC-A	7	1	0	1	....	....	....	18	....	....	....	....	....	....	....	....	....	....	....	....	....	....	....	....	....	....
1995-96	Adler Mannheim	Germany	47	0	3	3	....	....	....	40	....	....	....	....	....	....	....	....	....	....	8	0	0	0	4	....	....	....
	Germany	WJC-A	6	0	1	1	....	....	....	2	....	....	....	....	....	....	....	....	....	....	....	....	....	....	....	....	....	....
	Germany	WC-A	6	3	4	7	....	....	....	8	....	....	....	....	....	....	....	....	....	....	....	....	....	....	....	....	....	....
1996-97	Germany	W-Cup	3	0	1	1	....	....	....	2	....	....	....	....	....	....	....	....	....	....	....	....	....	....	....	....	....	....
	Kaufbeurer Adler	Germany	44	2	4	6	....	....	....	58	....	....	....	....	....	....	....	....	....	....	6	1	0	1	2	....	....	....
	Germany	WC-A	8	0	0	0	....	....	....	0	....	....	....	....	....	....	....	....	....	....	....	....	....	....	....	....	....	....
1997-98	Worcester IceCats	AHL	31	0	2	2	....	....	....	40	....	....	....	....	....	....	....	....	....	....	....	....	....	....	....	....	....	....
	Germany	Olympics	4	0	1	1	....	....	....	27	....	....	....	....	....	....	....	....	....	....	....	....	....	....	....	....	....	....
	Detroit Vipers	IHL	3	0	0	0	....	....	....	2	....	....	....	....	....	....	....	....	....	....	....	....	....	....	....	....	....	....
	Dayton Bombers	ECHL	3	0	2	2	....	....	....	5	....	....	....	....	....	....	....	....	....	....	5	0	0	0	8	....	....	....
	Germany	WC-A	6	0	0	0	....	....	....	16	....	....	....	....	....	....	....	....	....	....	....	....	....	....	....	....	....	....
1998-99	Hershey Bears	AHL	21	1	1	2	....	....	....	23	....	....	....	....	....	....	....	....	....	....	....	....	....	....	....	....	....	....
	Cincinnati Cyclones	IHL	5	0	1	1	....	....	....	7	....	....	....	....	....	....	....	....	....	....	....	....	....	....	....	....	....	....
	Cincinnati Mighty Ducks	AHL	32	0	2	2	....	....	....	18	....	....	....	....	....	....	....	....	....	....	3	0	0	0	2	....	....	....
99-2000	**Ottawa Senators**	**NHL**	**1**	**0**	**0**	**0**	**0**	**0**	**0**	**0**	**0**	**0**	**0**	**0**	**0.0**	**0**	**0**	**0**	**0**	**0**	....	....	....	....	....	....	....	....
	Grand Rapids Griffins	IHL	26	1	1	2	....	....	....	15	....	....	....	....	....	....	....	....	....	....	....	....	....	....	....	....	....	....
	Detroit Vipers	IHL	11	1	0	1	....	....	....	13	....	....	....	....	....	....	....	....	....	....	....	....	....	....	....	....	....	....
	NHL Totals		**1**	**0**	**0**	**0**	**0**	**0**	**0**	**0**	**0**	**0**	**0**	**0**	**0.0**	**0**	**0**	**0**	**0**		....	....	....	....	....	....	....	....

Loaned to **Cincinnati** (AHL) by **Ottawa** with Ratislav Pavlikovsky and Ivan Ciernik, January 12, 1999.

• GOLDSWORTHY, Bill

William Alfred "Goldie" RW – R. 6', 190 lbs. b: Waterloo, Ont., 8/24/1944 d: 3/29/1996.

Season	Club	League	GP	G	A	Pts	AG	AA	APts	PIM	PP	SH	GW	S	%	TGF	PGF	TGA	PGA	+/–	GP	G	A	Pts	PIM	PP	SH	GW
1962-63	Niagara Falls Flyers	OHA-Jr.	50	7	11	18	....	....	....	71	....	....	....	....	....	....	....	....	....	....	9	1	2	3	8	....	....	....
	Niagara Falls Flyers	Mem-Cup	16	3	7	10	....	....	....	39	....	....	....	....	....	....	....	....	....	....	....	....	....	....	....	....	....	....
1963-64	Niagara Falls Flyers	OHA-Jr.	56	21	47	68	....	....	....	91	....	....	....	....	....	....	....	....	....	....	4	0	3	3	4	....	....	....
1964-65	Niagara Falls Flyers	OHA-Jr.	54	28	27	55	....	....	....	164	....	....	....	....	....	....	....	....	....	....	11	5	11	16	26	....	....	....
	Boston Bruins	**NHL**	**2**	**0**	**0**	**0**	**0**	**0**	**0**	**0**	....	....	....	....	....	....	....	....	....	....	....	....	....	....	....	....	....	....
	Niagara Falls Flyers	Mem-Cup	13	11	7	18	....	....	....	37	....	....	....	....	....	....	....	....	....	....	....	....	....	....	....	....	....	....
1965-66	**Boston Bruins**	**NHL**	**13**	**3**	**1**	**4**	**3**	**1**	**4**	**6**	....	....	....	....	....	....	....	....	....	....	....	....	....	....	....	....	....	....
	Oklahoma City Blazers	CPHL	22	2	5	7	....	....	....	65	....	....	....	....	....	....	....	....	....	....	2	1	0	1	4	....	....	....
1966-67	**Boston Bruins**	**NHL**	**18**	**3**	**5**	**8**	**3**	**5**	**8**	**21**	....	....	....	....	....	....	....	....	....	....	....	....	....	....	....	....	....	....
	Oklahoma City Blazers	CPHL	11	4	1	5	....	....	....	14	....	....	....	....	....	....	....	....	....	....	....	....	....	....	....	....	....	....
	Buffalo Bisons	AHL	22	9	11	20	....	....	....	42	....	....	....	....	....	....	....	....	....	....	....	....	....	....	....	....	....	....
1967-68	**Minnesota North Stars**	**NHL**	**68**	**14**	**19**	**33**	**16**	**19**	**35**	**68**	**2**	**0**	**0**	**154**	**9.1**	**50**	**8**	**50**	**0**	**–8**	**14**	***8**	**7**	***15**	**12**	**1**	**0**	**1**
1968-69	**Minnesota North Stars**	**NHL**	**68**	**14**	**10**	**24**	**15**	**9**	**24**	**110**	**4**	**0**	**3**	**196**	**7.1**	**37**	**11**	**53**	**0**	**–27**	....	....	....	....	....	....	....	....
	Memphis South Stars	CHL	6	4	0	4	....	....	....	6	....	....	....	....	....	....	....	....	....	....	....	....	....	....	....	....	....	....
1969-70	**Minnesota North Stars**	**NHL**	**75**	**36**	**29**	**65**	**39**	**27**	**66**	**89**	**11**	**0**	**4**	**230**	**15.7**	**82**	**22**	**69**	**0**	**–9**	**6**	**4**	**3**	**7**	**6**	**3**	**2**	**0**
1970-71	**Minnesota North Stars**	**NHL**	**77**	**34**	**31**	**65**	**34**	**26**	**60**	**85**	**5**	**1**	**7**	**295**	**11.5**	**88**	**31**	**77**	**7**	**–13**	**7**	**2**	**4**	**6**	**6**	**0**	**0**	**0**
1971-72	**Minnesota North Stars**	**NHL**	**78**	**31**	**31**	**62**	**31**	**27**	**58**	**59**	**6**	**0**	**8**	**295**	**10.5**	**91**	**32**	**49**	**1**	**11**	**7**	**2**	**3**	**5**	**6**	**0**	**0**	**1**
1972-73	Team Canada	Summit-72	3	1	1	2	....	....	....	4	....	....	....	....	....	....	....	....	....	....	....	....	....	....	....	....	....	....
	Minnesota North Stars	**NHL**	**75**	**27**	**33**	**60**	**25**	**26**	**51**	**97**	**8**	**0**	**2**	**260**	**10.4**	**96**	**17**	**55**	**0**	**24**	**6**	**2**	**2**	**4**	**0**	**1**	**0**	**0**
1973-74	**Minnesota North Stars**	**NHL**	**74**	**48**	**26**	**74**	**46**	**21**	**67**	**73**	**12**	**1**	**4**	**321**	**15.0**	**106**	**24**	**93**	**14**	**3**	....	....	....	....	....	....	....	....
1974-75	**Minnesota North Stars**	**NHL**	**71**	**37**	**35**	**72**	**32**	**26**	**58**	**77**	**11**	**1**	**3**	**273**	**13.6**	**90**	**28**	**111**	**12**	**–37**	....	....	....	....	....	....	....	....
1975-76	**Minnesota North Stars**	**NHL**	**68**	**24**	**22**	**46**	**21**	**16**	**37**	**47**	**6**	**0**	**3**	**174**	**13.8**	**60**	**20**	**59**	**0**	**–19**	....	....	....	....	....	....	....	....
1976-77	**Minnesota North Stars**	**NHL**	**16**	**2**	**3**	**5**	**2**	**2**	**4**	**6**	**1**	**0**	**0**	**39**	**5.1**	**8**	**1**	**25**	**10**	**–8**	....	....	....	....	....	....	....	....
	New York Rangers	**NHL**	**61**	**10**	**12**	**22**	**9**	**9**	**18**	**43**	**0**	**0**	**2**	**96**	**10.4**	**34**	**4**	**57**	**10**	**–17**	....	....	....	....	....	....	....	....
1977-78	**New York Rangers**	**NHL**	**7**	**0**	**1**	**1**	**0**	**1**	**1**	**12**	**0**	**0**	**0**	**7**	**0.0**	**6**	**2**	**3**	**0**	**1**	....	....	....	....	....	....	....	....
	New Haven Nighthawks	AHL	4	1	2	3	....	....	....	4	....	....	....	....	....	....	....	....	....	....	....	....	....	....	....	....	....	....
	Indianapolis Racers	WHA	32	8	10	18	....	....	....	10	....	....	....	....	....	....	....	....	....	....	....	....	....	....	....	....	....	....
1978-79	Edmonton Oilers	WHA	17	4	2	6	....	....	....	14	....	....	....	....	....	....	....	....	....	....	4	1	1	2	11	....	....	....
	NHL Totals		**771**	**283**	**258**	**541**	**276**	**215**	**491**	**793**	....	....	....	....	....	....	....	....	....	....	**40**	**18**	**19**	**37**	**30**	....	....	....
	Other Major League Totals		49	12	12	24	....	....	....	24	....	....	....	....	....	....	....	....	....	....	4	1	1	2	11	....	....	....

Played in NHL All-Star Game (1970, 1972, 1974, 1976)

Claimed by **Minnesota** from **Boston** in Expansion Draft, June 6, 1967. Selected by **Minnesota** (WHA) in 1972 WHA General Player Draft, February 12, 1972. Traded to **NY Rangers** by **Minnesota** for Bill Fairbairn and Nick Beverley, November 11, 1976. Traded to **Indianapolis** (WHA) by **NY Rangers** for Frank Spring, December, 1977. Traded to **Edmonton** (WHA) by **Indianapolis** (WHA) for Juha Widing, June, 1978.

			REGULAR SEASON																		PLAYOFFS							
Season	Club	League	GP	G	A	Pts	AG	AA	APts	PIM	PP	SH	GW	S	%	TGF	PGF	TGA	PGA	+/–	GP	G	A	Pts	PIM	PP	SH	GW

• GOLDUP, Glenn

Glenn Michael RW – L. 6′, 190 lbs. b: St. Catharines, Ont., 4/26/1953. Montreal's 2nd, 17th overall, in 1973.

Season	Club	League	GP	G	A	Pts	AG	AA	APts	PIM	PP	SH	GW	S	%	TGF	PGF	TGA	PGA	+/–	GP	G	A	Pts	PIM	PP	SH	GW
1968-69	Toronto Marlboros	OHA-Jr.	35	20	20	40	....	....	....	....	....	....	....	....	....	....	....	....	....	....	....	....	....	....	....	....	....	....
1969-70	Markham Waxers	OHA-B	27	22	19	41	....	....	....	....	....	....	....	....	....	....	....	....	....	....	....	....	....	....	....	....	....	....
	Toronto Marlboros	OHA-Jr.	2	0	1	1	....	....	....	0	....	....	....	....	....	....	....	....	....	....	14	4	5	9	9	....	....	....
1970-71	Toronto Marlboros	OHA-Jr.	58	12	22	34	....	....	....	82	....	....	....	....	....	....	....	....	....	....	14	2	1	3	16	....	....	....
1971-72	Toronto Marlboros	OMJHL	63	24	34	58	....	....	....	161	....	....	....	....	....	....	....	....	....	....	10	2	2	4	30	....	....	....
1972-73	Toronto Marlboros	OMJHL	54	42	53	95	....	....	....	193	....	....	....	....	....	....	....	....	....	....	16	7	11	18	....	....	....	....
	Toronto Marlboros	Mem-Cup	3	3	2	5	....	....	....	2	....	....	....	....	....	....	....	....	....	....	....	....	....	....	....	....	....	....
1973-74	**Montreal Canadiens**	**NHL**	**6**	**0**	**0**	**0**	**0**	**0**	**0**	**0**	**0**	**0**	**0**	**2**	**0.0**	**0**	**0**	**1**	**0**	**–1**	....	....	....	....	....	....	....	....
	Nova Scotia Voyageurs	AHL	44	18	15	33	....	....	....	64	....	....	....	....	....	....	....	....	....	....	....	....	....	....	....	....	....	....
1974-75	**Montreal Canadiens**	**NHL**	**9**	**0**	**1**	**1**	**0**	**1**	**1**	**2**	**0**	**0**	**0**	**8**	**0.0**	**2**	**0**	**3**	**0**	**–1**	....	....	....	....	....	....	....	....
	Nova Scotia Voyageurs	AHL	49	15	16	31	....	....	....	140	....	....	....	....	....	....	....	....	....	....	5	1	4	5	36	....	....	....
1975-76	**Montreal Canadiens**	**NHL**	**3**	**0**	**0**	**0**	**0**	**0**	**0**	**2**	**0**	**0**	**0**	**1**	**0.0**	**0**	**0**	**1**	**0**	**–1**	....	....	....	....	....	....	....	....
	Nova Scotia Voyageurs	AHL	65	23	22	45	....	....	....	131	....	....	....	....	....	....	....	....	....	....	9	*8	3	11	*33	....	....	....
1976-77	**Los Angeles Kings**	**NHL**	**28**	**7**	**6**	**13**	**6**	**5**	**11**	**29**	**1**	**0**	**2**	**28**	**25.0**	**20**	**2**	**13**	**0**	**5**	**8**	**2**	**2**	**4**	**2**	**0**	**0**	**0**
	Fort Worth Texans	CHL	7	2	2	4	....	....	....	9	....	....	....	....	....	....	....	....	....	....	....	....	....	....	....	....	....	....
1977-78	**Los Angeles Kings**	**NHL**	**66**	**14**	**18**	**32**	**13**	**14**	**27**	**66**	**0**	**0**	**0**	**108**	**13.0**	**51**	**7**	**52**	**0**	**–8**	**2**	**1**	**0**	**1**	**11**	**0**	**0**	**0**
1978-79	**Los Angeles Kings**	**NHL**	**73**	**15**	**22**	**37**	**13**	**16**	**29**	**89**	**3**	**0**	**1**	**117**	**12.8**	**62**	**11**	**58**	**0**	**–7**	**2**	**0**	**1**	**1**	**9**	**0**	**0**	**0**
1979-80	**Los Angeles Kings**	**NHL**	**55**	**10**	**11**	**21**	**8**	**8**	**16**	**78**	**1**	**0**	**1**	**92**	**10.9**	**40**	**3**	**41**	**0**	**–4**	**4**	**1**	**0**	**1**	**0**	**0**	**0**	**0**
1980-81	**Los Angeles Kings**	**NHL**	**49**	**6**	**9**	**15**	**5**	**6**	**11**	**35**	**0**	**0**	**0**	**64**	**9.4**	**26**	**2**	**26**	**0**	**–2**	....	....	....	....	....	....	....	....
	New Haven Nighthawks	AHL	15	6	2	8	....	....	....	36	....	....	....	....	....	....	....	....	....	....	3	0	0	0	0	....	....	....
1981-82	**Los Angeles Kings**	**NHL**	**2**	**0**	**0**	**0**	**0**	**0**	**0**	**2**	**0**	**0**	**0**	**1**	**0.0**	**0**	**0**	**0**	**0**	**0**	....	....	....	....	....	....	....	....
	New Haven Nighthawks	AHL	51	14	17	31	....	....	....	91	....	....	....	....	....	....	....	....	....	....	4	3	1	4	2	....	....	....
1982-83	New Haven Nighthawks	AHL	28	0	8	8	....	....	....	39	....	....	....	....	....	....	....	....	....	....	....	....	....	....	....	....	....	....
1983-84	New Haven Nighthawks	AHL	1	0	0	0	....	....	....	0	....	....	....	....	....	....	....	....	....	....	....	....	....	....	....	....	....	....
	NHL Totals		**291**	**52**	**67**	**119**	**45**	**50**	**95**	**303**	**5**	**0**	**4**	**421**	**12.4**	**201**	**25**	**195**	**0**		**16**	**4**	**3**	**7**	**22**	**0**	**0**	**0**

• Son of Hank • AHL Second All-Star Team (1976)

Traded to **LA Kings** by **Montreal** with Montreal's 3rd round choice (later traded to Detroit — Detroit selected Doug Derkson) in 1978 Amateur Draft for LA Kings' 3rd round choice (Moe Robinson) in 1977 Amateur Draft and 1st round choice (Danny Geoffrion) in 1978 Amateur Draft, June 12, 1976.

• GOLUBOVSKY, Yan

D – R. 6′3″, 183 lbs. b: Novosibirsk, USSR, 3/9/1976. Detroit's 1st, 23rd overall, in 1994.

Season	Club	League	GP	G	A	Pts	AG	AA	APts	PIM	PP	SH	GW	S	%	TGF	PGF	TGA	PGA	+/–	GP	G	A	Pts	PIM	PP	SH	GW
1993-94	Dynamo Moscow-2	CIS-3	10	0	1	1	....	....	....	....	....	....	....	....	....	....	....	....	....	....	....	....	....	....	....	....	....	....
	Russian Penguins	IHL	8	0	0	0	....	....	....	23	....	....	....	....	....	....	....	....	....	....	....	....	....	....	....	....	....	....
1994-95	Adirondack Red Wings	AHL	57	4	2	6	....	....	....	39	....	....	....	....	....	....	....	....	....	....	....	....	....	....	....	....	....	....
1995-96	Adirondack Red Wings	AHL	71	5	16	21	....	....	....	97	....	....	....	....	....	....	....	....	....	....	3	0	0	0	2	....	....	....
1996-97	Adirondack Red Wings	AHL	62	2	11	13	....	....	....	67	....	....	....	....	....	....	....	....	....	....	4	0	0	0	0	....	....	....
1997-98	**Detroit Red Wings**	**NHL**	**12**	**0**	**2**	**2**	**0**	**2**	**2**	**6**	**0**	**0**	**0**	**9**	**0.0**	**3**	**0**	**2**	**0**	**1**	....	....	....	....	....	....	....	....
	Adirondack Red Wings	AHL	52	1	15	16	....	....	....	57	....	....	....	....	....	....	....	....	....	....	3	0	0	0	2	....	....	....
1998-99	**Detroit Red Wings**	**NHL**	**17**	**0**	**1**	**1**	**0**	**1**	**1**	**16**	**0**	**0**	**0**	**10**	**0.0**	**6**	**0**	**2**	**0**	**4**	....	....	....	....	....	....	....	....
	Adirondack Red Wings	AHL	43	2	2	4	....	....	....	32	....	....	....	....	....	....	....	....	....	....	2	0	0	0	4	....	....	....
99-2000	**Detroit Red Wings**	**NHL**	**21**	**1**	**2**	**3**	**1**	**2**	**3**	**8**	**0**	**0**	**0**	**7**	**14.3**	**6**	**0**	**3**	**0**	**3**	....	....	....	....	....	....	....	....
	NHL Totals		**50**	**1**	**5**	**6**	**1**	**5**	**6**	**30**	**0**	**0**	**0**	**26**	**3.8**	**15**	**0**	**7**	**0**		....	....	....	....	....	....	....	....

• GOMEZ, Scott

Scott Carlos C – L. 5′11″, 200 lbs. b: Anchorage, AK, 12/23/1979. New Jersey's 2nd, 27th overall, in 1998.

Season	Club	League	GP	G	A	Pts	AG	AA	APts	PIM	PP	SH	GW	S	%	TGF	PGF	TGA	PGA	+/–	GP	G	A	Pts	PIM	PP	SH	GW
1995-96	Anchorage All-Stars	AAHL	STATISTICS NOT AVAILABLE																									
1996-97	South Surrey Eagles	BCJHL	56	48	76	124	....	....	....	94	....	....	....	....	....	....	....	....	....	....	21	18	23	41	57	....	....	....
1997-98	Tri-City Americans	WHL	45	12	37	49	....	....	....	57	....	....	....	....	....	....	....	....	....	....	....	....	....	....	....	....	....	....
	United States	WJA-C	7	1	0	1	....	....	....	2	....	....	....	....	....	....	....	....	....	....	....	....	....	....	....	....	....	....
1998-99	Tri-City Americans	WHL	58	30	*78	108	....	....	....	55	....	....	....	....	....	....	....	....	....	....	10	6	13	19	31	....	....	....
	United States	WJC-A	6	3	7	10	....	....	....	4	....	....	....	....	....	....	....	....	....	....	....	....	....	....	....	....	....	....
99-2000♦	**New Jersey Devils**	**NHL**	**82**	**19**	**51**	**70**	**21**	**47**	**68**	**78**	**7**	**0**	**1**	**204**	**9.3**	**90**	**34**	**43**	**1**	**14**	**23**	**4**	**6**	**10**	**4**	**1**	**0**	**2**
	NHL Totals		**82**	**19**	**51**	**70**	**21**	**47**	**68**	**78**	**7**	**0**	**1**	**204**	**9.3**	**90**	**34**	**43**	**1**		**23**	**4**	**6**	**10**	**4**	**1**	**0**	**2**

WHL West First All-Star Team (1999) • NHL All-Rookie Team (2000) • Won Calder Memorial Trophy (2000) • Played in NHL All-Star Game (2000)

• GONCHAR, Sergei

D – L. 6′2″, 212 lbs. b: Chelyabinsk, USSR, 4/13/1974. Washington's 1st, 14th overall, in 1992.

Season	Club	League	GP	G	A	Pts	AG	AA	APts	PIM	PP	SH	GW	S	%	TGF	PGF	TGA	PGA	+/–	GP	G	A	Pts	PIM	PP	SH	GW
1991-92	Traktor Chelyabinsk	CIS	31	1	0	1	....	....	....	6	....	....	....	....	....	....	....	....	....	....	....	....	....	....	....	....	....	....
	Soviet Union	EJC-A	6	1	4	5	....	....	....	8	....	....	....	....	....	....	....	....	....	....	....	....	....	....	....	....	....	....
1992-93	Dynamo Moscow	CIS	31	1	3	4	....	....	....	70	....	....	....	....	....	....	....	....	....	....	10	0	0	0	12	....	....	....
	Russia	WJC-A	7	0	2	2	....	....	....	10	....	....	....	....	....	....	....	....	....	....	....	....	....	....	....	....	....	....
1993-94	Dynamo Moscow	CIS	44	4	5	9	....	....	....	36	....	....	....	....	....	....	....	....	....	....	10	0	3	3	14	....	....	....
	Portland Pirates	AHL	....	....	....	....	....	....	....	....	....	....	....	....	....	....	....	....	....	....	2	0	0	0	0	....	....	....
1994-95	Portland Pirates	AHL	61	10	32	42	....	....	....	67	....	....	....	....	....	....	....	....	....	....	....	....	....	....	....	....	....	....
	Washington Capitals	**NHL**	**31**	**2**	**5**	**7**	**4**	**7**	**11**	**22**	**0**	**0**	**0**	**38**	**5.3**	**16**	**2**	**11**	**1**	**4**	**7**	**2**	**2**	**4**	**2**	**0**	**0**	**1**
1995-96	**Washington Capitals**	**NHL**	**78**	**15**	**26**	**41**	**15**	**21**	**36**	**60**	**4**	**0**	**4**	**139**	**10.8**	**95**	**26**	**50**	**6**	**25**	**6**	**2**	**4**	**6**	**4**	**1**	**0**	**0**
1996-97	Russia	W-Cup	4	2	2	4	....	....	....	2	....	....	....	....	....	....	....	....	....	....	....	....	....	....	....	....	....	....
	Washington Capitals	**NHL**	**57**	**13**	**17**	**30**	**14**	**15**	**29**	**36**	**3**	**0**	**3**	**129**	**10.1**	**66**	**20**	**66**	**9**	**–11**	....	....	....	....	....	....	....	....
1997-98	Lada Togliatti	Russia	7	3	2	5	....	....	....	4	....	....	....	....	....	....	....	....	....	....	....	....	....	....	....	....	....	....
	Lada Togliatti	EuroHL	1	1	0	1	....	....	....	2	....	....	....	....	....	....	....	....	....	....	....	....	....	....	....	....	....	....
	Washington Capitals	**NHL**	**72**	**5**	**16**	**21**	**6**	**16**	**22**	**66**	**2**	**0**	**0**	**134**	**3.7**	**65**	**15**	**51**	**3**	**2**	**21**	**7**	**4**	**11**	**30**	**3**	**1**	**2**
	Russia	Olympics	6	0	2	2	....	....	....	0	....	....	....	....	....	....	....	....	....	....	....	....	....	....	....	....	....	....
1998-99	**Washington Capitals**	**NHL**	**53**	**21**	**10**	**31**	**25**	**10**	**35**	**57**	**13**	**1**	**3**	**180**	**11.7**	**68**	**26**	**47**	**6**	**1**	....	....	....	....	....	....	....	....
99-2000	**Washington Capitals**	**NHL**	**73**	**18**	**36**	**54**	**20**	**33**	**53**	**52**	**5**	**0**	**3**	**181**	**9.9**	**108**	**32**	**57**	**7**	**26**	**5**	**1**	**0**	**1**	**6**	**0**	**0**	**0**
	Russia	WC-A	6	1	0	1	....	....	....	2	....	....	....	....	....	....	....	....	....	....	....	....	....	....	....	....	....	....
	NHL Totals		**364**	**74**	**110**	**184**	**84**	**102**	**186**	**293**	**27**	**1**	**13**	**801**	**9.2**	**418**	**121**	**282**	**32**		**39**	**12**	**10**	**22**	**42**	**4**	**1**	**3**

• GONEAU, Daniel

LW – L. 6′, 194 lbs. b: Montreal, Que., 1/16/1976. NY Rangers' 2nd, 48th overall, in 1996.

Season	Club	League	GP	G	A	Pts	AG	AA	APts	PIM	PP	SH	GW	S	%	TGF	PGF	TGA	PGA	+/–	GP	G	A	Pts	PIM	PP	SH	GW
1990-91	Laval Leafs	QAAA	32	16	18	34	....	....	....	20	....	....	....	....	....	....	....	....	....	....	....	....	....	....	....	....	....	....
1991-92	Lac St-Louis Lions	QAAA	42	21	14	35	....	....	....	52	....	....	....	....	....	....	....	....	....	....	....	....	....	....	....	....	....	....
1992-93	Laval Titan	QMJHL	62	16	25	41	....	....	....	44	....	....	....	....	....	....	....	....	....	....	13	0	4	4	4	....	....	....
1993-94	Laval Titan	QMJHL	68	29	57	86	....	....	....	81	....	....	....	....	....	....	....	....	....	....	19	8	21	29	45	....	....	....
1994-95	Laval Titan	QMJHL	56	16	31	47	....	....	....	78	....	....	....	....	....	....	....	....	....	....	20	5	10	15	33	....	....	....
1995-96	Granby Bisons	QMJHL	67	54	51	105	....	....	....	115	....	....	....	....	....	....	....	....	....	....	21	11	22	33	40	....	....	....
1996-97	**New York Rangers**	**NHL**	**41**	**10**	**3**	**13**	**11**	**3**	**14**	**10**	**3**	**0**	**2**	**44**	**22.7**	**19**	**6**	**18**	**0**	**–5**	....	....	....	....	....	....	....	....
	Binghamton Rangers	AHL	39	15	15	30	....	....	....	10	....	....	....	....	....	....	....	....	....	....	....	....	....	....	....	....	....	....
1997-98	**New York Rangers**	**NHL**	**11**	**2**	**0**	**2**	**2**	**0**	**2**	**4**	**0**	**0**	**1**	**13**	**15.4**	**2**	**0**	**6**	**0**	**–4**	....	....	....	....	....	....	....	....
	Hartford Wolf Pack	AHL	66	21	26	47	....	....	....	44	....	....	....	....	....	....	....	....	....	....	13	1	4	5	18	....	....	....
1998-99	Hartford Wolf Pack	AHL	72	20	19	39	....	....	....	56	....	....	....	....	....	....	....	....	....	....	2	1	0	1	0	....	....	....
99-2000	**New York Rangers**	**NHL**	**1**	**0**	**0**	**0**	**0**	**0**	**0**	**0**	**0**	**0**	**0**	**3**	**0.0**	**0**	**0**	**1**	**0**	**–1**	....	....	....	....	....	....	....	....
	Hartford Wolf Pack	AHL	51	15	17	32	....	....	....	48	....	....	....	....	....	....	....	....	....	....	22	1	2	3	6	....	....	....
	NHL Totals		**53**	**12**	**3**	**15**	**13**	**3**	**16**	**14**	**3**	**0**	**3**	**60**	**20.0**	**21**	**6**	**25**	**0**		....	....	....	....	....	....	....	....

QMJHL First All-Star Team (1996)

• Re-entered NHL Entry Draft. Originally Boston's 2nd choice, 47th overall, in 1994 Entry Draft.

			REGULAR SEASON																		PLAYOFFS							
Season	Club	League	GP	G	A	Pts	AG	AA	APts	PIM	PP	SH	GW	S	%	TGF	PGF	TGA	PGA	+/–	GP	G	A	Pts	PIM	PP	SH	GW

• GOODENOUGH, Larry

Larry J. "Izzy" D – R. 6', 195 lbs. b: Toronto, Ont., 1/19/1953. Philadelphia's 1st, 20th overall, in 1973.

Season	Club	League	GP	G	A	Pts	AG	AA	APts	PIM	PP	SH	GW	S	%	TGF	PGF	TGA	PGA	+/–	GP	G	A	Pts	PIM	PP	SH	GW
1969-70	Etobicoke Indians	OMHA	STATISTICS NOT AVAILABLE																									
1970-71	Markham Waxers	OHA-B	STATISTICS NOT AVAILABLE																									
	Toronto Marlboros	OHA-Jr.	....	....	....	....	....	....	....	....	....	....	....	....	....	....	....	....	....	....	1	0	0	0	0	....	....	....
1971-72	Toronto Marlboros	OMJHL	62	3	35	38	....	....	....	61	....	....	....	....	....	....	....	....	....	....	10	2	6	8	10	....	....	....
1972-73	London Knights	OMJHL	59	15	51	66	....	....	....	153	....	....	....	....	....	....	....	....	....	....	10	2	7	9	10	....	....	....
1973-74	Richmond Robins	AHL	75	11	22	33	....	....	....	54	....	....	....	....	....	....	....	....	....	....	5	2	2	4	0	....	....	....
1974-75	Richmond Robins	AHL	57	10	40	50	....	....	....	76	....	....	....	....	....	....	....	....	....	....	....	....	....	....	....	....	....	....
	♦ **Philadelphia Flyers**	**NHL**	**20**	**3**	**9**	**12**	**3**	**7**	**10**	**0**	**1**	**0**	**0**	**37**	**8.1**	**39**	**17**	**11**	**1**	**12**	**5**	**0**	**4**	**4**	**2**	**0**	**0**	**0**
1975-76	**Philadelphia Flyers**	**NHL**	**77**	**8**	**34**	**42**	**7**	**25**	**32**	**83**	**5**	**1**	**2**	**149**	**5.4**	**127**	**47**	**52**	**17**	**45**	**16**	**3**	**11**	**14**	**6**	**1**	**0**	**0**
1976-77	**Philadelphia Flyers**	**NHL**	**32**	**4**	**13**	**17**	**4**	**10**	**14**	**21**	**1**	**0**	**0**	**52**	**7.7**	**45**	**9**	**26**	**5**	**15**	....	....	....	....	....	....	....	....
	Vancouver Canucks	**NHL**	**30**	**2**	**4**	**6**	**2**	**3**	**5**	**27**	**0**	**0**	**1**	**35**	**5.7**	**27**	**1**	**42**	**11**	**–5**	....	....	....	....	....	....	....	....
1977-78	**Vancouver Canucks**	**NHL**	**42**	**1**	**6**	**7**	**1**	**5**	**6**	**28**	**0**	**0**	**0**	**49**	**2.0**	**26**	**5**	**46**	**9**	**–16**	....	....	....	....	....	....	....	....
	Tulsa Oilers	CHL	32	5	18	23	....	....	....	26	....	....	....	....	....	....	....	....	....	....	5	0	3	3	11	....	....	....
1978-79	**Vancouver Canucks**	**NHL**	**36**	**4**	**9**	**13**	**3**	**7**	**10**	**18**	**2**	**0**	**0**	**75**	**5.3**	**34**	**14**	**37**	**3**	**–14**	**1**	**0**	**0**	**0**	**2**	**0**	**0**	**0**
	Dallas Black Hawks	CHL	31	3	16	19	....	....	....	23	....	....	....	....	....	....	....	....	....	....	....	....	....	....	....	....	....	....
1979-80	**Vancouver Canucks**	**NHL**	**5**	**0**	**2**	**2**	**0**	**1**	**1**	**2**	**0**	**0**	**0**	**9**	**0.0**	**3**	**1**	**3**	**1**	**0**	....	....	....	....	....	....	....	....
	Dallas Black Hawks	CHL	73	4	34	38	....	....	....	55	....	....	....	....	....	....	....	....	....	....	....	....	....	....	....	....	....	....
1980-81	Houston Apollos	CHL	13	2	3	5	....	....	....	2	....	....	....	....	....	....	....	....	....	....	....	....	....	....	....	....	....	....
	Saginaw Gears	IHL	54	10	43	53	....	....	....	32	....	....	....	....	....	....	....	....	....	....	13	1	12	13	20	....	....	....
1981-82	New Haven Nighthawks	AHL	76	3	27	30	....	....	....	60	....	....	....	....	....	....	....	....	....	....	2	0	1	1	9	....	....	....
1982-83	Binghamton Whalers	AHL	58	1	15	16	....	....	....	36	....	....	....	....	....	....	....	....	....	....	3	0	0	0	2	....	....	....
	NHL Totals		**242**	**22**	**77**	**99**	**20**	**58**	**78**	**179**	**9**	**1**	**3**	**406**	**5.4**	**301**	**94**	**217**	**47**		**22**	**3**	**15**	**18**	**10**	**1**	**0**	**0**

IHL First All-Star Team (1981) • Won Governors' Trophy (Top Defenseman - IHL) (1981)

Traded to **Vancouver** by **Philadelphia** with Jack McIlhargey for Bob Dailey, January 20, 1977. Signed as a free agent by **LA Kings**, August, 1980. Traded to **Chicago** by **LA Kings with LA Kings' 3rd round choice (Trent Yawney) in 1984 Entry Draft for Terry Ruskowski, October 24, 1982.**

• GORDIOUK, Viktor

LW – R. 5'10", 176 lbs. b: Odintsovo, USSR, 4/11/1970. Buffalo's 6th, 142nd overall, in 1990.

Season	Club	League	GP	G	A	Pts	AG	AA	APts	PIM	PP	SH	GW	S	%	TGF	PGF	TGA	PGA	+/–	GP	G	A	Pts	PIM	PP	SH	GW
1986-87	Krylja Sovetov Moscow	USSR	2	0	0	0	....	....	....	0	....	....	....	....	....	....	....	....	....	....	....	....	....	....	....	....	....	....
	Soviet Union	EJC-A	7	8	3	11	....	....	....	0	....	....	....	....	....	....	....	....	....	....	....	....	....	....	....	....	....	....
1987-88	Krylja Sovetov Moscow	USSR	26	2	2	4	....	....	....	6	....	....	....	....	....	....	....	....	....	....	....	....	....	....	....	....	....	....
	Soviet Union	EJC-A	6	2	1	3	....	....	....	4	....	....	....	....	....	....	....	....	....	....	....	....	....	....	....	....	....	....
1988-89	Krylja Sovetov Moscow	USSR	41	5	1	6	....	....	....	10	....	....	....	....	....	....	....	....	....	....	....	....	....	....	....	....	....	....
	Soviet Union	WJC-A	7	3	4	7	....	....	....	0	....	....	....	....	....	....	....	....	....	....	....	....	....	....	....	....	....	....
1989-90	Krylja Sovetov Moscow	USSR	48	11	4	15	....	....	....	24	....	....	....	....	....	....	....	....	....	....	....	....	....	....	....	....	....	....
	Soviet Union	WJC-A	7	3	6	9	....	....	....	2	....	....	....	....	....	....	....	....	....	....	....	....	....	....	....	....	....	....
1990-91	Krylja Sovetov Moscow	USSR	46	12	10	22	....	....	....	22	....	....	....	....	....	....	....	....	....	....	....	....	....	....	....	....	....	....
1991-92	Krylja Sovetov Moscow	CIS	42	16	7	23	....	....	....	24	....	....	....	....	....	....	....	....	....	....	....	....	....	....	....	....	....	....
1992-93	**Buffalo Sabres**	**NHL**	**16**	**3**	**6**	**9**	**2**	**4**	**6**	**0**	**0**	**0**	**0**	**24**	**12.5**	**14**	**1**	**9**	**0**	**4**	....	....	....	....	....	....	....	....
	Rochester Americans	AHL	35	11	14	25	....	....	....	8	....	....	....	....	....	....	....	....	....	....	17	9	9	18	4	....	....	....
1993-94	Rochester Americans	AHL	74	28	39	67	....	....	....	26	....	....	....	....	....	....	....	....	....	....	4	3	0	3	2	....	....	....
1994-95	**Buffalo Sabres**	**NHL**	**10**	**0**	**2**	**2**	**0**	**3**	**3**	**0**	**0**	**0**	**0**	**10**	**0.0**	**4**	**3**	**5**	**1**	**–3**	....	....	....	....	....	....	....	....
	Rochester Americans	AHL	63	31	30	61	....	....	....	36	....	....	....	....	....	....	....	....	....	....	3	0	2	2	0	....	....	....
1995-96	Los Angeles Ice Dogs	IHL	68	17	44	61	....	....	....	53	....	....	....	....	....	....	....	....	....	....	....	....	....	....	....	....	....	....
	Utah Grizzlies	IHL	13	4	4	8	....	....	....	6	....	....	....	....	....	....	....	....	....	....	22	4	6	10	14	....	....	....
1996-97	Dusseldorfer EG	Germany	47	20	16	36	....	....	....	26	....	....	....	....	....	....	....	....	....	....	4	0	2	2	2	....	....	....
1997-98	Dusseldorfer EG	Germany	46	14	17	31	....	....	....	20	....	....	....	....	....	....	....	....	....	....	3	0	0	0	2	....	....	....
1998-99	Dusseldorfer EG	Germany-2	65	36	59	95	....	....	....	44	....	....	....	....	....	....	....	....	....	....	....	....	....	....	....	....	....	....
99-2000	Dusseldorfer EG	Germany-2	45	19	28	47	....	....	....	85	....	....	....	....	....	....	....	....	....	....	16	7	13	20	14	....	....	....
	NHL Totals		**26**	**3**	**8**	**11**	**2**	**7**	**9**	**0**	**0**	**0**	**0**	**34**	**8.8**	**18**	**4**	**14**	**1**		....	....	....	....	....	....	....	....

• GORDON, Robb

C – R. 5'11", 190 lbs. b: Murrayville, B.C., 1/13/1976. Vancouver's 2nd, 39th overall, in 1994.

Season	Club	League	GP	G	A	Pts	AG	AA	APts	PIM	PP	SH	GW	S	%	TGF	PGF	TGA	PGA	+/–	GP	G	A	Pts	PIM	PP	SH	GW
1992-93	Powell River Paper Kings	BCJHL	60	55	38	93	....	....	....	76	....	....	....	....	....	....	....	....	....	....	....	....	....	....	....	....	....	....
1993-94	Powell River Paper Kings	BCJHL	60	69	*89	*158	....	....	....	141	....	....	....	....	....	....	....	....	....	....	....	....	....	....	....	....	....	....
1994-95	University of Michigan	CCHA	39	15	26	41	....	....	....	72	....	....	....	....	....	....	....	....	....	....	....	....	....	....	....	....	....	....
1995-96	Kelowna Rockets	WHL	58	51	63	114	....	....	....	84	....	....	....	....	....	....	....	....	....	....	6	3	6	9	19	....	....	....
	Canada	WJC-A	6	0	4	4	....	....	....	0	....	....	....	....	....	....	....	....	....	....	....	....	....	....	....	....	....	....
1996-97	Syracuse Crunch	AHL	63	11	14	25	....	....	....	72	....	....	....	....	....	....	....	....	....	....	3	0	0	0	7	....	....	....
1997-98	Syracuse Crunch	AHL	40	4	6	10	....	....	....	35	....	....	....	....	....	....	....	....	....	....	....	....	....	....	....	....	....	....
	Raleigh IceCaps	ECHL	7	3	10	13	....	....	....	28	....	....	....	....	....	....	....	....	....	....	....	....	....	....	....	....	....	....
1998-99	**Vancouver Canucks**	**NHL**	**4**	**0**	**0**	**0**	**0**	**0**	**0**	**2**	**0**	**0**	**0**	**1**	**0.0**	**0**	**0**	**0**	**0**	**0**	....	....	....	....	....	....	....	....
	Syracuse Crunch	AHL	68	16	22	38	....	....	....	98	....	....	....	....	....	....	....	....	....	....	....	....	....	....	....	....	....	....
99-2000	Long Beach Ice Dogs	IHL	50	7	11	18	....	....	....	54	....	....	....	....	....	....	....	....	....	....	1	0	0	0	0	....	....	....
	NHL Totals		**4**	**0**	**0**	**0**	**0**	**0**	**0**	**2**	**0**	**0**	**0**	**1**	**0.0**	**0**	**0**	**0**	**0**		....	....	....	....	....	....	....	....

WHL West First All-Star Team (1996) • Signed as a free agent by **Long Beach** (IHL), August 23, 1999.

• GORENCE, Tom

Thomas J. RW – R. 6', 190 lbs. b: St. Paul, MN, 3/11/1957. Philadelphia's 2nd, 35th overall, in 1977.

Season	Club	League	GP	G	A	Pts	AG	AA	APts	PIM	PP	SH	GW	S	%	TGF	PGF	TGA	PGA	+/–	GP	G	A	Pts	PIM	PP	SH	GW
1974-75	St. Paul Academy	Hi-School	STATISTICS NOT AVAILABLE																									
1975-76	University of Minnesota	WCHA	40	16	10	26	....	....	....	24	....	....	....	....	....	....	....	....	....	....	....	....	....	....	....	....	....	....
1976-77	University of Minnesota	WCHA	29	18	19	37	....	....	....	44	....	....	....	....	....	....	....	....	....	....	....	....	....	....	....	....	....	....
1977-78	Maine Mariners	AHL	79	28	25	53	....	....	....	23	....	....	....	....	....	....	....	....	....	....	12	*8	4	12	19	....	....	....
1978-79	Maine Mariners	AHL	31	11	13	24	....	....	....	23	....	....	....	....	....	....	....	....	....	....	....	....	....	....	....	....	....	....
	Philadelphia Flyers	**NHL**	**42**	**13**	**6**	**19**	**11**	**4**	**15**	**10**	**1**	**0**	**3**	**85**	**15.3**	**39**	**4**	**29**	**10**	**16**	**7**	**3**	**1**	**4**	**0**	**1**	**0**	**0**
1979-80	**Philadelphia Flyers**	**NHL**	**51**	**8**	**13**	**21**	**7**	**9**	**16**	**15**	**0**	**0**	**2**	**89**	**9.0**	**32**	**2**	**24**	**1**	**7**	**15**	**3**	**3**	**6**	**18**	**1**	**0**	**0**
1980-81	**Philadelphia Flyers**	**NHL**	**79**	**24**	**18**	**42**	**19**	**12**	**31**	**46**	**0**	**3**	**6**	**165**	**14.5**	**56**	**1**	**63**	**25**	**17**	**12**	**3**	**2**	**5**	**29**	**0**	**0**	**0**
1981-82	United States	Can-Cup	6	1	1	2	....	....	....	2	....	....	....	....	....	....	....	....	....	....	....	....	....	....	....	....	....	....
	Philadelphia Flyers	**NHL**	**66**	**5**	**8**	**13**	**4**	**5**	**9**	**8**	**0**	**1**	**0**	**88**	**5.7**	**23**	**0**	**67**	**27**	**–17**	**3**	**0**	**0**	**0**	**0**	**0**	**0**	**0**
	United States	WEC-A	7	1	1	2	....	....	....	2	....	....	....	....	....	....	....	....	....	....	....	....	....	....	....	....	....	....
1982-83	**Philadelphia Flyers**	**NHL**	**53**	**7**	**7**	**14**	**6**	**5**	**11**	**10**	**0**	**0**	**0**	**50**	**14.0**	**24**	**0**	**21**	**1**	**4**	....	....	....	....	....	....	....	....
	Maine Mariners	AHL	10	0	5	5	....	....	....	2	....	....	....	....	....	....	....	....	....	....	17	9	3	12	12	....	....	....
1983-84	**Edmonton Oilers**	**NHL**	**12**	**1**	**1**	**2**	**1**	**1**	**2**	**0**	**0**	**0**	**0**	**7**	**14.3**	**2**	**0**	**2**	**0**	**0**	....	....	....	....	....	....	....	....
	Moncton Alpines	AHL	53	13	14	27	....	....	....	17	....	....	....	....	....	....	....	....	....	....	....	....	....	....	....	....	....	....
1984-85	Maine Mariners	AHL	12	3	1	4	....	....	....	37	....	....	....	....	....	....	....	....	....	....	10	2	3	5	0	....	....	....
1985-86	Hershey Bears	AHL	1	0	0	0	....	....	....	0	....	....	....	....	....	....	....	....	....	....	....	....	....	....	....	....	....	....
	NHL Totals		**303**	**58**	**53**	**111**	**48**	**36**	**84**	**89**	**1**	**4**	**11**	**484**	**12.0**	**176**	**7**	**206**	**64**		**37**	**9**	**6**	**15**	**47**	**2**	**0**	**0**

Signed as a free agent by **Edmonton**, November 1, 1983. Signed as a free agent by **New Jersey**, March 5, 1985.

• GORING, Butch

Robert Thomas C – L. 5'9", 170 lbs. b: St. Boniface, Man., 10/22/1949. Los Angeles' 4th, 51st overall, in 1969.

Season	Club	League	GP	G	A	Pts	AG	AA	APts	PIM	PP	SH	GW	S	%	TGF	PGF	TGA	PGA	+/–	GP	G	A	Pts	PIM	PP	SH	GW
1965-66	West Kildonan North Stars	MJHL	STATISTICS NOT AVAILABLE																									
	Winnipeg Rangers	MJHL	3	0	0	0	....	....	....	0	....	....	....	....	....	....	....	....	....	....	3	0	1	1	0	....	....	....
1966-67	Winnipeg Rangers	MJHL	51	35	31	66	....	....	....	2	....	....	....	....	....	....	....	....	....	....	8	2	6	8	0	....	....	....
1967-68	Hull Nationals	QSHL	40	16	41	57	....	....	....	4	....	....	....	....	....	....	....	....	....	....	....	....	....	....	....	....	....	....
	Winnipeg Jets	MJHL	....	....	....	....	....	....	....	....	....	....	....	....	....	....	....	....	....	....	1	2	1	3	0	....	....	....
	St. Boniface Mohawks	Al-Cup	12	5	6	11	....	....	....	2	....	....	....	....	....	....	....	....	....	....	....	....	....	....	....	....	....	....
1968-69	Winnipeg Jets	WCJHL	39	42	33	75	....	....	....	0	....	....	....	....	....	....	....	....	....	....	....	....	....	....	....	....	....	....
	Dauphin Kings	Mem-Cup	12	8	8	16	....	....	....	5	....	....	....	....	....	....	....	....	....	....	....	....	....	....	....	....	....	....
	Regina Pats	Mem-Cup	2	2	3	5	....	....	....	0	....	....	....	....	....	....	....	....	....	....	....	....	....	....	....	....	....	....

Season	Club	League	REGULAR SEASON GP	G	A	Pts	AG	AA	APts	PIM	PP	SH	GW	S	%	TGF	PGF	TGA	PGA	+/-	PLAYOFFS GP	G	A	Pts	PIM	PP	SH	GW
1969-70	**Los Angeles Kings**	**NHL**	**59**	**13**	**23**	**36**	**14**	**22**	**36**	**8**	**2**	**0**	**0**	**125**	**10.4**	**48**	**10**	**59**	**6**	**–15**	....	....	....	....	....	....	....	....
	Springfield Kings	AHL	19	13	7	20	....	....	....	0	....	....	....	....	....	....	....	....	....	....	....	....	....	....	....	....	....	....
1970-71	**Los Angeles Kings**	**NHL**	**19**	**2**	**5**	**7**	**2**	**4**	**6**	**2**	**0**	**0**	**0**	**15**	**13.3**	**7**	**1**	**2**	**0**	**4**	....	....	....	....	....	....	....	....
	Springfield Kings	AHL	40	23	32	55	....	....	....	4	....	....	....	....	....	....	....	....	....	....	12	*11	*14	*25	0	....	....	....
1971-72	**Los Angeles Kings**	**NHL**	**74**	**21**	**29**	**50**	**21**	**25**	**46**	**2**	**3**	**0**	**2**	**137**	**15.3**	**65**	**15**	**64**	**4**	**–10**	....	....	....	....	....	....	....	....
1972-73	**Los Angeles Kings**	**NHL**	**67**	**28**	**31**	**59**	**26**	**25**	**51**	**2**	**4**	**1**	**1**	**148**	**18.9**	**74**	**12**	**63**	**1**	**0**	....	....	....	....	....	....	....	....
1973-74	**Los Angeles Kings**	**NHL**	**70**	**28**	**33**	**61**	**27**	**27**	**54**	**2**	**5**	**3**	**5**	**161**	**17.4**	**76**	**20**	**77**	**23**	**2**	**5**	**0**	**1**	**1**	**0**	**0**	**0**	**0**
1974-75	**Los Angeles Kings**	**NHL**	**60**	**27**	**33**	**60**	**24**	**25**	**49**	**6**	**6**	**3**	**7**	**134**	**20.1**	**77**	**26**	**51**	**26**	**26**	**3**	**0**	**0**	**0**	**0**	**0**	**0**	**0**
1975-76	**Los Angeles Kings**	**NHL**	**80**	**33**	**40**	**73**	**29**	**30**	**59**	**8**	**5**	**5**	**2**	**193**	**17.1**	**96**	**37**	**93**	**34**	**0**	**9**	**2**	**3**	**5**	**4**	**1**	**0**	**2**
1976-77	**Los Angeles Kings**	**NHL**	**78**	**30**	**55**	**85**	**27**	**42**	**69**	**6**	**13**	**0**	**3**	**216**	**13.9**	**120**	**56**	**82**	**28**	**10**	**9**	**7**	**5**	**12**	**0**	**3**	**0**	**2**
1977-78	**Los Angeles Kings**	**NHL**	**80**	**37**	**36**	**73**	**34**	**28**	**62**	**2**	**9**	**3**	**5**	**248**	**14.9**	**101**	**34**	**102**	**31**	**–4**	**2**	**0**	**0**	**0**	**2**	**0**	**0**	**0**
1978-79	**Los Angeles Kings**	**NHL**	**80**	**36**	**51**	**87**	**31**	**37**	**68**	**16**	**13**	**4**	**2**	**217**	**16.6**	**122**	**64**	**119**	**41**	**–20**	**2**	**0**	**0**	**0**	**0**	**0**	**0**	**0**
1979-80	**Los Angeles Kings**	**NHL**	**69**	**20**	**48**	**68**	**17**	**35**	**52**	**12**	**2**	**1**	**1**	**160**	**12.5**	**106**	**59**	**105**	**37**	**–21**	....	....	....	....	....	....	....	....
◆	**New York Islanders**	**NHL**	**12**	**6**	**5**	**11**	**5**	**4**	**9**	**2**	**0**	**1**	**0**	**20**	**30.0**	**16**	**3**	**9**	**3**	**7**	**21**	**7**	**12**	**19**	**2**	**1**	**0**	**0**
1980-81 ◆	**New York Islanders**	**NHL**	**78**	**23**	**37**	**60**	**18**	**25**	**43**	**0**	**4**	**1**	**1**	**152**	**15.1**	**82**	**24**	**88**	**34**	**4**	**18**	**10**	**10**	**20**	**6**	**4**	**2**	**2**
1981-82	Canada	Can-Cup	7	3	2	5	....	....	....	4	....	....	....	....	....	....	....	....	....	....	....	....	....	....	....	....	....	....
◆	**New York Islanders**	**NHL**	**67**	**15**	**17**	**32**	**12**	**11**	**23**	**10**	**1**	**5**	**1**	**63**	**23.8**	**54**	**10**	**76**	**29**	**–3**	**19**	**6**	**5**	**11**	**12**	**1**	**0**	**2**
1982-83 ◆	**New York Islanders**	**NHL**	**75**	**19**	**20**	**39**	**16**	**14**	**30**	**8**	**2**	**5**	**4**	**98**	**19.4**	**53**	**5**	**62**	**24**	**10**	**20**	**4**	**8**	**12**	**4**	**0**	**0**	**1**
1983-84	**New York Islanders**	**NHL**	**71**	**22**	**24**	**46**	**18**	**16**	**34**	**8**	**0**	**5**	**3**	**89**	**24.7**	**61**	**6**	**74**	**28**	**9**	**21**	**1**	**5**	**6**	**2**	**1**	**0**	**0**
1984-85	**New York Islanders**	**NHL**	**29**	**2**	**5**	**7**	**2**	**3**	**5**	**2**	**0**	**1**	**0**	**19**	**10.5**	**9**	**1**	**33**	**14**	**–11**	....	....	....	....	....	....	....	....
	Boston Bruins	**NHL**	**39**	**13**	**21**	**34**	**11**	**14**	**25**	**6**	**2**	**2**	**2**	**84**	**15.5**	**50**	**19**	**55**	**16**	**–8**	**5**	**1**	**1**	**2**	**0**	**0**	**0**	**0**
1985-86	**Boston Bruins**	**NHL**	DID NOT PLAY – COACHING																									
1986-87	**Boston Bruins**	**NHL**	DID NOT PLAY – COACHING																									
	Nova Scotia Oilers	AHL	10	3	5	8	....	....	....	2	....	....	....	....	....	....	....	....	....	....	....	....	....	....	....	....	....	....
1987-1989	Spokane Chiefs	WHL	DID NOT PLAY – COACHING																									
1989-1990			OUT OF HOCKEY – RETIRED																									
1990-1993	Capital District Islanders	AHL	DID NOT PLAY – COACHING																									
1993-1994	Las Vegas Thunder	IHL	DID NOT PLAY – COACHING																									
1994-1995	Denver Grizzlies	IHL	DID NOT PLAY – COACHING																									
1995-1999	Utah Grizzlies	IHL	DID NOT PLAY – COACHING																									
1999-2000	**New York Islanders**	**NHL**	DID NOT PLAY – COACHING																									
	NHL Totals		**1107**	**375**	**513**	**888**	**334**	**387**	**721**	**102**	**71**	**40**	**39**	**2279**	**16.5**	**1217**	**402**	**1214**	**379**		**134**	**38**	**50**	**88**	**32**	**11**	**2**	**9**

Won Bill Masterton Trophy (1978) • Won Lady Byng Trophy (1978) • Won Conn Smythe Trophy (1981) • Played in NHL All-Star Game (1980)

• Loaned to Dauphin (MJHL) and Regina (WCJHL) for Memorial Cup Playoffs, March, 1968. Traded to **NY Islanders** by **LA Kings** for Billy Harris and Dave Lewis, March 10, 1980. Claimed on waivers by **Boston** from **NY Islanders**, January 8, 1985.

• GORMAN, Dave

David Peter RW – R. 5'11", 185 lbs. b: Oshawa, Ont., 4/8/1955. Montreal's 7th, 70th overall, in 1975.

Season	Club	League	GP	G	A	Pts	AG	AA	APts	PIM	PP	SH	GW	S	%	TGF	PGF	TGA	PGA	+/-	GP	G	A	Pts	PIM	PP	SH	GW
1970-71	St. Catharines	OMHA	STATISTICS NOT AVAILABLE																									
	St. Catharines Black Hawks	OHA-Jr.	....	....	....	....	....	....	....	....	....	....	....	....	....	....	....	....	....	....	2	0	0	0	0	....	....	....
1971-72	St. Catharines Black Hawks	OMJHL	58	31	24	55	....	....	....	71	....	....	....	....	....	....	....	....	....	....	5	5	0	5	30	....	....	....
1972-73	St. Catharines Black Hawks	OMJHL	62	46	57	103	....	....	....	71	....	....	....	....	....	....	....	....	....	....	....	....	....	....	....	....	....	....
1973-74	St. Catharines Black Hawks	OMJHL	69	53	76	129	....	....	....	78	....	....	....	....	....	....	....	....	....	....	14	6	25	31	....	....	....	....
	St. Catharines Black Hawks	Mem-Cup	3	1	1	2	....	....	....	0	....	....	....	....	....	....	....	....	....	....	....	....	....	....	....	....	....	....
1974-75	Phoenix Roadrunners	WHA	13	3	5	8	....	....	....	10	....	....	....	....	....	....	....	....	....	....	....	....	....	....	....	....	....	....
	Tulsa Oilers	CHL	58	19	21	40	....	....	....	96	....	....	....	....	....	....	....	....	....	....	1	0	1	1	2	....	....	....
1975-76	Phoenix Roadrunners	WHA	67	11	20	31	....	....	....	28	....	....	....	....	....	....	....	....	....	....	5	0	2	2	24	....	....	....
1976-77	Phoenix Roadrunners	WHA	5	0	0	0	....	....	....	0	....	....	....	....	....	....	....	....	....	....	....	....	....	....	....	....	....	....
	Birmingham Bulls	WHA	52	9	13	22	....	....	....	38	....	....	....	....	....	....	....	....	....	....	....	....	....	....	....	....	....	....
1977-78	Birmingham Bulls	WHA	63	19	21	40	....	....	....	93	....	....	....	....	....	....	....	....	....	....	4	1	1	2	0	....	....	....
	Hampton Gulls	AHL	2	0	0	0	....	....	....	12	....	....	....	....	....	....	....	....	....	....	....	....	....	....	....	....	....	....
1978-79	Birmingham Bulls	WHA	60	14	24	38	....	....	....	18	....	....	....	....	....	....	....	....	....	....	....	....	....	....	....	....	....	....
1979-80	**Atlanta Flames**	**NHL**	**3**	**0**	**0**	**0**	**0**	**0**	**0**	**0**	**0**	**0**	**0**	**1**	**0.0**	**0**	**0**	**1**	**0**	**–1**	....	....	....	....	....	....	....	....
	Birmingham Bulls	CHL	75	22	43	65	....	....	....	75	....	....	....	....	....	....	....	....	....	....	4	1	1	2	2	....	....	....
1980-81	Nova Scotia Voyageurs	AHL	78	43	47	90	....	....	....	82	....	....	....	....	....	....	....	....	....	....	6	1	2	3	8	....	....	....
1981-82	Rochester Americans	AHL	77	26	41	67	....	....	....	131	....	....	....	....	....	....	....	....	....	....	8	3	4	7	11	....	....	....
1982-83	ZSC Zurich	Switz-2	28	48	19	67	....	....	....	....	....	....	....	....	....	....	....	....	....	....	....	....	....	....	....	....	....	....
1983-84	SC Herisau	Switz-2	28	36	26	62	....	....	....	....	....	....	....	....	....	....	....	....	....	....	10	5	12	17	....	....	....	....
1984-85	SC Herisau	Switz-2	28	47	54	101	....	....	....	....	....	....	....	....	....	....	....	....	....	....	....	....	....	....	....	....	....	....
	NHL Totals		**3**	**0**	**0**	**0**	**0**	**0**	**0**	**0**	**0**	**0**	**0**	**1**	**0.0**	**0**	**0**	**1**	**0**		....	....	....	....	....	....	....	....
	Other Major League Totals		260	56	83	139	....	....	....	187	....	....	....	....	....	....	....	....	....	....	9	1	3	4	24	....	....	....

OMJHL Second All-Star Team (1974) • AHL First All-Star Team (1981)

Selected by **Phoenix** (WHA) in1974 WHA Amateur Draft, June, 1974. Traded to **Birmingham** (WHA) by **Phoenix** (WHA) for Jerry Rollins, November, 1976. Signed as a free agent by **Atlanta**, August, 1979. Transferred to **Calgary** after **Atlanta** franchise relocated, June 24, 1980. Traded to **Montreal** by **Calgary** for Tim Burke, September, 1980. Signed as a free agent by **Buffalo**, June 30, 1981.

• GOSSELIN, Benoit

LW – L. 5'11", 190 lbs. b: Montreal, Que., 7/19/1957. NY Rangers' 6th, 80th overall, in 1977.

Season	Club	League	GP	G	A	Pts	AG	AA	APts	PIM	PP	SH	GW	S	%	TGF	PGF	TGA	PGA	+/-	GP	G	A	Pts	PIM	PP	SH	GW
1973-74	Shawinigan Bruins	QMJHL	64	12	17	29	....	....	....	134	....	....	....	....	....	....	....	....	....	....	....	....	....	....	....	....	....	....
1974-75	Shawinigan Bruins	QMJHL	60	48	49	97	....	....	....	153	....	....	....	....	....	....	....	....	....	....	....	....	....	....	....	....	....	....
1975-76	Sorel Black Hawks	QMJHL	63	40	52	92	....	....	....	144	....	....	....	....	....	....	....	....	....	....	3	2	0	2	51	....	....	....
1976-77	Trois-Rivieres Draveurs	QMJHL	74	64	62	126	....	....	....	145	....	....	....	....	....	....	....	....	....	....	6	3	5	8	10	....	....	....
1977-78	**New York Rangers**	**NHL**	**7**	**0**	**0**	**0**	**0**	**0**	**0**	**33**	**0**	**0**	**0**	**4**	**0.0**	**0**	**0**	**3**	**0**	**–3**	....	....	....	....	....	....	....	....
	New Haven Nighthawks	AHL	52	14	12	26	....	....	....	120	....	....	....	....	....	....	....	....	....	....	15	1	6	7	20	....	....	....
1978-79	New Haven Nighthawks	AHL	3	0	0	0	....	....	....	0	....	....	....	....	....	....	....	....	....	....	....	....	....	....	....	....	....	....
	Toledo Goaldiggers	IHL	8	5	3	8	....	....	....	18	....	....	....	....	....	....	....	....	....	....	....	....	....	....	....	....	....	....
	Kalamazoo Wings	IHL	65	35	24	59	....	....	....	81	....	....	....	....	....	....	....	....	....	....	15	8	6	14	60	....	....	....
1979-80	Dayton Gems	IHL	42	37	20	57	....	....	....	72	....	....	....	....	....	....	....	....	....	....	....	....	....	....	....	....	....	....
	Tulsa Oilers	CHL	37	21	15	36	....	....	....	24	....	....	....	....	....	....	....	....	....	....	3	0	0	0	11	....	....	....
1980-81	Tulsa Oilers	CHL	66	22	29	51	....	....	....	66	....	....	....	....	....	....	....	....	....	....	2	0	0	0	2	....	....	....
1981-82	Tulsa Oilers	CHL	71	31	23	54	....	....	....	29	....	....	....	....	....	....	....	....	....	....	....	....	....	....	....	....	....	....
1982-83	Sherbrooke Jets	AHL	21	5	2	7	....	....	....	6	....	....	....	....	....	....	....	....	....	....	....	....	....	....	....	....	....	....
1983-84	HC Caen	France	36	36	26	62	....	....	....	....	....	....	....	....	....	....	....	....	....	....	....	....	....	....	....	....	....	....
	NHL Totals		**7**	**0**	**0**	**0**	**0**	**0**	**0**	**33**	**0**	**0**	**0**	**4**	**0.0**	**0**	**0**	**3**	**0**		....	....	....	....	....	....	....	....

Signed as a free agent by **Winnipeg**, September 25, 1979.

• GOSSELIN, David

RW – R. 6', 180 lbs. b: Levis, Que., 6/22/1977. New Jersey's 4th, 78th overall, in 1995.

Season	Club	League	GP	G	A	Pts	AG	AA	APts	PIM	PP	SH	GW	S	%	TGF	PGF	TGA	PGA	+/-	GP	G	A	Pts	PIM	PP	SH	GW
1992-93	Richelieu Riverains	QAAA	40	5	12	17	....	....	....	....	....	....	....	....	....	....	....	....	....	....	....	....	....	....	....	....	....	....
1993-94	Richelieu Riverains	QAAA	44	26	19	45	....	....	....	62	....	....	....	....	....	....	....	....	....	....	....	....	....	....	....	....	....	....
1994-95	Sherbrooke Faucons	QMJHL	58	8	8	16	....	....	....	36	....	....	....	....	....	....	....	....	....	....	7	0	0	0	2	....	....	....
1995-96	Sherbrooke Faucons	QMJHL	55	24	24	48	....	....	....	147	....	....	....	....	....	....	....	....	....	....	7	2	2	4	4	....	....	....
1996-97	Sherbrooke Faucons	QMJHL	23	11	15	26	....	....	....	52	....	....	....	....	....	....	....	....	....	....	....	....	....	....	....	....	....	....
	Chicoutimi Sagueneens	QMJHL	28	16	33	49	....	....	....	65	....	....	....	....	....	....	....	....	....	....	12	9	7	16	16	....	....	....
1997-98	Chicoutimi Sagueneens	QMJHL	69	46	64	110	....	....	....	139	....	....	....	....	....	....	....	....	....	....	6	1	4	5	8	....	....	....
1998-99	Milwaukee Admirals	IHL	74	17	11	28	....	....	....	78	....	....	....	....	....	....	....	....	....	....	2	0	2	2	2	....	....	....
99-2000	**Nashville Predators**	**NHL**	**10**	**2**	**1**	**3**	**2**	**1**	**3**	**6**	**0**	**0**	**0**	**14**	**14.3**	**3**	**0**	**7**	**0**	**–4**	....	....	....	....	....	....	....	....
	Milwaukee Admirals	IHL	70	21	20	41	....	....	....	118	....	....	....	....	....	....	....	....	....	....	3	0	0	0	10	....	....	....
	NHL Totals		**10**	**2**	**1**	**3**	**2**	**1**	**3**	**6**	**0**	**0**	**0**	**14**	**14.3**	**3**	**0**	**7**	**0**		....	....	....	....	....	....	....	....

Signed as a free agent by **Nashville**, July 1, 1998.

			REGULAR SEASON																		PLAYOFFS							
Season	Club	League	GP	G	A	Pts	AG	AA	APts	PIM	PP	SH	GW	S	%	TGF	PGF	TGA	PGA	+/–	GP	G	A	Pts	PIM	PP	SH	GW

• GOSSELIN, Guy
Guy Gordon D – R. 5'10", 185 lbs. b: Rochester, MN, 1/6/1964. Winnipeg's 6th, 159th overall, in 1982.

Season	Club	League	GP	G	A	Pts	AG	AA	APts	PIM	PP	SH	GW	S	%	TGF	PGF	TGA	PGA	+/–	GP	G	A	Pts	PIM	PP	SH	GW
1981-82	John Marshall Rockets	Hi-School	22	14	15	29	....	....	....	48	....	....	....	....	....	....	....	....	....	....	....	....	....	....	....	....	....	....
1982-83	University of Minnesota-Duluth	WCHA	4	0	0	0	....	....	....	0	....	....	....	....	....	....	....	....	....	....	....	....	....	....	....	....	....	....
1983-84	University of Minnesota-Duluth	WCHA	37	3	3	6	....	....	....	26	....	....	....	....	....	....	....	....	....	....	....	....	....	....	....	....	....	....
1984-85	University of Minnesota-Duluth	WCHA	47	3	7	10	....	....	....	25	....	....	....	....	....	....	....	....	....	....	....	....	....	....	....	....	....	....
1985-86	University of Minnesota-Duluth	WCHA	39	2	16	18	....	....	....	53	....	....	....	....	....	....	....	....	....	....	....	....	....	....	....	....	....	....
	United States	WEC-A	8	0	0	0	....	....	....	10	....	....	....	....	....	....	....	....	....	....	....	....	....	....	....	....	....	....
1986-87	University of Minnesota-Duluth	WCHA	33	7	8	15	....	....	....	66	....	....	....	....	....	....	....	....	....	....	....	....	....	....	....	....	....	....
1987-88	United States	Nat-Team	50	3	19	22	....	....	....	82	....	....	....	....	....	....	....	....	....	....	....	....	....	....	....	....	....	....
	United States	Olympics	6	0	3	3	....	....	....	2	....	....	....	....	....	....	....	....	....	....	....	....	....	....	....	....	....	....
	Winnipeg Jets	**NHL**	**5**	**0**	**0**	**0**	**0**	**0**	**0**	**6**	**0**	**0**	**0**	**1**	**0.0**	**3**	**0**	**5**	**1**	**–1**	....	....	....	....	....	....	....	....
1988-89	Moncton Hawks	AHL	58	2	8	10	....	....	....	56	....	....	....	....	....	....	....	....	....	....	10	1	1	2	2	....	....	....
1989-90	Moncton Hawks	AHL	70	2	10	12	....	....	....	37	....	....	....	....	....	....	....	....	....	....	....	....	....	....	....	....	....	....
	United States	WEC-A	10	3	0	3	....	....	....	4	....	....	....	....	....	....	....	....	....	....	....	....	....	....	....	....	....	....
1990-91	Skelleftea AIK	Sweden 2	34	3	4	7	....	....	....	24	....	....	....	....	....	....	....	....	....	....	....	....	....	....	....	....	....	....
	United States	WEC-A	10	0	1	1	....	....	....	6	....	....	....	....	....	....	....	....	....	....	....	....	....	....	....	....	....	....
1991-92	United States	Nat-Team	18	1	3	4	....	....	....	20	....	....	....	....	....	....	....	....	....	....	....	....	....	....	....	....	....	....
	United States	Olympics	8	0	0	0	....	....	....	6	....	....	....	....	....	....	....	....	....	....	....	....	....	....	....	....	....	....
1992-93	Skelleftea AIK	Sweden	29	4	3	7	....	....	....	20	....	....	....	....	....	....	....	....	....	....	5	1	3	4	8	....	....	....
1993-94	Kansas City Blades	IHL	19	1	6	7	....	....	....	2	....	....	....	....	....	....	....	....	....	....	....	....	....	....	....	....	....	....
	NHL Totals		**5**	**0**	**0**	**0**	**0**	**0**	**0**	**6**	**0**	**0**	**0**	**1**	**0.0**	**3**	**0**	**5**	**1**		....	....	....	....	....	....	....	....

WCHA Second All-Star Team (1987)

Signed as a free agent by **San Jose**, August 25, 1993.

• GOTAAS, Steve
Steve P. C – R. 5'10", 180 lbs. b: Camrose, Alta., 5/10/1967. Pittsburgh's 4th, 86th overall, in 1985.

Season	Club	League	GP	G	A	Pts	AG	AA	APts	PIM	PP	SH	GW	S	%	TGF	PGF	TGA	PGA	+/–	GP	G	A	Pts	PIM	PP	SH	GW
1982-83	Camrose Bulldogs	AAHA	STATISTICS NOT AVAILABLE																									
1983-84	Prince Albert Raiders	WHL	65	10	22	32	....	....	....	47	....	....	....	....	....	....	....	....	....	....	5	0	1	1	0	....	....	....
1984-85	Prince Albert Raiders	WHL	72	32	41	73	....	....	....	66	....	....	....	....	....	....	....	....	....	....	13	3	6	9	17	....	....	....
	Prince Albert Raiders	Mem-Cup	5	4	1	5	....	....	....	0	....	....	....	....	....	....	....	....	....	....	....	....	....	....	....	....	....	....
1985-86	Prince Albert Raiders	WHL	61	40	61	101	....	....	....	31	....	....	....	....	....	....	....	....	....	....	20	8	14	22	8	....	....	....
1986-87	Prince Albert Raiders	WHL	68	53	55	108	....	....	....	94	....	....	....	....	....	....	....	....	....	....	8	5	6	11	16	....	....	....
1987-88	**Pittsburgh Penguins**	**NHL**	**36**	**5**	**6**	**11**	**4**	**4**	**8**	**45**	**0**	**0**	**1**	**27**	**18.5**	**13**	**0**	**34**	**10**	**–11**	....	....	....	....	....	....	....	....
	Muskegon Lumberjacks	IHL	34	16	22	38	....	....	....	4	....	....	....	....	....	....	....	....	....	....	....	....	....	....	....	....	....	....
1988-89	**Minnesota North Stars**	**NHL**	**12**	**1**	**3**	**4**	**1**	**2**	**3**	**6**	**1**	**0**	**0**	**18**	**5.6**	**5**	**2**	**4**	**0**	**–1**	**3**	**0**	**1**	**1**	**5**	**0**	**0**	**0**
	Muskegon Lumberjacks	IHL	19	9	16	25	....	....	....	34	....	....	....	....	....	....	....	....	....	....	....	....	....	....	....	....	....	....
	Kalamazoo Wings	IHL	30	24	22	46	....	....	....	12	....	....	....	....	....	....	....	....	....	....	5	2	3	5	2	....	....	....
1989-90	Kalamazoo Wings	IHL	1	1	0	1	....	....	....	0	....	....	....	....	....	....	....	....	....	....	2	0	0	0	2	....	....	....
1990-91	**Minnesota North Stars**	**NHL**	**1**	**0**	**0**	**0**	**0**	**0**	**0**	**2**	**0**	**0**	**0**	**2**	**0.0**	**0**	**0**	**1**	**0**	**–1**	....	....	....	....	....	....	....	....
	Kalamazoo Wings	IHL	78	30	49	79	....	....	....	88	....	....	....	....	....	....	....	....	....	....	7	3	5	8	4	....	....	....
1991-92	Kalamazoo Wings	IHL	72	34	29	63	....	....	....	115	....	....	....	....	....	....	....	....	....	....	12	4	10	14	20	....	....	....
1992-93	Dusseldorfer EG	Germany	30	4	16	20	....	....	....	20	....	....	....	....	....	....	....	....	....	....	....	....	....	....	....	....	....	....
	KAC Klagenfurt	Austria	11	3	4	7	....	....	....	....	....	....	....	....	....	....	....	....	....	....	....	....	....	....	....	....	....	....
1993-94	Las Vegas Thunder	IHL	39	4	13	17	....	....	....	43	....	....	....	....	....	....	....	....	....	....	4	0	0	0	28	....	....	....
	NHL Totals		**49**	**6**	**9**	**15**	**5**	**6**	**11**	**53**	**1**	**0**	**1**	**47**	**12.8**	**18**	**2**	**39**	**10**		**3**	**0**	**1**	**1**	**5**	**0**	**0**	**0**

Traded to **Minnesota** by **Pittsburgh** with Ville Siren for Gord Dineen and Scott Bjugstad, December 17, 1988.

• GOULD, Bobby
Robert Alexander RW – R. 6', 195 lbs. b: Petrolia, Ont., 9/2/1957. Atlanta's 7th, 118th overall, in 1977.

Season	Club	League	GP	G	A	Pts	AG	AA	APts	PIM	PP	SH	GW	S	%	TGF	PGF	TGA	PGA	+/–	GP	G	A	Pts	PIM	PP	SH	GW
1974-75	Petrolia Jets	OHA-B	STATISTICS NOT AVAILABLE																									
1975-76	University of New Hampshire	ECAC	31	13	14	27	....	....	....	16	....	....	....	....	....	....	....	....	....	....	....	....	....	....	....	....	....	....
1976-77	University of New Hampshire	ECAC	39	24	25	49	....	....	....	36	....	....	....	....	....	....	....	....	....	....	....	....	....	....	....	....	....	....
1977-78	University of New Hampshire	ECAC	30	23	34	57	....	....	....	40	....	....	....	....	....	....	....	....	....	....	....	....	....	....	....	....	....	....
1978-79	University of New Hampshire	ECAC	35	31	28	59	....	....	....	46	....	....	....	....	....	....	....	....	....	....	....	....	....	....	....	....	....	....
	Tulsa Oilers	CHL	5	2	0	2	....	....	....	4	....	....	....	....	....	....	....	....	....	....	....	....	....	....	....	....	....	....
1979-80	**Atlanta Flames**	**NHL**	**1**	**0**	**0**	**0**	**0**	**0**	**0**	**0**	**0**	**0**	**0**	**1**	**0.0**	**0**	**0**	**1**	**0**	**–1**	....	....	....	....	....	....	....	....
	Birmingham Bulls	CHL	79	27	33	60	....	....	....	73	....	....	....	....	....	....	....	....	....	....	4	2	4	6	0	....	....	....
1980-81	**Calgary Flames**	**NHL**	**3**	**0**	**0**	**0**	**0**	**0**	**0**	**0**	**0**	**0**	**0**	**5**	**0.0**	**1**	**0**	**1**	**0**	**0**	**11**	**3**	**1**	**4**	**4**	**0**	**0**	**0**
	Birmingham Bulls	CHL	58	25	25	50	....	....	....	43	....	....	....	....	....	....	....	....	....	....	....	....	....	....	....	....	....	....
	Fort Worth Texans	CHL	18	8	6	14	....	....	....	6	....	....	....	....	....	....	....	....	....	....	5	5	2	7	10	....	....	....
1981-82	**Calgary Flames**	**NHL**	**16**	**3**	**0**	**3**	**2**	**0**	**2**	**4**	**0**	**0**	**1**	**18**	**16.7**	**6**	**0**	**8**	**0**	**–2**	....	....	....	....	....	....	....	....
	Oklahoma City Stars	CHL	1	0	1	1	....	....	....	0	....	....	....	....	....	....	....	....	....	....	....	....	....	....	....	....	....	....
	Washington Capitals	**NHL**	**60**	**18**	**13**	**31**	**14**	**9**	**23**	**69**	**1**	**0**	**1**	**103**	**17.5**	**41**	**4**	**59**	**19**	**–3**	....	....	....	....	....	....	....	....
1982-83	**Washington Capitals**	**NHL**	**80**	**22**	**18**	**40**	**18**	**12**	**30**	**43**	**0**	**0**	**6**	**142**	**15.5**	**55**	**1**	**66**	**28**	**16**	**4**	**5**	**0**	**5**	**4**	**1**	**0**	**1**
1983-84	**Washington Capitals**	**NHL**	**78**	**21**	**19**	**40**	**17**	**13**	**30**	**74**	**4**	**0**	**4**	**155**	**13.5**	**53**	**7**	**64**	**16**	**–2**	**5**	**0**	**2**	**2**	**4**	**0**	**0**	**0**
1984-85	**Washington Capitals**	**NHL**	**78**	**14**	**19**	**33**	**11**	**13**	**24**	**69**	**0**	**1**	**3**	**114**	**12.3**	**45**	**0**	**56**	**21**	**10**	**5**	**0**	**1**	**1**	**2**	**0**	**0**	**0**
1985-86	**Washington Capitals**	**NHL**	**79**	**19**	**19**	**38**	**15**	**13**	**28**	**26**	**0**	**3**	**5**	**125**	**15.2**	**49**	**0**	**67**	**25**	**7**	**9**	**4**	**3**	**7**	**11**	**0**	**0**	**0**
1986-87	**Washington Capitals**	**NHL**	**78**	**23**	**27**	**50**	**20**	**20**	**40**	**74**	**1**	**1**	**2**	**156**	**14.7**	**66**	**1**	**74**	**27**	**18**	**7**	**0**	**3**	**3**	**8**	**0**	**0**	**0**
1987-88	**Washington Capitals**	**NHL**	**72**	**12**	**14**	**26**	**10**	**10**	**20**	**56**	**0**	**0**	**2**	**119**	**10.1**	**35**	**0**	**64**	**28**	**–1**	**14**	**3**	**1**	**4**	**21**	**0**	**2**	**0**
1988-89	**Washington Capitals**	**NHL**	**75**	**5**	**13**	**18**	**4**	**9**	**13**	**65**	**0**	**1**	**0**	**91**	**5.5**	**29**	**1**	**57**	**27**	**–2**	**6**	**0**	**2**	**2**	**0**	**0**	**0**	**0**
1989-90	**Boston Bruins**	**NHL**	**77**	**8**	**17**	**25**	**7**	**12**	**19**	**92**	**0**	**0**	**2**	**92**	**8.7**	**36**	**2**	**45**	**8**	**–3**	**17**	**0**	**0**	**0**	**4**	**0**	**0**	**0**
1990-91	Maine Mariners	AHL	71	10	15	25	....	....	....	30	....	....	....	....	....	....	....	....	....	....	2	0	0	0	0	....	....	....
	NHL Totals		**697**	**145**	**159**	**304**	**118**	**111**	**229**	**572**	**6**	**6**	**26**	**1121**	**12.9**	**416**	**16**	**562**	**199**		**78**	**15**	**13**	**28**	**58**	**1**	**2**	**1**

ECAC Second All-Star Team (1979)

Transferred to **Calgary** after **Atlanta** franchise relocated, June 24, 1980. Traded to **Washington** by **Calgary** with Randy Holt for Pat Ribble and Washington's 2nd round choice (later traded to Montreal — Montreal selected Todd Francis), November 25, 1981. Traded to **Boston** by **Washington** for Alain Cote, September 28, 1989.

• GOULD, John
John Milton RW – L. 5'11", 197 lbs. b: Beeton, Ont., 4/11/1949.

Season	Club	League	GP	G	A	Pts	AG	AA	APts	PIM	PP	SH	GW	S	%	TGF	PGF	TGA	PGA	+/–	GP	G	A	Pts	PIM	PP	SH	GW
1967-68	London Nationals/Knights	OHA-Jr.	54	19	27	46	....	....	....	14	....	....	....	....	....	....	....	....	....	....	5	1	2	3	13	....	....	....
1968-69	London Knights	OHA-Jr.	49	30	44	74	....	....	....	20	....	....	....	....	....	....	....	....	....	....	6	1	3	4	0	....	....	....
1969-70	Charlotte Checkers	EHL	69	25	48	73	....	....	....	18	....	....	....	....	....	....	....	....	....	....	11	10	6	16	6	....	....	....
	Tulsa Oilers	CHL	....	....	....	....	....	....	....	....	....	....	....	....	....	....	....	....	....	....	3	1	0	1	0	....	....	....
1970-71	Charlotte Checkers	EHL	72	48	52	100	....	....	....	50	....	....	....	....	....	....	....	....	....	....	13	10	8	18	6	....	....	....
1971-72	**Buffalo Sabres**	**NHL**	**2**	**1**	**0**	**1**	**1**	**0**	**1**	**0**	**0**	**0**	**0**	**3**	**33.3**	**1**	**0**	**2**	**0**	**–1**	....	....	....	....	....	....	....	....
	Cincinnati Swords	AHL	73	26	15	41	....	....	....	34	....	....	....	....	....	....	....	....	....	....	10	4	6	10	6	....	....	....
1972-73	**Buffalo Sabres**	**NHL**	**8**	**0**	**1**	**1**	**0**	**1**	**1**	**0**	**0**	**0**	**0**	**4**	**0.0**	**2**	**0**	**2**	**0**	**0**	....	....	....	....	....	....	....	....
	Cincinnati Swords	AHL	56	30	42	72	....	....	....	71	....	....	....	....	....	....	....	....	....	....	15	*10	6	16	9	....	....	....
1973-74	**Buffalo Sabres**	**NHL**	**30**	**4**	**2**	**6**	**4**	**2**	**6**	**2**	**0**	**0**	**1**	**48**	**8.3**	**12**	**2**	**21**	**4**	**–7**	....	....	....	....	....	....	....	....
	Vancouver Canucks	**NHL**	**45**	**9**	**10**	**19**	**9**	**8**	**17**	**8**	**2**	**0**	**4**	**127**	**7.1**	**38**	**9**	**45**	**12**	**–4**	....	....	....	....	....	....	....	....
1974-75	**Vancouver Canucks**	**NHL**	**78**	**34**	**31**	**65**	**30**	**23**	**53**	**27**	**6**	**0**	**6**	**230**	**14.8**	**101**	**32**	**81**	**19**	**7**	**5**	**2**	**2**	**4**	**0**	**1**	**0**	**0**
1975-76	**Vancouver Canucks**	**NHL**	**70**	**32**	**27**	**59**	**28**	**20**	**48**	**16**	**6**	**1**	**5**	**225**	**14.2**	**83**	**24**	**69**	**19**	**9**	**2**	**1**	**0**	**1**	**0**	**0**	**1**	**0**
1976-77	**Vancouver Canucks**	**NHL**	**25**	**7**	**8**	**15**	**6**	**6**	**12**	**2**	**1**	**0**	**2**	**65**	**10.8**	**21**	**3**	**30**	**3**	**–9**	....	....	....	....	....	....	....	....
	Atlanta Flames	**NHL**	**54**	**8**	**15**	**23**	**7**	**12**	**19**	**8**	**1**	**1**	**0**	**113**	**7.1**	**41**	**13**	**37**	**7**	**–2**	**3**	**0**	**0**	**0**	**2**	**0**	**0**	**0**
1977-78	**Atlanta Flames**	**NHL**	**79**	**19**	**28**	**47**	**17**	**22**	**39**	**21**	**2**	**0**	**4**	**133**	**14.3**	**73**	**16**	**88**	**38**	**7**	**2**	**0**	**0**	**0**	**2**	**0**	**0**	**0**

			REGULAR SEASON																		PLAYOFFS							
Season	Club	League	GP	G	A	Pts	AG	AA	APts	PIM	PP	SH	GW	S	%	TGF	PGF	TGA	PGA	+/–	GP	G	A	Pts	PIM	PP	SH	GW
1978-79	**Atlanta Flames**	**NHL**	**61**	**8**	**7**	**15**	**7**	**5**	**12**	**18**	**0**	**0**	**3**	**67**	**11.9**	**30**	**8**	**54**	**28**	**–4**	**2**	**0**	**0**	**0**	**0**	**0**	**0**	**0**
1979-80	**Buffalo Sabres**	**NHL**	**52**	**9**	**9**	**18**	**8**	**7**	**15**	**11**	**0**	**0**	**2**	**72**	**12.5**	**27**	**1**	**17**	**0**	**9**	....	....	....	....	....	....	....	....
	Rochester Americans	AHL	13	6	5	11	....	....	....	6	....	....	....	....	....	....	....	....	....	....	4	0	1	1	2	....	....	....
	NHL Totals		**504**	**131**	**138**	**269**	**117**	**106**	**223**	**113**	**18**	**2**	**27**	**1087**	**12.1**	**429**	**108**	**446**	**130**		**14**	**3**	**2**	**5**	**4**	**1**	**1**	**0**

• Brother of Larry • AHL Second All-Star Team (1973)

Signed as a free agent by **Buffalo**, August, 1971. Traded to **Vancouver** by **Buffalo** with Tracy Pratt for Jerry Korab, December 27, 1973. Traded to **Atlanta** by **Vancouver** with LA Kings' 2nd round choice (previously acquired, Atlanta selected Brian Hill) in 1977 Amateur Draft for Hilliard Graves and Larry Carriere, December 2, 1976. Claimed by **Edmonton** from **Atlanta** in Expansion Draft, June 13, 1979. Traded to **Buffalo** by **Edmonton** for Alex Tidey, November 13, 1979.

• GOULD, Larry

LW – L. 5'9", 170 lbs. b: Alliston, Ont., 8/16/1952.

Season	Club	League	GP	G	A	Pts	AG	AA	APts	PIM	PP	SH	GW	S	%	TGF	PGF	TGA	PGA	+/–	GP	G	A	Pts	PIM	PP	SH	GW
1969-70	Hamilton Red Wings	OHA-Jr.	49	21	19	40	....	....	....	81	....	....	....	....	....	....	....	....	....	....	....	....	....	....	....	....	....	....
1970-71	Hamilton Red Wings	OHA-Jr.	50	21	16	37	....	....	....	73	....	....	....	....	....	....	....	....	....	....	....	....	....	....	....	....	....	....
1971-72	Niagara Falls Flyers	OMJHL	61	14	20	34	....	....	....	92	....	....	....	....	....	....	....	....	....	....	6	2	1	3	30	....	....	....
1972-73	Des Moines Capitols	IHL	73	30	54	84	....	....	....	89	....	....	....	....	....	....	....	....	....	....	3	2	1	3	0	....	....	....
1973-74	**Vancouver Canucks**	**NHL**	**2**	**0**	**0**	**0**	**0**	**0**	**0**	**0**	**0**	**0**	**0**	**0**	**0.0**	**0**	**0**	**2**	**0**	**–2**	....	....	....	....	....	....	....	....
	Seattle Totems	WHL	53	17	32	49	....	....	....	49	....	....	....	....	....	....	....	....	....	....	....	....	....	....	....	....	....	....
1974-75	Seattle Totems	CHL	72	21	41	62	....	....	....	49	....	....	....	....	....	....	....	....	....	....	....	....	....	....	....	....	....	....
1975-76	Buffalo Norsemen	NAHL	71	32	68	100	....	....	....	22	....	....	....	....	....	....	....	....	....	....	....	....	....	....	....	....	....	....
1976-77	Port Huron Flags	IHL	74	35	71	106	....	....	....	37	....	....	....	....	....	....	....	....	....	....	....	....	....	....	....	....	....	....
1977-78	Port Huron Flags	IHL	80	36	69	105	....	....	....	86	....	....	....	....	....	....	....	....	....	....	....	....	....	....	....	....	....	....
1978-79	Port Huron Flags	IHL	59	30	36	66	....	....	....	32	....	....	....	....	....	....	....	....	....	....	....	....	....	....	....	....	....	....
1979-80	Port Huron Flags	IHL	75	25	57	82	....	....	....	35	....	....	....	....	....	....	....	....	....	....	11	3	12	15	4	....	....	....
1980-81	Port Huron Flags	IHL	71	30	63	93	....	....	....	51	....	....	....	....	....	....	....	....	....	....	4	1	1	2	0	....	....	....
1981-82	Muskegon Mohawks	IHL	15	2	15	17	....	....	....	2	....	....	....	....	....	....	....	....	....	....	....	....	....	....	....	....	....	....
	Flint Generals	IHL	59	31	45	76	....	....	....	22	....	....	....	....	....	....	....	....	....	....	4	2	2	4	2	....	....	....
	NHL Totals		**2**	**0**	**0**	**0**	**0**	**0**	**0**	**0**	**0**	**0**	**0**	**0**	**0.0**	**0**	**0**	**2**	**0**		....	....	....	....	....	....	....	....

• Brother of John • IHL Second All-Star Team (1977) • IHL First All-Star Team (1978)

Signed as a free agent by **Vancouver**, October, 1973. Traded to **Port Huron** (IHL) by **Toledo** (IHL) with Don O'Driscoll for Len Fontaine, October 7, 1976.

• GOULET, Michel

LW – L. 6'1", 195 lbs. b: Peribonka, Que., 4/21/1960. Quebec's 1st, 20th overall, in 1979. **HHOF**

Season	Club	League	GP	G	A	Pts	AG	AA	APts	PIM	PP	SH	GW	S	%	TGF	PGF	TGA	PGA	+/–	GP	G	A	Pts	PIM	PP	SH	GW
1976-77	Mistasinni Majors	QAAA	STATISTICS NOT AVAILABLE																									
	Quebec Remparts	QMJHL	37	17	18	35	....	....	....	9	....	....	....	....	....	....	....	....	....	....	14	3	8	11	19	....	....	....
1977-78	Quebec Remparts	QMJHL	72	73	62	135	....	....	....	109	....	....	....	....	....	....	....	....	....	....	1	0	1	1	0	....	....	....
1978-79	Birmingham Bulls	WHA	78	28	30	58	....	....	....	65	....	....	....	....	....	....	....	....	....	....	....	....	....	....	....	....	....	....
1979-80	**Quebec Nordiques**	**NHL**	**77**	**22**	**32**	**54**	**19**	**23**	**42**	**48**	**5**	**0**	**1**	**167**	**13.2**	**73**	**24**	**60**	**1**	**–10**	....	....	....	....	....	....	....	....
1980-81	**Quebec Nordiques**	**NHL**	**76**	**32**	**39**	**71**	**25**	**26**	**51**	**45**	**3**	**2**	**3**	**265**	**12.1**	**101**	**21**	**98**	**18**	**0**	**4**	**3**	**4**	**7**	**7**	**0**	**0**	**1**
1981-82	**Quebec Nordiques**	**NHL**	**80**	**42**	**42**	**84**	**33**	**28**	**61**	**48**	**7**	**6**	**3**	**251**	**16.7**	**122**	**21**	**96**	**30**	**35**	**16**	**8**	**5**	**13**	**6**	**2**	**2**	**0**
1982-83	**Quebec Nordiques**	**NHL**	**80**	**57**	**48**	**105**	**47**	**33**	**80**	**51**	**10**	**4**	**4**	**256**	**22.3**	**138**	**25**	**115**	**33**	**31**	**4**	**0**	**0**	**0**	**6**	**0**	**0**	**0**
	Canada	WEC-A	10	1	8	9	....	....	....	6	....	....	....	....	....	....	....	....	....	....	....	....	....	....	....	....	....	....
1983-84	**Quebec Nordiques**	**NHL**	**75**	**56**	**65**	**121**	**45**	**44**	**89**	**76**	**11**	**2**	**16**	**239**	**23.4**	**149**	**39**	**58**	**10**	**62**	**9**	**2**	**4**	**6**	**17**	**0**	**0**	**0**
1984-85	Canada	Can-Cup	8	5	6	11	....	....	....	0	....	....	....	....	....	....	....	....	....	....	....	....	....	....	....	....	....	....
	Quebec Nordiques	**NHL**	**69**	**55**	**40**	**95**	**45**	**27**	**72**	**55**	**17**	**0**	**6**	**257**	**21.4**	**120**	**40**	**71**	**1**	**10**	**17**	**11**	**10**	**21**	**17**	**7**	**0**	**0**
1985-86	**Quebec Nordiques**	**NHL**	**75**	**53**	**51**	**104**	**42**	**34**	**76**	**64**	**28**	**0**	**3**	**244**	**21.7**	**152**	**75**	**71**	**0**	**6**	**3**	**1**	**2**	**3**	**10**	**1**	**0**	**0**
1986-87	**Quebec Nordiques**	**NHL**	**75**	**49**	**47**	**96**	**42**	**34**	**76**	**61**	**17**	**0**	**6**	**276**	**17.8**	**139**	**63**	**92**	**4**	**–12**	**13**	**9**	**5**	**14**	**35**	**4**	**0**	**2**
	NHL All-Stars	RV-87	2	0	1	1	....	....	....	0	....	....	....	....	....	....	....	....	....	....	....	....	....	....	....	....	....	....
1987-88	Canada	Can-Cup	8	2	3	5	....	....	....	0	....	....	....	....	....	....	....	....	....	....	....	....	....	....	....	....	....	....
	Quebec Nordiques	**NHL**	**80**	**48**	**58**	**106**	**41**	**42**	**83**	**56**	**29**	**1**	**4**	**284**	**16.9**	**150**	**83**	**107**	**9**	**–31**	....	....	....	....	....	....	....	....
1988-89	**Quebec Nordiques**	**NHL**	**69**	**26**	**38**	**64**	**22**	**27**	**49**	**67**	**11**	**0**	**2**	**162**	**16.0**	**111**	**51**	**84**	**4**	**–20**	....	....	....	....	....	....	....	....
1989-90	**Quebec Nordiques**	**NHL**	**57**	**16**	**29**	**45**	**14**	**21**	**35**	**42**	**8**	**0**	**0**	**144**	**11.1**	**61**	**31**	**64**	**1**	**–33**	....	....	....	....	....	....	....	....
	Chicago Blackhawks	**NHL**	**8**	**4**	**1**	**5**	**3**	**1**	**4**	**9**	**1**	**1**	**0**	**10**	**40.0**	**6**	**2**	**4**	**1**	**1**	**14**	**2**	**4**	**6**	**6**	**0**	**0**	**0**
1990-91	**Chicago Blackhawks**	**NHL**	**74**	**27**	**38**	**65**	**25**	**29**	**54**	**65**	**9**	**0**	**1**	**167**	**16.2**	**93**	**36**	**31**	**1**	**27**	....	....	....	....	....	....	....	....
1991-92	**Chicago Blackhawks**	**NHL**	**75**	**22**	**41**	**63**	**20**	**31**	**51**	**69**	**9**	**0**	**4**	**176**	**12.5**	**89**	**34**	**40**	**5**	**20**	**9**	**3**	**4**	**7**	**6**	**0**	**0**	**1**
1992-93	**Chicago Blackhawks**	**NHL**	**63**	**23**	**21**	**44**	**19**	**14**	**33**	**43**	**10**	**0**	**5**	**125**	**18.4**	**62**	**29**	**25**	**2**	**10**	**3**	**0**	**1**	**1**	**0**	**0**	**0**	**0**
1993-94	**Chicago Blackhawks**	**NHL**	**56**	**16**	**14**	**30**	**15**	**11**	**26**	**26**	**3**	**0**	**6**	**120**	**13.3**	**49**	**19**	**29**	**0**	**1**	....	....	....	....	....	....	....	....
	NHL Totals		**1089**	**548**	**604**	**1152**	**457**	**425**	**882**	**825**	**178**	**16**	**64**	**3143**	**17.4**	**1615**	**593**	**1045**	**120**		**92**	**39**	**39**	**78**	**110**	**14**	**2**	**4**
	Other Major League Totals		78	28	30	58	....	....	....	65	....	....	....	....	....	....	....	....	....	....	....	....	....	....	....	....	....	....

QMJHL Second All-Star Team (1978) • NHL Second All-Star Team (1983, 1988) • NHL First All-Star Team (1984, 1986, 1987) • Played in NHL All-Star Game (1983, 1984, 1985, 1986, 1988)

Signed as an underage free agent by **Birmingham** (WHA), June, 1978. Traded to **Chicago** by **Quebec** with Greg Millen and Quebec's 6th round choice (Kevin St. Jacques) in 1991 Entry Draft for Mario Doyon, Everett Sanipass and Dan Vincelette, March 5, 1990. • Suffered career-ending head injury in game vs. Montreal, March 16, 1994.

• GOVEDARIS, Chris

Christopher LW – L. 6', 200 lbs. b: Toronto, Ont., 2/2/1970. Hartford's 1st, 11th overall, in 1988.

Season	Club	League	GP	G	A	Pts	AG	AA	APts	PIM	PP	SH	GW	S	%	TGF	PGF	TGA	PGA	+/–	GP	G	A	Pts	PIM	PP	SH	GW
1985-86	Toronto Young Nationals	MTHL	38	35	50	85	....	....	....	....	....	....	....	....	....	....	....	....	....	....	....	....	....	....	....	....	....	....
	St. Michael's Buzzers	OJHL-B	2	0	1	1	....	....	....	2	....	....	....	....	....	....	....	....	....	....	....	....	....	....	....	....	....	....
1986-87	Toronto Marlboros	OHL	64	36	28	64	....	....	....	148	....	....	....	....	....	....	....	....	....	....	....	....	....	....	....	....	....	....
1987-88	Toronto Marlboros	OHL	62	42	38	80	....	....	....	118	....	....	....	....	....	....	....	....	....	....	4	2	1	3	10	....	....	....
1988-89	Toronto Marlboros	OHL	49	41	38	79	....	....	....	117	....	....	....	....	....	....	....	....	....	....	6	2	3	5	0	....	....	....
1989-90	Dukes of Hamilton	OHL	23	11	21	32	....	....	....	53	....	....	....	....	....	....	....	....	....	....	....	....	....	....	....	....	....	....
	Hartford Whalers	**NHL**	**12**	**0**	**1**	**1**	**0**	**1**	**1**	**6**	**0**	**0**	**0**	**13**	**0.0**	**4**	**2**	**2**	**0**	**0**	**2**	**0**	**0**	**0**	**2**	**0**	**0**	**0**
	Binghamton Whalers	AHL	14	3	3	6	....	....	....	4	....	....	....	....	....	....	....	....	....	....	....	....	....	....	....	....	....	....
1990-91	**Hartford Whalers**	**NHL**	**14**	**1**	**3**	**4**	**1**	**2**	**3**	**4**	**0**	**0**	**1**	**10**	**10.0**	**7**	**2**	**10**	**1**	**–4**	....	....	....	....	....	....	....	....
	Springfield Indians	AHL	56	26	36	62	....	....	....	133	....	....	....	....	....	....	....	....	....	....	9	2	5	7	36	....	....	....
1991-92	Springfield Indians	AHL	43	14	25	39	....	....	....	55	....	....	....	....	....	....	....	....	....	....	11	3	2	5	25	....	....	....
1992-93	**Hartford Whalers**	**NHL**	**7**	**1**	**0**	**1**	**1**	**0**	**1**	**0**	**0**	**0**	**0**	**6**	**16.7**	**1**	**0**	**3**	**0**	**–2**	....	....	....	....	....	....	....	....
	Springfield Indians	AHL	65	31	24	55	....	....	....	58	....	....	....	....	....	....	....	....	....	....	15	7	4	11	18	....	....	....
1993-94	**Toronto Maple Leafs**	**NHL**	**12**	**2**	**2**	**4**	**2**	**2**	**4**	**14**	**0**	**0**	**0**	**16**	**12.5**	**5**	**0**	**1**	**0**	**4**	**2**	**0**	**0**	**0**	**0**	**0**	**0**	**0**
	St. John's Maple Leafs	AHL	62	35	35	70	....	....	....	76	....	....	....	....	....	....	....	....	....	....	11	6	5	11	22	....	....	....
1994-95	Milwaukee Admirals	IHL	54	34	25	59	....	....	....	71	....	....	....	....	....	....	....	....	....	....	....	....	....	....	....	....	....	....
	Adirondack Red Wings	AHL	24	19	11	30	....	....	....	34	....	....	....	....	....	....	....	....	....	....	4	2	1	3	10	....	....	....
	Canada	WC-A	8	1	0	1	....	....	....	6	....	....	....	....	....	....	....	....	....	....	....	....	....	....	....	....	....	....
1995-96	Minnesota Moose	IHL	81	31	36	67	....	....	....	133	....	....	....	....	....	....	....	....	....	....	....	....	....	....	....	....	....	....
1996-97	Eisbaren Berlin	Germany	48	24	22	46	....	....	....	115	....	....	....	....	....	....	....	....	....	....	8	4	2	6	10	....	....	....
1997-98	Eisbaren Berlin	Germany	45	19	24	43	....	....	....	40	....	....	....	....	....	....	....	....	....	....	10	2	6	8	10	....	....	....
1998-99	Eisbaren Berlin	Germany	49	24	21	45	....	....	....	50	....	....	....	....	....	....	....	....	....	....	8	3	2	5	8	....	....	....
	Eisbaren Berlin	EuroHL	6	2	2	4	....	....	....	6	....	....	....	....	....	....	....	....	....	....	6	1	3	4	8	....	....	....
99-2000	Eisbaren Berlin	Germany	47	19	25	44	....	....	....	47	....	....	....	....	....	....	....	....	....	....	....	....	....	....	....	....	....	....
	NHL Totals		**45**	**4**	**6**	**10**	**4**	**5**	**9**	**24**	**0**	**0**	**1**	**45**	**8.9**	**17**	**4**	**16**	**1**		**4**	**0**	**0**	**0**	**2**	**0**	**0**	**0**

Signed as a free agent by **Toronto**, September 16, 1993. Signed as a free agent by **Winnipeg**, August 14, 1995.

• GOYER, Gerry

Gerald Francis C – L. 6'2", 196 lbs. b: Belleville, Ont., 10/20/1936.

Season	Club	League	GP	G	A	Pts	AG	AA	APts	PIM	PP	SH	GW	S	%	TGF	PGF	TGA	PGA	+/–	GP	G	A	Pts	PIM	PP	SH	GW
1954-55	Pointe-Anne Hawks	OHA-I	STATISTICS NOT AVAILABLE																									
1955-56	Guelph Biltmores	OHA-Jr.	48	27	36	63	....	....	....	9	....	....	....	....	....	....	....	....	....	....	3	3	0	3	0	....	....	....
	Guelph Biltmores	Mem-Cup	6	0	1	1	....	....	....	0	....	....	....	....	....	....	....	....	....	....	....	....	....	....	....	....	....	....
1956-57	Guelph Biltmores	OHA-Jr.	52	17	20	37	....	....	....	12	....	....	....	....	....	....	....	....	....	....	10	4	5	9	8	....	....	....
	Belleville McFarlands	EOHL	1	0	0	0	....	....	....	0	....	....	....	....	....	....	....	....	....	....	....	....	....	....	....	....	....	....
	Guelph Biltmores	Mem-Cup	6	0	1	1	....	....	....	0	....	....	....	....	....	....	....	....	....	....	....	....	....	....	....	....	....	....
1957-58	Belleville McFarlands	EOHL	45	12	25	37	....	....	....	17	....	....	....	....	....	....	....	....	....	....	....	....	....	....	....	....	....	....
	Belleville McFarlands	Al-Cup	7	5	8	13	....	....	....	0	....	....	....	....	....	....	....	....	....	....	....	....	....	....	....	....	....	....

			REGULAR SEASON																		PLAYOFFS							
Season	Club	League	GP	G	A	Pts	AG	AA	APts	PIM	PP	SH	GW	S	%	TGF	PGF	TGA	PGA	+/–	GP	G	A	Pts	PIM	PP	SH	GW
1958-59	Kelowna Packers	OSHL	54	42	50	92				57																		
	Seattle Totems	WHL																			12	4	2	6	2			
1959-60	Seattle–Victoria Cougars	WHL	71	15	26	41				19											11	5	4	9	0			
1960-61	Victoria Cougars	WHL	70	31	46	77				28											5	0	4	4	0			
1961-62	Los Angeles Blades	WHL	53	29	41	70				24																		
1962-63	Portland Buckaroos	WHL	68	22	56	78				10											7	4	5	9	0			
1963-64	Portland Buckaroos	WHL	68	26	26	52				25											5	1	3	4	0			
1964-65	Portland Buckaroos	WHL	70	26	51	77				20											10	*7	8	*15	8			
1965-66	Portland Buckaroos	WHL	72	31	45	76				16											14	8	9	17	4			
1966-67	Portland Buckaroos	WHL	71	20	48	68				14											4	0	0	0	4			
1967-68	**Chicago Black Hawks**	**NHL**	**40**	**1**	**2**	**3**	**1**	**2**	**3**	**4**	**0**	**0**	**0**	**20**	**5.0**	**5**	**1**	**23**	**1**	**–18**	**3**	**0**	**0**	**0**	**2**	**0**	**0**	**0**
	Dallas Black Hawks	CPHL	5	1	5	6				2																		
1968-69	Portland Buckaroos	WHL	67	12	28	40				28											11	1	2	3	0			
1969-70	Portland Buckaroos	WHL	2	1	0	1				0																		
	Rochester Americans	AHL	5	2	5	7				2																		
	Vancouver Canucks	WHL	58	24	50	74				12											11	5	*16	*21	12			
1970-71	San Diego Gulls	WHL	72	24	67	91				39											6	1	4	5	8			
1971-72	San Diego Gulls	WHL	71	22	48	70				27											4	0	2	2	0			
1972-73	San Diego Gulls	WHL	70	28	41	69				36											6	0	1	1	13			
1973-74	San Diego Gulls	WHL	68	18	46	64				43											4	0	0	0	0			
1974-75	Cranbrook Royals	WIHL	45	23	57	80				49																		
1975-76	Cranbrook Royals	WIHL	25	6	23	29				23											12	6	16	22				
1976-77	Cranbrook Royals	WIHL	56	12	53	65				19																		
	NHL Totals		**40**	**1**	**2**	**3**	**1**	**2**	**3**	**4**	**0**	**0**	**0**	**20**	**5.0**	**5**	**1**	**23**	**1**		**3**	**0**	**0**	**0**	**2**	**0**	**0**	**0**

OSHL First All-Star Team (1959) • WHL Second All-Star Team (1971)

Claimed by **Toronto** from **LA Blades** (WHL) in Inter-League Draft, June 4, 1962. Traded to **Portland** (WHL) by **Toronto** for cash, September, 1962. Traded to **Chicago** by **Portland** (WHL) for cash, October, 1967. Traded to **Portland** (WHL) by **Chicago** for cash, July, 1968. Traded to **Vancouver** (WHL) by **Portland** (WHL) for cash, November 2, 1969. NHL rights transferred to **Vancouver** after NHL club purchased **Vancouver** (WHL) franchise, December 19, 1969. Traded to **San Diego** (WHL) by **Vancouver** for cash, September 4, 1970.

• GOYETTE, Phil

Philippe Joseph Georges C – L. 5'11", 170 lbs. b: Lachine, Que., 10/31/1933.

Season	Club	League	GP	G	A	Pts	AG	AA	APts	PIM	PP	SH	GW	S	%	TGF	PGF	TGA	PGA	+/–	GP	G	A	Pts	PIM	PP	SH	GW
1950-51	Montreal Nationale	QJHL	44	10	19	29				26											3	1	3	4	0			
1951-52	Montreal Nationale	QJHL	45	23	28	51				11											9	3	5	8	4			
1952-53	Montreal Jr. Canadiens	QJHL	44	23	36	59				13											7	2	4	6	0			
1953-54	Montreal Jr. Canadiens	QJHL	50	43	47	90				19											8	4	5	9	0			
1954-55	Cincinnati Mohawks	IHL	57	*41	51	*92				17											10	6	8	*14	2			
	Montreal Royals	QHL																			4	0	1	1	0			
1955-56	Montreal Royals	QHL	58	19	15	34				4											13	*10	7	17	0			
	Montreal Royals	Ed-Cup	6	1	3	4				0																		
1956-57♦	**Montreal Canadiens**	**NHL**	**14**	**3**	**4**	**7**	**4**	**4**	**8**	**0**											**10**	**2**	**1**	**3**	**4**			
	Montreal Royals	QHL	47	13	18	31				10																		
1957-58♦	**Montreal Canadiens**	**NHL**	**70**	**9**	**37**	**46**	**11**	**38**	**49**	**8**											**10**	**4**	**1**	**5**	**4**			
1958-59♦	**Montreal Canadiens**	**NHL**	**63**	**10**	**18**	**28**	**12**	**18**	**30**	**8**											**10**	**0**	**4**	**4**	**0**			
1959-60♦	**Montreal Canadiens**	**NHL**	**65**	**21**	**22**	**43**	**25**	**21**	**46**	**4**											**8**	**2**	**1**	**3**	**4**			
1960-61	**Montreal Canadiens**	**NHL**	**62**	**7**	**4**	**11**	**8**	**4**	**12**	**4**											**6**	**3**	**3**	**6**	**0**			
1961-62	**Montreal Canadiens**	**NHL**	**69**	**7**	**27**	**34**	**8**	**26**	**34**	**18**											**6**	**1**	**4**	**5**	**2**			
1962-63	**Montreal Canadiens**	**NHL**	**32**	**5**	**8**	**13**	**6**	**8**	**14**	**2**											**2**	**0**	**0**	**0**	**0**			
1963-64	**New York Rangers**	**NHL**	**67**	**24**	**41**	**65**	**30**	**43**	**73**	**15**																		
1964-65	**New York Rangers**	**NHL**	**52**	**12**	**34**	**46**	**14**	**35**	**49**	**6**																		
1965-66	**New York Rangers**	**NHL**	**60**	**11**	**31**	**42**	**12**	**30**	**42**	**6**																		
1966-67	**New York Rangers**	**NHL**	**70**	**12**	**49**	**61**	**14**	**48**	**62**	**6**											**4**	**1**	**0**	**1**	**0**			
1967-68	**New York Rangers**	**NHL**	**73**	**25**	**40**	**65**	**29**	**40**	**69**	**10**	**4**	**0**	**7**	**179**	**14.0**	**78**	**17**	**43**	**0**	**18**	**6**	**0**	**1**	**1**	**4**	**0**	**0**	**0**
1968-69	**New York Rangers**	**NHL**	**67**	**13**	**32**	**45**	**14**	**29**	**43**	**8**	**2**	**0**	**3**	**135**	**9.6**	**53**	**10**	**34**	**0**	**9**	**3**	**0**	**0**	**0**	**0**	**0**	**0**	**0**
1969-70	**St. Louis Blues**	**NHL**	**72**	**29**	**49**	**78**	**32**	**46**	**78**	**16**	**13**	**0**	**5**	**152**	**19.1**	**98**	**53**	**42**	**0**	**3**	**16**	**3**	**11**	**14**	**6**	**1**	**2**	**0**
1970-71	**Buffalo Sabres**	**NHL**	**60**	**15**	**46**	**61**	**15**	**39**	**54**	**6**	**9**	**0**	**1**	**119**	**12.6**	**75**	**39**	**53**	**2**	**–15**								
1971-72	**Buffalo Sabres**	**NHL**	**37**	**3**	**21**	**24**	**3**	**18**	**21**	**14**	**3**	**0**	**0**	**33**	**9.1**	**32**	**19**	**24**	**1**	**–10**								
	New York Rangers	**NHL**	**8**	**1**	**4**	**5**	**1**	**3**	**4**	**0**	**1**	**0**	**0**	**10**	**10.0**	**6**	**3**	**4**	**0**	**–1**	**13**	**1**	**3**	**4**	**2**	**1**	**0**	**0**
	NHL Totals		**941**	**207**	**467**	**674**	**238**	**450**	**688**	**131**											**94**	**17**	**29**	**46**	**26**			

IHL First All-Star Team (1955) • Won George H. Wilkinson Trophy (Top Scorer - IHL) (1955) • Won James Gatschene Memorial Trophy (MVP - IHL) (1955) • Won Lady Byng Trophy (1970)

Played in NHL All-Star Game (1957, 1958, 1959, 1961)

Claimed by **Montreal** from **Montreal Royals** (QHL) in Inter-League Draft, June 5, 1956. Traded to **NY Rangers** by **Montreal** with Don Marshall and Jacques Plante for Gump Worsley, Dave Balon, Leon Rochefort and Len Ronson, June 4, 1963. Traded to **St. Louis** by **NY Rangers** for St. Louis' 1st round choice (Andre Dupont) in 1969 Amateur Draft, June 10, 1969. Claimed by **Buffalo** from **St. Louis** in Expansion Draft, June 10, 1970. Traded to **NY Rangers** by **Buffalo** for cash, March 5, 1972.

• GRADIN, Thomas

Thomas K. C – R. 5'11", 176 lbs. b: Solleftea, Sweden, 2/18/1956. Chicago's 3rd, 45th overall, in 1976.

Season	Club	League	GP	G	A	Pts	AG	AA	APts	PIM	PP	SH	GW	S	%	TGF	PGF	TGA	PGA	+/–	GP	G	A	Pts	PIM	PP	SH	GW
1970-71	Langsele AIK	Sweden-3	14	11	2	13																						
1971-72	MoDo AIK	Sweden	DID NOT PLAY																									
1972-73	MoDo AIK	Sweden	11	5	1	6				4											6	3	1	4	2			
	MoDo AIK	Sweden-Q	8	6	4	10				2																		
	Sweden	EJC-A	5	2	1	3				2																		
1973-74	MoDo AIK	Sweden	14	4	4	8				2											13	5	8	13	2			
	MoDo AIK	Sweden-Q	13	5	8	13				2																		
	Sweden	WJC-A	5	3	3	6				2																		
	Sweden	EJC-A	5	5	5	10				2																		
1974-75	MoDo AIK	Sweden	29	16	15	31				16																		
	Sweden	WJC-A																										
	Sweden	EJC-A	5	4	4	8				0																		
	MoDo AIK	Sweden-Jr.																			2	2	4	6	2			
1975-76	MoDo AIK	Sweden	35	16	23	39				23																		
	Sweden	WJC-A	4	3	1	4				2																		
1976-77	AIK Solna Stockholm	Sweden	36	16	12	28				8																		
1977-78	AIK Solna Stockholm	Sweden	36	22	15	37				22											6	0	*5	5	14			
	Sweden	WEC-A	9	2	1	3				0																		
1978-79	**Vancouver Canucks**	**NHL**	**76**	**20**	**31**	**51**	**17**	**22**	**39**	**22**	**4**	**0**	**4**	**105**	**19.0**	**61**	**16**	**59**	**2**	**–12**	**3**	**4**	**1**	**5**	**4**	**0**	**0**	**0**
1979-80	**Vancouver Canucks**	**NHL**	**80**	**30**	**45**	**75**	**26**	**33**	**59**	**22**	**7**	**0**	**2**	**146**	**20.5**	**106**	**31**	**65**	**4**	**14**	**4**	**0**	**2**	**2**	**0**	**0**	**0**	**0**
1980-81	**Vancouver Canucks**	**NHL**	**79**	**21**	**48**	**69**	**16**	**32**	**48**	**34**	**4**	**0**	**1**	**158**	**13.3**	**92**	**23**	**67**	**0**	**2**	**3**	**1**	**3**	**4**	**0**	**0**	**0**	**0**
1981-82	Sweden	Can-Cup	5	1	2	3				4																		
	Vancouver Canucks	**NHL**	**76**	**37**	**49**	**86**	**29**	**33**	**62**	**32**	**6**	**3**	**4**	**183**	**20.2**	**116**	**33**	**91**	**23**	**15**	**17**	**9**	**10**	**19**	**10**	**4**	**0**	**0**
	Sweden	Nat-Team	11	3	4	7				4																		
1982-83	**Vancouver Canucks**	**NHL**	**80**	**32**	**54**	**86**	**26**	**38**	**64**	**61**	**12**	**2**	**4**	**175**	**18.3**	**120**	**46**	**105**	**14**	**–17**	**4**	**1**	**3**	**4**	**2**	**0**	**0**	**0**
1983-84	**Vancouver Canucks**	**NHL**	**75**	**21**	**57**	**78**	**17**	**39**	**56**	**32**	**11**	**1**	**5**	**170**	**12.4**	**117**	**39**	**97**	**17**	**–2**	**4**	**0**	**1**	**1**	**2**	**0**	**0**	**0**
1984-85	Sweden	Can-Cup	8	2	2	4				6																		
	Vancouver Canucks	**NHL**	**76**	**22**	**42**	**64**	**18**	**29**	**47**	**43**	**3**	**0**	**3**	**152**	**14.5**	**97**	**24**	**111**	**16**	**–22**								
1985-86	**Vancouver Canucks**	**NHL**	**71**	**14**	**27**	**41**	**11**	**18**	**29**	**34**	**2**	**1**	**3**	**121**	**11.6**	**77**	**20**	**97**	**24**	**–16**	**3**	**2**	**1**	**3**	**2**	**0**	**0**	**0**
1986-87	**Boston Bruins**	**NHL**	**64**	**12**	**31**	**43**	**10**	**23**	**33**	**18**	**2**	**3**	**3**	**87**	**13.8**	**60**	**12**	**55**	**11**	**4**	**4**	**0**	**4**	**4**	**0**	**0**	**0**	**0**
1987-88	AIK Solna Stockholm	Sweden	38	15	18	33				14											5	1	1	2	2			
1988-89	AIK Solna Stockholm	Sweden	33	11	21	32				40											2	0	1	1	2			
1989-90	AIK Solna Stockholm	Sweden	35	14	15	29				14											3	2	0	2	2			

Season	Club	League	REGULAR SEASON																		PLAYOFFS							
			GP	G	A	Pts	AG	AA	APts	PIM	PP	SH	GW	S	%	TGF	PGF	TGA	PGA	+/–	GP	G	A	Pts	PIM	PP	SH	GW
1990-1996			OUT OF HOCKEY – RETIRED																									
1996-97	Vasteras IK	Sweden	2	0	1	1	....	....	....	0	....	....	....	....	....	....	....	....	....	....	....	....	....	....	....	....	....	....
	Vasteras IK	Sweden-Q	10	1	2	3	....	....	....	2	....	....	....	....	....	....	....	....	....	....	....	....	....	....	....	....	....	....
	NHL Totals		**677**	**209**	**384**	**593**	**170**	**267**	**437**	**298**	**51**	**10**	**29**	**1297**	**16.1**	**846**	**244**	**747**	**111**		**42**	**17**	**25**	**42**	**20**	**4**	**0**	**0**

Named Best Forward at EJC-A (1974) • WJC-A All-Star Team (1974) • Played in NHL All-Star Game (1985)

• Missed entire 1971-72 Swedish Elite League season after transfer from Langsele AIK to MoDo AIK was refused (7 votes to 3) by Swedish ice Hockey Federation. Rights traded to **Vancouver** by **Chicago** for Vancouver's 2nd round choice (Steve Ludzik) in 1980 Entry Draft, June 14, 1978. Signed as a free agent by **Boston**, June 24, 1986.

• GRAHAM, Dirk

Dirk Milton W – R. 5'11", 198 lbs. b: Regina, Sask., 7/29/1959. Vancouver's 5th, 89th overall, in 1979.

Season	Club	League	GP	G	A	Pts	AG	AA	APts	PIM	PP	SH	GW	S	%	TGF	PGF	TGA	PGA	+/–	GP	G	A	Pts	PIM	PP	SH	GW
1975-76	Regina Blues	SJHL	54	36	32	68	....	....	....	82	....	....	....	....	....	....	....	....	....	....	....	....	....	....	....	....	....	....
	Regina Pats	WCJHL	2	0	0	0	....	....	....	0	....	....	....	....	....	....	....	....	....	....	6	1	1	2	5	....	....	....
1976-77	Regina Pats	WCJHL	65	37	28	65	....	....	....	66	....	....	....	....	....	....	....	....	....	....	....	....	....	....	....	....	....	....
1977-78	Regina Pats	WCJHL	72	49	61	110	....	....	....	87	....	....	....	....	....	....	....	....	....	....	13	15	19	34	37	....	....	....
1978-79	Regina Pats	WHL	71	48	60	108	....	....	....	252	....	....	....	....	....	....	....	....	....	....	....	....	....	....	....	....	....	....
1979-80	Dallas Black Hawks	CHL	62	17	15	32	....	....	....	96	....	....	....	....	....	....	....	....	....	....	....	....	....	....	....	....	....	....
1980-81	Fort Wayne Komets	IHL	6	1	2	3	....	....	....	12	....	....	....	....	....	....	....	....	....	....	....	....	....	....	....	....	....	....
	Toledo Goaldiggers	IHL	61	40	45	85	....	....	....	88	....	....	....	....	....	....	....	....	....	....	....	....	....	....	....	....	....	....
1981-82	Toledo Goaldiggers	IHL	72	49	56	105	....	....	....	68	....	....	....	....	....	....	....	....	....	....	13	10	11	*21	8	....	....	....
1982-83	Toledo Goaldiggers	IHL	78	70	55	125	....	....	....	88	....	....	....	....	....	....	....	....	....	....	11	13	7	*20	30	....	....	....
1983-84	**Minnesota North Stars**	**NHL**	**6**	**1**	**1**	**2**	**1**	**1**	**2**	**0**	**0**	**0**	**0**	**10**	**10.0**	**2**	**0**	**2**	**1**	**1**	**1**	**0**	**0**	**0**	**2**	**0**	**0**	**0**
	Salt Lake Golden Eagles	CHL	57	37	57	94	....	....	....	72	....	....	....	....	....	....	....	....	....	....	5	3	8	11	2	....	....	....
1984-85	**Minnesota North Stars**	**NHL**	**36**	**12**	**11**	**23**	**10**	**7**	**17**	**23**	**3**	**0**	**1**	**81**	**14.8**	**33**	**7**	**47**	**6**	**–15**	**9**	**0**	**4**	**4**	**7**	**0**	**0**	**0**
	Springfield Indians	AHL	37	20	28	48	....	....	....	41	....	....	....	....	....	....	....	....	....	....	....	....	....	....	....	....	....	....
1985-86	**Minnesota North Stars**	**NHL**	**80**	**22**	**33**	**55**	**18**	**22**	**40**	**87**	**0**	**4**	**3**	**173**	**12.7**	**77**	**13**	**105**	**35**	**–6**	**5**	**3**	**1**	**4**	**2**	**0**	**1**	**2**
1986-87	**Minnesota North Stars**	**NHL**	**76**	**25**	**29**	**54**	**22**	**21**	**43**	**142**	**6**	**5**	**2**	**197**	**12.7**	**73**	**17**	**100**	**42**	**–2**	....	....	....	....	....	....	....	....
	Canada	WEC-A	9	0	3	3	....	....	....	8	....	....	....	....	....	....	....	....	....	....	....	....	....	....	....	....	....	....
1987-88	**Minnesota North Stars**	**NHL**	**28**	**7**	**5**	**12**	**6**	**4**	**10**	**39**	**4**	**0**	**0**	**66**	**10.6**	**20**	**9**	**29**	**7**	**–11**	....	....	....	....	....	....	....	....
	Chicago Blackhawks	**NHL**	**42**	**17**	**19**	**36**	**14**	**14**	**28**	**32**	**6**	**1**	**2**	**107**	**15.9**	**48**	**13**	**47**	**16**	**4**	**4**	**1**	**2**	**3**	**4**	**0**	**0**	**0**
1988-89	**Chicago Blackhawks**	**NHL**	**80**	**33**	**45**	**78**	**28**	**32**	**60**	**89**	**5**	**10**	**5**	**217**	**15.2**	**106**	**23**	**127**	**52**	**8**	**16**	**2**	**4**	**6**	**38**	**1**	**0**	**0**
1989-90	**Chicago Blackhawks**	**NHL**	**73**	**22**	**32**	**54**	**19**	**23**	**42**	**102**	**2**	**3**	**1**	**180**	**12.2**	**83**	**19**	**95**	**32**	**1**	**5**	**1**	**5**	**6**	**2**	**0**	**1**	**0**
1990-91	**Chicago Blackhawks**	**NHL**	**80**	**24**	**21**	**45**	**22**	**16**	**38**	**88**	**4**	**6**	**7**	**189**	**12.7**	**71**	**16**	**74**	**31**	**12**	**6**	**1**	**2**	**3**	**17**	**0**	**0**	**0**
1991-92	Canada	Can-Cup	8	3	1	4	....	....	....	0	....	....	....	....	....	....	....	....	....	....	....	....	....	....	....	....	....	....
	Chicago Blackhawks	**NHL**	**80**	**17**	**30**	**47**	**15**	**23**	**38**	**89**	**6**	**1**	**1**	**222**	**7.7**	**68**	**20**	**92**	**39**	**–5**	**18**	**7**	**5**	**12**	**8**	**0**	**0**	**1**
1992-93	**Chicago Blackhawks**	**NHL**	**84**	**20**	**17**	**37**	**17**	**12**	**29**	**139**	**1**	**2**	**5**	**187**	**10.7**	**57**	**5**	**89**	**37**	**0**	**4**	**0**	**0**	**0**	**0**	**0**	**0**	**0**
1993-94	**Chicago Blackhawks**	**NHL**	**67**	**15**	**18**	**33**	**14**	**14**	**28**	**45**	**0**	**2**	**5**	**122**	**12.3**	**50**	**4**	**59**	**26**	**13**	**6**	**0**	**1**	**1**	**4**	**0**	**0**	**0**
1994-95	**Chicago Blackhawks**	**NHL**	**40**	**4**	**9**	**13**	**7**	**13**	**20**	**42**	**1**	**1**	**0**	**68**	**5.9**	**22**	**4**	**28**	**12**	**2**	**16**	**2**	**3**	**5**	**8**	**0**	**0**	**1**
	NHL Totals		**772**	**219**	**270**	**489**	**193**	**202**	**395**	**917**	**38**	**35**	**32**	**1819**	**12.0**	**710**	**150**	**894**	**336**		**90**	**17**	**27**	**44**	**92**	**1**	**2**	**4**

IHL Second All-Star Team (1981) • IHL First All-Star Team (1983) • CHL First All-Star Team (1984) • Won Frank J. Selke Trophy (1991)

Signed as a free agent by **Minnesota**, August 17, 1983. Traded to **Chicago** by **Minnesota** for Curt Fraser, January 4, 1988.

• GRAHAM, Pat

Pat Thomas LW – L. 6'1", 190 lbs. b: Toronto, Ont., 5/25/1961. Pittsburgh's 5th, 114th overall, in 1980.

Season	Club	League	GP	G	A	Pts	AG	AA	APts	PIM	PP	SH	GW	S	%	TGF	PGF	TGA	PGA	+/–	GP	G	A	Pts	PIM	PP	SH	GW
1976-77	St. Michael's Buzzers	OHA-B	30	20	28	48	....	....	....	100	....	....	....	....	....	....	....	....	....	....	....	....	....	....	....	....	....	....
1977-78	Toronto Marlboros	OMJHL	50	5	6	11	....	....	....	41	....	....	....	....	....	....	....	....	....	....	5	3	1	4	2	....	....	....
1978-79	Toronto Marlboros	OMJHL	49	10	12	22	....	....	....	102	....	....	....	....	....	....	....	....	....	....	3	0	1	1	0	....	....	....
1979-80	Toronto Marlboros	OMJHL	2	1	0	1	....	....	....	16	....	....	....	....	....	....	....	....	....	....	10	3	5	8	30	....	....	....
	Niagara Falls Flyers	OMJHL	59	31	32	63	....	....	....	75	....	....	....	....	....	....	....	....	....	....	....	....	....	....	....	....	....	....
1980-81	Niagara Falls Flyers	OMJHL	61	40	54	94	....	....	....	118	....	....	....	....	....	....	....	....	....	....	12	4	7	11	40	....	....	....
1981-82	**Pittsburgh Penguins**	**NHL**	**42**	**6**	**8**	**14**	**5**	**5**	**10**	**55**	**0**	**0**	**1**	**51**	**11.8**	**27**	**1**	**28**	**1**	**–1**	**4**	**0**	**0**	**0**	**2**	**0**	**0**	**0**
	Erie Blades	AHL	9	4	4	8	....	....	....	4	....	....	....	....	....	....	....	....	....	....	....	....	....	....	....	....	....	....
1982-83	**Pittsburgh Penguins**	**NHL**	**20**	**1**	**5**	**6**	**1**	**3**	**4**	**16**	**1**	**0**	**0**	**25**	**4.0**	**12**	**1**	**17**	**0**	**–6**	....	....	....	....	....	....	....	....
	Baltimore Skipjacks	AHL	57	16	16	32	....	....	....	32	....	....	....	....	....	....	....	....	....	....	....	....	....	....	....	....	....	....
1983-84	**Toronto Maple Leafs**	**NHL**	**41**	**4**	**4**	**8**	**3**	**3**	**6**	**65**	**0**	**0**	**0**	**46**	**8.7**	**12**	**0**	**21**	**0**	**–9**	....	....	....	....	....	....	....	....
	St. Catharines Saints	AHL	25	7	7	14	....	....	....	18	....	....	....	....	....	....	....	....	....	....	7	1	2	3	9	....	....	....
1984-85	HC Braunlage	Germany-2	24	12	8	20	....	....	....	57	....	....	....	....	....	....	....	....	....	....	....	....	....	....	....	....	....	....
	Adirondack Red Wings	AHL	27	5	5	10	....	....	....	19	....	....	....	....	....	....	....	....	....	....	....	....	....	....	....	....	....	....
	NHL Totals		**103**	**11**	**17**	**28**	**9**	**11**	**20**	**136**	**1**	**0**	**1**	**122**	**9.0**	**51**	**2**	**66**	**1**		**4**	**0**	**0**	**0**	**2**	**0**	**0**	**0**

Traded to **Toronto** by **Pittsburgh** with Nick Ricci for Rocky Saganiuk and Vincent Tremblay, August 15, 1983.

• GRAHAM, Rod

Rodney Douglas LW – L. 6', 185 lbs. b: London, Ont., 8/19/1946.

Season	Club	League	GP	G	A	Pts	AG	AA	APts	PIM	PP	SH	GW	S	%	TGF	PGF	TGA	PGA	+/–	GP	G	A	Pts	PIM	PP	SH	GW
1967-68	Kingston Aces	OHA-Sr.	37	15	23	38	....	....	....	46	....	....	....	....	....	....	....	....	....	....	....	....	....	....	....	....	....	....
	Oklahoma City Blazers	CPHL	....	....	....	....	....	....	....	....	....	....	....	....	....	....	....	....	....	....	4	0	2	2	2	....	....	....
1968-69	Kingston Aces	OHA-Sr.	39	26	32	58	....	....	....	94	....	....	....	....	....	....	....	....	....	....	....	....	....	....	....	....	....	....
1969-70	Kingston Aces	OHA-Sr.	32	11	14	25	....	....	....	81	....	....	....	....	....	....	....	....	....	....	....	....	....	....	....	....	....	....
1970-71	Kingston Aces	OHA-Sr.	32	24	19	43	....	....	....	65	....	....	....	....	....	....	....	....	....	....	....	....	....	....	....	....	....	....
1971-72	Woodstock Royals	OHA-Sr.	39	6	20	26	....	....	....	28	....	....	....	....	....	....	....	....	....	....	....	....	....	....	....	....	....	....
1972-73	Rochester Americans	AHL	70	16	22	38	....	....	....	83	....	....	....	....	....	....	....	....	....	....	6	2	1	3	5	....	....	....
1973-74	Rochester Americans	AHL	74	10	41	51	....	....	....	88	....	....	....	....	....	....	....	....	....	....	5	2	1	3	5	....	....	....
1974-75	**Boston Bruins**	**NHL**	**14**	**2**	**1**	**3**	**2**	**1**	**3**	**7**	**1**	**0**	**0**	**7**	**28.6**	**6**	**1**	**5**	**0**	**0**	....	....	....	....	....	....	....	....
	Rochester Americans	AHL	57	12	22	34	....	....	....	97	....	....	....	....	....	....	....	....	....	....	11	1	2	3	20	....	....	....
1975-76	Springfield Indians	AHL	70	20	35	55	....	....	....	74	....	....	....	....	....	....	....	....	....	....	....	....	....	....	....	....	....	....
1976-77	Rochester Americans	AHL	70	5	22	27	....	....	....	77	....	....	....	....	....	....	....	....	....	....	12	1	4	5	6	....	....	....
1977-78	Rochester Americans	AHL	73	7	12	19	....	....	....	39	....	....	....	....	....	....	....	....	....	....	6	0	2	2	9	....	....	....
	NHL Totals		**14**	**2**	**1**	**3**	**2**	**1**	**3**	**7**	**1**	**0**	**0**	**7**	**28.6**	**6**	**1**	**5**	**0**		....	....	....	....	....	....	....	....

Signed as a free agent by **Rochester** (AHL), September, 1972. Rights transferred to **Boston** after NHL club signed affiliate agreement with **Rochester** (AHL), June 14, 1974.

• GRANATO, Tony

Anthony Lewis RW – R. 5'10", 185 lbs. b: Downers Grove, IL, 7/25/1964. NY Rangers' 5th, 120th overall, in 1982.

Season	Club	League	GP	G	A	Pts	AG	AA	APts	PIM	PP	SH	GW	S	%	TGF	PGF	TGA	PGA	+/–	GP	G	A	Pts	PIM	PP	SH	GW
1982-83	Northwood Huskies	Hi-School	34	32	60	92	....	....	....	....	....	....	....	....	....	....	....	....	....	....	....	....	....	....	....	....	....	....
	United States	WJC-A	7	4	0	4	....	....	....	4	....	....	....	....	....	....	....	....	....	....	....	....	....	....	....	....	....	....
1983-84	University of Wisconsin	WCHA	35	14	17	31	....	....	....	48	....	....	....	....	....	....	....	....	....	....	....	....	....	....	....	....	....	....
	United States	WJC-A	7	1	3	4	....	....	....	6	....	....	....	....	....	....	....	....	....	....	....	....	....	....	....	....	....	....
1984-85	University of Wisconsin	WCHA	42	33	34	67	....	....	....	94	....	....	....	....	....	....	....	....	....	....	....	....	....	....	....	....	....	....
	United States	WEC-A	9	4	2	6	....	....	....	10	....	....	....	....	....	....	....	....	....	....	....	....	....	....	....	....	....	....
1985-86	University of Wisconsin	WCHA	33	25	24	49	....	....	....	36	....	....	....	....	....	....	....	....	....	....	....	....	....	....	....	....	....	....
	United States	WEC-A	8	2	7	9	....	....	....	8	....	....	....	....	....	....	....	....	....	....	....	....	....	....	....	....	....	....
1986-87	University of Wisconsin	WCHA	42	28	45	73	....	....	....	64	....	....	....	....	....	....	....	....	....	....	....	....	....	....	....	....	....	....
	United States	WEC-A	9	2	3	5	....	....	....	12	....	....	....	....	....	....	....	....	....	....	....	....	....	....	....	....	....	....
1987-88	United States	Nat-Team	49	40	31	71	....	....	....	55	....	....	....	....	....	....	....	....	....	....	....	....	....	....	....	....	....	....
	United States	Olympics	6	1	7	8	....	....	....	4	....	....	....	....	....	....	....	....	....	....	....	....	....	....	....	....	....	....
	Colorado Rangers	IHL	22	13	14	27	....	....	....	36	....	....	....	....	....	....	....	....	....	....	8	9	4	13	16	....	....	....
1988-89	**New York Rangers**	**NHL**	**78**	**36**	**27**	**63**	**31**	**19**	**50**	**140**	**4**	**4**	**3**	**234**	**15.4**	**88**	**13**	**92**	**34**	**17**	**4**	**1**	**1**	**2**	**21**	**0**	**0**	**0**
1989-90	**New York Rangers**	**NHL**	**37**	**7**	**18**	**25**	**6**	**13**	**19**	**77**	**1**	**0**	**0**	**79**	**8.9**	**36**	**11**	**35**	**11**	**1**								
	Los Angeles Kings	**NHL**	**19**	**5**	**6**	**11**	**4**	**4**	**8**	**45**	**1**	**0**	**0**	**41**	**12.2**	**21**	**6**	**23**	**6**	**–2**	**10**	**5**	**4**	**9**	**12**	**2**	**1**	**2**
1990-91	**Los Angeles Kings**	**NHL**	**68**	**30**	**34**	**64**	**28**	**26**	**54**	**154**	**11**	**1**	**3**	**197**	**15.2**	**100**	**26**	**66**	**14**	**22**	**12**	**1**	**4**	**5**	**28**	**0**	**0**	**0**
1991-92	United States	Can-Cup	7	1	2	3	....	....	....	12	....	....	....	....	....	....	....	....	....	....	....	....	....	....	....	....	....	....
	Los Angeles Kings	**NHL**	**80**	**39**	**29**	**68**	**36**	**22**	**58**	**187**	**7**	**2**	**8**	**223**	**17.5**	**103**	**30**	**85**	**16**	**4**	**6**	**1**	**5**	**6**	**10**	**0**	**0**	**0**
1992-93	**Los Angeles Kings**	**NHL**	**81**	**37**	**45**	**82**	**31**	**31**	**62**	**171**	**14**	**2**	**6**	**247**	**15.0**	**121**	**47**	**102**	**27**	**–1**	**24**	**6**	**11**	**17**	**50**	**1**	**0**	**1**
1993-94	**Los Angeles Kings**	**NHL**	**50**	**7**	**14**	**21**	**6**	**11**	**17**	**150**	**2**	**0**	**0**	**117**	**6.0**	**43**	**6**	**45**	**6**	**–2**	....	....	....	....	....	....	....	....

Season	Club	League	REGULAR SEASON GP	G	A	Pts	AG	AA	APts	PIM	PP	SH	GW	S	%	TGF	PGF	TGA	PGA	+/–	PLAYOFFS GP	G	A	Pts	PIM	PP	SH	GW
1994-95	**Los Angeles Kings**	**NHL**	**33**	**13**	**11**	**24**	**23**	**16**	**39**	**68**	**2**	**0**	**3**	**106**	**12.3**	**33**	**6**	**25**	**7**	**9**	....	....	....	....	....	....	....	....
1995-96	**Los Angeles Kings**	**NHL**	**49**	**17**	**18**	**35**	**17**	**15**	**32**	**46**	**5**	**0**	**1**	**156**	**10.9**	**45**	**14**	**45**	**9**	**–5**	....	....	....	....	....	....	....	....
1996-97	**San Jose Sharks**	**NHL**	**76**	**25**	**15**	**40**	**26**	**13**	**39**	**159**	**5**	**1**	**4**	**231**	**10.8**	**68**	**18**	**73**	**16**	**–7**	....	....	....	....	....	....	....	....
1997-98	**San Jose Sharks**	**NHL**	**59**	**16**	**9**	**25**	**19**	**9**	**28**	**70**	**3**	**0**	**2**	**119**	**13.4**	**41**	**8**	**36**	**6**	**3**	**1**	**0**	**0**	**0**	**0**	**0**	**0**	**0**
1998-99	**San Jose Sharks**	**NHL**	**35**	**6**	**6**	**12**	**7**	**6**	**13**	**54**	**0**	**1**	**1**	**65**	**9.2**	**20**	**5**	**11**	**0**	**4**	**6**	**1**	**1**	**2**	**2**	**0**	**0**	**0**
99-2000	**San Jose Sharks**	**NHL**	**48**	**6**	**7**	**13**	**7**	**6**	**13**	**39**	**1**	**0**	**0**	**67**	**9.0**	**19**	**1**	**16**	**0**	**2**	**12**	**0**	**1**	**1**	**14**	**0**	**0**	**0**
	NHL Totals		**713**	**244**	**239**	**483**	**241**	**191**	**432**	**1360**	**56**	**11**	**31**	**1882**	**13.0**	**738**	**191**	**654**	**152**		**75**	**15**	**27**	**42**	**137**	**3**	**1**	**3**

WCHA Second All-Star Team (1985, 1987) • NCAA West Second All-American Team (1985, 1987) • NHL All-Rookie Team (1989) • Won Bill Masterton Memorial Trophy (1997) • Played in NHL All-Star Game (1997)

Traded to **LA Kings** by **NY Rangers** with Tomas Sandstrom for Bernie Nicholls, January 20, 1990. Signed as a free agent by **San Jose**, August 15, 1996.

• GRAND-PIERRE, Jean-Luc

Jean-Luc D. D – R. 6'3", 207 lbs. b: Montreal, Que., 2/2/1977. St. Louis' 6th, 179th overall, in 1995.

Season	Club	League	GP	G	A	Pts	AG	AA	APts	PIM	PP	SH	GW	S	%	TGF	PGF	TGA	PGA	+/–	GP	G	A	Pts	PIM	PP	SH	GW
1993-94	Beauport Harfangs	QMJHL	46	1	4	5	....	....	....	27	....	....	....	....	....	....	....	....	....	....	1	0	0	0	0	....	....	....
1994-95	Val d'Or Foreurs	QMJHL	59	10	13	23	....	....	....	126	....	....	....	....	....	....	....	....	....	....	....	....	....	....	....	....	....	....
1995-96	Val d'Or Foreurs	QMJHL	67	13	21	34	....	....	....	209	....	....	....	....	....	....	....	....	....	....	13	1	4	5	47	....	....	....
1996-97	Val d'Or Foreurs	QMJHL	58	9	24	33	....	....	....	186	....	....	....	....	....	....	....	....	....	....	13	5	8	13	46	....	....	....
1997-98	Rochester Americans	AHL	75	4	6	10	....	....	....	211	....	....	....	....	....	....	....	....	....	....	4	0	0	0	2	....	....	....
1998-99	**Buffalo Sabres**	**NHL**	**16**	**0**	**1**	**1**	**0**	**1**	**1**	**17**	**0**	**0**	**0**	**11**	**0.0**	**9**	**0**	**9**	**0**	**0**	....	....	....	....	....	....	....	....
	Rochester Americans	AHL	55	5	4	9	....	....	....	90	....	....	....	....	....	....	....	....	....	....	....	....	....	....	....	....	....	....
99-2000	**Buffalo Sabres**	**NHL**	**11**	**0**	**0**	**0**	**0**	**0**	**0**	**15**	**0**	**0**	**0**	**11**	....	....	....	....	....	....	....	....	....	....	....	....	....	....
	Rochester Americans	AHL	62	5	8	13	....	....	....	124	....	....	....	....	....	....	....	....	....	....	17	0	1	1	40	....	....	....
	NHL Totals		**27**	**0**	**1**	**1**	**0**	**1**	**1**	**32**	**0**	**0**	**0**	**22**	**0.0**	**9**	**0**	**9**	**0**		....	....	....	....	....	....	....	....

Traded to **Buffalo** by **St. Louis** with Ottawa's 2nd round choice (previously acquired, Buffalo selected Cory Sarich) in 1996 Entry Draft and St. Louis' 3rd round choice (Maxim Afinogenov) in 1997 Entry Draft for Yuri Khmylev and Buffalo's 8th round choice (Andrei Podkonicky) in 1996 Entry Draft, March 20, 1996. Traded to **Columbus** by **Buffalo** with Matt Davidson, San Jose's 5th round choice (previously acquired, Columbus selected Tyler Kolarik) in 2000 Entry Draft and Buffalo's 5th round choice in 2001 Entry Draft to complete Expansion Draft agreement which had Columbus select Geoff Sanderson and Dwayne Roloson from Buffalo, June 23, 2000.

• GRANT, Danny

Daniel Frederick RW – L. 5'10", 188 lbs. b: Fredericton, N.B., 2/21/1946.

Season	Club	League	GP	G	A	Pts	AG	AA	APts	PIM	PP	SH	GW	S	%	TGF	PGF	TGA	PGA	+/–	GP	G	A	Pts	PIM	PP	SH	GW
1959-60	Barkers Point Aces	NBAHA	6	23	3	26	....	....	....	0	....	....	....	....	....	....	....	....	....	....	....	....	....	....	....	....	....	....
1960-61	Fredericton Bears	NBAHA	10	17	10	27	....	....	....	4	....	....	....	....	....	....	....	....	....	....	....	....	....	....	....	....	....	....
1961-62	Fredericton Canadians	YCHL	13	*12	2	*14	....	....	....	....	....	....	....	....	....	....	....	....	....	....	2	4	1	5	0	....	....	....
1962-63	Peterborough Petes	OHA-Jr.	50	12	9	21	....	....	....	8	....	....	....	....	....	....	....	....	....	....	6	0	1	1	0	....	....	....
1963-64	Peterborough Petes	OHA-Jr.	44	18	21	39	....	....	....	20	....	....	....	....	....	....	....	....	....	....	5	2	2	4	4	....	....	....
1964-65	Peterborough Petes	OHA-Jr.	56	47	59	106	....	....	....	23	....	....	....	....	....	....	....	....	....	....	12	7	7	14	4	....	....	....
	Quebec Aces	AHL	1	0	1	1	....	....	....	0	....	....	....	....	....	....	....	....	....	....	....	....	....	....	....	....	....	....
1965-66	Peterborough Petes	OHA-Jr.	48	*44	52	96	....	....	....	34	....	....	....	....	....	....	....	....	....	....	4	2	5	7	10	....	....	....
	Montreal Canadiens	**NHL**	**1**	**0**	**0**	**0**	**0**	**0**	**0**	**0**	....	....	....	....	....	....	....	....	....	....	....	....	....	....	....	....	....	....
1966-67	Houston Apollos	CPHL	64	22	28	50	....	....	....	29	....	....	....	....	....	....	....	....	....	....	6	4	4	8	2	....	....	....
1967-68♦	**Montreal Canadiens**	**NHL**	**22**	**3**	**4**	**7**	**3**	**4**	**7**	**10**	**0**	**0**	**0**	**16**	**18.8**	**11**	**2**	**6**	**0**	**3**	**10**	**0**	**3**	**3**	**5**	**0**	**0**	**0**
	Houston Apollos	CPHL	19	14	8	22	....	....	....	6	....	....	....	....	....	....	....	....	....	....	....	....	....	....	....	....	....	....
1968-69	**Minnesota North Stars**	**NHL**	**75**	**34**	**31**	**65**	**36**	**28**	**64**	**46**	**11**	**0**	**1**	**189**	**18.0**	**77**	**21**	**68**	**0**	**–12**	....	....	....	....	....	....	....	....
1969-70	**Minnesota North Stars**	**NHL**	**76**	**29**	**28**	**57**	**32**	**26**	**58**	**23**	**14**	**0**	**2**	**247**	**11.7**	**86**	**48**	**51**	**0**	**–13**	**6**	**0**	**2**	**2**	**4**	**0**	**0**	**0**
1970-71	**Minnesota North Stars**	**NHL**	**78**	**34**	**23**	**57**	**34**	**19**	**53**	**46**	**12**	**0**	**1**	**283**	**12.0**	**90**	**34**	**49**	**0**	**7**	**12**	**5**	**5**	**10**	**8**	**3**	**0**	**1**
1971-72	**Minnesota North Stars**	**NHL**	**78**	**18**	**25**	**43**	**18**	**22**	**40**	**18**	**6**	**0**	**0**	**212**	**8.5**	**73**	**29**	**44**	**0**	**0**	**7**	**2**	**1**	**3**	**0**	**0**	**0**	**0**
1972-73	**Minnesota North Stars**	**NHL**	**78**	**32**	**35**	**67**	**30**	**28**	**58**	**12**	**3**	**0**	**6**	**251**	**12.7**	**100**	**23**	**55**	**1**	**23**	**6**	**3**	**1**	**4**	**0**	**0**	**0**	**0**
1973-74	**Minnesota North Stars**	**NHL**	**78**	**29**	**35**	**64**	**28**	**29**	**57**	**16**	**3**	**0**	**3**	**185**	**15.7**	**92**	**21**	**72**	**0**	**–1**	....	....	....	....	....	....	....	....
1974-75	**Detroit Red Wings**	**NHL**	**80**	**50**	**37**	**87**	**44**	**28**	**72**	**28**	**19**	**1**	**5**	**241**	**20.7**	**134**	**52**	**119**	**26**	**–11**	....	....	....	....	....	....	....	....
1975-76	**Detroit Red Wings**	**NHL**	**39**	**10**	**13**	**23**	**9**	**10**	**19**	**20**	**4**	**1**	**0**	**70**	**14.3**	**32**	**13**	**46**	**10**	**–17**	....	....	....	....	....	....	....	....
1976-77	**Detroit Red Wings**	**NHL**	**42**	**2**	**10**	**12**	**2**	**8**	**10**	**4**	**0**	**0**	**0**	**62**	**3.2**	**14**	**5**	**45**	**2**	**–34**	....	....	....	....	....	....	....	....
1977-78	**Detroit Red Wings**	**NHL**	**13**	**2**	**2**	**4**	**2**	**2**	**4**	**6**	**1**	**0**	**0**	**9**	**22.2**	**7**	**4**	**5**	**0**	**–2**	....	....	....	....	....	....	....	....
	Los Angeles Kings	**NHL**	**41**	**10**	**19**	**29**	**9**	**15**	**24**	**2**	**4**	**0**	**0**	**97**	**10.3**	**45**	**13**	**34**	**0**	**–2**	**2**	**0**	**2**	**2**	**2**	**0**	**0**	**0**
1978-79	**Los Angeles Kings**	**NHL**	**35**	**10**	**11**	**21**	**9**	**8**	**17**	**8**	**4**	**0**	**1**	**47**	**21.3**	**30**	**13**	**12**	**0**	**5**	....	....	....	....	....	....	....	....
1979-80	Fredericton Capitals	YCHL	DID NOT PLAY – COACHING																									
1980-81	Fredericton Capitals	YCHL	DID NOT PLAY – COACHING																									
1981-82	Fredericton Express	AHL	18	2	7	9	....	....	....	4	....	....	....	....	....	....	....	....	....	....	....	....	....	....	....	....	....	....
	NHL Totals		**736**	**263**	**273**	**536**	**256**	**227**	**483**	**239**	....	....	....	....	....	....	....	....	....	....	**43**	**10**	**14**	**24**	**19**	....	....	....

OHA-Jr. Second All-Star Team (1965) • OHA-Jr. First All-Star Team (1966) • Won Calder Memorial Trophy (1969) • Played in NHL All-Star Game (1969, 1970, 1971)

Traded to **Minnesota** by **Montreal** with Claude Larose and future considerations (Bob Murdoch, May 25, 1971) for Minnesota's 1st round choice (Dave Gardner) in 1972 Amateur Draft, cash and future considerations (Marshall Johnston, May 25, 1971), June 10, 1968. Traded to **Detroit** by **Minnesota** for Henry Boucha, August 27, 1974. • Missed majority of 1975-76 season recovering from ruptured anterior thigh muscle suffered in game vs. Kansas City, December 19, 1975. Consecutive games played streak halted at 566. Traded to **LA Kings** by **Detroit** for Montreal's 3rd round choice (previously acquired, Detroit selected Doug Derkson) and the rights to Barry Long, January 9, 1978.

• GRATTON, Benoit

LW – L. 5'11", 194 lbs. b: Montreal, Que., 12/28/1976. Washington's 6th, 105th overall, in 1995.

Season	Club	League	GP	G	A	Pts	AG	AA	APts	PIM	PP	SH	GW	S	%	TGF	PGF	TGA	PGA	+/–	GP	G	A	Pts	PIM	PP	SH	GW
1992-93	Laval Regents	QAAA	40	19	38	57	....	....	....	74	....	....	....	....	....	....	....	....	....	....	13	1	9	10	27	....	....	....
1993-94	Laval Titan	QMJHL	51	9	14	23	....	....	....	70	....	....	....	....	....	....	....	....	....	....	20	2	1	3	19	....	....	....
1994-95	Laval Titan	QMJHL	71	30	58	88	....	....	....	199	....	....	....	....	....	....	....	....	....	....	20	8	*21	29	42	....	....	....
1995-96	Laval Titan	QMJHL	38	21	39	60	....	....	....	130	....	....	....	....	....	....	....	....	....	....	....	....	....	....	....	....	....	....
	Granby Bisons	QMJHL	27	12	46	58	....	....	....	97	....	....	....	....	....	....	....	....	....	....	21	13	26	39	68	....	....	....
	Granby Bisons	Mem-Cup	4	1	*5	6	....	....	....	12	....	....	....	....	....	....	....	....	....	....	....	....	....	....	....	....	....	....
1996-97	Portland Pirates	AHL	76	6	40	46	....	....	....	140	....	....	....	....	....	....	....	....	....	....	5	2	1	3	14	....	....	....
1997-98	**Washington Capitals**	**NHL**	**6**	**0**	**1**	**1**	**0**	**1**	**1**	**6**	**0**	**0**	**0**	**5**	**0.0**	**1**	**0**	**0**	**0**	**1**	....	....	....	....	....	....	....	....
	Portland Pirates	AHL	58	19	31	50	....	....	....	137	....	....	....	....	....	....	....	....	....	....	8	4	2	6	24	....	....	....
1998-99	**Washington Capitals**	**NHL**	**16**	**4**	**3**	**7**	**5**	**3**	**8**	**16**	**0**	**0**	**0**	**24**	**16.7**	**9**	**1**	**9**	**0**	**–1**	....	....	....	....	....	....	....	....
	Portland Pirates	AHL	64	18	42	60	....	....	....	135	....	....	....	....	....	....	....	....	....	....	....	....	....	....	....	....	....	....
99-2000	**Calgary Flames**	**NHL**	**10**	**0**	**2**	**2**	**0**	**2**	**2**	**10**	**0**	**0**	**0**	**4**	**0.0**	**3**	**0**	**2**	**0**	**1**	....	....	....	....	....	....	....	....
	Saint John Flames	AHL	65	17	49	66	....	....	....	137	....	....	....	....	....	....	....	....	....	....	3	0	1	1	4	....	....	....
	NHL Totals		**32**	**4**	**6**	**10**	**5**	**6**	**11**	**32**	**0**	**0**	**0**	**33**	**12.1**	**13**	**1**	**11**	**0**		....	....	....	....	....	....	....	....

Traded to **Calgary** by **Washington** for Steve Shirreffs, August 18, 1999.

• GRATTON, Chris

Chris A. C – L. 6'4", 218 lbs. b: Brantford, Ont., 7/5/1975. Tampa Bay's 1st, 3rd overall, in 1993.

Season	Club	League	GP	G	A	Pts	AG	AA	APts	PIM	PP	SH	GW	S	%	TGF	PGF	TGA	PGA	+/–	GP	G	A	Pts	PIM	PP	SH	GW
1989-90	Brantford Classics	OJHL-B	1	0	2	2	....	....	....	2	....	....	....	....	....	....	....	....	....	....	....	....	....	....	....	....	....	....
1990-91	Brantford Classics	OJHL-B	31	30	30	60	....	....	....	28	....	....	....	....	....	....	....	....	....	....	....	....	....	....	....	....	....	....
1991-92	Kingston Frontenacs	OHL	62	27	39	66	....	....	....	37	....	....	....	....	....	....	....	....	....	....	....	....	....	....	....	....	....	....
1992-93	Kingston Frontenacs	OHL	58	55	54	109	....	....	....	125	....	....	....	....	....	....	....	....	....	....	16	11	18	29	42	....	....	....
	Canada	WJC-A	7	2	2	4	....	....	....	6	....	....	....	....	....	....	....	....	....	....	....	....	....	....	....	....	....	....
1993-94	**Tampa Bay Lightning**	**NHL**	**84**	**13**	**29**	**42**	**12**	**22**	**34**	**123**	**5**	**1**	**2**	**161**	**8.1**	**59**	**27**	**58**	**1**	**–25**	....	....	....	....	....	....	....	....
1994-95	**Tampa Bay Lightning**	**NHL**	**46**	**7**	**20**	**27**	**12**	**30**	**42**	**89**	**2**	**0**	**0**	**91**	**7.7**	**37**	**11**	**28**	**0**	**–2**	....	....	....	....	....	....	....	....
1995-96	**Tampa Bay Lightning**	**NHL**	**82**	**17**	**21**	**38**	**17**	**17**	**34**	**105**	**7**	**0**	**3**	**183**	**9.3**	**64**	**28**	**50**	**1**	**–13**	**6**	**0**	**2**	**2**	**27**	**0**	**0**	**0**
1996-97	**Tampa Bay Lightning**	**NHL**	**82**	**30**	**32**	**62**	**32**	**28**	**60**	**201**	**9**	**0**	**4**	**230**	**13.0**	**81**	**29**	**81**	**1**	**–28**	....	....	....	....	....	....	....	....
	Canada	WC-A	11	0	5	5	....	....	....	14	....	....	....	....	....	....	....	....	....	....	....	....	....	....	....	....	....	....
1997-98	**Philadelphia Flyers**	**NHL**	**82**	**22**	**40**	**62**	**26**	**39**	**65**	**159**	**5**	**0**	**2**	**182**	**12.1**	**82**	**23**	**48**	**0**	**11**	**5**	**2**	**0**	**2**	**10**	**0**	**0**	**0**
	Canada	WC-A	4	1	0	1	....	....	....	4	....	....	....	....	....	....	....	....	....	....	....	....	....	....	....	....	....	....

Season	Club	League	REGULAR SEASON																		PLAYOFFS							
			GP	G	A	Pts	AG	AA	APts	PIM	PP	SH	GW	S	%	TGF	PGF	TGA	PGA	+/–	GP	G	A	Pts	PIM	PP	SH	GW
1998-99	**Philadelphia Flyers**	**NHL**	**26**	**1**	**7**	**8**	**1**	**7**	**8**	**41**	**0**	**0**	**0**	**54**	**1.9**	**14**	**4**	**18**	**0**	**–8**	....	....	....	....	....	....	....	....
	Tampa Bay Lightning	**NHL**	**52**	**7**	**19**	**26**	**8**	**18**	**26**	**102**	**1**	**0**	**1**	**127**	**5.5**	**38**	**11**	**50**	**3**	**–20**	....	....	....	....	....	....	....	....
99-2000	**Tampa Bay Lightning**	**NHL**	**58**	**14**	**27**	**41**	**16**	**25**	**41**	**121**	**4**	**0**	**1**	**168**	**8.3**	**59**	**23**	**65**	**5**	**–24**	....	....	....	....	....	....	....	....
	Buffalo Sabres	**NHL**	**14**	**1**	**7**	**8**	**1**	**6**	**7**	**15**	**0**	**0**	**0**	**34**	**2.9**	**14**	**5**	**8**	**0**	**1**	**5**	**0**	**1**	**1**	**4**	**0**	**0**	**0**
	NHL Totals		**526**	**112**	**202**	**314**	**125**	**192**	**317**	**956**	**33**	**1**	**13**	**1230**	**9.1**	**448**	**161**	**406**	**11**		**16**	**2**	**3**	**5**	**41**	**0**	**0**	**0**

Signed as a free agent by **Philadelphia**, August 14, 1997. Traded to **Tampa Bay** by **Philadelphia** with Mike Sillinger for Mikael Renberg and Daymond Langkow, December 12, 1998. Traded to **Buffalo** by **Tampa Bay** with Tampa Bay's 2nd round choice in 2001 Entry Draft for Cory Sarich, Wayne Primeau, Brian Holzinger and Buffalo's 3rd round choice (Alexandre Kharitonov) in 2000 Entry Draft, March 9, 2000.

• GRATTON, Dan

C – L. 6', 185 lbs. b: Brantford, Ont., 12/7/1966. Los Angeles' 2nd, 10th overall, in 1985.

Season	Club	League	GP	G	A	Pts	AG	AA	APts	PIM	PP	SH	GW	S	%	TGF	PGF	TGA	PGA	+/–	GP	G	A	Pts	PIM	PP	SH	GW
1980-81	Brantford Hawks	OMHA	5	4	4	8				2																		
1981-82	Guelph Midget Platers	OMHA	40	14	26	40	....	....	....	70	....	....	....	....	....	....	....	....	....	....	....	....	....	....	....	....	....	....
	Guelph Platers	OJHL	12	3	2	5	....	....	....	27	....	....	....	....	....	....	....	....	....	....	....	....	....	....	....	....	....	....
1982-83	Oshawa Generals	OHL	64	15	28	43	....	....	....	55	....	....	....	....	....	....	....	....	....	....	17	6	10	16	11	....	....	....
	Oshawa Generals	Mem-Cup	5	2	0	2	....	....	....	0	....	....	....	....	....	....	....	....	....	....	....	....	....	....	....	....	....	....
1983-84	Oshawa Generals	OHL	65	40	34	74	....	....	....	55	....	....	....	....	....	....	....	....	....	....	7	2	5	7	15	....	....	....
1984-85	Oshawa Generals	OHL	56	24	48	72	....	....	....	67	....	....	....	....	....	....	....	....	....	....	5	3	3	6	0	....	....	....
	Canada	WJC-A	7	2	3	5	....	....	....	16	....	....	....	....	....	....	....	....	....	....	....	....	....	....	....	....	....	....
1985-86	Oshawa Generals	OHL	10	3	5	8	....	....	....	15	....	....	....	....	....	....	....	....	....	....	....	....	....	....	....	....	....	....
	Ottawa 67's	OHL	25	18	18	36	....	....	....	19	....	....	....	....	....	....	....	....	....	....	....	....	....	....	....	....	....	....
	Belleville Bulls	OHL	20	12	14	26	....	....	....	11	....	....	....	....	....	....	....	....	....	....	24	*20	9	29	16	....	....	....
1986-87	New Haven Nighthawks	AHL	49	6	10	16	....	....	....	45	....	....	....	....	....	....	....	....	....	....	2	0	0	0	0	....	....	....
1987-88	**Los Angeles Kings**	**NHL**	**7**	**1**	**0**	**1**	**1**	**0**	**1**	**5**	**0**	**0**	**0**	**3**	**33.3**	**1**	**0**	**0**	**0**	**1**	....	....	....	....	....	....	....	....
	New Haven Nighthawks	AHL	57	18	28	46	....	....	....	77	....	....	....	....	....	....	....	....	....	....	....	....	....	....	....	....	....	....
1988-89	New Haven Nighthawks	AHL	29	5	13	18	....	....	....	41	....	....	....	....	....	....	....	....	....	....	....	....	....	....	....	....	....	....
	Flint Spirits	IHL	20	5	9	14	....	....	....	8	....	....	....	....	....	....	....	....	....	....	....	....	....	....	....	....	....	....
1989-90	Canada	Nat-Team	68	29	37	66	....	....	....	40	....	....	....	....	....	....	....	....	....	....	....	....	....	....	....	....	....	....
1990-91	Minnesota North Stars	Fr-Tour	3	0	1	1	....	....	....	0	....	....	....	....	....	....	....	....	....	....	....	....	....	....	....	....	....	....
	Canada	Nat-Team	8	6	2	8	....	....	....	4	....	....	....	....	....	....	....	....	....	....	....	....	....	....	....	....	....	....
	Kalamazoo Wings	IHL	44	9	11	20	....	....	....	32	....	....	....	....	....	....	....	....	....	....	6	1	0	1	14	....	....	....
1991-92	SC Lyss	Switz-2	11	6	5	11	....	....	....	12	....	....	....	....	....	....	....	....	....	....	....	....	....	....	....	....	....	....
	IEV Innsbruck	Austria	8	6	2	8	....	....	....	....	....	....	....	....	....	....	....	....	....	....	6	3	9	12	12	....	....	....
	Brantford Smoke	ColHL	17	8	12	20	....	....	....	6	....	....	....	....	....	....	....	....	....	....	....	....	....	....	....	....	....	....
1992-93	AAB Aalborg	Denmark	30	28	34	62	....	....	....	68	....	....	....	....	....	....	....	....	....	....	....	....	....	....	....	....	....	....
	Brantford Smoke	ColHL	13	9	8	17	....	....	....	0	....	....	....	....	....	....	....	....	....	....	10	2	11	13	4	....	....	....
1993-94	HC Fassa	Alpenliga	5	7	3	10	....	....	....	4	....	....	....	....	....	....	....	....	....	....	....	....	....	....	....	....	....	....
	HC Fassa	Italy	20	16	14	30	....	....	....	18	....	....	....	....	....	....	....	....	....	....	2	2	0	2	14	....	....	....
	Hamilton Canucks	AHL	2	0	0	0	....	....	....	12	....	....	....	....	....	....	....	....	....	....	....	....	....	....	....	....	....	....
	Brantford Smoke	ColHL	12	9	10	19	....	....	....	16	....	....	....	....	....	....	....	....	....	....	....	....	....	....	....	....	....	....
1994-95	EV Zeltweg	Austria	16	11	31	42	....	....	....	....	....	....	....	....	....	....	....	....	....	....	....	....	....	....	....	....	....	....
	Slough Jets	BH-Cup	10	14	15	29	....	....	....	48	....	....	....	....	....	....	....	....	....	....	....	....	....	....	....	....	....	....
	Slough Jets	Britain	39	84	87	171	....	....	....	142	....	....	....	....	....	....	....	....	....	....	6	12	11	23	8	....	....	....
1995-96	Slough Jets	BH-Cup	8	14	13	27	....	....	....	18	....	....	....	....	....	....	....	....	....	....	....	....	....	....	....	....	....	....
	Slough Jets	Britain	34	36	45	81	....	....	....	118	....	....	....	....	....	....	....	....	....	....	6	2	5	7	12	....	....	....
1996-97	Muskegon Fury	ColHL	60	14	35	49	....	....	....	36	....	....	....	....	....	....	....	....	....	....	2	1	0	1	19	....	....	....
1997-98	Muskegon Fury	UHL	4	0	1	1	....	....	....	0	....	....	....	....	....	....	....	....	....	....	....	....	....	....	....	....	....	....
	NHL Totals		**7**	**1**	**0**	**1**	**1**	**0**	**1**	**5**	**0**	**0**	**0**	**3**	**33.3**	**1**	**0**	**0**	**0**		....	....	....	....	....	....	....	....

Signed as a free agent by **Minnesota**, August 22, 1990.

• GRATTON, Norm

Normand Lionel LW – L. 5'11", 165 lbs. b: LaSalle, Que., 12/22/1950. NY Rangers' 1st, 11th overall, in 1970.

Season	Club	League	GP	G	A	Pts	AG	AA	APts	PIM	PP	SH	GW	S	%	TGF	PGF	TGA	PGA	+/–	GP	G	A	Pts	PIM	PP	SH	GW
1967-68	Thetford Mines Canadiens	QJHL	50	21	47	68	....	....	....	....	....	....	....	....	....	....	....	....	....	....	7	4	6	10	2	....	....	....
1968-69	Montreal Jr. Canadiens	OHA-Jr.	53	10	23	33	....	....	....	37	....	....	....	....	....	....	....	....	....	....	14	7	10	17	4	....	....	....
	Montreal Jr. Canadiens	Mem-Cup	8	2	6	8	....	....	....	16	....	....	....	....	....	....	....	....	....	....	....	....	....	....	....	....	....	....
1969-70	Montreal Jr. Canadiens	OHA-Jr.	54	32	41	73	....	....	....	65	....	....	....	....	....	....	....	....	....	....	16	10	14	24	12	....	....	....
	Montreal Jr. Canadiens	Mem-Cup	12	8	15	23	....	....	....	12	....	....	....	....	....	....	....	....	....	....	....	....	....	....	....	....	....	....
1970-71	Omaha Knights	CHL	70	19	31	50	....	....	....	52	....	....	....	....	....	....	....	....	....	....	11	6	2	8	0	....	....	....
1971-72	**New York Rangers**	**NHL**	**3**	**0**	**1**	**1**	**0**	**1**	**1**	**0**	**0**	**0**	**0**	**2**	**0.0**	**2**	**0**	**1**	**0**	**1**	....	....	....	....	....	....	....	....
	Omaha Knights	CHL	68	32	42	74	....	....	....	82	....	....	....	....	....	....	....	....	....	....	....	....	....	....	....	....	....	....
1972-73	**Atlanta Flames**	**NHL**	**29**	**3**	**6**	**9**	**3**	**5**	**8**	**12**	**1**	**0**	**0**	**26**	**11.5**	**14**	**6**	**7**	**0**	**1**	....	....	....	....	....	....	....	....
	Omaha Knights	CHL	11	5	8	13	....	....	....	4	....	....	....	....	....	....	....	....	....	....	....	....	....	....	....	....	....	....
	Buffalo Sabres	**NHL**	**21**	**6**	**5**	**11**	**6**	**4**	**10**	**12**	**2**	**0**	**1**	**26**	**23.1**	**22**	**11**	**11**	**0**	**0**	**6**	**0**	**1**	**1**	**2**	**0**	**0**	**0**
1973-74	**Buffalo Sabres**	**NHL**	**57**	**6**	**11**	**17**	**6**	**9**	**15**	**16**	**2**	**0**	**0**	**53**	**11.3**	**29**	**6**	**33**	**0**	**–10**	....	....	....	....	....	....	....	....
1974-75	**Buffalo Sabres**	**NHL**	**25**	**3**	**6**	**9**	**3**	**4**	**7**	**2**	**1**	**0**	**0**	**16**	**18.8**	**12**	**3**	**7**	**0**	**2**	....	....	....	....	....	....	....	....
	Minnesota North Stars	**NHL**	**34**	**14**	**12**	**26**	**12**	**9**	**21**	**8**	**4**	**0**	**1**	**88**	**15.9**	**34**	**8**	**37**	**0**	**–11**	....	....	....	....	....	....	....	....
1975-76	**Minnesota North Stars**	**NHL**	**32**	**7**	**3**	**10**	**6**	**2**	**8**	**14**	**3**	**0**	**0**	**51**	**13.7**	**18**	**6**	**24**	**0**	**–12**	....	....	....	....	....	....	....	....
	New Haven Nighthawks	AHL	29	7	7	14	....	....	....	4	....	....	....	....	....	....	....	....	....	....	3	0	0	0	0	....	....	....
1976-77	Maine Nordiques	NAHL	52	15	26	41	....	....	....	16	....	....	....	....	....	....	....	....	....	....	11	1	3	4	0	....	....	....
	NHL Totals		**201**	**39**	**44**	**83**	**36**	**34**	**70**	**64**	**13**	**0**	**2**	**262**	**14.9**	**131**	**40**	**120**	**0**		**6**	**0**	**1**	**1**	**2**	**0**	**0**	**0**

• Brother of Gilles • CHL Second All-Star Team (1972)

Claimed by **Atlanta** from **NY Rangers** in Expansion Draft, June 6, 1972. Traded to **Buffalo** by **Atlanta** for Butch Deadmarsh, February 14, 1973. Traded to **Minnesota** by **Buffalo** with Buffalo's 3rd round choice (Ron Zanussi) in 1976 Amateur Draft for Fred Stanfield, January 27, 1975.

• GRAVES, Adam

C – L. 6', 205 lbs. b: Toronto, Ont., 4/12/1968. Detroit's 2nd, 22nd overall, in 1986.

Season	Club	League	GP	G	A	Pts	AG	AA	APts	PIM	PP	SH	GW	S	%	TGF	PGF	TGA	PGA	+/–	GP	G	A	Pts	PIM	PP	SH	GW
1984-85	King City Dukes	OJHL-B	25	23	33	56	....	....	....	29	....	....	....	....	....	....	....	....	....	....	....	....	....	....	....	....	....	....
1985-86	Windsor Spitfires	OHL	62	27	37	64	....	....	....	35	....	....	....	....	....	....	....	....	....	....	16	5	11	16	10	....	....	....
1986-87	Windsor Spitfires	OHL	66	45	55	100	....	....	....	70	....	....	....	....	....	....	....	....	....	....	14	9	8	17	32	....	....	....
	Adirondack Red Wings	AHL	....	....	....	....	....	....	....	....	....	....	....	....	....	....	....	....	....	....	5	0	1	1	0	....	....	....
1987-88	Windsor Spitfires	OHL	37	28	32	60	....	....	....	107	....	....	....	....	....	....	....	....	....	....	12	14	18	*32	16	....	....	....
	Canada	WJC-A	7	5	0	5	....	....	....	4	....	....	....	....	....	....	....	....	....	....	....	....	....	....	....	....	....	....
	Detroit Red Wings	**NHL**	**9**	**0**	**1**	**1**	**0**	**1**	**1**	**8**	**0**	**0**	**0**	**9**	**0.0**	**3**	**0**	**6**	**1**	**–2**	....	....	....	....	....	....	....	....
	Windsor Spitfires	Mem-Cup	4	2	3	5	....	....	....	8	....	....	....	....	....	....	....	....	....	....	....	....	....	....	....	....	....	....
1988-89	**Detroit Red Wings**	**NHL**	**56**	**7**	**5**	**12**	**6**	**4**	**10**	**60**	**0**	**0**	**1**	**60**	**11.7**	**22**	**1**	**26**	**0**	**–5**	**5**	**0**	**0**	**0**	**4**	**0**	**0**	**0**
	Adirondack Red Wings	AHL	14	10	11	21	....	....	....	28	....	....	....	....	....	....	....	....	....	....	14	11	7	18	17	....	....	....
1989-90	**Detroit Red Wings**	**NHL**	**13**	**0**	**1**	**1**	**0**	**1**	**1**	**13**	**0**	**0**	**0**	**10**	**0.0**	**3**	**0**	**10**	**2**	**–5**	....	....	....	....	....	....	....	....
♦	**Edmonton Oilers**	**NHL**	**63**	**9**	**12**	**21**	**8**	**9**	**17**	**123**	**1**	**0**	**1**	**84**	**10.7**	**33**	**3**	**25**	**0**	**5**	**22**	**5**	**6**	**11**	**17**	**0**	**0**	**1**
1990-91	**Edmonton Oilers**	**NHL**	**76**	**7**	**18**	**25**	**6**	**14**	**20**	**127**	**2**	**0**	**1**	**126**	**5.6**	**42**	**10**	**56**	**3**	**–21**	**18**	**2**	**4**	**6**	**22**	**0**	**0**	**0**
1991-92	**New York Rangers**	**NHL**	**80**	**26**	**33**	**59**	**24**	**25**	**49**	**139**	**4**	**4**	**4**	**228**	**11.4**	**99**	**15**	**81**	**16**	**19**	**10**	**5**	**3**	**8**	**22**	**1**	**0**	**1**
1992-93	**New York Rangers**	**NHL**	**84**	**36**	**29**	**65**	**30**	**20**	**50**	**148**	**12**	**1**	**6**	**275**	**13.1**	**104**	**29**	**99**	**20**	**–4**	....	....	....	....	....	....	....	....
	Canada	WC-A	8	3	3	6	....	....	....	8	....	....	....	....	....	....	....	....	....	....	....	....	....	....	....	....	....	....
1993-94♦	**New York Rangers**	**NHL**	**84**	**52**	**27**	**79**	**49**	**21**	**70**	**127**	**20**	**4**	**4**	**291**	**17.9**	**137**	**54**	**85**	**29**	**27**	**23**	**10**	**7**	**17**	**24**	**3**	**0**	**0**
1994-95	**New York Rangers**	**NHL**	**47**	**17**	**14**	**31**	**30**	**21**	**51**	**51**	**9**	**0**	**3**	**185**	**9.2**	**69**	**30**	**43**	**13**	**9**	**10**	**4**	**4**	**8**	**8**	**2**	**0**	**0**
1995-96	**New York Rangers**	**NHL**	**82**	**22**	**36**	**58**	**22**	**30**	**52**	**100**	**9**	**1**	**2**	**266**	**8.3**	**121**	**48**	**96**	**41**	**18**	**10**	**7**	**1**	**8**	**4**	**6**	**0**	**2**
1996-97	Canada	W-Cup	7	0	1	1	....	....	....	2	....	....	....	....	....	....	....	....	....	....	....	....	....	....	....	....	....	....
	New York Rangers	**NHL**	**82**	**33**	**28**	**61**	**35**	**25**	**60**	**66**	**10**	**4**	**3**	**269**	**12.3**	**101**	**26**	**99**	**34**	**10**	**15**	**2**	**1**	**3**	**12**	**1**	**0**	**2**
1997-98	**New York Rangers**	**NHL**	**72**	**23**	**12**	**35**	**27**	**12**	**39**	**41**	**10**	**0**	**2**	**226**	**10.2**	**60**	**33**	**73**	**16**	**–30**	....	....	....	....	....	....	....	....

Season	Club	League	REGULAR SEASON																		PLAYOFFS							
			GP	G	A	Pts	AG	AA	APts	PIM	PP	SH	GW	S	%	TGF	PGF	TGA	PGA	+/-	GP	G	A	Pts	PIM	PP	SH	GW
1998-99	**New York Rangers**	**NHL**	**82**	**38**	**15**	**53**	**45**	**14**	**59**	**47**	**14**	**2**	**7**	**239**	**15.9**	**82**	**38**	**75**	**19**	**–12**	....	....	....	....	....	....	....	....
	Canada	WC-A	10	5	2	7	....	....	....	8	....	....	....	....	....	....	....	....	....	....	....	....	....	....	....	....	....	....
99-2000	**New York Rangers**	**NHL**	**77**	**23**	**17**	**40**	**26**	**16**	**42**	**14**	**11**	**0**	**4**	**194**	**11.9**	**71**	**25**	**75**	**14**	**–15**	....	....	....	....	....	....	....	....
	NHL Totals		**907**	**293**	**248**	**541**	**308**	**213**	**521**	**1064**	**102**	**16**	**38**	**2462**	**11.9**	**947**	**312**	**849**	**208**		**113**	**35**	**26**	**61**	**113**	**13**	**0**	**6**

NHL Second All-Star Team (1994) • Won King Clancy Memorial Trophy (1994) • Played in NHL All-Star Game (1994)

Traded to **Edmonton** by **Detroit** with Petr Klima, Joe Murphy and Jeff Sharples for Jimmy Carson, Kevin McClelland and Edmonton's 5th round choice (later traded to Montreal — Montreal selected Brad Layzell) in 1991 Entry Draft, November 2, 1989. Signed as a free agent by **NY Rangers**, September 3, 1991.

• GRAVES, Hilliard

Hilliard Donald RW – R. 5'11", 175 lbs. b: Saint John, N.B., 10/18/1950.

Season	Club	League	GP	G	A	Pts	AG	AA	APts	PIM	PP	SH	GW	S	%	TGF	PGF	TGA	PGA	+/-	GP	G	A	Pts	PIM	PP	SH	GW
1968-69	Charlottetown Islanders	MJrHL	38	16	26	42	....	....	....	69	....	....	....	....	....	....	....	....	....	....	14	10	*13	23	26	....	....	....
1969-70	Charlottetown Islanders	MJrHL	42	32	*65	*97	....	....	....	55	....	....	....	....	....	....	....	....	....	....	12	8	13	21	11	....	....	....
	Charlottetown Islanders	Mem-Cup	15	5	16	21	....	....	....	19	....	....	....	....	....	....	....	....	....	....	....	....	....	....	....	....	....	....
1970-71	**California Golden Seals**	**NHL**	**14**	**0**	**0**	**0**	**0**	**0**	**0**	**0**	**0**	**0**	**0**	**6**	**0.0**	**0**	**0**	**2**	**0**	**–2**	....	....	....	....	....	....	....	....
	Providence Reds	AHL	16	3	1	4	....	....	....	11	....	....	....	....	....	....	....	....	....	....	....	....	....	....	....	....	....	....
1971-72	Baltimore Clippers	AHL	76	14	18	32	....	....	....	67	....	....	....	....	....	....	....	....	....	....	18	5	4	9	33	....	....	....
1972-73	**California Golden Seals**	**NHL**	**75**	**27**	**25**	**52**	**25**	**20**	**45**	**34**	**3**	**0**	**3**	**128**	**21.1**	**62**	**11**	**66**	**0**	**–15**	....	....	....	....	....	....	....	....
1973-74	**California Golden Seals**	**NHL**	**64**	**11**	**18**	**29**	**11**	**15**	**26**	**48**	**1**	**0**	**1**	**91**	**12.1**	**42**	**5**	**70**	**1**	**–32**	....	....	....	....	....	....	....	....
1974-75	**Atlanta Flames**	**NHL**	**67**	**10**	**19**	**29**	**9**	**14**	**23**	**30**	**3**	**0**	**0**	**79**	**12.7**	**47**	**8**	**36**	**0**	**3**	....	....	....	....	....	....	....	....
1975-76	**Atlanta Flames**	**NHL**	**80**	**19**	**30**	**49**	**17**	**22**	**39**	**16**	**2**	**0**	**3**	**168**	**11.3**	**83**	**25**	**58**	**3**	**3**	**2**	**0**	**0**	**0**	**0**	**0**	**0**	**0**
1976-77	**Atlanta Flames**	**NHL**	**25**	**8**	**5**	**13**	**7**	**4**	**11**	**17**	**1**	**0**	**2**	**41**	**19.5**	**23**	**3**	**21**	**0**	**–1**	....	....	....	....	....	....	....	....
	Vancouver Canucks	**NHL**	**54**	**10**	**20**	**30**	**9**	**15**	**24**	**17**	**2**	**0**	**1**	**91**	**11.0**	**49**	**10**	**42**	**5**	**2**	....	....	....	....	....	....	....	....
1977-78	**Vancouver Canucks**	**NHL**	**80**	**21**	**26**	**47**	**19**	**20**	**39**	**18**	**4**	**1**	**2**	**138**	**15.2**	**68**	**12**	**96**	**23**	**–17**	....	....	....	....	....	....	....	....
1978-79	**Vancouver Canucks**	**NHL**	**62**	**11**	**15**	**26**	**9**	**11**	**20**	**14**	**2**	**0**	**2**	**112**	**9.8**	**46**	**10**	**74**	**23**	**–15**	....	....	....	....	....	....	....	....
	New Brunswick Hawks	AHL	18	8	15	23	....	....	....	22	....	....	....	....	....	....	....	....	....	....	5	4	5	9	10	....	....	....
1979-80	**Winnipeg Jets**	**NHL**	**35**	**1**	**5**	**6**	**1**	**4**	**5**	**15**	**0**	**0**	**0**	**27**	**3.7**	**12**	**1**	**30**	**6**	**–13**	....	....	....	....	....	....	....	....
	Tulsa Oilers	CHL	5	2	3	5	....	....	....	2	....	....	....	....	....	....	....	....	....	....	....	....	....	....	....	....	....	....
	New Brunswick Hawks	AHL	16	3	6	9	....	....	....	5	....	....	....	....	....	....	....	....	....	....	17	8	6	14	4	....	....	....
	NHL Totals		**556**	**118**	**163**	**281**	**107**	**125**	**232**	**209**	**18**	**1**	**14**	**881**	**13.4**	**432**	**85**	**495**	**61**		**2**	**0**	**0**	**0**	**0**	**0**	**0**	**0**

Signed as a free agent by **California**, October, 1970. Traded to **Atlanta** by **California** for John Stewart, July 18, 1974. Traded to **Vancouver** by **Atlanta** with Larry Carriere for John Gould and LA Kings' 2nd round choice (previously acquired, Atlanta selected Brian Hill) in 1977 Amateur Draft, December 2, 1976. Claimed by **Winnipeg** from **Vancouver** in Expansion Draft, June 13, 1979.

• GRAVES, Steve

LW – L. 5'10", 175 lbs. b: Trenton, Ont., 4/7/1964. Edmonton's 2nd, 41st overall, in 1982.

Season	Club	League	GP	G	A	Pts	AG	AA	APts	PIM	PP	SH	GW	S	%	TGF	PGF	TGA	PGA	+/-	GP	G	A	Pts	PIM	PP	SH	GW
1980-81	Ottawa Jr. Senators	OJHL	44	21	17	38	....	....	....	47	....	....	....	....	....	....	....	....	....	....	....	....	....	....	....	....	....	....
1981-82	Sault Ste. Marie Greyhounds	OHL	66	12	15	27	....	....	....	49	....	....	....	....	....	....	....	....	....	....	13	8	5	13	14	....	....	....
1982-83	Sault Ste. Marie Greyhounds	OHL	60	21	20	41	....	....	....	48	....	....	....	....	....	....	....	....	....	....	5	0	0	0	4	....	....	....
1983-84	Sault Ste. Marie Greyhounds	OHL	67	41	48	89	....	....	....	47	....	....	....	....	....	....	....	....	....	....	16	6	8	14	8	....	....	....
	Edmonton Oilers	**NHL**	**2**	**0**	**0**	**0**	**0**	**0**	**0**	**0**	**0**	**0**	**0**	**2**	**0.0**	**0**	**0**	**0**	**0**	**0**	....	....	....	....	....	....	....	....
1984-85	Nova Scotia Voyageurs	AHL	80	17	15	32	....	....	....	20	....	....	....	....	....	....	....	....	....	....	6	0	1	1	4	....	....	....
1985-86	Nova Scotia Oilers	AHL	78	19	18	37	....	....	....	22	....	....	....	....	....	....	....	....	....	....	....	....	....	....	....	....	....	....
1986-87	**Edmonton Oilers**	**NHL**	**12**	**2**	**0**	**2**	**2**	**0**	**2**	**0**	**0**	**0**	**1**	**12**	**16.7**	**2**	**0**	**4**	**0**	**–2**	....	....	....	....	....	....	....	....
	Nova Scotia Oilers	AHL	59	18	10	28	....	....	....	22	....	....	....	....	....	....	....	....	....	....	5	1	1	2	2	....	....	....
1987-88	**Edmonton Oilers**	**NHL**	**21**	**3**	**4**	**7**	**3**	**3**	**6**	**10**	**0**	**0**	**0**	**21**	**14.3**	**14**	**0**	**1**	**0**	**13**	....	....	....	....	....	....	....	....
	Nova Scotia Oilers	AHL	11	6	2	8	....	....	....	4	....	....	....	....	....	....	....	....	....	....	....	....	....	....	....	....	....	....
1988-89	Canada	Nat-Team	3	5	1	6	....	....	....	2	....	....	....	....	....	....	....	....	....	....	....	....	....	....	....	....	....	....
	TPS Turku	Finland	43	16	12	28	....	....	....	48	....	....	....	....	....	....	....	....	....	....	10	2	8	10	12	....	....	....
1989-90	Canada	Nat-Team	53	24	19	43	....	....	....	50	....	....	....	....	....	....	....	....	....	....	....	....	....	....	....	....	....	....
	HC Ajoie	Switz.	5	4	1	5	....	....	....	2	....	....	....	....	....	....	....	....	....	....	....	....	....	....	....	....	....	....
1990-91	New Haven Nighthawks	AHL	3	0	1	1	....	....	....	2	....	....	....	....	....	....	....	....	....	....	....	....	....	....	....	....	....	....
	Phoenix Roadrunners	IHL	56	11	20	31	....	....	....	64	....	....	....	....	....	....	....	....	....	....	5	1	3	4	2	....	....	....
1991-92	HC Asiago	Italy	12	4	6	10	....	....	....	4	....	....	....	....	....	....	....	....	....	....	....	....	....	....	....	....	....	....
	NHL Totals		**35**	**5**	**4**	**9**	**5**	**3**	**8**	**10**	**0**	**0**	**1**	**35**	**14.3**	**16**	**0**	**5**	**0**		....	....	....	....	....	....	....	....

OHL Third All-Star Team (1984)

Signed as a free agent by **LA Kings**, July 16, 1990.

• GRAY, Terry

Terrence Stanley RW – R. 6', 175 lbs. b: Montreal, Que., 3/21/1938.

Season	Club	League	GP	G	A	Pts	AG	AA	APts	PIM	PP	SH	GW	S	%	TGF	PGF	TGA	PGA	+/-	GP	G	A	Pts	PIM	PP	SH	GW
1953-54	Montreal Jr. Royals	QJHL	49	3	4	7	....	....	....	63	....	....	....	....	....	....	....	....	....	....	4	0	1	1	12	....	....	....
1954-55	Montreal Jr. Royals	QJHL	STATISTICS NOT AVAILABLE																									
1955-56	Montreal Nationale	QJHL	46	45	29	74	....	....	....	33	....	....	....	....	....	....	....	....	....	....	....	....	....	....	....	....	....	....
1956-57	Montreal Nationale	QJHL	30	30	24	54	....	....	....	59	....	....	....	....	....	....	....	....	....	....	....	....	....	....	....	....	....	....
	Hull-Ottawa Canadiens	OHA-Jr.	1	0	0	0	....	....	....	0	....	....	....	....	....	....	....	....	....	....	....	....	....	....	....	....	....	....
	Montreal Royals	QHL	3	1	0	1	....	....	....	0	....	....	....	....	....	....	....	....	....	....	....	....	....	....	....	....	....	....
1957-58	Hull-Ottawa Canadiens	OHA-Jr.	24	9	11	20	....	....	....	15	....	....	....	....	....	....	....	....	....	....	....	....	....	....	....	....	....	....
	Hull-Ottawa Canadiens	EOHL	33	13	13	26	....	....	....	15	....	....	....	....	....	....	....	....	....	....	....	....	....	....	....	....	....	....
	Montreal Royals	QHL	1	0	0	0	....	....	....	0	....	....	....	....	....	....	....	....	....	....	....	....	....	....	....	....	....	....
	Hull-Ottawa Canadiens	Mem-Cup	13	6	2	8	....	....	....	12	....	....	....	....	....	....	....	....	....	....	....	....	....	....	....	....	....	....
1958-59	Montreal Royals	QHL	19	11	9	20	....	....	....	33	....	....	....	....	....	....	....	....	....	....	....	....	....	....	....	....	....	....
	Rochester Americans	AHL	45	10	14	24	....	....	....	14	....	....	....	....	....	....	....	....	....	....	5	1	2	3	2	....	....	....
1959-60	Sault Ste. Marie Thunderbirds	EPHL	16	4	11	15	....	....	....	19	....	....	....	....	....	....	....	....	....	....	....	....	....	....	....	....	....	....
	Calgary Stampeders	WHL	49	20	14	34	....	....	....	29	....	....	....	....	....	....	....	....	....	....	....	....	....	....	....	....	....	....
	Buffalo Bisons	AHL	3	0	0	0	....	....	....	0	....	....	....	....	....	....	....	....	....	....	....	....	....	....	....	....	....	....
1960-61	Hull-Ottawa Canadiens	EPHL	69	40	37	77	....	....	....	63	....	....	....	....	....	....	....	....	....	....	14	8	*11	*19	13	....	....	....
1961-62	**Boston Bruins**	**NHL**	**42**	**8**	**7**	**15**	**9**	**7**	**16**	**15**	....	....	....	....	....	....	....	....	....	....	....	....	....	....	....	....	....	....
	Kingston Frontenacs	EPHL	24	9	11	20	....	....	....	24	....	....	....	....	....	....	....	....	....	....	9	*9	6	15	9	....	....	....
1962-63	Cleveland Barons	AHL	10	3	5	8	....	....	....	8	....	....	....	....	....	....	....	....	....	....	....	....	....	....	....	....	....	....
	Quebec Aces	AHL	58	22	20	42	....	....	....	53	....	....	....	....	....	....	....	....	....	....	....	....	....	....	....	....	....	....
1963-64	**Montreal Canadiens**	**NHL**	**4**	**0**	**0**	**0**	**0**	**0**	**0**	**6**	....	....	....	....	....	....	....	....	....	....	....	....	....	....	....	....	....	....
	Quebec Aces	AHL	55	25	22	47	....	....	....	65	....	....	....	....	....	....	....	....	....	....	4	0	1	1	6	....	....	....
1964-65	Quebec Aces	AHL	72	39	28	67	....	....	....	54	....	....	....	....	....	....	....	....	....	....	5	2	1	3	12	....	....	....
1965-66	Quebec Aces	AHL	56	26	29	55	....	....	....	6	....	....	....	....	....	....	....	....	....	....	....	....	....	....	....	....	....	....
	Pittsburgh Hornets	AHL	15	4	4	8	....	....	....	12	....	....	....	....	....	....	....	....	....	....	3	2	0	2	4	....	....	....
1966-67	Pittsburgh Hornets	AHL	63	25	29	54	....	....	....	52	....	....	....	....	....	....	....	....	....	....	9	3	4	7	11	....	....	....
1967-68	**Los Angeles Kings**	**NHL**	**65**	**12**	**16**	**28**	**14**	**16**	**30**	**22**	**3**	**0**	**0**	**113**	**10.6**	**40**	**6**	**39**	**2**	**–3**	**7**	**0**	**2**	**2**	**10**	**0**	**0**	**0**
1968-69	**St. Louis Blues**	**NHL**	**8**	**4**	**0**	**4**	**4**	**0**	**4**	**4**	**2**	**0**	**1**	**19**	**21.1**	**7**	**3**	**4**	**0**	**0**	**11**	**3**	**2**	**5**	**8**	**1**	**0**	**0**
	Kansas City Blues	CHL	53	22	28	50	....	....	....	84	....	....	....	....	....	....	....	....	....	....	....	....	....	....	....	....	....	....
1969-70	**St. Louis Blues**	**NHL**	**28**	**2**	**5**	**7**	**2**	**5**	**7**	**17**	**0**	**0**	**2**	**63**	**3.2**	**13**	**1**	**10**	**0**	**2**	**16**	**2**	**1**	**3**	**4**	**1**	**1**	**0**
	Kansas City Blues	CHL	22	15	15	30	....	....	....	89	....	....	....	....	....	....	....	....	....	....	....	....	....	....	....	....	....	....
1970-71	Montreal Voyageurs	AHL	63	24	22	46	....	....	....	78	....	....	....	....	....	....	....	....	....	....	3	1	1	2	4	....	....	....
	St. Louis Blues	**NHL**	....	....	....	....	....	....	....	....	....	....	....	....	....	....	....	....	....	....	**1**	**0**	**0**	**0**	**0**	**0**	**0**	**0**

Season	Club	League	REGULAR SEASON GP	G	A	Pts	AG	AA	APts	PIM	PP	SH	GW	S	%	TGF	PGF	TGA	PGA	+/-	PLAYOFFS GP	G	A	Pts	PIM	PP	SH	GW
1971-72	Columbus Seals	IHL	DID NOT PLAY – COACHING																									
1972-73	New Haven Nighthawks	AHL	71	25	25	50	....	....	....	40	....	....	....	....	....	....	....	....	....	....	....	....	....	....	....	....	....	....
1973-74	Fort Worth Wings	CHL	60	18	17	35	....	....	....	30	....	....	....	....	....	....	....	....	....	....	....	....	....	....	....	....	....	....
	NHL Totals		**147**	**26**	**28**	**54**	**29**	**28**	**57**	**64**	....	....	....	....	....	....	....	....	....	....	**35**	**5**	**5**	**10**	**22**	....	....	....

QJHL First All-Star Team (1957)

• Hull-Ottawa played partial schedule against OHA-Jr. teams in 1956-57 and 1957-58 that counted for opposition only. Traded to **Montreal** by **Chicago** with Glen Skov, the rights to Danny Lewicki, Lorne Ferguson and Bob Bailey for Cec Hoekstra, Reggie Fleming, Ab McDonald and Bob Courcy, June 7, 1960. Traded to **Boston** by **Montreal** with Cliff Pennington for Willie O'Ree and Stan Maxwell, June, 1961. Loaned to **Montreal** (Cleveland-AHL) by **Boston** for cash, July, 1962. Traded to **Quebec** (AHL) by **Montreal** (Cleveland-AHL) for Gary Bergman with Boston retaining NHL rights, November 1, 1962. Traded to **Springfield** (AHL) by **Boston** with Dale Rolfe, Bruce Gamble and Randy Miller for Bob McCord, June, 1963. Traded to **Montreal** by **Springfield** (AHL) with Ted Harris, Bruce Cline, Wayne Larkin and John Chasczewski for Wayne Boddy, Fred Hilts, Brian D. Smith, John Rodger and Lorne O'Donnell and the loan of Gary Bergman, June, 1963. Traded to **Detroit** (Pittsburgh-AHL) by **Quebec** (AHL) for Claude Laforge, March 1, 1966. Claimed by **LA Kings** from **Detroit** in Expansion Draft, June 6, 1967. Traded to **St. Louis** by **LA Kings** for Myron Stankiewicz, June 11, 1968. Loaned to **Montreal**by **St. Louis** and named Player/Assistant coach with **Montreal Voyageurs** (AHL), October 20, 1970.

• GREEN, Josh

LW – L. 6'4", 212 lbs. b: Camrose, Alta., 11/16/1977. Los Angeles' 1st, 30th overall, in 1996.

Season	Club	League	GP	G	A	Pts	AG	AA	APts	PIM	PP	SH	GW	S	%	TGF	PGF	TGA	PGA	+/-	GP	G	A	Pts	PIM	PP	SH	GW
1992-93	Camrose Bantam Kodiaks	AAHA	60	55	45	100	....	....	....	80	....	....	....	....	....	....	....	....	....	....	....	....	....	....	....	....	....	....
1993-94	Medicine Hat Tigers	WHL	63	22	22	44	....	....	....	43	....	....	....	....	....	....	....	....	....	....	3	0	0	0	4	....	....	....
1994-95	Medicine Hat Tigers	WHL	68	32	23	55	....	....	....	64	....	....	....	....	....	....	....	....	....	....	5	5	1	6	2	....	....	....
1995-96	Medicine Hat Tigers	WHL	46	18	25	43	....	....	....	55	....	....	....	....	....	....	....	....	....	....	5	2	2	4	4	....	....	....
1996-97	Medicine Hat Tigers	WHL	51	25	32	57	....	....	....	61	....	....	....	....	....	....	....	....	....	....	....	....	....	....	....	....	....	....
	Swift Current Broncos	WHL	23	10	15	25	....	....	....	33	....	....	....	....	....	....	....	....	....	....	10	9	7	16	19	....	....	....
1997-98	Swift Current Broncos	WHL	5	9	1	10	....	....	....	9	....	....	....	....	....	....	....	....	....	....	....	....	....	....	....	....	....	....
	Portland Winter Hawks	WHL	26	26	18	44	....	....	....	27	....	....	....	....	....	....	....	....	....	....	....	....	....	....	....	....	....	....
	Fredericton Canadiens	AHL	43	16	15	31	....	....	....	14	....	....	....	....	....	....	....	....	....	....	4	1	3	4	6	....	....	....
1998-99	**Los Angeles Kings**	**NHL**	**27**	**1**	**3**	**4**	**1**	**3**	**4**	**8**	**1**	**0**	**0**	**35**	**2.9**	**9**	**3**	**12**	**1**	**–5**	....	....	....	....	....	....	....	....
	Springfield Falcons	AHL	41	15	15	30	....	....	....	29	....	....	....	....	....	....	....	....	....	....	....	....	....	....	....	....	....	....
99-2000	**New York Islanders**	**NHL**	**49**	**12**	**14**	**26**	**13**	**13**	**26**	**41**	**2**	**0**	**3**	**109**	**11.0**	**40**	**15**	**32**	**0**	**–7**	....	....	....	....	....	....	....	....
	Lowell Lock Monsters	AHL	17	6	2	8	....	....	....	19	....	....	....	....	....	....	....	....	....	....	....	....	....	....	....	....	....	....
	NHL Totals		**76**	**13**	**17**	**30**	**14**	**16**	**30**	**49**	**3**	**0**	**3**	**144**	**9.0**	**49**	**18**	**44**	**1**		....	....	....	....	....	....	....	....

Traded to **NY Islanders** by **LA Kings** with Olli Jokinen, Mathieu Biron and LA Kings' 1st round choice (Taylor Pyatt) in 1999 Entry Draft for Zigmund Palffy, Brian Smolinski, Marcel Cousineau and New Jersey's 4th round choice (previously acquired, LA Kings selected Daniel Johanssen) in 1999 Entry Draft, June 20, 1999. Traded to **Edmonton** by **NY Islanders** with Eric Brewer and NY Islanders' 2nd round choice (Brad Winchester) in 2000 Entry Draft for Roman Hamrlik, June 24, 2000.

• GREEN, Rick

Richard Douglas D – L. 6'3", 220 lbs. b: Belleville, Ont., 2/20/1956. Washington's 1st, 1st overall, in 1976.

Season	Club	League	GP	G	A	Pts	AG	AA	APts	PIM	PP	SH	GW	S	%	TGF	PGF	TGA	PGA	+/-	GP	G	A	Pts	PIM	PP	SH	GW
1972-73	London Knights	OMJHL	8	0	1	1	....	....	....	2	....	....	....	....	....	....	....	....	....	....	....	....	....	....	....	....	....	....
1973-74	London Knights	OMJHL	65	6	30	36	....	....	....	45	....	....	....	....	....	....	....	....	....	....	....	....	....	....	....	....	....	....
1974-75	London Knights	OMJHL	65	8	45	53	....	....	....	68	....	....	....	....	....	....	....	....	....	....	....	....	....	....	....	....	....	....
1975-76	London Knights	OMJHL	61	13	47	60	....	....	....	69	....	....	....	....	....	....	....	....	....	....	5	1	0	1	4	....	....	....
1976-77	**Washington Capitals**	**NHL**	**45**	**3**	**12**	**15**	**3**	**9**	**12**	**16**	**1**	**0**	**0**	**89**	**3.4**	**45**	**10**	**58**	**3**	**–20**	....	....	....	....	....	....	....	....
1977-78	**Washington Capitals**	**NHL**	**60**	**5**	**14**	**19**	**5**	**11**	**16**	**67**	**4**	**0**	**1**	**84**	**6.0**	**62**	**20**	**97**	**20**	**–35**	....	....	....	....	....	....	....	....
1978-79	**Washington Capitals**	**NHL**	**71**	**8**	**33**	**41**	**7**	**24**	**31**	**62**	**2**	**1**	**0**	**133**	**6.0**	**103**	**30**	**163**	**45**	**–45**	....	....	....	....	....	....	....	....
	Canada	WEC-A	8	1	1	2	....	....	....	2	....	....	....	....	....	....	....	....	....	....	....	....	....	....	....	....	....	....
1979-80	**Washington Capitals**	**NHL**	**71**	**4**	**20**	**24**	**3**	**15**	**18**	**52**	**0**	**0**	**1**	**105**	**3.8**	**93**	**10**	**126**	**33**	**–10**	....	....	....	....	....	....	....	....
1980-81	**Washington Capitals**	**NHL**	**65**	**8**	**23**	**31**	**6**	**15**	**21**	**91**	**2**	**0**	**1**	**120**	**6.7**	**97**	**29**	**120**	**37**	**–15**	....	....	....	....	....	....	....	....
	Canada	WEC-A	7	1	3	4	....	....	....	2	....	....	....	....	....	....	....	....	....	....	....	....	....	....	....	....	....	....
1981-82	Washington Capitals	DN-Cup	4	0	1	1	....	....	....	....	....	....	....	....	....	....	....	....	....	....	....	....	....	....	....	....	....	....
	Washington Capitals	**NHL**	**65**	**3**	**25**	**28**	**2**	**17**	**19**	**93**	**1**	**0**	**0**	**91**	**3.3**	**108**	**23**	**129**	**32**	**–12**	....	....	....	....	....	....	....	....
	Canada	WEC-A	9	0	3	3	....	....	....	2	....	....	....	....	....	....	....	....	....	....	....	....	....	....	....	....	....	....
1982-83	**Montreal Canadiens**	**NHL**	**66**	**2**	**24**	**26**	**2**	**17**	**19**	**58**	**1**	**0**	**0**	**71**	**2.8**	**103**	**16**	**85**	**21**	**23**	**3**	**0**	**0**	**0**	**2**	**0**	**0**	**0**
1983-84	**Montreal Canadiens**	**NHL**	**7**	**0**	**1**	**1**	**0**	**1**	**1**	**7**	**0**	**0**	**0**	**10**	**0.0**	**5**	**1**	**10**	**1**	**–5**	**15**	**1**	**2**	**3**	**33**	**0**	**0**	**0**
1984-85	**Montreal Canadiens**	**NHL**	**77**	**1**	**18**	**19**	**1**	**12**	**13**	**30**	**1**	**0**	**0**	**63**	**1.6**	**63**	**9**	**93**	**28**	**–11**	**12**	**0**	**3**	**3**	**14**	**0**	**0**	**0**
1985-86♦	**Montreal Canadiens**	**NHL**	**46**	**3**	**2**	**5**	**2**	**1**	**3**	**20**	**0**	**0**	**0**	**45**	**6.7**	**45**	**1**	**75**	**22**	**–9**	**18**	**1**	**4**	**5**	**8**	**0**	**0**	**0**
1986-87	**Montreal Canadiens**	**NHL**	**72**	**1**	**9**	**10**	**1**	**7**	**8**	**10**	**0**	**0**	**0**	**38**	**2.6**	**47**	**2**	**83**	**37**	**–1**	**17**	**0**	**4**	**4**	**8**	**0**	**0**	**0**
	NHL All-Stars	RV-87	2	0	0	0	....	....	....	0	....	....	....	....	....	....	....	....	....	....	....	....	....	....	....	....	....	....
1987-88	**Montreal Canadiens**	**NHL**	**59**	**2**	**11**	**13**	**2**	**8**	**10**	**33**	**1**	**0**	**0**	**44**	**4.5**	**64**	**2**	**69**	**28**	**21**	**11**	**0**	**2**	**2**	**2**	**0**	**0**	**0**
1988-89	**Montreal Canadiens**	**NHL**	**72**	**1**	**14**	**15**	**1**	**10**	**11**	**25**	**0**	**0**	**0**	**42**	**2.4**	**66**	**2**	**57**	**12**	**19**	**21**	**1**	**1**	**2**	**6**	**0**	**0**	**0**
1989-90	HC Meran	Italy	9	2	6	8	....	....	....	2	....	....	....	....	....	....	....	....	....	....	10	3	6	9	4	....	....	....
	Canada	WEC-A	10	0	0	0	....	....	....	2	....	....	....	....	....	....	....	....	....	....	....	....	....	....	....	....	....	....
1990-91	**Detroit Red Wings**	**NHL**	**65**	**2**	**14**	**16**	**2**	**11**	**13**	**24**	**0**	**0**	**0**	**36**	**5.6**	**66**	**1**	**90**	**35**	**10**	**3**	**0**	**0**	**0**	**0**	**0**	**0**	**0**
1991-92	**New York Islanders**	**NHL**	**4**	**0**	**0**	**0**	**0**	**0**	**0**	**0**	**0**	**0**	**0**	**2**	**0.0**	**2**	**0**	**6**	**3**	**–1**	....	....	....	....	....	....	....	....
	NHL Totals		**845**	**43**	**220**	**263**	**37**	**158**	**195**	**588**	**13**	**1**	**3**	**973**	**4.4**	**969**	**156**	**1261**	**357**		**100**	**3**	**16**	**19**	**73**	**0**	**0**	**0**

OMJHL First All-Star Team (1976)

Traded to **Montreal** by **Washington** with Ryan Walter for Brian Engblom, Rod Langway, Doug Jarvis and Craig Laughlin, September 9, 1982. Traded to **Detroit** by **Montreal** for Edmonton's 5th round choice (previously acquired, Montreal selected Brad Layzell) in 1991 Entry Draft, June 15, 1990. Traded to **NY Islanders** by **Detroit** for Alan Kerr and future considerations, May 26, 1991.

• GREEN, Ted

Edward Joseph "Terrible Ted" D – R. 5'10", 200 lbs. b: Eriksdale, Man., 3/23/1940.

Season	Club	League	GP	G	A	Pts	AG	AA	APts	PIM	PP	SH	GW	S	%	TGF	PGF	TGA	PGA	+/-	GP	G	A	Pts	PIM	PP	SH	GW
1956-57	St. Boniface Canadiens	MJHL	17	1	2	3	....	....	....	76	....	....	....	....	....	....	....	....	....	....	7	0	0	0	10	....	....	....
1957-58	St. Boniface Canadiens	MJHL	23	1	4	5	....	....	....	*97	....	....	....	....	....	....	....	....	....	....	12	1	2	3	*32	....	....	....
	St. Boniface Canadiens	Mem-Cup	11	2	3	5	....	....	....	38	....	....	....	....	....	....	....	....	....	....	....	....	....	....	....	....	....	....
1958-59	St. Boniface Canadiens	MJHL	25	5	11	16	....	....	....	*120	....	....	....	....	....	....	....	....	....	....	9	1	5	6	32	....	....	....
	Winnipeg Braves	Mem-Cup	16	2	6	8	....	....	....	50	....	....	....	....	....	....	....	....	....	....	....	....	....	....	....	....	....	....
1959-60	Winnipeg Warriors	WHL	70	8	20	28	....	....	....	109	....	....	....	....	....	....	....	....	....	....	....	....	....	....	....	....	....	....
1960-61	**Boston Bruins**	**NHL**	**1**	**0**	**0**	**0**	**0**	**0**	**0**	**2**	....	....	....	....	....	....	....	....	....	....	....	....	....	....	....	....	....	....
	Kingston Frontenacs	EPHL	11	1	5	6	....	....	....	30	....	....	....	....	....	....	....	....	....	....	5	1	0	1	2	....	....	....
	Winnipeg Warriors	WHL	57	1	18	19	....	....	....	127	....	....	....	....	....	....	....	....	....	....	....	....	....	....	....	....	....	....
1961-62	**Boston Bruins**	**NHL**	**66**	**3**	**8**	**11**	**3**	**8**	**11**	**116**	....	....	....	....	....	....	....	....	....	....	....	....	....	....	....	....	....	....
1962-63	**Boston Bruins**	**NHL**	**70**	**1**	**11**	**12**	**1**	**11**	**12**	**117**	....	....	....	....	....	....	....	....	....	....	....	....	....	....	....	....	....	....
1963-64	**Boston Bruins**	**NHL**	**70**	**4**	**10**	**14**	**5**	**10**	**15**	**145**	....	....	....	....	....	....	....	....	....	....	....	....	....	....	....	....	....	....
1964-65	**Boston Bruins**	**NHL**	**70**	**8**	**27**	**35**	**10**	**28**	**38**	**156**	....	....	....	....	....	....	....	....	....	....	....	....	....	....	....	....	....	....
1965-66	**Boston Bruins**	**NHL**	**27**	**5**	**13**	**18**	**6**	**12**	**18**	**113**	....	....	....	....	....	....	....	....	....	....	....	....	....	....	....	....	....	....
1966-67	**Boston Bruins**	**NHL**	**47**	**6**	**10**	**16**	**7**	**10**	**17**	**67**	....	....	....	....	....	....	....	....	....	....	....	....	....	....	....	....	....	....
1967-68	**Boston Bruins**	**NHL**	**72**	**7**	**36**	**43**	**8**	**36**	**44**	**133**	**3**	**0**	**0**	**113**	**6.2**	**113**	**17**	**107**	**25**	**14**	**4**	**1**	**1**	**2**	**11**	**1**	**0**	**0**
1968-69	**Boston Bruins**	**NHL**	**65**	**8**	**38**	**46**	**8**	**34**	**42**	**99**	**3**	**0**	**0**	**131**	**6.1**	**126**	**41**	**95**	**19**	**9**	**10**	**2**	**7**	**9**	**18**	**0**	**0**	**0**
1969-70	**Boston Bruins**	**NHL**	DID NOT PLAY – INJURED																									
1970-71	**Boston Bruins**	**NHL**	**78**	**5**	**37**	**42**	**5**	**31**	**36**	**60**	**0**	**0**	**0**	**103**	**4.9**	**125**	**1**	**99**	**12**	**37**	**7**	**1**	**0**	**1**	**25**	**0**	**0**	**0**
1971-72♦	**Boston Bruins**	**NHL**	**54**	**1**	**16**	**17**	**1**	**14**	**15**	**21**	**0**	**0**	**0**	**41**	**2.4**	**60**	**0**	**58**	**8**	**10**	**10**	**0**	**0**	**0**	**0**	**0**	**0**	**0**
1972-73	New England Whalers	WHA	78	16	30	46	....	....	....	47	....	....	....	....	....	....	....	....	....	....	12	1	5	6	25	....	....	....
1973-74	New England Whalers	WHA	75	7	26	33	....	....	....	42	....	....	....	....	....	....	....	....	....	....	7	0	4	4	2	....	....	....
1974-75	New England Whalers	WHA	57	6	14	20	....	....	....	29	....	....	....	....	....	....	....	....	....	....	3	0	0	0	2	....	....	....
1975-76	Winnipeg Jets	WHA	79	5	23	28	....	....	....	73	....	....	....	....	....	....	....	....	....	....	11	0	2	2	16	....	....	....
1976-77	Winnipeg Jets	WHA	70	4	21	25	....	....	....	45	....	....	....	....	....	....	....	....	....	....	20	1	3	4	12	....	....	....
1977-78	Winnipeg Jets	WHA	73	4	22	26	....	....	....	52	....	....	....	....	....	....	....	....	....	....	8	0	2	2	2	....	....	....
1978-79	Winnipeg Jets	WHA	20	0	2	2	....	....	....	16	....	....	....	....	....	....	....	....	....	....	....	....	....	....	....	....	....	....
1979-1981	Carman Hornets	MAHA-I	DID NOT PLAY – COACHING																									
1981-1985	**Edmonton Oilers**	**NHL**	DID NOT PLAY – ASSISTANT COACH																									
1985-1986			OUT OF HOCKEY – RETIRED																									
1986-1991	**Edmonton Oilers**	**NHL**	DID NOT PLAY – ASSISTANT COACH																									

Season	Club	League	GP	G	A	Pts	AG	AA	APts	PIM	PP	SH	GW	S	%	TGF	PGF	TGA	PGA	+/-	Playoffs GP	G	A	Pts	PIM	PP	SH	GW
			REGULAR SEASON																		PLAYOFFS							
1991-1993	**Edmonton Oilers**	**NHL**	DID NOT PLAY – COACHING																									
1993-1997	**Edmonton Oilers**	**NHL**	DID NOT PLAY – ASSISTANT GENERAL MANAGER																									
1997-2000	**Edmonton Oilers**	**NHL**	DID NOT PLAY – ASSISTANT COACH																									
	NHL Totals		**620**	**48**	**206**	**254**	**54**	**194**	**248**	**1029**	....	....	....	....	....	....	....	....	....		**31**	**4**	**8**	**12**	**54**	....	....	....
	Other Major League Totals		452	42	138	180	....	....	....	304	....	....	....	....	....	....	....	....	....	....	61	2	16	18	59	....	....	....

NHL Second All-Star Team (1969) • Played in NHL All-Star Game (1965, 1969)

• Loaned to **Winnipeg Braves** by **St. Boniface** for Memorial Cup playoffs, April, 1959. Claimed by **Montreal** from **Winnipeg** (WHL) in Inter-League Draft, June 7, 1960. Claimed by **Boston** from **Montreal** in Intra-League Draft, June 8, 1960. • Missed entire 1969-70 season recovering from head injury suffered in exhibition game vs. St. Louis, September 19, 1969. Selected by **Winnipeg** (WHA) in 1972 WHA General Player Draft, February 12, 1972. Rights traded to **New England** (WHA) by **Winnipeg** (WHA) for cash, May, 1972. Traded to **Winnipeg** (WHA) by **New England** (WHA) for future considerations, May, 1975. • Named Assistant Coach of **NY Rangers**, July 12, 2000.

• GREEN, Travis

Travis Vernon C – R. 6'2", 196 lbs. b: Castlegar, B.C., 12/20/1970. NY Islanders' 2nd, 23rd overall, in 1989.

Season	Club	League	GP	G	A	Pts	AG	AA	APts	PIM	PP	SH	GW	S	%	TGF	PGF	TGA	PGA	+/-	Playoffs GP	G	A	Pts	PIM	PP	SH	GW
1985-86	Castlegar Rebels	KIJHL	35	30	40	70	....	....	....	41	....	....	....	....	....	....	....	....	....	....	....	....	....	....	....	....	....	....
1986-87	Spokane Chiefs	WHL	64	8	17	25	....	....	....	27	....	....	....	....	....	....	....	....	....	....	3	0	0	0	0	....	....	....
1987-88	Spokane Chiefs	WHL	72	33	54	87	....	....	....	42	....	....	....	....	....	....	....	....	....	....	15	10	10	20	13	....	....	....
1988-89	Spokane Chiefs	WHL	75	51	51	102	....	....	....	79	....	....	....	....	....	....	....	....	....	....	....	....	....	....	....	....	....	....
1989-90	Spokane Chiefs	WHL	50	45	44	89	....	....	....	80	....	....	....	....	....	....	....	....	....	....	....	....	....	....	....	....	....	....
	Medicine Hat Tigers	WHL	25	15	24	39	....	....	....	19	....	....	....	....	....	....	....	....	....	....	3	0	0	0	2	....	....	....
1990-91	Capital District Islanders	AHL	73	21	34	55	....	....	....	26	....	....	....	....	....	....	....	....	....	....	....	....	....	....	....	....	....	....
1991-92	Capital District Islanders	AHL	71	23	27	50	....	....	....	10	....	....	....	....	....	....	....	....	....	....	7	0	4	4	21	....	....	....
1992-93	**New York Islanders**	**NHL**	**61**	**7**	**18**	**25**	**6**	**12**	**18**	**43**	**1**	**0**	**0**	**115**	**6.1**	**42**	**2**	**37**	**1**	**4**	**12**	**3**	**1**	**4**	**6**	**0**	**0**	**0**
	Capital District Islanders	AHL	20	12	11	23	....	....	....	39	....	....	....	....	....	....	....	....	....	....	....	....	....	....	....	....	....	....
1993-94	**New York Islanders**	**NHL**	**83**	**18**	**22**	**40**	**17**	**17**	**34**	**44**	**1**	**0**	**2**	**164**	**11.0**	**62**	**7**	**48**	**9**	**16**	**4**	**0**	**0**	**0**	**2**	**0**	**0**	**0**
1994-95	**New York Islanders**	**NHL**	**42**	**5**	**7**	**12**	**9**	**10**	**19**	**25**	**0**	**0**	**0**	**59**	**8.5**	**18**	**2**	**37**	**11**	**–10**	....	....	....	....	....	....	....	....
1995-96	**New York Islanders**	**NHL**	**69**	**25**	**45**	**70**	**25**	**37**	**62**	**42**	**14**	**1**	**2**	**186**	**13.4**	**91**	**43**	**97**	**29**	**–20**	....	....	....	....	....	....	....	....
	Canada	WC-A	8	5	3	8	....	....	....	8	....	....	....	....	....	....	....	....	....	....	....	....	....	....	....	....	....	....
1996-97	**New York Islanders**	**NHL**	**79**	**23**	**41**	**64**	**24**	**37**	**61**	**38**	**10**	**0**	**3**	**177**	**13.0**	**98**	**28**	**82**	**7**	**–5**	....	....	....	....	....	....	....	....
	Canada	WC-A	11	3	6	9	....	....	....	12	....	....	....	....	....	....	....	....	....	....	....	....	....	....	....	....	....	....
1997-98	**New York Islanders**	**NHL**	**54**	**14**	**12**	**26**	**16**	**12**	**28**	**66**	**8**	**0**	**2**	**99**	**14.1**	**40**	**22**	**40**	**3**	**–19**	....	....	....	....	....	....	....	....
	Mighty Ducks of Anaheim	**NHL**	**22**	**5**	**11**	**16**	**6**	**11**	**17**	**16**	**1**	**0**	**0**	**42**	**11.9**	**23**	**10**	**26**	**3**	**–10**	....	....	....	....	....	....	....	....
	Canada	WC-A	6	0	3	3	....	....	....	2	....	....	....	....	....	....	....	....	....	....	....	....	....	....	....	....	....	....
1998-99	**Mighty Ducks of Anaheim**	**NHL**	**79**	**13**	**17**	**30**	**15**	**16**	**31**	**81**	**3**	**1**	**2**	**165**	**7.9**	**48**	**16**	**52**	**13**	**–7**	**4**	**0**	**1**	**1**	**4**	**0**	**0**	**0**
99-2000	**Phoenix Coyotes**	**NHL**	**78**	**25**	**21**	**46**	**28**	**19**	**47**	**45**	**6**	**0**	**2**	**157**	**15.9**	**70**	**22**	**52**	**0**	**–4**	**5**	**2**	**1**	**3**	**2**	**0**	**0**	**0**
	NHL Totals		**567**	**135**	**194**	**329**	**146**	**171**	**317**	**400**	**44**	**2**	**13**	**1164**	**11.6**	**492**	**152**	**471**	**76**		**25**	**5**	**3**	**8**	**14**	**0**	**0**	**0**

Traded to **Anaheim** by **NY Islanders** with Doug Houda and Tony Tuzzolino for Joe Sacco, J.J. Daigneault and Mark Janssens, February 6, 1998. Traded to **Phoenix** by **Anaheim** with Anaheim's 1st round choice (Scott Kelman) in 1999 Entry Draft for Oleg Tverdovsky, June 26, 1999.

• GREENLAW, Jeff

Jeff Carl "Charlie" LW – L. 6'1", 230 lbs. b: Toronto, Ont., 2/28/1968. Washington's 1st, 19th overall, in 1986.

Season	Club	League	GP	G	A	Pts	AG	AA	APts	PIM	PP	SH	GW	S	%	TGF	PGF	TGA	PGA	+/-	Playoffs GP	G	A	Pts	PIM	PP	SH	GW
1983-84	St. Catharines Falcons	OJHL-B	40	28	27	55	....	....	....	94	....	....	....	....	....	....	....	....	....	....	....	....	....	....	....	....	....	....
1984-85	St. Catharines Falcons	OJHL-B	33	21	29	50	....	....	....	141	....	....	....	....	....	....	....	....	....	....	....	....	....	....	....	....	....	....
1985-86	Canada	Nat-Team	57	3	16	19	....	....	....	81	....	....	....	....	....	....	....	....	....	....	....	....	....	....	....	....	....	....
	Canada	WJC-A	7	3	1	4	....	....	....	4	....	....	....	....	....	....	....	....	....	....	....	....	....	....	....	....	....	....
1986-87	**Washington Capitals**	**NHL**	**22**	**0**	**3**	**3**	**0**	**2**	**2**	**44**	**0**	**0**	**0**	**9**	**0.0**	**7**	**0**	**6**	**1**	**2**	....	....	....	....	....	....	....	....
	Binghamton Whalers	AHL	4	0	2	2	....	....	....	0	....	....	....	....	....	....	....	....	....	....	....	....	....	....	....	....	....	....
1987-88	Binghamton Whalers	AHL	56	8	7	15	....	....	....	142	....	....	....	....	....	....	....	....	....	....	1	0	0	0	2	....	....	....
	Washington Capitals	**NHL**	....	....	....	....	....	....	....	....	....	....	....	....	....	....	....	....	....	....	**1**	**0**	**0**	**0**	**19**	**0**	**0**	**0**
1988-89	Baltimore Skipjacks	AHL	55	12	15	27	....	....	....	115	....	....	....	....	....	....	....	....	....	....	....	....	....	....	....	....	....	....
1989-90	Baltimore Skipjacks	AHL	10	3	2	5	....	....	....	26	....	....	....	....	....	....	....	....	....	....	7	1	0	1	13	....	....	....
1990-91	**Washington Capitals**	**NHL**	**10**	**2**	**0**	**2**	**2**	**0**	**2**	**10**	**0**	**0**	**1**	**9**	**22.2**	**4**	**0**	**3**	**0**	**1**	**1**	**0**	**0**	**0**	**2**	**0**	**0**	**0**
	Baltimore Skipjacks	AHL	50	17	17	34	....	....	....	93	....	....	....	....	....	....	....	....	....	....	3	1	1	2	2	....	....	....
1991-92	**Washington Capitals**	**NHL**	**5**	**0**	**1**	**1**	**0**	**1**	**1**	**34**	**0**	**0**	**0**	**3**	**0.0**	**1**	**0**	**2**	**0**	**–1**	....	....	....	....	....	....	....	....
	Baltimore Skipjacks	AHL	37	6	8	14	....	....	....	57	....	....	....	....	....	....	....	....	....	....	....	....	....	....	....	....	....	....
1992-93	**Washington Capitals**	**NHL**	**16**	**1**	**1**	**2**	**1**	**1**	**2**	**18**	**0**	**0**	**0**	**15**	**6.7**	**2**	**0**	**6**	**1**	**–3**	....	....	....	....	....	....	....	....
	Baltimore Skipjacks	AHL	49	12	14	26	....	....	....	66	....	....	....	....	....	....	....	....	....	....	7	3	1	4	0	....	....	....
1993-94	**Florida Panthers**	**NHL**	**4**	**0**	**1**	**1**	**0**	**1**	**1**	**2**	**0**	**0**	**0**	**6**	**0.0**	**1**	**0**	**2**	**0**	**–1**	....	....	....	....	....	....	....	....
	Cincinnati Cyclones	IHL	55	14	15	29	....	....	....	85	....	....	....	....	....	....	....	....	....	....	11	2	2	4	28	....	....	....
1994-95	Cincinnati Cyclones	IHL	67	10	21	31	....	....	....	117	....	....	....	....	....	....	....	....	....	....	10	2	0	2	22	....	....	....
1995-96	Cincinnati Cyclones	IHL	64	17	15	32	....	....	....	112	....	....	....	....	....	....	....	....	....	....	17	2	4	6	36	....	....	....
1996-97	Cincinnati Cyclones	IHL	27	6	6	12	....	....	....	70	....	....	....	....	....	....	....	....	....	....	1	0	1	1	2	....	....	....
1997-98	Cincinnati Cyclones	IHL	70	6	9	15	....	....	....	130	....	....	....	....	....	....	....	....	....	....	9	0	2	2	36	....	....	....
1998-99	Austin Ice Bats	WPHL	52	25	15	40	....	....	....	183	....	....	....	....	....	....	....	....	....	....	....	....	....	....	....	....	....	....
99-2000	Austin Ice Bats	WPHL	52	19	23	42	....	....	....	150	....	....	....	....	....	....	....	....	....	....	10	2	3	5	12	....	....	....
	NHL Totals		**57**	**3**	**6**	**9**	**3**	**5**	**8**	**108**	**0**	**0**	**1**	**42**	**7.1**	**15**	**0**	**19**	**2**		**2**	**0**	**0**	**0**	**21**	**0**	**0**	**0**

Signed as a free agent by **Florida**, July 14, 1993.

• GREGG, Randy

Randall John D – L. 6'4", 215 lbs. b: Edmonton, Alta., 2/19/1956.

Season	Club	League	GP	G	A	Pts	AG	AA	APts	PIM	PP	SH	GW	S	%	TGF	PGF	TGA	PGA	+/-	Playoffs GP	G	A	Pts	PIM	PP	SH	GW
1975-76	University of Alberta	CWUAA	31	3	20	23	....	....	....	49	....	....	....	....	....	....	....	....	....	....	....	....	....	....	....	....	....	....
1976-77	University of Alberta	CWUAA	34	10	23	33	....	....	....	45	....	....	....	....	....	....	....	....	....	....	....	....	....	....	....	....	....	....
1977-78	University of Alberta	CWUAA	30	8	26	34	....	....	....	43	....	....	....	....	....	....	....	....	....	....	....	....	....	....	....	....	....	....
1978-79	University of Alberta	CWUAA	41	11	26	37	....	....	....	67	....	....	....	....	....	....	....	....	....	....	....	....	....	....	....	....	....	....
1979-80	Canada	Nat-Team	56	7	17	24	....	....	....	36	....	....	....	....	....	....	....	....	....	....	....	....	....	....	....	....	....	....
	Canada	Olympics	6	1	1	2	....	....	....	2	....	....	....	....	....	....	....	....	....	....	....	....	....	....	....	....	....	....
1980-81	Kokudo-Keikkau	Japan	35	12	18	30	....	....	....	30	....	....	....	....	....	....	....	....	....	....	....	....	....	....	....	....	....	....
1981-82	Kokudo-Keikkau	Japan	36	12	20	32	....	....	....	25	....	....	....	....	....	....	....	....	....	....	....	....	....	....	....	....	....	....
	Edmonton Oilers	**NHL**	....	....	....	....	....	....	....	....	....	....	....	....	....	....	....	....	....	....	**4**	**0**	**0**	**0**	**0**	**0**	**0**	**0**
1982-83	**Edmonton Oilers**	**NHL**	**80**	**6**	**22**	**28**	**5**	**15**	**20**	**54**	**0**	**2**	**2**	**94**	**6.4**	**93**	**8**	**106**	**36**	**15**	**16**	**2**	**4**	**6**	**13**	**0**	**1**	**1**
1983-84♦	**Edmonton Oilers**	**NHL**	**80**	**13**	**27**	**40**	**10**	**18**	**28**	**56**	**2**	**1**	**2**	**91**	**14.3**	**131**	**15**	**107**	**31**	**40**	**19**	**3**	**7**	**10**	**21**	**0**	**0**	**1**
1984-85	Canada	Can-Cup	3	0	1	1	....	....	....	4	....	....	....	....	....	....	....	....	....	....	....	....	....	....	....	....	....	....
♦	**Edmonton Oilers**	**NHL**	**57**	**3**	**20**	**23**	**2**	**14**	**16**	**32**	**0**	**0**	**0**	**58**	**5.2**	**78**	**12**	**54**	**15**	**27**	**17**	**0**	**6**	**6**	**12**	**0**	**0**	**0**
1985-86	**Edmonton Oilers**	**NHL**	**64**	**2**	**26**	**28**	**2**	**17**	**19**	**47**	**0**	**0**	**0**	**55**	**3.6**	**115**	**22**	**85**	**22**	**30**	**10**	**1**	**0**	**1**	**12**	**0**	**0**	**0**
1986-87♦	**Edmonton Oilers**	**NHL**	**52**	**8**	**16**	**24**	**7**	**12**	**19**	**42**	**0**	**0**	**2**	**59**	**13.6**	**90**	**12**	**70**	**28**	**36**	**18**	**3**	**6**	**9**	**17**	**1**	**0**	**1**
1987-88♦	**Edmonton Oilers**	**NHL**	**15**	**1**	**2**	**3**	**1**	**1**	**2**	**8**	**0**	**0**	**0**	**20**	**5.0**	**18**	**1**	**18**	**5**	**4**	**19**	**1**	**8**	**9**	**24**	**0**	**0**	**1**
	Canada	Nat-Team	37	2	6	8	....	....	....	37	....	....	....	....	....	....	....	....	....	....	....	....	....	....	....	....	....	....
	Canada	Olympics	8	1	2	3	....	....	....	8	....	....	....	....	....	....	....	....	....	....	....	....	....	....	....	....	....	....
1988-89	**Edmonton Oilers**	**NHL**	**57**	**3**	**15**	**18**	**3**	**11**	**14**	**28**	**1**	**0**	**1**	**42**	**7.1**	**60**	**13**	**74**	**18**	**–9**	**7**	**1**	**0**	**1**	**4**	**0**	**0**	**0**
1989-90♦	**Edmonton Oilers**	**NHL**	**48**	**4**	**20**	**24**	**3**	**14**	**17**	**42**	**0**	**0**	**0**	**41**	**9.8**	**72**	**14**	**52**	**18**	**24**	**20**	**2**	**6**	**8**	**16**	**1**	**0**	**0**
1990-91			OUT OF HOCKEY – RETIRED																									
1991-92	**Vancouver Canucks**	**NHL**	**21**	**1**	**4**	**5**	**1**	**3**	**4**	**24**	**0**	**0**	**0**	**19**	**5.3**	**17**	**2**	**27**	**9**	**–3**	**7**	**0**	**1**	**1**	**8**	**0**	**0**	**0**
	NHL Totals		**474**	**41**	**152**	**193**	**34**	**105**	**139**	**333**	**3**	**3**	**7**	**479**	**8.6**	**674**	**99**	**593**	**182**		**137**	**13**	**38**	**51**	**127**	**2**	**1**	**4**

CIAU Player of the Year (1979)

Signed as a free agent by **Edmonton**, October 18, 1982. Claimed by **Vancouver** from **Edmonton** in Waiver Draft, October 1, 1990.

• GREIG, Bruce

LW – L. 6'2", 220 lbs. b: High River, Alta., 5/9/1953. California's 6th, 114th overall, in 1973.

Season	Club	League	GP	G	A	Pts	AG	AA	APts	PIM	PP	SH	GW	S	%	TGF	PGF	TGA	PGA	+/-	Playoffs GP	G	A	Pts	PIM	PP	SH	GW
1971-72	Drumheller Miners	AJHL	5	0	1	1	....	....	....	6	....	....	....	....	....	....	....	....	....	....	....	....	....	....	....	....	....	....
	Medicine Hat Tigers	WCJHL	17	3	3	6	....	....	....	11	....	....	....	....	....	....	....	....	....	....	....	....	....	....	....	....	....	....
1972-73	Vancouver Nationals	WCJHL	24	3	3	6	....	....	....	79	....	....	....	....	....	....	....	....	....	....	....	....	....	....	....	....	....	....
1973-74	**California Golden Seals**	**NHL**	**1**	**0**	**0**	**0**	**0**	**0**	**0**	**4**	**0**	**0**	**0**	**0**	**0.0**	**0**	**0**	**0**	**0**	**0**	....	....	....	....	....	....	....	....
	Salt Lake Golden Eagles	WHL	13	1	2	3	....	....	....	36	....	....	....	....	....	....	....	....	....	....	....	....	....	....	....	....	....	....

Season	Club	League	REGULAR SEASON																		PLAYOFFS							
			GP	G	A	Pts	AG	AA	APts	PIM	PP	SH	GW	S	%	TGF	PGF	TGA	PGA	+/–	GP	G	A	Pts	PIM	PP	SH	GW
1974-75	**California Golden Seals**	**NHL**	8	0	1	1	0	1	1	42	0	0	0	5	0.0	1	0	4	0	–3	....	....	....	....	....	....	....	....
1975-76	Salt Lake Golden Eagles	CHL	1	0	0	0	....	....	....	11	....	....	....	....	....	....	....	....	....	....	....	....	....	....	....	....	....	....
	Flint Generals	IHL	10	0	5	5	....	....	....	77	....	....	....	....	....	....	....	....	....	....	....	....	....	....	....	....	....	....
1976-77	Calgary Cowboys	WHA	7	1	1	2	....	....	....	10	....	....	....	....	....	....	....	....	....	....	....	....	....	....	....	....	....	....
	Greensboro Generals	SHL	33	10	14	24	....	....	....	68	....	....	....	....	....	....	....	....	....	....	....	....	....	....	....	....	....	....
	Tidewater Sharks	SHL	2	0	0	0	....	....	....	2	....	....	....	....	....	....	....	....	....	....	....	....	....	....	....	....	....	....
1977-78	Cincinnati Stingers	WHA	32	3	1	4	....	....	....	57	....	....	....	....	....	....	....	....	....	....	....	....	....	....	....	....	....	....
1978-79	Indianapolis Racers	WHA	21	3	7	10	....	....	....	64	....	....	....	....	....	....	....	....	....	....	....	....	....	....	....	....	....	....
	San Diego Hawks	PHL	40	15	10	25	....	....	....	168	....	....	....	....	....	....	....	....	....	....	....	....	....	....	....	....	....	....
1979-80	Dayton Gems	IHL	42	12	17	29	....	....	....	112	....	....	....	....	....	....	....	....	....	....	....	....	....	....	....	....	....	....
	Toledo Goaldiggers	IHL	10	2	6	8	....	....	....	2	....	....	....	....	....	....	....	....	....	....	1	0	0	0	0	....	....	....
1980-81	Salem Raiders	EHL	58	20	32	52	....	....	....	213	....	....	....	....	....	....	....	....	....	....	6	2	2	4	2	....	....	....
1981-82	Dallas Black Hawks	CHL	9	0	3	3	....	....	....	10	....	....	....	....	....	....	....	....	....	....	....	....	....	....	....	....	....	....
	Salem Raiders	ACHL	37	12	20	32	....	....	....	212	....	....	....	....	....	....	....	....	....	....	11	1	6	7	28	....	....	....
1982-83	Virginia Raiders	ACHL	35	8	16	24	....	....	....	133	....	....	....	....	....	....	....	....	....	....	....	....	....	....	....	....	....	....
	Carolina Thunderbirds	ACHL	11	4	5	9	....	....	....	44	....	....	....	....	....	....	....	....	....	....	....	....	....	....	....	....	....	....
1983-84	Pine Bridge–Mohawk Valley	ACHL	37	12	12	24	....	....	....	206	....	....	....	....	....	....	....	....	....	....	5	0	2	2	49	....	....	....
	NHL Totals		9	0	1	1	0	1	1	46	0	0	0	5	0.0	1	0	4	0		....	....	....	....	....	....	....	....
	Other Major League Totals		60	7	9	16	....	....	....	131	....	....	....	....	....	....	....	....	....	....	....	....	....	....	....	....	....	....

• Brother of Mark

Selected by **Cleveland** (WHA) in 1973 WHA Amateur Draft, June, 1973. • Missed majority of 1973-74 season recovering from mononucleois, September, 1973. • Missed majority of 1974-75 season recovering from knee injury suffered in training camp, September 25, 1974. WHA rights traded to **Calgary** (WHA) by **Cleveland** (WHA) for cash, July, 1976. Signed as a free agent by **Cincinnati** (WHA) to 10-game trial contract, January, 1978. Signed as a free agent by **Indianapolis** (WHA), October, 1978.

• GREIG, Mark

RW – R. 5'11", 190 lbs. b: High River, Alta., 1/25/1970. Hartford's 1st, 15th overall, in 1990.

Season	Club	League	GP	G	A	Pts	AG	AA	APts	PIM	PP	SH	GW	S	%	TGF	PGF	TGA	PGA	+/–	GP	G	A	Pts	PIM	PP	SH	GW
1985-86	Blackie Bisons	AAHA	31	12	43	55	....	....	....	44	....	....	....	....	....	....	....	....	....	....	....	....	....	....	....	....	....	....
1986-87	Calgary North Stars	AAHA	18	9	28	37	....	....	....	30	....	....	....	....	....	....	....	....	....	....	....	....	....	....	....	....	....	....
	Calgary Wranglers	WHL	5	0	0	0	....	....	....	0	....	....	....	....	....	....	....	....	....	....	....	....	....	....	....	....	....	....
1987-88	Lethbridge Hurricanes	WHL	65	9	18	27	....	....	....	38	....	....	....	....	....	....	....	....	....	....	....	....	....	....	....	....	....	....
1988-89	Lethbridge Hurricanes	WHL	71	36	72	108	....	....	....	113	....	....	....	....	....	....	....	....	....	....	8	5	5	10	16	....	....	....
1989-90	Lethbridge Hurricanes	WHL	65	55	80	135	....	....	....	149	....	....	....	....	....	....	....	....	....	....	18	11	21	32	35	....	....	....
1990-91	**Hartford Whalers**	**NHL**	4	0	0	0	0	0	0	0	0	0	0	1	0.0	1	0	2	0	–1	....	....	....	....	....	....	....	....
	Springfield Indians	AHL	73	32	55	87	....	....	....	73	....	....	....	....	....	....	....	....	....	....	17	2	6	8	22	....	....	....
1991-92	**Hartford Whalers**	**NHL**	17	0	5	5	0	4	4	6	0	0	0	18	0.0	12	1	4	0	7	....	....	....	....	....	....	....	....
	Springfield Indians	AHL	50	20	27	47	....	....	....	38	....	....	....	....	....	....	....	....	....	....	9	1	1	2	20	....	....	....
1992-93	**Hartford Whalers**	**NHL**	22	1	7	8	1	5	6	27	0	0	0	16	6.3	9	2	18	0	–11	....	....	....	....	....	....	....	....
	Springfield Indians	AHL	55	20	38	58	....	....	....	86	....	....	....	....	....	....	....	....	....	....	....	....	....	....	....	....	....	....
1993-94	**Hartford Whalers**	**NHL**	31	4	5	9	4	4	8	31	0	0	0	41	9.8	14	3	17	0	–6	....	....	....	....	....	....	....	....
	Springfield Indians	AHL	4	0	4	4	....	....	....	21	....	....	....	....	....	....	....	....	....	....	....	....	....	....	....	....	....	....
	Toronto Maple Leafs	**NHL**	13	2	2	4	2	2	4	10	0	0	0	14	14.3	5	0	4	0	1	....	....	....	....	....	....	....	....
	St. John's Maple Leafs	AHL	9	4	6	10	....	....	....	0	....	....	....	....	....	....	....	....	....	....	11	4	2	6	26	....	....	....
1994-95	**Calgary Flames**	**NHL**	8	1	1	2	2	1	3	2	0	0	0	5	20.0	3	1	1	0	1	....	....	....	....	....	....	....	....
	Saint John Flames	AHL	67	31	50	81	....	....	....	82	....	....	....	....	....	....	....	....	....	....	2	0	1	1	0	....	....	....
1995-96	Atlanta Knights	IHL	71	25	48	73	....	....	....	104	....	....	....	....	....	....	....	....	....	....	3	2	1	3	4	....	....	....
1996-97	Quebec Rafales	IHL	5	1	2	3	....	....	....	0	....	....	....	....	....	....	....	....	....	....	....	....	....	....	....	....	....	....
	Houston Aeros	IHL	59	12	30	42	....	....	....	59	....	....	....	....	....	....	....	....	....	....	13	5	8	13	2	....	....	....
1997-98	Grand Rapids Griffins	IHL	69	26	36	62	....	....	....	103	....	....	....	....	....	....	....	....	....	....	3	0	4	4	4	....	....	....
1998-99	**Philadelphia Flyers**	**NHL**	7	1	3	4	1	3	4	2	0	0	0	9	11.1	4	2	1	0	1	2	0	1	1	0	0	0	0
	Philadelphia Phantoms	AHL	67	23	46	69	....	....	....	102	....	....	....	....	....	....	....	....	....	....	7	1	5	6	14	....	....	....
99-2000	**Philadelphia Flyers**	**NHL**	11	3	2	5	3	2	5	6	0	0	1	14	21.4	5	1	4	0	0	3	0	0	0	0	0	0	0
	Philadelphia Phantoms	AHL	68	34	48	82	....	....	....	116	....	....	....	....	....	....	....	....	....	....	5	3	2	5	6	....	....	....
	NHL Totals		113	12	25	37	13	21	34	84	0	0	1	118	10.2	53	10	51	0		5	0	1	1	0	0	0	0

• Brother of Bruce • WHL East First All-Star Team (1990)

Traded to **Toronto** by **Hartford** with Hartford's 6th round choice (Doug Bonner) in 1995 Entry Draft for Ted Crowley, January 25, 1994. Signed as a free agent by **Calgary**, August 9, 1994. Signed as a free agent by **Philadelphia**, July 28, 1998.

• GRENIER, Lucien

Lucien S.J. RW – L. 5'10", 163 lbs. b: Malartic, Que., 11/3/1946.

Season	Club	League	GP	G	A	Pts	AG	AA	APts	PIM	PP	SH	GW	S	%	TGF	PGF	TGA	PGA	+/–	GP	G	A	Pts	PIM	PP	SH	GW
1961-62	Quebec Citadelle	QJHL	STATISTICS NOT AVAILABLE																									
	Quebec Citadelle	Mem-Cup	9	0	4	4	....	....	....	12	....	....	....	....	....	....	....	....	....	....	....	....	....	....	....	....	....	....
1962-63	Quebec Citadelle	QJHL	STATISTICS NOT AVAILABLE																									
1963-64	Notre Dame Monarchs	MMJHL	44	19	29	48	....	....	....	19	....	....	....	....	....	....	....	....	....	....	18	9	7	16	15	....	....	....
	Notre Dame Monarchs	Mem-Cup	12	6	3	9	....	....	....	6	....	....	....	....	....	....	....	....	....	....	....	....	....	....	....	....	....	....
1964-65	Montreal Jr. Canadiens	OHA-Jr.	54	17	7	24	....	....	....	23	....	....	....	....	....	....	....	....	....	....	7	1	4	5	4	....	....	....
1965-66	Montreal Jr. Canadiens	OHA-Jr.	47	32	41	73	....	....	....	42	....	....	....	....	....	....	....	....	....	....	10	4	4	8	0	....	....	....
1966-67	Houston Apollos	CPHL	58	16	18	34	....	....	....	20	....	....	....	....	....	....	....	....	....	....	6	1	0	1	2	....	....	....
1967-68	Houston Apollos	CPHL	55	10	22	32	....	....	....	22	....	....	....	....	....	....	....	....	....	....	....	....	....	....	....	....	....	....
1968-69	Houston Apollos	CHL	56	17	23	40	....	....	....	22	....	....	....	....	....	....	....	....	....	....	3	1	0	1	0	....	....	....
♦	**Montreal Canadiens**	**NHL**	....	....	....	....	....	....	....	....	....	....	....	....	....	....	....	....	....	....	2	0	0	0	0	0	0	0
1969-70	**Montreal Canadiens**	**NHL**	23	2	3	5	2	3	5	2	0	0	1	25	8.0	12	0	12	1	1	....	....	....	....	....	....	....	....
	Montreal Voyageurs	AHL	25	12	8	20	....	....	....	4	....	....	....	....	....	....	....	....	....	....	....	....	....	....	....	....	....	....
1970-71	**Los Angeles Kings**	**NHL**	68	9	7	16	9	6	15	12	1	1	1	63	14.3	34	4	48	17	–1	....	....	....	....	....	....	....	....
1971-72	**Los Angeles Kings**	**NHL**	60	3	4	7	3	3	6	4	1	0	0	22	13.6	11	2	20	5	–6	....	....	....	....	....	....	....	....
1972-73	**Atlanta Flames**	**NHL**	DID NOT PLAY – INJURED																									
1973-74	Omaha Knights	CHL	56	5	5	10	....	....	....	15	....	....	....	....	....	....	....	....	....	....	5	0	1	1	0	....	....	....
1974-75	Omaha Knights	CHL	31	4	3	7	....	....	....	4	....	....	....	....	....	....	....	....	....	....	....	....	....	....	....	....	....	....
	NHL Totals		151	14	14	28	14	12	26	18	2	1	2	110	12.7	57	6	80	23		2	0	0	0	0	0	0	0

Traded to **LA Kings** by **Montreal** with Larry Mickey and Jack Norris for Leon Rochefort, Gregg Boddy and Wayne Thomas, May 22, 1970. Claimed by **Atlanta** from **LA Kings** in Expansion Draft, June 6, 1972. • Missed entire 1972-73 season recovering from ankle injury suffered in training camp, September, 1972.

• GRENIER, Richard

C – L. 5'11", 170 lbs. b: Montreal, Que., 9/18/1952. NY Islanders' 5th, 65th overall, in 1972.

Season	Club	League	GP	G	A	Pts	AG	AA	APts	PIM	PP	SH	GW	S	%	TGF	PGF	TGA	PGA	+/–	GP	G	A	Pts	PIM	PP	SH	GW
1969-70	St-Michael Cardinaux	QAAA	STATISTICS NOT AVAILABLE																									
1970-71	Quebec Remparts	QJHL	62	23	76	99	....	....	....	74	....	....	....	....	....	....	....	....	....	....	14	7	7	14	30	....	....	....
	Quebec Remparts	Mem-Cup	7	0	2	2	....	....	....	0	....	....	....	....	....	....	....	....	....	....	....	....	....	....	....	....	....	....
1971-72	Verdun Maple Leafs	QMJHL	61	46	56	102	....	....	....	83	....	....	....	....	....	....	....	....	....	....	4	2	1	3	4	....	....	....
1972-73	**New York Islanders**	**NHL**	10	1	1	2	1	1	2	2	0	0	1	18	5.6	2	0	4	0	–2	....	....	....	....	....	....	....	....
	New Haven Nighthawks	AHL	66	19	20	39	....	....	....	50	....	....	....	....	....	....	....	....	....	....	....	....	....	....	....	....	....	....
1973-74	Fort Worth Wings	CHL	70	28	26	54	....	....	....	39	....	....	....	....	....	....	....	....	....	....	5	2	2	7	6	....	....	....
1974-75	Fort Worth Texans	CHL	55	11	14	25	....	....	....	32	....	....	....	....	....	....	....	....	....	....	....	....	....	....	....	....	....	....
	New Haven Nighthawks	AHL	18	3	5	8	....	....	....	5	....	....	....	....	....	....	....	....	....	....	....	....	....	....	....	....	....	....
1975-76	Beauce Jaros	NAHL	73	77	83	160	....	....	....	82	....	....	....	....	....	....	....	....	....	....	12	14	4	18	12	....	....	....
1976-77	Quebec Nordiques	WHA	34	11	9	20	....	....	....	4	....	....	....	....	....	....	....	....	....	....	....	....	....	....	....	....	....	....
	Maine Nordiques	NAHL	41	25	23	48	....	....	....	12	....	....	....	....	....	....	....	....	....	....	12	*12	6	18	2	....	....	....
1977-78	Binghamton Whalers	AHL	75	*46	30	76	....	....	....	37	....	....	....	....	....	....	....	....	....	....	....	....	....	....	....	....	....	....
1978-79	Binghamton Whalers	AHL	68	37	27	64	....	....	....	36	....	....	....	....	....	....	....	....	....	....	10	6	4	10	13	....	....	....
1979-80	Nova Scotia Voyageurs	AHL	11	6	4	10	....	....	....	0	....	....	....	....	....	....	....	....	....	....	6	1	3	4	2	....	....	....
	VEU Feldkirch	Austria	34	60	43	103	....	....	....	68	....	....	....	....	....	....	....	....	....	....	....	....	....	....	....	....	....	....
1980-81	Kiekko-Reipas	Finland	36	29	21	50	....	....	....	36	....	....	....	....	....	....	....	....	....	....	....	....	....	....	....	....	....	....
1981-82	EHC Arosa	Switz.	36	*40	13	53	....	....	....	....	....	....	....	....	....	....	....	....	....	....	....	....	....	....	....	....	....	....
1982-83	EHC Arosa	Switz.	36	39	9	48	....	....	....	....	....	....	....	....	....	....	....	....	....	....	....	....	....	....	....	....	....	....

			REGULAR SEASON																		PLAYOFFS							
Season	Club	League	GP	G	A	Pts	AG	AA	APts	PIM	PP	SH	GW	S	%	TGF	PGF	TGA	PGA	+/–	GP	G	A	Pts	PIM	PP	SH	GW
1983-84	VSV Villach	Austria	28	42	47	89	....	....	....	....	....	....	....	....	....	....	....	....	....	....	....	....	....	....	....	....	....	....
1984-85	VSV Villach	Austria	32	29	45	74	....	....	....	38	....	....	....	....	....	....	....	....	....	....	....	....	....	....	....	....	....	....
1985-86	VSV Villach	Austria	41	36	52	88	....	....	....	30	....	....	....	....	....	....	....	....	....	....	....	....	....	....	....	....	....	....
1986-87	VSV Villach	Austria	20	14	21	35	....	....	....	22	....	....	....	....	....	....	....	....	....	....	....	....	....	....	....	....	....	....
	Austria	WC-B	7	3	4	7	....	....	....	2	....	....	....	....	....	....	....	....	....	....	....	....	....	....	....	....	....	....
1987-88	WEV Wien	Austria	34	19	26	45	....	....	....	24	....	....	....	....	....	....	....	....	....	....	....	....	....	....	....	....	....	....
1988-89	WEV Wien	Austria	38	11	25	36	....	....	....	....	....	....	....	....	....	....	....	....	....	....	....	....	....	....	....	....	....	....
1989-90	VEU Feldkirch	Austria	37	28	26	54	....	....	....	10	....	....	....	....	....	....	....	....	....	....	....	....	....	....	....	....	....	....
	NHL Totals		**10**	**1**	**1**	**2**	**1**	**1**	**2**	**2**	**0**	**0**	**1**	**18**	**5.6**	**2**	**0**	**4**	**0**		....	....	....	....	....	....	....	....
	Other Major League Totals		34	11	9	20	....	....	....	4	....	....	....	....	....	....	....	....	....	....	....	....	....	....	....	....	....	....

NAHL First All-Star Team (1976) • NAHL Second All-Star Team (1977)

Selected by **Miami-Philadelphia** (WHA) in 1972 WHA General Player Draft, February 13, 1972. WHA rights traded to **Quebec** (WHA) by **Calgary** (WHA) for future considerations, July, 1976,

• GRESCHNER, Ron

Ronald John D – L. 6'2", 205 lbs. b: Goodsoil, Sask., 12/22/1954. NY Rangers' 2nd, 32nd overall, in 1974.

Season	Club	League	GP	G	A	Pts	AG	AA	APts	PIM	PP	SH	GW	S	%	TGF	PGF	TGA	PGA	+/–	GP	G	A	Pts	PIM	PP	SH	GW
1971-72	Chilliwack Chiefs	BCJHL	STATISTICS NOT AVAILABLE																									
	New Westminster Bruins	WCJHL	44	1	9	10	....	....	....	126	....	....	....	....	....	....	....	....	....	....	5	·1	2	3	0	....	....	....
1972-73	New Westminster Bruins	WCJHL	68	22	47	69	....	....	....	169	....	....	....	....	....	....	....	....	....	....	5	2	4	6	19	....	....	....
1973-74	New Westminster Bruins	WCJHL	67	33	70	103	....	....	....	170	....	....	....	....	....	....	....	....	....	....	11	5	6	11	18	....	....	....
1974-75	**New York Rangers**	**NHL**	**70**	**8**	**37**	**45**	**7**	**28**	**35**	**93**	**0**	**0**	**2**	**122**	**6.6**	**128**	**28**	**108**	**16**	**8**	**3**	**0**	**1**	**1**	**2**	**0**	**0**	**0**
	Providence Reds	AHL	7	5	6	11	....	....	....	10	....	....	....	....	....	....	....	....	....	....	....	....	....	....	....	....	....	....
1975-76	**New York Rangers**	**NHL**	**77**	**6**	**21**	**27**	**5**	**16**	**21**	**93**	**2**	**0**	**0**	**176**	**3.4**	**85**	**21**	**135**	**20**	**–51**	....	....	....	....	....	....	....	....
1976-77	**New York Rangers**	**NHL**	**80**	**11**	**36**	**47**	**10**	**28**	**38**	**89**	**0**	**2**	**1**	**192**	**5.7**	**109**	**8**	**124**	**23**	**0**	....	....	....	....	....	....	....	....
1977-78	**New York Rangers**	**NHL**	**78**	**24**	**48**	**72**	**22**	**37**	**59**	**100**	**8**	**1**	**5**	**180**	**13.3**	**145**	**56**	**97**	**11**	**3**	**3**	**0**	**0**	**0**	**2**	**0**	**0**	**0**
1978-79	**New York Rangers**	**NHL**	**60**	**17**	**36**	**53**	**15**	**26**	**41**	**66**	**8**	**0**	**1**	**153**	**11.1**	**102**	**30**	**84**	**12**	**0**	**18**	**7**	**5**	**12**	**16**	**4**	**1**	**3**
	NHL All-Stars	Chal-Cup	DID NOT PLAY																									
1979-80	**New York Rangers**	**NHL**	**76**	**21**	**37**	**58**	**18**	**27**	**45**	**103**	**6**	**1**	**3**	**187**	**11.2**	**131**	**52**	**106**	**16**	**–11**	**9**	**0**	**6**	**6**	**10**	**0**	**0**	**0**
1980-81	**New York Rangers**	**NHL**	**74**	**27**	**41**	**68**	**21**	**27**	**48**	**112**	**6**	**0**	**1**	**193**	**14.0**	**135**	**42**	**106**	**13**	**0**	**14**	**4**	**8**	**12**	**17**	**1**	**0**	**0**
1981-82	New York Rangers	DN-Cup	3	1	0	1	....	....	....	....	....	....	....	....	....	....	....	....	....	....	....	....	....	....	....	....	....	....
	New York Rangers	**NHL**	**29**	**5**	**11**	**16**	**4**	**7**	**11**	**16**	**0**	**0**	**0**	**49**	**10.2**	**42**	**9**	**55**	**11**	**–11**	....	....	....	....	....	....	....	....
1982-83	**New York Rangers**	**NHL**	**10**	**3**	**5**	**8**	**2**	**3**	**5**	**0**	**1**	**0**	**0**	**12**	**25.0**	**9**	**3**	**6**	**0**	**0**	**8**	**2**	**2**	**4**	**12**	**2**	**0**	**0**
1983-84	**New York Rangers**	**NHL**	**77**	**12**	**44**	**56**	**10**	**30**	**40**	**117**	**5**	**0**	**0**	**130**	**9.2**	**109**	**39**	**67**	**2**	**5**	**2**	**1**	**0**	**1**	**2**	**0**	**0**	**0**
1984-85	**New York Rangers**	**NHL**	**48**	**16**	**29**	**45**	**13**	**20**	**33**	**42**	**8**	**0**	**2**	**88**	**18.2**	**73**	**32**	**62**	**2**	**–19**	**2**	**0**	**3**	**3**	**12**	**0**	**0**	**0**
1985-86	**New York Rangers**	**NHL**	**78**	**20**	**28**	**48**	**16**	**19**	**35**	**104**	**6**	**1**	**2**	**150**	**13.3**	**88**	**30**	**56**	**7**	**9**	**5**	**3**	**1**	**4**	**11**	**0**	**0**	**0**
1986-87	**New York Rangers**	**NHL**	**61**	**6**	**34**	**40**	**5**	**25**	**30**	**62**	**1**	**1**	**1**	**109**	**5.5**	**72**	**27**	**62**	**11**	**–6**	**6**	**0**	**5**	**5**	**0**	**0**	**0**	**0**
1987-88	**New York Rangers**	**NHL**	**51**	**1**	**5**	**6**	**1**	**4**	**5**	**82**	**0**	**0**	**0**	**67**	**1.5**	**48**	**12**	**64**	**19**	**–9**	....	....	....	....	....	....	....	....
1988-89	**New York Rangers**	**NHL**	**58**	**1**	**10**	**11**	**1**	**7**	**8**	**94**	**0**	**0**	**0**	**49**	**2.0**	**50**	**2**	**68**	**29**	**9**	**4**	**0**	**1**	**1**	**6**	**0**	**0**	**0**
1989-90	**New York Rangers**	**NHL**	**55**	**1**	**9**	**10**	**1**	**6**	**7**	**53**	**0**	**0**	**0**	**26**	**3.8**	**33**	**5**	**51**	**16**	**–7**	**10**	**0**	**0**	**0**	**16**	**0**	**0**	**0**
	NHL Totals		**982**	**179**	**431**	**610**	**151**	**310**	**461**	**1226**	**51**	**6**	**18**	**1883**	**9.5**	**1359**	**396**	**1251**	**208**		**84**	**17**	**32**	**49**	**106**	**7**	**1**	**3**

WCJHL First All-Star Team (1974) • Played in NHL All-Star Game (1980) • Missed majority of 1981-82 season recovering from back injury suffered in game vs. Philadelphia, November 18, 1981. • Missed majority of 1982-83 season recovering from back injury suffered in training camp, September, 1982.

• GRETZKY, Brent

C – L. 5'10", 160 lbs. b: Brantford, Ont., 2/20/1972. Tampa Bay's 3rd, 49th overall, in 1992.

Season	Club	League	GP	G	A	Pts	AG	AA	APts	PIM	PP	SH	GW	S	%	TGF	PGF	TGA	PGA	+/–	GP	G	A	Pts	PIM	PP	SH	GW
1987-88	Brantford Midget Classics	OMHA	40	49	70	119	....	....	....	....	....	....	....	....	....	....	....	....	....	....	....	....	....	....	....	....	....	....
	Brantford Classics	OJHL-B	14	4	11	15	....	....	....	2	....	....	....	....	....	....	....	....	....	....	....	....	....	....	....	....	....	....
1988-89	Brantford Classics	OJHL-B	40	29	47	76	....	....	....	57	....	....	....	....	....	....	....	....	....	....	....	....	....	....	....	....	....	....
1989-90	Belleville Bulls	OHL	66	15	32	47	....	....	....	30	....	....	....	....	....	....	....	....	....	....	11	0	0	0	0	....	....	....
1990-91	Belleville Bulls	OHL	66	26	56	82	....	....	....	25	....	....	....	....	....	....	....	....	....	....	6	3	3	6	2	....	....	....
1991-92	Belleville Bulls	OHL	62	43	78	121	....	....	....	37	....	....	....	....	....	....	....	....	....	....	....	....	....	....	....	....	....	....
1992-93	Atlanta Knights	IHL	77	20	34	54	....	....	....	84	....	....	....	....	....	....	....	....	....	....	9	3	2	5	8	....	....	....
1993-94	**Tampa Bay Lightning**	**NHL**	**10**	**1**	**2**	**3**	**1**	**2**	**3**	**2**	**0**	**0**	**0**	**14**	**7.1**	**3**	**0**	**3**	**0**	**0**	....	....	....	....	....	....	....	....
	Atlanta Knights	IHL	54	17	23	40	....	....	....	30	....	....	....	....	....	....	....	....	....	....	14	1	1	2	2	....	....	....
1994-95	**Tampa Bay Lightning**	**NHL**	**3**	**0**	**1**	**1**	**0**	**1**	**1**	**0**	**0**	**0**	**0**	**1**	**0.0**	**1**	**1**	**2**	**0**	**–2**	....	....	....	....	....	....	....	....
	Atlanta Knights	IHL	67	19	32	51	....	....	....	42	....	....	....	....	....	....	....	....	....	....	5	4	1	5	4	....	....	....
1995-96	St. John's Maple Leafs	AHL	68	13	28	41	....	....	....	40	....	....	....	....	....	....	....	....	....	....	4	0	6	6	0	....	....	....
1996-97	Las Vegas Thunder	IHL	40	5	12	17	....	....	....	8	....	....	....	....	....	....	....	....	....	....	....	....	....	....	....	....	....	....
	Quebec Rafales	IHL	1	0	0	0	....	....	....	0	....	....	....	....	....	....	....	....	....	....	....	....	....	....	....	....	....	....
	Pensacola Ice Pilots	ECHL	22	9	15	24	....	....	....	4	....	....	....	....	....	....	....	....	....	....	12	5	8	13	4	....	....	....
1997-98	EC Graz	Alpenliga	16	6	24	30	....	....	....	28	....	....	....	....	....	....	....	....	....	....	3	2	3	5	0	....	....	....
	EC Graz	Austria	18	11	16	27	....	....	....	8	....	....	....	....	....	....	....	....	....	....	....	....	....	....	....	....	....	....
1998-99	Asheville Smoke	UHL	32	28	42	70	....	....	....	29	....	....	....	....	....	....	....	....	....	....	....	....	....	....	....	....	....	....
	Hershey Bears	AHL	6	2	2	4	....	....	....	2	....	....	....	....	....	....	....	....	....	....	....	....	....	....	....	....	....	....
	Chicago Wolves	IHL	39	9	19	28	....	....	....	15	....	....	....	....	....	....	....	....	....	....	3	0	1	1	0	....	....	....
99-2000	Asheville Smoke	UHL	74	36	*92	*128	....	....	....	68	....	....	....	....	....	....	....	....	....	....	2	1	2	3	0	....	....	....
	Chicago Wolves	IHL	2	0	0	0	....	....	....	0	....	....	....	....	....	....	....	....	....	....	....	....	....	....	....	....	....	....
	NHL Totals		**13**	**1**	**3**	**4**	**1**	**3**	**4**	**2**	**0**	**0**	**0**	**15**	**6.7**	**4**	**1**	**5**	**0**		....	....	....	....	....	....	....	....

• Brother of Wayne • UHL First All-Star Team (2000)

Signed as a free agent by **Toronto**, September 20, 1995. Signed as a free agent by **Asheville** (UHL), August 18, 1998.

• GRETZKY, Wayne

Wayne Doug "The Great One" C – L. 6', 185 lbs. b: Brantford, Ont., 1/26/1961. **HHOF**

Season	Club	League	GP	G	A	Pts	AG	AA	APts	PIM	PP	SH	GW	S	%	TGF	PGF	TGA	PGA	+/–	GP	G	A	Pts	PIM	PP	SH	GW
1974-75	Brantford Charcon Chargers	OMHA	STATISTICS NOT AVAILABLE																									
1975-76	Vaughn Nationals	OHA-B	28	27	33	60	....	....	....	7	....	....	....	....	....	....	....	....	....	....	....	....	....	....	....	....	....	....
1976-77	Seneca Nationals	OHA-B	32	36	36	72	....	....	....	35	....	....	....	....	....	....	....	....	....	....	23	40	35	75	....	....	....	....
	Peterborough Petes	OMJHL	3	0	3	3	....	....	....	0	....	....	....	....	....	....	....	....	....	....	....	....	....	....	....	....	....	....
1977-78	Sault Ste. Marie Greyhounds	OMJHL	63	70	112	182	....	....	....	14	....	....	....	....	....	....	....	....	....	....	13	6	*20	26	0	....	....	....
	Canada	WJC-A	6	8	9	*17	....	....	....	2	....	....	....	....	....	....	....	....	....	....	....	....	....	....	....	....	....	....
1978-79	Indianapolis Racers	WHA	8	3	3	6	....	....	....	0	....	....	....	....	....	....	....	....	....	....	....	....	....	....	....	....	....	....
	Edmonton Oilers	WHA	72	43	61	104	....	....	....	19	....	....	....	....	....	....	....	....	....	....	13	*10	10	*20	2	....	....	....
1979-80	**Edmonton Oilers**	**NHL**	**79**	**51**	***86**	***137**	**44**	**63**	**107**	**21**	**13**	**1**	**6**	**284**	**18.0**	**155**	**42**	**116**	**18**	**15**	**3**	**2**	**1**	**3**	**0**	**0**	**0**	**0**
1980-81	**Edmonton Oilers**	**NHL**	**80**	**55**	***109**	***164**	**43**	**73**	**116**	**28**	**15**	**4**	**3**	**261**	**21.1**	**207**	**67**	**116**	**17**	**41**	**9**	**7**	**14**	**21**	**4**	**2**	**1**	**1**
1981-82	Canada	Can-Cup	7	5	7	*12	....	....	....	2	....	....	....	....	....	....	....	....	....	....	....	....	....	....	....	....	....	....
	Edmonton Oilers	**NHL**	**80**	***92**	***120**	***212**	**73**	**80**	**153**	**26**	**18**	**6**	**12**	**369**	**24.9**	**265**	**75**	**123**	**14**	**81**	**5**	**5**	**7**	**12**	**8**	**1**	**1**	**1**
	Canada	WEC-A	10	6	8	*14	....	....	....	0	....	....	....	....	....	....	....	....	....	....	....	....	....	....	....	....	....	....
1982-83	**Edmonton Oilers**	**NHL**	**80**	***71**	***125**	***196**	**59**	**87**	**146**	**59**	**18**	**6**	**9**	**348**	**20.4**	**236**	**77**	**134**	**35**	**60**	**16**	**12**	***26**	***38**	**4**	**2**	**3**	**3**
1983-84♦	**Edmonton Oilers**	**NHL**	**74**	***87**	***118**	***205**	**70**	**81**	**151**	**39**	**20**	**12**	**11**	**324**	**26.9**	**249**	**70**	**134**	**31**	**76**	**19**	**13**	***22**	***35**	**12**	**2**	**0**	**3**
1984-85	Canada	Can-Cup	8	5	7	*12	....	....	....	2	....	....	....	....	....	....	....	....	....	....	....	....	....	....	....	....	....	....
♦	**Edmonton Oilers**	**NHL**	**80**	***73**	***135**	***208**	**60**	**93**	**153**	**52**	**8**	**11**	**7**	**358**	**20.4**	**249**	**61**	**127**	**37**	**98**	**18**	**17**	***30**	***47**	**4**	**4**	**2**	**3**
1985-86	**Edmonton Oilers**	**NHL**	**80**	**52**	***163**	***215**	**42**	**111**	**153**	**46**	**11**	**3**	**6**	**350**	**14.9**	**260**	**69**	**162**	**42**	**71**	**10**	**8**	**11**	**19**	**2**	**4**	**1**	**2**
1986-87♦	**Edmonton Oilers**	**NHL**	**79**	***62**	***121**	***183**	**54**	**89**	**143**	**28**	**13**	**7**	**4**	**288**	**21.5**	**227**	**64**	**120**	**27**	**70**	**21**	**5**	***29**	***34**	**6**	**2**	**0**	**0**
	NHL All-Stars	RV-87	2	0	4	4	....	....	....	0	....	....	....	....	....	....	....	....	....	....	....	....	....	....	....	....	....	....
1987-88	Canada	Can-Cup	9	3	*18	*21	....	....	....	2	....	....	....	....	....	....	....	....	....	....	....	....	....	....	....	....	....	....
♦	**Edmonton Oilers**	**NHL**	**64**	**40**	***109**	**149**	**34**	**79**	**113**	**24**	**9**	**5**	**3**	**211**	**19.0**	**172**	**55**	**99**	**21**	**39**	**19**	**12**	***31**	***43**	**16**	**5**	**1**	**3**
1988-89	**Los Angeles Kings**	**NHL**	**78**	**54**	***114**	**168**	**46**	**81**	**127**	**26**	**11**	**5**	**5**	**303**	**17.8**	**213**	**72**	**169**	**43**	**15**	**11**	**5**	**17**	**22**	**0**	**1**	**1**	**0**
1989-90	**Los Angeles Kings**	**NHL**	**73**	**40**	***102**	***142**	**34**	**74**	**108**	**42**	**10**	**4**	**4**	**236**	**16.9**	**181**	**59**	**153**	**39**	**8**	**7**	**3**	**7**	**10**	**0**	**1**	**0**	**0**
1990-91	**Los Angeles Kings**	**NHL**	**78**	**41**	***122**	***163**	**38**	**94**	**132**	**16**	**8**	**0**	**5**	**212**	**19.3**	**200**	**70**	**110**	**10**	**30**	**12**	**4**	**11**	**15**	**2**	**1**	**0**	**2**
1991-92	Canada	Can-Cup	7	4	8	*12	....	....	....	2	....	....	....	....	....	....	....	....	....	....	....	....	....	....	....	....	....	....
	Los Angeles Kings	**NHL**	**74**	**31**	***90**	**121**	**28**	**68**	**96**	**34**	**12**	**2**	**2**	**215**	**14.4**	**151**	**65**	**114**	**16**	**–12**	**6**	**2**	**5**	**7**	**2**	**1**	**0**	**0**
1992-93	**Los Angeles Kings**	**NHL**	**45**	**16**	**49**	**65**	**13**	**34**	**47**	**6**	**0**	**2**	**1**	**141**	**11.3**	**90**	**36**	**60**	**12**	**6**	**24**	***15**	***25**	***40**	**4**	**4**	**1**	**3**
1993-94	**Los Angeles Kings**	**NHL**	**81**	**38**	***92**	***130**	**35**	**72**	**107**	**20**	**14**	**4**	**0**	**233**	**16.3**	**162**	**78**	**138**	**29**	**–25**	....	....	....	....	....	....	....	....
1994-95	**Los Angeles Kings**	**NHL**	**48**	**11**	**37**	**48**	**19**	**55**	**74**	**6**	**3**	**0**	**1**	**142**	**7.7**	**63**	**29**	**70**	**16**	**–20**	....	....	....	....	....	....	....	....

Season	Club	League	GP	G	A	Pts	AG	AA	APts	PIM	PP	SH	GW	S	%	TGF	PGF	TGA	PGA	+/-	GP	G	A	Pts	PIM	PP	SH	GW
			REGULAR SEASON																		PLAYOFFS							
1995-96	**Los Angeles Kings**	**NHL**	**62**	**15**	**66**	**81**	**15**	**54**	**69**	**32**	**5**	**0**	**2**	**144**	**10.4**	**97**	**42**	**76**	**14**	**-7**								
	St. Louis Blues	**NHL**	**18**	**8**	**13**	**21**	**8**	**11**	**19**	**2**	**1**	**1**	**1**	**51**	**15.7**	**27**	**13**	**25**	**5**	**-6**	**13**	**2**	**14**	**16**	**0**	**1**	**0**	**1**
1996-97	Canada	W-Cup	8	3	4	7				2																		
	New York Rangers	**NHL**	**82**	**25**	***72**	**97**	**26**	**64**	**90**	**28**	**6**	**0**	**2**	**286**	**8.7**	**125**	**41**	**83**	**11**	**12**	**15**	**10**	**10**	**20**	**2**	**3**	**0**	**2**
1997-98	**New York Rangers**	**NHL**	**82**	**23**	***67**	**90**	**27**	**66**	**93**	**28**	**6**	**0**	**4**	**201**	**11.4**	**110**	**41**	**85**	**5**	**-11**								
	Canada	Olympics	6	0	4	4				2																		
1998-99	**New York Rangers**	**NHL**	**70**	**9**	**53**	**62**	**11**	**51**	**62**	**14**	**3**	**0**	**3**	**132**	**6.8**	**81**	**38**	**71**	**5**	**-23**								
	NHL Totals		**1487**	**894**	**1963**	**2857**	**779**	**1480**	**2259**	**577**	**204**	**73**	**91**	**5089**	**17.6**	**3520**	**1164**	**2285**	**447**		**208**	**122**	**260**	**382**	**66**	**34**	**11**	**24**
	Other Major League Totals		80	46	64	110				19											13	10	10	20	2			

• Brother of Brent • Won Metro OHA-B Rookie-of-the-Year Award (1976) • WJC-A All-Star Team (1978) • Named Best Forward at WJC-A (1978) • OMJHL Second All-Star Team (1978) • WHA Second All-Star Team (1979) • Won Lou Kaplan Trophy (WHA Rookie of the Year) (1979) • Won Hart Trophy (1980, 1981, 1982, 1983, 1984, 1985, 1986, 1987, 1989) • Won Lady Byng Trophy (1980, 1991, 1992, 1994, 1999) • NHL Second All-Star Team (1980, 1988, 1989, 1990, 1994, 1997, 1998) • NHL First All-Star Team (1981, 1982, 1983, 1984, 1985, 1986, 1987, 1991) • Won Art Ross Trophy (1981, 1982, 1983, 1984, 1985, 1986, 1987, 1990, 1991, 1994) • NHL record for assists in regular season (1981, 1982, 1983, 1985, 1986) • NHL record for points in regular season (1981, 1982, 1986) • NHL record for goals in regular season (1982) • Won Lester B. Pearson Award (1982, 1983, 1984, 1985, 1987) • NHL Plus/Minus Leader (1982, 1984, 1985, 1987) • WEC-A All-Star Team (1982) • NHL record for assists in one playoff year (1983, 1985, 1988) • NHL record for points in one playoff year (1983, 1985) • Canada Cup All-Star Team (1984, 1987, 1991) • Won Conn Smythe Trophy (1985, 1988) • Selected Chrysler-Dodge/NHL Performer of the Year (1985, 1986, 1987) • Won Dodge Performance of the Year Award (1989) • Won Lester Patrick Trophy (1994)

Played in NHL All-Star Game (1980, 1981, 1982, 1983, 1984, 1985, 1986, 1988, 1989, 1990, 1991, 1992, 1993, 1994, 1996, 1997, 1998, 1999)

Signed as an underage free agent by **Indianapolis** (WHA), June 12, 1978. Traded to **Edmonton** (WHA) by **Indianapolis** (WHA) with Eddie Mio and Peter Driscoll for $700,000 and future considerations, November 2, 1978. Reclaimed by **Edmonton** as an under-age junior prior to Expansion Draft, June 9, 1979. Claimed as priority selection by **Edmonton**, June 9, 1979. Traded to **LA Kings** by **Edmonton** with Mike Krushelnyski and Marty McSorley for Jimmy Carson, Martin Gelinas, LA Kings' 1st round choices in 1989 (later traded to New Jersey — New Jersey selected Jason Miller), 1991 (Martin Rucinsky) and 1993 (Nick Stajduhar) Entry Drafts and cash, August 9, 1988. Traded to **St. Louis** by **LA Kings** for Craig Johnson, Patrice Tardif, Roman Vopat, St. Louis 5th round choice (Peter Hogan) in 1996 Entry Draft and 1st round choice (Matt Zultek) in 1997 Entry Draft, February 27, 1996. Signed as a free agent by **NY Rangers**, July 21, 1996. • Officially announced retirement, April 16, 1999.

• GRIER, Michael

Michael James RW – R. 6'1", 227 lbs. b: Detroit, MI, 1/5/1975. St. Louis' 7th, 219th overall, in 1993.

Season	Club	League	GP	G	A	Pts	AG	AA	APts	PIM	PP	SH	GW	S	%	TGF	PGF	TGA	PGA	+/-	GP	G	A	Pts	PIM	PP	SH	GW
1992-93	St. Sebastian's High	Hi-School	22	16	27	43				32																		
1993-94	Boston University	H-East	39	9	9	18				56																		
1994-95	Boston University	H-East	37	*29	26	55				85																		
	United States	WJC-A	7	0	2	2				12																		
1995-96	Boston University	H-East	38	21	25	46				82																		
1996-97	**Edmonton Oilers**	**NHL**	**79**	**15**	**17**	**32**	**16**	**15**	**31**	**45**	**4**	**0**	**2**	**89**	**16.9**	**52**	**8**	**37**	**0**	**7**	**12**	**3**	**1**	**4**	**4**	**1**	**0**	**1**
1997-98	**Edmonton Oilers**	**NHL**	**66**	**9**	**6**	**15**	**11**	**6**	**17**	**73**	**1**	**0**	**1**	**90**	**10.0**	**25**	**3**	**28**	**3**	**-3**	**12**	**2**	**2**	**4**	**13**	**0**	**0**	**1**
1998-99	**Edmonton Oilers**	**NHL**	**82**	**20**	**24**	**44**	**23**	**23**	**46**	**54**	**3**	**2**	**1**	**143**	**14.0**	**53**	**7**	**69**	**28**	**5**	**4**	**1**	**1**	**2**	**6**	**0**	**0**	**0**
99-2000	**Edmonton Oilers**	**NHL**	**65**	**9**	**22**	**31**	**10**	**20**	**30**	**68**	**0**	**3**	**2**	**115**														
	NHL Totals		**292**	**53**	**69**	**122**	**60**	**64**	**124**	**240**	**8**	**5**	**6**	**437**	**12.1**	**130**	**18**	**134**	**31**		**28**	**6**	**4**	**10**	**23**	**1**	**0**	**2**

Hockey East First All-Star Team (1995) • NCAA East First All-American Team (1995)

Rights traded to **Edmonton** by **St. Louis** with Curtis Joseph for St. Louis' 1st round choices (previously acquired) in 1996 (Marty Reasoner) and 1997 (later traded to LA Kings — LA Kings selected Matt Zultek) Entry Drafts, August 4, 1995.

• GRIEVE, Brent

Brent J. LW – L. 6'1", 202 lbs. b: Oshawa, Ont., 5/9/1969. NY Islanders' 4th, 65th overall, in 1989.

Season	Club	League	GP	G	A	Pts	AG	AA	APts	PIM	PP	SH	GW	S	%	TGF	PGF	TGA	PGA	+/-	GP	G	A	Pts	PIM	PP	SH	GW
1985-86	Oshawa Legionaires	OMHA	51	38	48	86				200																		
1986-87	Oshawa Generals	OHL	60	9	19	28				102											24	3	8	11	22			
	Oshawa Generals	Mem-Cup	4	0	2	2				16																		
1987-88	Oshawa Generals	OHL	55	19	20	39				122											7	0	1	1	8			
1988-89	Oshawa Generals	OHL	49	34	33	67				105											6	4	3	7	4			
1989-90	Oshawa Generals	OHL	62	46	47	93				125											17	10	10	20	26			
	Oshawa Generals	Mem-Cup	4	3	3	6				0																		
1990-91	Capital District Islanders	AHL	61	14	13	27				80																		
	Kansas City Blades	IHL	5	2	2	4				2																		
1991-92	Capital District Islanders	AHL	74	34	32	66				84											7	3	1	4	16			
1992-93	Capital District Islanders	AHL	79	34	28	62				122											4	1	1	2	10			
1993-94	**New York Islanders**	**NHL**	**3**	**0**	**0**	**0**	**0**	**0**	**0**	**7**	**0**	**0**	**0**	**1**	**0.0**	**0**	**0**	**1**	**1**	**0**								
	Salt Lake Golden Eagles	IHL	22	9	5	14				30																		
	Edmonton Oilers	**NHL**	**24**	**13**	**5**	**18**	**12**	**4**	**16**	**14**	**4**	**0**	**0**	**53**	**24.5**	**25**	**8**	**13**	**0**	**4**								
	Cape Breton Oilers	AHL	20	10	11	21				14											4	2	4	6	16			
1994-95	**Chicago Blackhawks**	**NHL**	**24**	**1**	**5**	**6**	**2**	**7**	**9**	**23**	**0**	**0**	**0**	**30**	**3.3**	**8**	**2**	**4**	**0**	**2**								
1995-96	**Chicago Blackhawks**	**NHL**	**28**	**2**	**4**	**6**	**2**	**3**	**5**	**28**	**0**	**0**	**0**	**22**	**9.1**	**11**	**0**	**6**	**0**	**5**								
	Indianapolis Ice	IHL	24	9	10	19				16																		
	Phoenix Roadrunners	IHL	13	8	11	19				14											4	2	1	3	18			
1996-97	**Los Angeles Kings**	**NHL**	**18**	**4**	**2**	**6**	**4**	**2**	**6**	**15**	**0**	**0**	**1**	**50**	**8.0**	**7**	**0**	**9**	**0**	**-2**								
	Phoenix Roadrunners	IHL	31	10	14	24				51																		
1997-98	Oshawa Generals	OHL	DID NOT PLAY – ASSISTANT COACH																									
	NHL Totals		**97**	**20**	**16**	**36**	**20**	**16**	**36**	**87**	**4**	**0**	**1**	**156**	**12.8**	**51**	**10**	**33**	**1**									

Traded to **Edmonton** by **NY Islanders** for Marc Laforge, December 15, 1993. Signed as a free agent by **Chicago**, July 7, 1994. Signed as a free agent by **LA Kings**, August 2, 1996.

• GRIMSON, Stu

"The Grim Reaper" LW – L. 6'5", 227 lbs. b: Kamloops, B.C., 5/20/1965. Calgary's 8th, 143rd overall, in 1985.

Season	Club	League	GP	G	A	Pts	AG	AA	APts	PIM	PP	SH	GW	S	%	TGF	PGF	TGA	PGA	+/-	GP	G	A	Pts	PIM	PP	SH	GW
1981-82	Kamloops Kolts	BCAHA	STATISTICS NOT AVAILABLE																									
1982-83	Regina Pats	WHL	48	0	1	1				105											5	0	0	0	14			
1983-84	Regina Pats	WHL	63	8	8	16				131											21	0	1	1	29			
1984-85	Regina Pats	WHL	71	24	32	56				248											8	1	2	3	14			
1985-86	University of Manitoba	CWUAA	12	7	4	11				113											8	1	1	2	24			
1986-87	University of Manitoba	CWUAA	29	8	8	16				67											14	4	2	6	28			
1987-88	Salt Lake Golden Eagles	IHL	38	9	5	14				268																		
1988-89	**Calgary Flames**	**NHL**	**1**	**0**	**0**	**0**	**0**	**0**	**0**	**5**	**0**	**0**	**0**	**0**	**0.0**	**0**	**0**	**0**	**0**	**0**								
	Salt Lake Golden Eagles	IHL	72	9	18	27				397											14	2	3	5	86			
1989-90	**Calgary Flames**	**NHL**	**3**	**0**	**0**	**0**	**0**	**0**	**0**	**17**	**0**	**0**	**0**	**0**	**0.0**	**0**	**0**	**1**	**0**	**-1**								
	Salt Lake Golden Eagles	IHL	62	8	8	16				319											4	0	0	0	8			
1990-91	**Chicago Blackhawks**	**NHL**	**35**	**0**	**1**	**1**	**0**	**1**	**1**	**183**	**0**	**0**	**0**	**14**	**0.0**	**4**	**0**	**7**	**0**	**-3**	**5**	**0**	**0**	**0**	**46**	**0**	**0**	**0**
1991-92	**Chicago Blackhawks**	**NHL**	**54**	**2**	**2**	**4**	**2**	**2**	**4**	**234**	**0**	**0**	**0**	**23**	**8.7**	**5**	**0**	**8**	**1**	**-2**	**14**	**0**	**1**	**1**	**10**	**0**	**0**	**0**
	Indianapolis Ice	IHL	5	1	1	2				17																		
1992-93	**Chicago Blackhawks**	**NHL**	**78**	**1**	**1**	**2**	**1**	**1**	**2**	**193**	**1**	**0**	**0**	**14**	**7.1**	**7**	**2**	**3**	**0**	**2**	**2**	**0**	**0**	**0**	**4**	**0**	**0**	**0**
1993-94	**Mighty Ducks of Anaheim**	**NHL**	**77**	**1**	**5**	**6**	**1**	**4**	**5**	**199**	**0**	**0**	**0**	**34**	**2.9**	**17**	**0**	**24**	**1**	**-6**								
1994-95	**Mighty Ducks of Anaheim**	**NHL**	**31**	**0**	**1**	**1**	**0**	**1**	**1**	**110**	**0**	**0**	**0**	**14**	**0.0**	**5**	**0**	**12**	**0**	**-7**								
	Detroit Red Wings	**NHL**	**11**	**0**	**0**	**0**	**0**	**0**	**0**	**37**	**0**	**0**	**0**	**4**	**0.0**	**2**	**0**	**6**	**0**	**-4**	**11**	**1**	**0**	**1**	**26**	**0**	**0**	**0**
1995-96	**Detroit Red Wings**	**NHL**	**56**	**0**	**1**	**1**	**0**	**1**	**1**	**128**	**0**	**0**	**0**	**19**	**0.0**	**6**	**0**	**16**	**0**	**-10**	**2**	**0**	**0**	**0**	**0**	**0**	**0**	**0**
1996-97	**Detroit Red Wings**	**NHL**	**1**	**0**	**0**	**0**	**0**	**0**	**0**	**0**	**0**	**0**	**0**	**0**	**0.0**	**0**	**0**	**1**	**0**	**-1**								
	Hartford Whalers	**NHL**	**75**	**2**	**2**	**4**	**2**	**2**	**4**	**218**	**0**	**0**	**0**	**17**	**11.8**	**8**	**0**	**15**	**0**	**-7**								
1997-98	**Carolina Hurricanes**	**NHL**	**82**	**3**	**4**	**7**	**4**	**4**	**8**	**204**	**0**	**0**	**1**	**17**	**17.6**	**10**	**0**	**10**	**0**	**0**								
1998-99	**Mighty Ducks of Anaheim**	**NHL**	**73**	**3**	**0**	**3**	**4**	**0**	**4**	**158**	**0**	**0**	**1**	**10**	**30.0**	**7**	**1**	**6**	**0**	**0**	**3**	**0**	**0**	**0**	**30**	**0**	**0**	**0**
99-2000	**Mighty Ducks of Anaheim**	**NHL**	**50**	**1**	**2**	**3**	**1**	**2**	**3**	**116**	**0**	**0**	**0**	**14**	**7.1**	**5**	**0**	**6**	**1**	**0**								
	NHL Totals		**627**	**13**	**19**	**32**	**15**	**18**	**33**	**1802**	**1**	**0**	**2**	**180**	**7.2**	**76**	**3**	**115**	**3**		**37**	**1**	**1**	**2**	**116**	**0**	**0**	**0**

• Re-entered NHL draft. Originally Detroit's 11th choice, 193rd overall, in 1983 Entry Draft.

Claimed on waivers by **Chicago** from **Calgary**, October 1, 1990. Claimed by **Anaheim** from **Chicago** in Expansion Draft, June 24, 1993. Traded to **Detroit** by **Anaheim** with Mark Ferner and Anaheim's 6th round choice (Magnus Nilsson) in 1996 Entry Draft for Mike Sillinger and Jason York, April 4, 1995. Claimed on waivers by **Hartford** from **Detroit**, October 13, 1996. Transferred to **Carolina** after **Hartford** franchise relocated, June 25, 1997. Traded to **Anaheim** by **Carolina** with Kevin Haller for David Karpa and Anaheim's 4th round choice (later traded to Atlanta - Atlanta selected Blake Robson) in 2000 Entry Draft, August 11, 1998. Signed as a free agent by **LA Kings**, July 6, 2000.

• GRISDALE, John

John Russell D – R. 6', 195 lbs. b: Geraldton, Ont., 8/23/1948.

			REGULAR SEASON																		PLAYOFFS							
Season	Club	League	GP	G	A	Pts	AG	AA	APts	PIM	PP	SH	GW	S	%	TGF	PGF	TGA	PGA	+/–	GP	G	A	Pts	PIM	PP	SH	GW
1966-67	Dixie Beehives	OHA-B	STATISTICS NOT AVAILABLE																									
1967-68	Michigan Tech Huskies	WCHA	DID NOT PLAY – FRESHMAN																									
1968-69	Michigan Tech Huskies	WCHA	30	7	7	14	....	....	....	45	....	....	....	....	....	....	....	....	....	....	....	....	....	....	....	....	....	....
1969-70	Michigan Tech Huskies	WCHA	33	2	11	13	....	....	....	62	....	....	....	....	....	....	....	....	....	....	....	....	....	....	....	....	....	....
1970-71	Michigan Tech Huskies	WCHA	31	2	23	25	....	....	....	61	....	....	....	....	....	....	....	....	....	....	....	....	....	....	....	....	....	....
	Tulsa Oilers	CHL	4	2	0	2	....	....	....	12	....	....	....	....	....	....	....	....	....	....	....	....	....	....	....	....	....	....
1971-72	Tulsa Oilers	CHL	59	0	15	15	....	....	....	105	....	....	....	....	....	....	....	....	....	....	13	1	3	4	23	....	....	....
1972-73	**Toronto Maple Leafs**	**NHL**	**49**	**1**	**7**	**8**	**1**	**6**	**7**	**76**	**0**	**0**	**0**	**49**	**2.0**	**47**	**2**	**76**	**9**	**–22**	....	....	....	....	....	....	....	....
1973-74	Tulsa Oilers	CHL	71	9	29	38	....	....	....	193	....	....	....	....	....	....	....	....	....	....	....	....	....	....	....	....	....	....
1974-75	**Toronto Maple Leafs**	**NHL**	**2**	**0**	**0**	**0**	**0**	**0**	**0**	**4**	**0**	**0**	**0**	**0**	**0.0**	**0**	**0**	**0**	**0**	**0**	....	....	....	....	....	....	....	....
	Vancouver Canucks	**NHL**	**58**	**1**	**12**	**13**	**1**	**9**	**10**	**91**	**0**	**0**	**0**	**41**	**2.4**	**68**	**6**	**73**	**14**	**3**	**5**	**0**	**1**	**1**	**13**	**0**	**0**	**0**
1975-76	**Vancouver Canucks**	**NHL**	**38**	**2**	**6**	**8**	**2**	**4**	**6**	**54**	**2**	**0**	**1**	**31**	**6.5**	**37**	**5**	**38**	**10**	**4**	**2**	**0**	**0**	**0**	**0**	**0**	**0**	**0**
	Tulsa Oilers	CHL	5	1	0	1	....	....	....	13	....	....	....	....	....	....	....	....	....	....	....	....	....	....	....	....	....	....
1976-77	**Vancouver Canucks**	**NHL**	**20**	**0**	**2**	**2**	**0**	**2**	**2**	**20**	**0**	**0**	**0**	**16**	**0.0**	**10**	**0**	**25**	**2**	**–13**	....	....	....	....	....	....	....	....
	Tulsa Oilers	CHL	47	2	23	25	....	....	....	132	....	....	....	....	....	....	....	....	....	....	9	2	4	6	11	....	....	....
1977-78	**Vancouver Canucks**	**NHL**	**42**	**0**	**9**	**9**	**0**	**7**	**7**	**47**	**0**	**0**	**0**	**44**	**0.0**	**45**	**2**	**57**	**16**	**2**	....	....	....	....	....	....	....	....
1978-79	**Vancouver Canucks**	**NHL**	**41**	**0**	**3**	**3**	**0**	**2**	**2**	**54**	**0**	**0**	**0**	**19**	**0.0**	**20**	**1**	**45**	**3**	**–23**	**3**	**0**	**0**	**0**	**2**	**0**	**0**	**0**
	Dallas Black Hawks	CHL	4	1	0	1	....	....	....	4	....	....	....	....	....	....	....	....	....	....	....	....	....	....	....	....	....	....
	NHL Totals		**250**	**4**	**39**	**43**	**4**	**30**	**34**	**346**	**2**	**0**	**1**	**200**	**2.0**	**227**	**16**	**314**	**54**		**10**	**0**	**1**	**1**	**15**	**0**	**0**	**0**

Signed as a free agent by **Toronto** (Tulsa-CHL) to four-game tryout contract, March, 1971. Traded to **Vancouver** by **Toronto** with Garry Monahan for Dave Dunn, October 16, 1974.

• GROLEAU, Francois

D – L. 6', 197 lbs. b: Longueuil, Que., 1/23/1973. Calgary's 2nd, 41st overall, in 1991.

Season	Club	League	GP	G	A	Pts	AG	AA	APts	PIM	PP	SH	GW	S	%	TGF	PGF	TGA	PGA	+/–	GP	G	A	Pts	PIM	PP	SH	GW
1988-89	Ste-Foy Gouverneurs	QAAA	42	3	24	27	....	....	....	42	....	....	....	....	....	....	....	....	....	....	....	....	....	....	....	....	....	....
1989-90	Shawinigan Cataractes	QMJHL	65	11	54	65	....	....	....	80	....	....	....	....	....	....	....	....	....	....	6	0	1	1	12	....	....	....
1990-91	Shawinigan Cataractes	QMJHL	70	9	60	69	....	....	....	70	....	....	....	....	....	....	....	....	....	....	6	0	3	3	2	....	....	....
1991-92	Shawinigan Cataractes	QMJHL	65	8	70	78	....	....	....	74	....	....	....	....	....	....	....	....	....	....	10	5	15	20	8	....	....	....
1992-93	St-Jean Lynx	QMJHL	48	7	38	45	....	....	....	66	....	....	....	....	....	....	....	....	....	....	4	0	1	1	14	....	....	....
1993-94	Saint John Flames	AHL	73	8	14	22	....	....	....	49	....	....	....	....	....	....	....	....	....	....	7	0	1	1	2	....	....	....
1994-95	Saint John Flames	AHL	65	6	34	40	....	....	....	28	....	....	....	....	....	....	....	....	....	....	....	....	....	....	....	....	....	....
	Cornwall Aces	AHL	8	1	2	3	....	....	....	7	....	....	....	....	....	....	....	....	....	....	14	2	7	9	16	....	....	....
1995-96	**Montreal Canadiens**	**NHL**	**2**	**0**	**1**	**1**	**0**	**1**	**1**	**2**	**0**	**0**	**0**	**1**	**0.0**	**2**	**0**	**0**	**0**	**2**	....	....	....	....	....	....	....	....
	San Francisco Spiders	IHL	63	6	26	32	....	....	....	60	....	....	....	....	....	....	....	....	....	....	....	....	....	....	....	....	....	....
	Fredericton Canadiens	AHL	12	3	5	8	....	....	....	10	....	....	....	....	....	....	....	....	....	....	10	1	6	7	14	....	....	....
1996-97	**Montreal Canadiens**	**NHL**	**5**	**0**	**0**	**0**	**0**	**0**	**0**	**4**	**0**	**0**	**0**	**3**	**0.0**	**3**	**0**	**3**	**0**	**0**	....	....	....	....	....	....	....	....
	Fredericton Canadiens	AHL	47	8	24	32	....	....	....	43	....	....	....	....	....	....	....	....	....	....	....	....	....	....	....	....	....	....
1997-98	**Montreal Canadiens**	**NHL**	**1**	**0**	**0**	**0**	**0**	**0**	**0**	**0**	**0**	**0**	**0**	**3**	**0.0**	**1**	**0**	**0**	**0**	**1**	....	....	....	....	....	....	....	....
	Fredericton Canadiens	AHL	63	14	26	40	....	....	....	70	....	....	....	....	....	....	....	....	....	....	4	0	2	2	4	....	....	....
1998-99	Augsburger Panther	Germany	52	9	21	30	....	....	....	67	....	....	....	....	....	....	....	....	....	....	5	0	4	4	4	....	....	....
99-2000	Quebec Citadelles	AHL	63	7	24	31	....	....	....	48	....	....	....	....	....	....	....	....	....	....	3	0	2	2	0	....	....	....
	NHL Totals		**8**	**0**	**1**	**1**	**0**	**1**	**1**	**6**	**0**	**0**	**0**	**7**	**0.0**	**6**	**0**	**3**	**0**		....	....	....	....	....	....	....	....

QMJHL Second All-Star Team (1990) • QMJHL First All-Star Team (1992)

Traded to **Quebec** by **Calgary** for Ed Ward, March 23, 1995. Signed as a free agent by **Montreal**, June 17, 1995.

• GRONMAN, Tuomas

D – R. 6'3", 219 lbs. b: Viitasaari, Finland, 3/22/1974. Quebec's 3rd, 29th overall, in 1992.

Season	Club	League	GP	G	A	Pts	AG	AA	APts	PIM	PP	SH	GW	S	%	TGF	PGF	TGA	PGA	+/–	GP	G	A	Pts	PIM	PP	SH	GW
1990-91	Lukko Rauma	Finn-Jr.	21	8	7	15	....	....	....	14	....	....	....	....	....	....	....	....	....	....	14	2	8	10	0	....	....	....
	Finland	EJC-A	5	1	0	1	....	....	....	4	....	....	....	....	....	....	....	....	....	....	....	....	....	....	....	....	....	....
1991-92	Tacoma Rockets	WHL	61	5	18	23	....	....	....	102	....	....	....	....	....	....	....	....	....	....	4	0	1	1	2	....	....	....
	Finland	WJC-A	7	1	0	1	....	....	....	10	....	....	....	....	....	....	....	....	....	....	....	....	....	....	....	....	....	....
1992-93	Lukko Rauma	Finn-Jr.	1	0	0	0	....	....	....	0	....	....	....	....	....	....	....	....	....	....	....	....	....	....	....	....	....	....
	Lukko Rauma	Finland	45	2	11	13	....	....	....	46	....	....	....	....	....	....	....	....	....	....	3	1	0	1	2	....	....	....
	Finland	WJC-A	7	1	2	3	....	....	....	14	....	....	....	....	....	....	....	....	....	....	....	....	....	....	....	....	....	....
1993-94	Lukko Rauma	Finland	44	4	12	16	....	....	....	60	....	....	....	....	....	....	....	....	....	....	9	0	1	1	14	....	....	....
	Finland	WJC-A	7	0	4	4	....	....	....	10	....	....	....	....	....	....	....	....	....	....	....	....	....	....	....	....	....	....
1994-95	TPS Turku	Finland-Jr.	1	0	0	0	....	....	....	0	....	....	....	....	....	....	....	....	....	....	....	....	....	....	....	....	....	....
	TPS Turku	Finland	47	4	20	24	....	....	....	66	....	....	....	....	....	....	....	....	....	....	13	2	2	4	43	....	....	....
1995-96	TPS Turku	Finland	32	5	7	12	....	....	....	85	....	....	....	....	....	....	....	....	....	....	11	1	4	5	*16	....	....	....
	Finland	Nat-Team	2	0	0	0	....	....	....	4	....	....	....	....	....	....	....	....	....	....	....	....	....	....	....	....	....	....
1996-97	**Chicago Blackhawks**	**NHL**	**16**	**0**	**1**	**1**	**0**	**1**	**1**	**13**	**0**	**0**	**0**	**9**	**0.0**	**2**	**0**	**7**	**1**	**–4**	....	....	....	....	....	....	....	....
	Indianapolis Ice	IHL	51	5	16	21	....	....	....	89	....	....	....	....	....	....	....	....	....	....	4	1	1	2	6	....	....	....
1997-98	Indianapolis Ice	IHL	6	0	3	3	....	....	....	6	....	....	....	....	....	....	....	....	....	....	....	....	....	....	....	....	....	....
	Pittsburgh Penguins	**NHL**	**22**	**1**	**2**	**3**	**1**	**2**	**3**	**25**	**1**	**0**	**1**	**33**	**3.0**	**15**	**5**	**7**	**0**	**3**	**1**	**0**	**0**	**0**	**0**	**0**	**0**	**0**
	Syracuse Crunch	AHL	33	6	14	20	....	....	....	45	....	....	....	....	....	....	....	....	....	....	....	....	....	....	....	....	....	....
	Finland	Nat-Team	2	0	0	0	....	....	....	0	....	....	....	....	....	....	....	....	....	....	....	....	....	....	....	....	....	....
	Finland	Olympics	4	0	0	0	....	....	....	2	....	....	....	....	....	....	....	....	....	....	....	....	....	....	....	....	....	....
1998-99	Kansas City Blades	IHL	4	0	0	0	....	....	....	0	....	....	....	....	....	....	....	....	....	....	....	....	....	....	....	....	....	....
99-2000	Jokerit Helsinki	Finland	51	1	9	10	....	....	....	72	....	....	....	....	....	....	....	....	....	....	1	0	0	0	0	....	....	....
	NHL Totals		**38**	**1**	**3**	**4**	**1**	**3**	**4**	**38**	**1**	**0**	**1**	**42**	**2.4**	**17**	**5**	**14**	**1**		**1**	**0**	**0**	**0**	**0**	**0**	**0**	**0**

Rights traded to **Chicago** by **Colorado** for Chicago's 2nd round choice (Phillippe Sauve) in 1998 Entry Draft, July 10, 1996. Traded to **Pittsburgh** by **Chicago** for Greg Johnson, October 27, 1997. • Missed majority of 1998-99 season recovering from knee injury suffered in game vs. Houston (IHL), October 16, 1998.

• GRONSTRAND, Jari

Jari V. D – L. 6'3", 195 lbs. b: Tampere, Finland, 11/14/1962. Minnesota's 8th, 96th overall, in 1986.

Season	Club	League	GP	G	A	Pts	AG	AA	APts	PIM	PP	SH	GW	S	%	TGF	PGF	TGA	PGA	+/–	GP	G	A	Pts	PIM	PP	SH	GW
1979-80	Tappara Tampere	Finn-Jr.	1	0	0	0	....	....	....	0	....	....	....	....	....	....	....	....	....	....	....	....	....	....	....	....	....	....
1980-81	Tappara Tampere	Finn-Jr.	32	5	12	17	....	....	....	20	....	....	....	....	....	....	....	....	....	....	....	....	....	....	....	....	....	....
1981-82	Tappara Tampere	Finn-Jr.	24	5	9	14	....	....	....	22	....	....	....	....	....	....	....	....	....	....	....	....	....	....	....	....	....	....
1982-83	Tappara Tampere	Finn-Jr.	11	1	2	3	....	....	....	18	....	....	....	....	....	....	....	....	....	....	....	....	....	....	....	....	....	....
	Tappara Tampere	Finland	35	2	2	4	....	....	....	18	....	....	....	....	....	....	....	....	....	....	8	0	0	0	4	....	....	....
1983-84	Tappara Tampere	Finland	32	2	4	6	....	....	....	14	....	....	....	....	....	....	....	....	....	....	9	0	2	2	4	....	....	....
1984-85	Tappara Tampere	Finland	36	1	9	10	....	....	....	27	....	....	....	....	....	....	....	....	....	....	....	....	....	....	....	....	....	....
1985-86	Tappara Tampere	Finland	36	9	5	14	....	....	....	32	....	....	....	....	....	....	....	....	....	....	8	1	2	3	4	....	....	....
	Finland	Nat-Team	10	1	0	1	....	....	....	2	....	....	....	....	....	....	....	....	....	....	....	....	....	....	....	....	....	....
	Finland	WEC-A	9	0	2	2	....	....	....	8	....	....	....	....	....	....	....	....	....	....	....	....	....	....	....	....	....	....
1986-87	**Minnesota North Stars**	**NHL**	**47**	**1**	**6**	**7**	**1**	**4**	**5**	**27**	**0**	**0**	**0**	**32**	**3.1**	**42**	**2**	**54**	**18**	**4**	....	....	....	....	....	....	....	....
1987-88	Finland	Can-Cup	4	0	0	0	....	....	....	0	....	....	....	....	....	....	....	....	....	....	....	....	....	....	....	....	....	....
	New York Rangers	**NHL**	**62**	**3**	**11**	**14**	**3**	**8**	**11**	**63**	**1**	**0**	**0**	**65**	**4.6**	**62**	**11**	**73**	**30**	**8**	....	....	....	....	....	....	....	....
	Colorado Rangers	IHL	3	1	3	4	....	....	....	0	....	....	....	....	....	....	....	....	....	....	....	....	....	....	....	....	....	....
	Finland	Nat-Team	6	0	0	0	....	....	....	19	....	....	....	....	....	....	....	....	....	....	....	....	....	....	....	....	....	....
1988-89	**Quebec Nordiques**	**NHL**	**25**	**1**	**3**	**4**	**1**	**2**	**3**	**14**	**0**	**0**	**0**	**18**	**5.6**	**20**	**4**	**28**	**3**	**–9**	....	....	....	....	....	....	....	....
	Halifax Citadels	AHL	8	0	1	1	....	....	....	5	....	....	....	....	....	....	....	....	....	....	....	....	....	....	....	....	....	....
1989-90	**Quebec Nordiques**	**NHL**	**7**	**0**	**1**	**1**	**0**	**1**	**1**	**2**	**0**	**0**	**0**	**3**	**0.0**	**3**	**0**	**8**	**4**	**–1**	....	....	....	....	....	....	....	....
	Halifax Citadels	AHL	2	0	0	0	....	....	....	0	....	....	....	....	....	....	....	....	....	....	....	....	....	....	....	....	....	....
	New York Islanders	**NHL**	**41**	**3**	**4**	**7**	**3**	**3**	**6**	**27**	**0**	**0**	**2**	**23**	**13.0**	**21**	**0**	**24**	**3**	**0**	**3**	**0**	**0**	**0**	**4**	**0**	**0**	**0**
	Springfield Indians	AHL	1	0	1	1	....	....	....	0	....	....	....	....	....	....	....	....	....	....	....	....	....	....	....	....	....	....
1990-91	**New York Islanders**	**NHL**	**3**	**0**	**1**	**1**	**0**	**1**	**1**	**2**	**0**	**0**	**0**	**1**	**0.0**	**3**	**1**	**4**	**0**	**–2**	....	....	....	....	....	....	....	....
	Capital District Islanders	AHL	63	13	22	35	....	....	....	40	....	....	....	....	....	....	....	....	....	....	....	....	....	....	....	....	....	....
1991-92	Tappara Tampere	Finland	38	3	7	10	....	....	....	52	....	....	....	....	....	....	....	....	....	....	3	1	2	3	2	....	....	....
1992-93	Tappara Tampere	Finland	46	5	5	10	....	....	....	76	....	....	....	....	....	....	....	....	....	....	....	....	....	....	....	....	....	....
1993-94	Tappara Tampere	Finland	48	5	6	11	....	....	....	34	....	....	....	....	....	....	....	....	....	....	....	....	....	....	....	....	....	....
1994-95	HC Saxonia	Germany-2	39	3	7	10	....	....	....	10	....	....	....	....	....	....	....	....	....	....	2	0	1	1	4	....	....	....

			REGULAR SEASON																		PLAYOFFS							
Season	Club	League	GP	G	A	Pts	AG	AA	APts	PIM	PP	SH	GW	S	%	TGF	PGF	TGA	PGA	+/–	GP	G	A	Pts	PIM	PP	SH	GW
1995-96	HC Chamonix	France	27	5	13	18	....	....	....	38	....	....	....	....	....	....	....	....	....	....	9	6	5	11	10	....	....	....
1996-97	HC Reims	France	27	4	8	12	....	....	....	30	....	....	....	....	....	....	....	....	....	....	3	0	0	0	0	....	....	....
1997-98	HC Reims	France	40	7	22	29	....	....	....	42	....	....	....	....	....	....	....	....	....	....	....	....	....	....	....	....	....	....
1998-99	HC Reims	France	35	6	11	17	....	....	....	....	....	....	....	....	....	....	....	....	....	....	11	1	1	2	....	....	....	....
99-2000	HC Reims	France	DID NOT PLAY – COACHING																									
	NHL Totals		**185**	**8**	**26**	**34**	**8**	**19**	**27**	**135**	**1**	**0**	**2**	**142**	**5.6**	**151**	**18**	**191**	**58**		**3**	**0**	**0**	**0**	**4**	**0**	**0**	**0**

Finnish First All-Star Team (1986)

Traded to **NY Rangers** by **Minnesota** with Paul Boutilier for Jay Caufield and Dave Gagner, October 8, 1987. Traded to **Quebec** by **NY Rangers** with Bruce Bell, Walt Poddubny and NY Rangers 4th round choice (Eric Dubois) in 1989 Entry Draft for Jason Lafreniere and Normand Rochefort, August 1, 1988. Claimed on waivers by **NY Islanders**, November 21, 1989.

• GROSEK, Michal

LW – R. 6'2", 207 lbs. b: Vyskov, Czech., 6/1/1975. Winnipeg's 7th, 145th overall, in 1993.

Season	Club	League	GP	G	A	Pts	AG	AA	APts	PIM	PP	SH	GW	S	%	TGF	PGF	TGA	PGA	+/–	GP	G	A	Pts	PIM	PP	SH	GW
1992-93	ZPS Zlin	Czech.	17	1	3	4	....	....	....	....	....	....	....	....	....	....	....	....	....	....	....	....	....	....	....	....	....	....
1993-94	Tacoma Rockets	WHL	30	25	20	45	....	....	....	106	....	....	....	....	....	....	....	....	....	....	7	2	2	4	30	....	....	....
	Winnipeg Jets	**NHL**	**3**	**1**	**0**	**1**	**1**	**0**	**1**	**0**	**0**	**0**	**0**	**4**	**25.0**	**1**	**0**	**2**	**0**	**–1**	....	....	....	....	....	....	....	....
	Moncton Hawks	AHL	20	1	2	3	....	....	....	47	....	....	....	....	....	....	....	....	....	....	2	0	0	0	0	....	....	....
1994-95	**Winnipeg Jets**	**NHL**	**24**	**2**	**2**	**4**	**4**	**3**	**7**	**21**	**0**	**0**	**1**	**27**	**7.4**	**10**	**2**	**11**	**0**	**–3**	....	....	....	....	....	....	....	....
	Springfield Falcons	AHL	45	10	22	32	....	....	....	98	....	....	....	....	....	....	....	....	....	....	....	....	....	....	....	....	....	....
1995-96	**Winnipeg Jets**	**NHL**	**1**	**0**	**0**	**0**	**0**	**0**	**0**	**0**	**0**	**0**	**0**	**1**	**0.0**	**0**	**0**	**1**	**0**	**–1**	....	....	....	....	....	....	....	....
	Springfield Falcons	AHL	39	16	19	35	....	....	....	68	....	....	....	....	....	....	....	....	....	....	....	....	....	....	....	....	....	....
	Buffalo Sabres	**NHL**	**22**	**6**	**4**	**10**	**6**	**3**	**9**	**31**	**2**	**0**	**1**	**33**	**18.2**	**15**	**6**	**11**	**2**	**0**	....	....	....	....	....	....	....	....
1996-97	**Buffalo Sabres**	**NHL**	**82**	**15**	**21**	**36**	**16**	**19**	**35**	**71**	**1**	**0**	**2**	**117**	**12.8**	**65**	**7**	**34**	**1**	**25**	**12**	**3**	**3**	**6**	**8**	**0**	**0**	**0**
1997-98	**Buffalo Sabres**	**NHL**	**67**	**10**	**20**	**30**	**12**	**20**	**32**	**60**	**2**	**0**	**1**	**114**	**8.8**	**41**	**8**	**24**	**0**	**9**	**15**	**6**	**4**	**10**	**28**	**2**	**0**	**3**
1998-99	**Buffalo Sabres**	**NHL**	**76**	**20**	**30**	**50**	**23**	**29**	**52**	**102**	**4**	**0**	**3**	**140**	**14.3**	**75**	**24**	**30**	**0**	**21**	**13**	**0**	**4**	**4**	**28**	**0**	**0**	**0**
99-2000	**Buffalo Sabres**	**NHL**	**61**	**11**	**23**	**34**	**12**	**21**	**33**	**35**	**2**	**0**	**2**	**96**	**11.5**	**52**	**9**	**31**	**0**	**12**	....	....	....	....	....	....	....	....
	Chicago Blackhawks	**NHL**	**14**	**2**	**4**	**6**	**2**	**4**	**6**	**12**	**1**	**0**	**0**	**18**	**11.1**	**8**	**1**	**8**	**0**	**–1**	....	....	....	....	....	....	....	....
	NHL Totals		**350**	**67**	**104**	**171**	**76**	**99**	**175**	**332**	**12**	**0**	**10**	**550**	**12.2**	**267**	**57**	**152**	**3**		**40**	**9**	**11**	**20**	**64**	**2**	**0**	**3**

Traded to **Buffalo** by **Winnipeg** with Darryl Shannon for Craig Muni, February 15, 1996. Traded to **Chicago** by **Buffalo** for Doug Gilmour, J.P. Dumont and future considerations, March 10, 2000.

• GROULX, Wayne

C – R. 6'1", 185 lbs. b: Welland, Ont., 2/2/1965. Quebec's 8th, 179th overall, in 1983.

Season	Club	League	GP	G	A	Pts	AG	AA	APts	PIM	PP	SH	GW	S	%	TGF	PGF	TGA	PGA	+/–	GP	G	A	Pts	PIM	PP	SH	GW
1980-81	Welland Cougars	OHA-B	38	44	32	76	....	....	....	44	....	....	....	....	....	....	....	....	....	....	....	....	....	....	....	....	....	....
1981-82	Sault Ste. Marie Greyhounds	OHL	66	25	41	66	....	....	....	66	....	....	....	....	....	....	....	....	....	....	13	6	8	14	8	....	....	....
1982-83	Sault Ste. Marie Greyhounds	OHL	67	44	86	130	....	....	....	54	....	....	....	....	....	....	....	....	....	....	16	7	9	16	13	....	....	....
1983-84	Sault Ste. Marie Greyhounds	OHL	70	59	78	137	....	....	....	48	....	....	....	....	....	....	....	....	....	....	16	14	0	*36	13	....	....	....
1984-85	Sault Ste. Marie Greyhounds	OHL	64	59	85	144	....	....	....	102	....	....	....	....	....	....	....	....	....	....	16	*18	18	*36	24	....	....	....
	Quebec Nordiques	**NHL**	**1**	**0**	**0**	**0**	**0**	**0**	**0**	**0**	**0**	**0**	**0**	**0**	**0.0**	**0**	**0**	**0**	**0**	**0**	....	....	....	....	....	....	....	....
	Sault Ste. Marie Greyhounds	Mem-Cup	4	2	2	4	....	....	....	7	....	....	....	....	....	....	....	....	....	....	....	....	....	....	....	....	....	....
1985-86	Fredericton Express	AHL	15	2	6	8	....	....	....	12	....	....	....	....	....	....	....	....	....	....	....	....	....	....	....	....	....	....
	Muskegon Lumberjacks	IHL	55	22	27	49	....	....	....	56	....	....	....	....	....	....	....	....	....	....	12	4	4	8	26	....	....	....
1986-87	Fredericton Express	AHL	30	11	7	18	....	....	....	8	....	....	....	....	....	....	....	....	....	....	....	....	....	....	....	....	....	....
	Muskegon Lumberjacks	IHL	38	18	22	40	....	....	....	49	....	....	....	....	....	....	....	....	....	....	....	....	....	....	....	....	....	....
	Canada	Nat-Team	9	3	4	7	....	....	....	8	....	....	....	....	....	....	....	....	....	....	....	....	....	....	....	....	....	....
1987-88	KalPa Kuopio	Finland	27	17	10	27	....	....	....	54	....	....	....	....	....	....	....	....	....	....	....	....	....	....	....	....	....	....
	Baltimore Skipjacks	AHL	5	5	0	5	....	....	....	15	....	....	....	....	....	....	....	....	....	....	....	....	....	....	....	....	....	....
1988-89	EHC Lustenau	Austria	40	40	47	87	....	....	....	....	....	....	....	....	....	....	....	....	....	....	....	....	....	....	....	....	....	....
1989-90	EC Graz	Austria	36	42	41	83	....	....	....	87	....	....	....	....	....	....	....	....	....	....	....	....	....	....	....	....	....	....
1990-91	EC Graz	Austria	32	26	22	48	....	....	....	85	....	....	....	....	....	....	....	....	....	....	....	....	....	....	....	....	....	....
1991-92	EC Graz	Austria	29	14	19	33	....	....	....	....	....	....	....	....	....	....	....	....	....	....	....	....	....	....	....	....	....	....
	Austria	WC-B	7	7	7	14	....	....	....	43	....	....	....	....	....	....	....	....	....	....	....	....	....	....	....	....	....	....
1992-93	EC Graz	Austria	55	*64	38	102	....	....	....	....	....	....	....	....	....	....	....	....	....	....	....	....	....	....	....	....	....	....
	Austria	WC-A	6	0	0	0	....	....	....	10	....	....	....	....	....	....	....	....	....	....	....	....	....	....	....	....	....	....
1993-94	EC Graz	Austria	44	20	17	37	....	....	....	....	....	....	....	....	....	....	....	....	....	....	....	....	....	....	....	....	....	....
1994-95	Lakeland Warriors	SunHL	13	7	12	19	....	....	....	22	....	....	....	....	....	....	....	....	....	....	....	....	....	....	....	....	....	....
	NHL Totals		**1**	**0**	**0**	**0**	**0**	**0**	**0**	**0**	**0**	**0**	**0**	**0**	**0.0**	**0**	**0**	**0**	**0**		....	....	....	....	....	....	....	....

OHL Second All-Star Team (1984) • OHL First All-Star Team (1985)

• GRUDEN, John

John D. D – L. 6', 203 lbs. b: Virginia, MN, 6/4/1970. Boston's 7th, 168th overall, in 1990.

Season	Club	League	GP	G	A	Pts	AG	AA	APts	PIM	PP	SH	GW	S	%	TGF	PGF	TGA	PGA	+/–	GP	G	A	Pts	PIM	PP	SH	GW
1989-90	Waterloo Black Hawks	USHL	47	7	39	46	....	....	....	35	....	....	....	....	....	....	....	....	....	....	....	....	....	....	....	....	....	....
1990-91	Ferris State Bulldogs	CCHA	37	4	11	15	....	....	....	27	....	....	....	....	....	....	....	....	....	....	....	....	....	....	....	....	....	....
1991-92	Ferris State Bulldogs	CCHA	37	9	14	23	....	....	....	24	....	....	....	....	....	....	....	....	....	....	....	....	....	....	....	....	....	....
1992-93	Ferris State Bulldogs	CCHA	41	16	14	30	....	....	....	58	....	....	....	....	....	....	....	....	....	....	....	....	....	....	....	....	....	....
1993-94	Ferris State Bulldogs	CCHA	38	11	25	36	....	....	....	52	....	....	....	....	....	....	....	....	....	....	....	....	....	....	....	....	....	....
	Boston Bruins	**NHL**	**7**	**0**	**1**	**1**	**0**	**1**	**1**	**2**	**0**	**0**	**0**	**8**	**0.0**	**2**	**0**	**6**	**1**	**–3**	....	....	....	....	....	....	....	....
1994-95	**Boston Bruins**	**NHL**	**38**	**0**	**6**	**6**	**0**	**9**	**9**	**22**	**0**	**0**	**0**	**30**	**0.0**	**26**	**0**	**23**	**0**	**3**	....	....	....	....	....	....	....	....
	Providence Bruins	AHL	1	0	1	1	....	....	....	0	....	....	....	....	....	....	....	....	....	....	....	....	....	....	....	....	....	....
1995-96	**Boston Bruins**	**NHL**	**14**	**0**	**0**	**0**	**0**	**0**	**0**	**4**	**0**	**0**	**0**	**12**	**0.0**	**2**	**0**	**5**	**0**	**–3**	**3**	**0**	**1**	**1**	**0**	**0**	**0**	**0**
	Providence Bruins	AHL	39	5	19	24	....	....	....	29	....	....	....	....	....	....	....	....	....	....	....	....	....	....	....	....	....	....
1996-97	Providence Bruins	AHL	78	18	27	45	....	....	....	52	....	....	....	....	....	....	....	....	....	....	10	3	6	9	4	....	....	....
1997-98	Detroit Vipers	IHL	76	13	42	55	....	....	....	74	....	....	....	....	....	....	....	....	....	....	21	1	8	9	14	....	....	....
1998-99	**Ottawa Senators**	**NHL**	**13**	**0**	**1**	**1**	**0**	**1**	**1**	**8**	**0**	**0**	**0**	**10**	**0.0**	**7**	**2**	**7**	**2**	**0**	....	....	....	....	....	....	....	....
	Detroit Vipers	IHL	59	10	28	38	....	....	....	52	....	....	....	....	....	....	....	....	....	....	10	0	1	1	6	....	....	....
99-2000	**Ottawa Senators**	**NHL**	**9**	**0**	**0**	**0**	**0**	**0**	**0**	**4**	**0**	**0**	**0**	**3**	**0.0**	**3**	**1**	**2**	**0**	**0**	....	....	....	....	....	....	....	....
	Grand Rapids Griffins	IHL	50	5	17	22	....	....	....	24	....	....	....	....	....	....	....	....	....	....	12	1	4	5	8	....	....	....
	NHL Totals		**81**	**0**	**8**	**8**	**0**	**11**	**11**	**40**	**0**	**0**	**0**	**63**	**0.0**	**40**	**3**	**43**	**3**		**3**	**0**	**1**	**1**	**0**	**0**	**0**	**0**

CCHA First All-Star Team (1994) • NCAA West First All-American Team (1994) • IHL Second All-Star Team (1998)

Signed as a free agent by **Ottawa**, August 7, 1998.

• GRUEN, Danny

Daniel Patrick LW – L. 5'11", 190 lbs. b: Thunder Bay, Ont., 6/26/1952. Detroit's 3rd, 58th overall, in 1972.

Season	Club	League	GP	G	A	Pts	AG	AA	APts	PIM	PP	SH	GW	S	%	TGF	PGF	TGA	PGA	+/–	GP	G	A	Pts	PIM	PP	SH	GW
1968-69	Fort William Canadiens	TBJHL	24	7	5	12	....	....	....	30	....	....	....	....	....	....	....	....	....	....	....	....	....	....	....	....	....	....
1969-70	Fort William Canadiens	TBJHL	23	11	16	27	....	....	....	66	....	....	....	....	....	....	....	....	....	....	....	....	....	....	....	....	....	....
1970-71	Thunder Bay Vulcans	TBJHL	STATISTICS NOT AVAILABLE																									
1971-72	Thunder Bay Vulcans	TBJHL	36	30	60	90	....	....	....	....	....	....	....	....	....	....	....	....	....	....	....	....	....	....	....	....	....	....
1972-73	**Detroit Red Wings**	**NHL**	**2**	**0**	**0**	**0**	**0**	**0**	**0**	**0**	**0**	**0**	**0**	**1**	**0.0**	**0**	**0**	**0**	**0**	**0**	....	....	....	....	....	....	....	....
	Fort Worth Wings	CHL	68	35	45	*80	....	....	....	*194	....	....	....	....	....	....	....	....	....	....	4	4	1	5	9	....	....	....
	Virginia Wings	AHL	3	1	1	2	....	....	....	0	....	....	....	....	....	....	....	....	....	....	....	....	....	....	....	....	....	....
1973-74	**Detroit Red Wings**	**NHL**	**18**	**1**	**3**	**4**	**1**	**2**	**3**	**7**	**0**	**0**	**0**	**18**	**5.6**	**9**	**0**	**9**	**0**	**0**	....	....	....	....	....	....	....	....
	Virginia Wings	AHL	57	25	27	52	....	....	....	64	....	....	....	....	....	....	....	....	....	....	....	....	....	....	....	....	....	....
1974-75	Michigan-Baltimore Stags	WHA	34	10	16	26	....	....	....	73	....	....	....	....	....	....	....	....	....	....	....	....	....	....	....	....	....	....
	Winnipeg Jets	WHA	32	9	12	21	....	....	....	21	....	....	....	....	....	....	....	....	....	....	....	....	....	....	....	....	....	....
1975-76	Cleveland Crusaders	WHA	80	26	24	50	....	....	....	72	....	....	....	....	....	....	....	....	....	....	3	2	0	2	0	....	....	....
1976-77	Minnesota Fighting Saints	WHA	34	10	9	19	....	....	....	19	....	....	....	....	....	....	....	....	....	....	....	....	....	....	....	....	....	....
	Calgary Cowboys	WHA	1	1	0	1	....	....	....	0	....	....	....	....	....	....	....	....	....	....	....	....	....	....	....	....	....	....
	Colorado Rockies	**NHL**	**29**	**8**	**10**	**18**	**7**	**8**	**15**	**12**	**2**	**0**	**1**	**60**	**13.3**	**28**	**6**	**31**	**3**	**–6**	....	....	....	....	....	....	....	....
1977-78	Kansas City Red Wings	CHL	30	15	20	35	....	....	....	40	....	....	....	....	....	....	....	....	....	....	....	....	....	....	....	....	....	....
1978-79	Kansas City Red Wings	CHL	65	19	27	46	....	....	....	82	....	....	....	....	....	....	....	....	....	....	4	0	3	3	0	....	....	....
1979-80	Dayton Gems	IHL	7	0	3	3	....	....	....	22	....	....	....	....	....	....	....	....	....	....	....	....	....	....	....	....	....	....
	Muskegon Mohawks	IHL	24	4	22	26	....	....	....	16	....	....	....	....	....	....	....	....	....	....	....	....	....	....	....	....	....	....
	Hampton Aces	EHL	32	12	9	21	....	....	....	20	....	....	....	....	....	....	....	....	....	....	....	....	....	....	....	....	....	....

Season	Club	League	GP	G	A	Pts	AG	AA	APts	PIM	PP	SH	GW	S	%	TGF	PGF	TGA	PGA	+/–	GP	G	A	Pts	PIM	PP	SH	GW
			REGULAR SEASON																		PLAYOFFS							
1980-81			DID NOT PLAY																									
1981-82			DID NOT PLAY																									
1982-83	Thunder Bay Twins	CASH	36	17	48	65																						
	NHL Totals		**49**	**9**	**13**	**22**	**8**	**10**	**18**	**19**	**2**	**0**	**1**	**79**	**11.4**	**37**	**6**	**40**	**3**									
	Other Major League Totals		181	56	61	117				185											3	2	0	2	0			

Selected by **Edmonton** (WHA) in 1973 WHA Professional Player Draft, June, 1973. Claimed by **Phoenix** (WHA) from **Edmonton** (WHA) in 1974 WHA Expansion Draft, May, 1974. Rights traded to **Michigan** (WHA) by **Phoenix** (WHA) for Jim Niecamp, May, 1974. Loaned to **Winnipeg** (WHA) by **Michigan-Baltimore** (WHA) for future considerations, February, 1975. Selected by **Cleveland** (WHA) from **Michigan-Baltimore** (WHA) in WHA Dispersal Draft, June 19, 1975. Transferred to **Minnesota** (WHA) after **Cleveland** (WHA) franchise relocated, July, 1976. Traded to **Calgary** (WHA) by **Minnesota** (WHA) with Butch Deadmarsh and John Arbour for cash, January, 1977. Rights traded to **Colorado** by **Detroit** for cash, February 11, 1977. Signed as a free agent by **Detroit**, August 17, 1977.

• GRUHL, Scott

Kenneth Scott LW – L. 5'11", 185 lbs. b: Port Colborne, Ont., 9/13/1959.

Season	Club	League	GP	G	A	Pts	AG	AA	APts	PIM	PP	SH	GW	S	%	TGF	PGF	TGA	PGA	+/–	GP	G	A	Pts	PIM	PP	SH	GW
1976-77	Northeastern University	H-East	17	6	4	10				0																		
1977-78	Northeastern University	H-East	28	21	38	59				46																		
1978-79	Sudbury Wolves	OMJHL	68	35	49	84				78											10	5	7	12	15			
1979-80	Binghamton Dusters	AHL	4	1	0	1				0																		
	Saginaw Gears	IHL	75	53	40	93				100											7	2	6	8	16			
1980-81	Houston Apollos	CHL	4	0	0	0				0																		
	Saginaw Gears	IHL	77	56	34	90				87											13	*11	8	*19	12			
1981-82	**Los Angeles Kings**	**NHL**	**7**	**2**	**1**	**3**	**2**	**1**	**3**	**2**	**0**	**0**	**0**	**8**	**25.0**	**5**	**0**	**4**	**0**	**1**								
	New Haven Nighthawks	AHL	73	28	41	69				107											4	0	4	4	2			
1982-83	**Los Angeles Kings**	**NHL**	**7**	**0**	**2**	**2**	**0**	**1**	**1**	**4**	**0**	**0**	**0**	**13**	**0.0**	**4**	**0**	**9**	**0**	**–5**								
	New Haven Nighthawks	AHL	68	25	38	63				114											12	3	3	6	22			
1983-84	Muskegon Mohawks	IHL	56	40	56	96				49																		
1984-85	Muskegon Mohawks	IHL	82	62	64	126				102											17	7	16	23	25			
1985-86	Muskegon Lumberjacks	IHL	82	*59	51	110				178											14	7	*13	20	22			
1986-87	Muskegon Lumberjacks	IHL	67	34	39	73				157											15	5	7	12	54			
1987-88	**Pittsburgh Penguins**	**NHL**	**6**	**1**	**0**	**1**	**1**	**0**	**1**	**0**	**0**	**0**	**0**	**7**	**14.3**	**1**	**0**	**1**	**0**	**0**								
	Muskegon Lumberjacks	IHL	55	28	47	75				115											6	5	1	6	12			
1988-89	Muskegon Lumberjacks	IHL	79	37	55	92				163											14	8	11	19	37			
1989-90	Muskegon Lumberjacks	IHL	80	41	51	92				206											15	8	6	14	26			
1990-91	Fort Wayne Komets	IHL	59	23	47	70				109											19	4	6	10	39			
1991-92	Fort Wayne Komets	IHL	78	44	61	105				196											6	2	2	4	48			
1992-93	Fort Wayne Komets	IHL	73	34	47	81				290											12	4	11	15	14			
1993-94	Milwaukee Admirals	IHL	28	6	9	15				102																		
	Kalamazoo Wings	IHL	30	15	12	27				85											5	1	4	5	26			
1994-95	Richmond Renegades	ECHL	49	31	40	71				288											17	9	9	18	68			
1995-96	Richmond Renegades	ECHL	60	46	39	85				236											7	3	5	8	18			
	Baltimore Bandits	AHL	1	0	0	0				0																		
	Fort Wayne Komets	IHL																			2	0	1	1	0			
1997-98	Richmond Renegades	ECHL	DID NOT PLAY – COACHING																									
	NHL Totals		**20**	**3**	**3**	**6**	**3**	**2**	**5**	**6**	**0**	**0**	**0**	**28**	**10.7**	**10**	**0**	**14**	**0**									

IHL Second All-Star Team (1980, 1986, 1992) • IHL First All-Star Team (1984, 1985) • Won James Gatschene Memorial Trophy (MVP - IHL) (1985)

Signed as a free agent by **LA Kings**, October 11, 1979. Signed as a free agent by **Pittsburgh**, December 14, 1987. • Played w/ RHI's San Diego Barracudas in 1994 (22-28-33-61-60).

• GRYP, Bob

Robert Douglas LW – L. 6'1", 190 lbs. b: Chatham, Ont., 5/6/1950. Toronto's 4th, 50th overall, in 1970.

Season	Club	League	GP	G	A	Pts	AG	AA	APts	PIM	PP	SH	GW	S	%	TGF	PGF	TGA	PGA	+/–	GP	G	A	Pts	PIM	PP	SH	GW
1967-68	Chatham Maroons	OHA-B	STATISTICS NOT AVAILABLE																									
1968-69	Boston University	ECAC	17	9	17	26				18																		
1969-70	Boston University	ECAC	27	12	17	29				20																		
1970-71	Boston University	ECAC	30	20	19	39				51																		
1971-72	Boston University	ECAC	31	9	36	45				14																		
1972-73	Boston Braves	AHL	76	38	28	66				99											7	3	1	4	4			
1973-74	**Boston Bruins**	**NHL**	**1**	**0**	**0**	**0**	**0**	**0**	**0**	**0**	**0**	**0**	**0**	**0**	**0.0**	**0**	**0**	**2**	**0**	**–2**								
	Boston Braves	AHL	66	30	18	48				62																		
1974-75	**Washington Capitals**	**NHL**	**27**	**5**	**8**	**13**	**4**	**6**	**10**	**21**	**0**	**0**	**0**	**43**	**11.6**	**21**	**6**	**44**	**5**	**–24**								
	Richmond Robins	AHL	49	10	11	21				94																		
1975-76	**Washington Capitals**	**NHL**	**46**	**6**	**5**	**11**	**5**	**4**	**9**	**12**	**0**	**0**	**0**	**52**	**11.5**	**14**	**2**	**45**	**15**	**–18**								
	Richmond Robins	AHL	9	2	2	4				10																		
	New Haven Nighthawks	AHL	22	10	9	19				28											3	0	0	0	14			
1976-77	Johnstown Jets	NAHL	2	1	0	1				0																		
1977-78	Long Beach Sharks-Rockets	PHL	5	1	0	1				14																		
	NHL Totals		**74**	**11**	**13**	**24**	**9**	**10**	**19**	**33**	**0**	**0**	**0**	**95**	**11.6**	**35**	**8**	**91**	**20**									

Claimed by **Boston** from **Tulsa** (CHL) in Reverse Draft, June, 1972. Claimed by **Washington** from **Boston** in Expansion Draft, June 12, 1974. Traded to **New Haven** (AHL) by **Washington** with Ron H. Anderson for Rich Nantais and Alain Langlais, February 23, 1976.

• GUAY, Francois

C – L. 6', 190 lbs. b: Gatineau, Que., 6/8/1968. Buffalo's 9th, 152nd overall, in 1986.

Season	Club	League	GP	G	A	Pts	AG	AA	APts	PIM	PP	SH	GW	S	%	TGF	PGF	TGA	PGA	+/–	GP	G	A	Pts	PIM	PP	SH	GW
1983-84	Richelieu Elites	QAAA	33	7	25	32																						
1984-85	Laval Voisins	QMJHL	66	13	18	31				21																		
1985-86	Laval Titan	QMJHL	71	19	55	74				46											14	5	6	11	15			
1986-87	Laval Titan	QMJHL	63	52	77	129				67											14	5	13	18	18			
1987-88	Laval Titan	QMJHL	66	60	84	144				142											14	10	15	25	10			
1988-89	Rochester Americans	AHL	45	6	20	26				34																		
1989-90	**Buffalo Sabres**	**NHL**	**1**	**0**	**0**	**0**	**0**	**0**	**0**	**0**	**0**	**0**	**0**	**0**	**0.0**	**0**	**0**	**0**	**0**	**0**								
	Rochester Americans	AHL	69	28	35	63				39											16	4	8	12	12			
1990-91	Rochester Americans	AHL	61	24	39	63				38											15	5	5	10	8			
1991-92	IEV Innsbruck	Austria	40	34	45	79																						
1992-93	IEV Innsbruck	Austria	53	43	59	102																						
1993-94	KAC Klagenfurt	Austria	46	30	50	80																						
1994-95	SC Herisau	Switz-2	36	23	44	67				83											4	1	2	3	14			
1995-96	SC Herisau	Switz-2	36	32	35	67				52											5	2	6	8	2			
1996-97	Adler Mannheim	Germany	14	2	8	10				10																		
1997-98	Adler Mannheim	Germany	39	8	13	21				41											10	0	4	4	6			
	Adler Mannheim	EuroHL	4	0	1	1				6																		
1998-99	Kassel Huskies	Germany	49	17	36	53				76																		
99-2000	Kassel Huskies	Germany	39	10	15	25				59											6	2	1	3	12			
	NHL Totals		**1**	**0**	**0**	**0**	**0**	**0**	**0**	**0**	**0**	**0**	**0**	**0**	**0.0**	**0**	**0**	**0**	**0**									

• GUAY, Paul

RW – R. 5'11", 185 lbs. b: Providence, RI, 9/2/1963. Minnesota's 10th, 118th overall, in 1981.

Season	Club	League	GP	G	A	Pts	AG	AA	APts	PIM	PP	SH	GW	S	%	TGF	PGF	TGA	PGA	+/–	GP	G	A	Pts	PIM	PP	SH	GW
1979-80	Mount St. Charles Mounties	Hi-School	23	18	19	37																						
1980-81	Mount St. Charles Mounties	Hi-School	23	28	38	66																						
1981-82	Providence College	ECAC	33	23	17	40				38																		
1982-83	Providence College	ECAC	42	34	31	65				83																		
1983-84	United States	Nat-Team	62	20	18	38				44																		
	United States	Olympics	6	1	0	1				8																		
	Philadelphia Flyers	**NHL**	**14**	**2**	**6**	**8**	**2**	**4**	**6**	**14**	**0**	**0**	**0**	**19**	**10.5**	**11**	**0**	**16**	**6**	**1**	**3**	**0**	**0**	**0**	**4**	**0**	**0**	**0**
1984-85	**Philadelphia Flyers**	**NHL**	**2**	**0**	**1**	**1**	**0**	**1**	**1**	**0**	**0**	**0**	**0**	**2**	**0.0**	**2**	**0**	**0**	**0**	**2**								
	Hershey Bears	AHL	74	23	30	53				123																		
1985-86	**Los Angeles Kings**	**NHL**	**23**	**3**	**3**	**6**	**2**	**2**	**4**	**18**	**0**	**0**	**0**	**18**	**16.7**	**11**	**1**	**20**	**4**	**–6**								
	New Haven Nighthawks	AHL	57	15	36	51				101											5	3	0	3	11			

Season	Club	League	GP	G	A	Pts	AG	AA	APts	PIM	PP	SH	GW	S	%	TGF	PGF	TGA	PGA	+/–	GP	G	A	Pts	PIM	PP	SH	GW
			REGULAR SEASON																		PLAYOFFS							
1986-87	**Los Angeles Kings**	**NHL**	**35**	**2**	**5**	**7**	**2**	**4**	**6**	**16**	**0**	**0**	**0**	**18**	**11.1**	**9**	**0**	**40**	**17**	**–14**	**2**	**0**	**0**	**0**	**0**	**0**	**0**	**0**
	New Haven Nighthawks	AHL	6	1	3	4	....	....	....	11	....	....	....	....	....	....	....	....	....	....	....	....	....	....	....	....	....	....
1987-88	**Los Angeles Kings**	**NHL**	**33**	**4**	**4**	**8**	**3**	**3**	**6**	**40**	**0**	**0**	**0**	**42**	**9.5**	**11**	**0**	**21**	**3**	**–7**	**4**	**0**	**1**	**1**	**8**	**0**	**0**	**0**
	New Haven Nighthawks	AHL	42	21	26	47	....	....	....	53	....	....	....	....	....	....	....	....	....	....	....	....	....	....	....	....	....	....
1988-89	**Los Angeles Kings**	**NHL**	**2**	**0**	**0**	**0**	**0**	**0**	**0**	**2**	**0**	**0**	**0**	**2**	**0.0**	**0**	**0**	**2**	**0**	**–2**	....	....	....	....	....	....	....	....
	New Haven Nighthawks	AHL	4	4	6	10	....	....	....	20	....	....	....	....	....	....	....	....	....	....	....	....	....	....	....	....	....	....
	Boston Bruins	**NHL**	**5**	**0**	**2**	**2**	**0**	**1**	**1**	**0**	**0**	**0**	**0**	**1**	**0.0**	**2**	**0**	**2**	**0**	**0**	....	....	....	....	....	....	....	....
	Maine Mariners	AHL	61	15	29	44	....	....	....	77	....	....	....	....	....	....	....	....	....	....	....	....	....	....	....	....	....	....
1989-90	Utica Devils	AHL	75	25	30	55	....	....	....	103	....	....	....	....	....	....	....	....	....	....	5	2	2	4	13	....	....	....
1990-91	**New York Islanders**	**NHL**	**3**	**0**	**2**	**2**	**0**	**2**	**2**	**2**	**0**	**0**	**0**	**5**	**0.0**	**3**	**0**	**1**	**0**	**2**	....	....	....	....	....	....	....	....
	Capital District Islanders	AHL	74	26	35	61	....	....	....	81	....	....	....	....	....	....	....	....	....	....	....	....	....	....	....	....	....	....
1991-92	Milwaukee Admirals	IHL	81	24	33	57	....	....	....	93	....	....	....	....	....	....	....	....	....	....	3	2	1	3	7	....	....	....
1992-93	Springfield Indians	AHL	65	10	32	42	....	....	....	90	....	....	....	....	....	....	....	....	....	....	11	1	2	3	6	....	....	....
	NHL Totals		**117**	**11**	**23**	**34**	**9**	**17**	**26**	**92**	**0**	**0**	**0**	**107**	**10.3**	**49**	**1**	**102**	**30**		**9**	**0**	**1**	**1**	**12**	**0**	**0**	**0**

ECAC Second All-Star Team (1983)

Rights traded to **Philadelphia** by **Minnesota** with Minnesota's 3rd round choice (Darryl Gilmour) in 1985 Entry Draft for Paul Holmgren, February 23, 1984. Traded to **LA Kings** by **Philadelphia** with Philadelphia's 4th round choice (Sylvain Couturier) in 1986 Entry Draft for Steve Seguin and LA Kings' 2nd round choice (Jukka Seppo) in 1986 Entry Draft, October 11, 1985. Traded to **Boston** by **LA Kings** for the rights to Dave Pasin, November 3, 1988. Signed as a free agent by **New Jersey**, August 14, 1989. Signed as a free agent by **NY Islanders**, August 13, 1990.

• GUERARD, Daniel

RW – R. 6'4", 215 lbs. b: LaSalle, Que., 4/9/1974. Ottawa's 5th, 98th overall, in 1992.

Season	Club	League	GP	G	A	Pts	AG	AA	APts	PIM	PP	SH	GW	S	%	TGF	PGF	TGA	PGA	+/–	GP	G	A	Pts	PIM	PP	SH	GW
1989-90	Lac St-Louis Lions	QAAA	32	6	7	13	....	....	....	30	....	....	....	....	....	....	....	....	....	....	....	....	....	....	....	....	....	....
1990-91	Verdun College-Francais	CEGEP	STATISTICS NOT AVAILABLE																									
1991-92	Victoriaville Tigres	QMJHL	31	5	16	21	....	....	....	66	....	....	....	....	....	....	....	....	....	....	....	....	....	....	....	....	....	....
1992-93	Verdun College-Francais	QMJHL	58	31	26	57	....	....	....	131	....	....	....	....	....	....	....	....	....	....	4	1	1	2	17	....	....	....
	New Haven Senators	AHL	2	2	1	3	....	....	....	0	....	....	....	....	....	....	....	....	....	....	....	....	....	....	....	....	....	....
1993-94	Verdun College-Francais	QMJHL	53	31	34	65	....	....	....	169	....	....	....	....	....	....	....	....	....	....	4	3	1	4	4	....	....	....
	P.E.I. Senators	AHL	3	0	0	0	....	....	....	17	....	....	....	....	....	....	....	....	....	....	....	....	....	....	....	....	....	....
1994-95	**Ottawa Senators**	**NHL**	**2**	**0**	**0**	**0**	**0**	**0**	**0**	**0**	**0**	**0**	**0**	**0**	**0.0**	**0**	**0**	**0**	**0**	**0**	....	....	....	....	....	....	....	....
	P.E.I. Senators	AHL	68	20	22	42	....	....	....	95	....	....	....	....	....	....	....	....	....	....	8	0	1	1	16	....	....	....
1995-96	P.E.I. Senators	AHL	42	3	7	10	....	....	....	56	....	....	....	....	....	....	....	....	....	....	....	....	....	....	....	....	....	....
1996-97	Worcester IceCats	AHL	49	8	8	16	....	....	....	50	....	....	....	....	....	....	....	....	....	....	....	....	....	....	....	....	....	....
1997-98	VEU Feldkirch	Alpenliga	16	8	17	25	....	....	....	41	....	....	....	....	....	....	....	....	....	....	....	....	....	....	....	....	....	....
	HK Acroni Jesenice	Slovenia	28	24	*30	54	....	....	....	....	....	....	....	....	....	....	....	....	....	....	11	14	1	15	....	....	....	....
1998-99	HC Straubing	Alpenliga	16	11	9	20	....	....	....	30	....	....	....	....	....	....	....	....	....	....	....	....	....	....	....	....	....	....
	CSG Grenoble	France	11	3	7	10	....	....	....	20	....	....	....	....	....	....	....	....	....	....	....	....	....	....	....	....	....	....
99-2000	LaSalle Rapides	QSPHL	38	19	33	52	....	....	....	53	....	....	....	....	....	....	....	....	....	....	16	10	8	18	12	....	....	....
	NHL Totals		**2**	**0**	**0**	**0**	**0**	**0**	**0**	**0**	**0**	**0**	**0**	**0**	**0.0**	**0**	**0**	**0**	**0**		....	....	....	....	....	....	....	....

• GUERARD, Stephane

D – L. 6'2", 198 lbs. b: Ste. Elizabeth, Que., 4/12/1968. Quebec's 3rd, 41st overall, in 1986.

Season	Club	League	GP	G	A	Pts	AG	AA	APts	PIM	PP	SH	GW	S	%	TGF	PGF	TGA	PGA	+/–	GP	G	A	Pts	PIM	PP	SH	GW
1984-85	Laval Laurentide	QAAA	36	6	12	18	....	....	....	140	....	....	....	....	....	....	....	....	....	....	....	....	....	....	....	....	....	....
1985-86	Shawinigan Cataracts	QMJHL	59	4	18	22	....	....	....	167	....	....	....	....	....	....	....	....	....	....	3	1	1	2	0	....	....	....
1986-87	Shawinigan Cataracts	QMJHL	31	5	16	21	....	....	....	57	....	....	....	....	....	....	....	....	....	....	12	2	9	11	36	....	....	....
1987-88	**Quebec Nordiques**	**NHL**	**30**	**0**	**0**	**0**	**0**	**0**	**0**	**34**	**0**	**0**	**0**	**12**	**0.0**	**14**	**0**	**24**	**3**	**–7**	....	....	....	....	....	....	....	....
1988-89	Halifax Citadels	AHL	37	1	9	10	....	....	....	140	....	....	....	....	....	....	....	....	....	....	4	0	0	0	8	....	....	....
1989-90	**Quebec Nordiques**	**NHL**	**4**	**0**	**0**	**0**	**0**	**0**	**0**	**6**	**0**	**0**	**0**	**9**	**0.0**	**1**	**0**	**8**	**2**	**–5**	....	....	....	....	....	....	....	....
	Halifax Citadels	AHL	1	0	0	0	....	....	....	5	....	....	....	....	....	....	....	....	....	....	....	....	....	....	....	....	....	....
1990-91	**Quebec Nordiques**	**NHL**	DID NOT PLAY – INJURED																									
1991-92	**Quebec Nordiques**	**NHL**	DID NOT PLAY – INJURED																									
	NHL Totals		**34**	**0**	**0**	**0**	**0**	**0**	**0**	**40**	**0**	**0**	**0**	**21**	**0.0**	**15**	**0**	**32**	**5**		....	....	....	....	....	....	....	....

• Missed majority of 1987-88 season recovering from knee injury suffered in game vs. St. Louis, November 3, 1987. • Missed entire 1990-91 season recovering from shoulder injury suffered in training camp, September, 1990. Traded to **NY Rangers** by **Quebec** for Miloslav Horava, May 25, 1991. Traded to **Quebec** by **NY Rangers** for cash, September 3, 1991. • Suffered eventual career-ending knee injury in training camp, September, 1991.

• GUERIN, Bill

William Robert RW – R. 6'2", 210 lbs. b: Wilbraham, MA, 11/9/1970. New Jersey's 1st, 5th overall, in 1989.

Season	Club	League	GP	G	A	Pts	AG	AA	APts	PIM	PP	SH	GW	S	%	TGF	PGF	TGA	PGA	+/–	GP	G	A	Pts	PIM	PP	SH	GW
1985-86	Springfield Jr. Blues	NEJHL	48	26	19	45	....	....	....	71	....	....	....	....	....	....	....	....	....	....	....	....	....	....	....	....	....	....
1986-87	Springfield Jr. Blues	NEJHL	32	34	20	54	....	....	....	40	....	....	....	....	....	....	....	....	....	....	....	....	....	....	....	....	....	....
1987-88	Springfield Jr. Blues	NEJHL	38	31	44	75	....	....	....	146	....	....	....	....	....	....	....	....	....	....	....	....	....	....	....	....	....	....
1988-89	Springfield Olympics	NEJHL	31	32	35	67	....	....	....	90	....	....	....	....	....	....	....	....	....	....	....	....	....	....	....	....	....	....
	United States	WJC-A	7	0	3	3	....	....	....	16	....	....	....	....	....	....	....	....	....	....	....	....	....	....	....	....	....	....
1989-90	Boston College	H-East	39	14	11	25	....	....	....	54	....	....	....	....	....	....	....	....	....	....	....	....	....	....	....	....	....	....
	United States	WJC-A	7	0	0	0	....	....	....	18	....	....	....	....	....	....	....	....	....	....	....	....	....	....	....	....	....	....
1990-91	Boston College	H-East	38	26	19	45	....	....	....	102	....	....	....	....	....	....	....	....	....	....	....	....	....	....	....	....	....	....
	United States	Nat-Team	46	12	15	27	....	....	....	67	....	....	....	....	....	....	....	....	....	....	....	....	....	....	....	....	....	....
1991-92	**New Jersey Devils**	**NHL**	**5**	**0**	**1**	**1**	**0**	**1**	**1**	**9**	**0**	**0**	**0**	**8**	**0.0**	**1**	**0**	**0**	**0**	**1**	**6**	**3**	**0**	**3**	**4**	**0**	**0**	**0**
	Utica Devils	AHL	22	13	10	23	....	....	....	6	....	....	....	....	....	....	....	....	....	....	4	1	3	4	14	....	....	....
1992-93	**New Jersey Devils**	**NHL**	**65**	**14**	**20**	**34**	**12**	**14**	**26**	**63**	**0**	**0**	**2**	**123**	**11.4**	**44**	**2**	**30**	**2**	**14**	**5**	**1**	**1**	**2**	**4**	**0**	**0**	**0**
	Utica Devils	AHL	18	10	7	17	....	....	....	47	....	....	....	....	....	....	....	....	....	....	....	....	....	....	....	....	....	....
1993-94	**New Jersey Devils**	**NHL**	**81**	**25**	**19**	**44**	**23**	**15**	**38**	**101**	**2**	**0**	**3**	**195**	**12.8**	**72**	**16**	**44**	**2**	**14**	**17**	**2**	**1**	**3**	**35**	**0**	**0**	**1**
1994-95♦	**New Jersey Devils**	**NHL**	**48**	**12**	**13**	**25**	**21**	**19**	**40**	**72**	**4**	**0**	**3**	**96**	**12.5**	**32**	**6**	**20**	**0**	**6**	**20**	**3**	**8**	**11**	**30**	**1**	**0**	**0**
1995-96	**New Jersey Devils**	**NHL**	**80**	**23**	**30**	**53**	**23**	**25**	**48**	**116**	**8**	**0**	**6**	**216**	**10.6**	**77**	**26**	**44**	**0**	**7**	....	....	....	....	....	....	....	....
1996-97	United States	W-Cup	7	0	2	2	....	....	....	17	....	....	....	....	....	....	....	....	....	....	....	....	....	....	....	....	....	....
	New Jersey Devils	**NHL**	**82**	**29**	**18**	**47**	**31**	**16**	**47**	**95**	**7**	**0**	**9**	**177**	**16.4**	**59**	**16**	**45**	**0**	**–2**	**8**	**2**	**1**	**3**	**18**	**1**	**0**	**1**
1997-98	**New Jersey Devils**	**NHL**	**19**	**5**	**5**	**10**	**6**	**5**	**11**	**13**	**1**	**0**	**2**	**48**	**10.4**	**14**	**4**	**10**	**0**	**0**	....	....	....	....	....	....	....	....
	Edmonton Oilers	**NHL**	**40**	**13**	**16**	**29**	**15**	**16**	**31**	**80**	**8**	**0**	**2**	**130**	**10.0**	**50**	**25**	**24**	**0**	**1**	**12**	**7**	**1**	**8**	**17**	**4**	**0**	**0**
	United States	Olympics	4	0	3	3	....	....	....	2	....	....	....	....	....	....	....	....	....	....	....	....	....	....	....	....	....	....
1998-99	**Edmonton Oilers**	**NHL**	**80**	**30**	**34**	**64**	**35**	**33**	**68**	**133**	**13**	**0**	**2**	**261**	**11.5**	**98**	**38**	**55**	**2**	**7**	**3**	**0**	**2**	**2**	**2**	**0**	**0**	**0**
99-2000	**Edmonton Oilers**	**NHL**	**70**	**24**	**22**	**46**	**27**	**20**	**47**	**123**	**11**	**0**	**2**	**188**	**12.8**	**74**	**27**	**43**	**0**	**4**	**5**	**3**	**2**	**5**	**9**	**1**	**0**	**0**
	NHL Totals		**570**	**175**	**178**	**353**	**193**	**164**	**357**	**805**	**54**	**0**	**31**	**1442**	**12.1**	**521**	**160**	**315**	**6**		**76**	**21**	**16**	**37**	**119**	**7**	**0**	**2**

Traded to **Edmonton** by **New Jersey** with Valeri Zelepukin for Jason Arnott and Bryan Muir, January 4, 1998.

• GUEVREMONT, Jocelyn

Jocelyn Marcel D – R. 6'2", 200 lbs. b: Montreal, Que., 3/1/1951. Vancouver's 1st, 3rd overall, in 1971.

Season	Club	League	GP	G	A	Pts	AG	AA	APts	PIM	PP	SH	GW	S	%	TGF	PGF	TGA	PGA	+/–	GP	G	A	Pts	PIM	PP	SH	GW
1967-68	Laval Saints	QJHL	50	10	20	30	....	....	....	....	....	....	....	....	....	....	....	....	....	....	....	....	....	....	....	....	....	....
1968-69	Montreal Jr. Canadiens	OHA-Jr.	54	11	40	51	....	....	....	79	....	....	....	....	....	....	....	....	....	....	14	6	*21	27	6	....	....	....
	Montreal Jr. Canadiens	Mem-Cup	8	2	5	7	....	....	....	6	....	....	....	....	....	....	....	....	....	....	....	....	....	....	....	....	....	....
1969-70	Montreal Jr. Canadiens	OHA-Jr.	54	13	45	58	....	....	....	46	....	....	....	....	....	....	....	....	....	....	16	5	*21	26	18	....	....	....
	Montreal Jr. Canadiens	Mem-Cup	12	4	24	28	....	....	....	10	....	....	....	....	....	....	....	....	....	....	....	....	....	....	....	....	....	....
1970-71	Montreal Jr. Canadiens	OHA-Jr.	60	22	66	88	....	....	....	112	....	....	....	....	....	....	....	....	....	....	11	7	13	20	26	....	....	....
1971-72	**Vancouver Canucks**	**NHL**	**75**	**13**	**38**	**51**	**13**	**33**	**46**	**44**	**3**	**0**	**1**	**210**	**6.2**	**118**	**41**	**137**	**32**	**–28**	....	....	....	....	....	....	....	....
1972-73	Team Canada	Summit-72	DID NOT PLAY																									
	Vancouver Canucks	**NHL**	**78**	**16**	**26**	**42**	**15**	**21**	**36**	**46**	**6**	**1**	**0**	**246**	**6.5**	**125**	**37**	**153**	**23**	**–42**	....	....	....	....	....	....	....	....
1973-74	**Vancouver Canucks**	**NHL**	**72**	**15**	**24**	**39**	**14**	**20**	**34**	**34**	**10**	**0**	**1**	**208**	**7.2**	**94**	**35**	**129**	**33**	**–37**	....	....	....	....	....	....	....	....
1974-75	**Vancouver Canucks**	**NHL**	**2**	**0**	**0**	**0**	**0**	**0**	**0**	**0**	**0**	**0**	**0**	**5**	**0.0**	**3**	**3**	**1**	**0**	**–1**	....	....	....	....	....	....	....	....
	Buffalo Sabres	**NHL**	**64**	**7**	**25**	**32**	**6**	**19**	**25**	**32**	**4**	**0**	**0**	**160**	**4.4**	**118**	**29**	**61**	**4**	**32**	**17**	**0**	**6**	**6**	**14**	**0**	**0**	**0**
1975-76	**Buffalo Sabres**	**NHL**	**80**	**12**	**40**	**52**	**11**	**30**	**41**	**57**	**6**	**0**	**3**	**229**	**5.2**	**173**	**41**	**105**	**20**	**47**	**9**	**0**	**5**	**5**	**2**	**0**	**0**	**0**
1976-77	**Buffalo Sabres**	**NHL**	**80**	**9**	**29**	**38**	**8**	**22**	**30**	**46**	**2**	**0**	**2**	**210**	**4.3**	**111**	**16**	**86**	**17**	**26**	**6**	**3**	**4**	**7**	**0**	**1**	**0**	**0**
1977-78	**Buffalo Sabres**	**NHL**	**66**	**7**	**28**	**35**	**6**	**22**	**28**	**46**	**0**	**0**	**1**	**162**	**4.3**	**98**	**22**	**59**	**8**	**25**	**8**	**1**	**2**	**3**	**2**	**0**	**0**	**0**

			REGULAR SEASON																		PLAYOFFS							
Season	Club	League	GP	G	A	Pts	AG	AA	APts	PIM	PP	SH	GW	S	%	TGF	PGF	TGA	PGA	+/–	GP	G	A	Pts	PIM	PP	SH	GW
1978-79	**Buffalo Sabres**	**NHL**	34	3	8	11	3	6	9	8	0	0	0	51	5.9	25	5	10	2	12	....	....	....	....	....	....	....	....
1979-80	**New York Rangers**	**NHL**	20	2	5	7	2	4	6	6	2	0	0	41	4.9	17	6	26	3	–12	....	....	....	....	....	....	....	....
	New Haven Nighthawks	AHL	36	7	27	34	....	....	....	18	....	....	....	....	....	....	....	....	....	....	10	0	10	10	10	....	....	....
	NHL Totals		571	84	223	307	78	177	255	319	33	1	8	1522	5.5	882	235	767	142		40	4	17	21	18	1	0	0

OHA-Jr. Second All-Star Team (1970) • OHA-Jr. First All-Star Team (1971) • Played in NHL All-Star Game (1974)

Traded to **Buffalo** by **Vancouver** with Bryan McSheffrey for Gerry Meehan and Mike Robitaille, October 14, 1974. Traded to **NY Rangers** by **Buffalo** for future considerations, March 12, 1979.

• GUINDON, Bobby

Robert Pierre LW – L. 5'9", 175 lbs. b: Labelle, Que., 11/19/1950. Detroit's 2nd, 26th overall, in 1970.

Season	Club	League	GP	G	A	Pts	AG	AA	APts	PIM	PP	SH	GW	S	%	TGF	PGF	TGA	PGA	+/–	GP	G	A	Pts	PIM	PP	SH	GW
1967-68	St-Jerome Alouettes	QJHL	50	25	35	60	....	....	....	....	....	....	....	....	....	....	....	....	....	....	....	....	....	....	....	....	....	....
1968-69	Montreal Jr. Canadiens	OHA-Jr.	54	38	40	78	....	....	....	29	....	....	....	....	....	....	....	....	....	....	14	3	6	9	10	....	....	....
	Montreal Jr. Canadiens	Mem-Cup	7	4	4	8	....	....	....	12	....	....	....	....	....	....	....	....	....	....	....	....	....	....	....	....	....	....
1969-70	Montreal Jr. Canadiens	OHA-Jr.	53	43	51	94	....	....	....	62	....	....	....	....	....	....	....	....	....	....	16	12	14	26	18	....	....	....
	Montreal Jr. Canadiens	Mem-Cup	10	7	12	19	....	....	....	8	....	....	....	....	....	....	....	....	....	....	....	....	....	....	....	....	....	....
1970-71	Fort Worth Wings	CHL	61	12	13	25	....	....	....	15	....	....	....	....	....	....	....	....	....	....	4	0	0	0	7	....	....	....
1971-72	Fort Worth Wings	CHL	72	22	26	48	....	....	....	36	....	....	....	....	....	....	....	....	....	....	7	2	6	8	14	....	....	....
1972-73	Quebec Nordiques	WHA	71	28	28	56	....	....	....	31	....	....	....	....	....	....	....	....	....	....	....	....	....	....	....	....	....	....
1973-74	Quebec Nordiques	WHA	77	31	39	70	....	....	....	30	....	....	....	....	....	....	....	....	....	....	....	....	....	....	....	....	....	....
1974-75	Quebec Nordiques	WHA	69	12	18	30	....	....	....	23	....	....	....	....	....	....	....	....	....	....	15	7	6	13	10	....	....	....
1975-76	Winnipeg Jets	WHA	29	3	3	6	....	....	....	14	....	....	....	....	....	....	....	....	....	....	13	3	3	6	9	....	....	....
1976-77	Winnipeg Jets	WHA	69	10	17	27	....	....	....	19	....	....	....	....	....	....	....	....	....	....	20	4	4	8	9	....	....	....
1977-78	Winnipeg Jets	WHA	77	20	22	42	....	....	....	18	....	....	....	....	....	....	....	....	....	....	9	8	5	13	5	....	....	....
1978-79	Winnipeg Jets	WHA	71	8	18	26	....	....	....	21	....	....	....	....	....	....	....	....	....	....	7	2	1	3	0	....	....	....
1979-80	**Winnipeg Jets**	**NHL**	6	0	1	1	0	1	1	0	0	0	0	10	0.0	4	0	2	0	2	....	....	....	....	....	....	....	....
	Tulsa Oilers	CHL	36	11	18	29	....	....	....	10	....	....	....	....	....	....	....	....	....	....	....	....	....	....	....	....	....	....
1980-81	Tulsa Oilers	CHL	25	7	2	9	....	....	....	27	....	....	....	....	....	....	....	....	....	....	....	....	....	....	....	....	....	....
	NHL Totals		6	0	1	1	0	1	1	0	0	0	0	10	0.0	4	0	2	0		....	....	....	....	....	....	....	....
	Other Major League Totals		463	112	145	257	....	....	....	156	....	....	....	....	....	....	....	....	....	....	64	24	19	43	33	....	....	....

OHA-Jr. Second All-Star Team (1970) • Won WHA Playoff MVP Trophy (1978)

Selected by **Quebec** (WHA) in 1972 WHA General Player Draft, February 13, 1972. Signed as a free agent by **Winnipeg** (WHA), November, 1975. Rights retained by **Winnipeg** prior to NHL Expansion Draft, June 9, 1979.

• GUOLLA, Stephen

LW – L. 6', 190 lbs. b: Scarborough, Ont., 3/15/1973. Ottawa's 1st, 3rd overall, in 1994 Supplemental Draft.

Season	Club	League	GP	G	A	Pts	AG	AA	APts	PIM	PP	SH	GW	S	%	TGF	PGF	TGA	PGA	+/–	GP	G	A	Pts	PIM	PP	SH	GW
1988-89	Toronto Red Wings	MTHL	25	14	20	34	....	....	....	....	....	....	....	....	....	....	....	....	....	....	....	....	....	....	....	....	....	....
1989-90	Toronto Red Wings	MTHL	40	42	47	89	....	....	....	....	....	....	....	....	....	....	....	....	....	....	....	....	....	....	....	....	....	....
1990-91	Wexford Raiders	OJHL-B	44	34	44	78	....	....	....	34	....	....	....	....	....	....	....	....	....	....	12	12	16	28	....	....	....	....
1991-92	Michigan State Spartans	CCHA	33	4	9	13	....	....	....	8	....	....	....	....	....	....	....	....	....	....	....	....	....	....	....	....	....	....
1992-93	Michigan State Spartans	CCHA	39	19	35	54	....	....	....	6	....	....	....	....	....	....	....	....	....	....	....	....	....	....	....	....	....	....
1993-94	Michigan State Spartans	CCHA	41	23	46	69	....	....	....	16	....	....	....	....	....	....	....	....	....	....	....	....	....	....	....	....	....	....
1994-95	Michigan State Spartans	CCHA	40	16	35	51	....	....	....	16	....	....	....	....	....	....	....	....	....	....	....	....	....	....	....	....	....	....
1995-96	P.E.I. Senators	AHL	72	32	48	80	....	....	....	28	....	....	....	....	....	....	....	....	....	....	3	0	0	0	0	....	....	....
1996-97	**San Jose Sharks**	**NHL**	43	13	8	21	14	7	21	14	2	0	1	81	16.0	35	7	40	2	–10	....	....	....	....	....	....	....	....
	Kentucky Thoroughblades	AHL	34	22	22	44	....	....	....	10	....	....	....	....	....	....	....	....	....	....	4	2	1	3	0	....	....	....
1997-98	**San Jose Sharks**	**NHL**	7	1	1	2	1	1	2	0	0	0	0	9	11.1	4	3	3	0	–2	....	....	....	....	....	....	....	....
	Kentucky Thoroughblades	AHL	69	37	63	100	....	....	....	45	....	....	....	....	....	....	....	....	....	....	3	0	0	0	0	....	....	....
1998-99	**San Jose Sharks**	**NHL**	14	2	2	4	2	2	4	6	0	0	1	22	9.1	6	0	3	0	3	....	....	....	....	....	....	....	....
	Kentucky Thoroughblades	AHL	53	29	47	76	....	....	....	33	....	....	....	....	....	....	....	....	....	....	....	....	....	....	....	....	....	....
99-2000	**Tampa Bay Lightning**	**NHL**	46	6	10	16	7	9	16	11	2	0	0	52	11.5	26	7	19	2	2	....	....	....	....	....	....	....	....
	Atlanta Thrashers	**NHL**	20	4	9	13	4	8	12	4	2	0	0	34	11.8	17	5	31	6	–13	....	....	....	....	....	....	....	....
	NHL Totals		130	26	30	56	28	27	55	35	6	0	2	198	13.1	88	22	96	10		....	....	....	....	....	....	....	....

CCHA Second All-Star Team (1994) • NCAA West Second All-American Team (1994) • AHL Second All-Star Team (1998, 1999) • Won Les Cunningham Award (MVP - AHL) (1998)

Signed as a free agent by **San Jose**, August 22, 1996. Traded to **Tampa Bay** by **San Jose** with Bill Houlder, Shawn Burr and Andrei Zyuzin for Niklas Sundstrom and NY Rangers' 3rd round choice (previously acquired, later traded to Chicago - Chicago selected Igor Radulov) in 2000 Entry Draft, August 4, 1999. Claimed on waivers by **Atlanta** from **Tampa Bay**, March 1, 2000.

• GUREN, Miloslav

D – L. 6'2", 209 lbs. b: Uherske Hradiste, Czech., 9/24/1976. Montreal's 2nd, 60th overall, in 1995.

Season	Club	League	GP	G	A	Pts	AG	AA	APts	PIM	PP	SH	GW	S	%	TGF	PGF	TGA	PGA	+/–	GP	G	A	Pts	PIM	PP	SH	GW
1993-94	ZPS Zlin	Czech-Rep	22	1	5	6	....	....	....	....	....	....	....	....	....	....	....	....	....	....	3	0	0	0	....	....	....	....
	Czech-Republic	EJC-A	5	1	3	4	....	....	....	2	....	....	....	....	....	....	....	....	....	....	....	....	....	....	....	....	....	....
1994-95	ZPS Zlin	Czech-Rep	32	3	7	10	....	....	....	10	....	....	....	....	....	....	....	....	....	....	12	1	0	1	6	....	....	....
	Czech-Republic	WJC-A	7	0	0	0	....	....	....	4	....	....	....	....	....	....	....	....	....	....	....	....	....	....	....	....	....	....
1995-96	ZPS Zlin	Czech-Rep	28	1	2	3	....	....	....	....	....	....	....	....	....	....	....	....	....	....	7	1	0	1	....	....	....	....
	Czech-Republic	WJC-A	6	0	2	2	....	....	....	2	....	....	....	....	....	....	....	....	....	....	....	....	....	....	....	....	....	....
1996-97	Fredericton Canadiens	AHL	79	6	26	32	....	....	....	26	....	....	....	....	....	....	....	....	....	....	....	....	....	....	....	....	....	....
1997-98	Fredericton Canadiens	AHL	78	15	36	51	....	....	....	36	....	....	....	....	....	....	....	....	....	....	4	1	2	3	0	....	....	....
1998-99	**Montreal Canadiens**	**NHL**	12	0	1	1	0	1	1	4	0	0	0	11	0.0	3	0	4	0	–1	....	....	....	....	....	....	....	....
	Fredericton Canadiens	AHL	63	5	16	21	....	....	....	24	....	....	....	....	....	....	....	....	....	....	15	4	7	11	10	....	....	....
99-2000	**Montreal Canadiens**	**NHL**	24	1	2	3	1	2	3	12	1	0	0	20	5.0	11	3	16	3	–5	....	....	....	....	....	....	....	....
	Quebec Citadelles	AHL	29	5	12	17	....	....	....	16	....	....	....	....	....	....	....	....	....	....	3	0	0	0	2	....	....	....
	NHL Totals		36	1	3	4	1	3	4	16	1	0	0	31	3.2	14	3	20	3		....	....	....	....	....	....	....	....

• GUSAROV, Alexei

D – L. 6'3", 185 lbs. b: Leningrad, USSR, 7/8/1964. Quebec's 11th, 213th overall, in 1988.

Season	Club	League	GP	G	A	Pts	AG	AA	APts	PIM	PP	SH	GW	S	%	TGF	PGF	TGA	PGA	+/–	GP	G	A	Pts	PIM	PP	SH	GW
1981-82	SKA Leningrad	USSR	20	1	2	3	....	....	....	16	....	....	....	....	....	....	....	....	....	....	....	....	....	....	....	....	....	....
	Soviet Union	EJC-A	5	1	1	2	....	....	....	6	....	....	....	....	....	....	....	....	....	....	....	....	....	....	....	....	....	....
1982-83	SKA Leningrad	USSR	42	2	1	3	....	....	....	32	....	....	....	....	....	....	....	....	....	....	....	....	....	....	....	....	....	....
1983-84	SKA Leningrad	USSR	43	2	3	5	....	....	....	32	....	....	....	....	....	....	....	....	....	....	....	....	....	....	....	....	....	....
	Soviet Union	WJC-A	7	4	5	9	....	....	....	8	....	....	....	....	....	....	....	....	....	....	....	....	....	....	....	....	....	....
1984-85	Soviet Union	Can-Cup	2	0	0	0	....	....	....	4	....	....	....	....	....	....	....	....	....	....	....	....	....	....	....	....	....	....
	CSKA Moscow	USSR	36	3	2	5	....	....	....	26	....	....	....	....	....	....	....	....	....	....	....	....	....	....	....	....	....	....
	Soviet Union	WEC-A	10	2	1	3	....	....	....	6	....	....	....	....	....	....	....	....	....	....	....	....	....	....	....	....	....	....
1985-86	CSKA Moscow	USSR	40	3	5	8	....	....	....	30	....	....	....	....	....	....	....	....	....	....	....	....	....	....	....	....	....	....
	CSKA Moscow	Super-S	6	1	3	4	....	....	....	4	....	....	....	....	....	....	....	....	....	....	....	....	....	....	....	....	....	....
	Soviet Union	WEC-A	9	1	2	3	....	....	....	8	....	....	....	....	....	....	....	....	....	....	....	....	....	....	....	....	....	....
1986-87	CSKA Moscow	USSR	38	4	7	11	....	....	....	24	....	....	....	....	....	....	....	....	....	....	....	....	....	....	....	....	....	....
	USSR	RV-87	2	0	0	0	....	....	....	0	....	....	....	....	....	....	....	....	....	....	....	....	....	....	....	....	....	....
	Soviet Union	WEC-A	10	1	2	3	....	....	....	8	....	....	....	....	....	....	....	....	....	....	....	....	....	....	....	....	....	....
1987-88	Soviet Union	Can-Cup	6	1	1	2	....	....	....	6	....	....	....	....	....	....	....	....	....	....	....	....	....	....	....	....	....	....
	CSKA Moscow	USSR	39	3	2	5	....	....	....	28	....	....	....	....	....	....	....	....	....	....	....	....	....	....	....	....	....	....
	Soviet Union	Olympics	8	1	3	4	....	....	....	6	....	....	....	....	....	....	....	....	....	....	....	....	....	....	....	....	....	....
1988-89	CSKA Moscow	USSR	42	5	4	9	....	....	....	37	....	....	....	....	....	....	....	....	....	....	....	....	....	....	....	....	....	....
	CSKA Moscow	Super-S	7	1	3	4	....	....	....	0	....	....	....	....	....	....	....	....	....	....	....	....	....	....	....	....	....	....
	Soviet Union	WEC-A	9	2	1	3	....	....	....	2	....	....	....	....	....	....	....	....	....	....	....	....	....	....	....	....	....	....
1989-90	CSKA Moscow	Fr-Tour	1	0	0	0	....	....	....	2	....	....	....	....	....	....	....	....	....	....	....	....	....	....	....	....	....	....
	CSKA Moscow	USSR	42	4	7	11	....	....	....	42	....	....	....	....	....	....	....	....	....	....	....	....	....	....	....	....	....	....
	CSKA Moscow	Super-S	2	1	1	2	....	....	....	15	....	....	....	....	....	....	....	....	....	....	....	....	....	....	....	....	....	....
	Soviet Union	WEC-A	10	1	3	4	....	....	....	6	....	....	....	....	....	....	....	....	....	....	....	....	....	....	....	....	....	....
1990-91	CSKA Moscow	Fr-Tour	1	0	0	0	....	....	....	0	....	....	....	....	....	....	....	....	....	....	....	....	....	....	....	....	....	....
	CSKA Moscow	USSR	15	0	0	0	....	....	....	12	....	....	....	....	....	....	....	....	....	....	....	....	....	....	....	....	....	....
	Quebec Nordiques	**NHL**	36	3	9	12	3	7	10	12	1	0	0	36	8.3	37	6	48	13	–4	....	....	....	....	....	....	....	....
	Halifax Citadels	AHL	2	0	3	3	....	....	....	2	....	....	....	....	....	....	....	....	....	....	....	....	....	....	....	....	....	....
	Soviet Union	WEC-A	10	1	4	5	....	....	....	2	....	....	....	....	....	....	....	....	....	....	....	....	....	....	....	....	....	....

Season	Club	League	GP	G	A	Pts	AG	AA	APts	PIM	PP	SH	GW	S	%	TGF	PGF	TGA	PGA	+/–	GP	G	A	Pts	PIM	PP	SH	GW
			REGULAR SEASON																		PLAYOFFS							
1991-92	Soviet Union	Can-Cup	5	0	2	2				0																		
	Quebec Nordiques	**NHL**	**68**	**5**	**18**	**23**	**5**	**14**	**19**	**22**	**3**	**0**	**1**	**66**	**7.6**	**79**	**16**	**112**	**40**	**–9**								
	Halifax Citadels	AHL	3	0	0	0				0																		
1992-93	**Quebec Nordiques**	**NHL**	**79**	**8**	**22**	**30**	**7**	**15**	**22**	**57**	**0**	**2**	**1**	**60**	**13.3**	**88**	**2**	**105**	**37**	**18**	**5**	**0**	**1**	**1**	**0**	**0**	**0**	**0**
1993-94	**Quebec Nordiques**	**NHL**	**76**	**5**	**20**	**25**	**5**	**16**	**21**	**38**	**0**	**1**	**0**	**84**	**6.0**	**87**	**15**	**112**	**43**	**3**								
1994-95	**Quebec Nordiques**	**NHL**	**14**	**1**	**2**	**3**	**2**	**3**	**5**	**6**	**0**	**0**	**1**	**7**	**14.3**	**11**	**0**	**12**	**0**	**–1**								
1995-96♦	**Colorado Avalanche**	**NHL**	**65**	**5**	**15**	**20**	**5**	**12**	**17**	**56**	**0**	**0**	**0**	**42**	**11.9**	**72**	**9**	**63**	**29**	**29**	**21**	**0**	**9**	**9**	**12**	**0**	**0**	**0**
1996-97	**Colorado Avalanche**	**NHL**	**58**	**2**	**12**	**14**	**2**	**11**	**13**	**28**	**0**	**0**	**0**	**33**	**6.1**	**52**	**3**	**63**	**18**	**4**	**17**	**0**	**3**	**3**	**14**	**0**	**0**	**0**
1997-98	**Colorado Avalanche**	**NHL**	**72**	**4**	**10**	**14**	**5**	**10**	**15**	**42**	**0**	**1**	**1**	**47**	**8.5**	**54**	**2**	**69**	**26**	**9**	**7**	**0**	**1**	**1**	**6**	**0**	**0**	**0**
	Russia	Olympics	6	0	1	1				8																		
1998-99	**Colorado Avalanche**	**NHL**	**54**	**3**	**10**	**13**	**4**	**10**	**14**	**24**	**1**	**0**	**0**	**28**	**10.7**	**49**	**9**	**45**	**17**	**12**	**5**	**0**	**0**	**0**	**2**	**0**	**0**	**0**
99-2000	**Colorado Avalanche**	**NHL**	**34**	**2**	**2**	**4**	**2**	**2**	**4**	**10**	**0**	**0**	**0**	**16**	**12.5**	**14**	**0**	**34**	**12**	**–8**								
	NHL Totals		**556**	**38**	**120**	**158**	**40**	**100**	**140**	**295**	**5**	**4**	**4**	**419**	**9.1**	**543**	**62**	**663**	**235**		**55**	**0**	**14**	**14**	**34**	**0**	**0**	**0**

EJC-A All-Star Team (1982) • Named Best Defenseman at EJC-A (1982) • WJC-A All-Star Team (1984) • Named Best Defenseman at WJC-A (1984)

• Transferred to **Colorado** after **Quebec** franchise relocated, June 21, 1995. • Missed remainder of 1999-2000 season recovering from leg injury suffered in game vs. Dallas, February 27, 2000.

• GUSEV, Sergey

Sergey V. D – L. 6'1", 195 lbs. b: Nizhny Tagil, USSR, 7/31/1975. Dallas' 4th, 69th overall, in 1995.

Season	Club	League	GP	G	A	Pts	AG	AA	APts	PIM	PP	SH	GW	S	%	TGF	PGF	TGA	PGA	+/–	GP	G	A	Pts	PIM	PP	SH	GW
1994-95	CSK Samara	CIS	50	3	5	8				58																		
	Russia	WJC-A	7	1	3	4				4																		
1995-96	Michigan K-Wings	IHL	73	11	17	28				76																		
1996-97	Michigan K-Wings	IHL	51	7	8	15				44											4	0	4	4	6			
1997-98	**Dallas Stars**	**NHL**	**9**	**0**	**0**	**0**	**0**	**0**	**0**	**2**	**0**	**0**	**0**	**5**	**0.0**	**1**	**1**	**5**	**0**	**–5**								
	Michigan K-Wings	IHL	36	3	6	9				36											4	0	2	2	6			
1998-99	**Dallas Stars**	**NHL**	**22**	**1**	**4**	**5**	**1**	**4**	**5**	**6**	**0**	**0**	**1**	**30**	**3.3**	**12**	**3**	**4**	**0**	**5**								
	Michigan K-Wings	IHL	12	0	6	6				14																		
	Tampa Bay Lightning	**NHL**	**14**	**0**	**3**	**3**	**0**	**3**	**3**	**10**	**0**	**0**	**0**	**16**	**0.0**	**9**	**5**	**14**	**2**	**–8**								
99-2000	**Tampa Bay Lightning**	**NHL**	**28**	**2**	**3**	**5**	**2**	**3**	**5**	**6**	**1**	**0**	**0**	**23**	**8.7**	**14**	**3**	**31**	**11**	**–9**								
	NHL Totals		**73**	**3**	**10**	**13**	**3**	**10**	**13**	**24**	**1**	**0**	**1**	**74**	**4.1**	**36**	**12**	**54**	**13**									

Traded to **Tampa Bay** by **Dallas** for Benoit Hogue and a conditional choice in 2001 Entry Draft, March 21, 1999. • Missed majority of 1999-2000 season recovering from knee injury suffered in game vs. NY Rangers, December 19, 1999.

• GUSMANOV, Ravil

LW – L. 6'3", 185 lbs. b: Naberezhnye Chelny, USSR, 7/25/1972. Winnipeg's 5th, 93rd overall, in 1993.

Season	Club	League	GP	G	A	Pts	AG	AA	APts	PIM	PP	SH	GW	S	%	TGF	PGF	TGA	PGA	+/–	GP	G	A	Pts	PIM	PP	SH	GW
1989-90	Traktor Chelyabinsk	USSR-Jr.	STATISTICS NOT AVAILABLE																									
	Soviet Union	EJC-A	6	3	1	4				0																		
1990-91	Traktor Chelyabinsk	USSR	15	0	0	0				10																		
1991-92	Traktor Chelyabinsk	CIS	38	4	4	8				20																		
	Russia	WJC-A	7	1	1	2				0																		
1992-93	Traktor Chelyabinsk	CIS	39	15	8	23				30											8	4	0	4	2			
1993-94	Traktor Chelyabinsk	CIS	43	18	9	27				51											6	4	3	7	10			
	Russia	Olympics	8	3	1	4				0																		
1994-95	Springfield Falcons	AHL	72	18	15	33				14																		
1995-96	**Winnipeg Jets**	**NHL**	**4**	**0**	**0**	**0**	**0**	**0**	**0**	**0**	**0**	**0**	**0**	**6**	**0.0**	**0**	**0**	**3**	**0**	**–3**								
	Springfield Falcons	AHL	60	36	32	68				20																		
	Indianapolis Ice	IHL	11	6	10	16				4											5	2	3	5	4			
1996-97	Indianapolis Ice	IHL	60	21	27	48				14																		
	Saint John Flames	AHL	12	4	4	8				2											3	0	1	1	2			
1997-98	Chicago Wolves	IHL	56	27	28	55				26											11	1	3	4	19			
1998-99	Metallurg Magnotogorsk	Russia	42	14	24	38				28											16	2	8	10	16			
	Metallurg Magnotogorsk	EuroHL	6	3	3	6				4											6	0	2	2	0			
	Russia	WC-A	6	2	3	5				2																		
99-2000	Metallurg Magnitogorsk	Russia	37	12	13	25				30											11	3	5	8	6			
	Metallurg Magnotogorsk	EuroHL	6	2	0	2				0											5	0	1	1	6			
	NHL Totals		**4**	**0**	**0**	**0**	**0**	**0**	**0**	**0**	**0**	**0**	**0**	**6**	**0.0**	**0**	**0**	**3**	**0**									

Traded to **Chicago** by **Winnipeg** for Chicago's 4th round choice (later traded to Toronto - Toronto selected Vladimir Antipov) in 1996 Entry Draft, March 20, 1996. Traded to **Calgary** by **Chicago** for Marc Hussey, March 18, 1997.

• GUSTAFSSON, Bengt-Ake

RW – L. 6', 185 lbs. b: Karlskoga, Sweden, 3/23/1958. Washington's 7th, 55th overall, in 1978.

Season	Club	League	GP	G	A	Pts	AG	AA	APts	PIM	PP	SH	GW	S	%	TGF	PGF	TGA	PGA	+/–	GP	G	A	Pts	PIM	PP	SH	GW
1973-74	KB Karlskoga	Sweden-2	8	1	4	5				0											6	1	1	2	0			
1974-75	KB Karlskoga	Sweden-2	18	4	5	9				2																		
	KB Karlskoga	Sweden-Jr.																			2	1	1	2	0			
1975-76	KB Karlskoga	Sweden-2	11	7	3	10																						
	Sweden	EJC-A	5	3	1	4				2																		
1976-77	KB Karlskoga/Bafors	Sweden-2	22	32	18	50															11	7	7	14				
1977-78	Farjestads BK Karlstad	Sweden	32	15	10	25				10											7	2	6	8	10			
	Sweden	WJC-A	7	2	6	8				10																		
1978-79	Farjestads BK Karlstad	Sweden	32	13	11	24				10											3	2	0	2	4			
	Sweden	WEC-A	8	4	2	6				0																		
	Edmonton Oilers	WHA																			2	1	2	3	0			
1979-80	**Washington Capitals**	**NHL**	**80**	**22**	**38**	**60**	**19**	**28**	**47**	**17**	**6**	**1**	**3**	**185**	**11.9**	**91**	**39**	**89**	**20**	**–17**								
1980-81	**Washington Capitals**	**NHL**	**72**	**21**	**34**	**55**	**16**	**23**	**39**	**26**	**4**	**2**	**1**	**170**	**12.4**	**89**	**31**	**61**	**14**	**11**								
	Sweden	WEC-A	6	3	1	4				8																		
1981-82	Washington Capitals	DN-Cup	4	2	0	2																						
	Washington Capitals	**NHL**	**70**	**26**	**34**	**60**	**21**	**23**	**44**	**40**	**3**	**0**	**2**	**142**	**18.3**	**87**	**29**	**84**	**6**	**–20**								
1982-83	**Washington Capitals**	**NHL**	**67**	**22**	**42**	**64**	**18**	**29**	**47**	**16**	**2**	**0**	**4**	**139**	**15.8**	**90**	**38**	**47**	**4**	**9**	**4**	**0**	**1**	**1**	**4**	**0**	**0**	**0**
	Sweden	WEC-A	10	2	7	9				6																		
1983-84	**Washington Capitals**	**NHL**	**69**	**32**	**43**	**75**	**26**	**29**	**55**	**16**	**8**	**0**	**5**	**146**	**21.9**	**100**	**33**	**38**	**0**	**29**	**5**	**2**	**3**	**5**	**0**	**2**	**0**	**0**
1984-85	Sweden	Can-Cup	5	1	3	4				2																		
	Washington Capitals	**NHL**	**51**	**14**	**29**	**43**	**11**	**20**	**31**	**8**	**6**	**1**	**3**	**98**	**14.3**	**58**	**20**	**32**	**7**	**13**	**5**	**1**	**3**	**4**	**0**	**1**	**0**	**0**
1985-86	**Washington Capitals**	**NHL**	**70**	**23**	**52**	**75**	**18**	**35**	**53**	**26**	**8**	**4**	**6**	**113**	**20.4**	**111**	**51**	**72**	**21**	**–9**								
1986-87	KB Karlskoga/Bafors	Sweden	28	16	26	42				22																		
	Sweden	WEC-A	10	3	8	11				4																		
1987-88	Sweden	Can-Cup	6	3	0	3				4																		
	Washington Capitals	**NHL**	**78**	**18**	**36**	**54**	**15**	**26**	**41**	**29**	**7**	**5**	**3**	**136**	**13.2**	**99**	**48**	**84**	**35**	**2**	**14**	**4**	**9**	**13**	**6**	**2**	**0**	**1**
1988-89	**Washington Capitals**	**NHL**	**72**	**18**	**51**	**69**	**15**	**36**	**51**	**18**	**5**	**4**	**6**	**107**	**16.8**	**96**	**36**	**78**	**31**	**13**	**4**	**2**	**3**	**5**	**6**	**1**	**0**	**0**
1989-90	Farjestads BK Karlstad	Sweden	37	22	24	46				14											10	4	*10	*14	18			
1990-91	Farjestads BK Karlstad	Sweden	37	9	21	30				6											8	3	6	9	2			
	Sweden	WEC-A	10	0	5	5				6																		
1991-92	Farjestads BK Karlstad	Sweden	35	12	20	32				30											6	2	5	7	2			
	Sweden	Olympics	8	0	1	1				0																		
1992-93	Farjestads BK Karlstad	Sweden	40	17	14	31				32											3	0	1	1	2			
1993-94	VEU Feldkirch	Alpenliga	28	9	32	41				8																		
	VEU Feldkirch	Austria	26	11	11	22				33																		
1994-95	VEU Feldkirch	Alpenliga	17	12	17	29				8																		
	VEU Feldkirch	Austria	24	9	25	34				14											13	9	13	22	2			
1995-96	VEU Feldkirch	Alpenliga	7	8	8	16				2																		
	VEU Feldkirch	Austria	36	20	46	66				12											4	1	5	6	2			
1996-97	VEU Feldkirch	Alpenliga	40	21	41	62				10																		
	VEU Feldkirch	Austria	11	3	13	16				0																		

			REGULAR SEASON																		PLAYOFFS							
Season	Club	League	GP	G	A	Pts	AG	AA	APts	PIM	PP	SH	GW	S	%	TGF	PGF	TGA	PGA	+/–	GP	G	A	Pts	PIM	PP	SH	GW
1997-98	VEU Feldkirch	Alpenliga	36	6	15	21				10																		
	VEU Feldkirch	Austria	18	4	15	19				6																		
	VEU Feldkirch	EuroHL	6	2	6	8				2											4	1	3	4	2			
1998-99	VEU Feldkirch	Alpenliga	2	0	0	0				0																		
	VEU Feldkirch	Austria	DID NOT PLAY – COACHING																									
99-2000	SC Langnau	Switz.	DID NOT PLAY – COACHING																									
	NHL Totals		**629**	**196**	**359**	**555**	**159**	**249**	**408**	**196**	**49**	**17**	**33**	**1236**	**15.9**	**821**	**325**	**585**	**138**		**32**	**9**	**19**	**28**	**16**	**6**	**0**	**1**
	Other Major League Totals																				2	1	2	3	0			

WJC-A All-Star Team (1977) • Swedish World All-Star Team (1983, 1987)

Signed as a free agent by **Edmonton** (WHA), March, 1979. Claimed by **Washington** from **Edmonton** prior to Expansion Draft, June 9, 1979.

• GUSTAFSSON, Per

D – L. 6'2", 190 lbs. b: Osterham, Sweden, 6/6/1970. Florida's 10th, 261st overall, in 1994.

Season	Club	League	GP	G	A	Pts	AG	AA	APts	PIM	PP	SH	GW	S	%	TGF	PGF	TGA	PGA	+/–	GP	G	A	Pts	PIM	PP	SH	GW
1986-87	IK Oskarshamn	Sweden-3	20	0	2	2																						
1987-88	IK Oskarshamn	Sweden-3	36	7	13	20																						
1988-89	HV-71 Jonkoping	Sweden	14	1	4	5				8											3	0	0	0	2			
1989-90	HV-71 Jonkoping	Sweden	27	4	3	7				16																		
1990-91	HV-71 Jonkoping	Sweden	31	3	5	8				16											2	0	0	0	4			
1991-92	HV-71 Jonkoping	Sweden	39	9	8	17				22											3	0	0	0	0			
1992-93	HV-71 Jonkoping	Sweden	40	6	3	9				28																		
1993-94	HV-71 Jonkoping	Sweden	34	9	7	16				10																		
1994-95	HV-71 Jonkoping	Sweden	38	10	6	16				14											13	7	5	12	8			
1995-96	HV-71 Jonkoping	Sweden	34	8	13	21				12											4	3	1	4	2			
	Sweden	WC-A	6	2	2	4				2																		
1996-97	**Florida Panthers**	**NHL**	**58**	**7**	**22**	**29**	**7**	**20**	**27**	**22**	**2**	**0**	**1**	**105**	**6.7**	**65**	**23**	**36**	**5**	**11**								
	Sweden	WC-A	6	0	0	0				0																		
1997-98	**Toronto Maple Leafs**	**NHL**	**22**	**1**	**4**	**5**	**1**	**4**	**5**	**10**	**0**	**0**	**0**	**24**	**4.2**	**15**	**5**	**15**	**0**	**–5**								
	St. John's Maple Leafs	AHL	25	7	18	25				10																		
	Ottawa Senators	**NHL**	**9**	**0**	**1**	**1**	**0**	**1**	**1**	**6**	**0**	**0**	**0**	**12**	**0.0**	**7**	**2**	**2**	**0**	**3**	**1**	**0**	**0**	**0**	**0**	**0**	**0**	**0**
1998-99	HV-71 Jonkoping	Sweden	50	12	16	28				52																		
99-2000	HV-71 Jonkoping	Sweden	40	6	15	21				47											6	1	4	5	10			
	NHL Totals		**89**	**8**	**27**	**35**	**8**	**25**	**33**	**38**	**2**	**0**	**1**	**141**	**5.7**	**87**	**30**	**53**	**5**		**1**	**0**	**0**	**0**	**0**	**0**	**0**	**0**

Swedish World All-Star Team (1996)

Traded to **Toronto** by **Florida** for Mike Lankshear, June 13, 1997. Traded to **Ottawa** by **Toronto** for Ottawa's 8th round choice (Dwight Wolfe) in 1998 Entry Draft, March 17, 1998.

• GUSTAVSSON, Peter

LW – L. 6'1", 188 lbs. b: Bollebygd, Sweden, 3/30/1958.

Season	Club	League	GP	G	A	Pts	AG	AA	APts	PIM	PP	SH	GW	S	%	TGF	PGF	TGA	PGA	+/–	GP	G	A	Pts	PIM	PP	SH	GW
1977-78	Vastra Frolunda	Sweden	16	1	5	6				0																		
1978-79	Vastra Frolunda	Sweden	35	2	1	3				4																		
1979-80	Vastra Frolunda	Sweden	36	14	8	22				12											8	2	1	3	0			
1980-81	Vastra Frolunda	Sweden	31	13	15	28				19											2	0	1	1	4			
1981-82	**Colorado Rockies**	**NHL**	**2**	**0**	**0**	**0**	**0**	**0**	**0**	**0**	**0**	**0**	**0**	**2**	**0.0**	**0**	**0**	**1**	**0**	**–1**								
	Fort Worth Texans	CHL	59	8	11	19				4																		
1982-83	Vastra Frolunda	Sweden	36	15	13	28				26																		
1983-84	Vastra Frolunda	Sweden	35	13	13	26				8																		
1984-85	Vastra Frolunda	Sweden-2	22	9	15	24				12																		
1985-86	Vastra Frolunda	Sweden-2	27	14	16	30				16											3	5	2	7	0			
1986-87	Vastra Frolunda	Sweden-2	29	22	16	38				18											2	0	0	0	0			
1987-88	Vastra Frolunda	Sweden-2	34	20	16	36				10											10	3	3	6	0			
1988-89	Vastra Frolunda	Sweden-2	34	16	19	35				14											11	2	5	7	2			
1989-90	Vastra Frolunda	Sweden	34	5	7	12				10																		
1990-1993			OUT OF HOCKEY – RETIRED																									
1993-94	Harryda HC	Sweden-3	29	13	25	38				6																		
	NHL Totals		**2**	**0**	**0**	**0**	**0**	**0**	**0**	**0**	**0**	**0**	**0**	**2**	**0.0**	**0**	**0**	**1**	**0**									

Signed as a free agent by **Colorado**, May 11, 1981.

• GUY, Kevan

Kevan Bruce D – R. 6'3", 202 lbs. b: Edmonton, Alta., 7/16/1965. Calgary's 5th, 73rd overall, in 1983.

Season	Club	League	GP	G	A	Pts	AG	AA	APts	PIM	PP	SH	GW	S	%	TGF	PGF	TGA	PGA	+/–	GP	G	A	Pts	PIM	PP	SH	GW
1981-82	Edmonton Athletic Club	AAHA	STATISTICS NOT AVAILABLE																									
1982-83	Medicine Hat Tigers	WHL	69	7	20	27				89											5	0	3	3	16			
1983-84	Medicine Hat Tigers	WHL	72	15	42	57				117											14	3	4	7	14			
1984-85	Medicine Hat Tigers	WHL	31	7	17	24				46											10	1	2	3	2			
1985-86	Moncton Golden Flames	AHL	73	4	20	24				56											10	0	2	2	6			
1986-87	**Calgary Flames**	**NHL**	**24**	**0**	**4**	**4**	**0**	**3**	**3**	**19**	**0**	**0**	**0**	**24**	**0.0**	**19**	**0**	**16**	**5**	**8**	**4**	**0**	**1**	**1**	**23**	**0**	**0**	**0**
	Moncton Golden Flames	AHL	46	2	10	12				38																		
1987-88	**Calgary Flames**	**NHL**	**11**	**0**	**3**	**3**	**0**	**2**	**2**	**8**	**0**	**0**	**0**	**4**	**0.0**	**12**	**0**	**14**	**3**	**1**								
	Salt Lake Golden Eagles	IHL	61	6	30	36				51											19	1	6	7	26			
1988-89	**Vancouver Canucks**	**NHL**	**45**	**2**	**2**	**4**	**2**	**1**	**3**	**34**	**0**	**0**	**0**	**40**	**5.0**	**19**	**2**	**34**	**3**	**–14**	**1**	**0**	**0**	**0**	**0**	**0**	**0**	**0**
1989-90	**Vancouver Canucks**	**NHL**	**30**	**2**	**5**	**7**	**2**	**4**	**6**	**32**	**0**	**0**	**0**	**44**	**4.5**	**14**	**3**	**27**	**4**	**–12**								
	Milwaukee Admirals	IHL	29	2	11	13				33																		
1990-91	**Vancouver Canucks**	**NHL**	**39**	**1**	**6**	**7**	**1**	**5**	**6**	**39**	**0**	**0**	**1**	**37**	**2.7**	**30**	**0**	**46**	**10**	**–6**								
	Calgary Flames	**NHL**	**4**	**0**	**0**	**0**	**0**	**0**	**0**	**4**	**0**	**0**	**0**	**6**	**0.0**	**5**	**0**	**6**	**2**	**1**								
1991-92	**Calgary Flames**	**NHL**	**3**	**0**	**0**	**0**	**0**	**0**	**0**	**2**	**0**	**0**	**0**	**3**	**0.0**	**3**	**0**	**2**	**1**	**2**								
	Salt Lake Golden Eagles	IHL	60	3	14	17				89											5	0	1	1	4			
1992-93	EC Graz	Austria	22	1	6	7																						
	Salt Lake Golden Eagles	IHL	33	1	9	10				50																		
1993-94	Salt Lake Golden Eagles	IHL	62	4	17	21				45																		
1994-95	Tallahassee Tiger Sharks	ECHL	6	0	5	5				0																		
	Denver Grizzlies	IHL	3	0	1	1				0																		
	NHL Totals		**156**	**5**	**20**	**25**	**5**	**15**	**20**	**138**	**0**	**0**	**1**	**158**	**3.2**	**102**	**5**	**145**	**28**		**5**	**0**	**1**	**1**	**23**	**0**	**0**	**0**

Traded to **Vancouver** by **Calgary** with Brian Bradley and Peter Bakovic for Craig Coxe, March 6, 1988. Traded to **Calgary** by **Vancouver** with Ron Stern for Dana Murzyn, March 5, 1991. Signed as a free agent by **NY Islanders**, September 18, 1993.

• HAANPAA, Ari

Ari Eerik RW – R. 6'1", 185 lbs. b: Nokla, Finland, 11/28/1965. NY Islanders' 5th, 83rd overall, in 1984.

Season	Club	League	GP	G	A	Pts	AG	AA	APts	PIM	PP	SH	GW	S	%	TGF	PGF	TGA	PGA	+/–	GP	G	A	Pts	PIM	PP	SH	GW
1982-83	Ilves Tampere	Finland-Jr.	21	9	9	18				54																		
	Finland	WJC-A	5	0	0	0				16																		
	Finland	EJC-A	5	3	0	3				12																		
1983-84	Ilves Tampere	Finland-Jr.	7	4	2	6				19																		
	Finland	WJC-A	7	5	3	8				8																		
	Ilves Tampere	Finland	27	0	1	1				8											2	0	0	0	2			
1984-85	Ilves Tampere	Finland	13	5	0	5				2											9	3	1	4	0			
	Finland	WJC-A	7	6	1	7				4																		
1985-86	**New York Islanders**	**NHL**	**18**	**0**	**7**	**7**	**0**	**5**	**5**	**20**	**0**	**0**	**0**	**16**	**0.0**	**8**	**0**	**8**	**0**	**0**								
	Springfield Indians	AHL	20	3	1	4				13																		
1986-87	**New York Islanders**	**NHL**	**41**	**6**	**4**	**10**	**5**	**3**	**8**	**17**	**0**	**0**	**3**	**45**	**13.3**	**23**	**1**	**14**	**0**	**8**	**6**	**0**	**0**	**0**	**10**	**0**	**0**	**0**
1987-88	**New York Islanders**	**NHL**	**1**	**0**	**0**	**0**	**0**	**0**	**0**	**0**	**0**	**0**	**0**	**0**	**0.0**	**0**	**0**	**2**	**0**	**–2**								
	Springfield Indians	AHL	61	14	19	33				34																		
1988-89	Lukko Rauma	Finland	42	28	19	47				36																		
	Finland	Nat-Team	2	0	0	0				4																		
1989-90	Lukko Rauma	Finland	24	17	9	26				59																		

Season	Club	League	GP	G	A	Pts	AG	AA	APts	PIM	PP	SH	GW	S	%	TGF	PGF	TGA	PGA	+/–	GP	G	A	Pts	PIM	PP	SH	GW
			REGULAR SEASON																		PLAYOFFS							
1990-91	JyP-HT Jyvaskyla	Finland	32	28	17	45	....	....	....	100	....	....	....	....	....	....	....	....	....	....	5	3	1	4	8	....	....	....
	Finland	Nat-Team	9	1	0	1	....	....	....	6	....	....	....	....	....	....	....	....	....	....	....	....	....	....	....	....	....	....
1991-92	JyP-HT Jyvaskyla	Finland	41	21	20	41	....	....	....	70	....	....	....	....	....	....	....	....	....	....	10	6	2	8	8	....	....	....
1992-93	JyP-HT Jyvaskyla	Finland	44	15	11	26	....	....	....	89	....	....	....	....	....	....	....	....	....	....	9	1	2	3	4	....	....	....
1993-94	Tappara Tampere	Finland	42	21	13	34	....	....	....	72	....	....	....	....	....	....	....	....	....	....	10	3	6	9	6	....	....	....
1994-95	Tappara Tampere	Finland	48	12	12	24	....	....	....	67	....	....	....	....	....	....	....	....	....	....	....	....	....	....	....	....	....	....
1995-96	Tappara Tampere	Finland	45	13	16	29	....	....	....	60	....	....	....	....	....	....	....	....	....	....	4	3	0	3	8	....	....	....
1996-97	WEV Wien	Alpenliga	25	9	6	15	....	....	....	39	....	....	....	....	....	....	....	....	....	....	....	....	....	....	....	....	....	....
	WEV Wien	Austria	4	6	7	13	....	....	....	0	....	....	....	....	....	....	....	....	....	....	....	....	....	....	....	....	....	....
	WEV Wien	EuroHL	4	0	0	0	....	....	....	0	....	....	....	....	....	....	....	....	....	....	....	....	....	....	....	....	....	....
1997-98	GEC Nordhorn	Germany-2	33	32	37	69	....	....	....	64	....	....	....	....	....	....	....	....	....	....	3	3	0	3	2	....	....	....
1998-99	HC Reims	France	24	16	9	25	....	....	....	....	....	....	....	....	....	....	....	....	....	....	11	3	6	9	....	....	....	....
	NHL Totals		**60**	**6**	**11**	**17**	**5**	**8**	**13**	**37**	**0**	**0**	**3**	**61**	**9.8**	**31**	**1**	**24**	**0**		**6**	**0**	**0**	**0**	**10**	**0**	**0**	**0**

Finnish First All-Star Team (1991)

• HAAS, David

"The Real Deal" LW – L. 6'2", 200 lbs. b: Toronto, Ont., 6/23/1968. Edmonton's 5th, 105th overall, in 1986.

Season	Club	League	GP	G	A	Pts	AG	AA	APts	PIM	PP	SH	GW	S	%	TGF	PGF	TGA	PGA	+/–	GP	G	A	Pts	PIM	PP	SH	GW
1984-85	Don Mills Flyers	MTHL	38	38	38	76	....	....	....	80	....	....	....	....	....	....	....	....	....	....	....	....	....	....	....	....	....	....
1985-86	London Knights	OHL	62	4	13	17	....	....	....	91	....	....	....	....	....	....	....	....	....	....	5	0	1	1	0	....	....	....
1986-87	London Knights	OHL	5	1	0	1	....	....	....	5	....	....	....	....	....	....	....	....	....	....	....	....	....	....	....	....	....	....
	Kitchener Rangers	OHL	4	0	1	1	....	....	....	4	....	....	....	....	....	....	....	....	....	....	....	....	....	....	....	....	....	....
	Belleville Bulls	OHL	55	10	13	23	....	....	....	86	....	....	....	....	....	....	....	....	....	....	6	3	0	3	13	....	....	....
1987-88	Belleville Bulls	OHL	5	1	1	2	....	....	....	9	....	....	....	....	....	....	....	....	....	....	....	....	....	....	....	....	....	....
	Windsor Spitfires	OHL	58	59	46	105	....	....	....	237	....	....	....	....	....	....	....	....	....	....	11	9	11	20	50	....	....	....
	Windsor Spitfires	Mem-Cup	4	2	2	4	....	....	....	6	....	....	....	....	....	....	....	....	....	....	....	....	....	....	....	....	....	....
1988-89	Cape Breton Oilers	AHL	61	9	9	18	....	....	....	325	....	....	....	....	....	....	....	....	....	....	....	....	....	....	....	....	....	....
1989-90	Cape Breton Oilers	AHL	53	6	12	18	....	....	....	230	....	....	....	....	....	....	....	....	....	....	4	2	2	4	15	....	....	....
1990-91	**Edmonton Oilers**	**NHL**	**5**	**1**	**0**	**1**	**1**	**0**	**1**	**0**	**0**	**0**	**0**	**4**	**25.0**	**1**	**0**	**3**	**0**	**–2**	....	....	....	....	....	....	....	....
	Cape Breton Oilers	AHL	60	24	23	47	....	....	....	137	....	....	....	....	....	....	....	....	....	....	3	0	2	2	12	....	....	....
1991-92	Cape Breton Oilers	AHL	16	3	7	10	....	....	....	32	....	....	....	....	....	....	....	....	....	....	....	....	....	....	....	....	....	....
	New Haven Nighthawks	AHL	50	13	23	36	....	....	....	97	....	....	....	....	....	....	....	....	....	....	5	3	0	3	13	....	....	....
1992-93	Cape Breton Oilers	AHL	73	22	56	78	....	....	....	121	....	....	....	....	....	....	....	....	....	....	16	11	13	24	36	....	....	....
1993-94	**Calgary Flames**	**NHL**	**2**	**1**	**1**	**2**	**1**	**1**	**2**	**7**	**0**	**0**	**0**	**3**	**33.3**	**4**	**0**	**2**	**0**	**2**	....	....	....	....	....	....	....	....
	Saint John Flames	AHL	37	11	17	28	....	....	....	108	....	....	....	....	....	....	....	....	....	....	....	....	....	....	....	....	....	....
	Phoenix Roadrunners	IHL	11	7	4	11	....	....	....	43	....	....	....	....	....	....	....	....	....	....	....	....	....	....	....	....	....	....
1994-95	HC Courmaosta	Italy	16	9	15	24	....	....	....	50	....	....	....	....	....	....	....	....	....	....	6	5	5	10	14	....	....	....
	Detroit Vipers	IHL	1	0	1	1	....	....	....	0	....	....	....	....	....	....	....	....	....	....	....	....	....	....	....	....	....	....
	Worcester IceCats	AHL	28	11	10	21	....	....	....	88	....	....	....	....	....	....	....	....	....	....	....	....	....	....	....	....	....	....
1995-96	HC Milano	Italy	10	9	8	17	....	....	....	55	....	....	....	....	....	....	....	....	....	....	....	....	....	....	....	....	....	....
1996-97	HK Olimpija Ljubljana	Alpenliga	45	*38	47	*85	....	....	....	88	....	....	....	....	....	....	....	....	....	....	....	....	....	....	....	....	....	....
	HK Olimpija Ljubljana	Slovenia	....	....	....	....	....	....	....	....	....	....	....	....	....	....	....	....	....	....	6	5	5	10	14	....	....	....
	HC Milano	Italy	4	6	5	11	....	....	....	31	....	....	....	....	....	....	....	....	....	....	6	3	3	6	24	....	....	....
1997-98	Hannover Scorpions	Germany	48	*25	28	53	....	....	....	105	....	....	....	....	....	....	....	....	....	....	4	1	1	2	10	....	....	....
1998-99	Hannover Scorpions	Germany	42	18	20	38	....	....	....	104	....	....	....	....	....	....	....	....	....	....	....	....	....	....	....	....	....	....
99-2000	Hannover Scorpions	Germany	40	12	19	31	....	....	....	106	....	....	....	....	....	....	....	....	....	....	....	....	....	....	....	....	....	....
	NHL Totals		**7**	**2**	**1**	**3**	**2**	**1**	**3**	**7**	**0**	**0**	**0**	**7**	**28.6**	**5**	**0**	**5**	**0**		....	....	....	....	....	....	....	....

OHL Second All-Star Team (1988) • Signed as a free agent by **Calgary**, August 10, 1993.

• HABSCHEID, Marc

Marc Joseph RW/C – R. 6', 185 lbs. b: Swift Current, Sask., 3/1/1963. Edmonton's 6th, 113th overall, in 1981.

Season	Club	League	GP	G	A	Pts	AG	AA	APts	PIM	PP	SH	GW	S	%	TGF	PGF	TGA	PGA	+/–	GP	G	A	Pts	PIM	PP	SH	GW
1979-80	Saskatoon Olympics	AJHL	STATISTICS NOT AVAILABLE																									
	Saskatoon Blades	WHL	15	2	3	5	....	....	....	2	....	....	....	....	....	....	....	....	....	....	....	....	....	....	....	....	....	....
1980-81	Saskatoon Blades	WHL	72	34	63	97	....	....	....	50	....	....	....	....	....	....	....	....	....	....	....	....	....	....	....	....	....	....
1981-82	Saskatoon Blades	WHL	55	64	87	151	....	....	....	74	....	....	....	....	....	....	....	....	....	....	5	3	4	7	4	....	....	....
	Canada	WJC-A	7	6	6	12	....	....	....	2	....	....	....	....	....	....	....	....	....	....	....	....	....	....	....	....	....	....
	Edmonton Oilers	**NHL**	**7**	**1**	**3**	**4**	**1**	**2**	**3**	**2**	**1**	**0**	**0**	**7**	**14.3**	**6**	**1**	**0**	**0**	**5**	....	....	....	....	....	....	....	....
	Wichita Wind	CHL	....	....	....	....	....	....	....	....	....	....	....	....	....	....	....	....	....	....	3	0	0	0	0	....	....	....
1982-83	Kamloops Blazers	WHL	6	7	16	23	....	....	....	8	....	....	....	....	....	....	....	....	....	....	....	....	....	....	....	....	....	....
	Edmonton Oilers	**NHL**	**32**	**3**	**10**	**13**	**2**	**7**	**9**	**14**	**0**	**0**	**0**	**19**	**15.8**	**22**	**2**	**7**	**1**	**14**	....	....	....	....	....	....	....	....
1983-84	**Edmonton Oilers**	**NHL**	**9**	**1**	**0**	**1**	**1**	**0**	**1**	**6**	**0**	**0**	**0**	**6**	**16.7**	**1**	**0**	**5**	**1**	**–3**	....	....	....	....	....	....	....	....
	Moncton Alpines	AHL	71	19	37	56	....	....	....	32	....	....	....	....	....	....	....	....	....	....	....	....	....	....	....	....	....	....
1984-85	**Edmonton Oilers**	**NHL**	**26**	**5**	**3**	**8**	**4**	**2**	**6**	**4**	**2**	**0**	**0**	**30**	**16.7**	**10**	**3**	**9**	**0**	**–2**	....	....	....	....	....	....	....	....
	Nova Scotia Voyageurs	AHL	48	29	29	58	....	....	....	65	....	....	....	....	....	....	....	....	....	....	6	4	3	7	9	....	....	....
1985-86	**Minnesota North Stars**	**NHL**	**6**	**2**	**3**	**5**	**2**	**2**	**4**	**0**	**1**	**0**	**0**	**8**	**25.0**	**7**	**3**	**6**	**0**	**–2**	**2**	**0**	**0**	**0**	**0**	**0**	**0**	**0**
	Springfield Indians	AHL	41	18	32	50	....	....	....	21	....	....	....	....	....	....	....	....	....	....	....	....	....	....	....	....	....	....
1986-87	Canada	Nat-Team	51	29	32	61	....	....	....	70	....	....	....	....	....	....	....	....	....	....	....	....	....	....	....	....	....	....
	Minnesota North Stars	**NHL**	**15**	**2**	**0**	**2**	**2**	**0**	**2**	**2**	**1**	**0**	**0**	**14**	**14.3**	**3**	**2**	**8**	**1**	**–6**	....	....	....	....	....	....	....	....
1987-88	Canada	Nat-Team	61	19	34	53	....	....	....	42	....	....	....	....	....	....	....	....	....	....	....	....	....	....	....	....	....	....
	Canada	Olympics	8	5	3	8	....	....	....	6	....	....	....	....	....	....	....	....	....	....	....	....	....	....	....	....	....	....
	Minnesota North Stars	**NHL**	**16**	**4**	**11**	**15**	**3**	**8**	**11**	**6**	**3**	**0**	**0**	**44**	**9.1**	**20**	**8**	**21**	**5**	**–4**	....	....	....	....	....	....	....	....
1988-89	**Minnesota North Stars**	**NHL**	**76**	**23**	**31**	**54**	**19**	**22**	**41**	**40**	**7**	**3**	**3**	**182**	**12.6**	**83**	**37**	**85**	**41**	**2**	**5**	**1**	**3**	**4**	**13**	**0**	**0**	**0**
1989-90	**Detroit Red Wings**	**NHL**	**66**	**15**	**11**	**26**	**13**	**8**	**21**	**33**	**0**	**0**	**0**	**114**	**13.2**	**46**	**7**	**48**	**10**	**1**	....	....	....	....	....	....	....	....
1990-91	**Detroit Red Wings**	**NHL**	**46**	**9**	**8**	**17**	**8**	**6**	**14**	**22**	**0**	**4**	**1**	**54**	**16.7**	**27**	**7**	**49**	**19**	**–10**	**5**	**0**	**0**	**0**	**0**	**0**	**0**	**0**
1991-92	**Calgary Flames**	**NHL**	**46**	**7**	**11**	**18**	**6**	**8**	**14**	**42**	**2**	**0**	**2**	**60**	**11.7**	**25**	**11**	**42**	**17**	**–11**	....	....	....	....	....	....	....	....
	Canada	WC-A	6	1	0	1	....	....	....	4	....	....	....	....	....	....	....	....	....	....	....	....	....	....	....	....	....	....
1992-93	SC Bern	Switz.	36	19	23	42	....	....	....	70	....	....	....	....	....	....	....	....	....	....	5	1	4	5	6	....	....	....
	Canada	Nat-Team	3	0	3	3	....	....	....	11	....	....	....	....	....	....	....	....	....	....	....	....	....	....	....	....	....	....
1993-94	Las Vegas Thunder	IHL	59	14	40	54	....	....	....	49	....	....	....	....	....	....	....	....	....	....	5	1	1	2	15	....	....	....
1994-95	Las Vegas Thunder	IHL	43	11	15	26	....	....	....	38	....	....	....	....	....	....	....	....	....	....	....	....	....	....	....	....	....	....
	EV Zug	Switz.	5	0	1	1	....	....	....	0	....	....	....	....	....	....	....	....	....	....	....	....	....	....	....	....	....	....
1995-96	Augsburger Panther	Germany	48	14	32	46	....	....	....	73	....	....	....	....	....	....	....	....	....	....	7	4	5	9	4	....	....	....
1996-97			OUT OF HOCKEY – RETIRED																									
1997-1999	Kamloops Blazers	WHL	DID NOT PLAY – COACHING																									
1999-2000	Kelowna Rockets	WHL	DID NOT PLAY – COACHING																									
	NHL Totals		**345**	**72**	**91**	**163**	**61**	**65**	**126**	**171**	**17**	**7**	**6**	**538**	**13.4**	**250**	**81**	**280**	**95**		**12**	**1**	**3**	**4**	**13**	**0**	**0**	**0**

WHL Second All-Star Team (1982)

• Suspended by Edmonton for refusing to report to Nova Scotia (AHL), October, 1985. Traded to **Minnesota** by **Edmonton** with Don Barber and Emanuel Viveiros for Gord Sherven and Don Biggs, December 20, 1985. Signed as a free agent by **Detroit**, June 9, 1989. Traded to **Calgary** by **Detroit** for Brian MacLellan, June 11, 1991.

• HACHBORN, Len

Leonard C – L. 5'10", 175 lbs. b: Brantford, Ont., 9/4/1961. Philadelphia's 12th, 184th overall, in 1981.

Season	Club	League	GP	G	A	Pts	AG	AA	APts	PIM	PP	SH	GW	S	%	TGF	PGF	TGA	PGA	+/–	GP	G	A	Pts	PIM	PP	SH	GW
1979-80	Hamilton Mountain A's	OJHL	43	25	20	45	....	....	....	42	....	....	....	....	....	....	....	....	....	....	....	....	....	....	....	....	....	....
	Brantford Alexanders	OMJHL	3	1	0	1	....	....	....	0	....	....	....	....	....	....	....	....	....	....	....	....	....	....	....	....	....	....
1980-81	Brantford Alexanders	OMJHL	66	34	52	86	....	....	....	94	....	....	....	....	....	....	....	....	....	....	6	1	5	6	15	....	....	....
1981-82	Brantford Alexanders	OHL	55	43	50	93	....	....	....	141	....	....	....	....	....	....	....	....	....	....	11	15	9	24	13	....	....	....
1982-83	Maine Mariners	AHL	75	28	55	83	....	....	....	32	....	....	....	....	....	....	....	....	....	....	17	2	7	9	2	....	....	....
1983-84	Springfield Indians	AHL	28	18	42	60	....	....	....	15	....	....	....	....	....	....	....	....	....	....	....	....	....	....	....	....	....	....
	Philadelphia Flyers	**NHL**	**38**	**11**	**21**	**32**	**9**	**14**	**23**	**4**	**1**	**0**	**2**	**69**	**15.9**	**41**	**8**	**26**	**1**	**8**	**3**	**0**	**0**	**0**	**7**	**0**	**0**	**0**
1984-85	**Philadelphia Flyers**	**NHL**	**40**	**5**	**17**	**22**	**4**	**12**	**16**	**23**	**0**	**0**	**0**	**48**	**10.4**	**30**	**2**	**12**	**0**	**16**	**4**	**0**	**3**	**3**	**0**	**0**	**0**	**0**
	Hershey Bears	AHL	14	6	7	13	....	....	....	14	....	....	....	....	....	....	....	....	....	....	....	....	....	....	....	....	....	....
1985-86	Hershey Bears	AHL	23	12	22	34	....	....	....	34	....	....	....	....	....	....	....	....	....	....	....	....	....	....	....	....	....	....
	Los Angeles Kings	**NHL**	**24**	**4**	**1**	**5**	**3**	**1**	**4**	**2**	**1**	**0**	**0**	**14**	**28.6**	**8**	**3**	**14**	**0**	**–9**	....	....	....	....	....	....	....	....
	New Haven Nighthawks	AHL	12	5	8	13	....	....	....	21	....	....	....	....	....	....	....	....	....	....	3	0	1	1	26	....	....	....

			REGULAR SEASON																		PLAYOFFS							
Season	Club	League	GP	G	A	Pts	AG	AA	APts	PIM	PP	SH	GW	S	%	TGF	PGF	TGA	PGA	+/–	GP	G	A	Pts	PIM	PP	SH	GW
1986-87	HC Bolzano	Italy	35	36	67	103				47																		
	Hershey Bears	AHL	17	4	10	14				2											5	0	2	2	2			
1987-88	IEV Innsbruck	Austria	34	32	38	70				14																		
	Maine Mariners	AHL	29	16	17	33				16											10	5	7	12	21			
1988-89	Rogle BK Angelholm	Sweden-2	32	21	21	42				56											3	2	2	4	26			
1989-90	ZSC Zurich	Switz.	5	6	3	9																						
	New Haven Nighthawks	AHL	32	13	27	40				15																		
1990-91	Binghamton Rangers	AHL	50	9	27	36				8											4	0	1	1	6			
1991-92	San Diego Gulls	IHL	70	34	73	107				124											4	0	2	2	17			
1992-93	Ayr Raiders	BH-Cup	8	16	20	36				28																		
	San Diego Gulls	IHL	59	23	36	59				49											10	2	2	4	2			
1993-94	Krefelder EV	Germany	2	1	1	2				0											3	2	0	2	2			
1994-95	Houston Aeros	IHL	53	12	30	42				10																		
	Springfield Indians	AHL	5	2	4	6				2																		
	Detroit Vipers	IHL																			1	0	1	1	0			
1995-96	Heilbronner EC	Germany-2	28	15	40	55				58											7	5	4	9	7			
1996-97	Grand Rapids Griffins	IHL	19	2	2	4				6																		
1997-98	San Diego Gulls	WCHL	45	27	63	90				62											12	7	7	14	10			
1998-99	San Diego Gulls	WCHL	49	23	64	87				36											12	4	*12	*16	4			
99-2000	Phoenix Mustangs	WCHL	12	4	14	18				2											12	3	10	13	8			
	NHL Totals		**102**	**20**	**39**	**59**	**16**	**27**	**43**	**29**	**2**	**0**	**2**	**131**	**15.3**	**79**	**13**	**52**	**1**		**7**	**0**	**3**	**3**	**7**	**0**	**0**	**0**

IHL Second All-Star Team (1992)

Traded to **LA Kings** by **Philadelphia** for cash, December 6, 1985. Signed as a free agent by **Phoenix Mustangs** (WCHL), February 29, 2000. • Played w/ RHI's New England Stingers in 1994 (14-13-27-40-8).

• HADFIELD, Vic

Victor Edward LW – L. 6', 190 lbs. b: Oakville, Ont., 10/4/1940.

Season	Club	League	GP	G	A	Pts	AG	AA	APts	PIM	PP	SH	GW	S	%	TGF	PGF	TGA	PGA	+/–	GP	G	A	Pts	PIM	PP	SH	GW
1958-59	St. Catharines Teepees	OHA-Jr.	51	6	14	20				72											7	1	2	3	12			
1959-60	St. Catharines Teepees	OHA-Jr.	48	19	34	53				130											17	11	13	24	*84			
	Buffalo Bisons	AHL	1	0	0	0				0																		
	St. Catharines Teepees	Mem-Cup	14	6	8	14				*60																		
1960-61	Buffalo Bisons	AHL	62	5	16	21				111											3	0	0	0	11			
1961-62	**New York Rangers**	**NHL**	**44**	**3**	**1**	**4**	**3**	**1**	**4**	**22**											**4**	**0**	**0**	**0**	**2**	**0**	**0**	**0**
1962-63	**New York Rangers**	**NHL**	**36**	**5**	**6**	**11**	**6**	**6**	**12**	**32**																		
	Baltimore Clippers	AHL	29	10	9	19				84																		
1963-64	**New York Rangers**	**NHL**	**69**	**14**	**11**	**25**	**17**	**11**	**28**	***151**																		
1964-65	**New York Rangers**	**NHL**	**70**	**18**	**20**	**38**	**22**	**20**	**42**	**102**																		
1965-66	**New York Rangers**	**NHL**	**67**	**16**	**19**	**35**	**18**	**18**	**36**	**112**																		
1966-67	**New York Rangers**	**NHL**	**69**	**13**	**20**	**33**	**15**	**20**	**35**	**80**											**4**	**1**	**0**	**1**	**17**	**0**	**0**	**0**
1967-68	**New York Rangers**	**NHL**	**59**	**20**	**19**	**39**	**23**	**19**	**42**	**45**	**7**	**0**	**7**	**177**	**11.3**	**59**	**21**	**40**	**0**	**–2**	**6**	**1**	**2**	**3**	**6**	**1**	**0**	**0**
1968-69	**New York Rangers**	**NHL**	**73**	**26**	**40**	**66**	**28**	**36**	**64**	**108**	**10**	**0**	**4**	**321**	**8.1**	**104**	**33**	**59**	**0**	**12**	**4**	**2**	**1**	**3**	**2**	**0**	**0**	**0**
1969-70	**New York Rangers**	**NHL**	**71**	**20**	**34**	**54**	**22**	**32**	**54**	**69**	**3**	**0**	**5**	**268**	**7.5**	**77**	**26**	**54**	**0**	**–3**								
1970-71	**New York Rangers**	**NHL**	**63**	**22**	**22**	**44**	**22**	**18**	**40**	**38**	**8**	**0**	**1**	**194**	**11.3**	**62**	**20**	**28**	**0**	**14**	**12**	**8**	**5**	**13**	**46**	**1**	**0**	**1**
1971-72	**New York Rangers**	**NHL**	**78**	**50**	**56**	**106**	**51**	**49**	**100**	**142**	**23**	**0**	**7**	**242**	**20.7**	**156**	**45**	**51**	**0**	**60**	**16**	**7**	**9**	**16**	**22**	**2**	**0**	**1**
1972-73	Team Canada	Summit-72	2	0	0	0				0																		
	New York Rangers	**NHL**	**63**	**28**	**34**	**62**	**26**	**27**	**53**	**60**	**9**	**0**	**4**	**214**	**13.1**	**93**	**26**	**54**	**0**	**13**	**9**	**2**	**2**	**4**	**11**	**0**	**0**	**1**
1973-74	**New York Rangers**	**NHL**	**77**	**27**	**28**	**55**	**26**	**23**	**49**	**75**	**12**	**0**	**4**	**201**	**13.4**	**91**	**37**	**54**	**1**	**1**	**6**	**1**	**0**	**1**	**0**	**0**	**0**	**0**
1974-75	**Pittsburgh Penguins**	**NHL**	**78**	**31**	**42**	**73**	**27**	**31**	**58**	**72**	**7**	**4**	**3**	**253**	**12.3**	**118**	**46**	**80**	**13**	**5**	**9**	**4**	**2**	**6**	**0**	**0**	**1**	**0**
1975-76	**Pittsburgh Penguins**	**NHL**	**76**	**30**	**35**	**65**	**26**	**26**	**52**	**46**	**3**	**0**	**2**	**203**	**14.8**	**107**	**38**	**77**	**5**	**–3**	**3**	**1**	**0**	**1**	**11**	**0**	**0**	**0**
1976-77	**Pittsburgh Penguins**	**NHL**	**9**	**0**	**2**	**2**	**0**	**2**	**2**	**0**	**0**	**0**	**0**	**9**	**0.0**	**6**	**4**	**1**	**0**	**1**								
	NHL Totals		**1002**	**323**	**389**	**712**	**332**	**339**	**671**	**1154**											**73**	**27**	**21**	**48**	**117**			

OHA-Jr. First All-Star Team (1960) • NHL Second All-Star Team (1972) • Played in NHL All-Star Game (1965, 1972)

Claimed by **NY Rangers** from **Chicago** in Intra-League Draft, June 13, 1961. Traded to **Pittsburgh** by **NY Rangers** for Nick Beverley, May 27, 1974. • Suffered eventual career-ending knee injury in game vs. Toronto, March 29, 1976.

• HAGGERTY, Sean

LW – L. 6'1", 186 lbs. b: Rye, NY, 2/11/1976. Toronto's 2nd, 48th overall, in 1994.

Season	Club	League	GP	G	A	Pts	AG	AA	APts	PIM	PP	SH	GW	S	%	TGF	PGF	TGA	PGA	+/–	GP	G	A	Pts	PIM	PP	SH	GW
1990-91	Westminster Wildcats	Hi-School	25	20	22	42																						
1991-92	Westminster Wildcats	Hi-School	25	24	36	60																						
1992-93	Boston Jr. Bruins	MBAHL	72	70	111	181				80																		
1993-94	Detroit Jr. Red Wings	OHL	60	31	32	63				21											17	9	10	19	11			
1994-95	Detroit Jr. Red Wings	OHL	61	40	49	89				37											21	13	24	37	18			
	United States	WJC-A	7	1	6	7				8																		
	Detroit Jr. Red Wings	Mem-Cup	5	*5	2	7				6																		
1995-96	Detroit Whalers	OHL	66	*60	51	111				78											17	15	9	24	30			
	Toronto Maple Leafs	**NHL**	**1**	**0**	**0**	**0**	**0**	**0**	**0**	**0**	**0**	**0**	**0**	**0**	**0.0**	**0**	**0**	**0**	**0**	**0**								
	Worcester IceCats	AHL																			1	0	0	0	2			
1996-97	Kentucky Thoroughblades	AHL	77	13	22	35				60											4	1	0	1	4			
1997-98	**New York Islanders**	**NHL**	**5**	**0**	**0**	**0**	**0**	**0**	**0**	**0**	**0**	**0**	**0**	**2**	**0.0**	**0**	**0**	**3**	**0**	**–3**								
	Kentucky Thoroughblades	AHL	63	33	20	53				64											3	0	2	2	4			
1998-99	Lowell Lock Monsters	AHL	77	19	27	46				40											3	0	1	1	0			
99-2000	**New York Islanders**	**NHL**	**5**	**1**	**1**	**2**	**1**	**1**	**2**	**4**	**0**	**0**	**0**	**2**	**50.0**	**5**	**0**	**2**	**0**	**3**								
	Kansas City Blades	IHL	76	27	33	60				94																		
	United States	WC-A	7	1	1	2				8																		
	NHL Totals		**11**	**1**	**1**	**2**	**1**	**1**	**2**	**4**	**0**	**0**	**0**	**4**	**25.0**	**5**	**0**	**5**	**0**									

Memorial Cup All-Star Team (1995) • OHL Second All-Star Team (1996) • AHL Second All-Star Team (1998)

Traded to **NY Islanders** by **Toronto** with Darby Hendrickson, Kenny Jonsson and Toronto's 1st round choice (Roberto Luongo) in 1997 Entry Draft for Wendel Clark, Mathieu Schneider and D.J. Smith, March 13, 1996. Claimed on waivers by **Nashville** from **NY Islanders**, May 23, 2000.

• HAGGLUND, Roger

"Bullen" D – L. 6'1", 175 lbs. b: Umea, Sweden, 7/2/1961 d: 6/6/1992. St. Louis' 6th, 138th overall, in 1980.

Season	Club	League	GP	G	A	Pts	AG	AA	APts	PIM	PP	SH	GW	S	%	TGF	PGF	TGA	PGA	+/–	GP	G	A	Pts	PIM	PP	SH	GW
1977-78	IF Bjorkloven Umea	Sweden-2	9	0	2	2				12																		
1978-79	IF Bjorkloven Umea	Sweden	24	2	3	5				23																		
1979-80	IF Bjorkloven Umea	Sweden	21	3	8	11				28																		
1980-81	IF Bjorkloven Umea	Sweden	27	1	7	8				21																		
	Sweden	WJC-A	5	3	4	7				6																		
1981-82	IF Bjorkloven Umea	Sweden	35	7	11	18				40											6	0	1	1	10			
	Sweden	WEC-A	7	0	0	0				0																		
1982-83	IF Bjorkloven Umea	Sweden	34	6	12	18				64											3	0	0	0	0			
	Sweden	WEC-A	7	0	3	3				4																		
1983-84	Vastra Frolunda	Sweden	27	8	7	15				10																		
1984-85	**Quebec Nordiques**	**NHL**	**3**	**0**	**0**	**0**	**0**	**0**	**0**	**0**	**0**	**0**	**0**	**5**	**0.0**	**2**	**1**	**1**	**0**	**0**								
	Fredericton Express	AHL	34	0	5	5				6																		
1985-86	IF Bjorkloven Umea	Sweden	31	4	17	21				50																		
1986-87	IF Bjorkloven Umea	Sweden	28	3	15	18				36											6	1	2	3	8			
1987-88	IF Bjorkloven Umea	Sweden	35	5	14	19				42											7	1	1	2	4			
1988-89	IF Bjorkloven Umea	Sweden	33	8	15	23				44																		

			REGULAR SEASON																		PLAYOFFS							
Season	Club	League	GP	G	A	Pts	AG	AA	APts	PIM	PP	SH	GW	S	%	TGF	PGF	TGA	PGA	+/-	GP	G	A	Pts	PIM	PP	SH	GW
1989-90	IF Bjorkloven Umea	Sweden-2	30	7	39	46	....	....	....	48	....	....	....	....	....	....	....	....	....	....	8	4	2	6	10	....	....	....
1990-91	IF Bjorkloven Umea	Sweden-2	34	11	36	47	....	....	....	36	....	....	....	....	....	....	....	....	....	....	2	0	0	0	2	....	....	....
1991-92	IF Bjorkloven Umea	Sweden-2	34	13	28	41	....	....	....	60	....	....	....	....	....	....	....	....	....	....	3	2	3	5	8	....	....	....
	NHL Totals		**3**	**0**	**0**	**0**	**0**	**0**	**0**	**0**	**0**	**0**	**0**	**5**	**0.0**	**2**	**1**	**1**	**0**		....	....	....	....	....	....	....	....

Traded to **Quebec** by **St. Louis** for cash, July, 1984. • Died of injuries suffered in automobile accident, June 6, 1992.

• HAGMAN, Matti

Matti Risto Tapio C – L. 6'1", 184 lbs. b: Helsinki, Finland, 9/21/1955. Boston's 6th, 104th overall, in 1975.

Season	Club	League	GP	G	A	Pts	AG	AA	APts	PIM	PP	SH	GW	S	%	TGF	PGF	TGA	PGA	+/-	GP	G	A	Pts	PIM	PP	SH	GW
1972-73	HIFK Helsinki	Finland	13	11	5	16	....	....	....	7	....	....	....	....	....	....	....	....	....	....	....	....	....	....	....	....	....	....
1973-74	HIFK Helsinki	Finn-Jr.	6	10	6	16	....	....	....	2	....	....	....	....	....	....	....	....	....	....	....	....	....	....	....	....	....	....
	HIFK Helsinki	Finland	35	30	9	39	....	....	....	20	....	....	....	....	....	....	....	....	....	....	....	....	....	....	....	....	....	....
1974-75	HIFK Helsinki	Finland	35	*30	16	46	....	....	....	27	....	....	....	....	....	....	....	....	....	....	....	....	....	....	....	....	....	....
	Finland	WJC-A	5	3	2	5	....	....	....	9	....	....	....	....	....	....	....	....	....	....	....	....	....	....	....	....	....	....
	Finland	Nat-Team	5	1	2	3	....	....	....	2	....	....	....	....	....	....	....	....	....	....	....	....	....	....	....	....	....	....
	Finland	EJC-A	5	10	2	12	....	....	....	0	....	....	....	....	....	....	....	....	....	....	....	....	....	....	....	....	....	....
	Finland	WEC-A	9	2	3	5	....	....	....	4	....	....	....	....	....	....	....	....	....	....	....	....	....	....	....	....	....	....
1975-76	HIFK Helsinki	Finland	36	24	34	58	....	....	....	39	....	....	....	....	....	....	....	....	....	....	4	1	1	2	5	....	....	....
	Finland	Nat-Team	16	1	4	5	....	....	....	2	....	....	....	....	....	....	....	....	....	....	....	....	....	....	....	....	....	....
	Finland	Olympics	6	1	4	5	....	....	....	2	....	....	....	....	....	....	....	....	....	....	....	....	....	....	....	....	....	....
	Finland	WEC-A	10	4	7	11	....	....	....	14	....	....	....	....	....	....	....	....	....	....	....	....	....	....	....	....	....	....
1976-77	Finland	Can-Cup	5	2	4	6	....	....	....	6	....	....	....	....	....	....	....	....	....	....	....	....	....	....	....	....	....	....
	Boston Bruins	**NHL**	**75**	**11**	**17**	**28**	**10**	**13**	**23**	**0**	**1**	**0**	**0**	**71**	**15.5**	**39**	**7**	**26**	**0**	**6**	**8**	**0**	**1**	**1**	**0**	**0**	**0**	**0**
	Finland	Nat-Team	4	0	0	0	....	....	....	2	....	....	....	....	....	....	....	....	....	....	....	....	....	....	....	....	....	....
1977-78	**Boston Bruins**	**NHL**	**15**	**4**	**1**	**5**	**4**	**1**	**5**	**2**	**3**	**0**	**1**	**13**	**30.8**	**9**	**6**	**4**	**0**	**–1**	....	....	....	....	....	....	....	....
	Quebec Nordiques	WHA	53	25	31	56	....	....	....	16	....	....	....	....	....	....	....	....	....	....	....	....	....	....	....	....	....	....
	Finland	Nat-Team	4	1	2	3	....	....	....	8	....	....	....	....	....	....	....	....	....	....	....	....	....	....	....	....	....	....
	Finland	WEC-A	5	1	2	3	....	....	....	8	....	....	....	....	....	....	....	....	....	....	....	....	....	....	....	....	....	....
1978-79	HIFK Helsinki	Finland	36	20	37	57	....	....	....	53	....	....	....	....	....	....	....	....	....	....	6	1	6	7	4	....	....	....
1979-80	HIFK Helsinki	Finland	36	*37	*50	*87	....	....	....	26	....	....	....	....	....	....	....	....	....	....	7	3	10	13	6	....	....	....
1980-81	**Edmonton Oilers**	**NHL**	**75**	**20**	**33**	**53**	**16**	**22**	**38**	**16**	**2**	**0**	**0**	**96**	**20.8**	**71**	**19**	**49**	**1**	**4**	**9**	**4**	**1**	**5**	**6**	**0**	**0**	**2**
1981-82	Finland	Can-Cup	5	1	2	3	....	....	....	4	....	....	....	....	....	....	....	....	....	....	....	....	....	....	....	....	....	....
	Edmonton Oilers	**NHL**	**72**	**21**	**38**	**59**	**17**	**25**	**42**	**18**	**5**	**0**	**2**	**94**	**22.3**	**92**	**22**	**56**	**1**	**15**	**3**	**1**	**0**	**1**	**0**	**0**	**0**	**0**
	Finland	Nat-Team	4	1	2	3	....	....	....	8	....	....	....	....	....	....	....	....	....	....	....	....	....	....	....	....	....	....
1982-83	HIFK Helsinki	Finland	36	23	*41	*64	....	....	....	50	....	....	....	....	....	....	....	....	....	....	9	*9	*8	*17	11	....	....	....
	Finland	Nat-Team	11	2	4	6	....	....	....	20	....	....	....	....	....	....	....	....	....	....	....	....	....	....	....	....	....	....
	Finland	WEC-A	10	2	5	7	....	....	....	4	....	....	....	....	....	....	....	....	....	....	....	....	....	....	....	....	....	....
1983-84	HIFK Helsinki	Finland	37	22	*47	*69	....	....	....	33	....	....	....	....	....	....	....	....	....	....	2	1	1	2	2	....	....	....
1984-85	HIFK Helsinki	Finland	34	23	*44	*67	....	....	....	24	....	....	....	....	....	....	....	....	....	....	....	....	....	....	....	....	....	....
1985-86	EV Landshut	Germany	36	25	49	74	....	....	....	24	....	....	....	....	....	....	....	....	....	....	3	1	1	2	2	....	....	....
1986-87	HIFK Helsinki	Finland	44	17	51	68	....	....	....	37	....	....	....	....	....	....	....	....	....	....	3	0	1	1	10	....	....	....
1987-88	Finland	Can-Cup	5	1	0	1	....	....	....	0	....	....	....	....	....	....	....	....	....	....	....	....	....	....	....	....	....	....
	HIFK Helsinki	Finland	44	17	43	60	....	....	....	37	....	....	....	....	....	....	....	....	....	....	6	4	5	9	6	....	....	....
	Finland	Nat-Team	6	0	2	2	....	....	....	8	....	....	....	....	....	....	....	....	....	....	....	....	....	....	....	....	....	....
1988-89	HIFK Helsinki	Finland	44	11	30	41	....	....	....	23	....	....	....	....	....	....	....	....	....	....	2	0	1	1	0	....	....	....
1989-90	H-Reipas Lahti	Finland-2	44	18	47	65	....	....	....	4	....	....	....	....	....	....	....	....	....	....	4	2	3	5	0	....	....	....
1990-91	H-Reipas Lahti	Finland	41	11	30	41	....	....	....	24	....	....	....	....	....	....	....	....	....	....	....	....	....	....	....	....	....	....
1991-92	HIFK Helsinki	Finland	42	8	20	28	....	....	....	20	....	....	....	....	....	....	....	....	....	....	8	1	3	4	2	....	....	....
	NHL Totals		**237**	**56**	**89**	**145**	**47**	**61**	**108**	**36**	**11**	**0**	**3**	**274**	**20.4**	**211**	**54**	**135**	**2**		**20**	**5**	**2**	**7**	**6**	**0**	**0**	**2**
	Other Major League Totals		53	25	31	56	....	....	....	16	....	....	....	....	....	....	....	....	....	....	....	....	....	....	....	....	....	....

Finnish Rookie of the Year (1974) • Finnish First All-Star Team (1980, 1983)

Traded to **Quebec** (WHA) by **Boston** for cash, December, 1977. Signed as a free agent by **Edmonton**, September 11, 1980.

• HAJDU, Richard

LW – L. 6'1", 185 lbs. b: Victoria, B.C., 5/10/1965. Buffalo's 5th, 34th overall, in 1983.

Season	Club	League	GP	G	A	Pts	AG	AA	APts	PIM	PP	SH	GW	S	%	TGF	PGF	TGA	PGA	+/-	GP	G	A	Pts	PIM	PP	SH	GW
1980-81	Cowichan Midget Caps	BCAHA	STATISTICS NOT AVAILABLE																									
1981-82	Kamloops Jr. Oilers	WHL	64	19	21	40	....	....	....	50	....	....	....	....	....	....	....	....	....	....	4	0	0	0	0	....	....	....
1982-83	Kamloops Jr. Oilers	WHL	70	22	36	58	....	....	....	101	....	....	....	....	....	....	....	....	....	....	5	0	0	0	4	....	....	....
1983-84	Victoria Cougars	WHL	42	17	10	27	....	....	....	106	....	....	....	....	....	....	....	....	....	....	....	....	....	....	....	....	....	....
1984-85	Victoria Cougars	WHL	24	12	16	28	....	....	....	33	....	....	....	....	....	....	....	....	....	....	....	....	....	....	....	....	....	....
	Rochester Americans	AHL	2	0	2	2	....	....	....	0	....	....	....	....	....	....	....	....	....	....	....	....	....	....	....	....	....	....
1985-86	**Buffalo Sabres**	**NHL**	**3**	**0**	**0**	**0**	**0**	**0**	**0**	**4**	**0**	**0**	**0**	**2**	**0.0**	**1**	**0**	**0**	**0**	**1**	....	....	....	....	....	....	....	....
	Rochester Americans	AHL	54	10	27	37	....	....	....	95	....	....	....	....	....	....	....	....	....	....	....	....	....	....	....	....	....	....
1986-87	**Buffalo Sabres**	**NHL**	**2**	**0**	**0**	**0**	**0**	**0**	**0**	**0**	**0**	**0**	**0**	**1**	**0.0**	**1**	**0**	**0**	**0**	**1**	....	....	....	....	....	....	....	....
	Rochester Americans	AHL	58	7	15	22	....	....	....	90	....	....	....	....	....	....	....	....	....	....	11	1	1	2	9	....	....	....
1987-88	Rochester Americans	AHL	37	7	11	18	....	....	....	24	....	....	....	....	....	....	....	....	....	....	1	0	0	0	0	....	....	....
	Flint Spirits	IHL	17	4	6	10	....	....	....	30	....	....	....	....	....	....	....	....	....	....	....	....	....	....	....	....	....	....
1988-89	Canada	Nat-Team	50	14	11	25	....	....	....	22	....	....	....	....	....	....	....	....	....	....	....	....	....	....	....	....	....	....
1989-90	Canada	Nat-Team	42	6	10	16	....	....	....	8	....	....	....	....	....	....	....	....	....	....	....	....	....	....	....	....	....	....
	EHC Lustenau	Austria	STATISTICS NOT AVAILABLE																									
1990-91	Gosser Ev	Austria	19	10	7	17	....	....	....	46	....	....	....	....	....	....	....	....	....	....	....	....	....	....	....	....	....	....
	Canada	Nat-Team	27	5	6	11	....	....	....	10	....	....	....	....	....	....	....	....	....	....	....	....	....	....	....	....	....	....
1991-92	HC Renon	Italy-2	24	19	24	43	....	....	....	14	....	....	....	....	....	....	....	....	....	....	....	....	....	....	....	....	....	....
1992-93	Dallas Freeze	CHL	21	10	14	24	....	....	....	57	....	....	....	....	....	....	....	....	....	....	....	....	....	....	....	....	....	....
	NHL Totals		**5**	**0**	**0**	**0**	**0**	**0**	**0**	**4**	**0**	**0**	**0**	**3**	**0.0**	**2**	**0**	**0**	**0**		....	....	....	....	....	....	....	....

• HAJT, Bill

William Albert D – L. 6'3", 215 lbs. b: Borden, Sask., 11/18/1951. Buffalo's 3rd, 33rd overall, in 1971.

Season	Club	League	GP	G	A	Pts	AG	AA	APts	PIM	PP	SH	GW	S	%	TGF	PGF	TGA	PGA	+/-	GP	G	A	Pts	PIM	PP	SH	GW
1967-68	Saskatoon Blades	WCJHL	60	4	10	14	....	....	....	35	....	....	....	....	....	....	....	....	....	....	7	0	1	1	2	....	....	....
1968-69	Saskatoon Blades	WCJHL	60	3	18	21	....	....	....	54	....	....	....	....	....	....	....	....	....	....	4	0	0	0	0	....	....	....
1969-70	Saskatoon Blades	WCJHL	60	10	21	31	....	....	....	40	....	....	....	....	....	....	....	....	....	....	7	2	3	5	8	....	....	....
1970-71	Saskatoon Blades	WCJHL	66	19	53	72	....	....	....	50	....	....	....	....	....	....	....	....	....	....	5	1	4	5	2	....	....	....
1971-72			DID NOT PLAY																									
1972-73	Cincinnati Swords	AHL	69	4	31	35	....	....	....	40	....	....	....	....	....	....	....	....	....	....	15	2	9	11	14	....	....	....
1973-74	**Buffalo Sabres**	**NHL**	**6**	**0**	**2**	**2**	**0**	**2**	**2**	**0**	**0**	**0**	**0**	**4**	**0.0**	**6**	**2**	**5**	**0**	**–1**	....	....	....	....	....	....	....	....
	Cincinnati Swords	AHL	66	5	30	35	....	....	....	66	....	....	....	....	....	....	....	....	....	....	5	0	4	4	4	....	....	....
1974-75	**Buffalo Sabres**	**NHL**	**76**	**3**	**26**	**29**	**3**	**19**	**22**	**68**	**1**	**0**	**0**	**107**	**2.8**	**132**	**9**	**92**	**16**	**47**	**17**	**1**	**4**	**5**	**18**	**0**	**0**	**0**
1975-76	**Buffalo Sabres**	**NHL**	**80**	**6**	**21**	**27**	**5**	**16**	**21**	**48**	**0**	**0**	**0**	**117**	**5.1**	**132**	**6**	**115**	**28**	**39**	**9**	**0**	**1**	**1**	**15**	**0**	**0**	**0**
1976-77	**Buffalo Sabres**	**NHL**	**79**	**6**	**20**	**26**	**5**	**15**	**20**	**56**	**0**	**0**	**1**	**106**	**5.7**	**123**	**8**	**94**	**18**	**39**	**6**	**0**	**1**	**1**	**4**	**0**	**0**	**0**
1977-78	**Buffalo Sabres**	**NHL**	**76**	**4**	**18**	**22**	**4**	**14**	**18**	**30**	**0**	**0**	**0**	**78**	**5.1**	**98**	**0**	**73**	**11**	**36**	**8**	**0**	**0**	**0**	**2**	**0**	**0**	**0**
1978-79	**Buffalo Sabres**	**NHL**	**40**	**3**	**8**	**11**	**3**	**6**	**9**	**20**	**0**	**1**	**1**	**53**	**5.7**	**39**	**1**	**55**	**13**	**–4**	....	....	....	....	....	....	....	....
1979-80	**Buffalo Sabres**	**NHL**	**75**	**4**	**12**	**16**	**3**	**9**	**12**	**24**	**0**	**1**	**0**	**63**	**6.3**	**76**	**1**	**69**	**30**	**36**	**14**	**0**	**5**	**5**	**4**	**0**	**0**	**0**
1980-81	**Buffalo Sabres**	**NHL**	**68**	**2**	**19**	**21**	**2**	**13**	**15**	**42**	**0**	**0**	**0**	**58**	**3.4**	**94**	**2**	**77**	**23**	**38**	**8**	**0**	**2**	**2**	**17**	**0**	**0**	**0**
1981-82	**Buffalo Sabres**	**NHL**	**65**	**2**	**9**	**11**	**2**	**6**	**8**	**44**	**0**	**0**	**0**	**58**	**3.4**	**61**	**1**	**80**	**31**	**11**	**2**	**0**	**0**	**0**	**0**	**0**	**0**	**0**
1982-83	**Buffalo Sabres**	**NHL**	**72**	**3**	**12**	**15**	**2**	**8**	**10**	**26**	**0**	**0**	**1**	**52**	**5.8**	**69**	**0**	**92**	**29**	**6**	**10**	**0**	**0**	**0**	**4**	**0**	**0**	**0**
1983-84	**Buffalo Sabres**	**NHL**	**79**	**3**	**24**	**27**	**2**	**16**	**18**	**32**	**0**	**1**	**0**	**53**	**5.7**	**92**	**2**	**99**	**34**	**25**	**3**	**0**	**0**	**0**	**0**	**0**	**0**	**0**
1984-85	**Buffalo Sabres**	**NHL**	**57**	**5**	**13**	**18**	**4**	**9**	**13**	**14**	**1**	**1**	**0**	**53**	**9.4**	**69**	**2**	**60**	**25**	**32**	**3**	**1**	**3**	**4**	**6**	**0**	**0**	**0**
1985-86	**Buffalo Sabres**	**NHL**	**58**	**1**	**16**	**17**	**1**	**11**	**12**	**25**	**0**	**0**	**0**	**42**	**2.4**	**67**	**2**	**83**	**35**	**17**	....	....	....	....	....	....	....	....
1986-87	**Buffalo Sabres**	**NHL**	**23**	**0**	**2**	**2**	**0**	**1**	**1**	**4**	**0**	**0**	**0**	**11**	**0.0**	**16**	**0**	**29**	**13**	**0**	....	....	....	....	....	....	....	....
	NHL Totals		**854**	**42**	**202**	**244**	**36**	**145**	**181**	**433**	**2**	**4**	**3**	**855**	**4.9**	**1074**	**36**	**1023**	**306**		**80**	**2**	**16**	**18**	**70**	**0**	**0**	**0**

• Sat out entire 1971-72 season after failing to come to contract terms with Buffalo.

• HAKANSSON, Anders

LW – L. 6'2", 190 lbs. b: Munkfors, Sweden, 4/27/1956. St. Louis' 15th, 134th overall, in 1976.

Season	Club	League	GP	G	A	Pts	AG	AA	APts	PIM	PP	SH	GW	S	%	TGF	PGF	TGA	PGA	+/–	GP	G	A	Pts	PIM	PP	SH	GW
			REGULAR SEASON																		PLAYOFFS							
1972-1975	Malmbergets AIF	Sweden-2	STATISTICS NOT AVAILABLE																									
1974-75	AIK Solna Stockholm	Sweden	2	0	0	0				0																		
1975-76	AIK Solna Stockholm	Sweden	18	4	4	8				6																		
	Sweden	WJC-A	4	3	1	4				8																		
1976-77	AIK Solna Stockholm	Sweden	2	0	0	0				0																		
1977-78	AIK Solna Stockholm	Sweden	27	8	4	12				10																		
1978-79	AIK Solna Stockholm	Sweden	36	12	8	20				37																		
1979-80	AIK Solna Stockholm	Sweden	36	14	10	24				32																		
	Sweden	Nat-Team	5	0	2	2				7																		
1980-81	AIK Solna Stockholm	DN-Cup	3	0	0	0				2																		
	AIK Solna Stockholm	Sweden	22	5	12	17				18												6	4	1	5	6			
	Sweden	Nat-Team	10	6	1	7				12																		
	Sweden	WEC-A	7	4	0	4				8																		
1981-82	Sweden	Can-Cup	5	1	1	2				4																		
	Minnesota North Stars	**NHL**	**72**	**12**	**4**	**16**	**9**	**3**	**12**	**29**	**0**	**4**	**1**	**76**	**15.8**	**31**	**1**	**55**	**13**	**–12**	**3**	**0**	**0**	**0**	**2**	**0**	**0**	**0**
1982-83	**Minnesota North Stars**	**NHL**	**5**	**0**	**0**	**0**	**0**	**0**	**0**	**9**	**0**	**0**	**0**	**3**	**0.0**	**2**	**0**	**5**	**4**	**1**								
	Pittsburgh Penguins	**NHL**	**62**	**9**	**12**	**21**	**7**	**8**	**15**	**26**	**0**	**0**	**1**	**67**	**13.4**	**27**	**0**	**52**	**14**	**–11**								
1983-84	**Los Angeles Kings**	**NHL**	**80**	**15**	**17**	**32**	**12**	**12**	**24**	**41**	**0**	**1**	**3**	**117**	**12.8**	**43**	**2**	**80**	**32**	**–7**								
1984-85	Sweden	Can-Cup	8	1	1	2				2																		
	Los Angeles Kings	**NHL**	**73**	**12**	**12**	**24**	**10**	**8**	**18**	**28**	**1**	**1**	**1**	**75**	**16.0**	**34**	**1**	**52**	**15**	**–4**	**3**	**0**	**0**	**0**	**0**	**0**	**0**	**0**
1985-86	**Los Angeles Kings**	**NHL**	**38**	**4**	**1**	**5**	**3**	**1**	**4**	**8**	**0**	**0**	**2**	**27**	**14.8**	**14**	**0**	**32**	**10**	**–8**								
	NHL Totals		**330**	**52**	**46**	**98**	**41**	**32**	**73**	**141**	**1**	**6**	**8**	**365**	**14.2**	**151**	**4**	**276**	**88**		**6**	**0**	**0**	**0**	**2**	**0**	**0**	**0**

Swedish World All-Star Team (1981)

Signed as a free agent by **Minnesota**, July 22, 1981. Traded to **Pittsburgh** by **Minnesota** with Ron Meighan and Minnesota's 1st round choice (Bob Errey) in 1983 Entry Draft for George Ferguson and Pittsburgh's 1st round choice (Brian Lawton) in 1983 Entry Draft, October 28, 1982. Traded to **LA Kings** by **Pittsburgh** for the rights to Kevin Stevens, September 9, 1983.

• HALE, Larry

Larry James D – L. 6'1", 180 lbs. b: Summerland, B.C., 10/9/1941.

Season	Club	League	GP	G	A	Pts	AG	AA	APts	PIM	PP	SH	GW	S	%	TGF	PGF	TGA	PGA	+/–	GP	G	A	Pts	PIM	PP	SH	GW
1960-61	Edmonton Oil Kings	CAHL	STATISTICS NOT AVAILABLE																									
	Edmonton Oil Kings	Mem-Cup	14	2	5	7				8																		
1961-62	Edmonton Oil Kings	CAHL	STATISTICS NOT AVAILABLE																									
	Edmonton Oil Kings	Mem-Cup	21	5	11	16				17																		
1962-63	Minneapolis Millers	IHL	70	5	30	35				49												12	1	4	5	14			
1963-64	Seattle Totems	WHL	70	5	16	21				46																			
1964-65	Seattle Totems	WHL	70	3	15	18				66												7	0	2	2	6			
1965-66	Seattle Totems	WHL	72	3	11	14				36																			
1966-67	Seattle Totems	WHL	72	3	23	26				50												10	2	4	6	13			
1967-68	Seattle Totems	WHL	70	9	19	28				41												9	1	8	9	10			
1968-69	**Philadelphia Flyers**	**NHL**	**67**	**3**	**16**	**19**	**3**	**14**	**17**	**28**	**0**	**0**	**0**	**62**	**4.8**	**55**	**1**	**94**	**16**	**–24**	**4**	**0**	**0**	**0**	**10**	**0**	**0**	**0**
1969-70	**Philadelphia Flyers**	**NHL**	**53**	**1**	**9**	**10**	**1**	**8**	**9**	**28**	**0**	**0**	**0**	**34**	**2.9**	**36**	**0**	**52**	**12**	**–4**								
	Quebec Aces	AHL	20	0	14	14				44																		
1970-71	**Philadelphia Flyers**	**NHL**	**70**	**1**	**11**	**12**	**1**	**9**	**10**	**34**	**0**	**0**	**1**	**51**	**2.0**	**46**	**1**	**77**	**14**	**–18**	**4**	**0**	**0**	**0**	**2**	**0**	**0**	**0**
1971-72	**Philadelphia Flyers**	**NHL**	**6**	**0**	**1**	**1**	**0**	**1**	**1**	**0**	**0**	**0**	**0**	**2**	**0.0**	**5**	**0**	**11**	**1**	**–5**								
	Richmond Robins	AHL	68	11	33	44				68																		
1972-73	Houston Aeros	WHA	68	4	26	30				65												10	1	2	3	2			
1973-74	Houston Aeros	WHA	69	2	14	16				39												14	3	2	5	6			
1974-75	Houston Aeros	WHA	76	2	18	20				40												13	0	4	4	0			
1975-76	Houston Aeros	WHA	77	2	12	14				30												17	0	5	5	8			
1976-77	Houston Aeros	WHA	67	0	14	14				18												11	0	2	2	6			
1977-78	Houston Aeros	WHA	56	2	11	13				22																		
1978-79	Spokane Flyers	PHL	54	0	18	18				30																		
	NHL Totals		**196**	**5**	**37**	**42**	**5**	**32**	**37**	**90**	**0**	**0**	**1**	**149**	**3.4**	**142**	**2**	**234**	**43**		**8**	**0**	**0**	**0**	**12**	**0**	**0**	**0**
	Other Major League Totals		413	12	95	107				214												65	4	15	19	22			

WHL Second All-Star Team (1968)

Traded to **Minneapolis** (IHL) by **Port Huron** (IHL) for Bill Lecaine, October, 1962. Claimed by **Minnesota** from **Seattle** (WHL) in Inter-League Draft, June 11, 1968. Claimed by **Philadelphia** from **Minnesota** in Intra-League Draft, June 12, 1968. Selected by **Houston** (WHA) in 1972 WHA General Player Draft, February 12, 1972. Claimed by **Atlanta** from **Philadelphia** in Expansion Draft, June 6, 1972.

• HALKIDIS, Bob

D – L. 5'11", 205 lbs. b: Toronto, Ont., 3/5/1966. Buffalo's 4th, 81st overall, in 1984.

Season	Club	League	GP	G	A	Pts	AG	AA	APts	PIM	PP	SH	GW	S	%	TGF	PGF	TGA	PGA	+/–	GP	G	A	Pts	PIM	PP	SH	GW
1981-82	Toronto Young Nationals	OMHA	40	9	27	36				54																		
1982-83	London Knights	OHL	37	3	12	15				52																		
1983-84	London Knights	OHL	51	9	22	31				123												8	0	2	2	27			
1984-85	London Knights	OHL	62	14	50	64				154												8	3	6	9	22			
	Buffalo Sabres	**NHL**																				**4**	**0**	**0**	**0**	**19**	**0**	**0**	**0**
1985-86	**Buffalo Sabres**	**NHL**	**37**	**1**	**9**	**10**	**1**	**6**	**7**	**115**	**0**	**0**	**0**	**19**	**5.3**	**27**	**2**	**28**	**0**	**–3**								
1986-87	**Buffalo Sabres**	**NHL**	**6**	**1**	**1**	**2**	**1**	**1**	**2**	**19**	**0**	**0**	**0**	**4**	**25.0**	**7**	**0**	**5**	**1**	**3**								
	Rochester Americans	AHL	59	1	8	9				144												8	0	0	0	43			
1987-88	**Buffalo Sabres**	**NHL**	**30**	**0**	**3**	**3**	**0**	**2**	**2**	**115**	**0**	**0**	**0**	**26**	**0.0**	**29**	**3**	**26**	**6**	**6**	**4**	**0**	**0**	**0**	**22**	**0**	**0**	**0**
	Rochester Americans	AHL	15	2	5	7				50																		
1988-89	**Buffalo Sabres**	**NHL**	**16**	**0**	**1**	**1**	**0**	**1**	**1**	**66**	**0**	**0**	**0**	**9**	**0.0**	**9**	**0**	**17**	**7**	**–1**								
	Rochester Americans	AHL	16	0	6	6				64																		
1989-90	Rochester Americans	AHL	18	1	13	14				70																		
	Los Angeles Kings	**NHL**	**20**	**0**	**4**	**4**	**0**	**3**	**3**	**56**	**0**	**0**	**0**	**19**	**0.0**	**23**	**2**	**23**	**6**	**4**	**8**	**0**	**1**	**1**	**8**	**0**	**0**	**0**
	New Haven Nighthawks	AHL	30	3	17	20				67																		
1990-91	**Los Angeles Kings**	**NHL**	**34**	**1**	**3**	**4**	**1**	**2**	**3**	**133**	**0**	**0**	**0**	**25**	**4.0**	**35**	**0**	**38**	**11**	**8**	**3**	**0**	**0**	**0**	**0**	**0**	**0**	**0**
	New Haven Nighthawks	AHL	7	1	3	4				10																		
	Phoenix Roadrunners	IHL	4	1	5	6				6																		
1991-92	**Toronto Maple Leafs**	**NHL**	**46**	**3**	**3**	**6**	**3**	**2**	**5**	**145**	**0**	**0**	**0**	**36**	**8.3**	**20**	**1**	**31**	**3**	**–9**								
1992-93	St. John's Maple Leafs	AHL	29	2	13	15				61																		
	Milwaukee Admirals	IHL	26	0	9	9				79												5	0	1	1	27			
1993-94	**Detroit Red Wings**	**NHL**	**28**	**1**	**4**	**5**	**1**	**3**	**4**	**93**	**0**	**0**	**0**	**35**	**2.9**	**14**	**0**	**18**	**3**	**–1**	**1**	**0**	**0**	**0**	**2**	**0**	**0**	**0**
	Adirondack Red Wings	AHL	15	0	6	6				46																		
1994-95	**Detroit Red Wings**	**NHL**	**4**	**0**	**1**	**1**	**0**	**1**	**1**	**6**	**0**	**0**	**0**	**0**	**0.0**	**3**	**0**	**2**	**1**	**2**								
	Tampa Bay Lightning	**NHL**	**27**	**1**	**3**	**4**	**2**	**4**	**6**	**40**	**0**	**0**	**0**	**25**	**4.0**	**10**	**0**	**23**	**1**	**–12**								
1995-96	**Tampa Bay Lightning**	**NHL**	**3**	**0**	**0**	**0**	**0**	**0**	**0**	**7**	**0**	**0**	**0**	**0**	**0.0**	**0**	**0**	**3**	**2**	**–1**								
	Atlanta Knights	IHL	21	1	7	8				62																		
	Indianapolis Ice	IHL	3	0	2	2				8																		
	New York Islanders	**NHL**	**5**	**0**	**0**	**0**	**0**	**0**	**0**	**30**	**0**	**0**	**0**	**2**	**0.0**	**0**	**0**	**3**	**0**	**–3**								
	Utah Grizzlies	IHL	27	0	7	7				72												12	1	1	2	36			
1996-97	Carolina Monarchs	AHL	41	5	13	18				47																		
1997-98	Winston-Salem IceHawks	UHL	3	0	1	1				15																		
	HIFK Helsinki	Finland	29	1	6	7				133												9	0	2	2	14			
1998-99	Kolner Haie	Germany	48	7	14	21				103												5	0	0	0	4			
	NHL Totals		**256**	**8**	**32**	**40**	**9**	**25**	**34**	**825**	**0**	**0**	**0**	**200**	**4.0**	**177**	**8**	**217**	**41**		**20**	**0**	**1**	**1**	**51**	**0**	**0**	**0**

OHL First All-Star Team (1985)

Traded to **LA Kings** by **Buffalo** with future considerations for Dale DeGray and future considerations, November 24, 1989. Signed as a free agent by **Toronto**, July 24, 1991. Signed as a free agent by **Detroit**, September 2, 1993. Claimed on waivers by **Tampa Bay** from **Detroit**, February 10, 1995. Claimed on waivers by **Chicago** from **Tampa Bay**, December 6, 1995. Traded to **NY Islanders** by **Chicago** for Danton Cole, February 2, 1996. Signed as a free agent by **Florida**, July 25, 1996.

• HALKO, Steven

Steven M. D – R. 6'1", 200 lbs. b: Etobicoke, Ont., 3/8/1974. Hartford's 10th, 225th overall, in 1992.

			REGULAR SEASON																		PLAYOFFS							
Season	**Club**	**League**	**GP**	**G**	**A**	**Pts**	**AG**	**AA**	**APts**	**PIM**	**PP**	**SH**	**GW**	**S**	**%**	**TGF**	**PGF**	**TGA**	**PGA**	**+/–**	**GP**	**G**	**A**	**Pts**	**PIM**	**PP**	**SH**	**GW**
1989-90	Newmarket 87's	OJHL-B	30	3	5	8	....	....	....	16	....	....	....	....	....	....	....	....	....	....	....	....	....	....	....	....	....	....
1990-91	Newmarket 87's	OJHL-B	35	2	13	15	....	....	....	37	....	....	....	....	....	....	....	....	....	....	....	....	....	....	....	....	....	....
	Markham Thunderbirds	OJHL-B	8	4	3	7	....	....	....	2	....	....	....	....	....	....	....	....	....	....	....	....	....	....	....	....	....	....
1991-92	Thornhill Islanders	OJHL	44	15	46	61	....	....	....	43	....	....	....	....	....	....	....	....	....	....	....	....	....	....	....	....	....	....
1992-93	University of Michigan	CCHA	39	1	12	13	....	....	....	12	....	....	....	....	....	....	....	....	....	....	....	....	....	....	....	....	....	....
1993-94	University of Michigan	CCHA	41	2	13	15	....	....	....	32	....	....	....	....	....	....	....	....	....	....	....	....	....	....	....	....	....	....
1994-95	University of Michigan	CCHA	39	2	14	16	....	....	....	20	....	....	....	....	....	....	....	....	....	....	....	....	....	....	....	....	....	....
1995-96	University of Michigan	CCHA	43	4	16	20	....	....	....	32	....	....	....	....	....	....	....	....	....	....	....	....	....	....	....	....	....	....
1996-97	Springfield Falcons	AHL	70	1	5	6	....	....	....	37	....	....	....	....	....	....	....	....	....	....	11	0	2	2	8	....	....	....
1997-98	**Carolina Hurricanes**	**NHL**	**18**	**0**	**2**	**2**	**0**	**2**	**2**	**10**	**0**	**0**	**0**	**7**	**0.0**	**8**	**0**	**12**	**3**	**–1**	....	....	....	....	....	....	....	....
	Beast of New Haven	AHL	65	1	19	20	....	....	....	44	....	....	....	....	....	....	....	....	....	....	1	0	0	0	0	....	....	....
1998-99	**Carolina Hurricanes**	**NHL**	**20**	**0**	**3**	**3**	**0**	**3**	**3**	**24**	**0**	**0**	**0**	**6**	**0.0**	**14**	**0**	**14**	**5**	**5**	**4**	**0**	**0**	**0**	**2**	**0**	**0**	**0**
	Beast of New Haven	AHL	42	2	7	9	....	....	....	58	....	....	....	....	....	....	....	....	....	....	....	....	....	....	....	....	....	....
99-2000	**Carolina Hurricanes**	**NHL**	**58**	**0**	**8**	**8**	**0**	**7**	**7**	**25**	**0**	**0**	**0**	**54**	**0.0**	**37**	**1**	**40**	**4**	**0**	....	....	....	....	....	....	....	....
	NHL Totals		**96**	**0**	**13**	**13**	**0**	**12**	**12**	**59**	**0**	**0**	**0**	**67**	**0.0**	**59**	**1**	**66**	**12**		**4**	**0**	**0**	**0**	**2**	**0**	**0**	**0**

CCHA Second All-Star Team (1995, 1996) • NCAA Championship All-Tournament Team (1996)

Transferred to **Carolina** after **Hartford** franchise relocated, June 25, 1997.

• HALL, Del

Del Allison C – L. 5'10", 170 lbs. b: Peterborough, Ont., 5/7/1949.

Season	**Club**	**League**	**GP**	**G**	**A**	**Pts**	**AG**	**AA**	**APts**	**PIM**	**PP**	**SH**	**GW**	**S**	**%**	**TGF**	**PGF**	**TGA**	**PGA**	**+/–**	**GP**	**G**	**A**	**Pts**	**PIM**	**PP**	**SH**	**GW**
1969-70	Chatham Maroons	OHA-B	40	*53	46	99	....	....	....		....	....	....	....	....	....	....	....	....	....	....	....	....	....	....	....	....	....
1970-71	St. Clair College	OUAA	22	23	30	53	....	....	....	26	....	....	....	....	....	....	....	....	....	....	....	....	....	....	....	....	....	....
1971-72	**California Golden Seals**	**NHL**	**1**	**0**	**0**	**0**	**0**	**0**	**0**	**0**	**0**	**0**	**0**	**1**	**0.0**	**0**	**0**	**1**	**0**	**–1**	....	....	....	....	....	....	....	....
	Columbus Seals	IHL	64	26	27	53	....	....	....	18	....	....	....	....	....	....	....	....	....	....	....	....	....	....	....	....	....	....
1972-73	**California Golden Seals**	**NHL**	**6**	**0**	**0**	**0**	**0**	**0**	**0**	**0**	**0**	**0**	**0**	**2**	**0.0**	**0**	**0**	**0**	**0**	**0**	....	....	....	....	....	....	....	....
	Salt Lake Golden Eagles	WHL	63	24	18	42	....	....	....	23	....	....	....	....	....	....	....	....	....	....	9	5	4	9	0	....	....	....
1973-74	**California Golden Seals**	**NHL**	**2**	**2**	**0**	**2**	**2**	**0**	**2**	**2**	**0**	**0**	**0**	**4**	**50.0**	**2**	**0**	**2**	**1**	**1**	....	....	....	....	....	....	....	....
	Salt Lake Golden Eagles	WHL	71	38	41	79	....	....	....	30	....	....	....	....	....	....	....	....	....	....	5	1	0	1	0	....	....	....
1974-75	Salt Lake Golden Eagles	CHL	70	32	32	64	....	....	....	4	....	....	....	....	....	....	....	....	....	....	11	7	8	15	6	....	....	....
1975-76	Phoenix Roadrunners	WHA	80	47	44	91	....	....	....	10	....	....	....	....	....	....	....	....	....	....	5	2	3	5	0	....	....	....
1976-77	Phoenix Roadrunners	WHA	80	38	41	79	....	....	....	30	....	....	....	....	....	....	....	....	....	....	....	....	....	....	....	....	....	....
1977-78	Cincinnati Stingers	WHA	25	4	3	7	....	....	....	4	....	....	....	....	....	....	....	....	....	....	....	....	....	....	....	....	....	....
	Edmonton Oilers	WHA	1	0	0	0	....	....	....	0	....	....	....	....	....	....	....	....	....	....	....	....	....	....	....	....	....	....
	NHL Totals		**9**	**2**	**0**	**2**	**2**	**0**	**2**	**2**	**0**	**0**	**0**	**7**	**28.6**	**2**	**0**	**3**	**1**		....	....	....	....	....	....	....	....
	Other Major League Totals		186	89	88	177	....	....	....	44	....	....	....	....	....	....	....	....	....	....	5	2	3	5	0	....	....	....

Signed as a free agent by **California**, October, 1971. Selected by **Edmonton** (WHA) in 1972 WHA General Player Draft, February 13, 1972. WHA rights traded to **Phoenix** (WHA) by **Edmonton** (WHA) for cash, June, 1974. Traded to **Cincinnati** (WHA) by **Phoenix** (WHA) for cash, April, 1977. Traded to **Edmonton** (WHA) by **Cincinnati** (WHA) for Butch Deadmarsh, December, 1977.

• HALL, Murray

Murray Winston RW – R. 6', 175 lbs. b: Kirkland Lake, Ont., 11/24/1940.

Season	**Club**	**League**	**GP**	**G**	**A**	**Pts**	**AG**	**AA**	**APts**	**PIM**	**PP**	**SH**	**GW**	**S**	**%**	**TGF**	**PGF**	**TGA**	**PGA**	**+/–**	**GP**	**G**	**A**	**Pts**	**PIM**	**PP**	**SH**	**GW**
1959-60	St. Catharines Teepees	OHA-Jr.	48	17	15	32	....	....	....	22	....	....	....	....	....	....	....	....	....	....	17	2	7	9	6	....	....	....
	St. Catharines Teepees	Mem-Cup	14	7	9	16	....	....	....	8	....	....	....	....	....	....	....	....	....	....	....	....	....	....	....	....	....	....
1960-61	St. Catharines Teepees	OHA-Jr.	48	35	41	76	....	....	....	60	....	....	....	....	....	....	....	....	....	....	6	3	1	4	2	....	....	....
	Sault Ste. Marie Thunderbirds	EPHL	....	....	....	....	....	....	....	....	....	....	....	....	....	....	....	....	....	....	8	0	2	2	2	....	....	....
1961-62	**Chicago Black Hawks**	**NHL**	**2**	**0**	**0**	**0**	**0**	**0**	**0**	**0**	....	....	....	....	....	....	....	....	....	....	....	....	....	....	....	....	....	....
	Buffalo Bisons	AHL	68	20	21	41	....	....	....	41	....	....	....	....	....	....	....	....	....	....	11	3	1	4	4	....	....	....
1962-63	St. Louis Braves	EPHL	71	29	*69	98	....	....	....	41	....	....	....	....	....	....	....	....	....	....	....	....	....	....	....	....	....	....
	Chicago Black Hawks	**NHL**	....	....	....	....	....	....	....	....	....	....	....	....	....	....	....	....	....	....	**4**	**0**	**0**	**0**	**0**	**0**	**0**	**0**
1963-64	**Chicago Black Hawks**	**NHL**	**23**	**2**	**0**	**2**	**2**	**0**	**2**	**4**	....	....	....	....	....	....	....	....	....	....	....	....	....	....	....	....	....	....
	St. Louis Braves	CPHL	28	17	40	57	....	....	....	35	....	....	....	....	....	....	....	....	....	....	6	2	4	6	0	....	....	....
1964-65	Pittsburgh Hornets	AHL	72	29	33	62	....	....	....	29	....	....	....	....	....	....	....	....	....	....	4	0	0	0	4	....	....	....
	Detroit Red Wings	**NHL**	....	....	....	....	....	....	....	....	....	....	....	....	....	....	....	....	....	....	**1**	**0**	**0**	**0**	**0**	**0**	**0**	**0**
1965-66	**Detroit Red Wings**	**NHL**	**1**	**0**	**0**	**0**	**0**	**0**	**0**	**0**	....	....	....	....	....	....	....	....	....	....	**1**	**0**	**0**	**0**	**0**	**0**	**0**	**0**
	Pittsburgh Hornets	AHL	70	28	45	73	....	....	....	102	....	....	....	....	....	....	....	....	....	....	3	0	3	3	0	....	....	....
1966-67	**Detroit Red Wings**	**NHL**	**12**	**4**	**3**	**7**	**5**	**3**	**8**	**4**	....	....	....	....	....	....	....	....	....	....	....	....	....	....	....	....	....	....
	Pittsburgh Hornets	AHL	12	5	11	16	....	....	....	10	....	....	....	....	....	....	....	....	....	....	....	....	....	....	....	....	....	....
	Los Angeles Blades	WHL	43	18	28	46	....	....	....	28	....	....	....	....	....	....	....	....	....	....	....	....	....	....	....	....	....	....
1967-68	**Minnesota North Stars**	**NHL**	**17**	**2**	**1**	**3**	**2**	**1**	**3**	**10**	**0**	**0**	**0**	**18**	**11.1**	**3**	**1**	**9**	**0**	**–7**	....	....	....	....	....	....	....	....
	Memphis South Stars	CPHL	12	3	8	11	....	....	....	23	....	....	....	....	....	....	....	....	....	....	....	....	....	....	....	....	....	....
	Rochester Americans	AHL	38	17	14	31	....	....	....	19	....	....	....	....	....	....	....	....	....	....	11	5	9	14	2	....	....	....
1968-69	Vancouver Canucks	WHL	69	28	37	65	....	....	....	34	....	....	....	....	....	....	....	....	....	....	8	2	3	5	0	....	....	....
1969-70	Vancouver Canucks	WHL	72	27	55	82	....	....	....	42	....	....	....	....	....	....	....	....	....	....	11	*10	11	*21	10	....	....	....
1970-71	**Vancouver Canucks**	**NHL**	**77**	**21**	**38**	**59**	**21**	**32**	**53**	**22**	**5**	**0**	**1**	**127**	**16.5**	**84**	**24**	**76**	**0**	**–16**	....	....	....	....	....	....	....	....
1971-72	**Vancouver Canucks**	**NHL**	**32**	**6**	**6**	**12**	**6**	**5**	**11**	**6**	**1**	**0**	**0**	**46**	**13.0**	**20**	**6**	**26**	**0**	**–12**	....	....	....	....	....	....	....	....
	Rochester Americans	AHL	37	10	32	42	....	....	....	70	....	....	....	....	....	....	....	....	....	....	....	....	....	....	....	....	....	....
1972-73	Houston Aeros	WHA	76	28	42	70	....	....	....	84	....	....	....	....	....	....	....	....	....	....	10	4	4	8	18	....	....	....
1973-74	Houston Aeros	WHA	78	30	28	58	....	....	....	25	....	....	....	....	....	....	....	....	....	....	14	9	6	15	6	....	....	....
1974-75	Houston Aeros	WHA	78	18	29	47	....	....	....	28	....	....	....	....	....	....	....	....	....	....	13	7	3	10	8	....	....	....
1975-76	Houston Aeros	WHA	80	20	26	46	....	....	....	18	....	....	....	....	....	....	....	....	....	....	17	1	4	5	0	....	....	....
1976-77	Oklahoma City Blazers	CHL	30	8	13	21	....	....	....	2	....	....	....	....	....	....	....	....	....	....	....	....	....	....	....	....	....	....
1977-78	Brantford Alexanders	OHA-Sr.	25	9	20	29	....	....	....	35	....	....	....	....	....	....	....	....	....	....	....	....	....	....	....	....	....	....
	NHL Totals		**164**	**35**	**48**	**83**	**36**	**41**	**77**	**46**	....	....	....	....	....	....	....	....	....	....	**6**	**0**	**0**	**0**	**0**	....	....	....
	Other Major League Totals		312	96	125	221	....	....	....	155	....	....	....	....	....	....	....	....	....	....	54	21	17	38	32	....	....	....

Played in NHL All-Star Game (1961)

Claimed by **Detroit** from **Chicago** in Intra-League Draft, June 10, 1964. Loaned to **Chicago** (LA Blades-WHL) by **Detroit** with Al Lebrun for remainder of 1966-67 season and future considerations (Murray Hall, Al Lebrun and Rick Morris, June, 1967) for Howie Young, December 20, 1966. Traded to **Chicago** by **Detroit** with Al Lebrun and Rick Morris to complete transaction that sent Howie Young to Detroit (December 20, 1966), June, 1967. Claimed by **Minnesota** from **Chicago** in Expansion Draft, June 6, 1967. Traded to **Toronto** (Rochester-AHL) by **Minnesota** with Ted Taylor, Len Lunde, Don Johns, Duke Harris and the loan of Carl Wetzel for Milan Marcetta and Jean-Paul Parise, December 23, 1967. Traded to **Rochester** (AHL) by **Toronto** for cash, June, 1968. Rights transferred to **Vancouver** (WHL) after WHL club purchased **Rochester** (AHL) franchise, August 13, 1968. NHL rights transferred to **Vancouver** after NHL club purchased **Vancouver** (WHL) franchise, December 19, 1969. Selected by **Houston** (WHA) in 1972 WHA General Player Draft, February 12, 1972.

• HALL, Taylor

"City" LW – L. 5'11", 180 lbs. b: Regina, Sask., 2/20/1964. Vancouver's 4th, 116th overall, in 1982.

Season	**Club**	**League**	**GP**	**G**	**A**	**Pts**	**AG**	**AA**	**APts**	**PIM**	**PP**	**SH**	**GW**	**S**	**%**	**TGF**	**PGF**	**TGA**	**PGA**	**+/–**	**GP**	**G**	**A**	**Pts**	**PIM**	**PP**	**SH**	**GW**
1980-81	Regina Pat Canadians	AAHA	65	93	71	164	....	....	....	94	....	....	....	....	....	....	....	....	....	....	....	....	....	....	....	....	....	....
	Regina Blues	AJHL	13	5	3	8	....	....	....	2	....	....	....	....	....	....	....	....	....	....	....	....	....	....	....	....	....	....
1981-82	Regina Pats	WHL	48	14	15	29	....	....	....	43	....	....	....	....	....	....	....	....	....	....	11	2	3	5	14	....	....	....
1982-83	Regina Pats	WHL	72	37	57	94	....	....	....	78	....	....	....	....	....	....	....	....	....	....	5	0	3	3	12	....	....	....
1983-84	Regina Pats	WHL	69	63	79	142	....	....	....	42	....	....	....	....	....	....	....	....	....	....	23	21	20	41	26	....	....	....
	Vancouver Canucks	**NHL**	**4**	**1**	**0**	**1**	**1**	**0**	**1**	**0**	**0**	**0**	**0**	**3**	**33.3**	**1**	**0**	**3**	**0**	**–2**	....	....	....	....	....	....	....	....
1984-85	**Vancouver Canucks**	**NHL**	**7**	**1**	**4**	**5**	**1**	**3**	**4**	**19**	**0**	**0**	**0**	**14**	**7.1**	**9**	**2**	**10**	**3**	**0**	....	....	....	....	....	....	....	....
1985-86	**Vancouver Canucks**	**NHL**	**19**	**5**	**5**	**10**	**4**	**3**	**7**	**6**	**1**	**0**	**0**	**30**	**16.7**	**12**	**4**	**20**	**1**	**–11**	....	....	....	....	....	....	....	....
	Fredericton Express	AHL	45	21	14	35	....	....	....	28	....	....	....	....	....	....	....	....	....	....	1	0	0	0	0	....	....	....
1986-87	**Vancouver Canucks**	**NHL**	**4**	**0**	**0**	**0**	**0**	**0**	**0**	**0**	**0**	**0**	**0**	**1**	**0.0**	**0**	**0**	**2**	**0**	**–2**	....	....	....	....	....	....	....	....
	Fredericton Express	AHL	36	21	20	41	....	....	....	23	....	....	....	....	....	....	....	....	....	....	....	....	....	....	....	....	....	....
1987-88	**Boston Bruins**	**NHL**	**7**	**0**	**0**	**0**	**0**	**0**	**0**	**4**	**0**	**0**	**0**	**5**	**0.0**	**3**	**1**	**6**	**1**	**–3**	....	....	....	....	....	....	....	....
	Maine Mariners	AHL	71	33	41	74	....	....	....	58	....	....	....	....	....	....	....	....	....	....	10	1	4	5	21	....	....	....
1988-89	Maine Mariners	AHL	8	0	1	1	....	....	....	7	....	....	....	....	....	....	....	....	....	....	....	....	....	....	....	....	....	....
	Newmarket Saints	AHL	9	5	5	10	....	....	....	14	....	....	....	....	....	....	....	....	....	....	....	....	....	....	....	....	....	....
	HC Asiago	Italy	26	25	21	46	....	....	....	60	....	....	....	....	....	....	....	....	....	....	....	....	....	....	....	....	....	....
1989-90	New Haven Nighthawks	AHL	51	14	23	37	....	....	....	10	....	....	....	....	....	....	....	....	....	....	....	....	....	....	....	....	....	....
	Canada	Nat-Team	4	4	2	6	....	....	....	0	....	....	....	....	....	....	....	....	....	....	....	....	....	....	....	....	....	....

			REGULAR SEASON																		PLAYOFFS							
Season	Club	League	GP	G	A	Pts	AG	AA	APts	PIM	PP	SH	GW	S	%	TGF	PGF	TGA	PGA	+/–	GP	G	A	Pts	PIM	PP	SH	GW
1990-91	San Diego Gulls	IHL	44	13	16	29	....	....	....	28	....	....	....	....	....	....	....	....	....	....	....	....	....	....	....	....	....	....
1991-92	Mannheimer ERC	Germany	15	4	6	10	....	....	....	4	....	....	....	....	....	....	....	....	....	....	....	....	....	....	....	....	....	....
	Fureset IF	Norway	29	13	16	29	....	....	....	22	....	....	....	....	....	....	....	....	....	....	....	....	....	....	....	....	....	....
1992-93	Tulsa Oilers	CHL	58	35	45	80	....	....	....	64	....	....	....	....	....	....	....	....	....	....	9	3	5	8	16	....	....	....
1993-94	Tulsa Oilers	CHL	64	33	26	59	....	....	....	95	....	....	....	....	....	....	....	....	....	....	11	3	5	8	14	....	....	....
1994-95	Tulsa Oilers	CHL	58	29	39	68	....	....	....	33	....	....	....	....	....	....	....	....	....	....	7	2	3	5	17	....	....	....
1995-96	Tulsa Oilers	CHL	63	27	35	62	....	....	....	52	....	....	....	....	....	....	....	....	....	....	6	1	1	2	14	....	....	....
1996-1998	New Mexico Scorpions	WPHL	DID NOT PLAY – COACHING																									
1998-2000	Corpus Christi Icerays	WPHL	DID NOT PLAY – COACHING																									
	NHL Totals		**41**	**7**	**9**	**16**	**6**	**6**	**12**	**29**	**1**	**0**	**0**	**53**	**13.2**	**25**	**7**	**41**	**5**		....	....	....	....	....	....	....	....

WHL East All-Star Team (1984)

• Missed remainder of 1984-85 season recovering from knee injury suffered in game vs. NY Islanders, October 23, 1984. Signed as a free agent by **Boston**, July, 1987. Signed as a free agent by **San Diego** (IHL), August, 1990. Traded to **Kansas City** (IHL) by **San Diego** (IHL) for Karl Vichorek, February 18, 1991.

• HALLER, Kevin

D – L. 6'2", 195 lbs. b: Trochu, Alta., 12/5/1970. Buffalo's 1st, 14th overall, in 1989.

Season	Club	League	GP	G	A	Pts	AG	AA	APts	PIM	PP	SH	GW	S	%	TGF	PGF	TGA	PGA	+/–	GP	G	A	Pts	PIM	PP	SH	GW
1986-87	Three Hills Braves	AAHA	12	10	11	21	....	....	....	8	....	....	....	....	....	....	....	....	....	....	....	....	....	....	....	....	....	....
1987-88	Olds Grizzlies	AJHL	51	13	31	44	....	....	....	58	....	....	....	....	....	....	....	....	....	....	....	....	....	....	....	....	....	....
	Regina Pats	WHL	5	0	1	1	....	....	....	2	....	....	....	....	....	....	....	....	....	....	4	1	1	2	2	....	....	....
1988-89	Regina Pats	WHL	72	10	31	41	....	....	....	99	....	....	....	....	....	....	....	....	....	....	....	....	....	....	....	....	....	....
1989-90	Regina Pats	WHL	58	16	37	53	....	....	....	93	....	....	....	....	....	....	....	....	....	....	11	2	9	11	16	....	....	....
	Canada	WJC-A	7	2	2	4	....	....	....	8	....	....	....	....	....	....	....	....	....	....	....	....	....	....	....	....	....	....
	Buffalo Sabres	**NHL**	**2**	**0**	**0**	**0**	**0**	**0**	**0**	**0**	**0**	**0**	**0**	**1**	**0.0**	**1**	**0**	**1**	**0**	**0**	....	....	....	....	....	....	....	....
1990-91	**Buffalo Sabres**	**NHL**	**21**	**1**	**8**	**9**	**1**	**6**	**7**	**20**	**1**	**0**	**0**	**42**	**2.4**	**33**	**8**	**20**	**4**	**9**	**6**	**1**	**4**	**5**	**10**	**0**	**0**	**0**
	Rochester Americans	AHL	52	2	8	10	....	....	....	53	....	....	....	....	....	....	....	....	....	....	10	2	1	3	6	....	....	....
1991-92	**Buffalo Sabres**	**NHL**	**58**	**6**	**15**	**21**	**5**	**11**	**16**	**75**	**2**	**0**	**1**	**76**	**7.9**	**62**	**17**	**66**	**8**	**–13**	....	....	....	....	....	....	....	....
	Rochester Americans	AHL	4	0	0	0	....	....	....	18	....	....	....	....	....	....	....	....	....	....	....	....	....	....	....	....	....	....
	Montreal Canadiens	**NHL**	**8**	**2**	**2**	**4**	**2**	**2**	**4**	**17**	**1**	**0**	**0**	**9**	**22.2**	**11**	**2**	**6**	**1**	**4**	**9**	**0**	**0**	**0**	**6**	**0**	**0**	**0**
1992-93♦	**Montreal Canadiens**	**NHL**	**73**	**11**	**14**	**25**	**9**	**10**	**19**	**117**	**6**	**0**	**1**	**126**	**8.7**	**91**	**24**	**72**	**12**	**7**	**17**	**1**	**6**	**7**	**16**	**1**	**0**	**0**
1993-94	**Montreal Canadiens**	**NHL**	**68**	**4**	**9**	**13**	**4**	**7**	**11**	**118**	**0**	**0**	**1**	**72**	**5.6**	**64**	**11**	**60**	**10**	**3**	**7**	**1**	**1**	**2**	**19**	**0**	**0**	**0**
1994-95	**Philadelphia Flyers**	**NHL**	**36**	**2**	**8**	**10**	**4**	**12**	**16**	**48**	**0**	**0**	**0**	**26**	**7.7**	**38**	**1**	**36**	**15**	**16**	**15**	**4**	**4**	**8**	**10**	**0**	**1**	**1**
1995-96	**Philadelphia Flyers**	**NHL**	**69**	**5**	**9**	**14**	**5**	**7**	**12**	**92**	**0**	**2**	**2**	**89**	**5.6**	**65**	**6**	**64**	**23**	**18**	**6**	**0**	**1**	**1**	**8**	**0**	**0**	**0**
1996-97	**Philadelphia Flyers**	**NHL**	**27**	**0**	**5**	**5**	**0**	**4**	**4**	**37**	**0**	**0**	**0**	**34**	**0.0**	**17**	**0**	**29**	**11**	**–1**	....	....	....	....	....	....	....	....
	Hartford Whalers	**NHL**	**35**	**2**	**6**	**8**	**2**	**5**	**7**	**48**	**0**	**0**	**0**	**43**	**4.7**	**26**	**6**	**43**	**12**	**–11**	....	....	....	....	....	....	....	....
1997-98	**Carolina Hurricanes**	**NHL**	**65**	**3**	**5**	**8**	**4**	**5**	**9**	**94**	**0**	**0**	**0**	**67**	**4.5**	**44**	**3**	**68**	**22**	**–5**	....	....	....	....	....	....	....	....
1998-99	**Mighty Ducks of Anaheim**	**NHL**	**82**	**1**	**6**	**7**	**1**	**6**	**7**	**122**	**0**	**0**	**0**	**64**	**1.6**	**52**	**2**	**83**	**32**	**–1**	**4**	**0**	**0**	**0**	**2**	**0**	**0**	**0**
99-2000	**Mighty Ducks of Anaheim**	**NHL**	**67**	**3**	**5**	**8**	**3**	**5**	**8**	**61**	**0**	**0**	**2**	**50**	**6.0**	**37**	**2**	**66**	**23**	**–8**	....	....	....	....	....	....	....	....
	NHL Totals		**611**	**40**	**92**	**132**	**40**	**80**	**120**	**849**	**10**	**2**	**7**	**699**	**5.7**	**541**	**82**	**614**	**173**		**64**	**7**	**16**	**23**	**71**	**1**	**1**	**1**

WHL East First All-Star Team (1990)

Traded to **Montreal** by **Buffalo** for Petr Svoboda, March 10, 1992. Traded to **Philadelphia** by **Montreal** for Yves Racine, June 29, 1994. Traded to **Hartford** by **Philadelphia** with Philadelphia's 1st round choice (later traded to San Jose — San Jose selected Scott Hannan) in 1997 Entry Draft and Hartford/Carolina's 7th round choice (previously acquired, Carolina selected Andrew Merrick) in 1997 Entry Draft for Paul Coffey and Hartford's 3rd round choice (Kris Mallette) in 1997 Entry Draft, December 15, 1996. Transferred to **Carolina** after **Hartford** franchise relocated, June 25, 1997. Traded to **Anaheim** by **Carolina** with Stu Grimson for David Karpa and Anaheim's 4th round choice (later traded to Atlanta - Atlanta selected Blake Robson) in 2000 Entry Draft, August 11, 1998. Signed as a free agent by **NY Islanders**, July 3, 2000.

• HALLIN, Mats

LW – L. 6'2", 200 lbs. b: Esklistuna, Sweden, 3/9/1958. Washington's 10th, 105th overall, in 1978.

Season	Club	League	GP	G	A	Pts	AG	AA	APts	PIM	PP	SH	GW	S	%	TGF	PGF	TGA	PGA	+/–	GP	G	A	Pts	PIM	PP	SH	GW
1974-75	Akers IF	Sweden-3	11	5	1	6	....	....	....	6	....	....	....	....	....	....	....	....	....	....	....	....	....	....	....	....	....	....
1975-76	Akers IF	Sweden-3	20	11	17	28	....	....	....	....	....	....	....	....	....	....	....	....	....	....	....	....	....	....	....	....	....	....
1976-77	Sodertalje SK	Sweden	15	2	5	7	....	....	....	23	....	....	....	....	....	....	....	....	....	....	....	....	....	....	....	....	....	....
1977-78	Sodertalje SK	Sweden	32	6	3	9	....	....	....	58	....	....	....	....	....	....	....	....	....	....	....	....	....	....	....	....	....	....
	Sweden	WJC-A	7	5	3	8	....	....	....	17	....	....	....	....	....	....	....	....	....	....	....	....	....	....	....	....	....	....
1978-79	Sodertalje SK	Sweden	14	4	7	11	....	....	....	18	....	....	....	....	....	....	....	....	....	....	....	....	....	....	....	....	....	....
1979-80	Sodertalje SK	Sweden-2	31	22	19	41	....	....	....	*84	....	....	....	....	....	....	....	....	....	....	9	8	5	13	36	....	....	....
1980-81	Sodertalje SK	Sweden	33	9	11	20	....	....	....	86	....	....	....	....	....	....	....	....	....	....	....	....	....	....	....	....	....	....
1981-82	Indianapolis Checkers	CHL	63	25	32	57	....	....	....	113	....	....	....	....	....	....	....	....	....	....	8	1	5	6	31	....	....	....
1982-83♦	**New York Islanders**	**NHL**	**30**	**7**	**7**	**14**	**6**	**5**	**11**	**26**	**0**	**0**	**0**	**37**	**18.9**	**25**	**6**	**15**	**0**	**4**	**7**	**1**	**0**	**1**	**6**	**0**	**0**	**1**
	Indianapolis Checkers	CHL	42	26	27	53	....	....	....	86	....	....	....	....	....	....	....	....	....	....	....	....	....	....	....	....	....	....
1983-84	**New York Islanders**	**NHL**	**40**	**2**	**5**	**7**	**2**	**3**	**5**	**27**	**0**	**0**	**0**	**31**	**6.5**	**12**	**1**	**13**	**0**	**–2**	**6**	**0**	**0**	**0**	**7**	**0**	**0**	**0**
1984-85	**New York Islanders**	**NHL**	**38**	**5**	**0**	**5**	**4**	**0**	**4**	**50**	**0**	**0**	**1**	**22**	**22.7**	**9**	**0**	**16**	**0**	**–7**	**1**	**0**	**0**	**0**	**0**	**0**	**0**	**0**
1985-86	**Minnesota North Stars**	**NHL**	**38**	**3**	**2**	**5**	**2**	**1**	**3**	**86**	**0**	**0**	**1**	**29**	**10.3**	**10**	**1**	**12**	**0**	**–3**	**1**	**0**	**0**	**0**	**0**	**0**	**0**	**0**
	Springfield Indians	AHL	2	1	1	2	....	....	....	0	....	....	....	....	....	....	....	....	....	....	....	....	....	....	....	....	....	....
1986-87	**Minnesota North Stars**	**NHL**	**6**	**0**	**0**	**0**	**0**	**0**	**0**	**4**	**0**	**0**	**0**	**5**	**0.0**	**0**	**0**	**3**	**0**	**–3**	....	....	....	....	....	....	....	....
	HC Lugano	Switz.	10	6	3	9	....	....	....	....	....	....	....	....	....	....	....	....	....	....	....	....	....	....	....	....	....	....
1987-88	Sodertalje SK	Sweden	30	10	13	23	....	....	....	50	....	....	....	....	....	....	....	....	....	....	2	0	1	1	6	....	....	....
1988-89	Sodertalje SK	Sweden	34	10	6	16	....	....	....	68	....	....	....	....	....	....	....	....	....	....	5	1	1	2	8	....	....	....
1989-90	Malmo IF	Sweden-2	24	10	8	18	....	....	....	40	....	....	....	....	....	....	....	....	....	....	3	1	3	4	2	....	....	....
1990-91	Malmo IF	Sweden	38	13	14	27	....	....	....	48	....	....	....	....	....	....	....	....	....	....	2	0	2	2	2	....	....	....
1991-92	Malmo IF	Sweden	34	4	9	13	....	....	....	68	....	....	....	....	....	....	....	....	....	....	10	1	1	2	10	....	....	....
	NHL Totals		**152**	**17**	**14**	**31**	**14**	**9**	**23**	**193**	**0**	**0**	**2**	**124**	**13.7**	**56**	**8**	**59**	**0**		**15**	**1**	**0**	**1**	**13**	**0**	**0**	**1**

Signed as a free agent by **NY Islanders**, June 12, 1981. Traded to **Minnesota** by **NY Islanders** for Minnesota's 7th round choice (Will Anderson) in 1986 Entry Draft, September 9, 1985.

• HALPERN, Jeff

C – R. 6', 195 lbs. b: Potomac, MD, 5/3/1976.

Season	Club	League	GP	G	A	Pts	AG	AA	APts	PIM	PP	SH	GW	S	%	TGF	PGF	TGA	PGA	+/–	GP	G	A	Pts	PIM	PP	SH	GW
1994-95	Stratford Cullitons	OJHL	44	29	54	83	....	....	....	43	....	....	....	....	....	....	....	....	....	....	....	....	....	....	....	....	....	....
1995-96	Princeton University	ECAC	29	3	11	14	....	....	....	30	....	....	....	....	....	....	....	....	....	....	....	....	....	....	....	....	....	....
1996-97	Princeton University	ECAC	33	7	24	31	....	....	....	35	....	....	....	....	....	....	....	....	....	....	....	....	....	....	....	....	....	....
1997-98	Princeton University	ECAC	36	*28	25	*53	....	....	....	46	....	....	....	....	....	....	....	....	....	....	....	....	....	....	....	....	....	....
1998-99	Princeton University	ECAC	33	*22	22	44	....	....	....	32	....	....	....	....	....	....	....	....	....	....	....	....	....	....	....	....	....	....
	Portland Pirates	AHL	6	2	1	3	....	....	....	4	....	....	....	....	....	....	....	....	....	....	....	....	....	....	....	....	....	....
99-2000	**Washington Capitals**	**NHL**	**79**	**18**	**11**	**29**	**20**	**10**	**30**	**39**	**4**	**4**	**1**	**108**	**16.7**	**48**	**11**	**26**	**10**	**21**	**5**	**2**	**1**	**3**	**0**	**1**	**0**	**1**
	United States	WC-A	7	1	1	2	....	....	....	4	....	....	....	....	....	....	....	....	....	....	....	....	....	....	....	....	....	....
	NHL Totals		**79**	**18**	**11**	**29**	**20**	**10**	**30**	**39**	**4**	**4**	**1**	**108**	**16.7**	**48**	**11**	**26**	**10**		**5**	**2**	**1**	**3**	**0**	**1**	**0**	**1**

ECAC Second All-Star Team (1998, 1999)

Signed as a free agent by **Washington**, March 29, 1999.

• HALVERSON, Trevor

LW – L. 6', 200 lbs. b: White River, Ont., 4/6/1971. Washington's 2nd, 21st overall, in 1991.

Season	Club	League	GP	G	A	Pts	AG	AA	APts	PIM	PP	SH	GW	S	%	TGF	PGF	TGA	PGA	+/–	GP	G	A	Pts	PIM	PP	SH	GW
1987-88	Sault Ste. Marie Elks	NOHA	33	29	35	64	....	....	....	34	....	....	....	....	....	....	....	....	....	....	....	....	....	....	....	....	....	....
	Thessalon Flyers	NOJHA	2	0	0	0	....	....	....	0	....	....	....	....	....	....	....	....	....	....	....	....	....	....	....	....	....	....
1988-89	Thessalon Flyers	NOJHA	2	0	0	0	....	....	....	0	....	....	....	....	....	....	....	....	....	....	....	....	....	....	....	....	....	....
	North Bay Centennials	OHL	52	8	10	18	....	....	....	7	....	....	....	....	....	....	....	....	....	....	....	....	....	....	....	....	....	....
1989-90	North Bay Centennials	OHL	54	22	20	42	....	....	....	162	....	....	....	....	....	....	....	....	....	....	2	2	1	3	2	....	....	....
1990-91	North Bay Centennials	OHL	54	22	20	42	....	....	....	172	....	....	....	....	....	....	....	....	....	....	2	2	1	3	2	....	....	....
1991-92	North Bay Centennials	OHL	64	59	36	95	....	....	....	128	....	....	....	....	....	....	....	....	....	....	10	3	6	9	4	....	....	....
1992-93	Hampton Roads Admirals	ECHL	9	7	5	12	....	....	....	6	....	....	....	....	....	....	....	....	....	....	....	....	....	....	....	....	....	....
	Baltimore Skipjacks	AHL	67	19	21	40	....	....	....	170	....	....	....	....	....	....	....	....	....	....	2	1	0	1	0	....	....	....
1993-94	San Diego Gulls	IHL	58	4	9	13	....	....	....	115	....	....	....	....	....	....	....	....	....	....	....	....	....	....	....	....	....	....
	Milwaukee Admirals	IHL	4	1	0	1	....	....	....	8	....	....	....	....	....	....	....	....	....	....	2	0	0	0	17	....	....	....
1994-95	Portland Pirates	AHL	5	0	1	1	....	....	....	9	....	....	....	....	....	....	....	....	....	....	....	....	....	....	....	....	....	....
	Hampton Roads Admirals	ECHL	42	14	26	40	....	....	....	194	....	....	....	....	....	....	....	....	....	....	....	....	....	....	....	....	....	....

			REGULAR SEASON																		PLAYOFFS							
Season	Club	League	GP	G	A	Pts	AG	AA	APts	PIM	PP	SH	GW	S	%	TGF	PGF	TGA	PGA	+/–	GP	G	A	Pts	PIM	PP	SH	GW
1995-96	Las Vegas Thunder	IHL	22	6	9	15	....	....	....	86	....	....	....	....	....	....	....	....	....	....	....	....	....	....	....	....	....	....
	Utah Grizzlies	IHL	1	0	1	1	....	....	....	0	....	....	....	....	....	....	....	....	....	....	....	....	....	....	....	....	....	....
	Hampton Roads Admirals	ECHL	38	34	27	61	....	....	....	152	....	....	....	....	....	....	....	....	....	....	....	....	....	....	....	....	....	....
	Portland Pirates	AHL	3	0	1	1	....	....	....	0	....	....	....	....	....	....	....	....	....	....	....	....	....	....	....	....	....	....
	Indianapolis Ice	IHL	12	0	1	1	....	....	....	18	....	....	....	....	....	....	....	....	....	....	5	0	0	0	4	....	....	....
1996-97	Portland Pirates	AHL	50	9	8	17	....	....	....	157	....	....	....	....	....	....	....	....	....	....	3	1	1	2	4	....	....	....
1997-98	Fort Wayne Comets	IHL	14	1	4	5	....	....	....	34	....	....	....	....	....	....	....	....	....	....	....	....	....	....	....	....	....	....
	Manitoba Moose	IHL	7	0	1	1	....	....	....	20	....	....	....	....	....	....	....	....	....	....	....	....	....	....	....	....	....	....
	Portland Pirates	AHL	43	14	13	27	....	....	....	181	....	....	....	....	....	....	....	....	....	....	10	2	4	6	20	....	....	....
1998-99	**Washington Capitals**	**NHL**	**17**	**0**	**4**	**4**	**0**	**4**	**4**	**28**	**0**	**0**	**0**	**16**	**0.0**	**6**	**0**	**11**	**0**	**–5**	....	....	....	....	....	....	....	....
	Portland Pirates	AHL	57	24	25	49	....	....	....	153	....	....	....	....	....	....	....	....	....	....	....	....	....	....	....	....	....	....
99-2000	**Washington Capitals**	**NHL**	DID NOT PLAY – INJURED																									
	NHL Totals		**17**	**0**	**4**	**4**	**0**	**4**	**4**	**28**	**0**	**0**	**0**	**16**	**0.0**	**6**	**0**	**11**	**0**		....	....	....	....	....	....	....	....

Claimed by **Anaheim** from **Washington** in Expansion Draft, June 24, 1993. Signed as a free agent by **Washington**, September, 1998. • Missed entire 1999-2000 season recovering from head injury suffered in training camp, September, 1999.

• HALWARD, Doug

Douglas Robert "Hawk" D – L. 6'1", 200 lbs. b: Toronto, Ont., 11/1/1955. Boston's 1st, 14th overall, in 1975.

Season	Club	League	GP	G	A	Pts	AG	AA	APts	PIM	PP	SH	GW	S	%	TGF	PGF	TGA	PGA	+/–	GP	G	A	Pts	PIM	PP	SH	GW
1973-74	Peterborough Petes	OMJHL	69	1	15	16	....	....	....	103	....	....	....	....	....	....	....	....	....	....	....	....	....	....	....	....	....	....
	Canada	WJC-A	5	0	0	0	....	....	....	2	....	....	....	....	....	....	....	....	....	....	....	....	....	....	....	....	....	....
1974-75	Peterborough Petes	OMJHL	68	11	52	63	....	....	....	97	....	....	....	....	....	....	....	....	....	....	3	1	2	3	5	....	....	....
1975-76	**Boston Bruins**	**NHL**	**22**	**1**	**5**	**6**	**1**	**4**	**5**	**6**	**1**	**0**	**0**	**30**	**3.3**	**21**	**4**	**25**	**4**	**–4**	**1**	**0**	**0**	**0**	**0**	**0**	**0**	**0**
	Rochester Americans	AHL	54	6	11	17	....	....	....	51	....	....	....	....	....	....	....	....	....	....	4	1	0	1	4	....	....	....
1976-77	**Boston Bruins**	**NHL**	**18**	**2**	**2**	**4**	**2**	**2**	**4**	**6**	**0**	**0**	**0**	**20**	**10.0**	**16**	**0**	**8**	**1**	**9**	**6**	**0**	**0**	**0**	**4**	**0**	**0**	**0**
	Rochester Americans	AHL	54	4	28	32	....	....	....	26	....	....	....	....	....	....	....	....	....	....	....	....	....	....	....	....	....	....
1977-78	**Boston Bruins**	**NHL**	**25**	**0**	**2**	**2**	**0**	**2**	**2**	**2**	**0**	**0**	**0**	**18**	**0.0**	**9**	**3**	**14**	**9**	**1**	....	....	....	....	....	....	....	....
	Rochester Americans	AHL	42	8	14	22	....	....	....	17	....	....	....	....	....	....	....	....	....	....	6	0	3	3	2	....	....	....
1978-79	**Los Angeles Kings**	**NHL**	**27**	**1**	**5**	**6**	**1**	**4**	**5**	**13**	**1**	**0**	**0**	**39**	**2.6**	**31**	**11**	**26**	**2**	**–4**	**1**	**0**	**0**	**0**	**12**	**0**	**0**	**0**
	Springfield Indians	AHL	14	5	1	6	....	....	....	10	....	....	....	....	....	....	....	....	....	....	....	....	....	....	....	....	....	....
1979-80	**Los Angeles Kings**	**NHL**	**63**	**11**	**45**	**56**	**9**	**33**	**42**	**52**	**8**	**0**	**0**	**165**	**6.7**	**141**	**49**	**118**	**40**	**14**	**1**	**0**	**0**	**0**	**2**	**0**	**0**	**0**
1980-81	**Los Angeles Kings**	**NHL**	**51**	**4**	**15**	**19**	**3**	**10**	**13**	**96**	**1**	**0**	**0**	**74**	**5.4**	**69**	**23**	**61**	**13**	**–2**	....	....	....	....	....	....	....	....
	Vancouver Canucks	**NHL**	**7**	**0**	**1**	**1**	**0**	**1**	**1**	**4**	**0**	**0**	**0**	**8**	**0.0**	**7**	**3**	**9**	**0**	**–5**	**2**	**0**	**1**	**1**	**6**	**0**	**0**	**0**
1981-82	**Vancouver Canucks**	**NHL**	**37**	**4**	**13**	**17**	**3**	**9**	**12**	**40**	**1**	**0**	**0**	**75**	**5.3**	**52**	**18**	**46**	**1**	**–11**	**15**	**2**	**4**	**6**	**44**	**0**	**0**	**1**
	Dallas Black Hawks	CHL	22	8	18	26	....	....	....	49	....	....	....	....	....	....	....	....	....	....	....	....	....	....	....	....	....	....
1982-83	**Vancouver Canucks**	**NHL**	**75**	**19**	**33**	**52**	**16**	**23**	**39**	**83**	**11**	**0**	**2**	**199**	**9.5**	**130**	**46**	**124**	**22**	**–18**	**4**	**1**	**0**	**1**	**21**	**0**	**0**	**0**
	Canada	WEC-A	10	1	2	3	....	....	....	6	....	....	....	....	....	....	....	....	....	....	....	....	....	....	....	....	....	....
1983-84	**Vancouver Canucks**	**NHL**	**54**	**7**	**16**	**23**	**6**	**11**	**17**	**35**	**2**	**0**	**1**	**108**	**6.5**	**78**	**27**	**70**	**20**	**1**	**4**	**3**	**1**	**4**	**2**	**2**	**0**	**0**
1984-85	**Vancouver Canucks**	**NHL**	**71**	**7**	**27**	**34**	**6**	**18**	**24**	**82**	**2**	**1**	**0**	**173**	**4.0**	**110**	**32**	**164**	**44**	**–42**	....	....	....	....	....	....	....	....
	Canada	WEC-A	10	1	2	3	....	....	....	4	....	....	....	....	....	....	....	....	....	....	....	....	....	....	....	....	....	....
1985-86	**Vancouver Canucks**	**NHL**	**70**	**8**	**25**	**33**	**6**	**17**	**23**	**111**	**3**	**0**	**0**	**122**	**6.6**	**98**	**29**	**112**	**24**	**–19**	**3**	**0**	**0**	**0**	**4**	**0**	**0**	**0**
1986-87	**Vancouver Canucks**	**NHL**	**10**	**0**	**3**	**3**	**0**	**2**	**2**	**34**	**0**	**0**	**0**	**21**	**0.0**	**8**	**0**	**22**	**6**	**–8**	....	....	....	....	....	....	....	....
	Detroit Red Wings	**NHL**	**11**	**0**	**3**	**3**	**0**	**2**	**2**	**19**	**0**	**0**	**0**	**8**	**0.0**	**11**	**2**	**5**	**0**	**4**	....	....	....	....	....	....	....	....
1987-88	**Detroit Red Wings**	**NHL**	**70**	**5**	**21**	**26**	**4**	**15**	**19**	**130**	**3**	**0**	**1**	**88**	**5.7**	**103**	**31**	**96**	**30**	**6**	**8**	**1**	**4**	**5**	**18**	**0**	**0**	**0**
1988-89	**Detroit Red Wings**	**NHL**	**18**	**0**	**1**	**1**	**0**	**1**	**1**	**36**	**0**	**0**	**0**	**5**	**0.0**	**14**	**1**	**30**	**6**	**–11**	....	....	....	....	....	....	....	....
	Adirondack Red Wings	AHL	4	1	0	1	....	....	....	0	....	....	....	....	....	....	....	....	....	....	....	....	....	....	....	....	....	....
	Edmonton Oilers	**NHL**	**24**	**0**	**7**	**7**	**0**	**5**	**5**	**25**	**0**	**0**	**0**	**8**	**0.0**	**17**	**1**	**23**	**4**	**–3**	**2**	**0**	**0**	**0**	**0**	**0**	**0**	**0**
	NHL Totals		**653**	**69**	**224**	**293**	**57**	**159**	**216**	**774**	**33**	**1**	**4**	**1161**	**5.9**	**915**	**280**	**953**	**226**		**47**	**7**	**10**	**17**	**113**	**2**	**0**	**1**

Traded to **LA Kings** by **Boston** for future considerations, September 18, 1978. Claimed by **LA Kings** as a fill-in during Expansion Draft, June 13, 1979. Traded to **Vancouver** by **LA Kings** for Vancouver's 5th round choice (Ulf Isaksson) in 1982 Entry Draft and future considerations (Gary Bromley, May 12, 1981) March 8, 1981. Traded to **Detroit** by **Vancouver** for Detroit's 6th round choice (Phil Von Stefanelli) in 1988 Entry Draft, November 21, 1986. Traded to **Edmonton** by **Detroit** for Edmonton's 12th round choice (Jason Glickman) in 1989 Entry Draft, January 23, 1989.

• HAMEL, Denis

Denis Jean LW – L. 6'2", 200 lbs. b: Lachute, Que., 5/10/1977. St. Louis' 5th, 153rd overall, in 1995.

Season	Club	League	GP	G	A	Pts	AG	AA	APts	PIM	PP	SH	GW	S	%	TGF	PGF	TGA	PGA	+/–	GP	G	A	Pts	PIM	PP	SH	GW
1992-93	Lachute Regents	QAAA	32	18	24	42	....	....	....	....	....	....	....	....	....	....	....	....	....	....	....	....	....	....	....	....	....	....
1993-94	Abitibi Forestiers	QAAA	15	5	7	12	....	....	....	29	....	....	....	....	....	....	....	....	....	....	....	....	....	....	....	....	....	....
1994-95	Chicoutimi Sagueneens	QMJHL	66	15	12	27	....	....	....	155	....	....	....	....	....	....	....	....	....	....	12	2	0	2	27	....	....	....
1995-96	Chicoutimi Sagueneens	QMJHL	65	40	49	89	....	....	....	199	....	....	....	....	....	....	....	....	....	....	17	10	14	24	64	....	....	....
1996-97	Chicoutimi Sagueneens	QMJHL	70	50	50	100	....	....	....	357	....	....	....	....	....	....	....	....	....	....	20	15	10	25	58	....	....	....
1997-98	Rochester Americans	AHL	74	10	15	25	....	....	....	98	....	....	....	....	....	....	....	....	....	....	4	1	2	3	0	....	....	....
1998-99	Rochester Americans	AHL	74	16	17	33	....	....	....	121	....	....	....	....	....	....	....	....	....	....	20	3	4	7	10	....	....	....
99-2000	**Buffalo Sabres**	**NHL**	**3**	**1**	**0**	**1**	**1**	**0**	**1**	**0**	**0**	**0**	**0**	**3**	**33.3**	**1**	**0**	**2**	**0**	**–1**	....	....	....	....	....	....	....	....
	Rochester Americans	AHL	76	34	24	58	....	....	....	122	....	....	....	....	....	....	....	....	....	....	21	6	7	13	49	....	....	....
	NHL Totals		**3**	**1**	**0**	**1**	**1**	**0**	**1**	**0**	**0**	**0**	**0**	**3**	**33.3**	**1**	**0**	**2**	**0**		....	....	....	....	....	....	....	....

Traded to **Buffalo** by **St. Louis** for Charlie Huddy and Buffalo's 7th round choice (Daniel Corso) in 1996 Entry Draft, March 19, 1996.

• HAMEL, Gilles

Gilles Julien LW – L. 6'3", 183 lbs. b: Asbestos, Que., 3/18/1960. Buffalo's 5th, 74th overall, in 1979.

Season	Club	League	GP	G	A	Pts	AG	AA	APts	PIM	PP	SH	GW	S	%	TGF	PGF	TGA	PGA	+/–	GP	G	A	Pts	PIM	PP	SH	GW
1976-77	Thetford Mines Fleur-de-Lys	QJHL	60	29	33	62	....	....	....	....	....	....	....	....	....	....	....	....	....	....	....	....	....	....	....	....	....	....
1977-78	Laval National	QMJHL	72	44	37	81	....	....	....	68	....	....	....	....	....	....	....	....	....	....	....	....	....	....	....	....	....	....
1978-79	Laval National	QMJHL	72	56	55	111	....	....	....	130	....	....	....	....	....	....	....	....	....	....	....	....	....	....	....	....	....	....
1979-80	Trois-Rivieres Draveurs	QMJHL	12	13	8	21	....	....	....	8	....	....	....	....	....	....	....	....	....	....	....	....	....	....	....	....	....	....
	Chicoutimi Sagueneens	QMJHL	57	73	62	135	....	....	....	87	....	....	....	....	....	....	....	....	....	....	12	10	6	16	20	....	....	....
	Rochester Americans	AHL	....	....	....	....	....	....	....	....	....	....	....	....	....	....	....	....	....	....	1	0	0	0	0	....	....	....
1980-81	**Buffalo Sabres**	**NHL**	**51**	**10**	**9**	**19**	**8**	**6**	**14**	**53**	**2**	**0**	**0**	**56**	**17.9**	**27**	**5**	**30**	**0**	**–8**	**5**	**0**	**1**	**1**	**4**	**0**	**0**	**0**
	Rochester Americans	AHL	14	8	7	15	....	....	....	7	....	....	....	....	....	....	....	....	....	....	....	....	....	....	....	....	....	....
1981-82	**Buffalo Sabres**	**NHL**	**16**	**2**	**7**	**9**	**2**	**5**	**7**	**2**	**0**	**0**	**1**	**17**	**11.8**	**9**	**0**	**10**	**0**	**–1**	....	....	....	....	....	....	....	....
	Rochester Americans	AHL	57	31	44	75	....	....	....	55	....	....	....	....	....	....	....	....	....	....	....	....	....	....	....	....	....	....
1982-83	**Buffalo Sabres**	**NHL**	**66**	**22**	**20**	**42**	**18**	**14**	**32**	**26**	**2**	**0**	**1**	**120**	**18.3**	**53**	**10**	**39**	**0**	**4**	**9**	**2**	**2**	**4**	**2**	**1**	**0**	**0**
1983-84	**Buffalo Sabres**	**NHL**	**75**	**21**	**23**	**44**	**17**	**16**	**33**	**37**	**4**	**2**	**1**	**135**	**15.6**	**66**	**14**	**53**	**5**	**4**	**3**	**0**	**2**	**2**	**2**	**0**	**0**	**0**
1984-85	**Buffalo Sabres**	**NHL**	**80**	**18**	**30**	**48**	**15**	**20**	**35**	**36**	**5**	**3**	**4**	**163**	**11.0**	**89**	**31**	**70**	**9**	**–3**	**1**	**0**	**0**	**0**	**0**	**0**	**0**	**0**
1985-86	**Buffalo Sabres**	**NHL**	**77**	**19**	**25**	**44**	**15**	**17**	**32**	**61**	**4**	**3**	**4**	**158**	**12.0**	**58**	**15**	**94**	**24**	**–27**	....	....	....	....	....	....	....	....
1986-87	**Winnipeg Jets**	**NHL**	**79**	**27**	**21**	**48**	**23**	**15**	**38**	**24**	**1**	**1**	**4**	**175**	**15.4**	**65**	**2**	**66**	**6**	**3**	**8**	**2**	**0**	**2**	**2**	**0**	**0**	**2**
1987-88	**Winnipeg Jets**	**NHL**	**63**	**8**	**11**	**19**	**7**	**8**	**15**	**35**	**1**	**0**	**0**	**106**	**7.5**	**30**	**3**	**44**	**1**	**–16**	**1**	**0**	**0**	**0**	**0**	**0**	**0**	**0**
1988-89	**Winnipeg Jets**	**NHL**	**1**	**0**	**0**	**0**	**0**	**0**	**0**	**0**	**0**	**0**	**0**	**0**	**0.0**	**0**	**0**	**0**	**0**	**0**	....	....	....	....	....	....	....	....
	Moncton Hawks	AHL	14	7	5	12	....	....	....	10	....	....	....	....	....	....	....	....	....	....	....	....	....	....	....	....	....	....
	Los Angeles Kings	**NHL**	**11**	**0**	**1**	**1**	**0**	**1**	**1**	**2**	**0**	**0**	**0**	**11**	**0.0**	**3**	**0**	**6**	**0**	**–3**	....	....	....	....	....	....	....	....
	New Haven Nighthawks	AHL	34	9	9	18	....	....	....	12	....	....	....	....	....	....	....	....	....	....	1	0	0	0	0	....	....	....
1989-90	HC Caen	France	8	8	7	15	....	....	....	10	....	....	....	....	....	....	....	....	....	....	....	....	....	....	....	....	....	....
	NHL Totals		**519**	**127**	**147**	**274**	**105**	**102**	**207**	**276**	**19**	**9**	**15**	**941**	**13.5**	**400**	**80**	**412**	**45**		**27**	**4**	**5**	**9**	**10**	**1**	**0**	**2**

• Brother of Jean • QMJHL Second All-Star Team (1979) • QMJHL First All-Star Team (1980)

Traded to **Winnipeg** by **Buffalo** for Scott Arniel, June 21, 1986. Traded to **LA Kings** by **Winnipeg** for Paul Fenton, Novemnber 25, 1988.

• HAMEL, Jean

Jean P. D – L. 5'11", 195 lbs. b: Asbestos, Que., 6/6/1952. St. Louis' 2nd, 41st overall, in 1972.

Season	Club	League	GP	G	A	Pts	AG	AA	APts	PIM	PP	SH	GW	S	%	TGF	PGF	TGA	PGA	+/–	GP	G	A	Pts	PIM	PP	SH	GW
1969-70	Drummondville Rangers	QJHL	56	4	11	15	....	....	....	75	....	....	....	....	....	....	....	....	....	....	6	1	1	2	20	....	....	....
1970-71	Drummondville Rangers	QJHL	61	7	23	30	....	....	....	109	....	....	....	....	....	....	....	....	....	....	6	1	1	2	8	....	....	....
1971-72	Drummondville Rangers	QMJHL	59	6	29	35	....	....	....	132	....	....	....	....	....	....	....	....	....	....	9	1	0	1	48	....	....	....
1972-73	**St. Louis Blues**	**NHL**	**55**	**2**	**7**	**9**	**2**	**6**	**8**	**24**	**0**	**0**	**0**	**56**	**3.6**	**41**	**1**	**51**	**6**	**–5**	**2**	**0**	**0**	**0**	**0**	**0**	**0**	**0**
	Denver Spurs	WHL	13	0	6	6	....	....	....	22	....	....	....	....	....	....	....	....	....	....	....	....	....	....	....	....	....	....
1973-74	**St. Louis Blues**	**NHL**	**23**	**1**	**1**	**2**	**1**	**1**	**2**	**6**	**0**	**0**	**0**	**21**	**4.8**	**12**	**0**	**17**	**2**	**–3**	....	....	....	....	....	....	....	....
	Denver Spurs	WHL	10	0	2	2	....	....	....	12	....	....	....	....	....	....	....	....	....	....	....	....	....	....	....	....	....	....
	Detroit Red Wings	**NHL**	**22**	**0**	**3**	**3**	**0**	**2**	**2**	**40**	**0**	**0**	**0**	**18**	**0.0**	**23**	**4**	**40**	**9**	**–12**	....	....	....	....	....	....	....	....

			REGULAR SEASON																		PLAYOFFS							
Season	Club	League	GP	G	A	Pts	AG	AA	APts	PIM	PP	SH	GW	S	%	TGF	PGF	TGA	PGA	+/–	GP	G	A	Pts	PIM	PP	SH	GW
1974-75	**Detroit Red Wings**	**NHL**	**80**	**5**	**19**	**24**	**4**	**14**	**18**	**136**	**0**	**0**	**0**	**112**	**4.5**	**95**	**12**	**157**	**34**	**–40**								
1975-76	**Detroit Red Wings**	**NHL**	**77**	**3**	**9**	**12**	**3**	**7**	**10**	**129**	**1**	**0**	**0**	**92**	**3.3**	**64**	**4**	**103**	**30**	**–13**								
1976-77	**Detroit Red Wings**	**NHL**	**71**	**1**	**10**	**11**	**1**	**8**	**9**	**63**	**0**	**0**	**0**	**85**	**1.2**	**44**	**0**	**85**	**23**	**–18**								
1977-78	**Detroit Red Wings**	**NHL**	**32**	**2**	**6**	**8**	**2**	**5**	**7**	**34**	**0**	**0**	**0**	**37**	**5.4**	**23**	**0**	**21**	**1**	**3**	**7**	**0**	**0**	**0**	**10**	**0**	**0**	**0**
	Kansas City Red Wings	CHL	28	2	10	12				29																		
1978-79	**Detroit Red Wings**	**NHL**	**52**	**2**	**4**	**6**	**2**	**3**	**5**	**72**	**0**	**0**	**0**	**41**	**4.9**	**28**	**3**	**35**	**1**	**–9**								
1979-80	**Detroit Red Wings**	**NHL**	**49**	**1**	**4**	**5**	**1**	**3**	**4**	**43**	**0**	**0**	**0**	**27**	**3.7**	**19**	**1**	**23**	**3**	**–2**								
1980-81	**Detroit Red Wings**	**NHL**	**68**	**5**	**7**	**12**	**4**	**5**	**9**	**57**	**0**	**0**	**0**	**47**	**10.6**	**32**	**0**	**46**	**13**	**–1**								
	Adirondack Red Wings	AHL	7	1	3	4				36																		
1981-82	**Quebec Nordiques**	**NHL**	**40**	**1**	**6**	**7**	**1**	**4**	**5**	**32**	**0**	**0**	**1**	**28**	**3.6**	**50**	**1**	**59**	**13**	**3**	**5**	**0**	**0**	**0**	**16**	**0**	**0**	**0**
	Fredericton Express	AHL	16	2	4	6				19																		
1982-83	**Quebec Nordiques**	**NHL**	**51**	**2**	**7**	**9**	**2**	**5**	**7**	**38**	**0**	**0**	**0**	**45**	**4.4**	**55**	**0**	**64**	**20**	**11**	**4**	**0**	**0**	**0**	**2**	**0**	**0**	**0**
1983-84	**Montreal Canadiens**	**NHL**	**79**	**1**	**12**	**13**	**1**	**8**	**9**	**92**	**0**	**0**	**0**	**68**	**1.5**	**84**	**0**	**91**	**14**	**7**	**15**	**0**	**2**	**2**	**16**	**0**	**0**	**0**
	NHL Totals		**699**	**26**	**95**	**121**	**24**	**71**	**95**	**766**	**1**	**0**	**1**	**677**	**3.8**	**570**	**26**	**792**	**169**		**33**	**0**	**2**	**2**	**44**	**0**	**0**	**0**

• Brother of Gilles • QMJHL Second All-Star Team (1972)

Traded to **Detroit** by **St. Louis** with Chris Evans and Bryan Watson for Ted Harris, Bill Collins and Garnet Bailey, February 14, 1974. Claimed as a fill-in by **Detroit** during Expansion Draft, June 13, 1979. Signed as a free agent by **Quebec**, October 6, 1981. Claimed by **Montreal** from **Quebec** in Waiver Draft, October 3, 1983.

• HAMILTON, Al

Allan Guy D – R. 6'1", 195 lbs. b: Flin Flon, Man., 8/20/1946.

Season	Club	League	GP	G	A	Pts	AG	AA	APts	PIM	PP	SH	GW	S	%	TGF	PGF	TGA	PGA	+/–	GP	G	A	Pts	PIM	PP	SH	GW
1962-63	Flin Flon Bombers	SJHL	STATISTICS NOT AVAILABLE																									
1963-64	Edmonton Oil Kings	CAHL	14	4	7	11				26											5	2	3	5	15			
	Edmonton Oil Kings	Mem-Cup	19	4	8	12				15																		
1964-65	Edmonton Oil Kings	CAHL	30	10	15	25																						
	St. Paul Rangers	CPHL	3	0	2	2				0																		
	Edmonton Oil Kings	Mem-Cup	20	4	12	16				40																		
1965-66	Edmonton Oil Kings	ASHL	28	15	22	37				*99											8	3	10	13	16			
	New York Rangers	**NHL**	**4**	**0**	**0**	**0**	**0**	**0**	**0**	**0**																		
	Edmonton Oil Kings	Mem-Cup	19	9	23	32				29																		
1966-67	Omaha Knights	CPHL	68	11	25	36				96											12	4	3	7	16			
1967-68	**New York Rangers**	**NHL**	**2**	**0**	**0**	**0**	**0**	**0**	**0**	**0**	**0**	**0**	**0**	**0**	**0.0**	**0**	**0**	**0**	**0**	**0**								
	Buffalo Bisons	AHL	72	9	21	30				82											5	0	4	4	23			
1968-69	**New York Rangers**	**NHL**	**16**	**0**	**0**	**0**	**0**	**0**	**0**	**8**	**0**	**0**	**0**	**9**	**0.0**	**2**	**0**	**3**	**1**	**0**	**1**	**0**	**0**	**0**	**0**	**0**	**0**	**0**
	Buffalo Bisons	AHL	41	4	14	18				61											6	0	4	4	12			
1969-70	**New York Rangers**	**NHL**	**59**	**0**	**5**	**5**	**0**	**5**	**5**	**54**	**0**	**0**	**0**	**42**	**0.0**	**24**	**3**	**38**	**9**	**–8**	**5**	**0**	**0**	**0**	**2**	**0**	**0**	**0**
1970-71	**Buffalo Sabres**	**NHL**	**69**	**2**	**28**	**30**	**2**	**23**	**25**	**71**	**0**	**0**	**0**	**98**	**2.0**	**81**	**13**	**114**	**23**	**–23**								
1971-72	**Buffalo Sabres**	**NHL**	**76**	**4**	**30**	**34**	**4**	**26**	**30**	**105**	**1**	**0**	**1**	**91**	**4.4**	**93**	**13**	**119**	**27**	**–12**								
1972-73	Alberta Oilers	WHA	78	11	50	61				124																		
1973-74	Edmonton Oilers	WHA	78	14	45	59				104											4	1	1	2	15			
1974-75	Team Canada	Summit-74	3	0	1	1				4																		
	Edmonton Oilers	WHA	25	1	13	14				42																		
1975-76	Edmonton Oilers	WHA	54	2	32	34				78											4	0	1	1	6			
1976-77	Edmonton Oilers	WHA	81	8	37	45				60											5	0	4	4	4			
1977-78	Edmonton Oilers	WHA	59	11	43	54				46																		
1978-79	Edmonton Oilers	WHA	80	6	38	44				38											13	4	5	9	4			
1979-80	**Edmonton Oilers**	**NHL**	**31**	**4**	**15**	**19**	**3**	**11**	**14**	**20**	**1**	**0**	**0**	**34**	**11.8**	**40**	**9**	**40**	**7**	**–2**	**1**	**0**	**0**	**0**	**0**	**0**	**0**	**0**
	Houston Apollos	CHL	4	0	0	0				0																		
	NHL Totals		**257**	**10**	**78**	**88**	**9**	**65**	**74**	**258**											**7**	**0**	**0**	**0**	**2**			
	Other Major League Totals		455	53	258	311				492											26	5	11	16	29			

CPHL Second All-Star Team (1967) • WHA Second All-Star Team (1974) • WHA First All-Star Team (1978)

Claimed by **Buffalo** from **NY Rangers** in Expansion Draft, June 10, 1970. Selected by **Alberta** (WHA) in 1972 WHA General Player Draft, February 12, 1972. Rights retained by **Edmonton** prior to Expansion Draft, June 9, 1979.

• HAMILTON, Chuck

Charles LW – L. 5'11", 175 lbs. b: Kirkland Lake, Ont., 1/18/1939.

Season	Club	League	GP	G	A	Pts	AG	AA	APts	PIM	PP	SH	GW	S	%	TGF	PGF	TGA	PGA	+/–	GP	G	A	Pts	PIM	PP	SH	GW
1956-57	Peterborough Petes	OHA-Jr.	52	7	11	18				15																		
1957-58	Peterborough Petes	OHA-Jr.	52	8	14	22				50											5	1	1	2	4			
1958-59	Peterborough Petes	OHA-Jr.	46	18	28	46				47											19	7	9	16	16			
	Peterborough Petes	Mem-Cup	12	1	3	4				48																		
1959-60	Hull-Ottawa Canadiens	EPHL	66	6	13	19				39											7	0	2	2	6			
1960-61	Hull-Ottawa Canadiens	EPHL	40	1	7	8				56											14	0	2	2	20			
1961-62	Hull-Ottawa Canadiens	EPHL	57	5	9	14				50											11	1	3	4	4			
	Montreal Canadiens	**NHL**	**1**	**0**	**0**	**0**	**0**	**0**	**0**	**0**																		
1962-63	Hull-Ottawa Canadiens	EPHL	64	17	33	50				51											3	0	1	1	6			
1963-64	Hershey Bears	AHL	72	8	30	38				31											6	0	3	3	2			
1964-65	Hershey Bears	AHL	55	7	15	22				47											15	2	0	2	4			
1965-66	Hershey Bears	AHL	67	7	16	23				24											3	0	2	2	0			
1966-67	Hershey Bears	AHL	62	9	12	21				20											5	0	0	0	0			
1967-68	Hershey Bears	AHL	69	8	22	30				65											5	0	1	1	18			
1968-69	Hershey Bears	AHL	74	28	46	74				46											11	2	4	6	16			
1969-70	Hershey Bears	AHL	60	10	20	30				8											7	1	4	5	0			
1970-71	Hershey Bears	AHL	DID NOT PLAY – INJURED																									
1971-72	Denver Spurs	WHL	70	14	18	32				29											9	1	3	4	4			
1972-73	**St. Louis Blues**	**NHL**	**3**	**0**	**2**	**2**	**0**	**2**	**2**	**2**	**0**	**0**	**0**	**2**	**0.0**	**5**	**0**	**1**	**0**	**4**								
	Denver Spurs	WHL	47	7	25	32				64											5	0	0	0	4			
	NHL Totals		**4**	**0**	**2**	**2**	**0**	**2**	**2**	**2**																		

Loaned to **Hershey** (AHL) by **Montreal** with the trade of Ralph Keller for Mark Reaume, June 11, 1963. Traded to **Hershey** (AHL) by **Montreal** for cash, October, 1964. Claimed by **Detroit** from **Hershey** (AHL) in Inter-League Draft, June 10, 1969. Traded to **Montreal** by **Detroit** for cash, June 11, 1969. Traded to **Hershey** (AHL) by **Montreal** for cash, October, 1969. • Missed entire 1970-71 season recovering from leg injury suffered in exhibition game vs. Baltimore (AHL), September 25, 1970. Traded to **St. Louis** (Denver-WHL) by **Hershey** (AHL) for cash, September, 1971.

• HAMILTON, Jim

James Neil RW – L. 6', 180 lbs. b: Barrie, Ont., 1/18/1957. Pittsburgh's 1st, 30th overall, in 1977.

Season	Club	League	GP	G	A	Pts	AG	AA	APts	PIM	PP	SH	GW	S	%	TGF	PGF	TGA	PGA	+/–	GP	G	A	Pts	PIM	PP	SH	GW
1973-74	London Knights	OMJHL	70	9	14	23				19																		
1974-75	London Knights	OMJHL	68	17	24	41				108																		
1975-76	London Knights	OMJHL	53	24	23	47				37											5	2	2	4	0			
1976-77	London Knights	OMJHL	65	39	53	92				40											19	6	5	11	16			
1977-78	**Pittsburgh Penguins**	**NHL**	**25**	**2**	**4**	**6**	**2**	**3**	**5**	**2**	**0**	**0**	**0**	**35**	**5.7**	**13**	**3**	**13**	**0**	**–3**								
	Binghamton Dusters	AHL	31	4	4	8				19																		
	Grand Rapids Owls	IHL	22	7	15	22				12																		
1978-79	**Pittsburgh Penguins**	**NHL**	**2**	**0**	**0**	**0**	**0**	**0**	**0**	**0**	**0**	**0**	**0**	**3**	**0.0**	**1**	**0**	**1**	**0**	**0**	**5**	**3**	**0**	**3**	**0**	**1**	**0**	**0**
	Binghamton Dusters	AHL	66	25	24	49				34											6	2	3	5	2			
1979-80	**Pittsburgh Penguins**	**NHL**	**10**	**2**	**0**	**2**	**2**	**0**	**2**	**0**	**0**	**0**	**0**	**12**	**16.7**	**5**	**0**	**11**	**0**	**–6**								
	Syracuse Firebirds	AHL	50	16	19	35				33											4	0	1	1	4			
1980-81	**Pittsburgh Penguins**	**NHL**	**20**	**1**	**6**	**7**	**1**	**4**	**5**	**18**	**0**	**0**	**0**	**26**	**3.8**	**10**	**1**	**7**	**0**	**2**	**1**	**0**	**0**	**0**	**0**	**0**	**0**	**0**
	Binghamton Whalers	AHL	28	16	18	34				31																		
1981-82	**Pittsburgh Penguins**	**NHL**	**11**	**5**	**3**	**8**	**4**	**2**	**6**	**2**	**0**	**0**	**1**	**15**	**33.3**	**9**	**0**	**7**	**0**	**2**								
	Erie Blades	AHL	57	27	17	44				51																		
1982-83	**Pittsburgh Penguins**	**NHL**	**5**	**0**	**2**	**2**	**0**	**1**	**1**	**2**	**0**	**0**	**0**	**12**	**0.0**	**2**	**0**	**4**	**0**	**–2**								
	Baltimore Skipjacks	AHL	45	32	10	42				36																		
1983-84	**Pittsburgh Penguins**	**NHL**	**11**	**2**	**2**	**4**	**2**	**1**	**3**	**4**	**1**	**0**	**0**	**21**	**9.5**	**10**	**2**	**6**	**0**	**2**								
	Baltimore Skipjacks	AHL	66	34	45	79				54											9	6	6	12	0			

Season	Club	League	GP	G	A	Pts	AG	AA	APts	PIM	PP	SH	GW	S	%	TGF	PGF	TGA	PGA	+/–	Playoffs GP	G	A	Pts	PIM	PP	SH	GW
1984-85	**Pittsburgh Penguins**	**NHL**	**11**	**2**	**1**	**3**	**2**	**1**	**3**	**0**	**0**	**0**	**0**	**19**	**10.5**	**6**	**0**	**15**	**3**	**–6**	....	....	....	....	....	....	....	....
	Baltimore Skipjacks	AHL	16	5	6	11	....	....	....	24	....	....	....	....	....	....	....	....	....	....	....	....	....	....	....	....	....	....
	Muskegon Mohawks	IHL	1	0	0	0	....	....	....	0	....	....	....	....	....	....	....	....	....	....	....	....	....	....	....	....	....	....
	ZSC Zurich	Switz.	14	17	4	21	....	....	....	....	....	....	....	....	....	....	....	....	....	....	1	0	1	1	....	....	....	....
	NHL Totals		**95**	**14**	**18**	**32**	**13**	**12**	**25**	**28**	**1**	**0**	**1**	**143**	**9.8**	**56**	**6**	**64**	**3**		**6**	**3**	**0**	**3**	**0**	**1**	**0**	**0**

• HAMMARSTROM, Inge Hans Inge LW – L. 6', 180 lbs. b: Sundsvall, Sweden, 1/20/1948.

Season	Club	League	GP	G	A	Pts	AG	AA	APts	PIM	PP	SH	GW	S	%	TGF	PGF	TGA	PGA	+/–	Playoffs GP	G	A	Pts	PIM	PP	SH	GW
1964-65	Wistra/Ostrand IF	Sweden	20	7	4	11	....	....	....	6	....	....	....	....	....	....	....	....	....	....	....	....	....	....	....	....	....	....
1965-66	Wistra/Ostrand IF	Sweden	21	9	8	17	....	....	....	2	....	....	....	....	....	....	....	....	....	....	2	0	0	0	0	....	....	....
1966-67	Timra IK	Sweden	19	14	11	25	....	....	....	4	....	....	....	....	....	....	....	....	....	....	....	....	....	....	....	....	....	....
1967-68	Timra IK	Sweden	21	14	10	24	....	....	....	....	....	....	....	....	....	....	....	....	....	....	....	....	....	....	....	....	....	....
1968-69	Brynas IF Gavle	Sweden	6	5	1	6	....	....	....	0	....	....	....	....	....	....	....	....	....	....	7	2	2	4	0	....	....	....
1969-70	Brynas IF Gavle	Sweden	14	7	4	11	....	....	....	2	....	....	....	....	....	....	....	....	....	....	14	7	1	8	2	....	....	....
1970-71	Brynas IF Gavle	Sweden	14	6	11	17	....	....	....	4	....	....	....	....	....	....	....	....	....	....	14	4	2	6	4	....	....	....
	Sweden	WEC-A	7	2	1	3	....	....	....	4	....	....	....	....	....	....	....	....	....	....	....	....	....	....	....	....	....	....
1971-72	Brynas IF Gavle	Sweden	28	19	9	28	....	....	....	10	....	....	....	....	....	....	....	....	....	....	10	6	0	6	0	....	....	....
	Sweden	Olympics	6	4	2	6	....	....	....	0	....	....	....	....	....	....	....	....	....	....	....	....	....	....	....	....	....	....
	Sweden	WEC-A	10	6	0	6	....	....	....	0	....	....	....	....	....	....	....	....	....	....	....	....	....	....	....	....	....	....
1972-73	Brynas IF Gavle	Sweden	28	18	11	29	....	....	....	14	....	....	....	....	....	....	....	....	....	....	14	10	6	16	8	....	....	....
	Sweden	WEC-A	10	6	3	9	....	....	....	2	....	....	....	....	....	....	....	....	....	....	....	....	....	....	....	....	....	....
1973-74	**Toronto Maple Leafs**	**NHL**	**66**	**20**	**23**	**43**	**19**	**19**	**38**	**14**	**4**	**0**	**4**	**135**	**14.8**	**79**	**21**	**41**	**0**	**17**	**4**	**1**	**0**	**1**	**0**	**0**	**0**	**0**
1974-75	**Toronto Maple Leafs**	**NHL**	**69**	**21**	**20**	**41**	**18**	**15**	**33**	**23**	**3**	**0**	**2**	**170**	**12.4**	**61**	**15**	**60**	**0**	**–14**	**7**	**1**	**3**	**4**	**4**	**0**	**0**	**1**
1975-76	**Toronto Maple Leafs**	**NHL**	**76**	**19**	**21**	**40**	**17**	**16**	**33**	**21**	**1**	**0**	**5**	**189**	**10.1**	**65**	**15**	**55**	**5**	**0**	....	....	....	....	....	....	....	....
1976-77	Sweden	Can-Cup	5	1	2	3	....	....	....	2	....	....	....	....	....	....	....	....	....	....	....	....	....	....	....	....	....	....
	Toronto Maple Leafs	**NHL**	**78**	**24**	**17**	**41**	**22**	**13**	**35**	**16**	**5**	**0**	**3**	**154**	**15.6**	**80**	**19**	**53**	**0**	**8**	**2**	**0**	**0**	**0**	**0**	**0**	**0**	**0**
1977-78	**Toronto Maple Leafs**	**NHL**	**3**	**1**	**1**	**2**	**1**	**1**	**2**	**0**	**1**	**0**	**0**	**6**	**16.7**	**3**	**2**	**0**	**0**	**1**	....	....	....	....	....	....	....	....
	St. Louis Blues	**NHL**	**70**	**19**	**19**	**38**	**17**	**15**	**32**	**4**	**3**	**0**	**2**	**165**	**11.5**	**55**	**16**	**60**	**0**	**–21**	....	....	....	....	....	....	....	....
1978-79	**St. Louis Blues**	**NHL**	**65**	**12**	**22**	**34**	**10**	**16**	**26**	**8**	**0**	**0**	**1**	**129**	**9.3**	**45**	**7**	**51**	**0**	**–13**	....	....	....	....	....	....	....	....
	Sweden	WEC-A	8	4	1	5	....	....	....	2	....	....	....	....	....	....	....	....	....	....	....	....	....	....	....	....	....	....
1979-80	Brynas IF Gavle	Sweden	34	16	10	26	....	....	....	30	....	....	....	....	....	....	....	....	....	....	7	*5	3	*8	6	....	....	....
1980-81	Brynas IF Gavle	Sweden	29	13	8	21	....	....	....	20	....	....	....	....	....	....	....	....	....	....	....	....	....	....	....	....	....	....
	Sweden	WEC-A	6	1	1	2	....	....	....	2	....	....	....	....	....	....	....	....	....	....	....	....	....	....	....	....	....	....
1981-82	Brynas IF Gavle	Sweden	34	10	12	22	....	....	....	20	....	....	....	....	....	....	....	....	....	....	....	....	....	....	....	....	....	....
	NHL Totals		**427**	**116**	**123**	**239**	**104**	**95**	**199**	**86**	**17**	**0**	**17**	**948**	**12.2**	**388**	**95**	**320**	**5**		**13**	**2**	**3**	**5**	**4**	**0**	**0**	**1**

• Playoff statistics for Brynas IF (1968-69) are Relegation Round totals. Signed as a free agent by **Toronto**, May 12, 1973. Traded to **St. Louis** by **Toronto** for Jerry Butler, November 1, 1977.

• HAMMOND, Ken Ken Paul D – L. 6'1", 190 lbs. b: Port Credit, Ont., 8/22/1963. Los Angeles' 8th, 152nd overall, in 1983.

Season	Club	League	GP	G	A	Pts	AG	AA	APts	PIM	PP	SH	GW	S	%	TGF	PGF	TGA	PGA	+/–	Playoffs GP	G	A	Pts	PIM	PP	SH	GW
1980-81	London Diamonds	OHA-B	40	12	16	28	....	....	....	89	....	....	....	....	....	....	....	....	....	....	4	1	1	2	0	....	....	....
1981-82	RPI Engineers	ECAC	24	2	3	5	....	....	....	54	....	....	....	....	....	....	....	....	....	....	....	....	....	....	....	....	....	....
1982-83	RPI Engineers	ECAC	28	17	26	43	....	....	....	8	....	....	....	....	....	....	....	....	....	....	....	....	....	....	....	....	....	....
1983-84	RPI Engineers	ECAC	34	5	11	16	....	....	....	72	....	....	....	....	....	....	....	....	....	....	....	....	....	....	....	....	....	....
1984-85	RPI Engineers	ECAC	38	11	28	39	....	....	....	90	....	....	....	....	....	....	....	....	....	....	....	....	....	....	....	....	....	....
	Los Angeles Kings	**NHL**	**3**	**1**	**0**	**1**	**1**	**0**	**1**	**0**	**0**	**0**	**1**	**3**	**33.3**	**4**	**0**	**5**	**3**	**2**	**3**	**0**	**0**	**0**	**4**	**0**	**0**	**0**
1985-86	**Los Angeles Kings**	**NHL**	**3**	**0**	**1**	**1**	**0**	**1**	**1**	**2**	**0**	**0**	**0**	**2**	**0.0**	**4**	**1**	**6**	**2**	**–1**	....	....	....	....	....	....	....	....
	New Haven Nighthawks	AHL	67	4	12	16	....	....	....	96	....	....	....	....	....	....	....	....	....	....	4	0	0	0	7	....	....	....
1986-87	**Los Angeles Kings**	**NHL**	**10**	**0**	**2**	**2**	**0**	**1**	**1**	**11**	....	....	....	....	....	....	....	....	....	....	....	....	....	....	....	....	....	....
	New Haven Nighthawks	AHL	66	1	15	16	....	....	....	76	....	....	....	....	....	....	....	....	....	....	6	0	1	1	21	....	....	....
1987-88	**Los Angeles Kings**	**NHL**	**46**	**7**	**9**	**16**	**6**	**6**	**12**	**69**	**1**	**0**	**1**	**52**	**13.5**	**47**	**8**	**53**	**13**	**–1**	**2**	**0**	**0**	**0**	**4**	**0**	**0**	**0**
	New Haven Nighthawks	AHL	26	3	8	11	....	....	....	27	....	....	....	....	....	....	....	....	....	....	....	....	....	....	....	....	....	....
1988-89	**Edmonton Oilers**	**NHL**	**5**	**0**	**1**	**1**	**0**	**1**	**1**	**8**	**0**	**0**	**0**	**1**	**0.0**	**2**	**0**	**4**	**0**	**–2**	....	....	....	....	....	....	....	....
	New York Rangers	**NHL**	**3**	**0**	**0**	**0**	**0**	**0**	**0**	**0**	**0**	**0**	**0**	**2**	**0.0**	**1**	**0**	**5**	**1**	**–3**	....	....	....	....	....	....	....	....
	Denver Rangers	IHL	38	5	18	23	....	....	....	24	....	....	....	....	....	....	....	....	....	....	....	....	....	....	....	....	....	....
	Toronto Maple Leafs	**NHL**	**14**	**0**	**2**	**2**	**0**	**1**	**1**	**12**	**0**	**0**	**0**	**9**	**0.0**	**6**	**0**	**23**	**4**	**–13**	....	....	....	....	....	....	....	....
1989-90	Newmarket Saints	AHL	75	9	45	54	....	....	....	106	....	....	....	....	....	....	....	....	....	....	....	....	....	....	....	....	....	....
1990-91	**Boston Bruins**	**NHL**	**1**	**1**	**0**	**1**	**1**	**0**	**1**	**2**	**0**	**0**	**0**	**3**	**33.3**	**2**	**0**	**0**	**0**	**2**	**8**	**0**	**0**	**0**	**10**	**0**	**0**	**0**
	Maine Mariners	AHL	80	10	41	51	....	....	....	159	....	....	....	....	....	....	....	....	....	....	2	0	1	1	16	....	....	....
1991-92	**San Jose Sharks**	**NHL**	**46**	**5**	**10**	**15**	**5**	**8**	**13**	**82**	**2**	**0**	**0**	**93**	**5.4**	**44**	**12**	**65**	**16**	**–17**	....	....	....	....	....	....	....	....
	Vancouver Canucks	**NHL**	....	....	....	....	....	....	....	....	....	....	....	....	....	....	....	....	....	....	**2**	**0**	**0**	**0**	**6**	**0**	**0**	**0**
1992-93	**Ottawa Senators**	**NHL**	**62**	**4**	**4**	**8**	**3**	**3**	**6**	**104**	**0**	**0**	**0**	**64**	**6.3**	**32**	**4**	**101**	**31**	**–42**	....	....	....	....	....	....	....	....
	New Haven Senators	AHL	4	0	1	1	....	....	....	4	....	....	....	....	....	....	....	....	....	....	....	....	....	....	....	....	....	....
1993-94	Providence Bruins	AHL	65	12	45	57	....	....	....	100	....	....	....	....	....	....	....	....	....	....	....	....	....	....	....	....	....	....
1994-95	Kansas City Blades	IHL	76	3	24	27	....	....	....	151	....	....	....	....	....	....	....	....	....	....	21	1	4	5	45	....	....	....
1995-96	Kansas City Blades	IHL	33	1	7	8	....	....	....	62	....	....	....	....	....	....	....	....	....	....	....	....	....	....	....	....	....	....
	NHL Totals		**193**	**18**	**29**	**47**	**16**	**21**	**37**	**290**	**3**	**0**	**2**	**229**	**7.9**	**142**	**25**	**262**	**70**		**15**	**0**	**0**	**0**	**24**	**0**	**0**	**0**

ECAC First All-Star Team (1985) • NCAA East First All-American Team (1985) • NCAA Championship All-Tournament Team (1985)

Claimed by **Edmonton** from **LA Kings** in Waiver Draft, October 3, 1988. Claimed on waivers by **NY Rangers** from **Edmonton**, November 1, 1988. Traded to **Toronto** by **NY Rangers** for Chris McRae, February 21, 1989. Traded to **Boston** by **Toronto** for cash, August 20, 1990. Signed as a free agent by **San Jose**, August 9, 1991. Traded to **Vancouver** by **San Jose** for Vancouver's 8th round choice (later traded to Detroit — Detroit selected C.J. Denomme) in 1992 Entry Draft, March 9, 1992. Claimed by **Ottawa** from **Vancouver** in Expansion Draft, June 18, 1992.

• HAMPSON, Gord Gordon LW – L. 6'3", 210 lbs. b: Vancouver, B.C., 2/13/1959.

Season	Club	League	GP	G	A	Pts	AG	AA	APts	PIM	PP	SH	GW	S	%	TGF	PGF	TGA	PGA	+/–	Playoffs GP	G	A	Pts	PIM	PP	SH	GW
1976-77	Edina High School	Hi-School	STATISTICS NOT AVAILABLE																									
1977-78	University of Michigan	WCHA	36	9	7	16	....	....	....	21	....	....	....	....	....	....	....	....	....	....	....	....	....	....	....	....	....	....
1978-79	University of Michigan	WCHA	36	6	6	12	....	....	....	24	....	....	....	....	....	....	....	....	....	....	....	....	....	....	....	....	....	....
1979-80	University of Michigan	WCHA	30	7	15	22	....	....	....	22	....	....	....	....	....	....	....	....	....	....	....	....	....	....	....	....	....	....
1980-81	University of Michigan	WCHA	40	15	23	38	....	....	....	40	....	....	....	....	....	....	....	....	....	....	....	....	....	....	....	....	....	....
1981-82	Oklahoma City Stars	CHL	71	11	23	34	....	....	....	48	....	....	....	....	....	....	....	....	....	....	1	0	0	0	0	....	....	....
1982-83	**Calgary Flames**	**NHL**	**4**	**0**	**0**	**0**	**0**	**0**	**0**	**5**	**0**	**0**	**0**	**4**	**0.0**	**0**	**0**	**2**	**0**	**–2**	....	....	....	....	....	....	....	....
	Colorado Flames	CHL	51	17	17	34	....	....	....	73	....	....	....	....	....	....	....	....	....	....	6	2	5	7	4	....	....	....
1983-84	Colorado Flames	CHL	62	19	25	44	....	....	....	89	....	....	....	....	....	....	....	....	....	....	....	....	....	....	....	....	....	....
	NHL Totals		**4**	**0**	**0**	**0**	**0**	**0**	**0**	**5**	**0**	**0**	**0**	**4**	**0.0**	**0**	**0**	**2**	**0**		....	....	....	....	....	....	....	....

• Son of Ted

Signed as a free agent by **Calgary**, June 8, 1981.

• HAMPSON, Ted Edward George C – L. 5'8", 173 lbs. b: Togo, Sask., 12/11/1936.

Season	Club	League	GP	G	A	Pts	AG	AA	APts	PIM	PP	SH	GW	S	%	TGF	PGF	TGA	PGA	+/–	Playoffs GP	G	A	Pts	PIM	PP	SH	GW
1953-54	Flin Flon Bombers	SJHL	....	....	....	....	....	....	....	....	....	....	....	....	....	....	....	....	....	....	1	1	0	1	0	....	....	....
	Flin Flon Bombers	Mem-Cup	2	1	1	2	....	....	....	0	....	....	....	....	....	....	....	....	....	....	....	....	....	....	....	....	....	....
1954-55	Flin Flon Bombers	SJHL	13	6	6	12	....	....	....	4	....	....	....	....	....	....	....	....	....	....	....	....	....	....	....	....	....	....
1955-56	Flin Flon Bombers	SJHL	48	51	*62	*113	....	....	....	16	....	....	....	....	....	....	....	....	....	....	12	*9	*12	*21	4	....	....	....
	Flin Flon Bombers	Mem-Cup	7	5	1	6	....	....	....	2	....	....	....	....	....	....	....	....	....	....	....	....	....	....	....	....	....	....
1956-57	Flin Flon Bombers	SJHL	55	48	*70	*118	....	....	....	37	....	....	....	....	....	....	....	....	....	....	10	6	*13	19	4	....	....	....
	Brandon Regals	WHL	2	1	3	4	....	....	....	0	....	....	....	....	....	....	....	....	....	....	....	....	....	....	....	....	....	....
	Flin Flon Bombers	Mem-Cup	17	7	*17	24	....	....	....	6	....	....	....	....	....	....	....	....	....	....	....	....	....	....	....	....	....	....
1957-58	Providence Reds	AHL	70	15	25	40	....	....	....	22	....	....	....	....	....	....	....	....	....	....	5	0	2	2	0	....	....	....
1958-59	Vancouver Canucks	WHL	66	27	41	68	....	....	....	23	....	....	....	....	....	....	....	....	....	....	9	1	4	5	0	....	....	....
1959-60	**Toronto Maple Leafs**	**NHL**	**41**	**2**	**8**	**10**	**2**	**8**	**10**	**17**	....	....	....	....	....	....	....	....	....	....	....	....	....	....	....	....	....	....
	Rochester Americans	AHL	29	6	18	24	....	....	....	9	....	....	....	....	....	....	....	....	....	....	12	2	4	6	2	....	....	....
1960-61	**New York Rangers**	**NHL**	**69**	**6**	**14**	**20**	**7**	**13**	**20**	**4**	....	....	....	....	....	....	....	....	....	....	....	....	....	....	....	....	....	....
1961-62	**New York Rangers**	**NHL**	**68**	**4**	**24**	**28**	**5**	**23**	**28**	**10**	....	....	....	....	....	....	....	....	....	....	**6**	**0**	**1**	**1**	**0**	**0**	**0**	**0**

			REGULAR SEASON																		PLAYOFFS							
Season	Club	League	GP	G	A	Pts	AG	AA	APts	PIM	PP	SH	GW	S	%	TGF	PGF	TGA	PGA	+/-	GP	G	A	Pts	PIM	PP	SH	GW
1962-63	**New York Rangers**	NHL	46	4	2	6	5	2	7	2																		
	Baltimore Clippers	AHL	22	12	14	26				4											3	1	2	3	0			
1963-64	**Detroit Red Wings**	NHL	7	0	1	1	0	1	1	0																		
	Pittsburgh Hornets	AHL	66	15	33	48				6											5	2	2	4	0			
1964-65	**Detroit Red Wings**	NHL	1	0	0	0	0	0	0	0																		
	Pittsburgh Hornets	AHL	64	15	39	54				39											4	1	2	3	2			
1965-66	Pittsburgh Hornets	AHL	72	20	29	49				6											3	1	0	1	0			
1966-67	**Detroit Red Wings**	NHL	65	13	35	48	15	34	49	4																		
	Pittsburgh Hornets	AHL	7	1	4	5				2																		
1967-68	**Detroit Red Wings**	NHL	37	9	18	27	10	18	28	10	0	0	2	75	12.0	38	6	27	3	8								
	Oakland Seals	NHL	34	8	19	27	9	19	28	4	2	0	1	72	11.1	35	14	39	8	–10								
1968-69	**Oakland Seals**	NHL	76	26	49	75	28	44	72	6	9	0	3	189	13.8	101	30	89	3	–15	7	3	4	7	2	2	0	0
1969-70	**Oakland Seals**	NHL	76	17	35	52	18	33	51	13	7	1	0	157	10.8	74	26	87	22	–17	4	1	1	2	0	0	0	0
1970-71	**California Golden Seals**	NHL	60	10	20	30	10	17	27	14	1	1	0	124	8.1	47	10	89	31	–21								
	Minnesota North Stars	NHL	18	4	6	10	4	5	9	4	1	3	2	34	11.8	11	2	15	5	–1	11	3	3	6	0	1	0	0
1971-72	**Minnesota North Stars**	NHL	78	5	14	19	5	12	17	6	0	2	0	100	5.0	26	1	61	35	–1	7	0	1	1	0	0	0	0
1972-73	Minnesota Fighting Saints	WHA	76	17	45	62				20											5	1	3	4	0			
1973-74	Minnesota Fighting Saints	WHA	77	17	38	55				9											11	4	4	8	8			
1974-75	Minnesota Fighting Saints	WHA	78	17	36	53				6											12	1	7	8	0			
1975-76	Minnesota Fighting Saints	WHA	59	5	15	20				14																		
	Quebec Nordiques	WHA	14	4	10	14				2											5	0	2	2	10			
1976-77	Bloomington Jr. Stars	MWJHL	DID NOT PLAY – COACHING																									
1977-78	Bloomington Jr. Stars	MWJHL	DID NOT PLAY – COACHING																									
1978-79	Oklahoma City Stars	CHL	23	2	7	9				4																		
1979-80	Oklahoma City Stars	CHL	3	0	1	1				0																		
1980-81	Oklahoma City Stars	CHL	6	0	0	0				12																		
	NHL Totals		676	108	245	353	118	229	347	94											35	7	10	17	2			
	Other Major League Totals		304	60	144	204				51											33	6	16	22	18			

• Father of Gord • SJHL First All-Star Team (1957) • Won Bill Masterton Trophy (1969) • Won Paul Daneau Trophy (WHA Most Gentlemanly Player) (1973) • Played in NHL All-Star Game (1969)

Claimed on waivers by **Toronto** from **NY Rangers**, September 18, 1959. Claimed by **NY Rangers** from **Toronto** in Intra-League Draft, June 8, 1960. Claimed by **Detroit** from **NY Rangers** in Intra-League Draft, June 4, 1963. Traded to **Oakland** by **Detroit** with John Brenneman and Bert Marshall for Kent Douglas, January 9, 1968. Traded to **Minnesota** by **California** with Wayne Muloin for Tom Williams and Dick Redmond, March 7, 1971. Selected by **Winnipeg** (WHA) in 1972 WHA General Player Draft, February 12, 1972. Claimed by **NY Islanders** from **Minnesota** in Expansion Draft, June 6, 1972. WHA rights traded to **Minnesota** (WHA) by **Winnipeg** (WHA) for cash, August, 1972. Signed as a free agent by **Quebec** (WHA) after **Minnesota** (WHA) franchise folded, February 27, 1976. Signed as a free agent by **Minnesota**, January 1, 1979.

• HAMPTON, Rick

Richard Charles LW/D – L. 6', 190 lbs. b: King City, Ont., 6/14/1956. California's 1st, 3rd overall, in 1974.

Season	Club	League	GP	G	A	Pts	AG	AA	APts	PIM	PP	SH	GW	S	%	TGF	PGF	TGA	PGA	+/-	GP	G	A	Pts	PIM	PP	SH	GW
1972-73	St. Catharines Black Hawks	OMJHL	50	1	20	21				98																		
1973-74	St. Catharines Black Hawks	OMJHL	65	25	25	50				110											12	3	8	11				
	St. Catharines Black Hawks	M-Cup	3	2	0	2				4																		
1974-75	**California Golden Seals**	NHL	78	8	17	25	7	13	20	39	1	1	0	99	8.1	64	25	88	9	–40								
1975-76	**California Golden Seals**	NHL	73	14	37	51	12	28	40	54	8	0	2	106	13.2	129	44	107	10	–12								
1976-77	**Cleveland Barons**	NHL	57	16	24	40	14	18	32	13	5	0	1	114	14.0	72	30	54	1	–11								
	Canada	WEC-A	10	1	2	3				4																		
1977-78	**Cleveland Barons**	NHL	77	18	18	36	16	14	30	19	3	0	0	159	11.3	62	23	81	18	–24								
	Canada	WEC-A	10	0	0	0				9																		
1978-79	**Los Angeles Kings**	NHL	49	3	17	20	3	12	15	22	0	0	0	70	4.3	62	8	65	11	0	2	0	0	0	0	0	0	0
1979-80	**Los Angeles Kings**	NHL	3	0	0	0	0	0	0	0	0	0	0	1	0.0	3	0	2	2	3								
	Binghamton Dusters	AHL	19	4	5	9				11																		
1980-81	Houston Apollos	CHL	33	11	13	24				17																		
	New Brunswick Hawks	AHL	36	4	23	27				37											13	0	1	1	30			
1981-82	HC Ambri-Piotta	Switz-2	STATISTICS NOT AVAILABLE																									
1982-83	HC Ambri-Piotta	Switz-2	32	3	8	11				7																		
1983-84	Rochester Americans	AHL	21	1	3	4				7																		
	NHL Totals		337	59	113	172	52	85	137	147	17	1	3	549	10.7	392	130	397	51		2	0	0	0	0	0	0	0

Transferred to **Cleveland** after **California** franchise relocated, August 26, 1976. Placed on **Minnesota** Reserve List prior to Minnesota-Cleveland Dispersal Draft, June 14, 1978. Transferred to **LA Kings** by **Minnesota** with Steve Jensen and Dave Gardner as compensation for Minnesota's signing of free agent Gary Sargent, July, 1978

• HAMR, Radek

D – L. 5'11", 175 lbs. b: Usti-Nad-Labem, Czech., 6/15/1974. Ottawa's 4th, 73rd overall, in 1992.

Season	Club	League	GP	G	A	Pts	AG	AA	APts	PIM	PP	SH	GW	S	%	TGF	PGF	TGA	PGA	+/-	GP	G	A	Pts	PIM	PP	SH	GW
1991-92	HC Sparta Praha	Czech.	3	0	0	0																						
	Czechoslovakia	EJC-A	6	1	2	3				6																		
1992-93	**Ottawa Senators**	NHL	4	0	0	0	0	0	0	0	0	0	0	2	0.0	0	0	5	1	–4								
	New Haven Senators	AHL	59	4	21	25				18																		
1993-94	**Ottawa Senators**	NHL	7	0	0	0	0	0	0	0	0	0	0	5	0.0	4	4	11	1	–10								
	P.E.I. Senators	AHL	69	10	26	36				44																		
1994-95	P.E.I. Senators	AHL	7	0	1	1				2																		
	Fort Wayne Komets	IHL	58	3	13	16				14											1	0	0	0	0			
1995-96	HC Sparta Praha	Czech-Rep	30	2	3	5															4	0	0	0				
1996-97	HC Sparta Praha	Czech-Rep	52	12	23	35				4											10	2	5	7	4			
	HC Sparta Praha	EuroHL	6	1	3	4				0											4	0	3	3	2			
1997-98	Vastra Frolunda	Sweden	46	2	12	14				36											7	1	2	3	29			
1998-99	Vastra Frolunda	Sweden	9	0	0	0				6																		
	Farjestads BK Karlstad	Sweden	38	6	11	17				26											4	1	0	1	0			
99-2000	Farjestads BK Karlstad	Sweden	50	7	14	21				46											7	0	1	1	6			
	NHL Totals		11	0	0	0	0	0	0	0	0	0	0	7	0.0	4	4	16	2									

• HAMRLIK, Roman

D – L. 6'2", 215 lbs. b: Gottwaldov, Czech., 4/12/1974. Tampa Bay's 1st, 1st overall, in 1992.

Season	Club	League	GP	G	A	Pts	AG	AA	APts	PIM	PP	SH	GW	S	%	TGF	PGF	TGA	PGA	+/-	GP	G	A	Pts	PIM	PP	SH	GW
1990-91	ZPS Zlin	Czech.	14	2	2	4				18																		
	Czechoslovakia	EJC-A	5	0	4	4				2																		
1991-92	ZPS Zlin	Czech.	34	5	5	10				50																		
	Czechoslovakia	WJC-A	7	3	0	3				8																		
	Czechoslovakia	EJC-A	6	1	1	2				8																		
1992-93	**Tampa Bay Lightning**	NHL	67	6	15	21	5	10	15	71	1	0	1	113	5.3	53	14	66	6	–21								
	Atlanta Knights	IHL	2	1	1	2				2																		
1993-94	**Tampa Bay Lightning**	NHL	64	3	18	21	3	14	17	135	0	0	0	158	1.9	58	18	59	5	–14								
	Czech-Republic	WC-A	1	0	0	0				0																		
1994-95	ZPS Zlin	Czech-Rep	2	1	0	1				10																		
	Tampa Bay Lightning	NHL	48	12	11	23	21	16	37	86	7	1	2	134	9.0	55	23	69	19	–18								
1995-96	**Tampa Bay Lightning**	NHL	82	16	49	65	16	40	56	103	12	0	2	281	5.7	130	66	109	21	–24	5	0	1	1	4	0	0	0
1996-97	Czech-Republic	W-Cup	3	0	0	0				4																		
	Tampa Bay Lightning	NHL	79	12	28	40	13	25	38	57	6	0	0	238	5.0	96	37	92	4	–29								
1997-98	**Tampa Bay Lightning**	NHL	37	3	12	15	4	12	16	22	1	0	0	86	3.5	34	14	45	7	–18								
	Edmonton Oilers	NHL	41	6	20	26	7	20	27	48	4	1	3	112	5.4	60	31	40	14	3	12	0	6	6	12	0	0	0
	Czech-Republic	Olympics	6	1	0	1				2																		

Season	Club	League	GP	G	A	Pts	AG	AA	APts	PIM	PP	SH	GW	S	%	TGF	PGF	TGA	PGA	+/–	GP	G	A	Pts	PIM	PP	SH	GW
			REGULAR SEASON																		PLAYOFFS							
1998-99	**Edmonton Oilers**	**NHL**	**75**	**8**	**24**	**32**	**9**	**23**	**32**	**70**	**3**	**0**	**0**	**172**	**4.7**	**97**	**28**	**87**	**27**	**9**	**3**	**0**	**0**	**0**	**2**	**0**	**0**	**0**
99-2000	HC Barum Zlin	Czech-Rep	6	0	3	3	....	....	....	4	....	....	....	....	....	....	....	....	....	....	....	....	....	....	....	....	....	....
	Edmonton Oilers	**NHL**	**80**	**8**	**37**	**45**	**9**	**34**	**43**	**68**	**5**	**0**	**0**	**180**	**4.4**	**98**	**37**	**76**	**16**	**1**	**5**	**0**	**1**	**1**	**4**	**0**	**0**	**0**
	NHL Totals		**573**	**74**	**214**	**288**	**87**	**194**	**281**	**660**	**39**	**2**	**8**	**1474**	**5.0**	**681**	**268**	**643**	**119**		**25**	**0**	**8**	**8**	**22**	**0**	**0**	**0**

Named Best Defenseman at EJC-A (1991) • EJC-A All-Star Team (1992) @FNOT = Played in NHL All-Star Game (1996, 1999)

Traded to **Edmonton** by **Tampa Bay** with Paul Comrie for Bryan Marchment, Steve Kelly and Jason Bonsignore, December 30, 1997. Traded to **NY Islanders** by **Edmonton** for Eric Brewer, Josh Green and NY Islanders' 2nd round choice (Brad Winchester) in 2000 Entry Draft, June 24, 2000.

• HAMWAY, Mark

RW – R. 6', 190 lbs. b: Detroit, MI, 8/9/1961. NY Islanders' 8th, 143rd overall, in 1980.

Season	Club	League	GP	G	A	Pts	AG	AA	APts	PIM	PP	SH	GW	S	%	TGF	PGF	TGA	PGA	+/–	GP	G	A	Pts	PIM	PP	SH	GW
1977-78	Detroit Nationals	MNHL	75	70	90	160	....	....	....	....	....	....	....	....	....	....	....	....	....	....	....	....	....	....	....	....	....	....
1978-79	Windsor Spitfires	OMJHL	66	27	42	69	....	....	....	29	....	....	....	....	....	....	....	....	....	....	....	....	....	....	....	....	....	....
1979-80	Michigan State Spartans	WCHA	38	16	28	44	....	....	....	28	....	....	....	....	....	....	....	....	....	....	....	....	....	....	....	....	....	....
1980-81	Michigan State Spartans	WCHA	35	18	15	33	....	....	....	20	....	....	....	....	....	....	....	....	....	....	....	....	....	....	....	....	....	....
1981-82	Michigan State Spartans	WCHA	41	34	31	65	....	....	....	37	....	....	....	....	....	....	....	....	....	....	....	....	....	....	....	....	....	....
1982-83	Michigan State Spartans	WCHA	32	22	21	43	....	....	....	10	....	....	....	....	....	....	....	....	....	....	....	....	....	....	....	....	....	....
1983-84	Indianapolis Checkers	CHL	71	22	32	54	....	....	....	38	....	....	....	....	....	....	....	....	....	....	9	1	1	2	0	....	....	....
1984-85	**New York Islanders**	**NHL**	**2**	**0**	**0**	**0**	**0**	**0**	**0**	**0**	**0**	**0**	**0**	**1**	**0.0**	**0**	**0**	**0**	**0**	**0**	....	....	....	....	....	....	....	....
	Springfield Indians	AHL	75	29	34	63	....	....	....	29	....	....	....	....	....	....	....	....	....	....	4	0	1	1	0	....	....	....
1985-86	**New York Islanders**	**NHL**	**49**	**5**	**12**	**17**	**4**	**8**	**12**	**9**	**1**	**0**	**1**	**50**	**10.0**	**21**	**1**	**26**	**1**	**–5**	**1**	**0**	**0**	**0**	**0**	**0**	**0**	**0**
	Springfield Indians	AHL	14	5	8	13	....	....	....	7	....	....	....	....	....	....	....	....	....	....	....	....	....	....	....	....	....	....
1986-87	**New York Islanders**	**NHL**	**2**	**0**	**1**	**1**	**0**	**1**	**1**	**0**	**0**	**0**	**0**	**1**	**0.0**	**1**	**0**	**2**	**0**	**–1**	....	....	....	....	....	....	....	....
	Springfield Indians	AHL	59	25	31	56	....	....	....	8	....	....	....	....	....	....	....	....	....	....	....	....	....	....	....	....	....	....
	NHL Totals		**53**	**5**	**13**	**18**	**4**	**9**	**13**	**9**	**1**	**0**	**1**	**52**	**9.6**	**22**	**1**	**28**	**1**		**1**	**0**	**0**	**0**	**0**	**0**	**0**	**0**

CCHA Second All-Star Team (1982)

• HANDY, Ron

Ronald LW – L. 5'11", 175 lbs. b: Toronto, Ont., 1/15/1963. NY Islanders' 3rd, 57th overall, in 1981.

Season	Club	League	GP	G	A	Pts	AG	AA	APts	PIM	PP	SH	GW	S	%	TGF	PGF	TGA	PGA	+/–	GP	G	A	Pts	PIM	PP	SH	GW
1979-80	Toronto Midget Marlboros	MTHL	39	48	60	108	....	....	....	....	....	....	....	....	....	....	....	....	....	....	....	....	....	....	....	....	....	....
	Port Credit Titans	OHA-B	3	2	3	5	....	....	....	0	....	....	....	....	....	....	....	....	....	....	....	....	....	....	....	....	....	....
1980-81	Sault Ste. Marie Greyhounds	OMJHL	66	43	43	86	....	....	....	45	....	....	....	....	....	....	....	....	....	....	18	3	5	8	25	....	....	....
1981-82	Sault Ste. Marie Greyhounds	OHL	20	15	10	25	....	....	....	20	....	....	....	....	....	....	....	....	....	....	....	....	....	....	....	....	....	....
	Kingston Canadians	OHL	44	35	38	73	....	....	....	23	....	....	....	....	....	....	....	....	....	....	4	1	1	2	16	....	....	....
1982-83	Kingston Canadians	OHL	67	52	96	148	....	....	....	64	....	....	....	....	....	....	....	....	....	....	....	....	....	....	....	....	....	....
	Indianapolis Checkers	CHL	9	2	7	9	....	....	....	0	....	....	....	....	....	....	....	....	....	....	10	3	8	11	18	....	....	....
1983-84	Indianapolis Checkers	CHL	66	29	46	75	....	....	....	40	....	....	....	....	....	....	....	....	....	....	10	2	5	7	0	....	....	....
1984-85	**New York Islanders**	**NHL**	**10**	**0**	**2**	**2**	**0**	**1**	**1**	**0**	**0**	**0**	**0**	**6**	**0.0**	**4**	**1**	**4**	**0**	**–1**	....	....	....	....	....	....	....	....
	Springfield Indians	AHL	69	29	35	64	....	....	....	38	....	....	....	....	....	....	....	....	....	....	3	2	2	4	0	....	....	....
1985-86	Springfield Indians	AHL	79	31	30	61	....	....	....	66	....	....	....	....	....	....	....	....	....	....	....	....	....	....	....	....	....	....
1986-87	Indianapolis Checkers	IHL	82	*55	80	135	....	....	....	57	....	....	....	....	....	....	....	....	....	....	6	4	3	7	2	....	....	....
1987-88	**St. Louis Blues**	**NHL**	**4**	**0**	**1**	**1**	**0**	**1**	**1**	**0**	**0**	**0**	**0**	**4**	**0.0**	**1**	**0**	**3**	**1**	**–1**	....	....	....	....	....	....	....	....
	Peoria Rivermen	IHL	78	53	63	116	....	....	....	61	....	....	....	....	....	....	....	....	....	....	7	2	3	5	4	....	....	....
1988-89	Indianapolis Ice	IHL	81	43	57	100	....	....	....	24	....	....	....	....	....	....	....	....	....	....	....	....	....	....	....	....	....	....
1989-90	Fort Wayne Komets	IHL	82	36	39	75	....	....	....	52	....	....	....	....	....	....	....	....	....	....	5	3	1	4	0	....	....	....
1990-91	Kansas City Blades	IHL	64	42	39	81	....	....	....	41	....	....	....	....	....	....	....	....	....	....	....	....	....	....	....	....	....	....
1991-92	Kansas City Blades	IHL	38	16	19	35	....	....	....	30	....	....	....	....	....	....	....	....	....	....	15	*13	8	*21	8	....	....	....
1992-93	Peoria Rivermen	IHL	18	0	7	7	....	....	....	16	....	....	....	....	....	....	....	....	....	....	....	....	....	....	....	....	....	....
	Kansas City Blades	IHL	6	1	1	2	....	....	....	2	....	....	....	....	....	....	....	....	....	....	....	....	....	....	....	....	....	....
	Wichita Thunder	CHL	11	6	12	18	....	....	....	20	....	....	....	....	....	....	....	....	....	....	....	....	....	....	....	....	....	....
1993-94	Wichita Thunder	CHL	57	29	80	109	....	....	....	98	....	....	....	....	....	....	....	....	....	....	11	12	10	22	12	....	....	....
1994-95	Sheffield Steelers	BH-Cup	12	10	10	20	....	....	....	31	....	....	....	....	....	....	....	....	....	....	....	....	....	....	....	....	....	....
	Sheffield Steelers	Britain	6	8	6	14	....	....	....	2	....	....	....	....	....	....	....	....	....	....	....	....	....	....	....	....	....	....
	Denver Grizzlies	IHL	1	0	0	0	....	....	....	0	....	....	....	....	....	....	....	....	....	....	....	....	....	....	....	....	....	....
	Wichita Thunder	CHL	46	24	45	69	....	....	....	72	....	....	....	....	....	....	....	....	....	....	11	*15	16	*31	4	....	....	....
1995-96	Huntsville Channel Cats	SHL	3	3	1	4	....	....	....	0	....	....	....	....	....	....	....	....	....	....	....	....	....	....	....	....	....	....
	Louisiana IceGators	ECHL	58	20	65	85	....	....	....	34	....	....	....	....	....	....	....	....	....	....	5	2	4	6	2	....	....	....
1996-97	Louisiana IceGators	ECHL	66	33	*67	100	....	....	....	58	....	....	....	....	....	....	....	....	....	....	17	5	17	22	0	....	....	....
1997-98	Huntsville Channel Cats	CHL	46	27	33	60	....	....	....	50	....	....	....	....	....	....	....	....	....	....	2	0	1	1	0	....	....	....
1998-99	Lake Charles Ice Pirates	WPHL	15	5	10	15	....	....	....	21	....	....	....	....	....	....	....	....	....	....	....	....	....	....	....	....	....	....
99-2000	Arkansas RiverBlades	ECHL	9	1	1	2	....	....	....	8	....	....	....	....	....	....	....	....	....	....	....	....	....	....	....	....	....	....
	NHL Totals		**14**	**0**	**3**	**3**	**0**	**2**	**2**	**0**	**0**	**0**	**0**	**10**	**0.0**	**5**	**1**	**7**	**1**		....	....	....	....	....	....	....	....

CHL Second All-Star Team (1984, 1994) • IHL Second All-Star Team (1987) • IHL First All-Star Team (1988) • Won "Bud" Poile Trophy (Playoff MVP - IHL) (1992) • Won President's Trophy (CHL's Playoff MVP) (1994, 1995)

Signed as a free agent by **St. Louis**, September, 1987. • Named Head Coach of **Arkansas** (ECHL), December 15, 2000. • Played w/ RHI's Utah Rollerbees in 1993 (6-7-10-17-12) and Chicago Cheetahs in 1994 (22-21-20-41-32).

• HANDZUS, Michal

"Zeus" C – L. 6'5", 210 lbs. b: Banska Bystrica, Czech., 3/11/1977. St. Louis' 3rd, 101st overall, in 1995.

Season	Club	League	GP	G	A	Pts	AG	AA	APts	PIM	PP	SH	GW	S	%	TGF	PGF	TGA	PGA	+/–	GP	G	A	Pts	PIM	PP	SH	GW
1993-94	Banska Bystrica	Slovakia-Jr.	40	23	36	59	....	....	....	....	....	....	....	....	....	....	....	....	....	....	....	....	....	....	....	....	....	....
1994-95	Banska Bystrica	Slovakia-2	22	15	14	29	....	....	....	10	....	....	....	....	....	....	....	....	....	....	....	....	....	....	....	....	....	....
	Slovakia	EJC-B	5	5	3	8	....	....	....	4	....	....	....	....	....	....	....	....	....	....	....	....	....	....	....	....	....	....
1995-96	Banska Bystrica	Slovakia	19	3	1	4	....	....	....	8	....	....	....	....	....	....	....	....	....	....	....	....	....	....	....	....	....	....
	Slovakia	WJC-A	6	0	3	3	....	....	....	2	....	....	....	....	....	....	....	....	....	....	....	....	....	....	....	....	....	....
1996-97	SKP Poprad	Slovakia	44	15	18	33	....	....	....	....	....	....	....	....	....	....	....	....	....	....	....	....	....	....	....	....	....	....
	Slovakia	WJC-A	6	2	4	6	....	....	....	2	....	....	....	....	....	....	....	....	....	....	....	....	....	....	....	....	....	....
1997-98	Worcester IceCats	AHL	69	27	36	63	....	....	....	54	....	....	....	....	....	....	....	....	....	....	11	2	6	8	10	....	....	....
1998-99	**St. Louis Blues**	**NHL**	**66**	**4**	**12**	**16**	**5**	**12**	**17**	**30**	**0**	**0**	**0**	**78**	**5.1**	**24**	**2**	**49**	**18**	**–9**	**11**	**0**	**2**	**2**	**8**	**0**	**0**	**0**
99-2000	**St. Louis Blues**	**NHL**	**81**	**25**	**28**	**53**	**28**	**26**	**54**	**44**	**3**	**4**	**5**	**166**	**15.1**	**71**	**15**	**51**	**14**	**19**	**7**	**0**	**3**	**3**	**6**	**0**	**0**	**0**
	Slovakia	WC-A	6	1	4	5	....	....	....	4	....	....	....	....	....	....	....	....	....	....	....	....	....	....	....	....	....	....
	NHL Totals		**147**	**29**	**40**	**69**	**33**	**38**	**71**	**74**	**3**	**4**	**5**	**244**	**11.9**	**95**	**17**	**100**	**32**		**18**	**0**	**5**	**5**	**14**	**0**	**0**	**0**

• HANGSLEBEN, Al

Alan William "Hank" D – L. 6'1", 195 lbs. b: Warroad, MN, 2/22/1953. Montreal's 6th, 56th overall, in 1973.

Season	Club	League	GP	G	A	Pts	AG	AA	APts	PIM	PP	SH	GW	S	%	TGF	PGF	TGA	PGA	+/–	GP	G	A	Pts	PIM	PP	SH	GW
1971-72	University of North Dakota	WCHA	36	13	21	34	....	....	....	49	....	....	....	....	....	....	....	....	....	....	....	....	....	....	....	....	....	....
1972-73	University of North Dakota	WCHA	36	15	18	33	....	....	....	77	....	....	....	....	....	....	....	....	....	....	....	....	....	....	....	....	....	....
	United States	WC-B	7	2	4	6	....	....	....	....	....	....	....	....	....	....	....	....	....	....	....	....	....	....	....	....	....	....
1973-74	University of North Dakota	WCHA	34	9	16	25	....	....	....	56	....	....	....	....	....	....	....	....	....	....	....	....	....	....	....	....	....	....
	United States	Nat-Team	7	2	3	5	....	....	....	10	....	....	....	....	....	....	....	....	....	....	....	....	....	....	....	....	....	....
1974-75	New England Whalers	WHA	26	0	5	5	....	....	....	8	....	....	....	....	....	....	....	....	....	....	6	0	3	3	19	....	....	....
	Cape Cod Codders	NAHL	55	4	39	43	....	....	....	130	....	....	....	....	....	....	....	....	....	....	....	....	....	....	....	....	....	....
1975-76	New England Whalers	WHA	78	2	23	25	....	....	....	62	....	....	....	....	....	....	....	....	....	....	13	2	3	5	20	....	....	....
	Cape Cod Codders	NAHL	1	0	0	0	....	....	....	9	....	....	....	....	....	....	....	....	....	....	....	....	....	....	....	....	....	....
1976-77	New England Whalers	WHA	74	13	9	22	....	....	....	79	....	....	....	....	....	....	....	....	....	....	4	0	0	0	9	....	....	....
1977-78	New England Whalers	WHA	79	11	18	29	....	....	....	140	....	....	....	....	....	....	....	....	....	....	14	1	4	5	37	....	....	....
1978-79	New England Whalers	WHA	77	10	19	29	....	....	....	148	....	....	....	....	....	....	....	....	....	....	10	1	2	3	12	....	....	....
1979-80	**Hartford Whalers**	**NHL**	**37**	**3**	**15**	**18**	**3**	**11**	**14**	**69**	**0**	**0**	**1**	**40**	**7.5**	**39**	**0**	**44**	**14**	**9**	....	....	....	....	....	....	....	....
	Washington Capitals	**NHL**	**37**	**10**	**7**	**17**	**8**	**5**	**13**	**45**	**2**	**0**	**1**	**67**	**14.9**	**43**	**7**	**37**	**2**	**1**	....	....	....	....	....	....	....	....
1980-81	**Washington Capitals**	**NHL**	**76**	**5**	**19**	**24**	**4**	**13**	**17**	**198**	**0**	**0**	**0**	**110**	**4.5**	**68**	**10**	**76**	**11**	**–7**	....	....	....	....	....	....	....	....
	United States	WEC-A	8	1	3	4	....	....	....	22	....	....	....	....	....	....	....	....	....	....	....	....	....	....	....	....	....	....

			REGULAR SEASON																		PLAYOFFS							
Season	Club	League	GP	G	A	Pts	AG	AA	APts	PIM	PP	SH	GW	S	%	TGF	PGF	TGA	PGA	+/-	GP	G	A	Pts	PIM	PP	SH	GW
1981-82	**Washington Capitals**	**NHL**	**17**	**1**	**1**	**2**	**1**	**1**	**2**	**19**	**0**	**0**	**0**	**13**	**7.7**	**6**	**0**	**14**	**5**	**–3**	....	....	....	....	....	....	....	....
	Hershey Bears	AHL	6	1	2	3	....	....	....	26	....	....	....	....	....	....	....	....	....	....	....	....	....	....	....	....	....	....
	Los Angeles Kings	**NHL**	**18**	**2**	**6**	**8**	**2**	**4**	**6**	**65**	**0**	**0**	**0**	**18**	**11.1**	**10**	**1**	**7**	**1**	**3**	....	....	....	....	....	....	....	....
	New Haven Nighthawks	AHL	18	5	4	9	....	....	....	28	....	....	....	....	....	....	....	....	....	....	4	0	0	0	4	....	....	....
1982-83	Moncton Alpines	AHL	71	10	16	26	....	....	....	127	....	....	....	....	....	....	....	....	....	....	....	....	....	....	....	....	....	....
1983-84	New Haven Nighthawks	AHL	58	1	23	24	....	....	....	88	....	....	....	....	....	....	....	....	....	....	....	....	....	....	....	....	....	....
	NHL Totals		**185**	**21**	**48**	**69**	**18**	**34**	**52**	**396**	**2**	**0**	**2**	**248**	**8.5**	**166**	**18**	**178**	**33**		....	....	....	....	....	....	....	....
	Other Major League Totals		334	36	74	110	....	....	....	437	....	....	....	....	....	....	....	....	....	....	47	4	12	16	97	....	....	....

WCHA First All-Star Team (1972) • NCAA West First All-American Team (1972)

Selected by **New England** (WHA) in 1973 WHA Amateur Draft, June, 1973. Reclaimed by **Montreal** from **Hartford** prior to Expansion Draft, June 9, 1976. Claimed by **Hartford** from **Montreal** in Expansion Draft, June 13, 1979. Traded to **Washington** by **Hartford** for Tom Rowe, January 17, 1980. Signed as a free agent by **LA Kings**, January 4, 1982. Traded to **Edmonton** by **LA Kings** for Rick Blight, December 7, 1982.

• HANKINSON, Ben

Benjamin J. RW – R. 6'2", 210 lbs. b: Edina, MN, 5/1/1969. New Jersey's 5th, 107th overall, in 1987.

Season	Club	League	GP	G	A	Pts	AG	AA	APts	PIM	PP	SH	GW	S	%	TGF	PGF	TGA	PGA	+/-	GP	G	A	Pts	PIM	PP	SH	GW
1985-86	Edina Hornets	Hi-School	26	9	21	30	....	....	....	....	....	....	....	....	....	....	....	....	....	....	....	....	....	....	....	....	....	....
1986-87	Edina Hornets	Hi-School	26	14	20	34	....	....	....	....	....	....	....	....	....	....	....	....	....	....	....	....	....	....	....	....	....	....
1987-88	University of Minnesota	WCHA	24	4	7	11	....	....	....	36	....	....	....	....	....	....	....	....	....	....	....	....	....	....	....	....	....	....
1988-89	University of Minnesota	WCHA	43	7	11	18	....	....	....	115	....	....	....	....	....	....	....	....	....	....	....	....	....	....	....	....	....	....
1989-90	University of Minnesota	WCHA	46	25	41	66	....	....	....	34	....	....	....	....	....	....	....	....	....	....	....	....	....	....	....	....	....	....
1990-91	University of Minnesota	WCHA	43	19	21	40	....	....	....	133	....	....	....	....	....	....	....	....	....	....	....	....	....	....	....	....	....	....
1991-92	Utica Devils	AHL	77	17	16	33	....	....	....	186	....	....	....	....	....	....	....	....	....	....	4	3	1	4	2	....	....	....
1992-93	**New Jersey Devils**	**NHL**	**4**	**2**	**1**	**3**	**2**	**1**	**3**	**9**	**0**	**0**	**0**	**3**	**66.7**	**4**	**0**	**2**	**0**	**2**	....	....	....	....	....	....	....	....
	Utica Devils	AHL	75	35	27	62	....	....	....	145	....	....	....	....	....	....	....	....	....	....	5	2	2	4	6	....	....	....
1993-94	**New Jersey Devils**	**NHL**	**13**	**1**	**0**	**1**	**1**	**0**	**1**	**23**	**0**	**0**	**1**	**14**	**7.1**	**4**	**0**	**4**	**0**	**0**	**2**	**1**	**0**	**1**	**4**	**0**	**0**	**0**
	Albany River Rats	AHL	29	9	14	23	....	....	....	80	....	....	....	....	....	....	....	....	....	....	5	3	1	4	6	....	....	....
1994-95	**New Jersey Devils**	**NHL**	**8**	**0**	**0**	**0**	**0**	**0**	**0**	**7**	**0**	**0**	**0**	**8**	**0.0**	**0**	**0**	**6**	**0**	**–6**	....	....	....	....	....	....	....	....
	Albany River Rats	AHL	1	1	0	1	....	....	....	6	....	....	....	....	....	....	....	....	....	....	....	....	....	....	....	....	....	....
	Tampa Bay Lightning	**NHL**	**18**	**0**	**2**	**2**	**0**	**3**	**3**	**6**	**0**	**0**	**0**	**18**	**0.0**	**5**	**0**	**4**	**0**	**1**	....	....	....	....	....	....	....	....
1995-96	Adirondack Red Wings	AHL	75	25	21	46	....	....	....	210	....	....	....	....	....	....	....	....	....	....	3	0	0	0	8	....	....	....
1996-97	Grand Rapids Griffins	IHL	68	16	13	29	....	....	....	219	....	....	....	....	....	....	....	....	....	....	5	2	2	4	4	....	....	....
1997-98	Orlando Solar Bears	IHL	80	15	15	30	....	....	....	221	....	....	....	....	....	....	....	....	....	....	14	0	4	4	47	....	....	....
	NHL Totals		**43**	**3**	**3**	**6**	**3**	**4**	**7**	**45**	**0**	**0**	**1**	**43**	**7.0**	**13**	**0**	**16**	**0**		**2**	**1**	**0**	**1**	**4**	**0**	**0**	**0**

WCHA First All-Star Team (1990)

Traded to **Tampa Bay** by **New Jersey** with Alexander Semak for Shawn Chambers and Danton Cole, March 14, 1995. Traded to **Detroit** by **Tampa Bay** with Marc Bergevin for Shawn Burr and Detroit's 3rd round choice (later traded to Boston — Boston selected Jason Doyle) in 1996 Entry Draft, August 17, 1995.

• HANNA, John

John Jack D – R. 5'11", 175 lbs. b: Sydney, N.S., 4/5/1935.

Season	Club	League	GP	G	A	Pts	AG	AA	APts	PIM	PP	SH	GW	S	%	TGF	PGF	TGA	PGA	+/-	GP	G	A	Pts	PIM	PP	SH	GW
1953-54	Sydney Bruins	CBJHL	STATISTICS NOT AVAILABLE																									
	North Sydney Franklins	Mem-Cup	5	1	1	2	....	....	....	4	....	....	....	....	....	....	....	....	....	....	....	....	....	....	....	....	....	....
1954-55	Trois-Rivieres Flambeaux	QJHL	42	3	6	9	....	....	....	107	....	....	....	....	....	....	....	....	....	....	9	0	1	1	10	....	....	....
1955-56	Philadelphia Ramblers	EHL	28	1	4	5	....	....	....	13	....	....	....	....	....	....	....	....	....	....	....	....	....	....	....	....	....	....
	Chicoutimi Sagueneens	QHL	40	3	14	17	....	....	....	101	....	....	....	....	....	....	....	....	....	....	5	0	0	0	4	....	....	....
1956-57	Chicoutimi Sagueneens	QHL	43	1	14	15	....	....	....	64	....	....	....	....	....	....	....	....	....	....	10	1	2	3	10	....	....	....
1957-58	Trois-Rivieres Lions	QHL	48	3	25	28	....	....	....	66	....	....	....	....	....	....	....	....	....	....	....	....	....	....	....	....	....	....
	Providence Reds	AHL	7	0	3	3	....	....	....	24	....	....	....	....	....	....	....	....	....	....	3	1	1	2	10	....	....	....
1958-59	**New York Rangers**	**NHL**	**70**	**1**	**10**	**11**	**1**	**10**	**11**	**83**	....	....	....	....	....	....	....	....	....	....	....	....	....	....	....	....	....	....
1959-60	**New York Rangers**	**NHL**	**61**	**4**	**8**	**12**	**5**	**8**	**13**	**87**	....	....	....	....	....	....	....	....	....	....	....	....	....	....	....	....	....	....
1960-61	**New York Rangers**	**NHL**	**46**	**1**	**8**	**9**	**1**	**8**	**9**	**34**	....	....	....	....	....	....	....	....	....	....	....	....	....	....	....	....	....	....
	Springfield Indians	AHL	18	2	2	4	....	....	....	14	....	....	....	....	....	....	....	....	....	....	....	....	....	....	....	....	....	....
1961-62	Quebec Aces	AHL	65	0	17	17	....	....	....	85	....	....	....	....	....	....	....	....	....	....	....	....	....	....	....	....	....	....
1962-63	Quebec Aces	AHL	70	7	21	28	....	....	....	61	....	....	....	....	....	....	....	....	....	....	....	....	....	....	....	....	....	....
1963-64	**Montreal Canadiens**	**NHL**	**6**	**0**	**0**	**0**	**0**	**0**	**0**	**2**	....	....	....	....	....	....	....	....	....	....	....	....	....	....	....	....	....	....
	Quebec Aces	AHL	58	4	14	18	....	....	....	54	....	....	....	....	....	....	....	....	....	....	9	0	4	4	10	....	....	....
1964-65	Quebec Aces	AHL	70	9	25	34	....	....	....	83	....	....	....	....	....	....	....	....	....	....	5	0	0	0	6	....	....	....
1965-66	Quebec Aces	AHL	69	4	22	26	....	....	....	93	....	....	....	....	....	....	....	....	....	....	6	0	1	1	20	....	....	....
1966-67	Quebec Aces	AHL	67	6	20	26	....	....	....	54	....	....	....	....	....	....	....	....	....	....	4	0	0	0	4	....	....	....
1967-68	**Philadelphia Flyers**	**NHL**	**15**	**0**	**0**	**0**	**0**	**0**	**0**	**0**	**0**	**0**	**0**	**4**	**0.0**	**2**	**1**	**0**	**0**	**1**	....	....	....	....	....	....	....	....
	Quebec Aces	AHL	24	1	12	13	....	....	....	27	....	....	....	....	....	....	....	....	....	....	14	2	6	8	34	....	....	....
1968-69	Seattle Totems	WHL	71	25	27	52	....	....	....	49	....	....	....	....	....	....	....	....	....	....	4	0	1	1	2	....	....	....
1969-70	Seattle Totems	WHL	66	9	33	42	....	....	....	38	....	....	....	....	....	....	....	....	....	....	6	0	1	1	11	....	....	....
1970-71	Seattle Totems	WHL	70	20	40	60	....	....	....	68	....	....	....	....	....	....	....	....	....	....	....	....	....	....	....	....	....	....
1971-72	Seattle Totems	WHL	36	5	10	15	....	....	....	16	....	....	....	....	....	....	....	....	....	....	....	....	....	....	....	....	....	....
1972-73	Cleveland Crusaders	WHA	66	6	20	26	....	....	....	68	....	....	....	....	....	....	....	....	....	....	....	....	....	....	....	....	....	....
1973-74	Jacksonville Barons	AHL	11	2	4	6	....	....	....	4	....	....	....	....	....	....	....	....	....	....	....	....	....	....	....	....	....	....
1974-75	Syracuse Eagles	AHL	1	0	0	0	....	....	....	0	....	....	....	....	....	....	....	....	....	....	....	....	....	....	....	....	....	....
1975-76	Tidewater Sharks	SHL	DID NOT PLAY – COACHING																									
	NHL Totals		**198**	**6**	**26**	**32**	**7**	**26**	**33**	**206**	....	....	....	....	....	....	....	....	....		....	....	....	....	....	....	....	....
	Other Major League Totals		66	6	20	26	....	....	....	68	....	....	....	....	....	....	....	....	....	....	....	....	....	....	....	....	....	....

QHL Second All-Star Team (1958) • WHL First All-Star Team (1969, 1971) • Won Hal Laycoe Cup (WHL Top Defenseman) (1969, 1971) • Won Leader Cup (WHL - MVP) (1969) • WHL Second All-Star Team (1970)

Claimed by **NY Rangers** from **Montreal** in Intra-League Draft, June 5, 1957. Traded to **Montreal** by **NY Rangers** for Albert Langlois, June 13, 1961. NHL rights transferred to **Philadelphia** after NHL club purchased **Quebec** (AHL) franchise, May 8, 1967. Traded to **Seattle** (WHL) by **Philadelphia** with Art Stratton to complete transaction that sent Earl Heiskala to Philadelphia (May 19, 1968), June, 1968. Selected by **LA Sharks** (WHA) in 1972 WHA General Player Draft, February 12, 1972. WHA rights traded to **Cleveland** (WHA) by **LA Sharks** (WHA) for future considerations, July, 1972.

• HANNAN, Dave

David Patrick C – L. 5'10", 180 lbs. b: Sudbury, Ont., 11/26/1961. Pittsburgh's 9th, 196th overall, in 1981.

Season	Club	League	GP	G	A	Pts	AG	AA	APts	PIM	PP	SH	GW	S	%	TGF	PGF	TGA	PGA	+/-	GP	G	A	Pts	PIM	PP	SH	GW
1976-77	Levack Midget Huskies	OMHA	94	109	88	197	....	....	....	....	....	....	....	....	....	....	....	....	....	....	....	....	....	....	....	....	....	....
	Levack Huskies	NOJHA	1	2	0	2	....	....	....	2	....	....	....	....	....	....	....	....	....	....	....	....	....	....	....	....	....	....
1977-78	Windsor Spitfires	OMJHL	68	14	16	30	....	....	....	43	....	....	....	....	....	....	....	....	....	....	6	0	1	1	2	....	....	....
1978-79	Sault Ste. Marie Greyhounds	OMJHL	26	7	8	15	....	....	....	13	....	....	....	....	....	....	....	....	....	....	....	....	....	....	....	....	....	....
1979-80	Sault Ste. Marie Greyhounds	OMJHL	28	11	10	21	....	....	....	31	....	....	....	....	....	....	....	....	....	....	....	....	....	....	....	....	....	....
	Brantford Alexanders	OMJHL	25	5	10	15	....	....	....	26	....	....	....	....	....	....	....	....	....	....	10	2	6	8	23	....	....	....
1980-81	Brantford Alexanders	OMJHL	56	46	35	81	....	....	....	155	....	....	....	....	....	....	....	....	....	....	6	2	4	6	20	....	....	....
1981-82	**Pittsburgh Penguins**	**NHL**	**1**	**0**	**0**	**0**	**0**	**0**	**0**	**0**	**0**	**0**	**0**	**0**	**0.0**	**0**	**0**	**2**	**0**	**–2**	....	....	....	....	....	....	....	....
	Erie Blades	AHL	76	33	37	70	....	....	....	129	....	....	....	....	....	....	....	....	....	....	....	....	....	....	....	....	....	....
1982-83	**Pittsburgh Penguins**	**NHL**	**74**	**11**	**22**	**33**	**9**	**15**	**24**	**127**	**2**	**0**	**3**	**95**	**11.6**	**44**	**5**	**77**	**10**	**–28**	....	....	....	....	....	....	....	....
	Baltimore Skipjacks	AHL	5	2	2	4	....	....	....	13	....	....	....	....	....	....	....	....	....	....	....	....	....	....	....	....	....	....
1983-84	**Pittsburgh Penguins**	**NHL**	**24**	**2**	**3**	**5**	**2**	**2**	**4**	**33**	**0**	**1**	**1**	**21**	**9.5**	**9**	**0**	**17**	**6**	**–2**	....	....	....	....	....	....	....	....
	Baltimore Skipjacks	AHL	47	18	24	42	....	....	....	98	....	....	....	....	....	....	....	....	....	....	10	2	6	8	27	....	....	....
1984-85	**Pittsburgh Penguins**	**NHL**	**30**	**6**	**7**	**13**	**5**	**5**	**10**	**43**	**0**	**1**	**1**	**38**	**15.8**	**15**	**0**	**30**	**7**	**–8**	....	....	....	....	....	....	....	....
	Baltimore Skipjacks	AHL	49	20	25	45	....	....	....	91	....	....	....	....	....	....	....	....	....	....	....	....	....	....	....	....	....	....
1985-86	**Pittsburgh Penguins**	**NHL**	**75**	**17**	**18**	**35**	**14**	**12**	**26**	**91**	**0**	**3**	**1**	**100**	**17.0**	**47**	**3**	**89**	**41**	**–4**	....	....	....	....	....	....	....	....
1986-87	**Pittsburgh Penguins**	**NHL**	**58**	**10**	**15**	**25**	**9**	**11**	**20**	**56**	**0**	**1**	**2**	**85**	**11.8**	**39**	**2**	**46**	**7**	**–2**	....	....	....	....	....	....	....	....
1987-88	**Pittsburgh Penguins**	**NHL**	**21**	**4**	**3**	**7**	**3**	**2**	**5**	**23**	**0**	**1**	**1**	**34**	**11.8**	**8**	**0**	**27**	**17**	**–2**	....	....	....	....	....	....	....	....
	♦ **Edmonton Oilers**	**NHL**	**51**	**9**	**11**	**20**	**8**	**8**	**16**	**43**	**0**	**2**	**2**	**62**	**14.5**	**31**	**0**	**28**	**9**	**12**	**12**	**1**	**1**	**2**	**8**	**0**	**0**	**1**
1988-89	**Pittsburgh Penguins**	**NHL**	**72**	**10**	**20**	**30**	**8**	**14**	**22**	**157**	**2**	**1**	**3**	**72**	**13.9**	**42**	**5**	**97**	**48**	**–12**	**8**	**0**	**1**	**1**	**4**	**0**	**0**	**0**
1989-90	**Toronto Maple Leafs**	**NHL**	**39**	**6**	**9**	**15**	**5**	**6**	**11**	**55**	**0**	**1**	**0**	**39**	**15.4**	**21**	**0**	**44**	**11**	**–12**	**3**	**1**	**0**	**1**	**4**	**0**	**0**	**1**
1990-91	**Toronto Maple Leafs**	**NHL**	**74**	**11**	**23**	**34**	**10**	**17**	**27**	**82**	**0**	**1**	**2**	**72**	**15.3**	**38**	**3**	**80**	**36**	**–9**	....	....	....	....	....	....	....	....

Season	Club	League	REGULAR SEASON GP	G	A	Pts	AG	AA	APts	PIM	PP	SH	GW	S	%	TGF	PGF	TGA	PGA	+/–	PLAYOFFS GP	G	A	Pts	PIM	PP	SH	GW
1991-92	**Toronto Maple Leafs**	**NHL**	**35**	**2**	**2**	**4**	**2**	**2**	**4**	**16**	**0**	**1**	**0**	**24**	**8.3**	**9**	**2**	**33**	**16**	**–10**	....	....	....	....	....	....	....	....
	Canada	Nat-Team	3	0	0	0	....	....	....	2	....	....	....	....	....	....	....	....	....	....	....	....	....	....	....	....	....	....
	Canada	Olympics	8	3	5	8	....	....	....	8	....	....	....	....	....	....	....	....	....	....	....	....	....	....	....	....	....	....
	Buffalo Sabres	**NHL**	**12**	**2**	**4**	**6**	**2**	**3**	**5**	**48**	**0**	**2**	**0**	**8**	**25.0**	**9**	**2**	**10**	**4**	**1**	**7**	**2**	**0**	**2**	**2**	**2**	**0**	**0**
1992-93	**Buffalo Sabres**	**NHL**	**55**	**5**	**15**	**20**	**4**	**10**	**14**	**43**	**0**	**0**	**0**	**43**	**11.6**	**31**	**3**	**44**	**24**	**8**	**8**	**1**	**1**	**2**	**18**	**0**	**0**	**0**
1993-94	**Buffalo Sabres**	**NHL**	**83**	**6**	**15**	**21**	**6**	**12**	**18**	**53**	**0**	**3**	**1**	**40**	**15.0**	**35**	**0**	**62**	**37**	**10**	**7**	**1**	**0**	**1**	**6**	**0**	**0**	**1**
1994-95	**Buffalo Sabres**	**NHL**	**42**	**4**	**12**	**16**	**7**	**18**	**25**	**32**	**0**	**2**	**0**	**36**	**11.1**	**23**	**1**	**30**	**11**	**3**	**5**	**0**	**2**	**2**	**2**	**0**	**0**	**0**
1995-96	**Buffalo Sabres**	**NHL**	**57**	**6**	**10**	**16**	**6**	**8**	**14**	**30**	**1**	**1**	**2**	**40**	**15.0**	**23**	**2**	**53**	**34**	**2**	....	....	....	....	....	....	....	....
♦	**Colorado Avalanche**	**NHL**	**4**	**1**	**0**	**1**	**1**	**0**	**1**	**2**	**0**	**0**	**0**	**41**	**2.4**	**1**	**0**	**2**	**2**	**1**	**13**	**0**	**2**	**2**	**2**	**0**	**0**	**0**
1996-97	**Ottawa Senators**	**NHL**	**34**	**2**	**2**	**4**	**2**	**2**	**4**	**8**	**0**	**1**	**1**	**16**	**12.5**	**9**	**0**	**22**	**12**	**–1**	....	....	....	....	....	....	....	....
	NHL Totals		**841**	**114**	**191**	**305**	**103**	**147**	**250**	**942**	**5**	**22**	**20**	**866**	**13.2**	**434**	**28**	**793**	**332**		**63**	**6**	**7**	**13**	**46**	**2**	**0**	**3**

Traded to **Edmonton** by **Pittsburgh** with Craig Simpson, Moe Mantha and Chris Joseph for Paul Coffey, Dave Hunter and Wayne Van Dorp, November 24, 1987. Claimed by **Pittsburgh** from **Edmonton** in Waiver Draft, October 3, 1988. Claimed by **Toronto** from **Pittsburgh** in Waiver Draft, October 2, 1989. Traded to **Buffalo** by **Toronto** for Minnesota's 5th round choice (previously acquired, Toronto selected Chris Deruiter) in 1992 Entry Draft, March 10, 1992. Traded to **Colorado** by **Buffalo** for Colorado's 6th round choice (Darren Mortier) in 1996 Entry Draft, March 20, 1996. Signed as a free agent by **Ottawa**, September 13, 1996.

• HANNAN, Scott

Kenneth Scott D – L. 6'2", 215 lbs. b: Richmond, B.C., 1/23/1979. San Jose's 2nd, 23rd overall, in 1997.

Season	Club	League	GP	G	A	Pts	AG	AA	APts	PIM	PP	SH	GW	S	%	TGF	PGF	TGA	PGA	+/–	GP	G	A	Pts	PIM	PP	SH	GW
1994-95	Surrey Wolves	BCAHA	70	54	54	108	....	....	....	200	....	....	....	....	....	....	....	....	....	....	....	....	....	....	....	....	....	....
	Tacoma Rockets	WHL	2	0	0	0	....	....	....	0	....	....	....	....	....	....	....	....	....	....	....	....	....	....	....	....	....	....
1995-96	Kelowna Rockets	WHL	69	4	5	9	....	....	....	76	....	....	....	....	....	....	....	....	....	....	6	0	1	1	4	....	....	....
1996-97	Kelowna Rockets	WHL	70	17	26	43	....	....	....	101	....	....	....	....	....	....	....	....	....	....	6	0	0	0	8	....	....	....
1997-98	Kelowna Rockets	WHL	47	10	30	40	....	....	....	70	....	....	....	....	....	....	....	....	....	....	7	2	7	9	14	....	....	....
1998-99	**San Jose Sharks**	**NHL**	**5**	**0**	**2**	**2**	**0**	**2**	**2**	**6**	**0**	**0**	**0**	**4**	**0.0**	**4**	**1**	**3**	**0**	**0**	....	....	....	....	....	....	....	....
	Kelowna Rockets	WHL	47	15	30	45	....	....	....	92	....	....	....	....	....	....	....	....	....	....	6	1	2	3	14	....	....	....
	Kentucky Thoroughblades	AHL	2	0	0	0	....	....	....	2	....	....	....	....	....	....	....	....	....	....	12	0	2	2	10	....	....	....
99-2000	**San Jose Sharks**	**NHL**	**30**	**1**	**2**	**3**	**1**	**2**	**3**	**10**	**0**	**0**	**0**	**28**	**3.6**	**24**	**1**	**20**	**4**	**7**	**1**	**0**	**1**	**1**	**0**	**0**	**0**	**0**
	Kentucky Thoroughblades	AHL	41	5	12	17	....	....	....	40	....	....	....	....	....	....	....	....	....	....	....	....	....	....	....	....	....	....
	NHL Totals		**35**	**1**	**4**	**5**	**1**	**4**	**5**	**16**	**0**	**0**	**0**	**32**	**3.1**	**28**	**2**	**23**	**4**		**1**	**0**	**1**	**1**	**0**	**0**	**0**	**0**

WHL West First All-Star Team (1999)

• HANNIGAN, Pat

Patrick Edward "Hopalong" LW – R. 5'10", 183 lbs. b: Timmins, Ont., 3/5/1936.

Season	Club	League	GP	G	A	Pts	AG	AA	APts	PIM	PP	SH	GW	S	%	TGF	PGF	TGA	PGA	+/–	GP	G	A	Pts	PIM	PP	SH	GW
1953-54	Schumacher Lions	NOJHA	STATISTICS NOT AVAILABLE																									
	St. Michael's Majors	OHA-Jr.	20	1	2	3	....	....	....	17	....	....	....	....	....	....	....	....	....	....	1	0	0	0	0	....	....	....
1954-55	St. Michael's Majors	OHA-Jr.	44	13	19	32	....	....	....	40	....	....	....	....	....	....	....	....	....	....	5	2	3	5	2	....	....	....
1955-56	St. Michael's Majors	OHA-Jr.	46	38	31	69	....	....	....	121	....	....	....	....	....	....	....	....	....	....	8	5	8	13	2	....	....	....
1956-57	Winnipeg Warriors	WHL	67	12	19	31	....	....	....	82	....	....	....	....	....	....	....	....	....	....	....	....	....	....	....	....	....	....
1957-58	New Westminster Royals	WHL	52	26	28	54	....	....	....	67	....	....	....	....	....	....	....	....	....	....	4	1	0	1	2	....	....	....
	Rochester Americans	AHL	8	0	4	4	....	....	....	4	....	....	....	....	....	....	....	....	....	....	....	....	....	....	....	....	....	....
1958-59	New Westminster Royals	WHL	69	37	46	83	....	....	....	73	....	....	....	....	....	....	....	....	....	....	....	....	....	....	....	....	....	....
	Rochester Americans	AHL	....	....	....	....	....	....	....	....	....	....	....	....	....	....	....	....	....	....	4	0	1	1	0	....	....	....
1959-60	**Toronto Maple Leafs**	**NHL**	**1**	**0**	**0**	**0**	**0**	**0**	**0**	**0**	....	....	....	....	....	....	....	....	....	....	....	....	....	....	....	....	....	....
	Rochester Americans	AHL	65	29	33	62	....	....	....	91	....	....	....	....	....	....	....	....	....	....	11	4	6	10	14	....	....	....
1960-61	Rochester Americans	AHL	13	5	6	11	....	....	....	4	....	....	....	....	....	....	....	....	....	....	....	....	....	....	....	....	....	....
	New York Rangers	**NHL**	**53**	**11**	**9**	**20**	**13**	**9**	**22**	**24**	....	....	....	....	....	....	....	....	....	....	....	....	....	....	....	....	....	....
1961-62	**New York Rangers**	**NHL**	**56**	**8**	**14**	**22**	**9**	**13**	**22**	**34**	....	....	....	....	....	....	....	....	....	....	**4**	**0**	**0**	**0**	**2**	**0**	**0**	**0**
1962-63	Baltimore Clippers	AHL	40	16	20	36	....	....	....	35	....	....	....	....	....	....	....	....	....	....	....	....	....	....	....	....	....	....
1963-64	Portland Buckaroos	WHL	34	12	8	20	....	....	....	43	....	....	....	....	....	....	....	....	....	....	....	....	....	....	....	....	....	....
	Buffalo Bisons	AHL	40	9	24	33	....	....	....	20	....	....	....	....	....	....	....	....	....	....	....	....	....	....	....	....	....	....
1964-65	Buffalo Bisons	AHL	72	38	54	92	....	....	....	118	....	....	....	....	....	....	....	....	....	....	9	3	4	7	23	....	....	....
1965-66	Buffalo Bisons	AHL	66	21	43	64	....	....	....	69	....	....	....	....	....	....	....	....	....	....	....	....	....	....	....	....	....	....
1966-67	Buffalo Bisons	AHL	68	18	38	56	....	....	....	37	....	....	....	....	....	....	....	....	....	....	....	....	....	....	....	....	....	....
1967-68	**Philadelphia Flyers**	**NHL**	**65**	**11**	**15**	**26**	**13**	**15**	**28**	**36**	**0**	**0**	**2**	**63**	**17.5**	**35**	**5**	**26**	**2**	**6**	**7**	**1**	**2**	**3**	**9**	**0**	**0**	**0**
1968-69	**Philadelphia Flyers**	**NHL**	**7**	**0**	**1**	**1**	**0**	**1**	**1**	**22**	**0**	**0**	**0**	**5**	**0.0**	**2**	**0**	**6**	**0**	**–4**	....	....	....	....	....	....	....	....
	Buffalo Bisons	AHL	31	14	25	39	....	....	....	37	....	....	....	....	....	....	....	....	....	....	....	....	....	....	....	....	....	....
	Vancouver Canucks	WHL	12	4	4	8	....	....	....	2	....	....	....	....	....	....	....	....	....	....	6	4	1	5	4	....	....	....
1969-70	Vancouver Canucks	WHL	69	28	42	70	....	....	....	47	....	....	....	....	....	....	....	....	....	....	....	....	....	....	....	....	....	....
1970-71	Phoenix Roadrunners	WHL	10	1	2	3	....	....	....	0	....	....	....	....	....	....	....	....	....	....	....	....	....	....	....	....	....	....
	NHL Totals		**182**	**30**	**39**	**69**	**35**	**38**	**73**	**116**	....	....	....	....	....	....	....	....	....		**11**	**1**	**2**	**3**	**11**	....	....	....

• Brother of Gord and Ray • WHL Coast Division First All-Star Team (1959) • AHL First All-Star Team (1965)

Traded to **NY Rangers** by **Toronto** with Johnny Wilson for Eddie Shack, November 7, 1960. Traded to **Portland** (WHL) by **NY Rangers** for Howie Glover, September 19, 1963. Traded to **Buffalo** (AHL) by **Portland** (WHL) for Cliff Schmautz, December, 1963. Claimed by **Detroit** from **Chicago** (Buffalo-AHL) in Inter-League Draft, June 8, 1965. Traded to **Chicago** (Buffalo-AHL) by **Detroit** for $15,000, November 15, 1965. Claimed by **Philadelphia** from **Chicago** in Expansion Draft, June 6, 1967. Traded to **Vancouver** (WHL) by **Philadelphia** for cash, March 2, 1969. NHL rights transferred to **Vancouver** after NHL club purchased **Vancouver** (WHL) franchise, December 19, 1969. Traded to **Toronto** (Phoenix-WHL) by **Vancouver** with Ted McCaskill for Andre Hinse, August, 1970.

• HANSEN, Richie

Richard John C – L. 5'10", 185 lbs. b: Bronx, NY, 10/30/1955. NY Islanders' 7th, 119th overall, in 1975.

Season	Club	League	GP	G	A	Pts	AG	AA	APts	PIM	PP	SH	GW	S	%	TGF	PGF	TGA	PGA	+/–	GP	G	A	Pts	PIM	PP	SH	GW
1971-72	Brooklyn Metros	NYJHL	30	19	*52	71	....	....	....	47	....	....	....	....	....	....	....	....	....	....	....	....	....	....	....	....	....	....
1972-73	Sudbury Wolves	OMJHL	39	13	21	34	....	....	....	26	....	....	....	....	....	....	....	....	....	....	4	0	2	2	0	....	....	....
1973-74	Sudbury Wolves	OMJHL	62	34	47	81	....	....	....	31	....	....	....	....	....	....	....	....	....	....	4	0	1	1	2	....	....	....
1974-75	Sudbury Wolves	OMJHL	69	26	46	72	....	....	....	28	....	....	....	....	....	....	....	....	....	....	15	4	13	17	10	....	....	....
1975-76	Erie Blades	NAHL	74	40	41	81	....	....	....	51	....	....	....	....	....	....	....	....	....	....	....	....	....	....	....	....	....	....
	Muskegon Mohawks	IHL	....	....	....	....	....	....	....	....	....	....	....	....	....	....	....	....	....	....	1	1	2	3	2	....	....	....
1976-77	**New York Islanders**	**NHL**	**4**	**1**	**0**	**1**	**1**	**0**	**1**	**0**	**0**	**0**	**0**	**9**	**11.1**	**1**	**0**	**2**	**0**	**–1**	....	....	....	....	....	....	....	....
	Fort Worth Texans	CHL	74	30	47	77	....	....	....	32	....	....	....	....	....	....	....	....	....	....	6	0	3	3	4	....	....	....
1977-78	**New York Islanders**	**NHL**	**2**	**0**	**0**	**0**	**0**	**0**	**0**	**0**	**0**	**0**	**0**	**2**	**0.0**	**1**	**0**	**1**	**0**	**0**	....	....	....	....	....	....	....	....
	Fort Worth Texans	CHL	67	25	53	78	....	....	....	36	....	....	....	....	....	....	....	....	....	....	14	7	*11	18	2	....	....	....
1978-79	**New York Islanders**	**NHL**	**12**	**1**	**6**	**7**	**1**	**4**	**5**	**4**	**0**	**0**	**0**	**10**	**10.0**	**12**	**1**	**2**	**0**	**9**	....	....	....	....	....	....	....	....
	Fort Worth Texans	CHL	20	4	8	12	....	....	....	4	....	....	....	....	....	....	....	....	....	....	5	1	0	1	0	....	....	....
1979-80	Salt Lake Golden Eagles	CHL	79	27	48	75	....	....	....	31	....	....	....	....	....	....	....	....	....	....	13	6	8	14	4	....	....	....
1980-81	Salt Lake Golden Eagles	CHL	72	27	51	78	....	....	....	43	....	....	....	....	....	....	....	....	....	....	17	5	18	23	19	....	....	....
1981-82	**St. Louis Blues**	**NHL**	**2**	**0**	**2**	**2**	**0**	**1**	**1**	**0**	**0**	**0**	**0**	**4**	**0.0**	**3**	**0**	**1**	**0**	**2**	....	....	....	....	....	....	....	....
	Salt Lake Golden Eagles	CHL	78	29	*81	110	....	....	....	52	....	....	....	....	....	....	....	....	....	....	10	1	9	10	0	....	....	....
1982-83	Wichita Wind	CHL	70	17	43	60	....	....	....	12	....	....	....	....	....	....	....	....	....	....	....	....	....	....	....	....	....	....
1983-84	Salt Lake Golden Eagles	CHL	63	24	32	56	....	....	....	22	....	....	....	....	....	....	....	....	....	....	5	0	0	0	2	....	....	....
	NHL Totals		**20**	**2**	**8**	**10**	**2**	**5**	**7**	**4**	**0**	**0**	**0**	**25**	**8.0**	**17**	**1**	**6**	**0**		....	....	....	....	....	....	....	....

CHL Second All-Star Team (1978)

Transferred to **Minnesota** by **NY Islanders** as compensation for NY Islander's signing of free agent Jean Potvin, June 10, 1979. Traded to **St. Louis** by **Minnesota** with Bryan Maxwell for St. Louis' 2nd round choice (later traded to Calgary — Calgary selected Dave Reierson) in 1982 Entry Draft, June 10, 1979. Signed as a free agent by **Minnesota**, July 30, 1983.

• HANSEN, Tavis

Tavis Svend C – R. 6'2", 204 lbs. b: Prince Albert, Sask., 6/17/1975. Winnipeg's 3rd, 58th overall, in 1994.

Season	Club	League	GP	G	A	Pts	AG	AA	APts	PIM	PP	SH	GW	S	%	TGF	PGF	TGA	PGA	+/–	GP	G	A	Pts	PIM	PP	SH	GW
1992-93	Shellbrook Steelers	SJHL	42	42	63	105	....	....	....	107	....	....	....	....	....	....	....	....	....	....	....	....	....	....	....	....	....	....
1993-94	Tacoma Rockets	WHL	71	23	31	54	....	....	....	122	....	....	....	....	....	....	....	....	....	....	8	1	3	4	17	....	....	....
1994-95	Tacoma Rockets	WHL	71	32	41	73	....	....	....	142	....	....	....	....	....	....	....	....	....	....	4	1	1	2	8	....	....	....
	Winnipeg Jets	**NHL**	**1**	**0**	**0**	**0**	**0**	**0**	**0**	**0**	**0**	**0**	**0**	**0**	**0.0**	**0**	**0**	**0**	**0**	**0**	....	....	....	....	....	....	....	....
1995-96	Springfield Falcons	AHL	67	6	16	22	....	....	....	85	....	....	....	....	....	....	....	....	....	....	5	1	2	3	2	....	....	....
1996-97	**Phoenix Coyotes**	**NHL**	**1**	**0**	**0**	**0**	**0**	**0**	**0**	**0**	**0**	**0**	**0**	**0**	**0.0**	**0**	**0**	**0**	**0**	**0**	....	....	....	....	....	....	....	....
	Springfield Falcons	AHL	12	3	1	4	....	....	....	23	....	....	....	....	....	....	....	....	....	....	....	....	....	....	....	....	....	....
1997-98	Springfield Falcons	AHL	73	20	14	34	....	....	....	70	....	....	....	....	....	....	....	....	....	....	4	1	2	3	18	....	....	....

			REGULAR SEASON																		PLAYOFFS							
Season	Club	League	GP	G	A	Pts	AG	AA	APts	PIM	PP	SH	GW	S	%	TGF	PGF	TGA	PGA	+/–	GP	G	A	Pts	PIM	PP	SH	GW
1998-99	**Phoenix Coyotes**	**NHL**	**20**	**2**	**1**	**3**	**2**	**1**	**3**	**12**	**0**	**0**	**0**	**14**	**14.3**	**4**	**0**	**8**	**0**	**–4**	**2**	**0**	**0**	**0**	**0**	**0**	**0**	**0**
	Springfield Falcons	AHL	63	23	11	34	....	....	....	85	....	....	....	....	....	....	....	....	....	....	3	0	1	1	5	....	....	....
99-2000	**Phoenix Coyotes**	**NHL**	**5**	**0**	**0**	**0**	**0**	**0**	**0**	**0**	**0**	**0**	**0**	**2**	**0.0**	**0**	**0**	**0**	**0**	**0**	....	....	....	....	....	....	....	....
	Springfield Falcons	AHL	59	21	27	48	....	....	....	164	....	....	....	....	....	....	....	....	....	....	5	2	1	3	4	....	....	....
	NHL Totals		**27**	**2**	**1**	**3**	**2**	**1**	**3**	**12**	**0**	**0**	**0**	**16**	**12.5**	**4**	**0**	**8**	**0**		**2**	**0**	**0**	**0**	**0**	**0**	**0**	**0**

Transferred to **Phoenix** after **Winnipeg** franchise relocated, July 1, 1996.

• HANSON, Dave

D – L. 6', 190 lbs. b: Cumberland, WI, 4/12/1954.

Season	Club	League	GP	G	A	Pts	AG	AA	APts	PIM	PP	SH	GW	S	%	TGF	PGF	TGA	PGA	+/–	GP	G	A	Pts	PIM	PP	SH	GW
1973-74	St. Paul Vulcans	MWJHL	56	9	13	22	....	....	....	*220	....	....	....	....	....	....	....	....	....	....	....	....	....	....	....	....	....	....
1974-75	Johnstown Jets	NAHL	72	10	24	34	....	....	....	249	....	....	....	....	....	....	....	....	....	....	....	....	....	....	....	....	....	....
1975-76	Johnstown Jets	NAHL	66	8	21	29	....	....	....	311	....	....	....	....	....	....	....	....	....	....	....	....	....	....	....	....	....	....
1976-77	Minnesota Fighting Saints	WHA	7	0	2	2	....	....	....	35	....	....	....	....	....	....	....	....	....	....	....	....	....	....	....	....	....	....
	Hampton Gulls	SHL	28	5	7	12	....	....	....	188	....	....	....	....	....	....	....	....	....	....	....	....	....	....	....	....	....	....
	Johnstown Jets	NAHL	6	0	3	3	....	....	....	27	....	....	....	....	....	....	....	....	....	....	....	....	....	....	....	....	....	....
	New England Whalers	WHA	1	0	0	0	....	....	....	9	....	....	....	....	....	....	....	....	....	....	1	0	0	0	0	....	....	....
	Rhode Island Reds	AHL	27	2	10	12	....	....	....	98	....	....	....	....	....	....	....	....	....	....	....	....	....	....	....	....	....	....
1977-78	Kansas City Red Wings	CHL	15	0	0	0	....	....	....	41	....	....	....	....	....	....	....	....	....	....	....	....	....	....	....	....	....	....
	Hampton Gulls	AHL	5	0	3	3	....	....	....	8	....	....	....	....	....	....	....	....	....	....	....	....	....	....	....	....	....	....
	Birmingham Bulls	WHA	42	7	16	23	....	....	....	241	....	....	....	....	....	....	....	....	....	....	5	0	1	1	48	....	....	....
1978-79	**Detroit Red Wings**	**NHL**	**11**	**0**	**0**	**0**	**0**	**0**	**0**	**26**	**0**	**0**	**0**	**5**	**0.0**	**2**	**0**	**3**	**0**	**–1**	....	....	....	....	....	....	....	....
	Birmingham Bulls	WHA	53	6	22	28	....	....	....	212	....	....	....	....	....	....	....	....	....	....	....	....	....	....	....	....	....	....
1979-80	Birmingham Bulls	CHL	33	4	6	10	....	....	....	174	....	....	....	....	....	....	....	....	....	....	....	....	....	....	....	....	....	....
	Minnesota North Stars	**NHL**	**22**	**1**	**1**	**2**	**1**	**1**	**2**	**39**	**0**	**0**	**0**	**11**	**9.1**	**2**	**0**	**7**	**0**	**–5**	....	....	....	....	....	....	....	....
	Oklahoma City Stars	CHL	6	0	0	0	....	....	....	12	....	....	....	....	....	....	....	....	....	....	....	....	....	....	....	....	....	....
1980-81	Adirondack Red Wings	AHL	77	11	21	32	....	....	....	267	....	....	....	....	....	....	....	....	....	....	18	1	4	5	30	....	....	....
1981-82	Adirondack Red Wings	AHL	75	11	23	34	....	....	....	206	....	....	....	....	....	....	....	....	....	....	5	1	3	4	23	....	....	....
1982-83	Indianapolis Checkers	CHL	80	18	21	39	....	....	....	285	....	....	....	....	....	....	....	....	....	....	5	1	3	4	2	....	....	....
1983-84	Indianapolis Checkers	CHL	1	0	0	0	....	....	....	0	....	....	....	....	....	....	....	....	....	....	....	....	....	....	....	....	....	....
	Toledo Goaldiggers	IHL	68	11	26	37	....	....	....	120	....	....	....	....	....	....	....	....	....	....	9	1	3	4	33	....	....	....
	NHL Totals		**33**	**1**	**1**	**2**	**1**	**1**	**2**	**65**	**0**	**0**	**0**	**16**	**6.3**	**4**	**0**	**10**	**0**		....	....	....	....	....	....	....	....
	Other Major League Totals		103	13	40	53	....	....	....	497	....	....	....	....	....	....	....	....	....	....	6	0	1	1	48	....	....	....

Selected by **Minnesota** (WHA) in 1974 WHA Amateur Draft, June, 1974. Signed as a free agent by **New England** (WHA) after **Minnesota** (WHA) franchise folded, March, 1977. Signed as a free agent by **Birmingham** (WHA), September, 1977. Signed as a free agent by **Detroit**, October 4, 1977. Loaned to **Birmingham** (WHA) by **Detroit** with the loan of Steve Durbano and future considerations for Vaclav Nedomansky and Tim Sheehy, November 18, 1977. Traded to **Birmingham** (WHA) by **Detroit** for cash, December, 1978. Traded to **Minnesota** by **Detroit** for future considerations, January 3, 1980. Claimed on waivers by **Detroit** from **Minnesota**, June 8, 1980. Signed as a free agent by **NY Islanders**, September 9, 1982.

• HANSON, Keith

Keith Francis D – R. 6'5", 215 lbs. b: Ada, MN, 4/26/1957. Minnesota's 8th, 145th overall, in 1977.

Season	Club	League	GP	G	A	Pts	AG	AA	APts	PIM	PP	SH	GW	S	%	TGF	PGF	TGA	PGA	+/–	GP	G	A	Pts	PIM	PP	SH	GW
1976-77	Austin Mavericks	MWJHL	44	11	38	49	....	....	....	71	....	....	....	....	....	....	....	....	....	....	....	....	....	....	....	....	....	....
	United States	WJC-A	DID NOT PLAY																									
1977-78	Northern Michigan University	CCHA	34	16	15	31	....	....	....	77	....	....	....	....	....	....	....	....	....	....	....	....	....	....	....	....	....	....
1978-79	Northern Michigan University	CCHA	DID NOT PLAY																									
1979-80	Northern Michigan University	CCHA	38	2	13	15	....	....	....	74	....	....	....	....	....	....	....	....	....	....	....	....	....	....	....	....	....	....
1980-81	Northern Michigan University	CCHA	43	8	24	32	....	....	....	95	....	....	....	....	....	....	....	....	....	....	....	....	....	....	....	....	....	....
1981-82	Toledo Goaldiggers	IHL	82	7	37	44	....	....	....	185	....	....	....	....	....	....	....	....	....	....	13	1	3	4	23	....	....	....
1982-83	Birmingham South Stars	CHL	69	4	21	25	....	....	....	187	....	....	....	....	....	....	....	....	....	....	12	0	3	3	29	....	....	....
1983-84	**Calgary Flames**	**NHL**	**25**	**0**	**2**	**2**	**0**	**1**	**1**	**77**	**0**	**0**	**0**	**19**	**0.0**	**15**	**0**	**32**	**4**	**–13**	....	....	....	....	....	....	....	....
	Colorado Flames	CHL	39	5	21	26	....	....	....	64	....	....	....	....	....	....	....	....	....	....	6	2	2	4	16	....	....	....
1984-85	Moncton Golden Flames	AHL	70	5	17	22	....	....	....	145	....	....	....	....	....	....	....	....	....	....	....	....	....	....	....	....	....	....
	NHL Totals		**25**	**0**	**2**	**2**	**0**	**1**	**1**	**77**	**0**	**0**	**0**	**19**	**0.0**	**15**	**0**	**32**	**4**		....	....	....	....	....	....	....	....

Traded to **Calgary** by **Minnesota** with Mike Eaves for Steve Christoff and Calgary's 2nd round choice (Frantisek Musil) in 1983 Entry Draft, June 8, 1983.

• HARBARUK, Nick

Mikolaj Nicholas RW – R. 6', 195 lbs. b: Drohiczyn, Poland, 8/16/1943.

Season	Club	League	GP	G	A	Pts	AG	AA	APts	PIM	PP	SH	GW	S	%	TGF	PGF	TGA	PGA	+/–	GP	G	A	Pts	PIM	PP	SH	GW
1960-61	Toronto Marlboros	OHA-Jr.	36	4	8	12	....	....	....	58	....	....	....	....	....	....	....	....	....	....	....	....	....	....	....	....	....	....
1961-62	Toronto Marlboros	OHA-Jr.	31	7	10	17	....	....	....	56	....	....	....	....	....	....	....	....	....	....	12	6	5	11	38	....	....	....
	Pittsburgh Hornets	AHL	1	0	0	0	....	....	....	0	....	....	....	....	....	....	....	....	....	....	....	....	....	....	....	....	....	....
1962-63	Toronto Marlboros	OHA-Jr.	16	12	8	20	....	....	....	23	....	....	....	....	....	....	....	....	....	....	....	....	....	....	....	....	....	....
1963-64	Toronto Marlboros	OHA-Jr.	54	15	25	40	....	....	....	71	....	....	....	....	....	....	....	....	....	....	9	2	2	4	9	....	....	....
	Toronto Marlboros	Mem-Cup	11	5	4	9	....	....	....	15	....	....	....	....	....	....	....	....	....	....	....	....	....	....	....	....	....	....
1964-65	Rochester Americans	AHL	2	0	0	0	....	....	....	0	....	....	....	....	....	....	....	....	....	....	....	....	....	....	....	....	....	....
	Tulsa Oilers	CPHL	67	27	43	70	....	....	....	65	....	....	....	....	....	....	....	....	....	....	12	5	8	13	25	....	....	....
1965-66	Tulsa Oilers	CPHL	70	20	46	66	....	....	....	97	....	....	....	....	....	....	....	....	....	....	11	1	4	5	10	....	....	....
1966-67	Tulsa Oilers	CPHL	70	14	26	40	....	....	....	84	....	....	....	....	....	....	....	....	....	....	....	....	....	....	....	....	....	....
1967-68	Tulsa Oilers	CPHL	54	20	30	50	....	....	....	96	....	....	....	....	....	....	....	....	....	....	11	1	6	7	14	....	....	....
1968-69	Vancouver Canucks	WHL	3	1	1	2	....	....	....	2	....	....	....	....	....	....	....	....	....	....	....	....	....	....	....	....	....	....
	Tulsa Oilers	CHL	69	26	19	45	....	....	....	89	....	....	....	....	....	....	....	....	....	....	7	2	5	7	18	....	....	....
1969-70	**Pittsburgh Penguins**	**NHL**	**74**	**5**	**17**	**22**	**5**	**16**	**21**	**56**	**2**	**0**	**1**	**119**	**4.2**	**39**	**11**	**57**	**22**	**–7**	**10**	**3**	**0**	**3**	**20**	**0**	**1**	**0**
1970-71	**Pittsburgh Penguins**	**NHL**	**78**	**13**	**12**	**25**	**13**	**10**	**23**	**108**	**2**	**1**	**1**	**147**	**8.8**	**40**	**4**	**61**	**16**	**–9**	....	....	....	....	....	....	....	....
1971-72	**Pittsburgh Penguins**	**NHL**	**78**	**12**	**17**	**29**	**12**	**15**	**27**	**46**	**3**	**0**	**1**	**140**	**8.6**	**43**	**7**	**72**	**23**	**–13**	**4**	**0**	**1**	**1**	**0**	**0**	**0**	**0**
1972-73	**Pittsburgh Penguins**	**NHL**	**78**	**10**	**15**	**25**	**9**	**12**	**21**	**47**	**0**	**2**	**1**	**96**	**10.4**	**35**	**2**	**63**	**19**	**–11**	....	....	....	....	....	....	....	....
1973-74	**St. Louis Blues**	**NHL**	**56**	**5**	**14**	**19**	**5**	**12**	**17**	**16**	**0**	**1**	**1**	**49**	**10.2**	**25**	**2**	**33**	**14**	**4**	....	....	....	....	....	....	....	....
1974-75	Indianapolis Racers	WHA	78	20	23	43	....	....	....	52	....	....	....	....	....	....	....	....	....	....	....	....	....	....	....	....	....	....
1975-76	Indianapolis Racers	WHA	76	23	19	42	....	....	....	24	....	....	....	....	....	....	....	....	....	....	7	2	0	2	10	....	....	....
1976-77	Indianapolis Racers	WHA	27	2	2	4	....	....	....	2	....	....	....	....	....	....	....	....	....	....	6	1	1	2	0	....	....	....
	Oklahoma City Blazers	CHL	42	17	18	35	....	....	....	22	....	....	....	....	....	....	....	....	....	....	....	....	....	....	....	....	....	....
	NHL Totals		**364**	**45**	**75**	**120**	**44**	**65**	**109**	**273**	**7**	**4**	**5**	**551**	**8.2**	**182**	**26**	**286**	**94**		**14**	**3**	**1**	**4**	**20**	**0**	**1**	**0**
	Other Major League Totals		181	45	44	89	....	....	....	78	....	....	....	....	....	....	....	....	....	....	13	3	1	4	10	....	....	....

Rights transferred to **Vancouver** (WHL) after WHL club purchased **Rochester** (AHL) franchise, August 13, 1968. Claimed by **Pittsburgh** from **Vancouver** (WHL) in Intra-League Draft, June 10, 1969. Traded to **St. Louis** by **Pittsburgh** for Bob Johnson, October 4, 1973. Selected by **New England** (WHA) in 1972 WHA General Player Draft, February 12, 1972. WHA rights traded to **Indianapolis** (WHA) by **New England** (WHA), June, 1974.

• HARDING, Jeff

Jeffrey James RW – R. 6'3", 220 lbs. b: Toronto, Ont., 4/6/1969. Philadelphia's 2nd, 30th overall, in 1987.

Season	Club	League	GP	G	A	Pts	AG	AA	APts	PIM	PP	SH	GW	S	%	TGF	PGF	TGA	PGA	+/–	GP	G	A	Pts	PIM	PP	SH	GW
1985-86	Henry Carr Crusaders	OJHL-B	23	14	10	24	....	....	....	30	....	....	....	....	....	....	....	....	....	....	....	....	....	....	....	....	....	....
1986-87	St. Michael's Buzzers	OJHL-B	22	22	8	30	....	....	....	97	....	....	....	....	....	....	....	....	....	....	....	....	....	....	....	....	....	....
1987-88	Michigan State Spartans	WCHA	43	17	10	27	....	....	....	129	....	....	....	....	....	....	....	....	....	....	....	....	....	....	....	....	....	....
1988-89	**Philadelphia Flyers**	**NHL**	**6**	**0**	**0**	**0**	**0**	**0**	**0**	**29**	**0**	**0**	**0**	**11**	**0.0**	**1**	**0**	**1**	**1**	**1**	....	....	....	....	....	....	....	....
	Hershey Bears	AHL	34	13	5	18	....	....	....	64	....	....	....	....	....	....	....	....	....	....	8	1	1	2	33	....	....	....
1989-90	**Philadelphia Flyers**	**NHL**	**9**	**0**	**0**	**0**	**0**	**0**	**0**	**18**	**0**	**0**	**0**	**11**	**0.0**	**1**	**0**	**2**	**0**	**–1**	....	....	....	....	....	....	....	....
	Canada	Nat-Team	21	5	6	11	....	....	....	50	....	....	....	....	....	....	....	....	....	....	....	....	....	....	....	....	....	....
	Hershey Bears	AHL	6	0	2	2	....	....	....	2	....	....	....	....	....	....	....	....	....	....	....	....	....	....	....	....	....	....
1990-91	Cape Breton Oilers	AHL	4	1	0	1	....	....	....	2	....	....	....	....	....	....	....	....	....	....	....	....	....	....	....	....	....	....
	Fort Wayne Komets	IHL	11	3	4	7	....	....	....	10	....	....	....	....	....	....	....	....	....	....	....	....	....	....	....	....	....	....
1991-92	Springfield Indians	AHL	17	1	4	5	....	....	....	27	....	....	....	....	....	....	....	....	....	....	....	....	....	....	....	....	....	....
	Kalamazoo K-Wings	IHL	6	1	0	1	....	....	....	63	....	....	....	....	....	....	....	....	....	....	....	....	....	....	....	....	....	....
	NHL Totals		**15**	**0**	**0**	**0**	**0**	**0**	**0**	**47**	**0**	**0**	**0**	**22**	**0.0**	**2**	**0**	**3**	**1**		....	....	....	....	....	....	....	....

• HARDY, Joe

Jocelyn Joseph "Gypsy Joe" C – L. 6', 185 lbs. b: Kenogami, Que., 12/5/1945.

			REGULAR SEASON																		PLAYOFFS							
Season	Club	League	GP	G	A	Pts	AG	AA	APts	PIM	PP	SH	GW	S	%	TGF	PGF	TGA	PGA	+/–	GP	G	A	Pts	PIM	PP	SH	GW
1964-65	Jonquiere Marquis	QJHL	STATISTICS NOT AVAILABLE																									
	Jonquiere Marquis	Mem-Cup	3	1	1	2	....	....	....	0	....	....	....	....	....	....	....	....	....	....	....	....	....	....	....	....	....	....
1965-66	Jonquierre Marquis	QJHL	STATISTICS NOT AVAILABLE																									
1966-67	New Haven Blades	EHL	72	28	51	79	....	....	....	77	....	....	....	....	....	....	....	....	....	....	....	....	....	....	....	....	....	....
1967-68	Victoriaville Tigers	QSHL	41	13	23	36	....	....	....	39	....	....	....	....	....	....	....	....	....	....	12	4	8	12	4	....	....	....
	Victoriaville Tigers	Al-Cup	13	7	6	13	....	....	....	16	....	....	....	....	....	....	....	....	....	....	....	....	....	....	....	....	....	....
1968-69	Victoriaville Tigers	QSHL	45	25	54	79	....	....	....	75	....	....	....	....	....	....	....	....	....	....	....	....	....	....	....	....	....	....
1969-70	**Oakland Seals**	**NHL**	**23**	**5**	**4**	**9**	**5**	**4**	**9**	**20**	**1**	**1**	**1**	**38**	**13.2**	**13**	**4**	**20**	**3**	**–8**	**4**	**0**	**0**	**0**	**0**	**0**	**0**	**0**
	Providence Reds	AHL	46	11	27	38	....	....	....	44	....	....	....	....	....	....	....	....	....	....	....	....	....	....	....	....	....	....
	Seattle Totems	WHL	....	....	....	....	....	....	....	....	....	....	....	....	....	....	....	....	....	....	2	1	0	1	4	....	....	....
1970-71	**California Golden Seals**	**NHL**	**40**	**4**	**10**	**14**	**4**	**8**	**12**	**31**	**1**	**0**	**0**	**43**	**9.3**	**18**	**4**	**34**	**6**	**–14**	....	....	....	....	....	....	....	....
1971-72	Nova Scotia Voyageurs	AHL	65	18	42	60	....	....	....	105	....	....	....	....	....	....	....	....	....	....	15	3	7	10	20	....	....	....
1972-73	Cleveland Crusaders	WHA	72	17	33	50	....	....	....	80	....	....	....	....	....	....	....	....	....	....	7	0	2	2	0	....	....	....
1973-74	Chicago Cougars	WHA	77	24	35	59	....	....	....	55	....	....	....	....	....	....	....	....	....	....	17	4	8	12	13	....	....	....
1974-75	Chicago Cougars	WHA	17	1	6	7	....	....	....	8	....	....	....	....	....	....	....	....	....	....	....	....	....	....	....	....	....	....
	Long Island Cougars	NAHL	4	1	2	3	....	....	....	2	....	....	....	....	....	....	....	....	....	....	....	....	....	....	....	....	....	....
	Indianapolis Racers	WHA	32	2	17	19	....	....	....	36	....	....	....	....	....	....	....	....	....	....	....	....	....	....	....	....	....	....
	San Diego Mariners	WHA	12	2	3	5	....	....	....	22	....	....	....	....	....	....	....	....	....	....	3	0	0	0	0	....	....	....
1975-76	Beauce Jaros	NAHL	72	60	*148	*208	....	....	....	98	....	....	....	....	....	....	....	....	....	....	14	4	24	28	44	....	....	....
1976-77	Beauce Jaros	NAHL	22	7	36	43	....	....	....	30	....	....	....	....	....	....	....	....	....	....	....	....	....	....	....	....	....	....
	Binghamton Dusters	NAHL	28	22	28	50	....	....	....	19	....	....	....	....	....	....	....	....	....	....	8	2	8	10	6	....	....	....
1977-78	Binghamton Dusters	AHL	73	24	*63	87	....	....	....	56	....	....	....	....	....	....	....	....	....	....	....	....	....	....	....	....	....	....
	NHL Totals		**63**	**9**	**14**	**23**	**9**	**12**	**21**	**51**	**2**	**1**	**1**	**81**	**11.1**	**31**	**8**	**54**	**9**		**4**	**0**	**0**	**0**	**0**	**0**	**0**	**0**
	Other Major League Totals		210	46	94	140	....	....	....	201	....	....	....	....	....	....	....	....	....	....	27	4	10	14	13	....	....	....

QSHL Second All-Star Team (1968) • QSHL First All-Star Team (1969) • NAHL First All-Star Team (1976)

Signed as a free agent by **Oakland**, September, 1969. Traded to **Montreal** by **Oakland** for cash, October, 1971. Selected by **Alberta** (WHA) in 1972 WHA General Player Draft, February 12, 1972. WHA rights traded to **Cleveland** (WHA) by **Alberta** (WHA) for future considerations, July, 1972. Traded to **Chicago** (WHA) by **Cleveland** (WHA) for Wayne Hillman, August, 1973. Traded to **Indianapolis** (WHA) by **Chicago** (WHA) for future considerations, December, 1974. Traded to **San Diego** (WHA) by **Indianapolis** (WHA) for future considerations, March, 1975. • Transferred to **Binghamton** (NAHL) when **Beauce** (NAHL) folded, December, 1976. • First professional hockey player to record 200 points in a single season (1975-76).

• HARDY, Mark

Mark Lea D – L. 5'11", 195 lbs. b: Semaden, Switz., 2/1/1959. Los Angeles' 3rd, 30th overall, in 1979.

Season	Club	League	GP	G	A	Pts	AG	AA	APts	PIM	PP	SH	GW	S	%	TGF	PGF	TGA	PGA	+/–	GP	G	A	Pts	PIM	PP	SH	GW
1975-76	Montreal Juniors	QMJHL	64	6	17	23	....	....	....	44	....	....	....	....	....	....	....	....	....	....	....	....	....	....	....	....	....	....
1976-77	Montreal Juniors	QMJHL	72	20	40	60	....	....	....	137	....	....	....	....	....	....	....	....	....	....	12	4	8	12	14	....	....	....
1977-78	Montreal Juniors	QMJHL	72	25	57	82	....	....	....	150	....	....	....	....	....	....	....	....	....	....	13	3	10	13	22	....	....	....
1978-79	Montreal Juniors	QMJHL	67	18	52	70	....	....	....	117	....	....	....	....	....	....	....	....	....	....	11	5	8	13	40	....	....	....
1979-80	**Los Angeles Kings**	**NHL**	**15**	**0**	**1**	**1**	**0**	**1**	**1**	**10**	**0**	**0**	**0**	**14**	**0.0**	**14**	**1**	**28**	**8**	**–7**	**4**	**1**	**1**	**2**	**9**	**0**	**0**	**0**
	Binghamton Dusters	AHL	56	3	13	16	....	....	....	32	....	....	....	....	....	....	....	....	....	....	....	....	....	....	....	....	....	....
1980-81	**Los Angeles Kings**	**NHL**	**77**	**5**	**20**	**25**	**4**	**13**	**17**	**77**	**3**	**0**	**1**	**90**	**5.6**	**111**	**23**	**108**	**34**	**14**	**4**	**1**	**2**	**3**	**4**	**1**	**0**	**0**
1981-82	**Los Angeles Kings**	**NHL**	**77**	**6**	**39**	**45**	**5**	**26**	**31**	**130**	**1**	**0**	**0**	**121**	**5.0**	**137**	**44**	**137**	**32**	**–12**	**10**	**1**	**2**	**3**	**9**	**0**	**0**	**0**
1982-83	**Los Angeles Kings**	**NHL**	**74**	**5**	**34**	**39**	**4**	**24**	**28**	**101**	**3**	**0**	**1**	**162**	**3.1**	**128**	**49**	**143**	**34**	**–30**	....	....	....	....	....	....	....	....
1983-84	**Los Angeles Kings**	**NHL**	**79**	**8**	**41**	**49**	**6**	**28**	**34**	**122**	**5**	**0**	**1**	**175**	**4.6**	**149**	**54**	**165**	**40**	**–30**	....	....	....	....	....	....	....	....
1984-85	**Los Angeles Kings**	**NHL**	**78**	**14**	**39**	**53**	**11**	**27**	**38**	**97**	**8**	**1**	**2**	**151**	**9.3**	**134**	**58**	**120**	**24**	**–20**	**3**	**0**	**1**	**1**	**2**	**0**	**0**	**0**
1985-86	**Los Angeles Kings**	**NHL**	**55**	**6**	**21**	**27**	**5**	**14**	**19**	**71**	**2**	**1**	**1**	**113**	**5.3**	**87**	**26**	**112**	**40**	**–11**	....	....	....	....	....	....	....	....
	Canada	WEC-A	10	3	2	5	....	....	....	12	....	....	....	....	....	....	....	....	....	....	....	....	....	....	....	....	....	....
1986-87	**Los Angeles Kings**	**NHL**	**73**	**3**	**27**	**30**	**3**	**20**	**23**	**120**	**0**	**0**	**0**	**97**	**3.1**	**114**	**33**	**98**	**33**	**16**	**5**	**1**	**2**	**3**	**10**	**0**	**0**	**0**
1987-88	**Los Angeles Kings**	**NHL**	**61**	**6**	**22**	**28**	**5**	**16**	**21**	**99**	**4**	**1**	**1**	**107**	**5.6**	**82**	**38**	**106**	**35**	**–27**	....	....	....	....	....	....	....	....
	New York Rangers	**NHL**	**19**	**2**	**2**	**4**	**2**	**1**	**3**	**31**	**0**	**0**	**0**	**27**	**7.4**	**12**	**2**	**26**	**11**	**–5**	....	....	....	....	....	....	....	....
1988-89	**Minnesota North Stars**	**NHL**	**15**	**2**	**4**	**6**	**2**	**3**	**5**	**26**	**0**	**0**	**1**	**19**	**10.5**	**14**	**5**	**20**	**10**	**–1**	....	....	....	....	....	....	....	....
	New York Rangers	**NHL**	**45**	**2**	**12**	**14**	**2**	**8**	**10**	**45**	**0**	**0**	**0**	**51**	**3.9**	**38**	**4**	**64**	**22**	**–8**	**4**	**0**	**1**	**1**	**31**	**0**	**0**	**0**
1989-90	**New York Rangers**	**NHL**	**54**	**0**	**15**	**15**	**0**	**11**	**11**	**94**	**0**	**0**	**0**	**55**	**0.0**	**53**	**10**	**64**	**25**	**4**	**3**	**0**	**1**	**1**	**2**	**0**	**0**	**0**
1990-91	**New York Rangers**	**NHL**	**70**	**1**	**5**	**6**	**1**	**4**	**5**	**89**	**0**	**0**	**0**	**63**	**1.6**	**60**	**4**	**85**	**28**	**–1**	**6**	**0**	**1**	**1**	**30**	**0**	**0**	**0**
1991-92	**New York Rangers**	**NHL**	**52**	**1**	**8**	**9**	**1**	**6**	**7**	**65**	**0**	**0**	**1**	**42**	**2.4**	**65**	**1**	**43**	**12**	**33**	**13**	**0**	**3**	**3**	**31**	**0**	**0**	**0**
1992-93	**New York Rangers**	**NHL**	**44**	**1**	**10**	**11**	**1**	**7**	**8**	**85**	**0**	**0**	**0**	**28**	**3.6**	**41**	**1**	**56**	**18**	**2**	....	....	....	....	....	....	....	....
	Los Angeles Kings	**NHL**	**11**	**0**	**3**	**3**	**0**	**2**	**2**	**4**	**0**	**0**	**0**	**20**	**0.0**	**6**	**2**	**14**	**6**	**–4**	**15**	**1**	**2**	**3**	**30**	**0**	**0**	**0**
1993-94	**Los Angeles Kings**	**NHL**	**16**	**0**	**3**	**3**	**0**	**2**	**2**	**27**	**0**	**0**	**0**	**8**	**0.0**	**10**	**0**	**17**	**2**	**–5**	....	....	....	....	....	....	....	....
	Phoenix Roadrunners	IHL	54	5	3	8	....	....	....	48	....	....	....	....	....	....	....	....	....	....	....	....	....	....	....	....	....	....
1994-95	Detroit Vipers	IHL	41	6	21	27	....	....	....	35	....	....	....	....	....	....	....	....	....	....	5	1	1	2	7	....	....	....
1995-96	Los Angeles Ice Dogs	IHL	69	4	18	22	....	....	....	128	....	....	....	....	....	....	....	....	....	....	....	....	....	....	....	....	....	....
	Detroit Vipers	IHL	10	0	4	4	....	....	....	8	....	....	....	....	....	....	....	....	....	....	12	1	1	2	16	....	....	....
1996-97	Long Beach Ice Dogs	IHL	DID NOT PLAY – ASSISTANT COACH																									
1997-98	Long Beach Ice Dogs	IHL	25	3	6	9	....	....	....	113	....	....	....	....	....	....	....	....	....	....	17	2	3	5	34	....	....	....
1998-99	Long Beach Ice Dogs	IHL	DID NOT PLAY – ASSISTANT COACH																									
99-2000	**Los Angeles Kings**	**NHL**	DID NOT PLAY – ASSISTANT COACH																									
	NHL Totals		**915**	**62**	**306**	**368**	**52**	**213**	**265**	**1293**	**26**	**3**	**9**	**1343**	**4.6**	**1255**	**355**	**1406**	**414**		**67**	**5**	**16**	**21**	**158**	**1**	**0**	**0**

QMJHL First All-Star Team (1978)

Traded to **NY Rangers** by **LA Kings** for Ron Duguay, February 23, 1988. Traded to **Minnesota** by **NY Rangers** for future considerations (Louie Debrusk) June 13, 1988. Traded to **NY Rangers** by **Minnesota** for Larry Bernard and NY Rangers' 5th round choice (Rhys Hollyman) in 1989 Entry Draft, December 9, 1988. Traded to **LA Kings** by **NY Rangers** with Ottawa's 5th round choice (previously acquired, LA Kings selected Frederick Beaubien) in 1993 Entry Draft for John McIntyre, March 22, 1993.

• HARGREAVES, Jim

James Albert "Cement Head" D – R. 5'11", 195 lbs. b: Winnipeg, Man., 5/2/1950. Vancouver's 2nd, 16th overall, in 1970.

Season	Club	League	GP	G	A	Pts	AG	AA	APts	PIM	PP	SH	GW	S	%	TGF	PGF	TGA	PGA	+/–	GP	G	A	Pts	PIM	PP	SH	GW
1968-69	Winnipeg Jets	WCJHL	56	10	19	29	....	....	....	107	....	....	....	....	....	....	....	....	....	....	....	....	....	....	....	....	....	....
1969-70	Winnipeg Jets	WCJHL	55	10	34	44	....	....	....	176	....	....	....	....	....	....	....	....	....	....	....	....	....	....	....	....	....	....
1970-71	**Vancouver Canucks**	**NHL**	**7**	**0**	**1**	**1**	**0**	**1**	**1**	**33**	**0**	**0**	**0**	**2**	**0.0**	**3**	**1**	**5**	**0**	**–3**	....	....	....	....	....	....	....	....
	Rochester Americans	AHL	42	1	10	11	....	....	....	109	....	....	....	....	....	....	....	....	....	....	....	....	....	....	....	....	....	....
1971-72	Rochester Americans	AHL	61	3	10	13	....	....	....	127	....	....	....	....	....	....	....	....	....	....	....	....	....	....	....	....	....	....
1972-73	**Vancouver Canucks**	**NHL**	**59**	**1**	**6**	**7**	**1**	**5**	**6**	**72**	**0**	**0**	**0**	**40**	**2.5**	**29**	**1**	**77**	**18**	**–31**	....	....	....	....	....	....	....	....
	Seattle Totems	WHL	17	1	11	12	....	....	....	43	....	....	....	....	....	....	....	....	....	....	....	....	....	....	....	....	....	....
1973-74	Winnipeg Jets	WHA	53	1	4	5	....	....	....	50	....	....	....	....	....	....	....	....	....	....	....	....	....	....	....	....	....	....
1974-75	Indianapolis Racers	WHA	37	2	5	7	....	....	....	30	....	....	....	....	....	....	....	....	....	....	....	....	....	....	....	....	....	....
	San Diego Mariners	WHA	41	8	10	18	....	....	....	45	....	....	....	....	....	....	....	....	....	....	10	1	0	1	6	....	....	....
1975-76	San Diego Mariners	WHA	43	1	1	2	....	....	....	26	....	....	....	....	....	....	....	....	....	....	5	0	0	0	2	....	....	....
	NHL Totals		**66**	**1**	**7**	**8**	**1**	**6**	**7**	**105**	**0**	**0**	**0**	**42**	**2.4**	**32**	**2**	**82**	**18**		....	....	....	....	....	....	....	....
	Other Major League Totals		174	12	20	32	....	....	....	151	....	....	....	....	....	....	....	....	....	....	15	1	0	1	8	....	....	....

Named WCJHL's Top Defenseman (1970) • WCJHL All-Star Team (1970)

Selected by **Winnipeg** (WHA) in 1972 WHA General Player Draft, February 12, 1972. Selected by **Indianapolis** (WHA) from **Winnipeg** (WHA) in 1974 WHA Expansion Draft, May 30, 1974. Traded to **San Diego** (WHA) by **Indianapolis** (WHA) for Ken Block, January, 1975.

• HARKINS, Brett

Brett A. LW – L. 6'1", 185 lbs. b: North Ridgeville, OH, 7/2/1970. NY Islanders' 9th, 133rd overall, in 1989.

Season	Club	League	GP	G	A	Pts	AG	AA	APts	PIM	PP	SH	GW	S	%	TGF	PGF	TGA	PGA	+/–	GP	G	A	Pts	PIM	PP	SH	GW
1986-87	St. Andrews College	Hi-School	30	47	60	107	....	....	....	....	....	....	....	....	....	....	....	....	....	....	....	....	....	....	....	....	....	....
1987-88	Brockville Braves	OJHL	55	21	55	76	....	....	....	36	....	....	....	....	....	....	....	....	....	....	....	....	....	....	....	....	....	....
1988-89	Detroit Compuware	NAJHL	38	23	46	69	....	....	....	94	....	....	....	....	....	....	....	....	....	....	....	....	....	....	....	....	....	....
1989-90	Bowling Green University	CCHA	41	11	43	54	....	....	....	45	....	....	....	....	....	....	....	....	....	....	....	....	....	....	....	....	....	....
1990-91	Bowling Green University	CCHA	40	22	38	60	....	....	....	30	....	....	....	....	....	....	....	....	....	....	....	....	....	....	....	....	....	....
1991-92	Bowling Green University	CCHA	34	8	39	47	....	....	....	32	....	....	....	....	....	....	....	....	....	....	....	....	....	....	....	....	....	....
1992-93	Bowling Green University	CCHA	35	19	28	47	....	....	....	28	....	....	....	....	....	....	....	....	....	....	....	....	....	....	....	....	....	....

Season	Club	League	GP	G	A	Pts	AG	AA	APts	PIM	PP	SH	GW	S	%	TGF	PGF	TGA	PGA	+/–	GP	G	A	Pts	PIM	PP	SH	GW
			REGULAR SEASON																		PLAYOFFS							
1993-94	Adirondack Red Wings	AHL	80	22	47	69	....	....	....	23	....	....	....	....	....	....	....	....	....	....	10	1	5	6	4	....	....	....
1994-95	**Boston Bruins**	**NHL**	**1**	**0**	**1**	**1**	**0**	**1**	**1**	**0**	**0**	**0**	**0**	**1**	**0.0**	**2**	**1**	**1**	**0**	**0**	....	....	....	....	....	....	....	....
	Providence Bruins	AHL	80	23	*69	92	....	....	....	32	....	....	....	....	....	....	....	....	....	....	13	8	14	22	4	....	....	....
1995-96	**Florida Panthers**	**NHL**	**8**	**0**	**3**	**3**	**0**	**2**	**2**	**6**	**0**	**0**	**0**	**4**	**0.0**	**6**	**3**	**5**	**0**	**–2**	....	....	....	....	....	....	....	....
	Carolina Monarchs	AHL	55	23	*71	94	....	....	....	44	....	....	....	....	....	....	....	....	....	....	....	....	....	....	....	....	....	....
1996-97	**Boston Bruins**	**NHL**	**44**	**4**	**14**	**18**	**4**	**12**	**16**	**8**	**3**	**0**	**2**	**52**	**7.7**	**28**	**9**	**22**	**0**	**–3**	....	....	....	....	....	....	....	....
	Providence Bruins	AHL	28	9	31	40	....	....	....	32	....	....	....	....	....	....	....	....	....	....	10	2	10	12	0	....	....	....
1997-98	Cleveland Lumberjacks	IHL	80	32	62	94	....	....	....	82	....	....	....	....	....	....	....	....	....	....	10	4	13	17	14	....	....	....
1998-99	Cleveland Lumberjacks	IHL	74	20	67	87	....	....	....	84	....	....	....	....	....	....	....	....	....	....	....	....	....	....	....	....	....	....
99-2000	Cleveland Lumberjacks	IHL	76	20	50	70	....	....	....	79	....	....	....	....	....	....	....	....	....	....	9	2	8	10	6	....	....	....
	NHL Totals		**53**	**4**	**18**	**22**	**4**	**15**	**19**	**14**	**3**	**0**	**2**	**57**	**7.0**	**36**	**13**	**28**	**0**		....	....	....	....	....	....	....	....

• Brother of Todd

Signed as a free agent by **Boston**, July 1, 1994. Signed as a free agent by **Florida**, July 24, 1995. Signed as a free agent by **Boston**, September 4, 1996. • Played w/ RHI's Utah Rollerbees in 1994 (6-5-10-15-8).

• HARKINS, Todd

Todd M. C – R. 6'3", 210 lbs. b: Cleveland, OH, 10/8/1968. Calgary's 2nd, 42nd overall, in 1988.

Season	Club	League	GP	G	A	Pts	AG	AA	APts	PIM	PP	SH	GW	S	%	TGF	PGF	TGA	PGA	+/–	GP	G	A	Pts	PIM	PP	SH	GW
1986-87	Aurora Eagles	OJHL	40	19	29	48	....	....	....	102	....	....	....	....	....	....	....	....	....	....	....	....	....	....	....	....	....	....
1987-88	University of Miami-Ohio	CCHA	34	9	7	16	....	....	....	133	....	....	....	....	....	....	....	....	....	....	....	....	....	....	....	....	....	....
1988-89	University of Miami-Ohio	CCHA	36	8	7	15	....	....	....	77	....	....	....	....	....	....	....	....	....	....	....	....	....	....	....	....	....	....
1989-90	University of Miami-Ohio	CCHA	40	27	17	44	....	....	....	78	....	....	....	....	....	....	....	....	....	....	....	....	....	....	....	....	....	....
1990-91	Salt Lake Golden Eagles	IHL	79	15	27	42	....	....	....	113	....	....	....	....	....	....	....	....	....	....	3	0	0	0	0	....	....	....
1991-92	**Calgary Flames**	**NHL**	**5**	**0**	**0**	**0**	**0**	**0**	**0**	**7**	**0**	**0**	**0**	**4**	**0.0**	**0**	**0**	**2**	**0**	**–2**	....	....	....	....	....	....	....	....
	Salt Lake Golden Eagles	IHL	72	32	30	62	....	....	....	67	....	....	....	....	....	....	....	....	....	....	5	1	1	2	6	....	....	....
	United States	WC-A	6	0	4	4	....	....	....	10	....	....	....	....	....	....	....	....	....	....	....	....	....	....	....	....	....	....
1992-93	**Calgary Flames**	**NHL**	**15**	**2**	**3**	**5**	**2**	**2**	**4**	**22**	**0**	**0**	**0**	**17**	**11.8**	**7**	**1**	**10**	**0**	**–4**	....	....	....	....	....	....	....	....
	Salt Lake Golden Eagles	IHL	53	13	21	34	....	....	....	90	....	....	....	....	....	....	....	....	....	....	....	....	....	....	....	....	....	....
1993-94	Saint John Flames	AHL	38	13	9	22	....	....	....	64	....	....	....	....	....	....	....	....	....	....	....	....	....	....	....	....	....	....
	Hartford Whalers	**NHL**	**28**	**1**	**0**	**1**	**1**	**0**	**1**	**49**	**0**	**0**	**0**	**15**	**6.7**	**3**	**0**	**7**	**0**	**–4**	....	....	....	....	....	....	....	....
	Springfield Indians	AHL	1	0	3	3	....	....	....	0	....	....	....	....	....	....	....	....	....	....	....	....	....	....	....	....	....	....
1994-95	Chicago Wolves	IHL	52	18	25	43	....	....	....	136	....	....	....	....	....	....	....	....	....	....	....	....	....	....	....	....	....	....
	Houston Aeros	IHL	25	9	10	19	....	....	....	77	....	....	....	....	....	....	....	....	....	....	4	1	1	2	28	....	....	....
	United States	WC-A	6	1	3	4	....	....	....	28	....	....	....	....	....	....	....	....	....	....	....	....	....	....	....	....	....	....
1995-96	Carolina Monarchs	AHL	69	27	28	55	....	....	....	172	....	....	....	....	....	....	....	....	....	....	....	....	....	....	....	....	....	....
1996-97	Fort Wayne Komets	IHL	60	12	13	25	....	....	....	131	....	....	....	....	....	....	....	....	....	....	....	....	....	....	....	....	....	....
	Phoenix Roadrunners	IHL	16	4	3	7	....	....	....	24	....	....	....	....	....	....	....	....	....	....	....	....	....	....	....	....	....	....
1997-98	Dusseldorfer EG	Germany	48	13	22	35	....	....	....	117	....	....	....	....	....	....	....	....	....	....	3	2	0	2	12	....	....	....
1998-99	Schwenningen Wild Wings	Germany	51	25	9	34	....	....	....	137	....	....	....	....	....	....	....	....	....	....	....	....	....	....	....	....	....	....
99-2000	Schwenningen Wild Wings	Germany	67	15	20	35	....	....	....	103	....	....	....	....	....	....	....	....	....	....	....	....	....	....	....	....	....	....
	NHL Totals		**48**	**3**	**3**	**6**	**3**	**2**	**5**	**78**	**0**	**0**	**0**	**36**	**8.3**	**10**	**1**	**19**	**0**		....	....	....	....	....	....	....	....

• Brother of Brett

Traded to **Hartford** by **Calgary** for Scott Morrow, January 24, 1994. Signed as a free agent by **Florida**, June 6, 1995. • Played w/ RHI's Utah Rollerbees in 1993 (9-14-7-21-58).

• HARLOCK, David

David A. D – L. 6'2", 220 lbs. b: Toronto, Ont., 3/16/1971. New Jersey's 2nd, 24th overall, in 1990.

Season	Club	League	GP	G	A	Pts	AG	AA	APts	PIM	PP	SH	GW	S	%	TGF	PGF	TGA	PGA	+/–	GP	G	A	Pts	PIM	PP	SH	GW
1986-87	Toronto Red Wings	MTHL	86	17	55	72	....	....	....	60	....	....	....	....	....	....	....	....	....	....	....	....	....	....	....	....	....	....
1987-88	Toronto Red Wings	MTHL	70	16	56	72	....	....	....	100	....	....	....	....	....	....	....	....	....	....	....	....	....	....	....	....	....	....
	Henry Carr Crusaders	OJHL-B	3	0	0	0	....	....	....	4	....	....	....	....	....	....	....	....	....	....	....	....	....	....	....	....	....	....
1988-89	St. Michael's Buzzers	OJHL-B	25	4	16	20	....	....	....	34	....	....	....	....	....	....	....	....	....	....	27	3	12	15	14	....	....	....
1989-90	University of Michigan	CCHA	42	2	13	15	....	....	....	44	....	....	....	....	....	....	....	....	....	....	....	....	....	....	....	....	....	....
1990-91	University of Michigan	CCHA	39	2	8	10	....	....	....	70	....	....	....	....	....	....	....	....	....	....	....	....	....	....	....	....	....	....
	Canada	WJC-A	7	0	2	2	....	....	....	2	....	....	....	....	....	....	....	....	....	....	....	....	....	....	....	....	....	....
1991-92	University of Michigan	CCHA	44	1	6	7	....	....	....	80	....	....	....	....	....	....	....	....	....	....	....	....	....	....	....	....	....	....
1992-93	University of Michigan	CCHA	38	3	9	12	....	....	....	58	....	....	....	....	....	....	....	....	....	....	....	....	....	....	....	....	....	....
	Canada	Nat-Team	4	0	0	0	....	....	....	2	....	....	....	....	....	....	....	....	....	....	....	....	....	....	....	....	....	....
1993-94	Canada	Nat-Team	41	0	3	3	....	....	....	28	....	....	....	....	....	....	....	....	....	....	....	....	....	....	....	....	....	....
	Canada	Olympics	8	0	0	0	....	....	....	8	....	....	....	....	....	....	....	....	....	....	....	....	....	....	....	....	....	....
	Toronto Maple Leafs	**NHL**	**6**	**0**	**0**	**0**	**0**	**0**	**0**	**0**	**0**	**0**	**0**	**2**	**0.0**	**3**	**0**	**6**	**1**	**–2**	....	....	....	....	....	....	....	....
	St. John's Maple Leafs	AHL	10	0	3	3	....	....	....	2	....	....	....	....	....	....	....	....	....	....	9	0	0	0	6	....	....	....
1994-95	**Toronto Maple Leafs**	**NHL**	**1**	**0**	**0**	**0**	**0**	**0**	**0**	**0**	**0**	**0**	**0**	**0**	**0.0**	**0**	**0**	**1**	**0**	**–1**	....	....	....	....	....	....	....	....
	St. John's Maple Leafs	AHL	58	0	6	6	....	....	....	44	....	....	....	....	....	....	....	....	....	....	5	0	0	0	0	....	....	....
1995-96	**Toronto Maple Leafs**	**NHL**	**1**	**0**	**0**	**0**	**0**	**0**	**0**	**0**	**0**	**0**	**0**	**0**	**0.0**	**0**	**0**	**0**	**0**	**0**	....	....	....	....	....	....	....	....
	St. John's Maple Leafs	AHL	77	0	12	12	....	....	....	92	....	....	....	....	....	....	....	....	....	....	4	0	1	1	2	....	....	....
1996-97	San Antonio Dragons	IHL	69	3	10	13	....	....	....	82	....	....	....	....	....	....	....	....	....	....	9	0	0	0	10	....	....	....
1997-98	**Washington Capitals**	**NHL**	**6**	**0**	**0**	**0**	**0**	**0**	**0**	**4**	**0**	**0**	**0**	**2**	**0.0**	**3**	**0**	**2**	**1**	**2**	....	....	....	....	....	....	....	....
	Portland Pirates	AHL	71	3	15	18	....	....	....	66	....	....	....	....	....	....	....	....	....	....	10	2	2	4	6	....	....	....
1998-99	**New York Islanders**	**NHL**	**70**	**2**	**6**	**8**	**2**	**6**	**8**	**68**	**0**	**0**	**0**	**35**	**5.7**	**34**	**0**	**74**	**24**	**–16**	....	....	....	....	....	....	....	....
99-2000	**Atlanta Thrashers**	**NHL**	**44**	**0**	**6**	**6**	**0**	**6**	**6**	**36**	**0**	**0**	**0**	**29**	**0.0**	**26**	**2**	**47**	**15**	**–8**	....	....	....	....	....	....	....	....
	NHL Totals		**128**	**2**	**12**	**14**	**2**	**12**	**14**	**108**	**0**	**0**	**0**	**68**	**2.9**	**66**	**2**	**130**	**41**		....	....	....	....	....	....	....	....

Signed as a free agent by **Toronto**, August 20, 1993. Signed as a free agent by **Washington**, August 20, 1997. Signed as a free agent by **NY Islanders**, August 24, 1998. Claimed by **Atlanta** from **NY Islanders** in Expansion Draft, June 25, 1999.

• HARLOW, Scott

LW – L. 6'1", 185 lbs. b: East Bridgewater, MA, 10/11/1963. Montreal's 6th, 61st overall, in 1982.

Season	Club	League	GP	G	A	Pts	AG	AA	APts	PIM	PP	SH	GW	S	%	TGF	PGF	TGA	PGA	+/–	GP	G	A	Pts	PIM	PP	SH	GW
1981-82	Bridgewater Bruins	NEJHL	24	36	38	74	....	....	....	....	....	....	....	....	....	....	....	....	....	....	....	....	....	....	....	....	....	....
1982-83	Boston College	ECAC	24	6	19	25	....	....	....	19	....	....	....	....	....	....	....	....	....	....	....	....	....	....	....	....	....	....
	United States	WJC-A	7	2	2	4	....	....	....	0	....	....	....	....	....	....	....	....	....	....	....	....	....	....	....	....	....	....
1983-84	Boston College	ECAC	39	27	20	47	....	....	....	17	....	....	....	....	....	....	....	....	....	....	....	....	....	....	....	....	....	....
1984-85	Boston College	H-East	44	34	38	72	....	....	....	45	....	....	....	....	....	....	....	....	....	....	....	....	....	....	....	....	....	....
1985-86	Boston College	H-East	42	38	41	79	....	....	....	48	....	....	....	....	....	....	....	....	....	....	....	....	....	....	....	....	....	....
1986-87	Sherbrooke Canadiens	AHL	66	22	26	48	....	....	....	6	....	....	....	....	....	....	....	....	....	....	15	5	6	11	6	....	....	....
1987-88	Sherbrooke Canadiens	AHL	18	6	12	18	....	....	....	8	....	....	....	....	....	....	....	....	....	....	....	....	....	....	....	....	....	....
	St. Louis Blues	**NHL**	**1**	**0**	**1**	**1**	**0**	**1**	**1**	**0**	**0**	**0**	**0**	**2**	**0.0**	**2**	**1**	**2**	**0**	**–1**	....	....	....	....	....	....	....	....
	Baltimore Skipjacks	AHL	29	24	27	51	....	....	....	21	....	....	....	....	....	....	....	....	....	....	....	....	....	....	....	....	....	....
	Peoria Rivermen	IHL	39	30	25	55	....	....	....	46	....	....	....	....	....	....	....	....	....	....	....	....	....	....	....	....	....	....
1988-89	Peoria Rivermen	IHL	45	16	26	42	....	....	....	22	....	....	....	....	....	....	....	....	....	....	....	....	....	....	....	....	....	....
	Maine Mariners	AHL	30	16	17	33	....	....	....	8	....	....	....	....	....	....	....	....	....	....	....	....	....	....	....	....	....	....
1989-90	Maine Mariners	AHL	80	31	32	63	....	....	....	68	....	....	....	....	....	....	....	....	....	....	....	....	....	....	....	....	....	....
1990-91	New Haven Nighthawks	AHL	73	28	28	56	....	....	....	92	....	....	....	....	....	....	....	....	....	....	....	....	....	....	....	....	....	....
	Phoenix Roadrunners	IHL	4	2	0	2	....	....	....	0	....	....	....	....	....	....	....	....	....	....	....	....	....	....	....	....	....	....
1991-92	Norwich-Peterborough Pirates	Britain	16	28	23	51	....	....	....	50	....	....	....	....	....	....	....	....	....	....	7	11	14	25	8	....	....	....
1992-1999	Bay City Sharks	MBAHL	DID NOT PLAY – COACHING																									
1999-2000	Stonehill College	NCAA-2	DID NOT PLAY – COACHING																									
	NHL Totals		**1**	**0**	**1**	**1**	**0**	**1**	**1**	**0**	**0**	**0**	**0**	**2**	**0.0**	**2**	**1**	**2**	**0**		....	....	....	....	....	....	....	....

Hockey East Second All-Star Team (1985) • Hockey East Player-of-the-Year (1986) • Hockey East First All-Star Team (1986) • NCAA East First All-American Team (1986)

Traded to **St. Louis** by **Montreal** for future considerations, January 21, 1988. Traded to **Boston** by **St. Louis** for Phil DeGaetano, February 3, 1989.

• HARPER, Terry — Terrance Victor — D – R. 6'1", 200 lbs. b: Regina, Sask., 1/27/1940.

Season	Club	League	GP	G	A	Pts	AG	AA	APts	PIM	PP	SH	GW	S	%	TGF	PGF	TGA	PGA	+/–	GP	G	A	Pts	PIM	PP	SH	GW
			REGULAR SEASON																		PLAYOFFS							
1957-58	Regina Pats	SJHL	51	6	10	16	....	....	....	74	....	....	....	....	....	....	....	....	....	....	12	2	3	5	12	....	....	....
	Regina Pats	Mem-Cup	16	3	2	5	....	....	....	8	....	....	....	....	....	....	....	....	....	....	....	....	....	....	....	....	....	....
1958-59	Regina Pats	SJHL	48	1	19	20	....	....	....	79	....	....	....	....	....	....	....	....	....	....	9	1	2	3	6	....	....	....
1959-60	Regina Pats	SJHL	59	17	21	38	....	....	....	56	....	....	....	....	....	....	....	....	....	....	13	3	7	10	6	....	....	....
1960-61	Montreal Royals	EPHL	69	3	14	17	....	....	....	85	....	....	....	....	....	....	....	....	....	....	....	....	....	....	....	....	....	....
1961-62	Hull-Ottawa Canadiens	EPHL	65	2	18	20	....	....	....	101	....	....	....	....	....	....	....	....	....	....	12	0	1	1	15	....	....	....
1962-63	**Montreal Canadiens**	**NHL**	**14**	**1**	**1**	**2**	**1**	**1**	**2**	**10**	....	....	....	....	....	....	....	....	....	....	**5**	**1**	**0**	**1**	**8**	**0**	**0**	**0**
	Hull-Ottawa Canadiens	EPHL	52	6	31	37	....	....	....	83	....	....	....	....	....	....	....	....	....	....	....	....	....	....	....	....	....	....
	Quebec Aces	AHL	3	0	0	0	....	....	....	0	....	....	....	....	....	....	....	....	....	....	....	....	....	....	....	....	....	....
1963-64	**Montreal Canadiens**	**NHL**	**70**	**2**	**15**	**17**	**2**	**16**	**18**	**149**	....	....	....	....	....	....	....	....	....	....	**7**	**0**	**0**	**0**	**6**	**0**	**0**	**0**
1964-65♦	**Montreal Canadiens**	**NHL**	**62**	**0**	**7**	**7**	**0**	**7**	**7**	**93**	....	....	....	....	....	....	....	....	....	....	**13**	**0**	**0**	**0**	**19**	**0**	**0**	**0**
1965-66♦	**Montreal Canadiens**	**NHL**	**69**	**1**	**11**	**12**	**1**	**10**	**11**	**91**	....	....	....	....	....	....	....	....	....	....	**10**	**2**	**3**	**5**	**18**	**0**	**0**	**1**
1966-67	**Montreal Canadiens**	**NHL**	**56**	**0**	**16**	**16**	**0**	**16**	**16**	**99**	....	....	....	....	....	....	....	....	....	....	**10**	**0**	**1**	**1**	**15**	**0**	**0**	**0**
1967-68♦	**Montreal Canadiens**	**NHL**	**57**	**3**	**8**	**11**	**3**	**8**	**11**	**66**	**0**	**0**	**1**	**47**	**6.4**	**67**	**1**	**48**	**3**	**21**	**13**	**0**	**1**	**1**	**8**	**0**	**0**	**0**
1968-69♦	**Montreal Canadiens**	**NHL**	**21**	**0**	**3**	**3**	**0**	**3**	**3**	**37**	**0**	**0**	**0**	**14**	**0.0**	**24**	**1**	**17**	**1**	**7**	**11**	**0**	**0**	**0**	**8**	**0**	**0**	**0**
	Cleveland Barons	AHL	28	2	4	6	....	....	....	21	....	....	....	....	....	....	....	....	....	....	....	....	....	....	....	....	....	....
1969-70	**Montreal Canadiens**	**NHL**	**75**	**4**	**18**	**22**	**4**	**17**	**21**	**109**	**0**	**0**	**0**	**60**	**6.7**	**90**	**1**	**94**	**32**	**27**	....	....	....	....	....	....	....	....
1970-71♦	**Montreal Canadiens**	**NHL**	**78**	**1**	**21**	**22**	**1**	**18**	**19**	**116**	**0**	**0**	**0**	**61**	**1.6**	**110**	**0**	**105**	**30**	**35**	**20**	**0**	**6**	**6**	**28**	**0**	**0**	**0**
1971-72	**Montreal Canadiens**	**NHL**	**52**	**2**	**12**	**14**	**2**	**10**	**12**	**35**	**0**	**0**	**0**	**39**	**5.1**	**53**	**0**	**54**	**10**	**9**	**5**	**1**	**1**	**2**	**6**	**0**	**0**	**0**
1972-73	**Los Angeles Kings**	**NHL**	**77**	**1**	**8**	**9**	**1**	**6**	**7**	**74**	**0**	**0**	**1**	**64**	**1.6**	**69**	**1**	**83**	**21**	**6**	....	....	....	....	....	....	....	....
1973-74	**Los Angeles Kings**	**NHL**	**77**	**0**	**17**	**17**	**0**	**14**	**14**	**119**	**0**	**0**	**0**	**114**	**0.0**	**100**	**1**	**102**	**28**	**25**	**5**	**0**	**0**	**0**	**16**	**0**	**0**	**0**
1974-75	**Los Angeles Kings**	**NHL**	**80**	**5**	**21**	**26**	**4**	**16**	**20**	**120**	**1**	**0**	**0**	**96**	**5.2**	**95**	**1**	**82**	**26**	**38**	**3**	**0**	**0**	**0**	**2**	**0**	**0**	**0**
1975-76	**Detroit Red Wings**	**NHL**	**69**	**8**	**25**	**33**	**7**	**19**	**26**	**59**	**4**	**0**	**0**	**111**	**7.2**	**102**	**26**	**112**	**42**	**6**	....	....	....	....	....	....	....	....
1976-77	**Detroit Red Wings**	**NHL**	**52**	**4**	**8**	**12**	**4**	**6**	**10**	**28**	**1**	**0**	**0**	**60**	**6.7**	**40**	**4**	**77**	**18**	**–23**	....	....	....	....	....	....	....	....
1977-78	**Detroit Red Wings**	**NHL**	**80**	**2**	**17**	**19**	**2**	**13**	**15**	**85**	**0**	**0**	**0**	**76**	**2.6**	**88**	**2**	**118**	**51**	**19**	**7**	**0**	**1**	**1**	**4**	**0**	**0**	**0**
1978-79	**Detroit Red Wings**	**NHL**	**51**	**0**	**6**	**6**	**0**	**4**	**4**	**58**	**0**	**0**	**0**	**33**	**0.0**	**43**	**2**	**68**	**24**	**–3**	....	....	....	....	....	....	....	....
	Kansas City Red Wings	CHL	22	0	13	13	....	....	....	36	....	....	....	....	....	....	....	....	....	....	....	....	....	....	....	....	....	....
1979-80	**St. Louis Blues**	**NHL**	**11**	**1**	**5**	**6**	**1**	**4**	**5**	**6**	**0**	**0**	**0**	**14**	**7.1**	**17**	**1**	**12**	**1**	**5**	**3**	**0**	**0**	**0**	**2**	**0**	**0**	**0**
1980-81	**Colorado Rockies**	**NHL**	**15**	**0**	**2**	**2**	**0**	**1**	**1**	**8**	**0**	**0**	**0**	**6**	**0.0**	**8**	**1**	**10**	**0**	**–3**	....	....	....	....	....	....	....	....
	NHL Totals		**1066**	**35**	**221**	**256**	**33**	**189**	**222**	**1362**	....	....	....	....	....	....	....	....	....	....	**112**	**4**	**13**	**17**	**140**	....	....	....

SJHL First All-Star Team (1960) • EPHL First All-Star Team (1962) • EPHL Second All-Star Team (1963) • Played in NHL All-Star Game (1965, 1967, 1973, 1975)

Traded to **LA Kings** by **Montreal** for LA Kings' 2nd round choice (Gary MacGregor) in 1974 Amateur Draft, 1st (Pierre Mondou) and 3rd (Paul Woods) round choices in 1975 Amateur Draft and 1st round choice (Rod Schutt) in 1976 Amateur Draft, August 22, 1972. Traded to **Detroit** by **LA Kings** with Dan Maloney and LA Kings' 2nd round choice (later traded to Minnesota — Minnesota selected Jim Roberts) in 1976 Amateur Draft for Bart Crashley and the rights to Marcel Dionne, June 23, 1975. Signed as a free agent by **St. Louis**, March 10, 1980. Signed as a free agent by **Colorado**, February 12, 1981.

• HARRER, Tim — RW – R. 6', 185 lbs. b: Bloomington, MN, 5/10/1957. Atlanta's 9th, 148th overall, in 1977.

Season	Club	League	GP	G	A	Pts	AG	AA	APts	PIM	PP	SH	GW	S	%	TGF	PGF	TGA	PGA	+/–	GP	G	A	Pts	PIM	PP	SH	GW
1975-76	Bloomington Jr. Stars	MWJHL	11	5	3	8	....	....	....	6	....	....	....	....	....	....	....	....	....	....	....	....	....	....	....	....	....	....
1976-77	University of Minnesota	WCHA	38	14	9	23	....	....	....	37	....	....	....	....	....	....	....	....	....	....	....	....	....	....	....	....	....	....
1977-78	University of Minnesota	WCHA	35	22	21	43	....	....	....	36	....	....	....	....	....	....	....	....	....	....	....	....	....	....	....	....	....	....
1978-79	University of Minnesota	WCHA	43	28	25	53	....	....	....	38	....	....	....	....	....	....	....	....	....	....	....	....	....	....	....	....	....	....
1979-80	University of Minnesota	WCHA	41	53	29	82	....	....	....	50	....	....	....	....	....	....	....	....	....	....	....	....	....	....	....	....	....	....
	United States	Nat-Team	4	1	3	4	....	....	....	0	....	....	....	....	....	....	....	....	....	....	....	....	....	....	....	....	....	....
1980-81	Birmingham Bulls	CHL	28	9	5	14	....	....	....	36	....	....	....	....	....	....	....	....	....	....	....	....	....	....	....	....	....	....
	Hershey Bears	AHL	39	7	6	13	....	....	....	12	....	....	....	....	....	....	....	....	....	....	2	0	0	0	0	....	....	....
1981-82	Oklahoma City Stars	CHL	77	29	27	56	....	....	....	36	....	....	....	....	....	....	....	....	....	....	4	2	2	4	0	....	....	....
1982-83	**Calgary Flames**	**NHL**	**3**	**0**	**0**	**0**	**0**	**0**	**0**	**2**	**0**	**0**	**0**	**3**	**0.0**	**1**	**0**	**1**	**0**	**0**	....	....	....	....	....	....	....	....
	Colorado Flames	CHL	69	33	29	62	....	....	....	28	....	....	....	....	....	....	....	....	....	....	6	3	3	6	4	....	....	....
1983-84	Salt Lake Golden Eagles	CHL	66	42	27	69	....	....	....	46	....	....	....	....	....	....	....	....	....	....	5	1	2	3	5	....	....	....
1984-85	Nova Scotia Voyageurs	AHL	7	0	0	0	....	....	....	0	....	....	....	....	....	....	....	....	....	....	....	....	....	....	....	....	....	....
	Toledo Goaldiggers	IHL	28	6	10	16	....	....	....	28	....	....	....	....	....	....	....	....	....	....	....	....	....	....	....	....	....	....
	EC Graz	Austria	4	3	1	4	....	....	....	2	....	....	....	....	....	....	....	....	....	....	....	....	....	....	....	....	....	....
	NHL Totals		**3**	**0**	**0**	**0**	**0**	**0**	**0**	**2**	**0**	**0**	**0**	**3**	**0.0**	**1**	**0**	**1**	**0**		....	....	....	....	....	....	....	....

WCHA First All-Star Team (1980) • NCAA West First All-American Team (1980)

Transferred to **Calgary** after **Atlanta** franchise relocated, June 24, 1980. Signed as a free agent by **Minnesota**, August 1, 1983.

• HARRIS, Billy — Billy Edward — RW – L. 6'2", 195 lbs. b: Toronto, Ont., 1/29/1952. NY Islanders' 1st, 1st overall, in 1972.

Season	Club	League	GP	G	A	Pts	AG	AA	APts	PIM	PP	SH	GW	S	%	TGF	PGF	TGA	PGA	+/–	GP	G	A	Pts	PIM	PP	SH	GW
1968-69	Toronto Marlboros	OHA-Jr.	41	9	18	27	....	....	....	14	....	....	....	....	....	....	....	....	....	....	6	2	2	4	....	....	....	....
1969-70	Toronto Marlboros	OHA-Jr.	46	13	17	30	....	....	....	75	....	....	....	....	....	....	....	....	....	....	18	4	9	13	26	....	....	....
1970-71	Toronto Marlboros	OHA-Jr.	48	34	48	82	....	....	....	61	....	....	....	....	....	....	....	....	....	....	13	8	9	17	14	....	....	....
1971-72	Toronto Marlboros	OMJHL	63	57	72	*129	....	....	....	87	....	....	....	....	....	....	....	....	....	....	10	13	10	23	26	....	....	....
1972-73	**New York Islanders**	**NHL**	**78**	**28**	**22**	**50**	**26**	**17**	**43**	**35**	**6**	**0**	**2**	**196**	**14.3**	**67**	**19**	**104**	**12**	**–44**	....	....	....	....	....	....	....	....
1973-74	**New York Islanders**	**NHL**	**78**	**23**	**27**	**50**	**22**	**22**	**44**	**34**	**4**	**0**	**3**	**190**	**12.1**	**67**	**21**	**58**	**1**	**–11**	....	....	....	....	....	....	....	....
1974-75	**New York Islanders**	**NHL**	**80**	**25**	**37**	**62**	**22**	**28**	**50**	**34**	**4**	**0**	**5**	**199**	**12.6**	**98**	**31**	**65**	**2**	**4**	**17**	**3**	**7**	**10**	**12**	**2**	**0**	**1**
1975-76	**New York Islanders**	**NHL**	**80**	**32**	**38**	**70**	**28**	**28**	**56**	**54**	**16**	**0**	**4**	**228**	**14.0**	**124**	**63**	**41**	**2**	**22**	**13**	**5**	**2**	**7**	**10**	**1**	**0**	**0**
1976-77	**New York Islanders**	**NHL**	**80**	**24**	**43**	**67**	**22**	**33**	**55**	**44**	**5**	**1**	**3**	**160**	**15.0**	**95**	**28**	**53**	**4**	**18**	**12**	**7**	**7**	**14**	**8**	**2**	**0**	**1**
1977-78	**New York Islanders**	**NHL**	**80**	**22**	**38**	**60**	**20**	**29**	**49**	**40**	**1**	**1**	**1**	**148**	**14.9**	**77**	**7**	**53**	**10**	**27**	**7**	**0**	**0**	**0**	**4**	**0**	**0**	**0**
1978-79	**New York Islanders**	**NHL**	**80**	**15**	**39**	**54**	**13**	**28**	**41**	**18**	**0**	**0**	**5**	**128**	**11.7**	**72**	**5**	**46**	**5**	**26**	**10**	**2**	**1**	**3**	**10**	**1**	**0**	**1**
1979-80	**New York Islanders**	**NHL**	**67**	**15**	**15**	**30**	**13**	**11**	**24**	**37**	**2**	**1**	**2**	**91**	**16.5**	**45**	**6**	**57**	**18**	**0**	....	....	....	....	....	....	....	....
	Los Angeles Kings	**NHL**	**11**	**4**	**3**	**7**	**3**	**2**	**5**	**6**	**1**	**0**	**1**	**22**	**18.2**	**12**	**2**	**9**	**3**	**4**	**4**	**0**	**0**	**0**	**2**	**0**	**0**	**0**
1980-81	**Los Angeles Kings**	**NHL**	**80**	**20**	**29**	**49**	**16**	**19**	**35**	**36**	**1**	**4**	**1**	**150**	**13.3**	**82**	**18**	**107**	**42**	**–1**	**4**	**2**	**1**	**3**	**0**	**0**	**0**	**0**
1981-82	**Los Angeles Kings**	**NHL**	**16**	**1**	**3**	**4**	**1**	**2**	**3**	**6**	**0**	**0**	**0**	**11**	**9.1**	**10**	**3**	**24**	**8**	**–9**	....	....	....	....	....	....	....	....
	Toronto Maple Leafs	**NHL**	**20**	**2**	**0**	**2**	**2**	**0**	**2**	**4**	**0**	**0**	**0**	**21**	**9.5**	**11**	**1**	**29**	**3**	**–16**	....	....	....	....	....	....	....	....
1982-83	**Toronto Maple Leafs**	**NHL**	**76**	**11**	**19**	**30**	**9**	**13**	**22**	**26**	**0**	**1**	**0**	**83**	**13.3**	**47**	**1**	**94**	**33**	**–15**	**4**	**0**	**1**	**1**	**2**	**0**	**0**	**0**
1983-84	**Toronto Maple Leafs**	**NHL**	**50**	**7**	**10**	**17**	**6**	**7**	**13**	**14**	**0**	**0**	**0**	**68**	**10.3**	**25**	**3**	**79**	**37**	**–20**	....	....	....	....	....	....	....	....
	St. Catharines Saints	AHL	2	0	1	1	....	....	....	0	....	....	....	....	....	....	....	....	....	....	....	....	....	....	....	....	....	....
	Los Angeles Kings	**NHL**	**21**	**2**	**4**	**6**	**2**	**3**	**5**	**6**	**0**	**0**	**0**	**19**	**10.5**	**9**	**0**	**24**	**12**	**–3**	....	....	....	....	....	....	....	....
	NHL Totals		**897**	**231**	**327**	**558**	**205**	**242**	**447**	**394**	**40**	**8**	**27**	**1714**	**13.5**	**841**	**208**	**843**	**192**		**71**	**19**	**19**	**38**	**48**	**6**	**0**	**3**

OHA-Jr. Second All-Star Team (1971) • OMJHL First All-Star Team (1972) • Played in NHL All-Star Game (1976)

Traded to **LA Kings** by **NY Islanders** with Dave Lewis for Butch Goring, March 10, 1980. Traded to **Toronto** by **LA Kings** with John Gibson for Ian Turnbull, November 11, 1981. Traded to **LA Kings** by **Toronto** for cash, February 15, 1984.

• HARRIS, Billy — William Edward "Hinky" — C – L. 6', 155 lbs. b: Toronto, Ont., 7/29/1935.

Season	Club	League	GP	G	A	Pts	AG	AA	APts	PIM	PP	SH	GW	S	%	TGF	PGF	TGA	PGA	+/–	GP	G	A	Pts	PIM	PP	SH	GW
1950-51	Weston Dukes	OHA-B	STATISTICS NOT AVAILABLE																									
	Toronto Marlboros	OHA-Jr.	2	0	1	1	....	....	....	0	....	....	....	....	....	....	....	....	....	....	....	....	....	....	....	....	....	....
1951-52	Weston Dukes	OHA-B	STATISTICS NOT AVAILABLE																									
	Toronto Marlboros	OHA-Jr.	3	0	1	1	....	....	....	0	....	....	....	....	....	....	....	....	....	....	....	....	....	....	....	....	....	....
1952-53	Toronto Marlboros	OHA-Jr.	56	20	31	51	....	....	....	4	....	....	....	....	....	....	....	....	....	....	7	2	1	3	4	....	....	....
1953-54	Toronto Marlboros	OHA-Jr.	59	25	39	64	....	....	....	27	....	....	....	....	....	....	....	....	....	....	15	4	6	10	20	....	....	....
1954-55	Toronto Marlboros	OHA-Jr.	47	37	29	66	....	....	....	26	....	....	....	....	....	....	....	....	....	....	13	*10	*18	*28	11	....	....	....
	Toronto Marlboros	Mem-Cup	11	5	6	11	....	....	....	0	....	....	....	....	....	....	....	....	....	....	....	....	....	....	....	....	....	....
1955-56	**Toronto Maple Leafs**	**NHL**	**70**	**9**	**13**	**22**	**12**	**15**	**27**	**8**	....	....	....	....	....	....	....	....	....	....	**5**	**1**	**0**	**1**	**4**	....	....	....
1956-57	**Toronto Maple Leafs**	**NHL**	**23**	**4**	**6**	**10**	**5**	**7**	**12**	**6**	....	....	....	....	....	....	....	....	....	....	....	....	....	....	....	....	....	....
	Rochester Americans	AHL	43	5	20	25	....	....	....	15	....	....	....	....	....	....	....	....	....	....	2	0	0	0	4	....	....	....
1957-58	**Toronto Maple Leafs**	**NHL**	**68**	**16**	**28**	**44**	**20**	**29**	**49**	**32**	....	....	....	....	....	....	....	....	....	....	....	....	....	....	....	....	....	....
1958-59	**Toronto Maple Leafs**	**NHL**	**70**	**22**	**30**	**52**	**26**	**30**	**56**	**29**	....	....	....	....	....	....	....	....	....	....	**12**	**3**	**4**	**7**	**16**	....	....	....
1959-60	**Toronto Maple Leafs**	**NHL**	**70**	**13**	**25**	**38**	**15**	**24**	**39**	**29**	....	....	....	....	....	....	....	....	....	....	**9**	**0**	**3**	**3**	**4**	....	....	....

			REGULAR SEASON																		PLAYOFFS							
Season	Club	League	GP	G	A	Pts	AG	AA	APts	PIM	PP	SH	GW	S	%	TGF	PGF	TGA	PGA	+/–	GP	G	A	Pts	PIM	PP	SH	GW
1960-61	**Toronto Maple Leafs**	**NHL**	66	12	27	39	14	26	40	30	....	....	....	....	....	....	....	....	....	....	5	1	0	1	0	....	....	....
1961-62♦	**Toronto Maple Leafs**	**NHL**	67	15	10	25	17	10	27	14	....	....	....	....	....	....	....	....	....	....	12	2	1	3	2	....	....	....
1962-63♦	**Toronto Maple Leafs**	**NHL**	65	8	24	32	9	24	33	22	....	....	....	....	....	....	....	....	....	....	10	0	1	1	0	....	....	....
1963-64♦	**Toronto Maple Leafs**	**NHL**	63	6	12	18	7	13	20	17	....	....	....	....	....	....	....	....	....	....	9	1	1	2	4	....	....	....
1964-65	**Toronto Maple Leafs**	**NHL**	48	1	6	7	1	6	7	0	....	....	....	....	....	....	....	....	....	....	....	....	....	....	....	....	....	....
	Rochester Americans	AHL	11	4	10	14	....	....	....	6	....	....	....	....	....	....	....	....	....	....	10	5	*12	*17	10	....	....	....
1965-66	**Detroit Red Wings**	**NHL**	24	1	4	5	1	4	5	6	....	....	....	....	....	....	....	....	....	....	....	....	....	....	....	....	....	....
	Pittsburgh Hornets	AHL	42	15	22	37	....	....	....	2	....	....	....	....	....	....	....	....	....	....	3	0	0	0	2	....	....	....
1966-67	Pittsburgh Hornets	AHL	70	34	36	70	....	....	....	29	....	....	....	....	....	....	....	....	....	....	9	2	6	8	6	....	....	....
1967-68	**Oakland Seals**	**NHL**	62	12	17	29	14	17	31	2	1	0	0	106	11.3	42	10	38	0	–6	....	....	....	....	....	....	....	....
1968-69	**Oakland Seals**	**NHL**	19	0	4	4	0	4	4	2	0	0	0	20	0.0	7	1	12	5	–1	....	....	....	....	....	....	....	....
	Pittsburgh Penguins	**NHL**	54	7	13	20	7	12	19	8	2	0	0	61	11.5	30	6	43	1	–18	....	....	....	....	....	....	....	....
1969-70	Canada	Nat-Team	STATISTICS NOT AVAILABLE																									
	NHL Totals		769	126	219	345	148	221	369	205	....	....	....	....	....	....	....	....	....	....	62	8	10	18	30	....	....	....

Played in NHL All-Star Game (1958, 1962, 1963, 1964)

Traded to **Detroit** by **Toronto** with Andy Bathgate and Gary Jarrett for Marcel Pronovost, Larry Jeffrey, Ed Joyal, Lowell MacDonald and Aut Erickson, May 20, 1965. Claimed by **Oakland** from **Detroit** in Expansion Draft, June 6, 1967. Traded to **Pittsburgh** by **Oakland** for Bob Dillabough, November 29, 1968.

• HARRIS, Duke

George Francis RW – R. 5'10", 180 lbs. b: Sarnia, Ont., 2/25/1942.

1958-59	St. Catharines Teepees	OHA-Jr.	51	11	16	27	....	....	....	26	....	....	....	....	....	....	....	....	....	....	7	0	1	1	0	....	....	....
1959-60	St. Catharines Teepees	OHA-Jr.	48	16	26	42	....	....	....	19	....	....	....	....	....	....	....	....	....	....	16	6	6	12	30	....	....	....
	St. Catharines Teepees	Mem-Cup	14	5	13	18	....	....	....	4	....	....	....	....	....	....	....	....	....	....	....	....	....	....	....	....	....	....
1960-61	St. Catharines Teepees	OHA-Jr.	48	15	22	37	....	....	....	30	....	....	....	....	....	....	....	....	....	....	6	0	3	3	4	....	....	....
1961-62	St. Catharines Teepees	OHA-Jr.	9	5	0	5	....	....	....	8	....	....	....	....	....	....	....	....	....	....	....	....	....	....	....	....	....	....
	Guelph Royals	OHA-Jr.	39	23	37	60	....	....	....	50	....	....	....	....	....	....	....	....	....	....	....	....	....	....	....	....	....	....
	Sault Ste. Marie Thunderbirds	EPHL	7	0	0	0	....	....	....	0	....	....	....	....	....	....	....	....	....	....	....	....	....	....	....	....	....	....
1962-63	St. Louis Braves	EPHL	72	28	31	59	....	....	....	38	....	....	....	....	....	....	....	....	....	....	....	....	....	....	....	....	....	....
1963-64	St. Louis Braves	CPHL	72	21	41	62	....	....	....	16	....	....	....	....	....	....	....	....	....	....	6	1	3	4	4	....	....	....
1964-65	Pittsburgh Hornets	AHL	72	19	31	50	....	....	....	16	....	....	....	....	....	....	....	....	....	....	4	0	3	3	6	....	....	....
1965-66	Pittsburgh Hornets	AHL	72	18	23	41	....	....	....	12	....	....	....	....	....	....	....	....	....	....	3	1	1	2	2	....	....	....
1966-67	Pittsburgh Hornets	AHL	70	27	27	54	....	....	....	24	....	....	....	....	....	....	....	....	....	....	9	1	3	4	4	....	....	....
1967-68	Fort Worth Wings	CPHL	3	1	1	2	....	....	....	0	....	....	....	....	....	....	....	....	....	....	....	....	....	....	....	....	....	....
	Minnesota North Stars	**NHL**	22	1	4	5	1	4	5	4	0	0	0	43	2.3	13	10	13	0	–10	....	....	....	....	....	....	....	....
	Toronto Maple Leafs	**NHL**	4	0	0	0	0	0	0	0	0	0	0	7	0.0	1	1	4	0	–4	....	....	....	....	....	....	....	....
	Rochester Americans	AHL	38	10	27	37	....	....	....	12	....	....	....	....	....	....	....	....	....	....	10	2	3	5	4	....	....	....
1968-69	Vancouver Canucks	WHL	74	23	17	40	....	....	....	18	....	....	....	....	....	....	....	....	....	....	8	3	0	3	2	....	....	....
1969-70	Vancouver Canucks	WHL	71	20	21	41	....	....	....	23	....	....	....	....	....	....	....	....	....	....	11	6	3	9	4	....	....	....
1970-71	Rochester Americans	AHL	70	29	25	54	....	....	....	42	....	....	....	....	....	....	....	....	....	....	....	....	....	....	....	....	....	....
1971-72	Rochester Americans	AHL	74	27	34	61	....	....	....	24	....	....	....	....	....	....	....	....	....	....	....	....	....	....	....	....	....	....
1972-73	Houston Aeros	WHA	75	30	12	42	....	....	....	14	....	....	....	....	....	....	....	....	....	....	10	1	1	2	4	....	....	....
1973-74	Chicago Cougars	WHA	64	14	16	30	....	....	....	20	....	....	....	....	....	....	....	....	....	....	18	6	6	12	2	....	....	....
1974-75	Chicago Cougars	WHA	54	9	19	28	....	....	....	18	....	....	....	....	....	....	....	....	....	....	....	....	....	....	....	....	....	....
	NHL Totals		26	1	4	5	1	4	5	4	0	0	0	50	2.0	14	11	17	0		....	....	....	....	....	....	....	....
	Other Major League Totals		193	53	47	100	....	....	....	52	....	....	....	....	....	....	....	....	....	....	28	7	7	14	6	....	....	....

Claimed by **Detroit** from **St. Louis** (CHL) in Intra-League Draft, June 10, 1964. Traded to **Minnesota** by **Detroit** with Bob McCord for Jean-Guy Talbot and Dave Richardson, October 19, 1967. Traded to **Toronto** (Rochester-AHL) by **Minnesota** with Don Johns, Murray Hall, Len Lunde, Ted Taylor and the loan of Carl Wetzel for Milan Marcetta and Jean-Paul Parise, December 23, 1967. Traded to **Rochester** (AHL) by **Toronto** for cash, March, 1968. Rights transferred to **Vancouver** (WHL) after WHL club purchased **Rochester** (AHL) franchise, August 13, 1968. NHL rights transferred to **Vancouver** after NHL club purchased **Vancouver** (WHL) franchise, December 19, 1969. Selected by **Houston** (WHA) in 1972 WHA General Player Draft, February 13, 1972. Traded to **Chicago** (WHA) by **Houston** (WHA) for cash, July, 1973. Selected by **Calgary** (WHA) from **Chicago** (WHA) in WHA Dispersal Draft, May 19, 1975.

• HARRIS, Hugh

Hugh Thomas C – L. 6'1", 195 lbs. b: Toronto, Ont., 6/7/1948.

1966-67	Weston Dodgers	OHA-B	STATISTICS NOT AVAILABLE																									
1967-68	Muskegon Mohawks	IHL	63	16	19	35	....	....	....	72	....	....	....	....	....	....	....	....	....	....	9	2	4	6	4	....	....	....
1968-69	Muskegon Mohawks	IHL	71	33	39	72	....	....	....	83	....	....	....	....	....	....	....	....	....	....	11	3	9	12	6	....	....	....
1969-70	Muskegon Mohawks	IHL	48	31	25	56	....	....	....	35	....	....	....	....	....	....	....	....	....	....	6	2	1	3	6	....	....	....
1970-71	Montreal Voyageurs	AHL	5	3	2	5	....	....	....	4	....	....	....	....	....	....	....	....	....	....	2	0	0	0	14	....	....	....
	Muskegon Mohawks	IHL	63	*39	47	86	....	....	....	86	....	....	....	....	....	....	....	....	....	....	6	3	3	6	0	....	....	....
1971-72	Cincinnati Swords	AHL	71	18	24	42	....	....	....	70	....	....	....	....	....	....	....	....	....	....	9	3	4	7	6	....	....	....
1972-73	**Buffalo Sabres**	**NHL**	60	12	26	38	11	21	32	17	0	0	0	121	9.9	54	4	41	0	9	3	0	0	0	0	0	0	0
	Cincinnati Swords	AHL	14	7	7	14	....	....	....	37	....	....	....	....	....	....	....	....	....	....	....	....	....	....	....	....	....	....
1973-74	New England Whalers	WHA	75	24	28	52	....	....	....	78	....	....	....	....	....	....	....	....	....	....	7	0	4	4	11	....	....	....
1974-75	Phoenix Roadrunners	WHA	22	10	10	20	....	....	....	15	....	....	....	....	....	....	....	....	....	....	....	....	....	....	....	....	....	....
	Vancouver Blazers	WHA	58	23	34	57	....	....	....	49	....	....	....	....	....	....	....	....	....	....	....	....	....	....	....	....	....	....
1975-76	Calgary Cowboys	WHA	30•	5	9	14	....	....	....	19	....	....	....	....	....	....	....	....	....	....	....	....	....	....	....	....	....	....
	Indianapolis Racers	WHA	41	12	27	39	....	....	....	23	....	....	....	....	....	....	....	....	....	....	7	2	5	7	8	....	....	....
1976-77	Indianapolis Racers	WHA	46	21	35	56	....	....	....	21	....	....	....	....	....	....	....	....	....	....	2	0	0	0	0	....	....	....
1977-78	Indianapolis Racers	WHA	19	1	7	8	....	....	....	6	....	....	....	....	....	....	....	....	....	....	....	....	....	....	....	....	....	....
	Cincinnati Stingers	WHA	45	11	23	34	....	....	....	30	....	....	....	....	....	....	....	....	....	....	....	....	....	....	....	....	....	....
	NHL Totals		60	12	26	38	11	21	32	17	0	0	0	121	9.9	54	4	41	0		3	0	0	0	0	0	0	0
	Other Major League Totals		336	107	173	280	....	....	....	241	....	....	....	....	....	....	....	....	....	....	16	2	9	11	19	....	....	....

IHL First All-Star Team (1971)

Claimed by **Buffalo** from **Montreal** in Intra-League Draft, June 8, 1971. Selected by **Minnesota** (WHA) in 1972 WHA General Player Draft, February 12, 1972. WHA rights traded to **New England** (WHA) by **Minnesota** (WHA) for cash, July, 1973. Traded to **Phoenix** (WHA) by **New England** (WHA) for future considerations, August, 1974. Traded to **Vancouver** (WHA) by **Phoenix** (WHA) for John Migneault, Serge Beaudoin and Pete McNamee, November, 1974. Transferred to **Calgary** (WHA) after **Vancouver** (WHA) franchise relocated, May 7, 1975. Traded to **Indianapolis** (WHA) by **Calgary** (WHA) for future considerations, January, 1976. Traded to **Cincinnati** (WHA) by **Indianapolis** (WHA) with Bryon Baltimore for Gilles Marotte and Blaine Stoughton, January, 1978.

• HARRIS, Ron

Ronald Thomas D – R. 5'10", 190 lbs. b: Verdun, Que., 6/30/1942.

1959-60	Lethbridge Lumber.	AAHA	STATISTICS NOT AVAILABLE																									
	Lethbridge Native Sons	Mem-Cup	3	2	1	3	....	....	....	4	....	....	....	....	....	....	....	....	....	....	....	....	....	....	....	....	....	....
1960-61	Hamilton Red Wings	OHA-Jr.	47	1	9	10	....	....	....	63	....	....	....	....	....	....	....	....	....	....	12	0	0	0	45	....	....	....
1961-62	Hamilton Red Wings	OHA-Jr.	50	7	29	36	....	....	....	85	....	....	....	....	....	....	....	....	....	....	10	3	2	5	25	....	....	....
	Hamilton Red Wings	Mem-Cup	14	2	8	10	....	....	....	28	....	....	....	....	....	....	....	....	....	....	....	....	....	....	....	....	....	....
1962-63	**Detroit Red Wings**	**NHL**	1	0	1	1	0	1	1	0	....	....	....	....	....	....	....	....	....	....	....	....	....	....	....	....	....	....
	Pittsburgh Hornets	AHL	62	3	18	21	....	....	....	88	....	....	....	....	....	....	....	....	....	....	....	....	....	....	....	....	....	....
1963-64	**Detroit Red Wings**	**NHL**	3	0	0	0	0	0	0	7	....	....	....	....	....	....	....	....	....	....	....	....	....	....	....	....	....	....
	Cincinnati Wings	CPHL	66	4	21	25	....	....	....	129	....	....	....	....	....	....	....	....	....	....	....	....	....	....	....	....	....	....
1964-65	Memphis Wings	CPHL	70	18	18	36	....	....	....	75	....	....	....	....	....	....	....	....	....	....	....	....	....	....	....	....	....	....
	Pittsburgh Hornets	AHL	....	....	....	....	....	....	....	....	....	....	....	....	....	....	....	....	....	....	1	0	0	0	0	....	....	....
1965-66	San Francisco Seals	WHL	54	12	16	28	....	....	....	74	....	....	....	....	....	....	....	....	....	....	7	2	1	3	15	....	....	....
1966-67	California Seals	WHL	31	8	9	17	....	....	....	40	....	....	....	....	....	....	....	....	....	....	6	1	0	1	12	....	....	....
1967-68	**Oakland Seals**	**NHL**	54	4	6	10	5	6	11	60	1	0	1	87	4.6	16	2	42	1	–27	....	....	....	....	....	....	....	....
1968-69	**Detroit Red Wings**	**NHL**	73	3	13	16	3	12	15	91	0	0	1	74	4.1	65	1	59	1	6	....	....	....	....	....	....	....	....
1969-70	**Detroit Red Wings**	**NHL**	72	2	19	21	2	18	20	99	0	0	0	126	1.6	74	10	59	9	14	4	0	0	0	8	0	0	0
1970-71	**Detroit Red Wings**	**NHL**	42	2	8	10	2	7	9	65	1	1	0	84	2.4	36	8	77	20	–29	....	....	....	....	....	....	....	....
1971-72	**Detroit Red Wings**	**NHL**	61	1	10	11	1	9	10	80	0	0	0	56	1.8	23	2	41	5	–15	....	....	....	....	....	....	....	....
1972-73	**Atlanta Flames**	**NHL**	24	2	4	6	2	3	5	8	1	0	0	36	5.6	12	2	16	1	–5	....	....	....	....	....	....	....	....
	New York Rangers	**NHL**	46	3	10	13	3	8	11	17	1	0	0	73	4.1	35	1	41	9	2	10	0	3	3	2	0	0	0

Season	Club	League	REGULAR SEASON																		PLAYOFFS							
			GP	G	A	Pts	AG	AA	APts	PIM	PP	SH	GW	S	%	TGF	PGF	TGA	PGA	+/–	GP	G	A	Pts	PIM	PP	SH	GW
1973-74	**New York Rangers**	**NHL**	63	2	12	14	2	10	12	25	0	0	0	75	2.7	38	1	48	9	–2	11	3	0	3	14	0	0	2
1974-75	**New York Rangers**	**NHL**	34	1	7	8	1	5	6	22	0	0	0	38	2.6	25	2	29	6	0	3	1	0	1	9	0	0	1
1975-76	**New York Rangers**	**NHL**	3	0	1	1	0	1	1	0	0	0	0	1	0.0	1	0	2	0	–1	....	....	....	....	....	....	....	....
	NHL Totals		476	20	91	111	21	80	101	474	....	....	....	....	....	....	....	....	....	....	28	4	3	7	33	....	....	....

OHA-Jr. First All-Star Team (1962)

Traded to **Boston** by **Detroit** with Albert Langlois, Parker MacDonald and Bob Dillabough for Ab McDonald, Bob McCord and Ken Stephanson, May 31, 1965. Claimed by **Oakland** from **Boston** in Expansion Draft, June 6, 1967. Traded to **Detroit** by **Oakland** with Bob Baun for Gary Jarrett, Doug Roberts, Howie Young and Chris Worthy, May 27, 1968. Claimed by **Atlanta** from **Detroit** in Expansion Draft, June 6, 1972. Traded to **NY Rangers** by **Atlanta** for Curt Bennett, November 28, 1972. • Suffered career-ending knee injury in game vs. NY Islanders, October 25, 1975.

• HARRIS, Ted

Edward Alexander D – L. 6'2", 183 lbs. b: Winnipeg, Man., 7/18/1936.

Season	Club	League	GP	G	A	Pts	AG	AA	APts	PIM	PP	SH	GW	S	%	TGF	PGF	TGA	PGA	+/–	GP	G	A	Pts	PIM	PP	SH	GW
1953-54	Winnipeg Monarchs	MJHL	36	4	5	9	....	....	....	94	....	....	....	....	....	....	....	....	....	....	5	1	1	2	10	....	....	....
1954-55	Winnipeg Monarchs	MJHL	32	2	15	17	....	....	....	*137	....	....	....	....	....	....	....	....	....	....	17	1	3	4	57	....	....	....
1955-56	Winnipeg Monarchs	MJHL	20	6	23	29	....	....	....	78	....	....	....	....	....	....	....	....	....	....	4	0	0	0	21	....	....	....
1956-57	Springfield Indians	AHL	2	0	0	0	....	....	....	4	....	....	....	....	....	....	....	....	....	....	....	....	....	....	....	....	....	....
	Philadelphia Ramblers	EHL	61	11	33	44	....	....	....	103	....	....	....	....	....	....	....	....	....	....	13	2	2	4	31	....	....	....
1957-58	Philadelphia Ramblers	EHL	62	10	19	29	....	....	....	82	....	....	....	....	....	....	....	....	....	....	....	....	....	....	....	....	....	....
1958-59	Springfield Indians	AHL	9	0	2	2	....	....	....	11	....	....	....	....	....	....	....	....	....	....	....	....	....	....	....	....	....	....
	Victoria Cougars	WHL	58	4	12	16	....	....	....	82	....	....	....	....	....	....	....	....	....	....	3	0	0	0	4	....	....	....
1959-60	Springfield Indians	AHL	63	4	13	17	....	....	....	100	....	....	....	....	....	....	....	....	....	....	10	0	2	2	16	....	....	....
1960-61	Springfield Indians	AHL	69	4	22	26	....	....	....	76	....	....	....	....	....	....	....	....	....	....	8	0	1	1	18	....	....	....
1961-62	Springfield Indians	AHL	70	2	29	31	....	....	....	142	....	....	....	....	....	....	....	....	....	....	11	3	3	6	14	....	....	....
1962-63	Springfield Indians	AHL	72	8	30	38	....	....	....	172	....	....	....	....	....	....	....	....	....	....	....	....	....	....	....	....	....	....
1963-64	**Montreal Canadiens**	**NHL**	4	0	1	1	0	1	1	0	....	....	....	....	....	....	....	....	....	....	....	....	....	....	....	....	....	....
	Cleveland Barons	AHL	67	6	23	29	....	....	....	109	....	....	....	....	....	....	....	....	....	....	9	0	5	5	20	....	....	....
1964-65♦	**Montreal Canadiens**	**NHL**	68	1	14	15	1	14	15	107	....	....	....	....	....	....	....	....	....	....	13	0	5	5	45	0	0	0
1965-66♦	**Montreal Canadiens**	**NHL**	53	0	13	13	0	12	12	87	....	....	....	....	....	....	....	....	....	....	10	0	0	0	38	0	0	0
1966-67	**Montreal Canadiens**	**NHL**	65	2	16	18	2	16	18	86	....	....	....	....	....	....	....	....	....	....	10	0	1	1	19	0	0	0
1967-68♦	**Montreal Canadiens**	**NHL**	67	5	16	21	6	16	22	78	0	0	1	56	8.9	74	0	59	8	23	13	0	4	4	22	0	0	0
1968-69♦	**Montreal Canadiens**	**NHL**	76	7	18	25	7	16	23	102	0	1	0	82	8.5	111	3	108	24	24	14	1	2	3	34	0	0	0
1969-70	**Montreal Canadiens**	**NHL**	74	3	17	20	3	16	19	116	0	0	0	65	4.6	80	1	89	19	9	....	....	....	....	....	....	....	....
1970-71	**Minnesota North Stars**	**NHL**	78	2	13	15	2	11	13	130	1	0	0	90	2.2	81	3	107	29	0	12	0	4	4	36	0	0	0
1971-72	**Minnesota North Stars**	**NHL**	78	2	15	17	2	13	15	77	0	0	0	89	2.2	74	3	97	26	0	7	0	1	1	17	0	0	0
1972-73	**Minnesota North Stars**	**NHL**	78	7	23	30	7	18	25	83	0	0	1	94	7.4	103	2	109	33	25	5	0	1	1	15	0	0	0
1973-74	**Minnesota North Stars**	**NHL**	12	0	1	1	0	1	1	4	0	0	0	10	0.0	6	0	17	3	–8	....	....	....	....	....	....	....	....
	Detroit Red Wings	**NHL**	41	0	11	11	0	9	9	66	0	0	0	32	0.0	62	5	70	9	–4	....	....	....	....	....	....	....	....
	St. Louis Blues	**NHL**	24	0	4	4	0	3	3	16	0	0	0	32	0.0	21	0	37	14	–2	....	....	....	....	....	....	....	....
1974-75♦	**Philadelphia Flyers**	**NHL**	70	1	6	7	1	4	5	48	0	0	1	38	2.6	52	1	26	2	27	16	0	4	4	4	0	0	0
	NHL Totals		788	30	168	198	31	150	181	1000	....	....	....	....	....	....	....	....	....	....	100	1	22	23	230	....	....	....

AHL First All-Star Team (1964) • Won Eddie Shore Award (Outstanding Defenseman - AHL) (1964) • NHL Second All-Star Team (1969) • Played in NHL All-Star Game (1965, 1967, 1969, 1971, 1972)

Loaned to **Victoria** (WHL) by **Springfield** (AHL) for cash, November 4, 1958. Traded to **Montreal** by **Springfield** (AHL) with Wayne Larkin, Terry Gray, Bruce Cline and John Chasczewski for Wayne Boddy, Fred Hilts, Brian Smith, John Rodger, Lorne O'Donnell and the loan of Gary Bergman, June, 1963. Claimed by **Minnesota** from **Montreal** in Intra-League Draft, June 9, 1970. Traded to **Detroit** by **Minnesota** for Gary Bergman, November 7, 1973. Traded to **St. Louis** by **Detroit** with Bill Collins and Garnet Bailey for Chris Evans, Bryan Watson and Jean Hamel, February 14, 1974. Traded to **Philadelphia** by **St. Louis** for cash, September 16, 1974.

• HARRISON, Jim

James David "Max" C – R. 5'11", 185 lbs. b: Bonnyville, Alta., 7/9/1947.

Season	Club	League	GP	G	A	Pts	AG	AA	APts	PIM	PP	SH	GW	S	%	TGF	PGF	TGA	PGA	+/–	GP	G	A	Pts	PIM	PP	SH	GW
1963-64	Kamloops Rockets	BCJHL	25	8	11	19	....	....	....	....	....	....	....	....	....	....	....	....	....	....	....	....	....	....	....	....	....	....
1964-65	Estevan Bruins	SJHL	25	2	5	7	....	....	....	40	....	....	....	....	....	....	....	....	....	....	....	....	....	....	....	....	....	....
1965-66	Estevan Bruins	SJHL	60	39	37	76	....	....	....	119	....	....	....	....	....	....	....	....	....	....	11	8	1	9	21	....	....	....
	Estevan Bruins	Mem-Cup	13	*10	5	15	....	....	....	*52	....	....	....	....	....	....	....	....	....	....	....	....	....	....	....	....	....	....
	Edmonton Oil Kings	Mem-Cup	6	2	3	5	....	....	....	11	....	....	....	....	....	....	....	....	....	....	....	....	....	....	....	....	....	....
1966-67	Estevan Bruins	CMJHL	47	34	40	74	....	....	....	179	....	....	....	....	....	....	....	....	....	....	8	2	4	6	38	....	....	....
1967-68	Estevan Bruins	WCJHL	46	32	43	75	....	....	....	222	....	....	....	....	....	....	....	....	....	....	14	*13	*22	*35	29	....	....	....
	Estevan Bruins	Mem-Cup	14	*19	15	*34	....	....	....	42	....	....	....	....	....	....	....	....	....	....	....	....	....	....	....	....	....	....
1968-69	**Boston Bruins**	**NHL**	16	1	2	3	1	2	3	21	0	0	0	12	8.3	4	0	9	0	–5	....	....	....	....	....	....	....	....
	Oklahoma City Blazers	CHL	43	13	13	26	....	....	....	130	....	....	....	....	....	....	....	....	....	....	9	3	2	5	6	....	....	....
1969-70	**Boston Bruins**	**NHL**	23	3	1	4	3	1	4	16	0	1	0	19	15.8	10	0	9	5	6	....	....	....	....	....	....	....	....
	Toronto Maple Leafs	**NHL**	31	7	10	17	8	9	17	36	1	0	0	43	16.3	21	2	24	7	2	....	....	....	....	....	....	....	....
1970-71	**Toronto Maple Leafs**	**NHL**	78	13	20	33	13	17	30	108	0	1	1	147	8.8	59	11	47	5	6	6	0	1	1	33	0	0	0
1971-72	**Toronto Maple Leafs**	**NHL**	66	19	17	36	19	15	34	104	5	0	0	149	12.8	49	10	46	3	–4	5	1	0	1	10	0	0	1
1972-73	Alberta Oilers	WHA	66	39	47	86	....	....	....	93	....	....	....	....	....	....	....	....	....	....	....	....	....	....	....	....	....	....
1973-74	Edmonton Oilers	WHA	47	24	45	69	....	....	....	99	....	....	....	....	....	....	....	....	....	....	....	....	....	....	....	....	....	....
1974-75	Team Canada	Summit-74	3	0	1	1	....	....	....	9	....	....	....	....	....	....	....	....	....	....	....	....	....	....	....	....	....	....
	Cleveland Crusaders	WHA	60	20	22	42	....	....	....	106	....	....	....	....	....	....	....	....	....	....	5	1	2	3	4	....	....	....
1975-76	Cleveland Crusaders	WHA	59	34	38	72	....	....	....	62	....	....	....	....	....	....	....	....	....	....	3	0	1	1	9	....	....	....
1976-77	**Chicago Black Hawks**	**NHL**	60	18	23	41	16	18	34	97	8	1	3	140	12.9	59	20	78	13	–26	2	0	0	0	0	0	0	0
1977-78	**Chicago Black Hawks**	**NHL**	26	2	8	10	2	6	8	31	1	0	0	43	4.7	18	2	21	2	–3	....	....	....	....	....	....	....	....
1978-79	**Chicago Black Hawks**	**NHL**	21	4	5	9	3	4	7	22	0	0	0	28	14.3	15	1	28	8	–6	....	....	....	....	....	....	....	....
	New Brunswick Hawks	AHL	2	0	0	0	....	....	....	0	....	....	....	....	....	....	....	....	....	....	....	....	....	....	....	....	....	....
1979-80	**Edmonton Oilers**	**NHL**	3	0	0	0	0	0	0	0	0	0	0	3	0.0	0	0	2	1	–1	....	....	....	....	....	....	....	....
	NHL Totals		324	67	86	153	65	72	137	435	15	3	4	584	11.5	235	46	264	44		13	1	1	2	43	0	0	1
	Other Major League Totals		232	117	152	269	....	....	....	360	....	....	....	....	....	....	....	....	....	....	8	1	3	4	13	....	....	....

WCJHL First All-Star Team (1968)

Traded to **Toronto** by **Boston** for Wayne Carlton, December 10, 1969. Selected by **Calgary-Cleveland** (WHA) in 1972 WHA General Player Draft, February 12, 1972. WHA rights traded to **Alberta** (WHA) by **Cleveland** (WHA) for cash, May, 1972. Traded to **Cleveland** (WHA) by **Edmonton** (WHA) for Ron Buchanan, October 14, 1974. Rights traded to **Chicago** by **Toronto** for Chicago's 2nd round choice (Bob Gladney) in 1977 Amateur Draft, September 28, 1976. Traded to **Edmonton** by **Chicago** for future considerations, September 24, 1979.

• HART, Gerry

Gerald William D – L. 5'9", 190 lbs. b: Flin Flon, Man., 1/1/1948.

Season	Club	League	GP	G	A	Pts	AG	AA	APts	PIM	PP	SH	GW	S	%	TGF	PGF	TGA	PGA	+/–	GP	G	A	Pts	PIM	PP	SH	GW
1964-65	Flin Flon Bombers	SJHL	2	0	0	0	....	....	....	0	....	....	....	....	....	....	....	....	....	....	1	0	0	0	2	....	....	....
1965-66	Flin Flon Bombers	SJHL	57	7	10	17	....	....	....	170	....	....	....	....	....	....	....	....	....	....	....	....	....	....	....	....	....	....
1966-67	Flin Flon Bombers	CMJHL	46	22	28	50	....	....	....	189	....	....	....	....	....	....	....	....	....	....	14	5	14	19	*90	....	....	....
	Flin Flon Bombers	Mem-Cup	6	1	2	3	....	....	....	48	....	....	....	....	....	....	....	....	....	....	....	....	....	....	....	....	....	....
	Port Arthur Marrs	Mem-Cup	5	0	2	2	....	....	....	23	....	....	....	....	....	....	....	....	....	....	....	....	....	....	....	....	....	....
1967-68	Flin Flon Bombers	WCJHL	58	13	38	51	....	....	....	290	....	....	....	....	....	....	....	....	....	....	15	1	7	8	43	....	....	....
1968-69	**Detroit Red Wings**	**NHL**	1	0	0	0	0	0	0	2	0	0	0	0	0.0	0	0	0	0	0	....	....	....	....	....	....	....	....
	Fort Worth Wings	CHL	26	2	3	5	....	....	....	52	....	....	....	....	....	....	....	....	....	....	....	....	....	....	....	....	....	....
	Baltimore Clippers	AHL	38	2	6	8	....	....	....	88	....	....	....	....	....	....	....	....	....	....	4	0	1	1	23	....	....	....
1969-70	**Detroit Red Wings**	**NHL**	3	0	0	0	0	0	0	2	0	0	0	0	0.0	0	0	0	0	0	....	....	....	....	....	....	....	....
	Fort Worth Wings	CHL	64	2	19	21	....	....	....	226	....	....	....	....	....	....	....	....	....	....	7	0	4	4	26	....	....	....
1970-71	**Detroit Red Wings**	**NHL**	64	2	7	9	2	6	8	148	1	0	1	62	3.2	55	2	73	17	–3	....	....	....	....	....	....	....	....
1971-72	**Detroit Red Wings**	**NHL**	3	0	0	0	0	0	0	0	0	0	0	2	0.0	1	0	3	0	–2	....	....	....	....	....	....	....	....
	Fort Worth Wings	CHL	14	1	4	5	....	....	....	84	....	....	....	....	....	....	....	....	....	....	....	....	....	....	....	....	....	....
	Tidewater Red Wings	AHL	28	4	9	13	....	....	....	146	....	....	....	....	....	....	....	....	....	....	....	....	....	....	....	....	....	....
1972-73	**New York Islanders**	**NHL**	47	1	11	12	1	9	10	158	0	0	0	72	1.4	50	4	79	15	–18	....	....	....	....	....	....	....	....
1973-74	**New York Islanders**	**NHL**	70	1	10	11	1	8	9	61	0	0	1	63	1.6	40	0	67	10	17	....	....	....	....	....	....	....	....
1974-75	**New York Islanders**	**NHL**	71	4	14	18	3	10	13	143	0	1	0	81	4.9	81	1	68	16	28	17	2	2	4	42	0	0	1
1975-76	**New York Islanders**	**NHL**	80	6	18	24	5	13	18	151	0	0	0	110	5.5	93	2	82	26	35	13	1	3	4	24	0	0	0
1976-77	**New York Islanders**	**NHL**	80	4	18	22	4	14	18	98	0	1	0	118	3.4	93	1	83	20	29	12	0	2	2	23	0	0	0

			REGULAR SEASON																		PLAYOFFS							
Season	Club	League	GP	G	A	Pts	AG	AA	APts	PIM	PP	SH	GW	S	%	TGF	PGF	TGA	PGA	+/–	GP	G	A	Pts	PIM	PP	SH	GW
1977-78	**New York Islanders**	**NHL**	**78**	**2**	**23**	**25**	**2**	**18**	**20**	**94**	**0**	**0**	**1**	**126**	**1.6**	**101**	**0**	**76**	**19**	**44**	**7**	**0**	**0**	**0**	**16**	**0**	**0**	**0**
1978-79	**New York Islanders**	**NHL**	**50**	**2**	**14**	**16**	**2**	**10**	**12**	**78**	**0**	**0**	**1**	**56**	**3.6**	**65**	**0**	**45**	**10**	**30**	**9**	**0**	**2**	**2**	**10**	**0**	**0**	**0**
1979-80	**Quebec Nordiques**	**NHL**	**71**	**3**	**23**	**26**	**3**	**17**	**20**	**59**	**1**	**0**	**0**	**53**	**5.7**	**70**	**9**	**116**	**42**	**–13**	....	....	....	....	....	....	....	....
1980-81	**Quebec Nordiques**	**NHL**	**6**	**0**	**0**	**0**	**0**	**0**	**0**	**10**	**0**	**0**	**0**	**6**	**0.0**	**5**	**0**	**12**	**5**	**–2**	....	....	....	....	....	....	....	....
	Nova Scotia Voyageurs	AHL	2	0	3	3	....	....	....	2	....	....	....	....	....	....	....	....	....	....	....	....	....	....	....	....	....	....
	St. Louis Blues	**NHL**	**63**	**4**	**11**	**15**	**3**	**7**	**10**	**132**	**0**	**0**	**0**	**44**	**9.1**	**67**	**1**	**69**	**12**	**9**	**10**	**0**	**0**	**0**	**27**	**0**	**0**	**0**
1981-82	**St. Louis Blues**	**NHL**	**35**	**0**	**1**	**1**	**0**	**1**	**1**	**102**	**0**	**0**	**0**	**15**	**0.0**	**32**	**0**	**50**	**13**	**–5**	**10**	**0**	**3**	**3**	**33**	**0**	**0**	**0**
1982-83	**St. Louis Blues**	**NHL**	**8**	**0**	**0**	**0**	**0**	**0**	**0**	**2**	**0**	**0**	**0**	**0**	**0.0**	**0**	**0**	**5**	**2**	**–3**	....	....	....	....	....	....	....	....
	NHL Totals		**730**	**29**	**150**	**179**	**26**	**113**	**139**	**1240**	**2**	**2**	**4**	**808**	**3.6**	**753**	**20**	**828**	**207**		**78**	**3**	**12**	**15**	**175**	**0**	**0**	**1**

WCJHL All-Star Team (1968)

Claimed by **NY Islanders** from **Detroit** in Expansion Draft, June 6, 1972. Claimed by **Quebec** from **NY Islanders** in Expansion Draft, June 13, 1979. Signed as a free agent by **St. Louis**, November 12, 1980. • Missed majority of 1981-82 season recovering from knee injury suffered in game vs. Detroit, October 15, 1981. • Officially announced retirement, December 1, 1982.

• HARTMAN, Mike

Michael J. LW – L. 6′, 190 lbs. b: Detroit, MI, 2/7/1967. Buffalo's 8th, 131st overall, in 1986.

Season	Club	League	GP	G	A	Pts	AG	AA	APts	PIM	PP	SH	GW	S	%	TGF	PGF	TGA	PGA	+/–	GP	G	A	Pts	PIM	PP	SH	GW
1983-84	North York Rangers	OJHL	37	17	26	43	....	....	....	141	....	....	....	....	....	....	....	....	....	....	....	....	....	....	....	....	....	....
1984-85	Belleville Bulls	OHL	49	13	12	25	....	....	....	119	....	....	....	....	....	....	....	....	....	....	....	....	....	....	....	....	....	....
1985-86	Belleville Bulls	OHL	4	2	1	3	....	....	....	5	....	....	....	....	....	....	....	....	....	....	....	....	....	....	....	....	....	....
	North Bay Centennials	OHL	53	19	16	35	....	....	....	205	....	....	....	....	....	....	....	....	....	....	10	2	4	6	34	....	....	....
1986-87	North Bay Centennials	OHL	32	15	24	39	....	....	....	144	....	....	....	....	....	....	....	....	....	....	19	7	8	15	88	....	....	....
	United States	WJC-A	6	2	1	3	....	....	....	4	....	....	....	....	....	....	....	....	....	....	....	....	....	....	....	....	....	....
	Buffalo Sabres	**NHL**	**17**	**3**	**3**	**6**	**3**	**2**	**5**	**69**	**0**	**0**	**0**	**19**	**15.8**	**9**	**0**	**7**	**0**	**2**	....	....	....	....	....	....	....	....
1987-88	**Buffalo Sabres**	**NHL**	**18**	**3**	**1**	**4**	**3**	**1**	**4**	**90**	**0**	**0**	**1**	**24**	**12.5**	**6**	**0**	**10**	**1**	**–3**	**6**	**0**	**0**	**0**	**35**	**0**	**0**	**0**
	Rochester Americans	AHL	57	13	14	27	....	....	....	283	....	....	....	....	....	....	....	....	....	....	4	1	0	1	22	....	....	....
1988-89	**Buffalo Sabres**	**NHL**	**70**	**8**	**9**	**17**	**7**	**6**	**13**	**316**	**1**	**0**	**0**	**91**	**8.8**	**29**	**1**	**20**	**1**	**9**	**5**	**0**	**0**	**0**	**34**	**0**	**0**	**0**
1989-90	**Buffalo Sabres**	**NHL**	**60**	**11**	**10**	**21**	**9**	**7**	**16**	**211**	**2**	**0**	**3**	**97**	**11.3**	**26**	**2**	**34**	**0**	**–10**	**6**	**0**	**0**	**0**	**18**	**0**	**0**	**0**
1990-91	**Buffalo Sabres**	**NHL**	**60**	**9**	**3**	**12**	**8**	**2**	**10**	**204**	**2**	**0**	**1**	**65**	**13.8**	**21**	**4**	**28**	**1**	**–10**	**2**	**0**	**0**	**0**	**17**	**0**	**0**	**0**
1991-92	**Winnipeg Jets**	**NHL**	**75**	**4**	**4**	**8**	**4**	**3**	**7**	**264**	**0**	**0**	**1**	**89**	**4.5**	**13**	**0**	**23**	**0**	**–10**	**2**	**0**	**0**	**0**	**2**	**0**	**0**	**0**
1992-93	**Tampa Bay Lightning**	**NHL**	**58**	**4**	**4**	**8**	**3**	**3**	**6**	**154**	**0**	**0**	**0**	**74**	**5.4**	**12**	**0**	**19**	**0**	**–7**	....	....	....	....	....	....	....	....
	New York Rangers	**NHL**	**3**	**0**	**0**	**0**	**0**	**0**	**0**	**6**	**0**	**0**	**0**	**3**	**0.0**	**0**	**0**	**0**	**0**	**0**	....	....	....	....	....	....	....	....
1993-94	**New York Rangers**	**NHL**	**35**	**1**	**1**	**2**	**1**	**1**	**2**	**70**	**0**	**0**	**0**	**19**	**5.3**	**3**	**0**	**8**	**0**	**–5**	....	....	....	....	....	....	....	....
1994-95	**New York Rangers**	**NHL**	**1**	**0**	**0**	**0**	**0**	**0**	**0**	**4**	**0**	**0**	**0**	**0**	**0.0**	**0**	**0**	**0**	**0**	**0**	....	....	....	....	....	....	....	....
	Detroit Vipers	IHL	6	1	0	1	....	....	....	52	....	....	....	....	....	....	....	....	....	....	1	0	0	0	0	....	....	....
1995-96	Orlando Solar Bears	IHL	77	14	10	24	....	....	....	243	....	....	....	....	....	....	....	....	....	....	21	2	2	4	31	....	....	....
1996-97	Hershey Bears	AHL	42	5	8	13	....	....	....	116	....	....	....	....	....	....	....	....	....	....	1	0	0	0	0	....	....	....
1997-98	Charlotte Checkers	ECHL	53	30	18	48	....	....	....	79	....	....	....	....	....	....	....	....	....	....	7	4	0	4	11	....	....	....
1998-99	Kolner Haie	Germany	43	6	3	9	....	....	....	156	....	....	....	....	....	....	....	....	....	....	....	....	....	....	....	....	....	....
	United States	WC-Q	3	2	4	6	....	....	....	0	....	....	....	....	....	....	....	....	....	....	....	....	....	....	....	....	....	....
	NHL Totals		**397**	**43**	**35**	**78**	**38**	**25**	**63**	**1388**	**5**	**0**	**6**	**481**	**8.9**	**119**	**7**	**149**	**3**		**21**	**0**	**0**	**0**	**106**	**0**	**0**	**0**

Traded to **Winnipeg** by **Buffalo** with Darrin Shannon and Dean Kennedy for Dave McLlwain, Gord Donnelly, Winnipeg's 5th round choice (Yuri Khmylev) in 1992 Entry Draft and future considerations, October 11, 1991. Claimed by **Tampa Bay** from **Winnipeg** in Expansion Draft, June 18, 1992. Traded to **NY Rangers** by **Tampa Bay** for Randy Gilhen, March 22, 1993. Signed as a free agent by **Colorado**, September 26, 1996.

• HARTSBURG, Craig

Craig William D – L. 6′1″, 200 lbs. b: Stratford, Ont., 6/29/1959. Minnesota's 1st, 6th overall, in 1979.

Season	Club	League	GP	G	A	Pts	AG	AA	APts	PIM	PP	SH	GW	S	%	TGF	PGF	TGA	PGA	+/–	GP	G	A	Pts	PIM	PP	SH	GW
1974-75	Guelph Biltmores	OJHL	25	7	23	30	....	....	....	....	....	....	....	....	....	....	....	....	....	....	....	....	....	....	....	....	....	....
1975-76	Sault Ste. Marie Greyhounds	OMJHL	64	9	19	28	....	....	....	65	....	....	....	....	....	....	....	....	....	....	12	1	0	1	16	....	....	....
1976-77	Sault Ste. Marie Greyhounds	OMJHL	61	29	64	93	....	....	....	142	....	....	....	....	....	....	....	....	....	....	9	0	11	11	27	....	....	....
1977-78	Sault Ste. Marie Greyhounds	OMJHL	36	15	42	57	....	....	....	101	....	....	....	....	....	....	....	....	....	....	13	4	8	12	24	....	....	....
	Canada	WJC-A	6	1	4	5	....	....	....	8	....	....	....	....	....	....	....	....	....	....	....	....	....	....	....	....	....	....
1978-79	Birmingham Bulls	WHA	77	9	40	49	....	....	....	73	....	....	....	....	....	....	....	....	....	....	....	....	....	....	....	....	....	....
1979-80	**Minnesota North Stars**	**NHL**	**79**	**14**	**30**	**44**	**12**	**22**	**34**	**81**	**7**	**0**	**2**	**202**	**6.9**	**140**	**45**	**116**	**19**	**–2**	**15**	**3**	**1**	**4**	**17**	**2**	**0**	**0**
1980-81	**Minnesota North Stars**	**NHL**	**74**	**13**	**30**	**43**	**10**	**20**	**30**	**124**	**8**	**0**	**2**	**207**	**6.3**	**109**	**48**	**86**	**16**	**–9**	**19**	**3**	**12**	**15**	**16**	**3**	**0**	**0**
1981-82	Canada	Can-Cup	7	0	1	1	....	....	....	6	....	....	....	....	....	....	....	....	....	....	....	....	....	....	....	....	....	....
	Minnesota North Stars	**NHL**	**76**	**17**	**60**	**77**	**13**	**40**	**53**	**117**	**5**	**0**	**2**	**204**	**8.3**	**159**	**48**	**115**	**15**	**11**	**4**	**1**	**2**	**3**	**14**	**0**	**0**	**0**
	Canada	WEC-A	10	3	3	6	....	....	....	12	....	....	....	....	....	....	....	....	....	....	....	....	....	....	....	....	....	....
1982-83	**Minnesota North Stars**	**NHL**	**78**	**12**	**50**	**62**	**10**	**35**	**45**	**109**	**3**	**1**	**1**	**200**	**6.0**	**143**	**43**	**121**	**28**	**7**	**9**	**3**	**8**	**11**	**7**	**2**	**0**	**0**
	Canada	WEC-A	5	1	2	3	....	....	....	2	....	....	....	....	....	....	....	....	....	....	....	....	....	....	....	....	....	....
1983-84	**Minnesota North Stars**	**NHL**	**26**	**7**	**7**	**14**	**6**	**5**	**11**	**37**	**5**	**0**	**0**	**54**	**13.0**	**53**	**22**	**46**	**13**	**–2**	....	....	....	....	....	....	....	....
1984-85	**Minnesota North Stars**	**NHL**	**32**	**7**	**11**	**18**	**6**	**7**	**13**	**54**	**1**	**1**	**1**	**93**	**7.5**	**51**	**18**	**50**	**12**	**–5**	**9**	**5**	**3**	**8**	**14**	**3**	**0**	**0**
1985-86	**Minnesota North Stars**	**NHL**	**75**	**10**	**47**	**57**	**8**	**32**	**40**	**127**	**4**	**0**	**2**	**185**	**5.4**	**161**	**78**	**87**	**11**	**7**	**5**	**0**	**1**	**1**	**2**	**0**	**0**	**0**
1986-87	**Minnesota North Stars**	**NHL**	**73**	**11**	**50**	**61**	**9**	**36**	**45**	**93**	**4**	**0**	**1**	**189**	**5.8**	**154**	**67**	**101**	**12**	**–2**	....	....	....	....	....	....	....	....
	Canada	WEC-A	10	0	1	1	....	....	....	14	....	....	....	....	....	....	....	....	....	....	....	....	....	....	....	....	....	....
1987-88	Canada	Can-Cup	9	0	2	2	....	....	....	6	....	....	....	....	....	....	....	....	....	....	....	....	....	....	....	....	....	....
	Minnesota North Stars	**NHL**	**27**	**3**	**16**	**19**	**3**	**11**	**14**	**29**	**2**	**0**	**1**	**83**	**3.6**	**42**	**23**	**30**	**9**	**–2**	....	....	....	....	....	....	....	....
1988-89	**Minnesota North Stars**	**NHL**	**30**	**4**	**14**	**18**	**3**	**10**	**13**	**47**	**1**	**0**	**0**	**75**	**5.3**	**42**	**15**	**37**	**2**	**–8**	....	....	....	....	....	....	....	....
1989-1990	**Minnesota North Stars**	**NHL**	DID NOT PLAY – ASSISTANT COACH																									
1990-1994	**Philadelphia Flyers**	**NHL**	DID NOT PLAY – ASSISTANT COACH																									
1994-1995	Guelph Platers	OHL	DID NOT PLAY – COACHING																									
1995-1998	**Chicago Blackhawks**	**NHL**	DID NOT PLAY – COACHING																									
1998-2000	**Mighty Ducks of Anaheim**	**NHL**	DID NOT PLAY – COACHING																									
	NHL Totals		**570**	**98**	**315**	**413**	**80**	**218**	**298**	**818**	**40**	**2**	**12**	**1492**	**6.6**	**1054**	**407**	**789**	**137**		**61**	**15**	**27**	**42**	**70**	**10**	**0**	**0**
	Other Major League Totals		77	9	40	49	....	....	....	73	....	....	....	....	....	....	....	....	....	....	....	....	....	....	....	....	....	....

OMJHL Second All-Star Team (1977) • Named Best Defenseman at WEC-A (1987) • Played in NHL All-Star Game (1980, 1982, 1983)

Signed as an underage free agent by **Birmingham** (WHA), June, 1978.

• HARVEY, Buster

Frederick John Charles RW – R. 6′, 185 lbs. b: Fredericton, N.B., 4/2/1950. Minnesota's 1st, 17th overall, in 1970.

Season	Club	League	GP	G	A	Pts	AG	AA	APts	PIM	PP	SH	GW	S	%	TGF	PGF	TGA	PGA	+/–	GP	G	A	Pts	PIM	PP	SH	GW
1964-65	Fredericton Red Wings	NBAHA	14	17	21	38	....	....	....	....	....	....	....	....	....	....	....	....	....	....	....	....	....	....	....	....	....	....
	Fredericton Lions	NBAHA	....	....	....	....	....	....	....	....	....	....	....	....	....	....	....	....	....	....	3	1	1	2	8	....	....	....
1965-66	Fredericton Hawks	NBAHA	25	*33	22	*55	....	....	....	....	....	....	....	....	....	....	....	....	....	....	....	....	....	....	....	....	....	....
1966-67	Halifax Canadians	MJrHL	51	23	51	74	....	....	....	50	....	....	....	....	....	....	....	....	....	....	17	9	18	27	10	....	....	....
1967-68	Fredericton Jr. Red Wings	NBJHL	4	2	4	6	....	....	....	2	....	....	....	....	....	....	....	....	....	....	6	2	4	6	16	....	....	....
	Fredericton Red Wings	SNBHL	6	2	8	10	....	....	....	34	....	....	....	....	....	....	....	....	....	....	5	0	7	7	11	....	....	....
	Fredericton Red Wings	M-Cup	6	6	4	10	....	....	....	2	....	....	....	....	....	....	....	....	....	....	....	....	....	....	....	....	....	....
	Halifax Jr. Canadians	M-Cup	3	2	3	5	....	....	....	2	....	....	....	....	....	....	....	....	....	....	....	....	....	....	....	....	....	....
1968-69	Hamilton Red Wings	OHA-Jr.	49	23	28	51	....	....	....	30	....	....	....	....	....	....	....	....	....	....	5	2	3	5	6	....	....	....
1969-70	Hamilton Red Wings	OHA-Jr.	54	26	34	60	....	....	....	39	....	....	....	....	....	....	....	....	....	....	....	....	....	....	....	....	....	....
1970-71	**Minnesota North Stars**	**NHL**	**59**	**12**	**8**	**20**	**12**	**7**	**19**	**36**	**4**	**0**	**3**	**154**	**7.8**	**47**	**18**	**42**	**0**	**–13**	**7**	**0**	**0**	**0**	**4**	**0**	**0**	**0**
1971-72	Cleveland Barons	AHL	73	41	54	95	....	....	....	72	....	....	....	....	....	....	....	....	....	....	6	1	2	3	34	....	....	....
	Minnesota North Stars	**NHL**	....	....	....	....	....	....	....	....	....	....	....	....	....	....	....	....	....	....	**1**	**0**	**0**	**0**	**0**	**0**	**0**	**0**
1972-73	**Minnesota North Stars**	**NHL**	**68**	**21**	**34**	**55**	**20**	**27**	**47**	**16**	**3**	**0**	**3**	**184**	**11.4**	**76**	**11**	**44**	**2**	**23**	**6**	**0**	**2**	**2**	**4**	**0**	**0**	**0**
1973-74	**Minnesota North Stars**	**NHL**	**72**	**16**	**17**	**33**	**15**	**14**	**29**	**14**	**1**	**0**	**3**	**190**	**8.4**	**55**	**2**	**64**	**0**	**–11**	....	....	....	....	....	....	....	....
1974-75	**Atlanta Flames**	**NHL**	**79**	**17**	**27**	**44**	**15**	**20**	**35**	**16**	**4**	**0**	**3**	**156**	**10.9**	**71**	**16**	**52**	**1**	**4**	....	....	....	....	....	....	....	....
1975-76	**Atlanta Flames**	**NHL**	**1**	**0**	**0**	**0**	**0**	**0**	**0**	**0**	**0**	**0**	**0**	**1**	**0.0**	**0**	**0**	**1**	**1**	**0**	....	....	....	....	....	....	....	....
	Kansas City Scouts	**NHL**	**39**	**5**	**12**	**17**	**4**	**9**	**13**	**6**	**0**	**0**	**0**	**76**	**6.6**	**26**	**4**	**54**	**1**	**–31**	....	....	....	....	....	....	....	....
	Detroit Red Wings	**NHL**	**35**	**8**	**9**	**17**	**7**	**7**	**14**	**25**	**1**	**0**	**0**	**71**	**11.3**	**27**	**4**	**41**	**10**	**–8**	....	....	....	....	....	....	....	....

			REGULAR SEASON																		PLAYOFFS							
Season	Club	League	GP	G	A	Pts	AG	AA	APts	PIM	PP	SH	GW	S	%	TGF	PGF	TGA	PGA	+/-	GP	G	A	Pts	PIM	PP	SH	GW
1976-77	Kansas City Blues	CHL	15	4	12	16	....	....	....	4	....	....	....	....	....	....	....	....	....	....	10	1	3	4	2	....	....	....
	Detroit Red Wings	**NHL**	**54**	**11**	**11**	**22**	**10**	**8**	**18**	**18**	**2**	**3**	**1**	**105**	**10.5**	**31**	**6**	**51**	**13**	**-13**	....	....	....	....	....	....	....	....
1977-78	Philadelphia Firebirds	AHL	71	10	17	27	....	....	....	31	....	....	....	....	....	....	....	....	....	....	4	1	0	1	2	....	....	....
	NHL Totals		**407**	**90**	**118**	**208**	**83**	**92**	**175**	**131**	**15**	**3**	**13**	**937**	**9.6**	**333**	**61**	**349**	**28**		**14**	**0**	**2**	**2**	**8**	**0**	**0**	**0**

OHA-Jr. Second All-Star Team (1970) • AHL Second All-Star Team (1972)

Traded to **Atlanta** by **Minnesota** with Jerry Byers for John Flesch and Don Martineau, May 27, 1974. Traded to **Kansas City** by **Atlanta** for Richard Lemieux and Kansas City's 2nd round choice (Miles Zaharko) in 1977 Amateur Draft, October 13, 1975. Traded to **Detroit** by **Kansas City** for Phil Roberto, January 14, 1976.

• HARVEY, Doug

Douglas Norman D – L. 5'11", 187 lbs. b: Montreal, Que., 12/19/1924 d: 12/26/1989. **HHOF**

Season	Club	League	GP	G	A	Pts	AG	AA	APts	PIM	PP	SH	GW	S	%	TGF	PGF	TGA	PGA	+/-	GP	G	A	Pts	PIM	PP	SH	GW
1942-43	Montreal Navy	MCHL	4	0	0	0	....	....	....	0	....	....	....	....	....	....	....	....	....	....	....	....	....	....	....	....	....	....
	Montreal Jr. Royals	QJHL	21	4	6	10	....	....	....	17	....	....	....	....	....	....	....	....	....	....	6	3	4	7	10	....	....	....
	Montreal Royals	QSHL	1	0	0	0	....	....	....	0	....	....	....	....	....	....	....	....	....	....	....	....	....	....	....	....	....	....
1943-44	Montreal Jr. Royals	QJHL	13	4	6	10	....	....	....	*34	....	....	....	....	....	....	....	....	....	....	4	2	*6	*8	10	....	....	....
	Montreal Royals	QSHL	1	1	1	2	....	....	....	2	....	....	....	....	....	....	....	....	....	....	....	....	....	....	....	....	....	....
	Montreal Navy	MCHL	15	4	1	5	....	....	....	24	....	....	....	....	....	....	....	....	....	....	5	3	1	4	15	....	....	....
	Montreal Jr. Royals	Mem-Cup	3	0	1	1	....	....	....	6	....	....	....	....	....	....	....	....	....	....	....	....	....	....	....	....	....	....
1944-45	Montreal Navy	MCHL	3	0	2	2	....	....	....	2	....	....	....	....	....	....	....	....	....	....	6	3	1	4	6	....	....	....
	Montreal Jr. Royals	QJHL	....	....	....	....	....	....	....	....	....	....	....	....	....	....	....	....	....	....	9	2	2	4	10	....	....	....
1945-46	Montreal Royals	QSHL	34	2	6	8	....	....	....	90	....	....	....	....	....	....	....	....	....	....	11	1	6	7	*37	....	....	....
1946-47	Montreal Royals	QSHL	40	2	26	28	....	....	....	*171	....	....	....	....	....	....	....	....	....	....	11	2	4	6	*62	....	....	....
	Montreal Royals	Al-Cup	14	4	9	13	....	....	....	26	....	....	....	....	....	....	....	....	....	....	....	....	....	....	....	....	....	....
1947-48	**Montreal Canadiens**	**NHL**	**35**	**4**	**4**	**8**	**5**	**5**	**10**	**32**	....	....	....	....	....	....	....	....	....	....	....	....	....	....	....	....	....	....
	Buffalo Bisons	AHL	24	1	7	8	....	....	....	38	....	....	....	....	....	....	....	....	....	....	....	....	....	....	....	....	....	....
1948-49	**Montreal Canadiens**	**NHL**	**55**	**3**	**13**	**16**	**4**	**18**	**22**	**87**	....	....	....	....	....	....	....	....	....	....	**7**	**0**	**1**	**1**	**10**	....	....	....
1949-50	**Montreal Canadiens**	**NHL**	**70**	**4**	**20**	**24**	**5**	**24**	**29**	**76**	....	....	....	....	....	....	....	....	....	....	**5**	**0**	**2**	**2**	**10**	....	....	....
1950-51	**Montreal Canadiens**	**NHL**	**70**	**5**	**24**	**29**	**6**	**29**	**35**	**93**	....	....	....	....	....	....	....	....	....	....	**11**	**0**	**5**	**5**	**12**	....	....	....
1951-52	**Montreal Canadiens**	**NHL**	**68**	**6**	**23**	**29**	**8**	**28**	**36**	**82**	....	....	....	....	....	....	....	....	....	....	**11**	**0**	**3**	**3**	**8**	....	....	....
1952-53♦	**Montreal Canadiens**	**NHL**	**69**	**4**	**30**	**34**	**5**	**37**	**42**	**67**	....	....	....	....	....	....	....	....	....	....	**12**	**0**	**5**	**5**	**8**	....	....	....
1953-54	**Montreal Canadiens**	**NHL**	**68**	**8**	**29**	**37**	**11**	**35**	**46**	**110**	....	....	....	....	....	....	....	....	....	....	**10**	**0**	**2**	**2**	**12**	....	....	....
1954-55	**Montreal Canadiens**	**NHL**	**70**	**6**	**43**	**49**	**8**	**50**	**58**	**58**	....	....	....	....	....	....	....	....	....	....	**12**	**0**	**8**	**8**	**6**	....	....	....
1955-56♦	**Montreal Canadiens**	**NHL**	**62**	**5**	**39**	**44**	**7**	**47**	**54**	**60**	....	....	....	....	....	....	....	....	....	....	**10**	**2**	**5**	**7**	**10**	....	....	....
1956-57♦	**Montreal Canadiens**	**NHL**	**70**	**6**	**44**	**50**	**8**	**49**	**57**	**92**	....	....	....	....	....	....	....	....	....	....	**10**	**0**	**7**	**7**	**10**	....	....	....
1957-58♦	**Montreal Canadiens**	**NHL**	**68**	**9**	**32**	**41**	**11**	**33**	**44**	**131**	....	....	....	....	....	....	....	....	....	....	**10**	**2**	**9**	**11**	**16**	....	....	....
1958-59♦	**Montreal Canadiens**	**NHL**	**61**	**4**	**16**	**20**	**5**	**16**	**21**	**61**	....	....	....	....	....	....	....	....	....	....	**11**	**1**	**11**	**12**	**22**	....	....	....
1959-60♦	**Montreal Canadiens**	**NHL**	**66**	**6**	**21**	**27**	**7**	**20**	**27**	**45**	....	....	....	....	....	....	....	....	....	....	**8**	**3**	**0**	**3**	**6**	....	....	....
1960-61	**Montreal Canadiens**	**NHL**	**58**	**6**	**33**	**39**	**7**	**32**	**39**	**48**	....	....	....	....	....	....	....	....	....	....	**6**	**0**	**1**	**1**	**8**	....	....	....
1961-62	**New York Rangers**	**NHL**	**69**	**6**	**24**	**30**	**7**	**23**	**30**	**42**	....	....	....	....	....	....	....	....	....	....	**6**	**0**	**1**	**1**	**2**	....	....	....
1962-63	**New York Rangers**	**NHL**	**68**	**4**	**35**	**39**	**5**	**35**	**40**	**92**	....	....	....	....	....	....	....	....	....	....	....	....	....	....	....	....	....	....
1963-64	St. Paul Rangers	CPHL	5	2	2	4	....	....	....	6	....	....	....	....	....	....	....	....	....	....	....	....	....	....	....	....	....	....
	New York Rangers	**NHL**	**14**	**0**	**2**	**2**	**0**	**2**	**2**	**10**	....	....	....	....	....	....	....	....	....	....	....	....	....	....	....	....	....	....
	Quebec Aces	AHL	52	6	36	42	....	....	....	30	....	....	....	....	....	....	....	....	....	....	9	0	4	4	10	....	....	....
1964-65	Quebec Aces	AHL	64	1	36	37	....	....	....	72	....	....	....	....	....	....	....	....	....	....	4	1	1	2	9	....	....	....
1965-66	Baltimore Clippers	AHL	67	7	32	39	....	....	....	80	....	....	....	....	....	....	....	....	....	....	....	....	....	....	....	....	....	....
1966-67	Baltimore Clippers	AHL	24	2	9	11	....	....	....	10	....	....	....	....	....	....	....	....	....	....	....	....	....	....	....	....	....	....
	Pittsburgh Hornets	AHL	28	0	9	9	....	....	....	22	....	....	....	....	....	....	....	....	....	....	9	0	0	0	2	....	....	....
	Detroit Red Wings	**NHL**	**2**	**0**	**0**	**0**	**0**	**0**	**0**	**0**	....	....	....	....	....	....	....	....	....	....	....	....	....	....	....	....	....	....
1967-68	Kansas City Blues	CPHL	59	4	16	20	....	....	....	12	....	....	....	....	....	....	....	....	....	....	7	0	6	6	6	....	....	....
	St. Louis Blues	**NHL**	....	....	....	....	....	....	....	....	....	....	....	....	....	....	....	....	....	....	**8**	**0**	**4**	**4**	**12**	....	....	....
1968-69	**St. Louis Blues**	**NHL**	**70**	**2**	**20**	**22**	**2**	**18**	**20**	**30**	**1**	**0**	**0**	**46**	**4.3**	**78**	**19**	**76**	**28**	**11**	....	....	....	....	....	....	....	....
1969-70	Laval Saints	QJHL	DID NOT PLAY – COACHING																									
	NHL Totals		**1113**	**88**	**452**	**540**	**111**	**501**	**612**	**1216**	....	....	....	....	....	....	....	....	....	....	**137**	**8**	**64**	**72**	**152**	....	....	....

NHL First All-Star Team (1952, 1953, 1954, 1955, 1956, 1957, 1958, 1960, 1961, 1962) • Won James Norris Trophy (1955, 1956, 1957, 1958, 1960, 1961, 1962) • NHL Second All-Star Team (1959) • AHL Second All-Star Team (1964) • Played in NHL All-Star Game (1951, 1952, 1953, 1954, 1955, 1956, 1957, 1958, 1959, 1960, 1961, 1962, 1969)

Traded to **NY Rangers** by **Montreal** for Lou Fontinato, June 13, 1961. Signed as a free agent by **Quebec** (AHL), November 26, 1963. Signed as a free agent by **Baltimore** (AHL), June 10, 1965. Traded to **Providence** (AHL) by **Baltimore** (AHL) for cash, December 23, 1966. • Activated contract clause that allowed him to become a free agent if traded by Baltimore and signed with **Detroit** (Pittsburgh-AHL), January 6, 1967. Signed as a free agent by **St. Louis** and named playing coach of Kansas City (CPHL), June, 1967.

• HARVEY, Hugh

Lionel Hugh C/LW – L. 6', 175 lbs. b: Kingston, Ont., 6/25/1949.

Season	Club	League	GP	G	A	Pts	AG	AA	APts	PIM	PP	SH	GW	S	%	TGF	PGF	TGA	PGA	+/-	GP	G	A	Pts	PIM	PP	SH	GW
1969-70	Kingston Aces	OHA-Sr.	27	17	16	33	....	....	....	51	....	....	....	....	....	....	....	....	....	....	....	....	....	....	....	....	....	....
1970-71	Oklahoma City Blazers	CHL	70	9	18	27	....	....	....	105	....	....	....	....	....	....	....	....	....	....	5	0	1	1	0	....	....	....
1971-72	Oklahoma City Blazers	CHL	10	2	3	5	....	....	....	20	....	....	....	....	....	....	....	....	....	....	....	....	....	....	....	....	....	....
	Dayton Gems	IHL	50	32	25	57	....	....	....	57	....	....	....	....	....	....	....	....	....	....	5	2	0	2	8	....	....	....
1972-73	Hershey Bears	AHL	70	23	27	50	....	....	....	89	....	....	....	....	....	....	....	....	....	....	7	6	2	8	2	....	....	....
1973-74	Hershey Bears	AHL	76	28	38	66	....	....	....	101	....	....	....	....	....	....	....	....	....	....	14	2	3	5	8	....	....	....
1974-75	**Kansas City Scouts**	**NHL**	**8**	**0**	**0**	**0**	**0**	**0**	**0**	**2**	**0**	**0**	**0**	**5**	**0.0**	**0**	**0**	**1**	**0**	**-1**	....	....	....	....	....	....	....	....
	Baltimore Clippers	AHL	36	4	11	15	....	....	....	30	....	....	....	....	....	....	....	....	....	....	....	....	....	....	....	....	....	....
	Fort Worth Texans	CHL	28	9	9	18	....	....	....	20	....	....	....	....	....	....	....	....	....	....	....	....	....	....	....	....	....	....
1975-76	**Kansas City Scouts**	**NHL**	**10**	**1**	**1**	**2**	**1**	**1**	**2**	**2**	**0**	**0**	**0**	**11**	**9.1**	**3**	**1**	**7**	**0**	**-5**	....	....	....	....	....	....	....	....
	Springfield Indians	AHL	44	15	9	24	....	....	....	49	....	....	....	....	....	....	....	....	....	....	....	....	....	....	....	....	....	....
	Baltimore Clippers	AHL	16	7	1	8	....	....	....	10	....	....	....	....	....	....	....	....	....	....	....	....	....	....	....	....	....	....
	NHL Totals		**18**	**1**	**1**	**2**	**1**	**1**	**2**	**4**	**0**	**0**	**0**	**16**	**6.3**	**3**	**1**	**8**	**0**		....	....	....	....	....	....	....	....

Signed as a free agent by **Philadelphia**, June, 1970. Claimed by **Hershey** (AHL) from **Philadelphia** in Reverse Draft, June 10, 1970. Claimed by **Kansas City** from **Hershey** (AHL) in Inter-League Draft, June 12, 1974.

• HARVEY, Todd

Todd Douglas Ross C – R. 6', 200 lbs. b: Hamilton, Ont., 2/17/1975. Dallas' 1st, 9th overall, in 1993.

Season	Club	League	GP	G	A	Pts	AG	AA	APts	PIM	PP	SH	GW	S	%	TGF	PGF	TGA	PGA	+/-	GP	G	A	Pts	PIM	PP	SH	GW
1989-90	Cambridge Winterhawks	OJHL-B	41	35	27	62	....	....	....	213	....	....	....	....	....	....	....	....	....	....	....	....	....	....	....	....	....	....
1990-91	Cambridge Winterhawks	OJHL-B	35	32	39	71	....	....	....	174	....	....	....	....	....	....	....	....	....	....	....	....	....	....	....	....	....	....
1991-92	Detroit Ambassadors	OHL	58	21	43	64	....	....	....	141	....	....	....	....	....	....	....	....	....	....	7	3	5	8	30	....	....	....
1992-93	Detroit Jr. Red Wings	OHL	55	50	50	100	....	....	....	83	....	....	....	....	....	....	....	....	....	....	15	9	12	21	39	....	....	....
1993-94	Detroit Jr. Red Wings	OHL	49	34	51	85	....	....	....	75	....	....	....	....	....	....	....	....	....	....	17	10	12	22	26	....	....	....
	Canada	WJC-A	7	4	3	7	....	....	....	6	....	....	....	....	....	....	....	....	....	....	....	....	....	....	....	....	....	....
1994-95	Detroit Jr. Red Wings	OHL	11	8	14	22	....	....	....	12	....	....	....	....	....	....	....	....	....	....	....	....	....	....	....	....	....	....
	Canada	WJC-A	7	6	0	6	....	....	....	4	....	....	....	....	....	....	....	....	....	....	....	....	....	....	....	....	....	....
	Dallas Stars	**NHL**	**40**	**11**	**9**	**20**	**19**	**13**	**32**	**67**	**2**	**0**	**1**	**64**	**17.2**	**26**	**10**	**19**	**0**	**-3**	**5**	**0**	**0**	**0**	**8**	**0**	**0**	**0**
1995-96	**Dallas Stars**	**NHL**	**69**	**9**	**20**	**29**	**9**	**16**	**25**	**136**	**3**	**0**	**1**	**101**	**8.9**	**59**	**21**	**51**	**0**	**-13**	....	....	....	....	....	....	....	....
	Michigan K-Wings	IHL	5	1	3	4	....	....	....	8	....	....	....	....	....	....	....	....	....	....	....	....	....	....	....	....	....	....
1996-97	**Dallas Stars**	**NHL**	**71**	**9**	**22**	**31**	**10**	**20**	**30**	**142**	**1**	**0**	**2**	**99**	**9.1**	**46**	**6**	**21**	**0**	**19**	**7**	**0**	**1**	**1**	**10**	**0**	**0**	**0**
1997-98	**Dallas Stars**	**NHL**	**59**	**9**	**10**	**19**	**11**	**10**	**21**	**104**	**0**	**0**	**1**	**88**	**10.2**	**25**	**4**	**16**	**0**	**5**	....	....	....	....	....	....	....	....
1998-99	**New York Rangers**	**NHL**	**37**	**11**	**17**	**28**	**13**	**16**	**29**	**72**	**6**	**0**	**2**	**58**	**19.0**	**43**	**24**	**26**	**6**	**-1**	....	....	....	....	....	....	....	....
99-2000	**New York Rangers**	**NHL**	**31**	**3**	**3**	**6**	**3**	**3**	**6**	**62**	**0**	**0**	**0**	**31**	**9.7**	**7**	**0**	**18**	**2**	**-9**	....	....	....	....	....	....	....	....
	San Jose Sharks	**NHL**	**40**	**8**	**4**	**12**	**9**	**4**	**13**	**78**	**2**	**0**	**0**	**59**	**13.6**	**19**	**5**	**16**	**0**	**-2**	**12**	**1**	**0**	**1**	**8**	**1**	**0**	**0**
	NHL Totals		**347**	**60**	**85**	**145**	**74**	**82**	**156**	**661**	**14**	**0**	**7**	**500**	**12.0**	**225**	**70**	**167**	**8**		**24**	**1**	**1**	**2**	**26**	**1**	**0**	**0**

Traded to **NY Rangers** by **Dallas** with Bob Errey and Dallas' 4th round choice (Boyd Kane) in 1998 Entry Draft for Brian Skrudland, Mike Keane and NY Rangers' 6th round choice (Pavel Patera) in 1998 Entry Draft, March 24, 1998. Traded to **San Jose** by **NY Rangers** with NY Rangers' 4th round choice in 2001 Entry Draft for Radek Dvorak, December 30, 1999.

• HATCHER, Derian
D – L. 6'5", 230 lbs. b: Sterling Heights, MI, 6/4/1972. Minnesota's 1st, 8th overall, in 1990.

			REGULAR SEASON																		PLAYOFFS							
Season	Club	League	GP	G	A	Pts	AG	AA	APts	PIM	PP	SH	GW	S	%	TGF	PGF	TGA	PGA	+/–	GP	G	A	Pts	PIM	PP	SH	GW
1987-88	Detroit G.P.D. Midgets	MNHL	25	5	13	18	....	....	....	52	....	....	....	....	....	....	....	....	....	....	....	....	....	....	....	....	....	....
1988-89	Detroit G.P.D. Midgets	MNHL	51	19	35	54	....	....	....	100	....	....	....	....	....	....	....	....	....	....	....	....	....	....	....	....	....	....
1989-90	North Bay Centennials	OHL	64	14	38	52	....	....	....	81	....	....	....	....	....	....	....	....	....	....	5	2	3	5	8	....	....	....
1990-91	North Bay Centennials	OHL	64	13	49	62	....	....	....	163	....	....	....	....	....	....	....	....	....	....	10	2	10	12	28	....	....	....
1991-92	**Minnesota North Stars**	**NHL**	**43**	**8**	**4**	**12**	**7**	**3**	**10**	**88**	**0**	**0**	**2**	**51**	**15.7**	**35**	**2**	**33**	**7**	**7**	**5**	**0**	**2**	**2**	**8**	**0**	**0**	**0**
1992-93	**Minnesota North Stars**	**NHL**	**67**	**4**	**15**	**19**	**3**	**10**	**13**	**178**	**0**	**0**	**1**	**73**	**5.5**	**69**	**13**	**109**	**26**	**–27**	....	....	....	....	....	....	....	....
	Kalamazoo Wings	IHL	2	1	2	3	....	....	....	21	....	....	....	....	....	....	....	....	....	....	....	....	....	....	....	....	....	....
	United States	WC-A	6	1	2	3	....	....	....	8	....	....	....	....	....	....	....	....	....	....	....	....	....	....	....	....	....	....
1993-94	**Dallas Stars**	**NHL**	**83**	**12**	**19**	**31**	**11**	**15**	**26**	**211**	**2**	**1**	**2**	**132**	**9.1**	**103**	**16**	**86**	**18**	**19**	**9**	**0**	**2**	**2**	**14**	**0**	**0**	**0**
1994-95	**Dallas Stars**	**NHL**	**43**	**5**	**11**	**16**	**9**	**16**	**25**	**105**	**2**	**0**	**2**	**74**	**6.8**	**47**	**15**	**43**	**14**	**3**	....	....	....	....	....	....	....	....
1995-96	**Dallas Stars**	**NHL**	**79**	**8**	**23**	**31**	**8**	**19**	**27**	**129**	**2**	**0**	**1**	**125**	**6.4**	**85**	**12**	**125**	**40**	**–12**	....	....	....	....	....	....	....	....
1996-97	United States	W-Cup	6	3	2	5	....	....	....	10	....	....	....	....	....	....	....	....	....	....	....	....	....	....	....	....	....	....
	Dallas Stars	**NHL**	**63**	**3**	**19**	**22**	**3**	**17**	**20**	**97**	**0**	**0**	**0**	**96**	**3.1**	**63**	**4**	**77**	**26**	**8**	**7**	**0**	**2**	**2**	**20**	**0**	**0**	**0**
1997-98	**Dallas Stars**	**NHL**	**70**	**6**	**25**	**31**	**7**	**24**	**31**	**132**	**3**	**0**	**2**	**74**	**8.1**	**72**	**17**	**62**	**16**	**9**	**17**	**3**	**3**	**6**	**39**	**2**	**0**	**0**
	United States	Olympics	4	0	0	0	....	....	....	0	....	....	....	....	....	....	....	....	....	....	....	....	....	....	....	....	....	....
1998-99♦	**Dallas Stars**	**NHL**	**80**	**9**	**21**	**30**	**11**	**20**	**31**	**102**	**3**	**0**	**2**	**125**	**7.2**	**91**	**12**	**85**	**27**	**21**	**18**	**1**	**6**	**7**	**24**	**0**	**0**	**0**
99-2000	**Dallas Stars**	**NHL**	**57**	**2**	**22**	**24**	**2**	**20**	**22**	**68**	**0**	**0**	**0**	**90**	**2.2**	**54**	**6**	**60**	**18**	**6**	**23**	**1**	**3**	**4**	**29**	**0**	**0**	**0**
	NHL Totals		**585**	**57**	**159**	**216**	**61**	**144**	**205**	**1110**	**12**	**1**	**12**	**840**	**6.8**	**619**	**97**	**680**	**192**		**79**	**5**	**18**	**23**	**134**	**2**	**0**	**0**

• Brother of Kevin • Played in NHL All-Star Game (1997)

Transferred to **Dallas** after **Minnesota** franchise relocated, June 9, 1993.

• HATCHER, Kevin
D – R. 6'3", 230 lbs. b: Detroit, MI, 9/9/1966. Washington's 1st, 17th overall, in 1984.

Season	Club	League	GP	G	A	Pts	AG	AA	APts	PIM	PP	SH	GW	S	%	TGF	PGF	TGA	PGA	+/–	GP	G	A	Pts	PIM	PP	SH	GW
1982-83	Detroit Compuware	MNHL	75	30	45	75	....	....	....	120	....	....	....	....	....	....	....	....	....	....	....	....	....	....	....	....	....	....
1983-84	North Bay Centennials	OHL	67	10	39	49	....	....	....	61	....	....	....	....	....	....	....	....	....	....	4	2	2	4	11	....	....	....
	United States	WJC-A	7	1	0	1	....	....	....	0	....	....	....	....	....	....	....	....	....	....	....	....	....	....	....	....	....	....
1984-85	North Bay Centennials	OHL	58	26	37	63	....	....	....	75	....	....	....	....	....	....	....	....	....	....	8	3	8	11	9	....	....	....
	Washington Capitals	**NHL**	**2**	**1**	**0**	**1**	**1**	**0**	**1**	**0**	**0**	**1**	**0**	**3**	**33.3**	**3**	**0**	**3**	**1**	**1**	**1**	**0**	**0**	**0**	**0**	**0**	**0**	**0**
1985-86	**Washington Capitals**	**NHL**	**79**	**9**	**10**	**19**	**7**	**7**	**14**	**119**	**1**	**0**	**1**	**132**	**6.8**	**80**	**6**	**91**	**23**	**6**	**9**	**1**	**1**	**2**	**19**	**0**	**0**	**0**
1986-87	**Washington Capitals**	**NHL**	**78**	**8**	**16**	**24**	**7**	**12**	**19**	**144**	**1**	**0**	**2**	**100**	**8.0**	**69**	**11**	**113**	**26**	**–29**	**7**	**1**	**0**	**1**	**20**	**0**	**0**	**0**
1987-88	United States	Can-Cup	5	0	0	0	....	....	....	4	....	....	....	....	....	....	....	....	....	....	....	....	....	....	....	....	....	....
	Washington Capitals	**NHL**	**71**	**14**	**27**	**41**	**12**	**19**	**31**	**137**	**5**	**0**	**3**	**181**	**7.7**	**86**	**28**	**94**	**37**	**1**	**14**	**5**	**7**	**12**	**55**	**1**	**0**	**1**
1988-89	**Washington Capitals**	**NHL**	**62**	**13**	**27**	**40**	**11**	**19**	**30**	**101**	**3**	**0**	**2**	**148**	**8.8**	**108**	**38**	**83**	**32**	**19**	**6**	**1**	**4**	**5**	**20**	**1**	**0**	**0**
1989-90	Washington Capitals	Fr-Tour	4	0	1	1	....	....	....	10	....	....	....	....	....	....	....	....	....	....	....	....	....	....	....	....	....	....
	Washington Capitals	**NHL**	**80**	**13**	**41**	**54**	**11**	**29**	**40**	**102**	**4**	**0**	**2**	**240**	**5.4**	**135**	**41**	**129**	**39**	**4**	**11**	**0**	**8**	**8**	**32**	**0**	**0**	**0**
1990-91	**Washington Capitals**	**NHL**	**79**	**24**	**50**	**74**	**22**	**38**	**60**	**69**	**9**	**2**	**3**	**267**	**9.0**	**138**	**49**	**125**	**26**	**–10**	**11**	**3**	**3**	**6**	**8**	**2**	**0**	**0**
1991-92	United States	Can-Cup	8	0	4	4	....	....	....	12	....	....	....	....	....	....	....	....	....	....	....	....	....	....	....	....	....	....
	Washington Capitals	**NHL**	**79**	**17**	**37**	**54**	**15**	**28**	**43**	**105**	**8**	**1**	**2**	**246**	**6.9**	**160**	**54**	**118**	**30**	**18**	**7**	**2**	**4**	**6**	**19**	**0**	**1**	**0**
1992-93	**Washington Capitals**	**NHL**	**83**	**34**	**45**	**79**	**28**	**31**	**59**	**114**	**13**	**1**	**6**	**329**	**10.3**	**162**	**56**	**162**	**49**	**–7**	**6**	**0**	**1**	**1**	**14**	**0**	**0**	**0**
1993-94	**Washington Capitals**	**NHL**	**72**	**16**	**24**	**40**	**15**	**19**	**34**	**108**	**6**	**0**	**3**	**217**	**7.4**	**100**	**33**	**122**	**42**	**–13**	**11**	**3**	**4**	**7**	**37**	**0**	**1**	**0**
1994-95	**Dallas Stars**	**NHL**	**47**	**10**	**19**	**29**	**18**	**28**	**46**	**66**	**3**	**0**	**2**	**138**	**7.2**	**72**	**27**	**64**	**15**	**–4**	**5**	**2**	**1**	**3**	**2**	**1**	**0**	**1**
1995-96	**Dallas Stars**	**NHL**	**74**	**15**	**26**	**41**	**15**	**21**	**36**	**58**	**7**	**0**	**3**	**237**	**6.3**	**105**	**45**	**104**	**20**	**–24**	....	....	....	....	....	....	....	....
1996-97	United States	W-Cup	7	0	3	3	....	....	....	4	....	....	....	....	....	....	....	....	....	....	....	....	....	....	....	....	....	....
	Pittsburgh Penguins	**NHL**	**80**	**15**	**39**	**54**	**16**	**35**	**51**	**103**	**9**	**0**	**1**	**199**	**7.5**	**144**	**47**	**117**	**31**	**11**	**5**	**1**	**1**	**2**	**4**	**1**	**0**	**0**
1997-98	**Pittsburgh Penguins**	**NHL**	**74**	**19**	**29**	**48**	**22**	**28**	**50**	**66**	**13**	**1**	**3**	**169**	**11.2**	**107**	**49**	**78**	**17**	**–3**	**6**	**1**	**0**	**1**	**12**	**1**	**0**	**0**
	United States	Olympics	3	0	2	2	....	....	....	0	....	....	....	....	....	....	....	....	....	....	....	....	....	....	....	....	....	....
1998-99	**Pittsburgh Penguins**	**NHL**	**66**	**11**	**27**	**38**	**13**	**26**	**39**	**24**	**4**	**2**	**3**	**131**	**8.4**	**103**	**31**	**87**	**26**	**11**	**13**	**2**	**3**	**5**	**4**	**1**	**0**	**0**
99-2000	**New York Rangers**	**NHL**	**74**	**4**	**19**	**23**	**4**	**18**	**22**	**38**	**2**	**0**	**0**	**112**	**3.6**	**70**	**25**	**79**	**24**	**–10**	....	....	....	....	....	....	....	....
	NHL Totals		**1100**	**223**	**436**	**659**	**217**	**358**	**575**	**1354**	**88**	**8**	**36**	**2849**	**7.8**	**1642**	**540**	**1569**	**438**		**112**	**22**	**37**	**59**	**246**	**8**	**2**	**2**

• Brother of Derian • OHL Second All-Star Team (1985) • Played in NHL All-Star Game (1990, 1991, 1992, 1996, 1997)

Traded to **Dallas** by **Washington** for Mark Tinordi and Rick Mrozik, January 18, 1995. Traded to **Pittsburgh** by **Dallas** for Sergei Zubov, June 22, 1996. Traded to **NY Rangers** by **Pittsburgh** for Peter Popovic, September 30, 1999.

• HATOUM, Ed
Edward RW – R. 5'10", 180 lbs. b: Beirut, Lebanon, 12/7/1947.

Season	Club	League	GP	G	A	Pts	AG	AA	APts	PIM	PP	SH	GW	S	%	TGF	PGF	TGA	PGA	+/–	GP	G	A	Pts	PIM	PP	SH	GW
1963-64	Ottawa Montagnards	OCJHL	STATISTICS NOT AVAILABLE																									
1964-65	Hamilton Red Wings	OHA-Jr.	17	0	3	3	....	....	....	8	....	....	....	....	....	....	....	....	....	....	....	....	....	....	....	....	....	....
1965-66	Hamilton Red Wings	OHA-Jr.	48	16	35	51	....	....	....	51	....	....	....	....	....	....	....	....	....	....	5	0	3	3	2	....	....	....
1966-67	Hamilton Red Wings	OHA-Jr.	45	19	25	44	....	....	....	89	....	....	....	....	....	....	....	....	....	....	17	5	11	16	16	....	....	....
1967-68	Hamilton Red Wings	OHA-Jr.	50	25	34	59	....	....	....	44	....	....	....	....	....	....	....	....	....	....	11	6	5	11	10	....	....	....
	Fort Worth Wings	CPHL	....	....	....	....	....	....	....	....	....	....	....	....	....	....	....	....	....	....	7	0	1	1	0	....	....	....
1968-69	**Detroit Red Wings**	**NHL**	**16**	**2**	**1**	**3**	**2**	**1**	**3**	**2**	**0**	**0**	**1**	**20**	**10.0**	**6**	**1**	**4**	**0**	**1**	....	....	....	....	....	....	....	....
	Fort Worth Wings	CHL	53	21	28	49	....	....	....	29	....	....	....	....	....	....	....	....	....	....	....	....	....	....	....	....	....	....
	Baltimore Clippers	AHL	3	0	1	1	....	....	....	2	....	....	....	....	....	....	....	....	....	....	4	1	1	2	0	....	....	....
1969-70	**Detroit Red Wings**	**NHL**	**5**	**0**	**2**	**2**	**0**	**2**	**2**	**2**	**0**	**0**	**0**	**1**	**0.0**	**2**	**0**	**1**	**0**	**1**	....	....	....	....	....	....	....	....
	Fort Worth Wings	CHL	69	15	40	55	....	....	....	32	....	....	....	....	....	....	....	....	....	....	6	2	3	5	0	....	....	....
1970-71	**Vancouver Canucks**	**NHL**	**26**	**1**	**3**	**4**	**1**	**2**	**3**	**21**	**0**	**1**	**0**	**27**	**3.7**	**9**	**4**	**26**	**7**	**–14**	....	....	....	....	....	....	....	....
	Seattle Totems	WHL	29	8	13	21	....	....	....	19	....	....	....	....	....	....	....	....	....	....	....	....	....	....	....	....	....	....
1971-72	Rochester Americans	AHL	67	9	23	32	....	....	....	29	....	....	....	....	....	....	....	....	....	....	....	....	....	....	....	....	....	....
1972-73	Chicago Cougars	WHA	16	1	1	2	....	....	....	2	....	....	....	....	....	....	....	....	....	....	....	....	....	....	....	....	....	....
	Seattle Totems	WHL	45	11	26	37	....	....	....	14	....	....	....	....	....	....	....	....	....	....	....	....	....	....	....	....	....	....
1973-74	Vancouver Blazers	WHA	37	3	12	15	....	....	....	8	....	....	....	....	....	....	....	....	....	....	....	....	....	....	....	....	....	....
	San Diego Gulls	WHL	5	1	0	1	....	....	....	4	....	....	....	....	....	....	....	....	....	....	....	....	....	....	....	....	....	....
1974-75	Nelson Maple Leafs	WIHL	48	25	53	78	....	....	....	18	....	....	....	....	....	....	....	....	....	....	....	....	....	....	....	....	....	....
1975-76	Nelson Maple Leafs	WIHL	4	0	3	3	....	....	....	0	....	....	....	....	....	....	....	....	....	....	....	....	....	....	....	....	....	....
	NHL Totals		**47**	**3**	**6**	**9**	**3**	**5**	**8**	**25**	**0**	**1**	**1**	**48**	**6.3**	**17**	**5**	**31**	**7**		....	....	....	....	....	....	....	....
	Other Major League Totals		53	4	13	17	....	....	....	10	....	....	....	....	....	....	....	....	....	....	....	....	....	....	....	....	....	....

Claimed by **Vancouver** from **Detroit** in Expansion Draft, June 10, 1970. Loaned to **Seattle** (WHL) by **Vancouver** with Jim Wiste for the remainder of the 1970-71 season for Bobby Schmautz, February 9, 1971. Selected by **LA Sharks** (WHA) in 1972 WHA General Player Draft, February 12, 1972. WHA rights traded to **Chicago** (WHA) by **LA Sharks** (WHA) for cash, October, 1972. Traded to **Vancouver** (WHA) by **Chicago** (WHA) for cash, September, 1973.

• HAUER, Brett
D – R. 6'2", 200 lbs. b: Richfield, MN, 7/11/1971. Vancouver's 3rd, 71st overall, in 1989.

Season	Club	League	GP	G	A	Pts	AG	AA	APts	PIM	PP	SH	GW	S	%	TGF	PGF	TGA	PGA	+/–	GP	G	A	Pts	PIM	PP	SH	GW
1987-88	Richfield Spartans	Hi-School	24	3	3	6	....	....	....	....	....	....	....	....	....	....	....	....	....	....	....	....	....	....	....	....	....	....
1988-89	Richfield Spartans	Hi-School	24	8	15	23	....	....	....	70	....	....	....	....	....	....	....	....	....	....	....	....	....	....	....	....	....	....
1989-90	University of Minnesota-Duluth	WCHA	37	2	6	8	....	....	....	44	....	....	....	....	....	....	....	....	....	....	....	....	....	....	....	....	....	....
1990-91	University of Minnesota-Duluth	WCHA	30	1	7	8	....	....	....	54	....	....	....	....	....	....	....	....	....	....	....	....	....	....	....	....	....	....
1991-92	University of Minnesota-Duluth	WCHA	33	8	14	22	....	....	....	40	....	....	....	....	....	....	....	....	....	....	....	....	....	....	....	....	....	....
1992-93	University of Minnesota-Duluth	WCHA	40	10	46	56	....	....	....	52	....	....	....	....	....	....	....	....	....	....	....	....	....	....	....	....	....	....
	United States	WC-A	6	0	0	0	....	....	....	8	....	....	....	....	....	....	....	....	....	....	....	....	....	....	....	....	....	....
1993-94	United States	Nat-Team	57	6	14	20	....	....	....	88	....	....	....	....	....	....	....	....	....	....	....	....	....	....	....	....	....	....
	United States	Olympics	8	0	0	0	....	....	....	10	....	....	....	....	....	....	....	....	....	....	....	....	....	....	....	....	....	....
	Las Vegas Thunder	IHL	21	0	7	7	....	....	....	8	....	....	....	....	....	....	....	....	....	....	1	0	0	0	0	....	....	....
1994-95	AIK Solna Stockholm	Sweden	37	1	3	4	....	....	....	38	....	....	....	....	....	....	....	....	....	....	....	....	....	....	....	....	....	....
	United States	WC-A	6	2	2	4	....	....	....	4	....	....	....	....	....	....	....	....	....	....	....	....	....	....	....	....	....	....
1995-96	**Edmonton Oilers**	**NHL**	**29**	**4**	**2**	**6**	**4**	**2**	**6**	**30**	**2**	**0**	**1**	**53**	**7.5**	**22**	**7**	**34**	**8**	**–11**	....	....	....	....	....	....	....	....
	Cape Breton Oilers	AHL	17	3	5	8	....	....	....	29	....	....	....	....	....	....	....	....	....	....	....	....	....	....	....	....	....	....
1996-97	Chicago Wolves	IHL	81	10	30	40	....	....	....	50	....	....	....	....	....	....	....	....	....	....	4	2	0	2	4	....	....	....
1997-98	Manitoba Moose	IHL	82	13	48	61	....	....	....	58	....	....	....	....	....	....	....	....	....	....	3	0	0	0	2	....	....	....

			REGULAR SEASON																		PLAYOFFS							
Season	Club	League	GP	G	A	Pts	AG	AA	APts	PIM	PP	SH	GW	S	%	TGF	PGF	TGA	PGA	+/–	GP	G	A	Pts	PIM	PP	SH	GW
1998-99	Manitoba Moose	IHL	81	15	56	71	....	....	....	66	....	....	....	....	....	....	....	....	....	....	5	0	5	5	4	....	....	....
99-2000	Edmonton Oilers	NHL	5	0	2	2	0	2	2	2	0	0	0	8	0.0	3	0	5	0	–2	....	....	....	....	....	....	....	....
	Manitoba Moose	IHL	77	13	47	60	....	....	....	92	....	....	....	....	....	....	....	....	....	....	2	0	1	1	2	....	....	....
	NHL Totals		34	4	4	8	4	4	8	32	2	0	1	61	6.6	25	7	39	8		....	....	....	....	....	....	....	....

WCHA First All-Star Team (1993) • NCAA West First All-American Team (1993) • IHL First All-Star Team (1999, 2000) • Won Larry D. Gordon Trophy (Top Defenseman - IHL) (2000)

Traded to **Edmonton** by **Vancouver** for Edmonton's 7th round choice (Larry Shapley) in 1997 Entry Draft, August 24, 1995. Signed as a free agent by **Manitoba** (IHL), September 15, 1997.

• HAVELID, Niclas

D – L. 5'11", 200 lbs. b: Enkoping, Sweden, 4/12/1973. Anaheim's 2nd, 83rd overall, in 1999.

Season	Club	League	GP	G	A	Pts	AG	AA	APts	PIM	PP	SH	GW	S	%	TGF	PGF	TGA	PGA	+/–	GP	G	A	Pts	PIM	PP	SH	GW
1991-92	AIK Solna Stockholm	Sweden	10	0	0	0	....	....	....	2	....	....	....	....	....	....	....	....	....	....	....	....	....	....	....	....	....	....
1992-93	AIK Solna Stockholm	Sweden	22	1	0	1	....	....	....	16	....	....	....	....	....	....	....	....	....	....	....	....	....	....	....	....	....	....
1993-94	AIK Solna Stockholm	Sweden-2	40	6	12	18	....	....	....	26	....	....	....	....	....	....	....	....	....	....	9	0	1	1	10	....	....	....
1994-95	AIK Solna Stockholm	Sweden	40	3	7	10	....	....	....	38	....	....	....	....	....	....	....	....	....	....	....	....	....	....	....	....	....	....
1995-96	AIK Solna Stockholm	Sweden	40	5	6	11	....	....	....	30	....	....	....	....	....	....	....	....	....	....	....	....	....	....	....	....	....	....
1996-97	AIK Solna Stockholm	Sweden	49	3	6	9	....	....	....	42	....	....	....	....	....	....	....	....	....	....	7	1	2	3	8	....	....	....
1997-98	AIK Solna Stockholm	Sweden	43	8	4	12	....	....	....	42	....	....	....	....	....	....	....	....	....	....	....	....	....	....	....	....	....	....
1998-99	Malmo IF	Sweden	50	10	12	22	....	....	....	42	....	....	....	....	....	....	....	....	....	....	8	0	4	4	10	....	....	....
99-2000	Mighty Ducks of Anaheim	NHL	50	2	7	9	2	6	8	20	0	0	2	70	2.9	36	4	42	10	0	....	....	....	....	....	....	....	....
	Cincinnati Mighty Ducks	AHL	2	0	0	0	....	....	....	0	....	....	....	....	....	....	....	....	....	....	....	....	....	....	....	....	....	....
	NHL Totals		50	2	7	9	2	6	8	20	0	0	2	70	2.9	36	4	42	10		....	....	....	....	....	....	....	....

• HAWERCHUK, Dale

Dale Martin C – L. 5'11", 190 lbs. b: Toronto, Ont., 4/4/1963. Winnipeg's 1st, 1st overall, in 1981.

Season	Club	League	GP	G	A	Pts	AG	AA	APts	PIM	PP	SH	GW	S	%	TGF	PGF	TGA	PGA	+/–	GP	G	A	Pts	PIM	PP	SH	GW
1978-79	Oshawa Legionnaires	OHA-B	36	32	52	84	....	....	....	....	....	....	....	....	....	....	....	....	....	....	....	....	....	....	....	....	....	....
1979-80	Cornwall Royals	QMJHL	72	37	66	103	....	....	....	21	....	....	....	....	....	....	....	....	....	....	18	20	25	45	0	....	....	....
	Cornwall Royals	Mem-Cup	5	1	5	6	....	....	....	0	....	....	....	....	....	....	....	....	....	....	....	....	....	....	....	....	....	....
1980-81	Cornwall Royals	QMJHL	72	81	102	183	....	....	....	69	....	....	....	....	....	....	....	....	....	....	19	15	20	35	8	....	....	....
	Canada	WJC-A	5	5	4	9	....	....	....	2	....	....	....	....	....	....	....	....	....	....	....	....	....	....	....	....	....	....
	Cornwall Royals	Mem-Cup	5	*8	4	*12	....	....	....	4	....	....	....	....	....	....	....	....	....	....	....	....	....	....	....	....	....	....
1981-82	Winnipeg Jets	NHL	80	45	58	103	36	39	75	47	12	0	2	339	13.3	144	55	97	4	–4	4	1	7	8	5	0	0	0
	Canada	WEC-A	10	3	1	4	....	....	....	0	....	....	....	....	....	....	....	....	....	....	....	....	....	....	....	....	....	....
1982-83	Winnipeg Jets	NHL	79	40	51	91	33	35	68	31	13	1	3	297	13.5	135	60	107	15	–17	3	1	4	5	8	1	0	0
1983-84	Winnipeg Jets	NHL	80	37	65	102	30	44	74	73	10	0	4	256	14.5	137	46	120	15	–14	3	1	1	2	0	1	0	0
1984-85	Winnipeg Jets	NHL	80	53	77	130	43	53	96	74	17	3	4	280	18.9	172	57	102	9	22	3	2	1	3	4	1	0	0
1985-86	Winnipeg Jets	NHL	80	46	59	105	37	40	77	44	18	2	2	313	14.7	130	53	128	24	–27	3	0	3	3	0	0	0	0
	Canada	WEC-A	8	2	4	6	....	....	....	4	....	....	....	....	....	....	....	....	....	....	....	....	....	....	....	....	....	....
1986-87	Winnipeg Jets	NHL	80	47	53	100	41	39	80	52	10	0	4	267	17.6	135	41	95	4	3	10	5	8	13	4	3	0	0
	NHL All-Stars	RV-87	2	0	1	1	....	....	....	2	....	....	....	....	....	....	....	....	....	....	....	....	....	....	....	....	....	....
1987-88	Canada	Can-Cup	9	4	2	6	....	....	....	0	....	....	....	....	....	....	....	....	....	....	....	....	....	....	....	....	....	....
	Winnipeg Jets	NHL	80	44	77	121	38	55	93	59	20	3	4	292	15.1	157	80	104	18	–9	5	3	4	7	16	2	0	0
1988-89	Winnipeg Jets	NHL	75	41	55	96	35	39	74	28	14	3	4	239	17.2	132	53	123	14	–30	....	....	....	....	....	....	....	....
	Canada	WEC-A	10	4	8	12	....	....	....	6	....	....	....	....	....	....	....	....	....	....	....	....	....	....	....	....	....	....
1989-90	Winnipeg Jets	NHL	79	26	55	81	22	39	61	60	8	0	2	211	12.3	117	44	91	7	–11	7	3	5	8	2	0	0	1
1990-91	Buffalo Sabres	NHL	80	31	58	89	28	44	72	32	12	0	1	194	16.0	116	47	69	2	2	6	2	4	6	10	1	0	0
1991-92	Canada	Can-Cup	8	2	3	5	....	....	....	0	....	....	....	....	....	....	....	....	....	....	....	....	....	....	....	....	....	....
	Buffalo Sabres	NHL	77	23	75	98	21	57	78	27	13	0	4	242	9.5	139	83	91	13	–22	7	2	5	7	0	0	0	0
1992-93	Buffalo Sabres	NHL	81	16	80	96	13	55	68	52	8	0	2	259	6.2	147	87	83	6	–17	8	5	9	14	2	3	0	0
1993-94	Buffalo Sabres	NHL	81	35	51	86	33	40	73	91	13	1	7	227	15.4	130	66	55	1	10	7	0	7	7	4	0	0	0
1994-95	Buffalo Sabres	NHL	23	5	11	16	9	16	25	2	2	0	2	56	8.9	20	13	9	0	–2	2	0	0	0	0	0	0	0
1995-96	St. Louis Blues	NHL	66	13	28	41	13	23	36	22	5	0	1	136	9.6	63	32	32	6	5	....	....	....	....	....	....	....	....
	Philadelphia Flyers	NHL	16	4	16	20	4	13	17	4	1	0	1	44	9.1	27	9	10	2	10	12	3	6	9	12	1	0	0
1996-97	Philadelphia Flyers	NHL	51	12	22	34	13	20	33	32	6	0	2	102	11.8	52	17	26	0	9	17	2	5	7	0	1	0	1
	NHL Totals		1188	518	891	1409	449	651	1100	730	182	13	49	3754	13.8	1953	843	1342	140		97	30	69	99	67	14	0	2

Memorial Cup All-Star Team (1980, 1981) • Won George Parsons Trophy (Memorial Cup Tournament Most Sportsmanlike Player) (1980) • QMJHL First All-Star Team (1981) • Canadian Major Junior Player of the Year (1981) • Won Stafford Smythe Memorial Trophy (Memorial Cup Tournament MVP) (1981) • Won Calder Memorial Trophy (1982) • NHL Second All-Star Team (1985)

Played in NHL All-Star Game (1982, 1985, 1986, 1988, 1997)

Traded to **Buffalo** by **Winnipeg** with Winnipeg's 1st round choice (Brad May) in 1990 Entry Draft and future considerations for Phil Housley, Scott Arniel, Jeff Parker and Buffalo's 1st round choice (Keith Tkachuk) in 1990 Entry Draft, June 16, 1990. Signed as a free agent by **St. Louis**, September 8, 1995. Traded to **Philadelphia** by **St. Louis** for Craig MacTavish, March 15, 1996.

• HAWGOOD, Greg

D – L. 5'10", 190 lbs. b: Edmonton, Alta., 8/10/1968. Boston's 9th, 202nd overall, in 1986.

Season	Club	League	GP	G	A	Pts	AG	AA	APts	PIM	PP	SH	GW	S	%	TGF	PGF	TGA	PGA	+/–	GP	G	A	Pts	PIM	PP	SH	GW
1982-83	St. Albert Sabres	AAHA	STATISTICS NOT AVAILABLE																									
1983-84	Kamloops Blazers	WHL	49	10	23	33	....	....	....	39	....	....	....	....	....	....	....	....	....	....	6	0	2	2	2	....	....	....
	Kamloops Blazers	Mem-Cup	3	0	1	1	....	....	....	0	....	....	....	....	....	....	....	....	....	....	....	....	....	....	....	....	....	....
1984-85	Kamloops Blazers	WHL	66	25	40	65	....	....	....	72	....	....	....	....	....	....	....	....	....	....	15	3	15	18	15	....	....	....
1985-86	Kamloops Blazers	WHL	71	34	85	119	....	....	....	86	....	....	....	....	....	....	....	....	....	....	16	9	22	31	16	....	....	....
	Kamloops Blazers	Mem-Cup	5	3	6	9	....	....	....	6	....	....	....	....	....	....	....	....	....	....	....	....	....	....	....	....	....	....
1986-87	Kamloops Blazers	WHL	61	30	93	123	....	....	....	139	....	....	....	....	....	....	....	....	....	....	13	7	16	23	18	....	....	....
	Canada	WJC-A	6	2	2	4	....	....	....	6	....	....	....	....	....	....	....	....	....	....	....	....	....	....	....	....	....	....
1987-88	Kamloops Blazers	WHL	63	48	85	133	....	....	....	142	....	....	....	....	....	....	....	....	....	....	16	10	16	26	33	....	....	....
	Canada	WJC-A	7	1	8	9	....	....	....	6	....	....	....	....	....	....	....	....	....	....	....	....	....	....	....	....	....	....
	Boston Bruins	NHL	1	0	0	0	0	0	0	0	0	0	0	1	0.0	0	0	1	0	–1	3	1	0	1	0	0	0	0
1988-89	Boston Bruins	NHL	56	16	24	40	14	17	31	84	5	0	0	132	12.1	88	31	63	10	4	10	0	2	2	2	0	0	0
	Maine Mariners	AHL	21	2	9	11	....	....	....	41	....	....	....	....	....	....	....	....	....	....	....	....	....	....	....	....	....	....
1989-90	Boston Bruins	NHL	77	11	27	38	9	19	28	76	2	0	1	127	8.7	67	14	43	2	12	15	1	3	4	12	1	0	0
1990-91	HC Asiago	Italy	2	3	0	3	....	....	....	9	....	....	....	....	....	....	....	....	....	....	....	....	....	....	....	....	....	....
	Maine Mariners	AHL	5	0	1	1	....	....	....	13	....	....	....	....	....	....	....	....	....	....	....	....	....	....	....	....	....	....
	Edmonton Oilers	NHL	6	0	1	1	0	1	1	6	0	0	0	9	0.0	3	2	4	1	–2	....	....	....	....	....	....	....	....
	Cape Breton Oilers	AHL	55	10	32	42	....	....	....	73	....	....	....	....	....	....	....	....	....	....	4	0	3	3	23	....	....	....
1991-92	Edmonton Oilers	NHL	20	2	11	13	2	8	10	22	0	0	0	24	8.3	34	4	16	5	19	13	0	3	3	23	0	0	0
	Cape Breton Oilers	AHL	56	20	55	75	....	....	....	26	....	....	....	....	....	....	....	....	....	....	3	2	2	4	0	....	....	....
1992-93	Edmonton Oilers	NHL	29	5	13	18	4	9	13	35	2	0	0	47	10.6	32	9	28	4	–1	....	....	....	....	....	....	....	....
	Philadelphia Flyers	NHL	40	6	22	28	5	15	20	39	5	0	1	91	6.6	57	33	32	1	–7	....	....	....	....	....	....	....	....
1993-94	Philadelphia Flyers	NHL	19	3	12	15	3	9	12	19	3	0	0	37	8.1	21	15	4	0	2	....	....	....	....	....	....	....	....
	Florida Panthers	NHL	33	2	14	16	2	11	13	9	0	0	1	55	3.6	38	20	10	0	8	....	....	....	....	....	....	....	....
	Pittsburgh Penguins	NHL	12	1	2	3	1	2	3	8	1	0	1	20	5.0	9	6	4	0	–1	1	0	0	0	0	0	0	0
1994-95	Pittsburgh Penguins	NHL	21	1	4	5	2	6	8	25	1	0	0	17	5.9	10	4	4	0	2	....	....	....	....	....	....	....	....
	Cleveland Lumberjacks	IHL	....	....	....	....	....	....	....	....	....	....	....	....	....	....	....	....	....	....	3	1	0	1	4	....	....	....
1995-96	Las Vegas Thunder	IHL	78	20	65	85	....	....	....	101	....	....	....	....	....	....	....	....	....	....	15	5	11	16	24	....	....	....
1996-97	San Jose Sharks	NHL	63	6	12	18	6	11	17	69	3	0	0	83	7.2	39	20	44	3	–22	....	....	....	....	....	....	....	....
1997-98	Kolner Haie	Germany	4	0	1	1	....	....	....	16	....	....	....	....	....	....	....	....	....	....	....	....	....	....	....	....	....	....
	Kolner Haie	EuroHL	1	0	0	0	....	....	....	2	....	....	....	....	....	....	....	....	....	....	....	....	....	....	....	....	....	....
	Houston Aeros	IHL	81	19	52	71	....	....	....	75	....	....	....	....	....	....	....	....	....	....	4	0	4	4	0	....	....	....
1998-99	Houston Aeros	IHL	76	17	57	74	....	....	....	90	....	....	....	....	....	....	....	....	....	....	19	4	8	12	24	....	....	....
99-2000	Vancouver Canucks	NHL	79	5	17	22	6	16	22	26	2	0	0	70	7.1	69	16	54	6	5	....	....	....	....	....	....	....	....
	NHL Totals		456	58	159	217	54	124	178	418	24	0	4	713	8.1	467	174	307	32		42	2	8	10	37	1	0	0

WHL West First All-Star Team (1986, 1987, 1988) • WJC-A All-Star Team (1988) • Canadian Major Junior Defenseman of the Year (1988) • AHL First All-Star Team (1992) • Won Eddie Shore Award (Top Defenseman - AHL) (1992) • IHL First All-Star Team (1996, 1998, 1999) • Won Governors' Trophy (Top Defenseman — IHL) (1996, 1999)

Traded to **Edmonton** by **Boston** for Vladimir Ruzicka, October 22, 1990. Traded to **Philadelphia** by **Edmonton** with Josef Beranek for Brian Benning, January 16, 1993. Traded to **Florida** by **Philadelphia** for cash, November 30, 1993. Traded to **Pittsburgh** by **Florida** for Jeff Daniels, March 19, 1994. Signed as a free agent by **San Jose**, September 25, 1996. Signed as a free agent by **Vancouver**, September 30, 1999.

• HAWKINS, Todd Todd D. W – R. 6'1", 195 lbs. b: Kingston, Ont., 8/2/1966. Vancouver's 10th, 217th overall, in 1986.

Season	Club	League	GP	G	A	Pts	AG	AA	APts	PIM	PP	SH	GW	S	%	TGF	PGF	TGA	PGA	+/-	Playoffs GP	G	A	Pts	PIM	PP	SH	GW
1983-84	Pembroke Lumber Kings	OJHL	53	28	22	50	....	....	....	117	....	....	....	....	....	....	....	....	....	....	....	....	....	....	....	....	....	....
1984-85	Belleville Bulls	OHL	58	7	16	23	....	....	....	117	....	....	....	....	....	....	....	....	....	....	12	1	0	1	10	....	....	....
1985-86	Belleville Bulls	OHL	60	14	13	27	....	....	....	172	....	....	....	....	....	....	....	....	....	....	24	9	7	16	60	....	....	....
1986-87	Belleville Bulls	OHL	60	47	40	87	....	....	....	187	....	....	....	....	....	....	....	....	....	....	6	3	5	8	16	....	....	....
1987-88	Flint Spirits	IHL	50	13	13	26	....	....	....	337	....	....	....	....	....	....	....	....	....	....	16	3	5	8	*174	....	....	....
	Fredericton Express	AHL	2	0	4	4	....	....	....	11	....	....	....	....	....	....	....	....	....	....	....	....	....	....	....	....	....	....
1988-89	**Vancouver Canucks**	**NHL**	**4**	**0**	**0**	**0**	**0**	**0**	**0**	**9**	**0**	**0**	**0**	**2**	**0.0**	**0**	**0**	**1**	**0**	**–1**	....	....	....	....	....	....	....	....
	Milwaukee Admirals	IHL	63	12	14	26	....	....	....	307	....	....	....	....	....	....	....	....	....	....	9	1	0	1	33	....	....	....
1989-90	**Vancouver Canucks**	**NHL**	**4**	**0**	**0**	**0**	**0**	**0**	**0**	**6**	**0**	**0**	**0**	**3**	**0.0**	**1**	**0**	**2**	**0**	**–1**	....	....	....	....	....	....	....	....
	Milwaukee Admirals	IHL	61	23	17	40	....	....	....	273	....	....	....	....	....	....	....	....	....	....	5	4	1	5	19	....	....	....
1990-91	Newmarket Saints	AHL	22	2	5	7	....	....	....	66	....	....	....	....	....	....	....	....	....	....	....	....	....	....	....	....	....	....
	Milwaukee Admirals	IHL	39	9	11	20	....	....	....	134	....	....	....	....	....	....	....	....	....	....	....	....	....	....	....	....	....	....
1991-92	**Toronto Maple Leafs**	**NHL**	**2**	**0**	**0**	**0**	**0**	**0**	**0**	**0**	**0**	**0**	**0**	**0**	**0.0**	**0**	**0**	**0**	**0**	**0**	....	....	....	....	....	....	....	....
	St. John's Maple Leafs	AHL	66	30	27	57	....	....	....	139	....	....	....	....	....	....	....	....	....	....	7	1	0	1	10	....	....	....
1992-93	St. John's Maple Leafs	AHL	72	21	41	62	....	....	....	103	....	....	....	....	....	....	....	....	....	....	9	1	3	4	10	....	....	....
1993-94	Cleveland Lumberjacks	IHL	76	19	14	33	....	....	....	115	....	....	....	....	....	....	....	....	....	....	....	....	....	....	....	....	....	....
1994-95	Cleveland Lumberjacks	IHL	4	2	0	2	....	....	....	29	....	....	....	....	....	....	....	....	....	....	....	....	....	....	....	....	....	....
	Minnesota Moose	IHL	47	10	8	18	....	....	....	95	....	....	....	....	....	....	....	....	....	....	3	0	1	1	12	....	....	....
1995-96	Cincinnati Cyclones	IHL	73	16	12	28	....	....	....	65	....	....	....	....	....	....	....	....	....	....	17	7	4	11	32	....	....	....
1996-97	Cincinnati Cyclones	IHL	81	13	13	26	....	....	....	162	....	....	....	....	....	....	....	....	....	....	3	0	1	1	2	....	....	....
1997-98	Cincinnati Cyclones	IHL	71	13	23	36	....	....	....	168	....	....	....	....	....	....	....	....	....	....	9	0	3	3	36	....	....	....
1998-99	Cincinnati Cyclones	IHL	82	20	32	52	....	....	....	171	....	....	....	....	....	....	....	....	....	....	3	2	1	3	8	....	....	....
99-2000	Cincinnati Cyclones	IHL	61	14	17	31	....	....	....	98	....	....	....	....	....	....	....	....	....	....	1	1	0	1	0	....	....	....
	NHL Totals		**10**	**0**	**0**	**0**	**0**	**0**	**0**	**15**	**0**	**0**	**0**	**5**	**0.0**	**1**	**0**	**3**	**0**		....	....	....	....	....	....	....	....

OHL Second All-Star Team (1987)

Traded to **Toronto** by **Vancouver** for Brian Blad, January 22, 1991. Signed as a free agent by **Pittsburgh**, August 20, 1993. Traded to **Cincinnati** (IHL) by **Cleveland** (IHL) with Dale Degray for Mike Stevens, September 9, 1995.

• HAWORTH, Alan Alan Joseph Gordon C – R. 5'10", 190 lbs. b: Drummondville, Que., 9/1/1960. Buffalo's 6th, 95th overall, in 1979.

Season	Club	League	GP	G	A	Pts	AG	AA	APts	PIM	PP	SH	GW	S	%	TGF	PGF	TGA	PGA	+/-	Playoffs GP	G	A	Pts	PIM	PP	SH	GW
1975-76	Drummondville Olympique	QAAA	STATISTICS NOT AVAILABLE																									
1976-77	Chicoutimi Sagueneens	QMJHL	68	11	18	29	....	....	....	15	....	....	....	....	....	....	....	....	....	....	....	....	....	....	....	....	....	....
1977-78	Chicoutimi Sagueneens	QMJHL	59	17	33	50	....	....	....	40	....	....	....	....	....	....	....	....	....	....	....	....	....	....	....	....	....	....
1978-79	Sherbrooke Beavers	QMJHL	70	50	70	120	....	....	....	63	....	....	....	....	....	....	....	....	....	....	12	6	10	16	8	....	....	....
1979-80	Sherbrooke Beavers	QMJHL	45	28	36	64	....	....	....	50	....	....	....	....	....	....	....	....	....	....	15	11	16	27	4	....	....	....
1980-81	**Buffalo Sabres**	**NHL**	**49**	**16**	**20**	**36**	**12**	**13**	**25**	**34**	**4**	**0**	**1**	**72**	**22.2**	**47**	**10**	**43**	**0**	**–6**	**7**	**4**	**4**	**8**	**2**	**3**	**0**	**1**
	Rochester Americans	AHL	21	14	18	32	....	....	....	19	....	....	....	....	....	....	....	....	....	....	....	....	....	....	....	....	....	....
1981-82	**Buffalo Sabres**	**NHL**	**57**	**21**	**18**	**39**	**17**	**12**	**29**	**30**	**3**	**0**	**1**	**114**	**18.4**	**62**	**9**	**47**	**0**	**6**	**3**	**0**	**1**	**1**	**2**	**0**	**0**	**0**
	Rochester Americans	AHL	14	5	12	17	....	....	....	10	....	....	....	....	....	....	....	....	....	....	....	....	....	....	....	....	....	....
1982-83	**Washington Capitals**	**NHL**	**74**	**23**	**27**	**50**	**19**	**19**	**38**	**34**	**5**	**0**	**2**	**145**	**15.9**	**74**	**21**	**58**	**0**	**–5**	**4**	**0**	**0**	**0**	**2**	**0**	**0**	**0**
1983-84	**Washington Capitals**	**NHL**	**75**	**24**	**31**	**55**	**19**	**21**	**40**	**52**	**7**	**0**	**5**	**164**	**14.6**	**75**	**20**	**41**	**0**	**14**	**8**	**3**	**2**	**5**	**4**	**1**	**0**	**0**
1984-85	**Washington Capitals**	**NHL**	**76**	**23**	**26**	**49**	**19**	**18**	**37**	**48**	**4**	**0**	**2**	**154**	**14.9**	**65**	**11**	**36**	**1**	**19**	**5**	**1**	**0**	**1**	**0**	**0**	**0**	**1**
1985-86	**Washington Capitals**	**NHL**	**71**	**34**	**39**	**73**	**27**	**26**	**53**	**72**	**7**	**0**	**5**	**194**	**17.5**	**92**	**17**	**40**	**1**	**36**	**9**	**4**	**6**	**10**	**11**	**1**	**0**	**0**
1986-87	**Washington Capitals**	**NHL**	**50**	**25**	**16**	**41**	**22**	**12**	**34**	**43**	**9**	**0**	**2**	**143**	**17.5**	**58**	**14**	**44**	**3**	**3**	**6**	**0**	**3**	**3**	**7**	**0**	**0**	**0**
1987-88	**Quebec Nordiques**	**NHL**	**72**	**23**	**34**	**57**	**20**	**24**	**44**	**112**	**6**	**0**	**2**	**171**	**13.5**	**77**	**26**	**59**	**3**	**–5**	....	....	....	....	....	....	....	....
1988-89	SC Bern	Switz.	36	24	29	53	....	....	....	....	....	....	....	....	....	....	....	....	....	....	11	*8	2	10	....	....	....	....
1989-90	SC Bern	Switz.	36	31	30	61	....	....	....	....	....	....	....	....	....	....	....	....	....	....	....	....	....	....	....	....	....	....
1990-91	SC Bern	Switz.	36	27	16	43	....	....	....	....	....	....	....	....	....	....	....	....	....	....	10	2	5	7	....	....	....	....
	Canada	Nat-Team	1	0	0	0	....	....	....	0	....	....	....	....	....	....	....	....	....	....	....	....	....	....	....	....	....	....
1991-92	SC Bern	Switz.	30	16	23	39	....	....	....	100	....	....	....	....	....	....	....	....	....	....	11	7	6	13	15	....	....	....
	NHL Totals		**524**	**189**	**211**	**400**	**155**	**145**	**300**	**425**	**45**	**0**	**20**	**1157**	**16.3**	**550**	**128**	**368**	**8**		**42**	**12**	**16**	**28**	**28**	**5**	**0**	**2**

• Son of Gord

Traded to **Washington** by **Buffalo** with Buffalo's 3rd round choice (Milan Novy) in 1982 Entry Draft for Washington's 2nd round choice (Mike Anderson) and 4th round choice (Timo Jutila) in 1982 Entry Draft, June 9, 1982. Traded to **Quebec** by **Washington** with Gaetan Duchesne and Washington's 1st round choice (Joe Sakic) in 1987 Entry Draft for Clint Malarchuk and Dale Hunter, June 13, 1987.

• HAWRYLIW, Neil RW – L. 5'11", 185 lbs. b: Fielding, Sask., 11/9/1955.

Season	Club	League	GP	G	A	Pts	AG	AA	APts	PIM	PP	SH	GW	S	%	TGF	PGF	TGA	PGA	+/-	Playoffs GP	G	A	Pts	PIM	PP	SH	GW
1972-73	Humboldt Broncos	SJHL	STATISTICS NOT AVAILABLE																									
1973-74	Saskatoon Blades	WCJHL	52	23	20	43	....	....	....	28	....	....	....	....	....	....	....	....	....	....	6	0	0	0	0	....	....	....
1974-75	Saskatoon Blades	WCJHL	68	29	38	67	....	....	....	51	....	....	....	....	....	....	....	....	....	....	17	2	10	12	13	....	....	....
1975-76	Saskatoon Blades	WCJHL	72	48	39	87	....	....	....	155	....	....	....	....	....	....	....	....	....	....	20	14	20	34	23	....	....	....
1976-77	Muskegon Mohawks	IHL	38	18	18	36	....	....	....	16	....	....	....	....	....	....	....	....	....	....	7	2	3	5	4	....	....	....
1977-78	Muskegon Mohawks	IHL	75	37	32	69	....	....	....	84	....	....	....	....	....	....	....	....	....	....	5	2	3	5	9	....	....	....
1978-79	Muskegon Mohawks	IHL	13	11	7	18	....	....	....	14	....	....	....	....	....	....	....	....	....	....	....	....	....	....	....	....	....	....
	Fort Worth Texans	CHL	57	9	15	24	....	....	....	87	....	....	....	....	....	....	....	....	....	....	....	....	....	....	....	....	....	....
1979-80	Indianapolis Checkers	CHL	70	26	19	45	....	....	....	56	....	....	....	....	....	....	....	....	....	....	7	4	2	6	6	....	....	....
1980-81	Indianapolis Checkers	CHL	80	37	42	79	....	....	....	61	....	....	....	....	....	....	....	....	....	....	5	0	2	2	7	....	....	....
1981-82	**New York Islanders**	**NHL**	**1**	**0**	**0**	**0**	**0**	**0**	**0**	**0**	**0**	**0**	**0**	**0**	**0.0**	**0**	**0**	**0**	**0**	**0**	....	....	....	....	....	....	....	....
	Indianapolis Checkers	CHL	58	20	14	34	....	....	....	89	....	....	....	....	....	....	....	....	....	....	13	3	11	14	6	....	....	....
1982-83	Muskegon Mohawks	IHL	68	33	24	57	....	....	....	42	....	....	....	....	....	....	....	....	....	....	4	0	1	1	4	....	....	....
	Wichita Wind	CHL	2	2	3	5	....	....	....	0	....	....	....	....	....	....	....	....	....	....	....	....	....	....	....	....	....	....
1983-84	Muskegon Mohawks	IHL	66	25	37	62	....	....	....	36	....	....	....	....	....	....	....	....	....	....	....	....	....	....	....	....	....	....
1984-85	Muskegon Mohawks	IHL	80	17	22	39	....	....	....	93	....	....	....	....	....	....	....	....	....	....	14	2	3	5	29	....	....	....
1985-86	Muskegon Lumberjacks	IHL	14	4	1	5	....	....	....	10	....	....	....	....	....	....	....	....	....	....	....	....	....	....	....	....	....	....
	Kalamazoo Wings	IHL	68	32	23	55	....	....	....	67	....	....	....	....	....	....	....	....	....	....	6	1	3	4	17	....	....	....
1986-87	Kalamazoo Wings	IHL	56	9	23	32	....	....	....	84	....	....	....	....	....	....	....	....	....	....	5	0	1	1	4	....	....	....
	NHL Totals		**1**	**0**	**0**	**0**	**0**	**0**	**0**	**0**	**0**	**0**	**0**	**0**	**0.0**	**0**	**0**	**0**	**0**		....	....	....	....	....	....	....	....

CHL First All-Star Team (1981)

Signed as a free agent by **NY Islanders**, October 10, 1978.

• HAY, Dwayne LW – L. 6', 219 lbs. b: London, Ont., 2/11/1977. Washington's 3rd, 43rd overall, in 1995.

Season	Club	League	GP	G	A	Pts	AG	AA	APts	PIM	PP	SH	GW	S	%	TGF	PGF	TGA	PGA	+/-	Playoffs GP	G	A	Pts	PIM	PP	SH	GW
1991-92	London Travellers	OMHA	86	70	56	126	....	....	....	104	....	....	....	....	....	....	....	....	....	....	....	....	....	....	....	....	....	....
1992-93	Listowel Cyclones	OJHL-B	50	19	33	52	....	....	....	40	....	....	....	....	....	....	....	....	....	....	....	....	....	....	....	....	....	....
1993-94	Listowel Cyclones	OJHL	48	10	24	34	....	....	....	56	....	....	....	....	....	....	....	....	....	....	....	....	....	....	....	....	....	....
1994-95	Guelph Storm	OHL	65	26	28	54	....	....	....	37	....	....	....	....	....	....	....	....	....	....	14	5	7	12	6	....	....	....
1995-96	Guelph Storm	OHL	60	28	30	58	....	....	....	49	....	....	....	....	....	....	....	....	....	....	16	4	9	13	18	....	....	....
	Guelph Storm	Mem-Cup	3	0	0	0	....	....	....	2	....	....	....	....	....	....	....	....	....	....	....	....	....	....	....	....	....	....
1996-97	Guelph Storm	OHL	32	17	17	34	....	....	....	21	....	....	....	....	....	....	....	....	....	....	11	4	6	10	0	....	....	....
	Canada	WJC-A	7	0	0	0	....	....	....	2	....	....	....	....	....	....	....	....	....	....	....	....	....	....	....	....	....	....
1997-98	**Washington Capitals**	**NHL**	**2**	**0**	**0**	**0**	**0**	**0**	**0**	**2**	**0**	**0**	**0**	**1**	**0.0**	**0**	**0**	**0**	**0**	**0**	....	....	....	....	....	....	....	....
	Portland Pirates	AHL	58	6	7	13	....	....	....	35	....	....	....	....	....	....	....	....	....	....	....	....	....	....	....	....	....	....
	Beast of New Haven	AHL	10	3	2	5	....	....	....	4	....	....	....	....	....	....	....	....	....	....	2	0	0	0	0	....	....	....
1998-99	**Florida Panthers**	**NHL**	**9**	**0**	**0**	**0**	**0**	**0**	**0**	**0**	**0**	**0**	**0**	**3**	**0.0**	**1**	**0**	**2**	**0**	**–1**	....	....	....	....	....	....	....	....
	Beast of New Haven	AHL	46	18	17	35	....	....	....	22	....	....	....	....	....	....	....	....	....	....	....	....	....	....	....	....	....	....

Season	Club	League	GP	G	A	Pts	AG	AA	APts	PIM	PP	SH	GW	S	%	TGF	PGF	TGA	PGA	+/–	GP	G	A	Pts	PIM	PP	SH	GW
			REGULAR SEASON																		PLAYOFFS							
99-2000	**Florida Panthers**	**NHL**	**6**	**0**	**0**	**0**	**0**	**0**	**0**	**2**	**0**	**0**	**0**	**3**	**0.0**	**1**	**0**	**3**	**0**	**–2**	....	....	....	....	....	....	....	....
	Louisville Panthers	AHL	41	11	20	31	....	....	....	18	....	....	....	....	....	....	....	....	....	....	....	....	....	....	....	....	....	....
	Tampa Bay Lightning	**NHL**	**13**	**1**	**1**	**2**	**1**	**1**	**2**	**2**	**0**	**0**	**0**	**11**	**9.1**	**2**	**0**	**2**	**0**	**0**	....	....	....	....	....	....	....	....
	NHL Totals		**30**	**1**	**1**	**2**	**1**	**1**	**2**	**6**	**0**	**0**	**0**	**18**	**5.6**	**4**	**0**	**7**	**0**		....	....	....	....	....	....	....	....

Traded to **Florida** by **Washington** with future considerations for Esa Tikkanen, March 9, 1998. Traded to **Tampa Bay** by **Florida** with Ryan Johnson for Mike Sillinger, March 14, 2000.

• HAYEK, Peter

D – L. 5'10", 200 lbs. b: Minneapolis, MN, 11/16/1957.

Season	Club	League	GP	G	A	Pts	AG	AA	APts	PIM	PP	SH	GW	S	%	TGF	PGF	TGA	PGA	+/–	GP	G	A	Pts	PIM	PP	SH	GW
1978-79	University of Minnesota	WCHA	6	0	0	0	....	....	....	8	....	....	....	....	....	....	....	....	....	....	....	....	....	....	....	....	....	....
1979-80	University of Minnesota	WCHA	41	8	14	22	....	....	....	110	....	....	....	....	....	....	....	....	....	....	....	....	....	....	....	....	....	....
	Baltimore Clippers	EHL	....	....	....	....	....	....	....	....	....	....	....	....	....	....	....	....	....	....	4	0	1	1	6	....	....	....
1980-81	Oklahoma City Stars	CHL	28	5	3	8	....	....	....	16	....	....	....	....	....	....	....	....	....	....	....	....	....	....	....	....	....	....
	Baltimore Clippers	EHL	47	18	22	40	....	....	....	55	....	....	....	....	....	....	....	....	....	....	4	0	1	1	0	....	....	....
1981-82	**Minnesota North Stars**	**NHL**	**1**	**0**	**0**	**0**	**0**	**0**	**0**	**0**	**0**	**0**	**0**	**0**	**0.0**	**0**	**0**	**1**	**0**	**–1**	....	....	....	....	....	....	....	....
	Nashville South Stars	CHL	68	3	12	15	....	....	....	131	....	....	....	....	....	....	....	....	....	....	3	1	0	1	4	....	....	....
1982-83	Birmingham South Stars	CHL	14	0	2	2	....	....	....	15	....	....	....	....	....	....	....	....	....	....	....	....	....	....	....	....	....	....
	NHL Totals		**1**	**0**	**0**	**0**	**0**	**0**	**0**	**0**	**0**	**0**	**0**	**0**	**0.0**	**0**	**0**	**1**	**0**		....	....	....	....	....	....	....	....

Signed as a free agent by **Minnesota**, September, 1981.

• HAYES, Chris

Christopher Joseph LW – L. 5'10", 180 lbs. b: Rouyn, Que., 8/24/1946.

Season	Club	League	GP	G	A	Pts	AG	AA	APts	PIM	PP	SH	GW	S	%	TGF	PGF	TGA	PGA	+/–	GP	G	A	Pts	PIM	PP	SH	GW
1963-64	Pembroke Lumber Kings	OHA-B	STATISTICS NOT AVAILABLE																									
1964-65	Oshawa Generals	OHA-Jr.	44	8	7	15	....	....	....	52	....	....	....	....	....	....	....	....	....	....	6	1	2	3	15	....	....	....
1965-66	Oshawa Generals	OHA-Jr.	44	8	14	22	....	....	....	92	....	....	....	....	....	....	....	....	....	....	17	0	2	2	26	....	....	....
	Oshawa Generals	Mem-Cup	14	10	14	24	....	....	....	20	....	....	....	....	....	....	....	....	....	....	....	....	....	....	....	....	....	....
1966-67	Oshawa Generals	OHA-Jr.	30	3	11	14	....	....	....	57	....	....	....	....	....	....	....	....	....	....	....	....	....	....	....	....	....	....
1967-68	Loyola College	OQAA	STATISTICS NOT AVAILABLE																									
1968-69	Loyola College	OQAA	STATISTICS NOT AVAILABLE																									
1969-70	Loyola College	OQAA	35	27	48	75	....	....	....	79	....	....	....	....	....	....	....	....	....	....	....	....	....	....	....	....	....	....
1970-71	Loyola College	OQAA	34	26	54	80	....	....	....	....	....	....	....	....	....	....	....	....	....	....	....	....	....	....	....	....	....	....
1971-72	Oklahoma City Blazers	CHL	72	15	38	53	....	....	....	59	....	....	....	....	....	....	....	....	....	....	6	5	4	9	2	....	....	....
	♦ **Boston Bruins**	**NHL**	....	....	....	....	....	....	....	....	....	....	....	....	....	....	....	....	....	....	**1**	**0**	**0**	**0**	**0**	**0**	**0**	**0**
1972-73	Boston Braves	AHL	63	9	19	28	....	....	....	31	....	....	....	....	....	....	....	....	....	....	10	2	5	7	4	....	....	....
1973-74	Albuquerque 6-Guns	CHL	71	20	28	48	....	....	....	118	....	....	....	....	....	....	....	....	....	....	....	....	....	....	....	....	....	....
1974-75			DID NOT PLAY																									
1975-76	Mohawk Valley Comets	NAHL	4	1	2	3	....	....	....	2	....	....	....	....	....	....	....	....	....	....	....	....	....	....	....	....	....	....
	NHL Totals		....	....	....	....	....	....	....	....	....	....	....	....	....	....	....	....	....		**1**	**0**	**0**	**0**	**0**	**0**	**0**	**0**

OQAA First All-Star Team (1970)

Signed as a free agent by **Boston**, September, 1971.

• HAYWARD, Rick

Rick Douglas D – L. 6', 180 lbs. b: Toledo, OH, 2/25/1966. Montreal's 9th, 162nd overall, in 1986.

Season	Club	League	GP	G	A	Pts	AG	AA	APts	PIM	PP	SH	GW	S	%	TGF	PGF	TGA	PGA	+/–	GP	G	A	Pts	PIM	PP	SH	GW
1983-84	Hull Olympiques	QMJHL	67	6	17	23	....	....	....	220	....	....	....	....	....	....	....	....	....	....	....	....	....	....	....	....	....	....
1984-85	Hull Olympiques	QMJHL	56	7	27	34	....	....	....	367	....	....	....	....	....	....	....	....	....	....	5	0	1	1	56	....	....	....
1985-86	Hull Olympiques	QMJHL	59	3	40	43	....	....	....	354	....	....	....	....	....	....	....	....	....	....	15	2	11	13	*98	....	....	....
	Hull Olympiques	Mem-Cup	5	0	1	1	....	....	....	*26	....	....	....	....	....	....	....	....	....	....	....	....	....	....	....	....	....	....
1986-87	Sherbrooke Canadiens	AHL	46	2	3	5	....	....	....	153	....	....	....	....	....	....	....	....	....	....	3	0	1	1	15	....	....	....
1987-88	Saginaw Hawks	IHL	24	3	4	7	....	....	....	129	....	....	....	....	....	....	....	....	....	....	....	....	....	....	....	....	....	....
	Salt Lake Golden Eagles	IHL	17	1	3	4	....	....	....	124	....	....	....	....	....	....	....	....	....	....	13	0	1	1	120	....	....	....
1988-89	Salt Lake Golden Eagles	IHL	72	4	20	24	....	....	....	313	....	....	....	....	....	....	....	....	....	....	10	4	3	7	42	....	....	....
1989-90	Salt Lake Golden Eagles	IHL	58	5	13	18	....	....	....	419	....	....	....	....	....	....	....	....	....	....	....	....	....	....	....	....	....	....
1990-91	**Los Angeles Kings**	**NHL**	**4**	**0**	**0**	**0**	**0**	**0**	**0**	**5**	**0**	**0**	**0**	**0**	**0.0**	**1**	**0**	**1**	**0**	**0**	....	....	....	....	....	....	....	....
	Phoenix Roadrunners	IHL	60	9	13	22	....	....	....	369	....	....	....	....	....	....	....	....	....	....	7	1	2	3	44	....	....	....
1991-92	Capital District Islanders	AHL	27	3	8	11	....	....	....	139	....	....	....	....	....	....	....	....	....	....	7	0	0	0	58	....	....	....
1992-93	Moncton Hawks	AHL	47	1	3	4	....	....	....	231	....	....	....	....	....	....	....	....	....	....	....	....	....	....	....	....	....	....
	Capital District Islanders	AHL	19	0	1	1	....	....	....	80	....	....	....	....	....	....	....	....	....	....	4	1	1	2	27	....	....	....
1993-94	Cincinnati Cyclones	IHL	61	2	6	8	....	....	....	302	....	....	....	....	....	....	....	....	....	....	8	0	1	1	*99	....	....	....
1994-95	Cleveland Lumberjacks	IHL	56	1	3	4	....	....	....	269	....	....	....	....	....	....	....	....	....	....	3	0	0	0	13	....	....	....
1995-96	Cleveland Lumberjacks	IHL	53	0	6	6	....	....	....	244	....	....	....	....	....	....	....	....	....	....	3	0	0	0	6	....	....	....
1996-97	Cleveland Lumberjacks	IHL	73	2	10	12	....	....	....	244	....	....	....	....	....	....	....	....	....	....	13	0	0	0	16	....	....	....
1997-98	Cleveland Lumberjacks	IHL	41	1	3	4	....	....	....	191	....	....	....	....	....	....	....	....	....	....	....	....	....	....	....	....	....	....
	Quebec Rafales	IHL	13	0	3	3	....	....	....	108	....	....	....	....	....	....	....	....	....	....	....	....	....	....	....	....	....	....
1998-99	Frankfurt Lions	Germany	22	0	0	0	....	....	....	113	....	....	....	....	....	....	....	....	....	....	1	0	0	0	27	....	....	....
99-2000	Frankfurt Lions	Germany	50	0	1	1	....	....	....	122	....	....	....	....	....	....	....	....	....	....	5	0	0	0	6	....	....	....
	NHL Totals		**4**	**0**	**0**	**0**	**0**	**0**	**0**	**5**	**0**	**0**	**0**	**0**	**0.0**	**1**	**0**	**1**	**0**		....	....	....	....	....	....	....	....

Traded to **Calgary** by **Montreal** for Martin Nicoletti, February 20, 1988. Signed as a free agent by **LA Kings**, July 15, 1990. Signed as a free agent by **Winnipeg**, July 30, 1992. Traded to **NY Islanders** by **Winnipeg** for future considerations, February 22, 1993. Signed as a free agent by **Cleveland** (IHL), June 24, 1994.

• HAZLETT, Steve

Stephen Edward LW – L. 5'9", 170 lbs. b: Sarnia, Ont., 12/12/1957. Vancouver's 6th, 76th overall, in 1977.

Season	Club	League	GP	G	A	Pts	AG	AA	APts	PIM	PP	SH	GW	S	%	TGF	PGF	TGA	PGA	+/–	GP	G	A	Pts	PIM	PP	SH	GW
1975-76	Hamilton Mountain A's	OJHL	60	50	45	95	....	....	....	30	....	....	....	....	....	....	....	....	....	....	....	....	....	....	....	....	....	....
	Hamilton Fincups	OMJHL	5	3	4	7	....	....	....	0	....	....	....	....	....	....	....	....	....	....	14	5	3	8	7	....	....	....
	Hamilton Fincups	Mem-Cup	3	*5	1	6	....	....	....	2	....	....	....	....	....	....	....	....	....	....	....	....	....	....	....	....	....	....
1976-77	St. Catharines Fincups	OMJHL	66	42	58	100	....	....	....	56	....	....	....	....	....	....	....	....	....	....	14	6	6	12	11	....	....	....
	Canada	WJC-A	7	6	0	6	....	....	....	6	....	....	....	....	....	....	....	....	....	....	....	....	....	....	....	....	....	....
1977-78	Hamilton Fincups	OMJHL	27	19	25	44	....	....	....	16	....	....	....	....	....	....	....	....	....	....	20	9	8	17	10	....	....	....
	Tulsa Oilers	CHL	15	1	2	3	....	....	....	10	....	....	....	....	....	....	....	....	....	....	....	....	....	....	....	....	....	....
	Fort Wayne Komets	IHL	4	3	1	4	....	....	....	4	....	....	....	....	....	....	....	....	....	....	....	....	....	....	....	....	....	....
1978-79	Dallas Black Hawks	CHL	76	*44	32	76	....	....	....	36	....	....	....	....	....	....	....	....	....	....	9	7	1	8	2	....	....	....
1979-80	**Vancouver Canucks**	**NHL**	**1**	**0**	**0**	**0**	**0**	**0**	**0**	**0**	**0**	**0**	**0**	**2**	**0.0**	**0**	**0**	**1**	**0**	**–1**	....	....	....	....	....	....	....	....
	Dallas Black Hawks	CHL	61	23	23	46	....	....	....	43	....	....	....	....	....	....	....	....	....	....	....	....	....	....	....	....	....	....
1980-81	Dallas Black Hawks	CHL	60	18	13	31	....	....	....	74	....	....	....	....	....	....	....	....	....	....	5	0	0	0	4	....	....	....
1981-82	Dallas Black Hawks	CHL	71	19	34	53	....	....	....	48	....	....	....	....	....	....	....	....	....	....	16	3	4	7	24	....	....	....
1982-83	Fort Wayne Komets	IHL	18	4	9	13	....	....	....	6	....	....	....	....	....	....	....	....	....	....	....	....	....	....	....	....	....	....
	NHL Totals		**1**	**0**	**0**	**0**	**0**	**0**	**0**	**0**	**0**	**0**	**0**	**2**	**0.0**	**0**	**0**	**1**	**0**		....	....	....	....	....	....	....	....

• HEAD, Galen

Galen Russell RW – R. 5'9", 160 lbs. b: Grande Prairie, Alta., 4/16/1947.

Season	Club	League	GP	G	A	Pts	AG	AA	APts	PIM	PP	SH	GW	S	%	TGF	PGF	TGA	PGA	+/–	GP	G	A	Pts	PIM	PP	SH	GW
1964-65	Edmonton Red Wings	AJHL-B	STATISTICS NOT AVAILABLE																									
	Edmonton Oil Kings	Mem-Cup	13	1	0	1	....	....	....	4	....	....	....	....	....	....	....	....	....	....	....	....	....	....	....	....	....	....
1965-66	Edmonton Oil Kings	ASHL	40	6	5	11	....	....	....	4	....	....	....	....	....	....	....	....	....	....	11	1	7	8	0	....	....	....
	Edmonton Oil Kings	Mem-Cup	19	12	4	16	....	....	....	19	....	....	....	....	....	....	....	....	....	....	....	....	....	....	....	....	....	....
1966-67	Edmonton Oil Kings	CMJHL	56	50	42	92	....	....	....	43	....	....	....	....	....	....	....	....	....	....	9	4	8	12	4	....	....	....
1967-68	**Detroit Red Wings**	**NHL**	**1**	**0**	**0**	**0**	**0**	**0**	**0**	**0**	**0**	**0**	**0**	**0**	**0.0**	**0**	**0**	**1**	**0**	**–1**	....	....	....	....	....	....	....	....
	Fort Worth Wings	CHL	4	3	1	4	....	....	....	4	....	....	....	....	....	....	....	....	....	....	2	1	0	1	0	....	....	....
	Johnstown Jets	EHL	70	53	52	105	....	....	....	31	....	....	....	....	....	....	....	....	....	....	3	2	0	2	0	....	....	....
1968-69	Johnstown Jets	EHL	72	*67	54	121	....	....	....	76	....	....	....	....	....	....	....	....	....	....	3	2	0	2	2	....	....	....
1969-70	Salt Lake Golden Eagles	WHL	43	9	12	21	....	....	....	6	....	....	....	....	....	....	....	....	....	....	....	....	....	....	....	....	....	....
1970-71	Johnstown Jets	EHL	67	31	27	58	....	....	....	42	....	....	....	....	....	....	....	....	....	....	10	7	3	10	2	....	....	....
1971-72	Johnstown Jets	EHL	75	37	34	71	....	....	....	43	....	....	....	....	....	....	....	....	....	....	11	2	5	7	2	....	....	....
1972-73	Johnstown Jets	EHL	72	44	33	77	....	....	....	37	....	....	....	....	....	....	....	....	....	....	12	4	6	10	6	....	....	....

			REGULAR SEASON																		PLAYOFFS							
Season	**Club**	**League**	**GP**	**G**	**A**	**Pts**	**AG**	**AA**	**APts**	**PIM**	**PP**	**SH**	**GW**	**S**	**%**	**TGF**	**PGF**	**TGA**	**PGA**	**+/–**	**GP**	**G**	**A**	**Pts**	**PIM**	**PP**	**SH**	**GW**
1973-74	Johnstown Jets	EHL	74	31	40	71	....	....	....	24	....	....	....	....	....	....	....	....	....	....	12	5	3	8	2	....	....	....
1974-75	Johnstown Jets	NAHL	58	18	23	41	....	....	....	30	....	....	....	....	....	....	....	....	....	....	15	8	10	18	....	....	....	....
1975-76	Johnstown Jets	NAHL	73	27	30	57	....	....	....	44	....	....	....	....	....	....	....	....	....	....	9	3	3	6	8	....	....	....
	NHL Totals		**1**	**0**	**0**	**0**	**0**	**0**	**0**	**0**	**0**	**0**	**0**	**0**	**0.0**	**0**	**0**	**1**	**0**		....	....	....	....	....	....	....	....

EHL North First All-Star Team (1969)

Claimed by **Salt Lake** (WHL) from **Detroit** in Reverse Draft, June 10, 1969.

• HEALEY, Paul

RW – R. 6'2", 185 lbs. b: Edmonton, Alta., 3/20/1975. Philadelphia's 7th, 192nd overall, in 1993.

Season	Club	League	GP	G	A	Pts	AG	AA	APts	PIM	PP	SH	GW	S	%	TGF	PGF	TGA	PGA	+/–	GP	G	A	Pts	PIM	PP	SH	GW
1991-92	Fort Saskatchewan Traders	AJHL	52	11	19	30	....	....	....	40	....	....	....	....	....	....	....	....	....	....	....	....	....	....	....	....	....	....
1992-93	Prince Albert Raiders	WHL	72	12	20	32	....	....	....	66	....	....	....	....	....	....	....	....	....	....	....	....	....	....	....	....	....	....
1993-94	Prince Albert Raiders	WHL	63	23	26	49	....	....	....	70	....	....	....	....	....	....	....	....	....	....	....	....	....	....	....	....	....	....
1994-95	Prince Albert Raiders	WHL	71	43	50	93	....	....	....	67	....	....	....	....	....	....	....	....	....	....	12	3	4	7	2	....	....	....
1995-96	Hershey Bears	AHL	60	7	15	22	....	....	....	35	....	....	....	....	....	....	....	....	....	....	....	....	....	....	....	....	....	....
1996-97	**Philadelphia Flyers**	**NHL**	**2**	**0**	**0**	**0**	**0**	**0**	**0**	**0**	**0**	**0**	**0**	**0**	**0.0**	**0**	**0**	**0**	**0**	**0**	....	....	....	....	....	....	....	....
	Philadelphia Phantoms	AHL	64	21	19	40	....	....	....	56	....	....	....	....	....	....	....	....	....	....	10	4	1	5	10	....	....	....
1997-98	**Philadelphia Flyers**	**NHL**	**4**	**0**	**0**	**0**	**0**	**0**	**0**	**12**	**0**	**0**	**0**	**0**	**0.0**	**0**	**0**	**0**	**0**	**0**	....	....	....	....	....	....	....	....
	Philadelphia Phantoms	AHL	71	34	18	52	....	....	....	48	....	....	....	....	....	....	....	....	....	....	20	6	2	8	4	....	....	....
1998-99	Philadelphia Phantoms	AHL	72	26	20	46	....	....	....	39	....	....	....	....	....	....	....	....	....	....	15	4	6	10	11	....	....	....
99-2000	Milwaukee Admirals	IHL	76	21	18	39	....	....	....	28	....	....	....	....	....	....	....	....	....	....	3	1	2	3	0	....	....	....
	NHL Totals		**6**	**0**	**0**	**0**	**0**	**0**	**0**	**12**	**0**	**0**	**0**	**0**	**0.0**	**0**	**0**	**0**	**0**		....	....	....	....	....	....	....	....

WHL East Second All-Star Team (1995)

Traded to **Nashville** by **Philadelphia** for Matt Henderson, September 27, 1999.

• HEAPHY, Shawn

C – L. 5'8", 180 lbs. b: Sudbury, Ont., 11/27/1968. Calgary's 1st, 26th overall, in 1989 Supplemental Draft.

Season	Club	League	GP	G	A	Pts	AG	AA	APts	PIM	PP	SH	GW	S	%	TGF	PGF	TGA	PGA	+/–	GP	G	A	Pts	PIM	PP	SH	GW
1984-85	Sudbury Legionaires	OMHA	70	*132	108	*240	....	....	....		....	....	....	....	....	....	....	....	....	....	....	....	....	....	....	....	....	....
1985-86	Stratford Cullitons	OJHL-B	35	50	32	82	....	....	....	75	....	....	....	....	....	....	....	....	....	....	....	....	....	....	....	....	....	....
1986-87	Stratford Cullitons	OJHL-B	40	*67	63	*130	....	....	....	172	....	....	....	....	....	....	....	....	....	....	....	....	....	....	....	....	....	....
1987-88	Michigan State Spartans	CCHA	44	19	24	43	....	....	....	48	....	....	....	....	....	....	....	....	....	....	....	....	....	....	....	....	....	....
1988-89	Michigan State Spartans	CCHA	47	26	17	43	....	....	....	80	....	....	....	....	....	....	....	....	....	....	....	....	....	....	....	....	....	....
1989-90	Michigan State Spartans	CCHA	45	28	31	59	....	....	....	54	....	....	....	....	....	....	....	....	....	....	....	....	....	....	....	....	....	....
1990-91	Michigan State Spartans	CCHA	39	30	19	49	....	....	....	57	....	....	....	....	....	....	....	....	....	....	....	....	....	....	....	....	....	....
	Salt Lake Golden Eagles	IHL	....	....	....	....	....	....	....	....	....	....	....	....	....	....	....	....	....	....	1	0	0	0	0	....	....	....
1991-92	Salt Lake Golden Eagles	IHL	76	41	36	77	....	....	....	85	....	....	....	....	....	....	....	....	....	....	5	2	2	4	2	....	....	....
1992-93	**Calgary Flames**	**NHL**	**1**	**0**	**0**	**0**	**0**	**0**	**0**	**0**	**0**	**0**	**0**	**2**	**0.0**	**0**	**0**	**0**	**0**	**0**	....	....	....	....	....	....	....	....
	Salt Lake Golden Eagles	IHL	78	29	36	65	....	....	....	63	....	....	....	....	....	....	....	....	....	....	....	....	....	....	....	....	....	....
1993-94	SG Brunico	Alpenliga	28	20	19	39	....	....	....	42	....	....	....	....	....	....	....	....	....	....	....	....	....	....	....	....	....	....
	SG Brunico	Italy	11	10	8	18	....	....	....	15	....	....	....	....	....	....	....	....	....	....	....	....	....	....	....	....	....	....
	Las Vegas Thunder	IHL	37	10	5	15	....	....	....	45	....	....	....	....	....	....	....	....	....	....	5	0	0	0	6	....	....	....
1994-95	Worcester IceCats	AHL	70	23	28	51	....	....	....	50	....	....	....	....	....	....	....	....	....	....	....	....	....	....	....	....	....	....
1995-96	P.E.I. Senators	AHL	77	40	42	82	....	....	....	65	....	....	....	....	....	....	....	....	....	....	6	4	6	10	6	....	....	....
1996-97	EHC Biel-Bienne	Switz-2	42	39	36	75	....	....	....	75	....	....	....	....	....	....	....	....	....	....	5	4	1	5	29	....	....	....
1997-98	EHC Biel-Bienne	Switz-2	40	44	52	96	....	....	....	60	....	....	....	....	....	....	....	....	....	....	11	8	6	14	26	....	....	....
1998-99	EHC Biel-Bienne	Switz-2	40	51	28	79	....	....	....	100	....	....	....	....	....	....	....	....	....	....	....	....	....	....	....	....	....	....
99-2000	HC Geneve-Servette	Switz-2	36	27	37	64	....	....	....	82	....	....	....	....	....	....	....	....	....	....	....	....	....	....	....	....	....	....
	NHL Totals		**1**	**0**	**0**	**0**	**0**	**0**	**0**	**0**	**0**	**0**	**0**	**2**	**0.0**	**0**	**0**	**0**	**0**		....	....	....	....	....	....	....	....

• Played w/ RHI's Las Vegas Flash in 1994 (10-2-5-7-8).

• HEASLIP, Mark

Mark Patrick RW – R. 5'10", 190 lbs. b: Duluth, MN, 12/26/1951.

Season	Club	League	GP	G	A	Pts	AG	AA	APts	PIM	PP	SH	GW	S	%	TGF	PGF	TGA	PGA	+/–	GP	G	A	Pts	PIM	PP	SH	GW
1969-1971	East Duluth Hounds	Hi-School	STATISTICS NOT AVAILABLE																									
1971-72	University of Minnesota-Duluth	WCHA	33	8	18	26	....	....	....	37	....	....	....	....	....	....	....	....	....	....	....	....	....	....	....	....	....	....
1972-73	University of Minnesota-Duluth	WCHA	36	25	20	45	....	....	....	46	....	....	....	....	....	....	....	....	....	....	....	....	....	....	....	....	....	....
1973-74	Springfield Kings	AHL	76	19	31	50	....	....	....	110	....	....	....	....	....	....	....	....	....	....	....	....	....	....	....	....	....	....
1974-75	Springfield Kings	AHL	75	18	39	57	....	....	....	86	....	....	....	....	....	....	....	....	....	....	17	2	11	13	15	....	....	....
1975-76	Fort Worth Texans	CHL	43	7	14	21	....	....	....	32	....	....	....	....	....	....	....	....	....	....	....	....	....	....	....	....	....	....
	Oklahoma City Blazers	CHL	33	3	8	11	....	....	....	16	....	....	....	....	....	....	....	....	....	....	4	0	0	0	12	....	....	....
1976-77	**New York Rangers**	**NHL**	**19**	**1**	**0**	**1**	**1**	**0**	**1**	**31**	**0**	**0**	**0**	**9**	**11.1**	**3**	**0**	**12**	**6**	**–3**	....	....	....	....	....	....	....	....
	New Haven Nighthawks	AHL	24	8	16	24	....	....	....	35	....	....	....	....	....	....	....	....	....	....	6	1	1	2	6	....	....	....
	United States	WEC-A	10	0	1	1	....	....	....	8	....	....	....	....	....	....	....	....	....	....	....	....	....	....	....	....	....	....
1977-78	**New York Rangers**	**NHL**	**29**	**5**	**10**	**15**	**5**	**8**	**13**	**34**	**0**	**0**	**0**	**32**	**15.6**	**23**	**1**	**22**	**3**	**3**	**3**	**0**	**0**	**0**	**0**	**0**	**0**	**0**
	New Haven Nighthawks	AHL	50	8	23	31	....	....	....	18	....	....	....	....	....	....	....	....	....	....	....	....	....	....	....	....	....	....
1978-79	**Los Angeles Kings**	**NHL**	**69**	**4**	**9**	**13**	**3**	**7**	**10**	**45**	**0**	**0**	**1**	**53**	**7.5**	**29**	**3**	**51**	**15**	**–10**	**2**	**0**	**0**	**0**	**2**	**0**	**0**	**0**
1979-80	Tulsa Oilers	CHL	68	14	18	32	....	....	....	33	....	....	....	....	....	....	....	....	....	....	3	0	0	0	4	....	....	....
	NHL Totals		**117**	**10**	**19**	**29**	**9**	**15**	**24**	**110**	**0**	**0**	**1**	**94**	**10.6**	**55**	**4**	**85**	**24**		**5**	**0**	**0**	**0**	**2**	**0**	**0**	**0**

Signed as a free agent by **LA Kings**, September, 1973. Traded to **NY Rangers** by **LA Kings** for John Campbell, May 28, 1976. Signed as a free agent by **LA Kings**, June 14, 1978. Claimed by **Winnipeg** from **LA Kings** in Expansion Draft, June 13, 1979.

• HEATH, Randy

Randy T. LW – L. 5'8", 160 lbs. b: Vancouver, B.C., 11/11/1964. NY Rangers' 2nd, 33rd overall, in 1983.

Season	Club	League	GP	G	A	Pts	AG	AA	APts	PIM	PP	SH	GW	S	%	TGF	PGF	TGA	PGA	+/–	GP	G	A	Pts	PIM	PP	SH	GW
1980-81	Vancouver Villas	BCJHL	50	35	35	70	....	....	....	30	....	....	....	....	....	....	....	....	....	....	....	....	....	....	....	....	....	....
	Portland Winter Hawks	WHL	2	1	0	1	....	....	....	0	....	....	....	....	....	....	....	....	....	....	....	....	....	....	....	....	....	....
1981-82	Portland Winter Hawks	WHL	65	52	47	99	....	....	....	65	....	....	....	....	....	....	....	....	....	....	15	13	19	32	4	....	....	....
	Portland Winter Hawks	Mem-Cup	4	2	3	5	....	....	....	2	....	....	....	....	....	....	....	....	....	....	....	....	....	....	....	....	....	....
1982-83	Portland Winter Hawks	WHL	72	82	69	151	....	....	....	52	....	....	....	....	....	....	....	....	....	....	14	6	12	18	12	....	....	....
	Portland Winter Hawks	Mem-Cup	4	*5	6	*11	....	....	....	2	....	....	....	....	....	....	....	....	....	....	....	....	....	....	....	....	....	....
1983-84	Portland Winter Hawks	WHL	60	44	46	90	....	....	....	107	....	....	....	....	....	....	....	....	....	....	14	9	12	21	10	....	....	....
	Canada	WJC-A	7	3	6	9	....	....	....	12	....	....	....	....	....	....	....	....	....	....	....	....	....	....	....	....	....	....
1984-85	**New York Rangers**	**NHL**	**12**	**2**	**3**	**5**	**2**	**2**	**4**	**15**	**1**	**0**	**0**	**18**	**11.1**	**8**	**2**	**7**	**0**	**–1**	....	....	....	....	....	....	....	....
	New Haven Nighthawks	AHL	60	23	26	49	....	....	....	29	....	....	....	....	....	....	....	....	....	....	....	....	....	....	....	....	....	....
1985-86	**New York Rangers**	**NHL**	**1**	**0**	**1**	**1**	**0**	**1**	**1**	**0**	**0**	**0**	**0**	**1**	**0.0**	**1**	**0**	**0**	**0**	**1**	....	....	....	....	....	....	....	....
	New Haven Nighthawks	AHL	77	36	38	74	....	....	....	53	....	....	....	....	....	....	....	....	....	....	5	3	2	5	7	....	....	....
1986-87	Skelleftea AIK	Sweden	36	12	14	26	....	....	....	40	....	....	....	....	....	....	....	....	....	....	....	....	....	....	....	....	....	....
1987-88	Vasteras IK	Sweden-2	31	26	25	51	....	....	....	50	....	....	....	....	....	....	....	....	....	....	14	11	9	20	12	....	....	....
1988-89	Vasteras IK	Sweden	22	5	10	15	....	....	....	14	....	....	....	....	....	....	....	....	....	....	....	....	....	....	....	....	....	....
	Vasteras IK	Sweden-R	14	1	3	4	....	....	....	4	....	....	....	....	....	....	....	....	....	....	4	2	0	2	0	....	....	....
	NHL Totals		**13**	**2**	**4**	**6**	**2**	**3**	**5**	**15**	**1**	**0**	**0**	**19**	**10.5**	**9**	**2**	**7**	**0**		....	....	....	....	....	....	....	....

WHL First All-Star Team (1983) • Memorial Cup All-Star Team (1983) • WHL West First All-Star Team (1984)

• HECHT, Jochen

C – L. 6'3", 196 lbs. b: Mannheim, West Germany, 6/21/1977. St. Louis' 1st, 49th overall, in 1995.

Season	Club	League	GP	G	A	Pts	AG	AA	APts	PIM	PP	SH	GW	S	%	TGF	PGF	TGA	PGA	+/–	GP	G	A	Pts	PIM	PP	SH	GW
1993-94	Adler Mannheim-Jr.	Germany	STATISTICS NOT AVAILABLE																									
	Germany	WJC-A	7	0	0	0	....	....	....	4	....	....	....	....	....	....	....	....	....	....	....	....	....	....	....	....	....	....
	Germany	EJC-A	5	6	2	8	....	....	....	18	....	....	....	....	....	....	....	....	....	....	....	....	....	....	....	....	....	....
1994-95	Adler Mannheim	Germany	43	11	12	23	....	....	....	68	....	....	....	....	....	....	....	....	....	....	10	5	4	9	12	....	....	....
	Germany	WJC-A	7	5	3	8	....	....	....	18	....	....	....	....	....	....	....	....	....	....	....	....	....	....	....	....	....	....
	Germany	EJC-A	5	3	3	6	....	....	....	18	....	....	....	....	....	....	....	....	....	....	....	....	....	....	....	....	....	....
1995-96	Adler Mannheim	Germany	44	12	16	28	....	....	....	68	....	....	....	....	....	....	....	....	....	....	8	3	2	5	6	....	....	....
	Germany	WJC-A	6	1	4	5	....	....	....	18	....	....	....	....	....	....	....	....	....	....	....	....	....	....	....	....	....	....
	Germany	WC-A	6	1	2	3	....	....	....	8	....	....	....	....	....	....	....	....	....	....	....	....	....	....	....	....	....	....

			REGULAR SEASON																		PLAYOFFS							
Season	Club	League	GP	G	A	Pts	AG	AA	APts	PIM	PP	SH	GW	S	%	TGF	PGF	TGA	PGA	+/–	GP	G	A	Pts	PIM	PP	SH	GW
1996-97	Germany	W-Cup	4	1	0	1	....	....	....	2	....	....	....	....	....	....	....	....	....	....	....	....	....	....	....	....	....	....
	Adler Mannheim	Germany	46	21	21	42	....	....	....	36	....	....	....	....	....	....	....	....	....	....	9	3	3	6	4	....	....	....
	Germany	WJC-A	6	0	2	2	....	....	....	4	....	....	....	....	....	....	....	....	....	....	....	....	....	....	....	....	....	....
	Germany	WC-A	8	2	0	2	....	....	....	6	....	....	....	....	....	....	....	....	....	....	....	....	....	....	....	....	....	....
1997-98	Adler Mannheim	Germany	44	7	19	26	....	....	....	42	....	....	....	....	....	....	....	....	....	....	10	1	1	2	14	....	....	....
	Adler Mannheim	EuroHL	5	0	4	4	....	....	....	8	....	....	....	....	....	....	....	....	....	....	....	....	....	....	....	....	....	....
	Germany	WC-A	6	1	1	2	....	....	....	2	....	....	....	....	....	....	....	....	....	....	....	....	....	....	....	....	....	....
	Germany	Olympics	4	1	0	1	....	....	....	6	....	....	....	....	....	....	....	....	....	....	....	....	....	....	....	....	....	....
1998-99	**St. Louis Blues**	**NHL**	**3**	**0**	**0**	**0**	**0**	**0**	**0**	**0**	**0**	**0**	**0**	**4**	**0.0**	**2**	**2**	**2**	**0**	**–2**	**5**	**2**	**0**	**2**	**0**	**0**	**0**	**0**
	Worcester IceCats	AHL	74	21	35	56	....	....	....	48	....	....	....	....	....	....	....	....	....	....	4	1	1	2	2	....	....	....
99-2000	**St. Louis Blues**	**NHL**	**63**	**13**	**21**	**34**	**15**	**19**	**34**	**28**	**5**	**0**	**1**	**140**	**9.3**	**61**	**20**	**21**	**0**	**20**	**7**	**4**	**6**	**10**	**2**	**1**	**0**	**1**
	NHL Totals		**66**	**13**	**21**	**34**	**15**	**19**	**34**	**28**	**5**	**0**	**1**	**144**	**9.0**	**63**	**22**	**23**	**0**		**12**	**6**	**6**	**12**	**2**	**1**	**0**	**1**

• HEDBERG, Anders

RW – L. 5'11", 175 lbs. b: Ornskoldsvik, Sweden, 2/25/1951.

Season	Club	League	GP	G	A	Pts	AG	AA	APts	PIM	PP	SH	GW	S	%	TGF	PGF	TGA	PGA	+/–	GP	G	A	Pts	PIM	PP	SH	GW
1966-67	Svedjeholmens IK	Sweden-3	16	*24	....	24	....	....	....	....	....	....	....	....	....	....	....	....	....	....	....	....	....	....	....	....	....	....
1967-68	MoDo AIK	Sweden	24	12	6	18	....	....	....	....	....	....	....	....	....	....	....	....	....	....	....	....	....	....	....	....	....	....
	Sweden	EJC-A	5	6	1	7	....	....	....	0	....	....	....	....	....	....	....	....	....	....	....	....	....	....	....	....	....	....
1968-69	MoDo AIK	Sweden	19	10	13	23	....	....	....	2	....	....	....	....	....	....	....	....	....	....	....	....	....	....	....	....	....	....
	Sweden	EJC-A	5	5	0	5	....	....	....	2	....	....	....	....	....	....	....	....	....	....	....	....	....	....	....	....	....	....
1969-70	MoDo AIK	Sweden	14	9	*14	23	....	....	....	2	....	....	....	....	....	....	....	....	....	....	....	....	....	....	....	....	....	....
	Sweden	EJC-A	5	6	....	....	....	....	....	....	....	....	....	....	....	....	....	....	....	....	....	....	....	....	....	....	....	....
	Sweden	WEC-A	9	2	3	5	....	....	....	0	....	....	....	....	....	....	....	....	....	....	....	....	....	....	....	....	....	....
1970-71	MoDo AIK	Sweden	14	7	6	13	....	....	....	0	....	....	....	....	....	....	....	....	....	....	....	....	....	....	....	....	....	....
1971-72	MoDo AIK	Sweden	2	1	0	1	....	....	....	0	....	....	....	....	....	....	....	....	....	....	6	3	5	8	0	....	....	....
	Sweden	WEC-A	10	6	5	11	....	....	....	4	....	....	....	....	....	....	....	....	....	....	....	....	....	....	....	....	....	....
1972-73	Djurgardens IF Stockholm	Sweden	12	6	3	9	....	....	....	2	....	....	....	....	....	....	....	....	....	....	14	6	7	13	4	....	....	....
	Sweden	WEC-A	10	2	5	7	....	....	....	0	....	....	....	....	....	....	....	....	....	....	....	....	....	....	....	....	....	....
1973-74	Djurgardens IF Stockholm	Sweden	14	10	6	16	....	....	....	2	....	....	....	....	....	....	....	....	....	....	14	7	7	14	4	....	....	....
	Sweden	WEC-A	10	7	3	10	....	....	....	2	....	....	....	....	....	....	....	....	....	....	....	....	....	....	....	....	....	....
1974-75	Winnipeg Jets	WHA	65	53	47	100	....	....	....	45	....	....	....	....	....	....	....	....	....	....	....	....	....	....	....	....	....	....
1975-76	Winnipeg Jets	WHA	76	50	55	105	....	....	....	48	....	....	....	....	....	....	....	....	....	....	13	*13	6	19	15	....	....	....
1976-77	Sweden	Can-Cup	5	3	2	5	....	....	....	4	....	....	....	....	....	....	....	....	....	....	....	....	....	....	....	....	....	....
	Winnipeg Jets	WHA	68	*70	61	131	....	....	....	48	....	....	....	....	....	....	....	....	....	....	20	13	16	29	13	....	....	....
1977-78	Winnipeg Jets	WHA	77	63	59	122	....	....	....	60	....	....	....	....	....	....	....	....	....	....	9	9	6	15	2	....	....	....
1978-79	**New York Rangers**	**NHL**	**80**	**33**	**45**	**78**	**28**	**33**	**61**	**33**	**6**	**0**	**5**	**214**	**15.4**	**121**	**41**	**72**	**11**	**19**	**18**	**4**	**5**	**9**	**12**	**0**	**1**	**1**
	NHL All-Stars	Chal-Cup	2	0	0	0	....	....	....	0	....	....	....	....	....	....	....	....	....	....	....	....	....	....	....	....	....	....
1979-80	**New York Rangers**	**NHL**	**80**	**32**	**39**	**71**	**27**	**28**	**55**	**21**	**7**	**0**	**4**	**241**	**13.3**	**106**	**35**	**64**	**6**	**13**	**9**	**3**	**2**	**5**	**7**	**0**	**0**	**1**
1980-81	**New York Rangers**	**NHL**	**80**	**30**	**40**	**70**	**23**	**27**	**50**	**52**	**7**	**1**	**3**	**243**	**12.3**	**110**	**34**	**91**	**15**	**0**	**14**	**8**	**8**	**16**	**6**	**3**	**0**	**0**
1981-82	Sweden	Can-Cup	5	4	2	6	....	....	....	0	....	....	....	....	....	....	....	....	....	....	....	....	....	....	....	....	....	....
	New York Rangers	DN-Cup	4	1	2	3	....	....	....	....	....	....	....	....	....	....	....	....	....	....	....	....	....	....	....	....	....	....
	New York Rangers	**NHL**	**4**	**0**	**1**	**1**	**0**	**1**	**1**	**0**	**0**	**0**	**0**	**8**	**0.0**	**2**	**0**	**6**	**2**	**–2**	....	....	....	....	....	....	....	....
1982-83	**New York Rangers**	**NHL**	**78**	**25**	**34**	**59**	**20**	**24**	**44**	**12**	**4**	**0**	**5**	**163**	**15.3**	**99**	**23**	**63**	**4**	**17**	**9**	**4**	**8**	**12**	**4**	**1**	**0**	**0**
1983-84	**New York Rangers**	**NHL**	**79**	**32**	**35**	**67**	**26**	**24**	**50**	**16**	**6**	**0**	**2**	**209**	**15.3**	**107**	**32**	**57**	**0**	**18**	**5**	**1**	**0**	**1**	**0**	**0**	**0**	**0**
1984-85	**New York Rangers**	**NHL**	**64**	**20**	**31**	**51**	**16**	**21**	**37**	**10**	**9**	**0**	**2**	**141**	**14.2**	**86**	**38**	**68**	**5**	**–15**	**3**	**2**	**1**	**3**	**2**	**0**	**0**	**0**
	NHL Totals		**465**	**172**	**225**	**397**	**140**	**158**	**298**	**144**	**39**	**1**	**21**	**1219**	**14.1**	**631**	**203**	**421**	**43**		**58**	**22**	**24**	**46**	**31**	**4**	**1**	**2**
	Other Major League Totals		286	236	222	458	....	....	....	201	....	....	....	....	....	....	....	....	....	....	42	35	28	63	30	....	....	....

Swedish Junior Player-of-the-Year (1969, 1970) • Named Best Forward at EJC-A (1970) • WHA Second All-Star Team (1975) • Won Lou Kaplan Trophy (WHA Rookie of the Year) (1975) • WHA First All-Star Team (1976, 1977) • WHA Second All-Star Team (1978) • Won Bill Masterton Trophy (1985) • Played in NHL All-Star Game (1985)

• Only goals and games played totals are available for 1966-67 season. Signed as a free agent by **Winnipeg** (WHA), May 3, 1974. Signed as a free agent by **NY Rangers**, June 5, 1978.

• HEDICAN, Bret

Bret M. D – L. 6'2", 205 lbs. b: St. Paul, MN, 8/10/1970. St. Louis' 10th, 198th overall, in 1988.

Season	Club	League	GP	G	A	Pts	AG	AA	APts	PIM	PP	SH	GW	S	%	TGF	PGF	TGA	PGA	+/–	GP	G	A	Pts	PIM	PP	SH	GW
1987-88	North St. Paul Dragons	Hi-School	23	15	19	34	....	....	....	16	....	....	....	....	....	....	....	....	....	....	....	....	....	....	....	....	....	....
1988-89	St. Cloud State Huskies	NCAA	28	5	3	8	....	....	....	28	....	....	....	....	....	....	....	....	....	....	....	....	....	....	....	....	....	....
1989-90	St. Cloud State Huskies	NCAA	36	4	17	21	....	....	....	37	....	....	....	....	....	....	....	....	....	....	....	....	....	....	....	....	....	....
1990-91	St. Cloud State Huskies	WCHA	41	21	26	47	....	....	....	26	....	....	....	....	....	....	....	....	....	....	....	....	....	....	....	....	....	....
1991-92	United States	Nat-Team	54	1	8	9	....	....	....	59	....	....	....	....	....	....	....	....	....	....	....	....	....	....	....	....	....	....
	United States	Olympics	8	0	0	0	....	....	....	4	....	....	....	....	....	....	....	....	....	....	....	....	....	....	....	....	....	....
	St. Louis Blues	**NHL**	**4**	**1**	**0**	**1**	**1**	**0**	**1**	**0**	**0**	**0**	**0**	**1**	**100.0**	**6**	**0**	**5**	**0**	**1**	**5**	**0**	**0**	**0**	**0**	**0**	**0**	**0**
1992-93	**St. Louis Blues**	**NHL**	**42**	**0**	**8**	**8**	**0**	**5**	**5**	**30**	**0**	**0**	**0**	**40**	**0.0**	**30**	**6**	**40**	**14**	**–2**	**10**	**0**	**0**	**0**	**14**	**0**	**0**	**0**
	Peoria Rivermen	IHL	19	0	8	8	....	....	....	10	....	....	....	....	....	....	....	....	....	....	....	....	....	....	....	....	....	....
1993-94	**St. Louis Blues**	**NHL**	**61**	**0**	**11**	**11**	**0**	**9**	**9**	**64**	**0**	**0**	**0**	**78**	**0.0**	**45**	**5**	**59**	**11**	**–8**	....	....	....	....	....	....	....	....
	Vancouver Canucks	**NHL**	**8**	**0**	**1**	**1**	**0**	**1**	**1**	**0**	**0**	**0**	**0**	**10**	**0.0**	**4**	**1**	**3**	**1**	**1**	**24**	**1**	**6**	**7**	**16**	**0**	**0**	**0**
1994-95	**Vancouver Canucks**	**NHL**	**45**	**2**	**11**	**13**	**4**	**16**	**20**	**34**	**0**	**0**	**0**	**56**	**3.6**	**41**	**6**	**54**	**16**	**–3**	**11**	**0**	**2**	**2**	**6**	**0**	**0**	**0**
1995-96	**Vancouver Canucks**	**NHL**	**77**	**6**	**23**	**29**	**6**	**19**	**25**	**83**	**1**	**0**	**0**	**113**	**5.3**	**84**	**13**	**85**	**22**	**8**	**6**	**0**	**1**	**1**	**10**	**0**	**0**	**0**
1996-97	**Vancouver Canucks**	**NHL**	**67**	**4**	**15**	**19**	**4**	**13**	**17**	**51**	**2**	**0**	**1**	**93**	**4.3**	**66**	**12**	**78**	**21**	**–3**	....	....	....	....	....	....	....	....
	United States	WC-A	8	0	5	5	....	....	....	10	....	....	....	....	....	....	....	....	....	....	....	....	....	....	....	....	....	....
1997-98	**Vancouver Canucks**	**NHL**	**71**	**3**	**24**	**27**	**4**	**24**	**28**	**79**	**1**	**0**	**0**	**84**	**3.6**	**68**	**10**	**79**	**24**	**3**	....	....	....	....	....	....	....	....
1998-99	**Vancouver Canucks**	**NHL**	**42**	**2**	**11**	**13**	**2**	**11**	**13**	**34**	**0**	**2**	**0**	**52**	**3.8**	**39**	**7**	**29**	**4**	**7**	....	....	....	....	....	....	....	....
	Florida Panthers	**NHL**	**25**	**3**	**7**	**10**	**4**	**7**	**11**	**17**	**0**	**0**	**1**	**38**	**7.9**	**17**	**0**	**29**	**10**	**–2**	....	....	....	....	....	....	....	....
	United States	WC-A	6	0	1	1	....	....	....	8	....	....	....	....	....	....	....	....	....	....	....	....	....	....	....	....	....	....
99-2000	**Florida Panthers**	**NHL**	**76**	**6**	**19**	**25**	**7**	**18**	**25**	**68**	**2**	**0**	**1**	**58**	**10.3**	**69**	**14**	**64**	**13**	**4**	**4**	**0**	**0**	**0**	**0**	**0**	**0**	**0**
	NHL Totals		**518**	**27**	**130**	**157**	**32**	**123**	**155**	**460**	**6**	**2**	**3**	**623**	**4.3**	**469**	**74**	**525**	**136**		**60**	**1**	**9**	**10**	**46**	**0**	**0**	**0**

WCHA First All-Star Team (1991)

Traded to **Vancouver** by **St. Louis** with Jeff Brown and Nathan Lafayette for Craig Janney, March 21, 1994. Traded to **Florida** by **Vancouver** with Pavel Bure, Brad Ference and Vancouver's 3rd round choice (Robert Fried) in 2000 Entry Draft for Ed Jovanovski, Dave Gagner, Mike Brown, Kevin Weekes and Florida's 1st round choice (Nathan Smith) in 2000 Entry Draft, January 17, 1999.

• HEIDT, Michael

D – L. 6'1", 190 lbs. b: Calgary, Alta., 11/4/1963. Los Angeles' 1st, 27th overall, in 1982.

Season	Club	League	GP	G	A	Pts	AG	AA	APts	PIM	PP	SH	GW	S	%	TGF	PGF	TGA	PGA	+/–	GP	G	A	Pts	PIM	PP	SH	GW
1980-81	Calgary Canucks	AJHL	56	28	63	91	....	....	....	104	....	....	....	....	....	....	....	....	....	....	....	....	....	....	....	....	....	....
	Calgary Wranglers	WHL	12	1	3	4	....	....	....	6	....	....	....	....	....	....	....	....	....	....	22	2	10	12	5	....	....	....
1981-82	Calgary Wranglers	WHL	70	13	44	57	....	....	....	142	....	....	....	....	....	....	....	....	....	....	9	2	3	5	21	....	....	....
1982-83	Calgary Wranglers	WHL	71	30	65	95	....	....	....	101	....	....	....	....	....	....	....	....	....	....	15	0	11	11	44	....	....	....
1983-84	**Los Angeles Kings**	**NHL**	**6**	**0**	**1**	**1**	**0**	**1**	**1**	**7**	**0**	**0**	**0**	**1**	**0.0**	**3**	**0**	**6**	**2**	**–1**	....	....	....	....	....	....	....	....
	New Haven Nighthawks	AHL	54	4	20	24	....	....	....	49	....	....	....	....	....	....	....	....	....	....	....	....	....	....	....	....	....	....
1984-85	New Haven Nighthawks	AHL	4	0	1	1	....	....	....	0	....	....	....	....	....	....	....	....	....	....	....	....	....	....	....	....	....	....
	Toledo Goaldiggers	IHL	4	0	0	0	....	....	....	0	....	....	....	....	....	....	....	....	....	....	....	....	....	....	....	....	....	....
	Nova Scotia Voyageurs	AHL	27	1	7	8	....	....	....	16	....	....	....	....	....	....	....	....	....	....	5	0	2	2	7	....	....	....
1985-86	Mount Royal College	ACAC	24	19	*51	*70	....	....	....	84	....	....	....	....	....	....	....	....	....	....	....	....	....	....	....	....	....	....
1986-87	EV Bayreuth	Germany-2	36	24	63	87	....	....	....	77	....	....	....	....	....	....	....	....	....	....	16	17	21	37	25	....	....	....
1987-88	EV Bayreuth	Germany-2	22	16	29	45	....	....	....	51	....	....	....	....	....	....	....	....	....	....	....	....	....	....	....	....	....	....
	EC Munchen	Germany	22	9	38	47	....	....	....	20	....	....	....	....	....	....	....	....	....	....	....	....	....	....	....	....	....	....
1988-89	Schwenninger ERC	Germany	36	10	22	32	....	....	....	42	....	....	....	....	....	....	....	....	....	....	2	1	1	2	2	....	....	....
1989-90	Schwenninger ERC	Germany	36	7	37	44	....	....	....	26	....	....	....	....	....	....	....	....	....	....	10	3	8	11	8	....	....	....
1990-91	SB Rosenheim	Germany	34	7	32	39	....	....	....	28	....	....	....	....	....	....	....	....	....	....	11	3	4	7	6	....	....	....
1991-92	SB Rosenheim	Germany	43	18	28	46	....	....	....	18	....	....	....	....	....	....	....	....	....	....	10	2	10	12	2	....	....	....
	Germany	Olympics	8	0	1	1	....	....	....	6	....	....	....	....	....	....	....	....	....	....	....	....	....	....	....	....	....	....
	Germany	WC-A	6	3	0	3	....	....	....	4	....	....	....	....	....	....	....	....	....	....	....	....	....	....	....	....	....	....
1992-93	Mannheimer ERC	Germany	42	10	27	37	....	....	....	28	....	....	....	....	....	....	....	....	....	....	8	4	3	7	6	....	....	....
1993-94	Adler Mannheim	Germany	44	14	33	47	....	....	....	28	....	....	....	....	....	....	....	....	....	....	4	0	2	2	4	....	....	....
1994-95	Adler Mannheim	Germany	37	9	25	34	....	....	....	36	....	....	....	....	....	....	....	....	....	....	10	1	9	10	6	....	....	....

			REGULAR SEASON																		PLAYOFFS							
Season	**Club**	**League**	**GP**	**G**	**A**	**Pts**	**AG**	**AA**	**APts**	**PIM**	**PP**	**SH**	**GW**	**S**	**%**	**TGF**	**PGF**	**TGA**	**PGA**	**+/–**	**GP**	**G**	**A**	**Pts**	**PIM**	**PP**	**SH**	**GW**
1995-96	Adler Mannheim	Germany	49	5	24	29	....	....	....	26	....	....	....	....	....	....	....	....	....	....	11	3	6	9	6	....	....	....
	Germany	WC-A	6	1	0	1	....	....	....	4	....	....	....	....	....	....	....	....	....	....	....	....	....	....	....	....	....	....
1996-97	Germany	W-Cup	4	0	1	1	....	....	....	2	....	....	....	....	....	....	....	....	....	....	....	....	....	....	....	....	....	....
	EV Landshut	Germany	36	4	16	20	....	....	....	18	....	....	....	....	....	....	....	....	....	....	7	1	2	3	8	....	....	....
1997-98	EV Landshut	Germany	14	2	6	8	....	....	....	12	....	....	....	....	....	....	....	....	....	....	....	....	....	....	....	....	....	....
	Germany	Olympics	DID NOT PLAY																									
	NHL Totals		**6**	**0**	**1**	**1**	**0**	**1**	**1**	**7**	**0**	**0**	**0**	**1**	**0.0**	**3**	**0**	**6**	**2**		....	....	....	....	....	....	....	....

WHL First All-Star Team (1983)

• HEINDL, Bill

William Wayne LW – L. 5'10", 175 lbs. b: Sherbrooke, Que., 5/13/1946 d: 3/1/1992.

Season	Club	League	GP	G	A	Pts	AG	AA	APts	PIM	PP	SH	GW	S	%	TGF	PGF	TGA	PGA	+/–	GP	G	A	Pts	PIM	PP	SH	GW
1963-64	Winnipeg Braves	MJHL	26	7	7	14	....	....	....	18	....	....	....	....	....	....	....	....	....	....	....	....	....	....	....	....	....	....
1964-65	Winnipeg Braves	MJHL	45	27	33	60	....	....	....	22	....	....	....	....	....	....	....	....	....	....	15	5	5	10	10	....	....	....
1965-66	Oshawa Generals	OHA-Jr.	48	15	26	41	....	....	....	46	....	....	....	....	....	....	....	....	....	....	17	4	5	9	10	....	....	....
	Oshawa Generals	Mem-Cup	14	13	8	21	....	....	....	8	....	....	....	....	....	....	....	....	....	....	....	....	....	....	....	....	....	....
1966-67	Clinton Comets	EHL	72	17	20	37	....	....	....	7	....	....	....	....	....	....	....	....	....	....	9	3	2	5	13	....	....	....
1967-68	Clinton Comets	EHL	72	52	53	105	....	....	....	20	....	....	....	....	....	....	....	....	....	....	14	10	5	15	7	....	....	....
1968-69	Canada	Nat-Team	STATISTICS NOT AVAILABLE																									
	Canada	WEC-A	9	4	1	5	....	....	....	2	....	....	....	....	....	....	....	....	....	....	....	....	....	....	....	....	....	....
1969-70	Canada	Nat-Team	STATISTICS NOT AVAILABLE																									
1970-71	**Minnesota North Stars**	**NHL**	**12**	**1**	**1**	**2**	**1**	**1**	**2**	**0**	**0**	**0**	**0**	**18**	**5.6**	**4**	**0**	**5**	**0**	**–1**	....	....	....	....	....	....	....	....
	Cleveland Barons	AHL	60	25	11	36	....	....	....	22	....	....	....	....	....	....	....	....	....	....	8	3	5	8	0	....	....	....
1971-72	**Minnesota North Stars**	**NHL**	**2**	**0**	**0**	**0**	**0**	**0**	**0**	**0**	**0**	**0**	**0**	**1**	**0.0**	**0**	**0**	**0**	**0**	**0**	....	....	....	....	....	....	....	....
	Cleveland Barons	AHL	70	22	25	47	....	....	....	19	....	....	....	....	....	....	....	....	....	....	6	0	3	3	2	....	....	....
1972-73	**New York Rangers**	**NHL**	**4**	**1**	**0**	**1**	**1**	**0**	**1**	**0**	**0**	**0**	**0**	**6**	**16.7**	**1**	**0**	**1**	**1**	**1**	....	....	....	....	....	....	....	....
	Providence Reds	AHL	66	21	43	64	....	....	....	10	....	....	....	....	....	....	....	....	....	....	4	1	0	1	2	....	....	....
1973-74	Cleveland Crusaders	WHA	67	4	14	18	....	....	....	4	....	....	....	....	....	....	....	....	....	....	5	0	1	1	2	....	....	....
	Jacksonville Barons	AHL	9	3	2	5	....	....	....	0	....	....	....	....	....	....	....	....	....	....	....	....	....	....	....	....	....	....
1974-75	Cape Cod Codders	NAHL	74	23	36	59	....	....	....	8	....	....	....	....	....	....	....	....	....	....	....	....	....	....	....	....	....	....
1975-76	BK Bracken	Sweden-2	20	16	16	32	....	....	....	48	....	....	....	....	....	....	....	....	....	....	....	....	....	....	....	....	....	....
1976-77	BK Bracken	Sweden-2	33	14	3	17	....	....	....	....	....	....	....	....	....	....	....	....	....	....	....	....	....	....	....	....	....	....
	NHL Totals		**18**	**2**	**1**	**3**	**2**	**1**	**3**	**0**	**0**	**0**	**0**	**25**	**8.0**	**5**	**0**	**6**	**1**		....	....	....	....	....	....	....	....
	Other Major League Totals		67	4	14	18	....	....	....	4	....	....	....	....	....	....	....	....	....	....	5	0	1	1	2	....	....	....

Claimed by **Minnesota** (Cleveland-AHL) from **Boston** in Reverse Draft, June, 1970. Selected by **Winnipeg** (WHA) in 1972 WHA General Player Draft, February 12, 1972. Claimed by **Atlanta** from **Minnesota** in Expansion Draft, June, 1972. Traded to **NY Rangers** by **Atlanta** for Bill Hogaboom, June 16, 1972. WHA rights traded to **Cleveland** (WHA) by **Winnipeg** (WHA) for cash, June, 1973.

• HEINS, Shawn

Shawn Joseph D – L. 6'4", 220 lbs. b: Eganville, Ont., 12/24/1973.

Season	Club	League	GP	G	A	Pts	AG	AA	APts	PIM	PP	SH	GW	S	%	TGF	PGF	TGA	PGA	+/–	GP	G	A	Pts	PIM	PP	SH	GW
1990-91	Wainwright Polar Kings	AAHA	STATISTICS NOT AVAILABLE																									
	Renfrew Timberwolves	OJHL-B	....	....	....	....	....	....	....	....	....	....	....	....	....	....	....	....	....	....	7	0	0	0	5	....	....	....
1991-92	Peterborough Petes	OHL	49	1	1	2	....	....	....	73	....	....	....	....	....	....	....	....	....	....	....	....	....	....	....	....	....	....
1992-93	Peterborough Petes	OHL	5	0	0	0	....	....	....	10	....	....	....	....	....	....	....	....	....	....	....	....	....	....	....	....	....	....
	Windsor Spitfires	OHL	53	7	10	17	....	....	....	107	....	....	....	....	....	....	....	....	....	....	....	....	....	....	....	....	....	....
1993-94	Renfrew Timberwolves	OJHL-B	32	16	34	50	....	....	....	250	....	....	....	....	....	....	....	....	....	....	....	....	....	....	....	....	....	....
1994-95	Renfrew Timberwolves	OJHL-B	35	30	49	79	....	....	....	188	....	....	....	....	....	....	....	....	....	....	....	....	....	....	....	....	....	....
1995-96	Mobile Mysticks	ECHL	62	7	20	27	....	....	....	152	....	....	....	....	....	....	....	....	....	....	....	....	....	....	....	....	....	....
	Cape Breton Oilers	AHL	1	0	0	0	....	....	....	0	....	....	....	....	....	....	....	....	....	....	....	....	....	....	....	....	....	....
1996-97	Mobile Mysticks	ECHL	56	6	17	23	....	....	....	253	....	....	....	....	....	....	....	....	....	....	3	0	2	2	2	....	....	....
	Kansas City Blades	IHL	6	0	0	0	....	....	....	9	....	....	....	....	....	....	....	....	....	....	....	....	....	....	....	....	....	....
1997-98	Kansas City Blades	IHL	82	22	28	50	....	....	....	303	....	....	....	....	....	....	....	....	....	....	11	1	0	1	49	....	....	....
1998-99	Canada	Nat-Team	36	5	16	21	....	....	....	66	....	....	....	....	....	....	....	....	....	....	....	....	....	....	....	....	....	....
	San Jose Sharks	**NHL**	**5**	**0**	**0**	**0**	**0**	**0**	**0**	**13**	**0**	**0**	**0**	**4**	**0.0**	**2**	**0**	**2**	**0**	**0**	....	....	....	....	....	....	....	....
	Kentucky Thoroughblades	AHL	18	2	2	4	....	....	....	108	....	....	....	....	....	....	....	....	....	....	12	2	7	9	10	....	....	....
99-2000	**San Jose Sharks**	**NHL**	**1**	**0**	**0**	**0**	**0**	**0**	**0**	**2**	**0**	**0**	**0**	**1**	**0.0**	**1**	**1**	**1**	**0**	**–1**	....	....	....	....	....	....	....	....
	Kentucky Thoroughblades	AHL	69	11	52	63	....	....	....	238	....	....	....	....	....	....	....	....	....	....	9	3	3	6	44	....	....	....
	NHL Totals		**6**	**0**	**0**	**0**	**0**	**0**	**0**	**15**	**0**	**0**	**0**	**5**	**0.0**	**3**	**1**	**3**	**0**		....	....	....	....	....	....	....	....

• AHL First All-Star Team (2000)

Signed as a free agent by **San Jose**, January 5, 1997.

• HEINZE, Steve

Stephen Herbert RW – R. 5'11", 202 lbs. b: Lawrence, MA, 1/30/1970. Boston's 2nd, 60th overall, in 1988.

Season	Club	League	GP	G	A	Pts	AG	AA	APts	PIM	PP	SH	GW	S	%	TGF	PGF	TGA	PGA	+/–	GP	G	A	Pts	PIM	PP	SH	GW
1986-87	Lawrence Academy	Hi-School	23	26	24	50	....	....	....	....	....	....	....	....	....	....	....	....	....	....	....	....	....	....	....	....	....	....
1987-88	Lawrence Academy	Hi-School	23	30	25	55	....	....	....	....	....	....	....	....	....	....	....	....	....	....	....	....	....	....	....	....	....	....
1988-89	Boston College	H-East	36	26	23	49	....	....	....	26	....	....	....	....	....	....	....	....	....	....	....	....	....	....	....	....	....	....
	United States	WJC-A	7	2	1	3	....	....	....	2	....	....	....	....	....	....	....	....	....	....	....	....	....	....	....	....	....	....
1989-90	Boston College	H-East	40	27	36	63	....	....	....	41	....	....	....	....	....	....	....	....	....	....	....	....	....	....	....	....	....	....
1990-91	Boston College	H-East	35	21	26	47	....	....	....	35	....	....	....	....	....	....	....	....	....	....	....	....	....	....	....	....	....	....
1991-92	United States	Nat-Team	49	18	15	33	....	....	....	38	....	....	....	....	....	....	....	....	....	....	....	....	....	....	....	....	....	....
	United States	Olympics	8	1	3	4	....	....	....	8	....	....	....	....	....	....	....	....	....	....	....	....	....	....	....	....	....	....
	Boston Bruins	**NHL**	**14**	**3**	**4**	**7**	**3**	**3**	**6**	**6**	**0**	**0**	**2**	**29**	**10.3**	**8**	**0**	**9**	**0**	**–1**	**7**	**0**	**3**	**3**	**17**	**0**	**0**	**0**
1992-93	**Boston Bruins**	**NHL**	**73**	**18**	**13**	**31**	**15**	**9**	**24**	**24**	**0**	**2**	**4**	**146**	**12.3**	**51**	**0**	**51**	**20**	**20**	**4**	**1**	**1**	**2**	**2**	**0**	**0**	**0**
1993-94	**Boston Bruins**	**NHL**	**77**	**10**	**11**	**21**	**9**	**9**	**18**	**32**	**0**	**2**	**1**	**183**	**5.5**	**37**	**1**	**54**	**16**	**–2**	**13**	**2**	**3**	**5**	**7**	**0**	**0**	**0**
1994-95	**Boston Bruins**	**NHL**	**36**	**7**	**9**	**16**	**12**	**13**	**25**	**23**	**0**	**1**	**0**	**70**	**10.0**	**19**	**0**	**29**	**10**	**0**	**5**	**0**	**0**	**0**	**0**	**0**	**0**	**0**
1995-96	**Boston Bruins**	**NHL**	**76**	**16**	**12**	**28**	**16**	**10**	**26**	**43**	**0**	**1**	**3**	**129**	**12.4**	**34**	**0**	**55**	**18**	**–3**	**5**	**1**	**1**	**2**	**4**	**0**	**1**	**0**
1996-97	**Boston Bruins**	**NHL**	**30**	**17**	**8**	**25**	**18**	**7**	**25**	**27**	**4**	**2**	**2**	**96**	**17.7**	**36**	**8**	**40**	**4**	**–8**	....	....	....	....	....	....	....	....
1997-98	**Boston Bruins**	**NHL**	**61**	**26**	**20**	**46**	**30**	**20**	**50**	**54**	**9**	**0**	**6**	**160**	**16.3**	**58**	**22**	**28**	**0**	**8**	**6**	**0**	**0**	**0**	**6**	**0**	**0**	**0**
1998-99	**Boston Bruins**	**NHL**	**73**	**22**	**18**	**40**	**26**	**17**	**43**	**30**	**9**	**0**	**3**	**146**	**15.1**	**65**	**23**	**35**	**0**	**7**	**12**	**4**	**3**	**7**	**0**	**2**	**0**	**0**
99-2000	**Boston Bruins**	**NHL**	**75**	**12**	**13**	**25**	**13**	**12**	**25**	**36**	**2**	**0**	**2**	**145**	**8.3**	**46**	**12**	**42**	**0**	**–8**	....	....	....	....	....	....	....	....
	United States	WC-A	7	0	3	3	....	....	....	8	....	....	....	....	....	....	....	....	....	....	....	....	....	....	....	....	....	....
	NHL Totals		**515**	**131**	**108**	**239**	**142**	**100**	**242**	**275**	**24**	**8**	**23**	**1104**	**11.9**	**354**	**66**	**343**	**68**		**52**	**8**	**11**	**19**	**36**	**2**	**1**	**0**

Hockey East First All-Star Team (1990) • NCAA East First All-American Team (1990)

Selected by **Columbus** from **Boston** in Expansion Draft, June 23, 2000.

• HEISKALA, Earl

Earl Waldemar LW – L. 6', 185 lbs. b: Kirkland Lake, Ont., 11/30/1942.

Season	Club	League	GP	G	A	Pts	AG	AA	APts	PIM	PP	SH	GW	S	%	TGF	PGF	TGA	PGA	+/–	GP	G	A	Pts	PIM	PP	SH	GW
1960-61	Hamilton Red Wings	OHA-Jr.	11	1	0	1	....	....	....	6	....	....	....	....	....	....	....	....	....	....	....	....	....	....	....	....	....	....
1961-62	Hamilton Red Wings	OHA-Jr.	50	10	20	30	....	....	....	71	....	....	....	....	....	....	....	....	....	....	10	1	4	5	10	....	....	....
	Hamilton Red Wings	Mem-Cup	14	4	3	7	....	....	....	23	....	....	....	....	....	....	....	....	....	....	....	....	....	....	....	....	....	....
1962-63	Hamilton Red Wings	OHA-Jr.	39	12	18	30	....	....	....	81	....	....	....	....	....	....	....	....	....	....	....	....	....	....	....	....	....	....
1963-64	Oakville Oaks	OHA-Sr.	1	0	1	1	....	....	....	2	....	....	....	....	....	....	....	....	....	....	....	....	....	....	....	....	....	....
	Cincinnati Wings	CPHL	2	0	0	0	....	....	....	6	....	....	....	....	....	....	....	....	....	....	....	....	....	....	....	....	....	....
1964-65	Knoxville Knights	EHL	70	25	39	64	....	....	....	156	....	....	....	....	....	....	....	....	....	....	10	1	4	5	23	....	....	....
1965-66	Seattle Totems	WHL	64	8	10	18	....	....	....	107	....	....	....	....	....	....	....	....	....	....	....	....	....	....	....	....	....	....
1966-67	Seattle Totems	WHL	65	18	22	40	....	....	....	147	....	....	....	....	....	....	....	....	....	....	10	1	2	3	*29	....	....	....
1967-68	Seattle Totems	WHL	71	26	18	44	....	....	....	*157	....	....	....	....	....	....	....	....	....	....	9	2	2	4	8	....	....	....
1968-69	**Philadelphia Flyers**	**NHL**	**21**	**3**	**3**	**6**	**3**	**3**	**6**	**51**	**0**	**0**	**0**	**38**	**7.9**	**9**	**0**	**13**	**0**	**–4**	....	....	....	....	....	....	....	....
	Quebec Aces	AHL	7	1	6	7	....	....	....	8	....	....	....	....	....	....	....	....	....	....	....	....	....	....	....	....	....	....
	Seattle Totems	WHL	34	14	9	23	....	....	....	69	....	....	....	....	....	....	....	....	....	....	4	1	0	1	6	....	....	....
1969-70	**Philadelphia Flyers**	**NHL**	**65**	**8**	**7**	**15**	**9**	**7**	**16**	**171**	**0**	**0**	**1**	**114**	**7.0**	**26**	**1**	**40**	**0**	**–15**	....	....	....	....	....	....	....	....
1970-71	**Philadelphia Flyers**	**NHL**	**41**	**2**	**1**	**3**	**2**	**1**	**3**	**72**	**0**	**0**	**1**	**39**	**5.1**	**6**	**0**	**15**	**0**	**–9**	....	....	....	....	....	....	....	....
	San Diego Gulls	WHL	21	6	5	11	....	....	....	34	....	....	....	....	....	....	....	....	....	....	5	1	0	1	4	....	....	....

Season	Club	League	GP	G	A	Pts	AG	AA	APts	PIM	PP	SH	GW	S	%	TGF	PGF	TGA	PGA	+/–	GP	G	A	Pts	PIM	PP	SH	GW
			REGULAR SEASON																		PLAYOFFS							
1971-72	San Diego Gulls	WHL	72	15	22	37	....	....	....	169	....	....	....	....	....	....	....	....	....	....	4	1	1	2	20	....	....	....
1972-73	Los Angeles Sharks	WHA	70	12	17	29	....	....	....	148	....	....	....	....	....	....	....	....	....	....	5	1	1	2	4	....	....	....
1973-74	Los Angeles Sharks	WHA	24	2	6	8	....	....	....	45	....	....	....	....	....	....	....	....	....	....	....	....	....	....	....	....	....	....
	Greensboro Generals	SHL	4	2	3	5	....	....	....	4	....	....	....	....	....	....	....	....	....	....	....	....	....	....	....	....	....	....
	NHL Totals		**127**	**13**	**11**	**24**	**14**	**11**	**25**	**294**	**0**	**0**	**1**	**191**	**6.8**	**41**	**1**	**68**	**0**		....	....	....	....	....	....	....	....
	Other Major League Totals		94	14	23	37	....	....	....	193	....	....	....	....	....	....	....	....	....	....	5	1	1	2	4	....	....	....

Traded to **Philadelphia** by **Seattle** (WHL) for the loan of Bob Courcy and Ray Larose and future considerations (the trade of Art Stratton and John Hanna, June, 1968), May 19, 1968. Loaned to **Seattle** (WHL) by **Philadelphia** for cash, December 23, 1968. Selected by **LA Sharks** (WHA) in 1972 WHA General Player Draft, February 12, 1972. Traded to **New York-New Jersey** (WHA) by **LA Sharks** (WHA) with Russ Gillow for Jim McLeod, January, 1974.

• HEJDUK, Milan

RW – R. 5'11", 185 lbs. b: Usti-nad-Labem, Czech., 2/14/1976. Quebec's 6th, 87th overall, in 1994.

Season	Club	League	GP	G	A	Pts	AG	AA	APts	PIM	PP	SH	GW	S	%	TGF	PGF	TGA	PGA	+/–	GP	G	A	Pts	PIM	PP	SH	GW
1993-94	HC Pardubice	Czech-Rep	22	6	3	9	....	....	....	....	....	....	....	....	....	....	....	....	....	....	10	5	1	6	....	....	....	....
1994-95	HC Pardubice	Czech-Rep	43	11	13	24	....	....	....	6	....	....	....	....	....	....	....	....	....	....	6	3	1	4	0	....	....	....
	Czech-Republic	WJC-A	7	1	3	4	....	....	....	14	....	....	....	....	....	....	....	....	....	....	....	....	....	....	....	....	....	....
1995-96	HC Pardubice	Czech-Rep	37	13	7	20	....	....	....	....	....	....	....	....	....	....	....	....	....	....	....	....	....	....	....	....	....	....
	Czech-Republic	WJC-A	6	0	0	0	....	....	....	0	....	....	....	....	....	....	....	....	....	....	....	....	....	....	....	....	....	....
1996-97	HC Pardubice	Czech-Rep	51	27	11	38	....	....	....	10	....	....	....	....	....	....	....	....	....	....	10	6	0	6	27	....	....	....
1997-98	Czech-Republic	WC-A	1	0	0	0	....	....	....	0	....	....	....	....	....	....	....	....	....	....	....	....	....	....	....	....	....	....
	HC Pardubice	Czech-Rep	48	26	19	45	....	....	....	20	....	....	....	....	....	....	....	....	....	....	3	0	0	0	2	....	....	....
	Czech-Republic	Olympics	4	0	0	0	....	....	....	2	....	....	....	....	....	....	....	....	....	....	....	....	....	....	....	....	....	....
1998-99	**Colorado Avalanche**	**NHL**	**82**	**14**	**34**	**48**	**16**	**33**	**49**	**26**	**4**	**0**	**5**	**178**	**7.9**	**66**	**19**	**41**	**2**	**8**	**16**	**6**	**6**	**12**	**4**	**1**	**0**	**3**
99-2000	**Colorado Avalanche**	**NHL**	**82**	**36**	**36**	**72**	**41**	**33**	**74**	**16**	**13**	**0**	**9**	**228**	**15.8**	**106**	**37**	**59**	**4**	**14**	**17**	**5**	**4**	**9**	**6**	**3**	**0**	**1**
	NHL Totals		**164**	**50**	**70**	**120**	**57**	**66**	**123**	**42**	**17**	**0**	**14**	**406**	**12.3**	**172**	**56**	**100**	**6**		**33**	**11**	**10**	**21**	**10**	**4**	**0**	**4**

NHL All-Rookie Team (1999) • Played in NHL All-Star Game (2000)

Rights transferred to **Colorado** after **Quebec** franchise relocated, June 21, 1995.

• HELANDER, Peter

Hans Peter D – L. 6'1", 185 lbs. b: Stockholm, Sweden, 12/4/1951. Los Angeles' 8th, 153rd overall, in 1982.

Season	Club	League	GP	G	A	Pts	AG	AA	APts	PIM	PP	SH	GW	S	%	TGF	PGF	TGA	PGA	+/–	GP	G	A	Pts	PIM	PP	SH	GW
1971-72	Ronnskars IF	Sweden-2	18	2	2	4	....	....	....	....	....	....	....	....	....	....	....	....	....	....	....	....	....	....	....	....	....	....
1972-73	Ronnskars IF	Sweden-2	17	5	2	7	....	....	....	....	....	....	....	....	....	....	....	....	....	....	....	....	....	....	....	....	....	....
1973-74	Ronnskars IF	Sweden-2	24	3	2	5	....	....	....	....	....	....	....	....	....	....	....	....	....	....	....	....	....	....	....	....	....	....
1974-75	Skelleftea AIK	Sweden	8	0	0	0	....	....	....	8	....	....	....	....	....	....	....	....	....	....	....	....	....	....	....	....	....	....
1975-76	Skelleftea AIK	Sweden	7	1	1	2	....	....	....	6	....	....	....	....	....	....	....	....	....	....	....	....	....	....	....	....	....	....
1976-77	Skelleftea AIK	Sweden	29	5	2	7	....	....	....	26	....	....	....	....	....	....	....	....	....	....	....	....	....	....	....	....	....	....
1977-78	Skelleftea AIK	Sweden	29	0	4	4	....	....	....	40	....	....	....	....	....	....	....	....	....	....	5	0	0	0	8	....	....	....
1978-79	Skelleftea AIK	Sweden	36	7	4	11	....	....	....	40	....	....	....	....	....	....	....	....	....	....	....	....	....	....	....	....	....	....
1979-80	Skelleftea AIK	Sweden-2	32	6	8	14	....	....	....	61	....	....	....	....	....	....	....	....	....	....	1	0	0	0	0	....	....	....
1980-81	Skelleftea AIK	Sweden	33	6	8	14	....	....	....	59	....	....	....	....	....	....	....	....	....	....	3	1	0	1	11	....	....	....
	Sweden	WEC-A	8	1	2	3	....	....	....	8	....	....	....	....	....	....	....	....	....	....	....	....	....	....	....	....	....	....
1981-82	Sweden	Can-Cup	5	0	2	2	....	....	....	8	....	....	....	....	....	....	....	....	....	....	....	....	....	....	....	....	....	....
	Skelleftea AIK	Sweden	30	6	2	8	....	....	....	50	....	....	....	....	....	....	....	....	....	....	....	....	....	....	....	....	....	....
	Sweden	WEC-A	10	1	2	3	....	....	....	14	....	....	....	....	....	....	....	....	....	....	....	....	....	....	....	....	....	....
1982-83	**Los Angeles Kings**	**NHL**	**7**	**0**	**1**	**1**	**0**	**1**	**1**	**0**	**0**	**0**	**0**	**2**	**0.0**	**4**	**0**	**10**	**4**	**–2**	....	....	....	....	....	....	....	....
	New Haven Nighthawks	AHL	9	1	3	4	....	....	....	0	....	....	....	....	....	....	....	....	....	....	....	....	....	....	....	....	....	....
	NHL Totals		**7**	**0**	**1**	**1**	**0**	**1**	**1**	**0**	**0**	**0**	**0**	**2**	**0.0**	**4**	**0**	**10**	**4**		....	....	....	....	....	....	....	....

Swedish World All-Star Team (1981, 1982)

• HELENIUS, Sami

D – L. 6'5", 225 lbs. b: Helsinki, Finland, 1/22/1974. Calgary's 5th, 102nd overall, in 1992.

Season	Club	League	GP	G	A	Pts	AG	AA	APts	PIM	PP	SH	GW	S	%	TGF	PGF	TGA	PGA	+/–	GP	G	A	Pts	PIM	PP	SH	GW
1990-91	Jokerit Helsinki	Finland-Jr.	2	0	0	0	....	....	....	6	....	....	....	....	....	....	....	....	....	....	....	....	....	....	....	....	....	....
1991-92	Jokerit Helsinki	Finland-Jr.	14	3	3	6	....	....	....	24	....	....	....	....	....	....	....	....	....	....	....	....	....	....	....	....	....	....
	Jokerit Helsinki	Finland-2	13	4	4	8	....	....	....	24	....	....	....	....	....	....	....	....	....	....	....	....	....	....	....	....	....	....
1992-93	Jokerit Helsinki	Finland-Jr.	13	2	3	5	....	....	....	18	....	....	....	....	....	....	....	....	....	....	....	....	....	....	....	....	....	....
	Vantaa HT	Finland-2	21	3	2	5	....	....	....	50	....	....	....	....	....	....	....	....	....	....	....	....	....	....	....	....	....	....
	Finland	WJC-A	7	0	1	1	....	....	....	6	....	....	....	....	....	....	....	....	....	....	....	....	....	....	....	....	....	....
	Jokerit Helsinki	Finland	1	0	0	0	....	....	....	0	....	....	....	....	....	....	....	....	....	....	....	....	....	....	....	....	....	....
1993-94	H-Reipas Lahti	Finland-Jr.	11	3	4	7	....	....	....	48	....	....	....	....	....	....	....	....	....	....	....	....	....	....	....	....	....	....
	H-Reipas Lahti	Finland	37	2	3	5	....	....	....	46	....	....	....	....	....	....	....	....	....	....	....	....	....	....	....	....	....	....
1994-95	Saint John Flames	AHL	69	2	5	7	....	....	....	217	....	....	....	....	....	....	....	....	....	....	....	....	....	....	....	....	....	....
1995-96	Saint John Flames	AHL	68	0	3	3	....	....	....	231	....	....	....	....	....	....	....	....	....	....	10	0	0	0	9	....	....	....
1996-97	**Calgary Flames**	**NHL**	**3**	**0**	**1**	**1**	**0**	**1**	**1**	**0**	**0**	**0**	**0**	**1**	**0.0**	**2**	**0**	**1**	**0**	**1**	....	....	....	....	....	....	....	....
	Saint John Flames	AHL	72	5	10	15	....	....	....	218	....	....	....	....	....	....	....	....	....	....	2	0	0	0	0	....	....	....
1997-98	Saint John Flames	AHL	63	1	2	3	....	....	....	185	....	....	....	....	....	....	....	....	....	....	....	....	....	....	....	....	....	....
	Las Vegas Thunder	IHL	10	0	1	1	....	....	....	19	....	....	....	....	....	....	....	....	....	....	4	0	0	0	25	....	....	....
1998-99	**Calgary Flames**	**NHL**	**4**	**0**	**0**	**0**	**0**	**0**	**0**	**8**	**0**	**0**	**0**	**1**	**0.0**	**0**	**0**	**3**	**1**	**–2**	....	....	....	....	....	....	....	....
	Las Vegas Thunder	IHL	42	2	3	5	....	....	....	193	....	....	....	....	....	....	....	....	....	....	....	....	....	....	....	....	....	....
	Tampa Bay Lightning	**NHL**	**4**	**1**	**0**	**1**	**1**	**0**	**1**	**15**	**0**	**1**	**0**	**3**	**33.3**	**1**	**0**	**6**	**2**	**–3**	....	....	....	....	....	....	....	....
	Chicago Wolves	IHL	4	0	0	0	....	....	....	11	....	....	....	....	....	....	....	....	....	....	....	....	....	....	....	....	....	....
	Hershey Bears	AHL	8	0	0	0	....	....	....	29	....	....	....	....	....	....	....	....	....	....	5	0	0	0	16	....	....	....
99-2000	**Colorado Avalanche**	**NHL**	**33**	**0**	**0**	**0**	**0**	**0**	**0**	**46**	**0**	**0**	**0**	**6**	**0.0**	**4**	**0**	**9**	**0**	**–5**	....	....	....	....	....	....	....	....
	Hershey Bears	AHL	12	0	1	1	....	....	....	31	....	....	....	....	....	....	....	....	....	....	9	0	0	0	40	....	....	....
	NHL Totals		**44**	**1**	**1**	**2**	**1**	**1**	**2**	**69**	**0**	**1**	**0**	**11**	**9.1**	**7**	**0**	**19**	**3**		....	....	....	....	....	....	....	....

Traded to **Tampa Bay** by **Calgary** for future considerations, January 29, 1999. Traded to **Colorado** by **Tampa Bay** for future considerations, March 23, 1999.

• HELMER, Bryan

Bryan Barry D – R. 6'1", 200 lbs. b: Sault Ste. Marie, Ont., 7/15/1972.

Season	Club	League	GP	G	A	Pts	AG	AA	APts	PIM	PP	SH	GW	S	%	TGF	PGF	TGA	PGA	+/–	GP	G	A	Pts	PIM	PP	SH	GW
1989-90	Wellington Dukes	OJHL-B	44	4	20	24	....	....	....	204	....	....	....	....	....	....	....	....	....	....	....	....	....	....	....	....	....	....
	Belleville Bulls	OHL	6	0	1	1	....	....	....	0	....	....	....	....	....	....	....	....	....	....	....	....	....	....	....	....	....	....
1990-91	Wellington Dukes	OJHL	50	11	14	25	....	....	....	109	....	....	....	....	....	....	....	....	....	....	....	....	....	....	....	....	....	....
1991-92	Wellington Dukes	OJHL	42	17	31	48	....	....	....	66	....	....	....	....	....	....	....	....	....	....	3	2	1	3	0	....	....	....
1992-93	Wellington Dukes	OJHL	48	21	54	75	....	....	....	84	....	....	....	....	....	....	....	....	....	....	9	4	8	12	22	....	....	....
1993-94	Albany River Rats	AHL	65	4	19	23	....	....	....	79	....	....	....	....	....	....	....	....	....	....	5	0	0	0	9	....	....	....
1994-95	Albany River Rats	AHL	77	7	36	43	....	....	....	101	....	....	....	....	....	....	....	....	....	....	7	1	0	1	0	....	....	....
1995-96	Albany River Rats	AHL	80	14	30	44	....	....	....	107	....	....	....	....	....	....	....	....	....	....	4	2	0	2	6	....	....	....
1996-97	Albany River Rats	AHL	77	12	27	39	....	....	....	113	....	....	....	....	....	....	....	....	....	....	16	1	7	8	10	....	....	....
1997-98	Albany River Rats	AHL	80	14	49	63	....	....	....	101	....	....	....	....	....	....	....	....	....	....	13	4	9	13	18	....	....	....
1998-99	**Phoenix Coyotes**	**NHL**	**11**	**0**	**0**	**0**	**0**	**0**	**0**	**23**	**0**	**0**	**0**	**11**	**0.0**	**4**	**0**	**2**	**0**	**2**	....	....	....	....	....	....	....	....
	Las Vegas Thunder	IHL	8	1	3	4	....	....	....	28	....	....	....	....	....	....	....	....	....	....	....	....	....	....	....	....	....	....
	St. Louis Blues	**NHL**	**29**	**0**	**4**	**4**	**0**	**4**	**4**	**19**	**0**	**0**	**0**	**38**	**0.0**	**23**	**1**	**25**	**6**	**3**	....	....	....	....	....	....	....	....
	Worcester IceCats	AHL	16	7	8	15	....	....	....	18	....	....	....	....	....	....	....	....	....	....	4	0	0	0	12	....	....	....
99-2000	**St. Louis Blues**	**NHL**	**15**	**1**	**1**	**2**	**1**	**1**	**2**	**10**	**1**	**0**	**1**	**19**	**5.3**	**5**	**1**	**9**	**2**	**–3**	....	....	....	....	....	....	....	....
	Worcester IceCats	AHL	54	10	25	35	....	....	....	124	....	....	....	....	....	....	....	....	....	....	9	1	4	5	10	....	....	....
	NHL Totals		**55**	**1**	**5**	**6**	**1**	**5**	**6**	**52**	**1**	**0**	**1**	**68**	**1.5**	**32**	**2**	**36**	**8**		....	....	....	....	....	....	....	....

AHL First All-Star Team (1998)

Signed as a free agent by **New Jersey**, July 10, 1994. Signed as a free agent by **Phoenix**, July 17, 1998. Claimed on waivers by **St. Louis** from **Phoenix**, December 19, 1998.

Season	Club	League	GP	G	A	Pts	AG	AA	APts	PIM	PP	SH	GW	S	%	TGF	PGF	TGA	PGA	+/–	GP	G	A	Pts	PIM	PP	SH	GW
			REGULAR SEASON																		PLAYOFFS							

• HELMINEN, Raimo

Raimo Ilmari C – L. 6', 185 lbs. b: Tampere, Finland, 3/11/1964. NY Rangers' 2nd, 35th overall, in 1984.

Season	Club	League	GP	G	A	Pts	AG	AA	APts	PIM	PP	SH	GW	S	%	TGF	PGF	TGA	PGA	+/–	GP	G	A	Pts	PIM	PP	SH	GW
1981-82	Ilves Tampere	Finland-Jr.	30	28	31	59				22											4	4	2	6	0			
1982-83	Ilves Tampere	Finland-Jr.	13	7	20	27				20											3	5	1	6	2			
	Finland	WJC-A	7	0	5	5				0																		
	Ilves Tampere	Finland	31	2	3	5				0											6	0	0	0	2			
1983-84	Ilves Tampere	Finland	37	17	13	30				14											2	0	0	0	2			
	Finland	WJC-A	7	11	11	22				4																		
	Finland	Nat-Team	8	2	0	2				0																		
	Finland	Olympics	6	0	2	2				2																		
1984-85	Ilves Tampere	Finland	36	21	36	57				20																		
	Finland	Nat-Team	18	7	6	13				0																		
	Finland	WEC-A	10	4	5	9				2																		
1985-86	**New York Rangers**	**NHL**	**66**	**10**	**30**	**40**	**8**	**20**	**28**	**10**	**4**	**0**	**2**	**125**	**8.0**	**62**	**26**	**37**	**0**	**–1**	**2**	**0**	**0**	**0**	**0**	**0**	**0**	**0**
1986-87	**New York Rangers**	**NHL**	**21**	**2**	**4**	**6**	**2**	**3**	**5**	**2**	**1**	**0**	**0**	**24**	**8.3**	**12**	**7**	**14**	**1**	**–8**								
	New Haven Nighthawks	AHL	6	0	2	2				0																		
	Minnesota North Stars	**NHL**	**6**	**0**	**1**	**1**	**0**	**1**	**1**	**0**	**0**	**0**	**0**	**6**	**0.0**	**3**	**2**	**4**	**0**	**–3**								
1987-88	Finland	Can-Cup	5	0	3	3				0																		
	Ilves Tampere	Finland	31	20	23	43				42											4	1	1	2	10			
	Finland	Nat-Team	22	5	5	10				12																		
	Finland	Olympics	7	2	8	10				4																		
1988-89	**New York Islanders**	**NHL**	**24**	**1**	**11**	**12**	**1**	**8**	**9**	**4**	**1**	**0**	**0**	**22**	**4.5**	**18**	**12**	**26**	**5**	**–15**								
	Springfield Indians	AHL	16	6	11	17				0																		
1989-90	Malmo IF	Sweden-2	29	26	30	56				16											3	2	1	3	2			
	Finland	Nat-Team	12	8	8	16				6																		
	Finland	WEC-A	4	0	0	0				0																		
1990-91	Malmo IF	Sweden	33	12	18	30				14											2	0	1	1	4			
	Finland	Nat-Team	10	0	6	6				2																		
1991-92	Malmo IF	Sweden	40	9	18	27				24											10	1	3	4	4			
	Finland	Nat-Team	4	0	3	3				0																		
	Finland	Olympics	8	1	2	3				0																		
1992-93	Malmo IF	Sweden	40	9	*33	42				59											6	1	0	1	8			
1993-94	Malmo IF	Sweden	38	20	34	*54				26											11	1	7	8	8			
	Finland	Nat-Team	11	3	3	6				0																		
	Finland	Olympics	8	1	5	6				8																		
	Finland	WC-A	8	1	5	6				0																		
1994-95	Malmo IF	Sweden	35	10	19	29				55											7	3	2	5	4			
	Finland	Nat-Team	12	0	5	5				0																		
	Finland	WC-A	8	1	7	8				2																		
1995-96	Malmo IF	Sweden	40	8	19	27				53											5	1	3	4	12			
	Finland	Nat-Team	17	0	8	8				8																		
	Finland	WC-A	6	0	4	4				0																		
1996-97	Finland	W-Cup	3	0	2	2				0																		
	Ilves Tampere	Finland	49	11	*39	50				8											8	1	5	6	2			
	Finland	Nat-Team	21	1	13	14				4																		
	Finland	WC-A	8	0	6	6				0																		
1997-98	Ilves Tampere	Finland	46	12	36	48				42											9	3	5	8	10			
	Finland	Nat-Team	12	2	10	12				0																		
	Finland	Olympics	6	2	0	2				2																		
	Finland	WC-A	10	2	9	11				0																		
1998-99	Ilves Tampere	Finland	53	12	38	50				44											4	0	3	3	2			
	Ilves Tampere	EuroHL	6	0	3	3				0											6	3	7	10	0			
	Finland	WC-A	12	1	3	4				2																		
99-2000	Ilves Tampere	Finland	51	7	38	45				68											3	1	0	1	12			
	Finland	WC-A	9	2	2	4				0																		
	NHL Totals		**117**	**13**	**46**	**59**	**11**	**32**	**43**	**16**	**6**	**0**	**2**	**177**	**7.3**	**95**	**47**	**81**	**6**		**2**	**0**	**0**	**0**	**0**	**0**	**0**	**0**

WJC-A All-Star Team (1984) • Named Best Forward at WJC-A (1984) • Finnish First All-Star Team (1988, 1997)

Traded to **Minnesota** by **NY Rangers** for future considerations, March 10, 1987. Signed as a free agent by **NY Islanders**, June 1, 1988.

• HENDERSON, Archie

Archie Robert RW – R. 6'6", 220 lbs. b: Calgary, Alta., 2/17/1957. Washington's 10th, 156th overall, in 1977.

Season	Club	League	GP	G	A	Pts	AG	AA	APts	PIM	PP	SH	GW	S	%	TGF	PGF	TGA	PGA	+/–	GP	G	A	Pts	PIM	PP	SH	GW
1973-74	Calgary Royals	AAHA	STATISTICS NOT AVAILABLE																									
1974-75	Lethbridge Broncos	WCJHL	65	3	10	13				177											8	0	0	0	22			
1975-76	Lethbridge Broncos	WCJHL	21	1	2	3				110																		
	Victoria Cougars	WCJHL	31	8	7	15				205											14	1	2	3	35			
1976-77	Victoria Cougars	WCJHL	47	14	10	24				208											3	1	0	1	29			
1977-78	Port Huron Flags	IHL	71	16	16	32				419											15	5	4	9	47			
1978-79	Hershey Bears	AHL	78	17	11	28				337											4	0	1	1	28			
1979-80	Hershey Bears	AHL	8	0	2	2				37																		
	Fort Worth Texans	CHL	49	8	9	17				199											12	2	1	3	*58			
1980-81	**Washington Capitals**	**NHL**	**7**	**1**	**0**	**1**	**1**	**0**	**1**	**28**	**0**	**0**	**0**	**4**	**25.0**	**2**	**0**	**3**	**0**	**–1**								
	Hershey Bears	AHL	60	3	5	8				251											5	0	0	0	6			
1981-82	**Minnesota North Stars**	**NHL**	**1**	**0**	**0**	**0**	**0**	**0**	**0**	**0**	**0**	**0**	**0**	**0**	**0.0**	**0**	**0**	**0**	**0**	**0**								
	Nashville South Stars	CHL	77	12	23	35				*320											3	0	0	0	17			
1982-83	**Hartford Whalers**	**NHL**	**15**	**2**	**1**	**3**	**2**	**1**	**3**	**64**	**0**	**0**	**0**	**7**	**28.6**	**4**	**0**	**6**	**0**	**–2**								
	Binghamton Whalers	AHL	50	8	9	17				172																		
1983-84	New Haven Nighthawks	AHL	48	1	8	9				164																		
1984-85	Nova Scotia Oilers	AHL	71	5	7	12				271											5	0	0	0	30			
1985-86	Maine Mariners	AHL	57	4	6	10				172											5	0	0	0	24			
1986-87	Maine Mariners	AHL	67	4	6	10				246																		
1987-88	Saginaw Hawks	IHL	55	4	9	13				231											10	0	0	0	66			
	NHL Totals		**23**	**3**	**1**	**4**	**3**	**1**	**4**	**92**	**0**	**0**	**0**	**11**	**27.3**	**6**	**0**	**9**	**0**									

Signed as a free agent by **Minnesota**, July 15, 1981. Signed as a free agent by **Hartford**, August 9, 1982. Signed as a free agent by **LA Kings**, August 29, 1983. Signed as a free agent by **New Jersey**, September 11, 1985.

• HENDERSON, Jay

Jay Elliot LW – L. 5'11", 188 lbs. b: Edmonton, Alta., 9/17/1978. Boston's 12th, 246th overall, in 1997.

Season	Club	League	GP	G	A	Pts	AG	AA	APts	PIM	PP	SH	GW	S	%	TGF	PGF	TGA	PGA	+/–	GP	G	A	Pts	PIM	PP	SH	GW
1993-94	Sherwood Park Crusaders	AAHA	31	12	21	33				36																		
1994-95	Red Deer Rebels	WHL	54	3	9	12				80																		
1995-96	Red Deer Rebels	WHL	71	15	13	28				139											10	1	1	2	11			
1996-97	Edmonton Ice	WHL	66	28	32	60				127																		
1997-98	Edmonton Ice	WHL	72	49	45	94				130																		
1998-99	**Boston Bruins**	**NHL**	**4**	**0**	**0**	**0**	**0**	**0**	**0**	**2**	**0**	**0**	**0**	**4**	**0.0**	**0**	**0**	**1**	**0**	**–1**								
	Providence Bruins	AHL	55	7	9	16				172											2	0	0	0	2			
99-2000	**Boston Bruins**	**NHL**	**16**	**1**	**3**	**4**	**1**	**3**	**4**	**9**	**0**	**0**	**0**	**18**	**5.6**	**5**	**0**	**4**	**0**	**1**								
	Providence Bruins	AHL	60	18	27	45				200											14	1	2	3	16			
	NHL Totals		**20**	**1**	**3**	**4**	**1**	**3**	**4**	**11**	**0**	**0**	**0**	**22**	**4.5**	**5**	**0**	**5**	**0**									

• HENDERSON, Matt

RW – L. 6'1", 200 lbs. b: White Bear Lake, MN, 6/22/1974.

Season	Club	League	GP	G	A	Pts	AG	AA	APts	PIM	PP	SH	GW	S	%	TGF	PGF	TGA	PGA	+/–	GP	G	A	Pts	PIM	PP	SH	GW
1991-92	White Bear Lake Bears	Hi-School	STATISTICS NOT AVAILABLE																									
1992-93	St. Paul Vulcans	USHL	STATISTICS NOT AVAILABLE																									
1993-94	St. Paul Vulcans	USHL	48	27	24	51																						

Season	Club	League	REGULAR SEASON																		PLAYOFFS							
			GP	G	A	Pts	AG	AA	APts	PIM	PP	SH	GW	S	%	TGF	PGF	TGA	PGA	+/–	GP	G	A	Pts	PIM	PP	SH	GW
1994-95	University of North Dakota	WCHA	19	1	3	4				16																		
1995-96	University of North Dakota	WCHA	36	9	10	19				34											2	0	1	1	0			
1996-97	University of North Dakota	WCHA	42	14	17	31				71											7	5	4	9	10			
1997-98	University of North Dakota	WCHA	38	24	14	38				74											5	2	2	4	4			
1998-99	**Nashville Predators**	**NHL**	2	0	0	0	0	0	0	2	0	0	0	0	0.0	0	0	1	0	–1								
	Milwaukee Admirals	IHL	77	19	19	38				117											2	0	0	0	0			
99-2000	Philadelphia Phantoms	AHL	51	4	8	12				37											5	0	0	0	4			
	Trenton Titans	ECHL	16	2	4	6				47																		
	NHL Totals		2	0	0	0	0	0	0	2	0	0	0	0	0.0	0	0	1	0									

NCAA Championship All-Tournament Team (1997) • NCAA Championship Tournament MVP (1997)

Signed as a free agent by **Nashville**, July 14, 1998. Traded to **Philadelphia** by **Nashville** for Paul Healey, September 27, 1999.

• HENDERSON, Paul

Paul Garnet RW – R. 5'11", 180 lbs. b: Kincardine, Ont., 1/28/1943.

Season	Club	League	GP	G	A	Pts	AG	AA	APts	PIM	PP	SH	GW	S	%	TGF	PGF	TGA	PGA	+/–	GP	G	A	Pts	PIM	PP	SH	GW
1960-61	Goderich Jets	OHA-B	STATISTICS NOT AVAILABLE																									
	Hamilton Red Wings	OHA-Jr.	30	1	3	4				9											12	1	1	2	4			
1961-62	Hamilton Red Wings	OHA-Jr.	50	24	19	43				68											10	4	6	10	13			
	Hamilton Red Wings	Mem-Cup	14	7	7	14				22																		
1962-63	**Detroit Red Wings**	**NHL**	2	0	0	0	0	0	0	9																		
	Hamilton Red Wings	OHA-Jr.	48	*49	27	76				53											3	2	0	2	0			
1963-64	**Detroit Red Wings**	**NHL**	32	3	3	6	4	3	7	14											14	2	3	5	6	0	0	0
	Pittsburgh Hornets	AHL	38	10	14	24				18																		
1964-65	**Detroit Red Wings**	**NHL**	70	8	13	21	10	13	23	30											7	0	2	2	0	0	0	0
1965-66	**Detroit Red Wings**	**NHL**	69	22	24	46	25	23	48	34											12	3	3	6	10	1	0	2
1966-67	**Detroit Red Wings**	**NHL**	46	21	19	40	24	19	43	10																		
1967-68	**Detroit Red Wings**	**NHL**	50	13	20	33	15	20	35	35	4	0	2	134	9.7	53	14	42	3	0								
	Toronto Maple Leafs	**NHL**	13	5	6	11	6	6	12	8	0	0	1	38	13.2	22	3	6	0	13								
1968-69	**Toronto Maple Leafs**	**NHL**	74	27	32	59	29	29	58	16	4	0	5	223	12.1	85	21	53	7	18	4	0	1	1	0	0	0	0
1969-70	**Toronto Maple Leafs**	**NHL**	67	20	22	42	22	21	43	18	5	0	4	213	9.4	71	16	41	0	14								
1970-71	**Toronto Maple Leafs**	**NHL**	72	30	30	60	30	25	55	34	8	0	2	213	14.1	86	25	48	1	14	6	5	1	6	4	1	0	2
1971-72	**Toronto Maple Leafs**	**NHL**	73	38	19	57	38	16	54	32	12	1	5	191	19.9	92	30	52	4	14	5	1	2	3	6	0	0	0
1972-73	Team Canada	Summit-72	8	*7	3	10				4																		
	Toronto Maple Leafs	**NHL**	40	18	16	34	17	13	30	18	2	0	3	105	17.1	47	10	36	1	2								
1973-74	**Toronto Maple Leafs**	**NHL**	69	24	31	55	23	26	49	40	5	0	2	159	15.1	85	23	58	5	9	4	0	2	2	2	0	0	0
1974-75	Team Canada	Summit-74	7	2	1	3				0																		
	Toronto Toros	WHA	58	30	33	63				18																		
1975-76	Toronto Toros	WHA	65	26	29	55				22																		
1976-77	Birmingham Bulls	WHA	81	23	25	48				30																		
1977-78	Birmingham Bulls	WHA	80	37	29	66				22											5	1	1	2	0			
1978-79	Birmingham Bulls	WHA	76	24	27	51				20																		
1979-80	**Atlanta Flames**	**NHL**	30	7	6	13	6	4	10	6	1	0	1	29	24.1	21	7	10	1	5	4	0	0	0	0	0	0	0
	Birmingham Bulls	CHL	47	17	18	35				10																		
1980-81	Birmingham Bulls	CHL	35	6	11	17				38																		
	NHL Totals		707	236	241	477	249	218	467	304											56	11	14	25	28			
	Other Major League Totals		360	140	143	283				112											5	1	1	2	0			

Played in NHL All-Star Game (1972, 1973)

Traded to **Toronto** by **Detroit** with Norm Ullman, Floyd Smith and Doug Barrie for Frank Mahovlich, Garry Unger, Pete Stemkowski and the rights to Carl Brewer, March 3, 1968. Selected by **Quebec** (WHA) in 1972 WHA General Player Draft, February 12, 1972. WHA rights traded to **Toronto** (WHA) by **Quebec** (WHA) for cash, June, 1974. Transferred to **Birmingham** (WHA) after **Toronto** (WHA) franchise reloctated, June 30, 1976. Signed as a free agent by **Atlanta**, September 17, 1979.

• HENDRICKSON, Darby

Darby J. C – L. 6', 195 lbs. b: Richfield, MN, 8/28/1972. Toronto's 3rd, 73rd overall, in 1990.

Season	Club	League	GP	G	A	Pts	AG	AA	APts	PIM	PP	SH	GW	S	%	TGF	PGF	TGA	PGA	+/–	GP	G	A	Pts	PIM	PP	SH	GW
1987-88	Richfield Spartans	Hi-School	22	12	9	21				10																		
1988-89	Richfield Spartans	Hi-School	22	22	20	42				12																		
1989-90	Richfield Spartans	Hi-School	24	23	27	50				49																		
1990-91	Richfield Spartans	Hi-School	27	32	29	61																						
1991-92	University of Minnesota	WCHA	41	25	28	53				61																		
1992-93	University of Minnesota	WCHA	31	12	15	27				35																		
1993-94	United States	Nat-Team	59	12	16	28				30																		
	United States	Olympics	8	0	0	0				6																		
	Toronto Maple Leafs	**NHL**																			2	0	0	0	0	0	0	0
	St. John's Maple Leafs	AHL	6	4	1	5				4											3	1	1	2	0			
1994-95	**Toronto Maple Leafs**	**NHL**	8	0	1	1	0	1	1	4	0	0	0	4	0.0	1	0	1	0	0								
	St. John's Maple Leafs	AHL	59	16	20	36				48																		
1995-96	**Toronto Maple Leafs**	**NHL**	46	6	6	12	6	5	11	47	0	0	0	43	14.0	20	1	23	2	–2								
	New York Islanders	**NHL**	16	1	4	5	1	3	4	33	0	0	1	30	3.3	9	2	18	5	–6								
	United States	WC-A	8	1	1	2				4																		
1996-97	**Toronto Maple Leafs**	**NHL**	64	11	6	17	12	5	17	47	0	1	0	105	10.5	24	1	63	20	–20								
	St. John's Maple Leafs	AHL	12	5	4	9				21																		
	United States	WC-A	8	0	1	1				8																		
1997-98	**Toronto Maple Leafs**	**NHL**	80	8	4	12	9	4	13	67	0	0	0	115	7.0	21	0	59	18	–20								
1998-99	**Toronto Maple Leafs**	**NHL**	35	2	3	5	2	3	5	30	0	0	0	34	5.9	10	0	23	9	–4								
	Vancouver Canucks	**NHL**	27	2	2	4	2	2	4	22	1	0	0	36	5.6	9	2	40	18	–15								
	United States	WC-A	6	0	2	2				0																		
99-2000	**Vancouver Canucks**	**NHL**	40	5	4	9	6	4	10	14	0	1	1	39	12.8	16	1	31	13	–3								
	Syracuse Crunch	AHL	20	5	8	13				16																		
	United States	WC-A	7	1	1	2				12																		
	NHL Totals		316	35	30	65	38	27	65	264	1	2	2	406	8.6	110	7	258	85		2	0	0	0	0	0	0	0

Traded to **NY Islanders** by **Toronto** with Sean Haggerty, Kenny Jonsson and Toronto's 1st round choice (Roberto Luongo) in 1997 Entry Draft for Wendel Clark, Mathieu Schneider and D.J. Smith, March 13, 1996. Traded to **Toronto** by **NY Islanders** for a conditional choice in 1998 Entry Draft, October 11, 1996. Traded to **Vancouver** by **Toronto** for Chris McAllister, February 16, 1999. Selected by **Minnesota** from **Vancouver** in Expansion Draft, June 23, 2000.

• HENNING, Lorne

Lorne Edward C – L. 5'11", 185 lbs. b: Melfort, Sask., 2/22/1952. NY Islanders' 2nd, 17th overall, in 1972.

Season	Club	League	GP	G	A	Pts	AG	AA	APts	PIM	PP	SH	GW	S	%	TGF	PGF	TGA	PGA	+/–	GP	G	A	Pts	PIM	PP	SH	GW
1967-68	North Battleford Beavers	SAHA	STATISTICS NOT AVAILABLE																									
1968-69	Estevan Bruins	WCJHL	60	27	27	54				20											10	3	3	6	0			
1969-70	Estevan Bruins	WCJHL	60	40	52	92				33											5	1	1	2	0			
1970-71	Estevan Bruins	WCJHL	66	64	66	130				41											7	5	10	15	7			
1971-72	New Westminster Bruins	WCJHL	60	51	63	114				29											5	3	1	4	7			
1972-73	**New York Islanders**	**NHL**	63	7	19	26	7	15	22	14	0	0	0	101	6.9	36	5	60	1	–28								
	New Haven Nighthawks	AHL	4	0	2	2				2																		
1973-74	**New York Islanders**	**NHL**	60	12	15	27	12	12	24	6	2	0	1	96	12.5	38	11	34	0	–7								
	Fort Worth Wings	CHL	8	4	6	10				4																		
1974-75	**New York Islanders**	**NHL**	61	5	6	11	4	4	8	6	0	4	0	45	11.1	18	2	26	17	7	17	0	2	2	0	0	0	0
1975-76	**New York Islanders**	**NHL**	80	7	10	17	6	7	13	16	0	4	0	84	8.3	25	0	57	38	6	13	2	0	2	2	1	1	0
1976-77	**New York Islanders**	**NHL**	80	13	18	31	12	14	26	10	0	6	2	103	12.6	48	0	65	38	21	12	0	1	1	0	0	0	0
1977-78	**New York Islanders**	**NHL**	79	12	15	27	11	12	23	6	0	2	4	79	15.2	34	0	65	41	10	7	0	0	0	4	0	0	0
1978-79	**New York Islanders**	**NHL**	73	13	20	33	11	14	25	14	0	2	2	70	18.6	41	1	70	47	17	10	2	0	2	0	0	1	0
1979-80♦	**New York Islanders**	**NHL**	39	3	6	9	3	4	7	6	0	0	0	45	6.7	11	0	44	23	–10	21	3	4	7	2	0	3	1
1980-81♦	**New York Islanders**	**NHL**	9	1	2	3	1	1	2	24	0	0	0	15	6.7	5	0	2	1	4	1	0	0	0	0	0	0	0
1981-1984	**New York Islanders**	**NHL**	DID NOT PLAY – ASSISTANT COACH																									
1984-1985	Springfield Indians	AHL	DID NOT PLAY – COACHING																									

			REGULAR SEASON																		PLAYOFFS							
Season	Club	League	GP	G	A	Pts	AG	AA	APts	PIM	PP	SH	GW	S	%	TGF	PGF	TGA	PGA	+/–	GP	G	A	Pts	PIM	PP	SH	GW
1985-1987	Minnesota North Stars	NHL	DID NOT PLAY – COACHING																									
1987-1989			OUT OF HOCKEY – RETIRED																									
1989-1994	New York Islanders	NHL	DID NOT PLAY – ASSISTANT GENERAL MANAGER																									
1994-1995	New York Islanders	NHL	DID NOT PLAY – COACHING																									
1995-1998	Chicago Blackhawks	NHL	DID NOT PLAY – ASSISTANT COACH																									
1998-2000	New York Islanders	NHL	DID NOT PLAY – ASSISTANT COACH																									
	NHL Totals		544	73	111	184	67	83	150	102	2	18	9	638	11.4	256	19	423	206		81	7	7	14	8	1	5	1

WCJHL Second All-Star Team (1971)

• HENRY, Camille

Camille Joseph Wilfred "The Eel" C – L. 5'9", 152 lbs. b: Quebec City, Que., 1/31/1933 d: 9/11/1997.

Season	Club	League	GP	G	A	Pts	AG	AA	APts	PIM	PP	SH	GW	S	%	TGF	PGF	TGA	PGA	+/–	GP	G	A	Pts	PIM	PP	SH	GW
1949-50	Quebec Citadelle	QJHL	1	0	0	0	....	....	....	0	....	....	....	....	....	....	....	....	....	....	....	....	....	....	....	....	....	....
1950-51	Quebec Citadelle	QJHL	46	25	23	48	....	....	....	26	....	....	....	....	....	....	....	....	....	....	22	13	12	25	22	....	....	....
1951-52	Quebec Citadelle	QJHL	50	*55	59	*114	....	....	....	59	....	....	....	....	....	....	....	....	....	....	6	*8	4	12	2	....	....	....
1952-53	Quebec Citadelle	QJHL	46	*46	30	76	....	....	....	43	....	....	....	....	....	....	....	....	....	....	9	*10	*8	*18	*21	....	....	....
	Quebec Citadeles	Mem-Cup	8	14	7	21	....	....	....	2	....	....	....	....	....	....	....	....	....	....	....	....	....	....	....	....	....	....
1953-54	New York Rangers	NHL	66	24	15	39	33	18	51	10	....	....	....	....	....	....	....	....	....	....	....	....	....	....	....	....	....	....
1954-55	New York Rangers	NHL	21	5	2	7	6	2	8	4	....	....	....	....	....	....	....	....	....	....	....	....	....	....	....	....	....	....
	Quebec Aces	QHL	37	20	18	38	....	....	....	2	....	....	....	....	....	....	....	....	....	....	8	3	1	4	0	....	....	....
1955-56	Providence Reds	AHL	59	*50	41	91	....	....	....	8	....	....	....	....	....	....	....	....	....	....	9	*10	6	16	2	....	....	....
1956-57	New York Rangers	NHL	36	14	15	29	18	16	34	2	....	....	....	....	....	....	....	....	....	....	5	2	3	5	0	1	0	0
	Providence Reds	AHL	29	31	16	47	....	....	....	8	....	....	....	....	....	....	....	....	....	....	....	....	....	....	....	....	....	....
1957-58	New York Rangers	NHL	70	32	24	56	40	25	65	2	....	....	....	....	....	....	....	....	....	....	6	1	4	5	5	1	0	0
1958-59	New York Rangers	NHL	70	23	35	58	28	36	64	2	....	....	....	....	....	....	....	....	....	....	....	....	....	....	....	....	....	....
1959-60	New York Rangers	NHL	49	12	15	27	14	15	29	6	....	....	....	....	....	....	....	....	....	....	....	....	....	....	....	....	....	....
1960-61	New York Rangers	NHL	53	28	25	53	32	24	56	8	....	....	....	....	....	....	....	....	....	....	....	....	....	....	....	....	....	....
1961-62	New York Rangers	NHL	60	23	15	38	26	14	40	8	....	....	....	....	....	....	....	....	....	....	5	0	0	0	0	0	0	0
1962-63	New York Rangers	NHL	60	37	23	60	44	23	67	8	....	....	....	....	....	....	....	....	....	....	....	....	....	....	....	....	....	....
1963-64	New York Rangers	NHL	68	29	26	55	36	27	63	8	....	....	....	....	....	....	....	....	....	....	....	....	....	....	....	....	....	....
1964-65	New York Rangers	NHL	48	21	15	36	25	15	40	20	....	....	....	....	....	....	....	....	....	....	....	....	....	....	....	....	....	....
	Chicago Black Hawks	NHL	22	5	3	8	6	3	9	2	....	....	....	....	....	....	....	....	....	....	14	1	0	1	2	1	0	0
1965-66	St. Louis Braves	CPHL	37	14	22	36	....	....	....	4	....	....	....	....	....	....	....	....	....	....	5	2	1	3	0	....	....	....
1966-67			OUT OF HOCKEY – RETIRED																									
1967-68	New York Rangers	NHL	36	8	12	20	9	12	21	0	1	0	0	39	20.5	36	7	21	0	8	6	0	0	0	0	0	0	0
	Buffalo Bisons	AHL	22	9	10	19	....	....	....	0	....	....	....	....	....	....	....	....	....	....	....	....	....	....	....	....	....	....
1968-69	St. Louis Blues	NHL	64	17	22	39	18	20	38	8	7	0	1	94	18.1	60	22	24	0	14	11	2	5	7	0	1	0	0
1969-70	St. Louis Blues	NHL	4	1	2	3	1	2	3	0	1	0	0	5	20.0	5	2	5	0	–2	....	....	....	....	....	....	....	....
	Kansas City Blues	CHL	15	5	7	12	....	....	....	4	....	....	....	....	....	....	....	....	....	....	....	....	....	....	....	....	....	....
	NHL Totals		727	279	249	528	336	252	588	88	....	....	....	....	....	....	....	....	....	....	47	6	12	18	7	....	....	....

QJHL First All-Star Team (1952, 1953) • Won Calder Memorial Trophy (1954) • AHL First All-Star Team (1956) • NHL Second All-Star Team (1958) • Won Lady Byng Trophy (1958) • Played in NHL All-Star Game (1958, 1963, 1964)

Traded to **Providence** (AHL) by **NY Rangers** for cash and the return of Earl Johnson (on loan), December 5, 1954. Loaned to **Quebec** (QHL) by **Providence** (AHL) for cash, December 5, 1954. Traded to **NY Rangers** by **Providence** (AHL) for cash, October 2, 1955. Traded to **Chicago** by **NY Rangers** with Don Johns, Wally Chevrier and Billy Taylor for Doug Robinson, Wayne Hillman and John Brenneman, February 4, 1965. Traded to **NY Rangers** by **Chicago** for Paul Shmyr, August 17, 1967. Traded to **St. Louis** by **NY Rangers** with Bill Plager and Robbie Irons for Don Caley and Wayne Rivers, June 13, 1968. Claimed by **Buffalo** (AHL) from **St. Louis** in Reverse Draft, June 12, 1969. Traded to **St. Louis** by **NY Rangers** (Buffalo-AHL) with Norm Beaudin for cash, June 27, 1969.

• HENRY, Dale

Dale T. LW – L. 6', 205 lbs. b: Prince Albert, Sask., 9/24/1964. NY Islanders' 10th, 163rd overall, in 1983.

Season	Club	League	GP	G	A	Pts	AG	AA	APts	PIM	PP	SH	GW	S	%	TGF	PGF	TGA	PGA	+/–	GP	G	A	Pts	PIM	PP	SH	GW
1981-82	Saskatoon Jays	SJHL	STATISTICS NOT AVAILABLE																									
	Saskatoon Blades	WHL	32	5	4	9	....	....	....	50	....	....	....	....	....	....	....	....	....	....	5	0	0	0	0	....	....	....
1982-83	Saskatoon Blades	WHL	63	21	19	40	....	....	....	213	....	....	....	....	....	....	....	....	....	....	3	0	0	0	12	....	....	....
1983-84	Saskatoon Blades	WHL	71	41	36	77	....	....	....	162	....	....	....	....	....	....	....	....	....	....	....	....	....	....	....	....	....	....
1984-85	New York Islanders	NHL	16	2	1	3	2	1	3	19	0	0	1	9	22.2	9	0	8	0	1	....	....	....	....	....	....	....	....
	Springfield Indians	AHL	67	11	20	31	....	....	....	133	....	....	....	....	....	....	....	....	....	....	4	0	0	0	13	....	....	....
1985-86	New York Islanders	NHL	7	1	3	4	1	2	3	15	0	0	0	5	20.0	6	0	6	0	0	....	....	....	....	....	....	....	....
	Springfield Indians	AHL	64	14	26	40	....	....	....	162	....	....	....	....	....	....	....	....	....	....	....	....	....	....	....	....	....	....
1986-87	New York Islanders	NHL	19	3	3	6	3	2	5	46	0	0	0	14	21.4	10	0	8	0	2	8	0	0	0	2	0	0	0
	Springfield Indians	AHL	23	9	14	23	....	....	....	49	....	....	....	....	....	....	....	....	....	....	....	....	....	....	....	....	....	....
1987-88	New York Islanders	NHL	48	5	15	20	4	11	15	115	0	0	0	53	9.4	31	5	18	0	8	6	1	0	1	17	0	1	0
	Springfield Indians	AHL	24	9	12	21	....	....	....	103	....	....	....	....	....	....	....	....	....	....	....	....	....	....	....	....	....	....
1988-89	New York Islanders	NHL	22	2	2	4	2	1	3	66	0	0	0	20	10.0	9	1	12	0	–4	....	....	....	....	....	....	....	....
	Springfield Indians	AHL	50	13	21	34	....	....	....	83	....	....	....	....	....	....	....	....	....	....	....	....	....	....	....	....	....	....
1989-90	New York Islanders	NHL	20	0	2	2	0	1	1	2	0	0	0	6	0.0	3	0	7	0	–4	....	....	....	....	....	....	....	....
	Springfield Indians	AHL	43	17	14	31	....	....	....	68	....	....	....	....	....	....	....	....	....	....	18	3	5	8	33	....	....	....
1990-91	Albany Choppers	IHL	55	16	22	38	....	....	....	87	....	....	....	....	....	....	....	....	....	....	....	....	....	....	....	....	....	....
	Springfield Indians	AHL	20	5	9	14	....	....	....	31	....	....	....	....	....	....	....	....	....	....	18	2	7	9	24	....	....	....
1991-92	Muskegon Lumberjacks	IHL	39	5	17	22	....	....	....	28	....	....	....	....	....	....	....	....	....	....	14	1	4	5	36	....	....	....
1992-93	SIJ Rotterdam	Holland	34	28	27	55	....	....	....	149	....	....	....	....	....	....	....	....	....	....	....	....	....	....	....	....	....	....
1993-94	Milwaukee Admirals	IHL	49	5	11	16	....	....	....	104	....	....	....	....	....	....	....	....	....	....	....	....	....	....	....	....	....	....
1994-95	San Antonio Iguanas	CHL	55	28	36	64	....	....	....	120	....	....	....	....	....	....	....	....	....	....	13	6	8	14	25	....	....	....
1995-96	San Antonio Iguanas	CHL	62	27	40	67	....	....	....	177	....	....	....	....	....	....	....	....	....	....	11	3	8	11	14	....	....	....
1996-97	San Antonio Iguanas	CHL	23	12	19	31	....	....	....	48	....	....	....	....	....	....	....	....	....	....	....	....	....	....	....	....	....	....
1997-98	Shreveport Mudbugs	WPHL	66	34	46	80	....	....	....	91	....	....	....	....	....	....	....	....	....	....	8	3	5	8	29	....	....	....
1998-99	Shreveport Mudbugs	WPHL	64	36	33	69	....	....	....	90	....	....	....	....	....	....	....	....	....	....	12	7	7	14	16	....	....	....
99-2000	Shreveport Mudbugs	WPHL	69	28	42	70	....	....	....	49	....	....	....	....	....	....	....	....	....	....	12	5	5	10	4	....	....	....
	NHL Totals		132	13	26	39	12	18	30	263	0	0	1	107	12.1	68	6	59	0		14	1	0	1	19	0	1	0

• Served as player/assistant coach with San Antonio (CHL) during 1996-97 season. • Played w/RHI's Oklahoma Coyotes in 1995 (24-10-23-33-13).

• HEPPLE, Alan

D – L. 5'9", 200 lbs. b: Blaydon-on-Tyne, England, 8/16/1963. New Jersey's 9th, 169th overall, in 1982.

Season	Club	League	GP	G	A	Pts	AG	AA	APts	PIM	PP	SH	GW	S	%	TGF	PGF	TGA	PGA	+/–	GP	G	A	Pts	PIM	PP	SH	GW
1979-80	Owen Sound Greys	OJHL-B	36	10	18	28	....	....	....	50	....	....	....	....	....	....	....	....	....	....	....	....	....	....	....	....	....	....
1980-81	Ottawa 67's	OMJHL	64	3	13	16	....	....	....	110	....	....	....	....	....	....	....	....	....	....	6	0	1	1	2	....	....	....
1981-82	Ottawa 67's	OHL	66	6	22	28	....	....	....	160	....	....	....	....	....	....	....	....	....	....	17	2	10	12	84	....	....	....
1982-83	Ottawa 67's	OHL	64	10	26	36	....	....	....	168	....	....	....	....	....	....	....	....	....	....	9	2	1	3	24	....	....	....
1983-84	New Jersey Devils	NHL	1	0	0	0	0	0	0	7	0	0	0	0	0.0	0	0	1	0	–1	....	....	....	....	....	....	....	....
	Maine Mariners	AHL	64	4	23	27	....	....	....	117	....	....	....	....	....	....	....	....	....	....	....	....	....	....	....	....	....	....
1984-85	New Jersey Devils	NHL	1	0	0	0	0	0	0	0	0	0	0	2	0.0	0	0	3	1	–2	....	....	....	....	....	....	....	....
	Maine Mariners	AHL	80	7	17	24	....	....	....	125	....	....	....	....	....	....	....	....	....	....	11	0	3	3	30	....	....	....
1985-86	New Jersey Devils	NHL	1	0	0	0	0	0	0	0	0	0	0	0	0.0	2	0	2	0	0	....	....	....	....	....	....	....	....
	Maine Mariners	AHL	69	4	21	25	....	....	....	104	....	....	....	....	....	....	....	....	....	....	5	0	0	0	11	....	....	....
1986-87	Maine Mariners	AHL	74	6	19	25	....	....	....	137	....	....	....	....	....	....	....	....	....	....	....	....	....	....	....	....	....	....
1987-88	Utica Devils	AHL	78	3	16	19	....	....	....	213	....	....	....	....	....	....	....	....	....	....	....	....	....	....	....	....	....	....
1988-89	Newmarket Saints	AHL	72	5	29	34	....	....	....	122	....	....	....	....	....	....	....	....	....	....	5	0	1	1	23	....	....	....
1989-90	Newmarket Saints	AHL	72	6	20	26	....	....	....	90	....	....	....	....	....	....	....	....	....	....	....	....	....	....	....	....	....	....
1990-91	Newmarket Saints	AHL	76	0	18	18	....	....	....	126	....	....	....	....	....	....	....	....	....	....	....	....	....	....	....	....	....	....
1991-92	San Diego Gulls	IHL	82	6	35	41	....	....	....	191	....	....	....	....	....	....	....	....	....	....	4	0	1	1	6	....	....	....
1992-93	San Diego Gulls	IHL	10	0	1	1	....	....	....	27	....	....	....	....	....	....	....	....	....	....	....	....	....	....	....	....	....	....
	Cincinnati Cyclones	IHL	70	7	31	38	....	....	....	201	....	....	....	....	....	....	....	....	....	....	....	....	....	....	....	....	....	....
	NHL Totals		3	0	0	0	0	0	0	7	0	0	0	2	0.0	2	0	6	1		....	....	....	....	....	....	....	....

Signed as a free agent by **Toronto**, June 24, 1988.

• HERBERS, Ian

Ian T. D – L. 6'4", 225 lbs. b: Jasper, Alta., 7/18/1967. Buffalo's 11th, 190th overall, in 1987.

			REGULAR SEASON																		PLAYOFFS							
Season	Club	League	GP	G	A	Pts	AG	AA	APts	PIM	PP	SH	GW	S	%	TGF	PGF	TGA	PGA	+/–	GP	G	A	Pts	PIM	PP	SH	GW
1983-84	Sherwood Park Sabres	AAHA	STATISTICS NOT AVAILABLE																									
1984-85	Kelowna Wings	WHL	68	3	14	17	....	....	....	120	....	....	....	....	....	....	....	....	....	....	6	0	1	1	9	....	....	....
1985-86	Spokane Chiefs	WHL	29	1	6	7	....	....	....	85	....	....	....	....	....	....	....	....	....	....	....	....	....	....	....	....	....	....
	Lethbridge Broncos	WHL	32	1	4	5	....	....	....	109	....	....	....	....	....	....	....	....	....	....	10	1	0	1	37	....	....	....
1986-87	Swift Current Broncos	WHL	72	5	8	13	....	....	....	230	....	....	....	....	....	....	....	....	....	....	4	1	1	2	12	....	....	....
1987-88	Swift Current Broncos	WHL	56	5	14	19	....	....	....	238	....	....	....	....	....	....	....	....	....	....	4	0	2	2	4	....	....	....
1988-89	University of Alberta	CWUAA	47	4	22	26	....	....	....	137	....	....	....	....	....	....	....	....	....	....	....	....	....	....	....	....	....	....
1989-90	University of Alberta	CWUAA	45	5	31	36	....	....	....	83	....	....	....	....	....	....	....	....	....	....	....	....	....	....	....	....	....	....
1990-91	University of Alberta	CWUAA	45	6	24	30	....	....	....	87	....	....	....	....	....	....	....	....	....	....	....	....	....	....	....	....	....	....
1991-92	University of Alberta	CWUAA	43	14	34	48	....	....	....	86	....	....	....	....	....	....	....	....	....	....	....	....	....	....	....	....	....	....
1992-93	Cape Breton Oilers	AHL	77	7	15	22	....	....	....	129	....	....	....	....	....	....	....	....	....	....	10	0	1	1	16	....	....	....
1993-94	**Edmonton Oilers**	**NHL**	**22**	**0**	**2**	**2**	**0**	**2**	**2**	**32**	**0**	**0**	**0**	**16**	**0.0**	**9**	**0**	**22**	**7**	**–6**	....	....	....	....	....	....	....	....
	Cape Breton Oilers	AHL	53	7	16	23	....	....	....	122	....	....	....	....	....	....	....	....	....	....	5	0	3	3	12	....	....	....
1994-95	Cape Breton Oilers	AHL	36	1	11	12	....	....	....	104	....	....	....	....	....	....	....	....	....	....	....	....	....	....	....	....	....	....
	Detroit Vipers	IHL	37	1	5	6	....	....	....	46	....	....	....	....	....	....	....	....	....	....	5	1	1	2	6	....	....	....
1995-96	Detroit Vipers	IHL	73	3	11	14	....	....	....	140	....	....	....	....	....	....	....	....	....	....	12	3	5	8	29	....	....	....
1996-97	Detroit Vipers	IHL	67	3	16	19	....	....	....	129	....	....	....	....	....	....	....	....	....	....	21	0	4	4	34	....	....	....
1997-98	Detroit Vipers	IHL	70	6	6	12	....	....	....	100	....	....	....	....	....	....	....	....	....	....	23	0	3	3	54	....	....	....
1998-99	Detroit Vipers	IHL	82	8	16	24	....	....	....	142	....	....	....	....	....	....	....	....	....	....	11	1	3	4	18	....	....	....
99-2000	**Tampa Bay Lightning**	**NHL**	**37**	**0**	**0**	**0**	**0**	**0**	**0**	**45**	**0**	**0**	**0**	**11**	**0.0**	**12**	**0**	**41**	**17**	**–12**	....	....	....	....	....	....	....	....
	Detroit Vipers	IHL	13	1	4	5	....	....	....	22	....	....	....	....	....	....	....	....	....	....	....	....	....	....	....	....	....	....
	New York Islanders	**NHL**	**6**	**0**	**3**	**3**	**0**	**3**	**3**	**2**	**0**	**0**	**0**	**3**	**0.0**	**7**	**0**	**3**	**2**	**6**	....	....	....	....	....	....	....	....
	NHL Totals		**65**	**0**	**5**	**5**	**0**	**5**	**5**	**79**	**0**	**0**	**0**	**30**	**0.0**	**28**	**0**	**66**	**26**		....	....	....	....	....	....	....	....

CIAU All-Canadian Team (1991, 1992)

Signed as a free agent by **Edmonton**, September 9, 1992. Signed as a free agent by **Tampa Bay**, September, 1999. Traded to **NY Islanders** by **Tampa Bay** for NY Islanders' 7th round choice (later traded back to NY Islanders - NY Islanders selected Ryan Caldwell) in 2000 Entry Draft, March 9, 2000. Selected by **Minnesota** from **NY Islanders** in Expansion Draft, June 23, 2000.

• HEROUX, Yves

RW – R. 5'11", 185 lbs. b: Terrebonne, Que., 4/27/1965. Quebec's 1st, 32nd overall, in 1983.

Season	Club	League	GP	G	A	Pts	AG	AA	APts	PIM	PP	SH	GW	S	%	TGF	PGF	TGA	PGA	+/–	GP	G	A	Pts	PIM	PP	SH	GW
1981-82	Boisbriand Laurentides	QAAA	48	53	53	106	....	....	....	84	....	....	....	....	....	....	....	....	....	....	....	....	....	....	....	....	....	....
1982-83	Chicoutimi Sagueneens	QMJHL	70	41	40	81	....	....	....	44	....	....	....	....	....	....	....	....	....	....	5	0	4	4	8	....	....	....
1983-84	Chicoutimi Sagueneens	QMJHL	56	28	25	53	....	....	....	67	....	....	....	....	....	....	....	....	....	....	....	....	....	....	....	....	....	....
	Fredericton Express	AHL	4	0	0	0	....	....	....	0	....	....	....	....	....	....	....	....	....	....	....	....	....	....	....	....	....	....
1984-85	Chicoutimi Sagueneens	QMJHL	66	42	54	96	....	....	....	123	....	....	....	....	....	....	....	....	....	....	14	5	8	13	16	....	....	....
1985-86	Fredericton Express	AHL	31	12	10	22	....	....	....	42	....	....	....	....	....	....	....	....	....	....	2	0	1	1	7	....	....	....
	Muskegon Lumberjacks	IHL	42	14	8	22	....	....	....	41	....	....	....	....	....	....	....	....	....	....	....	....	....	....	....	....	....	....
1986-87	**Quebec Nordiques**	**NHL**	**1**	**0**	**0**	**0**	**0**	**0**	**0**	**0**	**0**	**0**	**0**	**0**	**0.0**	**0**	**0**	**0**	**0**	**0**	....	....	....	....	....	....	....	....
	Fredericton Express	AHL	37	8	6	14	....	....	....	13	....	....	....	....	....	....	....	....	....	....	....	....	....	....	....	....	....	....
	Muskegon Lumberjacks	IHL	25	6	8	14	....	....	....	31	....	....	....	....	....	....	....	....	....	....	2	0	0	0	0	....	....	....
1987-88	Baltimore Skipjacks	AHL	5	0	2	2	....	....	....	2	....	....	....	....	....	....	....	....	....	....	....	....	....	....	....	....	....	....
1988-89	Flint Spirits	IHL	82	43	42	85	....	....	....	98	....	....	....	....	....	....	....	....	....	....	....	....	....	....	....	....	....	....
1989-90	Canada	Nat-Team	65	13	24	37	....	....	....	63	....	....	....	....	....	....	....	....	....	....	....	....	....	....	....	....	....	....
	Peoria Rivermen	IHL	14	3	2	5	....	....	....	4	....	....	....	....	....	....	....	....	....	....	5	2	2	4	0	....	....	....
1990-91	Albany Choppers	IHL	45	22	18	40	....	....	....	46	....	....	....	....	....	....	....	....	....	....	....	....	....	....	....	....	....	....
	Peoria Rivermen	IHL	33	16	8	24	....	....	....	26	....	....	....	....	....	....	....	....	....	....	17	4	4	8	16	....	....	....
1991-92	Peoria Rivermen	IHL	80	41	36	77	....	....	....	72	....	....	....	....	....	....	....	....	....	....	8	5	1	6	6	....	....	....
1992-93	Kalamazoo Wings	IHL	80	38	30	68	....	....	....	86	....	....	....	....	....	....	....	....	....	....	....	....	....	....	....	....	....	....
1993-94	Kalamazoo Wings	IHL	3	0	2	2	....	....	....	4	....	....	....	....	....	....	....	....	....	....	....	....	....	....	....	....	....	....
	Indianapolis Ice	IHL	74	28	30	58	....	....	....	113	....	....	....	....	....	....	....	....	....	....	....	....	....	....	....	....	....	....
1994-95	Worcester IceCats	AHL	7	3	1	4	....	....	....	2	....	....	....	....	....	....	....	....	....	....	....	....	....	....	....	....	....	....
	Atlanta Knights	IHL	66	31	24	55	....	....	....	56	....	....	....	....	....	....	....	....	....	....	5	2	3	5	6	....	....	....
1995-96	EHC Lustenau	Alpenliga	8	6	9	15	....	....	....	4	....	....	....	....	....	....	....	....	....	....	....	....	....	....	....	....	....	....
	EHC Lustenau	Austria	33	23	31	54	....	....	....	62	....	....	....	....	....	....	....	....	....	....	....	....	....	....	....	....	....	....
1996-97	Augsburger Panther	Germany	20	4	9	13	....	....	....	30	....	....	....	....	....	....	....	....	....	....	....	....	....	....	....	....	....	....
	Schwenningen Wild Wings	Germany	27	11	17	28	....	....	....	34	....	....	....	....	....	....	....	....	....	....	5	0	3	3	12	....	....	....
1997-98	Schwenningen Wild Wings	Germany	50	14	12	26	....	....	....	147	....	....	....	....	....	....	....	....	....	....	....	....	....	....	....	....	....	....
1998-99	HK Olimpija Ljubljana	Alpenliga	12	7	10	17	....	....	....	56	....	....	....	....	....	....	....	....	....	....	....	....	....	....	....	....	....	....
	EC Graz	Austria	STATISTICS NOT AVAILABLE																									
99-2000	Ayr Scottish Eagles	BH-Cup	8	7	3	10	....	....	....	2	....	....	....	....	....	....	....	....	....	....	....	....	....	....	....	....	....	....
	Ayr Scottish Eagles	Britain	37	17	20	37	....	....	....	90	....	....	....	....	....	....	....	....	....	....	7	0	0	0	14	....	....	....
	NHL Totals		**1**	**0**	**0**	**0**	**0**	**0**	**0**	**0**	**0**	**0**	**0**	**0**	**0.0**	**0**	**0**	**0**	**0**		....	....	....	....	....	....	....	....

Signed as a free agent by **St. Louis**, March 13, 1990. Signed as a free agent by **Minnesota**, August 10, 1992. • Played w/ RHI's New Jersey R@R in 1994 (21-24-19-43-77) and 1995 (9-7-3-10-20).

• HERPERGER, Chris

LW – L. 6', 190 lbs. b: Esterhazy, Sask., 2/24/1974. Philadelphia's 9th, 223rd overall, in 1992.

Season	Club	League	GP	G	A	Pts	AG	AA	APts	PIM	PP	SH	GW	S	%	TGF	PGF	TGA	PGA	+/–	GP	G	A	Pts	PIM	PP	SH	GW
1990-91	Swift Current Broncos	WHL	10	0	1	1	....	....	....	5	....	....	....	....	....	....	....	....	....	....	....	....	....	....	....	....	....	....
1991-92	Swift Current Broncos	WHL	72	14	19	33	....	....	....	44	....	....	....	....	....	....	....	....	....	....	8	0	1	1	9	....	....	....
1992-93	Swift Current Broncos	WHL	20	9	7	16	....	....	....	31	....	....	....	....	....	....	....	....	....	....	....	....	....	....	....	....	....	....
	Seattle Thunderbirds	WHL	46	20	11	31	....	....	....	30	....	....	....	....	....	....	....	....	....	....	5	1	1	2	6	....	....	....
1993-94	Seattle Thunderbirds	WHL	71	44	51	95	....	....	....	110	....	....	....	....	....	....	....	....	....	....	9	12	10	22	12	....	....	....
1994-95	Seattle Thunderbirds	WHL	59	49	52	101	....	....	....	106	....	....	....	....	....	....	....	....	....	....	4	4	0	4	6	....	....	....
	Hershey Bears	AHL	4	0	0	0	....	....	....	0	....	....	....	....	....	....	....	....	....	....	....	....	....	....	....	....	....	....
1995-96	Hershey Bears	AHL	46	8	12	20	....	....	....	36	....	....	....	....	....	....	....	....	....	....	....	....	....	....	....	....	....	....
	Baltimore Bandits	AHL	21	2	3	5	....	....	....	17	....	....	....	....	....	....	....	....	....	....	9	2	3	5	6	....	....	....
1996-97	Baltimore Bandits	AHL	67	19	22	41	....	....	....	88	....	....	....	....	....	....	....	....	....	....	3	0	0	0	0	....	....	....
1997-98	Canada	Nat-Team	63	20	30	50	....	....	....	102	....	....	....	....	....	....	....	....	....	....	....	....	....	....	....	....	....	....
1998-99	Indianapolis Ice	IHL	79	19	29	48	....	....	....	81	....	....	....	....	....	....	....	....	....	....	7	0	4	4	4	....	....	....
99-2000	**Chicago Blackhawks**	**NHL**	**9**	**0**	**0**	**0**	**0**	**0**	**0**	**5**	**0**	**0**	**0**	**2**	**0.0**	**1**	**0**	**3**	**0**	**–2**	....	....	....	....	....	....	....	....
	Cleveland Lumberjacks	IHL	73	22	26	48	....	....	....	122	....	....	....	....	....	....	....	....	....	....	9	3	3	6	8	....	....	....
	NHL Totals		**9**	**0**	**0**	**0**	**0**	**0**	**0**	**5**	**0**	**0**	**0**	**2**	**0.0**	**1**	**0**	**3**	**0**		....	....	....	....	....	....	....	....

WHL West Second All-Star Team (1995)

Traded to **Anaheim** by **Philadelphia** with Winnipeg's 7th round choice (previously acquired, Anaheim selected Tony Mohagen) in 1997 Entry Draft for Bob Corkum, February 6, 1996. Signed as a free agent by **Chicago**, September 2, 1998.

• HERR, Matt

Matthew C – L. 6'2", 204 lbs. b: Hackensack, NJ, 5/26/1976. Washington's 4th, 93rd overall, in 1994.

Season	Club	League	GP	G	A	Pts	AG	AA	APts	PIM	PP	SH	GW	S	%	TGF	PGF	TGA	PGA	+/–	GP	G	A	Pts	PIM	PP	SH	GW
1990-91	Hotchkiss Trojans	Hi-School	26	9	5	14	....	....	....	....	....	....	....	....	....	....	....	....	....	....	....	....	....	....	....	....	....	....
1991-92	Hotchkiss Trojans	Hi-School	25	17	16	33	....	....	....	....	....	....	....	....	....	....	....	....	....	....	....	....	....	....	....	....	....	....
1992-93	Hotchkiss Trojans	Hi-School	24	48	30	78	....	....	....	....	....	....	....	....	....	....	....	....	....	....	....	....	....	....	....	....	....	....
1993-94	Hotchkiss Trojans	Hi-School	24	28	19	47	....	....	....	....	....	....	....	....	....	....	....	....	....	....	....	....	....	....	....	....	....	....
1994-95	University of Michigan	CCHA	37	11	8	19	....	....	....	51	....	....	....	....	....	....	....	....	....	....	3	1	0	1	4	....	....	....
1995-96	University of Michigan	CCHA	40	18	13	31	....	....	....	55	....	....	....	....	....	....	....	....	....	....	7	0	4	4	0	....	....	....
	United States	WJC-A	6	1	0	1	....	....	....	0	....	....	....	....	....	....	....	....	....	....	....	....	....	....	....	....	....	....
1996-97	University of Michigan	CCHA	43	29	23	52	....	....	....	67	....	....	....	....	....	....	....	....	....	....	6	2	2	4	8	....	....	....
1997-98	University of Michigan	CCHA	31	14	17	31	....	....	....	62	....	....	....	....	....	....	....	....	....	....	....	....	....	....	....	....	....	....
1998-99	**Washington Capitals**	**NHL**	**30**	**2**	**2**	**4**	**2**	**2**	**4**	**8**	**1**	**0**	**0**	**40**	**5.0**	**6**	**3**	**14**	**4**	**–7**	....	....	....	....	....	....	....	....
	Portland Pirates	AHL	46	15	14	29	....	....	....	29	....	....	....	....	....	....	....	....	....	....	....	....	....	....	....	....	....	....
99-2000	Portland Pirates	AHL	77	22	21	43	....	....	....	51	....	....	....	....	....	....	....	....	....	....	4	1	1	2	4	....	....	....
	NHL Totals		**30**	**2**	**2**	**4**	**2**	**2**	**4**	**8**	**1**	**0**	**0**	**40**	**5.0**	**6**	**3**	**14**	**4**		....	....	....	....	....	....	....	....

• HERTER, Jason

D – R. 6'1", 190 lbs. b: Hafford, Sask., 10/2/1970. Vancouver's 1st, 8th overall, in 1989.

			REGULAR SEASON																		PLAYOFFS							
Season	Club	League	GP	G	A	Pts	AG	AA	APts	PIM	PP	SH	GW	S	%	TGF	PGF	TGA	PGA	+/–	GP	G	A	Pts	PIM	PP	SH	GW
1987-88	Notre Dame Hounds	SJHL	54	5	33	38	....	....	....	152	....	....	....	....	....	....	....	....	....	....	....	....	....	....	....	....	....	....
	Notre Dame Hounds	Cen-Cup	5	1	1	2	....	....	....	0	....	....	....	....	....	....	....	....	....	....	....	....	....	....	....	....	....	....
1988-89	University of North Dakota	WCHA	41	8	24	32	....	....	....	62	....	....	....	....	....	....	....	....	....	....	....	....	....	....	....	....	....	....
1989-90	University of North Dakota	WCHA	38	11	39	50	....	....	....	40	....	....	....	....	....	....	....	....	....	....	....	....	....	....	....	....	....	....
	Canada	WJC-A	7	0	1	1	....	....	....	2	....	....	....	....	....	....	....	....	....	....	....	....	....	....	....	....	....	....
1990-91	University of North Dakota	WCHA	39	11	26	37	....	....	....	52	....	....	....	....	....	....	....	....	....	....	....	....	....	....	....	....	....	....
1991-92	Milwaukee Admirals	IHL	56	7	18	25	....	....	....	34	....	....	....	....	....	....	....	....	....	....	1	0	0	0	2	....	....	....
1992-93	Hamilton Canucks	AHL	70	7	16	23	....	....	....	68	....	....	....	....	....	....	....	....	....	....	....	....	....	....	....	....	....	....
1993-94	Kalamazoo Wings	IHL	68	14	28	42	....	....	....	92	....	....	....	....	....	....	....	....	....	....	5	3	0	3	14	....	....	....
1994-95	Kalamazoo Wings	IHL	60	12	20	32	....	....	....	70	....	....	....	....	....	....	....	....	....	....	16	2	8	10	10	....	....	....
1995-96	**New York Islanders**	**NHL**	**1**	**0**	**1**	**1**	**0**	**1**	**1**	**0**	**0**	**0**	**0**	**1**	**0.0**	**3**	**2**	**0**	**0**	**1**	....	....	....	....	....	....	....	....
	Utah Grizzlies	IHL	74	14	31	45	....	....	....	58	....	....	....	....	....	....	....	....	....	....	20	4	10	14	8	....	....	....
1996-97	Kansas City Blades	IHL	71	9	26	35	....	....	....	62	....	....	....	....	....	....	....	....	....	....	3	0	1	1	0	....	....	....
1997-98	Kansas City Blades	IHL	57	6	19	25	....	....	....	55	....	....	....	....	....	....	....	....	....	....	....	....	....	....	....	....	....	....
	Orlando Solar Bears	IHL	8	1	3	4	....	....	....	8	....	....	....	....	....	....	....	....	....	....	17	5	7	12	20	....	....	....
1998-99	EV Landshut	Germany	46	14	16	30	....	....	....	66	....	....	....	....	....	....	....	....	....	....	3	1	1	2	29	....	....	....
99-2000	Munich Barons	Germany	44	6	14	20	....	....	....	74	....	....	....	....	....	....	....	....	....	....	11	1	3	4	43	....	....	....
	NHL Totals		**1**	**0**	**1**	**1**	**0**	**1**	**1**	**0**	**0**	**0**	**0**	**1**	**0.0**	**3**	**2**	**0**	**0**		....	....	....	....	....	....	....	....

WCHA Second All-Star Team (1990, 1991)

Signed as a free agent by **Dallas**, August 6, 1993. Traded to **NY Islanders** by **Dallas** for cash, September 21, 1995.

• HERVEY, Matt

D – R. 5'11", 205 lbs. b: Whittier, CA, 5/16/1968.

Season	Club	League	GP	G	A	Pts	AG	AA	APts	PIM	PP	SH	GW	S	%	TGF	PGF	TGA	PGA	+/–	GP	G	A	Pts	PIM	PP	SH	GW
1982-83	Richmond Sockeyes	BCJHL	STATISTICS NOT AVAILABLE																									
1983-84	Victoria Cougars	WHL	67	4	19	23	....	....	....	89	....	....	....	....	....	....	....	....	....	....	....	....	....	....	....	....	....	....
1984-85	Victoria Cougars	WHL	14	1	3	4	....	....	....	17	....	....	....	....	....	....	....	....	....	....	....	....	....	....	....	....	....	....
	Lethbridge Broncos	WHL	54	3	9	12	....	....	....	88	....	....	....	....	....	....	....	....	....	....	4	0	1	1	14	....	....	....
1985-86	Lethbridge Broncos	WHL	60	9	17	26	....	....	....	110	....	....	....	....	....	....	....	....	....	....	10	3	4	7	30	....	....	....
1986-87	Richmond Sockeyes	BCJHL	17	4	21	25	....	....	....	99	....	....	....	....	....	....	....	....	....	....	....	....	....	....	....	....	....	....
	Seattle Thunderbirds	WHL	9	4	5	9	....	....	....	59	....	....	....	....	....	....	....	....	....	....	....	....	....	....	....	....	....	....
	Richmond Sockeyes	Cen-Cup	5	2	*6	8	....	....	....	8	....	....	....	....	....	....	....	....	....	....	....	....	....	....	....	....	....	....
1987-88	Moncton Hawks	AHL	69	9	20	29	....	....	....	265	....	....	....	....	....	....	....	....	....	....	....	....	....	....	....	....	....	....
1988-89	**Winnipeg Jets**	**NHL**	**2**	**0**	**0**	**0**	**0**	**0**	**0**	**4**	**0**	**0**	**0**	**1**	**0.0**	**2**	**0**	**0**	**0**	**2**	....	....	....	....	....	....	....	....
	Moncton Hawks	AHL	73	8	28	36	....	....	....	295	....	....	....	....	....	....	....	....	....	....	10	1	2	3	42	....	....	....
1989-90	Moncton Hawks	AHL	47	3	13	16	....	....	....	168	....	....	....	....	....	....	....	....	....	....	....	....	....	....	....	....	....	....
1990-91	Moncton Hawks	AHL	71	4	28	32	....	....	....	132	....	....	....	....	....	....	....	....	....	....	7	0	1	1	23	....	....	....
1991-92	**Boston Bruins**	**NHL**	**16**	**0**	**1**	**1**	**0**	**1**	**1**	**55**	**0**	**0**	**0**	**8**	**0.0**	**5**	**0**	**13**	**3**	**–5**	**5**	**0**	**0**	**0**	**6**	**0**	**0**	**0**
	Maine Mariners	AHL	36	1	7	8	....	....	....	47	....	....	....	....	....	....	....	....	....	....	....	....	....	....	....	....	....	....
1992-93	**Tampa Bay Lightning**	**NHL**	**17**	**0**	**4**	**4**	**0**	**3**	**3**	**38**	**0**	**0**	**0**	**18**	**0.0**	**9**	**3**	**14**	**2**	**–6**	....	....	....	....	....	....	....	....
	Atlanta Knights	IHL	49	12	19	31	....	....	....	122	....	....	....	....	....	....	....	....	....	....	9	0	3	3	19	....	....	....
1993-94	Milwaukee Admirals	IHL	27	6	17	23	....	....	....	51	....	....	....	....	....	....	....	....	....	....	....	....	....	....	....	....	....	....
	NHL Totals		**35**	**0**	**5**	**5**	**0**	**4**	**4**	**97**	**0**	**0**	**0**	**27**	**0.0**	**16**	**3**	**27**	**5**		**5**	**0**	**0**	**0**	**6**	**0**	**0**	**0**

Centennial Cup All-Star Team (1987)

Signed as a free agent by **Winnipeg**, September 27, 1988. Signed as a free agent by **Boston**, August 15, 1991. Traded to **Tampa Bay** by **Boston** with Ken Hodge for Darin Kimble and future considerations, September 4, 1992.

• HESS, Bob

Robert George D – L. 5'11", 180 lbs. b: Middleton, N.S., 5/19/1955. St. Louis' 1st, 26th overall, in 1974.

Season	Club	League	GP	G	A	Pts	AG	AA	APts	PIM	PP	SH	GW	S	%	TGF	PGF	TGA	PGA	+/–	GP	G	A	Pts	PIM	PP	SH	GW
1971-72	Chilliwack Chiefs	BCJHL	STATISTICS NOT AVAILABLE																									
	New Westminster Bruins	WCJHL	5	0	0	0	....	....	....	0	....	....	....	....	....	....	....	....	....	....	1	0	0	0	0	....	....	....
1972-73	New Westminster Bruins	WCJHL	67	6	13	19	....	....	....	29	....	....	....	....	....	....	....	....	....	....	5	0	3	3	4	....	....	....
1973-74	New Westminster Bruins	WCJHL	68	10	30	40	....	....	....	104	....	....	....	....	....	....	....	....	....	....	11	3	3	6	6	....	....	....
1974-75	**St. Louis Blues**	**NHL**	**76**	**9**	**30**	**39**	**8**	**22**	**30**	**58**	**4**	**0**	**1**	**110**	**8.2**	**98**	**32**	**71**	**12**	**7**	**1**	**0**	**0**	**0**	**2**	**0**	**0**	**0**
1975-76	**St. Louis Blues**	**NHL**	**78**	**9**	**23**	**32**	**8**	**17**	**25**	**58**	**2**	**2**	**2**	**117**	**7.7**	**106**	**27**	**98**	**22**	**3**	**1**	**0**	**1**	**1**	**0**	**0**	**0**	**0**
1976-77	Kansas City Blues	CHL	10	1	8	9	....	....	....	16	....	....	....	....	....	....	....	....	....	....	....	....	....	....	....	....	....	....
	St. Louis Blues	**NHL**	**53**	**4**	**18**	**22**	**4**	**14**	**18**	**14**	**1**	**0**	**0**	**88**	**4.5**	**55**	**15**	**44**	**2**	**–2**	**1**	**0**	**0**	**0**	**0**	**0**	**0**	**0**
1977-78	**St. Louis Blues**	**NHL**	**55**	**2**	**12**	**14**	**2**	**9**	**11**	**16**	**0**	**0**	**0**	**101**	**2.0**	**48**	**7**	**45**	**4**	**0**	....	....	....	....	....	....	....	....
	Salt Lake Golden Eagles	CHL	7	1	3	4	....	....	....	4	....	....	....	....	....	....	....	....	....	....	....	....	....	....	....	....	....	....
1978-79	**St. Louis Blues**	**NHL**	**27**	**3**	**4**	**7**	**3**	**3**	**6**	**14**	**0**	**0**	**0**	**42**	**7.1**	**21**	**6**	**38**	**3**	**–20**	....	....	....	....	....	....	....	....
	Salt Lake Golden Eagles	CHL	45	19	29	48	....	....	....	22	....	....	....	....	....	....	....	....	....	....	9	4	6	10	9	....	....	....
1979-80	Salt Lake Golden Eagles	CHL	79	32	42	74	....	....	....	71	....	....	....	....	....	....	....	....	....	....	13	0	8	8	14	....	....	....
1980-81	**St. Louis Blues**	**NHL**	**4**	**0**	**0**	**0**	**0**	**0**	**0**	**4**	**0**	**0**	**0**	**3**	**0.0**	**4**	**0**	**8**	**1**	**–3**	....	....	....	....	....	....	....	....
	Rochester Americans	AHL	70	17	58	75	....	....	....	95	....	....	....	....	....	....	....	....	....	....	....	....	....	....	....	....	....	....
	Buffalo Sabres	**NHL**	**....**	**....**	**....**	**....**	....	....	....	....	....	....	....	....	....	....	....	....	....	....	**1**	**1**	**0**	**1**	**0**	**0**	**0**	**0**
1981-82	**Buffalo Sabres**	**NHL**	**33**	**0**	**8**	**8**	**0**	**5**	**5**	**14**	**0**	**0**	**0**	**33**	**0.0**	**40**	**10**	**28**	**4**	**6**	....	....	....	....	....	....	....	....
	Rochester Americans	AHL	22	6	13	19	....	....	....	10	....	....	....	....	....	....	....	....	....	....	9	1	3	4	2	....	....	....
1982-83	HC Lugano	Switz.	38	14	17	31	....	....	....	....	....	....	....	....	....	....	....	....	....	....	....	....	....	....	....	....	....	....
	Maine Mariners	AHL	13	5	3	8	....	....	....	10	....	....	....	....	....	....	....	....	....	....	17	0	9	9	15	....	....	....
1983-84	EHC Kloten	Switz.	23	6	10	16	....	....	....	....	....	....	....	....	....	....	....	....	....	....	....	....	....	....	....	....	....	....
	Hartford Whalers	**NHL**	**3**	**0**	**0**	**0**	**0**	**0**	**0**	**0**	**0**	**0**	**0**	**3**	**0.0**	**2**	**0**	**1**	**0**	**1**	....	....	....	....	....	....	....	....
	Indianapolis Checkers	CHL	9	2	6	8	....	....	....	10	....	....	....	....	....	....	....	....	....	....	9	2	4	6	6	....	....	....
1984-85	Salt Lake Golden Eagles	IHL	48	9	21	30	....	....	....	25	....	....	....	....	....	....	....	....	....	....	7	0	7	7	2	....	....	....
	NHL Totals		**329**	**27**	**95**	**122**	**25**	**70**	**95**	**178**	**7**	**2**	**3**	**497**	**5.4**	**374**	**97**	**333**	**48**		**4**	**1**	**1**	**2**	**2**	**0**	**0**	**0**

AHL First All-Star Team (1981)

Traded to **Buffalo** by **St. Louis** with St. Louis' 4th round choice (Anders Wickberg) in 1981 Entry Draft for Bill Stewart, October 30, 1980. Signed as a free agent by **Hartford**, December, 1984.

• HEWARD, Jamie

D – R. 6'2", 207 lbs. b: Regina, Sask., 3/30/1971. Pittsburgh's 1st, 16th overall, in 1989.

Season	Club	League	GP	G	A	Pts	AG	AA	APts	PIM	PP	SH	GW	S	%	TGF	PGF	TGA	PGA	+/–	GP	G	A	Pts	PIM	PP	SH	GW
1987-88	Regina Pats	WHL	68	10	17	27	....	....	....	17	....	....	....	....	....	....	....	....	....	....	4	1	1	2	2	....	....	....
1988-89	Regina Pats	WHL	52	31	28	59	....	....	....	29	....	....	....	....	....	....	....	....	....	....	....	....	....	....	....	....	....	....
1989-90	Regina Pats	WHL	72	14	44	58	....	....	....	42	....	....	....	....	....	....	....	....	....	....	11	2	2	4	10	....	....	....
1990-91	Regina Pats	WHL	71	23	61	84	....	....	....	41	....	....	....	....	....	....	....	....	....	....	8	2	9	11	6	....	....	....
1991-92	Muskegon Lumberjacks	IHL	54	6	21	27	....	....	....	37	....	....	....	....	....	....	....	....	....	....	14	1	4	5	4	....	....	....
1992-93	Cleveland Lumberjacks	IHL	58	9	18	27	....	....	....	64	....	....	....	....	....	....	....	....	....	....	....	....	....	....	....	....	....	....
1993-94	Cleveland Lumberjacks	IHL	73	8	16	24	....	....	....	72	....	....	....	....	....	....	....	....	....	....	....	....	....	....	....	....	....	....
1994-95	Canada	Nat-Team	51	11	35	46	....	....	....	32	....	....	....	....	....	....	....	....	....	....	....	....	....	....	....	....	....	....
	Canada	WC-A	8	0	5	5	....	....	....	6	....	....	....	....	....	....	....	....	....	....	....	....	....	....	....	....	....	....
1995-96	**Toronto Maple Leafs**	**NHL**	**5**	**0**	**0**	**0**	**0**	**0**	**0**	**0**	**0**	**0**	**0**	**8**	**0.0**	**0**	**0**	**1**	**0**	**–1**	....	....	....	....	....	....	....	....
	St. John's Maple Leafs	AHL	73	22	34	56	....	....	....	33	....	....	....	....	....	....	....	....	....	....	3	1	1	2	6	....	....	....
1996-97	**Toronto Maple Leafs**	**NHL**	**20**	**1**	**4**	**5**	**1**	**4**	**5**	**6**	**0**	**0**	**0**	**23**	**4.3**	**12**	**5**	**13**	**0**	**–6**	....	....	....	....	....	....	....	....
	St. John's Maple Leafs	AHL	27	8	19	27	....	....	....	26	....	....	....	....	....	....	....	....	....	....	9	1	3	4	6	....	....	....
1997-98	Philadelphia Phantoms	AHL	72	17	48	65	....	....	....	54	....	....	....	....	....	....	....	....	....	....	20	3	16	19	10	....	....	....
1998-99	**Nashville Predators**	**NHL**	**63**	**6**	**12**	**18**	**7**	**12**	**19**	**44**	**4**	**0**	**1**	**124**	**4.8**	**36**	**17**	**48**	**5**	**–24**	....	....	....	....	....	....	....	....
99-2000	**New York Islanders**	**NHL**	**54**	**6**	**11**	**17**	**7**	**10**	**17**	**26**	**2**	**0**	**1**	**92**	**6.5**	**46**	**14**	**49**	**8**	**–9**	....	....	....	....	....	....	....	....
	NHL Totals		**142**	**13**	**27**	**40**	**15**	**26**	**41**	**76**	**6**	**0**	**2**	**247**	**5.3**	**94**	**36**	**111**	**13**		....	....	....	....	....	....	....	....

WHL East First All-Star Team (1991) • AHL First All-Star Team (1996, 1998) • Won Eddie Shore Award (Outstanding Defenseman - AHL) (1998)

Signed as a free agent by **Toronto**, May 4, 1995. Signed as a free agent by **Philadelphia**, July 31, 1997. Signed as a free agent by **Nashville**, August 10, 1998. Signed as a free agent by **NY Islanders**, July 27, 1999. Claimed on waivers by **Columbus** from **NY Islanders**, May 26, 2000.

• HEXTALL, Bryan Jr.

Bryan Lee C – L. 5'11", 185 lbs. b: Winnipeg, Man., 5/23/1941.

			REGULAR SEASON																		PLAYOFFS							
Season	Club	League	GP	G	A	Pts	AG	AA	APts	PIM	PP	SH	GW	S	%	TGF	PGF	TGA	PGA	+/–	GP	G	A	Pts	PIM	PP	SH	GW
1958-59	Brandon Wheat Kings	MJHL	30	19	23	42				15											3	1	1	2	0			
1959-60	Brandon Wheat Kings	MJHL	29	22	25	47				33											22	*15	14	29	12			
1960-61	Brandon Wheat Kings	MJHL	31	22	35	57				54											9	7	7	14	10			
	Winnipeg Rangers	Mem-Cup	5	4	1	5				15																		
	Edmonton Oil Kings	Mem-Cup	5	2	2	4				0																		
1961-62	Kitchener-Waterloo Beavers	EPHL	56	22	23	45				48											7	1	0	1	0			
1962-63	**New York Rangers**	**NHL**	**21**	**0**	**2**	**2**	**0**	**2**	**2**	**10**																		
	Baltimore Clippers	AHL	50	8	14	22				26																		
1963-64	Baltimore Clippers	AHL	54	10	12	22				39																		
1964-65	Baltimore Clippers	AHL	71	13	30	43				46											5	0	2	2	6			
1965-66	Vancouver Canucks	WHL	41	8	20	28				37											7	3	1	4	23			
1966-67	Vancouver Canucks	WHL	61	14	42	56				60											8	3	5	8	11			
1967-68	Rochester Americans	AHL	72	24	47	71				134											11	4	10	14	13			
1968-69	Vancouver Canucks	WHL	70	22	56	78				104											8	4	7	11	22			
1969-70	**Pittsburgh Penguins**	**NHL**	**66**	**12**	**19**	**31**	**13**	**18**	**31**	**87**	**2**	**0**	**2**	**132**	**9.1**	**49**	**12**	**67**	**8**	**–22**	**10**	**0**	**1**	**1**	**34**	**0**	**0**	**0**
1970-71	**Pittsburgh Penguins**	**NHL**	**76**	**16**	**32**	**48**	**16**	**27**	**43**	**133**	**6**	**0**	**2**	**181**	**8.8**	**74**	**32**	**65**	**0**	**–23**								
1971-72	**Pittsburgh Penguins**	**NHL**	**78**	**20**	**24**	**44**	**20**	**21**	**41**	**126**	**5**	**0**	**5**	**145**	**13.8**	**60**	**14**	**72**	**0**	**–26**	**4**	**0**	**2**	**2**	**9**	**0**	**0**	**0**
1972-73	**Pittsburgh Penguins**	**NHL**	**78**	**21**	**33**	**54**	**20**	**26**	**46**	**113**	**6**	**0**	**3**	**169**	**12.4**	**78**	**22**	**79**	**0**	**–23**								
1973-74	**Pittsburgh Penguins**	**NHL**	**37**	**2**	**7**	**9**	**2**	**6**	**8**	**39**	**2**	**0**	**1**	**50**	**4.0**	**11**	**3**	**21**	**0**	**–13**								
	Atlanta Flames	**NHL**	**40**	**2**	**4**	**6**	**2**	**3**	**5**	**55**	**0**	**0**	**0**	**39**	**5.1**	**11**	**1**	**29**	**19**	**0**	**4**	**0**	**1**	**1**	**16**	**0**	**0**	**0**
1974-75	**Atlanta Flames**	**NHL**	**74**	**18**	**16**	**34**	**16**	**12**	**28**	**62**	**3**	**1**	**2**	**120**	**15.0**	**52**	**14**	**78**	**27**	**–13**								
1975-76	**Detroit Red Wings**	**NHL**	**21**	**0**	**4**	**4**	**0**	**3**	**3**	**29**	**0**	**0**	**0**	**17**	**0.0**	**8**	**3**	**22**	**13**	**–4**								
	Minnesota North Stars	**NHL**	**58**	**8**	**20**	**28**	**7**	**15**	**22**	**84**	**3**	**1**	**1**	**89**	**9.0**	**34**	**13**	**47**	**10**	**–16**								
1976-77			DID NOT PLAY																									
1977-78	Brandon Olympics	CSHL	30	7	34	41				45																		
	NHL Totals		**549**	**99**	**161**	**260**	**96**	**133**	**229**	**738**											**18**	**0**	**4**	**4**	**59**			

• Son of Bryan Sr. • Brother of Dennis • Father of Ron

• Loaned to **Winnipeg** (MJHL) and **Edmonton** (CAHL) by **Brandon** (MJHL) for Memorial Cup playoffs, March, 1961. Claimed by **Oakland** from **NY Rangers** in Expansion Draft, June 6, 1967. Traded to **Toronto** (Rochester-AHL) by **Oakland** with J.P. Parise for Gerry Ehman, October 12, 1967. Rights transferred to **Vancouver** (WHL) after WHL club purchased **Rochester** (AHL) franchise, August 13, 1968. Traded to **Pittsburgh** by **Vancouver** (WHL) for Paul Andrea, John Arbour and the loan of Andy Bathgate for the 1969-70 season, May 20, 1969. Claimed on waivers by **Atlanta** from **Pittsburgh**, January 6, 1974. Traded to **Detroit** by **Atlanta** for Dave Kryskow, June 5, 1975. Traded to **Minnesota** by **Detroit** for Rick Chinnick, November 21, 1975.

• HEXTALL, Dennis

Dennis Harold LW – L. 5'11", 175 lbs. b: Poplar Point, Man., 4/17/1943.

Season	Club	League	GP	G	A	Pts	AG	AA	APts	PIM	PP	SH	GW	S	%	TGF	PGF	TGA	PGA	+/–	GP	G	A	Pts	PIM	PP	SH	GW
1961-62	Brandon Wheat Kings	MJHL	39	11	18	29				24											9	0	3	3	4			
	Brandon Wheat Kings	Mem-Cup	11	2	3	5				9																		
1962-63	Brandon Wheat Kings	MJHL	39	21	*46	67				17											19	*16	10	26	12			
	Brandon Wheat Kings	Mem-Cup	9	5	6	11				8																		
1963-64	University of North Dakota	WCHA	DID NOT PLAY – FRESHMAN																									
1964-65	University of North Dakota	WCHA	33	17	36	53				33																		
1965-66	University of North Dakota	WCHA	30	19	29	48				30																		
1966-67	Knoxville Knights	EHL	61	20	56	76				202											4	3	2	5	21			
1967-68	Omaha Knights	CPHL	10	0	2	2				9																		
	Buffalo Bisons	AHL	51	15	33	48				114											5	1	5	6	12			
	New York Rangers	**NHL**																			**2**	**0**	**0**	**0**	**0**	**0**	**0**	**0**
1968-69	**New York Rangers**	**NHL**	**13**	**1**	**4**	**5**	**1**	**4**	**5**	**25**	**0**	**0**	**0**	**16**	**6.3**	**8**	**1**	**6**	**0**	**1**								
	Buffalo Bisons	AHL	60	21	44	65				179											6	1	3	4	6			
1969-70	**Los Angeles Kings**	**NHL**	**28**	**5**	**7**	**12**	**5**	**7**	**12**	**40**	**2**	**0**	**0**	**34**	**14.7**	**18**	**5**	**37**	**1**	**–23**								
	Springfield Indians	AHL	10	5	8	13				52																		
	Montreal Voyageurs	AHL	29	10	19	29				126											8	2	5	7	29			
1970-71	**California Golden Seals**	**NHL**	**78**	**21**	**31**	**52**	**21**	**26**	**47**	**217**	**1**	**0**	**3**	**153**	**13.7**	**85**	**12**	**103**	**10**	**–20**								
1971-72	**Minnesota North Stars**	**NHL**	**33**	**6**	**10**	**16**	**6**	**9**	**15**	**49**	**3**	**0**	**1**	**46**	**13.0**	**23**	**7**	**15**	**0**	**1**	**7**	**0**	**2**	**2**	**19**	**0**	**0**	**0**
	Cleveland Barons	AHL	5	1	1	2				18																		
1972-73	**Minnesota North Stars**	**NHL**	**78**	**30**	**52**	**82**	**28**	**41**	**69**	**140**	**3**	**0**	**4**	**140**	**21.4**	**109**	**19**	**64**	**3**	**29**	**6**	**2**	**0**	**2**	**16**	**0**	**0**	**2**
1973-74	**Minnesota North Stars**	**NHL**	**78**	**20**	**62**	**82**	**19**	**51**	**70**	**138**	**2**	**1**	**3**	**152**	**13.2**	**117**	**27**	**98**	**12**	**4**								
1974-75	**Minnesota North Stars**	**NHL**	**80**	**17**	**57**	**74**	**15**	**43**	**58**	**147**	**4**	**0**	**2**	**161**	**10.6**	**102**	**30**	**138**	**22**	**–44**								
1975-76	**Minnesota North Stars**	**NHL**	**59**	**11**	**35**	**46**	**10**	**26**	**36**	**93**	**2**	**0**	**0**	**93**	**11.8**	**55**	**17**	**72**	**5**	**–29**								
	Detroit Red Wings	**NHL**	**17**	**5**	**9**	**14**	**4**	**7**	**11**	**71**	**0**	**0**	**1**	**32**	**15.6**	**25**	**7**	**24**	**8**	**2**								
1976-77	**Detroit Red Wings**	**NHL**	**78**	**14**	**32**	**46**	**13**	**25**	**38**	**158**	**5**	**0**	**1**	**129**	**10.9**	**62**	**12**	**109**	**24**	**–35**								
1977-78	**Detroit Red Wings**	**NHL**	**78**	**16**	**33**	**49**	**15**	**26**	**41**	**195**	**2**	**2**	**3**	**89**	**18.0**	**61**	**11**	**89**	**34**	**–5**	**7**	**1**	**1**	**2**	**10**	**0**	**1**	**1**
1978-79	**Detroit Red Wings**	**NHL**	**20**	**4**	**8**	**12**	**3**	**6**	**9**	**33**	**2**	**0**	**0**	**16**	**25.0**	**17**	**4**	**14**	**4**	**3**								
	Washington Capitals	**NHL**	**26**	**2**	**9**	**11**	**2**	**7**	**9**	**43**	**0**	**0**	**0**	**22**	**9.1**	**17**	**4**	**35**	**9**	**–13**								
1979-80	**Washington Capitals**	**NHL**	**15**	**1**	**1**	**2**	**1**	**1**	**2**	**49**	**0**	**0**	**0**	**17**	**5.9**	**5**	**0**	**15**	**5**	**–5**								
	NHL Totals		**681**	**153**	**350**	**503**	**143**	**279**	**422**	**1398**	**26**	**3**	**18**	**1100**	**13.9**	**704**	**156**	**819**	**137**		**22**	**3**	**3**	**6**	**45**	**0**	**1**	**3**

• Son of Bryan Sr. • Brother of Bryan Jr. • WCHA Second All-Star Team (1965) • WCHA First All-Star Team (1966) • AHL Second All-Star Team (1969) • Played in NHL All-Star Game (1974, 1975)

Traded to **LA Kings** by **NY Rangers** with Leon Rochefort for Real Lemieux, June 9, 1969. Traded to **Montreal** by **LA Kings** for Dick Duff, January 23, 1970. Traded to **California** by **Montreal** for cash, May 22, 1970. Traded to **Minnesota** by **California** for Joey Johnston and Walt McKechnie, May 20, 1971. Traded to **Detroit** by **Minnesota** for Bill Hogaboam and LA Kings' 2nd round choice (previously acquired, Minnesota selected Jim Roberts) in 1976 Amateur Draft, February 27, 1976. Signed as a free agent by **Washington**, February 7, 1979.

• HICKE, Bill

William Lawrence RW – L. 5'8", 164 lbs. b: Regina, Sask., 3/31/1938.

Season	Club	League	GP	G	A	Pts	AG	AA	APts	PIM	PP	SH	GW	S	%	TGF	PGF	TGA	PGA	+/–	GP	G	A	Pts	PIM	PP	SH	GW
1954-55	Regina Pats	SJHL	8	3	9	12				7											14	6	8	14	4			
	Regina Pats	Mem-Cup	15	5	13	18				8																		
1955-56	Regina Pats	SJHL	36	33	9	42				51											10	6	8	14	10			
	Regina Pats	Mem-Cup	19	11	18	29				44																		
1956-57	Regina Pats	SJHL	53	52	48	100				94											7	5	5	10	14			
1957-58	Regina Pats	SJHL	49	*54	43	*97				144											12	9	10	19	20			
	Regina Pats	Mem-Cup	16	*18	8	26				31																		
1958-59	Rochester Americans	AHL	69	41	56	*97				41											5	1	1	2	12			
♦	**Montreal Canadiens**	**NHL**																			**1**	**0**	**0**	**0**	**0**	**0**	**0**	**0**
1959-60♦	**Montreal Canadiens**	**NHL**	**43**	**3**	**10**	**13**	**3**	**10**	**13**	**17**											**7**	**1**	**2**	**3**	**0**	**0**	**0**	**1**
	Rochester Americans	AHL	14	8	5	13				22																		
1960-61	**Montreal Canadiens**	**NHL**	**70**	**18**	**27**	**45**	**21**	**26**	**47**	**31**											**5**	**2**	**0**	**2**	**19**	**0**	**0**	**1**
1961-62	**Montreal Canadiens**	**NHL**	**70**	**20**	**31**	**51**	**23**	**30**	**53**	**42**											**6**	**0**	**2**	**2**	**14**	**0**	**0**	**0**
1962-63	**Montreal Canadiens**	**NHL**	**70**	**17**	**22**	**39**	**20**	**22**	**42**	**39**											**5**	**0**	**0**	**0**	**0**	**0**	**0**	**0**
1963-64	**Montreal Canadiens**	**NHL**	**48**	**11**	**9**	**20**	**14**	**9**	**23**	**41**											**7**	**0**	**2**	**2**	**2**	**0**	**0**	**0**
1964-65	**Montreal Canadiens**	**NHL**	**17**	**0**	**1**	**1**	**0**	**1**	**1**	**6**																		
	Cleveland Barons	AHL	6	3	2	5				2																		
	New York Rangers	**NHL**	**40**	**6**	**11**	**17**	**7**	**11**	**18**	**26**																		
1965-66	**New York Rangers**	**NHL**	**49**	**9**	**18**	**27**	**10**	**17**	**27**	**21**																		
	Minnesota Rangers	CPHL	3	2	0	2				4																		
1966-67	**New York Rangers**	**NHL**	**48**	**3**	**4**	**7**	**3**	**4**	**7**	**11**																		
	Baltimore Clippers	AHL	18	14	14	28				15											9	6	*8	*14	23			
1967-68	**Oakland Seals**	**NHL**	**52**	**21**	**19**	**40**	**24**	**19**	**43**	**32**	**12**	**0**	**4**	**142**	**14.8**	**50**	**23**	**51**	**2**	**–22**								
1968-69	**Oakland Seals**	**NHL**	**67**	**25**	**36**	**61**	**27**	**32**	**59**	**68**	**4**	**0**	**3**	**171**	**14.6**	**70**	**16**	**67**	**2**	**–11**	**7**	**0**	**3**	**3**	**4**	**0**	**0**	**0**
1969-70	**Oakland Seals**	**NHL**	**69**	**15**	**29**	**44**	**16**	**27**	**43**	**14**	**5**	**0**	**2**	**139**	**10.8**	**67**	**22**	**56**	**1**	**–10**	**4**	**0**	**1**	**1**	**2**	**0**	**0**	**0**
1970-71	**California Golden Seals**	**NHL**	**74**	**18**	**17**	**35**	**18**	**14**	**32**	**41**	**4**	**0**	**1**	**138**	**13.0**	**51**	**11**	**70**	**1**	**–29**								

			REGULAR SEASON																		PLAYOFFS							
Season	Club	League	GP	G	A	Pts	AG	AA	APts	PIM	PP	SH	GW	S	%	TGF	PGF	TGA	PGA	+/–	GP	G	A	Pts	PIM	PP	SH	GW
1971-72	**Pittsburgh Penguins**	**NHL**	**12**	**2**	**0**	**2**	**2**	**0**	**2**	**6**	**1**	**0**	**0**	**19**	**10.5**	**3**	**1**	**8**	**0**	**–6**	....	....	....	....	....	....	....	....
	Tidewater Red Wings	AHL	16	4	2	6	....	....	....	6	....	....	....	....	....	....	....	....	....	....	....	....	....	....	....	....	....	....
	Fort Worth Wings	CHL	34	9	10	19	....	....	....	51	....	....	....	....	....	....	....	....	....	....	7	0	5	5	12	....	....	....
1972-73	Alberta Oilers	WHA	73	14	24	38	....	....	....	20	....	....	....	....	....	....	....	....	....	....	....	....	....	....	....	....	....	....
	NHL Totals		**729**	**168**	**234**	**402**	**188**	**222**	**410**	**395**	....	....	....	....	....	....	....	....	....	....	**42**	**3**	**10**	**13**	**41**	....	....	....
	Other Major League Totals		73	14	24	38	....	....	....	20	....	....	....	....	....	....	....	....	....	....	....	....	....	....	....	....	....	....

• Brother of Ernie • AHL First All-Star Team (1959) • Won Dudley "Red" Garrett Memorial Award (Top Rookie - AHL) (1959) • Won John B. Sollenberger Trophy (Top Scorer - AHL) (1959) • Shared Les Cunningham Award (MVP - AHL) with Rudy Migay (1959) • Played in NHL All-Star Game (1959, 1960, 1969)

Traded to **NY Rangers** by **Montreal** with the loan of Jean-Guy Morissette for remainder of 1964-65 season for Dick Duff and Dave McComb, December 22, 1964. Claimed by **Oakland** from **NY Rangers** in Expansion Draft, June 6, 1967. Traded to **Pittsburgh** by **California** for cash, September 7, 1971. Traded to **Detroit** by **Pittsburgh** for cash, November 22, 1971. Signed as a free agent by **Alberta** (WHA), September, 1972.

• HICKE, Ernie

Ernest Allen LW – L. 5'11", 185 lbs. b: Regina, Sask., 11/7/1947.

Season	Club	League	GP	G	A	Pts	AG	AA	APts	PIM	PP	SH	GW	S	%	TGF	PGF	TGA	PGA	+/–	GP	G	A	Pts	PIM	PP	SH	GW
1963-64	Regina Pats	SJHL	41	10	16	26	....	....	....	22	....	....	....	....	....	....	....	....	....	....	19	11	11	22	44	....	....	....
1964-65	Regina Pats	SJHL	48	12	22	34	....	....	....	95	....	....	....	....	....	....	....	....	....	....	12	0	5	5	28	....	....	....
	Regina Pats	Mem-Cup	10	3	2	5	....	....	....	18	....	....	....	....	....	....	....	....	....	....	....	....	....	....	....	....	....	....
1965-66	Regina Pats	SJHL	51	39	62	101	....	....	....	151	....	....	....	....	....	....	....	....	....	....	5	3	3	6	10	....	....	....
1966-67	Regina Pats	CMJHL	55	37	66	103	....	....	....	184	....	....	....	....	....	....	....	....	....	....	16	7	12	19	60	....	....	....
1967-68	Houston Apollos	CPHL	67	16	20	36	....	....	....	142	....	....	....	....	....	....	....	....	....	....	....	....	....	....	....	....	....	....
1968-69	Houston Apollos	CPHL	72	29	43	72	....	....	....	146	....	....	....	....	....	....	....	....	....	....	3	0	0	0	7	....	....	....
1969-70	Salt Lake Golden Eagles	WHL	65	29	26	55	....	....	....	83	....	....	....	....	....	....	....	....	....	....	....	....	....	....	....	....	....	....
1970-71	**California Golden Seals**	**NHL**	**78**	**22**	**25**	**47**	**22**	**21**	**43**	**62**	**7**	**0**	**1**	**202**	**10.9**	**68**	**17**	**87**	**0**	**–36**	....	....	....	....	....	....	....	....
1971-72	**California Golden Seals**	**NHL**	**68**	**11**	**12**	**23**	**11**	**10**	**21**	**55**	**3**	**0**	**2**	**111**	**9.9**	**44**	**13**	**46**	**2**	**–13**	....	....	....	....	....	....	....	....
1972-73	**Atlanta Flames**	**NHL**	**58**	**14**	**23**	**37**	**13**	**18**	**31**	**37**	**2**	**0**	**2**	**120**	**11.7**	**51**	**19**	**34**	**0**	**–2**	....	....	....	....	....	....	....	....
	New York Islanders	**NHL**	**1**	**0**	**0**	**0**	**0**	**0**	**0**	**0**	**0**	**0**	**0**	**2**	**0.0**	**1**	**1**	**0**	**0**	**0**	....	....	....	....	....	....	....	....
1973-74	**New York Islanders**	**NHL**	**55**	**6**	**7**	**13**	**6**	**6**	**12**	**26**	**2**	**0**	**1**	**67**	**9.0**	**21**	**5**	**35**	**0**	**–19**	....	....	....	....	....	....	....	....
1974-75	**New York Islanders**	**NHL**	**20**	**2**	**6**	**8**	**2**	**4**	**6**	**40**	**0**	**0**	**0**	**17**	**11.8**	**15**	**1**	**7**	**0**	**7**	....	....	....	....	....	....	....	....
	Minnesota North Stars	**NHL**	**42**	**15**	**13**	**28**	**13**	**10**	**23**	**51**	**7**	**0**	**1**	**114**	**13.2**	**43**	**11**	**67**	**9**	**–26**	....	....	....	....	....	....	....	....
1975-76	**Minnesota North Stars**	**NHL**	**80**	**23**	**19**	**42**	**20**	**14**	**34**	**77**	**6**	**0**	**4**	**185**	**12.4**	**60**	**16**	**75**	**0**	**–31**	....	....	....	....	....	....	....	....
1976-77	**Minnesota North Stars**	**NHL**	**77**	**30**	**20**	**50**	**27**	**15**	**42**	**41**	**10**	**0**	**5**	**186**	**16.1**	**79**	**31**	**80**	**0**	**–32**	**2**	**1**	**0**	**1**	**0**	**0**	**0**	**0**
1977-78	**Los Angeles Kings**	**NHL**	**41**	**9**	**15**	**24**	**8**	**12**	**20**	**18**	**1**	**0**	**2**	**60**	**15.0**	**37**	**4**	**26**	**0**	**7**	....	....	....	....	....	....	....	....
	Binghamton Dusters	AHL	21	6	18	24	....	....	....	6	....	....	....	....	....	....	....	....	....	....	....	....	....	....	....	....	....	....
	Springfield Indians	AHL	7	0	1	1	....	....	....	2	....	....	....	....	....	....	....	....	....	....	....	....	....	....	....	....	....	....
1978-79	Dallas Black Hawks	CHL	39	8	24	32	....	....	....	69	....	....	....	....	....	....	....	....	....	....	....	....	....	....	....	....	....	....
1979-80	Dallas Black Hawks	CHL	72	11	26	37	....	....	....	67	....	....	....	....	....	....	....	....	....	....	....	....	....	....	....	....	....	....
	NHL Totals		**520**	**132**	**140**	**272**	**122**	**110**	**232**	**407**	**38**	**0**	**18**	**1064**	**12.4**	**419**	**118**	**457**	**11**		**2**	**1**	**0**	**1**	**0**	**0**	**0**	**0**

• Brother of Bill

Traded to **California** by **Montreal** with Montreal's 1st round choice (Chris Oddleifson) in 1970 Amateur Draft for Francois Lacombe and Oakland's 1st round choice (Guy Lafleur) in 1971 Amateur Draft, May 22, 1970. Claimed by **Atlanta** from **California** in Expansion Draft, June 6, 1972. Traded to **NY Islanders** by **Atlanta** with future considerations (Billy MacMillan, May 29, 1973) for Arnie Brown, February 13, 1973. Traded to **Minnesota** by **NY Islanders** with Doug Rombough for Jean-Paul Parise, January 5, 1975. Signed as a free agent by **LA Kings**, September 16, 1977.

• HICKEY, Greg

LW – L. 5'10", 160 lbs. b: Toronto, Ont., 3/8/1955. NY Rangers' 3rd, 48th overall, in 1975.

Season	Club	League	GP	G	A	Pts	AG	AA	APts	PIM	PP	SH	GW	S	%	TGF	PGF	TGA	PGA	+/–	GP	G	A	Pts	PIM	PP	SH	GW
1971-72	Hamilton Kilty B's	OHA-B	STATISTICS NOT AVAILABLE																									
1972-73	Hamilton Red Wings	OMJHL	53	13	9	22	....	....	....	65	....	....	....	....	....	....	....	....	....	....	....	....	....	....	....	....	....	....
1973-74	Hamilton Red Wings	OMJHL	67	30	28	58	....	....	....	63	....	....	....	....	....	....	....	....	....	....	....	....	....	....	....	....	....	....
1974-75	Hamilton Fincups	OMJHL	66	27	34	61	....	....	....	95	....	....	....	....	....	....	....	....	....	....	16	6	3	9	31	....	....	....
1975-76	Providence Reds	AHL	31	2	6	8	....	....	....	30	....	....	....	....	....	....	....	....	....	....	....	....	....	....	....	....	....	....
	Port Huron Flags	IHL	9	2	3	5	....	....	....	2	....	....	....	....	....	....	....	....	....	....	....	....	....	....	....	....	....	....
1976-77	New Haven Nighthawks	AHL	4	2	0	2	....	....	....	2	....	....	....	....	....	....	....	....	....	....	....	....	....	....	....	....	....	....
	Richmond Wildcats	SHL	28	8	16	24	....	....	....	65	....	....	....	....	....	....	....	....	....	....	....	....	....	....	....	....	....	....
	Charlotte Checkers	SHL	11	5	8	13	....	....	....	4	....	....	....	....	....	....	....	....	....	....	....	....	....	....	....	....	....	....
1977-78	**New York Rangers**	**NHL**	**1**	**0**	**0**	**0**	**0**	**0**	**0**	**0**	**0**	**0**	**0**	**2**	**0.0**	**1**	**0**	**2**	**0**	**–1**	....	....	....	....	....	....	....	....
	New Haven Nighthawks	AHL	68	18	17	35	....	....	....	40	....	....	....	....	....	....	....	....	....	....	15	3	3	6	14	....	....	....
1978-79	New Haven Nighthawks	AHL	76	23	40	63	....	....	....	75	....	....	....	....	....	....	....	....	....	....	10	3	7	10	4	....	....	....
1979-80	Fort Wayne Komets	IHL	51	21	23	44	....	....	....	34	....	....	....	....	....	....	....	....	....	....	15	6	6	12	12	....	....	....
1980-81	Springfield Indians	AHL	74	15	15	30	....	....	....	65	....	....	....	....	....	....	....	....	....	....	7	2	1	3	21	....	....	....
1981-82			DID NOT PLAY																									
1982-83	Hampton Roads Gulls	ACHL	19	9	13	22	....	....	....	16	....	....	....	....	....	....	....	....	....	....	....	....	....	....	....	....	....	....
	Virginia Raiders	ACHL	17	3	5	8	....	....	....	6	....	....	....	....	....	....	....	....	....	....	4	0	0	0	0	....	....	....
1983-84			OUT OF HOCKEY – RETIRED																									
1984-85			OUT OF HOCKEY – RETIRED																									
1985-86	New Haven Nighthawks	AHL	2	0	0	0	....	....	....	0	....	....	....	....	....	....	....	....	....	....	....	....	....	....	....	....	....	....
	NHL Totals		**1**	**0**	**0**	**0**	**0**	**0**	**0**	**0**	**0**	**0**	**0**	**2**	**0.0**	**1**	**0**	**2**	**0**		....	....	....	....	....	....	....	....

• Brother of Pat

• HICKEY, Pat

Patrick Joseph "Hitch" LW – L. 6'1", 190 lbs. b: Brantford, Ont., 5/15/1953. NY Rangers' 2nd, 30th overall, in 1973.

Season	Club	League	GP	G	A	Pts	AG	AA	APts	PIM	PP	SH	GW	S	%	TGF	PGF	TGA	PGA	+/–	GP	G	A	Pts	PIM	PP	SH	GW
1970-71	Hamilton Red Wings	OMJHL	55	15	17	32	....	....	....	46	....	....	....	....	....	....	....	....	....	....	7	0	1	1	2	....	....	....
1971-72	Hamilton Red Wings	OMJHL	58	21	39	60	....	....	....	78	....	....	....	....	....	....	....	....	....	....	....	....	....	....	....	....	....	....
1972-73	Hamilton Red Wings	OMJHL	61	32	47	79	....	....	....	80	....	....	....	....	....	....	....	....	....	....	....	....	....	....	....	....	....	....
1973-74	Toronto Toros	WHA	78	26	29	55	....	....	....	52	....	....	....	....	....	....	....	....	....	....	12	3	3	6	12	....	....	....
1974-75	Toronto Toros	WHA	74	35	34	69	....	....	....	50	....	....	....	....	....	....	....	....	....	....	5	0	1	1	4	....	....	....
1975-76	**New York Rangers**	**NHL**	**70**	**14**	**22**	**36**	**12**	**16**	**28**	**36**	**0**	**0**	**1**	**157**	**8.9**	**50**	**14**	**70**	**5**	**–29**	....	....	....	....	....	....	....	....
1976-77	**New York Rangers**	**NHL**	**80**	**23**	**17**	**40**	**21**	**13**	**34**	**35**	**4**	**1**	**1**	**130**	**17.7**	**57**	**12**	**62**	**6**	**–11**	....	....	....	....	....	....	....	....
1977-78	**New York Rangers**	**NHL**	**80**	**40**	**33**	**73**	**36**	**26**	**62**	**47**	**10**	**1**	**3**	**215**	**18.6**	**99**	**39**	**93**	**14**	**–19**	**3**	**2**	**0**	**2**	**0**	**1**	**0**	**0**
	Canada	WEC-A	10	5	1	6	....	....	....	4	....	....	....	....	....	....	....	....	....	....	....	....	....	....	....	....	....	....
1978-79	**New York Rangers**	**NHL**	**80**	**34**	**41**	**75**	**29**	**30**	**59**	**56**	**8**	**0**	**1**	**193**	**17.6**	**107**	**29**	**78**	**8**	**8**	**18**	**1**	**7**	**8**	**6**	**0**	**0**	**0**
1979-80	**New York Rangers**	**NHL**	**7**	**2**	**2**	**4**	**2**	**1**	**3**	**10**	**0**	**0**	**0**	**5**	**40.0**	**10**	**3**	**9**	**1**	**–1**	....	....	....	....	....	....	....	....
	Colorado Rockies	**NHL**	**24**	**7**	**9**	**16**	**6**	**7**	**13**	**10**	**0**	**0**	**0**	**52**	**13.5**	**32**	**5**	**34**	**5**	**–2**	....	....	....	....	....	....	....	....
	Toronto Maple Leafs	**NHL**	**45**	**22**	**16**	**38**	**19**	**12**	**31**	**16**	**6**	**0**	**3**	**99**	**22.2**	**66**	**20**	**46**	**1**	**1**	**3**	**0**	**0**	**0**	**2**	**0**	**0**	**0**
1980-81	**Toronto Maple Leafs**	**NHL**	**72**	**16**	**33**	**49**	**12**	**22**	**34**	**49**	**5**	**0**	**1**	**157**	**10.2**	**72**	**14**	**87**	**13**	**–16**	**2**	**0**	**0**	**0**	**0**	**0**	**0**	**0**
1981-82	**Toronto Maple Leafs**	**NHL**	**1**	**0**	**0**	**0**	**0**	**0**	**0**	**0**	**0**	**0**	**0**	**0**	**0.0**	**0**	**0**	**0**	**0**	**0**	....	....	....	....	....	....	....	....
	New York Rangers	**NHL**	**53**	**15**	**14**	**29**	**12**	**9**	**21**	**32**	**3**	**0**	**3**	**77**	**19.5**	**47**	**10**	**52**	**0**	**–15**	....	....	....	....	....	....	....	....
	Quebec Nordiques	**NHL**	**7**	**0**	**1**	**1**	**0**	**1**	**1**	**4**	**0**	**0**	**0**	**3**	**0.0**	**1**	**0**	**2**	**0**	**–1**	**15**	**1**	**3**	**4**	**21**	**1**	**0**	**0**
1982-83	**St. Louis Blues**	**NHL**	**1**	**0**	**0**	**0**	**0**	**0**	**0**	**0**	**0**	**0**	**0**	**1**	**0.0**	**0**	**0**	**0**	**0**	**0**	....	....	....	....	....	....	....	....
	Salt Lake Golden Eagles	CHL	36	13	12	25	....	....	....	28	....	....	....	....	....	....	....	....	....	....	6	1	0	1	2	....	....	....
1983-84	**St. Louis Blues**	**NHL**	**69**	**9**	**11**	**20**	**7**	**7**	**14**	**24**	**0**	**0**	**1**	**78**	**11.5**	**31**	**0**	**76**	**42**	**–3**	**11**	**1**	**1**	**2**	**6**	**0**	**1**	**0**
1984-85	**St. Louis Blues**	**NHL**	**57**	**10**	**13**	**23**	**8**	**9**	**17**	**32**	**0**	**3**	**1**	**53**	**18.9**	**29**	**0**	**47**	**14**	**–4**	**3**	**0**	**0**	**0**	**2**	**0**	**0**	**0**
	NHL Totals		**646**	**192**	**212**	**404**	**164**	**153**	**317**	**351**	**36**	**5**	**15**	**1220**	**15.7**	**601**	**146**	**656**	**109**		**55**	**5**	**11**	**16**	**37**	**2**	**1**	**0**
	Other Major League Totals		152	61	63	124	....	....	....	102	....	....	....	....	....	....	....	....	....	....	17	3	4	7	16	....	....	....

• Brother of Greg

Selected by **Toronto** (WHA) in 1973 WHA Amateur Draft, June, 1973. Traded to **Colorado** by **NY Rangers** with Lucien DeBlois, Mike McEwen, Dean Turner and future considerations (Bobby Crawford, January 15, 1980) for Barry Beck, November 2, 1979. Traded to **Toronto** by **Colorado** with Wilf Paiement for Lanny McDonald and Joel Quenneville, December 29, 1979. Traded to **NY Rangers** by **Toronto** for NY Rangers' 5th round choice (Sylvain Charland) in 1982 Entry Draft, October 16, 1981. Traded to **Quebec** by **NY Rangers** to complete transaction that sent Robbie Ftorek to NY Rangers (December 30, 1981), March 8, 1982. Traded to **St. Louis** by **Quebec** for Rick Lapointe, August 4, 1982.

• HICKS, Alex

Alex W. LW – L. 6', 190 lbs. b: Calgary, Alta., 9/4/1969.

Season	Club	League	REGULAR SEASON																		PLAYOFFS							
			GP	G	A	Pts	AG	AA	APts	PIM	PP	SH	GW	S	%	TGF	PGF	TGA	PGA	+/–	GP	G	A	Pts	PIM	PP	SH	GW
1987-88	Calgary Spurs	AJHL	STATISTICS NOT AVAILABLE																									
1988-89	U. of Wisconsin-Eau Claire	NCHA	30	21	26	47				42																		
1989-90	U. of Wisconsin-Eau Claire	NCHA	34	31	48	79				30																		
1990-91	U. of Wisconsin-Eau Claire	NCHA	26	22	35	57				43																		
1991-92	U. of Wisconsin-Eau Claire	NCHA	26	24	42	66				63																		
1992-93	Toledo Storm	ECHL	50	26	34	60				100											16	5	10	15	79			
	Adirondack Red Wings	AHL	3	0	0	0				0																		
1993-94	Toledo Storm	ECHL	60	31	49	80				240											14	10	10	20	56			
	Adirondack Red Wings	AHL	8	1	3	4				2											5	0	2	2	2			
1994-95	Las Vegas Thunder	IHL	79	24	42	66				212											9	2	4	6	47			
1995-96	**Mighty Ducks of Anaheim**	**NHL**	**64**	**10**	**11**	**21**	**10**	**9**	**19**	**37**	**0**	**0**	**2**	**83**	**12.0**	**36**	**3**	**29**	**7**	**11**								
	Baltimore Bandits	AHL	13	2	10	12				23																		
1996-97	**Mighty Ducks of Anaheim**	**NHL**	**18**	**2**	**6**	**8**	**2**	**5**	**7**	**14**	**0**	**0**	**0**	**21**	**9.5**	**11**	**0**	**14**	**4**	**1**								
	Pittsburgh Penguins	**NHL**	**55**	**5**	**15**	**20**	**5**	**13**	**18**	**76**	**0**	**0**	**3**	**57**	**8.8**	**26**	**0**	**42**	**10**	**–6**	**5**	**0**	**1**	**1**	**2**	**0**	**0**	**0**
1997-98	**Pittsburgh Penguins**	**NHL**	**58**	**7**	**13**	**20**	**8**	**13**	**21**	**54**	**0**	**0**	**1**	**78**	**9.0**	**28**	**1**	**31**	**8**	**4**	**6**	**0**	**0**	**0**	**2**	**0**	**0**	**0**
1998-99	**San Jose Sharks**	**NHL**	**4**	**0**	**1**	**1**	**0**	**1**	**1**	**4**	**0**	**0**	**0**	**4**	**0.0**	**1**	**0**	**2**	**0**	**–1**								
	Florida Panthers	**NHL**	**51**	**0**	**6**	**6**	**0**	**6**	**6**	**58**	**0**	**0**	**0**	**47**	**0.0**	**15**	**0**	**25**	**6**	**–4**								
99-2000	**Florida Panthers**	**NHL**	**8**	**1**	**2**	**3**	**1**	**2**	**3**	**4**	**0**	**0**	**0**	**6**	**16.7**	**4**	**0**	**1**	**0**	**3**	**4**	**0**	**1**	**1**	**4**	**0**	**0**	**0**
	Louisville Panthers	AHL	17	6	5	11				23																		
	NHL Totals		**258**	**25**	**54**	**79**	**26**	**49**	**75**	**247**	**0**	**0**	**6**	**296**	**8.4**	**121**	**4**	**144**	**35**		**15**	**0**	**2**	**2**	**8**	**0**	**0**	**0**

• Son of Wayne • NCHA West First All-American Team (1991, 1992)

Signed as a free agent by **Anaheim**, August 17, 1995. Traded to **Pittsburgh** by **Anaheim** with Fredrik Olausson for Shawn Antoski and Dmitri Mironov, November 19, 1996. Signed as a free agent by **San Jose**, October, 1998. Traded to **Florida** by **San Jose** with San Jose's 5th round choice (later traded to NY Islanders, NY Islanders selected Adam Johnson) in 1999 Entry Draft for Jeff Norton, November 11, 1998. • Missed majority of 1999-2000 season recovering from knee injury suffered in training camp after being re-assigned to minors, September 28, 1999. • Played w/ RHI's Buffalo Stampede in 1994 (22-19-32-51-62).

• HICKS, Doug

Douglas Allan D – L. 6', 185 lbs. b: Cold Lake, Alta., 5/28/1955. Minnesota's 1st, 6th overall, in 1974.

Season	Club	League	GP	G	A	Pts	AG	AA	APts	PIM	PP	SH	GW	S	%	TGF	PGF	TGA	PGA	+/–	GP	G	A	Pts	PIM	PP	SH	GW
1971-72	Flin Flon Bombers	WCJHL	50	1	4	5				80											7	0	0	0	21			
1972-73	Flin Flon Bombers	WCJHL	65	14	35	49				106											9	1	2	3	15			
1973-74	Flin Flon Bombers	WCJHL	68	13	48	61				102											1	0	1	1	4			
1974-75	**Minnesota North Stars**	**NHL**	**80**	**6**	**12**	**18**	**5**	**9**	**14**	**51**	**1**	**0**	**0**	**76**	**7.9**	**59**	**3**	**89**	**8**	**–25**								
1975-76	**Minnesota North Stars**	**NHL**	**80**	**5**	**13**	**18**	**4**	**10**	**14**	**54**	**3**	**0**	**1**	**102**	**4.9**	**78**	**16**	**81**	**2**	**–17**								
1976-77	**Minnesota North Stars**	**NHL**	**79**	**5**	**14**	**19**	**4**	**11**	**15**	**68**	**1**	**1**	**0**	**83**	**6.0**	**74**	**14**	**121**	**30**	**–31**	**2**	**0**	**0**	**0**	**7**	**0**	**0**	**0**
1977-78	**Minnesota North Stars**	**NHL**	**61**	**2**	**9**	**11**	**2**	**7**	**9**	**51**	**0**	**0**	**0**	**81**	**2.5**	**48**	**7**	**74**	**5**	**–28**								
	Chicago Black Hawks	**NHL**	**13**	**1**	**7**	**8**	**1**	**5**	**6**	**2**	**0**	**0**	**0**	**22**	**4.5**	**19**	**1**	**16**	**3**	**5**	**4**	**1**	**0**	**1**	**2**	**1**	**0**	**0**
1978-79	**Chicago Black Hawks**	**NHL**	**44**	**1**	**8**	**9**	**1**	**6**	**7**	**15**	**0**	**0**	**0**	**32**	**3.1**	**30**	**2**	**43**	**3**	**–12**								
	New Brunswick Hawks	AHL	6	0	1	1				12																		
	Dallas Black Hawks	CHL	16	1	10	11				60											9	3	6	9	11			
1979-80	**Edmonton Oilers**	**NHL**	**78**	**9**	**31**	**40**	**8**	**23**	**31**	**52**	**5**	**2**	**1**	**122**	**7.4**	**137**	**34**	**128**	**43**	**18**	**3**	**0**	**0**	**0**	**2**	**0**	**0**	**0**
1980-81	**Edmonton Oilers**	**NHL**	**59**	**5**	**16**	**21**	**4**	**11**	**15**	**76**	**1**	**1**	**0**	**109**	**4.6**	**86**	**16**	**76**	**27**	**21**	**9**	**1**	**1**	**2**	**4**	**0**	**0**	**0**
1981-82	**Edmonton Oilers**	**NHL**	**49**	**3**	**20**	**23**	**2**	**13**	**15**	**55**	**1**	**0**	**0**	**44**	**6.8**	**67**	**11**	**60**	**10**	**6**								
	Washington Capitals	**NHL**	**12**	**0**	**1**	**1**	**0**	**1**	**1**	**11**	**0**	**0**	**0**	**6**	**0.0**	**3**	**0**	**14**	**4**	**–7**								
1982-83	**Washington Capitals**	**NHL**	**6**	**0**	**0**	**0**	**0**	**0**	**0**	**7**	**0**	**0**	**0**	**6**	**0.0**	**0**	**0**	**6**	**3**	**–3**								
	Hershey Bears	AHL	75	2	35	37				44											5	0	2	2	0			
1983-84	St. Albert Saints	AJHL	DID NOT PLAY – COACHING																									
1984-85	Kolner EC	Germany	38	10	26	36				60											7	0	0	0	9			
1985-86			STATISTICS NOT AVAILABLE																									
1986-87	HC Salzburg	Austria	22	6	17	23				55																		
1987-88	HC Salzburg	Austria	33	4	21	25				63																		
	NHL Totals		**561**	**37**	**131**	**168**	**31**	**96**	**127**	**442**	**12**	**4**	**2**	**683**	**5.4**	**601**	**104**	**708**	**138**		**18**	**2**	**1**	**3**	**15**	**1**	**0**	**0**

• Brother of Glenn

Traded to **Chicago** by **Minnesota** with Minnesota's 3rd round choice (Marcel Frere) in 1980 Entry Draft for Eddie Mio and future considerations (Pierre Plante, May 4, 1978), March 14, 1978. Claimed by **Edmonton** from **Chicago** in Expansion Draft, June 13, 1979. Traded to **Washington** by **Edmonton** for Todd Bidner, March 9, 1982.

• HICKS, Glenn

LW – L. 5'10", 177 lbs. b: Red Deer, Alta., 8/28/1958. Detroit's 3rd, 28th overall, in 1978.

Season	Club	League	GP	G	A	Pts	AG	AA	APts	PIM	PP	SH	GW	S	%	TGF	PGF	TGA	PGA	+/–	GP	G	A	Pts	PIM	PP	SH	GW
1974-75	Red Deer Chiefs	AAHA	60	45	30	75				78																		
1975-76	Flin Flon Bombers	WCJHL	71	16	19	35				103																		
1976-77	Flin Flon Bombers	WCJHL	71	28	31	59				175																		
1977-78	Flin Flon Bombers	WCJHL	72	50	69	119				225																		
1978-79	Winnipeg Jets	WHA	69	6	10	16				48											7	1	1	2	4			
1979-80	**Detroit Red Wings**	**NHL**	**50**	**1**	**2**	**3**	**1**	**1**	**2**	**43**	**0**	**0**	**0**	**52**	**1.9**	**13**	**1**	**33**	**0**	**–21**								
1980-81	**Detroit Red Wings**	**NHL**	**58**	**5**	**10**	**15**	**4**	**7**	**11**	**84**	**1**	**0**	**0**	**71**	**7.0**	**28**	**1**	**31**	**4**	**0**								
	Adirondack Red Wings	AHL	19	10	6	16				56																		
1981-82	Tulsa Oilers	CHL	78	14	34	48				103											3	0	0	0	7			
1982-83	Birmingham South Stars	CHL	80	13	26	39				40											13	0	7	7	23			
1983-84	Salt Lake Golden Eagles	CHL	62	4	26	30				87											5	0	1	1	16			
1984-85	Springfield Indians	AHL	11	3	4	7				4																		
	EHC Kloten	Switz.	38	12	17	29																						
1985-86	Salt Lake Golden Eagles	IHL	82	14	40	54				75											5	0	4	4	6			
1986-87	EHC Chur	Switz-2	13	1	7	8																						
	NHL Totals		**108**	**6**	**12**	**18**	**5**	**8**	**13**	**127**	**1**	**0**	**0**	**123**	**4.9**	**41**	**2**	**64**	**4**									
	Other Major League Totals		69	6	10	16				48											7	1	1	2	4			

• Brother of Doug

Signed as an underage free agent by **Winnipeg** (WHA), June, 1978. Reclaimed by **Detroit** from **Winnipeg** prior to Expansion Draft, June 9, 1979. Signed as a free agent by **Minnesota**, September 2, 1983.

• HICKS, Wayne

Wayne Wilson RW – R. 5'11", 185 lbs. b: Aberdeen, WA, 4/9/1937.

Season	Club	League	GP	G	A	Pts	AG	AA	APts	PIM	PP	SH	GW	S	%	TGF	PGF	TGA	PGA	+/–	GP	G	A	Pts	PIM	PP	SH	GW
1953-54	Calgary Buffalos	WCJHL	8	1	1	2				4											5	0	0	0	0			
1954-55	Moose Jaw Canucks	WCJHL	35	4	5	9				12																		
1955-56	Yorkton Terriers	SJHL	48	28	25	53				81											5	2	1	3	2			
1956-57	Melville Millionaires	SJHL	50	42	38	80				76																		
	Calgary Stampeders	WHL	4	0	0	0				0																		
1957-58	Calgary Stampeders	WHL	60	7	14	21				19											14	0	1	1	6			
1958-59	Calgary Stampeders	WHL	64	15	20	35				41											8	1	2	3	5			
1959-60	Sault Ste. Marie Greyhounds	EPHL	69	30	47	77				64																		
	Chicago Black Hawks	**NHL**																			**1**	**0**	**1**	**1**	**0**	**0**	**0**	**0**
1960-61♦	**Chicago Black Hawks**	**NHL**	**1**	**0**	**0**	**0**	**0**	**0**	**0**	**0**											**1**	**0**	**0**	**0**	**2**	**0**	**0**	**0**
	Buffalo Bisons	AHL	72	20	35	55				57											4	2	2	4	6			
1961-62	Buffalo Bisons	AHL	70	22	42	64				74											11	3	3	6	8			
	Calgary Stampeders	WHL	4	1	0	1				0																		
1962-63	**Boston Bruins**	**NHL**	**65**	**7**	**9**	**16**	**8**	**9**	**17**	**14**																		
1963-64	**Montreal Canadiens**	**NHL**	**2**	**0**	**0**	**0**	**0**	**0**	**0**	**0**																		
	Quebec Aces	AHL	70	36	42	78				30											9	4	2	6	12			
1964-65	Quebec Aces	AHL	72	38	47	85				52											5	1	0	1	2			
1965-66	Quebec Aces	AHL	72	32	49	81				24											6	0	0	0	0			
1966-67	Quebec Aces	AHL	72	31	60	91				34											5	1	2	3	2			

Season	Club	League	GP	G	A	Pts	AG	AA	APts	PIM	PP	SH	GW	S	%	TGF	PGF	TGA	PGA	+/-	PO GP	PO G	PO A	PO Pts	PO PIM	PO PP	PO SH	PO GW
			REGULAR SEASON																		PLAYOFFS							
1967-68	**Philadelphia Flyers**	**NHL**	**32**	**2**	**7**	**9**	**2**	**7**	**9**	**6**	**1**	**0**	**0**	**41**	**4.9**	**15**	**11**	**9**	**0**	**–5**	....	....	....	....	....	....	....	....
	Quebec Aces	AHL	13	4	9	13	....	....	....	13	....	....	....	....	....	....	....	....	....	....	....	....	....	....	....	....	....	....
	Pittsburgh Penguins	**NHL**	**15**	**4**	**7**	**11**	**5**	**7**	**12**	**2**	**2**	**0**	**1**	**26**	**15.4**	**14**	**4**	**8**	**0**	**2**	....	....	....	....	....	....	....	....
1968-69	Baltimore Clippers	AHL	65	33	36	69	....	....	....	55	....	....	....	....	....	....	....	....	....	....	....	....	....	....	....	....	....	....
1969-70	Baltimore Clippers	AHL	64	14	21	35	....	....	....	58	....	....	....	....	....	....	....	....	....	....	3	0	0	0	0	....	....	....
1970-71	Salt Lake Golden Eagles	WHL	8	1	3	4	....	....	....	5	....	....	....	....	....	....	....	....	....	....	....	....	....	....	....	....	....	....
	Phoenix Roadrunners	WHL	67	29	32	61	....	....	....	36	....	....	....	....	....	....	....	....	....	....	10	1	8	9	2	....	....	....
1971-72	Phoenix Roadrunners	WHL	69	17	31	48	....	....	....	59	....	....	....	....	....	....	....	....	....	....	6	3	3	6	2	....	....	....
1972-73	Phoenix Roadrunners	WHL	67	17	33	50	....	....	....	31	....	....	....	....	....	....	....	....	....	....	10	4	*12	*16	4	....	....	....
1973-74	Phoenix Roadrunners	WHL	72	27	32	59	....	....	....	23	....	....	....	....	....	....	....	....	....	....	9	4	5	9	4	....	....	....
	NHL Totals		**115**	**13**	**23**	**36**	**15**	**23**	**38**	**22**	....	....	....	....	....	....	....	....	....	....	**2**	**0**	**1**	**1**	**2**	....	....	....

• Father of Alex • AHL Second All-Star Team (1965, 1969) • AHL First All-Star Team (1967)

Traded to **Montreal** by **Chicago** for Al MacNeil, May 30, 1962. Claimed by **Boston** from **Montreal** in Intra-League Draft, June 5, 1962. Traded to **Montreal** by **Boston** for cash, September 28, 1963. NHL rights transferred to **Philadelphia** after NHL club purchased **Quebec** (AHL) franchise, May 8, 1967. Traded to **Pittsburgh** by **Philadelphia** for Art Stratton, February 27, 1968. Traded to **Phoenix** (WHL) by **Salt Lake** (WHL) for Rick Charron, November, 1970.

• HIDI, Andre

Andre Lawrence LW – L. 6'2", 205 lbs. b: Toronto, Ont., 6/5/1960. Colorado's 7th, 148th overall, in 1980.

Season	Club	League	GP	G	A	Pts	AG	AA	APts	PIM	PP	SH	GW	S	%	TGF	PGF	TGA	PGA	+/-	PO GP	PO G	PO A	PO Pts	PO PIM	PO PP	PO SH	PO GW
1979-80	Peterborough Petes	OMJHL	68	30	35	65	....	....	....	49	....	....	....	....	....	....	....	....	....	....	14	4	8	12	31	....	....	....
	Canada	WJC-A	5	2	0	2	....	....	....	2	....	....	....	....	....	....	....	....	....	....	....	....	....	....	....	....	....	....
	Peterborough Petes	Mem-Cup	5	2	3	5	....	....	....	2	....	....	....	....	....	....	....	....	....	....	....	....	....	....	....	....	....	....
1980-81	University of Toronto	OUAA	22	12	13	25	....	....	....	32	....	....	....	....	....	....	....	....	....	....	....	....	....	....	....	....	....	....
	Peterborough Petes	OMJHL	3	1	1	2	....	....	....	2	....	....	....	....	....	....	....	....	....	....	5	2	3	5	11	....	....	....
1981-82	University of Toronto	OUAA	22	26	26	52	....	....	....	52	....	....	....	....	....	....	....	....	....	....	....	....	....	....	....	....	....	....
1982-83	University of Toronto	OUAA	24	23	29	52	....	....	....	50	....	....	....	....	....	....	....	....	....	....	....	....	....	....	....	....	....	....
1983-84	University of Toronto	OUAA	24	30	30	60	....	....	....	66	....	....	....	....	....	....	....	....	....	....	....	....	....	....	....	....	....	....
	Washington Capitals	**NHL**	**1**	**0**	**0**	**0**	**0**	**0**	**0**	**0**	**0**	**0**	**0**	**1**	**0.0**	**0**	**0**	**0**	**0**	**0**	**2**	**0**	**0**	**0**	**0**	**0**	**0**	**0**
1984-85	**Washington Capitals**	**NHL**	**6**	**2**	**1**	**3**	**2**	**1**	**3**	**9**	**1**	**0**	**0**	**7**	**28.6**	**9**	**5**	**2**	**0**	**2**	....	....	....	....	....	....	....	....
	Binghamton Whalers	AHL	55	12	17	29	....	....	....	57	....	....	....	....	....	....	....	....	....	....	3	0	1	1	5	....	....	....
1985-86	Binghamton Whalers	AHL	66	19	24	43	....	....	....	104	....	....	....	....	....	....	....	....	....	....	6	1	4	5	13	....	....	....
	NHL Totals		**7**	**2**	**1**	**3**	**2**	**1**	**3**	**9**	**1**	**0**	**0**	**8**	**25.0**	**9**	**5**	**2**	**0**		**2**	**0**	**0**	**0**	**0**	**0**	**0**	**0**

OUAA Second Team All-Star (1982) • OUAA First Team All-Star (1983) • CIAU Playoff MVP (1984)

Signed as a free agent by **Washington**, March 29, 1984.

• HIEMER, Uli

Ulrich D – L. 6'1", 190 lbs. b: Fussen, W. Germany, 9/21/1962. Colorado's 3rd, 48th overall, in 1981.

Season	Club	League	GP	G	A	Pts	AG	AA	APts	PIM	PP	SH	GW	S	%	TGF	PGF	TGA	PGA	+/-	PO GP	PO G	PO A	PO Pts	PO PIM	PO PP	PO SH	PO GW
1979-80	EV Fussen	Germany	44	6	10	16	....	....	....	84	....	....	....	....	....	....	....	....	....	....	....	....	....	....	....	....	....	....
	West Germany	WJC-A	5	1	4	5	....	....	....	12	....	....	....	....	....	....	....	....	....	....	....	....	....	....	....	....	....	....
1980-81	EV Fussen	Germany	34	11	11	22	....	....	....	84	....	....	....	....	....	....	....	....	....	....	....	....	....	....	....	....	....	....
	West Germany	WEC-A	6	0	1	1	....	....	....	14	....	....	....	....	....	....	....	....	....	....	....	....	....	....	....	....	....	....
1981-82	Kolner EC	Germany	43	10	23	33	....	....	....	85	....	....	....	....	....	....	....	....	....	....	9	3	0	3	27	....	....	....
	West Germany	WJC-A	7	1	2	3	....	....	....	21	....	....	....	....	....	....	....	....	....	....	....	....	....	....	....	....	....	....
	West Germany	WEC-A	2	0	0	0	....	....	....	2	....	....	....	....	....	....	....	....	....	....	....	....	....	....	....	....	....	....
1982-83	Kolner EC	Germany	35	8	17	25	....	....	....	69	....	....	....	....	....	....	....	....	....	....	8	2	6	8	23	....	....	....
	West Germany	WEC-A	9	1	3	4	....	....	....	8	....	....	....	....	....	....	....	....	....	....	....	....	....	....	....	....	....	....
1983-84	Kolner EC	Germany	50	23	23	46	....	....	....	93	....	....	....	....	....	....	....	....	....	....	....	....	....	....	....	....	....	....
	West Germany	Olympics	6	2	0	2	....	....	....	4	....	....	....	....	....	....	....	....	....	....	....	....	....	....	....	....	....	....
1984-85	West Germany	Can-Cup	3	0	0	0	....	....	....	4	....	....	....	....	....	....	....	....	....	....	....	....	....	....	....	....	....	....
	New Jersey Devils	**NHL**	**53**	**5**	**24**	**29**	**4**	**16**	**20**	**70**	**3**	**0**	**0**	**85**	**5.9**	**64**	**24**	**56**	**2**	**–14**	....	....	....	....	....	....	....	....
	West Germany	WEC-A	10	2	1	3	....	....	....	10	....	....	....	....	....	....	....	....	....	....	....	....	....	....	....	....	....	....
1985-86	**New Jersey Devils**	**NHL**	**50**	**8**	**16**	**24**	**6**	**11**	**17**	**61**	**6**	**0**	**1**	**100**	**8.0**	**70**	**22**	**59**	**10**	**–1**	....	....	....	....	....	....	....	....
	Maine Mariners	AHL	15	5	2	7	....	....	....	19	....	....	....	....	....	....	....	....	....	....	....	....	....	....	....	....	....	....
1986-87	**New Jersey Devils**	**NHL**	**40**	**6**	**14**	**20**	**5**	**10**	**15**	**45**	**2**	**0**	**1**	**80**	**7.5**	**53**	**16**	**46**	**3**	**–6**	....	....	....	....	....	....	....	....
	Maine Mariners	AHL	26	4	3	7	....	....	....	51	....	....	....	....	....	....	....	....	....	....	....	....	....	....	....	....	....	....
1987-88	Dusseldorfer EG	Germany	34	9	23	32	....	....	....	78	....	....	....	....	....	....	....	....	....	....	10	3	2	5	24	....	....	....
1988-89	Dusseldorfer EG	Germany	32	17	25	42	....	....	....	75	....	....	....	....	....	....	....	....	....	....	10	6	3	9	*46	....	....	....
	West Germany	WEC-A	10	2	1	3	....	....	....	8	....	....	....	....	....	....	....	....	....	....	....	....	....	....	....	....	....	....
1989-90	Dusseldorfer EG	Germany	35	13	29	42	....	....	....	67	....	....	....	....	....	....	....	....	....	....	11	1	9	10	16	....	....	....
	West Germany	WEC-A	10	0	1	1	....	....	....	6	....	....	....	....	....	....	....	....	....	....	....	....	....	....	....	....	....	....
1990-91	Dusseldorfer EG	Germany	44	18	32	50	....	....	....	43	....	....	....	....	....	....	....	....	....	....	13	3	11	14	22	....	....	....
1991-92	Dusseldorfer EG	Germany	42	8	27	35	....	....	....	67	....	....	....	....	....	....	....	....	....	....	9	4	6	10	12	....	....	....
	Germany	Olympics	8	0	1	1	....	....	....	12	....	....	....	....	....	....	....	....	....	....	....	....	....	....	....	....	....	....
	Germany	WC-A	6	3	1	4	....	....	....	26	....	....	....	....	....	....	....	....	....	....	....	....	....	....	....	....	....	....
1992-93	Dusseldorfer EG	Germany-2	44	11	28	39	....	....	....	57	....	....	....	....	....	....	....	....	....	....	....	....	....	....	....	....	....	....
	Germany	WC-A	5	0	1	1	....	....	....	22	....	....	....	....	....	....	....	....	....	....	....	....	....	....	....	....	....	....
1993-94	Dusseldorfer EG	Germany-2	44	17	22	39	....	....	....	60	....	....	....	....	....	....	....	....	....	....	....	....	....	....	....	....	....	....
	Germany	Olympics	6	0	0	0	....	....	....	0	....	....	....	....	....	....	....	....	....	....	....	....	....	....	....	....	....	....
1994-95	Dusseldorfer EG	Germany	40	9	19	28	....	....	....	54	....	....	....	....	....	....	....	....	....	....	10	1	9	10	20	....	....	....
	Germany	WC-A	5	0	2	2	....	....	....	2	....	....	....	....	....	....	....	....	....	....	....	....	....	....	....	....	....	....
1995-96	Dusseldorfer EG	Germany	47	9	22	31	....	....	....	98	....	....	....	....	....	....	....	....	....	....	13	3	6	9	24	....	....	....
	NHL Totals		**143**	**19**	**54**	**73**	**15**	**37**	**52**	**176**	**11**	**0**	**2**	**265**	**7.2**	**187**	**62**	**161**	**15**		....	....	....	....	....	....	....	....

Transferred to **New Jersey** after **Colorado** franchise relocated, June 30, 1982.

• HIGGINS, Matt

C – L. 6'2", 188 lbs. b: Calgary, Alta., 10/29/1977. Montreal's 1st, 18th overall, in 1996.

Season	Club	League	GP	G	A	Pts	AG	AA	APts	PIM	PP	SH	GW	S	%	TGF	PGF	TGA	PGA	+/-	PO GP	PO G	PO A	PO Pts	PO PIM	PO PP	PO SH	PO GW
1992-93	Vernon Bantam Lakers	BCAHA	70	53	76	129	....	....	....	54	....	....	....	....	....	....	....	....	....	....	....	....	....	....	....	....	....	....
1993-94	Moose Jaw Warriors	WHL	64	6	10	16	....	....	....	10	....	....	....	....	....	....	....	....	....	....	....	....	....	....	....	....	....	....
1994-95	Moose Jaw Warriors	WHL	72	36	34	70	....	....	....	26	....	....	....	....	....	....	....	....	....	....	10	1	2	3	2	....	....	....
1995-96	Moose Jaw Warriors	WHL	67	30	33	63	....	....	....	43	....	....	....	....	....	....	....	....	....	....	....	....	....	....	....	....	....	....
1996-97	Moose Jaw Warriors	WHL	71	33	57	90	....	....	....	51	....	....	....	....	....	....	....	....	....	....	12	3	5	8	2	....	....	....
1997-98	**Montreal Canadiens**	**NHL**	**1**	**0**	**0**	**0**	**0**	**0**	**0**	**0**	**0**	**0**	**0**	**1**	**0.0**	**0**	**0**	**1**	**0**	**–1**	....	....	....	....	....	....	....	....
	Fredericton Canadiens	AHL	50	5	22	27	....	....	....	12	....	....	....	....	....	....	....	....	....	....	4	1	2	3	2	....	....	....
1998-99	**Montreal Canadiens**	**NHL**	**25**	**1**	**0**	**1**	**1**	**0**	**1**	**0**	**0**	**0**	**0**	**12**	**8.3**	**2**	**0**	**7**	**3**	**–2**	....	....	....	....	....	....	....	....
	Fredericton Canadiens	AHL	11	3	4	7	....	....	....	6	....	....	....	....	....	....	....	....	....	....	5	0	2	2	0	....	....	....
99-2000	**Montreal Canadiens**	**NHL**	**25**	**0**	**2**	**2**	**0**	**2**	**2**	**4**	**0**	**0**	**0**	**9**	**0.0**	**2**	**0**	**8**	**0**	**–6**	....	....	....	....	....	....	....	....
	Quebec Citadelles	AHL	29	1	15	16	....	....	....	21	....	....	....	....	....	....	....	....	....	....	....	....	....	....	....	....	....	....
	NHL Totals		**51**	**1**	**2**	**3**	**1**	**2**	**3**	**4**	**0**	**0**	**0**	**22**	**4.5**	**4**	**0**	**16**	**3**		....	....	....	....	....	....	....	....

• HIGGINS, Paul

RW – R. 6'1", 195 lbs. b: St. John, N.B., 1/13/1962. Toronto's 10th, 200th overall, in 1980.

Season	Club	League	GP	G	A	Pts	AG	AA	APts	PIM	PP	SH	GW	S	%	TGF	PGF	TGA	PGA	+/-	PO GP	PO G	PO A	PO Pts	PO PIM	PO PP	PO SH	PO GW
1979-80	Henry Carr Crusaders	Hi-School	36	25	38	63	....	....	....	....	....	....	....	....	....	....	....	....	....	....	....	....	....	....	....	....	....	....
1980-81	Toronto Marlboros	OMJHL	46	4	4	8	....	....	....	178	....	....	....	....	....	....	....	....	....	....	5	0	0	0	52	....	....	....
1981-82	Toronto Marlboros	OHL	6	0	0	0	....	....	....	11	....	....	....	....	....	....	....	....	....	....	....	....	....	....	....	....	....	....
	Kitchener Rangers	OHL	29	3	5	8	....	....	....	119	....	....	....	....	....	....	....	....	....	....	....	....	....	....	....	....	....	....
	Toronto Maple Leafs	**NHL**	**3**	**0**	**0**	**0**	**0**	**0**	**0**	**17**	**0**	**0**	**0**	**0**	**0.0**	**0**	**0**	**1**	**0**	**–1**	....	....	....	....	....	....	....	....
1982-83	**Toronto Maple Leafs**	**NHL**	**22**	**0**	**0**	**0**	**0**	**0**	**0**	**135**	**0**	**0**	**0**	**1**	**0.0**	**1**	**0**	**4**	**0**	**–3**	**1**	**0**	**0**	**0**	**0**	**0**	**0**	**0**
1983-84	Carolina Thunderbirds	ACHL	4	0	1	1	....	....	....	18	....	....	....	....	....	....	....	....	....	....	....	....	....	....	....	....	....	....
	NHL Totals		**25**	**0**	**0**	**0**	**0**	**0**	**0**	**152**	**0**	**0**	**0**	**1**	**0.0**	**1**	**0**	**5**	**0**		**1**	**0**	**0**	**0**	**0**	**0**	**0**	**0**

● **HIGGINS, Tim** Timothy Raymond RW – . 6′, 185 lbs. b: Ottawa, Ont., 2/7/1958. Chicago's 1st, 10th overall, in 1978.

			REGULAR SEASON																		PLAYOFFS							
Season	Club	League	GP	G	A	Pts	AG	AA	APts	PIM	PP	SH	GW	S	%	TGF	PGF	TGA	PGA	+/–	GP	G	A	Pts	PIM	PP	SH	GW
1974-75	Ottawa Jr. Senators	OJHL	22	1	3	4	....	....	....	6	....	....	....	....	....	....	....	....	....	....	4	1	1	2	2	....	....	....
	Ottawa 67's	OMJHL	22	1	3	4	....	....	....	6	....	....	....	....	....	....	....	....	....	....	....	....	....	....	....	....	....	....
1975-76	Ottawa 67's	OMJHL	59	15	10	25	....	....	....	59	....	....	....	....	....	....	....	....	....	....	12	1	2	3	20	....	....	....
1976-77	Ottawa 67's	OMJHL	66	35	52	87	....	....	....	80	....	....	....	....	....	....	....	....	....	....	19	10	14	24	39	....	....	....
	Ottawa 67's	Mem-Cup	5	4	3	7	....	....	....	0	....	....	....	....	....	....	....	....	....	....	....	....	....	....	....	....	....	....
1977-78	Ottawa 67's	OMJHL	50	41	60	101	....	....	....	99	....	....	....	....	....	....	....	....	....	....	16	9	13	22	36	....	....	....
1978-79	**Chicago Black Hawks**	**NHL**	**36**	**7**	**16**	**23**	**6**	**12**	**18**	**30**	**0**	**0**	**1**	**64**	**10.9**	**36**	**7**	**24**	**1**	**6**	**4**	**0**	**0**	**0**	**0**	**0**	**0**	**0**
	New Brunswick Hawks	AHL	17	3	5	8	....	....	....	14	....	....	....	....	....	....	....	....	....	....	....	....	....	....	....	....	....	....
1979-80	**Chicago Black Hawks**	**NHL**	**74**	**13**	**12**	**25**	**11**	**9**	**20**	**50**	**2**	**0**	**0**	**110**	**11.8**	**37**	**4**	**49**	**1**	**–15**	**7**	**0**	**3**	**3**	**10**	**0**	**0**	**0**
1980-81	**Chicago Black Hawks**	**NHL**	**78**	**24**	**35**	**59**	**19**	**23**	**42**	**86**	**1**	**0**	**1**	**149**	**16.1**	**88**	**13**	**58**	**3**	**20**	**3**	**0**	**0**	**0**	**0**	**0**	**0**	**0**
1981-82	**Chicago Black Hawks**	**NHL**	**74**	**20**	**30**	**50**	**16**	**20**	**36**	**85**	**6**	**0**	**2**	**114**	**17.5**	**104**	**30**	**80**	**0**	**–6**	**12**	**3**	**1**	**4**	**15**	**0**	**0**	**0**
1982-83	**Chicago Black Hawks**	**NHL**	**64**	**14**	**9**	**23**	**11**	**6**	**17**	**63**	**0**	**0**	**2**	**71**	**19.7**	**33**	**0**	**39**	**2**	**–4**	**13**	**1**	**3**	**4**	**10**	**0**	**0**	**0**
1983-84	**Chicago Black Hawks**	**NHL**	**32**	**1**	**4**	**5**	**1**	**3**	**4**	**21**	**0**	**0**	**1**	**21**	**4.8**	**10**	**0**	**9**	**0**	**1**	....	....	....	....	....	....	....	....
	New Jersey Devils	**NHL**	**37**	**18**	**10**	**28**	**14**	**7**	**21**	**27**	**3**	**1**	**3**	**72**	**25.0**	**44**	**11**	**41**	**4**	**–4**	....	....	....	....	....	....	....	....
1984-85	**New Jersey Devils**	**NHL**	**71**	**19**	**29**	**48**	**15**	**20**	**35**	**30**	**5**	**0**	**2**	**147**	**12.9**	**73**	**26**	**58**	**1**	**–10**	....	....	....	....	....	....	....	....
1985-86	**New Jersey Devils**	**NHL**	**59**	**9**	**17**	**26**	**7**	**11**	**18**	**47**	**2**	**0**	**1**	**90**	**10.0**	**45**	**5**	**33**	**0**	**7**	....	....	....	....	....	....	....	....
1986-87	**Detroit Red Wings**	**NHL**	**77**	**12**	**14**	**26**	**10**	**10**	**20**	**124**	**0**	**1**	**1**	**110**	**10.9**	**43**	**1**	**68**	**24**	**–2**	**12**	**0**	**1**	**1**	**16**	**0**	**0**	**0**
1987-88	**Detroit Red Wings**	**NHL**	**62**	**12**	**13**	**25**	**10**	**9**	**19**	**94**	**0**	**1**	**1**	**63**	**19.0**	**35**	**1**	**37**	**8**	**5**	**13**	**1**	**0**	**1**	**26**	**0**	**0**	**1**
1988-89	**Detroit Red Wings**	**NHL**	**42**	**5**	**9**	**14**	**4**	**6**	**10**	**62**	**0**	**0**	**0**	**45**	**11.1**	**19**	**1**	**27**	**9**	**0**	**1**	**0**	**0**	**0**	**0**	**0**	**0**	**0**
	Adirondack Red Wings	AHL	14	7	4	11	....	....	....	24	....	....	....	....	....	....	....	....	....	....	....	....	....	....	....	....	....	....
	NHL Totals		**706**	**154**	**198**	**352**	**124**	**136**	**260**	**719**	**19**	**3**	**15**	**1056**	**14.6**	**567**	**99**	**523**	**53**		**65**	**5**	**8**	**13**	**77**	**0**	**0**	**1**

Traded to **New Jersey** by **Chicago** for Jeff Larmer, January 11, 1984. Traded to **Detroit** by **New Jersey** for Claude Loiselle, June 25, 1986.

● **HILL, Al** Alan Douglas C – L. 6′1″, 175 lbs. b: Nanaimo, B.C., 4/22/1955.

Season	Club	League	GP	G	A	Pts	AG	AA	APts	PIM	PP	SH	GW	S	%	TGF	PGF	TGA	PGA	+/–	GP	G	A	Pts	PIM	PP	SH	GW
1973-74	Nanaimo Clippers	BCJHL	64	29	41	70	....	....	....	60	....	....	....	....	....	....	....	....	....	....	....	....	....	....	....	....	....	....
1974-75	Victoria Cougars	WCJHL	70	21	36	57	....	....	....	75	....	....	....	....	....	....	....	....	....	....	12	5	2	7	21	....	....	....
1975-76	Victoria Cougars	WCJHL	68	26	40	66	....	....	....	172	....	....	....	....	....	....	....	....	....	....	15	5	10	15	94	....	....	....
1976-77	**Philadelphia Flyers**	**NHL**	**9**	**2**	**4**	**6**	**2**	**3**	**5**	**27**	**0**	**0**	**0**	**6**	**33.3**	**8**	**0**	**2**	**0**	**6**	....	....	....	....	....	....	....	....
	Springfield Indians	AHL	63	13	28	41	....	....	....	125	....	....	....	....	....	....	....	....	....	....	....	....	....	....	....	....	....	....
1977-78	**Philadelphia Flyers**	**NHL**	**3**	**0**	**0**	**0**	**0**	**0**	**0**	**2**	**0**	**0**	**0**	**3**	**0.0**	**0**	**0**	**0**	**0**	**0**	....	....	....	....	....	....	....	....
	Maine Mariners	AHL	80	32	59	91	....	....	....	118	....	....	....	....	....	....	....	....	....	....	12	2	7	9	49	....	....	....
1978-79	**Philadelphia Flyers**	**NHL**	**31**	**5**	**11**	**16**	**4**	**8**	**12**	**28**	**1**	**0**	**1**	**44**	**11.4**	**27**	**3**	**19**	**0**	**5**	**7**	**1**	**0**	**1**	**2**	**0**	**0**	**0**
	Maine Mariners	AHL	35	11	14	25	....	....	....	59	....	....	....	....	....	....	....	....	....	....	....	....	....	....	....	....	....	....
1979-80	**Philadelphia Flyers**	**NHL**	**61**	**16**	**10**	**26**	**14**	**7**	**21**	**53**	**0**	**0**	**2**	**79**	**20.3**	**50**	**3**	**39**	**6**	**14**	**19**	**3**	**5**	**8**	**19**	**1**	**0**	**0**
1980-81	**Philadelphia Flyers**	**NHL**	**57**	**10**	**15**	**25**	**8**	**10**	**18**	**45**	**0**	**0**	**2**	**70**	**14.3**	**37**	**4**	**28**	**6**	**11**	**12**	**2**	**4**	**6**	**18**	**0**	**0**	**1**
1981-82	**Philadelphia Flyers**	**NHL**	**41**	**6**	**13**	**19**	**5**	**9**	**14**	**58**	**0**	**0**	**0**	**50**	**12.0**	**24**	**2**	**42**	**16**	**–4**	**3**	**0**	**0**	**0**	**0**	**0**	**0**	**0**
1982-83	Moncton Alpines	AHL	78	22	22	44	....	....	....	78	....	....	....	....	....	....	....	....	....	....	....	....	....	....	....	....	....	....
1983-84	Maine Mariners	AHL	51	7	17	24	....	....	....	51	....	....	....	....	....	....	....	....	....	....	17	6	12	18	22	....	....	....
1984-85	Hershey Bears	AHL	73	11	30	41	....	....	....	77	....	....	....	....	....	....	....	....	....	....	....	....	....	....	....	....	....	....
1985-86	Hershey Bears	AHL	80	17	40	57	....	....	....	129	....	....	....	....	....	....	....	....	....	....	18	2	6	8	52	....	....	....
1986-87	**Philadelphia Flyers**	**NHL**	**7**	**0**	**2**	**2**	**0**	**1**	**1**	**4**	**0**	**0**	**0**	**2**	**0.0**	**2**	**0**	**1**	**0**	**1**	**9**	**2**	**1**	**3**	**0**	**0**	**0**	**0**
	Hershey Bears	AHL	76	13	35	48	....	....	....	124	....	....	....	....	....	....	....	....	....	....	5	0	1	1	2	....	....	....
1987-88	**Philadelphia Flyers**	**NHL**	**12**	**1**	**0**	**1**	**1**	**0**	**1**	**10**	**0**	**0**	**0**	**9**	**11.1**	**5**	**0**	**9**	**4**	**0**	**1**	**0**	**1**	**1**	**4**	**0**	**0**	**0**
	Hershey Bears	AHL	57	10	21	31	....	....	....	62	....	....	....	....	....	....	....	....	....	....	10	1	6	7	12	....	....	....
1988-89	Hershey Bears	AHL	62	13	20	33	....	....	....	63	....	....	....	....	....	....	....	....	....	....	8	2	0	2	10	....	....	....
1989-90	Hershey Bears	AHL	DID NOT PLAY – COACHING																									
	NHL Totals		**221**	**40**	**55**	**95**	**34**	**38**	**72**	**227**	**1**	**0**	**5**	**263**	**15.2**	**153**	**12**	**140**	**32**		**51**	**8**	**11**	**19**	**43**	**1**	**0**	**1**

AHL First All-Star Team (1978)

Signed as a free agent by **Philadelphia**, October 22, 1976. Signed as a free agent by **Edmonton**, November 10, 1982. Signed as a free agent by **Philadelphia**, October 8, 1984.

● **HILL, Brian** Brian Nelson RW – R. 6′, 175 lbs. b: Regina, Sask., 1/12/1957. Atlanta's 3rd, 31st overall, in 1977.

Season	Club	League	GP	G	A	Pts	AG	AA	APts	PIM	PP	SH	GW	S	%	TGF	PGF	TGA	PGA	+/–	GP	G	A	Pts	PIM	PP	SH	GW
1974-75	Estevan Bruins	SJHL	STATISTICS NOT AVAILABLE																									
	Medicine Hat Tigers	WCJHL	39	7	5	12	....	....	....	6	....	....	....	....	....	....	....	....	....	....	5	0	0	0	0	....	....	....
1975-76	Medicine Hat Tigers	WCJHL	70	22	24	46	....	....	....	98	....	....	....	....	....	....	....	....	....	....	9	2	3	5	2	....	....	....
1976-77	Medicine Hat Tigers	WCJHL	72	53	51	104	....	....	....	101	....	....	....	....	....	....	....	....	....	....	4	3	1	4	4	....	....	....
1977-78	Tulsa Oilers	CHL	75	13	26	39	....	....	....	46	....	....	....	....	....	....	....	....	....	....	7	2	2	4	6	....	....	....
1978-79	Tulsa Oilers	CHL	74	26	27	53	....	....	....	58	....	....	....	....	....	....	....	....	....	....	....	....	....	....	....	....	....	....
1979-80	**Hartford Whalers**	**NHL**	**19**	**1**	**1**	**2**	**1**	**1**	**2**	**4**	**0**	**0**	**0**	**17**	**5.9**	**9**	**0**	**10**	**0**	**–1**	....	....	....	....	....	....	....	....
	Springfield Indians	AHL	45	15	19	34	....	....	....	12	....	....	....	....	....	....	....	....	....	....	....	....	....	....	....	....	....	....
1980-81	EV Fussen	Germany	43	27	24	51	....	....	....	59	....	....	....	....	....	....	....	....	....	....	....	....	....	....	....	....	....	....
1981-82	VEU Feldkirch	Austria	28	20	22	42	....	....	....	....	....	....	....	....	....	....	....	....	....	....	10	6	16	22	....	....	....	....
1982-83	VEU Feldkirch	Austria	28	35	37	72	....	....	....	....	....	....	....	....	....	....	....	....	....	....	....	....	....	....	....	....	....	....
1983-84	VEU Feldkirch	Austria	STATISTICS NOT AVAILABLE																									
1984-85	VEU Feldkirch	Austria	37	36	31	67	....	....	....	40	....	....	....	....	....	....	....	....	....	....	....	....	....	....	....	....	....	....
1985-86	VEU Feldkirch	Austria	40	35	30	65	....	....	....	35	....	....	....	....	....	....	....	....	....	....	....	....	....	....	....	....	....	....
	Austria	WEC-B	7	3	1	4	....	....	....	2	....	....	....	....	....	....	....	....	....	....	....	....	....	....	....	....	....	....
1986-87	VEU Feldkirch	Austria	38	22	30	52	....	....	....	38	....	....	....	....	....	....	....	....	....	....	....	....	....	....	....	....	....	....
	Austria	WEC-B	5	1	0	1	....	....	....	2	....	....	....	....	....	....	....	....	....	....	....	....	....	....	....	....	....	....
1987-88	EHC Lustenau	Austria	17	3	18	21	....	....	....	30	....	....	....	....	....	....	....	....	....	....	....	....	....	....	....	....	....	....
	NHL Totals		**19**	**1**	**1**	**2**	**1**	**1**	**2**	**4**	**0**	**0**	**0**	**17**	**5.9**	**9**	**0**	**10**	**0**		....	....	....	....	....	....	....	....

Claimed by **Hartford** from **Atlanta** in Expansion Draft, June 13, 1979.

● **HILL, Sean** D – R. 6′, 205 lbs. b: Duluth, MN, 2/14/1970. Montreal's 9th, 167th overall, in 1988.

Season	Club	League	GP	G	A	Pts	AG	AA	APts	PIM	PP	SH	GW	S	%	TGF	PGF	TGA	PGA	+/–	GP	G	A	Pts	PIM	PP	SH	GW
1986-87	Lakefield Chiefs	OJHL-C	3	1	1	2	....	....	....	14	....	....	....	....	....	....	....	....	....	....	....	....	....	....	....	....	....	....
1987-88	East Duluth Hounds	Hi-School	24	10	17	27	....	....	....	....	....	....	....	....	....	....	....	....	....	....	....	....	....	....	....	....	....	....
1988-89	University of Wisconsin	WCHA	45	2	23	25	....	....	....	69	....	....	....	....	....	....	....	....	....	....	....	....	....	....	....	....	....	....
1989-90	University of Wisconsin	WCHA	42	14	39	53	....	....	....	78	....	....	....	....	....	....	....	....	....	....	....	....	....	....	....	....	....	....
	United States	WJC-A	7	0	3	3	....	....	....	10	....	....	....	....	....	....	....	....	....	....	....	....	....	....	....	....	....	....
1990-91	University of Wisconsin	WCHA	37	19	32	51	....	....	....	122	....	....	....	....	....	....	....	....	....	....	....	....	....	....	....	....	....	....
	Montreal Canadiens	**NHL**	....	....	....	....	....	....	....	....	....	....	....	....	....	....	....	....	....	....	**1**	**0**	**0**	**0**	**0**	**0**	**0**	**0**
	Fredericton Canadiens	AHL	....	....	....	....	....	....	....	....	....	....	....	....	....	....	....	....	....	....	3	0	2	2	2	....	....	....
1991-92	Fredericton Canadiens	AHL	42	7	20	27	....	....	....	65	....	....	....	....	....	....	....	....	....	....	7	1	3	4	6	....	....	....
	United States	Olympics	8	2	0	2	....	....	....	6	....	....	....	....	....	....	....	....	....	....	....	....	....	....	....	....	....	....
	United States	Nat-Team	12	4	3	7	....	....	....	16	....	....	....	....	....	....	....	....	....	....	....	....	....	....	....	....	....	....
	Montreal Canadiens	**NHL**	....	....	....	....	....	....	....	....	....	....	....	....	....	....	....	....	....	....	**4**	**1**	**0**	**1**	**2**	**0**	**0**	**0**
1992-93♦	**Montreal Canadiens**	**NHL**	**31**	**2**	**6**	**8**	**2**	**4**	**6**	**54**	**1**	**0**	**1**	**37**	**5.4**	**28**	**8**	**34**	**9**	**–5**	**3**	**0**	**0**	**0**	**4**	**0**	**0**	**0**
	Fredericton Canadiens	AHL	6	1	3	4	....	....	....	10	....	....	....	....	....	....	....	....	....	....	....	....	....	....	....	....	....	....
1993-94	**Mighty Ducks of Anaheim**	**NHL**	**68**	**7**	**20**	**27**	**6**	**16**	**22**	**78**	**2**	**1**	**1**	**165**	**4.2**	**72**	**25**	**74**	**15**	**–12**	....	....	....	....	....	....	....	....
	United States	WC-A	8	0	2	2	....	....	....	6	....	....	....	....	....	....	....	....	....	....	....	....	....	....	....	....	....	....
1994-95	**Ottawa Senators**	**NHL**	**45**	**1**	**14**	**15**	**2**	**21**	**23**	**30**	**0**	**0**	**0**	**107**	**0.9**	**50**	**14**	**66**	**19**	**–11**	....	....	....	....	....	....	....	....
1995-96	**Ottawa Senators**	**NHL**	**80**	**7**	**14**	**21**	**7**	**11**	**18**	**94**	**2**	**0**	**2**	**157**	**4.5**	**59**	**13**	**107**	**35**	**–26**	....	....	....	....	....	....	....	....
1996-97	**Ottawa Senators**	**NHL**	**5**	**0**	**0**	**0**	**0**	**0**	**0**	**4**	**0**	**0**	**0**	**9**	**0.0**	**2**	**0**	**3**	**2**	**1**	....	....	....	....	....	....	....	....

Season	Club	League	REGULAR SEASON GP	G	A	Pts	AG	AA	APts	PIM	PP	SH	GW	S	%	TGF	PGF	TGA	PGA	+/–	PLAYOFFS GP	G	A	Pts	PIM	PP	SH	GW
1997-98	Ottawa Senators	NHL	13	1	1	2	1	1	2	6	0	0	0	16	6.3	5	0	9	1	–3	....	....	....	....	....	....	....	....
	Carolina Hurricanes	NHL	42	0	5	5	0	5	5	48	0	0	0	37	0.0	24	1	31	6	–2	....	....	....	....	....	....	....	....
1998-99	Carolina Hurricanes	NHL	54	0	10	10	0	10	10	48	0	0	0	44	0.0	42	1	47	15	9	....	....	....	....	....	....	....	....
99-2000	Carolina Hurricanes	NHL	62	13	31	44	15	29	44	59	8	0	2	150	8.7	88	35	63	13	3	....	....	....	....	....	....	....	....
	NHL Totals		400	31	101	132	33	97	130	421	13	1	6	722	4.3	370	97	434	115		8	1	0	1	6	0	0	0

WCHA Second All-Star Team (1990, 1991) • NCAA West Second All-American Team (1991)

Claimed by **Anaheim** from **Montreal** in Expansion Draft, June 24, 1993. Traded to **Ottawa** by **Anaheim** with Anaheim's 9th round choice (Frederic Cassivi) in 1994 Entry Draft for Ottawa's 3rd round choice (later traded to Tampa Bay — Tampa Bay selected Vadim Epanchintsev) in 1994 Entry Draft, June 29, 1994. Traded to **Carolina** by **Ottawa** for Chris Murray, November 18, 1997. Signed as a free agent by **St. Louis**, July 1, 2000.

• HILLER, Jim

Jim A. RW – R. 6', 190 lbs. b: Port Alberni, B.C., 5/15/1969. Los Angeles' 10th, 207th overall, in 1989.

Season	Club	League	GP	G	A	Pts	AG	AA	APts	PIM	PP	SH	GW	S	%	TGF	PGF	TGA	PGA	+/–	GP	G	A	Pts	PIM	PP	SH	GW
1985-86	Kimberley Jr. Dynamiters	KIJHL	STATISTICS NOT AVAILABLE																									
1986-87	Melville Millionaires	SJHL	STATISTICS NOT AVAILABLE																									
	Prince Albert Raiders	WHL	3	0	0	0	....	....	....	12	....	....	....	....	....	....	....	....	....	....	....	....	....	....	....	....	....	....
1987-88	Melville Millionaires	SJHL	STATISTICS NOT AVAILABLE																									
1988-89	Melville Millionaires	SJHL	29	24	37	61	....	....	....	49	....	....	....	....	....	....	....	....	....	....	....	....	....	....	....	....	....	....
1989-90	Northern Michigan University	WCHA	39	23	33	56	....	....	....	52	....	....	....	....	....	....	....	....	....	....	....	....	....	....	....	....	....	....
1990-91	Northern Michigan University	WCHA	43	22	41	63	....	....	....	59	....	....	....	....	....	....	....	....	....	....	....	....	....	....	....	....	....	....
1991-92	Northern Michigan University	WCHA	39	28	52	80	....	....	....	115	....	....	....	....	....	....	....	....	....	....	....	....	....	....	....	....	....	....
1992-93	Los Angeles Kings	NHL	40	6	6	12	5	4	9	90	1	0	2	59	10.2	24	4	20	0	0	....	....	....	....	....	....	....	....
	Phoenix Roadrunners	IHL	3	0	2	2	....	....	....	2	....	....	....	....	....	....	....	....	....	....	....	....	....	....	....	....	....	....
	Detroit Red Wings	NHL	21	2	6	8	2	4	6	19	0	0	0	24	8.3	12	0	5	0	7	2	0	0	0	4	0	0	0
1993-94	New York Rangers	NHL	2	0	0	0	0	0	0	7	0	0	0	0	0.0	2	1	0	0	1	....	....	....	....	....	....	....	....
	Binghamton Rangers	AHL	67	27	34	61	....	....	....	61	....	....	....	....	....	....	....	....	....	....	....	....	....	....	....	....	....	....
1994-95	Binghamton Rangers	AHL	49	15	13	28	....	....	....	44	....	....	....	....	....	....	....	....	....	....	....	....	....	....	....	....	....	....
	Atlanta Knights	IHL	17	5	10	15	....	....	....	28	....	....	....	....	....	....	....	....	....	....	5	0	3	3	8	....	....	....
1995-96	Canada	Nat-Team	53	17	26	43	....	....	....	68	....	....	....	....	....	....	....	....	....	....	....	....	....	....	....	....	....	....
1996-97	Star Bulls Rosenheim	Germany	47	22	27	49	....	....	....	*187	....	....	....	....	....	....	....	....	....	....	3	0	1	1	45	....	....	....
1997-98	Star Bulls Rosenheim	Germany	42	8	19	27	....	....	....	83	....	....	....	....	....	....	....	....	....	....	....	....	....	....	....	....	....	....
1998-99	Star Bulls Rosenheim	Germany	52	23	44	67	....	....	....	65	....	....	....	....	....	....	....	....	....	....	....	....	....	....	....	....	....	....
99-2000	Berlin Capitals	Germany	48	16	16	32	....	....	....	90	....	....	....	....	....	....	....	....	....	....	6	3	1	4	38	....	....	....
	NHL Totals		63	8	12	20	7	8	15	116	1	0	2	83	9.6	38	5	25	0		2	0	0	0	4	0	0	0

WCHA Second All-Star Team (1992) • NCAA West Second All-American Team (1992)

Traded to **Detroit** by **LA Kings** with Paul Coffey and Sylvain Couturier for Jimmy Carson, Marc Potvin and Gary Shuchuk, January 29, 1993. Claimed on waivers by **NY Rangers** from **Detroit**, October 12, 1993.

• HILLIER, Randy

Randy George D – L. 6'1", 192 lbs. b: Toronto, Ont., 3/30/1960. Boston's 4th, 102nd overall, in 1980.

Season	Club	League	GP	G	A	Pts	AG	AA	APts	PIM	PP	SH	GW	S	%	TGF	PGF	TGA	PGA	+/–	GP	G	A	Pts	PIM	PP	SH	GW
1976-77	Lido Bruins	MTHL	38	8	22	30	....	....	....	36	....	....	....	....	....	....	....	....	....	....	....	....	....	....	....	....	....	....
1977-78	Sudbury Wolves	OMJHL	60	1	14	15	....	....	....	67	....	....	....	....	....	....	....	....	....	....	....	....	....	....	....	....	....	....
1978-79	Sudbury Wolves	OMJHL	61	8	25	33	....	....	....	173	....	....	....	....	....	....	....	....	....	....	10	2	5	7	21	....	....	....
1979-80	Sudbury Wolves	OMJHL	60	16	49	65	....	....	....	143	....	....	....	....	....	....	....	....	....	....	9	3	6	9	14	....	....	....
1980-81	Springfield Indians	AHL	64	3	17	20	....	....	....	105	....	....	....	....	....	....	....	....	....	....	6	0	2	2	36	....	....	....
1981-82	Boston Bruins	NHL	25	0	8	8	0	5	5	29	0	0	0	17	0.0	29	0	25	2	6	8	0	1	1	16	0	0	0
	Erie Blades	AHL	35	6	13	19	....	....	....	52	....	....	....	....	....	....	....	....	....	....	....	....	....	....	....	....	....	....
1982-83	Boston Bruins	NHL	70	0	10	10	0	7	7	99	0	0	0	45	0.0	51	2	42	3	10	3	0	0	0	4	0	0	0
1983-84	Boston Bruins	NHL	69	3	12	15	2	8	10	125	0	0	0	62	4.8	46	0	55	4	–5	....	....	....	....	....	....	....	....
1984-85	Pittsburgh Penguins	NHL	45	2	19	21	2	13	15	56	1	0	1	58	3.4	49	4	70	13	–12	....	....	....	....	....	....	....	....
1985-86	Pittsburgh Penguins	NHL	28	0	3	3	0	2	2	53	0	0	0	22	0.0	22	2	27	4	–3	....	....	....	....	....	....	....	....
	Baltimore Skipjacks	AHL	8	0	5	5	....	....	....	14	....	....	....	....	....	....	....	....	....	....	....	....	....	....	....	....	....	....
1986-87	Pittsburgh Penguins	NHL	55	4	8	12	3	6	9	97	0	0	0	51	7.8	46	2	45	13	12	....	....	....	....	....	....	....	....
1987-88	Pittsburgh Penguins	NHL	55	1	12	13	1	9	10	144	0	0	0	44	2.3	52	10	76	28	–6	....	....	....	....	....	....	....	....
1988-89	Pittsburgh Penguins	NHL	68	1	23	24	1	16	17	141	0	1	0	37	2.7	73	1	107	31	–4	9	0	1	1	49	0	0	0
1989-90	Pittsburgh Penguins	NHL	61	3	12	15	3	9	12	71	0	0	1	45	6.7	71	2	82	24	11	....	....	....	....	....	....	....	....
1990-91 ♦	Pittsburgh Penguins	NHL	31	2	2	4	2	2	4	32	0	0	0	14	14.3	31	0	46	12	–3	8	0	0	0	24	0	0	0
1991-92	New York Islanders	NHL	8	0	0	0	0	0	0	11	0	0	0	5	0.0	4	0	10	3	–3	....	....	....	....	....	....	....	....
	Buffalo Sabres	NHL	28	0	1	1	0	1	1	48	0	0	0	18	0.0	16	1	37	8	–14	....	....	....	....	....	....	....	....
	San Diego Gulls	IHL	6	0	2	2	....	....	....	4	....	....	....	....	....	....	....	....	....	....	....	....	....	....	....	....	....	....
1992-93	KAC Klagenfurt	Austria	23	2	9	11																						
	NHL Totals		543	16	110	126	14	78	92	906	1	1	2	418	3.8	490	24	622	145		28	0	2	2	93	0	0	0

Traded to **Pittsburgh** by **Boston** for Pittsburgh's 4th round choice (later traded to Quebec — Quebec selected Greg Polak) in 1985 Entry Draft, October 15, 1984. Signed as a free agent by **NY Islanders**, June 30, 1984. Traded to **Buffalo** by **NY Islanders** with Pat LaFontaine, Randy Wood and NY Islanders' 4th round choice (Dean Melanson) in 1992 Entry Draft for Pierre Turgeon, Uwe Krupp, Benoit Hogue and Dave McLlwain, October 25, 1991.

• HILLMAN, Larry

Larry Morley D – L. 6', 185 lbs. b: Kirkland Lake, Ont., 2/5/1937.

Season	Club	League	GP	G	A	Pts	AG	AA	APts	PIM	PP	SH	GW	S	%	TGF	PGF	TGA	PGA	+/–	GP	G	A	Pts	PIM	PP	SH	GW
1952-53	Windsor Spitfires	OHA-Jr.	56	2	4	6	....	....	....	39	....	....	....	....	....	....	....	....	....	....	....	....	....	....	....	....	....	....
1953-54	Hamilton Tiger Cubs	OHA-Jr.	58	6	14	20	....	....	....	99	....	....	....	....	....	....	....	....	....	....	7	0	2	2	10	....	....	....
1954-55	Hamilton Tiger Cubs	OHA-Jr.	49	5	20	25	....	....	....	106	....	....	....	....	....	....	....	....	....	....	3	0	1	1	9	....	....	....
♦	Detroit Red Wings	NHL	6	0	0	0	0	0	0	2	....	....	....	....	....	....	....	....	....	....	3	0	0	0	0	0	0	0
1955-56	Detroit Red Wings	NHL	47	0	3	3	0	4	4	53	....	....	....	....	....	....	....	....	....	....	10	0	1	1	6	0	0	0
	Buffalo Bisons	AHL	15	1	3	4	....	....	....	21	....	....	....	....	....	....	....	....	....	....	....	....	....	....	....	....	....	....
1956-57	Detroit Red Wings	NHL	16	1	2	3	1	2	3	4	....	....	....	....	....	....	....	....	....	....	....	....	....	....	....	....	....	....
	Edmonton Flyers	WHL	46	4	2	6	....	....	....	87	....	....	....	....	....	....	....	....	....	....	8	0	4	4	2	....	....	....
1957-58	Boston Bruins	NHL	70	3	19	22	4	20	24	60	....	....	....	....	....	....	....	....	....	....	11	0	2	2	6	0	0	0
1958-59	Boston Bruins	NHL	55	3	10	13	4	10	14	19	....	....	....	....	....	....	....	....	....	....	7	0	1	1	0	0	0	0
1959-60	Boston Bruins	NHL	2	0	1	1	0	1	1	2	....	....	....	....	....	....	....	....	....	....	....	....	....	....	....	....	....	....
	Providence Reds	AHL	70	12	31	43	....	....	....	159	....	....	....	....	....	....	....	....	....	....	5	0	1	1	4	....	....	....
1960-61	Toronto Maple Leafs	NHL	62	3	10	13	3	10	13	59	....	....	....	....	....	....	....	....	....	....	5	0	0	0	0	0	0	0
1961-62	Toronto Maple Leafs	NHL	5	0	0	0	0	0	0	4	....	....	....	....	....	....	....	....	....	....	....	....	....	....	....	....	....	....
	Rochester Americans	AHL	26	1	14	15	....	....	....	16	....	....	....	....	....	....	....	....	....	....	....	....	....	....	....	....	....	....
1962-63	Toronto Maple Leafs	NHL	5	0	0	0	0	0	0	2	....	....	....	....	....	....	....	....	....	....	....	....	....	....	....	....	....	....
	Springfield Indians	AHL	65	5	23	28	....	....	....	56	....	....	....	....	....	....	....	....	....	....	....	....	....	....	....	....	....	....
1963-64 ♦	Toronto Maple Leafs	NHL	33	0	4	4	0	4	4	31	....	....	....	....	....	....	....	....	....	....	11	0	0	0	2	0	0	0
	Rochester Americans	AHL	32	1	18	19	....	....	....	48	....	....	....	....	....	....	....	....	....	....	....	....	....	....	....	....	....	....
1964-65	Toronto Maple Leafs	NHL	2	0	0	0	0	0	0	2	....	....	....	....	....	....	....	....	....	....	....	....	....	....	....	....	....	....
	Rochester Americans	AHL	71	9	43	52	....	....	....	98	....	....	....	....	....	....	....	....	....	....	10	3	5	8	31	....	....	....
1965-66	Toronto Maple Leafs	NHL	48	3	25	28	3	24	27	34	....	....	....	....	....	....	....	....	....	....	4	1	1	2	6	0	0	0
	Rochester Americans	AHL	22	2	20	22	....	....	....	34	....	....	....	....	....	....	....	....	....	....	....	....	....	....	....	....	....	....
1966-67 ♦	Toronto Maple Leafs	NHL	55	4	19	23	5	19	24	40	....	....	....	....	....	....	....	....	....	....	12	1	2	3	0	0	0	0
	Rochester Americans	AHL	12	1	12	13	....	....	....	16	....	....	....	....	....	....	....	....	....	....	....	....	....	....	....	....	....	....
1967-68	Toronto Maple Leafs	NHL	55	3	17	20	3	17	20	13	2	0	1	92	3.3	69	19	50	7	7	....	....	....	....	....	....	....	....
	Rochester Americans	AHL	6	0	1	1	....	....	....	0	....	....	....	....	....	....	....	....	....	....	....	....	....	....	....	....	....	....
1968-69	Minnesota North Stars	NHL	12	1	5	6	1	4	5	0	1	0	0	20	5.0	13	9	12	0	–8	....	....	....	....	....	....	....	....
♦	Montreal Canadiens	NHL	25	0	5	5	0	4	4	17	0	0	0	14	0.0	13	0	15	0	–2	1	0	0	0	0	0	0	0
1969-70	Philadelphia Flyers	NHL	76	5	26	31	5	24	29	73	0	0	0	252	2.0	62	4	87	31	2	....	....	....	....	....	....	....	....
1970-71	Philadelphia Flyers	NHL	73	3	13	16	3	11	14	39	0	0	0	177	1.7	68	4	79	24	9	4	0	2	2	2	0	0	0
1971-72	Los Angeles Kings	NHL	22	1	2	3	1	2	3	11	0	0	0	13	7.7	7	0	17	3	–7	....	....	....	....	....	....	....	....
	Buffalo Sabres	NHL	43	1	11	12	1	9	10	58	0	0	0	78	1.3	65	19	82	15	–21	....	....	....	....	....	....	....	....
1972-73	Buffalo Sabres	NHL	78	5	24	29	5	19	24	56	2	0	0	102	4.9	93	36	71	11	–3	6	0	0	0	8	0	0	0

Season	Club	League	REGULAR SEASON																		PLAYOFFS							
			GP	G	A	Pts	AG	AA	APts	PIM	PP	SH	GW	S	%	TGF	PGF	TGA	PGA	+/–	GP	G	A	Pts	PIM	PP	SH	GW
1973-74	Cleveland Crusaders	WHA	44	5	21	26				37																		
1974-75	Cleveland Crusaders	WHA	77	0	16	16				83											5	1	3	4	8			
1975-76	Winnipeg Jets	WHA	71	1	12	13				62											12	0	2	2	32			
	NHL Totals		**790**	**36**	**196**	**232**	**39**	**184**	**223**	**579**											**74**	**2**	**9**	**11**	**30**			
	Other Major League Totals		192	6	49	55				182											17	1	5	6	40			

• Brother of Floyd and Wayne • AHL First All-Star Team (1960, 1965) • Won Eddie Shore Award (Outstanding Defenseman - AHL) (1960) • Played in NHL All-Star Game (1955, 1962, 1963, 1964, 1968)

Claimed by **Chicago** from **Detroit** in Intra-League Draft, June 5, 1957. Claimed on waivers by **Boston** from **Chicago**, October 14, 1957. Claimed by **Toronto** from **Boston** in Intra-League Draft, June 8, 1960. Claimed by **NY Rangers** from **Toronto** in Intra-League Draft, June 12, 1968. Claimed by **Minnesota** from **NY Rangers** in Intra-League Draft, June 12, 1968. Claimed on waivers by **Pittsburgh** from **Minnesota**, November 22, 1968. Traded to **Montreal** by **Pittsburgh** for Jean-Guy Lagace and cash, November 22, 1968. Claimed by **Philadelphia** from **Montreal** in Intra-League Draft, June 11, 1969. Traded to **LA Kings** by **Philadelphia** for Larry Mickey, June 13, 1971. Traded to **Buffalo** by **LA Kings** with Mike Byers for Doug Barrie and Mike Keeler, December 16, 1971. Selected by **Ontario-Ottawa** (WHA) in 1972 WHA General Player Draft, February 12, 1972. WHA rights traded to **Cleveland** (WHA) by **Ottawa** (WHA) for cash, June, 1973. Claimed by **Winnipeg** (WHA) from **Cleveland** (WHA) in WHA Intra-League Draft, June 19, 1975.

• HILLMAN, Wayne

Wayne James D – R. 6'1", 205 lbs. b: Kirkland Lake, Ont., 11/13/1938 d: 11/24/1990.

Season	Club	League	GP	G	A	Pts	AG	AA	APts	PIM	PP	SH	GW	S	%	TGF	PGF	TGA	PGA	+/–	GP	G	A	Pts	PIM	PP	SH	GW
1955-56	St. Catharines Teepees	OHA-Jr.	43	2	2	4				23											6	1	0	1	4			
1956-57	St. Catharines Teepees	OHA-Jr.	49	5	9	14				83											14	0	13	13	32			
	Buffalo Bisons	AHL	1	0	0	0				0																		
1957-58	St. Catharines Teepees	OHA-Jr.	52	13	26	39				160											8	1	5	6	18			
1958-59	St. Catharines Teepees	OHA-Jr.	49	8	30	38				115											7	0	0	0	21			
	Buffalo Bisons	AHL	1	0	1	1				0																		
1959-60	Buffalo Bisons	AHL	64	1	13	14				48																		
1960-61	Buffalo Bisons	AHL	72	0	18	18				40											4	0	1	1	0			
♦	**Chicago Black Hawks**	**NHL**																			**1**	**0**	**0**	**0**	**0**	**0**	**0**	**0**
1961-62	**Chicago Black Hawks**	**NHL**	**19**	**0**	**2**	**2**	**0**	**2**	**2**	**14**																		
	Buffalo Bisons	AHL	50	2	16	18				43											9	0	1	1	10			
1962-63	**Chicago Black Hawks**	**NHL**	**67**	**3**	**5**	**8**	**3**	**5**	**8**	**74**											**6**	**0**	**2**	**2**	**2**	**0**	**0**	**0**
1963-64	**Chicago Black Hawks**	**NHL**	**59**	**1**	**4**	**5**	**1**	**4**	**5**	**51**											**7**	**0**	**1**	**1**	**15**	**0**	**0**	**0**
1964-65	**Chicago Black Hawks**	**NHL**	**19**	**0**	**1**	**1**	**0**	**1**	**1**	**8**																		
	St. Louis Braves	CPHL	29	7	12	19				19																		
	New York Rangers	**NHL**	**22**	**1**	**7**	**8**	**1**	**7**	**8**	**26**																		
1965-66	**New York Rangers**	**NHL**	**68**	**3**	**17**	**20**	**3**	**16**	**19**	**70**																		
1966-67	**New York Rangers**	**NHL**	**67**	**2**	**12**	**14**	**2**	**12**	**14**	**43**											**4**	**0**	**0**	**0**	**2**	**0**	**0**	**0**
1967-68	**New York Rangers**	**NHL**	**62**	**0**	**5**	**5**	**0**	**5**	**5**	**46**	**0**	**0**	**0**	**39**	**0.0**	**49**	**0**	**49**	**9**	**9**	**2**	**0**	**0**	**0**	**0**	**0**	**0**	**0**
1968-69	**Minnesota North Stars**	**NHL**	**50**	**0**	**8**	**8**	**0**	**7**	**7**	**32**	**0**	**0**	**0**	**44**	**0.0**	**34**	**1**	**73**	**15**	**–25**								
1969-70	**Philadelphia Flyers**	**NHL**	**68**	**3**	**5**	**8**	**3**	**5**	**8**	**69**	**2**	**0**	**0**	**79**	**3.8**	**88**	**17**	**111**	**31**	**–9**								
1970-71	**Philadelphia Flyers**	**NHL**	**69**	**5**	**7**	**12**	**5**	**6**	**11**	**47**	**0**	**0**	**1**	**71**	**7.0**	**57**	**1**	**62**	**18**	**12**								
1971-72	**Philadelphia Flyers**	**NHL**	**47**	**0**	**3**	**3**	**0**	**3**	**3**	**21**	**0**	**0**	**0**	**18**	**0.0**	**14**	**2**	**38**	**10**	**–16**								
1972-73	**Philadelphia Flyers**	**NHL**	**74**	**0**	**10**	**10**	**0**	**8**	**8**	**33**	**0**	**0**	**0**	**41**	**0.0**	**63**	**1**	**59**	**13**	**16**	**8**	**0**	**0**	**0**	**0**	**0**	**0**	**0**
1973-74	Cleveland Crusaders	WHA	66	1	7	8				51											5	0	0	0	16			
1974-75	Cleveland Crusaders	WHA	60	2	9	11				37											5	0	2	2	2			
	NHL Totals		**691**	**18**	**86**	**104**	**18**	**81**	**99**	**534**											**28**	**0**	**3**	**3**	**19**			
	Other Major League Totals		126	3	16	19				88											10	0	2	2	18			

• Brother of Floyd and Larry • OHA-Jr. First All-Star Team (1958)

Traded to **NY Rangers** by **Chicago** with Doug Robinson and John Brenneman for Camille Henry, Don Johns, Billy Taylor and Wally Chevrier, February 4, 1965. Traded to **Minnesota** by **NY Rangers** with Dan Seguin and Joey Johnston for Dave Balon, June 12, 1968. Traded to **Philadelphia** by **Minnesota** for John Miszuk, May 14, 1969. Signed as a free agent by **Cleveland** (WHA), September, 1973.

• HILWORTH, John

D – R. 6'4", 205 lbs. b: Jasper, Alta., 5/23/1957. Detroit's 3rd, 55th overall, in 1977.

Season	Club	League	GP	G	A	Pts	AG	AA	APts	PIM	PP	SH	GW	S	%	TGF	PGF	TGA	PGA	+/–	GP	G	A	Pts	PIM	PP	SH	GW
1973-74	Drumheller Falcons	AJHL	57	10	28	38				161																		
	Medicine Hat Tigers	WCJHL	13	0	2	2				11											6	0	0	0	12			
1974-75	Medicine Hat Tigers	WCJHL	70	1	12	13				146											5	0	3	3	10			
1975-76	Medicine Hat Tigers	WCJHL	67	3	17	20				257											5	1	1	2	33			
1976-77	Medicine Hat Tigers	WCJHL	70	6	28	34				268											4	0	0	0	10			
1977-78	**Detroit Red Wings**	**NHL**	**5**	**0**	**0**	**0**	**0**	**0**	**0**	**12**	**0**	**0**	**0**	**0**	**0.0**	**3**	**0**	**3**	**0**	**0**								
	Kansas City Red Wings	CHL	63	3	8	11				119																		
1978-79	**Detroit Red Wings**	**NHL**	**37**	**1**	**1**	**2**	**1**	**1**	**2**	**66**	**0**	**0**	**0**	**25**	**4.0**	**5**	**1**	**17**	**0**	**–13**								
	Kansas City Red Wings	CHL	42	2	14	16				107											3	0	0	0	16			
	Kalamazoo Wings	IHL	2	1	2	3				7																		
1979-80	**Detroit Red Wings**	**NHL**	**15**	**0**	**0**	**0**	**0**	**0**	**0**	**11**	**0**	**0**	**0**	**7**	**0.0**	**0**	**0**	**2**	**0**	**–2**								
	Adirondack Red Wings	AHL	29	0	2	2				83																		
	Johnstown Red Wings	EHL	4	0	4	4				11																		
	Houston Apollos	CHL	12	2	2	4				36											6	0	3	3	12			
1980-81	Wichita Wind	CHL	64	3	12	15				144											13	1	3	4	42			
1981-82			DID NOT PLAY																									
1982-83	Fort Wayne Komets	IHL	82	16	46	62				171											10	2	6	8	33			
1983-84	Fort Wayne Komets	IHL	75	10	20	30				124											6	0	0	0	11			
1984-85	Toledo Goaldiggers	IHL	24	2	5	7				48											6	0	0	0	9			
	NHL Totals		**57**	**1**	**1**	**2**	**1**	**1**	**2**	**89**	**0**	**0**	**0**	**32**	**3.1**	**8**	**1**	**22**	**0**									

Claimed on waivers by **Edmonton** from **Detroit**, March, 1980.

• HINDMARCH, Dave

David RW – R. 5'11", 182 lbs. b: Vancouver, B.C., 10/15/1958. Atlanta's 6th, 114th overall, in 1978.

Season	Club	League	GP	G	A	Pts	AG	AA	APts	PIM	PP	SH	GW	S	%	TGF	PGF	TGA	PGA	+/–	GP	G	A	Pts	PIM	PP	SH	GW
1976-77	University of Alberta	CWUAA	30	16	19	35				8																		
1977-78	University of Alberta	CWUAA	25	11	18	29				13																		
1978-79	University of Alberta	CWUAA	41	33	29	62				40																		
1979-80	Canada	Nat-Team	44	12	11	23				30																		
	Canada	Olympics	6	3	4	7				4																		
1980-81	**Calgary Flames**	**NHL**	**1**	**1**	**0**	**1**	**1**	**0**	**1**	**0**	**0**	**0**	**0**	**1**	**100.0**	**1**	**0**	**1**	**0**	**0**	**6**	**0**	**0**	**0**	**2**	**0**	**0**	**0**
	Birmingham Bulls	CHL	48	15	14	29				18																		
	Rochester Americans	AHL	18	6	2	8				6																		
1981-82	**Calgary Flames**	**NHL**	**9**	**3**	**0**	**3**	**2**	**0**	**2**	**0**	**0**	**0**	**0**	**10**	**30.0**	**4**	**0**	**9**	**1**	**–4**								
	Oklahoma City Stars	CHL	63	27	21	48				21											4	0	1	1	6			
1982-83	**Calgary Flames**	**NHL**	**60**	**11**	**12**	**23**	**9**	**8**	**17**	**23**	**0**	**0**	**1**	**86**	**12.8**	**40**	**0**	**68**	**20**	**–8**	**4**	**0**	**0**	**0**	**4**	**0**	**0**	**0**
1983-84	**Calgary Flames**	**NHL**	**29**	**6**	**5**	**11**	**5**	**3**	**8**	**2**	**0**	**0**	**0**	**49**	**12.2**	**17**	**0**	**27**	**8**	**–2**								
	NHL Totals		**99**	**21**	**17**	**38**	**17**	**11**	**28**	**25**	**0**	**0**	**1**	**146**	**14.4**	**62**	**0**	**105**	**29**		**10**	**0**	**0**	**0**	**6**	**0**	**0**	**0**

Transferred to **Calgary** after **Atlanta** franchise relocated, June 24, 1980. • Suffered career-ending knee injury in game vs. Vancouver, December 16, 1983.

• HINOTE, Dan

RW – R. 6', 187 lbs. b: Leesburg, FL, 1/30/1977. Colorado's 9th, 167th overall, in 1996.

Season	Club	League	GP	G	A	Pts	AG	AA	APts	PIM	PP	SH	GW	S	%	TGF	PGF	TGA	PGA	+/–	GP	G	A	Pts	PIM	PP	SH	GW
1994-95	Army Black Knights	NCAA	33	20	24	44				20																		
1995-96	Army Black Knights	NCAA	34	21	24	45				22																		
1996-97	Oshawa Generals	OHL	60	15	13	28				58											18	4	5	9	8			
	Oshawa Generals	Mem-Cup	4	0	1	1				0																		
1997-98	Oshawa Generals	OHL	35	12	15	27				39											5	2	2	4	7			
	Hershey Bears	AHL	24	1	4	5				25																		
1998-99	Hershey Bears	AHL	65	4	16	20				95											5	3	1	4	6			
99-2000	**Colorado Avalanche**	**NHL**	**27**	**1**	**3**	**4**	**1**	**3**	**4**	**10**	**0**	**0**	**0**	**14**	**7.1**	**7**	**1**	**6**	**0**	**0**								
	Hershey Bears	AHL	55	28	31	59				96											14	4	5	9	19			
	NHL Totals		**27**	**1**	**3**	**4**	**1**	**3**	**4**	**10**	**0**	**0**	**0**	**14**	**7.1**	**7**	**1**	**6**	**0**									

• HINSE, Andre

Joseph Charles Andre "Gypsy Joe" LW – L. 5'9", 175 lbs. b: Trois-Rivieres, Que., 4/19/1945.

			REGULAR SEASON																		PLAYOFFS							
Season	Club	League	GP	G	A	Pts	AG	AA	APts	PIM	PP	SH	GW	S	%	TGF	PGF	TGA	PGA	+/–	GP	G	A	Pts	PIM	PP	SH	GW
1962-63	Shawinigan Cataractes	QJHL	....	....	....	....	....	....	....	....	....	....	....	....	....	....	....	....	....	....	6	1	4	5	14	....	....	....
1963-64	Shawinigan Cataractes	QJHL	STATISTICS NOT AVAILABLE																									
	Trois-Rivieres Reds	QJHL	....	....	....	....	....	....	....	....	....	....	....	....	....	....	....	....	....	....	11	8	18	26	6	....	....	....
1964-65	Trois-Rivieres Reds	QJHL	36	31	*46	*77	....	....	....	....	....	....	....	....	....	....	....	....	....	....	....	....	....	....	....	....	....	....
1965-66	Charlotte Checkers	EHL	69	33	30	63	....	....	....	67	....	....	....	....	....	....	....	....	....	....	9	3	4	7	23	....	....	....
1966-67	Charlotte Checkers	EHL	72	41	37	78	....	....	....	33	....	....	....	....	....	....	....	....	....	....	8	5	8	13	17	....	....	....
1967-68	**Toronto Maple Leafs**	**NHL**	**4**	**0**	**0**	**0**	**0**	**0**	**0**	**0**	**0**	**0**	**0**	**1**	**0.0**	**1**	**0**	**3**	**0**	**–2**	....	....	....	....	....	....	....	....
	Tulsa Oilers	CHL	61	31	34	65	....	....	....	35	....	....	....	....	....	....	....	....	....	....	11	*6	6	12	14	....	....	....
1968-69	Tulsa Oilers	CHL	42	19	23	42	....	....	....	22	....	....	....	....	....	....	....	....	....	....	7	4	1	5	0	....	....	....
1969-70	Phoenix Roadrunners	WHL	72	32	36	68	....	....	....	35	....	....	....	....	....	....	....	....	....	....	....	....	....	....	....	....	....	....
1970-71	Phoenix Roadrunners	WHL	67	44	49	93	....	....	....	34	....	....	....	....	....	....	....	....	....	....	5	0	3	3	2	....	....	....
1971-72	Phoenix Roadrunners	WHL	66	33	43	76	....	....	....	61	....	....	....	....	....	....	....	....	....	....	6	3	3	6	9	....	....	....
1972-73	Phoenix Roadrunners	WHL	72	34	42	76	....	....	....	25	....	....	....	....	....	....	....	....	....	....	10	*8	7	15	7	....	....	....
1973-74	Houston Aeros	WHA	69	24	56	80	....	....	....	39	....	....	....	....	....	....	....	....	....	....	14	8	9	17	18	....	....	....
1974-75	Houston Aeros	WHA	75	39	47	86	....	....	....	12	....	....	....	....	....	....	....	....	....	....	11	5	4	9	8	....	....	....
1975-76	Houston Aeros	WHA	70	35	38	73	....	....	....	6	....	....	....	....	....	....	....	....	....	....	17	2	3	5	2	....	....	....
1976-77	Houston Aeros	WHA	26	2	3	5	....	....	....	8	....	....	....	....	....	....	....	....	....	....	....	....	....	....	....	....	....	....
	Phoenix Roadrunners	WHA	16	2	7	9	....	....	....	14	....	....	....	....	....	....	....	....	....	....	....	....	....	....	....	....	....	....
	NHL Totals		**4**	**0**	**0**	**0**	**0**	**0**	**0**	**0**	**0**	**0**	**0**	**1**	**0.0**	**1**	**0**	**3**	**0**		....	....	....	....	....	....	....	....
	Other Major League Totals		256	102	151	253	....	....	....	79	....	....	....	....	....	....	....	....	....	....	42	15	16	31	28	....	....	....

QJHL First All-Star Team (1965) • QJHL Second All-Star Team (1964) • WHL First All-Star Team (1971, 1972, 1973)

Signed as a free agent by **Toronto**, September, 1966. Traded to **Vancouver** by **Toronto** (Phoenix-WHL) for Ted McCaskill and Pat Hannigan, August, 1970. Loaned to **Toronto** (Phoenix-WHL) by **Vancouver** for cash, September, 1970. Traded to **Toronto** by **Vancouver** for Doug Brindley, September 27, 1971. Selected by **Houston** (WHA) in 1972 WHA General Player Draft, February 12, 1972. Traded to **Phoenix** (WHA) by **Houston** (WHA) with Frank Hughes for Al McLeod, John Gray and Neil Lyseng, December, 1976.

• HINTON, Dan

Daniel Anthony LW – L. 6'1", 180 lbs. b: Toronto, Ont., 5/24/1953. Chicago's 5th, 77th overall, in 1973.

Season	Club	League	GP	G	A	Pts	AG	AA	APts	PIM	PP	SH	GW	S	%	TGF	PGF	TGA	PGA	+/–	GP	G	A	Pts	PIM	PP	SH	GW
1971-72	Kitchener Rangers	OMJHL	56	15	14	29	....	....	....	89	....	....	....	....	....	....	....	....	....	....	5	1	1	2	11	....	....	....
1972-73	Sault Ste. Marie Greyhounds	OMJHL	47	22	38	60	....	....	....	99	....	....	....	....	....	....	....	....	....	....	....	....	....	....	....	....	....	....
1973-74	Dallas Black Hawks	CHL	65	11	7	18	....	....	....	51	....	....	....	....	....	....	....	....	....	....	10	2	5	7	9	....	....	....
1974-75	Dallas Black Hawks	CHL	74	24	13	37	....	....	....	107	....	....	....	....	....	....	....	....	....	....	10	8	3	11	26	....	....	....
1975-76	Dallas Black Hawks	CHL	75	20	32	52	....	....	....	105	....	....	....	....	....	....	....	....	....	....	10	*5	3	8	23	....	....	....
1976-77	**Chicago Black Hawks**	**NHL**	**14**	**0**	**0**	**0**	**0**	**0**	**0**	**16**	**0**	**0**	**0**	**11**	**0.0**	**4**	**0**	**10**	**1**	**–5**	....	....	....	....	....	....	....	....
	Dallas Black Hawks	CHL	60	13	22	35	....	....	....	77	....	....	....	....	....	....	....	....	....	....	5	1	2	3	6	....	....	....
1977-78	Dallas Black Hawks	CHL	64	20	13	33	....	....	....	57	....	....	....	....	....	....	....	....	....	....	13	2	1	3	12	....	....	....
1978-79	New Brunswick Hawks	AHL	79	21	31	52	....	....	....	56	....	....	....	....	....	....	....	....	....	....	4	2	0	2	7	....	....	....
	NHL Totals		**14**	**0**	**0**	**0**	**0**	**0**	**0**	**16**	**0**	**0**	**0**	**11**	**0.0**	**4**	**0**	**10**	**1**		....	....	....	....	....	....	....	....

• HIRSCH, Tom

Thomas W. D – R. 6'4", 210 lbs. b: Minneapolis, MN, 1/27/1963. Minnesota's 4th, 33rd overall, in 1981.

Season	Club	League	GP	G	A	Pts	AG	AA	APts	PIM	PP	SH	GW	S	%	TGF	PGF	TGA	PGA	+/–	GP	G	A	Pts	PIM	PP	SH	GW
1980-81	Patrick Henry High	Hi-School	23	42	35	77	....	....	....	....	....	....	....	....	....	....	....	....	....	....	....	....	....	....	....	....	....	....
1981-82	University of Minnesota	WCHA	36	7	16	23	....	....	....	53	....	....	....	....	....	....	....	....	....	....	....	....	....	....	....	....	....	....
	United States	WEC-A	6	1	1	2	....	....	....	0	....	....	....	....	....	....	....	....	....	....	....	....	....	....	....	....	....	....
1982-83	University of Minnesota	WCHA	37	8	23	31	....	....	....	70	....	....	....	....	....	....	....	....	....	....	....	....	....	....	....	....	....	....
1983-84	United States	Nat-Team	56	8	25	33	....	....	....	72	....	....	....	....	....	....	....	....	....	....	....	....	....	....	....	....	....	....
	United States	Olympics	6	1	0	1	....	....	....	10	....	....	....	....	....	....	....	....	....	....	....	....	....	....	....	....	....	....
	Minnesota North Stars	**NHL**	**15**	**1**	**3**	**4**	**1**	**2**	**3**	**20**	**0**	**1**	**0**	**24**	**4.2**	**11**	**4**	**13**	**3**	**–3**	**12**	**0**	**0**	**0**	**6**	**0**	**0**	**0**
1984-85	United States	Can-Cup	5	0	0	0	....	....	....	0	....	....	....	....	....	....	....	....	....	....	....	....	....	....	....	....	....	....
	Minnesota North Stars	**NHL**	**15**	**0**	**4**	**4**	**0**	**3**	**3**	**10**	**0**	**0**	**0**	**14**	**0.0**	**11**	**2**	**27**	**5**	**–13**	....	....	....	....	....	....	....	....
	Springfield Indians	AHL	19	4	5	9	....	....	....	2	....	....	....	....	....	....	....	....	....	....	....	....	....	....	....	....	....	....
1985-86	**Minnesota North Stars**	**NHL**	DID NOT PLAY – INJURED																									
1986-87	**Minnesota North Stars**	**NHL**	DID NOT PLAY – INJURED																									
1987-88	**Minnesota North Stars**	**NHL**	**1**	**0**	**0**	**0**	**0**	**0**	**0**	**0**	**0**	**0**	**0**	**0**	**0.0**	**1**	**0**	**0**	**0**	**1**	....	....	....	....	....	....	....	....
	NHL Totals		**31**	**1**	**7**	**8**	**1**	**5**	**6**	**30**	**0**	**1**	**0**	**38**	**2.6**	**23**	**6**	**40**	**8**		**12**	**0**	**0**	**0**	**6**	**0**	**0**	**0**

• Missed entire 1985-86 and 1986-87 seasons recovering from shoulder surgery, October, 1985.

• HISLOP, Jamie

James Donald RW – R. 5'10", 180 lbs. b: Sarnia, Ont., 1/20/1954. Montreal's 13th, 140th overall, in 1974.

Season	Club	League	GP	G	A	Pts	AG	AA	APts	PIM	PP	SH	GW	S	%	TGF	PGF	TGA	PGA	+/–	GP	G	A	Pts	PIM	PP	SH	GW
1971-72	Stratford Cullitons	OHA-B	38	26	30	56	....	....	....	....	....	....	....	....	....	....	....	....	....	....	....	....	....	....	....	....	....	....
1972-73	University of New Hampshire	ECAC	26	5	16	21	....	....	....	12	....	....	....	....	....	....	....	....	....	....	....	....	....	....	....	....	....	....
1973-74	University of New Hampshire	ECAC	31	21	*35	56	....	....	....	30	....	....	....	....	....	....	....	....	....	....	....	....	....	....	....	....	....	....
1974-75	University of New Hampshire	ECAC	31	28	38	66	....	....	....	12	....	....	....	....	....	....	....	....	....	....	....	....	....	....	....	....	....	....
1975-76	University of New Hampshire	ECAC	31	23	43	66	....	....	....	20	....	....	....	....	....	....	....	....	....	....	....	....	....	....	....	....	....	....
1976-77	Cincinnati Stingers	WHA	46	7	19	26	....	....	....	6	....	....	....	....	....	....	....	....	....	....	4	0	1	1	4	....	....	....
	Hampton Gulls	SHL	37	16	17	33	....	....	....	11	....	....	....	....	....	....	....	....	....	....	....	....	....	....	....	....	....	....
1977-78	Cincinnati Stingers	WHA	80	24	43	67	....	....	....	17	....	....	....	....	....	....	....	....	....	....	....	....	....	....	....	....	....	....
1978-79	Cincinnati Stingers	WHA	80	30	40	70	....	....	....	45	....	....	....	....	....	....	....	....	....	....	3	2	4	6	0	....	....	....
1979-80	**Quebec Nordiques**	**NHL**	**80**	**19**	**20**	**39**	**16**	**15**	**31**	**6**	**0**	**1**	**3**	**124**	**15.3**	**64**	**11**	**80**	**14**	**–13**	....	....	....	....	....	....	....	....
1980-81	**Quebec Nordiques**	**NHL**	**50**	**19**	**22**	**41**	**15**	**15**	**30**	**15**	**5**	**0**	**1**	**86**	**22.1**	**66**	**14**	**73**	**17**	**–4**	....	....	....	....	....	....	....	....
	Calgary Flames	**NHL**	**29**	**6**	**9**	**15**	**5**	**6**	**11**	**11**	**0**	**0**	**0**	**31**	**19.4**	**19**	**0**	**36**	**14**	**–3**	**16**	**3**	**0**	**3**	**5**	**1**	**0**	**1**
1981-82	**Calgary Flames**	**NHL**	**80**	**16**	**25**	**41**	**13**	**17**	**30**	**35**	**0**	**2**	**1**	**113**	**14.2**	**60**	**0**	**87**	**28**	**1**	**3**	**0**	**0**	**0**	**0**	**0**	**0**	**0**
1982-83	**Calgary Flames**	**NHL**	**79**	**14**	**19**	**33**	**11**	**13**	**24**	**17**	**1**	**1**	**0**	**80**	**17.5**	**56**	**1**	**80**	**20**	**–5**	**9**	**0**	**2**	**2**	**6**	**0**	**0**	**0**
1983-84	**Calgary Flames**	**NHL**	**27**	**1**	**8**	**9**	**1**	**5**	**6**	**2**	**0**	**0**	**1**	**18**	**5.6**	**12**	**0**	**15**	**3**	**0**	....	....	....	....	....	....	....	....
1984-1985	**Calgary Flames**	**NHL**	DID NOT PLAY – ASSISTANT COACH																									
1985-1989			OUT OF HOCKEY – RETIRED																									
1989-1991	Salt Lake Golden Eagles	IHL	DID NOT PLAY – ASSISTANT COACH																									
1991-1998	**Calgary Flames**	**NHL**	DID NOT PLAY – SCOUTING																									
1998-2000	**Calgary Flames**	**NHL**	DID NOT PLAY – ASSISTANT COACH																									
	NHL Totals		**345**	**75**	**103**	**178**	**61**	**71**	**132**	**86**	**6**	**4**	**6**	**452**	**16.6**	**277**	**26**	**371**	**96**		**28**	**3**	**2**	**5**	**11**	**1**	**0**	**1**
	Other Major League Totals		206	61	102	163	....	....	....	68	....	....	....	....	....	....	....	....	....	....	7	2	5	7	4	....	....	....

ECAC First All-Star Team (1975, 1976) • NCAA East First All-American Team (1976)

Signed as a free agent by **Cincinnati** (WHA), July, 1976. Claimed by **Winnipeg** from **Cincinnati** (WHA) in WHA Dispersal Draft, June 22, 1979. Traded to **Quebec** by **Winnipeg** with Barry Legge for Barry Melrose, June 28, 1979. Traded to **Calgary** by **Quebec** for Daniel Bouchard, January 30, 1981. • Suffered eventual career-ending eye injury in game vs. NY Islanders, December 1, 1983.

• HLAVAC, Jan

LW – L. 6', 183 lbs. b: Prague, Czech., 9/20/1976. NY Islanders' 2nd, 28th overall, in 1995.

Season	Club	League	GP	G	A	Pts	AG	AA	APts	PIM	PP	SH	GW	S	%	TGF	PGF	TGA	PGA	+/–	GP	G	A	Pts	PIM	PP	SH	GW
1993-94	HC Sparta Praha	Czech-Rep	9	1	1	2	....	....	....	....	....	....	....	....	....	....	....	....	....	....	....	....	....	....	....	....	....	....
	Czech-Republic	EJC-A	5	0	1	1	....	....	....	0	....	....	....	....	....	....	....	....	....	....	....	....	....	....	....	....	....	....
1994-95	HC Sparta Praha	Czech-Rep	38	7	6	13	....	....	....	18	....	....	....	....	....	....	....	....	....	....	5	0	2	2	0	....	....	....
	Czech-Republic	WJC-A	7	2	3	5	....	....	....	4	....	....	....	....	....	....	....	....	....	....	....	....	....	....	....	....	....	....
1995-96	HC Sparta Praha	Czech-Rep	34	8	5	13	....	....	....	....	....	....	....	....	....	....	....	....	....	....	12	1	2	3	....	....	....	....
	Czech-Republic	WJC-A	6	0	0	0	....	....	....	2	....	....	....	....	....	....	....	....	....	....	....	....	....	....	....	....	....	....
1996-97	HC Sparta Praha	Czech-Rep	38	8	13	21	....	....	....	24	....	....	....	....	....	....	....	....	....	....	10	5	2	7	2	....	....	....
	HC Sparta Praha	EuroHL	3	4	0	4	....	....	....	6	....	....	....	....	....	....	....	....	....	....	....	....	....	....	....	....	....	....
1997-98	HC Sparta Praha	EuroHL	5	0	3	3	....	....	....	4	....	....	....	....	....	....	....	....	....	....	....	....	....	....	....	....	....	....
	HC Sparta Praha	Czech-Rep	48	17	30	47	....	....	....	40	....	....	....	....	....	....	....	....	....	....	5	1	0	1	2	....	....	....
	Czech-Republic	WC-A	8	1	3	4	....	....	....	2	....	....	....	....	....	....	....	....	....	....	....	....	....	....	....	....	....	....

Season	Club	League	REGULAR SEASON																		PLAYOFFS							
			GP	G	A	Pts	AG	AA	APts	PIM	PP	SH	GW	S	%	TGF	PGF	TGA	PGA	+/–	GP	G	A	Pts	PIM	PP	SH	GW
1998-99	HC Sparta Praha	Czech-Rep	49	*33	20	53	....	....	....	52	....	....	....	....	....	....	....	....	....	....	6	1	3	4	....	....	....	....
	HC Sparta Praha	EuroHL	5	4	2	6	....	....	....	0	....	....	....	....	....	....	....	....	....	....	1	1	1	2	0	....	....	....
	Czech-Republic	WC-A	12	5	5	10	....	....	....	4	....	....	....	....	....	....	....	....	....	....	....	....	....	....	....	....	....	....
99-2000	**New York Rangers**	**NHL**	**67**	**19**	**23**	**42**	**21**	**21**	**42**	**16**	**6**	**0**	**2**	**134**	**14.2**	**62**	**19**	**40**	**0**	**3**	....	....	....	....	....	....	....	....
	Hartford Wolf Pack	AHL	3	1	0	1	....	....	....	0	....	....	....	....	....	....	....	....	....	....	....	....	....	....	....	....	....	....
	NHL Totals		**67**	**19**	**23**	**42**	**21**	**21**	**42**	**16**	**6**	**0**	**2**	**134**	**14.2**	**62**	**19**	**40**	**0**		....	....	....	....	....	....	....	....

Rights traded to **NY Rangers** by **Calgary** with Calgary's 1st (Jamie Lundmark) and 3rd (later traded back to Calgary - Calgary selected Craig Andersson) round choices in 1999 Entry Draft for Marc Savard and NY Rangers' 1st round choice (Oleg Saprykin) in 1999 Entry Draft, June 26, 1999.

• HLINKA, Ivan

C – L. 6'2", 220 lbs. b: Most, Czech., 1/26/1950.

Season	Club	League	GP	G	A	Pts	AG	AA	APts	PIM	PP	SH	GW	S	%	TGF	PGF	TGA	PGA	+/–	GP	G	A	Pts	PIM	PP	SH	GW
1966-67	CHZ Litvinov	Czech.	14	4	0	4	....	....	....	....	....	....	....	....	....	....	....	....	....	....	....	....	....	....	....	....	....	....
1967-68	CHZ Litvinov	Czech.	32	15	14	29	....	....	....	....	....	....	....	....	....	....	....	....	....	....	....	....	....	....	....	....	....	....
1968-69	CHZ Litvinov	Czech.	36	21	17	38	....	....	....	....	....	....	....	....	....	....	....	....	....	....	....	....	....	....	....	....	....	....
1969-70	CHZ Litvinov	Czech.	33	17	17	34	....	....	....	20	....	....	....	....	....	....	....	....	....	....	....	....	....	....	....	....	....	....
	Czechoslovakia	WEC-A	4	0	0	0	....	....	....	2	....	....	....	....	....	....	....	....	....	....	....	....	....	....	....	....	....	....
1970-71	CHZ Litvinov	Czech.	36	20	20	40	....	....	....	....	....	....	....	....	....	....	....	....	....	....	....	....	....	....	....	....	....	....
	Czechoslovakia	WEC-A	10	4	2	6	....	....	....	2	....	....	....	....	....	....	....	....	....	....	....	....	....	....	....	....	....	....
1971-72	CHZ Litvinov	Czech.	36	31	23	54	....	....	....	....	....	....	....	....	....	....	....	....	....	....	....	....	....	....	....	....	....	....
	Czechoslovakia	Olympics	6	5	3	8	....	....	....	2	....	....	....	....	....	....	....	....	....	....	....	....	....	....	....	....	....	....
	Czechoslovakia	WEC-A	5	2	3	5	....	....	....	0	....	....	....	....	....	....	....	....	....	....	....	....	....	....	....	....	....	....
1972-73	CHZ Litvinov	Czech.	36	24	11	35	....	....	....	....	....	....	....	....	....	....	....	....	....	....	....	....	....	....	....	....	....	....
	Czechoslovakia	WEC-A	8	2	1	3	....	....	....	0	....	....	....	....	....	....	....	....	....	....	....	....	....	....	....	....	....	....
1973-74	CHZ Litvinov	Czech.	39	27	27	54	....	....	....	....	....	....	....	....	....	....	....	....	....	....	....	....	....	....	....	....	....	....
	Czechoslovakia	WEC-A	10	9	4	13	....	....	....	2	....	....	....	....	....	....	....	....	....	....	....	....	....	....	....	....	....	....
1974-75	CHZ Litvinov	Czech.	44	36	*42	*78	....	....	....	....	....	....	....	....	....	....	....	....	....	....	....	....	....	....	....	....	....	....
	Czechoslovakia	WEC-A	6	2	4	6	....	....	....	2	....	....	....	....	....	....	....	....	....	....	....	....	....	....	....	....	....	....
1975-76	CHZ Litvinov	Czech.	30	25	18	43	....	....	....	6	....	....	....	....	....	....	....	....	....	....	....	....	....	....	....	....	....	....
	Czechoslovakia	Olympics	5	3	3	6	....	....	....	7	....	....	....	....	....	....	....	....	....	....	....	....	....	....	....	....	....	....
	Czechoslovakia	WEC-A	10	7	8	15	....	....	....	4	....	....	....	....	....	....	....	....	....	....	....	....	....	....	....	....	....	....
1976-77	Czechoslovakia	Can-Cup	7	2	2	4	....	....	....	12	....	....	....	....	....	....	....	....	....	....	....	....	....	....	....	....	....	....
	CHZ Litvinov	Czech.	42	39	19	58	....	....	....	....	....	....	....	....	....	....	....	....	....	....	....	....	....	....	....	....	....	....
	Czechoslovakia	WEC-A	10	9	3	12	....	....	....	5	....	....	....	....	....	....	....	....	....	....	....	....	....	....	....	....	....	....
1977-78	CHZ Litvinov	Czech.	43	32	39	71	....	....	....	30	....	....	....	....	....	....	....	....	....	....	....	....	....	....	....	....	....	....
	Czechoslovakia	WEC-A	10	4	10	14	....	....	....	4	....	....	....	....	....	....	....	....	....	....	....	....	....	....	....	....	....	....
1978-79	Dukla Trencin	Czech.	8	2	3	5	....	....	....	0	....	....	....	....	....	....	....	....	....	....	....	....	....	....	....	....	....	....
	CHZ Litvinov	Czech.	23	15	17	32	....	....	....	14	....	....	....	....	....	....	....	....	....	....	....	....	....	....	....	....	....	....
	Czechoslovakia	WEC-A	8	3	5	8	....	....	....	6	....	....	....	....	....	....	....	....	....	....	....	....	....	....	....	....	....	....
1979-80	CHZ Litvinov	Czech.	33	14	16	30	....	....	....	8	....	....	....	....	....	....	....	....	....	....	2	1	1	2	0	....	....	....
1980-81	CHZ Litvinov	Czech.	40	21	31	52	....	....	....	38	....	....	....	....	....	....	....	....	....	....	28	5	15	20	....	....	....	....
	Czechoslovakia	WEC-A	8	0	3	3	....	....	....	0	....	....	....	....	....	....	....	....	....	....	....	....	....	....	....	....	....	....
1981-82	**Vancouver Canucks**	**NHL**	**72**	**23**	**37**	**60**	**18**	**25**	**43**	**16**	**7**	**0**	**2**	**152**	**15.1**	**81**	**17**	**43**	**0**	**21**	**12**	**2**	**6**	**8**	**4**	**2**	**0**	**0**
1982-83	**Vancouver Canucks**	**NHL**	**65**	**19**	**44**	**63**	**16**	**31**	**47**	**12**	**8**	**0**	**0**	**147**	**12.9**	**91**	**46**	**48**	**0**	**–3**	**4**	**1**	**4**	**5**	**4**	**0**	**0**	**0**
1983-84	EV Zug	Switz-2	41	46	43	89	....	....	....	....	....	....	....	....	....	....	....	....	....	....	....	....	....	....	....	....	....	....
1984-85	EV Zug	Switz-2	39	30	43	73	....	....	....	....	....	....	....	....	....	....	....	....	....	....	....	....	....	....	....	....	....	....
1985-86	CHZ Litvonov	Czech.	DID NOT PLAY – COACHING																									
1986-87	CHZ Litvonov	Czech.	19	5	18	23	....	....	....	12	....	....	....	....	....	....	....	....	....	....	....	....	....	....	....	....	....	....
1987-1990	CHZ Litvonov	Czech.	DID NOT PLAY – COACHING																									
1990-91			OUT OF HOCKEY – RETIRED																									
1991-1993	Czechoslovakia	Nat-Team	DID NOT PLAY – COACHING																									
1993-94	Czech-Republic	Nat-Team	DID NOT PLAY – COACHING																									
1994-1997			OUT OF HOCKEY – RETIRED																									
1997-2000	Czech-Republic	Nat-Team	DID NOT PLAY – COACHING																									
1999-2000	**Pittsburgh Penguins**	**NHL**	DID NOT PLAY – ASSISTANT COACH																									
	NHL Totals		**137**	**42**	**81**	**123**	**34**	**56**	**90**	**28**	**15**	**0**	**2**	**299**	**14.0**	**172**	**63**	**91**	**0**		**16**	**3**	**10**	**13**	**8**	**2**	**0**	**0**

Czechoslovakian Player of the Year (1978) • WEC-A All-Star Team (1978)

Claimed in Special Czechoslovakian Entry Draft by **Winnipeg**, May 28, 1981. Rights traded to **Vancouver** by **Winnipeg** for Brent Ashton and Vancouver's 4th round choice (Tom Martin), July 15, 1981. • Named Head Coach of **Pittsburgh**, June 28, 2000.

• HLUSHKO, Todd

C – L. 5'11", 185 lbs. b: Toronto, Ont., 2/7/1970. Washington's 14th, 240th overall, in 1990.

Season	Club	League	GP	G	A	Pts	AG	AA	APts	PIM	PP	SH	GW	S	%	TGF	PGF	TGA	PGA	+/–	GP	G	A	Pts	PIM	PP	SH	GW
1987-88	Guelph Jr. B's	OJHL-B	44	36	47	83	....	....	....	94	....	....	....	....	....	....	....	....	....	....	....	....	....	....	....	....	....	....
1988-89	Guelph Platers	OHL	66	28	18	46	....	....	....	71	....	....	....	....	....	....	....	....	....	....	7	5	3	8	18	....	....	....
1989-90	Owen Sound Platers	OHL	25	9	17	26	....	....	....	31	....	....	....	....	....	....	....	....	....	....	....	....	....	....	....	....	....	....
	London Knights	OHL	40	27	17	44	....	....	....	39	....	....	....	....	....	....	....	....	....	....	6	2	4	6	10	....	....	....
1990-91	Baltimore Skipjacks	AHL	66	9	14	23	....	....	....	55	....	....	....	....	....	....	....	....	....	....	....	....	....	....	....	....	....	....
1991-92	Baltimore Skipjacks	AHL	74	16	35	51	....	....	....	113	....	....	....	....	....	....	....	....	....	....	....	....	....	....	....	....	....	....
1992-93	Canada	Nat-Team	58	22	26	48	....	....	....	10	....	....	....	....	....	....	....	....	....	....	....	....	....	....	....	....	....	....
1993-94	Canada	Nat-Team	55	22	6	28	....	....	....	61	....	....	....	....	....	....	....	....	....	....	....	....	....	....	....	....	....	....
	Canada	Olympics	8	5	0	5	....	....	....	6	....	....	....	....	....	....	....	....	....	....	....	....	....	....	....	....	....	....
	Philadelphia Flyers	**NHL**	**2**	**1**	**0**	**1**	**1**	**0**	**1**	**0**	**0**	**0**	**0**	**2**	**50.0**	**1**	**0**	**0**	**0**	**1**	....	....	....	....	....	....	....	....
	Hershey Bears	AHL	9	6	0	6	....	....	....	4	....	....	....	....	....	....	....	....	....	....	6	2	1	3	4	....	....	....
1994-95	**Calgary Flames**	**NHL**	**2**	**0**	**1**	**1**	**0**	**1**	**1**	**2**	**0**	**0**	**0**	**3**	**0.0**	**1**	**0**	**0**	**0**	**1**	**1**	**0**	**0**	**0**	**2**	**0**	**0**	**0**
	Saint John Flames	AHL	46	22	10	32	....	....	....	36	....	....	....	....	....	....	....	....	....	....	4	2	2	4	22	....	....	....
	Canada	WC-A	8	4	0	4	....	....	....	4	....	....	....	....	....	....	....	....	....	....	....	....	....	....	....	....	....	....
1995-96	**Calgary Flames**	**NHL**	**4**	**0**	**0**	**0**	**0**	**0**	**0**	**6**	**0**	**0**	**0**	**6**	**0.0**	**1**	**0**	**3**	**2**	**0**	....	....	....	....	....	....	....	....
	Saint John Flames	AHL	35	14	13	27	....	....	....	70	....	....	....	....	....	....	....	....	....	....	16	8	1	9	26	....	....	....
1996-97	**Calgary Flames**	**NHL**	**58**	**7**	**11**	**18**	**7**	**10**	**17**	**49**	**0**	**0**	**0**	**76**	**9.2**	**20**	**0**	**36**	**14**	**–2**	....	....	....	....	....	....	....	....
1997-98	**Calgary Flames**	**NHL**	**13**	**0**	**1**	**1**	**0**	**1**	**1**	**27**	**0**	**0**	**0**	**7**	**0.0**	**3**	**0**	**5**	**2**	**0**	....	....	....	....	....	....	....	....
	Saint John Flames	AHL	33	10	14	24	....	....	....	48	....	....	....	....	....	....	....	....	....	....	21	*13	4	17	61	....	....	....
1998-99	Grand Rapids Griffins	IHL	82	24	26	50	....	....	....	78	....	....	....	....	....	....	....	....	....	....	....	....	....	....	....	....	....	....
	Pittsburgh Penguins	**NHL**	....	....	....	....	....	....	....	....	....	....	....	....	....	....	....	....	....	....	**2**	**0**	**0**	**0**	**0**	**0**	**0**	**0**
99-2000	Kolner Haie	Germany	55	13	28	41	....	....	....	78	....	....	....	....	....	....	....	....	....	....	10	5	2	7	20	....	....	....
	NHL Totals		**79**	**8**	**13**	**21**	**8**	**12**	**20**	**84**	**0**	**0**	**0**	**94**	**8.5**	**26**	**0**	**44**	**18**		**3**	**0**	**0**	**0**	**2**	**0**	**0**	**0**

Signed as a free agent by **Philadelphia**, March 7, 1994. Signed as a free agent by **Calgary**, June 17, 1994. Traded to **Pittsburgh** by **Calgary** with German Titov for Ken Wregget and Dave Roche, June 17, 1998.

• HOCKING, Justin

Justin R. D – R. 6'4", 205 lbs. b: Stettler, Alta., 1/9/1974. Los Angeles' 1st, 39th overall, in 1992.

Season	Club	League	GP	G	A	Pts	AG	AA	APts	PIM	PP	SH	GW	S	%	TGF	PGF	TGA	PGA	+/–	GP	G	A	Pts	PIM	PP	SH	GW
1990-91	Fort Saskatchewan Traders	AJHL	38	4	6	10	....	....	....	84	....	....	....	....	....	....	....	....	....	....	....	....	....	....	....	....	....	....
1991-92	Spokane Chiefs	WHL	71	4	6	10	....	....	....	309	....	....	....	....	....	....	....	....	....	....	10	0	3	3	28	....	....	....
1992-93	Spokane Chiefs	WHL	16	0	1	1	....	....	....	75	....	....	....	....	....	....	....	....	....	....	....	....	....	....	....	....	....	....
	Medicine Hat Tigers	WHL	54	1	9	10	....	....	....	119	....	....	....	....	....	....	....	....	....	....	10	0	1	1	13	....	....	....
1993-94	Medicine Hat Tigers	WHL	68	7	26	33	....	....	....	236	....	....	....	....	....	....	....	....	....	....	3	0	0	0	6	....	....	....
	Los Angeles Kings	**NHL**	**1**	**0**	**0**	**0**	**0**	**0**	**0**	**0**	**0**	**0**	**0**	**0**	**0.0**	**0**	**0**	**0**	**0**	**0**	....	....	....	....	....	....	....	....
	Phoenix Roadrunners	IHL	3	0	0	0	....	....	....	15	....	....	....	....	....	....	....	....	....	....	....	....	....	....	....	....	....	....
1994-95	Syracuse Crunch	AHL	7	0	0	0	....	....	....	24	....	....	....	....	....	....	....	....	....	....	....	....	....	....	....	....	....	....
	Portland Pirates	AHL	9	0	1	1	....	....	....	34	....	....	....	....	....	....	....	....	....	....	....	....	....	....	....	....	....	....
	Knoxville Cherokees	ECHL	20	0	6	6	....	....	....	70	....	....	....	....	....	....	....	....	....	....	4	0	0	0	26	....	....	....
	Phoenix Roadrunners	IHL	20	1	1	2	....	....	....	50	....	....	....	....	....	....	....	....	....	....	1	0	0	0	0	....	....	....
1995-96	P.E.I. Senators	AHL	74	4	8	12	....	....	....	251	....	....	....	....	....	....	....	....	....	....	4	0	2	2	5	....	....	....
1996-97	Worcester IceCats	AHL	68	1	10	11	....	....	....	198	....	....	....	....	....	....	....	....	....	....	5	0	3	3	2	....	....	....

			REGULAR SEASON																		PLAYOFFS							
Season	Club	League	GP	G	A	Pts	AG	AA	APts	PIM	PP	SH	GW	S	%	TGF	PGF	TGA	PGA	+/–	GP	G	A	Pts	PIM	PP	SH	GW
1997-98	Worcester IceCats	AHL	79	5	12	17	....	....	....	198	....	....	....	....	....	....	....	....	....	....	11	1	2	3	19	....	....	....
1998-99	Indianapolis Ice	IHL	34	2	4	6	....	....	....	111	....	....	....	....	....	....	....	....	....	....	....	....	....	....	....	....	....	....
	St. John's Maple Leafs	AHL	44	4	6	10	....	....	....	99	....	....	....	....	....	....	....	....	....	....	5	0	0	0	2	....	....	....
99-2000	St. John's Maple Leafs	AHL	68	4	9	13	....	....	....	175	....	....	....	....	....	....	....	....	....	....	....	....	....	....	....	....	....	....
	NHL Totals		**1**	**0**	**0**	**0**	**0**	**0**	**0**	**0**	**0**	**0**	**0**	**0**	**0.0**	**0**	**0**	**0**	**0**		....	....	....	....	....	....	....	....

WHL East Second All-Star Team (1994)

Claimed by **Ottawa** from **LA Kings** in Waiver Draft, October 2, 1995. Traded to **Chicago** by **Ottawa** for Brian Felsner, August 21, 1998. Signed as a free agent by **Toronto**, July 23, 1999.

• HODGE, Ken
Kenneth Raymond RW – R. 6'2", 210 lbs. b: Birmingham, England, 6/25/1944.

Season	Club	League	GP	G	A	Pts	AG	AA	APts	PIM	PP	SH	GW	S	%	TGF	PGF	TGA	PGA	+/–	GP	G	A	Pts	PIM	PP	SH	GW
1961-62	Lakeshore Bruins	OHA-B	STATISTICS NOT AVAILABLE																									
	St. Catharines Teepees	OHA-Jr.	31	4	3	7	....	....	....	6	....	....	....	....	....	....	....	....	....	....	6	1	0	1	6	....	....	....
1962-63	St. Catharines Black Hawks	OHA-Jr.	50	23	23	46	....	....	....	97	....	....	....	....	....	....	....	....	....	....	....	....	....	....	....	....	....	....
1963-64	St. Catharines Black Hawks	OHA-Jr.	56	37	51	88	....	....	....	110	....	....	....	....	....	....	....	....	....	....	13	6	19	25	28	....	....	....
1964-65	St. Catharines Black Hawks	OHA-Jr.	55	*63	60	*123	....	....	....	107	....	....	....	....	....	....	....	....	....	....	5	3	7	10	8	....	....	....
	Chicago Black Hawks	**NHL**	**1**	**0**	**0**	**0**	**0**	**0**	**0**	**2**	....	....	....	....	....	....	....	....	....	....	....	....	....	....	....	....	....	....
	Buffalo Bisons	AHL	2	0	2	2	....	....	....	0	....	....	....	....	....	....	....	....	....	....	4	0	0	0	4	....	....	....
1965-66	**Chicago Black Hawks**	**NHL**	**63**	**6**	**17**	**23**	**7**	**16**	**23**	**47**	....	....	....	....	....	....	....	....	....	....	**5**	**0**	**0**	**0**	**8**	**0**	**0**	**0**
1966-67	**Chicago Black Hawks**	**NHL**	**69**	**10**	**25**	**35**	**12**	**24**	**36**	**59**	....	....	....	....	....	....	....	....	....	....	**6**	**0**	**0**	**0**	**4**	**0**	**0**	**0**
1967-68	**Boston Bruins**	**NHL**	**74**	**25**	**31**	**56**	**29**	**31**	**60**	**31**	**5**	**0**	**3**	**188**	**13.3**	**75**	**12**	**53**	**3**	**13**	**4**	**3**	**0**	**3**	**2**	**0**	**0**	**0**
1968-69	**Boston Bruins**	**NHL**	**75**	**45**	**45**	**90**	**48**	**40**	**88**	**75**	**9**	**1**	**7**	**236**	**19.1**	**125**	**22**	**60**	**6**	**49**	**10**	**5**	**7**	**12**	**4**	**2**	**0**	**0**
1969-70♦	**Boston Bruins**	**NHL**	**72**	**25**	**29**	**54**	**27**	**27**	**54**	**87**	**6**	**0**	**5**	**198**	**12.6**	**82**	**21**	**53**	**7**	**15**	**14**	**3**	**10**	**13**	**7**	**0**	**1**	**0**
1970-71	**Boston Bruins**	**NHL**	**78**	**43**	**62**	**105**	**43**	**52**	**95**	**113**	**4**	**0**	**7**	**232**	**18.5**	**147**	**20**	**58**	**2**	**71**	**7**	**2**	**5**	**7**	**6**	**0**	**0**	**0**
1971-72♦	**Boston Bruins**	**NHL**	**60**	**16**	**40**	**56**	**16**	**35**	**51**	**81**	**0**	**1**	**2**	**140**	**11.4**	**86**	**7**	**40**	**2**	**41**	**15**	**9**	**8**	**17**	***62**	**2**	**1**	**3**
1972-73	**Boston Bruins**	**NHL**	**73**	**37**	**44**	**81**	**35**	**35**	**70**	**58**	**16**	**0**	**5**	**197**	**18.8**	**136**	**55**	**77**	**6**	**10**	**5**	**1**	**0**	**1**	**7**	**1**	**0**	**0**
1973-74	**Boston Bruins**	**NHL**	**76**	**50**	**55**	**105**	**48**	**46**	**94**	**43**	**15**	**0**	**11**	**251**	**19.9**	**174**	**60**	**75**	**1**	**40**	**16**	**6**	**10**	**16**	**16**	**1**	**0**	**1**
1974-75	**Boston Bruins**	**NHL**	**72**	**23**	**43**	**66**	**20**	**32**	**52**	**90**	**16**	**0**	**2**	**175**	**13.1**	**124**	**58**	**59**	**0**	**7**	**3**	**1**	**1**	**2**	**0**	**1**	**0**	**0**
1975-76	**Boston Bruins**	**NHL**	**72**	**25**	**36**	**61**	**22**	**27**	**49**	**42**	**8**	**0**	**5**	**161**	**15.5**	**100**	**47**	**34**	**0**	**19**	**12**	**4**	**6**	**10**	**4**	**4**	**0**	**1**
1976-77	**New York Rangers**	**NHL**	**78**	**21**	**41**	**62**	**19**	**32**	**51**	**43**	**6**	**0**	**5**	**141**	**14.9**	**95**	**36**	**78**	**1**	**–18**	....	....	....	....	....	....	....	....
1977-78	**New York Rangers**	**NHL**	**18**	**2**	**4**	**6**	**2**	**3**	**5**	**8**	**1**	**0**	**1**	**13**	**15.4**	**9**	**4**	**11**	**0**	**–6**	....	....	....	....	....	....	....	....
	New Haven Nighthawks	AHL	52	17	29	46	....	....	....	13	....	....	....	....	....	....	....	....	....	....	15	3	4	7	20	....	....	....
1978-79			DID NOT PLAY – INJURED																									
1979-80	Binghamton Dusters	AHL	37	10	20	30	....	....	....	24	....	....	....	....	....	....	....	....	....	....	....	....	....	....	....	....	....	....
	NHL Totals		**881**	**328**	**472**	**800**	**328**	**400**	**728**	**779**	....	....	....	....	....	....	....	....	....	....	**97**	**34**	**47**	**81**	**120**	....	....	....

• Father of Ken Jr. • OHA-Jr. First All-Star Team (1965) • NHL First All-Star Team (1971, 1974) • Played in NHL All-Star Game (1971, 1973, 1974)

Traded to **Boston** by **Chicago** with Phil Esposito and Fred Stanfield for Gilles Marotte, Pit Martin and Jack Norris, May 15, 1967. Traded to **NY Rangers** by **Boston** for Rick Middleton, May 26, 1976. • Missed entire 1978-79 season recovering from elbow surgery, August, 1978.

• HODGE, Ken
Kenneth David C/RW – L. 6'1", 200 lbs. b: Windsor, Ont., 4/13/1966. Minnesota's 2nd, 46th overall, in 1984.

Season	Club	League	GP	G	A	Pts	AG	AA	APts	PIM	PP	SH	GW	S	%	TGF	PGF	TGA	PGA	+/–	GP	G	A	Pts	PIM	PP	SH	GW
1982-83	St. John's Prep School	Hi-School	22	22	33	55	....	....	....	....	....	....	....	....	....	....	....	....	....	....	....	....	....	....	....	....	....	....
1983-84	St. John's Prep School	Hi-School	22	25	38	63	....	....	....	....	....	....	....	....	....	....	....	....	....	....	....	....	....	....	....	....	....	....
1984-85	Boston College	H-East	41	20	44	64	....	....	....	28	....	....	....	....	....	....	....	....	....	....	....	....	....	....	....	....	....	....
1985-86	Boston College	H-East	21	11	17	28	....	....	....	16	....	....	....	....	....	....	....	....	....	....	....	....	....	....	....	....	....	....
1986-87	Boston College	H-East	37	29	33	62	....	....	....	30	....	....	....	....	....	....	....	....	....	....	....	....	....	....	....	....	....	....
1987-88	Kalamazoo Wings	IHL	70	15	35	50	....	....	....	24	....	....	....	....	....	....	....	....	....	....	....	....	....	....	....	....	....	....
1988-89	**Minnesota North Stars**	**NHL**	**5**	**1**	**1**	**2**	**1**	**1**	**2**	**0**	**0**	**0**	**0**	**6**	**16.7**	**3**	**0**	**2**	**0**	**1**	....	....	....	....	....	....	....	....
	Kalamazoo Wings	IHL	72	26	45	71	....	....	....	34	....	....	....	....	....	....	....	....	....	....	6	1	5	6	16	....	....	....
1989-90	Kalamazoo Wings	IHL	68	33	53	86	....	....	....	19	....	....	....	....	....	....	....	....	....	....	10	5	13	18	2	....	....	....
1990-91	**Boston Bruins**	**NHL**	**70**	**30**	**29**	**59**	**28**	**22**	**50**	**20**	**12**	**2**	**4**	**137**	**21.9**	**80**	**26**	**57**	**14**	**11**	**15**	**4**	**6**	**10**	**6**	**1**	**0**	**1**
	Maine Mariners	AHL	8	7	10	17	....	....	....	2	....	....	....	....	....	....	....	....	....	....	....	....	....	....	....	....	....	....
1991-92	**Boston Bruins**	**NHL**	**42**	**6**	**11**	**17**	**5**	**8**	**13**	**10**	**3**	**1**	**3**	**62**	**9.7**	**29**	**11**	**41**	**15**	**–8**	....	....	....	....	....	....	....	....
	Maine Mariners	AHL	19	6	11	17	....	....	....	4	....	....	....	....	....	....	....	....	....	....	....	....	....	....	....	....	....	....
1992-93	**Tampa Bay Lightning**	**NHL**	**25**	**2**	**7**	**9**	**2**	**5**	**7**	**2**	**0**	**0**	**1**	**32**	**6.3**	**14**	**7**	**22**	**9**	**–6**	....	....	....	....	....	....	....	....
	Atlanta Knights	IHL	16	10	17	27	....	....	....	0	....	....	....	....	....	....	....	....	....	....	....	....	....	....	....	....	....	....
	San Diego Gulls	IHL	30	11	24	35	....	....	....	16	....	....	....	....	....	....	....	....	....	....	14	4	6	10	6	....	....	....
1993-94	Binghamton Rangers	AHL	79	22	56	78	....	....	....	51	....	....	....	....	....	....	....	....	....	....	....	....	....	....	....	....	....	....
1994-95	Kansas City Blades	IHL	62	15	25	40	....	....	....	18	....	....	....	....	....	....	....	....	....	....	17	4	6	10	4	....	....	....
1995-96	Minnesota Moose	IHL	75	14	40	54	....	....	....	28	....	....	....	....	....	....	....	....	....	....	....	....	....	....	....	....	....	....
1996-97	Ratingen Lowen	Germany	6	1	3	4	....	....	....	0	....	....	....	....	....	....	....	....	....	....	....	....	....	....	....	....	....	....
	Cardiff Devils	Britain	34	16	29	45	....	....	....	6	....	....	....	....	....	....	....	....	....	....	7	1	4	5	2	....	....	....
1997-98	Cardiff Devils	BH-Cup	15	4	13	17	....	....	....	8	....	....	....	....	....	....	....	....	....	....	....	....	....	....	....	....	....	....
	Cardiff Devils	Britain	32	10	19	29	....	....	....	18	....	....	....	....	....	....	....	....	....	....	9	4	10	14	0	....	....	....
	NHL Totals		**142**	**39**	**48**	**87**	**36**	**36**	**72**	**32**	**15**	**3**	**8**	**237**	**16.5**	**126**	**44**	**122**	**38**		**15**	**4**	**6**	**10**	**6**	**1**	**0**	**1**

• Son of Ken • NHL All-Rookie Team (1991)

Traded to **Boston** by **Minnesota** for Boston's 4th round choice (Jere Lehtinen) in 1992 Entry Draft, August 21, 1990. Traded to **Tampa Bay** by **Boston** with Matt Hervey for Darin Kimble and future considerations, September 4, 1992. Signed as a free agent by **NY Rangers**, September 2, 1993.

• HODGSON, Dan
Daniel W. C – R. 5'10", 175 lbs. b: Fort Vermillon, Alta., 8/29/1965. Toronto's 4th, 85th overall, in 1983.

Season	Club	League	GP	G	A	Pts	AG	AA	APts	PIM	PP	SH	GW	S	%	TGF	PGF	TGA	PGA	+/–	GP	G	A	Pts	PIM	PP	SH	GW
1980-81	Cowichan Valley Capitals	BCJHL	39	32	42	74	....	....	....	26	....	....	....	....	....	....	....	....	....	....	....	....	....	....	....	....	....	....
	Spokane Chiefs	WHL	2	0	0	0	....	....	....	0	....	....	....	....	....	....	....	....	....	....	....	....	....	....	....	....	....	....
1981-82	Cowichan Valley Capitals	BCJHL	46	45	75	120	....	....	....	30	....	....	....	....	....	....	....	....	....	....	....	....	....	....	....	....	....	....
1982-83	Prince Albert Raiders	WHL	72	56	74	130	....	....	....	66	....	....	....	....	....	....	....	....	....	....	....	....	....	....	....	....	....	....
1983-84	Prince Albert Raiders	WHL	66	62	*119	181	....	....	....	65	....	....	....	....	....	....	....	....	....	....	5	5	3	8	7	....	....	....
	Canada	WJC-A	7	1	4	5	....	....	....	4	....	....	....	....	....	....	....	....	....	....	....	....	....	....	....	....	....	....
1984-85	Prince Albert Raiders	WHL	64	70	*112	182	....	....	....	86	....	....	....	....	....	....	....	....	....	....	13	10	*26	*36	32	....	....	....
	Canada	WJC-A	7	5	2	7	....	....	....	0	....	....	....	....	....	....	....	....	....	....	....	....	....	....	....	....	....	....
	Prince Albert Raiders	Mem-Cup	5	1	*13	*14	....	....	....	6	....	....	....	....	....	....	....	....	....	....	....	....	....	....	....	....	....	....
1985-86	**Toronto Maple Leafs**	**NHL**	**40**	**13**	**12**	**25**	**10**	**8**	**18**	**12**	**2**	**0**	**0**	**54**	**24.1**	**33**	**9**	**32**	**3**	**–5**	....	....	....	....	....	....	....	....
	St. Catharines Saints	AHL	22	13	16	29	....	....	....	15	....	....	....	....	....	....	....	....	....	....	13	3	9	12	14	....	....	....
1986-87	Newmarket Saints	AHL	20	7	12	19	....	....	....	16	....	....	....	....	....	....	....	....	....	....	....	....	....	....	....	....	....	....
	Vancouver Canucks	**NHL**	**43**	**9**	**13**	**22**	**8**	**9**	**17**	**25**	**4**	**0**	**0**	**42**	**21.4**	**37**	**17**	**29**	**0**	**–9**	....	....	....	....	....	....	....	....
1987-88	**Vancouver Canucks**	**NHL**	**8**	**3**	**7**	**10**	**3**	**5**	**8**	**2**	**1**	**0**	**1**	**7**	**42.9**	**13**	**7**	**5**	**0**	**1**	....	....	....	....	....	....	....	....
	Fredericton Express	AHL	13	8	18	26	....	....	....	16	....	....	....	....	....	....	....	....	....	....	....	....	....	....	....	....	....	....
1988-89	**Vancouver Canucks**	**NHL**	**23**	**4**	**13**	**17**	**3**	**9**	**12**	**25**	**0**	**0**	**1**	**38**	**10.5**	**29**	**10**	**16**	**0**	**3**	....	....	....	....	....	....	....	....
	Milwaukee Admirals	IHL	47	27	55	82	....	....	....	47	....	....	....	....	....	....	....	....	....	....	11	6	7	13	10	....	....	....
1989-90	EHC Lustenau	Austria	2	1	1	2	....	....	....	0	....	....	....	....	....	....	....	....	....	....	....	....	....	....	....	....	....	....
	HC Fribourg-Gotteron	Switz.	36	17	22	39	....	....	....	....	....	....	....	....	....	....	....	....	....	....	3	4	0	4	....	....	....	....
1990-91	ECH Munich	Germany	22	10	17	27	....	....	....	12	....	....	....	....	....	....	....	....	....	....	4	1	0	1	11	....	....	....
1991-92	ECH Munich	Germany	44	24	22	46	....	....	....	31	....	....	....	....	....	....	....	....	....	....	6	4	5	9	6	....	....	....
	HC Ajoie	Switz-2	1	1	1	2	....	....	....	0	....	....	....	....	....	....	....	....	....	....	....	....	....	....	....	....	....	....
1992-93	SC Langnau	Switz-2	36	33	39	72	....	....	....	35	....	....	....	....	....	....	....	....	....	....	5	3	5	8	20	....	....	....
1993-94	SC Langnau	Switz-2	8	6	7	13	....	....	....	6	....	....	....	....	....	....	....	....	....	....	....	....	....	....	....	....	....	....
1994-95	HC Davos	Switz.	35	23	27	50	....	....	....	32	....	....	....	....	....	....	....	....	....	....	5	1	2	3	4	....	....	....
1995-96	HC Davos	Switz.	33	16	32	48	....	....	....	59	....	....	....	....	....	....	....	....	....	....	5	3	4	7	2	....	....	....
1996-97	HC Davos	Switz.	46	29	32	61	....	....	....	69	....	....	....	....	....	....	....	....	....	....	6	2	3	5	2	....	....	....
1997-98	HC Davos	Switz.	28	11	29	40	....	....	....	18	....	....	....	....	....	....	....	....	....	....	....	....	....	....	....	....	....	....

Season	Club	League	GP	G	A	Pts	AG	AA	APts	PIM	PP	SH	GW	S	%	TGF	PGF	TGA	PGA	+/–	GP	G	A	Pts	PIM	PP	SH	GW
			REGULAR SEASON																		PLAYOFFS							
1998-99	ZSC Lions Zurich	Switz.	43	10	39	49	....	....	....	42	....	....	....	....	....	....	....	....	....	....	7	2	7	9	6	....	....	....
	Canada	Nat-Team	3	2	4	6	....	....	....	0	....	....	....	....	....	....	....	....	....	....	....	....	....	....	....	....	....	....
99-2000	ZSC Lions Zurich	Switz.	40	11	30	41	....	....	....	64	....	....	....	....	....	....	....	....	....	....	15	3	5	8	10	....	....	....
	NHL Totals		**114**	**29**	**45**	**74**	**24**	**31**	**55**	**64**	**7**	**0**	**2**	**141**	**20.6**	**112**	**43**	**82**	**3**	....	....	....	....	....	....	....	....	....

WHL East First All-Star Team (1985) • Memorial Cup All-Star Team (1985) • Canadian Major Junior Player of the Year (1985) • Won Stafford Smythe Memorial Trophy (Memorial Cup Tournament MVP) (1985)

Traded to **Vancouver** by **Toronto** with Jim Benning for Rick Lanz, December 2, 1986.

• HODGSON, Rick

Richard S. D – R. 6', 175 lbs. b: Medicine Hat, Alta., 5/23/1956. Atlanta's 4th, 46th overall, in 1976.

Season	Club	League	GP	G	A	Pts	AG	AA	APts	PIM	PP	SH	GW	S	%	TGF	PGF	TGA	PGA	+/–	GP	G	A	Pts	PIM	PP	SH	GW
1972-73	Kamloops Blazers	BCJHL	STATISTICS NOT AVAILABLE																									
1973-74	Calgary Centennials	WCJHL	65	8	44	52	....	....	....	174	....	....	....	....	....	....	....	....	....	....	14	1	9	10	34	....	....	....
1974-75	Calgary Centennials	WCJHL	56	7	36	43	....	....	....	221	....	....	....	....	....	....	....	....	....	....	....	....	....	....	....	....	....	....
	Canada	WJC-A	3	0	1	1	....	....	....	0	....	....	....	....	....	....	....	....	....	....	....	....	....	....	....	....	....	....
1975-76	Calgary Centennials	WCJHL	50	7	48	55	....	....	....	168	....	....	....	....	....	....	....	....	....	....	....	....	....	....	....	....	....	....
1976-77	Tulsa Oilers	CHL	62	3	18	21	....	....	....	101	....	....	....	....	....	....	....	....	....	....	6	0	0	0	6	....	....	....
1977-78	Tulsa Oilers	CHL	76	7	20	27	....	....	....	180	....	....	....	....	....	....	....	....	....	....	7	0	3	3	19	....	....	....
1978-79	Tulsa Oilers	CHL	75	9	17	26	....	....	....	167	....	....	....	....	....	....	....	....	....	....	....	....	....	....	....	....	....	....
1979-80	**Hartford Whalers**	**NHL**	**6**	**0**	**0**	**0**	**0**	**0**	**0**	**6**	**0**	**0**	**0**	**1**	**0.0**	**4**	**0**	**10**	**1**	**–5**	**1**	**0**	**0**	**0**	**0**	**0**	**0**	**0**
	Springfield Indians	AHL	75	7	26	33	....	....	....	186	....	....	....	....	....	....	....	....	....	....	....	....	....	....	....	....	....	....
	NHL Totals		**6**	**0**	**0**	**0**	**0**	**0**	**0**	**6**	**0**	**0**	**0**	**1**	**0.0**	**4**	**0**	**10**	**1**		**1**	**0**	**0**	**0**	**0**	**0**	**0**	**0**

Claimed by **Hartford** from **Atlanta** in Expansion Draft, June 13, 1979.

• HOEKSTRA, Ed

Edward Adrian C – R. 5'11", 170 lbs. b: Winnipeg, Man., 11/4/1937.

Season	Club	League	GP	G	A	Pts	AG	AA	APts	PIM	PP	SH	GW	S	%	TGF	PGF	TGA	PGA	+/–	GP	G	A	Pts	PIM	PP	SH	GW
1954-55	St. Catharines Teepees	OHA-Jr.	49	17	21	38	....	....	....	20	....	....	....	....	....	....	....	....	....	....	11	3	2	5	21	....	....	....
1955-56	St. Catharines Teepees	OHA-Jr.	48	22	31	53	....	....	....	18	....	....	....	....	....	....	....	....	....	....	6	2	0	2	4	....	....	....
1956-57	St. Catharines Teepees	OHA-Jr.	52	28	42	70	....	....	....	22	....	....	....	....	....	....	....	....	....	....	14	11	*15	26	2	....	....	....
1957-58	St. Catharines Teepees	OHA-Jr.	49	35	*58	93	....	....	....	28	....	....	....	....	....	....	....	....	....	....	8	2	6	8	4	....	....	....
1958-59	Trois-Rivieres Lions	QHL	58	19	37	56	....	....	....	8	....	....	....	....	....	....	....	....	....	....	8	3	4	7	0	....	....	....
1959-60	Cleveland Barons	AHL	66	20	38	58	....	....	....	4	....	....	....	....	....	....	....	....	....	....	7	4	3	7	0	....	....	....
1960-61	Kitchener-Waterloo Beavers	EPHL	70	32	33	65	....	....	....	18	....	....	....	....	....	....	....	....	....	....	7	2	3	5	0	....	....	....
1961-62	Kitchener-Waterloo Beavers	EPHL	44	23	27	50	....	....	....	16	....	....	....	....	....	....	....	....	....	....	....	....	....	....	....	....	....	....
	Quebec Aces	AHL	22	6	10	16	....	....	....	2	....	....	....	....	....	....	....	....	....	....	....	....	....	....	....	....	....	....
1962-63	Quebec Aces	AHL	30	6	8	14	....	....	....	2	....	....	....	....	....	....	....	....	....	....	....	....	....	....	....	....	....	....
1963-64	Quebec Aces	AHL	71	20	44	64	....	....	....	22	....	....	....	....	....	....	....	....	....	....	6	2	2	4	2	....	....	....
1964-65	Quebec Aces	AHL	71	28	51	79	....	....	....	16	....	....	....	....	....	....	....	....	....	....	5	0	3	3	6	....	....	....
1965-66	Quebec Aces	AHL	61	24	50	74	....	....	....	10	....	....	....	....	....	....	....	....	....	....	6	5	0	5	4	....	....	....
1966-67	Quebec Aces	AHL	7	1	0	1	....	....	....	0	....	....	....	....	....	....	....	....	....	....	....	....	....	....	....	....	....	....
	California Seals	WHL	31	11	7	18	....	....	....	4	....	....	....	....	....	....	....	....	....	....	6	1	3	4	2	....	....	....
1967-68	**Philadelphia Flyers**	**NHL**	**70**	**15**	**21**	**36**	**17**	**21**	**38**	**6**	**5**	**0**	**4**	**126**	**11.9**	**51**	**10**	**51**	**16**	**6**	**7**	**0**	**1**	**1**	**0**	**0**	**0**	**0**
1968-69	Denver Spurs	WHL	62	20	49	69	....	....	....	4	....	....	....	....	....	....	....	....	....	....	....	....	....	....	....	....	....	....
1969-70	Denver Spurs	WHL	27	9	18	27	....	....	....	2	....	....	....	....	....	....	....	....	....	....	....	....	....	....	....	....	....	....
	Buffalo Bisons	AHL	1	0	0	0	....	....	....	0	....	....	....	....	....	....	....	....	....	....	....	....	....	....	....	....	....	....
1970-71	Denver Spurs	WHL	30	11	11	22	....	....	....	0	....	....	....	....	....	....	....	....	....	....	....	....	....	....	....	....	....	....
	Springfield Kings	AHL	44	13	22	35	....	....	....	4	....	....	....	....	....	....	....	....	....	....	12	4	2	6	4	....	....	....
1971-72	Springfield Kings	AHL	74	16	*69	85	....	....	....	32	....	....	....	....	....	....	....	....	....	....	5	1	1	2	0	....	....	....
1972-73	Houston Aeros	WHA	78	11	28	39	....	....	....	12	....	....	....	....	....	....	....	....	....	....	9	1	2	3	0	....	....	....
1973-74	Houston Aeros	WHA	19	2	0	2	....	....	....	0	....	....	....	....	....	....	....	....	....	....	....	....	....	....	....	....	....	....
	Macon Whoopees	SHL	2	0	5	5	....	....	....	0	....	....	....	....	....	....	....	....	....	....	....	....	....	....	....	....	....	....
	Jacksonville Barons	AHL	29	11	12	23	....	....	....	2	....	....	....	....	....	....	....	....	....	....	....	....	....	....	....	....	....	....
	NHL Totals		**70**	**15**	**21**	**36**	**17**	**21**	**38**	**6**	**5**	**0**	**4**	**126**	**11.9**	**51**	**10**	**51**	**16**		**7**	**0**	**1**	**1**	**0**	**0**	**0**	**0**
	Other Major League Totals		97	13	28	41	....	....	....	12	....	....	....	....	....	....	....	....	....	....	9	1	2	3	0	....	....	....

• Brother of Cec • Won William Northey Trophy (Top Rookie - QHL) (1959)

Claimed by **NY Rangers** from **Chicago** (Calgary-WHL) in Inter-League Draft, June 9, 1959. Traded to **Cleveland** (AHL) by **NY Rangers** with Aldo Guidolin for Art Stratton with NY Rangers holding right of recall, June, 1959. Loaned to **California** (WHL) by **Quebec** (AHL) for the loan of Jean-Guy Morissette, January, 1967. NHL rights transferred to **Philadelphia** after NHL club purchased **Quebec** (AHL) franchise, May 8, 1967. Claimed by **Denver** (WHL) from **Philadelphia** in Reverse Draft, June 13, 1968. Traded to **LA Kings** by **Denver** (WHL) for Jimmy Peters Jr. with LA Kings holding right of recall, December, 1970. Selected by **Houston** (WHA) in 1972 WHA General Player Draft, February 13, 1972.

• HOENE, Phil

Phil George LW – L. 5'9", 175 lbs. b: Duluth, MN, 3/15/1949.

Season	Club	League	GP	G	A	Pts	AG	AA	APts	PIM	PP	SH	GW	S	%	TGF	PGF	TGA	PGA	+/–	GP	G	A	Pts	PIM	PP	SH	GW
1968-69	University of Minnesota-Duluth	WCHA	18	8	6	14	....	....	....	4	....	....	....	....	....	....	....	....	....	....	....	....	....	....	....	....	....	....
1969-70	University of Minnesota-Duluth	WCHA	18	5	6	11	....	....	....	8	....	....	....	....	....	....	....	....	....	....	....	....	....	....	....	....	....	....
1970-71	University of Minnesota-Duluth	WCHA	34	14	13	27	....	....	....	37	....	....	....	....	....	....	....	....	....	....	....	....	....	....	....	....	....	....
1971-72	Springfield Kings	AHL	65	15	11	26	....	....	....	17	....	....	....	....	....	....	....	....	....	....	2	0	0	0	0	....	....	....
1972-73	**Los Angeles Kings**	**NHL**	**4**	**0**	**1**	**1**	**0**	**1**	**1**	**0**	**0**	**0**	**0**	**3**	**0.0**	**2**	**1**	**0**	**0**	**1**	....	....	....	....	....	....	....	....
	Springfield Kings	AHL	70	36	44	80	....	....	....	17	....	....	....	....	....	....	....	....	....	....	....	....	....	....	....	....	....	....
1973-74	**Los Angeles Kings**	**NHL**	**31**	**2**	**3**	**5**	**2**	**2**	**4**	**22**	**0**	**0**	**1**	**20**	**10.0**	**6**	**0**	**19**	**8**	**–5**	....	....	....	....	....	....	....	....
	Springfield Kings	AHL	42	19	23	42	....	....	....	20	....	....	....	....	....	....	....	....	....	....	....	....	....	....	....	....	....	....
1974-75	**Los Angeles Kings**	**NHL**	**2**	**0**	**0**	**0**	**0**	**0**	**0**	**0**	**0**	**0**	**0**	**0**	**0.0**	**0**	**0**	**1**	**1**	**0**	....	....	....	....	....	....	....	....
	Springfield Indians	AHL	70	25	30	55	....	....	....	10	....	....	....	....	....	....	....	....	....	....	17	*12	10	*22	8	....	....	....
1975-76	Fort Worth Texans	CHL	76	13	22	35	....	....	....	14	....	....	....	....	....	....	....	....	....	....	....	....	....	....	....	....	....	....
1976-1988	Sun Valley Suns	X-Games	144	89	122	211	....	....	....	30	....	....	....	....	....	....	....	....	....	....	....	....	....	....	....	....	....	....
	NHL Totals		**37**	**2**	**4**	**6**	**2**	**3**	**5**	**22**	**0**	**0**	**1**	**23**	**8.7**	**8**	**1**	**20**	**9**		....	....	....	....	....	....	....	....

Signed as a free agent by **LA Kings**, June, 1971. • **Sun Valley Suns** statistics represent the player's entire career - 1976-1988 - with the team.

• HOFFMAN, Mike

Michael LW – L. 5'11", 190 lbs. b: Barrie, Ont., 2/26/1963. Hartford's 3rd, 67th overall, in 1981.

Season	Club	League	GP	G	A	Pts	AG	AA	APts	PIM	PP	SH	GW	S	%	TGF	PGF	TGA	PGA	+/–	GP	G	A	Pts	PIM	PP	SH	GW
1979-80	Barrie Colts	OJHL	60	40	35	75	....	....	....	....	....	....	....	....	....	....	....	....	....	....	....	....	....	....	....	....	....	....
1980-81	Brantford Alexanders	OMJHL	68	15	19	34	....	....	....	71	....	....	....	....	....	....	....	....	....	....	6	1	0	1	5	....	....	....
1981-82	Brantford Alexanders	OHL	66	34	47	81	....	....	....	169	....	....	....	....	....	....	....	....	....	....	11	5	8	13	9	....	....	....
1982-83	Brantford Alexanders	OHL	63	26	49	75	....	....	....	128	....	....	....	....	....	....	....	....	....	....	8	5	4	9	18	....	....	....
	Hartford Whalers	**NHL**	**2**	**0**	**1**	**1**	**0**	**1**	**1**	**0**	**0**	**0**	**0**	**2**	**0.0**	**2**	**0**	**4**	**0**	**–2**	....	....	....	....	....	....	....	....
	Binghamton Whalers	AHL	1	0	0	0	....	....	....	0	....	....	....	....	....	....	....	....	....	....	3	0	1	1	0	....	....	....
1983-84	Binghamton Whalers	AHL	64	11	13	24	....	....	....	92	....	....	....	....	....	....	....	....	....	....	....	....	....	....	....	....	....	....
1984-85	**Hartford Whalers**	**NHL**	**1**	**0**	**0**	**0**	**0**	**0**	**0**	**0**	**0**	**0**	**0**	**0**	**0.0**	**0**	**0**	**0**	**0**	**0**	....	....	....	....	....	....	....	....
	Binghamton Whalers	AHL	76	19	26	45	....	....	....	95	....	....	....	....	....	....	....	....	....	....	8	4	1	5	23	....	....	....
1985-86	**Hartford Whalers**	**NHL**	**6**	**1**	**2**	**3**	**1**	**1**	**2**	**2**	**0**	**0**	**0**	**7**	**14.3**	**3**	**0**	**5**	**0**	**–2**	....	....	....	....	....	....	....	....
	Binghamton Whalers	AHL	40	14	14	28	....	....	....	79	....	....	....	....	....	....	....	....	....	....	2	1	0	1	2	....	....	....
1986-87	Binghamton Whalers	AHL	74	9	32	41	....	....	....	120	....	....	....	....	....	....	....	....	....	....	13	2	2	4	23	....	....	....
1987-88	Flint Spirits	IHL	64	35	28	63	....	....	....	49	....	....	....	....	....	....	....	....	....	....	14	3	7	10	36	....	....	....
1988-89	Flint Spirits	IHL	76	33	39	72	....	....	....	46	....	....	....	....	....	....	....	....	....	....	....	....	....	....	....	....	....	....
1989-90	EV Landsberg	Germany-2	13	6	12	18	....	....	....	14	....	....	....	....	....	....	....	....	....	....	....	....	....	....	....	....	....	....
	NHL Totals		**9**	**1**	**3**	**4**	**1**	**2**	**3**	**2**	**0**	**0**	**0**	**9**	**11.1**	**5**	**0**	**9**	**0**		....	....	....	....	....	....	....	....

• HOFFMEYER, Bob

Robert Frank D – L. 6', 182 lbs. b: Dodsland, Sask., 7/27/1955. Chicago's 5th, 79th overall, in 1975.

Season	Club	League	GP	G	A	Pts	AG	AA	APts	PIM	PP	SH	GW	S	%	TGF	PGF	TGA	PGA	+/–	GP	G	A	Pts	PIM	PP	SH	GW
1972-73	Prince Albert Raiders	SJHL	46	3	20	23	....	....	....	....	....	....	....	....	....	....	....	....	....	....	....	....	....	....	....	....	....	....
1973-74	Saskatoon Blades	WCJHL	62	2	10	12	....	....	....	198	....	....	....	....	....	....	....	....	....	....	6	0	1	1	20	....	....	....
1974-75	Saskatoon Blades	WCJHL	64	4	38	42	....	....	....	242	....	....	....	....	....	....	....	....	....	....	17	2	10	12	69	....	....	....
1975-76	Dallas Black Hawks	CHL	5	0	0	0	....	....	....	11	....	....	....	....	....	....	....	....	....	....	....	....	....	....	....	....	....	....
	Flint Generals	IHL	67	3	13	16	....	....	....	145	....	....	....	....	....	....	....	....	....	....	4	1	1	2	5	....	....	....

			REGULAR SEASON																		PLAYOFFS							
Season	Club	League	GP	G	A	Pts	AG	AA	APts	PIM	PP	SH	GW	S	%	TGF	PGF	TGA	PGA	+/–	GP	G	A	Pts	PIM	PP	SH	GW
1976-77	Flint Generals	IHL	78	12	51	63	....	....	....	213	....	....	....	....	....	....	....	....	....	....	5	0	7	7	22	....	....	....
1977-78	**Chicago Black Hawks**	**NHL**	**5**	**0**	**1**	**1**	**0**	**1**	**1**	**12**	**0**	**0**	**0**	**3**	**0.0**	**3**	**0**	**5**	**0**	**–2**	....	....	....	....	....	....	....	....
	Dallas Black Hawks	CHL	67	5	11	16	....	....	....	172	....	....	....	....	....	....	....	....	....	....	13	1	3	4	40	....	....	....
1978-79	**Chicago Black Hawks**	**NHL**	**6**	**0**	**2**	**2**	**0**	**1**	**1**	**5**	**0**	**0**	**0**	**3**	**0.0**	**3**	**0**	**8**	**1**	**–4**	....	....	....	....	....	....	....	....
	New Brunswick Hawks	AHL	41	3	6	9	....	....	....	104	....	....	....	....	....	....	....	....	....	....	....	....	....	....	....	....	....	....
1979-80	New Brunswick Hawks	AHL	77	3	20	23	....	....	....	161	....	....	....	....	....	....	....	....	....	....	17	0	3	3	38	....	....	....
1980-81	Schwenninger ERC	Germany	39	22	30	52	....	....	....	122	....	....	....	....	....	....	....	....	....	....	....	....	....	....	....	....	....	....
	Maine Mariners	AHL	2	1	1	2	....	....	....	0	....	....	....	....	....	....	....	....	....	....	20	2	11	13	68	....	....	....
1981-82	**Philadelphia Flyers**	**NHL**	**57**	**7**	**20**	**27**	**6**	**13**	**19**	**142**	**4**	**0**	**0**	**88**	**8.0**	**90**	**28**	**68**	**19**	**13**	**2**	**0**	**1**	**1**	**25**	**0**	**0**	**0**
	Maine Mariners	AHL	21	6	8	14	....	....	....	57	....	....	....	....	....	....	....	....	....	....	....	....	....	....	....	....	....	....
1982-83	**Philadelphia Flyers**	**NHL**	**35**	**2**	**11**	**13**	**2**	**8**	**10**	**40**	**1**	**0**	**0**	**50**	**4.0**	**38**	**4**	**44**	**17**	**7**	**1**	**0**	**0**	**0**	**0**	**0**	**0**	**0**
	Maine Mariners	AHL	23	5	10	15	....	....	....	79	....	....	....	....	....	....	....	....	....	....	....	....	....	....	....	....	....	....
1983-84	Maine Mariners	AHL	14	3	1	4	....	....	....	27	....	....	....	....	....	....	....	....	....	....	....	....	....	....	....	....	....	....
	New Jersey Devils	**NHL**	**58**	**4**	**12**	**16**	**3**	**8**	**11**	**61**	**0**	**0**	**0**	**80**	**5.0**	**45**	**2**	**91**	**28**	**–20**	....	....	....	....	....	....	....	....
1984-85	**New Jersey Devils**	**NHL**	**37**	**1**	**6**	**7**	**1**	**4**	**5**	**65**	**0**	**0**	**0**	**37**	**2.7**	**20**	**0**	**50**	**15**	**–15**	....	....	....	....	....	....	....	....
1985-86	Maine Mariners	AHL	8	0	0	0	....	....	....	6	....	....	....	....	....	....	....	....	....	....	5	0	0	0	6	....	....	....
	NHL Totals		**198**	**14**	**52**	**66**	**12**	**35**	**47**	**325**	**5**	**0**	**0**	**261**	**5.4**	**199**	**34**	**266**	**80**		**3**	**0**	**1**	**1**	**25**	**0**	**0**	**0**

Signed as a free agent by **Philadelphia**, November 22, 1981. Claimed by **Edmonton** from **Philadelphia** in Waiver Draft, October 4, 1982. Traded to **Philadelphia** by **Edmonton** for Peter Dineen, October 22, 1982. Signed as a free agent by **New Jersey**, August 15, 1983.

• HOFFORD, Jim

James D – R. 6', 190 lbs. b: Sudbury, Ont., 10/4/1964. Buffalo's 8th, 118th overall, in 1983.

Season	Club	League	GP	G	A	Pts	AG	AA	APts	PIM	PP	SH	GW	S	%	TGF	PGF	TGA	PGA	+/–	GP	G	A	Pts	PIM	PP	SH	GW
1980-81	Sudbury Toppazzini Midgets	NOHA	52	18	39	57	....	....	....	....	....	....	....	....	....	....	....	....	....	....	....	....	....	....	....	....	....	....
1981-82	Windsor Spitfires	OHA-Jr.	67	5	9	14	....	....	....	214	....	....	....	....	....	....	....	....	....	....	....	....	....	....	....	....	....	....
1982-83	Windsor Spitfires	OHL	63	8	20	28	....	....	....	173	....	....	....	....	....	....	....	....	....	....	3	0	1	1	15	....	....	....
1983-84	Windsor Spitfires	OHL	1	0	0	0	....	....	....	2	....	....	....	....	....	....	....	....	....	....	....	....	....	....	....	....	....	....
1984-85	Rochester Americans	AHL	71	2	13	15	....	....	....	166	....	....	....	....	....	....	....	....	....	....	5	0	0	0	16	....	....	....
1985-86	**Buffalo Sabres**	**NHL**	**5**	**0**	**0**	**0**	**0**	**0**	**0**	**5**	**0**	**0**	**0**	**3**	**0.0**	**3**	**0**	**5**	**1**	**–1**	....	....	....	....	....	....	....	....
	Rochester Americans	AHL	40	2	7	9	....	....	....	148	....	....	....	....	....	....	....	....	....	....	....	....	....	....	....	....	....	....
1986-87	**Buffalo Sabres**	**NHL**	**12**	**0**	**0**	**0**	**0**	**0**	**0**	**40**	**0**	**0**	**0**	**8**	**0.0**	**8**	**0**	**10**	**1**	**–1**	....	....	....	....	....	....	....	....
	Rochester Americans	AHL	54	1	8	9	....	....	....	204	....	....	....	....	....	....	....	....	....	....	13	1	0	1	57	....	....	....
1987-88	Rochester Americans	AHL	69	3	15	18	....	....	....	322	....	....	....	....	....	....	....	....	....	....	7	0	0	0	28	....	....	....
1988-89	**Los Angeles Kings**	**NHL**	**1**	**0**	**0**	**0**	**0**	**0**	**0**	**2**	**0**	**0**	**0**	**0**	**0.0**	**2**	**0**	**0**	**0**	**2**	....	....	....	....	....	....	....	....
	Rochester Americans	AHL	34	1	9	10	....	....	....	13	....	....	....	....	....	....	....	....	....	....	....	....	....	....	....	....	....	....
1989-90	Rochester Americans	AHL	52	1	9	10	....	....	....	233	....	....	....	....	....	....	....	....	....	....	17	1	1	2	56	....	....	....
	NHL Totals		**18**	**0**	**0**	**0**	**0**	**0**	**0**	**47**	**0**	**0**	**0**	**11**	**0.0**	**13**	**0**	**15**	**2**		....	....	....	....	....	....	....	....

• Missed remainder of 1983-84 season recovering from knee injury suffered in game vs. Sudbury (OHL), September 29, 1983. Claimed by **LA Kings** from **Buffalo**, in Waiver Draft, October 3, 1988.

• HOGABOAM, Bill

William Harold C – R. 5'11", 170 lbs. b: Swift Current, Sask., 9/5/1949.

Season	Club	League	GP	G	A	Pts	AG	AA	APts	PIM	PP	SH	GW	S	%	TGF	PGF	TGA	PGA	+/–	GP	G	A	Pts	PIM	PP	SH	GW
1965-66	Swift Current Crusaders	SIHA	STATISTICS NOT AVAILABLE																									
1966-67	Swift Current Broncos	X-Games	26	30	30	60	....	....	....	....	....	....	....	....	....	....	....	....	....	....	....	....	....	....	....	....	....	....
1967-68	Swift Current Broncos	WCJHL	40	27	26	53	....	....	....	34	....	....	....	....	....	....	....	....	....	....	....	....	....	....	....	....	....	....
1968-69	Swift Current Broncos	WCJHL	5	5	4	9	....	....	....	2	....	....	....	....	....	....	....	....	....	....	....	....	....	....	....	....	....	....
	Sorel Black Hawks	MMJHL	STATISTICS NOT AVAILABLE																									
	Sorel Black Hawks	Mem-Cup	....	....	....	....	....	....	....	....	....	....	....	....	....	....	....	....	....	....	....	....	....	....	....	....	....	....
1969-70	Saskatoon Blades	WCJHL	53	27	42	69	....	....	....	8	....	....	....	....	....	....	....	....	....	....	7	3	2	5	2	....	....	....
1970-71	Omaha Knights	CHL	63	12	18	30	....	....	....	12	....	....	....	....	....	....	....	....	....	....	11	2	3	5	6	....	....	....
1971-72	Phoenix Roadrunners	WHL	1	0	1	1	....	....	....	2	....	....	....	....	....	....	....	....	....	....	....	....	....	....	....	....	....	....
	Omaha Knights	CHL	70	30	52	82	....	....	....	36	....	....	....	....	....	....	....	....	....	....	4	1	5	6	0	....	....	....
1972-73	**Atlanta Flames**	**NHL**	**2**	**0**	**0**	**0**	**0**	**0**	**0**	**0**	**0**	**0**	**0**	**0**	**0.0**	**0**	**0**	**0**	**0**	**0**	....	....	....	....	....	....	....	....
	Detroit Red Wings	**NHL**	**4**	**1**	**0**	**1**	**1**	**0**	**1**	**2**	**0**	**0**	**0**	**1**	**100.0**	**1**	**0**	**2**	**0**	**–1**	....	....	....	....	....	....	....	....
	Virginia Wings	AHL	50	16	28	44	....	....	....	14	....	....	....	....	....	....	....	....	....	....	13	6	10	16	10	....	....	....
1973-74	**Detroit Red Wings**	**NHL**	**47**	**18**	**23**	**41**	**17**	**19**	**36**	**12**	**6**	**0**	**0**	**100**	**18.0**	**57**	**20**	**40**	**0**	**–3**	....	....	....	....	....	....	....	....
	Virginia Wings	AHL	23	8	11	19	....	....	....	15	....	....	....	....	....	....	....	....	....	....	....	....	....	....	....	....	....	....
1974-75	**Detroit Red Wings**	**NHL**	**60**	**14**	**27**	**41**	**12**	**20**	**32**	**16**	**6**	**1**	**1**	**129**	**10.9**	**56**	**24**	**79**	**13**	**–34**	....	....	....	....	....	....	....	....
1975-76	**Detroit Red Wings**	**NHL**	**50**	**21**	**16**	**37**	**18**	**12**	**30**	**30**	**6**	**2**	**0**	**116**	**18.1**	**53**	**15**	**54**	**8**	**–8**	....	....	....	....	....	....	....	....
	Minnesota North Stars	**NHL**	**18**	**7**	**7**	**14**	**6**	**5**	**11**	**6**	**1**	**0**	**0**	**44**	**15.9**	**17**	**4**	**17**	**0**	**–4**	....	....	....	....	....	....	....	....
1976-77	**Minnesota North Stars**	**NHL**	**73**	**10**	**15**	**25**	**9**	**12**	**21**	**16**	**0**	**0**	**0**	**120**	**8.3**	**39**	**3**	**53**	**0**	**–17**	**2**	**0**	**0**	**0**	**0**	**0**	**0**	**0**
1977-78	**Minnesota North Stars**	**NHL**	**8**	**1**	**2**	**3**	**1**	**2**	**3**	**4**	**0**	**0**	**0**	**6**	**16.7**	**4**	**0**	**9**	**0**	**–5**	....	....	....	....	....	....	....	....
	Fort Worth Texans	CHL	60	22	44	66	....	....	....	43	....	....	....	....	....	....	....	....	....	....	10	0	7	7	6	....	....	....
1978-79	**Minnesota North Stars**	**NHL**	**10**	**1**	**1**	**2**	**1**	**1**	**2**	**0**	**0**	**0**	**0**	**6**	**16.7**	**4**	**0**	**7**	**2**	**–1**	....	....	....	....	....	....	....	....
	Oklahoma City Stars	CHL	40	21	29	50	....	....	....	18	....	....	....	....	....	....	....	....	....	....	....	....	....	....	....	....	....	....
	Detroit Red Wings	**NHL**	**18**	**4**	**6**	**10**	**3**	**4**	**7**	**4**	**1**	**0**	**1**	**29**	**13.8**	**13**	**3**	**15**	**0**	**–5**	....	....	....	....	....	....	....	....
1979-80	**Detroit Red Wings**	**NHL**	**42**	**3**	**12**	**15**	**3**	**9**	**12**	**10**	**0**	**0**	**1**	**26**	**11.5**	**18**	**0**	**30**	**4**	**–8**	....	....	....	....	....	....	....	....
	Adirondack Red Wings	AHL	25	11	15	26	....	....	....	4	....	....	....	....	....	....	....	....	....	....	....	....	....	....	....	....	....	....
1980-81	Adirondack Red Wings	AHL	73	19	37	56	....	....	....	78	....	....	....	....	....	....	....	....	....	....	18	0	15	15	4	....	....	....
1981-82	Dallas Black Hawks	CHL	67	20	47	67	....	....	....	24	....	....	....	....	....	....	....	....	....	....	16	1	9	10	8	....	....	....
1982-83	Adirondack Red Wings	AHL	77	20	38	58	....	....	....	14	....	....	....	....	....	....	....	....	....	....	6	3	5	8	0	....	....	....
	NHL Totals		**332**	**80**	**109**	**189**	**71**	**84**	**155**	**100**	**20**	**3**	**3**	**577**	**13.9**	**262**	**69**	**306**	**27**		**2**	**0**	**0**	**0**	**0**	**0**	**0**	**0**

Traded to **Atlanta** by **NY Rangers** for Bill Heindl, June 16, 1972. Traded to **Detroit** by **Atlanta** for Leon Rochefort, November 28, 1972. Traded to **Minnesota** by **Detroit** with LA Kings' 2nd round choice (previously acquired, Minnesota selected Jim Roberts) in 1976 Amateur Draft for Dennis Hextall, February 27, 1976. Signed as a free agent by **Detroit**, February 12, 1979.

• HOGANSON, Dale

Dale Gordon "Red" D – L. 5'10", 190 lbs. b: North Battleford, Sask., 7/8/1949. Los Angeles' 1st, 16th overall, in 1969.

Season	Club	League	GP	G	A	Pts	AG	AA	APts	PIM	PP	SH	GW	S	%	TGF	PGF	TGA	PGA	+/–	GP	G	A	Pts	PIM	PP	SH	GW
1964-65	Estevan Bruins	SJHL	3	0	0	0	....	....	....	0	....	....	....	....	....	....	....	....	....	....	2	0	0	0	4	....	....	....
1965-66	Estevan Bruins	SJHL	56	15	18	33	....	....	....	19	....	....	....	....	....	....	....	....	....	....	12	0	0	0	6	....	....	....
	Estevan Bruins	Mem-Cup	11	3	4	7	....	....	....	10	....	....	....	....	....	....	....	....	....	....	....	....	....	....	....	....	....	....
1966-67	Estevan Bruins	WCJHL	55	3	17	20	....	....	....	35	....	....	....	....	....	....	....	....	....	....	13	2	3	5	21	....	....	....
1967-68	Estevan Bruins	WCJHL	56	19	40	59	....	....	....	36	....	....	....	....	....	....	....	....	....	....	14	9	13	22	4	....	....	....
	Estevan Bruins	Mem-Cup	14	7	10	17	....	....	....	8	....	....	....	....	....	....	....	....	....	....	....	....	....	....	....	....	....	....
1968-69	Estevan Bruins	WCJHL	54	16	44	60	....	....	....	67	....	....	....	....	....	....	....	....	....	....	10	0	3	3	....	....	....	....
	Estevan Bruins	Mem-Cup	14	7	9	16	....	....	....	8	....	....	....	....	....	....	....	....	....	....	....	....	....	....	....	....	....	....
1969-70	**Los Angeles Kings**	**NHL**	**49**	**1**	**7**	**8**	**1**	**7**	**8**	**37**	**0**	**0**	**0**	**57**	**1.8**	**37**	**6**	**59**	**7**	**–21**	....	....	....	....	....	....	....	....
	Springfield Kings	AHL	19	2	5	7	....	....	....	43	....	....	....	....	....	....	....	....	....	....	....	....	....	....	....	....	....	....
1970-71	**Los Angeles Kings**	**NHL**	**70**	**4**	**10**	**14**	**4**	**8**	**12**	**52**	**0**	**0**	**0**	**72**	**5.6**	**68**	**5**	**97**	**18**	**–16**	....	....	....	....	....	....	....	....
1971-72	**Los Angeles Kings**	**NHL**	**10**	**1**	**2**	**3**	**1**	**2**	**3**	**14**	**0**	**0**	**0**	**17**	**5.9**	**8**	**1**	**9**	**0**	**–2**	....	....	....	....	....	....	....	....
	Montreal Canadiens	**NHL**	**21**	**0**	**0**	**0**	**0**	**0**	**0**	**2**	**0**	**0**	**0**	**11**	**0.0**	**11**	**0**	**7**	**1**	**5**	....	....	....	....	....	....	....	....
	Nova Scotia Voyageurs	AHL	13	3	4	7	....	....	....	11	....	....	....	....	....	....	....	....	....	....	....	....	....	....	....	....	....	....
1972-73	**Montreal Canadiens**	**NHL**	**25**	**0**	**2**	**2**	**0**	**2**	**2**	**2**	**0**	**0**	**0**	**17**	**0.0**	**17**	**0**	**13**	**0**	**4**	....	....	....	....	....	....	....	....
1973-74	Quebec Nordiques	WHA	62	8	33	41	....	....	....	27	....	....	....	....	....	....	....	....	....	....	....	....	....	....	....	....	....	....
1974-75	Quebec Nordiques	WHA	78	9	35	44	....	....	....	47	....	....	....	....	....	....	....	....	....	....	13	1	3	4	4	....	....	....
1975-76	Quebec Nordiques	WHA	45	3	14	17	....	....	....	18	....	....	....	....	....	....	....	....	....	....	5	1	3	4	2	....	....	....
1976-77	Birmingham Bulls	WHA	81	7	48	55	....	....	....	48	....	....	....	....	....	....	....	....	....	....	....	....	....	....	....	....	....	....
1977-78	Birmingham Bulls	WHA	43	1	12	13	....	....	....	29	....	....	....	....	....	....	....	....	....	....	5	0	0	0	7	....	....	....
1978-79	Quebec Nordiques	WHA	69	2	19	21	....	....	....	17	....	....	....	....	....	....	....	....	....	....	4	0	0	0	2	....	....	....
1979-80	**Quebec Nordiques**	**NHL**	**77**	**4**	**36**	**40**	**3**	**26**	**29**	**31**	**0**	**0**	**0**	**99**	**4.0**	**104**	**35**	**140**	**29**	**–42**	....	....	....	....	....	....	....	....

			REGULAR SEASON																		PLAYOFFS							
Season	Club	League	GP	G	A	Pts	AG	AA	APts	PIM	PP	SH	GW	S	%	TGF	PGF	TGA	PGA	+/–	GP	G	A	Pts	PIM	PP	SH	GW
1980-81	**Quebec Nordiques**	**NHL**	**61**	**3**	**14**	**17**	**2**	**9**	**11**	**32**	**1**	**0**	**0**	**56**	**5.4**	**85**	**16**	**114**	**37**	**–8**	**5**	**0**	**3**	**3**	**10**	**0**	**0**	**0**
1981-82	**Quebec Nordiques**	**NHL**	**30**	**0**	**6**	**6**	**0**	**4**	**4**	**16**	**0**	**0**	**0**	**14**	**0.0**	**29**	**1**	**61**	**9**	**–24**	**6**	**0**	**0**	**0**	**2**	**0**	**0**	**0**
	Fredericton Express	AHL	19	2	4	6				18																		
	NHL Totals		**343**	**13**	**77**	**90**	**11**	**58**	**69**	**186**	**1**	**0**	**0**	**343**	**3.8**	**359**	**64**	**500**	**101**		**11**	**0**	**3**	**3**	**12**	**0**	**0**	**0**
	Other Major League Totals		378	30	161	191				186											27	2	6	8	15			

WCJHL All-Star Team (1968, 1969)

Traded to **Montreal** by **LA Kings** with Denis DeJordy, Noel Price and Doug Robinson for Rogie Vachon, November 4, 1971. Selected by **Calgary-Cleveland** (WHA) in 1972 WHA General Player Draft, February 12, 1972. WHA rights traded to **Quebec** (WHA) by **Cleveland** (WHA) for future considerations, June, 1973. Rights traded to **Atlanta** by **Montreal** for cash, May 29, 1973. Traded to **Birmingham** (WHA) by **Quebec** (WHA) for future considerations (Jim Dorey, October, 1976), June 30, 1976. Traded to **Quebec** (WHA) by **Birmingham** (WHA) for cash, July 7, 1978. Rights retained by **Quebec** prior to Expansion Draft, June 9, 1979.

• HOGLUND, Jonas

RW – R. 6'3", 215 lbs. b: Hammaro, Swe., 8/29/1972. Calgary's 11th, 222nd overall, in 1992.

Season	Club	League	GP	G	A	Pts	AG	AA	APts	PIM	PP	SH	GW	S	%	TGF	PGF	TGA	PGA	+/–	GP	G	A	Pts	PIM	PP	SH	GW
1988-89	Farjestads BK Karlstad	Sweden	1	0	0	0				0																		
1989-90	Farjestads BK Karlstad	Sweden	1	0	0					0																		
	Sweden	EJC-A	6	2	0	2				0																		
1990-91	Farjestads BK Karlstad	Sweden	40	5	5	10				4											8	1	0	1	0			
1991-92	Farjestads BK Karlstad	Sweden	40	14	11	25				6											6	2	4	6	2			
	Sweden	WJC-A	7	3	2	5				0																		
1992-93	Farjestads BK Karlstad	Sweden	40	13	13	26				14											3	1	0	1	0			
1993-94	Farjestads BK Karlstad	Sweden	22	7	2	9				10																		
1994-95	Farjestads BK Karlstad	Sweden	40	14	12	26				16											4	3	2	5	0			
1995-96	Farjestads BK Karlstad	Sweden	40	32	11	43				18											8	2	1	3	6			
1996-97	**Calgary Flames**	**NHL**	**68**	**19**	**16**	**35**	**20**	**14**	**34**	**12**	**3**	**0**	**6**	**189**	**10.1**	**58**	**22**	**41**	**1**	**–4**								
	Sweden	WC-A	11	4	3	7				4																		
1997-98	**Calgary Flames**	**NHL**	**50**	**6**	**8**	**14**	**7**	**8**	**15**	**16**	**0**	**0**	**0**	**124**	**4.8**	**25**	**4**	**30**	**0**	**–9**								
	Montreal Canadiens	**NHL**	**28**	**6**	**5**	**11**	**7**	**5**	**12**	**6**	**4**	**0**	**0**	**62**	**9.7**	**18**	**9**	**7**	**0**	**2**	**10**	**2**	**0**	**2**	**0**	**0**	**0**	**0**
1998-99	**Montreal Canadiens**	**NHL**	**74**	**8**	**10**	**18**	**9**	**10**	**19**	**16**	**1**	**0**	**0**	**122**	**6.6**	**34**	**10**	**29**	**0**	**–5**								
99-2000	**Toronto Maple Leafs**	**NHL**	**82**	**29**	**27**	**56**	**33**	**25**	**58**	**10**	**9**	**1**	**3**	**215**	**13.5**	**85**	**29**	**72**	**14**	**–2**	**12**	**2**	**4**	**6**	**2**	**0**	**0**	**0**
	NHL Totals		**302**	**68**	**66**	**134**	**76**	**62**	**138**	**60**	**17**	**1**	**9**	**712**	**9.6**	**220**	**74**	**179**	**15**		**22**	**4**	**4**	**8**	**2**	**0**	**0**	**0**

Traded to **Montreal** by **Calgary** with Zarley Zalapski for Valeri Bure and Montreal's 4th round choice (Shaun Sutter) in 1998 Entry Draft, February 1, 1998. Signed as a free agent by **Toronto**, July 13, 1999.

• HOGUE, Benoit

Benoit G. C – L. 5'10", 194 lbs. b: Repentigny, Que., 10/28/1966. Buffalo's 2nd, 35th overall, in 1985.

Season	Club	League	GP	G	A	Pts	AG	AA	APts	PIM	PP	SH	GW	S	%	TGF	PGF	TGA	PGA	+/–	GP	G	A	Pts	PIM	PP	SH	GW
1982-83	Bourassa Angevins	QAAA	40	20	20	40																						
1983-84	St-Jean Castors	QMJHL	59	14	11	25				42																		
1984-85	St-Jean Castors	QMJHL	63	46	44	90				92																		
1985-86	St-Jean Castors	QMJHL	65	54	54	108				115											9	6	4	10	26			
1986-87	Rochester Americans	AHL	52	14	20	34				52											12	5	4	9	8			
1987-88	**Buffalo Sabres**	**NHL**	**3**	**1**	**1**	**2**	**1**	**1**	**2**	**0**	**0**	**0**	**1**	**3**	**33.3**	**3**	**0**	**0**	**0**	**3**								
	Rochester Americans	AHL	62	24	31	55				141											7	6	1	7	46			
1988-89	**Buffalo Sabres**	**NHL**	**69**	**14**	**30**	**44**	**12**	**21**	**33**	**120**	**1**	**2**	**0**	**114**	**12.3**	**65**	**11**	**79**	**20**	**–5**	**5**	**0**	**0**	**0**	**17**	**0**	**0**	**0**
1989-90	**Buffalo Sabres**	**NHL**	**45**	**11**	**7**	**18**	**9**	**5**	**14**	**79**	**1**	**0**	**1**	**73**	**15.1**	**22**	**2**	**24**	**4**	**0**	**3**	**0**	**0**	**0**	**10**	**0**	**0**	**0**
1990-91	**Buffalo Sabres**	**NHL**	**76**	**19**	**28**	**47**	**17**	**21**	**38**	**76**	**1**	**0**	**2**	**134**	**14.2**	**64**	**16**	**61**	**5**	**–8**	**5**	**3**	**1**	**4**	**10**	**0**	**0**	**0**
1991-92	**Buffalo Sabres**	**NHL**	**3**	**0**	**1**	**1**	**0**	**1**	**1**	**0**	**0**	**0**	**0**	**6**	**0.0**	**2**	**0**	**2**	**0**	**0**								
	New York Islanders	**NHL**	**72**	**30**	**45**	**75**	**27**	**34**	**61**	**67**	**8**	**0**	**5**	**143**	**21.0**	**98**	**20**	**65**	**17**	**30**								
1992-93	**New York Islanders**	**NHL**	**70**	**33**	**42**	**75**	**27**	**29**	**56**	**108**	**5**	**3**	**5**	**147**	**22.4**	**90**	**19**	**88**	**30**	**13**	**18**	**6**	**6**	**12**	**31**	**0**	**0**	**0**
1993-94	**New York Islanders**	**NHL**	**83**	**36**	**33**	**69**	**34**	**26**	**60**	**73**	**9**	**5**	**3**	**218**	**16.5**	**95**	**30**	**98**	**26**	**–7**	**4**	**0**	**1**	**1**	**4**	**0**	**0**	**0**
1994-95	**New York Islanders**	**NHL**	**33**	**6**	**4**	**10**	**11**	**6**	**17**	**34**	**1**	**0**	**1**	**50**	**12.0**	**25**	**5**	**33**	**13**	**0**								
	Toronto Maple Leafs	**NHL**	**12**	**3**	**3**	**6**	**5**	**4**	**9**	**0**	**1**	**0**	**1**	**16**	**18.8**	**11**	**2**	**9**	**0**	**0**	**7**	**0**	**0**	**0**	**6**	**0**	**0**	**0**
1995-96	**Toronto Maple Leafs**	**NHL**	**44**	**12**	**25**	**37**	**12**	**20**	**32**	**68**	**3**	**0**	**5**	**94**	**12.8**	**49**	**15**	**39**	**11**	**6**								
	Dallas Stars	**NHL**	**34**	**7**	**20**	**27**	**7**	**16**	**23**	**36**	**2**	**0**	**0**	**61**	**11.5**	**42**	**14**	**29**	**5**	**4**								
1996-97	**Dallas Stars**	**NHL**	**73**	**19**	**24**	**43**	**20**	**21**	**41**	**54**	**5**	**0**	**5**	**131**	**14.5**	**70**	**15**	**47**	**0**	**8**	**7**	**2**	**2**	**4**	**6**	**1**	**0**	**0**
1997-98	**Dallas Stars**	**NHL**	**53**	**6**	**16**	**22**	**7**	**16**	**23**	**35**	**3**	**0**	**1**	**55**	**10.9**	**38**	**9**	**22**	**0**	**7**	**17**	**4**	**2**	**6**	**16**	**1**	**0**	**2**
1998-99	**Tampa Bay**	**NHL**	**62**	**11**	**14**	**25**	**13**	**13**	**26**	**50**	**2**	**0**	**3**	**101**	**10.9**	**42**	**10**	**59**	**15**	**–12**								
	♦ **Dallas Stars**	**NHL**	**12**	**1**	**3**	**4**	**1**	**3**	**4**	**4**	**0**	**0**	**0**	**20**	**5.0**	**6**	**1**	**3**	**0**	**2**	**14**	**0**	**2**	**2**	**16**	**0**	**0**	**0**
99-2000	**Phoenix Coyotes**	**NHL**	**27**	**3**	**10**	**13**	**3**	**9**	**12**	**10**	**0**	**0**	**0**	**39**	**7.7**	**17**	**2**	**16**	**0**	**–1**	**5**	**1**	**2**	**3**	**2**	**0**	**0**	**0**
	NHL Totals		**771**	**212**	**306**	**518**	**206**	**246**	**452**	**814**	**42**	**10**	**33**	**1405**	**15.1**	**739**	**171**	**674**	**146**		**85**	**16**	**16**	**32**	**118**	**2**	**0**	**2**

Traded to **NY Islanders** by **Buffalo** with Pierre Turgeon, Uwe Krupp and Dave McLlwain for Pat LaFontaine, Randy Hillier, Randy Wood and NY Islanders' 4th round choice (Dean Melanson) in 1992 Entry Draft, October 25, 1991. Traded to **Toronto** by **NY Islanders** with NY Islanders' 3rd round choice (Ryan Pepperall) in 1995 Entry Draft and 5th round choice (Brandon Sugden) in 1996 Entry Draft for Eric Fichaud, April 6, 1995. Traded to **Dallas** by **Toronto** with Randy Wood for Dave Gagner and Dallas' 6th round choice (Dmitriy Yakushin) in 1996 Entry Draft, January 29, 1996. Signed as a free agent by **Tampa Bay**, August 19, 1998. Traded to **Dallas** by **Tampa Bay** with a conditional choice in 2001 Entry Draft for Sergey Gusev, March 21, 1999. Signed as a free agent by **Phoenix**, February 3, 2000.

• HOLAN, Milos

D – L. 5'11", 191 lbs. b: Bilovec, Czech., 4/22/1971. Philadelphia's 3rd, 77th overall, in 1993.

Season	Club	League	GP	G	A	Pts	AG	AA	APts	PIM	PP	SH	GW	S	%	TGF	PGF	TGA	PGA	+/–	GP	G	A	Pts	PIM	PP	SH	GW
1988-89	TJ Vitkovice	Czech.	7	0	0	0				0																		
1989-90	TJ Vitkovice	Czech.	43	6	7	13															7	2	1	3				
	Czechoslovakia	WJC-A	4	2	0	2				2																		
1990-91	Dukla Trencin	Czech.	53	6	13	19																						
	Czechoslovakia	WJC-A	6	0	2	2				0																		
1991-92	Dukla Trencin	Czech.	51	13	22	35				32																		
1992-93	TJ Vitkovice	Czech.	53	35	33	68																						
	Czechoslovakia	WC-A	8	1	3	4				10																		
1993-94	**Philadelphia Flyers**	**NHL**	**8**	**1**	**1**	**2**	**1**	**1**	**2**	**4**	**1**	**0**	**0**	**26**	**3.8**	**9**	**6**	**7**	**0**	**–4**								
	Hershey Bears	AHL	27	7	22	29				16																		
	Czech-Republic	WC-A	6	0	3	3				8																		
1994-95	Hershey Bears	AHL	55	22	27	49				75																		
	Mighty Ducks of Anaheim	**NHL**	**25**	**2**	**8**	**10**	**4**	**12**	**16**	**14**	**1**	**0**	**1**	**93**	**2.2**	**26**	**9**	**17**	**4**	**4**								
1995-96	**Mighty Ducks of Anaheim**	**NHL**	**16**	**2**	**2**	**4**	**2**	**2**	**4**	**24**	**0**	**0**	**0**	**47**	**4.3**	**10**	**3**	**20**	**1**	**–12**								
1996-97			DID NOT PLAY																									
1997-98			DID NOT PLAY																									
1998-99	HC Vitkovice	Czech-Rep	30	9	13	22				26											4	0	2	2				
99-2000	HC Trinec	Czech-2	10	1	6	7																						
	HC Ocelari Trinec	Czech-Rep	11	1	5	6				6																		
	EHC Freiburg	Germany-2	5	1	3	4				16																		
	NHL Totals		**49**	**5**	**11**	**16**	**7**	**15**	**22**	**42**	**2**	**0**	**1**	**166**	**3.0**	**45**	**18**	**44**	**5**									

Czechoslovakian Player of the Year (1993)

Traded to **Anaheim** by **Philadelphia** for Anatoli Semenov, March 8, 1995. • Missed entire 1996-97 and 1997-98 seasons after being diagnosed with Chronic Granulocytic Leukemia, February 21, 1996.

• HOLBROOK, Terry

Terry Eugene RW – R. 6', 185 lbs. b: Petrolia, Ont., 7/11/1950. Los Angeles' 2nd, 38th overall, in 1970.

Season	Club	League	GP	G	A	Pts	AG	AA	APts	PIM	PP	SH	GW	S	%	TGF	PGF	TGA	PGA	+/–	GP	G	A	Pts	PIM	PP	SH	GW
1969-70	London Knights	OHA-Jr.	54	13	15	28				13											12	5	1	6	11			
1970-71	Springfield Kings	AHL	40	2	8	10				8																		
	Cleveland Barons	AHL	17	1	7	8				0											8	0	0	0	0			
1971-72	Cleveland Barons	AHL	76	7	22	29				16											6	1	0	1	7			
1972-73	Cleveland-Jacksonville Barons	AHL	51	22	21	43				12																		
	Minnesota North Stars	**NHL**	**21**	**2**	**3**	**5**	**2**	**2**	**4**	**0**	**0**	**0**	**1**	**18**	**11.1**	**6**	**0**	**10**	**0**	**–4**	**6**	**0**	**0**	**0**	**0**	**0**	**0**	**0**

			REGULAR SEASON																		PLAYOFFS							
Season	Club	League	GP	G	A	Pts	AG	AA	APts	PIM	PP	SH	GW	S	%	TGF	PGF	TGA	PGA	+/–	GP	G	A	Pts	PIM	PP	SH	GW
1973-74	**Minnesota North Stars**	**NHL**	**22**	**1**	**3**	**4**	**1**	**2**	**3**	**4**	**1**	**0**	**0**	**19**	**5.3**	**8**	**2**	**16**	**7**	**–3**								
	New Haven Nighthawks	AHL	37	15	21	36				18																		
1974-75	Cleveland Crusaders	WHA	78	10	13	23				7											5	0	1	1	0			
1975-76	Cleveland Crusaders	WHA	15	1	2	3				6											3	0	0	0	0			
	NHL Totals		**43**	**3**	**6**	**9**	**3**	**4**	**7**	**4**	**1**	**0**	**1**	**37**	**8.1**	**14**	**2**	**26**	**7**		**6**	**0**	**0**	**0**	**0**	**0**	**0**	**0**
	Other Major League Totals		93	11	15	26				13											8	0	1	1	0			

Traded to **Minnesota** by **LA Kings** for Wayne Schultz and the rights to Steve Sutherland, March, 1971. Selected by **Calgary-Cleveland** (WHA) in 1972 WHA General Player Draft, February 12, 1972.

• HOLDEN, Josh

C – L. 6', 190 lbs. b: Calgary, Alta., 1/18/1978. Vancouver's 1st, 12th overall, in 1996.

Season	Club	League	GP	G	A	Pts	AG	AA	APts	PIM	PP	SH	GW	S	%	TGF	PGF	TGA	PGA	+/–	GP	G	A	Pts	PIM	PP	SH	GW
1993-94	Calgary Buffaloes	AAHA	34	14	15	29				82																		
1994-95	Regina Pats	WHL	62	20	23	43				45											4	3	1	4	0			
1995-96	Regina Pats	WHL	70	57	55	112				105											11	4	5	9	23			
1996-97	Regina Pats	WHL	58	49	49	98				148											5	3	2	5	10			
1997-98	Regina Pats	WHL	56	41	58	99				134											2	2	2	4	10			
	Canada	WJC-A	7	4	0	4				14																		
1998-99	**Vancouver Canucks**	**NHL**	**30**	**2**	**4**	**6**	**2**	**4**	**6**	**10**	**1**	**0**	**0**	**44**	**4.5**	**11**	**1**	**22**	**2**	**–10**								
	Syracuse Crunch	AHL	38	14	15	29				48																		
99-2000	**Vancouver Canucks**	**NHL**	**6**	**1**	**5**	**6**	**1**	**5**	**6**	**2**	**0**	**0**	**0**	**5**	**20.0**	**6**	**0**	**4**	**0**	**2**								
	Syracuse Crunch	AHL	45	19	32	51				113											4	1	0	1	10			
	NHL Totals		**36**	**3**	**9**	**12**	**3**	**9**	**12**	**12**	**1**	**0**	**0**	**49**	**6.1**	**17**	**1**	**26**	**2**									

WHL East Second All-Star Team (1998)

• HOLIK, Bobby

Robert LW – R. 6'4", 230 lbs. b: Jihlava, Czech., 1/1/1971. Hartford's 1st, 10th overall, in 1989.

Season	Club	League	GP	G	A	Pts	AG	AA	APts	PIM	PP	SH	GW	S	%	TGF	PGF	TGA	PGA	+/–	GP	G	A	Pts	PIM	PP	SH	GW
1987-88	Dukla Jihlava	Czech.	31	5	9	14				16																		
	Czechoslovakia	EJC-A	6	5	2	7				2																		
1988-89	Dukla Jihlava	Czech.	24	7	10	17				32																		
	Czechoslovakia	WJC-A	7	5	3	8				2																		
	Czechoslovakia	EJC-A	6	3	11	14				2																		
1989-90	Dukla Jihlava	Czech.	42	15	26	41																						
	Czechoslovakia	WJC-A	7	6	5	11				12																		
1990-91	**Hartford Whalers**	**NHL**	**78**	**21**	**22**	**43**	**19**	**17**	**36**	**113**	**8**	**0**	**3**	**173**	**12.1**	**59**	**14**	**49**	**1**	**–3**	**6**	**0**	**0**	**0**	**7**	**0**	**0**	**0**
1991-92	**Hartford Whalers**	**NHL**	**76**	**21**	**24**	**45**	**19**	**18**	**37**	**44**	**1**	**0**	**2**	**207**	**10.1**	**63**	**6**	**54**	**1**	**4**	**7**	**0**	**1**	**1**	**6**	**0**	**0**	**0**
1992-93	**New Jersey Devils**	**NHL**	**61**	**20**	**19**	**39**	**17**	**13**	**30**	**76**	**7**	**0**	**4**	**180**	**11.1**	**62**	**24**	**44**	**0**	**–6**	**5**	**1**	**1**	**2**	**6**	**0**	**0**	**0**
	Utica Devils	AHL	1							2																		
1993-94	**New Jersey Devils**	**NHL**	**70**	**13**	**20**	**33**	**12**	**16**	**28**	**72**	**2**	**0**	**3**	**130**	**10.0**	**49**	**3**	**18**	**0**	**28**	**20**	**0**	**3**	**3**	**6**	**0**	**0**	**0**
1994-95♦	**New Jersey Devils**	**NHL**	**48**	**10**	**10**	**20**	**18**	**15**	**33**	**18**	**0**	**0**	**2**	**84**	**11.9**	**26**	**2**	**16**	**1**	**9**	**20**	**4**	**4**	**8**	**22**	**2**	**0**	**1**
1995-96	**New Jersey Devils**	**NHL**	**63**	**13**	**17**	**30**	**13**	**14**	**27**	**58**	**1**	**0**	**1**	**157**	**8.3**	**39**	**8**	**23**	**1**	**9**								
1996-97	Czech-Republic	W-Cup	3	0	0	0				0																		
	New Jersey Devils	**NHL**	**82**	**23**	**39**	**62**	**24**	**35**	**59**	**54**	**5**	**0**	**6**	**192**	**12.0**	**80**	**17**	**39**	**0**	**24**	**10**	**2**	**3**	**5**	**4**	**1**	**0**	**0**
1997-98	**New Jersey Devils**	**NHL**	**82**	**29**	**36**	**65**	**34**	**35**	**69**	**100**	**8**	**0**	**8**	**238**	**12.2**	**89**	**37**	**29**	**0**	**23**	**5**	**0**	**0**	**0**	**8**	**0**	**0**	**0**
1998-99	**New Jersey Devils**	**NHL**	**78**	**27**	**37**	**64**	**32**	**36**	**68**	**119**	**5**	**0**	**8**	**253**	**10.7**	**78**	**19**	**43**	**0**	**16**	**7**	**0**	**7**	**7**	**6**	**0**	**0**	**0**
99-2000♦	**New Jersey Devils**	**NHL**	**79**	**23**	**23**	**46**	**26**	**21**	**47**	**106**	**7**	**0**	**4**	**257**	**8.9**	**71**	**20**	**45**	**1**	**7**	**23**	**3**	**7**	**10**	**14**	**0**	**0**	**1**
	NHL Totals		**717**	**200**	**247**	**447**	**214**	**220**	**434**	**760**	**44**	**0**	**41**	**1871**	**10.7**	**616**	**150**	**360**	**5**		**103**	**10**	**26**	**36**	**79**	**3**	**0**	**2**

Played in NHL All-Star Game (1998, 1999)

Traded to **New Jersey** by **Hartford** with Hartford's 2nd round choice (Jay Pandolfo) in 1993 Entry Draft for Sean Burke and Eric Weinrich, August 28, 1992.

• HOLLAND, Jason

Jason Ryan D – R. 6'2", 193 lbs. b: Morinville, Alta., 4/30/1976. NY Islanders' 2nd, 38th overall, in 1994.

Season	Club	League	GP	G	A	Pts	AG	AA	APts	PIM	PP	SH	GW	S	%	TGF	PGF	TGA	PGA	+/–	GP	G	A	Pts	PIM	PP	SH	GW
1991-92	St. Albert Eagle Raiders	AAHA	38	9	29	38				94																		
1992-93	St. Albert Eagle Raiders	AAHA	31	11	25	36				36																		
	Kamloops Blazers	WHL	4	0	0	0				2																		
1993-94	Kamloops Blazers	WHL	59	14	15	29				80											18	2	3	5	4			
	Kamloops Blazers	Mem-Cup	4	0	2	2				0																		
1994-95	Kamloops Blazers	WHL	71	9	32	41				65											21	2	7	9	9			
	Kamloops Blazers	Mem-Cup	4	0	4	4				2																		
1995-96	Kamloops Blazers	WHL	63	24	33	57				98											16	4	9	13	22			
	Canada	WJC-A	6	2	1	3				4																		
1996-97	**New York Islanders**	**NHL**	**4**	**1**	**0**	**1**	**1**	**0**	**1**	**0**	**0**	**0**	**0**	**3**	**33.3**	**3**	**0**	**2**	**0**	**1**								
	Kentucky Thoroughblades	AHL	72	14	25	39				46											4	0	2	2	0			
1997-98	**New York Islanders**	**NHL**	**8**	**0**	**0**	**0**	**0**	**0**	**0**	**4**	**0**	**0**	**0**	**6**	**0.0**	**2**	**0**	**7**	**1**	**–4**								
	Kentucky Thoroughblades	AHL	50	10	16	26				29																		
	Rochester Americans	AHL	9	0	4	4				10											4	0	3	3	4			
1998-99	**Buffalo Sabres**	**NHL**	**3**	**0**	**0**	**0**	**0**	**0**	**0**	**8**	**0**	**0**	**0**	**2**	**0.0**	**0**	**0**	**2**	**1**	**–1**								
	Rochester Americans	AHL	74	4	25	29				36											20	2	5	7	8			
99-2000	**Buffalo Sabres**	**NHL**	**9**	**0**	**1**	**1**	**0**	**1**	**1**	**0**	**0**	**0**	**0**	**8**	**0.0**	**8**	**2**	**6**	**0**	**0**	**1**	**0**	**0**	**0**	**0**	**0**	**0**	**0**
	Rochester Americans	AHL	54	3	15	18				24											12	1	0	1	2			
	NHL Totals		**24**	**1**	**1**	**2**	**1**	**1**	**2**	**12**	**0**	**0**	**0**	**19**	**5.3**	**13**	**2**	**17**	**2**		**1**	**0**	**0**	**0**	**0**	**0**	**0**	**0**

WHL West First All-Star Team (1996)

Traded to **Buffalo** by **NY Islanders** with Paul Kruse for Jason Dawe, March 24, 1998.

• HOLLAND, Jerry

Jerry Allan LW – L. 5'10", 180 lbs. b: Beaverlodge, Alta., 8/25/1954. NY Rangers' 3rd, 50th overall, in 1974.

Season	Club	League	GP	G	A	Pts	AG	AA	APts	PIM	PP	SH	GW	S	%	TGF	PGF	TGA	PGA	+/–	GP	G	A	Pts	PIM	PP	SH	GW
1970-71	Kamloops Rockets	BCJHL	60	33	39	72				50																		
1971-72	St. Albert Saints	AJHL	STATISTICS NOT AVAILABLE																									
	Calgary Centennials	WCJHL	33	17	13	30				23											13	5	4	9	4			
1972-73	Calgary Centennials	WCJHL	67	51	54	105				66											6	2	5	7	9			
1973-74	Calgary Centennials	WCJHL	67	55	65	120				54											14	15	8	23	4			
1974-75	**New York Rangers**	**NHL**	**1**	**1**	**0**	**1**	**1**	**0**	**1**	**0**	**0**	**0**	**0**	**1**	**100.0**	**1**	**0**	**0**	**0**	**1**								
	Providence Reds	AHL	67	*44	35	79				44											6	1	2	3	11			
1975-76	**New York Rangers**	**NHL**	**36**	**7**	**4**	**11**	**6**	**3**	**9**	**6**	**2**	**0**	**1**	**50**	**14.0**	**18**	**4**	**19**	**0**	**–5**								
	Providence Reds	AHL	28	9	11	20				11											3	0	1	1	0			
1976-77	New Haven Nighthawks	AHL	72	28	34	62				35											6	0	3	3	0			
1977-78	Edmonton Oilers	WHA	22	2	1	3				14																		
	Salt Lake Golden Eagles	CHL	11	5	6	11				11																		
1978-79	Spokane Flyers	PHL	52	*38	23	61				20																		
	NHL Totals		**37**	**8**	**4**	**12**	**7**	**3**	**10**	**6**	**2**	**0**	**1**	**51**	**15.7**	**19**	**4**	**19**	**0**									
	Other Major League Totals		22	2	1	3				14																		

AHL First All-Star Team (1975) • Won Dudley "Red" Garrett Memorial Award (Top Rookie - AHL) (1975)

Selected by **Cincinnati** (WHA) in 1974 WHA Amateur Draft, June, 1974. Signed as a free agent by **Edmonton** (WHA), September, 1977.

• HOLLINGER, Terry

Terry J. D – L. 6'1", 200 lbs. b: Regina, Sask., 2/24/1971. St. Louis' 7th, 153rd overall, in 1991.

Season	Club	League	GP	G	A	Pts	AG	AA	APts	PIM	PP	SH	GW	S	%	TGF	PGF	TGA	PGA	+/–	GP	G	A	Pts	PIM	PP	SH	GW
1986-87	Regina Cougars	SAHA	31	37	36	73				59																		
1987-88	Regina Pat Canadians	AAHA	30	13	36	49				74																		
	Regina Pats	WHL	7	1	1	2				4																		
1988-89	Regina Pats	WHL	65	2	27	29				49																		
1989-90	Regina Pats	WHL	70	14	43	57				40											11	1	3	4	10			

Season	Club	League	GP	G	A	Pts	AG	AA	APts	PIM	PP	SH	GW	S	%	TGF	PGF	TGA	PGA	+/–	GP	G	A	Pts	PIM	PP	SH	GW
			REGULAR SEASON																		PLAYOFFS							
1990-91	Regina Pats	WHL	8	1	6	7	....	....	....	6	....	....	....	....	....	....	....	....	....	....	....	....	....	....	....	....	....	....
	Lethbridge Hurricanes	WHL	62	9	32	41	....	....	....	113	....	....	....	....	....	....	....	....	....	....	16	3	14	17	22	....	....	....
1991-92	Lethbridge Hurricanes	WHL	65	23	62	85	....	....	....	155	....	....	....	....	....	....	....	....	....	....	5	1	2	3	13	....	....	....
	Peoria Rivermen	IHL	1	0	2	2	....	....	....	0	....	....	....	....	....	....	....	....	....	....	5	0	1	1	0	....	....	....
1992-93	Peoria Rivermen	IHL	72	2	28	30	....	....	....	67	....	....	....	....	....	....	....	....	....	....	4	1	1	2	0	....	....	....
1993-94	**St. Louis Blues**	**NHL**	**2**	**0**	**0**	**0**	**0**	**0**	**0**	**0**	**0**	**0**	**0**	**0**	**0.0**	**1**	**0**	**1**	**1**	**1**	....	....	....	....	....	....	....	....
	Peoria Rivermen	IHL	78	12	31	43	....	....	....	96	....	....	....	....	....	....	....	....	....	....	6	0	3	3	31	....	....	....
1994-95	**St. Louis Blues**	**NHL**	**5**	**0**	**0**	**0**	**0**	**0**	**0**	**2**	**0**	**0**	**0**	**1**	**0.0**	**2**	**0**	**4**	**1**	**–1**	....	....	....	....	....	....	....	....
	Peoria Rivermen	IHL	69	7	25	32	....	....	....	137	....	....	....	....	....	....	....	....	....	....	4	2	4	6	8	....	....	....
1995-96	Rochester Americans	AHL	62	5	50	55	....	....	....	71	....	....	....	....	....	....	....	....	....	....	19	3	11	14	12	....	....	....
1996-97	Rochester Americans	AHL	73	12	51	63	....	....	....	54	....	....	....	....	....	....	....	....	....	....	10	2	7	9	27	....	....	....
1997-98	Worcester IceCats	AHL	55	8	24	32	....	....	....	34	....	....	....	....	....	....	....	....	....	....	....	....	....	....	....	....	....	....
	Houston Aeros	IHL	8	1	1	2	....	....	....	6	....	....	....	....	....	....	....	....	....	....	4	1	2	3	11	....	....	....
1998-99	Utah Grizzlies	IHL	58	4	19	23	....	....	....	40	....	....	....	....	....	....	....	....	....	....	....	....	....	....	....	....	....	....
	Orlando Solar Bears	IHL	21	9	9	18	....	....	....	18	....	....	....	....	....	....	....	....	....	....	17	3	5	8	14	....	....	....
99-2000	Orlando Solar Bears	IHL	20	4	4	8	....	....	....	13	....	....	....	....	....	....	....	....	....	....	....	....	....	....	....	....	....	....
	Manitoba Moose	IHL	18	3	10	13	....	....	....	4	....	....	....	....	....	....	....	....	....	....	....	....	....	....	....	....	....	....
	Providence Bruins	AHL	4	0	3	3	....	....	....	2	....	....	....	....	....	....	....	....	....	....	10	1	4	5	6	....	....	....
	NHL Totals		**7**	**0**	**0**	**0**	**0**	**0**	**0**	**2**	**0**	**0**	**0**	**1**	**0.0**	**3**	**0**	**5**	**2**		....	....	....	....	....	....	....	....

AHL Second All-Star Team (1996) • AHL First All-Star Team (1997)

Signed as a free agent by **Buffalo**, August 23, 1995. Signed as a free agent by **St. Louis**, July 28, 1997. Traded to **Orlando** (IHL) by **Utah** (IHL) for Rob Bonneau and Mike Nicholishen, March 1, 1999. Traded to **Manitoba** (IHL) by **Orlando** (IHL) for Jason McDonald, January 10, 2000. Traded to **Providence** (AHL) by **Manitoba** (IHL) for Sean Pronger and Keith McCambridge, March 16, 2000.

• HOLLOWAY, Bruce

D – L. 6', 200 lbs. b: Revelstoke, B.C., 6/27/1963. Vancouver's 6th, 136th overall, in 1981.

Season	Club	League	GP	G	A	Pts	AG	AA	APts	PIM	PP	SH	GW	S	%	TGF	PGF	TGA	PGA	+/–	GP	G	A	Pts	PIM	PP	SH	GW
1978-79	Revelstoke Bruins	BCJHL	61	4	14	18	....	....	....	52	....	....	....	....	....	....	....	....	....	....	....	....	....	....	....	....	....	....
	Billings Bighorns	WHL	9	0	1	1	....	....	....	0	....	....	....	....	....	....	....	....	....	....	4	0	0	0	0	....	....	....
1979-80	Melville Millionaires	SJHL	9	3	2	5	....	....	....	10	....	....	....	....	....	....	....	....	....	....	....	....	....	....	....	....	....	....
	Billings Bighorns	WHL	49	1	9	10	....	....	....	6	....	....	....	....	....	....	....	....	....	....	....	....	....	....	....	....	....	....
1980-81	Billings Bighorns	WHL	2	0	2	2	....	....	....	0	....	....	....	....	....	....	....	....	....	....	....	....	....	....	....	....	....	....
	Regina Pats	WHL	66	6	27	33	....	....	....	61	....	....	....	....	....	....	....	....	....	....	11	2	5	7	4	....	....	....
1981-82	Regina Pats	WHL	69	4	28	32	....	....	....	111	....	....	....	....	....	....	....	....	....	....	2	0	2	2	17	....	....	....
1982-83	Brandon Wheat Kings	WHL	7	0	5	5	....	....	....	8	....	....	....	....	....	....	....	....	....	....	....	....	....	....	....	....	....	....
	Kamloops Junior Oilers	WHL	51	6	53	59	....	....	....	82	....	....	....	....	....	....	....	....	....	....	7	1	4	5	6	....	....	....
1983-84	Fredericton Express	AHL	66	3	30	33	....	....	....	29	....	....	....	....	....	....	....	....	....	....	5	0	0	0	0	....	....	....
1984-85	**Vancouver Canucks**	**NHL**	**2**	**0**	**0**	**0**	**0**	**0**	**0**	**0**	**0**	**0**	**0**	**0**	**0.0**	**0**	**0**	**1**	**0**	**–1**	....	....	....	....	....	....	....	....
	Fredericton Express	AHL	31	2	4	6	....	....	....	16	....	....	....	....	....	....	....	....	....	....	....	....	....	....	....	....	....	....
	St. Catharines Saints	AHL	13	1	0	1	....	....	....	0	....	....	....	....	....	....	....	....	....	....	....	....	....	....	....	....	....	....
1985-86	Kalamazoo Wings	IHL	38	7	11	18	....	....	....	45	....	....	....	....	....	....	....	....	....	....	....	....	....	....	....	....	....	....
	Peoria Rivermen	IHL	29	4	13	17	....	....	....	47	....	....	....	....	....	....	....	....	....	....	7	2	3	5	2	....	....	....
	NHL Totals		**2**	**0**	**0**	**0**	**0**	**0**	**0**	**0**	**0**	**0**	**0**	**0**	**0.0**	**0**	**0**	**1**	**0**		....	....	....	....	....	....	....	....

• HOLMES, Warren

C – L. 6'1", 195 lbs. b: Beeton, Ont., 2/18/1957. Los Angeles' 2nd, 85th overall, in 1977.

Season	Club	League	GP	G	A	Pts	AG	AA	APts	PIM	PP	SH	GW	S	%	TGF	PGF	TGA	PGA	+/–	GP	G	A	Pts	PIM	PP	SH	GW
1974-75	Ottawa 67's	OMJHL	54	9	17	26	....	....	....	47	....	....	....	....	....	....	....	....	....	....	7	6	2	8	6	....	....	....
1975-76	Ottawa 67's	OMJHL	28	3	11	14	....	....	....	6	....	....	....	....	....	....	....	....	....	....	....	....	....	....	....	....	....	....
1976-77	Ottawa 67's	OMJHL	36	18	29	47	....	....	....	31	....	....	....	....	....	....	....	....	....	....	19	11	10	21	23	....	....	....
	Ottawa 67's	Mem-Cup	5	3	2	5	....	....	....	4	....	....	....	....	....	....	....	....	....	....	....	....	....	....	....	....	....	....
1977-78	Saginaw Gears	IHL	78	48	33	81	....	....	....	51	....	....	....	....	....	....	....	....	....	....	5	3	3	6	14	....	....	....
1978-79	Springfield Indians	AHL	4	0	0	0	....	....	....	0	....	....	....	....	....	....	....	....	....	....	....	....	....	....	....	....	....	....
	Milwaukee Admirals	IHL	31	11	17	28	....	....	....	33	....	....	....	....	....	....	....	....	....	....	....	....	....	....	....	....	....	....
	Saginaw Gears	IHL	38	11	18	29	....	....	....	30	....	....	....	....	....	....	....	....	....	....	4	1	3	4	8	....	....	....
1979-80	Binghamton Dusters	AHL	2	0	0	0	....	....	....	0	....	....	....	....	....	....	....	....	....	....	....	....	....	....	....	....	....	....
	Saginaw Gears	IHL	72	37	55	92	....	....	....	62	....	....	....	....	....	....	....	....	....	....	7	5	3	8	21	....	....	....
1980-81	Houston Apollos	CHL	25	7	7	14	....	....	....	18	....	....	....	....	....	....	....	....	....	....	....	....	....	....	....	....	....	....
	Saginaw Gears	IHL	40	21	26	47	....	....	....	27	....	....	....	....	....	....	....	....	....	....	13	8	9	17	19	....	....	....
1981-82	**Los Angeles Kings**	**NHL**	**3**	**0**	**2**	**2**	**0**	**1**	**1**	**0**	**0**	**0**	**0**	**6**	**0.0**	**3**	**0**	**3**	**1**	**1**	....	....	....	....	....	....	....	....
	New Haven Nighthawks	AHL	73	28	28	56	....	....	....	29	....	....	....	....	....	....	....	....	....	....	4	1	5	6	0	....	....	....
1982-83	**Los Angeles Kings**	**NHL**	**39**	**8**	**16**	**24**	**7**	**11**	**18**	**7**	**2**	**0**	**0**	**66**	**12.1**	**36**	**12**	**56**	**24**	**–8**	....	....	....	....	....	....	....	....
	New Haven Nighthawks	AHL	35	17	18	35	....	....	....	26	....	....	....	....	....	....	....	....	....	....	....	....	....	....	....	....	....	....
1983-84	**Los Angeles Kings**	**NHL**	**3**	**0**	**0**	**0**	**0**	**0**	**0**	**0**	**0**	**0**	**0**	**3**	**0.0**	**0**	**0**	**4**	**1**	**–3**	....	....	....	....	....	....	....	....
	New Haven Nighthawks	AHL	76	26	35	61	....	....	....	25	....	....	....	....	....	....	....	....	....	....	....	....	....	....	....	....	....	....
1984-85	Flint Generals	IHL	80	23	44	67	....	....	....	70	....	....	....	....	....	....	....	....	....	....	7	3	3	6	11	....	....	....
1985-86	Saginaw Generals	IHL	65	17	20	37	....	....	....	88	....	....	....	....	....	....	....	....	....	....	....	....	....	....	....	....	....	....
	NHL Totals		**45**	**8**	**18**	**26**	**7**	**12**	**19**	**7**	**2**	**0**	**0**	**75**	**10.7**	**39**	**12**	**63**	**26**		....	....	....	....	....	....	....	....

• HOLMGREN, Paul

Paul Howard RW – R. 6'3", 210 lbs. b: St. Paul, MN, 12/2/1955. Philadelphia's 5th, 108th overall, in 1975.

Season	Club	League	GP	G	A	Pts	AG	AA	APts	PIM	PP	SH	GW	S	%	TGF	PGF	TGA	PGA	+/–	GP	G	A	Pts	PIM	PP	SH	GW
1973-74	St. Paul Vulcans	MWJHL	55	22	59	81	....	....	....	183	....	....	....	....	....	....	....	....	....	....	....	....	....	....	....	....	....	....
	United States	WJC-A	4	0	0	0	....	....	....	8	....	....	....	....	....	....	....	....	....	....	....	....	....	....	....	....	....	....
1974-75	University of Minnesota	WCHA	37	10	21	31	....	....	....	108	....	....	....	....	....	....	....	....	....	....	....	....	....	....	....	....	....	....
1975-76	Minnesota Fighting Saints	WHA	51	14	16	30	....	....	....	121	....	....	....	....	....	....	....	....	....	....	....	....	....	....	....	....	....	....
	Johnstown Jets	NAHL	6	3	12	15	....	....	....	12	....	....	....	....	....	....	....	....	....	....	....	....	....	....	....	....	....	....
	Philadelphia Flyers	**NHL**	**1**	**0**	**0**	**0**	**0**	**0**	**0**	**2**	**0**	**0**	**0**	**1**	**0.0**	**0**	**0**	**0**	**0**	**0**	....	....	....	....	....	....	....	....
	Richmond Robins	AHL	6	4	4	8	....	....	....	23	....	....	....	....	....	....	....	....	....	....	....	....	....	....	....	....	....	....
1976-77	**Philadelphia Flyers**	**NHL**	**59**	**14**	**12**	**26**	**13**	**9**	**22**	**201**	**0**	**0**	**2**	**74**	**18.9**	**43**	**6**	**28**	**1**	**10**	**10**	**1**	**1**	**2**	**25**	**0**	**0**	**0**
1977-78	**Philadelphia Flyers**	**NHL**	**62**	**16**	**18**	**34**	**15**	**14**	**29**	**190**	**2**	**0**	**1**	**91**	**17.6**	**66**	**11**	**34**	**2**	**23**	**12**	**1**	**4**	**5**	**26**	**0**	**0**	**0**
1978-79	**Philadelphia Flyers**	**NHL**	**57**	**19**	**10**	**29**	**16**	**7**	**23**	**168**	**4**	**0**	**3**	**122**	**15.6**	**50**	**11**	**37**	**0**	**2**	**8**	**1**	**5**	**6**	**22**	**0**	**0**	**0**
1979-80	**Philadelphia Flyers**	**NHL**	**74**	**30**	**35**	**65**	**26**	**26**	**52**	**267**	**9**	**0**	**3**	**153**	**19.6**	**99**	**26**	**44**	**6**	**35**	**18**	**10**	**10**	**20**	**47**	**3**	**0**	**1**
1980-81	**Philadelphia Flyers**	**NHL**	**77**	**22**	**37**	**59**	**17**	**25**	**42**	**306**	**3**	**0**	**2**	**159**	**13.8**	**102**	**30**	**62**	**2**	**12**	**12**	**5**	**9**	**14**	**49**	**2**	**0**	**1**
1981-82	**Philadelphia Flyers**	**NHL**	**41**	**9**	**22**	**31**	**7**	**15**	**22**	**183**	**4**	**0**	**3**	**71**	**12.7**	**47**	**11**	**27**	**1**	**10**	**4**	**1**	**2**	**3**	**6**	**0**	**0**	**0**
1982-83	**Philadelphia Flyers**	**NHL**	**77**	**19**	**24**	**43**	**16**	**17**	**33**	**178**	**3**	**0**	**2**	**122**	**15.6**	**77**	**19**	**40**	**0**	**18**	**3**	**0**	**0**	**0**	**6**	**0**	**0**	**0**
1983-84	**Philadelphia Flyers**	**NHL**	**52**	**9**	**13**	**22**	**7**	**9**	**16**	**105**	**1**	**0**	**1**	**75**	**12.0**	**34**	**1**	**32**	**0**	**1**	....	....	....	....	....	....	....	....
	Minnesota North Stars	**NHL**	**11**	**2**	**5**	**7**	**2**	**3**	**5**	**46**	**0**	**0**	**0**	**17**	**11.8**	**7**	**0**	**9**	**0**	**–2**	**12**	**0**	**1**	**1**	**6**	**0**	**0**	**0**
1984-85	**Minnesota North Stars**	**NHL**	**16**	**4**	**3**	**7**	**3**	**2**	**5**	**38**	**2**	**0**	**0**	**13**	**30.8**	**10**	**5**	**9**	**0**	**–4**	**3**	**0**	**0**	**0**	**8**	**0**	**0**	**0**
	NHL Totals		**527**	**144**	**179**	**323**	**122**	**127**	**249**	**1684**	**28**	**0**	**17**	**898**	**16.0**	**535**	**120**	**322**	**12**		**82**	**19**	**32**	**51**	**195**	**5**	**0**	**2**
	Other Major League Totals		51	14	16	30	....	....	....	121	....	....	....	....	....	....	....	....	....	....	....	....	....	....	....	....	....	....

Played in NHL All-Star Game (1981)

Selected by **Edmonton** (WHA) in 1974 WHA Amateur Draft, June, 1974. WHA rights traded to **Minnesota** (WHA) by **Edmonton** (WHA) for cash, July, 1975. Traded to **Minnesota** by **Philadelphia** for the rights to Paul Guay and Minnesota's 3rd round choice (Darryl Gilmour) in 1985 Entry Draft, February 23, 1984.

• HOLMSTROM, Tomas

LW – L. 6', 200 lbs. b: Pitea, Sweden, 1/23/1973. Detroit's 9th, 257th overall, in 1994.

Season	Club	League	GP	G	A	Pts	AG	AA	APts	PIM	PP	SH	GW	S	%	TGF	PGF	TGA	PGA	+/–	GP	G	A	Pts	PIM	PP	SH	GW
1989-90	Pitea HC	Sweden-2	9	1	0	1	....	....	....	4	....	....	....	....	....	....	....	....	....	....	....	....	....	....	....	....	....	....
1990-91	Pitea HC	Sweden-2	26	5	4	9	....	....	....	16	....	....	....	....	....	....	....	....	....	....	....	....	....	....	....	....	....	....
1991-92	Pitea HC	Sweden-2	31	15	12	27	....	....	....	44	....	....	....	....	....	....	....	....	....	....	....	....	....	....	....	....	....	....
1992-93	Pitea HC	Sweden-2	32	17	15	32	....	....	....	30	....	....	....	....	....	....	....	....	....	....	....	....	....	....	....	....	....	....
1993-94	Bodens IK	Sweden-2	34	23	16	39	....	....	....	86	....	....	....	....	....	....	....	....	....	....	9	3	3	6	24	....	....	....
1994-95	Lulea HF	Sweden	40	14	14	28	....	....	....	56	....	....	....	....	....	....	....	....	....	....	8	1	2	3	20	....	....	....
1995-96	Lulea HF	Sweden	34	12	11	23	....	....	....	78	....	....	....	....	....	....	....	....	....	....	11	6	2	8	22	....	....	....
	Sweden	WC-A	6	1	0	1	....	....	....	12	....	....	....	....	....	....	....	....	....	....	....	....	....	....	....	....	....	....

			REGULAR SEASON																		PLAYOFFS							
Season	Club	League	GP	G	A	Pts	AG	AA	APts	PIM	PP	SH	GW	S	%	TGF	PGF	TGA	PGA	+/–	GP	G	A	Pts	PIM	PP	SH	GW
1996-97	Sweden	W-Cup	DID NOT PLAY																									
	♦ **Detroit Red Wings**	**NHL**	**47**	**6**	**3**	**9**	**6**	**3**	**9**	**33**	**3**	**0**	**0**	**53**	**11.3**	**19**	**10**	**19**	**0**	**–10**	**1**	**0**	**0**	**0**	**0**	**0**	**0**	**0**
	Adirondack Red Wings	AHL	6	3	1	4	....	....	....	7	....	....	....	....	....	....	....	....	....	....	....	....	....	....	....	....	....	....
1997-98♦	**Detroit Red Wings**	**NHL**	**57**	**5**	**17**	**22**	**6**	**17**	**23**	**44**	**1**	**0**	**1**	**48**	**10.4**	**33**	**10**	**17**	**0**	**6**	**22**	**7**	**12**	**19**	**16**	**2**	**0**	**0**
1998-99	**Detroit Red Wings**	**NHL**	**82**	**13**	**21**	**34**	**15**	**20**	**35**	**69**	**5**	**0**	**4**	**100**	**13.0**	**55**	**27**	**39**	**0**	**–11**	**10**	**4**	**3**	**7**	**4**	**2**	**0**	**1**
99-2000	**Detroit Red Wings**	**NHL**	**72**	**13**	**22**	**35**	**15**	**20**	**35**	**43**	**4**	**0**	**1**	**71**	**18.3**	**58**	**25**	**30**	**1**	**4**	**9**	**3**	**1**	**4**	**16**	**1**	**0**	**1**
	NHL Totals		**258**	**37**	**63**	**100**	**42**	**60**	**102**	**189**	**13**	**0**	**6**	**272**	**13.6**	**165**	**72**	**105**	**1**		**42**	**14**	**16**	**30**	**36**	**5**	**0**	**2**

• HOLST, Greg

Gregory C – L. 5'10", 170 lbs. b: Montreal, Que., 2/21/1954. NY Rangers' 8th, 139th overall, in 1974.

Season	Club	League	GP	G	A	Pts	AG	AA	APts	PIM	PP	SH	GW	S	%	TGF	PGF	TGA	PGA	+/–	GP	G	A	Pts	PIM	PP	SH	GW
1971-72	University of New Brunswick	AUAA	18	7	7	14	....	....	....	38	....	....	....	....	....	....	....	....	....	....	....	....	....	....	....	....	....	....
1972-73	University of New Brunswick	AUAA	19	21	11	32	....	....	....	82	....	....	....	....	....	....	....	....	....	....	....	....	....	....	....	....	....	....
1973-74	Kingston Canadians	OMJHL	62	33	47	80	....	....	....	121	....	....	....	....	....	....	....	....	....	....	....	....	....	....	....	....	....	....
1974-75	Port Huron Flags	IHL	8	1	0	1	....	....	....	6	....	....	....	....	....	....	....	....	....	....	....	....	....	....	....	....	....	....
	Winston-Salem Polar Bears	SHL	62	33	37	70	....	....	....	112	....	....	....	....	....	....	....	....	....	....	7	5	6	11	42	....	....	....
1975-76	**New York Rangers**	**NHL**	**2**	**0**	**0**	**0**	**0**	**0**	**0**	**0**	**0**	**0**	**0**	**0**	**0.0**	**0**	**0**	**3**	**0**	**–3**	....	....	....	....	....	....	....	....
	Providence Reds	AHL	69	37	44	81	....	....	....	77	....	....	....	....	....	....	....	....	....	....	3	0	0	0	22	....	....	....
1976-77	**New York Rangers**	**NHL**	**5**	**0**	**0**	**0**	**0**	**0**	**0**	**0**	**0**	**0**	**0**	**7**	**0.0**	**0**	**0**	**2**	**0**	**–2**	....	....	....	....	....	....	....	....
	New Haven Nighthawks	AHL	65	21	25	46	....	....	....	90	....	....	....	....	....	....	....	....	....	....	6	2	3	5	2	....	....	....
1977-78	**New York Rangers**	**NHL**	**4**	**0**	**0**	**0**	**0**	**0**	**0**	**0**	**0**	**0**	**0**	**2**	**0.0**	**0**	**0**	**1**	**0**	**–1**	....	....	....	....	....	....	....	....
	New Haven Nighthawks	AHL	65	15	25	40	....	....	....	44	....	....	....	....	....	....	....	....	....	....	15	6	7	13	6	....	....	....
1978-79	IEV Innsbruck	Austria	34	42	26	68	....	....	....	....	....	....	....	....	....	....	....	....	....	....	....	....	....	....	....	....	....	....
1979-80	IEV Innsbruck	Austria	39	37	34	71	....	....	....	63	....	....	....	....	....	....	....	....	....	....	....	....	....	....	....	....	....	....
1980-81	IEV Innsbruck	Austria	33	28	*48	76	....	....	....	70	....	....	....	....	....	....	....	....	....	....	....	....	....	....	....	....	....	....
1981-82	WEV Wien	Austria	38	41	19	60	....	....	....	....	....	....	....	....	....	....	....	....	....	....	10	14	15	*29	....	....	....	....
	Austria	WC-B	7	2	3	5	....	....	....	6	....	....	....	....	....	....	....	....	....	....	....	....	....	....	....	....	....	....
1982-83	IEV Innsbruck	Austria-2	STATISTICS NOT AVAILABLE																									
	Austria	WC-B	7	*8	8	*16	....	....	....	0	....	....	....	....	....	....	....	....	....	....	....	....	....	....	....	....	....	....
1983-84	IEV Innsbruck	Austria	28	36	32	68	....	....	....	....	....	....	....	....	....	....	....	....	....	....	7	7	*13	20	....	....	....	....
1984-85	IEV Innsbruck	Austria	39	44	57	101	....	....	....	36	....	....	....	....	....	....	....	....	....	....	....	....	....	....	....	....	....	....
	Austria	WEC-B	7	2	1	3	....	....	....	10	....	....	....	....	....	....	....	....	....	....	....	....	....	....	....	....	....	....
1985-86	IEV Innsbruck	Austria	36	27	24	51	....	....	....	83	....	....	....	....	....	....	....	....	....	....	....	....	....	....	....	....	....	....
	Austria	WEC-B	7	3	3	6	....	....	....	0	....	....	....	....	....	....	....	....	....	....	....	....	....	....	....	....	....	....
1986-87	IEV Innsbruck	Austria	38	39	36	75	....	....	....	50	....	....	....	....	....	....	....	....	....	....	....	....	....	....	....	....	....	....
1987-88	HC Salzburger	Austria	34	31	20	51	....	....	....	24	....	....	....	....	....	....	....	....	....	....	....	....	....	....	....	....	....	....
1988-89	VSV Villach	Austria	46	38	41	79	....	....	....	....	....	....	....	....	....	....	....	....	....	....	....	....	....	....	....	....	....	....
1989-90	IEV Innsbruck	Austria	33	36	39	75	....	....	....	55	....	....	....	....	....	....	....	....	....	....	....	....	....	....	....	....	....	....
1990-91	IEV Innsbruck	Austria	34	19	22	41	....	....	....	....	....	....	....	....	....	....	....	....	....	....	....	....	....	....	....	....	....	....
	Gosser EV	Austria	34	19	22	41	....	....	....	45	....	....	....	....	....	....	....	....	....	....	....	....	....	....	....	....	....	....
1991-92	IEV Innsbruck	Austria	42	21	30	51	....	....	....	....	....	....	....	....	....	....	....	....	....	....	....	....	....	....	....	....	....	....
1992-93	EC Graz	Austria	25	4	9	13	....	....	....	....	....	....	....	....	....	....	....	....	....	....	....	....	....	....	....	....	....	....
	NHL Totals		**11**	**0**	**0**	**0**	**0**	**0**	**0**	**0**	**0**	**0**	**0**	**9**	**0.0**	**0**	**0**	**6**	**0**		....	....	....	....	....	....	....	....

AUAA Second All-Star Team (1973)

Won Dudley "Red" Garrett Memorial Award (Top Rookie - AHL) (1976)

• HOLT, Gary

Gary Ray LW – L. 5'9", 175 lbs. b: Sarnia, Ont., 1/1/1952.

Season	Club	League	GP	G	A	Pts	AG	AA	APts	PIM	PP	SH	GW	S	%	TGF	PGF	TGA	PGA	+/–	GP	G	A	Pts	PIM	PP	SH	GW
1969-70	Sudbury Wolves	NOJHA	46	37	40	77	....	....	....	106	....	....	....	....	....	....	....	....	....	....	....	....	....	....	....	....	....	....
1970-71	Niagara Falls Flyers	OHA-Jr.	35	10	14	24	....	....	....	48	....	....	....	....	....	....	....	....	....	....	....	....	....	....	....	....	....	....
1971-72	Niagara Falls Flyers	OMJHL	64	11	12	23	....	....	....	27	....	....	....	....	....	....	....	....	....	....	6	1	3	4	4	....	....	....
1972-73	Columbus–Port Huron	IHL	75	30	30	60	....	....	....	82	....	....	....	....	....	....	....	....	....	....	11	1	6	7	6	....	....	....
1973-74	**California Golden Seals**	**NHL**	**1**	**0**	**0**	**0**	**0**	**0**	**0**	**0**	**0**	**0**	**0**	**1**	**0.0**	**0**	**0**	**0**	**0**	**0**	....	....	....	....	....	....	....	....
	Salt Lake Golden Eagles	WHL	71	21	26	47	....	....	....	197	....	....	....	....	....	....	....	....	....	....	5	0	0	0	11	....	....	....
1974-75	**California Golden Seals**	**NHL**	**1**	**0**	**1**	**1**	**0**	**1**	**1**	**0**	**0**	**0**	**0**	**2**	**0.0**	**1**	**0**	**0**	**0**	**1**	....	....	....	....	....	....	....	....
	Salt Lake Golden Eagles	CHL	78	26	39	65	....	....	....	200	....	....	....	....	....	....	....	....	....	....	11	6	4	10	57	....	....	....
1975-76	**California Golden Seals**	**NHL**	**48**	**6**	**5**	**11**	**5**	**4**	**9**	**50**	**1**	**0**	**0**	**59**	**10.2**	**18**	**4**	**24**	**0**	**–10**	....	....	....	....	....	....	....	....
	Salt Lake Golden Eagles	CHL	21	9	6	15	....	....	....	30	....	....	....	....	....	....	....	....	....	....	4	1	1	2	45	....	....	....
1976-77	**Cleveland Barons**	**NHL**	**2**	**0**	**1**	**1**	**0**	**1**	**1**	**2**	**0**	**0**	**0**	**4**	**0.0**	**1**	**0**	**2**	**0**	**–1**	....	....	....	....	....	....	....	....
	Salt Lake Golden Eagles	CHL	68	17	21	38	....	....	....	*226	....	....	....	....	....	....	....	....	....	....	....	....	....	....	....	....	....	....
1977-78	**St. Louis Blues**	**NHL**	**49**	**7**	**4**	**11**	**6**	**3**	**9**	**81**	**0**	**0**	**1**	**57**	**12.3**	**20**	**1**	**27**	**2**	**–6**	....	....	....	....	....	....	....	....
	Salt Lake Golden Eagles	CHL	24	8	7	15	....	....	....	89	....	....	....	....	....	....	....	....	....	....	....	....	....	....	....	....	....	....
1978-79	Salt Lake Golden Eagles	CHL	72	14	17	31	....	....	....	143	....	....	....	....	....	....	....	....	....	....	8	2	1	3	12	....	....	....
	NHL Totals		**101**	**13**	**11**	**24**	**11**	**9**	**20**	**133**	**1**	**0**	**1**	**123**	**10.6**	**40**	**5**	**53**	**2**		....	....	....	....	....	....	....	....

• Brother of Randy

Traded to **Port Huron** (IHL) by **Columbus** (IHL) with Dave Haley for Marty Reynolds, Randy Prior and loan of Brian Skinner, December, 1972. Signed as a free agent by **California**, September, 1973. Signed as a free agent by **St. Louis**, October 20, 1977.

• HOLT, Randy

Stewart Randall D – R. 5'11", 185 lbs. b: Pembroke, Ont., 1/15/1953. Chicago's 3rd, 45th overall, in 1973.

Season	Club	League	GP	G	A	Pts	AG	AA	APts	PIM	PP	SH	GW	S	%	TGF	PGF	TGA	PGA	+/–	GP	G	A	Pts	PIM	PP	SH	GW
1970-71	Sudbury Wolves	NOJHA	STATISTICS NOT AVAILABLE																									
	Niagara Falls Flyers	OHA-Jr.	35	5	7	12	....	....	....	178	....	....	....	....	....	....	....	....	....	....	....	....	....	....	....	....	....	....
1971-72	Niagara Falls Flyers	OMJHL	27	3	5	8	....	....	....	118	....	....	....	....	....	....	....	....	....	....	6	0	3	3	31	....	....	....
1972-73	Sudbury Wolves	OMJHL	55	7	42	49	....	....	....	294	....	....	....	....	....	....	....	....	....	....	4	2	0	2	34	....	....	....
1973-74	Dallas Black Hawks	CHL	66	3	15	18	....	....	....	222	....	....	....	....	....	....	....	....	....	....	10	1	2	3	*51	....	....	....
1974-75	**Chicago Black Hawks**	**NHL**	**12**	**0**	**1**	**1**	**0**	**1**	**1**	**13**	**0**	**0**	**0**	**8**	**0.0**	**5**	**1**	**6**	**1**	**–1**	....	....	....	....	....	....	....	....
	Dallas Black Hawks	CHL	65	8	32	40	....	....	....	*411	....	....	....	....	....	....	....	....	....	....	10	0	7	7	*86	....	....	....
1975-76	**Chicago Black Hawks**	**NHL**	**12**	**0**	**0**	**0**	**0**	**0**	**0**	**13**	**0**	**0**	**0**	**5**	**0.0**	**2**	**0**	**15**	**1**	**–12**	....	....	....	....	....	....	....	....
	Dallas Black Hawks	CHL	64	6	46	52	....	....	....	161	....	....	....	....	....	....	....	....	....	....	8	3	2	5	51	....	....	....
1976-77	**Chicago Black Hawks**	**NHL**	**12**	**0**	**3**	**3**	**0**	**2**	**2**	**14**	**0**	**0**	**0**	**7**	**0.0**	**8**	**0**	**17**	**5**	**–4**	**2**	**0**	**0**	**0**	**7**	**0**	**0**	**0**
	Dallas Black Hawks	CHL	30	0	10	10	....	....	....	90	....	....	....	....	....	....	....	....	....	....	3	0	1	1	25	....	....	....
1977-78	**Chicago Black Hawks**	**NHL**	**6**	**0**	**0**	**0**	**0**	**0**	**0**	**20**	**0**	**0**	**0**	**4**	**0.0**	**3**	**0**	**10**	**3**	**–4**	....	....	....	....	....	....	....	....
	Cleveland Barons	**NHL**	**48**	**1**	**4**	**5**	**1**	**3**	**4**	**229**	**0**	**0**	**0**	**23**	**4.3**	**15**	**1**	**40**	**2**	**–24**	....	....	....	....	....	....	....	....
1978-79	**Vancouver Canucks**	**NHL**	**22**	**1**	**3**	**4**	**1**	**2**	**3**	**80**	**0**	**0**	**0**	**17**	**5.9**	**19**	**0**	**30**	**10**	**–1**	....	....	....	....	....	....	....	....
	Los Angeles Kings	**NHL**	**36**	**0**	**6**	**6**	**0**	**4**	**4**	**202**	**0**	**0**	**0**	**21**	**0.0**	**16**	**0**	**21**	**3**	**–2**	**2**	**0**	**0**	**0**	**4**	**0**	**0**	**0**
1979-80	**Los Angeles Kings**	**NHL**	**42**	**0**	**1**	**1**	**0**	**1**	**1**	**94**	**0**	**0**	**0**	**10**	**0.0**	**8**	**0**	**11**	**0**	**–3**	....	....	....	....	....	....	....	....
1980-81	**Calgary Flames**	**NHL**	**48**	**0**	**5**	**5**	**0**	**3**	**3**	**165**	**0**	**0**	**0**	**14**	**0.0**	**11**	**0**	**17**	**0**	**–6**	**13**	**2**	**2**	**4**	**52**	**0**	**0**	**1**
1981-82	**Calgary Flames**	**NHL**	**8**	**0**	**0**	**0**	**0**	**0**	**0**	**9**	**0**	**0**	**0**	**1**	**0.0**	**0**	**0**	**4**	**0**	**–4**	....	....	....	....	....	....	....	....
	Washington Capitals	**NHL**	**53**	**2**	**6**	**8**	**2**	**4**	**6**	**250**	**0**	**0**	**0**	**32**	**6.3**	**37**	**0**	**48**	**4**	**–7**	....	....	....	....	....	....	....	....
1982-83	**Washington Capitals**	**NHL**	**70**	**0**	**8**	**8**	**0**	**6**	**6**	***275**	**0**	**0**	**0**	**30**	**0.0**	**45**	**0**	**66**	**14**	**–7**	**4**	**0**	**1**	**1**	**20**	**0**	**0**	**0**
1983-84	**Philadelphia Flyers**	**NHL**	**26**	**0**	**0**	**0**	**0**	**0**	**0**	**74**	**0**	**0**	**0**	**4**	**0.0**	**2**	**0**	**16**	**13**	**–1**	....	....	....	....	....	....	....	....
	NHL Totals		**395**	**4**	**37**	**41**	**4**	**26**	**30**	**1438**	**0**	**0**	**0**	**176**	**2.3**	**171**	**2**	**301**	**56**		**21**	**2**	**3**	**5**	**83**	**0**	**0**	**1**

• Brother of Gary • CHL First All-Star Team (1975)

Traded to **Cleveland** by **Chicago** for Reg Kerr, November 23, 1977. Claimed by **Vancouver** in **Cleveland-Minnesota** Dispersal Draft, June 15, 1978. Traded to **LA Kings** by **Vancouver** for Don Kozak, December 31, 1978. Traded to **Calgary** by **LA Kings** with Bert Wilson for Gary Unger, June 6, 1980. Traded to **Washington** by **Calgary** with Bobby Gould for Washington's 2nd round choice (later traded to Montreal — Montreal selected Todd Francis) in 1983 Entry Draft and Pat Ribble, November 25, 1981. Signed as a free agent by **Philadelphia**, August 30, 1983.

• HOLZINGER, Brian

Brian Alan C – R. 5'11", 190 lbs. b: Parma, OH, 10/10/1972. Buffalo's 7th, 124th overall, in 1991.

Season	Club	League	GP	G	A	Pts	AG	AA	APts	PIM	PP	SH	GW	S	%	TGF	PGF	TGA	PGA	+/–	GP	G	A	Pts	PIM	PP	SH	GW
1988-89	Padua Franciscan High	Hi-School	35	73	65	138	....	....	....	....	....	....	....	....	....	....	....	....	....	....	....	....	....	....	....	....	....	....
1989-90	Detroit Compuware	NAJHL	44	36	37	73	....	....	....	....	....	....	....	....	....	....	....	....	....	....	....	....	....	....	....	....	....	....
1990-91	Detroit Compuware	NAJHL	37	45	41	86	....	....	....	16	....	....	....	....	....	....	....	....	....	....	....	....	....	....	....	....	....	....

Season	Club	League	REGULAR SEASON																		PLAYOFFS							
			GP	G	A	Pts	AG	AA	APts	PIM	PP	SH	GW	S	%	TGF	PGF	TGA	PGA	+/–	GP	G	A	Pts	PIM	PP	SH	GW
1991-92	Bowling Green University	CCHA	30	14	8	22	....	....	....	36	....	....	....	....	....	....	....	....	....	....	....	....	....	....	....	....	....	....
	United States	WJC-A	7	1	1	2	....	....	....	2	....	....	....	....	....	....	....	....	....	....	....	....	....	....	....	....	....	....
1992-93	Bowling Green University	CCHA	41	31	26	57	....	....	....	44	....	....	....	....	....	....	....	....	....	....	....	....	....	....	....	....	....	....
1993-94	Bowling Green University	CCHA	38	22	15	37	....	....	....	24	....	....	....	....	....	....	....	....	....	....	....	....	....	....	....	....	....	....
1994-95	Bowling Green University	CCHA	38	35	33	68	....	....	....	42	....	....	....	....	....	....	....	....	....	....	....	....	....	....	....	....	....	....
	Buffalo Sabres	**NHL**	**4**	**0**	**3**	**3**	**0**	**4**	**4**	**0**	**0**	**0**	**0**	**3**	**0.0**	**4**	**0**	**2**	**0**	**2**	**4**	**2**	**1**	**3**	**2**	**1**	**0**	**0**
1995-96	**Buffalo Sabres**	**NHL**	**58**	**10**	**10**	**20**	**10**	**8**	**18**	**37**	**5**	**0**	**1**	**71**	**14.1**	**26**	**9**	**47**	**9**	**–21**	....	....	....	....	....	....	....	....
	Rochester Americans	AHL	17	10	11	21	....	....	....	14	....	....	....	....	....	....	....	....	....	....	19	10	14	24	10	....	....	....
1996-97	**Buffalo Sabres**	**NHL**	**81**	**22**	**29**	**51**	**23**	**26**	**49**	**54**	**2**	**2**	**6**	**142**	**15.5**	**75**	**17**	**67**	**18**	**9**	**12**	**2**	**5**	**7**	**8**	**0**	**1**	**0**
1997-98	**Buffalo Sabres**	**NHL**	**69**	**14**	**21**	**35**	**16**	**21**	**37**	**36**	**4**	**2**	**1**	**116**	**12.1**	**54**	**16**	**58**	**18**	**–2**	**15**	**4**	**7**	**11**	**18**	**1**	**1**	**0**
1998-99	**Buffalo Sabres**	**NHL**	**81**	**17**	**17**	**34**	**20**	**16**	**36**	**45**	**5**	**0**	**2**	**143**	**11.9**	**49**	**14**	**51**	**18**	**2**	**21**	**3**	**5**	**8**	**33**	**1**	**0**	**0**
99-2000	**Buffalo Sabres**	**NHL**	**59**	**7**	**17**	**24**	**8**	**16**	**24**	**30**	**0**	**1**	**2**	**81**	**8.6**	**33**	**3**	**42**	**16**	**4**	....	....	....	....	....	....	....	....
	Tampa Bay Lightning	**NHL**	**14**	**3**	**3**	**6**	**3**	**3**	**6**	**21**	**1**	**1**	**0**	**23**	**13.0**	**9**	**3**	**21**	**8**	**–7**	....	....	....	....	....	....	....	....
	NHL Totals		**366**	**73**	**100**	**173**	**80**	**94**	**174**	**223**	**17**	**6**	**12**	**579**	**12.6**	**250**	**62**	**288**	**87**		**52**	**11**	**18**	**29**	**61**	**3**	**2**	**0**

CCHA Second All-Star Team (1993) • CCHA First All-Star Team (1995) • NCAA West First All-American Team (1995) • Won Hobey Baker Memorial Award (Top U.S. Collegiate Player) (1995)

Traded to **Tampa Bay** by **Buffalo** with Cory Sarich, Wayne Primeau and Buffalo's 3rd round choice (Alexandre Kharitonov) in 2000 Entry Draft for Chris Gratton and Tampa Bay's 2nd round choice in 2001 Entry Draft, March 9, 2000.

• HOMENUKE, Ron

Ronald Wayne RW – R. 5'10", 180 lbs. b: Hazelton, B.C., 1/5/1952. Vancouver's 4th, 51st overall, in 1972.

Season	Club	League	GP	G	A	Pts	AG	AA	APts	PIM	PP	SH	GW	S	%	TGF	PGF	TGA	PGA	+/–	GP	G	A	Pts	PIM	PP	SH	GW
1968-69	Calgary Centennials	WCJHL	37	1	6	7	....	....	....	19	....	....	....	....	....	....	....	....	....	....	....	....	....	....	....	....	....	....
1969-70	Calgary Centennials	WCJHL	56	17	14	31	....	....	....	54	....	....	....	....	....	....	....	....	....	....	16	5	2	7	35	....	....	....
1970-71	Calgary Centennials	WCJHL	63	27	33	60	....	....	....	114	....	....	....	....	....	....	....	....	....	....	11	2	3	5	18	....	....	....
1971-72	Calgary Centennials	WCJHL	68	33	62	95	....	....	....	57	....	....	....	....	....	....	....	....	....	....	13	6	5	11	14	....	....	....
1972-73	**Vancouver Canucks**	**NHL**	**1**	**0**	**0**	**0**	**0**	**0**	**0**	**0**	**0**	**0**	**0**	**1**	**0.0**	**0**	**0**	**3**	**0**	**–3**	....	....	....	....	....	....	....	....
	Seattle Totems	WHL	67	13	24	37	....	....	....	46	....	....	....	....	....	....	....	....	....	....	....	....	....	....	....	....	....	....
1973-74	Albuquerque 6-Guns	CHL	47	12	15	27	....	....	....	39	....	....	....	....	....	....	....	....	....	....	....	....	....	....	....	....	....	....
1974-75	Seattle Totems	CHL	69	8	27	35	....	....	....	60	....	....	....	....	....	....	....	....	....	....	....	....	....	....	....	....	....	....
1975-76	Nelson Maple Leafs	WIHL	27	8	16	24	....	....	....	30	....	....	....	....	....	....	....	....	....	....	....	....	....	....	....	....	....	....
	NHL Totals		**1**	**0**	**0**	**0**	**0**	**0**	**0**	**0**	**0**	**0**	**0**	**1**	**0.0**	**0**	**0**	**3**	**0**		....	....	....	....	....	....	....	....

• HOOVER, Ron

Ron Kenneth C – L. 6'1", 185 lbs. b: Oakville, Ont., 10/28/1966. Hartford's 7th, 158th overall, in 1986.

Season	Club	League	GP	G	A	Pts	AG	AA	APts	PIM	PP	SH	GW	S	%	TGF	PGF	TGA	PGA	+/–	GP	G	A	Pts	PIM	PP	SH	GW
1983-84	Oakville Blades	OJHL-B	40	33	26	59	....	....	....	47	....	....	....	....	....	....	....	....	....	....	....	....	....	....	....	....	....	....
	Richmond Hill Dynes	OJHL	1	1	0	1	....	....	....	2	....	....	....	....	....	....	....	....	....	....	....	....	....	....	....	....	....	....
1984-85	Oakville Blades	OJHL-B	38	29	41	70	....	....	....	76	....	....	....	....	....	....	....	....	....	....	....	....	....	....	....	....	....	....
1985-86	Western Michigan University	CCHA	43	10	23	33	....	....	....	36	....	....	....	....	....	....	....	....	....	....	....	....	....	....	....	....	....	....
1986-87	Western Michigan University	CCHA	34	7	10	17	....	....	....	22	....	....	....	....	....	....	....	....	....	....	....	....	....	....	....	....	....	....
1987-88	Western Michigan University	CCHA	42	39	23	62	....	....	....	40	....	....	....	....	....	....	....	....	....	....	....	....	....	....	....	....	....	....
1988-89	Western Michigan University	CCHA	42	32	27	59	....	....	....	66	....	....	....	....	....	....	....	....	....	....	....	....	....	....	....	....	....	....
1989-90	**Boston Bruins**	**NHL**	**2**	**0**	**0**	**0**	**0**	**0**	**0**	**0**	**0**	**0**	**0**	**2**	**0.0**	**0**	**0**	**2**	**0**	**–2**	....	....	....	....	....	....	....	....
	Maine Mariners	AHL	75	28	26	54	....	....	....	57	....	....	....	....	....	....	....	....	....	....	....	....	....	....	....	....	....	....
1990-91	**Boston Bruins**	**NHL**	**15**	**4**	**0**	**4**	**4**	**0**	**4**	**31**	**0**	**0**	**1**	**17**	**23.5**	**6**	**0**	**6**	**0**	**0**	**8**	**0**	**0**	**0**	**18**	**0**	**0**	**0**
	Maine Mariners	AHL	62	28	16	44	....	....	....	40	....	....	....	....	....	....	....	....	....	....	....	....	....	....	....	....	....	....
1991-92	**St. Louis Blues**	**NHL**	**1**	**0**	**0**	**0**	**0**	**0**	**0**	**0**	**0**	**0**	**0**	**1**	**0.0**	**0**	**0**	**0**	**0**	**0**	....	....	....	....	....	....	....	....
	Peoria Rivermen	IHL	71	27	34	61	....	....	....	30	....	....	....	....	....	....	....	....	....	....	10	4	4	8	4	....	....	....
1992-93	Peoria Rivermen	IHL	58	17	13	30	....	....	....	28	....	....	....	....	....	....	....	....	....	....	4	1	1	2	2	....	....	....
1993-94	Peoria Rivermen	IHL	80	26	24	50	....	....	....	89	....	....	....	....	....	....	....	....	....	....	6	0	1	1	10	....	....	....
1994-95	Peoria Rivermen	IHL	76	22	20	42	....	....	....	70	....	....	....	....	....	....	....	....	....	....	9	2	1	3	12	....	....	....
1995-96	Peoria Rivermen	IHL	74	22	15	37	....	....	....	94	....	....	....	....	....	....	....	....	....	....	12	0	3	3	8	....	....	....
1996-97	Cincinnati Cyclones	IHL	4	1	1	2	....	....	....	0	....	....	....	....	....	....	....	....	....	....	....	....	....	....	....	....	....	....
	San Antonio Dragons	IHL	21	2	3	5	....	....	....	18	....	....	....	....	....	....	....	....	....	....	8	1	1	2	0	....	....	....
1997-98	San Antonio Dragons	IHL	21	1	3	4	....	....	....	20	....	....	....	....	....	....	....	....	....	....	....	....	....	....	....	....	....	....
	Brantford Smoke	UHL	41	27	24	51	....	....	....	20	....	....	....	....	....	....	....	....	....	....	9	2	8	10	18	....	....	....
	NHL Totals		**18**	**4**	**0**	**4**	**4**	**0**	**4**	**31**	**0**	**0**	**1**	**20**	**20.0**	**6**	**0**	**8**	**0**		**8**	**0**	**0**	**0**	**18**	**0**	**0**	**0**

CCHA Second All-Star Team (1988)

Signed as a free agent by **Boston**, September 1, 1989. Signed as a free agent by **St. Louis**, July 23, 1991.

• HOPKINS, Dean

Dean Robert RW – R. 6'1", 210 lbs. b: Cobourg, Ont., 6/6/1959. Los Angeles' 2nd, 29th overall, in 1979.

Season	Club	League	GP	G	A	Pts	AG	AA	APts	PIM	PP	SH	GW	S	%	TGF	PGF	TGA	PGA	+/–	GP	G	A	Pts	PIM	PP	SH	GW
1974-75	Owen Sound Greys	OHA-B	38	21	20	41	....	....	....	44	....	....	....	....	....	....	....	....	....	....	....	....	....	....	....	....	....	....
1975-76	London Knights	OMJHL	53	4	14	18	....	....	....	50	....	....	....	....	....	....	....	....	....	....	....	....	....	....	....	....	....	....
1976-77	London Knights	OMJHL	63	19	26	45	....	....	....	67	....	....	....	....	....	....	....	....	....	....	19	4	8	12	17	....	....	....
1977-78	London Knights	OMJHL	67	19	34	53	....	....	....	70	....	....	....	....	....	....	....	....	....	....	11	1	5	6	24	....	....	....
1978-79	London Knights	OMJHL	65	37	55	92	....	....	....	149	....	....	....	....	....	....	....	....	....	....	7	6	0	6	27	....	....	....
1979-80	**Los Angeles Kings**	**NHL**	**60**	**8**	**6**	**14**	**7**	**4**	**11**	**39**	**1**	**0**	**2**	**57**	**14.0**	**19**	**2**	**33**	**0**	**–16**	**4**	**0**	**1**	**1**	**5**	**0**	**0**	**0**
1980-81	**Los Angeles Kings**	**NHL**	**67**	**8**	**18**	**26**	**6**	**12**	**18**	**118**	**2**	**0**	**1**	**60**	**13.3**	**42**	**2**	**34**	**0**	**6**	**4**	**1**	**0**	**1**	**9**	**0**	**0**	**1**
1981-82	**Los Angeles Kings**	**NHL**	**41**	**2**	**13**	**15**	**2**	**9**	**11**	**102**	**0**	**0**	**0**	**55**	**3.6**	**21**	**2**	**46**	**7**	**–20**	**10**	**0**	**4**	**4**	**15**	**0**	**0**	**0**
1982-83	**Los Angeles Kings**	**NHL**	**49**	**5**	**12**	**17**	**4**	**8**	**12**	**43**	**0**	**0**	**0**	**50**	**10.0**	**27**	**1**	**32**	**1**	**–5**	....	....	....	....	....	....	....	....
	New Haven Nighthawks	AHL	20	9	8	17	....	....	....	58	....	....	....	....	....	....	....	....	....	....	....	....	....	....	....	....	....	....
1983-84	New Haven Nighthawks	AHL	79	35	47	82	....	....	....	162	....	....	....	....	....	....	....	....	....	....	....	....	....	....	....	....	....	....
1984-85	New Haven Nighthawks	AHL	20	7	10	17	....	....	....	38	....	....	....	....	....	....	....	....	....	....	....	....	....	....	....	....	....	....
	Nova Scotia Voyageurs	AHL	49	13	17	30	....	....	....	93	....	....	....	....	....	....	....	....	....	....	6	1	2	3	20	....	....	....
1985-86	**Edmonton Oilers**	**NHL**	**1**	**0**	**0**	**0**	**0**	**0**	**0**	**0**	**0**	**0**	**0**	**0**	**0.0**	**0**	**0**	**0**	**0**	**0**	....	....	....	....	....	....	....	....
	Nova Scotia Oilers	AHL	60	23	32	55	....	....	....	131	....	....	....	....	....	....	....	....	....	....	....	....	....	....	....	....	....	....
1986-87	Nova Scotia Oilers	AHL	59	20	25	45	....	....	....	84	....	....	....	....	....	....	....	....	....	....	1	0	0	0	5	....	....	....
1987-88	Nova Scotia Oilers	AHL	44	20	22	42	....	....	....	122	....	....	....	....	....	....	....	....	....	....	5	2	5	7	16	....	....	....
1988-89	**Quebec Nordiques**	**NHL**	**5**	**0**	**2**	**2**	**0**	**1**	**1**	**4**	**0**	**0**	**0**	**6**	**0.0**	**2**	**0**	**1**	**0**	**1**	....	....	....	....	....	....	....	....
	Halifax Citadels	AHL	53	18	31	49	....	....	....	116	....	....	....	....	....	....	....	....	....	....	3	0	1	1	6	....	....	....
1989-90	Halifax Citadels	AHL	54	23	32	55	....	....	....	167	....	....	....	....	....	....	....	....	....	....	6	1	4	5	8	....	....	....
1990-91	Halifax Citadels	AHL	3	2	0	2	....	....	....	2	....	....	....	....	....	....	....	....	....	....	....	....	....	....	....	....	....	....
	NHL Totals		**223**	**23**	**51**	**74**	**19**	**34**	**53**	**306**	**3**	**0**	**3**	**228**	**10.1**	**111**	**7**	**146**	**8**		**18**	**1**	**5**	**6**	**29**	**0**	**0**	**1**

Traded to **Edmonton** by **LA Kings** for cash, November 27, 1984. Traded to **LA Kings** by **Edmonton** for future considerations, May 31, 1985. Signed as a free agent by **Edmonton**, September 27, 1985. Signed as a free agent by **Quebec**, July 30, 1988.

• HOPKINS, Larry

Larry Harold LW – L. 6'1", 215 lbs. b: Oshawa, Ont., 3/17/1954. Atlanta's 9th, 152nd overall, in 1974.

Season	Club	League	GP	G	A	Pts	AG	AA	APts	PIM	PP	SH	GW	S	%	TGF	PGF	TGA	PGA	+/–	GP	G	A	Pts	PIM	PP	SH	GW
1972-73	Oshawa Generals	OMJHL	50	5	17	22	....	....	....	9	....	....	....	....	....	....	....	....	....	....	....	....	....	....	....	....	....	....
1973-74	University of Toronto	OUAA	18	3	8	11	....	....	....	10	....	....	....	....	....	....	....	....	....	....	....	....	....	....	....	....	....	....
1974-75	University of Toronto	OUAA	20	1	4	5	....	....	....	2	....	....	....	....	....	....	....	....	....	....	....	....	....	....	....	....	....	....
1975-76	University of Toronto	OUAA	20	7	12	19	....	....	....	6	....	....	....	....	....	....	....	....	....	....	....	....	....	....	....	....	....	....
1976-77	University of Toronto	OUAA	20	12	20	32	....	....	....	10	....	....	....	....	....	....	....	....	....	....	....	....	....	....	....	....	....	....
1977-78	University of Toronto	OUAA	20	14	26	40	....	....	....	12	....	....	....	....	....	....	....	....	....	....	....	....	....	....	....	....	....	....
	Toronto Maple Leafs	**NHL**	**2**	**0**	**0**	**0**	**0**	**0**	**0**	**0**	**0**	**0**	**0**	**0**	**0.0**	**0**	**0**	**0**	**0**	**0**	....	....	....	....	....	....	....	....
	Dallas Black Hawks	CHL	....	....	....	....	....	....	....	....	....	....	....	....	....	....	....	....	....	....	11	0	1	1	7	....	....	....
1978-79	Saginaw Gears	IHL	80	36	41	77	....	....	....	67	....	....	....	....	....	....	....	....	....	....	....	....	....	....	....	....	....	....
1979-80	**Winnipeg Jets**	**NHL**	**5**	**0**	**0**	**0**	**0**	**0**	**0**	**0**	**0**	**0**	**0**	**3**	**0.0**	**0**	**0**	**3**	**0**	**–3**	....	....	....	....	....	....	....	....
	Tulsa Oilers	CHL	72	29	31	60	....	....	....	33	....	....	....	....	....	....	....	....	....	....	3	0	0	0	0	....	....	....
1980-81	Tulsa Oilers	CHL	79	16	44	60	....	....	....	45	....	....	....	....	....	....	....	....	....	....	8	1	4	5	11	....	....	....

			REGULAR SEASON																			PLAYOFFS							
Season	**Club**	**League**	**GP**	**G**	**A**	**Pts**	**AG**	**AA**	**APts**	**PIM**	**PP**	**SH**	**GW**	**S**	**%**	**TGF**	**PGF**	**TGA**	**PGA**	**+/–**	**GP**	**G**	**A**	**Pts**	**PIM**	**PP**	**SH**	**GW**
1981-82	**Winnipeg Jets**	**NHL**	**41**	**10**	**15**	**25**	**8**	**10**	**18**	**22**	**0**	**0**	**3**	**52**	**19.2**	**40**	**1**	**46**	**15**	**8**	**4**	**0**	**0**	**0**	**2**	**0**	**0**	**0**
	Tulsa Oilers	CHL	31	12	18	30	....	....	....	9	....	....	....	....	....	....	....	....	....	....	....	....	....	....	....	....	....	....
1982-83	**Winnipeg Jets**	**NHL**	**12**	**3**	**1**	**4**	**2**	**1**	**3**	**4**	**0**	**0**	**1**	**16**	**18.8**	**10**	**0**	**6**	**1**	**5**	**2**	**0**	**0**	**0**	**0**	**0**	**0**	**0**
	Sherbrooke Jets	AHL	66	18	30	48	....	....	....	42	....	....	....	....	....	....	....	....	....	....	....	....	....	....	....	....	....	....
	NHL Totals		**60**	**13**	**16**	**29**	**10**	**11**	**21**	**26**	**0**	**0**	**4**	**71**	**18.3**	**50**	**1**	**55**	**16**		**6**	**0**	**0**	**0**	**2**	**0**	**0**	**0**

Signed to an amateur try-out contract by **Toronto**, March 8, 1978. Signed as a free agent by **Winnipeg**, August 15, 1979.

• HORACEK, Tony

Tony S. LW – L. 6'4", 210 lbs. b: Vancouver, B.C., 2/3/1967. Philadelphia's 8th, 147th overall, in 1985.

Season	Club	League	GP	G	A	Pts	AG	AA	APts	PIM	PP	SH	GW	S	%	TGF	PGF	TGA	PGA	+/–	GP	G	A	Pts	PIM	PP	SH	GW
1983-84	Vancouver Grandview IWA	BCAHA	STATISTICS NOT AVAILABLE																									
1984-85	Kelowna Wings	WHL	67	9	18	27	....	....	....	114	....	....	....	....	....	....	....	....	....	....	6	0	1	1	11	....	....	....
1985-86	Spokane Chiefs	WHL	64	19	28	47	....	....	....	129	....	....	....	....	....	....	....	....	....	....	9	4	5	9	29	....	....	....
1986-87	Spokane Chiefs	WHL	64	23	37	60	....	....	....	177	....	....	....	....	....	....	....	....	....	....	5	1	3	4	18	....	....	....
	Hershey Bears	AHL	....	....	....	....	....	....	....	....	....	....	....	....	....	....	....	....	....	....	1	0	0	0	0	....	....	....
1987-88	Spokane Chiefs	WHL	24	17	23	40	....	....	....	63	....	....	....	....	....	....	....	....	....	....	....	....	....	....	....	....	....	....
	Kamloops Blazers	WHL	26	14	17	31	....	....	....	51	....	....	....	....	....	....	....	....	....	....	18	6	4	10	73	....	....	....
	Hershey Bears	AHL	1	0	0	0	....	....	....	0	....	....	....	....	....	....	....	....	....	....	....	....	....	....	....	....	....	....
1988-89	Hershey Bears	AHL	10	0	0	0	....	....	....	38	....	....	....	....	....	....	....	....	....	....	....	....	....	....	....	....	....	....
	Indianapolis Ice	IHL	43	11	13	24	....	....	....	138	....	....	....	....	....	....	....	....	....	....	....	....	....	....	....	....	....	....
1989-90	**Philadelphia Flyers**	**NHL**	**48**	**5**	**5**	**10**	**4**	**4**	**8**	**117**	**0**	**0**	**1**	**31**	**16.1**	**19**	**0**	**13**	**0**	**6**	....	....	....	....	....	....	....	....
	Hershey Bears	AHL	12	0	5	5	....	....	....	25	....	....	....	....	....	....	....	....	....	....	....	....	....	....	....	....	....	....
1990-91	**Philadelphia Flyers**	**NHL**	**34**	**3**	**6**	**9**	**3**	**5**	**8**	**49**	**0**	**0**	**1**	**35**	**8.6**	**17**	**0**	**11**	**0**	**6**	....	....	....	....	....	....	....	....
	Hershey Bears	AHL	19	5	3	8	....	....	....	35	....	....	....	....	....	....	....	....	....	....	4	2	0	2	14	....	....	....
1991-92	**Philadelphia Flyers**	**NHL**	**34**	**1**	**3**	**4**	**1**	**2**	**3**	**51**	**0**	**0**	**0**	**22**	**4.5**	**5**	**0**	**14**	**0**	**–9**	....	....	....	....	....	....	....	....
	Chicago Blackhawks	**NHL**	**12**	**1**	**4**	**5**	**1**	**3**	**4**	**21**	**0**	**0**	**0**	**10**	**10.0**	**5**	**0**	**4**	**1**	**2**	**2**	**1**	**0**	**1**	**2**	**0**	**0**	**0**
1992-93	Indianapolis Ice	IHL	6	1	1	2	....	....	....	28	....	....	....	....	....	....	....	....	....	....	5	3	2	5	18	....	....	....
1993-94	**Chicago Blackhawks**	**NHL**	**7**	**0**	**0**	**0**	**0**	**0**	**0**	**53**	**0**	**0**	**0**	**2**	**0.0**	**1**	**0**	**0**	**0**	**1**	....	....	....	....	....	....	....	....
	Indianapolis Ice	IHL	29	6	7	13	....	....	....	63	....	....	....	....	....	....	....	....	....	....	....	....	....	....	....	....	....	....
1994-95	**Chicago Blackhawks**	**NHL**	**19**	**0**	**1**	**1**	**0**	**1**	**1**	**25**	**0**	**0**	**0**	**6**	**0.0**	**1**	**0**	**5**	**0**	**–4**	....	....	....	....	....	....	....	....
	Indianapolis Ice	IHL	51	7	19	26	....	....	....	201	....	....	....	....	....	....	....	....	....	....	....	....	....	....	....	....	....	....
1995-96	Hershey Bears	AHL	34	4	9	13	....	....	....	75	....	....	....	....	....	....	....	....	....	....	5	1	1	2	4	....	....	....
1996-97	Cincinnati Cyclones	IHL	60	4	5	9	....	....	....	158	....	....	....	....	....	....	....	....	....	....	2	0	1	1	2	....	....	....
1997-98	Utah Grizzlies	IHL	5	0	0	0	....	....	....	7	....	....	....	....	....	....	....	....	....	....	....	....	....	....	....	....	....	....
	NHL Totals		**154**	**10**	**19**	**29**	**9**	**15**	**24**	**316**	**0**	**0**	**2**	**106**	**9.4**	**48**	**0**	**47**	**1**		**2**	**1**	**0**	**1**	**2**	**0**	**0**	**0**

Traded to **Chicago** by **Philadelphia** for Ryan McGill, February 7, 1992.

• HORAVA, Miloslav

D – L. 6', 193 lbs. b: Kladno, Czech., 8/14/1961. Edmonton's 8th, 176th overall, in 1981.

Season	Club	League	GP	G	A	Pts	AG	AA	APts	PIM	PP	SH	GW	S	%	TGF	PGF	TGA	PGA	+/–	GP	G	A	Pts	PIM	PP	SH	GW
1969-1977	PZ Kladno	Czech-Jr.	STATISTICS NOT AVAILABLE																									
1977-78	Poldi Kladno	Czech.	STATISTICS NOT AVAILABLE																									
1978-79	Poldi Kladno	Czech.	22	1	5	6	....	....	....	2	....	....	....	....	....	....	....	....	....	....	....	....	....	....	....	....	....	....
	Czechoslovakia	EJC-A	5	2	0	2	....	....	....	0	....	....	....	....	....	....	....	....	....	....	....	....	....	....	....	....	....	....
1979-80	Poldi Kladno	Czech.	44	19	15	34	....	....	....	10	....	....	....	....	....	....	....	....	....	....	....	....	....	....	....	....	....	....
	Czechoslovakia	WJC-A	5	0	1	1	....	....	....	2	....	....	....	....	....	....	....	....	....	....	....	....	....	....	....	....	....	....
1980-81	Poldi Kladno	Czech.	40	13	16	29	....	....	....	22	....	....	....	....	....	....	....	....	....	....	....	....	....	....	....	....	....	....
	Czechoslovakia	WJC-A	5	2	3	5	....	....	....	6	....	....	....	....	....	....	....	....	....	....	....	....	....	....	....	....	....	....
	Czechoslovakia	WEC-A	8	0	6	6	....	....	....	8	....	....	....	....	....	....	....	....	....	....	....	....	....	....	....	....	....	....
1981-82	Czechoslovakia	Can-Cup	6	2	0	2	....	....	....	2	....	....	....	....	....	....	....	....	....	....	....	....	....	....	....	....	....	....
	Poldi Kladno	Czech.	42	10	12	22	....	....	....	18	....	....	....	....	....	....	....	....	....	....	....	....	....	....	....	....	....	....
	Czechoslovakia	WEC-A	10	0	1	1	....	....	....	2	....	....	....	....	....	....	....	....	....	....	....	....	....	....	....	....	....	....
1982-83	Poldi Kladno	Czech.	40	12	16	28	....	....	....	26	....	....	....	....	....	....	....	....	....	....	....	....	....	....	....	....	....	....
1983-84	Dukla Trencin	Czech.	44	2	15	17	....	....	....	8	....	....	....	....	....	....	....	....	....	....	....	....	....	....	....	....	....	....
	Czechoslovakia	Olympics	7	0	4	4	....	....	....	2	....	....	....	....	....	....	....	....	....	....	....	....	....	....	....	....	....	....
1984-85	Czechoslovakia	Can-Cup	4	0	1	1	....	....	....	5	....	....	....	....	....	....	....	....	....	....	....	....	....	....	....	....	....	....
	Dukla Trencin	Czech.	42	20	22	42	....	....	....	22	....	....	....	....	....	....	....	....	....	....	....	....	....	....	....	....	....	....
	Czechoslovakia	WEC-A	9	3	2	5	....	....	....	4	....	....	....	....	....	....	....	....	....	....	....	....	....	....	....	....	....	....
1985-86	Poldi Kladno	Czech.	38	17	26	43	....	....	....	14	....	....	....	....	....	....	....	....	....	....	....	....	....	....	....	....	....	....
1986-87	Poldi Kladno	Czech.	29	7	11	18	....	....	....	10	....	....	....	....	....	....	....	....	....	....	....	....	....	....	....	....	....	....
	Czechoslovakia	WEC-A	10	1	4	5	....	....	....	4	....	....	....	....	....	....	....	....	....	....	....	....	....	....	....	....	....	....
1987-88	Czechoslovakia	Can-Cup	6	1	2	3	....	....	....	4	....	....	....	....	....	....	....	....	....	....	....	....	....	....	....	....	....	....
	Poldi Kladno	Czech.	29	10	18	28	....	....	....	18	....	....	....	....	....	....	....	....	....	....	....	....	....	....	....	....	....	....
	Czechoslovakia	Olympics	8	1	2	3	....	....	....	14	....	....	....	....	....	....	....	....	....	....	....	....	....	....	....	....	....	....
1988-89	Poldi Kladno	Czech.	35	10	16	26	....	....	....	24	....	....	....	....	....	....	....	....	....	....	....	....	....	....	....	....	....	....
	New York Rangers	**NHL**	**6**	**0**	**1**	**1**	**0**	**1**	**1**	**0**	**0**	**0**	**0**	**7**	**0.0**	**2**	**1**	**3**	**0**	**–2**	....	....	....	....	....	....	....	....
1989-90	**New York Rangers**	**NHL**	**45**	**4**	**10**	**14**	**3**	**7**	**10**	**26**	**1**	**0**	**1**	**50**	**8.0**	**44**	**13**	**21**	**0**	**10**	**2**	**0**	**1**	**1**	**0**	**0**	**0**	**0**
1990-91	**New York Rangers**	**NHL**	**29**	**1**	**6**	**7**	**1**	**5**	**6**	**12**	**0**	**0**	**0**	**27**	**3.7**	**22**	**6**	**15**	**1**	**2**	....	....	....	....	....	....	....	....
1991-92	MoDo AIK	Sweden	40	3	21	24	....	....	....	60	....	....	....	....	....	....	....	....	....	....	....	....	....	....	....	....	....	....
	Czechoslovakia	Olympics	6	1	0	1	....	....	....	0	....	....	....	....	....	....	....	....	....	....	....	....	....	....	....	....	....	....
1992-93	MoDo AIK	Sweden	38	8	27	35	....	....	....	52	....	....	....	....	....	....	....	....	....	....	....	....	....	....	....	....	....	....
	Czechoslovakia	WC-A	8	0	3	3	....	....	....	0	....	....	....	....	....	....	....	....	....	....	....	....	....	....	....	....	....	....
1993-94	MoDo AIK	Sweden	29	5	14	19	....	....	....	38	....	....	....	....	....	....	....	....	....	....	....	....	....	....	....	....	....	....
	Czech-Republic	Olympics	7	0	0	0	....	....	....	8	....	....	....	....	....	....	....	....	....	....	....	....	....	....	....	....	....	....
1994-95	Slavia Praha	Czech-Rep	38	7	17	24	....	....	....	....	....	....	....	....	....	....	....	....	....	....	....	....	....	....	....	....	....	....
1995-96	Slavia Praha	Czech-Rep	37	7	31	38	....	....	....	....	....	....	....	....	....	....	....	....	....	....	7	0	7	7	....	....	....	....
1996-97	Slavia Praha	Czech-Rep	43	3	23	26	....	....	....	62	....	....	....	....	....	....	....	....	....	....	3	0	1	1	0	....	....	....
1997-98	Karlovy Vary	Czech-Rep	26	4	6	10	....	....	....	8	....	....	....	....	....	....	....	....	....	....	....	....	....	....	....	....	....	....
1998-99	HC Chemopetrol Litvinov	Cze-Rep	28	3	12	15	....	....	....	24	....	....	....	....	....	....	....	....	....	....	....	....	....	....	....	....	....	....
	HKM Zvolen	Slovakia-2	19	1	2	3	....	....	....	14	....	....	....	....	....	....	....	....	....	....	....	....	....	....	....	....	....	....
99-2000	HC Chemopetrol Litvinov	Czech-Rep	44	3	16	19	....	....	....	30	....	....	....	....	....	....	....	....	....	....	....	....	....	....	....	....	....	....
	NHL Totals		**80**	**5**	**17**	**22**	**4**	**13**	**17**	**38**	**1**	**0**	**1**	**84**	**6.0**	**68**	**20**	**39**	**1**		**2**	**0**	**1**	**1**	**0**	**0**	**0**	**0**

WJC-A All-Star Team (1981) • Named Best Defenseman at WJC-A (1981)

Traded to **NY Rangers** by **Edmonton** with Don Jackson, Mike Golden and future considerations (Stu Kulak, March 10, 1987) for Reijo Ruotsalainen, Ville Kentala, Clark Donatelli and Jim Wiemer, October 23, 1986. Traded to **Quebec** by **NY Rangers** for Stephane Guerard, May 25, 1991.

• HORBUL, Doug

Douglas George LW – L. 5'9", 170 lbs. b: Nokomis, Sask., 7/27/1952. NY Rangers' 6th, 63rd overall, in 1972.

Season	Club	League	GP	G	A	Pts	AG	AA	APts	PIM	PP	SH	GW	S	%	TGF	PGF	TGA	PGA	+/–	GP	G	A	Pts	PIM	PP	SH	GW
1969-70	Saskatoon Blades	WCJHL	60	22	30	52	....	....	....	22	....	....	....	....	....	....	....	....	....	....	7	1	1	2	2	....	....	....
1970-71	Saskatoon Blades	WCJHL	40	17	18	35	....	....	....	20	....	....	....	....	....	....	....	....	....	....	....	....	....	....	....	....	....	....
	Calgary Centennials	WCJHL	25	15	8	23	....	....	....	16	....	....	....	....	....	....	....	....	....	....	11	3	4	7	6	....	....	....
1971-72	Calgary Centennials	WCJHL	68	39	32	71	....	....	....	38	....	....	....	....	....	....	....	....	....	....	13	9	8	17	6	....	....	....
1972-73	Providence Reds	AHL	10	1	4	5	....	....	....	2	....	....	....	....	....	....	....	....	....	....	....	....	....	....	....	....	....	....
	Omaha Knights	CHL	53	15	11	26	....	....	....	19	....	....	....	....	....	....	....	....	....	....	11	*7	3	*10	2	....	....	....
1973-74	Providence Reds	AHL	75	34	29	63	....	....	....	31	....	....	....	....	....	....	....	....	....	....	15	9	4	13	8	....	....	....
1974-75	**Kansas City Scouts**	**NHL**	**4**	**1**	**0**	**1**	**1**	**0**	**1**	**2**	**0**	**0**	**0**	**5**	**20.0**	**2**	**1**	**4**	**0**	**–3**	....	....	....	....	....	....	....	....
	Baltimore Clippers	AHL	38	16	8	24	....	....	....	11	....	....	....	....	....	....	....	....	....	....	....	....	....	....	....	....	....	....
	Providence Reds	AHL	32	13	12	25	....	....	....	16	....	....	....	....	....	....	....	....	....	....	6	1	2	3	0	....	....	....
1975-76	Springfield Indians	AHL	25	2	1	3	....	....	....	8	....	....	....	....	....	....	....	....	....	....	....	....	....	....	....	....	....	....
	Baltimore Clippers	AHL	43	7	10	17	....	....	....	16	....	....	....	....	....	....	....	....	....	....	....	....	....	....	....	....	....	....

			REGULAR SEASON																		PLAYOFFS							
Season	Club	League	GP	G	A	Pts	AG	AA	APts	PIM	PP	SH	GW	S	%	TGF	PGF	TGA	PGA	+/–	GP	G	A	Pts	PIM	PP	SH	GW
1976-77	Rhode Island Reds	AHL	16	3	4	7	....	....	....	2	....	....	....	....	....	....	....	....	....	....	....	....	....	....	....	....	....	....
	Fort Wayne Komets	IHL	45	14	21	35	....	....	....	14	....	....	....	....	....	....	....	....	....	....	9	4	6	10	0	....	....	....
1977-78	Trail Smoke Eaters	WIHL	45	12	29	41	....	....	....	8	....	....	....	....	....	....	....	....	....	....	....	....	....	....	....	....	....	....
1978-1981	Trail Smoke Eaters	WIHL	STATISTICS NOT AVAILABLE																									
	NHL Totals		**4**	**1**	**0**	**1**	**1**	**0**	**1**	**2**	**0**	**0**	**0**	**5**	**20.0**	**2**	**1**	**4**	**0**		....	....	....	....	....	....	....	....

Claimed by **Kansas City** from **NY Rangers** in Expansion Draft, June 12, 1974.

• HORDY, Mike

Michael D – R. 5'10", 180 lbs. b: Thunder Bay, Ont., 10/10/1956. NY Islanders' 5th, 86th overall, in 1976.

Season	Club	League	GP	G	A	Pts	AG	AA	APts	PIM	PP	SH	GW	S	%	TGF	PGF	TGA	PGA	+/–	GP	G	A	Pts	PIM	PP	SH	GW
1973-74	Thunder Bay Hurricanes	MWJHL	59	11	39	50	....	....	....	34	....	....	....	....	....	....	....	....	....	....	....	....	....	....	....	....	....	....
1974-75	Sault Ste. Marie Greyhounds	OMJHL	70	18	33	51	....	....	....	59	....	....	....	....	....	....	....	....	....	....	....	....	....	....	....	....	....	....
1975-76	Sault Ste. Marie Greyhounds	OMJHL	63	17	51	68	....	....	....	84	....	....	....	....	....	....	....	....	....	....	12	2	8	10	8	....	....	....
1976-77	Fort Worth Texans	CHL	2	0	0	0	....	....	....	5	....	....	....	....	....	....	....	....	....	....	3	0	0	0	0	....	....	....
	Muskegon Mohawks	IHL	77	16	45	61	....	....	....	38	....	....	....	....	....	....	....	....	....	....	7	2	4	6	2	....	....	....
1977-78	Fort Worth Texans	CHL	76	14	35	49	....	....	....	87	....	....	....	....	....	....	....	....	....	....	14	2	9	11	15	....	....	....
1978-79	**New York Islanders**	**NHL**	**2**	**0**	**0**	**0**	**0**	**0**	**0**	**0**	**0**	**0**	**0**	**2**	**0.0**	**2**	**0**	**2**	**0**	**0**	....	....	....	....	....	....	....	....
	Fort Worth Texans	CHL	74	17	48	65	....	....	....	71	....	....	....	....	....	....	....	....	....	....	5	0	3	3	6	....	....	....
1979-80	**New York Islanders**	**NHL**	**9**	**0**	**0**	**0**	**0**	**0**	**0**	**7**	**0**	**0**	**0**	**8**	**0.0**	**8**	**0**	**9**	**1**	**0**	....	....	....	....	....	....	....	....
	Indianapolis Checkers	CHL	64	4	32	36	....	....	....	43	....	....	....	....	....	....	....	....	....	....	7	0	4	4	2	....	....	....
1980-81	Indianapolis Checkers	CHL	70	10	48	58	....	....	....	103	....	....	....	....	....	....	....	....	....	....	5	1	3	4	6	....	....	....
1981-82	Indianapolis Checkers	CHL	79	17	49	66	....	....	....	86	....	....	....	....	....	....	....	....	....	....	10	4	6	10	15	....	....	....
1982-83	ZSC Zurich	Switz.	27	16	10	26	....	....	....	40	....	....	....	....	....	....	....	....	....	....	....	....	....	....	....	....	....	....
1983-84	Maine Mariners	AHL	72	11	40	51	....	....	....	31	....	....	....	....	....	....	....	....	....	....	17	2	6	8	4	....	....	....
1984-85	Maine Mariners	AHL	68	1	18	19	....	....	....	46	....	....	....	....	....	....	....	....	....	....	....	....	....	....	....	....	....	....
	NHL Totals		**11**	**0**	**0**	**0**	**0**	**0**	**0**	**7**	**0**	**0**	**0**	**10**	**0.0**	**10**	**0**	**11**	**1**		....	....	....	....	....	....	....	....

CHL Second All-Star Team (1979, 1980, 1981) • CHL First All-Star Team (1982)

Signed as a free agent by **New Jersey**, August 23, 1983.

• HORNUNG, Larry

Larry John D – L. 6', 190 lbs. b: Weyburn, Sask., 11/10/1945.

Season	Club	League	GP	G	A	Pts	AG	AA	APts	PIM	PP	SH	GW	S	%	TGF	PGF	TGA	PGA	+/–	GP	G	A	Pts	PIM	PP	SH	GW
1963-64	Flin Flon Bombers	SJHL	57	4	13	17	....	....	....	96	....	....	....	....	....	....	....	....	....	....	7	0	3	3	8	....	....	....
1964-65	Moose Jaw Canucks	SSHL	17	0	7	7	....	....	....	22	....	....	....	....	....	....	....	....	....	....	7	0	0	0	12	....	....	....
1965-66	Weyburn Red Wings	SJHL	58	16	46	62	....	....	....	90	....	....	....	....	....	....	....	....	....	....	18	1	9	10	20	....	....	....
1966-67	Toledo Blades	IHL	72	8	29	37	....	....	....	34	....	....	....	....	....	....	....	....	....	....	10	1	6	7	20	....	....	....
1967-68	Kansas City Blues	CPHL	70	7	30	37	....	....	....	74	....	....	....	....	....	....	....	....	....	....	7	0	1	1	0	....	....	....
1968-69	Kansas City Blues	CHL	2	0	1	1	....	....	....	2	....	....	....	....	....	....	....	....	....	....	....	....	....	....	....	....	....	....
	Buffalo Bisons	AHL	60	7	18	25	....	....	....	38	....	....	....	....	....	....	....	....	....	....	6	0	0	0	2	....	....	....
1969-70	Kansas City Blues	CHL	12	2	6	8	....	....	....	10	....	....	....	....	....	....	....	....	....	....	....	....	....	....	....	....	....	....
	Buffalo Bisons	AHL	54	6	26	32	....	....	....	24	....	....	....	....	....	....	....	....	....	....	14	2	4	6	20	....	....	....
1970-71	**St. Louis Blues**	**NHL**	**1**	**0**	**0**	**0**	**0**	**0**	**0**	**0**	**0**	**0**	**0**	**1**	**0.0**	**3**	**0**	**2**	**0**	**1**	....	....	....	....	....	....	....	....
	Kansas City Blues	CHL	70	3	17	20	....	....	....	49	....	....	....	....	....	....	....	....	....	....	....	....	....	....	....	....	....	....
1971-72	**St. Louis Blues**	**NHL**	**47**	**2**	**9**	**11**	**2**	**8**	**10**	**10**	**0**	**0**	**1**	**60**	**3.3**	**37**	**5**	**50**	**17**	**–1**	**11**	**0**	**2**	**2**	**2**	**0**	**0**	**0**
	Kansas City Blues	CHL	26	2	20	22	....	....	....	23	....	....	....	....	....	....	....	....	....	....	....	....	....	....	....	....	....	....
1972-73	Winnipeg Jets	WHA	77	13	45	58	....	....	....	28	....	....	....	....	....	....	....	....	....	....	14	2	9	11	0	....	....	....
1973-74	Winnipeg Jets	WHA	51	4	19	23	....	....	....	18	....	....	....	....	....	....	....	....	....	....	4	0	0	0	0	....	....	....
1974-75	Winnipeg Jets	WHA	69	7	25	32	....	....	....	21	....	....	....	....	....	....	....	....	....	....	....	....	....	....	....	....	....	....
1975-76	Winnipeg Jets	WHA	76	3	18	21	....	....	....	26	....	....	....	....	....	....	....	....	....	....	13	0	3	3	6	....	....	....
1976-77	Edmonton Oilers	WHA	21	2	1	3	....	....	....	0	....	....	....	....	....	....	....	....	....	....	....	....	....	....	....	....	....	....
	San Diego Mariners	WHA	58	4	9	13	....	....	....	8	....	....	....	....	....	....	....	....	....	....	6	0	0	0	0	....	....	....
1977-78	Winnipeg Jets	WHA	19	1	4	5	....	....	....	2	....	....	....	....	....	....	....	....	....	....	....	....	....	....	....	....	....	....
	NHL Totals		**48**	**2**	**9**	**11**	**2**	**8**	**10**	**10**	**0**	**0**	**1**	**61**	**3.3**	**40**	**5**	**52**	**17**		**11**	**0**	**2**	**2**	**2**	**0**	**0**	**0**
	Other Major League Totals		371	34	121	155	....	....	....	103	....	....	....	....	....	....	....	....	....	....	37	2	12	14	6	....	....	....

SJHL First All-Star Team (1966) • WHA Second All-Star Team (1973)

Traded to **St. Louis** by **Detroit** with Craig Cameron and Dan Giesebrecht for John Brenneman, October 9, 1967. Loaned to **NY Rangers** by **St. Louis** for the remainder of the 1969-70 season for the loan of Sheldon Kannegiesser for the remainder of the 1969-70 season, November, 1969. Selected by **Winnipeg** (WHA) in 1972 WHA General Player Draft, February 12, 1972. Claimed by **NY Islanders** from **St. Louis** in Expansion Draft, June 6, 1972. Rights traded to **Kansas City** by **NY Islanders** with future considerations (Bart Crashley, September 16, 1974) for Bob Bourne, September 10, 1974. Claimed by **Edmonton** (WHA) from **Winnipeg** (WHA) in 1976 WHA Intra-League Draft, June, 1976. Traded to **San Diego** (WHA) by **Edmonton** (WHA) for Gregg Boddy, November, 1976. Signed as a free agent by **Winnipeg** (WHA) after **San Diego** (WHA) franchise folded, May, 1977.

• HORTON, Tim

Miles Gilbert D – R. 5'10", 180 lbs. b: Cochrane, Ont., 1/12/1930 d: 2/21/1974. **HHOF**

Season	Club	League	GP	G	A	Pts	AG	AA	APts	PIM	PP	SH	GW	S	%	TGF	PGF	TGA	PGA	+/–	GP	G	A	Pts	PIM	PP	SH	GW
1946-47	Copper Cliff Redmen	NOJHA	9	0	0	0	....	....	....	14	....	....	....	....	....	....	....	....	....	....	5	0	1	1	0	....	....	....
1947-48	St. Michael's Majors	OHA-Jr.	32	6	7	13	....	....	....	*137	....	....	....	....	....	....	....	....	....	....	....	....	....	....	....	....	....	....
1948-49	St. Michael's Majors	OHA-Jr.	32	9	18	27	....	....	....	95	....	....	....	....	....	....	....	....	....	....	....	....	....	....	....	....	....	....
1949-50	**Toronto Maple Leafs**	**NHL**	**1**	**0**	**0**	**0**	**0**	**0**	**0**	**2**	....	....	....	....	....	....	....	....	....	....	**1**	**0**	**0**	**0**	**2**	....	....	....
	Pittsburgh Hornets	AHL	60	5	18	23	....	....	....	83	....	....	....	....	....	....	....	....	....	....	....	....	....	....	....	....	....	....
1950-51	Pittsburgh Hornets	AHL	68	8	26	34	....	....	....	129	....	....	....	....	....	....	....	....	....	....	13	0	9	9	16	....	....	....
1951-52	**Toronto Maple Leafs**	**NHL**	**4**	**0**	**0**	**0**	**0**	**0**	**0**	**8**	....	....	....	....	....	....	....	....	....	....	....	....	....	....	....	....	....	....
	Pittsburgh Hornets	AHL	64	12	19	31	....	....	....	146	....	....	....	....	....	....	....	....	....	....	11	1	3	4	16	....	....	....
1952-53	**Toronto Maple Leafs**	**NHL**	**70**	**2**	**14**	**16**	**3**	**17**	**20**	**85**	....	....	....	....	....	....	....	....	....	....	....	....	....	....	....	....	....	....
1953-54	**Toronto Maple Leafs**	**NHL**	**70**	**7**	**24**	**31**	**9**	**29**	**38**	**94**	....	....	....	....	....	....	....	....	....	....	**5**	**1**	**1**	**2**	**4**	....	....	....
1954-55	**Toronto Maple Leafs**	**NHL**	**67**	**5**	**9**	**14**	**6**	**10**	**16**	**84**	....	....	....	....	....	....	....	....	....	....	....	....	....	....	....	....	....	....
1955-56	**Toronto Maple Leafs**	**NHL**	**35**	**0**	**5**	**5**	**0**	**6**	**6**	**36**	....	....	....	....	....	....	....	....	....	....	**2**	**0**	**0**	**0**	**4**	....	....	....
1956-57	**Toronto Maple Leafs**	**NHL**	**66**	**6**	**19**	**25**	**8**	**21**	**29**	**72**	....	....	....	....	....	....	....	....	....	....	....	....	....	....	....	....	....	....
1957-58	**Toronto Maple Leafs**	**NHL**	**53**	**6**	**20**	**26**	**7**	**21**	**28**	**39**	....	....	....	....	....	....	....	....	....	....	....	....	....	....	....	....	....	....
1958-59	**Toronto Maple Leafs**	**NHL**	**70**	**5**	**21**	**26**	**6**	**21**	**27**	**76**	....	....	....	....	....	....	....	....	....	....	**12**	**0**	**3**	**3**	**16**	....	....	....
1959-60	**Toronto Maple Leafs**	**NHL**	**70**	**3**	**29**	**32**	**3**	**28**	**31**	**69**	....	....	....	....	....	....	....	....	....	....	**10**	**0**	**1**	**1**	**6**	....	....	....
1960-61	**Toronto Maple Leafs**	**NHL**	**57**	**6**	**15**	**21**	**7**	**14**	**21**	**75**	....	....	....	....	....	....	....	....	....	....	**5**	**0**	**0**	**0**	**0**	....	....	....
1961-62 ♦	**Toronto Maple Leafs**	**NHL**	**70**	**10**	**28**	**38**	**11**	**27**	**38**	**88**	....	....	....	....	....	....	....	....	....	....	**12**	**3**	**13**	**16**	**16**	....	....	....
1962-63 ♦	**Toronto Maple Leafs**	**NHL**	**70**	**6**	**19**	**25**	**7**	**19**	**26**	**69**	....	....	....	....	....	....	....	....	....	....	**10**	**1**	**3**	**4**	**10**	....	....	....
1963-64 ♦	**Toronto Maple Leafs**	**NHL**	**70**	**9**	**20**	**29**	**11**	**21**	**32**	**71**	....	....	....	....	....	....	....	....	....	....	**14**	**0**	**4**	**4**	**20**	....	....	....
1964-65	**Toronto Maple Leafs**	**NHL**	**70**	**12**	**16**	**28**	**14**	**16**	**30**	**95**	....	....	....	....	....	....	....	....	....	....	**6**	**0**	**2**	**2**	**13**	....	....	....
1965-66	**Toronto Maple Leafs**	**NHL**	**70**	**6**	**22**	**28**	**7**	**21**	**28**	**76**	....	....	....	....	....	....	....	....	....	....	**4**	**1**	**0**	**1**	**12**	....	....	....
1966-67 ♦	**Toronto Maple Leafs**	**NHL**	**70**	**8**	**17**	**25**	**9**	**17**	**26**	**70**	....	....	....	....	....	....	....	....	....	....	**12**	**3**	**5**	**8**	**25**	....	....	....
1967-68	**Toronto Maple Leafs**	**NHL**	**69**	**4**	**23**	**27**	**5**	**23**	**28**	**82**	**1**	**1**	**0**	**179**	**2.2**	**99**	**15**	**82**	**18**	**20**	....	....	....	....	....	....	....	....
1968-69	**Toronto Maple Leafs**	**NHL**	**74**	**11**	**29**	**40**	**12**	**26**	**38**	**107**	**3**	**0**	**1**	**169**	**6.5**	**130**	**23**	**119**	**26**	**14**	**4**	**0**	**0**	**0**	**7**	**0**	**0**	**0**
1969-70	**Toronto Maple Leafs**	**NHL**	**59**	**3**	**19**	**22**	**3**	**18**	**21**	**91**	**1**	**0**	**1**	**116**	**2.6**	**82**	**11**	**90**	**23**	**4**	....	....	....	....	....	....	....	....
	New York Rangers	**NHL**	**15**	**1**	**5**	**6**	**1**	**5**	**6**	**16**	**1**	**0**	**0**	**41**	**2.4**	**11**	**3**	**21**	**6**	**–7**	**6**	**1**	**1**	**2**	**28**	**0**	**0**	**0**
1970-71	**New York Rangers**	**NHL**	**78**	**2**	**18**	**20**	**2**	**15**	**17**	**57**	**1**	**0**	**1**	**124**	**1.6**	**92**	**17**	**62**	**15**	**28**	**13**	**1**	**4**	**5**	**14**	**0**	**0**	**0**
1971-72	**Pittsburgh Penguins**	**NHL**	**44**	**2**	**9**	**11**	**2**	**8**	**10**	**40**	**0**	**0**	**1**	**84**	**2.4**	**50**	**7**	**54**	**16**	**5**	**4**	**0**	**1**	**1**	**2**	**0**	**0**	**0**
1972-73	**Buffalo Sabres**	**NHL**	**69**	**1**	**16**	**17**	**1**	**13**	**14**	**56**	**0**	**0**	**0**	**73**	**1.4**	**81**	**3**	**91**	**25**	**12**	**6**	**0**	**1**	**1**	**4**	**0**	**0**	**0**
1973-74	**Buffalo Sabres**	**NHL**	**55**	**0**	**6**	**6**	**0**	**5**	**5**	**53**	**0**	**0**	**0**	**59**	**0.0**	**71**	**1**	**86**	**21**	**5**	....	....	....	....	....	....	....	....
	NHL Totals		**1446**	**115**	**403**	**518**	**134**	**401**	**535**	**1611**	....	....	....	....	....	....	....	....	....	....	**126**	**11**	**39**	**50**	**183**	....	....	....

AHL First All-Star Team (1952) • NHL Second All-Star Team (1954, 1963, 1967) • NHL First All-Star Team (1964, 1968, 1969) • Played in NHL All-Star Game (1954, 1961, 1962, 1963, 1964, 1968, 1969)

Traded to **NY Rangers** by **Toronto** for future considerations (Denis Dupere, May 18, 1970), March 3, 1970. Claimed by **Pittsburgh** from **NY Rangers** in Intra-League Draft, June 8, 1971. Claimed by **Buffalo** from **Pittsburgh** in Intra-League Draft, June 5, 1972. • Died from injuries suffered in automobile acccient, February 21, 1974.

• HORVATH, Bronco

Bronco Joseph C – L. 5'11", 185 lbs. b: Port Colborne, Ont., 3/12/1930.

			REGULAR SEASON																		PLAYOFFS							
Season	Club	League	GP	G	A	Pts	AG	AA	APts	PIM	PP	SH	GW	S	%	TGF	PGF	TGA	PGA	+/–	GP	G	A	Pts	PIM	PP	SH	GW
1948-49	Galt Black Hawks	OHA-Jr.	33	22	18	40	....	....	....	45	....	....	....	....	....	....	....	....	....	....	....	....	....	....	....	....	....	....
1949-50	Galt Black Hawks	OHA-Jr.	47	20	33	53	....	....	....	91	....	....	....	....	....	....	....	....	....	....	....	....	....	....	....	....	....	....
	Grand Rapids Rockets	EAHL	5	6	1	7	....	....	....	12	....	....	....	....	....	....	....	....	....	....	6	2	6	8	8	....	....	....
1950-51	Springfield Indians	AHL	43	12	26	38	....	....	....	37	....	....	....	....	....	....	....	....	....	....	2	0	0	0	0	....	....	....
1951-52	Syracuse Warriors	AHL	50	12	36	48	....	....	....	56	....	....	....	....	....	....	....	....	....	....	....	....	....	....	....	....	....	....
1952-53	Syracuse Warriors	AHL	52	19	40	59	....	....	....	44	....	....	....	....	....	....	....	....	....	....	4	0	0	0	2	....	....	....
1953-54	Springfield Indians	QHL	19	11	14	25	....	....	....	25	....	....	....	....	....	....	....	....	....	....	....	....	....	....	....	....	....	....
	Syracuse Warriors	AHL	46	21	39	60	....	....	....	54	....	....	....	....	....	....	....	....	....	....	....	....	....	....	....	....	....	....
1954-55	Edmonton Flyers	WHL	67	*50	60	*110	....	....	....	71	....	....	....	....	....	....	....	....	....	....	9	*7	4	*11	12	....	....	....
	Edmonton Flyers	Ed-Cup	7	*5	3	*8	....	....	....	28	....	....	....	....	....	....	....	....	....	....	....	....	....	....	....	....	....	....
1955-56	**New York Rangers**	**NHL**	**66**	**12**	**17**	**29**	**16**	**20**	**36**	**40**	....	....	....	....	....	....	....	....	....	....	**5**	**1**	**2**	**3**	**4**	....	....	....
1956-57	**New York Rangers**	**NHL**	**7**	**1**	**2**	**3**	**1**	**2**	**3**	**4**	....	....	....	....	....	....	....	....	....	....	....	....	....	....	....	....	....	....
	Montreal Canadiens	**NHL**	**1**	**0**	**0**	**0**	**0**	**0**	**0**	**0**	....	....	....	....	....	....	....	....	....	....	....	....	....	....	....	....	....	....
	Rochester Americans	AHL	56	37	44	81	....	....	....	39	....	....	....	....	....	....	....	....	....	....	10	6	7	13	14	....	....	....
1957-58	**Boston Bruins**	**NHL**	**67**	**30**	**36**	**66**	**37**	**37**	**74**	**71**	....	....	....	....	....	....	....	....	....	....	**12**	**5**	**3**	**8**	**8**	....	....	....
1958-59	**Boston Bruins**	**NHL**	**45**	**19**	**20**	**39**	**23**	**20**	**43**	**58**	....	....	....	....	....	....	....	....	....	....	**7**	**2**	**3**	**5**	**0**	....	....	....
1959-60	**Boston Bruins**	**NHL**	**68**	***39**	**41**	**80**	**47**	**40**	**87**	**60**	....	....	....	....	....	....	....	....	....	....	....	....	....	....	....	....	....	....
1960-61	**Boston Bruins**	**NHL**	**47**	**15**	**15**	**30**	**17**	**14**	**31**	**15**	....	....	....	....	....	....	....	....	....	....	....	....	....	....	....	....	....	....
1961-62	**Chicago Black Hawks**	**NHL**	**68**	**17**	**29**	**46**	**19**	**28**	**47**	**21**	....	....	....	....	....	....	....	....	....	....	**12**	**4**	**1**	**5**	**6**	....	....	....
1962-63	**New York Rangers**	**NHL**	**41**	**7**	**15**	**22**	**8**	**15**	**23**	**34**	....	....	....	....	....	....	....	....	....	....	....	....	....	....	....	....	....	....
	Toronto Maple Leafs	**NHL**	**10**	**0**	**4**	**4**	**0**	**4**	**4**	**12**	....	....	....	....	....	....	....	....	....	....	....	....	....	....	....	....	....	....
	Rochester Americans	AHL	18	7	15	22	....	....	....	6	....	....	....	....	....	....	....	....	....	....	....	....	....	....	....	....	....	....
1963-64	Rochester Americans	AHL	70	25	59	84	....	....	....	28	....	....	....	....	....	....	....	....	....	....	2	0	0	0	2	....	....	....
1964-65	Rochester Americans	AHL	72	38	68	106	....	....	....	24	....	....	....	....	....	....	....	....	....	....	10	4	5	9	16	....	....	....
1965-66	Rochester Americans	AHL	70	27	48	75	....	....	....	34	....	....	....	....	....	....	....	....	....	....	12	3	7	10	22	....	....	....
1966-67	Rochester Americans	AHL	72	29	49	78	....	....	....	54	....	....	....	....	....	....	....	....	....	....	12	2	7	9	2	....	....	....
1967-68	Tulsa Oilers	CPHL	4	1	2	3	....	....	....	0	....	....	....	....	....	....	....	....	....	....	....	....	....	....	....	....	....	....
	Rochester Americans	AHL	44	15	29	44	....	....	....	10	....	....	....	....	....	....	....	....	....	....	10	0	7	7	0	....	....	....
	Minnesota North Stars	**NHL**	**14**	**1**	**6**	**7**	**1**	**6**	**7**	**4**	**0**	**0**	**0**	**12**	**8.3**	**14**	**11**	**9**	**0**	**–6**	....	....	....	....	....	....	....	....
1968-69	Rochester Americans	AHL	66	18	30	48	....	....	....	30	....	....	....	....	....	....	....	....	....	....	....	....	....	....	....	....	....	....
1969-70	Rochester Americans	AHL	5	3	1	4	....	....	....	0	....	....	....	....	....	....	....	....	....	....	....	....	....	....	....	....	....	....
	NHL Totals		**434**	**141**	**185**	**326**	**169**	**186**	**355**	**319**	....	....	....	....	....	....	....	....	....	....	**36**	**12**	**9**	**21**	**18**	....	....	....

WHL First All-Star Team (1955) • AHL First All-Star Team (1957) • NHL Second All-Star Team (1960) • AHL Second All-Star Team (1964, 1965) • Played in NHL All-Star Game (1960, 1961)

Traded to **NY Rangers** by **Detroit** with Dave Creighton for Billy Dea, Aggie Kukulwicz and cash, August 18, 1955. Traded to **Montreal** by **NY Rangers** for cash, November 4, 1956. Claimed by **Boston** from **Montreal** in Intra-League Draft, June 5, 1957. Claimed by **Chicago** from **Boston** in Intra-League Draft, June 13, 1961. Claimed by **NY Rangers** from **Chicago** in Intra-League Draft, June 4, 1962. Claimed on waivers by **Toronto** from **NY Rangers**, January 23, 1963. Loaned to **Minnesota** by **Toronto** as injury replacement for Bill Masterton, January 21, 1968. Returned to **Rochester** (AHL) by **Minnesota** when trade negotiations failed, February 27, 1968. Rights transferred to **Vancouver** (WHL) after WHL club purchased **Rochester** (AHL) franchise, August 13, 1968.

• HOSPODAR, Ed

Edward David "Boxcar" D – R. 6'2", 210 lbs. b: Bowling Green, OH, 2/9/1959. NY Rangers' 2nd, 34th overall, in 1979.

Season	Club	League	GP	G	A	Pts	AG	AA	APts	PIM	PP	SH	GW	S	%	TGF	PGF	TGA	PGA	+/–	GP	G	A	Pts	PIM	PP	SH	GW
1975-76	Markham Waxers	OHA-B	STATISTICS NOT AVAILABLE																									
1976-77	Ottawa 67's	OMJHL	51	3	19	22	....	....	....	140	....	....	....	....	....	....	....	....	....	....	19	3	9	12	*113	....	....	....
	Ottawa 67's	Mem-Cup	5	1	2	3	....	....	....	8	....	....	....	....	....	....	....	....	....	....	....	....	....	....	....	....	....	....
1977-78	Ottawa 67's	OMJHL	62	7	26	33	....	....	....	172	....	....	....	....	....	....	....	....	....	....	16	3	6	9	78	....	....	....
	United States	WJC-A	6	3	4	7	....	....	....	10	....	....	....	....	....	....	....	....	....	....	....	....	....	....	....	....	....	....
1978-79	Ottawa 67's	OMJHL	45	7	16	23	....	....	....	131	....	....	....	....	....	....	....	....	....	....	5	0	1	1	39	....	....	....
1979-80	**New York Rangers**	**NHL**	**20**	**0**	**1**	**1**	**0**	**1**	**1**	**76**	**0**	**0**	**0**	**9**	**0.0**	**5**	**0**	**7**	**0**	**–2**	**7**	**1**	**0**	**1**	**42**	**0**	**0**	**1**
	New Haven Nighthawks	AHL	25	3	9	12	....	....	....	131	....	....	....	....	....	....	....	....	....	....	5	0	1	1	39	....	....	....
1980-81	**New York Rangers**	**NHL**	**61**	**5**	**14**	**19**	**4**	**9**	**13**	**214**	**0**	**0**	**0**	**49**	**10.2**	**40**	**4**	**30**	**4**	**10**	**12**	**2**	**0**	**2**	***93**	**0**	**0**	**0**
1981-82	**New York Rangers**	**NHL**	**41**	**3**	**8**	**11**	**2**	**5**	**7**	**152**	**0**	**0**	**0**	**29**	**10.3**	**32**	**0**	**44**	**4**	**–8**	....	....	....	....	....	....	....	....
1982-83	**Hartford Whalers**	**NHL**	**72**	**1**	**9**	**10**	**1**	**6**	**7**	**199**	**0**	**0**	**0**	**54**	**1.9**	**39**	**0**	**86**	**15**	**–32**	....	....	....	....	....	....	....	....
1983-84	**Hartford Whalers**	**NHL**	**59**	**0**	**9**	**9**	**0**	**6**	**6**	**163**	**0**	**0**	**0**	**55**	**0.0**	**44**	**1**	**69**	**9**	**–17**	....	....	....	....	....	....	....	....
1984-85	**Philadelphia Flyers**	**NHL**	**50**	**3**	**4**	**7**	**2**	**3**	**5**	**130**	**0**	**0**	**0**	**51**	**5.9**	**34**	**1**	**27**	**1**	**7**	**18**	**1**	**1**	**2**	**69**	**0**	**0**	**0**
1985-86	**Philadelphia Flyers**	**NHL**	**17**	**3**	**1**	**4**	**2**	**1**	**3**	**55**	**0**	**1**	**0**	**11**	**27.3**	**8**	**0**	**9**	**1**	**0**	....	....	....	....	....	....	....	....
	Minnesota North Stars	**NHL**	**43**	**0**	**2**	**2**	**0**	**1**	**1**	**91**	**0**	**0**	**0**	**33**	**0.0**	**24**	**0**	**19**	**3**	**8**	**2**	**0**	**0**	**0**	**2**	**0**	**0**	**0**
1986-87	**Philadelphia Flyers**	**NHL**	**45**	**2**	**2**	**4**	**2**	**1**	**3**	**136**	**0**	**0**	**1**	**17**	**11.8**	**16**	**0**	**26**	**2**	**–8**	**5**	**0**	**0**	**0**	**2**	**0**	**0**	**0**
1987-88	**Buffalo Sabres**	**NHL**	**42**	**0**	**1**	**1**	**0**	**1**	**1**	**98**	**0**	**0**	**0**	**15**	**0.0**	**11**	**0**	**14**	**2**	**–1**	....	....	....	....	....	....	....	....
1988-89	Rochester Americans	AHL	5	0	0	0	....	....	....	10	....	....	....	....	....	....	....	....	....	....	....	....	....	....	....	....	....	....
	NHL Totals		**450**	**17**	**51**	**68**	**13**	**34**	**47**	**1314**	**0**	**1**	**1**	**323**	**5.3**	**253**	**6**	**331**	**41**		**44**	**4**	**1**	**5**	**208**	**0**	**0**	**1**

OMJHL Second All-Star Team (1979)

Traded to **Hartford** by **NY Rangers** for Kent-Erik Andersson, October 1, 1982. Signed as a free agent by **Philadelphia**, July 25, 1984. Traded to **Minnesota** by **Philadelphia** with Todd Bergen for Bo Berglund and Dave Richter, November 29, 1985. Signed as a free agent by **Philadelphia**, June 12, 1986. Claimed by **Buffalo** from **Philadelphia** in Waiver Draft, October 5, 1987.

• HOSSA, Marian

LW – L. 6'1", 199 lbs. b: Stara Lubovna, Czech., 1/12/1979. Ottawa's 1st, 12th overall, in 1997.

Season	Club	League	GP	G	A	Pts	AG	AA	APts	PIM	PP	SH	GW	S	%	TGF	PGF	TGA	PGA	+/–	GP	G	A	Pts	PIM	PP	SH	GW
1995-96	Dukla Trencin	Slovakia-Jr.	53	42	49	91	....	....	....	26	....	....	....	....	....	....	....	....	....	....	....	....	....	....	....	....	....	....
1996-97	Dukla Trencin	Slovakia	46	25	19	44	....	....	....	33	....	....	....	....	....	....	....	....	....	....	7	5	5	10	....	....	....	....
	Slovakia	WJC-A	6	5	2	7	....	....	....	2	....	....	....	....	....	....	....	....	....	....	....	....	....	....	....	....	....	....
	Slovakia	WC-A	8	0	2	2	....	....	....	0	....	....	....	....	....	....	....	....	....	....	....	....	....	....	....	....	....	....
1997-98	Portland Winter Hawks	WHL	53	45	40	85	....	....	....	50	....	....	....	....	....	....	....	....	....	....	16	13	6	19	6	....	....	....
	Slovakia	WJC-A	6	4	4	8	....	....	....	12	....	....	....	....	....	....	....	....	....	....	....	....	....	....	....	....	....	....
	Ottawa Senators	**NHL**	**7**	**0**	**1**	**1**	**0**	**1**	**1**	**0**	**0**	**0**	**0**	**10**	**0.0**	**2**	**1**	**2**	**0**	**–1**	....	....	....	....	....	....	....	....
	Portland Winter Hawks	Mem-Cup	4	5	4	9	....	....	....	4	....	....	....	....	....	....	....	....	....	....	....	....	....	....	....	....	....	....
1998-99	**Ottawa Senators**	**NHL**	**60**	**15**	**15**	**30**	**18**	**14**	**32**	**37**	**1**	**0**	**2**	**124**	**12.1**	**44**	**5**	**21**	**0**	**18**	**4**	**0**	**2**	**2**	**4**	**0**	**0**	**0**
	Slovakia	WC-A	6	5	2	7	....	....	....	8	....	....	....	....	....	....	....	....	....	....	....	....	....	....	....	....	....	....
99-2000	**Ottawa Senators**	**NHL**	**78**	**29**	**27**	**56**	**33**	**25**	**58**	**32**	**5**	**0**	**4**	**240**	**12.1**	**80**	**23**	**52**	**0**	**5**	**6**	**0**	**0**	**0**	**2**	**0**	**0**	**0**
	NHL Totals		**145**	**44**	**43**	**87**	**51**	**40**	**91**	**69**	**6**	**0**	**6**	**374**	**11.8**	**126**	**29**	**75**	**0**		**10**	**0**	**2**	**2**	**6**	**0**	**0**	**0**

• WHL West First All-Star Team (1998) • Canadian Major Junior First All-Star Team (1998) • Memorial Cup All-Star Team (1998) • NHL All-Rookie Team (1999)

• HOSTAK, Martin

C – L. 6'3", 198 lbs. b: Hradec Kralove, Czech., 11/11/1967. Philadelphia's 3rd, 62nd overall, in 1987.

Season	Club	League	GP	G	A	Pts	AG	AA	APts	PIM	PP	SH	GW	S	%	TGF	PGF	TGA	PGA	+/–	GP	G	A	Pts	PIM	PP	SH	GW
1984-85	Hradec Kralove	Czech-2	STATISTICS NOT AVAILABLE																									
	Czechoslovakia	EJC-A	5	3	2	5	....	....	....	6	....	....	....	....	....	....	....	....	....	....	....	....	....	....	....	....	....	....
1985-86	Hradec Kralove	Czech-2	STATISTICS NOT AVAILABLE																									
1986-87	HC Sparta Praha	Czech.	40	7	2	9	....	....	....	2	....	....	....	....	....	....	....	....	....	....	....	....	....	....	....	....	....	....
	Czechoslovakia	WJC-A	7	7	3	10	....	....	....	4	....	....	....	....	....	....	....	....	....	....	....	....	....	....	....	....	....	....
1987-88	HC Sparta Praha	Czech.	26	8	9	17	....	....	....	4	....	....	....	....	....	....	....	....	....	....	....	....	....	....	....	....	....	....
1988-89	HC Sparta Praha	Czech.	35	11	15	26	....	....	....	10	....	....	....	....	....	....	....	....	....	....	....	....	....	....	....	....	....	....
1989-90	HC Sparta Praha	Czech.	44	26	27	53	....	....	....	....	....	....	....	....	....	....	....	....	....	....	11	4	7	11	....	....	....	....
	Czechoslovakia	WEC-A	4	0	0	0	....	....	....	4	....	....	....	....	....	....	....	....	....	....	....	....	....	....	....	....	....	....
1990-91	**Philadelphia Flyers**	**NHL**	**50**	**3**	**10**	**13**	**3**	**8**	**11**	**22**	**1**	**0**	**0**	**64**	**4.7**	**24**	**7**	**17**	**1**	**1**	....	....	....	....	....	....	....	....
	Hershey Bears	AHL	11	6	2	8	....	....	....	2	....	....	....	....	....	....	....	....	....	....	3	1	0	1	0	....	....	....
1991-92	**Philadelphia Flyers**	**NHL**	**5**	**0**	**1**	**1**	**0**	**1**	**1**	**2**	**0**	**0**	**0**	**8**	**0.0**	**1**	**0**	**2**	**0**	**–1**	....	....	....	....	....	....	....	....
	Hershey Bears	AHL	63	27	36	63	....	....	....	77	....	....	....	....	....	....	....	....	....	....	6	1	2	3	2	....	....	....
1992-93	MoDo AIK	Sweden	40	15	19	34	....	....	....	42	....	....	....	....	....	....	....	....	....	....	3	2	1	3	4	....	....	....
	Czech-Republic	WC-A	8	4	4	8	....	....	....	0	....	....	....	....	....	....	....	....	....	....	....	....	....	....	....	....	....	....
1993-94	MoDo AIK	Sweden	34	16	17	33	....	....	....	28	....	....	....	....	....	....	....	....	....	....	....	....	....	....	....	....	....	....
	Czech-Republic	Olympics	7	1	0	1	....	....	....	0	....	....	....	....	....	....	....	....	....	....	....	....	....	....	....	....	....	....
1994-95	MoDo Hockey	Sweden	40	14	17	31	....	....	....	30	....	....	....	....	....	....	....	....	....	....	....	....	....	....	....	....	....	....
	Czech-Republic	WC-A	4	0	0	0	....	....	....	2	....	....	....	....	....	....	....	....	....	....	....	....	....	....	....	....	....	....

Season	Club	League	GP	G	A	Pts	AG	AA	APts	PIM	PP	SH	GW	S	%	TGF	PGF	TGA	PGA	+/-	GP	G	A	Pts	PIM	PP	SH	GW
			REGULAR SEASON																		PLAYOFFS							
1995-96	MoDo Hockey	Sweden	36	12	15	27	....	....	....	28	....	....	....	....	....	....	....	....	....	....	8	0	2	2	4	....	....	....
1996-97	HC Sparta Praha	Czech-Rep	27	6	14	20	....	....	....	12	....	....	....	....	....	....	....	....	....	....	....	....	....	....	....	....	....	....
	HC Sparta Praha	EuroHL	6	0	1	1	....	....	....	2	....	....	....	....	....	....	....	....	....	....	....	....	....	....	....	....	....	....
	Sodertalje SK	Sweden	21	12	8	20	....	....	....	6	....	....	....	....	....	....	....	....	....	....	....	....	....	....	....	....	....	....
1997-98	Sodertalje SK	Sweden	46	16	18	34	....	....	....	30	....	....	....	....	....	....	....	....	....	....	....	....	....	....	....	....	....	....
1998-99	Lulea HF	Sweden	49	19	21	40	....	....	....	34	....	....	....	....	....	....	....	....	....	....	9	3	1	4	10	....	....	....
99-2000	Lulea HF	Sweden	50	23	16	39	....	....	....	60	....	....	....	....	....	....	....	....	....	....	9	0	1	1	12	....	....	....
	NHL Totals		**55**	**3**	**11**	**14**	**3**	**9**	**12**	**24**	**1**	**0**	**0**	**72**	**4.2**	**25**	**7**	**19**	**1**		....	....	....	....	....	....	....	....

• HOTHAM, Greg

Gregory S. D – R. 5'11", 183 lbs. b: London, Ont., 3/7/1956. Toronto's 5th, 84th overall, in 1976.

Season	Club	League	GP	G	A	Pts	AG	AA	APts	PIM	PP	SH	GW	S	%	TGF	PGF	TGA	PGA	+/-	GP	G	A	Pts	PIM	PP	SH	GW
1973-74	Aurora Tigers	OJHL	44	10	22	32	....	....	....	120	....	....	....	....	....	....	....	....	....	....	....	....	....	....	....	....	....	....
1974-75	Aurora Tigers	OJHL	27	14	10	24	....	....	....	46	....	....	....	....	....	....	....	....	....	....	....	....	....	....	....	....	....	....
	Kingston Canadians	OHA-Jr.	31	1	14	15	....	....	....	49	....	....	....	....	....	....	....	....	....	....	8	5	4	9	0	....	....	....
1975-76	Kingston Canadians	OHA-Jr.	49	10	32	42	....	....	....	72	....	....	....	....	....	....	....	....	....	....	7	1	2	3	10	....	....	....
1976-77	Saginaw Gears	IHL	60	4	33	37	....	....	....	100	....	....	....	....	....	....	....	....	....	....	....	....	....	....	....	....	....	....
1977-78	Saginaw Gears	IHL	80	13	59	72	....	....	....	56	....	....	....	....	....	....	....	....	....	....	....	....	....	....	....	....	....	....
	Dallas Black Hawks	CHL	....	....	....	....	....	....	....	....	....	....	....	....	....	....	....	....	....	....	5	0	2	2	7	....	....	....
1978-79	New Brunswick Hawks	AHL	76	9	27	36	....	....	....	86	....	....	....	....	....	....	....	....	....	....	5	0	2	2	6	....	....	....
1979-80	**Toronto Maple Leafs**	**NHL**	**46**	**3**	**10**	**13**	**3**	**7**	**10**	**10**	**0**	**0**	**0**	**46**	**6.5**	**49**	**2**	**56**	**5**	**–4**	....	....	....	....	....	....	....	....
	New Brunswick Hawks	AHL	21	1	6	7	....	....	....	10	....	....	....	....	....	....	....	....	....	....	17	2	8	10	26	....	....	....
1980-81	**Toronto Maple Leafs**	**NHL**	**11**	**1**	**1**	**2**	**1**	**1**	**2**	**11**	**0**	**0**	**0**	**8**	**12.5**	**14**	**0**	**13**	**3**	**4**	....	....	....	....	....	....	....	....
	New Brunswick Hawks	AHL	68	8	48	56	....	....	....	80	....	....	....	....	....	....	....	....	....	....	11	1	6	7	16	....	....	....
1981-82	**Toronto Maple Leafs**	**NHL**	**3**	**0**	**0**	**0**	**0**	**0**	**0**	**0**	**0**	**0**	**0**	**4**	**0.0**	**1**	**0**	**8**	**2**	**–5**	....	....	....	....	....	....	....	....
	Cincinnati Tigers	CHL	46	10	33	43	....	....	....	94	....	....	....	....	....	....	....	....	....	....	....	....	....	....	....	....	....	....
	Pittsburgh Penguins	**NHL**	**25**	**4**	**6**	**10**	**3**	**4**	**7**	**16**	**2**	**0**	**0**	**38**	**10.5**	**34**	**18**	**28**	**6**	**–6**	**5**	**0**	**3**	**3**	**6**	**0**	**0**	**0**
1982-83	**Pittsburgh Penguins**	**NHL**	**58**	**2**	**30**	**32**	**2**	**21**	**23**	**39**	**0**	**0**	**0**	**75**	**2.7**	**78**	**26**	**102**	**36**	**–14**	....	....	....	....	....	....	....	....
1983-84	**Pittsburgh Penguins**	**NHL**	**76**	**5**	**25**	**30**	**4**	**17**	**21**	**59**	**3**	**0**	**0**	**120**	**4.2**	**101**	**30**	**146**	**50**	**–25**	....	....	....	....	....	....	....	....
1984-85	**Pittsburgh Penguins**	**NHL**	**11**	**0**	**2**	**2**	**0**	**1**	**1**	**4**	**0**	**0**	**0**	**6**	**0.0**	**7**	**2**	**9**	**1**	**–3**	....	....	....	....	....	....	....	....
	Baltimore Skipjacks	AHL	44	4	27	31	....	....	....	43	....	....	....	....	....	....	....	....	....	....	15	4	4	8	34	....	....	....
1985-86	Baltimore Skipjacks	AHL	78	2	26	28	....	....	....	94	....	....	....	....	....	....	....	....	....	....	....	....	....	....	....	....	....	....
1986-87	Newmarket Saints	AHL	51	4	9	13	....	....	....	60	....	....	....	....	....	....	....	....	....	....	....	....	....	....	....	....	....	....
1987-88	Newmarket Saints	AHL	78	12	27	39	....	....	....	102	....	....	....	....	....	....	....	....	....	....	....	....	....	....	....	....	....	....
1988-89	Newmarket Saints	AHL	73	9	42	51	....	....	....	62	....	....	....	....	....	....	....	....	....	....	5	1	4	5	0	....	....	....
1989-90	Newmarket Saints	AHL	24	0	8	8	....	....	....	31	....	....	....	....	....	....	....	....	....	....	....	....	....	....	....	....	....	....
	NHL Totals		**230**	**15**	**74**	**89**	**13**	**51**	**64**	**139**	**5**	**0**	**0**	**297**	**5.1**	**284**	**78**	**362**	**103**		**5**	**0**	**3**	**3**	**6**	**0**	**0**	**0**

IHL Second All-Star Team (1978)

Traded to **Pittsburgh** by **Toronto** for Pittsburgh's 6th round choice (Craig Kales) in 1982 Entry Draft, February 3, 1982.

• HOUCK, Paul

RW – R. 5'11", 185 lbs. b: N. Vancouver, B.C., 8/12/1963. Edmonton's 3rd, 71st overall, in 1981.

Season	Club	League	GP	G	A	Pts	AG	AA	APts	PIM	PP	SH	GW	S	%	TGF	PGF	TGA	PGA	+/-	GP	G	A	Pts	PIM	PP	SH	GW
1980-81	Kelowna Buckaroos	BCJHL	52	*65	51	*116	....	....	....	39	....	....	....	....	....	....	....	....	....	....	....	....	....	....	....	....	....	....
1981-82	University of Wisconsin	WCHA	43	9	16	25	....	....	....	38	....	....	....	....	....	....	....	....	....	....	....	....	....	....	....	....	....	....
1982-83	University of Wisconsin	WCHA	47	38	33	71	....	....	....	36	....	....	....	....	....	....	....	....	....	....	....	....	....	....	....	....	....	....
1983-84	University of Wisconsin	WCHA	37	20	20	40	....	....	....	29	....	....	....	....	....	....	....	....	....	....	....	....	....	....	....	....	....	....
1984-85	University of Wisconsin	WCHA	39	16	24	40	....	....	....	54	....	....	....	....	....	....	....	....	....	....	....	....	....	....	....	....	....	....
	Nova Scotia Voyageurs	AHL	10	1	0	1	....	....	....	0	....	....	....	....	....	....	....	....	....	....	....	....	....	....	....	....	....	....
1985-86	**Minnesota North Stars**	**NHL**	**3**	**1**	**0**	**1**	**1**	**0**	**1**	**0**	**0**	**0**	**0**	**3**	**33.3**	**1**	**0**	**0**	**0**	**1**	....	....	....	....	....	....	....	....
	Springfield Indians	AHL	61	15	17	32	....	....	....	27	....	....	....	....	....	....	....	....	....	....	....	....	....	....	....	....	....	....
1986-87	**Minnesota North Stars**	**NHL**	**12**	**0**	**2**	**2**	**0**	**1**	**1**	**2**	**0**	**0**	**0**	**10**	**0.0**	**3**	**0**	**9**	**4**	**–2**	....	....	....	....	....	....	....	....
	Springfield Indians	AHL	64	29	18	47	....	....	....	58	....	....	....	....	....	....	....	....	....	....	....	....	....	....	....	....	....	....
1987-88	**Minnesota North Stars**	**NHL**	**1**	**0**	**0**	**0**	**0**	**0**	**0**	**0**	**0**	**0**	**0**	**1**	**0.0**	**0**	**0**	**0**	**0**	**0**	....	....	....	....	....	....	....	....
	Kalamazoo Wings	IHL	74	27	29	56	....	....	....	73	....	....	....	....	....	....	....	....	....	....	7	3	4	7	8	....	....	....
1988-89	Springfield Indians	AHL	2	1	0	1	....	....	....	0	....	....	....	....	....	....	....	....	....	....	....	....	....	....	....	....	....	....
	Indianapolis Ice	IHL	81	22	37	59	....	....	....	51	....	....	....	....	....	....	....	....	....	....	....	....	....	....	....	....	....	....
1989-90	IJC Utrecht	Holland	40	35	46	81	....	....	....	....	....	....	....	....	....	....	....	....	....	....	....	....	....	....	....	....	....	....
1990-91	IJC Utrecht	Holland	41	37	40	77	....	....	....	49	....	....	....	....	....	....	....	....	....	....	....	....	....	....	....	....	....	....
	NHL Totals		**16**	**1**	**2**	**3**	**1**	**1**	**2**	**2**	**0**	**0**	**0**	**14**	**7.1**	**4**	**0**	**9**	**4**		....	....	....	....	....	....	....	....

WCHA Second All-Star Team (1983) • NCAA Championship All-Tournament Team (1983)

Traded to **Minnesota** by **Edmonton** for Gilles Meloche, May 31, 1985.

• HOUDA, Doug

Doug Harold D – R. 6'2", 190 lbs. b: Blairmore, Alta., 6/3/1966. Detroit's 2nd, 28th overall, in 1984.

Season	Club	League	GP	G	A	Pts	AG	AA	APts	PIM	PP	SH	GW	S	%	TGF	PGF	TGA	PGA	+/-	GP	G	A	Pts	PIM	PP	SH	GW
1981-82	Calgary Royals	AAHA	STATISTICS NOT AVAILABLE																									
	Calgary Wranglers	WHL	3	0	0	0	....	....	....	2	....	....	....	....	....	....	....	....	....	....	....	....	....	....	....	....	....	....
1982-83	Calgary Wranglers	WHL	71	5	23	28	....	....	....	99	....	....	....	....	....	....	....	....	....	....	16	1	3	4	44	....	....	....
1983-84	Calgary Wranglers	WHL	69	6	30	36	....	....	....	195	....	....	....	....	....	....	....	....	....	....	4	0	0	0	7	....	....	....
1984-85	Calgary Wranglers	WHL	65	20	54	74	....	....	....	182	....	....	....	....	....	....	....	....	....	....	8	3	4	7	29	....	....	....
	Kalamazoo Wings	IHL	....	....	....	....	....	....	....	....	....	....	....	....	....	....	....	....	....	....	7	0	2	2	10	....	....	....
1985-86	Calgary Wranglers	WHL	16	4	10	14	....	....	....	60	....	....	....	....	....	....	....	....	....	....	....	....	....	....	....	....	....	....
	Medicine Hat Tigers	WHL	35	9	23	32	....	....	....	80	....	....	....	....	....	....	....	....	....	....	25	4	19	23	64	....	....	....
	Detroit Red Wings	**NHL**	**6**	**0**	**0**	**0**	**0**	**0**	**0**	**4**	**0**	**0**	**0**	**5**	**0.0**	**3**	**0**	**11**	**1**	**–7**	....	....	....	....	....	....	....	....
1986-87	Adirondack Red Wings	AHL	77	6	23	29	....	....	....	142	....	....	....	....	....	....	....	....	....	....	11	1	8	9	50	....	....	....
1987-88	**Detroit Red Wings**	**NHL**	**11**	**1**	**1**	**2**	**1**	**1**	**2**	**10**	**0**	**0**	**0**	**10**	**10.0**	**8**	**0**	**9**	**1**	**0**	....	....	....	....	....	....	....	....
	Adirondack Red Wings	AHL	71	10	32	42	....	....	....	169	....	....	....	....	....	....	....	....	....	....	11	0	3	3	44	....	....	....
1988-89	**Detroit Red Wings**	**NHL**	**57**	**2**	**11**	**13**	**2**	**8**	**10**	**67**	**0**	**0**	**0**	**38**	**5.3**	**57**	**0**	**47**	**7**	**17**	**6**	**0**	**1**	**1**	**0**	**0**	**0**	**0**
	Adirondack Red Wings	AHL	7	0	3	3	....	....	....	8	....	....	....	....	....	....	....	....	....	....	....	....	....	....	....	....	....	....
1989-90	**Detroit Red Wings**	**NHL**	**73**	**2**	**9**	**11**	**2**	**6**	**8**	**127**	**0**	**0**	**0**	**59**	**3.4**	**51**	**0**	**64**	**8**	**–5**	....	....	....	....	....	....	....	....
1990-91	**Detroit Red Wings**	**NHL**	**22**	**0**	**4**	**4**	**0**	**3**	**3**	**43**	**0**	**0**	**0**	**21**	**0.0**	**18**	**2**	**24**	**6**	**–2**	....	....	....	....	....	....	....	....
	Adirondack Red Wings	AHL	38	9	17	26	....	....	....	67	....	....	....	....	....	....	....	....	....	....	....	....	....	....	....	....	....	....
	Hartford Whalers	**NHL**	**19**	**1**	**2**	**3**	**1**	**2**	**3**	**41**	**0**	**0**	**0**	**21**	**4.8**	**14**	**0**	**22**	**5**	**–3**	**6**	**0**	**0**	**0**	**8**	**0**	**0**	**0**
1991-92	**Hartford Whalers**	**NHL**	**56**	**3**	**6**	**9**	**3**	**5**	**8**	**125**	**1**	**0**	**1**	**40**	**7.5**	**38**	**1**	**59**	**20**	**–2**	**6**	**0**	**2**	**2**	**13**	**0**	**0**	**0**
1992-93	**Hartford Whalers**	**NHL**	**60**	**2**	**6**	**8**	**2**	**4**	**6**	**167**	**0**	**0**	**0**	**43**	**4.7**	**42**	**2**	**79**	**20**	**–19**	....	....	....	....	....	....	....	....
1993-94	**Hartford Whalers**	**NHL**	**7**	**0**	**0**	**0**	**0**	**0**	**0**	**23**	**0**	**0**	**0**	**1**	**0.0**	**1**	**0**	**6**	**1**	**–4**	....	....	....	....	....	....	....	....
	Los Angeles Kings	**NHL**	**54**	**2**	**6**	**8**	**2**	**5**	**7**	**165**	**0**	**0**	**0**	**31**	**6.5**	**28**	**0**	**56**	**13**	**–15**	....	....	....	....	....	....	....	....
1994-95	**Buffalo Sabres**	**NHL**	**28**	**1**	**2**	**3**	**2**	**3**	**5**	**68**	**0**	**0**	**0**	**21**	**4.8**	**12**	**1**	**17**	**7**	**1**	....	....	....	....	....	....	....	....
1995-96	**Buffalo Sabres**	**NHL**	**38**	**1**	**3**	**4**	**1**	**2**	**3**	**52**	**0**	**0**	**0**	**21**	**4.8**	**27**	**0**	**29**	**5**	**3**	....	....	....	....	....	....	....	....
	Rochester Americans	AHL	21	1	6	7	....	....	....	41	....	....	....	....	....	....	....	....	....	....	19	3	5	8	30	....	....	....
1996-97	**New York Islanders**	**NHL**	**70**	**2**	**8**	**10**	**2**	**7**	**9**	**99**	**0**	**0**	**0**	**29**	**6.9**	**32**	**2**	**42**	**13**	**1**	....	....	....	....	....	....	....	....
	Utah Grizzlies	IHL	3	0	0	0	....	....	....	7	....	....	....	....	....	....	....	....	....	....	....	....	....	....	....	....	....	....
1997-98	**New York Islanders**	**NHL**	**31**	**1**	**2**	**3**	**1**	**2**	**3**	**47**	**0**	**0**	**0**	**15**	**6.7**	**14**	**2**	**20**	**2**	**–6**	....	....	....	....	....	....	....	....
	Mighty Ducks of Anaheim	**NHL**	**24**	**1**	**2**	**3**	**1**	**2**	**3**	**52**	**0**	**1**	**0**	**9**	**11.1**	**13**	**0**	**24**	**6**	**–5**	....	....	....	....	....	....	....	....
1998-99	**Detroit Red Wings**	**NHL**	**3**	**0**	**1**	**1**	**0**	**1**	**1**	**0**	**0**	**0**	**0**	**1**	**0.0**	**1**	**0**	**3**	**0**	**–2**	....	....	....	....	....	....	....	....
	Adirondack Red Wings	AHL	73	7	21	28	....	....	....	122	....	....	....	....	....	....	....	....	....	....	3	0	1	1	4	....	....	....
99-2000	**Buffalo Sabres**	**NHL**	**1**	**0**	**0**	**0**	**0**	**0**	**0**	**12**	**0**	**0**	**0**	**0**	**0.0**	**0**	**0**	**2**	**2**	**0**	....	....	....	....	....	....	....	....
	Rochester Americans	AHL	79	7	17	24	....	....	....	175	....	....	....	....	....	....	....	....	....	....	21	1	8	9	39	....	....	....
	NHL Totals		**560**	**19**	**63**	**82**	**20**	**51**	**71**	**1102**	**1**	**1**	**1**	**365**	**5.2**	**359**	**10**	**514**	**117**		**18**	**0**	**3**	**3**	**21**	**0**	**0**	**0**

WHL East Second All-Star Team (1985) • AHL First All-Star Team (1988)

Traded to **Hartford** by **Detroit** for Doug Crossman, February 20, 1991. Traded to **LA Kings** by **Hartford** for Marc Potvin, November 3, 1993. Traded to **Buffalo** by **LA Kings** for Sean O'Donnell, July 26, 1994. Signed as a free agent by **NY Islanders**, October 26, 1996. Traded to **Anaheim** by **NY Islanders** with Travis Green and Tony Tuzzolino for Joe Sacco, J.J. Daigneault and Mark Janssens, February 6, 1998. Traded to **Detroit** by **Anaheim** for future considerations, October 9, 1998. Signed as a free agent by **Buffalo**, July 13, 1999.

• HOUDE, Claude
Claude Daniel D – L. 6'1", 188 lbs. b: Drummondville, Que., 11/8/1947.

Season	Club	League	GP	G	A	Pts	AG	AA	APts	PIM	PP	SH	GW	S	%	TGF	PGF	TGA	PGA	+/–	GP	G	A	Pts	PIM	PP	SH	GW
			REGULAR SEASON																		PLAYOFFS							
1965-1968	Arvida Indians	SLJHL	STATISTICS NOT AVAILABLE																									
1968-69	Granby Bisons	QSHL	51	15	30	45	....	....	....	....	....	....	....	....	....	....	....	....	....	....	....	....	....	....	....	....	....	....
1969-70	Granby Bisons	QSHL	STATISTICS NOT AVAILABLE																									
1970-71	Syracuse Blazers	EHL	65	15	19	34	....	....	....	62	....	....	....	....	....	....	....	....	....	....	6	1	0	1	0	....	....	....
1971-72	Providence Reds	AHL	54	3	9	12	....	....	....	26	....	....	....	....	....	....	....	....	....	....	5	0	0	0	5	....	....	....
1972-73	Toledo Hornets	IHL	22	7	4	11	....	....	....	20	....	....	....	....	....	....	....	....	....	....	....	....	....	....	....	....	....	....
	Providence Reds	AHL	55	9	14	23	....	....	....	22	....	....	....	....	....	....	....	....	....	....	3	0	1	1	10	....	....	....
1973-74	Baltimore Clippers	AHL	62	7	17	24	....	....	....	30	....	....	....	....	....	....	....	....	....	....	....	....	....	....	....	....	....	....
	Virginia Wings	AHL	14	2	3	5	....	....	....	6	....	....	....	....	....	....	....	....	....	....	....	....	....	....	....	....	....	....
1974-75	Virginia Wings	AHL	25	1	2	3	....	....	....	26	....	....	....	....	....	....	....	....	....	....	....	....	....	....	....	....	....	....
	Kansas City Scouts	**NHL**	**34**	**3**	**4**	**7**	**3**	**3**	**6**	**20**	**2**	**0**	**1**	**43**	**7.0**	**22**	**7**	**49**	**3**	**–31**	....	....	....	....	....	....	....	....
1975-76	**Kansas City Scouts**	**NHL**	**25**	**0**	**2**	**2**	**0**	**1**	**1**	**20**	**0**	**0**	**0**	**16**	**0.0**	**8**	**0**	**28**	**7**	**–13**	....	....	....	....	....	....	....	....
	Springfield Indians	AHL	29	5	9	14	....	....	....	24	....	....	....	....	....	....	....	....	....	....	....	....	....	....	....	....	....	....
1976-77	Beauce Jaros	NAHL	22	6	16	22	....	....	....	10	....	....	....	....	....	....	....	....	....	....	....	....	....	....	....	....	....	....
	NHL Totals		**59**	**3**	**6**	**9**	**3**	**4**	**7**	**40**	**2**	**0**	**1**	**59**	**5.1**	**30**	**7**	**77**	**10**		....	....	....	....	....	....	....	....

SLJHL Second All-Star Team (1968)

Traded to **Detroit** by **NY Rangers** for Brian Lavender, February 28, 1974. Traded to **Kansas City** by **Detroit** with Guy Charron for Bart Crashley, Ted Snell and Larry Giroux, December 14, 1974.

• HOUDE, Eric
C – L. 5'11", 191 lbs. b: Montreal, Que., 12/19/1976. Montreal's 9th, 216th overall, in 1995.

Season	Club	League	GP	G	A	Pts	AG	AA	APts	PIM	PP	SH	GW	S	%	TGF	PGF	TGA	PGA	+/–	GP	G	A	Pts	PIM	PP	SH	GW
1992-93	St-Hubert Selects	QAAA	35	45	40	85	....	....	....	....	....	....	....	....	....	....	....	....	....	....	....	....	....	....	....	....	....	....
1993-94	St-Jean Lynx	QMJHL	71	16	16	32	....	....	....	14	....	....	....	....	....	....	....	....	....	....	5	1	1	2	4	....	....	....
1994-95	St-Jean Lynx	QMJHL	40	10	13	23	....	....	....	23	....	....	....	....	....	....	....	....	....	....	....	....	....	....	....	....	....	....
	Halifax Mooseheads	QMJHL	28	13	23	36	....	....	....	8	....	....	....	....	....	....	....	....	....	....	3	2	1	3	4	....	....	....
1995-96	Halifax Mooseheads	QMJHL	69	40	48	88	....	....	....	35	....	....	....	....	....	....	....	....	....	....	6	3	4	7	2	....	....	....
1996-97	**Montreal Canadiens**	**NHL**	**13**	**0**	**2**	**2**	**0**	**2**	**2**	**2**	**0**	**0**	**0**	**1**	**0.0**	**2**	**0**	**1**	**0**	**1**	....	....	....	....	....	....	....	....
	Fredericton Canadiens	AHL	66	30	36	66	....	....	....	20	....	....	....	....	....	....	....	....	....	....	....	....	....	....	....	....	....	....
1997-98	**Montreal Canadiens**	**NHL**	**9**	**1**	**0**	**1**	**1**	**0**	**1**	**0**	**0**	**0**	**1**	**4**	**25.0**	**1**	**0**	**4**	**0**	**–3**	....	....	....	....	....	....	....	....
	Fredericton Canadiens	AHL	71	28	42	70	....	....	....	24	....	....	....	....	....	....	....	....	....	....	4	5	2	7	4	....	....	....
1998-99	**Montreal Canadiens**	**NHL**	**8**	**1**	**1**	**2**	**1**	**1**	**2**	**2**	**0**	**0**	**1**	**4**	**25.0**	**2**	**0**	**4**	**0**	**–2**	....	....	....	....	....	....	....	....
	Fredericton Canadiens	AHL	69	27	37	64	....	....	....	32	....	....	....	....	....	....	....	....	....	....	14	2	7	9	4	....	....	....
99-2000	Hamilton Bulldogs	AHL	18	3	4	7	....	....	....	10	....	....	....	....	....	....	....	....	....	....	....	....	....	....	....	....	....	....
	Springfield Falcons	AHL	57	28	34	62	....	....	....	43	....	....	....	....	....	....	....	....	....	....	5	2	2	4	2	....	....	....
	NHL Totals		**30**	**2**	**3**	**5**	**2**	**3**	**5**	**4**	**0**	**0**	**2**	**9**	**22.2**	**5**	**0**	**9**	**0**		....	....	....	....	....	....	....	....

Signed as a free agent by **Edmonton**, August 11, 1999. Traded to **Phoenix** by **Edmonton** for Rob Murray, November 30, 1999.

• HOUGH, Mike
Michael Lloyd LW – L. 6'1", 197 lbs. b: Montreal, Que., 2/6/1963. Quebec's 7th, 181st overall, in 1982.

Season	Club	League	GP	G	A	Pts	AG	AA	APts	PIM	PP	SH	GW	S	%	TGF	PGF	TGA	PGA	+/–	GP	G	A	Pts	PIM	PP	SH	GW
1978-79	Mississagua Reps	MTHL	STATISTICS NOT AVAILABLE																									
1979-80	Toronto Midget Marlboros	MTHL	44	20	50	70	....	....	....	....	....	....	....	....	....	....	....	....	....	....	....	....	....	....	....	....	....	....
1980-81	Dixie Beehives	OJHL	24	15	20	35	....	....	....	84	....	....	....	....	....	....	....	....	....	....	....	....	....	....	....	....	....	....
1981-82	Kitchener Rangers	OHL	58	14	24	38	....	....	....	172	....	....	....	....	....	....	....	....	....	....	14	4	1	5	16	....	....	....
	Kitchener Rangers	Mem-Cup	5	1	1	2	....	....	....	11	....	....	....	....	....	....	....	....	....	....	....	....	....	....	....	....	....	....
1982-83	Kitchener Rangers	OHL	61	17	27	44	....	....	....	156	....	....	....	....	....	....	....	....	....	....	12	5	4	9	30	....	....	....
1983-84	Fredericton Express	AHL	69	11	16	27	....	....	....	142	....	....	....	....	....	....	....	....	....	....	1	0	0	0	7	....	....	....
1984-85	Fredericton Express	AHL	76	21	27	48	....	....	....	49	....	....	....	....	....	....	....	....	....	....	6	1	1	2	2	....	....	....
1985-86	Fredericton Express	AHL	74	21	33	54	....	....	....	68	....	....	....	....	....	....	....	....	....	....	6	0	3	3	8	....	....	....
1986-87	**Quebec Nordiques**	**NHL**	**56**	**6**	**8**	**14**	**5**	**6**	**11**	**79**	**1**	**1**	**0**	**60**	**10.0**	**25**	**4**	**35**	**6**	**–8**	**9**	**0**	**3**	**3**	**26**	**0**	**0**	**0**
	Fredericton Express	AHL	10	1	3	4	....	....	....	20	....	....	....	....	....	....	....	....	....	....	....	....	....	....	....	....	....	....
1987-88	**Quebec Nordiques**	**NHL**	**17**	**3**	**2**	**5**	**3**	**1**	**4**	**2**	**0**	**0**	**1**	**23**	**13.0**	**7**	**0**	**15**	**0**	**–8**	....	....	....	....	....	....	....	....
	Fredericton Express	AHL	46	16	25	41	....	....	....	133	....	....	....	....	....	....	....	....	....	....	15	4	8	12	55	....	....	....
1988-89	**Quebec Nordiques**	**NHL**	**46**	**9**	**10**	**19**	**8**	**7**	**15**	**39**	**1**	**3**	**3**	**51**	**17.6**	**24**	**2**	**34**	**5**	**–7**	....	....	....	....	....	....	....	....
	Halifax Citadels	AHL	22	11	10	21	....	....	....	87	....	....	....	....	....	....	....	....	....	....	....	....	....	....	....	....	....	....
1989-90	**Quebec Nordiques**	**NHL**	**43**	**13**	**13**	**26**	**11**	**9**	**20**	**84**	**3**	**1**	**0**	**93**	**14.0**	**43**	**16**	**57**	**6**	**–24**	....	....	....	....	....	....	....	....
1990-91	**Quebec Nordiques**	**NHL**	**63**	**13**	**20**	**33**	**12**	**15**	**27**	**111**	**1**	**1**	**1**	**106**	**12.3**	**57**	**8**	**90**	**34**	**–7**	....	....	....	....	....	....	....	....
1991-92	**Quebec Nordiques**	**NHL**	**61**	**16**	**22**	**38**	**15**	**17**	**32**	**77**	**6**	**2**	**1**	**92**	**17.4**	**75**	**26**	**69**	**19**	**–1**	....	....	....	....	....	....	....	....
1992-93	**Quebec Nordiques**	**NHL**	**77**	**8**	**22**	**30**	**7**	**15**	**22**	**69**	**2**	**1**	**2**	**98**	**8.2**	**53**	**9**	**76**	**21**	**–11**	**6**	**0**	**1**	**1**	**2**	**0**	**0**	**0**
1993-94	**Florida Panthers**	**NHL**	**78**	**6**	**23**	**29**	**6**	**18**	**24**	**62**	**0**	**1**	**1**	**106**	**5.7**	**43**	**0**	**59**	**19**	**3**	....	....	....	....	....	....	....	....
1994-95	**Florida Panthers**	**NHL**	**48**	**6**	**7**	**13**	**11**	**10**	**21**	**38**	**0**	**0**	**2**	**58**	**10.3**	**20**	**1**	**29**	**11**	**1**	....	....	....	....	....	....	....	....
1995-96	**Florida Panthers**	**NHL**	**64**	**7**	**16**	**23**	**7**	**13**	**20**	**37**	**0**	**1**	**1**	**66**	**10.6**	**35**	**0**	**45**	**14**	**4**	**22**	**4**	**1**	**5**	**8**	**0**	**0**	**2**
1996-97	**Florida Panthers**	**NHL**	**69**	**8**	**6**	**14**	**8**	**5**	**13**	**48**	**0**	**0**	**2**	**85**	**9.4**	**30**	**0**	**35**	**17**	**12**	**5**	**1**	**0**	**1**	**2**	**0**	**0**	**0**
1997-98	**New York Islanders**	**NHL**	**74**	**5**	**7**	**12**	**6**	**7**	**13**	**27**	**0**	**0**	**0**	**44**	**11.4**	**21**	**1**	**41**	**17**	**–4**	....	....	....	....	....	....	....	....
1998-99	**New York Islanders**	**NHL**	**11**	**0**	**0**	**0**	**0**	**0**	**0**	**2**	**0**	**0**	**0**	**4**	**0.0**	**2**	**0**	**7**	**3**	**–2**	....	....	....	....	....	....	....	....
	Utah Grizzlies	IHL	26	5	7	12	....	....	....	8	....	....	....	....	....	....	....	....	....	....	....	....	....	....	....	....	....	....
	Lowell Lock Monsters	AHL	11	0	3	3	....	....	....	21	....	....	....	....	....	....	....	....	....	....	....	....	....	....	....	....	....	....
	NHL Totals		**707**	**100**	**156**	**256**	**99**	**123**	**222**	**675**	**14**	**11**	**14**	**886**	**11.3**	**435**	**67**	**592**	**172**		**42**	**5**	**5**	**10**	**38**	**0**	**0**	**2**

Traded to **Washington** by **Quebec** for Reggie Savage and Paul MacDermid, June 20, 1993. Claimed by **Florida** from **Washington** in Expansion Draft, June 24, 1993. Signed as a free agent by **NY Islanders**, July 21, 1997.

• HOULDER, Bill
D – L. 6'2", 211 lbs. b: Thunder Bay, Ont., 3/11/1967. Washington's 4th, 82nd overall, in 1985.

Season	Club	League	GP	G	A	Pts	AG	AA	APts	PIM	PP	SH	GW	S	%	TGF	PGF	TGA	PGA	+/–	GP	G	A	Pts	PIM	PP	SH	GW
1983-84	Thunder Bay Beavers	TBJHL	23	4	18	22	....	....	....	37	....	....	....	....	....	....	....	....	....	....	....	....	....	....	....	....	....	....
1984-85	North Bay Centennials	OHL	66	4	20	24	....	....	....	37	....	....	....	....	....	....	....	....	....	....	8	0	0	0	2	....	....	....
1985-86	North Bay Centennials	OHL	59	5	30	35	....	....	....	97	....	....	....	....	....	....	....	....	....	....	10	1	6	7	12	....	....	....
1986-87	North Bay Centennials	OHL	62	17	51	68	....	....	....	68	....	....	....	....	....	....	....	....	....	....	22	4	19	23	20	....	....	....
1987-88	**Washington Capitals**	**NHL**	**30**	**1**	**2**	**3**	**1**	**1**	**2**	**10**	**0**	**0**	**0**	**20**	**5.0**	**13**	**0**	**15**	**0**	**–2**	....	....	....	....	....	....	....	....
	Fort Wayne Komets	IHL	43	10	14	24	....	....	....	32	....	....	....	....	....	....	....	....	....	....	....	....	....	....	....	....	....	....
1988-89	**Washington Capitals**	**NHL**	**8**	**0**	**3**	**3**	**0**	**2**	**2**	**4**	**0**	**0**	**0**	**5**	**0.0**	**11**	**1**	**3**	**0**	**7**	....	....	....	....	....	....	....	....
	Baltimore Skipjacks	AHL	65	10	36	46	....	....	....	50	....	....	....	....	....	....	....	....	....	....	....	....	....	....	....	....	....	....
1989-90	Washington Capitals	Fr-Tour	4	0	0	0	....	....	....	2	....	....	....	....	....	....	....	....	....	....	....	....	....	....	....	....	....	....
	Washington Capitals	**NHL**	**41**	**1**	**11**	**12**	**1**	**8**	**9**	**28**	**0**	**0**	**0**	**49**	**2.0**	**56**	**8**	**41**	**1**	**8**	....	....	....	....	....	....	....	....
	Baltimore Skipjacks	AHL	26	3	7	10	....	....	....	12	....	....	....	....	....	....	....	....	....	....	7	0	2	2	2	....	....	....
1990-91	**Buffalo Sabres**	**NHL**	**7**	**0**	**2**	**2**	**0**	**2**	**2**	**4**	**0**	**0**	**0**	**7**	**0.0**	**3**	**2**	**3**	**0**	**–2**	....	....	....	....	....	....	....	....
	Rochester Americans	AHL	69	13	53	66	....	....	....	28	....	....	....	....	....	....	....	....	....	....	15	5	13	18	4	....	....	....
1991-92	**Buffalo Sabres**	**NHL**	**10**	**1**	**0**	**1**	**1**	**0**	**1**	**8**	**0**	**0**	**0**	**18**	**5.6**	**6**	**1**	**8**	**1**	**–2**	....	....	....	....	....	....	....	....
	Rochester Americans	AHL	42	8	26	34	....	....	....	16	....	....	....	....	....	....	....	....	....	....	16	5	6	11	4	....	....	....
1992-93	**Buffalo Sabres**	**NHL**	**15**	**3**	**5**	**8**	**2**	**3**	**5**	**6**	**0**	**0**	**0**	**29**	**10.3**	**17**	**2**	**13**	**3**	**5**	**8**	**0**	**2**	**2**	**4**	**0**	**0**	**0**
	San Diego Gulls	IHL	64	24	48	72	....	....	....	39	....	....	....	....	....	....	....	....	....	....	....	....	....	....	....	....	....	....
1993-94	**Mighty Ducks of Anaheim**	**NHL**	**80**	**14**	**25**	**39**	**13**	**19**	**32**	**40**	**3**	**0**	**3**	**187**	**7.5**	**77**	**31**	**89**	**25**	**–18**	....	....	....	....	....	....	....	....
1994-95	**St. Louis Blues**	**NHL**	**41**	**5**	**13**	**18**	**9**	**19**	**28**	**20**	**1**	**0**	**0**	**59**	**8.5**	**48**	**7**	**28**	**3**	**16**	**4**	**1**	**1**	**2**	**0**	**0**	**0**	**0**
1995-96	**Tampa Bay Lightning**	**NHL**	**61**	**5**	**23**	**28**	**5**	**19**	**24**	**22**	**3**	**0**	**0**	**90**	**5.6**	**60**	**24**	**58**	**23**	**1**	**6**	**0**	**1**	**1**	**4**	**0**	**0**	**0**
1996-97	**Tampa Bay Lightning**	**NHL**	**79**	**4**	**21**	**25**	**4**	**19**	**23**	**30**	**0**	**0**	**2**	**116**	**3.4**	**92**	**14**	**93**	**31**	**16**	....	....	....	....	....	....	....	....
1997-98	**San Jose Sharks**	**NHL**	**82**	**7**	**25**	**32**	**8**	**24**	**32**	**48**	**4**	**0**	**2**	**102**	**6.9**	**86**	**25**	**80**	**32**	**13**	**6**	**1**	**2**	**3**	**2**	**0**	**0**	**0**

Season	Club	League	GP	G	A	Pts	AG	AA	APts	PIM	PP	SH	GW	S	%	TGF	PGF	TGA	PGA	+/–	GP	G	A	Pts	PIM	PP	SH	GW
			REGULAR SEASON																		PLAYOFFS							
1998-99	San Jose Sharks	NHL	76	9	23	32	11	22	33	40	7	0	5	115	7.8	78	32	69	31	8	6	3	0	3	4	3	0	0
99-2000	Tampa Bay Lightning	NHL	14	1	2	3	1	2	3	2	1	0	0	21	4.8	12	4	17	6	–3	....	....	....	....	....	....	....	....
	Nashville Predators	NHL	57	2	12	14	2	11	13	24	1	0	1	68	2.9	48	4	62	12	–6	....	....	....	....	....	....	....	....
	NHL Totals		601	53	167	220	58	151	209	286	20	0	13	886	6.0	607	155	579	168		30	5	6	11	14	3	0	0

AHL First All-Star Team (1991) • Won Governor's Trophy (Outstanding Defenseman - IHL) (1993) • IHL First All-Star Team (1993)

Traded to **Buffalo** by **Washington** for Shawn Anderson, September 30, 1990. Claimed by **Anaheim** from **Buffalo** in Expansion Draft, June 24, 1993. Traded to **St. Louis** by **Anaheim** for Jason Marshall, August 29, 1994. Signed as a free agent by **Tampa Bay**, July 26, 1995. Signed as a free agent by **San Jose**, July 16, 1997. Traded to **Tampa Bay** by **San Jose** with Andrei Zyuzin, Shawn Burr and Steve Guolla for Niklas Sundstrom and NY Rangers' 3rd round choice (previously acquired, later traded to Chicago - Chicago selected Igor Radulov) in 2000 Entry Draft, August 4, 1999. Claimed on waivers by **Nashville** from **Tampa Bay**, November 10, 1999.

• HOULE, Rejean

"Reggie" W – L. 5'11", 170 lbs. b: Rouyn, Que., 10/25/1949. Montreal's 1st, 1st overall, in 1969.

Season	Club	League	GP	G	A	Pts	AG	AA	APts	PIM	PP	SH	GW	S	%	TGF	PGF	TGA	PGA	+/–	GP	G	A	Pts	PIM	PP	SH	GW
1966-67	Thetford Canadiens	QJHL	43	30	30	60	....	....	....	80	....	....	....	....	....	....	....	....	....	....	11	10	12	22	27	....	....	....
	Thetford Canadiens	Mem-Cup	19	14	16	30	....	....	....	12	....	....	....	....	....	....	....	....	....	....	....	....	....	....	....	....	....	....
1967-68	Montreal Jr. Canadiens	OHA-Jr.	45	27	38	65	....	....	....	102	....	....	....	....	....	....	....	....	....	....	11	12	8	20	10	....	....	....
1968-69	Montreal Jr. Canadiens	OHA-Jr.	54	53	55	*108	....	....	....	76	....	....	....	....	....	....	....	....	....	....	14	13	10	23	13	....	....	....
	Montreal Jr. Canadiens	Mem-Cup	8	6	2	8	....	....	....	20	....	....	....	....	....	....	....	....	....	....	....	....	....	....	....	....	....	....
1969-70	Montreal Canadiens	NHL	9	0	1	1	0	1	1	0	0	0	0	1	0.0	2	0	1	0	1	....	....	....	....	....	....	....	....
	Montreal Voyageurs	AHL	27	9	16	25	....	....	....	23	....	....	....	....	....	....	....	....	....	....	8	3	2	5	4	....	....	....
1970-71 ♦	Montreal Canadiens	NHL	66	10	9	19	10	7	17	28	1	0	1	87	11.5	37	5	25	0	7	20	2	5	7	20	0	0	1
1971-72	Montreal Canadiens	NHL	77	11	17	28	11	15	26	21	1	0	1	145	7.6	49	5	38	3	9	6	0	0	0	2	0	0	0
1972-73 ♦	Montreal Canadiens	NHL	72	13	35	48	12	28	40	36	3	0	1	117	11.1	68	11	35	2	24	17	3	6	9	0	0	0	0
1973-74	Quebec Nordiques	WHA	69	27	35	62	....	....	....	17	....	....	....	....	....	....	....	....	....	....	....	....	....	....	....	....	....	....
1974-75	Team Canada	Summit-74	7	1	1	2	....	....	....	2	....	....	....	....	....	....	....	....	....	....	....	....	....	....	....	....	....	....
	Quebec Nordiques	WHA	64	40	52	92	....	....	....	37	....	....	....	....	....	....	....	....	....	....	15	*10	6	16	2	....	....	....
1975-76	Quebec Nordiques	WHA	81	51	52	103	....	....	....	61	....	....	....	....	....	....	....	....	....	....	5	2	0	2	8	....	....	....
1976-77 ♦	Montreal Canadiens	NHL	65	22	30	52	20	23	43	24	2	0	3	131	16.8	76	12	30	5	39	6	0	1	1	4	0	0	0
1977-78 ♦	Montreal Canadiens	NHL	76	30	28	58	27	22	49	50	3	0	5	143	21.0	96	23	41	7	39	15	3	8	11	14	0	0	0
1978-79 ♦	Montreal Canadiens	NHL	66	17	34	51	15	25	40	43	6	0	4	105	16.2	78	18	52	8	16	7	1	5	6	2	0	0	0
1979-80	Montreal Canadiens	NHL	60	18	27	45	15	20	35	68	2	0	3	115	15.7	63	13	55	8	3	10	4	5	9	12	1	0	0
1980-81	Montreal Canadiens	NHL	77	27	31	58	21	21	42	83	6	1	3	158	17.1	88	18	63	13	20	3	1	0	1	6	0	0	0
1981-82	Montreal Canadiens	NHL	51	11	32	43	9	21	30	34	2	1	1	81	13.6	59	16	29	4	18	5	0	4	4	6	0	0	0
1982-83	Montreal Canadiens	NHL	16	2	3	5	2	2	4	8	1	0	0	18	11.1	8	2	3	1	4	1	0	0	0	0	0	0	0
1983-1995			OUT OF HOCKEY – RETIRED																									
1995-2000	Montreal Canadiens	NHL	DID NOT PLAY – GENERAL MANAGER																									
	NHL Totals		635	161	247	408	142	185	327	395	27	2	22	1101	14.6	624	123	372	51		90	14	34	48	66	1	0	1
	Other Major League Totals		214	118	139	257	....	....	....	115	....	....	....	....	....	....	....	....	....	....	20	12	6	18	10	....	....	....

OHA-Jr. First All-Star Team (1969)

Selected by **Quebec** (WHA) in 1972 WHA General Player Draft, February 13, 1972. Signed as a free agent by **Montreal**, June 10, 1976. • Worked as an executive with Molson Breweries, 1983-1995.

• HOUSLEY, Phil

Phil F. D – L. 5'10", 185 lbs. b: St. Paul, MN, 3/9/1964. Buffalo's 1st, 6th overall, in 1982.

Season	Club	League	GP	G	A	Pts	AG	AA	APts	PIM	PP	SH	GW	S	%	TGF	PGF	TGA	PGA	+/–	GP	G	A	Pts	PIM	PP	SH	GW
1980-81	South St. Paul High School	Hi-School	STATISTICS NOT AVAILABLE																									
	St. Paul Vulcans	USHL	6	7	7	14	....	....	....	6	....	....	....	....	....	....	....	....	....	....	10	5	5	10	0	....	....	....
1981-82	St. Paul High School	Hi-School	22	31	34	65	....	....	....	18	....	....	....	....	....	....	....	....	....	....	....	....	....	....	....	....	....	....
	United States	WJC-A	7	1	0	1	....	....	....	6	....	....	....	....	....	....	....	....	....	....	....	....	....	....	....	....	....	....
	United States	WEC-A	7	1	0	1	....	....	....	4	....	....	....	....	....	....	....	....	....	....	....	....	....	....	....	....	....	....
1982-83	Buffalo Sabres	NHL	77	19	47	66	16	33	49	39	11	0	2	183	10.4	141	53	98	6	–4	10	3	4	7	2	1	0	0
1983-84	Buffalo Sabres	NHL	75	31	46	77	25	31	56	33	13	2	6	234	13.2	143	57	87	4	3	3	0	0	0	6	0	0	0
1984-85	United States	Can-Cup	6	0	2	2	....	....	....	0	....	....	....	....	....	....	....	....	....	....	....	....	....	....	....	....	....	....
	Buffalo Sabres	NHL	73	16	53	69	13	36	49	28	3	0	4	188	8.5	106	45	48	2	15	5	3	2	5	2	0	0	0
1985-86	Buffalo Sabres	NHL	79	15	47	62	12	32	44	54	7	0	2	180	8.3	111	53	70	3	–9	....	....	....	....	....	....	....	....
	United States	WEC-A	10	2	6	8	....	....	....	4	....	....	....	....	....	....	....	....	....	....	....	....	....	....	....	....	....	....
1986-87	Buffalo Sabres	NHL	78	21	46	67	18	33	51	57	8	1	2	202	10.4	132	48	100	14	–2	....	....	....	....	....	....	....	....
1987-88	United States	Can-Cup	5	0	2	2	....	....	....	4	....	....	....	....	....	....	....	....	....	....	....	....	....	....	....	....	....	....
	Buffalo Sabres	NHL	74	29	37	66	25	26	51	96	6	0	1	231	12.6	137	61	103	10	–17	6	2	4	6	6	1	0	0
1988-89	Buffalo Sabres	NHL	72	26	44	70	22	31	53	47	5	0	3	178	14.6	148	65	92	15	6	5	1	3	4	2	0	0	0
	United States	WEC-A	7	3	4	7	....	....	....	2	....	....	....	....	....	....	....	....	....	....	....	....	....	....	....	....	....	....
1989-90	Buffalo Sabres	NHL	80	21	60	81	18	43	61	32	8	1	4	201	10.4	159	68	86	6	11	6	1	4	5	4	1	0	0
1990-91	Winnipeg Jets	NHL	78	23	53	76	21	40	61	24	12	1	3	206	11.2	134	57	103	13	–13	....	....	....	....	....	....	....	....
1991-92	Winnipeg Jets	NHL	74	23	63	86	21	48	69	92	11	0	4	234	9.8	138	77	81	15	–5	7	1	4	5	0	1	0	1
1992-93	Winnipeg Jets	NHL	80	18	79	97	15	55	70	52	6	0	2	249	7.2	187	91	120	10	–14	6	0	7	7	2	0	0	0
1993-94	St. Louis Blues	NHL	26	7	15	22	6	12	18	12	4	0	1	60	11.7	45	27	30	7	–5	4	2	1	3	4	2	0	0
1994-95	ZSC Lions Zurich	Switz.	10	6	8	14	....	....	....	34	....	....	....	....	....	....	....	....	....	....	....	....	....	....	....	....	....	....
	Calgary Flames	NHL	43	8	35	43	14	52	66	18	3	0	0	135	5.9	86	34	36	1	17	7	0	9	9	0	0	0	0
1995-96	Calgary Flames	NHL	59	16	36	52	16	30	46	22	6	0	1	155	10.3	91	43	59	9	–2	....	....	....	....	....	....	....	....
	New Jersey Devils	NHL	22	1	15	16	1	12	13	8	0	0	0	50	2.0	28	11	22	1	–4	....	....	....	....	....	....	....	....
1996-97	United States	W-Cup	1	0	1	1	....	....	....	0	....	....	....	....	....	....	....	....	....	....	....	....	....	....	....	....	....	....
	Washington Capitals	NHL	77	11	29	40	12	26	38	24	3	1	2	167	6.6	97	44	68	5	–10	....	....	....	....	....	....	....	....
1997-98	Washington Capitals	NHL	64	6	25	31	7	24	31	24	4	1	0	116	5.2	75	40	48	3	–10	18	0	4	4	4	0	0	0
1998-99	Calgary Flames	NHL	79	11	43	54	13	42	55	52	4	0	1	193	5.7	113	44	58	3	14	....	....	....	....	....	....	....	....
99-2000	Calgary Flames	NHL	78	11	44	55	12	41	53	24	5	0	2	176	6.3	101	51	71	9	–12	....	....	....	....	....	....	....	....
	United States	WC-A	7	2	3	5	....	....	....	0	....	....	....	....	....	....	....	....	....	....	....	....	....	....	....	....	....	....
	NHL Totals		1288	313	817	1130	287	647	934	738	119	7	40	3338	9.4	2172	969	1380	136		77	13	42	55	32	6	0	1

NHL All-Rookie Team (1983) • NHL Second All-Star Team (1992) • Played in NHL All-Star Game (1984, 1989, 1990, 1991, 1992, 1993, 2000)

Traded to **Winnipeg** by **Buffalo** with Scott Arniel, Jeff Parker and Buffalo's 1st round choice (Keith Tkachuk) in 1990 Entry Draft for Dale Hawerchuk, Winnipeg's 1st round choice (Brad May) in 1990 Entry Draft and future considerations, June 16, 1990. Traded to **St. Louis** by **Winnipeg** for Nelson Emerson and Stephane Quintal, September 24, 1993. Traded to **Calgary** by **St. Louis** with St. Louis' 2nd round choices in 1996 (Steve Begin) and 1997 (John Tripp) Entry Drafts for Al MacInnis and Calgary's 4th round choice (Didier Tremblay) in 1997 Entry Draft, July 4, 1994. Traded to **New Jersey** by **Calgary** with Dan Keczmer for Tommy Albelin, Cale Hulse and Jocelyn Lemieux, February 26, 1996. Signed as a free agent by **Washington**, July 22, 1996. Claimed on waivers by **Calgary** from **Washington**, July 21, 1998.

• HOUSTON, Ken

Kenneth Lyle RW – R. 6'2", 210 lbs. b: Dresden, Ont., 9/15/1953. Atlanta's 6th, 85th overall, in 1973.

Season	Club	League	GP	G	A	Pts	AG	AA	APts	PIM	PP	SH	GW	S	%	TGF	PGF	TGA	PGA	+/–	GP	G	A	Pts	PIM	PP	SH	GW
1971-72	Chatham Maroons	OHA-B	48	8	24	32	....	....	....	213	....	....	....	....	....	....	....	....	....	....	....	....	....	....	....	....	....	....
1972-73	Chatham Maroons	OHA-B	52	14	41	55	....	....	....	60	....	....	....	....	....	....	....	....	....	....	....	....	....	....	....	....	....	....
1973-74	Omaha Knights	CHL	71	8	22	30	....	....	....	144	....	....	....	....	....	....	....	....	....	....	5	1	1	2	6	....	....	....
1974-75	Omaha Knights	CHL	78	9	32	41	....	....	....	158	....	....	....	....	....	....	....	....	....	....	6	1	7	8	8	....	....	....
1975-76	Atlanta Flames	NHL	38	5	6	11	4	4	8	11	1	0	0	49	10.2	18	1	20	0	–3	2	0	0	0	0	0	0	0
	Nova Scotia Voyageurs	AHL	27	14	15	29	....	....	....	56	....	....	....	....	....	....	....	....	....	....	....	....	....	....	....	....	....	....
1976-77	Atlanta Flames	NHL	78	20	24	44	18	18	36	35	3	0	2	151	13.2	67	8	54	0	5	3	0	0	0	4	0	0	0
1977-78	Atlanta Flames	NHL	74	22	16	38	20	12	32	51	2	0	2	147	15.0	54	4	46	0	4	2	0	0	0	0	0	0	0
1978-79	Atlanta Flames	NHL	80	21	31	52	18	22	40	135	2	0	2	140	15.0	83	11	68	0	4	1	0	0	0	16	0	0	0
1979-80	Atlanta Flames	NHL	80	23	31	54	20	23	43	100	4	0	4	155	14.8	85	15	72	1	–1	4	1	1	2	10	0	0	0
1980-81	Calgary Flames	NHL	42	15	15	30	12	10	22	93	4	0	4	78	19.2	58	27	32	1	0	16	7	8	15	28	5	0	1
1981-82	Calgary Flames	NHL	70	22	22	44	17	15	32	91	3	0	0	165	13.3	76	14	64	0	–2	3	1	0	1	4	0	0	0

Season	Club	League	REGULAR SEASON																		PLAYOFFS							
			GP	G	A	Pts	AG	AA	APts	PIM	PP	SH	GW	S	%	TGF	PGF	TGA	PGA	+/–	GP	G	A	Pts	PIM	PP	SH	GW
1982-83	**Washington Capitals**	**NHL**	71	25	14	39	20	10	30	93	9	0	0	139	18.0	70	27	51	0	–8	4	1	0	1	4	0	0	0
1983-84	**Washington Capitals**	**NHL**	4	0	0	0	0	0	0	4	0	0	0	3	0.0	1	0	3	0	–2	....	....	....	....	....	....	....	....
	Los Angeles Kings	**NHL**	33	8	8	16	6	5	11	11	0	0	0	35	22.9	23	3	23	0	–3	....	....	....	....	....	....	....	....
	NHL Totals		570	161	167	328	135	119	254	624	28	0	14	1062	15.2	535	110	433	2		35	10	9	19	66	5	0	1

OHA-B First All-Star Team (1973)

Transferred to **Calgary** after **Atlanta** franchise relocated, June 24, 1980. Traded to **Washington** by **Calgary** with Pat Riggin for Howard Walker, George White, Washington's 6th round choice (Mats Kihlstron) in 1982 Entry Draft, 3rd round choice (Parry Berezan) in 1983 Entry Draft and 2nd round choice (Paul Ranheim) in 1984 Entry Draft, June 9, 1982. Traded to **LA Kings** by **Washington** with Brian Engblom for Larry Murphy, October 18, 1983.

• HOWATT, Garry

Garry Robert Charles LW – R. 5'9", 175 lbs. b: Grand Center, Alta., 9/26/1952. NY Islanders' 13th, 144th overall, in 1972.

Season	Club	League	GP	G	A	Pts	AG	AA	APts	PIM	PP	SH	GW	S	%	TGF	PGF	TGA	PGA	+/–	GP	G	A	Pts	PIM	PP	SH	GW
1971-72	Kamloops Rockets	BCJHL	36	19	35	54	....	....	....	....	....	....	....	....	....	....	....	....	....	....	....	....	....	....	....	....	....	....
	Victoria Cougars	WCJHL	24	5	15	20	....	....	....	36	....	....	....	....	....	....	....	....	....	....	....	....	....	....	....	....	....	....
	Flin Flon Bombers	WCJHL	36	24	35	59	....	....	....	109	....	....	....	....	....	....	....	....	....	....	7	4	1	5	30	....	....	....
1972-73	**New York Islanders**	**NHL**	8	0	1	1	0	1	1	18	0	0	0	2	0.0	2	0	7	0	–5	....	....	....	....	....	....	....	....
	New Haven Nighthawks	AHL	65	22	27	49	....	....	....	157	....	....	....	....	....	....	....	....	....	....	....	....	....	....	....	....	....	....
1973-74	**New York Islanders**	**NHL**	78	6	11	17	6	9	15	204	0	0	0	84	7.1	43	3	54	1	–13	....	....	....	....	....	....	....	....
1974-75	**New York Islanders**	**NHL**	77	18	30	48	16	22	38	121	1	0	3	126	14.3	75	5	38	0	32	17	3	3	6	59	0	0	1
1975-76	**New York Islanders**	**NHL**	80	21	13	34	18	10	28	197	0	0	2	115	18.3	60	2	32	0	26	13	5	5	10	23	0	0	1
1976-77	**New York Islanders**	**NHL**	70	13	15	28	12	12	24	182	1	0	4	91	14.3	48	3	31	0	14	12	1	1	2	28	0	0	0
1977-78	**New York Islanders**	**NHL**	61	7	12	19	6	9	15	146	0	0	0	60	11.7	38	0	31	0	7	7	0	1	1	62	0	0	0
1978-79	**New York Islanders**	**NHL**	75	16	12	28	14	9	23	205	0	0	2	81	19.8	49	1	43	1	6	9	0	1	1	18	0	0	0
1979-80♦	**New York Islanders**	**NHL**	77	8	11	19	7	8	15	219	0	0	1	62	12.9	32	1	47	13	–3	21	3	1	4	84	0	0	1
1980-81♦	**New York Islanders**	**NHL**	70	4	15	19	3	10	13	174	0	0	0	48	8.3	33	1	20	0	12	8	0	2	2	15	0	0	0
1981-82	**Hartford Whalers**	**NHL**	80	18	32	50	14	21	35	242	1	0	2	111	16.2	89	11	84	1	–5	....	....	....	....	....	....	....	....
1982-83	**New Jersey Devils**	**NHL**	38	1	4	5	1	3	4	114	0	0	0	30	3.3	9	1	41	4	–29	....	....	....	....	....	....	....	....
	Wichita Wind	CHL	11	0	5	5	....	....	....	4	....	....	....	....	....	....	....	....	....	....	....	....	....	....	....	....	....	....
1983-84	**New Jersey Devils**	**NHL**	6	0	0	0	0	0	0	14	0	0	0	5	0.0	2	0	4	1	–1	....	....	....	....	....	....	....	....
	Maine Mariners	AHL	63	12	20	32	....	....	....	124	....	....	....	....	....	....	....	....	....	....	17	4	7	11	46	....	....	....
	NHL Totals		720	112	156	268	97	114	211	1836	3	0	14	815	13.7	480	28	432	21		87	12	14	26	289	0	0	3

Traded to **Hartford** by **NY Islanders** for Hartford's 5th round choice (Bob Caulfield) in 1983 Entry Draft, October 2, 1981. Traded to **New Jersey** by **Hartford** with Rick Meagher for Merlin Malinowski and the rights to Scott Fusco, October 15, 1982.

• HOWE, Gordie

Gordon "Mr. Hockey" RW – R. 6', 205 lbs. b: Floral, Sask., 3/31/1928. **HHOF**

Season	Club	League	GP	G	A	Pts	AG	AA	APts	PIM	PP	SH	GW	S	%	TGF	PGF	TGA	PGA	+/–	GP	G	A	Pts	PIM	PP	SH	GW
1942-43	King George High	Hi-School	STATISTICS NOT AVAILABLE																									
1943-44	Saskatoon Lions	SAHA	5	6	*5	11	....	....	....	4	....	....	....	....	....	....	....	....	....	....	2	0	0	0	6	....	....	....
1944-45	Galt Red Wings	OHA-Jr.	PLAYED EXHIBITION SEASON ONLY																									
1945-46	Omaha Knights	USHL	51	22	26	48	....	....	....	53	....	....	....	....	....	....	....	....	....	....	6	2	1	3	15	....	....	....
1946-47	**Detroit Red Wings**	**NHL**	58	7	15	22	8	18	26	52	....	....	....	....	....	....	....	....	....	....	5	0	0	0	18	....	....	....
1947-48	**Detroit Red Wings**	**NHL**	60	16	28	44	21	37	58	63	....	....	....	....	....	....	....	....	....	....	10	1	1	2	11	....	....	....
1948-49	**Detroit Red Wings**	**NHL**	40	12	25	37	17	36	53	57	....	....	....	....	....	....	....	....	....	....	11	*8	3	*11	19	....	....	....
1949-50♦	**Detroit Red Wings**	**NHL**	70	35	33	68	45	40	85	69	....	....	....	....	....	....	....	....	....	....	1	0	0	0	7	....	....	....
1950-51	**Detroit Red Wings**	**NHL**	70	*43	*43	*86	56	53	109	74	....	....	....	....	....	....	....	....	....	....	6	4	3	7	4	....	....	....
1951-52♦	**Detroit Red Wings**	**NHL**	70	*47	39	*86	64	49	113	78	....	....	....	....	....	....	....	....	....	....	8	2	*5	*7	2	....	....	....
1952-53	**Detroit Red Wings**	**NHL**	70	*49	*46	*95	67	57	124	57	....	....	....	....	....	....	....	....	....	....	6	2	5	7	2	....	....	....
1953-54♦	**Detroit Red Wings**	**NHL**	70	33	*48	*81	45	59	104	109	....	....	....	....	....	....	....	....	....	....	12	4	5	9	*31	....	....	....
1954-55♦	**Detroit Red Wings**	**NHL**	64	29	33	62	38	38	76	68	....	....	....	....	....	....	....	....	....	....	11	*9	*11	*20	24	....	....	....
1955-56	**Detroit Red Wings**	**NHL**	70	38	41	79	53	49	102	100	....	....	....	....	....	....	....	....	....	....	10	3	9	12	8	....	....	....
1956-57	**Detroit Red Wings**	**NHL**	70	*44	45	*89	58	50	108	72	....	....	....	....	....	....	....	....	....	....	5	2	5	7	6	....	....	....
1957-58	**Detroit Red Wings**	**NHL**	64	33	44	77	41	46	87	40	....	....	....	....	....	....	....	....	....	....	4	1	1	2	0	....	....	....
1958-59	**Detroit Red Wings**	**NHL**	70	32	46	78	39	47	86	57	....	....	....	....	....	....	....	....	....	....	....	....	....	....	....	....	....	....
1959-60	**Detroit Red Wings**	**NHL**	70	28	45	73	33	44	77	46	....	....	....	....	....	....	....	....	....	....	6	1	5	6	4	....	....	....
1960-61	**Detroit Red Wings**	**NHL**	64	23	49	72	27	48	75	30	....	....	....	....	....	....	....	....	....	....	11	4	11	*15	10	....	....	....
1961-62	**Detroit Red Wings**	**NHL**	70	33	44	77	38	43	81	54	....	....	....	....	....	....	....	....	....	....	....	....	....	....	....	....	....	....
1962-63	**Detroit Red Wings**	**NHL**	70	*38	48	*86	45	48	93	100	....	....	....	....	....	....	....	....	....	....	11	7	9	*16	22	....	....	....
1963-64	**Detroit Red Wings**	**NHL**	69	26	47	73	33	50	83	70	....	....	....	....	....	....	....	....	....	....	14	*9	10	*19	16	....	....	....
1964-65	**Detroit Red Wings**	**NHL**	70	29	47	76	35	49	84	104	....	....	....	....	....	....	....	....	....	....	7	4	2	6	20	....	....	....
1965-66	**Detroit Red Wings**	**NHL**	70	29	46	75	33	44	77	83	....	....	....	....	....	....	....	....	....	....	12	4	6	10	12	....	....	....
1966-67	**Detroit Red Wings**	**NHL**	69	25	40	65	29	39	68	53	....	....	....	....	....	....	....	....	....	....	....	....	....	....	....	....	....	....
1967-68	**Detroit Red Wings**	**NHL**	74	39	43	82	46	43	89	53	10	0	4	301	13.0	117	34	83	12	12	....	....	....	....	....	....	....	....
1968-69	**Detroit Red Wings**	**NHL**	76	44	59	103	47	53	100	58	9	0	6	283	15.5	134	35	66	12	45	....	....	....	....	....	....	....	....
1969-70	**Detroit Red Wings**	**NHL**	76	31	40	71	34	38	72	58	11	4	5	268	11.6	105	38	54	10	23	4	2	0	2	2	1	0	0
1970-71	**Detroit Red Wings**	**NHL**	63	23	29	52	23	24	47	38	7	1	3	195	11.8	76	24	65	11	–2	....	....	....	....	....	....	....	....
1971-72			OUT OF HOCKEY – RETIRED																									
1972-73			OUT OF HOCKEY – RETIRED																									
1973-74	Houston Aeros	WHA	70	31	69	100	....	....	....	46	....	....	....	....	....	....	....	....	....	....	13	3	*14	17	34	....	....	....
1974-75	Canada	Summit	7	3	4	7	....	....	....	2	....	....	....	....	....	....	....	....	....	....	....	....	....	....	....	....	....	....
	Houston Aeros	WHA	75	34	65	99	....	....	....	84	....	....	....	....	....	....	....	....	....	....	13	8	12	20	20	....	....	....
1975-76	Houston Aeros	WHA	78	32	70	102	....	....	....	76	....	....	....	....	....	....	....	....	....	....	17	4	8	12	31	....	....	....
1976-77	Houston Aeros	WHA	62	24	44	68	....	....	....	57	....	....	....	....	....	....	....	....	....	....	11	5	3	8	11	....	....	....
1977-78	New England Whalers	WHA	76	34	62	96	....	....	....	85	....	....	....	....	....	....	....	....	....	....	14	5	5	10	15	....	....	....
1978-79	New England Whalers	WHA	58	19	24	43	....	....	....	51	....	....	....	....	....	....	....	....	....	....	10	3	1	4	4	....	....	....
1979-80	**Hartford Whalers**	**NHL**	80	15	26	41	13	19	32	42	2	0	0	94	16.0	66	11	46	0	9	3	1	1	2	2	0	0	0
1980-1997			OUT OF HOCKEY – RETIRED																									
1997-98	Detroit Vipers	IHL	1	0	0	0	....	....	....	0	....	....	....	....	....	....	....	....	....	....	....	....	....	....	....	....	....	....
	NHL Totals		1767	801	1049	1850	988	1121	2109	1685	....	....	....	....	....	....	....	....	....	....	157	68	92	160	220	....	....	....
	Other Major League Totals		419	174	334	508	....	....	....	399	....	....	....	....	....	....	....	....	....	....	78	28	43	71	115	....	....	....

• Brother of Vic • Father of Marty and Mark • USHL Second All-Star Team (1946) • NHL Second All-Star Team (1949, 1950, 1956, 1959, 1961, 1962, 1964, 1965, 1967) • NHL First All-Star Team (1951, 1952, 1953, 1954, 1957, 1958, 1960, 1963, 1966, 1968, 1969, 1970) • Won Art Ross Trophy (1951, 1952, 1953, 1954, 1957, 1963) • Won Hart Trophy (1952, 1953, 1957, 1958, 1960, 1963) • Won Lester Patrick Trophy (1967) • WHA First All-Star Team (1974, 1975) • Won Gary Davidson Trophy (WHA MVP) (1974) • Played in NHL All-Star Game (1948, 1949, 1950, 1951, 1952, 1953, 1954, 1955, 1957, 1958, 1959, 1960, 1961, 1962, 1963, 1964, 1965, 1967, 1968, 1969, 1970, 1971, 1980)

• Played exhibition schedule only with **Galt Red Wings** (OHA-Jr.) in 1944-45 season after OHA rejected transfer request. Signed as a free agent by **Omaha** (USHL), November 1, 1945. Signed as a free agent by **Detroit**, October 8, 1946. Signed as a free agent by **Houston** (WHA), June 5, 1973. Signed as a free agent by **New England** (WHA), June, 1977. Rights retained by **Hartford** prior to Expansion Draft, June 9, 1979. • Oldest player (52 years, 10 days) to play in a NHL game, April 11, 1980. (Montreal 4, Hartford 3). Signed to a one-game contract by **Detroit** (IHL), September, 1997.

• HOWE, Mark

Mark Steven D – L. 5'11", 185 lbs. b: Detroit, MI, 5/28/1955. Boston's 2nd, 25th overall, in 1974.

Season	Club	League	GP	G	A	Pts	AG	AA	APts	PIM	PP	SH	GW	S	%	TGF	PGF	TGA	PGA	+/–	GP	G	A	Pts	PIM	PP	SH	GW
1969-70	Detroit Olympia	MNHL	40	30	39	69	....	....	....	21	....	....	....	....	....	....	....	....	....	....	....	....	....	....	....	....	....	....
1970-71	Detroit Jr. Red Wings	OJHL	44	37	*70	*107	....	....	....	....	....	....	....	....	....	....	....	....	....	....	....	....	....	....	....	....	....	....
	Detroit Jr. Red Wings	Cen-Cup	10	5	19	24	....	....	....	0	....	....	....	....	....	....	....	....	....	....	....	....	....	....	....	....	....	....
1971-72	Detroit Jr. Red Wings	OJHL	9	5	9	14	....	....	....	....	....	....	....	....	....	....	....	....	....	....	....	....	....	....	....	....	....	....
	United States	Olympics	6	0	0	0	....	....	....	0	....	....	....	....	....	....	....	....	....	....	....	....	....	....	....	....	....	....
1972-73	Toronto Marlboros	OMJHL	60	38	66	104	....	....	....	27	....	....	....	....	....	....	....	....	....	....	....	....	....	....	....	....	....	....
	Toronto Marlboros	Mem-Cup	3	*4	*4	*8	....	....	....	6	....	....	....	....	....	....	....	....	....	....	....	....	....	....	....	....	....	....
1973-74	Houston Aeros	WHA	76	38	41	79	....	....	....	20	....	....	....	....	....	....	....	....	....	....	14	9	10	19	4	....	....	....
1974-75	Team Canada	Summit-74	7	2	4	6	....	....	....	4	....	....	....	....	....	....	....	....	....	....	....	....	....	....	....	....	....	....
	Houston Aeros	WHA	74	36	40	76	....	....	....	30	....	....	....	....	....	....	....	....	....	....	13	*10	12	*22	0	....	....	....
1975-76	Houston Aeros	WHA	72	39	37	76	....	....	....	38	....	....	....	....	....	....	....	....	....	....	17	6	10	16	18	....	....	....
1976-77	Houston Aeros	WHA	57	23	52	75	....	....	....	46	....	....	....	....	....	....	....	....	....	....	10	4	10	14	2	....	....	....
1977-78	New England Whalers	WHA	70	30	61	91	....	....	....	32	....	....	....	....	....	....	....	....	....	....	14	8	7	15	18	....	....	....

Season	Club	League	REGULAR SEASON																		PLAYOFFS							
			GP	G	A	Pts	AG	AA	APts	PIM	PP	SH	GW	S	%	TGF	PGF	TGA	PGA	+/–	GP	G	A	Pts	PIM	PP	SH	GW
1978-79	New England Whalers	WHA	77	42	65	107	....	....	....	32	....	....	....	....	....	....	....	....	....	....	6	4	2	6	6	....	....	....
1979-80	**Hartford Whalers**	**NHL**	74	24	56	80	20	41	61	20	5	2	3	178	13.5	137	32	120	29	14	3	1	2	3	2	0	0	0
1980-81	**Hartford Whalers**	**NHL**	63	19	46	65	15	31	46	54	7	2	3	172	11.0	137	38	118	29	10	....	....	....	....	....	....	....	....
1981-82	United States	Can-Cup	6	0	4	4	....	....	....	2	....	....	....	....	....	....	....	....	....	....	....	....	....	....	....	....	....	....
	Hartford Whalers	**NHL**	76	8	45	53	6	30	36	18	3	0	1	220	3.6	127	41	119	25	–8	....	....	....	....	....	....	....	....
1982-83	**Philadelphia Flyers**	**NHL**	76	20	47	67	16	33	49	18	5	5	4	219	9.1	148	40	78	17	47	3	0	2	2	4	0	0	0
1983-84	**Philadelphia Flyers**	**NHL**	71	19	34	53	15	23	38	44	3	3	2	184	10.3	114	28	82	26	30	3	0	0	0	2	0	0	0
1984-85	**Philadelphia Flyers**	**NHL**	73	18	39	57	15	27	42	31	3	2	1	213	8.5	146	29	98	32	51	19	3	8	11	6	1	0	1
1985-86	**Philadelphia Flyers**	**NHL**	77	24	58	82	19	39	58	36	4	7	3	193	12.4	188	46	93	36	85	5	0	4	4	0	0	0	0
1986-87	**Philadelphia Flyers**	**NHL**	69	15	43	58	13	31	44	37	2	4	0	148	10.1	152	42	82	29	57	26	2	10	12	4	0	0	0
1987-88	**Philadelphia Flyers**	**NHL**	75	19	43	62	16	31	47	62	8	1	4	177	10.7	137	47	108	41	23	7	3	6	9	4	0	0	0
1988-89	**Philadelphia Flyers**	**NHL**	52	9	29	38	8	21	29	45	5	1	1	95	9.5	97	44	73	27	7	19	0	15	15	10	0	0	0
1989-90	**Philadelphia Flyers**	**NHL**	40	7	21	28	6	15	21	24	3	1	1	63	11.1	65	16	45	18	22	....	....	....	....	....	....	....	....
1990-91	**Philadelphia Flyers**	**NHL**	19	0	10	10	0	8	8	8	0	0	0	40	0.0	29	9	23	12	9	....	....	....	....	....	....	....	....
1991-92	**Philadelphia Flyers**	**NHL**	42	7	18	25	6	14	20	18	6	0	0	63	11.1	65	20	40	13	18	....	....	....	....	....	....	....	....
1992-93	**Detroit Red Wings**	**NHL**	60	3	31	34	2	21	23	22	3	0	0	72	4.2	88	29	52	15	22	7	1	3	4	2	0	0	0
1993-94	**Detroit Red Wings**	**NHL**	44	4	20	24	4	16	20	8	1	0	0	72	5.6	54	9	36	7	16	6	0	1	1	0	0	0	0
1994-95	**Detroit Red Wings**	**NHL**	18	1	5	6	2	7	9	10	0	0	1	14	7.1	12	6	11	2	–3	3	0	0	0	0	0	0	0
	NHL Totals		929	197	545	742	163	388	551	455	58	28	24	2123	9.3	1696	476	1178	358		101	10	51	61	34	1	0	1
	Other Major League Totals		426	208	296	504	....	....	....	198	....	....	....	....	....	....	....	....	....	....	74	41	51	92	48	....	....	....

• Son of Gordie • Brother of Marty •OJHL First All-Star Team (1971) • Won Stafford Smythe Memorial Trophy (Memorial Cup Tournament MVP) (1973) • WHA Second All-Star Team (1974) • Won Lou Kaplan Trophy (WHA Rookie of the Year) (1974) • WHA First All-Star Team (1979) • NHL First All-Star Team (1983, 1986, 1987) • NHL Plus/Minus Leader (1986) • Played in NHL All-Star Game (1981, 1983, 1986, 1988)

• Missed majority of 1971-72 season recovering from knee surgery, June, 1971. Selected by **Houston** (WHA) in 1973 WHA Professional Player Draft, June, 1973. Signed as a free agent by **New England** (WHA), June, 1977. Reclaimed by **Boston** from **Hartford** prior to Expansion Draft, June 9, 1979. Claimed as a priority selection by **Hartford**, June 9, 1979. Traded to **Philadelphia** by **Hartford** with Hartford's 3rd round choice (Derrick Smith) in 1983 Entry Draft for Ken Linseman, Greg C. Adams and Philadelphia's 1st (David Jensen) and 3rd (Leif Karlsson) round choices in 1982 Entry Draft, August 19, 1982. • Missed majority of 1990-91 season recovering from back injury originally suffered in game vs. Chicago, November 3, 1990. Signed as a free agent by **Detroit**, July 7, 1992.

• HOWE, Marty

Marty Gordon D – L. 6'1", 195 lbs. b: Detroit, MI, 2/18/1954. Montreal's 8th, 51st overall, in 1974.

Season	Club	League	GP	G	A	Pts	AG	AA	APts	PIM	PP	SH	GW	S	%	TGF	PGF	TGA	PGA	+/–	GP	G	A	Pts	PIM	PP	SH	GW
1970-71	Detroit Jr. Red Wings	OJHL	STATISTICS NOT AVAILABLE																									
	Detroit Jr. Red Wings	Cen-Cup	12	1	9	10	....	....	....	18	....	....	....	....	....	....	....	....	....	....	....	....	....	....	....	....	....	....
1971-72	Toronto Marlboros	OMJHL	56	7	21	28	....	....	....	122	....	....	....	....	....	....	....	....	....	....	10	1	8	9	38	....	....	....
1972-73	Toronto Marlboros	OMJHL	38	11	17	28	....	....	....	81	....	....	....	....	....	....	....	....	....	....	....	....	....	....	....	....	....	....
	Toronto	Mem-Cup	3	0	1	1	....	....	....	0	....	....	....	....	....	....	....	....	....	....	....	....	....	....	....	....	....	....
1973-74	Houston Aeros	WHA	73	4	20	24	....	....	....	90	....	....	....	....	....	....	....	....	....	....	14	1	5	6	31	....	....	....
1974-75	Team Canada	Summit-74	4	0	0	0	....	....	....	12	....	....	....	....	....	....	....	....	....	....	....	....	....	....	....	....	....	....
	Houston Aeros	WHA	75	13	21	34	....	....	....	89	....	....	....	....	....	....	....	....	....	....	11	0	2	2	11	....	....	....
1975-76	Houston Aeros	WHA	80	14	23	37	....	....	....	81	....	....	....	....	....	....	....	....	....	....	16	4	4	8	12	....	....	....
1976-77	Houston Aeros	WHA	80	17	28	45	....	....	....	103	....	....	....	....	....	....	....	....	....	....	11	3	1	4	10	....	....	....
1977-78	New England Whalers	WHA	75	10	10	20	....	....	....	66	....	....	....	....	....	....	....	....	....	....	14	1	1	2	13	....	....	....
1978-79	New England Whalers	WHA	66	9	15	24	....	....	....	31	....	....	....	....	....	....	....	....	....	....	9	0	1	1	8	....	....	....
1979-80	**Hartford Whalers**	**NHL**	6	0	1	1	0	1	1	4	0	0	0	6	0.0	4	0	6	0	–2	3	1	1	2	0	0	0	0
	Springfield Indians	AHL	31	8	5	13	....	....	....	12	....	....	....	....	....	....	....	....	....	....	....	....	....	....	....	....	....	....
1980-81	**Hartford Whalers**	**NHL**	12	0	1	1	0	1	1	25	0	0	0	3	0.0	6	1	12	2	–5	....	....	....	....	....	....	....	....
	Binghamton Whalers	AHL	37	4	10	14	....	....	....	34	....	....	....	....	....	....	....	....	....	....	6	0	2	2	6	....	....	....
1981-82	**Hartford Whalers**	**NHL**	13	0	4	4	0	3	3	2	0	0	0	25	0.0	16	4	21	5	–4	....	....	....	....	....	....	....	....
	Binghamton Whalers	AHL	61	8	38	46	....	....	....	42	....	....	....	....	....	....	....	....	....	....	15	0	8	8	4	....	....	....
1982-83	**Boston Bruins**	**NHL**	78	1	11	12	1	8	9	24	0	0	0	68	1.5	59	0	38	0	21	12	0	1	1	9	0	0	0
1983-84	**Hartford Whalers**	**NHL**	69	0	11	11	0	7	7	34	0	0	0	58	0.0	58	4	60	7	1	....	....	....	....	....	....	....	....
1984-85	**Hartford Whalers**	**NHL**	19	1	1	2	1	1	2	10	0	0	0	23	4.3	19	2	25	4	–4	....	....	....	....	....	....	....	....
	Binghamton Whalers	AHL	44	7	12	19	....	....	....	22	....	....	....	....	....	....	....	....	....	....	8	3	2	5	6	....	....	....
1985-1992			OUT OF HOCKEY – RETIRED																									
1992-1993	Flint Bulldogs	ColHL	3	0	1	1	....	....	....	4	....	....	....	....	....	....	....	....	....	....	....	....	....	....	....	....	....	....
1993-1994	Utica Bulldogs	ColHL	DID NOT PLAY – COACHING																									
1994-1997			OUT OF HOCKEY – RETIRED																									
1997-1998	Gaylord Grizzlies	NAJHL	DID NOT PLAY – COACHING																									
1998-1999			OUT OF HOCKEY – RETIRED																									
1999-2000	Chicago Wolves	IHL	DID NOT PLAY – ASSISTANT COACH																									
	NHL Totals		197	2	29	31	2	21	23	99	0	0	0	183	1.1	162	11	162	18		15	1	2	3	9	0	0	0
	Other Major League Totals		449	67	117	184	....	....	....	460	....	....	....	....	....	....	....	....	....	....	75	9	14	23	85	....	....	....

• Son of Gordie • Brother of Mark • OJHL Second All-Star Team (1971) • WHA Second All-Star Team (1977)

Selected by **Houston** (WHA) in 1973 WHA Professional Player Draft, June, 1973. Rights traded to **Detroit** by **Montreal** for cash and future considerations, February 25, 1977. Signed as a free agent by **New England** (WHA), June, 1977. Rights retained by **Hartford** prior to Expansion Draft, June 9, 1979. Traded to **Boston** by **Hartford** for future considerations, October 1, 1982. Traded to **Hartford** by **Boston** for future considerations, September 29, 1983.

• HOWELL, Harry

Henry Vernon "Horse" D – L. 6'1", 195 lbs. b: Hamilton, Ont., 12/28/1932. **HHOF**

Season	Club	League	GP	G	A	Pts	AG	AA	APts	PIM	PP	SH	GW	S	%	TGF	PGF	TGA	PGA	+/–	GP	G	A	Pts	PIM	PP	SH	GW
1949-50	Guelph Biltmores	OHA-Jr.	3	0	1	1	....	....	....	2	....	....	....	....	....	....	....	....	....	....	5	0	1	1	14	....	....	....
	Guelph Biltmores	Mem-Cup	5	0	1	1	....	....	....	14	....	....	....	....	....	....	....	....	....	....	....	....	....	....	....	....	....	....
1950-51	Guelph Biltmores	OHA-Jr.	50	6	16	22	....	....	....	77	....	....	....	....	....	....	....	....	....	....	5	1	0	1	6	....	....	....
	Guelph Biltmores	Mem-Cup	12	5	5	10	....	....	....	24	....	....	....	....	....	....	....	....	....	....	....	....	....	....	....	....	....	....
1951-52	Guelph Biltmores	OHA-Jr.	51	17	20	37	....	....	....	79	....	....	....	....	....	....	....	....	....	....	23	7	9	16	36	....	....	....
	Cincinnati Mohawks	AHL	1	0	0	0	....	....	....	0	....	....	....	....	....	....	....	....	....	....	....	....	....	....	....	....	....	....
1952-53	**New York Rangers**	**NHL**	67	3	8	11	4	10	14	46	....	....	....	....	....	....	....	....	....	....	....	....	....	....	....	....	....	....
	Guelph Biltmores	Mem-Cup	12	5	5	10	....	....	....	24	....	....	....	....	....	....	....	....	....	....	....	....	....	....	....	....	....	....
1953-54	**New York Rangers**	**NHL**	67	7	9	16	9	11	20	58	....	....	....	....	....	....	....	....	....	....	....	....	....	....	....	....	....	....
1954-55	**New York Rangers**	**NHL**	70	2	14	16	3	16	19	87	....	....	....	....	....	....	....	....	....	....	....	....	....	....	....	....	....	....
1955-56	**New York Rangers**	**NHL**	70	3	15	18	4	18	22	77	....	....	....	....	....	....	....	....	....	....	5	0	1	1	4	....	....	....
1956-57	**New York Rangers**	**NHL**	65	2	10	12	3	11	14	70	....	....	....	....	....	....	....	....	....	....	5	1	0	1	6	....	....	....
1957-58	**New York Rangers**	**NHL**	70	4	7	11	5	7	12	62	....	....	....	....	....	....	....	....	....	....	6	1	0	1	8	....	....	....
1958-59	**New York Rangers**	**NHL**	70	4	10	14	5	10	15	101	....	....	....	....	....	....	....	....	....	....	....	....	....	....	....	....	....	....
1959-60	**New York Rangers**	**NHL**	67	7	6	13	8	6	14	58	....	....	....	....	....	....	....	....	....	....	....	....	....	....	....	....	....	....
1960-61	**New York Rangers**	**NHL**	70	7	10	17	8	10	18	62	....	....	....	....	....	....	....	....	....	....	....	....	....	....	....	....	....	....
1961-62	**New York Rangers**	**NHL**	66	6	15	21	7	14	21	89	....	....	....	....	....	....	....	....	....	....	6	0	1	1	8	....	....	....
1962-63	**New York Rangers**	**NHL**	70	5	20	25	6	20	26	55	....	....	....	....	....	....	....	....	....	....	....	....	....	....	....	....	....	....
1963-64	**New York Rangers**	**NHL**	70	5	31	36	6	33	39	75	....	....	....	....	....	....	....	....	....	....	....	....	....	....	....	....	....	....
1964-65	**New York Rangers**	**NHL**	68	2	20	22	2	20	22	63	....	....	....	....	....	....	....	....	....	....	....	....	....	....	....	....	....	....
1965-66	**New York Rangers**	**NHL**	70	4	29	33	4	28	32	92	....	....	....	....	....	....	....	....	....	....	....	....	....	....	....	....	....	....
1966-67	**New York Rangers**	**NHL**	70	12	28	40	14	27	41	54	....	....	....	....	....	....	....	....	....	....	4	0	0	0	4	....	....	....
1967-68	**New York Rangers**	**NHL**	74	5	24	29	6	24	30	62	1	0	2	220	2.3	102	17	99	26	12	6	1	0	1	0	1	0	1
1968-69	**New York Rangers**	**NHL**	56	4	7	11	4	6	10	36	1	0	1	140	2.9	63	13	59	11	2	2	0	0	0	0	0	0	0
1969-70	**Oakland Seals**	**NHL**	55	4	16	20	4	15	19	52	3	0	3	147	2.7	57	15	75	19	–14	4	0	1	1	2	0	0	0
1970-71	**California Golden Seals**	**NHL**	28	0	9	9	0	7	7	14	0	0	0	51	0.0	17	4	44	11	–20	....	....	....	....	....	....	....	....
	Los Angeles Kings	**NHL**	18	3	8	11	3	7	10	4	1	0	0	33	9.1	25	5	23	4	1	....	....	....	....	....	....	....	....
1971-72	**Los Angeles Kings**	**NHL**	77	1	17	18	1	15	16	53	0	0	0	138	0.7	83	5	139	27	–34	....	....	....	....	....	....	....	....
1972-73	**Los Angeles Kings**	**NHL**	73	4	11	15	4	9	13	28	0	0	0	97	4.1	64	4	68	4	–4	....	....	....	....	....	....	....	....

Season	Club	League	GP	G	A	Pts	AG	AA	APts	PIM	PP	SH	GW	S	%	TGF	PGF	TGA	PGA	+/-	GP	G	A	Pts	PIM	PP	SH	GW
			REGULAR SEASON																		PLAYOFFS							
1973-74	New York-Jersey Knights	WHA	65	3	23	26	....	....	....	24	....	....	....	....	....	....	....	....	....	....	....	....	....	....	....	....	....	....
1974-75	San Diego Mariners	WHA	74	4	10	14	....	....	....	28	....	....	....	....	....	....	....	....	....	....	5	1	0	1	10	....	....	....
1975-76	Calgary Cowboys	WHA	31	0	3	3	....	....	....	6	....	....	....	....	....	....	....	....	....	....	2	0	0	0	2	....	....	....
	NHL Totals		**1411**	**94**	**324**	**418**	**110**	**324**	**434**	**1298**	....	....	....	....	....	....	....	....	....		**38**	**3**	**3**	**6**	**32**	....	....	....
	Other Major League Totals		170	7	36	43	....	....	....	58	....	....	....	....	....	....	....	....	....	....	7	1	0	1	12	....	....	....

• Brother of Ron • NHL First All-Star Team (1967) • Won James Norris Trophy (1967) • Played in NHL All-Star Game (1954, 1963, 1964, 1965, 1967, 1968, 1970)

Traded to **Oakland** by **NY Rangers** for cash, June 10, 1969. Traded to **LA Kings** by **California** for cash, February 5, 1971. Selected by **NY Raiders** (WHA) in 1972 WHA General Player Draft, February 12, 1972. Transferred to **San Diego** (WHA) after **New York-Jersey** (WHA) franchise relocated, April 30, 1974. Signed as a free agent by **Calgary** (WHA), January, 1976.

• HOWSE, Don

Donald Gordon LW – L. 6', 182 lbs. b: Grand Falls, Nfld., 7/28/1952.

Season	Club	League	GP	G	A	Pts	AG	AA	APts	PIM	PP	SH	GW	S	%	TGF	PGF	TGA	PGA	+/-	GP	G	A	Pts	PIM	PP	SH	GW
1968-69	Grand Falls Cataracts	Nfld-Jr.	STATISTICS NOT AVAILABLE																									
1969-70	Ottawa 67's	OHA-Jr.	50	3	3	6	....	....	....	4	....	....	....	....	....	....	....	....	....	....	....	....	....	....	....	....	....	....
1970-71	Ottawa 67's	OMJHL	58	5	12	17	....	....	....	4	....	....	....	....	....	....	....	....	....	....	....	....	....	....	....	....	....	....
1971-72	Grand Falls Flyers	Nfld-Sr.	27	23	18	41	....	....	....	18	....	....	....	....	....	....	....	....	....	....	13	10	16	26	9	....	....	....
1972-73	Greensboro Generals	EHL	64	35	54	89	....	....	....	39	....	....	....	....	....	....	....	....	....	....	7	0	2	2	0	....	....	....
1973-74	Nova Scotia Voyageurs	AHL	40	6	12	18	....	....	....	2	....	....	....	....	....	....	....	....	....	....	5	0	3	3	9	....	....	....
1974-75	Nova Scotia Voyageurs	AHL	68	30	43	73	....	....	....	50	....	....	....	....	....	....	....	....	....	....	6	1	1	2	2	....	....	....
1975-76	Nova Scotia Voyageurs	AHL	68	24	36	60	....	....	....	34	....	....	....	....	....	....	....	....	....	....	9	2	5	7	9	....	....	....
1976-77	Nova Scotia Voyageurs	AHL	58	13	24	37	....	....	....	39	....	....	....	....	....	....	....	....	....	....	12	2	3	5	8	....	....	....
1977-78	Nova Scotia Voyageurs	AHL	48	7	22	29	....	....	....	12	....	....	....	....	....	....	....	....	....	....	11	1	3	4	18	....	....	....
1978-79	Nova Scotia Voyageurs	AHL	58	19	15	34	....	....	....	65	....	....	....	....	....	....	....	....	....	....	10	4	3	7	6	....	....	....
1979-80	Binghamton Dusters	AHL	38	12	30	42	....	....	....	32	....	....	....	....	....	....	....	....	....	....	....	....	....	....	....	....	....	....
	Los Angeles Kings	**NHL**	**33**	**2**	**5**	**7**	**2**	**4**	**6**	**6**	**0**	**0**	**0**	**46**	**4.3**	**10**	**1**	**36**	**11**	**–16**	**2**	**0**	**0**	**0**	**0**	**0**	**0**	**0**
1980-81	Houston Apollos	CHL	33	5	9	14	....	....	....	27	....	....	....	....	....	....	....	....	....	....	....	....	....	....	....	....	....	....
	Hershey Bears	AHL	37	9	10	19	....	....	....	22	....	....	....	....	....	....	....	....	....	....	10	1	4	5	11	....	....	....
1981-82	Port-aux-Basques Mariners	Nfld-Sr.	STATISTICS NOT AVAILABLE																									
	Stephenville Jets	Nfld-Sr.	PLAYER/COACH – STATISTICS UNAVAILABLE																									
	NHL Totals		**33**	**2**	**5**	**7**	**2**	**4**	**6**	**6**	**0**	**0**	**0**	**46**	**4.3**	**10**	**1**	**36**	**11**		**2**	**0**	**0**	**0**	**0**	**0**	**0**	**0**

Nfld-Sr. Rookie of the Year (1972)

Signed as a free agent by **Montreal**, June, 1973. Signed as a free agent by **LA Kings**, October, 1979.

• HOWSON, Scott

Donald Scott C – R. 5'11", 160 lbs. b: Toronto, Ont., 4/9/1960.

Season	Club	League	GP	G	A	Pts	AG	AA	APts	PIM	PP	SH	GW	S	%	TGF	PGF	TGA	PGA	+/-	GP	G	A	Pts	PIM	PP	SH	GW
1977-78	North York Rangers	OJHL	55	27	31	58	....	....	....	30	....	....	....	....	....	....	....	....	....	....	....	....	....	....	....	....	....	....
1978-79	Kingston Canadians	OMJHL	58	27	47	74	....	....	....	45	....	....	....	....	....	....	....	....	....	....	11	0	10	10	12	....	....	....
1979-80	Kingston Canadians	OMJHL	68	38	50	88	....	....	....	52	....	....	....	....	....	....	....	....	....	....	3	0	4	4	0	....	....	....
1980-81	Kingston Canadians	OMJHL	66	57	83	140	....	....	....	53	....	....	....	....	....	....	....	....	....	....	14	9	10	19	2	....	....	....
1981-82	Indianapolis Checkers	CHL	8	2	1	3	....	....	....	5	....	....	....	....	....	....	....	....	....	....	....	....	....	....	....	....	....	....
	Toledo Goaldiggers	IHL	71	55	65	120	....	....	....	14	....	....	....	....	....	....	....	....	....	....	12	10	9	19	6	....	....	....
1982-83	Indianapolis Checkers	CHL	67	34	40	74	....	....	....	22	....	....	....	....	....	....	....	....	....	....	13	12	9	21	21	....	....	....
1983-84	Indianapolis Checkers	CHL	71	34	34	68	....	....	....	40	....	....	....	....	....	....	....	....	....	....	7	1	3	4	2	....	....	....
1984-85	**New York Islanders**	**NHL**	**8**	**4**	**1**	**5**	**3**	**1**	**4**	**2**	**1**	**0**	**0**	**6**	**66.7**	**6**	**1**	**1**	**0**	**4**	....	....	....	....	....	....	....	....
	Springfield Indians	AHL	57	20	40	60	....	....	....	31	....	....	....	....	....	....	....	....	....	....	4	1	3	4	2	....	....	....
1985-86	**New York Islanders**	**NHL**	**10**	**1**	**2**	**3**	**1**	**1**	**2**	**2**	**0**	**0**	**0**	**8**	**12.5**	**4**	**0**	**2**	**0**	**2**	....	....	....	....	....	....	....	....
	Springfield Indians	AHL	53	15	19	34	....	....	....	10	....	....	....	....	....	....	....	....	....	....	....	....	....	....	....	....	....	....
	NHL Totals		**18**	**5**	**3**	**8**	**4**	**2**	**6**	**4**	**1**	**0**	**0**	**14**	**35.7**	**10**	**1**	**3**	**0**		....	....	....	....	....	....	....	....

Won Garry F. Longman Memorial Trophy (Top Rookie - IHL) (1982)

Signed as a free agent by **NY Islanders**, August 25, 1981.

• HOYDA, Dave

David Allan LW – L. 6'1", 205 lbs. b: Edmonton, Alta., 5/20/1957. Philadelphia's 3rd, 53rd overall, in 1977.

Season	Club	League	GP	G	A	Pts	AG	AA	APts	PIM	PP	SH	GW	S	%	TGF	PGF	TGA	PGA	+/-	GP	G	A	Pts	PIM	PP	SH	GW
1973-74	Edmonton Mets	AJHL	28	0	1	1	....	....	....	56	....	....	....	....	....	....	....	....	....	....	....	....	....	....	....	....	....	....
1974-75	Spruce Grove Mets	AJHL	59	25	31	56	....	....	....	141	....	....	....	....	....	....	....	....	....	....	12	7	6	13	42	....	....	....
	Edmonton Oil Kings	WCJHL	1	0	0	0	....	....	....	2	....	....	....	....	....	....	....	....	....	....	....	....	....	....	....	....	....	....
	Spruce Grove Mets	Cen-Cup	....	....	....	....	....	....	....	....	....	....	....	....	....	....	....	....	....	....	....	....	....	....	....	....	....	....
1975-76	Spruce Grove Mets	AJHL	4	3	3	6	....	....	....	37	....	....	....	....	....	....	....	....	....	....	....	....	....	....	....	....	....	....
	Edmonton Oil Kings	WCJHL	43	5	18	23	....	....	....	170	....	....	....	....	....	....	....	....	....	....	5	0	1	1	23	....	....	....
1976-77	Portland Winterhawks	WCJHL	61	16	26	42	....	....	....	220	....	....	....	....	....	....	....	....	....	....	10	7	2	9	22	....	....	....
1977-78	**Philadelphia Flyers**	**NHL**	**41**	**1**	**3**	**4**	**1**	**2**	**3**	**119**	**0**	**0**	**0**	**8**	**12.5**	**7**	**0**	**12**	**0**	**–5**	**9**	**0**	**0**	**0**	**17**	**0**	**0**	**0**
	Maine Mariners	AHL	31	4	5	9	....	....	....	112	....	....	....	....	....	....	....	....	....	....	....	....	....	....	....	....	....	....
1978-79	**Philadelphia Flyers**	**NHL**	**67**	**3**	**13**	**16**	**3**	**9**	**12**	**138**	**0**	**0**	**0**	**37**	**8.1**	**28**	**0**	**26**	**0**	**2**	**3**	**0**	**0**	**0**	**0**	**0**	**0**	**0**
1979-80	**Winnipeg Jets**	**NHL**	**15**	**1**	**1**	**2**	**1**	**1**	**2**	**35**	**0**	**0**	**0**	**7**	**14.3**	**2**	**0**	**6**	**0**	**–4**	....	....	....	....	....	....	....	....
	Tulsa Oilers	CHL	32	11	6	17	....	....	....	89	....	....	....	....	....	....	....	....	....	....	....	....	....	....	....	....	....	....
1980-81	**Winnipeg Jets**	**NHL**	**9**	**1**	**0**	**1**	**1**	**0**	**1**	**7**	**0**	**0**	**0**	**2**	**50.0**	**3**	**0**	**3**	**0**	**0**	....	....	....	....	....	....	....	....
	Tulsa Oilers	CHL	42	13	22	35	....	....	....	118	....	....	....	....	....	....	....	....	....	....	....	....	....	....	....	....	....	....
	NHL Totals		**132**	**6**	**17**	**23**	**6**	**12**	**18**	**299**	**0**	**0**	**0**	**54**	**11.1**	**40**	**0**	**47**	**0**		**12**	**0**	**0**	**0**	**17**	**0**	**0**	**0**

Claimed by **Winnipeg** from **Philadelphia** in Expansion Draft, June 13, 1979.

• HRDINA, Jan

C – R. 6', 197 lbs. b: Hradec Kralove, Czech., 2/5/1976. Pittsburgh's 4th, 128th overall, in 1995.

Season	Club	League	GP	G	A	Pts	AG	AA	APts	PIM	PP	SH	GW	S	%	TGF	PGF	TGA	PGA	+/-	GP	G	A	Pts	PIM	PP	SH	GW
1993-94	HC Stadion Kralove	Czech-Jr.	10	1	6	7	....	....	....	0	....	....	....	....	....	....	....	....	....	....	....	....	....	....	....	....	....	....
	HC Stadion Kralove	Czech-Rep	23	1	5	6	....	....	....	....	....	....	....	....	....	....	....	....	....	....	4	0	1	1	....	....	....	....
	Czech-Republic	EJC-A	5	1	1	2	....	....	....	0	....	....	....	....	....	....	....	....	....	....	....	....	....	....	....	....	....	....
1994-95	Seattle Thunderbirds	WHL	69	41	59	100	....	....	....	79	....	....	....	....	....	....	....	....	....	....	4	0	1	1	8	....	....	....
	Czech-Republic	WJC-A	7	2	1	3	....	....	....	4	....	....	....	....	....	....	....	....	....	....	....	....	....	....	....	....	....	....
1995-96	Seattle Thunderbirds	WHL	30	19	28	47	....	....	....	37	....	....	....	....	....	....	....	....	....	....	....	....	....	....	....	....	....	....
	Spokane Chiefs	WHL	18	10	16	26	....	....	....	25	....	....	....	....	....	....	....	....	....	....	18	5	14	19	49	....	....	....
1996-97	Cleveland Lumberjacks	IHL	68	23	31	54	....	....	....	82	....	....	....	....	....	....	....	....	....	....	13	1	2	3	8	....	....	....
1997-98	Syracuse Crunch	AHL	72	20	24	44	....	....	....	82	....	....	....	....	....	....	....	....	....	....	5	1	3	4	10	....	....	....
1998-99	**Pittsburgh Penguins**	**NHL**	**82**	**13**	**29**	**42**	**15**	**28**	**43**	**40**	**3**	**0**	**2**	**94**	**13.8**	**60**	**18**	**56**	**12**	**–2**	**13**	**4**	**1**	**5**	**12**	**1**	**0**	**1**
99-2000	**Pittsburgh Penguins**	**NHL**	**70**	**13**	**33**	**46**	**15**	**31**	**46**	**43**	**3**	**0**	**1**	**84**	**15.5**	**65**	**11**	**59**	**18**	**13**	**9**	**4**	**8**	**12**	**2**	**1**	**0**	**0**
	NHL Totals		**152**	**26**	**62**	**88**	**30**	**59**	**89**	**83**	**6**	**0**	**3**	**178**	**14.6**	**125**	**29**	**115**	**30**		**22**	**8**	**9**	**17**	**14**	**2**	**0**	**1**

• HRDINA, Jiri

C – L. 6', 195 lbs. b: Prague, Czech., 1/5/1958. Calgary's 8th, 159th overall, in 1984.

Season	Club	League	GP	G	A	Pts	AG	AA	APts	PIM	PP	SH	GW	S	%	TGF	PGF	TGA	PGA	+/-	GP	G	A	Pts	PIM	PP	SH	GW
1964-1977	Autoskoda Mlada Bodes	Czech-Jr.	STATISTICS NOT AVAILABLE																									
1977-78	Sparta CKD Praha	Czech-Jr.	35	6	8	14	....	....	....	20	....	....	....	....	....	....	....	....	....	....	....	....	....	....	....	....	....	....
	Czechoslovakia	WJC-A	6	1	3	4	....	....	....	0	....	....	....	....	....	....	....	....	....	....	....	....	....	....	....	....	....	....
1978-79	Sparta CKD Praha	Czech-2	39	7	8	15	....	....	....	18	....	....	....	....	....	....	....	....	....	....	....	....	....	....	....	....	....	....
1979-80	Sparta CKD Praha	Czech-2	44	7	7	14	....	....	....	24	....	....	....	....	....	....	....	....	....	....	....	....	....	....	....	....	....	....
1980-81	Sparta CKD Praha	Czech.	42	14	20	34	....	....	....	54	....	....	....	....	....	....	....	....	....	....	....	....	....	....	....	....	....	....
1981-82	Dukla Trencin	Czech.	44	11	27	38	....	....	....	36	....	....	....	....	....	....	....	....	....	....	....	....	....	....	....	....	....	....
	Czechoslovakia	WEC-A	9	1	0	1	....	....	....	4	....	....	....	....	....	....	....	....	....	....	....	....	....	....	....	....	....	....
1982-83	Dukla Trencin	Czech-2	36	40	24	64	....	....	....	....	....	....	....	....	....	....	....	....	....	....	....	....	....	....	....	....	....	....
	Czechoslovakia	WEC-A	9	1	0	1	....	....	....	4	....	....	....	....	....	....	....	....	....	....	....	....	....	....	....	....	....	....
1983-84	Sparta CKD Praha	Czech.	44	16	*33	49	....	....	....	28	....	....	....	....	....	....	....	....	....	....	....	....	....	....	....	....	....	....
	Czechoslovakia	Olympics	7	4	6	10	....	....	....	10	....	....	....	....	....	....	....	....	....	....	....	....	....	....	....	....	....	....
1984-85	Czechoslovakia	Can-Cup	5	0	1	1	....	....	....	4	....	....	....	....	....	....	....	....	....	....	....	....	....	....	....	....	....	....
	Sparta CKD Praha	Czech.	44	18	19	37	....	....	....	30	....	....	....	....	....	....	....	....	....	....	....	....	....	....	....	....	....	....
	Czechoslovakia	WEC-A	10	2	2	4	....	....	....	4	....	....	....	....	....	....	....	....	....	....	....	....	....	....	....	....	....	....

			REGULAR SEASON																		PLAYOFFS							
Season	**Club**	**League**	**GP**	**G**	**A**	**Pts**	**AG**	**AA**	**APts**	**PIM**	**PP**	**SH**	**GW**	**S**	**%**	**TGF**	**PGF**	**TGA**	**PGA**	**+/–**	**GP**	**G**	**A**	**Pts**	**PIM**	**PP**	**SH**	**GW**
1985-86	Sparta CKD Praha	Czech.	34	26	19	45				30											6	2	2	4				
	Czechoslovakia	WEC-A	10	7	5	12				14																		
1986-87	Sparta CKD Praha	Czech.	31	18	18	36				50											6	2	5	7				
	Czechoslovakia	WEC-A	10	3	3	6				6																		
1987-88	Czechoslovakia	Can-Cup	6	1	2	3				0																		
	Sparta CKD Praha	Czech.	22	7	15	22				30																		
	Czechoslovakia	Olympics	8	2	5	7				4																		
	Calgary Flames	**NHL**	**9**	**2**	**5**	**7**	**2**	**4**	**6**	**2**	**0**	**0**	**0**	**13**	**15.4**	**11**	**1**	**3**	**0**	**7**	**1**	**0**	**0**	**0**	**0**	**0**	**0**	**0**
1988-89♦	**Calgary Flames**	**NHL**	**70**	**22**	**32**	**54**	**19**	**23**	**42**	**26**	**6**	**0**	**2**	**147**	**15.0**	**85**	**37**	**29**	**0**	**19**	**4**	**0**	**0**	**0**	**0**	**0**	**0**	**0**
1989-90	Calgary Flames	Fr-Tour	3	1	0	1				0																		
	Calgary Flames	**NHL**	**64**	**12**	**18**	**30**	**10**	**13**	**23**	**31**	**0**	**0**	**3**	**96**	**12.5**	**48**	**7**	**33**	**2**	**10**	**6**	**0**	**1**	**1**	**2**	**0**	**0**	**0**
	Czechoslovakia	WEC-A	9	1	5	6				8																		
1990-91	**Calgary Flames**	**NHL**	**14**	**0**	**3**	**3**	**0**	**2**	**2**	**4**	**0**	**0**	**0**	**8**	**0.0**	**5**	**0**	**9**	**0**	**–4**								
♦	**Pittsburgh Penguins**	**NHL**	**37**	**6**	**14**	**20**	**5**	**11**	**16**	**13**	**1**	**1**	**0**	**58**	**10.3**	**34**	**7**	**32**	**3**	**–2**	**14**	**2**	**2**	**4**	**6**	**0**	**0**	**1**
1991-92♦	**Pittsburgh Penguins**	**NHL**	**56**	**3**	**13**	**16**	**3**	**10**	**13**	**16**	**0**	**0**	**1**	**51**	**5.9**	**31**	**0**	**30**	**3**	**4**	**21**	**0**	**2**	**2**	**16**	**0**	**0**	**0**
	NHL Totals		**250**	**45**	**85**	**130**	**39**	**63**	**102**	**92**	**7**	**1**	**6**	**373**	**12.1**	**214**	**52**	**136**	**8**		**46**	**2**	**5**	**7**	**24**	**0**	**0**	**1**

Traded to **Pittsburgh** by **Calgary** for Jim Kyte, December 13, 1990.

• HRECHKOSY, Dave

David John LW – L. 6'2", 195 lbs. b: Winnipeg, Man., 11/1/1951.

Season	Club	League	GP	G	A	Pts	AG	AA	APts	PIM	PP	SH	GW	S	%	TGF	PGF	TGA	PGA	+/–	GP	G	A	Pts	PIM	PP	SH	GW
1969-70	West Kildonen North Stars	MJHL	48	28	15	43				36																		
	Dauphin Kings	Mem-Cup	5	1	1	2				2																		
1970-71	Winnipeg Jets	WCJHL	57	16	21	37				70											12	4	3	7	24			
1971-72	New Haven Blades	EHL	75	31	34	65				66											7	4	5	9	16			
	Providence Reds	AHL	7	3	0	3				2																		
1972-73	Rochester Americans	AHL	70	15	24	39				48											4	0	2	2	8			
1973-74	**California Golden Seals**	**NHL**	**2**	**0**	**0**	**0**	**0**	**0**	**0**	**0**	**0**	**0**	**0**	**3**	**0.0**	**1**	**0**	**0**	**0**	**1**								
	Salt Lake Golden Eagles	WHL	78	36	35	71				58											5	2	1	3	10			
1974-75	**California Golden Seals**	**NHL**	**72**	**29**	**14**	**43**	**25**	**10**	**35**	**25**	**8**	**2**	**6**	**178**	**16.3**	**56**	**12**	**63**	**2**	**–17**								
1975-76	**California Golden Seals**	**NHL**	**38**	**9**	**5**	**14**	**8**	**4**	**12**	**14**	**4**	**0**	**1**	**75**	**12.0**	**26**	**10**	**31**	**0**	**–15**								
	Salt Lake Golden Eagles	CHL	16	8	3	11				6																		
	St. Louis Blues	**NHL**	**13**	**3**	**3**	**6**	**3**	**2**	**5**	**0**	**1**	**0**	**0**	**20**	**15.0**	**12**	**4**	**6**	**0**	**2**	**3**	**1**	**0**	**1**	**2**	**0**	**0**	**0**
1976-77	**St. Louis Blues**	**NHL**	**15**	**1**	**2**	**3**	**1**	**2**	**3**	**2**	**0**	**0**	**0**	**9**	**11.1**	**5**	**1**	**4**	**0**	**0**								
	Kansas City Blues	CHL	45	9	12	21				4											10	3	3	6	0			
1977-78	Salt Lake Golden Eagles	CHL	55	5	12	17				11																		
1978-79	Saginaw Gears	IHL	2	0	2	2				0																		
	New Haven Nighthawks	AHL	61	15	20	35				21											10	6	7	13	8			
1979-80	New Haven Nighthawks	AHL	1	0	0	0				0																		
	NHL Totals		**140**	**42**	**24**	**66**	**37**	**18**	**55**	**41**	**13**	**2**	**7**	**285**	**14.7**	**100**	**27**	**104**	**2**		**3**	**1**	**0**	**1**	**2**	**0**	**0**	**0**

Traded to **California** by **NY Rangers** with Gary Coalter to complete transaction that sent Bert Marshall to NY Rangers (March 4, 1973), May 17, 1973. Traded to **St. Louis** by **California** for St. Louis' 5th round choice (Cal Sandbeck) in 1976 Amateur Draft and California's 3rd round choice (previously acquired, California selected Reg Kerr) in 1977 Amateur Draft, March 9, 1976.

• HRKAC, Tony

Anthony J. C – L. 5'11", 170 lbs. b: Thunder Bay, Ont., 7/7/1966. St. Louis' 2nd, 32nd overall, in 1984.

Season	Club	League	GP	G	A	Pts	AG	AA	APts	PIM	PP	SH	GW	S	%	TGF	PGF	TGA	PGA	+/–	GP	G	A	Pts	PIM	PP	SH	GW
1982-83	Thunder Bay Kings	TBAHA	STATISTICS NOT AVAILABLE																									
1983-84	Orillia Travelways	OJHL	42	*52	54	*106				20																		
1984-85	University of North Dakota	WCHA	36	18	36	54				16																		
1985-86	Canada	Nat-Team	62	19	30	49				36																		
1986-87	University of North Dakota	WCHA	48	46	79	125				48																		
	St. Louis Blues	**NHL**																			**3**	**0**	**0**	**0**	**0**	**0**	**0**	**0**
1987-88	**St. Louis Blues**	**NHL**	**67**	**11**	**37**	**48**	**9**	**26**	**35**	**22**	**2**	**1**	**3**	**86**	**12.8**	**60**	**16**	**63**	**24**	**5**	**10**	**6**	**1**	**7**	**4**	**3**	**1**	**1**
1988-89	**St. Louis Blues**	**NHL**	**70**	**17**	**28**	**45**	**14**	**20**	**34**	**8**	**5**	**0**	**1**	**133**	**12.8**	**66**	**27**	**81**	**32**	**–10**	**4**	**1**	**1**	**2**	**0**	**0**	**0**	**1**
1989-90	**St. Louis Blues**	**NHL**	**28**	**5**	**12**	**17**	**4**	**9**	**13**	**8**	**1**	**0**	**0**	**41**	**12.2**	**28**	**11**	**16**	**0**	**1**								
	Quebec Nordiques	**NHL**	**22**	**4**	**8**	**12**	**3**	**6**	**9**	**2**	**2**	**0**	**0**	**29**	**13.8**	**17**	**9**	**13**	**0**	**–5**								
	Halifax Citadels	AHL	20	12	21	33				4											6	5	9	14	4			
1990-91	**Quebec Nordiques**	**NHL**	**70**	**16**	**32**	**48**	**15**	**24**	**39**	**16**	**6**	**0**	**0**	**122**	**13.1**	**69**	**27**	**68**	**4**	**–22**								
	Halifax Citadels	AHL	3	4	1	5				2																		
1991-92	**San Jose Sharks**	**NHL**	**22**	**2**	**10**	**12**	**2**	**8**	**10**	**4**	**0**	**0**	**0**	**31**	**6.5**	**19**	**8**	**15**	**2**	**–2**								
	Chicago Blackhawks	**NHL**	**18**	**1**	**2**	**3**	**1**	**2**	**3**	**6**	**0**	**0**	**0**	**22**	**4.5**	**11**	**1**	**8**	**2**	**4**	**3**	**0**	**0**	**0**	**2**	**0**	**0**	**0**
1992-93	Indianapolis Ice	IHL	80	45	*87	*132				70											5	0	2	2	2			
1993-94	**St. Louis Blues**	**NHL**	**36**	**6**	**5**	**11**	**6**	**4**	**10**	**8**	**1**	**1**	**1**	**43**	**14.0**	**13**	**3**	**25**	**4**	**–11**	**4**	**0**	**0**	**0**	**0**	**0**	**0**	**0**
	Peoria Rivermen	IHL	45	30	51	81				25											1	1	2	3	0			
1994-95	Milwaukee Admirals	IHL	71	24	67	91				26											15	4	9	13	16			
1995-96	Milwaukee Admirals	IHL	43	14	28	42				18											5	1	3	4	4			
1996-97	Milwaukee Admirals	IHL	81	27	61	88				20											3	1	1	2	2			
1997-98	**Dallas Stars**	**NHL**	**13**	**5**	**3**	**8**	**6**	**3**	**9**	**0**	**3**	**0**	**0**	**14**	**35.7**	**9**	**5**	**4**	**0**	**0**								
	Michigan K-Wings	IHL	20	7	15	22				6																		
	Edmonton Oilers	**NHL**	**36**	**8**	**11**	**19**	**9**	**11**	**20**	**10**	**4**	**0**	**1**	**43**	**18.6**	**25**	**10**	**12**	**0**	**3**	**12**	**0**	**3**	**3**	**2**	**0**	**0**	**0**
1998-99♦	**Dallas Stars**	**NHL**	**69**	**13**	**14**	**27**	**15**	**13**	**28**	**26**	**2**	**0**	**2**	**67**	**19.4**	**31**	**8**	**21**	**0**	**2**	**5**	**0**	**2**	**2**	**4**	**0**	**0**	**0**
99-2000	**New York Islanders**	**NHL**	**7**	**0**	**2**	**2**	**0**	**2**	**2**	**0**	**0**	**0**	**0**	**2**	**0.0**	**4**	**1**	**9**	**5**	**–1**								
	Mighty Ducks of Anaheim	**NHL**	**60**	**4**	**7**	**11**	**4**	**6**	**10**	**8**	**1**	**0**	**0**	**37**	**10.8**	**18**	**2**	**18**	**0**	**–2**								
	NHL Totals		**518**	**92**	**171**	**263**	**88**	**134**	**222**	**118**	**27**	**2**	**8**	**670**	**13.7**	**370**	**128**	**353**	**73**		**41**	**7**	**7**	**14**	**12**	**3**	**1**	**2**

WCHA First All-Star Team (1987) • NCAA West First All-American Team (1987) • NCAA Championship All-Tournament Team (1987) • NCAA Championship Tournament MVP (1987) • Won 1987 Hobey Baker Memorial Award (Top U.S. Collegiate Player) (1987) • Won James Gatschene Memorial Trophy (MVP - IHL) (1993) • Won Leo P. Lamoureux Memorial Trophy (Leading Scorer - IHL) (1993) • IHL First All-Star Team (1993)

Traded to **Quebec** by **St. Louis** with Greg Millen for Jeff Brown, December 13, 1989. Traded to **San Jose** by **Quebec** for Greg Paslawski, May 31, 1991. Traded to **Chicago** by **San Jose** for Chicago's 6th round choice (Fredrik Oduya) in 1993 Entry Draft, February 7, 1992. Signed as a free agent by **St. Louis**, July 30, 1993. Signed as a free agent by **Dallas**, August 12, 1997. Claimed on waivers by **Edmonton** from **Dallas**, January 6, 1998. Traded to **Pittsburgh** by **Edmonton** with Bobby Dollas for Josef Beranek, June 16, 1998. Claimed by **Nashville** from **Pittsburgh** in Expansion Draft, June 26, 1998. Traded to **Dallas** by **Nashville** for future considerations, July 9, 1998. Signed as a free agent by **NY Islanders**, July 29, 1999. Traded to **Anaheim** by **NY Islanders** with Dean Malkoc for Ted Drury, October 29, 1999.

• HRYCUIK, Jim

James Peter C – L. 5'10", 180 lbs. b: Rosthern, Sask., 10/7/1949.

Season	Club	League	GP	G	A	Pts	AG	AA	APts	PIM	PP	SH	GW	S	%	TGF	PGF	TGA	PGA	+/–	GP	G	A	Pts	PIM	PP	SH	GW
1970-71	Moose Jaw Canucks	SJHL	STATISTICS NOT AVAILABLE																									
1971-72	Regina Caps	ASHL	38	21	*39	*60				36																		
1972-73	Hershey Bears	AHL	36	3	7	10				22																		
	Fort Wayne Komets	IHL	25	12	11	23				35											9	7	5	12	6			
1973-74	Hershey Bears	AHL	74	26	49	75				75											14	3	11	14	28			
1974-75	**Washington Capitals**	**NHL**	**21**	**5**	**5**	**10**	**4**	**4**	**8**	**12**	**1**	**0**	**0**	**29**	**17.2**	**11**	**4**	**19**	**0**	**–12**								
	Richmond Robins	AHL	7	4	3	7				2																		
1975-76	Richmond Robins	AHL	56	6	13	19				43											8	3	1	4	0			
	NHL Totals		**21**	**5**	**5**	**10**	**4**	**4**	**8**	**12**	**1**	**0**	**0**	**29**	**17.2**	**11**	**4**	**19**	**0**									

Signed as a free agent by **Hershey** (AHL), September, 1972. Claimed by **Washington** from **Hershey** (AHL) in Intra-League Draft, June 12, 1974.

• HRYNEWICH, Tim

LW – L. 5'11", 190 lbs. b: Leamington, Ont., 10/2/1963. Pittsburgh's 2nd, 38th overall, in 1982.

Season	Club	League	GP	G	A	Pts	AG	AA	APts	PIM	PP	SH	GW	S	%	TGF	PGF	TGA	PGA	+/–	GP	G	A	Pts	PIM	PP	SH	GW
1979-80	Petrolia Jets	OJHL-B	41	29	25	54				50																		
1980-81	Sudbury Wolves	OMJHL	65	25	17	42				104																		
1981-82	Sudbury Wolves	OHL	64	29	41	70				144																		
1982-83	Sudbury Wolves	OHL	23	21	16	37				65																		
	Pittsburgh Penguins	**NHL**	**30**	**2**	**3**	**5**	**2**	**2**	**4**	**48**	**0**	**0**	**0**	**22**	**9.1**	**9**	**0**	**15**	**0**	**–6**								
	Baltimore Skipjacks	AHL	9	2	1	3				6																		

			REGULAR SEASON																		PLAYOFFS							
Season	Club	League	GP	G	A	Pts	AG	AA	APts	PIM	PP	SH	GW	S	%	TGF	PGF	TGA	PGA	+/–	GP	G	A	Pts	PIM	PP	SH	GW
1983-84	**Pittsburgh Penguins**	**NHL**	**25**	**4**	**5**	**9**	**3**	**3**	**6**	**34**	**0**	**0**	**2**	**24**	**16.7**	**18**	**1**	**27**	**0**	**–10**	....	....	....	....	....	....	....	....
	Baltimore Skipjacks	AHL	52	13	17	30	....	....	....	65	....	....	....	....	....	....	....	....	....	....	....	....	....	....	....	....	....	....
1984-85	Baltimore Skipjacks	AHL	21	4	3	7	....	....	....	31	....	....	....	....	....	....	....	....	....	....	....	....	....	....	....	....	....	....
	Muskegon Mohawks	IHL	30	10	13	23	....	....	....	42	....	....	....	....	....	....	....	....	....	....	17	8	7	15	39	....	....	....
1985-86	Muskegon Lumberjacks	IHL	67	25	26	51	....	....	....	110	....	....	....	....	....	....	....	....	....	....	....	....	....	....	....	....	....	....
	Toledo Goaldiggers	IHL	13	8	13	21	....	....	....	25	....	....	....	....	....	....	....	....	....	....	....	....	....	....	....	....	....	....
1986-87	Milwaukee Admirals	IHL	82	39	37	76	....	....	....	78	....	....	....	....	....	....	....	....	....	....	6	2	3	5	2	....	....	....
1987-88	Milwaukee Admirals	IHL	28	6	8	14	....	....	....	39	....	....	....	....	....	....	....	....	....	....	....	....	....	....	....	....	....	....
	SaiPa Lappeenranta	Finland-2	21	13	5	18	....	....	....	48	....	....	....	....	....	....	....	....	....	....	....	....	....	....	....	....	....	....
1988-89	Flint Spirits	IHL	5	0	1	1	....	....	....	4	....	....	....	....	....	....	....	....	....	....	....	....	....	....	....	....	....	....
	Fort Wayne Komets	IHL	4	0	1	1	....	....	....	8	....	....	....	....	....	....	....	....	....	....	....	....	....	....	....	....	....	....
	NHL Totals		**55**	**6**	**8**	**14**	**5**	**5**	**10**	**82**	**0**	**0**	**2**	**46**	**13.0**	**27**	**1**	**42**	**0**		....	....	....	....	....	....	....	....

Traded to **Edmonton** by **Pittsburgh** with Marty McSorley and future considerations (Craig Muni, October 6, 1986) for Gilles Meloche, September 11, 1985.

• HUARD, Bill

William John LW – L. 6'1", 215 lbs. b: Welland, Ont., 6/24/1967.

Season	Club	League	GP	G	A	Pts	AG	AA	APts	PIM	PP	SH	GW	S	%	TGF	PGF	TGA	PGA	+/–	GP	G	A	Pts	PIM	PP	SH	GW
1984-85	Fort Erie Meteors	OJHL-B	41	4	9	13	....	....	....	114	....	....	....	....	....	....	....	....	....	....	....	....	....	....	....	....	....	....
1985-86	Welland Cougars	OJHL-B	28	8	17	25	....	....	....	123	....	....	....	....	....	....	....	....	....	....	....	....	....	....	....	....	....	....
	Peterborough Petes	OHL	7	1	1	2	....	....	....	2	....	....	....	....	....	....	....	....	....	....	....	....	....	....	....	....	....	....
1986-87	Peterborough Petes	OHL	61	14	11	25	....	....	....	61	....	....	....	....	....	....	....	....	....	....	12	5	2	7	19	....	....	....
1987-88	Peterborough Petes	OHL	66	28	33	61	....	....	....	132	....	....	....	....	....	....	....	....	....	....	12	7	8	15	33	....	....	....
1988-89	Carolina Thunderbirds	ECHL	40	27	21	48	....	....	....	177	....	....	....	....	....	....	....	....	....	....	10	7	2	9	70	....	....	....
1989-90	Utica Devils	AHL	27	1	7	8	....	....	....	67	....	....	....	....	....	....	....	....	....	....	5	0	1	1	33	....	....	....
	Nashville Knights	ECHL	34	24	27	51	....	....	....	212	....	....	....	....	....	....	....	....	....	....	....	....	....	....	....	....	....	....
1990-91	Utica Devils	AHL	72	11	16	27	....	....	....	359	....	....	....	....	....	....	....	....	....	....	....	....	....	....	....	....	....	....
1991-92	Utica Devils	AHL	62	9	11	20	....	....	....	233	....	....	....	....	....	....	....	....	....	....	4	1	1	2	4	....	....	....
1992-93	**Boston Bruins**	**NHL**	**2**	**0**	**0**	**0**	**0**	**0**	**0**	**0**	**0**	**0**	**0**	**0**	**0.0**	**0**	**0**	**0**	**0**	**0**	....	....	....	....	....	....	....	....
	Providence Bruins	AHL	72	18	19	37	....	....	....	302	....	....	....	....	....	....	....	....	....	....	6	3	0	3	9	....	....	....
1993-94	**Ottawa Senators**	**NHL**	**63**	**2**	**2**	**4**	**2**	**2**	**4**	**162**	**0**	**0**	**0**	**24**	**8.3**	**7**	**0**	**27**	**1**	**–19**	....	....	....	....	....	....	....	....
1994-95	**Ottawa Senators**	**NHL**	**26**	**1**	**1**	**2**	**2**	**1**	**3**	**64**	**0**	**0**	**0**	**15**	**6.7**	**6**	**0**	**8**	**0**	**–2**	....	....	....	....	....	....	....	....
	Quebec Nordiques	**NHL**	**7**	**2**	**2**	**4**	**4**	**3**	**7**	**13**	**0**	**0**	**0**	**6**	**33.3**	**5**	**0**	**3**	**0**	**2**	**1**	**0**	**0**	**0**	**0**	**0**	**0**	**0**
1995-96	**Dallas Stars**	**NHL**	**51**	**6**	**6**	**12**	**6**	**5**	**11**	**176**	**0**	**0**	**0**	**34**	**17.6**	**18**	**0**	**15**	**0**	**3**	....	....	....	....	....	....	....	....
	Michigan K-Wings	IHL	12	1	1	2	....	....	....	74	....	....	....	....	....	....	....	....	....	....	....	....	....	....	....	....	....	....
1996-97	**Dallas Stars**	**NHL**	**40**	**5**	**6**	**11**	**5**	**5**	**10**	**105**	**0**	**0**	**0**	**34**	**14.7**	**11**	**0**	**6**	**0**	**5**	....	....	....	....	....	....	....	....
1997-98	**Edmonton Oilers**	**NHL**	**30**	**0**	**1**	**1**	**0**	**1**	**1**	**72**	**0**	**0**	**0**	**12**	**0.0**	**5**	**1**	**9**	**0**	**–5**	**4**	**0**	**0**	**0**	**2**	**0**	**0**	**0**
1998-99	**Edmonton Oilers**	**NHL**	**3**	**0**	**0**	**0**	**0**	**0**	**0**	**0**	**0**	**0**	**0**	**2**	**0.0**	**0**	**0**	**0**	**0**	**0**	....	....	....	....	....	....	....	....
	Houston Aeros	IHL	38	9	5	14	....	....	....	201	....	....	....	....	....	....	....	....	....	....	10	0	0	0	8	....	....	....
99-2000	**Los Angeles Kings**	**NHL**	**1**	**0**	**0**	**0**	**0**	**0**	**0**	**2**	**0**	**0**	**0**	**0**	**0.0**	**0**	**0**	**0**	**0**	**0**	....	....	....	....	....	....	....	....
	Lowell Lock Monsters	AHL	13	2	2	4	....	....	....	65	....	....	....	....	....	....	....	....	....	....	....	....	....	....	....	....	....	....
	Orlando Solar Bears	IHL	19	4	2	6	....	....	....	85	....	....	....	....	....	....	....	....	....	....	3	0	0	0	10	....	....	....
	NHL Totals		**223**	**16**	**18**	**34**	**19**	**17**	**36**	**594**	**0**	**0**	**0**	**127**	**12.6**	**52**	**1**	**68**	**1**		**5**	**0**	**0**	**0**	**2**	**0**	**0**	**0**

Signed as a free agent by **New Jersey**, October 1, 1989. Signed as a free agent by **Boston**, December 4, 1992. Signed as a free agent by **Ottawa**, June 30, 1993. Traded to **Quebec** by **Ottawa** for the rights to Mika Stromberg and Quebec's 4th round choice (Kevin Boyd) in 1995 Entry Draft, April 7, 1995. Transferred to **Colorado** after **Quebec** franchise relocated, July 1, 1995. Claimed by **Dallas** from **Colorado** in NHL Waiver Draft, October 2, 1995. Signed as a free agent by **Edmonton**, July 22, 1997. Signed as a free agent by **Houston** (IHL), January 23, 1999. Signed as a free agent by **LA Kings**, July 19, 1999. Traded to **Atlanta** by **LA Kings** for future considerations, January 25, 2000.

• HUBER, Willie

Wilhelm Heinrich D – R. 6'5", 228 lbs. b: Strasskirchen, Germany, 1/15/1958. Detroit's 1st, 9th overall, in 1978.

Season	Club	League	GP	G	A	Pts	AG	AA	APts	PIM	PP	SH	GW	S	%	TGF	PGF	TGA	PGA	+/–	GP	G	A	Pts	PIM	PP	SH	GW
1975-76	Hamilton Fincups	OMJHL	58	2	8	10	....	....	....	64	....	....	....	....	....	....	....	....	....	....	14	2	11	13	28	....	....	....
	Hamilton Fincups	Mem-Cup	3	0	0	0	....	....	....	8	....	....	....	....	....	....	....	....	....	....	....	....	....	....	....	....	....	....
1976-77	St. Catharines Fincups	OMJHL	36	10	24	34	....	....	....	111	....	....	....	....	....	....	....	....	....	....	10	2	4	6	29	....	....	....
	Canada	WJC-A	7	1	2	3	....	....	....	13	....	....	....	....	....	....	....	....	....	....	....	....	....	....	....	....	....	....
1977-78	Hamilton Fincups	OMJHL	61	12	45	57	....	....	....	168	....	....	....	....	....	....	....	....	....	....	20	6	12	18	45	....	....	....
	Canada	WJC-A	6	0	2	2	....	....	....	2	....	....	....	....	....	....	....	....	....	....	....	....	....	....	....	....	....	....
1978-79	**Detroit Red Wings**	**NHL**	**68**	**7**	**24**	**31**	**6**	**17**	**23**	**114**	**4**	**0**	**2**	**153**	**4.6**	**87**	**38**	**79**	**5**	**–25**	....	....	....	....	....	....	....	....
	Kansas City Red Wings	CHL	10	2	7	9	....	....	....	12	....	....	....	....	....	....	....	....	....	....	....	....	....	....	....	....	....	....
1979-80	**Detroit Red Wings**	**NHL**	**76**	**17**	**23**	**40**	**14**	**17**	**31**	**164**	**4**	**2**	**2**	**197**	**8.6**	**105**	**26**	**125**	**20**	**–26**	....	....	....	....	....	....	....	....
	Adirondack Red Wings	AHL	4	1	3	4	....	....	....	2	....	....	....	....	....	....	....	....	....	....	....	....	....	....	....	....	....	....
1980-81	**Detroit Red Wings**	**NHL**	**80**	**15**	**34**	**49**	**12**	**23**	**35**	**130**	**3**	**0**	**0**	**207**	**7.2**	**138**	**42**	**158**	**34**	**–28**	....	....	....	....	....	....	....	....
	Canada	WEC-A	7	0	2	2	....	....	....	10	....	....	....	....	....	....	....	....	....	....	....	....	....	....	....	....	....	....
1981-82	**Detroit Red Wings**	**NHL**	**74**	**15**	**30**	**45**	**12**	**20**	**32**	**98**	**5**	**0**	**2**	**270**	**5.6**	**134**	**25**	**163**	**38**	**–16**	....	....	....	....	....	....	....	....
1982-83	**Detroit Red Wings**	**NHL**	**74**	**14**	**29**	**43**	**11**	**20**	**31**	**106**	**3**	**0**	**1**	**241**	**5.8**	**113**	**26**	**154**	**33**	**–34**	....	....	....	....	....	....	....	....
1983-84	**New York Rangers**	**NHL**	**42**	**9**	**14**	**23**	**7**	**10**	**17**	**60**	**4**	**1**	**1**	**92**	**9.8**	**57**	**14**	**72**	**15**	**–14**	**4**	**1**	**1**	**2**	**9**	**0**	**0**	**0**
1984-85	**New York Rangers**	**NHL**	**49**	**3**	**11**	**14**	**2**	**7**	**9**	**55**	**1**	**0**	**0**	**75**	**4.0**	**46**	**10**	**81**	**25**	**–20**	**2**	**1**	**0**	**1**	**2**	**1**	**0**	**0**
1985-86	**New York Rangers**	**NHL**	**70**	**7**	**8**	**15**	**6**	**5**	**11**	**85**	**1**	**0**	**2**	**124**	**5.6**	**62**	**13**	**93**	**33**	**–11**	**16**	**3**	**2**	**5**	**16**	**2**	**0**	**0**
1986-87	**New York Rangers**	**NHL**	**66**	**8**	**22**	**30**	**7**	**16**	**23**	**68**	**3**	**1**	**0**	**117**	**6.8**	**86**	**29**	**88**	**18**	**–13**	**6**	**0**	**2**	**2**	**6**	**0**	**0**	**0**
1987-88	**New York Rangers**	**NHL**	**11**	**1**	**3**	**4**	**1**	**2**	**3**	**14**	**0**	**0**	**0**	**18**	**5.6**	**9**	**2**	**19**	**8**	**–4**	....	....	....	....	....	....	....	....
	Vancouver Canucks	**NHL**	**35**	**4**	**10**	**14**	**3**	**7**	**10**	**40**	**2**	**0**	**0**	**79**	**5.1**	**44**	**17**	**54**	**17**	**–10**	....	....	....	....	....	....	....	....
	Philadelphia Flyers	**NHL**	**10**	**4**	**9**	**13**	**3**	**6**	**9**	**16**	**3**	**0**	**0**	**14**	**28.6**	**19**	**12**	**18**	**9**	**–2**	**5**	**0**	**0**	**0**	**2**	**0**	**0**	**0**
	NHL Totals		**655**	**104**	**217**	**321**	**84**	**150**	**234**	**950**	**33**	**4**	**10**	**1587**	**6.6**	**900**	**254**	**1104**	**255**		**33**	**5**	**5**	**10**	**35**	**3**	**0**	**0**

OMJHL Second All-Star Team (1978) • Played in NHL All-Star Game (1983)

Traded to **NY Rangers** by **Detroit** with Mike Blaisdell and Mark Osborne for Ron Duguay, Eddie Mio and Eddie Johnstone, June 13, 1983. Traded to **Vancouver** by **NY Rangers** with Larry Melynk for Michel Petit, November 4, 1987. Traded to **Philadelphia** by **Vancouver** for Paul Lawless and Vancouver's 5th round choice (previously acquired, later traded to Edmonton — Edmonton selected Peter White) in 1989 Entry Draft, March 1, 1988.

• HUBICK, Greg

Gregory Wayne D – L. 5'11", 185 lbs. b: Strasbourg, Sask., 11/12/1951. Montreal's 9th, 53rd overall, in 1971.

Season	Club	League	GP	G	A	Pts	AG	AA	APts	PIM	PP	SH	GW	S	%	TGF	PGF	TGA	PGA	+/–	GP	G	A	Pts	PIM	PP	SH	GW
1969-70	Weyburn Red Wings	SJHL	35	9	21	30	....	....	....	61	....	....	....	....	....	....	....	....	....	....	....	....	....	....	....	....	....	....
	Weyburn Red Wings	Mem-Cup	21	6	11	17	....	....	....	29	....	....	....	....	....	....	....	....	....	....	....	....	....	....	....	....	....	....
1970-71	University of Minnesota-Duluth	WCHA	31	7	15	22	....	....	....	69	....	....	....	....	....	....	....	....	....	....	....	....	....	....	....	....	....	....
1971-72	University of Minnesota-Duluth	WCHA	35	7	14	21	....	....	....	36	....	....	....	....	....	....	....	....	....	....	....	....	....	....	....	....	....	....
1972-73	Nova Scotia Voyageurs	AHL	49	6	14	20	....	....	....	17	....	....	....	....	....	....	....	....	....	....	13	2	7	9	13	....	....	....
1973-74	Nova Scotia Voyageurs	AHL	75	11	26	37	....	....	....	44	....	....	....	....	....	....	....	....	....	....	6	0	2	2	0	....	....	....
1974-75	Nova Scotia Voyageurs	AHL	74	9	27	36	....	....	....	93	....	....	....	....	....	....	....	....	....	....	6	4	1	5	0	....	....	....
1975-76	**Toronto Maple Leafs**	**NHL**	**72**	**6**	**8**	**14**	**5**	**6**	**11**	**10**	**0**	**0**	**1**	**54**	**11.1**	**24**	**1**	**31**	**8**	**0**	....	....	....	....	....	....	....	....
1976-77	Dallas Black Hawks	CHL	70	13	22	35	....	....	....	12	....	....	....	....	....	....	....	....	....	....	5	0	1	1	4	....	....	....
1977-78	Dallas Black Hawks	CHL	76	6	15	21	....	....	....	64	....	....	....	....	....	....	....	....	....	....	13	2	2	4	8	....	....	....
1978-79	Dallas Black Hawks	CHL	69	10	16	26	....	....	....	52	....	....	....	....	....	....	....	....	....	....	9	0	5	5	6	....	....	....
1979-80	**Vancouver Canucks**	**NHL**	**5**	**0**	**1**	**1**	**0**	**1**	**1**	**0**	**0**	**0**	**0**	**4**	**0.0**	**1**	**0**	**2**	**0**	**–1**	....	....	....	....	....	....	....	....
	Dallas Black Hawks	CHL	68	3	22	25	....	....	....	59	....	....	....	....	....	....	....	....	....	....	....	....	....	....	....	....	....	....
1980-81	Dallas Black Hawks	CHL	74	8	51	59	....	....	....	46	....	....	....	....	....	....	....	....	....	....	6	0	3	3	8	....	....	....
1981-82	Wichita Wind	CHL	27	0	6	6	....	....	....	26	....	....	....	....	....	....	....	....	....	....	7	1	3	4	12	....	....	....
	NHL Totals		**77**	**6**	**9**	**15**	**5**	**7**	**12**	**10**	**0**	**0**	**1**	**58**	**10.3**	**25**	**1**	**33**	**8**		....	....	....	....	....	....	....	....

CHL First All-Star Team (1979, 1981) • Named CHL's Top Defenseman (1979)

Traded to **Toronto** by **Montreal** for Doug Jarvis, June 26, 1975. Signed as a free agent by **Vancouver**, September 7, 1979.

• HUCK, Fran

Anthony Francis "Golden Hawk" C – L. 5'7", 165 lbs. b: Regina, Sask., 12/4/1945.

Season	Club	League	GP	G	A	Pts	AG	AA	APts	PIM	PP	SH	GW	S	%	TGF	PGF	TGA	PGA	+/–	GP	G	A	Pts	PIM	PP	SH	GW
1962-63	Regina Pats	SJHL	28	4	11	15	....	....	....	20	....	....	....	....	....	....	....	....	....	....	6	4	2	6	8	....	....	....
1963-64	Regina Pats	SJHL	62	*86	67	*153	....	....	....	104	....	....	....	....	....	....	....	....	....	....	19	*22	18	*40	60	....	....	....
	Estevan Bruins	Mem-Cup	5	3	0	3	....	....	....	4	....	....	....	....	....	....	....	....	....	....	....	....	....	....	....	....	....	....
	Edmonton Oil Kings	Mem-Cup	4	2	3	5	....	....	....	0	....	....	....	....	....	....	....	....	....	....	....	....	....	....	....	....	....	....

			REGULAR SEASON																		PLAYOFFS							
Season	Club	League	GP	G	A	Pts	AG	AA	APts	PIM	PP	SH	GW	S	%	TGF	PGF	TGA	PGA	+/–	GP	G	A	Pts	PIM	PP	SH	GW
1964-65	Regina Pats	SJHL	56	*77	59	136				36											12	10	13	23	18			
	Edmonton Oil Kings	Mem-Cup	10	*15	10	25				4																		
1965-66	Canada	Nat-Team	STATISTICS NOT AVAILABLE																									
	Canada	WEC-A	7	4	4	8				8																		
1966-67	Canada	Nat-Team	STATISTICS NOT AVAILABLE																									
	Canada	WEC-A	7	5	6	11				6																		
1967-68	Ottawa Nationals	OHA-Sr.	18	8	17	25				24																		
	Canada	Olympics	7	4	5	9				10																		
1968-69	Canada	Nat-Team	STATISTICS NOT AVAILABLE																									
	Canada	WEC-A	10	3	2	5				12																		
1969-70	Canada	Nat-Team	STATISTICS NOT AVAILABLE																									
	Montreal Canadiens	**NHL**	**2**	**0**	**0**	**0**	**0**	**0**	**0**	**0**	**0**	**0**	**0**	**2**	**0.0**	**0**	**0**	**0**	**0**	**0**								
	Montreal Voyageurs	AHL	2	1	2	3				0																		
1970-71	**Montreal Canadiens**	**NHL**	**5**	**1**	**2**	**3**	**1**	**2**	**3**	**0**	**0**	**0**	**0**	**8**	**12.5**	**4**	**0**	**1**	**0**	**3**								
	Montreal Voyageurs	AHL	31	12	17	29				18																		
	St. Louis Blues	**NHL**	**29**	**7**	**8**	**15**	**7**	**7**	**14**	**18**	**2**	**0**	**1**	**43**	**16.3**	**21**	**9**	**11**	**0**	**1**	**6**	**1**	**2**	**3**	**2**	**0**	**0**	**0**
1971-72	Denver Spurs	WHL	72	28	63	91				83											9	*9	4	*13	16			
1972-73	**St. Louis Blues**	**NHL**	**58**	**16**	**20**	**36**	**15**	**16**	**31**	**20**	**2**	**0**	**2**	**82**	**19.5**	**49**	**10**	**47**	**7**	**–1**	**5**	**2**	**2**	**4**	**0**	**1**	**0**	**0**
1973-74	Winnipeg Jets	WHA	74	26	48	74				68											4	0	0	0	2			
1974-75	Minnesota Fighting Saints	WHA	78	22	45	67				26											12	3	*13	16	6			
1975-76	Minnesota Fighting Saints	WHA	59	17	32	49				27																		
1976-77	ZSC Zurich	Switz-2	PLAYER/COACH – STATISTICS UNAVAILABLE																									
	Winnipeg Jets	WHA	12	2	2	4				10											7	0	2	2	6			
1977-78	Winnipeg Jets	WHA	5	0	0	0				2																		
	NHL Totals		**94**	**24**	**30**	**54**	**23**	**25**	**48**	**38**	**4**	**0**	**3**	**135**	**17.8**	**74**	**19**	**59**	**7**		**11**	**3**	**4**	**7**	**2**	**1**	**0**	**0**
	Other Major League Totals		228	67	127	194				133											23	3	15	18	14			

SJHL First All-Star Team (1964) • SJHL Second All-Star Team (1965) • WEC-A All-Star Team (1966) • WHL Second All-Star Team (1972) • Won Leader Cup (WHL - MVP) (1972)

Loaned to **Estevan** and **Edmonton** by **Regina** for Memorial Cup playoffs, April, 1963. Loaned to **Edmonton** by **Regina** for Memorial Cup playoffs, April, 1965. Signed as a free agent by **Montreal**, March, 1970. Traded to **St. Louis** by **Montreal** for St. Louis' 2nd round choice (Michel Deguise) in 1971 Amateur Draft, January 28, 1971. Selected by **Winnipeg** (WHA) in 1972 WHA General Player Draft, February 12, 1972. Traded to **Minnesota** (WHA) by **Winnipeg** (WHA) for cash, June, 1974. Signed as a free agent by **Winnipeg** (WHA) after **Minnesota** (WHA) franchise folded, June, 1976.

• HUCUL, Fred

Frederick Albert D – L. 5'10", 170 lbs. b: Tubrose, Sask., 12/4/1931.

Season	Club	League	GP	G	A	Pts	AG	AA	APts	PIM	PP	SH	GW	S	%	TGF	PGF	TGA	PGA	+/–	GP	G	A	Pts	PIM	PP	SH	GW
1948-49	Westaskiwin Canadians	EJrHL	STATISTICS NOT AVAILABLE																									
	Westaskiwin Canadians	M-Cup	3	1	2	3				14																		
1949-50	Moose Jaw Canucks	WCJHL	27	8	11	19				59											4	1	2	3	8			
1950-51	Moose Jaw Canucks	WCJHL	37	19	27	46				165																		
	Chicago Black Hawks	**NHL**	**3**	**1**	**0**	**1**	**1**	**0**	**1**	**2**																		
	Regina Caps	WCSHL	5	0	2	2				4																		
1951-52	**Chicago Black Hawks**	**NHL**	**34**	**3**	**7**	**10**	**4**	**9**	**13**	**37**																		
	St. Louis Flyers	AHL	9	2	3	5				8																		
1952-53	**Chicago Black Hawks**	**NHL**	**57**	**5**	**7**	**12**	**7**	**8**	**15**	**25**											**6**	**1**	**0**	**1**	**10**			
1953-54	**Chicago Black Hawks**	**NHL**	**27**	**0**	**3**	**3**	**0**	**4**	**4**	**19**																		
	Calgary Stampeders	WHL	15	7	4	11				12																		
	Quebec Aces	QHL	13	4	6	10				26											12	1	3	4	10			
	Quebec Aces	Ed-Cup	5	1	1	2				2																		
1954-55	Calgary Stampeders	WHL	51	12	23	35				59																		
1955-56	Calgary Stampeders	WHL	70	21	38	59				85											8	1	4	5	19			
1956-57	Buffalo Bisons	AHL	9	0	6	6				11																		
1957-58	Calgary Stampeders	WHL	61	18	40	58				51											14	1	4	5	27			
1958-59	Calgary Stampeders	WHL	64	7	36	43				61											8	1	0	1	9			
1959-60	Calgary Stampeders	WHL	66	7	46	53				32																		
1960-61	Calgary Stampeders	WHL	67	9	42	51				55											5	0	0	0	9			
1961-62	Calgary Stampeders	WHL	53	19	37	56				42											7	0	4	4	2			
1962-63	Calgary Stampeders	WHL	70	16	41	57				56																		
1963-64	Denver Invaders	WHL	69	8	49	57				58											6	3	4	7	6			
1964-65	Victoria Maple Leafs	WHL	51	8	20	28				67											12	1	4	5	*28			
1965-66	Tulsa Oilers	CPHL	7	1	0	1				4																		
	Victoria Maple Leafs	WHL	61	16	43	59				56											14	8	7	15	14			
1966-67	Victoria Maple Leafs	WHL	13	3	6	9				12																		
1967-68	**St. Louis Blues**	**NHL**	**43**	**2**	**13**	**15**	**2**	**13**	**15**	**30**	**1**	**0**	**0**	**85**	**2.4**	**46**	**14**	**41**	**6**	**–3**								
1968-69	Kansas City Blues	CHL	2	0	1	1				0																		
	NHL Totals		**164**	**11**	**30**	**41**	**14**	**34**	**48**	**113**											**6**	**1**	**0**	**1**	**10**			

WCJHL Second All-Star Team (1950) • WHL First All-Star Team (1956, 1963, 1964, 1966) • WHL Prairie Division First All-Star Team (1958, 1959) • WHL Second All-Star Team (1961, 1962)

Traded to **Calgary** (WHL) by **Chicago** for cash, September, 1954. Traded to **Toronto** by **Calgary** (WHL) for cash, August, 1963. Claimed by **St. Louis** from **Toronto** in Expansion Draft, June 6, 1967. • Named playing-coach of Kansas City (CHL), June 5, 1968.

• HUDDY, Charlie

Charles William D – L. 6', 210 lbs. b: Oshawa, Ont., 6/2/1959.

Season	Club	League	GP	G	A	Pts	AG	AA	APts	PIM	PP	SH	GW	S	%	TGF	PGF	TGA	PGA	+/–	GP	G	A	Pts	PIM	PP	SH	GW
1976-77	Marham Waxers	OHA-B	48	14	20	34				80																		
1977-78	Oshawa Generals	OMJHL	59	17	18	35				81											6	2	1	3	10			
1978-79	Oshawa Generals	OMJHL	64	20	38	58				108											5	3	4	7	12			
1979-80	Houston Apollos	CHL	79	14	34	48				46											6	1	0	1	2			
1980-81	**Edmonton Oilers**	**NHL**	**12**	**2**	**5**	**7**	**2**	**3**	**5**	**6**	**1**	**0**	**0**	**23**	**8.7**	**18**	**4**	**20**	**7**	**1**								
	Wichita Wind	CHL	47	8	36	44				71											17	3	11	14	10			
1981-82	**Edmonton Oilers**	**NHL**	**41**	**4**	**11**	**15**	**3**	**7**	**10**	**46**	**0**	**0**	**0**	**84**	**4.8**	**51**	**7**	**37**	**10**	**17**	**5**	**1**	**2**	**3**	**14**	**0**	**1**	**0**
	Wichita Wind	CHL	32	7	19	26				51																		
1982-83	**Edmonton Oilers**	**NHL**	**76**	**20**	**37**	**57**	**16**	**26**	**42**	**58**	**7**	**0**	**2**	**151**	**13.2**	**194**	**54**	**98**	**20**	**62**	**15**	**1**	**6**	**7**	**10**	**0**	**0**	**0**
1983-84♦	**Edmonton Oilers**	**NHL**	**75**	**8**	**34**	**42**	**6**	**23**	**29**	**43**	**3**	**0**	**0**	**161**	**5.0**	**172**	**36**	**103**	**17**	**50**	**12**	**1**	**9**	**10**	**8**	**0**	**0**	**0**
1984-85	Canada	Can-Cup	7	0	2	2				2																		
♦	**Edmonton Oilers**	**NHL**	**80**	**7**	**44**	**51**	**6**	**30**	**36**	**46**	**3**	**0**	**1**	**146**	**4.8**	**189**	**42**	**123**	**26**	**50**	**18**	**3**	**17**	**20**	**17**	**1**	**0**	**0**
1985-86	**Edmonton Oilers**	**NHL**	**76**	**6**	**35**	**41**	**5**	**24**	**29**	**55**	**1**	**0**	**0**	**151**	**4.0**	**173**	**44**	**128**	**29**	**30**	**7**	**0**	**2**	**2**	**0**	**0**	**0**	**0**
1986-87♦	**Edmonton Oilers**	**NHL**	**58**	**4**	**15**	**19**	**3**	**11**	**14**	**35**	**0**	**0**	**0**	**75**	**5.3**	**89**	**19**	**61**	**18**	**27**	**21**	**1**	**7**	**8**	**21**	**0**	**0**	**0**
1987-88♦	**Edmonton Oilers**	**NHL**	**77**	**13**	**28**	**41**	**11**	**20**	**31**	**71**	**2**	**0**	**2**	**163**	**8.0**	**117**	**31**	**94**	**31**	**23**	**13**	**4**	**5**	**9**	**10**	**2**	**0**	**0**
1988-89	**Edmonton Oilers**	**NHL**	**76**	**11**	**33**	**44**	**9**	**23**	**32**	**52**	**5**	**2**	**0**	**178**	**6.2**	**131**	**42**	**115**	**26**	**0**	**7**	**2**	**0**	**2**	**4**	**1**	**0**	**0**
1989-90♦	**Edmonton Oilers**	**NHL**	**70**	**1**	**23**	**24**	**1**	**16**	**17**	**56**	**1**	**0**	**1**	**119**	**0.8**	**74**	**19**	**93**	**25**	**–13**	**22**	**0**	**6**	**6**	**11**	**0**	**0**	**0**
1990-91	**Edmonton Oilers**	**NHL**	**53**	**5**	**22**	**27**	**5**	**17**	**22**	**32**	**2**	**0**	**0**	**90**	**5.6**	**59**	**9**	**61**	**15**	**4**	**18**	**3**	**7**	**10**	**10**	**1**	**0**	**0**
1991-92	**Los Angeles Kings**	**NHL**	**56**	**4**	**19**	**23**	**4**	**14**	**18**	**43**	**2**	**1**	**0**	**109**	**3.7**	**80**	**24**	**93**	**27**	**–10**	**6**	**1**	**1**	**2**	**10**	**0**	**0**	**1**
1992-93	**Los Angeles Kings**	**NHL**	**82**	**2**	**25**	**27**	**2**	**17**	**19**	**64**	**0**	**0**	**1**	**106**	**1.9**	**90**	**5**	**123**	**54**	**16**	**23**	**1**	**4**	**5**	**12**	**0**	**0**	**0**
1993-94	**Los Angeles Kings**	**NHL**	**79**	**5**	**13**	**18**	**5**	**10**	**15**	**71**	**1**	**0**	**0**	**134**	**3.7**	**79**	**7**	**107**	**39**	**4**								
1994-95	**Los Angeles Kings**	**NHL**	**9**	**0**	**1**	**1**	**0**	**1**	**1**	**6**	**0**	**0**	**0**	**11**	**0.0**	**4**	**0**	**11**	**1**	**–6**								
	Buffalo Sabres	**NHL**	**32**	**2**	**4**	**6**	**4**	**6**	**10**	**36**	**1**	**0**	**0**	**40**	**5.0**	**21**	**2**	**27**	**7**	**–1**	**3**	**0**	**0**	**0**	**0**	**0**	**0**	**0**
1995-96	**Buffalo Sabres**	**NHL**	**52**	**5**	**5**	**10**	**5**	**4**	**9**	**59**	**2**	**0**	**1**	**57**	**8.8**	**35**	**5**	**43**	**8**	**–5**								
	St. Louis Blues	**NHL**	**12**	**0**	**0**	**0**	**0**	**0**	**0**	**6**	**0**	**0**	**0**	**13**	**0.0**	**6**	**0**	**16**	**3**	**–7**	**13**	**1**	**0**	**1**	**8**	**0**	**0**	**0**

			REGULAR SEASON																		PLAYOFFS							
Season	Club	League	GP	G	A	Pts	AG	AA	APts	PIM	PP	SH	GW	S	%	TGF	PGF	TGA	PGA	+/–	GP	G	A	Pts	PIM	PP	SH	GW
1996-97	**Buffalo Sabres**	**NHL**	1	0	0	0	0	0	0	0	0	0	0	0	0.0	0	0	1	0	–1	....	....	....	....	....	....	....	....
	Rochester Americans	AHL	63	6	8	14	....	....	....	36	....	....	....	....	....	....	....	....	....	....	4	0	0	0	0	....	....	....
1997-98	Huntington Blizzard	ECHL	DID NOT PLAY – COACHING																									
1998-2000	**New York Rangers**	**NHL**	DID NOT PLAY – ASSISTANT COACH																									
	NHL Totals		1017	99	354	453	87	252	339	785	31	3	8	1811	5.5	1582	350	1354	363		183	19	66	85	135	5	1	1

NHL Plus/Minus Leader (1983)

Signed as a free agent by **Edmonton**, September 14, 1979. Claimed by **Minnesota** from **Edmonton** in Expansion Draft, May 30, 1991. Traded to **LA Kings** by **Minnesota** with Randy Gilhen, Jim Thomson and NY Rangers' 4th round choice (previously acquired, LA Kings selected Alexei Zhitnik) in 1991 Entry Draft for Todd Elik, June 22, 1991. Traded to **Buffalo** by **LA Kings** with Alexei Zhitnik, Robb Stauber and LA Kings' 5th round choice (Marian Menhart) in 1995 Entry Draft for Philippe Boucher, Denis Tsygurov and Grant Fuhr, February 14, 1995. Traded to **St. Louis** by **Buffalo** with Buffalo's 7th round choice (Daniel Corso) in 1996 Entry Draft for Denis Hamel, March 19, 1996. Signed as a free agent by **Buffalo**, September 26, 1996.

• HUDSON, Dave

David Richard C – L. 6', 185 lbs. b: St. Thomas, Ont., 12/28/1949. Chicago's 6th, 71st overall, in 1969.

Season	Club	League	GP	G	A	Pts	AG	AA	APts	PIM	PP	SH	GW	S	%	TGF	PGF	TGA	PGA	+/–	GP	G	A	Pts	PIM	PP	SH	GW
1967-68	University of North Dakota	WCHA	33	8	6	14	....	....	....	6	....	....	....	....	....	....	....	....	....	....	....	....	....	....	....	....	....	....
1968-69	University of North Dakota	WCHA	29	16	14	30	....	....	....	16	....	....	....	....	....	....	....	....	....	....	....	....	....	....	....	....	....	....
1969-70	University of North Dakota	WCHA	30	16	13	29	....	....	....	28	....	....	....	....	....	....	....	....	....	....	....	....	....	....	....	....	....	....
1970-71	Dallas Black Hawks	CHL	69	17	37	54	....	....	....	57	....	....	....	....	....	....	....	....	....	....	7	0	1	1	19	....	....	....
1971-72	Dallas Black Hawks	CHL	63	29	34	63	....	....	....	49	....	....	....	....	....	....	....	....	....	....	12	7	7	14	12	....	....	....
1972-73	**New York Islanders**	**NHL**	69	12	19	31	11	15	26	17	4	0	0	111	10.8	40	13	66	0	–39	....	....	....	....	....	....	....	....
1973-74	**New York Islanders**	**NHL**	63	2	10	12	2	8	10	7	0	0	0	43	4.7	19	1	24	0	–6	....	....	....	....	....	....	....	....
	Fort Worth Wings	CHL	10	5	3	8	....	....	....	19	....	....	....	....	....	....	....	....	....	....	....	....	....	....	....	....	....	....
1974-75	**Kansas City Scouts**	**NHL**	70	9	32	41	8	24	32	27	2	0	1	115	7.8	55	17	71	14	–19	....	....	....	....	....	....	....	....
1975-76	**Kansas City Scouts**	**NHL**	74	11	20	31	10	15	25	12	2	0	0	114	9.6	48	9	85	18	–28	....	....	....	....	....	....	....	....
1976-77	**Colorado Rockies**	**NHL**	73	15	21	36	13	16	29	14	1	0	2	89	16.9	51	5	72	23	–3	....	....	....	....	....	....	....	....
	Rhode Island Reds	AHL	5	0	2	2	....	....	....	2	....	....	....	....	....	....	....	....	....	....	....	....	....	....	....	....	....	....
1977-78	**Colorado Rockies**	**NHL**	60	10	22	32	9	17	26	12	1	0	0	89	11.2	44	6	63	20	–5	2	1	1	2	0	0	0	0
	NHL Totals		409	59	124	183	53	95	148	89	10	0	3	561	10.5	257	51	381	75		2	1	1	2	0	0	0	0

Claimed by **Chicago** (Portland-WHL) from **Chicago** in Reverse Draft, June 10, 1970. Claimed by **NY Islanders** from **Chicago** in Expansion Draft, June 6, 1972. Claimed by **Kansas City** from **NY Islanders** in Expansion Draft, June 12, 1974. Transferred to **Colorado** after **Kansas City** franchise relocated, June, 1976.

• HUDSON, Lex

Alexander D – L. 6'3", 184 lbs. b: Winnipeg, Man., 12/31/1955. Pittsburgh's 12th, 196th overall, in 1975.

Season	Club	League	GP	G	A	Pts	AG	AA	APts	PIM	PP	SH	GW	S	%	TGF	PGF	TGA	PGA	+/–	GP	G	A	Pts	PIM	PP	SH	GW
1973-74	West Kildonan North Stars	MJHL	46	9	28	37	....	....	....	50	....	....	....	....	....	....	....	....	....	....	....	....	....	....	....	....	....	....
1974-75	University of Denver	WCHA	35	2	3	5	....	....	....	29	....	....	....	....	....	....	....	....	....	....	....	....	....	....	....	....	....	....
1975-76	University of Denver	WCHA	35	1	13	14	....	....	....	34	....	....	....	....	....	....	....	....	....	....	....	....	....	....	....	....	....	....
1976-77	University of Denver	WCHA	29	0	9	9	....	....	....	32	....	....	....	....	....	....	....	....	....	....	....	....	....	....	....	....	....	....
1977-78	University of Denver	WCHA	40	1	12	13	....	....	....	46	....	....	....	....	....	....	....	....	....	....	....	....	....	....	....	....	....	....
1978-79	**Pittsburgh Penguins**	**NHL**	2	0	0	0	0	0	0	0	0	0	0	1	0.0	2	0	4	2	0	2	0	0	0	0	0	0	0
	Binghamton Dusters	AHL	2	0	0	0	....	....	....	0	....	....	....	....	....	....	....	....	....	....	....	....	....	....	....	....	....	....
	Grand Rapids Owls	IHL	69	6	29	35	....	....	....	63	....	....	....	....	....	....	....	....	....	....	18	2	6	8	18	....	....	....
1979-80	Cincinnati Stingers	CHL	32	1	6	7	....	....	....	21	....	....	....	....	....	....	....	....	....	....	....	....	....	....	....	....	....	....
	Grand Rapids Owls	IHL	8	1	5	6	....	....	....	0	....	....	....	....	....	....	....	....	....	....	....	....	....	....	....	....	....	....
	NHL Totals		2	0	0	0	0	0	0	0	0	0	0	1	0.0	2	0	4	2		2	0	0	0	0	0	0	0

WCHA Second All-Star Team (1978)

• HUDSON, Mike

C/LW – L. 6'1", 205 lbs. b: Guelph, Ont., 2/6/1967. Chicago's 6th, 140th overall, in 1986.

Season	Club	League	GP	G	A	Pts	AG	AA	APts	PIM	PP	SH	GW	S	%	TGF	PGF	TGA	PGA	+/–	GP	G	A	Pts	PIM	PP	SH	GW
1983-84	Guelph Midget Platers	OMHA	23	14	13	27	....	....	....	20	....	....	....	....	....	....	....	....	....	....	....	....	....	....	....	....	....	....
1984-85	Hamilton Steelhawks	OHL	50	10	12	22	....	....	....	13	....	....	....	....	....	....	....	....	....	....	....	....	....	....	....	....	....	....
1985-86	Hamilton Steelhawks	OHL	7	3	2	5	....	....	....	4	....	....	....	....	....	....	....	....	....	....	....	....	....	....	....	....	....	....
	Sudbury Wolves	OHL	59	35	42	77	....	....	....	20	....	....	....	....	....	....	....	....	....	....	4	2	5	7	7	....	....	....
1986-87	Sudbury Wolves	OHL	63	40	57	97	....	....	....	18	....	....	....	....	....	....	....	....	....	....	....	....	....	....	....	....	....	....
1987-88	Saginaw Hawks	IHL	75	18	30	48	....	....	....	44	....	....	....	....	....	....	....	....	....	....	10	2	3	5	20	....	....	....
1988-89	**Chicago Blackhawks**	**NHL**	41	7	16	23	6	11	17	20	0	1	0	45	15.6	28	5	41	6	–12	10	1	2	3	18	1	0	0
	Saginaw Hawks	IHL	30	15	17	32	....	....	....	10	....	....	....	....	....	....	....	....	....	....	....	....	....	....	....	....	....	....
1989-90	**Chicago Blackhawks**	**NHL**	49	9	12	21	8	9	17	56	0	0	3	51	17.6	32	3	38	6	–3	4	0	0	0	2	0	0	0
1990-91	**Chicago Blackhawks**	**NHL**	55	7	9	16	6	7	13	62	0	0	1	53	13.2	24	1	24	6	5	6	0	2	2	8	0	0	0
	Indianapolis Ice	IHL	3	1	2	3	....	....	....	0	....	....	....	....	....	....	....	....	....	....	....	....	....	....	....	....	....	....
1991-92	**Chicago Blackhawks**	**NHL**	76	14	15	29	13	11	24	92	2	1	2	97	14.4	38	5	59	15	–11	16	3	5	8	26	0	0	0
1992-93	**Chicago Blackhawks**	**NHL**	36	1	6	7	1	4	5	44	0	0	0	33	3.0	13	1	20	2	–6	....	....	....	....	....	....	....	....
	Edmonton Oilers	**NHL**	5	0	1	1	0	1	1	2	0	0	0	2	0.0	2	0	7	4	–1	....	....	....	....	....	....	....	....
1993-94♦	**New York Rangers**	**NHL**	48	4	7	11	4	5	9	47	0	0	1	48	8.3	18	1	22	0	–5	....	....	....	....	....	....	....	....
1994-95	**Pittsburgh Penguins**	**NHL**	40	2	9	11	4	13	17	34	0	0	1	33	6.1	17	0	27	9	–1	11	0	0	0	6	0	0	0
1995-96	**Toronto Maple Leafs**	**NHL**	27	2	0	2	2	0	2	29	0	0	0	27	7.4	3	0	11	3	–5	....	....	....	....	....	....	....	....
	St. Louis Blues	**NHL**	32	3	12	15	3	10	13	26	0	0	0	32	9.4	18	2	12	3	7	2	0	1	1	4	0	0	0
1996-97	Phoenix Roadrunners	IHL	33	6	9	15	....	....	....	10	....	....	....	....	....	....	....	....	....	....	....	....	....	....	....	....	....	....
	Phoenix Coyotes	**NHL**	7	0	0	0	0	0	0	2	0	0	0	9	0.0	1	0	5	0	–4	....	....	....	....	....	....	....	....
1997-98	Augsburger Panther	Germany	15	1	5	6	....	....	....	16	....	....	....	....	....	....	....	....	....	....	....	....	....	....	....	....	....	....
	Adler Mannheim	Germany	14	4	3	7	....	....	....	2	....	....	....	....	....	....	....	....	....	....	10	2	5	7	12	....	....	....
	Adler Mannheim	EuroHL	1	0	0	0	....	....	....	0	....	....	....	....	....	....	....	....	....	....	....	....	....	....	....	....	....	....
1998-99	Adler Mannheim	Germany	45	6	18	24	....	....	....	44	....	....	....	....	....	....	....	....	....	....	12	0	3	3	14	....	....	....
	Adler Mannheim	EuroHL	5	0	2	2	....	....	....	8	....	....	....	....	....	....	....	....	....	....	2	0	0	0	0	....	....	....
	NHL Totals		416	49	87	136	47	71	118	414	2	2	8	430	11.4	194	18	266	54		49	4	10	14	64	1	0	0

Traded to **Edmonton** by **Chicago** for Craig Muni, March 22, 1993. Claimed by **NY Rangers** from **Edmonton** in NHL Waiver Draft, October 3, 1993. Claimed by **Pittsburgh** from **NY Rangers** in NHL Waiver Draft, January 18, 1995. Signed as a free agent by **Toronto**, September 22, 1995. Claimed on waivers by **St. Louis** from **Toronto**, January 4, 1996. Signed as a free agent by **Phoenix**, November 12, 1996.

• HUFFMAN, Kerry

D – L. 6'2", 200 lbs. b: Peterborough, Ont., 1/3/1968. Philadelphia's 1st, 20th overall, in 1986.

Season	Club	League	GP	G	A	Pts	AG	AA	APts	PIM	PP	SH	GW	S	%	TGF	PGF	TGA	PGA	+/–	GP	G	A	Pts	PIM	PP	SH	GW
1984-85	Peterborough Jr. Bees	OJHL-B	24	2	5	7	....	....	....	53	....	....	....	....	....	....	....	....	....	....	....	....	....	....	....	....	....	....
1985-86	Guelph Platers	OHL	56	3	24	27	....	....	....	35	....	....	....	....	....	....	....	....	....	....	20	1	10	11	10	....	....	....
	Guelph Platers	Mem-Cup	4	0	3	3	....	....	....	2	....	....	....	....	....	....	....	....	....	....	....	....	....	....	....	....	....	....
1986-87	Guelph Platers	OHL	44	4	31	35	....	....	....	20	....	....	....	....	....	....	....	....	....	....	5	0	2	2	8	....	....	....
	Canada	WJC-A	6	0	1	1	....	....	....	4	....	....	....	....	....	....	....	....	....	....	....	....	....	....	....	....	....	....
	Philadelphia Flyers	**NHL**	9	0	0	0	0	0	0	2	0	0	0	3	0.0	6	1	0	0	5	....	....	....	....	....	....	....	....
	Hershey Bears	AHL	3	0	1	1	....	....	....	0	....	....	....	....	....	....	....	....	....	....	4	0	0	0	0	....	....	....
1987-88	**Philadelphia Flyers**	**NHL**	52	6	17	23	5	12	17	34	3	0	2	84	7.1	52	19	48	4	–11	2	0	0	0	0	0	0	0
1988-89	**Philadelphia Flyers**	**NHL**	29	0	11	11	0	8	8	31	0	0	0	23	0.0	32	14	18	0	0	....	....	....	....	....	....	....	....
	Hershey Bears	AHL	29	2	13	15	....	....	....	16	....	....	....	....	....	....	....	....	....	....	....	....	....	....	....	....	....	....
1989-90	**Philadelphia Flyers**	**NHL**	43	1	12	13	1	9	10	34	0	0	0	70	1.4	56	19	41	1	–3	....	....	....	....	....	....	....	....
1990-91	**Philadelphia Flyers**	**NHL**	10	1	2	3	1	2	3	10	0	0	1	14	7.1	12	1	10	0	1	....	....	....	....	....	....	....	....
	Hershey Bears	AHL	45	5	29	34	....	....	....	20	....	....	....	....	....	....	....	....	....	....	7	1	2	3	0	....	....	....
1991-92	**Philadelphia Flyers**	**NHL**	60	14	18	32	13	14	27	41	4	0	2	123	11.4	66	20	57	12	1	....	....	....	....	....	....	....	....
	Canada	WC-A	6	1	0	1	....	....	....	2	....	....	....	....	....	....	....	....	....	....	....	....	....	....	....	....	....	....
1992-93	**Quebec Nordiques**	**NHL**	52	4	18	22	3	12	15	54	3	0	0	86	4.7	64	22	56	14	0	3	0	0	0	0	0	0	0
1993-94	**Quebec Nordiques**	**NHL**	28	0	6	6	0	5	5	28	0	0	0	44	0.0	30	9	20	1	2	....	....	....	....	....	....	....	....
	Ottawa Senators	**NHL**	34	4	8	12	4	6	10	12	2	1	0	68	5.9	25	12	57	14	–30	....	....	....	....	....	....	....	....
1994-95	**Ottawa Senators**	**NHL**	37	2	4	6	4	6	10	46	2	0	0	68	2.9	30	9	50	12	–17	....	....	....	....	....	....	....	....
1995-96	**Ottawa Senators**	**NHL**	43	4	11	15	4	9	13	63	3	0	0	88	4.5	42	22	44	6	–18	....	....	....	....	....	....	....	....
	Philadelphia Flyers	**NHL**	4	1	1	2	1	1	2	6	0	0	1	3	33.3	5	3	2	0	0	6	0	0	0	2	0	0	0

Season	Club	League	GP	G	A	Pts	AG	AA	APts	PIM	PP	SH	GW	S	%	TGF	PGF	TGA	PGA	+/–	GP	G	A	Pts	PIM	PP	SH	GW
			REGULAR SEASON																		PLAYOFFS							
1996-97	Las Vegas Thunder	IHL	44	5	19	24	....	....	....	38	....	....	....	....	....	....	....	....	....	....	3	0	0	0	2	....	....	....
1997-98	Grand Rapids Griffins	IHL	73	4	23	27	....	....	....	60	....	....	....	....	....	....	....	....	....	....	3	0	0	0	2	....	....	....
1998-99	Grand Rapids Griffins	IHL	4	0	1	1	....	....	....	6	....	....	....	....	....	....	....	....	....	....	....	....	....	....	....	....	....	....
	NHL Totals		**401**	**37**	**108**	**145**	**36**	**84**	**120**	**361**	**17**	**1**	**6**	**674**	**5.5**	**420**	**151**	**403**	**64**		**11**	**0**	**0**	**0**	**2**	**0**	**0**	**0**

Won George Parsons Trophy (Memorial Cup Tournament Most Sportsmanlike Player) (1986) • OHL First All-Star Team (1987)

Traded to **Quebec** by **Philadelphia** with Steve Duchesne, Peter Forsberg, Mike Ricci, Ron Hextall, Philadelphia's 1st round choice (Jocelyn Thibault) in 1993 Entry Draft, $15,000,000 and future considerations (Chris Simon and Philadelphia's 1st round choice (later traded to Toronto — later traded to Washington — Washington selected Nolan Baumgartner) in 1994 Entry Draft, July 21, 1992) for Eric Lindros, June 30, 1992. Claimed on waivers by **Ottawa** from **Quebec**, January 15, 1994. Traded to **Philadelphia** by **Ottawa** for future considerations, March 19, 1996. Signed as a free agent by Las Vegas (IHL), October 12, 1996. Signed as a free agent by **Grand Rapids** (IHL), October 16, 1997.

• HUGHES, Brent

Brent Alexander D – L. 6', 205 lbs. b: Bowmanville, Ont., 6/17/1943.

Season	Club	League	GP	G	A	Pts	AG	AA	APts	PIM	PP	SH	GW	S	%	TGF	PGF	TGA	PGA	+/–	GP	G	A	Pts	PIM	PP	SH	GW
1959-60	Toronto Midget Marlboros	MTHL	STATISTICS NOT AVAILABLE																									
	Toronto Marlboros	OHA-Jr.	16	0	1	1	....	....	....	4	....	....	....	....	....	....	....	....	....	....	....	....	....	....	....	....	....	....
1960-61			STATISTICS NOT AVAILABLE																									
1961-62	St. Catharines Teepees	OHA-Jr.	41	1	7	8	....	....	....	46	....	....	....	....	....	....	....	....	....	....	6	1	1	2	6	....	....	....
1962-63	St. Catharines Teepees	OHA-Jr.	50	9	18	27	....	....	....	78	....	....	....	....	....	....	....	....	....	....	....	....	....	....	....	....	....	....
1963-64	New Haven Blades	EHL	53	6	25	31	....	....	....	100	....	....	....	....	....	....	....	....	....	....	5	0	1	1	0	....	....	....
1964-65	Minneapolis Bruins	CPHL	68	2	16	18	....	....	....	79	....	....	....	....	....	....	....	....	....	....	5	2	0	2	13	....	....	....
1965-66	Memphis Wings	CPHL	70	4	21	25	....	....	....	50	....	....	....	....	....	....	....	....	....	....	....	....	....	....	....	....	....	....
1966-67	Pittsburgh Hornets	AHL	5	2	4	6	....	....	....	4	....	....	....	....	....	....	....	....	....	....	....	....	....	....	....	....	....	....
	Memphis Wings	CPHL	52	3	15	18	....	....	....	49	....	....	....	....	....	....	....	....	....	....	7	0	2	2	6	....	....	....
1967-68	**Los Angeles Kings**	**NHL**	**44**	**4**	**10**	**14**	**5**	**10**	**15**	**36**	**2**	**0**	**0**	**72**	**5.6**	**55**	**7**	**44**	**11**	**15**	**7**	**0**	**0**	**0**	**10**	**0**	**0**	**0**
	Springfield Kings	AHL	25	5	14	19	....	....	....	30	....	....	....	....	....	....	....	....	....	....	....	....	....	....	....	....	....	....
1968-69	**Los Angeles Kings**	**NHL**	**72**	**2**	**19**	**21**	**2**	**17**	**19**	**73**	**0**	**0**	**0**	**116**	**1.7**	**74**	**13**	**101**	**24**	**–16**	**11**	**1**	**3**	**4**	**37**	**0**	**0**	**0**
1969-70	**Los Angeles Kings**	**NHL**	**52**	**1**	**7**	**8**	**1**	**7**	**8**	**108**	**0**	**0**	**0**	**64**	**1.6**	**33**	**3**	**83**	**20**	**–33**	....	....	....	....	....	....	....	....
	Springfield Kings	AHL	3	0	0	0	....	....	....	10	....	....	....	....	....	....	....	....	....	....	12	0	3	3	51	....	....	....
1970-71	**Philadelphia Flyers**	**NHL**	**30**	**1**	**10**	**11**	**1**	**8**	**9**	**21**	**0**	**0**	**0**	**37**	**2.7**	**37**	**14**	**33**	**4**	**–6**	**4**	**0**	**0**	**0**	**6**	**0**	**0**	**0**
	Quebec Aces	AHL	25	4	20	24	....	....	....	34	....	....	....	....	....	....	....	....	....	....	....	....	....	....	....	....	....	....
1971-72	**Philadelphia Flyers**	**NHL**	**63**	**2**	**20**	**22**	**2**	**17**	**19**	**35**	**0**	**0**	**0**	**93**	**2.2**	**77**	**17**	**67**	**13**	**6**	....	....	....	....	....	....	....	....
	Baltimore Clippers	AHL	10	2	4	6	....	....	....	6	....	....	....	....	....	....	....	....	....	....	....	....	....	....	....	....	....	....
1972-73	**Philadelphia Flyers**	**NHL**	**29**	**2**	**11**	**13**	**2**	**9**	**11**	**32**	**0**	**0**	**0**	**40**	**5.0**	**36**	**11**	**43**	**10**	**–8**	....	....	....	....	....	....	....	....
	St. Louis Blues	**NHL**	**8**	**1**	**1**	**2**	**1**	**1**	**2**	**0**	**0**	**0**	**0**	**16**	**6.3**	**13**	**2**	**12**	**2**	**1**	....	....	....	....	....	....	....	....
1973-74	**St. Louis Blues**	**NHL**	**2**	**0**	**0**	**0**	**0**	**0**	**0**	**0**	**0**	**0**	**0**	**0**	**0.0**	**0**	**0**	**0**	**0**	**0**	....	....	....	....	....	....	....	....
	Detroit Red Wings	**NHL**	**69**	**1**	**21**	**22**	**1**	**17**	**18**	**92**	**0**	**0**	**0**	**74**	**1.4**	**83**	**20**	**108**	**17**	**–28**	....	....	....	....	....	....	....	....
1974-75	**Kansas City Scouts**	**NHL**	**66**	**1**	**18**	**19**	**1**	**13**	**14**	**43**	**0**	**0**	**0**	**80**	**1.3**	**73**	**11**	**142**	**29**	**–51**	....	....	....	....	....	....	....	....
1975-76	San Diego Mariners	WHA	78	7	28	35	....	....	....	63	....	....	....	....	....	....	....	....	....	....	10	1	5	6	6	....	....	....
1976-77	San Diego Mariners	WHA	62	4	13	17	....	....	....	48	....	....	....	....	....	....	....	....	....	....	7	1	4	5	0	....	....	....
1977-78	Birmingham Bulls	WHA	80	9	35	44	....	....	....	48	....	....	....	....	....	....	....	....	....	....	5	0	0	0	12	....	....	....
1978-79	Birmingham Bulls	WHA	48	3	3	6	....	....	....	21	....	....	....	....	....	....	....	....	....	....	....	....	....	....	....	....	....	....
	Binghamton Dusters	AHL	8	1	2	3	....	....	....	8	....	....	....	....	....	....	....	....	....	....	....	....	....	....	....	....	....	....
1979-80	Cincinnati Stingers	CHL	11	0	1	1	....	....	....	0	....	....	....	....	....	....	....	....	....	....	....	....	....	....	....	....	....	....
	NHL Totals		**435**	**15**	**117**	**132**	**16**	**99**	**115**	**440**	**2**	**0**	**0**	**592**	**2.5**	**481**	**98**	**633**	**130**		**22**	**1**	**3**	**4**	**53**	**0**	**0**	**0**
	Other Major League Totals		268	23	79	102	....	....	....	180	....	....	....	....	....	....	....	....	....	....	22	2	9	11	18	....	....	....

Claimed by **Detroit** (Springfield-AHL) from **Boston** in Reverse Draft, June 9, 1965. Claimed by **LA Kings** from **Detroit** in Expansion Draft, June 6, 1967. Traded to **Philadelphia** by **LA Kings** for Mike Byers, May 20, 1970. Selected by **NY Raiders** (WHA) in 1972 WHA General Player Draft, February 12, 1972. Traded to **St. Louis** by **Philadelphia** with Pierre Plante for Andre Dupont and St. Louis' 3rd round choice (Bob Stumpf) in 1973 Amateur Draft, December 14, 1972. Traded to **Detroit** by **St. Louis** for cash, October 27, 1973. Transferred to **San Diego** (WHA) after **New York-New Jersey** (WHA) franchise relocated, April 30, 1974. Claimed by **Kansas City** from **Detroit** in Expansion Draft, June 12, 1974. Signed as a free agent by **Birmingham** (WHA) after **San Diego** (WHA) franchise folded, June, 1977.

• HUGHES, Brent

Brent Alexander LW – L. 5'11", 195 lbs. b: New Westminster, B.C., 4/5/1966.

Season	Club	League	GP	G	A	Pts	AG	AA	APts	PIM	PP	SH	GW	S	%	TGF	PGF	TGA	PGA	+/–	GP	G	A	Pts	PIM	PP	SH	GW
1983-84	New Westminster Bruins	WHL	67	21	18	39	....	....	....	133	....	....	....	....	....	....	....	....	....	....	9	2	2	4	27	....	....	....
1984-85	New Westminster Bruins	WHL	64	25	32	57	....	....	....	135	....	....	....	....	....	....	....	....	....	....	11	2	1	3	37	....	....	....
1985-86	New Westminster Bruins	WHL	71	28	52	80	....	....	....	180	....	....	....	....	....	....	....	....	....	....	....	....	....	....	....	....	....	....
1986-87	New Westminster Bruins	WHL	8	5	4	9	....	....	....	22	....	....	....	....	....	....	....	....	....	....	....	....	....	....	....	....	....	....
	Victoria Cougars	WHL	61	38	61	99	....	....	....	146	....	....	....	....	....	....	....	....	....	....	5	4	1	5	8	....	....	....
1987-88	Moncton Hawks	AHL	73	13	19	32	....	....	....	206	....	....	....	....	....	....	....	....	....	....	....	....	....	....	....	....	....	....
1988-89	**Winnipeg Jets**	**NHL**	**28**	**3**	**2**	**5**	**3**	**1**	**4**	**82**	**0**	**1**	**0**	**37**	**8.1**	**12**	**1**	**18**	**0**	**–7**	....	....	....	....	....	....	....	....
	Moncton Hawks	AHL	54	34	34	68	....	....	....	286	....	....	....	....	....	....	....	....	....	....	10	9	4	13	40	....	....	....
1989-90	**Winnipeg Jets**	**NHL**	**11**	**1**	**2**	**3**	**1**	**1**	**2**	**33**	**0**	**0**	**1**	**7**	**14.3**	**4**	**0**	**8**	**0**	**–4**	....	....	....	....	....	....	....	....
	Moncton Hawks	AHL	65	31	29	60	....	....	....	277	....	....	....	....	....	....	....	....	....	....	....	....	....	....	....	....	....	....
1990-91	Moncton Hawks	AHL	63	21	22	43	....	....	....	144	....	....	....	....	....	....	....	....	....	....	3	0	0	0	7	....	....	....
1991-92	Baltimore Skipjacks	AHL	55	25	29	54	....	....	....	190	....	....	....	....	....	....	....	....	....	....	....	....	....	....	....	....	....	....
	Boston Bruins	**NHL**	**8**	**1**	**1**	**2**	**1**	**1**	**2**	**38**	**0**	**0**	**1**	**10**	**10.0**	**4**	**0**	**4**	**1**	**1**	**10**	**2**	**0**	**2**	**20**	**0**	**0**	**0**
	Maine Mariners	AHL	12	6	4	10	....	....	....	34	....	....	....	....	....	....	....	....	....	....	....	....	....	....	....	....	....	....
1992-93	**Boston Bruins**	**NHL**	**62**	**5**	**4**	**9**	**4**	**3**	**7**	**191**	**0**	**0**	**0**	**54**	**9.3**	**17**	**0**	**22**	**1**	**–4**	**1**	**0**	**0**	**0**	**2**	**0**	**0**	**0**
1993-94	**Boston Bruins**	**NHL**	**77**	**13**	**11**	**24**	**12**	**9**	**21**	**143**	**1**	**0**	**1**	**100**	**13.0**	**38**	**1**	**27**	**0**	**10**	**13**	**2**	**1**	**3**	**27**	**0**	**0**	**1**
	Providence Bruins	AHL	6	2	5	7	....	....	....	4	....	....	....	....	....	....	....	....	....	....	....	....	....	....	....	....	....	....
1994-95	**Boston Bruins**	**NHL**	**44**	**6**	**6**	**12**	**11**	**9**	**20**	**139**	**0**	**0**	**0**	**75**	**8.0**	**19**	**0**	**13**	**0**	**6**	**5**	**0**	**0**	**0**	**4**	**0**	**0**	**0**
1995-96	**Buffalo Sabres**	**NHL**	**76**	**5**	**10**	**15**	**5**	**8**	**13**	**148**	**0**	**0**	**0**	**56**	**8.9**	**21**	**0**	**30**	**0**	**–9**	....	....	....	....	....	....	....	....
1996-97	**New York Islanders**	**NHL**	**51**	**7**	**3**	**10**	**7**	**3**	**10**	**57**	**0**	**0**	**0**	**47**	**14.9**	**12**	**0**	**17**	**1**	**–4**	....	....	....	....	....	....	....	....
	Utah Grizzlies	IHL	5	2	2	4	....	....	....	11	....	....	....	....	....	....	....	....	....	....	....	....	....	....	....	....	....	....
1997-98	Houston Aeros	IHL	79	19	12	31	....	....	....	128	....	....	....	....	....	....	....	....	....	....	4	0	3	3	20	....	....	....
1998-99	Houston Aeros	IHL	29	4	2	6	....	....	....	87	....	....	....	....	....	....	....	....	....	....	....	....	....	....	....	....	....	....
	Utah Grizzlies	IHL	51	13	11	24	....	....	....	80	....	....	....	....	....	....	....	....	....	....	....	....	....	....	....	....	....	....
99-2000	Austin Ice Bats	WCHL	DID NOT PLAY – COACHING																									
	NHL Totals		**357**	**41**	**39**	**80**	**44**	**35**	**79**	**831**	**1**	**1**	**3**	**386**	**10.6**	**127**	**2**	**139**	**3**		**29**	**4**	**1**	**5**	**53**	**0**	**0**	**1**

Signed as a free agent by **Winnipeg**, June 13, 1988. Traded to **Washington** by **Winnipeg** with Craig Duncanson and Simon Wheeldon for Bob Joyce, Tyler Larter and Kent Paynter, May 21, 1991. Traded to **Boston** by **Washington** with future considerations for John Byce and Dennis Smith, February 24, 1992. Claimed By **Buffalo** from **Boston** in NHL Waiver Draft, October 2, 1995. Signed as a free agent by **NY Islanders**, August 9, 1996. • Officially announced retirement and named Head Coach of **Austin** (WPHL), June 10, 1999.

• HUGHES, Frank

LW – L. 5'10", 180 lbs. b: Fernie, B.C., 10/1/1949. Toronto's 4th, 43rd overall, in 1969.

Season	Club	League	GP	G	A	Pts	AG	AA	APts	PIM	PP	SH	GW	S	%	TGF	PGF	TGA	PGA	+/–	GP	G	A	Pts	PIM	PP	SH	GW
1967-68	Edmonton Oil Kings	WCJHL	....	....	....	....	....	....	....	....	....	....	....	....	....	....	....	....	....	....	1	0	0	0	0	....	....	....
1968-69	Edmonton Oil Kings	WCJHL	50	18	10	28	....	....	....	10	....	....	....	....	....	....	....	....	....	....	17	10	7	17	....	....	....	....
1969-70	Phoenix Roadrunners	WHL	71	26	42	68	....	....	....	44	....	....	....	....	....	....	....	....	....	....	....	....	....	....	....	....	....	....
1970-71	Phoenix Roadrunners	WHL	68	30	38	68	....	....	....	67	....	....	....	....	....	....	....	....	....	....	10	4	4	8	14	....	....	....
1971-72	**California Golden Seals**	**NHL**	**5**	**0**	**0**	**0**	**0**	**0**	**0**	**0**	**0**	**0**	**0**	**1**	**0.0**	**1**	**1**	**2**	**0**	**–2**	....	....	....	....	....	....	....	....
	Phoenix Roadrunners	WHL	53	34	28	62	....	....	....	41	....	....	....	....	....	....	....	....	....	....	6	2	3	5	13	....	....	....
1972-73	Houston Aeros	WHA	76	22	19	41	....	....	....	41	....	....	....	....	....	....	....	....	....	....	10	4	4	8	2	....	....	....
1973-74	Houston Aeros	WHA	73	42	42	84	....	....	....	47	....	....	....	....	....	....	....	....	....	....	14	9	5	14	9	....	....	....
1974-75	Houston Aeros	WHA	76	48	35	83	....	....	....	35	....	....	....	....	....	....	....	....	....	....	13	6	6	12	2	....	....	....
1975-76	Houston Aeros	WHA	80	31	45	76	....	....	....	26	....	....	....	....	....	....	....	....	....	....	17	5	1	6	20	....	....	....
1976-77	Houston Aeros	WHA	27	3	8	11	....	....	....	2	....	....	....	....	....	....	....	....	....	....	....	....	....	....	....	....	....	....
	Phoenix Roadrunners	WHA	48	24	29	53	....	....	....	20	....	....	....	....	....	....	....	....	....	....	....	....	....	....	....	....	....	....

			REGULAR SEASON																		PLAYOFFS							
Season	Club	League	GP	G	A	Pts	AG	AA	APts	PIM	PP	SH	GW	S	%	TGF	PGF	TGA	PGA	+/–	GP	G	A	Pts	PIM	PP	SH	GW
1977-78	Houston Aeros	WHA	11	3	2	5	....	....	....	2	....	....	....	....	....	....	....	....	....	....	....	....	....	....	....	....	....	....
	Phoenix Roadrunners	PHL	40	*33	*41	*74	....	....	....	44	....	....	....	....	....	....	....	....	....	....	....	....	....	....	....	....	....	....
1978-79	Tucson Rustlers	PHL	58	35	49	84	....	....	....	32	....	....	....	....	....	....	....	....	....	....	....	....	....	....	....	....	....	....
	NHL Totals		**5**	**0**	**0**	**0**	**0**	**0**	**0**	**0**	**0**	**0**	**0**	**1**	**0.0**	**1**	**1**	**2**	**0**		....	....	....	....	....	....	....	....
	Other Major League Totals		391	173	180	353	....	....	....	173	....	....	....	....	....	....	....	....	....	....	54	24	16	40	33	....	....	....

PHL First All-Star Team (1978) • PHL MVP (1978) • PHL Second All-Star Team (1979)

Claimed by **California** from **Toronto** in Intra-League Draft, June 8, 1971. Selected by **Dayton-Houston** (WHA) in 1972 WHA General Player Draft, February 12, 1972. Claimed by **Atlanta** from **California** in Expansion Draft, June 6, 1972. Traded to **Phoenix** (WHA) by **Houston** (WHA) with Andre Hinse for John Gray, Al McLeod and Neil Lyseng, December, 1976. Signed as a free agent by **Houston** (WHA) after **Phoenix** (WHA) franchise folded, July, 1977.

• HUGHES, Howie
Howard Duncan RW – L. 5'9", 180 lbs. b: St. Boniface, Man., 4/4/1939.

Season	Club	League	GP	G	A	Pts	AG	AA	APts	PIM	PP	SH	GW	S	%	TGF	PGF	TGA	PGA	+/–	GP	G	A	Pts	PIM	PP	SH	GW
1955-56	St. Boniface Braves	MAHA	STATISTICS NOT AVAILABLE																									
	St. Boniface Canadiens	MJHL	....	....	....	....	....	....	....	....	....	....	....	....	....	....	....	....	....	....	1	0	0	0	0	....	....	....
1956-57	St. Boniface Canadiens	MJHL	21	9	13	22	....	....	....	0	....	....	....	....	....	....	....	....	....	....	3	0	0	0	0	....	....	....
1957-58	St. Boniface Canadiens	MJHL	30	18	15	33	....	....	....	26	....	....	....	....	....	....	....	....	....	....	12	4	*6	10	4	....	....	....
	St. Boniface Canadiens	Mem-Cup	9	1	1	2	....	....	....	2	....	....	....	....	....	....	....	....	....	....	....	....	....	....	....	....	....	....
1958-59	St. Boniface Canadiens	MJHL	27	10	18	28	....	....	....	35	....	....	....	....	....	....	....	....	....	....	6	1	2	3	14	....	....	....
	Winnipeg Braves	Mem-Cup	16	8	5	13	....	....	....	10	....	....	....	....	....	....	....	....	....	....	....	....	....	....	....	....	....	....
1959-60	St. Paul Saints	IHL	68	35	44	79	....	....	....	33	....	....	....	....	....	....	....	....	....	....	13	5	8	13	12	....	....	....
1960-61	Winnipeg Warriors	WHL	68	12	23	35	....	....	....	26	....	....	....	....	....	....	....	....	....	....	....	....	....	....	....	....	....	....
1961-62	Seattle Totems	WHL	64	17	22	39	....	....	....	22	....	....	....	....	....	....	....	....	....	....	2	0	2	2	2	....	....	....
1962-63	Vancouver Canucks	WHL	40	5	10	15	....	....	....	12	....	....	....	....	....	....	....	....	....	....	7	0	0	0	2	....	....	....
1963-64	St. Paul Rangers	CPHL	66	30	34	64	....	....	....	37	....	....	....	....	....	....	....	....	....	....	8	1	3	4	2	....	....	....
1964-65	Vancouver Canucks	WHL	67	24	26	50	....	....	....	26	....	....	....	....	....	....	....	....	....	....	5	0	0	0	2	....	....	....
1965-66	Vancouver Canucks	WHL	65	37	35	72	....	....	....	24	....	....	....	....	....	....	....	....	....	....	7	3	2	5	0	....	....	....
1966-67	Seattle Totems	WHL	70	26	45	71	....	....	....	27	....	....	....	....	....	....	....	....	....	....	10	*6	5	*11	4	....	....	....
1967-68	**Los Angeles Kings**	**NHL**	**74**	**9**	**14**	**23**	**10**	**14**	**24**	**20**	**1**	**1**	**2**	**119**	**7.6**	**32**	**2**	**58**	**29**	**1**	**7**	**2**	**0**	**2**	**0**	**1**	**0**	**0**
1968-69	**Los Angeles Kings**	**NHL**	**73**	**16**	**14**	**30**	**17**	**12**	**29**	**10**	**5**	**0**	**3**	**161**	**9.9**	**48**	**8**	**47**	**4**	**–3**	**7**	**0**	**0**	**0**	**2**	**0**	**0**	**0**
1969-70	**Los Angeles Kings**	**NHL**	**21**	**0**	**4**	**4**	**0**	**4**	**4**	**0**	**0**	**0**	**0**	**18**	**0.0**	**9**	**4**	**21**	**10**	**–6**	....	....	....	....	....	....	....	....
1970-71	Springfield Kings	AHL	2	0	1	1	....	....	....	4	....	....	....	....	....	....	....	....	....	....	....	....	....	....	....	....	....	....
	Denver Spurs	WHL	62	19	21	40	....	....	....	19	....	....	....	....	....	....	....	....	....	....	5	2	2	4	8	....	....	....
1971-72	Seattle Totems	WHL	71	17	29	46	....	....	....	26	....	....	....	....	....	....	....	....	....	....	....	....	....	....	....	....	....	....
1972-73	San Diego Gulls	WHL	68	23	25	48	....	....	....	23	....	....	....	....	....	....	....	....	....	....	6	4	1	5	2	....	....	....
1973-74	Portland Buckaroos	WHL	75	41	36	77	....	....	....	22	....	....	....	....	....	....	....	....	....	....	10	3	4	7	2	....	....	....
1974-75	Seattle Totems	CHL	48	11	15	26	....	....	....	16	....	....	....	....	....	....	....	....	....	....	....	....	....	....	....	....	....	....
	NHL Totals		**168**	**25**	**32**	**57**	**27**	**30**	**57**	**30**	**6**	**1**	**5**	**298**	**8.4**	**89**	**14**	**126**	**43**		**14**	**2**	**0**	**2**	**2**	**1**	**0**	**0**

WHL Second All-Star Team (1967) • WHL First All-Star Team (1974)

Traded to **Vancouver** (WHL) by **Winnipeg** (WHL) for cash, June, 1961. Traded to **Seattle** (WHL) by **Vancouver** with Don Bambaruk for Emile Gillies, October 22, 1961. Traded to **Vancouver** (WHL) by **Seattle** (WHL) with Don Bambaruk for Emile Gillies, October 18, 1962. Claimed by **LA Kings** from **Montreal** in Expansion Draft, June 6, 1967. Loaned to **Denver** (WHL) by **LA Kings** for cash, November, 1970. Claimed by **San Diego** (WHL) from **LA Kings** (Seattle-WHL) in Reverse Draft, June, 1972.

• HUGHES, Jack
John Francis D – R. 6'1", 205 lbs. b: Somerville, MA, 7/20/1957. Colorado's 8th, 142nd overall, in 1977.

Season	Club	League	GP	G	A	Pts	AG	AA	APts	PIM	PP	SH	GW	S	%	TGF	PGF	TGA	PGA	+/–	GP	G	A	Pts	PIM	PP	SH	GW
1976-77	Harvard University	ECAC	26	5	16	21	....	....	....	16	....	....	....	....	....	....	....	....	....	....	....	....	....	....	....	....	....	....
1977-78	Harvard University	ECAC	23	8	19	27	....	....	....	33	....	....	....	....	....	....	....	....	....	....	....	....	....	....	....	....	....	....
1978-79	Harvard University	ECAC	25	3	29	32	....	....	....	51	....	....	....	....	....	....	....	....	....	....	....	....	....	....	....	....	....	....
1979-80	United States	Nat-Team	49	3	15	18	....	....	....	62	....	....	....	....	....	....	....	....	....	....	....	....	....	....	....	....	....	....
	Fort Worth Texans	CHL	29	1	7	8	....	....	....	70	....	....	....	....	....	....	....	....	....	....	15	1	11	12	40	....	....	....
1980-81	**Colorado Rockies**	**NHL**	**38**	**2**	**5**	**7**	**2**	**3**	**5**	**91**	**1**	**0**	**0**	**20**	**10.0**	**28**	**2**	**57**	**9**	**–22**	....	....	....	....	....	....	....	....
	Fort Worth Texans	CHL	27	1	7	8	....	....	....	36	....	....	....	....	....	....	....	....	....	....	5	0	5	5	16	....	....	....
1981-82	**Colorado Rockies**	**NHL**	**8**	**0**	**0**	**0**	**0**	**0**	**0**	**13**	**0**	**0**	**0**	**1**	**0.0**	**2**	**0**	**9**	**0**	**–7**	....	....	....	....	....	....	....	....
	Fort Worth Texans	CHL	65	7	25	32	....	....	....	158	....	....	....	....	....	....	....	....	....	....	....	....	....	....	....	....	....	....
	NHL Totals		**46**	**2**	**5**	**7**	**2**	**3**	**5**	**104**	**1**	**0**	**0**	**21**	**9.5**	**30**	**2**	**66**	**9**		....	....	....	....	....	....	....	....

ECAC First All-Star Team (1977) • ECAC Second All-Star Team (1978)

• HUGHES, John
John Spencer D – L. 5'11", 200 lbs. b: Charlottetown, P.E.I., 3/18/1954. Vancouver's 2nd, 41st overall, in 1974.

Season	Club	League	GP	G	A	Pts	AG	AA	APts	PIM	PP	SH	GW	S	%	TGF	PGF	TGA	PGA	+/–	GP	G	A	Pts	PIM	PP	SH	GW
1970-71	Charlottetown Islanders	MJrHL	STATISTICS NOT AVAILABLE																									
	Markham Waxers	OHA-B	STATISTICS NOT AVAILABLE																									
1971-72	Markham Waxers	OHA-B	STATISTICS NOT AVAILABLE																									
	Toronto Marlboros	OMJHL	2	0	0	0	....	....	....	0	....	....	....	....	....	....	....	....	....	....	1	0	0	0	0	....	....	....
1972-73	Toronto Marlboros	OMJHL	63	13	42	55	....	....	....	195	....	....	....	....	....	....	....	....	....	....	....	....	....	....	....	....	....	....
	Toronto Marlboros	Mem-Cup	3	0	0	0	....	....	....	15	....	....	....	....	....	....	....	....	....	....	....	....	....	....	....	....	....	....
1973-74	Toronto Marlboros	OMJHL	67	6	34	40	....	....	....	189	....	....	....	....	....	....	....	....	....	....	....	....	....	....	....	....	....	....
1974-75	Phoenix Roadrunners	WHA	72	4	25	29	....	....	....	201	....	....	....	....	....	....	....	....	....	....	....	....	....	....	....	....	....	....
1975-76	Cincinnati Stingers	WHA	79	3	34	37	....	....	....	204	....	....	....	....	....	....	....	....	....	....	....	....	....	....	....	....	....	....
1976-77	Cincinnati Stingers	WHA	79	3	27	30	....	....	....	113	....	....	....	....	....	....	....	....	....	....	4	0	0	0	8	....	....	....
1977-78	Houston Aeros	WHA	79	3	25	28	....	....	....	130	....	....	....	....	....	....	....	....	....	....	6	1	1	2	6	....	....	....
1978-79	Indianapolis Racers	WHA	22	3	4	7	....	....	....	48	....	....	....	....	....	....	....	....	....	....	....	....	....	....	....	....	....	....
	Edmonton Oilers	WHA	41	2	15	17	....	....	....	81	....	....	....	....	....	....	....	....	....	....	13	1	0	1	35	....	....	....
1979-80	**Vancouver Canucks**	**NHL**	**52**	**2**	**11**	**13**	**2**	**8**	**10**	**181**	**0**	**0**	**0**	**49**	**4.1**	**40**	**1**	**49**	**10**	**0**	**4**	**0**	**0**	**0**	**10**	**0**	**0**	**0**
1980-81	**Edmonton Oilers**	**NHL**	**18**	**0**	**3**	**3**	**0**	**2**	**2**	**30**	**0**	**0**	**0**	**9**	**0.0**	**13**	**1**	**26**	**8**	**–6**	....	....	....	....	....	....	....	....
	Wichita Wind	CHL	23	2	4	6	....	....	....	88	....	....	....	....	....	....	....	....	....	....	....	....	....	....	....	....	....	....
	New Haven Nighthawks	AHL	14	3	6	9	....	....	....	50	....	....	....	....	....	....	....	....	....	....	2	0	0	0	8	....	....	....
	New York Rangers	**NHL**	....	....	....	....	....	....	....	....	....	....	....	....	....	....	....	....	....	....	**3**	**0**	**1**	**1**	**6**	**0**	**0**	**0**
1981-82	Springfield Indians	AHL	76	1	33	34	....	....	....	174	....	....	....	....	....	....	....	....	....	....	....	....	....	....	....	....	....	....
	NHL Totals		**70**	**2**	**14**	**16**	**2**	**10**	**12**	**211**	**0**	**0**	**0**	**58**	**3.4**	**53**	**2**	**75**	**18**		**7**	**0**	**1**	**1**	**16**	**0**	**0**	**0**
	Other Major League Totals		372	18	130	148	....	....	....	777	....	....	....	....	....	....	....	....	....	....	23	2	1	3	49	....	....	....

Selected by **Cincinnati** (WHA) in 1974 WHA Amateur Draft, June, 1974. Loaned to **Phoenix** (WHA) by **Cincinnati** (WHA) for 1974-75 season, July, 1974. Traded to **Houston** (WHA) by **Cincinnati** (WHA) for Craig Norwich and the rights to Dave Taylor, May, 1977. Traded to **Indianapolis** (WHA) by **Houston** (WHA) for cash, July, 1978. Signed as a free agent by **Edmonton** (WHA) after **Indianapolis** (WHA) franchise folded, January, 1979. Reclaimed by **Vancouver** from **Edmonton** prior to Expansion Draft, June 9, 1979. Claimed on waivers by **Edmonton** from **Vancouver**, December 15, 1980. Traded to **NY Rangers** by **Edmonton** for Ray Markham, March 10, 1981.

• HUGHES, Pat
Patrick James RW – R. 6'1", 180 lbs. b: Calgary, Alta., 3/25/1955. Montreal's 6th, 52nd overall, in 1975.

Season	Club	League	GP	G	A	Pts	AG	AA	APts	PIM	PP	SH	GW	S	%	TGF	PGF	TGA	PGA	+/–	GP	G	A	Pts	PIM	PP	SH	GW
1972-73	Richmond Hill Dynes	OHA-B	STATISTICS NOT AVAILABLE																									
1973-74	University of Michigan	WCHA	38	13	7	20	....	....	....	34	....	....	....	....	....	....	....	....	....	....	....	....	....	....	....	....	....	....
1974-75	University of Michigan	WCHA	38	24	19	43	....	....	....	64	....	....	....	....	....	....	....	....	....	....	....	....	....	....	....	....	....	....
1975-76	University of Michigan	WCHA	35	16	18	34	....	....	....	70	....	....	....	....	....	....	....	....	....	....	....	....	....	....	....	....	....	....
1976-77	Nova Scotia Voyageurs	AHL	77	29	39	68	....	....	....	144	....	....	....	....	....	....	....	....	....	....	12	2	2	4	8	....	....	....
1977-78	**Montreal Canadiens**	**NHL**	**3**	**0**	**0**	**0**	**0**	**0**	**0**	**2**	**0**	**0**	**0**	**5**	**0.0**	**0**	**0**	**2**	**0**	**–2**	....	....	....	....	....	....	....	....
	Nova Scotia Voyageurs	AHL	74	40	28	68	....	....	....	128	....	....	....	....	....	....	....	....	....	....	11	5	9	14	24	....	....	....
1978-79♦	**Montreal Canadiens**	**NHL**	**41**	**9**	**8**	**17**	**8**	**6**	**14**	**22**	**1**	**0**	**1**	**51**	**17.6**	**19**	**2**	**10**	**0**	**7**	**8**	**1**	**2**	**3**	**4**	**0**	**0**	**0**
1979-80	**Pittsburgh Penguins**	**NHL**	**76**	**18**	**14**	**32**	**15**	**10**	**25**	**78**	**5**	**0**	**0**	**159**	**11.3**	**45**	**12**	**72**	**1**	**–38**	**5**	**0**	**0**	**0**	**21**	**0**	**0**	**0**
1980-81	**Pittsburgh Penguins**	**NHL**	**58**	**10**	**9**	**19**	**8**	**6**	**14**	**161**	**0**	**0**	**2**	**89**	**11.2**	**32**	**2**	**39**	**0**	**–9**	....	....	....	....	....	....	....	....
	Edmonton Oilers	**NHL**	**2**	**0**	**0**	**0**	**0**	**0**	**0**	**0**	**0**	**0**	**0**	**3**	**0.0**	**0**	**0**	**3**	**0**	**–3**	**5**	**0**	**5**	**5**	**16**	**0**	**0**	**0**
1981-82	**Edmonton Oilers**	**NHL**	**68**	**24**	**22**	**46**	**19**	**15**	**34**	**99**	**4**	**2**	**0**	**167**	**14.4**	**66**	**6**	**63**	**24**	**21**	**5**	**2**	**1**	**3**	**6**	**0**	**0**	**0**
1982-83	**Edmonton Oilers**	**NHL**	**80**	**25**	**20**	**45**	**20**	**14**	**34**	**85**	**2**	**5**	**7**	**144**	**17.4**	**64**	**6**	**81**	**23**	**0**	**16**	**2**	**5**	**7**	**14**	**0**	**0**	**1**
1983-84♦	**Edmonton Oilers**	**NHL**	**77**	**27**	**28**	**55**	**22**	**19**	**41**	**61**	**2**	**3**	**3**	**164**	**16.5**	**78**	**7**	**76**	**23**	**18**	**19**	**2**	**11**	**13**	**12**	**0**	**0**	**0**
1984-85♦	**Edmonton Oilers**	**NHL**	**73**	**12**	**13**	**25**	**10**	**9**	**19**	**85**	**1**	**1**	**0**	**98**	**12.2**	**43**	**2**	**62**	**14**	**–7**	**10**	**1**	**1**	**2**	**4**	**0**	**0**	**0**

			REGULAR SEASON																		PLAYOFFS							
Season	Club	League	GP	G	A	Pts	AG	AA	APts	PIM	PP	SH	GW	S	%	TGF	PGF	TGA	PGA	+/–	GP	G	A	Pts	PIM	PP	SH	GW
1985-86	Buffalo Sabres	NHL	50	4	9	13	3	6	9	25	0	0	0	51	7.8	26	1	42	11	–6								
	Rochester Americans	AHL	10	3	3	6				7																		
1986-87	St. Louis Blues	NHL	43	1	5	6	1	4	5	26	0	0	0	30	3.3	10	0	27	11	–6								
	Hartford Whalers	NHL	2	0	0	0	0	0	0	2	0	0	0	3	0.0	0	0	1	0	–1	3	0	0	0	0	0	0	0
	NHL Totals		573	130	128	258	106	89	195	646	15	11	13	964	13.5	383	38	478	107		71	8	25	33	77	0	0	1

AHL Second All-Star Team (1978)

Traded to **Pittsburgh** by **Montreal** with Robbie Holland for Denis Herron and Pittsburgh's 2nd round choice (Jocelyn Gauvreau) in 1982 Entry Draft, August 30, 1979. Traded to **Edmonton** by **Pittsburgh** for Pat Price, March 10, 1981. Traded to **Pittsburgh** by **Edmonton** for Mike Moller, October 4, 1985. Traded to **Buffalo** by **Pittsburgh** for Mike Moller and Randy Cunneyworth, October 4, 1985. Claimed by **St. Louis** from **Buffalo** in Waiver Draft, October 6, 1986. Traded to **Hartford** by **St. Louis** for Hartford's 10th round choice (Andy Cesarski) in 1987 Entry Draft, March 10, 1987.

• HUGHES, Ryan

C – L. 6'2", 196 lbs. b: Montreal, Que., 1/17/1972. Quebec's 2nd, 22nd overall, in 1990.

Season	Club	League	GP	G	A	Pts	AG	AA	APts	PIM	PP	SH	GW	S	%	TGF	PGF	TGA	PGA	+/–	GP	G	A	Pts	PIM	PP	SH	GW
1986-87	West Island Selects	QAAA	14	14	18	32																						
1987-88	Lac St-Louis Lions	QAAA	36	19	32	51															2	1	0	1				
1988-89	Lac St-Louis Lions	QAAA	42	25	62	87				48																		
	Canada	Nat-Team	3	0	0	0				2																		
1989-90	Cornell University	ECAC	27	7	16	23				35																		
1990-91	Cornell University	ECAC	32	18	34	52				28																		
1991-92	Cornell University	ECAC	27	8	13	21				36																		
	Canada	WJC-A	7	0	1	1				0																		
1992-93	Cornell University	ECAC	26	8	14	22				30																		
1993-94	Cornwall Aces	AHL	54	17	12	29				24											13	2	4	6	6			
1994-95	Cornwall Aces	AHL	72	15	24	39				48											14	0	7	7	10			
1995-96	Boston Bruins	NHL	3	0	0	0	0	0	0	0	0	0	0	2	0.0	0	0	0	0	0								
	Providence Bruins	AHL	78	22	52	74				89											4	1	2	3	20			
1996-97	Chicago Wolves	IHL	14	2	6	8				12																		
	Quebec Rafales	IHL	30	2	3	5				24											8	1	1	2	4			
	NHL Totals		3	0	0	0	0	0	0	0	0	0	0	2	0.0	0	0	0	0									

Signed as a free agent by **Boston**, October 6, 1995.

• HULBIG, Joe

Joseph Allan LW – L. 6'3", 215 lbs. b: Norwood, MA, 9/29/1973. Edmonton's 1st, 13th overall, in 1992.

Season	Club	League	GP	G	A	Pts	AG	AA	APts	PIM	PP	SH	GW	S	%	TGF	PGF	TGA	PGA	+/–	GP	G	A	Pts	PIM	PP	SH	GW
1988-89	South Shore Kings	MBHL	STATISTICS NOT AVAILABLE																									
1989-90	St. Sebastian's Academy	Hi-School	30	13	12	25																						
1990-91	St. Sebastian's Academy	Hi-School	30	23	19	42																						
1991-92	St. Sebastian's Academy	Hi-School	17	19	24	43				30																		
1992-93	Providence College	H-East	26	3	13	16				22																		
1993-94	Providence College	H-East	28	6	4	10				36																		
1994-95	Providence College	H-East	37	14	21	35				36																		
1995-96	Providence College	H-East	31	14	22	36				56																		
1996-97	Edmonton Oilers	NHL	6	0	0	0	0	0	0	0	0	0	0	4	0.0	1	0	2	0	–1	6	0	1	1	2	0	0	0
	Hamilton Bulldogs	AHL	73	18	28	46				59											16	6	10	16	6			
1997-98	Edmonton Oilers	NHL	17	2	2	4	2	2	4	2	0	0	1	8	25.0	6	2	5	0	–1								
	Hamilton Bulldogs	AHL	46	15	16	31				52											3	0	1	1	2			
1998-99	Edmonton Oilers	NHL	1	0	0	0	0	0	0	2	0	0	0	2	0.0	1	0	0	0	1								
	Hamilton Bulldogs	AHL	76	22	24	46				68											11	4	2	6	18			
99-2000	Boston Bruins	NHL	24	2	2	4	2	2	4	8	0	0	0	15	13.3	6	0	14	0	–8								
	Providence Bruins	AHL	15	4	5	9				17																		
	NHL Totals		48	4	4	8	4	4	8	12	0	0	1	29	13.8	14	2	21	0		6	0	1	1	2	0	0	0

Signed as a free agent by **Boston**, July 23, 1999.

• HULL, Bobby

Robert Marvin "The Golden Jet" LW – L. 5'10", 195 lbs. b: Point Anne, Ont., 1/3/1939. **HHOF**

Season	Club	League	GP	G	A	Pts	AG	AA	APts	PIM	PP	SH	GW	S	%	TGF	PGF	TGA	PGA	+/–	GP	G	A	Pts	PIM	PP	SH	GW
1954-55	Woodstock Athletics	OHA-B	STATISTICS NOT AVAILABLE																									
	Galt Black Hawks	OHA-Jr.	6	0	0	0				0																		
1955-56	St. Catharines Teepees	OHA-Jr.	48	11	7	18				79											6	0	2	2	9			
1956-57	St. Catharines Teepees	OHA-Jr.	52	33	28	61				95											13	8	8	16	24			
1957-58	Chicago Black Hawks	NHL	70	13	34	47	16	35	51	62																		
1958-59	Chicago Black Hawks	NHL	70	18	32	50	21	32	53	50											6	1	1	2	2			
1959-60	Chicago Black Hawks	NHL	70	*39	42	*81	47	41	88	68											3	1	0	1	2			
1960-61 ♦	Chicago Black Hawks	NHL	67	31	25	56	36	24	60	43											12	4	10	14	4			
1961-62	Chicago Black Hawks	NHL	70	*50	34	*84	59	33	92	35											12	*8	6	14	12			
1962-63	Chicago Black Hawks	NHL	65	31	31	62	36	31	67	27											5	*8	2	10	4			
1963-64	Chicago Black Hawks	NHL	70	*43	44	87	55	47	102	50											7	2	5	7	2			
1964-65	Chicago Black Hawks	NHL	61	39	32	71	48	33	81	32											14	*10	7	*17	27			
1965-66	Chicago Black Hawks	NHL	65	*54	43	*97	63	41	104	70											6	2	2	4	10			
1966-67	Chicago Black Hawks	NHL	66	*52	28	80	62	27	89	52											6	4	2	6	0			
1967-68	Chicago Black Hawks	NHL	71	*44	31	75	52	31	83	39	8	2	6	364	12.1	105	28	73	10	14	11	4	6	10	15	1	1	1
1968-69	Chicago Black Hawks	NHL	74	*58	49	107	62	44	106	48	20	2	11	414	14.0	132	49	99	9	–7								
1969-70	Chicago Black Hawks	NHL	61	38	29	67	42	27	69	8	10	2	8	289	13.1	90	29	50	9	20	8	3	8	11	2	0	0	0
1970-71	Chicago Black Hawks	NHL	78	44	52	96	44	44	88	32	11	0	11	378	11.6	129	49	54	8	34	18	11	14	25	16	6	0	4
1971-72	Chicago Black Hawks	NHL	78	50	43	93	51	37	88	24	8	3	9	336	14.9	126	37	47	12	54	8	4	4	8	6	0	1	0
1972-73	Winnipeg Jets	WHA	63	51	52	103				37											14	9	*16	25	16			
1973-74	Winnipeg Jets	WHA	75	53	42	95				38											4	1	1	2	4			
1974-75	Team Canada	Summit-74	8	7	2	9				0																		
	Winnipeg Jets	WHA	78	*77	65	142				41																		
1975-76	Winnipeg Jets	WHA	80	53	70	123				30											13	12	8	20	4			
1976-77	Canada	Can-Cup	7	5	3	8				2																		
	Winnipeg Jets	WHA	34	21	32	53				14											20	13	9	22	2			
1977-78	Winnipeg Jets	WHA	77	46	71	117				23											9	8	3	11	12			
1978-79	Winnipeg Jets	WHA	4	2	3	5				0																		
1979-80	Winnipeg Jets	NHL	18	4	6	10	3	4	7	0	1	0	0	25	16.0	18	4	21	0	–7								
	Hartford Whalers	NHL	9	2	5	7	2	4	6	0	1	0	0	13	15.4	9	2	10	0	–3	3	0	0	0	0	0	0	0
1980-81			OUT OF HOCKEY – RETIRED																									
1981-82	New York Rangers	DN-Cup	4	1	1	2				0																		
	NHL Totals		1063	610	560	1170	699	535	1234	640											119	62	67	129	102			
	Other Major League Totals		411	303	335	638				183											60	43	37	80	38			

• Brother of Dennis • Father of Brett • NHL First All-Star Team (1960, 1962, 1964, 1965, 1966, 1967, 1968, 1969, 1970, 1972) • Won Art Ross Trophy (1960, 1962, 1966) • NHL Second All-Star Team (1963, 1971) • Won Lady Byng Trophy (1965) • Won Hart Trophy (1965, 1966) • Won Lester Patrick Trophy (1969) • WHA First All-Star Team (1973, 1974, 1975) • Won Gary Davidson Trophy (WHA MVP) (1973, 1975) • WHA Second All-Star Team (1976, 1978) • Played in NHL All-Star Game (1960, 1961, 1962, 1963, 1964, 1965, 1967, 1968, 1969, 1970, 1971, 1972)

Selected by **Winnipeg** (WHA) in 1972 WHA General Player Draft, February 12, 1972. • Missed majority of 1976-77 season recovering from wrist injury suffered in pre-season game vs. St. Louis (NHL), September 26, 1976. • Missed majority of 1978-79 season after announcing retirement, November 1, 1978. Reclaimed by **Chicago** from **Winnipeg** prior to Expansion Draft, June 9, 1979. Claimed by **Winnipeg** from **Chicago** in Expansion Draft, June 13, 1979. Traded to **Hartford** by **Winnipeg** for future considerations, February 27, 1980. • Played with NY Rangers in 1981 Dagen Nyheter Cup Challenge in Sweden, September 17-23, 1981.

• HULL, Brett

Brett A. RW – R. 5'11", 203 lbs. b: Belleville, Ont., 8/9/1964. Calgary's 6th, 117th overall, in 1984.

Season	Club	League	GP	G	A	Pts	AG	AA	APts	PIM	PP	SH	GW	S	%	TGF	PGF	TGA	PGA	+/–	GP	G	A	Pts	PIM	PP	SH	GW
1982-83	Penticton Knights	BCJHL	50	48	56	104				27																		
1983-84	Penticton Knights	BCJHL	56	*105	83	*188				20																		
1984-85	University of Minnesota-Duluth	WCHA	48	32	28	60				24																		

Season	Club	League	REGULAR SEASON																		PLAYOFFS							
			GP	G	A	Pts	AG	AA	APts	PIM	PP	SH	GW	S	%	TGF	PGF	TGA	PGA	+/–	GP	G	A	Pts	PIM	PP	SH	GW
1985-86	University of Minnesota-Duluth	WCHA	42	52	32	84	....	....	....	46	....	....	....	....	....	....	....	....	....	....	....	....	....	....	....	....	....	....
	United States	WEC-A	10	7	4	11	....	....	....	18	....	....	....	....	....	....	....	....	....	....	....	....	....	....	....	....	....	....
	Calgary Flames	**NHL**	....	....	....	....	....	....	....	....	....	....	....	....	....	....	....	....	....	....	**2**	**0**	**0**	**0**	**0**	**0**	**0**	**0**
1986-87	**Calgary Flames**	**NHL**	**5**	**1**	**0**	**1**	**1**	**0**	**1**	**0**	**0**	**0**	**1**	**5**	**20.0**	**2**	**0**	**3**	**0**	**–1**	**4**	**2**	**1**	**3**	**0**	**0**	**0**	**0**
	Moncton Golden Flames	AHL	67	50	42	92	....	....	....	16	....	....	....	....	....	....	....	....	....	....	3	2	2	4	2	....	....	....
1987-88	**Calgary Flames**	**NHL**	**52**	**26**	**24**	**50**	**22**	**17**	**39**	**12**	**4**	**0**	**3**	**153**	**17.0**	**72**	**27**	**35**	**0**	**10**	....	....	....	....	....	....	....	....
	St. Louis Blues	**NHL**	**13**	**6**	**8**	**14**	**5**	**6**	**11**	**4**	**2**	**0**	**0**	**58**	**10.3**	**23**	**8**	**11**	**0**	**4**	**10**	**7**	**2**	**9**	**4**	**4**	**0**	**3**
1988-89	**St. Louis Blues**	**NHL**	**78**	**41**	**43**	**84**	**35**	**30**	**65**	**33**	**16**	**0**	**6**	**305**	**13.4**	**114**	**58**	**73**	**0**	**–17**	**10**	**5**	**5**	**10**	**6**	**1**	**0**	**2**
1989-90	**St. Louis Blues**	**NHL**	**80**	***72**	**41**	**113**	**62**	**29**	**91**	**24**	**27**	**0**	**12**	**385**	**18.7**	**154**	**66**	**90**	**1**	**–1**	**12**	**13**	**8**	**21**	**17**	**7**	**0**	**3**
1990-91	**St. Louis Blues**	**NHL**	**78**	***86**	**45**	**131**	**80**	**34**	**114**	**22**	**29**	**0**	**11**	**389**	**22.1**	**170**	**62**	**86**	**1**	**23**	**13**	**11**	**8**	**19**	**4**	**3**	**0**	**2**
1991-92	United States	Can-Cup	8	2	7	9	....	....	....	0	....	....	....	....	....	....	....	....	....	....	....	....	....	....	....	....	....	....
	St. Louis Blues	**NHL**	**73**	***70**	**39**	**109**	**64**	**29**	**93**	**48**	**20**	**5**	**9**	**408**	**17.2**	**146**	**52**	**100**	**4**	**–2**	**6**	**4**	**4**	**8**	**4**	**1**	**1**	**1**
1992-93	**St. Louis Blues**	**NHL**	**80**	**54**	**47**	**101**	**45**	**32**	**77**	**41**	**29**	**0**	**2**	**390**	**13.8**	**140**	**77**	**95**	**5**	**–27**	**11**	**8**	**5**	**13**	**2**	**5**	**0**	**2**
1993-94	**St. Louis Blues**	**NHL**	**81**	**57**	**40**	**97**	**53**	**31**	**84**	**38**	**25**	**3**	**6**	**392**	**14.5**	**136**	**67**	**94**	**22**	**–3**	**4**	**2**	**1**	**3**	**0**	**1**	**0**	**0**
1994-95	**St. Louis Blues**	**NHL**	**48**	**29**	**21**	**50**	**51**	**31**	**82**	**10**	**9**	**3**	**6**	**200**	**14.5**	**77**	**29**	**57**	**22**	**13**	**7**	**6**	**2**	**8**	**0**	**2**	**0**	**0**
1995-96	**St. Louis Blues**	**NHL**	**70**	**43**	**40**	**83**	**42**	**33**	**75**	**30**	**16**	**5**	**6**	**327**	**13.1**	**110**	**47**	**91**	**32**	**4**	**13**	**6**	**5**	**11**	**10**	**2**	**1**	**1**
1996-97	United States	W-Cup	7	*7	4	*11	....	....	....	4	....	....	....	....	....	....	....	....	....	....	....	....	....	....	....	....	....	....
	St. Louis Blues	**NHL**	**77**	**42**	**40**	**82**	**45**	**36**	**81**	**10**	**12**	**2**	**6**	**302**	**13.9**	**100**	**34**	**91**	**16**	**–9**	**6**	**2**	**7**	**9**	**2**	**0**	**0**	**0**
1997-98	**St. Louis Blues**	**NHL**	**66**	**27**	**45**	**72**	**32**	**44**	**76**	**26**	**10**	**0**	**6**	**211**	**12.8**	**94**	**37**	**60**	**2**	**–1**	**10**	**3**	**3**	**6**	**2**	**1**	**0**	**1**
	United States	Olympics	4	2	1	3	....	....	....	0	....	....	....	....	....	....	....	....	....	....	....	....	....	....	....	....	....	....
1998-99♦	**Dallas Stars**	**NHL**	**60**	**32**	**26**	**58**	**38**	**25**	**63**	**30**	**15**	**0**	**11**	**192**	**16.7**	**78**	**30**	**31**	**2**	**19**	**22**	**8**	**7**	**15**	**4**	**3**	**0**	**2**
99-2000	**Dallas Stars**	**NHL**	**79**	**24**	**35**	**59**	**27**	**32**	**59**	**43**	**11**	**0**	**3**	**223**	**10.8**	**80**	**38**	**67**	**4**	**–21**	**23**	***11**	***13**	***24**	**4**	**3**	**0**	**4**
	NHL Totals		**940**	**610**	**494**	**1104**	**602**	**409**	**1011**	**371**	**225**	**18**	**88**	**3940**	**15.5**	**1496**	**632**	**984**	**111**		**153**	**88**	**71**	**159**	**59**	**33**	**2**	**21**

• Son of Bobby • WCHA First All-Star Team (1986) • AHL First All-Star Team (1987) • Won Dudley "Red" Garrett Memorial Trophy (Top Rookie - AHL) (1987) • NHL First All-Star Team (1990, 1991, 1992) • Won Lady Byng Trophy (1990) • Won Dodge Ram Tough Award (1990, 1991) • Won Hart Memorial Trophy (1991) • Won Lester B. Pearson Award (1991) • Won ProSet/NHL Player of the Year Award (1991) • World Cup All-Star Team (1996) • Played in NHL All-Star Game (1989, 1990, 1992, 1993, 1994, 1996, 1997)

Traded to **St. Louis** by **Calgary** with Steve Bozek for Rob Ramage and Rick Wamsley, March 7, 1988. Signed as a free agent by **Dallas**, July 3, 1998.

• HULL, Dennis

Dennis William LW – L. 5'11", 198 lbs. b: Pointe Anne, Ont., 11/19/1944.

Season	Club	League	GP	G	A	Pts	AG	AA	APts	PIM	PP	SH	GW	S	%	TGF	PGF	TGA	PGA	+/–	GP	G	A	Pts	PIM	PP	SH	GW
1960-61	St. Catharines Teepees	OHA-Jr.	47	6	4	10	....	....	....	33	....	....	....	....	....	....	....	....	....	....	6	0	1	1	2	....	....	....
1961-62	St. Catharines Teepees	OHA-Jr.	50	6	12	18	....	....	....	29	....	....	....	....	....	....	....	....	....	....	2	0	0	0	0	....	....	....
1962-63	St. Catharines Black Hawks	OHA-Jr.	50	19	29	48	....	....	....	73	....	....	....	....	....	....	....	....	....	....	....	....	....	....	....	....	....	....
1963-64	St. Catharines Black Hawks	OHA-Jr.	55	48	49	97	....	....	....	123	....	....	....	....	....	....	....	....	....	....	12	4	11	15	50	....	....	....
1964-65	**Chicago Black Hawks**	**NHL**	**55**	**10**	**4**	**14**	**12**	**4**	**16**	**18**	....	....	....	....	....	....	....	....	....	....	**6**	**0**	**0**	**0**	**0**	**0**	**0**	**0**
1965-66	**Chicago Black Hawks**	**NHL**	**25**	**1**	**5**	**6**	**1**	**5**	**6**	**6**	....	....	....	....	....	....	....	....	....	....	**3**	**0**	**0**	**0**	**0**	**0**	**0**	**0**
	St. Louis Braves	CPHL	40	11	16	27	....	....	....	14	....	....	....	....	....	....	....	....	....	....	5	2	1	3	0	....	....	....
1966-67	**Chicago Black Hawks**	**NHL**	**70**	**25**	**17**	**42**	**29**	**17**	**46**	**33**	....	....	....	....	....	....	....	....	....	....	**6**	**0**	**1**	**1**	**12**	**0**	**0**	**0**
1967-68	**Chicago Black Hawks**	**NHL**	**74**	**18**	**15**	**33**	**21**	**15**	**36**	**34**	**0**	**0**	**2**	**197**	**9.1**	**40**	**1**	**71**	**12**	**–20**	**11**	**1**	**3**	**4**	**6**	**0**	**0**	**1**
1968-69	**Chicago Black Hawks**	**NHL**	**72**	**30**	**34**	**64**	**32**	**30**	**62**	**25**	**3**	**0**	**3**	**233**	**12.9**	**95**	**21**	**71**	**4**	**7**	....	....	....	....	....	....	....	....
1969-70	**Chicago Black Hawks**	**NHL**	**76**	**17**	**35**	**52**	**18**	**33**	**51**	**31**	**5**	**0**	**3**	**223**	**7.6**	**74**	**15**	**57**	**2**	**4**	**8**	**5**	**2**	**7**	**0**	**0**	**1**	**0**
1970-71	**Chicago Black Hawks**	**NHL**	**78**	**40**	**26**	**66**	**40**	**22**	**62**	**16**	**10**	**0**	**7**	**229**	**17.5**	**92**	**27**	**41**	**4**	**28**	**18**	**7**	**6**	**13**	**2**	**2**	**0**	**1**
1971-72	**Chicago Black Hawks**	**NHL**	**78**	**30**	**39**	**69**	**30**	**34**	**64**	**10**	**8**	**1**	**2**	**270**	**11.1**	**51**	**9**	**30**	**0**	**12**	**8**	**4**	**2**	**6**	**4**	**1**	**0**	**0**
1972-73	Team Canada	Summit-72	4	2	2	4	....	....	....	4	....	....	....	....	....	....	....	....	....	....	....	....	....	....	....	....	....	....
	Chicago Black Hawks	**NHL**	**78**	**39**	**51**	**90**	**37**	**41**	**78**	**27**	**8**	**0**	**7**	**263**	**14.8**	**130**	**30**	**74**	**2**	**28**	**16**	**9**	***15**	**24**	**4**	**4**	**0**	**1**
1973-74	**Chicago Black Hawks**	**NHL**	**74**	**29**	**39**	**68**	**28**	**32**	**60**	**15**	**5**	**1**	**6**	**220**	**13.2**	**96**	**26**	**46**	**1**	**25**	**10**	**6**	**3**	**9**	**0**	**1**	**0**	**1**
1974-75	**Chicago Black Hawks**	**NHL**	**69**	**16**	**21**	**37**	**14**	**16**	**30**	**10**	**4**	**0**	**2**	**199**	**8.0**	**56**	**16**	**59**	**5**	**–14**	**5**	**0**	**2**	**2**	**0**	**0**	**0**	**0**
1975-76	**Chicago Black Hawks**	**NHL**	**80**	**27**	**39**	**66**	**24**	**29**	**53**	**28**	**1**	**4**	**4**	**225**	**12.0**	**87**	**21**	**108**	**25**	**–17**	**4**	**0**	**0**	**0**	**0**	**0**	**0**	**0**
1976-77	**Chicago Black Hawks**	**NHL**	**75**	**16**	**17**	**33**	**14**	**13**	**27**	**2**	**3**	**0**	**0**	**207**	**7.7**	**69**	**21**	**82**	**14**	**–20**	**2**	**1**	**0**	**1**	**0**	**1**	**0**	**0**
1977-78	**Detroit Red Wings**	**NHL**	**55**	**5**	**9**	**14**	**5**	**7**	**12**	**6**	**2**	**0**	**1**	**72**	**6.9**	**22**	**8**	**34**	**0**	**–20**	**7**	**0**	**0**	**0**	**2**	**0**	**0**	**0**
	NHL Totals		**959**	**303**	**351**	**654**	**305**	**298**	**603**	**261**	....	....	....	....	....	....	....	....	....		**104**	**33**	**34**	**67**	**30**	....	....	....

• Brother of Bobby OHA-Jr. First All-Star Team (1964) • NHL Second All-Star Team (1973) • Played in NHL All-Star Game (1969, 1971, 1972, 1973, 1974)

Traded to **Detroit** by **Chicago** for Detroit's 4th round choice (Carey Wilson) in 1980 Entry Draft, December 2, 1977.

• HULL, Jody

RW – R. 6'2", 200 lbs. b: Petrolia, Ont., 2/2/1969. Hartford's 1st, 18th overall, in 1987.

Season	Club	League	GP	G	A	Pts	AG	AA	APts	PIM	PP	SH	GW	S	%	TGF	PGF	TGA	PGA	+/–	GP	G	A	Pts	PIM	PP	SH	GW
1984-85	Cambridge Winterhawks	OJHL-B	38	13	17	30	....	....	....	39	....	....	....	....	....	....	....	....	....	....	....	....	....	....	....	....	....	....
1985-86	Peterborough Petes	OHL	61	20	22	42	....	....	....	29	....	....	....	....	....	....	....	....	....	....	16	1	5	6	4	....	....	....
1986-87	Peterborough Petes	OHL	49	18	34	52	....	....	....	22	....	....	....	....	....	....	....	....	....	....	12	4	9	13	14	....	....	....
1987-88	Peterborough Petes	OHL	60	50	44	94	....	....	....	33	....	....	....	....	....	....	....	....	....	....	12	10	8	18	8	....	....	....
	Canada	WJC-A	7	2	1	3	....	....	....	2	....	....	....	....	....	....	....	....	....	....	....	....	....	....	....	....	....	....
1988-89	**Hartford Whalers**	**NHL**	**60**	**16**	**18**	**34**	**14**	**13**	**27**	**10**	**6**	**0**	**2**	**82**	**19.5**	**53**	**12**	**35**	**0**	**6**	**1**	**0**	**0**	**0**	**2**	**0**	**0**	**0**
1989-90	**Hartford Whalers**	**NHL**	**38**	**7**	**10**	**17**	**6**	**7**	**13**	**21**	**2**	**0**	**0**	**46**	**15.2**	**18**	**3**	**26**	**5**	**–6**	**5**	**0**	**1**	**1**	**2**	**0**	**0**	**0**
	Binghamton Whalers	AHL	21	7	10	17	....	....	....	6	....	....	....	....	....	....	....	....	....	....	....	....	....	....	....	....	....	....
1990-91	**New York Rangers**	**NHL**	**47**	**5**	**8**	**13**	**5**	**6**	**11**	**10**	**0**	**0**	**0**	**57**	**8.8**	**20**	**0**	**27**	**9**	**2**	....	....	....	....	....	....	....	....
1991-92	**New York Rangers**	**NHL**	**3**	**0**	**0**	**0**	**0**	**0**	**0**	**2**	**0**	**0**	**0**	**4**	**0.0**	**0**	**0**	**5**	**1**	**–4**	....	....	....	....	....	....	....	....
	Binghamton Rangers	AHL	69	34	31	65	....	....	....	28	....	....	....	....	....	....	....	....	....	....	11	5	2	7	4	....	....	....
1992-93	**Ottawa Senators**	**NHL**	**69**	**13**	**21**	**34**	**11**	**14**	**25**	**14**	**5**	**1**	**0**	**134**	**9.7**	**56**	**26**	**72**	**18**	**–24**	....	....	....	....	....	....	....	....
1993-94	**Florida Panthers**	**NHL**	**69**	**13**	**13**	**26**	**12**	**10**	**22**	**8**	**0**	**1**	**5**	**100**	**13.0**	**38**	**1**	**53**	**22**	**6**	....	....	....	....	....	....	....	....
1994-95	**Florida Panthers**	**NHL**	**46**	**11**	**8**	**19**	**19**	**12**	**31**	**8**	**0**	**0**	**4**	**63**	**17.5**	**23**	**2**	**35**	**13**	**–1**	....	....	....	....	....	....	....	....
1995-96	**Florida Panthers**	**NHL**	**78**	**20**	**17**	**37**	**20**	**14**	**34**	**25**	**2**	**0**	**3**	**120**	**16.7**	**43**	**4**	**60**	**26**	**5**	**14**	**3**	**2**	**5**	**0**	**0**	**0**	**0**
1996-97	**Florida Panthers**	**NHL**	**67**	**10**	**6**	**16**	**11**	**5**	**16**	**4**	**0**	**1**	**2**	**92**	**10.9**	**20**	**3**	**20**	**4**	**1**	**5**	**0**	**0**	**0**	**0**	**0**	**0**	**0**
1997-98	**Florida Panthers**	**NHL**	**21**	**2**	**0**	**2**	**2**	**0**	**2**	**4**	**0**	**1**	**0**	**23**	**8.7**	**5**	**0**	**11**	**7**	**1**	....	....	....	....	....	....	....	....
	Tampa Bay Lightning	**NHL**	**28**	**2**	**4**	**6**	**2**	**4**	**6**	**4**	**0**	**0**	**2**	**28**	**7.1**	**13**	**1**	**22**	**12**	**2**	....	....	....	....	....	....	....	....
1998-99	**Philadelphia Flyers**	**NHL**	**72**	**3**	**11**	**14**	**4**	**11**	**15**	**12**	**0**	**0**	**1**	**73**	**4.1**	**22**	**0**	**46**	**22**	**–2**	**6**	**0**	**0**	**0**	**4**	**0**	**0**	**0**
99-2000	Orlando Solar Bears	IHL	1	0	0	0	....	....	....	0	....	....	....	....	....	....	....	....	....	....	....	....	....	....	....	....	....	....
	Philadelphia Flyers	**NHL**	**67**	**10**	**3**	**13**	**11**	**3**	**14**	**4**	**0**	**2**	**2**	**63**	**15.9**	**23**	**0**	**27**	**12**	**8**	**18**	**0**	**1**	**1**	**0**	**0**	**0**	**0**
	NHL Totals		**665**	**112**	**119**	**231**	**117**	**99**	**216**	**126**	**15**	**6**	**21**	**885**	**12.7**	**334**	**52**	**439**	**151**		**49**	**3**	**4**	**7**	**8**	**0**	**0**	**0**

OHL Second All-Star Team (1988)

Traded to **NY Rangers** by **Hartford** for Carey Wilson and NY Rangers' 3rd round choice (Michael Nylander) in the 1991 Entry Draft, July 9, 1990. Traded to **Ottawa** by **NY Rangers** for future considerations, July 28, 1992. Signed as a free agent by **Florida**, August 10, 1993. Traded to **Tampa Bay** by **Florida** with Mark Fitzpatrick for Dino Ciccarelli and Jeff Norton, January 15, 1998. Signed as a free agent by **Philadelphia**, October 7, 1998. Claimed by **Atlanta** from **Philadelphia** in Expansion Draft, June 25, 1999. Traded to **Philadelphia** by **Atlanta** for cash, October 15, 1999.

• HULSE, Cale

Cale D. D – R. 6'3", 215 lbs. b: Edmonton, Alta., 11/10/1973. New Jersey's 3rd, 66th overall, in 1992.

Season	Club	League	GP	G	A	Pts	AG	AA	APts	PIM	PP	SH	GW	S	%	TGF	PGF	TGA	PGA	+/–	GP	G	A	Pts	PIM	PP	SH	GW
1990-91	Calgary Royals	AJHL	49	3	23	26	....	....	....	220	....	....	....	....	....	....	....	....	....	....	....	....	....	....	....	....	....	....
1991-92	Portland Winter Hawks	WHL	70	4	18	22	....	....	....	230	....	....	....	....	....	....	....	....	....	....	6	0	2	2	27	....	....	....
1992-93	Portland Winter Hawks	WHL	72	10	26	36	....	....	....	284	....	....	....	....	....	....	....	....	....	....	16	4	4	8	65	....	....	....
1993-94	Albany River Rats	AHL	79	7	14	21	....	....	....	186	....	....	....	....	....	....	....	....	....	....	5	0	3	3	11	....	....	....
1994-95	Albany River Rats	AHL	77	5	13	18	....	....	....	215	....	....	....	....	....	....	....	....	....	....	12	1	1	2	17	....	....	....
1995-96	**New Jersey Devils**	**NHL**	**8**	**0**	**0**	**0**	**0**	**0**	**0**	**15**	**0**	**0**	**0**	**5**	**0.0**	**3**	**0**	**5**	**0**	**–2**	....	....	....	....	....	....	....	....
	Albany River Rats	AHL	42	4	23	27	....	....	....	107	....	....	....	....	....	....	....	....	....	....	....	....	....	....	....	....	....	....
	Calgary Flames	**NHL**	**3**	**0**	**0**	**0**	**0**	**0**	**0**	**5**	**0**	**0**	**0**	**4**	**0.0**	**3**	**0**	**0**	**0**	**3**	**1**	**0**	**0**	**0**	**0**	**0**	**0**	**0**
	Saint John Flames	AHL	13	2	7	9	....	....	....	39	....	....	....	....	....	....	....	....	....	....	....	....	....	....	....	....	....	....
1996-97	**Calgary Flames**	**NHL**	**63**	**1**	**6**	**7**	**1**	**5**	**6**	**91**	**0**	**1**	**0**	**58**	**1.7**	**34**	**2**	**51**	**17**	**–2**	....	....	....	....	....	....	....	....

			REGULAR SEASON																		PLAYOFFS							
Season	Club	League	GP	G	A	Pts	AG	AA	APts	PIM	PP	SH	GW	S	%	TGF	PGF	TGA	PGA	+/–	GP	G	A	Pts	PIM	PP	SH	GW
1997-98	**Calgary Flames**	**NHL**	**79**	**5**	**22**	**27**	**6**	**22**	**28**	**169**	**1**	**1**	**0**	**117**	**4.3**	**66**	**14**	**76**	**25**	**1**	....	....	....	....	....	....	....	....
1998-99	**Calgary Flames**	**NHL**	**73**	**3**	**9**	**12**	**4**	**9**	**13**	**117**	**0**	**0**	**0**	**83**	**3.6**	**34**	**4**	**66**	**28**	**–8**	....	....	....	....	....	....	....	....
99-2000	**Calgary Flames**	**NHL**	**47**	**1**	**6**	**7**	**1**	**6**	**7**	**47**	**0**	**0**	**0**	**41**	**2.4**	**19**	**0**	**35**	**5**	**–11**	....	....	....	....	....	....	....	....
	NHL Totals		**273**	**10**	**43**	**53**	**12**	**42**	**54**	**444**	**1**	**2**	**0**	**308**	**3.2**	**159**	**20**	**233**	**75**		**1**	**0**	**0**	**0**	**0**	**0**	**0**	**0**

Traded to **Calgary** by **New Jersey** with Tommy Albelin and Jocelyn Lemieux for Phil Housley and Dan Keczmer, February 26, 1996. Traded to **Nashville** by **Calgary** with Calgary's 3rd round choice in 2001 Entry Draft for Sergei Krivokrasov, March 14, 2000. • Missed remainder of 1999-2000 season recovering from ankle injury suffered in game vs. San Jose, March 12, 2000.

• HUNTER, Dale

Dale Robert C – L. 5'10", 198 lbs. b: Petrolia, Ont., 7/31/1960. Quebec's 2nd, 41st overall, in 1979.

Season	Club	League	GP	G	A	Pts	AG	AA	APts	PIM	PP	SH	GW	S	%	TGF	PGF	TGA	PGA	+/–	GP	G	A	Pts	PIM	PP	SH	GW
1976-77	Strathroy Blades	OHA-B	42	25	30	55	....	....	....	....	....	....	....	....	....	....	....	....	....	....	....	....	....	....	....	....	....	....
1977-78	Kitchener Rangers	OMJHL	68	22	42	64	....	....	....	115	....	....	....	....	....	....	....	....	....	....	9	1	0	1	32	....	....	....
1978-79	Sudbury Wolves	OMJHL	59	42	68	110	....	....	....	188	....	....	....	....	....	....	....	....	....	....	10	4	12	16	47	....	....	....
1979-80	Sudbury Wolves	OMJHL	61	34	51	85	....	....	....	189	....	....	....	....	....	....	....	....	....	....	9	6	9	15	45	....	....	....
1980-81	**Quebec Nordiques**	**NHL**	**80**	**19**	**44**	**63**	**15**	**29**	**44**	**226**	**2**	**0**	**2**	**152**	**12.5**	**83**	**9**	**107**	**38**	**5**	**5**	**4**	**2**	**6**	**34**	**0**	**0**	**1**
1981-82	**Quebec Nordiques**	**NHL**	**80**	**22**	**50**	**72**	**17**	**33**	**50**	**272**	**0**	**2**	**1**	**124**	**17.7**	**95**	**9**	**96**	**36**	**26**	**16**	**3**	**7**	**10**	**52**	**1**	**0**	**2**
1982-83	**Quebec Nordiques**	**NHL**	**80**	**17**	**46**	**63**	**14**	**32**	**46**	**206**	**1**	**2**	**1**	**125**	**13.6**	**92**	**4**	**122**	**44**	**10**	**4**	**2**	**1**	**3**	**24**	**0**	**1**	**0**
1983-84	**Quebec Nordiques**	**NHL**	**77**	**24**	**55**	**79**	**19**	**38**	**57**	**232**	**7**	**2**	**1**	**123**	**19.5**	**108**	**20**	**76**	**23**	**35**	**9**	**2**	**3**	**5**	**41**	**0**	**0**	**0**
1984-85	**Quebec Nordiques**	**NHL**	**80**	**20**	**52**	**72**	**16**	**35**	**51**	**209**	**3**	**3**	**3**	**115**	**17.4**	**104**	**21**	**87**	**27**	**23**	**17**	**4**	**6**	**10**	***97**	**0**	**1**	**2**
1985-86	**Quebec Nordiques**	**NHL**	**80**	**28**	**42**	**70**	**22**	**28**	**50**	**265**	**7**	**0**	**4**	**152**	**18.4**	**98**	**23**	**84**	**15**	**6**	**3**	**0**	**0**	**0**	**15**	**0**	**0**	**0**
1986-87	**Quebec Nordiques**	**NHL**	**46**	**10**	**29**	**39**	**9**	**21**	**30**	**135**	**0**	**0**	**0**	**53**	**18.9**	**61**	**14**	**52**	**9**	**4**	**13**	**1**	**7**	**8**	**56**	**1**	**0**	**0**
1987-88	**Washington Capitals**	**NHL**	**79**	**22**	**37**	**59**	**19**	**26**	**45**	**240**	**11**	**0**	**1**	**126**	**17.5**	**109**	**54**	**56**	**8**	**7**	**14**	**7**	**5**	**12**	**98**	**4**	**0**	**1**
1988-89	**Washington Capitals**	**NHL**	**80**	**20**	**37**	**57**	**17**	**26**	**43**	**219**	**9**	**0**	**3**	**138**	**14.5**	**95**	**46**	**58**	**6**	**–3**	**6**	**0**	**4**	**4**	**29**	**0**	**0**	**0**
1989-90	Washington Capitals	Fr-Tour	4	1	2	3	....	....	....	4	....	....	....	....	....	....	....	....	....	....	....	....	....	....	....	....	....	....
	Washington Capitals	**NHL**	**80**	**23**	**39**	**62**	**20**	**28**	**48**	**233**	**9**	**1**	**6**	**123**	**18.7**	**104**	**37**	**52**	**2**	**17**	**15**	**4**	**8**	**12**	**61**	**1**	**0**	**0**
1990-91	**Washington Capitals**	**NHL**	**76**	**16**	**30**	**46**	**15**	**23**	**38**	**234**	**9**	**0**	**2**	**106**	**15.1**	**71**	**31**	**63**	**1**	**–22**	**11**	**1**	**9**	**10**	**41**	**0**	**0**	**0**
1991-92	**Washington Capitals**	**NHL**	**80**	**28**	**50**	**78**	**25**	**38**	**63**	**205**	**13**	**0**	**4**	**110**	**25.5**	**124**	**53**	**75**	**2**	**–2**	**7**	**1**	**4**	**5**	**16**	**0**	**0**	**0**
1992-93	**Washington Capitals**	**NHL**	**84**	**20**	**59**	**79**	**17**	**41**	**58**	**198**	**10**	**0**	**2**	**120**	**16.7**	**109**	**50**	**58**	**2**	**3**	**6**	**7**	**1**	**8**	**35**	**4**	**0**	**1**
1993-94	**Washington Capitals**	**NHL**	**52**	**9**	**29**	**38**	**8**	**22**	**30**	**131**	**1**	**0**	**1**	**61**	**14.8**	**58**	**16**	**51**	**5**	**–4**	**7**	**0**	**3**	**3**	**14**	**0**	**0**	**0**
1994-95	**Washington Capitals**	**NHL**	**45**	**8**	**15**	**23**	**14**	**22**	**36**	**101**	**3**	**0**	**1**	**73**	**11.0**	**36**	**13**	**27**	**0**	**–4**	**7**	**4**	**4**	**8**	**24**	**2**	**0**	**0**
1995-96	**Washington Capitals**	**NHL**	**82**	**13**	**24**	**37**	**13**	**20**	**33**	**112**	**4**	**0**	**3**	**128**	**10.2**	**48**	**15**	**29**	**1**	**5**	**6**	**1**	**5**	**6**	**24**	**0**	**0**	**0**
1996-97	**Washington Capitals**	**NHL**	**82**	**14**	**32**	**46**	**15**	**28**	**43**	**125**	**3**	**0**	**5**	**110**	**12.7**	**63**	**18**	**47**	**0**	**–2**	....	....	....	....	....	....	....	....
1997-98	**Washington Capitals**	**NHL**	**82**	**8**	**18**	**26**	**9**	**18**	**27**	**103**	**0**	**0**	**1**	**82**	**9.8**	**38**	**2**	**42**	**7**	**1**	**21**	**0**	**4**	**4**	**30**	**0**	**0**	**0**
1998-99	**Washington Capitals**	**NHL**	**50**	**0**	**5**	**5**	**0**	**5**	**5**	**102**	**0**	**0**	**0**	**18**	**0.0**	**10**	**0**	**21**	**4**	**–7**	....	....	....	....	....	....	....	....
	Colorado Avalanche	**NHL**	**12**	**2**	**4**	**6**	**2**	**4**	**6**	**17**	**0**	**0**	**0**	**6**	**33.3**	**9**	**3**	**7**	**1**	**0**	**19**	**1**	**3**	**4**	**38**	**0**	**0**	**0**
99-2000	**Washington Capitals**	**NHL**	DID NOT PLAY – FRONT OFFICE STAFF																									
	NHL Totals		**1407**	**323**	**697**	**1020**	**286**	**517**	**803**	**3565**	**92**	**10**	**41**	**2045**	**15.8**	**1515**	**438**	**1210**	**231**		**186**	**42**	**76**	**118**	**729**	**13**	**2**	**7**

• Brother of Dave and Mark • Played in NHL All-Star Game (1997)

Traded to **Washington** by **Quebec** with Clint Malarchuk for Gaetan Duchesne, Alan Haworth and Washington's 1st round choice (Joe Sakic) in 1987 Entry Draft, June 13, 1987. Traded to **Colorado** by **Washington** with Washington's 3rd round choice (Sergei Kliazmine) in 2000 Entry Draft for Vancouver's 2nd round choice (previously acquired, Washington selected Charlie Stephens) in 1999 Entry Draft, March 23, 1999.

• HUNTER, Dave

David P. LW – L. 5'11", 195 lbs. b: Petrolia, Ont., 1/1/1958. Montreal's 2nd, 17th overall, in 1978.

Season	Club	League	GP	G	A	Pts	AG	AA	APts	PIM	PP	SH	GW	S	%	TGF	PGF	TGA	PGA	+/–	GP	G	A	Pts	PIM	PP	SH	GW
1974-75	Petroilia Jets	OHA-B	STATISTICS NOT AVAILABLE																									
1975-76	Sudbury Wolves	OMJHL	53	7	21	28	....	....	....	117	....	....	....	....	....	....	....	....	....	....	17	0	9	9	53	....	....	....
1976-77	Sudbury Wolves	OMJHL	62	30	56	86	....	....	....	140	....	....	....	....	....	....	....	....	....	....	6	1	3	4	9	....	....	....
	Canada	WJC-A	7	6	2	8	....	....	....	2	....	....	....	....	....	....	....	....	....	....	....	....	....	....	....	....	....	....
1977-78	Sudbury Wolves	OMJHL	68	44	44	88	....	....	....	156	....	....	....	....	....	....	....	....	....	....	....	....	....	....	....	....	....	....
1978-79	Edmonton Oilers	WHA	72	7	25	32	....	....	....	134	....	....	....	....	....	....	....	....	....	....	13	2	3	5	42	....	....	....
	Dallas Black Hawks	CHL	6	3	4	7	....	....	....	6	....	....	....	....	....	....	....	....	....	....	....	....	....	....	....	....	....	....
1979-80	**Edmonton Oilers**	**NHL**	**80**	**12**	**31**	**43**	**10**	**23**	**33**	**103**	**1**	**2**	**3**	**109**	**11.0**	**71**	**3**	**78**	**17**	**7**	**3**	**0**	**0**	**0**	**7**	**0**	**0**	**0**
1980-81	**Edmonton Oilers**	**NHL**	**78**	**12**	**16**	**28**	**9**	**11**	**20**	**98**	**0**	**0**	**3**	**104**	**11.5**	**51**	**1**	**91**	**29**	**–12**	**9**	**0**	**0**	**0**	**28**	**0**	**0**	**0**
1981-82	**Edmonton Oilers**	**NHL**	**63**	**16**	**22**	**38**	**13**	**15**	**28**	**63**	**0**	**0**	**3**	**124**	**12.9**	**72**	**7**	**47**	**15**	**33**	**5**	**0**	**1**	**1**	**26**	**0**	**0**	**0**
1982-83	**Edmonton Oilers**	**NHL**	**80**	**13**	**18**	**31**	**11**	**12**	**23**	**120**	**0**	**1**	**0**	**113**	**11.5**	**59**	**1**	**67**	**21**	**12**	**16**	**4**	**7**	**11**	**60**	**0**	**0**	**0**
1983-84♦	**Edmonton Oilers**	**NHL**	**80**	**22**	**26**	**48**	**18**	**18**	**36**	**90**	**1**	**1**	**3**	**117**	**18.8**	**75**	**3**	**67**	**20**	**25**	**17**	**5**	**5**	**10**	**14**	**1**	**1**	**0**
1984-85♦	**Edmonton Oilers**	**NHL**	**80**	**17**	**19**	**36**	**14**	**13**	**27**	**122**	**1**	**1**	**1**	**119**	**14.3**	**51**	**2**	**68**	**18**	**–1**	**18**	**2**	**5**	**7**	**33**	**0**	**0**	**0**
1985-86	**Edmonton Oilers**	**NHL**	**62**	**15**	**22**	**37**	**12**	**15**	**27**	**77**	**0**	**0**	**1**	**110**	**13.6**	**69**	**0**	**45**	**13**	**37**	**10**	**2**	**3**	**5**	**23**	**0**	**0**	**0**
1986-87♦	**Edmonton Oilers**	**NHL**	**77**	**6**	**9**	**15**	**5**	**7**	**12**	**79**	**0**	**1**	**1**	**84**	**7.1**	**32**	**0**	**53**	**22**	**1**	**21**	**3**	**3**	**6**	**20**	**0**	**0**	**0**
1987-88	**Edmonton Oilers**	**NHL**	**21**	**3**	**3**	**6**	**3**	**2**	**5**	**6**	**0**	**0**	**0**	**18**	**16.7**	**8**	**0**	**15**	**8**	**1**	....	....	....	....	....	....	....	....
	Pittsburgh Penguins	**NHL**	**59**	**11**	**18**	**29**	**9**	**13**	**22**	**77**	**0**	**2**	**1**	**115**	**9.6**	**50**	**2**	**85**	**45**	**8**	....	....	....	....	....	....	....	....
1988-89	**Winnipeg Jets**	**NHL**	**34**	**3**	**1**	**4**	**3**	**1**	**4**	**61**	**0**	**1**	**0**	**43**	**7.0**	**9**	**0**	**18**	**6**	**–3**	....	....	....	....	....	....	....	....
	Edmonton Oilers	**NHL**	**32**	**3**	**5**	**8**	**3**	**4**	**7**	**22**	**0**	**0**	**0**	**44**	**6.8**	**12**	**0**	**30**	**13**	**–5**	**6**	**0**	**0**	**0**	**0**	**0**	**0**	**0**
	NHL Totals		**746**	**133**	**190**	**323**	**110**	**134**	**244**	**918**	**3**	**9**	**16**	**1100**	**12.1**	**559**	**19**	**664**	**227**		**105**	**16**	**24**	**40**	**211**	**1**	**1**	**0**
	Other Major League Totals		72	7	25	32	....	....	....	134	....	....	....	....	....	....	....	....	....	....	13	2	3	5	42	....	....	....

• Brother of Dale and Mark

Signed as an underage free agent by **Edmonton** (WHA), June, 1978. Claimed by **Edmonton** from **Montreal** in Expansion Draft, June 13, 1979. Traded to **Pittsburgh** by **Edmonton** with Paul Coffey and Wayne Van Dorp for Craig Simpson, Dave Hannan, Moe Mantha and Chris Joseph, November 24, 1987. Transferred to **Edmonton** by **Pittsburgh** as compensation for Pittsburgh's claiming Dave Hannan in Waiver Draft, October 3, 1988. Claimed by **Winnipeg** from **Edmonton** in Waiver Draft, October 3, 1988. Claimed on waivers by **Edmonton** from **Winnipeg**, January 14, 1989.

• HUNTER, Mark

Mark William RW – R. 6', 200 lbs. b: Petrolia, Ont., 11/12/1962. Montreal's 1st, 7th overall, in 1981.

Season	Club	League	GP	G	A	Pts	AG	AA	APts	PIM	PP	SH	GW	S	%	TGF	PGF	TGA	PGA	+/–	GP	G	A	Pts	PIM	PP	SH	GW
1978-79	Petrolia Jets	OJHL	44	35	44	79	....	....	....	160	....	....	....	....	....	....	....	....	....	....	....	....	....	....	....	....	....	....
1979-80	Brantford Alexanders	OMJHL	66	34	56	90	....	....	....	171	....	....	....	....	....	....	....	....	....	....	11	2	8	10	27	....	....	....
1980-81	Brantford Alexanders	OMJHL	53	39	40	79	....	....	....	157	....	....	....	....	....	....	....	....	....	....	6	3	3	6	27	....	....	....
1981-82	**Montreal Canadiens**	**NHL**	**71**	**18**	**11**	**29**	**14**	**7**	**21**	**143**	**0**	**0**	**5**	**79**	**22.8**	**43**	**4**	**29**	**0**	**10**	**5**	**0**	**0**	**0**	**20**	**0**	**0**	**0**
1982-83	**Montreal Canadiens**	**NHL**	**31**	**8**	**8**	**16**	**7**	**6**	**13**	**73**	**1**	**0**	**2**	**39**	**20.5**	**25**	**2**	**18**	**0**	**5**	....	....	....	....	....	....	....	....
1983-84	**Montreal Canadiens**	**NHL**	**22**	**6**	**4**	**10**	**5**	**3**	**8**	**42**	**1**	**0**	**0**	**24**	**25.0**	**14**	**1**	**15**	**0**	**–2**	**14**	**2**	**1**	**3**	**69**	**0**	**0**	**0**
1984-85	**Montreal Canadiens**	**NHL**	**72**	**21**	**12**	**33**	**17**	**8**	**25**	**123**	**6**	**0**	**3**	**108**	**19.4**	**49**	**11**	**51**	**0**	**–13**	**11**	**0**	**3**	**3**	**13**	**0**	**0**	**0**
1985-86	**St. Louis Blues**	**NHL**	**78**	**44**	**30**	**74**	**35**	**20**	**55**	**171**	**11**	**2**	**3**	**204**	**21.6**	**108**	**36**	**64**	**7**	**15**	**19**	**7**	**7**	**14**	**48**	**2**	**0**	**1**
1986-87	**St. Louis Blues**	**NHL**	**74**	**36**	**33**	**69**	**31**	**24**	**55**	**167**	**12**	**0**	**4**	**178**	**20.2**	**98**	**44**	**74**	**1**	**–19**	**5**	**0**	**3**	**3**	**10**	**0**	**0**	**0**
1987-88	**St. Louis Blues**	**NHL**	**66**	**32**	**31**	**63**	**27**	**22**	**49**	**136**	**14**	**0**	**0**	**164**	**19.5**	**92**	**39**	**60**	**1**	**–6**	**5**	**2**	**3**	**5**	**24**	**1**	**0**	**0**
1988-89♦	**Calgary Flames**	**NHL**	**66**	**22**	**8**	**30**	**19**	**6**	**25**	**194**	**12**	**0**	**2**	**116**	**19.0**	**56**	**25**	**27**	**0**	**4**	**10**	**2**	**2**	**4**	**23**	**0**	**0**	**0**
1989-90	Calgary Flames	Fr-Tour	4	2	0	2	....	....	....	4	....	....	....	....	....	....	....	....	....	....	....	....	....	....	....	....	....	....
	Calgary Flames	**NHL**	**10**	**2**	**3**	**5**	**2**	**2**	**4**	**39**	**2**	**0**	**0**	**15**	**13.3**	**9**	**4**	**5**	**0**	**0**	....	....	....	....	....	....	....	....
1990-91	**Calgary Flames**	**NHL**	**57**	**10**	**15**	**25**	**9**	**11**	**20**	**125**	**6**	**0**	**0**	**90**	**11.1**	**39**	**16**	**24**	**0**	**–1**	....	....	....	....	....	....	....	....
	Hartford Whalers	**NHL**	**11**	**4**	**3**	**7**	**4**	**2**	**6**	**40**	**1**	**0**	**0**	**20**	**20.0**	**12**	**3**	**6**	**0**	**3**	**6**	**5**	**1**	**6**	**17**	**3**	**0**	**0**
1991-92	**Hartford Whalers**	**NHL**	**63**	**10**	**13**	**23**	**9**	**10**	**19**	**159**	**5**	**0**	**0**	**92**	**10.9**	**37**	**12**	**39**	**6**	**–8**	**4**	**0**	**0**	**0**	**6**	**0**	**0**	**0**
1992-93	**Washington Capitals**	**NHL**	**7**	**0**	**0**	**0**	**0**	**0**	**0**	**14**	**0**	**0**	**0**	**5**	**0.0**	**1**	**0**	**0**	**0**	**1**	....	....	....	....	....	....	....	....
	Baltimore Skipjacks	AHL	28	13	18	31	....	....	....	66	....	....	....	....	....	....	....	....	....	....	7	3	1	4	12	....	....	....
1993-1996	Sarnia Sting	OHL	DID NOT PLAY – COACHING																									

Season	Club	League	REGULAR SEASON GP	G	A	Pts	AG	AA	APts	PIM	PP	SH	GW	S	%	TGF	PGF	TGA	PGA	+/–	PLAYOFFS GP	G	A	Pts	PIM	PP	SH	GW
1996-1997	St. John's Maple Leafs	AHL	DID NOT PLAY – COACHING																									
1997-1999	Sarnia Sting	OHL	DID NOT PLAY – COACHING																									
1999-2000	Michigan K-Wings	IHL	DID NOT PLAY – ASSISTANT COACH																									
	NHL Totals		**628**	**213**	**171**	**384**	**179**	**121**	**300**	**1426**	**71**	**2**	**19**	**1134**	**18.8**	**583**	**197**	**412**	**15**		**79**	**18**	**20**	**38**	**230**	**6**	**0**	**1**

• Brother of Dave and Dale • Played in NHL All-Star Game (1986)

• Missed majority of 1982-83 season recovering from knee injury suffered in game vs. Quebec, December 26, 1982. • Missed majority of 1983-84 season recovering from knee surgery, September, 1983. Traded to **St. Louis** by **Montreal** with Michael Dark and Montreal's 2nd (Herb Raglan), 3rd (Nelson Emerson), 5th (Dan Brooks) and 6th (Rick Burchill) round choices in 1985 Entry Draft for St. Louis' 1st (Jose Charbonneau), 2nd (Todd Richards), 4th (Martin Desjardins), 5th (Tom Sagissor) and 6th (Donald Dufresne) round choices in 1985 Entry Draft, June 15, 1985. Traded to **Calgary** by **St. Louis** with Doug Gilmour, Steve Bozek and Michael Dark for Mike Bullard, Craig Coxe and Tim Corkery, September 6, 1988. • Missed majority of 1989-90 season recovering from knee surgery, December 15, 1989. Traded to **Hartford** by **Calgary** for Carey Wilson, March 5, 1991. Traded to **Wasington** by **Hartford** with future considerations (Yvon Corriveau, August 20, 1992) for Nick Kypreos, June 15, 1992.

• HUNTER, Tim

Timothy Robert RW – R. 6'2", 202 lbs. b: Calgary, Alta., 9/10/1960. Atlanta's 4th, 54th overall, in 1979.

Season	Club	League	GP	G	A	Pts	AG	AA	APts	PIM	PP	SH	GW	S	%	TGF	PGF	TGA	PGA	+/–	GP	G	A	Pts	PIM	PP	SH	GW
1977-78	Kamloops Chiefs	BCJHL	51	9	28	37	....	....	....	266	....	....	....	....	....	....	....	....	....	....	....	....	....	....	....	....	....	....
	Seattle Breakers	WCJHL	3	1	2	3	....	....	....	4	....	....	....	....	....	....	....	....	....	....	....	....	....	....	....	....	....	....
1978-79	Seattle Breakers	WHL	70	8	41	49	....	....	....	300	....	....	....	....	....	....	....	....	....	....	....	....	....	....	....	....	....	....
1979-80	Seattle Breakers	WHL	72	14	53	67	....	....	....	311	....	....	....	....	....	....	....	....	....	....	12	1	2	3	41	....	....	....
1980-81	Birmingham Bulls	CHL	58	3	5	8	....	....	....	*236	....	....	....	....	....	....	....	....	....	....	....	....	....	....	....	....	....	....
	Nova Scotia Voyageurs	AHL	17	0	0	0	....	....	....	62	....	....	....	....	....	....	....	....	....	....	6	0	1	1	45	....	....	....
1981-82	**Calgary Flames**	**NHL**	**2**	**0**	**0**	**0**	**0**	**0**	**0**	**9**	**0**	**0**	**0**	**0**	**0.0**	**1**	**0**	**1**	**0**	**0**	....	....	....	....	....	....	....	....
	Oklahoma City Stars	CHL	55	4	12	16	....	....	....	222	....	....	....	....	....	....	....	....	....	....	....	....	....	....	....	....	....	....
1982-83	**Calgary Flames**	**NHL**	**16**	**1**	**0**	**1**	**1**	**0**	**1**	**54**	**0**	**0**	**0**	**7**	**14.3**	**3**	**0**	**5**	**0**	**–2**	**9**	**1**	**0**	**1**	***70**	**1**	**0**	**0**
	Colorado Flames	CHL	46	5	12	17	....	....	....	225	....	....	....	....	....	....	....	....	....	....	....	....	....	....	....	....	....	....
1983-84	**Calgary Flames**	**NHL**	**43**	**4**	**4**	**8**	**3**	**3**	**6**	**130**	**0**	**0**	**0**	**22**	**18.2**	**20**	**2**	**18**	**0**	**0**	**7**	**0**	**0**	**0**	**21**	**0**	**0**	**0**
1984-85	**Calgary Flames**	**NHL**	**71**	**11**	**11**	**22**	**9**	**7**	**16**	**259**	**1**	**0**	**1**	**68**	**16.2**	**42**	**4**	**24**	**0**	**14**	**4**	**0**	**0**	**0**	**24**	**0**	**0**	**0**
1985-86	**Calgary Flames**	**NHL**	**66**	**8**	**7**	**15**	**6**	**5**	**11**	**291**	**2**	**0**	**2**	**65**	**12.3**	**25**	**7**	**27**	**0**	**–9**	**19**	**0**	**3**	**3**	**108**	**0**	**0**	**0**
1986-87	**Calgary Flames**	**NHL**	**73**	**6**	**15**	**21**	**5**	**11**	**16**	***361**	**0**	**0**	**1**	**66**	**9.1**	**52**	**4**	**52**	**3**	**–1**	**6**	**0**	**0**	**0**	**51**	**0**	**0**	**0**
1987-88	**Calgary Flames**	**NHL**	**68**	**8**	**5**	**13**	**7**	**4**	**11**	**337**	**0**	**0**	**0**	**60**	**13.3**	**22**	**0**	**30**	**0**	**–8**	**9**	**4**	**0**	**4**	**32**	**0**	**0**	**2**
1988-89♦	**Calgary Flames**	**NHL**	**75**	**3**	**9**	**12**	**3**	**6**	**9**	***375**	**0**	**0**	**1**	**67**	**4.5**	**43**	**0**	**21**	**0**	**22**	**19**	**0**	**4**	**4**	**32**	**0**	**0**	**0**
1989-90	Calgary Flames	Fr-Tour	3	2	0	2	....	....	....	0	....	....	....	....	....	....	....	....	....	....	....	....	....	....	....	....	....	....
	Calgary Flames	**NHL**	**67**	**2**	**3**	**5**	**2**	**2**	**4**	**279**	**0**	**0**	**0**	**69**	**2.9**	**18**	**0**	**28**	**1**	**–9**	**6**	**0**	**0**	**0**	**4**	**0**	**0**	**0**
1990-91	**Calgary Flames**	**NHL**	**34**	**5**	**2**	**7**	**5**	**2**	**7**	**143**	**0**	**0**	**1**	**29**	**17.2**	**16**	**0**	**15**	**0**	**1**	**7**	**0**	**0**	**0**	**10**	**0**	**0**	**0**
1991-92	**Calgary Flames**	**NHL**	**30**	**1**	**3**	**4**	**1**	**2**	**3**	**167**	**0**	**0**	**0**	**19**	**5.3**	**10**	**0**	**8**	**0**	**2**	....	....	....	....	....	....	....	....
1992-93	**Quebec Nordiques**	**NHL**	**48**	**5**	**3**	**8**	**4**	**2**	**6**	**94**	**0**	**0**	**0**	**28**	**17.9**	**13**	**0**	**17**	**0**	**–4**	....	....	....	....	....	....	....	....
	Vancouver Canucks	**NHL**	**26**	**0**	**4**	**4**	**0**	**3**	**3**	**99**	**0**	**0**	**0**	**12**	**0.0**	**13**	**0**	**12**	**0**	**1**	**11**	**0**	**0**	**0**	**26**	**0**	**0**	**0**
1993-94	**Vancouver Canucks**	**NHL**	**56**	**3**	**4**	**7**	**3**	**3**	**6**	**171**	**0**	**1**	**1**	**41**	**7.3**	**11**	**1**	**37**	**20**	**–7**	**24**	**0**	**0**	**0**	**26**	**0**	**0**	**0**
1994-95	**Vancouver Canucks**	**NHL**	**34**	**3**	**2**	**5**	**5**	**3**	**8**	**120**	**0**	**0**	**0**	**17**	**17.6**	**8**	**0**	**10**	**3**	**1**	**11**	**0**	**0**	**0**	**22**	**0**	**0**	**0**
1995-96	**Vancouver Canucks**	**NHL**	**60**	**2**	**0**	**2**	**2**	**0**	**2**	**122**	**0**	**0**	**1**	**26**	**7.7**	**10**	**2**	**16**	**0**	**–8**	....	....	....	....	....	....	....	....
1996-97	**San Jose Sharks**	**NHL**	**46**	**0**	**4**	**4**	**0**	**4**	**4**	**135**	**0**	**0**	**0**	**13**	**0.0**	**6**	**0**	**7**	**1**	**0**	....	....	....	....	....	....	....	....
1997-2000	**Washington Capitals**	**NHL**	DID NOT PLAY – ASSISTANT COACH																									
	NHL Totals		**815**	**62**	**76**	**138**	**56**	**57**	**113**	**3146**	**3**	**1**	**8**	**609**	**10.2**	**313**	**20**	**328**	**28**		**132**	**5**	**7**	**12**	**426**	**1**	**0**	**2**

Claimed by **Tampa Bay** from **Calgary** in Expansion Draft, June 18, 1992. Traded to **Quebec** by **Tampa Bay** for future considerations (Martin Simard, September 14, 1992), June 19, 1992. Claimed on waivers by **Vancouver** from **Quebec**, February 12, 1993. Signed as a free agent by **San Jose**, July 23, 1996.

• HURAS, Larry

Larry Robert D – L. 6'2", 200 lbs. b: Listowel, Ont., 7/8/1955. NY Rangers' 5th, 84th overall, in 1975.

Season	Club	League	GP	G	A	Pts	AG	AA	APts	PIM	PP	SH	GW	S	%	TGF	PGF	TGA	PGA	+/–	GP	G	A	Pts	PIM	PP	SH	GW
1971-72	Elmira Sugar Kings	OHA-B	STATISTICS NOT AVAILABLE																									
1972-73	Kitchener Rangers	OMJHL	60	0	7	7	....	....	....	55	....	....	....	....	....	....	....	....	....	....	....	....	....	....	....	....	....	....
1973-74	Kitchener Rangers	OMJHL	67	4	22	26	....	....	....	83	....	....	....	....	....	....	....	....	....	....	....	....	....	....	....	....	....	....
1974-75	Kitchener Rangers	OMJHL	68	4	28	32	....	....	....	166	....	....	....	....	....	....	....	....	....	....	....	....	....	....	....	....	....	....
1975-76	Providence Reds	AHL	55	0	12	12	....	....	....	102	....	....	....	....	....	....	....	....	....	....	3	0	1	1	9	....	....	....
	Port Huron Flags	IHL	17	3	9	12	....	....	....	49	....	....	....	....	....	....	....	....	....	....	....	....	....	....	....	....	....	....
1976-77	**New York Rangers**	**NHL**	**2**	**0**	**0**	**0**	**0**	**0**	**0**	**0**	**0**	**0**	**0**	**0**	**0.0**	**0**	**0**	**0**	**0**	**0**	....	....	....	....	....	....	....	....
	New Haven Nighthawks	AHL	48	0	6	6	....	....	....	82	....	....	....	....	....	....	....	....	....	....	4	0	0	0	0	....	....	....
1977-78	Salt Lake Golden Eagles	CHL	52	5	7	12	....	....	....	55	....	....	....	....	....	....	....	....	....	....	1	0	0	0	0	....	....	....
1978-79	Dallas Black Hawks	CHL	6	0	1	1	....	....	....	21	....	....	....	....	....	....	....	....	....	....	....	....	....	....	....	....	....	....
	Salt Lake Golden Eagles	CHL	32	1	9	10	....	....	....	52	....	....	....	....	....	....	....	....	....	....	7	0	0	0	15	....	....	....
1979-80	Port Huron Flags	IHL	77	3	28	31	....	....	....	106	....	....	....	....	....	....	....	....	....	....	11	1	1	2	27	....	....	....
1980-81	CSG Grenoble	France	10	1	8	9	....	....	....	....	....	....	....	....	....	....	....	....	....	....	....	....	....	....	....	....	....	....
1981-82	CSG Grenoble	France	28	5	16	21	....	....	....	....	....	....	....	....	....	....	....	....	....	....	....	....	....	....	....	....	....	....
1982-83	CSG Grenoble	France	27	5	15	20	....	....	....	....	....	....	....	....	....	....	....	....	....	....	....	....	....	....	....	....	....	....
1983-84	HC Gap	France	28	6	14	20	....	....	....	....	....	....	....	....	....	....	....	....	....	....	....	....	....	....	....	....	....	....
1984-85	HC Gap	France	32	4	14	18	....	....	....	....	....	....	....	....	....	....	....	....	....	....	....	....	....	....	....	....	....	....
1985-86	HC Gap	France	24	8	4	12	....	....	....	....	....	....	....	....	....	....	....	....	....	....	....	....	....	....	....	....	....	....
1986-87	HC Gap	France	32	8	22	30	....	....	....	....	....	....	....	....	....	....	....	....	....	....	....	....	....	....	....	....	....	....
1987-88	HC Gap	France	33	5	13	18	....	....	....	44	....	....	....	....	....	....	....	....	....	....	....	....	....	....	....	....	....	....
1988-89	HC Rouen	France	42	2	21	23	....	....	....	48	....	....	....	....	....	....	....	....	....	....	....	....	....	....	....	....	....	....
1989-90	HC Rouen	France	25	1	5	6	....	....	....	18	....	....	....	....	....	....	....	....	....	....	2	0	0	0	0	....	....	....
1990-91	HC Rouen	France	28	1	6	7	....	....	....	18	....	....	....	....	....	....	....	....	....	....	9	2	2	4	15	....	....	....
1991-92	HC Rouen	France	24	0	4	4	....	....	....	30	....	....	....	....	....	....	....	....	....	....	....	....	....	....	....	....	....	....
1992-93	HC Rouen	France	1	0	0	0	....	....	....	0	....	....	....	....	....	....	....	....	....	....	....	....	....	....	....	....	....	....
1993-94	HC Rouen	France	9	0	2	2	....	....	....	12	....	....	....	....	....	....	....	....	....	....	....	....	....	....	....	....	....	....
1994-1996	HC Rouen	France	DID NOT PLAY – COACHING																									
1996-2000	EHC Biel-Bienne	Switz-2	DID NOT PLAY – COACHING																									
	NHL Totals		**2**	**0**	**0**	**0**	**0**	**0**	**0**	**0**	**0**	**0**	**0**	**0**	**0.0**	**0**	**0**	**0**	**0**		....	....	....	....	....	....	....	....

Signed as a free agent by **St. Louis**, October 12, 1977. • Named NLB (Switz-2) Coach-of-the-Year (1998-99)

• HURLBURT, Bob

Robert George LW – L. 5'11", 185 lbs. b: Toronto, Ont., 5/1/1950.

Season	Club	League	GP	G	A	Pts	AG	AA	APts	PIM	PP	SH	GW	S	%	TGF	PGF	TGA	PGA	+/–	GP	G	A	Pts	PIM	PP	SH	GW
1967-68	North York Rangers	OHA-B	35	19	11	30	....	....	....	54	....	....	....	....	....	....	....	....	....	....	....	....	....	....	....	....	....	....
1968-69	Kitchener Rangers	OHA-Jr.	53	9	14	23	....	....	....	76	....	....	....	....	....	....	....	....	....	....	....	....	....	....	....	....	....	....
1969-70	Kitchener Rangers	OHA-Jr.	54	9	13	22	....	....	....	126	....	....	....	....	....	....	....	....	....	....	5	0	0	0	6	....	....	....
1970-71	Quebec Aces	AHL	72	10	21	31	....	....	....	51	....	....	....	....	....	....	....	....	....	....	1	0	1	1	0	....	....	....
1971-72	Richmond Robins	AHL	69	5	13	18	....	....	....	69	....	....	....	....	....	....	....	....	....	....	....	....	....	....	....	....	....	....
1972-73	Richmond Robins	AHL	71	2	11	13	....	....	....	64	....	....	....	....	....	....	....	....	....	....	2	0	0	0	2	....	....	....
1973-74	San Diego Gulls	WHL	75	20	27	47	....	....	....	51	....	....	....	....	....	....	....	....	....	....	4	0	3	3	2	....	....	....
1974-75	**Vancouver Canucks**	**NHL**	**1**	**0**	**0**	**0**	**0**	**0**	**0**	**2**	**0**	**0**	**0**	**0**	**0.0**	**1**	**0**	**1**	**0**	**0**	....	....	....	....	....	....	....	....
	Seattle Totems	CHL	74	16	23	39	....	....	....	68	....	....	....	....	....	....	....	....	....	....	....	....	....	....	....	....	....	....
1975-76			REINSTATED AS AN AMATEUR																									
1976-77	Whitby Warriors	OHA-Sr.	12	3	4	7	....	....	....	6	....	....	....	....	....	....	....	....	....	....	....	....	....	....	....	....	....	....
	NHL Totals		**1**	**0**	**0**	**0**	**0**	**0**	**0**	**2**	**0**	**0**	**0**	**0**	**0.0**	**1**	**0**	**1**	**0**		....	....	....	....	....	....	....	....

Traded to **San Diego** (WHL) by **Philadelphia** with Tom Trevelyan, Bob Currier and Jim Stanfield for Bruce Cowick, May 25, 1973. Traded to **Vancouver** by **San Diego** (WHL) for cash, July 23, 1974.

• HURLBUT, Mike

Michael R. D – L. 6'2", 200 lbs. b: Massena, NY, 10/7/1966. NY Rangers' 1st, 5th overall, in 1988 Supplemental Draft.

Season	Club	League	GP	G	A	Pts	AG	AA	APts	PIM	PP	SH	GW	S	%	TGF	PGF	TGA	PGA	+/–	GP	G	A	Pts	PIM	PP	SH	GW
1983-84	Massena Central High School	Hi-School	27	22	31	53	....	....	....	15	....	....	....	....	....	....	....	....	....	....	....	....	....	....	....	....	....	....
1984-85	Northwood Prep	Hi-School	34	20	27	47	....	....	....	30	....	....	....	....	....	....	....	....	....	....	....	....	....	....	....	....	....	....
1985-86	St. Lawrence University	ECAC	25	2	10	12	....	....	....	40	....	....	....	....	....	....	....	....	....	....	....	....	....	....	....	....	....	....
1986-87	St. Lawrence University	ECAC	35	8	15	23	....	....	....	44	....	....	....	....	....	....	....	....	....	....	....	....	....	....	....	....	....	....
1987-88	St. Lawrence University	ECAC	38	6	12	18	....	....	....	18	....	....	....	....	....	....	....	....	....	....	....	....	....	....	....	....	....	....

			REGULAR SEASON																		PLAYOFFS							
Season	Club	League	GP	G	A	Pts	AG	AA	APts	PIM	PP	SH	GW	S	%	TGF	PGF	TGA	PGA	+/-	GP	G	A	Pts	PIM	PP	SH	GW
1988-89	St. Lawrence University	ECAC	36	8	25	33	....	....	....	30	....	....	....	....	....	....	....	....	....	....	....	....	....	....	....	....	....	....
	Denver Rangers	IHL	8	0	2	2	....	....	....	13	....	....	....	....	....	....	....	....	....	....	4	1	2	3	2	....	....	....
1989-90	Flint Spirits	IHL	74	3	34	37	....	....	....	38	....	....	....	....	....	....	....	....	....	....	3	0	1	1	2	....	....	....
1990-91	San Diego Gulls	IHL	2	1	0	1	....	....	....	0	....	....	....	....	....	....	....	....	....	....	....	....	....	....	....	....	....	....
	Binghamton Rangers	AHL	33	2	11	13	....	....	....	27	....	....	....	....	....	....	....	....	....	....	3	0	1	1	0	....	....	....
1991-92	Binghamton Rangers	AHL	79	16	39	55	....	....	....	64	....	....	....	....	....	....	....	....	....	....	11	2	7	9	8	....	....	....
1992-93	**New York Rangers**	**NHL**	**23**	**1**	**8**	**9**	**1**	**5**	**6**	**16**	**1**	**0**	**0**	**26**	**3.8**	**27**	**7**	**20**	**4**	**4**	....	....	....	....	....	....	....	....
	Binghamton Rangers	AHL	45	11	25	36	....	....	....	46	....	....	....	....	....	....	....	....	....	....	14	2	5	7	12	....	....	....
1993-94	**Quebec Nordiques**	**NHL**	**1**	**0**	**0**	**0**	**0**	**0**	**0**	**0**	**0**	**0**	**0**	**1**	**0.0**	**0**	**0**	**1**	**0**	**–1**	....	....	....	....	....	....	....	....
	Cornwall Aces	AHL	77	13	33	46	....	....	....	100	....	....	....	....	....	....	....	....	....	....	13	3	7	10	12	....	....	....
1994-95	Cornwall Aces	AHL	74	11	49	60	....	....	....	69	....	....	....	....	....	....	....	....	....	....	3	1	0	1	15	....	....	....
1995-96	Minnesota Moose	IHL	22	1	4	5	....	....	....	22	....	....	....	....	....	....	....	....	....	....	....	....	....	....	....	....	....	....
	Houston Aeros	IHL	38	3	12	15	....	....	....	33	....	....	....	....	....	....	....	....	....	....	....	....	....	....	....	....	....	....
1996-97	Houston Aeros	IHL	70	11	24	35	....	....	....	62	....	....	....	....	....	....	....	....	....	....	13	5	8	13	12	....	....	....
1997-98	**Buffalo Sabres**	**NHL**	**3**	**0**	**0**	**0**	**0**	**0**	**0**	**2**	**0**	**0**	**0**	**3**	**0.0**	**0**	**0**	**2**	**1**	**–1**	....	....	....	....	....	....	....	....
	Rochester Americans	AHL	45	10	20	30	....	....	....	48	....	....	....	....	....	....	....	....	....	....	4	1	1	2	2	....	....	....
1998-99	**Buffalo Sabres**	**NHL**	**1**	**0**	**0**	**0**	**0**	**0**	**0**	**0**	**0**	**0**	**0**	**2**	**0.0**	**2**	**0**	**0**	**0**	**2**	....	....	....	....	....	....	....	....
	Rochester Americans	AHL	72	15	39	54	....	....	....	46	....	....	....	....	....	....	....	....	....	....	20	4	5	9	12	....	....	....
99-2000	**Buffalo Sabres**	**NHL**	**1**	**0**	**0**	**0**	**0**	**0**	**0**	**2**	**0**	**0**	**0**	**1**	**0.0**	**1**	**0**	**0**	**0**	**1**	....	....	....	....	....	....	....	....
	Rochester Americans	AHL	74	10	29	39	....	....	....	83	....	....	....	....	....	....	....	....	....	....	21	5	6	11	14	....	....	....
	NHL Totals		**29**	**1**	**8**	**9**	**1**	**5**	**6**	**20**	**1**	**0**	**0**	**33**	**3.0**	**30**	**7**	**23**	**5**		....	....	....	....	....	....	....	....

ECAC First All-Star Team (1989) • NCAA East First All-American Team (1989) • AHL Second All-Star Team (1995)

Traded to **Quebec** by **NY Rangers** for Alexander Karpovtsev, September 7, 1993. Signed as a free agent by **Buffalo**, September 9, 1997.

• HURLEY, Paul

Paul Michael D – R. 5'11", 185 lbs. b: Melrose, MA, 7/12/1946.

Season	Club	League	GP	G	A	Pts	AG	AA	APts	PIM	PP	SH	GW	S	%	TGF	PGF	TGA	PGA	+/-	GP	G	A	Pts	PIM	PP	SH	GW
1962-63	Melrose High School	Hi-School	STATISTICS NOT AVAILABLE																									
1963-64	Deerfield Academy	Hi-School	STATISTICS NOT AVAILABLE																									
1964-65	Boston College	ECAC	18	22	13	35	....	....	....	....	....	....	....	....	....	....	....	....	....	....	....	....	....	....	....	....	....	....
1965-66	Boston College	ECAC	27	9	26	35	....	....	....	22	....	....	....	....	....	....	....	....	....	....	....	....	....	....	....	....	....	....
1966-67	Boston College	ECAC	28	32	23	55	....	....	....	19	....	....	....	....	....	....	....	....	....	....	....	....	....	....	....	....	....	....
1967-68	Concord Eastern Olympics	NESHL	21	9	7	16	....	....	....	6	....	....	....	....	....	....	....	....	....	....	....	....	....	....	....	....	....	....
	United States	Olympics	7	3	3	6	....	....	....	0	....	....	....	....	....	....	....	....	....	....	....	....	....	....	....	....	....	....
1968-69	Boston College	ECAC	26	14	28	42	....	....	....	22	....	....	....	....	....	....	....	....	....	....	....	....	....	....	....	....	....	....
	Boston Bruins	**NHL**	**1**	**0**	**1**	**1**	**0**	**1**	**1**	**0**	**0**	**0**	**0**	**5**	**0.0**	**2**	**0**	**2**	**1**	**1**	....	....	....	....	....	....	....	....
	Oklahoma City Blazers	CHL	6	2	1	3	....	....	....	4	....	....	....	....	....	....	....	....	....	....	....	....	....	....	....	....	....	....
1969-70	Oklahoma City Blazers	CHL	69	6	26	32	....	....	....	109	....	....	....	....	....	....	....	....	....	....	....	....	....	....	....	....	....	....
1970-71	Oklahoma City Blazers	CHL	43	5	12	17	....	....	....	47	....	....	....	....	....	....	....	....	....	....	5	0	1	1	8	....	....	....
1971-72	Boston Braves	AHL	74	7	28	35	....	....	....	65	....	....	....	....	....	....	....	....	....	....	9	0	4	4	8	....	....	....
1972-73	New England Whalers	WHA	78	3	15	18	....	....	....	58	....	....	....	....	....	....	....	....	....	....	15	0	7	7	14	....	....	....
1973-74	New England Whalers	WHA	52	3	11	14	....	....	....	21	....	....	....	....	....	....	....	....	....	....	....	....	....	....	....	....	....	....
1974-75	New England Whalers	WHA	75	3	26	29	....	....	....	36	....	....	....	....	....	....	....	....	....	....	6	0	1	1	4	....	....	....
1975-76	New England Whalers	WHA	10	0	14	14	....	....	....	20	....	....	....	....	....	....	....	....	....	....	4	0	0	0	0	....	....	....
	Edmonton Oilers	WHA	26	1	4	5	....	....	....	14	....	....	....	....	....	....	....	....	....	....	....	....	....	....	....	....	....	....
1976-77	Calgary Cowboys	WHA	34	0	6	6	....	....	....	32	....	....	....	....	....	....	....	....	....	....	....	....	....	....	....	....	....	....
	NHL Totals		**1**	**0**	**1**	**1**	**0**	**1**	**1**	**0**	**0**	**0**	**0**	**5**	**0.0**	**2**	**0**	**2**	**1**		....	....	....	....	....	....	....	....
	Other Major League Totals		275	10	76	86	....	....	....	181	....	....	....	....	....	....	....	....	....	....	25	0	8	8	18	....	....	....

ECAC First All-Star Team (1969) • NCAA East First All-American Team (1969)

Signed as a free agent by **Boston**, March, 1969. Selected by **New England** (WHA) in 1972 WHA General Player Draft, February 12, 1972. Traded to **Edmonton** (WHA) by **New England** (WHA) with the rights to Clarke Jantze for Kerry Ketter and Steve Carlyle, February 2, 1976. Signed as a free agent by **Calgary** (WHA), September, 1976.

• HUSCROFT, Jamie

D – R. 6'3", 210 lbs. b: Creston, B.C., 1/9/1967. New Jersey's 9th, 171st overall, in 1985.

Season	Club	League	GP	G	A	Pts	AG	AA	APts	PIM	PP	SH	GW	S	%	TGF	PGF	TGA	PGA	+/-	GP	G	A	Pts	PIM	PP	SH	GW
1982-83	Creston Clippers	RMJHL	STATISTICS NOT AVAILABLE																									
1983-84	Portland Winter Hawks	WHL	18	0	5	5	....	....	....	15	....	....	....	....	....	....	....	....	....	....	....	....	....	....	....	....	....	....
	Seattle Breakers	WHL	45	0	7	7	....	....	....	62	....	....	....	....	....	....	....	....	....	....	5	0	0	0	15	....	....	....
1984-85	Seattle Breakers	WHL	69	3	13	16	....	....	....	273	....	....	....	....	....	....	....	....	....	....	....	....	....	....	....	....	....	....
1985-86	Seattle Thunderbirds	WHL	66	6	20	26	....	....	....	394	....	....	....	....	....	....	....	....	....	....	5	0	1	1	18	....	....	....
1986-87	Seattle Thunderbirds	WHL	21	1	18	19	....	....	....	99	....	....	....	....	....	....	....	....	....	....	....	....	....	....	....	....	....	....
	Medicine Hat Tigers	WHL	14	3	3	6	....	....	....	71	....	....	....	....	....	....	....	....	....	....	20	0	3	3	*125	....	....	....
	Medicine Hat Tigers	Mem-Cup	5	0	1	1	....	....	....	25	....	....	....	....	....	....	....	....	....	....	....	....	....	....	....	....	....	....
1987-88	Utica Devils	AHL	71	5	7	12	....	....	....	316	....	....	....	....	....	....	....	....	....	....	....	....	....	....	....	....	....	....
	Flint Spirits	IHL	3	1	0	1	....	....	....	2	....	....	....	....	....	....	....	....	....	....	16	0	1	1	110	....	....	....
1988-89	**New Jersey Devils**	**NHL**	**15**	**0**	**2**	**2**	**0**	**1**	**1**	**51**	**0**	**0**	**0**	**9**	**0.0**	**6**	**0**	**13**	**4**	**–3**	....	....	....	....	....	....	....	....
	Utica Devils	AHL	41	2	10	12	....	....	....	215	....	....	....	....	....	....	....	....	....	....	5	0	0	0	40	....	....	....
1989-90	**New Jersey Devils**	**NHL**	**42**	**2**	**3**	**5**	**2**	**2**	**4**	**149**	**0**	**0**	**0**	**19**	**10.5**	**7**	**0**	**9**	**0**	**–2**	**5**	**0**	**0**	**0**	**16**	**0**	**0**	**0**
	Utica Devils	AHL	22	3	6	9	....	....	....	122	....	....	....	....	....	....	....	....	....	....	....	....	....	....	....	....	....	....
1990-91	**New Jersey Devils**	**NHL**	**8**	**0**	**1**	**1**	**0**	**1**	**1**	**27**	**0**	**0**	**0**	**3**	**0.0**	**1**	**0**	**0**	**0**	**1**	**3**	**0**	**0**	**0**	**6**	**0**	**0**	**0**
	Utica Devils	AHL	59	3	15	18	....	....	....	339	....	....	....	....	....	....	....	....	....	....	....	....	....	....	....	....	....	....
1991-92	Utica Devils	AHL	50	4	7	11	....	....	....	224	....	....	....	....	....	....	....	....	....	....	....	....	....	....	....	....	....	....
1992-93	Providence Bruins	AHL	69	2	15	17	....	....	....	257	....	....	....	....	....	....	....	....	....	....	2	0	1	1	6	....	....	....
1993-94	**Boston Bruins**	**NHL**	**36**	**0**	**1**	**1**	**0**	**1**	**1**	**144**	**0**	**0**	**0**	**13**	**0.0**	**8**	**1**	**9**	**0**	**–2**	**4**	**0**	**0**	**0**	**9**	**0**	**0**	**0**
	Providence Bruins	AHL	32	1	10	11	....	....	....	157	....	....	....	....	....	....	....	....	....	....	....	....	....	....	....	....	....	....
1994-95	**Boston Bruins**	**NHL**	**34**	**0**	**6**	**6**	**0**	**9**	**9**	**103**	**0**	**0**	**0**	**30**	**0.0**	**16**	**0**	**21**	**2**	**–3**	**5**	**0**	**0**	**0**	**11**	**0**	**0**	**0**
	Fresno Falcons	SunHL	3	1	1	2	....	....	....	7	....	....	....	....	....	....	....	....	....	....	....	....	....	....	....	....	....	....
1995-96	**Calgary Flames**	**NHL**	**70**	**3**	**9**	**12**	**3**	**7**	**10**	**162**	**0**	**0**	**1**	**57**	**5.3**	**37**	**0**	**28**	**5**	**14**	**4**	**0**	**1**	**1**	**4**	**0**	**0**	**0**
1996-97	**Calgary Flames**	**NHL**	**39**	**0**	**4**	**4**	**0**	**4**	**4**	**117**	**0**	**0**	**0**	**33**	**0.0**	**15**	**0**	**18**	**5**	**2**	....	....	....	....	....	....	....	....
	Tampa Bay Lightning	**NHL**	**13**	**0**	**1**	**1**	**0**	**1**	**1**	**34**	**0**	**0**	**0**	**7**	**0.0**	**3**	**0**	**8**	**1**	**–4**	....	....	....	....	....	....	....	....
1997-98	**Tampa Bay Lightning**	**NHL**	**44**	**0**	**3**	**3**	**0**	**3**	**3**	**122**	**0**	**0**	**0**	**21**	**0.0**	**11**	**0**	**23**	**8**	**–4**	....	....	....	....	....	....	....	....
	Vancouver Canucks	**NHL**	**7**	**0**	**1**	**1**	**0**	**1**	**1**	**55**	**0**	**0**	**0**	**5**	**0.0**	**3**	**0**	**2**	**1**	**2**	....	....	....	....	....	....	....	....
1998-99	**Vancouver Canucks**	**NHL**	**26**	**0**	**1**	**1**	**0**	**1**	**1**	**63**	**0**	**0**	**0**	**20**	**0.0**	**7**	**0**	**12**	**2**	**–3**	....	....	....	....	....	....	....	....
	Phoenix Coyotes	**NHL**	**11**	**0**	**1**	**1**	**0**	**1**	**1**	**27**	**0**	**0**	**0**	**7**	**0.0**	**2**	**0**	**5**	**2**	**–1**	....	....	....	....	....	....	....	....
99-2000	**Washington Capitals**	**NHL**	**7**	**0**	**0**	**0**	**0**	**0**	**0**	**11**	**0**	**0**	**0**	**4**	**0.0**	**2**	**0**	**7**	**0**	**–5**	....	....	....	....	....	....	....	....
	Portland Pirates	AHL	56	0	12	12	....	....	....	154	....	....	....	....	....	....	....	....	....	....	4	0	0	0	14	....	....	....
	NHL Totals		**352**	**5**	**33**	**38**	**5**	**32**	**37**	**1065**	**0**	**0**	**1**	**228**	**2.2**	**118**	**1**	**155**	**30**		**21**	**0**	**1**	**1**	**46**	**0**	**0**	**0**

Signed as a free agent by **Boston**, July 23, 1992. Signed as a free agent by **Calgary**, August 22, 1995. Traded to **Tampa Bay** by **Calgary** for Tyler Moss, March 18, 1997. Traded to **Vancouver** by **Tampa Bay** for Enrico Ciccone, March 14, 1998. Traded to **Phoenix** by **Vancouver** for future considerations, March 8, 1999. Signed as a free agent by **Washington**, August 9, 1999.

• HUSKA, Ryan

LW – L. 6'2", 194 lbs. b: Cranbrook, B.C., 7/2/1975. Chicago's 4th, 76th overall, in 1993.

Season	Club	League	GP	G	A	Pts	AG	AA	APts	PIM	PP	SH	GW	S	%	TGF	PGF	TGA	PGA	+/-	GP	G	A	Pts	PIM	PP	SH	GW
1990-91	Trail Selects	BCAHA	37	65	70	135	....	....	....	18	....	....	....	....	....	....	....	....	....	....	....	....	....	....	....	....	....	....
1991-92	Kamloops Blazers	WHL	44	4	5	9	....	....	....	23	....	....	....	....	....	....	....	....	....	....	6	0	1	1	0	....	....	....
	Kamloops Blazers	Mem-Cup	2	0	0	0	....	....	....	0	....	....	....	....	....	....	....	....	....	....	....	....	....	....	....	....	....	....
1992-93	Kamloops Blazers	WHL	68	17	15	32	....	....	....	50	....	....	....	....	....	....	....	....	....	....	13	2	6	8	4	....	....	....
1993-94	Kamloops Blazers	WHL	69	23	31	54	....	....	....	66	....	....	....	....	....	....	....	....	....	....	19	9	5	14	23	....	....	....
	Kamloops Blazers	Mem-Cup	4	2	1	3	....	....	....	17	....	....	....	....	....	....	....	....	....	....	....	....	....	....	....	....	....	....
1994-95	Kamloops Blazers	WHL	66	27	40	67	....	....	....	78	....	....	....	....	....	....	....	....	....	....	17	7	8	15	12	....	....	....
	Kamloops Blazers	Mem-Cup	4	2	5	7	....	....	....	6	....	....	....	....	....	....	....	....	....	....	....	....	....	....	....	....	....	....
1995-96	Indianapolis Ice	IHL	28	2	3	5	....	....	....	15	....	....	....	....	....	....	....	....	....	....	5	1	1	2	27	....	....	....
1996-97	Indianapolis Ice	IHL	80	18	12	30	....	....	....	100	....	....	....	....	....	....	....	....	....	....	4	0	0	0	4	....	....	....

			REGULAR SEASON																		PLAYOFFS							
Season	Club	League	GP	G	A	Pts	AG	AA	APts	PIM	PP	SH	GW	S	%	TGF	PGF	TGA	PGA	+/–	GP	G	A	Pts	PIM	PP	SH	GW
1997-98	**Chicago Blackhawks**	**NHL**	**1**	**0**	**0**	**0**	**0**	**0**	**0**	**0**	**0**	**0**	**0**	**0**	**0.0**	**0**	**0**	**0**	**0**	**0**	....	....	....	....	....	....	....	....
	Indianapolis Ice	IHL	80	19	16	35	....	....	....	115	....	....	....	....	....	....	....	....	....	....	5	0	3	3	10	....	....	....
1998-99	Lowell Lock Monsters	AHL	60	5	13	18	....	....	....	70	....	....	....	....	....	....	....	....	....	....	2	0	0	0	0	....	....	....
99-2000	Springfield Falcons	AHL	61	12	9	21	....	....	....	77	....	....	....	....	....	....	....	....	....	....	4	0	1	1	0	....	....	....
	NHL Totals		**1**	**0**	**0**	**0**	**0**	**0**	**0**	**0**	**0**	**0**	**0**	**0**	**0.0**	**0**	**0**	**0**	**0**		....	....	....	....	....	....	....	....

Signed as a free agent by **NY Islanders**, September 9, 1998. Signed as a free agent by **Phoenix**, August 15, 1999.

• HUSTON, Ron

Ronald Earle "Spike" C – R. 5'9", 170 lbs. b: Manitou, Man., 4/8/1945.

Season	Club	League	GP	G	A	Pts	AG	AA	APts	PIM	PP	SH	GW	S	%	TGF	PGF	TGA	PGA	+/–	GP	G	A	Pts	PIM	PP	SH	GW
1962-63	Brandon Wheat Kings	MJHL	20	5	9	14	....	....	....	4	....	....	....	....	....	....	....	....	....	....	4	0	1	1	0	....	....	....
	Brandon Wheat Kings	Mem-Cup	4	0	1	1	....	....	....	0	....	....	....	....	....	....	....	....	....	....	....	....	....	....	....	....	....	....
1963-64	Brandon Wheat Kings	MJHL	30	20	30	50	....	....	....	15	....	....	....	....	....	....	....	....	....	....	20	6	9	15	4	....	....	....
1964-65	Brandon Wheat Kings	MJHL	52	18	21	39	....	....	....	20	....	....	....	....	....	....	....	....	....	....	8	5	1	6	2	....	....	....
1965-66	Cranbrook Royals	WIHL	49	39	42	81	....	....	....	4	....	....	....	....	....	....	....	....	....	....	....	....	....	....	....	....	....	....
1966-67	Cranbrook Royals	WIHL	39	23	36	59	....	....	....	12	....	....	....	....	....	....	....	....	....	....	....	....	....	....	....	....	....	....
	Jersey Devils	EHL	4	1	0	1	....	....	....	0	....	....	....	....	....	....	....	....	....	....	....	....	....	....	....	....	....	....
1967-68	Cranbrook Royals	WIHL	44	38	43	81	....	....	....	4	....	....	....	....	....	....	....	....	....	....	....	....	....	....	....	....	....	....
	Spokane Jets	Al-Cup	7	2	0	2	....	....	....	0	....	....	....	....	....	....	....	....	....	....	....	....	....	....	....	....	....	....
1968-69	Portland Buckaroos	WHL	3	0	0	0	....	....	....	0	....	....	....	....	....	....	....	....	....	....	....	....	....	....	....	....	....	....
	Cranbrook Royals	WIHL	47	*45	43	*88	....	....	....	4	....	....	....	....	....	....	....	....	....	....	....	....	....	....	....	....	....	....
	Spokane Jets	Al-Cup	6	1	3	4	....	....	....	0	....	....	....	....	....	....	....	....	....	....	....	....	....	....	....	....	....	....
1969-70	Seattle Totems	WHL	5	0	2	2	....	....	....	0	....	....	....	....	....	....	....	....	....	....	....	....	....	....	....	....	....	....
	Cranbrook Royals	WIHL	47	*36	*53	*89	....	....	....	10	....	....	....	....	....	....	....	....	....	....	5	5	2	7	2	....	....	....
	Spokane Jets	Al-Cup	13	*13	7	*20	....	....	....	2	....	....	....	....	....	....	....	....	....	....	....	....	....	....	....	....	....	....
1970-71	Calgary Stampeders	ASHL	40	23	19	42	....	....	....	2	....	....	....	....	....	....	....	....	....	....	....	....	....	....	....	....	....	....
1971-72	Spokane Jets	WIHL	49	39	47	*86	....	....	....	30	....	....	....	....	....	....	....	....	....	....	....	....	....	....	....	....	....	....
1972-73	Salt Lake Golden Eagles	WHL	72	42	42	84	....	....	....	21	....	....	....	....	....	....	....	....	....	....	9	6	7	13	2	....	....	....
1973-74	**California Golden Seals**	**NHL**	**23**	**3**	**10**	**13**	**3**	**8**	**11**	**0**	**0**	**0**	**1**	**29**	**10.3**	**22**	**4**	**34**	**4**	**–12**	....	....	....	....	....	....	....	....
	Salt Lake Golden Eagles	WHL	50	20	32	52	....	....	....	4	....	....	....	....	....	....	....	....	....	....	5	0	2	2	2	....	....	....
1974-75	**California Golden Seals**	**NHL**	**56**	**12**	**21**	**33**	**10**	**16**	**26**	**8**	**0**	**0**	**2**	**111**	**10.8**	**44**	**7**	**63**	**11**	**–15**	....	....	....	....	....	....	....	....
1975-76	Phoenix Roadrunners	WHA	79	22	44	66	....	....	....	4	....	....	....	....	....	....	....	....	....	....	5	1	1	2	0	....	....	....
1976-77	Phoenix Roadrunners	WHA	80	20	39	59	....	....	....	10	....	....	....	....	....	....	....	....	....	....	....	....	....	....	....	....	....	....
1977-78	Spokane Flyers	WIHL	56	33	*86	*119	....	....	....	....	....	....	....	....	....	....	....	....	....	....	....	....	....	....	....	....	....	....
1978-79	Spokane Flyers	PHL	49	19	35	54	....	....	....	8	....	....	....	....	....	....	....	....	....	....	....	....	....	....	....	....	....	....
1979-80			DID NOT PLAY																									
1980-1983	Elk Valley Blazers	WIHL	STATISTICS NOT AVAILABLE																									
	NHL Totals		**79**	**15**	**31**	**46**	**13**	**24**	**37**	**8**	**0**	**0**	**3**	**140**	**10.7**	**66**	**11**	**97**	**15**		....	....	....	....	....	....	....	....
	Other Major League Totals		159	42	83	125	....	....	....	14	....	....	....	....	....	....	....	....	....	....	5	1	1	2	0	....	....	....

WIHL First All-Star Team (1969, 1970, 1972, 1978) • WHL Second All-Star Team (1973) • Won WHL Rookie of the Year Award (1973)

Loaned to **Spokane** (WIHL) by **Cranbrook** (WIHL) for Allan Cup playoffs, April, 1970. Signed as a free agent by **California**, September, 1972. Rights traded to **Phoenix** (WHA) by **California** with the rights to Del Hall for the rights to Gary Holt, June, 1975.

• HUTCHISON, Dave

David Joseph D – L. 6'3", 205 lbs. b: London, Ont., 5/2/1952. Los Angeles' 2nd, 36th overall, in 1972.

Season	Club	League	GP	G	A	Pts	AG	AA	APts	PIM	PP	SH	GW	S	%	TGF	PGF	TGA	PGA	+/–	GP	G	A	Pts	PIM	PP	SH	GW
1969-70	London Diamonds	OHA-B	STATISTICS NOT AVAILABLE																									
	London Knights	OHA-Jr.	7	1	2	3	....	....	....	30	....	....	....	....	....	....	....	....	....	....	12	0	4	4	60	....	....	....
1970-71	London Knights	OHA-Jr.	54	2	13	15	....	....	....	154	....	....	....	....	....	....	....	....	....	....	....	....	....	....	....	....	....	....
1971-72	London Knights	OMJHL	46	3	11	14	....	....	....	151	....	....	....	....	....	....	....	....	....	....	3	0	1	1	15	....	....	....
1972-73	Philadelphia Blazers	WHA	28	0	2	2	....	....	....	34	....	....	....	....	....	....	....	....	....	....	3	0	0	0	2	....	....	....
	Rhode Island Eagles	EHL	32	7	18	25	....	....	....	158	....	....	....	....	....	....	....	....	....	....	....	....	....	....	....	....	....	....
1973-74	Vancouver Blazers	WHA	69	0	13	13	....	....	....	151	....	....	....	....	....	....	....	....	....	....	....	....	....	....	....	....	....	....
1974-75	**Los Angeles Kings**	**NHL**	**68**	**0**	**6**	**6**	**0**	**4**	**4**	**133**	**0**	**0**	**0**	**55**	**0.0**	**30**	**0**	**30**	**5**	**5**	**2**	**0**	**0**	**0**	**22**	**0**	**0**	**0**
1975-76	**Los Angeles Kings**	**NHL**	**50**	**0**	**10**	**10**	**0**	**7**	**7**	**181**	**0**	**0**	**0**	**61**	**0.0**	**37**	**0**	**40**	**7**	**4**	**9**	**0**	**3**	**3**	**29**	**0**	**0**	**0**
1976-77	**Los Angeles Kings**	**NHL**	**70**	**6**	**11**	**17**	**5**	**8**	**13**	**220**	**1**	**0**	**3**	**115**	**5.2**	**78**	**6**	**80**	**15**	**7**	**9**	**1**	**4**	**5**	**17**	**0**	**0**	**0**
1977-78	**Los Angeles Kings**	**NHL**	**44**	**0**	**10**	**10**	**0**	**8**	**8**	**71**	**0**	**0**	**0**	**60**	**0.0**	**43**	**0**	**37**	**5**	**11**	....	....	....	....	....	....	....	....
1978-79	**Toronto Maple Leafs**	**NHL**	**79**	**4**	**15**	**19**	**3**	**11**	**14**	**235**	**0**	**0**	**0**	**117**	**3.4**	**84**	**2**	**65**	**19**	**36**	**6**	**0**	**3**	**3**	**23**	**0**	**0**	**0**
1979-80	**Toronto Maple Leafs**	**NHL**	**31**	**1**	**6**	**7**	**1**	**4**	**5**	**28**	**0**	**0**	**0**	**21**	**4.8**	**18**	**0**	**21**	**4**	**1**	....	....	....	....	....	....	....	....
	Chicago Black Hawks	**NHL**	**38**	**0**	**5**	**5**	**0**	**4**	**4**	**73**	**0**	**0**	**0**	**57**	**0.0**	**23**	**0**	**29**	**6**	**0**	**6**	**0**	**0**	**0**	**12**	**0**	**0**	**0**
1980-81	**Chicago Black Hawks**	**NHL**	**59**	**2**	**9**	**11**	**2**	**6**	**8**	**124**	**0**	**0**	**0**	**58**	**3.4**	**53**	**1**	**50**	**10**	**12**	**2**	**0**	**0**	**0**	**2**	**0**	**0**	**0**
1981-82	**Chicago Black Hawks**	**NHL**	**66**	**5**	**18**	**23**	**4**	**12**	**16**	**246**	**0**	**1**	**0**	**72**	**6.9**	**78**	**0**	**110**	**36**	**4**	**14**	**1**	**2**	**3**	**44**	**0**	**0**	**0**
1982-83	**New Jersey Devils**	**NHL**	**32**	**1**	**4**	**5**	**1**	**3**	**4**	**102**	**0**	**0**	**0**	**21**	**4.8**	**11**	**0**	**38**	**7**	**–20**	....	....	....	....	....	....	....	....
	Wichita Wind	CHL	2	0	0	0	....	....	....	0	....	....	....	....	....	....	....	....	....	....	....	....	....	....	....	....	....	....
1983-84	**Toronto Maple Leafs**	**NHL**	**47**	**0**	**3**	**3**	**0**	**2**	**2**	**137**	**0**	**0**	**0**	**16**	**0.0**	**22**	**0**	**31**	**14**	**5**	....	....	....	....	....	....	....	....
	NHL Totals		**584**	**19**	**97**	**116**	**16**	**69**	**85**	**1550**	**1**	**1**	**3**	**653**	**2.9**	**477**	**9**	**531**	**128**		**48**	**2**	**12**	**14**	**149**	**0**	**0**	**0**
	Other Major League Totals		97	0	15	15	....	....	....	185	....	....	....	....	....	....	....	....	....	....	3	0	0	0	2	....	....	....

Selected by **Miami-Philadelphia** (WHA) in 1972 WHA General Player Draft, February 13, 1972. Transferred to **Vancouver** (WHA) after **Philadelphia** (WHA) franchise relocated, May, 1973. Traded to **Toronto** by **LA Kings** with Lorne Stamler for Brian Glennie, Kurt Walker, Scott Garland and Toronto's 2nd round choice (Mark Hardy) in 1979 Entry Draft, June 14, 1978. Traded to **Chicago** by **Toronto** for Pat Ribble, January 10, 1980. Traded to **Washington** by **Chicago** with Ted Bulley for Washington's 6th round choice (Jari Torkii) in 1983 Entry Draft and Washington's 5th round choice (Darin Sceviour) in 1984 Entry Draft, August 12, 1982. Claimed by **New Jersey** from **Washington** in Waiver Draft, October 4, 1982. Signed as a free agent by **Toronto**, November 15, 1983.

• HYNES, Dave

LW – L. 5'9", 182 lbs. b: Cambridge, MA, 4/17/1951. Boston's 5th, 56th overall, in 1971.

Season	Club	League	GP	G	A	Pts	AG	AA	APts	PIM	PP	SH	GW	S	%	TGF	PGF	TGA	PGA	+/–	GP	G	A	Pts	PIM	PP	SH	GW
1970-71	Harvard University	ECAC	27	26	26	52	....	....	....	16	....	....	....	....	....	....	....	....	....	....	....	....	....	....	....	....	....	....
1971-72	Harvard University	ECAC	25	23	31	54	....	....	....	40	....	....	....	....	....	....	....	....	....	....	....	....	....	....	....	....	....	....
1972-73	Harvard University	ECAC	12	15	19	34	....	....	....	12	....	....	....	....	....	....	....	....	....	....	....	....	....	....	....	....	....	....
	United States	Nat-Team	7	*9	6	15	....	....	....	....	....	....	....	....	....	....	....	....	....	....	....	....	....	....	....	....	....	....
1973-74	**Boston Bruins**	**NHL**	**3**	**0**	**0**	**0**	**0**	**0**	**0**	**0**	**0**	**0**	**0**	**1**	**0.0**	**0**	**0**	**0**	**0**	**0**	....	....	....	....	....	....	....	....
	Boston Braves	AHL	73	35	37	72	....	....	....	22	....	....	....	....	....	....	....	....	....	....	....	....	....	....	....	....	....	....
1974-75	**Boston Bruins**	**NHL**	**19**	**4**	**0**	**4**	**3**	**0**	**3**	**2**	**0**	**0**	**0**	**15**	**26.7**	**6**	**0**	**3**	**0**	**3**	....	....	....	....	....	....	....	....
	Rochester Americans	AHL	59	42	35	77	....	....	....	33	....	....	....	....	....	....	....	....	....	....	12	2	7	9	6	....	....	....
1975-76	Rochester Americans	AHL	63	37	30	67	....	....	....	20	....	....	....	....	....	....	....	....	....	....	7	3	2	5	11	....	....	....
1976-77	New England Whalers	WHA	22	5	4	9	....	....	....	4	....	....	....	....	....	....	....	....	....	....	....	....	....	....	....	....	....	....
	Rhode Island Reds	AHL	46	22	15	37	....	....	....	8	....	....	....	....	....	....	....	....	....	....	....	....	....	....	....	....	....	....
	United States	WEC-A	10	3	4	7	....	....	....	10	....	....	....	....	....	....	....	....	....	....	....	....	....	....	....	....	....	....
1977-78	Springfield Indians	AHL	46	16	30	46	....	....	....	6	....	....	....	....	....	....	....	....	....	....	4	1	0	1	0	....	....	....
	NHL Totals		**22**	**4**	**0**	**4**	**3**	**0**	**3**	**2**	**0**	**0**	**0**	**16**	**25.0**	**6**	**0**	**3**	**0**		....	....	....	....	....	....	....	....
	Other Major League Totals		22	5	4	9	....	....	....	4	....	....	....	....	....	....	....	....	....	....	....	....	....	....	....	....	....	....

ECAC Second All-Star Team (1972) • NCAA East First All-American Team (1972) • AHL First All-Star Team (1976)

Signed as a free agent by **New England** (WHA), August, 1976.

• HYNES, Gord

Gordon R. D – L. 6'1", 170 lbs. b: Montreal, Que., 7/22/1966. Boston's 5th, 115th overall, in 1985.

Season	Club	League	GP	G	A	Pts	AG	AA	APts	PIM	PP	SH	GW	S	%	TGF	PGF	TGA	PGA	+/–	GP	G	A	Pts	PIM	PP	SH	GW
1982-83	St. Albert Sabres	AAHA	STATISTICS NOT AVAILABLE																									
1983-84	Medicine Hat Tigers	WHL	72	5	14	19	....	....	....	39	....	....	....	....	....	....	....	....	....	....	14	0	0	0	0	....	....	....
1984-85	Medicine Hat Tigers	WHL	70	18	45	63	....	....	....	61	....	....	....	....	....	....	....	....	....	....	10	6	9	15	17	....	....	....
1985-86	Medicine Hat Tigers	WHL	58	22	39	61	....	....	....	45	....	....	....	....	....	....	....	....	....	....	25	8	15	23	32	....	....	....
1986-87	Moncton Golden Flames	AHL	69	2	19	21	....	....	....	21	....	....	....	....	....	....	....	....	....	....	4	0	0	0	2	....	....	....
1987-88	Maine Mariners	AHL	69	5	30	35	....	....	....	65	....	....	....	....	....	....	....	....	....	....	7	1	3	4	4	....	....	....
1988-89	Canada	Nat-Team	61	8	38	46	....	....	....	44	....	....	....	....	....	....	....	....	....	....	....	....	....	....	....	....	....	....
1989-90	Canada	Nat-Team	11	3	1	4	....	....	....	4	....	....	....	....	....	....	....	....	....	....	....	....	....	....	....	....	....	....
	HC Varese	Italy	29	13	36	49	....	....	....	16	....	....	....	....	....	....	....	....	....	....	6	3	3	6	0	....	....	....

Season	Club	League	REGULAR SEASON																		PLAYOFFS							
			GP	G	A	Pts	AG	AA	APts	PIM	PP	SH	GW	S	%	TGF	PGF	TGA	PGA	+/-	GP	G	A	Pts	PIM	PP	SH	GW
1990-91	Canada	Nat-Team	57	12	30	42				62																		
1991-92	Canada	Nat-Team	48	12	22	34				50																		
	Canada	Olympics	8	3	3	6				6																		
	Boston Bruins	**NHL**	**15**	**0**	**5**	**5**	**0**	**4**	**4**	**6**	**0**	**0**	**0**	**16**	**0.0**	**17**	**0**	**9**	**0**	**8**	**12**	**1**	**2**	**3**	**6**	**0**	**0**	**0**
1992-93	**Philadelphia Flyers**	**NHL**	**37**	**3**	**4**	**7**	**2**	**3**	**5**	**16**	**0**	**0**	**0**	**39**	**7.7**	**31**	**5**	**31**	**2**	**-3**								
	Hershey Bears	AHL	9	1	3	4				4																		
1993-94	Cincinnati Cyclones	IHL	80	15	43	58				50											11	2	6	8	24			
1994-95	Detroit Vipers	IHL	62	4	35	39				32																		
1995-96	Schwenningen Wild Wings	Germany	49	9	32	41				61											4	0	2	2	10			
1996-97	Schwenningen Wild Wings	Germany	47	15	41	56				82											5	2	5	7	18			
	Hershey Bears	AHL	9	1	3	4				4																		
1997-98	Adler Mannheim	Germany	40	5	24	29				95											10	3	4	7	22			
	Adler Mannheim	EuroHL	4	1	4	5				2																		
1998-99	Adler Mannheim	Germany	52	15	28	43				86											12	1	8	9	14			
	Adler Mannheim	EuroHL	5	2	3	5				10											4	3	2	5	2			
99-2000	Adler Mannheim	Germany	50	11	26	37				66											5	1	1	2	4			
	Adler Mannheim	EuroHL	5	0	1	1				6																		
	NHL Totals		**52**	**3**	**9**	**12**	**2**	**7**	**9**	**22**	**0**	**0**	**0**	**55**	**5.5**	**48**	**5**	**40**	**2**		**12**	**1**	**2**	**3**	**6**	**0**	**0**	**0**

Signed as a free agent by **Philadelphia**, August 25, 1992. Claimed by **Florida** from **Philadelphia** in Expansion Draft, June 24, 1993.

• IAFRATE, Al

Albert Anthony "Wild Thing" D – L. 6'3", 235 lbs. b: Dearborn, MI, 3/21/1966. Toronto's 1st, 4th overall, in 1984.

Season	Club	League	GP	G	A	Pts	AG	AA	APts	PIM	PP	SH	GW	S	%	TGF	PGF	TGA	PGA	+/-	GP	G	A	Pts	PIM	PP	SH	GW
1981-82	Detroit Adrays	MNHL	STATISTICS NOT AVAILABLE																									
1982-83	Detroit Compuware	MNHL	66	30	45	75				90																		
1983-84	United States	Nat-Team	55	4	17	21				26																		
	United States	Olympics	6	0	0	0				2																		
	Belleville Bulls	OHL	10	2	4	6				2											3	0	1	1	5			
1984-85	**Toronto Maple Leafs**	**NHL**	**68**	**5**	**16**	**21**	**4**	**11**	**15**	**51**	**3**	**0**	**0**	**88**	**5.7**	**67**	**18**	**83**	**15**	**-19**								
1985-86	**Toronto Maple Leafs**	**NHL**	**65**	**8**	**25**	**33**	**6**	**17**	**23**	**40**	**2**	**0**	**2**	**94**	**8.5**	**92**	**23**	**92**	**13**	**-10**	**10**	**0**	**3**	**3**	**4**	**0**	**0**	**0**
1986-87	**Toronto Maple Leafs**	**NHL**	**80**	**9**	**21**	**30**	**8**	**15**	**23**	**55**	**0**	**0**	**3**	**132**	**6.8**	**103**	**12**	**141**	**32**	**-18**	**13**	**1**	**3**	**4**	**11**	**1**	**0**	**0**
1987-88	**Toronto Maple Leafs**	**NHL**	**77**	**22**	**30**	**52**	**19**	**21**	**40**	**80**	**4**	**3**	**4**	**169**	**13.0**	**105**	**26**	**141**	**41**	**-21**	**6**	**3**	**4**	**7**	**6**	**2**	**0**	**0**
1988-89	**Toronto Maple Leafs**	**NHL**	**65**	**13**	**20**	**33**	**11**	**14**	**25**	**72**	**1**	**2**	**3**	**105**	**12.4**	**89**	**15**	**91**	**20**	**3**								
1989-90	**Toronto Maple Leafs**	**NHL**	**75**	**21**	**42**	**63**	**18**	**30**	**48**	**135**	**6**	**1**	**0**	**153**	**13.7**	**118**	**33**	**126**	**37**	**-4**								
1990-91	**Toronto Maple Leafs**	**NHL**	**42**	**3**	**15**	**18**	**3**	**11**	**14**	**113**	**2**	**0**	**0**	**51**	**5.9**	**40**	**12**	**57**	**14**	**-15**								
	Washington Capitals	**NHL**	**30**	**6**	**8**	**14**	**5**	**6**	**11**	**124**	**0**	**1**	**1**	**55**	**10.9**	**36**	**4**	**38**	**5**	**-1**	**10**	**1**	**3**	**4**	**22**	**0**	**0**	**1**
1991-92	**Washington Capitals**	**NHL**	**78**	**17**	**34**	**51**	**15**	**26**	**41**	**180**	**6**	**0**	**1**	**151**	**11.3**	**126**	**36**	**112**	**23**	**1**	**7**	**4**	**2**	**6**	**14**	**1**	**0**	**0**
1992-93	**Washington Capitals**	**NHL**	**81**	**25**	**41**	**66**	**21**	**28**	**49**	**169**	**11**	**1**	**4**	**289**	**8.7**	**145**	**48**	**115**	**33**	**15**	**6**	**6**	**0**	**6**	**4**	**3**	**0**	**1**
1993-94	**Washington Capitals**	**NHL**	**67**	**10**	**35**	**45**	**9**	**27**	**36**	**143**	**4**	**0**	**3**	**252**	**4.0**	**101**	**32**	**78**	**19**	**10**								
	Boston Bruins	**NHL**	**12**	**5**	**8**	**13**	**5**	**6**	**11**	**20**	**2**	**0**	**1**	**47**	**10.6**	**26**	**6**	**17**	**3**	**6**	**13**	**3**	**1**	**4**	**6**	**1**	**0**	**1**
1994-95	**Boston Bruins**	**NHL**	DID NOT PLAY – INJURED																									
1995-96	**Boston Bruins**	**NHL**	DID NOT PLAY – INJURED																									
1996-97	**San Jose Sharks**	**NHL**	**38**	**6**	**9**	**15**	**6**	**8**	**14**	**91**	**3**	**0**	**0**	**91**	**6.6**	**32**	**9**	**40**	**7**	**-10**								
1997-98	**San Jose Sharks**	**NHL**	**21**	**2**	**7**	**9**	**2**	**7**	**9**	**28**	**2**	**0**	**0**	**37**	**5.4**	**19**	**5**	**15**	**0**	**-1**	**6**	**1**	**0**	**1**	**10**	**1**	**0**	**0**
	United States	WC-A	4	0	2	2				6																		
1998-99	**Carolina Hurricanes**	**NHL**	DID NOT PLAY – INJURED																									
	NHL Totals		**799**	**152**	**311**	**463**	**132**	**227**	**359**	**1301**	**46**	**8**	**22**	**1714**	**8.9**	**1099**	**279**	**1146**	**262**		**71**	**19**	**16**	**35**	**77**	**9**	**0**	**3**

NHL Second All-Star Team (1993) • Played in NHL All-Star Game (1988, 1990, 1993, 1994)

Traded to **Washington** by **Toronto** for Peter Zezel and Bob Rouse, January 16, 1991. Traded to **Boston** by **Washington** for Joe Juneau, March 21, 1994. • Missed entire 1994-95 and 1995-96 seasons recovering from knee surgery. Traded to **San Jose** by **Boston** for Jeff Odgers and Pittsburgh's 5th round choice (previously acquired, Boston selected Elias Abrahamsson) in 1996 Entry Draft, June 21, 1996. Claimed by **Nashville** from **San Jose** in Expansion Draft, June 26, 1998. Signed as a free agent by **Carolina**, July 14, 1998. • Officially announced retirement, September 1, 1998.

• IGINLA, Jarome

RW – R. 6'1", 202 lbs. b: Edmonton, Alta., 7/1/1977. Dallas' 1st, 11th overall, in 1995.

Season	Club	League	GP	G	A	Pts	AG	AA	APts	PIM	PP	SH	GW	S	%	TGF	PGF	TGA	PGA	+/-	GP	G	A	Pts	PIM	PP	SH	GW
1991-92	St. Albert Eagle Raiders	AAHA	36	26	30	56				22																		
1992-93	St. Albert Midget Raiders	AAHA	36	34	53	87				20																		
1993-94	Kamloops Blazers	WHL	48	6	23	29				33											19	3	6	9	10			
	Kamloops Blazers	Mem-Cup	4	0	2	2				4																		
1994-95	Kamloops Blazers	WHL	72	33	38	71				111											21	7	11	18	34			
	Kamloops Blazers	Mem-Cup	4	4	2	6				7																		
1995-96	Kamloops Blazers	WHL	63	63	73	136				120											16	16	13	29	44			
	Canada	WJC-A	6	5	7	*12				4																		
	Calgary Flames	**NHL**																			**2**	**1**	**1**	**2**	**0**	**0**	**0**	**0**
1996-97	**Calgary Flames**	**NHL**	**82**	**21**	**29**	**50**	**22**	**26**	**48**	**37**	**8**	**1**	**3**	**169**	**12.4**	**71**	**24**	**70**	**19**	**-4**								
	Canada	WC-A	11	2	3	5				2																		
1997-98	**Calgary Flames**	**NHL**	**70**	**13**	**19**	**32**	**15**	**19**	**34**	**29**	**0**	**2**	**1**	**154**	**8.4**	**44**	**9**	**53**	**8**	**-10**								
1998-99	**Calgary Flames**	**NHL**	**82**	**28**	**23**	**51**	**33**	**22**	**55**	**58**	**7**	**0**	**4**	**211**	**13.3**	**78**	**25**	**54**	**2**	**1**								
99-2000	**Calgary Flames**	**NHL**	**77**	**29**	**34**	**63**	**33**	**32**	**65**	**26**	**12**	**0**	**4**	**256**	**11.3**	**87**	**37**	**58**	**8**	**0**								
	NHL Totals		**311**	**91**	**105**	**196**	**103**	**99**	**202**	**150**	**27**	**3**	**12**	**790**	**11.5**	**280**	**95**	**235**	**37**		**2**	**1**	**1**	**2**	**0**	**0**	**0**	**0**

Won George Parsons Trophy (Memorial Cup Tournament Most Sportsmanlike Player) (1995) • WJC-A All-Star Team (1996) • Named Best Forward at WJC-A (1996) • WHL West First All-Star Team (1996) • Canadian Major Junior First All-Star Team (1996) • NHL All-Rookie Team (1997)

Traded to **Calgary** by **Dallas** with Corey Millen for Joe Nieuwendyk, December 19, 1995.

• IGNATJEV, Victor

D – L. 6'4", 215 lbs. b: Riga, USSR, 4/26/1970. San Jose's 11th, 243rd overall, in 1992.

Season	Club	League	GP	G	A	Pts	AG	AA	APts	PIM	PP	SH	GW	S	%	TGF	PGF	TGA	PGA	+/-	GP	G	A	Pts	PIM	PP	SH	GW
1989-90	Dynamo Riga	USSR	40	0	0	0				26																		
1990-91	Dynamo Riga	USSR	10	0	0	0				2																		
1991-92	Dynamo Riga	CIS	22	4	5	9				22																		
1992-93	Kansas City Blades	IHL	64	5	16	21				68											4	1	2	3	24			
1993-94	Kansas City Blades	IHL	67	1	24	25				123																		
1994-95	Oklahoma City Blazers	CHL	47	11	35	46				66																		
	Denver Grizzlies	IHL	23	2	11	13				4											17	3	8	11	8			
1995-96	Utah Grizzlies	IHL	73	9	29	38				67											21	3	8	11	22			
1996-97	Long Beach Ice Dogs	IHL	82	16	53	69				112											16	3	4	7	26			
1997-98	Long Beach Ice Dogs	IHL	71	12	33	45				102											17	3	11	14	16			
1998-99	**Pittsburgh Penguins**	**NHL**	**11**	**0**	**1**	**1**	**0**	**1**	**1**	**6**	**0**	**0**	**0**	**15**	**0.0**	**6**	**3**	**7**	**1**	**-3**	**1**	**0**	**0**	**0**	**2**	**0**	**0**	**0**
99-2000	Nurnberg Ice Tigers	Germany	60	3	15	18				56																		
	Nurnberg Ice Tigers	EuroHL	4	0	3	3				22											2	0	0	0	6			
	Latvia	WC-A	7	0	0	0				18																		
	NHL Totals		**11**	**0**	**1**	**1**	**0**	**1**	**1**	**6**	**0**	**0**	**0**	**15**	**0.0**	**6**	**3**	**7**	**1**		**1**	**0**	**0**	**0**	**2**	**0**	**0**	**0**

IHL Second All-Star Team (1997)

Signed as a free agent by **Pittsburgh**, August 11, 1998. • Missed majority of 1998-99 season recovering from shoulder injury that required surgery, November, 1998. • Played w/ RHI's Sacramento River Rats in 1996 (21-15-23-38-27).

• IHNACAK, Miroslav

LW – L. 5'11", 175 lbs. b: Poprad, CSSR, 11/19/1962. Toronto's 12th, 171st overall, in 1982.

Season	Club	League	GP	G	A	Pts	AG	AA	APts	PIM	PP	SH	GW	S	%	TGF	PGF	TGA	PGA	+/-	GP	G	A	Pts	PIM	PP	SH	GW
1978-79	SST Poprad	Czech-2	STATISTICS NOT AVAILABLE																									
	Czechoslovakia	EJC-A	5	3	3	6				10																		
1979-80	SST Poprad	Czech-2	STATISTICS NOT AVAILABLE																									
	Czechoslovakia	EJC-A	5	4	4	8				0																		
1980-81	SST Poprad	Czech-2	STATISTICS NOT AVAILABLE																									
1981-82	VSZ Kosice	Czech.	41	22	11	33				28																		

			REGULAR SEASON																		PLAYOFFS							
Season	Club	League	GP	G	A	Pts	AG	AA	APts	PIM	PP	SH	GW	S	%	TGF	PGF	TGA	PGA	+/–	GP	G	A	Pts	PIM	PP	SH	GW
1982-83	VSZ Kosice	Czech.	42	20	17	37	....	....	....	32	....	....	....	....	....	....	....	....	....	....	....	....	....	....	....	....	....	....
1983-84	VSZ Kosice	Czech.	42	19	25	44	....	....	....	34	....	....	....	....	....	....	....	....	....	....	....	....	....	....	....	....	....	....
1984-85	VSZ Kosice	Czech.	43	35	31	*66	....	....	....	68	....	....	....	....	....	....	....	....	....	....	....	....	....	....	....	....	....	....
1985-86	VSZ Kosice	Czech.	21	16	16	32	....	....	....	....	....	....	....	....	....	....	....	....	....	....	....	....	....	....	....	....	....	....
	Toronto Maple Leafs	**NHL**	**21**	**2**	**4**	**6**	**2**	**3**	**5**	**27**	**1**	**0**	**0**	**25**	**8.0**	**11**	**2**	**16**	**1**	**–6**	....	....	....	....	....	....	....	....
	St. Catharines Saints	AHL	13	4	4	8	....	....	....	2	....	....	....	....	....	....	....	....	....	....	13	8	3	11	10	....	....	....
1986-87	**Toronto Maple Leafs**	**NHL**	**34**	**6**	**5**	**11**	**5**	**4**	**9**	**12**	**0**	**0**	**0**	**65**	**9.2**	**24**	**1**	**20**	**0**	**3**	**1**	**0**	**0**	**0**	**0**	**0**	**0**	**0**
	Newmarket Saints	AHL	32	11	17	28	....	....	....	6	....	....	....	....	....	....	....	....	....	....	....	....	....	....	....	....	....	....
1987-88	Newmarket Saints	AHL	51	11	17	28	....	....	....	24	....	....	....	....	....	....	....	....	....	....	....	....	....	....	....	....	....	....
1988-89	**Detroit Red Wings**	**NHL**	**1**	**0**	**0**	**0**	**0**	**0**	**0**	**0**	**0**	**0**	**0**	**1**	**0.0**	**1**	**0**	**1**	**0**	**0**	....	....	....	....	....	....	....	....
	Adirondack Red Wings	AHL	62	34	37	71	....	....	....	32	....	....	....	....	....	....	....	....	....	....	13	4	3	7	16	....	....	....
1989-90	Halifax Citadels	AHL	57	33	37	70	....	....	....	43	....	....	....	....	....	....	....	....	....	....	5	1	4	5	6	....	....	....
1990-91	Halifax Citadels	AHL	77	38	57	95	....	....	....	42	....	....	....	....	....	....	....	....	....	....	....	....	....	....	....	....	....	....
1991-92	BSC Preussen Berlin	Germany	26	8	12	20	....	....	....	24	....	....	....	....	....	....	....	....	....	....	7	4	3	7	18	....	....	....
1992-93	Mannheimer ERC	Germany	8	2	7	9	....	....	....	2	....	....	....	....	....	....	....	....	....	....	....	....	....	....	....	....	....	....
	SKP Poprad	Czech.	10	7	2	9	....	....	....	2	....	....	....	....	....	....	....	....	....	....	....	....	....	....	....	....	....	....
	EV Zug	Switz.	7	6	3	9	....	....	....	8	....	....	....	....	....	....	....	....	....	....	....	....	....	....	....	....	....	....
1993-94	Milwaukee Admirals	IHL	1	0	0	0	....	....	....	0	....	....	....	....	....	....	....	....	....	....	....	....	....	....	....	....	....	....
1994-95	HC Kosice	Slovakia	20	13	17	30	....	....	....	16	....	....	....	....	....	....	....	....	....	....	4	6	*14	*20	6	....	....	....
	Heilbronner ERC	Germany-2	11	9	9	18	....	....	....	8	....	....	....	....	....	....	....	....	....	....	....	....	....	....	....	....	....	....
	Slovakia	WC-B	7	7	1	8	....	....	....	2	....	....	....	....	....	....	....	....	....	....	....	....	....	....	....	....	....	....
1995-96	ERC Selb	Germany-2	44	39	68	107	....	....	....	63	....	....	....	....	....	....	....	....	....	....	....	....	....	....	....	....	....	....
1996-97	ERC Selb	Germany-2	41	25	46	71	....	....	....	69	....	....	....	....	....	....	....	....	....	....	....	....	....	....	....	....	....	....
1997-98	ERC Selb	Germany-2	24	14	16	30	....	....	....	6	....	....	....	....	....	....	....	....	....	....	22	15	20	35	6	....	....	....
1998-99	HC Kosice	Slovakia	42	12	29	41	....	....	....	20	....	....	....	....	....	....	....	....	....	....	11	5	4	9	4	....	....	....
99-2000	HC Kosice	Slovakia	49	15	22	37	....	....	....	34	....	....	....	....	....	....	....	....	....	....	....	....	....	....	....	....	....	....
	NHL Totals		**56**	**8**	**9**	**17**	**7**	**7**	**14**	**39**	**1**	**0**	**0**	**91**	**8.8**	**36**	**3**	**37**	**1**		**1**	**0**	**0**	**0**	**0**	**0**	**0**	**0**

• Brother of Peter • EJC-A All-Star Team (1979)

Signed as a free agent by **Detroit**, November 18, 1988.

• IHNACAK, Peter

C – R. 5'11", 180 lbs. b: Poprad, Czech., 5/3/1957. Toronto's 3rd, 25th overall, in 1982.

Season	Club	League	GP	G	A	Pts	AG	AA	APts	PIM	PP	SH	GW	S	%	TGF	PGF	TGA	PGA	+/–	GP	G	A	Pts	PIM	PP	SH	GW
1976-77	Dukla Jihlava	Czech-Jr.	STATISTICS NOT AVAILABLE																									
	Czechoslovakia	WJC-A	4	2	2	4	....	....	....	0	....	....	....	....	....	....	....	....	....	....	....	....	....	....	....	....	....	....
1977-78	Dukla Jihlava	Czech.	5	0	1	1	....	....	....	4	....	....	....	....	....	....	....	....	....	....	3	0	2	2	2	....	....	....
1978-79	Dukla Jihlava	Czech.	44	22	12	34	....	....	....	....	....	....	....	....	....	....	....	....	....	....	....	....	....	....	....	....	....	....
1979-80	HC Sparta Praha	Czech.	44	19	28	47	....	....	....	....	....	....	....	....	....	....	....	....	....	....	....	....	....	....	....	....	....	....
1980-81	HC Sparta Praha	Czech.	44	23	22	45	....	....	....	....	....	....	....	....	....	....	....	....	....	....	....	....	....	....	....	....	....	....
1981-82	HC Sparta Praha	Czech.	39	16	22	38	....	....	....	50	....	....	....	....	....	....	....	....	....	....	....	....	....	....	....	....	....	....
	Czechoslovakia	WEC-A	5	0	0	0	....	....	....	0	....	....	....	....	....	....	....	....	....	....	....	....	....	....	....	....	....	....
1982-83	**Toronto Maple Leafs**	**NHL**	**80**	**28**	**38**	**66**	**23**	**26**	**49**	**44**	**6**	**0**	**2**	**162**	**17.3**	**95**	**24**	**66**	**1**	**6**	....	....	....	....	....	....	....	....
1983-84	**Toronto Maple Leafs**	**NHL**	**47**	**10**	**13**	**23**	**8**	**9**	**17**	**24**	**5**	**0**	**0**	**76**	**13.2**	**42**	**13**	**50**	**0**	**–21**	....	....	....	....	....	....	....	....
1984-85	**Toronto Maple Leafs**	**NHL**	**70**	**22**	**22**	**44**	**18**	**15**	**33**	**24**	**8**	**0**	**1**	**115**	**19.1**	**56**	**21**	**61**	**0**	**–26**	....	....	....	....	....	....	....	....
1985-86	**Toronto Maple Leafs**	**NHL**	**63**	**18**	**27**	**45**	**14**	**18**	**32**	**16**	**5**	**0**	**1**	**96**	**18.8**	**65**	**17**	**57**	**0**	**–9**	**10**	**2**	**3**	**5**	**12**	**0**	**0**	**1**
1986-87	**Toronto Maple Leafs**	**NHL**	**58**	**12**	**27**	**39**	**10**	**20**	**30**	**16**	**4**	**0**	**1**	**98**	**12.2**	**61**	**11**	**55**	**10**	**5**	**13**	**2**	**4**	**6**	**9**	**0**	**0**	**0**
	Newmarket Saints	AHL	8	2	6	8	....	....	....	0	....	....	....	....	....	....	....	....	....	....	....	....	....	....	....	....	....	....
1987-88	**Toronto Maple Leafs**	**NHL**	**68**	**10**	**20**	**30**	**9**	**14**	**23**	**41**	**0**	**0**	**0**	**75**	**13.3**	**48**	**6**	**60**	**12**	**–6**	**5**	**0**	**3**	**3**	**4**	**0**	**0**	**0**
1988-89	**Toronto Maple Leafs**	**NHL**	**26**	**2**	**16**	**18**	**2**	**11**	**13**	**10**	**0**	**0**	**0**	**30**	**6.7**	**26**	**0**	**25**	**2**	**3**	....	....	....	....	....	....	....	....
	Newmarket Saints	AHL	38	14	16	30	....	....	....	8	....	....	....	....	....	....	....	....	....	....	....	....	....	....	....	....	....	....
1989-90	**Toronto Maple Leafs**	**NHL**	**5**	**0**	**2**	**2**	**0**	**1**	**1**	**0**	**0**	**0**	**0**	**5**	**0.0**	**5**	**1**	**1**	**0**	**3**	....	....	....	....	....	....	....	....
	Newmarket Saints	AHL	72	26	47	73	....	....	....	40	....	....	....	....	....	....	....	....	....	....	....	....	....	....	....	....	....	....
1990-91	ECH Munich	Germany	20	6	17	23	....	....	....	23	....	....	....	....	....	....	....	....	....	....	....	....	....	....	....	....	....	....
	EHC Freiburg	Germany	10	5	5	10	....	....	....	12	....	....	....	....	....	....	....	....	....	....	5	1	5	6	4	....	....	....
1991-92	EHC Freiburg	Germany	41	21	26	47	....	....	....	34	....	....	....	....	....	....	....	....	....	....	4	0	0	0	4	....	....	....
	EHC Kloten	Switz.	1	0	0	0	....	....	....	0	....	....	....	....	....	....	....	....	....	....	....	....	....	....	....	....	....	....
1992-93	HC Ajoie	Switz.	13	3	8	11	....	....	....	10	....	....	....	....	....	....	....	....	....	....	....	....	....	....	....	....	....	....
	Krefelder EV	Germany	15	5	5	10	....	....	....	10	....	....	....	....	....	....	....	....	....	....	....	....	....	....	....	....	....	....
1993-94	Krefelder EV	Germany	42	10	25	35	....	....	....	25	....	....	....	....	....	....	....	....	....	....	....	....	....	....	....	....	....	....
1994-95	Krefeld Pinguine	Germany	19	7	6	13	....	....	....	8	....	....	....	....	....	....	....	....	....	....	15	2	4	6	6	....	....	....
1995-96	Krefeld Pinguine	Germany	47	9	34	43	....	....	....	22	....	....	....	....	....	....	....	....	....	....	6	0	0	0	2	....	....	....
1996-97	Krefeld Pinguine	Germany	51	21	17	38	....	....	....	34	....	....	....	....	....	....	....	....	....	....	3	1	0	1	4	....	....	....
1997-2000	Nurnberg Ice Tigers	Germany	DID NOT PLAY – COACHING																									
	NHL Totals		**417**	**102**	**165**	**267**	**84**	**114**	**198**	**175**	**28**	**0**	**5**	**657**	**15.5**	**398**	**93**	**375**	**25**		**28**	**4**	**10**	**14**	**25**	**0**	**0**	**1**

• Brother of Miroslav

• INGARFIELD, Earl

Earl Thompson C – L. 5'11", 185 lbs. b: Lethbridge, Alta., 10/25/1934.

Season	Club	League	GP	G	A	Pts	AG	AA	APts	PIM	PP	SH	GW	S	%	TGF	PGF	TGA	PGA	+/–	GP	G	A	Pts	PIM	PP	SH	GW
1951-52	Lethbridge Native Sons	WCJHL	44	32	15	47	....	....	....	28	....	....	....	....	....	....	....	....	....	....	....	....	....	....	....	....	....	....
1952-53	Lethbridge Native Sons	WCJHL	30	22	25	47	....	....	....	37	....	....	....	....	....	....	....	....	....	....	14	6	3	9	9	....	....	....
	Lethbridge Native Sons	Mem-Cup	11	6	2	8	....	....	....	12	....	....	....	....	....	....	....	....	....	....	....	....	....	....	....	....	....	....
1953-54	Lethbridge Native Sons	WCJHL	36	46	42	88	....	....	....	48	....	....	....	....	....	....	....	....	....	....	4	0	2	2	0	....	....	....
	Great Falls Americans	AMHL	STATISTICS NOT AVAILABLE																									
1954-55	Lethbridge Native Sons	WCJHL	36	*45	31	*76	....	....	....	45	....	....	....	....	....	....	....	....	....	....	11	5	6	11	4	....	....	....
	Vancouver Canucks	WHL	2	0	0	0	....	....	....	0	....	....	....	....	....	....	....	....	....	....	....	....	....	....	....	....	....	....
	Regina Pats	Mem-Cup	2	0	1	1	....	....	....	0	....	....	....	....	....	....	....	....	....	....	....	....	....	....	....	....	....	....
1955-56	Saskatoon Quakers	WHL	70	15	23	38	....	....	....	46	....	....	....	....	....	....	....	....	....	....	3	0	0	0	0	....	....	....
1956-57	Winnipeg Warriors	WHL	69	21	27	48	....	....	....	41	....	....	....	....	....	....	....	....	....	....	....	....	....	....	....	....	....	....
1957-58	Winnipeg Warriors	WHL	64	39	41	80	....	....	....	25	....	....	....	....	....	....	....	....	....	....	7	2	2	4	2	....	....	....
1958-59	**New York Rangers**	**NHL**	**35**	**1**	**2**	**3**	**1**	**2**	**3**	**10**	....	....	....	....	....	....	....	....	....	....	....	....	....	....	....	....	....	....
1959-60	**New York Rangers**	**NHL**	**20**	**1**	**2**	**3**	**1**	**2**	**3**	**2**	....	....	....	....	....	....	....	....	....	....	....	....	....	....	....	....	....	....
	Cleveland Barons	AHL	40	25	40	65	....	....	....	17	....	....	....	....	....	....	....	....	....	....	7	3	6	9	6	....	....	....
1960-61	**New York Rangers**	**NHL**	**66**	**13**	**21**	**34**	**15**	**20**	**35**	**18**	....	....	....	....	....	....	....	....	....	....	....	....	....	....	....	....	....	....
1961-62	**New York Rangers**	**NHL**	**70**	**26**	**31**	**57**	**30**	**30**	**60**	**18**	....	....	....	....	....	....	....	....	....	....	**6**	**3**	**2**	**5**	**2**	**1**	**0**	**0**
1962-63	**New York Rangers**	**NHL**	**69**	**19**	**24**	**43**	**22**	**24**	**46**	**40**	....	....	....	....	....	....	....	....	....	....	....	....	....	....	....	....	....	....
1963-64	**New York Rangers**	**NHL**	**63**	**15**	**11**	**26**	**19**	**11**	**30**	**26**	....	....	....	....	....	....	....	....	....	....	....	....	....	....	....	....	....	....
1964-65	**New York Rangers**	**NHL**	**69**	**15**	**13**	**28**	**18**	**13**	**31**	**40**	....	....	....	....	....	....	....	....	....	....	....	....	....	....	....	....	....	....
1965-66	**New York Rangers**	**NHL**	**68**	**20**	**16**	**36**	**23**	**15**	**38**	**35**	....	....	....	....	....	....	....	....	....	....	....	....	....	....	....	....	....	....
1966-67	**New York Rangers**	**NHL**	**67**	**12**	**22**	**34**	**14**	**21**	**35**	**12**	....	....	....	....	....	....	....	....	....	....	**4**	**1**	**0**	**1**	**2**	**0**	**0**	**0**
1967-68	**Pittsburgh Penguins**	**NHL**	**50**	**15**	**22**	**37**	**17**	**22**	**39**	**12**	**2**	**1**	**0**	**110**	**13.6**	**51**	**11**	**53**	**6**	**–7**	....	....	....	....	....	....	....	....
1968-69	**Pittsburgh Penguins**	**NHL**	**40**	**8**	**15**	**23**	**8**	**13**	**21**	**4**	**3**	**0**	**0**	**71**	**11.3**	**27**	**8**	**36**	**0**	**–17**	....	....	....	....	....	....	....	....
	Oakland Seals	**NHL**	**26**	**8**	**15**	**23**	**8**	**13**	**21**	**8**	**3**	**0**	**0**	**60**	**13.3**	**32**	**8**	**29**	**4**	**–1**	**7**	**4**	**6**	**10**	**2**	**0**	**1**	**1**
1969-70	**Oakland Seals**	**NHL**	**54**	**21**	**24**	**45**	**23**	**22**	**45**	**10**	**9**	**0**	**3**	**130**	**16.2**	**56**	**22**	**60**	**19**	**–7**	**4**	**1**	**0**	**1**	**4**	**1**	**0**	**0**
1970-71	**California Golden Seals**	**NHL**	**49**	**5**	**8**	**13**	**5**	**7**	**12**	**4**	**0**	**0**	**0**	**76**	**6.6**	**25**	**4**	**59**	**30**	**–8**	....	....	....	....	....	....	....	....
1971-72	Regina Pats	WCJHL	DID NOT PLAY – COACHING																									
	NHL Totals		**746**	**179**	**226**	**405**	**204**	**215**	**419**	**239**	....	....	....	....	....	....	....	....	....		**21**	**9**	**8**	**17**	**10**	....	....	....

• Father of Earl Jr.

Traded to **Montreal** by **NY Rangers** with Noel Price, Gord Labossiere, Dave McComb and cash for Cesare Maniago and Garry Peters, June 8, 1965. Claimed by **NY Rangers** from **Montreal** in Intra-League Draft, June 9, 1965. Claimed by **Pittsburgh** from **NY Rangers** in Expansion Draft, June 6, 1967. Traded to **Oakland** by **Pittsburgh** with Gene Ubriaco and Dick Mattiussi for Bryan Watson, George Swarbrick and Tracy Pratt, January 30, 1969.

• INGARFIELD, Earl Jr.

Earl Thompson C – L. 5'11", 180 lbs. b: New York, NY, 1/30/1959.

Season	Club	League	REGULAR SEASON																		PLAYOFFS							
			GP	G	A	Pts	AG	AA	APts	PIM	PP	SH	GW	S	%	TGF	PGF	TGA	PGA	+/–	GP	G	A	Pts	PIM	PP	SH	GW
1975-76	Swift Current Broncos	SJHL	54	36	30	66	....	....	....	128	....	....	....	....	....	....	....	....	....	....	....	....	....	....	....	....	....	....
1976-77	Regina Pats	WCJHL	25	1	0	1	....	....	....	38	....	....	....	....	....	....	....	....	....	....	....	....	....	....	....	....	....	....
	Lethbridge Broncos	WCJHL	1	0	0	0	....	....	....	0	....	....	....	....	....	....	....	....	....	....	....	....	....	....	....	....	....	....
1977-78	Lethbridge Broncos	WCJHL	65	25	25	50	....	....	....	127	....	....	....	....	....	....	....	....	....	....	....	....	....	....	....	....	....	....
1978-79	Lethbridge Broncos	WHL	70	43	46	89	....	....	....	84	....	....	....	....	....	....	....	....	....	....	19	8	10	18	10	....	....	....
1979-80	**Atlanta Flames**	**NHL**	**1**	**0**	**0**	**0**	**0**	**0**	**0**	**0**	**0**	**0**	**0**	**7**	**0.0**	**0**	**0**	**1**	**0**	**–1**	**2**	**0**	**1**	**1**	**0**	**0**	**0**	**0**
	Birmingham Bulls	CHL	75	27	30	57	....	....	....	160	....	....	....	....	....	....	....	....	....	....	2	4	1	5	0	....	....	....
1980-81	**Calgary Flames**	**NHL**	**16**	**2**	**3**	**5**	**2**	**2**	**4**	**6**	**0**	**0**	**0**	**20**	**10.0**	**6**	**0**	**8**	**3**	**1**	....	....	....	....	....	....	....	....
	Birmingham Bulls	CHL	23	7	9	16	....	....	....	47	....	....	....	....	....	....	....	....	....	....	....	....	....	....	....	....	....	....
	Detroit Red Wings	**NHL**	**22**	**2**	**1**	**3**	**2**	**1**	**3**	**16**	**0**	**0**	**0**	**18**	**11.1**	**5**	**0**	**3**	**0**	**2**	....	....	....	....	....	....	....	....
1981-82	Adirondack Red Wings	AHL	68	24	19	43	....	....	....	86	....	....	....	....	....	....	....	....	....	....	2	0	1	1	4	....	....	....
1982-83	Adirondack Red Wings	AHL	65	11	26	37	....	....	....	60	....	....	....	....	....	....	....	....	....	....	1	0	1	1	2	....	....	....
1983-84			DID NOT PLAY																									
1984-85			DID NOT PLAY																									
1985-86	Springfield Indians	AHL	18	2	3	5	....	....	....	27	....	....	....	....	....	....	....	....	....	....	....	....	....	....	....	....	....	....
	Indianapolis Checkers	IHL	20	11	6	17	....	....	....	17	....	....	....	....	....	....	....	....	....	....	5	2	3	5	11	....	....	....
1986-87	Peoria Rivermen	IHL	33	8	11	19	....	....	....	18	....	....	....	....	....	....	....	....	....	....	....	....	....	....	....	....	....	....
	NHL Totals		**39**	**4**	**4**	**8**	**4**	**3**	**7**	**22**	**0**	**0**	**0**	**45**	**8.9**	**11**	**0**	**12**	**3**		**2**	**0**	**1**	**1**	**0**	**0**	**0**	**0**

• Son of Earl

Signed as a free agent by **Atlanta**, October 9, 1979. Transferred to **Calgary** after **Atlanta** franchise relocated, June 30, 1980. Traded to **Detroit** by **Calgary** for Dan Labraaten, February 3, 1981.

• INGLIS, Billy

William John C – L. 5'9", 160 lbs. b: Ottawa, Ont., 5/11/1943.

Season	Club	League	REGULAR SEASON																		PLAYOFFS							
			GP	G	A	Pts	AG	AA	APts	PIM	PP	SH	GW	S	%	TGF	PGF	TGA	PGA	+/–	GP	G	A	Pts	PIM	PP	SH	GW
1960-61	Pembroke Lumber Kings	OVJHL	18	10	17	27	....	....	....	16	....	....	....	....	....	....	....	....	....	....	13	*24	16	*40	8	....	....	....
	Pembroke Lumber Kings	Mem-Cup	4	4	6	10	....	....	....	0	....	....	....	....	....	....	....	....	....	....	....	....	....	....	....	....	....	....
1961-62	Montreal Jr. Canadiens	OHA-Jr.	50	22	28	50	....	....	....	27	....	....	....	....	....	....	....	....	....	....	6	3	4	7	2	....	....	....
1962-63	Montreal Jr. Canadiens	OHA-Jr.	50	30	39	69	....	....	....	64	....	....	....	....	....	....	....	....	....	....	10	5	3	8	2	....	....	....
	Hull-Ottawa Canadiens	EPHL	1	1	0	1	....	....	....	0	....	....	....	....	....	....	....	....	....	....	....	....	....	....	....	....	....	....
1963-64	Omaha Knights	CPHL	60	20	16	36	....	....	....	19	....	....	....	....	....	....	....	....	....	....	10	3	3	6	8	....	....	....
1964-65	Omaha Knights	CPHL	70	29	34	63	....	....	....	44	....	....	....	....	....	....	....	....	....	....	6	3	0	3	10	....	....	....
1965-66	Houston Apollos	CPHL	69	34	36	70	....	....	....	61	....	....	....	....	....	....	....	....	....	....	....	....	....	....	....	....	....	....
1966-67	Houston Apollos	CPHL	70	33	34	67	....	....	....	50	....	....	....	....	....	....	....	....	....	....	6	2	4	6	2	....	....	....
1967-68	**Los Angeles Kings**	**NHL**	**12**	**1**	**1**	**2**	**1**	**1**	**2**	**0**	**0**	**0**	**0**	**17**	**5.9**	**5**	**0**	**20**	**9**	**–6**	....	....	....	....	....	....	....	....
	Springfield Kings	AHL	59	22	24	46	....	....	....	44	....	....	....	....	....	....	....	....	....	....	4	0	0	0	7	....	....	....
1968-69	**Los Angeles Kings**	**NHL**	**10**	**0**	**1**	**1**	**0**	**1**	**1**	**0**	**0**	**0**	**0**	**18**	**0.0**	**2**	**0**	**6**	**2**	**–2**	**11**	**1**	**2**	**3**	**4**	**0**	**0**	**0**
	Springfield Kings	AHL	57	26	30	56	....	....	....	22	....	....	....	....	....	....	....	....	....	....	....	....	....	....	....	....	....	....
1969-70	Springfield Kings	AHL	72	31	44	75	....	....	....	25	....	....	....	....	....	....	....	....	....	....	14	5	4	9	6	....	....	....
1970-71	**Buffalo Sabres**	**NHL**	**14**	**0**	**1**	**1**	**0**	**1**	**1**	**4**	**0**	**0**	**0**	**9**	**0.0**	**1**	**1**	**5**	**1**	**–4**	....	....	....	....	....	....	....	....
	Salt Lake Golden Eagles	WHL	6	3	0	3	....	....	....	2	....	....	....	....	....	....	....	....	....	....	....	....	....	....	....	....	....	....
1971-72	Salt Lake Golden Eagles	WHL	71	24	36	60	....	....	....	29	....	....	....	....	....	....	....	....	....	....	....	....	....	....	....	....	....	....
1972-73	Cincinnati Swords	AHL	75	40	57	97	....	....	....	29	....	....	....	....	....	....	....	....	....	....	15	8	7	15	12	....	....	....
1973-74	Cincinnati Swords	AHL	76	35	36	71	....	....	....	48	....	....	....	....	....	....	....	....	....	....	5	2	1	3	4	....	....	....
1974-75	Hershey Bears	AHL	72	27	43	70	....	....	....	42	....	....	....	....	....	....	....	....	....	....	12	4	6	10	4	....	....	....
1975-76	Springfield Indians	AHL	70	19	48	67	....	....	....	8	....	....	....	....	....	....	....	....	....	....	....	....	....	....	....	....	....	....
1976-77	Hershey Bears	AHL	75	21	47	68	....	....	....	10	....	....	....	....	....	....	....	....	....	....	6	0	1	1	0	....	....	....
1977-78	Phoenix Roadrunners	CHL	9	3	4	7	....	....	....	0	....	....	....	....	....	....	....	....	....	....	....	....	....	....	....	....	....	....
	Binghamton Dusters	AHL	11	3	3	6	....	....	....	2	....	....	....	....	....	....	....	....	....	....	....	....	....	....	....	....	....	....
	New Haven Nighthawks	AHL	20	1	1	2	....	....	....	0	....	....	....	....	....	....	....	....	....	....	....	....	....	....	....	....	....	....
	NHL Totals		**36**	**1**	**3**	**4**	**1**	**3**	**4**	**4**	**0**	**0**	**0**	**44**	**2.3**	**8**	**1**	**31**	**12**		**11**	**1**	**2**	**3**	**4**	**0**	**0**	**0**

AHL First All-Star Team (1973) • Won Les Cunningham Award (MVP - AHL) (1973)

Claimed by **LA Kings** from **Montreal** in Expansion Draft, June 6, 1967. Claimed by **Montreal** from **LA Kings** in Intra-League Draft, June 9, 1970. Claimed by **Buffalo** from **Montreal** in Intra-League Draft, June 9, 1970.

• INTRANUOVO, Ralph

C – L. 5'8", 185 lbs. b: East York, Ont., 12/11/1973. Edmonton's 5th, 96th overall, in 1992.

Season	Club	League	REGULAR SEASON																		PLAYOFFS							
			GP	G	A	Pts	AG	AA	APts	PIM	PP	SH	GW	S	%	TGF	PGF	TGA	PGA	+/–	GP	G	A	Pts	PIM	PP	SH	GW
1989-90	Toronto Young Nationals	MTHL	37	33	26	59	....	....	....	20	....	....	....	....	....	....	....	....	....	....	....	....	....	....	....	....	....	....
1990-91	Sault Ste. Marie Greyhounds	OHL	63	25	42	67	....	....	....	22	....	....	....	....	....	....	....	....	....	....	14	7	13	20	17	....	....	....
	Sault Ste. Marie Greyhounds	Mem-Cup	3	0	0	0	....	....	....	0	....	....	....	....	....	....	....	....	....	....	....	....	....	....	....	....	....	....
1991-92	Sault Ste. Marie Greyhounds	OHL	65	50	63	113	....	....	....	44	....	....	....	....	....	....	....	....	....	....	18	10	14	24	12	....	....	....
	Sault Ste. Marie Greyhounds	Mem-Cup	4	1	3	4	....	....	....	4	....	....	....	....	....	....	....	....	....	....	....	....	....	....	....	....	....	....
1992-93	Sault Ste. Marie Greyhounds	OHL	54	31	47	78	....	....	....	61	....	....	....	....	....	....	....	....	....	....	18	10	16	26	30	....	....	....
	Canada	WJC-A	7	3	2	5	....	....	....	4	....	....	....	....	....	....	....	....	....	....	....	....	....	....	....	....	....	....
	Sault Ste. Marie Greyhounds	Mem-Cup	4	3	4	7	....	....	....	8	....	....	....	....	....	....	....	....	....	....	....	....	....	....	....	....	....	....
1993-94	Cape Breton Oilers	AHL	66	21	31	52	....	....	....	39	....	....	....	....	....	....	....	....	....	....	4	1	2	3	2	....	....	....
1994-95	**Edmonton Oilers**	**NHL**	**1**	**0**	**1**	**1**	**0**	**1**	**1**	**0**	**0**	**0**	**0**	**1**	**0.0**	**1**	**0**	**0**	**0**	**1**	....	....	....	....	....	....	....	....
	Cape Breton Oilers	AHL	70	46	47	93	....	....	....	62	....	....	....	....	....	....	....	....	....	....	....	....	....	....	....	....	....	....
	Canada	WC-A	8	5	1	6	....	....	....	6	....	....	....	....	....	....	....	....	....	....	....	....	....	....	....	....	....	....
1995-96	**Edmonton Oilers**	**NHL**	**13**	**1**	**2**	**3**	**1**	**2**	**3**	**4**	**0**	**0**	**1**	**19**	**5.3**	**6**	**3**	**6**	**0**	**–3**	....	....	....	....	....	....	....	....
	Cape Breton Oilers	AHL	52	34	39	73	....	....	....	84	....	....	....	....	....	....	....	....	....	....	....	....	....	....	....	....	....	....
1996-97	**Toronto Maple Leafs**	**NHL**	**3**	**0**	**1**	**1**	**0**	**1**	**1**	**0**	**0**	**0**	**0**	**4**	**0.0**	**2**	**0**	**3**	**0**	**–1**	....	....	....	....	....	....	....	....
	Edmonton Oilers	**NHL**	**5**	**1**	**0**	**1**	**1**	**0**	**1**	**0**	**0**	**0**	**0**	**2**	**50.0**	**1**	**0**	**1**	**0**	**0**	....	....	....	....	....	....	....	....
	Hamilton Bulldogs	AHL	68	36	40	76	....	....	....	88	....	....	....	....	....	....	....	....	....	....	22	8	4	12	30	....	....	....
1997-98	Manitoba Moose	IHL	81	26	35	61	....	....	....	68	....	....	....	....	....	....	....	....	....	....	3	2	0	2	4	....	....	....
1998-99	Manitoba Moose	IHL	71	29	31	60	....	....	....	70	....	....	....	....	....	....	....	....	....	....	5	2	1	3	4	....	....	....
99-2000	Adler Mannheim	Germany	54	14	19	33	....	....	....	20	....	....	....	....	....	....	....	....	....	....	5	1	0	1	2	....	....	....
	Adler Mannheim	EuroHL	5	1	4	5	....	....	....	0	....	....	....	....	....	....	....	....	....	....	....	....	....	....	....	....	....	....
	NHL Totals		**22**	**2**	**4**	**6**	**2**	**4**	**6**	**4**	**0**	**0**	**1**	**26**	**7.7**	**10**	**3**	**10**	**0**		....	....	....	....	....	....	....	....

Memorial Cup All-Star Team (1993) • Won Stafford Smythe Memorial Trophy (Memorial Cup Tournament MVP) (1993) • AHL Second All-Star Team (1995, 1997)

Claimed by **Toronto** from **Edmonton** in Waiver Draft, September 30, 1996. Claimed on waivers by **Edmonton** from **Toronto**, October 25, 1996.

• IRVINE, Ted

Edward Amos LW – L. 6'2", 195 lbs. b: Winnipeg, Man., 12/8/1944.

Season	Club	League	REGULAR SEASON																		PLAYOFFS							
			GP	G	A	Pts	AG	AA	APts	PIM	PP	SH	GW	S	%	TGF	PGF	TGA	PGA	+/–	GP	G	A	Pts	PIM	PP	SH	GW
1961-62	St. Boniface Canadiens	MJHL	36	6	7	13	....	....	....	4	....	....	....	....	....	....	....	....	....	....	4	5	0	5	0	....	....	....
1962-63	St. Boniface Canadiens	MJHL	32	*31	23	54	....	....	....	13	....	....	....	....	....	....	....	....	....	....	8	7	5	12	6	....	....	....
	Brandon Wheat Kings	Mem-Cup	5	2	2	4	....	....	....	4	....	....	....	....	....	....	....	....	....	....	....	....	....	....	....	....	....	....
1963-64	St. Boniface Canadiens	MJHL	19	17	11	28	....	....	....	19	....	....	....	....	....	....	....	....	....	....	....	....	....	....	....	....	....	....
	Winnipeg Braves	MJHL	10	3	5	8	....	....	....	2	....	....	....	....	....	....	....	....	....	....	....	....	....	....	....	....	....	....
	Boston Bruins	**NHL**	**1**	**0**	**0**	**0**	**0**	**0**	**0**	**0**	....	....	....	....	....	....	....	....	....	....	....	....	....	....	....	....	....	....
	Minneapolis Bruins	CPHL	3	1	5	6	....	....	....	0	....	....	....	....	....	....	....	....	....	....	4	1	1	2	2	....	....	....
1964-65	Minneapolis Bruins	CPHL	68	15	16	31	....	....	....	40	....	....	....	....	....	....	....	....	....	....	5	0	1	1	6	....	....	....
1965-66	Oklahoma City Blazers	CPHL	69	26	20	46	....	....	....	27	....	....	....	....	....	....	....	....	....	....	9	*6	3	9	4	....	....	....
1966-67	Oklahoma City Blazers	CPHL	63	15	17	32	....	....	....	54	....	....	....	....	....	....	....	....	....	....	11	6	1	7	0	....	....	....
1967-68	**Los Angeles Kings**	**NHL**	**73**	**18**	**22**	**40**	**21**	**22**	**43**	**26**	**4**	**1**	**3**	**136**	**13.2**	**56**	**9**	**58**	**1**	**–10**	**6**	**1**	**3**	**4**	**2**	**0**	**0**	**0**
1968-69	**Los Angeles Kings**	**NHL**	**76**	**15**	**24**	**39**	**16**	**21**	**37**	**47**	**0**	**0**	**3**	**206**	**7.3**	**55**	**8**	**65**	**1**	**–17**	**11**	**5**	**1**	**6**	**7**	**1**	**1**	**0**
1969-70	**Los Angeles Kings**	**NHL**	**58**	**11**	**13**	**24**	**12**	**12**	**24**	**28**	**2**	**0**	**0**	**120**	**9.2**	**32**	**4**	**48**	**0**	**–20**	....	....	....	....	....	....	....	....
	New York Rangers	**NHL**	**17**	**0**	**3**	**3**	**0**	**3**	**3**	**10**	**0**	**0**	**0**	**28**	**0.0**	**5**	**1**	**11**	**1**	**–6**	**6**	**1**	**2**	**3**	**8**	**0**	**1**	**0**
1970-71	**New York Rangers**	**NHL**	**76**	**20**	**18**	**38**	**20**	**15**	**35**	**137**	**2**	**0**	**6**	**150**	**13.3**	**57**	**8**	**32**	**1**	**18**	**12**	**1**	**2**	**3**	**28**	**0**	**0**	**0**
1971-72	**New York Rangers**	**NHL**	**78**	**15**	**21**	**36**	**15**	**18**	**33**	**66**	**0**	**0**	**1**	**164**	**9.1**	**56**	**3**	**45**	**0**	**8**	**16**	**4**	**5**	**9**	**19**	**0**	**0**	**0**
1972-73	**New York Rangers**	**NHL**	**53**	**8**	**12**	**20**	**7**	**9**	**16**	**54**	**1**	**0**	**1**	**91**	**8.8**	**33**	**5**	**24**	**0**	**4**	**10**	**1**	**3**	**4**	**20**	**1**	**0**	**0**
1973-74	**New York Rangers**	**NHL**	**75**	**26**	**20**	**46**	**25**	**16**	**41**	**105**	**2**	**0**	**5**	**142**	**18.3**	**80**	**4**	**75**	**1**	**2**	**13**	**3**	**5**	**8**	**16**	**0**	**0**	**0**

			REGULAR SEASON																		PLAYOFFS							
Season	Club	League	GP	G	A	Pts	AG	AA	APts	PIM	PP	SH	GW	S	%	TGF	PGF	TGA	PGA	+/–	GP	G	A	Pts	PIM	PP	SH	GW
1974-75	**New York Rangers**	**NHL**	**79**	**17**	**17**	**34**	**15**	**13**	**28**	**66**	**4**	**0**	**3**	**174**	**9.8**	**72**	**11**	**76**	**0**	**–15**	**3**	**0**	**1**	**1**	**11**	**0**	**0**	**0**
1975-76	**St. Louis Blues**	**NHL**	**69**	**10**	**13**	**23**	**9**	**10**	**19**	**80**	**2**	**0**	**2**	**105**	**9.5**	**41**	**5**	**50**	**2**	**–12**	**3**	**0**	**2**	**2**	**2**	**0**	**0**	**0**
1976-77	**St. Louis Blues**	**NHL**	**69**	**14**	**14**	**28**	**13**	**11**	**24**	**38**	**1**	**0**	**2**	**122**	**11.5**	**46**	**3**	**59**	**0**	**–16**	**3**	**0**	**0**	**0**	**2**	**0**	**0**	**0**
1977-78	St. James Braves	CCHL	12	6	6	12	....	....	....	30	....	....	....	....	....	....	....	....	....	....	....	....	....	....	....	....	....	....
	NHL Totals		**724**	**154**	**177**	**331**	**153**	**150**	**303**	**657**	....	....	....	....	....	....	....	....	....	....	**83**	**16**	**24**	**40**	**115**	....	....	....

Claimed by **LA Kings** from **Boston** in Expansion Draft, June 6, 1967. Traded to **NY Rangers** by **LA Kings** for Real Lemieux and Juha Widing, February 28, 1970. Traded to **St. Louis** by **NY Rangers** with Bert Wilson and Jerry Butler for Bill Collins and John Davidson, June 18, 1975.

• ISAKSSON, Ulf

Ulf Erik LW – L. 6'1", 185 lbs. b: Norrsunda, Sweden, 3/19/1954. Los Angeles' 6th, 95th overall, in 1982.

Season	Club	League	GP	G	A	Pts	AG	AA	APts	PIM	PP	SH	GW	S	%	TGF	PGF	TGA	PGA	+/–	GP	G	A	Pts	PIM	PP	SH	GW
1971-72	Rosersberg IK	Sweden	18	*23	....	23	....	....	....	....	....	....	....	....	....	....	....	....	....	....	....	....	....	....	....	....	....	....
1972-73			STATISTICS NOT AVAILABLE																									
1973-74	AIK Solna Stockholm	Sweden	4	0	0	0	....	....	....	0	....	....	....	....	....	....	....	....	....	....	18	5	3	8	6	....	....	....
1974-75	AIK Solna Stockholm	Sweden	30	15	10	25	....	....	....	12	....	....	....	....	....	....	....	....	....	....	....	....	....	....	....	....	....	....
1975-76	AIK Solna Stockholm	Sweden	36	11	7	18	....	....	....	6	....	....	....	....	....	....	....	....	....	....	....	....	....	....	....	....	....	....
1976-77	AIK Solna Stockholm	Sweden	36	14	5	19	....	....	....	8	....	....	....	....	....	....	....	....	....	....	....	....	....	....	....	....	....	....
1977-78	AIK Solna Stockholm	Sweden	34	11	10	21	....	....	....	16	....	....	....	....	....	....	....	....	....	....	6	3	2	5	2	....	....	....
1978-79	AIK Solna Stockholm	Sweden	34	15	14	29	....	....	....	14	....	....	....	....	....	....	....	....	....	....	....	....	....	....	....	....	....	....
1979-80	AIK Solna Stockholm	Sweden	36	9	11	20	....	....	....	12	....	....	....	....	....	....	....	....	....	....	....	....	....	....	....	....	....	....
1980-81	AIK Solna Stockholm	DN-Cup	3	1	0	1	....	....	....	2	....	....	....	....	....	....	....	....	....	....	....	....	....	....	....	....	....	....
	AIK Solna Stockholm	Sweden	35	13	8	21	....	....	....	26	....	....	....	....	....	....	....	....	....	....	6	3	0	3	2	....	....	....
	Sweden	WEC-A	5	0	1	1	....	....	....	4	....	....	....	....	....	....	....	....	....	....	....	....	....	....	....	....	....	....
1981-82	AIK Solna Stockholm	Sweden	24	9	8	17	....	....	....	16	....	....	....	....	....	....	....	....	....	....	7	*5	2	*7	4	....	....	....
	Sweden	Nat-Team	32	16	14	30	....	....	....	26	....	....	....	....	....	....	....	....	....	....	....	....	....	....	....	....	....	....
	Sweden	WEC-A	10	1	2	3	....	....	....	4	....	....	....	....	....	....	....	....	....	....	....	....	....	....	....	....	....	....
1982-83	**Los Angeles Kings**	**NHL**	**50**	**7**	**15**	**22**	**6**	**10**	**16**	**10**	**0**	**0**	**1**	**71**	**9.9**	**35**	**4**	**32**	**2**	**1**	....	....	....	....	....	....	....	....
	New Haven Nighthawks	AHL	14	1	3	4	....	....	....	2	....	....	....	....	....	....	....	....	....	....	2	0	0	0	0	....	....	....
1983-84	AIK Solna Stockholm	Sweden	36	11	11	22	....	....	....	12	....	....	....	....	....	....	....	....	....	....	6	3	2	5	6	....	....	....
1984-85	AIK Solna Stockholm	Sweden	33	7	8	15	....	....	....	20	....	....	....	....	....	....	....	....	....	....	....	....	....	....	....	....	....	....
1985-86	RA-73	Sweden-3	28	25	22	*47	....	....	....	....	....	....	....	....	....	....	....	....	....	....	....	....	....	....	....	....	....	....
1986-87	RA-73	Sweden-2	30	20	14	34	....	....	....	10	....	....	....	....	....	....	....	....	....	....	....	....	....	....	....	....	....	....
1987-88	RA-73	Sweden-2	12	4	8	12	....	....	....	8	....	....	....	....	....	....	....	....	....	....	....	....	....	....	....	....	....	....
	NHL Totals		**50**	**7**	**15**	**22**	**6**	**10**	**16**	**10**	**0**	**0**	**1**	**71**	**9.9**	**35**	**4**	**32**	**2**		....	....	....	....	....	....	....	....

Swedish World All-Star Team (1982) • Only goals and games played totals available for 1971-72 season.

• ISBISTER, Brad

RW – R. 6'3", 222 lbs. b: Edmonton, Alta., 5/7/1977. Winnipeg's 4th, 67th overall, in 1995.

Season	Club	League	GP	G	A	Pts	AG	AA	APts	PIM	PP	SH	GW	S	%	TGF	PGF	TGA	PGA	+/–	GP	G	A	Pts	PIM	PP	SH	GW
1992-93	Calgary Bantam Canadians	AAHA	35	24	25	49	....	....	....	74	....	....	....	....	....	....	....	....	....	....	....	....	....	....	....	....	....	....
1993-94	Portland Winter Hawks	WHL	64	7	10	17	....	....	....	45	....	....	....	....	....	....	....	....	....	....	10	0	2	2	0	....	....	....
1994-95	Portland Winter Hawks	WHL	67	16	20	36	....	....	....	123	....	....	....	....	....	....	....	....	....	....	....	....	....	....	....	....	....	....
1995-96	Portland Winter Hawks	WHL	71	45	44	89	....	....	....	184	....	....	....	....	....	....	....	....	....	....	7	2	4	6	20	....	....	....
1996-97	Portland Winter Hawks	WHL	24	15	18	33	....	....	....	45	....	....	....	....	....	....	....	....	....	....	6	2	1	3	16	....	....	....
	Canada	WJC-A	7	4	3	7	....	....	....	8	....	....	....	....	....	....	....	....	....	....	....	....	....	....	....	....	....	....
	Springfield Falcons	AHL	7	3	1	4	....	....	....	14	....	....	....	....	....	....	....	....	....	....	9	1	2	3	10	....	....	....
1997-98	**Phoenix Coyotes**	**NHL**	**66**	**9**	**8**	**17**	**11**	**8**	**19**	**102**	**1**	**0**	**1**	**115**	**7.8**	**35**	**7**	**27**	**3**	**4**	**5**	**0**	**0**	**0**	**2**	**0**	**0**	**0**
	Springfield Falcons	AHL	9	8	2	10	....	....	....	36	....	....	....	....	....	....	....	....	....	....	....	....	....	....	....	....	....	....
1998-99	**Phoenix Coyotes**	**NHL**	**32**	**4**	**4**	**8**	**5**	**4**	**9**	**46**	**0**	**0**	**2**	**48**	**8.3**	**11**	**0**	**10**	**0**	**1**	....	....	....	....	....	....	....	....
	Springfield Falcons	AHL	4	1	1	2	....	....	....	12	....	....	....	....	....	....	....	....	....	....	....	....	....	....	....	....	....	....
	Las Vegas Thunder	IHL	2	0	0	0	....	....	....	9	....	....	....	....	....	....	....	....	....	....	....	....	....	....	....	....	....	....
99-2000	**New York Islanders**	**NHL**	**64**	**22**	**20**	**42**	**25**	**19**	**44**	**100**	**9**	**0**	**1**	**135**	**16.3**	**60**	**23**	**55**	**0**	**–18**	....	....	....	....	....	....	....	....
	Canada	WC-A	9	4	3	7	....	....	....	18	....	....	....	....	....	....	....	....	....	....	....	....	....	....	....	....	....	....
	NHL Totals		**162**	**35**	**32**	**67**	**41**	**31**	**72**	**248**	**10**	**0**	**4**	**298**	**11.7**	**106**	**30**	**92**	**3**		**5**	**0**	**0**	**0**	**2**	**0**	**0**	**0**

WHL West Second All-Star Team (1997)

Rights transferred to **Phoenix** after **Winnipeg** franchise relocated, July 1, 1996. Traded to **NY Islanders** by **Phoenix** with Phoenix's 3rd round choice (Brian Collins) in 1999 Entry Draft for Robert Reichel, NY Islanders' 3rd round choice (Jason Jaspers) in 1999 Entry Draft and Ottawa's 4th round choice (previously acquired, Phoenix selected Preston Mizzi) in 1999 Entry Draft, March 20, 1999.

• ISSEL, Kim

Kim D. RW – R. 6'4", 196 lbs. b: Calgary, Alberta, 9/25/1967. Edmonton's 1st, 21st overall, in 1986.

Season	Club	League	GP	G	A	Pts	AG	AA	APts	PIM	PP	SH	GW	S	%	TGF	PGF	TGA	PGA	+/–	GP	G	A	Pts	PIM	PP	SH	GW
1981-82	Calgary Bantam Blazers	AAHA	STATISTICS NOT AVAILABLE																									
1982-83	Calgary North Stars	AAHA	STATISTICS NOT AVAILABLE																									
1983-84	Prince Albert Raiders	WHL	31	9	9	18	....	....	....	24	....	....	....	....	....	....	....	....	....	....	5	4	0	4	9	....	....	....
1984-85	Prince Albert Raiders	WHL	44	8	15	23	....	....	....	43	....	....	....	....	....	....	....	....	....	....	12	6	4	10	8	....	....	....
	Prince Albert Raiders	Mem-Cup	3	0	0	0	....	....	....	16	....	....	....	....	....	....	....	....	....	....	....	....	....	....	....	....	....	....
1985-86	Prince Albert Raiders	WHL	68	29	39	68	....	....	....	41	....	....	....	....	....	....	....	....	....	....	19	6	7	13	6	....	....	....
1986-87	Prince Albert Raiders	WHL	70	31	44	75	....	....	....	55	....	....	....	....	....	....	....	....	....	....	6	1	2	3	17	....	....	....
1987-88	Nova Scotia Oilers	AHL	68	2	25	27	....	....	....	31	....	....	....	....	....	....	....	....	....	....	2	1	0	1	10	....	....	....
1988-89	**Edmonton Oilers**	**NHL**	**4**	**0**	**0**	**0**	**0**	**0**	**0**	**0**	**0**	**0**	**0**	**1**	**0.0**	**1**	**0**	**2**	**0**	**–1**	....	....	....	....	....	....	....	....
	Cape Breton Oilers	AHL	65	34	28	62	....	....	....	4	....	....	....	....	....	....	....	....	....	....	....	....	....	....	....	....	....	....
1989-90	Cape Breton Oilers	AHL	62	36	32	68	....	....	....	46	....	....	....	....	....	....	....	....	....	....	6	1	3	4	10	....	....	....
1990-91	Cape Breton Oilers	AHL	24	6	4	10	....	....	....	28	....	....	....	....	....	....	....	....	....	....	....	....	....	....	....	....	....	....
	Kansas City Blades	IHL	13	7	2	9	....	....	....	2	....	....	....	....	....	....	....	....	....	....	....	....	....	....	....	....	....	....
1991-92	VSV Villach	Austria	45	42	49	91	....	....	....	....	....	....	....	....	....	....	....	....	....	....	....	....	....	....	....	....	....	....
1992-93	VSV Villach	Austria	54	39	48	87	....	....	....	....	....	....	....	....	....	....	....	....	....	....	....	....	....	....	....	....	....	....
1993-94	VSV Villach	Austria	33	23	27	50	....	....	....	....	....	....	....	....	....	....	....	....	....	....	....	....	....	....	....	....	....	....
1994-95	EK Zell-am-Zee	Austria	30	31	20	51	....	....	....	80	....	....	....	....	....	....	....	....	....	....	2	3	5	8	6	....	....	....
	HC Bolzano	Italy	5	0	2	2	....	....	....	2	....	....	....	....	....	....	....	....	....	....	....	....	....	....	....	....	....	....
1995-96	Durham Wasps	BH-Cup	6	8	7	15	....	....	....	12	....	....	....	....	....	....	....	....	....	....	....	....	....	....	....	....	....	....
	Durham Wasps	Britain	27	31	27	58	....	....	....	63	....	....	....	....	....	....	....	....	....	....	5	4	4	8	8	....	....	....
1996-97	HK Olimpija Ljubljana	Slovenia	52	27	27	54	....	....	....	....	....	....	....	....	....	....	....	....	....	....	....	....	....	....	....	....	....	....
1997-98	Schwenningen Wild Wings	Germany	6	1	0	1	....	....	....	4	....	....	....	....	....	....	....	....	....	....	....	....	....	....	....	....	....	....
	ERC Inglostadt	Germany-2	9	4	6	10	....	....	....	8	....	....	....	....	....	....	....	....	....	....	....	....	....	....	....	....	....	....
	HK Olimpija Ljubljana	Slovenia	....	....	....	....	....	....	....	....	....	....	....	....	....	....	....	....	....	....	10	10	9	19	2	....	....	....
1998-99	HK Olimpija Ljubljana	Alpenliga	STATISTICS NOT AVAILABLE																									
	HK Olimpija Ljubljana	Slovenia	STATISTICS NOT AVAILABLE																									
	NHL Totals		**4**	**0**	**0**	**0**	**0**	**0**	**0**	**0**	**0**	**0**	**0**	**1**	**0.0**	**1**	**0**	**2**	**0**		....	....	....	....	....	....	....	....

WHL East Second All-Star Team (1986)

Traded to **Pittsburgh** by **Edmonton** for Brad Aitken, March 5, 1991. Signed as a free agent by **Vancouver**, August, 1991. • Officially announced retirement, July 1, 1999.

• JACKMAN, Richard

D – R. 6'2", 192 lbs. b: Toronto, Ont., 6/28/1978. Dallas' 1st, 5th overall, in 1996.

Season	Club	League	GP	G	A	Pts	AG	AA	APts	PIM	PP	SH	GW	S	%	TGF	PGF	TGA	PGA	+/–	GP	G	A	Pts	PIM	PP	SH	GW
1993-94	Mississauga Senators	MTHL	81	35	53	88	....	....	....	156	....	....	....	....	....	....	....	....	....	....	....	....	....	....	....	....	....	....
1994-95	Mississauga Senators	MTHL	53	20	37	57	....	....	....	120	....	....	....	....	....	....	....	....	....	....	....	....	....	....	....	....	....	....
	Richmond Hill Dynes	OJHL	10	2	9	11	....	....	....	16	....	....	....	....	....	....	....	....	....	....	....	....	....	....	....	....	....	....
1995-96	Sault Ste. Marie Greyhounds	OHL	66	13	29	42	....	....	....	97	....	....	....	....	....	....	....	....	....	....	4	1	0	1	15	....	....	....
1996-97	Sault Ste. Marie Greyhounds	OHL	53	13	34	47	....	....	....	116	....	....	....	....	....	....	....	....	....	....	10	2	6	8	24	....	....	....
	Canada	WJC-A	7	2	0	2	....	....	....	0	....	....	....	....	....	....	....	....	....	....	....	....	....	....	....	....	....	....
1997-98	Sault Ste. Marie Greyhoinds	OHL	60	33	40	73	....	....	....	111	....	....	....	....	....	....	....	....	....	....	....	....	....	....	....	....	....	....
	Michigan K-Wings	IHL	14	1	5	6	....	....	....	10	....	....	....	....	....	....	....	....	....	....	4	0	0	0	10	....	....	....

			REGULAR SEASON																		PLAYOFFS							
Season	Club	League	GP	G	A	Pts	AG	AA	APts	PIM	PP	SH	GW	S	%	TGF	PGF	TGA	PGA	+/–	GP	G	A	Pts	PIM	PP	SH	GW
1998-99	Michigan K-Wings	IHL	71	13	17	30	....	....	....	106	....	....	....	....	....	....	....	....	....	....	5	0	4	4	6	....	....	....
99-2000	**Dallas Stars**	**NHL**	**22**	**1**	**2**	**3**	**1**	**2**	**3**	**6**	**1**	**0**	**0**	**16**	**6.3**	**5**	**3**	**3**	**0**	**–1**	....	....	....	....	....	....	....	....
	Michigan K-Wings	IHL	50	3	16	19	....	....	....	51	....	....	....	....	....	....	....	....	....	....	....	....	....	....	....	....	....	....
	NHL Totals		**22**	**1**	**2**	**3**	**1**	**2**	**3**	**6**	**1**	**0**	**0**	**16**	**6.3**	**5**	**3**	**3**	**0**		....	....	....	....	....	....	....	....

OHL Second All-Star Team (1998)

• JACKSON, Dane

Dane K. RW – R. 6'1", 200 lbs. b: Castlegar, B.C., 5/17/1970. Vancouver's 3rd, 44th overall, in 1988.

Season	Club	League	GP	G	A	Pts	AG	AA	APts	PIM	PP	SH	GW	S	%	TGF	PGF	TGA	PGA	+/–	GP	G	A	Pts	PIM	PP	SH	GW
1985-86	Castlegar Rebels	KIJHL	39	22	38	60	....	....	....	53	....	....	....	....	....	....	....	....	....	....	....	....	....	....	....	....	....	....
1986-87	Castlegar Rebels	KIJHL	STATISTICS NOT AVAILABLE																									
1987-88	Vernon Lakers	BCJHL	49	24	30	54	....	....	....	95	....	....	....	....	....	....	....	....	....	....	13	7	10	17	49	....	....	....
1988-89	University of North Dakota	WCHA	30	4	5	9	....	....	....	33	....	....	....	....	....	....	....	....	....	....	....	....	....	....	....	....	....	....
1989-90	University of North Dakota	WCHA	44	15	11	26	....	....	....	56	....	....	....	....	....	....	....	....	....	....	....	....	....	....	....	....	....	....
1990-91	University of North Dakota	WCHA	37	17	9	26	....	....	....	79	....	....	....	....	....	....	....	....	....	....	....	....	....	....	....	....	....	....
1991-92	University of North Dakota	WCHA	39	23	19	42	....	....	....	81	....	....	....	....	....	....	....	....	....	....	....	....	....	....	....	....	....	....
1992-93	Hamilton Canucks	AHL	68	23	20	43	....	....	....	59	....	....	....	....	....	....	....	....	....	....	....	....	....	....	....	....	....	....
1993-94	**Vancouver Canucks**	**NHL**	**12**	**5**	**1**	**6**	**5**	**1**	**6**	**9**	**0**	**0**	**0**	**18**	**27.8**	**10**	**1**	**6**	**0**	**3**	....	....	....	....	....	....	....	....
	Hamilton Canucks	AHL	60	25	35	60	....	....	....	75	....	....	....	....	....	....	....	....	....	....	4	2	2	4	16	....	....	....
1994-95	**Vancouver Canucks**	**NHL**	**3**	**1**	**0**	**1**	**2**	**0**	**2**	**4**	**0**	**0**	**0**	**6**	**16.7**	**2**	**0**	**3**	**1**	**0**	**6**	**0**	**0**	**0**	**10**	**0**	**0**	**0**
	Syracuse Crunch	AHL	78	30	28	58	....	....	....	162	....	....	....	....	....	....	....	....	....	....	....	....	....	....	....	....	....	....
1995-96	**Buffalo Sabres**	**NHL**	**22**	**5**	**4**	**9**	**5**	**3**	**8**	**41**	**0**	**0**	**1**	**20**	**25.0**	**16**	**2**	**11**	**0**	**3**	....	....	....	....	....	....	....	....
	Rochester Americans	AHL	50	27	19	46	....	....	....	132	....	....	....	....	....	....	....	....	....	....	19	4	6	10	53	....	....	....
1996-97	Rochester Americans	AHL	78	24	34	58	....	....	....	111	....	....	....	....	....	....	....	....	....	....	10	7	4	11	14	....	....	....
1997-98	**New York Islanders**	**NHL**	**8**	**1**	**1**	**2**	**1**	**1**	**2**	**4**	**0**	**0**	**1**	**5**	**20.0**	**3**	**0**	**2**	**0**	**1**	....	....	....	....	....	....	....	....
	Rochester Americans	AHL	28	10	13	23	....	....	....	55	....	....	....	....	....	....	....	....	....	....	3	2	2	4	4	....	....	....
1998-99	Lowell Lock Monsters	AHL	80	16	27	43	....	....	....	103	....	....	....	....	....	....	....	....	....	....	3	0	1	1	16	....	....	....
99-2000	Rochester Americans	AHL	21	6	9	15	....	....	....	8	....	....	....	....	....	....	....	....	....	....	....	....	....	....	....	....	....	....
	NHL Totals		**45**	**12**	**6**	**18**	**13**	**5**	**18**	**58**	**0**	**0**	**2**	**49**	**24.5**	**31**	**3**	**22**	**1**		**6**	**0**	**0**	**0**	**10**	**0**	**0**	**0**

Signed as a free agent by **Buffalo**, September 20, 1995. Signed as a free agent by **NY Islanders**, July 21, 1997. Signed as a free agent by **Rochester** (AHL), August 29, 1999. • Suffered season-ending knee injury in game vs. Springfield (AHL), January 21, 2000.

• JACKSON, Don

Donald Clinton D – L. 6'3", 210 lbs. b: Minneapolis, MN, 9/2/1956. Minnesota's 3rd, 39th overall, in 1976.

Season	Club	League	GP	G	A	Pts	AG	AA	APts	PIM	PP	SH	GW	S	%	TGF	PGF	TGA	PGA	+/–	GP	G	A	Pts	PIM	PP	SH	GW
1973-74	Kennedy Eagles	Hi-School	STATISTICS NOT AVAILABLE																									
1974-75	University of Notre Dame	WCHA	35	2	7	9	....	....	....	29	....	....	....	....	....	....	....	....	....	....	....	....	....	....	....	....	....	....
1975-76	University of Notre Dame	WCHA	30	4	5	9	....	....	....	22	....	....	....	....	....	....	....	....	....	....	....	....	....	....	....	....	....	....
1976-77	University of Notre Dame	WCHA	38	2	9	11	....	....	....	52	....	....	....	....	....	....	....	....	....	....	....	....	....	....	....	....	....	....
1977-78	University of Notre Dame	WCHA	37	10	23	33	....	....	....	69	....	....	....	....	....	....	....	....	....	....	....	....	....	....	....	....	....	....
	Minnesota North Stars	**NHL**	**2**	**0**	**0**	**0**	**0**	**0**	**0**	**2**	**0**	**0**	**0**	**3**	**0.0**	**2**	**0**	**2**	**1**	**1**	....	....	....	....	....	....	....	....
	United States	WEC-A	10	1	1	2	....	....	....	4	....	....	....	....	....	....	....	....	....	....	....	....	....	....	....	....	....	....
1978-79	**Minnesota North Stars**	**NHL**	**5**	**0**	**0**	**0**	**0**	**0**	**0**	**2**	**0**	**0**	**0**	**6**	**0.0**	**2**	**0**	**4**	**1**	**–1**	....	....	....	....	....	....	....	....
	Oklahoma City Stars	CHL	73	8	23	31	....	....	....	108	....	....	....	....	....	....	....	....	....	....	....	....	....	....	....	....	....	....
	United States	WEC-A	8	0	1	1	....	....	....	16	....	....	....	....	....	....	....	....	....	....	....	....	....	....	....	....	....	....
1979-80	**Minnesota North Stars**	**NHL**	**10**	**0**	**4**	**4**	**0**	**3**	**3**	**18**	**0**	**0**	**0**	**8**	**0.0**	**9**	**0**	**8**	**3**	**4**	**1**	**0**	**0**	**0**	**0**	**0**	**0**	**0**
	Oklahoma City Stars	CHL	33	5	9	14	....	....	....	54	....	....	....	....	....	....	....	....	....	....	....	....	....	....	....	....	....	....
1980-81	**Minnesota North Stars**	**NHL**	**10**	**0**	**3**	**3**	**0**	**2**	**2**	**19**	**0**	**0**	**0**	**14**	**0.0**	**8**	**0**	**8**	**3**	**3**	....	....	....	....	....	....	....	....
	Oklahoma City Stars	CHL	59	5	33	38	....	....	....	67	....	....	....	....	....	....	....	....	....	....	3	0	0	0	0	....	....	....
1981-82	**Edmonton Oilers**	**NHL**	**8**	**0**	**0**	**0**	**0**	**0**	**0**	**18**	**0**	**0**	**0**	**4**	**0.0**	**6**	**1**	**6**	**1**	**0**	....	....	....	....	....	....	....	....
	Wichita Wind	CHL	71	7	37	44	....	....	....	116	....	....	....	....	....	....	....	....	....	....	7	0	1	1	21	....	....	....
1982-83	**Edmonton Oilers**	**NHL**	**71**	**2**	**8**	**10**	**2**	**6**	**8**	**136**	**0**	**1**	**1**	**72**	**2.8**	**73**	**2**	**81**	**22**	**12**	**16**	**3**	**3**	**6**	**30**	**0**	**0**	**0**
	Birmingham South Stars	CHL	4	1	4	5	....	....	....	8	....	....	....	....	....	....	....	....	....	....	....	....	....	....	....	....	....	....
1983-84♦	**Edmonton Oilers**	**NHL**	**60**	**8**	**12**	**20**	**6**	**8**	**14**	**120**	**0**	**1**	**2**	**57**	**14.0**	**77**	**0**	**66**	**17**	**28**	**19**	**1**	**2**	**3**	**32**	**0**	**0**	**0**
1984-85♦	**Edmonton Oilers**	**NHL**	**78**	**3**	**17**	**20**	**2**	**12**	**14**	**141**	**0**	**0**	**0**	**47**	**6.4**	**81**	**1**	**64**	**11**	**27**	**9**	**0**	**0**	**0**	**64**	**0**	**0**	**0**
1985-86	**Edmonton Oilers**	**NHL**	**45**	**2**	**8**	**10**	**2**	**5**	**7**	**93**	**0**	**0**	**0**	**34**	**5.9**	**42**	**3**	**42**	**5**	**2**	**8**	**0**	**0**	**0**	**21**	**0**	**0**	**0**
1986-87	**New York Rangers**	**NHL**	**22**	**1**	**0**	**1**	**1**	**0**	**1**	**91**	**0**	**0**	**0**	**4**	**25.0**	**11**	**0**	**14**	**2**	**–1**	....	....	....	....	....	....	....	....
1987-88			OUT OF HOCKEY – RETIRED																									
1988-1989	Knoxville Cherokees	ECHL	DID NOT PLAY – ASSISTANT COACH																									
1989-1991	Knoxville Cherokees	ECHL	DID NOT PLAY – COACHING																									
1991-1994	**Quebec Nordiques**	**NHL**	DID NOT PLAY – ASSISTANT COACH																									
1994-1995	Cincinnati Cyclones	IHL	DID NOT PLAY – COACHING																									
1995-1996	Wichita Thunder	CHL	DID NOT PLAY – COACHING																									
1996-1997	Kansas City Blades	IHL	DID NOT PLAY – COACHING																									
1997-2000	**Pittsburgh Penguins**	**NHL**	DID NOT PLAY – ASSISTANT COACH																									
	NHL Totals		**311**	**16**	**52**	**68**	**13**	**36**	**49**	**640**	**0**	**2**	**3**	**249**	**6.4**	**311**	**7**	**295**	**66**		**53**	**4**	**5**	**9**	**147**	**0**	**0**	**0**

Traded to **Edmonton** by **Minnesota** with Edmonton's 3rd round choice (previously acquired, Edmonton selected Wally Chapman) in 1982 Entry Draft for the rights to Don Murdoch, August 21, 1981. Traded to **NY Rangers** by **Edmonton** with Mike Golden, Miroslav Horava and future considerations (Stu Kulak, March 10, 1987) for Reijo Ruotsalainen, Ville Kentala, Clark Donatelli and Jim Wiemer, October 23, 1986. • Named Assistant Coach of **Chicago**, July 3, 2000.

• JACKSON, Jeff

LW – L. 6'1", 195 lbs. b: Dresden, Ont., 4/24/1965. Toronto's 2nd, 28th overall, in 1983.

Season	Club	League	GP	G	A	Pts	AG	AA	APts	PIM	PP	SH	GW	S	%	TGF	PGF	TGA	PGA	+/–	GP	G	A	Pts	PIM	PP	SH	GW
1981-82	Newmarket Flyers	OJHL	45	30	39	69	....	....	....	105	....	....	....	....	....	....	....	....	....	....	....	....	....	....	....	....	....	....
1982-83	Brantford Alexanders	OHL	64	18	25	43	....	....	....	63	....	....	....	....	....	....	....	....	....	....	8	1	1	2	27	....	....	....
1983-84	Brantford Alexanders	OHL	58	27	42	69	....	....	....	78	....	....	....	....	....	....	....	....	....	....	2	0	1	1	0	....	....	....
1984-85	Hamilton Steelhawks	OHL	20	13	14	27	....	....	....	51	....	....	....	....	....	....	....	....	....	....	17	8	12	20	26	....	....	....
	Canada	WJC-A	7	1	7	8	....	....	....	10	....	....	....	....	....	....	....	....	....	....	....	....	....	....	....	....	....	....
	Toronto Maple Leafs	**NHL**	**17**	**0**	**1**	**1**	**0**	**1**	**1**	**24**	**0**	**0**	**0**	**12**	**0.0**	**2**	**0**	**8**	**2**	**–4**	....	....	....	....	....	....	....	....
1985-86	**Toronto Maple Leafs**	**NHL**	**5**	**1**	**2**	**3**	**1**	**1**	**2**	**2**	**0**	**0**	**0**	**2**	**50.0**	**4**	**0**	**1**	**0**	**3**	....	....	....	....	....	....	....	....
	St. Catharines Saints	AHL	74	17	28	45	....	....	....	122	....	....	....	....	....	....	....	....	....	....	13	5	2	7	30	....	....	....
1986-87	**Toronto Maple Leafs**	**NHL**	**55**	**8**	**7**	**15**	**7**	**5**	**12**	**64**	**0**	**0**	**0**	**42**	**19.0**	**19**	**0**	**36**	**6**	**–11**	....	....	....	....	....	....	....	....
	Newmarket Saints	AHL	7	3	6	9	....	....	....	13	....	....	....	....	....	....	....	....	....	....	....	....	....	....	....	....	....	....
	New York Rangers	**NHL**	**9**	**5**	**1**	**6**	**4**	**1**	**5**	**15**	**2**	**0**	**1**	**16**	**31.3**	**8**	**2**	**10**	**1**	**–3**	**6**	**1**	**1**	**2**	**16**	**0**	**0**	**0**
1987-88	**Quebec Nordiques**	**NHL**	**68**	**9**	**18**	**27**	**8**	**13**	**21**	**103**	**0**	**2**	**3**	**98**	**9.2**	**36**	**1**	**36**	**6**	**5**	....	....	....	....	....	....	....	....
1988-89	**Quebec Nordiques**	**NHL**	**33**	**4**	**6**	**10**	**3**	**4**	**7**	**28**	**0**	**1**	**2**	**40**	**10.0**	**16**	**2**	**38**	**9**	**–15**	....	....	....	....	....	....	....	....
1989-90	**Quebec Nordiques**	**NHL**	**65**	**8**	**12**	**20**	**7**	**9**	**16**	**71**	**0**	**1**	**0**	**73**	**11.0**	**34**	**3**	**79**	**27**	**–21**	....	....	....	....	....	....	....	....
1990-91	**Quebec Nordiques**	**NHL**	**10**	**3**	**1**	**4**	**3**	**1**	**4**	**4**	**0**	**0**	**0**	**13**	**23.1**	**9**	**0**	**13**	**7**	**3**	....	....	....	....	....	....	....	....
	Halifax Citadels	AHL	25	8	17	25	....	....	....	45	....	....	....	....	....	....	....	....	....	....	....	....	....	....	....	....	....	....
1991-92	New Haven Nighthawks	AHL	30	10	14	24	....	....	....	60	....	....	....	....	....	....	....	....	....	....	5	0	5	5	6	....	....	....
	Chicago Blackhawks	**NHL**	**1**	**0**	**0**	**0**	**0**	**0**	**0**	**2**	**0**	**0**	**0**	**0**	**0.0**	**0**	**0**	**0**	**0**	**0**	....	....	....	....	....	....	....	....
	Indianapolis Ice	IHL	18	3	7	10	....	....	....	41	....	....	....	....	....	....	....	....	....	....	....	....	....	....	....	....	....	....
	NHL Totals		**263**	**38**	**48**	**86**	**33**	**35**	**68**	**313**	**2**	**4**	**6**	**296**	**12.8**	**128**	**8**	**221**	**58**		**6**	**1**	**1**	**2**	**16**	**0**	**0**	**0**

Traded to **NY Rangers** by **Toronto** with Toronto's 3rd round choice (Rob Zamuner) in 1989 Entry Draft for Mark Osborne, March 5, 1987. Traded to **Quebec** by **NY Rangers** with Terry Carkner for John Ogrodnick and David Shaw, September 30, 1987. Signed as a free agent by **Chicago**, February 19, 1992.

• JACKSON, Jim

James Kenneth LW – R. 5'9", 190 lbs. b: Oshawa, Ont., 2/1/1960.

Season	Club	League	GP	G	A	Pts	AG	AA	APts	PIM	PP	SH	GW	S	%	TGF	PGF	TGA	PGA	+/–	GP	G	A	Pts	PIM	PP	SH	GW
1975-76	Parkway AAA Selects	OMHA	77	47	55	102	....	....	....	50	....	....	....	....	....	....	....	....	....	....	....	....	....	....	....	....	....	....
1976-77	Oshawa Generals	OMJHL	65	13	40	53	....	....	....	26	....	....	....	....	....	....	....	....	....	....	....	....	....	....	....	....	....	....
1977-78	Oshawa Generals	OMJHL	68	33	47	80	....	....	....	60	....	....	....	....	....	....	....	....	....	....	6	2	2	4	26	....	....	....
1978-79	Niagara Falls Flyers	OMJHL	62	26	39	65	....	....	....	73	....	....	....	....	....	....	....	....	....	....	20	6	9	15	16	....	....	....
1979-80	Niagara Falls Flyers	OMJHL	66	29	57	86	....	....	....	55	....	....	....	....	....	....	....	....	....	....	10	7	8	15	8	....	....	....
1980-81	Richmond Rifles	EHL	58	17	43	60	....	....	....	42	....	....	....	....	....	....	....	....	....	....	10	1	0	1	4	....	....	....
1981-82	Muskegon Mohawks	IHL	82	24	51	75	....	....	....	72	....	....	....	....	....	....	....	....	....	....	....	....	....	....	....	....	....	....

			REGULAR SEASON																		PLAYOFFS							
Season	Club	League	GP	G	A	Pts	AG	AA	APts	PIM	PP	SH	GW	S	%	TGF	PGF	TGA	PGA	+/–	GP	G	A	Pts	PIM	PP	SH	GW
1982-83	**Calgary Flames**	**NHL**	**48**	**8**	**12**	**20**	**7**	**8**	**15**	**7**	**1**	**0**	**1**	**85**	**9.4**	**38**	**4**	**25**	**0**	**9**	**8**	**2**	**1**	**3**	**2**	**0**	**0**	**0**
	Colorado Flames	CHL	30	10	16	26	....	....	....	4	....	....	....	....	....	....	....	....	....	....	....	....	....	....	....	....	....	....
1983-84	**Calgary Flames**	**NHL**	**49**	**6**	**14**	**20**	**5**	**10**	**15**	**13**	**0**	**1**	**0**	**66**	**9.1**	**33**	**0**	**41**	**9**	**1**	**6**	**1**	**1**	**2**	**4**	**0**	**1**	**0**
	Colorado Flames	CHL	25	5	27	32	....	....	....	4	....	....	....	....	....	....	....	....	....	....	....	....	....	....	....	....	....	....
1984-85	**Calgary Flames**	**NHL**	**10**	**1**	**4**	**5**	**1**	**3**	**4**	**0**	**0**	**1**	**1**	**10**	**10.0**	**6**	**0**	**8**	**3**	**1**	....	....	....	....	....	....	....	....
	Moncton Golden Flames	AHL	24	2	5	7	....	....	....	6	....	....	....	....	....	....	....	....	....	....	....	....	....	....	....	....	....	....
1985-86	Rochester Americans	AHL	65	16	32	48	....	....	....	10	....	....	....	....	....	....	....	....	....	....	....	....	....	....	....	....	....	....
1986-87	Rochester Americans	AHL	71	19	38	57	....	....	....	48	....	....	....	....	....	....	....	....	....	....	16	5	4	9	6	....	....	....
1987-88	**Buffalo Sabres**	**NHL**	**5**	**2**	**0**	**2**	**2**	**0**	**2**	**0**	**1**	**0**	**1**	**11**	**18.2**	**3**	**1**	**3**	**1**	**0**	....	....	....	....	....	....	....	....
	Rochester Americans	AHL	74	23	48	71	....	....	....	23	....	....	....	....	....	....	....	....	....	....	7	2	6	8	4	....	....	....
1988-89	Rochester Americans	AHL	73	19	50	69	....	....	....	14	....	....	....	....	....	....	....	....	....	....	....	....	....	....	....	....	....	....
1989-90	Rochester Americans	AHL	77	16	37	53	....	....	....	14	....	....	....	....	....	....	....	....	....	....	9	1	5	6	4	....	....	....
	NHL Totals		**112**	**17**	**30**	**47**	**15**	**21**	**36**	**20**	**2**	**2**	**3**	**172**	**9.9**	**80**	**5**	**77**	**13**		**14**	**3**	**2**	**5**	**6**	**0**	**1**	**0**

EHL Second All-Star Team (1981) • IHL Second All-Star Team (1982)

Signed as a free agent by **Calgary**, October 8, 1982. Signed as a free agent by **Buffalo**, September 26, 1985.

• JACOBS, Tim

Timothy James D – L. 5'10", 180 lbs. b: Espanola, Ont., 3/28/1952. California's 5th, 70th overall, in 1972.

Season	Club	League	GP	G	A	Pts	AG	AA	APts	PIM	PP	SH	GW	S	%	TGF	PGF	TGA	PGA	+/–	GP	G	A	Pts	PIM	PP	SH	GW
1969-70	St. Catharines Legionnaires	OHA-B	STATISTICS NOT AVAILABLE																									
	St. Catharines Black Hawks	OHA-Jr.	26	0	0	0	....	....	....	6	....	....	....	....	....	....	....	....	....	....	6	0	0	0	4	....	....	....
1970-71	St. Catharines Black Hawks	OHA-Jr.	60	1	10	11	....	....	....	23	....	....	....	....	....	....	....	....	....	....	15	2	4	6	4	....	....	....
1971-72	St. Catharines Black Hawks	OMJHL	58	6	19	25	....	....	....	46	....	....	....	....	....	....	....	....	....	....	5	0	0	0	4	....	....	....
1972-73	Salt Lake Golden Eagles	WHL	72	7	14	21	....	....	....	33	....	....	....	....	....	....	....	....	....	....	9	0	1	1	18	....	....	....
1973-74	Salt Lake Golden Eagles	WHL	75	2	26	28	....	....	....	46	....	....	....	....	....	....	....	....	....	....	5	1	2	3	2	....	....	....
1974-75	Springfield Indians	AHL	73	3	31	34	....	....	....	57	....	....	....	....	....	....	....	....	....	....	17	2	13	15	28	....	....	....
1975-76	**California Golden Seals**	**NHL**	**46**	**0**	**10**	**10**	**0**	**7**	**7**	**35**	**0**	**0**	**0**	**46**	**0.0**	**53**	**11**	**61**	**17**	**–2**	....	....	....	....	....	....	....	....
	Salt Lake Golden Eagles	CHL	30	4	12	16	....	....	....	22	....	....	....	....	....	....	....	....	....	....	....	....	....	....	....	....	....	....
1976-77	Salt Lake Golden Eagles	CHL	71	1	19	20	....	....	....	34	....	....	....	....	....	....	....	....	....	....	....	....	....	....	....	....	....	....
1977-78	Springfield Indians	AHL	78	6	20	26	....	....	....	16	....	....	....	....	....	....	....	....	....	....	4	0	1	1	0	....	....	....
1978-79	Springfield Indians	AHL	80	7	35	42	....	....	....	33	....	....	....	....	....	....	....	....	....	....	....	....	....	....	....	....	....	....
	NHL Totals		**46**	**0**	**10**	**10**	**0**	**7**	**7**	**35**	**0**	**0**	**0**	**46**	**0.0**	**53**	**11**	**61**	**17**		....	....	....	....	....	....	....	....

• JAGR, Jaromir

RW – L. 6'2", 230 lbs. b: Kladno, Czech., 2/15/1972. Pittsburgh's 1st, 5th overall, in 1990.

Season	Club	League	GP	G	A	Pts	AG	AA	APts	PIM	PP	SH	GW	S	%	TGF	PGF	TGA	PGA	+/–	GP	G	A	Pts	PIM	PP	SH	GW
1984-85	Poldi Kladno	Czech-Jr.	34	24	17	41	....	....	....	....	....	....	....	....	....	....	....	....	....	....	....	....	....	....	....	....	....	....
1985-86	Poldi Kladno	Czech-Jr.	36	41	29	70	....	....	....	....	....	....	....	....	....	....	....	....	....	....	....	....	....	....	....	....	....	....
1986-87	Poldi Kladno	Czech-Jr.	30	35	35	70	....	....	....	....	....	....	....	....	....	....	....	....	....	....	....	....	....	....	....	....	....	....
1987-88	Poldi Kladno	Czech-Jr.	35	57	27	84	....	....	....	....	....	....	....	....	....	....	....	....	....	....	....	....	....	....	....	....	....	....
1988-89	Poldi Kladno	Czech.	29	3	3	6	....	....	....	4	....	....	....	....	....	....	....	....	....	....	10	5	7	12	0	....	....	....
	Czechoslovakia	EJC-A	5	8	4	12	....	....	....	2	....	....	....	....	....	....	....	....	....	....	....	....	....	....	....	....	....	....
1989-90	Poldi Kladno	Czech.	42	22	28	50	....	....	....	....	....	....	....	....	....	....	....	....	....	....	9	*8	2	10	....	....	....	....
	Czechoslovakia	WJC-A	7	5	13	18	....	....	....	6	....	....	....	....	....	....	....	....	....	....	....	....	....	....	....	....	....	....
	Czechoslovakia	WEC-A	10	3	2	5	....	....	....	2	....	....	....	....	....	....	....	....	....	....	....	....	....	....	....	....	....	....
1990-91 ♦	**Pittsburgh Penguins**	**NHL**	**80**	**27**	**30**	**57**	**25**	**23**	**48**	**42**	**7**	**0**	**4**	**136**	**19.9**	**68**	**15**	**57**	**0**	**–4**	**24**	**3**	**10**	**13**	**6**	**1**	**0**	**1**
1991-92	Czechoslovakia	Can-Cup	5	1	0	1	....	....	....	0	....	....	....	....	....	....	....	....	....	....	....	....	....	....	....	....	....	....
♦	**Pittsburgh Penguins**	**NHL**	**70**	**32**	**37**	**69**	**29**	**28**	**57**	**34**	**4**	**0**	**4**	**194**	**16.5**	**98**	**18**	**69**	**1**	**12**	**21**	**11**	**13**	**24**	**6**	**2**	**0**	**4**
1992-93	**Pittsburgh Penguins**	**NHL**	**81**	**34**	**60**	**94**	**28**	**41**	**69**	**61**	**10**	**1**	**9**	**242**	**14.0**	**131**	**43**	**61**	**3**	**30**	**12**	**5**	**4**	**9**	**23**	**1**	**0**	**1**
1993-94	**Pittsburgh Penguins**	**NHL**	**80**	**32**	**67**	**99**	**30**	**52**	**82**	**61**	**9**	**0**	**6**	**298**	**10.7**	**133**	**41**	**81**	**4**	**15**	**6**	**2**	**4**	**6**	**16**	**0**	**0**	**1**
	Czech-Republic	WC-A	3	0	2	2	....	....	....	2	....	....	....	....	....	....	....	....	....	....	....	....	....	....	....	....	....	....
1994-95	Poldi Kladno	Czech-Rep	11	8	14	22	....	....	....	10	....	....	....	....	....	....	....	....	....	....	....	....	....	....	....	....	....	....
	HC Bolzano	Alpenliga	5	8	8	16	....	....	....	4	....	....	....	....	....	....	....	....	....	....	....	....	....	....	....	....	....	....
	HC Bolzano	Italy	1	0	0	0	....	....	....	0	....	....	....	....	....	....	....	....	....	....	....	....	....	....	....	....	....	....
	EHC Schalke	Germany-2	1	1	10	11	....	....	....	0	....	....	....	....	....	....	....	....	....	....	....	....	....	....	....	....	....	....
	Pittsburgh Penguins	**NHL**	**48**	**32**	**38**	***70**	**57**	**56**	**113**	**37**	**8**	**3**	**7**	**192**	**16.7**	**89**	**29**	**46**	**9**	**23**	**12**	**10**	**5**	**15**	**6**	**2**	**1**	**1**
1995-96	**Pittsburgh Penguins**	**NHL**	**82**	**62**	**87**	**149**	**61**	**72**	**133**	**96**	**20**	**1**	**12**	**403**	**15.4**	**205**	**90**	**102**	**18**	**31**	**18**	**11**	**12**	**23**	**18**	**5**	**1**	**1**
1996-97	Czech-Republic	W-Cup	3	1	0	1	....	....	....	2	....	....	....	....	....	....	....	....	....	....	....	....	....	....	....	....	....	....
	Pittsburgh Penguins	**NHL**	**63**	**47**	**48**	**95**	**50**	**43**	**93**	**40**	**11**	**2**	**6**	**234**	**20.1**	**128**	**41**	**71**	**6**	**22**	**5**	**4**	**4**	**8**	**4**	**2**	**0**	**0**
1997-98	**Pittsburgh Penguins**	**NHL**	**77**	**35**	***67**	***102**	**41**	**66**	**107**	**64**	**7**	**0**	**8**	**262**	**13.4**	**123**	**46**	**63**	**3**	**17**	**6**	**4**	**5**	**9**	**2**	**1**	**0**	**0**
	Czech-Republic	Olympics	6	1	4	5	....	....	....	2	....	....	....	....	....	....	....	....	....	....	....	....	....	....	....	....	....	....
1998-99	**Pittsburgh Penguins**	**NHL**	**81**	**44**	***83**	***127**	**52**	**80**	**132**	**66**	**10**	**1**	**7**	**343**	**12.8**	**159**	**55**	**94**	**7**	**17**	**9**	**5**	**7**	**12**	**16**	**1**	**0**	**1**
99-2000	**Pittsburgh Penguins**	**NHL**	**63**	**42**	**54**	***96**	**47**	**50**	**97**	**50**	**10**	**0**	**5**	**290**	**14.5**	**118**	**38**	**60**	**5**	**25**	**11**	**8**	**8**	**16**	**6**	**2**	**0**	**4**
	NHL Totals		**725**	**387**	**571**	**958**	**420**	**511**	**931**	**551**	**96**	**8**	**68**	**2594**	**14.9**	**1252**	**416**	**704**	**56**		**124**	**63**	**72**	**135**	**103**	**17**	**2**	**14**

• WJC-A All-Star Team (1990) • NHL All-Rookie Team (1991) • NHL First All-Star Team (1995, 1996, 1998, 1999, 2000) • Won Art Ross Trophy (1995, 1998, 1999, 2000) • NHL Second All-Star Team (1997) • Won Lester B. Pearson Award (1999, 2000) • Won Hart Trophy (1999) • Played in NHL All-Star Game (1992, 1993, 1996, 1998, 1999, 2000)

• JAKOPIN, John

D – R. 6'5", 239 lbs. b: Toronto, Ont., 5/16/1975. Detroit's 4th, 97th overall, in 1993.

Season	Club	League	GP	G	A	Pts	AG	AA	APts	PIM	PP	SH	GW	S	%	TGF	PGF	TGA	PGA	+/–	GP	G	A	Pts	PIM	PP	SH	GW
1992-93	St. Michael's Buzzers	OJHL	45	9	21	30	....	....	....	42	....	....	....	....	....	....	....	....	....	....	13	3	2	5	4	....	....	....
1993-94	Merrimack College	H-East	36	2	8	10	....	....	....	64	....	....	....	....	....	....	....	....	....	....	....	....	....	....	....	....	....	....
1994-95	Merrimack College	H-East	37	4	10	14	....	....	....	42	....	....	....	....	....	....	....	....	....	....	....	....	....	....	....	....	....	....
1995-96	Merrimack College	H-East	32	10	15	25	....	....	....	68	....	....	....	....	....	....	....	....	....	....	....	....	....	....	....	....	....	....
1996-97	Merrimack College	H-East	31	4	12	16	....	....	....	68	....	....	....	....	....	....	....	....	....	....	....	....	....	....	....	....	....	....
	Adirondack Red Wings	AHL	3	0	0	0	....	....	....	9	....	....	....	....	....	....	....	....	....	....	....	....	....	....	....	....	....	....
1997-98	**Florida Panthers**	**NHL**	**2**	**0**	**0**	**0**	**0**	**0**	**0**	**4**	**0**	**0**	**0**	**1**	**0.0**	**0**	**0**	**4**	**1**	**–3**	....	....	....	....	....	....	....	....
	Beast of New Haven	AHL	60	2	18	20	....	....	....	151	....	....	....	....	....	....	....	....	....	....	3	0	0	0	0	....	....	....
1998-99	**Florida Panthers**	**NHL**	**3**	**0**	**0**	**0**	**0**	**0**	**0**	**0**	**0**	**0**	**0**	**0**	**0.0**	**1**	**0**	**2**	**0**	**–1**	....	....	....	....	....	....	....	....
	Beast of New Haven	AHL	60	2	7	9	....	....	....	154	....	....	....	....	....	....	....	....	....	....	....	....	....	....	....	....	....	....
99-2000	**Florida Panthers**	**NHL**	**17**	**0**	**0**	**0**	**0**	**0**	**0**	**26**	**0**	**0**	**0**	**1**	**0.0**	**6**	**0**	**9**	**1**	**–2**	....	....	....	....	....	....	....	....
	Louisville Panthers	AHL	23	4	6	10	....	....	....	47	....	....	....	....	....	....	....	....	....	....	....	....	....	....	....	....	....	....
	NHL Totals		**22**	**0**	**0**	**0**	**0**	**0**	**0**	**30**	**0**	**0**	**0**	**2**	**0.0**	**7**	**0**	**15**	**2**		....	....	....	....	....	....	....	....

Signed as a free agent by **Florida**, May 14, 1997. • Missed remainder of 1999-2000 season recovering from groin injury suffered in game vs. Carolina, February 1, 2000.

• JALO, Risto

C – L. 5'11", 185 lbs. b: Tampere, Finland, 7/18/1962. Washington's 7th, 131st overall, in 1981.

Season	Club	League	GP	G	A	Pts	AG	AA	APts	PIM	PP	SH	GW	S	%	TGF	PGF	TGA	PGA	+/–	GP	G	A	Pts	PIM	PP	SH	GW
1979-80	KooVee Tampere	Finland	32	13	10	23	....	....	....	16	....	....	....	....	....	....	....	....	....	....	....	....	....	....	....	....	....	....
	KooVee Tampere	Finland-2	....	....	....	....	....	....	....	....	....	....	....	....	....	....	....	....	....	....	6	4	3	7	2	....	....	....
	Finland	EJC-A	5	5	2	7	....	....	....	4	....	....	....	....	....	....	....	....	....	....	....	....	....	....	....	....	....	....
1980-81	Ilves Tampere	Finland-Jr.	14	11	19	30	....	....	....	29	....	....	....	....	....	....	....	....	....	....	5	*6	*5	*11	2	....	....	....
	Finland	WJC-A	5	1	5	6	....	....	....	6	....	....	....	....	....	....	....	....	....	....	....	....	....	....	....	....	....	....
	Ilves Tampere	Finland	16	3	3	6	....	....	....	2	....	....	....	....	....	....	....	....	....	....	....	....	....	....	....	....	....	....
1981-82	Ilves Tampere	Finland-Jr.	1	1	1	2	....	....	....	0	....	....	....	....	....	....	....	....	....	....	2	2	*4	6	0	....	....	....
	Finland	WJC-A	7	7	8	15	....	....	....	2	....	....	....	....	....	....	....	....	....	....	....	....	....	....	....	....	....	....
	Ilves Tampere	Finland	34	17	20	37	....	....	....	8	....	....	....	....	....	....	....	....	....	....	....	....	....	....	....	....	....	....
1982-83	Ilves Tampere	Finland	33	14	36	50	....	....	....	20	....	....	....	....	....	....	....	....	....	....	2	0	2	2	0	....	....	....
	Finland	Nat-Team	12	1	2	3	....	....	....	2	....	....	....	....	....	....	....	....	....	....	....	....	....	....	....	....	....	....
	Finland	WEC-A	10	1	2	3	....	....	....	4	....	....	....	....	....	....	....	....	....	....	....	....	....	....	....	....	....	....
1983-84	Ilves Tampere	Finland	30	13	32	45	....	....	....	30	....	....	....	....	....	....	....	....	....	....	2	2	2	4	0	....	....	....
	Finland	Nat-Team	12	5	5	10	....	....	....	4	....	....	....	....	....	....	....	....	....	....	....	....	....	....	....	....	....	....
	Finland	Olympics	6	2	6	8	....	....	....	4	....	....	....	....	....	....	....	....	....	....	....	....	....	....	....	....	....	....
1984-85	Ilves Tampere	Finland	35	17	21	38	....	....	....	18	....	....	....	....	....	....	....	....	....	....	9	3	4	7	5	....	....	....
	Finland	Nat-Team	8	4	2	6	....	....	....	2	....	....	....	....	....	....	....	....	....	....	....	....	....	....	....	....	....	....
	Finland	WEC-A	10	2	2	4	....	....	....	2	....	....	....	....	....	....	....	....	....	....	....	....	....	....	....	....	....	....

Season	Club	League	REGULAR SEASON																		PLAYOFFS							
			GP	G	A	Pts	AG	AA	APts	PIM	PP	SH	GW	S	%	TGF	PGF	TGA	PGA	+/–	GP	G	A	Pts	PIM	PP	SH	GW
1985-86	Ilves Tampere	Finland	30	17	31	48	....	....	....	30	....	....	....	....	....	....	....	....	....	....	....	....	....	....	....	....	....	....
	Edmonton Oilers	**NHL**	**3**	**0**	**3**	**3**	**0**	**2**	**2**	**0**	**0**	**0**	**0**	**3**	**0.0**	**5**	**1**	**2**	**0**	**2**	....	....	....	....	....	....	....	....
1986-87	Ilves Tampere	Finland	44	23	31	54	....	....	....	38	....	....	....	....	....	....	....	....	....	....	....	....	....	....	....	....	....	....
	Finland	Nat-Team	16	7	5	12	....	....	....	8	....	....	....	....	....	....	....	....	....	....	....	....	....	....	....	....	....	....
	Finland	WEC-A	9	0	4	4	....	....	....	10	....	....	....	....	....	....	....	....	....	....	....	....	....	....	....	....	....	....
1987-88	Ilves Tampere	Finland	35	25	35	60	....	....	....	24	....	....	....	....	....	....	....	....	....	....	3	0	2	2	2	....	....	....
1988-89	Ilves Tampere	Finland	22	5	15	20	....	....	....	6	....	....	....	....	....	....	....	....	....	....	5	4	8	12	2	....	....	....
1989-90	Ilves Tampere	Finland	43	18	41	59	....	....	....	36	....	....	....	....	....	....	....	....	....	....	7	1	4	5	4	....	....	....
	Finland	Nat-Team	12	4	5	9	....	....	....	4	....	....	....	....	....	....	....	....	....	....	....	....	....	....	....	....	....	....
	Finland	WEC-A	10	1	2	3	....	....	....	0	....	....	....	....	....	....	....	....	....	....	....	....	....	....	....	....	....	....
1990-91	Vita Hasten	Sweden-2	33	15	23	38	....	....	....	34	....	....	....	....	....	....	....	....	....	....	6	1	1	2	2	....	....	....
1991-92	Ilves Tampere	Finland	40	14	18	32	....	....	....	16	....	....	....	....	....	....	....	....	....	....	....	....	....	....	....	....	....	....
1992-93	HC Fassa	Alpenliga	29	20	22	42	....	....	....	6	....	....	....	....	....	....	....	....	....	....	....	....	....	....	....	....	....	....
	HC Fassa	Italy	15	13	13	26	....	....	....	2	....	....	....	....	....	....	....	....	....	....	3	1	1	2	2	....	....	....
1993-94	Ilves Tampere	Finland	46	12	23	35	....	....	....	32	....	....	....	....	....	....	....	....	....	....	4	0	2	2	2	....	....	....
1994-95	HPK Hameenlinna	Finland	50	12	33	45	....	....	....	30	....	....	....	....	....	....	....	....	....	....	....	....	....	....	....	....	....	....
1995-96	HPK Hameenlinna	Finland	34	10	21	31	....	....	....	40	....	....	....	....	....	....	....	....	....	....	9	1	3	4	18	....	....	....
1996-97	HPK Hameenlinna	Finland	38	16	26	42	....	....	....	26	....	....	....	....	....	....	....	....	....	....	7	2	3	5	4	....	....	....
1997-98	HPK Hameenlinna	Finland	21	4	10	14	....	....	....	53	....	....	....	....	....	....	....	....	....	....	....	....	....	....	....	....	....	....
	HPK Hameenlinna	EuroHL	3	0	2	2	....	....	....	0	....	....	....	....	....	....	....	....	....	....	....	....	....	....	....	....	....	....
	NHL Totals		**3**	**0**	**3**	**3**	**0**	**2**	**2**	**0**	**0**	**0**	**0**	**3**	**0.0**	**5**	**1**	**2**	**0**		....	....	....	....	....	....	....	....

Finnish First All-Star Team (1984)

Traded to **Edmonton** by **Washington** for Edmonton's 4th round choice (Larry Shaw) in 1985 Entry Draft, March 6, 1984.

• JALONEN, Kari

C – R. 6'3", 190 lbs. b: Oulu, Finland, 1/6/1960.

Season	Club	League	GP	G	A	Pts	AG	AA	APts	PIM	PP	SH	GW	S	%	TGF	PGF	TGA	PGA	+/–	GP	G	A	Pts	PIM	PP	SH	GW
1976-77	Karpat Oulu	Finland-Jr.	24	21	10	31	....	....	....	32	....	....	....	....	....	....	....	....	....	....	6	4	3	7	6	....	....	....
1977-78	Karpat Oulu	Finland-Jr.	23	23	18	41	....	....	....	52	....	....	....	....	....	....	....	....	....	....	5	2	3	5	16	....	....	....
	Finland	EJC-A	5	2	2	4	....	....	....	2	....	....	....	....	....	....	....	....	....	....	....	....	....	....	....	....	....	....
1978-79	Karpat Oulu	Finland	36	13	13	26	....	....	....	30	....	....	....	....	....	....	....	....	....	....	....	....	....	....	....	....	....	....
	Finland	WJC-A	6	3	3	6	....	....	....	2	....	....	....	....	....	....	....	....	....	....	....	....	....	....	....	....	....	....
1979-80	Karpat Oulu	Finland	28	23	24	47	....	....	....	16	....	....	....	....	....	....	....	....	....	....	6	3	5	8	2	....	....	....
	Finland	WJC-A	5	3	5	8	....	....	....	0	....	....	....	....	....	....	....	....	....	....	....	....	....	....	....	....	....	....
1980-81	Karpat Oulu	Finland	35	16	34	50	....	....	....	22	....	....	....	....	....	....	....	....	....	....	12	*7	*14	*21	14	....	....	....
	Finland	Nat-Team	16	5	1	6	....	....	....	10	....	....	....	....	....	....	....	....	....	....	....	....	....	....	....	....	....	....
	Finland	WEC-A	8	4	3	7	....	....	....	5	....	....	....	....	....	....	....	....	....	....	....	....	....	....	....	....	....	....
1981-82	Finland	Can-Cup	5	0	1	1	....	....	....	4	....	....	....	....	....	....	....	....	....	....	....	....	....	....	....	....	....	....
	Karpat Oulu	Finland	33	21	26	47	....	....	....	24	....	....	....	....	....	....	....	....	....	....	3	2	5	7	2	....	....	....
	Finland	Nat-Team	16	5	1	6	....	....	....	10	....	....	....	....	....	....	....	....	....	....	....	....	....	....	....	....	....	....
	Finland	WEC-A	7	3	4	7	....	....	....	0	....	....	....	....	....	....	....	....	....	....	....	....	....	....	....	....	....	....
1982-83	**Calgary Flames**	**NHL**	**25**	**9**	**3**	**12**	**7**	**2**	**9**	**4**	**0**	**0**	**1**	**32**	**28.1**	**20**	**0**	**12**	**0**	**8**	**5**	**1**	**0**	**1**	**0**	**0**	**0**	**0**
	Colorado Flames	CHL	33	12	32	44	....	....	....	8	....	....	....	....	....	....	....	....	....	....	....	....	....	....	....	....	....	....
	Finland	WEC-A	6	3	2	5	....	....	....	0	....	....	....	....	....	....	....	....	....	....	....	....	....	....	....	....	....	....
1983-84	**Calgary Flames**	**NHL**	**9**	**0**	**3**	**3**	**0**	**2**	**2**	**0**	**0**	**0**	**0**	**4**	**0.0**	**5**	**0**	**6**	**0**	**–1**	....	....	....	....	....	....	....	....
	Colorado Flames	CHL	1	0	0	0	....	....	....	0	....	....	....	....	....	....	....	....	....	....	....	....	....	....	....	....	....	....
	Edmonton Oilers	**NHL**	**3**	**0**	**0**	**0**	**0**	**0**	**0**	**0**	**0**	**0**	**0**	**0**	**0.0**	**0**	**0**	**2**	**0**	**–2**	....	....	....	....	....	....	....	....
	Karpat Oulu	Finland	14	6	15	21	....	....	....	17	....	....	....	....	....	....	....	....	....	....	10	5	*12	*17	10	....	....	....
1984-85	HIFK Helsinki	Finland	21	9	9	18	....	....	....	10	....	....	....	....	....	....	....	....	....	....	....	....	....	....	....	....	....	....
	Finland	Nat-Team	4	0	3	3	....	....	....	0	....	....	....	....	....	....	....	....	....	....	....	....	....	....	....	....	....	....
1985-86	Karpat Oulu	Finland	36	19	35	54	....	....	....	46	....	....	....	....	....	....	....	....	....	....	5	2	3	5	14	....	....	....
	Finland	Nat-Team	11	2	5	7	....	....	....	10	....	....	....	....	....	....	....	....	....	....	....	....	....	....	....	....	....	....
	Finland	WEC-A	9	4	6	10	....	....	....	6	....	....	....	....	....	....	....	....	....	....	....	....	....	....	....	....	....	....
1986-87	Karpat Oulu	Finland	44	29	*64	*93	....	....	....	30	....	....	....	....	....	....	....	....	....	....	9	3	*7	10	12	....	....	....
	Finland	Nat-Team	17	2	2	4	....	....	....	6	....	....	....	....	....	....	....	....	....	....	....	....	....	....	....	....	....	....
	Finland	WEC-A	10	2	3	5	....	....	....	0	....	....	....	....	....	....	....	....	....	....	....	....	....	....	....	....	....	....
1987-88	Skelleftea AIK	Sweden	38	18	33	51	....	....	....	33	....	....	....	....	....	....	....	....	....	....	8	5	4	9	6	....	....	....
	Finland	Nat-Team	9	2	3	5	....	....	....	4	....	....	....	....	....	....	....	....	....	....	....	....	....	....	....	....	....	....
1988-89	TPS Turku	Finland	44	18	*56	74	....	....	....	40	....	....	....	....	....	....	....	....	....	....	10	4	*14	*18	8	....	....	....
	Finland	Nat-Team	13	5	4	9	....	....	....	4	....	....	....	....	....	....	....	....	....	....	....	....	....	....	....	....	....	....
	Finland	WEC-A	10	5	9	14	....	....	....	0	....	....	....	....	....	....	....	....	....	....	....	....	....	....	....	....	....	....
1989-90	TPS Turku	Finland	37	19	31	50	....	....	....	12	....	....	....	....	....	....	....	....	....	....	9	5	8	13	10	....	....	....
	Finland	Nat-Team	8	1	1	2	....	....	....	2	....	....	....	....	....	....	....	....	....	....	....	....	....	....	....	....	....	....
1990-91	TPS Turku	Finland	26	4	22	26	....	....	....	18	....	....	....	....	....	....	....	....	....	....	9	3	4	7	2	....	....	....
	Finland	Nat-Team	5	1	2	3	....	....	....	0	....	....	....	....	....	....	....	....	....	....	....	....	....	....	....	....	....	....
1991-92	TPS Turku	Finland	44	10	21	31	....	....	....	8	....	....	....	....	....	....	....	....	....	....	3	0	1	1	0	....	....	....
1992-93	Junkkarit Kalajoki	Finland-2	26	21	45	66	....	....	....	28	....	....	....	....	....	....	....	....	....	....	....	....	....	....	....	....	....	....
	TPS Turku	Finland	6	0	0	0	....	....	....	6	....	....	....	....	....	....	....	....	....	....	9	2	3	5	2	....	....	....
1993-94	Karpat Oulu	Finland-2	28	21	*46	*67	....	....	....	22	....	....	....	....	....	....	....	....	....	....	....	....	....	....	....	....	....	....
	Lukko Rauma	Finland	18	3	10	13	....	....	....	2	....	....	....	....	....	....	....	....	....	....	9	1	2	3	4	....	....	....
1994-95	HC Rouen	France	23	16	18	34	....	....	....	4	....	....	....	....	....	....	....	....	....	....	8	5	*13	18	4	....	....	....
1995-96	HC Rouen	France	18	8	26	34	....	....	....	27	....	....	....	....	....	....	....	....	....	....	5	4	4	8	0	....	....	....
	NHL Totals		**37**	**9**	**6**	**15**	**7**	**4**	**11**	**4**	**0**	**0**	**1**	**36**	**25.0**	**25**	**0**	**20**	**0**		**5**	**1**	**0**	**1**	**0**	**0**	**0**	**0**

Finnish Rookie of the Year (1979) • Finnish First All-Star Team (1987, 1989)

Signed as a free agent by **Calgary**, January 21, 1982. Signed as a free agent by **Edmonton**, December, 1983.

• JAMES, Val

Valmore Edwin LW – L. 6'2", 205 lbs. b: Ocala, FL, 2/14/1957. Detroit's 15th, 184th overall, in 1977.

Season	Club	League	GP	G	A	Pts	AG	AA	APts	PIM	PP	SH	GW	S	%	TGF	PGF	TGA	PGA	+/–	GP	G	A	Pts	PIM	PP	SH	GW
1975-76	Quebec Remparts	QMJHL	72	14	19	33	....	....	....	83	....	....	....	....	....	....	....	....	....	....	15	0	6	6	52	....	....	....
	Quebec Remparts	Mem-Cup	3	1	0	1	....	....	....	2	....	....	....	....	....	....	....	....	....	....	....	....	....	....	....	....	....	....
1976-77	Quebec Remparts	QMJHL	68	16	16	32	....	....	....	99	....	....	....	....	....	....	....	....	....	....	10	1	1	2	48	....	....	....
1977-78	Mississauga Reps	OHA-Sr.	11	1	0	1	....	....	....	2	....	....	....	....	....	....	....	....	....	....	....	....	....	....	....	....	....	....
1978-79	Erie Blades	NEHL	67	14	26	40	....	....	....	112	....	....	....	....	....	....	....	....	....	....	....	....	....	....	....	....	....	....
1979-80	Erie Blades	EHL	69	12	13	25	....	....	....	117	....	....	....	....	....	....	....	....	....	....	9	0	1	1	34	....	....	....
1980-81	Rochester Americans	AHL	3	0	0	0	....	....	....	12	....	....	....	....	....	....	....	....	....	....	....	....	....	....	....	....	....	....
	Erie Blades	EHL	70	3	18	21	....	....	....	179	....	....	....	....	....	....	....	....	....	....	6	1	3	4	30	....	....	....
1981-82	**Buffalo Sabres**	**NHL**	**7**	**0**	**0**	**0**	**0**	**0**	**0**	**16**	**0**	**0**	**0**	**5**	**0.0**	**0**	**0**	**1**	**0**	**–1**	....	....	....	....	....	....	....	....
	Rochester Americans	AHL	65	5	4	9	....	....	....	204	....	....	....	....	....	....	....	....	....	....	6	0	2	2	16	....	....	....
1982-83	Rochester Americans	AHL	68	3	4	7	....	....	....	88	....	....	....	....	....	....	....	....	....	....	16	1	0	1	27	....	....	....
1983-84	Rochester Americans	AHL	62	1	2	3	....	....	....	122	....	....	....	....	....	....	....	....	....	....	....	....	....	....	....	....	....	....
1984-85	Rochester Americans	AHL	55	1	4	5	....	....	....	70	....	....	....	....	....	....	....	....	....	....	3	0	0	0	15	....	....	....
1985-86	St. Catharines Saints	AHL	80	0	3	3	....	....	....	162	....	....	....	....	....	....	....	....	....	....	13	1	1	2	53	....	....	....
1986-87	**Toronto Maple Leafs**	**NHL**	**4**	**0**	**0**	**0**	**0**	**0**	**0**	**14**	**0**	**0**	**0**	**0**	**0.0**	**0**	**0**	**0**	**0**	**0**	....	....	....	....	....	....	....	....
	Newmarket Saints	AHL	74	4	3	7	....	....	....	71	....	....	....	....	....	....	....	....	....	....	....	....	....	....	....	....	....	....
1987-88	Baltimore Skipjacks	AHL	9	0	0	0	....	....	....	11	....	....	....	....	....	....	....	....	....	....	....	....	....	....	....	....	....	....
	Flint Spirits	IHL	8	2	0	2	....	....	....	26	....	....	....	....	....	....	....	....	....	....	....	....	....	....	....	....	....	....
	NHL Totals		**11**	**0**	**0**	**0**	**0**	**0**	**0**	**30**	**0**	**0**	**0**	**5**	**0.0**	**0**	**0**	**1**	**0**		....	....	....	....	....	....	....	....

Signed as a free agent by **Buffalo**, July 22, 1981. Signed as a free agent by **Toronto**, October 3, 1985.

• JANNEY, Craig

Craig H. C – L. 6'1", 190 lbs. b: Hartford, CT, 9/26/1967. Boston's 1st, 13th overall, in 1986.

			REGULAR SEASON																		PLAYOFFS							
Season	Club	League	GP	G	A	Pts	AG	AA	APts	PIM	PP	SH	GW	S	%	TGF	PGF	TGA	PGA	+/–	GP	G	A	Pts	PIM	PP	SH	GW
1984-85	Deerfield Warriors	Hi-School	17	33	35	68	....	....	....	6	....	....	....	....	....	....	....	....	....	....	....	....	....	....	....	....	....	....
	United States	WJC-A	7	4	2	6	....	....	....	0	....	....	....	....	....	....	....	....	....	....	....	....	....	....	....	....	....	....
1985-86	Boston College	H-East	34	13	14	27	....	....	....	8	....	....	....	....	....	....	....	....	....	....	....	....	....	....	....	....	....	....
	United States	WJC-A	3	1	1	2	....	....	....	2	....	....	....	....	....	....	....	....	....	....	....	....	....	....	....	....	....	....
1986-87	Boston College	H-East	37	26	55	81	....	....	....	6	....	....	....	....	....	....	....	....	....	....	....	....	....	....	....	....	....	....
	United States	WEC-A	10	1	0	1	....	....	....	0	....	....	....	....	....	....	....	....	....	....	....	....	....	....	....	....	....	....
1987-88	United States	Nat-Team	52	26	44	70	....	....	....	6	....	....	....	....	....	....	....	....	....	....	....	....	....	....	....	....	....	....
	United States	Olympics	5	3	3	6	....	....	....	2	....	....	....	....	....	....	....	....	....	....	....	....	....	....	....	....	....	....
	Boston Bruins	**NHL**	**15**	**7**	**9**	**16**	**6**	**6**	**12**	**0**	**1**	**0**	**1**	**29**	**24.1**	**18**	**7**	**5**	**0**	**6**	**23**	**6**	**10**	**16**	**11**	**4**	**0**	**1**
1988-89	**Boston Bruins**	**NHL**	**62**	**16**	**46**	**62**	**14**	**33**	**47**	**12**	**2**	**0**	**2**	**95**	**16.8**	**92**	**32**	**41**	**1**	**20**	**10**	**4**	**9**	**13**	**21**	**0**	**0**	**0**
1989-90	**Boston Bruins**	**NHL**	**55**	**24**	**38**	**62**	**21**	**27**	**48**	**4**	**11**	**0**	**5**	**105**	**22.9**	**88**	**47**	**41**	**3**	**3**	**18**	**3**	**19**	**22**	**2**	**1**	**0**	**2**
1990-91	**Boston Bruins**	**NHL**	**77**	**26**	**66**	**92**	**24**	**50**	**74**	**8**	**9**	**1**	**5**	**133**	**19.5**	**128**	**54**	**62**	**3**	**15**	**18**	**4**	**18**	**22**	**11**	**4**	**0**	**0**
1991-92	United States	Can-Cup	8	4	2	6	....	....	....	0	....	....	....	....	....	....	....	....	....	....	....	....	....	....	....	....	....	....
	Boston Bruins	**NHL**	**53**	**12**	**39**	**51**	**11**	**29**	**40**	**20**	**3**	**0**	**1**	**90**	**13.3**	**74**	**30**	**44**	**1**	**1**	....	....	....	....	....	....	....	....
	St. Louis Blues	**NHL**	**25**	**6**	**30**	**36**	**5**	**23**	**28**	**2**	**3**	**0**	**1**	**37**	**16.2**	**44**	**16**	**23**	**0**	**5**	**6**	**0**	**6**	**6**	**0**	**0**	**0**	**0**
1992-93	**St. Louis Blues**	**NHL**	**84**	**24**	**82**	**106**	**20**	**57**	**77**	**12**	**8**	**0**	**6**	**137**	**17.5**	**154**	**79**	**80**	**1**	**–4**	**11**	**2**	**9**	**11**	**0**	**1**	**0**	**2**
1993-94	**St. Louis Blues**	**NHL**	**69**	**16**	**68**	**84**	**15**	**53**	**68**	**24**	**8**	**0**	**7**	**95**	**16.8**	**121**	**63**	**72**	**0**	**–14**	**4**	**1**	**3**	**4**	**0**	**0**	**0**	**0**
	United States	WC-A	7	2	5	7	....	....	....	0	....	....	....	....	....	....	....	....	....	....	....	....	....	....	....	....	....	....
1994-95	**St. Louis Blues**	**NHL**	**8**	**2**	**5**	**7**	**4**	**7**	**11**	**0**	**1**	**0**	**0**	**9**	**22.2**	**10**	**4**	**4**	**1**	**3**	....	....	....	....	....	....	....	....
	San Jose Sharks	**NHL**	**27**	**5**	**15**	**20**	**9**	**22**	**31**	**10**	**2**	**0**	**1**	**31**	**16.1**	**30**	**10**	**24**	**0**	**–4**	**11**	**3**	**4**	**7**	**4**	**0**	**0**	**1**
1995-96	**San Jose Sharks**	**NHL**	**71**	**13**	**49**	**62**	**13**	**40**	**53**	**26**	**5**	**0**	**1**	**78**	**16.7**	**87**	**37**	**85**	**0**	**–35**	....	....	....	....	....	....	....	....
	Winnipeg Jets	**NHL**	**13**	**7**	**13**	**20**	**7**	**11**	**18**	**0**	**2**	**0**	**1**	**13**	**53.8**	**24**	**11**	**12**	**1**	**2**	**6**	**1**	**2**	**3**	**0**	**0**	**0**	**0**
1996-97	**Phoenix Coyotes**	**NHL**	**77**	**15**	**38**	**53**	**16**	**34**	**50**	**26**	**5**	**0**	**1**	**88**	**17.0**	**74**	**21**	**55**	**1**	**–1**	**7**	**0**	**3**	**3**	**4**	**0**	**0**	**0**
1997-98	**Phoenix Coyotes**	**NHL**	**68**	**10**	**43**	**53**	**12**	**42**	**54**	**12**	**4**	**0**	**0**	**72**	**13.9**	**78**	**22**	**52**	**1**	**5**	**6**	**0**	**3**	**3**	**0**	**0**	**0**	**0**
1998-99	**Tampa Bay Lightning**	**NHL**	**38**	**4**	**18**	**22**	**5**	**17**	**22**	**10**	**2**	**0**	**0**	**36**	**11.1**	**34**	**15**	**32**	**0**	**–13**	....	....	....	....	....	....	....	....
	New York Islanders	**NHL**	**18**	**1**	**4**	**5**	**1**	**4**	**5**	**4**	**0**	**0**	**0**	**9**	**11.1**	**10**	**2**	**10**	**0**	**–2**	....	....	....	....	....	....	....	....
	NHL Totals		**760**	**188**	**563**	**751**	**183**	**455**	**638**	**170**	**66**	**1**	**32**	**1057**	**17.8**	**1066**	**450**	**642**	**13**		**120**	**24**	**86**	**110**	**53**	**10**	**0**	**6**

Hockey East First All-Star Team (1987) • NCAA East First All-American Team (1987)

Traded to **St. Louis** by **Boston** with Stephane Quintal for Adam Oates, February 7, 1992. Acquired by **Vancouver** from **St. Louis** with St. Louis' 2nd round choice (Dave Scathard) in 1994 Entry Draft as compensation for St. Louis' signing of free agent Petr Nedved, March 14, 1994. Traded to **St. Louis** by **Vancouver** for Jeff Brown, Bret Hedican and Nathan Lafayette, March 21, 1994. Traded to **San Jose** by **St. Louis** with cash for Jeff Norton and future considerations, March 6, 1995. Traded to **Winnipeg** by **San Jose** for Darren Turcotte and Dallas' 2nd round choice (previously acquired, later traded to Chicago — Chicago selected Remi Royer) in 1996 Entry Draft, March 18, 1996. Transferred to **Phoenix** after **Winnipeg** franchise relocated, July 1, 1996. Traded to **Tampa Bay** by **Phoenix** for Louie Debrusk and Tampa Bay's 5th round choice (Jay Leach) in 1998 Entry Draft, June 11, 1998. Traded to **NY Islanders** by **Tampa Bay** for Toronto's 6th round choice (previously acquired, Tampa Bay selected Fedor Fedorov) in 1999 Entry Draft, January 18, 1999.

• JANSSENS, Mark

Mark Francis C – L. 6'3", 212 lbs. b: Surrey, B.C., 5/19/1968. NY Rangers' 4th, 72nd overall, in 1986.

Season	Club	League	GP	G	A	Pts	AG	AA	APts	PIM	PP	SH	GW	S	%	TGF	PGF	TGA	PGA	+/–	GP	G	A	Pts	PIM	PP	SH	GW
1983-84	Surrey Midget Eagles	BCAHA	40	40	58	98	....	....	....	64	....	....	....	....	....	....	....	....	....	....	....	....	....	....	....	....	....	....
1984-85	Regina Pats	WHL	70	8	22	30	....	....	....	51	....	....	....	....	....	....	....	....	....	....	5	1	1	2	0	....	....	....
1985-86	Regina Pats	WHL	71	25	38	63	....	....	....	146	....	....	....	....	....	....	....	....	....	....	9	0	2	2	17	....	....	....
1986-87	Regina Pats	WHL	68	24	38	62	....	....	....	209	....	....	....	....	....	....	....	....	....	....	3	0	1	1	14	....	....	....
1987-88	Regina Pats	WHL	71	39	51	90	....	....	....	202	....	....	....	....	....	....	....	....	....	....	4	3	4	7	6	....	....	....
	New York Rangers	**NHL**	**1**	**0**	**0**	**0**	**0**	**0**	**0**	**0**	**0**	**0**	**0**	**0**	**0.0**	**0**	**0**	**0**	**0**	**0**	....	....	....	....	....	....	....	....
	Colorado Rangers	IHL	6	2	2	4	....	....	....	24	....	....	....	....	....	....	....	....	....	....	12	3	2	5	20	....	....	....
1988-89	**New York Rangers**	**NHL**	**5**	**0**	**0**	**0**	**0**	**0**	**0**	**0**	**0**	**0**	**0**	**4**	**0.0**	**1**	**1**	**5**	**1**	**–4**	....	....	....	....	....	....	....	....
	Denver Rangers	IHL	38	19	19	38	....	....	....	104	....	....	....	....	....	....	....	....	....	....	4	3	0	3	18	....	....	....
1989-90	**New York Rangers**	**NHL**	**80**	**5**	**8**	**13**	**4**	**6**	**10**	**161**	**0**	**0**	**0**	**61**	**8.2**	**20**	**1**	**66**	**21**	**–26**	**9**	**2**	**1**	**3**	**10**	**0**	**0**	**1**
1990-91	**New York Rangers**	**NHL**	**67**	**9**	**7**	**16**	**8**	**5**	**13**	**172**	**0**	**0**	**1**	**45**	**20.0**	**23**	**0**	**33**	**9**	**–1**	**6**	**3**	**0**	**3**	**6**	**0**	**0**	**0**
1991-92	**New York Rangers**	**NHL**	**4**	**0**	**0**	**0**	**0**	**0**	**0**	**5**	**0**	**0**	**0**	**0**	**0.0**	**0**	**0**	**1**	**0**	**–1**	....	....	....	....	....	....	....	....
	Binghamton Rangers	AHL	55	10	23	33	....	....	....	109	....	....	....	....	....	....	....	....	....	....	....	....	....	....	....	....	....	....
	Minnesota North Stars	**NHL**	**3**	**0**	**0**	**0**	**0**	**0**	**0**	**0**	**0**	**0**	**0**	**1**	**0.0**	**0**	**0**	**1**	**0**	**–1**	....	....	....	....	....	....	....	....
	Kalamazoo Wings	IHL	2	0	0	0	....	....	....	2	....	....	....	....	....	....	....	....	....	....	11	1	2	3	22	....	....	....
1992-93	**Hartford Whalers**	**NHL**	**76**	**12**	**17**	**29**	**10**	**12**	**22**	**237**	**0**	**0**	**1**	**63**	**19.0**	**43**	**0**	**83**	**25**	**–15**	....	....	....	....	....	....	....	....
1993-94	**Hartford Whalers**	**NHL**	**84**	**2**	**10**	**12**	**2**	**8**	**10**	**137**	**0**	**0**	**0**	**52**	**3.8**	**28**	**1**	**69**	**29**	**–13**	....	....	....	....	....	....	....	....
1994-95	**Hartford Whalers**	**NHL**	**46**	**2**	**5**	**7**	**4**	**7**	**11**	**93**	**0**	**0**	**0**	**33**	**6.1**	**13**	**0**	**29**	**8**	**–8**	....	....	....	....	....	....	....	....
1995-96	**Hartford Whalers**	**NHL**	**81**	**2**	**7**	**9**	**2**	**6**	**8**	**155**	**0**	**0**	**0**	**63**	**3.2**	**14**	**0**	**38**	**11**	**–13**	....	....	....	....	....	....	....	....
1996-97	**Hartford Whalers**	**NHL**	**54**	**2**	**4**	**6**	**2**	**4**	**6**	**90**	**0**	**0**	**0**	**30**	**6.7**	**9**	**1**	**31**	**13**	**–10**	....	....	....	....	....	....	....	....
	Mighty Ducks of Anaheim	**NHL**	**12**	**0**	**2**	**2**	**0**	**2**	**2**	**47**	**0**	**0**	**0**	**9**	**0.0**	**4**	**0**	**9**	**2**	**–3**	**11**	**0**	**0**	**0**	**15**	**0**	**0**	**0**
1997-98	**Mighty Ducks of Anaheim**	**NHL**	**55**	**4**	**5**	**9**	**5**	**5**	**10**	**116**	**0**	**0**	**1**	**43**	**9.3**	**17**	**1**	**49**	**11**	**–22**	....	....	....	....	....	....	....	....
	New York Islanders	**NHL**	**12**	**0**	**0**	**0**	**0**	**0**	**0**	**34**	**0**	**0**	**0**	**4**	**0.0**	**1**	**0**	**5**	**1**	**–3**	....	....	....	....	....	....	....	....
	Phoenix Coyotes	**NHL**	**7**	**1**	**2**	**3**	**1**	**2**	**3**	**4**	**0**	**0**	**0**	**6**	**16.7**	**6**	**0**	**3**	**1**	**4**	**1**	**0**	**0**	**0**	**2**	**0**	**0**	**0**
1998-99	**Chicago Blackhawks**	**NHL**	**60**	**1**	**0**	**1**	**1**	**0**	**1**	**65**	**0**	**0**	**0**	**27**	**3.7**	**8**	**0**	**28**	**9**	**–11**	....	....	....	....	....	....	....	....
99-2000	**Chicago Blackhawks**	**NHL**	**36**	**0**	**6**	**6**	**0**	**6**	**6**	**73**	**0**	**0**	**0**	**14**	**0.0**	**11**	**0**	**15**	**2**	**–2**	....	....	....	....	....	....	....	....
	NHL Totals		**683**	**40**	**73**	**113**	**39**	**63**	**102**	**1389**	**0**	**0**	**3**	**455**	**8.8**	**198**	**5**	**465**	**143**		**27**	**5**	**1**	**6**	**33**	**0**	**0**	**1**

Traded to **Minnesota** by **NY Rangers** for Mario Thyer and Minnesota's 3rd round choice (Maxim Galanov) in 1993 Entry Draft, March 10, 1992. Traded to **Hartford** by **Minnesota** for James Black, September 3, 1992. Traded to **Anaheim** by **Hartford** for Bates Battaglia and Anaheim's 4th round choice (Carolina selected Josef Vasicek) in 1998 Entry Draft, March 18, 1997. Traded to **NY Islanders** by **Anaheim** with Joe Sacco and J.J. Daigneault for Travis Green, Doug Houda and Tony Tuzzolino, February 6, 1998. Traded to **Phoenix** by **NY Islanders** for Phoenix's 9th round choice (Jason Doyle) in 1998 Entry Draft, March 24, 1998. Signed as a free agent by **Chicago**, July 28, 1998. • Missed majority of 1999-2000 season recovering from back injury suffered in game vs. Edmonton, December 3, 1999. Traded to **Philadelphia** by **Chicago** for Philadelphia's 9th round choice (Arne Ramholt) in 2000 Entry Draft, June 12, 2000. Claimed on waivers by **Chicago** from **Philadelphia**, July 6, 2000.

• JANTUNEN, Marko

C – L. 5'10", 185 lbs. b: Lahti, Finland, 2/14/1971. Calgary's 13th, 239th overall, in 1991.

Season	Club	League	GP	G	A	Pts	AG	AA	APts	PIM	PP	SH	GW	S	%	TGF	PGF	TGA	PGA	+/–	GP	G	A	Pts	PIM	PP	SH	GW
1988-89	H-Reipas Lahti	Finland-Jr.	15	4	10	14	....	....	....	30	....	....	....	....	....	....	....	....	....	....	....	....	....	....	....	....	....	....
	Finland	EJC-A	6	3	3	6	....	....	....	6	....	....	....	....	....	....	....	....	....	....	....	....	....	....	....	....	....	....
1989-90	Army Sport Academy	Finland-Jr.	8	4	9	13	....	....	....	6	....	....	....	....	....	....	....	....	....	....	....	....	....	....	....	....	....	....
	H-Reipas Lahti	Finland-Jr.	8	6	5	11	....	....	....	40	....	....	....	....	....	....	....	....	....	....	....	....	....	....	....	....	....	....
	H-Reipas Lahti	Finland-2	31	11	19	30	....	....	....	20	....	....	....	....	....	....	....	....	....	....	4	1	2	3	6	....	....	....
1990-91	H-Reipas Lahti	Finland	39	9	20	29	....	....	....	20	....	....	....	....	....	....	....	....	....	....	....	....	....	....	....	....	....	....
	Finland	WJC-A	7	3	10	13	....	....	....	12	....	....	....	....	....	....	....	....	....	....	....	....	....	....	....	....	....	....
1991-92	H-Reipas Lahti	Finland	42	10	14	24	....	....	....	46	....	....	....	....	....	....	....	....	....	....	....	....	....	....	....	....	....	....
1992-93	KalPa Kuopio	Finland	48	21	27	48	....	....	....	63	....	....	....	....	....	....	....	....	....	....	....	....	....	....	....	....	....	....
1993-94	TPS Turku	Finland	48	*29	29	58	....	....	....	22	....	....	....	....	....	....	....	....	....	....	11	2	6	8	12	....	....	....
	Finland	Nat-Team	5	0	0	0	....	....	....	2	....	....	....	....	....	....	....	....	....	....	....	....	....	....	....	....	....	....
1994-95	Vastra Frolunda	Sweden	18	14	*16	*30	....	....	....	20	....	....	....	....	....	....	....	....	....	....	5	4	4	8	6	....	....	....
	Vastra Frolunda	Sweden-2	23	18	20	38	....	....	....	26	....	....	....	....	....	....	....	....	....	....	....	....	....	....	....	....	....	....
	Finland	Nat-Team	17	3	4	7	....	....	....	12	....	....	....	....	....	....	....	....	....	....	....	....	....	....	....	....	....	....
1995-96	Vastra Frolunda	Sweden	40	17	14	31	....	....	....	66	....	....	....	....	....	....	....	....	....	....	13	8	8	16	10	....	....	....
	Finland	Nat-Team	8	4	1	5	....	....	....	12	....	....	....	....	....	....	....	....	....	....	....	....	....	....	....	....	....	....
1996-97	Vastra Frolunda	Sweden	13	4	7	11	....	....	....	16	....	....	....	....	....	....	....	....	....	....	3	2	0	2	16	....	....	....
	Vastra Frolunda	EuroHL	2	0	0	0	....	....	....	0	....	....	....	....	....	....	....	....	....	....	....	....	....	....	....	....	....	....
	Calgary Flames	**NHL**	**3**	**0**	**0**	**0**	**0**	**0**	**0**	**0**	**0**	**0**	**0**	**7**	**0.0**	**0**	**0**	**1**	**0**	**–1**	....	....	....	....	....	....	....	....
	Saint John Flames	AHL	23	8	16	24	....	....	....	18	....	....	....	....	....	....	....	....	....	....	....	....	....	....	....	....	....	....
	Finland	WC-A	8	1	0	1	....	....	....	6	....	....	....	....	....	....	....	....	....	....	....	....	....	....	....	....	....	....
1997-98	Vasteras IK	Sweden	43	14	20	34	....	....	....	61	....	....	....	....	....	....	....	....	....	....	7	1	2	3	2	....	....	....
1998-99	Vasteras IK	Sweden	47	12	21	33	....	....	....	57	....	....	....	....	....	....	....	....	....	....	4	4	0	4	4	....	....	....
99-2000	Farjestads BK Karlstad	Sweden	50	18	18	36	....	....	....	36	....	....	....	....	....	....	....	....	....	....	7	0	2	2	8	....	....	....
	NHL Totals		**3**	**0**	**0**	**0**	**0**	**0**	**0**	**0**	**0**	**0**	**0**	**7**	**0.0**	**0**	**0**	**1**	**0**		....	....	....	....	....	....	....	....

• JARRETT, Doug　Douglas William　D – L. 6'3", 205 lbs.　b: London, Ont., 4/22/1944.

Season	Club	League	GP	G	A	Pts	AG	AA	APts	PIM	PP	SH	GW	S	%	TGF	PGF	TGA	PGA	+/-	GP	G	A	Pts	PIM	PP	SH	GW
			REGULAR SEASON																		PLAYOFFS							
1960-61	St. Catharines Teepees	OHA-Jr.	36	2	2	4	....	....	....	78	....	....	....	....	....	....	....	....	....	....	6	0	0	0	16	....	....	....
1961-62	St. Catharines Teepees	OHA-Jr.	49	4	6	10	....	....	....	103	....	....	....	....	....	....	....	....	....	....	6	0	1	1	10	....	....	....
1962-63	St. Catharines Black Hawks	OHA-Jr.	50	9	18	27	....	....	....	88	....	....	....	....	....	....	....	....	....	....	....	....	....	....	....	....	....	....
	Buffalo Bisons	AHL	1	0	0	0	....	....	....	4	....	....	....	....	....	....	....	....	....	....	....	....	....	....	....	....	....	....
1963-64	St. Catharines Black Hawks	OHA-Jr.	54	10	51	61	....	....	....	144	....	....	....	....	....	....	....	....	....	....	13	5	12	17	22	....	....	....
	Buffalo Bisons	AHL	1	0	0	0	....	....	....	0	....	....	....	....	....	....	....	....	....	....	....	....	....	....	....	....	....	....
1964-65	**Chicago Black Hawks**	**NHL**	**46**	**2**	**15**	**17**	**2**	**15**	**17**	**34**	....	....	....	....	....	....	....	....	....	....	**11**	**1**	**0**	**1**	**10**	**0**	**0**	**0**
	St. Louis Braves	CPHL	17	3	7	10	....	....	....	23	....	....	....	....	....	....	....	....	....	....	....	....	....	....	....	....	....	....
	Buffalo Bisons	AHL	1	0	0	0	....	....	....	0	....	....	....	....	....	....	....	....	....	....	....	....	....	....	....	....	....	....
1965-66	**Chicago Black Hawks**	**NHL**	**66**	**4**	**12**	**16**	**4**	**11**	**15**	**71**	....	....	....	....	....	....	....	....	....	....	**5**	**0**	**1**	**1**	**9**	**0**	**0**	**0**
1966-67	**Chicago Black Hawks**	**NHL**	**70**	**5**	**21**	**26**	**6**	**20**	**26**	**76**	....	....	....	....	....	....	....	....	....	....	**6**	**0**	**3**	**3**	**8**	**0**	**0**	**0**
1967-68	**Chicago Black Hawks**	**NHL**	**74**	**4**	**19**	**23**	**5**	**19**	**24**	**48**	**0**	**1**	**2**	**148**	**2.7**	**71**	**0**	**110**	**24**	**-15**	**11**	**4**	**0**	**4**	**9**	**0**	**0**	**0**
1968-69	**Chicago Black Hawks**	**NHL**	**69**	**0**	**13**	**13**	**0**	**12**	**12**	**58**	**0**	**0**	**0**	**116**	**0.0**	**71**	**0**	**83**	**19**	**7**	....	....	....	....	....	....	....	....
1969-70	**Chicago Black Hawks**	**NHL**	**72**	**4**	**20**	**24**	**4**	**19**	**23**	**78**	**1**	**0**	**2**	**134**	**3.0**	**81**	**4**	**60**	**16**	**33**	**8**	**1**	**0**	**1**	**4**	**0**	**0**	**0**
1970-71	**Chicago Black Hawks**	**NHL**	**51**	**1**	**12**	**13**	**1**	**10**	**11**	**46**	**0**	**1**	**0**	**75**	**1.3**	**43**	**4**	**40**	**11**	**10**	**18**	**1**	**6**	**7**	**14**	**0**	**0**	**0**
1971-72	**Chicago Black Hawks**	**NHL**	**78**	**6**	**23**	**29**	**6**	**20**	**26**	**68**	**2**	**0**	**1**	**123**	**4.9**	**100**	**2**	**71**	**12**	**39**	**8**	**0**	**2**	**2**	**16**	**0**	**0**	**0**
1972-73	**Chicago Black Hawks**	**NHL**	**49**	**2**	**11**	**13**	**2**	**9**	**11**	**18**	**1**	**0**	**0**	**74**	**2.7**	**53**	**3**	**54**	**13**	**9**	**15**	**0**	**3**	**3**	**2**	**0**	**0**	**0**
1973-74	**Chicago Black Hawks**	**NHL**	**67**	**5**	**11**	**16**	**5**	**9**	**14**	**45**	**1**	**0**	**1**	**54**	**9.3**	**55**	**5**	**52**	**7**	**5**	**10**	**0**	**1**	**1**	**6**	**0**	**0**	**0**
1974-75	**Chicago Black Hawks**	**NHL**	**79**	**5**	**21**	**26**	**4**	**16**	**20**	**66**	**0**	**0**	**0**	**124**	**4.0**	**81**	**6**	**90**	**28**	**13**	**7**	**0**	**0**	**0**	**4**	**0**	**0**	**0**
1975-76	**New York Rangers**	**NHL**	**45**	**0**	**4**	**4**	**0**	**3**	**3**	**19**	**0**	**0**	**0**	**45**	**0.0**	**32**	**0**	**73**	**15**	**-26**	....	....	....	....	....	....	....	....
1976-77	**New York Rangers**	**NHL**	**9**	**0**	**0**	**0**	**0**	**0**	**0**	**4**	**0**	**0**	**0**	**3**	**0.0**	**2**	**0**	**11**	**3**	**-6**	....	....	....	....	....	....	....	....
	New Haven Nighthawks	AHL	40	2	7	9	....	....	....	10	....	....	....	....	....	....	....	....	....	....	....	....	....	....	....	....	....	....
	NHL Totals		**775**	**38**	**182**	**220**	**39**	**163**	**202**	**631**	....	....	....	....	....	....	....	....	....	....	**99**	**7**	**16**	**23**	**82**	....	....	....

OHA-Jr. First All-Star Team (1964) • Played in NHL All-Star Game (1975)

Traded to **NY Rangers** by **Chicago** for Gilles Villemure, October 28, 1975.

• JARRETT, Gary　Gary Walter　LW – L. 5'8", 170 lbs.　b: Toronto, Ont., 9/3/1942.

Season	Club	League	GP	G	A	Pts	AG	AA	APts	PIM	PP	SH	GW	S	%	TGF	PGF	TGA	PGA	+/-	GP	G	A	Pts	PIM	PP	SH	GW
1959-60	Toronto Marlboros	OHA-Jr.	48	24	28	52	....	....	....	12	....	....	....	....	....	....	....	....	....	....	4	1	3	4	14	....	....	....
1960-61	Toronto Marlboros	OHA-Jr.	46	30	20	50	....	....	....	90	....	....	....	....	....	....	....	....	....	....	....	....	....	....	....	....	....	....
	Sudbury Wolves	EPHL	1	0	0	0	....	....	....	0	....	....	....	....	....	....	....	....	....	....	....	....	....	....	....	....	....	....
	Toronto Maple Leafs	**NHL**	**1**	**0**	**0**	**0**	**0**	**0**	**0**	**0**	....	....	....	....	....	....	....	....	....	....	....	....	....	....	....	....	....	....
	Rochester Americans	AHL	6	0	0	0	....	....	....	2	....	....	....	....	....	....	....	....	....	....	....	....	....	....	....	....	....	....
1961-62	Toronto Marlboros	MTJHL	31	*28	27	55	....	....	....	80	....	....	....	....	....	....	....	....	....	....	12	11	*15	26	41	....	....	....
	Rochester Americans	AHL	5	3	1	4	....	....	....	6	....	....	....	....	....	....	....	....	....	....	....	....	....	....	....	....	....	....
1962-63	Sudbury Wolves	EPHL	21	13	14	27	....	....	....	14	....	....	....	....	....	....	....	....	....	....	....	....	....	....	....	....	....	....
	Rochester Americans	AHL	47	6	22	28	....	....	....	19	....	....	....	....	....	....	....	....	....	....	2	1	3	4	0	....	....	....
1963-64	Denver Invaders	WHL	64	22	35	57	....	....	....	37	....	....	....	....	....	....	....	....	....	....	6	2	0	2	6	....	....	....
	Rochester Americans	AHL	5	0	1	1	....	....	....	0	....	....	....	....	....	....	....	....	....	....	....	....	....	....	....	....	....	....
1964-65	Tulsa Oilers	CPHL	67	27	29	56	....	....	....	60	....	....	....	....	....	....	....	....	....	....	12	*8	5	13	10	....	....	....
1965-66	Pittsburgh Hornets	AHL	71	24	26	50	....	....	....	30	....	....	....	....	....	....	....	....	....	....	3	1	0	1	4	....	....	....
1966-67	**Detroit Red Wings**	**NHL**	**4**	**0**	**0**	**0**	**0**	**0**	**0**	**0**	....	....	....	....	....	....	....	....	....	....	....	....	....	....	....	....	....	....
	Pittsburgh Hornets	AHL	68	29	42	71	....	....	....	28	....	....	....	....	....	....	....	....	....	....	9	6	3	9	11	....	....	....
1967-68	**Detroit Red Wings**	**NHL**	**68**	**18**	**21**	**39**	**21**	**21**	**42**	**20**	**1**	**0**	**2**	**207**	**8.7**	**52**	**8**	**44**	**4**	**4**	....	....	....	....	....	....	....	....
1968-69	**Oakland Seals**	**NHL**	**63**	**22**	**23**	**45**	**23**	**20**	**43**	**22**	**3**	**0**	**1**	**201**	**10.9**	**56**	**13**	**52**	**1**	**-8**	**7**	**2**	**1**	**3**	**4**	**0**	**1**	**0**
1969-70	**Oakland Seals**	**NHL**	**75**	**12**	**19**	**31**	**13**	**18**	**31**	**31**	**2**	**0**	**4**	**229**	**5.2**	**45**	**6**	**63**	**0**	**-24**	**4**	**1**	**0**	**1**	**5**	**1**	**0**	**0**
1970-71	**California Golden Seals**	**NHL**	**75**	**15**	**19**	**34**	**15**	**16**	**31**	**40**	**2**	**0**	**2**	**169**	**8.9**	**51**	**9**	**69**	**0**	**-27**	....	....	....	....	....	....	....	....
1971-72	**California Golden Seals**	**NHL**	**55**	**5**	**10**	**15**	**5**	**9**	**14**	**18**	**2**	**0**	**0**	**64**	**7.8**	**21**	**4**	**18**	**1**	**0**	....	....	....	....	....	....	....	....
1972-73	Cleveland Crusaders	WHA	77	40	38	78	....	....	....	79	....	....	....	....	....	....	....	....	....	....	9	8	3	11	19	....	....	....
1973-74	Cleveland Crusaders	WHA	75	31	39	70	....	....	....	68	....	....	....	....	....	....	....	....	....	....	5	1	1	2	13	....	....	....
1974-75	Cleveland Crusaders	WHA	77	17	24	41	....	....	....	70	....	....	....	....	....	....	....	....	....	....	5	0	1	1	0	....	....	....
1975-76	Cleveland Crusaders	WHA	69	16	17	33	....	....	....	22	....	....	....	....	....	....	....	....	....	....	3	0	3	3	2	....	....	....
	NHL Totals		**341**	**72**	**92**	**164**	**77**	**84**	**161**	**131**	....	....	....	....	....	....	....	....	....	....	**11**	**3**	**1**	**4**	**9**	....	....	....
	Other Major League Totals		298	104	118	222	....	....	....	239	....	....	....	....	....	....	....	....	....	....	22	9	8	17	34	....	....	....

OHA-Jr. First All-Star Team (1961) • WHA Second All-Star Team (1973)

Traded to **Detroit** by **Toronto** with Billy Harris and Andy Bathgate for Lowell MacDonald, Marcel Pronovost, Eddie Joyal, Larry Jeffrey and Aut Erickson, May 20, 1965. Traded to **Oakland** by **Detroit** with Doug Roberts, Howie Young and Chris Worthy for Bob Baun and Ron Harris, May 27, 1968. Selected by **Alberta** (WHA) in 1972 WHA General Player Draft, February 12, 1972. WHA rights traded to **Cleveland** (WHA) by **Alberta** (WHA) for cash, August, 1972.

• JARRY, Pierre　Pierre Joseph Reynald　LW – L. 5'11", 190 lbs.　b: Montreal, Que., 3/30/1949. NY Rangers' 2nd, 12th overall, in 1969.

Season	Club	League	GP	G	A	Pts	AG	AA	APts	PIM	PP	SH	GW	S	%	TGF	PGF	TGA	PGA	+/-	GP	G	A	Pts	PIM	PP	SH	GW
1966-67	Sherbrooke Castors	QJHL	26	18	15	33	....	....	....	....	....	....	....	....	....	....	....	....	....	....	....	....	....	....	....	....	....	....
1967-68	Ottawa 67's	OHA-Jr.	50	36	21	57	....	....	....	61	....	....	....	....	....	....	....	....	....	....	....	....	....	....	....	....	....	....
	St. Catharines Black Hawks	OHA-Jr.	....	....	....	....	....	....	....	....	....	....	....	....	....	....	....	....	....	....	5	3	1	4	0	....	....	....
1968-69	Ottawa 67's	OHA-Jr.	53	41	57	98	....	....	....	74	....	....	....	....	....	....	....	....	....	....	7	5	8	13	11	....	....	....
1969-70	Omaha Knights	CHL	70	26	27	53	....	....	....	62	....	....	....	....	....	....	....	....	....	....	8	1	2	3	22	....	....	....
1970-71	Omaha Knights	CHL	71	*46	46	*92	....	....	....	94	....	....	....	....	....	....	....	....	....	....	11	4	5	9	8	....	....	....
1971-72	**New York Rangers**	**NHL**	**34**	**3**	**3**	**6**	**3**	**3**	**6**	**20**	**0**	**0**	**0**	**32**	**9.4**	**12**	**3**	**7**	**0**	**2**	....	....	....	....	....	....	....	....
	Toronto Maple Leafs	**NHL**	**18**	**3**	**4**	**7**	**3**	**3**	**6**	**13**	**0**	**0**	**1**	**42**	**7.1**	**8**	**1**	**10**	**0**	**-3**	**5**	**0**	**1**	**1**	**0**	**0**	**0**	**0**
1972-73	**Toronto Maple Leafs**	**NHL**	**74**	**19**	**18**	**37**	**18**	**14**	**32**	**42**	**2**	**0**	**2**	**188**	**10.1**	**47**	**5**	**55**	**0**	**-13**	....	....	....	....	....	....	....	....
1973-74	**Toronto Maple Leafs**	**NHL**	**12**	**2**	**8**	**10**	**2**	**7**	**9**	**10**	**0**	**0**	**0**	**31**	**6.5**	**16**	**1**	**7**	**0**	**8**	....	....	....	....	....	....	....	....
	Detroit Red Wings	**NHL**	**52**	**15**	**23**	**38**	**14**	**19**	**33**	**17**	**2**	**0**	**0**	**139**	**10.8**	**54**	**16**	**49**	**0**	**-11**	....	....	....	....	....	....	....	....
1974-75	**Detroit Red Wings**	**NHL**	**39**	**8**	**13**	**21**	**7**	**10**	**17**	**4**	**0**	**0**	**1**	**90**	**8.9**	**32**	**15**	**29**	**0**	**-12**	....	....	....	....	....	....	....	....
	Virginia Wings	AHL	20	11	12	23	....	....	....	17	....	....	....	....	....	....	....	....	....	....	....	....	....	....	....	....	....	....
1975-76	**Minnesota North Stars**	**NHL**	**59**	**21**	**18**	**39**	**18**	**13**	**31**	**32**	**3**	**0**	**0**	**143**	**14.7**	**61**	**17**	**53**	**2**	**-7**	....	....	....	....	....	....	....	....
	New Haven Nighthawks	AHL	13	5	7	12	....	....	....	18	....	....	....	....	....	....	....	....	....	....	....	....	....	....	....	....	....	....
1976-77	**Minnesota North Stars**	**NHL**	**21**	**8**	**13**	**21**	**7**	**10**	**17**	**2**	**4**	**0**	**1**	**52**	**15.4**	**26**	**12**	**21**	**1**	**-6**	....	....	....	....	....	....	....	....
1977-78	**Minnesota North Stars**	**NHL**	**35**	**9**	**17**	**26**	**8**	**13**	**21**	**2**	**1**	**0**	**1**	**77**	**11.7**	**32**	**10**	**31**	**0**	**-9**	....	....	....	....	....	....	....	....
	Fort Worth Texans	CHL	15	4	8	12	....	....	....	14	....	....	....	....	....	....	....	....	....	....	....	....	....	....	....	....	....	....
	Edmonton Oilers	WHA	18	4	10	14	....	....	....	4	....	....	....	....	....	....	....	....	....	....	5	1	0	1	4	....	....	....
	NHL Totals		**344**	**88**	**117**	**205**	**80**	**92**	**172**	**142**	**12**	**0**	**6**	**794**	**11.1**	**288**	**80**	**262**	**3**	....	**5**	**0**	**1**	**1**	**0**	**0**	**0**	**0**
	Other Major League Totals		18	4	10	14	....	....	....	4	....	....	....	....	....	....	....	....	....	....	5	1	0	1	4	....	....	....

CHL First All-Star Team (1971)

• Loaned to **St. Catharines** (OHA-Jr.) by **Ottawa** (OHA-Jr.) for the 1968 OHA-Jr. Finals, February, 1968. Selected by **Chicago** (WHA) in 1972 WHA General Player Draft, February 12, 1972. Traded to **Toronto** by **NY Rangers** for Jim Dorey, February 20, 1972. Traded to **Detroit** by **Toronto** for Tim Ecclestone, November 29, 1973. Traded to **Minnesota** by **Detroit** for Don Martineau, November 25, 1975. • Missed majority of 1976-77 season recovering from knee injury suffered in game vs. Toronto, November 20, 1976. Traded to **Edmonton** (WHA) by **Minnesota** with Chris Ahrens for future considerations, March, 1978.

• JARVENPAA, Hannu　RW – L. 6', 195 lbs.　b: Ilves, Finland, 5/19/1963. Winnipeg's 4th, 71st overall, in 1986.

Season	Club	League	GP	G	A	Pts	AG	AA	APts	PIM	PP	SH	GW	S	%	TGF	PGF	TGA	PGA	+/-	GP	G	A	Pts	PIM	PP	SH	GW
1980-81	Karpat Oulu	Finland-Jr.	31	26	21	47	....	....	....	40	....	....	....	....	....	....	....	....	....	....	4	4	1	5	4	....	....	....
1981-82	Karpat Oulu	Finland-Jr.	17	19	18	37	....	....	....	46	....	....	....	....	....	....	....	....	....	....	....	....	....	....	....	....	....	....
	Finland	WJC-A	7	4	4	8	....	....	....	6	....	....	....	....	....	....	....	....	....	....	....	....	....	....	....	....	....	....
	Karpat Oulu	Finland	14	11	2	13	....	....	....	18	....	....	....	....	....	....	....	....	....	....	3	1	1	2	4	....	....	....
1982-83	Karpat Oulu	Finland	34	15	8	23	....	....	....	56	....	....	....	....	....	....	....	....	....	....	5	3	1	4	0	....	....	....
	Finland	WJC-A	6	0	1	1	....	....	....	4	....	....	....	....	....	....	....	....	....	....	....	....	....	....	....	....	....	....
1983-84	Karpat Oulu	Finland-Jr.	4	4	4	8	....	....	....	28	....	....	....	....	....	....	....	....	....	....	....	....	....	....	....	....	....	....
	Karpat Oulu	Finland	37	15	13	28	....	....	....	46	....	....	....	....	....	....	....	....	....	....	10	3	3	6	10	....	....	....
1984-85	Karpat Oulu	Finland	34	12	12	24	....	....	....	45	....	....	....	....	....	....	....	....	....	....	7	2	2	4	2	....	....	....
	Finland	WEC-A	9	1	5	6	....	....	....	6	....	....	....	....	....	....	....	....	....	....	....	....	....	....	....	....	....	....

Season	Club	League	REGULAR SEASON																		PLAYOFFS							
			GP	G	A	Pts	AG	AA	APts	PIM	PP	SH	GW	S	%	TGF	PGF	TGA	PGA	+/–	GP	G	A	Pts	PIM	PP	SH	GW
1985-86	Karpat Oulu	Finland	36	26	9	35				48											5	*5	2	7	12			
	Finland	WEC-A	9	5	4	9				12																		
1986-87	**Winnipeg Jets**	**NHL**	**20**	**1**	**8**	**9**	**1**	**6**	**7**	**8**	**0**	**0**	**0**	**36**	**2.8**	**14**	**2**	**16**	**0**	**–4**								
1987-88	**Winnipeg Jets**	**NHL**	**41**	**6**	**11**	**17**	**5**	**8**	**13**	**34**	**1**	**0**	**0**	**52**	**11.5**	**28**	**4**	**25**	**1**	**0**								
	Moncton Hawks	AHL	5	3	1	4				2																		
1988-89	**Winnipeg Jets**	**NHL**	**53**	**4**	**7**	**11**	**3**	**5**	**8**	**41**	**1**	**0**	**0**	**27**	**14.8**	**15**	**2**	**27**	**0**	**–14**								
	Moncton Hawks	AHL	4	1	0	1				0																		
	Finland	WEC-A	7	2	1	3				4																		
1989-90	Lukko Rauma	Finland	38	12	15	27				48																		
1990-91	Lukko Rauma	Finland	43	27	18	45				54																		
	Finland	WEC-A	9	2	2	4				22																		
1991-92	Finland	Can-Cup	6	0	1	1				4																		
	Leksands IF	Sweden	22	4	4	8				28											11	1	3	4	12			
	Finland	Olympics	8	5	6	11				14																		
	Finland	WC-A	8	1	3	4				14																		
1992-93	Jokerit Helsinki	Finland	44	6	8	14				36											3	0	1	1	0			
1993-94	Kiekoo-Espoo	Finland	44	15	16	31				40																		
1994-95	Kiekoo-Espoo	Finland	45	9	6	15				20											4	0	0	0	2			
	NHL Totals		**114**	**11**	**26**	**37**	**9**	**19**	**28**	**83**	**2**	**0**	**0**	**115**	**9.6**	**57**	**8**	**68**	**1**									

• Re-entered NHL draft. Originally Montreal's 11th choice, 145th overall, in 1982 Entry Draft.

• JARVI, Iiro

RW – L. 6'1", 198 lbs. b: Helsinki, Finland, 3/23/1965. Quebec's 3rd, 55th overall, in 1983.

Season	Club	League	GP	G	A	Pts	AG	AA	APts	PIM	PP	SH	GW	S	%	TGF	PGF	TGA	PGA	+/–	GP	G	A	Pts	PIM	PP	SH	GW
1981-82	HIFK Helsinki	Finland-Jr.	30	9	9	18				22											3	0	0	0	0			
1982-83	HIFK Helsinki	Finland-Jr.	31	24	17	41				89																		
	Finland	WJC-A	7	3	1	4				2																		
	Finland	EJC-A	5	3	1	4				22																		
1983-84	HIFK Helsinki	Finland-Jr.	11	8	12	20				14											5	*5	3	8	17			
	Finland	WJC-A	7	4	3	7				8																		
	HIFK Helsinki	Finland	27	0	6	6				6																		
1984-85	HIFK Helsinki	Finland	9	0	1	1				2																		
	Finland	WJC-A	7	1	1	2				2																		
	H-Reipas Lahti	Finland	15	2	3	5				10																		
1985-86	HIFK Helsinki	Finland-Jr.	1	0	1	1				4											2	1	0	1	4			
	HIFK Helsinki	Finland	29	7	6	13				19											10	4	6	10	2			
1986-87	HIFK Helsinki	Finland	43	23	30	53				82											5	1	5	6	9			
	Finland	Nat-Team	17	0	1	1				6																		
	Finland	WEC-A	8	2	0	2				10																		
1987-88	Finland	Can-Cup	4	0	0	0				2																		
	HIFK Helsinki	Finland	44	21	20	41				68											5	2	1	3	7			
	Finland	Nat-Team	22	5	2	7				18																		
	Finland	Olympics	8	2	5	7				10																		
1988-89	**Quebec Nordiques**	**NHL**	**75**	**11**	**30**	**41**	**9**	**21**	**30**	**40**	**1**	**0**	**1**	**109**	**10.1**	**61**	**11**	**65**	**2**	**–13**								
	Finland	Nat-Team	1	0	0	0				2																		
	Finland	WEC-A	9	0	2	2				10																		
1989-90	**Quebec Nordiques**	**NHL**	**41**	**7**	**13**	**20**	**6**	**9**	**15**	**18**	**1**	**0**	**1**	**52**	**13.5**	**29**	**3**	**37**	**0**	**–11**								
	Halifax Citadels	AHL	26	4	13	17				4																		
1990-91	KAC Klagenfurt	Austria	26	12	21	33																						
	Halifax Citadels	AHL	5	0	2	2				2																		
1991-92	Finland	Can-Cup	6	0	0	0				6																		
	HIFK Helsinki	Finland	43	14	23	37				64											9	3	4	7	2			
	Finland	Nat-Team	8	0	1	1				8																		
1992-93	HIFK Helsinki	Finland	47	7	23	30				64											4	3	3	6	4			
1993-94	HIFK Helsinki	Finland	47	13	24	37				113											3	0	2	2	4			
1994-95	HIFK Helsinki	Finland	50	14	29	43				50											3	0	0	0	2			
1995-96	HIFK Helsinki	Finland	50	13	30	43				88											3	0	2	2	0			
	Finland	Nat-Team	2	1	0	1				0																		
1996-97	Frankfurt Lions	Germany	48	13	23	36				44											9	2	8	10	14			
1997-98	KAC Klagenfurt	Alpenliga	21	6	16	22				16																		
	KAC Klagenfurt	Austria	28	7	11	18				30																		
1998-99	SaiPa Lappeenranta	Finland	32	3	9	12				26											7	0	2	2	33			
99-2000	Newcastle Riverkings	BH-Cup	2	0	1	1				0																		
	Newcastle Riverkings	Britain	39	14	26	40				51											8	2	2	4	4			
	NHL Totals		**116**	**18**	**43**	**61**	**15**	**30**	**45**	**58**	**2**	**0**	**2**	**161**	**11.2**	**90**	**14**	**102**	**2**									

• JARVIS, Doug

Douglas M. C – L. 5'9", 170 lbs. b: Brantford, Ont., 3/24/1955. Toronto's 2nd, 24th overall, in 1975.

Season	Club	League	GP	G	A	Pts	AG	AA	APts	PIM	PP	SH	GW	S	%	TGF	PGF	TGA	PGA	+/–	GP	G	A	Pts	PIM	PP	SH	GW
1971-72	Brantford Legionaires	OMHA	11	2	10	12				0																		
1972-73	Peterborough Petes	OMJHL	63	20	49	69				14																		
1973-74	Peterborough Petes	OMJHL	70	31	53	84				27																		
	Canada	WJC-A	5	4	1	5				2																		
1974-75	Peterborough Petes	OMJHL	64	45	88	133				38											11	4	11	15	8			
1975-76♦	**Montreal Canadiens**	**NHL**	**80**	**5**	**30**	**35**	**4**	**22**	**26**	**16**	**0**	**1**	**1**	**92**	**5.4**	**45**	**7**	**45**	**24**	**17**	**13**	**2**	**1**	**3**	**2**	**0**	**0**	**0**
1976-77♦	**Montreal Canadiens**	**NHL**	**80**	**16**	**22**	**38**	**14**	**17**	**31**	**14**	**0**	**0**	**2**	**88**	**18.2**	**55**	**0**	**38**	**13**	**30**	**14**	**0**	**7**	**7**	**2**	**0**	**0**	**0**
1977-78♦	**Montreal Canadiens**	**NHL**	**80**	**11**	**28**	**39**	**10**	**22**	**32**	**23**	**2**	**2**	**1**	**129**	**8.5**	**52**	**6**	**59**	**25**	**12**	**15**	**3**	**5**	**8**	**12**	**1**	**0**	**1**
1978-79♦	**Montreal Canadiens**	**NHL**	**80**	**10**	**13**	**23**	**9**	**9**	**18**	**16**	**0**	**1**	**1**	**117**	**8.5**	**49**	**1**	**60**	**17**	**5**	**12**	**1**	**3**	**4**	**4**	**0**	**0**	**0**
1979-80	**Montreal Canadiens**	**NHL**	**80**	**13**	**11**	**24**	**11**	**8**	**19**	**28**	**0**	**1**	**3**	**130**	**10.0**	**39**	**1**	**72**	**29**	**–5**	**10**	**4**	**4**	**8**	**2**	**0**	**1**	**0**
1980-81	**Montreal Canadiens**	**NHL**	**80**	**16**	**22**	**38**	**12**	**15**	**27**	**34**	**0**	**2**	**1**	**122**	**13.1**	**52**	**1**	**71**	**32**	**12**	**3**	**0**	**0**	**0**	**0**	**0**	**0**	**0**
1981-82	**Montreal Canadiens**	**NHL**	**80**	**20**	**28**	**48**	**16**	**19**	**35**	**20**	**1**	**0**	**4**	**127**	**15.7**	**69**	**4**	**67**	**36**	**34**	**5**	**1**	**0**	**1**	**4**	**0**	**1**	**0**
1982-83	**Washington Capitals**	**NHL**	**80**	**8**	**22**	**30**	**7**	**15**	**22**	**10**	**0**	**1**	**0**	**95**	**8.4**	**42**	**1**	**79**	**26**	**–12**	**4**	**0**	**1**	**1**	**0**	**0**	**0**	**0**
1983-84	**Washington Capitals**	**NHL**	**80**	**13**	**29**	**42**	**10**	**20**	**30**	**12**	**0**	**2**	**0**	**122**	**10.7**	**68**	**14**	**70**	**23**	**7**	**8**	**2**	**3**	**5**	**6**	**0**	**0**	**0**
1984-85	**Washington Capitals**	**NHL**	**80**	**9**	**28**	**37**	**7**	**19**	**26**	**32**	**1**	**1**	**1**	**103**	**8.7**	**58**	**3**	**73**	**37**	**19**	**5**	**1**	**0**	**1**	**2**	**0**	**0**	**0**
1985-86	**Washington Capitals**	**NHL**	**25**	**1**	**2**	**3**	**1**	**1**	**2**	**16**	**0**	**0**	**0**	**19**	**5.3**	**7**	**0**	**15**	**3**	**–5**								
	Hartford Whalers	**NHL**	**57**	**8**	**16**	**24**	**6**	**11**	**17**	**20**	**0**	**3**	**0**	**55**	**14.5**	**36**	**0**	**60**	**31**	**7**	**10**	**0**	**3**	**3**	**4**	**0**	**0**	**0**
1986-87	**Hartford Whalers**	**NHL**	**80**	**9**	**13**	**22**	**8**	**9**	**17**	**20**	**0**	**2**	**2**	**88**	**10.2**	**34**	**1**	**66**	**33**	**0**	**6**	**0**	**0**	**0**	**4**	**0**	**0**	**0**
1987-88	**Hartford Whalers**	**NHL**	**2**	**0**	**0**	**0**	**0**	**0**	**0**	**2**	**0**	**0**	**0**	**2**	**0.0**	**0**	**0**	**2**	**2**	**0**								
	Binghamton Whalers	AHL	24	5	4	9				4																		
	Binghamton Whalers	AHL	DID NOT PLAY – COACHING																									
1988-1993	**Minnesota North Stars**	**NHL**	DID NOT PLAY – ASSISTANT COACH																									
1993-2000	**Dallas Stars**	**NHL**	DID NOT PLAY – ASSISTANT COACH																									
	NHL Totals		**964**	**139**	**264**	**403**	**115**	**187**	**302**	**263**	**4**	**16**	**16**	**1289**	**10.8**	**606**	**39**	**777**	**331**		**105**	**14**	**27**	**41**	**42**	**1**	**2**	**1**

OMJHL Second All-Star Team (1975) • Won Frank J. Selke Trophy (1984) • Won Bill Masterton Trophy (1987)

Traded to **Montreal** by **Toronto** for Greg Hubick, June 26, 1975. Traded to **Washington** by **Montreal** with Rod Langway, Craig Laughlin and Brian Engblom for Ryan Walter and Rick Green, September 9, 1982. Traded to **Hartford** by **Washington** for Jorgen Pettersson, December 6, 1985.

• JARVIS, Wes

Wesley Herbert C – L. 5'11", 185 lbs. b: Toronto, Ont., 5/30/1958. Washington's 18th, 213th overall, in 1978.

Season	Club	League	GP	G	A	Pts	AG	AA	APts	PIM	PP	SH	GW	S	%	TGF	PGF	TGA	PGA	+/–	GP	G	A	Pts	PIM	PP	SH	GW
1974-75	Weston Dodgers	OHA-B	38	20	27	47				18																		
1975-76	Sudbury Wolves	OMJHL	64	26	48	74				22											17	9	*28	*37	4			
1976-77	Sudbury Wolves	OMJHL	65	36	60	96				24											6	3	2	5	7			
1977-78	Sudbury Wolves	OMJHL	21	7	16	23				16																		
	Windsor Spitfires	OMJHL	44	27	51	78				37											6	0	2	2	0			
1978-79	Port Huron Flags	IHL	73	44	65	109				39											7	4	4	8	2			

Season	Club	League	GP	G	A	Pts	AG	AA	APts	PIM	PP	SH	GW	S	%	TGF	PGF	TGA	PGA	+/–	GP	G	A	Pts	PIM	PP	SH	GW
			REGULAR SEASON																		PLAYOFFS							
1979-80	**Washington Capitals**	**NHL**	**63**	**11**	**15**	**26**	**9**	**11**	**20**	**8**	**0**	**0**	**0**	**43**	**25.6**	**30**	**0**	**48**	**15**	**–3**	....	....	....	....	....	....	....	....
	Hershey Bears	AHL	16	6	14	20	....	....	....	4	....	....	....	....	....	....	....	....	....	....	....	....	....	....	....	....	....	....
1980-81	**Washington Capitals**	**NHL**	**55**	**9**	**14**	**23**	**7**	**9**	**16**	**30**	**0**	**1**	**0**	**61**	**14.8**	**29**	**1**	**58**	**21**	**–9**	....	....	....	....	....	....	....	....
	Hershey Bears	AHL	24	15	25	40	....	....	....	39	....	....	....	....	....	....	....	....	....	....	10	3	13	16	2	....	....	....
1981-82	**Washington Capitals**	**NHL**	**26**	**1**	**12**	**13**	**1**	**8**	**9**	**18**	**0**	**0**	**0**	**22**	**4.5**	**24**	**3**	**25**	**9**	**5**	....	....	....	....	....	....	....	....
	Hershey Bears	AHL	56	31	61	92	....	....	....	44	....	....	....	....	....	....	....	....	....	....	5	3	4	7	4	....	....	....
1982-83	**Minnesota North Stars**	**NHL**	**3**	**0**	**0**	**0**	**0**	**0**	**0**	**2**	**0**	**0**	**0**	**2**	**0.0**	**0**	**0**	**2**	**0**	**–2**	....	....	....	....	....	....	....	....
	Birmingham South Stars	CHL	75	40	*68	*108	....	....	....	36	....	....	....	....	....	....	....	....	....	....	13	8	8	16	4	....	....	....
1983-84	**Los Angeles Kings**	**NHL**	**61**	**9**	**13**	**22**	**7**	**9**	**16**	**36**	**1**	**1**	**0**	**63**	**14.3**	**24**	**1**	**53**	**23**	**–7**	....	....	....	....	....	....	....	....
1984-85	**Toronto Maple Leafs**	**NHL**	**26**	**0**	**1**	**1**	**0**	**1**	**1**	**2**	**0**	**0**	**0**	**12**	**0.0**	**3**	**0**	**12**	**3**	**–6**	....	....	....	....	....	....	....	....
	St. Catharines Saints	AHL	52	29	44	73	....	....	....	22	....	....	....	....	....	....	....	....	....	....	....	....	....	....	....	....	....	....
1985-86	**Toronto Maple Leafs**	**NHL**	**2**	**1**	**0**	**1**	**1**	**0**	**1**	**2**	**0**	**0**	**0**	**2**	**50.0**	**1**	**0**	**2**	**0**	**–1**	....	....	....	....	....	....	....	....
	St. Catharines Saints	AHL	74	36	60	96	....	....	....	38	....	....	....	....	....	....	....	....	....	....	....	....	....	....	....	....	....	....
1986-87	Newmarket Saints	AHL	70	28	50	78	....	....	....	32	....	....	....	....	....	....	....	....	....	....	13	5	8	13	12	....	....	....
	Toronto Maple Leafs	**NHL**	....	....	....	....	....	....	....	....	....	....	....	....	....	....	....	....	....	....	**2**	**0**	**0**	**0**	**2**	**0**	**0**	**0**
1987-88	**Toronto Maple Leafs**	**NHL**	**1**	**0**	**0**	**0**	**0**	**0**	**0**	**0**	**0**	**0**	**0**	**0**	**0.0**	**0**	**0**	**0**	**0**	**0**	....	....	....	....	....	....	....	....
	Newmarket Saints	AHL	79	25	59	84	....	....	....	48	....	....	....	....	....	....	....	....	....	....	....	....	....	....	....	....	....	....
1988-89	Newmarket Saints	AHL	52	22	31	53	....	....	....	38	....	....	....	....	....	....	....	....	....	....	5	2	4	6	4	....	....	....
1989-90	Newmarket Saints	AHL	36	13	22	35	....	....	....	18	....	....	....	....	....	....	....	....	....	....	....	....	....	....	....	....	....	....
	NHL Totals		**237**	**31**	**55**	**86**	**25**	**38**	**63**	**98**	**1**	**2**	**0**	**205**	**15.1**	**111**	**5**	**200**	**71**		**2**	**0**	**0**	**0**	**2**	**0**	**0**	**0**

IHL Second All-Star Team (1979) • Won Garry F. Longman Memorial Trophy (Top Rookie - IHL) (1979) • CHL First All-Star Team (1983)

Traded to **Minnesota** by **Washington** with Rollie Boutin for Robbie Moore and Minnesota's 11th round choice (Anders Huss) in 1983 Entry Draft, August 4, 1982. Signed as a free agent by **LA Kings**, August 10, 1983. Signed as a free agent by **Toronto**, October 2, 1984.

• JAVANAINEN, Arto

RW – R. 6′, 185 lbs. b: Pori, Finland, 4/8/1959. Pittsburgh's 5th, 85th overall, in 1984.

Season	Club	League	GP	G	A	Pts	AG	AA	APts	PIM	PP	SH	GW	S	%	TGF	PGF	TGA	PGA	+/–	GP	G	A	Pts	PIM	PP	SH	GW
1975-76	Assat Pori	Finland-Jr.	29	10	3	13	....	....	....	41	....	....	....	....	....	....	....	....	....	....	....	....	....	....	....	....	....	....
	Assat Pori	Finland	27	0	0	0	....	....	....	0	....	....	....	....	....	....	....	....	....	....	3	0	0	0	0	....	....	....
1976-77	Assat Pori	Finland-Jr.	4	3	1	4	....	....	....	16	....	....	....	....	....	....	....	....	....	....	....	....	....	....	....	....	....	....
	Assat Pori	Finland	34	9	5	14	....	....	....	8	....	....	....	....	....	....	....	....	....	....	....	....	....	....	....	....	....	....
	Finland	WJC-A	7	4	2	6	....	....	....	4	....	....	....	....	....	....	....	....	....	....	....	....	....	....	....	....	....	....
1977-78	Assat Pori	Finland-Jr.	13	13	7	20	....	....	....	12	....	....	....	....	....	....	....	....	....	....	....	....	....	....	....	....	....	....
	Finland	WJC-A	6	1	7	8	....	....	....	6	....	....	....	....	....	....	....	....	....	....	....	....	....	....	....	....	....	....
	Assat Pori	Finland	35	8	8	16	....	....	....	0	....	....	....	....	....	....	....	....	....	....	9	5	4	9	5	....	....	....
1978-79	Assat Pori	Finland-Jr.	1	1	0	1	....	....	....	7	....	....	....	....	....	....	....	....	....	....	....	....	....	....	....	....	....	....
	Finland	Nat-Team	1	1	0	1	....	....	....	0	....	....	....	....	....	....	....	....	....	....	....	....	....	....	....	....	....	....
	Finland	WJC-A	6	2	3	5	....	....	....	0	....	....	....	....	....	....	....	....	....	....	....	....	....	....	....	....	....	....
	Assat Pori	Finland	36	31	18	49	....	....	....	36	....	....	....	....	....	....	....	....	....	....	8	7	4	11	7	....	....	....
1979-80	Assat Pori	Finland	36	28	29	57	....	....	....	48	....	....	....	....	....	....	....	....	....	....	7	*7	2	9	10	....	....	....
	Finland	Nat-Team	5	1	0	1	....	....	....	0	....	....	....	....	....	....	....	....	....	....	....	....	....	....	....	....	....	....
1980-81	Assat Pori	Finland	36	*37	27	64	....	....	....	40	....	....	....	....	....	....	....	....	....	....	2	1	0	1	2	....	....	....
	Finland	Nat-Team	6	0	0	0	....	....	....	0	....	....	....	....	....	....	....	....	....	....	....	....	....	....	....	....	....	....
1981-82	Finland	Can-Cup	5	1	0	1	....	....	....	2	....	....	....	....	....	....	....	....	....	....	....	....	....	....	....	....	....	....
	Assat Pori	Finland	36	29	27	56	....	....	....	50	....	....	....	....	....	....	....	....	....	....	9	5	4	9	8	....	....	....
	Finland	Nat-Team	10	5	0	5	....	....	....	8	....	....	....	....	....	....	....	....	....	....	....	....	....	....	....	....	....	....
	Finland	WEC-A	5	2	1	3	....	....	....	4	....	....	....	....	....	....	....	....	....	....	....	....	....	....	....	....	....	....
1982-83	Assat Pori	Finland	36	28	23	51	....	....	....	56	....	....	....	....	....	....	....	....	....	....	....	....	....	....	....	....	....	....
	Finland	Nat-Team	13	4	2	6	....	....	....	24	....	....	....	....	....	....	....	....	....	....	....	....	....	....	....	....	....	....
	Finland	WEC-A	10	1	2	3	....	....	....	8	....	....	....	....	....	....	....	....	....	....	....	....	....	....	....	....	....	....
1983-84	Assat Pori	Finland	37	*37	25	62	....	....	....	62	....	....	....	....	....	....	....	....	....	....	9	4	2	6	10	....	....	....
	Finland	Nat-Team	13	4	1	5	....	....	....	12	....	....	....	....	....	....	....	....	....	....	....	....	....	....	....	....	....	....
	Finland	Olympics	5	2	3	5	....	....	....	4	....	....	....	....	....	....	....	....	....	....	....	....	....	....	....	....	....	....
1984-85	**Pittsburgh Penguins**	**NHL**	**14**	**4**	**1**	**5**	**3**	**1**	**4**	**2**	**0**	**0**	**0**	**20**	**20.0**	**11**	**0**	**10**	**0**	**1**	....	....	....	....	....	....	....	....
	Baltimore Skipjacks	AHL	59	26	29	55	....	....	....	15	....	....	....	....	....	....	....	....	....	....	15	5	4	9	2	....	....	....
1985-86	Assat Pori	Finland	36	*44	27	*71	....	....	....	26	....	....	....	....	....	....	....	....	....	....	....	....	....	....	....	....	....	....
	Finland	Nat-Team	9	1	2	3	....	....	....	2	....	....	....	....	....	....	....	....	....	....	....	....	....	....	....	....	....	....
1986-87	Assat Pori	Finland	44	37	24	61	....	....	....	80	....	....	....	....	....	....	....	....	....	....	....	....	....	....	....	....	....	....
1987-88	TPS Turku	Finland	44	47	20	67	....	....	....	42	....	....	....	....	....	....	....	....	....	....	....	....	....	....	....	....	....	....
1988-89	TPS Turku	Finland	44	32	23	55	....	....	....	38	....	....	....	....	....	....	....	....	....	....	6	5	3	8	2	....	....	....
1989-90	Assat Pori	Finland-2	36	59	39	98	....	....	....	30	....	....	....	....	....	....	....	....	....	....	3	2	1	3	6	....	....	....
1990-91	Assat Pori	Finland	44	*35	18	53	....	....	....	38	....	....	....	....	....	....	....	....	....	....	....	....	....	....	....	....	....	....
1991-92	Assat Pori	Finland	44	20	14	34	....	....	....	22	....	....	....	....	....	....	....	....	....	....	8	1	2	3	8	....	....	....
1992-93	Assat Pori	Finland	45	17	17	34	....	....	....	26	....	....	....	....	....	....	....	....	....	....	8	2	3	5	8	....	....	....
1993-94	Assat Pori	Finland	48	22	19	41	....	....	....	46	....	....	....	....	....	....	....	....	....	....	5	1	0	1	4	....	....	....
1994-95	Rungsted IK	Denmark	23	33	18	51	....	....	....	6	....	....	....	....	....	....	....	....	....	....	6	3	1	4	0	....	....	....
	NHL Totals		**14**	**4**	**1**	**5**	**3**	**1**	**4**	**2**	**0**	**0**	**0**	**20**	**20.0**	**11**	**0**	**10**	**0**		....	....	....	....	....	....	....	....

Finnish First All-Star Team (1982, 1986, 1987, 1988) • Re-entered NHL draft. Originally Montreal's 8th choice, 122nd overall, in 1983 Entry Draft.

• JAY, Bob

D – R. 5′11″, 190 lbs. b: Burlington, MA, 11/18/1965.

Season	Club	League	GP	G	A	Pts	AG	AA	APts	PIM	PP	SH	GW	S	%	TGF	PGF	TGA	PGA	+/–	GP	G	A	Pts	PIM	PP	SH	GW
1984-85	Merrimack College	NCAA-2	23	3	5	8	....	....	....	20	....	....	....	....	....	....	....	....	....	....	....	....	....	....	....	....	....	....
1985-86	Merrimack College	NCAA-2	30	6	18	24	....	....	....	33	....	....	....	....	....	....	....	....	....	....	....	....	....	....	....	....	....	....
1986-87	Merrimack College	NCAA-2	36	4	21	25	....	....	....	42	....	....	....	....	....	....	....	....	....	....	....	....	....	....	....	....	....	....
1987-88	Merrimack College	NCAA-2	27	4	19	23	....	....	....	20	....	....	....	....	....	....	....	....	....	....	....	....	....	....	....	....	....	....
1988-89			DID NOT PLAY																									
1989-90			DID NOT PLAY																									
1990-91	Fort Wayne Komets	IHL	40	1	8	9	....	....	....	24	....	....	....	....	....	....	....	....	....	....	14	0	3	3	16	....	....	....
1991-92	Fort Wayne Komets	IHL	76	1	19	20	....	....	....	119	....	....	....	....	....	....	....	....	....	....	7	0	2	2	4	....	....	....
1992-93	Fort Wayne Komets	IHL	78	5	21	26	....	....	....	100	....	....	....	....	....	....	....	....	....	....	8	0	2	2	14	....	....	....
1993-94	**Los Angeles Kings**	**NHL**	**3**	**0**	**1**	**1**	**0**	**1**	**1**	**0**	**0**	**0**	**0**	**2**	**0.0**	**1**	**0**	**4**	**1**	**–2**	....	....	....	....	....	....	....	....
	Phoenix Roadrunners	IHL	65	7	15	22	....	....	....	54	....	....	....	....	....	....	....	....	....	....	....	....	....	....	....	....	....	....
1994-95	Detroit Vipers	IHL	57	3	8	11	....	....	....	51	....	....	....	....	....	....	....	....	....	....	5	0	0	0	10	....	....	....
1995-96	Detroit Vipers	IHL	17	2	2	4	....	....	....	22	....	....	....	....	....	....	....	....	....	....	6	0	1	1	16	....	....	....
1996-97	Detroit Vipers	IHL	71	3	11	14	....	....	....	44	....	....	....	....	....	....	....	....	....	....	21	1	1	2	21	....	....	....
1997-98	Detroit Vipers	IHL	66	5	12	17	....	....	....	88	....	....	....	....	....	....	....	....	....	....	8	1	3	4	8	....	....	....
1998-99	Detroit Vipers	IHL	44	1	3	4	....	....	....	51	....	....	....	....	....	....	....	....	....	....	....	....	....	....	....	....	....	....
99-2000	Detroit Vipers	IHL	DID NOT PLAY – ASSISTANT COACH																		....	....	....	....	....	....	....	....
	NHL Totals		**3**	**0**	**1**	**1**	**0**	**1**	**1**	**0**	**0**	**0**	**0**	**2**	**0.0**	**1**	**0**	**4**	**1**		....	....	....	....	....	....	....	....

Signed as a free agent by **LA Kings**, July 16, 1993. Signed as a free agent by **Detroit Vipers** (IHL), July 20, 1994.

• JEFFREY, Larry

Lawrence Joseph LW – L. 5′11″, 189 lbs. b: Goderich, Ont., 10/12/1940.

Season	Club	League	GP	G	A	Pts	AG	AA	APts	PIM	PP	SH	GW	S	%	TGF	PGF	TGA	PGA	+/–	GP	G	A	Pts	PIM	PP	SH	GW
1957-58	Hamilton Kilty B's	OHA-B	STATISTICS NOT AVAILABLE																									
	Hamilton Red Wings	OHA-Jr.	....	....	....	....	....	....	....	....	....	....	....	....	....	....	....	....	....	....	9	0	0	0	0	....	....	....
1958-59	Hamilton Red Wings	OHA-Jr.	54	21	20	41	....	....	....	149	....	....	....	....	....	....	....	....	....	....	....	....	....	....	....	....	....	....
1959-60	Hamilton Red Wings	OHA-Jr.	46	14	24	38	....	....	....	84	....	....	....	....	....	....	....	....	....	....	....	....	....	....	....	....	....	....
	Hershey Bears	AHL	5	0	3	3	....	....	....	2	....	....	....	....	....	....	....	....	....	....	....	....	....	....	....	....	....	....
1960-61	Hamilton Red Wings	OHA-Jr.	48	28	32	60	....	....	....	105	....	....	....	....	....	....	....	....	....	....	12	6	3	9	39	....	....	....
1961-62	**Detroit Red Wings**	**NHL**	**18**	**5**	**3**	**8**	**6**	**3**	**9**	**20**	....	....	....	....	....	....	....	....	....	....	....	....	....	....	....	....	....	....
	Edmonton Flyers	WHL	48	20	22	42	....	....	....	80	....	....	....	....	....	....	....	....	....	....	....	....	....	....	....	....	....	....
1962-63	**Detroit Red Wings**	**NHL**	**53**	**5**	**11**	**16**	**6**	**11**	**17**	**62**	....	....	....	....	....	....	....	....	....	....	**9**	**3**	**3**	**6**	**8**	**1**	**0**	**0**
	Pittsburgh Hornets	AHL	21	14	7	21	....	....	....	12	....	....	....	....	....	....	....	....	....	....	....	....	....	....	....	....	....	....
1963-64	**Detroit Red Wings**	**NHL**	**58**	**10**	**18**	**28**	**12**	**19**	**31**	**87**	....	....	....	....	....	....	....	....	....	....	**14**	**1**	**6**	**7**	**28**	**0**	**0**	**1**

			REGULAR SEASON																		PLAYOFFS							
Season	Club	League	GP	G	A	Pts	AG	AA	APts	PIM	PP	SH	GW	S	%	TGF	PGF	TGA	PGA	+/-	GP	G	A	Pts	PIM	PP	SH	GW
1964-65	Detroit Red Wings	NHL	41	4	2	6	5	2	7	48	....	....	....	....	....	....	....	....	....	....	2	0	0	0	0	0	0	0
1965-66	Toronto Maple Leafs	NHL	20	1	1	2	1	1	2	22	....	....	....	....	....	....	....	....	....	....	....	....	....	....	....	....	....	....
	Rochester Americans	AHL	51	10	20	30	....	....	....	36	....	....	....	....	....	....	....	....	....	....	12	6	5	11	4	....	....	....
1966-67♦	Toronto Maple Leafs	NHL	56	11	17	28	13	17	30	27	....	....	....	....	....	....	....	....	....	....	6	0	1	1	4	0	0	0
1967-68	New York Rangers	NHL	47	2	4	6	2	4	6	15	0	0	0	48	4.2	10	1	29	7	–13	3	0	0	0	0	0	0	0
1968-69	New York Rangers	NHL	75	1	6	7	1	5	6	12	0	0	0	31	3.2	10	0	33	23	0	4	0	0	0	2	0	0	0
1969-70	Detroit Red Wings	NHL	DID NOT PLAY – INJURED																									
	NHL Totals		368	39	62	101	46	62	108	293	....	....	....	....	....	....	....	....	....	....	38	4	10	14	42	....	....	....

Traded to **Toronto** by **Detroit** with Marcel Pronovost, Ed Joyal, Aut Erickson and Lowell MacDonald for Andy Bathgate, Billy Harris and Gary Jarrett, May 20, 1965. Claimed by **Pittsburgh** from **Toronto** in Expansion Draft, June 6, 1967. Traded to **NY Rangers** by **Pittsburgh** for George Konik, Paul Andrea, Dunc McCallum and Frank Francis, June 6, 1967. Traded to **Detroit** by **NY Rangers** for Sandy Snow and Terry Sawchuk, June 17, 1969. • Suffered career-ending leg injury in automobile accident, October 5, 1969.

• JELINEK, Tomas

RW – L. 5'9", 189 lbs. b: Prague, Czech., 4/29/1962. Ottawa's 11th, 242nd overall, in 1992.

Season	Club	League	GP	G	A	Pts	AG	AA	APts	PIM	PP	SH	GW	S	%	TGF	PGF	TGA	PGA	+/-	GP	G	A	Pts	PIM	PP	SH	GW
1979-80	HC Sparta Praha	Czech.	7	0	1	1	....	....	....	....	....	....	....	....	....	....	....	....	....	....	....	....	....	....	....	....	....	....
	Czechoslovakia	EJC-A	5	0	1	1	....	....	....	8	....	....	....	....	....	....	....	....	....	....	....	....	....	....	....	....	....	....
1980-81	Dukla Trencin	Czech.	34	5	6	11	....	....	....	....	....	....	....	....	....	....	....	....	....	....	....	....	....	....	....	....	....	....
	Czechoslovakia	WJC-A	5	3	1	4	....	....	....	8	....	....	....	....	....	....	....	....	....	....	....	....	....	....	....	....	....	....
1981-82	Dukla Trencin	Czech.	36	9	3	12	....	....	....	46	....	....	....	....	....	....	....	....	....	....	....	....	....	....	....	....	....	....
	Czechoslovakia	WJC-A	7	2	2	4	....	....	....	6	....	....	....	....	....	....	....	....	....	....	....	....	....	....	....	....	....	....
1982-83	HC Sparta Praha	Czech.	40	20	25	45	....	....	....	....	....	....	....	....	....	....	....	....	....	....	....	....	....	....	....	....	....	....
1983-84	HC Sparta Praha	Czech.	43	13	5	18	....	....	....	48	....	....	....	....	....	....	....	....	....	....	....	....	....	....	....	....	....	....
1984-85	HC Sparta Praha	Czech.	44	15	4	19	....	....	....	70	....	....	....	....	....	....	....	....	....	....	....	....	....	....	....	....	....	....
1985-86	HC Sparta Praha	Czech.	40	7	2	9	....	....	....	....	....	....	....	....	....	....	....	....	....	....	....	....	....	....	....	....	....	....
1986-87	HC Sparta Praha	Czech.	36	7	5	12	....	....	....	58	....	....	....	....	....	....	....	....	....	....	....	....	....	....	....	....	....	....
1987-88	HC Sparta Praha	Czech.	45	14	11	25	....	....	....	45	....	....	....	....	....	....	....	....	....	....	....	....	....	....	....	....	....	....
1988-89	HC Sparta Praha	Czech.	45	15	17	32	....	....	....	87	....	....	....	....	....	....	....	....	....	....	....	....	....	....	....	....	....	....
	Czechoslovakia	WEC-A	5	1	1	2	....	....	....	2	....	....	....	....	....	....	....	....	....	....	....	....	....	....	....	....	....	....
1989-90	Motor Ceske Budejovice	Czech.	38	21	17	38	....	....	....	....	....	....	....	....	....	....	....	....	....	....	5	2	3	5	....	....	....	....
	Czechoslovakia	WEC-A	10	1	4	5	....	....	....	14	....	....	....	....	....	....	....	....	....	....	....	....	....	....	....	....	....	....
1990-91	Motor Ceske Budejovice	Czech.	51	24	23	47	....	....	....	102	....	....	....	....	....	....	....	....	....	....	....	....	....	....	....	....	....	....
1991-92	Czechoslovakia	Can-Cup	5	2	3	5	....	....	....	10	....	....	....	....	....	....	....	....	....	....	....	....	....	....	....	....	....	....
	HPK Hameenlinna	Finland	41	24	23	47	....	....	....	*98	....	....	....	....	....	....	....	....	....	....	....	....	....	....	....	....	....	....
	Czechoslovakia	Olympics	8	3	2	5	....	....	....	12	....	....	....	....	....	....	....	....	....	....	....	....	....	....	....	....	....	....
	Czechoslovakia	WC-A	8	4	5	9	....	....	....	10	....	....	....	....	....	....	....	....	....	....	....	....	....	....	....	....	....	....
1992-93	Ottawa Senators	NHL	49	7	6	13	6	4	10	52	0	0	0	60	11.7	24	7	38	0	–21	....	....	....	....	....	....	....	....
1993-94	P.E.I. Senators	AHL	2	0	0	0	....	....	....	0	....	....	....	....	....	....	....	....	....	....	....	....	....	....	....	....	....	....
	ZSC Lions Zurich	Switz.	8	3	3	6	....	....	....	18	....	....	....	....	....	....	....	....	....	....	....	....	....	....	....	....	....	....
1994-95	Slavia Praha	Czech-Rep	41	11	17	28	....	....	....	....	....	....	....	....	....	....	....	....	....	....	3	0	0	0	0	....	....	....
1995-96	Skoda Plzen	Czech-Rep	37	19	25	44	....	....	....	....	....	....	....	....	....	....	....	....	....	....	3	1	3	4	....	....	....	....
1996-97	ZKZ Plzen	Czech-Rep	51	22	26	48	....	....	....	66	....	....	....	....	....	....	....	....	....	....	....	....	....	....	....	....	....	....
1997-98	Skoda Plzen	Czech-Rep	14	2	5	7	....	....	....	20	....	....	....	....	....	....	....	....	....	....	....	....	....	....	....	....	....	....
	HC Sparta Praha	Czech-Rep	37	10	13	23	....	....	....	114	....	....	....	....	....	....	....	....	....	....	10	0	5	5	38	....	....	....
1998-99	HC Vitkovice	Czech-Rep	19	4	6	10	....	....	....	34	....	....	....	....	....	....	....	....	....	....	....	....	....	....	....	....	....	....
	EV Weiden	Germany-2	14	10	16	26	....	....	....	34	....	....	....	....	....	....	....	....	....	....	....	....	....	....	....	....	....	....
	HC Sparta Praha	Czech-Rep	1	0	0	0	....	....	....	0	....	....	....	....	....	....	....	....	....	....	....	....	....	....	....	....	....	....
	HC Opava	Czech-Rep	7	1	0	1	....	....	....	8	....	....	....	....	....	....	....	....	....	....	....	....	....	....	....	....	....	....
99-2000	Calgary Flames	NHL	DID NOT PLAY – SCOUTING																									
	NHL Totals		49	7	6	13	6	4	10	52	0	0	0	60	11.7	24	7	38	0		....	....	....	....	....	....	....	....

• JENKINS, Dean

RW – R. 6', 190 lbs. b: Billerica, MA, 11/21/1959.

Season	Club	League	GP	G	A	Pts	AG	AA	APts	PIM	PP	SH	GW	S	%	TGF	PGF	TGA	PGA	+/-	GP	G	A	Pts	PIM	PP	SH	GW
1977-78	U. of Massachusetts-Lowell	ECAC	24	11	7	18	....	....	....	28	....	....	....	....	....	....	....	....	....	....	....	....	....	....	....	....	....	....
1978-79	U. of Massachusetts-Lowell	ECAC	33	16	37	53	....	....	....	75	....	....	....	....	....	....	....	....	....	....	....	....	....	....	....	....	....	....
1979-80	U. of Massachusetts-Lowell	ECAC	29	23	42	65	....	....	....	83	....	....	....	....	....	....	....	....	....	....	....	....	....	....	....	....	....	....
1980-81	U. of Massachusetts-Lowell	ECAC	31	23	32	55	....	....	....	83	....	....	....	....	....	....	....	....	....	....	....	....	....	....	....	....	....	....
1981-82	New Haven Nighthawks	AHL	78	13	22	35	....	....	....	147	....	....	....	....	....	....	....	....	....	....	....	....	....	....	....	....	....	....
1982-83	New Haven Nighthawks	AHL	80	29	43	72	....	....	....	50	....	....	....	....	....	....	....	....	....	....	12	6	2	8	40	....	....	....
1983-84	Los Angeles Kings	NHL	5	0	0	0	0	0	0	2	0	0	0	3	0.0	1	1	3	2	–1	....	....	....	....	....	....	....	....
	New Haven Nighthawks	AHL	64	24	26	50	....	....	....	131	....	....	....	....	....	....	....	....	....	....	....	....	....	....	....	....	....	....
1984-85	Hershey Bears	AHL	64	14	32	46	....	....	....	135	....	....	....	....	....	....	....	....	....	....	....	....	....	....	....	....	....	....
	NHL Totals		5	0	0	0	0	0	0	2	0	0	0	3	0.0	1	1	3	2		....	....	....	....	....	....	....	....

ECAC First All-Star Team (1980) • ECAC Second All-Star Team (1981)

Signed as a free agent by **LA Kings**, April 30, 1981. Signed as a free agent by **Boston**, October 10, 1984.

• JENNINGS, Grant

Grant Curtis D – L. 6'3", 210 lbs. b: Hudson Bay, Sask., 5/5/1965.

Season	Club	League	GP	G	A	Pts	AG	AA	APts	PIM	PP	SH	GW	S	%	TGF	PGF	TGA	PGA	+/-	GP	G	A	Pts	PIM	PP	SH	GW
1982-83	Humboldt Broncos	SJHL	60	4	22	26	....	....	....	199	....	....	....	....	....	....	....	....	....	....	....	....	....	....	....	....	....	....
1983-84	Saskatoon Blades	WHL	64	5	13	18	....	....	....	102	....	....	....	....	....	....	....	....	....	....	....	....	....	....	....	....	....	....
1984-85	Saskatoon Blades	WHL	46	10	24	34	....	....	....	134	....	....	....	....	....	....	....	....	....	....	2	1	0	1	2	....	....	....
1985-86	Binghamton Whalers	AHL	51	0	4	4	....	....	....	109	....	....	....	....	....	....	....	....	....	....	....	....	....	....	....	....	....	....
1986-87	Fort Wayne Komets	IHL	3	0	0	0	....	....	....	0	....	....	....	....	....	....	....	....	....	....	....	....	....	....	....	....	....	....
	Binghamton Whalers	AHL	47	1	5	6	....	....	....	125	....	....	....	....	....	....	....	....	....	....	13	0	2	2	17	....	....	....
1987-88	Binghamton Whalers	AHL	56	2	12	14	....	....	....	195	....	....	....	....	....	....	....	....	....	....	3	1	0	1	15	....	....	....
	Washington Capitals	NHL	....	....	....	....	....	....	....	....	....	....	....	....	....	....	....	....	....	....	1	0	0	0	0	0	0	0
1988-89	Hartford Whalers	NHL	55	3	10	13	3	7	10	159	0	0	0	39	7.7	50	1	51	19	17	4	1	0	1	17	1	0	0
	Binghamton Whalers	AHL	2	0	0	0	....	....	....	2	....	....	....	....	....	....	....	....	....	....	....	....	....	....	....	....	....	....
1989-90	Hartford Whalers	NHL	64	3	6	9	3	4	7	171	0	0	0	45	6.7	39	0	72	29	–4	7	0	0	0	13	0	0	0
1990-91	Hartford Whalers	NHL	44	1	4	5	1	3	4	82	0	0	0	28	3.6	17	0	46	16	–13	....	....	....	....	....	....	....	....
♦	Pittsburgh Penguins	NHL	13	1	3	4	1	2	3	26	0	0	0	8	12.5	10	0	10	2	2	13	1	1	2	16	0	0	0
1991-92♦	Pittsburgh Penguins	NHL	53	4	5	9	4	4	8	104	0	2	2	35	11.4	28	0	41	12	–1	10	0	0	0	12	0	0	0
1992-93	Pittsburgh Penguins	NHL	58	0	5	5	0	3	3	65	0	0	0	32	0.0	31	0	26	1	6	12	0	0	0	8	0	0	0
1993-94	Pittsburgh Penguins	NHL	61	2	4	6	2	3	5	126	0	1	1	49	4.1	25	0	44	9	–10	3	0	0	0	2	0	0	0
1994-95	Pittsburgh Penguins	NHL	25	0	4	4	0	6	6	36	0	0	0	16	0.0	20	0	28	10	2	....	....	....	....	....	....	....	....
	Toronto Maple Leafs	NHL	10	0	2	2	0	3	3	7	0	0	0	9	0.0	2	0	8	0	–6	4	0	0	0	0	0	0	0
1995-96	Buffalo Sabres	NHL	6	0	0	0	0	0	0	28	0	0	0	3	0.0	1	0	1	1	1	....	....	....	....	....	....	....	....
	Rochester Americans	AHL	9	0	1	1	....	....	....	28	....	....	....	....	....	....	....	....	....	....	....	....	....	....	....	....	....	....
	Atlanta Knights	IHL	3	0	0	0	....	....	....	19	....	....	....	....	....	....	....	....	....	....	3	0	0	0	20	....	....	....
1996-97	Quebec Rafales	IHL	42	2	10	12	....	....	....	79	....	....	....	....	....	....	....	....	....	....	....	....	....	....	....	....	....	....
1997-98	San Antonio Dragons	IHL	44	1	4	5	....	....	....	116	....	....	....	....	....	....	....	....	....	....	....	....	....	....	....	....	....	....
	NHL Totals		389	14	43	57	14	35	49	804	0	3	3	264	5.3	223	1	327	99		54	2	1	3	68	1	0	0

Signed as a free agent by **Washington**, June 25, 1985. Traded to **Hartford** by **Washington** with Ed Kastelic for Mike Millar and Neil Sheehy, July 6, 1988. Traded to **Pittsburgh** by **Hartford** with Ron Francis and Ulf Samuelsson for John Cullen, Jeff Parker and Zarley Zalapski, March 4, 1991. Traded to **Toronto** by **Pittsburgh** for Drake Berehowsky, April 7, 1995. Signed as a free agent by **Buffalo**, September 20, 1995.

• JENSEN, Chris

RW – R. 5'11", 180 lbs. b: Fort St. John, B.C., 10/28/1963. NY Rangers' 4th, 78th overall, in 1982.

Season	Club	League	GP	G	A	Pts	AG	AA	APts	PIM	PP	SH	GW	S	%	TGF	PGF	TGA	PGA	+/-	GP	G	A	Pts	PIM	PP	SH	GW
1980-81	Kelowna Buckaroos	BCJHL	50	48	43	91	....	....	....	66	....	....	....	....	....	....	....	....	....	....	3	3	2	5	6	....	....	....
1981-82	Kelowna Buckaroos	BCJHL	41	39	37	76	....	....	....	92	....	....	....	....	....	....	....	....	....	....	7	7	9	16	120	....	....	....
1982-83	University of North Dakota	WCHA	13	3	3	6	....	....	....	28	....	....	....	....	....	....	....	....	....	....	....	....	....	....	....	....	....	....
1983-84	University of North Dakota	WCHA	44	24	25	49	....	....	....	100	....	....	....	....	....	....	....	....	....	....	....	....	....	....	....	....	....	....
1984-85	University of North Dakota	WCHA	40	25	27	52	....	....	....	80	....	....	....	....	....	....	....	....	....	....	....	....	....	....	....	....	....	....

Season	Club	League	GP	G	A	Pts	AG	AA	APts	PIM	PP	SH	GW	S	%	TGF	PGF	TGA	PGA	+/–	GP	G	A	Pts	PIM	PP	SH	GW
			REGULAR SEASON																		PLAYOFFS							
1985-86	University of North Dakota	WCHA	34	25	40	65				53																		
	New York Rangers	**NHL**	**9**	**1**	**3**	**4**	**1**	**2**	**3**	**0**	**0**	**0**	**1**	**18**	**5.6**	**6**	**3**	**2**	**0**	**1**								
1986-87	**New York Rangers**	**NHL**	**37**	**6**	**7**	**13**	**5**	**5**	**10**	**21**	**0**	**1**	**2**	**70**	**8.6**	**23**	**2**	**22**	**0**	**–1**								
	New Haven Nighthawks	AHL	14	4	9	13				41																		
1987-88	**New York Rangers**	**NHL**	**7**	**0**	**1**	**1**	**0**	**1**	**1**	**2**	**0**	**0**	**0**	**11**	**0.0**	**2**	**0**	**3**	**0**	**–1**								
	Colorado Rangers	IHL	43	10	23	33				68											10	3	7	10	8			
1988-89	Hershey Bears	AHL	45	27	31	58				66											10	4	5	9	29			
1989-90	**Philadelphia Flyers**	**NHL**	**1**	**0**	**0**	**0**	**0**	**0**	**0**	**2**	**0**	**0**	**0**	**0**	**0.0**	**0**	**0**	**1**	**0**	**–1**								
	Hershey Bears	AHL	43	16	26	42				101																		
1990-91	**Philadelphia Flyers**	**NHL**	**18**	**2**	**1**	**3**	**2**	**1**	**3**	**2**	**0**	**0**	**0**	**22**	**9.1**	**7**	**1**	**11**	**0**	**–5**								
	Hershey Bears	AHL	50	26	20	46				83											6	2	2	4	10			
1991-92	**Philadelphia Flyers**	**NHL**	**2**	**0**	**0**	**0**	**0**	**0**	**0**	**0**	**0**	**0**	**0**	**2**	**0.0**	**0**	**0**	**1**	**0**	**–1**								
	Hershey Bears	AHL	71	38	33	71				134											6	0	1	1	2			
1992-93	Hershey Bears	AHL	74	33	47	80				95																		
1993-94	Portland Pirates	AHL	56	33	28	61				52											16	6	10	16	22			
1994-95	Portland Pirates	AHL	67	35	42	77				89											7	4	3	7	0			
1995-96	Minnesota Moose	IHL	52	25	19	44				109																		
	Michigan K-Wings	IHL	13	5	5	10				7											6	0	2	2	6			
1996-97	Manitoba Moose	IHL	16	6	4	10				23																		
	Long Beach Ice Dogs	IHL	16	3	5	8				10											18	2	2	4	28			
1997-98	Wheeling Nailers	ECHL	39	14	14	28				120											15	8	4	12	26			
1998-99	Wheeling Nailers	ECHL	DID NOT PLAY – COACHING																									
	NHL Totals		**74**	**9**	**12**	**21**	**8**	**9**	**17**	**27**	**0**	**1**	**3**	**123**	**7.3**	**38**	**6**	**40**	**0**									

Traded to **Philadelphia** by **NY Rangers** for Michael Boyce, September 28, 1988.

• JENSEN, David

David Henry D – L. 6'1", 185 lbs. b: Minneapolis, MN, 5/3/1961. Minnesota's 5th, 100th overall, in 1980.

Season	Club	League	GP	G	A	Pts	AG	AA	APts	PIM	PP	SH	GW	S	%	TGF	PGF	TGA	PGA	+/–	GP	G	A	Pts	PIM	PP	SH	GW
1978-79	Armstrong High School	Hi-School	STATISTICS NOT AVAILABLE																									
1979-80	University of Minnesota	WCHA	33	0	5	5				32																		
	United States	WJC-A	5	0	3	3				4																		
1980-81	University of Minnesota	WCHA	35	0	13	13				64																		
	United States	WJC-A	5	0	0	0				4																		
1981-82	University of Minnesota	WCHA	32	3	13	16				68																		
1982-83	University of Minnesota	WCHA	25	4	14	18				38																		
	Birmingham South Stars	CHL																			2	0	0	0	0			
1983-84	United States	Nat-Team	47	3	15	18				38																		
	Minnesota North Stars	**NHL**	**8**	**0**	**1**	**1**	**0**	**1**	**1**	**0**	**0**	**0**	**0**	**5**	**0.0**	**6**	**0**	**5**	**1**	**2**								
	Salt Lake Golden Eagles	CHL	13	0	7	7				6											5	0	1	1	5			
1984-85	**Minnesota North Stars**	**NHL**	**5**	**0**	**1**	**1**	**0**	**1**	**1**	**4**	**0**	**0**	**0**	**3**	**0.0**	**2**	**0**	**8**	**1**	**–5**								
	Springfield Indians	AHL	69	13	27	40				63											4	0	1	1	0			
1985-86	**Minnesota North Stars**	**NHL**	**5**	**0**	**0**	**0**	**0**	**0**	**0**	**7**	**0**	**0**	**0**	**1**	**0.0**	**1**	**0**	**3**	**0**	**–2**								
	United States	WC-A	10	1	0	1				12																		
	Springfield Indians	AHL	40	4	18	22				31																		
1986-87	HC Ritten	Italy	40	21	38	59				53																		
1987-88	ASG Tours	France	30	7	19	26				46																		
1988-89	HC Renon	Italy-2	29	20	35	55				22																		
	NHL Totals		**18**	**0**	**2**	**2**	**0**	**2**	**2**	**11**	**0**	**0**	**0**	**9**	**0.0**	**9**	**0**	**16**	**2**									

• JENSEN, David

David Allan C – L. 6'1", 195 lbs. b: Newton, MA, 8/19/1965. Hartford's 2nd, 20th overall, in 1983.

Season	Club	League	GP	G	A	Pts	AG	AA	APts	PIM	PP	SH	GW	S	%	TGF	PGF	TGA	PGA	+/–	GP	G	A	Pts	PIM	PP	SH	GW
1980-1982	Belmont Hill Hillies	Hi-School	STATISTICS NOT AVAILABLE																									
1982-83	Lawrence Academy	Hi-School	25	41	48	89																						
1983-84	United States	Nat-Team	61	22	56	78				6																		
	United States	Olympics	6	2	7	9				6																		
1984-85	United States	Can-Cup	6	2	1	3				2																		
	Hartford Whalers	**NHL**	**13**	**0**	**4**	**4**	**0**	**3**	**3**	**6**	**0**	**0**	**0**	**11**	**0.0**	**6**	**0**	**7**	**0**	**–1**								
	Binghamton Whalers	AHL	40	8	9	17				2																		
1985-86	**Washington Capitals**	**NHL**	**5**	**1**	**0**	**1**	**1**	**0**	**1**	**0**	**0**	**0**	**0**	**5**	**20.0**	**2**	**0**	**1**	**0**	**1**	**4**	**0**	**0**	**0**	**0**	**0**	**0**	**0**
	Binghamton Whalers	AHL	41	17	14	31				4											4	2	4	6	0			
1986-87	**Washington Capitals**	**NHL**	**46**	**8**	**8**	**16**	**7**	**6**	**13**	**12**	**2**	**0**	**0**	**49**	**16.3**	**21**	**5**	**26**	**0**	**–10**	**7**	**0**	**0**	**0**	**2**	**0**	**0**	**0**
	Binghamton Whalers	AHL	6	2	5	7				0																		
1987-88	**Washington Capitals**	**NHL**	**5**	**0**	**1**	**1**	**0**	**1**	**1**	**4**	**0**	**0**	**0**	**1**	**0.0**	**1**	**0**	**1**	**0**	**0**								
	Binghamton Whalers	AHL	9	5	2	7				2																		
	Fort Wayne Komets	IHL	32	10	13	23				8											5	1	1	2	0			
1988-89	Maine Mariners	AHL	18	12	8	20				2																		
1989-90	Maine Mariners	AHL	4	0	2	2				0																		
1990-91	Maine Mariners	AHL	15	2	5	7				0																		
	SC Cortina	Italy	35	27	18	45				8											6	7	7	14	4			
1991-92	Maine Mariners	AHL	15	2	5	7				0																		
	NHL Totals		**69**	**9**	**13**	**22**	**8**	**10**	**18**	**22**	**2**	**0**	**0**	**66**	**13.6**	**30**	**5**	**35**	**0**		**11**	**0**	**0**	**0**	**2**	**0**	**0**	**0**

Traded to **Washington** by **Hartford** for Dean Evason and Peter Sidorkiewicz, March 12, 1985. Signed as a free agent by **Boston**, August 1, 1988.

• JENSEN, Steve

Steven Allan LW – L. 6'2", 190 lbs. b: Minneapolis, MN, 4/14/1955. Minnesota's 4th, 58th overall, in 1975.

Season	Club	League	GP	G	A	Pts	AG	AA	APts	PIM	PP	SH	GW	S	%	TGF	PGF	TGA	PGA	+/–	GP	G	A	Pts	PIM	PP	SH	GW
1973-74	Michigan Tech Huskies	WCHA	40	17	9	26				32																		
1974-75	Michigan Tech Huskies	WCHA	41	16	32	48				18																		
	United States	Nat-Team	17	4	1	5																						
	United States	WEC-A	9	2	0	2				2																		
1975-76	United States	Nat-Team	64	52	44	96				42																		
	United States	Olympics	6	6	0	6				6																		
	United States	WEC-A	7	4	5	9				8																		
	Minnesota North Stars	**NHL**	**19**	**7**	**6**	**13**	**6**	**4**	**10**	**6**	**1**	**0**	**1**	**49**	**14.3**	**20**	**4**	**23**	**2**	**–5**								
1976-77	United States	Can-Cup	5	1	0	1				2																		
	Minnesota North Stars	**NHL**	**78**	**22**	**23**	**45**	**20**	**18**	**38**	**62**	**4**	**2**	**1**	**160**	**13.8**	**72**	**11**	**81**	**14**	**–6**	**2**	**0**	**1**	**1**	**0**	**0**	**0**	**0**
1977-78	**Minnesota North Stars**	**NHL**	**74**	**13**	**17**	**30**	**12**	**13**	**25**	**73**	**2**	**0**	**1**	**132**	**9.8**	**47**	**5**	**80**	**8**	**–30**								
	Fort Worth Texans	CHL	3	0	1	1				2																		
	United States	WEC-A	10	3	0	3				2																		
1978-79	**Los Angeles Kings**	**NHL**	**72**	**23**	**8**	**31**	**20**	**6**	**26**	**57**	**2**	**0**	**4**	**114**	**20.2**	**40**	**5**	**64**	**1**	**–28**	**2**	**0**	**0**	**0**	**0**	**0**	**0**	**0**
	United States	WEC-A	DID NOT PLAY																									
1979-80	**Los Angeles Kings**	**NHL**	**76**	**21**	**15**	**36**	**18**	**11**	**29**	**13**	**4**	**2**	**2**	**149**	**14.1**	**58**	**16**	**90**	**9**	**–39**	**4**	**0**	**0**	**0**	**2**	**0**	**0**	**0**
1980-81	**Los Angeles Kings**	**NHL**	**74**	**19**	**19**	**38**	**15**	**13**	**28**	**88**	**5**	**1**	**4**	**118**	**16.1**	**57**	**9**	**69**	**15**	**–6**	**4**	**0**	**2**	**2**	**7**	**0**	**0**	**0**
1981-82	**Los Angeles Kings**	**NHL**	**45**	**8**	**19**	**27**	**6**	**13**	**19**	**19**	**1**	**0**	**1**	**78**	**10.3**	**41**	**6**	**69**	**20**	**–14**								
	New Haven Nighthawks	AHL	14	5	8	13				4											1	0	0	0	0			
1982-83			STATISTICS NOT AVAILABLE																									
1983-84	EV Zug	Switz-2	STATISTICS NOT AVAILABLE																									
1984-85	EV Zug	Switz-2	36	38	19	57																						
1985-86	Springfield Indians	AHL	4	3	3	6				2																		
	NHL Totals		**438**	**113**	**107**	**220**	**97**	**78**	**175**	**318**	**19**	**5**	**14**	**800**	**14.1**	**335**	**56**	**476**	**69**		**12**	**0**	**3**	**3**	**9**	**0**	**0**	**0**

NCAA Championship All-Tournament Team (1974, 1975)

Transferred to **LA Kings** by **Minnesota** with Dave Gardner and Rick Hampton as compensation for Minnesota's signing of Gary Sargent, July 15, 1978.

• JERRARD, Paul
Paul C. D – R. 5'10", 185 lbs. b: Winnipeg, Man., 4/20/1965. NY Rangers' 10th, 180th overall, in 1983.

			REGULAR SEASON																		PLAYOFFS							
Season	Club	League	GP	G	A	Pts	AG	AA	APts	PIM	PP	SH	GW	S	%	TGF	PGF	TGA	PGA	+/–	GP	G	A	Pts	PIM	PP	SH	GW
1982-83	Notre Dame Hounds	Hi-School	60	34	37	71	....	....	....	150	....	....	....	....	....	....	....	....	....	....	....	....	....	....	....	....	....	....
1983-84	Lake Superior State	CCHA	40	8	18	26	....	....	....	48	....	....	....	....	....	....	....	....	....	....	....	....	....	....	....	....	....	....
1984-85	Lake Superior State	CCHA	43	9	25	34	....	....	....	61	....	....	....	....	....	....	....	....	....	....	....	....	....	....	....	....	....	....
1985-86	Lake Superior State	CCHA	40	13	11	24	....	....	....	34	....	....	....	....	....	....	....	....	....	....	....	....	....	....	....	....	....	....
1986-87	Lake Superior State	CCHA	35	10	19	29	....	....	....	56	....	....	....	....	....	....	....	....	....	....	....	....	....	....	....	....	....	....
1987-88	Colorado Rangers	IHL	77	20	28	48	....	....	....	182	....	....	....	....	....	....	....	....	....	....	11	2	4	6	40	....	....	....
1988-89	Denver Rangers	IHL	2	1	1	2	....	....	....	21	....	....	....	....	....	....	....	....	....	....	....	....	....	....	....	....	....	....
	Minnesota North Stars	**NHL**	**5**	**0**	**0**	**0**	**0**	**0**	**0**	**4**	**0**	**0**	**0**	**8**	**0.0**	**1**	**0**	**0**	**0**	**1**	....	....	....	....	....	....	....	....
	Kalamazoo Wings	IHL	68	15	25	40	....	....	....	195	....	....	....	....	....	....	....	....	....	....	6	2	1	3	37	....	....	....
1989-90	Kalamazoo Wings	IHL	60	9	18	27	....	....	....	134	....	....	....	....	....	....	....	....	....	....	7	1	1	2	11	....	....	....
1990-91	Albany Choppers	IHL	7	0	3	3	....	....	....	30	....	....	....	....	....	....	....	....	....	....	....	....	....	....	....	....	....	....
	Kalamazoo Wings	IHL	62	10	23	33	....	....	....	111	....	....	....	....	....	....	....	....	....	....	7	0	0	0	13	....	....	....
1991-92	Kalamazoo Wings	IHL	76	4	24	28	....	....	....	123	....	....	....	....	....	....	....	....	....	....	12	1	7	8	31	....	....	....
1992-93	Kalamazoo Wings	IHL	80	8	11	19	....	....	....	187	....	....	....	....	....	....	....	....	....	....	....	....	....	....	....	....	....	....
1993-94	Kalamazoo Wings	IHL	24	0	2	2	....	....	....	60	....	....	....	....	....	....	....	....	....	....	....	....	....	....	....	....	....	....
	Milwaukee Admirals	IHL	28	6	3	9	....	....	....	58	....	....	....	....	....	....	....	....	....	....	2	0	0	0	8	....	....	....
1994-95	Hershey Bears	AHL	66	17	11	28	....	....	....	118	....	....	....	....	....	....	....	....	....	....	6	0	1	....	18	....	....	....
1995-96	Hershey Bears	AHL	25	1	7	8	....	....	....	63	....	....	....	....	....	....	....	....	....	....	....	....	....	....	....	....	....	....
	Fort Wayne Komets	IHL	19	0	1	1	....	....	....	43	....	....	....	....	....	....	....	....	....	....	4	0	0	0	2	....	....	....
1996-97	Hershey Bears	AHL	62	3	13	16	....	....	....	144	....	....	....	....	....	....	....	....	....	....	22	1	5	6	24	....	....	....
1997-1998	Lake Superior State	CCHA	DID NOT PLAY – ASSISTANT COACH																									
1998-1999	Lowell Lockmonsters	AHL	DID NOT PLAY – ASSISTANT COACH																									
1999-2000	Lake Superior State	CCHA	DID NOT PLAY – ASSISTANT COACH																									
	NHL Totals		**5**	**0**	**0**	**0**	**0**	**0**	**0**	**4**	**0**	**0**	**0**	**8**	**0.0**	**1**	**0**	**0**	**0**		....	....	....	....	....	....	....	....

Traded to **Minnesota** by **NY Rangers** with Mark Tinordi, the rights to Bret Barnett and Mike Sullivan and LA Kings' 3rd round choice (previously acquired, Minnesota selected Murray Garbutt) in 1989 Entry Draft for Brian Lawton, Igor Liba and the rights to Rick Bennett, October 11, 1988.

• JIRIK, Jaroslav
LW – L. 5'11", 170 lbs. b: Vojnuv Mestec, Czech., 12/10/1939.

Season	Club	League	GP	G	A	Pts	AG	AA	APts	PIM	PP	SH	GW	S	%	TGF	PGF	TGA	PGA	+/–	GP	G	A	Pts	PIM	PP	SH	GW
1951-1957	SONP Kladno	Czech-Jr.	STATISTICS NOT AVAILABLE																									
1957-58	SONP Kladno	Czech.	STATISTICS NOT AVAILABLE																									
1958-59	SONP Kladno	Czech.	22	16	....	16	....	....	....	....	....	....	....	....	....	....	....	....	....	....	....	....	....	....	....	....	....	....
	Czechoslovakia	WC-A	8	6	2	8	....	....	....	....	....	....	....	....	....	....	....	....	....	....	....	....	....	....	....	....	....	....
1959-60	SONP Kladno	Czech.	STATISTICS NOT AVAILABLE																									
	Czechoslovakia	Olympics	5	1	3	4	....	....	....	2	....	....	....	....	....	....	....	....	....	....	....	....	....	....	....	....	....	....
1960-61	SONP Kladno	Czech.	STATISTICS NOT AVAILABLE																									
1961-62	RH Brno	Czech.	32	28	....	28	....	....	....	....	....	....	....	....	....	....	....	....	....	....	....	....	....	....	....	....	....	....
1962-63	ZKL Brno	Czech.	32	23	....	23	....	....	....	....	....	....	....	....	....	....	....	....	....	....	....	....	....	....	....	....	....	....
	Czechoslovakia	WEC-A	7	4	3	7	....	....	....	9	....	....	....	....	....	....	....	....	....	....	....	....	....	....	....	....	....	....
1963-64	ZKL Brno	Czech.	STATISTICS NOT AVAILABLE																									
	Czechoslovakia	Olympics	7	3	1	4	....	....	....	6	....	....	....	....	....	....	....	....	....	....	....	....	....	....	....	....	....	....
1964-65	ZKL Brno	Czech.	32	23	....	23	....	....	....	....	....	....	....	....	....	....	....	....	....	....	....	....	....	....	....	....	....	....
	Czechoslovakia	WEC-A	7	8	4	12	....	....	....	5	....	....	....	....	....	....	....	....	....	....	....	....	....	....	....	....	....	....
1965-66	ZKL Brno	Czech.	STATISTICS NOT AVAILABLE																									
	Czechoslovakia	WEC-A	7	4	1	5	....	....	....	2	....	....	....	....	....	....	....	....	....	....	....	....	....	....	....	....	....	....
1966-67	ZKL Brno	Czech.	STATISTICS NOT AVAILABLE																									
	Czechoslovakia	WEC-A	6	5	3	8	....	....	....	2	....	....	....	....	....	....	....	....	....	....	....	....	....	....	....	....	....	....
1967-68	ZKL Brno	Czech.	32	25	12	37	....	....	....	....	....	....	....	....	....	....	....	....	....	....	....	....	....	....	....	....	....	....
	Czechoslovakia	Olympics	4	3	3	6	....	....	....	0	....	....	....	....	....	....	....	....	....	....	....	....	....	....	....	....	....	....
1968-69	ZKL Brno	Czech.	36	*36	7	43	....	....	....	....	....	....	....	....	....	....	....	....	....	....	....	....	....	....	....	....	....	....
	Czechoslovakia	WEC-A	5	2	3	5	....	....	....	0	....	....	....	....	....	....	....	....	....	....	....	....	....	....	....	....	....	....
1969-70	**St. Louis Blues**	**NHL**	**3**	**0**	**0**	**0**	**0**	**0**	**0**	**0**	**0**	**0**	**0**	**4**	**0.0**	**1**	**0**	**0**	**0**	**1**	....	....	....	....	....	....	....	....
	Kansas City Blues	CHL	53	19	16	35	....	....	....	11	....	....	....	....	....	....	....	....	....	....	....	....	....	....	....	....	....	....
1970-71	ZKL Brno	Czech.	36	26	12	38	....	....	....	....	....	....	....	....	....	....	....	....	....	....	....	....	....	....	....	....	....	....
1971-72	ZKL Brno	Czech.	STATISTICS NOT AVAILABLE																									
1972-73	ZKL Brno	Czech.	STATISTICS NOT AVAILABLE																									
1973-74	ZKL Brno	Czech.	....	8	7	15	....	....	....	....	....	....	....	....	....	....	....	....	....	....	....	....	....	....	....	....	....	....
1974-75	ZKL Brno	Czech.	STATISTICS NOT AVAILABLE																									
	NHL Totals		**3**	**0**	**0**	**0**	**0**	**0**	**0**	**0**	**0**	**0**	**0**	**4**	**0.0**	**1**	**0**	**0**	**0**		....	....	....	....	....	....	....	....

WEC-A All-Star Team (1965)

Signed as a free agent by **St. Louis**,September 11, 1969. • First player from Iron Curtain country to play in NHL. • Played 17 seasons in Czechoslovakian Premier League (13 w/ Brno and 4 w/ Kladno) scoring a total of 300 goals in 450 games. • Only goals and games played totals available for 1958-59; 1961-62; 1962-63 and 1964-65 seasons.

• JODZIO, Rick
Richard Joseph LW – L. 6'1", 190 lbs. b: Edmonton, Alta., 6/3/1954. Buffalo's 9th, 153rd overall, in 1974.

Season	Club	League	GP	G	A	Pts	AG	AA	APts	PIM	PP	SH	GW	S	%	TGF	PGF	TGA	PGA	+/–	GP	G	A	Pts	PIM	PP	SH	GW
1972-73	Downsview Beavers	OHA-B	STATISTICS NOT AVAILABLE																									
1973-74	Downsview Beavers	OHA-B	30	7	12	19	....	....	....	166	....	....	....	....	....	....	....	....	....	....	....	....	....	....	....	....	....	....
	Hamilton Red Wings	OMJHL	30	1	8	9	....	....	....	86	....	....	....	....	....	....	....	....	....	....	....	....	....	....	....	....	....	....
1974-75	Vancouver Blazers	WHA	44	1	3	4	....	....	....	59	....	....	....	....	....	....	....	....	....	....	....	....	....	....	....	....	....	....
	Charlotte Checkers	SHL	37	9	8	17	....	....	....	109	....	....	....	....	....	....	....	....	....	....	1	0	2	2	0	....	....	....
1975-76	Calgary Cowboys	WHA	47	10	7	17	....	....	....	137	....	....	....	....	....	....	....	....	....	....	2	0	0	0	14	....	....	....
	Springfield Indians	AHL	24	2	3	5	....	....	....	37	....	....	....	....	....	....	....	....	....	....	....	....	....	....	....	....	....	....
1976-77	Calgary Cowboys	WHA	46	4	6	10	....	....	....	61	....	....	....	....	....	....	....	....	....	....	....	....	....	....	....	....	....	....
	Tidewater Sharks	SHL	7	3	3	6	....	....	....	4	....	....	....	....	....	....	....	....	....	....	....	....	....	....	....	....	....	....
	Erie Blades	NAHL	15	5	5	10	....	....	....	32	....	....	....	....	....	....	....	....	....	....	9	2	7	9	21	....	....	....
1977-78	**Colorado Rockies**	**NHL**	**32**	**0**	**5**	**5**	**0**	**4**	**4**	**28**	**0**	**0**	**0**	**25**	**0.0**	**14**	**1**	**18**	**0**	**–5**	....	....	....	....	....	....	....	....
	Cleveland Barons	**NHL**	**38**	**2**	**3**	**5**	**2**	**2**	**4**	**43**	**0**	**0**	**1**	**23**	**8.7**	**9**	**0**	**18**	**0**	**–9**	....	....	....	....	....	....	....	....
1978-79	Oklahoma City Stars	CHL	62	4	21	25	....	....	....	117	....	....	....	....	....	....	....	....	....	....	....	....	....	....	....	....	....	....
1979-80	New Brunswick Hawks	AHL	79	13	25	38	....	....	....	113	....	....	....	....	....	....	....	....	....	....	17	2	4	6	43	....	....	....
	NHL Totals		**70**	**2**	**8**	**10**	**2**	**6**	**8**	**71**	**0**	**0**	**1**	**48**	**4.2**	**23**	**1**	**36**	**0**		....	....	....	....	....	....	....	....
	Other Major League Totals		137	15	16	31	....	....	....	257	....	....	....	....	....	....	....	....	....	....	2	0	0	0	14	....	....	....

Signed as a free agent by **Vancouver** (WHA), January, 1975. • Suspended for remainder of 1975-76 season by WHA for intentionally injuring Marc Tardif in playoff game, April 11, 1976. Traded to **Colorado** by **Buffalo** for cash, September 22, 1977. Traded to **Cleveland** by **Colorado** with Chuck Arnason for Ralph Klassen and Fred Ahern, January 9, 1978. Placed on Reserve List by **Minnesota** after **Cleveland-Minnesota** Dispersal Draft, June 15, 1978.

• JOHANNESEN, Glenn
LW – R. 6'2", 220 lbs. b: Lac La Ronge, Sask., 2/15/1962. NY Islanders' 11th, 206th overall, in 1980.

Season	Club	League	GP	G	A	Pts	AG	AA	APts	PIM	PP	SH	GW	S	%	TGF	PGF	TGA	PGA	+/–	GP	G	A	Pts	PIM	PP	SH	GW
1979-80	Red Deer Rustlers	AJHL	STATISTICS NOT AVAILABLE																									
1980-81	Western Michigan University	CCHA	35	2	18	20	....	....	....	65	....	....	....	....	....	....	....	....	....	....	....	....	....	....	....	....	....	....
1981-82	Western Michigan University	CCHA	33	3	10	13	....	....	....	37	....	....	....	....	....	....	....	....	....	....	....	....	....	....	....	....	....	....
1982-83	Western Michigan University	CCHA	32	1	9	10	....	....	....	36	....	....	....	....	....	....	....	....	....	....	....	....	....	....	....	....	....	....
1983-84	Western Michigan University	CCHA	41	4	16	20	....	....	....	80	....	....	....	....	....	....	....	....	....	....	....	....	....	....	....	....	....	....
	Kalamazoo Wings	IHL	3	0	0	0	....	....	....	0	....	....	....	....	....	....	....	....	....	....	....	....	....	....	....	....	....	....
1984-85	Indianapolis Checkers	IHL	51	10	19	29	....	....	....	130	....	....	....	....	....	....	....	....	....	....	....	....	....	....	....	....	....	....
	Springfield Indians	AHL	21	1	3	4	....	....	....	59	....	....	....	....	....	....	....	....	....	....	....	....	....	....	....	....	....	....
1985-86	**New York Islanders**	**NHL**	**2**	**0**	**0**	**0**	**0**	**0**	**0**	**0**	**0**	**0**	**0**	**2**	**0.0**	**0**	**0**	**1**	**0**	**–1**	....	....	....	....	....	....	....	....
	Springfield Indians	AHL	78	8	21	29	....	....	....	187	....	....	....	....	....	....	....	....	....	....	....	....	....	....	....	....	....	....
1986-87	Springfield Indians	AHL	54	10	6	16	....	....	....	156	....	....	....	....	....	....	....	....	....	....	....	....	....	....	....	....	....	....

Season	Club	League	REGULAR SEASON																		PLAYOFFS							
			GP	G	A	Pts	AG	AA	APts	PIM	PP	SH	GW	S	%	TGF	PGF	TGA	PGA	+/–	GP	G	A	Pts	PIM	PP	SH	GW
1987-88	Springfield Indians	AHL	1	0	0	0	....	....	....	0	....	....	....	....	....	....	....	....	....	....	....	....	....	....	....	....	....	....
	Peoria Rivermen	IHL	73	24	29	53	....	....	....	172	....	....	....	....	....	....	....	....	....	....	7	4	3	7	32	....	....	....
1988-89	Springfield Indians	AHL	5	1	1	2	....	....	....	20	....	....	....	....	....	....	....	....	....	....	....	....	....	....	....	....	....	....
	Indianapolis Ice	IHL	76	18	23	41	....	....	....	235	....	....	....	....	....	....	....	....	....	....	....	....	....	....	....	....	....	....
	NHL Totals		**2**	**0**	**0**	**0**	**0**	**0**	**0**	**0**	**0**	**0**	**0**	**2**	**0.0**	**0**	**0**	**1**	**0**		....	....	....	....	....	....	....	....

• JOHANNSON, John

C – L. 6'1", 175 lbs. b: Rochester, MN, 10/18/1961. Colorado's 10th, 192nd overall, in 1981.

Season	Club	League	GP	G	A	Pts	AG	AA	APts	PIM	PP	SH	GW	S	%	TGF	PGF	TGA	PGA	+/–	GP	G	A	Pts	PIM	PP	SH	GW
1980-81	University of Wisconsin	WCHA	38	6	12	18	....	....	....	32	....	....	....	....	....	....	....	....	....	....	....	....	....	....	....	....	....	....
	United States	WJC-A	4	3	0	3	....	....	....	0	....	....	....	....	....	....	....	....	....	....	....	....	....	....	....	....	....	....
1981-82	University of Wisconsin	WCHA	47	15	34	49	....	....	....	46	....	....	....	....	....	....	....	....	....	....	....	....	....	....	....	....	....	....
1982-83	University of Wisconsin	WCHA	47	22	41	63	....	....	....	68	....	....	....	....	....	....	....	....	....	....	10	6	11	17	....	....	....	....
1983-84	University of Wisconsin	WCHA	39	21	25	46	....	....	....	32	....	....	....	....	....	....	....	....	....	....	....	....	....	....	....	....	....	....
	New Jersey Devils	**NHL**	**5**	**0**	**0**	**0**	**0**	**0**	**0**	**0**	**0**	**0**	**0**	**4**	**0.0**	**0**	**0**	**2**	**0**	**–2**	....	....	....	....	....	....	....	....
1984-85	WEV Wien	Austria	23	41	43	84	....	....	....	34	....	....	....	....	....	....	....	....	....	....	....	....	....	....	....	....	....	....
	NHL Totals		**5**	**0**	**0**	**0**	**0**	**0**	**0**	**0**	**0**	**0**	**0**	**4**	**0.0**	**0**	**0**	**2**	**0**		....	....	....	....	....	....	....	....

Rights transferred to **New Jersey** after **Colorado** franchise relocated, June 30, 1982.

• JOHANSEN, Trevor

Trevor Daniel D – R. 5'9", 200 lbs. b: Thunder Bay, Ont., 3/30/1957. Toronto's 2nd, 12th overall, in 1977.

Season	Club	League	GP	G	A	Pts	AG	AA	APts	PIM	PP	SH	GW	S	%	TGF	PGF	TGA	PGA	+/–	GP	G	A	Pts	PIM	PP	SH	GW
1973-74	Thunder Bay Hurricanes	MWJHL	59	13	31	44	....	....	....	137	....	....	....	....	....	....	....	....	....	....	....	....	....	....	....	....	....	....
1974-75	Toronto Marlboros	OMJHL	50	9	30	39	....	....	....	175	....	....	....	....	....	....	....	....	....	....	22	2	8	10	48	....	....	....
	Toronto Marlboros	Mem-Cup	4	0	2	2	....	....	....	4	....	....	....	....	....	....	....	....	....	....	....	....	....	....	....	....	....	....
1975-76	Toronto Marlboros	OMJHL	61	5	25	30	....	....	....	141	....	....	....	....	....	....	....	....	....	....	1	0	0	0	0	....	....	....
1976-77	Toronto Marlboros	OMJHL	61	2	34	36	....	....	....	177	....	....	....	....	....	....	....	....	....	....	....	....	....	....	....	....	....	....
	Canada	WJC-A	5	0	0	0	....	....	....	5	....	....	....	....	....	....	....	....	....	....	....	....	....	....	....	....	....	....
1977-78	**Toronto Maple Leafs**	**NHL**	**79**	**2**	**14**	**16**	**2**	**11**	**13**	**82**	**0**	**0**	**0**	**82**	**2.4**	**86**	**0**	**96**	**13**	**3**	**13**	**0**	**3**	**3**	**21**	**0**	**0**	**0**
1978-79	**Toronto Maple Leafs**	**NHL**	**40**	**1**	**4**	**5**	**1**	**3**	**4**	**48**	**0**	**0**	**0**	**31**	**3.2**	**31**	**2**	**37**	**9**	**1**	....	....	....	....	....	....	....	....
	New Brunswick Hawks	AHL	24	1	7	8	....	....	....	49	....	....	....	....	....	....	....	....	....	....	....	....	....	....	....	....	....	....
	Colorado Rockies	**NHL**	**11**	**1**	**3**	**4**	**1**	**2**	**3**	**16**	**0**	**0**	**0**	**14**	**7.1**	**5**	**0**	**14**	**1**	**–8**	....	....	....	....	....	....	....	....
	Canada	WEC-A	8	2	1	3	....	....	....	4	....	....	....	....	....	....	....	....	....	....	....	....	....	....	....	....	....	....
1979-80	**Colorado Rockies**	**NHL**	**62**	**3**	**8**	**11**	**3**	**6**	**9**	**45**	**1**	**0**	**0**	**43**	**7.0**	**47**	**1**	**80**	**17**	**–17**	....	....	....	....	....	....	....	....
1980-81	**Colorado Rockies**	**NHL**	**35**	**0**	**7**	**7**	**0**	**5**	**5**	**18**	**0**	**0**	**0**	**33**	**0.0**	**28**	**1**	**61**	**14**	**–20**	....	....	....	....	....	....	....	....
1981-82	**Los Angeles Kings**	**NHL**	**46**	**3**	**7**	**10**	**2**	**5**	**7**	**69**	**0**	**0**	**0**	**40**	**7.5**	**38**	**1**	**68**	**17**	**–14**	....	....	....	....	....	....	....	....
	Toronto Maple Leafs	**NHL**	**13**	**1**	**3**	**4**	**1**	**2**	**3**	**4**	**0**	**0**	**0**	**14**	**7.1**	**9**	**0**	**34**	**9**	**–16**	....	....	....	....	....	....	....	....
1982-83	Springfield Indians	AHL	6	0	0	0	....	....	....	16	....	....	....	....	....	....	....	....	....	....	....	....	....	....	....	....	....	....
	NHL Totals		**286**	**11**	**46**	**57**	**10**	**34**	**44**	**282**	**1**	**0**	**0**	**257**	**4.3**	**244**	**5**	**390**	**80**		**13**	**0**	**3**	**3**	**21**	**0**	**0**	**0**

• Son of Bill • OMJHL First All-Star Team (1977)

Traded to **Colorado** by **Toronto** with Don Ashby for Paul Gardner, March 13, 1979. Claimed by **LA Kings** from **Colorado** in Waiver Draft, October 5, 1981. Claimed on waivers by **Toronto** from **LA Kings**, February 19, 1982.

• JOHANSSON, Andreas

C – L. 6', 202 lbs. b: Hofors, Sweden, 5/19/1973. NY Islanders' 7th, 136th overall, in 1991.

Season	Club	League	GP	G	A	Pts	AG	AA	APts	PIM	PP	SH	GW	S	%	TGF	PGF	TGA	PGA	+/–	GP	G	A	Pts	PIM	PP	SH	GW
1987-88	Hofors HC	Sweden-3	1	0	0	0	....	....	....	0	....	....	....	....	....	....	....	....	....	....	....	....	....	....	....	....	....	....
1988-89	Hofors HC	Sweden-3	28	19	11	30	....	....	....	....	....	....	....	....	....	....	....	....	....	....	....	....	....	....	....	....	....	....
1989-90	Falu IF	Sweden-2	21	3	1	4	....	....	....	14	....	....	....	....	....	....	....	....	....	....	....	....	....	....	....	....	....	....
1990-91	Falu IF	Sweden 2	31	12	10	22	....	....	....	38	....	....	....	....	....	....	....	....	....	....	....	....	....	....	....	....	....	....
1991-92	Farjestads BK Karlstad	Sweden	30	3	1	4	....	....	....	10	....	....	....	....	....	....	....	....	....	....	6	0	0	0	4	....	....	....
	Sweden	WJC-A	7	1	2	3	....	....	....	4	....	....	....	....	....	....	....	....	....	....	....	....	....	....	....	....	....	....
1992-93	Farjestads BK Karlstad	Sweden	38	4	7	11	....	....	....	38	....	....	....	....	....	....	....	....	....	....	2	0	0	0	0	....	....	....
	Sweden	WJC-A	7	1	5	6	....	....	....	14	....	....	....	....	....	....	....	....	....	....	....	....	....	....	....	....	....	....
1993-94	Farjestads BK Karlstad	Sweden	20	3	6	9	....	....	....	6	....	....	....	....	....	....	....	....	....	....	....	....	....	....	....	....	....	....
1994-95	Farjestads BK Karlstad	Sweden	36	9	10	19	....	....	....	42	....	....	....	....	....	....	....	....	....	....	4	0	0	0	10	....	....	....
	Sweden	WC-A	8	3	6	9	....	....	....	8	....	....	....	....	....	....	....	....	....	....	....	....	....	....	....	....	....	....
1995-96	**New York Islanders**	**NHL**	**3**	**0**	**1**	**1**	**0**	**1**	**1**	**0**	**0**	**0**	**0**	**6**	**0.0**	**1**	**0**	**0**	**0**	**1**	....	....	....	....	....	....	....	....
	Worcester IceCats	AHL	29	5	5	10	....	....	....	32	....	....	....	....	....	....	....	....	....	....	....	....	....	....	....	....	....	....
	Utah Grizzlies	IHL	22	4	13	17	....	....	....	28	....	....	....	....	....	....	....	....	....	....	12	0	5	5	6	....	....	....
1996-97	Sweden	W-Cup	2	0	0	0	....	....	....	2	....	....	....	....	....	....	....	....	....	....	....	....	....	....	....	....	....	....
	New York Islanders	**NHL**	**15**	**2**	**2**	**4**	**2**	**2**	**4**	**0**	**1**	**0**	**0**	**21**	**9.5**	**5**	**2**	**9**	**0**	**–6**	....	....	....	....	....	....	....	....
	Pittsburgh Penguins	**NHL**	**27**	**2**	**7**	**9**	**2**	**6**	**8**	**20**	**0**	**0**	**0**	**38**	**5.3**	**11**	**0**	**20**	**3**	**–6**	....	....	....	....	....	....	....	....
	Cleveland Lumberjacks	IHL	10	2	4	6	....	....	....	42	....	....	....	....	....	....	....	....	....	....	11	1	5	6	8	....	....	....
1997-98	**Pittsburgh Penguins**	**NHL**	**50**	**5**	**10**	**15**	**6**	**10**	**16**	**20**	**0**	**1**	**0**	**49**	**10.2**	**23**	**2**	**22**	**5**	**4**	**1**	**0**	**0**	**0**	**0**	**0**	**0**	**0**
	Sweden	Olympics	3	0	0	0	....	....	....	2	....	....	....	....	....	....	....	....	....	....	....	....	....	....	....	....	....	....
1998-99	**Ottawa Senators**	**NHL**	**69**	**21**	**16**	**37**	**25**	**15**	**40**	**34**	**7**	**0**	**6**	**144**	**14.6**	**59**	**23**	**35**	**0**	**1**	**2**	**0**	**0**	**0**	**0**	**0**	**0**	**0**
99-2000	**Tampa Bay Lightning**	**NHL**	**12**	**2**	**3**	**5**	**2**	**3**	**5**	**8**	**0**	**0**	**0**	**11**	**18.2**	**9**	**2**	**8**	**2**	**1**	....	....	....	....	....	....	....	....
	Calgary Flames	**NHL**	**28**	**3**	**7**	**10**	**3**	**6**	**9**	**14**	**1**	**0**	**0**	**47**	**6.4**	**13**	**5**	**11**	**0**	**–3**	....	....	....	....	....	....	....	....
	NHL Totals		**204**	**35**	**46**	**81**	**40**	**43**	**83**	**96**	**9**	**1**	**6**	**316**	**11.1**	**121**	**34**	**105**	**10**		**3**	**0**	**0**	**0**	**0**	**0**	**0**	**0**

Swedish World All-Star Team (1995)

Traded to **Pittsburgh** by **NY Islanders** with Darius Kasparaitis for Bryan Smolinski, November 17, 1996. Signed as a free agent by **Ottawa**, September 29, 1998. Traded to **Tampa Bay** by **Ottawa** for Rob Zamuner and future considerations, June 29, 1999. Traded to **Calgary** by **Tampa Bay** for Nils Ekman and Calgary's 4th round choice (later traded to NY Islanders - NY Islanders selected Vladimir Gorbunov) in 2000 Entry Draft, November 13, 1999. • Missed remainder of 1999-2000 season recovering from back injury suffered in game vs. Vancouver, January 2, 2000.

• JOHANSSON, Bjorn

D – L. 6', 195 lbs. b: Orebro, Sweden, 1/15/1956. California's 1st, 5th overall, in 1976.

Season	Club	League	GP	G	A	Pts	AG	AA	APts	PIM	PP	SH	GW	S	%	TGF	PGF	TGA	PGA	+/–	GP	G	A	Pts	PIM	PP	SH	GW
1971-72	Orebro IK	Sweden-2	9	2	2	4	....	....	....	....	....	....	....	....	....	....	....	....	....	....	....	....	....	....	....	....	....	....
1972-73	Orebro IK	Sweden-2	8	2	2	4	....	....	....	4	....	....	....	....	....	....	....	....	....	....	....	....	....	....	....	....	....	....
1973-74	Orebro IK	Sweden	36	15	17	32	....	....	....	10	....	....	....	....	....	....	....	....	....	....	....	....	....	....	....	....	....	....
	Sweden	WJC-A	5	0	1	1	....	....	....	2	....	....	....	....	....	....	....	....	....	....	....	....	....	....	....	....	....	....
	Sweden	EJC-A	5	0	1	1	....	....	....	6	....	....	....	....	....	....	....	....	....	....	....	....	....	....	....	....	....	....
1974-75	Orebro IK	Sweden	30	13	1	14	....	....	....	22	....	....	....	....	....	....	....	....	....	....	13	2	1	3	23	....	....	....
	Sweden	WJC-A	....	1	2	3	....	....	....	....	....	....	....	....	....	....	....	....	....	....	....	....	....	....	....	....	....	....
	Sweden	EJC-A	5	3	2	5	....	....	....	2	....	....	....	....	....	....	....	....	....	....	....	....	....	....	....	....	....	....
1975-76	Orebro IK	Sweden	36	30	21	51	....	....	....	30	....	....	....	....	....	....	....	....	....	....	....	....	....	....	....	....	....	....
	Sweden	WJC-A	4	3	2	5	....	....	....	0	....	....	....	....	....	....	....	....	....	....	....	....	....	....	....	....	....	....
1976-77	**Cleveland Barons**	**NHL**	**10**	**1**	**1**	**2**	**1**	**1**	**2**	**4**	**0**	**0**	**0**	**8**	**12.5**	**5**	**0**	**17**	**1**	**–11**	....	....	....	....	....	....	....	....
	Salt Lake Golden Eagles	CHL	56	8	16	24	....	....	....	10	....	....	....	....	....	....	....	....	....	....	....	....	....	....	....	....	....	....
1977-78	**Cleveland Barons**	**NHL**	**5**	**0**	**0**	**0**	**0**	**0**	**0**	**6**	**0**	**0**	**0**	**1**	**0.0**	**1**	**0**	**3**	**0**	**–2**	....	....	....	....	....	....	....	....
	Phoenix Roadrunners	CHL	13	0	3	3	....	....	....	15	....	....	....	....	....	....	....	....	....	....	....	....	....	....	....	....	....	....
	Binghamton Dusters	AHL	24	0	10	10	....	....	....	6	....	....	....	....	....	....	....	....	....	....	....	....	....	....	....	....	....	....
	Rochester Americans	AHL	25	2	10	12	....	....	....	20	....	....	....	....	....	....	....	....	....	....	....	....	....	....	....	....	....	....
1978-79	Orebro IK	Sweden	36	7	15	22	....	....	....	37	....	....	....	....	....	....	....	....	....	....	....	....	....	....	....	....	....	....
1979-80	Vastra Frolunda	Sweden	33	8	10	18	....	....	....	46	....	....	....	....	....	....	....	....	....	....	8	2	1	3	8	....	....	....
1980-81	Djurgardens IF Stockholm	Sweden	20	1	3	4	....	....	....	11	....	....	....	....	....	....	....	....	....	....	....	....	....	....	....	....	....	....
1981-82	Orebro IK	Sweden-2	36	18	18	36	....	....	....	63	....	....	....	....	....	....	....	....	....	....	....	....	....	....	....	....	....	....
1982-83	Orebro IK	Sweden-2	31	9	18	27	....	....	....	50	....	....	....	....	....	....	....	....	....	....	....	....	....	....	....	....	....	....
1983-84	Orebro IK	Sweden-2	29	18	18	36	....	....	....	24	....	....	....	....	....	....	....	....	....	....	....	....	....	....	....	....	....	....
1984-85	Orebro IK	Sweden-2	32	7	13	20	....	....	....	40	....	....	....	....	....	....	....	....	....	....	....	....	....	....	....	....	....	....
1985-86	Orebro IK	Sweden-2	31	9	14	23	....	....	....	24	....	....	....	....	....	....	....	....	....	....	4	1	3	4	6	....	....	....

Season	Club	League	REGULAR SEASON GP	G	A	Pts	AG	AA	APts	PIM	PP	SH	GW	S	%	TGF	PGF	TGA	PGA	+/–	PLAYOFFS GP	G	A	Pts	PIM	PP	SH	GW
1986-87	Orebro IK	Sweden-2	30	6	19	25	....	....	....	24	....	....	....	....	....	....	....	....	....	....	6	3	2	5	10	....	....	....
1987-88	Orebro IK	Sweden-2	34	4	24	28	....	....	....	32	....	....	....	....	....	....	....	....	....	....	7	0	5	5	12	....	....	....
1988-89	Orebro IK	Sweden-2	29	5	22	27	....	....	....	38	....	....	....	....	....	....	....	....	....	....	12	1	3	4	12	....	....	....
	NHL Totals		**15**	**1**	**1**	**2**	**1**	**1**	**2**	**10**	**0**	**0**	**0**	**9**	**11.1**	**6**	**0**	**20**	**1**		....	....	....	....	....	....	....	....

WJC-A All-Star Team (1976)

Transferred to **Cleveland** after **California** franchise relocated, August 26, 1976. Traded to **Rochester** by **Binghamton** (AHL) for Peter McNamee, February, 1978.

• JOHANSSON, Calle

D – L. 5'11", 200 lbs. b: Goteborg, Sweden, 2/14/1967. Buffalo's 1st, 14th overall, in 1985.

Season	Club	League	GP	G	A	Pts	AG	AA	APts	PIM	PP	SH	GW	S	%	TGF	PGF	TGA	PGA	+/–	GP	G	A	Pts	PIM	PP	SH	GW
1981-82	KBA-67	Sweden-3	27	3	3	6	....	....	....	....	....	....	....	....	....	....	....	....	....	....	....	....	....	....	....	....	....	....
1982-83	KBA-67	Sweden-3	29	12	11	23	....	....	....	....	....	....	....	....	....	....	....	....	....	....	....	....	....	....	....	....	....	....
1983-84	Vastra Frolunda	Sweden	28	4	4	8	....	....	....	10	....	....	....	....	....	....	....	....	....	....	....	....	....	....	....	....	....	....
	Sweden	EJC-A	5	2	3	5	....	....	....	6	....	....	....	....	....	....	....	....	....	....	....	....	....	....	....	....	....	....
1984-85	Vastra Frolunda	Sweden-2	25	8	13	21	....	....	....	16	....	....	....	....	....	....	....	....	....	....	6	1	2	3	4	....	....	....
	Sweden	EJC-A	5	4	0	4	....	....	....	4	....	....	....	....	....	....	....	....	....	....	....	....	....	....	....	....	....	....
1985-86	Bjorkloven Umea	Sweden	17	1	2	3	....	....	....	4	....	....	....	....	....	....	....	....	....	....	....	....	....	....	....	....	....	....
	Sweden	WJC-A	7	1	1	2	....	....	....	6	....	....	....	....	....	....	....	....	....	....	....	....	....	....	....	....	....	....
1986-87	Bjorkloven Umea	Sweden	30	2	13	15	....	....	....	20	....	....	....	....	....	....	....	....	....	....	6	1	3	4	6	....	....	....
	Sweden	WJC-A	6	0	8	8	....	....	....	6	....	....	....	....	....	....	....	....	....	....	....	....	....	....	....	....	....	....
1987-88	**Buffalo Sabres**	**NHL**	**71**	**4**	**38**	**42**	**3**	**27**	**30**	**37**	**2**	**0**	**0**	**93**	**4.3**	**96**	**33**	**90**	**39**	**12**	**6**	**0**	**1**	**1**	**0**	**0**	**0**	**0**
1988-89	**Buffalo Sabres**	**NHL**	**47**	**2**	**11**	**13**	**2**	**8**	**10**	**33**	**0**	**0**	**1**	**53**	**3.8**	**50**	**12**	**65**	**20**	**–7**	....	....	....	....	....	....	....	....
	Washington Capitals	**NHL**	**12**	**1**	**7**	**8**	**1**	**5**	**6**	**4**	**1**	**0**	**0**	**22**	**4.5**	**13**	**4**	**8**	**0**	**1**	**6**	**1**	**2**	**3**	**0**	**1**	**0**	**0**
1989-90	Washington Capitals	Fr-Tour	2	0	0	0	....	....	....	0	....	....	....	....	....	....	....	....	....	....	....	....	....	....	....	....	....	....
	Washington Capitals	**NHL**	**70**	**8**	**31**	**39**	**7**	**22**	**29**	**25**	**4**	**0**	**2**	**103**	**7.8**	**93**	**36**	**60**	**10**	**7**	**15**	**1**	**6**	**7**	**4**	**0**	**0**	**0**
1990-91	**Washington Capitals**	**NHL**	**80**	**11**	**41**	**52**	**10**	**31**	**41**	**23**	**2**	**1**	**2**	**128**	**8.6**	**111**	**41**	**82**	**10**	**–2**	**10**	**2**	**7**	**9**	**8**	**1**	**0**	**0**
	Sweden	WEC-A	4	1	1	2	....	....	....	6	....	....	....	....	....	....	....	....	....	....	....	....	....	....	....	....	....	....
1991-92	Sweden	Can-Cup	6	1	2	3	....	....	....	0	....	....	....	....	....	....	....	....	....	....	....	....	....	....	....	....	....	....
	Washington Capitals	**NHL**	**80**	**14**	**42**	**56**	**13**	**32**	**45**	**49**	**5**	**2**	**2**	**119**	**11.8**	**140**	**52**	**103**	**17**	**2**	**7**	**0**	**5**	**5**	**4**	**0**	**0**	**0**
	Sweden	WC-A	5	0	0	0	....	....	....	4	....	....	....	....	....	....	....	....	....	....	....	....	....	....	....	....	....	....
1992-93	**Washington Capitals**	**NHL**	**77**	**7**	**38**	**45**	**6**	**26**	**32**	**56**	**6**	**0**	**0**	**133**	**5.3**	**119**	**42**	**107**	**33**	**3**	**6**	**0**	**5**	**5**	**4**	**0**	**0**	**0**
1993-94	**Washington Capitals**	**NHL**	**84**	**9**	**33**	**42**	**8**	**26**	**34**	**59**	**4**	**0**	**1**	**141**	**6.4**	**100**	**28**	**111**	**42**	**3**	**6**	**1**	**3**	**4**	**4**	**0**	**0**	**1**
1994-95	EHC Kloten	Switz.	5	1	2	3	....	....	....	8	....	....	....	....	....	....	....	....	....	....	....	....	....	....	....	....	....	....
	Washington Capitals	**NHL**	**46**	**5**	**26**	**31**	**9**	**38**	**47**	**35**	**4**	**0**	**2**	**112**	**4.5**	**61**	**33**	**51**	**17**	**–6**	**7**	**3**	**1**	**4**	**0**	**1**	**0**	**0**
1995-96	**Washington Capitals**	**NHL**	**78**	**10**	**25**	**35**	**10**	**20**	**30**	**50**	**4**	**0**	**0**	**182**	**5.5**	**82**	**31**	**75**	**37**	**13**	....	....	....	....	....	....	....	....
1996-97	Sweden	W-Cup	4	1	5	6	....	....	....	8	....	....	....	....	....	....	....	....	....	....	....	....	....	....	....	....	....	....
	Washington Capitals	**NHL**	**65**	**6**	**11**	**17**	**6**	**10**	**16**	**16**	**2**	**0**	**0**	**133**	**4.5**	**57**	**15**	**68**	**24**	**–2**	....	....	....	....	....	....	....	....
1997-98	**Washington Capitals**	**NHL**	**73**	**15**	**20**	**35**	**18**	**20**	**38**	**30**	**10**	**1**	**1**	**163**	**9.2**	**80**	**35**	**79**	**23**	**–11**	**21**	**2**	**8**	**10**	**16**	**0**	**0**	**0**
	Sweden	Olympics	4	0	0	0	....	....	....	2	....	....	....	....	....	....	....	....	....	....	....	....	....	....	....	....	....	....
1998-99	**Washington Capitals**	**NHL**	**67**	**8**	**21**	**29**	**9**	**20**	**29**	**22**	**2**	**0**	**2**	**145**	**5.5**	**81**	**27**	**64**	**20**	**10**	....	....	....	....	....	....	....	....
99-2000	**Washington Capitals**	**NHL**	**82**	**7**	**25**	**32**	**8**	**23**	**31**	**24**	**1**	**0**	**3**	**138**	**5.1**	**80**	**14**	**83**	**30**	**13**	**5**	**1**	**2**	**3**	**0**	**1**	**0**	**0**
	NHL Totals		**932**	**107**	**369**	**476**	**110**	**308**	**418**	**463**	**47**	**4**	**16**	**1665**	**6.4**	**1163**	**403**	**1046**	**322**		**89**	**11**	**40**	**51**	**40**	**4**	**0**	**1**

Named Best Defenseman at WJC-A (1987) • NHL All-Rookie Team (1988) • World Cup All-Star Team (1996)

Traded to **Washington** by **Buffalo** with Buffalo's 2nd round choice (Byron Dafoe) in 1989 Entry Draft for Clint Malarchuk, Grant Ledyard and Washington's 6th round choice (Brian Holzinger) in 1991 Entry Draft, March 7, 1989.

• JOHANSSON, Roger

D – L. 6'1", 190 lbs. b: Ljungby, Sweden, 4/17/1967. Calgary's 5th, 80th overall, in 1985.

Season	Club	League	GP	G	A	Pts	AG	AA	APts	PIM	PP	SH	GW	S	%	TGF	PGF	TGA	PGA	+/–	GP	G	A	Pts	PIM	PP	SH	GW
1983-84	HK Troja-Ljungby	Sweden-2	11	2	2	4	....	....	....	12	....	....	....	....	....	....	....	....	....	....	....	....	....	....	....	....	....	....
1984-85	HK Troja-Ljungby	Sweden-2	30	1	6	7	....	....	....	20	....	....	....	....	....	....	....	....	....	....	9	0	4	4	8	....	....	....
1985-86	HK Troja-Ljungby	Sweden-2	32	5	16	21	....	....	....	42	....	....	....	....	....	....	....	....	....	....	....	....	....	....	....	....	....	....
	Sweden	WJC-A	7	1	1	2	....	....	....	8	....	....	....	....	....	....	....	....	....	....	....	....	....	....	....	....	....	....
1986-87	Farjestads BK Karlstad	Sweden	31	6	11	17	....	....	....	20	....	....	....	....	....	....	....	....	....	....	7	1	1	2	8	....	....	....
	Sweden	WJC-A	7	2	4	6	....	....	....	2	....	....	....	....	....	....	....	....	....	....	....	....	....	....	....	....	....	....
1987-88	Farjestads BK Karlstad	Sweden	24	3	11	14	....	....	....	20	....	....	....	....	....	....	....	....	....	....	9	1	6	7	12	....	....	....
1988-89	Farjestads BK Karlstad	Sweden	40	5	15	20	....	....	....	38	....	....	....	....	....	....	....	....	....	....	....	....	....	....	....	....	....	....
1989-90	Calgary Flames	Fr-Tour	4	0	1	1	....	....	....	6	....	....	....	....	....	....	....	....	....	....	....	....	....	....	....	....	....	....
	Calgary Flames	**NHL**	**35**	**0**	**5**	**5**	**0**	**4**	**4**	**48**	**0**	**0**	**0**	**23**	**0.0**	**22**	**0**	**18**	**5**	**9**	....	....	....	....	....	....	....	....
1990-91	**Calgary Flames**	**NHL**	**38**	**4**	**13**	**17**	**4**	**10**	**14**	**47**	**0**	**0**	**0**	**41**	**9.8**	**40**	**4**	**35**	**8**	**9**	....	....	....	....	....	....	....	....
1991-92	Leksands IF	Sweden	22	3	9	12	....	....	....	42	....	....	....	....	....	....	....	....	....	....	....	....	....	....	....	....	....	....
1992-93	**Calgary Flames**	**NHL**	**77**	**4**	**16**	**20**	**3**	**11**	**14**	**62**	**1**	**0**	**0**	**101**	**4.0**	**54**	**7**	**47**	**13**	**13**	**5**	**0**	**1**	**1**	**2**	**0**	**0**	**0**
1993-94	Leksands IF	Sweden	38	6	15	21	....	....	....	56	....	....	....	....	....	....	....	....	....	....	4	0	1	1	0	....	....	....
	Sweden	Olympics	8	2	0	2	....	....	....	8	....	....	....	....	....	....	....	....	....	....	....	....	....	....	....	....	....	....
	Sweden	WC-A	8	0	3	3	....	....	....	4	....	....	....	....	....	....	....	....	....	....	....	....	....	....	....	....	....	....
1994-95	Leksands IF	Sweden	7	0	0	0	....	....	....	14	....	....	....	....	....	....	....	....	....	....	....	....	....	....	....	....	....	....
	Chicago Blackhawks	**NHL**	**11**	**1**	**0**	**1**	**2**	**0**	**2**	**6**	**0**	**0**	**0**	**10**	**10.0**	**4**	**0**	**3**	**0**	**1**	....	....	....	....	....	....	....	....
1995-96	Farjestads BK Karlstad	Sweden	34	3	4	7	....	....	....	46	....	....	....	....	....	....	....	....	....	....	8	3	1	4	16	....	....	....
	Sweden	WC-A	6	1	1	2	....	....	....	6	....	....	....	....	....	....	....	....	....	....	....	....	....	....	....	....	....	....
1996-97	Sweden	W-Cup	3	0	0	0	....	....	....	0	....	....	....	....	....	....	....	....	....	....	....	....	....	....	....	....	....	....
	Farjestads BK Karlstad	Sweden	46	8	15	23	....	....	....	52	....	....	....	....	....	....	....	....	....	....	14	3	5	8	38	....	....	....
	Farjestads BK Karlstad	EuroHL	4	0	1	1	....	....	....	6	....	....	....	....	....	....	....	....	....	....	....	....	....	....	....	....	....	....
	Sweden	WC-A	10	0	1	1	....	....	....	16	....	....	....	....	....	....	....	....	....	....	....	....	....	....	....	....	....	....
1997-98	Farjestads BK Karlstad	Sweden	46	12	27	39	....	....	....	44	....	....	....	....	....	....	....	....	....	....	10	2	7	9	8	....	....	....
	Farjestads BK Karlstad	EuroHL	6	1	1	2	....	....	....	6	....	....	....	....	....	....	....	....	....	....	....	....	....	....	....	....	....	....
1998-99	Farjestads BK Karlstad	Sweden	39	11	11	22	....	....	....	42	....	....	....	....	....	....	....	....	....	....	4	0	1	1	4	....	....	....
99-2000	Farjestads BK Karlstad	Sweden	43	5	13	18	....	....	....	58	....	....	....	....	....	....	....	....	....	....	7	0	1	1	12	....	....	....
	NHL Totals		**161**	**9**	**34**	**43**	**9**	**25**	**34**	**163**	**1**	**0**	**0**	**175**	**5.1**	**120**	**11**	**103**	**26**		**5**	**0**	**1**	**1**	**2**	**0**	**0**	**0**

Claimed by **Chicago** from **Calgary** in Waiver Draft, January 18, 1995.

• JOHNS, Don

Donald Ernest D – R. 6', 180 lbs. b: St. George, Ont., 12/13/1937.

Season	Club	League	GP	G	A	Pts	AG	AA	APts	PIM	PP	SH	GW	S	%	TGF	PGF	TGA	PGA	+/–	GP	G	A	Pts	PIM	PP	SH	GW
1956-57	Hull-Ottawa Canadiens	OHA-Jr.	27	2	3	5	....	....	....	12	....	....	....	....	....	....	....	....	....	....	....	....	....	....	....	....	....	....
	Hull-Ottawa Canadiens	QHL	15	0	0	0	....	....	....	0	....	....	....	....	....	....	....	....	....	....	....	....	....	....	....	....	....	....
	Hull-Ottawa Canadiens	EOHL	8	0	2	2	....	....	....	2	....	....	....	....	....	....	....	....	....	....	....	....	....	....	....	....	....	....
	Hull-Ottawa Canadiens	Mem-Cup	13	0	0	0	....	....	....	2	....	....	....	....	....	....	....	....	....	....	....	....	....	....	....	....	....	....
1957-58	Fort William Canadiens	TBJHL	50	3	14	17	....	....	....	56	....	....	....	....	....	....	....	....	....	....	4	1	1	2	8	....	....	....
	Fort William Canadiens	Mem-Cup	5	0	2	2	....	....	....	12	....	....	....	....	....	....	....	....	....	....	....	....	....	....	....	....	....	....
1958-59	Winnipeg Warriors	WHL	60	4	18	22	....	....	....	112	....	....	....	....	....	....	....	....	....	....	7	1	0	1	18	....	....	....
1959-60	Winnipeg Warriors	WHL	70	3	21	24	....	....	....	72	....	....	....	....	....	....	....	....	....	....	....	....	....	....	....	....	....	....
1960-61	**New York Rangers**	**NHL**	**63**	**1**	**7**	**8**	**1**	**7**	**8**	**34**	....	....	....	....	....	....	....	....	....	....	....	....	....	....	....	....	....	....
1961-62	Springfield Indians	AHL	59	3	10	13	....	....	....	14	....	....	....	....	....	....	....	....	....	....	11	1	4	5	10	....	....	....
1962-63	**New York Rangers**	**NHL**	**6**	**0**	**4**	**4**	**0**	**4**	**4**	**6**	....	....	....	....	....	....	....	....	....	....	....	....	....	....	....	....	....	....
	Baltimore Clippers	AHL	69	9	17	26	....	....	....	30	....	....	....	....	....	....	....	....	....	....	3	1	3	4	2	....	....	....
1963-64	**New York Rangers**	**NHL**	**57**	**1**	**9**	**10**	**1**	**9**	**10**	**26**	....	....	....	....	....	....	....	....	....	....	....	....	....	....	....	....	....	....
	Baltimore Clippers	AHL	12	0	1	1	....	....	....	10	....	....	....	....	....	....	....	....	....	....	....	....	....	....	....	....	....	....
1964-65	**New York Rangers**	**NHL**	**22**	**0**	**1**	**1**	**0**	**1**	**1**	**4**	....	....	....	....	....	....	....	....	....	....	....	....	....	....	....	....	....	....
	Baltimore Clippers	AHL	26	2	10	12	....	....	....	28	....	....	....	....	....	....	....	....	....	....	9	0	2	2	14	....	....	....
	St. Louis Braves	CPHL	23	1	5	6	....	....	....	10	....	....	....	....	....	....	....	....	....	....	....	....	....	....	....	....	....	....
1965-66	**Montreal Canadiens**	**NHL**	**1**	**0**	**0**	**0**	**0**	**0**	**0**	**0**	....	....	....	....	....	....	....	....	....	....	....	....	....	....	....	....	....	....
	Quebec Aces	AHL	63	2	24	26	....	....	....	78	....	....	....	....	....	....	....	....	....	....	....	....	....	....	....	....	....	....
1966-67	Quebec Aces	AHL	69	1	15	16	....	....	....	54	....	....	....	....	....	....	....	....	....	....	....	....	....	....	....	....	....	....

			REGULAR SEASON																		PLAYOFFS							
Season	Club	League	GP	G	A	Pts	AG	AA	APts	PIM	PP	SH	GW	S	%	TGF	PGF	TGA	PGA	+/-	GP	G	A	Pts	PIM	PP	SH	GW
1967-68	**Minnesota North Stars**	**NHL**	**4**	**0**	**0**	**0**	**0**	**0**	**0**	**6**	**0**	**0**	**0**	**4**	**0.0**	**4**	**0**	**6**	**1**	**–1**	....	....	....	....	....	....	....	....
	Memphis South Stars	CPHL	27	0	9	9	....	....	....	22	....	....	....	....	....	....	....	....	....	....	....	....	....	....	....	....	....	....
	Rochester Americans	AHL	42	1	13	14	....	....	....	32	....	....	....	....	....	....	....	....	....	....	11	1	1	2	18	....	....	....
1968-69	Vancouver Canucks	WHL	66	1	22	23	....	....	....	102	....	....	....	....	....	....	....	....	....	....	7	0	3	3	18	....	....	....
	NHL Totals		**153**	**2**	**21**	**23**	**2**	**21**	**23**	**76**	....	....	....	....	....	....	....	....	....	....	....	....	....	....	....	....	....	....

• Hull-Ottawa played partial schedule against OHA-Jr. teams that counted for opposition only. Claimed by **NY Rangers** from **Winnipeg** (WHL) in Inter-League Draft, June 7, 1960. Traded to **Chicago** by **NY Rangers** with Camille Henry, Billy Taylor and Wally Chevrier for Doug Robinson, Wayne Hillman and John Brenneman, February 4, 1965. Traded to **Montreal** by **Chicago** for Bryan Watson, June 8, 1965. Traded to **Minnesota** by **Montreal** for cash, October 5, 1967. Traded to **Toronto** (Rochester-AHL) by **Minnesota** with Duke Harris, Murray Hall, Ted Taylor, Len Lunde and the loan of Carl Wetzel for Jean-Paul Parise and Milan Marcetta, December 23, 1967. Rights transferred to **Vancouver** (WHL) after WHL club purchased **Rochester** (AHL) franchise, August 13, 1968.

• JOHNSON, Brian

RW – R. 6'1", 185 lbs. b: Montreal, Que., 4/1/1960. Hartford's 7th, 107th overall, in 1983.

Season	Club	League	GP	G	A	Pts	AG	AA	APts	PIM	PP	SH	GW	S	%	TGF	PGF	TGA	PGA	+/-	GP	G	A	Pts	PIM	PP	SH	GW
1977-78	Verdun Eperviers	QMJHL	50	11	14	25	....	....	....	145	....	....	....	....	....	....	....	....	....	....	....	....	....	....	....	....	....	....
1978-79	Verdun Eperviers	QMJHL	71	32	36	68	....	....	....	192	....	....	....	....	....	....	....	....	....	....	11	1	6	7	61	....	....	....
1979-80	Verdun Eperviers	QMJHL	21	8	27	35	....	....	....	68	....	....	....	....	....	....	....	....	....	....	....	....	....	....	....	....	....	....
	Sherbrooke Castors	QMJHL	49	32	52	84	....	....	....	144	....	....	....	....	....	....	....	....	....	....	15	11	15	26	66	....	....	....
1980-81	Adirondack Red Wings	AHL	65	10	21	31	....	....	....	193	....	....	....	....	....	....	....	....	....	....	8	0	0	0	33	....	....	....
1981-82	Dallas Black Hawks	CHL	79	18	36	54	....	....	....	223	....	....	....	....	....	....	....	....	....	....	16	4	3	7	*129	....	....	....
1982-83	Adirondack Red Wings	AHL	67	6	16	22	....	....	....	250	....	....	....	....	....	....	....	....	....	....	6	1	2	3	15	....	....	....
1983-84	**Detroit Red Wings**	**NHL**	**3**	**0**	**0**	**0**	**0**	**0**	**0**	**5**	**0**	**0**	**0**	**4**	**0.0**	**0**	**0**	**3**	**0**	**–3**	....	....	....	....	....	....	....	....
	Adirondack Red Wings	AHL	58	4	27	31	....	....	....	233	....	....	....	....	....	....	....	....	....	....	7	0	0	0	40	....	....	....
1984-85			DID NOT PLAY																									
1985-86	Indianapolis Checkers	IHL	13	0	1	1	....	....	....	57	....	....	....	....	....	....	....	....	....	....	....	....	....	....	....	....	....	....
	Carolina Thunderbirds	ACHL	22	8	11	19	....	....	....	167	....	....	....	....	....	....	....	....	....	....	....	....	....	....	....	....	....	....
	NHL Totals		**3**	**0**	**0**	**0**	**0**	**0**	**0**	**5**	**0**	**0**	**0**	**4**	**0.0**	**0**	**0**	**3**	**0**		....	....	....	....	....	....	....	....

QMJHL Second All-Star Team (1980)

Signed as a free agent by **Detroit**, October 30, 1979.

• JOHNSON, Craig

LW – L. 6'2", 200 lbs. b: St. Paul, MN, 3/8/1972. St. Louis' 1st, 33rd overall, in 1990.

Season	Club	League	GP	G	A	Pts	AG	AA	APts	PIM	PP	SH	GW	S	%	TGF	PGF	TGA	PGA	+/-	GP	G	A	Pts	PIM	PP	SH	GW
1987-88	Hill-Murray Pioneers	Hi-School	28	14	20	34	....	....	....	4	....	....	....	....	....	....	....	....	....	....	....	....	....	....	....	....	....	....
1988-89	Hill-Murray Pioneers	Hi-School	24	22	30	52	....	....	....	10	....	....	....	....	....	....	....	....	....	....	....	....	....	....	....	....	....	....
1989-90	Hill-Murray Pioneers	Hi-School	23	15	36	51	....	....	....	0	....	....	....	....	....	....	....	....	....	....	....	....	....	....	....	....	....	....
1990-91	University of Minnesota	WCHA	33	13	18	31	....	....	....	34	....	....	....	....	....	....	....	....	....	....	....	....	....	....	....	....	....	....
	United States	WJC-A	2	0	2	2	....	....	....	0	....	....	....	....	....	....	....	....	....	....	....	....	....	....	....	....	....	....
1991-92	University of Minnesota	WCHA	41	17	38	55	....	....	....	66	....	....	....	....	....	....	....	....	....	....	....	....	....	....	....	....	....	....
1992-93	University of Minnesota	WCHA	42	22	24	46	....	....	....	70	....	....	....	....	....	....	....	....	....	....	....	....	....	....	....	....	....	....
	Jacksonville Bullets	SunHL	23	2	9	11	....	....	....	38	....	....	....	....	....	....	....	....	....	....	....	....	....	....	....	....	....	....
	United States	WC-A	6	1	1	2	....	....	....	4	....	....	....	....	....	....	....	....	....	....	....	....	....	....	....	....	....	....
1993-94	United States	Nat-Team	54	25	26	51	....	....	....	64	....	....	....	....	....	....	....	....	....	....	....	....	....	....	....	....	....	....
	United States	Olympics	8	0	4	4	....	....	....	4	....	....	....	....	....	....	....	....	....	....	....	....	....	....	....	....	....	....
1994-95	**St. Louis Blues**	**NHL**	**15**	**3**	**3**	**6**	**5**	**4**	**9**	**6**	**0**	**0**	**0**	**19**	**15.8**	**11**	**1**	**7**	**1**	**4**	**1**	**0**	**0**	**0**	**2**	**0**	**0**	**0**
	Peoria Rivermen	IHL	16	2	6	8	....	....	....	25	....	....	....	....	....	....	....	....	....	....	9	0	4	4	10	....	....	....
1995-96	**St. Louis Blues**	**NHL**	**49**	**8**	**7**	**15**	**8**	**6**	**14**	**30**	**1**	**0**	**0**	**69**	**11.6**	**22**	**2**	**29**	**5**	**–4**	....	....	....	....	....	....	....	....
	Worcester IceCats	AHL	5	3	0	3	....	....	....	2	....	....	....	....	....	....	....	....	....	....	....	....	....	....	....	....	....	....
	Los Angeles Kings	**NHL**	**11**	**5**	**4**	**9**	**5**	**3**	**8**	**6**	**3**	**0**	**0**	**28**	**17.9**	**10**	**3**	**12**	**1**	**–4**	....	....	....	....	....	....	....	....
	United States	WC-A	6	1	1	2	....	....	....	2	....	....	....	....	....	....	....	....	....	....	....	....	....	....	....	....	....	....
1996-97	**Los Angeles Kings**	**NHL**	**31**	**4**	**3**	**7**	**4**	**3**	**7**	**26**	**1**	**0**	**0**	**30**	**13.3**	**12**	**2**	**17**	**0**	**–7**	....	....	....	....	....	....	....	....
1997-98	**Los Angeles Kings**	**NHL**	**74**	**17**	**21**	**38**	**20**	**21**	**41**	**42**	**6**	**0**	**2**	**125**	**13.6**	**54**	**14**	**43**	**12**	**9**	**4**	**1**	**0**	**1**	**4**	**0**	**0**	**0**
1998-99	**Los Angeles Kings**	**NHL**	**69**	**7**	**12**	**19**	**8**	**12**	**20**	**32**	**2**	**0**	**2**	**94**	**7.4**	**30**	**5**	**38**	**1**	**–12**	....	....	....	....	....	....	....	....
	United States	WC-A	6	0	3	3	....	....	....	0	....	....	....	....	....	....	....	....	....	....	....	....	....	....	....	....	....	....
99-2000	**Los Angeles Kings**	**NHL**	**76**	**9**	**14**	**23**	**10**	**13**	**23**	**28**	**1**	**0**	**1**	**106**	**8.5**	**34**	**2**	**61**	**19**	**–10**	**4**	**1**	**0**	**1**	**2**	**0**	**0**	**0**
	NHL Totals		**325**	**53**	**64**	**117**	**60**	**62**	**122**	**170**	**14**	**0**	**5**	**471**	**11.3**	**173**	**29**	**207**	**39**		**9**	**2**	**0**	**2**	**8**	**0**	**0**	**0**

Traded to **LA Kings** by **St. Louis** with Patrice Tardif, Roman Vopat, St. Louis 5th round choice (Peter Hogan) in 1996 Entry Draft and 1st round choice (Matt Zultek) in 1997 Entry Draft for Wayne Gretzky, February 27, 1996.

• JOHNSON, Danny

Daniel Douglas C – L. 5'11", 170 lbs. b: Winnipegosis, Man., 10/1/1944 d: 3/6/1993.

Season	Club	League	GP	G	A	Pts	AG	AA	APts	PIM	PP	SH	GW	S	%	TGF	PGF	TGA	PGA	+/-	GP	G	A	Pts	PIM	PP	SH	GW
1962-63	Flin Flon Bombers	SJHL	45	5	14	19	....	....	....	26	....	....	....	....	....	....	....	....	....	....	6	2	4	6	2	....	....	....
1963-64	Fort Frances Royals	MJHL	26	8	11	19	....	....	....	49	....	....	....	....	....	....	....	....	....	....	9	6	2	8	24	....	....	....
1964-65	Brandon Wheat Kings	MJHL	56	26	29	55	....	....	....	90	....	....	....	....	....	....	....	....	....	....	....	....	....	....	....	....	....	....
1965-66	Tulsa Oilers	CPHL	67	6	23	29	....	....	....	40	....	....	....	....	....	....	....	....	....	....	10	2	0	2	4	....	....	....
1966-67	Omaha Knights	CPHL	38	9	11	20	....	....	....	20	....	....	....	....	....	....	....	....	....	....	....	....	....	....	....	....	....	....
	Tulsa Oilers	CPHL	22	2	6	8	....	....	....	10	....	....	....	....	....	....	....	....	....	....	12	1	4	5	4	....	....	....
1967-68	Tulsa Oilers	CPHL	69	19	37	56	....	....	....	42	....	....	....	....	....	....	....	....	....	....	11	3	2	5	21	....	....	....
1968-69	Tulsa Oilers	CHL	72	34	38	72	....	....	....	63	....	....	....	....	....	....	....	....	....	....	7	2	6	8	12	....	....	....
1969-70	**Toronto Maple Leafs**	**NHL**	**1**	**0**	**0**	**0**	**0**	**0**	**0**	**0**	**0**	**0**	**0**	**0**	**0.0**	**0**	**0**	**0**	**0**	**0**	....	....	....	....	....	....	....	....
	Tulsa Oilers	CHL	72	33	46	79	....	....	....	56	....	....	....	....	....	....	....	....	....	....	6	3	4	7	4	....	....	....
1970-71	**Vancouver Canucks**	**NHL**	**66**	**15**	**11**	**26**	**15**	**9**	**24**	**16**	**1**	**0**	**2**	**76**	**19.7**	**34**	**3**	**51**	**5**	**–15**	....	....	....	....	....	....	....	....
	Rochester Americans	AHL	7	2	2	4	....	....	....	4	....	....	....	....	....	....	....	....	....	....	....	....	....	....	....	....	....	....
1971-72	**Vancouver Canucks**	**NHL**	**11**	**1**	**3**	**4**	**1**	**3**	**4**	**0**	**0**	**0**	**1**	**10**	**10.0**	**5**	**0**	**8**	**0**	**–3**	....	....	....	....	....	....	....	....
	Detroit Red Wings	**NHL**	**43**	**2**	**5**	**7**	**2**	**4**	**6**	**8**	**0**	**0**	**0**	**28**	**7.1**	**12**	**0**	**14**	**0**	**–2**	....	....	....	....	....	....	....	....
1972-73	Winnipeg Jets	WHA	76	19	23	42	....	....	....	17	....	....	....	....	....	....	....	....	....	....	14	4	1	5	0	....	....	....
1973-74	Winnipeg Jets	WHA	78	16	21	37	....	....	....	20	....	....	....	....	....	....	....	....	....	....	4	1	0	1	5	....	....	....
1974-75	Winnipeg Jets	WHA	78	18	14	32	....	....	....	25	....	....	....	....	....	....	....	....	....	....	....	....	....	....	....	....	....	....
	NHL Totals		**121**	**18**	**19**	**37**	**18**	**16**	**34**	**24**	**1**	**0**	**3**	**114**	**15.8**	**51**	**3**	**73**	**5**		....	....	....	....	....	....	....	....
	Other Major League Totals		232	53	58	111	....	....	....	62	....	....	....	....	....	....	....	....	....	....	18	5	1	6	5	....	....	....

CHL Second All-Star Team (1969, 1970) • Won Tommy Ivan Trophy (MVP - CHL) (1970)

Claimed by **Toronto** from **Tulsa** (CHL) in Inter-League Draft, June, 1966. Claimed by **Toronto** (Rochester-AHL) from **Toronto** in Reverse Draft, June 15, 1966. Claimed by **Vancouver** from **Toronto** in Expansion Draft, June 10, 1970. Claimed on waivers by **Detroit** from **Vancouver**, November 22, 1971. Selected by **NY Raiders** (WHA) in 1972 WHA General Player Draft, February 12, 1972. Rights traded to **Winnipeg** (WHA) by **NY Raiders** (WHA) for the rights to Mark Dufour, June, 1972.

• JOHNSON, Greg

Greg C. C – L. 5'10", 194 lbs. b: Thunder Bay, Ont., 3/16/1971. Philadelphia's 1st, 33rd overall, in 1989.

Season	Club	League	GP	G	A	Pts	AG	AA	APts	PIM	PP	SH	GW	S	%	TGF	PGF	TGA	PGA	+/-	GP	G	A	Pts	PIM	PP	SH	GW
1987-88	Thunder Bay Kings	TBAHA	STATISTICS NOT AVAILABLE																									
1988-89	Thunder Bay Flyers	USHL	47	32	64	96	....	....	....	4	....	....	....	....	....	....	....	....	....	....	12	5	13	18	0	....	....	....
	Thunder Bay Flyers	Cen-Cup	STATISTICS NOT AVAILABLE																									
1989-90	University of North Dakota	WCHA	44	17	38	55	....	....	....	11	....	....	....	....	....	....	....	....	....	....	....	....	....	....	....	....	....	....
1990-91	University of North Dakota	WCHA	38	18	*61	79	....	....	....	6	....	....	....	....	....	....	....	....	....	....	....	....	....	....	....	....	....	....
	Canada	WJC-A	7	4	2	6	....	....	....	0	....	....	....	....	....	....	....	....	....	....	....	....	....	....	....	....	....	....
1991-92	University of North Dakota	WCHA	39	20	*54	74	....	....	....	8	....	....	....	....	....	....	....	....	....	....	....	....	....	....	....	....	....	....
1992-93	University of North Dakota	WCHA	34	19	45	64	....	....	....	18	....	....	....	....	....	....	....	....	....	....	....	....	....	....	....	....	....	....
	Canada	Nat-Team	23	6	14	20	....	....	....	2	....	....	....	....	....	....	....	....	....	....	....	....	....	....	....	....	....	....
	Canada	WC-A	8	1	2	3	....	....	....	2	....	....	....	....	....	....	....	....	....	....	....	....	....	....	....	....	....	....
1993-94	**Detroit Red Wings**	**NHL**	**52**	**6**	**11**	**17**	**6**	**9**	**15**	**22**	**1**	**1**	**0**	**48**	**12.5**	**22**	**2**	**37**	**10**	**–7**	**7**	**2**	**2**	**4**	**2**	**1**	**0**	**0**
	Adirondack Red Wings	AHL	3	2	4	6	....	....	....	0	....	....	....	....	....	....	....	....	....	....	4	0	4	4	2	....	....	....
	Canada	Nat-Team	6	2	6	8	....	....	....	4	....	....	....	....	....	....	....	....	....	....	....	....	....	....	....	....	....	....
	Canada	Olympics	8	0	3	3	....	....	....	0	....	....	....	....	....	....	....	....	....	....	....	....	....	....	....	....	....	....
1994-95	**Detroit Red Wings**	**NHL**	**22**	**3**	**5**	**8**	**5**	**7**	**12**	**14**	**2**	**0**	**0**	**32**	**9.4**	**11**	**2**	**9**	**1**	**1**	**1**	**0**	**0**	**0**	**0**	**0**	**0**	**0**
1995-96	**Detroit Red Wings**	**NHL**	**60**	**18**	**22**	**40**	**18**	**18**	**36**	**30**	**5**	**0**	**2**	**87**	**20.7**	**47**	**16**	**25**	**0**	**6**	**13**	**3**	**1**	**4**	**8**	**0**	**0**	**0**

			REGULAR SEASON																		PLAYOFFS							
Season	Club	League	GP	G	A	Pts	AG	AA	APts	PIM	PP	SH	GW	S	%	TGF	PGF	TGA	PGA	+/–	GP	G	A	Pts	PIM	PP	SH	GW
1996-97	**Detroit Red Wings**	**NHL**	43	6	10	16	6	9	15	12	0	0	0	56	10.7	19	4	20	0	–5	....	....	....	....	....	....	....	....
	Pittsburgh Penguins	**NHL**	32	7	9	16	7	8	15	14	1	0	0	52	13.5	23	5	38	7	–13	5	1	0	1	2	0	0	0
1997-98	**Pittsburgh Penguins**	**NHL**	5	1	0	1	1	0	1	2	0	0	0	4	25.0	1	0	2	1	0	....	....	....	....	....	....	....	....
	Chicago Blackhawks	**NHL**	69	11	22	33	13	22	35	38	4	0	3	85	12.9	54	13	56	13	–2	....	....	....	....	....	....	....	....
1998-99	**Nashville Predators**	**NHL**	68	16	34	50	19	33	52	24	2	3	0	120	13.3	61	15	77	23	–8	....	....	....	....	....	....	....	....
99-2000	**Nashville Predators**	**NHL**	82	11	33	44	12	31	43	40	2	0	1	133	8.3	62	8	87	18	–15	....	....	....	....	....	....	....	....
	NHL Totals		433	79	146	225	87	137	224	196	17	4	6	617	12.8	300	65	351	73		26	6	3	9	12	1	0	0

• Brother of Ryan • Centennial Cup All-Star Team (1989) • WCHA First All-Star Team (1991, 1992, 1993) • NCAA West First All-American Team (1991, 1993) • NCAA West Second All-American Team (1992)

Traded to **Detroit** by **Philadelphia** with Philadelphia's 5th round choice (Frederic Deschenes) in 1994 Entry Draft for Jim Cummins and Philadelphia's 4th round choice (previously acquired by Detroit — later traded to Boston — Boston selected Charles Paquette) in 1993 Entry Draft, June 20, 1993. Traded to **Pittsburgh** by **Detroit** for Tomas Sandstrom, January 27, 1997. Traded to **Chicago** by **Pittsburgh** for Tuomas Gronman, October 27, 1997. Claimed by **Nashville** from **Chicago** in Expansion Draft, June 26, 1998.

• JOHNSON, Jim

D – L. 6'1", 190 lbs. b: New Hope, MN, 8/9/1962.

Season	Club	League	GP	G	A	Pts	AG	AA	APts	PIM	PP	SH	GW	S	%	TGF	PGF	TGA	PGA	+/–	GP	G	A	Pts	PIM	PP	SH	GW
1980-81	St. Paul Vulcans	USHL	48	7	25	32	....	....	....	92	....	....	....	....	....	....	....	....	....	....	6	1	3	4	8	....	....	....
1981-82	University of Minnesota-Duluth	WCHA	40	0	10	10	....	....	....	62	....	....	....	....	....	....	....	....	....	....	....	....	....	....	....	....	....	....
1982-83	University of Minnesota-Duluth	WCHA	44	3	18	21	....	....	....	118	....	....	....	....	....	....	....	....	....	....	....	....	....	....	....	....	....	....
1983-84	University of Minnesota-Duluth	WCHA	43	3	13	16	....	....	....	116	....	....	....	....	....	....	....	....	....	....	....	....	....	....	....	....	....	....
1984-85	University of Minnesota-Duluth	WCHA	47	7	29	36	....	....	....	49	....	....	....	....	....	....	....	....	....	....	....	....	....	....	....	....	....	....
	United States	WEC-A	9	0	1	1	....	....	....	22	....	....	....	....	....	....	....	....	....	....	....	....	....	....	....	....	....	....
1985-86	**Pittsburgh Penguins**	**NHL**	80	3	26	29	2	17	19	115	0	0	0	118	2.5	115	22	119	38	12	....	....	....	....	....	....	....	....
	United States	WEC-A	9	0	0	0	....	....	....	12	....	....	....	....	....	....	....	....	....	....	....	....	....	....	....	....	....	....
1986-87	**Pittsburgh Penguins**	**NHL**	80	5	25	30	4	18	22	116	0	0	1	89	5.6	92	18	115	35	–6	....	....	....	....	....	....	....	....
	United States	WEC-A	10	0	0	0	....	....	....	28	....	....	....	....	....	....	....	....	....	....	....	....	....	....	....	....	....	....
1987-88	**Pittsburgh Penguins**	**NHL**	55	1	12	13	1	9	10	87	0	0	0	44	2.3	40	4	74	34	–4	....	....	....	....	....	....	....	....
1988-89	**Pittsburgh Penguins**	**NHL**	76	2	14	16	2	10	12	163	1	0	0	70	2.9	85	13	114	49	7	11	0	5	5	44	0	0	0
1989-90	**Pittsburgh Penguins**	**NHL**	75	3	13	16	3	9	12	154	1	0	0	72	4.2	68	10	111	33	–20	....	....	....	....	....	....	....	....
	United States	WEC-A	10	0	5	5	....	....	....	16	....	....	....	....	....	....	....	....	....	....	....	....	....	....	....	....	....	....
1990-91	**Pittsburgh Penguins**	**NHL**	24	0	5	5	0	4	4	23	0	0	0	22	0.0	23	0	35	9	–3	....	....	....	....	....	....	....	....
	Minnesota North Stars	**NHL**	44	1	9	10	1	7	8	100	0	0	0	61	1.6	40	0	42	11	9	14	0	1	1	52	0	0	0
1991-92	United States	Can-Cup	8	0	0	0	....	....	....	20	....	....	....	....	....	....	....	....	....	....	....	....	....	....	....	....	....	....
	Minnesota North Stars	**NHL**	71	4	10	14	4	8	12	102	0	0	1	86	4.7	72	13	80	32	11	7	1	3	4	18	0	0	0
1992-93	**Minnesota North Stars**	**NHL**	79	3	20	23	2	14	16	105	1	0	0	67	4.5	74	4	100	39	9	....	....	....	....	....	....	....	....
1993-94	**Dallas Stars**	**NHL**	53	0	7	7	0	5	5	51	0	0	0	44	0.0	32	0	62	24	–6	....	....	....	....	....	....	....	....
	Washington Capitals	**NHL**	8	0	0	0	0	0	0	12	0	0	0	5	0.0	6	0	8	1	–1	....	....	....	....	....	....	....	....
1994-95	**Washington Capitals**	**NHL**	47	0	13	13	0	19	19	43	0	0	0	46	0.0	34	3	34	9	6	7	0	2	2	8	0	0	0
1995-96	**Washington Capitals**	**NHL**	66	2	4	6	2	3	5	34	0	0	0	49	4.1	25	0	32	4	–3	6	0	0	0	6	0	0	0
1996-97	**Phoenix Coyotes**	**NHL**	55	3	7	10	3	6	9	74	0	0	0	51	5.9	36	0	39	8	5	6	0	0	0	4	0	0	0
1997-98	**Phoenix Coyotes**	**NHL**	16	2	1	3	2	1	3	18	0	0	0	17	11.8	10	0	11	1	0	....	....	....	....	....	....	....	....
	NHL Totals		829	29	166	195	26	130	156	1197	3	0	2	841	3.4	752	87	976	327		51	1	11	12	132	0	0	0

Signed as a free agent by **Pittsburgh**, June 9, 1985. Traded to **Minnesota** by **Pittsburgh** with Chris Dahlquist for Larry Murphy and Peter Taglianetti, December 11, 1990. Transferred to **Dallas** after **Minnesota** franchise relocated, June 9, 1993. Traded to **Washington** by **Dallas** for Alan May and Washington's 7th round choice (Jeff Dewar) in 1995 Entry Draft, March 21, 1994. Signed as a free agent by **Phoenix**, July 6, 1996. • Suffered career-ending head injury in game vs. Tampa Bay, November 11, 1997. • Officially announced retirement, July 21, 1998.

• JOHNSON, Jim

Norman James C – L. 5'9", 190 lbs. b: Winnipeg, Man., 11/7/1942.

Season	Club	League	GP	G	A	Pts	AG	AA	APts	PIM	PP	SH	GW	S	%	TGF	PGF	TGA	PGA	+/–	GP	G	A	Pts	PIM	PP	SH	GW
1960-61	Winnipeg Rangers	MJHL	29	15	21	36	....	....	....	12	....	....	....	....	....	....	....	....	....	....	....	....	....	....	....	....	....	....
1961-62	Winnipeg Rangers	MJHL	39	22	23	45	....	....	....	48	....	....	....	....	....	....	....	....	....	....	3	1	1	2	0	....	....	....
1962-63	Sudbury Wolves	EPHL	70	16	36	52	....	....	....	16	....	....	....	....	....	....	....	....	....	....	8	1	4	5	2	....	....	....
1963-64	St. Paul Rangers	CPHL	70	21	33	54	....	....	....	14	....	....	....	....	....	....	....	....	....	....	11	3	5	8	0	....	....	....
1964-65	**New York Rangers**	**NHL**	1	0	0	0	0	0	0	0	....	....	....	....	....	....	....	....	....	....	....	....	....	....	....	....	....	....
	St. Paul Rangers	CPHL	61	19	45	64	....	....	....	14	....	....	....	....	....	....	....	....	....	....	11	4	6	10	7	....	....	....
1965-66	**New York Rangers**	**NHL**	5	1	0	1	1	0	1	0	....	....	....	....	....	....	....	....	....	....	....	....	....	....	....	....	....	....
	Minnesota Rangers	CPHL	62	24	46	70	....	....	....	12	....	....	....	....	....	....	....	....	....	....	7	3	2	5	0	....	....	....
1966-67	**New York Rangers**	**NHL**	2	0	0	0	0	0	0	0	....	....	....	....	....	....	....	....	....	....	....	....	....	....	....	....	....	....
	Omaha Knights	CPHL	64	26	46	72	....	....	....	20	....	....	....	....	....	....	....	....	....	....	12	2	5	7	2	....	....	....
1967-68	**Philadelphia Flyers**	**NHL**	13	2	1	3	2	1	3	2	0	0	0	12	16.7	3	0	4	0	–1	....	....	....	....	....	....	....	....
	Quebec Aces	AHL	59	27	45	72	....	....	....	14	....	....	....	....	....	....	....	....	....	....	15	5	8	13	10	....	....	....
1968-69	**Philadelphia Flyers**	**NHL**	69	17	27	44	18	24	42	20	1	1	5	146	11.6	55	7	71	18	–5	3	0	0	0	2	0	0	0
1969-70	**Philadelphia Flyers**	**NHL**	72	18	30	48	20	28	48	17	2	2	1	168	10.7	64	11	65	13	1	....	....	....	....	....	....	....	....
1970-71	**Philadelphia Flyers**	**NHL**	66	16	29	45	16	24	40	16	2	0	2	121	13.2	62	11	73	12	–10	4	0	2	2	0	0	0	0
	Quebec Aces	AHL	5	0	1	1	....	....	....	0	....	....	....	....	....	....	....	....	....	....	....	....	....	....	....	....	....	....
1971-72	**Philadelphia Flyers**	**NHL**	46	13	15	28	13	13	26	12	5	2	1	86	15.1	34	12	58	15	–21	....	....	....	....	....	....	....	....
	Los Angeles Kings	**NHL**	28	8	9	17	8	8	16	6	3	2	0	53	15.1	27	5	30	7	–1	....	....	....	....	....	....	....	....
1972-73	Minnesota Fighting Saints	WHA	33	9	14	23	....	....	....	12	....	....	....	....	....	....	....	....	....	....	5	2	1	3	2	....	....	....
1973-74	Minnesota Fighting Saints	WHA	71	15	39	54	....	....	....	30	....	....	....	....	....	....	....	....	....	....	11	1	4	5	4	....	....	....
1974-75	Minnesota Fighting Saints	WHA	11	1	3	4	....	....	....	0	....	....	....	....	....	....	....	....	....	....	....	....	....	....	....	....	....	....
	Indianapolis Racers	WHA	42	7	15	22	....	....	....	12	....	....	....	....	....	....	....	....	....	....	....	....	....	....	....	....	....	....
	NHL Totals		302	75	111	186	78	98	176	73	....	....	....	....	....	....	....	....	....	....	7	0	2	2	2	....	....	....
	Other Major League Totals		157	32	71	103	....	....	....	54	....	....	....	....	....	....	....	....	....	....	16	3	5	8	6	....	....	....

Claimed by **NY Rangers** from **Baltimore** (AHL) in Inter-League Draft, June 8, 1964. Claimed by **Philadelphia** from **NY Rangers** in Expansion Draft, June 6, 1967. Traded to **LA Kings** by **Philadelphia** with Bill Lesuk and Serge Bernier for Bill Flett, Eddie Joyal, Jean Potvin and Ross Lonsberry, January 28, 1972. Selected by **Minnesota** (WHA) in 1972 WHA General Player Draft, February 12, 1972. Traded to **Indianapolis** (WHA) by **Minnesota** (WHA) for Joe Robertson, November, 1974.

• JOHNSON, Mark

Mark E. C – L. 5'9", 170 lbs. b: Madison, WI, 9/22/1957. Pittsburgh's 3rd, 66th overall, in 1977.

Season	Club	League	GP	G	A	Pts	AG	AA	APts	PIM	PP	SH	GW	S	%	TGF	PGF	TGA	PGA	+/–	GP	G	A	Pts	PIM	PP	SH	GW
1975-76	Memorial High School	Hi-School	30	65	56	121	....	....	....	....	....	....	....	....	....	....	....	....	....	....	....	....	....	....	....	....	....	....
	United States	Nat-Team	11	5	6	11	....	....	....	0	....	....	....	....	....	....	....	....	....	....	....	....	....	....	....	....	....	....
1976-77	University of Wisconsin	WCHA	43	36	44	80	....	....	....	16	....	....	....	....	....	....	....	....	....	....	....	....	....	....	....	....	....	....
1977-78	University of Wisconsin	WCHA	42	*48	38	86	....	....	....	24	....	....	....	....	....	....	....	....	....	....	....	....	....	....	....	....	....	....
	United States	WEC-A	10	0	2	2	....	....	....	0	....	....	....	....	....	....	....	....	....	....	....	....	....	....	....	....	....	....
1978-79	University of Wisconsin	WCHA	40	*41	49	*90	....	....	....	34	....	....	....	....	....	....	....	....	....	....	....	....	....	....	....	....	....	....
	United States	WEC-A	2	0	0	0	....	....	....	0	....	....	....	....	....	....	....	....	....	....	....	....	....	....	....	....	....	....
1979-80	United States	Nat-Team	53	33	48	81	....	....	....	25	....	....	....	....	....	....	....	....	....	....	....	....	....	....	....	....	....	....
	United States	Olympics	7	5	6	11	....	....	....	6	....	....	....	....	....	....	....	....	....	....	....	....	....	....	....	....	....	....
	Pittsburgh Penguins	**NHL**	17	3	5	8	3	4	7	4	1	0	1	32	9.4	12	6	10	0	–4	5	2	2	4	0	1	0	1
1980-81	**Pittsburgh Penguins**	**NHL**	73	10	23	33	8	15	23	50	0	0	1	109	9.2	61	14	71	28	4	5	2	1	3	6	1	0	0
	United States	WEC-A	5	0	2	2	....	....	....	2	....	....	....	....	....	....	....	....	....	....	....	....	....	....	....	....	....	....
1981-82	United States	Can-Cup	6	1	3	4	....	....	....	2	....	....	....	....	....	....	....	....	....	....	....	....	....	....	....	....	....	....
	Pittsburgh Penguins	**NHL**	46	10	11	21	8	7	15	30	1	1	0	93	10.8	34	7	54	13	–14	....	....	....	....	....	....	....	....
	Minnesota North Stars	**NHL**	10	2	2	4	2	1	3	10	1	0	0	18	11.1	4	3	7	2	–4	4	2	0	2	0	1	0	0
	United States	WEC-A	7	1	1	2	....	....	....	6	....	....	....	....	....	....	....	....	....	....	....	....	....	....	....	....	....	....
1982-83	**Hartford Whalers**	**NHL**	73	31	38	69	25	26	51	28	5	3	5	167	18.6	92	22	116	41	–5	....	....	....	....	....	....	....	....
1983-84	**Hartford Whalers**	**NHL**	79	35	52	87	28	35	63	27	13	1	2	184	19.0	117	41	94	4	–14	....	....	....	....	....	....	....	....
1984-85	United States	Can-Cup	6	2	3	5	....	....	....	0	....	....	....	....	....	....	....	....	....	....	....	....	....	....	....	....	....	....
	Hartford Whalers	**NHL**	49	19	28	47	15	19	34	21	10	0	2	107	17.8	65	34	58	3	–24	....	....	....	....	....	....	....	....
	St. Louis Blues	**NHL**	17	4	6	10	3	4	7	2	2	0	0	36	11.1	16	6	19	7	–2	3	0	1	1	0	0	0	0
	United States	WEC-A	10	4	1	5	....	....	....	6	....	....	....	....	....	....	....	....	....	....	....	....	....	....	....	....	....	....
1985-86	**New Jersey Devils**	**NHL**	80	21	41	62	17	28	45	16	6	1	3	167	12.6	91	45	89	30	–13	....	....	....	....	....	....	....	....
	United States	WEC-A	10	5	3	8	....	....	....	10	....	....	....	....	....	....	....	....	....	....	....	....	....	....	....	....	....	....
1986-87	**New Jersey Devils**	**NHL**	68	25	26	51	22	19	41	22	11	2	0	193	13.0	86	57	81	31	–21	....	....	....	....	....	....	....	....
	United States	WEC-A	10	3	6	9	....	....	....	8	....	....	....	....	....	....	....	....	....	....	....	....	....	....	....	....	....	....

Season	Club	League	GP	G	A	Pts	AG	AA	APts	PIM	PP	SH	GW	S	%	TGF	PGF	TGA	PGA	+/–	GP	G	A	Pts	PIM	PP	SH	GW
			REGULAR SEASON																		PLAYOFFS							
1987-88	United States	Can-Cup	5	0	1	1	....	....	....	0	....	....	....	....	....	....	....	....	....	....	....	....	....	....	....	....	....	....
	New Jersey Devils	**NHL**	**54**	**14**	**19**	**33**	**12**	**14**	**26**	**14**	**2**	**3**	**3**	**121**	**11.6**	**60**	**33**	**53**	**16**	**–10**	**18**	**10**	**8**	**18**	**4**	**5**	**0**	**1**
1988-89	**New Jersey Devils**	**NHL**	**40**	**13**	**25**	**38**	**11**	**18**	**29**	**24**	**4**	**0**	**2**	**95**	**13.7**	**56**	**26**	**41**	**10**	**–1**	....	....	....	....	....	....	....	....
1989-90	**New Jersey Devils**	**NHL**	**63**	**16**	**29**	**45**	**14**	**21**	**35**	**12**	**4**	**0**	**1**	**82**	**19.5**	**72**	**16**	**71**	**7**	**–8**	**2**	**0**	**0**	**0**	**0**	**0**	**0**	**0**
	United States	WEC-A	9	2	3	5	....	....	....	2	....	....	....	....	....	....	....	....	....	....	....	....	....	....	....	....	....	....
1990-91	HC Milano Saima	Italy	36	32	45	77	....	....	....	15	....	....	....	....	....	....	....	....	....	....	10	7	16	23	6	....	....	....
1991-92	HC Milano Saima	Italy	2	1	3	4	....	....	....	0	....	....	....	....	....	....	....	....	....	....	....	....	....	....	....	....	....	....
	HK Zell-am-Zee	Alpenliga	18	13	28	41	....	....	....	8	....	....	....	....	....	....	....	....	....	....	....	....	....	....	....	....	....	....
	HK Zell-am-Zee	Austria	15	10	21	31	....	....	....	6	....	....	....	....	....	....	....	....	....	....	....	....	....	....	....	....	....	....
1992-1994	Madison Memorial High	Hi-School	DID NOT PLAY – COACHING																									
1994-1995	Verona High School	Hi-School	DID NOT PLAY – COACHING																									
1995-1996	Madison Monsters	ColHL	DID NOT PLAY – COACHING																									
1996-1999	University of Wisconsin	WCHA	DID NOT PLAY – ASSISTANT COACH																									
1998-1999	United States	WC-Q	2	0	0	0	....	....	....	0	....	....	....	....	....	....	....	....	....	....	....	....	....	....	....	....	....	....
1999-2000	University of Wisconsin	WCHA	DID NOT PLAY – ASSISTANT COACH																									
	NHL Totals		**669**	**203**	**305**	**508**	**168**	**211**	**379**	**260**	**60**	**11**	**20**	**1404**	**14.5**	**766**	**310**	**764**	**192**		**37**	**16**	**12**	**28**	**10**	**8**	**0**	**2**

WCHA First All-Star Team (1978, 1979) • NCAA West First All-American Team (1978, 1979) • Played in NHL All-Star Game (1984)

Traded to **Minnesota** by **Pittsburgh** for Minnesota's 2nd round choice (Tim Hrynewich) in 1982 Entry Draft, March 2, 1982. Traded to **Hartford** by **Minnesota** with Kent-Erik Andersson for Jordy Douglas and Hartford's 5th round choice (Jiri Poner) in 1984 Entry Draft, October 1, 1982. Traded to **St. Louis** by **Hartford** with Greg Millen for Mike Luit and Jorgen Petterson, February 21, 1985. Traded to **New Jersey** by **St. Louis** for Shawn Evans and New Jersey's 5th round choice (Michael Wolak) in 1986 Entry Draft, September 19, 1985.

• JOHNSON, Matt

LW – L. 6'5", 232 lbs. b: Welland, Ont., 11/23/1975. Los Angeles' 2nd, 33rd overall, in 1994.

Season	Club	League	GP	G	A	Pts	AG	AA	APts	PIM	PP	SH	GW	S	%	TGF	PGF	TGA	PGA	+/–	GP	G	A	Pts	PIM	PP	SH	GW
1991-92	Welland Aerostars	OJHL-B	38	6	19	25	....	....	....	214	....	....	....	....	....	....	....	....	....	....	....	....	....	....	....	....	....	....
	Ajax Axemen	OJHL-B	1	0	0	0	....	....	....	0	....	....	....	....	....	....	....	....	....	....	....	....	....	....	....	....	....	....
1992-93	Peterborough Petes	OHL	66	8	17	25	....	....	....	211	....	....	....	....	....	....	....	....	....	....	16	1	1	2	56	....	....	....
	Peterborough Petes	Mem-Cup	4	0	0	0	....	....	....	2	....	....	....	....	....	....	....	....	....	....	....	....	....	....	....	....	....	....
1993-94	Peterborough Petes	OHL	50	13	24	37	....	....	....	233	....	....	....	....	....	....	....	....	....	....	....	....	....	....	....	....	....	....
1994-95	Peterborough Petes	OHL	14	1	2	3	....	....	....	43	....	....	....	....	....	....	....	....	....	....	....	....	....	....	....	....	....	....
	Los Angeles Kings	**NHL**	**14**	**1**	**0**	**1**	**2**	**0**	**2**	**102**	**0**	**0**	**0**	**4**	**25.0**	**1**	**0**	**1**	**0**	**0**	....	....	....	....	....	....	....	....
1995-96	**Los Angeles Kings**	**NHL**	**1**	**0**	**0**	**0**	**0**	**0**	**0**	**5**	**0**	**0**	**0**	**1**	**0.0**	**0**	**0**	**0**	**0**	**0**	....	....	....	....	....	....	....	....
	Phoenix Roadrunners	IHL	29	4	4	8	....	....	....	87	....	....	....	....	....	....	....	....	....	....	....	....	....	....	....	....	....	....
1996-97	**Los Angeles Kings**	**NHL**	**52**	**1**	**3**	**4**	**1**	**3**	**4**	**194**	**0**	**0**	**0**	**20**	**5.0**	**7**	**0**	**11**	**0**	**–4**	....	....	....	....	....	....	....	....
1997-98	**Los Angeles Kings**	**NHL**	**66**	**2**	**4**	**6**	**2**	**4**	**6**	**249**	**0**	**0**	**0**	**18**	**11.1**	**9**	**0**	**17**	**0**	**–8**	**4**	**0**	**0**	**0**	**6**	**0**	**0**	**0**
1998-99	**Los Angeles Kings**	**NHL**	**49**	**2**	**1**	**3**	**2**	**1**	**3**	**131**	**0**	**0**	**0**	**14**	**14.3**	**6**	**0**	**11**	**0**	**–5**	....	....	....	....	....	....	....	....
99-2000	**Atlanta Thrashers**	**NHL**	**64**	**2**	**5**	**7**	**2**	**5**	**7**	**144**	**0**	**0**	**0**	**54**	**3.7**	**12**	**0**	**24**	**1**	**–11**	....	....	....	....	....	....	....	....
	NHL Totals		**246**	**8**	**13**	**21**	**9**	**13**	**22**	**825**	**0**	**0**	**0**	**111**	**7.2**	**35**	**0**	**64**	**1**		**4**	**0**	**0**	**0**	**6**	**0**	**0**	**0**

Claimed by **Atlanta** from **Los Angeles** in Expansion Draft, June 25, 1999.

• JOHNSON, Mike

Michael Paul RW – R. 6'2", 197 lbs. b: Scarborough, Ont., 10/3/1974.

Season	Club	League	GP	G	A	Pts	AG	AA	APts	PIM	PP	SH	GW	S	%	TGF	PGF	TGA	PGA	+/–	GP	G	A	Pts	PIM	PP	SH	GW
1991-92	Hillcrest Summits	MTHL	45	43	66	109	....	....	....	....	....	....	....	....	....	....	....	....	....	....	20	10	19	29	....	....	....	....
1992-93	Aurora Eagles	OJHL	48	25	40	65	....	....	....	18	....	....	....	....	....	....	....	....	....	....	7	7	15	22	....	....	....	....
1993-94	Bowling Green University	CCHA	38	6	14	20	....	....	....	18	....	....	....	....	....	....	....	....	....	....	....	....	....	....	....	....	....	....
1994-95	Bowling Green University	CCHA	37	16	33	49	....	....	....	35	....	....	....	....	....	....	....	....	....	....	....	....	....	....	....	....	....	....
1995-96	Bowling Green University	CCHA	30	12	19	31	....	....	....	22	....	....	....	....	....	....	....	....	....	....	....	....	....	....	....	....	....	....
1996-97	Bowling Green University	CCHA	38	30	32	62	....	....	....	46	....	....	....	....	....	....	....	....	....	....	....	....	....	....	....	....	....	....
	Toronto Maple Leafs	**NHL**	**13**	**2**	**2**	**4**	**2**	**2**	**4**	**4**	**0**	**1**	**1**	**27**	**7.4**	**8**	**1**	**11**	**2**	**–2**	....	....	....	....	....	....	....	....
1997-98	**Toronto Maple Leafs**	**NHL**	**82**	**15**	**32**	**47**	**18**	**31**	**49**	**24**	**5**	**0**	**0**	**143**	**10.5**	**71**	**23**	**65**	**13**	**–4**	....	....	....	....	....	....	....	....
1998-99	**Toronto Maple Leafs**	**NHL**	**79**	**20**	**24**	**44**	**23**	**23**	**46**	**35**	**5**	**3**	**2**	**149**	**13.4**	**67**	**16**	**51**	**13**	**13**	**17**	**3**	**2**	**5**	**4**	**0**	**0**	**1**
99-2000	**Toronto Maple Leafs**	**NHL**	**52**	**11**	**14**	**25**	**12**	**13**	**25**	**23**	**2**	**1**	**3**	**89**	**12.4**	**37**	**5**	**34**	**10**	**8**	....	....	....	....	....	....	....	....
	Tampa Bay Lightning	**NHL**	**28**	**10**	**12**	**22**	**11**	**11**	**22**	**4**	**4**	**0**	**0**	**43**	**23.3**	**29**	**12**	**26**	**7**	**–2**	....	....	....	....	....	....	....	....
	Canada	WC-A	9	1	1	2	....	....	....	10	....	....	....	....	....	....	....	....	....	....	....	....	....	....	....	....	....	....
	NHL Totals		**254**	**58**	**84**	**142**	**66**	**80**	**146**	**90**	**16**	**5**	**6**	**451**	**12.9**	**212**	**57**	**187**	**45**		**17**	**3**	**2**	**5**	**4**	**0**	**0**	**1**

NHL All-Rookie Team (1998)

Signed as a free agent by **Toronto**, March 16, 1997. Traded to **Tampa Bay** by **Toronto** with Marek Posmyk, Toronto's 5th (Pavel Sedov) and 6th (Aaron Gionet) round choices in 2000 Entry Draft and future considerations for Darcy Tucker, Tampa Bay's 4th round choice (Miguel Delisle) in 2000 Entry Draft and future considerations, February 9, 2000.

• JOHNSON, Ryan

Ryan M. C – L. 6'1", 200 lbs. b: Thunder Bay, Ont., 6/14/1976. Florida's 4th, 36th overall, in 1994.

Season	Club	League	GP	G	A	Pts	AG	AA	APts	PIM	PP	SH	GW	S	%	TGF	PGF	TGA	PGA	+/–	GP	G	A	Pts	PIM	PP	SH	GW
1992-93	Thunder Bay Kings	TBAHA	60	25	33	58	....	....	....	....	....	....	....	....	....	....	....	....	....	....								
1993-94	Thunder Bay Flyers	USHL	48	14	36	50	....	....	....	28	....	....	....	....	....	....	....	....	....	....	....	....	....	....	....	....	....	....
1994-95	University of North Dakota	WCHA	38	6	22	28	....	....	....	39	....	....	....	....	....	....	....	....	....	....	....	....	....	....	....	....	....	....
1995-96	University of North Dakota	WCHA	21	2	17	19	....	....	....	14	....	....	....	....	....	....	....	....	....	....	....	....	....	....	....	....	....	....
	Canada	Nat-Team	28	5	12	17	....	....	....	14	....	....	....	....	....	....	....	....	....	....	....	....	....	....	....	....	....	....
1996-97	Carolina Monarchs	AHL	79	18	24	42	....	....	....	28	....	....	....	....	....	....	....	....	....	....	....	....	....	....	....	....	....	....
1997-98	**Florida Panthers**	**NHL**	**10**	**0**	**2**	**2**	**0**	**2**	**2**	**0**	**0**	**0**	**0**	**6**	**0.0**	**2**	**0**	**9**	**3**	**–4**	....	....	....	....	....	....	....	....
	Beast of New Haven	AHL	64	19	48	67	....	....	....	12	....	....	....	....	....	....	....	....	....	....	3	0	1	1	0	....	....	....
1998-99	**Florida Panthers**	**NHL**	**1**	**1**	**0**	**1**	**1**	**0**	**1**	**0**	**0**	**0**	**0**	**1**	**100.0**	**1**	**0**	**1**	**0**	**0**	....	....	....	....	....	....	....	....
	Beast of New Haven	AHL	37	8	19	27	....	....	....	18	....	....	....	....	....	....	....	....	....	....	....	....	....	....	....	....	....	....
99-2000	**Florida Panthers**	**NHL**	**66**	**4**	**12**	**16**	**4**	**11**	**15**	**14**	**0**	**0**	**0**	**44**	**9.1**	**24**	**1**	**37**	**15**	**1**	....	....	....	....	....	....	....	....
	Tampa Bay Lightning	**NHL**	**14**	**0**	**2**	**2**	**0**	**2**	**2**	**2**	**0**	**0**	**0**	**5**	**0.0**	**2**	**0**	**16**	**5**	**–9**	....	....	....	....	....	....	....	....
	NHL Totals		**91**	**5**	**16**	**21**	**5**	**15**	**20**	**16**	**0**	**0**	**0**	**56**	**8.9**	**29**	**1**	**63**	**23**		....	....	....	....	....	....	....	....

• Brother of Greg

Traded to **Tampa Bay** by **Florida**. with Dwayne Hay for Mike Sillinger, March 14, 2000.

• JOHNSON, Terry

D – L. 6'3", 210 lbs. b: Calgary, Alta., 11/28/1958.

Season	Club	League	GP	G	A	Pts	AG	AA	APts	PIM	PP	SH	GW	S	%	TGF	PGF	TGA	PGA	+/–	GP	G	A	Pts	PIM	PP	SH	GW
1975-76	Calgary Canucks	AJHL	55	3	13	16	....	....	....	100	....	....	....	....	....	....	....	....	....	....	....	....	....	....	....	....	....	....
1976-77	Calgary Canucks	AJHL	60	5	26	31	....	....	....	31	....	....	....	....	....	....	....	....	....	....	....	....	....	....	....	....	....	....
1977-78	Saskatoon Blades	WCJHL	70	2	20	22	....	....	....	195	....	....	....	....	....	....	....	....	....	....	....	....	....	....	....	....	....	....
1978-79	University of Calgary	CWUAA	24	2	4	6	....	....	....	81	....	....	....	....	....	....	....	....	....	....	3	1	0	1	2	....	....	....
1979-80	**Quebec Nordiques**	**NHL**	**3**	**0**	**0**	**0**	**0**	**0**	**0**	**2**	**0**	**0**	**0**	**0**	**0.0**	**1**	**0**	**1**	**0**	**0**	....	....	....	....	....	....	....	....
	Syracuse Firebirds	AHL	74	0	13	13	....	....	....	163	....	....	....	....	....	....	....	....	....	....	4	0	0	0	7	....	....	....
1980-81	**Quebec Nordiques**	**NHL**	**13**	**0**	**1**	**1**	**0**	**1**	**1**	**46**	**0**	**0**	**0**	**5**	**0.0**	**7**	**0**	**9**	**1**	**–1**	**2**	**0**	**0**	**0**	**0**	**0**	**0**	**0**
	Hershey Bears	AHL	63	1	7	8	....	....	....	207	....	....	....	....	....	....	....	....	....	....	9	0	1	1	14	....	....	....
1981-82	**Quebec Nordiques**	**NHL**	**6**	**0**	**1**	**1**	**0**	**1**	**1**	**5**	**0**	**0**	**0**	**0**	**0.0**	**2**	**0**	**3**	**0**	**–1**	....	....	....	....	....	....	....	....
	Fredericton Express	AHL	43	0	7	7	....	....	....	132	....	....	....	....	....	....	....	....	....	....	....	....	....	....	....	....	....	....
1982-83	**Quebec Nordiques**	**NHL**	**3**	**0**	**0**	**0**	**0**	**0**	**0**	**2**	**0**	**0**	**0**	**0**	**0.0**	**0**	**0**	**0**	**0**	**0**	....	....	....	....	....	....	....	....
	Fredericton Express	AHL	78	2	15	17	....	....	....	181	....	....	....	....	....	....	....	....	....	....	12	1	1	2	12	....	....	....
1983-84	**St. Louis Blues**	**NHL**	**65**	**2**	**6**	**8**	**2**	**4**	**6**	**143**	**0**	**0**	**0**	**38**	**5.3**	**51**	**1**	**78**	**33**	**5**	**11**	**0**	**1**	**1**	**25**	**0**	**0**	**0**
1984-85	**St. Louis Blues**	**NHL**	**74**	**0**	**7**	**7**	**0**	**5**	**5**	**120**	....	....	....	....	....	....	....	....	....	....	**3**	**0**	**0**	**0**	**19**	**0**	**0**	**0**
1985-86	**St. Louis Blues**	**NHL**	**49**	**0**	**4**	**4**	**0**	**3**	**3**	**87**	**0**	**0**	**0**	**21**	**0.0**	**42**	**1**	**72**	**25**	**–6**	....	....	....	....	....	....	....	....
	Calgary Flames	**NHL**	**24**	**1**	**4**	**5**	**1**	**3**	**4**	**71**	**0**	**0**	**0**	**11**	**9.1**	**19**	**0**	**34**	**12**	**–3**	**17**	**0**	**3**	**3**	**64**	**0**	**0**	**0**

			REGULAR SEASON																		PLAYOFFS							
Season	Club	League	GP	G	A	Pts	AG	AA	APts	PIM	PP	SH	GW	S	%	TGF	PGF	TGA	PGA	+/-	GP	G	A	Pts	PIM	PP	SH	GW
1986-87	**Toronto Maple Leafs**	**NHL**	**48**	**0**	**1**	**1**	**0**	**1**	**1**	**104**	**0**	**0**	**0**	**10**	**0.0**	**27**	**0**	**38**	**6**	**-5**	**2**	**0**	**0**	**0**	**0**	**0**	**0**	**0**
	Newmarket Saints	AHL	24	0	1	1				37																		
1987-88	Newmarket Saints	AHL	72	3	3	6				174																		
	Toronto Maple Leafs	**NHL**																			**3**	**0**	**0**	**0**	**10**	**0**	**0**	**0**
	NHL Totals		**285**	**3**	**24**	**27**	**3**	**18**	**21**	**580**	**0**	**0**	**0**	**85**	**3.5**	**149**	**2**	**235**	**77**		**38**	**0**	**4**	**4**	**118**	**0**	**0**	**0**

Signed as a free agent by **Quebec**, October 1, 1978. Claimed by **St. Louis** from **Quebec** in Waiver Draft, October 3, 1983. Traded to **Calgary** by **St. Louis** with Joe Mullen and Rik Wilson for Eddy Beers, Charlie Bourgeois and Gino Cavallini, February 1, 1986. Traded to **Toronto** by **Calgary** for Jim Korn, October 3, 1986.

● JOHNSSON, Kim

D – L. 6'1", 175 lbs. b: Malmo, Sweden, 3/16/1976. NY Rangers' 15th, 286th overall, in 1994.

Season	Club	League	GP	G	A	Pts	AG	AA	APts	PIM	PP	SH	GW	S	%	TGF	PGF	TGA	PGA	+/-	GP	G	A	Pts	PIM	PP	SH	GW
1993-94	Malmo IF	Sweden-Jr.	14	5	3	8				14																		
	Malmo IF	Sweden	2	0	0	0				0																		
1994-95	Malmo IF	Sweden-Jr.	29	6	15	21				40																		
	Malmo IF	Sweden	13	0	0	0				4											1	0	0	0	0			
1995-96	Malmo IF	Sweden	38	2	0	2				30											4	0	1	1	8			
	Sweden	WJC-A	7	1	2	3				6																		
1996-97	Malmo IF	Sweden	49	4	9	13				42											4	0	0	0	2			
1997-98	Malmo IF	Sweden	45	5	9	14				29																		
	Sweden	WC-A	10	1	0	1				4																		
1998-99	Malmo IF	Sweden	49	9	8	17				76											8	2	3	5	12			
	Sweden	WC-A	10	0	0	0				4																		
99-2000	**New York Rangers**	**NHL**	**76**	**6**	**15**	**21**	**7**	**14**	**21**	**46**	**1**	**0**	**1**	**101**	**5.9**	**61**	**13**	**69**	**8**	**-13**								
	NHL Totals		**76**	**6**	**15**	**21**	**7**	**14**	**21**	**46**	**1**	**0**	**1**	**101**	**5.9**	**61**	**13**	**69**	**8**									

● JOHNSTON, Bernie

C – L. 5'11", 185 lbs. b: Toronto, Ont., 9/15/1956.

Season	Club	League	GP	G	A	Pts	AG	AA	APts	PIM	PP	SH	GW	S	%	TGF	PGF	TGA	PGA	+/-	GP	G	A	Pts	PIM	PP	SH	GW
1972-73	Ajax Waxers	OHA-B	30	28	42	70				32																		
1973-74	Toronto Marlboros	OMJHL	65	10	11	21				21																		
1974-75	Toronto Marlboros	OMJHL	47	9	29	38				20											3	1	2	3	4			
	Toronto Marlboros	Mem-Cup	4	0	4	4				2																		
1975-76	Toronto Marlboros	OMJHL	60	22	39	61				44											10	0	4	4	8			
1976-77	Syracuse Blazers	NAHL	73	53	71	124				40											9	1	9	10	2			
1977-78	Maine Mariners	AHL	68	28	29	57				35											11	2	7	9	6			
1978-79	Maine Mariners	AHL	70	29	*66	*95				40											10	2	5	7	8			
1979-80	**Hartford Whalers**	**NHL**	**32**	**8**	**13**	**21**	**7**	**9**	**16**	**8**	**0**	**0**	**0**	**54**	**14.8**	**33**	**0**	**24**	**0**	**9**	**3**	**0**	**1**	**1**	**0**	**0**	**0**	**0**
	Springfield Indians	AHL	41	18	36	54				25																		
1980-81	**Hartford Whalers**	**NHL**	**25**	**4**	**11**	**15**	**3**	**7**	**10**	**8**	**0**	**0**	**0**	**34**	**11.8**	**18**	**1**	**21**	**0**	**-4**								
	Binghamton Whalers	AHL	38	14	22	36				36											3	0	0	0	0			
1981-82	EHC Kloten	Switz.	38	24	22	46																						
	Maine Mariners	AHL																			4	0	5	5	0			
1982-83	EHC Kloten	Switz.	38	36	32	68																						
	Maine Mariners	AHL	11	7	2	9				2											8	4	1	5	4			
1983-84	EHC Kloten	Switz.	38	31	34	65																						
1984-85	EHC Basel	Switz.	32	33	46	79																						
1985-86	EHC Basel	Switz-2	36	25	33	58																						
	Hershey Bears	AHL	15	2	9	11				6											18	2	3	5	11			
1986-87			DID NOT PLAY																									
1987-88			DID NOT PLAY																									
1988-89	Maine Mariners	AHL	11	2	3	5				0																		
	NHL Totals		**57**	**12**	**24**	**36**	**10**	**16**	**26**	**16**	**0**	**0**	**0**	**88**	**13.6**	**51**	**1**	**45**	**0**		**3**	**0**	**1**	**1**	**0**	**0**	**0**	**0**

AHL First All-Star Team (1979) • Won John B. Sollenberger Trophy (Top Scorer - AHL) (1979) • Won Fred T. Hunt Memorial Trophy (Sportsmanship - AHL) (1979)

Signed as a free agent by **Philadelphia**, September 28, 1977. Claimed by **Hartford** from **Philadelphia** in Expansion Draft, June 13, 1979.

● JOHNSTON, Greg

Gregory Norman "Magic" RW – R. 6'1", 205 lbs. b: Barrie, Ont., 1/14/1965. Boston's 2nd, 42nd overall, in 1983.

Season	Club	League	GP	G	A	Pts	AG	AA	APts	PIM	PP	SH	GW	S	%	TGF	PGF	TGA	PGA	+/-	GP	G	A	Pts	PIM	PP	SH	GW
1981-82	Barrie Midget Colts	OMHA	42	31	46	77				74																		
1982-83	Toronto Marlboros	OHL	58	18	19	37				58											4	1	0	1	4			
1983-84	Toronto Marlboros	OHL	57	38	35	73				67											9	4	2	6	13			
	Boston Bruins	**NHL**	**15**	**2**	**1**	**3**	**2**	**1**	**3**	**2**	**0**	**0**	**1**	**15**	**13.3**	**8**	**1**	**10**	**0**	**-3**								
1984-85	Toronto Marlboros	OHL	42	22	28	50				55											5	1	3	4	4			
	Canada	WJC-A	7	2	0	2				2																		
	Boston Bruins	**NHL**	**6**	**0**	**0**	**0**	**0**	**0**	**0**	**0**	**0**	**0**	**0**	**1**	**0.0**	**1**	**0**	**2**	**0**	**-1**								
	Hershey Bears	AHL	3	1	0	1				0																		
1985-86	**Boston Bruins**	**NHL**	**20**	**0**	**2**	**2**	**0**	**1**	**1**	**0**	**0**	**0**	**0**	**11**	**0.0**	**5**	**0**	**12**	**6**	**-1**								
	Moncton Golden Flames	AHL	60	19	26	45				56											10	4	6	10	4			
1986-87	**Boston Bruins**	**NHL**	**76**	**12**	**15**	**27**	**10**	**11**	**21**	**79**	**0**	**0**	**1**	**131**	**9.2**	**45**	**3**	**75**	**26**	**-7**	**4**	**0**	**0**	**0**	**0**	**0**	**0**	**0**
1987-88	Maine Mariners	AHL	75	21	32	53				106											10	6	4	10	23			
	Boston Bruins	**NHL**																			**3**	**0**	**1**	**1**	**2**	**0**	**0**	**0**
1988-89	**Boston Bruins**	**NHL**	**57**	**11**	**9**	**20**	**9**	**6**	**15**	**32**	**0**	**1**	**5**	**89**	**12.4**	**39**	**2**	**48**	**18**	**7**	**10**	**1**	**0**	**1**	**6**	**0**	**1**	**0**
	Maine Mariners	AHL	15	5	7	12				31																		
1989-90	**Boston Bruins**	**NHL**	**9**	**1**	**1**	**2**	**1**	**1**	**2**	**6**	**0**	**0**	**0**	**9**	**11.1**	**2**	**0**	**3**	**0**	**-1**	**5**	**1**	**0**	**1**	**4**	**0**	**0**	**1**
	Maine Mariners	AHL	52	16	26	42				45																		
1990-91	**Toronto Maple Leafs**	**NHL**	**1**	**0**	**0**	**0**	**0**	**0**	**0**	**0**	**0**	**0**	**0**	**0**	**0.0**	**0**	**0**	**0**	**0**	**0**								
	Newmarket Saints	AHL	73	32	50	82				54																		
1991-92	**Toronto Maple Leafs**	**NHL**	**3**	**0**	**1**	**1**	**0**	**1**	**1**	**5**	**0**	**0**	**0**	**2**	**0.0**	**2**	**0**	**3**	**0**	**-1**								
	St. John's Maple Leafs	AHL	63	28	45	73				33											16	8	6	14	10			
1992-93	ECD Sauerland	Germany-2	47	49	59	108				70																		
1993-94	ECD Sauerland	Germany-2	51	40	60	100				74																		
1994-95	Kassel Huskies	Germany	42	17	27	44				26											9	4	6	10	6			
1995-96	Kassel Huskies	Germany	49	16	23	39				75											8	0	1	1	12			
1996-97	Kassel Huskies	Germany	49	19	22	41				98											10	*8	4	12	14			
1997-98	Kassel Huskies	Germany	43	9	28	37				73																		
	Kassel Huskies	EuroHL	6	2	2	4				6																		
1998-99	Kassel Huskies	Germany	52	11	16	27				28																		
99-2000	Berlin Capitals	Germany	56	19	21	40				68											7	1	4	5	14			
	NHL Totals		**187**	**26**	**29**	**55**	**22**	**21**	**43**	**124**	**0**	**1**	**7**	**258**	**10.1**	**102**	**6**	**153**	**50**		**22**	**2**	**1**	**3**	**12**	**0**	**1**	**1**

Traded to **NY Rangers** by **Boston** with future considerations for Chris Nilan, June 28, 1990. Traded to **Toronto** by **NY Rangers** for Tie Domi and Mark LaForest, June 28, 1990.

● JOHNSTON, Jay

Jay John Timothy D – L. 5'11", 195 lbs. b: Hamilton, Ont., 2/28/1958. Washington's 6th, 45th overall, in 1978.

Season	Club	League	GP	G	A	Pts	AG	AA	APts	PIM	PP	SH	GW	S	%	TGF	PGF	TGA	PGA	+/-	GP	G	A	Pts	PIM	PP	SH	GW
1975-76	Hamilton Tigers	OJHL	36	1	25	26				70																		
1976-77	St. Catharines Fincups	OMJHL	65	8	20	28				146											14	0	6	6	49			
1977-78	Hamilton Fincups	OMJHL	48	2	12	14				163											18	0	3	3	59			
1978-79	Port Huron Flags	IHL	75	5	19	24				409											6	0	1	1	21			
1979-80	Hershey Bears	AHL	69	3	20	23				229											14	0	4	4	42			
1980-81	**Washington Capitals**	**NHL**	**2**	**0**	**0**	**0**	**0**	**0**	**0**	**9**	**0**	**0**	**0**	**0**	**0.0**	**1**	**0**	**1**	**0**	**0**								
	Hershey Bears	AHL	61	1	11	12				187											4	0	0	0	4			
1981-82	**Washington Capitals**	**NHL**	**6**	**0**	**0**	**0**	**0**	**0**	**0**	**4**	**0**	**0**	**0**	**3**	**0.0**	**1**	**0**	**5**	**2**	**-2**								
	Hershey Bears	AHL	67	4	9	13				228											5	0	0	0	22			
1982-83	Hershey Bears	AHL	76	3	13	16				148											5	0	0	0	14			
1983-84	Hershey Bears	AHL	69	1	9	10				231																		

			REGULAR SEASON																		PLAYOFFS							
Season	Club	League	GP	G	A	Pts	AG	AA	APts	PIM	PP	SH	GW	S	%	TGF	PGF	TGA	PGA	+/–	GP	G	A	Pts	PIM	PP	SH	GW
1984-85	Fort Wayne Komets	IHL	69	1	12	13	....	....	....	211	....	....	....	....	....	....	....	....	....	....	13	1	4	5	36	....	....	....
1985-86	Fort Wayne Komets	IHL	78	1	13	14	....	....	....	176	....	....	....	....	....	....	....	....	....	....	15	0	1	1	47	....	....	....
1986-87	Fort Wayne Komets	IHL	31	0	8	8	....	....	....	92	....	....	....	....	....	....	....	....	....	....	....	....	....	....	....	....	....	....
	NHL Totals		**8**	**0**	**0**	**0**	**0**	**0**	**0**	**13**	**0**	**0**	**0**	**3**	**0.0**	**2**	**0**	**6**	**2**		....	....	....	....	....	....	....	....

• JOHNSTON, Joey

Joseph John LW – L. 5'10", 180 lbs. b: Peterborough, Ont., 3/3/1949. NY Rangers' 2nd, 8th overall, in 1966.

Season	Club	League	GP	G	A	Pts	AG	AA	APts	PIM	PP	SH	GW	S	%	TGF	PGF	TGA	PGA	+/–	GP	G	A	Pts	PIM	PP	SH	GW
1964-65	Peterborough Jr. Bees	OHA-B	STATISTICS NOT AVAILABLE																									
	Peterborough Petes	OHA-Jr.	3	0	0	0	....	....	....	0	....	....	....	....	....	....	....	....	....	....	....	....	....	....	....	....	....	....
1965-66	Peterborough Petes	OHA-Jr.	44	8	15	23	....	....	....	91	....	....	....	....	....	....	....	....	....	....	6	0	0	0	10	....	....	....
1966-67	Peterborough Petes	OHA-Jr.	32	8	19	27	....	....	....	114	....	....	....	....	....	....	....	....	....	....	6	1	3	4	28	....	....	....
1967-68	Buffalo Bisons	AHL	1	0	0	0	....	....	....	0	....	....	....	....	....	....	....	....	....	....	....	....	....	....	....	....	....	....
	Omaha Knights	CPHL	70	24	22	46	....	....	....	131	....	....	....	....	....	....	....	....	....	....	....	....	....	....	....	....	....	....
1968-69	**Minnesota North Stars**	**NHL**	**11**	**1**	**0**	**1**	**1**	**0**	**1**	**6**	**0**	**0**	**0**	**17**	**5.9**	**2**	**0**	**3**	**0**	**–1**	....	....	....	....	....	....	....	....
	Memphis South Stars	CHL	58	20	37	57	....	....	....	91	....	....	....	....	....	....	....	....	....	....	....	....	....	....	....	....	....	....
1969-70	Iowa Stars	CHL	62	20	37	57	....	....	....	115	....	....	....	....	....	....	....	....	....	....	11	4	6	10	38	....	....	....
1970-71	Cleveland Barons	AHL	72	27	47	74	....	....	....	142	....	....	....	....	....	....	....	....	....	....	8	7	4	11	24	....	....	....
1971-72	**California Golden Seals**	**NHL**	**77**	**15**	**17**	**32**	**15**	**15**	**30**	**107**	**0**	**0**	**3**	**154**	**9.7**	**49**	**3**	**96**	**22**	**–28**	....	....	....	....	....	....	....	....
1972-73	**California Golden Seals**	**NHL**	**71**	**28**	**21**	**49**	**26**	**17**	**43**	**62**	**8**	**1**	**2**	**170**	**16.5**	**74**	**20**	**81**	**8**	**–19**	....	....	....	....	....	....	....	....
1973-74	**California Golden Seals**	**NHL**	**78**	**27**	**40**	**67**	**26**	**33**	**59**	**67**	**10**	**2**	**0**	**202**	**13.4**	**83**	**21**	**105**	**6**	**–37**	....	....	....	....	....	....	....	....
1974-75	**California Golden Seals**	**NHL**	**62**	**14**	**23**	**37**	**12**	**17**	**29**	**72**	**5**	**0**	**0**	**133**	**10.5**	**47**	**19**	**63**	**5**	**–30**	....	....	....	....	....	....	....	....
1975-76	**Chicago Black Hawks**	**NHL**	**32**	**0**	**5**	**5**	**0**	**4**	**4**	**6**	**0**	**0**	**0**	**20**	**0.0**	**9**	**4**	**11**	**1**	**–5**	....	....	....	....	....	....	....	....
	Dallas Black Hawks	CHL	11	4	2	6	....	....	....	4	....	....	....	....	....	....	....	....	....	....	....	....	....	....	....	....	....	....
	NHL Totals		**331**	**85**	**106**	**191**	**80**	**86**	**166**	**320**	**23**	**3**	**5**	**696**	**12.2**	**264**	**67**	**359**	**42**		....	....	....	....	....	....	....	....

AHL First All-Star Team (1971) • Played in NHL All-Star Game (1973, 1974, 1975)

Traded to **Minnesota** by **NY Rangers** with Wayne Hillman and Dan Seguin for Dave Balon, June 12, 1968. Traded to **California** by **Minnesota** with Walt McKechnie for Dennis Hextall, May 20, 1971. Traded to **Chicago** by **California** for Jim Pappin and Chicago's 3rd round choice (Guy Lash) in 1977 Amateur Draft, June 1, 1975.

• JOHNSTON, Larry

Larry Roy D – R. 5'11", 195 lbs. b: Kitchener, Ont., 7/20/1943.

Season	Club	League	GP	G	A	Pts	AG	AA	APts	PIM	PP	SH	GW	S	%	TGF	PGF	TGA	PGA	+/–	GP	G	A	Pts	PIM	PP	SH	GW
1962-63	Waterloo Warriors	OHA-B	STATISTICS NOT AVAILABLE																									
1963-64	Johnstown Jets	EHL	71	7	39	46	....	....	....	*356	....	....	....	....	....	....	....	....	....	....	10	3	5	8	*50	....	....	....
1964-65	Tulsa Oilers	CPHL	57	4	16	20	....	....	....	*262	....	....	....	....	....	....	....	....	....	....	12	0	4	4	41	....	....	....
1965-66	Springfield Indians	AHL	29	2	5	7	....	....	....	58	....	....	....	....	....	....	....	....	....	....	....	....	....	....	....	....	....	....
	Tulsa Oilers	CPHL	36	2	6	8	....	....	....	129	....	....	....	....	....	....	....	....	....	....	10	2	2	4	*26	....	....	....
1966-67	Springfield Indians	AHL	59	4	14	18	....	....	....	93	....	....	....	....	....	....	....	....	....	....	....	....	....	....	....	....	....	....
1967-68	**Los Angeles Kings**	**NHL**	**4**	**0**	**0**	**0**	**0**	**0**	**0**	**4**	**0**	**0**	**0**	**2**	**0.0**	**0**	**0**	**8**	**1**	**–7**	....	....	....	....	....	....	....	....
	Springfield Kings	AHL	60	2	22	24	....	....	....	*197	....	....	....	....	....	....	....	....	....	....	4	0	2	2	22	....	....	....
1968-69	Springfield Kings	AHL	74	3	21	24	....	....	....	*240	....	....	....	....	....	....	....	....	....	....	....	....	....	....	....	....	....	....
1969-70	Springfield Kings	AHL	52	3	24	27	....	....	....	150	....	....	....	....	....	....	....	....	....	....	....	....	....	....	....	....	....	....
	Fort Worth Wings	CHL	13	1	0	1	....	....	....	60	....	....	....	....	....	....	....	....	....	....	7	0	1	1	7	....	....	....
1970-71	Baltimore Clippers	AHL	58	2	14	16	....	....	....	198	....	....	....	....	....	....	....	....	....	....	6	0	1	1	12	....	....	....
1971-72	**Detroit Red Wings**	**NHL**	**65**	**4**	**20**	**24**	**4**	**17**	**21**	**111**	**0**	**0**	**0**	**59**	**6.8**	**87**	**0**	**83**	**16**	**20**	....	....	....	....	....	....	....	....
	Tidewater Red Wings	AHL	12	1	1	2	....	....	....	45	....	....	....	....	....	....	....	....	....	....	....	....	....	....	....	....	....	....
1972-73	**Detroit Red Wings**	**NHL**	**73**	**1**	**12**	**13**	**1**	**9**	**10**	**169**	**0**	**0**	**1**	**53**	**1.9**	**79**	**0**	**87**	**14**	**6**	....	....	....	....	....	....	....	....
1973-74	**Detroit Red Wings**	**NHL**	**65**	**2**	**12**	**14**	**2**	**10**	**12**	**139**	**0**	**0**	**1**	**47**	**4.3**	**67**	**0**	**116**	**23**	**–26**	....	....	....	....	....	....	....	....
1974-75	Michigan-Baltimore Stags	WHA	49	0	9	9	....	....	....	93	....	....	....	....	....	....	....	....	....	....	....	....	....	....	....	....	....	....
	Kansas City Scouts	**NHL**	**16**	**0**	**7**	**7**	**0**	**5**	**5**	**10**	**0**	**0**	**0**	**12**	**0.0**	**16**	**1**	**36**	**4**	**–17**	....	....	....	....	....	....	....	....
1975-76	**Kansas City Scouts**	**NHL**	**72**	**2**	**10**	**12**	**2**	**7**	**9**	**112**	**1**	**0**	**0**	**77**	**2.6**	**64**	**8**	**150**	**33**	**–61**	....	....	....	....	....	....	....	....
1976-77	**Colorado Rockies**	**NHL**	**25**	**0**	**3**	**3**	**0**	**2**	**2**	**35**	**0**	**0**	**0**	**22**	**0.0**	**13**	**0**	**42**	**4**	**–25**	....	....	....	....	....	....	....	....
	Maine Nordiques	NAHL	51	4	22	26	....	....	....	62	....	....	....	....	....	....	....	....	....	....	....	....	....	....	....	....	....	....
	NHL Totals		**320**	**9**	**64**	**73**	**9**	**50**	**59**	**580**	**1**	**0**	**2**	**272**	**3.3**	**326**	**9**	**522**	**95**		....	....	....	....	....	....	....	....
	Other Major League Totals		49	0	9	9	....	....	....	93	....	....	....	....	....	....	....	....	....	....	....	....	....	....	....	....	....	....

Claimed by **Toronto** from **Tulsa** (CPHL) in Inter-League Draft, June 8, 1965. Traded to **Springfield** (AHL) by **Toronto** with Bill Smith for Bruce Gamble, September, 1965. NHL rights transferred to **LA Kings** after NHL club purchased **Springfield** (AHL) franchise, May, 1967. Traded to **Detroit** by **LA Kings** with Dale Rolfe and Gary Croteau for Garry Monahan, Brian Gibbons and Matt Ravlich, February 20, 1970. Signed as a free agent by **Michigan** (WHA), July, 1974. Signed as a free agent by **Kansas City** after **Michigan-Baltimore** (WHA) franchise folded, March 1, 1975. Transferred to **Colorado** after **Kansas City** franchise relocated, June, 1976.

• JOHNSTON, Marshall

Lawrence Marshall D – R. 5'11", 175 lbs. b: Birch Hills, Sask., 6/6/1941.

Season	Club	League	GP	G	A	Pts	AG	AA	APts	PIM	PP	SH	GW	S	%	TGF	PGF	TGA	PGA	+/–	GP	G	A	Pts	PIM	PP	SH	GW
1957-58	Prince Albert Mintos	SJHL	49	20	29	49	....	....	....	21	....	....	....	....	....	....	....	....	....	....	5	0	0	0	2	....	....	....
1958-59	Prince Albert Mintos	SJHL	48	31	24	55	....	....	....	17	....	....	....	....	....	....	....	....	....	....	5	1	0	1	4	....	....	....
1959-60	University of Denver	WCHA	DID NOT PLAY – FRESHMAN																									
1960-61	University of Denver	WCHA	14	4	7	11	....	....	....	....	....	....	....	....	....	....	....	....	....	....	....	....	....	....	....	....	....	....
1961-62	University of Denver	WCHA	12	7	11	18	....	....	....	2	....	....	....	....	....	....	....	....	....	....	....	....	....	....	....	....	....	....
1962-63	University of Denver	WCHA	14	6	12	18	....	....	....	8	....	....	....	....	....	....	....	....	....	....	....	....	....	....	....	....	....	....
1963-64	Canada	Nat-Team	STATISTICS NOT AVAILABLE																									
	Canada	Olympics	7	0	3	3	....	....	....	6	....	....	....	....	....	....	....	....	....	....	....	....	....	....	....	....	....	....
1964-65	Canada	Nat-Team	STATISTICS NOT AVAILABLE																									
	Winnipeg Maroons	SSHL	2	1	2	3	....	....	....	0	....	....	....	....	....	....	....	....	....	....	....	....	....	....	....	....	....	....
1965-66	Canada	Nat-Team	STATISTICS NOT AVAILABLE																									
	Canada	WEC-A	7	3	3	6	....	....	....	4	....	....	....	....	....	....	....	....	....	....	....	....	....	....	....	....	....	....
1966-67	Canada	Nat-Team	STATISTICS NOT AVAILABLE																									
	Canada	WEC-A	7	2	2	4	....	....	....	0	....	....	....	....	....	....	....	....	....	....	....	....	....	....	....	....	....	....
1967-68	Winnipeg Nationals	WCSHL	....	5	13	18	....	....	....	10	....	....	....	....	....	....	....	....	....	....	....	....	....	....	....	....	....	....
	Canada	Olympics	7	2	5	7	....	....	....	2	....	....	....	....	....	....	....	....	....	....	....	....	....	....	....	....	....	....
	Minnesota North Stars	**NHL**	**7**	**0**	**0**	**0**	**0**	**0**	**0**	**0**	**0**	**0**	**0**	**5**	**0.0**	**4**	**2**	**1**	**0**	**1**	....	....	....	....	....	....	....	....
1968-69	**Minnesota North Stars**	**NHL**	**13**	**0**	**0**	**0**	**0**	**0**	**0**	**2**	**0**	**0**	**0**	**12**	**0.0**	**1**	**0**	**3**	**0**	**–2**	....	....	....	....	....	....	....	....
	Cleveland Barons	AHL	53	6	20	26	....	....	....	31	....	....	....	....	....	....	....	....	....	....	5	0	4	4	4	....	....	....
1969-70	**Minnesota North Stars**	**NHL**	**28**	**0**	**5**	**5**	**0**	**5**	**5**	**14**	**0**	**0**	**0**	**48**	**0.0**	**31**	**5**	**37**	**12**	**1**	**6**	**0**	**0**	**0**	**2**	**0**	**0**	**0**
	Iowa Stars	CHL	50	1	25	26	....	....	....	42	....	....	....	....	....	....	....	....	....	....	....	....	....	....	....	....	....	....
1970-71	**Minnesota North Stars**	**NHL**	**1**	**0**	**0**	**0**	**0**	**0**	**0**	**0**	**0**	**0**	**0**	**0**	**0.0**	**0**	**0**	**0**	**0**	**0**	....	....	....	....	....	....	....	....
	Cleveland Barons	AHL	69	11	45	56	....	....	....	45	....	....	....	....	....	....	....	....	....	....	8	0	6	6	4	....	....	....
1971-72	**California Golden Seals**	**NHL**	**74**	**2**	**11**	**13**	**2**	**9**	**11**	**4**	**2**	**0**	**0**	**52**	**3.8**	**49**	**17**	**78**	**19**	**–27**	....	....	....	....	....	....	....	....
1972-73	**California Golden Seals**	**NHL**	**78**	**10**	**20**	**30**	**9**	**16**	**25**	**14**	**0**	**1**	**0**	**93**	**10.8**	**69**	**25**	**73**	**28**	**–1**	....	....	....	....	....	....	....	....
1973-1974	**California Golden Seals**	**NHL**	**50**	**2**	**16**	**18**	**2**	**13**	**15**	**24**	**2**	**0**	**0**	**51**	**3.9**	**50**	**12**	**101**	**18**	**–45**	....	....	....	....	....	....	....	....
	California Golden Seals	**NHL**	DID NOT PLAY – COACHING																									
1974-1975	**California Golden Seals**	**NHL**	DID NOT PLAY – COACHING																									
1975-1979	Denver University	WCHA	DID NOT PLAY – COACHING																									
1979-1981			OUT OF HOCKEY – RETIRED																									
1981-1982	**Colorado Rockies**	**NHL**	DID NOT PLAY – ASSISTANT GENERAL MANAGER																									
	Colorado Rockies	**NHL**	DID NOT PLAY – COACHING																									
1982-1985	**New Jersey Devils**	**NHL**	DID NOT PLAY – ASSISTANT COACH																									
1985-1993	**New Jersey Devils**	**NHL**	DID NOT PLAY – FRONT OFFICE STAFF																									
1993-1995			DID NOT PLAY																									

Season	Club	League	GP	G	A	Pts	AG	AA	APts	PIM	PP	SH	GW	S	%	TGF	PGF	TGA	PGA	+/–	GP	G	A	Pts	PIM	PP	SH	GW
			REGULAR SEASON																		PLAYOFFS							
1995-1996	**New York Islanders**	**NHL**	DID NOT PLAY – SCOUTING																									
1996-1999	**Ottawa Senators**	**NHL**	DID NOT PLAY – FRONT OFFICE STAFF																									
1999-2000	**Ottawa Senators**	**NHL**	DID NOT PLAY – GENERAL MANAGER																									
	NHL Totals		**251**	**14**	**52**	**66**	**13**	**43**	**56**	**58**	**4**	**1**	**0**	**261**	**5.4**	**204**	**61**	**293**	**77**		**6**	**0**	**0**	**0**	**2**	**0**	**0**	**0**

AHL First All-Star Team (1971) • Won Eddie Shore Award (Outstanding Defenseman - AHL) (1971)

Rights traded to **Minnesota** by **NY Rangers** for cash, June, 1967. Traded to **Montreal** by **Minnesota** with Bob Murdoch to complete transaction that sent Danny Grant and Claude Larose to Minnesota (June 10, 1968), May 25, 1971. Traded to **California** by **Montreal** for cash, August 31, 1971. • Served as Director of Playing Personnel for New Jersey, 1985-1993. • Spent 1993-1995 as CEO of CIPRO, a professional scouting network jointly owned by the NHL's Dallas, Philadelphia, Hartford and Winnipeg franchises. • Served as Director of Player Personnel for Ottawa, 1996-1999.

• JOHNSTON, Randy

Randy John D – L. 6', 190 lbs. b: Brampton, Ont., 6/2/1958. NY Islanders' 2nd, 34th overall, in 1978.

Season	Club	League	GP	G	A	Pts	AG	AA	APts	PIM	PP	SH	GW	S	%	TGF	PGF	TGA	PGA	+/–	GP	G	A	Pts	PIM	PP	SH	GW
1975-76	Peterborough Petes	OMJHL	46	0	5	5	....	....	....	57	....	....	....	....	....	....	....	....	....	....	....	....	....	....	....	....	....	....
1976-77	Peterborough Petes	OMJHL	66	4	21	25	....	....	....	141	....	....	....	....	....	....	....	....	....	....	4	0	0	0	8	....	....	....
1977-78	Peterborough Petes	OMJHL	63	4	31	35	....	....	....	79	....	....	....	....	....	....	....	....	....	....	20	1	4	5	34	....	....	....
1978-79	Fort Worth Texans	CHL	76	3	15	18	....	....	....	80	....	....	....	....	....	....	....	....	....	....	5	0	0	0	6	....	....	....
1979-80	**New York Islanders**	**NHL**	**4**	**0**	**0**	**0**	**0**	**0**	**0**	**4**	**0**	**0**	**0**	**2**	**0.0**	**2**	**0**	**4**	**0**	**–2**	....	....	....	....	....	....	....	....
	Indianapolis Checkers	CHL	69	3	27	30	....	....	....	45	....	....	....	....	....	....	....	....	....	....	7	1	0	1	18	....	....	....
1980-81	Indianapolis Checkers	CHL	76	3	20	23	....	....	....	69	....	....	....	....	....	....	....	....	....	....	5	0	0	0	6	....	....	....
1981-82	Indianapolis Checkers	CHL	78	7	34	41	....	....	....	71	....	....	....	....	....	....	....	....	....	....	11	1	5	6	17	....	....	....
1982-83	Indianapolis Checkers	CHL	66	2	15	17	....	....	....	63	....	....	....	....	....	....	....	....	....	....	10	1	2	3	16	....	....	....
	NHL Totals		**4**	**0**	**0**	**0**	**0**	**0**	**0**	**4**	**0**	**0**	**0**	**2**	**0.0**	**2**	**0**	**4**	**0**		....	....	....	....	....	....	....	....

• JOHNSTONE, Eddie

Eddie Lavern RW – R. 5'9", 175 lbs. b: Brandon, Man., 3/2/1954. NY Rangers' 6th, 104th overall, in 1974.

Season	Club	League	GP	G	A	Pts	AG	AA	APts	PIM	PP	SH	GW	S	%	TGF	PGF	TGA	PGA	+/–	GP	G	A	Pts	PIM	PP	SH	GW
1970-71	Vernon Essos	BCJHL	50	45	49	94	....	....	....	79	....	....	....	....	....	....	....	....	....	....	....	....	....	....	....	....	....	....
1971-72	Vernon Essos	BCJHL	STATISTICS NOT AVAILABLE																									
	Medicine Hat Tigers	WCJHL	27	14	15	29	....	....	....	46	....	....	....	....	....	....	....	....	....	....	7	2	2	4	6	....	....	....
1972-73	Medicine Hat Tigers	WCJHL	68	58	44	102	....	....	....	70	....	....	....	....	....	....	....	....	....	....	17	13	10	23	21	....	....	....
	Medicine Hat Tigers	Mem-Cup	2	3	0	3	....	....	....	0	....	....	....	....	....	....	....	....	....	....	....	....	....	....	....	....	....	....
1973-74	Medicine Hat Tigers	WCJHL	68	64	54	118	....	....	....	164	....	....	....	....	....	....	....	....	....	....	5	5	0	5	10	....	....	....
1974-75	Michigan-Baltimore Stags	WHA	23	4	4	8	....	....	....	43	....	....	....	....	....	....	....	....	....	....	....	....	....	....	....	....	....	....
	Greensboro Generals	SHL	25	21	25	46	....	....	....	21	....	....	....	....	....	....	....	....	....	....	....	....	....	....	....	....	....	....
	Providence Reds	AHL	23	7	10	17	....	....	....	35	....	....	....	....	....	....	....	....	....	....	5	0	0	0	0	....	....	....
1975-76	**New York Rangers**	**NHL**	**10**	**2**	**1**	**3**	**2**	**1**	**3**	**4**	**0**	**0**	**0**	**6**	**33.3**	**5**	**0**	**1**	**0**	**4**	....	....	....	....	....	....	....	....
	Providence Reds	AHL	58	23	33	56	....	....	....	102	....	....	....	....	....	....	....	....	....	....	3	0	0	0	14	....	....	....
1976-77	New Haven Nighthawks	AHL	80	40	58	98	....	....	....	79	....	....	....	....	....	....	....	....	....	....	6	3	6	9	7	....	....	....
1977-78	**New York Rangers**	**NHL**	**53**	**13**	**13**	**26**	**12**	**10**	**22**	**44**	**2**	**1**	**0**	**93**	**14.0**	**38**	**11**	**40**	**10**	**–3**	....	....	....	....	....	....	....	....
	New Haven Nighthawks	AHL	17	10	12	22	....	....	....	20	....	....	....	....	....	....	....	....	....	....	....	....	....	....	....	....	....	....
1978-79	**New York Rangers**	**NHL**	**30**	**5**	**3**	**8**	**4**	**2**	**6**	**27**	**0**	**0**	**0**	**18**	**27.8**	**11**	**1**	**19**	**4**	**–5**	**17**	**5**	**0**	**5**	**10**	**0**	**1**	**1**
1979-80	**New York Rangers**	**NHL**	**78**	**14**	**21**	**35**	**12**	**15**	**27**	**60**	**0**	**0**	**3**	**121**	**11.6**	**59**	**4**	**69**	**17**	**3**	**9**	**0**	**1**	**1**	**25**	**0**	**0**	**0**
1980-81	**New York Rangers**	**NHL**	**80**	**30**	**38**	**68**	**23**	**25**	**48**	**100**	**4**	**3**	**5**	**187**	**16.0**	**97**	**21**	**85**	**24**	**15**	**8**	**2**	**2**	**4**	**4**	**0**	**0**	**1**
1981-82	New York Rangers	DN-Cup	4	*6	1	*7	....	....	....	....	....	....	....	....	....	....	....	....	....	....	....	....	....	....	....	....	....	....
	New York Rangers	**NHL**	**68**	**30**	**28**	**58**	**24**	**19**	**43**	**57**	**4**	**0**	**3**	**141**	**21.3**	**92**	**17**	**89**	**9**	**–5**	**10**	**2**	**6**	**8**	**25**	**1**	**0**	**0**
1982-83	**New York Rangers**	**NHL**	**52**	**15**	**21**	**36**	**12**	**15**	**27**	**27**	**2**	**1**	**1**	**98**	**15.3**	**63**	**23**	**50**	**6**	**–4**	**9**	**4**	**1**	**5**	**19**	**1**	**1**	**0**
1983-84	**Detroit Red Wings**	**NHL**	**46**	**12**	**11**	**23**	**10**	**7**	**17**	**54**	**4**	**0**	**0**	**50**	**24.0**	**39**	**8**	**34**	**6**	**3**	**2**	**0**	**0**	**0**	**0**	**0**	**0**	**0**
1984-85	Adirondack Red Wings	AHL	69	27	28	55	....	....	....	70	....	....	....	....	....	....	....	....	....	....	....	....	....	....	....	....	....	....
1985-86	**Detroit Red Wings**	**NHL**	**3**	**1**	**0**	**1**	**1**	**0**	**1**	**2**	**0**	**0**	**0**	**3**	**33.3**	**1**	**0**	**2**	**1**	**0**	....	....	....	....	....	....	....	....
	Adirondack Red Wings	AHL	62	29	31	60	....	....	....	74	....	....	....	....	....	....	....	....	....	....	17	5	7	12	4	....	....	....
1986-87	**Detroit Red Wings**	**NHL**	**6**	**0**	**0**	**0**	**0**	**0**	**0**	**0**	**0**	**0**	**0**	**0**	**0.0**	**2**	**0**	**2**	**1**	**1**	....	....	....	....	....	....	....	....
	Adirondack Red Wings	AHL	61	30	22	52	....	....	....	83	....	....	....	....	....	....	....	....	....	....	5	1	0	1	2	....	....	....
1987-1988	New Westminster Royals	WHL	DID NOT PLAY – ASSISTANT COACH																									
1988-1989	Vernon Lakers	BCJHL	DID NOT PLAY – ASSISTANT COACH																									
1989-1992	Vernon Lakers	BCJHL	DID NOT PLAY – COACHING																									
1992-1995	Johnstown Chiefs	ECHL	DID NOT PLAY – COACHING																									
1995-1997	Mobile Mysticks	ECHL	DID NOT PLAY – COACHING																									
1997-2000	Cincinnati Mighty Ducks	AHL	DID NOT PLAY – ASSISTANT COACH																									
	NHL Totals		**426**	**122**	**136**	**258**	**100**	**94**	**194**	**375**	**16**	**5**	**12**	**717**	**17.0**	**407**	**85**	**391**	**78**		**55**	**13**	**10**	**23**	**83**	**2**	**2**	**2**
	Other Major League Totals		23	4	4	8	....	....	....	43	....	....	....	....	....	....	....	....	....	....	....	....	....	....	....	....	....	....

AHL First All-Star Team (1977) • Played in NHL All-Star Game (1981)

Selected by **Michigan** (WHA) in 1974 WHA Amateur Draft, June, 1974. Claimed by **NY Rangers** as a fill-in during Expansion Draft, June 13, 1979. Traded to **Detroit** by **NY Rangers** with Eddie Mio and Ron Duguay for Mike Blaisdell, Mark Osborne and Willie Huber, June 13, 1983.

• JOKINEN, Olli

C – L. 6'3", 208 lbs. b: Kuopio, Finland, 12/5/1978. Los Angeles' 1st, 3rd overall, in 1997.

Season	Club	League	GP	G	A	Pts	AG	AA	APts	PIM	PP	SH	GW	S	%	TGF	PGF	TGA	PGA	+/–	GP	G	A	Pts	PIM	PP	SH	GW
1992-93	KalPa Kuopio-C	Finland-Jr.	14	8	3	11	....	....	....	12	....	....	....	....	....	....	....	....	....	....	....	....	....	....	....	....	....	....
1993-94	KalPa Kuopio-C	Finland-Jr.	31	27	25	52	....	....	....	62	....	....	....	....	....	....	....	....	....	....	....	....	....	....	....	....	....	....
1994-95	KalPa Kuopio-B	Finland-Jr.	12	9	14	23	....	....	....	46	....	....	....	....	....	....	....	....	....	....	....	....	....	....	....	....	....	....
	KalPa Kuopio	Finland-2	30	22	28	50	....	....	....	92	....	....	....	....	....	....	....	....	....	....	....	....	....	....	....	....	....	....
1995-96	KalPa Kuopio	Finland-Jr.	25	20	14	34	....	....	....	47	....	....	....	....	....	....	....	....	....	....	7	4	4	8	20	....	....	....
	KalPa Kuopio	Finland	15	1	1	2	....	....	....	2	....	....	....	....	....	....	....	....	....	....	....	....	....	....	....	....	....	....
	Finland	EJC-A	5	5	2	7	....	....	....	2	....	....	....	....	....	....	....	....	....	....	....	....	....	....	....	....	....	....
1996-97	HIFK Helsinki	Finland-Jr.	2	1	0	1	....	....	....	6	....	....	....	....	....	....	....	....	....	....	....	....	....	....	....	....	....	....
	HIFK Helsinki	Finland	50	14	27	41	....	....	....	88	....	....	....	....	....	....	....	....	....	....	....	....	....	....	....	....	....	....
	Finland	WJC-A	6	5	0	5	....	....	....	12	....	....	....	....	....	....	....	....	....	....	....	....	....	....	....	....	....	....
	Finland	Nat-Team	12	4	3	7	....	....	....	4	....	....	....	....	....	....	....	....	....	....	....	....	....	....	....	....	....	....
	Finland	WC-A	8	4	2	6	....	....	....	6	....	....	....	....	....	....	....	....	....	....	....	....	....	....	....	....	....	....
1997-98	**Los Angeles Kings**	**NHL**	**8**	**0**	**0**	**0**	**0**	**0**	**0**	**6**	**0**	**0**	**0**	**12**	**0.0**	**2**	**0**	**7**	**0**	**–5**	....	....	....	....	....	....	....	....
	HIFK Helsinki	Finland	30	11	28	39	....	....	....	8	....	....	....	....	....	....	....	....	....	....	9	*7	2	9	2	....	....	....
	Finland	WJC-A	7	4	6	10	....	....	....	6	....	....	....	....	....	....	....	....	....	....	....	....	....	....	....	....	....	....
	Finland	Nat-Team	5	1	1	2	....	....	....	33	....	....	....	....	....	....	....	....	....	....	....	....	....	....	....	....	....	....
	Finland	WC-A	10	0	1	1	....	....	....	6	....	....	....	....	....	....	....	....	....	....	....	....	....	....	....	....	....	....
1998-99	**Los Angeles Kings**	**NHL**	**66**	**9**	**12**	**21**	**11**	**12**	**23**	**44**	**3**	**1**	**1**	**87**	**10.3**	**35**	**9**	**41**	**5**	**–10**	....	....	....	....	....	....	....	....
	Springfield Falcons	AHL	9	3	6	9	....	....	....	6	....	....	....	....	....	....	....	....	....	....	....	....	....	....	....	....	....	....
	Finland	WC-A	12	3	1	4	....	....	....	14	....	....	....	....	....	....	....	....	....	....	....	....	....	....	....	....	....	....
99-2000	**New York Islanders**	**NHL**	**82**	**11**	**10**	**21**	**12**	**9**	**21**	**80**	**1**	**2**	**3**	**138**	**8.0**	**46**	**4**	**66**	**24**	**0**	....	....	....	....	....	....	....	....
	Finland	WC-A	9	1	3	4	....	....	....	6	....	....	....	....	....	....	....	....	....	....	....	....	....	....	....	....	....	....
	NHL Totals		**156**	**20**	**22**	**42**	**23**	**21**	**44**	**130**	**4**	**3**	**4**	**237**	**8.4**	**83**	**13**	**114**	**29**		....	....	....	....	....	....	....	....

Finnish Rookie of the Year (1997) • WJC-A All-Star Team (1998) • Named Best Forward at WJC-A (1998)

Traded to **NY Islanders** by **LA Kings** with Josh Green, Mathieu Biron and LA Kings' 1st round choice (Taylor Pyatt) in 1999 Entry Draft for Zigmund Palffy, Brian Smolinski, Marcel Cousineau and New Jersey's 4th round choice (previously acquired, LA Kings selected Daniel Johanssen) in 1999 Entry Draft, June 20, 1999. Traded to **Florida** by **NY Islanders** with Roberto Luongo for Mark Parrish and Oleg Kvasha, June 24, 2000.

• JOLY, Greg

Gregory James D – L. 6'1", 190 lbs. b: Calgary, Alta., 5/30/1954. Washington's 1st, 1st overall, in 1974.

Season	Club	League	GP	G	A	Pts	AG	AA	APts	PIM	PP	SH	GW	S	%	TGF	PGF	TGA	PGA	+/–	GP	G	A	Pts	PIM	PP	SH	GW
1971-72	Regina Pats	WCJHL	67	6	38	44	....	....	....	41	....	....	....	....	....	....	....	....	....	....	15	0	3	3	10	....	....	....
1972-73	Regina Pats	WCJHL	67	14	54	68	....	....	....	94	....	....	....	....	....	....	....	....	....	....	4	0	3	3	4	....	....	....
1973-74	Regina Pats	WCJHL	67	21	71	92	....	....	....	103	....	....	....	....	....	....	....	....	....	....	16	7	13	20	8	....	....	....
	Regina Pats	Mem-Cup	3	2	3	5	....	....	....	4	....	....	....	....	....	....	....	....	....	....	....	....	....	....	....	....	....	....
1974-75	**Washington Capitals**	**NHL**	**44**	**1**	**7**	**8**	**1**	**5**	**6**	**44**	**1**	**0**	**0**	**72**	**1.4**	**49**	**19**	**107**	**9**	**–68**	....	....	....	....	....	....	....	....
1975-76	**Washington Capitals**	**NHL**	**54**	**8**	**17**	**25**	**7**	**13**	**20**	**28**	**3**	**1**	**1**	**81**	**9.9**	**62**	**17**	**105**	**14**	**–46**	....	....	....	....	....	....	....	....
	Richmond Robins	AHL	3	3	2	5	....	....	....	4	....	....	....	....	....	....	....	....	....	....	....	....	....	....	....	....	....	....

Season	Club	League	REGULAR SEASON																		PLAYOFFS							
			GP	G	A	Pts	AG	AA	APts	PIM	PP	SH	GW	S	%	TGF	PGF	TGA	PGA	+/-	GP	G	A	Pts	PIM	PP	SH	GW
1976-77	**Detroit Red Wings**	**NHL**	**53**	**1**	**11**	**12**	**1**	**8**	**9**	**14**	**1**	**0**	**0**	**73**	**1.4**	**32**	**16**	**44**	**6**	**-22**	....	....	....	....	....	....	....	....
	Springfield Indians	AHL	22	0	8	8	....	....	....	16	....	....	....	....	....	....	....	....	....	....	....	....	....	....	....	....	....	....
1977-78	**Detroit Red Wings**	**NHL**	**79**	**7**	**20**	**27**	**6**	**15**	**21**	**73**	**2**	**0**	**2**	**134**	**5.2**	**82**	**11**	**87**	**12**	**-4**	**5**	**0**	**0**	**0**	**8**	**0**	**0**	**0**
1978-79	**Detroit Red Wings**	**NHL**	**20**	**0**	**4**	**4**	**0**	**3**	**3**	**6**	**0**	**0**	**0**	**13**	**0.0**	**13**	**0**	**21**	**0**	**-8**	....	....	....	....	....	....	....	....
1979-80	**Detroit Red Wings**	**NHL**	**59**	**3**	**10**	**13**	**3**	**7**	**10**	**45**	**0**	**0**	**0**	**50**	**6.0**	**45**	**0**	**54**	**7**	**-2**	....	....	....	....	....	....	....	....
	Adirondack Red Wings	AHL	8	3	3	6	....	....	....	10	....	....	....	....	....	....	....	....	....	....	....	....	....	....	....	....	....	....
1980-81	**Detroit Red Wings**	**NHL**	**17**	**0**	**2**	**2**	**0**	**1**	**1**	**10**	**0**	**0**	**0**	**8**	**0.0**	**15**	**0**	**25**	**2**	**-8**	....	....	....	....	....	....	....	....
	Adirondack Red Wings	AHL	62	3	34	37	....	....	....	158	....	....	....	....	....	....	....	....	....	....	17	4	12	16	38	....	....	....
1981-82	**Detroit Red Wings**	**NHL**	**37**	**1**	**5**	**6**	**1**	**3**	**4**	**30**	**0**	**1**	**0**	**30**	**3.3**	**24**	**1**	**31**	**3**	**-5**	....	....	....	....	....	....	....	....
	Adirondack Red Wings	AHL	36	3	22	25	....	....	....	59	....	....	....	....	....	....	....	....	....	....	....	....	....	....	....	....	....	....
1982-83	**Detroit Red Wings**	**NHL**	**2**	**0**	**0**	**0**	**0**	**0**	**0**	**0**	**0**	**0**	**0**	**3**	**0.0**	**1**	**0**	**1**	**0**	**0**	....	....	....	....	....	....	....	....
	Adirondack Red Wings	AHL	71	8	40	48	....	....	....	118	....	....	....	....	....	....	....	....	....	....	6	1	0	1	0	....	....	....
1983-84	Adirondack Red Wings	AHL	78	10	33	43	....	....	....	133	....	....	....	....	....	....	....	....	....	....	7	0	1	1	19	....	....	....
1984-85	Adirondack Red Wings	AHL	76	9	40	49	....	....	....	111	....	....	....	....	....	....	....	....	....	....	....	....	....	....	....	....	....	....
1985-86	Adirondack Red Wings	AHL	65	0	22	22	....	....	....	68	....	....	....	....	....	....	....	....	....	....	16	0	4	4	38	....	....	....
	NHL Totals		**365**	**21**	**76**	**97**	**19**	**55**	**74**	**250**	**7**	**2**	**3**	**464**	**4.5**	**323**	**64**	**475**	**53**	....	**5**	**0**	**0**	**0**	**8**	**0**	**0**	**0**

WCJHL First All-Star Team (1973, 1974) • Won Stafford Smythe Memorial Trophy (Memorial Cup Tournament MVP) (1974) • AHL Second All-Star Team (1984) • AHL First All-Star Team (1985)
Traded to **Detroit** by **Washington** for Bryan Watson, November 30, 1976.

• JOLY, Yvan

Yvan Joseph Rene RW – R. 5'8", 175 lbs. b: Hawkesbury, Ont., 2/6/1960. Montreal's 7th, 100th overall, in 1979.

Season	Club	League	GP	G	A	Pts	AG	AA	APts	PIM	PP	SH	GW	S	%	TGF	PGF	TGA	PGA	+/-	GP	G	A	Pts	PIM	PP	SH	GW
1976-77	Ottawa 67's	OMJHL	62	30	26	56	....	....	....	36	....	....	....	....	....	....	....	....	....	....	....	....	....	....	....	....	....	....
1977-78	Ottawa 67's	OMJHL	64	34	37	71	....	....	....	67	....	....	....	....	....	....	....	....	....	....	16	7	8	15	24	....	....	....
1978-79	Ottawa 67's	OMJHL	63	53	59	112	....	....	....	45	....	....	....	....	....	....	....	....	....	....	4	0	2	2	6	....	....	....
	Canada	WJC-A	5	2	0	2	....	....	....	2	....	....	....	....	....	....	....	....	....	....	....	....	....	....	....	....	....	....
1979-80	Ottawa 67's	OMJHL	67	*66	93	159	....	....	....	47	....	....	....	....	....	....	....	....	....	....	11	4	12	16	13	....	....	....
	Canada	WJC-A	5	3	0	3	....	....	....	8	....	....	....	....	....	....	....	....	....	....	....	....	....	....	....	....	....	....
	Montreal Canadiens	**NHL**	....	....	....	....	....	....	....	....	....	....	....	....	....	....	....	....	....	....	**1**	**0**	**0**	**0**	**0**	**0**	**0**	**0**
1980-81	**Montreal Canadiens**	**NHL**	**1**	**0**	**0**	**0**	**0**	**0**	**0**	**0**	**0**	**0**	**0**	**0**	**0.0**	**0**	**0**	**0**	**0**	**0**	....	....	....	....	....	....	....	....
	Nova Scotia Voyageurs	AHL	68	14	27	41	....	....	....	74	....	....	....	....	....	....	....	....	....	....	4	1	0	1	0	....	....	....
1981-82	Nova Scotia Voyageurs	AHL	71	20	30	50	....	....	....	75	....	....	....	....	....	....	....	....	....	....	9	2	3	5	8	....	....	....
1982-83	**Montreal Canadiens**	**NHL**	**1**	**0**	**0**	**0**	**0**	**0**	**0**	**0**	**0**	**0**	**0**	**1**	**0.0**	**0**	**0**	**1**	**0**	**-1**	....	....	....	....	....	....	....	....
	Nova Scotia Voyageurs	AHL	76	43	37	80	....	....	....	52	....	....	....	....	....	....	....	....	....	....	7	2	1	3	2	....	....	....
1983-84	HC Gardena-Groden	Italy	19	15	18	33	....	....	....	10	....	....	....	....	....	....	....	....	....	....	....	....	....	....	....	....	....	....
	Maine Mariners	AHL	39	12	17	29	....	....	....	25	....	....	....	....	....	....	....	....	....	....	14	0	5	5	4	....	....	....
1984-85			OUT OF HOCKEY – RETIRED																									
1985-86	Indianapolis Checkers	IHL	17	1	6	7	....	....	....	28	....	....	....	....	....	....	....	....	....	....	....	....	....	....	....	....	....	....
	NHL Totals		**2**	**0**	**0**	**0**	**0**	**0**	**0**	**0**	**0**	**0**	**0**	**1**	**0.0**	**0**	**0**	**1**	**0**		**1**	**0**	**0**	**0**	**0**	**0**	**0**	**0**

OMJHL Second All-Star Team (1979) • OMJHL First All-Star Team (1980)

• JOMPHE, Jean-Francois

C – L. 6'1", 195 lbs. b: Harve' St. Pierre, Que., 12/28/1972.

Season	Club	League	GP	G	A	Pts	AG	AA	APts	PIM	PP	SH	GW	S	%	TGF	PGF	TGA	PGA	+/-	GP	G	A	Pts	PIM	PP	SH	GW
1990-91	Shawinigan Cataractes	QMJHL	42	17	22	39	....	....	....	14	....	....	....	....	....	....	....	....	....	....	6	2	1	3	2	....	....	....
1991-92	Shawinigan Cataractes	QMJHL	44	28	33	61	....	....	....	69	....	....	....	....	....	....	....	....	....	....	10	6	10	16	10	....	....	....
1992-93	Sherbrooke Faucons	QMJHL	60	43	43	86	....	....	....	86	....	....	....	....	....	....	....	....	....	....	15	10	13	23	18	....	....	....
1993-94	San Diego Gulls	IHL	29	2	3	5	....	....	....	12	....	....	....	....	....	....	....	....	....	....	....	....	....	....	....	....	....	....
	Greensboro Monarchs	ECHL	25	9	9	18	....	....	....	41	....	....	....	....	....	....	....	....	....	....	1	1	0	1	0	....	....	....
1994-95	Canada	Nat-Team	52	33	25	58	....	....	....	85	....	....	....	....	....	....	....	....	....	....	....	....	....	....	....	....	....	....
	Canada	WC-A	8	4	0	4	....	....	....	6	....	....	....	....	....	....	....	....	....	....	....	....	....	....	....	....	....	....
1995-96	**Mighty Ducks of Anaheim**	**NHL**	**31**	**2**	**12**	**14**	**2**	**10**	**12**	**39**	**2**	**0**	**0**	**46**	**4.3**	**19**	**4**	**14**	**6**	**7**	....	....	....	....	....	....	....	....
	Baltimore Bandits	AHL	47	21	34	55	....	....	....	75	....	....	....	....	....	....	....	....	....	....	....	....	....	....	....	....	....	....
	Canada	WC-A	8	0	1	1	....	....	....	4	....	....	....	....	....	....	....	....	....	....	....	....	....	....	....	....	....	....
1996-97	**Mighty Ducks of Anaheim**	**NHL**	**64**	**7**	**14**	**21**	**7**	**12**	**19**	**53**	**0**	**1**	**0**	**81**	**8.6**	**28**	**4**	**49**	**16**	**-9**	....	....	....	....	....	....	....	....
1997-98	**Mighty Ducks of Anaheim**	**NHL**	**9**	**1**	**3**	**4**	**1**	**3**	**4**	**8**	**0**	**0**	**0**	**8**	**12.5**	**4**	**0**	**8**	**5**	**1**	....	....	....	....	....	....	....	....
	Cincinnati Mighty Ducks	AHL	38	9	19	28	....	....	....	32	....	....	....	....	....	....	....	....	....	....	....	....	....	....	....	....	....	....
	Quebec Rafales	IHL	17	6	4	10	....	....	....	24	....	....	....	....	....	....	....	....	....	....	....	....	....	....	....	....	....	....
1998-99	**Phoenix Coyotes**	**NHL**	**1**	**0**	**0**	**0**	**0**	**0**	**0**	**2**	**0**	**0**	**0**	**0**	**0.0**	**0**	**0**	**0**	**0**	**0**	....	....	....	....	....	....	....	....
	Springfield Falcons	AHL	29	10	18	28	....	....	....	36	....	....	....	....	....	....	....	....	....	....	....	....	....	....	....	....	....	....
	Las Vegas Thunder	IHL	32	6	14	20	....	....	....	63	....	....	....	....	....	....	....	....	....	....	....	....	....	....	....	....	....	....
	Montreal Canadiens	**NHL**	**6**	**0**	**0**	**0**	**0**	**0**	**0**	**0**	**0**	**0**	**0**	**4**	**0.0**	**0**	**0**	**0**	**0**	**0**	....	....	....	....	....	....	....	....
	Fredericton Canadiens	AHL	3	1	3	4	....	....	....	6	....	....	....	....	....	....	....	....	....	....	15	5	11	16	49	....	....	....
99-2000	Krefeld Pinguine	Germany	47	12	33	45	....	....	....	109	....	....	....	....	....	....	....	....	....	....	4	0	1	1	6	....	....	....
	NHL Totals		**111**	**10**	**29**	**39**	**10**	**25**	**35**	**102**	**2**	**1**	**0**	**139**	**7.2**	**51**	**8**	**71**	**27**		....	....	....	....	....	....	....	....

Signed as a free agent by **Anaheim**, September 7, 1993. Traded to **Phoenix** by **Anaheim** for Jim McKenzie, June 18, 1998. Traded to **Montreal** by **Phoenix** for cash, March 23, 1999.

• JONATHAN, Stan

Stanley Carl LW – L. 5'8", 175 lbs. b: Ohsweken, Ont., 9/5/1955. Boston's 5th, 86th overall, in 1975.

Season	Club	League	GP	G	A	Pts	AG	AA	APts	PIM	PP	SH	GW	S	%	TGF	PGF	TGA	PGA	+/-	GP	G	A	Pts	PIM	PP	SH	GW
1972-73	Peterborough Petes	OMJHL	64	14	35	49	....	....	....	107	....	....	....	....	....	....	....	....	....	....	....	....	....	....	....	....	....	....
1973-74	Peterborough Petes	OMJHL	70	19	33	52	....	....	....	127	....	....	....	....	....	....	....	....	....	....	11	4	5	9	14	....	....	....
1974-75	Peterborough Petes	OMJHL	70	36	39	75	....	....	....	138	....	....	....	....	....	....	....	....	....	....	11	4	5	9	14	....	....	....
1975-76	**Boston Bruins**	**NHL**	**1**	**0**	**0**	**0**	**0**	**0**	**0**	**0**	**0**	**0**	**0**	**0**	**0.0**	**0**	**0**	**0**	**0**	**0**	....	....	....	....	....	....	....	....
	Rochester Americans	AHL	6	1	1	2	....	....	....	0	....	....	....	....	....	....	....	....	....	....	....	....	....	....	....	....	....	....
	Dayton Gems	IHL	69	26	47	73	....	....	....	192	....	....	....	....	....	....	....	....	....	....	15	*13	8	*21	54	....	....	....
1976-77	**Boston Bruins**	**NHL**	**69**	**17**	**13**	**30**	**15**	**10**	**25**	**69**	**1**	**0**	**2**	**71**	**23.9**	**42**	**2**	**39**	**0**	**1**	**14**	**4**	**2**	**6**	**24**	**0**	**0**	**1**
	Rochester Americans	AHL	3	0	0	0	....	....	....	7	....	....	....	....	....	....	....	....	....	....	....	....	....	....	....	....	....	....
1977-78	**Boston Bruins**	**NHL**	**68**	**27**	**25**	**52**	**25**	**19**	**44**	**116**	**0**	**0**	**2**	**121**	**22.3**	**78**	**11**	**46**	**13**	**34**	**15**	**0**	**1**	**1**	**36**	**0**	**0**	**0**
1978-79	**Boston Bruins**	**NHL**	**33**	**6**	**9**	**15**	**5**	**7**	**12**	**96**	**0**	**0**	**1**	**32**	**18.8**	**30**	**2**	**22**	**2**	**8**	**11**	**4**	**1**	**5**	**12**	**0**	**0**	**0**
1979-80	**Boston Bruins**	**NHL**	**79**	**21**	**19**	**40**	**18**	**14**	**32**	**208**	**0**	**0**	**3**	**108**	**19.4**	**80**	**4**	**58**	**2**	**20**	**9**	**0**	**0**	**0**	**29**	**0**	**0**	**0**
1980-81	**Boston Bruins**	**NHL**	**74**	**14**	**24**	**38**	**11**	**16**	**27**	**192**	**0**	**0**	**2**	**85**	**16.5**	**61**	**4**	**53**	**1**	**5**	**3**	**0**	**0**	**0**	**30**	**0**	**0**	**0**
1981-82	**Boston Bruins**	**NHL**	**67**	**6**	**17**	**23**	**5**	**11**	**16**	**57**	**1**	**0**	**0**	**50**	**12.0**	**35**	**1**	**30**	**2**	**6**	**11**	**0**	**0**	**0**	**6**	**0**	**0**	**0**
1982-83	**Boston Bruins**	**NHL**	**1**	**0**	**0**	**0**	**0**	**0**	**0**	**0**	**0**	**0**	**0**	**1**	**0.0**	**0**	**0**	**0**	**0**	**0**	....	....	....	....	....	....	....	....
	Pittsburgh Penguins	**NHL**	**19**	**0**	**3**	**3**	**0**	**2**	**2**	**13**	**0**	**0**	**0**	**16**	**0.0**	**11**	**0**	**19**	**0**	**-8**	....	....	....	....	....	....	....	....
	Baltimore Skipjacks	AHL	48	13	23	36	....	....	....	86	....	....	....	....	....	....	....	....	....	....	....	....	....	....	....	....	....	....
1983-1985			OUT OF HOCKEY – RETIRED																									
1985-86	Flamboro Flames	OHA-Sr.	STATISTICS NOT AVAILABLE																									
1986-87	Brantford Mott's Clamatos	OHA-Sr.	1	0	0	0	....	....	....	2	....	....	....	....	....	....	....	....	....	....	....	....	....	....	....	....	....	....
	NHL Totals		**411**	**91**	**110**	**201**	**79**	**79**	**158**	**751**	**2**	**0**	**10**	**484**	**18.8**	**337**	**24**	**267**	**20**		**63**	**8**	**4**	**12**	**137**	**0**	**0**	**1**

IHL First All-Star Team (1976)
Traded to **Pittsburgh** by **Boston** for cash, November 8, 1982.

• JONES, Bob

Robert Charles LW – L. 6'1", 185 lbs. b: Espanola, Ont., 11/27/1945. Detroit's 9th, 179th overall, in 1989.

Season	Club	League	GP	G	A	Pts	AG	AA	APts	PIM	PP	SH	GW	S	%	TGF	PGF	TGA	PGA	+/-	GP	G	A	Pts	PIM	PP	SH	GW
1962-63	Guelph Royals	OHA-Jr.	49	5	7	12	....	....	....	13	....	....	....	....	....	....	....	....	....	....	....	....	....	....	....	....	....	....
1963-64	Kitchener Rangers	OHA-Jr.	56	6	12	18	....	....	....	50	....	....	....	....	....	....	....	....	....	....	....	....	....	....	....	....	....	....
1964-65	Kitchener Rangers	OHA-Jr.	56	39	53	92	....	....	....	59	....	....	....	....	....	....	....	....	....	....	....	....	....	....	....	....	....	....
1965-66	Kitchener Rangers	OHA-Jr.	48	24	25	49	....	....	....	57	....	....	....	....	....	....	....	....	....	....	19	11	14	25	18	....	....	....
1966-67	Omaha Knights	CPHL	19	0	2	2	....	....	....	10	....	....	....	....	....	....	....	....	....	....	....	....	....	....	....	....	....	....
	Vancouver Canucks	WHL	47	8	9	17	....	....	....	24	....	....	....	....	....	....	....	....	....	....	8	3	2	5	8	....	....	....
1967-68	Buffalo Bisons	AHL	72	21	32	53	....	....	....	38	....	....	....	....	....	....	....	....	....	....	5	2	4	6	4	....	....	....
1968-69	**New York Rangers**	**NHL**	**2**	**0**	**0**	**0**	**0**	**0**	**0**	**0**	**0**	**0**	**0**	**2**	**0.0**	**0**	**0**	**0**	**0**	**0**	....	....	....	....	....	....	....	....
	Buffalo Bisons	AHL	70	19	37	56	....	....	....	92	....	....	....	....	....	....	....	....	....	....	6	2	4	6	4	....	....	....
1969-70	Buffalo Bisons	AHL	71	25	37	62	....	....	....	40	....	....	....	....	....	....	....	....	....	....	14	5	10	15	14	....	....	....

			REGULAR SEASON																		PLAYOFFS							
Season	Club	League	GP	G	A	Pts	AG	AA	APts	PIM	PP	SH	GW	S	%	TGF	PGF	TGA	PGA	+/–	GP	G	A	Pts	PIM	PP	SH	GW
1970-71	Seattle Totems	WHL	72	17	43	60				61																		
1971-72	Salt Lake Golden Eagles	WHL	27	9	7	16				10																		
	Portland Buckaroos	WHL	18	4	4	8				9											11	2	3	5	16			
1972-73	Los Angeles Sharks	WHA	20	2	7	9				8																		
	New York Raiders	WHA	56	11	12	23				24																		
1973-74	New York-Jersey Knights	WHA	78	17	28	45				20																		
1974-75	Baltimore Stags	WHA	5	0	1	1				8																		
	Syracuse Blazers	NAHL	67	38	*76	*114				52																		
1975-76	Indianapolis Racers	WHA	2	0	0	0				0																		
	Mohawk Valley Comets	NAHL	69	39	70	109				38											4	3	1	4	7			
	NHL Totals		**2**	**0**	**0**	**0**	**0**	**0**	**0**	**0**	**0**	**0**	**0**	**2**	**0.0**	**0**	**0**	**0**	**0**									
	Other Major League Totals		161	30	48	78				60																		

• Brother of Jim • NAHL First All-Star Team (1975)

Traded to **Salt Lake** (WHL) by **NY Rangers** for Rick Charron, May, 1971. Traded to **Portland** (WHL) by **Salt Lake** (WHL) for cash, February, 1972. Selected by **Dayton-Houston** (WHA) in 1972 WHA General Player Draft, February 12, 1972. WHA rights traded to **LA Sharks** (WHA) by **Houston** (WHA) for future considerations, September, 1972. Traded to **NY Raiders** (WHA) by **LA Sharks** (WHA) with Jarda Krupicka for Alton White, November, 1972. Transferred to **San Diego** (WHA) after **New York-Jersey** (WHA) franchise relocated, April 30, 1974. Claimed by **Phoenix** (WHA) from **San Diego** in 1974 WHA Expansion Draft, May, 1974. Claimed by **Indianapolis** (WHA) from **Michigan-Baltimore** (WHA) in 1975 WHA Dispersal Draft, June, 1975.

• JONES, Brad

Bradley Scott LW – L. 6', 195 lbs. b: Sterling Heights, MI, 6/26/1965. Winnipeg's 8th, 156th overall, in 1984.

Season	Club	League	GP	G	A	Pts	AG	AA	APts	PIM	PP	SH	GW	S	%	TGF	PGF	TGA	PGA	+/–	GP	G	A	Pts	PIM	PP	SH	GW
1981-82	Utica Ford High School	Hi-School	STATISTICS NOT AVAILABLE																									
1982-83	Markham Waxers	OJHL-B	46	20	36	56				75																		
1983-84	University of Michigan	CCHA	37	8	26	34				32																		
1984-85	University of Michigan	CCHA	34	21	27	48				66																		
1985-86	University of Michigan	CCHA	36	28	39	67				40																		
1986-87	University of Michigan	CCHA	40	32	46	78				64																		
	Winnipeg Jets	**NHL**	**4**	**1**	**0**	**1**	**1**	**0**	**1**	**0**	**0**	**0**	**0**	**8**	**12.5**	**2**	**0**	**0**	**0**	**2**								
1987-88	United States	Nat-Team	50	27	23	50				59																		
	Winnipeg Jets	**NHL**	**19**	**2**	**5**	**7**	**2**	**4**	**6**	**15**	**0**	**0**	**1**	**33**	**6.1**	**9**	**0**	**10**	**3**	**2**	**1**	**0**	**0**	**0**	**0**	**0**	**0**	**0**
1988-89	**Winnipeg Jets**	**NHL**	**22**	**6**	**5**	**11**	**5**	**4**	**9**	**6**	**0**	**1**	**0**	**25**	**24.0**	**18**	**0**	**20**	**2**	**0**								
	Moncton Hawks	AHL	44	20	19	39				62											7	0	1	1	22			
1989-90	**Winnipeg Jets**	**NHL**	**2**	**0**	**0**	**0**	**0**	**0**	**0**	**0**	**0**	**0**	**0**	**0**	**0.0**	**0**	**0**	**2**	**0**	**–2**								
	Moncton Hawks	AHL	15	5	6	11				47																		
	New Haven Nighthawks	AHL	36	8	11	19				71																		
1990-91	**Los Angeles Kings**	**NHL**	**53**	**9**	**11**	**20**	**8**	**8**	**16**	**57**	**0**	**1**	**1**	**47**	**19.1**	**31**	**1**	**34**	**15**	**11**	**8**	**1**	**1**	**2**	**2**	**0**	**0**	**1**
1991-92	**Philadelphia Flyers**	**NHL**	**48**	**7**	**10**	**17**	**6**	**8**	**14**	**44**	**0**	**0**	**1**	**67**	**10.4**	**23**	**0**	**38**	**13**	**–2**								
1992-93	Ilves Tampere	Finland	26	10	7	17				62											4	0	1	1	4			
	New Haven Senators	AHL	4	2	1	3				6																		
1993-94	HC Ajoie	Switz.	19	9	12	21				22																		
1994-95	Springfield Falcons	AHL	61	23	22	45				47																		
	Fort Wayne Komets	IHL	4	1	1	2				6																		
	United States	WC-A	5	0	2	2				2																		
1995-96	Binghamton Rangers	AHL	62	25	27	52				36											4	1	1	2	0			
1996-97	Frankfurt Lions	Germany	37	14	11	25				89											9	5	3	8	8			
1997-98	Binghamton Icemen	UHL	55	37	28	65				58											5	2	3	5	6			
1998-2000	Binghamton Icemen	UHL	DID NOT PLAY – COACHING																									
	NHL Totals		**148**	**25**	**31**	**56**	**22**	**24**	**46**	**122**	**0**	**2**	**3**	**180**	**13.9**	**83**	**1**	**104**	**33**		**9**	**1**	**1**	**2**	**2**	**0**	**0**	**1**

CCHA Second All-Star Team (1986) • CCHA First All-Star Team (1987) • NCAA West Second All-American Team (1987)

Traded to **LA Kings** by **Winnipeg** for Phil Sykes, December 1, 1989. Signed as a free agent by **Philadelphia**, August 6, 1991.

• JONES, Jim

James William D – L. 5'10", 185 lbs. b: Espanola, Ont., 7/27/1949. Boston's 8th, 69th overall, in 1969.

Season	Club	League	GP	G	A	Pts	AG	AA	APts	PIM	PP	SH	GW	S	%	TGF	PGF	TGA	PGA	+/–	GP	G	A	Pts	PIM	PP	SH	GW
1965-66	Espanola Eagles	NOJHA	STATISTICS NOT AVAILABLE																									
1966-67	Kitchener Rangers	OHA-Jr.	44	1	2	3				10											13	0	0	0	0			
1967-68	Kitchener Rangers	OHA-Jr.	11	3	1	4				6																		
	Peterborough Petes	OHA-Jr.	42	6	19	25				31											5	1	3	4	2			
1968-69	Peterborough Petes	OHA-Jr.	54	10	42	52				73											10	0	5	5	2			
1969-70	Oklahoma City Blazers	CHL	63	4	10	14				54																		
1970-71	Oklahoma City Blazers	CHL	36	1	2	3				26																		
1971-72	**California Golden Seals**	**NHL**	**2**	**0**	**0**	**0**	**0**	**0**	**0**	**0**	**0**	**0**	**0**	**0**	**0.0**	**1**	**0**	**1**	**0**	**0**								
	Salt Lake Golden Eagles	WHL	28	2	7	9				20																		
1972-73	Baltimore Clippers	AHL	16	1	2	3				12																		
	Columbus Seals	IHL	40	3	15	18				52																		
	Salt Lake Golden Eagles	WHL	17	0	3	3				16											9	1	1	2	0			
1973-74	Chicago Cougars	WHA	1	0	0	0				0																		
	Winston-Salem Polar Bears	SHL	49	2	17	19				35											7	1	5	6	6			
1974-75	Port Huron–Des Moines	IHL	17	1	5	6				14																		
	Greensboro Generals	SHL	35	7	20	27				18																		
	Philadelphia Firebirds	NAHL	12	0	1	1				16											4	0	1	1	0			
1975-76	Roanoke Valley Rebels	SHL	8	0	2	2				4																		
	NHL Totals		**2**	**0**	**0**	**0**	**0**	**0**	**0**	**0**	**0**	**0**	**0**	**0**	**0.0**	**1**	**0**	**1**	**0**									
	Other Major League Totals		1	0	0	0				0																		

• Brother of Bob • Signed as a free agent by **California**, June, 1971. Signed as a free agent by **Chicago** (WHA), September, 1973.

• JONES, Jimmy

James Harrison RW – R. 5'9", 180 lbs. b: Woodbridge, Ont., 1/2/1953. Boston's 2nd, 31st overall, in 1973.

Season	Club	League	GP	G	A	Pts	AG	AA	APts	PIM	PP	SH	GW	S	%	TGF	PGF	TGA	PGA	+/–	GP	G	A	Pts	PIM	PP	SH	GW
1970-71	Peterborough Petes	OMJHL	11	0	2	2				2																		
1971-72	Peterborough Jr. Bees	OHA-B	STATISTICS NOT AVAILABLE																									
	Peterborough Petes	OMJHL	4	1	2	3				8											15	4	10	14	19			
	Peterborough Petes	Mem-Cup	3	1	1	2				6																		
1972-73	Peterborough Petes	OMJHL	63	37	33	70				73											13	11	6	17	38			
1973-74	Vancouver Blazers	WHA	18	3	2	5				23																		
	Roanoke Valley Rebels	SHL	60	24	38	62				97																		
1974-75	Vancouver Blazers	WHA	63	11	7	18				39																		
	Tulsa Oilers	CHL	9	6	7	13				17																		
1975-76	Rochester Americans	AHL	66	16	22	38				71											7	1	0	1	11			
1976-77	Rochester Americans	AHL	74	24	34	58				66																		
1977-78	**Toronto Maple Leafs**	**NHL**	**78**	**4**	**9**	**13**	**4**	**7**	**11**	**23**	**0**	**2**	**1**	**54**	**7.4**	**15**	**1**	**53**	**40**	**1**	**13**	**1**	**5**	**6**	**7**	**0**	**0**	**0**
1978-79	**Toronto Maple Leafs**	**NHL**	**69**	**9**	**9**	**18**	**8**	**7**	**15**	**45**	**0**	**0**	**0**	**63**	**14.3**	**26**	**0**	**64**	**40**	**2**	**6**	**0**	**0**	**0**	**4**	**0**	**0**	**0**
1979-80	**Toronto Maple Leafs**	**NHL**	**1**	**0**	**0**	**0**	**0**	**0**	**0**	**0**	**0**	**0**	**0**	**1**	**0.0**	**0**	**0**	**1**	**0**	**–1**								
	New Brunswick Hawks	AHL	48	17	17	34				31																		
1980-81	Rochester Americans	AHL	73	13	15	28				83																		
	NHL Totals		**148**	**13**	**18**	**31**	**12**	**14**	**26**	**68**	**0**	**2**	**1**	**118**	**11.0**	**41**	**1**	**118**	**80**		**19**	**1**	**5**	**6**	**11**	**0**	**0**	**0**
	Other Major League Totals		81	14	9	23				62																		

Selected by **Vancouver** (WHA) in 1973 WHA Amateur Draft, June, 1973. Signed as a free agent by **Toronto**, October 25, 1977. Claimed as a fill-in by **Toronto** during Expansion Draft, June 13, 1979.

• JONES, Keith

RW – L. 6'2", 200 lbs. b: Brantford, Ont., 11/8/1968. Washington's 7th, 141st overall, in 1988.

Season	Club	League	GP	G	A	Pts	AG	AA	APts	PIM	PP	SH	GW	S	%	TGF	PGF	TGA	PGA	+/–	GP	G	A	Pts	PIM	PP	SH	GW
1985-86	Paris Mounties	OJHL-C	30	26	13	39				61																		
1986-87	Paris Mounties	OJHL-C	30	39	38	77				136																		
1987-88	Niagara Falls Canucks	OJHL-B	40	50	80	130				113																		

			REGULAR SEASON																		PLAYOFFS							
Season	Club	League	GP	G	A	Pts	AG	AA	APts	PIM	PP	SH	GW	S	%	TGF	PGF	TGA	PGA	+/-	GP	G	A	Pts	PIM	PP	SH	GW
1988-89	Western Michigan University	CCHA	37	9	12	21	....	....	....	51	....	....	....	....	....	....	....	....	....	....	....	....	....	....	....	....	....	....
1989-90	Western Michigan University	CCHA	40	19	18	37	....	....	....	82	....	....	....	....	....	....	....	....	....	....	....	....	....	....	....	....	....	....
1990-91	Western Michigan University	CCHA	41	30	19	49	....	....	....	106	....	....	....	....	....	....	....	....	....	....	....	....	....	....	....	....	....	....
1991-92	Western Michigan University	CCHA	35	25	31	56	....	....	....	77	....	....	....	....	....	....	....	....	....	....	....	....	....	....	....	....	....	....
	Baltimore Skipjacks	AHL	6	2	4	6	....	....	....	0	....	....	....	....	....	....	....	....	....	....	....	....	....	....	....	....	....	....
1992-93	**Washington Capitals**	**NHL**	**71**	**12**	**14**	**26**	**10**	**10**	**20**	**124**	**0**	**0**	**3**	**73**	**16.4**	**46**	**4**	**24**	**0**	**18**	**6**	**0**	**0**	**0**	**10**	**0**	**0**	**0**
	Baltimore Skipjacks	AHL	8	7	3	10	....	....	....	4	....	....	....	....	....	....	....	....	....	....	....	....	....	....	....	....	....	....
1993-94	**Washington Capitals**	**NHL**	**68**	**16**	**19**	**35**	**15**	**15**	**30**	**149**	**5**	**0**	**1**	**97**	**16.5**	**52**	**15**	**33**	**0**	**4**	**11**	**0**	**1**	**1**	**36**	**0**	**0**	**0**
	Portland Pirates	AHL	6	5	7	12	....	....	....	4	....	....	....	....	....	....	....	....	....	....	....	....	....	....	....	....	....	....
1994-95	**Washington Capitals**	**NHL**	**40**	**14**	**6**	**20**	**25**	**9**	**34**	**65**	**1**	**0**	**4**	**85**	**16.5**	**24**	**6**	**20**	**0**	**–2**	**7**	**4**	**4**	**8**	**22**	**1**	**0**	**0**
1995-96	**Washington Capitals**	**NHL**	**68**	**18**	**23**	**41**	**18**	**19**	**37**	**103**	**5**	**0**	**2**	**155**	**11.6**	**70**	**26**	**38**	**2**	**8**	**2**	**0**	**0**	**0**	**7**	**0**	**0**	**0**
1996-97	**Washington Capitals**	**NHL**	**11**	**2**	**3**	**5**	**2**	**3**	**5**	**13**	**1**	**0**	**0**	**12**	**16.7**	**8**	**2**	**8**	**0**	**–2**	....	....	....	....	....	....	....	....
	Colorado Avalanche	**NHL**	**67**	**23**	**20**	**43**	**24**	**18**	**42**	**105**	**13**	**1**	**7**	**158**	**14.6**	**73**	**35**	**35**	**2**	**5**	**6**	**3**	**3**	**6**	**4**	**1**	**0**	**0**
1997-98	**Colorado Avalanche**	**NHL**	**23**	**3**	**7**	**10**	**4**	**7**	**11**	**22**	**1**	**0**	**2**	**31**	**9.7**	**18**	**9**	**13**	**0**	**–4**	**7**	**0**	**0**	**0**	**13**	**0**	**0**	**0**
	Hershey Bears	AHL	4	2	1	3	....	....	....	2	....	....	....	....	....	....	....	....	....	....	....	....	....	....	....	....	....	....
1998-99	**Colorado Avalanche**	**NHL**	**12**	**2**	**2**	**4**	**2**	**2**	**4**	**20**	**1**	**0**	**0**	**11**	**18.2**	**7**	**3**	**10**	**0**	**–6**	....	....	....	....	....	....	....	....
	Philadelphia Flyers	**NHL**	**66**	**18**	**31**	**49**	**21**	**30**	**51**	**78**	**2**	**0**	**3**	**124**	**14.5**	**87**	**17**	**41**	**0**	**29**	**6**	**2**	**1**	**3**	**14**	**0**	**0**	**0**
99-2000	**Philadelphia Flyers**	**NHL**	**57**	**9**	**16**	**25**	**10**	**15**	**25**	**82**	**1**	**0**	**0**	**92**	**9.8**	**40**	**7**	**25**	**0**	**8**	**18**	**3**	**3**	**6**	**14**	**1**	**0**	**0**
	NHL Totals		**483**	**117**	**141**	**258**	**131**	**128**	**259**	**761**	**30**	**1**	**22**	**838**	**14.0**	**425**	**124**	**247**	**4**		**63**	**12**	**12**	**24**	**120**	**3**	**0**	**0**

CCHA First All-Star Team (1992)

Traded to **Colorado** by **Washington** with Washington's 1st round choice (Scott Parker) in 1998 Entry Draft and future considerations for Curtis Leschyshyn and Chris Simon, November 2, 1996. Traded to **Philadelphia** by **Colorado** for Shjon Podein, November 12, 1998.

• JONES, Ron

Ronald Perry D – L. 6'1", 195 lbs. b: Vermillion, Alta., 4/11/1951. Boston's 1st, 6th overall, in 1971.

			REGULAR SEASON																		PLAYOFFS							
Season	Club	League	GP	G	A	Pts	AG	AA	APts	PIM	PP	SH	GW	S	%	TGF	PGF	TGA	PGA	+/-	GP	G	A	Pts	PIM	PP	SH	GW
1967-68	Edmonton Oil Kings	WCJHL	48	1	5	6	....	....	....	29	....	....	....	....	....	....	....	....	....	....	4	0	0	0	0	....	....	....
1968-69	Edmonton Oil Kings	WCJHL	46	2	11	13	....	....	....	37	....	....	....	....	....	....	....	....	....	....	17	0	2	2	8	....	....	....
1969-70	Edmonton Oil Kings	WCJHL	52	7	33	40	....	....	....	82	....	....	....	....	....	....	....	....	....	....	18	1	6	7	10	....	....	....
	Edmonton Oil Kings	Mem-Cup	2	0	1	1	....	....	....	6	....	....	....	....	....	....	....	....	....	....	....	....	....	....	....	....	....	....
1970-71	Edmonton Oil Kings	WCJHL	63	11	40	51	....	....	....	46	....	....	....	....	....	....	....	....	....	....	17	2	13	15	16	....	....	....
	Edmonton Oil Kings	Mem-Cup	2	0	1	1	....	....	....	6	....	....	....	....	....	....	....	....	....	....	....	....	....	....	....	....	....	....
1971-72	**Boston Bruins**	**NHL**	**1**	**0**	**0**	**0**	**0**	**0**	**0**	**0**	**0**	**0**	**0**	**3**	**0.0**	**1**	**0**	**0**	**0**	**1**	....	....	....	....	....	....	....	....
	Boston Braves	AHL	74	6	11	17	....	....	....	36	....	....	....	....	....	....	....	....	....	....	9	0	0	0	7	....	....	....
1972-73	**Boston Bruins**	**NHL**	**7**	**0**	**0**	**0**	**0**	**0**	**0**	**0**	**0**	**0**	**0**	**0**	**0.0**	**3**	**0**	**2**	**0**	**1**	....	....	....	....	....	....	....	....
	Boston Braves	AHL	55	3	25	28	....	....	....	34	....	....	....	....	....	....	....	....	....	....	5	0	1	1	2	....	....	....
1973-74	**Pittsburgh Penguins**	**NHL**	**25**	**0**	**3**	**3**	**0**	**2**	**2**	**15**	**0**	**0**	**0**	**18**	**0.0**	**21**	**3**	**36**	**4**	**–14**	....	....	....	....	....	....	....	....
	Hershey Bears	AHL	34	0	12	12	....	....	....	23	....	....	....	....	....	....	....	....	....	....	14	0	3	3	6	....	....	....
1974-75	**Washington Capitals**	**NHL**	**19**	**1**	**1**	**2**	**1**	**1**	**2**	**16**	**1**	**0**	**0**	**13**	**7.7**	**21**	**6**	**38**	**9**	**–14**	....	....	....	....	....	....	....	....
	Hershey Bears	AHL	25	0	6	6	....	....	....	37	....	....	....	....	....	....	....	....	....	....	....	....	....	....	....	....	....	....
1975-76	**Washington Capitals**	**NHL**	**2**	**0**	**0**	**0**	**0**	**0**	**0**	**0**	**0**	**0**	**0**	**0**	**0.0**	**0**	**0**	**1**	**0**	**–1**	....	....	....	....	....	....	....	....
	Richmond Robins	AHL	20	0	7	7	....	....	....	8	....	....	....	....	....	....	....	....	....	....	....	....	....	....	....	....	....	....
	Hershey Bears	AHL	53	7	23	30	....	....	....	34	....	....	....	....	....	....	....	....	....	....	10	1	5	6	9	....	....	....
1976-77	Hershey Bears	AHL	36	0	9	9	....	....	....	18	....	....	....	....	....	....	....	....	....	....	6	0	3	3	4	....	....	....
	NHL Totals		**54**	**1**	**4**	**5**	**1**	**3**	**4**	**31**	**1**	**0**	**0**	**34**	**2.9**	**46**	**9**	**77**	**13**		....	....	....	....	....	....	....	....

WCJHL All-Star Team (1971)

Claimed by **Pittsburgh** from **Boston** in Intra-League Draft, June 12, 1973. Traded to **Washington** by **Pittsburgh** for Pete Laframboise, January 21, 1975. • Missed majority of 1976-77 in retirement.

• JONES, Ty

RW – R. 6'3", 218 lbs. b: Richland, WA, 2/22/1979. Chicago's 2nd, 16th overall, in 1997.

			REGULAR SEASON																		PLAYOFFS							
Season	Club	League	GP	G	A	Pts	AG	AA	APts	PIM	PP	SH	GW	S	%	TGF	PGF	TGA	PGA	+/-	GP	G	A	Pts	PIM	PP	SH	GW
1993-94	Alaska All-Stars	AAHL	64	84	104	188	....	....	....	126	....	....	....	....	....	....	....	....	....	....	....	....	....	....	....	....	....	....
1994-95	Alaska All-Stars	AAHL	42	33	35	68	....	....	....	98	....	....	....	....	....	....	....	....	....	....	....	....	....	....	....	....	....	....
1995-96	Spokane Chiefs	WHL	34	1	0	1	....	....	....	77	....	....	....	....	....	....	....	....	....	....	3	0	0	0	6	....	....	....
1996-97	Spokane Chiefs	WHL	67	20	34	54	....	....	....	202	....	....	....	....	....	....	....	....	....	....	9	2	4	6	10	....	....	....
1997-98	Spokane Chiefs	WHL	60	36	48	84	....	....	....	161	....	....	....	....	....	....	....	....	....	....	18	2	14	16	35	....	....	....
	United States	WJC-A	7	0	2	2	....	....	....	6	....	....	....	....	....	....	....	....	....	....	....	....	....	....	....	....	....	....
1998-99	Spokane Chiefs	WHL	26	15	12	27	....	....	....	98	....	....	....	....	....	....	....	....	....	....	....	....	....	....	....	....	....	....
	Kamloops Blazers	WHL	20	3	16	19	....	....	....	84	....	....	....	....	....	....	....	....	....	....	14	5	3	8	22	....	....	....
	Chicago Blackhawks	**NHL**	**8**	**0**	**0**	**0**	**0**	**0**	**0**	**12**	**0**	**0**	**0**	**3**	**0.0**	**0**	**0**	**1**	**0**	**–1**	....	....	....	....	....	....	....	....
99-2000	Cleveland Lumberjacks	IHL	10	1	1	2	....	....	....	34	....	....	....	....	....	....	....	....	....	....	....	....	....	....	....	....	....	....
	Florida Everblades	ECHL	48	11	26	37	....	....	....	81	....	....	....	....	....	....	....	....	....	....	5	1	1	2	17	....	....	....
	NHL Totals		**8**	**0**	**0**	**0**	**0**	**0**	**0**	**12**	**0**	**0**	**0**	**3**	**0.0**	**0**	**0**	**1**	**0**		....	....	....	....	....	....	....	....

• JONSSON, Hans

D – L. 6'1", 183 lbs. b: Jarved, Sweden, 8/2/1973. Pittsburgh's 11th, 286th overall, in 1993.

			REGULAR SEASON																		PLAYOFFS							
Season	Club	League	GP	G	A	Pts	AG	AA	APts	PIM	PP	SH	GW	S	%	TGF	PGF	TGA	PGA	+/-	GP	G	A	Pts	PIM	PP	SH	GW
1991-92	MoDo AIK	Sweden	6	0	1	1	....	....	....	4	....	....	....	....	....	....	....	....	....	....	....	....	....	....	....	....	....	....
1992-93	MoDo AIK	Sweden	40	2	2	4	....	....	....	24	....	....	....	....	....	....	....	....	....	....	3	0	1	1	2	....	....	....
	Sweden	WJC-A	7	2	1	3	....	....	....	24	....	....	....	....	....	....	....	....	....	....	....	....	....	....	....	....	....	....
1993-94	MoDo Hockey	Sweden	23	4	1	5	....	....	....	18	....	....	....	....	....	....	....	....	....	....	10	0	1	1	12	....	....	....
1994-95	MoDo Hockey	Sweden	39	4	6	10	....	....	....	30	....	....	....	....	....	....	....	....	....	....	....	....	....	....	....	....	....	....
1995-96	MoDo Hockey	Sweden	36	10	6	16	....	....	....	30	....	....	....	....	....	....	....	....	....	....	8	2	1	3	24	....	....	....
	Sweden	WC-A	6	1	0	1	....	....	....	4	....	....	....	....	....	....	....	....	....	....	....	....	....	....	....	....	....	....
1996-97	MoDo Hockey	Sweden	27	7	5	12	....	....	....	18	....	....	....	....	....	....	....	....	....	....	....	....	....	....	....	....	....	....
1997-98	MoDo Hockey	Sweden	40	8	6	14	....	....	....	40	....	....	....	....	....	....	....	....	....	....	8	1	1	2	12	....	....	....
	Sweden	WC-A	10	0	1	1	....	....	....	2	....	....	....	....	....	....	....	....	....	....	....	....	....	....	....	....	....	....
	Sweden	WC-A	10	0	0	0	....	....	....	16	....	....	....	....	....	....	....	....	....	....	....	....	....	....	....	....	....	....
1998-99	MoDo Hockey	Sweden	41	3	4	7	....	....	....	40	....	....	....	....	....	....	....	....	....	....	13	2	4	6	22	....	....	....
99-2000	**Pittsburgh Penguins**	**NHL**	**68**	**3**	**11**	**14**	**3**	**10**	**13**	**12**	**0**	**1**	**1**	**49**	**6.1**	**54**	**10**	**65**	**16**	**–5**	**11**	**0**	**1**	**1**	**6**	**0**	**0**	**0**
	NHL Totals		**68**	**3**	**11**	**14**	**3**	**10**	**13**	**12**	**0**	**1**	**1**	**49**	**6.1**	**54**	**10**	**65**	**16**		**11**	**0**	**1**	**1**	**6**	**0**	**0**	**0**

• JONSSON, Jorgen

LW – L. 6', 185 lbs. b: Angelholm, Sweden, 9/29/1972. Calgary's 11th, 227th overall, in 1994.

			REGULAR SEASON																		PLAYOFFS							
Season	Club	League	GP	G	A	Pts	AG	AA	APts	PIM	PP	SH	GW	S	%	TGF	PGF	TGA	PGA	+/-	GP	G	A	Pts	PIM	PP	SH	GW
1989-90	Rogle BK Angelholm	Sweden-2	1	0	0	0	....	....	....	0	....	....	....	....	....	....	....	....	....	....	4	0	0	0	0	....	....	....
1990-91	Rogle BK Angelholm	Sweden-2	21	4	2	6	....	....	....	2	....	....	....	....	....	....	....	....	....	....	12	2	1	3	2	....	....	....
1991-92	Rogle BK Angelholm	Sweden-2	27	1	8	9	....	....	....	6	....	....	....	....	....	....	....	....	....	....	5	0	0	0	0	....	....	....
1992-93	Rogle BK Angelholm	Sweden	40	17	11	28	....	....	....	28	....	....	....	....	....	....	....	....	....	....	....	....	....	....	....	....	....	....
1993-94	Rogle BK Angelholm	Sweden	40	17	14	31	....	....	....	46	....	....	....	....	....	....	....	....	....	....	....	....	....	....	....	....	....	....
	Sweden	Olympics	6	0	0	0	....	....	....	0	....	....	....	....	....	....	....	....	....	....	....	....	....	....	....	....	....	....
	Sweden	WC-A	7	3	2	5	....	....	....	4	....	....	....	....	....	....	....	....	....	....	....	....	....	....	....	....	....	....
1994-95	Rogle BK Angelholm	Sweden	22	4	6	10	....	....	....	18	....	....	....	....	....	....	....	....	....	....	....	....	....	....	....	....	....	....
1995-96	Farjestads BK Karlstad	Sweden	39	11	15	26	....	....	....	36	....	....	....	....	....	....	....	....	....	....	8	0	4	4	6	....	....	....
1996-97	Farjestads BK Karlstad	Sweden	49	12	21	33	....	....	....	58	....	....	....	....	....	....	....	....	....	....	14	9	5	14	14	....	....	....
	Farjestads BK Karlstad	EuroHL	4	2	1	3	....	....	....	2	....	....	....	....	....	....	....	....	....	....	....	....	....	....	....	....	....	....
	Sweden	WC-A	11	5	2	7	....	....	....	6	....	....	....	....	....	....	....	....	....	....	....	....	....	....	....	....	....	....
1997-98	Farjestads BK Karlstad	Sweden	45	22	25	47	....	....	....	53	....	....	....	....	....	....	....	....	....	....	12	2	*9	11	12	....	....	....
	Farjestads BK Karlstad	EuroHL	7	2	4	6	....	....	....	6	....	....	....	....	....	....	....	....	....	....	....	....	....	....	....	....	....	....
	Sweden	Olympics	1	0	0	0	....	....	....	0	....	....	....	....	....	....	....	....	....	....	....	....	....	....	....	....	....	....
	Sweden	WC-A	10	2	1	3	....	....	....	6	....	....	....	....	....	....	....	....	....	....	....	....	....	....	....	....	....	....
1998-99	Farjestads BK Karlstad	Sweden	48	17	24	41	....	....	....	44	....	....	....	....	....	....	....	....	....	....	4	0	2	2	4	....	....	....
	Farjestads BK Karlstad	EuroHL	5	2	4	6	....	....	....	4	....	....	....	....	....	....	....	....	....	....	2	1	0	1	4	....	....	....
	Sweden	WC-A	10	3	1	4	....	....	....	10	....	....	....	....	....	....	....	....	....	....	....	....	....	....	....	....	....	....

			REGULAR SEASON																		PLAYOFFS							
Season	Club	League	GP	G	A	Pts	AG	AA	APts	PIM	PP	SH	GW	S	%	TGF	PGF	TGA	PGA	+/–	GP	G	A	Pts	PIM	PP	SH	GW
99-2000	**New York Islanders**	**NHL**	68	11	17	28	12	16	28	16	1	2	0	95	11.6	46	11	65	24	–6	....	....	....	....	....	....	....	....
	Mighty Ducks of Anaheim	**NHL**	13	1	2	3	1	2	3	0	0	0	1	21	4.8	4	0	8	2	–2	....	....	....	....	....	....	....	....
	Sweden	WC-A	6	0	2	2	....	....	....	2	....	....	....	....	....	....	....	....	....	....	....	....	....	....	....	....	....	....
	NHL Totals		81	12	19	31	13	18	31	16	1	2	1	116	10.3	50	11	73	26		....	....	....	....	....	....	....	....

• Brother of Kenny. Traded to **Anaheim** by **NY Islanders** for Johan Davidsson and future considerations, March 11, 2000.

• JONSSON, Kenny

D – L. 6'3", 195 lbs. b: Angelholm, Sweden, 10/6/1974. Toronto's 1st, 12th overall, in 1993.

Season	Club	League	GP	G	A	Pts	AG	AA	APts	PIM	PP	SH	GW	S	%	TGF	PGF	TGA	PGA	+/–	GP	G	A	Pts	PIM	PP	SH	GW
1991-92	Rogle BK Angelholm	Sweden-2	30	4	11	15	....	....	....	24	....	....	....	....	....	....	....	....	....	....	5	0	0	0	0	....	....	....
	Sweden	EJC-A	6	1	2	3	....	....	....	10	....	....	....	....	....	....	....	....	....	....	....	....	....	....	....	....	....	....
1992-93	Rogle BK Angelholm	Sweden-Jr.	2	1	2	3	....	....	....	25	....	....	....	....	....	....	....	....	....	....	....	....	....	....	....	....	....	....
	Rogle BK Angelholm	Sweden	39	3	10	13	....	....	....	42	....	....	....	....	....	....	....	....	....	....	....	....	....	....	....	....	....	....
	Sweden	WJC-A	7	2	3	5	....	....	....	14	....	....	....	....	....	....	....	....	....	....	....	....	....	....	....	....	....	....
1993-94	Rogle BK Angelholm	Sweden	36	4	13	17	....	....	....	40	....	....	....	....	....	....	....	....	....	....	3	1	1	2	2	....	....	....
	Sweden	WJC-A	7	3	5	8	....	....	....	8	....	....	....	....	....	....	....	....	....	....	....	....	....	....	....	....	....	....
	Sweden	Olympics	3	1	0	1	....	....	....	0	....	....	....	....	....	....	....	....	....	....	....	....	....	....	....	....	....	....
	Sweden	WC-A	7	0	1	1	....	....	....	6	....	....	....	....	....	....	....	....	....	....	....	....	....	....	....	....	....	....
1994-95	Rogle BK Angelholm	Sweden	8	3	1	4	....	....	....	20	....	....	....	....	....	....	....	....	....	....	....	....	....	....	....	....	....	....
	Toronto Maple Leafs	**NHL**	39	2	7	9	4	10	14	16	0	0	1	50	4.0	25	9	26	2	–8	4	0	0	0	0	0	0	0
	St. John's Maple Leafs	AHL	10	2	5	7	....	....	....	2	....	....	....	....	....	....	....	....	....	....	....	....	....	....	....	....	....	....
1995-96	**Toronto Maple Leafs**	**NHL**	50	4	22	26	4	18	22	22	3	0	1	90	4.4	64	30	26	4	12	....	....	....	....	....	....	....	....
	New York Islanders	**NHL**	16	0	4	4	0	3	3	10	0	0	0	40	0.0	17	7	20	5	–5	....	....	....	....	....	....	....	....
	Sweden	WC-A	6	0	1	1	....	....	....	8	....	....	....	....	....	....	....	....	....	....	....	....	....	....	....	....	....	....
1996-97	Sweden	W-Cup	1	0	0	0	....	....	....	4	....	....	....	....	....	....	....	....	....	....	....	....	....	....	....	....	....	....
	New York Islanders	**NHL**	81	3	18	21	3	16	19	24	1	0	0	92	3.3	92	16	94	28	10	....	....	....	....	....	....	....	....
1997-98	**New York Islanders**	**NHL**	81	14	26	40	16	25	41	58	6	0	2	108	13.0	98	40	92	32	–2	....	....	....	....	....	....	....	....
1998-99	**New York Islanders**	**NHL**	63	8	18	26	9	17	26	34	6	0	0	91	8.8	58	27	65	16	–18	....	....	....	....	....	....	....	....
99-2000	**New York Islanders**	**NHL**	65	1	24	25	1	22	23	32	1	0	0	84	1.2	71	26	94	34	–15	....	....	....	....	....	....	....	....
	NHL Totals		395	32	119	151	37	111	148	196	17	0	4	555	5.8	425	155	417	121		4	0	0	0	0	0	0	0

• Brother of Jorgen • WJC-A All-Star Team (1993, 1994) • Swedish Rookie of the Year (1993) • Named Best Defenseman at WJC-A (1994) • NHL All-Rookie Team (1995)

Traded to **NY Islanders** by **Toronto** with Sean Haggerty, Darby Hendrickson and Toronto's 1st round choice (Roberto Luongo) in 1997 Entry Draft for Wendel Clark, Mathieu Schneider and D.J. Smith, March 13, 1996.

• JONSSON, Tomas

D – L. 5'10", 185 lbs. b: Falun, Sweden, 4/12/1960. NY Islanders' 2nd, 25th overall, in 1979.

Season	Club	League	GP	G	A	Pts	AG	AA	APts	PIM	PP	SH	GW	S	%	TGF	PGF	TGA	PGA	+/–	GP	G	A	Pts	PIM	PP	SH	GW
1974-75	Falu IF	Sweden-2	8	0	0	0	....	....	....	0	....	....	....	....	....	....	....	....	....	....	....	....	....	....	....	....	....	....
1975-76	Falu IF	Sweden-2	20	0	4	4	....	....	....	....	....	....	....	....	....	....	....	....	....	....	....	....	....	....	....	....	....	....
1976-77	Falu IF	Sweden-2	19	3	7	10	....	....	....	....	....	....	....	....	....	....	....	....	....	....	....	....	....	....	....	....	....	....
	Sweden	EJC-A	6	2	3	5	....	....	....	16	....	....	....	....	....	....	....	....	....	....	....	....	....	....	....	....	....	....
1977-78	MoDo AIK	Sweden	35	8	9	17	....	....	....	45	....	....	....	....	....	....	....	....	....	....	2	0	0	0	4	....	....	....
	Sweden	WJC-A	7	1	2	3	....	....	....	10	....	....	....	....	....	....	....	....	....	....	....	....	....	....	....	....	....	....
1978-79	MoDo AIK	Sweden	34	11	9	20	....	....	....	77	....	....	....	....	....	....	....	....	....	....	5	1	2	3	13	....	....	....
	Sweden	WJC-A	6	1	1	2	....	....	....	4	....	....	....	....	....	....	....	....	....	....	....	....	....	....	....	....	....	....
	Sweden	Nat-Team	15	2	3	5	....	....	....	16	....	....	....	....	....	....	....	....	....	....	....	....	....	....	....	....	....	....
	Sweden	WEC-A	8	1	3	4	....	....	....	8	....	....	....	....	....	....	....	....	....	....	....	....	....	....	....	....	....	....
1979-80	MoDo AIK	Sweden	36	3	13	16	....	....	....	42	....	....	....	....	....	....	....	....	....	....	....	....	....	....	....	....	....	....
	Sweden	WJC-A	5	2	1	3	....	....	....	10	....	....	....	....	....	....	....	....	....	....	....	....	....	....	....	....	....	....
	Sweden	Nat-Team	18	2	4	6	....	....	....	24	....	....	....	....	....	....	....	....	....	....	....	....	....	....	....	....	....	....
	Sweden	Olympics	7	2	2	4	....	....	....	6	....	....	....	....	....	....	....	....	....	....	....	....	....	....	....	....	....	....
1980-81	MoDo AIK	Sweden	35	8	12	20	....	....	....	58	....	....	....	....	....	....	....	....	....	....	....	....	....	....	....	....	....	....
	Sweden	Nat-Team	19	0	2	2	....	....	....	2	....	....	....	....	....	....	....	....	....	....	....	....	....	....	....	....	....	....
	Sweden	WEC-A	1	0	0	0	....	....	....	0	....	....	....	....	....	....	....	....	....	....	....	....	....	....	....	....	....	....
1981-82	Sweden	Can-Cup	3	0	1	1	....	....	....	4	....	....	....	....	....	....	....	....	....	....	....	....	....	....	....	....	....	....
	MoDo AIK	Sweden	7	0	2	2	....	....	....	8	....	....	....	....	....	....	....	....	....	....	....	....	....	....	....	....	....	....
♦	**New York Islanders**	**NHL**	70	9	25	34	7	17	24	51	0	0	1	89	10.1	104	20	60	2	26	10	0	2	2	21	0	0	0
1982-83♦	**New York Islanders**	**NHL**	72	13	35	48	11	24	35	50	1	0	3	100	13.0	118	27	60	9	40	20	2	10	12	18	0	0	0
1983-84	**New York Islanders**	**NHL**	72	11	36	47	9	25	34	54	2	0	1	122	9.0	112	34	82	16	12	21	3	5	8	22	2	0	0
1984-85	**New York Islanders**	**NHL**	69	16	34	50	13	23	36	58	8	0	4	128	12.5	125	47	97	18	–1	7	1	2	3	10	1	0	0
1985-86	**New York Islanders**	**NHL**	77	14	30	44	11	20	31	62	5	1	1	119	11.8	132	44	87	15	16	3	0	1	1	4	0	0	0
	Sweden	WEC-A	8	0	5	5	....	....	....	10	....	....	....	....	....	....	....	....	....	....	....	....	....	....	....	....	....	....
1986-87	**New York Islanders**	**NHL**	47	6	25	31	5	18	23	36	1	1	0	99	6.1	82	42	60	12	–8	10	1	4	5	6	1	0	0
1987-88	Sweden	Can-Cup	6	1	1	2	....	....	....	2	....	....	....	....	....	....	....	....	....	....	....	....	....	....	....	....	....	....
	New York Islanders	**NHL**	72	6	41	47	5	29	34	115	1	0	1	121	5.0	119	55	72	14	6	5	2	2	4	10	1	0	0
1988-89	**New York Islanders**	**NHL**	53	9	23	32	8	16	24	34	4	1	1	103	8.7	75	42	64	18	–13	....	....	....	....	....	....	....	....
	Edmonton Oilers	**NHL**	20	1	10	11	1	7	8	22	1	0	0	46	2.2	34	20	26	0	–12	4	2	0	2	6	2	0	0
1989-90	Leksands IF	Sweden	40	11	15	26	....	....	....	54	....	....	....	....	....	....	....	....	....	....	3	1	1	2	4	....	....	....
	Sweden	WEC-A	8	0	1	1	....	....	....	8	....	....	....	....	....	....	....	....	....	....	....	....	....	....	....	....	....	....
1990-91	Leksands IF	Sweden	22	7	7	14	....	....	....	16	....	....	....	....	....	....	....	....	....	....	....	....	....	....	....	....	....	....
	Sweden	WEC-A	10	0	4	4	....	....	....	8	....	....	....	....	....	....	....	....	....	....	....	....	....	....	....	....	....	....
1991-92	Leksands IF	Sweden	22	6	7	13	....	....	....	26	....	....	....	....	....	....	....	....	....	....	....	....	....	....	....	....	....	....
1992-93	Leksands IF	Sweden	38	8	15	23	....	....	....	90	....	....	....	....	....	....	....	....	....	....	2	1	1	2	4	....	....	....
1993-94	Leksands IF	Sweden	33	4	14	18	....	....	....	38	....	....	....	....	....	....	....	....	....	....	4	0	1	1	6	....	....	....
	Sweden	Olympics	8	1	3	4	....	....	....	10	....	....	....	....	....	....	....	....	....	....	....	....	....	....	....	....	....	....
1994-95	Leksands IF	Sweden	37	8	17	25	....	....	....	38	....	....	....	....	....	....	....	....	....	....	4	1	3	4	27	....	....	....
	Sweden	WC-A	8	0	2	2	....	....	....	12	....	....	....	....	....	....	....	....	....	....	....	....	....	....	....	....	....	....
1995-96	Leksands IF	Sweden	34	5	17	22	....	....	....	24	....	....	....	....	....	....	....	....	....	....	5	0	4	4	2	....	....	....
1996-97	Leksands IF	Sweden	38	8	13	21	....	....	....	42	....	....	....	....	....	....	....	....	....	....	9	2	1	3	4	....	....	....
1997-98	Leksands IF	Sweden	38	7	10	17	....	....	....	34	....	....	....	....	....	....	....	....	....	....	4	0	0	0	12	....	....	....
	Leksands IF	EuroHL	5	1	3	4	....	....	....	6	....	....	....	....	....	....	....	....	....	....	....	....	....	....	....	....	....	....
1998-99	Falu IF	Sweden-5	1	0	0	0	....	....	....	0	....	....	....	....	....	....	....	....	....	....	....	....	....	....	....	....	....	....
	NHL Totals		552	85	259	344	70	179	249	482	23	3	12	927	9.2	901	331	608	104		80	11	26	37	97	7	0	0

Swedish World All-Star Team (1979, 1980, 1990, 1995) • WJC-A All-Star Team (1980) • Swedish Player of the Year (1995)

Traded to **Edmonton** by **NY Islanders** for future considerations, February 15, 1989.

• JOSEPH, Chris

Robin Christopher D – R. 6'2", 212 lbs. b: Burnaby, B.C., 9/10/1969. Pittsburgh's 1st, 5th overall, in 1987.

Season	Club	League	GP	G	A	Pts	AG	AA	APts	PIM	PP	SH	GW	S	%	TGF	PGF	TGA	PGA	+/–	GP	G	A	Pts	PIM	PP	SH	GW
1984-85	Burnaby Winter Beavers	BCAHA	52	18	48	66	....	....	....	52	....	....	....	....	....	....	....	....	....	....	....	....	....	....	....	....	....	....
1985-86	Seattle Thunderbirds	WHL	72	4	8	12	....	....	....	50	....	....	....	....	....	....	....	....	....	....	5	0	3	3	12	....	....	....
1986-87	Seattle Thunderbirds	WHL	67	13	45	58	....	....	....	155	....	....	....	....	....	....	....	....	....	....	....	....	....	....	....	....	....	....
	Canada	WJC-A	6	1	1	2	....	....	....	12	....	....	....	....	....	....	....	....	....	....	....	....	....	....	....	....	....	....
1987-88	**Pittsburgh Penguins**	**NHL**	17	0	4	4	0	3	3	12	0	0	0	13	0.0	18	6	10	0	2	....	....	....	....	....	....	....	....
	Edmonton Oilers	**NHL**	7	0	4	4	0	3	3	6	0	0	0	1	0.0	8	5	6	0	–3	....	....	....	....	....	....	....	....
	Seattle Thunderbirds	WHL	23	5	14	19	....	....	....	49	....	....	....	....	....	....	....	....	....	....	....	....	....	....	....	....	....	....
	Canada	WJC-A	7	1	2	3	....	....	....	6	....	....	....	....	....	....	....	....	....	....	....	....	....	....	....	....	....	....
	Nova Scotia Oilers	AHL	8	0	2	2	....	....	....	8	....	....	....	....	....	....	....	....	....	....	4	0	0	0	9	....	....	....
1988-89	**Edmonton Oilers**	**NHL**	44	4	5	9	3	4	7	54	0	0	0	36	11.1	43	6	50	4	–9	....	....	....	....	....	....	....	....
	Cape Breton Oilers	AHL	5	1	1	2	....	....	....	18	....	....	....	....	....	....	....	....	....	....	....	....	....	....	....	....	....	....
1989-90	**Edmonton Oilers**	**NHL**	4	0	2	2	0	1	1	2	0	0	0	5	0.0	3	3	2	0	–2	....	....	....	....	....	....	....	....
	Cape Breton Oilers	AHL	61	10	20	30	....	....	....	69	....	....	....	....	....	....	....	....	....	....	6	2	1	3	4	....	....	....
1990-91	**Edmonton Oilers**	**NHL**	49	5	17	22	5	13	18	59	2	0	0	74	6.8	59	18	42	4	3	....	....	....	....	....	....	....	....
1991-92	**Edmonton Oilers**	**NHL**	7	0	0	0	0	0	0	8	0	0	0	5	0.0	5	0	6	0	–1	5	1	3	4	2	0	0	0
	Cape Breton Oilers	AHL	63	14	29	43	....	....	....	72	....	....	....	....	....	....	....	....	....	....	5	0	2	2	8	....	....	....

Season	Club	League	REGULAR SEASON																		PLAYOFFS							
			GP	G	A	Pts	AG	AA	APts	PIM	PP	SH	GW	S	%	TGF	PGF	TGA	PGA	+/–	GP	G	A	Pts	PIM	PP	SH	GW
1992-93	**Edmonton Oilers**	**NHL**	**33**	**2**	**10**	**12**	**2**	**7**	**9**	**48**	**1**	**0**	**0**	**49**	**4.1**	**31**	**10**	**36**	**6**	**–9**	....	....	....	....	....	....	....	....
1993-94	**Edmonton Oilers**	**NHL**	**10**	**1**	**1**	**2**	**1**	**1**	**2**	**28**	**1**	**0**	**0**	**25**	**4.0**	**11**	**4**	**18**	**3**	**–8**	....	....	....	....	....	....	....	....
	Tampa Bay Lightning	**NHL**	**66**	**10**	**19**	**29**	**9**	**15**	**24**	**108**	**7**	**0**	**0**	**154**	**6.5**	**93**	**38**	**73**	**5**	**–13**	....	....	....	....	....	....	....	....
1994-95	**Pittsburgh Penguins**	**NHL**	**33**	**5**	**10**	**15**	**9**	**15**	**24**	**46**	**3**	**0**	**0**	**73**	**6.8**	**33**	**9**	**24**	**3**	**3**	**10**	**1**	**1**	**2**	**12**	**0**	**0**	**0**
1995-96	**Pittsburgh Penguins**	**NHL**	**70**	**5**	**14**	**19**	**5**	**11**	**16**	**71**	**0**	**0**	**1**	**94**	**5.3**	**61**	**5**	**62**	**12**	**6**	**15**	**1**	**0**	**1**	**8**	**0**	**0**	**0**
1996-97	**Vancouver Canucks**	**NHL**	**63**	**3**	**13**	**16**	**3**	**12**	**15**	**62**	**2**	**0**	**1**	**99**	**3.0**	**69**	**24**	**83**	**17**	**–21**	....	....	....	....	....	....	....	....
1997-98	**Philadelphia Flyers**	**NHL**	**15**	**1**	**0**	**1**	**1**	**0**	**1**	**19**	**0**	**0**	**1**	**20**	**5.0**	**10**	**3**	**8**	**2**	**1**	**1**	**0**	**0**	**0**	**2**	**0**	**0**	**0**
	Philadelphia Phantoms	AHL	6	2	3	5	....	....	....	2	....	....	....	....	....	....	....	....	....	....	....	....	....	....	....	....	....	....
1998-99	**Philadelphia Flyers**	**NHL**	**2**	**0**	**0**	**0**	**0**	**0**	**0**	**2**	**0**	**0**	**0**	**1**	**0.0**	**0**	**0**	**0**	**0**	**0**	....	....	....	....	....	....	....	....
	Cincinnati Cyclones	IHL	27	11	19	30	....	....	....	38	....	....	....	....	....	....	....	....	....	....	....	....	....	....	....	....	....	....
	Philadelphia Phantoms	AHL	51	9	29	38	....	....	....	26	....	....	....	....	....	....	....	....	....	....	16	3	10	13	8	....	....	....
99-2000	**Vancouver Canucks**	**NHL**	**38**	**2**	**9**	**11**	**2**	**8**	**10**	**6**	**1**	**0**	**0**	**73**	**2.7**	**28**	**6**	**30**	**4**	**–4**	....	....	....	....	....	....	....	....
	Phoenix Coyotes	**NHL**	**9**	**0**	**0**	**0**	**0**	**0**	**0**	**0**	**0**	**0**	**0**	**13**	**0.0**	**2**	**0**	**7**	**0**	**–5**	....	....	....	....	....	....	....	....
	NHL Totals		**467**	**38**	**108**	**146**	**40**	**93**	**133**	**531**	**17**	**0**	**3**	**735**	**5.2**	**474**	**137**	**457**	**60**		**31**	**3**	**4**	**7**	**24**	**0**	**0**	**0**

WHL West Second All-Star Team (1987) • Won King Clancy Memorial Trophy (2000)

Traded to **Edmonton** by **Pittsburgh** with Craig Simpson, Dave Hannan and Moe Mantha for Paul Coffey, Dave Hunter and Wayne Van Dorp, November 24, 1987. Traded to **Tampa Bay** by **Edmonton** for Bob Beers, November 11, 1993. Claimed by **Pittsburgh** from **Tampa Bay** in NHL Waiver Draft, January 18, 1995. Claimed by **Vancouver** from **Pittsburgh** in NHL Waiver Draft, September 30, 1996. Signed as a free agent by **Philadelphia**, September 11, 1997. Signed as a free agent by **Ottawa**, August 18, 1999. Claimed on waivers by **Vancouver** from **Ottawa**, September 27, 1999. Claimed on waivers by **Phoenix** from **Vancouver**, March 14, 2000.

• JOSEPH, Tony

Anthony RW – R. 6′4″, 203 lbs. b: Cornwall, Ont., 3/1/1969. Winnipeg's 5th, 94th overall, in 1988.

Season	Club	League	GP	G	A	Pts	AG	AA	APts	PIM	PP	SH	GW	S	%	TGF	PGF	TGA	PGA	+/–	GP	G	A	Pts	PIM	PP	SH	GW
1984-85	Cornwall Midget Royals	OMHA	37	33	30	63	....	....	....	48	....	....	....	....	....	....	....	....	....	....	....	....	....	....	....	....	....	....
1985-86	Oshawa Generals	OHL	41	3	1	4	....	....	....	28	....	....	....	....	....	....	....	....	....	....	....	....	....	....	....	....	....	....
1986-87	Oshawa Generals	OHL	44	2	5	7	....	....	....	93	....	....	....	....	....	....	....	....	....	....	19	0	0	0	58	....	....	....
	Oshawa Generals	Mem-Cup	1	0	0	0	....	....	....	26	....	....	....	....	....	....	....	....	....	....	....	....	....	....	....	....	....	....
1987-88	Oshawa Generals	OHL	49	9	18	27	....	....	....	126	....	....	....	....	....	....	....	....	....	....	7	0	0	0	9	....	....	....
1988-89	Oshawa Generals	OHL	52	20	16	36	....	....	....	106	....	....	....	....	....	....	....	....	....	....	6	4	2	6	22	....	....	....
	Winnipeg Jets	**NHL**	**2**	**1**	**0**	**1**	**1**	**0**	**1**	**0**	**0**	**0**	**0**	**4**	**25.0**	**1**	**0**	**0**	**0**	**1**	....	....	....	....	....	....	....	....
1989-90	Tappara Tampere	Finland	5	0	0	0	....	....	....	2	....	....	....	....	....	....	....	....	....	....	....	....	....	....	....	....	....	....
	Moncton Hawks	AHL	61	9	9	18	....	....	....	74	....	....	....	....	....	....	....	....	....	....	....	....	....	....	....	....	....	....
1990-91	Moncton Hawks	AHL	16	4	2	6	....	....	....	79	....	....	....	....	....	....	....	....	....	....	8	0	1	1	31	....	....	....
1991-92	Kalamazoo Wings	IHL	15	2	0	2	....	....	....	51	....	....	....	....	....	....	....	....	....	....	....	....	....	....	....	....	....	....
	Moncton Hawks	AHL	42	6	5	11	....	....	....	118	....	....	....	....	....	....	....	....	....	....	6	0	1	1	25	....	....	....
1992-93			DID NOT PLAY																									
1993-94	Salt Lake Golden Eagles	IHL	43	4	2	6	....	....	....	213	....	....	....	....	....	....	....	....	....	....	....	....	....	....	....	....	....	....
	NHL Totals		**2**	**1**	**0**	**1**	**1**	**0**	**1**	**0**	**0**	**0**	**0**	**4**	**25.0**	**1**	**0**	**0**	**0**		....	....	....	....	....	....	....	....

Traded to **Minnesota** by **Winnipeg** for Tyler Larter, October 15, 1991. Traded to **Winnipeg** by **Minnesota** with future considerations for Warren Rychel, December 30, 1991.

• JOVANOVSKI, Ed

D – L. 6′2″, 210 lbs. b: Windsor, Ont., 6/26/1976. Florida's 1st, 1st overall, in 1994.

Season	Club	League	GP	G	A	Pts	AG	AA	APts	PIM	PP	SH	GW	S	%	TGF	PGF	TGA	PGA	+/–	GP	G	A	Pts	PIM	PP	SH	GW
1991-92	Windsor Bantam Bulldogs	OMHA	50	25	40	65	....	....	....	88	....	....	....	....	....	....	....	....	....	....	....	....	....	....	....	....	....	....
1992-93	Windsor Bulldogs	OJHL-B	48	7	46	53	....	....	....	88	....	....	....	....	....	....	....	....	....	....	....	....	....	....	....	....	....	....
1993-94	Windsor Spitfires	OHL	62	15	36	51	....	....	....	221	....	....	....	....	....	....	....	....	....	....	4	0	0	0	15	....	....	....
1994-95	Windsor Spitfires	OHL	50	23	42	65	....	....	....	198	....	....	....	....	....	....	....	....	....	....	9	2	7	9	39	....	....	....
	Canada	WJC-A	7	2	0	2	....	....	....	4	....	....	....	....	....	....	....	....	....	....	....	....	....	....	....	....	....	....
1995-96	**Florida Panthers**	**NHL**	**70**	**10**	**11**	**21**	**10**	**9**	**19**	**137**	**2**	**0**	**2**	**116**	**8.6**	**60**	**17**	**50**	**4**	**–3**	**22**	**1**	**8**	**9**	**52**	**0**	**0**	**0**
1996-97	Canada	W-Cup	DID NOT PLAY																									
	Florida Panthers	**NHL**	**61**	**7**	**16**	**23**	**7**	**14**	**21**	**172**	**3**	**0**	**1**	**80**	**8.8**	**57**	**16**	**44**	**2**	**–1**	**5**	**0**	**0**	**0**	**4**	**0**	**0**	**0**
1997-98	**Florida Panthers**	**NHL**	**81**	**9**	**14**	**23**	**11**	**14**	**25**	**158**	**2**	**1**	**3**	**142**	**6.3**	**64**	**15**	**69**	**8**	**–12**	....	....	....	....	....	....	....	....
	Canada	WC-A	6	2	1	3	....	....	....	6	....	....	....	....	....	....	....	....	....	....	....	....	....	....	....	....	....	....
1998-99	**Florida Panthers**	**NHL**	**41**	**3**	**13**	**16**	**4**	**13**	**17**	**82**	**1**	**0**	**1**	**68**	**4.4**	**39**	**13**	**42**	**12**	**–4**	....	....	....	....	....	....	....	....
	Vancouver Canucks	**NHL**	**31**	**2**	**9**	**11**	**2**	**9**	**11**	**44**	**0**	**0**	**0**	**41**	**4.9**	**23**	**2**	**39**	**13**	**–5**	....	....	....	....	....	....	....	....
99-2000	**Vancouver Canucks**	**NHL**	**75**	**5**	**21**	**26**	**6**	**19**	**25**	**54**	**1**	**0**	**1**	**109**	**4.6**	**74**	**4**	**102**	**29**	**–3**	....	....	....	....	....	....	....	....
	Canada	WC-A	9	1	1	2	....	....	....	8	....	....	....	....	....	....	....	....	....	....	....	....	....	....	....	....	....	....
	NHL Totals		**359**	**36**	**84**	**120**	**40**	**78**	**118**	**647**	**9**	**1**	**8**	**556**	**6.5**	**317**	**67**	**346**	**68**		**27**	**1**	**8**	**9**	**56**	**0**	**0**	**0**

OHL Second All-Star Team (1994) • OHL First All-Star Team (1995) • NHL All-Rookie Team (1996)

Traded to **Vancouver** by **Florida** with Dave Gagner, Mike Brown, Kevin Weekes and Florida's 1st round choice (Nathan Smith) in 2000 Entry Draft for Pavel Bure, Bret Hedican, Brad Ference and Vancouver's 3rd round choice (Robert Fried) in 2000 Entry Draft, January 17, 1999.

• JOYAL, Eddie

Edward Abel C – L. 6′, 178 lbs. b: Edmonton, Alta., 5/8/1940.

Season	Club	League	GP	G	A	Pts	AG	AA	APts	PIM	PP	SH	GW	S	%	TGF	PGF	TGA	PGA	+/–	GP	G	A	Pts	PIM	PP	SH	GW
1958-59	Edmonton Oil Kings	CAHL	35	23	23	46	....	....	....	8	....	....	....	....	....	....	....	....	....	....	....	....	....	....	....	....	....	....
	Edmonton Oil Kings	Mem-Cup	4	4	1	5	....	....	....	0	....	....	....	....	....	....	....	....	....	....	....	....	....	....	....	....	....	....
1959-60	Edmonton Oil Kings	CAHL	23	16	22	38	....	....	....	10	....	....	....	....	....	....	....	....	....	....	....	....	....	....	....	....	....	....
	Calgary Stampeders	WHL	1	0	0	0	....	....	....	0	....	....	....	....	....	....	....	....	....	....	....	....	....	....	....	....	....	....
	Edmonton Oil Kings	Mem-Cup	22	*22	14	36	....	....	....	10	....	....	....	....	....	....	....	....	....	....	....	....	....	....	....	....	....	....
1960-61	Edmonton Flyers	WHL	64	20	27	47	....	....	....	12	....	....	....	....	....	....	....	....	....	....	....	....	....	....	....	....	....	....
1961-62	Edmonton Flyers	WHL	70	37	32	69	....	....	....	14	....	....	....	....	....	....	....	....	....	....	12	*10	8	18	4	....	....	....
1962-63	**Detroit Red Wings**	**NHL**	**14**	**2**	**8**	**10**	**2**	**8**	**10**	**0**	....	....	....	....	....	....	....	....	....	....	**11**	**1**	**0**	**1**	**2**	**1**	**0**	**0**
	Pittsburgh Hornets	AHL	54	29	27	56	....	....	....	6	....	....	....	....	....	....	....	....	....	....	....	....	....	....	....	....	....	....
1963-64	**Detroit Red Wings**	**NHL**	**47**	**10**	**7**	**17**	**12**	**7**	**19**	**6**	....	....	....	....	....	....	....	....	....	....	**14**	**2**	**3**	**5**	**10**	**0**	**0**	**1**
	Pittsburgh Hornets	AHL	5	3	3	6	....	....	....	6	....	....	....	....	....	....	....	....	....	....	....	....	....	....	....	....	....	....
1964-65	**Detroit Red Wings**	**NHL**	**46**	**8**	**14**	**22**	**10**	**14**	**24**	**4**	....	....	....	....	....	....	....	....	....	....	**7**	**1**	**1**	**2**	**4**	**1**	**0**	**0**
	Pittsburgh Hornets	AHL	6	5	3	8	....	....	....	0	....	....	....	....	....	....	....	....	....	....	....	....	....	....	....	....	....	....
1965-66	**Toronto Maple Leafs**	**NHL**	**14**	**0**	**2**	**2**	**0**	**2**	**2**	**2**	....	....	....	....	....	....	....	....	....	....	....	....	....	....	....	....	....	....
	Rochester Americans	AHL	9	9	1	10	....	....	....	6	....	....	....	....	....	....	....	....	....	....	....	....	....	....	....	....	....	....
	Tulsa Oilers	CPHL	41	32	25	57	....	....	....	38	....	....	....	....	....	....	....	....	....	....	11	2	5	7	2	....	....	....
1966-67	Rochester Americans	AHL	70	32	51	83	....	....	....	10	....	....	....	....	....	....	....	....	....	....	13	*10	3	13	4	....	....	....
1967-68	**Los Angeles Kings**	**NHL**	**74**	**23**	**34**	**57**	**27**	**34**	**61**	**20**	**5**	**0**	**3**	**226**	**10.2**	**69**	**17**	**55**	**1**	**–2**	**7**	**4**	**1**	**5**	**2**	**3**	**0**	**1**
1968-69	**Los Angeles Kings**	**NHL**	**73**	**33**	**19**	**52**	**35**	**17**	**52**	**24**	**9**	**0**	**5**	**222**	**14.9**	**71**	**20**	**81**	**0**	**–30**	**11**	**3**	**3**	**6**	**0**	**1**	**0**	**0**
1969-70	**Los Angeles Kings**	**NHL**	**59**	**18**	**22**	**40**	**20**	**21**	**41**	**8**	**6**	**1**	**1**	**173**	**10.4**	**47**	**14**	**57**	**7**	**–17**	....	....	....	....	....	....	....	....
1970-71	**Los Angeles Kings**	**NHL**	**69**	**20**	**21**	**41**	**20**	**18**	**38**	**14**	**3**	**0**	**1**	**168**	**11.9**	**57**	**13**	**55**	**1**	**–10**	....	....	....	....	....	....	....	....
1971-72	**Los Angeles Kings**	**NHL**	**44**	**11**	**3**	**14**	**11**	**3**	**14**	**17**	**1**	**0**	**2**	**70**	**15.7**	**22**	**2**	**50**	**0**	**–30**	....	....	....	....	....	....	....	....
	Philadelphia Flyers	**NHL**	**26**	**3**	**4**	**7**	**3**	**3**	**6**	**8**	**2**	**0**	**0**	**41**	**7.3**	**11**	**4**	**20**	**0**	**–13**	....	....	....	....	....	....	....	....
1972-73	Alberta Oilers	WHA	71	22	16	38	....	....	....	16	....	....	....	....	....	....	....	....	....	....	....	....	....	....	....	....	....	....
1973-74	Edmonton Oilers	WHA	45	8	10	18	....	....	....	2	....	....	....	....	....	....	....	....	....	....	5	2	0	2	4	....	....	....
1974-75	Edmonton Oilers	WHA	78	22	25	47	....	....	....	2	....	....	....	....	....	....	....	....	....	....	....	....	....	....	....	....	....	....
1975-76	Edmonton Oilers	WHA	45	5	4	9	....	....	....	6	....	....	....	....	....	....	....	....	....	....	....	....	....	....	....	....	....	....
	NHL Totals		**466**	**128**	**134**	**262**	**140**	**127**	**267**	**103**	....	....	....	....	....	....	....	....	....		**50**	**11**	**8**	**19**	**18**	....	....	....
	Other Major League Totals		239	57	55	112	....	....	....	26	....	....	....	....	....	....	....	....	....	....	5	2	0	2	4	....	....	....

CPHL Second All-Star Team (1966)

Traded to **Toronto** by **Detroit** with Marcel Pronovost, Larry Jeffrey, Lowell MacDonald and Aut Erickson for Andy Bathgate, Billy Harris and Gary Jarrett, May 20, 1965. Claimed by **LA Kings** from **Toronto** in Expansion Draft, June 6, 1967. Traded to **Philadelphia** by **LA Kings** with Bill Flett, Jean Potvin and Ross Lonsberry for Bill Lesuk, Jim Johnson and Serge Bernier, January 28, 1972. Selected by **Alberta** (WHA) in 1972 WHA General Player Draft, February 12, 1972.

• JOYCE, Bob

Robert Thomas LW – L. 6′, 195 lbs. b: St. John, N.B., 7/11/1966. Boston's 4th, 82nd overall, in 1984.

Season	Club	League	GP	G	A	Pts	AG	AA	APts	PIM	PP	SH	GW	S	%	TGF	PGF	TGA	PGA	+/–	GP	G	A	Pts	PIM	PP	SH	GW
1983-84	Notre Dame Hounds	Hi-School	30	33	37	70	....	....	....	....	....	....	....	....	....	....	....	....	....	....	20	13	14	27	....	....	....	....
1984-85	University of North Dakota	WCHA	41	18	16	34	....	....	....	10	....	....	....	....	....	....	....	....	....	....	....	....	....	....	....	....	....	....
1985-86	University of North Dakota	WCHA	38	31	28	59	....	....	....	40	....	....	....	....	....	....	....	....	....	....	....	....	....	....	....	....	....	....
1986-87	University of North Dakota	WCHA	48	*52	37	89	....	....	....	42	....	....	....	....	....	....	....	....	....	....	....	....	....	....	....	....	....	....

			REGULAR SEASON																		PLAYOFFS							
Season	**Club**	**League**	**GP**	**G**	**A**	**Pts**	**AG**	**AA**	**APts**	**PIM**	**PP**	**SH**	**GW**	**S**	**%**	**TGF**	**PGF**	**TGA**	**PGA**	**+/–**	**GP**	**G**	**A**	**Pts**	**PIM**	**PP**	**SH**	**GW**
1987-88	Canada	Nat-Team	46	12	10	22	....	....	....	28	....	....	....	....	....	....	....	....	....	....	....	....	....	....	....	....	....	....
	Canada	Olympics	4	1	0	1	....	....	....	0	....	....	....	....	....	....	....	....	....	....	....	....	....	....	....	....	....	....
	Boston Bruins	**NHL**	**15**	**7**	**5**	**12**	**6**	**4**	**10**	**10**	**2**	**0**	**0**	**30**	**23.3**	**17**	**5**	**8**	**0**	**4**	**23**	**8**	**6**	**14**	**18**	**3**	**0**	**1**
1988-89	**Boston Bruins**	**NHL**	**77**	**18**	**31**	**49**	**15**	**22**	**37**	**46**	**7**	**0**	**3**	**142**	**12.7**	**86**	**28**	**51**	**1**	**8**	**9**	**5**	**2**	**7**	**2**	**0**	**0**	**0**
1989-90	**Boston Bruins**	**NHL**	**23**	**1**	**2**	**3**	**1**	**1**	**2**	**22**	**0**	**0**	**0**	**32**	**3.1**	**7**	**1**	**16**	**2**	**–8**	....	....	....	....	....	....	....	....
	Washington Capitals	**NHL**	**24**	**5**	**8**	**13**	**4**	**6**	**10**	**4**	**1**	**0**	**1**	**30**	**16.7**	**19**	**4**	**13**	**0**	**2**	**14**	**2**	**1**	**3**	**9**	**0**	**0**	**0**
1990-91	**Washington Capitals**	**NHL**	**17**	**3**	**3**	**6**	**3**	**2**	**5**	**8**	**0**	**0**	**1**	**30**	**10.0**	**11**	**0**	**8**	**0**	**3**	....	....	....	....	....	....	....	....
	Baltimore Skipjacks	AHL	36	10	8	18	....	....	....	14	....	....	....	....	....	....	....	....	....	....	6	1	0	1	4	....	....	....
1991-92	**Winnipeg Jets**	**NHL**	**1**	**0**	**0**	**0**	**0**	**0**	**0**	**0**	**0**	**0**	**0**	**0**	**0.0**	**0**	**0**	**0**	**0**	**0**	....	....	....	....	....	....	....	....
	Moncton Hawks	AHL	66	19	29	48	....	....	....	51	....	....	....	....	....	....	....	....	....	....	10	0	5	5	9	....	....	....
1992-93	**Winnipeg Jets**	**NHL**	**1**	**0**	**0**	**0**	**0**	**0**	**0**	**0**	**0**	**0**	**0**	**0**	**0.0**	**0**	**0**	**0**	**0**	**0**	....	....	....	....	....	....	....	....
	Moncton Hawks	AHL	75	25	32	57	....	....	....	52	....	....	....	....	....	....	....	....	....	....	5	0	0	0	2	....	....	....
1993-94	Las Vegas Thunder	IHL	63	15	18	33	....	....	....	45	....	....	....	....	....	....	....	....	....	....	5	2	1	3	8	....	....	....
1994-95	Las Vegas Thunder	IHL	60	15	12	27	....	....	....	52	....	....	....	....	....	....	....	....	....	....	10	4	3	7	26	....	....	....
1995-96	Orlando Solar Bears	IHL	55	7	11	18	....	....	....	81	....	....	....	....	....	....	....	....	....	....	18	2	1	3	12	....	....	....
1996-97	Orlando Solar Bears	IHL	76	15	33	48	....	....	....	98	....	....	....	....	....	....	....	....	....	....	5	0	0	0	2	....	....	....
1997-98	Dusseldorfer EG	Germany	39	6	7	13	....	....	....	26	....	....	....	....	....	....	....	....	....	....	3	0	1	1	6	....	....	....
1998-99	EV Landshut	Germany	52	4	11	15	....	....	....	26	....	....	....	....	....	....	....	....	....	....	....	....	....	....	....	....	....	....
99-2000	Munich Barons	Germany	42	4	4	8	....	....	....	34	....	....	....	....	....	....	....	....	....	....	4	1	2	3	2	....	....	....
	NHL Totals		**158**	**34**	**49**	**83**	**29**	**35**	**64**	**90**	**10**	**0**	**5**	**264**	**12.9**	**140**	**38**	**96**	**3**		**46**	**15**	**9**	**24**	**29**	**3**	**0**	**1**

WCHA First All-Star Team (1987) • NCAA West First All-American Team (1987) • NCAA Championship All-Tournament Team (1987)

Traded to **Washington** by **Boston** for Dave Christian, December 13, 1989. Traded to **Winnipeg** by **Washington** with Tyler Larter and Kent Paynter for Craig Duncanson, Brent Hughes and Simon Wheeldon, May 21, 1991.

• JOYCE, Duane

Duane A. D – R. 6'2", 203 lbs. b: Pembroke, MA, 5/5/1965.

1983-1985	Union College	NCAA-2	50	16	20	36	....	....	....	....	....	....	....	....	....	....	....	....	....	....	....	....	....	....	....	....	....	....
1985-86	Union College	NCAA-2	25	7	12	19	....	....	....	....	....	....	....	....	....	....	....	....	....	....	....	....	....	....	....	....	....	....
1986-87	Union College	NCAA-2	25	8	11	19	....	....	....	....	....	....	....	....	....	....	....	....	....	....	....	....	....	....	....	....	....	....
1987-88	Virginia Lancers	AAHL	42	22	45	67	....	....	....	73	....	....	....	....	....	....	....	....	....	....	8	3	5	8	6	....	....	....
	Springfield Indians	AHL	1	1	1	2	....	....	....	0	....	....	....	....	....	....	....	....	....	....	....	....	....	....	....	....	....	....
1988-89	Springfield Indians	AHL	3	0	0	0	....	....	....	0	....	....	....	....	....	....	....	....	....	....	....	....	....	....	....	....	....	....
1989-90	Kalamazoo Wings	IHL	2	0	0	0	....	....	....	2	....	....	....	....	....	....	....	....	....	....	....	....	....	....	....	....	....	....
	Fort Wayne Komets	IHL	66	10	26	36	....	....	....	53	....	....	....	....	....	....	....	....	....	....	....	....	....	....	....	....	....	....
	Muskegon Lumberjacks	IHL	13	3	10	13	....	....	....	8	....	....	....	....	....	....	....	....	....	....	12	3	7	10	13	....	....	....
1990-91	Kalamazoo Wings	IHL	80	12	32	44	....	....	....	53	....	....	....	....	....	....	....	....	....	....	11	0	3	3	6	....	....	....
1991-92	Kansas City Blades	IHL	80	12	32	44	....	....	....	62	....	....	....	....	....	....	....	....	....	....	15	6	11	17	8	....	....	....
1992-93	Kansas City Blades	IHL	75	15	25	40	....	....	....	30	....	....	....	....	....	....	....	....	....	....	12	1	2	3	6	....	....	....
1993-94	**Dallas Stars**	**NHL**	**3**	**0**	**0**	**0**	**0**	**0**	**0**	**0**	**0**	**0**	**0**	**1**	**0.0**	**0**	**0**	**0**	**0**	**0**	....	....	....	....	....	....	....	....
	Kansas City Blades	IHL	43	9	23	32	....	....	....	40	....	....	....	....	....	....	....	....	....	....	....	....	....	....	....	....	....	....
1994-95	Kansas City Blades	IHL	71	9	21	30	....	....	....	31	....	....	....	....	....	....	....	....	....	....	21	2	5	7	4	....	....	....
1995-96	Cincinnati Cyclones	IHL	49	11	25	36	....	....	....	36	....	....	....	....	....	....	....	....	....	....	....	....	....	....	....	....	....	....
	Orlando Solar Bears	IHL	34	3	17	20	....	....	....	18	....	....	....	....	....	....	....	....	....	....	21	4	6	10	2	....	....	....
1996-97	Carolina Monarchs	AHL	34	6	18	24	....	....	....	27	....	....	....	....	....	....	....	....	....	....	....	....	....	....	....	....	....	....
	Cincinnati Cyclones	IHL	38	3	16	19	....	....	....	12	....	....	....	....	....	....	....	....	....	....	3	1	2	3	0	....	....	....
1997-98	Adirondack Red Wings	AHL	66	7	21	28	....	....	....	30	....	....	....	....	....	....	....	....	....	....	....	....	....	....	....	....	....	....
	Detroit Vipers	IHL	7	0	2	2	....	....	....	4	....	....	....	....	....	....	....	....	....	....	15	5	4	9	4	....	....	....
1998-2000	Pembroke Pythons	PYHL	DID NOT PLAY – COACHING																									
	NHL Totals		**3**	**0**	**0**	**0**	**0**	**0**	**0**	**0**	**0**	**0**	**0**	**1**	**0.0**	**0**	**0**	**0**	**0**		....	....	....	....	....	....	....	....

Signed as a free agent by **San Jose**, August 13, 1991. Signed as a free agent by **Dallas**, December 3, 1993. Traded to **Cincinnati** (IHL) by **Kansas City** (IHL) for future considerations, July 26, 1995.

• JUHLIN, Patrik

LW – L. 6', 194 lbs. b: Huddinge, Sweden, 4/24/1970. Philadelphia's 2nd, 34th overall, in 1989.

1987-88	Vasteras IK	Sweden-2	2	0	0	0	....	....	....	0	....	....	....	....	....	....	....	....	....	....	3	2	1	3	0	....	....	....
1988-89	Vasteras IK	Sweden-2	30	29	13	42	....	....	....	....	....	....	....	....	....	....	....	....	....	....	....	....	....	....	....	....	....	....
1989-90	Vasteras IK	Sweden	35	10	13	23	....	....	....	18	....	....	....	....	....	....	....	....	....	....	2	0	0	0	0	....	....	....
	Sweden	WJC-A	6	1	0	1	....	....	....	0	....	....	....	....	....	....	....	....	....	....	....	....	....	....	....	....	....	....
1990-91	Vasteras IK	Sweden	40	13	9	22	....	....	....	24	....	....	....	....	....	....	....	....	....	....	4	3	1	4	0	....	....	....
1991-92	Vasteras IK	Sweden	39	15	12	27	....	....	....	40	....	....	....	....	....	....	....	....	....	....	....	....	....	....	....	....	....	....
1992-93	Vasteras IK	Sweden	34	14	12	26	....	....	....	22	....	....	....	....	....	....	....	....	....	....	3	0	1	1	2	....	....	....
	Sweden	WC-A	8	2	1	3	....	....	....	4	....	....	....	....	....	....	....	....	....	....	....	....	....	....	....	....	....	....
1993-94	Vasteras IK	Sweden	40	15	16	31	....	....	....	20	....	....	....	....	....	....	....	....	....	....	4	1	1	2	2	....	....	....
	Sweden	Olympics	8	7	1	8	....	....	....	16	....	....	....	....	....	....	....	....	....	....	....	....	....	....	....	....	....	....
	Sweden	WC-A	1	0	0	0	....	....	....	0	....	....	....	....	....	....	....	....	....	....	....	....	....	....	....	....	....	....
1994-95	Vasteras IK	Sweden	11	5	9	14	....	....	....	8	....	....	....	....	....	....	....	....	....	....	....	....	....	....	....	....	....	....
	Philadelphia Flyers	**NHL**	**42**	**4**	**3**	**7**	**7**	**4**	**11**	**6**	**0**	**0**	**1**	**44**	**9.1**	**10**	**1**	**22**	**0**	**–13**	**13**	**1**	**0**	**1**	**2**	**0**	**0**	**0**
1995-96	**Philadelphia Flyers**	**NHL**	**14**	**3**	**3**	**6**	**3**	**2**	**5**	**17**	**1**	**0**	**0**	**14**	**21.4**	**7**	**1**	**2**	**0**	**4**	....	....	....	....	....	....	....	....
	Hershey Bears	AHL	14	5	2	7	....	....	....	8	....	....	....	....	....	....	....	....	....	....	1	0	0	0	0	....	....	....
1996-97	Sweden	W-Cup	4	0	0	0	....	....	....	2	....	....	....	....	....	....	....	....	....	....	....	....	....	....	....	....	....	....
	Philadelphia Phantoms	AHL	78	31	60	91	....	....	....	24	....	....	....	....	....	....	....	....	....	....	9	7	6	13	4	....	....	....
1997-98	Jokerit Helsinki	Finland	47	19	9	28	....	....	....	20	....	....	....	....	....	....	....	....	....	....	7	5	0	5	4	....	....	....
	Jokerit Helsinki	EuroHL	6	2	3	5	....	....	....	2	....	....	....	....	....	....	....	....	....	....	....	....	....	....	....	....	....	....
1998-99	Jokerit Helsinki	Finland	54	17	12	29	....	....	....	30	....	....	....	....	....	....	....	....	....	....	3	0	0	0	2	....	....	....
	Jokerit Heksinki	EuroHL	6	1	....	1	....	....	....	10	....	....	....	....	....	....	....	....	....	....	2	0	0	0	0	....	....	....
99-2000	Jokerit Helsinki	Finland	10	0	0	0	....	....	....	2	....	....	....	....	....	....	....	....	....	....	....	....	....	....	....	....	....	....
	SC Bern	Switz.	33	17	14	31	....	....	....	12	....	....	....	....	....	....	....	....	....	....	5	0	1	1	4	....	....	....
	NHL Totals		**56**	**7**	**6**	**13**	**10**	**6**	**16**	**23**	**1**	**0**	**1**	**58**	**12.1**	**17**	**2**	**24**	**0**		**13**	**1**	**0**	**1**	**2**	**0**	**0**	**0**

AHL First All-Star Team (1997)

• JULIEN, Claude

D – R. 6', 198 lbs. b: Blind River, Ont., 4/23/1960.

1977-78	Newmarket Flyers	OJHL	45	18	26	44	....	....	....	137	....	....	....	....	....	....	....	....	....	....	....	....	....	....	....	....	....	....
	Oshawa Generals	OMJHL	11	0	5	5	....	....	....	14	....	....	....	....	....	....	....	....	....	....	2	0	0	0	2	....	....	....
1978-79	Windsor Spitfires	OMJHL	40	6	20	26	....	....	....	69	....	....	....	....	....	....	....	....	....	....	....	....	....	....	....	....	....	....
1979-80	Windsor Spitfires	OMJHL	68	14	37	51	....	....	....	148	....	....	....	....	....	....	....	....	....	....	16	5	11	16	23	....	....	....
1980-81	Windsor Spitfires	OMJHL	3	1	2	3	....	....	....	21	....	....	....	....	....	....	....	....	....	....	....	....	....	....	....	....	....	....
	Port Huron Flags	IHL	77	15	40	55	....	....	....	153	....	....	....	....	....	....	....	....	....	....	4	1	1	2	4	....	....	....
1981-82	Salt Lake Golden Eagles	CHL	70	4	18	22	....	....	....	134	....	....	....	....	....	....	....	....	....	....	5	1	4	5	0	....	....	....
1982-83	Salt Lake Golden Eagles	CHL	76	14	47	61	....	....	....	176	....	....	....	....	....	....	....	....	....	....	6	3	3	6	16	....	....	....
1983-84	Milwaukee Admirals	IHL	5	0	3	3	....	....	....	2	....	....	....	....	....	....	....	....	....	....	....	....	....	....	....	....	....	....
	Fredericton Express	AHL	57	7	22	29	....	....	....	58	....	....	....	....	....	....	....	....	....	....	7	0	4	4	6	....	....	....
1984-85	**Quebec Nordiques**	**NHL**	**1**	**0**	**0**	**0**	**0**	**0**	**0**	**0**	**0**	**0**	**0**	**0**	**0.0**	**0**	**0**	**0**	**0**	**0**	....	....	....	....	....	....	....	....
	Fredericton Express	AHL	77	6	28	34	....	....	....	97	....	....	....	....	....	....	....	....	....	....	6	2	4	6	13	....	....	....
1985-86	**Quebec Nordiques**	**NHL**	**13**	**0**	**1**	**1**	**0**	**1**	**1**	**25**	**0**	**0**	**0**	**4**	**0.0**	**5**	**0**	**4**	**1**	**2**	....	....	....	....	....	....	....	....
	Fredericton Express	AHL	49	3	18	21	....	....	....	74	....	....	....	....	....	....	....	....	....	....	6	1	4	5	19	....	....	....
1986-87	Fredericton Express	AHL	17	1	6	7	....	....	....	22	....	....	....	....	....	....	....	....	....	....	....	....	....	....	....	....	....	....
	Paris Francais Volants	France	36	15	50	65	....	....	....	....	....	....	....	....	....	....	....	....	....	....	....	....	....	....	....	....	....	....
1987-88	Baltimore Skipjacks	AHL	30	6	14	20	....	....	....	22	....	....	....	....	....	....	....	....	....	....	....	....	....	....	....	....	....	....
	Fredericton Express	AHL	35	1	14	15	....	....	....	52	....	....	....	....	....	....	....	....	....	....	13	1	3	4	30	....	....	....
1988-89	Halifax Citadels	AHL	79	8	52	60	....	....	....	72	....	....	....	....	....	....	....	....	....	....	4	0	2	2	4	....	....	....
1989-90	Halifax Citadels	AHL	77	6	37	43	....	....	....	65	....	....	....	....	....	....	....	....	....	....	4	0	1	1	7	....	....	....
1990-91	Kansas City Blades	IHL	54	7	16	23	....	....	....	43	....	....	....	....	....	....	....	....	....	....	....	....	....	....	....	....	....	....

			REGULAR SEASON																		PLAYOFFS							
Season	Club	League	GP	G	A	Pts	AG	AA	APts	PIM	PP	SH	GW	S	%	TGF	PGF	TGA	PGA	+/–	GP	G	A	Pts	PIM	PP	SH	GW
1991-92	Moncton Hawks	AHL	48	2	15	17				10											4	0	1	1	4			
1992-93			OUT OF HOCKEY – RETIRED																									
1993-1994	Ottawa Jr. Senators	OJHL	DID NOT PLAY – COACHING																									
1994-1996	Hull Olympiques	QMJHL	DID NOT PLAY – ASSISTANT COACH																									
1996-2000	Hull Olympiques	QMJHL	DID NOT PLAY – COACHING																									
	NHL Totals		**14**	**0**	**1**	**1**	**0**	**1**	**1**	**25**	**0**	**0**	**0**	**4**	**0.0**	**5**	**0**	**4**	**1**									

CHL Second All-Star Team (1983) • AHL Second All-Star Team (1969)

Signed as a free agent by **St. Louis**, September 28, 1981. Transferred to **Quebec** by **St. Louis** with the rights to Gord Donnelly as compensation for St. Louis' signing of Jacques Demers as coach, August 19, 1983.

• JUNEAU, Joe

Joseph C – L. 6', 199 lbs. b: Pont-Rouge, Que., 1/5/1968. Boston's 3rd, 81st overall, in 1988.

Season	Club	League	GP	G	A	Pts	AG	AA	APts	PIM	PP	SH	GW	S	%	TGF	PGF	TGA	PGA	+/–	GP	G	A	Pts	PIM	PP	SH	GW
1983-84	Ste-Foy Gouverneurs	QAAA	30	3	7	10																						
1984-85	Ste-Foy Gouverneurs	QAAA	41	25	46	71																						
1985-86	Levis-Lauzon College	CEGEP	STATISTICS NOT AVAILABLE																									
1986-87	Levis-Lauzon College	CEGEP	38	27	57	84																						
1987-88	RPI Engineers	ECAC	31	16	29	45				18																		
1988-89	RPI Engineers	ECAC	30	12	23	35				40																		
1989-90	RPI Engineers	ECAC	34	18	*52	*70				31																		
	Canada	Nat-Team	3	0	2	2				4																		
1990-91	RPI Engineers	ECAC	29	23	40	63				68																		
	Canada	Nat-Team	7	2	3	5				0																		
1991-92	Canada	Nat-Team	60	20	49	69				35																		
	Canada	Olympics	8	6	*9	*15				4																		
	Boston Bruins	**NHL**	**14**	**5**	**14**	**19**	**5**	**11**	**16**	**4**	**2**	**0**	**0**	**38**	**13.2**	**30**	**14**	**11**	**1**	**6**	**15**	**4**	**8**	**12**	**21**	**2**	**0**	**0**
1992-93	**Boston Bruins**	**NHL**	**84**	**32**	**70**	**102**	**27**	**48**	**75**	**33**	**9**	**0**	**3**	**229**	**14.0**	**150**	**64**	**64**	**1**	**23**	**4**	**2**	**4**	**6**	**6**	**2**	**0**	**0**
1993-94	**Boston Bruins**	**NHL**	**63**	**14**	**58**	**72**	**13**	**45**	**58**	**35**	**4**	**0**	**2**	**142**	**9.9**	**115**	**53**	**54**	**3**	**11**								
	Washington Capitals	**NHL**	**11**	**5**	**8**	**13**	**5**	**6**	**11**	**6**	**2**	**0**	**0**	**22**	**22.7**	**16**	**7**	**9**	**0**	**0**	**11**	**4**	**5**	**9**	**6**	**2**	**0**	**1**
1994-95	**Washington Capitals**	**NHL**	**44**	**5**	**38**	**43**	**9**	**56**	**65**	**8**	**3**	**0**	**0**	**70**	**7.1**	**58**	**33**	**26**	**0**	**–1**	**7**	**2**	**6**	**8**	**2**	**0**	**0**	**0**
1995-96	**Washington Capitals**	**NHL**	**80**	**14**	**50**	**64**	**14**	**41**	**55**	**30**	**7**	**2**	**2**	**176**	**8.0**	**82**	**38**	**69**	**22**	**–3**	**5**	**0**	**7**	**7**	**6**	**0**	**0**	**0**
1996-97	**Washington Capitals**	**NHL**	**58**	**15**	**27**	**42**	**16**	**24**	**40**	**8**	**9**	**1**	**3**	**124**	**12.1**	**60**	**26**	**59**	**14**	**–11**								
1997-98	**Washington Capitals**	**NHL**	**56**	**9**	**22**	**31**	**11**	**22**	**33**	**26**	**4**	**1**	**1**	**87**	**10.3**	**42**	**16**	**43**	**9**	**–8**	**21**	**7**	**10**	**17**	**8**	**1**	**1**	**4**
1998-99	**Washington Capitals**	**NHL**	**63**	**14**	**27**	**41**	**16**	**26**	**42**	**20**	**2**	**1**	**3**	**142**	**9.9**	**62**	**25**	**56**	**16**	**–3**								
	Buffalo Sabres	**NHL**	**9**	**1**	**1**	**2**	**1**	**1**	**2**	**2**	**0**	**0**	**0**	**8**	**12.5**	**3**	**1**	**5**	**2**	**–1**	**20**	**3**	**8**	**11**	**10**	**0**	**1**	**0**
99-2000	**Ottawa Senators**	**NHL**	**65**	**13**	**24**	**37**	**15**	**22**	**37**	**22**	**2**	**0**	**2**	**126**	**10.3**	**55**	**15**	**48**	**11**	**3**	**6**	**2**	**1**	**3**	**0**	**0**	**0**	**0**
	NHL Totals		**547**	**127**	**339**	**466**	**132**	**302**	**434**	**194**	**44**	**5**	**16**	**1164**	**10.9**	**673**	**292**	**444**	**79**		**89**	**24**	**49**	**73**	**59**	**7**	**2**	**5**

NCAA East First All-American Team (1990) • ECAC Second All-Star Team (1991) • NCAA East Second All-American Team (1991) • NHL All-Rookie Team (1993)

Traded to **Washington** by **Boston** for Al Iafrate, March 21, 1994. Traded to **Buffalo** by **Washington** with Washington's 3rd round choice (Tim Preston) in 1999 Entry Draft for Alexei Tezikov and Buffalo's 4th round compensatory choice (later traded to Calgary - Calgary selected Levente Szuper) in 2000 Entry Draft, March 22, 1999. Signed as a free agent by **Ottawa**, October 25, 1999. Selected by **Minnesota** from **Ottawa** in Expansion Draft, June 23, 2000. Traded to **Phoenix** by **Minnesota** for the rights to Rickard Wallin, June 23, 2000.

• JUNKER, Steve

LW – L. 6', 184 lbs. b: Castlegar, B.C., 6/26/1972. NY Islanders' 5th, 92nd overall, in 1991.

Season	Club	League	GP	G	A	Pts	AG	AA	APts	PIM	PP	SH	GW	S	%	TGF	PGF	TGA	PGA	+/–	GP	G	A	Pts	PIM	PP	SH	GW
1987-88	Castlegar Bantam Rebels	BCAHA	32	45	47	92				48																		
1988-89	Spokane Chiefs	WHL	68	19	15	34				40																		
1989-90	Spokane Chiefs	WHL	69	20	36	56				76											6	0	4	4	2			
1990-91	Spokane Chiefs	WHL	71	39	38	77				86											15	5	13	18	6			
	Spokane Chiefs	Mem-Cup	4	0	3	3				2																		
1991-92	Spokane Chiefs	WHL	58	28	32	60				110											10	6	7	13	18			
	Canada	WJC-A	7	2	2	4				4																		
1992-93	Capital District Islanders	AHL	79	16	31	47				20											4	0	0	0	0			
	New York Islanders	**NHL**																			**3**	**0**	**1**	**1**	**0**	**0**	**0**	**0**
1993-94	**New York Islanders**	**NHL**	**5**	**0**	**0**	**0**	**0**	**0**	**0**	**0**	**0**	**0**	**0**	**2**	**0.0**	**0**	**0**	**2**	**2**	**0**								
	Salt Lake Golden Eagles	IHL	71	9	14	23				36																		
1994-95	Denver Grizzlies	IHL	72	13	16	29				37											11	3	4	7	4			
1995-96	Rochester Americans	AHL	29	5	2	7				31																		
	Detroit Vipers	IHL	22	4	5	9				14																		
	Los Angeles Ice Dogs	IHL	7	0	3	3				4																		
1996-97	Canada	Nat-Team	55	15	23	38				24																		
1997-98	EV Landshut	Germany	39	3	4	7				6											6	0	0	0	6			
1998-99	EV Landshut	Germany	52	12	6	18				22											3	0	0	0	18			
99-2000	Adler Mannheim	Germany	52	4	16	20				24											5	1	0	1	0			
	Adler Mannheim	EuroHL	6	0	0	0				2																		
	NHL Totals		**5**	**0**	**0**	**0**	**0**	**0**	**0**	**0**	**0**	**0**	**0**	**2**	**0.0**	**0**	**0**	**2**	**2**		**3**	**0**	**1**	**1**	**0**	**0**	**0**	**0**

• JUTILA, Timo

D – L. 5'7", 175 lbs. b: Turku, Finland, 12/24/1963. Buffalo's 6th, 68th overall, in 1982.

Season	Club	League	GP	G	A	Pts	AG	AA	APts	PIM	PP	SH	GW	S	%	TGF	PGF	TGA	PGA	+/–	GP	G	A	Pts	PIM	PP	SH	GW
1979-80	Tappara Tampere	Finland-Jr.	26	7	15	22				38																		
1980-81	Tappara Tampere	Finland	36	9	12	21				44											8	3	2	5	6			
	Finland	WJC-A	5	1	0	1				2																		
1981-82	Tappara Tampere	Finland	36	8	11	19				41											11	0	0	0	16			
	Finland	WJC-A	7	1	6	7				14																		
1982-83	Tappara Tampere	Finland	36	8	14	22				46											8	1	3	4	24			
	Finland	WJC-A	7	1	1	2				14																		
1983-84	Tappara Tampere	Finland	37	5	22	27				57											9	0	5	5	18			
	Finland	Nat-Team	13	0	1	1				8																		
	Finland	Olympics	5	0	0	0				8																		
1984-85	**Buffalo Sabres**	**NHL**	**10**	**1**	**5**	**6**	**1**	**3**	**4**	**13**	**1**	**0**	**0**	**28**	**3.6**	**15**	**7**	**13**	**0**	**–5**								
	Rochester Americans	AHL	56	13	30	43				26											5	2	5	7	2			
1985-86	Tappara Tampere	Finland	30	8	11	19				16											8	3	6	9	2			
	Finland	Nat-Team	2	0	0	0				0																		
1986-87	Tappara Tampere	Finland	44	10	28	38				60											9	1	5	6	18			
	Finland	Nat-Team	17	3	3	6				14																		
	Finland	WEC-A	9	1	3	4				4																		
1987-88	Finland	Can-Cup	5	1	0	1				6																		
	Tappara Tampere	Finland	44	12	34	46				52											10	6	6	12	16			
	Finland	Nat-Team	8	0	1	1				10																		
1988-89	Lulea HF	Sweden	35	7	19	26				42											3	0	0	0	2			
1989-90	Lulea HF	Sweden	36	6	23	29				42											5	1	2	3	0			
1990-91	Lulea HF	Sweden	40	8	25	33				55											5	0	2	2	8			
	Finland	Nat-Team	19	2	4	6				14																		
	Finland	WEC-A	10	0	1	1				14																		
1991-92	Finland	Can-Cup	6	0	0	0				2																		
	Lulea HF	Sweden	40	11	26	37				48											2	1	0	1	4			
	Finland	Olympics	8	2	2	4				2																		
	Finland	Nat-Team	17	2	4	6				12																		
	Finland	WC-A	8	2	5	7				10																		
1992-93	Tappara Tampere	Finland	47	10	33	43				54																		
	Finland	Nat-Team	17	2	7	9				10																		
	Finland	WC-A	6	1	2	3				8																		

			REGULAR SEASON																		PLAYOFFS							
Season	Club	League	GP	G	A	Pts	AG	AA	APts	PIM	PP	SH	GW	S	%	TGF	PGF	TGA	PGA	+/–	GP	G	A	Pts	PIM	PP	SH	GW
1993-94	Tappara Tampere	Finland	48	13	36	49				30											10	2	5	7	12			
	Finland	Olympics	8	1	2	3				6																		
	Finland	Nat-Team	11	0	4	4				8																		
	Finland	WC-A	8	3	4	7				6																		
1994-95	Tappara Tampere	Finland	50	11	30	41				66																		
	Finland	Nat-Team	19	8	6	14				4																		
	Finland	WC-A	8	5	2	7				10																		
1995-96	Tappara Tampere	Finland	49	14	37	51				62											4	0	0	0	6			
	Finland	Nat-Team	16	4	12	16				6																		
	Finland	WC-A	6	0	1	1				4																		
1996-97	SC Bern	Switz.	29	8	20	28				26																		
	SC Bern	EuroHL	6	1	5	6				2																		
	Finland	Nat-Team	12	2	1	3				12																		
	Finland	WC-A	8	1	3	4				6																		
1997-98	Tappara Tampere	Finland	48	7	20	27				77											4	1	1	2	2			
1998-99	Tappara Tampere	Finland	48	9	18	27				50																		
	NHL Totals		**10**	**1**	**5**	**6**	**1**	**3**	**4**	**13**	**1**	**0**	**0**	**28**	**3.6**	**15**	**7**	**13**	**0**									

Finnish First All-Star Team (1987, 1988, 1993, 1994, 1996) • WC-A All-Star Team (1992, 1994, 1995)

• KABERLE, Frantisek

D – L. 6', 185 lbs. b: Kladno, Czech., 11/8/1973. Los Angeles' 3rd, 76th overall, in 1999.

Season	Club	League	GP	G	A	Pts	AG	AA	APts	PIM	PP	SH	GW	S	%	TGF	PGF	TGA	PGA	+/–	GP	G	A	Pts	PIM	PP	SH	GW
1991-92	Poldi Kladno	Czech.	37	1	4	5				8											8	0	1	1	0			
1992-93	Poldi Kladno	Czech.	40	4	5	9															9	2	4	6				
1993-94	HC Kladno	Czech-Rep	41	4	16	20															11	1	1	2				
1994-95	HC Kladno	Czech-Rep	40	7	17	24				20											8	0	3	3	12			
1995-96	MoDo Hockey	Sweden	40	5	7	12				34											8	0	1	1	0			
1996-97	MoDo Hockey	Sweden	50	3	11	14				28																		
1997-98	MoDo Hockey	Sweden	46	5	4	9				22											9	1	1	2	4			
1998-99	MoDo Hockey	Sweden	45	15	18	33				4											13	2	5	7	8			
	Czech-Republic	WC-A	12	3	3	6				0																		
99-2000	**Los Angeles Kings**	**NHL**	**37**	**0**	**9**	**9**	**0**	**8**	**8**	**4**	**0**	**0**	**0**	**41**	**0.0**	**35**	**15**	**20**	**3**	**3**								
	Long Beach Ice Dogs	IHL	18	2	8	10				8																		
	Atlanta Thrashers	**NHL**	**14**	**1**	**6**	**7**	**1**	**6**	**7**	**6**	**0**	**1**	**0**	**35**	**2.9**	**15**	**8**	**23**	**3**	**–13**								
	Lowell Lock Monsters	AHL	4	0	2	2				0																		
	Czech-Republic	WC-A	8	2	3	5				6																		
	NHL Totals		**51**	**1**	**15**	**16**	**1**	**14**	**15**	**10**	**0**	**1**	**0**	**76**	**1.3**	**50**	**23**	**43**	**6**									

• Brother of Tomas

Traded to **Atlanta** by **Los Angeles** with Donald Audette for Kelly Buchberger and Nelson Emerson, March 13, 2000.

• KABERLE, Tomas

D – L. 6'2", 200 lbs. b: Rakovnik, Czech., 3/2/1978. Toronto's 13th, 204th overall, in 1996.

Season	Club	League	GP	G	A	Pts	AG	AA	APts	PIM	PP	SH	GW	S	%	TGF	PGF	TGA	PGA	+/–	GP	G	A	Pts	PIM	PP	SH	GW
1994-95	Poldi Kladno-Jr.	Czech-Rep	37	7	10	17																						
	Poldi Kladno	Czech-Rep	4	0	1	1				0																		
1995-96	Poldi Kladno	Czech-Jr.	23	6	13	19																						
	Poldi Kladno	Czech-Rep	23	0	1	1				2											2	0	0	0	0			
1996-97	Poldi Kladno	Czech-Rep	49	0	5	5				26											3	0	0	0	0			
1997-98	Poldi Kladno	Czech-Rep	47	4	19	23				12																		
	Czech-Republic	WJC-A	7	1	1	2				2																		
	St. John's Maple Leafs	AHL	2	0	0	0				0																		
1998-99	**Toronto Maple Leafs**	**NHL**	**57**	**4**	**18**	**22**	**5**	**17**	**22**	**12**	**0**	**0**	**2**	**71**	**5.6**	**60**	**15**	**55**	**13**	**3**	**14**	**0**	**3**	**3**	**2**	**0**	**0**	**0**
99-2000	**Toronto Maple Leafs**	**NHL**	**82**	**7**	**33**	**40**	**8**	**31**	**39**	**24**	**2**	**0**	**0**	**82**	**8.5**	**106**	**30**	**102**	**29**	**3**	**12**	**1**	**4**	**5**	**0**	**0**	**0**	**1**
	NHL Totals		**139**	**11**	**51**	**62**	**13**	**48**	**61**	**36**	**2**	**0**	**2**	**153**	**7.2**	**166**	**45**	**157**	**42**		**26**	**1**	**7**	**8**	**2**	**0**	**0**	**1**

• Brother of Frantisek

• KACHOWSKI, Mark

Mark Edward LW – L. 5'11", 200 lbs. b: Edmonton, Alta., 2/20/1965.

Season	Club	League	GP	G	A	Pts	AG	AA	APts	PIM	PP	SH	GW	S	%	TGF	PGF	TGA	PGA	+/–	GP	G	A	Pts	PIM	PP	SH	GW
1982-83	Williams Lake Mustangs	PCJHL	STATISTICS NOT AVAILABLE																									
1983-84	Kamloops Blazers	WHL	57	6	9	15				156											16	4	2	6	29			
	Kamloops Blazers	Mem-Cup	4	0	1	1				*42																		
1984-85	Kamloops Blazers	WHL	68	22	15	37				185											14	6	8	14	38			
1985-86	Kamloops Blazers	WHL	61	21	31	52				182											16	7	8	15	51			
	Kamloops Blazers	Mem-Cup	5	1	5	6				11																		
1986-87	Flint Spirits	IHL	75	18	13	31				273											6	1	1	2	21			
1987-88	**Pittsburgh Penguins**	**NHL**	**38**	**5**	**3**	**8**	**4**	**2**	**6**	**126**	**0**	**0**	**1**	**21**	**23.8**	**9**	**0**	**8**	**0**	**1**								
	Muskegon Lumberjacks	IHL	25	3	6	9				72											5	0	2	2	11			
1988-89	**Pittsburgh Penguins**	**NHL**	**12**	**1**	**1**	**2**	**1**	**1**	**2**	**43**	**0**	**0**	**0**	**3**	**33.3**	**3**	**0**	**2**	**0**	**1**								
	Muskegon Lumberjacks	IHL	57	8	8	16				167											8	1	2	3	17			
1989-90	**Pittsburgh Penguins**	**NHL**	**14**	**0**	**1**	**1**	**0**	**1**	**1**	**40**	**0**	**0**	**0**	**4**	**0.0**	**4**	**1**	**2**	**0**	**1**								
	Muskegon Lumberjacks	IHL	61	23	8	31				129											12	2	4	6	21			
1990-91	Muskegon Lumberjacks	IHL	80	19	21	40				108											5	1	1	2	9			
1991-92	Muskegon Lumberjacks	IHL	6	0	0	0				9											4	2	0	2	16			
	NHL Totals		**64**	**6**	**5**	**11**	**5**	**4**	**9**	**209**	**0**	**0**	**1**	**28**	**21.4**	**16**	**1**	**12**	**0**									

Signed as a free agent by **Pittsburgh**, August 31, 1987.

• KAESE, Trent

RW – R. 5'11", 225 lbs. b: Nanaimo, B.C., 9/9/1967. Buffalo's 8th, 161st overall, in 1985.

Season	Club	League	GP	G	A	Pts	AG	AA	APts	PIM	PP	SH	GW	S	%	TGF	PGF	TGA	PGA	+/–	GP	G	A	Pts	PIM	PP	SH	GW
1983-84	Lethbridge Broncos	WHL	64	6	6	12				33											1	0	0	0	0			
1984-85	Lethbridge Broncos	WHL	67	20	18	38				107											4	0	1	1	7			
1985-86	Lethbridge Broncos	WHL	67	24	41	65				67											10	5	3	8	8			
1986-87	Swift Current Broncos	WHL	2	1	0	1				4																		
	Calgary Wranglers	WHL	68	30	24	54				117																		
	Flint Spirits	IHL	1	0	0	0				0											6	4	1	5	9			
1987-88	Rochester Americans	AHL	37	6	11	17				32											3	1	2	3	2			
	Flint Spirits	IHL	43	11	26	37				58											12	6	6	12	21			
1988-89	**Buffalo Sabres**	**NHL**	**1**	**0**	**0**	**0**	**0**	**0**	**0**	**0**	**0**	**0**	**0**	**5**	**0.0**	**0**	**0**	**0**	**0**	**0**								
	Rochester Americans	AHL	45	9	11	20				68																		
	Flint Spirits	IHL	9	2	3	5				61																		
1989-90	Phoenix Roadrunners	IHL	2	0	1	1				2																		
	Winston-Salem Thunderbirds	ECHL	57	56	51	107				110											8	5	1	6	18			
1990-91	Peterborough Pirates	Aut-Cup	8	17	12	29				85																		
	Peterborough Pirates	Britain	28	68	32	100				81											18	18	7	25	14			
1991-92	Norwich-Peterborough Pirates	Aut-Cup	8	16	10	26				14																		
	Columbus Chill	ECHL	28	28	22	50				56																		
	Norwich-Peterborough Pirates	Britain	15	18	18	36				36																		
1992-93	Norich-Peterborough Pirates	BH-Cup	8	19	6	25				12																		
	Norich-Peterborough Pirates	Britain	36	81	45	126				126											6	14	13	27	12			
1993-94	Milton-Keynes Kings	BH-Cup	4	8	2	10				6																		
	Milton-Keynes Kings	Britain	43	96	92	188				157											6	15	12	27	6			
1994-95	Milton-Keynes Kings	BH-Cup	8	9	14	23				12																		
	Milton-Keynes Kings	Britain	11	7	10	17				22																		
	Blackburn Black Hawks	Britain	28	50	50	100				80																		
1995-96			OUT OF HOCKEY – RETIRED																									

			REGULAR SEASON																		PLAYOFFS							
Season	Club	League	GP	G	A	Pts	AG	AA	APts	PIM	PP	SH	GW	S	%	TGF	PGF	TGA	PGA	+/–	GP	G	A	Pts	PIM	PP	SH	GW
1996-97			OUT OF HOCKEY – RETIRED																									
1997-98	Powell River Regals	CHHL	STATISTICS NOT AVAILABLE																									
	Powell River Regals	CHHL	STATISTICS NOT AVAILABLE																									
	Powell River Regals	Al-Cup	3	2	0	2	....	....	....	0	....	....	....	....	....	....	....	....	....	....	....	....	....	....	....	....	....	....
1998-99	Powell River Regals	CHHL	STATISTICS NOT AVAILABLE																									
99-2000	Nanimo Clippers	BCJHL	DID NOT PLAY – ASSISTANT COACH																									
	Powell River Regals	Al-Cup	4	3	3	6	....	....	....	4	....	....	....	....	....	....	....	....	....	....	....	....	....	....	....	....	....	....
	NHL Totals		**1**	**0**	**0**	**0**	**0**	**0**	**0**	**0**	**0**	**0**	**0**	**5**	**0.0**	**0**	**0**	**0**	**0**		....	....	....	....	....	....	....	....

ECHL First All-Star Team (1990) • Named Allan Cup MVP (2000)

• KALININ, Dmitri

D – L. 6'2", 198 lbs. b: Chelyabinsk, USSR, 7/22/1980. Buffalo's 1st, 18th overall, in 1998.

Season	Club	League	GP	G	A	Pts	AG	AA	APts	PIM	PP	SH	GW	S	%	TGF	PGF	TGA	PGA	+/–	GP	G	A	Pts	PIM	PP	SH	GW
1995-96	Traktor Chelyabinsk	Russia-Jr.	30	10	10	20	....	....	....	60	....	....	....	....	....	....	....	....	....	....	....	....	....	....	....	....	....	....
	Traktor Chelyabinsk	Russia-2	20	0	3	3	....	....	....	10	....	....	....	....	....	....	....	....	....	....	....	....	....	....	....	....	....	....
1996-97	Traktor Chelyabinsk	Russia	2	0	0	0	....	....	....	0	....	....	....	....	....	....	....	....	....	....	2	0	0	0	0	....	....	....
	Traktor Chelyabinsk-2	Russia-3	20	0	0	0	....	....	....	10	....	....	....	....	....	....	....	....	....	....	....	....	....	....	....	....	....	....
1997-98	Traktor Chelyabinsk	Russia	26	0	2	2	....	....	....	24	....	....	....	....	....	....	....	....	....	....	....	....	....	....	....	....	....	....
	Russia	EJC-A	6	0	2	2	....	....	....	6	....	....	....	....	....	....	....	....	....	....	....	....	....	....	....	....	....	....
1998-99	Moncton Wildcats	QMJHL	39	7	18	25	....	....	....	44	....	....	....	....	....	....	....	....	....	....	4	1	1	2	0	....	....	....
	Rochester Americans	AHL	3	0	1	1	....	....	....	14	....	....	....	....	....	....	....	....	....	....	7	0	0	0	6	....	....	....
99-2000	**Buffalo Sabres**	**NHL**	**4**	**0**	**0**	**0**	**0**	**0**	**0**	**4**	**0**	**0**	**0**	**3**	**0.0**	....	....	....	....	....	....	....	....	....	....	....	....	....
	Rochester Americans	AHL	75	2	19	21	....	....	....	52	....	....	....	....	....	....	....	....	....	....	21	2	9	11	8	....	....	....
1999-99	Russia	EJC-A	6	0	2	2	....	....	....	6	....	....	....	....	....	....	....	....	....	....	....	....	....	....	....	....	....	....
	NHL Totals		**4**	**0**	**0**	**0**	**0**	**0**	**0**	**4**	**0**	**0**	**0**	**3**	**0.0**	....	....	....	....	....	....	....	....	....	....	....	....	....

• KALLUR, Anders

"Andy" RW – L. 5'11", 185 lbs. b: Ludvika, Sweden, 7/6/1952.

Season	Club	League	GP	G	A	Pts	AG	AA	APts	PIM	PP	SH	GW	S	%	TGF	PGF	TGA	PGA	+/–	GP	G	A	Pts	PIM	PP	SH	GW
1970-71	Falu IF	Sweden-2	18	6	....	6	....	....	....	....	....	....	....	....	....	....	....	....	....	....	....	....	....	....	....	....	....	....
1971-72	Falu IF	Sweden-2	18	15	....	15	....	....	....	....	....	....	....	....	....	....	....	....	....	....	....	....	....	....	....	....	....	....
1972-73	HC Tunabro	Sweden	14	3	3	6	....	....	....	4	....	....	....	....	....	....	....	....	....	....	6	3	1	4	0	....	....	....
1973-74	HC Tunabro	Sweden	14	5	3	8	....	....	....	4	....	....	....	....	....	....	....	....	....	....	13	8	7	15	22	....	....	....
1974-75	MoDo AIK	Sweden	30	*30	16	46	....	....	....	26	....	....	....	....	....	....	....	....	....	....	....	....	....	....	....	....	....	....
1975-76	MoDo AIK	Sweden	36	11	16	27	....	....	....	33	....	....	....	....	....	....	....	....	....	....	....	....	....	....	....	....	....	....
1976-77	Sodertalje SK	Sweden	31	14	9	23	....	....	....	26	....	....	....	....	....	....	....	....	....	....	....	....	....	....	....	....	....	....
1977-78	Sodertalje SK	Sweden	30	5	7	12	....	....	....	10	....	....	....	....	....	....	....	....	....	....	....	....	....	....	....	....	....	....
1978-79	Djurgardens IF Stockholm	Sweden	36	25	21	46	....	....	....	32	....	....	....	....	....	....	....	....	....	....	4	3	3	6	2	....	....	....
1979-80 ♦	**New York Islanders**	**NHL**	**76**	**22**	**30**	**52**	**19**	**22**	**41**	**16**	**5**	**4**	**2**	**138**	**15.9**	**85**	**31**	**70**	**28**	**12**	....	....	....	....	....	....	....	....
	Indianapolis Checkers	CHL	2	0	2	2	....	....	....	0	....	....	....	....	....	....	....	....	....	....	....	....	....	....	....	....	....	....
1980-81 ♦	**New York Islanders**	**NHL**	**78**	**36**	**28**	**64**	**28**	**19**	**47**	**32**	**7**	**6**	**4**	**163**	**22.1**	**88**	**21**	**79**	**37**	**25**	**12**	**4**	**3**	**7**	**10**	**0**	**2**	**0**
1981-82	Sweden	Can-Cup	5	3	1	4	....	....	....	0	....	....	....	....	....	....	....	....	....	....	....	....	....	....	....	....	....	....
♦	**New York Islanders**	**NHL**	**58**	**18**	**22**	**40**	**14**	**15**	**29**	**18**	**2**	**3**	**3**	**74**	**24.3**	**49**	**8**	**49**	**13**	**5**	**19**	**1**	**6**	**7**	**8**	**0**	**1**	**0**
1982-83 ♦	**New York Islanders**	**NHL**	**55**	**6**	**8**	**14**	**5**	**6**	**11**	**33**	**1**	**1**	**0**	**77**	**7.8**	**35**	**9**	**32**	**15**	**9**	**20**	**3**	**12**	**15**	**12**	**1**	**1**	**0**
1983-84	**New York Islanders**	**NHL**	**65**	**9**	**14**	**23**	**7**	**10**	**17**	**24**	**2**	**3**	**1**	**70**	**12.9**	**41**	**8**	**47**	**14**	**0**	**17**	**2**	**2**	**4**	**2**	**0**	**1**	**1**
1984-85	**New York Islanders**	**NHL**	**51**	**10**	**8**	**18**	**8**	**5**	**13**	**26**	**0**	**2**	**2**	**72**	**13.9**	**25**	**2**	**44**	**12**	**–9**	**10**	**2**	**0**	**2**	**0**	**0**	**0**	**0**
	NHL Totals		**383**	**101**	**110**	**211**	**81**	**77**	**158**	**149**	**17**	**19**	**12**	**594**	**17.0**	**323**	**79**	**321**	**119**		**78**	**12**	**23**	**35**	**32**	**1**	**5**	**1**

Swedish World All-Star Team (1979) • Swedish Player of the Year (1979)

• Only goals and games played totals are available for 1970-71 and 1971-72 season. Signed as a free agent by **NY Islanders**, August 15, 1979.

• KAMENSKY, Valeri

LW – R. 6'2", 198 lbs. b: Voskresensk, USSR, 4/18/1966. Quebec's 8th, 129th overall, in 1988.

Season	Club	League	GP	G	A	Pts	AG	AA	APts	PIM	PP	SH	GW	S	%	TGF	PGF	TGA	PGA	+/–	GP	G	A	Pts	PIM	PP	SH	GW
1982-83	Khimik Voskresensk	USSR	5	0	0	0	....	....	....	0	....	....	....	....	....	....	....	....	....	....	....	....	....	....	....	....	....	....
1983-84	Khimik Voskresensk	USSR	20	2	2	4	....	....	....	6	....	....	....	....	....	....	....	....	....	....	....	....	....	....	....	....	....	....
	Soviet Union	EJC-A	5	1	3	4	....	....	....	0	....	....	....	....	....	....	....	....	....	....	....	....	....	....	....	....	....	....
1984-85	Khimik Voskresensk	USSR	45	9	3	12	....	....	....	24	....	....	....	....	....	....	....	....	....	....	....	....	....	....	....	....	....	....
	Soviet Union	WJC-A	7	2	2	4	....	....	....	8	....	....	....	....	....	....	....	....	....	....	....	....	....	....	....	....	....	....
1985-86	CSKA Moscow	USSR	40	15	9	24	....	....	....	8	....	....	....	....	....	....	....	....	....	....	....	....	....	....	....	....	....	....
	Soviet Union	WJC-A	7	7	6	13	....	....	....	6	....	....	....	....	....	....	....	....	....	....	....	....	....	....	....	....	....	....
	Soviet Union	WEC-A	9	2	0	2	....	....	....	8	....	....	....	....	....	....	....	....	....	....	....	....	....	....	....	....	....	....
1986-87	CSKA Moscow	USSR	37	13	8	21	....	....	....	16	....	....	....	....	....	....	....	....	....	....	....	....	....	....	....	....	....	....
	USSR	RV-87	2	2	1	3	....	....	....	2	....	....	....	....	....	....	....	....	....	....	....	....	....	....	....	....	....	....
	Soviet Union	WEC-A	10	5	3	8	....	....	....	6	....	....	....	....	....	....	....	....	....	....	....	....	....	....	....	....	....	....
1987-88	Soviet Union	Can-Cup	9	6	1	7	....	....	....	6	....	....	....	....	....	....	....	....	....	....	....	....	....	....	....	....	....	....
	CSKA Moscow	USSR	51	26	20	46	....	....	....	40	....	....	....	....	....	....	....	....	....	....	....	....	....	....	....	....	....	....
	Soviet Union	Olympics	8	4	2	6	....	....	....	4	....	....	....	....	....	....	....	....	....	....	....	....	....	....	....	....	....	....
1988-89	CSKA Moscow	USSR	40	18	10	28	....	....	....	30	....	....	....	....	....	....	....	....	....	....	....	....	....	....	....	....	....	....
	CSKA Moscow	Super-S	7	2	4	6	....	....	....	4	....	....	....	....	....	....	....	....	....	....	....	....	....	....	....	....	....	....
	Soviet Union	WEC-A	10	4	4	8	....	....	....	8	....	....	....	....	....	....	....	....	....	....	....	....	....	....	....	....	....	....
1989-90	CSKA Moscow	Fr-Tour	1	0	0	0	....	....	....	0	....	....	....	....	....	....	....	....	....	....	....	....	....	....	....	....	....	....
	CSKA Moscow	USSR	45	19	18	37	....	....	....	40	....	....	....	....	....	....	....	....	....	....	....	....	....	....	....	....	....	....
	CSKA Moscow	Super-S	5	1	2	3	....	....	....	6	....	....	....	....	....	....	....	....	....	....	....	....	....	....	....	....	....	....
	Soviet Union	WEC-A	10	7	2	9	....	....	....	20	....	....	....	....	....	....	....	....	....	....	....	....	....	....	....	....	....	....
1990-91	CSKA Moscow	Fr-Tour	1	0	0	0	....	....	....	0	....	....	....	....	....	....	....	....	....	....	....	....	....	....	....	....	....	....
	CSKA Moscow	USSR	46	20	26	46	....	....	....	66	....	....	....	....	....	....	....	....	....	....	....	....	....	....	....	....	....	....
	CSKA Moscow	Super-S	4	2	2	4	....	....	....	0	....	....	....	....	....	....	....	....	....	....	....	....	....	....	....	....	....	....
	Soviet Union	WEC-A	10	6	5	11	....	....	....	10	....	....	....	....	....	....	....	....	....	....	....	....	....	....	....	....	....	....
1991-92	**Quebec Nordiques**	**NHL**	**23**	**7**	**14**	**21**	**6**	**11**	**17**	**14**	**2**	**0**	**1**	**42**	**16.7**	**31**	**13**	**23**	**4**	**–1**	....	....	....	....	....	....	....	....
1992-93	**Quebec Nordiques**	**NHL**	**32**	**15**	**22**	**37**	**12**	**15**	**27**	**14**	**2**	**3**	**0**	**94**	**16.0**	**50**	**13**	**26**	**2**	**13**	**6**	**0**	**1**	**1**	**6**	**0**	**0**	**0**
1993-94	**Quebec Nordiques**	**NHL**	**76**	**28**	**37**	**65**	**26**	**29**	**55**	**42**	**6**	**0**	**1**	**170**	**16.5**	**90**	**23**	**61**	**6**	**12**	....	....	....	....	....	....	....	....
	Russia	WC-A	6	5	5	10	....	....	....	12	....	....	....	....	....	....	....	....	....	....	....	....	....	....	....	....	....	....
1994-95	HC Ambri-Piotta	Switz.	12	13	6	19	....	....	....	2	....	....	....	....	....	....	....	....	....	....	....	....	....	....	....	....	....	....
	Quebec Nordiques	**NHL**	**40**	**10**	**20**	**30**	**18**	**30**	**48**	**22**	**5**	**1**	**5**	**70**	**14.3**	**41**	**16**	**26**	**4**	**3**	**2**	**1**	**0**	**1**	**0**	**0**	**0**	**0**
1995-96 ♦	**Colorado Avalanche**	**NHL**	**81**	**38**	**47**	**85**	**37**	**39**	**76**	**85**	**18**	**1**	**5**	**220**	**17.3**	**125**	**47**	**69**	**5**	**14**	**22**	**10**	**12**	**22**	**28**	**3**	**0**	**2**
1996-97	**Colorado Avalanche**	**NHL**	**68**	**28**	**38**	**66**	**30**	**34**	**64**	**38**	**8**	**0**	**4**	**165**	**17.0**	**100**	**43**	**52**	**0**	**5**	**17**	**8**	**14**	**22**	**16**	**5**	**0**	**2**
1997-98	**Colorado Avalanche**	**NHL**	**75**	**26**	**40**	**66**	**30**	**39**	**69**	**60**	**8**	**0**	**4**	**173**	**15.0**	**104**	**48**	**60**	**2**	**–2**	**7**	**2**	**3**	**5**	**18**	**1**	**0**	**0**
	Russia	Olympics	6	1	2	3	....	....	....	0	....	....	....	....	....	....	....	....	....	....	....	....	....	....	....	....	....	....
1998-99	**Colorado Avalanche**	**NHL**	**65**	**14**	**30**	**44**	**16**	**29**	**45**	**28**	**2**	**0**	**2**	**123**	**11.4**	**62**	**20**	**41**	**0**	**1**	**10**	**4**	**5**	**9**	**4**	**1**	**0**	**1**
99-2000	**New York Rangers**	**NHL**	**58**	**13**	**19**	**32**	**15**	**18**	**33**	**24**	**3**	**0**	**1**	**88**	**14.8**	**43**	**13**	**43**	**0**	**–13**	....	....	....	....	....	....	....	....
	Russia	WC-A	6	0	0	0	....	....	....	10	....	....	....	....	....	....	....	....	....	....	....	....	....	....	....	....	....	....
	NHL Totals		**518**	**179**	**267**	**446**	**190**	**244**	**434**	**327**	**54**	**5**	**23**	**1145**	**15.6**	**646**	**236**	**401**	**23**		**64**	**25**	**35**	**60**	**72**	**10**	**0**	**5**

USSR First All-Star Team (1990, 1991) • USSR Player of the Year (1991) • WEC-A All-Star Team (1991) • Named Best Forward at WEC-A (1991) • Played in NHL All-Star Game (1998)

• Missed majority of 1991-92 season recovering from ankle injury suffered in game vs. Tampa Bay, October 27, 1991. Transferred to **Colorado** after **Quebec** franchise relocated, June 21, 1995. Signed as a free agent by **NY Rangers**, July 7, 1999.

• KAMINSKI, Kevin

Kevin S. C – L. 5'10", 190 lbs. b: Churchbridge, Sask., 3/13/1969. Minnesota's 3rd, 48th overall, in 1987.

Season	Club	League	GP	G	A	Pts	AG	AA	APts	PIM	PP	SH	GW	S	%	TGF	PGF	TGA	PGA	+/–	GP	G	A	Pts	PIM	PP	SH	GW
1984-85	Saskatoon Blazers	SAHA	STATISTICS NOT AVAILABLE																									
	Saskatoon Blades	WHL	5	0	1	1	....	....	....	17	....	....	....	....	....	....	....	....	....	....	....	....	....	....	....	....	....	....
1985-86	Saskatoon Blazers	SAHA	32	39	64	103	....	....	....	106	....	....	....	....	....	....	....	....	....	....	....	....	....	....	....	....	....	....
	Saskatoon Blades	WHL	4	1	1	2	....	....	....	35	....	....	....	....	....	....	....	....	....	....	2	0	0	0	5	....	....	....
1986-87	Saskatoon Blades	WHL	67	26	44	70	....	....	....	325	....	....	....	....	....	....	....	....	....	....	11	5	6	11	45	....	....	....
1987-88	Saskatoon Blades	WHL	55	38	61	99	....	....	....	247	....	....	....	....	....	....	....	....	....	....	10	5	7	12	37	....	....	....

			REGULAR SEASON																		PLAYOFFS							
Season	**Club**	**League**	**GP**	**G**	**A**	**Pts**	**AG**	**AA**	**APts**	**PIM**	**PP**	**SH**	**GW**	**S**	**%**	**TGF**	**PGF**	**TGA**	**PGA**	**+/–**	**GP**	**G**	**A**	**Pts**	**PIM**	**PP**	**SH**	**GW**
1988-89	Saskatoon Blades	WHL	52	25	43	68	....	....	....	199	....	....	....	....	....	....	....	....	....	....	8	4	9	13	25	....	....	....
	Minnesota North Stars	**NHL**	**1**	**0**	**0**	**0**	**0**	**0**	**0**	**0**	**0**	**0**	**0**	**0**	**0.0**	**0**	**0**	**0**	**0**	**0**	....	....	....	....	....	....	....	....
	Saskatoon Blades	Mem-Cup	4	0	4	4	....	....	....	9	....	....	....	....	....	....	....	....	....	....	....	....	....	....	....	....	....	....
1989-90	**Quebec Nordiques**	**NHL**	**1**	**0**	**0**	**0**	**0**	**0**	**0**	**0**	**0**	**0**	**0**	**0**	**0.0**	**0**	**0**	**1**	**0**	**–1**	....	....	....	....	....	....	....	....
	Halifax Citadels	AHL	19	3	4	7	....	....	....	128	....	....	....	....	....	....	....	....	....	....	2	0	0	0	5	....	....	....
1990-91	Halifax Citadels	AHL	7	1	0	1	....	....	....	44	....	....	....	....	....	....	....	....	....	....	....	....	....	....	....	....	....	....
	Fort Wayne Komets	IHL	56	9	15	24	....	....	....	*455	....	....	....	....	....	....	....	....	....	....	19	4	2	6	*169	....	....	....
1991-92	**Quebec Nordiques**	**NHL**	**5**	**0**	**0**	**0**	**0**	**0**	**0**	**45**	**0**	**0**	**0**	**6**	**0.0**	**0**	**0**	**2**	**0**	**–2**	....	....	....	....	....	....	....	....
	Halifax Citadels	AHL	63	18	27	45	....	....	....	329	....	....	....	....	....	....	....	....	....	....	....	....	....	....	....	....	....	....
1992-93	Halifax Citadels	AHL	79	27	37	64	....	....	....	*345	....	....	....	....	....	....	....	....	....	....	....	....	....	....	....	....	....	....
1993-94	**Washington Capitals**	**NHL**	**13**	**0**	**5**	**5**	**0**	**4**	**4**	**87**	**0**	**0**	**0**	**9**	**0.0**	**6**	**0**	**4**	**0**	**2**	....	....	....	....	....	....	....	....
	Portland Pirates	AHL	39	10	22	32	....	....	....	263	....	....	....	....	....	....	....	....	....	....	16	4	5	9	*91	....	....	....
1994-95	Portland Pirates	AHL	34	15	20	35	....	....	....	292	....	....	....	....	....	....	....	....	....	....	....	....	....	....	....	....	....	....
	Washington Capitals	**NHL**	**27**	**1**	**1**	**2**	**2**	**1**	**3**	**102**	**0**	**0**	**1**	**12**	**8.3**	**6**	**1**	**11**	**0**	**–6**	**5**	**0**	**0**	**0**	**36**	**0**	**0**	**0**
1995-96	**Washington Capitals**	**NHL**	**54**	**1**	**2**	**3**	**1**	**2**	**3**	**164**	**0**	**0**	**0**	**17**	**5.9**	**6**	**1**	**6**	**0**	**–1**	**3**	**0**	**0**	**0**	**16**	**0**	**0**	**0**
1996-97	**Washington Capitals**	**NHL**	**38**	**1**	**2**	**3**	**1**	**2**	**3**	**130**	**0**	**0**	**0**	**12**	**8.3**	**7**	**1**	**6**	**0**	**0**	....	....	....	....	....	....	....	....
1997-98	Portland Pirates	AHL	40	8	12	20	....	....	....	242	....	....	....	....	....	....	....	....	....	....	8	2	1	3	69	....	....	....
1998-99	Las Vegas Thunder	IHL	39	7	10	17	....	....	....	217	....	....	....	....	....	....	....	....	....	....	....	....	....	....	....	....	....	....
99-2000	Providence Bruins	AHL	5	0	2	2	....	....	....	17	....	....	....	....	....	....	....	....	....	....	....	....	....	....	....	....	....	....
	Orlando Solar Bears	IHL	5	0	0	0	....	....	....	9	....	....	....	....	....	....	....	....	....	....	....	....	....	....	....	....	....	....
	NHL Totals		**139**	**3**	**10**	**13**	**4**	**9**	**13**	**528**	**0**	**0**	**1**	**56**	**5.4**	**25**	**3**	**30**	**0**		**8**	**0**	**0**	**0**	**52**	**0**	**0**	**0**

Traded to **Quebec** by **Minnesota** for Gaetan Duchesne, June 19, 1989. Traded to **Washington** by **Quebec** for Mark Matier, June 15, 1993. Signed as a free agent by **Las Vegas** (IHL), September 4, 1998. IHL rights acquired by **Utah** (IHL) from **Las Vegas** (IHL) with Russ Romaniuk, Scott Hollis and Brad Miller after Las Vegas franchise folded, July 6, 1999. Signed as a free agent by **Providence** (AHL), September 9, 1999. Traded to **Orlando** (IHL) by **Providence** (AHL) for cash, November 11, 1999. • Missed remainder of 1999-2000 season recovering from head injury suffered in game vs. Grand Rapids (IHL), November 20, 1999. • Played w/ RHI's New England Stingers in 1994 (13-16-30-46-30).

• KAMINSKY, Yan

RW – L. 6'1", 176 lbs. b: Penza, USSR, 7/28/1971. Winnipeg's 4th, 99th overall, in 1991.

Season	Club	League	GP	G	A	Pts	AG	AA	APts	PIM	PP	SH	GW	S	%	TGF	PGF	TGA	PGA	+/–	GP	G	A	Pts	PIM	PP	SH	GW
1988-89	Dynamo Moscow	USSR-Jr.	STATISTICS NOT AVAILABLE																									
	Soviet Union	EJC-A	6	2	2	4	....	....	....	6	....	....	....	....	....	....	....	....	....	....	....	....	....	....	....	....	....	....
1989-90	Dynamo Moscow	USSR	6	1	0	1	....	....	....	4	....	....	....	....	....	....	....	....	....	....	....	....	....	....	....	....	....	....
	Soviet Union	WJC-A	7	2	0	2	....	....	....	0	....	....	....	....	....	....	....	....	....	....	....	....	....	....	....	....	....	....
1990-91	Dynamo Moscow	USSR	25	10	5	15	....	....	....	2	....	....	....	....	....	....	....	....	....	....	....	....	....	....	....	....	....	....
	Soviet Union	WJC-A	6	1	1	2	....	....	....	6	....	....	....	....	....	....	....	....	....	....	....	....	....	....	....	....	....	....
1991-92	Dynamo Moscow	CIS	42	9	7	16	....	....	....	22	....	....	....	....	....	....	....	....	....	....	....	....	....	....	....	....	....	....
	HC Fribourg	Switz.	1	0	0	0	....	....	....	0	....	....	....	....	....	....	....	....	....	....	....	....	....	....	....	....	....	....
1992-93	Dynamo Moscow	CIS	39	15	14	29	....	....	....	12	....	....	....	....	....	....	....	....	....	....	10	2	5	7	8	....	....	....
	Russia	WC-A	8	2	2	4	....	....	....	4	....	....	....	....	....	....	....	....	....	....	....	....	....	....	....	....	....	....
1993-94	**Winnipeg Jets**	**NHL**	**1**	**0**	**0**	**0**	**0**	**0**	**0**	**0**	**0**	**0**	**0**	**0**	**0.0**	**1**	**0**	**0**	**0**	**1**	....	....	....	....	....	....	....	....
	Moncton Hawks	AHL	33	9	13	22	....	....	....	6	....	....	....	....	....	....	....	....	....	....	....	....	....	....	....	....	....	....
	New York Islanders	**NHL**	**23**	**2**	**1**	**3**	**2**	**1**	**3**	**4**	**0**	**0**	**0**	**23**	**8.7**	**7**	**0**	**3**	**0**	**4**	**2**	**0**	**0**	**0**	**4**	**0**	**0**	**0**
1994-95	Denver Grizzlies	IHL	38	17	16	33	....	....	....	14	....	....	....	....	....	....	....	....	....	....	15	6	6	12	0	....	....	....
	New York Islanders	**NHL**	**2**	**1**	**1**	**2**	**2**	**1**	**3**	**0**	**0**	**0**	**0**	**4**	**25.0**	**2**	**0**	**0**	**0**	**2**	....	....	....	....	....	....	....	....
1995-96	Utah Grizzlies	IHL	16	3	3	6	....	....	....	8	....	....	....	....	....	....	....	....	....	....	21	3	5	8	4	....	....	....
1996-97	Utah Grizzlies	IHL	77	28	27	55	....	....	....	18	....	....	....	....	....	....	....	....	....	....	7	1	4	5	0	....	....	....
1997-98	Lukko Rauma	Finland	38	5	8	13	....	....	....	33	....	....	....	....	....	....	....	....	....	....	....	....	....	....	....	....	....	....
1998-99	Utah Grizzlies	IHL	56	11	17	28	....	....	....	12	....	....	....	....	....	....	....	....	....	....	....	....	....	....	....	....	....	....
	Grand Rapids Griffins	IHL	7	0	2	2	....	....	....	0	....	....	....	....	....	....	....	....	....	....	....	....	....	....	....	....	....	....
	NHL Totals		**26**	**3**	**2**	**5**	**4**	**2**	**6**	**4**	**0**	**0**	**0**	**27**	**11.1**	**10**	**0**	**3**	**0**		**2**	**0**	**0**	**0**	**4**	**0**	**0**	**0**

Traded to **NY Islanders** by **Winnipeg** for Wayne McBean, February 1, 1994.

• KANNEGIESSER, Gord

Gordon Cameron D – L. 6', 190 lbs. b: North Bay, Ont., 12/21/1945.

Season	Club	League	GP	G	A	Pts	AG	AA	APts	PIM	PP	SH	GW	S	%	TGF	PGF	TGA	PGA	+/–	GP	G	A	Pts	PIM	PP	SH	GW
1962-63	Guelph Royals	OHA-Jr.	45	2	4	6	....	....	....	4	....	....	....	....	....	....	....	....	....	....	....	....	....	....	....	....	....	....
1963-64	Kitchener Rangers	OHA-Jr.	56	5	7	12	....	....	....	39	....	....	....	....	....	....	....	....	....	....	....	....	....	....	....	....	....	....
1964-65	Kitchener Rangers	OHA-Jr.	56	1	9	10	....	....	....	49	....	....	....	....	....	....	....	....	....	....	....	....	....	....	....	....	....	....
1965-66	Kitchener Rangers	OHA-Jr.	46	4	10	14	....	....	....	53	....	....	....	....	....	....	....	....	....	....	19	3	8	11	34	....	....	....
1966-67	Des Moines Oak Leafs	IHL	72	7	30	37	....	....	....	56	....	....	....	....	....	....	....	....	....	....	7	3	2	5	4	....	....	....
1967-68	**St. Louis Blues**	**NHL**	**19**	**0**	**1**	**1**	**0**	**1**	**1**	**13**	**0**	**0**	**0**	**12**	**0.0**	**6**	**1**	**11**	**3**	**–3**	....	....	....	....	....	....	....	....
	Kansas City Blues	CPHL	44	5	9	14	....	....	....	29	....	....	....	....	....	....	....	....	....	....	7	0	1	1	8	....	....	....
1968-69	Kansas City Blues	CHL	72	9	18	27	....	....	....	74	....	....	....	....	....	....	....	....	....	....	4	1	0	1	4	....	....	....
1969-70	Kansas City Blues	CHL	68	1	12	13	....	....	....	68	....	....	....	....	....	....	....	....	....	....	....	....	....	....	....	....	....	....
1970-71	Seattle Totems	WHL	39	6	7	13	....	....	....	18	....	....	....	....	....	....	....	....	....	....	....	....	....	....	....	....	....	....
	Omaha Knights	CHL	....	....	....	....	....	....	....	....	....	....	....	....	....	....	....	....	....	....	5	2	1	3	0	....	....	....
1971-72	**St. Louis Blues**	**NHL**	**4**	**0**	**0**	**0**	**0**	**0**	**0**	**2**	**0**	**0**	**0**	**4**	**0.0**	**1**	**0**	**2**	**0**	**–1**	....	....	....	....	....	....	....	....
	Denver Spurs	WHL	70	8	25	33	....	....	....	57	....	....	....	....	....	....	....	....	....	....	9	0	3	3	9	....	....	....
1972-73	Houston Aeros	WHA	45	0	10	10	....	....	....	37	....	....	....	....	....	....	....	....	....	....	9	0	1	1	11	....	....	....
1973-74	Houston Aeros	WHA	78	0	20	20	....	....	....	26	....	....	....	....	....	....	....	....	....	....	3	0	2	2	2	....	....	....
1974-75	Indianapolis Racers	WHA	4	1	4	5	....	....	....	4	....	....	....	....	....	....	....	....	....	....	....	....	....	....	....	....	....	....
	NHL Totals		**23**	**0**	**1**	**1**	**0**	**1**	**1**	**15**	**0**	**0**	**0**	**16**	**0.0**	**7**	**1**	**13**	**3**		....	....	....	....	....	....	....	....
	Other Major League Totals		127	1	34	35	....	....	....	67	....	....	....	....	....	....	....	....	....	....	12	0	3	3	13	....	....	....

• Brother of Sheldon

Traded to **St. Louis** by **NY Rangers** with Gary Sabourin, Bob Plager and Tim Ecclestone for Rod Seiling, June 6, 1967. Selected by **Dayton-Houston** (WHA) in 1972 WHA General Player Draft, February 12, 1972. Claimed by **Indianapolis** (WHA) from **Houston** (WHA) in WHA Supplemental Draft, June, 1974.

• KANNEGIESSER, Sheldon

Sheldon Bruce D – L. 6', 198 lbs. b: North Bay, Ont., 8/15/1947.

Season	Club	League	GP	G	A	Pts	AG	AA	APts	PIM	PP	SH	GW	S	%	TGF	PGF	TGA	PGA	+/–	GP	G	A	Pts	PIM	PP	SH	GW
1963-64	North Bay Trappers	NOJHA	STATISTICS NOT AVAILABLE																									
	North Bay Trappers	Mem-Cup	4	0	3	3	....	....	....	0	....	....	....	....	....	....	....	....	....	....	....	....	....	....	....	....	....	....
1964-65	North Bay Trappers	NOJHA	STATISTICS NOT AVAILABLE																									
1965-66	Kitchener Rangers	OHA-Jr.	45	1	8	9	....	....	....	19	....	....	....	....	....	....	....	....	....	....	19	1	3	4	29	....	....	....
1966-67	Kitchener Rangers	OHA-Jr.	48	7	16	23	....	....	....	81	....	....	....	....	....	....	....	....	....	....	13	2	5	7	16	....	....	....
1967-68	Omaha Knights	CPHL	20	1	2	3	....	....	....	11	....	....	....	....	....	....	....	....	....	....	....	....	....	....	....	....	....	....
	Buffalo Bisons	AHL	47	4	2	6	....	....	....	20	....	....	....	....	....	....	....	....	....	....	5	0	0	0	0	....	....	....
1968-69	Omaha Knights	CHL	70	8	13	21	....	....	....	104	....	....	....	....	....	....	....	....	....	....	7	1	1	2	6	....	....	....
1969-70	Buffalo Bisons	AHL	17	1	2	3	....	....	....	14	....	....	....	....	....	....	....	....	....	....	....	....	....	....	....	....	....	....
	Kansas City Blues	CHL	36	0	7	7	....	....	....	44	....	....	....	....	....	....	....	....	....	....	....	....	....	....	....	....	....	....
1970-71	Omaha Knights	CHL	46	4	10	14	....	....	....	75	....	....	....	....	....	....	....	....	....	....	....	....	....	....	....	....	....	....
	Pittsburgh Penguins	**NHL**	**18**	**0**	**2**	**2**	**0**	**2**	**2**	**29**	**0**	**0**	**0**	**14**	**0.0**	**10**	**0**	**23**	**4**	**–9**	....	....	....	....	....	....	....	....
	Amarillo Wranglers	CHL	7	2	2	4	....	....	....	4	....	....	....	....	....	....	....	....	....	....	....	....	....	....	....	....	....	....
1971-72	**Pittsburgh Penguins**	**NHL**	**54**	**2**	**4**	**6**	**2**	**3**	**5**	**47**	**0**	**0**	**0**	**49**	**4.1**	**30**	**0**	**49**	**5**	**–14**	....	....	....	....	....	....	....	....
1972-73	**Pittsburgh Penguins**	**NHL**	**3**	**0**	**0**	**0**	**0**	**0**	**0**	**0**	**0**	**0**	**0**	**4**	**0.0**	**0**	**0**	**1**	**0**	**–1**	....	....	....	....	....	....	....	....
	Hershey Bears	AHL	36	3	12	15	....	....	....	31	....	....	....	....	....	....	....	....	....	....	....	....	....	....	....	....	....	....
	New York Rangers	**NHL**	**3**	**0**	**1**	**1**	**0**	**1**	**1**	**4**	**0**	**0**	**0**	**2**	**0.0**	**3**	**0**	**0**	**0**	**3**	**1**	**0**	**0**	**0**	**2**	**0**	**0**	**0**
1973-74	**New York Rangers**	**NHL**	**12**	**1**	**3**	**4**	**1**	**2**	**3**	**6**	**0**	**0**	**0**	**6**	**16.7**	**12**	**1**	**8**	**1**	**4**	....	....	....	....	....	....	....	....
	Los Angeles Kings	**NHL**	**51**	**3**	**17**	**20**	**3**	**14**	**17**	**49**	**1**	**0**	**0**	**76**	**3.9**	**60**	**16**	**50**	**9**	**3**	**5**	**0**	**1**	**1**	**0**	**0**	**0**	**0**
1974-75	**Los Angeles Kings**	**NHL**	**74**	**2**	**23**	**25**	**2**	**17**	**19**	**57**	**0**	**0**	**0**	**84**	**2.4**	**99**	**13**	**60**	**15**	**41**	**3**	**0**	**1**	**1**	**4**	**0**	**0**	**0**
1975-76	**Los Angeles Kings**	**NHL**	**70**	**4**	**9**	**13**	**3**	**7**	**10**	**36**	**2**	**0**	**0**	**79**	**5.1**	**84**	**15**	**78**	**19**	**10**	**9**	**0**	**0**	**0**	**4**	**0**	**0**	**0**

			REGULAR SEASON																		PLAYOFFS							
Season	Club	League	GP	G	A	Pts	AG	AA	APts	PIM	PP	SH	GW	S	%	TGF	PGF	TGA	PGA	+/-	GP	G	A	Pts	PIM	PP	SH	GW
1976-77	**Los Angeles Kings**	**NHL**	**39**	**1**	**1**	**2**	**1**	**1**	**2**	**28**	**0**	**0**	**1**	**18**	**5.6**	**22**	**1**	**37**	**9**	**–7**	....	....	....	....	....	....	....	....
	Fort Worth Texans	CHL	24	1	7	8	....	....	....	16	....	....	....	....	....	....	....	....	....	....	....	....	....	....	....	....	....	....
1977-78	**Vancouver Canucks**	**NHL**	**42**	**1**	**7**	**8**	**1**	**5**	**6**	**36**	**0**	**0**	**0**	**21**	**4.8**	**41**	**0**	**63**	**15**	**–7**	....	....	....	....	....	....	....	....
	Springfield Indians	AHL	14	2	8	10	....	....	....	19	....	....	....	....	....	....	....	....	....	....	....	....	....	....	....	....	....	....
	NHL Totals		**366**	**14**	**67**	**81**	**13**	**52**	**65**	**292**	**3**	**0**	**1**	**353**	**4.0**	**361**	**46**	**369**	**77**		**18**	**0**	**2**	**2**	**10**	**0**	**0**	**0**

• Brother of Gord

Loaned to **St. Louis** by **NY Rangers** for the remainder of the 1969-70 season for the loan of Larry Hornung for the remainder of the 1969-70 season, November, 1969. Traded to **Pittsburgh** by **NY Rangers** with Syl Apps Jr. for Glen Sather, January 26, 1971. Traded to **NY Rangers** by **Pittsburgh** for future considerations (Steve Andrascik, May 16, 1973), March 2, 1973. Traded to **LA Kings** by **NY Rangers** with Mike Murphy and Tom Williams for Gilles Marotte and Real Lemieux, November 30, 1973. Traded to **Vancouver** by **LA Kings** for Larry Carriere, November 21, 1977.

• KAPANEN, Sami

LW – L. 5'10", 195 lbs. b: Vantaa, Finland, 6/14/1973. Hartford's 4th, 87th overall, in 1995.

Season	Club	League	GP	G	A	Pts	AG	AA	APts	PIM	PP	SH	GW	S	%	TGF	PGF	TGA	PGA	+/-	GP	G	A	Pts	PIM	PP	SH	GW
1989-90	KalPa Kuopio	Finland-Jr.	30	14	13	27	....	....	....	4	....	....	....	....	....	....	....	....	....	....	....	....	....	....	....	....	....	....
1990-91	KalPa Kuopio	Finland-Jr.	31	9	27	36	....	....	....	10	....	....	....	....	....	....	....	....	....	....	....	....	....	....	....	....	....	....
	KalPa Kuopio	Finland	14	1	2	3	....	....	....	2	....	....	....	....	....	....	....	....	....	....	8	2	1	3	2	....	....	....
	Finland	EJC-A	5	6	4	10	....	....	....	0	....	....	....	....	....	....	....	....	....	....	....	....	....	....	....	....	....	....
1991-92	KalPa Kuopio	Finland-Jr.	8	1	3	4	....	....	....	12	....	....	....	....	....	....	....	....	....	....	....	....	....	....	....	....	....	....
	KalPa Kuopio	Finland	42	15	10	25	....	....	....	8	....	....	....	....	....	....	....	....	....	....	....	....	....	....	....	....	....	....
	Finland	WJC-A	7	1	5	6	....	....	....	8	....	....	....	....	....	....	....	....	....	....	....	....	....	....	....	....	....	....
1992-93	KalPa Kuopio	Finland-Jr.	7	11	14	25	....	....	....	2	....	....	....	....	....	....	....	....	....	....	....	....	....	....	....	....	....	....
	Finland	WJC-A	7	1	2	3	....	....	....	2	....	....	....	....	....	....	....	....	....	....	....	....	....	....	....	....	....	....
	KalPa Kuopio	Finland	37	4	17	21	....	....	....	12	....	....	....	....	....	....	....	....	....	....	....	....	....	....	....	....	....	....
1993-94	KalPa Kuopio	Finland	48	23	32	55	....	....	....	16	....	....	....	....	....	....	....	....	....	....	....	....	....	....	....	....	....	....
	Finland	Nat-Team	20	9	3	12	....	....	....	0	....	....	....	....	....	....	....	....	....	....	....	....	....	....	....	....	....	....
	Finland	Olympics	8	1	0	1	....	....	....	2	....	....	....	....	....	....	....	....	....	....	....	....	....	....	....	....	....	....
	Finland	WC-A	8	4	2	6	....	....	....	0	....	....	....	....	....	....	....	....	....	....	....	....	....	....	....	....	....	....
1994-95	HIFK Helsinki	Finland	49	14	28	42	....	....	....	42	....	....	....	....	....	....	....	....	....	....	3	0	0	0	0	....	....	....
	Finland	Nat-Team	19	3	1	4	....	....	....	8	....	....	....	....	....	....	....	....	....	....	....	....	....	....	....	....	....	....
	Finland	WC-A	8	2	2	4	....	....	....	6	....	....	....	....	....	....	....	....	....	....	....	....	....	....	....	....	....	....
1995-96	**Hartford Whalers**	**NHL**	**35**	**5**	**4**	**9**	**5**	**3**	**8**	**6**	**0**	**0**	**0**	**46**	**10.9**	**14**	**1**	**14**	**1**	**0**	....	....	....	....	....	....	....	....
	Springfield Falcons	AHL	28	14	17	31	....	....	....	4	....	....	....	....	....	....	....	....	....	....	3	1	2	3	0	....	....	....
	Finland	Nat-Team	2	0	1	1	....	....	....	0	....	....	....	....	....	....	....	....	....	....	....	....	....	....	....	....	....	....
	Finland	WC-A	6	2	3	5	....	....	....	2	....	....	....	....	....	....	....	....	....	....	....	....	....	....	....	....	....	....
1996-97	Finland	W-Cup	3	0	0	0	....	....	....	4	....	....	....	....	....	....	....	....	....	....	....	....	....	....	....	....	....	....
	Hartford Whalers	**NHL**	**45**	**13**	**12**	**25**	**14**	**11**	**25**	**2**	**3**	**0**	**2**	**82**	**15.9**	**43**	**7**	**31**	**1**	**6**	....	....	....	....	....	....	....	....
	Finland	Nat-Team	4	1	0	1	....	....	....	4	....	....	....	....	....	....	....	....	....	....	....	....	....	....	....	....	....	....
1997-98	**Carolina Hurricanes**	**NHL**	**81**	**26**	**37**	**63**	**30**	**36**	**66**	**16**	**4**	**0**	**5**	**190**	**13.7**	**94**	**31**	**59**	**5**	**9**	....	....	....	....	....	....	....	....
	Finland	Olympics	6	0	1	1	....	....	....	0	....	....	....	....	....	....	....	....	....	....	....	....	....	....	....	....	....	....
	Finland	WC-A	10	4	3	7	....	....	....	2	....	....	....	....	....	....	....	....	....	....	....	....	....	....	....	....	....	....
1998-99	**Carolina Hurricanes**	**NHL**	**81**	**24**	**35**	**59**	**28**	**34**	**62**	**10**	**5**	**0**	**7**	**254**	**9.4**	**80**	**27**	**58**	**4**	**–1**	**5**	**1**	**1**	**2**	**0**	**0**	**0**	**0**
99-2000	**Carolina Hurricanes**	**NHL**	**76**	**24**	**24**	**48**	**27**	**22**	**49**	**12**	**7**	**0**	**5**	**229**	**10.5**	**79**	**32**	**38**	**1**	**10**	....	....	....	....	....	....	....	....
	NHL Totals		**318**	**92**	**112**	**204**	**104**	**106**	**210**	**46**	**19**	**0**	**19**	**801**	**11.5**	**310**	**98**	**200**	**12**		**5**	**1**	**1**	**2**	**0**	**0**	**0**	**0**

Finnish First All-Star Team (1994) • Played in NHL All-Star Game (2000)

Transferred to **Carolina** after **Hartford** franchise relocated, June 25, 1997.

• KARABIN, Ladislav

LW – L. 6'1", 189 lbs. b: Spisska Nova Ves, Czech., 2/16/1970. Pittsburgh's 11th, 173rd overall, in 1990.

Season	Club	League	GP	G	A	Pts	AG	AA	APts	PIM	PP	SH	GW	S	%	TGF	PGF	TGA	PGA	+/-	GP	G	A	Pts	PIM	PP	SH	GW
1987-88	Slovan Bratislava	Czech-2	STATISTICS NOT AVAILABLE																									
	Czechoslovakia	EJC-A	6	1	4	5	....	....	....	12	....	....	....	....	....	....	....	....	....	....	....	....	....	....	....	....	....	....
1988-89	Slovan Bratislava	Czech.	31	7	2	9	....	....	....	10	....	....	....	....	....	....	....	....	....	....	....	....	....	....	....	....	....	....
1989-90	Slovan Bratislava	Czech-2	STATISTICS NOT AVAILABLE																									
	Czechoslovakia	WJC-A	6	2	1	3	....	....	....	6	....	....	....	....	....	....	....	....	....	....	....	....	....	....	....	....	....	....
1990-91	Slovan Bratislava	Czech.	49	21	7	28	....	....	....	57	....	....	....	....	....	....	....	....	....	....	....	....	....	....	....	....	....	....
1991-92	Slovan Bratislava	Czech.	27	4	8	12	....	....	....	10	....	....	....	....	....	....	....	....	....	....	....	....	....	....	....	....	....	....
1992-93	Slovan Bratislava	Czech.	39	21	23	44	....	....	....	....	....	....	....	....	....	....	....	....	....	....	....	....	....	....	....	....	....	....
1993-94	**Pittsburgh Penguins**	**NHL**	**9**	**0**	**0**	**0**	**0**	**0**	**0**	**2**	**0**	**0**	**0**	**3**	**0.0**	**2**	**0**	**2**	**0**	**0**	....	....	....	....	....	....	....	....
	Cleveland Lumberjacks	IHL	58	13	26	39	....	....	....	48	....	....	....	....	....	....	....	....	....	....	....	....	....	....	....	....	....	....
1994-95	Cleveland Lumberjacks	IHL	47	15	25	40	....	....	....	26	....	....	....	....	....	....	....	....	....	....	4	0	0	0	2	....	....	....
1995-96	Rochester Americans	AHL	21	3	5	8	....	....	....	18	....	....	....	....	....	....	....	....	....	....	....	....	....	....	....	....	....	....
	Los Angeles Ice Dogs	IHL	32	6	8	14	....	....	....	58	....	....	....	....	....	....	....	....	....	....	....	....	....	....	....	....	....	....
1996-97	Slovan Bratislava	Slovakia	33	4	10	14	....	....	....	....	....	....	....	....	....	....	....	....	....	....	....	....	....	....	....	....	....	....
	HC Sparta Praha	EuroHL	5	1	2	3	....	....	....	6	....	....	....	....	....	....	....	....	....	....	2	0	0	0	0	....	....	....
1997-98	Spartak Dubnica	Slovakia-2	9	7	6	13	....	....	....	0	....	....	....	....	....	....	....	....	....	....	....	....	....	....	....	....	....	....
	Slovan Bratislava	Slovakia	6	0	0	0	....	....	....	0	....	....	....	....	....	....	....	....	....	....	5	1	0	1	4	....	....	....
	Slovan Bratislava	EuroHL	2	0	0	0	....	....	....	0	....	....	....	....	....	....	....	....	....	....	....	....	....	....	....	....	....	....
1998-99	VTJ Nova Ves	Slovakia	47	25	28	53	....	....	....	70	....	....	....	....	....	....	....	....	....	....	1	0	0	0	*50	....	....	....
99-2000	Revier Lowen	Germany	55	14	13	27	....	....	....	28	....	....	....	....	....	....	....	....	....	....	....	....	....	....	....	....	....	....
	NHL Totals		**9**	**0**	**0**	**0**	**0**	**0**	**0**	**2**	**0**	**0**	**0**	**3**	**0.0**	**2**	**0**	**2**	**0**		....	....	....	....	....	....	....	....

Signed as a free agent by **Buffalo**, September 20, 1995.

• KARALAHTI, Jere

D – R. 6'2", 210 lbs. b: Helsinki, Finland, 3/25/1975. Los Angeles' 7th, 146th overall, in 1993.

Season	Club	League	GP	G	A	Pts	AG	AA	APts	PIM	PP	SH	GW	S	%	TGF	PGF	TGA	PGA	+/-	GP	G	A	Pts	PIM	PP	SH	GW
1991-92	HIFK Helsinki	Finland-Jr.	30	12	5	17	....	....	....	36	....	....	....	....	....	....	....	....	....	....	1	0	0	0	2	....	....	....
1992-93	HIFK Helsinki-B	Finland-Jr.	7	3	1	4	....	....	....	4	....	....	....	....	....	....	....	....	....	....	....	....	....	....	....	....	....	....
	HIFK Helsinki	Finland-Jr.	30	2	13	15	....	....	....	49	....	....	....	....	....	....	....	....	....	....	2	0	0	0	0	....	....	....
1993-94	HIFK Helsinki	Finland-Jr.	3	0	0	0	....	....	....	0	....	....	....	....	....	....	....	....	....	....	....	....	....	....	....	....	....	....
	HIFK Helsinki	Finland	46	1	10	11	....	....	....	36	....	....	....	....	....	....	....	....	....	....	3	0	0	0	6	....	....	....
	Finland	WJC-A	7	3	2	5	....	....	....	4	....	....	....	....	....	....	....	....	....	....	....	....	....	....	....	....	....	....
1994-95	HIFK Helsinki	Finland-Jr.	1	0	0	0	....	....	....	8	....	....	....	....	....	....	....	....	....	....	....	....	....	....	....	....	....	....
	HIFK Helsinki	Finland	37	1	7	8	....	....	....	42	....	....	....	....	....	....	....	....	....	....	3	0	0	0	0	....	....	....
	Finland	WJC-A	7	2	4	6	....	....	....	8	....	....	....	....	....	....	....	....	....	....	....	....	....	....	....	....	....	....
1995-96	HIFK Helsinki	Finland-Jr.	3	1	2	3	....	....	....	2	....	....	....	....	....	....	....	....	....	....	....	....	....	....	....	....	....	....
	HIFK Helsinki	Finland	36	4	6	10	....	....	....	102	....	....	....	....	....	....	....	....	....	....	3	0	0	0	4	....	....	....
1996-97	HIFK Helsinki	Finland	18	3	5	8	....	....	....	20	....	....	....	....	....	....	....	....	....	....	....	....	....	....	....	....	....	....
1997-98	HIFK Helsinki	Finland	43	14	16	30	....	....	....	32	....	....	....	....	....	....	....	....	....	....	9	2	0	2	8	....	....	....
	Finland	WC-A	10	4	3	7	....	....	....	6	....	....	....	....	....	....	....	....	....	....	....	....	....	....	....	....	....	....
1998-99	HIFK Helsinki	Finland	49	11	22	33	....	....	....	65	....	....	....	....	....	....	....	....	....	....	11	1	1	2	10	....	....	....
	HIFK Helsinki	EuroHL	6	2	1	3	....	....	....	2	....	....	....	....	....	....	....	....	....	....	4	....	2	....	....	....	....	....
	Finland	WC-A	12	5	3	8	....	....	....	2	....	....	....	....	....	....	....	....	....	....	....	....	....	....	....	....	....	....
99-2000	HIFK Helsinki	Finland	13	2	2	4	....	....	....	55	....	....	....	....	....	....	....	....	....	....	....	....	....	....	....	....	....	....
	Los Angeles Kings	**NHL**	**48**	**6**	**10**	**16**	**7**	**9**	**16**	**18**	**4**	**0**	**1**	**69**	**8.7**	**39**	**10**	**34**	**8**	**3**	**4**	**0**	**1**	**1**	**2**	**0**	**0**	**0**
	Long Beach Ice Dogs	IHL	10	0	3	3	....	....	....	4	....	....	....	....	....	....	....	....	....	....	....	....	....	....	....	....	....	....
	Finland	WC-A	9	1	1	2	....	....	....	8	....	....	....	....	....	....	....	....	....	....	....	....	....	....	....	....	....	....
	NHL Totals		**48**	**6**	**10**	**16**	**7**	**9**	**16**	**18**	**4**	**0**	**1**	**69**	**8.7**	**39**	**10**	**34**	**8**		**4**	**0**	**1**	**1**	**2**	**0**	**0**	**0**

WC-A All-Star Team (1999)

• KARAMNOV, Vitali

LW – L. 6'2", 185 lbs. b: Moscow, USSR, 7/6/1968. St. Louis' 2nd, 62nd overall, in 1992.

Season	Club	League	GP	G	A	Pts	AG	AA	APts	PIM	PP	SH	GW	S	%	TGF	PGF	TGA	PGA	+/-	GP	G	A	Pts	PIM	PP	SH	GW
1986-87	Dynamo Moscow	USSR	4	0	0	0	....	....	....	0	....	....	....	....	....	....	....	....	....	....	....	....	....	....	....	....	....	....
1987-88	Dynamo Moscow	USSR	2	0	1	1	....	....	....	0	....	....	....	....	....	....	....	....	....	....	....	....	....	....	....	....	....	....
1988-89	Dynamo Kharkov	USSR	23	4	1	5	....	....	....	19	....	....	....	....	....	....	....	....	....	....	....	....	....	....	....	....	....	....

Season	Club	League	GP	G	A	Pts	AG	AA	APts	PIM	PP	SH	GW	S	%	TGF	PGF	TGA	PGA	+/–	GP	G	A	Pts	PIM	PP	SH	GW
			REGULAR SEASON																		PLAYOFFS							
1989-90	Torpedo Yaroslavl	USSR	47	6	7	13	....	....	....	32	....	....	....	....	....	....	....	....	....	....	....	....	....	....	....	....	....	....
1990-91	Torpedo Yaroslavl	Fr-Tour	1	0	1	1	....	....	....	0	....	....	....	....	....	....	....	....	....	....	....	....	....	....	....	....	....	....
	Torpedo Yaroslavl	USSR	45	14	7	21	....	....	....	30	....	....	....	....	....	....	....	....	....	....	....	....	....	....	....	....	....	....
1991-92	Dynamo Moscow	CIS	40	13	19	32	....	....	....	25	....	....	....	....	....	....	....	....	....	....	....	....	....	....	....	....	....	....
1992-93	**St. Louis Blues**	**NHL**	**7**	**0**	**1**	**1**	**0**	**1**	**1**	**0**	**0**	**0**	**0**	**7**	**0.0**	**1**	**0**	**3**	**0**	**–2**	....	....	....	....	....	....	....	....
	Peoria Rivermen	IHL	23	8	12	20	....	....	....	47	....	....	....	....	....	....	....	....	....	....	....	....	....	....	....	....	....	....
1993-94	**St. Louis Blues**	**NHL**	**59**	**9**	**12**	**21**	**8**	**9**	**17**	**51**	**2**	**0**	**1**	**66**	**13.6**	**27**	**3**	**27**	**0**	**–3**	....	....	....	....	....	....	....	....
	Peoria Rivermen	IHL	3	0	1	1	....	....	....	2	....	....	....	....	....	....	....	....	....	....	1	0	1	1	0	....	....	....
1994-95	**St. Louis Blues**	**NHL**	**26**	**3**	**7**	**10**	**5**	**10**	**15**	**14**	**0**	**0**	**0**	**22**	**13.6**	**17**	**1**	**9**	**0**	**7**	**2**	**0**	**0**	**0**	**2**	**0**	**0**	**0**
	Peoria Rivermen	IHL	15	6	9	15	....	....	....	7	....	....	....	....	....	....	....	....	....	....	....	....	....	....	....	....	....	....
1995-96	JyP-HT Jyvaskyla	Finland	24	8	7	15	....	....	....	36	....	....	....	....	....	....	....	....	....	....	....	....	....	....	....	....	....	....
	Russia	WC-A	8	0	2	2	....	....	....	0	....	....	....	....	....	....	....	....	....	....	....	....	....	....	....	....	....	....
1996-97	Berlin Capitals	Germany	4	2	1	3	....	....	....	27	....	....	....	....	....	....	....	....	....	....	....	....	....	....	....	....	....	....
	Berlin Capitals	EuroHL	1	0	0	0	....	....	....	2	....	....	....	....	....	....	....	....	....	....	....	....	....	....	....	....	....	....
	Krefeld Pinguine	Germany	28	7	13	20	....	....	....	80	....	....	....	....	....	....	....	....	....	....	3	1	1	2	25	....	....	....
1997-98	Krefeld Pinguine	Germany	31	8	13	21	....	....	....	38	....	....	....	....	....	....	....	....	....	....	3	0	2	2	2	....	....	....
1998-99	Krefeld Pinguine	Germany	40	11	17	28	....	....	....	61	....	....	....	....	....	....	....	....	....	....	2	1	0	1	4	....	....	....
99-2000	HC Slovnaft Vsetin	Czech-Rep	5	0	0	0	....	....	....	10	....	....	....	....	....	....	....	....	....	....	....	....	....	....	....	....	....	....
	NHL Totals		**92**	**12**	**20**	**32**	**13**	**20**	**33**	**65**	**2**	**0**	**1**	**95**	**12.6**	**45**	**4**	**39**	**0**		**2**	**0**	**0**	**0**	**2**	**0**	**0**	**0**

• KARIYA, Paul

LW – L. 5'11", 180 lbs. b: Vancouver, B.C., 10/16/1974. Anaheim's 1st, 4th overall, in 1993.

Season	Club	League	GP	G	A	Pts	AG	AA	APts	PIM	PP	SH	GW	S	%	TGF	PGF	TGA	PGA	+/–	GP	G	A	Pts	PIM	PP	SH	GW
1990-91	Penticton Panthers	BCJHL	54	45	67	112	....	....	....	8	....	....	....	....	....	....	....	....	....	....	....	....	....	....	....	....	....	....
1991-92	Penticton Panthers	BCJHL	40	46	86	132	....	....	....	18	....	....	....	....	....	....	....	....	....	....	....	....	....	....	....	....	....	....
	Canada	WJC-A	6	1	1	2	....	....	....	2	....	....	....	....	....	....	....	....	....	....	....	....	....	....	....	....	....	....
1992-93	University of Maine	H-East	39	25	*75	*100	....	....	....	12	....	....	....	....	....	....	....	....	....	....	....	....	....	....	....	....	....	....
	Canada	WJC-A	7	2	6	8	....	....	....	2	....	....	....	....	....	....	....	....	....	....	....	....	....	....	....	....	....	....
	Canada	WC-A	8	2	7	9	....	....	....	0	....	....	....	....	....	....	....	....	....	....	....	....	....	....	....	....	....	....
1993-94	University of Maine	H-East	12	8	16	24	....	....	....	4	....	....	....	....	....	....	....	....	....	....	....	....	....	....	....	....	....	....
	Canada	Nat-Team	23	7	34	41	....	....	....	2	....	....	....	....	....	....	....	....	....	....	....	....	....	....	....	....	....	....
	Canada	Olympics	8	3	4	7	....	....	....	2	....	....	....	....	....	....	....	....	....	....	....	....	....	....	....	....	....	....
	Canada	WC-A	8	5	7	12	....	....	....	2	....	....	....	....	....	....	....	....	....	....	....	....	....	....	....	....	....	....
1994-95	**Mighty Ducks of Anaheim**	**NHL**	**47**	**18**	**21**	**39**	**32**	**31**	**63**	**4**	**7**	**1**	**3**	**134**	**13.4**	**50**	**22**	**51**	**6**	**–17**	....	....	....	....	....	....	....	....
1995-96	**Mighty Ducks of Anaheim**	**NHL**	**82**	**50**	**58**	**108**	**49**	**48**	**97**	**20**	**20**	**3**	**9**	**349**	**14.3**	**132**	**52**	**87**	**16**	**9**	....	....	....	....	....	....	....	....
	Canada	WC-A	8	4	3	7	....	....	....	2	....	....	....	....	....	....	....	....	....	....	....	....	....	....	....	....	....	....
1996-97	**Mighty Ducks of Anaheim**	**NHL**	**69**	**44**	**55**	**99**	**47**	**49**	**96**	**6**	**15**	**3**	**10**	**340**	**12.9**	**133**	**47**	**63**	**13**	**36**	**11**	**7**	**6**	**13**	**4**	**4**	**0**	**1**
1997-98	**Mighty Ducks of Anaheim**	**NHL**	**22**	**17**	**14**	**31**	**20**	**14**	**34**	**23**	**3**	**0**	**2**	**103**	**16.5**	**41**	**8**	**25**	**4**	**12**	....	....	....	....	....	....	....	....
1998-99	**Mighty Ducks of Anaheim**	**NHL**	**82**	**39**	**62**	**101**	**46**	**60**	**106**	**40**	**11**	**2**	**4**	**429**	**9.1**	**155**	**79**	**83**	**24**	**17**	**3**	**1**	**3**	**4**	**0**	**0**	**0**	**0**
99-2000	**Mighty Ducks of Anaheim**	**NHL**	**74**	**42**	**44**	**86**	**47**	**41**	**88**	**24**	**11**	**3**	**3**	**324**	**13.0**	**124**	**42**	**79**	**19**	**22**	....	....	....	....	....	....	....	....
	NHL Totals		**376**	**210**	**254**	**464**	**241**	**243**	**484**	**117**	**67**	**12**	**31**	**1679**	**12.5**	**635**	**250**	**388**	**82**		**14**	**8**	**9**	**17**	**4**	**4**	**0**	**1**

• Brother of Steve • WJC-A All-Star Team (1993) • Hockey East First All-Star Team (1993) • NCAA East First All-American Team (1993) • NCAA Championship All-Tournament Team (1993) • Won Hobey Baker Memorial Award (Top U.S. Collegiate Player) (1993) • WC-A All-Star Team (1994, 1996) • Named Best Forward at WC-A (1994, 1996) • NHL All-Rookie Team (1995) • NHL First All-Star Team (1996, 1997, 1999) • Won Lady Byng Trophy (1996, 1997) • NHL Second All-Star Team (2000) • Played in NHL All-Star Game (1996, 1997, 1999, 2000)

• KARIYA, Steve

LW – R. 5'9", 165 lbs. b: North Vancouver, B.C., 12/22/1977.

Season	Club	League	GP	G	A	Pts	AG	AA	APts	PIM	PP	SH	GW	S	%	TGF	PGF	TGA	PGA	+/–	GP	G	A	Pts	PIM	PP	SH	GW
1993-94	North Vancouver Canucks	BCAHA	STATISTICS NOT AVAILABLE																									
1994-95	Nanaimo Clippers	BCJHL	60	36	60	96	....	....	....	4	....	....	....	....	....	....	....	....	....	....	....	....	....	....	....	....	....	....
1995-96	University of Maine	H-East	39	7	16	23	....	....	....	8	....	....	....	....	....	....	....	....	....	....	....	....	....	....	....	....	....	....
1996-97	University of Maine	H-East	35	19	31	50	....	....	....	10	....	....	....	....	....	....	....	....	....	....	....	....	....	....	....	....	....	....
1997-98	University of Maine	H-East	35	25	25	50	....	....	....	22	....	....	....	....	....	....	....	....	....	....	....	....	....	....	....	....	....	....
1998-99	University of Maine	H-East	41	27	38	65	....	....	....	24	....	....	....	....	....	....	....	....	....	....	....	....	....	....	....	....	....	....
99-2000	**Vancouver Canucks**	**NHL**	**45**	**8**	**11**	**19**	**9**	**10**	**19**	**22**	**0**	**0**	**0**	**41**	**19.5**	**31**	**5**	**17**	**0**	**9**	....	....	....	....	....	....	....	....
	Syracuse Crunch	AHL	29	18	23	41	....	....	....	22	....	....	....	....	....	....	....	....	....	....	4	2	1	3	0	....	....	....
	NHL Totals		**45**	**8**	**11**	**19**	**9**	**10**	**19**	**22**	**0**	**0**	**0**	**41**	**19.5**	**31**	**5**	**17**	**0**		....	....	....	....	....	....	....	....

• Brother of Paul • BCJHL First Team All-Star (1995) • BCJHL Most Sportsmanlike Player (1985) • Hockey East First All-Star Team (1999) • NCAA East First All-American Team (1999)

Signed as a free agent by **Vancouver**, April 21, 1999.

• KARJALAINEN, Kyosti

RW – R. 6'2", 190 lbs. b: Gavle, Sweden, 6/19/1967. Los Angeles' 6th, 132nd overall, in 1987.

Season	Club	League	GP	G	A	Pts	AG	AA	APts	PIM	PP	SH	GW	S	%	TGF	PGF	TGA	PGA	+/–	GP	G	A	Pts	PIM	PP	SH	GW
1986-87	Brynas IF Gavle	Sweden	11	3	2	5	....	....	....	0	....	....	....	....	....	....	....	....	....	....	....	....	....	....	....	....	....	....
1987-88	Brynas IF Gavle	Sweden	20	2	1	3	....	....	....	10	....	....	....	....	....	....	....	....	....	....	....	....	....	....	....	....	....	....
1988-89	Brynas IF Gavle	Sweden	39	20	17	37	....	....	....	16	....	....	....	....	....	....	....	....	....	....	....	....	....	....	....	....	....	....
1989-90	Brynas IF Gavle	Sweden	38	17	15	32	....	....	....	16	....	....	....	....	....	....	....	....	....	....	5	0	3	3	0	....	....	....
1990-91	Phoenix Roadrunners	IHL	70	14	35	49	....	....	....	10	....	....	....	....	....	....	....	....	....	....	6	2	3	5	6	....	....	....
1991-92	**Los Angeles Kings**	**NHL**	**28**	**1**	**8**	**9**	**1**	**6**	**7**	**12**	**0**	**0**	**0**	**20**	**5.0**	**15**	**0**	**11**	**0**	**4**	**3**	**0**	**1**	**1**	**2**	**0**	**0**	**0**
	Phoenix Roadrunners	IHL	43	14	22	36	....	....	....	30	....	....	....	....	....	....	....	....	....	....	....	....	....	....	....	....	....	....
1992-93	Lulea HF	Sweden	39	7	5	12	....	....	....	44	....	....	....	....	....	....	....	....	....	....	11	0	1	1	0	....	....	....
1993-94	Lulea HF	Sweden	36	2	5	7	....	....	....	8	....	....	....	....	....	....	....	....	....	....	....	....	....	....	....	....	....	....
1994-95	MoDo Hockey	Sweden	35	7	9	16	....	....	....	20	....	....	....	....	....	....	....	....	....	....	....	....	....	....	....	....	....	....
1995-96	MoDo Hockey	Sweden	35	6	7	13	....	....	....	28	....	....	....	....	....	....	....	....	....	....	8	4	3	7	12	....	....	....
1996-97	Timra IK	Sweden-2	32	17	26	43	....	....	....	22	....	....	....	....	....	....	....	....	....	....	2	0	1	1	2	....	....	....
1997-98	HC Sodertalje	Sweden	46	10	17	27	....	....	....	18	....	....	....	....	....	....	....	....	....	....	10	2	4	6	20	....	....	....
1998-99	Augsburger Panther	Germany	52	17	28	45	....	....	....	20	....	....	....	....	....	....	....	....	....	....	5	1	2	3	2	....	....	....
99-2000	Augsburger Panther	Germany	43	9	7	16	....	....	....	24	....	....	....	....	....	....	....	....	....	....	2	0	0	0	27	....	....	....
	NHL Totals		**28**	**1**	**8**	**9**	**1**	**6**	**7**	**12**	**0**	**0**	**0**	**20**	**5.0**	**15**	**0**	**11**	**0**		**3**	**0**	**1**	**1**	**2**	**0**	**0**	**0**

• KARLANDER, Al

Allan David C – L. 5'8", 170 lbs. b: Lac La H'ache, B.C., 11/5/1946. Detroit's 2nd, 17th overall, in 1967.

Season	Club	League	GP	G	A	Pts	AG	AA	APts	PIM	PP	SH	GW	S	%	TGF	PGF	TGA	PGA	+/–	GP	G	A	Pts	PIM	PP	SH	GW
1964-65	Notre Dame Hounds	Hi-School	STATISTICS NOT AVAILABLE																									
1965-66	Michigan Tech JV Huskies	WCHA	8	9	10	19	....	....	....	6	....	....	....	....	....	....	....	....	....	....	....	....	....	....	....	....	....	....
1966-67	Michigan Tech Huskies	WCHA	29	5	12	17	....	....	....	10	....	....	....	....	....	....	....	....	....	....	....	....	....	....	....	....	....	....
1967-68	Michigan Tech Huskies	WCHA	32	22	13	35	....	....	....	24	....	....	....	....	....	....	....	....	....	....	....	....	....	....	....	....	....	....
1968-69	Michigan Tech Huskies	WCHA	32	31	13	44	....	....	....	24	....	....	....	....	....	....	....	....	....	....	....	....	....	....	....	....	....	....
1969-70	**Detroit Red Wings**	**NHL**	**41**	**5**	**10**	**15**	**5**	**9**	**14**	**6**	**0**	**0**	**0**	**41**	**12.2**	**23**	**2**	**13**	**0**	**8**	**4**	**0**	**1**	**1**	**0**	**0**	**0**	**0**
	Fort Worth Wings	CHL	24	15	14	29	....	....	....	12	....	....	....	....	....	....	....	....	....	....	....	....	....	....	....	....	....	....
1970-71	**Detroit Red Wings**	**NHL**	**23**	**1**	**4**	**5**	**1**	**3**	**4**	**10**	**1**	**0**	**0**	**9**	**11.1**	**9**	**2**	**3**	**1**	**5**	....	....	....	....	....	....	....	....
	Fort Worth Wings	CHL	48	30	28	58	....	....	....	40	....	....	....	....	....	....	....	....	....	....	4	2	1	3	2	....	....	....
1971-72	**Detroit Red Wings**	**NHL**	**71**	**15**	**20**	**35**	**15**	**17**	**32**	**29**	**0**	**0**	**5**	**93**	**16.1**	**61**	**9**	**51**	**13**	**14**	....	....	....	....	....	....	....	....
1972-73	**Detroit Red Wings**	**NHL**	**77**	**15**	**22**	**37**	**14**	**17**	**31**	**25**	**4**	**0**	**4**	**99**	**15.2**	**51**	**5**	**51**	**7**	**2**	....	....	....	....	....	....	....	....
1973-74	New England Whalers	WHA	77	20	41	61	....	....	....	46	....	....	....	....	....	....	....	....	....	....	7	1	3	4	2	....	....	....
1974-75	New England Whalers	WHA	51	7	14	21	....	....	....	2	....	....	....	....	....	....	....	....	....	....	5	0	3	3	0	....	....	....
	Cape Cod Codders	NAHL	3	1	2	3	....	....	....	0	....	....	....	....	....	....	....	....	....	....	....	....	....	....	....	....	....	....
1975-76	Indianapolis Racers	WHA	79	16	28	44	....	....	....	36	....	....	....	....	....	....	....	....	....	....	3	0	0	0	4	....	....	....
1976-77	Indianapolis Racers	WHA	65	17	28	45	....	....	....	23	....	....	....	....	....	....	....	....	....	....	6	2	1	3	0	....	....	....
	NHL Totals		**212**	**36**	**56**	**92**	**35**	**46**	**81**	**70**	**5**	**0**	**9**	**242**	**14.9**	**144**	**18**	**118**	**21**		**4**	**0**	**1**	**1**	**0**	**0**	**0**	**0**
	Other Major League Totals		272	60	111	171	....	....	....	107	....	....	....	....	....	....	....	....	....	....	21	3	7	10	6	....	....	....

WCHA Second All-Star Team (1968) • WCHA First All-Star Team (1969) • NCAA West First All-American Team (1969)

Selected by **New England** (WHA) in 1972 WHA General Player Draft, February 12, 1972. Claimed by **Indianapolis** (WHA) from **New England** (WHA) in WHA Intra-League Draft, June 19, 1975.

			REGULAR SEASON																		PLAYOFFS							
Season	**Club**	**League**	**GP**	**G**	**A**	**Pts**	**AG**	**AA**	**APts**	**PIM**	**PP**	**SH**	**GW**	**S**	**%**	**TGF**	**PGF**	**TGA**	**PGA**	**+/–**	**GP**	**G**	**A**	**Pts**	**PIM**	**PP**	**SH**	**GW**

• KARLSSON, Andreas

C – L. 6'3", 195 lbs. b: Luvicka, Sweden, 8/19/1975. Calgary's 8th, 148th overall, in 1993.

Season	Club	League	GP	G	A	Pts	AG	AA	APts	PIM	PP	SH	GW	S	%	TGF	PGF	TGA	PGA	+/–	GP	G	A	Pts	PIM	PP	SH	GW
1992-93	Leksands IF	Sweden	13	0	0	0	....	....	....	6	....	....	....	....	....	....	....	....	....	....	....	....	....	....	....	....	....	....
1993-94	Leksands IF	Sweden	21	0	0	0	....	....	....	10	....	....	....	....	....	....	....	....	....	....	3	0	0	0	0	....	....	....
1994-95	Leksands IF	Sweden	24	7	8	15	....	....	....	0	....	....	....	....	....	....	....	....	....	....	4	0	1	1	0	....	....	....
	Sweden	WJC-A	7	2	2	4	....	....	....	0	....	....	....	....	....	....	....	....	....	....	....	....	....	....	....	....	....	....
1995-96	Leksands IF	Sweden	40	10	13	23	....	....	....	10	....	....	....	....	....	....	....	....	....	....	....	....	....	....	....	....	....	....
	Sweden	WC-A	5	0	0	0	....	....	....	4	....	....	....	....	....	....	....	....	....	....	....	....	....	....	....	....	....	....
1996-97	Leksands IF	Sweden	49	13	11	24	....	....	....	39	....	....	....	....	....	....	....	....	....	....	9	2	0	2	2	....	....	....
1997-98	Leksands IF	Sweden	33	9	14	23	....	....	....	20	....	....	....	....	....	....	....	....	....	....	4	1	0	1	0	....	....	....
	Leksands IF	EuroHL	6	2	3	5	....	....	....	2	....	....	....	....	....	....	....	....	....	....	....	....	....	....	....	....	....	....
1998-99	Leksands IF	Sweden	49	18	15	33	....	....	....	18	....	....	....	....	....	....	....	....	....	....	4	1	0	1	6	....	....	....
	Leksands IF	EuroHL	6	1	3	4	....	....	....	2	....	....	....	....	....	....	....	....	....	....	2	1	1	2	2	....	....	....
99-2000	**Atlanta Thrashers**	**NHL**	**51**	**5**	**9**	**14**	**6**	**8**	**14**	**14**	**1**	**0**	**0**	**74**	**6.8**	**18**	**2**	**40**	**7**	**–17**	....	....	....	....	....	....	....	....
	Orlando Solar Bears	IHL	18	5	5	10	....	....	....	6	....	....	....	....	....	....	....	....	....	....	....	....	....	....	....	....	....	....
	NHL Totals		**51**	**5**	**9**	**14**	**6**	**8**	**14**	**14**	**1**	**0**	**0**	**74**	**6.8**	**18**	**2**	**40**	**7**		....	....	....	....	....	....	....	....

Traded to **Atlanta** by **Calgary** for future considerations, June 25, 1999.

• KARPA, Dave

David J. D – R. 6'1", 210 lbs. b: Regina, Sask., 5/7/1971. Quebec's 4th, 68th overall, in 1991.

Season	Club	League	GP	G	A	Pts	AG	AA	APts	PIM	PP	SH	GW	S	%	TGF	PGF	TGA	PGA	+/–	GP	G	A	Pts	PIM	PP	SH	GW
1988-89	Notre Dame Hounds	SJHL	41	16	37	53	....	....	....	....	....	....	....	....	....	....	....	....	....	....	....	....	....	....	....	....	....	....
1989-90	Notre Dame Hounds	SJHL	43	9	19	28	....	....	....	271	....	....	....	....	....	....	....	....	....	....	....	....	....	....	....	....	....	....
1990-91	Ferris State Bulldogs	CCHA	41	6	19	25	....	....	....	109	....	....	....	....	....	....	....	....	....	....	....	....	....	....	....	....	....	....
1991-92	Ferris State Bulldogs	CCHA	34	7	12	19	....	....	....	124	....	....	....	....	....	....	....	....	....	....	....	....	....	....	....	....	....	....
	Quebec Nordiques	**NHL**	**4**	**0**	**0**	**0**	**0**	**0**	**0**	**14**	**0**	**0**	**0**	**2**	**0.0**	**2**	**0**	**0**	**0**	**2**	....	....	....	....	....	....	....	....
	Halifax Citadels	AHL	2	0	0	0	....	....	....	4	....	....	....	....	....	....	....	....	....	....	....	....	....	....	....	....	....	....
1992-93	**Quebec Nordiques**	**NHL**	**12**	**0**	**1**	**1**	**0**	**1**	**1**	**13**	**0**	**0**	**0**	**2**	**0.0**	**4**	**0**	**10**	**0**	**–6**	**3**	**0**	**0**	**0**	**0**	**0**	**0**	**0**
	Halifax Citadels	AHL	71	4	27	31	....	....	....	167	....	....	....	....	....	....	....	....	....	....	....	....	....	....	....	....	....	....
1993-94	**Quebec Nordiques**	**NHL**	**60**	**5**	**12**	**17**	**5**	**9**	**14**	**148**	**2**	**0**	**0**	**48**	**10.4**	**45**	**8**	**43**	**6**	**0**	....	....	....	....	....	....	....	....
	Cornwall Aces	AHL	1	0	0	0	....	....	....	0	....	....	....	....	....	....	....	....	....	....	12	2	2	4	27	....	....	....
1994-95	**Quebec Nordiques**	**NHL**	**2**	**0**	**0**	**0**	**0**	**0**	**0**	**0**	**0**	**0**	**0**	**1**	**0.0**	**1**	**0**	**2**	**0**	**–1**	....	....	....	....	....	....	....	....
	Cornwall Aces	AHL	6	0	2	2	....	....	....	19	....	....	....	....	....	....	....	....	....	....	....	....	....	....	....	....	....	....
	Mighty Ducks of Anaheim	**NHL**	**26**	**1**	**5**	**6**	**2**	**7**	**9**	**91**	**0**	**0**	**0**	**32**	**3.1**	**22**	**0**	**34**	**12**	**0**	....	....	....	....	....	....	....	....
1995-96	**Mighty Ducks of Anaheim**	**NHL**	**72**	**3**	**16**	**19**	**3**	**13**	**16**	**270**	**0**	**1**	**1**	**62**	**4.8**	**52**	**4**	**77**	**26**	**–3**	....	....	....	....	....	....	....	....
1996-97	**Mighty Ducks of Anaheim**	**NHL**	**69**	**2**	**11**	**13**	**2**	**10**	**12**	**210**	**0**	**0**	**1**	**90**	**2.2**	**54**	**3**	**67**	**27**	**11**	**8**	**1**	**1**	**2**	**20**	**0**	**0**	**1**
1997-98	**Mighty Ducks of Anaheim**	**NHL**	**78**	**1**	**11**	**12**	**1**	**11**	**12**	**217**	**0**	**0**	**0**	**64**	**1.6**	**59**	**2**	**88**	**28**	**–3**	....	....	....	....	....	....	....	....
1998-99	**Carolina Hurricanes**	**NHL**	**33**	**0**	**2**	**2**	**0**	**2**	**2**	**55**	**0**	**0**	**0**	**21**	**0.0**	**22**	**1**	**21**	**1**	**1**	**2**	**0**	**0**	**0**	**2**	**0**	**0**	**0**
99-2000	**Carolina Hurricanes**	**NHL**	**27**	**1**	**4**	**5**	**1**	**4**	**5**	**52**	**0**	**0**	**0**	**24**	**4.2**	**21**	**0**	**18**	**6**	**9**	....	....	....	....	....	....	....	....
	Cincinnati Cyclones	IHL	39	1	8	9	....	....	....	147	....	....	....	....	....	....	....	....	....	....	....	....	....	....	....	....	....	....
	NHL Totals		**383**	**13**	**62**	**75**	**14**	**57**	**71**	**1070**	**2**	**1**	**2**	**346**	**3.8**	**282**	**18**	**360**	**106**		**13**	**1**	**1**	**2**	**22**	**0**	**0**	**1**

Traded to **Anaheim** by **Quebec** for Anaheim's 4th round choice (later traded to St. Louis — St. Louis selected Jan Horacek) in 1997 Entry Draft, March 9, 1995. Traded to **Carolina** by **Anaheim** with Anaheim's 4th round choice (later traded to Atlanta - Atlanta selected Blake Robson) in 2000 Entry Draft for Stu Grimson and Kevin Haller, August 11, 1998.

• KARPOV, Valeri

Valeri E. RW – L. 5'10", 176 lbs. b: Chelyabinsk, USSR, 8/5/1971. Anaheim's 3rd, 56th overall, in 1993.

Season	Club	League	GP	G	A	Pts	AG	AA	APts	PIM	PP	SH	GW	S	%	TGF	PGF	TGA	PGA	+/–	GP	G	A	Pts	PIM	PP	SH	GW
1988-89	Traktor Chelyabinsk	USSR	5	0	0	0	....	....	....	0	....	....	....	....	....	....	....	....	....	....	....	....	....	....	....	....	....	....
	Soviet Union	EJC-A	6	2	2	4	....	....	....	6	....	....	....	....	....	....	....	....	....	....	....	....	....	....	....	....	....	....
1989-90	Traktor Chelyabinsk	USSR	24	1	2	3	....	....	....	6	....	....	....	....	....	....	....	....	....	....	....	....	....	....	....	....	....	....
1990-91	Traktor Chelyabinsk	USSR	25	8	4	12	....	....	....	15	....	....	....	....	....	....	....	....	....	....	....	....	....	....	....	....	....	....
	Soviet Union	WJC-A	7	0	4	4	....	....	....	2	....	....	....	....	....	....	....	....	....	....	....	....	....	....	....	....	....	....
1991-92	Traktor Chelyabinsk	CIS	44	16	10	26	....	....	....	34	....	....	....	....	....	....	....	....	....	....	....	....	....	....	....	....	....	....
1992-93	CSKA Moscow	CIS	9	2	6	8	....	....	....	0	....	....	....	....	....	....	....	....	....	....	....	....	....	....	....	....	....	....
	Traktor Chelyabinsk	CIS	29	10	15	25	....	....	....	6	....	....	....	....	....	....	....	....	....	....	8	0	1	1	10	....	....	....
	Russia	WC-A	8	4	5	9	....	....	....	0	....	....	....	....	....	....	....	....	....	....	....	....	....	....	....	....	....	....
1993-94	Traktor Chelyabinsk	CIS	32	13	16	29	....	....	....	....	....	....	....	....	....	....	....	....	....	....	6	2	5	7	2	....	....	....
	Russia	Olympics	8	3	1	4	....	....	....	2	....	....	....	....	....	....	....	....	....	....	....	....	....	....	....	....	....	....
1994-95	Traktor Chelyabinsk	CIS	10	6	8	14	....	....	....	8	....	....	....	....	....	....	....	....	....	....	....	....	....	....	....	....	....	....
	Mighty Ducks of Anaheim	**NHL**	**30**	**4**	**7**	**11**	**7**	**10**	**17**	**6**	**0**	**0**	**0**	**48**	**8.3**	**17**	**1**	**20**	**0**	**–4**	....	....	....	....	....	....	....	....
	San Diego Gulls	IHL	5	3	3	6	....	....	....	0	....	....	....	....	....	....	....	....	....	....	....	....	....	....	....	....	....	....
1995-96	**Mighty Ducks of Anaheim**	**NHL**	**37**	**9**	**8**	**17**	**9**	**7**	**16**	**10**	**0**	**0**	**1**	**42**	**21.4**	**20**	**4**	**17**	**0**	**–1**	....	....	....	....	....	....	....	....
	Russia	WC-A	8	3	0	3	....	....	....	6	....	....	....	....	....	....	....	....	....	....	....	....	....	....	....	....	....	....
1996-97	**Mighty Ducks of Anaheim**	**NHL**	**9**	**1**	**0**	**1**	**1**	**0**	**1**	**16**	**0**	**0**	**0**	**4**	**25.0**	**1**	**0**	**4**	**1**	**–2**	....	....	....	....	....	....	....	....
	Baltimore Bandits	AHL	10	4	8	12	....	....	....	8	....	....	....	....	....	....	....	....	....	....	....	....	....	....	....	....	....	....
	Long Beach Ice Dogs	IHL	30	18	17	35	....	....	....	19	....	....	....	....	....	....	....	....	....	....	18	8	7	15	18	....	....	....
1997-98	Metallurg Magnitogorsk	Russia	34	11	14	25	....	....	....	20	....	....	....	....	....	....	....	....	....	....	....	....	....	....	....	....	....	....
1998-99	Metallurg Magnitogorsk	Russia	40	16	14	30	....	....	....	38	....	....	....	....	....	....	....	....	....	....	16	6	*10	*16	14	....	....	....
	Metallurg Magnitogorsk	EuroHL	6	1	1	2	....	....	....	2	....	....	....	....	....	....	....	....	....	....	6	2	1	3	2	....	....	....
	Russia	WC-A	6	0	0	0	....	....	....	0	....	....	....	....	....	....	....	....	....	....	....	....	....	....	....	....	....	....
99-2000	Metallurg Magnitogorsk	Russia	38	9	14	23	....	....	....	22	....	....	....	....	....	....	....	....	....	....	10	3	4	7	8	....	....	....
	Metallurg Magnitogorsk	EuroHL	6	3	4	7	....	....	....	4	....	....	....	....	....	....	....	....	....	....	3	0	1	1	0	....	....	....
	NHL Totals		**76**	**14**	**15**	**29**	**17**	**17**	**34**	**32**	**0**	**0**	**1**	**94**	**14.9**	**38**	**5**	**41**	**1**		....	....	....	....	....	....	....	....

CIS First All-Star Team (1993, 1994)

Signed as a free agent by **Calgary**, September 3, 1997.

• KARPOVTSEV, Alexander

D – R. 6'1", 205 lbs. b: Moscow, USSR, 4/7/1970. Quebec's 7th, 158th overall, in 1990.

Season	Club	League	GP	G	A	Pts	AG	AA	APts	PIM	PP	SH	GW	S	%	TGF	PGF	TGA	PGA	+/–	GP	G	A	Pts	PIM	PP	SH	GW
1987-88	Soviet Union	EJC-A	6	0	2	2	....	....	....	4	....	....	....	....	....	....	....	....	....	....	....	....	....	....	....	....	....	....
1989-90	Dynamo Moscow	USSR	35	1	1	2	....	....	....	27	....	....	....	....	....	....	....	....	....	....	....	....	....	....	....	....	....	....
	Soviet Union	WJC-A	7	0	1	1	....	....	....	8	....	....	....	....	....	....	....	....	....	....	....	....	....	....	....	....	....	....
1990-91	Dynamo Moscow	Fr-Tour	1	0	0	0	....	....	....	2	....	....	....	....	....	....	....	....	....	....	....	....	....	....	....	....	....	....
	Dynamo Moscow	USSR	40	0	5	5	....	....	....	15	....	....	....	....	....	....	....	....	....	....	....	....	....	....	....	....	....	....
	Dynamo Moscow	Super-S	7	0	0	0	....	....	....	6	....	....	....	....	....	....	....	....	....	....	....	....	....	....	....	....	....	....
1991-92	Dynamo Moscow	CIS	35	4	2	6	....	....	....	26	....	....	....	....	....	....	....	....	....	....	....	....	....	....	....	....	....	....
1992-93	Dynamo Moscow	CIS	36	3	11	14	....	....	....	100	....	....	....	....	....	....	....	....	....	....	7	2	1	3	0	....	....	....
	Russia	WC-A	8	0	1	1	....	....	....	10	....	....	....	....	....	....	....	....	....	....	....	....	....	....	....	....	....	....
1993-94♦	**New York Rangers**	**NHL**	**67**	**3**	**15**	**18**	**3**	**12**	**15**	**58**	**1**	**0**	**1**	**78**	**3.8**	**52**	**10**	**41**	**11**	**12**	**17**	**0**	**4**	**4**	**12**	**0**	**0**	**0**
1994-95	Dynamo Moscow	CIS	13	0	2	2	....	....	....	10	....	....	....	....	....	....	....	....	....	....	....	....	....	....	....	....	....	....
	New York Rangers	**NHL**	**47**	**4**	**8**	**12**	**7**	**12**	**19**	**30**	**1**	**0**	**1**	**82**	**4.9**	**29**	**6**	**34**	**7**	**–4**	**8**	**1**	**0**	**1**	**0**	**0**	**0**	**0**
1995-96	**New York Rangers**	**NHL**	**40**	**2**	**16**	**18**	**2**	**13**	**15**	**26**	**1**	**0**	**1**	**71**	**2.8**	**51**	**18**	**24**	**3**	**12**	**6**	**0**	**1**	**1**	**4**	**0**	**0**	**0**
1996-97	Russia	W-Cup	1	0	0	0	....	....	....	0	....	....	....	....	....	....	....	....	....	....	....	....	....	....	....	....	....	....
	New York Rangers	**NHL**	**77**	**9**	**29**	**38**	**10**	**26**	**36**	**59**	**6**	**1**	**0**	**84**	**10.7**	**88**	**28**	**78**	**19**	**1**	**13**	**1**	**3**	**4**	**20**	**1**	**0**	**0**
1997-98	**New York Rangers**	**NHL**	**47**	**3**	**7**	**10**	**4**	**7**	**11**	**38**	**1**	**0**	**1**	**46**	**6.5**	**31**	**7**	**35**	**10**	**–1**	....	....	....	....	....	....	....	....
1998-99	**New York Rangers**	**NHL**	**2**	**1**	**0**	**1**	**1**	**0**	**1**	**0**	**0**	**0**	**0**	**4**	**25.0**	**2**	**0**	**2**	**1**	**1**	....	....	....	....	....	....	....	....
	Toronto Maple Leafs	**NHL**	**56**	**2**	**25**	**27**	**2**	**24**	**26**	**52**	**1**	**0**	**1**	**61**	**3.3**	**81**	**22**	**39**	**18**	**38**	**14**	**1**	**3**	**4**	**12**	**1**	**0**	**0**
99-2000	**Toronto Maple Leafs**	**NHL**	**69**	**3**	**14**	**17**	**3**	**13**	**16**	**54**	**3**	**0**	**0**	**51**	**5.9**	**68**	**21**	**57**	**19**	**9**	**11**	**0**	**3**	**3**	**4**	**0**	**0**	**0**
	NHL Totals		**405**	**27**	**114**	**141**	**32**	**107**	**139**	**317**	**14**	**1**	**5**	**477**	**5.7**	**402**	**112**	**310**	**88**		**69**	**3**	**14**	**17**	**52**	**2**	**0**	**0**

Traded to **NY Rangers** by **Quebec** for Mike Hurlbut, September 7, 1993. Traded to **Toronto** by **NY Rangers** with NY Rangers' 4th round choice (Mirko Murovic) in 1999 Entry Draft for Mathieu Schneider, October 14, 1998.

• KASATONOV, Alexei

D – L. 6'1", 215 lbs. b: Leningrad, USSR, 10/14/1959. New Jersey's 10th, 234th overall, in 1983.

Season	Club	League	GP	G	A	Pts	AG	AA	APts	PIM	PP	SH	GW	S	%	TGF	PGF	TGA	PGA	+/-	GP	G	A	Pts	PIM	PP	SH	GW
			REGULAR SEASON																		PLAYOFFS							
1976-77	SKA Leningrad	USSR	7	0	0	0	....	....	....	0	....	....	....	....	....	....	....	....	....	....	....	....	....	....	....	....	....	....
	Soviet Union	EJC-A	6	3	1	4	....	....	....	6	....	....	....	....	....	....	....	....	....	....	....	....	....	....	....	....	....	....
1977-78	SKA Leningrad	USSR	35	4	7	11	....	....	....	15	....	....	....	....	....	....	....	....	....	....	....	....	....	....	....	....	....	....
	Soviet Union	WJC-A	7	1	2	3	....	....	....	2	....	....	....	....	....	....	....	....	....	....	....	....	....	....	....	....	....	....
1978-79	CSKA Moscow	USSR	40	5	14	19	....	....	....	30	....	....	....	....	....	....	....	....	....	....	....	....	....	....	....	....	....	....
	Soviet Union	WJC-A	6	3	4	7	....	....	....	6	....	....	....	....	....	....	....	....	....	....	....	....	....	....	....	....	....	....
	USSR	Chal-Cup	DID NOT PLAY																									
1979-80	CSKA Moscow	USSR	37	5	8	13	....	....	....	26	....	....	....	....	....	....	....	....	....	....	....	....	....	....	....	....	....	....
	CSKA Moscow	Super-S	5	0	4	4	....	....	....	6	....	....	....	....	....	....	....	....	....	....	....	....	....	....	....	....	....	....
	Soviet Union	Olympics	7	2	5	7	....	....	....	8	....	....	....	....	....	....	....	....	....	....	....	....	....	....	....	....	....	....
1980-81	CSKA Moscow	USSR	47	10	12	22	....	....	....	38	....	....	....	....	....	....	....	....	....	....	....	....	....	....	....	....	....	....
	Soviet Union	WEC-A	8	1	3	4	....	....	....	8	....	....	....	....	....	....	....	....	....	....	....	....	....	....	....	....	....	....
1981-82	Soviet Union	Can-Cup	7	1	*10	11	....	....	....	8	....	....	....	....	....	....	....	....	....	....	....	....	....	....	....	....	....	....
	CSKA Moscow	USSR	46	12	27	39	....	....	....	45	....	....	....	....	....	....	....	....	....	....	....	....	....	....	....	....	....	....
	Soviet Union	WEC-A	10	0	3	3	....	....	....	6	....	....	....	....	....	....	....	....	....	....	....	....	....	....	....	....	....	....
1982-83	CSKA Moscow	USSR	44	12	19	31	....	....	....	37	....	....	....	....	....	....	....	....	....	....	....	....	....	....	....	....	....	....
	CSKA Moscow	Super-S	6	0	3	3	....	....	....	8	....	....	....	....	....	....	....	....	....	....	....	....	....	....	....	....	....	....
	Soviet Union	WEC-A	10	1	10	11	....	....	....	14	....	....	....	....	....	....	....	....	....	....	....	....	....	....	....	....	....	....
1983-84	CSKA Moscow	USSR	39	12	24	36	....	....	....	20	....	....	....	....	....	....	....	....	....	....	....	....	....	....	....	....	....	....
	Soviet Union	Olympics	7	3	3	6	....	....	....	0	....	....	....	....	....	....	....	....	....	....	....	....	....	....	....	....	....	....
1984-85	Soviet Union	Can-Cup	6	1	4	5	....	....	....	2	....	....	....	....	....	....	....	....	....	....	....	....	....	....	....	....	....	....
	CSKA Moscow	USSR	40	18	18	36	....	....	....	26	....	....	....	....	....	....	....	....	....	....	....	....	....	....	....	....	....	....
	Soviet Union	WEC-A	9	5	6	11	....	....	....	19	....	....	....	....	....	....	....	....	....	....	....	....	....	....	....	....	....	....
1985-86	CSKA Moscow	USSR	40	6	17	23	....	....	....	27	....	....	....	....	....	....	....	....	....	....	....	....	....	....	....	....	....	....
	CSKA Moscow	Super-S	6	1	3	4	....	....	....	4	....	....	....	....	....	....	....	....	....	....	....	....	....	....	....	....	....	....
	Soviet Union	WEC-A	10	3	4	7	....	....	....	4	....	....	....	....	....	....	....	....	....	....	....	....	....	....	....	....	....	....
1986-87	CSKA Moscow	USSR	40	13	17	30	....	....	....	16	....	....	....	....	....	....	....	....	....	....	....	....	....	....	....	....	....	....
	USSR	RV-87	2	1	0	1	....	....	....	2	....	....	....	....	....	....	....	....	....	....	....	....	....	....	....	....	....	....
	Soviet Union	WEC-A	10	3	5	8	....	....	....	8	....	....	....	....	....	....	....	....	....	....	....	....	....	....	....	....	....	....
1987-88	Soviet Union	Can-Cup	9	1	4	5	....	....	....	4	....	....	....	....	....	....	....	....	....	....	....	....	....	....	....	....	....	....
	CSKA Moscow	USSR	43	8	12	20	....	....	....	8	....	....	....	....	....	....	....	....	....	....	....	....	....	....	....	....	....	....
	Soviet Union	Olympics	7	2	6	8	....	....	....	0	....	....	....	....	....	....	....	....	....	....	....	....	....	....	....	....	....	....
1988-89	CSKA Moscow	USSR	41	8	14	22	....	....	....	8	....	....	....	....	....	....	....	....	....	....	....	....	....	....	....	....	....	....
	CSKA Moscow	Super-S	7	3	2	5	....	....	....	0	....	....	....	....	....	....	....	....	....	....	....	....	....	....	....	....	....	....
	Soviet Union	WEC-A	10	2	0	2	....	....	....	2	....	....	....	....	....	....	....	....	....	....	....	....	....	....	....	....	....	....
1989-90	CSKA Moscow	Fr-Tour	1	1	0	1	....	....	....	0	....	....	....	....	....	....	....	....	....	....	....	....	....	....	....	....	....	....
	CSKA Moscow	USSR	30	6	7	13	....	....	....	16	....	....	....	....	....	....	....	....	....	....	....	....	....	....	....	....	....	....
	New Jersey Devils	**NHL**	**39**	**6**	**15**	**21**	**5**	**11**	**16**	**16**	**1**	**0**	**0**	**60**	**10.0**	**53**	**10**	**46**	**18**	**15**	**6**	**0**	**3**	**3**	**14**	**0**	**0**	**0**
	Utica Devils	AHL	3	0	2	2	....	....	....	7	....	....	....	....	....	....	....	....	....	....	....	....	....	....	....	....	....	....
1990-91	**New Jersey Devils**	**NHL**	**78**	**10**	**31**	**41**	**9**	**24**	**33**	**76**	**1**	**0**	**3**	**122**	**8.2**	**88**	**15**	**94**	**44**	**23**	**7**	**1**	**3**	**4**	**10**	**0**	**0**	**0**
	Soviet Union	WEC-A	10	3	3	6	....	....	....	8	....	....	....	....	....	....	....	....	....	....	....	....	....	....	....	....	....	....
1991-92	Soviet Union	Can-Cup	5	0	1	1	....	....	....	6	....	....	....	....	....	....	....	....	....	....	....	....	....	....	....	....	....	....
	New Jersey Devils	**NHL**	**76**	**12**	**28**	**40**	**11**	**21**	**32**	**70**	**3**	**2**	**1**	**107**	**11.2**	**106**	**28**	**88**	**24**	**14**	**7**	**1**	**1**	**2**	**12**	**0**	**0**	**0**
1992-93	**New Jersey Devils**	**NHL**	**64**	**3**	**14**	**17**	**2**	**10**	**12**	**57**	**0**	**0**	**0**	**63**	**4.8**	**67**	**3**	**90**	**30**	**4**	**4**	**0**	**0**	**0**	**0**	**0**	**0**	**0**
1993-94	**Mighty Ducks of Anaheim**	**NHL**	**55**	**4**	**18**	**22**	**4**	**14**	**18**	**43**	**1**	**0**	**1**	**81**	**4.9**	**54**	**16**	**60**	**14**	**–8**	....	....	....	....	....	....	....	....
	St. Louis Blues	**NHL**	**8**	**0**	**2**	**2**	**0**	**2**	**2**	**19**	**0**	**0**	**0**	**6**	**0.0**	**13**	**1**	**11**	**4**	**5**	**4**	**2**	**0**	**2**	**2**	**0**	**0**	**0**
1994-95	CSKA Moscow	CIS	9	2	3	5	....	....	....	6	....	....	....	....	....	....	....	....	....	....	....	....	....	....	....	....	....	....
	Boston Bruins	**NHL**	**44**	**2**	**14**	**16**	**4**	**21**	**25**	**33**	**0**	**1**	**0**	**50**	**4.0**	**52**	**19**	**40**	**5**	**–2**	**5**	**0**	**0**	**0**	**2**	**0**	**0**	**0**
1995-96	**Boston Bruins**	**NHL**	**19**	**1**	**0**	**1**	**1**	**0**	**1**	**12**	**0**	**0**	**0**	**15**	**6.7**	**21**	**0**	**23**	**3**	**1**	....	....	....	....	....	....	....	....
	Providence Bruins	AHL	16	3	6	9	....	....	....	10	....	....	....	....	....	....	....	....	....	....	....	....	....	....	....	....	....	....
1996-97	CSKA Moscow	Russia	38	3	20	23	....	....	....	68	....	....	....	....	....	....	....	....	....	....	1	0	0	0	0	....	....	....
	CSKA Moscow	EuroHL	6	0	4	4	....	....	....	2	....	....	....	....	....	....	....	....	....	....	....	....	....	....	....	....	....	....
	NHL Totals		**383**	**38**	**122**	**160**	**36**	**103**	**139**	**326**	**6**	**3**	**5**	**504**	**7.5**	**454**	**92**	**452**	**142**		**33**	**4**	**7**	**11**	**40**	**0**	**0**	**0**

WJC-A All-Star Team (1979) • Named Best Defenseman at WJC-A (1979) • USSR First All-Star Team (1981, 1982, 1983, 1984, 1985, 1986, 1987, 1988) • Canada Cup All-Star Team (1981) • WEC-A All-Star Team (1982, 1983, 1985, 1986, 1991) • Named Best Defenseman at WEC-A (1983) • Played in NHL All-Star Game (1994)

Claimed by **Anaheim** from **New Jersey** in Expansion Draft, June 24, 1993. Traded to **St. Louis** by **Anaheim** for the rights to Maxim Bets and St.Louis' 6th round choice (later traded back to St. Louis — St. Louis selected Denis Hamel) in 1995 Entry Draft, March 21, 1994. Signed as a free agent by **Boston**, June 22, 1994.

• KASPARAITIS, Darius

D – L. 5'11", 212 lbs. b: Elektrenai, USSR, 10/16/1972. NY Islanders' 1st, 5th overall, in 1992.

Season	Club	League	GP	G	A	Pts	AG	AA	APts	PIM	PP	SH	GW	S	%	TGF	PGF	TGA	PGA	+/-	GP	G	A	Pts	PIM	PP	SH	GW
1988-89	Dynamo Moscow	USSR	3	0	0	0	....	....	....	0	....	....	....	....	....	....	....	....	....	....	....	....	....	....	....	....	....	....
1989-90	Dynamo Moscow	USSR	1	0	0	0	....	....	....	0	....	....	....	....	....	....	....	....	....	....	....	....	....	....	....	....	....	....
	Soviet Union	EJC-A	6	1	6	7	....	....	....	12	....	....	....	....	....	....	....	....	....	....	....	....	....	....	....	....	....	....
1990-91	Dynamo Moscow	USSR	17	0	1	1	....	....	....	10	....	....	....	....	....	....	....	....	....	....	....	....	....	....	....	....	....	....
	Soviet Union	WJC-A	6	1	3	4	....	....	....	16	....	....	....	....	....	....	....	....	....	....	....	....	....	....	....	....	....	....
1991-92	Dynamo Moscow	CIS	31	2	10	12	....	....	....	14	....	....	....	....	....	....	....	....	....	....	....	....	....	....	....	....	....	....
	Russia	WJC-A	7	1	5	6	....	....	....	8	....	....	....	....	....	....	....	....	....	....	....	....	....	....	....	....	....	....
	Russia	WC-A	6	2	1	3	....	....	....	4	....	....	....	....	....	....	....	....	....	....	....	....	....	....	....	....	....	....
1992-93	Dynamo Moscow	CIS	7	1	3	4	....	....	....	8	....	....	....	....	....	....	....	....	....	....	....	....	....	....	....	....	....	....
	New York Islanders	**NHL**	**79**	**4**	**17**	**21**	**3**	**12**	**15**	**166**	**0**	**0**	**0**	**92**	**4.3**	**83**	**0**	**97**	**29**	**15**	**18**	**0**	**5**	**5**	**31**	**0**	**0**	**0**
1993-94	**New York Islanders**	**NHL**	**76**	**1**	**10**	**11**	**1**	**8**	**9**	**142**	**0**	**0**	**0**	**81**	**1.2**	**57**	**3**	**96**	**36**	**–6**	**4**	**0**	**0**	**0**	**8**	**0**	**0**	**0**
1994-95	**New York Islanders**	**NHL**	**13**	**0**	**1**	**1**	**0**	**1**	**1**	**22**	**0**	**0**	**0**	**8**	**0.0**	**5**	**0**	**17**	**1**	**–11**	....	....	....	....	....	....	....	....
1995-96	**New York Islanders**	**NHL**	**46**	**1**	**7**	**8**	**1**	**6**	**7**	**93**	**0**	**0**	**0**	**34**	**2.9**	**34**	**2**	**59**	**15**	**–12**	....	....	....	....	....	....	....	....
	Russia	WC-A	8	0	2	2	....	....	....	2	....	....	....	....	....	....	....	....	....	....	....	....	....	....	....	....	....	....
1996-97	Russia	W-Cup	5	0	2	2	....	....	....	14	....	....	....	....	....	....	....	....	....	....	....	....	....	....	....	....	....	....
	New York Islanders	**NHL**	**18**	**0**	**5**	**5**	**0**	**4**	**4**	**16**	**0**	**0**	**0**	**12**	**0.0**	**14**	**0**	**27**	**6**	**–7**	....	....	....	....	....	....	....	....
	Pittsburgh Penguins	**NHL**	**57**	**2**	**16**	**18**	**2**	**14**	**16**	**84**	**0**	**0**	**0**	**46**	**4.3**	**71**	**4**	**69**	**26**	**24**	**5**	**0**	**0**	**0**	**6**	**0**	**0**	**0**
1997-98	**Pittsburgh Penguins**	**NHL**	**81**	**4**	**8**	**12**	**5**	**8**	**13**	**127**	**0**	**2**	**0**	**71**	**5.6**	**50**	**5**	**58**	**16**	**3**	**5**	**0**	**0**	**0**	**8**	**0**	**0**	**0**
	Russia	Olympics	6	0	2	2	....	....	....	6	....	....	....	....	....	....	....	....	....	....	....	....	....	....	....	....	....	....
1998-99	**Pittsburgh Penguins**	**NHL**	**48**	**1**	**4**	**5**	**1**	**4**	**5**	**70**	**0**	**0**	**0**	**32**	**3.1**	**31**	**1**	**26**	**8**	**12**	....	....	....	....	....	....	....	....
99-2000	**Pittsburgh Penguins**	**NHL**	**73**	**3**	**12**	**15**	**3**	**11**	**14**	**146**	**1**	**0**	**1**	**76**	**3.9**	**42**	**3**	**71**	**20**	**–12**	**11**	**1**	**1**	**2**	**10**	**0**	**0**	**0**
	NHL Totals		**491**	**16**	**80**	**96**	**16**	**68**	**84**	**866**	**1**	**2**	**1**	**452**	**3.5**	**387**	**18**	**520**	**157**		**43**	**1**	**6**	**7**	**63**	**0**	**0**	**0**

EJC-A All-Star Team (1990) • Named Best Defenseman at WJC-A (1992)

Traded to **Pittsburgh** by **NY Islanders** with Andreas Johansson for Bryan Smolinski, November 17, 1996.

• KASPER, Steve

Stephen Neil "The Friendly Ghost" C – L. 5'8", 175 lbs. b: Montreal, Que., 9/28/1961. Boston's 3rd, 81st overall, in 1980.

Season	Club	League	GP	G	A	Pts	AG	AA	APts	PIM	PP	SH	GW	S	%	TGF	PGF	TGA	PGA	+/-	GP	G	A	Pts	PIM	PP	SH	GW
1977-78	Verdun Epeviers	QMJHL	63	26	45	71	....	....	....	16	....	....	....	....	....	....	....	....	....	....	....	....	....	....	....	....	....	....
1978-79	Verdun Epeviers	QMJHL	67	37	67	104	....	....	....	53	....	....	....	....	....	....	....	....	....	....	11	7	6	13	22	....	....	....
1979-80	Sorel Black Hawks	QMJHL	70	57	65	122	....	....	....	117	....	....	....	....	....	....	....	....	....	....	....	....	....	....	....	....	....	....
1980-81	Sorel Black Hawks	QMJHL	2	5	2	7	....	....	....	0	....	....	....	....	....	....	....	....	....	....	....	....	....	....	....	....	....	....
	Boston Bruins	**NHL**	**76**	**21**	**35**	**56**	**16**	**23**	**39**	**94**	**5**	**0**	**1**	**165**	**12.7**	**82**	**15**	**67**	**9**	**9**	**3**	**0**	**1**	**1**	**0**	**0**	**0**	**0**
1981-82	**Boston Bruins**	**NHL**	**73**	**20**	**31**	**51**	**16**	**21**	**37**	**72**	**1**	**3**	**3**	**151**	**13.2**	**68**	**7**	**101**	**22**	**–18**	**11**	**3**	**6**	**9**	**22**	**1**	**0**	**0**
1982-83	**Boston Bruins**	**NHL**	**24**	**2**	**6**	**8**	**2**	**4**	**6**	**24**	**0**	**0**	**1**	**26**	**7.7**	**11**	**0**	**26**	**7**	**–8**	**12**	**2**	**1**	**3**	**10**	**0**	**1**	**0**
1983-84	**Boston Bruins**	**NHL**	**27**	**3**	**11**	**14**	**2**	**7**	**9**	**19**	**0**	**0**	**0**	**39**	**7.7**	**18**	**0**	**19**	**4**	**3**	**3**	**0**	**0**	**0**	**7**	**0**	**0**	**0**
1984-85	**Boston Bruins**	**NHL**	**77**	**16**	**24**	**40**	**13**	**16**	**29**	**33**	**0**	**5**	**1**	**144**	**11.1**	**52**	**0**	**95**	**31**	**–12**	**5**	**1**	**0**	**1**	**9**	**0**	**0**	**0**
1985-86	**Boston Bruins**	**NHL**	**80**	**17**	**23**	**40**	**14**	**15**	**29**	**73**	**1**	**3**	**1**	**149**	**11.4**	**57**	**2**	**117**	**52**	**–10**	**3**	**1**	**0**	**1**	**4**	**0**	**1**	**0**
1986-87	**Boston Bruins**	**NHL**	**79**	**20**	**30**	**50**	**17**	**22**	**39**	**51**	**4**	**2**	**2**	**110**	**18.2**	**67**	**6**	**103**	**38**	**–4**	**3**	**0**	**2**	**2**	**0**	**0**	**0**	**0**
1987-88	**Boston Bruins**	**NHL**	**79**	**26**	**44**	**70**	**22**	**32**	**54**	**35**	**9**	**3**	**5**	**166**	**15.7**	**100**	**32**	**109**	**40**	**–1**	**23**	**7**	**6**	**13**	**10**	**0**	**1**	**0**
1988-89	**Boston Bruins**	**NHL**	**49**	**10**	**16**	**26**	**8**	**11**	**19**	**49**	**2**	**0**	**0**	**82**	**12.2**	**38**	**6**	**61**	**27**	**–2**	....	....	....	....	....	....	....	....
	Los Angeles Kings	**NHL**	**29**	**9**	**15**	**24**	**8**	**11**	**19**	**14**	**3**	**2**	**2**	**48**	**18.8**	**27**	**8**	**26**	**7**	**0**	**11**	**1**	**5**	**6**	**10**	**0**	**0**	**0**

Season	Club	League	GP	G	A	Pts	AG	AA	APts	PIM	PP	SH	GW	S	%	TGF	PGF	TGA	PGA	+/-	GP	G	A	Pts	PIM	PP	SH	GW
			REGULAR SEASON																		PLAYOFFS							
1989-90	Los Angeles Kings	NHL	77	17	28	45	15	20	35	27	1	1	4	72	23.6	59	3	102	50	4	10	1	1	2	2	0	0	0
1990-91	Los Angeles Kings	NHL	67	9	19	28	8	14	22	33	0	1	1	70	12.9	42	1	70	32	3	10	4	6	10	8	0	1	0
1991-92	Philadelphia Flyers	NHL	16	3	2	5	3	2	5	10	0	1	0	13	23.1	9	0	20	8	–3	....	....	....	....	....	....	....	....
1992-93	Philadelphia Flyers	NHL	21	1	3	4	1	2	3	2	0	1	0	9	11.1	6	0	25	15	–4	....	....	....	....	....	....	....	....
	Tampa Bay Lightning	NHL	47	3	4	7	2	3	5	18	0	0	0	23	13.0	10	0	45	22	–13	....	....	....	....	....	....	....	....
	NHL Totals		821	177	291	468	147	203	350	554	26	22	21	1267	14.0	646	80	986	364		94	20	28	48	82	1	4	0

Won Frank J. Selke Trophy (1982)

Traded to **LA Kings** by **Boston** for Bob Carpenter to complete transaction that sent Jay Miller to LA Kings (January 22, 1989), January 23, 1989. Traded to **Philadelphia** by **LA Kings** with Steve Duchesne and LA Kings' 4th round choice (Aris Brimanis) in 1991 Entry Draft for Jari Kurri and Jeff Chychrun, May 30, 1991. • Missed remainder of 1991-92 season recovering from knee injury suffered in game vs. Pittsburgh, November 20, 1991. Traded to **Tampa Bay** by **Philadelphia** for Dan Vincelette, December 8, 1992.

• KASTELIC, Ed

Edward P. W – R. 6'4", 215 lbs. b: Toronto, Ont., 1/29/1964. Washington's 4th, 110th overall, in 1982.

Season	Club	League	GP	G	A	Pts	AG	AA	APts	PIM	PP	SH	GW	S	%	TGF	PGF	TGA	PGA	+/-	GP	G	A	Pts	PIM	PP	SH	GW
1980-81	Mississauga Reps	MTHL	51	4	10	14	....	....	....	164	....	....	....	....	....	....	....	....	....	....	....	....	....	....	....	....	....	....
1981-82	London Knights	OHL	68	5	18	23	....	....	....	63	....	....	....	....	....	....	....	....	....	....	4	0	1	1	4	....	....	....
1982-83	London Knights	OHL	68	12	11	23	....	....	....	96	....	....	....	....	....	....	....	....	....	....	3	0	0	0	5	....	....	....
1983-84	London Knights	OHL	68	17	16	33	....	....	....	218	....	....	....	....	....	....	....	....	....	....	8	0	2	2	41	....	....	....
1984-85	Moncton Golden Flames	AHL	62	5	11	16	....	....	....	187	....	....	....	....	....	....	....	....	....	....	....	....	....	....	....	....	....	....
	Binghamton Whalers	AHL	4	0	0	0	....	....	....	7	....	....	....	....	....	....	....	....	....	....	....	....	....	....	....	....	....	....
	Fort Wayne Komets	IHL	5	1	0	1	....	....	....	37	....	....	....	....	....	....	....	....	....	....	....	....	....	....	....	....	....	....
1985-86	Washington Capitals	NHL	15	0	0	0	0	0	0	73	0	0	0	2	0.0	3	0	3	0	0	....	....	....	....	....	....	....	....
	Binghamton Whalers	AHL	23	7	9	16	....	....	....	76	....	....	....	....	....	....	....	....	....	....	....	....	....	....	....	....	....	....
1986-87	Washington Capitals	NHL	23	1	1	2	1	1	2	83	1	0	0	15	6.7	9	5	7	0	–3	5	1	0	1	13	1	0	0
	Binghamton Whalers	AHL	48	17	11	28	....	....	....	124	....	....	....	....	....	....	....	....	....	....	....	....	....	....	....	....	....	....
1987-88	Washington Capitals	NHL	35	1	0	1	1	0	1	78	0	0	0	20	5.0	6	0	9	0	–3	1	0	0	0	19	0	0	0
	Binghamton Whalers	AHL	6	4	1	5	....	....	....	6	....	....	....	....	....	....	....	....	....	....	....	....	....	....	....	....	....	....
1988-89	Hartford Whalers	NHL	10	0	2	2	0	1	1	15	0	0	0	6	0.0	2	0	2	0	0	....	....	....	....	....	....	....	....
	Binghamton Whalers	AHL	35	9	6	15	....	....	....	124	....	....	....	....	....	....	....	....	....	....	....	....	....	....	....	....	....	....
1989-90	Hartford Whalers	NHL	67	6	2	8	5	1	6	198	0	0	0	35	17.1	18	1	20	0	–3	2	0	0	0	0	0	0	0
1990-91	Hartford Whalers	NHL	45	2	2	4	2	2	4	211	0	0	0	15	13.3	5	1	11	0	–7	....	....	....	....	....	....	....	....
1991-92	Hartford Whalers	NHL	25	1	3	4	1	2	3	61	0	0	0	4	25.0	7	1	10	0	–4	....	....	....	....	....	....	....	....
1992-93	Phoenix Roadrunners	IHL	57	11	7	18	....	....	....	158	....	....	....	....	....	....	....	....	....	....	....	....	....	....	....	....	....	....
1993-94	Binghamton Rangers	AHL	44	3	6	9	....	....	....	119	....	....	....	....	....	....	....	....	....	....	....	....	....	....	....	....	....	....
1994-95	HK Olimpija Ljubljana	Slovenia	30	20	15	35	....	....	....	48	....	....	....	....	....	....	....	....	....	....	....	....	....	....	....	....	....	....
1995-96	HK Olimpija Ljubljana	Alpenliga	10	5	5	10	....	....	....	79	....	....	....	....	....	....	....	....	....	....	....	....	....	....	....	....	....	....
	HK Olimpija Ljubljana	Slovenia	31	13	17	30	....	....	....	82	....	....	....	....	....	....	....	....	....	....	....	....	....	....	....	....	....	....
1996-97	HK Olimpija Ljubljana	Slovenia	32	25	24	49	....	....	....	76	....	....	....	....	....	....	....	....	....	....	16	3	2	5	73	....	....	....
1997-98	Star Bulls Rosenheim	Germany	42	2	4	6	....	....	....	108	....	....	....	....	....	....	....	....	....	....	....	....	....	....	....	....	....	....
1998-99	HK Olimpija Ljubljana	Alpenliga	17	4	5	9	....	....	....	47	....	....	....	....	....	....	....	....	....	....	....	....	....	....	....	....	....	....
	Slovenia	WC-Q	3	1	0	1	....	....	....	27	....	....	....	....	....	....	....	....	....	....	....	....	....	....	....	....	....	....
	HC Arcroni Jesenice	Slovenia	STATISTICS NOT AVAILABLE																									
	NHL Totals		220	11	10	21	10	7	17	719	1	0	0	97	11.3	50	8	62	0		8	1	0	1	32	1	0	0

Traded to **Hartford** by **Washington** with Grant Jennings for Mike Millar and Neil Sheehy, July 6, 1988.

• KASZYCKI, Mike

Michael John C – L. 5'9", 190 lbs. b: Milton, Ont., 2/27/1956. NY Islanders' 2nd, 32nd overall, in 1976.

Season	Club	League	GP	G	A	Pts	AG	AA	APts	PIM	PP	SH	GW	S	%	TGF	PGF	TGA	PGA	+/-	GP	G	A	Pts	PIM	PP	SH	GW
1971-72	St. Michael's Midget Majors	MTHL	STATISTICS NOT AVAILABLE																									
1972-73	Dixie Beehives	OHA-B	44	35	54	89	....	....	....	33	....	....	....	....	....	....	....	....	....	....	....	....	....	....	....	....	....	....
1973-74	Dixie Beehives	OHA-B	43	44	55	*99	....	....	....	34	....	....	....	....	....	....	....	....	....	....	....	....	....	....	....	....	....	....
1974-75	Toronto Marlboros	OMJHL	70	41	44	85	....	....	....	48	....	....	....	....	....	....	....	....	....	....	23	11	15	26	21	....	....	....
	Toronto Marlboros	Mem-Cup	4	2	0	2	....	....	....	0	....	....	....	....	....	....	....	....	....	....	....	....	....	....	....	....	....	....
1975-76	Sault Ste. Marie Greyhounds	OMJHL	66	51	*119	*170	....	....	....	38	....	....	....	....	....	....	....	....	....	....	12	10	10	20	8	....	....	....
1976-77	Fort Worth Texans	CHL	76	32	55	87	....	....	....	50	....	....	....	....	....	....	....	....	....	....	6	3	3	6	10	....	....	....
1977-78	New York Islanders	NHL	58	13	29	42	12	22	34	24	3	0	2	85	15.3	59	7	37	0	15	7	1	3	4	4	0	0	0
	Rochester Americans	AHL	6	4	2	6	....	....	....	2	....	....	....	....	....	....	....	....	....	....	....	....	....	....	....	....	....	....
1978-79	New York Islanders	NHL	71	16	18	34	14	13	27	37	2	0	4	89	18.0	46	6	34	1	7	10	1	3	4	4	0	0	0
1979-80	New York Islanders	NHL	16	1	4	5	1	3	4	15	0	0	0	13	7.7	13	3	7	0	3	....	....	....	....	....	....	....	....
	Washington Capitals	NHL	28	7	10	17	6	7	13	10	1	0	0	34	20.6	29	10	24	0	–5	....	....	....	....	....	....	....	....
	Toronto Maple Leafs	NHL	25	4	4	8	3	3	6	10	0	0	0	17	23.5	10	1	25	12	–4	2	0	0	0	2	0	0	0
1980-81	Toronto Maple Leafs	NHL	6	0	2	2	0	1	1	2	0	0	0	3	0.0	2	0	1	1	2	....	....	....	....	....	....	....	....
	Dallas Black Hawks	CHL	42	15	21	36	....	....	....	42	....	....	....	....	....	....	....	....	....	....	6	2	2	4	9	....	....	....
1981-82	New Brunswick Hawks	AHL	80	36	*82	*118	....	....	....	67	....	....	....	....	....	....	....	....	....	....	15	8	*13	*21	17	....	....	....
1982-83	Toronto Maple Leafs	NHL	22	1	13	14	1	9	10	10	0	0	0	19	5.3	20	3	20	3	0	....	....	....	....	....	....	....	....
	St. Catharines Saints	AHL	56	26	42	68	....	....	....	30	....	....	....	....	....	....	....	....	....	....	....	....	....	....	....	....	....	....
1983-84	St. Catharines Saints	AHL	72	39	71	110	....	....	....	51	....	....	....	....	....	....	....	....	....	....	5	1	1	2	7	....	....	....
1984-85	HC Langnau	Switz.	22	12	13	25	....	....	....	....	....	....	....	....	....	....	....	....	....	....	....	....	....	....	....	....	....	....
	Moncton Golden Flames	AHL	30	9	15	24	....	....	....	8	....	....	....	....	....	....	....	....	....	....	....	....	....	....	....	....	....	....
1985-86	HC Ambri-Piotta	Switz.	36	19	19	38	....	....	....	....	....	....	....	....	....	....	....	....	....	....	....	....	....	....	....	....	....	....
1986-87	HC Ambri-Piotta	Switz.	36	23	24	47	....	....	....	....	....	....	....	....	....	....	....	....	....	....	4	1	2	3	0	....	....	....
1987-88	HC Ambri-Piotta	Switz.	30	17	19	36	....	....	....	....	....	....	....	....	....	....	....	....	....	....	4	5	2	7	0	....	....	....
1988-89	EV Zug	Switz.	36	25	22	47	....	....	....	....	....	....	....	....	....	....	....	....	....	....	3	1	2	3	....	....	....	....
	NHL Totals		226	42	80	122	37	58	95	108	6	0	6	260	16.2	179	30	148	17		19	2	6	8	10	0	0	0

OMJHL Second All-Star Team (1976) • AHL First All-Star Team (1982) • Won Fred T. Hunt Memorial Trophy (Sportsmanship - AHL) (1982) • Won John B. Sollenberger Trophy (Top Scorer - AHL) (1982) • Won Les Cunningham Award (MVP - AHL) (1982) • AHL Second All-Star Team (1984)

Traded to **Washington** by **NY Islanders** for Gord Lane, December 7, 1979. Traded to **Toronto** by **Washington** for Pat Ribble, February 16, 1980.

• KEA, Ed

Adrian Joseph D – L. 6'3", 200 lbs. b: Weesp, Holland, 1/19/1948 d: 8/31/1999.

Season	Club	League	GP	G	A	Pts	AG	AA	APts	PIM	PP	SH	GW	S	%	TGF	PGF	TGA	PGA	+/-	GP	G	A	Pts	PIM	PP	SH	GW
1967-68	Collingwood Legionaires	OHA-C	STATISTICS NOT AVAILABLE																									
	Collingwood Kings	OHA-Sr.	2	0	1	1	....	....	....	0	....	....	....	....	....	....	....	....	....	....	....	....	....	....	....	....	....	....
1968-69	Collingwood Legionaires	OHA-C	STATISTICS NOT AVAILABLE																									
	Collingwood Kings	OHA-Sr.	8	0	1	1	....	....	....	4	....	....	....	....	....	....	....	....	....	....	....	....	....	....	....	....	....	....
1969-70	New Jersey Devils	EHL	52	4	18	22	....	....	....	130	....	....	....	....	....	....	....	....	....	....	....	....	....	....	....	....	....	....
1970-71	Seattle Totems	WHL	5	0	0	0	....	....	....	2	....	....	....	....	....	....	....	....	....	....	....	....	....	....	....	....	....	....
	New Jersey Devils	EHL	74	8	26	34	....	....	....	148	....	....	....	....	....	....	....	....	....	....	....	....	....	....	....	....	....	....
1971-72	St. Petersburg Suns	EHL	63	10	39	49	....	....	....	107	....	....	....	....	....	....	....	....	....	....	6	2	2	4	20	....	....	....
1972-73	Omaha Knights	CHL	68	10	22	32	....	....	....	145	....	....	....	....	....	....	....	....	....	....	11	3	3	6	10	....	....	....
1973-74	Atlanta Flames	NHL	3	0	2	2	0	2	2	0	0	0	0	3	0.0	3	0	1	0	2	....	....	....	....	....	....	....	....
	Tulsa Oilers	CHL	51	6	17	23	....	....	....	38	....	....	....	....	....	....	....	....	....	....	....	....	....	....	....	....	....	....
	Omaha Knights	CHL	7	2	1	3	....	....	....	13	....	....	....	....	....	....	....	....	....	....	....	....	....	....	....	....	....	....
1974-75	Atlanta Flames	NHL	50	1	9	10	1	7	8	39	0	0	0	61	1.6	43	2	40	6	7	....	....	....	....	....	....	....	....
	Omaha Knights	CHL	21	6	6	12	....	....	....	26	....	....	....	....	....	....	....	....	....	....	....	....	....	....	....	....	....	....
1975-76	Atlanta Flames	NHL	78	8	19	27	7	14	21	101	1	0	0	125	6.4	93	8	83	19	21	2	0	0	0	7	0	0	0
1976-77	Atlanta Flames	NHL	72	4	21	25	4	16	20	63	0	0	0	112	3.6	73	4	90	21	0	3	0	1	1	2	0	0	0
1977-78	Atlanta Flames	NHL	60	3	23	26	3	18	21	40	0	0	0	78	3.8	79	4	63	13	25	1	0	0	0	0	0	0	0
1978-79	Atlanta Flames	NHL	53	6	18	24	5	13	18	40	2	0	1	53	11.3	57	4	64	9	–2	2	0	0	0	0	0	0	0
	Tulsa Oilers	CHL	2	0	3	3	....	....	....	0	....	....	....	....	....	....	....	....	....	....	....	....	....	....	....	....	....	....
1979-80	St. Louis Blues	NHL	69	3	16	19	3	12	15	79	0	0	1	73	4.1	85	2	90	16	9	3	0	0	0	2	0	0	0
1980-81	St. Louis Blues	NHL	74	3	18	21	2	12	14	60	0	0	0	59	5.1	81	2	97	33	15	11	1	2	3	12	0	0	0

			REGULAR SEASON																		PLAYOFFS							
Season	Club	League	GP	G	A	Pts	AG	AA	APts	PIM	PP	SH	GW	S	%	TGF	PGF	TGA	PGA	+/-	GP	G	A	Pts	PIM	PP	SH	GW
1981-82	**St. Louis Blues**	**NHL**	**78**	**2**	**14**	**16**	**2**	**9**	**11**	**62**	**0**	**0**	**0**	**89**	**2.2**	**87**	**1**	**105**	**38**	**19**	**10**	**1**	**1**	**2**	**16**	**0**	**0**	**0**
1982-83	**St. Louis Blues**	**NHL**	**46**	**0**	**5**	**5**	**0**	**3**	**3**	**24**	**0**	**0**	**0**	**42**	**0.0**	**28**	**0**	**47**	**12**	**–7**	....	....	....	....	....	....	....	....
	Salt Lake Golden Eagles	CHL	9	1	4	5	....	....	....	10	....	....	....	....	....	....	....	....	....	....	....	....	....	....	....	....	....	....
	NHL Totals		**583**	**30**	**145**	**175**	**27**	**106**	**133**	**508**	**3**	**0**	**2**	**695**	**4.3**	**629**	**27**	**680**	**167**		**32**	**2**	**4**	**6**	**39**	**0**	**0**	**0**

CHL Second All-Star Team (1974)

Signed as a free agent by **Atlanta**, October 6, 1972. Traded to **St. Louis** by **Atlanta** with Don Laurence and Atlanta's 2nd round choice (Hakan Nordin) in 1981 Entry Draft for Garry Unger, October 10, 1979. • Suffered career-ending head injury in game vs. Tulsa (CHL), March 9, 1983.

• KEANE, Mike

Michael J. RW – R. 6', 185 lbs. b: Winnipeg, Man., 5/29/1967.

Season	Club	League	GP	G	A	Pts	AG	AA	APts	PIM	PP	SH	GW	S	%	TGF	PGF	TGA	PGA	+/-	GP	G	A	Pts	PIM	PP	SH	GW
1983-84	Winnipeg Monarchs	MAHA	21	17	19	36	....	....	....	59	....	....	....	....	....	....	....	....	....	....	....	....	....	....	....	....	....	....
	Winnipeg Warriors	WHL	1	0	0	0	....	....	....	0	....	....	....	....	....	....	....	....	....	....	....	....	....	....	....	....	....	....
1984-85	Moose Jaw Warriors	WHL	65	17	26	43	....	....	....	141	....	....	....	....	....	....	....	....	....	....	....	....	....	....	....	....	....	....
1985-86	Moose Jaw Warriors	WHL	67	34	49	83	....	....	....	162	....	....	....	....	....	....	....	....	....	....	13	6	8	14	9	....	....	....
1986-87	Moose Jaw Warriors	WHL	53	25	45	70	....	....	....	107	....	....	....	....	....	....	....	....	....	....	9	3	9	12	11	....	....	....
	Sherbrooke Canadiens	AHL	....	....	....	....	....	....	....	....	....	....	....	....	....	....	....	....	....	....	9	2	2	4	16	....	....	....
	Canada	WJC-A	6	0	1	1	....	....	....	4	....	....	....	....	....	....	....	....	....	....	....	....	....	....	....	....	....	....
1987-88	Sherbrooke Canadiens	AHL	78	25	43	68	....	....	....	70	....	....	....	....	....	....	....	....	....	....	6	1	1	2	18	....	....	....
1988-89	**Montreal Canadiens**	**NHL**	**69**	**16**	**19**	**35**	**14**	**13**	**27**	**69**	**5**	**0**	**1**	**90**	**17.8**	**62**	**17**	**43**	**7**	**9**	**21**	**4**	**3**	**7**	**17**	**2**	**0**	**0**
1989-90	**Montreal Canadiens**	**NHL**	**74**	**9**	**15**	**24**	**8**	**11**	**19**	**78**	**1**	**0**	**1**	**92**	**9.8**	**41**	**6**	**52**	**17**	**0**	**11**	**0**	**1**	**1**	**8**	**0**	**0**	**0**
1990-91	Montreal Canadiens	Fr-Tour	3	0	0	0	....	....	....	6	....	....	....	....	....	....	....	....	....	....	....	....	....	....	....	....	....	....
	Montreal Canadiens	**NHL**	**73**	**13**	**23**	**36**	**12**	**17**	**29**	**50**	**2**	**1**	**2**	**109**	**11.9**	**54**	**6**	**54**	**12**	**6**	**12**	**3**	**2**	**5**	**6**	**0**	**0**	**0**
1991-92	**Montreal Canadiens**	**NHL**	**67**	**11**	**30**	**41**	**10**	**23**	**33**	**64**	**2**	**0**	**2**	**116**	**9.5**	**71**	**16**	**51**	**12**	**16**	**8**	**1**	**1**	**2**	**16**	**0**	**0**	**0**
1992-93♦	**Montreal Canadiens**	**NHL**	**77**	**15**	**45**	**60**	**12**	**31**	**43**	**95**	**0**	**0**	**1**	**120**	**12.5**	**79**	**2**	**74**	**26**	**29**	**19**	**2**	**13**	**15**	**6**	**0**	**0**	**0**
1993-94	**Montreal Canadiens**	**NHL**	**80**	**16**	**30**	**46**	**15**	**23**	**38**	**119**	**6**	**2**	**2**	**129**	**12.4**	**78**	**21**	**77**	**26**	**6**	**6**	**3**	**1**	**4**	**4**	**0**	**0**	**0**
1994-95	**Montreal Canadiens**	**NHL**	**48**	**10**	**10**	**20**	**18**	**15**	**33**	**15**	**1**	**0**	**0**	**75**	**13.3**	**30**	**3**	**37**	**15**	**5**	....	....	....	....	....	....	....	....
1995-96	**Montreal Canadiens**	**NHL**	**18**	**0**	**7**	**7**	**0**	**6**	**6**	**6**	**0**	**0**	**0**	**17**	**0.0**	**12**	**3**	**21**	**6**	**–6**	....	....	....	....	....	....	....	....
♦	**Colorado Avalanche**	**NHL**	**55**	**10**	**10**	**20**	**10**	**8**	**18**	**40**	**0**	**2**	**2**	**67**	**14.9**	**29**	**0**	**40**	**12**	**1**	**22**	**3**	**2**	**5**	**16**	**0**	**0**	**1**
1996-97	**Colorado Avalanche**	**NHL**	**81**	**10**	**17**	**27**	**11**	**15**	**26**	**63**	**0**	**1**	**1**	**91**	**11.0**	**43**	**1**	**55**	**15**	**2**	**17**	**3**	**1**	**4**	**24**	**0**	**0**	**1**
1997-98	**New York Rangers**	**NHL**	**70**	**8**	**10**	**18**	**9**	**10**	**19**	**47**	**2**	**0**	**0**	**113**	**7.1**	**25**	**5**	**56**	**24**	**–12**	....	....	....	....	....	....	....	....
	Dallas Stars	**NHL**	**13**	**2**	**3**	**5**	**2**	**3**	**5**	**5**	**0**	**0**	**1**	**15**	**13.3**	**6**	**0**	**8**	**2**	**0**	**17**	**4**	**4**	**8**	**0**	**0**	**1**	**1**
1998-99♦	**Dallas Stars**	**NHL**	**81**	**6**	**23**	**29**	**7**	**22**	**29**	**62**	**1**	**1**	**1**	**106**	**5.7**	**36**	**3**	**42**	**7**	**–2**	**23**	**5**	**2**	**7**	**6**	**0**	**1**	**1**
99-2000	**Dallas Stars**	**NHL**	**81**	**13**	**21**	**34**	**15**	**19**	**34**	**41**	**0**	**4**	**3**	**85**	**15.3**	**44**	**0**	**47**	**12**	**9**	**23**	**2**	**4**	**6**	**14**	**0**	**0**	**0**
	NHL Totals		**887**	**139**	**263**	**402**	**143**	**216**	**359**	**754**	**20**	**11**	**17**	**1225**	**11.3**	**610**	**83**	**657**	**193**		**179**	**30**	**34**	**64**	**117**	**2**	**2**	**4**

Signed as a free agent by **Montreal**, September 25, 1985. Traded to **Colorado** by **Montreal** with Patrick Roy for Andrei Kovalenko, Martin Rucinsky and Jocelyn Thibault, December 6, 1995. Signed as a free agent by **NY Rangers**, July 30, 1997. Traded to **Dallas** by **NY Rangers** with Brian Skrudland and NY Rangers' 6th round choice (Pavel Patera) in 1998 Entry Draft for Todd Harvey, Bob Errey and Dallas' 4th round choice (Boyd Kane) in 1998 Entry Draft, March 24, 1998.

• KEARNS, Dennis

Dennis McAleer D – L. 5'9", 185 lbs. b: Kingston, Ont., 9/27/1945.

Season	Club	League	GP	G	A	Pts	AG	AA	APts	PIM	PP	SH	GW	S	%	TGF	PGF	TGA	PGA	+/-	GP	G	A	Pts	PIM	PP	SH	GW
1965-66	Kingston Canadians	OHA-B	STATISTICS NOT AVAILABLE																									
1966-67	Kingston Aces	OHA-Sr.	40	17	14	31	....	....	....	47	....	....	....	....	....	....	....	....	....	....	....	....	....	....	....	....	....	....
1967-68	Portland Buckaroos	WHL	68	5	15	20	....	....	....	62	....	....	....	....	....	....	....	....	....	....	12	2	4	6	2	....	....	....
1968-69	Portland Buckaroos	WHL	74	2	42	44	....	....	....	81	....	....	....	....	....	....	....	....	....	....	11	2	6	8	13	....	....	....
1969-70	Portland Buckaroos	WHL	72	11	42	53	....	....	....	67	....	....	....	....	....	....	....	....	....	....	8	1	6	7	9	....	....	....
1970-71	Dallas Black Hawks	CHL	65	8	44	52	....	....	....	65	....	....	....	....	....	....	....	....	....	....	10	2	5	7	14	....	....	....
1971-72	**Vancouver Canucks**	**NHL**	**73**	**3**	**26**	**29**	**3**	**22**	**25**	**59**	**2**	**0**	**0**	**103**	**2.9**	**79**	**34**	**77**	**5**	**–27**	....	....	....	....	....	....	....	....
1972-73	**Vancouver Canucks**	**NHL**	**72**	**4**	**33**	**37**	**4**	**26**	**30**	**51**	**2**	**0**	**0**	**113**	**3.5**	**98**	**21**	**116**	**13**	**–26**	....	....	....	....	....	....	....	....
1973-74	**Vancouver Canucks**	**NHL**	**52**	**4**	**13**	**17**	**4**	**11**	**15**	**30**	**2**	**0**	**0**	**61**	**6.6**	**52**	**23**	**51**	**11**	**–11**	....	....	....	....	....	....	....	....
1974-75	**Vancouver Canucks**	**NHL**	**49**	**1**	**11**	**12**	**1**	**8**	**9**	**31**	**1**	**0**	**0**	**71**	**1.4**	**73**	**23**	**56**	**11**	**5**	**4**	**0**	**0**	**0**	**4**	**0**	**0**	**0**
1975-76	**Vancouver Canucks**	**NHL**	**80**	**5**	**46**	**51**	**4**	**34**	**38**	**48**	**1**	**0**	**0**	**118**	**4.2**	**126**	**46**	**101**	**15**	**–6**	**2**	**0**	**1**	**1**	**0**	**0**	**0**	**0**
1976-77	**Vancouver Canucks**	**NHL**	**80**	**5**	**55**	**60**	**4**	**42**	**46**	**60**	**2**	**1**	**1**	**121**	**4.1**	**116**	**39**	**116**	**14**	**–25**	....	....	....	....	....	....	....	....
	Canada	WEC-A	10	0	1	1	....	....	....	2	....	....	....	....	....	....	....	....	....	....	....	....	....	....	....	....	....	....
1977-78	**Vancouver Canucks**	**NHL**	**80**	**4**	**43**	**47**	**4**	**33**	**37**	**27**	**1**	**0**	**2**	**101**	**4.0**	**115**	**48**	**142**	**35**	**–40**	....	....	....	....	....	....	....	....
	Canada	WEC-A	10	0	1	1	....	....	....	14	....	....	....	....	....	....	....	....	....	....	....	....	....	....	....	....	....	....
1978-79	**Vancouver Canucks**	**NHL**	**78**	**3**	**31**	**34**	**3**	**22**	**25**	**28**	**0**	**0**	**0**	**102**	**2.9**	**95**	**22**	**103**	**7**	**–23**	**3**	**1**	**1**	**2**	**2**	**1**	**0**	**0**
1979-80	**Vancouver Canucks**	**NHL**	**67**	**1**	**18**	**19**	**1**	**13**	**14**	**24**	**0**	**0**	**0**	**66**	**1.5**	**70**	**10**	**67**	**9**	**2**	**2**	**0**	**0**	**0**	**2**	**0**	**0**	**0**
1980-81	**Vancouver Canucks**	**NHL**	**46**	**1**	**14**	**15**	**1**	**9**	**10**	**28**	**0**	**0**	**0**	**43**	**2.3**	**43**	**10**	**43**	**3**	**–7**	....	....	....	....	....	....	....	....
	NHL Totals		**677**	**31**	**290**	**321**	**29**	**220**	**249**	**386**	**11**	**1**	**3**	**899**	**3.4**	**867**	**276**	**872**	**123**		**11**	**1**	**2**	**3**	**8**	**1**	**0**	**0**

WHL Second All-Star Team (1969) • WHL First All-Star Team (1970) • CHL First All-Star Team (1971)

Traded to **Chicago** (Dallas-CHL) by **Portland** (WHL) for cash, August, 1970. Claimed by **Vancouver** from **Chicago** in Intra-League Draft, June 8, 1971.

• KEATING, Mike

Mike Joseph LW – L. 6', 185 lbs. b: Toronto, Ont., 1/21/1957. NY Rangers' 3rd, 26th overall, in 1977.

Season	Club	League	GP	G	A	Pts	AG	AA	APts	PIM	PP	SH	GW	S	%	TGF	PGF	TGA	PGA	+/-	GP	G	A	Pts	PIM	PP	SH	GW
1973-74	Seneca Flyers	OHA-B	44	38	51	89	....	....	....	66	....	....	....	....	....	....	....	....	....	....	....	....	....	....	....	....	....	....
1974-75	Hamilton Fincups	OMJHL	53	31	24	55	....	....	....	83	....	....	....	....	....	....	....	....	....	....	16	3	5	8	41	....	....	....
1975-76	Hamilton Fincups	OMJHL	66	42	37	79	....	....	....	82	....	....	....	....	....	....	....	....	....	....	14	7	4	11	8	....	....	....
	Hamilton Fincups	Mem-Cup	3	1	1	2	....	....	....	0	....	....	....	....	....	....	....	....	....	....	....	....	....	....	....	....	....	....
1976-77	St. Catharines Fincups	OMJHL	65	52	61	113	....	....	....	96	....	....	....	....	....	....	....	....	....	....	11	5	4	9	19	....	....	....
	Canada	WJC-A	7	0	2	2	....	....	....	4	....	....	....	....	....	....	....	....	....	....	....	....	....	....	....	....	....	....
1977-78	**New York Rangers**	**NHL**	**1**	**0**	**0**	**0**	**0**	**0**	**0**	**0**	**0**	**0**	**0**	**2**	**0.0**	**0**	**0**	**1**	**0**	**–1**	....	....	....	....	....	....	....	....
	New Haven Nighthawks	AHL	62	15	9	24	....	....	....	12	....	....	....	....	....	....	....	....	....	....	2	0	0	0	0	....	....	....
1978-79	New Haven Nighthawks	AHL	1	0	0	0	....	....	....	0	....	....	....	....	....	....	....	....	....	....	....	....	....	....	....	....	....	....
	Toledo Goaldiggers	IHL	66	26	27	53	....	....	....	54	....	....	....	....	....	....	....	....	....	....	6	4	2	6	14	....	....	....
1979-80	Dayton Gems	IHL	3	1	2	3	....	....	....	0	....	....	....	....	....	....	....	....	....	....	....	....	....	....	....	....	....	....
	Toledo Goaldiggers	IHL	63	31	29	60	....	....	....	58	....	....	....	....	....	....	....	....	....	....	4	2	0	2	8	....	....	....
	NHL Totals		**1**	**0**	**0**	**0**	**0**	**0**	**0**	**0**	**0**	**0**	**0**	**2**	**0.0**	**0**	**0**	**1**	**0**		....	....	....	....	....	....	....	....

• KECZMER, Dan

Daniel L. D – L. 6'1", 190 lbs. b: Mt. Clemens, MI, 5/25/1968. Minnesota's 11th, 201st overall, in 1986.

Season	Club	League	GP	G	A	Pts	AG	AA	APts	PIM	PP	SH	GW	S	%	TGF	PGF	TGA	PGA	+/-	GP	G	A	Pts	PIM	PP	SH	GW
1985-86	Detroit Little Caesars	NAJHL	65	6	48	54	....	....	....	116	....	....	....	....	....	....	....	....	....	....	....	....	....	....	....	....	....	....
1986-87	Lake Superior State	CCHA	38	3	5	8	....	....	....	26	....	....	....	....	....	....	....	....	....	....	....	....	....	....	....	....	....	....
1987-88	Lake Superior State	CCHA	41	2	15	17	....	....	....	34	....	....	....	....	....	....	....	....	....	....	....	....	....	....	....	....	....	....
1988-89	Lake Superior State	CCHA	46	3	26	29	....	....	....	68	....	....	....	....	....	....	....	....	....	....	....	....	....	....	....	....	....	....
1989-90	Lake Superior State	CCHA	43	13	23	36	....	....	....	48	....	....	....	....	....	....	....	....	....	....	....	....	....	....	....	....	....	....
	United States	WEC-A	10	0	0	0	....	....	....	2	....	....	....	....	....	....	....	....	....	....	....	....	....	....	....	....	....	....
1990-91	**Minnesota North Stars**	**NHL**	**9**	**0**	**1**	**1**	**0**	**1**	**1**	**6**	**0**	**0**	**0**	**6**	**0.0**	**2**	**0**	**2**	**0**	**0**	....	....	....	....	....	....	....	....
	Kalamazoo Wings	IHL	60	4	20	24	....	....	....	60	....	....	....	....	....	....	....	....	....	....	9	1	2	3	10	....	....	....
1991-92	United States	Nat-Team	51	3	11	14	....	....	....	56	....	....	....	....	....	....	....	....	....	....	....	....	....	....	....	....	....	....
	Hartford Whalers	**NHL**	**1**	**0**	**0**	**0**	**0**	**0**	**0**	**0**	**0**	**0**	**0**	**2**	**0.0**	**1**	**1**	**1**	**0**	**–1**	....	....	....	....	....	....	....	....
	Springfield Indians	AHL	18	3	4	7	....	....	....	10	....	....	....	....	....	....	....	....	....	....	4	0	0	0	6	....	....	....
1992-93	**Hartford Whalers**	**NHL**	**23**	**4**	**4**	**8**	**3**	**3**	**6**	**28**	**2**	**0**	**1**	**38**	**10.5**	**24**	**4**	**23**	**0**	**–3**	....	....	....	....	....	....	....	....
	Springfield Indians	AHL	37	1	13	14	....	....	....	38	....	....	....	....	....	....	....	....	....	....	12	0	4	4	14	....	....	....
1993-94	**Hartford Whalers**	**NHL**	**12**	**0**	**1**	**1**	**0**	**1**	**1**	**12**	**0**	**0**	**0**	**12**	**0.0**	**8**	**4**	**11**	**1**	**–6**	....	....	....	....	....	....	....	....
	Springfield Indians	AHL	7	0	1	1	....	....	....	4	....	....	....	....	....	....	....	....	....	....	....	....	....	....	....	....	....	....
	Calgary Flames	**NHL**	**57**	**1**	**20**	**21**	**1**	**16**	**17**	**48**	**0**	**0**	**0**	**104**	**1.0**	**72**	**37**	**45**	**8**	**–2**	**3**	**0**	**0**	**0**	**4**	**0**	**0**	**0**
1994-95	**Calgary Flames**	**NHL**	**28**	**2**	**3**	**5**	**4**	**4**	**8**	**10**	**0**	**0**	**0**	**33**	**6.1**	**18**	**2**	**13**	**4**	**7**	**7**	**0**	**1**	**1**	**2**	**0**	**0**	**0**
1995-96	**Calgary Flames**	**NHL**	**13**	**0**	**0**	**0**	**0**	**0**	**0**	**14**	**0**	**0**	**0**	**13**	**0.0**	**3**	**1**	**8**	**0**	**–6**	....	....	....	....	....	....	....	....
	Saint John Flames	AHL	22	3	11	14	....	....	....	14	....	....	....	....	....	....	....	....	....	....	....	....	....	....	....	....	....	....
	Albany River Rats	AHL	17	0	4	4	....	....	....	4	....	....	....	....	....	....	....	....	....	....	1	0	0	0	0	....	....	....
1996-97	**Dallas Stars**	**NHL**	**13**	**0**	**1**	**1**	**0**	**1**	**1**	**6**	**0**	**0**	**0**	**10**	**0.0**	**8**	**0**	**6**	**1**	**3**	....	....	....	....	....	....	....	....
	Michigan K-Wings	IHL	42	3	17	20	....	....	....	24	....	....	....	....	....	....	....	....	....	....	....	....	....	....	....	....	....	....

			REGULAR SEASON																		PLAYOFFS							
Season	Club	League	GP	G	A	Pts	AG	AA	APts	PIM	PP	SH	GW	S	%	TGF	PGF	TGA	PGA	+/–	GP	G	A	Pts	PIM	PP	SH	GW
1997-98	**Dallas Stars**	**NHL**	17	1	2	3	1	2	3	26	0	0	0	9	11.1	11	1	5	0	5	2	0	0	0	2	0	0	0
	Michigan K-Wings	IHL	44	1	11	12	....	....	....	29	....	....	....	....	....	....	....	....	....	....	....	....	....	....	....	....	....	....
1998-99	**Dallas Stars**	**NHL**	22	0	1	1	0	1	1	22	0	0	0	12	0.0	2	0	4	0	–2	....	....	....	....	....	....	....	....
	Michigan K-Wings	IHL	5	0	1	1	....	....	....	2	....	....	....	....	....	....	....	....	....	....	....	....	....	....	....	....	....	....
	Nashville Predators	**NHL**	16	0	0	0	0	0	0	12	0	0	0	12	0.0	7	0	14	4	–3	....	....	....	....	....	....	....	....
	United States	WC-A	6	2	0	2	....	....	....	6	....	....	....	....	....	....	....	....	....	....	....	....	....	....	....	....	....	....
99-2000	**Nashville Predators**	**NHL**	24	0	5	5	0	5	5	28	0	0	0	21	0.0	14	0	27	11	–2	....	....	....	....	....	....	....	....
	Milwaukee Admirals	IHL	18	1	3	4	....	....	....	10	....	....	....	....	....	....	....	....	....	....	....	....	....	....	....	....	....	....
	Worcester IceCats	AHL	25	•1	9	10	....	....	....	12	....	....	....	....	....	....	....	....	....	....	9	0	1	1	10	....	....	....
	NHL Totals		235	8	38	46	9	34	43	212	2	0	1	272	2.9	170	50	159	29		12	0	1	1	8	0	0	0

CCHA Second All-Star Team (1990)

Claimed by **San Jose** from **Minnesota** in Dispersal Draft, May 30, 1991. Traded to **Hartford** by **San Jose** for Dean Evason, October 2, 1991. Traded to **Calgary** by **Hartford** for Jeff Reese, November 19, 1993. Traded to **New Jersey** by **Calgary** with Phil Housley for Tommy Albelin, Cale Hulse and Jocelyn Lemieux, February 26, 1996. Signed as a free agent by **Dallas**, August 19, 1996. Claimed on waivers by **Nashville** from **Dallas**, March 12, 1999. Traded to **St. Louis** by **Nashville** for Rory Fitzpatrick, February 9, 2000.

• KEENAN, Larry

Lawrence Christopher LW – L. 5'11", 175 lbs. b: North Bay, Ont., 10/1/1940.

Season	Club	League	GP	G	A	Pts	AG	AA	APts	PIM	PP	SH	GW	S	%	TGF	PGF	TGA	PGA	+/–	GP	G	A	Pts	PIM	PP	SH	GW
1957-58	St. Michael's Buzzers	OHA-B	STATISTICS NOT AVAILABLE																									
	St. Michael's Majors	OHA-Jr.	3	0	1	1	....	....	....	2	....	....	....	....	....	....	....	....	....	....	....	....	....	....	....	....	....	....
1958-59	St. Michael's Majors	OHA-Jr.	48	17	12	29	....	....	....	24	....	....	....	....	....	....	....	....	....	....	15	5	4	9	0	....	....	....
1959-60	St. Michael's Majors	OHA-Jr.	48	21	20	41	....	....	....	34	....	....	....	....	....	....	....	....	....	....	10	8	10	18	0	....	....	....
1960-61	St. Michael's Majors	OHA-Jr.	48	31	38	69	....	....	....	41	....	....	....	....	....	....	....	....	....	....	20	24	13	37	8	....	....	....
	St. Michael's Majors	Mem-Cup	9	7	6	13	....	....	....	4	....	....	....	....	....	....	....	....	....	....	....	....	....	....	....	....	....	....
1961-62	**Toronto Maple Leafs**	**NHL**	2	0	0	0	0	0	0	0	....	....	....	....	....	....	....	....	....	....	....	....	....	....	....	....	....	....
	Rochester Americans	AHL	57	11	19	30	....	....	....	12	....	....	....	....	....	....	....	....	....	....	2	0	0	0	0	....	....	....
1962-63	Rochester Americans	AHL	64	11	28	39	....	....	....	24	....	....	....	....	....	....	....	....	....	....	2	0	1	1	0	....	....	....
1963-64	Denver Invaders	WHL	66	25	30	55	....	....	....	22	....	....	....	....	....	....	....	....	....	....	6	2	2	4	4	....	....	....
1964-65	Victoria Maple Leafs	WHL	67	35	20	55	....	....	....	27	....	....	....	....	....	....	....	....	....	....	12	5	2	7	8	....	....	....
1965-66	Victoria Maple Leafs	WHL	36	8	18	26	....	....	....	6	....	....	....	....	....	....	....	....	....	....	14	2	4	6	2	....	....	....
1966-67	Victoria Maple Leafs	WHL	17	4	10	14	....	....	....	6	....	....	....	....	....	....	....	....	....	....	....	....	....	....	....	....	....	....
1967-68	**St. Louis Blues**	**NHL**	40	12	8	20	14	8	22	4	4	0	2	102	11.8	26	9	24	0	–7	18	4	5	9	4	1	0	2
1968-69	**St. Louis Blues**	**NHL**	46	5	9	14	5	8	13	6	0	0	2	73	6.8	30	3	8	0	19	12	4	5	9	8	1	2	0
	Kansas City Blues	CHL	7	3	1	4	....	....	....	0	....	....	....	....	....	....	....	....	....	....	....	....	....	....	....	....	....	....
1969-70	**St. Louis Blues**	**NHL**	56	10	23	33	11	22	33	8	3	0	0	113	8.8	60	26	44	2	–8	16	7	6	13	0	4	2	0
	Kansas City Blues	CHL	6	6	2	8	....	....	....	0	....	....	....	....	....	....	....	....	....	....	....	....	....	....	....	....	....	....
1970-71	**St. Louis Blues**	**NHL**	10	1	3	4	1	2	3	0	0	0	0	24	4.2	7	3	1	0	3	....	....	....	....	....	....	....	....
	Buffalo Sabres	**NHL**	51	7	20	27	7	17	24	6	3	0	2	67	10.4	41	9	44	2	–10	....	....	....	....	....	....	....	....
1971-72	**Buffalo Sabres**	**NHL**	14	2	0	2	2	0	2	2	0	0	0	15	13.3	5	1	8	1	–3	....	....	....	....	....	....	....	....
	Philadelphia Flyers	**NHL**	14	1	1	2	1	1	2	2	1	0	1	13	7.7	4	2	7	1	–4	....	....	....	....	....	....	....	....
	Richmond Robins	AHL	23	3	6	9	....	....	....	0	....	....	....	....	....	....	....	....	....	....	....	....	....	....	....	....	....	....
1972-73	Richmond Robins	AHL	35	15	18	33	....	....	....	8	....	....	....	....	....	....	....	....	....	....	3	1	0	1	0	....	....	....
1973-74	Richmond Robins	AHL	68	22	37	59	....	....	....	28	....	....	....	....	....	....	....	....	....	....	5	1	0	1	0	....	....	....
	NHL Totals		233	38	64	102	41	58	99	28	....	....	....	....	....	....	....	....	....		46	15	16	31	12	....	....	....

• Missed majority of 1966-67 season recovering from ankle injury suffered in game vs. San Francisco (WHL), December 3, 1966. Claimed by **St. Louis** from **Toronto** in Expansion Draft, June 6, 1967. Traded to **Buffalo** by **St. Louis** with Jean-Guy Talbot for Bob Baun, November 4, 1970. Traded to **Philadelphia** by **Buffalo** for Larry Mickey, November 16, 1971.

• KEHOE, Rick

Rick Thomas RW – R. 5'11", 180 lbs. b: Windsor, Ont., 7/15/1951. Toronto's 1st, 22nd overall, in 1971.

Season	Club	League	GP	G	A	Pts	AG	AA	APts	PIM	PP	SH	GW	S	%	TGF	PGF	TGA	PGA	+/–	GP	G	A	Pts	PIM	PP	SH	GW
1969-70	London Knights	OHA-Jr.	23	3	2	5	....	....	....	6	....	....	....	....	....	....	....	....	....	....	....	....	....	....	....	....	....	....
	Hamilton Red Wings	OHA-Jr.	32	2	4	6	....	....	....	77	....	....	....	....	....	....	....	....	....	....	....	....	....	....	....	....	....	....
1970-71	Hamilton Red Wings	OHA-Jr.	58	39	41	80	....	....	....	43	....	....	....	....	....	....	....	....	....	....	7	4	0	4	2	....	....	....
1971-72	**Toronto Maple Leafs**	**NHL**	38	8	8	16	8	7	15	4	2	0	0	70	11.4	24	5	20	0	–1	2	0	0	0	2	0	0	0
	Tulsa Oilers	CHL	32	18	21	39	....	....	....	20	....	....	....	....	....	....	....	....	....	....	....	....	....	....	....	....	....	....
1972-73	**Toronto Maple Leafs**	**NHL**	77	33	42	75	31	33	64	20	2	0	5	204	16.2	98	22	87	0	–11	....	....	....	....	....	....	....	....
1973-74	**Toronto Maple Leafs**	**NHL**	69	18	22	40	17	18	35	8	3	0	3	197	9.1	72	12	41	0	19	....	....	....	....	....	....	....	....
1974-75	**Pittsburgh Penguins**	**NHL**	76	32	31	63	28	23	51	22	3	1	0	240	13.3	98	17	64	1	18	9	0	2	2	0	0	0	0
1975-76	**Pittsburgh Penguins**	**NHL**	71	29	47	76	25	35	60	6	5	0	2	180	16.1	102	18	75	0	9	3	0	0	0	0	0	0	0
1976-77	**Pittsburgh Penguins**	**NHL**	80	30	27	57	27	21	48	10	7	0	5	250	12.0	88	22	71	0	–5	3	0	2	2	0	0	0	0
1977-78	**Pittsburgh Penguins**	**NHL**	70	29	21	50	26	16	42	10	7	0	2	177	16.4	72	20	75	5	–18	....	....	....	....	....	....	....	....
1978-79	**Pittsburgh Penguins**	**NHL**	57	27	18	45	23	13	36	2	7	0	3	165	16.4	73	24	36	1	14	7	0	2	2	0	0	0	0
1979-80	**Pittsburgh Penguins**	**NHL**	79	30	30	60	26	22	48	4	7	0	3	239	12.6	86	23	66	0	–3	5	2	5	7	0	2	0	0
1980-81	**Pittsburgh Penguins**	**NHL**	80	55	33	88	43	22	65	6	20	0	5	299	18.4	135	65	79	0	–9	5	0	3	3	0	0	0	0
1981-82	**Pittsburgh Penguins**	**NHL**	71	33	52	85	26	35	61	8	17	0	1	249	13.3	119	67	80	1	–27	5	2	3	5	2	0	0	2
1982-83	**Pittsburgh Penguins**	**NHL**	75	29	36	65	24	25	49	12	15	0	2	203	14.3	99	61	83	0	–45	....	....	....	....	....	....	....	....
1983-84	**Pittsburgh Penguins**	**NHL**	57	18	27	45	14	18	32	8	7	0	3	156	11.5	58	25	54	1	–20	....	....	....	....	....	....	....	....
1984-85	**Pittsburgh Penguins**	**NHL**	6	0	2	2	0	1	1	0	0	0	0	7	0.0	3	0	3	0	0	....	....	....	....	....	....	....	....
1985-1987	**Pittsburgh Penguins**	**NHL**	DID NOT PLAY – SCOUTING																									
1987-1997	**Pittsburgh Penguins**	**NHL**	DID NOT PLAY – ASSISTANT COACH																									
1997-1999	**Pittsburgh Penguins**	**NHL**	DID NOT PLAY – SCOUTING																									
1999-2000	**Pittsburgh Penguins**	**NHL**	DID NOT PLAY – SCOUTING																									
	Wilkes-Barre Penguins	AHL	DID NOT PLAY – ASSISTANT COACH																									
	Pittsburgh Penguins	**NHL**	DID NOT PLAY – ASSISTANT COACH																									
	NHL Totals		906	371	396	767	318	289	607	120	102	1	34	2636	14.1	1127	381	834	9		39	4	17	21	4	2	0	2

Won Lady Byng Trophy (1981) • Played in NHL All-Star Game (1981, 1983)

Traded to **Pittsburgh** by **Toronto** for Blaine Stoughton and future considerations, September 13, 1974. • Suffered eventual career-ending neck injury in game vs. Quebec, February 13, 1984. • Named interim Assistant Coach of **Pittsburgh**, November 2, 1999. • Named Assistant Coach of **Pittsburgh**, June 22, 2000.

• KEKALAINEN, Jarmo

LW – L. 6', 190 lbs. b: Tampere, Finland, 7/3/1966.

Season	Club	League	GP	G	A	Pts	AG	AA	APts	PIM	PP	SH	GW	S	%	TGF	PGF	TGA	PGA	+/–	GP	G	A	Pts	PIM	PP	SH	GW
1985-86	Ilves Tampere	Finland	29	6	6	12	....	....	....	8	....	....	....	....	....	....	....	....	....	....	....	....	....	....	....	....	....	....
	Finland	WJC-A	7	4	3	7	....	....	....	4	....	....	....	....	....	....	....	....	....	....	....	....	....	....	....	....	....	....
1986-87	Ilves Tampere	Finland	42	3	4	7	....	....	....	4	....	....	....	....	....	....	....	....	....	....	....	....	....	....	....	....	....	....
1987-88	Clarkson University	ECAC	32	7	11	18	....	....	....	38	....	....	....	....	....	....	....	....	....	....	....	....	....	....	....	....	....	....
1988-89	Clarkson University	ECAC	31	19	25	44	....	....	....	47	....	....	....	....	....	....	....	....	....	....	....	....	....	....	....	....	....	....
1989-90	Clarkson University	ECAC	8	9	9	18	....	....	....	4	....	....	....	....	....	....	....	....	....	....	....	....	....	....	....	....	....	....
	Boston Bruins	**NHL**	11	2	2	4	2	1	3	8	0	0	1	7	28.6	4	1	1	0	2	....	....	....	....	....	....	....	....
	Maine Mariners	AHL	18	5	11	16	....	....	....	6	....	....	....	....	....	....	....	....	....	....	....	....	....	....	....	....	....	....
1990-91	**Boston Bruins**	**NHL**	16	2	1	3	2	1	3	6	0	0	0	12	16.7	7	0	7	0	0	....	....	....	....	....	....	....	....
	Maine Mariners	AHL	11	2	4	6	....	....	....	4	....	....	....	....	....	....	....	....	....	....	1	0	1	1	0	....	....	....
1991-92	Finland	Can-Cup	5	0	1	1	....	....	....	0	....	....	....	....	....	....	....	....	....	....	....	....	....	....	....	....	....	....
	KalPa Kuopio	Finland	24	2	8	10	....	....	....	24	....	....	....	....	....	....	....	....	....	....	....	....	....	....	....	....	....	....
1992-93	Tappara Tampere	Finland	47	15	12	27	....	....	....	34	....	....	....	....	....	....	....	....	....	....	....	....	....	....	....	....	....	....
1993-94	**Ottawa Senators**	**NHL**	28	1	5	6	1	4	5	14	0	0	0	18	5.6	11	1	30	12	–8	....	....	....	....	....	....	....	....
	P.E.I. Senators	AHL	18	6	6	12	....	....	....	18	....	....	....	....	....	....	....	....	....	....	....	....	....	....	....	....	....	....
1994-95	Vasteras IK	Sweden	23	1	5	6	....	....	....	24	....	....	....	....	....	....	....	....	....	....	1	0	0	0	0	....	....	....
	NHL Totals		55	5	8	13	5	6	11	28	0	0	1	37	13.5	22	2	38	12		....	....	....	....	....	....	....	....

ECAC First All-Star Team (1989)

Signed as a free agent by **Boston**, May 3, 1989. Signed as a free agent by **Ottawa**, August 13, 1993.

• KELLGREN, Christer

RW – L. 6', 173 lbs. b: Goteborg, Sweden, 8/15/1958.

			REGULAR SEASON																		PLAYOFFS							
Season	Club	League	GP	G	A	Pts	AG	AA	APts	PIM	PP	SH	GW	S	%	TGF	PGF	TGA	PGA	+/–	GP	G	A	Pts	PIM	PP	SH	GW
1974-75	Vastra Frolunda	Sweden-Jr.	....	....	....	....	....	....	....	....	....	....	....	....	....	....	....	....	....	....	2	0	0	0	*12	....	....	....
1975-76	Vastra Frolunda	Sweden-Jr.	STATISTICS NOT AVAILABLE																									
1976-77	Vastra Frolunda	Swede-Jr.	STATISTICS NOT AVAILABLE																									
	Vastra Frolunda	Sweden	1	0	0	0	....	....	....	0	....	....	....	....	....	....	....	....	....	....	....	....	....	....	....	....	....	....
1977-78	Vastra Frolunda	Swede-Jr.	STATISTICS NOT AVAILABLE																									
	Vastra Frolunda	Sweden	3	0	0	0	....	....	....	0	....	....	....	....	....	....	....	....	....	....	....	....	....	....	....	....	....	....
1978-79	Vastra Frolunda	Sweden	14	1	0	1	....	....	....	2	....	....	....	....	....	....	....	....	....	....	....	....	....	....	....	....	....	....
1979-80	Vastra Frolunda	Sweden	27	3	4	7	....	....	....	4	....	....	....	....	....	....	....	....	....	....	8	1	*4	5	2	....	....	....
1980-81	Vastra Frolunda	Sweden	36	20	10	30	....	....	....	20	....	....	....	....	....	....	....	....	....	....	2	1	1	2	4	....	....	....
1981-82	**Colorado Rockies**	**NHL**	**5**	**0**	**0**	**0**	**0**	**0**	**0**	**0**	**0**	**0**	**0**	**4**	**0.0**	**1**	**0**	**5**	**0**	**–4**	....	....	....	....	....	....	....	....
	Fort Worth Texans	CHL	60	9	10	19	....	....	....	6	....	....	....	....	....	....	....	....	....	....	....	....	....	....	....	....	....	....
1982-83	Vastra Frolunda	Sweden	36	16	9	25	....	....	....	26	....	....	....	....	....	....	....	....	....	....	....	....	....	....	....	....	....	....
1983-84	Vastra Frolunda	Sweden	36	17	12	29	....	....	....	32	....	....	....	....	....	....	....	....	....	....	....	....	....	....	....	....	....	....
1984-85	Vastra Frolunda	Sweden-2	32	22	18	40	....	....	....	24	....	....	....	....	....	....	....	....	....	....	....	....	....	....	....	....	....	....
1985-86	Vastra Frolunda	Sweden-2	32	20	19	39	....	....	....	14	....	....	....	....	....	....	....	....	....	....	3	0	7	7	0	....	....	....
1986-87	Vastra Frolunda	Sweden-2	30	24	24	48	....	....	....	24	....	....	....	....	....	....	....	....	....	....	2	0	0	0	6	....	....	....
1987-88	Vastra Frolunda	Sweden-2	35	25	27	52	....	....	....	26	....	....	....	....	....	....	....	....	....	....	9	2	2	4	14	....	....	....
1988-89	Vastra Frolunda	Sweden-2	24	9	5	14	....	....	....	14	....	....	....	....	....	....	....	....	....	....	8	0	3	3	2	....	....	....
	NHL Totals		**5**	**0**	**0**	**0**	**0**	**0**	**0**	**0**	**0**	**0**	**0**	**4**	**0.0**	**1**	**0**	**5**	**0**		....	....	....	....	....	....	....	....

Signed as a free agent by **Colorado**, May 11, 1981.

• KELLY, Bob

John Robert "Houndog" LW – L. 6'2", 195 lbs. b: Fort William, Ont., 6/6/1946. Toronto's 1st, 16th overall, in 1967.

Season	Club	League	GP	G	A	Pts	AG	AA	APts	PIM	PP	SH	GW	S	%	TGF	PGF	TGA	PGA	+/–	GP	G	A	Pts	PIM	PP	SH	GW
1966-67	Port Arthur Marrs	TBJHL	5	0	2	2	....	....	....	13	....	....	....	....	....	....	....	....	....	....	....	....	....	....	....	....	....	....
	Port Arthur Marrs	Mem-Cup	6	3	1	4	....	....	....	2	....	....	....	....	....	....	....	....	....	....	....	....	....	....	....	....	....	....
1967-68	Port Huron Flags	IHL	65	11	26	37	....	....	....	216	....	....	....	....	....	....	....	....	....	....	....	....	....	....	....	....	....	....
1968-69	Port Huron–Columbus	IHL	59	9	15	24	....	....	....	55	....	....	....	....	....	....	....	....	....	....	3	1	1	2	2	....	....	....
1969-70	Providence Reds	AHL	65	2	5	7	....	....	....	28	....	....	....	....	....	....	....	....	....	....	....	....	....	....	....	....	....	....
1970-71	Providence Reds	AHL	26	1	0	1	....	....	....	31	....	....	....	....	....	....	....	....	....	....	....	....	....	....	....	....	....	....
	Des Moines Oak Leafs	IHL	24	3	14	17	....	....	....	58	....	....	....	....	....	....	....	....	....	....	....	....	....	....	....	....	....	....
1971-72	Omaha Knights	CHL	3	2	2	4	....	....	....	4	....	....	....	....	....	....	....	....	....	....	....	....	....	....	....	....	....	....
	Oklahoma City Blazers	CHL	6	1	2	3	....	....	....	22	....	....	....	....	....	....	....	....	....	....	....	....	....	....	....	....	....	....
	Des Moines Oak Leafs	IHL	55	26	23	49	....	....	....	123	....	....	....	....	....	....	....	....	....	....	3	0	1	1	0	....	....	....
1972-73	Rochester Americans	AHL	70	27	35	62	....	....	....	206	....	....	....	....	....	....	....	....	....	....	6	4	4	8	18	....	....	....
1973-74	**St. Louis Blues**	**NHL**	**37**	**9**	**8**	**17**	**9**	**7**	**16**	**45**	**2**	**0**	**0**	**70**	**12.9**	**26**	**5**	**20**	**0**	**1**	....	....	....	....	....	....	....	....
	Pittsburgh Penguins	**NHL**	**30**	**7**	**10**	**17**	**7**	**8**	**15**	**78**	**1**	**0**	**2**	**101**	**6.9**	**29**	**1**	**38**	**5**	**–5**	....	....	....	....	....	....	....	....
1974-75	**Pittsburgh Penguins**	**NHL**	**69**	**27**	**24**	**51**	**24**	**18**	**42**	**120**	**5**	**0**	**1**	**223**	**12.1**	**85**	**18**	**63**	**2**	**6**	**9**	**5**	**3**	**8**	**17**	**1**	**0**	**0**
1975-76	**Pittsburgh Penguins**	**NHL**	**77**	**25**	**30**	**55**	**22**	**22**	**44**	**149**	**5**	**0**	**4**	**193**	**13.0**	**89**	**11**	**75**	**1**	**4**	**3**	**0**	**0**	**0**	**2**	**0**	**0**	**0**
1976-77	**Pittsburgh Penguins**	**NHL**	**74**	**10**	**21**	**31**	**9**	**16**	**25**	**115**	**1**	**0**	**1**	**136**	**7.4**	**53**	**4**	**38**	**2**	**13**	**3**	**1**	**0**	**1**	**4**	**0**	**0**	**0**
1977-78	**Chicago Black Hawks**	**NHL**	**75**	**7**	**11**	**18**	**6**	**8**	**14**	**95**	**0**	**0**	**2**	**155**	**4.5**	**26**	**6**	**47**	**1**	**–26**	**4**	**0**	**0**	**0**	**8**	**0**	**0**	**0**
1978-79	**Chicago Black Hawks**	**NHL**	**63**	**2**	**5**	**7**	**2**	**4**	**6**	**85**	**0**	**0**	**0**	**59**	**3.4**	**11**	**1**	**20**	**0**	**–10**	**4**	**0**	**0**	**0**	**9**	**0**	**0**	**0**
	New Brunswick Hawks	AHL	7	0	0	0	....	....	....	60	....	....	....	....	....	....	....	....	....	....	....	....	....	....	....	....	....	....
1979-80	Cincinnati Stingers	CHL	2	0	0	0	....	....	....	5	....	....	....	....	....	....	....	....	....	....	....	....	....	....	....	....	....	....
	Houston Apollos	CHL	2	0	0	0	....	....	....	10	....	....	....	....	....	....	....	....	....	....	....	....	....	....	....	....	....	....
	NHL Totals		**425**	**87**	**109**	**196**	**79**	**83**	**162**	**687**	**14**	**0**	**10**	**937**	**9.3**	**319**	**46**	**301**	**11**		**23**	**6**	**3**	**9**	**40**	**1**	**0**	**0**

Traded to **Columbus** (IHL) by **Port Huron** (IHL) for cash, November, 1968. Signed as a free agent by **Providence** (AHL), October, 1969. Traded to **NY Rangers** by **Columbus** (IHL) for cash, October, 1970. Traded to **Rochester** (AHL) by **NY Rangers** for $7,500, October, 1972. Traded to **NY Rangers** by **Rochester** (AHL) for Bill Knibbs and $20,000, June, 1973. Traded to **St. Louis** by **NY Rangers** for Norm Dennis and Don Borgeson, September 8, 1973. Traded to **Pittsburgh** by **St. Louis** with Steve Durbano and Ab DeMarco Jr. for Bryan Watson, Greg Polis and Pittsburgh's 2nd round choice (Bob Hess) in 1974 Amateur Draft, January 17, 1974. Signed as a free agent by **Chicago**, August 17, 1977.

• KELLY, Bob

Robert James "Battleship" LW – L. 5'10", 200 lbs. b: Oakville, Ont., 11/25/1950. Philadelphia's 2nd, 32nd overall, in 1970.

Season	Club	League	GP	G	A	Pts	AG	AA	APts	PIM	PP	SH	GW	S	%	TGF	PGF	TGA	PGA	+/–	GP	G	A	Pts	PIM	PP	SH	GW
1968-69	Oshawa Generals	OHA-Jr.	54	21	23	44	....	....	....	128	....	....	....	....	....	....	....	....	....	....	....	....	....	....	....	....	....	....
1969-70	Oshawa Generals	OHA-Jr.	53	21	31	52	....	....	....	117	....	....	....	....	....	....	....	....	....	....	6	2	1	3	7	....	....	....
1970-71	**Philadelphia Flyers**	**NHL**	**76**	**14**	**18**	**32**	**14**	**15**	**29**	**70**	**1**	**0**	**2**	**178**	**7.9**	**52**	**6**	**40**	**1**	**7**	**4**	**1**	**0**	**1**	**2**	**0**	**0**	**0**
1971-72	**Philadelphia Flyers**	**NHL**	**78**	**14**	**15**	**29**	**14**	**13**	**27**	**157**	**0**	**0**	**3**	**117**	**12.0**	**41**	**1**	**25**	**1**	**16**	....	....	....	....	....	....	....	....
1972-73	**Philadelphia Flyers**	**NHL**	**77**	**10**	**11**	**21**	**9**	**9**	**18**	**238**	**0**	**0**	**2**	**125**	**8.0**	**35**	**0**	**35**	**1**	**1**	**11**	**0**	**1**	**1**	**8**	**0**	**0**	**0**
1973-74♦	**Philadelphia Flyers**	**NHL**	**65**	**4**	**10**	**14**	**4**	**8**	**12**	**130**	**0**	**0**	**1**	**59**	**6.8**	**20**	**0**	**10**	**0**	**10**	**5**	**0**	**0**	**0**	**11**	**0**	**0**	**0**
1974-75♦	**Philadelphia Flyers**	**NHL**	**67**	**11**	**18**	**29**	**10**	**13**	**23**	**99**	**0**	**0**	**1**	**106**	**10.4**	**40**	**0**	**19**	**0**	**21**	**16**	**3**	**3**	**6**	**15**	**0**	**0**	**1**
1975-76	**Philadelphia Flyers**	**NHL**	**79**	**12**	**8**	**20**	**11**	**6**	**17**	**125**	**0**	**0**	**3**	**103**	**11.7**	**36**	**2**	**31**	**0**	**3**	**16**	**0**	**2**	**2**	**44**	**0**	**0**	**0**
1976-77	**Philadelphia Flyers**	**NHL**	**73**	**22**	**24**	**46**	**20**	**18**	**38**	**117**	**2**	**0**	**5**	**102**	**21.6**	**62**	**3**	**32**	**0**	**27**	**10**	**0**	**1**	**1**	**18**	**0**	**0**	**0**
1977-78	**Philadelphia Flyers**	**NHL**	**74**	**19**	**13**	**32**	**17**	**10**	**27**	**95**	**0**	**0**	**5**	**96**	**19.8**	**45**	**1**	**29**	**0**	**15**	**12**	**3**	**5**	**8**	**26**	**0**	**0**	**0**
1978-79	**Philadelphia Flyers**	**NHL**	**77**	**7**	**31**	**38**	**6**	**22**	**28**	**132**	**1**	**0**	**0**	**85**	**8.2**	**53**	**5**	**33**	**0**	**15**	**8**	**1**	**1**	**2**	**10**	**1**	**0**	**0**
1979-80	**Philadelphia Flyers**	**NHL**	**75**	**15**	**20**	**35**	**13**	**15**	**28**	**122**	**2**	**0**	**2**	**112**	**13.4**	**57**	**5**	**33**	**0**	**19**	**19**	**1**	**1**	**2**	**38**	**0**	**0**	**0**
1980-81	**Washington Capitals**	**NHL**	**80**	**26**	**36**	**62**	**20**	**24**	**44**	**157**	**8**	**0**	**4**	**125**	**20.8**	**92**	**26**	**79**	**0**	**–13**	....	....	....	....	....	....	....	....
1981-82	Washington Capitals	DN-Cup	4	1	0	1	....	....	....	....	....	....	....	....	....	....	....	....	....	....	....	....	....	....	....	....	....	....
	Washington Capitals	**NHL**	**16**	**0**	**4**	**4**	**0**	**3**	**3**	**12**	**0**	**0**	**0**	**24**	**0.0**	**7**	**3**	**16**	**0**	**–12**	....	....	....	....	....	....	....	....
	NHL Totals		**837**	**154**	**208**	**362**	**138**	**156**	**294**	**1454**	**14**	**0**	**28**	**1232**	**12.5**	**540**	**52**	**382**	**3**		**101**	**9**	**14**	**23**	**172**	**1**	**0**	**1**

Traded to **Washington** by **Philadelphia** for Washington's 3rd round choice (Bill Campbell) in 1982 Entry Draft, August 21, 1980.

• KELLY, Dave

David Leslie RW – R. 6'2", 205 lbs. b: Chatham, Ont., 9/20/1952.

Season	Club	League	GP	G	A	Pts	AG	AA	APts	PIM	PP	SH	GW	S	%	TGF	PGF	TGA	PGA	+/–	GP	G	A	Pts	PIM	PP	SH	GW
1969-70	Dresden Kings	OJHL	36	35	21	56	....	....	....	109	....	....	....	....	....	....	....	....	....	....	....	....	....	....	....	....	....	....
1970-71	Streetsville Derbys	OHA-B	STATISTICS NOT AVAILABLE																									
1971-72	Providence College	ECAC	DID NOT PLAY – FRESHMAN																									
1972-73	Providence College	ECAC	22	11	12	23	....	....	....	54	....	....	....	....	....	....	....	....	....	....	....	....	....	....	....	....	....	....
1973-74	Providence College	ECAC	25	10	8	18	....	....	....	56	....	....	....	....	....	....	....	....	....	....	....	....	....	....	....	....	....	....
1974-75	Providence College	ECAC	27	21	22	43	....	....	....	66	....	....	....	....	....	....	....	....	....	....	....	....	....	....	....	....	....	....
1975-76	Richmond Robins	AHL	74	21	19	40	....	....	....	149	....	....	....	....	....	....	....	....	....	....	8	3	4	7	19	....	....	....
1976-77	Springfield Indians	AHL	3	0	1	1	....	....	....	0	....	....	....	....	....	....	....	....	....	....	....	....	....	....	....	....	....	....
	Rhode Island Reds	AHL	45	16	19	35	....	....	....	95	....	....	....	....	....	....	....	....	....	....	....	....	....	....	....	....	....	....
	Detroit Red Wings	**NHL**	**16**	**2**	**0**	**2**	**2**	**0**	**2**	**4**	**0**	**0**	**1**	**17**	**11.8**	**3**	**0**	**11**	**0**	**–8**	....	....	....	....	....	....	....	....
	Kansas City Blues	CHL	....	....	....	....	....	....	....	....	....	....	....	....	....	....	....	....	....	....	10	*4	1	5	6	....	....	....
1977-78	Philadelphia Firebirds	AHL	74	15	13	28	....	....	....	89	....	....	....	....	....	....	....	....	....	....	4	3	2	5	2	....	....	....
	NHL Totals		**16**	**2**	**0**	**2**	**2**	**0**	**2**	**4**	**0**	**0**	**1**	**17**	**11.8**	**3**	**0**	**11**	**0**		....	....	....	....	....	....	....	....

Signed as a free agent by **Philadelphia**, August 12, 1975. Traded to **Detroit** by **Philadelphia** with Terry Murray, Bob Ritchie and Steve Coates for Rick Lapointe and Mike Korney, February 17, 1977.

• KELLY, John Paul

John Paul "Jeep" LW – L. 6'1", 215 lbs. b: Edmonton, Alta., 11/15/1959. Los Angeles' 4th, 50th overall, in 1979.

Season	Club	League	GP	G	A	Pts	AG	AA	APts	PIM	PP	SH	GW	S	%	TGF	PGF	TGA	PGA	+/–	GP	G	A	Pts	PIM	PP	SH	GW
1975-76	Maple Ridge Blazers	BCJHL	64	34	35	69	....	....	....	68	....	....	....	....	....	....	....	....	....	....	....	....	....	....	....	....	....	....
	New Westminster Bruins	WCJHL	2	0	0	0	....	....	....	2	....	....	....	....	....	....	....	....	....	....	....	....	....	....	....	....	....	....
1976-77	New Westminster Bruins	WCJHL	68	35	24	59	....	....	....	62	....	....	....	....	....	....	....	....	....	....	5	2	2	4	0	....	....	....
	New Westminster Bruins	Mem-Cup	DID NOT PLAY																									
1977-78	New Westminster Bruins	WCJHL	70	26	30	56	....	....	....	124	....	....	....	....	....	....	....	....	....	....	20	10	15	25	51	....	....	....
	New Westminster Bruins	Mem-Cup	5	3	0	3	....	....	....	2	....	....	....	....	....	....	....	....	....	....	....	....	....	....	....	....	....	....
1978-79	New Westminster Bruins	WHL	70	25	22	47	....	....	....	207	....	....	....	....	....	....	....	....	....	....	5	0	1	1	15	....	....	....
	Canada	WJC-A	5	0	0	0	....	....	....	10	....	....	....	....	....	....	....	....	....	....	....	....	....	....	....	....	....	....
1979-80	**Los Angeles Kings**	**NHL**	**40**	**2**	**5**	**7**	**2**	**4**	**6**	**28**	**0**	**0**	**0**	**31**	**6.5**	**12**	**0**	**18**	**0**	**–6**	**3**	**0**	**0**	**0**	**2**	**0**	**0**	**0**

Season	Club	League	REGULAR SEASON																		PLAYOFFS							
			GP	G	A	Pts	AG	AA	APts	PIM	PP	SH	GW	S	%	TGF	PGF	TGA	PGA	+/–	GP	G	A	Pts	PIM	PP	SH	GW
1980-81	**Los Angeles Kings**	**NHL**	**19**	**3**	**6**	**9**	**2**	**4**	**6**	**8**	**0**	**0**	**0**	**18**	**16.7**	**11**	**0**	**7**	**0**	**4**	**4**	**0**	**1**	**1**	**25**	**0**	**0**	**0**
	Houston Apollos	CHL	33	11	17	28	....	....	....	31	....	....	....	....	....	....	....	....	....	....	....	....	....	....	....	....	....	....
	Rochester Americans	AHL	16	5	10	15	....	....	....	32	....	....	....	....	....	....	....	....	....	....	....	....	....	....	....	....	....	....
1981-82	**Los Angeles Kings**	**NHL**	**70**	**12**	**11**	**23**	**9**	**7**	**16**	**100**	**0**	**0**	**0**	**92**	**13.0**	**38**	**3**	**61**	**5**	**–21**	**10**	**1**	**0**	**1**	**14**	**1**	**0**	**0**
1982-83	**Los Angeles Kings**	**NHL**	**65**	**16**	**15**	**31**	**13**	**10**	**23**	**52**	**4**	**1**	**2**	**102**	**15.7**	**53**	**9**	**59**	**1**	**–14**	....	....	....	....	....	....	....	....
1983-84	**Los Angeles Kings**	**NHL**	**72**	**7**	**14**	**21**	**6**	**10**	**16**	**73**	**0**	**0**	**0**	**86**	**8.1**	**35**	**1**	**68**	**0**	**–34**	....	....	....	....	....	....	....	....
1984-85	**Los Angeles Kings**	**NHL**	**73**	**8**	**10**	**18**	**6**	**7**	**13**	**55**	**0**	**0**	**2**	**70**	**11.4**	**28**	**2**	**35**	**0**	**–9**	**1**	**0**	**0**	**0**	**0**	**0**	**0**	**0**
1985-86	**Los Angeles Kings**	**NHL**	**61**	**6**	**9**	**15**	**5**	**6**	**11**	**50**	**0**	**0**	**0**	**38**	**15.8**	**27**	**5**	**39**	**0**	**–17**	....	....	....	....	....	....	....	....
	NHL Totals		**400**	**54**	**70**	**124**	**43**	**48**	**91**	**366**	**4**	**1**	**4**	**437**	**12.4**	**204**	**20**	**287**	**6**		**18**	**1**	**1**	**2**	**41**	**1**	**0**	**0**

• KELLY, Steve

C – L. 6'2", 210 lbs. b: Vancouver, B.C., 10/26/1976. Edmonton's 1st, 6th overall, in 1995.

Season	Club	League	GP	G	A	Pts	AG	AA	APts	PIM	PP	SH	GW	S	%	TGF	PGF	TGA	PGA	+/–	GP	G	A	Pts	PIM	PP	SH	GW
1991-92	Westbank Westsides	BCAHA	30	25	60	85	....	....	....	75	....	....	....	....	....	....	....	....	....	....	....	....	....	....	....	....	....	....
1992-93	Prince Albert Raiders	WHL	65	11	9	20	....	....	....	75	....	....	....	....	....	....	....	....	....	....	....	....	....	....	....	....	....	....
1993-94	Prince Albert Raiders	WHL	65	19	42	61	....	....	....	106	....	....	....	....	....	....	....	....	....	....	....	....	....	....	....	....	....	....
1994-95	Prince Albert Raiders	WHL	68	31	41	72	....	....	....	153	....	....	....	....	....	....	....	....	....	....	15	7	9	16	35	....	....	....
1995-96	Prince Albert Raiders	WHL	70	27	74	101	....	....	....	203	....	....	....	....	....	....	....	....	....	....	18	13	18	31	47	....	....	....
1996-97	**Edmonton Oilers**	**NHL**	**8**	**1**	**0**	**1**	**1**	**0**	**1**	**6**	**0**	**0**	**1**	**6**	**16.7**	**2**	**0**	**3**	**0**	**–1**	**6**	**0**	**0**	**0**	**2**	**0**	**0**	**0**
	Hamilton Bulldogs	AHL	48	9	29	38	....	....	....	111	....	....	....	....	....	....	....	....	....	....	11	3	3	6	24	....	....	....
1997-98	**Edmonton Oilers**	**NHL**	**19**	**0**	**2**	**2**	**0**	**2**	**2**	**8**	**0**	**0**	**0**	**5**	**0.0**	**5**	**0**	**9**	**0**	**–4**	....	....	....	....	....	....	....	....
	Hamilton Bulldogs	AHL	11	2	8	10	....	....	....	18	....	....	....	....	....	....	....	....	....	....	....	....	....	....	....	....	....	....
	Tampa Bay Lightning	**NHL**	**24**	**2**	**1**	**3**	**2**	**1**	**3**	**15**	**1**	**0**	**0**	**17**	**11.8**	**6**	**1**	**14**	**0**	**–9**	....	....	....	....	....	....	....	....
	Milwaukee Admirals	IHL	5	0	1	1	....	....	....	19	....	....	....	....	....	....	....	....	....	....	....	....	....	....	....	....	....	....
	Cleveland Lumberjacks	IHL	5	1	1	2	....	....	....	29	....	....	....	....	....	....	....	....	....	....	1	0	1	1	0	....	....	....
1998-99	**Tampa Bay Lighning**	**NHL**	**34**	**1**	**3**	**4**	**1**	**3**	**4**	**27**	**0**	**0**	**1**	**15**	**6.7**	**7**	**0**	**25**	**3**	**–15**	....	....	....	....	....	....	....	....
	Cleveland Lumberjacks	IHL	18	6	7	13	....	....	....	36	....	....	....	....	....	....	....	....	....	....	....	....	....	....	....	....	....	....
99-2000	Detroit Vipers	IHL	1	0	0	0	....	....	....	4	....	....	....	....	....	....	....	....	....	....	....	....	....	....	....	....	....	....
	New Jersey Devils	**NHL**	**1**	**0**	**0**	**0**	**0**	**0**	**0**	**0**	**0**	**0**	**0**	**0**	**0.0**	**0**	**0**	**0**	**0**	**0**	**10**	**0**	**0**	**0**	**4**	**0**	**0**	**0**
	Albany River Rats	AHL	76	21	36	57	....	....	....	131	....	....	....	....	....	....	....	....	....	....	3	1	1	2	2	....	....	....
	NHL Totals		**86**	**4**	**6**	**10**	**4**	**6**	**10**	**56**	**1**	**0**	**2**	**43**	**9.3**	**20**	**1**	**51**	**3**		**16**	**0**	**0**	**0**	**6**	**0**	**0**	**0**

Traded to **Tampa Bay** by **Edmonton** with Bryan Marchment and Jason Bonsignore for Roman Hamrlik and Paul Comrie, December 30, 1997. Traded to **New Jersey** by **Tampa Bay** for New Jersey's 7th round choice (Brian Eklund) in 2000 Entry Draft, October 7, 1999.

• KEMP, Kevin

Kevin Glen D – L. 6', 188 lbs. b: Ottawa, Ont., 5/3/1954 d: 8/25/1999. Toronto's 8th, 138th overall, in 1974.

Season	Club	League	GP	G	A	Pts	AG	AA	APts	PIM	PP	SH	GW	S	%	TGF	PGF	TGA	PGA	+/–	GP	G	A	Pts	PIM	PP	SH	GW
1973-74	Ottawa 67's	OMJHL	59	4	8	12	....	....	....	205	....	....	....	....	....	....	....	....	....	....	7	0	2	2	24	....	....	....
1974-75	Milwaukee Admirals	USHL	33	4	14	18	....	....	....	59	....	....	....	....	....	....	....	....	....	....	....	....	....	....	....	....	....	....
	Saginaw Gears	IHL	3	0	0	0	....	....	....	0	....	....	....	....	....	....	....	....	....	....	....	....	....	....	....	....	....	....
	Hampton Gulls	SHL	5	0	0	0	....	....	....	17	....	....	....	....	....	....	....	....	....	....	....	....	....	....	....	....	....	....
1975-76	Oklahoma City Blazers	CHL	33	0	1	1	....	....	....	31	....	....	....	....	....	....	....	....	....	....	3	1	0	1	2	....	....	....
1976-77	Saginaw Gears	IHL	50	2	11	13	....	....	....	186	....	....	....	....	....	....	....	....	....	....	19	1	3	4	99	....	....	....
1977-78	Saginaw Gears	IHL	78	10	18	28	....	....	....	267	....	....	....	....	....	....	....	....	....	....	5	0	0	0	28	....	....	....
1978-79	New Brunswick Hawks	AHL	44	1	4	5	....	....	....	113	....	....	....	....	....	....	....	....	....	....	....	....	....	....	....	....	....	....
	Saginaw Gears	IHL	13	0	4	4	....	....	....	28	....	....	....	....	....	....	....	....	....	....	4	1	1	2	6	....	....	....
1979-80	Springfield Indians	AHL	77	0	19	19	....	....	....	180	....	....	....	....	....	....	....	....	....	....	....	....	....	....	....	....	....	....
1980-81	**Hartford Whalers**	**NHL**	**3**	**0**	**0**	**0**	**0**	**0**	**0**	**4**	**0**	**0**	**0**	**5**	**0.0**	**3**	**0**	**4**	**0**	**–1**	....	....	....	....	....	....	....	....
	Binghamton Whalers	AHL	75	0	5	5	....	....	....	204	....	....	....	....	....	....	....	....	....	....	5	0	2	2	4	....	....	....
	NHL Totals		**3**	**0**	**0**	**0**	**0**	**0**	**0**	**4**	**0**	**0**	**0**	**5**	**0.0**	**3**	**0**	**4**	**0**		....	....	....	....	....	....	....	....

Claimed by **Hartford** from **Toronto** in Expansion Draft, June 13, 1979.

• KENADY, Chris

Christopher RW – R. 6'2", 195 lbs. b: Mound, MN, 4/10/1973. St. Louis' 8th, 175th overall, in 1991.

Season	Club	League	GP	G	A	Pts	AG	AA	APts	PIM	PP	SH	GW	S	%	TGF	PGF	TGA	PGA	+/–	GP	G	A	Pts	PIM	PP	SH	GW
1990-91	St. Paul Vulcans	USHL	45	16	20	36	....	....	....	57	....	....	....	....	....	....	....	....	....	....	....	....	....	....	....	....	....	....
1991-92	University of Denver	WCHA	36	8	5	13	....	....	....	56	....	....	....	....	....	....	....	....	....	....	....	....	....	....	....	....	....	....
1992-93	University of Denver	WCHA	38	8	16	24	....	....	....	95	....	....	....	....	....	....	....	....	....	....	....	....	....	....	....	....	....	....
1993-94	University of Denver	WCHA	37	14	11	25	....	....	....	125	....	....	....	....	....	....	....	....	....	....	....	....	....	....	....	....	....	....
1994-95	University of Denver	WCHA	39	21	17	38	....	....	....	113	....	....	....	....	....	....	....	....	....	....	....	....	....	....	....	....	....	....
1995-96	Worcester IceCats	AHL	43	9	10	19	....	....	....	58	....	....	....	....	....	....	....	....	....	....	2	0	0	0	0	....	....	....
1996-97	Worcester IceCats	AHL	73	23	26	49	....	....	....	131	....	....	....	....	....	....	....	....	....	....	5	0	1	1	2	....	....	....
1997-98	**St. Louis Blues**	**NHL**	**5**	**0**	**2**	**2**	**0**	**2**	**2**	**0**	**0**	**0**	**0**	**3**	**0.0**	**2**	**0**	**1**	**0**	**1**	....	....	....	....	....	....	....	....
	Worcester IceCats	AHL	63	23	22	45	....	....	....	84	....	....	....	....	....	....	....	....	....	....	11	1	5	6	26	....	....	....
1998-99	Utah Grizzlies	IHL	35	7	6	13	....	....	....	68	....	....	....	....	....	....	....	....	....	....	....	....	....	....	....	....	....	....
	Long Beach Ice Dogs	IHL	19	1	6	7	....	....	....	47	....	....	....	....	....	....	....	....	....	....	....	....	....	....	....	....	....	....
	Hartford Wolf Pack	AHL	22	2	6	8	....	....	....	52	....	....	....	....	....	....	....	....	....	....	2	0	1	1	6	....	....	....
99-2000	**New York Rangers**	**NHL**	**2**	**0**	**0**	**0**	**0**	**0**	**0**	**0**	**0**	**0**	**0**	**1**	**0.0**	**0**	**0**	**1**	**0**	**–1**	....	....	....	....	....	....	....	....
	Hartford Wolf Pack	AHL	71	15	16	31	....	....	....	196	....	....	....	....	....	....	....	....	....	....	21	8	3	11	40	....	....	....
	NHL Totals		**7**	**0**	**2**	**2**	**0**	**2**	**2**	**0**	**0**	**0**	**0**	**4**	**0.0**	**2**	**0**	**2**	**0**		....	....	....	....	....	....	....	....

Traded to **NY Rangers** by **St. Louis** to complete transaction that sent sent Jeff Finley and Geoff Smith to St. Louis (February 13, 1999), February 22, 1999.

• KENNEDY, Dean

Edward Dean D – R. 6'2", 208 lbs. b: Redvers, Sask., 1/18/1963. Los Angeles' 2nd, 39th overall, in 1981.

Season	Club	League	GP	G	A	Pts	AG	AA	APts	PIM	PP	SH	GW	S	%	TGF	PGF	TGA	PGA	+/–	GP	G	A	Pts	PIM	PP	SH	GW
1979-80	Weyburn Red Wings	SJHL	57	12	20	32	....	....	....	64	....	....	....	....	....	....	....	....	....	....	....	....	....	....	....	....	....	....
	Brandon Wheat Kings	WHL	1	0	0	0	....	....	....	0	....	....	....	....	....	....	....	....	....	....	....	....	....	....	....	....	....	....
1980-81	Brandon Wheat Kings	WHL	71	3	29	32	....	....	....	157	....	....	....	....	....	....	....	....	....	....	5	0	2	2	7	....	....	....
1981-82	Brandon Wheat Kings	WHL	49	5	38	43	....	....	....	103	....	....	....	....	....	....	....	....	....	....	....	....	....	....	....	....	....	....
1982-83	Brandon Wheat Kings	WHL	14	2	15	17	....	....	....	22	....	....	....	....	....	....	....	....	....	....	....	....	....	....	....	....	....	....
	Los Angeles Kings	**NHL**	**55**	**0**	**12**	**12**	**0**	**8**	**8**	**97**	**0**	**0**	**0**	**53**	**0.0**	**44**	**0**	**72**	**11**	**–17**	....	....	....	....	....	....	....	....
	Saskatoon Blades	WHL	....	....	....	....	....	....	....	....	....	....	....	....	....	....	....	....	....	....	4	0	3	3	0	....	....	....
1983-84	**Los Angeles Kings**	**NHL**	**37**	**1**	**5**	**6**	**1**	**3**	**4**	**50**	**0**	**0**	**0**	**22**	**4.5**	**21**	**0**	**30**	**4**	**–5**	....	....	....	....	....	....	....	....
	New Haven Nighthawks	AHL	26	1	7	8	....	....	....	23	....	....	....	....	....	....	....	....	....	....	....	....	....	....	....	....	....	....
1984-85	New Haven Nighthawks	AHL	76	3	14	17	....	....	....	104	....	....	....	....	....	....	....	....	....	....	....	....	....	....	....	....	....	....
1985-86	**Los Angeles Kings**	**NHL**	**78**	**2**	**10**	**12**	**2**	**7**	**9**	**132**	**0**	**0**	**0**	**59**	**3.4**	**59**	**2**	**90**	**23**	**–10**	....	....	....	....	....	....	....	....
1986-87	**Los Angeles Kings**	**NHL**	**66**	**6**	**14**	**20**	**5**	**10**	**15**	**91**	**0**	**0**	**1**	**59**	**10.2**	**67**	**1**	**85**	**28**	**9**	**5**	**0**	**2**	**2**	**10**	**0**	**0**	**0**
1987-88	**Los Angeles Kings**	**NHL**	**58**	**1**	**11**	**12**	**1**	**8**	**9**	**158**	**0**	**0**	**0**	**40**	**2.5**	**46**	**0**	**89**	**21**	**–22**	**4**	**0**	**1**	**1**	**10**	**0**	**0**	**0**
1988-89	**Los Angeles Kings**	**NHL**	**25**	**2**	**5**	**7**	**2**	**4**	**6**	**23**	....	....	....	....	....	....	....	....	....	....	....	....	....	....	....	....	....	....
	New York Rangers	**NHL**	**16**	**0**	**1**	**1**	**0**	**1**	**1**	**40**	**0**	**0**	**0**	**7**	**0.0**	**8**	**0**	**9**	**0**	**–1**	....	....	....	....	....	....	....	....
	Los Angeles Kings	**NHL**	**26**	**1**	**3**	**4**	**1**	**2**	**3**	**40**	**0**	**0**	**1**	**38**	**2.6**	**59**	**1**	**61**	**21**	**18**	**11**	**0**	**2**	**2**	**8**	**0**	**0**	**0**
1989-90	**Buffalo Sabres**	**NHL**	**80**	**2**	**12**	**14**	**2**	**9**	**11**	**53**	**0**	**0**	**0**	**51**	**3.9**	**38**	**1**	**75**	**26**	**–12**	**6**	**1**	**1**	**2**	**12**	**0**	**0**	**0**
1990-91	**Buffalo Sabres**	**NHL**	**64**	**4**	**8**	**12**	**4**	**6**	**10**	**119**	**0**	**0**	**2**	**46**	**8.7**	**57**	**0**	**66**	**14**	**5**	**2**	**0**	**1**	**1**	**17**	**0**	**0**	**0**
1991-92	**Winnipeg Jets**	**NHL**	**18**	**2**	**4**	**6**	**2**	**3**	**5**	**21**	**0**	**0**	**1**	**20**	**10.0**	**14**	**0**	**21**	**9**	**2**	**2**	**0**	**0**	**0**	**0**	**0**	**0**	**0**
1992-93	**Winnipeg Jets**	**NHL**	**78**	**1**	**7**	**8**	**1**	**5**	**6**	**105**	**0**	**0**	**1**	**50**	**2.0**	**48**	**0**	**80**	**29**	**–3**	**2**	**0**	**0**	**0**	**0**	**0**	**0**	**0**
1993-94	**Winnipeg Jets**	**NHL**	**76**	**2**	**8**	**10**	**2**	**6**	**8**	**164**	**0**	**0**	**1**	**38**	**5.3**	**30**	**0**	**71**	**19**	**–22**	**6**	**0**	**0**	**0**	**2**	**0**	**0**	**0**
1994-95	**Edmonton Oilers**	**NHL**	**40**	**2**	**8**	**10**	**4**	**12**	**16**	**25**	**0**	**0**	**1**	**45**	**4.4**	**29**	**0**	**41**	**14**	**2**	....	....	....	....	....	....	....	....
	NHL Totals		**717**	**26**	**108**	**134**	**27**	**84**	**111**	**1118**	**0**	**0**	**8**	**528**	**4.9**	**520**	**5**	**790**	**219**		**36**	**1**	**7**	**8**	**59**	**0**	**0**	**0**

Traded to **NY Rangers** by **LA Kings** with Denis Larocque for Igor Liba, Michael Boyce, Todd Elik and future considerations, December 12, 1988. Traded to **LA Kings** by **NY Rangers** for LA Kings' 4th round choice (later traded to Minnesota — Minnesota selected Cal McGowan) in 1990 Entry Draft, February 3, 1989. Traded to **Buffalo** by **LA Kings** for Buffalo's 4th round choice (Keith Redmond) in 1991 Entry Draft, October 4, 1989. Traded to **Winnipeg** by **Buffalo** with Darrin Shannon and Mike Hartman for Dave McLlwain, Gord Donnelly, Winnipeg's 5th round choice (Yuri Khmylev) in 1992 Entry Draft and future considerations, October 11, 1991. • Missed majority of 1991-92 season recovering from knee injury suffered in game vs. NY Islanders, November 20, 1991. Claimed by **Edmonton** from **Winnipeg** in NHL Waiver Draft, January 18, 1995.

• KENNEDY, Forbes

Forbes Taylor C – L. 5'8", 150 lbs. b: Dorchester, N.B., 8/18/1935.

			REGULAR SEASON																		PLAYOFFS							
Season	Club	League	GP	G	A	Pts	AG	AA	APts	PIM	PP	SH	GW	S	%	TGF	PGF	TGA	PGA	+/-	GP	G	A	Pts	PIM	PP	SH	GW
1951-52	Charlottetown Abbies	PEIHA	6	*16	8	*24	....	....	....	20	....	....	....	....	....	....	....	....	....	....	6	*23	*14	*37	*21	....	....	....
1952-53	Halifax St. Mary's	MJrHL	25	16	11	27	....	....	....	....	....	....	....	....	....	....	....	....	....	....	....	....	....	....	....	....	....	....
	Halifax St. Mary's	NSSHL	11	16	11	27	....	....	....	24	....	....	....	....	....	....	....	....	....	....	....	....	....	....	....	....	....	....
	Halifax St. Mary's	Mem-Cup	12	12	7	19	....	....	....	25	....	....	....	....	....	....	....	....	....	....	....	....	....	....	....	....	....	....
1953-54	Montreal Jr. Canadiens	QJHL	54	19	19	38	....	....	....	43	....	....	....	....	....	....	....	....	....	....	8	1	8	9	6	....	....	....
1954-55	Montreal Jr. Canadiens	QJHL	46	7	14	21	....	....	....	118	....	....	....	....	....	....	....	....	....	....	4	0	2	2	4	....	....	....
1955-56	Montreal Jr. Canadiens	QJHL	STATISTICS NOT AVAILABLE																									
	Montreal–Shawinigan	QHL	3	0	3	3	....	....	....	2	....	....	....	....	....	....	....	....	....	....	....	....	....	....	....	....	....	....
	Montreal Jr. Canadiens	Mem-Cup	10	3	5	8	....	....	....	19	....	....	....	....	....	....	....	....	....	....	....	....	....	....	....	....	....	....
1956-57	**Chicago Black Hawks**	**NHL**	**69**	**8**	**13**	**21**	**10**	**14**	**24**	**102**	....	....	....	....	....	....	....	....	....	....	....	....	....	....	....	....	....	....
1957-58	**Detroit Red Wings**	**NHL**	**70**	**11**	**16**	**27**	**14**	**16**	**30**	**135**	....	....	....	....	....	....	....	....	....	....	**4**	**1**	**0**	**1**	**12**	**0**	**0**	**1**
1958-59	**Detroit Red Wings**	**NHL**	**67**	**1**	**4**	**5**	**1**	**4**	**5**	**149**	....	....	....	....	....	....	....	....	....	....	....	....	....	....	....	....	....	....
1959-60	**Detroit Red Wings**	**NHL**	**17**	**1**	**2**	**3**	**1**	**2**	**3**	**8**	....	....	....	....	....	....	....	....	....	....	....	....	....	....	....	....	....	....
	Edmonton Flyers	WHL	30	6	10	16	....	....	....	39	....	....	....	....	....	....	....	....	....	....	....	....	....	....	....	....	....	....
	Hershey Bears	AHL	21	3	11	14	....	....	....	50	....	....	....	....	....	....	....	....	....	....	....	....	....	....	....	....	....	....
1960-61	Spokane Comets	WHL	70	23	38	61	....	....	....	165	....	....	....	....	....	....	....	....	....	....	4	2	1	3	0	....	....	....
1961-62	**Detroit Red Wings**	**NHL**	**14**	**1**	**0**	**1**	**1**	**0**	**1**	**8**	....	....	....	....	....	....	....	....	....	....	....	....	....	....	....	....	....	....
	Edmonton Flyers	WHL	58	23	31	54	....	....	....	124	....	....	....	....	....	....	....	....	....	....	....	....	....	....	....	....	....	....
1962-63	Edmonton Flyers	WHL	23	7	15	22	....	....	....	38	....	....	....	....	....	....	....	....	....	....	....	....	....	....	....	....	....	....
	Boston Bruins	**NHL**	**49**	**12**	**18**	**30**	**14**	**18**	**32**	**46**	....	....	....	....	....	....	....	....	....	....	....	....	....	....	....	....	....	....
1963-64	**Boston Bruins**	**NHL**	**70**	**8**	**17**	**25**	**10**	**18**	**28**	**95**	....	....	....	....	....	....	....	....	....	....	....	....	....	....	....	....	....	....
1964-65	**Boston Bruins**	**NHL**	**52**	**6**	**4**	**10**	**7**	**4**	**11**	**41**	....	....	....	....	....	....	....	....	....	....	....	....	....	....	....	....	....	....
1965-66	**Boston Bruins**	**NHL**	**50**	**4**	**6**	**10**	**4**	**6**	**10**	**55**	....	....	....	....	....	....	....	....	....	....	....	....	....	....	....	....	....	....
	San Francisco Seals	WHL	6	3	3	6	....	....	....	48	....	....	....	....	....	....	....	....	....	....	....	....	....	....	....	....	....	....
1966-67	California Seals	WHL	71	25	41	66	....	....	....	91	....	....	....	....	....	....	....	....	....	....	6	2	0	2	4	....	....	....
1967-68	**Philadelphia Flyers**	**NHL**	**73**	**10**	**18**	**28**	**12**	**18**	**30**	**130**	**1**	**1**	**3**	**100**	**10.0**	**33**	**1**	**50**	**22**	**4**	**7**	**1**	**4**	**5**	**14**	**0**	**1**	**0**
1968-69	**Philadelphia Flyers**	**NHL**	**59**	**8**	**7**	**15**	**8**	**6**	**14**	***195**	**0**	**0**	**0**	**64**	**12.5**	**21**	**1**	**51**	**6**	**–25**	....	....	....	....	....	....	....	....
	Toronto Maple Leafs	**NHL**	**13**	**0**	**3**	**3**	**0**	**3**	**3**	***24**	**0**	**0**	**0**	**7**	**0.0**	**3**	**0**	**4**	**0**	**–1**	**1**	**0**	**0**	**0**	**38**	**0**	**0**	**0**
1969-70	Buffalo Bisons	AHL	19	2	1	3	....	....	....	42	....	....	....	....	....	....	....	....	....	....	4	0	0	0	0	....	....	....
	Omaha Knights	CHL	....	....	....	....	....	....	....	....	....	....	....	....	....	....	....	....	....	....	6	0	1	1	7	....	....	....
1970-71	Halifax Jr. Canadians	MJrHL	DID NOT PLAY – COACHING																									
	NHL Totals		**603**	**70**	**108**	**178**	**82**	**109**	**191**	**988**	....	....	....	....	....	....	....	....	....	....	**12**	**2**	**4**	**6**	**64**	....	....	....

Traded to **Chicago** by **Montreal** with Ed Kachur for $50,000, May 24, 1956. Traded to **Detroit** by **Chicago** with Johnny Wilson, Hank Bassen and Bill Preston for Ted Lindsay and Glenn Hall, July 23, 1957. Traded to **Boston** by **Detroit** for Andre Pronovost, December 3, 1962. Claimed by **Philadelphia** from **Boston** in Expansion Draft, June 6, 1967. Traded to **Toronto** by **Philadelphia** with Brit Selby for Gerry Meehan, Mike Byers and Bill Sutherland, March 2, 1969. Traded to **Pittsburgh** by **Toronto** for cash, May 30, 1969. Claimed by **NY Rangers** from **Pittsburgh** in Intra-League Draft, June 11, 1969.

• KENNEDY, Mike

C – R. 6'1", 195 lbs. b: Vancouver, B.C., 4/13/1972. Minnesota's 3rd, 97th overall, in 1991.

Season	Club	League	GP	G	A	Pts	AG	AA	APts	PIM	PP	SH	GW	S	%	TGF	PGF	TGA	PGA	+/-	GP	G	A	Pts	PIM	PP	SH	GW
1989-90	University of British Columbia	CWUAA	9	5	7	12	....	....	....	0	....	....	....	....	....	....	....	....	....	....	....	....	....	....	....	....	....	....
1990-91	University of British Columbia	CWUAA	28	17	17	34	....	....	....	18	....	....	....	....	....	....	....	....	....	....	....	....	....	....	....	....	....	....
1991-92	Seattle Thunderbirds	WHL	71	42	47	89	....	....	....	134	....	....	....	....	....	....	....	....	....	....	15	11	6	17	20	....	....	....
1992-93	Kalamazoo Wings	IHL	77	21	30	51	....	....	....	39	....	....	....	....	....	....	....	....	....	....	....	....	....	....	....	....	....	....
1993-94	Kalamazoo Wings	IHL	63	20	18	38	....	....	....	42	....	....	....	....	....	....	....	....	....	....	3	1	2	3	2	....	....	....
1994-95	**Dallas Stars**	**NHL**	**44**	**6**	**12**	**18**	**11**	**18**	**29**	**33**	**2**	**0**	**0**	**76**	**7.9**	**30**	**5**	**21**	**0**	**4**	**5**	**0**	**0**	**0**	**9**	**0**	**0**	**0**
	Kalamazoo Wings	IHL	42	20	28	48	....	....	....	29	....	....	....	....	....	....	....	....	....	....	....	....	....	....	....	....	....	....
1995-96	**Dallas Stars**	**NHL**	**61**	**9**	**17**	**26**	**9**	**14**	**23**	**48**	**4**	**0**	**1**	**111**	**8.1**	**38**	**8**	**41**	**4**	**–7**	....	....	....	....	....	....	....	....
1996-97	**Dallas Stars**	**NHL**	**24**	**1**	**6**	**7**	**1**	**5**	**6**	**13**	**0**	**0**	**1**	**26**	**3.8**	**8**	**0**	**5**	**0**	**3**	....	....	....	....	....	....	....	....
	Michigan K-Wings	IHL	2	0	1	1	....	....	....	2	....	....	....	....	....	....	....	....	....	....	....	....	....	....	....	....	....	....
1997-98	**Toronto Maple Leafs**	**NHL**	**13**	**0**	**1**	**1**	**0**	**1**	**1**	**14**	**0**	**0**	**0**	**12**	**0.0**	**3**	**0**	**5**	**0**	**–2**	....	....	....	....	....	....	....	....
	St. John's Maple Leafs	AHL	49	11	17	28	....	....	....	86	....	....	....	....	....	....	....	....	....	....	....	....	....	....	....	....	....	....
	Dallas Stars	**NHL**	**2**	**0**	**0**	**0**	**0**	**0**	**0**	**2**	**0**	**0**	**0**	**0**	**0.0**	**1**	**0**	**0**	**0**	**1**	....	....	....	....	....	....	....	....
1998-99	**New York Islanders**	**NHL**	**1**	**0**	**0**	**0**	**0**	**0**	**0**	**2**	**0**	**0**	**0**	**0**	**0.0**	**0**	**0**	**0**	**0**	**0**	....	....	....	....	....	....	....	....
	Lowell Lock Monsters	AHL	62	14	26	40	....	....	....	52	....	....	....	....	....	....	....	....	....	....	3	1	0	1	0	....	....	....
99-2000	Munich Barons	Germany	13	2	5	7	....	....	....	6	....	....	....	....	....	....	....	....	....	....	12	4	4	8	28	....	....	....
	NHL Totals		**145**	**16**	**36**	**52**	**21**	**38**	**59**	**112**	**6**	**0**	**2**	**225**	**7.1**	**80**	**13**	**72**	**4**		**5**	**0**	**0**	**0**	**9**	**0**	**0**	**0**

WHL West Second All-Star Team (1992)

Rights transferred to **Dallas** after **Minnesota** franchise relocated, June 9, 1993. Signed as a free agent by **Toronto**, July 2, 1997. Traded to **Dallas** by **Toronto** for Dallas' 8th round choice (Mikhail Travnicek) in 1998 Entry Draft, March 24, 1998. Signed as a free agent by **NY Islanders**, July 1, 1998. • Missed majority of 1999-2000 season recovering from ankle injury suffered in game vs. Moskitos Essen (DEL), September 17, 1999. • Played w/ RHI's Vancouver Voodoo in 1993 (11-10-16-26-14) and 1994 (17-22-36-58-4); Oklahoma Coyotes in 1995 (1-0-0-0-0).

• KENNEDY, Sheldon

RW – R. 5'10", 180 lbs. b: Elkhorn, Man., 6/15/1969. Detroit's 5th, 80th overall, in 1988.

Season	Club	League	GP	G	A	Pts	AG	AA	APts	PIM	PP	SH	GW	S	%	TGF	PGF	TGA	PGA	+/-	GP	G	A	Pts	PIM	PP	SH	GW
1985-86	Winnipeg South Blues	MJHL	43	37	38	75	....	....	....	103	....	....	....	....	....	....	....	....	....	....	....	....	....	....	....	....	....	....
1986-87	Swift Current Broncos	WHL	49	23	41	64	....	....	....	43	....	....	....	....	....	....	....	....	....	....	4	0	3	3	4	....	....	....
1987-88	Swift Current Broncos	WHL	59	53	64	117	....	....	....	45	....	....	....	....	....	....	....	....	....	....	10	8	9	17	12	....	....	....
	Canada	WJC-A	7	4	2	6	....	....	....	6	....	....	....	....	....	....	....	....	....	....	....	....	....	....	....	....	....	....
1988-89	Swift Current Broncos	WHL	51	58	48	106	....	....	....	92	....	....	....	....	....	....	....	....	....	....	12	9	15	24	22	....	....	....
	Canada	WJC-A	7	3	4	7	....	....	....	14	....	....	....	....	....	....	....	....	....	....	....	....	....	....	....	....	....	....
	Swift Current Broncos	Mem-Cup	5	4	5	*9	....	....	....	6	....	....	....	....	....	....	....	....	....	....	....	....	....	....	....	....	....	....
1989-90	**Detroit Red Wings**	**NHL**	**20**	**2**	**7**	**9**	**2**	**5**	**7**	**10**	**0**	**0**	**1**	**23**	**8.7**	**13**	**3**	**11**	**1**	**0**	....	....	....	....	....	....	....	....
	Adirondack Red Wings	AHL	26	11	15	26	....	....	....	35	....	....	....	....	....	....	....	....	....	....	....	....	....	....	....	....	....	....
1990-91	**Detroit Red Wings**	**NHL**	**7**	**1**	**0**	**1**	**1**	**0**	**1**	**12**	**0**	**0**	**0**	**11**	**9.1**	**4**	**0**	**5**	**0**	**–1**	....	....	....	....	....	....	....	....
	Adirondack Red Wings	AHL	11	1	3	4	....	....	....	8	....	....	....	....	....	....	....	....	....	....	....	....	....	....	....	....	....	....
1991-92	**Detroit Red Wings**	**NHL**	**27**	**3**	**8**	**11**	**3**	**6**	**9**	**24**	**0**	**0**	**1**	**33**	**9.1**	**15**	**1**	**16**	**0**	**–2**	....	....	....	....	....	....	....	....
	Adirondack Red Wings	AHL	46	25	24	49	....	....	....	56	....	....	....	....	....	....	....	....	....	....	16	5	9	14	12	....	....	....
1992-93	**Detroit Red Wings**	**NHL**	**68**	**19**	**11**	**30**	**16**	**8**	**24**	**46**	**1**	**0**	**2**	**110**	**17.3**	**32**	**1**	**37**	**5**	**–1**	**7**	**1**	**1**	**2**	**2**	**0**	**0**	**0**
1993-94	**Detroit Red Wings**	**NHL**	**61**	**6**	**7**	**13**	**6**	**5**	**11**	**30**	**0**	**1**	**0**	**60**	**10.0**	**22**	**0**	**29**	**5**	**–2**	**7**	**1**	**2**	**3**	**0**	**0**	**0**	**0**
1994-95	**Calgary Flames**	**NHL**	**30**	**7**	**8**	**15**	**12**	**12**	**24**	**45**	**1**	**0**	**0**	**44**	**15.9**	**20**	**2**	**18**	**5**	**5**	**7**	**3**	**1**	**4**	**16**	**0**	**1**	**0**
1995-96	**Calgary Flames**	**NHL**	**41**	**3**	**7**	**10**	**3**	**6**	**9**	**36**	**0**	**0**	**1**	**54**	**5.6**	**20**	**3**	**14**	**0**	**3**	**3**	**1**	**0**	**1**	**2**	**0**	**0**	**0**
	Saint John Flames	AHL	3	4	0	4	....	....	....	8	....	....	....	....	....	....	....	....	....	....	....	....	....	....	....	....	....	....
1996-97	**Boston Bruins**	**NHL**	**56**	**8**	**10**	**18**	**8**	**9**	**17**	**30**	**0**	**4**	**0**	**65**	**12.3**	**24**	**0**	**54**	**13**	**–17**	....	....	....	....	....	....	....	....
	Providence Bruins	AHL	3	0	1	1	....	....	....	2	....	....	....	....	....	....	....	....	....	....	....	....	....	....	....	....	....	....
1997-98			DID NOT PLAY – INJURED																									
1998-99	Manitoba Moose	IHL	24	7	7	14	....	....	....	14	....	....	....	....	....	....	....	....	....	....	....	....	....	....	....	....	....	....
	EV Landshut	Germany	13	0	3	3	....	....	....	0	....	....	....	....	....	....	....	....	....	....	3	0	0	0	4	....	....	....
	NHL Totals		**310**	**49**	**58**	**107**	**51**	**51**	**102**	**233**	**2**	**5**	**5**	**400**	**12.3**	**150**	**10**	**184**	**29**		**24**	**6**	**4**	**10**	**20**	**0**	**1**	**0**

WHL East Second All-Star Team (1989) • Memorial Cup All-Star Team (1989)

• Missed majority of 1990-91 season recovering from arm injury suffered in automobile accident, July, 1990. Traded to **Winnipeg** by **Detroit** for Winnipeg's 3rd round choice (Darryl Laplante) in 1995 Entry Draft, May 25, 1994. Claimed by **Calgary** from **Winnipeg** in NHL Waiver Draft, January 18, 1995. Signed as free agent by **Boston**, August 7, 1996. • Missed entire 1997-98 season recovering from leg injury suffered in cycling accident, July, 1997.

• KEON, Dave

David Michael C – L. 5'9", 165 lbs. b: Noranda, Que., 3/22/1940. **HHOF**

Season	Club	League	GP	G	A	Pts	AG	AA	APts	PIM	PP	SH	GW	S	%	TGF	PGF	TGA	PGA	+/-	GP	G	A	Pts	PIM	PP	SH	GW
1956-57	St. Michael's Buzzers	OHA-B	36	20	23	43	....	....	....	14	....	....	....	....	....	....	....	....	....	....	....	....	....	....	....	....	....	....
	St. Michael's Majors	OHA-Jr.	4	1	3	4	....	....	....	0	....	....	....	....	....	....	....	....	....	....	....	....	....	....	....	....	....	....
1957-58	St. Michael's Majors	OHA-Jr.	45	23	27	50	....	....	....	29	....	....	....	....	....	....	....	....	....	....	9	8	5	13	10	....	....	....
1958-59	St. Michael's Majors	OHA-Jr.	47	33	38	71	....	....	....	31	....	....	....	....	....	....	....	....	....	....	15	4	9	13	8	....	....	....
1959-60	St. Michael's Majors	OHA-Jr.	46	16	29	45	....	....	....	8	....	....	....	....	....	....	....	....	....	....	10	8	10	18	2	....	....	....
	Kitchener-Waterloo Dutchmen	OHA-Sr.	1	1	0	1	....	....	....	0	....	....	....	....	....	....	....	....	....	....	....	....	....	....	....	....	....	....
	Sudbury Wolves	EPHL	....	....	....	....	....	....	....	....	....	....	....	....	....	....	....	....	....	....	4	2	2	4	2	....	....	....

Season	Club	League	REGULAR SEASON GP	G	A	Pts	AG	AA	APts	PIM	PP	SH	GW	S	%	TGF	PGF	TGA	PGA	+/–	PLAYOFFS GP	G	A	Pts	PIM	PP	SH	GW
1960-61	Toronto Maple Leafs	NHL	70	20	25	45	23	24	47	6	....	....	....	....	....	....	....	....	....	....	5	1	1	2	0	....	....	....
1961-62♦	Toronto Maple Leafs	NHL	64	26	35	61	30	34	64	2	....	....	....	....	....	....	....	....	....	....	12	5	3	8	0	....	....	....
1962-63♦	Toronto Maple Leafs	NHL	68	28	28	56	33	28	61	2	....	....	....	....	....	....	....	....	....	....	10	7	5	12	0	....	....	....
1963-64♦	Toronto Maple Leafs	NHL	70	23	37	60	29	39	68	6	....	....	....	....	....	....	....	....	....	....	14	7	2	9	2	....	....	....
1964-65	Toronto Maple Leafs	NHL	65	21	29	50	25	30	55	10	....	....	....	....	....	....	....	....	....	....	6	2	2	4	2	....	....	....
1965-66	Toronto Maple Leafs	NHL	69	24	30	54	27	29	56	4	....	....	....	....	....	....	....	....	....	....	4	0	2	2	0	....	....	....
1966-67♦	Toronto Maple Leafs	NHL	66	19	33	52	22	32	54	2	....	....	....	....	....	....	....	....	....	....	12	3	5	8	0	....	....	....
1967-68	Toronto Maple Leafs	NHL	67	11	37	48	13	37	50	4	1	0	3	196	5.6	72	15	52	11	16	....	....	....	....	....	....	....	....
1968-69	Toronto Maple Leafs	NHL	75	27	34	61	29	30	59	12	3	6	6	281	9.6	82	12	69	16	17	4	1	3	4	2	0	0	1
1969-70	Toronto Maple Leafs	NHL	72	32	30	62	35	28	63	6	9	2	4	284	11.3	84	34	82	17	–15	....	....	....	....	....	....	....	....
1970-71	Toronto Maple Leafs	NHL	76	38	38	76	38	32	70	4	5	8	9	277	13.7	97	27	63	17	24	6	3	2	5	0	0	0	0
1971-72	Toronto Maple Leafs	NHL	72	18	30	48	18	26	44	4	2	2	5	265	6.8	74	33	60	20	1	5	2	3	5	0	0	0	0
1972-73	Toronto Maple Leafs	NHL	76	37	36	73	35	29	64	2	8	2	6	277	13.4	104	38	81	19	4	....	....	....	....	....	....	....	....
1973-74	Toronto Maple Leafs	NHL	74	25	28	53	24	23	47	7	1	2	3	244	10.2	68	14	58	17	13	4	1	2	3	0	0	0	0
1974-75	Toronto Maple Leafs	NHL	78	16	43	59	14	32	46	4	1	1	2	183	8.7	84	22	89	30	3	7	0	5	5	0	0	0	0
1975-76	Minnesota Fighting Saints	WHA	57	26	38	64	....	....	....	4	....	....	....	....	....	....	....	....	....	....	....	....	....	....	....	....	....	....
	Indianapolis Racers	WHA	12	3	7	10	....	....	....	2	....	....	....	....	....	....	....	....	....	....	7	2	2	4	2	....	....	....
1976-77	Minnesota Fighting Saints	WHA	42	13	38	51	....	....	....	2	....	....	....	....	....	....	....	....	....	....	....	....	....	....	....	....	....	....
	New England Whalers	WHA	34	14	25	39	....	....	....	8	....	....	....	....	....	....	....	....	....	....	5	3	1	4	0	....	....	....
1977-78	New England Whalers	WHA	77	24	38	62	....	....	....	2	....	....	....	....	....	....	....	....	....	....	14	5	11	16	4	....	....	....
1978-79	New England Whalers	WHA	79	22	43	65	....	....	....	2	....	....	....	....	....	....	....	....	....	....	10	3	9	12	2	....	....	....
1979-80	Hartford Whalers	NHL	76	10	52	62	8	38	46	10	0	0	0	146	6.8	87	18	107	25	–13	3	0	1	1	0	0	0	0
1980-81	Hartford Whalers	NHL	80	13	34	47	10	23	33	26	2	0	1	131	9.9	69	15	116	31	–31	....	....	....	....	....	....	....	....
1981-82	Hartford Whalers	NHL	78	8	11	19	6	7	13	6	0	1	1	84	9.5	26	0	68	11	–31	....	....	....	....	....	....	....	....
	NHL Totals		1296	396	590	986	419	521	940	117	....	....	....	....	....	....	....	....	....	....	92	32	36	68	6	....	....	....
	Other Major League Totals		301	102	189	291	....	....	....	20	....	....	....	....	....	....	....	....	....	....	36	13	23	36	8	....	....	....

Won OHA-B Rookie-of-the-Year Award (1957) 195 Won Calder Memorial Trophy (1961) • NHL Second All-Star Team (1962, 1971) • Won Lady Byng Trophy (1962, 1963) • Won Conn Smythe Trophy (1967) • Won Paul Daneau Trophy (WHA Most Gentlemanly Player) (1977, 1978) • Played in NHL All-Star Game (1962, 1963, 1964, 1967, 1968, 1970, 1971, 1973)

Selected by **Ontario-Ottawa** (WHA) in 1972 WHA General Player Draft, February 12, 1972. WHA rights transferred to **Toronto** (WHA) after **Ottawa** (WHA) franchise relocated, May, 1973. WHA rights traded to **Minnesota** (WHA) by **Toronto** (WHA) for future considerations, May, 1975. Signed as a free agent by **Indianapolis** (WHA) after **Minnesota** (WHA) franchise folded, March 10, 1976. Traded to **Minnesota** (WHA) by **Indianapolis** (WHA) for Gary MacGregor and future considerations, September, 1976. Traded to **Edmonton** (WHA) by **Minnesota** (WHA) with Mike Antonovich, Bill Butters, Jack Carlson, Steve Carlson, Jean-Louis Levasseur and John McKenzie, January, 1977. Traded to **New England** (WHA) by **Edmonton** (WHA) with Jack Carlson, Steve Carlson, Dave Dryden and John McKenzie for future considerations (Dave Debol, June, 1977), Dan Arndt and cash, January, 1977. Rights retained by **Hartford** prior to Expansion Draft, June 9, 1979.

• KERCH, Alexander

LW – R. 5′10″, 190 lbs. b: Arkhangelsk, USSR, 3/16/1967. Edmonton's 5th, 60th overall, in 1993.

Season	Club	League	GP	G	A	Pts	AG	AA	APts	PIM	PP	SH	GW	S	%	TGF	PGF	TGA	PGA	+/–	GP	G	A	Pts	PIM	PP	SH	GW
1984-85	Dynamo Riga	USSR	8	0	0	0	....	....	....	6	....	....	....	....	....	....	....	....	....	....	....	....	....	....	....	....	....	....
1985-86	Dynamo Riga	USSR	23	5	2	7	....	....	....	16	....	....	....	....	....	....	....	....	....	....	....	....	....	....	....	....	....	....
1986-87	Dynamo Riga	USSR	26	5	4	9	....	....	....	10	....	....	....	....	....	....	....	....	....	....	....	....	....	....	....	....	....	....
1987-88	Dynamo Riga	USSR	50	14	4	18	....	....	....	28	....	....	....	....	....	....	....	....	....	....	....	....	....	....	....	....	....	....
1988-89	Dynamo Riga	USSR	39	6	7	13	....	....	....	41	....	....	....	....	....	....	....	....	....	....	....	....	....	....	....	....	....	....
	Dynamo Riga	Super-S	7	1	1	2	....	....	....	4	....	....	....	....	....	....	....	....	....	....	....	....	....	....	....	....	....	....
1989-90	Dynamo Riga	Fr-Tour	1	0	0	0	....	....	....	0	....	....	....	....	....	....	....	....	....	....	....	....	....	....	....	....	....	....
	Dynamo Riga	USSR	46	9	11	20	....	....	....	22	....	....	....	....	....	....	....	....	....	....	....	....	....	....	....	....	....	....
1990-91	Dynamo Riga	Fr-Tour	1	0	0	0	....	....	....	0	....	....	....	....	....	....	....	....	....	....	....	....	....	....	....	....	....	....
	HC Riga	USSR	46	16	17	33	....	....	....	46	....	....	....	....	....	....	....	....	....	....	....	....	....	....	....	....	....	....
1991-92	HC Riga	CIS	27	7	9	16	....	....	....	20	....	....	....	....	....	....	....	....	....	....	....	....	....	....	....	....	....	....
1992-93	HC Riga	CIS	42	23	14	37	....	....	....	28	....	....	....	....	....	....	....	....	....	....	2	1	2	3	2	....	....	....
	Latvia	WC-C	7	8	13	21	....	....	....	4	....	....	....	....	....	....	....	....	....	....	....	....	....	....	....	....	....	....
1993-94	Edmonton Oilers	NHL	5	0	0	0	0	0	0	2	0	0	0	4	0.0	1	1	8	0	–8	....	....	....	....	....	....	....	....
	Cape Breton Oilers	AHL	57	24	38	62	....	....	....	16	....	....	....	....	....	....	....	....	....	....	4	1	1	2	2	....	....	....
1994-95	HC Riga	CIS	11	4	0	4	....	....	....	4	....	....	....	....	....	....	....	....	....	....	....	....	....	....	....	....	....	....
	Providence Bruins	AHL	1	0	0	0	....	....	....	15	....	....	....	....	....	....	....	....	....	....	4	0	2	2	0	....	....	....
1995-96	HC Riga	Latvia	29	28	21	49	....	....	....	42	....	....	....	....	....	....	....	....	....	....	8	*7	6	13	....	....	....	....
	Latvia	WC-B	7	3	6	9	....	....	....	20	....	....	....	....	....	....	....	....	....	....	....	....	....	....	....	....	....	....
1996-97	EV Landsberg	Germany-2	45	36	49	85	....	....	....	52	....	....	....	....	....	....	....	....	....	....	6	6	5	11	....	....	....	....
	Latvia	WC-A	8	4	4	8	....	....	....	6	....	....	....	....	....	....	....	....	....	....	....	....	....	....	....	....	....	....
1997-98	Tappara Tampere	Finland	46	14	17	31	....	....	....	57	....	....	....	....	....	....	....	....	....	....	4	1	0	1	2	....	....	....
	Latvia	WC-A	6	3	1	4	....	....	....	2	....	....	....	....	....	....	....	....	....	....	....	....	....	....	....	....	....	....
1998-99	Revier Lowen	Germany	38	10	23	33	....	....	....	18	....	....	....	....	....	....	....	....	....	....	....	....	....	....	....	....	....	....
	Latvia	WC-A	6	2	1	3	....	....	....	12	....	....	....	....	....	....	....	....	....	....	....	....	....	....	....	....	....	....
99-2000	Revier Lowen	Germany	67	17	36	53	....	....	....	66	....	....	....	....	....	....	....	....	....	....	....	....	....	....	....	....	....	....
	Latvia	WC-A	7	1	2	3	....	....	....	0	....	....	....	....	....	....	....	....	....	....	....	....	....	....	....	....	....	....
	NHL Totals		5	0	0	0	0	0	0	2	0	0	0	4	0.0	1	1	8	0		....	....	....	....	....	....	....	....

• KERR, Alan

Alan G. RW – R. 5′11″, 195 lbs. b: Hazelton, B.C., 3/28/1964. NY Islanders' 4th, 84th overall, in 1982.

Season	Club	League	GP	G	A	Pts	AG	AA	APts	PIM	PP	SH	GW	S	%	TGF	PGF	TGA	PGA	+/–	GP	G	A	Pts	PIM	PP	SH	GW
1980-81	Merritt Centennials	BCJHL	STATISTICS NOT AVAILABLE																									
1981-82	Seattle Breakers	WHL	68	15	18	33	....	....	....	107	....	....	....	....	....	....	....	....	....	....	10	6	6	12	32	....	....	....
1982-83	Seattle Breakers	WHL	71	38	53	91	....	....	....	183	....	....	....	....	....	....	....	....	....	....	4	2	3	5	0	....	....	....
1983-84	Seattle Breakers	WHL	66	46	66	112	....	....	....	141	....	....	....	....	....	....	....	....	....	....	5	1	4	5	12	....	....	....
1984-85	New York Islanders	NHL	19	3	1	4	2	1	3	24	0	0	0	17	17.6	6	0	13	0	–7	4	1	0	1	4	1	0	0
	Springfield Indians	AHL	62	32	27	59	....	....	....	140	....	....	....	....	....	....	....	....	....	....	4	1	2	3	2	....	....	....
1985-86	New York Islanders	NHL	7	0	1	1	0	1	1	16	0	0	0	9	0.0	2	0	1	0	1	1	0	0	0	0	0	0	0
	Springfield Indians	AHL	71	35	36	71	....	....	....	127	....	....	....	....	....	....	....	....	....	....	....	....	....	....	....	....	....	....
1986-87	New York Islanders	NHL	72	7	10	17	6	7	13	175	0	1	1	97	7.2	28	1	50	13	–10	14	1	4	5	25	0	0	0
1987-88	New York Islanders	NHL	80	24	34	58	20	24	44	198	4	0	2	196	12.2	95	17	74	26	30	6	1	0	1	14	0	0	0
1988-89	New York Islanders	NHL	71	20	18	38	17	13	30	144	6	0	4	147	13.6	52	8	59	10	–5	....	....	....	....	....	....	....	....
1989-90	New York Islanders	NHL	75	15	21	36	13	15	28	129	3	0	1	127	11.8	65	15	51	0	–1	4	0	0	0	10	0	0	0
1990-91	New York Islanders	NHL	2	0	0	0	0	0	0	5	0	0	0	2	0.0	0	0	0	0	0	....	....	....	....	....	....	....	....
	Capital District Islanders	AHL	43	11	21	32	....	....	....	131	....	....	....	....	....	....	....	....	....	....	....	....	....	....	....	....	....	....
1991-92	Detroit Red Wings	NHL	58	3	8	11	3	6	9	133	0	0	1	41	7.3	22	0	23	2	1	9	2	0	2	17	0	0	0
1992-93	Winnipeg Jets	NHL	7	0	1	1	0	1	1	2	0	0	0	1	0.0	1	0	5	0	–4	....	....	....	....	....	....	....	....
	Moncton Hawks	AHL	36	6	10	16	....	....	....	85	....	....	....	....	....	....	....	....	....	....	5	0	2	2	11	....	....	....
	NHL Totals		391	72	94	166	61	68	129	826	13	1	9	637	11.3	271	41	276	51		38	5	4	9	70	1	0	0

WHL West All-Star Team (1984)

Traded to **Detroit** by **NY Islanders** with future considerations for Rick Green, May 26, 1991. Traded to **Winnipeg** by **Detroit** to complete transaction that sent Aaron Ward to Detroit (June 11, 1993), June 19, 1993.

• KERR, Reg

Reginald John LW – L. 5′10″, 180 lbs. b: Oxbow, Sask., 10/16/1957. Cleveland's 3rd, 41st overall, in 1977.

Season	Club	League	GP	G	A	Pts	AG	AA	APts	PIM	PP	SH	GW	S	%	TGF	PGF	TGA	PGA	+/–	GP	G	A	Pts	PIM	PP	SH	GW
1973-74	Penticton Broncos	BCJHL	60	15	36	51				130											....	....	....	....	....	....	....	....
1974-75	Kamloops Chiefs	WCJHL	70	28	57	85	....	....	....	87	....	....	....	....	....	....	....	....	....	....	6	1	7	8	9	....	....	....
1975-76	Kamloops Chiefs	WCJHL	70	23	58	81	....	....	....	147	....	....	....	....	....	....	....	....	....	....	12	6	11	17	18	....	....	....
1976-77	Kamloops Chiefs	WCJHL	72	47	54	101	....	....	....	172	....	....	....	....	....	....	....	....	....	....	5	2	2	4	16	....	....	....
1977-78	Cleveland Barons	NHL	7	0	2	2	0	2	2	7	0	0	0	9	0.0	2	0	2	0	0	....	....	....	....	....	....	....	....
	Phoenix Roadrunners	CHL	11	4	1	5	....	....	....	15	....	....	....	....	....	....	....	....	....	....	....	....	....	....	....	....	....	....
	Chicago Black Hawks	NHL	2	0	2	2	0	2	2	0	0	0	0	2	0.0	3	1	0	0	2	....	....	....	....	....	....	....	....
	Dallas Black Hawks	CHL	55	20	21	41	....	....	....	40	....	....	....	....	....	....	....	....	....	....	13	1	2	3	20	....	....	....
1978-79	Chicago Black Hawks	NHL	73	16	24	40	14	17	31	50	2	2	4	111	14.4	54	6	74	19	–7	4	1	0	1	5	0	0	0
1979-80	Chicago Black Hawks	NHL	49	9	8	17	8	6	14	17	1	1	0	69	13.0	22	3	36	7	–10	....	....	....	....	....	....	....	....
1980-81	Chicago Black Hawks	NHL	70	30	30	60	23	20	43	56	6	0	4	154	19.5	85	18	64	7	10	3	0	0	0	2	0	0	0

			REGULAR SEASON																		PLAYOFFS							
Season	Club	League	GP	G	A	Pts	AG	AA	APts	PIM	PP	SH	GW	S	%	TGF	PGF	TGA	PGA	+/–	GP	G	A	Pts	PIM	PP	SH	GW
1981-82	**Chicago Black Hawks**	**NHL**	**59**	**11**	**28**	**39**	**9**	**19**	**28**	**39**	**1**	**0**	**1**	**106**	**10.4**	**54**	**3**	**63**	**2**	**–10**	....	....	....	....	....	....	....	....
1982-83	Springfield Indians	AHL	45	7	18	25	....	....	....	13	....	....	....	....	....	....	....	....	....	....	....	....	....	....	....	....	....	....
1983-84	**Edmonton Oilers**	**NHL**	**3**	**0**	**0**	**0**	**0**	**0**	**0**	**0**	**0**	**0**	**0**	**3**	**0.0**	**0**	**0**	**4**	**1**	**–3**	....	....	....	....	....	....	....	....
	Moncton Alpines	AHL	63	13	29	42	....	....	....	43	....	....	....	....	....	....	....	....	....	....	....	....	....	....	....	....	....	....
	NHL Totals		**263**	**66**	**94**	**160**	**54**	**66**	**120**	**169**	**10**	**3**	**9**	**454**	**14.5**	**220**	**31**	**243**	**36**		**7**	**1**	**0**	**1**	**7**	**0**	**0**	**0**

WCJHL All-Star Team (1977)

Traded to **Chicago** by **Cleveland** for Randy Holt, November 23, 1977. Signed as a free agent by **Edmonton**, November 9, 1983.

• KERR, Tim

Timothy E. C/RW – R. 6'3", 230 lbs. b: Windsor, Ont., 1/5/1960.

Season	Club	League	GP	G	A	Pts	AG	AA	APts	PIM	PP	SH	GW	S	%	TGF	PGF	TGA	PGA	+/–	GP	G	A	Pts	PIM	PP	SH	GW
1976-77	Windsor Royals	OHA-B	38	34	28	62	....	....	....	85	....	....	....	....	....	....	....	....	....	....	....	....	....	....	....	....	....	....
	Windsor Spitfires	OMJHL	9	2	4	6	....	....	....	7	....	....	....	....	....	....	....	....	....	....	3	0	0	0	0	....	....	....
1977-78	Kingston Canadians	OMJHL	67	14	25	39	....	....	....	33	....	....	....	....	....	....	....	....	....	....	5	0	0	0	0	....	....	....
1978-79	Kingston Canadians	OMJHL	57	17	25	42	....	....	....	27	....	....	....	....	....	....	....	....	....	....	6	1	1	2	2	....	....	....
1979-80	Kingston Canadians	OMJHL	63	40	33	73	....	....	....	39	....	....	....	....	....	....	....	....	....	....	3	0	1	1	16	....	....	....
	Maine Mariners	AHL	7	2	4	6	....	....	....	2	....	....	....	....	....	....	....	....	....	....	....	....	....	....	....	....	....	....
1980-81	**Philadelphia Flyers**	**NHL**	**68**	**22**	**23**	**45**	**17**	**15**	**32**	**84**	**6**	**0**	**7**	**95**	**23.2**	**55**	**19**	**33**	**0**	**3**	**10**	**1**	**3**	**4**	**2**	**1**	**0**	**0**
1981-82	**Philadelphia Flyers**	**NHL**	**61**	**21**	**30**	**51**	**17**	**20**	**37**	**138**	**7**	**0**	**2**	**118**	**17.8**	**74**	**15**	**58**	**5**	**6**	**4**	**0**	**2**	**2**	**2**	**0**	**0**	**0**
1982-83	**Philadelphia Flyers**	**NHL**	**24**	**11**	**8**	**19**	**9**	**6**	**15**	**6**	**0**	**0**	**1**	**49**	**22.4**	**22**	**3**	**15**	**0**	**4**	**2**	**2**	**0**	**2**	**0**	**0**	**0**	**0**
1983-84	**Philadelphia Flyers**	**NHL**	**79**	**54**	**39**	**93**	**44**	**27**	**71**	**29**	**9**	**0**	**5**	**286**	**18.9**	**138**	**29**	**79**	**0**	**30**	**3**	**0**	**0**	**0**	**0**	**0**	**0**	**0**
1984-85	**Philadelphia Flyers**	**NHL**	**74**	**54**	**44**	**98**	**44**	**30**	**74**	**57**	**21**	**0**	**9**	**267**	**20.2**	**135**	**52**	**54**	**0**	**29**	**12**	**10**	**4**	**14**	**13**	**4**	**0**	**1**
1985-86	**Philadelphia Flyers**	**NHL**	**76**	**58**	**26**	**84**	**46**	**17**	**63**	**79**	**34**	**0**	**8**	**285**	**20.4**	**141**	**78**	**68**	**0**	**–5**	**5**	**3**	**3**	**6**	**8**	**1**	**0**	**0**
1986-87	**Philadelphia Flyers**	**NHL**	**75**	**58**	**37**	**95**	**50**	**27**	**77**	**57**	**26**	**0**	**10**	**261**	**22.2**	**139**	**55**	**48**	**2**	**38**	**12**	**8**	**5**	**13**	**2**	**5**	**0**	**3**
	NHL All-Stars	RV-87	DID NOT PLAY																									
1987-88	**Philadelphia Flyers**	**NHL**	**8**	**3**	**2**	**5**	**3**	**1**	**4**	**12**	**2**	**0**	**0**	**34**	**8.8**	**17**	**11**	**6**	**0**	**0**	**6**	**1**	**3**	**4**	**4**	**1**	**0**	**0**
1988-89	**Philadelphia Flyers**	**NHL**	**69**	**48**	**40**	**88**	**41**	**28**	**69**	**73**	**25**	**0**	**2**	**236**	**20.3**	**121**	**62**	**64**	**1**	**–4**	**19**	**14**	**11**	**25**	**27**	**8**	**0**	**2**
1989-90	**Philadelphia Flyers**	**NHL**	**40**	**24**	**24**	**48**	**21**	**17**	**38**	**34**	**9**	**0**	**2**	**162**	**14.8**	**75**	**34**	**44**	**0**	**–3**	....	....	....	....	....	....	....	....
1990-91	**Philadelphia Flyers**	**NHL**	**27**	**10**	**14**	**24**	**9**	**11**	**20**	**8**	**6**	**0**	**0**	**74**	**13.5**	**33**	**18**	**23**	**0**	**–8**	....	....	....	....	....	....	....	....
1991-92	**New York Rangers**	**NHL**	**32**	**7**	**11**	**18**	**6**	**8**	**14**	**12**	**5**	**0**	**2**	**56**	**12.5**	**27**	**13**	**19**	**0**	**–5**	**8**	**1**	**0**	**1**	**0**	**1**	**0**	**0**
1992-93	**Hartford Whalers**	**NHL**	**22**	**0**	**6**	**6**	**0**	**4**	**4**	**7**	**0**	**0**	**0**	**48**	**0.0**	**17**	**7**	**21**	**0**	**–11**	....	....	....	....	....	....	....	....
	NHL Totals		**655**	**370**	**304**	**674**	**307**	**211**	**518**	**596**	**150**	**0**	**48**	**1971**	**18.8**	**994**	**396**	**532**	**8**		**81**	**40**	**31**	**71**	**58**	**21**	**0**	**6**

NHL Second All-Star Team (1987) • Won Bill Masterton Trophy (1989) • Played in NHL All-Star Game (1984, 1985, 1986)

Signed as a free agent by **Philadelphia**, October 25, 1979. • Missed majority of 1982-83 season recovering from knee injury suffered in game vs. Buffalo, November 24, 1982. • Missed majority of 1987-88 season recovering from shoulder surgery, December, 1987. Claimed by **San Jose** from **Philadelphia** in Expansion Draft, May 30, 1991. Traded to **NY Rangers** by **San Jose** for Brian Mullen, May 30, 1991. Traded to **Hartford** by **NY Rangers** for future considerations, July 9, 1992.

• KESA, Dan

RW – R. 6', 198 lbs. b: Vancouver, B.C., 11/23/1971. Vancouver's 4th, 95th overall, in 1991.

Season	Club	League	GP	G	A	Pts	AG	AA	APts	PIM	PP	SH	GW	S	%	TGF	PGF	TGA	PGA	+/–	GP	G	A	Pts	PIM	PP	SH	GW
1988-89	Richmond Sockeyes	BCJHL	44	21	21	42	....	....	....	71	....	....	....	....	....	....	....	....	....	....	....	....	....	....	....	....	....	....
1989-90	Richmond Sockeyes	BCJHL	54	39	38	77	....	....	....	103	....	....	....	....	....	....	....	....	....	....	....	....	....	....	....	....	....	....
1990-91	Prince Albert Raiders	WHL	69	30	23	53	....	....	....	116	....	....	....	....	....	....	....	....	....	....	3	1	1	2	0	....	....	....
1991-92	Prince Albert Raiders	WHL	62	46	51	97	....	....	....	201	....	....	....	....	....	....	....	....	....	....	10	9	10	19	27	....	....	....
1992-93	Hamilton Canucks	AHL	62	16	24	40	....	....	....	76	....	....	....	....	....	....	....	....	....	....	....	....	....	....	....	....	....	....
1993-94	**Vancouver Canucks**	**NHL**	**19**	**2**	**4**	**6**	**2**	**3**	**5**	**18**	**1**	**0**	**1**	**18**	**11.1**	**8**	**1**	**15**	**5**	**–3**	....	....	....	....	....	....	....	....
	Hamilton Canucks	AHL	53	37	33	70	....	....	....	33	....	....	....	....	....	....	....	....	....	....	4	1	4	5	4	....	....	....
1994-95	Syracuse Crunch	AHL	70	34	44	78	....	....	....	81	....	....	....	....	....	....	....	....	....	....	....	....	....	....	....	....	....	....
1995-96	**Dallas Stars**	**NHL**	**3**	**0**	**0**	**0**	**0**	**0**	**0**	**0**	**0**	**0**	**0**	**0**	**0.0**	**0**	**0**	**3**	**2**	**–1**	....	....	....	....	....	....	....	....
	Michigan K-Wings	IHL	15	4	11	15	....	....	....	33	....	....	....	....	....	....	....	....	....	....	....	....	....	....	....	....	....	....
	Springfield Falcons	AHL	22	10	5	15	....	....	....	13	....	....	....	....	....	....	....	....	....	....	....	....	....	....	....	....	....	....
	Detroit Vipers	IHL	27	9	6	15	....	....	....	22	....	....	....	....	....	....	....	....	....	....	12	6	4	10	4	....	....	....
1996-97	Detroit Vipers	IHL	60	22	21	43	....	....	....	19	....	....	....	....	....	....	....	....	....	....	20	7	5	12	20	....	....	....
1997-98	Detroit Vipers	IHL	76	40	37	77	....	....	....	40	....	....	....	....	....	....	....	....	....	....	20	*13	5	18	14	....	....	....
1998-99	**Pittsburgh Penguins**	**NHL**	**67**	**2**	**8**	**10**	**2**	**8**	**10**	**27**	**0**	**0**	**0**	**33**	**6.1**	**16**	**2**	**39**	**16**	**–9**	**13**	**1**	**0**	**1**	**0**	**1**	**0**	**1**
	Detroit Vipers	IHL	8	3	5	8	....	....	....	12	....	....	....	....	....	....	....	....	....	....	....	....	....	....	....	....	....	....
99-2000	**Tampa Bay Lightning**	**NHL**	**50**	**4**	**10**	**14**	**4**	**9**	**13**	**21**	**0**	**1**	**1**	**55**	**7.3**	**18**	**0**	**49**	**20**	**–11**	....	....	....	....	....	....	....	....
	Manitoba Moose	IHL	1	0	0	0	....	....	....	0	....	....	....	....	....	....	....	....	....	....	....	....	....	....	....	....	....	....
	Detroit Vipers	IHL	5	3	0	3	....	....	....	2	....	....	....	....	....	....	....	....	....	....	....	....	....	....	....	....	....	....
	NHL Totals		**139**	**8**	**22**	**30**	**8**	**20**	**28**	**66**	**1**	**1**	**2**	**106**	**7.5**	**42**	**3**	**106**	**43**		**13**	**1**	**0**	**1**	**0**	**1**	**0**	**1**

Traded to **Dallas** by **Vancouver** with Greg Adams and Vancouver's 5th round choice (later traded to LA Kings — LA Kings selected Jason Morgan) in 1995 Entry Draft for Russ Courtnall, April 7, 1995. Traded to **Hartford** by **Dallas** for Robert Petrovicky, November 29, 1995. Signed as a free agent by **Pittsburgh**, August 20, 1998. Signed as a free agent by **Tampa Bay**, September 6, 1999.

• KESSELL, Rick

Richard John C – L. 5'10", 175 lbs. b: Toronto, Ont., 7/27/1949. Pittsburgh's 1st, 15th overall, in 1969.

Season	Club	League	GP	G	A	Pts	AG	AA	APts	PIM	PP	SH	GW	S	%	TGF	PGF	TGA	PGA	+/–	GP	G	A	Pts	PIM	PP	SH	GW
1965-66	Toronto Midget Marlboros	MTHL	STATISTICS NOT AVAILABLE																									
	Toronto Marlboros	OHA-Jr.	....	....	....	....	....	....	....	....	....	....	....	....	....	....	....	....	....	....	2	0	0	0	0	....	....	....
1966-67	Markham Marauders	OHA-B	35	29	27	56	....	....	....	....	....	....	....	....	....	....	....	....	....	....	....	....	....	....	....	....	....	....
1967-68	Markham Waxers	OHA-B	STATISTICS NOT AVAILABLE																									
	Toronto Marlboros	OHA-Jr.	14	1	3	4	....	....	....	2	....	....	....	....	....	....	....	....	....	....	....	....	....	....	....	....	....	....
	London Nationals/Knights	OHA-Jr.	16	2	2	4	....	....	....	0	....	....	....	....	....	....	....	....	....	....	....	....	....	....	....	....	....	....
1968-69	Oshawa Generals	OHA-Jr.	53	26	*66	92	....	....	....	8	....	....	....	....	....	....	....	....	....	....	....	....	....	....	....	....	....	....
1969-70	**Pittsburgh Penguins**	**NHL**	**8**	**1**	**2**	**3**	**1**	**2**	**3**	**0**	**0**	**0**	**0**	**15**	**6.7**	**5**	**2**	**3**	**0**	**0**	....	....	....	....	....	....	....	....
	Baltimore Clippers	AHL	52	15	21	36	....	....	....	6	....	....	....	....	....	....	....	....	....	....	5	1	1	2	0	....	....	....
1970-71	**Pittsburgh Penguins**	**NHL**	**6**	**0**	**2**	**2**	**0**	**2**	**2**	**2**	**0**	**0**	**0**	**15**	**0.0**	**4**	**0**	**3**	**0**	**1**	....	....	....	....	....	....	....	....
	Amarillo Wranglers	CHL	62	31	38	69	....	....	....	10	....	....	....	....	....	....	....	....	....	....	....	....	....	....	....	....	....	....
1971-72	**Pittsburgh Penguins**	**NHL**	**3**	**0**	**1**	**1**	**0**	**1**	**1**	**0**	**0**	**0**	**0**	**3**	**0.0**	**1**	**1**	**1**	**0**	**–1**	....	....	....	....	....	....	....	....
	Hershey Bears	AHL	54	24	19	43	....	....	....	12	....	....	....	....	....	....	....	....	....	....	....	....	....	....	....	....	....	....
1972-73	**Pittsburgh Penguins**	**NHL**	**67**	**1**	**13**	**14**	**1**	**10**	**11**	**0**	**0**	**0**	**0**	**35**	**2.9**	**16**	**2**	**26**	**3**	**–9**	....	....	....	....	....	....	....	....
1973-74	**California Golden Seals**	**NHL**	**51**	**2**	**6**	**8**	**2**	**5**	**7**	**4**	**1**	**0**	**0**	**31**	**6.5**	**10**	**1**	**33**	**20**	**–4**	....	....	....	....	....	....	....	....
1974-75	Salt Lake Golden Eagles	CHL	8	1	4	5	....	....	....	2	....	....	....	....	....	....	....	....	....	....	....	....	....	....	....	....	....	....
	New Haven Nighthawks	AHL	60	21	46	67	....	....	....	16	....	....	....	....	....	....	....	....	....	....	16	4	9	13	2	....	....	....
1975-76	Salt Lake Golden Eagles	CHL	54	16	39	55	....	....	....	19	....	....	....	....	....	....	....	....	....	....	5	2	3	5	2	....	....	....
1976-77	Whitby Warriors	OHA-Sr.	34	9	17	26	....	....	....	6	....	....	....	....	....	....	....	....	....	....	....	....	....	....	....	....	....	....
1977-78	Whitby Warriors	OHA-Sr.	32	12	17	29	....	....	....	18	....	....	....	....	....	....	....	....	....	....	....	....	....	....	....	....	....	....
1978-79			STATISTICS NOT AVAILABLE																									
1979-80	Georgetown Gyros	GBSHL	STATISTICS NOT AVAILABLE																									
1980-81	Georgetown Gyros	OHA-Sr.	36	18	49	67	....	....	....	....	....	....	....	....	....	....	....	....	....	....	....	....	....	....	....	....	....	....
	NHL Totals		**135**	**4**	**24**	**28**	**4**	**20**	**24**	**6**	**1**	**0**	**0**	**99**	**4.0**	**36**	**6**	**66**	**23**		....	....	....	....	....	....	....	....

Claimed by **California** (Salt Lake-CHL) from **Pittsburgh** in Reverse Draft, June 13, 1973.

• KETOLA, Veli-Pekka

C – L. 6'3", 220 lbs. b: Pori, Finland, 3/28/1948.

Season	Club	League	GP	G	A	Pts	AG	AA	APts	PIM	PP	SH	GW	S	%	TGF	PGF	TGA	PGA	+/–	GP	G	A	Pts	PIM	PP	SH	GW
1963-64	Karpat Pori	Finland	2	0	0	0	....	....	....	0	....	....	....	....	....	....	....	....	....	....	....	....	....	....	....	....	....	....
1964-65	Karpat Pori	Finland	18	4	1	5	....	....	....	2	....	....	....	....	....	....	....	....	....	....	....	....	....	....	....	....	....	....
1965-66	Karpat Pori	Finland	19	8	3	11	....	....	....	12	....	....	....	....	....	....	....	....	....	....	....	....	....	....	....	....	....	....
	Karpat Pori	Finland	STATISTICS NOT AVAILABLE																									
1966-67	Karpat Pori	Finland	22	15	10	25	....	....	....	30	....	....	....	....	....	....	....	....	....	....	....	....	....	....	....	....	....	....
1967-68	Assat Pori	Finland	20	12	13	25	....	....	....	16	....	....	....	....	....	....	....	....	....	....	....	....	....	....	....	....	....	....
	Finland	Nat-Team	13	10	7	17	....	....	....	13	....	....	....	....	....	....	....	....	....	....	....	....	....	....	....	....	....	....
	Finland	Olympics	7	2	1	3	....	....	....	10	....	....	....	....	....	....	....	....	....	....	....	....	....	....	....	....	....	....

Season	Club	League	GP	G	A	Pts	AG	AA	APts	PIM	PP	SH	GW	S	%	TGF	PGF	TGA	PGA	+/–	GP	G	A	Pts	PIM	PP	SH	GW
			REGULAR SEASON																		PLAYOFFS							
1968-69	Assat Pori	Finland	20	15	9	24	....	....	....	22	....	....	....	....	....	....	....	....	....	....	....	....	....	....	....	....	....	....
	Finland	Nat-Team	11	1	4	5	....	....	....	10	....	....	....	....	....	....	....	....	....	....	....	....	....	....	....	....	....	....
	Finland	WEC-A	8	0	2	2	....	....	....	2	....	....	....	....	....	....	....	....	....	....	....	....	....	....	....	....	....	....
1969-70	Jokerit Helsinki	Finland	22	25	12	37	....	....	....	26	....	....	....	....	....	....	....	....	....	....	....	....	....	....	....	....	....	....
	Finalnd	WEC-A	10	4	3	7	....	....	....	32	....	....	....	....	....	....	....	....	....	....	....	....	....	....	....	....	....	....
1970-71	Assat Pori	Finland	31	25	17	42	....	....	....	31	....	....	....	....	....	....	....	....	....	....	....	....	....	....	....	....	....	....
	Finland	Nat-Team	17	6	7	13	....	....	....	16	....	....	....	....	....	....	....	....	....	....	....	....	....	....	....	....	....	....
	Finland	WEC-A	6	5	1	6	....	....	....	4	....	....	....	....	....	....	....	....	....	....	....	....	....	....	....	....	....	....
1971-72	Assat Pori	Finland	32	16	14	30	....	....	....	25	....	....	....	....	....	....	....	....	....	....	....	....	....	....	....	....	....	....
	Finland	Nat-Team	9	1	1	2	....	....	....	2	....	....	....	....	....	....	....	....	....	....	....	....	....	....	....	....	....	....
	Finland	Olympics	6	1	3	4	....	....	....	7	....	....	....	....	....	....	....	....	....	....	....	....	....	....	....	....	....	....
	Finland	WEC-A	9	4	3	7	....	....	....	4	....	....	....	....	....	....	....	....	....	....	....	....	....	....	....	....	....	....
1972-73	Assat Pori	Finland	36	25	16	41	....	....	....	*74	....	....	....	....	....	....	....	....	....	....	10	2	2	4	12	....	....	....
	Finland	Nat-Team	8	1	0	1	....	....	....	11	....	....	....	....	....	....	....	....	....	....	....	....	....	....	....	....	....	....
	Finland	WEC-A	10	2	2	4	....	....	....	12	....	....	....	....	....	....	....	....	....	....	....	....	....	....	....	....	....	....
1973-74	Assat Pori	Finland	35	23	21	44	....	....	....	44	....	....	....	....	....	....	....	....	....	....	10	7	3	10	4	....	....	....
	Finland	Nat-Team	18	4	1	5	....	....	....	6	....	....	....	....	....	....	....	....	....	....	....	....	....	....	....	....	....	....
	Finland	WEC-A	10	7	3	10	....	....	....	4	....	....	....	....	....	....	....	....	....	....	....	....	....	....	....	....	....	....
1974-75	Winnipeg Jets	WHA	74	23	28	51	....	....	....	25	....	....	....	....	....	....	....	....	....	....	....	....	....	....	....	....	....	....
1975-76	Winnipeg Jets	WHA	80	32	36	68	....	....	....	32	....	....	....	....	....	....	....	....	....	....	13	7	5	12	2	....	....	....
1976-77	Finland	Can-Cup	5	0	0	0	....	....	....	2	....	....	....	....	....	....	....	....	....	....	....	....	....	....	....	....	....	....
	Calgary Cowboys	WHA	17	4	6	10	....	....	....	2	....	....	....	....	....	....	....	....	....	....	....	....	....	....	....	....	....	....
	Winnipeg Jets	WHA	64	25	29	54	....	....	....	59	....	....	....	....	....	....	....	....	....	....	....	....	....	....	....	....	....	....
	Finland	Nat-Team	5	0	0	0	....	....	....	6	....	....	....	....	....	....	....	....	....	....	....	....	....	....	....	....	....	....
1977-78	Assat Pori	Finland	36	27	29	56	....	....	....	59	....	....	....	....	....	....	....	....	....	....	9	*10	*10	*20	22	....	....	....
	Finland	Nat-Team	6	1	1	2	....	....	....	20	....	....	....	....	....	....	....	....	....	....	....	....	....	....	....	....	....	....
1978-79	Assat Pori	Finland	36	23	*49	*72	....	....	....	66	....	....	....	....	....	....	....	....	....	....	8	1	6	7	30	....	....	....
1979-80	Assat Pori	Finland	36	22	38	60	....	....	....	61	....	....	....	....	....	....	....	....	....	....	7	3	7	10	*40	....	....	....
1980-81	Assat Pori	Finland	36	23	39	62	....	....	....	61	....	....	....	....	....	....	....	....	....	....	2	0	0	0	2	....	....	....
1981-82	Finland	Can-Cup	5	0	0	0	....	....	....	6	....	....	....	....	....	....	....	....	....	....	....	....	....	....	....	....	....	....
	Colorado Rockies	**NHL**	**44**	**9**	**5**	**14**	**7**	**3**	**10**	**4**	**4**	**0**	**1**	**42**	**21.4**	**26**	**10**	**33**	**0**	**–17**	....	....	....	....	....	....	....	....
	Finland	Nat-Team	5	1	2	3	....	....	....	2	....	....	....	....	....	....	....	....	....	....	....	....	....	....	....	....	....	....
1982-83	KalPa Kuopio	Finland-2	6	4	8	12	....	....	....	6	....	....	....	....	....	....	....	....	....	....	....	....	....	....	....	....	....	....
	NHL Totals		**44**	**9**	**5**	**14**	**7**	**3**	**10**	**4**	**4**	**0**	**1**	**42**	**21.4**	**26**	**10**	**33**	**0**		....	....	....	....	....	....	....	....
	Other Major League Totals		235	84	99	183	....	....	....	118	....	....	....	....	....	....	....	....	....	....	13	7	5	12	2	....	....	....

Finnish First All-Star Team (1968, 1970, 1971, 1974, 1978, 1979)

Selected by **Calgary-Cleveland** (WHA) in 1972 WHA General Player Draft, February 12, 1972. WHA rights traded to **Winnipeg** (WHA) by **Cleveland** (WHA) for future considerations, August, 1974. Traded to **Calgary** (WHA) by **Winnipeg** (WHA) with Ron Ward and Heikki Riihiranta for Mike Ford and Danny Lawson and future considerations, March, 1977. Signed as a free agent by **Colorado**, July 8, 1981.

• KETTER, Kerry

Kerry Kenneth D – L. 6'1", 202 lbs. b: Prince George, B.C., 9/20/1947.

Season	Club	League	GP	G	A	Pts	AG	AA	APts	PIM	PP	SH	GW	S	%	TGF	PGF	TGA	PGA	+/–	GP	G	A	Pts	PIM	PP	SH	GW
1965-66	Edmonton Oil Kings	ASHL	50	3	5	8	....	....	....	14	....	....	....	....	....	....	....	....	....	....	11	1	4	5	18	....	....	....
	Edmonton Oil Kings	Mem-Cup	12	1	2	3	....	....	....	13	....	....	....	....	....	....	....	....	....	....	....	....	....	....	....	....	....	....
1966-67	Edmonton Oil Kings	CMJHL	56	4	26	30	....	....	....	99	....	....	....	....	....	....	....	....	....	....	9	1	4	5	22	....	....	....
1967-68	Edmonton Oil Kings	WCJHL	59	11	28	39	....	....	....	169	....	....	....	....	....	....	....	....	....	....	13	1	5	6	26	....	....	....
	Edmonton Nuggets	ASHL	1	1	0	1	....	....	....	0	....	....	....	....	....	....	....	....	....	....	3	0	1	1	12	....	....	....
	Estevan Bruins	Mem-Cup	5	0	0	0	....	....	....	12	....	....	....	....	....	....	....	....	....	....	....	....	....	....	....	....	....	....
1968-69	Fort Worth Wings	CHL	62	2	10	12	....	....	....	80	....	....	....	....	....	....	....	....	....	....	....	....	....	....	....	....	....	....
1969-70	Fort Worth Wings	CHL	61	4	8	12	....	....	....	79	....	....	....	....	....	....	....	....	....	....	7	0	0	0	7	....	....	....
1970-71	Baltimore Clippers	AHL	71	2	20	22	....	....	....	102	....	....	....	....	....	....	....	....	....	....	6	2	1	3	10	....	....	....
1971-72	Nova Scotia Voyageurs	AHL	69	2	8	10	....	....	....	108	....	....	....	....	....	....	....	....	....	....	15	2	5	7	50	....	....	....
1972-73	**Atlanta Flames**	**NHL**	**41**	**0**	**2**	**2**	**0**	**2**	**2**	**58**	**0**	**0**	**0**	**31**	**0.0**	**19**	**1**	**26**	**2**	**–6**	....	....	....	....	....	....	....	....
1973-74	Dallas Black Hawks	CHL	65	5	20	25	....	....	....	84	....	....	....	....	....	....	....	....	....	....	5	0	0	0	4	....	....	....
1974-75	Baltimore Clippers	AHL	44	1	7	8	....	....	....	44	....	....	....	....	....	....	....	....	....	....	....	....	....	....	....	....	....	....
	Omaha Knights	CHL	31	2	11	13	....	....	....	36	....	....	....	....	....	....	....	....	....	....	5	0	4	4	2	....	....	....
1975-76	Edmonton Oilers	WHA	48	1	9	10	....	....	....	20	....	....	....	....	....	....	....	....	....	....	....	....	....	....	....	....	....	....
	NHL Totals		**41**	**0**	**2**	**2**	**0**	**2**	**2**	**58**	**0**	**0**	**0**	**31**	**0.0**	**19**	**1**	**26**	**2**		....	....	....	....	....	....	....	....
	Other Major League Totals		48	1	9	10	....	....	....	20	....	....	....	....	....	....	....	....	....	....	....	....	....	....	....	....	....	....

Loaned to **Estevan** by **Edmonton** for Memorial Cup playoffs, April, 1968. Traded to **Montreal** by **Detroit** with cash for Leon Rochefort, May 25, 1971. Selected by **Edmonton** (WHA) in 1972 WHA General Player Draft, February 12, 1972. Claimed by **Atlanta** from **Montreal** in Expansion Draft, June 6, 1972. Claimed by **Kansas City** from **Atlanta** in Expansion Draft, June 12, 1974. Traded to **New England** (WHA) by **Edmonton** (WHA) with Steve Carlyle for Paul Hurley and the rights to Clarke Jantze, February 2, 1976. • Suspended by **New England** (WHA) for refusing to report to team, February, 1976.

• KHARIN, Sergei

RW – L. 5'11", 180 lbs. b: Odintsovo, USSR, 2/20/1963. Winnipeg's 15th, 240th overall, in 1989.

Season	Club	League	GP	G	A	Pts	AG	AA	APts	PIM	PP	SH	GW	S	%	TGF	PGF	TGA	PGA	+/–	GP	G	A	Pts	PIM	PP	SH	GW
1980-81	Krylja Sovetov Moscow	USSR	2	0	0	0	....	....	....	0	....	....	....	....	....	....	....	....	....	....	....	....	....	....	....	....	....	....
	Soviet Union	EJC-A	5	6	6	12	....	....	....	2	....	....	....	....	....	....	....	....	....	....	....	....	....	....	....	....	....	....
1981-82	Krylja Sovetov Moscow	USSR	34	4	3	7	....	....	....	10	....	....	....	....	....	....	....	....	....	....	....	....	....	....	....	....	....	....
1982-83	Krylja Sovetov Moscow	USSR	49	5	5	10	....	....	....	20	....	....	....	....	....	....	....	....	....	....	....	....	....	....	....	....	....	....
	Soviet Union	WJC-A	7	8	2	10	....	....	....	2	....	....	....	....	....	....	....	....	....	....	....	....	....	....	....	....	....	....
1983-84	Krylja Sovetov Moscow	USSR	33	5	3	8	....	....	....	18	....	....	....	....	....	....	....	....	....	....	....	....	....	....	....	....	....	....
1984-85	Krylja Sovetov Moscow	USSR	34	12	8	20	....	....	....	6	....	....	....	....	....	....	....	....	....	....	....	....	....	....	....	....	....	....
1985-86	Krylja Sovetov Moscow	USSR	38	15	14	29	....	....	....	19	....	....	....	....	....	....	....	....	....	....	....	....	....	....	....	....	....	....
1986-87	Krylja Sovetov Moscow	USSR	40	16	11	27	....	....	....	14	....	....	....	....	....	....	....	....	....	....	....	....	....	....	....	....	....	....
1987-88	Krylja Sovetov Moscow	USSR	45	17	13	30	....	....	....	20	....	....	....	....	....	....	....	....	....	....	....	....	....	....	....	....	....	....
1988-89	Krylja Sovetov Moscow	USSR	44	15	9	24	....	....	....	14	....	....	....	....	....	....	....	....	....	....	....	....	....	....	....	....	....	....
1989-90	Krylja Sovetov Moscow	Fr-Tour	1	0	1	1	....	....	....	0	....	....	....	....	....	....	....	....	....	....	....	....	....	....	....	....	....	....
	Krylja Sovetov Moscow	USSR	47	12	5	17	....	....	....	28	....	....	....	....	....	....	....	....	....	....	....	....	....	....	....	....	....	....
	Krylja Sovetov Moscow	Super-S	5	0	2	2	....	....	....	4	....	....	....	....	....	....	....	....	....	....	....	....	....	....	....	....	....	....
1990-91	**Winnipeg Jets**	**NHL**	**7**	**2**	**3**	**5**	**2**	**2**	**4**	**2**	**0**	**0**	**0**	**13**	**15.4**	**8**	**2**	**4**	**0**	**2**	....	....	....	....	....	....	....	....
	Moncton Hawks	AHL	66	22	18	40	....	....	....	38	....	....	....	....	....	....	....	....	....	....	5	1	0	1	2	....	....	....
1991-92	Halifax Citadels	AHL	40	10	12	22	....	....	....	15	....	....	....	....	....	....	....	....	....	....	....	....	....	....	....	....	....	....
1992-93	Birmingham Bulls	ECHL	2	0	3	3	....	....	....	0	....	....	....	....	....	....	....	....	....	....	....	....	....	....	....	....	....	....
	Cincinnati Cyclones	IHL	60	13	18	31	....	....	....	25	....	....	....	....	....	....	....	....	....	....	....	....	....	....	....	....	....	....
1993-94	Dayton Bombers	ECHL	59	30	59	89	....	....	....	56	....	....	....	....	....	....	....	....	....	....	....	....	....	....	....	....	....	....
1994-95	Cincinnati Cyclones	IHL	56	14	29	43	....	....	....	24	....	....	....	....	....	....	....	....	....	....	3	2	0	2	4	....	....	....
1995-96	Dayton Bombers	ECHL	25	7	9	16	....	....	....	25	....	....	....	....	....	....	....	....	....	....	1	0	0	0	0	....	....	....
	Worcester IceCats	AHL	28	7	12	19	....	....	....	10	....	....	....	....	....	....	....	....	....	....	....	....	....	....	....	....	....	....
1996-97	Port Huron Border Cats	ColHL	49	20	24	44	....	....	....	20	....	....	....	....	....	....	....	....	....	....	3	1	1	2	2	....	....	....
	Muskegon Fury	ColHL	19	12	16	28	....	....	....	12	....	....	....	....	....	....	....	....	....	....	....	....	....	....	....	....	....	....
1997-98	Muskegon Fury	UHL	74	36	86	122	....	....	....	38	....	....	....	....	....	....	....	....	....	....	3	2	1	3	6	....	....	....
1998-99	Muskegon Fury	UHL	70	37	63	100	....	....	....	77	....	....	....	....	....	....	....	....	....	....	11	4	15	19	0	....	....	....
99-2000	Muskegon Fury	UHL	59	11	50	61	....	....	....	13	....	....	....	....	....	....	....	....	....	....	18	7	*17	24	10	....	....	....
	NHL Totals		**7**	**2**	**3**	**5**	**2**	**2**	**4**	**2**	**0**	**0**	**0**	**13**	**15.4**	**8**	**2**	**4**	**0**		....	....	....	....	....	....	....	....

UHL Second All-Star Team (1998, 1999)

Traded to **Quebec** by **Winnipeg** for Shawn Anderson, October 22, 1991.

Season	Club	League	GP	G	A	Pts	AG	AA	APts	PIM	PP	SH	GW	S	%	TGF	PGF	TGA	PGA	+/–	GP	G	A	Pts	PIM	PP	SH	GW
			REGULAR SEASON																		PLAYOFFS							

• KHMYLEV, Yuri

LW – R. 6'1", 189 lbs. b: Moscow, USSR, 8/9/1964. Buffalo's 7th, 108th overall, in 1992.

Season	Club	League	GP	G	A	Pts	AG	AA	APts	PIM	PP	SH	GW	S	%	TGF	PGF	TGA	PGA	+/–	GP	G	A	Pts	PIM	PP	SH	GW
1981-82	Krylja Sovetov Moscow	USSR	8	2	2	4	....	....	....	2	....	....	....	....	....	....	....	....	....	....	....	....	....	....	....	....	....	....
	Soviet Union	EJC-A	5	2	3	5	....	....	....	4	....	....	....	....	....	....	....	....	....	....	....	....	....	....	....	....	....	....
1982-83	Krylja Sovetov Moscow	USSR	51	9	7	16	....	....	....	14	....	....	....	....	....	....	....	....	....	....	....	....	....	....	....	....	....	....
1983-84	Krylja Sovetov Moscow	USSR	43	7	8	15	....	....	....	10	....	....	....	....	....	....	....	....	....	....	....	....	....	....	....	....	....	....
	Soviet Union	WJC-A	7	2	7	9	....	....	....	0	....	....	....	....	....	....	....	....	....	....	....	....	....	....	....	....	....	....
1984-85	Krylja Sovetov Moscow	USSR	30	11	4	15	....	....	....	24	....	....	....	....	....	....	....	....	....	....	....	....	....	....	....	....	....	....
1985-86	Krylja Sovetov Moscow	USSR	40	24	9	33	....	....	....	22	....	....	....	....	....	....	....	....	....	....	....	....	....	....	....	....	....	....
	Soviet Union	WEC-A	6	2	1	3	....	....	....	4	....	....	....	....	....	....	....	....	....	....	....	....	....	....	....	....	....	....
1986-87	Krylja Sovetov Moscow	USSR	40	15	15	30	....	....	....	48	....	....	....	....	....	....	....	....	....	....	....	....	....	....	....	....	....	....
	Team USSR	RV-87	2	0	0	0	....	....	....	0	....	....	....	....	....	....	....	....	....	....	....	....	....	....	....	....	....	....
	Soviet Union	WEC-A	10	1	1	2	....	....	....	8	....	....	....	....	....	....	....	....	....	....	....	....	....	....	....	....	....	....
1987-88	Soviet Union	Can-Cup	9	0	1	1	....	....	....	2	....	....	....	....	....	....	....	....	....	....	....	....	....	....	....	....	....	....
	Krylja Sovetov Moscow	USSR	48	21	8	29	....	....	....	46	....	....	....	....	....	....	....	....	....	....	....	....	....	....	....	....	....	....
1988-89	Krylja Sovetov Moscow	USSR	44	16	18	34	....	....	....	38	....	....	....	....	....	....	....	....	....	....	....	....	....	....	....	....	....	....
	CSKA Moscow	Super-S	2	1	0	1	....	....	....	2	....	....	....	....	....	....	....	....	....	....	....	....	....	....	....	....	....	....
	Soviet Union	WEC-A	8	1	3	4	....	....	....	0	....	....	....	....	....	....	....	....	....	....	....	....	....	....	....	....	....	....
1989-90	Krylja Sovetov Moscow	Fr-Tour	1	1	0	1	....	....	....	0	....	....	....	....	....	....	....	....	....	....	....	....	....	....	....	....	....	....
	Krylja Sovetov Moscow	USSR	44	14	13	27	....	....	....	30	....	....	....	....	....	....	....	....	....	....	....	....	....	....	....	....	....	....
	Krylja Sovetov Moscow	Super-S	5	4	1	5	....	....	....	0	....	....	....	....	....	....	....	....	....	....	....	....	....	....	....	....	....	....
1990-91	Krylja Sovetov Moscow	Fr-Tour	1	0	0	0	....	....	....	0	....	....	....	....	....	....	....	....	....	....	....	....	....	....	....	....	....	....
	Krylja Sovetov Moscow	USSR	45	25	14	39	....	....	....	26	....	....	....	....	....	....	....	....	....	....	....	....	....	....	....	....	....	....
	CSKA Moscow	Super-S	7	3	3	6	....	....	....	0	....	....	....	....	....	....	....	....	....	....	....	....	....	....	....	....	....	....
1991-92	Krylja Sovetov Moscow	CIS	42	19	17	36	....	....	....	20	....	....	....	....	....	....	....	....	....	....	....	....	....	....	....	....	....	....
	Russia	Olympics	8	4	6	10	....	....	....	4	....	....	....	....	....	....	....	....	....	....	....	....	....	....	....	....	....	....
	Russia	WC-A	5	0	1	1	....	....	....	0	....	....	....	....	....	....	....	....	....	....	....	....	....	....	....	....	....	....
1992-93	Buffalo Sabres	NHL	68	20	19	39	17	13	30	28	0	3	3	122	16.4	75	12	66	9	6	8	4	3	7	4	1	0	1
1993-94	Buffalo Sabres	NHL	72	27	31	58	25	24	49	49	11	0	4	171	15.8	97	45	54	15	13	7	3	1	4	8	0	0	0
1994-95	Krylja Sovetov Moscow	IHL	11	2	2	4	....	....	....	4	....	....	....	....	....	....	....	....	....	....	....	....	....	....	....	....	....	....
	Buffalo Sabres	NHL	48	8	17	25	14	25	39	14	2	1	1	71	11.3	34	5	33	12	8	5	0	1	1	8	0	0	0
1995-96	Buffalo Sabres	NHL	66	8	20	28	8	16	24	40	5	1	1	123	6.5	48	20	64	24	–12	....	....	....	....	....	....	....	....
	St. Louis Blues	NHL	7	0	1	1	0	1	1	0	0	0	0	13	0.0	1	0	7	1	–5	6	1	1	2	4	0	0	1
1996-97	St. Louis Blues	NHL	2	1	0	1	1	0	1	2	0	0	0	3	33.3	1	0	2	0	–1	....	....	....	....	....	....	....	....
	Quebec Rafales	IHL	15	1	7	8	....	....	....	4	....	....	....	....	....	....	....	....	....	....	....	....	....	....	....	....	....	....
	Hamilton Bulldogs	AHL	52	5	19	24	....	....	....	43	....	....	....	....	....	....	....	....	....	....	22	6	7	13	12	....	....	....
1997-98	HC Fribourg-Gotteron	Switz.	17	5	6	11	....	....	....	2	....	....	....	....	....	....	....	....	....	....	2	1	0	1	0	....	....	....
1998-99	St. John's Maple Leafs	AHL	48	12	21	33	....	....	....	19	....	....	....	....	....	....	....	....	....	....	5	2	1	3	4	....	....	....
	NHL Totals		263	64	88	152	65	79	144	133	18	5	9	503	12.7	256	82	226	61		26	8	6	14	24	1	0	2

Traded to **St. Louis** by **Buffalo** with Buffalo's 8th round choice (Andrei Podkonicky) in 1996 Entry Draft for Jean-Luc Grand Pierre, Ottawa's 2nd round choice (previously acquired, Buffalo selected Cory Sarich) in 1996 Entry Draft and St. Louis' 3rd round choice (Maxim Afinogenov) in 1997 Entry Draft, March 20, 1996.

• KHRISTICH, Dmitri

LW/C – R. 6'2", 195 lbs. b: Kiev, USSR, 7/23/1969. Washington's 6th, 120th overall, in 1988.

Season	Club	League	GP	G	A	Pts	AG	AA	APts	PIM	PP	SH	GW	S	%	TGF	PGF	TGA	PGA	+/–	GP	G	A	Pts	PIM	PP	SH	GW
1985-86	Sokol Kiev	USSR	4	0	0	0	....	....	....	0	....	....	....	....	....	....	....	....	....	....	....	....	....	....	....	....	....	....
1986-87	Sokol Kiev	USSR	20	3	0	3	....	....	....	4	....	....	....	....	....	....	....	....	....	....	....	....	....	....	....	....	....	....
	Soviet Union	EJC-A	7	7	0	7	....	....	....	2	....	....	....	....	....	....	....	....	....	....	....	....	....	....	....	....	....	....
1987-88	Sokol Kiev	USSR	37	9	1	10	....	....	....	18	....	....	....	....	....	....	....	....	....	....	....	....	....	....	....	....	....	....
1988-89	Sokol Kiev	USSR	42	17	10	27	....	....	....	15	....	....	....	....	....	....	....	....	....	....	....	....	....	....	....	....	....	....
	Soviet Union	WJC-A	7	6	2	8	....	....	....	2	....	....	....	....	....	....	....	....	....	....	....	....	....	....	....	....	....	....
1989-90	Sokol Kiev	USSR	47	14	22	36	....	....	....	32	....	....	....	....	....	....	....	....	....	....	....	....	....	....	....	....	....	....
	Soviet Union	WEC-A	7	2	3	5	....	....	....	4	....	....	....	....	....	....	....	....	....	....	....	....	....	....	....	....	....	....
1990-91	Sokol Kiev	USSR	28	10	12	22	....	....	....	20	....	....	....	....	....	....	....	....	....	....	....	....	....	....	....	....	....	....
	Washington Capitals	NHL	40	13	14	27	12	11	23	21	1	0	0	77	16.9	39	5	36	1	–1	11	1	3	4	6	0	0	0
	Baltimore Skipjacks	AHL	3	0	0	0	....	....	....	0	....	....	....	....	....	....	....	....	....	....	....	....	....	....	....	....	....	....
1991-92	Washington Capitals	NHL	80	36	37	73	33	28	61	35	14	1	7	188	19.1	122	53	51	6	24	7	3	2	5	15	3	0	1
1992-93	Washington Capitals	NHL	64	31	35	66	26	24	50	28	9	1	1	127	24.4	116	40	53	6	29	6	2	5	7	2	1	0	0
1993-94	Washington Capitals	NHL	83	29	29	58	27	22	49	73	10	0	4	195	14.9	99	36	72	7	–2	11	2	3	5	10	0	0	0
1994-95	Washington Capitals	NHL	48	12	14	26	21	21	42	41	8	0	2	92	13.0	50	27	27	4	0	7	1	4	5	0	0	0	0
1995-96	Los Angeles Kings	NHL	76	27	37	64	27	30	57	44	12	0	3	204	13.2	90	36	57	3	0	....	....	....	....	....	....	....	....
1996-97	Los Angeles Kings	NHL	75	19	37	56	20	33	53	38	3	0	2	135	14.1	84	20	66	10	8	....	....	....	....	....	....	....	....
1997-98	Boston Bruins	NHL	82	29	37	66	34	36	70	42	13	2	1	144	20.1	99	37	42	5	25	6	2	2	4	2	2	0	0
1998-99	Boston Bruins	NHL	79	29	42	71	34	41	75	48	13	1	6	144	20.1	98	35	57	5	11	12	3	4	7	6	0	0	1
99-2000	Toronto Maple Leafs	NHL	53	12	18	30	13	17	30	24	3	0	0	79	15.2	46	12	35	9	8	12	1	2	3	0	1	0	0
	NHL Totals		680	237	300	537	247	263	510	394	86	5	26	1385	17.1	843	301	496	56		72	15	25	40	41	7	0	2

Played in NHL All-Star Game (1997, 1999)

Traded to **LA Kings** by **Washington** with Byron Dafoe for LA Kings' 1st round choice (Alexander Volchkov) and Dallas' 4th round choice (previously acquired, Washington selected Justin Davis) in 1996 Entry Draft, July 8, 1995. Traded to **Boston** by **LA Kings** with Byron Dafoe for Jozef Stumpel, Sandy Moger and Boston's 4th round choice (later traded to New Jersey - New Jersey selected Pierre Dagenais) in 1998 Entry Draft, August 29, 1997. Traded to **Toronto** by **Boston** for Toronto's 2nd round choice (Ivan Huml) in 2000 Entry Draft, October 20, 1999.

• KIDD, Ian

D – R. 5'11", 195 lbs. b: Gresham, OR, 5/11/1964.

Season	Club	League	GP	G	A	Pts	AG	AA	APts	PIM	PP	SH	GW	S	%	TGF	PGF	TGA	PGA	+/–	GP	G	A	Pts	PIM	PP	SH	GW
1982-83	Penticton Knights	BCJHL	42	18	26	44	....	....	....	214	....	....	....	....	....	....	....	....	....	....	....	....	....	....	....	....	....	....
1983-84	Penticton Knights	BCJHL	55	31	52	83	....	....	....	188	....	....	....	....	....	....	....	....	....	....	....	....	....	....	....	....	....	....
1984-85	Penticton Knights	BCJHL	46	31	77	108	....	....	....	177	....	....	....	....	....	....	....	....	....	....	....	....	....	....	....	....	....	....
	Penticton Knights	Cen-Cup	4	1	2	3	....	....	....	12	....	....	....	....	....	....	....	....	....	....	....	....	....	....	....	....	....	....
1985-86	University of North Dakota	WCHA	37	6	16	22	....	....	....	65	....	....	....	....	....	....	....	....	....	....	....	....	....	....	....	....	....	....
1986-87	University of North Dakota	WCHA	47	13	47	60	....	....	....	58	....	....	....	....	....	....	....	....	....	....	....	....	....	....	....	....	....	....
1987-88	Vancouver Canucks	NHL	19	4	7	11	3	5	8	25	3	0	0	22	18.2	19	7	15	0	–3	....	....	....	....	....	....	....	....
	Fredericton Express	AHL	53	1	21	22	....	....	....	70	....	....	....	....	....	....	....	....	....	....	12	0	4	4	22	....	....	....
1988-89	Vancouver Canucks	NHL	1	0	0	0	0	0	0	0	0	0	0	0	0.0	0	0	1	0	–1	....	....	....	....	....	....	....	....
	Milwaukee Admirals	IHL	76	13	40	53	....	....	....	124	....	....	....	....	....	....	....	....	....	....	4	0	2	2	7	....	....	....
1989-90	Milwaukee Admirals	IHL	65	11	36	47	....	....	....	86	....	....	....	....	....	....	....	....	....	....	6	2	5	7	0	....	....	....
1990-91	Milwaukee Admirals	IHL	72	5	26	31	....	....	....	41	....	....	....	....	....	....	....	....	....	....	6	0	1	1	2	....	....	....
1991-92	Milwaukee Admirals	IHL	80	9	24	33	....	....	....	75	....	....	....	....	....	....	....	....	....	....	5	0	1	1	11	....	....	....
1992-93	Milwaukee Admirals	IHL	32	3	10	13	....	....	....	36	....	....	....	....	....	....	....	....	....	....	....	....	....	....	....	....	....	....
	Cincinnati Cyclones	IHL	23	6	23	29	....	....	....	10	....	....	....	....	....	....	....	....	....	....	....	....	....	....	....	....	....	....
1993-94	Cincinnati Cyclones	IHL	79	8	30	38	....	....	....	93	....	....	....	....	....	....	....	....	....	....	8	0	3	3	10	....	....	....
1994-95	Chicago Wolves	IHL	22	2	0	2	....	....	....	20	....	....	....	....	....	....	....	....	....	....	....	....	....	....	....	....	....	....
	Cincinnati Cyclones	IHL	13	1	1	2	....	....	....	10	....	....	....	....	....	....	....	....	....	....	8	1	3	4	6	....	....	....
	NHL Totals		20	4	7	11	3	5	8	25	3	0	0	22	18.2	19	7	16	0		....	....	....	....	....	....	....	....

WCHA First All-Star Team (1987) • NCAA West First All-American Team (1987) • NCAA Championship All-Tournament Team (1987)

Signed as a free agent by **Vancouver**, July 30, 1987. Signed as a free agent by **Milwaukee** (IHL), June 19, 1992. Traded to **Cincinnati** (IHL) by **Milwaukee** (IHL) for Jeff Madill, February 25, 1993.

• KIESSLING, Udo

D – L. 5'10", 180 lbs. b: Crimmitschau, Germany, 5/21/1955.

Season	Club	League	GP	G	A	Pts	AG	AA	APts	PIM	PP	SH	GW	S	%	TGF	PGF	TGA	PGA	+/–	GP	G	A	Pts	PIM	PP	SH	GW
1972-73	SC Riessersee	Germany	40	8	6	14	....	....	....	44	....	....	....	....	....	....	....	....	....	....	....	....	....	....	....	....	....	....
	West Germany	WEC-A	10	0	0	0	....	....	....	6	....	....	....	....	....	....	....	....	....	....	....	....	....	....	....	....	....	....
1973-74	Augsburger EV Panther	Germany	36	16	6	22	....	....	....	52	....	....	....	....	....	....	....	....	....	....	....	....	....	....	....	....	....	....
	West Germany	WEC-B	7	1	2	3	....	....	....	8	....	....	....	....	....	....	....	....	....	....	....	....	....	....	....	....	....	....
1974-75	SB Rosenheim	Germany-3	34	20	18	38	....	....	....	73	....	....	....	....	....	....	....	....	....	....	....	....	....	....	....	....	....	....
	West Germany	WEC-B	7	1	3	4	....	....	....	8	....	....	....	....	....	....	....	....	....	....	....	....	....	....	....	....	....	....

			REGULAR SEASON																		PLAYOFFS							
Season	**Club**	**League**	**GP**	**G**	**A**	**Pts**	**AG**	**AA**	**APts**	**PIM**	**PP**	**SH**	**GW**	**S**	**%**	**TGF**	**PGF**	**TGA**	**PGA**	**+/–**	**GP**	**G**	**A**	**Pts**	**PIM**	**PP**	**SH**	**GW**
1975-76	SB Rosenheim	Germany	34	30	22	52	....	....	....	72	....	....	....	....	....	....	....	....	....	....	....	....	....	....	....	....	....	....
	West Germany	Olympics	6	0	1	1	....	....	....	8	....	....	....	....	....	....	....	....	....	....	....	....	....	....	....	....	....	....
	West Germany	WEC-A	10	0	1	1	....	....	....	8	....	....	....	....	....	....	....	....	....	....	....	....	....	....	....	....	....	....
1976-77	Kolner EC	Germany	46	13	21	34	....	....	....	143	....	....	....	....	....	....	....	....	....	....	....	....	....	....	....	....	....	....
	West Germany	WEC-A	10	1	2	3	....	....	....	6	....	....	....	....	....	....	....	....	....	....	....	....	....	....	....	....	....	....
1977-78	Kolner EC	Germany	39	16	18	34	....	....	....	48	....	....	....	....	....	....	....	....	....	....	....	....	....	....	....	....	....	....
	West Germany	WEC-A	10	0	5	5	....	....	....	10	....	....	....	....	....	....	....	....	....	....	....	....	....	....	....	....	....	....
1978-79	Kolner EC	Germany	40	28	32	60	....	....	....	78	....	....	....	....	....	....	....	....	....	....	....	....	....	....	....	....	....	....
	West Germany	WEC-A	8	2	4	6	....	....	....	14	....	....	....	....	....	....	....	....	....	....	....	....	....	....	....	....	....	....
1979-80	Dusseldorfer EG	Germany	48	39	44	83	....	....	....	84	....	....	....	....	....	....	....	....	....	....	7	2	2	4	10	....	....	....
	West Germany	Olympics	5	2	2	4	....	....	....	6	....	....	....	....	....	....	....	....	....	....	....	....	....	....	....	....	....	....
1980-81	Dusseldorfer EG	Germany	39	14	29	43	....	....	....	93	....	....	....	....	....	....	....	....	....	....	11	8	4	12	22	....	....	....
1981-82	Dusseldorfer EG	Germany	38	15	22	37	....	....	....	54	....	....	....	....	....	....	....	....	....	....	2	0	0	0	7	....	....	....
	West Germany	WEC-A	7	1	3	4	....	....	....	12	....	....	....	....	....	....	....	....	....	....	....	....	....	....	....	....	....	....
	Minnesota North Stars	**NHL**	**1**	**0**	**0**	**0**	**0**	**0**	**0**	**2**	**0**	**0**	**0**	**1**	**0.0**	**1**	**1**	**0**	**0**	**0**	....	....	....	....	....	....	....	....
1982-83	EV Fussen	Germany	21	12	13	25	....	....	....	52	....	....	....	....	....	....	....	....	....	....	....	....	....	....	....	....	....	....
	Kolner EC	Germany	9	4	0	4	....	....	....	2	....	....	....	....	....	....	....	....	....	....	9	3	7	10	18	....	....	....
	West Germany	WEC-A	4	0	1	1	....	....	....	10	....	....	....	....	....	....	....	....	....	....	....	....	....	....	....	....	....	....
1983-84	Kolner EC	Germany	45	9	19	28	....	....	....	74	....	....	....	....	....	....	....	....	....	....	....	....	....	....	....	....	....	....
	West Germany	Olympics	6	3	1	4	....	....	....	4	....	....	....	....	....	....	....	....	....	....	....	....	....	....	....	....	....	....
1984-85	West Germany	Can-Cup	4	0	1	1	....	....	....	4	....	....	....	....	....	....	....	....	....	....	....	....	....	....	....	....	....	....
	Kolner EC	Germany	36	14	26	40	....	....	....	38	....	....	....	....	....	....	....	....	....	....	9	4	*10	14	22	....	....	....
	West Germany	WEC-A	10	0	3	3	....	....	....	16	....	....	....	....	....	....	....	....	....	....	....	....	....	....	....	....	....	....
1985-86	Kolner EC	Germany	37	18	27	45	....	....	....	41	....	....	....	....	....	....	....	....	....	....	....	....	....	....	....	....	....	....
	West Germany	WEC-A	10	4	2	6	....	....	....	22	....	....	....	....	....	....	....	....	....	....	....	....	....	....	....	....	....	....
1986-87	Kolner EC	Germany	42	10	34	44	....	....	....	70	....	....	....	....	....	....	....	....	....	....	9	4	11	15	....	....	....	....
	West Germany	WEC-A	10	5	3	8	....	....	....	18	....	....	....	....	....	....	....	....	....	....	....	....	....	....	....	....	....	....
1987-88	Kolner EC	Germany	46	12	27	39	....	....	....	76	....	....	....	....	....	....	....	....	....	....	....	....	....	....	....	....	....	....
	West Germany	Olympics	8	1	5	6	....	....	....	20	....	....	....	....	....	....	....	....	....	....	....	....	....	....	....	....	....	....
1988-89	Kolner EC	Germany	31	11	24	35	....	....	....	38	....	....	....	....	....	....	....	....	....	....	9	6	4	10	8	....	....	....
	West Germany	WEC-A	10	2	0	2	....	....	....	12	....	....	....	....	....	....	....	....	....	....	....	....	....	....	....	....	....	....
1989-90	Kolner EC	Germany	35	7	15	22	....	....	....	45	....	....	....	....	....	....	....	....	....	....	8	1	2	3	10	....	....	....
	West Germany	WEC-A	10	2	1	3	....	....	....	10	....	....	....	....	....	....	....	....	....	....	....	....	....	....	....	....	....	....
1990-91	Kolner EC	Germany	35	7	13	20	....	....	....	36	....	....	....	....	....	....	....	....	....	....	12	2	4	6	18	....	....	....
	Germany	WEC-A	10	0	1	1	....	....	....	6	....	....	....	....	....	....	....	....	....	....	....	....	....	....	....	....	....	....
1991-92	Kolner EC	Germany	42	11	23	34	....	....	....	38	....	....	....	....	....	....	....	....	....	....	4	2	0	2	2	....	....	....
	Germany	Olympics	8	0	0	0	....	....	....	6	....	....	....	....	....	....	....	....	....	....	....	....	....	....	....	....	....	....
1992-93	EV Landshut	Germany	44	9	19	28	....	....	....	50	....	....	....	....	....	....	....	....	....	....	....	....	....	....	....	....	....	....
1993-94	EV Landshut	Germany	44	3	16	19	....	....	....	74	....	....	....	....	....	....	....	....	....	....	....	....	....	....	....	....	....	....
1994-95	EV Landshut	Germany	41	7	15	22	....	....	....	40	....	....	....	....	....	....	....	....	....	....	18	3	7	10	22	....	....	....
1995-96	EV Landshut	Germany	50	3	19	22	....	....	....	44	....	....	....	....	....	....	....	....	....	....	7	0	2	2	4	....	....	....
	NHL Totals		**1**	**0**	**0**	**0**	**0**	**0**	**0**	**2**	**0**	**0**	**0**	**1**	**0.0**	**1**	**1**	**0**	**0**		....	....	....	....	....	....	....	....

German Player of the Year (1977, 1984, 1986) • WEC-A All-Star Team (1987)

Signed as a free agent by **Minnesota**, March 5, 1982.

• KILGER, Chad

Chad William Lawrence C – L. 6'3", 215 lbs. b: Cornwall, Ont., 11/27/1976. Anaheim's 1st, 4th overall, in 1995.

Season	**Club**	**League**	**GP**	**G**	**A**	**Pts**	**AG**	**AA**	**APts**	**PIM**	**PP**	**SH**	**GW**	**S**	**%**	**TGF**	**PGF**	**TGA**	**PGA**	**+/–**	**GP**	**G**	**A**	**Pts**	**PIM**	**PP**	**SH**	**GW**
1992-93	Cornwall Colts	OJHL	55	30	36	66	....	....	....	26	....	....	....	....	....	....	....	....	....	....	6	0	0	0	0	....	....	....
1993-94	Kingston Frontenacs	OHL	66	17	35	52	....	....	....	23	....	....	....	....	....	....	....	....	....	....	6	7	2	9	8	....	....	....
1994-95	Kingston Frontenacs	OHL	65	42	53	95	....	....	....	95	....	....	....	....	....	....	....	....	....	....	6	5	2	7	10	....	....	....
1995-96	**Mighty Ducks of Anaheim**	**NHL**	**45**	**5**	**7**	**12**	**5**	**6**	**11**	**22**	**0**	**0**	**1**	**38**	**13.2**	**26**	**4**	**24**	**0**	**–2**	....	....	....	....	....	....	....	....
	Winnipeg Jets	**NHL**	**29**	**2**	**3**	**5**	**2**	**2**	**4**	**12**	**0**	**0**	**0**	**19**	**10.5**	**8**	**0**	**10**	**0**	**–2**	**4**	**1**	**0**	**1**	**0**	**0**	**0**	**1**
1996-97	**Phoenix Coyotes**	**NHL**	**24**	**4**	**3**	**7**	**4**	**3**	**7**	**13**	**1**	**0**	**0**	**30**	**13.3**	**8**	**1**	**12**	**0**	**–5**	....	....	....	....	....	....	....	....
	Springfield Falcons	AHL	52	17	28	45	....	....	....	36	....	....	....	....	....	....	....	....	....	....	16	5	7	12	56	....	....	....
1997-98	**Phoenix Coyotes**	**NHL**	**10**	**0**	**1**	**1**	**0**	**1**	**1**	**4**	**0**	**0**	**0**	**9**	**0.0**	**1**	**0**	**3**	**0**	**–2**	....	....	....	....	....	....	....	....
	Springfield Falcons	AHL	35	14	14	28	....	....	....	33	....	....	....	....	....	....	....	....	....	....	....	....	....	....	....	....	....	....
	Chicago Blackhawks	**NHL**	**22**	**3**	**8**	**11**	**4**	**8**	**12**	**6**	**2**	**0**	**1**	**23**	**13.0**	**17**	**5**	**10**	**0**	**2**	....	....	....	....	....	....	....	....
1998-99	**Chicago Blackhawks**	**NHL**	**64**	**14**	**11**	**25**	**16**	**11**	**27**	**30**	**2**	**1**	**1**	**68**	**20.6**	**33**	**4**	**39**	**9**	**–1**	....	....	....	....	....	....	....	....
	Edmonton Oilers	**NHL**	**13**	**1**	**1**	**2**	**1**	**1**	**2**	**4**	**0**	**0**	**0**	**13**	**7.7**	**4**	**2**	**5**	**0**	**–3**	**4**	**0**	**0**	**0**	**4**	**0**	**0**	**0**
99-2000	**Edmonton Oilers**	**NHL**	**40**	**3**	**2**	**5**	**3**	**2**	**5**	**18**	**0**	**0**	**0**	**32**	**9.4**	**7**	**0**	**14**	**1**	**–6**	**3**	**0**	**0**	**0**	**0**	**0**	**0**	**0**
	Hamilton Bulldogs	AHL	7	4	2	6	....	....	....	4	....	....	....	....	....	....	....	....	....	....	....	....	....	....	....	....	....	....
	NHL Totals		**247**	**32**	**36**	**68**	**35**	**34**	**69**	**109**	**5**	**1**	**3**	**232**	**13.8**	**104**	**16**	**117**	**10**		**11**	**1**	**0**	**1**	**4**	**0**	**0**	**1**

Traded to **Winnipeg** by **Anaheim** with Oleg Tverdovsky and Anaheim's 3rd round choice (Per-Anton Lundstrom) in 1996 Entry Draft for Teemu Selanne, Marc Chouinard and Winnipeg's 4th round choice (later traded to Toronto — later traded to Montreal — Montreal selected Kim Staal) in 1996 Entry Draft, February 7, 1996. Transferred to **Phoenix** after **Winnipeg** franchise relocated, July 1, 1996. Traded to **Chicago** by **Phoenix** with Jayson More for Keith Carney and Jim Cummins, March 4, 1998. Traded to **Edmonton** by **Chicago** with Daniel Cleary, Ethan Moreau and Christian Laflamme for Boris Mironov, Dean McAmmond and Jonas Elofsson, March 20, 1999.

• KILREA, Brian

Brian Blair C – R. 5'11", 175 lbs. b: Ottawa, Ont., 10/21/1934.

Season	**Club**	**League**	**GP**	**G**	**A**	**Pts**	**AG**	**AA**	**APts**	**PIM**	**PP**	**SH**	**GW**	**S**	**%**	**TGF**	**PGF**	**TGA**	**PGA**	**+/–**	**GP**	**G**	**A**	**Pts**	**PIM**	**PP**	**SH**	**GW**
1953-54	Hamilton Tiger Cubs	OHA-Jr.	58	26	34	60	....	....	....	69	....	....	....	....	....	....	....	....	....	....	6	1	2	3	6	....	....	....
1954-55	Hamilton Tiger Cubs	OHA-Jr.	49	27	25	52	....	....	....	56	....	....	....	....	....	....	....	....	....	....	3	1	1	2	7	....	....	....
1955-56	Troy Bruins	IHL	60	16	36	52	....	....	....	22	....	....	....	....	....	....	....	....	....	....	5	0	0	0	2	....	....	....
1956-57	Troy Bruins	IHL	60	9	35	44	....	....	....	46	....	....	....	....	....	....	....	....	....	....	....	....	....	....	....	....	....	....
1957-58	**Detroit Red Wings**	**NHL**	**1**	**0**	**0**	**0**	**0**	**0**	**0**	**0**	....	....	....	....	....	....	....	....	....	....	....	....	....	....	....	....	....	....
	Edmonton Flyers	WHL	3	0	0	0	....	....	....	0	....	....	....	....	....	....	....	....	....	....	....	....	....	....	....	....	....	....
	Troy Bruins	IHL	58	30	35	65	....	....	....	25	....	....	....	....	....	....	....	....	....	....	....	....	....	....	....	....	....	....
1958-59	Troy Bruins	IHL	54	33	60	93	....	....	....	44	....	....	....	....	....	....	....	....	....	....	5	2	3	5	17	....	....	....
1959-60	Springfield Indians	AHL	63	14	27	41	....	....	....	26	....	....	....	....	....	....	....	....	....	....	8	0	1	1	4	....	....	....
1960-61	Springfield Indians	AHL	70	20	67	87	....	....	....	47	....	....	....	....	....	....	....	....	....	....	8	1	5	6	2	....	....	....
1961-62	Springfield Indians	AHL	70	20	*73	93	....	....	....	28	....	....	....	....	....	....	....	....	....	....	2	0	1	1	0	....	....	....
1962-63	Springfield Indians	AHL	72	25	50	75	....	....	....	34	....	....	....	....	....	....	....	....	....	....	....	....	....	....	....	....	....	....
1963-64	Springfield Indians	AHL	72	22	61	83	....	....	....	28	....	....	....	....	....	....	....	....	....	....	....	....	....	....	....	....	....	....
1964-65	Springfield Indians	AHL	71	23	54	77	....	....	....	18	....	....	....	....	....	....	....	....	....	....	....	....	....	....	....	....	....	....
1965-66	Springfield Indians	AHL	70	13	47	60	....	....	....	14	....	....	....	....	....	....	....	....	....	....	6	3	1	4	0	....	....	....
1966-67	Springfield Indians	AHL	63	25	38	63	....	....	....	29	....	....	....	....	....	....	....	....	....	....	....	....	....	....	....	....	....	....
1967-68	**Los Angeles Kings**	**NHL**	**25**	**3**	**5**	**8**	**3**	**5**	**8**	**12**	**0**	**0**	**0**	**24**	**12.5**	**11**	**2**	**17**	**4**	**–4**	....	....	....	....	....	....	....	....
	Springfield Kings	AHL	38	7	25	32	....	....	....	14	....	....	....	....	....	....	....	....	....	....	4	0	3	3	0	....	....	....
1968-69	Vancouver Canucks	WHL	1	0	1	1	....	....	....	0	....	....	....	....	....	....	....	....	....	....	....	....	....	....	....	....	....	....
	Rochester Americans	AHL	33	2	11	13	....	....	....	4	....	....	....	....	....	....	....	....	....	....	....	....	....	....	....	....	....	....
	Tulsa Oilers	CHL	24	11	25	36	....	....	....	12	....	....	....	....	....	....	....	....	....	....	4	0	1	1	0	....	....	....
1969-70	Denver Spurs	WHL	32	5	14	19	....	....	....	18	....	....	....	....	....	....	....	....	....	....	....	....	....	....	....	....	....	....
	NHL Totals		**26**	**3**	**5**	**8**	**3**	**5**	**8**	**12**	....	....	....	....	....	....	....	....	....	....	....	....	....	....	....	....	....	....

IHL Second All-Star Team (1959)

NHL rights transferred to **LA Kings** after NHL club purchased **Springfield** (AHL) franchise, May, 1967. Claimed by **Vancouver** (WHL) from **LA Kings** in Reverse Draft, June 13, 1968. Claimed on waivers by **Denver** (WHL) from **Vancouver** (WHL), January, 1970.

			REGULAR SEASON																		PLAYOFFS							
Season	Club	League	GP	G	A	Pts	AG	AA	APts	PIM	PP	SH	GW	S	%	TGF	PGF	TGA	PGA	+/–	GP	G	A	Pts	PIM	PP	SH	GW

• KIMBLE, Darin

RW – R. 6'2", 210 lbs. b: Lucky Lake, Sask., 11/22/1968. Quebec's 5th, 66th overall, in 1988.

Season	Club	League	GP	G	A	Pts	AG	AA	APts	PIM	PP	SH	GW	S	%	TGF	PGF	TGA	PGA	+/–	GP	G	A	Pts	PIM	PP	SH	GW
1984-85	Swift Current Broncos	SJHL	59	28	32	60				264																		
	Calgary Wranglers	WHL																			1	0	0	0	0			
1985-86	Calgary Wranglers	WHL	37	14	8	22				93																		
	New Westminster Bruins	WHL	11	1	1	2				22																		
	Brandon Wheat Kings	WHL	15	1	6	7				39																		
1986-87	Prince Albert Raiders	WHL	68	17	13	30				190											8	1	5	6	22			
1987-88	Prince Albert Raiders	WHL	67	35	36	71				307											8	2	2	4	32			
1988-89	**Quebec Nordiques**	**NHL**	**26**	**3**	**1**	**4**	**3**	**1**	**4**	**149**	**0**	**0**	**0**	**21**	**14.3**	**9**	**1**	**13**	**0**	**–5**								
	Halifax Citadels	AHL	39	8	6	14				188																		
1989-90	**Quebec Nordiques**	**NHL**	**44**	**5**	**5**	**10**	**4**	**4**	**8**	**185**	**2**	**0**	**1**	**40**	**12.5**	**23**	**8**	**35**	**0**	**–20**								
	Halifax Citadels	AHL	18	6	6	12				37											6	1	1	2	61			
1990-91	**Quebec Nordiques**	**NHL**	**35**	**2**	**5**	**7**	**2**	**4**	**6**	**114**	**0**	**0**	**0**	**14**	**14.3**	**9**	**0**	**14**	**0**	**–5**								
	Halifax Citadels	AHL	7	1	4	5				20																		
	St. Louis Blues	**NHL**	**26**	**1**	**1**	**2**	**1**	**1**	**2**	**128**	**0**	**0**	**1**	**14**	**7.1**	**6**	**0**	**4**	**0**	**2**	**13**	**0**	**0**	**0**	**38**	**0**	**0**	**0**
1991-92	**St. Louis Blues**	**NHL**	**46**	**1**	**3**	**4**	**1**	**2**	**3**	**166**	**0**	**0**	**0**	**12**	**8.3**	**5**	**0**	**9**	**1**	**–3**	**5**	**0**	**0**	**0**	**7**	**0**	**0**	**0**
1992-93	**Boston Bruins**	**NHL**	**55**	**7**	**3**	**10**	**6**	**2**	**8**	**177**	**0**	**0**	**0**	**20**	**35.0**	**16**	**0**	**12**	**0**	**4**	**4**	**0**	**0**	**0**	**2**	**0**	**0**	**0**
	Providence Bruins	AHL	12	1	4	5				34																		
1993-94	**Chicago Blackhawks**	**NHL**	**65**	**4**	**2**	**6**	**4**	**2**	**6**	**133**	**0**	**0**	**0**	**17**	**23.5**	**12**	**0**	**10**	**0**	**2**	**1**	**0**	**0**	**0**	**5**	**0**	**0**	**0**
1994-95	**Chicago Blackhawks**	**NHL**	**14**	**0**	**0**	**0**	**0**	**0**	**0**	**30**	**0**	**0**	**0**	**2**	**0.0**	**1**	**0**	**6**	**0**	**–5**								
1995-96	Indianapolis Ice	IHL	9	1	0	1				15																		
	Albany River Rats	AHL	60	4	15	19				144											3	0	0	0	2			
1996-97	Manitoba Moose	IHL	39	3	4	7				115																		
	Kansas City Blades	IHL	33	9	9	18				106											2	0	0	0	0			
1997-98	Kansas City Blades	IHL	16	1	3	4				60																		
	San Antonio Dragons	IHL	56	6	14	20				143																		
1998-99	Shreveport Mudbugs	WPHL	9	1	2	3				13																		
	Arkansas Glaciercats	WPHL	51	9	17	26				133											3	0	0	0	8			
99-2000	Peoria Rivermen	ECHL	10	0	0	0				21																		
	Missouri River Otters	UHL	24	10	13	23				49											3	1	0	1	4			
	NHL Totals		**311**	**23**	**20**	**43**	**21**	**16**	**37**	**1082**	**2**	**0**	**2**	**140**	**16.4**	**81**	**9**	**103**	**1**		**23**	**0**	**0**	**0**	**52**	**0**	**0**	**0**

Traded to **St. Louis** by **Quebec** for Herb Raglan, Tony Twist and Andy Rymsha, February 4, 1991. Traded to **Tampa Bay** by **St. Louis** with Pat Jablonski, Steve Tuttle and Rob Robinson for future considerations, June 19, 1992. Traded to **Boston** by **Tampa Bay** with future considerations for Ken Hodge and Matt Hervey, September 4, 1992. Signed as a free agent by **Florida**, July 9, 1993. Traded to **Chicago** by **Florida** for Keith Brown, September 30, 1993. Traded to **New Jersey** by **Chicago** for Michael Vukonich and Bill Armstrong, November 1, 1995. Signed as a free agent by **Phoenix**, July 28, 1997. Signed as a free agent by **Peoria** (ECHL), October 15, 1999. Signed as a free agent by **Missouri** (UHL) following release by **Peoria** (ECHL), February 6, 2000.

• KINDRACHUK, Orest

Orest Michael C – L. 5'10", 175 lbs. b: Nanton, Alta., 9/14/1950.

Season	Club	League	GP	G	A	Pts	AG	AA	APts	PIM	PP	SH	GW	S	%	TGF	PGF	TGA	PGA	+/–	GP	G	A	Pts	PIM	PP	SH	GW
1967-68	Saskatoon Blades	WCJHL	58	24	37	61				44											7	1	3	4	20			
1968-69	Saskatoon Blades	WCJHL	41	21	25	46				33											4	1	1	2	0			
1969-70	Saskatoon Blades	WCJHL	4	3	4	7				5											5	2	4	6	25			
1970-71	Saskatoon Blades	WCJHL	61	49	*100	149				103											5	2	4	6	25			
1971-72	San Diego Gulls	WHL	61	18	36	54				71											4	1	1	2	0			
1972-73	**Philadelphia Flyers**	**NHL**	**2**	**0**	**0**	**0**	**0**	**0**	**0**	**0**	**0**	**0**	**0**	**0**	**0.0**	**0**	**0**	**0**	**0**	**0**								
	Richmond Robins	AHL	72	35	51	86				133											3	0	1	1	10			
1973-74♦	**Philadelphia Flyers**	**NHL**	**71**	**11**	**30**	**41**	**11**	**25**	**36**	**85**	**3**	**1**	**3**	**106**	**10.4**	**49**	**11**	**19**	**0**	**19**	**17**	**5**	**4**	**9**	**17**	**0**	**0**	**0**
1974-75♦	**Philadelphia Flyers**	**NHL**	**60**	**10**	**21**	**31**	**9**	**16**	**25**	**72**	**1**	**0**	**2**	**104**	**9.6**	**44**	**8**	**33**	**5**	**8**	**14**	**0**	**2**	**2**	**12**	**0**	**0**	**0**
1975-76	**Philadelphia Flyers**	**NHL**	**76**	**26**	**49**	**75**	**23**	**37**	**60**	**101**	**5**	**2**	**2**	**181**	**14.4**	**100**	**31**	**61**	**24**	**32**	**16**	**4**	**7**	**11**	**4**	**1**	**0**	**2**
1976-77	**Philadelphia Flyers**	**NHL**	**78**	**15**	**36**	**51**	**13**	**28**	**41**	**79**	**1**	**1**	**3**	**147**	**10.2**	**75**	**11**	**58**	**16**	**22**	**10**	**2**	**1**	**3**	**0**	**1**	**0**	**0**
1977-78	**Philadelphia Flyers**	**NHL**	**73**	**17**	**45**	**62**	**15**	**35**	**50**	**128**	**1**	**1**	**4**	**170**	**10.0**	**87**	**14**	**56**	**18**	**35**	**12**	**5**	**5**	**10**	**13**	**2**	**0**	**1**
1978-79	**Pittsburgh Penguins**	**NHL**	**79**	**18**	**42**	**60**	**15**	**30**	**45**	**84**	**4**	**1**	**0**	**145**	**12.4**	**87**	**26**	**81**	**23**	**3**	**7**	**4**	**1**	**5**	**7**	**0**	**0**	**1**
1979-80	**Pittsburgh Penguins**	**NHL**	**52**	**17**	**29**	**46**	**14**	**21**	**35**	**63**	**2**	**2**	**1**	**94**	**18.1**	**58**	**14**	**56**	**16**	**4**								
1980-81	**Pittsburgh Penguins**	**NHL**	**13**	**3**	**9**	**12**	**2**	**6**	**8**	**34**	**1**	**0**	**0**	**35**	**8.6**	**18**	**8**	**17**	**10**	**3**								
1981-82	**Washington Capitals**	**NHL**	**4**	**1**	**0**	**1**	**1**	**0**	**1**	**2**	**1**	**0**	**0**	**8**	**12.5**	**2**	**1**	**6**	**1**	**–4**								
	NHL Totals		**508**	**118**	**261**	**379**	**103**	**198**	**301**	**648**	**19**	**8**	**15**	**990**	**11.9**	**520**	**124**	**387**	**113**		**76**	**20**	**20**	**40**	**53**	**4**	**0**	**4**

WCJHL First All-Star Team (1971)

Signed as a free agent by **Philadelphia**, July, 1971. Traded to **Pittsburgh** by **Philadelphia** with Tom Bladon and Ross Lonsberry for Pittsburgh's 1st round choice (Behn Wilson) in 1978 Amateur Draft, June 14, 1978. Signed as a free agent by **Washington**, September 4, 1981.

• KING, Derek

LW – L. 6', 210 lbs. b: Hamilton, Ont., 2/11/1967. NY Islanders' 2nd, 13th overall, in 1985.

Season	Club	League	GP	G	A	Pts	AG	AA	APts	PIM	PP	SH	GW	S	%	TGF	PGF	TGA	PGA	+/–	GP	G	A	Pts	PIM	PP	SH	GW
1982-83	Hamilton Mountain A's	OJHL	8	1	2	3				0																		
1983-84	Hamilton Mountain A's	OJHL	37	10	14	24				142																		
1984-85	Sault Ste. Marie Greyhounds	OHL	63	35	38	73				106											16	3	13	16	11			
	Sault Ste. Marie Greyhounds	Mem-Cup	4	2	2	4				8																		
1985-86	Sault Ste. Marie Greyhounds	OHL	25	12	17	29				33																		
	Oshawa Generals	OHL	19	8	13	21				15											6	3	2	5	13			
1986-87	Oshawa Generals	OHL	57	53	53	106				74											17	14	10	24	40			
	New York Islanders	**NHL**	**2**	**0**	**0**	**0**	**0**	**0**	**0**	**0**	**0**	**0**	**0**	**5**	**0.0**	**1**	**0**	**1**	**0**	**0**								
	Oshawa Generals	Mem-Cup	4	0	3	3				7																		
1987-88	**New York Islanders**	**NHL**	**55**	**12**	**24**	**36**	**10**	**17**	**27**	**30**	**1**	**0**	**4**	**94**	**12.8**	**62**	**19**	**36**	**0**	**7**	**5**	**0**	**2**	**2**	**2**	**0**	**0**	**0**
	Springfield Indians	AHL	10	7	6	13				6																		
1988-89	**New York Islanders**	**NHL**	**60**	**14**	**29**	**43**	**12**	**21**	**33**	**14**	**4**	**0**	**0**	**103**	**13.6**	**65**	**21**	**34**	**0**	**10**								
	Springfield Indians	AHL	4	4	0	4				0																		
1989-90	**New York Islanders**	**NHL**	**46**	**13**	**27**	**40**	**11**	**19**	**30**	**20**	**5**	**0**	**1**	**91**	**14.3**	**55**	**19**	**34**	**0**	**2**	**4**	**0**	**0**	**0**	**4**	**0**	**0**	**0**
	Springfield Indians	AHL	21	11	12	23				33																		
1990-91	**New York Islanders**	**NHL**	**66**	**19**	**26**	**45**	**17**	**20**	**37**	**44**	**2**	**0**	**2**	**130**	**14.6**	**63**	**20**	**42**	**0**	**1**								
1991-92	**New York Islanders**	**NHL**	**80**	**40**	**38**	**78**	**36**	**29**	**65**	**46**	**21**	**0**	**6**	**189**	**21.2**	**107**	**49**	**68**	**0**	**–10**								
	Canada	WC-A	6	1	1	2				6																		
1992-93	**New York Islanders**	**NHL**	**77**	**38**	**38**	**76**	**32**	**26**	**58**	**47**	**21**	**0**	**7**	**201**	**18.9**	**132**	**66**	**70**	**0**	**–4**	**18**	**3**	**11**	**14**	**14**	**0**	**0**	**0**
1993-94	**New York Islanders**	**NHL**	**78**	**30**	**40**	**70**	**28**	**31**	**59**	**59**	**10**	**0**	**7**	**171**	**17.5**	**112**	**43**	**51**	**0**	**18**	**4**	**0**	**1**	**1**	**0**	**0**	**0**	**0**
1994-95	**New York Islanders**	**NHL**	**43**	**10**	**16**	**26**	**18**	**24**	**42**	**41**	**7**	**0**	**0**	**118**	**8.5**	**44**	**16**	**34**	**1**	**–5**								
1995-96	**New York Islanders**	**NHL**	**61**	**12**	**20**	**32**	**12**	**16**	**28**	**23**	**5**	**1**	**0**	**154**	**7.8**	**50**	**13**	**52**	**5**	**–10**								
1996-97	**New York Islanders**	**NHL**	**70**	**23**	**30**	**53**	**24**	**27**	**51**	**20**	**5**	**0**	**3**	**153**	**15.0**	**83**	**21**	**68**	**0**	**–6**								
	Hartford Whalers	**NHL**	**12**	**3**	**3**	**6**	**3**	**3**	**6**	**2**	**1**	**0**	**0**	**28**	**10.7**	**13**	**5**	**8**	**0**	**0**								
1997-98	**Toronto Maple Leafs**	**NHL**	**77**	**21**	**25**	**46**	**25**	**24**	**49**	**43**	**4**	**0**	**3**	**166**	**12.7**	**61**	**20**	**48**	**0**	**–7**								
1998-99	**Toronto Maple Leafs**	**NHL**	**81**	**24**	**28**	**52**	**28**	**27**	**55**	**20**	**8**	**0**	**4**	**150**	**16.0**	**74**	**21**	**38**	**0**	**15**	**16**	**1**	**3**	**4**	**4**	**0**	**0**	**0**
99-2000	**Toronto Maple Leafs**	**NHL**	**3**	**0**	**0**	**0**	**0**	**0**	**0**	**2**	**0**	**0**	**0**	**4**	**0.0**	**1**	**1**	**2**	**0**	**–2**								
	St. Louis Blues	**NHL**	**19**	**2**	**7**	**9**	**2**	**6**	**8**	**6**	**1**	**0**	**0**	**29**	**6.9**	**11**	**4**	**7**	**0**	**0**								
	Grand Rapids Griffins	IHL	52	19	30	49				25											17	7	8	15	8			
	NHL Totals		**830**	**261**	**351**	**612**	**258**	**290**	**548**	**417**	**95**	**1**	**37**	**1786**	**14.6**	**934**	**338**	**593**	**6**		**47**	**4**	**17**	**21**	**24**	**0**	**0**	**0**

OHL First All-Star Team (1987)

Traded to **Hartford** by **NY Islanders** for Hartford's 5th round choice (Adam Edinger) in 1997 Entry Draft, March 18, 1997. Signed as a free agent by **Toronto**, July 4, 1997. Traded to **St. Louis** by **Toronto** with a conditional choice in 2000 Entry Draft for Tyler Harlton and a conditional choice in 2000 Entry Draft, October 20, 1999.

• KING, Kris

Kristopher LW – L. 5'11", 208 lbs. b: Bracebridge, Ont., 2/18/1966. Washington's 4th, 80th overall, in 1984.

Season	Club	League	GP	G	A	Pts	AG	AA	APts	PIM	PP	SH	GW	S	%	TGF	PGF	TGA	PGA	+/–	GP	G	A	Pts	PIM	PP	SH	GW
1982-83	Gravenhurst Indians	OJHL-C	32	*72	53	*125				115																		
1983-84	Peterborough Petes	OHL	62	13	18	31				168											8	3	3	6	14			
1984-85	Peterborough Petes	OHL	61	18	35	53				222											16	2	8	10	28			
1985-86	Peterborough Petes	OHL	58	19	40	59				254											8	4	0	4	21			

			REGULAR SEASON																		PLAYOFFS							
Season	Club	League	GP	G	A	Pts	AG	AA	APts	PIM	PP	SH	GW	S	%	TGF	PGF	TGA	PGA	+/–	GP	G	A	Pts	PIM	PP	SH	GW
1986-87	Peterborough Petes	OHL	46	23	33	56	....	....	....	160	....	....	....	....	....	....	....	....	....	....	12	5	8	13	41	....	....	....
	Binghamton Whalers	AHL	7	0	0	0	....	....	....	18	....	....	....	....	....	....	....	....	....	....	....	....	....	....	....	....	....	....
1987-88	**Detroit Red Wings**	**NHL**	**3**	**1**	**0**	**1**	**1**	**0**	**1**	**2**	**0**	**0**	**0**	**3**	**33.3**	**1**	**0**	**0**	**0**	**1**	....	....	....	....	....	....	....	....
	Adirondack Red Wings	AHL	76	21	32	53	....	....	....	337	....	....	....	....	....	....	....	....	....	....	10	4	4	8	53	....	....	....
1988-89	**Detroit Red Wings**	**NHL**	**55**	**2**	**3**	**5**	**2**	**2**	**4**	**168**	**0**	**0**	**0**	**34**	**5.9**	**9**	**0**	**16**	**0**	**–7**	**2**	**0**	**0**	**0**	**2**	**0**	**0**	**0**
1989-90	**New York Rangers**	**NHL**	**68**	**6**	**7**	**13**	**5**	**5**	**10**	**286**	**0**	**0**	**0**	**49**	**12.2**	**30**	**0**	**28**	**0**	**2**	**10**	**0**	**1**	**1**	**38**	**0**	**0**	**0**
1990-91	**New York Rangers**	**NHL**	**72**	**11**	**14**	**25**	**10**	**11**	**21**	**154**	**0**	**0**	**0**	**107**	**10.3**	**35**	**0**	**36**	**0**	**–1**	**6**	**2**	**0**	**2**	**36**	**0**	**0**	**1**
1991-92	**New York Rangers**	**NHL**	**79**	**10**	**9**	**19**	**9**	**7**	**16**	**224**	**0**	**0**	**2**	**97**	**10.3**	**45**	**0**	**32**	**0**	**13**	**13**	**4**	**1**	**5**	**14**	**0**	**0**	**3**
1992-93	**New York Rangers**	**NHL**	**30**	**0**	**3**	**3**	**0**	**2**	**2**	**67**	**0**	**0**	**0**	**23**	**0.0**	**11**	**0**	**12**	**0**	**–1**	....	....	....	....	....	....	....	....
	Winnipeg Jets	**NHL**	**48**	**8**	**8**	**16**	**7**	**5**	**12**	**136**	**0**	**0**	**1**	**51**	**15.7**	**25**	**0**	**23**	**3**	**5**	**6**	**1**	**1**	**2**	**4**	**0**	**0**	**0**
1993-94	**Winnipeg Jets**	**NHL**	**83**	**4**	**8**	**12**	**4**	**6**	**10**	**205**	**0**	**0**	**1**	**86**	**4.7**	**20**	**0**	**42**	**0**	**–22**	....	....	....	....	....	....	....	....
1994-95	**Winnipeg Jets**	**NHL**	**48**	**4**	**2**	**6**	**7**	**3**	**10**	**85**	**0**	**0**	**0**	**58**	**6.9**	**22**	**0**	**23**	**1**	**0**	....	....	....	....	....	....	....	....
1995-96	**Winnipeg Jets**	**NHL**	**81**	**9**	**11**	**20**	**9**	**9**	**18**	**151**	**0**	**1**	**2**	**89**	**10.1**	**38**	**0**	**62**	**17**	**–7**	**5**	**0**	**1**	**1**	**4**	**0**	**0**	**0**
1996-97	**Phoenix Coyotes**	**NHL**	**81**	**3**	**11**	**14**	**3**	**10**	**13**	**185**	**0**	**0**	**0**	**57**	**5.3**	**22**	**3**	**31**	**5**	**–7**	**7**	**0**	**0**	**0**	**17**	**0**	**0**	**0**
1997-98	**Toronto Maple Leafs**	**NHL**	**82**	**3**	**3**	**6**	**4**	**3**	**7**	**199**	**0**	**0**	**2**	**53**	**5.7**	**14**	**0**	**40**	**13**	**–13**	....	....	....	....	....	....	....	....
1998-99	**Toronto Maple Leafs**	**NHL**	**67**	**2**	**2**	**4**	**2**	**2**	**4**	**105**	**0**	**1**	**1**	**34**	**5.9**	**9**	**0**	**44**	**19**	**–16**	**17**	**1**	**1**	**2**	**25**	**0**	**0**	**0**
99-2000	**Toronto Maple Leafs**	**NHL**	**39**	**2**	**4**	**6**	**2**	**4**	**6**	**55**	**0**	**0**	**0**	**24**	**8.3**	**14**	**0**	**11**	**1**	**4**	**1**	**0**	**0**	**0**	**2**	**0**	**0**	**0**
	Chicago Wolves	IHL	15	2	4	6	....	....	....	19	....	....	....	....	....	....	....	....	....	....	....	....	....	....	....	....	....	....
	NHL Totals		**836**	**65**	**85**	**150**	**65**	**69**	**134**	**2022**	**0**	**2**	**9**	**765**	**8.5**	**295**	**3**	**400**	**59**		**67**	**8**	**5**	**13**	**142**	**0**	**0**	**4**

Won King Clancy Memorial Trophy (1996)

Signed as a free agent by **Detroit**, March 23, 1987. Traded to **NY Rangers** by **Detroit** for Chris McRae and Detroit's 5th round choice (previously acquired, Detroit selected Tony Burns) in 1990 Entry Draft, September 7, 1989. Traded to **Winnipeg** by **NY Rangers** with Tie Domi for Ed Olczyk, December 28, 1992. Transferred to **Phoenix** after **Winnipeg** franchise relocated, July 1, 1996. Signed as a free agent by **Toronto**, July 23, 1997.

• KING, Steven

Steven A. RW – R. 6', 195 lbs. b: Greenwich, RI, 7/22/1969. NY Rangers' 1st, 21st overall, in 1991 Supplemental Draft.

Season	Club	League	GP	G	A	Pts	AG	AA	APts	PIM	PP	SH	GW	S	%	TGF	PGF	TGA	PGA	+/–	GP	G	A	Pts	PIM	PP	SH	GW
1986-87	Bishop Hendrickson Hawks	Hi-School	STATISTICS NOT AVAILABLE																									
1987-88	Brown University	ECAC	24	10	5	15	....	....	....	30	....	....	....	....	....	....	....	....	....	....	....	....	....	....	....	....	....	....
1988-89	Brown University	ECAC	26	8	5	13	....	....	....	73	....	....	....	....	....	....	....	....	....	....	....	....	....	....	....	....	....	....
1989-90	Brown University	ECAC	27	19	8	27	....	....	....	53	....	....	....	....	....	....	....	....	....	....	....	....	....	....	....	....	....	....
1990-91	Brown University	ECAC	27	19	15	34	....	....	....	76	....	....	....	....	....	....	....	....	....	....	....	....	....	....	....	....	....	....
1991-92	Binghamton Rangers	AHL	66	27	15	42	....	....	....	56	....	....	....	....	....	....	....	....	....	....	10	2	0	2	14	....	....	....
1992-93	**New York Rangers**	**NHL**	**24**	**7**	**5**	**12**	**6**	**3**	**9**	**16**	**5**	**0**	**2**	**42**	**16.7**	**25**	**9**	**12**	**0**	**4**	....	....	....	....	....	....	....	....
	Binghamton Rangers	AHL	53	35	33	68	....	....	....	100	....	....	....	....	....	....	....	....	....	....	14	7	9	16	26	....	....	....
1993-94	**Mighty Ducks of Anaheim**	**NHL**	**36**	**8**	**3**	**11**	**7**	**2**	**9**	**44**	**3**	**0**	**1**	**50**	**16.0**	**16**	**5**	**18**	**0**	**–7**	....	....	....	....	....	....	....	....
1994-95	**Mighty Ducks of Anaheim**	**NHL**	DID NOT PLAY – INJURED																									
1995-96	**Mighty Ducks of Anaheim**	**NHL**	**7**	**2**	**0**	**2**	**2**	**0**	**2**	**15**	**1**	**0**	**1**	**5**	**40.0**	**3**	**1**	**3**	**0**	**–1**	....	....	....	....	....	....	....	....
	Baltimore Bandits	AHL	68	40	21	61	....	....	....	95	....	....	....	....	....	....	....	....	....	....	12	7	5	12	20	....	....	....
1996-97	Philadelphia Phantoms	AHL	39	17	10	27	....	....	....	47	....	....	....	....	....	....	....	....	....	....	....	....	....	....	....	....	....	....
	Michigan K-Wings	IHL	39	15	11	26	....	....	....	39	....	....	....	....	....	....	....	....	....	....	4	1	2	3	12	....	....	....
1997-98	Cincinnati Cyclones	IHL	41	17	9	26	....	....	....	22	....	....	....	....	....	....	....	....	....	....	....	....	....	....	....	....	....	....
	Rochester Americans	AHL	28	15	15	30	....	....	....	28	....	....	....	....	....	....	....	....	....	....	4	1	1	2	4	....	....	....
1998-99	Providence Bruins	AHL	3	1	0	1	....	....	....	0	....	....	....	....	....	....	....	....	....	....	13	7	4	11	12	....	....	....
99-2000	Springfield Falcons	AHL	23	10	6	16	....	....	....	20	....	....	....	....	....	....	....	....	....	....	....	....	....	....	....	....	....	....
	NHL Totals		**67**	**17**	**8**	**25**	**15**	**5**	**20**	**75**	**9**	**0**	**4**	**97**	**17.5**	**44**	**15**	**33**	**0**		....	....	....	....	....	....	....	....

Claimed by **Anaheim** from **NY Rangers** in Expansion Draft, June 24, 1993. • Missed majority of 1993-94 and entire 1994-95 seasons recovering from shoulder surgery, January 5, 1994. Signed as a free agent by **Philadelphia**, July 31, 1996. • Missed remainder of 1998-99 and majority of 1999-2000 seasons recovering from shoulder surgery, August, 1998. Signed as a free agent by **Phoenix**, July 28, 1999.

• KING, Wayne

Wayne Gordon C – R. 5'10", 185 lbs. b: Midland, Ont., 9/4/1951.

Season	Club	League	GP	G	A	Pts	AG	AA	APts	PIM	PP	SH	GW	S	%	TGF	PGF	TGA	PGA	+/–	GP	G	A	Pts	PIM	PP	SH	GW
1968-69	Niagara Falls Canucks	OJHL	STATISTICS NOT AVAILABLE																									
	Niagara Falls Flyers	OHA-Jr.	4	1	0	1	....	....	....	0	....	....	....	....	....	....	....	....	....	....	....	....	....	....	....	....	....	....
1969-70	Niagara Falls Flyers	OHA-Jr.	54	8	26	34	....	....	....	61	....	....	....	....	....	....	....	....	....	....	....	....	....	....	....	....	....	....
1970-71	Niagara Falls Flyers	OHA-Jr.	59	14	18	32	....	....	....	112	....	....	....	....	....	....	....	....	....	....	....	....	....	....	....	....	....	....
1971-72	Columbus Seals	IHL	72	22	29	51	....	....	....	29	....	....	....	....	....	....	....	....	....	....	....	....	....	....	....	....	....	....
1972-73	Salt Lake Golden Eagles	WHL	72	16	27	43	....	....	....	55	....	....	....	....	....	....	....	....	....	....	9	2	5	7	11	....	....	....
1973-74	**California Golden Seals**	**NHL**	**2**	**0**	**0**	**0**	**0**	**0**	**0**	**0**	**0**	**0**	**0**	**2**	**0.0**	**0**	**0**	**2**	**2**	**0**	....	....	....	....	....	....	....	....
	Salt Lake Golden Eagles	WHL	76	34	34	68	....	....	....	72	....	....	....	....	....	....	....	....	....	....	5	1	0	1	9	....	....	....
1974-75	**California Golden Seals**	**NHL**	**25**	**4**	**7**	**11**	**3**	**5**	**8**	**8**	**1**	**0**	**0**	**29**	**13.8**	**20**	**2**	**28**	**0**	**–10**	....	....	....	....	....	....	....	....
1975-76	**California Golden Seals**	**NHL**	**46**	**1**	**11**	**12**	**1**	**8**	**9**	**26**	**1**	**0**	**0**	**46**	**2.2**	**19**	**5**	**17**	**0**	**–3**	....	....	....	....	....	....	....	....
	Salt Lake Golden Eagles	CHL	20	9	8	17	....	....	....	21	....	....	....	....	....	....	....	....	....	....	5	1	0	1	10	....	....	....
1976-77	Salt Lake Golden Eagles	CHL	51	12	13	25	....	....	....	36	....	....	....	....	....	....	....	....	....	....	....	....	....	....	....	....	....	....
1977-78	Barrie Flyers	OHA-Sr.	40	24	16	40	....	....	....	47	....	....	....	....	....	....	....	....	....	....	....	....	....	....	....	....	....	....
	NHL Totals		**73**	**5**	**18**	**23**	**4**	**13**	**17**	**34**	**2**	**0**	**0**	**77**	**6.5**	**39**	**7**	**47**	**2**		....	....	....	....	....	....	....	....

WHL Second All-Star Team (1974)

Signed as a free agent by **California**, October, 1971.

• KINNEAR, Geordie

D – L. 6'1", 195 lbs. b: Simcoe, Ont., 7/9/1973. New Jersey's 8th, 162nd overall, in 1992.

Season	Club	League	GP	G	A	Pts	AG	AA	APts	PIM	PP	SH	GW	S	%	TGF	PGF	TGA	PGA	+/–	GP	G	A	Pts	PIM	PP	SH	GW
1989-90	Norwich Merchants	OJHL-C	1	0	0	0	....	....	....	19	....	....	....	....	....	....	....	....	....	....	....	....	....	....	....	....	....	....
	Tillsonburg Titans	OJHL-B	34	2	5	7	....	....	....	153	....	....	....	....	....	....	....	....	....	....	....	....	....	....	....	....	....	....
1990-91	Peterborough Jr. Petes	OJHL-B	6	0	6	6	....	....	....	51	....	....	....	....	....	....	....	....	....	....	....	....	....	....	....	....	....	....
	Peterborough Petes	OHL	37	1	0	1	....	....	....	76	....	....	....	....	....	....	....	....	....	....	2	0	0	0	10	....	....	....
1991-92	Peterborough Petes	OHL	63	5	16	21	....	....	....	195	....	....	....	....	....	....	....	....	....	....	10	0	2	2	36	....	....	....
1992-93	Peterborough Petes	OHL	58	6	22	28	....	....	....	161	....	....	....	....	....	....	....	....	....	....	19	1	5	6	43	....	....	....
1993-94	Albany River Rats	AHL	59	3	12	15	....	....	....	197	....	....	....	....	....	....	....	....	....	....	5	0	0	0	21	....	....	....
1994-95	Albany River Rats	AHL	68	5	11	16	....	....	....	136	....	....	....	....	....	....	....	....	....	....	9	1	1	2	7	....	....	....
1995-96	Albany River Rats	AHL	73	4	7	11	....	....	....	170	....	....	....	....	....	....	....	....	....	....	4	0	1	1	2	....	....	....
1996-97	Albany River Rats	AHL	59	2	9	11	....	....	....	175	....	....	....	....	....	....	....	....	....	....	10	0	1	1	15	....	....	....
1997-98	Albany River Rats	AHL	78	1	15	16	....	....	....	206	....	....	....	....	....	....	....	....	....	....	13	1	1	2	68	....	....	....
1998-99	Albany River Rats	AHL	55	1	13	14	....	....	....	162	....	....	....	....	....	....	....	....	....	....	5	0	1	1	0	....	....	....
99-2000	**Atlanta Thrashers**	**NHL**	**4**	**0**	**0**	**0**	**0**	**0**	**0**	**13**	**0**	**0**	**0**	**2**	**0.0**	**1**	**0**	**4**	**2**	**–1**	....	....	....	....	....	....	....	....
	Orlando Solar Bears	IHL	69	1	5	6	....	....	....	231	....	....	....	....	....	....	....	....	....	....	6	0	0	0	9	....	....	....
	NHL Totals		**4**	**0**	**0**	**0**	**0**	**0**	**0**	**13**	**0**	**0**	**0**	**2**	**0.0**	**1**	**0**	**4**	**2**		....	....	....	....	....	....	....	....

Signed as a free agent by **Atlanta**, August 12, 1999.

• KINSELLA, Brian

Brian Edward C – R. 5'11", 180 lbs. b: Barrie, Ont., 2/11/1954. Washington's 6th, 91st overall, in 1974.

Season	Club	League	GP	G	A	Pts	AG	AA	APts	PIM	PP	SH	GW	S	%	TGF	PGF	TGA	PGA	+/–	GP	G	A	Pts	PIM	PP	SH	GW
1971-72	Oshawa Generals	OMJHL	44	13	19	32	....	....	....	48	....	....	....	....	....	....	....	....	....	....	12	5	4	9	32	....	....	....
1972-73	Oshawa Generals	OMJHL	48	28	57	85	....	....	....	49	....	....	....	....	....	....	....	....	....	....	....	....	....	....	....	....	....	....
1973-74	Oshawa Generals	OMJHL	64	36	43	79	....	....	....	95	....	....	....	....	....	....	....	....	....	....	....	....	....	....	....	....	....	....
1974-75	Richmond Robins	AHL	4	0	0	0	....	....	....	6	....	....	....	....	....	....	....	....	....	....	....	....	....	....	....	....	....	....
	Dayton Gems	IHL	40	15	15	30	....	....	....	35	....	....	....	....	....	....	....	....	....	....	....	....	....	....	....	....	....	....
	Kalamazoo Wings	IHL	10	3	7	10	....	....	....	36	....	....	....	....	....	....	....	....	....	....	....	....	....	....	....	....	....	....
1975-76	**Washington Capitals**	**NHL**	**4**	**0**	**1**	**1**	**0**	**1**	**1**	**0**	**0**	**0**	**0**	**11**	**0.0**	**1**	**0**	**3**	**0**	**–2**	....	....	....	....	....	....	....	....
	Springfield Indians	AHL	1	0	0	0	....	....	....	0	....	....	....	....	....	....	....	....	....	....	....	....	....	....	....	....	....	....
	Dayton Gems	IHL	74	43	45	88	....	....	....	43	....	....	....	....	....	....	....	....	....	....	15	10	7	17	12	....	....	....
1976-77	**Washington Capitals**	**NHL**	**6**	**0**	**0**	**0**	**0**	**0**	**0**	**0**	**0**	**0**	**0**	**3**	**0.0**	**0**	**0**	**4**	**2**	**–2**	....	....	....	....	....	....	....	....
	Springfield Indians	AHL	59	26	16	42	....	....	....	36	....	....	....	....	....	....	....	....	....	....	....	....	....	....	....	....	....	....
1977-78	Port Huron Flags	IHL	34	11	19	30	....	....	....	16	....	....	....	....	....	....	....	....	....	....	....	....	....	....	....	....	....	....
1978-79	Port Huron Flags	IHL	72	16	52	68	....	....	....	94	....	....	....	....	....	....	....	....	....	....	7	2	5	7	8	....	....	....

			REGULAR SEASON																		PLAYOFFS							
Season	**Club**	**League**	**GP**	**G**	**A**	**Pts**	**AG**	**AA**	**APts**	**PIM**	**PP**	**SH**	**GW**	**S**	**%**	**TGF**	**PGF**	**TGA**	**PGA**	**+/–**	**GP**	**G**	**A**	**Pts**	**PIM**	**PP**	**SH**	**GW**
1979-80	Port Huron Flags	IHL	73	43	40	83	....	....	....	61	....	....	....	....	....	....	....	....	....	....	11	7	3	10	16	....	....	....
1980-81	Port Huron Flags	IHL	79	36	40	76	....	....	....	71	....	....	....	....	....	....	....	....	....	....	4	2	0	2	4	....	....	....
1981-82	Toledo Goaldiggers	IHL	80	36	45	81	....	....	....	71	....	....	....	....	....	....	....	....	....	....	12	8	7	15	10	....	....	....
1982-83	Toledo Goaldiggers	IHL	73	31	35	66	....	....	....	37	....	....	....	....	....	....	....	....	....	....	11	6	5	11	2	....	....	....
1983-84	Toledo Goaldiggers	IHL	41	18	19	37	....	....	....	27	....	....	....	....	....	....	....	....	....	....	....	....	....	....	....	....	....	....
	NHL Totals		**10**	**0**	**1**	**1**	**0**	**1**	**1**	**0**	**0**	**0**	**0**	**14**	**0.0**	**1**	**0**	**7**	**2**		....	....	....	....	....	....	....	....
• KIPRUSOFF, Marko D – L. 6', 195 lbs. b: Turku, Finland, 6/6/1972. Montreal's 4th, 70th overall, in 1994.																												
1988-89	TPS Turku	Finland-Jr.	19	3	5	8	....	....	....	4	....	....	....	....	....	....	....	....	....	....	....	....	....	....	....	....	....	....
1989-90	TPS Turku	Finland-Jr.	23	4	9	13	....	....	....	2	....	....	....	....	....	....	....	....	....	....	....	....	....	....	....	....	....	....
1990-91	TPS Turku	Finland-Jr.	17	2	9	11	....	....	....	2	....	....	....	....	....	....	....	....	....	....	....	....	....	....	....	....	....	....
	TuTo Turku	Finland-2	22	4	8	12	....	....	....	0	....	....	....	....	....	....	....	....	....	....	....	....	....	....	....	....	....	....
	TPS Turku	Finland	3	0	0	0	....	....	....	0	....	....	....	....	....	....	....	....	....	....	....	....	....	....	....	....	....	....
1991-92	TPS Turku	Finland	23	0	2	2	....	....	....	0	....	....	....	....	....	....	....	....	....	....	....	....	....	....	....	....	....	....
	Kiekko-67 Turku	Finland-2	4	0	0	0	....	....	....	2	....	....	....	....	....	....	....	....	....	....	....	....	....	....	....	....	....	....
	HPK Hameenlinna	Finland	3	0	0	0	....	....	....	0	....	....	....	....	....	....	....	....	....	....	....	....	....	....	....	....	....	....
	Finland	WJC-A	7	2	2	4	....	....	....	2	....	....	....	....	....	....	....	....	....	....	....	....	....	....	....	....	....	....
1992-93	Kiekko-67 Turku	Finland-2	1	0	1	1	....	....	....	2	....	....	....	....	....	....	....	....	....	....	....	....	....	....	....	....	....	....
	TPS Turku	Finland	43	3	7	10	....	....	....	14	....	....	....	....	....	....	....	....	....	....	12	2	3	5	6	....	....	....
	Finland	Nat-Team	7	0	0	0	....	....	....	0	....	....	....	....	....	....	....	....	....	....	....	....	....	....	....	....	....	....
1993-94	TPS Turku	Finland	48	5	19	24	....	....	....	8	....	....	....	....	....	....	....	....	....	....	11	0	6	6	4	....	....	....
	Finland	Nat-Team	13	0	2	2	....	....	....	10	....	....	....	....	....	....	....	....	....	....	....	....	....	....	....	....	....	....
	Finland	Olympics	8	3	3	6	....	....	....	4	....	....	....	....	....	....	....	....	....	....	....	....	....	....	....	....	....	....
	Finland	WC-A	8	2	1	3	....	....	....	2	....	....	....	....	....	....	....	....	....	....	....	....	....	....	....	....	....	....
1994-95	TPS Turku	Finland	50	10	21	31	....	....	....	16	....	....	....	....	....	....	....	....	....	....	13	0	9	9	2	....	....	....
	Finland	Nat-Team	15	2	2	4	....	....	....	2	....	....	....	....	....	....	....	....	....	....	....	....	....	....	....	....	....	....
	Finland	WC-A	8	0	3	3	....	....	....	0	....	....	....	....	....	....	....	....	....	....	....	....	....	....	....	....	....	....
1995-96	**Montreal Canadiens**	**NHL**	**24**	**0**	**4**	**4**	**0**	**3**	**3**	**8**	**0**	**0**	**0**	**36**	**0.0**	**15**	**4**	**18**	**4**	**–3**	....	....	....	....	....	....	....	....
	Fredericton Canadiens	AHL	28	4	10	14	....	....	....	2	....	....	....	....	....	....	....	....	....	....	10	2	5	7	2	....	....	....
1996-97	Finland	W-Cup	4	0	1	1	....	....	....	0	....	....	....	....	....	....	....	....	....	....	....	....	....	....	....	....	....	....
	Malmo IF	Sweden	50	10	18	28	....	....	....	24	....	....	....	....	....	....	....	....	....	....	4	0	0	0	0	....	....	....
	Finland	Nat-Team	25	5	7	12	....	....	....	6	....	....	....	....	....	....	....	....	....	....	....	....	....	....	....	....	....	....
	Finland	WC-A	8	0	2	2	....	....	....	2	....	....	....	....	....	....	....	....	....	....	....	....	....	....	....	....	....	....
1997-98	Malmo IF	Sweden	46	7	16	23	....	....	....	23	....	....	....	....	....	....	....	....	....	....	....	....	....	....	....	....	....	....
	Finland	Nat-Team	16	2	6	8	....	....	....	2	....	....	....	....	....	....	....	....	....	....	....	....	....	....	....	....	....	....
	Finland	WC-A	10	2	1	3	....	....	....	4	....	....	....	....	....	....	....	....	....	....	....	....	....	....	....	....	....	....
1998-99	TPS Turku	Finland	49	15	22	37	....	....	....	12	....	....	....	....	....	....	....	....	....	....	10	3	6	9	0	....	....	....
	Finland	WC-A	12	1	4	5	....	....	....	4	....	....	....	....	....	....	....	....	....	....	....	....	....	....	....	....	....	....
99-2000	TPS Turku	Finland	53	6	27	33	....	....	....	10	....	....	....	....	....	....	....	....	....	....	11	0	3	3	0	....	....	....
	TPS Turku	EuroHL	5	1	2	3	....	....	....	2	....	....	....	....	....	....	....	....	....	....	5	2	0	2	2	....	....	....
	NHL Totals		**24**	**0**	**4**	**4**	**0**	**3**	**3**	**8**	**0**	**0**	**0**	**36**	**0.0**	**15**	**4**	**18**	**4**		....	....	....	....	....	....	....	....

Finnish League First All-Star Team (1994, 1995)

• KIRTON, Mark Mark Robert C – L. 5'10", 170 lbs. b: Regina, Sask., 2/3/1958. Toronto's 2nd, 48th overall, in 1978.																												
1974-75	Wexford Warriors	OJHL	38	18	29	47	....	....	....	26	....	....	....	....	....	....	....	....	....	....	....	....	....	....	....	....	....	....
1975-76	Peterborough Petes	OMJHL	65	22	38	60	....	....	....	10	....	....	....	....	....	....	....	....	....	....	....	....	....	....	....	....	....	....
1976-77	Peterborough Petes	OMJHL	48	18	24	42	....	....	....	41	....	....	....	....	....	....	....	....	....	....	4	6	1	7	0	....	....	....
1977-78	Peterborough Petes	OMJHL	68	27	44	71	....	....	....	29	....	....	....	....	....	....	....	....	....	....	21	12	14	26	14	....	....	....
	Peterborough Petes	Mem-Cup	5	4	5	9	....	....	....	0	....	....	....	....	....	....	....	....	....	....	....	....	....	....	....	....	....	....
1978-79	New Brunswick Hawks	AHL	80	20	30	50	....	....	....	14	....	....	....	....	....	....	....	....	....	....	5	0	0	0	2	....	....	....
1979-80	**Toronto Maple Leafs**	**NHL**	**2**	**1**	**0**	**1**	**1**	**0**	**1**	**2**	**0**	**0**	**0**	**3**	**33.3**	**1**	**0**	**2**	**1**	**0**	....	....	....	....	....	....	....	....
	New Brunswick Hawks	AHL	61	19	42	61	....	....	....	33	....	....	....	....	....	....	....	....	....	....	17	7	11	18	16	....	....	....
1980-81	**Toronto Maple Leafs**	**NHL**	**11**	**0**	**0**	**0**	**0**	**0**	**0**	**0**	**0**	**0**	**0**	**5**	**0.0**	**1**	**0**	**8**	**6**	**–1**	....	....	....	....	....	....	....	....
	Detroit Red Wings	**NHL**	**50**	**18**	**13**	**31**	**14**	**9**	**23**	**24**	**6**	**1**	**3**	**97**	**18.6**	**41**	**12**	**78**	**19**	**–30**	....	....	....	....	....	....	....	....
1981-82	**Detroit Red Wings**	**NHL**	**74**	**14**	**28**	**42**	**11**	**19**	**30**	**62**	**0**	**1**	**0**	**121**	**11.6**	**65**	**3**	**112**	**32**	**–18**	....	....	....	....	....	....	....	....
1982-83	**Detroit Red Wings**	**NHL**	**10**	**1**	**1**	**2**	**1**	**1**	**2**	**6**	**0**	**0**	**0**	**15**	**6.7**	**4**	**0**	**6**	**1**	**–1**	....	....	....	....	....	....	....	....
	Vancouver Canucks	**NHL**	**31**	**4**	**6**	**10**	**3**	**4**	**7**	**4**	**0**	**0**	**1**	**34**	**11.8**	**17**	**0**	**25**	**13**	**5**	**4**	**1**	**2**	**3**	**7**	**0**	**0**	**0**
1983-84	**Vancouver Canucks**	**NHL**	**26**	**2**	**3**	**5**	**2**	**2**	**4**	**2**	**0**	**0**	**0**	**26**	**7.7**	**6**	**0**	**33**	**19**	**–8**	....	....	....	....	....	....	....	....
	Fredericton Express	AHL	35	8	10	18	....	....	....	8	....	....	....	....	....	....	....	....	....	....	7	2	3	5	6	....	....	....
1984-85	**Vancouver Canucks**	**NHL**	**62**	**17**	**5**	**22**	**14**	**3**	**17**	**21**	**0**	**1**	**1**	**92**	**18.5**	**28**	**0**	**84**	**34**	**–22**	....	....	....	....	....	....	....	....
	Fredericton Express	AHL	15	5	9	14	....	....	....	18	....	....	....	....	....	....	....	....	....	....	....	....	....	....	....	....	....	....
1985-86	Fredericton Express	AHL	77	23	36	59	....	....	....	33	....	....	....	....	....	....	....	....	....	....	6	2	2	4	4	....	....	....
1986-87	Fredericton Express	AHL	80	27	37	64	....	....	....	20	....	....	....	....	....	....	....	....	....	....	....	....	....	....	....	....	....	....
1987-88	Newmarket Saints	AHL	73	17	30	47	....	....	....	42	....	....	....	....	....	....	....	....	....	....	....	....	....	....	....	....	....	....
1988-89	Newmarket Saints	AHL	37	4	8	12	....	....	....	18	....	....	....	....	....	....	....	....	....	....	....	....	....	....	....	....	....	....
	NHL Totals		**266**	**57**	**56**	**113**	**46**	**38**	**84**	**121**	**6**	**3**	**5**	**393**	**14.5**	**163**	**15**	**348**	**125**		**4**	**1**	**2**	**3**	**7**	**0**	**0**	**0**

Memorial Cup All-Star Team (1978) • Won George Parsons Trophy (Memorial Cup Tournament Most Sportsmanlike Player) (1978)

Traded to **Detroit** by **Toronto** for Jim Rutherford, December 4, 1980. Traded to **Vancouver** by **Detroit** for Ivan Boldirev, January 17, 1983. Signed as a free agent by **Toronto**, August 15, 1987.

• KISIO, Kelly Kelvin Wade C – R. 5'10", 185 lbs. b: Peace River, Alta., 9/18/1959.																												
1976-77	Red Deer Rustlers	AJHL	60	53	48	101	....	....	....	101	....	....	....	....	....	....	....	....	....	....	....	....	....	....	....	....	....	....
1977-78	Red Deer Rustlers	AJHL	58	74	68	142	....	....	....	66	....	....	....	....	....	....	....	....	....	....	....	....	....	....	....	....	....	....
1978-79	Calgary Wranglers	WHL	70	60	61	121	....	....	....	73	....	....	....	....	....	....	....	....	....	....	15	12	16	28	4	....	....	....
1979-80	Calgary Wranglers	WHL	71	65	73	138	....	....	....	64	....	....	....	....	....	....	....	....	....	....	2	1	0	1	4	....	....	....
1980-81	Adirondack Red Wings	AHL	41	10	14	24	....	....	....	43	....	....	....	....	....	....	....	....	....	....	....	....	....	....	....	....	....	....
	Kalamazoo Wings	IHL	31	27	16	43	....	....	....	48	....	....	....	....	....	....	....	....	....	....	8	7	7	14	13	....	....	....
1981-82	Dallas Black Hawks	CHL	78	*62	39	101	....	....	....	59	....	....	....	....	....	....	....	....	....	....	16	*12	*17	*29	38	....	....	....
1982-83	HC Davos	Switz.	35	40	33	73	....	....	....	....	....	....	....	....	....	....	....	....	....	....	3	9	2	11	0	....	....	....
	Detroit Red Wings	**NHL**	**15**	**4**	**3**	**7**	**3**	**2**	**5**	**0**	**0**	**0**	**0**	**16**	**25.0**	**13**	**1**	**14**	**0**	**–2**	....	....	....	....	....	....	....	....
1983-84	**Detroit Red Wings**	**NHL**	**70**	**23**	**37**	**60**	**18**	**25**	**43**	**34**	**1**	**0**	**2**	**146**	**15.8**	**81**	**19**	**47**	**1**	**16**	**4**	**1**	**0**	**1**	**4**	**0**	**0**	**0**
1984-85	**Detroit Red Wings**	**NHL**	**75**	**20**	**41**	**61**	**16**	**28**	**44**	**56**	**5**	**0**	**0**	**126**	**15.9**	**80**	**19**	**59**	**0**	**2**	**3**	**0**	**2**	**2**	**2**	**0**	**0**	**0**
1985-86	**Detroit Red Wings**	**NHL**	**76**	**21**	**48**	**69**	**17**	**32**	**49**	**85**	**7**	**3**	**0**	**140**	**15.0**	**94**	**37**	**85**	**7**	**–21**	....	....	....	....	....	....	....	....
1986-87	**New York Rangers**	**NHL**	**70**	**24**	**40**	**64**	**21**	**29**	**50**	**73**	**4**	**2**	**1**	**137**	**17.5**	**87**	**21**	**89**	**18**	**–5**	**4**	**0**	**1**	**1**	**2**	**0**	**0**	**0**
1987-88	**New York Rangers**	**NHL**	**77**	**23**	**55**	**78**	**20**	**39**	**59**	**88**	**9**	**1**	**1**	**145**	**15.9**	**104**	**41**	**80**	**25**	**8**	....	....	....	....	....	....	....	....
1988-89	**New York Rangers**	**NHL**	**70**	**26**	**36**	**62**	**22**	**25**	**47**	**91**	**2**	**0**	**4**	**128**	**20.3**	**83**	**13**	**70**	**14**	**14**	**4**	**0**	**0**	**0**	**9**	**0**	**0**	**0**
1989-90	**New York Rangers**	**NHL**	**68**	**22**	**44**	**66**	**19**	**32**	**51**	**105**	**7**	**2**	**1**	**128**	**17.2**	**101**	**43**	**70**	**23**	**11**	**10**	**2**	**8**	**10**	**8**	**0**	**1**	**0**
1990-91	**New York Rangers**	**NHL**	**51**	**15**	**20**	**35**	**14**	**15**	**29**	**58**	**7**	**1**	**2**	**74**	**20.3**	**46**	**18**	**35**	**10**	**3**	....	....	....	....	....	....	....	....
1991-92	**San Jose Sharks**	**NHL**	**48**	**11**	**26**	**37**	**10**	**20**	**30**	**54**	**2**	**3**	**2**	**68**	**16.2**	**50**	**18**	**59**	**20**	**–7**	....	....	....	....	....	....	....	....
1992-93	**San Jose Sharks**	**NHL**	**78**	**26**	**52**	**78**	**22**	**36**	**58**	**90**	**9**	**2**	**2**	**152**	**17.1**	**104**	**46**	**101**	**28**	**–15**	....	....	....	....	....	....	....	....
1993-94	**Calgary Flames**	**NHL**	**51**	**7**	**23**	**30**	**6**	**18**	**24**	**28**	**1**	**0**	**1**	**62**	**11.3**	**44**	**21**	**35**	**6**	**–6**	**7**	**0**	**2**	**2**	**8**	**0**	**0**	**0**

			REGULAR SEASON																		PLAYOFFS							
Season	Club	League	GP	G	A	Pts	AG	AA	APts	PIM	PP	SH	GW	S	%	TGF	PGF	TGA	PGA	+/–	GP	G	A	Pts	PIM	PP	SH	GW
1994-95	**Calgary Flames**	**NHL**	12	7	4	11	12	6	18	6	5	1	0	26	26.9	13	5	8	2	2	7	3	2	5	19	1	0	0
1995-1998	**Calgary Flames**	**NHL**	DID NOT PLAY – SCOUTING																									
1998-2000	Calgary Hitmen	WHL	DID NOT PLAY – ASSISTANT COACH																									
	NHL Totals		**761**	**229**	**429**	**658**	**200**	**307**	**507**	**768**	**59**	**15**	**16**	**1348**	**17.0**	**900**	**302**	**752**	**154**		**39**	**6**	**15**	**21**	**52**	**1**	**1**	**0**

Played in NHL All-Star Game (1993)

Signed as a free agent by **Detroit**, March 2, 1983. Traded to **NY Rangers** by **Detroit** with Lane Lambert, Jim Leavins and Detroit's 5th round choice (later traded to Winnipeg–Winnipeg selected Benoit LeBeau) in 1988 Entry Draft for Glen Hanlon and NY Rangers' 3rd round choices in 1987 (Dennis Holland) and 1988 (Guy Dupuis) Entry Drafts, July 29, 1986. Claimed by **Minnesota** from **NY Rangers** in Expansion Draft, May 30, 1991. Traded to **San Jose** by **Minnesota** for Shane Churla, June 3, 1991. Signed as a free agent by **Calgary**, August 18, 1993. • Missed majority of 1994-95 season recovering from shoulder injury suffered in game vs. Washington, January 22, 1995.

• KITCHEN, Bill

William D – L. 6'1", 200 lbs. b: Schomberg, Ont., 10/2/1960.

Season	Club	League	GP	G	A	Pts	AG	AA	APts	PIM	PP	SH	GW	S	%	TGF	PGF	TGA	PGA	+/–	GP	G	A	Pts	PIM	PP	SH	GW
1976-77	Aurora Eagles	OJHL	44	3	24	27				87																		
	Windsor Spitfires	OMJHL	2	1	0	1				0																		
1977-78	Ottawa 67's	OMJHL	67	5	6	11				54											15	1	2	3	9			
1978-79	Ottawa 67's	OMJHL	55	3	16	19				188											4	0	1	1	14			
1979-80	Ottawa 67's	OMJHL	63	7	19	26				195											11	1	8	9	21			
	Canada	WJC-A	5	0	1	1				10																		
	Nova Scotia Voyageurs	AHL																			2	0	1	1	0			
1980-81	Nova Scotia Voyageurs	AHL	65	2	7	9				135											6	0	1	1	5			
1981-82	**Montreal Canadiens**	**NHL**	**1**	**0**	**0**	**0**	**0**	**0**	**0**	**7**	**0**	**0**	**0**	**0**	**0.0**	**0**	**0**	**2**	**2**	**0**	**3**	**0**	**1**	**1**	**0**	**0**	**0**	**0**
	Nova Scotia Voyageurs	AHL	71	3	17	20				135											6	2	0	2	11			
1982-83	**Montreal Canadiens**	**NHL**	**8**	**0**	**0**	**0**	**0**	**0**	**0**	**4**	**0**	**0**	**0**	**2**	**0.0**	**2**	**1**	**3**	**0**	**–2**								
	Nova Scotia Voyageurs	AHL	53	3	11	14				71																		
1983-84	**Montreal Canadiens**	**NHL**	**3**	**0**	**0**	**0**	**0**	**0**	**0**	**2**	**0**	**0**	**0**	**3**	**0.0**	**2**	**1**	**4**	**3**	**0**								
	Nova Scotia Voyageurs	AHL	68	4	20	24				193											10	1	1	2	8			
1984-85	**Toronto Maple Leafs**	**NHL**	**29**	**1**	**4**	**5**	**1**	**3**	**4**	**27**	**0**	**0**	**0**	**21**	**4.8**	**30**	**0**	**48**	**12**	**–6**								
	St. Catharines Saints	AHL	31	3	7	10				52																		
1985-86	St. Catharines Saints	AHL	72	7	32	39				109											12	0	2	2	19			
	NHL Totals		**41**	**1**	**4**	**5**	**1**	**3**	**4**	**40**	**0**	**0**	**0**	**26**	**3.8**	**34**	**2**	**57**	**17**		**3**	**0**	**1**	**1**	**0**	**0**	**0**	**0**

• Brother of Mike

Signed as a free agent by **Montreal**, October 23, 1979. Signed as a free agent by **Toronto**, August 16, 1984.

• KITCHEN, Mike

Michael Elwin D – L. 5'10", 185 lbs. b: Newmarket, Ont., 2/1/1956. Kansas City's 2nd, 38th overall, in 1976.

Season	Club	League	GP	G	A	Pts	AG	AA	APts	PIM	PP	SH	GW	S	%	TGF	PGF	TGA	PGA	+/–	GP	G	A	Pts	PIM	PP	SH	GW
1973-74	Toronto Marlboros	OMJHL	69	3	17	20				145																		
1974-75	Toronto Marlboros	OMJHL	68	5	30	35				136											21	1	9	10	35			
	Toronto Marlboros	Mem-Cup	4	0	4	4				8																		
1975-76	Toronto Marlboros	OMJHL	65	6	18	24				148											10	0	2	2	26			
1976-77	**Colorado Rockies**	**NHL**	**60**	**1**	**8**	**9**	**1**	**6**	**7**	**36**	**0**	**0**	**0**	**46**	**2.2**	**58**	**6**	**57**	**3**	**–2**								
	Rhode Island Reds	AHL	14	0	10	10				14																		
1977-78	**Colorado Rockies**	**NHL**	**61**	**2**	**17**	**19**	**2**	**13**	**15**	**45**	**0**	**0**	**1**	**57**	**3.5**	**54**	**3**	**75**	**12**	**–12**	**2**	**0**	**0**	**0**	**2**	**0**	**0**	**0**
1978-79	**Colorado Rockies**	**NHL**	**53**	**1**	**4**	**5**	**1**	**3**	**4**	**28**	**0**	**0**	**0**	**22**	**4.5**	**25**	**1**	**51**	**8**	**–19**								
1979-80	**Colorado Rockies**	**NHL**	**42**	**1**	**6**	**7**	**1**	**4**	**5**	**25**	**0**	**0**	**0**	**31**	**3.2**	**16**	**1**	**29**	**4**	**–10**								
	Fort Worth Texans	CHL	30	0	9	9				22											15	0	1	1	16			
1980-81	**Colorado Rockies**	**NHL**	**75**	**1**	**7**	**8**	**1**	**5**	**6**	**100**	**0**	**0**	**0**	**49**	**2.0**	**47**	**2**	**104**	**21**	**–38**								
1981-82	**Colorado Rockies**	**NHL**	**63**	**1**	**8**	**9**	**1**	**5**	**6**	**60**	**0**	**0**	**0**	**35**	**2.9**	**59**	**0**	**95**	**18**	**–18**								
	Fort Worth Texans	CHL	13	1	5	6				16																		
1982-83	**New Jersey Devils**	**NHL**	**77**	**4**	**8**	**12**	**3**	**6**	**9**	**52**	**0**	**1**	**0**	**46**	**8.7**	**47**	**0**	**106**	**34**	**–25**								
1983-84	**New Jersey Devils**	**NHL**	**43**	**1**	**4**	**5**	**1**	**3**	**4**	**24**	**0**	**0**	**0**	**37**	**2.7**	**21**	**2**	**45**	**11**	**–15**								
1984-85	Maine Mariners	AHL	12	0	1	1				10																		
1985-1988			OUT OF HOCKEY – RETIRED																									
1988-1989	Newmarket Saints	AHL	DID NOT PLAY – ASSISTANT COACH																									
1989-1998	**Toronto Maple Leafs**	**NHL**	DID NOT PLAY – ASSISTANT COACH																									
1998-2000	**St. Louis Blues**	**NHL**	DID NOT PLAY – ASSISTANT COACH																									
	NHL Totals		**474**	**12**	**62**	**74**	**11**	**45**	**56**	**370**	**0**	**1**	**1**	**323**	**3.7**	**327**	**15**	**562**	**111**		**2**	**0**	**0**	**0**	**2**	**0**	**0**	**0**

• Brother of Bill • OMJHL First All-Star Team (1975) • Memorial Cup All-Star Team (1975)

Rights transferred to **Colorado** when **Kansas City** franchise relocated, July 15, 1976. Transferred to **New Jersey** after **Colorado** franchise relocated, June 30, 1982.

• KJELLBERG, Patrik

Patrik G. LW – L. 6'2", 186 lbs. b: Falun, Sweden, 6/7/1969. Montreal's 4th, 83rd overall, in 1988.

Season	Club	League	GP	G	A	Pts	AG	AA	APts	PIM	PP	SH	GW	S	%	TGF	PGF	TGA	PGA	+/–	GP	G	A	Pts	PIM	PP	SH	GW
1985-86	Falun IF	Sweden-2	5	0	2	2				0																		
1986-87	Falun IF	Sweden-2	32	11	13	24				16																		
	Sweden	EJC-A	7	8	3	11				2																		
1987-88	Falun IF	Sweden-2	29	15	10	25				6																		
1988-89	AIK Solna Stockholm	Sweden	25	7	9	16				8																		
	Sweden	WJC-A	7	3	4	7				4																		
1989-90	AIK Solna Stockholm	Sweden	33	8	16	24				6											3	1	0	1	0			
1990-91	AIK Solna Stockholm	Sweden	38	4	11	15				18																		
1991-92	AIK Solna Stockholm	Sweden	40	20	13	33				14											3	1	0	1	2			
	Sweden	Olympics	8	1	3	4				0																		
	Sweden	WC-A	8	2	2	4				2																		
1992-93	**Montreal Canadiens**	**NHL**	**7**	**0**	**0**	**0**	**0**	**0**	**0**	**2**	**0**	**0**	**0**	**7**	**0.0**	**0**	**0**	**5**	**2**	**–3**								
	Fredericton Canadiens	AHL	41	10	27	37				14											5	2	2	4	0			
1993-94	HV-71 Jonkoping	Sweden	40	11	17	28				18																		
	Sweden	Olympics	8	0	1	1				2																		
1994-95	HV-71 Jonkoping	Sweden	29	5	15	20				12																		
1995-96	Djurgardens IF Stockholm	Sweden	40	9	7	16				10											4	0	2	2	2			
1996-97	Djurgardens IF Stockholm	Sweden	49	29	11	40				18											4	2	3	5	4			
1997-98	Djurgardens IF Stockholm	Sweden	46	*30	18	48				16											15	7	3	10	12			
1998-99	**Nashville Predators**	**NHL**	**71**	**11**	**20**	**31**	**13**	**19**	**32**	**24**	**2**	**0**	**2**	**103**	**10.7**	**50**	**18**	**47**	**2**	**–13**								
99-2000	**Nashville Predators**	**NHL**	**82**	**23**	**23**	**46**	**26**	**21**	**47**	**14**	**9**	**0**	**3**	**129**	**17.8**	**79**	**29**	**61**	**0**	**–11**								
	NHL Totals		**160**	**34**	**43**	**77**	**39**	**40**	**79**	**40**	**11**	**0**	**5**	**239**	**14.2**	**129**	**47**	**113**	**4**									

EJC-A All-Star Team (1987)

Signed as a free agent by **Nashville**, July 7, 1998.

• KLASSEN, Ralph

Ralph L. C – L. 5'11", 175 lbs. b: Humboldt, Sask., 9/15/1955. California's 1st, 3rd overall, in 1975.

Season	Club	League	GP	G	A	Pts	AG	AA	APts	PIM	PP	SH	GW	S	%	TGF	PGF	TGA	PGA	+/–	GP	G	A	Pts	PIM	PP	SH	GW
1970-71	Saskatoon Blades	WCJHL	61	1	8	9				29											3	0	0	0	0			
1971-72	Saskatoon Blades	WCJHL	62	17	38	55				64											8	1	5	6	7			
1972-73	Saskatoon Blades	WCJHL	68	19	47	66				80											16	5	3	8	16			
1973-74	Saskatoon Blades	WCJHL	68	23	54	77				110											6	0	3	3	7			
1974-75	Saskatoon Blades	WCJHL	41	21	47	68				34											17	5	*23	*28	14			
	Canada	WJC-A	4	0	3	3				0																		
1975-76	**California Golden Seals**	**NHL**	**71**	**6**	**15**	**21**	**5**	**11**	**16**	**26**	**2**	**0**	**0**	**96**	**6.3**	**35**	**11**	**71**	**21**	**–26**								
	Salt Lake Golden Eagles	CHL	4	3	3	6				4																		
1976-77	**Cleveland Barons**	**NHL**	**80**	**14**	**18**	**32**	**13**	**14**	**27**	**23**	**4**	**1**	**1**	**131**	**10.7**	**50**	**10**	**100**	**35**	**–25**								
	Canada	WEC-A	10	1	5	6				0																		
1977-78	**Cleveland Barons**	**NHL**	**13**	**2**	**1**	**3**	**2**	**1**	**3**	**6**	**0**	**1**	**0**	**14**	**14.3**	**6**	**0**	**17**	**9**	**–2**								
	Colorado Rockies	**NHL**	**44**	**6**	**9**	**15**	**5**	**7**	**12**	**8**	**3**	**0**	**0**	**47**	**12.8**	**37**	**11**	**55**	**10**	**–19**	**2**	**0**	**0**	**0**	**0**	**0**	**0**	**0**

Season	Club	League	GP	G	A	Pts	AG	AA	APts	PIM	PP	SH	GW	S	%	TGF	PGF	TGA	PGA	+/–	PO GP	PO G	PO A	PO Pts	PO PIM	PO PP	PO SH	PO GW
			REGULAR SEASON																		PLAYOFFS							
1978-79	Colorado Rockies	NHL	64	6	13	19	5	9	14	12	1	1	2	100	6.0	32	2	87	32	–25								
	Philadelphia Firebirds	AHL	18	3	9	12				2																		
1979-80	St. Louis Blues	NHL	80	9	16	25	8	12	20	10	0	0	3	100	9.0	39	0	78	20	–19	3	0	0	0	0	0	0	0
1980-81	St. Louis Blues	NHL	66	6	12	18	5	8	13	23	0	1	0	65	9.2	29	0	60	26	–5	11	2	0	2	2	0	0	0
1981-82	St. Louis Blues	NHL	45	3	7	10	2	5	7	6	0	1	1	25	12.0	16	2	40	23	–3	10	2	2	4	10	0	0	0
1982-83	St. Louis Blues	NHL	29	0	2	2	0	1	1	6	0	0	0	14	0.0	4	0	13	6	–3								
	Salt Lake Golden Eagles	CHL	21	9	10	19				8											6	2	6	8	5			
1983-84	St. Louis Blues	NHL	5	0	0	0	0	0	0	0	0	0	0	5	0.0	0	0	5	0	–5								
	NHL Totals		497	52	93	145	45	68	113	120	10	5	7	597	8.7	248	36	526	182		26	4	2	6	12	0	0	0

Transferred to **Cleveland** after **California** franchise relocated, June, 1976. Traded to **Colorado** by **Cleveland** with Fred Ahern for Rick Jodzio and Chuck Arnason, January 9, 1978. Claimed by **Hartford** from **Colorado** in Expansion Draft, June 13, 1979. Traded to **NY Islanders** by **Hartford** for Terry Richardson, June 14, 1979. Traded to **St. Louis** by **NY Islanders** as part of three-team transaction that sent Barry Gibbs and Tom Williams to NY Islanders (June 9, 1979) and Tom Williams to LA Kings (August 16, 1979), June 14, 1979.

• KLATT, Trent

Trent T. RW – R. 6'1", 205 lbs. b: Robbinsdale, MN, 1/30/1971. Washington's 5th, 82nd overall, in 1989.

Season	Club	League	GP	G	A	Pts	AG	AA	APts	PIM	PP	SH	GW	S	%	TGF	PGF	TGA	PGA	+/–	PO GP	PO G	PO A	PO Pts	PO PIM	PO PP	PO SH	PO GW
1986-87	Osseo Orioles	Hi-School	22	9	27	36																						
1987-88	Osseo Orioles	Hi-School	22	19	17	36																						
1988-89	Osseo Orioles	Hi-School	22	24	39	63																						
	St. Paul Vulcans	USHL	STATISTICS NOT AVAILABLE																									
1989-90	University of Minnesota	WCHA	38	22	14	36				16																		
1990-91	University of Minnesota	WCHA	39	16	28	44				58																		
	United States	WJC-A	8	6	6	12				6																		
1991-92	University of Minnesota	WCHA	41	27	36	63				76																		
	Minnesota North Stars	NHL	1	0	0	0	0	0	0	0	0	0	0	1	0.0	1	0	1	0	0	6	0	0	0	2	0	0	0
1992-93	Minnesota North Stars	NHL	47	4	19	23	3	13	16	38	1	0	0	69	5.8	31	4	26	1	2								
	Kalamazoo Wings	IHL	31	8	11	19				18																		
1993-94	Dallas Stars	NHL	61	14	24	38	13	19	32	30	3	0	2	86	16.3	55	12	30	0	13	9	2	1	3	4	1	0	0
	Kalamazoo Wings	IHL	6	3	2	5				4																		
1994-95	Dallas Stars	NHL	47	12	10	22	21	15	36	26	5	0	3	91	13.2	39	18	23	0	–2	5	1	0	1	0	1	0	0
1995-96	Dallas Stars	NHL	22	4	4	8	4	3	7	23	0	0	1	37	10.8	14	6	8	0	0								
	Michigan K-Wings	IHL	2	1	2	3				5																		
	Philadelphia Flyers	NHL	49	3	8	11	3	7	10	21	0	0	1	64	4.7	13	1	15	5	2	12	4	1	5	0	0	0	0
1996-97	Philadelphia Flyers	NHL	76	24	21	45	25	19	44	20	5	5	5	131	18.3	63	10	57	13	9	19	4	3	7	12	0	0	2
1997-98	Philadelphia Flyers	NHL	82	14	28	42	16	27	43	16	5	0	3	143	9.8	63	18	63	20	2	5	0	0	0	0	0	0	0
1998-99	Philadelphia Flyers	NHL	2	0	0	0	0	0	0	0	0	0	0	2	0.0	0	0	0	0	0								
	Vancouver Canucks	NHL	73	4	10	14	5	10	15	12	0	0	0	58	6.9	27	0	46	16	–3								
	United States	WC-A	6	3	0	3				0																		
99-2000	Vancouver Canucks	NHL	47	10	10	20	11	9	20	26	8	0	0	100	10.0	40	22	30	4	–8								
	Syracuse Crunch	AHL	24	13	10	23				6																		
	NHL Totals		507	89	134	223	101	122	223	212	27	5	15	782	11.4	346	91	299	59		56	11	5	16	18	2	0	2

Traded to **Minnesota** by **Washington** with Steve Maltais for Shawn Chambers, June 21, 1991. Transferred to **Dallas** after **Minnesota** franchise relocated, June 9, 1993. Traded to **Philadelphia** by **Dallas** for Brent Fedyk, December 13, 1995. Traded to **Vancouver** by **Philadelphia** for Vancouver's 6th round choice (later traded to Atlanta - Atlanta selected Jeff Dwyer) in 2000 Entry Draft, October 19, 1998.

• KLEE, Ken

D – R. 6'1", 212 lbs. b: Indianapolis, IN, 4/24/1971. Washington's 11th, 177th overall, in 1990.

Season	Club	League	GP	G	A	Pts	AG	AA	APts	PIM	PP	SH	GW	S	%	TGF	PGF	TGA	PGA	+/–	PO GP	PO G	PO A	PO Pts	PO PIM	PO PP	PO SH	PO GW
1988-89	St. Michael's Buzzers	OJHL-B	40	9	23	32				64											27	5	12	17	54			
1989-90	Bowling Green University	CCHA	39	0	5	5				52																		
1990-91	Bowling Green University	CCHA	37	7	28	35				50																		
	United States	WJC-A	8	1	1	2				2																		
1991-92	Bowling Green University	CCHA	10	0	1	1				14																		
	United States	WC-A	2	0	0	0				0																		
1992-93	Baltimore Skipjacks	AHL	77	4	14	18				93											7	0	1	1	15			
1993-94	Portland Pirates	AHL	65	2	9	11				87											17	1	2	3	14			
1994-95	Washington Capitals	NHL	23	3	1	4	5	1	6	41	0	0	0	18	16.7	11	0	9	0	2	7	0	0	0	4	0	0	0
	Portland Pirates	AHL	49	5	7	12				89																		
1995-96	Washington Capitals	NHL	66	8	3	11	8	2	10	60	0	1	2	76	10.5	28	3	29	3	–1	1	0	0	0	0	0	0	0
1996-97	Washington Capitals	NHL	80	3	8	11	3	7	10	115	0	0	2	108	2.8	39	0	60	16	–5								
	United States	WC-A	8	1	0	1				12																		
1997-98	Washington Capitals	NHL	51	4	2	6	5	2	7	46	0	0	1	44	9.1	16	0	22	3	–3	9	1	0	1	10	0	0	0
1998-99	Washington Capitals	NHL	78	7	13	20	8	13	21	80	0	0	1	132	5.3	53	10	69	17	–9								
99-2000	Washington Capitals	NHL	80	7	13	20	8	12	20	79	0	0	2	113	6.2	58	5	62	17	8	5	0	1	1	10	0	0	0
	NHL Totals		378	32	40	72	37	37	74	421	0	1	8	491	6.5	205	18	251	56		22	1	1	2	24	0	0	0

• KLEINENDORST, Scot

Scot B. D – L. 6'3", 215 lbs. b: Grand Rapids, MN, 1/16/1960. NY Rangers' 4th, 98th overall, in 1980.

Season	Club	League	GP	G	A	Pts	AG	AA	APts	PIM	PP	SH	GW	S	%	TGF	PGF	TGA	PGA	+/–	PO GP	PO G	PO A	PO Pts	PO PIM	PO PP	PO SH	PO GW
1978-79	Providence College	ECAC	25	4	4	8				27																		
1979-80	Providence College	ECAC	30	1	12	13				38																		
1980-81	Providence College	ECAC	32	3	31	34				75																		
1981-82	Providence College	ECAC	33	11	27	38				85																		
	United States	WEC-A	4	0	0	0				2																		
	Springfield Indians	AHL	5	0	4	4				11																		
1982-83	New York Rangers	NHL	30	2	9	11	2	6	8	8	1	0	0	16	12.5	31	5	24	5	7	6	0	2	2	2	0	0	0
	Tulsa Oilers	CHL	10	0	7	7				2																		
1983-84	New York Rangers	NHL	23	0	2	2	0	1	1	35	0	0	0	13	0.0	11	1	23	3	–10								
	Tulsa Oilers	CHL	10	4	5	9				4																		
1984-85	Hartford Whalers	NHL	35	1	8	9	1	5	6	69	0	0	0	16	6.3	29	1	49	11	–10								
	Binghamton Whalers	AHL	30	3	7	10				42																		
1985-86	Hartford Whalers	NHL	41	2	7	9	2	5	7	62	0	0	0	26	7.7	46	0	56	18	8	10	0	1	1	18	0	0	0
1986-87	Hartford Whalers	NHL	66	3	9	12	3	7	10	130	0	0	0	50	6.0	54	0	90	40	4	4	1	3	4	20	0	0	0
1987-88	Hartford Whalers	NHL	44	3	6	9	3	4	7	86	0	0	0	44	6.8	25	0	44	14	–5	3	1	1	2	0	0	0	0
1988-89	Hartford Whalers	NHL	24	0	1	1	0	1	1	36	0	0	0	7	0.0	7	0	24	6	–11								
	Binghamton Whalers	AHL	4	0	1	1				19																		
	Washington Capitals	NHL	3	0	1	1	0	1	1	10	0	0	0	0	0.0	3	0	4	1	0								
1989-90	Washington Capitals	Fr-Tour	3	1	0	1				0																		
	Washington Capitals	NHL	15	1	3	4	1	2	3	16	0	0	0	13	7.7	8	0	7	3	4	3	0	0	0	0	0	0	0
	Baltimore Skipjacks	AHL	2	2	0	2				6																		
	NHL Totals		281	12	46	58	12	32	44	452	1	0	0	185	6.5	214	7	321	101		26	2	7	9	40	0	0	0

ECAC Second All-Star Team (1980) • ECAC First All-Star Team (1982)

Traded to **Hartford** by **NY Rangers** for Blaine Stoughton, February 27, 1984. Traded to **Washington** by **Hartford** for Jim Thomson, March 6, 1989.

• KLEMM, Jon

D – R. 6'3", 200 lbs. b: Cranbrook, B.C., 1/8/1970.

Season	Club	League	GP	G	A	Pts	AG	AA	APts	PIM	PP	SH	GW	S	%	TGF	PGF	TGA	PGA	+/–	PO GP	PO G	PO A	PO Pts	PO PIM	PO PP	PO SH	PO GW
1986-87	Cranbrook Colts	KIJHL	59	20	51	71				54																		
1987-88	Seattle Thunderbirds	WHL	68	6	7	13				24																		
1988-89	Seattle Thunderbirds	WHL	2	1	1	2				0																		
	Spokane Chiefs	WHL	66	6	34	40				42																		
1989-90	Spokane Chiefs	WHL	66	3	28	31				100											6	1	1	2	5			
1990-91	Spokane Chiefs	WHL	72	7	58	65				65											15	3	6	9	8			
	Spokane Chiefs	Mem-Cup	4	1	4	5				17																		
1991-92	Quebec Nordiques	NHL	4	0	1	1	0	1	1	0	0	0	0	2	0.0	3	0	4	3	2								
	Halifax Citadels	AHL	70	6	13	19				40																		
1992-93	Halifax Citadels	AHL	80	3	20	23				32																		

			REGULAR SEASON																		PLAYOFFS							
Season	Club	League	GP	G	A	Pts	AG	AA	APts	PIM	PP	SH	GW	S	%	TGF	PGF	TGA	PGA	+/–	GP	G	A	Pts	PIM	PP	SH	GW
1993-94	**Quebec Nordiques**	**NHL**	**7**	**0**	**0**	**0**	**0**	**0**	**0**	**4**	**0**	**0**	**0**	**11**	**0.0**	**1**	**0**	**2**	**0**	**–1**	....	....	....	....	....	....	....	....
	Cornwall Aces	AHL	66	4	26	30	....	....	....	78	....	....	....	....	....	....	....	....	....	....	13	1	2	3	6	....	....	....
1994-95	**Quebec Nordiques**	**NHL**	**4**	**1**	**0**	**1**	**2**	**0**	**2**	**2**	**0**	**0**	**0**	**5**	**20.0**	**3**	**0**	**1**	**1**	**3**	....	....	....	....	....	....	....	....
	Cornwall Aces	AHL	65	6	13	19	....	....	....	84	....	....	....	....	....	....	....	....	....	....	....	....	....	....	....	....	....	....
1995-96♦	**Colorado Avalanche**	**NHL**	**56**	**3**	**12**	**15**	**3**	**10**	**13**	**20**	**0**	**1**	**1**	**61**	**4.9**	**43**	**1**	**40**	**10**	**12**	**15**	**2**	**1**	**3**	**0**	**1**	**0**	**0**
1996-97	**Colorado Avalanche**	**NHL**	**80**	**9**	**15**	**24**	**10**	**13**	**23**	**37**	**1**	**2**	**1**	**103**	**8.7**	**61**	**5**	**61**	**17**	**12**	**17**	**1**	**1**	**2**	**6**	**0**	**0**	**0**
1997-98	**Colorado Avalanche**	**NHL**	**67**	**6**	**8**	**14**	**7**	**8**	**15**	**30**	**0**	**0**	**0**	**60**	**10.0**	**27**	**0**	**48**	**18**	**–3**	**4**	**0**	**0**	**0**	**0**	**0**	**0**	**0**
1998-99	**Colorado Avalanche**	**NHL**	**39**	**1**	**2**	**3**	**1**	**2**	**3**	**31**	**0**	**0**	**0**	**28**	**3.6**	**21**	**2**	**18**	**3**	**4**	**19**	**0**	**1**	**1**	**10**	**0**	**0**	**0**
99-2000	**Colorado Avalanche**	**NHL**	**73**	**5**	**7**	**12**	**6**	**6**	**12**	**34**	**0**	**0**	**0**	**64**	**7.8**	**54**	**1**	**44**	**17**	**26**	**17**	**2**	**1**	**3**	**9**	**0**	**0**	**0**
	NHL Totals		**330**	**25**	**45**	**70**	**29**	**40**	**69**	**158**	**1**	**3**	**2**	**334**	**7.5**	**213**	**9**	**218**	**69**		**72**	**5**	**4**	**9**	**25**	**1**	**0**	**0**

WHL West Second All-Star Team (1991)

Signed as a free agent by **Quebec**, May 14, 1991. Transferred to **Colorado** after **Quebec** franchise relocated, June 21, 1995. • Missed majority of 1998-99 season recovering from knee injury suffered in game vs. Phoenix, November 10, 1998.

• KLIMA, Petr

W – R. 6', 190 lbs. b: Chomutov, Czech., 12/23/1964. Detroit's 5th, 88th overall, in 1983.

Season	Club	League	GP	G	A	Pts	AG	AA	APts	PIM	PP	SH	GW	S	%	TGF	PGF	TGA	PGA	+/–	GP	G	A	Pts	PIM	PP	SH	GW
1981-82	CHZ Litvinov	Czech.	18	7	3	10	....	....	....	8	....	....	....	....	....	....	....	....	....	....	....	....	....	....	....	....	....	....
	Czechoslovakia	EJC-A	5	7	2	9	....	....	....	12	....	....	....	....	....	....	....	....	....	....	....	....	....	....	....	....	....	....
1982-83	CHZ Litvinov	Czech.	44	19	17	36	....	....	....	74	....	....	....	....	....	....	....	....	....	....	....	....	....	....	....	....	....	....
	Czechoslovakia	WJC-A	7	4	4	8	....	....	....	6	....	....	....	....	....	....	....	....	....	....	....	....	....	....	....	....	....	....
1983-84	Dukla Jihlava	Czech.	41	20	16	36	....	....	....	46	....	....	....	....	....	....	....	....	....	....	....	....	....	....	....	....	....	....
	Czechoslovakia	WJC-A	7	6	4	10	....	....	....	22	....	....	....	....	....	....	....	....	....	....	....	....	....	....	....	....	....	....
1984-85	Czechoslovakia	Can-Cup	5	2	1	3	....	....	....	4	....	....	....	....	....	....	....	....	....	....	....	....	....	....	....	....	....	....
	Dukla Jihlava	Czech.	35	23	22	45	....	....	....	76	....	....	....	....	....	....	....	....	....	....	....	....	....	....	....	....	....	....
1985-86	**Detroit Red Wings**	**NHL**	**74**	**32**	**24**	**56**	**26**	**16**	**42**	**16**	**8**	**0**	**4**	**174**	**18.4**	**82**	**26**	**106**	**11**	**–39**	....	....	....	....	....	....	....	....
1986-87	**Detroit Red Wings**	**NHL**	**77**	**30**	**23**	**53**	**26**	**17**	**43**	**42**	**6**	**0**	**5**	**209**	**14.4**	**78**	**24**	**70**	**7**	**–9**	**13**	**1**	**2**	**3**	**4**	**0**	**0**	**0**
1987-88	**Detroit Red Wings**	**NHL**	**78**	**37**	**25**	**62**	**32**	**18**	**50**	**46**	**6**	**5**	**5**	**174**	**21.3**	**87**	**20**	**76**	**13**	**4**	**12**	**10**	**8**	**18**	**10**	**2**	**1**	**4**
1988-89	**Detroit Red Wings**	**NHL**	**51**	**25**	**16**	**41**	**21**	**11**	**32**	**44**	**1**	**0**	**3**	**145**	**17.2**	**52**	**5**	**49**	**7**	**5**	**6**	**2**	**4**	**6**	**19**	**1**	**0**	**0**
	Adirondack Red Wings	AHL	5	5	1	6	....	....	....	4	....	....	....	....	....	....	....	....	....	....	....	....	....	....	....	....	....	....
1989-90	**Detroit Red Wings**	**NHL**	**13**	**5**	**5**	**10**	**4**	**4**	**8**	**6**	**2**	**0**	**0**	**37**	**13.5**	**11**	**5**	**14**	**0**	**–8**	....	....	....	....	....	....	....	....
♦	**Edmonton Oilers**	**NHL**	**63**	**25**	**28**	**53**	**21**	**20**	**41**	**66**	**7**	**0**	**3**	**149**	**16.8**	**86**	**35**	**53**	**1**	**–1**	**21**	**5**	**0**	**5**	**8**	**1**	**0**	**1**
1990-91	**Edmonton Oilers**	**NHL**	**70**	**40**	**28**	**68**	**37**	**21**	**58**	**113**	**7**	**1**	**5**	**204**	**19.6**	**97**	**30**	**44**	**1**	**24**	**18**	**7**	**6**	**13**	**16**	**1**	**0**	**3**
1991-92	**Edmonton Oilers**	**NHL**	**57**	**21**	**13**	**34**	**19**	**10**	**29**	**52**	**5**	**0**	**0**	**107**	**19.6**	**46**	**18**	**48**	**2**	**–18**	**15**	**1**	**4**	**5**	**8**	**0**	**0**	**0**
1992-93	**Edmonton Oilers**	**NHL**	**68**	**32**	**16**	**48**	**27**	**11**	**38**	**100**	**13**	**0**	**2**	**175**	**18.3**	**75**	**33**	**58**	**1**	**–15**	....	....	....	....	....	....	....	....
1993-94	**Tampa Bay Lightning**	**NHL**	**75**	**28**	**27**	**55**	**26**	**21**	**47**	**76**	**10**	**0**	**2**	**167**	**16.8**	**79**	**32**	**62**	**0**	**–15**	....	....	....	....	....	....	....	....
1994-95	EHC Wolfsburg	Germany-2	12	27	11	38	....	....	....	28	....	....	....	....	....	....	....	....	....	....	....	....	....	....	....	....	....	....
	ZPS Zlin	Czech-Rep	1	1	0	1	....	....	....	0	....	....	....	....	....	....	....	....	....	....	....	....	....	....	....	....	....	....
	Tampa Bay Lightning	**NHL**	**47**	**13**	**13**	**26**	**23**	**19**	**42**	**26**	**4**	**0**	**3**	**75**	**17.3**	**36**	**12**	**37**	**0**	**–13**	....	....	....	....	....	....	....	....
1995-96	**Tampa Bay Lightning**	**NHL**	**67**	**22**	**30**	**52**	**22**	**25**	**47**	**68**	**8**	**0**	**3**	**164**	**13.4**	**85**	**53**	**57**	**0**	**–25**	**4**	**2**	**0**	**2**	**14**	**2**	**0**	**0**
1996-97	**Los Angeles Kings**	**NHL**	**8**	**0**	**4**	**4**	**0**	**4**	**4**	**2**	**0**	**0**	**0**	**12**	**0.0**	**6**	**4**	**9**	**0**	**–7**	....	....	....	....	....	....	....	....
	Pittsburgh Penguins	**NHL**	**9**	**1**	**3**	**4**	**1**	**3**	**4**	**4**	**0**	**0**	**0**	**21**	**4.8**	**7**	**6**	**5**	**0**	**–4**	....	....	....	....	....	....	....	....
	Cleveland Lumberjacks	IHL	19	7	14	21	....	....	....	6	....	....	....	....	....	....	....	....	....	....	....	....	....	....	....	....	....	....
	Edmonton Oilers	**NHL**	**16**	**1**	**5**	**6**	**1**	**4**	**5**	**6**	**0**	**0**	**0**	**22**	**4.5**	**11**	**6**	**6**	**0**	**–1**	**6**	**0**	**0**	**0**	**4**	**0**	**0**	**0**
1997-98	Krefelder Pinguine	Germany	38	7	12	19	....	....	....	18	....	....	....	....	....	....	....	....	....	....	....	....	....	....	....	....	....	....
1998-99	**Detroit Red Wings**	**NHL**	**13**	**1**	**0**	**1**	**1**	**0**	**1**	**4**	**0**	**0**	**1**	**12**	**8.3**	**1**	**0**	**4**	**0**	**–3**	....	....	....	....	....	....	....	....
	Adirondack Red Wings	AHL	15	2	6	8	....	....	....	8	....	....	....	....	....	....	....	....	....	....	....	....	....	....	....	....	....	....
	NHL Totals		**786**	**313**	**260**	**573**	**287**	**204**	**491**	**671**	**77**	**6**	**36**	**1847**	**16.9**	**839**	**309**	**698**	**43**		**95**	**28**	**24**	**52**	**83**	**7**	**1**	**8**

Traded to **Edmonton** by **Detroit** with Joe Murphy, Adam Graves and Jeff Sharples for Jimmy Carson, Kevin McClelland and Edmonton's 5th round choice (later traded to Montreal — Montreal selected Brad Layzell) in 1991 Entry Draft, November 2, 1989. Traded to **Tampa Bay** by **Edmonton** for Tampa Bay's 3rd round choice (Brad Symes) in 1994 Entry Draft, June 16, 1993. Traded to **LA Kings** by **Tampa Bay** for LA Kings' 5th round choice (Jan Sulc) in 1997 Entry Draft, August 22, 1996. Traded to **Pittsburgh** by **LA Kings** for conditional draft pick, October 25, 1996. Klima failed to meet conditions specified in the trade agreement and conditional pick was forfeited. Signed as a free agent by **Edmonton**, February 26, 1997. Signed as a free agent by **Detroit**, January 11, 1999.

• KLIMOVICH, Sergei

C – R. 6'3", 189 lbs. b: Novosibirsk, USSR, 3/8/1974. Chicago's 3rd, 41st overall, in 1992.

Season	Club	League	GP	G	A	Pts	AG	AA	APts	PIM	PP	SH	GW	S	%	TGF	PGF	TGA	PGA	+/–	GP	G	A	Pts	PIM	PP	SH	GW
1991-92	Dynamo Moscow	CIS-Jr.	STATISTICS NOT AVAILABLE																									
	Dynamo Moscow	CIS	3	0	0	0	....	....	....	0	....	....	....	....	....	....	....	....	....	....	....	....	....	....	....	....	....	....
	Russia	EJC-A	6	3	3	6	....	....	....	2	....	....	....	....	....	....	....	....	....	....	....	....	....	....	....	....	....	....
1992-93	Dynamo Moscow	CIS	30	4	1	5	....	....	....	14	....	....	....	....	....	....	....	....	....	....	10	1	0	1	2	....	....	....
	Russia	WJC-A	7	2	2	4	....	....	....	10	....	....	....	....	....	....	....	....	....	....	....	....	....	....	....	....	....	....
1993-94	Dynamo Moscow	CIS	39	7	4	11	....	....	....	14	....	....	....	....	....	....	....	....	....	....	12	2	3	5	6	....	....	....
1994-95	Dynamo Moscow	CIS	4	1	0	1	....	....	....	2	....	....	....	....	....	....	....	....	....	....	....	....	....	....	....	....	....	....
	Indianapolis Ice	IHL	71	14	30	44	....	....	....	20	....	....	....	....	....	....	....	....	....	....	....	....	....	....	....	....	....	....
1995-96	Indianapolis Ice	IHL	68	17	21	38	....	....	....	28	....	....	....	....	....	....	....	....	....	....	5	1	1	2	6	....	....	....
1996-97	**Chicago Blackhawks**	**NHL**	**1**	**0**	**0**	**0**	**0**	**0**	**0**	**2**	**0**	**0**	**0**	**0**	**0.0**	**0**	**0**	**1**	**1**	**0**	....	....	....	....	....	....	....	....
	Indianapolis Ice	IHL	75	20	37	57	....	....	....	98	....	....	....	....	....	....	....	....	....	....	3	1	2	3	0	....	....	....
1997-98	Las Vegas Thunder	IHL	25	2	8	10	....	....	....	6	....	....	....	....	....	....	....	....	....	....	....	....	....	....	....	....	....	....
	Quebec Rafales	IHL	21	1	7	8	....	....	....	8	....	....	....	....	....	....	....	....	....	....	....	....	....	....	....	....	....	....
	Idaho Steelheads	WCHL	13	5	9	14	....	....	....	18	....	....	....	....	....	....	....	....	....	....	1	0	0	0	0	....	....	....
1998-99	EC Graz	Alpenliga	13	13	7	20	....	....	....	23	....	....	....	....	....	....	....	....	....	....	....	....	....	....	....	....	....	....
	Augsburger Panther	Germany	31	7	8	15	....	....	....	30	....	....	....	....	....	....	....	....	....	....	5	2	0	2	6	....	....	....
99-2000	Augsburger Panther	Germany	47	5	14	19	....	....	....	91	....	....	....	....	....	....	....	....	....	....	3	0	0	0	0	....	....	....
	NHL Totals		**1**	**0**	**0**	**0**	**0**	**0**	**0**	**2**	**0**	**0**	**0**	**0**	**0.0**	**0**	**0**	**1**	**1**		....	....	....	....	....	....	....	....

• KLUZAK, Gord

Gordon Glen D – L. 6'4", 220 lbs. b: Climax, Sask., 3/4/1964. Boston's 1st, 1st overall, in 1982.

Season	Club	League	GP	G	A	Pts	AG	AA	APts	PIM	PP	SH	GW	S	%	TGF	PGF	TGA	PGA	+/–	GP	G	A	Pts	PIM	PP	SH	GW
1980-81	Billings Bighorns	WHL	68	4	34	38	....	....	....	160	....	....	....	....	....	....	....	....	....	....	5	0	1	1	4	....	....	....
1981-82	Billings Bighorns	WHL	38	9	24	33	....	....	....	110	....	....	....	....	....	....	....	....	....	....	....	....	....	....	....	....	....	....
	Canada	WJC-A	7	0	1	1	....	....	....	4	....	....	....	....	....	....	....	....	....	....	....	....	....	....	....	....	....	....
1982-83	**Boston Bruins**	**NHL**	**70**	**1**	**6**	**7**	**1**	**4**	**5**	**105**	**0**	**0**	**0**	**49**	**2.0**	**37**	**2**	**32**	**3**	**6**	**17**	**1**	**4**	**5**	**54**	**0**	**0**	**0**
1983-84	**Boston Bruins**	**NHL**	**80**	**10**	**27**	**37**	**8**	**18**	**26**	**135**	**5**	**0**	**3**	**125**	**8.0**	**117**	**40**	**75**	**7**	**9**	**3**	**0**	**0**	**0**	**0**	**0**	**0**	**0**
1984-85	**Boston Bruins**	**NHL**	DID NOT PLAY – INJURED																									
1985-86	**Boston Bruins**	**NHL**	**70**	**8**	**31**	**39**	**6**	**21**	**27**	**155**	**3**	**0**	**0**	**114**	**7.0**	**94**	**30**	**85**	**24**	**3**	**3**	**1**	**1**	**2**	**16**	**1**	**0**	**0**
1986-87	**Boston Bruins**	**NHL**	DID NOT PLAY – INJURED																									
1987-88	**Boston Bruins**	**NHL**	**66**	**6**	**31**	**37**	**5**	**22**	**27**	**135**	**0**	**1**	**0**	**168**	**3.6**	**100**	**29**	**78**	**25**	**18**	**23**	**4**	**8**	**12**	**59**	**0**	**1**	**1**
1988-89	**Boston Bruins**	**NHL**	**3**	**0**	**1**	**1**	**0**	**1**	**1**	**2**	**0**	**0**	**0**	**4**	**0.0**	**3**	**1**	**5**	**1**	**–2**	....	....	....	....	....	....	....	....
1989-90	**Boston Bruins**	**NHL**	**8**	**0**	**2**	**2**	**0**	**1**	**1**	**11**	**0**	**0**	**0**	**8**	**0.0**	**10**	**2**	**5**	**1**	**4**	....	....	....	....	....	....	....	....
1990-91	**Boston Bruins**	**NHL**	**2**	**0**	**0**	**0**	**0**	**0**	**0**	**0**	**0**	**0**	**0**	**3**	**0.0**	**3**	**0**	**1**	**0**	**2**	....	....	....	....	....	....	....	....
	NHL Totals		**299**	**25**	**98**	**123**	**20**	**67**	**87**	**543**	**8**	**1**	**3**	**471**	**5.3**	**364**	**104**	**281**	**61**		**46**	**6**	**13**	**19**	**129**	**1**	**1**	**1**

WHL Second All-Star Team (1982) • WJC-A All-Star Team (1982) • Named Best Defenseman at WJC-A (1982) • Won Bill Masterton Trophy (1990)

• Missed entire 1984-85 season recovering from knee injury suffered in pre-season game vs. New Jersey, October 7, 1984. • Missed entire 1986-87 season recovering from knee surgery, September, 1986. • Missed majority of 1988-89 season recovering from 8th knee surgery, September 17, 1988. • Missed majority of 1989-90 season recovering from 10th knee surgery, October 27, 1989.

• KNIPSCHEER, Fred

C – L. 5'11", 185 lbs. b: Ft. Wayne, IN, 9/3/1969.

Season	Club	League	GP	G	A	Pts	AG	AA	APts	PIM	PP	SH	GW	S	%	TGF	PGF	TGA	PGA	+/–	GP	G	A	Pts	PIM	PP	SH	GW
1988-89	Omaha Lancers	USHL	47	32	33	65	....	....	....	123	....	....	....	....	....	....	....	....	....	....	....	....	....	....	....	....	....	....
1989-90	Omaha Lancers	USHL	48	38	46	84	....	....	....	66	....	....	....	....	....	....	....	....	....	....	....	....	....	....	....	....	....	....
1990-91	St. Cloud State Huskies	WCHA	40	9	10	19	....	....	....	57	....	....	....	....	....	....	....	....	....	....	....	....	....	....	....	....	....	....
1991-92	St. Cloud State Huskies	WCHA	33	15	17	32	....	....	....	48	....	....	....	....	....	....	....	....	....	....	....	....	....	....	....	....	....	....
1992-93	St. Cloud State Huskies	WCHA	36	34	26	60	....	....	....	68	....	....	....	....	....	....	....	....	....	....	....	....	....	....	....	....	....	....

			REGULAR SEASON																		PLAYOFFS							
Season	Club	League	GP	G	A	Pts	AG	AA	APts	PIM	PP	SH	GW	S	%	TGF	PGF	TGA	PGA	+/–	GP	G	A	Pts	PIM	PP	SH	GW
1993-94	**Boston Bruins**	**NHL**	**11**	**3**	**2**	**5**	**3**	**2**	**5**	**14**	**0**	**0**	**1**	**15**	**20.0**	**7**	**0**	**5**	**1**	**3**	**12**	**2**	**1**	**3**	**6**	**0**	**0**	**1**
	Providence Bruins	AHL	62	26	13	39	....	....	....	50	....	....	....	....	....	....	....	....	....	....	....	....	....	....	....	....	....	....
1994-95	**Boston Bruins**	**NHL**	**16**	**3**	**1**	**4**	**5**	**1**	**6**	**2**	**0**	**0**	**1**	**20**	**15.0**	**9**	**0**	**8**	**0**	**1**	**4**	**0**	**0**	**0**	**0**	**0**	**0**	**0**
	Providence Bruins	AHL	71	29	34	63	....	....	....	81	....	....	....	....	....	....	....	....	....	....	....	....	....	....	....	....	....	....
1995-96	**St. Louis Blues**	**NHL**	**1**	**0**	**0**	**0**	**0**	**0**	**0**	**2**	**0**	**0**	**0**	**2**	**0.0**	**0**	**0**	**0**	**0**	**0**	....	....	....	....	....	....	....	....
	Worcester IceCats	AHL	68	36	37	73	....	....	....	93	....	....	....	....	....	....	....	....	....	....	3	0	0	0	2	....	....	....
1996-97	Phoenix Roadrunners	IHL	24	5	11	16	....	....	....	19	....	....	....	....	....	....	....	....	....	....	....	....	....	....	....	....	....	....
	Indianapolis Ice	IHL	41	10	9	19	....	....	....	46	....	....	....	....	....	....	....	....	....	....	4	0	2	2	10	....	....	....
1997-98	Kentucky Thoroughblades	AHL	17	0	7	7	....	....	....	8	....	....	....	....	....	....	....	....	....	....	3	0	1	1	7	....	....	....
	Utah Grizzlies	IHL	58	21	32	53	....	....	....	69	....	....	....	....	....	....	....	....	....	....	2	0	0	0	4	....	....	....
1998-99	Utah Grizzlies	IHL	21	4	9	13	....	....	....	20	....	....	....	....	....	....	....	....	....	....	....	....	....	....	....	....	....	....
	Cincinnati Cyclones	IHL	43	14	15	29	....	....	....	44	....	....	....	....	....	....	....	....	....	....	3	2	1	3	4	....	....	....
99-2000	Cincinnati Cyclones	IHL	8	1	0	1	....	....	....	2	....	....	....	....	....	....	....	....	....	....	....	....	....	....	....	....	....	....
	Milwaukee Admirals	IHL	40	8	23	31	....	....	....	26	....	....	....	....	....	....	....	....	....	....	3	2	2	4	0	....	....	....
	NHL Totals		**28**	**6**	**3**	**9**	**8**	**3**	**11**	**18**	**0**	**0**	**2**	**37**	**16.2**	**16**	**0**	**13**	**1**		**16**	**2**	**1**	**3**	**6**	**0**	**0**	**1**

WCHA First All-Star Team (1993) • NCAA West Second All-American Team (1993)

Signed as a free agent by **Boston**, April 30, 1993. Traded to **St. Louis** by **Boston** for Rick Zombo, October 2, 1995. Signed as a free agent by **Chicago**, August 16, 1996. Traded to **Cincinnati** (IHL) by **Utah** (IHL) for Don Biggs, December 3, 1998. Signed as a free agent by **Milwaukee** (IHL), December 10, 1999.

• KNUBLE, Mike

RW – R. 6'3", 208 lbs. b: Toronto, Ont., 7/4/1972. Detroit's 4th, 76th overall, in 1991.

1988-89	East Kentwood High	Hi-School	28	52	37	89	....	....	....	60	....	....	....	....	....	....	....	....	....	....	....	....	....	....	....	....	....	....
1989-90	East Kentwood High	Hi-School	29	63	40	103	....	....	....	40	....	....	....	....	....	....	....	....	....	....	....	....	....	....	....	....	....	....
1990-91	Kalamazoo Jr. K-Wings	NAJHL	36	18	24	42	....	....	....	30	....	....	....	....	....	....	....	....	....	....	....	....	....	....	....	....	....	....
1991-92	University of Michigan	CCHA	43	7	8	15	....	....	....	48	....	....	....	....	....	....	....	....	....	....	....	....	....	....	....	....	....	....
1992-93	University of Michigan	CCHA	39	26	16	42	....	....	....	57	....	....	....	....	....	....	....	....	....	....	....	....	....	....	....	....	....	....
1993-94	University of Michigan	CCHA	41	32	26	58	....	....	....	71	....	....	....	....	....	....	....	....	....	....	....	....	....	....	....	....	....	....
1994-95	University of Michigan	CCHA	34	*38	22	60	....	....	....	62	....	....	....	....	....	....	....	....	....	....	....	....	....	....	....	....	....	....
	Adirondack Red Wings	AHL	....	....	....	....	....	....	....	....	....	....	....	....	....	....	....	....	....	....	3	0	0	0	0	....	....	....
	United States	WC-A	6	1	2	3	....	....	....	2	....	....	....	....	....	....	....	....	....	....	....	....	....	....	....	....	....	....
1995-96	Adirondack Red Wings	AHL	80	22	23	45	....	....	....	59	....	....	....	....	....	....	....	....	....	....	3	1	0	1	0	....	....	....
1996-97	**Detroit Red Wings**	**NHL**	**9**	**1**	**0**	**1**	**1**	**0**	**1**	**0**	**0**	**0**	**0**	**10**	**10.0**	**3**	**0**	**4**	**0**	**–1**	....	....	....	....	....	....	....	....
	Adirondack Red Wings	AHL	68	28	35	63	....	....	....	54	....	....	....	....	....	....	....	....	....	....	....	....	....	....	....	....	....	....
1997-98♦	**Detroit Red Wings**	**NHL**	**53**	**7**	**6**	**13**	**8**	**6**	**14**	**16**	**0**	**0**	**0**	**54**	**13.0**	**22**	**0**	**20**	**0**	**2**	**3**	**0**	**1**	**1**	**0**	**0**	**0**	**0**
1998-99	**New York Rangers**	**NHL**	**82**	**15**	**20**	**35**	**18**	**19**	**37**	**26**	**3**	**0**	**1**	**113**	**13.3**	**58**	**15**	**50**	**0**	**–7**	....	....	....	....	....	....	....	....
	United States	WC-A	6	0	0	0	....	....	....	10	....	....	....	....	....	....	....	....	....	....	....	....	....	....	....	....	....	....
99-2000	**New York Rangers**	**NHL**	**59**	**9**	**5**	**14**	**10**	**5**	**15**	**18**	**1**	**0**	**1**	**50**	**18.0**	**18**	**1**	**22**	**0**	**–5**	....	....	....	....	....	....	....	....
	Boston Bruins	**NHL**	**14**	**3**	**3**	**6**	**3**	**3**	**6**	**8**	**1**	**0**	**1**	**28**	**10.7**	**9**	**3**	**11**	**3**	**–2**	....	....	....	....	....	....	....	....
	NHL Totals		**217**	**35**	**34**	**69**	**40**	**33**	**73**	**68**	**5**	**0**	**3**	**255**	**13.7**	**110**	**19**	**107**	**3**		**3**	**0**	**1**	**1**	**0**	**0**	**0**	**0**

CCHA Second All-Star Team (1994, 1995) • NCAA West Second All-American Team (1995)

Traded to **NY Rangers** by **Detroit** for NY Rangers' 3rd round choice in 2000 Entry Draft, October 1, 1998. Traded to **Boston** by **NY Rangers** for Rob DiMaio, March 10, 2000.

• KNUTSEN, Espen

C – L. 5'11", 180 lbs. b: Oslo, Norway, 1/12/1972. Hartford's 9th, 204th overall, in 1990.

1988-89	Valerengen IF Oslo	Norway-Jr.	36	14	7	21	....	....	....	18	....	....	....	....	....	....	....	....	....	....	....	....	....	....	....	....	....	....
	Norway	WJC-A	6	0	2	2	....	....	....	6	....	....	....	....	....	....	....	....	....	....	....	....	....	....	....	....	....	....
	Norway	EJC-A	5	8	4	12	....	....	....	10	....	....	....	....	....	....	....	....	....	....	....	....	....	....	....	....	....	....
1989-90	Valerengen IF Oslo	Norway	40	25	28	53	....	....	....	44	....	....	....	....	....	....	....	....	....	....	....	....	....	....	....	....	....	....
	Norway	WJC-A	7	2	7	9	....	....	....	6	....	....	....	....	....	....	....	....	....	....	....	....	....	....	....	....	....	....
	Norway	EJC-A	6	6	11	17	....	....	....	10	....	....	....	....	....	....	....	....	....	....	....	....	....	....	....	....	....	....
1990-91	Valerengen IF Oslo	Norway	31	30	24	54	....	....	....	42	....	....	....	....	....	....	....	....	....	....	5	3	4	7	....	....	....	....
	Norway	WJC-A	7	1	2	3	....	....	....	4	....	....	....	....	....	....	....	....	....	....	....	....	....	....	....	....	....	....
1991-92	Valerengen IF Oslo	Norway	30	28	26	54	....	....	....	37	....	....	....	....	....	....	....	....	....	....	8	7	8	15	....	....	....	....
1992-93	Valerengen IF Oslo	Norway	13	11	13	24	....	....	....	4	....	....	....	....	....	....	....	....	....	....	....	....	....	....	....	....	....	....
1993-94	Valerengen IF Oslo	Norway	38	32	26	58	....	....	....	20	....	....	....	....	....	....	....	....	....	....	....	....	....	....	....	....	....	....
	Norway	Olympics	7	1	3	4	....	....	....	2	....	....	....	....	....	....	....	....	....	....	....	....	....	....	....	....	....	....
	Norway	WC-A	6	3	2	5	....	....	....	0	....	....	....	....	....	....	....	....	....	....	....	....	....	....	....	....	....	....
1994-95	Djurgardens IF Stockholm	Sweden	30	6	14	20	....	....	....	18	....	....	....	....	....	....	....	....	....	....	3	0	1	1	0	....	....	....
	Norway	WC-A	5	2	1	3	....	....	....	0	....	....	....	....	....	....	....	....	....	....	....	....	....	....	....	....	....	....
1995-96	Djurgardens IF Stockholm	Sweden	32	10	23	33	....	....	....	50	....	....	....	....	....	....	....	....	....	....	4	1	0	1	2	....	....	....
	Norway	WC-A	5	3	0	3	....	....	....	0	....	....	....	....	....	....	....	....	....	....	....	....	....	....	....	....	....	....
1996-97	Djurgardens IF Stockholm	Sweden	39	16	33	49	....	....	....	20	....	....	....	....	....	....	....	....	....	....	4	2	4	6	6	....	....	....
	Norway	WC-A	8	0	5	5	....	....	....	4	....	....	....	....	....	....	....	....	....	....	....	....	....	....	....	....	....	....
1997-98	**Mighty Ducks of Anaheim**	**NHL**	**19**	**3**	**0**	**3**	**4**	**0**	**4**	**6**	**1**	**0**	**0**	**21**	**14.3**	**6**	**4**	**12**	**0**	**–10**	....	....	....	....	....	....	....	....
	Cincinnati Mighty Ducks	AHL	41	4	13	17	....	....	....	18	....	....	....	....	....	....	....	....	....	....	....	....	....	....	....	....	....	....
1998-99	Djurgardens IF Stockholm	Sweden	39	18	24	42	....	....	....	32	....	....	....	....	....	....	....	....	....	....	4	0	1	1	2	....	....	....
	Djurgardens IF Stockholm	EuroHL	4	2	2	4	....	....	....	2	....	....	....	....	....	....	....	....	....	....	....	....	....	....	....	....	....	....
99-2000	Djurgardens IF Stockholm	Sweden	48	18	35	53	....	....	....	65	....	....	....	....	....	....	....	....	....	....	13	5	*16	*21	2	....	....	....
	NHL Totals		**19**	**3**	**0**	**3**	**4**	**0**	**4**	**6**	**1**	**0**	**0**	**21**	**14.3**	**6**	**4**	**12**	**0**		....	....	....	....	....	....	....	....

Norwegian Player of the Year (1994)

Rights traded to **Anaheim** by **Hartford** for Kevin Brown, October 1, 1996. Traded to **Columbus** by **Anaheim** for Columbus' 4th round choice in 2001 Entry Draft, May 25, 2000.

• KOCUR, Joe

Joseph George RW – R. 6', 205 lbs. b: Calgary, Alta., 12/21/1964. Detroit's 6th, 91st overall, in 1983.

1980-81	Yorkton Terriers	SJHL	48	6	9	15	....	....	....	307	....	....	....	....	....	....	....	....	....	....	....	....	....	....	....	....	....	....
1981-82	Yorkton Terriers	SJHL	47	20	21	41	....	....	....	199	....	....	....	....	....	....	....	....	....	....	....	....	....	....	....	....	....	....
1982-83	Saskatoon Blades	WHL	62	23	17	40	....	....	....	289	....	....	....	....	....	....	....	....	....	....	6	2	3	5	25	....	....	....
1983-84	Saskatoon Blades	WHL	69	40	41	81	....	....	....	258	....	....	....	....	....	....	....	....	....	....	....	....	....	....	....	....	....	....
	Adirondack Red Wings	AHL	....	....	....	....	....	....	....	....	....	....	....	....	....	....	....	....	....	....	5	0	0	0	20	....	....	....
1984-85	**Detroit Red Wings**	**NHL**	**17**	**1**	**0**	**1**	**1**	**0**	**1**	**64**	**0**	**0**	**0**	**7**	**14.3**	**3**	**1**	**6**	**0**	**–4**	**3**	**1**	**0**	**1**	**5**	**0**	**0**	**0**
	Adirondack Red Wings	AHL	47	12	7	19	....	....	....	171	....	....	....	....	....	....	....	....	....	....	....	....	....	....	....	....	....	....
1985-86	**Detroit Red Wings**	**NHL**	**59**	**9**	**6**	**15**	**7**	**4**	**11**	***377**	**2**	**0**	**0**	**65**	**13.8**	**25**	**9**	**40**	**0**	**–24**	....	....	....	....	....	....	....	....
	Adirondack Red Wings	AHL	9	6	2	8	....	....	....	34	....	....	....	....	....	....	....	....	....	....	....	....	....	....	....	....	....	....
1986-87	**Detroit Red Wings**	**NHL**	**77**	**9**	**9**	**18**	**8**	**7**	**15**	**276**	**2**	**0**	**2**	**81**	**11.1**	**36**	**8**	**39**	**1**	**–10**	**16**	**2**	**3**	**5**	**71**	**1**	**0**	**2**
1987-88	**Detroit Red Wings**	**NHL**	**63**	**7**	**7**	**14**	**6**	**5**	**11**	**263**	**0**	**0**	**1**	**41**	**17.1**	**21**	**2**	**30**	**0**	**–11**	**10**	**0**	**1**	**1**	**13**	**0**	**0**	**0**
1988-89	**Detroit Red Wings**	**NHL**	**60**	**9**	**9**	**18**	**8**	**6**	**14**	**213**	**1**	**0**	**1**	**76**	**11.8**	**30**	**3**	**31**	**0**	**–4**	**3**	**0**	**1**	**1**	**6**	**0**	**0**	**0**
1989-90	**Detroit Red Wings**	**NHL**	**71**	**16**	**20**	**36**	**14**	**14**	**28**	**268**	**1**	**0**	**5**	**128**	**12.5**	**67**	**4**	**67**	**0**	**–4**	....	....	....	....	....	....	....	....
1990-91	**Detroit Red Wings**	**NHL**	**52**	**5**	**4**	**9**	**5**	**3**	**8**	**253**	**0**	**0**	**0**	**67**	**7.5**	**23**	**3**	**27**	**1**	**–6**	....	....	....	....	....	....	....	....
	New York Rangers	**NHL**	**5**	**0**	**0**	**0**	**0**	**0**	**0**	**36**	**0**	**0**	**0**	**6**	**0.0**	**1**	**0**	**2**	**0**	**–1**	**6**	**0**	**2**	**2**	**21**	**0**	**0**	**0**
1991-92	**New York Rangers**	**NHL**	**51**	**7**	**4**	**11**	**6**	**3**	**9**	**121**	**0**	**0**	**2**	**72**	**9.7**	**21**	**0**	**25**	**0**	**–4**	**12**	**1**	**1**	**2**	**38**	**0**	**0**	**0**
1992-93	**New York Rangers**	**NHL**	**65**	**3**	**6**	**9**	**2**	**4**	**6**	**131**	**2**	**0**	**0**	**43**	**7.0**	**22**	**3**	**28**	**0**	**–9**	....	....	....	....	....	....	....	....
1993-94♦	**New York Rangers**	**NHL**	**71**	**2**	**1**	**3**	**2**	**1**	**3**	**129**	**0**	**0**	**0**	**43**	**4.7**	**12**	**1**	**20**	**0**	**–9**	**20**	**1**	**1**	**2**	**17**	**0**	**0**	**0**
1994-95	**New York Rangers**	**NHL**	**48**	**1**	**2**	**3**	**2**	**3**	**5**	**71**	**0**	**0**	**0**	**25**	**4.0**	**9**	**0**	**14**	**1**	**–4**	**10**	**0**	**0**	**0**	**8**	**0**	**0**	**0**
1995-96	**New York Rangers**	**NHL**	**38**	**1**	**2**	**3**	**1**	**2**	**3**	**49**	**0**	**0**	**0**	**19**	**5.3**	**4**	**0**	**8**	**0**	**–4**	....	....	....	....	....	....	....	....
	Vancouver Canucks	**NHL**	**7**	**0**	**1**	**1**	**0**	**1**	**1**	**19**	**0**	**0**	**0**	**1**	**0.0**	**1**	**0**	**4**	**0**	**–3**	**1**	**0**	**0**	**0**	**0**	**0**	**0**	**0**
1996-97	San Antonio Dragons	IHL	5	1	1	2	....	....	....	24	....	....	....	....	....	....	....	....	....	....	....	....	....	....	....	....	....	....
♦	**Detroit Red Wings**	**NHL**	**34**	**2**	**1**	**3**	**2**	**1**	**3**	**70**	**0**	**0**	**1**	**38**	**5.3**	**5**	**0**	**12**	**0**	**–7**	**19**	**1**	**3**	**4**	**22**	**0**	**0**	**0**

Season	Club	League	REGULAR SEASON GP	G	A	Pts	AG	AA	APts	PIM	PP	SH	GW	S	%	TGF	PGF	TGA	PGA	+/–	PLAYOFFS GP	G	A	Pts	PIM	PP	SH	GW
1997-98♦	**Detroit Red Wings**	**NHL**	**63**	**6**	**5**	**11**	**7**	**5**	**12**	**92**	**0**	**0**	**2**	**53**	**11.3**	**28**	**1**	**20**	**0**	**7**	**18**	**4**	**0**	**4**	**30**	**0**	**0**	**0**
1998-99	**Detroit Red Wings**	**NHL**	**39**	**2**	**5**	**7**	**2**	**5**	**7**	**87**	**0**	**0**	**0**	**20**	**10.0**	**9**	**0**	**9**	**0**	**0**								
99-2000	**Detroit Red Wings**	**NHL**	DID NOT PLAY – INJURED																									
	NHL Totals		**820**	**80**	**82**	**162**	**73**	**64**	**137**	**2519**	**8**	**0**	**14**	**785**	**10.2**	**317**	**35**	**382**	**3**		**118**	**10**	**12**	**22**	**231**	**1**	**0**	**2**

Traded to **NY Rangers** by **Detroit** with Per Djoos for Kevin Miller, Jim Cummins and Dennis Vial, March 5, 1991. Traded to **Vancouver** by **NY Rangers** for Kay Whitmore, March 20, 1996. Signed as a free agent by **Detroit**, December 27, 1996. • Missed remainder of 1998-99 and entire 1999-2000 seasons recovering from hernia injury and surgery, May, 1999.

• KOHN, Ladislav

RW – L. 5'11", 194 lbs. b: Uherske Hradiste, Czech., 3/4/1975. Calgary's 9th, 175th overall, in 1994.

Season	Club	League	GP	G	A	Pts	AG	AA	APts	PIM	PP	SH	GW	S	%	TGF	PGF	TGA	PGA	+/–	GP	G	A	Pts	PIM	PP	SH	GW
1993-94	Brandon Wheat Kings	WHL	2	0	0	0				0																		
	Swift Current Broncos	WHL	69	33	35	68				68											7	5	4	9	8			
1994-95	Swift Current Broncos	WHL	65	32	60	92				122											6	2	6	8	14			
	Czech-Republic	WJC-A	7	0	4	4				8																		
	Saint John Flames	AHL	1	0	0	0				0																		
1995-96	**Calgary Flames**	**NHL**	**5**	**1**	**0**	**1**	**1**	**0**	**1**	**2**	**0**	**0**	**0**	**8**	**12.5**	**1**	**0**	**2**	**0**	**–1**								
	Saint John Flames	AHL	73	28	45	73				97											16	6	5	11	12			
1996-97	Saint John Flames	AHL	76	28	29	57				81											5	0	0	0	0			
1997-98	**Calgary Flames**	**NHL**	**4**	**0**	**1**	**1**	**0**	**1**	**1**	**0**	**0**	**0**	**0**	**2**	**0.0**	**2**	**0**	**0**	**0**	**2**								
	Saint John Flames	AHL	65	25	31	56				90											21	14	6	20	20			
1998-99	**Toronto Maple Leafs**	**NHL**	**16**	**1**	**3**	**4**	**1**	**3**	**4**	**4**	**0**	**0**	**0**	**23**	**4.3**	**6**	**0**	**6**	**1**	**1**	**2**	**0**	**0**	**0**	**5**	**0**	**0**	**0**
	St. John's Maple Leafs	AHL	61	27	42	69				90																		
99-2000	**Mighty Ducks of Anaheim**	**NHL**	**77**	**5**	**16**	**21**	**6**	**15**	**21**	**27**	**1**	**0**	**1**	**123**	**4.1**	**25**	**2**	**41**	**1**	**–17**								
	NHL Totals		**102**	**7**	**20**	**27**	**8**	**19**	**27**	**33**	**1**	**0**	**1**	**156**	**4.5**	**34**	**2**	**49**	**2**		**2**	**0**	**0**	**0**	**5**	**0**	**0**	**0**

Traded to **Toronto** by **Calgary** for David Cooper, July 2, 1998. Claimed by **Atlanta** from **Toronto** in Waiver Draft, September 27, 1999. Traded to **Anaheim** by **Atlanta** for Anaheim's 8th round choice (Evan Nielsen) in 2000 Entry Draft, September 27, 1999.

• KOIVU, Saku

C – L. 5'10", 183 lbs. b: Turku, Finland, 11/23/1974. Montreal's 1st, 21st overall, in 1993.

Season	Club	League	GP	G	A	Pts	AG	AA	APts	PIM	PP	SH	GW	S	%	TGF	PGF	TGA	PGA	+/–	GP	G	A	Pts	PIM	PP	SH	GW
1990-91	TPS Turku-B	Finland-Jr.	24	20	28	48				26																		
1991-92	TPS Turku-B	Finland-Jr.	12	3	7	10				6																		
	TPS Turku	Finland-Jr.	34	25	28	53				57											8	5	*9	*14	6			
	Finland	EJC-A	6	3	5	8				18																		
1992-93	TPS Turku	Finland	46	3	7	10				28											11	3	2	5	2			
	Finland	WJC-A	7	1	8	9				6																		
	Finland	Nat-Team	4	2	2	4				2																		
	Finland	WC-A	6	0	1	1				2																		
1993-94	TPS Turku	Finland	47	23	30	53				42											11	4	8	12	16			
	Finland	WJC-A	7	3	6	9				12																		
	Finland	Nat-Team	7	2	3	5				12																		
	Finland	Olympics	8	4	3	7				12																		
	Finland	WC-A	8	5	6	11				4																		
1994-95	TPS Turku	Finland	45	27	*47	*74				73											13	*7	10	17	16			
	Finland	Nat-Team	7	1	5	6				8																		
	Finland	WC-A	8	5	5	10				18																		
1995-96	**Montreal Canadiens**	**NHL**	**82**	**20**	**25**	**45**	**20**	**20**	**40**	**40**	**8**	**3**	**2**	**136**	**14.7**	**63**	**22**	**76**	**28**	**–7**	**6**	**3**	**1**	**4**	**8**	**0**	**0**	**0**
1996-97	Finland	W-Cup	4	1	3	4				4																		
	Montreal Canadiens	**NHL**	**50**	**17**	**39**	**56**	**18**	**35**	**53**	**38**	**5**	**0**	**3**	**135**	**12.6**	**68**	**21**	**51**	**11**	**7**	**5**	**1**	**3**	**4**	**10**	**0**	**0**	**0**
	Finland	Nat-Team	7	1	5	6				8																		
	Finland	WC-A	6	2	2	4				2																		
1997-98	**Montreal Canadiens**	**NHL**	**69**	**14**	**43**	**57**	**16**	**42**	**58**	**48**	**2**	**2**	**3**	**145**	**9.7**	**78**	**30**	**51**	**11**	**8**	**6**	**2**	**3**	**5**	**2**	**1**	**0**	**0**
	Finland	Olympics	6	2	*8	*10				4																		
1998-99	**Montreal Canadiens**	**NHL**	**65**	**14**	**30**	**44**	**16**	**29**	**45**	**38**	**4**	**2**	**0**	**145**	**9.7**	**68**	**27**	**54**	**6**	**–7**								
	Finland	WC-A	10	4	12	16				4																		
99-2000	**Montreal Canadiens**	**NHL**	**24**	**3**	**18**	**21**	**3**	**17**	**20**	**14**	**1**	**0**	**0**	**53**	**5.7**	**27**	**10**	**11**	**1**	**7**								
	NHL Totals		**290**	**68**	**155**	**223**	**73**	**143**	**216**	**178**	**20**	**7**	**8**	**614**	**11.1**	**304**	**110**	**243**	**57**		**17**	**6**	**7**	**13**	**20**	**1**	**0**	**0**

WC-A All-Star Team (1994, 1995, 1999) • Finnish First All-Star Team (1995) • Finnish Player of the Year (1995) • Named Best Forward at WC-A (1995, 1999) • Played in NHL All-Star Game (1998)

• Missed majority of 1999-2000 season recovering from shoulder injury suffered in game vs. NY Rangers, October 30, 1999.

• KOLESAR, Mark

Mark Timothy LW – R. 6'1", 188 lbs. b: Brampton, Ont., 1/23/1973.

Season	Club	League	GP	G	A	Pts	AG	AA	APts	PIM	PP	SH	GW	S	%	TGF	PGF	TGA	PGA	+/–	GP	G	A	Pts	PIM	PP	SH	GW
1990-91	Neepawa Natives	MJHL	44	24	30	54				58																		
1991-92	Brandon Wheat Kings	WHL	56	6	7	13				36																		
1992-93	Brandon Wheat Kings	WHL	68	27	33	60				110											4	0	0	0	4			
1993-94	Brandon Wheat Kings	WHL	59	29	37	66				131											14	8	3	11	48			
1994-95	St. John's Maple Leafs	AHL	65	12	18	30				62											5	1	0	1	2			
1995-96	**Toronto Maple Leafs**	**NHL**	**21**	**2**	**2**	**4**	**2**	**2**	**4**	**14**	**0**	**0**	**0**	**10**	**20.0**	**4**	**0**	**9**	**5**	**0**	**3**	**1**	**0**	**1**	**2**	**0**	**1**	**0**
	St. John's Maple Leafs	AHL	52	22	13	35				47																		
1996-97	**Toronto Maple Leafs**	**NHL**	**7**	**0**	**0**	**0**	**0**	**0**	**0**	**0**	**0**	**0**	**0**	**3**	**0.0**	**0**	**0**	**3**	**0**	**–3**								
	St. John's Maple Leafs	AHL	62	22	28	50				64											10	1	3	4	6			
1997-98	St. John's Maple Leafs	AHL	2	0	0	0				2																		
	Manitoba Moose	IHL	30	1	9	10				29																		
	Hamilton Bulldogs	AHL	27	2	12	14				47											6	1	1	2	0			
1998-99	Nottingham Panthers	BH-Cup	13	5	6	11				4																		
	Nottingham Panthers	Britain	39	15	27	42				54											7	3	6	9	0			
99-2000	Schwenningen Wild Wings	Germany	67	11	14	25				78																		
	NHL Totals		**28**	**2**	**2**	**4**	**2**	**2**	**4**	**14**	**0**	**0**	**0**	**13**	**15.4**	**4**	**0**	**12**	**5**		**3**	**1**	**0**	**1**	**2**	**0**	**1**	**0**

Signed as a free agent by **Toronto**, May 24, 1994.

• KOLSTAD, Dean

D – L. 6'6", 220 lbs. b: Edmonton, Alta., 6/16/1968. Minnesota's 3rd, 33rd overall, in 1986.

Season	Club	League	GP	G	A	Pts	AG	AA	APts	PIM	PP	SH	GW	S	%	TGF	PGF	TGA	PGA	+/–	GP	G	A	Pts	PIM	PP	SH	GW
1983-84	Langley Eagles	BCJHL	STATISTICS NOT AVAILABLE																									
	New Westminster Bruins	WHL	4	1	0	1				0											2	0	0	0	0			
1984-85	Langley Eagles	BCJHL	25	3	11	14				61																		
	New Westminster Bruins	WHL	13	0	0	0				16																		
1985-86	New Westminster Bruins	WHL	16	0	5	5				19																		
	Prince Albert Raiders	WHL	54	2	15	17				80											20	5	3	8	26			
1986-87	Prince Albert Raiders	WHL	72	17	37	54				112											8	1	5	6	8			
1987-88	Prince Albert Raiders	WHL	72	14	37	51				121											10	0	9	9	20			
1988-89	**Minnesota North Stars**	**NHL**	**25**	**1**	**5**	**6**	**1**	**4**	**5**	**42**	**1**	**0**	**0**	**41**	**2.4**	**28**	**12**	**28**	**7**	**–5**								
	Kalamazoo Wings	IHL	51	10	23	33				91											6	1	0	1	23			
1989-90	Kalamazoo Wings	IHL	77	10	40	50				172											10	3	4	7	14			
1990-91	Minnesota North Stars	Fr-Tour	3	0	0	0				6																		
	Minnesota North Stars	**NHL**	**5**	**0**	**0**	**0**	**0**	**0**	**0**	**15**	**0**	**0**	**0**	**9**	**0.0**	**1**	**1**	**2**	**0**	**–2**								
	Kalamazoo Wings	IHL	33	4	8	12				50											9	1	6	7	4			
1991-92	Kansas City Blades	IHL	74	9	20	29				83											15	3	6	9	8			
1992-93	**San Jose Sharks**	**NHL**	**10**	**0**	**2**	**2**	**0**	**1**	**1**	**12**	**0**	**0**	**0**	**22**	**0.0**	**5**	**4**	**11**	**1**	**–9**								
	Kansas City Blades	IHL	63	9	21	30				79											3	0	0	0	2			
1993-94	Binghamton Rangers	AHL	68	7	26	33				92																		
1994-95	Minnesota Moose	IHL	73	6	18	24				71											1	0	0	0	2			

			REGULAR SEASON																		PLAYOFFS							
Season	Club	League	GP	G	A	Pts	AG	AA	APts	PIM	PP	SH	GW	S	%	TGF	PGF	TGA	PGA	+/–	GP	G	A	Pts	PIM	PP	SH	GW
1995-96	Portland Pirates	AHL	12	1	1	2	....	....	....	14	....	....	....	....	....	....	....	....	....	....	....	....	....	....	....	....	....	....
1996-97	Central Texas Stampede	WPHL	17	2	10	12	....	....	....	44	....	....	....	....	....	....	....	....	....	....	11	4	7	11	12	....	....	....
1997-98	Central Texas Stampede	WPHL	66	14	59	73	....	....	....	92	....	....	....	....	....	....	....	....	....	....	4	2	2	4	10	....	....	....
	NHL Totals		**40**	**1**	**7**	**8**	**1**	**5**	**6**	**69**	**1**	**0**	**0**	**72**	**1.4**	**34**	**17**	**41**	**8**		....	....	....	....	....	....	....	....

WHL East Second All-Star Team (1987, 1988) • IHL Second All-Star Team (1990)

Claimed by **San Jose** from **Minnesota** in Dispersal Draft, May 30, 1991.

• KOMADOSKI, Neil

Neil George D – L. 6', 200 lbs. b: Winnipeg, Man., 11/5/1951. Los Angeles' 2nd, 48th overall, in 1971.

Season	Club	League	GP	G	A	Pts	AG	AA	APts	PIM	PP	SH	GW	S	%	TGF	PGF	TGA	PGA	+/–	GP	G	A	Pts	PIM	PP	SH	GW
1968-69	Winnipeg Jets	WCJHL	58	2	8	10	....	....	....	83	....	....	....	....	....	....	....	....	....	....	7	0	0	0	0	....	....	....
1969-70	Winnipeg Jets	WCJHL	53	7	10	17	....	....	....	104	....	....	....	....	....	....	....	....	....	....	14	5	3	8	72	....	....	....
1970-71	Winnipeg Jets	WCJHL	52	15	24	39	....	....	....	116	....	....	....	....	....	....	....	....	....	....	12	6	5	11	15	....	....	....
1971-72	Springfield Kings	AHL	64	7	20	27	....	....	....	87	....	....	....	....	....	....	....	....	....	....	5	0	0	0	8	....	....	....
1972-73	**Los Angeles Kings**	**NHL**	**62**	**1**	**8**	**9**	**1**	**6**	**7**	**67**	**1**	**0**	**0**	**47**	**2.1**	**50**	**3**	**76**	**7**	**–22**	....	....	....	....	....	....	....	....
1973-74	**Los Angeles Kings**	**NHL**	**68**	**2**	**4**	**6**	**2**	**3**	**5**	**43**	**0**	**0**	**0**	**53**	**3.8**	**32**	**2**	**40**	**6**	**–4**	**2**	**0**	**0**	**0**	**12**	**0**	**0**	**0**
1974-75	**Los Angeles Kings**	**NHL**	**75**	**4**	**12**	**16**	**3**	**9**	**12**	**69**	**3**	**0**	**0**	**66**	**6.1**	**54**	**13**	**38**	**7**	**10**	**3**	**0**	**0**	**0**	**2**	**0**	**0**	**0**
1975-76	**Los Angeles Kings**	**NHL**	**80**	**3**	**15**	**18**	**3**	**11**	**14**	**165**	**1**	**0**	**0**	**94**	**3.2**	**92**	**5**	**103**	**23**	**7**	**9**	**0**	**0**	**0**	**18**	**0**	**0**	**0**
1976-77	**Los Angeles Kings**	**NHL**	**68**	**3**	**9**	**12**	**3**	**7**	**10**	**109**	**0**	**0**	**1**	**76**	**3.9**	**57**	**4**	**47**	**11**	**17**	**9**	**0**	**2**	**2**	**15**	**0**	**0**	**0**
1977-78	**Los Angeles Kings**	**NHL**	**25**	**0**	**6**	**6**	**0**	**5**	**5**	**24**	**0**	**0**	**0**	**14**	**0.0**	**23**	**0**	**19**	**5**	**9**	....	....	....	....	....	....	....	....
	Springfield Indians	AHL	5	0	1	1	....	....	....	6	....	....	....	....	....	....	....	....	....	....	....	....	....	....	....	....	....	....
	St. Louis Blues	**NHL**	**33**	**2**	**8**	**10**	**2**	**6**	**8**	**73**	**0**	**0**	**0**	**26**	**7.7**	**23**	**4**	**50**	**2**	**–29**	....	....	....	....	....	....	....	....
1978-79	**St. Louis Blues**	**NHL**	**42**	**1**	**2**	**3**	**1**	**1**	**2**	**30**	**0**	**0**	**0**	**28**	**3.6**	**41**	**0**	**46**	**5**	**0**	....	....	....	....	....	....	....	....
	Salt Lake Golden Eagles	CHL	23	0	2	2	....	....	....	36	....	....	....	....	....	....	....	....	....	....	....	....	....	....	....	....	....	....
1979-80	**St. Louis Blues**	**NHL**	**49**	**0**	**12**	**12**	**0**	**9**	**9**	**52**	**0**	**0**	**0**	**22**	**0.0**	**30**	**0**	**62**	**10**	**–22**	....	....	....	....	....	....	....	....
1980-81	Salt Lake Golden Eagles	CHL	12	0	3	3	....	....	....	12	....	....	....	....	....	....	....	....	....	....	....	....	....	....	....	....	....	....
	Oklahoma City Stars	CHL	28	0	10	10	....	....	....	20	....	....	....	....	....	....	....	....	....	....	....	....	....	....	....	....	....	....
	NHL Totals		**502**	**16**	**76**	**92**	**15**	**57**	**72**	**632**	**5**	**0**	**1**	**426**	**3.8**	**402**	**31**	**481**	**76**		**23**	**0**	**2**	**2**	**47**	**0**	**0**	**0**

Traded to **St. Louis** by **LA Kings** for St. Louis' 2nd round choice (Greg Terrion) in 1980 Entry Draft, January 14, 1978. Claimed by **St. Louis** as a fill-in during Expansion Draft, June 13, 1979.

• KOMARNISKI, Zenith

D – L. 6', 200 lbs. b: Edmonton, Alta., 8/13/1978. Vancouver's 2nd, 75th overall, in 1996.

Season	Club	League	GP	G	A	Pts	AG	AA	APts	PIM	PP	SH	GW	S	%	TGF	PGF	TGA	PGA	+/–	GP	G	A	Pts	PIM	PP	SH	GW
1993-94	Fort Saskatchewan Rangers	AAHA	32	14	32	46	....	....	....	42	....	....	....	....	....	....	....	....	....	....	....	....	....	....	....	....	....	....
1994-95	Tri-City Americans	WHL	66	5	19	24	....	....	....	110	....	....	....	....	....	....	....	....	....	....	17	1	2	3	47	....	....	....
1995-96	Tri-City Americans	WHL	42	5	21	26	....	....	....	85	....	....	....	....	....	....	....	....	....	....	....	....	....	....	....	....	....	....
1996-97	Tri-City Americans	WHL	58	12	44	56	....	....	....	112	....	....	....	....	....	....	....	....	....	....	....	....	....	....	....	....	....	....
1997-98	Tri-City Americans	WHL	3	0	4	4	....	....	....	18	....	....	....	....	....	....	....	....	....	....	....	....	....	....	....	....	....	....
	Spokane	WHL	43	7	20	27	....	....	....	90	....	....	....	....	....	....	....	....	....	....	18	4	6	10	49	....	....	....
	Canada	WJC-A	7	0	0	0	....	....	....	26	....	....	....	....	....	....	....	....	....	....	....	....	....	....	....	....	....	....
1998-99	Syracuse Crunch	AHL	58	9	19	28	....	....	....	89	....	....	....	....	....	....	....	....	....	....	....	....	....	....	....	....	....	....
99-2000	**Vancouver Canucks**	**NHL**	**18**	**1**	**1**	**2**	**1**	**1**	**2**	**8**	**0**	**0**	**0**	**21**	**4.8**	**9**	**0**	**17**	**7**	**–1**	....	....	....	....	....	....	....	....
	Syracuse Crunch	AHL	42	4	12	16	....	....	....	130	....	....	....	....	....	....	....	....	....	....	4	2	0	2	6	....	....	....
	NHL Totals		**18**	**1**	**1**	**2**	**1**	**1**	**2**	**8**	**0**	**0**	**0**	**21**	**4.8**	**9**	**0**	**17**	**7**		....	....	....	....	....	....	....	....

WHL West First All-Star Team (1997)

• KONIK, George

George Samuel D/LW – L. 5'11", 190 lbs. b: Flin Flon, Man., 5/4/1937.

Season	Club	League	GP	G	A	Pts	AG	AA	APts	PIM	PP	SH	GW	S	%	TGF	PGF	TGA	PGA	+/–	GP	G	A	Pts	PIM	PP	SH	GW
1952-53	Flin Flon Bombers	SJHL	5	0	0	0	....	....	....	4	....	....	....	....	....	....	....	....	....	....	....	....	....	....	....	....	....	....
1953-54	Flin Flon Bombers	SJHL	4	0	2	2	....	....	....	4	....	....	....	....	....	....	....	....	....	....	2	0	0	0	0	....	....	....
	Flin Flon Bombers	Mem-Cup	2	0	0	0	....	....	....	2	....	....	....	....	....	....	....	....	....	....	....	....	....	....	....	....	....	....
1954-55	Flin Flon Bombers	SJHL	12	9	5	14	....	....	....	18	....	....	....	....	....	....	....	....	....	....	....	....	....	....	....	....	....	....
1955-56	Flin Flon Bombers	SJHL	37	13	21	34	....	....	....	83	....	....	....	....	....	....	....	....	....	....	12	4	6	10	12	....	....	....
	Flin Flon Bombers	Mem-Cup	7	3	2	5	....	....	....	2	....	....	....	....	....	....	....	....	....	....	....	....	....	....	....	....	....	....
1956-57	Flin Flon Bombers	SJHL	53	35	41	76	....	....	....	73	....	....	....	....	....	....	....	....	....	....	10	5	7	12	7	....	....	....
	Flin Flon Bombers	Mem-Cup	16	6	3	9	....	....	....	44	....	....	....	....	....	....	....	....	....	....	....	....	....	....	....	....	....	....
1957-58	University of Denver	WCHA	DID NOT PLAY – FRESHMAN																									
	Flin Flon Bombers	Mem-Cup	16	6	4	10	....	....	....	42	....	....	....	....	....	....	....	....	....	....	....	....	....	....	....	....	....	....
1958-59	University of Denver	WCHA	28	21	23	44	....	....	....	75	....	....	....	....	....	....	....	....	....	....	....	....	....	....	....	....	....	....
1959-60	University of Denver	WCHA	34	13	28	41	....	....	....	50	....	....	....	....	....	....	....	....	....	....	....	....	....	....	....	....	....	....
1960-61	University of Denver	WCHA	27	12	19	31	....	....	....	40	....	....	....	....	....	....	....	....	....	....	....	....	....	....	....	....	....	....
1961-62	Los Angeles Blades	WHL	43	3	8	11	....	....	....	38	....	....	....	....	....	....	....	....	....	....	....	....	....	....	....	....	....	....
1962-63	Seattle Totems	WHL	42	7	12	19	....	....	....	50	....	....	....	....	....	....	....	....	....	....	17	4	1	5	38	....	....	....
1963-64	Baltimore Clippers	AHL	72	19	22	41	....	....	....	80	....	....	....	....	....	....	....	....	....	....	....	....	....	....	....	....	....	....
1964-65	St. Paul Saints	USHL	STATISTICS NOT AVAILABLE																									
1965-66	Minnesota Rangers	CPHL	38	10	20	30	....	....	....	35	....	....	....	....	....	....	....	....	....	....	7	2	5	7	6	....	....	....
1966-67	Omaha Knights	CPHL	66	27	47	74	....	....	....	109	....	....	....	....	....	....	....	....	....	....	12	4	8	12	24	....	....	....
1967-68	**Pittsburgh Penguins**	**NHL**	**52**	**7**	**8**	**15**	**8**	**8**	**16**	**26**	**1**	**0**	**1**	**50**	**14.0**	**19**	**4**	**27**	**3**	**–9**	....	....	....	....	....	....	....	....
	Baltimore Clippers	AHL	5	0	2	2	....	....	....	7	....	....	....	....	....	....	....	....	....	....	....	....	....	....	....	....	....	....
1968-69	Rochester Mustangs	USHL	STATISTICS NOT AVAILABLE																									
1969-70	United States	Nat-Team	6	3	*5	*8	....	....	....	4	....	....	....	....	....	....	....	....	....	....	....	....	....	....	....	....	....	....
	United States	WEC-B	7	4	7	11	....	....	....	4	....	....	....	....	....	....	....	....	....	....	....	....	....	....	....	....	....	....
1970-71	United States	Nat-Team	....	....	....	....	....	....	....	....	....	....	....	....	....	....	....	....	....	....	....	....	....	....	....	....	....	....
	United States	WEC-A	9	1	1	2	....	....	....	8	....	....	....	....	....	....	....	....	....	....	....	....	....	....	....	....	....	....
1971-72			OUT OF HOCKEY – RETIRED																									
1972-73	Minnesota Fighting Saints	WHA	54	4	12	16	....	....	....	34	....	....	....	....	....	....	....	....	....	....	....	....	....	....	....	....	....	....
	NHL Totals		**52**	**7**	**8**	**15**	**8**	**8**	**16**	**26**	**1**	**0**	**1**	**50**	**14.0**	**19**	**4**	**27**	**3**		....	....	....	....	....	....	....	....
	Other Major League Totals		54	4	12	16	....	....	....	34	....	....	....	....	....	....	....	....	....	....	....	....	....	....	....	....	....	....

WCHA Second All-Star Team (1960) • NCAA West First All-American Team (1960) • NCAA Championship All-Tournament Team (1960) • WCHA First All-Star Team (1961) • CHL First All-Star Team (1967) • WEC-B All-Star Team (1970) • Named Best Defenseman at WEC-B (1970)

Traded to **Pittsburgh** by **NY Rangers** with Paul Andrea, Dunc McCallum and Frank Francis for Larry Jeffrey, June 6, 1967. Traded to **Oakland** by **Pittsburgh** for cash, July 4, 1968. Selected by **Minnesota** (WHA) in 1972 WHA General Player Draft, February 12, 1972.

• KONOWALCHUK, Steve

C – L. 6'2", 207 lbs. b: Salt Lake City, UT, 11/11/1972. Washington's 5th, 58th overall, in 1991.

Season	Club	League	GP	G	A	Pts	AG	AA	APts	PIM	PP	SH	GW	S	%	TGF	PGF	TGA	PGA	+/–	GP	G	A	Pts	PIM	PP	SH	GW
1989-90	Prince Albert Midget Raiders	SAHA	36	30	28	58	....	....	....	22	....	....	....	....	....	....	....	....	....	....	....	....	....	....	....	....	....	....
1990-91	Portland Winter Hawks	WHL	72	43	49	92	....	....	....	78	....	....	....	....	....	....	....	....	....	....	....	....	....	....	....	....	....	....
1991-92	Portland Winter Hawks	WHL	64	51	53	104	....	....	....	95	....	....	....	....	....	....	....	....	....	....	6	3	6	9	12	....	....	....
	United States	WJC-A	7	4	0	4	....	....	....	8	....	....	....	....	....	....	....	....	....	....	....	....	....	....	....	....	....	....
	Washington Capitals	**NHL**	**1**	**0**	**0**	**0**	**0**	**0**	**0**	**0**	**0**	**0**	**0**	**1**	**0.0**	**0**	**0**	**0**	**0**	**0**	....	....	....	....	....	....	....	....
	Baltimore Skipjacks	AHL	3	1	1	2	....	....	....	0	....	....	....	....	....	....	....	....	....	....	....	....	....	....	....	....	....	....
1992-93	**Washington Capitals**	**NHL**	**36**	**4**	**7**	**11**	**3**	**5**	**8**	**16**	**1**	**0**	**1**	**34**	**11.8**	**14**	**2**	**8**	**0**	**4**	**2**	**0**	**1**	**1**	**0**	**0**	**0**	**0**
	Baltimore Skipjacks	AHL	37	18	28	46	....	....	....	74	....	....	....	....	....	....	....	....	....	....	....	....	....	....	....	....	....	....
1993-94	**Washington Capitals**	**NHL**	**62**	**12**	**14**	**26**	**11**	**11**	**22**	**33**	**0**	**0**	**0**	**63**	**19.0**	**37**	**6**	**29**	**7**	**9**	**11**	**0**	**1**	**1**	**10**	**0**	**0**	**0**
	Portland Pirates	AHL	8	11	4	15	....	....	....	4	....	....	....	....	....	....	....	....	....	....	....	....	....	....	....	....	....	....
1994-95	**Washington Capitals**	**NHL**	**46**	**11**	**14**	**25**	**19**	**21**	**40**	**44**	**3**	**3**	**3**	**88**	**12.5**	**31**	**3**	**31**	**10**	**7**	**7**	**2**	**5**	**7**	**12**	**0**	**1**	**0**
1995-96	**Washington Capitals**	**NHL**	**70**	**23**	**22**	**45**	**23**	**18**	**41**	**92**	**7**	**1**	**3**	**197**	**11.7**	**69**	**25**	**55**	**24**	**13**	**2**	**0**	**2**	**2**	**0**	**0**	**0**	**0**
1996-97	United States	W-Cup	1	0	0	0	....	....	....	0	....	....	....	....	....	....	....	....	....	....	....	....	....	....	....	....	....	....
	Washington Capitals	**NHL**	**78**	**17**	**25**	**42**	**18**	**22**	**40**	**67**	**2**	**1**	**3**	**155**	**11.0**	**52**	**10**	**61**	**16**	**–3**	....	....	....	....	....	....	....	....
1997-98	**Washington Capitals**	**NHL**	**80**	**10**	**24**	**34**	**12**	**24**	**36**	**80**	**2**	**0**	**2**	**131**	**7.6**	**57**	**7**	**53**	**12**	**9**	....	....	....	....	....	....	....	....

Season	Club	League	REGULAR SEASON GP	G	A	Pts	AG	AA	APts	PIM	PP	SH	GW	S	%	TGF	PGF	TGA	PGA	+/–	PLAYOFFS GP	G	A	Pts	PIM	PP	SH	GW
1998-99	**Washington Capitals**	**NHL**	**45**	**12**	**12**	**24**	**14**	**12**	**26**	**26**	**4**	**1**	**2**	**98**	**12.2**	**35**	**14**	**32**	**11**	**0**	....	....	....	....	....	....	....	....
99-2000	**Washington Capitals**	**NHL**	**82**	**16**	**27**	**43**	**18**	**25**	**43**	**80**	**3**	**0**	**1**	**146**	**11.0**	**66**	**8**	**51**	**12**	**19**	**5**	**1**	**0**	**1**	**2**	**0**	**1**	**0**
	United States	WC-A	7	2	1	3	....	....	....	2	....	....	....	....	....	....	....	....	....	....	....	....	....	....	....	....	....	....
	NHL Totals		**500**	**105**	**145**	**250**	**118**	**138**	**256**	**438**	**22**	**6**	**15**	**913**	**11.5**	**361**	**75**	**320**	**92**		**27**	**3**	**9**	**12**	**24**	**0**	**2**	**0**

WHL First All-Star Team (1992)

• KONROYD, Steve

Stephen Mark D – L. 6'1", 195 lbs. b: Scarborough, Ont., 2/10/1961. Calgary's 4th, 39th overall, in 1980.

Season	Club	League	GP	G	A	Pts	AG	AA	APts	PIM	PP	SH	GW	S	%	TGF	PGF	TGA	PGA	+/–	GP	G	A	Pts	PIM	PP	SH	GW
1977-78	Markham Waxers	OHA-B	28	4	15	19	....	....	....	28	....	....	....	....	....	....	....	....	....	....	....	....	....	....	....	....	....	....
1978-79	Oshawa Generals	OMJHL	65	4	19	23	....	....	....	63	....	....	....	....	....	....	....	....	....	....	5	1	2	3	14	....	....	....
1979-80	Oshawa Generals	OMJHL	62	11	23	34	....	....	....	133	....	....	....	....	....	....	....	....	....	....	7	0	2	2	14	....	....	....
1980-81	**Calgary Flames**	**NHL**	**4**	**0**	**0**	**0**	**0**	**0**	**0**	**4**	**0**	**0**	**0**	**0**	**0.0**	**1**	**0**	**1**	**0**	**0**	....	....	....	....	....	....	....	....
	Oshawa Generals	OHA	59	19	49	68	....	....	....	232	....	....	....	....	....	....	....	....	....	....	11	3	11	14	35	....	....	....
1981-82	**Calgary Flames**	**NHL**	**63**	**3**	**14**	**17**	**2**	**9**	**11**	**78**	**0**	**0**	**1**	**57**	**5.3**	**71**	**7**	**73**	**3**	**–6**	**3**	**0**	**0**	**0**	**12**	**0**	**0**	**0**
	Oklahoma City Stars	CHL	14	2	3	5	....	....	....	15	....	....	....	....	....	....	....	....	....	....	....	....	....	....	....	....	....	....
1982-83	**Calgary Flames**	**NHL**	**79**	**4**	**13**	**17**	**3**	**9**	**12**	**73**	**0**	**0**	**0**	**80**	**5.0**	**87**	**1**	**111**	**28**	**3**	**9**	**2**	**1**	**3**	**18**	**0**	**0**	**0**
1983-84	**Calgary Flames**	**NHL**	**80**	**1**	**13**	**14**	**1**	**9**	**10**	**94**	**0**	**1**	**0**	**94**	**1.1**	**81**	**0**	**131**	**42**	**–8**	**8**	**1**	**2**	**3**	**8**	**0**	**0**	**0**
1984-85	**Calgary Flames**	**NHL**	**64**	**3**	**23**	**26**	**2**	**16**	**18**	**73**	**0**	**0**	**0**	**121**	**2.5**	**86**	**15**	**101**	**42**	**12**	**4**	**1**	**4**	**5**	**2**	**0**	**1**	**0**
	Canada	WEC-A	10	0	3	3	....	....	....	0	....	....	....	....	....	....	....	....	....	....	....	....	....	....	....	....	....	....
1985-86	**Calgary Flames**	**NHL**	**59**	**7**	**20**	**27**	**6**	**13**	**19**	**64**	**1**	**0**	**1**	**111**	**6.3**	**93**	**17**	**91**	**35**	**20**	....	....	....	....	....	....	....	....
	New York Islanders	**NHL**	**14**	**0**	**5**	**5**	**0**	**3**	**3**	**16**	**0**	**0**	**0**	**13**	**0.0**	**15**	**0**	**13**	**2**	**4**	**3**	**0**	**0**	**0**	**6**	**0**	**0**	**0**
1986-87	**New York Islanders**	**NHL**	**72**	**5**	**16**	**21**	**4**	**12**	**16**	**70**	**3**	**0**	**0**	**119**	**4.2**	**79**	**13**	**106**	**36**	**–4**	**14**	**1**	**4**	**5**	**10**	**0**	**0**	**0**
1987-88	**New York Islanders**	**NHL**	**62**	**2**	**15**	**17**	**2**	**11**	**13**	**99**	**1**	**0**	**0**	**105**	**1.9**	**81**	**13**	**94**	**42**	**16**	**6**	**1**	**0**	**1**	**4**	**0**	**1**	**0**
1988-89	**New York Islanders**	**NHL**	**21**	**1**	**5**	**6**	**1**	**4**	**5**	**2**	**0**	**0**	**0**	**30**	**3.3**	**18**	**3**	**42**	**22**	**–5**	....	....	....	....	....	....	....	....
	Chicago Blackhawks	**NHL**	**57**	**5**	**7**	**12**	**4**	**5**	**9**	**40**	**0**	**0**	**1**	**102**	**4.9**	**54**	**1**	**101**	**37**	**–11**	**16**	**2**	**0**	**2**	**10**	**0**	**1**	**0**
1989-90	**Chicago Blackhawks**	**NHL**	**75**	**3**	**14**	**17**	**3**	**10**	**13**	**34**	**1**	**0**	**0**	**93**	**3.2**	**78**	**1**	**96**	**25**	**6**	**20**	**1**	**3**	**4**	**19**	**0**	**0**	**0**
1990-91	**Chicago Blackhawks**	**NHL**	**70**	**0**	**12**	**12**	**0**	**9**	**9**	**40**	**0**	**0**	**0**	**93**	**0.0**	**54**	**3**	**59**	**19**	**11**	**6**	**1**	**0**	**1**	**8**	**0**	**0**	**0**
	Canada	WEC-A	10	1	3	4	....	....	....	0	....	....	....	....	....	....	....	....	....	....	....	....	....	....	....	....	....	....
1991-92	**Chicago Blackhawks**	**NHL**	**49**	**2**	**14**	**16**	**2**	**11**	**13**	**65**	**0**	**0**	**0**	**70**	**2.9**	**45**	**8**	**52**	**19**	**4**	....	....	....	....	....	....	....	....
	Hartford Whalers	**NHL**	**33**	**2**	**10**	**12**	**2**	**8**	**10**	**32**	**1**	**0**	**0**	**56**	**3.6**	**32**	**8**	**52**	**23**	**–5**	**7**	**0**	**1**	**1**	**2**	**0**	**0**	**0**
1992-93	**Hartford Whalers**	**NHL**	**59**	**3**	**11**	**14**	**2**	**8**	**10**	**63**	**0**	**0**	**0**	**62**	**4.8**	**49**	**3**	**90**	**28**	**–16**	....	....	....	....	....	....	....	....
	Detroit Red Wings	**NHL**	**6**	**0**	**1**	**1**	**0**	**1**	**1**	**4**	**0**	**0**	**0**	**4**	**0.0**	**3**	**0**	**5**	**3**	**1**	**1**	**0**	**0**	**0**	**0**	**0**	**0**	**0**
1993-94	**Detroit Red Wings**	**NHL**	**19**	**0**	**0**	**0**	**0**	**0**	**0**	**10**	**0**	**0**	**0**	**12**	**0.0**	**11**	**1**	**10**	**1**	**1**	....	....	....	....	....	....	....	....
	Ottawa Senators	**NHL**	**8**	**0**	**2**	**2**	**0**	**2**	**2**	**2**	**0**	**0**	**0**	**9**	**0.0**	**7**	**0**	**12**	**1**	**–4**	....	....	....	....	....	....	....	....
1994-95	Chicago Wolves	IHL	16	2	2	4	....	....	....	4	....	....	....	....	....	....	....	....	....	....	3	0	1	1	2	....	....	....
	Calgary Flames	**NHL**	**1**	**0**	**0**	**0**	**0**	**0**	**0**	**0**	**0**	**0**	**0**	**0**	**0.0**	**1**	**0**	**1**	**0**	**0**	....	....	....	....	....	....	....	....
	NHL Totals		**895**	**41**	**195**	**236**	**34**	**140**	**174**	**863**	**7**	**1**	**3**	**1231**	**3.3**	**946**	**94**	**1241**	**408**		**97**	**10**	**15**	**25**	**99**	**0**	**3**	**0**

• Original family name was Koniarski • OMJHL Second All-Star Team (1981)

Traded to **NY Islanders** by **Calgary** with Richard Kromm for John Tonelli, March 11, 1986. Traded to **Chicago** by **NY Islanders** with Bob Bassen for Marc Bergevin and Gary Nylund, November 25, 1988. Traded to **Hartford** by **Chicago** for Rob Brown, January 24, 1992. Traded to **Detroit** by **Hartford** for Detroit's 6th round choice (traded back to Detroit — Detroit selected Tim Spitzig) in 1993 Entry Draft, March 22, 1993. Traded to **Ottawa** by **Detroit** for Daniel Berthiaume, March 21, 1994. Signed as a free agent by **Calgary**, April 7, 1995.

• KONSTANTINOV, Vladimir

Vladimir N. D – R. 5'11", 190 lbs. b: Murmansk, USSR, 3/19/1967. Detroit's 12th, 221st overall, in 1989.

Season	Club	League	GP	G	A	Pts	AG	AA	APts	PIM	PP	SH	GW	S	%	TGF	PGF	TGA	PGA	+/–	GP	G	A	Pts	PIM	PP	SH	GW
1984-85	CSKA Moscow	USSR	40	1	4	5	....	....	....	10	....	....	....	....	....	....	....	....	....	....	....	....	....	....	....	....	....	....
	Soviet Union	EJC-A	5	1	0	1	....	....	....	8	....	....	....	....	....	....	....	....	....	....	....	....	....	....	....	....	....	....
1985-86	CSKA Moscow	USSR	26	4	3	7	....	....	....	12	....	....	....	....	....	....	....	....	....	....	....	....	....	....	....	....	....	....
	Soviet Union	WJC-A	7	2	4	6	....	....	....	4	....	....	....	....	....	....	....	....	....	....	....	....	....	....	....	....	....	....
	Soviet Union	WEC-A	10	1	1	2	....	....	....	8	....	....	....	....	....	....	....	....	....	....	....	....	....	....	....	....	....	....
1986-87	CSKA Moscow	USSR	35	2	2	4	....	....	....	19	....	....	....	....	....	....	....	....	....	....	....	....	....	....	....	....	....	....
1987-88	CSKA Moscow	USSR	50	3	6	9	....	....	....	32	....	....	....	....	....	....	....	....	....	....	....	....	....	....	....	....	....	....
1988-89	CSKA Moscow	USSR	37	7	8	15	....	....	....	20	....	....	....	....	....	....	....	....	....	....	....	....	....	....	....	....	....	....
	CSKA Moscow	Super-S	7	1	1	2	....	....	....	8	....	....	....	....	....	....	....	....	....	....	....	....	....	....	....	....	....	....
	Soviet Union	WEC-A	8	2	1	3	....	....	....	2	....	....	....	....	....	....	....	....	....	....	....	....	....	....	....	....	....	....
1989-90	CSKA Moscow	Fr-Tour	1	0	0	0	....	....	....	2	....	....	....	....	....	....	....	....	....	....	....	....	....	....	....	....	....	....
	CSKA Moscow	USSR	47	14	14	28	....	....	....	44	....	....	....	....	....	....	....	....	....	....	....	....	....	....	....	....	....	....
	CSKA Moscow	Super-S	5	0	2	2	....	....	....	6	....	....	....	....	....	....	....	....	....	....	....	....	....	....	....	....	....	....
	Soviet Union	WEC-A	10	2	2	4	....	....	....	12	....	....	....	....	....	....	....	....	....	....	....	....	....	....	....	....	....	....
1990-91	CSKA Moscow	Fr-Tour	1	0	0	0	....	....	....	2	....	....	....	....	....	....	....	....	....	....	....	....	....	....	....	....	....	....
	CSKA Moscow	USSR	45	5	12	17	....	....	....	42	....	....	....	....	....	....	....	....	....	....	....	....	....	....	....	....	....	....
	CSKA Moscow	Super-S	7	1	5	6	....	....	....	10	....	....	....	....	....	....	....	....	....	....	....	....	....	....	....	....	....	....
	Soviet Union	WEC-A	10	0	2	2	....	....	....	37	....	....	....	....	....	....	....	....	....	....	....	....	....	....	....	....	....	....
1991-92	**Detroit Red Wings**	**NHL**	**79**	**8**	**26**	**34**	**7**	**20**	**27**	**172**	**1**	**0**	**2**	**108**	**7.4**	**103**	**7**	**103**	**32**	**25**	**11**	**0**	**1**	**1**	**16**	**0**	**0**	**0**
1992-93	**Detroit Red Wings**	**NHL**	**82**	**5**	**17**	**22**	**4**	**12**	**16**	**137**	**0**	**0**	**0**	**85**	**5.9**	**86**	**1**	**99**	**36**	**22**	**7**	**0**	**1**	**1**	**8**	**0**	**0**	**0**
1993-94	**Detroit Red Wings**	**NHL**	**80**	**12**	**21**	**33**	**11**	**16**	**27**	**138**	**1**	**3**	**3**	**97**	**12.4**	**93**	**10**	**81**	**28**	**30**	**7**	**0**	**2**	**2**	**4**	**0**	**0**	**0**
1994-95	EHC Wedemark	Germany-2	15	13	17	30	....	....	....	51	....	....	....	....	....	....	....	....	....	....	....	....	....	....	....	....	....	....
	Detroit Red Wings	**NHL**	**47**	**3**	**11**	**14**	**5**	**16**	**21**	**101**	**0**	**0**	**0**	**57**	**5.3**	**44**	**6**	**37**	**9**	**10**	**18**	**1**	**1**	**2**	**22**	**0**	**0**	**1**
1995-96	**Detroit Red Wings**	**NHL**	**81**	**14**	**20**	**34**	**14**	**16**	**30**	**139**	**3**	**1**	**3**	**168**	**8.3**	**113**	**19**	**51**	**17**	**60**	**19**	**4**	**5**	**9**	**28**	**0**	**1**	**0**
1996-97♦	**Detroit Red Wings**	**NHL**	**77**	**5**	**33**	**38**	**5**	**29**	**34**	**151**	**0**	**0**	**0**	**141**	**3.5**	**92**	**15**	**59**	**20**	**38**	**20**	**0**	**4**	**4**	**29**	**0**	**0**	**0**
1997-98	**Detroit Red Wings**	**NHL**	DID NOT PLAY – INJURED																									
	NHL Totals		**446**	**47**	**128**	**175**	**46**	**109**	**155**	**838**	**5**	**4**	**8**	**656**	**7.2**	**531**	**58**	**430**	**142**		**82**	**5**	**14**	**19**	**107**	**0**	**1**	**1**

NHL All-Rookie Team (1992) • NHL Second All-Star Team (1996) • Won Alka-Seltzer Plus Award (1996)

• Suffered career-ending injuries in automobile accident, July 13, 1997.

• KONTOS, Chris

Christopher T. LW/C – L. 6'1", 195 lbs. b: Toronto, Ont., 12/10/1963. NY Rangers' 1st, 15th overall, in 1982.

Season	Club	League	GP	G	A	Pts	AG	AA	APts	PIM	PP	SH	GW	S	%	TGF	PGF	TGA	PGA	+/–	GP	G	A	Pts	PIM	PP	SH	GW
1979-80	North York Flames	OJHL	42	39	55	94	....	....	....	37	....	....	....	....	....	....	....	....	....	....	....	....	....	....	....	....	....	....
1980-81	Sudbury Wolves	OMJHL	57	17	27	44	....	....	....	36	....	....	....	....	....	....	....	....	....	....	....	....	....	....	....	....	....	....
1981-82	Sudbury Wolves	OHL	12	6	6	12	....	....	....	18	....	....	....	....	....	....	....	....	....	....	....	....	....	....	....	....	....	....
	Toronto Marlboros	OHL	59	36	56	92	....	....	....	68	....	....	....	....	....	....	....	....	....	....	10	7	9	16	2	....	....	....
1982-83	Toronto Marlboros	OHL	28	21	33	54	....	....	....	23	....	....	....	....	....	....	....	....	....	....	....	....	....	....	....	....	....	....
	New York Rangers	**NHL**	**44**	**8**	**7**	**15**	**7**	**5**	**12**	**33**	**0**	**0**	**0**	**63**	**12.7**	**26**	**1**	**24**	**0**	**1**	....	....	....	....	....	....	....	....
1983-84	**New York Rangers**	**NHL**	**6**	**0**	**1**	**1**	**0**	**1**	**1**	**8**	**0**	**0**	**0**	**1**	**0.0**	**1**	**0**	**1**	**0**	**0**	....	....	....	....	....	....	....	....
	Tulsa Oilers	CHL	21	5	13	18	....	....	....	8	....	....	....	....	....	....	....	....	....	....	....	....	....	....	....	....	....	....
1984-85	**New York Rangers**	**NHL**	**28**	**4**	**8**	**12**	**3**	**5**	**8**	**24**	**1**	**0**	**0**	**50**	**8.0**	**17**	**4**	**25**	**0**	**–12**	....	....	....	....	....	....	....	....
	New Haven Nighthawks	AHL	48	19	24	43	....	....	....	30	....	....	....	....	....	....	....	....	....	....	....	....	....	....	....	....	....	....
1985-86	Ilves Tampere	Finland	36	16	15	31	....	....	....	30	....	....	....	....	....	....	....	....	....	....	....	....	....	....	....	....	....	....
	New Haven Nighthawks	AHL	21	8	15	23	....	....	....	12	....	....	....	....	....	....	....	....	....	....	5	4	2	6	4	....	....	....
1986-87	**Pittsburgh Penguins**	**NHL**	**31**	**8**	**9**	**17**	**7**	**7**	**14**	**6**	**1**	**0**	**1**	**38**	**21.1**	**24**	**6**	**25**	**1**	**–6**	....	....	....	....	....	....	....	....
	New Haven Nighthawks	AHL	36	14	17	31	....	....	....	29	....	....	....	....	....	....	....	....	....	....	....	....	....	....	....	....	....	....
1987-88	**Pittsburgh Penguins**	**NHL**	**36**	**1**	**7**	**8**	**1**	**5**	**6**	**12**	**0**	**0**	**0**	**17**	**5.9**	**8**	**0**	**23**	**12**	**–3**	....	....	....	....	....	....	....	....
	Muskegon Lumberjacks	IHL	10	3	6	9	....	....	....	8	....	....	....	....	....	....	....	....	....	....	....	....	....	....	....	....	....	....
	Los Angeles Kings	**NHL**	**6**	**2**	**10**	**12**	**2**	**7**	**9**	**2**	**1**	**0**	**0**	**19**	**10.5**	**18**	**10**	**10**	**3**	**1**	**4**	**1**	**0**	**1**	**4**	**0**	**0**	**0**
	New Haven Nighthawks	AHL	16	8	16	24	....	....	....	4	....	....	....	....	....	....	....	....	....	....	....	....	....	....	....	....	....	....
1988-89	EHC Kloten	Switz.	36	33	22	55	....	....	....	....	....	....	....	....	....	....	....	....	....	....	6	5	4	9	....	....	....	....
	Los Angeles Kings	**NHL**	**7**	**2**	**1**	**3**	**2**	**1**	**3**	**2**	**1**	**0**	**0**	**9**	**22.2**	**7**	**1**	**4**	**0**	**2**	**11**	**9**	**0**	**9**	**8**	**6**	**0**	**1**
1989-90	**Los Angeles Kings**	**NHL**	**6**	**2**	**2**	**4**	**2**	**1**	**3**	**4**	**0**	**0**	**0**	**9**	**22.2**	**7**	**1**	**3**	**0**	**3**	**5**	**1**	**0**	**1**	**0**	**0**	**1**	**0**
	New Haven Nighthawks	AHL	42	10	20	30	....	....	....	25	....	....	....	....	....	....	....	....	....	....	....	....	....	....	....	....	....	....
1990-91	Phoenix Roadrunners	IHL	69	26	36	62	....	....	....	19	....	....	....	....	....	....	....	....	....	....	11	9	12	21	0	....	....	....
1991-92	Canada	Nat-Team	26	10	10	20	....	....	....	4	....	....	....	....	....	....	....	....	....	....	....	....	....	....	....	....	....	....
1992-93	**Tampa Bay Lightning**	**NHL**	**66**	**27**	**24**	**51**	**22**	**17**	**39**	**12**	**12**	**1**	**3**	**136**	**19.9**	**74**	**34**	**58**	**11**	**–7**	....	....	....	....	....	....	....	....

			REGULAR SEASON																		PLAYOFFS							
Season	Club	League	GP	G	A	Pts	AG	AA	APts	PIM	PP	SH	GW	S	%	TGF	PGF	TGA	PGA	+/–	GP	G	A	Pts	PIM	PP	SH	GW
1993-94	Canada	Nat-Team	35	16	16	32	....	....	....	12	....	....	....	....	....	....	....	....	....	....	....	....	....	....	....	....	....	....
	Canada	Olympics	8	3	1	4	....	....	....	2	....	....	....	....	....	....	....	....	....	....	....	....	....	....	....	....	....	....
1994-95	Skelleftea AIK	Sweden-2	36	21	27	48	....	....	....	30	....	....	....	....	....	....	....	....	....	....	5	2	3	5	4	....	....	....
	Canada	Nat-Team	3	0	1	1	....	....	....	4	....	....	....	....	....	....	....	....	....	....	....	....	....	....	....	....	....	....
1995-96	Cincinnati Cyclones	IHL	81	26	44	70	....	....	....	13	....	....	....	....	....	....	....	....	....	....	17	5	8	13	0	....	....	....
1996-97	Cincinnati Cyclones	IHL	11	1	3	4	....	....	....	4	....	....	....	....	....	....	....	....	....	....	....	....	....	....	....	....	....	....
	Quebec Rafales	IHL	19	8	3	11	....	....	....	0	....	....	....	....	....	....	....	....	....	....	....	....	....	....	....	....	....	....
	Manitoba Moose	IHL	40	17	18	35	....	....	....	12	....	....	....	....	....	....	....	....	....	....	....	....	....	....	....	....	....	....
1997-98	Revier Lowen	Germany	26	10	4	14	....	....	....	14	....	....	....	....	....	....	....	....	....	....	....	....	....	....	....	....	....	....
	NHL Totals		**230**	**54**	**69**	**123**	**46**	**49**	**95**	**103**	**16**	**1**	**4**	**342**	**15.8**	**182**	**57**	**173**	**27**		**20**	**11**	**0**	**11**	**12**	**6**	**1**	**1**

Traded to **Pittsburgh** by **NY Rangers** for Ron Duguay, January 21, 1987. Traded to **LA Kings** by **Pittsburgh** with Pittsburgh's 6th round choice (Micah Aivazoff) in 1988 Entry Draft for Bryan Erickson, February 5, 1988. Signed as a free agent by **Tampa Bay**, July 21, 1992. Signed as a free agent by **Florida**, July 7, 1995.

• KORAB, Jerry

Gerald Joseph "Kong" D – L. 6'3", 220 lbs. b: Sault Ste. Marie, Ont., 9/15/1948.

Season	Club	League	GP	G	A	Pts	AG	AA	APts	PIM	PP	SH	GW	S	%	TGF	PGF	TGA	PGA	+/–	GP	G	A	Pts	PIM	PP	SH	GW
1965-66	Sault Ste-Marie Greyhounds	NOJHA	STATISTICS NOT AVAILABLE																									
1966-67	St. Catharines Black Hawks	OHA-Jr.	43	3	10	13	....	....	....	57	....	....	....	....	....	....	....	....	....	....	4	0	1	1	12	....	....	....
1967-68	St. Catharines Black Hawks	OHA-Jr.	54	10	34	44	....	....	....	*244	....	....	....	....	....	....	....	....	....	....	5	0	3	3	26	....	....	....
1968-69	Port Huron Flags	IHL	71	18	46	64	....	....	....	284	....	....	....	....	....	....	....	....	....	....	....	....	....	....	....	....	....	....
1969-70	Portland Buckaroos	WHL	65	9	12	21	....	....	....	169	....	....	....	....	....	....	....	....	....	....	....	....	....	....	....	....	....	....
1970-71	**Chicago Black Hawks**	**NHL**	46	4	14	18	4	12	16	152	1	0	1	97	4.1	47	1	35	3	14	7	1	0	1	20	0	0	0
	Portland Buckaroos	WHL	20	3	5	8	....	....	....	78	....	....	....	....	....	....	....	....	....	....	....	....	....	....	....	....	....	....
1971-72	**Chicago Black Hawks**	**NHL**	73	9	5	14	9	4	13	95	2	0	1	97	9.3	37	12	27	3	1	8	0	1	1	20	0	0	0
1972-73	**Chicago Black Hawks**	**NHL**	77	12	15	27	11	12	23	94	0	1	1	127	9.4	49	7	53	16	5	15	0	0	0	22	0	0	0
1973-74	**Vancouver Canucks**	**NHL**	31	4	7	11	4	6	10	64	3	0	0	75	5.3	26	13	42	8	–21	....	....	....	....	....	....	....	....
	Buffalo Sabres	**NHL**	45	6	12	18	6	10	16	73	2	0	0	106	5.7	44	6	67	6	–23	....	....	....	....	....	....	....	....
1974-75	**Buffalo Sabres**	**NHL**	79	12	44	56	10	33	43	184	3	2	1	218	5.5	189	61	126	39	41	16	3	2	5	32	1	0	0
1975-76	**Buffalo Sabres**	**NHL**	65	13	28	41	11	21	32	85	3	0	1	146	8.9	122	29	100	25	18	9	1	3	4	12	0	0	0
1976-77	**Buffalo Sabres**	**NHL**	77	14	33	47	13	25	38	120	4	0	1	185	7.6	140	40	96	18	22	6	2	4	6	8	1	0	1
1977-78	**Buffalo Sabres**	**NHL**	77	7	34	41	6	26	32	119	3	0	2	204	3.4	135	26	113	23	19	8	0	5	5	6	0	0	0
1978-79	**Buffalo Sabres**	**NHL**	78	11	40	51	9	29	38	104	8	1	0	204	5.4	131	40	125	39	5	3	1	0	1	4	0	0	0
1979-80	**Buffalo Sabres**	**NHL**	43	1	10	11	1	7	8	74	0	0	1	55	1.8	45	6	46	7	0	....	....	....	....	....	....	....	....
	Los Angeles Kings	**NHL**	11	1	2	3	1	1	2	34	0	0	0	30	3.3	10	3	14	4	–3	3	0	1	1	11	0	0	0
1980-81	**Los Angeles Kings**	**NHL**	78	9	43	52	7	29	36	139	3	0	2	120	7.5	146	55	118	37	10	4	0	0	0	33	0	0	0
1981-82	**Los Angeles Kings**	**NHL**	50	5	13	18	4	9	13	91	3	0	0	71	7.0	70	22	81	14	–19	10	0	2	2	26	0	0	0
1982-83	**Los Angeles Kings**	**NHL**	72	3	26	29	2	18	20	90	1	0	0	132	2.3	83	15	109	35	–6	....	....	....	....	....	....	....	....
1983-84	**Buffalo Sabres**	**NHL**	48	2	9	11	2	6	8	82	1	0	1	41	4.9	46	3	45	6	4	3	0	0	0	5	0	0	0
	Rochester Americans	AHL	4	0	4	4	....	....	....	2	....	....	....	....	....	....	....	....	....	....	....	....	....	....	....	....	....	....
1984-85	**Buffalo Sabres**	**NHL**	25	1	6	7	1	4	5	29	0	0	1	30	3.3	23	9	27	4	–9	1	0	0	0	2	0	0	0
	Rochester Americans	AHL	3	1	2	3	....	....	....	6	....	....	....	....	....	....	....	....	....	....	....	....	....	....	....	....	....	....
	NHL Totals		**975**	**114**	**341**	**455**	**101**	**252**	**353**	**1629**	**37**	**4**	**13**	**1938**	**5.9**	**1343**	**348**	**1224**	**287**		**93**	**8**	**18**	**26**	**201**	**2**	**0**	**1**

Played in NHL All-Star Game (1975, 1976)

Traded to **Vancouver** by **Chicago** with Gary Smith for Dale Tallon, May 14, 1973. Traded to **Buffalo** by **Vancouver** for John Gould and Tracy Pratt, December 27, 1973. Traded to **LA Kings** by **Buffalo** for LA Kings' 1st round choice (Phil Housley) in 1982 Entry Draft, March 10, 1980. Signed as a free agent by **Minnesota**, October 17, 1983. Claimed on waivers by **Buffalo** from **Minnesota**, October 20, 1983.

• KORDIC, Dan

LW – L. 6'5", 234 lbs. b: Edmonton, Alta., 4/18/1971. Philadelphia's 9th, 88th overall, in 1990.

Season	Club	League	GP	G	A	Pts	AG	AA	APts	PIM	PP	SH	GW	S	%	TGF	PGF	TGA	PGA	+/–	GP	G	A	Pts	PIM	PP	SH	GW
1986-87	Edmonton Pats	AAHA	42	1	16	17	....	....	....	88	....	....	....	....	....	....	....	....	....	....	....	....	....	....	....	....	....	....
1987-88	Medicine Hat Tigers	WHL	63	1	5	6	....	....	....	75	....	....	....	....	....	....	....	....	....	....	16	0	0	0	2	....	....	....
	Medicine Hat Tigers	Mem-Cup	5	0	0	0	....	....	....	0	....	....	....	....	....	....	....	....	....	....	....	....	....	....	....	....	....	....
1988-89	Medicine Hat Tigers	WHL	70	1	13	14	....	....	....	190	....	....	....	....	....	....	....	....	....	....	3	0	0	0	10	....	....	....
1989-90	Medicine Hat Tigers	WHL	59	4	12	16	....	....	....	182	....	....	....	....	....	....	....	....	....	....	3	0	0	0	9	....	....	....
1990-91	Medicine Hat Tigers	WHL	67	8	15	23	....	....	....	150	....	....	....	....	....	....	....	....	....	....	12	2	6	8	42	....	....	....
1991-92	**Philadelphia Flyers**	**NHL**	46	1	3	4	1	2	3	126	0	0	0	27	3.7	23	0	32	10	1	....	....	....	....	....	....	....	....
1992-93	Hershey Bears	AHL	14	0	2	2	....	....	....	17	....	....	....	....	....	....	....	....	....	....	....	....	....	....	....	....	....	....
1993-94	**Philadelphia Flyers**	**NHL**	4	0	0	0	0	0	0	5	0	0	0	0	0.0	1	0	1	0	0	....	....	....	....	....	....	....	....
	Hershey Bears	AHL	64	0	4	4	....	....	....	164	....	....	....	....	....	....	....	....	....	....	11	0	3	3	26	....	....	....
1994-95	Hershey Bears	AHL	37	0	2	2	....	....	....	121	....	....	....	....	....	....	....	....	....	....	6	0	1	1	21	....	....	....
1995-96	**Philadelphia Flyers**	**NHL**	9	1	0	1	1	0	1	31	0	0	0	2	50.0	4	0	3	0	1	....	....	....	....	....	....	....	....
	Hershey Bears	AHL	52	2	6	8	....	....	....	101	....	....	....	....	....	....	....	....	....	....	....	....	....	....	....	....	....	....
1996-97	**Philadelphia Flyers**	**NHL**	75	1	4	5	1	4	5	210	0	0	0	21	4.8	11	0	12	0	–1	12	1	0	1	22	0	0	0
1997-98	**Philadelphia Flyers**	**NHL**	61	1	1	2	1	1	2	210	0	0	0	12	8.3	4	0	8	0	–4	....	....	....	....	....	....	....	....
1998-99	**Philadelphia Flyers**	**NHL**	2	0	0	0	0	0	0	2	0	0	0	0	0.0	0	0	1	0	–1	....	....	....	....	....	....	....	....
	Grand Rapids Griffins	IHL	3	0	0	0	....	....	....	0	....	....	....	....	....	....	....	....	....	....	....	....	....	....	....	....	....	....
	Philadelphia Phantoms	AHL	9	1	1	2	....	....	....	43	....	....	....	....	....	....	....	....	....	....	1	0	0	0	0	....	....	....
1999-2000			DID NOT PLAY – REFEREE																									
	NHL Totals		**197**	**4**	**8**	**12**	**4**	**7**	**11**	**584**	**0**	**0**	**0**	**62**	**6.5**	**43**	**0**	**57**	**10**		**12**	**1**	**0**	**1**	**22**	**0**	**0**	**0**

• Brother of John

• KORDIC, John

John Nick RW – R. 6'2", 210 lbs. b: Edmonton, Alta., 3/22/1965 d: 8/8/1992. Montreal's 6th, 80th overall, in 1983.

Season	Club	League	GP	G	A	Pts	AG	AA	APts	PIM	PP	SH	GW	S	%	TGF	PGF	TGA	PGA	+/–	GP	G	A	Pts	PIM	PP	SH	GW
1981-82	Edmonton Pats	AAHA	48	23	41	64	....	....	....	178	....	....	....	....	....	....	....	....	....	....	....	....	....	....	....	....	....	....
1982-83	Portland Winter Hawks	WHL	72	3	22	25	....	....	....	235	....	....	....	....	....	....	....	....	....	....	14	1	6	7	30	....	....	....
	Portland Winter Hawks	Mem-Cup	4	0	1	1	....	....	....	6	....	....	....	....	....	....	....	....	....	....	....	....	....	....	....	....	....	....
1983-84	Portland Winter Hawks	WHL	67	9	50	59	....	....	....	232	....	....	....	....	....	....	....	....	....	....	14	0	13	13	56	....	....	....
1984-85	Portland Winter Hawks	WHL	25	6	22	28	....	....	....	73	....	....	....	....	....	....	....	....	....	....	....	....	....	....	....	....	....	....
	Seattle Breakers	WHL	46	17	36	53	....	....	....	154	....	....	....	....	....	....	....	....	....	....	....	....	....	....	....	....	....	....
	Sherbrooke Canadiens	AHL	4	0	0	0	....	....	....	4	....	....	....	....	....	....	....	....	....	....	4	0	0	0	11	....	....	....
1985-86♦	**Montreal Canadiens**	**NHL**	5	0	1	1	0	1	1	12	0	0	0	0	0.0	1	0	0	0	1	18	0	0	0	53	0	0	0
	Sherbrooke Canadiens	AHL	68	3	14	17	....	....	....	238	....	....	....	....	....	....	....	....	....	....	....	....	....	....	....	....	....	....
1986-87	**Montreal Canadiens**	**NHL**	44	5	3	8	4	2	6	151	0	0	0	32	15.6	11	0	18	0	–7	11	2	0	2	19	0	0	1
	Sherbrooke Canadiens	AHL	10	4	4	8	....	....	....	49	....	....	....	....	....	....	....	....	....	....	....	....	....	....	....	....	....	....
1987-88	**Montreal Canadiens**	**NHL**	60	2	6	8	2	4	6	159	0	0	0	17	11.8	12	0	12	0	0	7	2	2	4	26	0	0	0
1988-89	**Montreal Canadiens**	**NHL**	6	0	0	0	0	0	0	13	0	0	0	2	0.0	1	0	2	0	–1	....	....	....	....	....	....	....	....
	Toronto Maple Leafs	**NHL**	46	1	2	3	1	1	2	185	0	0	0	33	3.0	7	0	20	0	–13	....	....	....	....	....	....	....	....
1989-90	**Toronto Maple Leafs**	**NHL**	55	9	4	13	8	3	11	252	3	0	0	48	18.8	20	4	24	0	–8	5	0	1	1	33	0	0	0
1990-91	**Toronto Maple Leafs**	**NHL**	3	0	0	0	0	0	0	9	0	0	0	1	0.0	0	0	0	0	0	....	....	....	....	....	....	....	....
	Newmarket Saints	AHL	8	1	1	2	....	....	....	79	....	....	....	....	....	....	....	....	....	....	....	....	....	....	....	....	....	....
	Washington Capitals	**NHL**	7	0	0	0	0	0	0	101	0	0	0	0	0.0	2	0	1	0	1	....	....	....	....	....	....	....	....
1991-92	**Quebec Nordiques**	**NHL**	18	0	2	2	0	2	2	115	0	0	0	3	0.0	2	0	5	0	–3	....	....	....	....	....	....	....	....
	Cape Breton Oilers	AHL	12	2	1	3	....	....	....	141	....	....	....	....	....	....	....	....	....	....	5	0	1	1	53	....	....	....
	NHL Totals		**244**	**17**	**18**	**35**	**15**	**13**	**28**	**997**	**3**	**0**	**0**	**136**	**12.5**	**56**	**4**	**82**	**0**		**41**	**4**	**3**	**7**	**131**	**0**	**0**	**1**

• Brother of Dan • WHL West Second All-Star Team (1985)

Traded to **Toronto** by **Montreal** with Montreal's 6th round choice (Michael Doers) in 1989 Entry Draft for Russ Courtnall, November 7, 1988. Traded to **Washington** by **Toronto** with Paul Fenton for Washington's 5th round choice (Alexei Kudashov) in 1991 Entry Draft, January 24, 1991. Signed as a free agent by **Quebec**, October 4, 1991.

Season	Club	League	REGULAR SEASON																		PLAYOFFS							
			GP	G	A	Pts	AG	AA	APts	PIM	PP	SH	GW	S	%	TGF	PGF	TGA	PGA	+/–	GP	G	A	Pts	PIM	PP	SH	GW

• KORN, Jim James Allen D/LW – L. 6'4", 220 lbs. b: Hopkins, MN, 7/28/1957. Detroit's 4th, 73rd overall, in 1977.

Season	Club	League	GP	G	A	Pts	AG	AA	APts	PIM	PP	SH	GW	S	%	TGF	PGF	TGA	PGA	+/–	GP	G	A	Pts	PIM	PP	SH	GW
1975-76	Providence College	ECAC	20	2	0	2				10																		
1976-77	Providence College	ECAC	29	6	9	15				73																		
1977-78	Providence College	ECAC	33	7	14	21				47																		
1978-79	Providence College	ECAC	27	5	19	24				72																		
	United States	WEC-A	8	0	1	1				8																		
1979-80	**Detroit Red Wings**	**NHL**	**63**	**5**	**13**	**18**	**4**	**9**	**13**	**108**	**1**	**0**	**1**	**58**	**8.6**	**62**	**5**	**64**	**3**	**–4**								
	Adirondack Red Wings	AHL	14	2	7	9				40																		
1980-81	**Detroit Red Wings**	**NHL**	**63**	**5**	**15**	**20**	**4**	**10**	**14**	**246**	**1**	**1**	**1**	**82**	**6.1**	**71**	**10**	**82**	**16**	**–5**								
	Adirondack Red Wings	AHL	9	3	7	10				53																		
	United States	WEC-A	5	0	1	1				6																		
1981-82	**Detroit Red Wings**	**NHL**	**59**	**1**	**7**	**8**	**1**	**5**	**6**	**104**	**0**	**0**	**0**	**41**	**2.4**	**28**	**2**	**55**	**10**	**–19**								
	Toronto Maple Leafs	**NHL**	**11**	**1**	**3**	**4**	**1**	**2**	**3**	**44**	**0**	**0**	**0**	**10**	**10.0**	**16**	**2**	**23**	**10**	**1**								
1982-83	**Toronto Maple Leafs**	**NHL**	**80**	**8**	**21**	**29**	**7**	**15**	**22**	**236**	**0**	**3**	**1**	**101**	**7.9**	**93**	**6**	**162**	**48**	**–27**	**3**	**0**	**0**	**0**	**26**	**0**	**0**	**0**
1983-84	**Toronto Maple Leafs**	**NHL**	**65**	**12**	**14**	**26**	**10**	**10**	**20**	**257**	**0**	**0**	**1**	**94**	**12.8**	**61**	**3**	**121**	**30**	**–33**								
1984-85	**Toronto Maple Leafs**	**NHL**	**41**	**5**	**5**	**10**	**4**	**3**	**7**	**171**	**2**	**0**	**1**	**48**	**10.4**	**25**	**7**	**35**	**0**	**–17**								
1985-86	**Toronto Maple Leafs**	**NHL**	DID NOT PLAY – INJURED																									
1986-87	**Buffalo Sabres**	**NHL**	**52**	**4**	**10**	**14**	**3**	**7**	**10**	**158**	**0**	**0**	**0**	**35**	**11.4**	**24**	**0**	**30**	**3**	**–3**								
1987-88	**New Jersey Devils**	**NHL**	**52**	**8**	**13**	**21**	**7**	**9**	**16**	**140**	**3**	**0**	**0**	**49**	**16.3**	**29**	**13**	**38**	**0**	**–22**	**9**	**0**	**2**	**2**	**71**	**0**	**0**	**0**
1988-89	**New Jersey Devils**	**NHL**	**65**	**15**	**16**	**31**	**13**	**11**	**24**	**212**	**4**	**0**	**3**	**65**	**23.1**	**53**	**11**	**50**	**5**	**–3**								
1989-90	**New Jersey Devils**	**NHL**	**37**	**2**	**3**	**5**	**2**	**2**	**4**	**99**	**0**	**0**	**0**	**18**	**11.1**	**9**	**0**	**14**	**4**	**–1**								
	Calgary Flames	**NHL**	**9**	**0**	**2**	**2**	**0**	**1**	**1**	**26**	**0**	**0**	**0**	**3**	**0.0**	**5**	**0**	**4**	**0**	**1**	**4**	**1**	**0**	**1**	**12**	**0**	**0**	**0**
	NHL Totals		**597**	**66**	**122**	**188**	**56**	**84**	**140**	**1801**	**11**	**4**	**8**	**604**	**10.9**	**476**	**59**	**678**	**129**		**16**	**1**	**2**	**3**	**109**	**0**	**0**	**0**

ECAC Second All-Star Team (1979)

Traded to **Toronto** by **Detroit** for Toronto's 4th round choice (Craig Coxe) in 1982 Entry Draft and Toronto's 5th round choice (Joey Kocur) in 1983 Entry Draft, March 8, 1982. • Missed entire 1985-86 season recovering from knee injury suffered in training camp, September 29, 1985. Traded to **Calgary** by **Toronto** for Terry Johnson, October 3, 1986. Traded to **Buffalo** by **Calgary** for Brian Engblom, October 3, 1986. Traded to **New Jersey** by **Buffalo** for Jan Ludwig, May 22, 1987. Traded to **Calgary** by **New Jersey** for Calgary's 5th round choice (Peter Kuchyna) in 1990 Entry Draft, March 6, 1990.

• KORNEY, Mike Michael Wayne RW – R. 6'3", 195 lbs. b: Dauphin, Man., 9/15/1953. Detroit's 4th, 59th overall, in 1973.

Season	Club	League	GP	G	A	Pts	AG	AA	APts	PIM	PP	SH	GW	S	%	TGF	PGF	TGA	PGA	+/–	GP	G	A	Pts	PIM	PP	SH	GW
1970-71	Dauphin Kings	MJHL	45	15	31	46				38																		
1971-72	Dauphin Kings	MJHL	41	16	33	49				64																		
1972-73	Winnipeg Jets	WCJHL	68	20	29	49				92																		
1973-74	**Detroit Red Wings**	**NHL**	**2**	**0**	**0**	**0**	**0**	**0**	**0**	**0**	**0**	**0**	**0**	**1**	**0.0**	**1**	**0**	**4**	**0**	**–3**								
	Virginia Wings	AHL	19	1	1	2				15																		
	Port Huron Wings	IHL	7	1	0	1				9																		
	London Lions	Britain	31	15	10	25				33																		
1974-75	**Detroit Red Wings**	**NHL**	**30**	**8**	**2**	**10**	**7**	**1**	**8**	**18**	**2**	**0**	**1**	**50**	**16.0**	**20**	**3**	**26**	**0**	**–9**								
	Virginia Wings	AHL	2	0	0	0				0																		
	Providence Reds	AHL	3	1	0	1				0																		
	Springfield Indians	AHL	1	0	0	0				0																		
	Hampton Gulls	SHL	13	0	1	1				35																		
1975-76	**Detroit Red Wings**	**NHL**	**27**	**1**	**7**	**8**	**1**	**5**	**6**	**23**	**0**	**0**	**0**	**21**	**4.8**	**12**	**3**	**17**	**0**	**–8**								
	New Haven Nighthawks	AHL	21	8	9	17				31																		
	Oklahoma City Blazers	CHL	18	8	6	14				20											4	0	0	0	2			
1976-77	Kansas City Blues	CHL	74	17	24	41				82											10	1	6	7	13			
1977-78	Milwaukee Admirals	IHL	3	0	0	0				2																		
	Maine Mariners	AHL	15	2	4	6				20																		
	Salt Lake Golden Eagles	CHL	54	12	8	20				75											6	2	4	6	6			
1978-79	**New York Rangers**	**NHL**	**18**	**0**	**1**	**1**	**0**	**1**	**1**	**18**	**0**	**0**	**0**	**20**	**0.0**	**14**	**2**	**11**	**3**	**4**								
	New Haven Nighthawks	AHL	5	1	3	4				0																		
	Tulsa Oilers	CHL	11	0	9	9				36																		
1979-80	Syracuse Firebirds	AHL	73	11	16	27				87											4	1	2	3	18			
1980-81	Cranbrook Royals	WIHL	PLAYER/COACH – STATISTICS UNAVAILABLE																									
1981-82	Cranbrook Royals	WIHL	PLAYER/COACH – STATISTICS UNAVAILABLE																									
	Cranbrook Royals	Al-Cup	5	1	*6	7				2																		
	NHL Totals		**77**	**9**	**10**	**19**	**8**	**7**	**15**	**59**	**2**	**0**	**1**	**92**	**9.8**	**47**	**8**	**58**	**3**									

Traded to **Philadelphia** by **Detroit** with Rick Lapointe for Terry Murray, Bob Ritchie, Steve Coates and Dave Kelly, February 17, 1977. Signed as a free agent by **St. Louis**, July 22, 1978. Traded to **Montreal** by **St. Louis** for Gord McTavish, October 7, 1978. Claimed by **NY Rangers** from **Montreal** in Waiver Draft, October 9, 1978.

• KOROLEV, Evgeny D – L. 6'1", 186 lbs. b: Moscow, USSR, 7/24/1978. NY Islanders' 6th, 182nd overall, in 1998.

Season	Club	League	GP	G	A	Pts	AG	AA	APts	PIM	PP	SH	GW	S	%	TGF	PGF	TGA	PGA	+/–	GP	G	A	Pts	PIM	PP	SH	GW
1995-96	Peterborough Petes	OHL	60	2	12	14				60											6	0	0	0	2			
1996-97	Peterborough Petes	OHL	64	5	17	22				60											11	1	1	2	8			
1997-98	Peterborough Petes	OHL	37	5	21	26				39																		
	London Knights	OHL	27	4	10	14				36											15	2	7	9	29			
1998-99	Roanoke Express	ECHL	2	0	1	1				0																		
	Lowell Lock Monsters	AHL	54	2	6	8				48											2	0	1	1	0			
99-2000	**New York Islanders**	**NHL**	**17**	**1**	**2**	**3**	**1**	**2**	**3**	**8**	**0**	**0**	**0**	**7**	**14.3**	**7**	**1**	**16**	**0**	**–10**								
	Lowell Lock Monsters	AHL	57	1	10	11				61											6	0	0	0	4			
	NHL Totals		**17**	**1**	**2**	**3**	**1**	**2**	**3**	**8**	**0**	**0**	**0**	**7**	**14.3**	**7**	**1**	**16**	**0**									

• KOROLEV, Igor C/LW – L. 6'1", 195 lbs. b: Moscow, USSR, 9/6/1970. St. Louis' 1st, 38th overall, in 1992.

Season	Club	League	GP	G	A	Pts	AG	AA	APts	PIM	PP	SH	GW	S	%	TGF	PGF	TGA	PGA	+/–	GP	G	A	Pts	PIM	PP	SH	GW
1987-88	Soviet Union	EJC-A	6	3	2	5				2																		
1988-89	Dynamo Moscow	USSR	1	0	0	0				2																		
1989-90	Dynamo Moscow	USSR	17	3	2	5				2																		
1990-91	Dynamo Moscow	Fr-Tour	1	0	2	2				0																		
	Dynamo Moscow	USSR	38	12	4	16				12																		
	Dynamo Moscow	Super-S	7	0	1	1				4																		
1991-92	Soviet Union	Can-Cup	5	0	0	0				0																		
	Dynamo Moscow	CIS	39	15	12	27				16																		
	Russia	WC-A	6	2	1	3				2																		
1992-93	Dynamo Moscow	CIS	5	1	2	3				4																		
	St. Louis Blues	**NHL**	**74**	**4**	**23**	**27**	**3**	**16**	**19**	**20**	**2**	**0**	**0**	**76**	**5.3**	**38**	**9**	**31**	**1**	**–1**	**3**	**0**	**0**	**0**	**0**	**0**	**0**	**0**
1993-94	**St. Louis Blues**	**NHL**	**73**	**6**	**10**	**16**	**6**	**8**	**14**	**40**	**0**	**0**	**1**	**93**	**6.5**	**33**	**2**	**45**	**2**	**–12**	**2**	**0**	**0**	**0**	**0**	**0**	**0**	**0**
1994-95	Dynamo Moscow	CIS	13	4	6	10				18																		
	Winnipeg Jets	**NHL**	**45**	**8**	**22**	**30**	**14**	**33**	**47**	**10**	**1**	**0**	**1**	**85**	**9.4**	**47**	**9**	**37**	**0**	**1**								
1995-96	**Winnipeg Jets**	**NHL**	**73**	**22**	**29**	**51**	**22**	**24**	**46**	**42**	**8**	**0**	**5**	**165**	**13.3**	**77**	**27**	**51**	**2**	**1**	**6**	**0**	**3**	**3**	**0**	**0**	**0**	**0**
1996-97	**Phoenix Coyotes**	**NHL**	**41**	**3**	**7**	**10**	**3**	**6**	**9**	**28**	**2**	**0**	**0**	**41**	**7.3**	**22**	**7**	**20**	**0**	**–5**	**1**	**0**	**0**	**0**	**0**	**0**	**0**	**0**
	Michigan K-Wings	IHL	4	2	2	4				0																		
	Phoenix Roadrunners	IHL	4	2	6	8				4																		
1997-98	**Toronto Maple Leafs**	**NHL**	**78**	**17**	**22**	**39**	**20**	**22**	**42**	**22**	**6**	**3**	**5**	**97**	**17.5**	**57**	**16**	**69**	**10**	**–18**								
1998-99	**Toronto Maple Leafs**	**NHL**	**66**	**13**	**34**	**47**	**15**	**33**	**48**	**46**	**1**	**0**	**2**	**99**	**13.1**	**66**	**15**	**57**	**17**	**11**	**1**	**0**	**0**	**0**	**0**	**0**	**0**	**0**
99-2000	**Toronto Maple Leafs**	**NHL**	**80**	**20**	**26**	**46**	**22**	**24**	**46**	**22**	**5**	**3**	**4**	**101**	**19.8**	**65**	**17**	**60**	**24**	**12**	**12**	**0**	**4**	**4**	**6**	**0**	**0**	**0**
	NHL Totals		**530**	**93**	**173**	**266**	**105**	**166**	**271**	**230**	**25**	**6**	**18**	**757**	**12.3**	**405**	**102**	**370**	**56**		**25**	**0**	**7**	**7**	**6**	**0**	**0**	**0**

Claimed by **Winnipeg** from **St. Louis** in NHL Waiver Draft, January 18, 1995. Transferred to **Phoenix** after **Winnipeg** franchise relocated, July 1, 1996. Signed as a free agent by **Toronto**, September 29, 1997.

• KOROLL, Cliff

Clifford Eugene RW – R. 6'1", 195 lbs. b: Canora, Sask., 10/1/1946.

			REGULAR SEASON																		PLAYOFFS							
Season	Club	League	GP	G	A	Pts	AG	AA	APts	PIM	PP	SH	GW	S	%	TGF	PGF	TGA	PGA	+/–	GP	G	A	Pts	PIM	PP	SH	GW
1965-66	University of Denver	WCHA	32	21	10	31	....	....	....	23	....	....	....	....	....	....	....	....	....	....	....	....	....	....	....	....	....	....
1966-67	University of Denver	WCHA	25	18	19	37	....	....	....	34	....	....	....	....	....	....	....	....	....	....	....	....	....	....	....	....	....	....
1967-68	University of Denver	WCHA	34	18	22	40	....	....	....	55	....	....	....	....	....	....	....	....	....	....	....	....	....	....	....	....	....	....
1968-69	Dallas Black Hawks	CHL	67	28	34	62	....	....	....	50	....	....	....	....	....	....	....	....	....	....	11	2	8	10	15	....	....	....
1969-70	**Chicago Black Hawks**	**NHL**	73	18	19	37	20	18	38	44	0	0	3	160	11.3	58	7	39	3	15	8	1	4	5	9	0	0	0
1970-71	**Chicago Black Hawks**	**NHL**	72	16	34	50	16	28	44	85	4	0	3	124	12.9	85	23	37	3	28	18	7	9	16	18	3	0	1
1971-72	**Chicago Black Hawks**	**NHL**	76	22	23	45	22	20	42	51	4	0	6	136	16.2	70	16	34	0	20	8	0	0	0	11	0	0	0
1972-73	**Chicago Black Hawks**	**NHL**	77	33	24	57	31	19	50	38	6	1	6	151	21.9	87	19	57	6	17	16	4	6	10	6	0	0	0
1973-74	**Chicago Black Hawks**	**NHL**	78	21	25	46	20	21	41	32	7	0	3	151	13.9	82	18	37	0	27	11	2	5	7	13	1	0	0
1974-75	**Chicago Black Hawks**	**NHL**	80	27	32	59	24	24	48	27	11	0	9	164	16.5	105	40	61	16	20	8	3	5	8	8	2	0	0
1975-76	**Chicago Black Hawks**	**NHL**	80	25	33	58	22	25	47	29	11	1	2	185	13.5	94	37	66	15	6	4	1	0	1	0	1	0	0
1976-77	**Chicago Black Hawks**	**NHL**	80	15	26	41	13	20	33	25	8	1	1	138	10.9	82	28	104	25	–25	2	0	0	0	0	0	0	0
1977-78	**Chicago Black Hawks**	**NHL**	73	16	15	31	15	12	27	19	1	0	4	100	16.0	48	7	45	12	8	4	1	0	1	0	0	0	0
1978-79	**Chicago Black Hawks**	**NHL**	78	12	19	31	10	14	24	20	1	2	2	109	11.0	62	9	85	35	3	4	0	0	0	0	0	0	0
1979-80	**Chicago Black Hawks**	**NHL**	47	3	4	7	3	3	6	6	0	0	0	40	7.5	11	0	34	13	–10	2	0	0	0	2	0	0	0
	NHL Totals		814	208	254	462	196	204	400	376	53	5	39	1458	14.3	784	204	599	128		85	19	29	48	67	7	0	1

WCHA Second All-Star Team (1968)

Rights traded to **Chicago** by **LA Blades** (WHL) for cash, August, 1967.

• KOROLYUK, Alexander

Alexander Ivanovich RW – L. 5'9", 190 lbs. b: Moscow, USSR, 1/15/1976. San Jose's 6th, 141st overall, in 1994.

Season	Club	League	GP	G	A	Pts	AG	AA	APts	PIM	PP	SH	GW	S	%	TGF	PGF	TGA	PGA	+/–	GP	G	A	Pts	PIM	PP	SH	GW
1993-94	Krylja Sovetov Moscow	CIS	22	4	4	8	....	....	....	20	....	....	....	....	....	....	....	....	....	....	3	1	0	1	4	....	....	....
	Russia	EJC-A	5	2	3	5	....	....	....	0	....	....	....	....	....	....	....	....	....	....	....	....	....	....	....	....	....	....
1994-95	Krylja Sovetov Moscow	CIS	52	16	13	29	....	....	....	62	....	....	....	....	....	....	....	....	....	....	4	1	2	3	4	....	....	....
	Russia	WJC-A	7	8	2	10	....	....	....	47	....	....	....	....	....	....	....	....	....	....	....	....	....	....	....	....	....	....
1995-96	Krylja Sovetov Moscow	CIS	50	30	19	49	....	....	....	77	....	....	....	....	....	....	....	....	....	....	....	....	....	....	....	....	....	....
	Russia	WJC-A	7	5	2	7	....	....	....	4	....	....	....	....	....	....	....	....	....	....	....	....	....	....	....	....	....	....
1996-97	Krylja Sovetov Moscow	Russia	17	8	5	13	....	....	....	46	....	....	....	....	....	....	....	....	....	....	....	....	....	....	....	....	....	....
	Manitoba Moose	IHL	42	20	16	36	....	....	....	71	....	....	....	....	....	....	....	....	....	....	....	....	....	....	....	....	....	....
	Russia	WC-A	6	2	3	5	....	....	....	6	....	....	....	....	....	....	....	....	....	....	....	....	....	....	....	....	....	....
1997-98	**San Jose Sharks**	**NHL**	19	2	3	5	2	3	5	6	1	0	0	23	8.7	9	2	12	0	–5	....	....	....	....	....	....	....	....
	Kentucky Thoroughblades	AHL	44	16	23	39	....	....	....	96	....	....	....	....	....	....	....	....	....	....	3	0	0	0	0	....	....	....
1998-99	**San Jose Sharks**	**NHL**	55	12	18	30	14	17	31	26	2	0	0	96	12.5	40	12	25	0	3	6	1	3	4	2	0	0	1
	Kentucky Thoroughblades	AHL	23	9	13	22	....	....	....	16	....	....	....	....	....	....	....	....	....	....	....	....	....	....	....	....	....	....
99-2000	**San Jose Sharks**	**NHL**	57	14	21	35	16	19	35	35	3	0	1	124	11.3	41	9	28	0	4	9	0	3	3	6	0	0	0
	NHL Totals		131	28	42	70	32	39	71	67	6	0	1	243	11.5	90	23	65	0		15	1	6	7	8	0	0	1

• KORTKO, Roger

C – L. 5'11", 195 lbs. b: Hafford, Sask., 2/1/1963. NY Islanders' 6th, 126th overall, in 1982.

Season	Club	League	GP	G	A	Pts	AG	AA	APts	PIM	PP	SH	GW	S	%	TGF	PGF	TGA	PGA	+/–	GP	G	A	Pts	PIM	PP	SH	GW
1980-81	Humboldt Broncos	SJHL	60	43	82	125	....	....	....	52	....	....	....	....	....	....	....	....	....	....	....	....	....	....	....	....	....	....
	Saskatoon Blades	WHL	2	0	1	1	....	....	....	2	....	....	....	....	....	....	....	....	....	....	....	....	....	....	....	....	....	....
1981-82	Saskatoon Blades	WHL	65	33	51	84	....	....	....	82	....	....	....	....	....	....	....	....	....	....	4	1	4	5	7	....	....	....
1982-83	Saskatoon Blades	WHL	72	62	99	161	....	....	....	79	....	....	....	....	....	....	....	....	....	....	1	1	1	2	5	....	....	....
1983-84	Indianapolis Checkers	CHL	64	16	27	43	....	....	....	48	....	....	....	....	....	....	....	....	....	....	9	1	5	6	9	....	....	....
1984-85	**New York Islanders**	**NHL**	27	2	9	11	2	6	8	9	1	0	0	20	10.0	16	2	24	7	–3	10	0	3	3	17	0	0	0
	Springfield Indians	AHL	30	8	30	38	....	....	....	6	....	....	....	....	....	....	....	....	....	....	....	....	....	....	....	....	....	....
1985-86	**New York Islanders**	**NHL**	52	5	8	13	4	5	9	19	0	0	1	49	10.2	23	0	49	15	–11	....	....	....	....	....	....	....	....
	Springfield Indians	AHL	12	2	10	12	....	....	....	10	....	....	....	....	....	....	....	....	....	....	....	....	....	....	....	....	....	....
1986-87	Springfield Indians	AHL	75	16	30	46	....	....	....	54	....	....	....	....	....	....	....	....	....	....	....	....	....	....	....	....	....	....
1987-88	Binghamton Whalers	AHL	72	26	45	71	....	....	....	46	....	....	....	....	....	....	....	....	....	....	4	1	1	2	2	....	....	....
1988-89	Binghamton Whalers	AHL	79	22	36	58	....	....	....	28	....	....	....	....	....	....	....	....	....	....	....	....	....	....	....	....	....	....
1989-90	EV Fussen	Germany-2	36	18	53	71	....	....	....	31	....	....	....	....	....	....	....	....	....	....	12	19	30	49	6	....	....	....
1990-91	Tilburg Trappers	Holland	21	27	22	49	....	....	....	22	....	....	....	....	....	....	....	....	....	....	17	9	22	31	8	....	....	....
1991-92	Tilburg Trappers	Holland	34	25	*51	76	....	....	....	....	....	....	....	....	....	....	....	....	....	....	....	....	....	....	....	....	....	....
	NHL Totals		79	7	17	24	6	11	17	28	1	0	1	69	10.1	39	2	73	22		10	0	3	3	17	0	0	0

Signed as a free agent by **Hartford**, September 15, 1987.

• KOSTYNSKI, Doug

Douglas C – R. 6'1", 170 lbs. b: Castlegar, B.C., 2/23/1963. Boston's 9th, 186th overall, in 1982.

Season	Club	League	GP	G	A	Pts	AG	AA	APts	PIM	PP	SH	GW	S	%	TGF	PGF	TGA	PGA	+/–	GP	G	A	Pts	PIM	PP	SH	GW
1979-80	Abbotsford Flyers	BCJHL	STATISTICS NOT AVAILABLE																									
	New Westminster Bruins	WHL	11	1	4	5	....	....	....	12	....	....	....	....	....	....	....	....	....	....	....	....	....	....	....	....	....	....
1980-81	New Westminster Bruins	WHL	64	18	40	58	....	....	....	51	....	....	....	....	....	....	....	....	....	....	....	....	....	....	....	....	....	....
1981-82	Kamloops Jr. Oilers	WHL	53	39	42	81	....	....	....	57	....	....	....	....	....	....	....	....	....	....	3	1	0	1	0	....	....	....
1982-83	Kamloops Jr. Oilers	WHL	75	57	59	116	....	....	....	55	....	....	....	....	....	....	....	....	....	....	7	2	7	9	6	....	....	....
1983-84	**Boston Bruins**	**NHL**	9	3	1	4	2	1	3	2	0	0	0	8	37.5	9	0	7	0	2	....	....	....	....	....	....	....	....
	Hershey Bears	AHL	67	13	27	40	....	....	....	8	....	....	....	....	....	....	....	....	....	....	....	....	....	....	....	....	....	....
1984-85	**Boston Bruins**	**NHL**	6	0	0	0	0	0	0	2	0	0	0	4	0.0	2	0	2	0	0	....	....	....	....	....	....	....	....
	Hershey Bears	AHL	55	17	27	44	....	....	....	26	....	....	....	....	....	....	....	....	....	....	....	....	....	....	....	....	....	....
1985-86	Moncton Golden Flames	AHL	72	18	36	54	....	....	....	24	....	....	....	....	....	....	....	....	....	....	8	3	1	4	9	....	....	....
1986-87	Moncton Golden Flames	AHL	74	21	45	66	....	....	....	22	....	....	....	....	....	....	....	....	....	....	6	2	1	3	0	....	....	....
1987-88	Adirondack Red Wings	AHL	10	3	3	6	....	....	....	10	....	....	....	....	....	....	....	....	....	....	1	0	0	0	2	....	....	....
1988-89	SaiPa Lappeenranta	Finland	44	20	32	52	....	....	....	16	....	....	....	....	....	....	....	....	....	....	....	....	....	....	....	....	....	....
1989-90	SaiPa Lappeenranta	Finland	38	13	17	30	....	....	....	34	....	....	....	....	....	....	....	....	....	....	....	....	....	....	....	....	....	....
	NHL Totals		15	3	1	4	2	1	3	4	0	0	0	12	25.0	11	0	9	0		....	....	....	....	....	....	....	....

• KOTSOPOULOS, Chris

Christopher D – R. 6'3", 215 lbs. b: Scarborough, Ont., 11/27/1958.

Season	Club	League	GP	G	A	Pts	AG	AA	APts	PIM	PP	SH	GW	S	%	TGF	PGF	TGA	PGA	+/–	GP	G	A	Pts	PIM	PP	SH	GW
1974-75	Wexford Raiders	OHA-B	30	0	5	5	....	....	....	128	....	....	....	....	....	....	....	....	....	....	....	....	....	....	....	....	....	....
1975-76	Windsor Spitfires	OMJHL	59	3	13	16	....	....	....	169	....	....	....	....	....	....	....	....	....	....	....	....	....	....	....	....	....	....
1976-77	Acadia University	AUAA	DID NOT PLAY – ACADEMICALLY INELIGIBLE																									
1977-78	Acadia University	AUAA	17	0	7	7	....	....	....	72	....	....	....	....	....	....	....	....	....	....	....	....	....	....	....	....	....	....
1978-79	Toledo Goaldiggers	IHL	62	6	22	28	....	....	....	153	....	....	....	....	....	....	....	....	....	....	6	1	7	8	48	....	....	....
1979-80	New Haven Nighthawks	AHL	75	7	27	34	....	....	....	149	....	....	....	....	....	....	....	....	....	....	10	4	5	9	28	....	....	....
1980-81	**New York Rangers**	**NHL**	54	4	12	16	3	8	11	153	0	0	0	104	3.8	46	8	62	14	–10	14	0	3	3	63	0	0	0
1981-82	**Hartford Whalers**	**NHL**	68	13	20	33	10	13	23	147	5	0	1	153	8.5	87	33	108	29	–25	....	....	....	....	....	....	....	....
1982-83	**Hartford Whalers**	**NHL**	68	6	24	30	5	17	22	125	3	0	0	122	4.9	89	17	114	21	–21	....	....	....	....	....	....	....	....
1983-84	**Hartford Whalers**	**NHL**	72	5	13	18	4	9	13	118	3	0	0	96	5.2	83	11	112	38	–2	....	....	....	....	....	....	....	....
1984-85	**Hartford Whalers**	**NHL**	33	5	3	8	4	2	6	53	1	0	0	39	12.8	33	1	55	25	2	....	....	....	....	....	....	....	....
1985-86	**Toronto Maple Leafs**	**NHL**	61	6	11	17	5	7	12	83	0	0	0	69	8.7	76	8	98	25	–5	10	1	0	1	14	0	0	0
1986-87	**Toronto Maple Leafs**	**NHL**	43	2	10	12	2	7	9	75	0	0	0	43	4.7	49	4	54	17	8	7	0	0	0	14	0	0	0
1987-88	**Toronto Maple Leafs**	**NHL**	21	2	2	4	2	1	3	19	0	0	0	22	9.1	16	1	27	9	–3	....	....	....	....	....	....	....	....
1988-89	**Toronto Maple Leafs**	**NHL**	57	1	14	15	1	10	11	44	0	0	0	66	1.5	59	17	72	26	–4	....	....	....	....	....	....	....	....
1989-90	**Detroit Red Wings**	**NHL**	2	0	0	0	0	0	0	10	0	0	0	0	0.0	1	0	3	1	–1	....	....	....	....	....	....	....	....
	Adirondack Red Wings	AHL	24	2	4	6	....	....	....	4	....	....	....	....	....	....	....	....	....	....	4	0	0	0	2	....	....	....
	NHL Totals		479	44	109	153	36	74	110	827	12	0	1	714	6.2	539	100	705	205		31	1	3	4	91	0	0	0

Signed as a free agent by **NY Rangers**, July 10, 1980. Traded to **Hartford** by **NY Rangers** with Gerry McDonald and Doug Sulliman for Mike Rogers and Hartford's 10th round choice (Simo Saarinen) in 1982 Entry Draft, October 2, 1981. Traded to **Toronto** by **Hartford** for Stew Gavin, October 7, 1985. Signed as a free agent by **Detroit**, June 23, 1989.

• KOVALENKO, Andrei

RW – L. 5'10", 215 lbs. b: Balakovo, USSR, 6/7/1970. Quebec's 6th, 148th overall, in 1990.

			REGULAR SEASON																		PLAYOFFS							
Season	Club	League	GP	G	A	Pts	AG	AA	APts	PIM	PP	SH	GW	S	%	TGF	PGF	TGA	PGA	+/-	GP	G	A	Pts	PIM	PP	SH	GW
1987-88	Torpedo Gorky	USSR	2	1	0	1	....	....	....	0	....	....	....	....	....	....	....	....	....	....	....	....	....	....	....	....	....	....
1988-89	SKA Kalinin	USSR-2	30	8	7	15	....	....	....	29	....	....	....	....	....	....	....	....	....	....	....	....	....	....	....	....	....	....
	CSKA Moscow	USSR	10	1	0	1	....	....	....	0	....	....	....	....	....	....	....	....	....	....	....	....	....	....	....	....	....	....
1989-90	CSKA Moscow	Fr-Tour	1	0	0	0	....	....	....	4	....	....	....	....	....	....	....	....	....	....	....	....	....	....	....	....	....	....
	CSKA Moscow	USSR	48	8	5	13	....	....	....	20	....	....	....	....	....	....	....	....	....	....	....	....	....	....	....	....	....	....
	Soviet Union	WJC-A	7	5	6	11	....	....	....	8	....	....	....	....	....	....	....	....	....	....	....	....	....	....	....	....	....	....
1990-91	CSKA Moscow	Fr-Tour	1	1	0	1	....	....	....	2	....	....	....	....	....	....	....	....	....	....	....	....	....	....	....	....	....	....
	CSKA Moscow	USSR	45	13	8	21	....	....	....	26	....	....	....	....	....	....	....	....	....	....	....	....	....	....	....	....	....	....
	CSKA Moscow	Super-S	7	6	3	9	....	....	....	2	....	....	....	....	....	....	....	....	....	....	....	....	....	....	....	....	....	....
1991-92	Soviet Union	Can-Cup	5	1	2	3	....	....	....	10	....	....	....	....	....	....	....	....	....	....	....	....	....	....	....	....	....	....
	CSKA Moscow	CIS	44	19	13	32	....	....	....	32	....	....	....	....	....	....	....	....	....	....	....	....	....	....	....	....	....	....
	Russia	Olympics	8	1	1	2	....	....	....	2	....	....	....	....	....	....	....	....	....	....	....	....	....	....	....	....	....	....
	Russia	WC-A	6	3	1	4	....	....	....	2	....	....	....	....	....	....	....	....	....	....	....	....	....	....	....	....	....	....
1992-93	CSKA Moscow	CIS	3	3	1	4	....	....	....	4	....	....	....	....	....	....	....	....	....	....	....	....	....	....	....	....	....	....
	Quebec Nordiques	**NHL**	**81**	**27**	**41**	**68**	**22**	**28**	**50**	**57**	**8**	**1**	**4**	**153**	**17.6**	**102**	**29**	**62**	**2**	**13**	**4**	**1**	**0**	**1**	**2**	**0**	**0**	**0**
1993-94	**Quebec Nordiques**	**NHL**	**58**	**16**	**17**	**33**	**15**	**13**	**28**	**46**	**5**	**0**	**4**	**92**	**17.4**	**47**	**17**	**35**	**0**	**–5**	....	....	....	....	....	....	....	....
	Russia	WC-A	6	5	4	9	....	....	....	2	....	....	....	....	....	....	....	....	....	....	....	....	....	....	....	....	....	....
1994-95	Lada Togliatti	CIS	11	9	2	11	....	....	....	14	....	....	....	....	....	....	....	....	....	....	....	....	....	....	....	....	....	....
	Quebec Nordiques	**NHL**	**45**	**14**	**10**	**24**	**25**	**15**	**40**	**31**	**1**	**0**	**3**	**63**	**22.2**	**42**	**10**	**36**	**0**	**–4**	**6**	**0**	**1**	**1**	**2**	**0**	**0**	**0**
1995-96	**Colorado Avalanche**	**NHL**	**26**	**11**	**11**	**22**	**11**	**9**	**20**	**16**	**3**	**0**	**3**	**46**	**23.9**	**31**	**12**	**8**	**0**	**11**	....	....	....	....	....	....	....	....
	Montreal Canadiens	**NHL**	**51**	**17**	**17**	**34**	**17**	**14**	**31**	**33**	**3**	**0**	**3**	**85**	**20.0**	**56**	**15**	**32**	**0**	**9**	**6**	**0**	**0**	**0**	**6**	**0**	**0**	**0**
1996-97	Russia	W-Cup	5	2	0	2	....	....	....	4	....	....	....	....	....	....	....	....	....	....	....	....	....	....	....	....	....	....
	Edmonton Oilers	**NHL**	**74**	**32**	**27**	**59**	**34**	**24**	**58**	**81**	**14**	**0**	**2**	**163**	**19.6**	**93**	**47**	**51**	**0**	**–5**	**12**	**4**	**3**	**7**	**6**	**3**	**0**	**0**
1997-98	**Edmonton Oilers**	**NHL**	**59**	**6**	**17**	**23**	**7**	**17**	**24**	**28**	**1**	**0**	**2**	**89**	**6.7**	**38**	**19**	**33**	**0**	**–14**	**1**	**0**	**0**	**0**	**2**	**0**	**0**	**0**
	Russia	Olympics	6	4	1	5	....	....	....	14	....	....	....	....	....	....	....	....	....	....	....	....	....	....	....	....	....	....
1998-99	**Edmonton Oilers**	**NHL**	**43**	**13**	**14**	**27**	**15**	**13**	**28**	**30**	**2**	**0**	**3**	**75**	**17.3**	**43**	**17**	**30**	**0**	**–4**	....	....	....	....	....	....	....	....
	Philadelphia Flyers	**NHL**	**13**	**0**	**1**	**1**	**0**	**1**	**1**	**2**	**0**	**0**	**0**	**8**	**0.0**	**1**	**1**	**5**	**0**	**–5**	....	....	....	....	....	....	....	....
	Carolina Hurricanes	**NHL**	**18**	**6**	**6**	**12**	**7**	**6**	**13**	**0**	**1**	**0**	**1**	**21**	**28.6**	**16**	**3**	**10**	**0**	**3**	**4**	**0**	**2**	**2**	**2**	**0**	**0**	**0**
99-2000	**Carolina Hurricanes**	**NHL**	**76**	**15**	**24**	**39**	**17**	**22**	**39**	**38**	**2**	**0**	**3**	**114**	**13.2**	**53**	**10**	**56**	**0**	**–13**	....	....	....	....	....	....	....	....
	Russia	WC-A	6	0	0	0	....	....	....	0	....	....	....	....	....	....	....	....	....	....	....	....	....	....	....	....	....	....
	NHL Totals		**544**	**157**	**185**	**342**	**170**	**162**	**332**	**362**	**40**	**1**	**28**	**909**	**17.3**	**522**	**180**	**358**	**2**		**33**	**5**	**6**	**11**	**20**	**3**	**0**	**0**

Transferred to **Colorado** after **Quebec** franchise relocated, June 21, 1995. Traded to **Montreal** by **Colorado** with Martin Rucinsky and Jocelyn Thibault for Patrick Roy and Mike Keane, December 6, 1995. Traded to **Edmonton** by **Montreal** for Scott Thornton, September 6, 1996. Traded to **Philadelphia** by **Edmonton** for Alexandre Daigle, January 29, 1999. Traded to **Carolina** by **Philadelphia** for Adam Burt, March 6, 1999.

• KOVALEV, Alexei

RW – L. 6'2", 215 lbs. b: Togliatti, USSR, 2/24/1973. NY Rangers' 1st, 15th overall, in 1991.

Season	Club	League	GP	G	A	Pts	AG	AA	APts	PIM	PP	SH	GW	S	%	TGF	PGF	TGA	PGA	+/-	GP	G	A	Pts	PIM	PP	SH	GW
1989-90	Dynamo Moscow	USSR	1	0	0	0	....	....	....	0	....	....	....	....	....	....	....	....	....	....	....	....	....	....	....	....	....	....
	Soviet Union	EJC-A	6	4	3	7	....	....	....	6	....	....	....	....	....	....	....	....	....	....	....	....	....	....	....	....	....	....
1990-91	Dynamo Moscow	Fr-Tour	1	0	0	0	....	....	....	0	....	....	....	....	....	....	....	....	....	....	....	....	....	....	....	....	....	....
	Dynamo Moscow	USSR	18	1	2	3	....	....	....	4	....	....	....	....	....	....	....	....	....	....	....	....	....	....	....	....	....	....
	Dynamo Moscow	Super-S	1	0	0	0	....	....	....	0	....	....	....	....	....	....	....	....	....	....	....	....	....	....	....	....	....	....
	Soviet Union	EJC-A	5	8	3	11	....	....	....	8	....	....	....	....	....	....	....	....	....	....	....	....	....	....	....	....	....	....
1991-92	Dynamo Moscow	CIS	33	16	9	25	....	....	....	20	....	....	....	....	....	....	....	....	....	....	....	....	....	....	....	....	....	....
	Russia	WJC-A	7	5	5	10	....	....	....	2	....	....	....	....	....	....	....	....	....	....	....	....	....	....	....	....	....	....
	Russia	Olympics	8	1	2	3	....	....	....	14	....	....	....	....	....	....	....	....	....	....	....	....	....	....	....	....	....	....
	Russia	WC-A	6	0	1	1	....	....	....	0	....	....	....	....	....	....	....	....	....	....	....	....	....	....	....	....	....	....
1992-93	**New York Rangers**	**NHL**	**65**	**20**	**18**	**38**	**17**	**12**	**29**	**79**	**3**	**0**	**3**	**134**	**14.9**	**54**	**15**	**50**	**1**	**–10**	....	....	....	....	....	....	....	....
	Binghamton Rangers	AHL	13	13	11	24	....	....	....	35	....	....	....	....	....	....	....	....	....	....	9	3	5	8	14	....	....	....
1993-94♦	**New York Rangers**	**NHL**	**76**	**23**	**33**	**56**	**21**	**26**	**47**	**154**	**7**	**0**	**3**	**184**	**12.5**	**80**	**22**	**47**	**7**	**18**	**23**	**9**	**12**	**21**	**18**	**5**	**0**	**2**
1994-95	Lada Togliatti	CIS	12	8	8	16	....	....	....	49	....	....	....	....	....	....	....	....	....	....	....	....	....	....	....	....	....	....
	New York Rangers	**NHL**	**48**	**13**	**15**	**28**	**23**	**22**	**45**	**30**	**1**	**1**	**1**	**103**	**12.6**	**42**	**11**	**39**	**2**	**–6**	**10**	**4**	**7**	**11**	**10**	**0**	**0**	**0**
1995-96	**New York Rangers**	**NHL**	**81**	**24**	**34**	**58**	**24**	**28**	**52**	**98**	**8**	**1**	**7**	**206**	**11.7**	**85**	**28**	**60**	**8**	**5**	**11**	**3**	**4**	**7**	**14**	**0**	**0**	**1**
1996-97	Russia	W-Cup	5	2	1	3	....	....	....	8	....	....	....	....	....	....	....	....	....	....	....	....	....	....	....	....	....	....
	New York Rangers	**NHL**	**45**	**13**	**22**	**35**	**14**	**20**	**34**	**42**	**1**	**0**	**0**	**110**	**11.8**	**50**	**15**	**33**	**9**	**11**	....	....	....	....	....	....	....	....
1997-98	**New York Rangers**	**NHL**	**73**	**23**	**30**	**53**	**27**	**29**	**56**	**44**	**8**	**0**	**3**	**173**	**13.3**	**83**	**40**	**65**	**0**	**–22**	....	....	....	....	....	....	....	....
	Russia	WC-A	6	5	2	7	....	....	....	14	....	....	....	....	....	....	....	....	....	....	....	....	....	....	....	....	....	....
1998-99	**New York Rangers**	**NHL**	**14**	**3**	**4**	**7**	**4**	**4**	**8**	**12**	**1**	**0**	**1**	**35**	**8.6**	**10**	**4**	**12**	**0**	**–6**	....	....	....	....	....	....	....	....
	Pittsburgh Penguins	**NHL**	**63**	**20**	**26**	**46**	**23**	**25**	**48**	**37**	**5**	**1**	**4**	**156**	**12.8**	**88**	**30**	**53**	**3**	**8**	**10**	**5**	**7**	**12**	**14**	**0**	**0**	**1**
	Belarus	WC-A	6	2	2	4	....	....	....	2	....	....	....	....	....	....	....	....	....	....	....	....	....	....	....	....	....	....
99-2000	**Pittsburgh Penguins**	**NHL**	**82**	**26**	**40**	**66**	**29**	**37**	**66**	**94**	**9**	**2**	**4**	**254**	**10.2**	**96**	**42**	**68**	**11**	**–3**	**11**	**1**	**5**	**6**	**10**	**0**	**0**	**0**
	NHL Totals		**547**	**165**	**222**	**387**	**182**	**203**	**385**	**590**	**43**	**5**	**26**	**1355**	**12.2**	**588**	**207**	**427**	**41**		**65**	**22**	**35**	**57**	**66**	**5**	**0**	**4**

WJC-A All-Star Team (1992)

Traded to **Pittsburgh** by **NY Rangers** with Harry York for Petr Nedved, Chris Tamer and Sean Pronger, November 25, 1998.

• KOWAL, Joe

Joseph Douglas LW – L. 6'5", 212 lbs. b: Toronto, Ont., 2/3/1956. Buffalo's 1st, 33rd overall, in 1976.

Season	Club	League	GP	G	A	Pts	AG	AA	APts	PIM	PP	SH	GW	S	%	TGF	PGF	TGA	PGA	+/-	GP	G	A	Pts	PIM	PP	SH	GW
1973-74	Whitby Knob Hill Farms	OHA-B	38	12	13	25	....	....	....	47	....	....	....	....	....	....	....	....	....	....	....	....	....	....	....	....	....	....
1974-75	Oshawa Generals	OMJHL	61	18	26	44	....	....	....	93	....	....	....	....	....	....	....	....	....	....	5	1	0	1	12	....	....	....
1975-76	Oshawa Generals	OMJHL	4	0	2	2	....	....	....	13	....	....	....	....	....	....	....	....	....	....	....	....	....	....	....	....	....	....
	Hamilton Fincups	OMJHL	52	32	45	77	....	....	....	100	....	....	....	....	....	....	....	....	....	....	10	5	4	9	39	....	....	....
	Hamilton Fincups	Mem-Cup	3	1	0	1	....	....	....	17	....	....	....	....	....	....	....	....	....	....	....	....	....	....	....	....	....	....
1976-77	**Buffalo Sabres**	**NHL**	**16**	**0**	**5**	**5**	**0**	**4**	**4**	**6**	**0**	**0**	**0**	**6**	**0.0**	**11**	**0**	**8**	**0**	**3**	....	....	....	....	....	....	....	....
	Hershey Bears	AHL	46	13	17	30	....	....	....	75	....	....	....	....	....	....	....	....	....	....	2	0	0	0	8	....	....	....
1977-78	**Buffalo Sabres**	**NHL**	**6**	**0**	**0**	**0**	**0**	**0**	**0**	**7**	**0**	**0**	**0**	**3**	**0.0**	**1**	**1**	**0**	**0**	**0**	**2**	**0**	**0**	**0**	**0**	**0**	**0**	**0**
	Hershey Bears	AHL	45	14	16	30	....	....	....	48	....	....	....	....	....	....	....	....	....	....	....	....	....	....	....	....	....	....
1978-79	Springfield Indians	AHL	12	3	3	6	....	....	....	10	....	....	....	....	....	....	....	....	....	....	....	....	....	....	....	....	....	....
	Binghamton Dusters	AHL	52	17	31	48	....	....	....	75	....	....	....	....	....	....	....	....	....	....	10	1	1	2	16	....	....	....
1979-80	Rochester Americans	AHL	66	20	27	47	....	....	....	139	....	....	....	....	....	....	....	....	....	....	3	0	0	0	4	....	....	....
1980-81	Nova Scotia Voyageurs	AHL	34	1	10	11	....	....	....	166	....	....	....	....	....	....	....	....	....	....	....	....	....	....	....	....	....	....
	NHL Totals		**22**	**0**	**5**	**5**	**0**	**4**	**4**	**13**	**0**	**0**	**0**	**9**	**0.0**	**12**	**1**	**8**	**0**		**2**	**0**	**0**	**0**	**0**	**0**	**0**	**0**

• KOZAK, Don

Donald RW – R. 5'11", 190 lbs. b: Saskatoon, Sask., 2/2/1952. Los Angeles' 1st, 20th overall, in 1972.

Season	Club	League	GP	G	A	Pts	AG	AA	APts	PIM	PP	SH	GW	S	%	TGF	PGF	TGA	PGA	+/-	GP	G	A	Pts	PIM	PP	SH	GW
1967-68	Saskatoon Blades	WCJHL	35	9	5	14	....	....	....	10	....	....	....	....	....	....	....	....	....	....	7	0	1	1	8	....	....	....
1968-69	Saskatoon Blades	WCJHL	26	5	6	11	....	....	....	43	....	....	....	....	....	....	....	....	....	....	4	0	0	0	0	....	....	....
1969-70	Swift Current Broncos	WCJHL	56	40	34	74	....	....	....	67	....	....	....	....	....	....	....	....	....	....	5	1	3	4	4	....	....	....
1970-71	Edmonton Oil Kings	WCJHL	66	60	61	121	....	....	....	122	....	....	....	....	....	....	....	....	....	....	17	9	16	25	49	....	....	....
	Edmonton Oil Kings	Mem-Cup	2	0	1	1	....	....	....	2	....	....	....	....	....	....	....	....	....	....	....	....	....	....	....	....	....	....
1971-72	Edmonton Oil Kings	WCJHL	68	55	50	105	....	....	....	183	....	....	....	....	....	....	....	....	....	....	16	7	7	14	18	....	....	....
	Edmonton Oil Kings	Mem-Cup	2	1	1	2	....	....	....	2	....	....	....	....	....	....	....	....	....	....	....	....	....	....	....	....	....	....
1972-73	**Los Angeles Kings**	**NHL**	**72**	**14**	**6**	**20**	**13**	**5**	**18**	**104**	**4**	**0**	**4**	**78**	**17.9**	**27**	**6**	**47**	**1**	**–25**	....	....	....	....	....	....	....	....
1973-74	**Los Angeles Kings**	**NHL**	**76**	**21**	**14**	**35**	**20**	**12**	**32**	**54**	**1**	**0**	**2**	**109**	**19.3**	**55**	**7**	**41**	**0**	**7**	**5**	**0**	**0**	**0**	**33**	**0**	**0**	**0**
1974-75	**Los Angeles Kings**	**NHL**	**77**	**16**	**15**	**31**	**14**	**11**	**25**	**64**	**2**	**0**	**6**	**109**	**14.7**	**48**	**13**	**30**	**0**	**5**	**3**	**1**	**1**	**2**	**7**	**0**	**0**	**0**
1975-76	**Los Angeles Kings**	**NHL**	**62**	**20**	**24**	**44**	**18**	**18**	**36**	**94**	**7**	**0**	**4**	**81**	**24.7**	**52**	**11**	**45**	**0**	**–4**	**9**	**1**	**0**	**1**	**12**	**0**	**0**	**1**
1976-77	**Los Angeles Kings**	**NHL**	**79**	**15**	**17**	**32**	**13**	**13**	**26**	**89**	**1**	**0**	**1**	**98**	**15.3**	**46**	**5**	**50**	**0**	**–9**	**9**	**4**	**1**	**5**	**17**	**1**	**0**	**0**
1977-78	**Los Angeles Kings**	**NHL**	**43**	**8**	**5**	**13**	**7**	**4**	**11**	**45**	**0**	**0**	**1**	**54**	**14.8**	**20**	**1**	**15**	**0**	**4**	....	....	....	....	....	....	....	....
	Springfield Indians	AHL	7	1	4	5	....	....	....	0	....	....	....	....	....	....	....	....	....	....	....	....	....	....	....	....	....	....
1978-79	Tulsa Oilers	CHL	29	15	10	25	....	....	....	44	....	....	....	....	....	....	....	....	....	....	....	....	....	....	....	....	....	....
	Vancouver Canucks	**NHL**	**28**	**2**	**5**	**7**	**2**	**4**	**6**	**30**	**1**	**0**	**0**	**29**	**6.9**	**13**	**2**	**27**	**1**	**–15**	**3**	**1**	**0**	**1**	**0**	**0**	**0**	**0**
	Dallas Black Hawks	CHL	7	2	4	6	....	....	....	9	....	....	....	....	....	....	....	....	....	....	....	....	....	....	....	....	....	....

Season	Club	League	GP	G	A	Pts	AG	AA	APts	PIM	PP	SH	GW	S	%	TGF	PGF	TGA	PGA	+/-	GP	G	A	Pts	PIM	PP	SH	GW
			REGULAR SEASON																		**PLAYOFFS**							
1979-80	Cincinnati Stingers	CHL	33	10	7	17				68																		
	Springfield Indians	AHL	51	9	17	26				48																		
1980-81	Binghamton Whalers	AHL	41	5	10	15				37																		
1981-82	EHC Straubing	Germany-3	21	19	11	30				16																		
	NHL Totals		**437**	**96**	**86**	**182**	**87**	**67**	**154**	**480**	**16**	**0**	**18**	**558**	**17.2**	**261**	**45**	**255**	**2**		**29**	**7**	**2**	**9**	**69**	**1**	**0**	**1**

WCJHL Second All-Star Team (1971, 1972)

Traded to **Vancouver** by **LA Kings** for Randy Holt, December 31, 1978. Claimed by **Hartford** from **Vancouver** in Expansion Draft, June 13, 1979.

• KOZLOV, Viktor

C – R. 6'5", 232 lbs. b: Togliatti, USSR, 2/14/1975. San Jose's 1st, 6th overall, in 1993.

Season	Club	League	GP	G	A	Pts	AG	AA	APts	PIM	PP	SH	GW	S	%	TGF	PGF	TGA	PGA	+/-	GP	G	A	Pts	PIM	PP	SH	GW
1990-91	Lada Togliatti	USSR 2	2	2	0	2				0																		
1991-92	Lada Togliatti	CIS	3	0	0	0				0																		
	Russia	EJC-A	6	3	3	6				2																		
1992-93	Dynamo Moscow	CIS	30	6	5	11				4											10	3	0	3	0			
	Russia	WJC-A	7	2	1	3				2																		
	Russia	EJC-A	6	3	3	6				4																		
1993-94	Dynamo Moscow	CIS	42	16	9	25				14											7	3	2	5	0			
1994-95	Dynamo Moscow	CIS	3	1	1	2				2																		
	San Jose Sharks	**NHL**	**16**	**2**	**0**	**2**	**4**	**0**	**4**	**2**	**0**	**0**	**0**	**23**	**8.7**	**6**	**3**	**8**	**0**	**–5**								
	Kansas City Blades	IHL	4	1	1	2				0											13	4	5	9	12			
1995-96	**San Jose Sharks**	**NHL**	**62**	**6**	**13**	**19**	**6**	**11**	**17**	**6**	**1**	**0**	**0**	**107**	**5.6**	**35**	**6**	**45**	**1**	**–15**								
	Kansas City Blades	IHL	15	4	7	11				12																		
	Russia	WC-A	8	0	3	3				0																		
1996-97	**San Jose Sharks**	**NHL**	**78**	**16**	**25**	**41**	**17**	**22**	**39**	**40**	**4**	**0**	**4**	**184**	**8.7**	**59**	**18**	**59**	**2**	**–16**								
1997-98	**San Jose Sharks**	**NHL**	**18**	**5**	**2**	**7**	**6**	**2**	**8**	**2**	**2**	**0**	**0**	**51**	**9.8**	**11**	**4**	**9**	**0**	**–2**								
	Florida Panthers	**NHL**	**46**	**12**	**11**	**23**	**14**	**11**	**25**	**14**	**3**	**2**	**0**	**114**	**10.5**	**38**	**11**	**35**	**7**	**–1**								
	Russia	WC-A	6	4	5	9				0																		
1998-99	**Florida Panthers**	**NHL**	**65**	**16**	**35**	**51**	**19**	**34**	**53**	**24**	**5**	**1**	**1**	**209**	**7.7**	**74**	**27**	**41**	**7**	**13**								
99-2000	**Florida Panthers**	**NHL**	**80**	**17**	**53**	**70**	**19**	**49**	**68**	**16**	**6**	**0**	**2**	**223**	**7.6**	**97**	**27**	**57**	**11**	**24**	**4**	**0**	**1**	**1**	**0**	**0**	**0**	**0**
	Russia	WC-A	6	1	3	4				2																		
	NHL Totals		**365**	**74**	**139**	**213**	**85**	**129**	**214**	**104**	**21**	**3**	**7**	**911**	**8.1**	**320**	**96**	**254**	**28**		**4**	**0**	**1**	**1**	**0**	**0**	**0**	**0**

EJC-A All-Star Team (1993) • Played in NHL All-Star Game (2000)

Traded to **Florida** by **San Jose** with Florida's 5th round choice (previously acquired, Florida selected Jaroslav Spacek) in 1998 Entry Draft for Dave Lowry and Florida's 1st round choice (later traded to Tampa Bay - Tampa Bay selected Vincent Lecavalier) in 1998 Entry Draft, November 13, 1997.

• KOZLOV, Vyacheslav

C – L. 5'10", 180 lbs. b: Voskresensk, USSR, 5/3/1972. Detroit's 2nd, 45th overall, in 1990.

Season	Club	League	GP	G	A	Pts	AG	AA	APts	PIM	PP	SH	GW	S	%	TGF	PGF	TGA	PGA	+/-	GP	G	A	Pts	PIM	PP	SH	GW
1987-88	Khimik Voskresensk	USSR	2	0	0	0				0																		
	Soviet Union	EJC-A	5	2	1	3				4																		
1988-89	Khimik Voskresensk	USSR	14	0	1	1				2																		
	Soviet Union	EJC-A	6	5	7	12				8																		
1989-90	Khimik Voskresensk	Fr-Tour	DID NOT PLAY																									
	Khimik Voskresensk	USSR	45	14	12	26				38																		
	Soviet Union	WJC-A	7	4	7	11				0																		
	Soviet Union	EJC-A	6	9	10	19				11																		
1990-91	Khimik Voskresensk	Fr-Tour	1	2	0	2				0																		
	Khimik Voskresensk	USSR	45	11	13	24				46																		
	Soviet Union	WJC-A	7	3	9	12				12																		
	Soviet Union	WEC-A	10	3	4	7				10																		
1991-92	Soviet Union	Can-Cup	5	1	2	3				6																		
	CSKA Moscow	CIS	11	6	5	11				12																		
	Detroit Red Wings	**NHL**	**7**	**0**	**2**	**2**	**0**	**2**	**2**	**2**	**0**	**0**	**0**	**9**	**0.0**	**2**	**0**	**4**	**0**	**–2**								
1992-93	**Detroit Red Wings**	**NHL**	**17**	**4**	**1**	**5**	**3**	**1**	**4**	**14**	**0**	**0**	**0**	**26**	**15.4**	**12**	**2**	**11**	**0**	**–1**	**4**	**0**	**2**	**2**	**2**	**0**	**0**	**0**
	Adirondack Red Wings	AHL	45	23	36	59				54											4	1	1	2	4			
1993-94	**Detroit Red Wings**	**NHL**	**77**	**34**	**39**	**73**	**32**	**30**	**62**	**50**	**8**	**2**	**6**	**202**	**16.8**	**104**	**28**	**57**	**8**	**27**	**7**	**2**	**5**	**7**	**12**	**0**	**0**	**0**
	Adirondack Red Wings	AHL	3	0	1	1				15																		
	Russia	WC-A	1	0	0	0				4																		
1994-95	CSKA Moscow	CIS	10	3	4	7				14																		
	Detroit Red Wings	**NHL**	**46**	**13**	**20**	**33**	**23**	**30**	**53**	**45**	**5**	**0**	**3**	**97**	**13.4**	**53**	**18**	**23**	**0**	**12**	**18**	**9**	**7**	**16**	**10**	**1**	**0**	**4**
1995-96	**Detroit Red Wings**	**NHL**	**82**	**36**	**37**	**73**	**35**	**30**	**65**	**70**	**9**	**0**	**7**	**237**	**15.2**	**101**	**28**	**43**	**3**	**33**	**19**	**5**	**7**	**12**	**10**	**2**	**0**	**1**
1996-97	Russia	W-Cup	5	1	2	3				8																		
♦	**Detroit Red Wings**	**NHL**	**75**	**23**	**22**	**45**	**24**	**20**	**44**	**46**	**3**	**0**	**6**	**211**	**10.9**	**67**	**11**	**35**	**0**	**21**	**20**	**8**	**5**	**13**	**14**	**4**	**0**	**2**
1997-98♦	**Detroit Red Wings**	**NHL**	**80**	**25**	**27**	**52**	**29**	**26**	**55**	**46**	**6**	**0**	**1**	**221**	**11.3**	**84**	**27**	**45**	**2**	**14**	**22**	**6**	**8**	**14**	**10**	**1**	**0**	**4**
1998-99	**Detroit Red Wings**	**NHL**	**79**	**29**	**29**	**58**	**34**	**28**	**62**	**45**	**6**	**1**	**4**	**209**	**13.9**	**76**	**30**	**37**	**1**	**10**	**10**	**6**	**1**	**7**	**4**	**3**	**0**	**0**
99-2000	**Detroit Red Wings**	**NHL**	**72**	**18**	**18**	**36**	**20**	**17**	**37**	**28**	**4**	**0**	**3**	**165**	**10.9**	**62**	**15**	**42**	**6**	**11**	**8**	**2**	**1**	**3**	**12**	**1**	**0**	**1**
	NHL Totals		**535**	**182**	**195**	**377**	**200**	**184**	**384**	**346**	**41**	**3**	**30**	**1377**	**13.2**	**561**	**159**	**297**	**20**		**108**	**38**	**36**	**74**	**74**	**12**	**0**	**12**

USSR Rookie of the Year (1990)

• KRAKE, Skip

Philip Gordon C – R. 5'11", 170 lbs. b: North Battleford, Sask., 10/14/1943.

Season	Club	League	GP	G	A	Pts	AG	AA	APts	PIM	PP	SH	GW	S	%	TGF	PGF	TGA	PGA	+/-	GP	G	A	Pts	PIM	PP	SH	GW
1960-61	Estevan Bruins	SJHL	11	3	1	4				4											11	0	3	3	0			
1961-62	Estevan Bruins	SJHL	42	25	15	40				42											10	3	4	7	10			
1962-63	Estevan Bruins	SJHL	54	26	37	63				126											11	11	10	21	35			
	Estevan Bruins	Mem-Cup	6	2	1	3				2																		
1963-64	Estevan Bruins	SJHL	60	59	56	115				142											10	13	9	22	16			
	Boston Bruins	**NHL**	**2**	**0**	**0**	**0**	**0**	**0**	**0**	**0**																		
	Estevan Bruins	Mem-Cup	6	0	2	2				14																		
1964-65	Minneapolis Bruins	CHL	69	22	24	46				33											5	1	2	3	11			
1965-66	**Boston Bruins**	**NHL**	**2**	**0**	**0**	**0**	**0**	**0**	**0**	**0**																		
	Oklahoma City Blazers	CHL	70	24	37	61				97											9	4	6	10	11			
1966-67	**Boston Bruins**	**NHL**	**15**	**6**	**2**	**8**	**7**	**2**	**9**	**4**																		
	Oklahoma City Blazers	CHL	49	15	18	33				107																		
1967-68	**Boston Bruins**	**NHL**	**68**	**5**	**7**	**12**	**6**	**7**	**13**	**13**	**0**	**3**	**0**	**48**	**10.4**	**23**	**2**	**25**	**13**	**9**	**4**	**0**	**0**	**0**	**2**	**0**	**0**	**0**
1968-69	**Los Angeles Kings**	**NHL**	**30**	**3**	**9**	**12**	**3**	**8**	**11**	**11**	**1**	**0**	**0**	**52**	**5.8**	**15**	**7**	**25**	**7**	**–10**	**6**	**1**	**0**	**1**	**15**	**0**	**0**	**0**
	Springfield Kings	AHL	43	8	23	31				67																		
1969-70	**Los Angeles Kings**	**NHL**	**58**	**5**	**17**	**22**	**5**	**16**	**21**	**86**	**2**	**1**	**0**	**101**	**5.0**	**30**	**8**	**60**	**13**	**–25**								
1970-71	**Buffalo Sabres**	**NHL**	**74**	**4**	**5**	**9**	**4**	**4**	**8**	**68**	**1**	**0**	**0**	**64**	**6.3**	**15**	**1**	**58**	**23**	**–21**								
1971-72	Salt Lake Golden Eagles	WHL	53	15	36	51				59																		
1972-73	Cleveland Crusaders	WHA	26	9	10	19				61											9	1	2	3	27			
1973-74	Cleveland Crusaders	WHA	69	20	36	56				94											5	0	1	1	39			
1974-75	Cleveland Crusaders	WHA	71	15	23	38				108											5	1	1	2	0			
1975-76	Edmonton Oilers	WHA	41	8	8	16				55																		
	NHL Totals		**249**	**23**	**40**	**63**	**25**	**37**	**62**	**182**											**10**	**1**	**0**	**1**	**17**			
	Other Major League Totals		207	52	77	129				318											19	2	4	6	66			

SJHL Second All-Star Team (1964)

Traded to **LA Kings** by **Boston** for LA Kings' 1st round choice (Reggie Leach) in 1970 Amateur Draft, May 20, 1968. Claimed by **Buffalo** from **LA Kings** in Expansion Draft, June 10, 1970. Selected by **Calgary-Cleveland** (WHA) in 1972 WHA General Player Draft, February 12, 1972. Traded to **Edmonton** (WHA) by **Cleveland** (WHA) for Ray McKay, August, 1975.

• KRAVCHUK, Igor

D – L. 6'1", 218 lbs. b: Ufa, USSR, 9/13/1966. Chicago's 5th, 71st overall, in 1991.

			REGULAR SEASON																		PLAYOFFS							
Season	Club	League	GP	G	A	Pts	AG	AA	APts	PIM	PP	SH	GW	S	%	TGF	PGF	TGA	PGA	+/-	GP	G	A	Pts	PIM	PP	SH	GW
1983-84	Salavat Yulayev	USSR-Jr.	STATISTICS NOT AVAILABLE																									
	Soviet Union	EJC-A	5	1	1	2	....	....	....	6	....	....	....	....	....	....	....	....	....	....	....	....	....	....	....	....	....	....
1984-85	Salavat Yulayev	USSR-2	50	3	2	5	....	....	....	22	....	....	....	....	....	....	....	....	....	....	....	....	....	....	....	....	....	....
	Soviet Union	WJC-A	7	0	3	3	....	....	....	6	....	....	....	....	....	....	....	....	....	....	....	....	....	....	....	....	....	....
1985-86	Salavat Yulayev	USSR	21	2	2	4	....	....	....	6	....	....	....	....	....	....	....	....	....	....	....	....	....	....	....	....	....	....
	Soviet Union	WJC-A	7	0	2	2	....	....	....	4	....	....	....	....	....	....	....	....	....	....	....	....	....	....	....	....	....	....
1986-87	Salavat Yulayev	USSR	22	0	1	1	....	....	....	8	....	....	....	....	....	....	....	....	....	....	....	....	....	....	....	....	....	....
1987-88	Soviet Union	Can-Cup	5	0	4	4	....	....	....	2	....	....	....	....	....	....	....	....	....	....	....	....	....	....	....	....	....	....
	CSKA Moscow	USSR	48	1	8	9	....	....	....	12	....	....	....	....	....	....	....	....	....	....	....	....	....	....	....	....	....	....
	Soviet Union	Olympics	6	1	0	1	....	....	....	0	....	....	....	....	....	....	....	....	....	....	....	....	....	....	....	....	....	....
1988-89	CSKA Moscow	USSR	22	3	3	6	....	....	....	2	....	....	....	....	....	....	....	....	....	....	....	....	....	....	....	....	....	....
1989-90	CSKA Moscow	Fr-Tour	1	0	0	0	....	....	....	2	....	....	....	....	....	....	....	....	....	....	....	....	....	....	....	....	....	....
	CSKA Moscow	USSR	48	1	3	4	....	....	....	16	....	....	....	....	....	....	....	....	....	....	....	....	....	....	....	....	....	....
	CSKA Moscow	Super-S	5	0	3	3	....	....	....	0	....	....	....	....	....	....	....	....	....	....	....	....	....	....	....	....	....	....
	Soviet Union	WEC-A	10	1	4	5	....	....	....	8	....	....	....	....	....	....	....	....	....	....	....	....	....	....	....	....	....	....
1990-91	CSKA Moscow	Fr-Tour	1	0	0	0	....	....	....	0	....	....	....	....	....	....	....	....	....	....	....	....	....	....	....	....	....	....
	CSKA Moscow	USSR	41	6	5	11	....	....	....	16	....	....	....	....	....	....	....	....	....	....	....	....	....	....	....	....	....	....
	CSKA Moscow	Super-S	7	0	2	2	....	....	....	0	....	....	....	....	....	....	....	....	....	....	....	....	....	....	....	....	....	....
	Soviet Union	WEC-A	10	1	3	4	....	....	....	8	....	....	....	....	....	....	....	....	....	....	....	....	....	....	....	....	....	....
1991-92	Soviet Union	Can-Cup	5	0	0	0	....	....	....	2	....	....	....	....	....	....	....	....	....	....	....	....	....	....	....	....	....	....
	CSKA Moscow	CIS	30	3	8	11	....	....	....	6	....	....	....	....	....	....	....	....	....	....	....	....	....	....	....	....	....	....
	Russia	Olympics	8	3	2	5	....	....	....	6	....	....	....	....	....	....	....	....	....	....	....	....	....	....	....	....	....	....
	Chicago Blackhawks	**NHL**	**18**	**1**	**8**	**9**	**1**	**6**	**7**	**4**	**0**	**0**	**1**	**40**	**2.5**	**22**	**9**	**20**	**4**	**–3**	**18**	**2**	**6**	**8**	**8**	**1**	**0**	**0**
1992-93	**Chicago Blackhawks**	**NHL**	**38**	**6**	**9**	**15**	**5**	**6**	**11**	**30**	**3**	**0**	**0**	**101**	**5.9**	**39**	**9**	**29**	**10**	**11**	....	....	....	....	....	....	....	....
	Edmonton Oilers	**NHL**	**17**	**4**	**8**	**12**	**3**	**5**	**8**	**2**	**1**	**0**	**0**	**42**	**9.5**	**19**	**5**	**28**	**6**	**–8**	....	....	....	....	....	....	....	....
1993-94	**Edmonton Oilers**	**NHL**	**81**	**12**	**38**	**50**	**11**	**30**	**41**	**16**	**5**	**0**	**2**	**197**	**6.1**	**109**	**37**	**113**	**29**	**–12**	....	....	....	....	....	....	....	....
1994-95	**Edmonton Oilers**	**NHL**	**36**	**7**	**11**	**18**	**12**	**16**	**28**	**29**	**3**	**1**	**0**	**93**	**7.5**	**48**	**25**	**52**	**14**	**–15**	....	....	....	....	....	....	....	....
1995-96	**Edmonton Oilers**	**NHL**	**26**	**4**	**4**	**8**	**4**	**3**	**7**	**10**	**3**	**0**	**0**	**59**	**6.8**	**30**	**16**	**35**	**8**	**–13**	....	....	....	....	....	....	....	....
	St. Louis Blues	**NHL**	**40**	**3**	**12**	**15**	**3**	**10**	**13**	**24**	**0**	**0**	**1**	**114**	**2.6**	**47**	**13**	**55**	**15**	**–6**	**10**	**1**	**5**	**6**	**4**	**0**	**0**	**1**
1996-97	**St. Louis Blues**	**NHL**	**82**	**4**	**24**	**28**	**4**	**21**	**25**	**35**	**1**	**0**	**0**	**142**	**2.8**	**95**	**20**	**93**	**25**	**7**	**2**	**0**	**0**	**0**	**2**	**0**	**0**	**0**
1997-98	**Ottawa Senators**	**NHL**	**81**	**8**	**27**	**35**	**9**	**26**	**35**	**8**	**3**	**1**	**1**	**191**	**4.2**	**85**	**31**	**89**	**16**	**–19**	**11**	**2**	**3**	**5**	**4**	**0**	**0**	**0**
	Russia	Olympics	6	0	2	2	....	....	....	2	....	....	....	....	....	....	....	....	....	....	....	....	....	....	....	....	....	....
1998-99	**Ottawa Senators**	**NHL**	**79**	**4**	**21**	**25**	**5**	**20**	**25**	**32**	**3**	**0**	**0**	**171**	**2.3**	**96**	**35**	**57**	**10**	**14**	**4**	**0**	**0**	**0**	**0**	**0**	**0**	**0**
99-2000	**Ottawa Senators**	**NHL**	**64**	**6**	**12**	**18**	**7**	**11**	**18**	**20**	**5**	**0**	**1**	**126**	**4.8**	**61**	**22**	**49**	**5**	**–5**	**6**	**1**	**1**	**2**	**0**	**0**	**0**	**0**
	Russia	WC-A	6	0	0	0	....	....	....	0	....	....	....	....	....	....	....	....	....	....	....	....	....	....	....	....	....	....
	NHL Totals		**562**	**59**	**174**	**233**	**64**	**154**	**218**	**210**	**27**	**2**	**6**	**1276**	**4.6**	**651**	**222**	**620**	**142**		**51**	**6**	**15**	**21**	**18**	**1**	**0**	**1**

Played in NHL All-Star Game (1999)

Traded to **Edmonton** by **Chicago** with Dean McAmmond for Joe Murphy, February 24, 1993. Traded to **St. Louis** by **Edmonton** with Ken Sutton for Jeff Norton and Donald Dufresne, January 4, 1996. Traded to **Ottawa** by **St. Louis** for Steve Duchesne, August 25, 1997.

• KRAVETS, Mikhail

RW – L. 5'10", 195 lbs. b: Leningrad, USSR, 11/12/1963. San Jose's 13th, 243rd overall, in 1991.

Season	Club	League	GP	G	A	Pts	AG	AA	APts	PIM	PP	SH	GW	S	%	TGF	PGF	TGA	PGA	+/-	GP	G	A	Pts	PIM	PP	SH	GW
1985-86	SKA Leningrad	USSR	38	14	7	21	....	....	....	20	....	....	....	....	....	....	....	....	....	....	....	....	....	....	....	....	....	....
1986-87	SKA Leningrad	USSR	36	16	11	27	....	....	....	37	....	....	....	....	....	....	....	....	....	....	....	....	....	....	....	....	....	....
1987-88	SKA Leningrad	USSR	44	9	5	14	....	....	....	36	....	....	....	....	....	....	....	....	....	....	....	....	....	....	....	....	....	....
1988-89	SKA Leningrad	USSR	43	8	18	26	....	....	....	20	....	....	....	....	....	....	....	....	....	....	....	....	....	....	....	....	....	....
1989-90	SKA Leningrad	Fr-Tour	1	0	0	0	....	....	....	2	....	....	....	....	....	....	....	....	....	....	....	....	....	....	....	....	....	....
	SKA Leningrad	USSR	30	10	14	24	....	....	....	36	....	....	....	....	....	....	....	....	....	....	....	....	....	....	....	....	....	....
1990-91	Torpedo Yaroslavl	Fr-Tour	1	0	0	0	....	....	....	0	....	....	....	....	....	....	....	....	....	....	....	....	....	....	....	....	....	....
	SKA Leningrad	USSR	25	8	8	16	....	....	....	28	....	....	....	....	....	....	....	....	....	....	....	....	....	....	....	....	....	....
1991-92	**San Jose Sharks**	**NHL**	**1**	**0**	**0**	**0**	**0**	**0**	**0**	**0**	**0**	**0**	**0**	**2**	**0.0**	**0**	**0**	**0**	**0**	**0**	....	....	....	....	....	....	....	....
	Kansas City Blades	IHL	74	10	32	42	....	....	....	172	....	....	....	....	....	....	....	....	....	....	15	6	8	14	12	....	....	....
1992-93	**San Jose Sharks**	**NHL**	**1**	**0**	**0**	**0**	**0**	**0**	**0**	**0**	**0**	**0**	**0**	**0**	**0.0**	**0**	**0**	**1**	**0**	**–1**	....	....	....	....	....	....	....	....
	Kansas City Blades	IHL	71	19	49	68	....	....	....	153	....	....	....	....	....	....	....	....	....	....	10	2	5	7	55	....	....	....
1993-94	Kansas City Blades	IHL	63	14	44	58	....	....	....	171	....	....	....	....	....	....	....	....	....	....	....	....	....	....	....	....	....	....
1994-95	Detroit Vipers	IHL	7	0	0	0	....	....	....	4	....	....	....	....	....	....	....	....	....	....	....	....	....	....	....	....	....	....
	Minnesota Moose	IHL	37	7	15	22	....	....	....	25	....	....	....	....	....	....	....	....	....	....	....	....	....	....	....	....	....	....
	Syracuse Crunch	AHL	7	2	2	4	....	....	....	8	....	....	....	....	....	....	....	....	....	....	....	....	....	....	....	....	....	....
1995-96	Wichita Thunder	CHL	37	14	57	71	....	....	....	89	....	....	....	....	....	....	....	....	....	....	....	....	....	....	....	....	....	....
	Milwaukee Admirals	IHL	7	0	1	1	....	....	....	4	....	....	....	....	....	....	....	....	....	....	....	....	....	....	....	....	....	....
1996-97	Louisiana IceGators	ECHL	57	22	45	67	....	....	....	93	....	....	....	....	....	....	....	....	....	....	17	4	9	13	18	....	....	....
1997-98	Baton Rouge Kingfish	ECHL	11	2	9	11	....	....	....	37	....	....	....	....	....	....	....	....	....	....	....	....	....	....	....	....	....	....
	Louisiana IceGators	ECHL	28	8	18	26	....	....	....	41	....	....	....	....	....	....	....	....	....	....	....	....	....	....	....	....	....	....
	New Orleans Brass	ECHL	4	1	0	1	....	....	....	2	....	....	....	....	....	....	....	....	....	....	....	....	....	....	....	....	....	....
	Mississippi Sea Wolves	ECHL	10	4	10	14	....	....	....	25	....	....	....	....	....	....	....	....	....	....	....	....	....	....	....	....	....	....
1998-99	Mississippi Sea Wolves	ECHL	59	17	42	59	....	....	....	136	....	....	....	....	....	....	....	....	....	....	18	5	8	13	10	....	....	....
99-2000	Arkansas RiverBlades	ECHL	30	10	17	27	....	....	....	64	....	....	....	....	....	....	....	....	....	....	....	....	....	....	....	....	....	....
	Mississippi Sea Wolves	ECHL	23	7	20	27	....	....	....	27	....	....	....	....	....	....	....	....	....	....	7	1	6	7	8	....	....	....
	NHL Totals		**2**	**0**	**0**	**0**	**0**	**0**	**0**	**0**	**0**	**0**	**0**	**2**	**0.0**	**0**	**0**	**1**	**0**		....	....	....	....	....	....	....	....

Signed to 25-game try-out contract by **Mississippi** (ECHL) after release by **Arkansas** (ECHL), February 4, 2000. Signed as a free agent by **Mississippi** (ECHL), June 6, 2000.

• KRENTZ, Dale

Dale M. LW – L. 5'11", 190 lbs. b: Steinbach, Man., 12/19/1961.

Season	Club	League	GP	G	A	Pts	AG	AA	APts	PIM	PP	SH	GW	S	%	TGF	PGF	TGA	PGA	+/-	GP	G	A	Pts	PIM	PP	SH	GW
1981-82	Selkirk Steelers	MJHL	48	37	69	106	....	....	....	....	....	....	....	....	....	....	....	....	....	....	....	....	....	....	....	....	....	....
1982-83	Michigan State Spartans	CCHA	42	11	24	35	....	....	....	50	....	....	....	....	....	....	....	....	....	....	....	....	....	....	....	....	....	....
1983-84	Michigan State Spartans	CCHA	44	12	20	32	....	....	....	34	....	....	....	....	....	....	....	....	....	....	....	....	....	....	....	....	....	....
1984-85	Michigan State Spartans	CCHA	44	24	30	54	....	....	....	26	....	....	....	....	....	....	....	....	....	....	....	....	....	....	....	....	....	....
1985-86	Adirondack Red Wings	AHL	79	19	27	46	....	....	....	27	....	....	....	....	....	....	....	....	....	....	13	2	6	8	9	....	....	....
1986-87	**Detroit Red Wings**	**NHL**	**8**	**0**	**0**	**0**	**0**	**0**	**0**	**0**	**0**	**0**	**0**	**5**	**0.0**	**1**	**0**	**3**	**0**	**–2**	....	....	....	....	....	....	....	....
	Adirondack Red Wings	AHL	71	32	39	71	....	....	....	68	....	....	....	....	....	....	....	....	....	....	11	3	4	7	10	....	....	....
1987-88	**Detroit Red Wings**	**NHL**	**6**	**2**	**0**	**2**	**2**	**0**	**2**	**5**	**0**	**0**	**1**	**5**	**40.0**	**5**	**0**	**6**	**3**	**2**	**2**	**0**	**0**	**0**	**0**	**0**	**0**	**0**
	Adirondack Red Wings	AHL	67	39	43	82	....	....	....	65	....	....	....	....	....	....	....	....	....	....	8	11	4	15	8	....	....	....
1988-89	**Detroit Red Wings**	**NHL**	**16**	**3**	**3**	**6**	**3**	**2**	**5**	**4**	**0**	**0**	**1**	**27**	**11.1**	**9**	**2**	**11**	**1**	**–3**	....	....	....	....	....	....	....	....
	Adirondack Red Wings	AHL	36	21	20	41	....	....	....	30	....	....	....	....	....	....	....	....	....	....	....	....	....	....	....	....	....	....
1989-90	Adirondack Red Wings	AHL	74	38	50	88	....	....	....	36	....	....	....	....	....	....	....	....	....	....	6	2	3	5	11	....	....	....
1990-91	Mannheimer ERC	Germany	44	28	29	57	....	....	....	24	....	....	....	....	....	....	....	....	....	....	3	1	0	1	2	....	....	....
1991-92	Mannheimer ERC	Germany	44	25	30	55	....	....	....	24	....	....	....	....	....	....	....	....	....	....	7	1	2	3	6	....	....	....
1992-93	Mannheimer ERC	Germany	43	20	21	41	....	....	....	48	....	....	....	....	....	....	....	....	....	....	8	4	1	5	6	....	....	....
1993-94	Mannheimer ERC	Germany	44	22	22	44	....	....	....	53	....	....	....	....	....	....	....	....	....	....	4	2	1	3	8	....	....	....
1994-95	Mannheimer ERC	Germany	42	14	25	39	....	....	....	55	....	....	....	....	....	....	....	....	....	....	10	3	8	11	12	....	....	....
1995-96	Star Bulls Rosenheim	Germany	49	24	29	53	....	....	....	62	....	....	....	....	....	....	....	....	....	....	4	0	1	1	6	....	....	....
	NHL Totals		**30**	**5**	**3**	**8**	**5**	**2**	**7**	**9**	**0**	**0**	**2**	**37**	**13.5**	**15**	**2**	**20**	**4**		**2**	**0**	**0**	**0**	**0**	**0**	**0**	**0**

AHL Second All-Star Team (1988)

Signed as a free agent by **Detroit**, June 5, 1985.

• KRIVOKRASOV, Sergei

RW – L. 5'10", 185 lbs. b: Angarsk, USSR, 4/15/1974. Chicago's 1st, 12th overall, in 1992.

Season	Club	League	GP	G	A	Pts	AG	AA	APts	PIM	PP	SH	GW	S	%	TGF	PGF	TGA	PGA	+/-	GP	G	A	Pts	PIM	PP	SH	GW
1990-91	CSKA Moscow	Fr-Tour	1	0	0	0	....	....	....	0	....	....	....	....	....	....	....	....	....	....	....	....	....	....	....	....	....	....
	CSKA Moscow	USSR	41	4	0	4	....	....	....	8	....	....	....	....	....	....	....	....	....	....	....	....	....	....	....	....	....	....
	Soviet Union	EJC-A	5	4	1	5	....	....	....	4	....	....	....	....	....	....	....	....	....	....	....	....	....	....	....	....	....	....

			REGULAR SEASON																		PLAYOFFS							
Season	Club	League	GP	G	A	Pts	AG	AA	APts	PIM	PP	SH	GW	S	%	TGF	PGF	TGA	PGA	+/–	GP	G	A	Pts	PIM	PP	SH	GW
1991-92	CSKA Moscow	CIS	42	10	8	18	....	....	....	35	....	....	....	....	....	....	....	....	....	....	....	....	....	....	....	....	....	....
	Russia	WJC-A	7	3	3	6	....	....	....	22	....	....	....	....	....	....	....	....	....	....	....	....	....	....	....	....	....	....
1992-93	**Chicago Blackhawks**	**NHL**	**4**	**0**	**0**	**0**	**0**	**0**	**0**	**2**	**0**	**0**	**0**	**0**	**0.0**	**0**	**0**	**2**	**0**	**–2**	....	....	....	....	....	....	....	....
	Indianapolis Ice	IHL	78	36	33	69	....	....	....	157	....	....	....	....	....	....	....	....	....	....	5	3	1	4	2	....	....	....
1993-94	**Chicago Blackhawks**	**NHL**	**9**	**1**	**0**	**1**	**1**	**0**	**1**	**4**	**0**	**0**	**0**	**7**	**14.3**	**1**	**0**	**3**	**0**	**–2**	....	....	....	....	....	....	....	....
	Indianapolis Ice	IHL	53	19	26	45	....	....	....	145	....	....	....	....	....	....	....	....	....	....	....	....	....	....	....	....	....	....
1994-95	Indianapolis Ice	IHL	29	12	15	27	....	....	....	41	....	....	....	....	....	....	....	....	....	....	....	....	....	....	....	....	....	....
	Chicago Blackhawks	**NHL**	**41**	**12**	**7**	**19**	**21**	**10**	**31**	**33**	**6**	**0**	**2**	**72**	**16.7**	**27**	**7**	**12**	**1**	**9**	**10**	**0**	**0**	**0**	**8**	**0**	**0**	**0**
1995-96	**Chicago Blackhawks**	**NHL**	**46**	**6**	**10**	**16**	**6**	**8**	**14**	**32**	**0**	**0**	**1**	**52**	**11.5**	**26**	**1**	**15**	**0**	**10**	**5**	**1**	**0**	**1**	**2**	**0**	**0**	**1**
	Indianapolis Ice	IHL	9	4	5	9	....	....	....	28	....	....	....	....	....	....	....	....	....	....	....	....	....	....	....	....	....	....
1996-97	**Chicago Blackhawks**	**NHL**	**67**	**13**	**11**	**24**	**14**	**10**	**24**	**42**	**2**	**0**	**3**	**104**	**12.5**	**31**	**3**	**29**	**0**	**–1**	**6**	**1**	**0**	**1**	**4**	**0**	**0**	**0**
1997-98	**Chicago Blackhawks**	**NHL**	**58**	**10**	**13**	**23**	**12**	**13**	**25**	**33**	**1**	**0**	**2**	**127**	**7.9**	**33**	**7**	**27**	**0**	**–1**	....	....	....	....	....	....	....	....
	Russia	Olympics	6	0	0	0	....	....	....	4	....	....	....	....	....	....	....	....	....	....	....	....	....	....	....	....	....	....
1998-99	**Nashville Predators**	**NHL**	**70**	**25**	**23**	**48**	**29**	**22**	**51**	**42**	**10**	**0**	**6**	**208**	**12.0**	**54**	**18**	**41**	**0**	**–5**	....	....	....	....	....	....	....	....
99-2000	**Nashville Predators**	**NHL**	**63**	**9**	**17**	**26**	**10**	**16**	**26**	**40**	**3**	**0**	**2**	**132**	**6.8**	**42**	**15**	**34**	**0**	**–7**	....	....	....	....	....	....	....	....
	Calgary Flames	**NHL**	**12**	**1**	**10**	**11**	**1**	**9**	**10**	**4**	**0**	**0**	**0**	**27**	**3.7**	**11**	**3**	**6**	**0**	**2**	....	....	....	....	....	....	....	....
	NHL Totals		**370**	**77**	**91**	**168**	**94**	**88**	**182**	**232**	**22**	**0**	**16**	**729**	**10.6**	**225**	**54**	**169**	**1**		**21**	**2**	**0**	**2**	**14**	**0**	**0**	**1**

Played in NHL All-Star Game (1999)

Traded to **Nashville** by **Chicago** for future considerations, June 26, 1998. Traded to **Calgary** by **Nashville** for Cale Hulse and Calgary's 3rd round choice in 2001 Entry Draft, March 14, 2000. Selected by **Minnesota** from **Calgary** in Expansion Draft, June 23, 2000.

• KROG, Jason

C – R. 5′11″, 191 lbs. b: Fernie, B.C., 10/9/1975.

Season	Club	League	GP	G	A	Pts	AG	AA	APts	PIM	PP	SH	GW	S	%	TGF	PGF	TGA	PGA	+/–	GP	G	A	Pts	PIM	PP	SH	GW
1992-93	Chilliwack Chiefs	BCJHL	52	30	27	57	....	....	....	52	....	....	....	....	....	....	....	....	....	....	....	....	....	....	....	....	....	....
1993-94	Chilliwack Chiefs	BCJHL	42	19	36	55	....	....	....	20	....	....	....	....	....	....	....	....	....	....	....	....	....	....	....	....	....	....
1994-95	Chilliwack Chiefs	BCJHL	60	47	81	128	....	....	....	36	....	....	....	....	....	....	....	....	....	....	....	....	....	....	....	....	....	....
1995-96	University of New Hampshire	H-East	34	4	16	20	....	....	....	20	....	....	....	....	....	....	....	....	....	....	....	....	....	....	....	....	....	....
1996-97	University of New Hampshire	H-East	39	23	*44	*67	....	....	....	28	....	....	....	....	....	....	....	....	....	....	....	....	....	....	....	....	....	....
1997-98	University of New Hampshire	H-East	38	*33	33	66	....	....	....	44	....	....	....	....	....	....	....	....	....	....	....	....	....	....	....	....	....	....
1998-99	University of New Hampshire	H-East	41	*34	*51	*85	....	....	....	38	....	....	....	....	....	....	....	....	....	....	....	....	....	....	....	....	....	....
99-2000	**New York Islanders**	**NHL**	**17**	**2**	**4**	**6**	**2**	**4**	**6**	**6**	**1**	**0**	**0**	**22**	**9.1**	**12**	**8**	**6**	**1**	**–1**	....	....	....	....	....	....	....	....
	Lowell Lock Monsters	AHL	45	6	21	27	....	....	....	22	....	....	....	....	....	....	....	....	....	....	....	....	....	....	....	....	....	....
	Providence Bruins	AHL	11	9	8	17	....	....	....	4	....	....	....	....	....	....	....	....	....	....	6	2	2	4	0	....	....	....
	NHL Totals		**17**	**2**	**4**	**6**	**2**	**4**	**6**	**6**	**1**	**0**	**0**	**22**	**9.1**	**12**	**8**	**6**	**1**		....	....	....	....	....	....	....	....

Hockey East All-Star Team (1997) • NCAA East Second All-American Team (1997) • Hockey East First All-Star Team (1998, 1999) • NCAA East First All-American Team (1999) • NCAA Championship All-Tournament Team (1999) • Won Hobey Baker Memorial Award (Top U.S. Collegiate Player) (1999)

Signed as a free agent by **NY Islanders**, May 14, 1999. Loaned to **Providence** (AHL) by **NY Islanders**, March 1, 2000.

• KROMM, Rich

Richard Gordon LW – L. 5′11″, 180 lbs. b: Trail, B.C., 3/29/1964. Calgary's 2nd, 37th overall, in 1982.

Season	Club	League	GP	G	A	Pts	AG	AA	APts	PIM	PP	SH	GW	S	%	TGF	PGF	TGA	PGA	+/–	GP	G	A	Pts	PIM	PP	SH	GW
1980-81	Windsor Royals	OHA-B	39	22	31	53	....	....	....	40	....	....	....	....	....	....	....	....	....	....	....	....	....	....	....	....	....	....
1981-82	Portland Winter Hawks	WHL	60	16	38	54	....	....	....	30	....	....	....	....	....	....	....	....	....	....	14	0	3	3	17	....	....	....
	Portland Winter Hawks	Mem-Cup	4	4	1	5	....	....	....	12	....	....	....	....	....	....	....	....	....	....	....	....	....	....	....	....	....	....
1982-83	Portland Winter Hawks	WHL	72	35	68	103	....	....	....	64	....	....	....	....	....	....	....	....	....	....	14	7	13	20	12	....	....	....
	Portland Winter Hawks	Mem-Cup	4	2	5	7	....	....	....	2	....	....	....	....	....	....	....	....	....	....	....	....	....	....	....	....	....	....
1983-84	Portland Winter Hawks	WHL	10	10	4	14	....	....	....	13	....	....	....	....	....	....	....	....	....	....	....	....	....	....	....	....	....	....
	Calgary Flames	**NHL**	**53**	**11**	**12**	**23**	**9**	**8**	**17**	**27**	**0**	**0**	**3**	**66**	**16.7**	**42**	**0**	**30**	**2**	**14**	**11**	**1**	**1**	**2**	**9**	**0**	**0**	**0**
1984-85	**Calgary Flames**	**NHL**	**73**	**20**	**32**	**52**	**16**	**22**	**38**	**32**	**1**	**0**	**2**	**140**	**14.3**	**71**	**1**	**58**	**7**	**19**	**3**	**0**	**1**	**1**	**4**	**0**	**0**	**0**
1985-86	**Calgary Flames**	**NHL**	**63**	**12**	**17**	**29**	**10**	**11**	**21**	**31**	**0**	**0**	**2**	**97**	**12.4**	**51**	**0**	**45**	**3**	**9**	....	....	....	....	....	....	....	....
	New York Islanders	**NHL**	**14**	**7**	**7**	**14**	**6**	**5**	**11**	**4**	**0**	**0**	**0**	**23**	**30.4**	**22**	**5**	**9**	**0**	**8**	**3**	**0**	**1**	**1**	**0**	**0**	**0**	**0**
1986-87	**New York Islanders**	**NHL**	**70**	**12**	**17**	**29**	**10**	**12**	**22**	**20**	**0**	**0**	**0**	**110**	**10.9**	**46**	**5**	**68**	**29**	**2**	**14**	**1**	**3**	**4**	**4**	**0**	**0**	**0**
1987-88	**New York Islanders**	**NHL**	**71**	**5**	**10**	**15**	**4**	**7**	**11**	**20**	**0**	**1**	**1**	**84**	**6.0**	**30**	**1**	**48**	**21**	**2**	**5**	**0**	**0**	**0**	**5**	**0**	**0**	**0**
1988-89	**New York Islanders**	**NHL**	**20**	**1**	**6**	**7**	**1**	**4**	**5**	**4**	**0**	**0**	**0**	**12**	**8.3**	**7**	**0**	**15**	**5**	**–3**	....	....	....	....	....	....	....	....
	Springfield Indians	AHL	48	21	26	47	....	....	....	15	....	....	....	....	....	....	....	....	....	....	....	....	....	....	....	....	....	....
1989-90	Leksands IF	Sweden	40	8	16	24	....	....	....	28	....	....	....	....	....	....	....	....	....	....	3	3	1	4	0	....	....	....
	Springfield Indians	AHL	9	3	4	7	....	....	....	4	....	....	....	....	....	....	....	....	....	....	16	1	5	6	4	....	....	....
1990-91	**New York Islanders**	**NHL**	**6**	**1**	**0**	**1**	**1**	**0**	**1**	**0**	**0**	**1**	**0**	**6**	**16.7**	**1**	**0**	**3**	**0**	**–2**	....	....	....	....	....	....	....	....
	Capital District Islanders	AHL	76	19	36	55	....	....	....	18	....	....	....	....	....	....	....	....	....	....	....	....	....	....	....	....	....	....
1991-92	**New York Islanders**	**NHL**	**1**	**0**	**0**	**0**	**0**	**0**	**0**	**0**	**0**	**0**	**0**	**0**	**0.0**	**0**	**0**	**0**	**0**	**0**	....	....	....	....	....	....	....	....
	Capital District Islanders	AHL	76	16	39	55	....	....	....	36	....	....	....	....	....	....	....	....	....	....	7	2	3	5	6	....	....	....
1992-93	**New York Islanders**	**NHL**	**1**	**1**	**2**	**3**	**1**	**1**	**2**	**0**	**0**	**0**	**0**	**2**	**50.0**	**3**	**0**	**1**	**1**	**3**	....	....	....	....	....	....	....	....
	Capital District Islanders	AHL	79	20	34	54	....	....	....	28	....	....	....	....	....	....	....	....	....	....	3	0	0	0	0	....	....	....
1993-1995	Cincinnati Cyclones	IHL	DID NOT PLAY – COACHING																									
1995-1997	Carolina Monarchs	AHL	DID NOT PLAY – COACHING																									
1997-1998	Chicago Wolves	IHL	DID NOT PLAY – ASSISTANT COACH																									
1998-2000	Muskegon Fury	UHL	DID NOT PLAY – COACHING																									
	NHL Totals		**372**	**70**	**103**	**173**	**58**	**70**	**128**	**138**	**1**	**2**	**8**	**540**	**13.0**	**273**	**12**	**277**	**68**		**36**	**2**	**6**	**8**	**22**	**0**	**0**	**0**

Traded to **NY Islanders** by **Calgary** with Steve Konroyd for John Tonelli, March 11, 1986.

• KRON, Robert

LW – L. 5′11″, 185 lbs. b: Brno, Czech., 2/27/1967. Vancouver's 5th, 88th overall, in 1985.

Season	Club	League	GP	G	A	Pts	AG	AA	APts	PIM	PP	SH	GW	S	%	TGF	PGF	TGA	PGA	+/–	GP	G	A	Pts	PIM	PP	SH	GW
1983-84	Ingstav Brno	Czech-2	3	0	1	1	....	....	....	0	....	....	....	....	....	....	....	....	....	....	....	....	....	....	....	....	....	....
	Czechoslovakia	EJC-A	5	2	2	4	....	....	....	6	....	....	....	....	....	....	....	....	....	....	....	....	....	....	....	....	....	....
1984-85	Zetor Brno	Czech.	40	6	8	14	....	....	....	6	....	....	....	....	....	....	....	....	....	....	....	....	....	....	....	....	....	....
	Czechoslovakia	WJC-A	7	3	5	8	....	....	....	4	....	....	....	....	....	....	....	....	....	....	....	....	....	....	....	....	....	....
	Czechoslovakia	EJC-A	5	3	4	7	....	....	....	0	....	....	....	....	....	....	....	....	....	....	....	....	....	....	....	....	....	....
1985-86	Zetor Brno	Czech.	44	5	6	11	....	....	....	....	....	....	....	....	....	....	....	....	....	....	....	....	....	....	....	....	....	....
	Czechoslovakia	WJC-A	7	3	1	4	....	....	....	6	....	....	....	....	....	....	....	....	....	....	....	....	....	....	....	....	....	....
1986-87	Zetor Brno	Czech.	34	18	11	29	....	....	....	10	....	....	....	....	....	....	....	....	....	....	....	....	....	....	....	....	....	....
	Czechoslovakia	WJC-A	5	1	2	3	....	....	....	4	....	....	....	....	....	....	....	....	....	....	....	....	....	....	....	....	....	....
1987-88	Zetor Brno	Czech.	44	14	7	21	....	....	....	30	....	....	....	....	....	....	....	....	....	....	....	....	....	....	....	....	....	....
1988-89	Dukla Trencin	Czech.	43	28	19	47	....	....	....	26	....	....	....	....	....	....	....	....	....	....	....	....	....	....	....	....	....	....
	Czechoslovakia	WEC-A	10	2	2	4	....	....	....	2	....	....	....	....	....	....	....	....	....	....	....	....	....	....	....	....	....	....
1989-90	Dukla Trencin	Czech.	39	22	22	44	....	....	....	....	....	....	....	....	....	....	....	....	....	....	....	....	....	....	....	....	....	....
	Czechoslovakia	WEC-A	10	0	1	1	....	....	....	0	....	....	....	....	....	....	....	....	....	....	....	....	....	....	....	....	....	....
1990-91	**Vancouver Canucks**	**NHL**	**76**	**12**	**20**	**32**	**11**	**15**	**26**	**21**	**2**	**3**	**0**	**124**	**9.7**	**50**	**5**	**77**	**21**	**–11**	....	....	....	....	....	....	....	....
1991-92	Czechoslovakia	Can-Cup	5	0	0	0	....	....	....	0	....	....	....	....	....	....	....	....	....	....	....	....	....	....	....	....	....	....
	Vancouver Canucks	**NHL**	**36**	**2**	**2**	**4**	**2**	**2**	**4**	**2**	**0**	**0**	**0**	**49**	**4.1**	**10**	**1**	**25**	**7**	**–9**	**11**	**1**	**2**	**3**	**2**	**0**	**1**	**0**
1992-93	**Vancouver Canucks**	**NHL**	**32**	**10**	**11**	**21**	**8**	**8**	**16**	**14**	**2**	**2**	**2**	**60**	**16.7**	**29**	**3**	**29**	**13**	**10**	....	....	....	....	....	....	....	....
	Hartford Whalers	**NHL**	**13**	**4**	**2**	**6**	**3**	**1**	**4**	**4**	**2**	**0**	**0**	**37**	**10.8**	**8**	**3**	**13**	**3**	**–5**	....	....	....	....	....	....	....	....
1993-94	**Hartford Whalers**	**NHL**	**77**	**24**	**26**	**50**	**22**	**20**	**42**	**8**	**2**	**1**	**3**	**194**	**12.4**	**81**	**19**	**90**	**28**	**0**	....	....	....	....	....	....	....	....
1994-95	**Hartford Whalers**	**NHL**	**37**	**10**	**8**	**18**	**18**	**12**	**30**	**10**	**3**	**1**	**1**	**88**	**11.4**	**29**	**9**	**36**	**13**	**–3**	....	....	....	....	....	....	....	....
1995-96	**Hartford Whalers**	**NHL**	**77**	**22**	**28**	**50**	**22**	**23**	**45**	**6**	**8**	**1**	**3**	**203**	**10.8**	**79**	**30**	**70**	**20**	**–1**	....	....	....	....	....	....	....	....
1996-97	**Hartford Whalers**	**NHL**	**68**	**10**	**12**	**22**	**11**	**11**	**22**	**10**	**2**	**0**	**4**	**182**	**5.5**	**40**	**9**	**56**	**7**	**–18**	....	....	....	....	....	....	....	....

			REGULAR SEASON																		PLAYOFFS							
Season	Club	League	GP	G	A	Pts	AG	AA	APts	PIM	PP	SH	GW	S	%	TGF	PGF	TGA	PGA	+/–	GP	G	A	Pts	PIM	PP	SH	GW
1997-98	**Carolina Hurricanes**	**NHL**	81	16	20	36	19	20	39	12	4	0	2	175	9.1	55	13	67	17	–8	....	....	....	....	....	....	....	....
1998-99	**Carolina Hurricanes**	**NHL**	75	9	16	25	11	15	26	10	3	1	2	134	6.7	41	11	52	9	–13	5	2	0	2	0	0	0	1
99-2000	**Carolina Hurricanes**	**NHL**	81	13	27	40	15	25	40	8	2	1	3	134	9.7	56	11	57	8	–4	....	....	....	....	....	....	....	....
	NHL Totals		653	132	172	304	142	152	294	105	30	10	20	1380	9.6	478	114	572	146		16	3	2	5	2	0	1	1

Named Best Forward at WJC-A (1987)

Traded to **Hartford** by **Vancouver** with Vancouver's 3rd round choice (Marek Malik) in 1993 Entry Draft and future considerations (Jim Sandlak, May 17, 1993) for Murray Craven and Vancouver's 5th round choice (previously acquired, Vancouver selected Scott Walker) in 1993 Entry Draft, March 22, 1993. Transferred to **Carolina** after **Hartford** franchise relocated, June 25, 1997. Selected by **Columbus** from **Carolina** in Expansion Draft, June 23, 2000.

• KROOK, Kevin

Kevin Bradley D – L. 5'11", 187 lbs. b: Cold Lake, Alta., 4/5/1958. Colorado's 10th, 142nd overall, in 1978.

Season	Club	League	GP	G	A	Pts	AG	AA	APts	PIM	PP	SH	GW	S	%	TGF	PGF	TGA	PGA	+/–	GP	G	A	Pts	PIM	PP	SH	GW
1974-75	Bellingham Blazers	BCJHL	46	18	52	70	....	....	....	250	....	....	....	....	....	....	....	....	....	....	....	....	....	....	....	....	....	....
1975-76	New Westminster Bruins	WCJHL	44	0	9	9	....	....	....	17	....	....	....	....	....	....	....	....	....	....	17	0	1	1	2	....	....	....
1976-77	Calgary Centennials	WCJHL	25	2	8	10	....	....	....	18	....	....	....	....	....	....	....	....	....	....	....	....	....	....	....	....	....	....
	Regina Pats	WCJHL	49	5	26	31	....	....	....	118	....	....	....	....	....	....	....	....	....	....	....	....	....	....	....	....	....	....
1977-78	Regina Pats	WCJHL	57	8	43	51	....	....	....	203	....	....	....	....	....	....	....	....	....	....	13	2	11	13	28	....	....	....
1978-79	**Colorado Rockies**	**NHL**	3	0	0	0	0	0	0	2	0	0	0	0	0.0	0	0	0	0	0	....	....	....	....	....	....	....	....
	Muskegon Mohawks	IHL	39	2	13	15	....	....	....	39	....	....	....	....	....	....	....	....	....	....	....	....	....	....	....	....	....	....
	NHL Totals		3	0	0	0	0	0	0	2	0	0	0	0	0.0	0	0	0	0		....	....	....	....	....	....	....	....

• KROUPA, Vlastimil

D – L. 6'3", 215 lbs. b: Most, Czech., 4/27/1975. San Jose's 3rd, 45th overall, in 1993.

Season	Club	League	GP	G	A	Pts	AG	AA	APts	PIM	PP	SH	GW	S	%	TGF	PGF	TGA	PGA	+/–	GP	G	A	Pts	PIM	PP	SH	GW
1991-92	CHZ Litvinov	Czech-Jr.	37	9	16	25	....	....	....	....	....	....	....	....	....	....	....	....	....	....	....	....	....	....	....	....	....	....
1992-93	CHZ Litvinov	Czech.	9	0	1	1	....	....	....	....	....	....	....	....	....	....	....	....	....	....	....	....	....	....	....	....	....	....
	Czech-Republic	EJC-A	6	1	0	1	....	....	....	4	....	....	....	....	....	....	....	....	....	....	....	....	....	....	....	....	....	....
1993-94	**San Jose Sharks**	**NHL**	27	1	3	4	1	2	3	20	0	0	0	16	6.3	19	1	30	6	–6	14	1	2	3	21	0	0	1
	Kansas City Blades	IHL	39	3	12	15	....	....	....	12	....	....	....	....	....	....	....	....	....	....	....	....	....	....	....	....	....	....
1994-95	**San Jose Sharks**	**NHL**	14	0	2	2	0	3	3	16	0	0	0	4	0.0	7	0	20	6	–7	6	0	0	0	4	0	0	0
	Czech-Republic	WJC-A	7	4	2	6	....	....	....	10	....	....	....	....	....	....	....	....	....	....	....	....	....	....	....	....	....	....
	Kansas City Blades	IHL	51	4	8	12	....	....	....	49	....	....	....	....	....	....	....	....	....	....	12	2	4	6	22	....	....	....
1995-96	**San Jose Sharks**	**NHL**	27	1	7	8	1	6	7	18	0	0	0	11	9.1	18	2	37	4	–17	....	....	....	....	....	....	....	....
	Kansas City Blades	IHL	39	5	22	27	....	....	....	44	....	....	....	....	....	....	....	....	....	....	5	0	1	1	6	....	....	....
1996-97	**San Jose Sharks**	**NHL**	35	2	6	8	2	5	7	12	2	0	1	24	8.3	22	7	35	3	–17	....	....	....	....	....	....	....	....
	Kentucky Thoroughblades	AHL	5	0	3	3	....	....	....	0	....	....	....	....	....	....	....	....	....	....	....	....	....	....	....	....	....	....
	Czech-Republic	WC-A	9	0	4	4	....	....	....	10	....	....	....	....	....	....	....	....	....	....	....	....	....	....	....	....	....	....
1997-98	**New Jersey Devils**	**NHL**	2	0	1	1	0	1	1	0	0	0	0	1	0.0	2	0	1	0	1	....	....	....	....	....	....	....	....
	Albany River Rats	AHL	71	5	29	34	....	....	....	48	....	....	....	....	....	....	....	....	....	....	12	0	3	3	6	....	....	....
1998-99	Albany River Rats	AHL	2	0	1	1	....	....	....	4	....	....	....	....	....	....	....	....	....	....	....	....	....	....	....	....	....	....
	Kansas City Blades	IHL	77	6	32	38	....	....	....	52	....	....	....	....	....	....	....	....	....	....	3	0	1	1	0	....	....	....
99-2000	Albany River Rats	AHL	1	1	0	1	....	....	....	0	....	....	....	....	....	....	....	....	....	....	....	....	....	....	....	....	....	....
	Moskitos Essen	Germany	56	6	13	19	....	....	....	56	....	....	....	....	....	....	....	....	....	....	....	....	....	....	....	....	....	....
	NHL Totals		105	4	19	23	4	17	21	66	2	0	1	56	7.1	68	10	123	19		20	1	2	3	25	0	0	1

Traded to **New Jersey** by **San Jose** for New Jersey's 3rd round choice (later traded to Nashville — Nashville selected Geoff Koch) in 1998 Entry Draft, August 22, 1997.

• KRULICKI, Jim

James John LW – L. 5'11", 180 lbs. b: Kitchener, Ont., 3/9/1948.

Season	Club	League	GP	G	A	Pts	AG	AA	APts	PIM	PP	SH	GW	S	%	TGF	PGF	TGA	PGA	+/–	GP	G	A	Pts	PIM	PP	SH	GW
1964-65	Kitchener Greenshirts	OHA-B	STATISTICS NOT AVAILABLE																									
	Kitchener Rangers	OHA-Jr.	2	0	0	0	....	....	....	0	....	....	....	....	....	....	....	....	....	....	....	....	....	....	....	....	....	....
1965-66	Kitchener Rangers	OHA-Jr.	48	16	8	24	....	....	....	41	....	....	....	....	....	....	....	....	....	....	19	4	4	8	4	....	....	....
1966-67	Kitchener Rangers	OHA-Jr.	48	25	24	49	....	....	....	50	....	....	....	....	....	....	....	....	....	....	13	10	3	13	19	....	....	....
	Omaha Knights	CPHL	....	....	....	....	....	....	....	....	....	....	....	....	....	....	....	....	....	....	3	0	0	0	0	....	....	....
1967-68	Kitchener Rangers	OHA-Jr.	51	28	31	59	....	....	....	49	....	....	....	....	....	....	....	....	....	....	19	3	13	16	32	....	....	....
1968-69	Omaha Knights	CHL	32	3	6	9	....	....	....	10	....	....	....	....	....	....	....	....	....	....	....	....	....	....	....	....	....	....
1969-70	Omaha Knights	CHL	72	9	19	28	....	....	....	26	....	....	....	....	....	....	....	....	....	....	12	5	7	12	22	....	....	....
	Buffalo Bisons	AHL	....	....	....	....	....	....	....	....	....	....	....	....	....	....	....	....	....	....	7	3	2	5	5	....	....	....
1970-71	**New York Rangers**	**NHL**	27	0	2	2	0	2	2	6	0	0	0	13	0.0	2	1	9	7	–1	....	....	....	....	....	....	....	....
	Omaha Knights	CHL	9	2	4	6	....	....	....	7	....	....	....	....	....	....	....	....	....	....	....	....	....	....	....	....	....	....
	Detroit Red Wings	**NHL**	14	0	1	1	0	1	1	0	0	0	0	7	0.0	1	1	7	1	–6	....	....	....	....	....	....	....	....
	NHL Totals		41	0	3	3	0	3	3	6	0	0	0	20	0.0	3	2	16	8		....	....	....	....	....	....	....	....

Traded to **Detroit** by **NY Rangers** for Dale Rolfe, March 2, 1971.

• KRUPP, Uwe

Uwe G. D – R. 6'6", 235 lbs. b: Cologne, West Germany, 6/24/1965. Buffalo's 13th, 223rd overall, in 1983.

Season	Club	League	GP	G	A	Pts	AG	AA	APts	PIM	PP	SH	GW	S	%	TGF	PGF	TGA	PGA	+/–	GP	G	A	Pts	PIM	PP	SH	GW
1982-83	Kolner EC	Germany	11	0	0	0	....	....	....	0	....	....	....	....	....	....	....	....	....	....	....	....	....	....	....	....	....	....
	West Germany	WJC-A	7	0	0	0	....	....	....	0	....	....	....	....	....	....	....	....	....	....	....	....	....	....	....	....	....	....
	West Germany	EJC-A	5	3	4	7	....	....	....	2	....	....	....	....	....	....	....	....	....	....	....	....	....	....	....	....	....	....
1983-84	Kolner EC	Germany	26	0	4	4	....	....	....	22	....	....	....	....	....	....	....	....	....	....	....	....	....	....	....	....	....	....
1984-85	Kolner EC	Germany	31	7	7	14	....	....	....	....	....	....	....	....	....	....	....	....	....	....	9	4	1	5	....	....	....	....
	West Germany	WJC-A	7	0	1	1	....	....	....	8	....	....	....	....	....	....	....	....	....	....	....	....	....	....	....	....	....	....
1985-86	Kolner EC	Germany	35	6	18	24	....	....	....	83	....	....	....	....	....	....	....	....	....	....	10	4	3	7	....	....	....	....
	West Germany	WEC-A	3	2	1	3	....	....	....	2	....	....	....	....	....	....	....	....	....	....	....	....	....	....	....	....	....	....
1986-87	**Buffalo Sabres**	**NHL**	26	1	4	5	1	3	4	23	0	0	0	34	2.9	27	5	34	3	–9	....	....	....	....	....	....	....	....
	Rochester Americans	AHL	42	3	19	22	....	....	....	50	....	....	....	....	....	....	....	....	....	....	17	1	11	12	16	....	....	....
1987-88	**Buffalo Sabres**	**NHL**	75	2	9	11	2	6	8	151	0	0	0	84	2.4	83	10	123	49	–1	6	0	0	0	15	0	0	0
1988-89	**Buffalo Sabres**	**NHL**	70	5	13	18	4	9	13	55	0	1	0	51	9.8	66	1	106	41	0	5	0	1	1	4	0	0	0
1989-90	**Buffalo Sabres**	**NHL**	74	3	20	23	3	14	17	85	0	1	1	69	4.3	75	4	86	30	15	6	0	0	0	4	0	0	0
	West Germany	WEC-A	2	0	0	0	....	....	....	2	....	....	....	....	....	....	....	....	....	....	....	....	....	....	....	....	....	....
1990-91	**Buffalo Sabres**	**NHL**	74	12	32	44	11	24	35	66	6	0	0	138	8.7	126	40	107	35	14	6	1	1	2	6	1	0	0
1991-92	**Buffalo Sabres**	**NHL**	8	2	0	2	2	0	2	6	0	0	0	13	15.4	9	3	15	9	0	....	....	....	....	....	....	....	....
	New York Islanders	**NHL**	59	6	29	35	5	22	27	43	2	0	0	115	5.2	110	29	102	34	13	....	....	....	....	....	....	....	....
1992-93	**New York Islanders**	**NHL**	80	9	29	38	7	20	27	67	2	0	2	116	7.8	106	35	95	30	6	18	1	5	6	12	0	0	0
1993-94	**New York Islanders**	**NHL**	41	7	14	21	6	11	17	30	3	0	0	82	8.5	59	16	40	8	11	4	0	1	1	4	0	0	0
1994-95	EV Landshut	Germany	5	1	2	3	....	....	....	6	....	....	....	....	....	....	....	....	....	....	....	....	....	....	....	....	....	....
	Quebec Nordiques	**NHL**	44	6	17	23	11	25	36	20	3	0	1	102	5.9	70	25	45	14	14	5	0	2	2	2	0	0	0
1995-96♦	**Colorado Avalanche**	**NHL**	6	0	3	3	0	2	2	4	0	0	0	9	0.0	10	3	3	0	4	22	4	12	16	33	1	0	2
1996-97	**Colorado Avalanche**	**NHL**	60	4	17	21	4	15	19	48	2	0	1	107	3.7	70	20	51	13	12	....	....	....	....	....	....	....	....
1997-98	**Colorado Avalanche**	**NHL**	78	9	22	31	11	22	33	38	5	0	2	149	6.0	82	29	50	18	21	7	0	1	1	4	0	0	0
	Germany	Olympics	2	0	2	2	....	....	....	4	....	....	....	....	....	....	....	....	....	....	....	....	....	....	....	....	....	....
1998-99	**Detroit Red Wings**	**NHL**	22	3	2	5	4	2	6	6	0	0	0	32	9.4	24	4	25	5	0	....	....	....	....	....	....	....	....
99-2000	**Detroit Red Wings**	**NHL**	DID NOT PLAY – INJURED																									
	NHL Totals		717	69	211	280	71	175	246	642	23	2	7	1101	6.3	917	224	882	289		79	6	23	29	84	2	0	2

Played in NHL All-Star Game (1991)

Traded to **NY Islanders** by **Buffalo** with Pierre Turgeon, Benoit Hogue and Dave McLlwain for Pat LaFontaine, Randy Hillier, Randy Wood and NY Islanders' 4th round choice (Dean Melanson) in 1992 Entry Draft, October 25, 1991. Traded to **Quebec** by **NY Islanders** with NY Islanders' 1st round choice (Wade Belak) in 1994 Entry Draft for Ron Sutter and Quebec's 1st round choice (Brett Lindros) in 1994 Entry Draft, June 28, 1994. Transferred to **Colorado** after **Quebec** franchise relocated, June 21, 1995. Claimed by **Nashville** from **Colorado** in Expansion Draft, June 26, 1998. Signed as a free agent by **Detroit**, July 7, 1998. • Missed remainder of 1998-99 and entire 1999-2000 seasons recovering from back injury suffered prior to game vs. Phoenix, December 19, 1998.

• KRUPPKE, Gord

Gord W. D – R. 6'1", 215 lbs. b: Slave Lake, Alta., 4/2/1969. Detroit's 2nd, 32nd overall, in 1987.

			REGULAR SEASON																			PLAYOFFS							
Season	Club	League	GP	G	A	Pts	AG	AA	APts	PIM	PP	SH	GW	S	%	TGF	PGF	TGA	PGA	+/–	GP	G	A	Pts	PIM	PP	SH	GW
1984-85	Calgary Buffaloes	AAHA	36	3	22	25	....	....	....	77	....	....	....	....	....	....	....	....	....	....	....	....	....	....	....	....	....	....
1985-86	Prince Albert Raiders	WHL	62	1	8	9	....	....	....	81	....	....	....	....	....	....	....	....	....	....	20	4	4	8	22	....	....	....
1986-87	Prince Albert Raiders	WHL	49	2	10	12	....	....	....	129	....	....	....	....	....	....	....	....	....	....	8	0	0	0	9	....	....	....
1987-88	Prince Albert Raiders	WHL	54	8	8	16	....	....	....	113	....	....	....	....	....	....	....	....	....	....	10	0	0	0	46	....	....	....
1988-89	Prince Albert Raiders	WHL	62	6	26	32	....	....	....	254	....	....	....	....	....	....	....	....	....	....	3	0	0	0	11	....	....	....
1989-90	Adirondack Red Wings	AHL	59	2	12	14	....	....	....	103	....	....	....	....	....	....	....	....	....	....	....	....	....	....	....	....	....	....
1990-91	**Detroit Red Wings**	**NHL**	**4**	**0**	**0**	**0**	**0**	**0**	**0**	**0**	**0**	**0**	**0**	**0**	**0.0**	**2**	**0**	**1**	**0**	**1**	....	....	....	....	....	....	....	....
	Adirondack Red Wings	AHL	45	1	8	9	....	....	....	153	....	....	....	....	....	....	....	....	....	....	....	....	....	....	....	....	....	....
1991-92	Adirondack Red Wings	AHL	65	3	9	12	....	....	....	208	....	....	....	....	....	....	....	....	....	....	16	0	1	1	52	....	....	....
1992-93	**Detroit Red Wings**	**NHL**	**10**	**0**	**0**	**0**	**0**	**0**	**0**	**20**	**0**	**0**	**0**	**7**	**0.0**	**6**	**0**	**6**	**1**	**1**	....	....	....	....	....	....	....	....
	Adirondack Red Wings	AHL	41	2	12	14	....	....	....	197	....	....	....	....	....	....	....	....	....	....	9	1	2	3	20	....	....	....
1993-94	**Detroit Red Wings**	**NHL**	**9**	**0**	**0**	**0**	**0**	**0**	**0**	**12**	**0**	**0**	**0**	**5**	**0.0**	**4**	**0**	**11**	**3**	**–4**	....	....	....	....	....	....	....	....
	Adirondack Red Wings	AHL	54	2	9	11	....	....	....	210	....	....	....	....	....	....	....	....	....	....	12	1	3	4	32	....	....	....
1994-95	Adirondack Red Wings	AHL	48	2	9	11	....	....	....	157	....	....	....	....	....	....	....	....	....	....	....	....	....	....	....	....	....	....
	St. John's Maple Leafs	AHL	3	0	1	1	....	....	....	6	....	....	....	....	....	....	....	....	....	....	....	....	....	....	....	....	....	....
1995-96	Houston Aeros	IHL	50	0	4	4	....	....	....	119	....	....	....	....	....	....	....	....	....	....	....	....	....	....	....	....	....	....
1996-97	Houston Aeros	IHL	43	0	5	5	....	....	....	91	....	....	....	....	....	....	....	....	....	....	9	0	1	1	14	....	....	....
1997-98	Houston Aeros	IHL	71	2	6	8	....	....	....	171	....	....	....	....	....	....	....	....	....	....	4	0	0	0	27	....	....	....
1998-99	Houston Aeros	IHL	19	0	2	2	....	....	....	58	....	....	....	....	....	....	....	....	....	....	....	....	....	....	....	....	....	....
	Grand Rapids Griffins	IHL	42	0	5	5	....	....	....	93	....	....	....	....	....	....	....	....	....	....	....	....	....	....	....	....	....	....
	NHL Totals		**23**	**0**	**0**	**0**	**0**	**0**	**0**	**32**	**0**	**0**	**0**	**12**	**0.0**	**12**	**0**	**18**	**4**		....	....	....	....	....	....	....	....

WHL East Second All-Star Team (1989)

Traded to **Toronto** by **Detroit** for future considerations, April 7, 1995. • Traded to **Grand Rapids** (IHL) by **Houston** (IHL) for Anders Bjork, January 8, 1999.

• KRUSE, Paul

Paul Johannes LW – L. 6', 202 lbs. b: Merritt, B.C., 3/15/1970. Calgary's 6th, 83rd overall, in 1990.

Season	Club	League	GP	G	A	Pts	AG	AA	APts	PIM	PP	SH	GW	S	%	TGF	PGF	TGA	PGA	+/–	GP	G	A	Pts	PIM	PP	SH	GW
1985-86	Merritt Bantam Reps	BCAHA	STATISTICS NOT AVAILABLE																									
1986-87	Merritt Centennials	BCJHL	35	8	15	23	....	....	....	120	....	....	....	....	....	....	....	....	....	....	....	....	....	....	....	....	....	....
1987-88	Merritt Centennials	BCJHL	44	12	32	44	....	....	....	223	....	....	....	....	....	....	....	....	....	....	4	1	4	5	18	....	....	....
	Moose Jaw Warriors	WHL	1	0	0	0	....	....	....	0	....	....	....	....	....	....	....	....	....	....	....	....	....	....	....	....	....	....
1988-89	Kamloops Blazers	WHL	68	8	15	23	....	....	....	209	....	....	....	....	....	....	....	....	....	....	16	0	0	0	36	....	....	....
1989-90	Kamloops Blazers	WHL	67	22	23	45	....	....	....	291	....	....	....	....	....	....	....	....	....	....	17	3	5	8	79	....	....	....
1990-91	**Calgary Flames**	**NHL**	**1**	**0**	**0**	**0**	**0**	**0**	**0**	**7**	**0**	**0**	**0**	**0**	**0.0**	**0**	**0**	**1**	**0**	**–1**	....	....	....	....	....	....	....	....
	Salt Lake Golden Eagles	IHL	83	24	20	44	....	....	....	313	....	....	....	....	....	....	....	....	....	....	4	1	1	2	4	....	....	....
1991-92	**Calgary Flames**	**NHL**	**16**	**3**	**1**	**4**	**3**	**1**	**4**	**65**	**0**	**0**	**0**	**12**	**25.0**	**10**	**1**	**9**	**1**	**1**	....	....	....	....	....	....	....	....
	Salt Lake Golden Eagles	IHL	57	14	15	29	....	....	....	267	....	....	....	....	....	....	....	....	....	....	5	1	2	3	19	....	....	....
1992-93	**Calgary Flames**	**NHL**	**27**	**2**	**3**	**5**	**2**	**2**	**4**	**41**	**0**	**0**	**0**	**17**	**11.8**	**11**	**0**	**9**	**0**	**2**	....	....	....	....	....	....	....	....
	Salt Lake Golden Eagles	IHL	35	1	4	5	....	....	....	206	....	....	....	....	....	....	....	....	....	....	....	....	....	....	....	....	....	....
1993-94	**Calgary Flames**	**NHL**	**68**	**3**	**8**	**11**	**3**	**6**	**9**	**185**	**0**	**0**	**0**	**52**	**5.8**	**21**	**0**	**29**	**2**	**–6**	**7**	**0**	**0**	**0**	**14**	**0**	**0**	**0**
1994-95	**Calgary Flames**	**NHL**	**45**	**11**	**5**	**16**	**19**	**7**	**26**	**141**	**0**	**0**	**2**	**52**	**21.2**	**28**	**0**	**16**	**1**	**13**	**7**	**4**	**2**	**6**	**10**	**0**	**1**	**0**
1995-96	**Calgary Flames**	**NHL**	**75**	**3**	**12**	**15**	**3**	**10**	**13**	**145**	**0**	**0**	**0**	**83**	**3.6**	**26**	**0**	**31**	**0**	**–5**	**3**	**0**	**0**	**0**	**4**	**0**	**0**	**0**
1996-97	**Calgary Flames**	**NHL**	**14**	**2**	**0**	**2**	**2**	**0**	**2**	**30**	**0**	**0**	**1**	**10**	**20.0**	**3**	**0**	**7**	**0**	**–4**	....	....	....	....	....	....	....	....
	New York Islanders	**NHL**	**48**	**4**	**2**	**6**	**4**	**2**	**6**	**111**	**0**	**0**	**0**	**39**	**10.3**	**16**	**1**	**20**	**0**	**–5**	....	....	....	....	....	....	....	....
1997-98	**New York Islanders**	**NHL**	**62**	**6**	**1**	**7**	**7**	**1**	**8**	**138**	**0**	**0**	**2**	**44**	**13.6**	**10**	**0**	**22**	**0**	**–12**	....	....	....	....	....	....	....	....
	Buffalo Sabres	**NHL**	**12**	**1**	**1**	**2**	**1**	**1**	**2**	**49**	**0**	**0**	**0**	**8**	**12.5**	**2**	**0**	**1**	**0**	**1**	**1**	**1**	**0**	**1**	**4**	**0**	**0**	**0**
1998-99	**Buffalo Sabres**	**NHL**	**43**	**3**	**0**	**3**	**4**	**0**	**4**	**114**	**0**	**0**	**0**	**33**	**9.1**	**5**	**0**	**5**	**0**	**0**	**10**	**0**	**0**	**0**	**4**	**0**	**0**	**0**
99-2000	**Buffalo Sabres**	**NHL**	**11**	**0**	**0**	**0**	**0**	**0**	**0**	**43**	**0**	**0**	**0**	**7**	**0.0**	**1**	**0**	**3**	**0**	**–2**	....	....	....	....	....	....	....	....
	Utah Grizzlies	IHL	44	10	13	23	....	....	....	71	....	....	....	....	....	....	....	....	....	....	5	0	3	3	28	....	....	....
	NHL Totals		**422**	**38**	**33**	**71**	**48**	**30**	**78**	**1069**	**0**	**0**	**5**	**357**	**10.6**	**133**	**2**	**153**	**4**		**28**	**5**	**2**	**7**	**36**	**0**	**1**	**0**

Traded to **NY Islanders** by **Calgary** for Colorado's 3rd round choice (previously acquired by NY Islanders — later traded to Hartford — Hartford selected Francis Lessard) in 1997 Entry Draft, November 27, 1996. Traded to **Buffalo** by **NY Islanders** with Jason Holland for Jason Dawe, March 24, 1998. Loaned to **Utah** (IHL) by **Buffalo** after clearing NHL waivers, January 11, 2000.

• KRUSHELNYSKI, Mike

"Krusher" LW/C – L. 6'2", 200 lbs. b: Montreal, Que., 4/27/1960. Boston's 7th, 120th overall, in 1979.

Season	Club	League	GP	G	A	Pts	AG	AA	APts	PIM	PP	SH	GW	S	%	TGF	PGF	TGA	PGA	+/–	GP	G	A	Pts	PIM	PP	SH	GW
1978-79	Montreal Juniors	QMJHL	46	15	29	44	....	....	....	42	....	....	....	....	....	....	....	....	....	....	11	3	4	7	8	....	....	....
1979-80	Montreal Juniors	QMJHL	72	39	60	99	....	....	....	78	....	....	....	....	....	....	....	....	....	....	6	2	3	5	2	....	....	....
1980-81	Springfield Indians	AHL	80	25	28	53	....	....	....	47	....	....	....	....	....	....	....	....	....	....	7	1	1	2	29	....	....	....
1981-82	**Boston Bruins**	**NHL**	**17**	**3**	**3**	**6**	**2**	**2**	**4**	**2**	**0**	**1**	**0**	**19**	**15.8**	**8**	**0**	**8**	**0**	**0**	**1**	**0**	**0**	**0**	**2**	**0**	**0**	**0**
	Erie Blades	AHL	62	31	52	83	....	....	....	44	....	....	....	....	....	....	....	....	....	....	....	....	....	....	....	....	....	....
1982-83	**Boston Bruins**	**NHL**	**79**	**23**	**42**	**65**	**19**	**29**	**48**	**43**	**4**	**2**	**1**	**153**	**15.0**	**104**	**10**	**84**	**28**	**38**	**17**	**8**	**6**	**14**	**12**	**2**	**0**	**0**
1983-84	**Boston Bruins**	**NHL**	**66**	**25**	**20**	**45**	**20**	**14**	**34**	**55**	**3**	**2**	**1**	**152**	**16.4**	**74**	**19**	**72**	**26**	**9**	**2**	**0**	**0**	**0**	**0**	**0**	**0**	**0**
1984-85♦	**Edmonton Oilers**	**NHL**	**80**	**43**	**45**	**88**	**35**	**31**	**66**	**60**	**13**	**0**	**4**	**187**	**23.0**	**161**	**38**	**74**	**7**	**56**	**18**	**5**	**8**	**13**	**22**	**2**	**0**	**2**
1985-86	**Edmonton Oilers**	**NHL**	**54**	**16**	**24**	**40**	**13**	**16**	**29**	**22**	**3**	**0**	**1**	**98**	**16.3**	**74**	**20**	**48**	**5**	**11**	**10**	**4**	**5**	**9**	**16**	**1**	**0**	**2**
1986-87♦	**Edmonton Oilers**	**NHL**	**80**	**16**	**35**	**51**	**14**	**25**	**39**	**67**	**4**	**1**	**2**	**89**	**18.0**	**85**	**17**	**46**	**4**	**26**	**21**	**3**	**4**	**7**	**18**	**0**	**0**	**1**
1987-88♦	**Edmonton Oilers**	**NHL**	**76**	**20**	**27**	**47**	**17**	**19**	**36**	**64**	**4**	**0**	**0**	**124**	**16.1**	**68**	**11**	**40**	**9**	**26**	**19**	**4**	**6**	**10**	**12**	**0**	**0**	**0**
1988-89	**Los Angeles Kings**	**NHL**	**78**	**26**	**36**	**62**	**22**	**25**	**47**	**110**	**5**	**0**	**8**	**143**	**18.2**	**109**	**29**	**86**	**15**	**9**	**11**	**1**	**4**	**5**	**4**	**1**	**0**	**0**
1989-90	**Los Angeles Kings**	**NHL**	**63**	**16**	**25**	**41**	**14**	**18**	**32**	**50**	**2**	**2**	**2**	**101**	**15.8**	**66**	**8**	**67**	**16**	**7**	**10**	**1**	**3**	**4**	**12**	**0**	**0**	**1**
1990-91	**Los Angeles Kings**	**NHL**	**15**	**1**	**5**	**6**	**1**	**4**	**5**	**10**	**1**	**0**	**0**	**11**	**9.1**	**9**	**1**	**4**	**3**	**7**	....	....	....	....	....	....	....	....
	Toronto Maple Leafs	**NHL**	**59**	**17**	**22**	**39**	**16**	**17**	**33**	**48**	**2**	**2**	**1**	**98**	**17.3**	**55**	**12**	**55**	**6**	**–6**	....	....	....	....	....	....	....	....
1991-92	**Toronto Maple Leafs**	**NHL**	**72**	**9**	**15**	**24**	**8**	**11**	**19**	**72**	**0**	**2**	**1**	**100**	**9.0**	**50**	**4**	**59**	**8**	**–5**	....	....	....	....	....	....	....	....
1992-93	**Toronto Maple Leafs**	**NHL**	**84**	**19**	**20**	**39**	**16**	**14**	**30**	**62**	**6**	**2**	**3**	**130**	**14.6**	**65**	**25**	**49**	**12**	**3**	**16**	**3**	**7**	**10**	**8**	**1**	**0**	**0**
1993-94	**Toronto Maple Leafs**	**NHL**	**54**	**5**	**6**	**11**	**5**	**5**	**10**	**28**	**1**	**0**	**1**	**71**	**7.0**	**22**	**1**	**41**	**15**	**–5**	**6**	**0**	**0**	**0**	**0**	**0**	**0**	**0**
1994-95	**Detroit Red Wings**	**NHL**	**20**	**2**	**3**	**5**	**4**	**4**	**8**	**6**	**0**	**0**	**0**	**20**	**10.0**	**8**	**0**	**8**	**3**	**3**	**8**	**0**	**0**	**0**	**0**	**0**	**0**	**0**
1995-96	Cape Breton Oilers	AHL	50	16	25	41	....	....	....	78	....	....	....	....	....	....	....	....	....	....	....	....	....	....	....	....	....	....
1996-97	HC Milano	Alpenliga	2	0	0	0	....	....	....	0	....	....	....	....	....	....	....	....	....	....	....	....	....	....	....	....	....	....
1997-98	Fort Worth Fire	CHL	DID NOT PLAY – COACHING																									
	NHL Totals		**897**	**241**	**328**	**569**	**206**	**234**	**440**	**699**	**48**	**14**	**25**	**1496**	**16.1**	**958**	**195**	**741**	**157**		**139**	**29**	**43**	**72**	**106**	**7**	**0**	**6**

Played in NHL All-Star Game (1985)

Traded to **Edmonton** by **Boston** for Ken Linseman, June 21, 1984. Traded to **LA Kings** by **Edmonton** with Wayne Gretzky and Marty McSorley for Jimmy Carson, Martin Gelinas, LA Kings' 1st round choices in 1989 (later traded to New Jersey — New Jersey selected Jason Miller), 1991 (Martin Rucinsky) and 1993 (Nick Stajduhar) Entry Drafts and cash, August 9, 1988. Traded to **Toronto** by **LA Kings** for John McIntyre, November 9, 1990. Signed as a free agent by **Detroit**, August 1, 1994.

• KRUTOV, Vladimir

"The Tank" LW – L. 5'9", 195 lbs. b: Moscow, Soviet Union, 6/1/1960. Vancouver's 11th, 238th overall, in 1986.

Season	Club	League	GP	G	A	Pts	AG	AA	APts	PIM	PP	SH	GW	S	%	TGF	PGF	TGA	PGA	+/–	GP	G	A	Pts	PIM	PP	SH	GW
1977-78	CSKA Moscow	USSR	1	0	0	0	....	....	....	0	....	....	....	....	....	....	....	....	....	....	....	....	....	....	....	....	....	....
	Soviet Union	EJC-A	5	6	7	13	....	....	....	4	....	....	....	....	....	....	....	....	....	....	....	....	....	....	....	....	....	....
1978-79	CSKA Moscow	USSR	24	8	3	11	....	....	....	6	....	....	....	....	....	....	....	....	....	....	....	....	....	....	....	....	....	....
	Soviet Union	WJC-A	6	8	6	*14	....	....	....	2	....	....	....	....	....	....	....	....	....	....	....	....	....	....	....	....	....	....
1979-80	CSKA Moscow	USSR	40	30	12	42	....	....	....	16	....	....	....	....	....	....	....	....	....	....	....	....	....	....	....	....	....	....
	Soviet Union	WJC-A	5	7	4	*11	....	....	....	5	....	....	....	....	....	....	....	....	....	....	....	....	....	....	....	....	....	....
	Soviet Union	Olympics	7	6	5	11	....	....	....	4	....	....	....	....	....	....	....	....	....	....	....	....	....	....	....	....	....	....
1980-81	CSKA Moscow	USSR	47	25	15	40	....	....	....	20	....	....	....	....	....	....	....	....	....	....	....	....	....	....	....	....	....	....
	Soviet Union	WEC-A	8	6	3	9	....	....	....	8	....	....	....	....	....	....	....	....	....	....	....	....	....	....	....	....	....	....
1981-82	Soviet Union	Can-Cup	7	4	4	8	....	....	....	10	....	....	....	....	....	....	....	....	....	....	....	....	....	....	....	....	....	....
	CSKA Moscow	USSR	46	37	29	66	....	....	....	30	....	....	....	....	....	....	....	....	....	....	....	....	....	....	....	....	....	....
	Soviet Union	WEC-A	10	4	3	7	....	....	....	6	....	....	....	....	....	....	....	....	....	....	....	....	....	....	....	....	....	....
1982-83	CSKA Moscow	USSR	44	32	21	53	....	....	....	34	....	....	....	....	....	....	....	....	....	....	....	....	....	....	....	....	....	....
	USSR	Super-S	6	5	3	8	....	....	....	2	....	....	....	....	....	....	....	....	....	....	....	....	....	....	....	....	....	....
	Soviet Union	WEC-A	10	8	7	15	....	....	....	12	....	....	....	....	....	....	....	....	....	....	....	....	....	....	....	....	....	....
1983-84	CSKA Moscow	USSR	44	37	20	57	....	....	....	20	....	....	....	....	....	....	....	....	....	....	....	....	....	....	....	....	....	....
	Soviet Union	Olympics	7	4	1	5	....	....	....	2	....	....	....	....	....	....	....	....	....	....	....	....	....	....	....	....	....	....

Season	Club	League	GP	G	A	Pts	AG	AA	APts	PIM	PP	SH	GW	S	%	TGF	PGF	TGA	PGA	+/–	GP	G	A	Pts	PIM	PP	SH	GW
			REGULAR SEASON																		PLAYOFFS							
1984-85	Soviet Union	Can-Cup	6	3	5	8				4																		
	CSKA Moscow	USSR	40	23	30	53				26																		
	Soviet Union	WEC-A	10	3	5	8				8																		
1985-86	CSKA Moscow	USSR	40	31	17	48				10																		
	CSKA Moscow	Super-S	6	3	6	9				0																		
	Soviet Union	WEC-A	10	7	10	17				14																		
1986-87	CSKA Moscow	USSR	39	26	24	50				16																		
	USSR	RV-87	2	2	0	2				2																		
	Soviet Union	WEC-A	10	11	3	14				8																		
1987-88	Soviet Union	Can-Cup	9	7	7	14				4																		
	CSKA Moscow	USSR	38	19	23	42				20																		
	Soviet Union	Olympics	8	6	*9	*15				0																		
1988-89	CSKA Moscow	USSR	35	20	21	41				12																		
	CSKA Moscow	Super-S	5	2	2	4				2																		
	Soviet Union	WEC-A	10	4	2	6				12																		
1989-90	**Vancouver Canucks**	**NHL**	**61**	**11**	**23**	**34**	**9**	**16**	**25**	**20**	**2**	**0**	**1**	**81**	**13.6**	**53**	**18**	**45**	**5**	**–5**								
1990-91	ZSC Lions Zurich	Swiz.	1	0	1	1				0											3	3	6	9	0			
1991-92	ZSC Lions Zurich	Switz.	28	13	19	32				4											6	4	3	7	4			
1992-93	Ostersunds IK	Sweden-3	19	*25	24	*49				12																		
1993-94	Ostersunds IK	Sweden-2	28	18	22	40				14																		
1994-95	Ostersunds IK	Sweden-2	27	9	9	18				31																		
1995-96	Brunflo IK	Sweden-3	18	7	9	16				6																		
	NHL Totals		**61**	**11**	**23**	**34**	**9**	**16**	**25**	**20**	**2**	**0**	**1**	**81**	**13.6**	**53**	**18**	**45**	**5**									

WJC-A All-Star Team (1979, 1980) • Named Best Forward at WJC-A (1979, 1980) • USSR First All-Star Team (1982, 1983, 1984, 1985, 1986, 1987, 1988) • WEC-A All-Star Team (1983, 1985, 1986, 1987) • Named Best Forward at WEC-A (1986, 1987) • USSR Player of the Year (1987) • Canada Cup All-Star Team (1987)

• KRYGIER, Todd

Todd A. LW – L. 6', 185 lbs. b: Chicago Heights, IL, 10/12/1965. Hartford's 1st, 16th overall, in 1988 Supplemental Draft.

Season	Club	League	GP	G	A	Pts	AG	AA	APts	PIM	PP	SH	GW	S	%	TGF	PGF	TGA	PGA	+/–	GP	G	A	Pts	PIM	PP	SH	GW
1983-84	Buffalo Regals	NAJHL	STATISTICS NOT AVAILABLE																									
1984-85	University of Connecticut	ECAC-2	14	14	11	25				12																		
1985-86	University of Connecticut	ECAC-2	32	29	27	56				46																		
1986-87	University of Connecticut	ECAC-2	28	24	24	48				44																		
1987-88	University of Connecticut	ECAC-2	27	32	39	71				28																		
	New Haven Nighthawks	AHL	13	1	5	6				34																		
1988-89	Binghamton Whalers	AHL	76	26	42	68				77																		
1989-90	**Hartford Whalers**	**NHL**	**58**	**18**	**12**	**30**	**15**	**9**	**24**	**52**	**5**	**1**	**3**	**103**	**17.5**	**52**	**9**	**45**	**6**	**4**	**7**	**2**	**1**	**3**	**4**	**0**	**0**	**0**
	Binghamton Whalers	AHL	12	1	9	10				16																		
1990-91	**Hartford Whalers**	**NHL**	**72**	**13**	**17**	**30**	**12**	**13**	**25**	**95**	**3**	**0**	**2**	**113**	**11.5**	**42**	**8**	**50**	**17**	**1**	**6**	**0**	**2**	**2**	**0**	**0**	**0**	**0**
	United States	WEC-A	10	4	4	8				12																		
1991-92	**Washington Capitals**	**NHL**	**67**	**13**	**17**	**30**	**12**	**13**	**25**	**107**	**1**	**0**	**1**	**127**	**10.2**	**39**	**2**	**39**	**1**	**–1**	**5**	**2**	**1**	**3**	**4**	**0**	**0**	**0**
	United States	WC-A	1	0	0	0				2																		
1992-93	**Washington Capitals**	**NHL**	**77**	**11**	**12**	**23**	**9**	**8**	**17**	**60**	**0**	**2**	**0**	**133**	**8.3**	**41**	**2**	**64**	**12**	**–13**	**6**	**1**	**1**	**2**	**4**	**0**	**1**	**0**
1993-94	**Washington Capitals**	**NHL**	**66**	**12**	**18**	**30**	**11**	**14**	**25**	**60**	**0**	**1**	**3**	**146**	**8.2**	**41**	**1**	**58**	**14**	**–4**	**5**	**2**	**0**	**2**	**10**	**0**	**0**	**0**
1994-95	**Mighty Ducks of Anaheim**	**NHL**	**35**	**11**	**11**	**22**	**19**	**16**	**35**	**10**	**1**	**0**	**1**	**90**	**12.2**	**31**	**6**	**30**	**6**	**1**								
1995-96	**Mighty Ducks of Anaheim**	**NHL**	**60**	**9**	**28**	**37**	**9**	**23**	**32**	**70**	**2**	**1**	**0**	**153**	**5.9**	**46**	**8**	**53**	**6**	**–9**								
	Washington Capitals	**NHL**	**16**	**6**	**5**	**11**	**6**	**4**	**10**	**12**	**1**	**0**	**0**	**28**	**21.4**	**16**	**2**	**6**	**0**	**8**	**6**	**2**	**0**	**2**	**12**	**0**	**0**	**1**
1996-97	**Washington Capitals**	**NHL**	**47**	**5**	**11**	**16**	**5**	**10**	**15**	**37**	**1**	**0**	**1**	**121**	**4.1**	**24**	**7**	**27**	**0**	**–10**								
	United States	WC-A	8	1	1	2				6																		
1997-98	**Washington Capitals**	**NHL**	**45**	**2**	**12**	**14**	**2**	**12**	**14**	**30**	**0**	**0**	**1**	**71**	**2.8**	**24**	**6**	**23**	**2**	**–3**	**13**	**1**	**2**	**3**	**6**	**0**	**0**	**1**
	Portland Pirates	AHL	6	3	4	7				6																		
1998-99	Orlando Solar Bears	IHL	65	19	40	59				82											17	9	10	19	16			
99-2000	Orlando Solar Bears	IHL	28	7	13	20				12											6	2	1	3	2			
	NHL Totals		**543**	**100**	**143**	**243**	**100**	**122**	**222**	**533**	**14**	**5**	**12**	**1085**	**9.2**	**356**	**51**	**395**	**64**		**48**	**10**	**7**	**17**	**40**	**0**	**1**	**2**

NCAA (College Div.) East Second All-American Team (1987)

Traded to **Washington** by **Hartford** for Washington's 4th round choice (later traded to Calgary — Calgary selected Jason Smith) in 1993 Entry Draft, October 3, 1991. Traded to **Anaheim** by **Washington** for Anaheim's 4th round choice (later traded to Dallas — Dallas selected Mike Hurley) in 1996 Entry Draft, February 2, 1995. Traded to **Washington** by **Anaheim** for Mike Torchia, March 8, 1996. Signed as a free agent by **Orlando** (IHL), November 11, 1999.

• KRYSKOW, Dave

David Roy LW – L. 5'10", 175 lbs. b: Edmonton, Alta., 12/25/1957. Chicago's 2nd, 26th overall, in 1971.

Season	Club	League	GP	G	A	Pts	AG	AA	APts	PIM	PP	SH	GW	S	%	TGF	PGF	TGA	PGA	+/–	GP	G	A	Pts	PIM	PP	SH	GW
1969-70	Saskatoon Blades	WCJHL	28	4	25	29				57																		
	Edmonton Oil Kings	WCJHL	22	8	8	16				24											6	0	6	6	24			
1970-71	Edmonton Oil Kings	WCJHL	65	42	45	87				149											17	16	17	33	30			
	Edmonton Oil Kings	Mem-Cup	2	0	0	0				10																		
1971-72	Dallas Black Hawks	CHL	55	9	18	27				85											3	0	0	0	0			
1972-73	**Chicago Black Hawks**	**NHL**	**11**	**1**	**0**	**1**	**1**	**0**	**1**	**0**	**0**	**0**	**0**	**4**	**25.0**	**3**	**0**	**4**	**0**	**–1**	**3**	**2**	**0**	**2**	**0**	**0**	**0**	**0**
	Dallas Black Hawks	CHL	52	34	28	62				110											7	2	3	5	4			
1973-74	**Chicago Black Hawks**	**NHL**	**72**	**7**	**12**	**19**	**7**	**10**	**17**	**22**	**0**	**1**	**0**	**60**	**11.7**	**29**	**0**	**28**	**4**	**5**	**7**	**0**	**0**	**0**	**2**	**0**	**0**	**0**
1974-75	**Washington Capitals**	**NHL**	**51**	**9**	**15**	**24**	**8**	**11**	**19**	**83**	**1**	**1**	**0**	**98**	**9.2**	**40**	**12**	**71**	**15**	**–28**								
	Detroit Red Wings	**NHL**	**18**	**1**	**4**	**5**	**1**	**3**	**4**	**4**	**0**	**0**	**0**	**7**	**14.3**	**4**	**0**	**6**	**0**	**–2**								
1975-76	**Atlanta Flames**	**NHL**	**79**	**15**	**25**	**40**	**13**	**19**	**32**	**65**	**1**	**0**	**2**	**120**	**12.5**	**57**	**6**	**60**	**3**	**–6**	**2**	**0**	**0**	**0**	**2**	**0**	**0**	**0**
1976-77	Calgary Cowboys	WHA	45	16	17	33				47																		
	Tidewater Sharks	SHL	37	16	23	39				95																		
1977-78	Winnipeg Jets	WHA	71	20	21	41				16											9	4	4	8	2			
	NHL Totals		**231**	**33**	**56**	**89**	**30**	**43**	**73**	**174**	**2**	**2**	**2**	**289**	**11.4**	**133**	**18**	**169**	**22**		**12**	**2**	**0**	**2**	**4**	**0**	**0**	**0**
	Other Major League Totals		116	36	38	74				63											9	4	4	8	2			

CHL First All-Star Team (1973)

Selected by **Edmonton** (WHA) in 1972 WHA General Player Draft, February 12, 1972. Claimed by **Washington** from **Chicago** in Expansion Draft, June 12, 1974. Traded to **Detroit** by **Washington** for Jack Lynch, February 8, 1975. Traded to **Atlanta** by **Detroit** for Bryan Hextall Jr., June 5, 1975. WHA rights traded to **Calgary** (WHA) by **Edmonton** (WHA) for future considerations, September, 1976. Signed as a free agent by **Winnipeg** (WHA) after **Calgary** (WHA) franchise folded, November, 1977.

• KUBA, Filip

D – L. 6'3", 202 lbs. b: Ostrava, Czech., 12/29/1976. Florida's 8th, 192nd overall, in 1995.

Season	Club	League	GP	G	A	Pts	AG	AA	APts	PIM	PP	SH	GW	S	%	TGF	PGF	TGA	PGA	+/–	GP	G	A	Pts	PIM	PP	SH	GW
1994-95	HC Vitkovice	Czech-Jr.	35	10	15	25																						
	HC Vitkovice	Czech-Rep																			4	0	0	0	2			
1995-96	HC Vitkovice	Czech-Rep	19	0	1	1																						
1996-97	Carolina Monarchs	AHL	51	0	12	12				38																		
1997-98	Beast of New Haven	AHL	77	4	13	17				58											3	1	1	2	0			
1998-99	**Florida Panthers**	**NHL**	**5**	**0**	**1**	**1**	**0**	**1**	**1**	**0**	**0**	**0**	**0**	**5**	**0.0**	**4**	**0**	**2**	**0**	**2**								
	Kentucky Thoroughblades	AHL	45	2	8	10				33											10	0	1	1	4			
99-2000	**Florida Panthers**	**NHL**	**13**	**1**	**5**	**6**	**1**	**5**	**6**	**2**	**1**	**0**	**1**	**16**	**6.3**	**10**	**6**	**8**	**1**	**–3**								
	Houston Aeros	IHL	27	3	6	9				13											11	1	2	3	4			
	NHL Totals		**18**	**1**	**6**	**7**	**1**	**6**	**7**	**2**	**1**	**0**	**1**	**21**	**4.8**	**14**	**6**	**10**	**1**									

Traded to **Calgary** by **Florida** for Rocky Thompson, March 16, 2000. Selected by **Minnesota** from **Calgary** in Expansion Draft, June 23, 2000.

• KUBINA, Pavel

D – R. 6'3", 213 lbs. b: Celadna, Czech., 4/15/1977. Tampa Bay's 6th, 179th overall, in 1996.

Season	Club	League	GP	G	A	Pts	AG	AA	APts	PIM	PP	SH	GW	S	%	TGF	PGF	TGA	PGA	+/–	GP	G	A	Pts	PIM	PP	SH	GW
1993-94	HC Vitkovice	Czech-Jr.	35	4	3	7																						
	HC Vitkovice	Czech-Rep	1	0	0	0																						
1994-95	HC Vitkovice	Czech-Jr.	20	6	10	16																						
	HC Vitkovice	Czech-Rep	8	2	0	2				10											4	0	0	0	0			

			REGULAR SEASON																		PLAYOFFS							
Season	**Club**	**League**	**GP**	**G**	**A**	**Pts**	**AG**	**AA**	**APts**	**PIM**	**PP**	**SH**	**GW**	**S**	**%**	**TGF**	**PGF**	**TGA**	**PGA**	**+/–**	**GP**	**G**	**A**	**Pts**	**PIM**	**PP**	**SH**	**GW**
1995-96	HC Vitkovice	Czech-Rep	33	3	4	7	....	....	....	32	....	....	....	....	....	....	....	....	....	....	4	0	0	0	0	....	....	....
	Czech-Republic	WJC-A	6	0	2	2	....	....	....	8	....	....	....	....	....	....	....	....	....	....	....	....	....	....	....	....	....	....
	HC Vitkovice	Czech-Jr.	16	5	10	15	....	....	....	....	....	....	....	....	....	....	....	....	....	....	....	....	....	....	....	....	....	....
1996-97	HC Vitkovice	Czech-Rep	1	0	0	0	....	....	....	0	....	....	....	....	....	....	....	....	....	....	....	....	....	....	....	....	....	....
	Moose Jaw Warriors	WHL	61	12	32	44	....	....	....	116	....	....	....	....	....	....	....	....	....	....	11	2	5	7	27	....	....	....
1997-98	**Tampa Bay Lightning**	**NHL**	**10**	**1**	**2**	**3**	**1**	**2**	**3**	**22**	**0**	**0**	**0**	**8**	**12.5**	**7**	**0**	**12**	**4**	**–1**	....	....	....	....	....	....	....	....
	Adirondack Red Wings	AHL	55	4	8	12	....	....	....	86	....	....	....	....	....	....	....	....	....	....	1	1	0	1	14	....	....	....
1998-99	**Tampa Bay Lighning**	**NHL**	**68**	**9**	**12**	**21**	**11**	**12**	**23**	**80**	**3**	**1**	**1**	**119**	**7.6**	**54**	**13**	**89**	**15**	**–33**	....	....	....	....	....	....	....	....
	Cleveland Lumberjacks	IHL	6	2	2	4	....	....	....	16	....	....	....	....	....	....	....	....	....	....	....	....	....	....	....	....	....	....
	Czech-Republic	WC-A	12	2	6	8	....	....	....	12	....	....	....	....	....	....	....	....	....	....	....	....	....	....	....	....	....	....
99-2000	**Tampa Bay Lightning**	**NHL**	**69**	**8**	**18**	**26**	**9**	**17**	**26**	**93**	**6**	**0**	**3**	**128**	**6.3**	**87**	**30**	**89**	**13**	**–19**	....	....	....	....	....	....	....	....
	NHL Totals		**147**	**18**	**32**	**50**	**21**	**31**	**52**	**195**	**9**	**1**	**4**	**255**	**7.1**	**148**	**43**	**190**	**32**		....	....	....	....	....	....	....	....

WC-A All-Star Team (1999)

• KUCERA, Frantisek

D – R. 6′2″, 205 lbs. b: Prague, Czech., 2/3/1968. Chicago's 3rd, 77th overall, in 1986.

Season	Club	League	GP	G	A	Pts	AG	AA	APts	PIM	PP	SH	GW	S	%	TGF	PGF	TGA	PGA	+/–	GP	G	A	Pts	PIM	PP	SH	GW
1984-85	HC Sparta Praha	Czech-2	STATISTICS NOT AVAILABLE																									
	Czechoslovakia	EJC-A	5	0	2	2	....	....	....	2	....	....	....	....	....	....	....	....	....	....	....	....	....	....	....	....	....	....
1985-86	HC Sparta Praha	Czech.	15	0	0	0	....	....	....	....	....	....	....	....	....	....	....	....	....	....	....	....	....	....	....	....	....	....
	Czechoslovakia	EJC-A	5	1	2	3	....	....	....	4	....	....	....	....	....	....	....	....	....	....	....	....	....	....	....	....	....	....
1986-87	HC Sparta Praha	Czech.	40	5	2	7	....	....	....	14	....	....	....	....	....	....	....	....	....	....	....	....	....	....	....	....	....	....
	Czechoslovakia	WJC-A	7	1	2	3	....	....	....	2	....	....	....	....	....	....	....	....	....	....	....	....	....	....	....	....	....	....
1987-88	HC Sparta Praha	Czech.	46	7	2	9	....	....	....	30	....	....	....	....	....	....	....	....	....	....	....	....	....	....	....	....	....	....
	Czechoslovakia	WJC-A	7	1	2	3	....	....	....	2	....	....	....	....	....	....	....	....	....	....	....	....	....	....	....	....	....	....
1988-89	Dukla Jihlava	Czech.	45	10	9	19	....	....	....	28	....	....	....	....	....	....	....	....	....	....	....	....	....	....	....	....	....	....
	Czechoslovakia	WEC-A	6	0	1	1	....	....	....	6	....	....	....	....	....	....	....	....	....	....	....	....	....	....	....	....	....	....
1989-90	Dukla Jihlava	Czech.	42	8	10	18	....	....	....	....	....	....	....	....	....	....	....	....	....	....	1	1	0	1	....	....	....	....
1990-91	**Chicago Blackhawks**	**NHL**	**40**	**2**	**12**	**14**	**2**	**9**	**11**	**32**	**1**	**0**	**0**	**65**	**3.1**	**38**	**9**	**38**	**12**	**3**	....	....	....	....	....	....	....	....
	Indianapolis Ice	IHL	35	8	19	27	....	....	....	23	....	....	....	....	....	....	....	....	....	....	7	0	1	1	15	....	....	....
1991-92	Czechoslovakia	Can-Cup	5	0	0	0	....	....	....	4	....	....	....	....	....	....	....	....	....	....	....	....	....	....	....	....	....	....
	Chicago Blackhawks	**NHL**	**61**	**3**	**10**	**13**	**3**	**8**	**11**	**36**	**1**	**0**	**1**	**82**	**3.7**	**50**	**12**	**58**	**23**	**3**	**6**	**0**	**0**	**0**	**0**	**0**	**0**	**0**
	Indianapolis Ice	IHL	7	1	2	3	....	....	....	4	....	....	....	....	....	....	....	....	....	....	....	....	....	....	....	....	....	....
1992-93	**Chicago Blackhawks**	**NHL**	**71**	**5**	**14**	**19**	**4**	**10**	**14**	**59**	**1**	**0**	**1**	**117**	**4.3**	**57**	**8**	**54**	**12**	**7**	....	....	....	....	....	....	....	....
1993-94	**Chicago Blackhawks**	**NHL**	**60**	**4**	**13**	**17**	**4**	**10**	**14**	**34**	**2**	**0**	**0**	**90**	**4.4**	**53**	**6**	**48**	**10**	**9**	....	....	....	....	....	....	....	....
	Hartford Whalers	**NHL**	**16**	**1**	**3**	**4**	**1**	**2**	**3**	**14**	**1**	**0**	**0**	**32**	**3.1**	**15**	**7**	**27**	**7**	**–12**	....	....	....	....	....	....	....	....
	Czech-Republic	WC-A	4	0	0	0	....	....	....	2	....	....	....	....	....	....	....	....	....	....	....	....	....	....	....	....	....	....
1994-95	HC Sparta Praha	Czech-Rep	16	1	2	3	....	....	....	14	....	....	....	....	....	....	....	....	....	....	....	....	....	....	....	....	....	....
	Hartford Whalers	**NHL**	**48**	**3**	**17**	**20**	**5**	**25**	**30**	**30**	**0**	**0**	**1**	**73**	**4.1**	**38**	**7**	**38**	**10**	**3**	....	....	....	....	....	....	....	....
1995-96	**Hartford Whalers**	**NHL**	**30**	**2**	**6**	**8**	**2**	**5**	**7**	**10**	**0**	**0**	**1**	**43**	**4.7**	**22**	**3**	**25**	**3**	**–3**	....	....	....	....	....	....	....	....
	Vancouver Canucks	**NHL**	**24**	**1**	**0**	**1**	**1**	**0**	**1**	**10**	**0**	**0**	**0**	**34**	**2.9**	**20**	**5**	**13**	**3**	**5**	**6**	**0**	**1**	**1**	**0**	**0**	**0**	**0**
1996-97	**Vancouver Canucks**	**NHL**	**2**	**0**	**0**	**0**	**0**	**0**	**0**	**0**	**0**	**0**	**0**	**3**	**0.0**	**0**	**0**	**1**	**1**	**0**	....	....	....	....	....	....	....	....
	Syracuse Crunch	AHL	42	6	29	35	....	....	....	36	....	....	....	....	....	....	....	....	....	....	....	....	....	....	....	....	....	....
	Houston Aeros	IHL	12	0	3	3	....	....	....	20	....	....	....	....	....	....	....	....	....	....	....	....	....	....	....	....	....	....
	Philadelphia Flyers	**NHL**	**2**	**0**	**0**	**0**	**0**	**0**	**0**	**2**	**0**	**0**	**0**	**2**	**0.0**	**1**	**1**	**2**	**0**	**–2**	....	....	....	....	....	....	....	....
	Philadelphia Phantoms	AHL	9	1	5	6	....	....	....	2	....	....	....	....	....	....	....	....	....	....	10	1	6	7	20	....	....	....
1997-98	HC Sparta Praha	Czech-Rep	43	8	12	20	....	....	....	49	....	....	....	....	....	....	....	....	....	....	9	3	1	4	*53	....	....	....
	HC Sparta Praha	EuroHL	4	0	1	1	....	....	....	2	....	....	....	....	....	....	....	....	....	....	....	....	....	....	....	....	....	....
	Czech-Republic	Olympics	6	0	0	0	....	....	....	0	....	....	....	....	....	....	....	....	....	....	....	....	....	....	....	....	....	....
1998-99	HC Sparta Praha	Czech-Rep	42	3	12	15	....	....	....	92	....	....	....	....	....	....	....	....	....	....	8	0	2	2	....	....	....	....
	HC Sparta Praha	EuroHL	6	0	2	2	....	....	....	10	....	....	....	....	....	....	....	....	....	....	2	0	0	0	2	....	....	....
	Czech-Republic	WC-A	12	0	6	6	....	....	....	6	....	....	....	....	....	....	....	....	....	....	....	....	....	....	....	....	....	....
99-2000	HC Sparta Praha	Czech-Rep	51	7	26	33	....	....	....	40	....	....	....	....	....	....	....	....	....	....	9	1	9	10	4	....	....	....
	HC Sparta Praha	EuroHL	6	0	2	2	....	....	....	4	....	....	....	....	....	....	....	....	....	....	4	0	1	1	2	....	....	....
	Czech Republic	WC-A	9	2	2	4	....	....	....	6	....	....	....	....	....	....	....	....	....	....	....	....	....	....	....	....	....	....
	NHL Totals		**354**	**21**	**75**	**96**	**22**	**69**	**91**	**227**	**6**	**0**	**4**	**541**	**3.9**	**294**	**58**	**304**	**81**		**12**	**0**	**1**	**1**	**0**	**0**	**0**	**0**

EJC-A All-Star Team (1986) • Named Best Defenseman at WC-A (1999)

Traded to **Hartford** by **Chicago** with Jocelyn Lemieux for Gary Suter, Randy Cunneyworth and Hartford's 3rd round choice (later traded to Vancouver — Vancouver selected Larry Courville) in 1995 Entry Draft, March 11, 1994. Traded to **Vancouver** by **Hartford** with Jim Dowd and Hartford's 2nd round choice (Ryan Bonni) in 1997 Entry Draft for Jeff Brown and Vancouver's 3rd round choice (later traded to Calgary — Calgary selected Paul Manning) in 1998 Entry Draft, December 19, 1995. Traded to **Philadelphia** by **Vancouver** for future considerations, March 18, 1997. Signed as a free agent by **Columbus**, July 7, 2000.

• KUDASHOV, Alexei

C – R. 6′, 183 lbs. b: Elektrostal, USSR, 7/21/1971. Toronto's 3rd, 102nd overall, in 1991.

Season	Club	League	GP	G	A	Pts	AG	AA	APts	PIM	PP	SH	GW	S	%	TGF	PGF	TGA	PGA	+/–	GP	G	A	Pts	PIM	PP	SH	GW
1988-89	Krylja Sovetov Moscow	USSR-2	STATISTICS NOT AVAILABLE																									
	Soviet Union	EJC-A	6	5	1	6	....	....	....	2	....	....	....	....	....	....	....	....	....	....	....	....	....	....	....	....	....	....
1989-90	Krylja Sovetov Moscow	Fr-Tour	1	0	0	0	....	....	....	0	....	....	....	....	....	....	....	....	....	....	....	....	....	....	....	....	....	....
	Krylja Sovetov Moscow	USSR	45	0	5	5	....	....	....	14	....	....	....	....	....	....	....	....	....	....	....	....	....	....	....	....	....	....
	Soviet Union	WJC-A	7	2	1	3	....	....	....	0	....	....	....	....	....	....	....	....	....	....	....	....	....	....	....	....	....	....
1990-91	Krylja Sovetov Moscow	Fr-Tour	1	0	0	0	....	....	....	0	....	....	....	....	....	....	....	....	....	....	....	....	....	....	....	....	....	....
	Krylja Sovetov Moscow	USSR	45	9	5	14	....	....	....	10	....	....	....	....	....	....	....	....	....	....	....	....	....	....	....	....	....	....
	Soviet Union	WJC-A	7	2	8	10	....	....	....	6	....	....	....	....	....	....	....	....	....	....	....	....	....	....	....	....	....	....
1991-92	Krylja Sovetov Moscow	CIS	42	9	16	25	....	....	....	14	....	....	....	....	....	....	....	....	....	....	....	....	....	....	....	....	....	....
1992-93	Krylja Sovetov Moscow	CIS	41	8	20	28	....	....	....	24	....	....	....	....	....	....	....	....	....	....	7	1	3	4	4	....	....	....
1993-94	Krylja Sovetov Moscow	CIS	1	2	0	2	....	....	....	0	....	....	....	....	....	....	....	....	....	....	....	....	....	....	....	....	....	....
	Toronto Maple Leafs	**NHL**	**25**	**1**	**0**	**1**	**1**	**0**	**1**	**4**	**0**	**0**	**0**	**24**	**4.2**	**2**	**0**	**6**	**1**	**–3**	....	....	....	....	....	....	....	....
	St. John's Maple Leafs	AHL	27	7	15	22	....	....	....	21	....	....	....	....	....	....	....	....	....	....	....	....	....	....	....	....	....	....
1994-95	St. John's Maple Leafs	AHL	75	25	54	79	....	....	....	17	....	....	....	....	....	....	....	....	....	....	5	1	4	5	2	....	....	....
1995-96	Carolina Monarchs	AHL	33	7	22	29	....	....	....	18	....	....	....	....	....	....	....	....	....	....	....	....	....	....	....	....	....	....
	Dusseldorfer EG	Germany	9	7	8	15	....	....	....	4	....	....	....	....	....	....	....	....	....	....	13	5	5	10	14	....	....	....
1996-97	Dusseldorfer EG	Germany	48	13	16	29	....	....	....	16	....	....	....	....	....	....	....	....	....	....	4	3	1	4	2	....	....	....
1997-98	TPS Turku	Finland	48	8	31	39	....	....	....	34	....	....	....	....	....	....	....	....	....	....	4	0	0	0	4	....	....	....
	TPS Turku	EuroHL	6	0	2	2	....	....	....	0	....	....	....	....	....	....	....	....	....	....	....	....	....	....	....	....	....	....
	Russia	WC-A	3	1	2	3	....	....	....	2	....	....	....	....	....	....	....	....	....	....	....	....	....	....	....	....	....	....
1998-99	AK Bars Kazan	Russia	41	8	8	16	....	....	....	32	....	....	....	....	....	....	....	....	....	....	9	5	1	6	2	....	....	....
	AK Bars Kazan	EuroHL	6	1	1	2	....	....	....	2	....	....	....	....	....	....	....	....	....	....	2	2	0	2	0	....	....	....
	Russia	WC-A	6	0	2	2	....	....	....	6	....	....	....	....	....	....	....	....	....	....	....	....	....	....	....	....	....	....
99-2000	Dynamo Moscow	Russia	37	12	12	24	....	....	....	20	....	....	....	....	....	....	....	....	....	....	14	0	4	4	20	....	....	....
	Russia	WC-A	6	0	1	1	....	....	....	4	....	....	....	....	....	....	....	....	....	....	....	....	....	....	....	....	....	....
	NHL Totals		**25**	**1**	**0**	**1**	**1**	**0**	**1**	**4**	**0**	**0**	**0**	**24**	**4.2**	**2**	**0**	**6**	**1**		....	....	....	....	....	....	....	....

Signed as a free agent by **Florida**, September 10, 1995.

• KUDELSKI, Bob

Robert RW – R. 6′1″, 205 lbs. b: Springfield, MA, 3/3/1964. Los Angeles' 1st, 2nd overall, in 1986 Supplemental Draft.

Season	Club	League	GP	G	A	Pts	AG	AA	APts	PIM	PP	SH	GW	S	%	TGF	PGF	TGA	PGA	+/–	GP	G	A	Pts	PIM	PP	SH	GW
1981-82	Feeding Hills High School	Hi-School	STATISTICS NOT AVAILABLE																									
1982-83	Springfield Jr. Pics	EJHL-B	STATISTICS NOT AVAILABLE																									
1983-84	Yale University	ECAC	21	14	12	26	....	....	....	12	....	....	....	....	....	....	....	....	....	....	....	....	....	....	....	....	....	....
1984-85	Yale University	ECAC	32	21	23	44	....	....	....	38	....	....	....	....	....	....	....	....	....	....	....	....	....	....	....	....	....	....
1985-86	Yale University	ECAC	31	18	23	41	....	....	....	48	....	....	....	....	....	....	....	....	....	....	....	....	....	....	....	....	....	....
1986-87	Yale University	ECAC	30	25	22	47	....	....	....	34	....	....	....	....	....	....	....	....	....	....	....	....	....	....	....	....	....	....
1987-88	**Los Angeles Kings**	**NHL**	**26**	**0**	**1**	**1**	**0**	**1**	**1**	**8**	**0**	**0**	**0**	**18**	**0.0**	**3**	**1**	**30**	**18**	**–10**	....	....	....	....	....	....	....	....
	New Haven Nighthawks	AHL	50	15	19	34	....	....	....	41	....	....	....	....	....	....	....	....	....	....	....	....	....	....	....	....	....	....
1988-89	**Los Angeles Kings**	**NHL**	**14**	**1**	**3**	**4**	**1**	**2**	**3**	**17**	**0**	**0**	**0**	**15**	**6.7**	**6**	**0**	**11**	**0**	**–5**	....	....	....	....	....	....	....	....
	New Haven Nighthawks	AHL	60	32	19	51	....	....	....	43	....	....	....	....	....	....	....	....	....	....	17	8	5	13	12	....	....	....

			REGULAR SEASON																		PLAYOFFS							
Season	Club	League	GP	G	A	Pts	AG	AA	APts	PIM	PP	SH	GW	S	%	TGF	PGF	TGA	PGA	+/-	GP	G	A	Pts	PIM	PP	SH	GW
1989-90	Los Angeles Kings	NHL	62	23	13	36	20	9	29	49	2	2	3	135	17.0	53	11	60	11	-7	8	1	2	3	2	0	0	0
1990-91	Los Angeles Kings	NHL	72	23	13	36	21	10	31	46	2	3	3	137	16.8	57	7	62	21	9	8	3	2	5	2	0	0	0
1991-92	Los Angeles Kings	NHL	80	22	21	43	20	16	36	42	2	1	2	155	14.2	58	10	82	19	-15	6	0	0	0	0	0	0	0
1992-93	Los Angeles Kings	NHL	15	3	3	6	2	2	4	8	0	0	1	12	25.0	11	4	12	2	-3	....	....	....	....	....	....	....	....
	Ottawa Senators	NHL	48	21	14	35	17	10	27	22	12	0	2	125	16.8	54	31	45	0	-22	....	....	....	....	....	....	....	....
1993-94	Ottawa Senators	NHL	42	26	15	41	24	12	36	14	12	0	1	127	20.5	57	25	58	1	-25	....	....	....	....	....	....	....	....
	Florida Panthers	NHL	44	14	15	29	13	12	25	10	5	0	2	124	11.3	41	15	34	0	-8	....	....	....	....	....	....	....	....
1994-95	Florida Panthers	NHL	26	6	3	9	11	4	15	2	3	0	1	29	20.7	15	6	7	0	2	....	....	....	....	....	....	....	....
1995-96	Florida Panthers	NHL	13	0	1	1	0	1	1	0	0	0	0	23	0.0	5	1	3	0	1	....	....	....	....	....	....	....	....
	Carolina Monarchs	AHL	4	1	0	1	....	....	....	0	....	....	....	....	....	....	....	....	....	....	....	....	....	....	....	....	....	....
	NHL Totals		442	139	102	241	129	79	208	218	38	6	15	900	15.4	360	111	404	72		22	4	4	8	4	0	0	0

ECAC First All-Star Team (1987) • Played in NHL All-Star Game (1994)

Traded to **Ottawa** by **LA Kings** with Shawn McCosh for Marc Fortier and Jim Thomson, December 19, 1992. Traded to **Florida** by **Ottawa** for Evgeny Davydov, Scott Levins, Florida's 6th round choice (Mike Gaffney) in 1994 Entry Draft and Dallas' 4th round choice (previously acquired, Ottawa selected Kevin Bolibruck) in 1995 Entry Draft, January 6, 1994.

• KULAK, Stu

Stuart RW – R. 5'10", 180 lbs. b: Edmonton, Alta., 3/10/1963. Vancouver's 5th, 115th overall, in 1981.

Season	Club	League	GP	G	A	Pts	AG	AA	APts	PIM	PP	SH	GW	S	%	TGF	PGF	TGA	PGA	+/-	GP	G	A	Pts	PIM	PP	SH	GW
1979-80	Sherwood Park Crusaders	AJHL	53	30	23	53	....	....	....	111	....	....	....	....	....	....	....	....	....	....	....	....	....	....	....	....	....	....
	Victoria Cougars	WHL	3	0	0	0	....	....	....	0	....	....	....	....	....	....	....	....	....	....	....	....	....	....	....	....	....	....
1980-81	Victoria Cougars	WHL	72	23	24	47	....	....	....	43	....	....	....	....	....	....	....	....	....	....	15	3	5	8	19	....	....	....
	Victoria Cougars	Mem-Cup	4	0	0	0	....	....	....	7	....	....	....	....	....	....	....	....	....	....	....	....	....	....	....	....	....	....
1981-82	Victoria Cougars	WHL	71	38	50	88	....	....	....	92	....	....	....	....	....	....	....	....	....	....	4	1	2	3	43	....	....	....
1982-83	**Vancouver Canucks**	**NHL**	4	1	1	2	1	1	2	0	0	0	0	2	50.0	2	0	1	0	1	....	....	....	....	....	....	....	....
	Victoria Cougars	WHL	50	29	33	62	....	....	....	130	....	....	....	....	....	....	....	....	....	....	10	10	9	19	29	....	....	....
1983-84	Fredericton Express	AHL	52	12	16	28	....	....	....	55	....	....	....	....	....	....	....	....	....	....	5	0	0	0	59	....	....	....
1984-85	Fredericton Express	AHL	DID NOT PLAY – INJURED																									
1985-86	Fredericton Express	AHL	3	1	0	1	....	....	....	0	....	....	....	....	....	....	....	....	....	....	6	2	1	3	0	....	....	....
	Kalamazoo Wings	IHL	30	14	8	22	....	....	....	38	....	....	....	....	....	....	....	....	....	....	2	2	0	2	0	....	....	....
1986-87	**Vancouver Canucks**	**NHL**	28	1	1	2	1	1	2	37	1	0	1	24	4.2	2	1	13	1	-11	....	....	....	....	....	....	....	....
	Edmonton Oilers	**NHL**	23	3	1	4	3	1	4	41	0	0	1	30	10.0	11	0	8	0	3	....	....	....	....	....	....	....	....
	New York Rangers	**NHL**	3	0	0	0	0	0	0	0	0	0	0	2	0.0	1	0	2	0	-1	3	0	0	0	2	0	0	0
1987-88	**Quebec Nordiques**	**NHL**	14	1	1	2	1	1	2	28	0	0	0	22	4.5	2	0	7	0	-5	....	....	....	....	....	....	....	....
	Moncton Hawks	AHL	37	9	12	21	....	....	....	58	....	....	....	....	....	....	....	....	....	....	....	....	....	....	....	....	....	....
1988-89	**Winnipeg Jets**	**NHL**	18	2	0	2	2	0	2	24	1	0	0	18	11.1	2	1	7	0	-6	....	....	....	....	....	....	....	....
	Moncton Hawks	AHL	51	30	29	59	....	....	....	98	....	....	....	....	....	....	....	....	....	....	10	5	6	11	16	....	....	....
1989-90	Moncton Hawks	AHL	36	14	23	37	....	....	....	72	....	....	....	....	....	....	....	....	....	....	....	....	....	....	....	....	....	....
1990-91	Kansas City Blades	IHL	47	13	28	41	....	....	....	20	....	....	....	....	....	....	....	....	....	....	....	....	....	....	....	....	....	....
1991-92	TIJ Tilburg	Holland	18	14	17	31	....	....	....	44	....	....	....	....	....	....	....	....	....	....	....	....	....	....	....	....	....	....
1992-93	Erie Panthers	ECHL	21	13	8	21	....	....	....	23	....	....	....	....	....	....	....	....	....	....	....	....	....	....	....	....	....	....
1993-94	Tulsa Oilers	CHL	59	17	29	46	....	....	....	101	....	....	....	....	....	....	....	....	....	....	8	0	0	0	28	....	....	....
1994-95	San Antonio Iguanas	CHL	65	30	38	68	....	....	....	97	....	....	....	....	....	....	....	....	....	....	13	3	3	6	36	....	....	....
1995-96	Reno Renegades	WCHL	43	16	25	41	....	....	....	60	....	....	....	....	....	....	....	....	....	....	3	1	1	2	0	....	....	....
1996-97	Reno Renegades	WCHL	36	12	18	30	....	....	....	60	....	....	....	....	....	....	....	....	....	....	....	....	....	....	....	....	....	....
	New Mexico Scorpions	WCHL	5	0	0	0	....	....	....	0	....	....	....	....	....	....	....	....	....	....	6	1	1	2	8	....	....	....
1997-98	Reno Renegades	WCHL	63	16	25	41	....	....	....	54	....	....	....	....	....	....	....	....	....	....	3	3	2	5	4	....	....	....
1998-99	Tucson Gila Monsters	WCHL	21	8	15	23	....	....	....	16	....	....	....	....	....	....	....	....	....	....	....	....	....	....	....	....	....	....
	Phoenix Mustangs	WCHL	20	3	15	18	....	....	....	18	....	....	....	....	....	....	....	....	....	....	....	....	....	....	....	....	....	....
	Fresno Fighting Falcons	WCHL	9	5	6	11	....	....	....	8	....	....	....	....	....	....	....	....	....	....	7	2	2	4	6	....	....	....
99-2000	Austin Ice Bats	WPHL	42	4	10	14	....	....	....	16	....	....	....	....	....	....	....	....	....	....	....	....	....	....	....	....	....	....
	NHL Totals		90	8	4	12	8	4	12	130	2	0	2	98	8.2	20	2	38	1		3	0	0	0	2	0	0	0

• Missed entire 1984-85 season recovering from abdominal injury suffered in training camp, September, 1984. Traded to **Edmonton** by **Vancouver** for cash December 11, 1986. Traded to **NY Rangers** by **Edmonton** to complete transaction that sent Reijo Ruotsalanien, Clark Donatelli, Velle Kentala and Jim Wiemer to Edmonton (October 23, 1986), March 10, 1987. Claimed by **Quebec** from **NY Rangers** in Waiver Draft, October 5, 1987. Traded to **Winnipeg** by **Quebec** for Bobby Dollas, December 17,1987. • Played w/ RHI's Las Vegas Flash (19-9-13-22-44) and Oakland Skates (5-1-1-2-2) in 1994; Sacremento River Rats in 1997 (21-7-8-15-50).

• KUMPEL, Mark

Mark Alan RW – R. 6', 190 lbs. b: Wakefield, MA, 3/7/1961. Quebec's 4th, 108th overall, in 1980.

Season	Club	League	GP	G	A	Pts	AG	AA	APts	PIM	PP	SH	GW	S	%	TGF	PGF	TGA	PGA	+/-	GP	G	A	Pts	PIM	PP	SH	GW
1979-80	U. of Massachusetts-Lowell	ECAC	30	18	18	36	....	....	....	12	....	....	....	....	....	....	....	....	....	....	....	....	....	....	....	....	....	....
1980-81	U. of Massachusetts-Lowell	ECAC	1	2	0	2	....	....	....	0	....	....	....	....	....	....	....	....	....	....	....	....	....	....	....	....	....	....
1981-82	U. of Massachusetts-Lowell	ECAC	35	17	13	30	....	....	....	23	....	....	....	....	....	....	....	....	....	....	....	....	....	....	....	....	....	....
1982-83	U. of Massachusetts-Lowell	ECAC	7	8	5	13	....	....	....	0	....	....	....	....	....	....	....	....	....	....	....	....	....	....	....	....	....	....
	United States	Nat-Team	30	14	18	32	....	....	....	6	....	....	....	....	....	....	....	....	....	....	....	....	....	....	....	....	....	....
1983-84	United States	Nat-Team	61	14	19	33	....	....	....	19	....	....	....	....	....	....	....	....	....	....	....	....	....	....	....	....	....	....
	United States	Olympics	6	1	0	1	....	....	....	2	....	....	....	....	....	....	....	....	....	....	....	....	....	....	....	....	....	....
	Fredericton Express	AHL	16	1	1	2	....	....	....	5	....	....	....	....	....	....	....	....	....	....	3	0	0	0	15	....	....	....
1984-85	**Quebec Nordiques**	**NHL**	42	8	7	15	6	5	11	26	1	0	0	52	15.4	23	1	18	0	4	18	3	4	7	4	0	0	1
	Fredericton Express	AHL	18	9	6	15	....	....	....	17	....	....	....	....	....	....	....	....	....	....	....	....	....	....	....	....	....	....
1985-86	**Quebec Nordiques**	**NHL**	47	10	12	22	8	8	16	17	0	0	3	76	13.2	37	3	25	1	10	2	1	0	1	0	0	0	0
	Fredericton Express	AHL	7	4	2	6	....	....	....	4	....	....	....	....	....	....	....	....	....	....	....	....	....	....	....	....	....	....
1986-87	**Quebec Nordiques**	**NHL**	40	1	8	9	1	6	7	16	0	0	0	47	2.1	15	2	25	0	-12	....	....	....	....	....	....	....	....
	Detroit Red Wings	**NHL**	5	0	1	1	0	1	1	0	0	0	0	1	0.0	2	0	0	0	2	8	0	0	0	4	0	0	0
	Adirondack Red Wings	AHL	7	2	3	5	....	....	....	0	....	....	....	....	....	....	....	....	....	....	1	1	0	1	0	....	....	....
1987-88	**Detroit Red Wings**	**NHL**	13	0	2	2	0	1	1	4	0	0	0	6	0.0	2	0	2	0	0	....	....	....	....	....	....	....	....
	Adirondack Red Wings	AHL	4	5	0	5	....	....	....	2	....	....	....	....	....	....	....	....	....	....	....	....	....	....	....	....	....	....
	Winnipeg Jets	**NHL**	32	4	4	8	3	3	6	19	0	0	0	36	11.1	13	0	11	2	4	4	0	0	0	4	0	0	0
1988-89	Moncton Hawks	AHL	53	22	23	45	....	....	....	25	....	....	....	....	....	....	....	....	....	....	10	3	4	7	0	....	....	....
1989-90	**Winnipeg Jets**	**NHL**	56	8	9	17	7	6	13	21	0	1	1	74	10.8	29	2	40	8	-5	7	2	0	2	2	0	0	0
1990-91	**Winnipeg Jets**	**NHL**	53	7	3	10	6	2	8	10	0	0	0	65	10.8	22	0	39	7	-10	....	....	....	....	....	....	....	....
1991-92	Moncton Hawks	AHL	41	11	18	29	....	....	....	12	....	....	....	....	....	....	....	....	....	....	2	0	0	0	0	....	....	....
1992-93	Providence Bruins	AHL	30	5	3	8	....	....	....	14	....	....	....	....	....	....	....	....	....	....	....	....	....	....	....	....	....	....
1993-1994	Providence Bruins	AHL	DID NOT PLAY – ASSISTANT COACH																									
1994-1996	Nashville Knights	ECHL	DID NOT PLAY – COACHING																									
1996-1998	Dayton Bombers	ECHL	DID NOT PLAY – COACHING																									
1998-1999	Portland Pirates	AHL	DID NOT PLAY – COACHING																									
1999-2000	Portland Pirates	AHL	DID NOT PLAY – ASSISTANT COACH																									
	NHL Totals		288	38	46	84	31	32	63	113	1	1	4	357	10.6	143	8	160	18		39	6	4	10	14	0	0	1

• Missed majority of 1980-81 season recovering from knee injury suffered in opening game of season, October, 1980. Traded to **Detroit** by **Quebec** with Brent Ashton and Gilbert Delorme for Basil McRae, John Ogrodnick and Doug Sheddon, January 17, 1987. Traded to **Winnipeg** by **Detroit** for Jim Nill, January 11, 1988.

• KUNTZ, Murray

Murray Robert LW – L. 5'10", 180 lbs. b: Ottawa, Ont., 12/19/1945.

Season	Club	League	GP	G	A	Pts	AG	AA	APts	PIM	PP	SH	GW	S	%	TGF	PGF	TGA	PGA	+/-	GP	G	A	Pts	PIM	PP	SH	GW
1964-65	Brockville Braves	OHA-B	STATISTICS NOT AVAILABLE																									
1965-66	Ottawa Jr. Montagnards	OJHL	STATISTICS NOT AVAILABLE																									
1966-67	Toledo Blades	IHL	10	5	4	9	....	....	....	4	....	....	....	....	....	....	....	....	....	....	....	....	....	....	....	....	....	....
	New Haven Blades	EHL	36	13	10	23	....	....	....	11	....	....	....	....	....	....	....	....	....	....	....	....	....	....	....	....	....	....
1967-68	New Haven Blades	EHL	72	40	60	100	....	....	....	34	....	....	....	....	....	....	....	....	....	....	10	5	5	10	7	....	....	....
1968-69	New Haven Blades	EHL	25	28	31	59	....	....	....	25	....	....	....	....	....	....	....	....	....	....	10	4	6	10	2	....	....	....
1969-70	New Haven Blades	EHL	74	51	47	98	....	....	....	68	....	....	....	....	....	....	....	....	....	....	11	1	5	6	2	....	....	....
1970-71	Salt Lake Golden Eagles	WHL	68	18	22	40	....	....	....	14	....	....	....	....	....	....	....	....	....	....	....	....	....	....	....	....	....	....
1971-72	Cincinnati Swords	AHL	45	4	9	13	....	....	....	20	....	....	....	....	....	....	....	....	....	....	....	....	....	....	....	....	....	....
1972-73	Cincinnati Swords	AHL	63	35	30	65	....	....	....	10	....	....	....	....	....	....	....	....	....	....	13	4	4	8	6	....	....	....
1973-74	Rochester Americans	AHL	73	*51	31	82	....	....	....	33	....	....	....	....	....	....	....	....	....	....	6	0	3	3	2	....	....	....

Season	Club	League	REGULAR SEASON																		PLAYOFFS							
			GP	G	A	Pts	AG	AA	APts	PIM	PP	SH	GW	S	%	TGF	PGF	TGA	PGA	+/–	GP	G	A	Pts	PIM	PP	SH	GW
1974-75	St. Louis Blues	NHL	7	1	2	3	1	1	2	0	0	0	0	16	6.3	11	2	3	0	6	....	....	....	....	....	....	....	....
	Denver Spurs	CHL	26	11	16	27	....	....	....	10	....	....	....	....	....	....	....	....	....	....	....	....	....	....	....	....	....	....
	Syracuse Eagles	AHL	33	14	16	30	....	....	....	38	....	....	....	....	....	....	....	....	....	....	1	1	0	1	0	....	....	....
1975-76	Springfield Indians	AHL	39	17	12	29	....	....	....	10	....	....	....	....	....	....	....	....	....	....	....	....	....	....	....	....	....	....
	Baltimore Clippers	AHL	39	11	6	17	....	....	....	2	....	....	....	....	....	....	....	....	....	....	....	....	....	....	....	....	....	....
1976-77	Maine Nordiques	NAHL	46	19	17	36	....	....	....	8	....	....	....	....	....	....	....	....	....	....	11	2	5	7	2	....	....	....
	Beauce Jaros	NAHL	23	9	17	26	....	....	....	14	....	....	....	....	....	....	....	....	....	....	....	....	....	....	....	....	....	....
	NHL Totals		7	1	2	3	1	1	2	0	0	0	0	16	6.3	11	2	3	0		....	....	....	....	....	....	....	....

AHL First All-Star Team (1974)

Signed as a free agent by **Buffalo**, September, 1970. Claimed by **Rochester** (AHL) from **Buffalo** in Reverse Draft, June 12, 1973. Traded to **St. Louis** by **Rochester** (AHL) for cash, June, 1974.

• KURRI, Jari

RW – R. 6'1", 195 lbs. b: Helsinki, Finland, 5/18/1960. Edmonton's 3rd, 69th overall, in 1980.

Season	Club	League	GP	G	A	Pts	AG	AA	APts	PIM	PP	SH	GW	S	%	TGF	PGF	TGA	PGA	+/–	GP	G	A	Pts	PIM	PP	SH	GW
1976-77	Jokerit Helsinki	Finland-Jr.	18	4	6	10	....	....	....	4	....	....	....	....	....	....	....	....	....	....	....	....	....	....	....	....	....	....
1977-78	Jokerit Helsinki	Finland-Jr.	5	5	4	9	....	....	....	2	....	....	....	....	....	....	....	....	....	....	....	....	....	....	....	....	....	....
	Jokerit Helsinki	Finland	29	2	9	11	....	....	....	12	....	....	....	....	....	....	....	....	....	....	....	....	....	....	....	....	....	....
	Finland	EJC-A	4	6	2	8	....	....	....	4	....	....	....	....	....	....	....	....	....	....	....	....	....	....	....	....	....	....
1978-79	Jokerit Helsinki	Finland-Jr.	2	1	1	2	....	....	....	2	....	....	....	....	....	....	....	....	....	....	....	....	....	....	....	....	....	....
	Jokerit Helsinki	Finland	33	16	14	30	....	....	....	12	....	....	....	....	....	....	....	....	....	....	....	....	....	....	....	....	....	....
	Finland	WJC-A	6	2	3	5	....	....	....	2	....	....	....	....	....	....	....	....	....	....	....	....	....	....	....	....	....	....
1979-80	Jokerit Helsinki	Finland-Jr.	6	7	2	9	....	....	....	13	....	....	....	....	....	....	....	....	....	....	....	....	....	....	....	....	....	....
	Jokerit Helsinki	Finland	33	23	16	39	....	....	....	22	....	....	....	....	....	....	....	....	....	....	....	....	....	....	....	....	....	....
	Finland	WJC-A	5	4	7	*11	....	....	....	0	....	....	....	....	....	....	....	....	....	....	....	....	....	....	....	....	....	....
	Finland	Nat-Team	8	3	1	4	....	....	....	0	....	....	....	....	....	....	....	....	....	....	....	....	....	....	....	....	....	....
	Finland	Olympics	7	2	1	3	....	....	....	6	....	....	....	....	....	....	....	....	....	....	....	....	....	....	....	....	....	....
1980-81	Edmonton Oilers	NHL	75	32	43	75	25	29	54	40	9	0	1	202	15.8	127	36	66	1	26	9	5	7	12	4	0	0	0
1981-82	Finland	Can-Cup	5	0	1	1	....	....	....	0	....	....	....	....	....	....	....	....	....	....	....	....	....	....	....	....	....	....
	Edmonton Oilers	NHL	71	32	54	86	25	36	61	32	6	1	5	211	15.2	122	26	65	7	38	5	2	5	7	10	0	0	0
	Finland	Nat-Team	5	1	2	3	....	....	....	2	....	....	....	....	....	....	....	....	....	....	....	....	....	....	....	....	....	....
	Finland	WEC-A	7	4	3	7	....	....	....	2	....	....	....	....	....	....	....	....	....	....	....	....	....	....	....	....	....	....
1982-83	Edmonton Oilers	NHL	80	45	59	104	37	41	78	22	10	1	3	218	20.6	148	33	89	21	47	16	8	15	23	8	2	2	0
1983-84♦	Edmonton Oilers	NHL	64	52	61	113	42	42	84	14	10	5	4	194	26.8	158	42	95	17	38	19	*14	14	28	13	4	0	0
1984-85♦	Edmonton Oilers	NHL	73	71	64	135	58	44	102	30	14	3	13	261	27.2	178	38	85	21	76	18	*19	12	31	6	1	2	2
1985-86	Edmonton Oilers	NHL	78	*68	63	131	55	42	97	22	16	6	9	236	28.8	187	46	123	27	45	10	2	10	12	4	0	1	0
1986-87♦	Edmonton Oilers	NHL	79	54	54	108	47	39	86	41	7	3	5	211	25.6	75	23	38	5	19	21	*15	10	25	20	4	1	5
	NHL All-Stars	RV-87	2	1	1	2	....	....	....	0	....	....	....	....	....	....	....	....	....	....	....	....	....	....	....	....	....	....
1987-88	Finland	Nat-Team	6	2	2	4	....	....	....	2	....	....	....	....	....	....	....	....	....	....	....	....	....	....	....	....	....	....
	Finland	Can-Cup	5	1	1	2	....	....	....	4	....	....	....	....	....	....	....	....	....	....	....	....	....	....	....	....	....	....
♦	Edmonton Oilers	NHL	80	43	53	96	37	38	75	30	10	3	5	207	20.8	137	39	85	12	25	19	*14	17	31	12	5	0	3
1988-89	Edmonton Oilers	NHL	76	44	58	102	37	41	78	69	10	5	8	214	20.6	138	44	102	27	19	7	3	5	8	6	0	1	0
	Finland	WEC-A	7	5	4	9	....	....	....	4	....	....	....	....	....	....	....	....	....	....	....	....	....	....	....	....	....	....
1989-90♦	Edmonton Oilers	NHL	78	33	60	93	28	43	71	48	10	2	2	201	16.4	127	44	89	24	18	22	10	15	25	18	6	0	3
1990-91	HC Milano	Italy	30	27	48	75	....	....	....	6	....	....	....	....	....	....	....	....	....	....	10	10	12	22	2	....	....	....
	Finland	Nat-Team	6	4	4	8	....	....	....	2	....	....	....	....	....	....	....	....	....	....	....	....	....	....	....	....	....	....
	Finland	WEC-A	10	6	6	12	....	....	....	2	....	....	....	....	....	....	....	....	....	....	....	....	....	....	....	....	....	....
1991-92	Finland	Nat-Team	5	0	2	2	....	....	....	2	....	....	....	....	....	....	....	....	....	....	....	....	....	....	....	....	....	....
	Finland	Can-Cup	6	2	0	2	....	....	....	7	....	....	....	....	....	....	....	....	....	....	....	....	....	....	....	....	....	....
	Los Angeles Kings	NHL	73	23	37	60	21	28	49	24	10	1	3	167	13.8	97	41	94	14	–24	4	1	2	3	4	1	0	0
1992-93	Los Angeles Kings	NHL	82	27	60	87	22	41	63	38	12	2	3	210	12.9	138	53	95	29	19	24	9	8	17	12	2	2	0
	Finland	Nat-Team	1	0	0	0	....	....	....	2	....	....	....	....	....	....	....	....	....	....	....	....	....	....	....	....	....	....
1993-94	Los Angeles Kings	NHL	81	31	46	77	29	36	65	48	14	4	3	198	15.7	121	56	124	35	–24	....	....	....	....	....	....	....	....
	Finland	WC-A	8	4	6	10	....	....	....	2	....	....	....	....	....	....	....	....	....	....	....	....	....	....	....	....	....	....
1994-95	Jokerit Helsinki	Finland	20	10	9	19	....	....	....	10	....	....	....	....	....	....	....	....	....	....	....	....	....	....	....	....	....	....
	Los Angeles Kings	NHL	38	10	19	29	18	28	46	24	2	0	0	84	11.9	37	18	48	12	–17	....	....	....	....	....	....	....	....
	Finland	Nat-Team	1	0	0	0	....	....	....	0	....	....	....	....	....	....	....	....	....	....	....	....	....	....	....	....	....	....
1995-96	Los Angeles Kings	NHL	57	17	23	40	17	19	36	37	5	1	0	131	13.0	66	30	62	14	–12	....	....	....	....	....	....	....	....
	New York Rangers	NHL	14	1	4	5	1	3	4	2	0	0	0	27	3.7	8	3	15	6	–4	11	3	5	8	2	0	1	1
1996-97	Finland	Nat-Team	4	0	0	0	....	....	....	0	....	....	....	....	....	....	....	....	....	....	....	....	....	....	....	....	....	....
	Finland	W-Cup	4	1	0	1	....	....	....	0	....	....	....	....	....	....	....	....	....	....	....	....	....	....	....	....	....	....
	Mighty Ducks of Anaheim	NHL	82	13	22	35	14	20	34	12	3	0	3	109	11.9	56	13	77	21	–13	11	1	2	3	4	0	0	0
1997-98	Colorado Avalanche	NHL	70	5	17	22	6	17	23	12	2	0	0	61	8.2	38	10	38	16	6	4	0	0	0	0	0	0	0
	Finland	Olympics	6	1	4	5	....	....	....	2	....	....	....	....	....	....	....	....	....	....	....	....	....	....	....	....	....	....
	NHL Totals		1251	601	797	1398	519	587	1106	545	150	37	67	3142	19.1	1958	595	1390	309		200	106	127	233	123	25	10	14

NHL Second All-Star Team (1984, 1986, 1989) • Won Lady Byng Memorial Trophy (1985) • NHL First All-Star Team (1985, 1987) • WEC-A All-Star Team (1991) • WC-A All-Star Team (1994) • Played in NHL All-Star Game (1983, 1985, 1986, 1988, 1989, 1990, 1993, 1998)

Traded to **Philadelphia** by **Edmonton** with Dave Brown and Corey Foster for Craig Fisher, Scott Mellanby and Craig Berube, May 30, 1991. Traded to **LA Kings** by **Philadelphia** with Jeff Chychrun for Steve Duchesne, Steve Kasper and LA Kings' 4th round choice (Aris Brimanis) in 1991 Entry Draft, May 30, 1991. Traded to **NY Rangers** by **LA Kings** with Marty McSorley and Shane Churla for Ray Ferraro, Ian Laperriere, Mattias Norstrom, Nathan Lafayette and NY Rangers' 4th round choice (Sean Blanchard) in 1997 Entry Draft, March 14, 1996. Signed as a free agent by **Anaheim**, September 10, 1996. Signed as a free agent by **Colorado**, September 15, 1997.

• KURTENBACH, Orland

Orland John C – L. 6'2", 180 lbs. b: Cudworth, Sask., 9/7/1936.

Season	Club	League	GP	G	A	Pts	AG	AA	APts	PIM	PP	SH	GW	S	%	TGF	PGF	TGA	PGA	+/–	GP	G	A	Pts	PIM	PP	SH	GW
1953-54	Prince Albert Mintos	SJHL	47	29	*40	69	....	....	....	48	....	....	....	....	....	....	....	....	....	....	15	11	10	21	14	....	....	....
1954-55	Prince Albert Mintos	SJHL	48	30	41	71	....	....	....	57	....	....	....	....	....	....	....	....	....	....	10	8	7	15	0	....	....	....
	Saskatoon Quakers	WHL	1	0	0	0	....	....	....	0	....	....	....	....	....	....	....	....	....	....	....	....	....	....	....	....	....	....
1955-56	Prince Albert Mintos	SJHL	43	41	38	79	....	....	....	66	....	....	....	....	....	....	....	....	....	....	12	5	12	17	13	....	....	....
	Saskatoon Quakers	WHL	3	0	0	0	....	....	....	4	....	....	....	....	....	....	....	....	....	....	2	0	0	0	0	....	....	....
	Flin Flon Bombers	Mem-Cup	5	1	3	4	....	....	....	2	....	....	....	....	....	....	....	....	....	....	....	....	....	....	....	....	....	....
1956-57	Prince Albert Mintos	SJHL	50	48	54	102	....	....	....	115	....	....	....	....	....	....	....	....	....	....	13	5	11	16	13	....	....	....
	Flin Flon Bombers	Mem-Cup	5	1	3	4	....	....	....	2	....	....	....	....	....	....	....	....	....	....	....	....	....	....	....	....	....	....
1957-58	Vancouver Canucks	WHL	52	15	39	54	....	....	....	58	....	....	....	....	....	....	....	....	....	....	8	3	3	6	8	....	....	....
1958-59	Buffalo Bisons	AHL	70	9	14	23	....	....	....	73	....	....	....	....	....	....	....	....	....	....	7	0	0	0	0	....	....	....
1959-60	Springfield Indians	AHL	14	0	6	6	....	....	....	17	....	....	....	....	....	....	....	....	....	....	....	....	....	....	....	....	....	....
	Vancouver Canucks	WHL	42	11	27	38	....	....	....	51	....	....	....	....	....	....	....	....	....	....	11	1	5	6	11	....	....	....
1960-61	New York Rangers	NHL	10	0	6	6	0	6	6	2	....	....	....	....	....	....	....	....	....	....	....	....	....	....	....	....	....	....
	Vancouver Canucks	WHL	55	20	27	47	....	....	....	31	....	....	....	....	....	....	....	....	....	....	....	....	....	....	....	....	....	....
1961-62	Boston Bruins	NHL	8	0	0	0	0	0	0	6	....	....	....	....	....	....	....	....	....	....	....	....	....	....	....	....	....	....
	Providence Reds	AHL	64	31	33	64	....	....	....	51	....	....	....	....	....	....	....	....	....	....	3	1	1	2	5	....	....	....
1962-63	San Francisco Seals	WHL	70	30	57	87	....	....	....	94	....	....	....	....	....	....	....	....	....	....	17	4	13	17	*51	....	....	....
1963-64	Boston Bruins	NHL	70	12	25	37	15	26	41	91	....	....	....	....	....	....	....	....	....	....	....	....	....	....	....	....	....	....
1964-65	Boston Bruins	NHL	64	6	20	26	7	20	27	86	....	....	....	....	....	....	....	....	....	....	....	....	....	....	....	....	....	....
1965-66	Toronto Maple Leafs	NHL	70	9	6	15	10	6	16	54	....	....	....	....	....	....	....	....	....	....	4	0	0	0	20	0	0	0
1966-67	New York Rangers	NHL	60	11	25	36	13	24	37	58	....	....	....	....	....	....	....	....	....	....	3	0	2	2	0	0	0	0
1967-68	New York Rangers	NHL	73	15	20	35	17	20	37	82	2	0	2	175	8.6	44	4	52	17	5	6	1	0	1	26	0	0	0
1968-69	New York Rangers	NHL	2	0	0	0	0	0	0	2	0	0	0	3	0.0	0	0	0	0	0	....	....	....	....	....	....	....	....
	Omaha Knights	CHL	1	0	0	0	....	....	....	0	....	....	....	....	....	....	....	....	....	....	....	....	....	....	....	....	....	....
1969-70	New York Rangers	NHL	53	4	10	14	4	9	13	47	1	0	0	89	4.5	26	3	23	4	4	6	1	2	3	24	0	0	0
	Buffalo Bisons	AHL	6	1	5	6	....	....	....	2	....	....	....	....	....	....	....	....	....	....	....	....	....	....	....	....	....	....
1970-71	Vancouver Canucks	NHL	52	21	32	53	21	27	48	84	8	1	4	129	16.3	72	21	74	22	–1	....	....	....	....	....	....	....	....
1971-72	Vancouver Canucks	NHL	78	24	37	61	24	32	56	48	5	3	1	160	15.0	85	25	86	24	–2	....	....	....	....	....	....	....	....

			REGULAR SEASON																		PLAYOFFS							
Season	Club	League	GP	G	A	Pts	AG	AA	APts	PIM	PP	SH	GW	S	%	TGF	PGF	TGA	PGA	+/–	GP	G	A	Pts	PIM	PP	SH	GW
1972-73	**Vancouver Canucks**	**NHL**	**47**	**9**	**19**	**28**	**8**	**15**	**23**	**38**	**4**	**0**	**1**	**78**	**11.5**	**43**	**9**	**59**	**11**	**–14**	....	....	....	....	....	....	....	....
1973-74	**Vancouver Canucks**	**NHL**	**52**	**8**	**13**	**21**	**8**	**11**	**19**	**30**	**1**	**0**	**2**	**77**	**10.4**	**32**	**11**	**55**	**4**	**–30**	....	....	....	....	....	....	....	....
1974-75	Seattle Totems	WHL	DID NOT PLAY – COACHING																									
	NHL Totals		**639**	**119**	**213**	**332**	**127**	**196**	**323**	**628**	....	....	....	....	....	....	....	....	....		**19**	**2**	**4**	**6**	**70**	....	....	....

Won WHL Coast Division Rookie of the Year Award (1958)

Claimed by **Boston** from **NY Rangers** in Intra-League Draft, June 13, 1961. Traded to **San Francisco** (WHL) by **Boston** with Ed Panagabko and future considerations (Gerry Ouelette, July 7, 1963) for Larry McNabb and cash, July 26, 1962. Traded to **Boston** by **San Francisco** (WHL) for cash, October, 1963. Traded to **Toronto** by **Boston** with Pat Stapleton and Andy Hebenton for Ron Stewart, June 8, 1965. Claimed by **NY Rangers** from **Toronto** in Intra-league Draft, June 15, 1966. Claimed by **Vancouver** from **NY Rangers** in Expansion Draft, June 10, 1970.

• KURVERS, Tom

Thomas J. D – L. 6'2", 195 lbs. b: Minneapolis, MN, 9/14/1962. Montreal's 10th, 145th overall, in 1981.

Season	Club	League	GP	G	A	Pts	AG	AA	APts	PIM	PP	SH	GW	S	%	TGF	PGF	TGA	PGA	+/–	GP	G	A	Pts	PIM	PP	SH	GW
1980-81	University of Minnesota-Duluth	WCHA	39	6	24	30	....	....	....	48	....	....	....	....	....	....	....	....	....	....	....	....	....	....	....	....	....	....
1981-82	University of Minnesota-Duluth	WCHA	37	11	31	42	....	....	....	18	....	....	....	....	....	....	....	....	....	....	....	....	....	....	....	....	....	....
	United States	WJC-A	7	3	3	6	....	....	....	16	....	....	....	....	....	....	....	....	....	....	....	....	....	....	....	....	....	....
1982-83	University of Minnesota-Duluth	WCHA	26	4	23	27	....	....	....	24	....	....	....	....	....	....	....	....	....	....	....	....	....	....	....	....	....	....
1983-84	University of Minnesota-Duluth	WCHA	43	18	58	76	....	....	....	46	....	....	....	....	....	....	....	....	....	....	....	....	....	....	....	....	....	....
1984-85	**Montreal Canadiens**	**NHL**	**75**	**10**	**35**	**45**	**8**	**24**	**32**	**30**	**6**	**1**	**3**	**136**	**7.4**	**117**	**45**	**80**	**5**	**–3**	**12**	**0**	**6**	**6**	**6**	**0**	**0**	**0**
1985-86♦	**Montreal Canadiens**	**NHL**	**62**	**7**	**23**	**30**	**6**	**15**	**21**	**36**	**3**	**0**	**1**	**69**	**10.1**	**76**	**22**	**47**	**2**	**9**	....	....	....	....	....	....	....	....
1986-87	**Montreal Canadiens**	**NHL**	**1**	**0**	**0**	**0**	**0**	**0**	**0**	**0**	**0**	**0**	**0**	**2**	**0.0**	**1**	**0**	**0**	**0**	**1**	....	....	....	....	....	....	....	....
	Buffalo Sabres	**NHL**	**55**	**6**	**17**	**23**	**5**	**12**	**17**	**22**	**1**	**0**	**1**	**71**	**8.5**	**70**	**16**	**86**	**22**	**–10**	....	....	....	....	....	....	....	....
	United States	WEC-A	10	3	1	4	....	....	....	11	....	....	....	....	....	....	....	....	....	....	....	....	....	....	....	....	....	....
1987-88	**New Jersey Devils**	**NHL**	**56**	**5**	**29**	**34**	**4**	**21**	**25**	**46**	**2**	**0**	**1**	**88**	**5.7**	**82**	**29**	**61**	**14**	**6**	**19**	**6**	**9**	**15**	**38**	**3**	**0**	**1**
1988-89	**New Jersey Devils**	**NHL**	**74**	**16**	**50**	**66**	**14**	**35**	**49**	**38**	**5**	**0**	**0**	**190**	**8.4**	**143**	**61**	**81**	**10**	**11**	....	....	....	....	....	....	....	....
	United States	WEC-A	10	2	2	4	....	....	....	8	....	....	....	....	....	....	....	....	....	....	....	....	....	....	....	....	....	....
1989-90	**New Jersey Devils**	**NHL**	**1**	**0**	**0**	**0**	**0**	**0**	**0**	**0**	**0**	**0**	**0**	**0**	**0.0**	**0**	**0**	**1**	**0**	**–1**	....	....	....	....	....	....	....	....
	Toronto Maple Leafs	**NHL**	**70**	**15**	**37**	**52**	**13**	**27**	**40**	**29**	**9**	**1**	**1**	**156**	**9.6**	**132**	**56**	**117**	**33**	**–8**	**5**	**0**	**3**	**3**	**4**	**0**	**0**	**0**
1990-91	**Toronto Maple Leafs**	**NHL**	**19**	**0**	**3**	**3**	**0**	**2**	**2**	**8**	**0**	**0**	**0**	**23**	**0.0**	**12**	**3**	**22**	**1**	**–12**	....	....	....	....	....	....	....	....
	Vancouver Canucks	**NHL**	**32**	**4**	**23**	**27**	**4**	**17**	**21**	**20**	**3**	**0**	**0**	**76**	**5.3**	**51**	**25**	**49**	**10**	**–13**	**6**	**2**	**2**	**4**	**12**	**1**	**0**	**0**
1991-92	**New York Islanders**	**NHL**	**74**	**9**	**47**	**56**	**8**	**36**	**44**	**30**	**6**	**0**	**1**	**132**	**6.8**	**125**	**71**	**87**	**15**	**–18**	....	....	....	....	....	....	....	....
1992-93	**New York Islanders**	**NHL**	**52**	**8**	**30**	**38**	**7**	**21**	**28**	**38**	**3**	**0**	**0**	**128**	**6.3**	**91**	**44**	**38**	**0**	**9**	**12**	**0**	**2**	**2**	**6**	**0**	**0**	**0**
	Capital District Islanders	AHL	7	3	4	7	....	....	....	8	....	....	....	....	....	....	....	....	....	....	....	....	....	....	....	....	....	....
1993-94	**New York Islanders**	**NHL**	**66**	**9**	**31**	**40**	**8**	**24**	**32**	**47**	**5**	**0**	**1**	**141**	**6.4**	**94**	**50**	**39**	**2**	**7**	**3**	**0**	**0**	**0**	**2**	**0**	**0**	**0**
1994-95	**Mighty Ducks of Anaheim**	**NHL**	**22**	**4**	**3**	**7**	**7**	**4**	**11**	**6**	**1**	**0**	**1**	**44**	**9.1**	**16**	**4**	**28**	**3**	**–13**	....	....	....	....	....	....	....	....
1995-96	Seibu-Tetsudo	Japan	20	18	34	52	....	....	....	....	....	....	....	....	....	....	....	....	....	....	....	....	....	....	....	....	....	....
	NHL Totals		**659**	**93**	**328**	**421**	**84**	**238**	**322**	**350**	**44**	**2**	**10**	**1256**	**7.4**	**1010**	**426**	**736**	**117**		**57**	**8**	**22**	**30**	**68**	**4**	**0**	**1**

WCHA First All-Star Team (1984) • NCAA West First All-American Team (1984) • Won Hobey Baker Memorial Award (Top U.S. Collegiate Player) (1984)

Traded to **Buffalo** by **Montreal** for Buffalo's 2nd round choice (Martin St. Amour) in 1988 Entry Draft, November 18, 1986. Traded to **New Jersey** by **Buffalo** for Detroit's 3rd round choice (previously acquired, Buffalo selected Andrew McVicar) in 1987 Entry Draft, June 13, 1987. Traded to **Toronto** by **New Jersey** for Toronto's 1st round choice (Scott Niedermayer) in 1991 Entry Draft, October 16, 1989. Traded to **Vancouver** by **Toronto** for Brian Bradley, January 12, 1991. Traded to **Minnesota** by **Vancouver** for Dave Babych, June 22, 1991. Traded to **NY Islanders** by **Minnesota** for Craig Ludwig, June 22, 1991. Traded to **Anaheim** by **NY Islanders** for Troy Loney, June 29, 1994.

• KUSHNER, Dale

Dale T. RW – L. 6'1", 195 lbs. b: Terrace, B.C., 6/13/1966.

Season	Club	League	GP	G	A	Pts	AG	AA	APts	PIM	PP	SH	GW	S	%	TGF	PGF	TGA	PGA	+/–	GP	G	A	Pts	PIM	PP	SH	GW
1983-84	Fort McMurray Oil Barons	AJHL	44	15	6	21	....	....	....	139	....	....	....	....	....	....	....	....	....	....	....	....	....	....	....	....	....	....
	Prince Albert Raiders	WHL	1	0	0	0	....	....	....	5	....	....	....	....	....	....	....	....	....	....	....	....	....	....	....	....	....	....
1984-85	Prince Albert Raiders	WHL	2	0	0	0	....	....	....	2	....	....	....	....	....	....	....	....	....	....	....	....	....	....	....	....	....	....
	Moose Jaw Warriors	WHL	17	5	2	7	....	....	....	23	....	....	....	....	....	....	....	....	....	....	....	....	....	....	....	....	....	....
	Medicine Hat Tigers	WHL	48	23	17	40	....	....	....	173	....	....	....	....	....	....	....	....	....	....	10	3	3	6	18	....	....	....
1985-86	Medicine Hat Tigers	WHL	66	25	19	44	....	....	....	218	....	....	....	....	....	....	....	....	....	....	25	0	5	5	114	....	....	....
1986-87	Medicine Hat Tigers	WHL	63	34	34	68	....	....	....	250	....	....	....	....	....	....	....	....	....	....	20	8	13	21	57	....	....	....
	Medicine Hat Tigers	Mem-Cup	5	3	2	5	....	....	....	32	....	....	....	....	....	....	....	....	....	....	....	....	....	....	....	....	....	....
1987-88	Springfield Indians	AHL	68	13	23	36	....	....	....	201	....	....	....	....	....	....	....	....	....	....	....	....	....	....	....	....	....	....
1988-89	Springfield Indians	AHL	45	5	8	13	....	....	....	132	....	....	....	....	....	....	....	....	....	....	....	....	....	....	....	....	....	....
1989-90	**New York Islanders**	**NHL**	**2**	**0**	**0**	**0**	**0**	**0**	**0**	**2**	**0**	**0**	**0**	**0**	**0.0**	**0**	**0**	**0**	**0**	**0**	....	....	....	....	....	....	....	....
	Springfield Indians	AHL	45	14	11	25	....	....	....	163	....	....	....	....	....	....	....	....	....	....	7	2	3	5	61	....	....	....
1990-91	**Philadelphia Flyers**	**NHL**	**63**	**7**	**11**	**18**	**6**	**8**	**14**	**195**	**1**	**0**	**0**	**59**	**11.9**	**23**	**2**	**25**	**0**	**–4**	....	....	....	....	....	....	....	....
	Hershey Bears	AHL	5	3	4	7	....	....	....	14	....	....	....	....	....	....	....	....	....	....	....	....	....	....	....	....	....	....
1991-92	**Philadelphia Flyers**	**NHL**	**19**	**3**	**2**	**5**	**3**	**2**	**5**	**18**	**0**	**0**	**1**	**19**	**15.8**	**7**	**0**	**12**	**0**	**–5**	....	....	....	....	....	....	....	....
	Hershey Bears	AHL	46	9	7	16	....	....	....	98	....	....	....	....	....	....	....	....	....	....	6	0	2	2	23	....	....	....
1992-93	Hershey Bears	AHL	26	1	7	8	....	....	....	98	....	....	....	....	....	....	....	....	....	....	....	....	....	....	....	....	....	....
	Capital District Islanders	AHL	7	0	1	1	....	....	....	29	....	....	....	....	....	....	....	....	....	....	2	1	0	1	29	....	....	....
1993-94	Saint John Flames	AHL	73	20	17	37	....	....	....	199	....	....	....	....	....	....	....	....	....	....	7	2	1	3	28	....	....	....
1994-95	Saint John Flames	AHL	38	13	10	23	....	....	....	97	....	....	....	....	....	....	....	....	....	....	5	0	3	3	14	....	....	....
1995-96	Michigan K-Wings	IHL	49	5	12	17	....	....	....	108	....	....	....	....	....	....	....	....	....	....	6	0	0	0	20	....	....	....
	NHL Totals		**84**	**10**	**13**	**23**	**9**	**10**	**19**	**215**	**1**	**0**	**1**	**78**	**12.8**	**30**	**2**	**37**	**0**		....	....	....	....	....	....	....	....

Memorial Cup All-Star Team (1987)

Signed as a free agent by **NY Islanders**, April 7, 1987. Signed as a free agent by **Philadelphia**, July 31, 1990.

• KUZYK, Ken

Kenneth Michael RW – R. 6'1", 195 lbs. b: Toronto, Ont., 8/11/1953.

Season	Club	League	GP	G	A	Pts	AG	AA	APts	PIM	PP	SH	GW	S	%	TGF	PGF	TGA	PGA	+/–	GP	G	A	Pts	PIM	PP	SH	GW
1972-73	Boston University	ECAC	28	10	15	25	....	....	....	8	....	....	....	....	....	....	....	....	....	....	....	....	....	....	....	....	....	....
1973-74	Boston University	ECAC	31	8	7	15	....	....	....	26	....	....	....	....	....	....	....	....	....	....	....	....	....	....	....	....	....	....
1974-75	Boston University	ECAC	32	8	16	24	....	....	....	46	....	....	....	....	....	....	....	....	....	....	....	....	....	....	....	....	....	....
1975-76	Boston University	ECAC	30	15	8	23	....	....	....	30	....	....	....	....	....	....	....	....	....	....	....	....	....	....	....	....	....	....
1976-77	**Cleveland Barons**	**NHL**	**13**	**0**	**5**	**5**	**0**	**4**	**4**	**2**	**0**	**0**	**0**	**19**	**0.0**	**9**	**4**	**4**	**0**	**1**	....	....	....	....	....	....	....	....
	Salt Lake Golden Eagles	CHL	62	33	27	60	....	....	....	10	....	....	....	....	....	....	....	....	....	....	....	....	....	....	....	....	....	....
1977-78	**Cleveland Barons**	**NHL**	**28**	**5**	**4**	**9**	**5**	**3**	**8**	**6**	**0**	**0**	**0**	**49**	**10.2**	**16**	**1**	**16**	**0**	**–1**	....	....	....	....	....	....	....	....
	Binghamton Dusters	AHL	14	1	1	2	....	....	....	2	....	....	....	....	....	....	....	....	....	....	....	....	....	....	....	....	....	....
	Phoenix Roadrunners	CHL	17	10	11	21	....	....	....	2	....	....	....	....	....	....	....	....	....	....	....	....	....	....	....	....	....	....
	Salt Lake Golden Eagles	CHL	14	4	8	12	....	....	....	0	....	....	....	....	....	....	....	....	....	....	6	1	0	1	0	....	....	....
1978-79	Tulsa Oilers	CHL	74	31	32	63	....	....	....	22	....	....	....	....	....	....	....	....	....	....	....	....	....	....	....	....	....	....
1979-80	Cincinnati Stingers	CHL	17	3	7	10	....	....	....	0	....	....	....	....	....	....	....	....	....	....	....	....	....	....	....	....	....	....
	Baltimore Clippers	EHL	1	0	0	0	....	....	....	0	....	....	....	....	....	....	....	....	....	....	....	....	....	....	....	....	....	....
	Oklahoma City Stars	CHL	41	10	12	22	....	....	....	11	....	....	....	....	....	....	....	....	....	....	....	....	....	....	....	....	....	....
1980-1983			OUT OF HOCKEY – RETIRED																									
1982-1985	RPI Engineers	ECAC	DID NOT PLAY – ASSISTANT COACH																									
1985-2000	St. Anselm State Hawks	ECAC-3	DID NOT PLAY – COACHING																									
	NHL Totals		**41**	**5**	**9**	**14**	**5**	**7**	**12**	**8**	**0**	**0**	**0**	**68**	**7.4**	**25**	**5**	**20**	**0**		....	....	....	....	....	....	....	....

CHL Second All-Star Team (1977)

Signed as a free agent by **Cleveland**, September, 1976. Placed on **Minnesota** Reserve List after **Cleveland-Minnesota** Dispersal Draft, June 15, 1978. Claimed by **Quebec** from **Minnesota** in Expansion Draft, June 13, 1979. Signed as a free agent by **Minnesota**, February 1, 1980.

• KVARTALNOV, Dmitri

LW – L. 5'11", 180 lbs. b: Voskresensk, USSR, 3/25/1966. Boston's 1st, 16th overall, in 1992.

Season	Club	League	GP	G	A	Pts	AG	AA	APts	PIM	PP	SH	GW	S	%	TGF	PGF	TGA	PGA	+/–	GP	G	A	Pts	PIM	PP	SH	GW
1982-83	Khimik Voskresensk	USSR	7	0	0	0	....	....	....	0	....	....	....	....	....	....	....	....	....	....	....	....	....	....	....	....	....	....
1983-84	Khimik Voskresensk	USSR	2	0	0	0	....	....	....	0	....	....	....	....	....	....	....	....	....	....	....	....	....	....	....	....	....	....
1984-85	SKA Kalinen	USSR-2	STATISTICS NOT AVAILABLE																									
1985-86	SKA Kalinen	USSR-2	STATISTICS NOT AVAILABLE																									
1986-87	Khimik Voskresensk	USSR	40	11	6	17	....	....	....	28	....	....	....	....	....	....	....	....	....	....	....	....	....	....	....	....	....	....
1987-88	Khimik Voskresensk	USSR	43	16	11	27	....	....	....	16	....	....	....	....	....	....	....	....	....	....	....	....	....	....	....	....	....	....

Season	Club	League	GP	G	A	Pts	AG	AA	APts	PIM	PP	SH	GW	S	%	TGF	PGF	TGA	PGA	+/–	GP	G	A	Pts	PIM	PP	SH	GW
			REGULAR SEASON																		PLAYOFFS							
1988-89	Khimik Voskresensk	USSR	44	20	12	32				18																		
	Soviet Union	WEC-A	10	3	3	6				6																		
1989-90	Khimik Voskresensk	Fr-Tour	1	0	0	0				0																		
	Khimik Voskresensk	USSR	46	25	29	*54				33																		
	Khimik Voskresensk	Super-S	6	3	4	7				2																		
1990-91	Khimik Voskresensk	USSR	42	12	10	22				18																		
	Khimik Voskresensk	Super-S	7	3	5	8				2																		
	Soviet Union	WEC-A	7	0	1	1				0																		
1991-92	San Diego Gulls	IHL	77	*60	58	*118				16											4	2	0	2	2			
1992-93	Khimik Voskresensk	CIS	3	0	0	0				0																		
	Boston Bruins	**NHL**	**73**	**30**	**42**	**72**	**25**	**29**	**54**	**16**	**11**	**0**	**4**	**226**	**13.3**	**111**	**48**	**54**	**0**	**9**	**4**	**0**	**0**	**0**	**0**	**0**	**0**	**0**
1993-94	**Boston Bruins**	**NHL**	**39**	**12**	**7**	**19**	**11**	**5**	**16**	**10**	**4**	**0**	**0**	**68**	**17.6**	**24**	**11**	**22**	**0**	**–9**								
	Providence Bruins	AHL	23	13	13	26				8																		
1994-95	HC Ambri-Piotta	Switz.	27	24	18	42				30											3	2	0	2	2			
1995-96	HC Ambri-Piotta	Switz.	30	21	37	58				36											7	6	7	13	10			
	Russia	WC-A	8	4	4	8				2																		
1996-97	HC Ambri-Piotta	Switz.	44	30	32	62				30																		
1997-98	KAC Klagenfurt	Alpenliga	21	18	19	37				6																		
	KAC Klagenfurt	Austria	24	*16	19	*35				47											12	10	9	19	6			
1998-99	KAC Klagenfurt	Alpenliga	32	34	21	55				18																		
	KAC Klagenfurt	Austria	22	16	18	34				4																		
99-2000	Adler Mannheim	Germany	15	4	4	8				10																		
	Adler Mannheim	EuroHL	4	1	0	1				0																		
	Jokerit Helsinki	Finland	27	9	8	17				10											11	4	4	8	4			
	NHL Totals		**112**	**42**	**49**	**91**	**36**	**34**	**70**	**26**	**15**	**0**	**4**	**294**	**14.3**	**135**	**59**	**76**	**0**		**4**	**0**	**0**	**0**	**0**	**0**	**0**	**0**

Won Izvestia Trophy (USSR Top Scorer) (1990) • IHL First All-Star Team (1992) • Won Garry F. Longman Memorial Trophy (Top Rookie - IHL) (1992) • Won Leo P. Lamoureux Memorial Trophy (Top Scorer - IHL) (1992) • Won James Gatschene Memorial Trophy (MVP - IHL) (1992)

• KVASHA, Oleg

LW – R. 6'5", 216 lbs. b: Moscow, USSR, 7/26/1978. Florida's 3rd, 65th overall, in 1996.

Season	Club	League	GP	G	A	Pts	AG	AA	APts	PIM	PP	SH	GW	S	%	TGF	PGF	TGA	PGA	+/–	GP	G	A	Pts	PIM	PP	SH	GW
1995-96	CSKA Moscow	CIS	38	2	3	5				14											2	0	0	0	0			
	Russia	EJC-A	5	4	2	6				6																		
1996-97	CSKA Moscow	Russia	44	20	22	42				115																		
	Russia	WJC-A	6	2	0	2				4																		
1997-98	Beast of New Haven	AHL	57	13	16	29				46											3	2	1	3	0			
	Russia	WJC-A	7	4	2	6				4																		
1998-99	**Florida Panthers**	**NHL**	**68**	**12**	**13**	**25**	**14**	**13**	**27**	**45**	**4**	**0**	**2**	**138**	**8.7**	**42**	**12**	**25**	**0**	**5**								
99-2000	**Florida Panthers**	**NHL**	**78**	**5**	**20**	**25**	**6**	**19**	**25**	**34**	**2**	**0**	**0**	**110**	**4.5**	**41**	**8**	**30**	**0**	**3**	**4**	**0**	**0**	**0**	**0**	**0**	**0**	**0**
	NHL Totals		**146**	**17**	**33**	**50**	**20**	**32**	**52**	**79**	**6**	**0**	**2**	**248**	**6.9**	**83**	**20**	**55**	**0**		**4**	**0**	**0**	**0**	**0**	**0**	**0**	**0**

Traded to **NY Islanders** by **Florida** with Mark Parrish for Roberto Luongo and Olli Jokinen, June 24, 2000.

• KYLLONEN, Markku

LW – L. 6'2", 200 lbs. b: Joensuu, Finland, 2/15/1962. Winnipeg's 8th, 163rd overall, in 1987.

Season	Club	League	GP	G	A	Pts	AG	AA	APts	PIM	PP	SH	GW	S	%	TGF	PGF	TGA	PGA	+/–	GP	G	A	Pts	PIM	PP	SH	GW
1980-81	JoKP Joensuu	Finland-2	33	7	6	13				12																		
1981-82	JoKP Joensuu	Finland-2	31	13	16	29				20																		
1982-83	JoKP Joensuu	Finland-2	35	16	23	39				8																		
1983-84	JoKP Joensuu	Finland-2	33	16	12	28				4																		
1984-85	JoKP Joensuu	Finland-2	43	28	27	55				22																		
1985-86	SaiPa Lappeenranta	Finland-2	34	15	13	28				14																		
1986-87	Karpat Oulu	Finland	43	24	16	40				14											9	3	2	5	4			
1987-88	Karpat Oulu	Finland	43	8	24	32				32																		
1988-89	Finland	Can-Cup	5	0	2	2				0																		
	Winnipeg Jets	**NHL**	**9**	**0**	**2**	**2**	**0**	**1**	**1**	**2**	**0**	**0**	**0**	**7**	**0.0**	**4**	**2**	**5**	**0**	**–3**								
	Moncton Hawks	AHL	60	14	20	34				16											5	1	0	1	0			
1989-90	JoKP Joensuu	Finland-2	42	16	12	28				22																		
1990-91	JoKP Joensuu	Finland-2	44	42	37	79				22																		
1991-92	JoKP Joensuu	Finland-2	37	11	15	26				22																		
1992-93	JoKP Joensuu	Finland-2	44	26	42	68				68											5	1	2	3	2			
1993-94	JoKP Joensuu	Finland-2	29	9	22	31				34																		
	JoKP Joensuu	Finland-3	6	3	5	8				4																		
1994-95	Kiekko-Karhut	Finland-3	13	*22	20	42				20											15	*20	19	*39	16			
1995-96			OUT OF HOCKEY – RETIRED																									
1996-97	Newcastle Cobras	BH-Cup	6	3	4	7				0																		
	Newcastle Cobras	Britain	25	5	7	12				6											6	1	0	1	2			
1997-98	EV Landsberg	Germany-2	34	15	18	33				24																		
1998-99	Odense IK	Denmark	42	22	12	34				51																		
99-2000	Odense IK	Denmark	41	26	19	45				54																		
	NHL Totals		**9**	**0**	**2**	**2**	**0**	**1**	**1**	**2**	**0**	**0**	**0**	**7**	**0.0**	**4**	**2**	**5**	**0**									

• KYPREOS, Nick

LW – L. 6', 205 lbs. b: Toronto, Ont., 6/4/1966.

Season	Club	League	GP	G	A	Pts	AG	AA	APts	PIM	PP	SH	GW	S	%	TGF	PGF	TGA	PGA	+/–	GP	G	A	Pts	PIM	PP	SH	GW
1982-83	North York Civics	MTHL	STATISTICS NOT AVAILABLE																									
1983-84	Dixie Beehives	OJHL	9	3	7	10				12																		
	Kitchener Rangers	OHL	4	2	0	2				0																		
	North Bay Centennials	OHL	47	10	11	21				36											4	3	2	5	9			
1984-85	North Bay Centennials	OHL	64	41	36	77				71											8	2	2	4	15			
1985-86	North Bay Centennials	OHL	64	62	35	97				112																		
1986-87	North Bay Centennials	OHL	46	49	41	90				54											24	11	5	16	78			
	Hershey Bears	AHL	10	0	1	1				4																		
1987-88	Hershey Bears	AHL	71	24	20	44				101											12	0	2	2	17			
1988-89	Hershey Bears	AHL	28	12	15	27				19											12	4	5	9	11			
1989-90	**Washington Capitals**	**NHL**	**31**	**5**	**4**	**9**	**4**	**3**	**7**	**82**	**0**	**0**	**2**	**27**	**18.5**	**13**	**1**	**10**	**0**	**2**	**7**	**1**	**0**	**1**	**15**	**0**	**0**	**0**
	Baltimore Skipjacks	AHL	14	6	5	11				6											7	4	1	5	17			
1990-91	**Washington Capitals**	**NHL**	**79**	**9**	**9**	**18**	**8**	**7**	**15**	**196**	**0**	**0**	**3**	**60**	**15.0**	**28**	**0**	**33**	**1**	**–4**	**9**	**0**	**1**	**1**	**38**	**0**	**0**	**0**
1991-92	**Washington Capitals**	**NHL**	**65**	**4**	**6**	**10**	**4**	**5**	**9**	**206**	**0**	**0**	**0**	**28**	**14.3**	**16**	**0**	**19**	**0**	**–3**								
1992-93	**Hartford Whalers**	**NHL**	**75**	**17**	**10**	**27**	**14**	**7**	**21**	**325**	**0**	**0**	**2**	**81**	**21.0**	**44**	**0**	**60**	**11**	**–5**								
1993-94	**Hartford Whalers**	**NHL**	**10**	**0**	**0**	**0**	**0**	**0**	**0**	**37**	**0**	**0**	**0**	**5**	**0.0**	**0**	**0**	**11**	**3**	**–8**								
	♦ **New York Rangers**	**NHL**	**46**	**3**	**5**	**8**	**3**	**4**	**7**	**102**	**0**	**0**	**1**	**29**	**10.3**	**11**	**0**	**19**	**0**	**–8**	**3**	**0**	**0**	**0**	**2**	**0**	**0**	**0**
1994-95	**New York Rangers**	**NHL**	**40**	**1**	**3**	**4**	**2**	**4**	**6**	**93**	**0**	**0**	**0**	**16**	**6.3**	**6**	**0**	**6**	**0**	**0**	**10**	**0**	**2**	**2**	**6**	**0**	**0**	**0**
1995-96	**New York Rangers**	**NHL**	**42**	**3**	**4**	**7**	**3**	**3**	**6**	**77**	**0**	**0**	**1**	**35**	**8.6**	**9**	**0**	**8**	**0**	**1**								
	Toronto Maple Leafs	**NHL**	**19**	**1**	**1**	**2**	**1**	**1**	**2**	**30**	**0**	**0**	**0**	**14**	**7.1**	**2**	**0**	**2**	**0**	**0**	**5**	**0**	**0**	**0**	**4**	**0**	**0**	**0**
1996-97	**Toronto Maple Leafs**	**NHL**	**35**	**3**	**2**	**5**	**3**	**2**	**5**	**62**	**0**	**0**	**0**	**18**	**16.7**	**7**	**0**	**6**	**0**	**1**								
	St. John's Maple Leafs	AHL	4	0	0	0				4																		
1997-98	**Toronto Maple Leafs**	**NHL**	DID NOT PLAY – INJURED																									
	NHL Totals		**442**	**46**	**44**	**90**	**42**	**36**	**78**	**1210**	**0**	**0**	**9**	**313**	**14.7**	**136**	**1**	**174**	**15**		**34**	**1**	**3**	**4**	**65**	**0**	**0**	**0**

OHL First All-Star Team (1986) • OHL Second All-Star Team (1987)

Signed as a free agent by **Philadelphia,** September 30, 1984. Claimed by **Washington** from **Philadelphia** in NHL Waiver Draft, October 2, 1989. Traded to **Hartford** by **Washington** for Mark Hunter and future considerations (Yvon Corriveau, August 20, 1992), June 15, 1992. Traded to **NY Rangers** by **Hartford** with Steve Larmer, Barry Richter and Hartford's 6th round choice (Yuri Litvinov) in 1994 Entry Draft for Darren Turcotte and James Patrick, November 2, 1993. Traded to **Toronto** by **NY Rangers** for Bill Berg, February 29, 1996. • Suffered career-ending head injury in exhibition game vs. NY Rangers, September 17, 1997.

• KYTE, Jim
James G. D – L. 6'5", 210 lbs. b: Ottawa, Ont., 3/21/1964. Winnipeg's 1st, 12th overall, in 1982.

			REGULAR SEASON																		PLAYOFFS							
Season	Club	League	GP	G	A	Pts	AG	AA	APts	PIM	PP	SH	GW	S	%	TGF	PGF	TGA	PGA	+/–	GP	G	A	Pts	PIM	PP	SH	GW
1980-81	Hawkesbury Hawks	OJHL	42	2	24	26	....	....	....	133	....	....	....	....	....	....	....	....	....	....	....	....	....	....	....	....	....	....
1981-82	Cornwall Royals	OHL	52	4	13	17	....	....	....	148	....	....	....	....	....	....	....	....	....	....	5	0	0	0	10	....	....	....
1982-83	Cornwall Royals	OHL	65	6	30	36	....	....	....	195	....	....	....	....	....	....	....	....	....	....	8	0	2	2	24	....	....	....
	Winnipeg Jets	**NHL**	**2**	**0**	**0**	**0**	**0**	**0**	**0**	**0**	**0**	**0**	**0**	**0**	**0.0**	**0**	**0**	**1**	**0**	**–1**	....	....	....	....	....	....	....	....
1983-84	**Winnipeg Jets**	**NHL**	**58**	**1**	**2**	**3**	**1**	**1**	**2**	**55**	**0**	**0**	**0**	**7**	**14.3**	**23**	**0**	**32**	**2**	**–7**	**3**	**0**	**0**	**0**	**11**	**0**	**0**	**0**
1984-85	**Winnipeg Jets**	**NHL**	**71**	**0**	**3**	**3**	**0**	**2**	**2**	**111**	**0**	**0**	**0**	**32**	**0.0**	**27**	**0**	**56**	**3**	**–26**	**8**	**0**	**0**	**0**	**14**	**0**	**0**	**0**
1985-86	**Winnipeg Jets**	**NHL**	**71**	**1**	**3**	**4**	**1**	**2**	**3**	**126**	**0**	**0**	**0**	**28**	**3.6**	**27**	**2**	**52**	**6**	**–21**	**3**	**0**	**0**	**0**	**12**	**0**	**0**	**0**
1986-87	**Winnipeg Jets**	**NHL**	**72**	**5**	**5**	**10**	**4**	**4**	**8**	**162**	**0**	**0**	**1**	**62**	**8.1**	**61**	**1**	**81**	**25**	**4**	**10**	**0**	**4**	**4**	**36**	**0**	**0**	**0**
1987-88	**Winnipeg Jets**	**NHL**	**51**	**1**	**3**	**4**	**1**	**2**	**3**	**128**	**0**	**0**	**0**	**59**	**1.7**	**38**	**0**	**74**	**37**	**1**	....	....	....	....	....	....	....	....
1988-89	**Winnipeg Jets**	**NHL**	**74**	**3**	**9**	**12**	**3**	**6**	**9**	**190**	**0**	**0**	**0**	**56**	**5.4**	**38**	**0**	**90**	**27**	**–25**	....	....	....	....	....	....	....	....
1989-90	**Pittsburgh Penguins**	**NHL**	**56**	**3**	**1**	**4**	**3**	**1**	**4**	**125**	**0**	**0**	**0**	**23**	**13.0**	**34**	**1**	**57**	**14**	**–10**	....	....	....	....	....	....	....	....
1990-91	**Pittsburgh Penguins**	**NHL**	**1**	**0**	**0**	**0**	**0**	**0**	**0**	**2**	**0**	**0**	**0**	**0**	**0.0**	**0**	**0**	**0**	**0**	**0**	....	....	....	....	....	....	....	....
	Muskegon Lumberjacks	IHL	25	2	5	7	....	....	....	157	....	....	....	....	....	....	....	....	....	....	....	....	....	....	....	....	....	....
	Calgary Flames	**NHL**	**42**	**0**	**9**	**9**	**0**	**7**	**7**	**153**	**0**	**0**	**0**	**29**	**0.0**	**32**	**0**	**25**	**3**	**10**	**7**	**0**	**0**	**0**	**7**	**0**	**0**	**0**
1991-92	**Calgary Flames**	**NHL**	**21**	**0**	**1**	**1**	**0**	**1**	**1**	**107**	**0**	**0**	**0**	**13**	**0.0**	**16**	**0**	**18**	**4**	**2**	....	....	....	....	....	....	....	....
	Salt Lake Golden Eagles	IHL	6	0	1	1	....	....	....	9	....	....	....	....	....	....	....	....	....	....	....	....	....	....	....	....	....	....
1992-93	**Ottawa Senators**	**NHL**	**4**	....	**1**	**1**	**0**	**1**	**1**	**4**	**0**	**0**	**0**	**1**	**0.0**	**1**	**0**	**3**	**2**	**0**	....	....	....	....	....	....	....	....
	New Haven Senators	AHL	63	6	18	24	....	....	....	163	....	....	....	....	....	....	....	....	....	....	....	....	....	....	....	....	....	....
1993-94	Las Vegas Thunder	IHL	75	2	16	18	....	....	....	246	....	....	....	....	....	....	....	....	....	....	4	0	1	1	51	....	....	....
1994-95	Las Vegas Thunder	IHL	76	3	17	20	....	....	....	195	....	....	....	....	....	....	....	....	....	....	....	....	....	....	....	....	....	....
	San Jose Sharks	**NHL**	**18**	**2**	**5**	**7**	**4**	**7**	**11**	**33**	**0**	**0**	**1**	**14**	**14.3**	**12**	**1**	**23**	**5**	**–7**	**11**	**0**	**2**	**2**	**14**	**0**	**0**	**0**
1995-96	**San Jose Sharks**	**NHL**	**57**	**1**	**7**	**8**	**1**	**6**	**7**	**146**	**0**	**0**	**0**	**32**	**3.1**	**33**	**0**	**65**	**20**	**–12**	....	....	....	....	....	....	....	....
1996-97	Kansas City Blades	IHL	76	3	8	11	....	....	....	259	....	....	....	....	....	....	....	....	....	....	3	0	0	0	2	....	....	....
	NHL Totals		**598**	**17**	**49**	**66**	**18**	**40**	**58**	**1342**	**0**	**0**	**2**	**356**	**4.8**	**342**	**5**	**577**	**148**		**42**	**0**	**6**	**6**	**94**	**0**	**0**	**0**

Traded to **Pittsburgh** by **Winnipeg** with Andrew McBain and Randy Gilhen for Randy Cunneyworth, Rick Tabaracci and Dave McLlwain, June 17, 1989. Traded to **Calgary** by **Pittsburgh** for Jiri Hrdina, December 13, 1990. Signed as a free agent by **Ottawa**, September 10, 1992. Signed as a free agent by **San Jose**, March 31, 1995.

• LAAKSONEN, Antti
Antti Akseli LW – L. 6', 180 lbs. b: Tammela, Finland, 10/3/1973. Boston's 10th, 191st overall, in 1997.

Season	Club	League	GP	G	A	Pts	AG	AA	APts	PIM	PP	SH	GW	S	%	TGF	PGF	TGA	PGA	+/–	GP	G	A	Pts	PIM	PP	SH	GW
1990-91	FoPS Forssa-2	Finland-Jr.	STATISTICS NOT AVAILABLE																									
	FoPS Forssa	Finland-2	3	0	0	0	....	....	....	0	....	....	....	....	....	....	....	....	....	....	2	0	0	0	0	....	....	....
1991-92	FoPS Forssa	Finland-Jr.	24	19	23	42	....	....	....	22	....	....	....	....	....	....	....	....	....	....	....	....	....	....	....	....	....	....
	FoPS Forssa	Finland-2	41	16	15	31	....	....	....	8	....	....	....	....	....	....	....	....	....	....	....	....	....	....	....	....	....	....
1992-93	FoPS Forssa	Finland-Jr.	9	5	3	8	....	....	....	10	....	....	....	....	....	....	....	....	....	....	....	....	....	....	....	....	....	....
	HPK Hameenlinna	Finland-Jr.	1	1	1	2	....	....	....	0	....	....	....	....	....	....	....	....	....	....	....	....	....	....	....	....	....	....
	FoPS Forssa	Finland-2	34	11	19	30	....	....	....	36	....	....	....	....	....	....	....	....	....	....	....	....	....	....	....	....	....	....
	HPK Hameenlinna	Finland	2	0	0	0	....	....	....	0	....	....	....	....	....	....	....	....	....	....	....	....	....	....	....	....	....	....
1993-94	University of Denver	WCHA	36	12	9	21	....	....	....	38	....	....	....	....	....	....	....	....	....	....	....	....	....	....	....	....	....	....
1994-95	University of Denver	WCHA	40	17	18	35	....	....	....	42	....	....	....	....	....	....	....	....	....	....	....	....	....	....	....	....	....	....
1995-96	University of Denver	WCHA	39	25	28	53	....	....	....	71	....	....	....	....	....	....	....	....	....	....	....	....	....	....	....	....	....	....
1996-97	University of Denver	WCHA	39	21	17	38	....	....	....	63	....	....	....	....	....	....	....	....	....	....	....	....	....	....	....	....	....	....
1997-98	Providence Bruins	AHL	38	3	2	5	....	....	....	14	....	....	....	....	....	....	....	....	....	....	....	....	....	....	....	....	....	....
	Charlotte Checkers	ECHL	15	4	3	7	....	....	....	12	....	....	....	....	....	....	....	....	....	....	6	0	3	3	0	....	....	....
1998-99	**Boston Bruins**	**NHL**	**11**	**1**	**2**	**3**	**1**	**2**	**3**	**2**	**0**	**0**	**0**	**8**	**12.5**	**4**	**1**	**4**	**0**	**–1**	....	....	....	....	....	....	....	....
	Providence Bruins	AHL	66	25	33	58	....	....	....	52	....	....	....	....	....	....	....	....	....	....	19	7	2	9	28	....	....	....
99-2000	**Boston Bruins**	**NHL**	**27**	**6**	**3**	**9**	**7**	**3**	**10**	**2**	**0**	**0**	**1**	**23**	**26.1**	**12**	**0**	**10**	**1**	**3**	....	....	....	....	....	....	....	....
	Providence Bruins	AHL	40	10	12	22	....	....	....	57	....	....	....	....	....	....	....	....	....	....	14	5	4	9	4	....	....	....
	NHL Totals		**38**	**7**	**5**	**12**	**8**	**5**	**13**	**4**	**0**	**0**	**1**	**31**	**22.6**	**16**	**1**	**14**	**1**		....	....	....	....	....	....	....	....

WCHA Second All-Star Team (1996)

• LABATTE, Neil
Neil Joseph Henry C/D – L. 6'2", 178 lbs. b: Toronto, Ont., 4/24/1957. St. Louis' 2nd, 27th overall, in 1977.

Season	Club	League	GP	G	A	Pts	AG	AA	APts	PIM	PP	SH	GW	S	%	TGF	PGF	TGA	PGA	+/–	GP	G	A	Pts	PIM	PP	SH	GW
1974-75	Brown University	ECAC	16	9	6	15	....	....	....	94	....	....	....	....	....	....	....	....	....	....	....	....	....	....	....	....	....	....
1975-76	Brown University	ECAC	13	7	14	21	....	....	....	51	....	....	....	....	....	....	....	....	....	....	....	....	....	....	....	....	....	....
1976-77	Toronto Marlboros	OMJHL	66	21	32	53	....	....	....	114	....	....	....	....	....	....	....	....	....	....	6	1	0	1	4	....	....	....
1977-78	Salt Lake Golden Eagles	CHL	75	11	25	36	....	....	....	116	....	....	....	....	....	....	....	....	....	....	6	0	2	2	8	....	....	....
1978-79	**St. Louis Blues**	**NHL**	**22**	**0**	**2**	**2**	**0**	**1**	**1**	**13**	**0**	**0**	**0**	**15**	**0.0**	**18**	**0**	**20**	**1**	**–1**	....	....	....	....	....	....	....	....
	Salt Lake Golden Eagles	CHL	37	2	13	15	....	....	....	90	....	....	....	....	....	....	....	....	....	....	....	....	....	....	....	....	....	....
1979-80	Salt Lake Golden Eagles	CHL	70	1	26	27	....	....	....	79	....	....	....	....	....	....	....	....	....	....	10	1	7	8	17	....	....	....
1980-81	Salt Lake Golden Eagles	CHL	55	8	18	26	....	....	....	55	....	....	....	....	....	....	....	....	....	....	....	....	....	....	....	....	....	....
1981-82	**St. Louis Blues**	**NHL**	**4**	**0**	**0**	**0**	**0**	**0**	**0**	**6**	**0**	**0**	**0**	**3**	**0.0**	**0**	**0**	**3**	**0**	**–3**	....	....	....	....	....	....	....	....
	Salt Lake Golden Eagles	CHL	72	7	24	31	....	....	....	86	....	....	....	....	....	....	....	....	....	....	9	2	5	7	21	....	....	....
	NHL Totals		**26**	**0**	**2**	**2**	**0**	**1**	**1**	**19**	**0**	**0**	**0**	**18**	**0.0**	**18**	**0**	**23**	**1**		....	....	....	....	....	....	....	....

• L'ABBE, Moe
Maurice Joseph RW – L. 5'9", 170 lbs. b: Montreal, Que., 8/12/1947. Chicago's 4th, 22nd overall, in 1964.

Season	Club	League	GP	G	A	Pts	AG	AA	APts	PIM	PP	SH	GW	S	%	TGF	PGF	TGA	PGA	+/–	GP	G	A	Pts	PIM	PP	SH	GW
1964-65	St. Catharines Black Hawks	OHA-Jr.	17	3	4	7	....	....	....	7	....	....	....	....	....	....	....	....	....	....	....	....	....	....	....	....	....	....
1965-66	St. Catharines Black Hawks	OHA-Jr.	11	0	2	2	....	....	....	32	....	....	....	....	....	....	....	....	....	....	6	0	2	2	0	....	....	....
1966-67	St. Catharines Black Hawks	OHA-Jr.	48	14	17	31	....	....	....	18	....	....	....	....	....	....	....	....	....	....	6	5	4	9	2	....	....	....
1967-68	St. Catharines Black Hawks	OHA-Jr.	50	27	23	50	....	....	....	28	....	....	....	....	....	....	....	....	....	....	5	3	3	6	0	....	....	....
1968-69	Dallas Black Hawks	CHL	1	0	0	0	....	....	....	0	....	....	....	....	....	....	....	....	....	....	....	....	....	....	....	....	....	....
	Greensboro Generals	EHL	47	20	29	49	....	....	....	22	....	....	....	....	....	....	....	....	....	....	8	5	2	7	2	....	....	....
1969-70	Dallas Black Hawks	CHL	3	1	2	3	....	....	....	2	....	....	....	....	....	....	....	....	....	....	....	....	....	....	....	....	....	....
	Greensboro Generals	EHL	69	52	39	91	....	....	....	28	....	....	....	....	....	....	....	....	....	....	16	7	10	17	2	....	....	....
1970-71	Dallas Black Hawks	CHL	69	17	24	41	....	....	....	8	....	....	....	....	....	....	....	....	....	....	10	1	1	2	4	....	....	....
1971-72	Portland Buckaroos	WHL	5	0	2	2	....	....	....	0	....	....	....	....	....	....	....	....	....	....	....	....	....	....	....	....	....	....
	Flint Generals	IHL	41	17	17	34	....	....	....	10	....	....	....	....	....	....	....	....	....	....	....	....	....	....	....	....	....	....
1972-73	**Chicago Black Hawks**	**NHL**	**5**	**0**	**1**	**1**	**0**	**1**	**1**	**0**	**0**	**0**	**0**	**4**	**0.0**	**2**	**0**	**1**	**0**	**1**	....	....	....	....	....	....	....	....
	Dallas Black Hawks	CHL	67	28	34	62	....	....	....	18	....	....	....	....	....	....	....	....	....	....	7	4	6	*10	0	....	....	....
1973-74	Dallas Black Hawks	CHL	72	24	30	54	....	....	....	8	....	....	....	....	....	....	....	....	....	....	10	4	*7	*11	0	....	....	....
1974-75	Dallas Black Hawks	CHL	28	9	13	22	....	....	....	11	....	....	....	....	....	....	....	....	....	....	....	....	....	....	....	....	....	....
1975-76	Dallas Black Hawks	CHL	76	38	38	76	....	....	....	10	....	....	....	....	....	....	....	....	....	....	10	4	3	7	2	....	....	....
	NHL Totals		**5**	**0**	**1**	**1**	**0**	**1**	**1**	**0**	**0**	**0**	**0**	**4**	**0.0**	**2**	**0**	**1**	**0**		....	....	....	....	....	....	....	....

EHL South First All-Star Team (1970) • CHL First All-Star Team (1973)

• LABELLE, Marc
LW – L. 6'1", 215 lbs. b: Maniwaki, Que., 12/20/1969.

Season	Club	League	GP	G	A	Pts	AG	AA	APts	PIM	PP	SH	GW	S	%	TGF	PGF	TGA	PGA	+/–	GP	G	A	Pts	PIM	PP	SH	GW
1986-87	Hull Olympiques	QMJHL	58	1	4	5	....	....	....	91	....	....	....	....	....	....	....	....	....	....	7	0	2	2	12	....	....	....
1987-88	Victoriaville Tigres	QMJHL	63	11	14	25	....	....	....	236	....	....	....	....	....	....	....	....	....	....	5	2	4	6	20	....	....	....
1988-89	Victoriaville Tigres	QMJHL	62	9	26	35	....	....	....	202	....	....	....	....	....	....	....	....	....	....	15	6	3	9	30	....	....	....
1989-90	Victoriaville Tigres	QMJHL	56	18	21	39	....	....	....	192	....	....	....	....	....	....	....	....	....	....	16	4	8	12	42	....	....	....
1990-91	Fredericton Canadiens	AHL	25	1	4	5	....	....	....	95	....	....	....	....	....	....	....	....	....	....	4	0	2	2	25	....	....	....
	Richmond Renegades	ECHL	5	1	1	2	....	....	....	37	....	....	....	....	....	....	....	....	....	....	....	....	....	....	....	....	....	....
1991-92	Fredericton Canadiens	AHL	62	7	10	17	....	....	....	238	....	....	....	....	....	....	....	....	....	....	3	0	0	0	6	....	....	....
1992-93	San Diego Gulls	IHL	5	0	2	2	....	....	....	5	....	....	....	....	....	....	....	....	....	....	....	....	....	....	....	....	....	....
	New Haven Senators	AHL	31	5	4	9	....	....	....	124	....	....	....	....	....	....	....	....	....	....	....	....	....	....	....	....	....	....
	Thunder Bay Thunder Hawks	ColHL	9	0	5	5	....	....	....	17	....	....	....	....	....	....	....	....	....	....	7	0	1	1	11	....	....	....
1993-94	Cincinnati Cyclones	IHL	37	2	1	3	....	....	....	133	....	....	....	....	....	....	....	....	....	....	4	0	1	1	6	....	....	....
1994-95	Cincinnati Cyclones	IHL	54	3	4	7	....	....	....	173	....	....	....	....	....	....	....	....	....	....	8	0	0	0	7	....	....	....
1995-96	Cincinnati Cyclones	IHL	57	6	11	17	....	....	....	218	....	....	....	....	....	....	....	....	....	....	....	....	....	....	....	....	....	....
	Milwaukee Admirals	IHL	20	5	3	8	....	....	....	50	....	....	....	....	....	....	....	....	....	....	5	1	1	2	4	....	....	....

Season	Club	League	REGULAR SEASON GP	G	A	Pts	AG	AA	APts	PIM	PP	SH	GW	S	%	TGF	PGF	TGA	PGA	+/–	PLAYOFFS GP	G	A	Pts	PIM	PP	SH	GW
1996-97	**Dallas Stars**	**NHL**	**9**	**0**	**0**	**0**	**0**	**0**	**0**	**46**	**0**	**0**	**0**	**2**	**0.0**	**0**	**0**	**4**	**0**	**–4**	....	....	....	....	....	....	....	....
	Milwaukee Admirals	IHL	14	1	1	2	....	....	....	33	....	....	....	....	....	....	....	....	....	....	....	....	....	....	....	....	....	....
	Michigan K-Wings	IHL	46	4	7	11	....	....	....	148	....	....	....	....	....	....	....	....	....	....	3	0	0	0	6	....	....	....
1997-98	Lachute Rapides	QSPHL	1	0	0	0	....	....	....	0	....	....	....	....	....	....	....	....	....	....	....	....	....	....	....	....	....	....
	Cincinnati Cyclones	IHL	60	2	1	3	....	....	....	160	....	....	....	....	....	....	....	....	....	....	9	0	1	1	38	....	....	....
1998-99	El Paso Buzzards	WPHL	47	11	25	36	....	....	....	182	....	....	....	....	....	....	....	....	....	....	3	1	0	1	0	....	....	....
99-2000	El Paso Buzzards	WPHL	39	0	9	9	....	....	....	186	....	....	....	....	....	....	....	....	....	....	2	0	0	0	7	....	....	....
	NHL Totals		**9**	**0**	**0**	**0**	**0**	**0**	**0**	**46**	**0**	**0**	**0**	**2**	**0.0**	**0**	**0**	**4**	**0**		....	....	....	....	....	....	....	....

Signed as a free agent by **Montreal**, January 21, 1991. Signed as a free agent by **Ottawa**, July 30, 1992. Claimed by **Florida** from **Ottawa** in Expansion Draft, June 24, 1993. Signed as a free agent by **Dallas**, April 15, 1996. Signed as a free agent by **Ottawa**, July 14, 1997. • Named playing/associate coach of **El Paso** (WPHL), September 10, 1999. • Missed majority of 1999-2000 season recovering from hand injury suffered in game vs. New Mexico (WPHL), November 28, 1999.

• LABOSSIERE, Gord

Gordon William C – R. 6'1", 190 lbs. b: St. Boniface, Man., 1/2/1940.

Season	Club	League	GP	G	A	Pts	AG	AA	APts	PIM	PP	SH	GW	S	%	TGF	PGF	TGA	PGA	+/–	GP	G	A	Pts	PIM	PP	SH	GW
1956-57	Winnipeg Rangers	MJHL	29	20	13	33	....	....	....	57	....	....	....	....	....	....	....	....	....	....	4	1	0	1	6	....	....	....
1957-58	Brandon Rangers	MJHL	30	*44	35	*79	....	....	....	*97	....	....	....	....	....	....	....	....	....	....	....	....	....	....	....	....	....	....
	Saskatoon-St. Paul Regals	WHL	2	0	0	0	....	....	....	2	....	....	....	....	....	....	....	....	....	....	....	....	....	....	....	....	....	....
	St. Boniface Canadiens	Mem-Cup	11	10	5	15	....	....	....	*38	....	....	....	....	....	....	....	....	....	....	....	....	....	....	....	....	....	....
1958-59	Saskatoon Quakers	WHL	64	25	19	44	....	....	....	83	....	....	....	....	....	....	....	....	....	....	....	....	....	....	....	....	....	....
1959-60	Edmonton Flyers	WHL	65	20	18	38	....	....	....	72	....	....	....	....	....	....	....	....	....	....	4	0	1	1	4	....	....	....
1960-61	Edmonton Flyers	WHL	20	5	11	16	....	....	....	20	....	....	....	....	....	....	....	....	....	....	....	....	....	....	....	....	....	....
	Winnipeg Warriors	WHL	43	17	17	34	....	....	....	62	....	....	....	....	....	....	....	....	....	....	....	....	....	....	....	....	....	....
1961-62	Sudbury Wolves	EPHL	30	10	11	21	....	....	....	44	....	....	....	....	....	....	....	....	....	....	....	....	....	....	....	....	....	....
	Seattle Totems	WHL	21	4	4	8	....	....	....	12	....	....	....	....	....	....	....	....	....	....	2	0	0	0	0	....	....	....
1962-63	Sudbury Wolves	EPHL	72	34	67	*101	....	....	....	94	....	....	....	....	....	....	....	....	....	....	8	4	5	9	*23	....	....	....
1963-64	**New York Rangers**	**NHL**	**15**	**0**	**0**	**0**	**0**	**0**	**0**	**12**	....	....	....	....	....	....	....	....	....	....	....	....	....	....	....	....	....	....
	Baltimore Clippers	AHL	48	17	17	34	....	....	....	20	....	....	....	....	....	....	....	....	....	....	....	....	....	....	....	....	....	....
1964-65	**New York Rangers**	**NHL**	**1**	**0**	**0**	**0**	**0**	**0**	**0**	**0**	....	....	....	....	....	....	....	....	....	....	....	....	....	....	....	....	....	....
	Baltimore Clippers	AHL	72	38	41	79	....	....	....	72	....	....	....	....	....	....	....	....	....	....	5	1	1	2	6	....	....	....
1965-66	Quebec Aces	AHL	63	31	51	82	....	....	....	137	....	....	....	....	....	....	....	....	....	....	6	0	1	1	14	....	....	....
1966-67	Quebec Aces	AHL	72	40	55	*95	....	....	....	71	....	....	....	....	....	....	....	....	....	....	5	2	3	5	18	....	....	....
1967-68	**Los Angeles Kings**	**NHL**	**68**	**13**	**27**	**40**	**15**	**27**	**42**	**31**	**1**	**0**	**3**	**153**	**8.5**	**53**	**6**	**41**	**0**	**6**	**7**	**2**	**3**	**5**	**24**	**0**	**0**	**0**
1968-69	**Los Angeles Kings**	**NHL**	**48**	**10**	**18**	**28**	**11**	**16**	**27**	**12**	**2**	**0**	**0**	**97**	**10.3**	**29**	**3**	**33**	**0**	**–7**	....	....	....	....	....	....	....	....
	Springfield Kings	AHL	25	13	23	36	....	....	....	40	....	....	....	....	....	....	....	....	....	....	....	....	....	....	....	....	....	....
1969-70	Springfield Kings	AHL	60	30	59	89	....	....	....	94	....	....	....	....	....	....	....	....	....	....	14	2	5	7	21	....	....	....
1970-71	**Los Angeles Kings**	**NHL**	**45**	**11**	**10**	**21**	**11**	**8**	**19**	**16**	**1**	**0**	**0**	**88**	**12.5**	**29**	**4**	**48**	**1**	**–22**	....	....	....	....	....	....	....	....
	Minnesota North Stars	**NHL**	**29**	**8**	**4**	**12**	**8**	**3**	**11**	**4**	**0**	**0**	**1**	**45**	**17.8**	**15**	**2**	**16**	**0**	**–3**	**3**	**0**	**0**	**0**	**4**	**0**	**0**	**0**
1971-72	**Minnesota North Stars**	**NHL**	**9**	**2**	**3**	**5**	**2**	**3**	**5**	**0**	**0**	**0**	**0**	**23**	**8.7**	**7**	**0**	**5**	**0**	**2**	....	....	....	....	....	....	....	....
	Cleveland Barons	AHL	66	40	45	85	....	....	....	71	....	....	....	....	....	....	....	....	....	....	6	4	2	6	4	....	....	....
1972-73	Houston Aeros	WHA	77	36	60	96	....	....	....	56	....	....	....	....	....	....	....	....	....	....	6	1	4	5	8	....	....	....
1973-74	Houston Aeros	WHA	67	19	36	55	....	....	....	30	....	....	....	....	....	....	....	....	....	....	14	7	9	16	20	....	....	....
1974-75	Houston Aeros	WHA	76	23	34	57	....	....	....	40	....	....	....	....	....	....	....	....	....	....	13	6	7	13	4	....	....	....
1975-76	Houston Aeros	WHA	80	24	32	56	....	....	....	18	....	....	....	....	....	....	....	....	....	....	17	2	8	10	14	....	....	....
	NHL Totals		**215**	**44**	**62**	**106**	**47**	**57**	**104**	**75**	....	....	....	....	....	....	....	....	....	....	**10**	**2**	**3**	**5**	**28**	....	....	....
	Other Major League Totals		300	102	162	264	....	....	....	144	....	....	....	....	....	....	....	....	....	....	50	16	28	44	46	....	....	....

EPHL First All-Star Team (1963) • AHL First All-Star Team (1967) • Won John B. Sollenberger Trophy (Top Scorer - AHL) (1967) • AHL Second All-Star Team (1970)

Claimed by **Detroit** from **NY Rangers** (Saskatoon-WHL) in Inter-League Draft, June 9, 1959. Loaned to **Winnipeg** (WHL) by **Detroit** (Edmonton-WHL) for the loan of Ray Brunel, December, 1960. Claimed by **NY Rangers** from **Detroit** (Sudbury-EPHL) in Inter-League Draft, June 4, 1963. Traded to **Montreal** by **NY Rangers** with Earl Ingarfield, Noel Price, Dave McComb and cash for Garry Peters and Cesare Maniago, June 8, 1965. Claimed by **LA Kings** from **Montreal** in Expansion Draft, June 6, 1967. Traded to **Montreal** by **LA Kings** with Ray Fortin for Ralph Backstrom, January 26, 1971. Traded to **Minnesota** by **Montreal** for Rey Comeau, January 26, 1971. Selected by **Houston** (WHA) in 1972 WHA General Player Draft, February 12, 1972. Traded to **NY Islanders** by **Minnesota** for future considerations for cash, June 6, 1972. Claimed by **Quebec** (WHA) from **Houston** (WHA) in 1976 WHA Intra-League Draft, June, 1976.

• LABRAATEN, Dan

Daniel "Rusty" LW – R. 6', 190 lbs. b: Leksand, Sweden, 6/9/1951.

Season	Club	League	GP	G	A	Pts	AG	AA	APts	PIM	PP	SH	GW	S	%	TGF	PGF	TGA	PGA	+/–	GP	G	A	Pts	PIM	PP	SH	GW
1966-67	Grums IK	Sweden-2	22	7	....	7	....	....	....	....	....	....	....	....	....	....	....	....	....	....	....	....	....	....	....	....	....	....
1967-68	Grums IK	Sweden-2	19	14	9	23	....	....	....	....	....	....	....	....	....	....	....	....	....	....	....	....	....	....	....	....	....	....
	Sweden	EJC-A	5	5	2	7	....	....	....	0	....	....	....	....	....	....	....	....	....	....	....	....	....	....	....	....	....	....
1968-69	Grums IK	Sweden-2	21	18	9	27	....	....	....	....	....	....	....	....	....	....	....	....	....	....	....	....	....	....	....	....	....	....
	Sweden	EJC-A	5	0	0	0	....	....	....	0	....	....	....	....	....	....	....	....	....	....	....	....	....	....	....	....	....	....
1969-70	Leksands IF	Sweden	14	8	4	12	....	....	....	0	....	....	....	....	....	....	....	....	....	....	14	6	5	11	4	....	....	....
	Sweden	EJC-A	5	6	....	....	....	....	....	....	....	....	....	....	....	....	....	....	....	....	....	....	....	....	....	....	....	....
1970-71	Leksands IF	Sweden	14	7	8	15	....	....	....	2	....	....	....	....	....	....	....	....	....	....	9	6	6	12	9	....	....	....
1971-72	Leksands IF	Sweden	28	12	8	20	....	....	....	12	....	....	....	....	....	....	....	....	....	....	....	....	....	....	....	....	....	....
1972-73	Leksands IF	Sweden	14	8	5	13	....	....	....	20	....	....	....	....	....	....	....	....	....	....	14	9	5	14	5	....	....	....
1973-74	Sweden	Nat-Team	10	3	0	3	....	....	....	8	....	....	....	....	....	....	....	....	....	....	....	....	....	....	....	....	....	....
	Sweden	WEC-A	10	2	0	2	....	....	....	8	....	....	....	....	....	....	....	....	....	....	....	....	....	....	....	....	....	....
1974-75	Leksands IF	Sweden	30	24	14	38	....	....	....	40	....	....	....	....	....	....	....	....	....	....	5	2	0	2	2	....	....	....
	Sweden	WEC-A	10	9	1	10	....	....	....	12	....	....	....	....	....	....	....	....	....	....	....	....	....	....	....	....	....	....
1975-76	Leksands IF	Sweden	16	13	9	22	....	....	....	6	....	....	....	....	....	....	....	....	....	....	4	2	2	4	0	....	....	....
	Sweden	WEC-A	10	5	3	8	....	....	....	6	....	....	....	....	....	....	....	....	....	....	....	....	....	....	....	....	....	....
1976-77	Sweden	Can-Cup	5	0	1	1	....	....	....	2	....	....	....	....	....	....	....	....	....	....	....	....	....	....	....	....	....	....
	Winnipeg Jets	WHA	64	24	27	51	....	....	....	21	....	....	....	....	....	....	....	....	....	....	20	7	17	24	15	....	....	....
1977-78	Winnipeg Jets	WHA	47	18	16	34	....	....	....	30	....	....	....	....	....	....	....	....	....	....	4	1	1	2	8	....	....	....
1978-79	**Detroit Red Wings**	**NHL**	**78**	**19**	**19**	**38**	**16**	**14**	**30**	**8**	**7**	**0**	**3**	**112**	**17.0**	**58**	**18**	**57**	**0**	**–17**	....	....	....	....	....	....	....	....
	Sweden	WEC-A	8	1	1	2	....	....	....	4	....	....	....	....	....	....	....	....	....	....	....	....	....	....	....	....	....	....
1979-80	**Detroit Red Wings**	**NHL**	**76**	**30**	**27**	**57**	**26**	**20**	**46**	**8**	**6**	**0**	**5**	**152**	**19.7**	**91**	**26**	**60**	**0**	**5**	....	....	....	....	....	....	....	....
1980-81	**Detroit Red Wings**	**NHL**	**44**	**3**	**8**	**11**	**2**	**5**	**7**	**12**	**0**	**0**	**0**	**43**	**7.0**	**17**	**3**	**33**	**0**	**–19**	....	....	....	....	....	....	....	....
	Calgary Flames	**NHL**	**27**	**9**	**7**	**16**	**7**	**5**	**12**	**13**	**1**	**0**	**0**	**39**	**23.1**	**32**	**8**	**23**	**0**	**1**	**5**	**1**	**0**	**1**	**4**	**1**	**0**	**1**
1981-82	**Calgary Flames**	**NHL**	**43**	**10**	**12**	**22**	**8**	**8**	**16**	**6**	**1**	**0**	**0**	**60**	**16.7**	**32**	**6**	**31**	**1**	**–4**	**3**	**0**	**0**	**0**	**0**	**0**	**0**	**0**
1982-83	Leksands IF	Sweden	30	9	10	19	....	....	....	26	....	....	....	....	....	....	....	....	....	....	....	....	....	....	....	....	....	....
1983-84	Leksands IF	Sweden	36	23	21	*44	....	....	....	14	....	....	....	....	....	....	....	....	....	....	....	....	....	....	....	....	....	....
1984-85	Leksands IF	Sweden	27	15	14	29	....	....	....	14	....	....	....	....	....	....	....	....	....	....	....	....	....	....	....	....	....	....
	Sweden	WEC-A	10	2	2	4	....	....	....	6	....	....	....	....	....	....	....	....	....	....	....	....	....	....	....	....	....	....
1985-86	Leksands IF	Sweden	36	20	12	32	....	....	....	18	....	....	....	....	....	....	....	....	....	....	....	....	....	....	....	....	....	....
	Sweden	WEC-A	8	0	3	3	....	....	....	4	....	....	....	....	....	....	....	....	....	....	....	....	....	....	....	....	....	....
1986-87	Leksands IF	Sweden	31	17	14	31	....	....	....	14	....	....	....	....	....	....	....	....	....	....	....	....	....	....	....	....	....	....
1987-88	Leksands IF	Sweden	24	9	7	16	....	....	....	10	....	....	....	....	....	....	....	....	....	....	3	0	0	0	2	....	....	....
	NHL Totals		**268**	**71**	**73**	**144**	**59**	**52**	**111**	**47**	**15**	**0**	**8**	**406**	**17.5**	**230**	**61**	**204**	**1**		**8**	**1**	**0**	**1**	**4**	**1**	**0**	**1**
	Other Major League Totals		111	42	43	85	....	....	....	51	....	....	....	....	....	....	....	....	....	....	24	8	18	26	23	....	....	....

• Only goals and games played totals are available for 1966-67 season. Signed as a free agent by **Winnipeg** (WHA), June, 1976. Signed as a free agent by **Detroit**, October 12, 1978. Traded to **Calgary** by **Detroit** for Earl Ingarfield Jr., February 3, 1981.

• LABRE, Yvon

Yvon Jules D – L. 5'11", 190 lbs. b: Sudbury, Ont., 11/29/1949. Pittsburgh's 3rd, 38th overall, in 1969.

Season	Club	League	GP	G	A	Pts	AG	AA	APts	PIM	PP	SH	GW	S	%	TGF	PGF	TGA	PGA	+/–	GP	G	A	Pts	PIM	PP	SH	GW
1966-67	Markham Waxers	OHA-B	32	0	14	14	....	....	....	....	....	....	....	....	....	....	....	....	....	....	....	....	....	....	....	....	....	....
1967-68	Toronto Marlboros	OHA-Jr.	43	4	8	12	....	....	....	107	....	....	....	....	....	....	....	....	....	....	5	0	0	0	18	....	....	....
1968-69	Toronto Marlboros	OHA-Jr.	54	1	16	17	....	....	....	185	....	....	....	....	....	....	....	....	....	....	6	1	1	2	26	....	....	....
1969-70	Baltimore Clippers	AHL	64	1	8	9	....	....	....	111	....	....	....	....	....	....	....	....	....	....	5	0	2	2	38	....	....	....
1970-71	**Pittsburgh Penguins**	**NHL**	**21**	**1**	**1**	**2**	**1**	**1**	**2**	**19**	**0**	**0**	**0**	**30**	**3.3**	**13**	**2**	**11**	**2**	**2**	....	....	....	....	....	....	....	....
	Amarillo Wranglers	CHL	42	2	9	11	....	....	....	125	....	....	....	....	....	....	....	....	....	....	....	....	....	....	....	....	....	....
1971-72	Hershey Bears	AHL	59	3	9	12	....	....	....	134	....	....	....	....	....	....	....	....	....	....	4	2	1	3	20	....	....	....
1972-73	Hershey Bears	AHL	72	8	29	37	....	....	....	170	....	....	....	....	....	....	....	....	....	....	7	1	3	4	35	....	....	....

Season	Club	League	REGULAR SEASON																		PLAYOFFS							
			GP	G	A	Pts	AG	AA	APts	PIM	PP	SH	GW	S	%	TGF	PGF	TGA	PGA	+/–	GP	G	A	Pts	PIM	PP	SH	GW
1973-74	**Pittsburgh Penguins**	**NHL**	**16**	**1**	**2**	**3**	**1**	**2**	**3**	**13**	**0**	**0**	**0**	**12**	**8.3**	**9**	**0**	**17**	**1**	**–7**	....	....	....	....	....	....	....	....
	Hershey Bears	AHL	56	6	23	29	....	....	....	135	....	....	....	....	....	....	....	....	....	....	14	1	5	6	42	....	....	....
1974-75	**Washington Capitals**	**NHL**	**76**	**4**	**23**	**27**	**3**	**17**	**20**	**182**	**0**	**0**	**0**	**72**	**5.6**	**67**	**11**	**136**	**26**	**–54**	....	....	....	....	....	....	....	....
1975-76	**Washington Capitals**	**NHL**	**80**	**2**	**20**	**22**	**2**	**15**	**17**	**146**	**0**	**0**	**0**	**110**	**1.8**	**83**	**8**	**141**	**28**	**–38**	....	....	....	....	....	....	....	....
1976-77	**Washington Capitals**	**NHL**	**62**	**3**	**11**	**14**	**3**	**8**	**11**	**169**	**0**	**2**	**0**	**99**	**3.0**	**54**	**4**	**76**	**21**	**–5**	....	....	....	....	....	....	....	....
1977-78	**Washington Capitals**	**NHL**	**22**	**0**	**8**	**8**	**0**	**6**	**6**	**41**	**0**	**0**	**0**	**21**	**0.0**	**17**	**0**	**22**	**5**	**0**	....	....	....	....	....	....	....	....
	Hershey Bears	AHL	21	1	6	7	....	....	....	72	....	....	....	....	....	....	....	....	....	....	....	....	....	....	....	....	....	....
1978-79	**Washington Capitals**	**NHL**	**51**	**1**	**13**	**14**	**1**	**9**	**10**	**80**	**0**	**0**	**0**	**36**	**2.8**	**44**	**2**	**50**	**15**	**7**	....	....	....	....	....	....	....	....
1979-80	**Washington Capitals**	**NHL**	**18**	**0**	**5**	**5**	**0**	**4**	**4**	**38**	**0**	**0**	**0**	**5**	**0.0**	**13**	**0**	**16**	**6**	**3**	....	....	....	....	....	....	....	....
1980-81	**Washington Capitals**	**NHL**	**25**	**2**	**4**	**6**	**2**	**3**	**5**	**100**	**0**	**0**	**0**	**13**	**15.4**	**20**	**1**	**24**	**3**	**–2**	....	....	....	....	....	....	....	....
	NHL Totals		**371**	**14**	**87**	**101**	**13**	**65**	**78**	**788**	**0**	**2**	**0**	**398**	**3.5**	**320**	**28**	**493**	**107**		....	....	....	....	....	....	....	....

Claimed by **Washington** from **Pittsburgh** in Expansion Draft, June 12, 1974.

• LACHANCE, Michel

D – R. 6′, 190 lbs. b: Quebec City, Que., 4/11/1955. Montreal's 9th, 106th overall, in 1975.

Season	Club	League	GP	G	A	Pts	AG	AA	APts	PIM	PP	SH	GW	S	%	TGF	PGF	TGA	PGA	+/–	GP	G	A	Pts	PIM	PP	SH	GW
1972-73	Quebec Remparts	QMJHL	51	1	8	9	....	....	....	49	....	....	....	....	....	....	....	....	....	....	....	....	....	....	....	....	....	....
1973-74	Quebec Remparts	QMJHL	70	9	63	72	....	....	....	170	....	....	....	....	....	....	....	....	....	....	....	....	....	....	....	....	....	....
	Quebec Remparts	Mem-Cup	4	1	4	5	....	....	....	4	....	....	....	....	....	....	....	....	....	....	....	....	....	....	....	....	....	....
1974-75	Quebec–Montreal	QMJHL	65	13	44	57	....	....	....	145	....	....	....	....	....	....	....	....	....	....	....	....	....	....	....	....	....	....
1975-76			STATISTICS NOT AVAILABLE																									
1976-77	Greensboro Generals	EHL	40	7	10	17	....	....	....	108	....	....	....	....	....	....	....	....	....	....	....	....	....	....	....	....	....	....
	Baltimore Clippers	AHL	10	0	4	4	....	....	....	16	....	....	....	....	....	....	....	....	....	....	....	....	....	....	....	....	....	....
	Maine Nordiques	NAHL	4	1	0	1	....	....	....	5	....	....	....	....	....	....	....	....	....	....	....	....	....	....	....	....	....	....
	Milwaukee Admirals	USHL	7	1	2	3	....	....	....	33	....	....	....	....	....	....	....	....	....	....	....	....	....	....	....	....	....	....
1977-78	Milwaukee Admirals	IHL	72	19	23	42	....	....	....	210	....	....	....	....	....	....	....	....	....	....	....	....	....	....	....	....	....	....
1978-79	**Colorado Rockies**	**NHL**	**21**	**0**	**4**	**4**	**0**	**3**	**3**	**22**	**0**	**0**	**0**	**22**	**0.0**	**7**	**1**	**18**	**3**	**–9**	....	....	....	....	....	....	....	....
	Philadelphia Firebirds	AHL	22	1	5	6	....	....	....	42	....	....	....	....	....	....	....	....	....	....	....	....	....	....	....	....	....	....
	Tulsa Oilers	CHL	22	2	5	7	....	....	....	35	....	....	....	....	....	....	....	....	....	....	....	....	....	....	....	....	....	....
	New Brunswick Hawks	AHL	10	4	1	5	....	....	....	0	....	....	....	....	....	....	....	....	....	....	5	0	2	2	4	....	....	....
1979-80	Fort Worth Texans	CHL	76	12	25	37	....	....	....	95	....	....	....	....	....	....	....	....	....	....	....	....	....	....	....	....	....	....
1980-81	HC Caen	France	26	11	4	15	....	....	....	....	....	....	....	....	....	....	....	....	....	....	....	....	....	....	....	....	....	....
	NHL Totals		**21**	**0**	**4**	**4**	**0**	**3**	**3**	**22**	**0**	**0**	**0**	**22**	**0.0**	**7**	**1**	**18**	**3**		....	....	....	....	....	....	....	....

IHL First All-Star Team (1978) • Won Governors' Trophy (Top Defenseman - IHL) (1978)

Signed as a free agent by **Colorado**, October 13, 1978.

• LACHANCE, Scott

Scott J. D – L. 6′1″, 209 lbs. b: Charlottesville, VA, 10/22/1972. NY Islanders' 1st, 4th overall, in 1991.

Season	Club	League	GP	G	A	Pts	AG	AA	APts	PIM	PP	SH	GW	S	%	TGF	PGF	TGA	PGA	+/–	GP	G	A	Pts	PIM	PP	SH	GW
1988-89	Springfield Jr. Blues	NEJHL	36	8	28	36	....	....	....	20	....	....	....	....	....	....	....	....	....	....	....	....	....	....	....	....	....	....
1989-90	Springfield Jr. Blues	NEJHL	34	25	41	66	....	....	....	62	....	....	....	....	....	....	....	....	....	....	....	....	....	....	....	....	....	....
1990-91	Boston University	H-East	31	5	19	24	....	....	....	48	....	....	....	....	....	....	....	....	....	....	....	....	....	....	....	....	....	....
	United States	WJC-A	8	2	1	3	....	....	....	2	....	....	....	....	....	....	....	....	....	....	....	....	....	....	....	....	....	....
1991-92	United States	Nat-Team	36	1	10	11	....	....	....	34	....	....	....	....	....	....	....	....	....	....	....	....	....	....	....	....	....	....
	United States	WJC-A	7	1	4	5	....	....	....	0	....	....	....	....	....	....	....	....	....	....	....	....	....	....	....	....	....	....
	United States	Olympics	8	0	1	1	....	....	....	6	....	....	....	....	....	....	....	....	....	....	....	....	....	....	....	....	....	....
	New York Islanders	**NHL**	**17**	**1**	**4**	**5**	**1**	**3**	**4**	**9**	**0**	**0**	**0**	**20**	**5.0**	**22**	**3**	**9**	**3**	**13**	....	....	....	....	....	....	....	....
1992-93	**New York Islanders**	**NHL**	**75**	**7**	**17**	**24**	**6**	**12**	**18**	**67**	**0**	**1**	**2**	**62**	**11.3**	**69**	**2**	**100**	**32**	**–1**	....	....	....	....	....	....	....	....
1993-94	**New York Islanders**	**NHL**	**74**	**3**	**11**	**14**	**3**	**9**	**12**	**70**	**0**	**0**	**1**	**59**	**5.1**	**67**	**10**	**89**	**27**	**–5**	**3**	**0**	**0**	**0**	**0**	**0**	**0**	**0**
1994-95	**New York Islanders**	**NHL**	**26**	**6**	**7**	**13**	**11**	**10**	**21**	**26**	**3**	**0**	**0**	**56**	**10.7**	**33**	**14**	**29**	**12**	**2**	....	....	....	....	....	....	....	....
1995-96	**New York Islanders**	**NHL**	**55**	**3**	**10**	**13**	**3**	**8**	**11**	**54**	**1**	**0**	**0**	**81**	**3.7**	**58**	**17**	**89**	**29**	**–19**	....	....	....	....	....	....	....	....
	United States	WC-A	8	0	0	0	....	....	....	2	....	....	....	....	....	....	....	....	....	....	....	....	....	....	....	....	....	....
1996-97	**New York Islanders**	**NHL**	**81**	**3**	**11**	**14**	**3**	**10**	**13**	**47**	**1**	**0**	**0**	**97**	**3.1**	**72**	**8**	**90**	**19**	**–7**	....	....	....	....	....	....	....	....
	United States	WC-A	8	0	2	2	....	....	....	4	....	....	....	....	....	....	....	....	....	....	....	....	....	....	....	....	....	....
1997-98	**New York Islanders**	**NHL**	**63**	**2**	**11**	**13**	**2**	**11**	**13**	**45**	**1**	**0**	**0**	**62**	**3.2**	**47**	**11**	**64**	**17**	**–11**	....	....	....	....	....	....	....	....
1998-99	**New York Islanders**	**NHL**	**59**	**1**	**8**	**9**	**1**	**8**	**9**	**30**	**1**	**0**	**0**	**37**	**2.7**	**43**	**7**	**75**	**20**	**–19**	....	....	....	....	....	....	....	....
	Montreal Canadiens	**NHL**	**17**	**1**	**1**	**2**	**1**	**1**	**2**	**11**	**0**	**0**	**0**	**22**	**4.5**	**7**	**1**	**11**	**3**	**–2**	....	....	....	....	....	....	....	....
	United States	WC-A	6	0	0	0	....	....	....	4	....	....	....	....	....	....	....	....	....	....	....	....	....	....	....	....	....	....
99-2000	**Montreal Canadiens**	**NHL**	**57**	**0**	**6**	**6**	**0**	**6**	**6**	**22**	**0**	**0**	**0**	**41**	**0.0**	**28**	**0**	**38**	**6**	**–4**	....	....	....	....	....	....	....	....
	NHL Totals		**524**	**27**	**86**	**113**	**31**	**78**	**109**	**381**	**7**	**1**	**3**	**537**	**5.0**	**446**	**73**	**594**	**168**		**3**	**0**	**0**	**0**	**0**	**0**	**0**	**0**

WJC-A All-Star Team (1991) • Played in NHL All-Star Game (1997)

Traded to **Montreal** by **NY Islanders** for Montreal's 3rd round choice (Mattias Weinhandl) in 1999 Entry Draft, March 9, 1999.

• LACOMBE, Francois

D – L. 5′10″, 185 lbs. b: Montreal, Que., 2/24/1948.

Season	Club	League	GP	G	A	Pts	AG	AA	APts	PIM	PP	SH	GW	S	%	TGF	PGF	TGA	PGA	+/–	GP	G	A	Pts	PIM	PP	SH	GW
1965-66	Lachine Maroons	QJHL	40	2	14	16	....	....	....	70	....	....	....	....	....	....	....	....	....	....	....	....	....	....	....	....	....	....
1966-67	Lachine Maroons	QJHL	STATISTICS NOT AVAILABLE																									
	Thetford Mines Canadiens	Mem-Cup	4	0	0	0	....	....	....	0	....	....	....	....	....	....	....	....	....	....	....	....	....	....	....	....	....	....
1967-68	Montreal Jr. Canadiens	OHA-Jr.	51	1	10	11	....	....	....	59	....	....	....	....	....	....	....	....	....	....	11	0	3	3	4	....	....	....
1968-69	**Oakland Seals**	**NHL**	**72**	**2**	**16**	**18**	**2**	**14**	**16**	**50**	**1**	**0**	**0**	**103**	**1.9**	**80**	**14**	**82**	**6**	**–10**	**3**	**1**	**0**	**1**	**0**	**0**	**0**	**0**
1969-70	**Oakland Seals**	**NHL**	**2**	**0**	**0**	**0**	**0**	**0**	**0**	**0**	**0**	**0**	**0**	**1**	**0.0**	**2**	**0**	**1**	**0**	**1**	....	....	....	....	....	....	....	....
	Providence Reds	AHL	70	9	16	25	....	....	....	64	....	....	....	....	....	....	....	....	....	....	....	....	....	....	....	....	....	....
1970-71	**Buffalo Sabres**	**NHL**	**1**	**0**	**1**	**1**	**0**	**1**	**1**	**2**	**0**	**0**	**0**	**1**	**0.0**	**1**	**1**	**2**	**0**	**–2**	....	....	....	....	....	....	....	....
	Salt Lake Golden Eagles	WHL	70	11	39	50	....	....	....	89	....	....	....	....	....	....	....	....	....	....	....	....	....	....	....	....	....	....
1971-72	Salt Lake Golden Eagles	WHL	11	2	3	5	....	....	....	22	....	....	....	....	....	....	....	....	....	....	....	....	....	....	....	....	....	....
	Fort Worth Wings	CHL	19	3	5	8	....	....	....	26	....	....	....	....	....	....	....	....	....	....	....	....	....	....	....	....	....	....
	Cincinnati Swords	AHL	35	4	10	14	....	....	....	26	....	....	....	....	....	....	....	....	....	....	10	1	6	7	20	....	....	....
1972-73	Quebec Nordiques	WHA	62	10	18	28	....	....	....	123	....	....	....	....	....	....	....	....	....	....	....	....	....	....	....	....	....	....
1973-74	Quebec Nordiques	WHA	71	9	26	35	....	....	....	41	....	....	....	....	....	....	....	....	....	....	....	....	....	....	....	....	....	....
1974-75	Maine Nordiques	NAHL	4	0	3	3	....	....	....	12	....	....	....	....	....	....	....	....	....	....	....	....	....	....	....	....	....	....
	Quebec Nordiques	WHA	55	7	17	24	....	....	....	54	....	....	....	....	....	....	....	....	....	....	15	0	2	2	14	....	....	....
1975-76	Calgary Cowboys	WHA	71	3	28	31	....	....	....	62	....	....	....	....	....	....	....	....	....	....	8	0	0	0	2	....	....	....
1976-77	Quebec Nordiques	WHA	81	5	22	27	....	....	....	86	....	....	....	....	....	....	....	....	....	....	17	4	3	7	16	....	....	....
1977-78	Quebec Nordiques	WHA	22	1	7	8	....	....	....	12	....	....	....	....	....	....	....	....	....	....	10	1	4	5	2	....	....	....
1978-79	Quebec Nordiques	WHA	78	3	21	24	....	....	....	44	....	....	....	....	....	....	....	....	....	....	4	0	1	1	2	....	....	....
1979-80	**Quebec Nordiques**	**NHL**	**3**	**0**	**0**	**0**	**0**	**0**	**0**	**2**	**0**	**0**	**0**	**2**	**0.0**	**3**	**0**	**5**	**1**	**–1**	....	....	....	....	....	....	....	....
	Syracuse Firebirds	AHL	50	3	26	29	....	....	....	34	....	....	....	....	....	....	....	....	....	....	1	0	0	0	0	....	....	....
	NHL Totals		**78**	**2**	**17**	**19**	**2**	**15**	**17**	**54**	**1**	**0**	**0**	**107**	**1.9**	**86**	**15**	**90**	**7**		**3**	**1**	**0**	**1**	**0**	**0**	**0**	**0**
	Other Major League Totals		440	38	139	177	....	....	....	422	....	....	....	....	....	....	....	....	....	....	54	5	10	15	36	....	....	....

Traded to **Oakland** by **Montreal** with Michel Jacques to complete transaction that sent Wally Boyer to Montreal (May 21, 1968), June, 1968. Traded to **Montreal** by **California** with cash and California's 1st round choice (Guy Lafleur) in 1971 Amateur Draft for Ernie Hicke and Montreal's 1st round choice (Chris Oddleifson) in 1970 Amateur Draft, May 22, 1970. Claimed by **Buffalo** from **Montreal** in Expansion Draft, June 10, 1970. Selected by **Alberta** (WHA) in 1972 WHA General Player Draft, February 12, 1972. WHA rights traded to **Quebec** (WHA) by **Alberta** (WHA) for future considerations, June, 1972. Claimed by **Calgary** (WHA) from **Quebec** (WHA) in WHA Intra-League Draft, May 19, 1975. Traded to **Quebec** (WHA) by **Calgary** (WHA) for future considerations, August, 1976. Rights retained by **Quebec** prior to Expansion Draft, June 9, 1979.

• LACOMBE, Normand

RW – R. 6′, 205 lbs. b: Pierrefonds, Que., 10/18/1964. Buffalo's 2nd, 10th overall, in 1983.

Season	Club	League	GP	G	A	Pts	AG	AA	APts	PIM	PP	SH	GW	S	%	TGF	PGF	TGA	PGA	+/–	GP	G	A	Pts	PIM	PP	SH	GW
1979-80	Lac St-Louis Lions	QAAA	42	20	33	53	....	....	....	....	....	....	....	....	....	....	....	....	....	....	....	....	....	....	....	....	....	....
1980-81	Lac St-Louis Lions	QAAA	47	36	59	95	....	....	....	....	....	....	....	....	....	....	....	....	....	....	....	....	....	....	....	....	....	....
1981-82	University of New Hampshire	ECAC	35	18	16	34	....	....	....	38	....	....	....	....	....	....	....	....	....	....	....	....	....	....	....	....	....	....
1982-83	University of New Hampshire	ECAC	35	18	25	43	....	....	....	48	....	....	....	....	....	....	....	....	....	....	....	....	....	....	....	....	....	....
1983-84	Rochester Americans	AHL	44	10	16	26	....	....	....	45	....	....	....	....	....	....	....	....	....	....	....	....	....	....	....	....	....	....
1984-85	**Buffalo Sabres**	**NHL**	**30**	**2**	**4**	**6**	**2**	**3**	**5**	**25**	**0**	**0**	**0**	**30**	**6.7**	**10**	**1**	**12**	**0**	**–3**	....	....	....	....	....	....	....	....
	Rochester Americans	AHL	33	13	16	29	....	....	....	33	....	....	....	....	....	....	....	....	....	....	5	3	1	4	4	....	....	....

			REGULAR SEASON																		PLAYOFFS							
Season	Club	League	GP	G	A	Pts	AG	AA	APts	PIM	PP	SH	GW	S	%	TGF	PGF	TGA	PGA	+/–	GP	G	A	Pts	PIM	PP	SH	GW
1985-86	Buffalo Sabres	NHL	25	6	7	13	5	5	10	13	3	0	2	38	15.8	32	9	16	2	9								
	Rochester Americans	AHL	32	10	13	23				56																		
1986-87	Buffalo Sabres	NHL	39	4	7	11	3	5	8	8	1	0	0	48	8.3	18	2	27	2	–9								
	Rochester Americans	AHL	13	6	5	11				4																		
	Edmonton Oilers	NHL	1	0	0	0	0	0	0	2	0	0	0	0	0.0	1	0	2	0	–1								
	Nova Scotia Oilers	AHL	10	3	5	8				4											5	1	1	2	6			
1987-88♦	Edmonton Oilers	NHL	53	8	9	17	7	6	13	36	1	0	2	44	18.2	26	2	27	0	–3	19	3	0	3	28	0	0	1
1988-89	Edmonton Oilers	NHL	64	17	11	28	14	8	22	57	2	0	1	71	23.9	45	4	39	0	2	7	2	1	3	21	0	0	0
1989-90	Edmonton Oilers	NHL	15	5	2	7	4	1	5	21	0	0	0	15	33.3	9	0	5	0	4								
	Philadelphia Flyers	NHL	18	0	2	2	0	1	1	7	0	0	0	21	0.0	9	0	9	0	0								
1990-91	Philadelphia Flyers	NHL	74	11	20	31	10	15	25	27	1	0	1	91	12.1	37	1	47	10	–1								
1991-92	Canada	Nat-Team	11	1	4	5				16																		
	NHL Totals		319	53	62	115	45	44	89	196	8	0	6	358	14.8	187	19	184	14		26	5	1	6	49	0	0	1

ECAC Second All-Star Team (1983)

Traded to **Edmonton** by **Buffalo** with Wayne Van Dorp and Buffalo's 4th round choice (Peter Ericksson) in 1987 Entry Draft for Lee Fogolin, Mark Napier and Edmonton's 4th round choice (John Bradley) in 1987 Entry Draft, March 6, 1987. Traded to **Philadelphia** by **Edmonton** for future considerations, January 5, 1990.

• LaCOUTURE, Dan

Daniel Scott LW – L. 6'3", 210 lbs. b: Hyannis, MA, 4/18/1977. NY Islanders' 2nd, 29th overall, in 1996.

Season	Club	League	GP	G	A	Pts	AG	AA	APts	PIM	PP	SH	GW	S	%	TGF	PGF	TGA	PGA	+/–	GP	G	A	Pts	PIM	PP	SH	GW
1992-93	Natick Redmen	Hi-School	20	38	34	72				46																		
1993-94	Natick Redmen	Hi-School	21	52	49	101				58																		
1994-95	Springfield Jr. Pics	IJHL	52	44	56	100				98																		
1995-96	Springfield Jr. Whalers	NAJHL	41	36	41	77				87											13	12	13	25	23			
1996-97	Boston University	H-East	31	13	12	25				18																		
1997-98	Hamilton Bulldogs	AHL	77	15	10	25				31											5	1	0	1	0			
1998-99	Edmonton Oilers	NHL	3	0	0	0	0	0	0	0	0	0	0	0	0.0	1	0	0	0	1								
	Hamilton Bulldogs	AHL	72	17	14	31				73											9	2	1	3	2			
99-2000	Edmonton Oilers	NHL	5	0	0	0	0	0	0	10	0	0	0	2	0.0	0	0	0	0	0	1	0	0	0	0	0	0	0
	Hamilton Bulldogs	AHL	70	23	17	40				85											6	2	1	3	0			
	NHL Totals		8	0	0	0	0	0	0	10	0	0	0	2	0.0	1	0	0	0		1	0	0	0	0	0	0	0

Traded to **Edmonton** by **NY Islanders** for Mariusz Czerkawski, August 25, 1997.

• LACROIX, Andre

Andre Joseph C – L. 5'8", 175 lbs. b: Lauzon, Que., 6/5/1945.

Season	Club	League	GP	G	A	Pts	AG	AA	APts	PIM	PP	SH	GW	S	%	TGF	PGF	TGA	PGA	+/–	GP	G	A	Pts	PIM	PP	SH	GW
1961-62	Quebec Citadelle	QJHL	STATISTICS NOT AVAILABLE																									
	Quebec Citadelle	Mem-Cup	2	0	0	0				4																		
1962-63	Quebec Citadelle	QJHL	50	45	50	95															12	10	13	23	8			
1963-64	Montreal Jr. Canadiens	OHA-Jr.	34	12	18	30				13											17	8	13	21	8			
1964-65	Peterborough Petes	OHA-Jr.	49	45	*74	119				24											12	8	12	20	4			
	Quebec Aces	AHL	1	0	0	0				0																		
1965-66	Peterborough Petes	OHA-Jr.	48	40	*80	*120				20											6	4	8	12	6			
	Quebec Aces	AHL	2	1	3	4				0																		
1966-67	Quebec Aces	AHL	67	25	24	49				14											5	2	3	5	2			
1967-68	Philadelphia Flyers	NHL	18	6	8	14	7	8	15	6	0	0	1	51	11.8	17	4	13	0	0	7	2	3	5	0	1	0	0
	Quebec Aces	AHL	54	41	46	87				18																		
1968-69	Philadelphia Flyers	NHL	75	24	32	56	25	29	54	4	13	0	1	217	11.1	75	32	55	0	–12	4	0	0	0	0	0	0	0
1969-70	Philadelphia Flyers	NHL	74	22	36	58	24	34	58	14	6	0	4	175	12.6	71	31	46	0	–6								
1970-71	Philadelphia Flyers	NHL	78	20	22	42	20	18	38	12	9	0	4	180	11.1	56	30	35	0	–9	4	0	2	2	0	0	0	0
1971-72	Chicago Black Hawks	NHL	51	4	7	11	4	6	10	6	1	0	1	34	11.8	18	4	10	0	4	1	0	0	0	0	0	0	0
1972-73	Philadelphia Blazers	WHA	78	50	74	*124				83											4	0	2	2	18			
1973-74	New York-Jersey Knights	WHA	78	31	*80	111				54																		
1974-75	Team Canada	Summit-74	8	1	6	7				6																		
	San Diego Mariners	WHA	78	41	*106	*147				63											10	3	9	12	2			
1975-76	San Diego Mariners	WHA	80	29	72	101				42											11	4	6	10	4			
1976-77	San Diego Mariners	WHA	81	32	82	114				79											7	1	6	7	6			
1977-78	Houston Aeros	WHA	78	36	77	113				57											6	2	2	4	0			
1978-79	New England Whalers	WHA	78	32	56	88				34											10	4	4	8	0			
1979-80	Hartford Whalers	NHL	29	3	14	17	3	10	13	2	1	0	0	45	6.7	22	3	27	2	–6								
	NHL Totals		325	79	119	198	83	105	188	44	30	0	11	702	11.3	259	104	186	2		16	2	5	7	0	1	0	0
	Other Major League Totals		551	251	547	798				412											48	14	29	43	30			

OHA-Jr. First All-Star Team (1965, 1966) • WHA First All-Star Team (1973, 1974, 1975) • Won W. D. (Bill) Hunter Trophy (WHA Scoring Leader) (1973, 1975)

NHL rights transferred to **Philadelphia** after NHL club purchased **Quebec** (AHL) franchise, May 8, 1967. Traded to **Chicago** by **Philadelphia** for Rick Foley, October 15, 1971. Selected by **Quebec** (WHA) in 1972 WHA General Player Draft, February 12, 1972. WHA rights traded to **Miami-Philadelphia** (WHA) by **Quebec** (WHA) for cash, March, 1972. Transferred to **Vancouver** (WHA) after **Philadelphia** franchise relocated, May, 1973. Traded to **NY Raiders** (WHA) by **Vancouver** (WHA) with Dan Herriman and Bernie Parent for Ron Ward and Pete Donnelly, June, 1973. Transferred to **San Diego** (WHA) after **New York-Jersey** (WHA) franchise relocated, April 30, 1974. Signed as a free agent by **Houston** (WHA) after **San Diego** (WHA) franchise folded, May 30, 1977. Signed as a free agent by **Winnipeg** (WHA) after **Houston** (WHA) franchise folded, July, 1978. Traded to **New England** (WHA) by **Winnipeg** (WHA) for future considerations, August, 1978. Rights retained by **Hartford** prior to Expansion Draft, June 9, 1979.

• LACROIX, Daniel

LW – L. 6'2", 205 lbs. b: Montreal, Que., 3/11/1969. NY Rangers' 2nd, 31st overall, in 1987.

Season	Club	League	GP	G	A	Pts	AG	AA	APts	PIM	PP	SH	GW	S	%	TGF	PGF	TGA	PGA	+/–	GP	G	A	Pts	PIM	PP	SH	GW
1985-86	Hull Frontaliers	QAAA	37	10	13	23				46																		
1986-87	Granby Bisons	QMJHL	54	9	16	25				311											8	1	2	3	22			
1987-88	Granby Bisons	QMJHL	58	24	50	74				468											5	0	4	4	12			
1988-89	Granby Bisons	QMJHL	70	45	49	94				320											4	1	1	2	57			
	Denver Rangers	IHL	2	0	1	1				0											2	0	1	1	0			
1989-90	Flint Spirits	IHL	61	12	16	28				128											4	2	0	2	24			
1990-91	Binghamton Rangers	AHL	54	7	12	19				237											5	1	0	1	24			
1991-92	Binghamton Rangers	AHL	52	12	20	32				149											11	2	4	6	28			
1992-93	Binghamton Rangers	AHL	73	21	22	43				255																		
1993-94	New York Rangers	NHL	4	0	0	0	0	0	0	0	0	0	0	0	0.0	0	0	0	0	0								
	Binghamton Rangers	AHL	59	20	23	43				278																		
1994-95	Providence Bruins	AHL	40	15	11	26				266																		
	Boston Bruins	NHL	23	1	0	1	2	0	2	38	0	0	0	14	7.1	3	0	7	2	–2								
	New York Rangers	NHL	1	0	0	0	0	0	0	0	0	0	0	0	0.0	0	0	0	0	0								
1995-96	New York Rangers	NHL	25	2	2	4	2	2	4	30	0	0	0	14	14.3	6	0	9	2	–1								
	Binghamton Rangers	AHL	26	12	15	27				155																		
1996-97	Philadelphia Flyers	NHL	74	7	1	8	7	1	8	163	1	0	0	54	13.0	21	1	23	2	–1	12	0	1	1	22	0	0	0
1997-98	Philadelphia Flyers	NHL	56	1	4	5	1	4	5	135	0	0	0	28	3.6	6	0	6	0	0	4	0	0	0	4	0	0	0
1998-99	Edmonton Oilers	NHL	4	0	0	0	0	0	0	13	0	0	0	5	0.0	1	0	1	0	0								
	Hamilton Bulldogs	AHL	46	13	9	22				260											11	3	1	4	65			
99-2000	New York Islanders	NHL	1	0	0	0	0	0	0	0	0	0	0	0	0.0	0	0	3	2	–1								
	Chicago Wolves	IHL	61	3	10	13				194											7	0	0	0	28			
	NHL Totals		188	11	7	18	12	7	19	379	1	0	0	115	9.6	37	1	49	8		16	0	1	1	26	0	0	0

Traded to **Boston** by **NY Rangers** for Glen Featherstone, August 19, 1994. Claimed on waivers by **NY Rangers** from **Boston**, March 23, 1995. Signed as a free agent by **Philadelphia**, July 18, 1996. Traded to **Edmonton** by **Philadelphia** for Valeri Zelepukin, October 5, 1998. Signed as a free agent by **NY Islanders**, August 11, 1999.

• LACROIX, Eric

LW – L. 6'2", 210 lbs. b: Montreal, Que., 7/15/1971. Toronto's 6th, 136th overall, in 1990.

Season	Club	League	GP	G	A	Pts	AG	AA	APts	PIM	PP	SH	GW	S	%	TGF	PGF	TGA	PGA	+/–	GP	G	A	Pts	PIM	PP	SH	GW
1989-90	Governor Dummer Academy	Hi-School	25	23	18	41																						
1990-91	St. Lawrence University	ECAC	35	13	11	24				35																		
1991-92	St. Lawrence University	ECAC	34	11	20	31				40																		
1992-93	St. John's Maple Leafs	AHL	76	15	19	34				59											9	5	3	8	4			

Season	Club	League	REGULAR SEASON GP	G	A	Pts	AG	AA	APts	PIM	PP	SH	GW	S	%	TGF	PGF	TGA	PGA	+/–	PLAYOFFS GP	G	A	Pts	PIM	PP	SH	GW
1993-94	**Toronto Maple Leafs**	**NHL**	**3**	**0**	**0**	**0**	**0**	**0**	**0**	**2**	**0**	**0**	**0**	**3**	**0.0**	**1**	**0**	**1**	**0**	**0**	**2**	**0**	**0**	**0**	**0**	**0**	**0**	**0**
	St. John's Maple Leafs	AHL	59	17	22	39	....	....	....	69	....	....	....	....	....	....	....	....	....	....	11	5	3	8	6	....	....	....
1994-95	St. John's Maple Leafs	AHL	1	0	0	0	....	....	....	2	....	....	....	....	....	....	....	....	....	....	....	....	....	....	....	....	....	....
	Phoenix Roadrunners	IHL	25	7	1	8	....	....	....	31	....	....	....	....	....	....	....	....	....	....	....	....	....	....	....	....	....	....
	Los Angeles Kings	**NHL**	**45**	**9**	**7**	**16**	**16**	**10**	**26**	**54**	**2**	**1**	**1**	**64**	**14.1**	**28**	**3**	**23**	**0**	**2**	....	....	....	....	....	....	....	....
1995-96	**Los Angeles Kings**	**NHL**	**72**	**16**	**16**	**32**	**16**	**13**	**29**	**110**	**3**	**0**	**1**	**107**	**15.0**	**53**	**12**	**57**	**5**	**–11**	....	....	....	....	....	....	....	....
1996-97	**Colorado Avalanche**	**NHL**	**81**	**18**	**18**	**36**	**19**	**16**	**35**	**26**	**2**	**0**	**4**	**141**	**12.8**	**53**	**9**	**32**	**4**	**16**	**17**	**1**	**4**	**5**	**19**	**0**	**0**	**0**
1997-98	**Colorado Avalanche**	**NHL**	**82**	**16**	**15**	**31**	**19**	**15**	**34**	**84**	**5**	**0**	**6**	**126**	**12.7**	**41**	**10**	**38**	**7**	**0**	**7**	**0**	**0**	**0**	**6**	**0**	**0**	**0**
1998-99	**Colorado Avalanche**	**NHL**	**7**	**0**	**0**	**0**	**0**	**0**	**0**	**2**	**0**	**0**	**0**	**4**	**0.0**	**0**	**0**	**7**	**5**	**–2**	....	....	....	....	....	....	....	....
	Los Angeles Kings	**NHL**	**27**	**0**	**1**	**1**	**0**	**1**	**1**	**12**	**0**	**0**	**0**	**17**	**0.0**	**2**	**0**	**8**	**1**	**–5**	....	....	....	....	....	....	....	....
	New York Rangers	**NHL**	**30**	**2**	**1**	**3**	**2**	**1**	**3**	**4**	**0**	**0**	**1**	**17**	**11.8**	**4**	**1**	**8**	**0**	**–5**	....	....	....	....	....	....	....	....
99-2000	**New York Rangers**	**NHL**	**70**	**4**	**8**	**12**	**4**	**7**	**11**	**24**	**0**	**0**	**1**	**46**	**8.7**	**16**	**1**	**33**	**6**	**–12**	....	....	....	....	....	....	....	....
	NHL Totals		**417**	**65**	**66**	**131**	**76**	**63**	**139**	**318**	**12**	**1**	**14**	**525**	**12.4**	**198**	**36**	**207**	**28**		**26**	**1**	**4**	**5**	**25**	**0**	**0**	**0**

Traded to **LA Kings** by **Toronto** with Chris Snell and Toronto's 4th round choice (Eric Belanger) in 1996 Entry Draft for Dixon Ward, Guy Leveque, Kelly Fairchild and Shayne Toporowski, October 3, 1994. Traded to **Colorado** by **LA Kings** with LA Kings' 1st round choice (Martin Skoula) in 1998 Entry Draft for Stephane Fiset and Colorado's 1st round choice (Mathieu Biron) in 1998 Entry Draft, June 20, 1996. Traded to **Los Angeles** by **Colorado** for Roman Vopat and Los Angeles' 6th round choice (later traded to Ottawa - Ottawa selected Martin Brusek) in 1999 Entry Draft, October 29, 1998. Traded to **NY Rangers** by **Los Angeles** for Sean Pronger, February 12, 1999.

• LACROIX, Pierre

D – L. 5'11", 185 lbs. b: Quebec City, Que., 4/11/1959. Quebec's 5th, 104th overall, in 1979.

Season	Club	League	GP	G	A	Pts	AG	AA	APts	PIM	PP	SH	GW	S	%	TGF	PGF	TGA	PGA	+/–	GP	G	A	Pts	PIM	PP	SH	GW
1975-76	Quebec Remparts	QMJHL	72	7	30	37	....	....	....	90	....	....	....	....	....	....	....	....	....	....	....	....	....	....	....	....	....	....
	Quebec Remparts	Mem-Cup	3	0	1	1	....	....	....	2	....	....	....	....	....	....	....	....	....	....	....	....	....	....	....	....	....	....
1976-77	Quebec Remparts	QMJHL	69	10	43	53	....	....	....	61	....	....	....	....	....	....	....	....	....	....	....	....	....	....	....	....	....	....
1977-78	Quebec Remparts	QMJHL	38	11	30	41	....	....	....	35	....	....	....	....	....	....	....	....	....	....	....	....	....	....	....	....	....	....
	Trois-Rivieres Draveurs	QMJHL	30	6	24	30	....	....	....	20	....	....	....	....	....	....	....	....	....	....	5	3	5	8	4	....	....	....
	Trois-Rivieres Draveurs	Mem-Cup	4	0	3	3	....	....	....	2	....	....	....	....	....	....	....	....	....	....	....	....	....	....	....	....	....	....
1978-79	Trois-Rivieres Draveurs	QMJHL	72	37	100	137	....	....	....	57	....	....	....	....	....	....	....	....	....	....	13	2	10	12	6	....	....	....
	Trois-Rivieres Draveurs	Mem-Cup	4	0	4	4	....	....	....	6	....	....	....	....	....	....	....	....	....	....	....	....	....	....	....	....	....	....
1979-80	**Quebec Nordiques**	**NHL**	**76**	**9**	**21**	**30**	**8**	**15**	**23**	**45**	**4**	**0**	**0**	**86**	**10.5**	**78**	**23**	**63**	**2**	**–6**	....	....	....	....	....	....	....	....
1980-81	**Quebec Nordiques**	**NHL**	**61**	**5**	**34**	**39**	**4**	**23**	**27**	**54**	**4**	**0**	**0**	**96**	**5.2**	**110**	**39**	**80**	**18**	**9**	**5**	**0**	**2**	**2**	**10**	**0**	**0**	**0**
1981-82	**Quebec Nordiques**	**NHL**	**68**	**4**	**23**	**27**	**3**	**15**	**18**	**74**	**1**	**0**	**0**	**73**	**5.5**	**87**	**19**	**73**	**6**	**1**	**3**	**0**	**0**	**0**	**0**	**0**	**0**	**0**
1982-83	**Quebec Nordiques**	**NHL**	**13**	**0**	**5**	**5**	**0**	**3**	**3**	**6**	**0**	**0**	**0**	**8**	**0.0**	**14**	**3**	**11**	**4**	**4**	....	....	....	....	....	....	....	....
	Fredericton Express	AHL	6	0	5	5	....	....	....	0	....	....	....	....	....	....	....	....	....	....	....	....	....	....	....	....	....	....
	Hartford Whalers	**NHL**	**56**	**6**	**25**	**31**	**5**	**17**	**22**	**18**	**1**	**0**	**0**	**89**	**6.7**	**81**	**15**	**102**	**17**	**–19**	....	....	....	....	....	....	....	....
1983-84			STATISTICS NOT AVAILABLE																									
1984-85			STATISTICS NOT AVAILABLE																									
1985-86	EHC Arosa	Switz.	15	5	7	12	....	....	....																			
1986-87	Paris Francais Volants	France	STATISTICS NOT AVAILABLE																									
1987-88	HC Fribourg-Gotteron	Switz.	35	8	15	23	....	....	....	....	....	....	....	....	....	....	....	....	....	....	....	....	....	....	....	....	....	....
1988-89	HC Fribourg-Gotteron	Switz.	35	11	9	20	....	....	....	....	....	....	....	....	....	....	....	....	....	....	....	....	....	....	....	....	....	....
1989-90	CS Villard-de-Lans	France	35	7	32	39	....	....	....	22	....	....	....	....	....	....	....	....	....	....	....	....	....	....	....	....	....	....
1990-91	ASG Tours	France	7	5	5	10	....	....	....	10	....	....	....	....	....	....	....	....	....	....	....	....	....	....	....	....	....	....
1991-92	OHC Viry-Essone	France	33	5	17	22	....	....	....	26	....	....	....	....	....	....	....	....	....	....	....	....	....	....	....	....	....	....
1992-93	OHC Viry-Essone	France	DID NOT PLAY – COACHING																									
	NHL Totals		**274**	**24**	**108**	**132**	**20**	**73**	**93**	**197**	**10**	**0**	**0**	**352**	**6.8**	**370**	**99**	**329**	**47**		**8**	**0**	**2**	**2**	**10**	**0**	**0**	**0**

QMJHL First All-Star Team (1979) • Canadian Major Junior Player of the Year (1979)

Traded to **Hartford** by **Quebec** for Blake Wesley, December 3, 1982.

• LADOUCEUR, Randy

Randy J. D – L. 6'2", 220 lbs. b: Brockville, Ont., 6/30/1960.

Season	Club	League	GP	G	A	Pts	AG	AA	APts	PIM	PP	SH	GW	S	%	TGF	PGF	TGA	PGA	+/–	GP	G	A	Pts	PIM	PP	SH	GW
1976-77	Brockville Blackhawks	OMHA	50	25	56	81	....	....	....	....	....	....	....	....	....	....	....	....	....	....	....	....	....	....	....	....	....	....
1977-78	Hamilton Fincups	OMJHL	64	8	20	28	....	....	....	82	....	....	....	....	....	....	....	....	....	....	20	0	0	0	9	....	....	....
1978-79	Brantford Alexanders	OMJHL	64	3	17	20	....	....	....	141	....	....	....	....	....	....	....	....	....	....	....	....	....	....	....	....	....	....
1979-80	Brantford Alexanders	OMJHL	37	6	15	21	....	....	....	125	....	....	....	....	....	....	....	....	....	....	8	0	5	5	18	....	....	....
1980-81	Kalamazoo Wings	IHL	80	7	30	37	....	....	....	52	....	....	....	....	....	....	....	....	....	....	8	1	3	4	10	....	....	....
1981-82	Adirondack Red Wings	AHL	78	4	28	32	....	....	....	78	....	....	....	....	....	....	....	....	....	....	5	1	1	2	6	....	....	....
1982-83	**Detroit Red Wings**	**NHL**	**27**	**0**	**4**	**4**	**0**	**3**	**3**	**16**	**0**	**0**	**0**	**17**	**0.0**	**18**	**2**	**29**	**3**	**–10**	....	....	....	....	....	....	....	....
	Adirondack Red Wings	AHL	48	11	21	32	....	....	....	54	....	....	....	....	....	....	....	....	....	....	....	....	....	....	....	....	....	....
1983-84	**Detroit Red Wings**	**NHL**	**71**	**3**	**17**	**20**	**2**	**12**	**14**	**58**	**0**	**0**	**0**	**89**	**3.4**	**75**	**8**	**107**	**28**	**–12**	**4**	**1**	**0**	**1**	**6**	**0**	**1**	**0**
	Adirondack Red Wings	AHL	11	3	5	8	....	....	....	12	....	....	....	....	....	....	....	....	....	....	....	....	....	....	....	....	....	....
1984-85	**Detroit Red Wings**	**NHL**	**80**	**3**	**27**	**30**	**2**	**18**	**20**	**108**	**1**	**0**	**1**	**83**	**3.6**	**119**	**18**	**147**	**49**	**3**	**3**	**1**	**0**	**1**	**0**	**0**	**0**	**0**
1985-86	**Detroit Red Wings**	**NHL**	**78**	**5**	**13**	**18**	**4**	**9**	**13**	**196**	**0**	**0**	**1**	**92**	**5.4**	**76**	**12**	**168**	**50**	**–54**	....	....	....	....	....	....	....	....
1986-87	**Detroit Red Wings**	**NHL**	**34**	**3**	**6**	**9**	**3**	**4**	**7**	**70**	**1**	**0**	**1**	**25**	**12.0**	**29**	**3**	**40**	**10**	**–4**	....	....	....	....	....	....	....	....
	Hartford Whalers	**NHL**	**36**	**2**	**3**	**5**	**2**	**2**	**4**	**51**	**0**	**0**	**0**	**29**	**6.9**	**36**	**1**	**38**	**9**	**6**	**6**	**0**	**2**	**2**	**12**	**0**	**0**	**0**
1987-88	**Hartford Whalers**	**NHL**	**67**	**1**	**7**	**8**	**1**	**5**	**6**	**91**	**0**	**0**	**1**	**37**	**2.7**	**53**	**3**	**64**	**21**	**7**	**6**	**1**	**1**	**2**	**4**	**0**	**0**	**0**
1988-89	**Hartford Whalers**	**NHL**	**75**	**2**	**5**	**7**	**2**	**4**	**6**	**95**	**0**	**0**	**0**	**56**	**3.6**	**66**	**0**	**115**	**26**	**–23**	**1**	**0**	**0**	**0**	**10**	**0**	**0**	**0**
1989-90	**Hartford Whalers**	**NHL**	**71**	**3**	**12**	**15**	**3**	**9**	**12**	**126**	**0**	**0**	**0**	**45**	**6.7**	**53**	**2**	**87**	**30**	**–6**	**7**	**1**	**0**	**1**	**10**	**0**	**0**	**1**
1990-91	**Hartford Whalers**	**NHL**	**67**	**1**	**3**	**4**	**1**	**2**	**3**	**118**	**0**	**0**	**0**	**44**	**2.3**	**47**	**0**	**85**	**28**	**–10**	**6**	**1**	**4**	**5**	**6**	**0**	**0**	**0**
1991-92	**Hartford Whalers**	**NHL**	**74**	**1**	**9**	**10**	**1**	**7**	**8**	**127**	**0**	**0**	**0**	**59**	**1.7**	**44**	**1**	**77**	**33**	**–1**	**7**	**0**	**1**	**1**	**11**	**0**	**0**	**0**
1992-93	**Hartford Whalers**	**NHL**	**62**	**2**	**4**	**6**	**2**	**3**	**5**	**109**	**0**	**0**	**0**	**37**	**5.4**	**41**	**0**	**85**	**26**	**–18**	....	....	....	....	....	....	....	....
1993-94	**Mighty Ducks of Anaheim**	**NHL**	**81**	**1**	**9**	**10**	**1**	**7**	**8**	**74**	**0**	**0**	**0**	**66**	**1.5**	**59**	**0**	**78**	**26**	**7**	....	....	....	....	....	....	....	....
1994-95	**Mighty Ducks of Anaheim**	**NHL**	**44**	**2**	**4**	**6**	**4**	**6**	**10**	**36**	**0**	**0**	**0**	**42**	**4.8**	**29**	**1**	**41**	**15**	**2**	....	....	....	....	....	....	....	....
1995-96	**Mighty Ducks of Anaheim**	**NHL**	**63**	**1**	**3**	**4**	**1**	**2**	**3**	**47**	**0**	**0**	**0**	**48**	**2.1**	**45**	**0**	**66**	**26**	**5**	....	....	....	....	....	....	....	....
	NHL Totals		**930**	**30**	**126**	**156**	**29**	**93**	**122**	**1322**	**2**	**0**	**4**	**769**	**3.9**	**790**	**51**	**1227**	**380**		**40**	**5**	**8**	**13**	**59**	**0**	**1**	**1**

Signed as a free agent by **Detroit**, November 1, 1979. Traded to **Hartford** by **Detroit** for Dave Barr, January 12, 1987. Claimed by **Anaheim** from **Hartford** in Expansion Draft, June 24, 1993.

• LaFAYETTE, Nathan

C – R. 6'1", 205 lbs. b: New Westminster, B.C., 2/17/1973. St. Louis' 3rd, 65th overall, in 1991.

Season	Club	League	GP	G	A	Pts	AG	AA	APts	PIM	PP	SH	GW	S	%	TGF	PGF	TGA	PGA	+/–	GP	G	A	Pts	PIM	PP	SH	GW
1988-89	Toronto Midget Marlboros	MTHL	69	38	68	106	....	....	....	24	....	....	....	....	....	....	....	....	....	....	....	....	....	....	....	....	....	....
	Pickering Panthers	OJHL-B	1	0	0	0	....	....	....	0	....	....	....	....	....	....	....	....	....	....	....	....	....	....	....	....	....	....
1989-90	Kingston Frontenacs	OHL	53	6	8	14	....	....	....	14	....	....	....	....	....	....	....	....	....	....	7	0	1	1	0	....	....	....
1990-91	Kingston Frontenacs	OHL	35	13	13	26	....	....	....	10	....	....	....	....	....	....	....	....	....	....	....	....	....	....	....	....	....	....
	Cornwall Royals	OHL	28	16	22	38	....	....	....	25	....	....	....	....	....	....	....	....	....	....	....	....	....	....	....	....	....	....
1991-92	Cornwall Royals	OHL	66	28	45	73	....	....	....	26	....	....	....	....	....	....	....	....	....	....	6	2	5	7	15	....	....	....
1992-93	Newmarket Royals	OHL	58	49	38	87	....	....	....	26	....	....	....	....	....	....	....	....	....	....	7	4	5	9	19	....	....	....
	Canada	WJC-A	7	3	1	4	....	....	....	0	....	....	....	....	....	....	....	....	....	....	....	....	....	....	....	....	....	....
1993-94	**St. Louis Blues**	**NHL**	**38**	**2**	**3**	**5**	**2**	**2**	**4**	**14**	**0**	**0**	**0**	**23**	**8.7**	**10**	**0**	**22**	**3**	**–9**	....	....	....	....	....	....	....	....
	Peoria Rivermen	IHL	27	13	11	24	....	....	....	20	....	....	....	....	....	....	....	....	....	....	....	....	....	....	....	....	....	....
	Vancouver Canucks	**NHL**	**11**	**1**	**1**	**2**	**1**	**1**	**2**	**4**	**0**	**0**	**0**	**11**	**9.1**	**7**	**1**	**10**	**6**	**2**	**20**	**2**	**7**	**9**	**4**	**0**	**0**	**0**
1994-95	Syracuse Crunch	AHL	27	9	9	18	....	....	....	10	....	....	....	....	....	....	....	....	....	....	....	....	....	....	....	....	....	....
	Vancouver Canucks	**NHL**	**27**	**4**	**4**	**8**	**7**	**6**	**13**	**2**	**0**	**1**	**0**	**30**	**13.3**	**12**	**1**	**19**	**10**	**2**	....	....	....	....	....	....	....	....
	New York Rangers	**NHL**	**12**	**0**	**0**	**0**	**0**	**0**	**0**	**0**	**0**	**0**	**0**	**5**	**0.0**	**3**	**0**	**2**	**0**	**1**	**8**	**0**	**0**	**0**	**2**	**0**	**0**	**0**
1995-96	**New York Rangers**	**NHL**	**5**	**0**	**0**	**0**	**0**	**0**	**0**	**2**	**0**	**0**	**0**	**5**	**0.0**	**0**	**0**	**2**	**1**	**–1**	....	....	....	....	....	....	....	....
	Binghamton Rangers	AHL	57	21	27	48	....	....	....	32	....	....	....	....	....	....	....	....	....	....	....	....	....	....	....	....	....	....
	Los Angeles Kings	**NHL**	**12**	**2**	**4**	**6**	**2**	**3**	**5**	**6**	**1**	**0**	**0**	**23**	**8.7**	**7**	**1**	**11**	**2**	**–3**	....	....	....	....	....	....	....	....
1996-97	**Los Angeles Kings**	**NHL**	**15**	**1**	**3**	**4**	**1**	**3**	**4**	**8**	**0**	**1**	**1**	**26**	**3.8**	**5**	**0**	**14**	**1**	**–8**	....	....	....	....	....	....	....	....
	Phoenix Roadrunners	IHL	31	2	5	7	....	....	....	16	....	....	....	....	....	....	....	....	....	....	....	....	....	....	....	....	....	....
	Syracuse Crunch	AHL	26	14	11	25	....	....	....	18	....	....	....	....	....	....	....	....	....	....	3	1	0	1	2	....	....	....
1997-98	**Los Angeles Kings**	**NHL**	**34**	**5**	**3**	**8**	**6**	**3**	**9**	**32**	**1**	**0**	**1**	**60**	**8.3**	**13**	**1**	**12**	**2**	**2**	**4**	**0**	**0**	**0**	**2**	**0**	**0**	**0**
	Fredericton Canadiens	AHL	28	7	8	15	....	....	....	36	....	....	....	....	....	....	....	....	....	....	....	....	....	....	....	....	....	....

			REGULAR SEASON																		PLAYOFFS							
Season	Club	League	GP	G	A	Pts	AG	AA	APts	PIM	PP	SH	GW	S	%	TGF	PGF	TGA	PGA	+/–	GP	G	A	Pts	PIM	PP	SH	GW
1998-99	**Los Angeles Kings**	**NHL**	**33**	**2**	**2**	**4**	**2**	**2**	**4**	**35**	**0**	**1**	**1**	**42**	**4.8**	**11**	**1**	**14**	**4**	**0**								
	Long Beach Ice Dogs	IHL	41	9	13	22				24											7	1	0	1	8			
99-2000	Lowell Lock Monsters	AHL	42	7	15	22				33																		
	NHL Totals		**187**	**17**	**20**	**37**	**21**	**20**	**41**	**103**	**2**	**3**	**3**	**225**	**7.6**	**68**	**5**	**106**	**29**		**32**	**2**	**7**	**9**	**8**	**0**	**0**	**0**

Canadian Major Junior Scholastic Player of the Year (1992)

Traded to **Vancouver** by **St. Louis** with Jeff Brown and Bret Hedican for Craig Janney, March 21, 1994. Traded to **NY Rangers** by **Vancouver** for Corey Hirsch, April 7, 1995. Traded to **LA Kings** by **NY Rangers** with Ray Ferraro, Mattias Norstrom, Ian Laperriere and NY Rangers' 4th round choice (Sean Blanchard) in 1997 Entry Draft for Marty McSorley, Jari Kurri and Shane Churla, March 14, 1996.

• LAFLAMME, Christian

D – R. 6'1", 210 lbs. b: St. Charles, Que., 11/24/1976. Chicago's 2nd, 45th overall, in 1995.

Season	Club	League	GP	G	A	Pts	AG	AA	APts	PIM	PP	SH	GW	S	%	TGF	PGF	TGA	PGA	+/–	GP	G	A	Pts	PIM	PP	SH	GW
1991-92	Ste-Foy Gouverneurs	QAAA	42	5	27	32				100																		
1992-93	Verdun College-Francais	QMJHL	69	2	17	19				85											3	0	2	2	6			
1993-94	Verdun College-Francais	QMJHL	72	4	34	38				85											4	0	3	3	4			
1994-95	Beauport Harfangs	QMJHL	67	6	41	47				82											8	1	4	5	6			
1995-96	Beauport Harfangs	QMJHL	41	13	23	36				63											20	7	17	24	32			
1996-97	**Chicago Blackhawks**	**NHL**	**4**	**0**	**1**	**1**	**0**	**1**	**1**	**2**	**0**	**0**	**0**	**3**	**0.0**	**4**	**0**	**1**	**0**	**3**								
	Indianapolis Ice	IHL	62	5	15	20				60											4	1	1	2	16			
1997-98	**Chicago Blackhawks**	**NHL**	**72**	**0**	**11**	**11**	**0**	**11**	**11**	**59**	**0**	**0**	**0**	**75**	**0.0**	**37**	**3**	**25**	**5**	**14**								
1998-99	**Chicago Blackhawks**	**NHL**	**62**	**2**	**11**	**13**	**2**	**11**	**13**	**70**	**0**	**0**	**0**	**53**	**3.8**	**40**	**5**	**58**	**23**	**0**								
	Portland Pirates	AHL	2	0	1	1				2																		
	Edmonton Oilers	**NHL**	**11**	**0**	**1**	**1**	**0**	**1**	**1**	**0**	**0**	**0**	**0**	**15**	**0.0**	**8**	**4**	**8**	**1**	**–3**	**4**	**0**	**1**	**1**	**2**	**0**	**0**	**0**
99-2000	**Edmonton Oilers**	**NHL**	**50**	**0**	**5**	**5**	**0**	**5**	**5**	**32**	**0**	**0**	**0**	**18**	**0.0**	**29**	**1**	**37**	**5**	**–4**								
	Montreal Canadiens	**NHL**	**15**	**0**	**2**	**2**	**0**	**2**	**2**	**8**	**0**	**0**	**0**	**6**	**0.0**	**6**	**0**	**12**	**1**	**–5**								
	NHL Totals		**214**	**2**	**31**	**33**	**2**	**31**	**33**	**171**	**0**	**0**	**0**	**170**	**1.2**	**124**	**13**	**141**	**35**		**4**	**0**	**1**	**1**	**2**	**0**	**0**	**0**

QMJHL Second All-Star Team (1995)

Traded to **Edmonton** by **Chicago** with Daniel Cleary, Ethan Moreau and Chad Kilger for Boris Mironov, Dean McAmmond and Jonas Elofsson, March 20, 1999. Traded to **Montreal** by **Edmonton** with Matthieu Descoteaux for Igor Ulanov and Alain Nasreddine, March 9, 2000.

• LAFLEUR, Guy

Guy Damien "The Flower" RW – R. 6', 185 lbs. b: Thurso, Que., 9/20/1951. Montreal's 1st, 1st overall, in 1971. **HHOF**

Season	Club	League	GP	G	A	Pts	AG	AA	APts	PIM	PP	SH	GW	S	%	TGF	PGF	TGA	PGA	+/–	GP	G	A	Pts	PIM	PP	SH	GW
1966-67	Quebec Canadian Tire	QAHA	STATISTICS NOT AVAILABLE																									
	Quebec Aces	QJHL	8	1	1	2				0																		
1967-68	Quebec Aces	QJHL	43	30	19	49																						
1968-69	Quebec Aces	QJHL	49	50	60	110				83																		
1969-70	Quebec Remparts	QJHL	56	*103	67	170				105											15	*25	18	*43	34			
	Quebec Remparts	Mem-Cup	12	18	18	36				23																		
1970-71	Quebec Remparts	QMJHL	62	*130	79	*209				135											14	*22	*21	*43	24			
	Quebec Remparts	Mem-Cup	7	9	5	14				18																		
1971-72	**Montreal Canadiens**	**NHL**	**73**	**29**	**35**	**64**	**29**	**30**	**59**	**48**	**5**	**0**	**5**	**187**	**15.5**	**99**	**27**	**45**	**0**	**27**	**6**	**1**	**4**	**5**	**2**	**0**	**0**	**0**
1972-73♦	**Montreal Canadiens**	**NHL**	**69**	**28**	**27**	**55**	**26**	**21**	**47**	**51**	**9**	**0**	**7**	**176**	**15.9**	**80**	**26**	**39**	**1**	**16**	**17**	**3**	**5**	**8**	**9**	**2**	**0**	**1**
1973-74	**Montreal Canadiens**	**NHL**	**73**	**21**	**35**	**56**	**20**	**29**	**49**	**29**	**3**	**1**	**2**	**167**	**12.6**	**87**	**25**	**54**	**2**	**10**	**6**	**0**	**1**	**1**	**4**	**0**	**0**	**0**
1974-75	**Montreal Canadiens**	**NHL**	**70**	**53**	**66**	**119**	**47**	**50**	**97**	**37**	**15**	**2**	**11**	**260**	**20.4**	**166**	**59**	**65**	**10**	**52**	**11**	***12**	**7**	**19**	**15**	**4**	**0**	**4**
1975-76♦	**Montreal Canadiens**	**NHL**	**80**	**56**	**69**	***125**	**49**	**52**	**101**	**36**	**18**	**0**	**12**	**303**	**18.5**	**179**	**63**	**49**	**1**	**68**	**13**	**7**	**10**	**17**	**2**	**0**	**0**	**3**
1976-77	Canada	Can-Cup	7	1	5	6				12																		
♦	**Montreal Canadiens**	**NHL**	**80**	**56**	***80**	***136**	**51**	**62**	**113**	**20**	**14**	**0**	**8**	**291**	**19.2**	**179**	**47**	**43**	**0**	**89**	**14**	**9**	***17**	***26**	**6**	**1**	**0**	**2**
1977-78♦	**Montreal Canadiens**	**NHL**	**78**	***60**	**72**	***132**	**55**	**56**	**111**	**26**	**15**	**0**	**12**	**307**	**19.5**	**186**	**57**	**57**	**1**	**73**	**15**	***10**	**11**	***21**	**16**	**3**	**0**	**2**
1978-79♦	**Montreal Canadiens**	**NHL**	**80**	**52**	**77**	**129**	**45**	**56**	**101**	**28**	**13**	**0**	**12**	**342**	**15.2**	**178**	**59**	**64**	**1**	**56**	**16**	**10**	***13**	***23**	**0**	**2**	**0**	**2**
	NHL All-Stars	Chal-Cup	3	1	2	3				0																		
1979-80	**Montreal Canadiens**	**NHL**	**74**	**50**	**75**	**125**	**43**	**55**	**98**	**12**	**15**	**0**	**7**	**323**	**15.5**	**187**	**70**	**81**	**4**	**40**	**3**	**3**	**1**	**4**	**0**	**0**	**0**	**0**
1980-81	**Montreal Canadiens**	**NHL**	**51**	**27**	**43**	**70**	**21**	**29**	**50**	**29**	**7**	**0**	**7**	**191**	**14.1**	**100**	**44**	**36**	**4**	**24**	**3**	**0**	**1**	**1**	**2**	**0**	**0**	**0**
	Canada	WEC-A	7	1	0	1				2																		
1981-82	Canada	Can-Cup	7	2	9	11				0																		
	Montreal Canadiens	**NHL**	**66**	**27**	**57**	**84**	**21**	**38**	**59**	**24**	**9**	**0**	**3**	**233**	**11.6**	**111**	**35**	**46**	**3**	**33**	**5**	**2**	**1**	**3**	**4**	**2**	**0**	**0**
1982-83	**Montreal Canadiens**	**NHL**	**68**	**27**	**49**	**76**	**22**	**34**	**56**	**12**	**9**	**0**	**1**	**177**	**15.3**	**114**	**42**	**66**	**0**	**6**	**3**	**0**	**2**	**2**	**2**	**0**	**0**	**0**
1983-84	**Montreal Canadiens**	**NHL**	**80**	**30**	**40**	**70**	**24**	**27**	**51**	**19**	**6**	**0**	**6**	**217**	**13.8**	**113**	**46**	**83**	**2**	**–14**	**12**	**0**	**3**	**3**	**5**	**0**	**0**	**0**
1984-85	**Montreal Canadiens**	**NHL**	**19**	**2**	**3**	**5**	**2**	**2**	**4**	**10**	**0**	**0**	**0**	**35**	**5.7**	**13**	**4**	**12**	**0**	**–3**								
1985-1988			OUT OF HOCKEY – RETIRED																									
1988-89	**New York Rangers**	**NHL**	**67**	**18**	**27**	**45**	**15**	**19**	**34**	**12**	**6**	**0**	**2**	**122**	**14.8**	**73**	**31**	**41**	**0**	**1**	**4**	**1**	**0**	**1**	**0**	**1**	**0**	**0**
1989-90	**Quebec Nordiques**	**NHL**	**39**	**12**	**22**	**34**	**10**	**16**	**26**	**4**	**6**	**0**	**2**	**100**	**12.0**	**50**	**27**	**38**	**0**	**–15**								
1990-91	**Quebec Nordiques**	**NHL**	**59**	**12**	**16**	**28**	**11**	**12**	**23**	**2**	**3**	**0**	**0**	**90**	**13.3**	**49**	**15**	**44**	**0**	**–10**								
	NHL Totals		**1126**	**560**	**793**	**1353**	**491**	**588**	**1079**	**399**	**153**	**3**	**97**	**3521**	**15.9**	**1964**	**677**	**863**	**29**		**128**	**58**	**76**	**134**	**67**	**15**	**0**	**14**

QJHL First All-Star Team (1970, 1971) • NHL First All-Star Team (1975, 1976, 1977, 1978, 1979, 1980) • Won Art Ross Trophy (1976, 1977, 1978) • Won Lester B. Pearson Award (1976, 1977, 1978) • Won Hart Trophy (1977, 1978) • Won Conn Smythe Trophy (1977) • NHL Plus/Minus Leader (1978) • Played in NHL All-Star Game (1975, 1976, 1977, 1978, 1980, 1991)

Signed as a free agent by **NY Rangers**, September 26, 1988. Signed as a free agent by **Quebec**, July 14, 1989. NY Rangers received Quebec's 5th round choice (Sergei Zubov) as compensation. Claimed by **Minnesota** from **Quebec** in Expansion Draft, May 30, 1991. Traded to **Quebec** by **Minnesota** for Alan Haworth, May 31, 1991.

• LaFONTAINE, Pat

C – R. 5'10", 182 lbs. b: St. Louis, MO, 2/22/1965. NY Islanders' 1st, 3rd overall, in 1983.

Season	Club	League	GP	G	A	Pts	AG	AA	APts	PIM	PP	SH	GW	S	%	TGF	PGF	TGA	PGA	+/–	GP	G	A	Pts	PIM	PP	SH	GW
1981-82	Detroit Compuware	MNHL	79	175	149	324																						
1982-83	Verdun Juniors	QMJHL	70	*104	*130	*234				10											15	11	*24	*35	4			
	Verdun Juniors	Mem-Cup	4	3	2	5				2																		
1983-84	United States	Nat-Team	58	56	55	111				22																		
	United States	Olympics	6	5	3	8				0																		
	New York Islanders	**NHL**	**15**	**13**	**6**	**19**	**10**	**4**	**14**	**6**	**1**	**0**	**0**	**35**	**37.1**	**23**	**2**	**12**	**0**	**9**	**16**	**3**	**6**	**9**	**8**	**0**	**0**	**0**
1984-85	**New York Islanders**	**NHL**	**67**	**19**	**35**	**54**	**15**	**24**	**39**	**32**	**1**	**0**	**1**	**173**	**11.0**	**82**	**14**	**60**	**1**	**9**	**9**	**1**	**2**	**3**	**4**	**0**	**0**	**0**
1985-86	**New York Islanders**	**NHL**	**65**	**30**	**23**	**53**	**24**	**15**	**39**	**43**	**2**	**0**	**4**	**172**	**17.4**	**74**	**14**	**46**	**2**	**16**	**3**	**1**	**0**	**1**	**0**	**1**	**0**	**0**
1986-87	**New York Islanders**	**NHL**	**80**	**38**	**32**	**70**	**33**	**23**	**56**	**70**	**19**	**1**	**6**	**219**	**17.4**	**104**	**53**	**71**	**10**	**–10**	**14**	**5**	**7**	**12**	**10**	**1**	**0**	**2**
1987-88	United States	Can-Cup	5	3	0	3				0																		
	New York Islanders	**NHL**	**75**	**47**	**45**	**92**	**40**	**32**	**72**	**52**	**15**	**0**	**7**	**242**	**19.4**	**125**	**52**	**67**	**6**	**12**	**6**	**4**	**5**	**9**	**8**	**1**	**0**	**1**
1988-89	**New York Islanders**	**NHL**	**79**	**45**	**43**	**88**	**38**	**30**	**68**	**26**	**16**	**0**	**4**	**288**	**15.6**	**115**	**52**	**77**	**6**	**–8**								
	United States	WEC-A	10	5	3	8				8																		
1989-90	**New York Islanders**	**NHL**	**74**	**54**	**51**	**105**	**47**	**37**	**84**	**38**	**13**	**2**	**8**	**286**	**18.9**	**141**	**66**	**98**	**10**	**–13**	**2**	**0**	**1**	**1**	**0**	**0**	**0**	**0**
1990-91	**New York Islanders**	**NHL**	**75**	**41**	**44**	**85**	**38**	**34**	**72**	**42**	**12**	**2**	**5**	**225**	**18.2**	**117**	**45**	**91**	**13**	**–6**								
1991-92	United States	Can-Cup	6	3	1	4				2																		
	Buffalo Sabres	**NHL**	**57**	**46**	**47**	**93**	**42**	**36**	**78**	**98**	**23**	**0**	**5**	**203**	**22.7**	**136**	**70**	**67**	**11**	**10**	**7**	**8**	**3**	**11**	**4**	**5**	**1**	**1**
1992-93	**Buffalo Sabres**	**NHL**	**84**	**53**	**95**	**148**	**44**	**66**	**110**	**63**	**20**	**2**	**7**	**306**	**17.3**	**200**	**88**	**105**	**4**	**11**	**7**	**2**	**10**	**12**	**0**	**1**	**0**	**0**
1993-94	**Buffalo Sabres**	**NHL**	**16**	**5**	**13**	**18**	**5**	**10**	**15**	**2**	**1**	**0**	**0**	**40**	**12.5**	**30**	**11**	**28**	**5**	**–4**								
1994-95	**Buffalo Sabres**	**NHL**	**22**	**12**	**15**	**27**	**21**	**22**	**43**	**4**	**6**	**1**	**3**	**54**	**22.2**	**41**	**22**	**18**	**1**	**2**	**5**	**2**	**2**	**4**	**2**	**1**	**0**	**0**
1995-96	**Buffalo Sabres**	**NHL**	**76**	**40**	**51**	**91**	**39**	**42**	**81**	**36**	**15**	**3**	**7**	**224**	**17.9**	**133**	**68**	**90**	**17**	**–8**								
1996-97	United States	W-Cup	5	2	2	4				2																		
	Buffalo Sabres	**NHL**	**13**	**2**	**6**	**8**	**2**	**5**	**7**	**4**	**1**	**0**	**0**	**38**	**5.3**	**11**	**6**	**13**	**0**	**–8**								
1997-98	**New York Rangers**	**NHL**	**67**	**23**	**39**	**62**	**27**	**38**	**65**	**36**	**11**	**0**	**2**	**160**	**14.4**	**75**	**38**	**56**	**3**	**–16**								
	United States	Olympics	4	1	1	2				0																		
	NHL Totals		**865**	**468**	**545**	**1013**	**425**	**418**	**843**	**552**	**156**	**11**	**59**	**2665**	**17.6**	**1407**	**601**	**899**	**89**		**69**	**26**	**36**	**62**	**36**	**10**	**1**	**4**

QMJHL First All-Star Team (1983) • Canadian Major Junior Player of the Year (1983) • Won Dodge Performer of the Year Award (1990) • NHL Second All-Star Team (1993) • Won Bill Masterton Memorial Trophy (1995) • Played in NHL All-Star Game (1988, 1989, 1990, 1991, 1993)

Traded to **Buffalo** by **NY Islanders** with Randy Hillier, Randy Wood and NY Islanders' 4th round choice (Dean Melanson) in 1992 Entry Draft for Pierre Turgeon, Uwe Krupp, Benoit Hogue and Dave McLlwain, October 25, 1991. Traded to **NY Rangers** by **Buffalo** for NY Rangers' 2nd round choice (Andrew Peters) in 1998 Entry Draft and future considerations, September 29, 1997. • Suffered career-ending head injury in game vs. Ottawa, March 16, 1998. • Officially announced retirement, October 12, 1999.

• LAFOREST, Bob

Robert RW – R. 5'10", 195 lbs. b: Sault Ste. Marie, Ont., 5/19/1963. Los Angeles' 3rd, 89th overall, in 1983.

Season	Club	League	GP	G	A	Pts	AG	AA	APts	PIM	PP	SH	GW	S	%	TGF	PGF	TGA	PGA	+/–	GP	G	A	Pts	PIM	PP	SH	GW
			REGULAR SEASON																		PLAYOFFS							
1979-80	Welland Cougars	OJHL	43	30	32	62	....	....	....	6	....	....	....	....	....	....	....	....	....	....	....	....	....	....	....	....	....	....
1980-81	Niagara Falls Flyers	OMJHL	47	10	6	16	....	....	....	21	....	....	....	....	....	....	....	....	....	....	11	1	3	4	18	....	....	....
1981-82	Niagara Falls Flyers	OHL	66	31	40	71	....	....	....	40	....	....	....	....	....	....	....	....	....	....	5	4	5	9	0	....	....	....
1982-83	North Bay Centennials	OHL	65	58	38	96	....	....	....	32	....	....	....	....	....	....	....	....	....	....	8	5	2	7	8	....	....	....
1983-84	**Los Angeles Kings**	**NHL**	**5**	**1**	**0**	**1**	**1**	**0**	**1**	**2**	**1**	**0**	**0**	**15**	**6.7**	**6**	**3**	**6**	**0**	**–3**	....	....	....	....	....	....	....	....
	New Haven Nighthawks	AHL	26	2	7	9	....	....	....	0	....	....	....	....	....	....	....	....	....	....	....	....	....	....	....	....	....	....
	Hershey Bears	AHL	42	11	16	27	....	....	....	10	....	....	....	....	....	....	....	....	....	....	....	....	....	....	....	....	....	....
1984-85	Indianapolis Checkers	IHL	18	3	6	9	....	....	....	0	....	....	....	....	....	....	....	....	....	....	....	....	....	....	....	....	....	....
	Fort Wayne Komets	IHL	3	1	0	1	....	....	....	0	....	....	....	....	....	....	....	....	....	....	....	....	....	....	....	....	....	....
1985-86	Milwaukee Admirals	IHL	3	0	0	0	....	....	....	0	....	....	....	....	....	....	....	....	....	....	....	....	....	....	....	....	....	....
1986-87	Dundas Real McCoys	OHA-Sr.	36	19	24	43	....	....	....	19	....	....	....	....	....	....	....	....	....	....	....	....	....	....	....	....	....	....
	NHL Totals		**5**	**1**	**0**	**1**	**1**	**0**	**1**	**2**	**1**	**0**	**0**	**15**	**6.7**	**6**	**3**	**6**	**0**		....	....	....	....	....	....	....	....

• Brother of Mark

Traded to **Boston** by **LA Kings** for Marco Baron, January 3, 1984.

• LAFORGE, Claude

Claude Roger LW – L. 5'9", 172 lbs. b: Sorel, Que., 7/1/1936.

Season	Club	League	GP	G	A	Pts	AG	AA	APts	PIM	PP	SH	GW	S	%	TGF	PGF	TGA	PGA	+/–	GP	G	A	Pts	PIM	PP	SH	GW
1954-55	Montreal Jr. Canadiens	QJHL	45	18	4	22	....	....	....	43	....	....	....	....	....	....	....	....	....	....	5	1	0	1	0	....	....	....
1955-56	Montreal Jr. Canadiens	QJHL	STATISTICS NOT AVAILABLE																									
	Montreal Royals	QHL	2	0	0	0	....	....	....	2	....	....	....	....	....	....	....	....	....	....	....	....	....	....	....	....	....	....
	Montreal Jr. Canadiens	Mem-Cup	10	1	4	5	....	....	....	11	....	....	....	....	....	....	....	....	....	....	....	....	....	....	....	....	....	....
1956-57	Shawinigan Cataracts	QHL	60	12	13	25	....	....	....	10	....	....	....	....	....	....	....	....	....	....	....	....	....	....	....	....	....	....
	Cincinnati Mohawks	IHL	8	5	5	10	....	....	....	2	....	....	....	....	....	....	....	....	....	....	....	....	....	....	....	....	....	....
1957-58	**Montreal Canadiens**	**NHL**	**5**	**0**	**0**	**0**	**0**	**0**	**0**	**0**	....	....	....	....	....	....	....	....	....	....	....	....	....	....	....	....	....	....
	Shawinigan Cataracts	QHL	52	26	27	53	....	....	....	45	....	....	....	....	....	....	....	....	....	....	....	....	....	....	....	....	....	....
	Rochester Americans	AHL	14	7	6	13	....	....	....	10	....	....	....	....	....	....	....	....	....	....	....	....	....	....	....	....	....	....
1958-59	**Detroit Red Wings**	**NHL**	**57**	**2**	**5**	**7**	**2**	**5**	**7**	**18**	....	....	....	....	....	....	....	....	....	....	....	....	....	....	....	....	....	....
	Hershey Bears	AHL	10	4	5	9	....	....	....	16	....	....	....	....	....	....	....	....	....	....	....	....	....	....	....	....	....	....
1959-60	Hershey Bears	AHL	68	27	31	58	....	....	....	38	....	....	....	....	....	....	....	....	....	....	....	....	....	....	....	....	....	....
1960-61	**Detroit Red Wings**	**NHL**	**10**	**1**	**0**	**1**	**1**	**0**	**1**	**2**	....	....	....	....	....	....	....	....	....	....	....	....	....	....	....	....	....	....
	Hershey Bears	AHL	49	20	30	50	....	....	....	55	....	....	....	....	....	....	....	....	....	....	8	2	1	3	*35	....	....	....
1961-62	**Detroit Red Wings**	**NHL**	**38**	**10**	**9**	**19**	**11**	**9**	**20**	**20**	....	....	....	....	....	....	....	....	....	....	....	....	....	....	....	....	....	....
	Hershey Bears	AHL	31	13	13	26	....	....	....	59	....	....	....	....	....	....	....	....	....	....	....	....	....	....	....	....	....	....
1962-63	Pittsburgh Hornets	AHL	50	10	23	33	....	....	....	73	....	....	....	....	....	....	....	....	....	....	....	....	....	....	....	....	....	....
1963-64	**Detroit Red Wings**	**NHL**	**17**	**2**	**3**	**5**	**2**	**3**	**5**	**4**	....	....	....	....	....	....	....	....	....	....	....	....	....	....	....	....	....	....
	Pittsburgh Hornets	AHL	51	19	23	42	....	....	....	59	....	....	....	....	....	....	....	....	....	....	5	1	3	4	4	....	....	....
1964-65	**Detroit Red Wings**	**NHL**	**1**	**0**	**0**	**0**	**0**	**0**	**0**	**2**	....	....	....	....	....	....	....	....	....	....	....	....	....	....	....	....	....	....
	Pittsburgh Hornets	AHL	67	23	32	55	....	....	....	26	....	....	....	....	....	....	....	....	....	....	4	4	2	6	2	....	....	....
1965-66	Pittsburgh Hornets	AHL	55	11	20	31	....	....	....	38	....	....	....	....	....	....	....	....	....	....	....	....	....	....	....	....	....	....
	Quebec Aces	AHL	9	2	6	8	....	....	....	0	....	....	....	....	....	....	....	....	....	....	....	....	....	....	....	....	....	....
1966-67	Quebec Aces	AHL	60	16	25	41	....	....	....	46	....	....	....	....	....	....	....	....	....	....	5	4	2	6	0	....	....	....
1967-68	**Philadelphia Flyers**	**NHL**	**63**	**9**	**16**	**25**	**10**	**16**	**26**	**36**	**0**	**0**	**2**	**106**	**8.5**	**39**	**3**	**38**	**10**	**8**	**5**	**1**	**2**	**3**	**15**	**0**	**0**	**0**
	Quebec Aces	AHL	8	5	4	9	....	....	....	2	....	....	....	....	....	....	....	....	....	....	....	....	....	....	....	....	....	....
1968-69	**Philadelphia Flyers**	**NHL**	**2**	**0**	**0**	**0**	**0**	**0**	**0**	**0**	**0**	**0**	**0**	**1**	**0.0**	**0**	**0**	**3**	**1**	**–2**	....	....	....	....	....	....	....	....
	Quebec Aces	AHL	57	21	31	52	....	....	....	24	....	....	....	....	....	....	....	....	....	....	11	0	7	7	2	....	....	....
1969-70	Quebec Aces	AHL	72	28	39	67	....	....	....	44	....	....	....	....	....	....	....	....	....	....	6	0	2	2	6	....	....	....
1970-71	Denver Spurs	WHL	64	25	28	53	....	....	....	34	....	....	....	....	....	....	....	....	....	....	5	2	3	5	4	....	....	....
1971-72	Denver Spurs	WHL	56	15	31	46	....	....	....	12	....	....	....	....	....	....	....	....	....	....	9	1	5	6	6	....	....	....
1972-73	Denver Spurs	WHL	25	8	11	19	....	....	....	12	....	....	....	....	....	....	....	....	....	....	....	....	....	....	....	....	....	....
	NHL Totals		**193**	**24**	**33**	**57**	**26**	**33**	**59**	**82**	....	....	....	....	....	....	....	....	....	....	**5**	**1**	**2**	**3**	**15**	....	....	....

QHL Second All-Star Team (1958)

Traded to **Detroit** by **Montreal** with Gene Achtymichuk and Bud MacPherson for cash, June 3, 1958. Traded to **Quebec** (AHL) by **Detroit** (Pittsburgh-AHL) for Terry Gray, March 1, 1966. NHL rights transferred to **Philadelphia** after NHL club purchased **Quebec** (AHL) franchise, May 8, 1967. Traded to **Denver** (WHL) by **Philadelphia** for cash, August, 1970.

• LAFORGE, Marc

Marc F. LW – L. 6'2", 210 lbs. b: Sudbury, Ont., 1/3/1968. Hartford's 2nd, 32nd overall, in 1986.

Season	Club	League	GP	G	A	Pts	AG	AA	APts	PIM	PP	SH	GW	S	%	TGF	PGF	TGA	PGA	+/–	GP	G	A	Pts	PIM	PP	SH	GW
1983-84	Sudbury Midget Wolves	NOHA	55	6	24	30	....	....	....	42	....	....	....	....	....	....	....	....	....	....	....	....	....	....	....	....	....	....
1984-85	Kingston Canadians	OHL	57	1	5	6	....	....	....	214	....	....	....	....	....	....	....	....	....	....	....	....	....	....	....	....	....	....
1985-86	Kingston Canadians	OHL	60	1	13	14	....	....	....	248	....	....	....	....	....	....	....	....	....	....	10	0	1	1	30	....	....	....
1986-87	Kingston Canadians	OHL	53	2	10	12	....	....	....	224	....	....	....	....	....	....	....	....	....	....	12	1	0	1	79	....	....	....
	Binghamton Whalers	AHL	....	....	....	....	....	....	....	....	....	....	....	....	....	....	....	....	....	....	4	0	0	0	7	....	....	....
1987-88	Sudbury Wolves	OHL	14	0	2	2	....	....	....	68	....	....	....	....	....	....	....	....	....	....	....	....	....	....	....	....	....	....
1988-89	Binghamton Whalers	AHL	38	2	2	4	....	....	....	179	....	....	....	....	....	....	....	....	....	....	....	....	....	....	....	....	....	....
	Indianapolis Ice	IHL	14	0	2	2	....	....	....	138	....	....	....	....	....	....	....	....	....	....	....	....	....	....	....	....	....	....
1989-90	**Hartford Whalers**	**NHL**	**9**	**0**	**0**	**0**	**0**	**0**	**0**	**43**	**0**	**0**	**0**	**0**	**0.0**	**0**	**0**	**1**	**0**	**–1**	....	....	....	....	....	....	....	....
	Binghamton Whalers	AHL	25	2	6	8	....	....	....	111	....	....	....	....	....	....	....	....	....	....	....	....	....	....	....	....	....	....
	Cape Breton Oilers	AHL	3	0	1	1	....	....	....	24	....	....	....	....	....	....	....	....	....	....	3	0	0	0	27	....	....	....
1990-91	Cape Breton Oilers	AHL	49	1	7	8	....	....	....	217	....	....	....	....	....	....	....	....	....	....	....	....	....	....	....	....	....	....
1991-92	Cape Breton Oilers	AHL	59	0	14	14	....	....	....	341	....	....	....	....	....	....	....	....	....	....	4	0	0	0	24	....	....	....
1992-93	Cape Breton Oilers	AHL	77	1	12	13	....	....	....	208	....	....	....	....	....	....	....	....	....	....	15	1	2	3	*78	....	....	....
1993-94	**Edmonton Oilers**	**NHL**	**5**	**0**	**0**	**0**	**0**	**0**	**0**	**21**	**0**	**0**	**0**	**0**	**0.0**	**3**	**0**	**7**	**2**	**–2**	....	....	....	....	....	....	....	....
	Cape Breton Oilers	AHL	14	0	0	0	....	....	....	91	....	....	....	....	....	....	....	....	....	....	....	....	....	....	....	....	....	....
	Salt Lake Golden Eagles	IHL	43	0	2	2	....	....	....	242	....	....	....	....	....	....	....	....	....	....	....	....	....	....	....	....	....	....
1994-95	Cape Breton Oilers	AHL	18	0	1	1	....	....	....	80	....	....	....	....	....	....	....	....	....	....	....	....	....	....	....	....	....	....
	Syracuse Crunch	AHL	39	1	5	6	....	....	....	202	....	....	....	....	....	....	....	....	....	....	....	....	....	....	....	....	....	....
1995-96	Minnesota Moose	IHL	20	0	2	2	....	....	....	102	....	....	....	....	....	....	....	....	....	....	....	....	....	....	....	....	....	....
1996-97	San Antonio Dragons	IHL	67	1	7	8	....	....	....	311	....	....	....	....	....	....	....	....	....	....	7	0	0	0	26	....	....	....
1997-98	Manitoba Moose	IHL	7	0	0	0	....	....	....	4	....	....	....	....	....	....	....	....	....	....	....	....	....	....	....	....	....	....
	Anchorage Aces	WCHL	27	1	10	11	....	....	....	124	....	....	....	....	....	....	....	....	....	....	8	1	2	3	14	....	....	....
1998-99	San Antonio Iguanas	CHL	58	0	8	8	....	....	....	302	....	....	....	....	....	....	....	....	....	....	7	0	0	0	43	....	....	....
99-2000	San Antonio Iguanas	CHL	61	2	15	17	....	....	....	243	....	....	....	....	....	....	....	....	....	....	....	....	....	....	....	....	....	....
	NHL Totals		**14**	**0**	**0**	**0**	**0**	**0**	**0**	**64**	**0**	**0**	**0**	**0**	**0.0**	**3**	**0**	**8**	**2**		....	....	....	....	....	....	....	....

• Suspened for life by OHL for on-ice incident in game vs. Guelph, November 6, 1987. Traded to **Edmonton** by **Hartford** for the rights to Cam Brauer, March 6, 1990. Traded to **NY Islanders** by **Edmonton** for Brent Grieve, December 15, 1993.

• LAFRAMBOISE, Pete

Peter Alfred LW/C – L. 6'2", 185 lbs. b: Ottawa, Ont., 1/18/1950. California's 2nd, 19th overall, in 1970.

Season	Club	League	GP	G	A	Pts	AG	AA	APts	PIM	PP	SH	GW	S	%	TGF	PGF	TGA	PGA	+/–	GP	G	A	Pts	PIM	PP	SH	GW
1966-67	Oshawa Legionnaires	OMHA	STATISTICS NOT AVAILABLE																									
	Oshawa Generals	OHA-Jr.	1	0	0	0	....	....	....	0	....	....	....	....	....	....	....	....	....	....	....	....	....	....	....	....	....	....
1967-68	Ottawa 67's	OHA-Jr.	35	6	5	11	....	....	....	36	....	....	....	....	....	....	....	....	....	....	....	....	....	....	....	....	....	....
1968-69	Ottawa 67's	OHA-Jr.	47	31	39	70	....	....	....	98	....	....	....	....	....	....	....	....	....	....	7	10	4	14	12	....	....	....
1969-70	Ottawa 67's	OHA-Jr.	54	26	46	72	....	....	....	68	....	....	....	....	....	....	....	....	....	....	5	0	1	1	2	....	....	....
1970-71	Providence Reds	AHL	64	13	19	32	....	....	....	36	....	....	....	....	....	....	....	....	....	....	10	0	2	2	4	....	....	....
1971-72	**California Golden Seals**	**NHL**	**5**	**0**	**0**	**0**	**0**	**0**	**0**	**0**	**0**	**0**	**0**	**3**	**0.0**	**1**	**1**	**6**	**1**	**–5**	....	....	....	....	....	....	....	....
	Baltimore Clippers	AHL	72	37	44	81	....	....	....	95	....	....	....	....	....	....	....	....	....	....	18	5	8	13	24	....	....	....
1972-73	**California Golden Seals**	**NHL**	**77**	**16**	**25**	**41**	**15**	**20**	**35**	**26**	**2**	**0**	**1**	**113**	**14.2**	**56**	**8**	**72**	**0**	**–24**	....	....	....	....	....	....	....	....
1973-74	**California Golden Seals**	**NHL**	**65**	**7**	**7**	**14**	**7**	**6**	**13**	**14**	**0**	**0**	**0**	**67**	**10.4**	**21**	**1**	**52**	**4**	**–28**	....	....	....	....	....	....	....	....
1974-75	**Washington Capitals**	**NHL**	**45**	**5**	**10**	**15**	**4**	**7**	**11**	**22**	**0**	**0**	**0**	**86**	**5.8**	**20**	**3**	**56**	**2**	**–37**	....	....	....	....	....	....	....	....
	Pittsburgh Penguins	**NHL**	**35**	**5**	**13**	**18**	**4**	**10**	**14**	**8**	**3**	**0**	**0**	**33**	**15.2**	**30**	**12**	**18**	**3**	**3**	**9**	**1**	**0**	**1**	**0**	**0**	**0**	**0**
1975-76	Hershey Bears	AHL	69	18	47	65	....	....	....	79	....	....	....	....	....	....	....	....	....	....	7	2	3	5	6	....	....	....

Season	Club	League	GP	G	A	Pts	AG	AA	APts	PIM	PP	SH	GW	S	%	TGF	PGF	TGA	PGA	+/–	GP	G	A	Pts	PIM	PP	SH	GW
			REGULAR SEASON																		PLAYOFFS							
1976-77	Edmonton Oilers	WHA	17	0	5	5				12																		
	Springfield Indians	AHL	53	18	50	68				87																		
1977-78	Springfield Indians	AHL	68	20	50	70				73											4	1	1	2	2			
1978-79	Binghamton Dusters	AHL	39	8	25	33				18																		
	NHL Totals		**227**	**33**	**55**	**88**	**30**	**43**	**73**	**70**	**5**	**0**	**1**	**302**	**10.9**	**128**	**25**	**204**	**10**		**9**	**1**	**0**	**1**	**0**	**0**	**0**	**0**
	Other Major League Totals		17	0	5	5				12																		

AHL First All-Star Team (1972)

Selected by **LA Sharks** in 1972 WHA General Player Draft, February 12, 1972. Claimed by **Washington** from **California** in Expansion Draft, June 12, 1974. Traded to **Pittsburgh** by **Washington** for Ron Jones, January 21, 1975. Signed as a free agent by **Edmonton** (WHA) after **LA Sharks** (WHA) franchise folded, May, 1975. Traded to **Birmingham** (WHA) by **Edmonton** (WHA) with Dan Arndt and Chris Evans for Lou Nistico and Jeff Jacques, September, 1977.

• LAFRENIERE, Jason

Jason Roger "Hawk" C – R. 5′11″, 185 lbs. b: St. Catharines, Ont., 12/6/1966. Quebec's 2nd, 36th overall, in 1985.

Season	Club	League	GP	G	A	Pts	AG	AA	APts	PIM	PP	SH	GW	S	%	TGF	PGF	TGA	PGA	+/–	GP	G	A	Pts	PIM	PP	SH	GW
1982-83	Orillia Travelways	OJHL-B	48	17	40	57				9																		
1983-84	Brantford Alexanders	OHL	70	24	57	81				4											6	2	4	6	2			
1984-85	Hamilton Steelhawks	OHL	59	26	69	95				10											17	12	16	28	0			
1985-86	Hamilton Steelhawks	OHL	14	12	10	22				2																		
	Belleville Bulls	OHL	48	37	73	110				2											23	10	*22	*32	6			
1986-87	**Quebec Nordiques**	**NHL**	**56**	**13**	**15**	**28**	**11**	**11**	**22**	**8**	**7**	**0**	**1**	**55**	**23.6**	**40**	**23**	**20**	**0**	**–3**	**12**	**1**	**5**	**6**	**2**	**1**	**0**	**0**
	Fredericton Express	AHL	11	3	11	14				0																		
1987-88	**Quebec Nordiques**	**NHL**	**40**	**10**	**19**	**29**	**9**	**14**	**23**	**4**	**5**	**0**	**1**	**54**	**18.5**	**43**	**22**	**22**	**0**	**–1**								
	Fredericton Express	AHL	32	12	19	31				38																		
1988-89	**New York Rangers**	**NHL**	**38**	**8**	**16**	**24**	**7**	**11**	**18**	**6**	**3**	**0**	**0**	**42**	**19.0**	**34**	**15**	**22**	**0**	**–3**	**3**	**0**	**0**	**0**	**17**	**0**	**0**	**0**
	Denver Rangers	IHL	24	10	19	29				17																		
1989-90	Flint Spirits	IHL	41	9	25	34				34																		
	Phoenix Roadrunners	IHL	14	4	9	13				0																		
1990-91	Canada	Nat-Team	59	26	33	59				50																		
1991-92	San Diego Gulls	IHL	5	1	2	3				2																		
	EV Landshut	Germany	23	7	22	29				16											9	5	4	9	16			
	Canada	Nat-Team	8	3	4	7				6																		
1992-93	**Tampa Bay Lightning**	**NHL**	**11**	**3**	**3**	**6**	**2**	**2**	**4**	**4**	**1**	**0**	**0**	**17**	**17.6**	**7**	**3**	**10**	**0**	**–6**								
	Atlanta Knights	IHL	63	23	47	70				34											9	3	4	7	22			
1993-94	**Tampa Bay Lightning**	**NHL**	**1**	**0**	**0**	**0**	**0**	**0**	**0**	**0**	**0**	**0**	**0**	**2**	**0.0**	**0**	**0**	**1**	**0**	**–1**								
	Milwaukee Admirals	IHL	52	14	47	61				16																		
1994-95	HC Courmaosta	Alpenliga	17	12	15	27				20																		
	HC Courmaosta	Italy	35	23	33	56				12											6	2	14	16	12			
1995-96	VSV Villach	Alpenliga	10	10	10	20				6																		
	VSV Villach	Austria	34	30	26	56				42																		
1996-97	HK Olimpija Ljubljana	Alpenliga	4	3	4	7				0																		
	Sheffield Steelers	Britain	22	11	18	29				18											7	4	2	6	4			
	Michigan K-Wings	IHL	17	4	2	6				18																		
1997-98	Hamburg Scorpions	Germany	49	15	45	60				62											4	1	1	2	10			
1998-99	Hamburg Scorpions	Germany	47	7	31	38				20																		
99-2000	EHC Hamburg	Germany-2	8	1	5	6				4																		
	Topeka Scare Crows	CHL	3	3	1	4				2																		
	CH Hielo Barcelona	Spain	1	3	0	3				0																		
	Bakersfield Condors	WCHL	10	3	4	7				0											4	0	1	1	10			
	NHL Totals		**146**	**34**	**53**	**87**	**29**	**38**	**67**	**22**	**16**	**0**	**2**	**170**	**20.0**	**124**	**63**	**75**	**0**		**15**	**1**	**5**	**6**	**19**	**1**	**0**	**0**

• Son of Roger • OHL First All-Star Team (1986)

Traded to **NY Rangers** by **Quebec** with Normand Rochefort for Bruce Bell, Jari Gronstrand, Walt Poddubny and NY Rangers' 4th round choice (Eric Dubois) in 1989 Entry Draft, August 1, 1988. Signed as a free agent by **Tampa Bay**, July 29, 1992. Signed as a free agent by **Topeka** (CHL), November 17, 1999. Signed as a free agent by **Bakersfield** (WCHL), February 22, 2000.

• LAFRENIERE, Roger

Roger Joseph LW – L. 6′, 190 lbs. b: Montreal, Que., 7/24/1942.

Season	Club	League	GP	G	A	Pts	AG	AA	APts	PIM	PP	SH	GW	S	%	TGF	PGF	TGA	PGA	+/–	GP	G	A	Pts	PIM	PP	SH	GW
1961-62	Hamilton Red Wings	OHA-Jr.	48	4	19	23				76											10	2	4	6	15			
	Hamilton Red Wings	Mem-Cup	14	0	8	8				16																		
1962-63	**Detroit Red Wings**	**NHL**	**3**	**0**	**0**	**0**	**0**	**0**	**0**	**4**																		
	Pittsburgh Hornets	AHL	65	2	14	16				123																		
1963-64	Cincinnati Wings	CPHL	66	3	24	27				112																		
1964-65	Memphis Wings	CPHL	2	0	1	1				0																		
	Providence Reds	AHL	57	4	13	17				96																		
1965-66	Buffalo Bisons	AHL	72	1	16	17				76																		
1966-67	Buffalo Bisons	AHL	71	2	16	18				72																		
1967-68	Buffalo Bisons	AHL	5	0	1	1				0																		
	Omaha Knights	CPHL	65	10	25	35				129																		
1968-69	Omaha Knights	CHL	70	14	29	43				122											7	1	5	6	16			
1969-70	Denver Spurs	WHL	61	4	19	23				85																		
1970-71	Denver Spurs	WHL	58	5	13	18				47											5	0	1	1	12			
1971-72	Denver Spurs	WHL	71	10	24	34				87											9	0	1	1	8			
1972-73	**St. Louis Blues**	**NHL**	**10**	**0**	**0**	**0**	**0**	**0**	**0**	**0**	**0**	**0**	**0**	**3**	**0.0**	**0**	**0**	**3**	**2**	**–1**								
	Denver Spurs	WHL	53	9	20	29				100											5	0	2	2	8			
1973-74	San Diego Gulls	WHL	70	9	14	23				75											4	1	0	1	0			
1974-75	Roanoke Valley Rebels	SHL	29	2	18	20				24																		
	NHL Totals		**13**	**0**	**0**	**0**	**0**	**0**	**0**	**4**																		

• Father of Jason

Claimed by **Buffalo** (AHL) from **Detroit** in Reverse Draft, June 9, 1965. Traded to **St. Louis** (Denver-WHL) by **Buffalo** for cash, October, 1969. Traded to **San Diego** (WHL) by **St. Louis** for cash, September, 1973.

• LAGACE, Jean-Guy

D – R. 5′10″, 185 lbs. b: L'Abord A Plouffe, Que., 2/5/1945.

Season	Club	League	GP	G	A	Pts	AG	AA	APts	PIM	PP	SH	GW	S	%	TGF	PGF	TGA	PGA	+/–	GP	G	A	Pts	PIM	PP	SH	GW
1963-64	Laval College	QUAA	STATISTICS NOT AVAILABLE																									
1964-65	Montreal Jr. Canadiens	OHA-Jr.	4	0	0	0				0																		
1965-66	Muskegon Zephyrs	IHL	66	10	33	43				163											4	0	0	0	8			
1966-67	Muskegon Mohawks	IHL	72	14	25	39				162																		
1967-68	Muskegon Mohawks	IHL	65	14	48	62				157											9	2	5	7	42			
1968-69	**Pittsburgh Penguins**	**NHL**	**17**	**0**	**1**	**1**	**0**	**1**	**1**	**14**	**0**	**0**	**0**	**15**	**0.0**	**5**	**0**	**16**	**3**	**–8**								
	Amarillo Wranglers	CHL	49	9	19	28				96																		
1969-70	Baltimore Clippers	AHL	68	7	21	28				138											4	1	2	3	2			
1970-71	**Buffalo Sabres**	**NHL**	**3**	**0**	**0**	**0**	**0**	**0**	**0**	**2**	**0**	**0**	**0**	**3**	**0.0**	**1**	**1**	**1**	**1**	**0**								
	Amarillo Wranglers	CHL	19	1	15	16				61																		
	Salt Lake Golden Eagles	WHL	39	2	13	15				83																		
1971-72	Hershey Bears	AHL	61	11	30	41				117											4	0	0	0	8			
1972-73	**Pittsburgh Penguins**	**NHL**	**31**	**1**	**5**	**6**	**1**	**4**	**5**	**32**	**0**	**0**	**0**	**33**	**3.0**	**23**	**1**	**32**	**2**	**–8**								
	Hershey Bears	AHL	37	7	14	21				54																		
1973-74	**Pittsburgh Penguins**	**NHL**	**31**	**2**	**6**	**8**	**2**	**5**	**7**	**34**	**1**	**1**	**0**	**28**	**7.1**	**15**	**2**	**30**	**5**	**–12**								

Season	Club	League	REGULAR SEASON																		PLAYOFFS							
			GP	G	A	Pts	AG	AA	APts	PIM	PP	SH	GW	S	%	TGF	PGF	TGA	PGA	+/–	GP	G	A	Pts	PIM	PP	SH	GW
1974-75	Pittsburgh Penguins	NHL	27	1	8	9	1	6	7	39	0	0	1	31	3.2	33	4	27	3	5	....	....	....	....	....	....	....	....
	Kansas City Scouts	NHL	19	2	9	11	2	7	9	22	2	0	0	40	5.0	26	13	39	6	–20	....	....	....	....	....	....	....	....
	Hershey Bears	AHL	6	0	7	7	....	....	....	8	....	....	....	....	....	....	....	....	....	....	....	....	....	....	....	....	....	....
1975-76	Kansas City Scouts	NHL	69	3	10	13	3	7	10	108	1	1	1	75	4.0	65	12	125	34	–38	....	....	....	....	....	....	....	....
1976-77	Birmingham Bulls	WHA	78	2	25	27	....	....	....	110	....	....	....	....	....	....	....	....	....	....	....	....	....	....	....	....	....	....
	NHL Totals		197	9	39	48	9	30	39	251	4	2	2	225	4.0	168	33	270	54		....	....	....	....	....	....	....	....
	Other Major League Totals		78	2	25	27	....	....	....	110	....	....	....	....	....	....	....	....	....	....	....	....	....	....	....	....	....	....

Traded to **Pittsburgh** by **Montreal** for Larry Hillman, November 22, 1968. Claimed by **Minnesota** from **Pittsburgh** in Intra-League Draft, June 9, 1970. Claimed by **Buffalo** from **Minnesota** in Expansion Draft, June 10, 1970. Traded to **Pittsburgh** by **Buffalo** for Terry Ball, January 24, 1971. Selected by **LA Sharks** (WHA) in 1972 WHA General Player Draft, February 12, 1972. Traded to **Kansas City** by **Pittsburgh** with Denis Herron for Michel Plasse, January 10, 1975. Signed as a free agent by **Birmingham** (WHA) after **LA Sharks** (WHA) franchise folded, September, 1976.

• LAIDLAW, Tom

Thomas J. "Cowboy" D – L. 6'2", 215 lbs. b: Brampton, Ont., 4/15/1958. NY Rangers' 7th, 93rd overall, in 1978.

Season	Club	League	GP	G	A	Pts	AG	AA	APts	PIM	PP	SH	GW	S	%	TGF	PGF	TGA	PGA	+/–	GP	G	A	Pts	PIM	PP	SH	GW
1973-1976	Bramalea Blues	OHA-B	STATISTICS NOT AVAILABLE																									
1976-77	Northern Michigan University	CCHA	32	1	13	14	....	....	....	95	....	....	....	....	....	....	....	....	....	....	....	....	....	....	....	....	....	....
1977-78	Northern Michigan University	CCHA	24	1	7	8	....	....	....	95	....	....	....	....	....	....	....	....	....	....	....	....	....	....	....	....	....	....
1978-79	Northern Michigan University	CCHA	29	10	20	30	....	....	....	137	....	....	....	....	....	....	....	....	....	....	....	....	....	....	....	....	....	....
1979-80	Northern Michigan University	CCHA	39	8	30	38	....	....	....	83	....	....	....	....	....	....	....	....	....	....	....	....	....	....	....	....	....	....
	New Haven Nighthawks	AHL	1	0	0	0	....	....	....	0	....	....	....	....	....	....	....	....	....	....	10	1	6	7	27	....	....	....
1980-81	New York Rangers	NHL	80	6	23	29	5	15	20	100	1	0	0	101	5.9	95	5	113	23	0	14	1	4	5	18	0	0	1
1981-82	New York Rangers	NHL	79	3	18	21	2	12	14	104	0	0	0	62	4.8	88	5	113	37	7	10	0	3	3	14	0	0	0
1982-83	New York Rangers	NHL	80	0	10	10	0	7	7	75	0	0	0	44	0.0	61	1	107	36	–11	9	1	1	2	10	0	0	0
1983-84	New York Rangers	NHL	79	3	15	18	2	10	12	62	0	0	1	61	4.9	72	2	132	52	–10	5	0	0	0	8	0	0	0
1984-85	New York Rangers	NHL	61	1	11	12	1	7	8	52	0	0	0	37	2.7	58	3	96	29	–12	3	0	2	2	4	0	0	0
1985-86	New York Rangers	NHL	68	6	12	18	5	8	13	103	0	1	0	50	12.0	60	0	104	41	–3	7	0	2	2	12	0	0	0
1986-87	New York Rangers	NHL	63	1	10	11	1	7	8	65	1	0	1	36	2.8	58	2	109	35	–18	....	....	....	....	....	....	....	....
	Los Angeles Kings	NHL	11	0	3	3	0	2	2	4	0	0	0	7	0.0	10	1	12	4	1	5	0	0	0	2	0	0	0
1987-88	Los Angeles Kings	NHL	57	1	12	13	1	9	10	47	0	0	0	30	3.3	64	10	85	34	3	5	0	2	2	4	0	0	0
1988-89	Los Angeles Kings	NHL	70	3	17	20	3	12	15	63	0	0	1	31	9.7	105	4	110	39	30	11	2	3	5	6	0	0	0
1989-90	Los Angeles Kings	NHL	57	1	8	9	1	6	7	42	0	0	0	27	3.7	61	0	86	29	4	....	....	....	....	....	....	....	....
1990-91	Phoenix Roadrunners	IHL	4	0	1	1	....	....	....	2	....	....	....	....	....	....	....	....	....	....	....	....	....	....	....	....	....	....
	NHL Totals		705	25	139	164	21	95	116	717	2	1	3	486	5.1	732	33	1067	359		69	4	17	21	78	0	0	1

CCHA First All-Star Team (1979, 1980) • NCAA Championship All-Tournament Team (1980)

Traded to **LA Kings** by **NY Rangers** with Bob Carpenter for Jeff Crossman, Marcel Dionne and LA Kings' 3rd round choice (later traded to Minnesota — Minnesota selected Murray Garbut) in 1989 Entry Draft, March 10, 1987.

• LAIRD, Robbie

Glenn Robert LW – L. 5'9", 165 lbs. b: Regina, Sask., 12/29/1954. Pittsburgh's 6th, 116th overall, in 1974.

Season	Club	League	GP	G	A	Pts	AG	AA	APts	PIM	PP	SH	GW	S	%	TGF	PGF	TGA	PGA	+/–	GP	G	A	Pts	PIM	PP	SH	GW
1971-72	Regina Pat Blues	SJHL	STATISTICS NOT AVAILABLE																									
	Regina Pats	WCJHL	1	1	0	1	....	....	....	0	....	....	....	....	....	....	....	....	....	....	....	....	....	....	....	....	....	....
1972-73	Regina Pats	WCJHL	68	14	18	32	....	....	....	102	....	....	....	....	....	....	....	....	....	....	4	0	0	0	13	....	....	....
1973-74	Regina Pats	WCJHL	68	39	45	84	....	....	....	243	....	....	....	....	....	....	....	....	....	....	16	11	15	26	69	....	....	....
	Regina Pats	Mem-Cup	3	2	3	5	....	....	....	*33	....	....	....	....	....	....	....	....	....	....	....	....	....	....	....	....	....	....
1974-75	Fort Wayne Komets	IHL	62	15	28	43	....	....	....	115	....	....	....	....	....	....	....	....	....	....	....	....	....	....	....	....	....	....
1975-76	Fort Wayne Komets	IHL	78	30	38	68	....	....	....	127	....	....	....	....	....	....	....	....	....	....	9	8	4	12	15	....	....	....
1976-77	Fort Wayne Komets	IHL	78	43	46	89	....	....	....	151	....	....	....	....	....	....	....	....	....	....	9	3	3	6	10	....	....	....
1977-78	Fort Wayne Komets	IHL	64	20	22	42	....	....	....	202	....	....	....	....	....	....	....	....	....	....	11	3	6	9	48	....	....	....
1978-79	Fort Wayne Komets	IHL	80	45	62	107	....	....	....	296	....	....	....	....	....	....	....	....	....	....	13	7	10	17	30	....	....	....
1979-80	Minnesota North Stars	NHL	1	0	0	0	0	0	0	0	0	0	0	0	0.0	0	0	2	0	–2	....	....	....	....	....	....	....	....
	Oklahoma City Stars	CHL	61	26	19	45	....	....	....	160	....	....	....	....	....	....	....	....	....	....	....	....	....	....	....	....	....	....
1980-81	Oklahoma City Stars	CHL	55	24	23	47	....	....	....	137	....	....	....	....	....	....	....	....	....	....	3	1	1	2	8	....	....	....
1981-82	Nashville South Stars	CHL	35	5	13	18	....	....	....	55	....	....	....	....	....	....	....	....	....	....	3	0	1	1	15	....	....	....
1982-83			OUT OF HOCKEY – RETIRED																									
1983-84	Fort Wayne Komets	IHL	77	37	46	83	....	....	....	137	....	....	....	....	....	....	....	....	....	....	4	0	1	1	17	....	....	....
1984-85	Fort Wayne Komets	IHL	79	33	34	67	....	....	....	157	....	....	....	....	....	....	....	....	....	....	13	7	5	12	25	....	....	....
1985-86	Fort Wayne Komets	IHL	2	0	0	0	....	....	....	15	....	....	....	....	....	....	....	....	....	....	....	....	....	....	....	....	....	....
1986-87	Fort Wayne Komets	IHL	DID NOT PLAY – COACHING																									
	NHL Totals		1	0	0	0	0	0	0	0	0	0	0	0	0.0	0	0	2	0		....	....	....	....	....	....	....	....

IHL First All-Star Team (1979)

Signed as a free agent by **Minnesota**, September 15, 1979.

• LAJEUNESSE, Serge

D/RW – L. 5'10", 185 lbs. b: Montreal, Que., 6/11/1950. Detroit's 1st, 12th overall, in 1970.

Season	Club	League	GP	G	A	Pts	AG	AA	APts	PIM	PP	SH	GW	S	%	TGF	PGF	TGA	PGA	+/–	GP	G	A	Pts	PIM	PP	SH	GW
1967-68	Montreal Beavers	QJHL	40	5	14	19	....	....	....	....	....	....	....	....	....	....	....	....	....	....	....	....	....	....	....	....	....	....
1968-69	Montreal Jr. Canadiens	OHA-Jr.	54	2	20	22	....	....	....	172	....	....	....	....	....	....	....	....	....	....	14	1	4	5	19	....	....	....
	Montreal Jr. Canadiens	Mem-Cup	8	1	4	5	....	....	....	19	....	....	....	....	....	....	....	....	....	....	....	....	....	....	....	....	....	....
1969-70	Montreal Jr. Canadiens	OHA-Jr.	54	2	27	29	....	....	....	87	....	....	....	....	....	....	....	....	....	....	16	0	8	8	22	....	....	....
	Montreal Jr. Canadiens	Mem-Cup	12	3	9	12	....	....	....	21	....	....	....	....	....	....	....	....	....	....	....	....	....	....	....	....	....	....
1970-71	Detroit Red Wings	NHL	62	1	3	4	1	2	3	55	0	1	0	76	1.3	37	0	70	5	–28	....	....	....	....	....	....	....	....
	Fort Worth Wings	CHL	12	1	5	6	....	....	....	21	....	....	....	....	....	....	....	....	....	....	....	....	....	....	....	....	....	....
1971-72	Detroit Red Wings	NHL	7	0	0	0	0	0	0	20	0	0	0	2	0.0	4	0	5	0	–1	....	....	....	....	....	....	....	....
	Tidewater Red Wings	AHL	26	4	7	11	....	....	....	26	....	....	....	....	....	....	....	....	....	....	....	....	....	....	....	....	....	....
	Fort Worth Wings	CHL	36	8	11	19	....	....	....	53	....	....	....	....	....	....	....	....	....	....	7	0	2	2	16	....	....	....
1972-73	Detroit Red Wings	NHL	28	0	1	1	0	1	1	26	0	0	0	10	0.0	7	1	24	3	–15	....	....	....	....	....	....	....	....
	Virginia Wings	AHL	39	7	16	23	....	....	....	69	....	....	....	....	....	....	....	....	....	....	13	2	5	7	23	....	....	....
1973-74	Philadelphia Flyers	NHL	1	0	0	0	0	0	0	0	0	0	0	2	0.0	0	0	0	0	0	....	....	....	....	....	....	....	....
	Richmond Robins	AHL	75	28	17	45	....	....	....	96	....	....	....	....	....	....	....	....	....	....	5	0	5	5	2	....	....	....
1974-75	Philadelphia Flyers	NHL	5	0	0	0	0	0	0	2	0	0	0	6	0.0	1	0	0	0	1	....	....	....	....	....	....	....	....
	Richmond Robins	AHL	66	11	18	29	....	....	....	58	....	....	....	....	....	....	....	....	....	....	7	1	2	3	4	....	....	....
1975-76	Richmond Robins	AHL	57	7	17	24	....	....	....	42	....	....	....	....	....	....	....	....	....	....	3	0	0	0	2	....	....	....
	NHL Totals		103	1	4	5	1	3	4	103	0	1	0	96	1.0	49	1	99	8		....	....	....	....	....	....	....	....

OHA-Jr. Second All-Star Team (1969, 1970)

Traded to **Philadelphia** by **Detroit** for Rick Foley, May 15, 1973.

• LAKOVIC, Sasha

Sasha Gordon "The Basha" RW – L. 6', 220 lbs. b: Vancouver, B.C., 9/7/1971.

Season	Club	League	GP	G	A	Pts	AG	AA	APts	PIM	PP	SH	GW	S	%	TGF	PGF	TGA	PGA	+/–	GP	G	A	Pts	PIM	PP	SH	GW
1991-92	Kelowna Spartans	BCJHL	4	1	0	1	....	....	....	14	....	....	....	....	....	....	....	....	....	....	....	....	....	....	....	....	....	....
	Bellingham Ice Hawks	BCJHL	24	8	3	11	....	....	....	67	....	....	....	....	....	....	....	....	....	....	....	....	....	....	....	....	....	....
1992-93	Brantford Wheels	ColHL	28	7	5	12	....	....	....	235	....	....	....	....	....	....	....	....	....	....	....	....	....	....	....	....	....	....
	Columbus Chill	ECHL	27	7	9	16	....	....	....	162	....	....	....	....	....	....	....	....	....	....	....	....	....	....	....	....	....	....
	Binghamton Rangers	AHL	3	0	0	0	....	....	....	0	....	....	....	....	....	....	....	....	....	....	....	....	....	....	....	....	....	....
	Brantford Smoke	ColHL	....	....	....	....	....	....	....	....	....	....	....	....	....	....	....	....	....	....	5	2	1	3	66	....	....	....
1993-94	Toledo Storm	ECHL	24	5	10	15	....	....	....	198	....	....	....	....	....	....	....	....	....	....	....	....	....	....	....	....	....	....
	Chatham Wheels	ColHL	13	11	7	18	....	....	....	61	....	....	....	....	....	....	....	....	....	....	....	....	....	....	....	....	....	....
1994-95	Tulsa Oilers	CHL	40	20	24	44	....	....	....	214	....	....	....	....	....	....	....	....	....	....	5	1	3	4	88	....	....	....
1995-96	Las Vegas Thunder	IHL	49	1	2	3	....	....	....	416	....	....	....	....	....	....	....	....	....	....	13	1	1	2	*57	....	....	....
1996-97	Calgary Flames	NHL	19	0	1	1	0	1	1	54	0	0	0	10	0.0	2	0	3	0	–1	....	....	....	....	....	....	....	....
	Saint John Flames	AHL	18	1	8	9	....	....	....	182	....	....	....	....	....	....	....	....	....	....	....	....	....	....	....	....	....	....
	Las Vegas Thunder	IHL	10	0	0	0	....	....	....	81	....	....	....	....	....	....	....	....	....	....	2	0	0	0	14	....	....	....
1997-98	New Jersey Devils	NHL	2	0	0	0	0	0	0	5	0	0	0	2	0.0	0	0	0	0	0	....	....	....	....	....	....	....	....
	Albany River Rats	AHL	30	7	6	13	....	....	....	158	....	....	....	....	....	....	....	....	....	....	13	3	4	7	*84	....	....	....

			REGULAR SEASON																		PLAYOFFS							
Season	Club	League	GP	G	A	Pts	AG	AA	APts	PIM	PP	SH	GW	S	%	TGF	PGF	TGA	PGA	+/–	GP	G	A	Pts	PIM	PP	SH	GW
1998-99	**New Jersey Devils**	**NHL**	16	0	3	3	0	3	3	59	0	0	0	10	0.0	4	0	4	0	0	....	....	....	....	....	....	....	....
	Albany River Rats	AHL	10	1	1	2	....	....	....	93	....	....	....	....	....	....	....	....	....	....	....	....	....	....	....	....	....	....
99-2000	Albany River Rats	AHL	51	10	16	26	....	....	....	144	....	....	....	....	....	....	....	....	....	....	5	0	0	0	14	....	....	....
	NHL Totals		37	0	4	4	0	4	4	118	0	0	0	22	0.0	6	0	7	0		....	....	....	....	....	....	....	....

Signed as a free agent by **Calgary**, October 10, 1996. Signed as a free agent by **New Jersey**, September 24, 1997. • Played w/ RHI's Vancouver Voodoo in 1993 (11-14-10-24-83) and 1994 (3-2-5-7-0); Oakland Skates in 1994 (4-4-3-7-40) and 1995 (17-17-14-31-80); San Jose Sting in 1997 (21-18-13-31-108) and MLRH's Philadelphia Sting in 1998 (3-5-5-10-23).

• LALONDE, Bobby

Robert Patrick C – L. 5'5", 155 lbs. b: Montreal, Que., 3/27/1951. Vancouver's 2nd, 17th overall, in 1971.

Season	Club	League	GP	G	A	Pts	AG	AA	APts	PIM	PP	SH	GW	S	%	TGF	PGF	TGA	PGA	+/–	GP	G	A	Pts	PIM	PP	SH	GW
1967-68	Shawinigan Bruins	QJHL	44	29	29	58	....	....	....	....	....	....	....	....	....	....	....	....	....	....	12	5	3	8	6	....	....	....
1968-69	Montreal Jr. Canadiens	OHA-Jr.	54	17	27	44	....	....	....	18	....	....	....	....	....	....	....	....	....	....	13	0	5	5	0	....	....	....
	Montreal Jr. Canadiens	Mem-Cup	8	4	4	8	....	....	....	17	....	....	....	....	....	....	....	....	....	....	....	....	....	....	....	....	....	....
1969-70	Montreal Jr. Canadiens	OHA-Jr.	54	42	42	84	....	....	....	73	....	....	....	....	....	....	....	....	....	....	16	6	10	16	17	....	....	....
	Montreal Jr. Canadiens	Mem-Cup	12	6	19	25	....	....	....	19	....	....	....	....	....	....	....	....	....	....	....	....	....	....	....	....	....	....
1970-71	Montreal Jr. Canadiens	OHA-Jr.	61	59	68	127	....	....	....	71	....	....	....	....	....	....	....	....	....	....	11	8	13	21	35	....	....	....
1971-72	**Vancouver Canucks**	**NHL**	27	1	5	6	1	4	5	2	0	0	0	24	4.2	9	1	16	0	–8	....	....	....	....	....	....	....	....
	Rochester Americans	AHL	42	14	11	25	....	....	....	19	....	....	....	....	....	....	....	....	....	....	....	....	....	....	....	....	....	....
1972-73	**Vancouver Canucks**	**NHL**	77	20	27	47	19	21	40	32	7	0	6	126	15.9	67	21	80	2	–32	....	....	....	....	....	....	....	....
1973-74	**Vancouver Canucks**	**NHL**	36	3	4	7	3	3	6	18	1	0	1	42	7.1	14	3	18	4	–3	....	....	....	....	....	....	....	....
1974-75	**Vancouver Canucks**	**NHL**	74	17	30	47	15	22	37	48	4	0	1	135	12.6	51	10	46	5	0	5	0	0	0	0	0	0	0
1975-76	**Vancouver Canucks**	**NHL**	71	14	36	50	12	27	39	46	2	0	2	143	9.8	63	8	64	5	–4	1	0	0	0	2	0	0	0
	Tulsa Oilers	CHL	4	3	2	5	....	....	....	2	....	....	....	....	....	....	....	....	....	....	....	....	....	....	....	....	....	....
1976-77	**Vancouver Canucks**	**NHL**	68	17	15	32	15	12	27	39	3	0	1	115	14.8	48	16	44	0	–12	....	....	....	....	....	....	....	....
	Tulsa Oilers	CHL	7	2	2	4	....	....	....	0	....	....	....	....	....	....	....	....	....	....	....	....	....	....	....	....	....	....
1977-78	**Atlanta Flames**	**NHL**	73	14	23	37	13	18	31	28	0	0	0	94	14.9	53	10	38	0	5	1	1	0	1	0	0	0	0
1978-79	**Atlanta Flames**	**NHL**	78	24	32	56	21	23	44	24	6	0	1	135	17.8	74	22	68	13	–3	2	1	0	1	0	1	0	0
1979-80	**Atlanta Flames**	**NHL**	3	0	1	1	0	1	1	2	0	0	0	2	0.0	2	1	2	0	–1	....	....	....	....	....	....	....	....
	Boston Bruins	**NHL**	71	10	25	35	8	18	26	28	1	2	0	91	11.0	50	4	55	23	14	4	0	1	1	2	0	0	0
1980-81	**Boston Bruins**	**NHL**	62	4	12	16	3	8	11	31	0	1	0	42	9.5	25	4	49	31	3	3	2	1	3	2	0	2	0
1981-82	**Calgary Flames**	**NHL**	1	0	0	0	0	0	0	0	0	0	0	1	0.0	2	0	0	0	2	....	....	....	....	....	....	....	....
	Oklahoma City Stars	CHL	19	6	11	17	....	....	....	36	....	....	....	....	....	....	....	....	....	....	....	....	....	....	....	....	....	....
	HC Davos	Switz-2	15	8	21	29	....	....	....	....	....	....	....	....	....	....	....	....	....	....	12	13	13	26	....	....	....	....
	NHL Totals		641	124	210	334	110	157	267	298	24	3	12	950	13.1	458	100	480	83		16	4	2	6	6	1	2	0

Signed as a free agent by **Atlanta**, September 20, 1977. Claimed by **Atlanta** as a fill-in during Expansion Draft, June 13, 1979. Traded to **Boston** by **Atlanta** for future considerations, October 23, 1979. Signed as a free agent by **Calgary**, October 25, 1981.

• LALONDE, Ron

Ronald Leo C – L. 5'10", 170 lbs. b: Toronto, Ont., 10/30/1952. Pittsburgh's 4th, 56th overall, in 1972.

Season	Club	League	GP	G	A	Pts	AG	AA	APts	PIM	PP	SH	GW	S	%	TGF	PGF	TGA	PGA	+/–	GP	G	A	Pts	PIM	PP	SH	GW
1969-70	North York Rangers	OHA-B	STATISTICS NOT AVAILABLE																									
1970-71	Peterborough Petes	OHA-Jr.	44	21	25	46	....	....	....	13	....	....	....	....	....	....	....	....	....	....	5	2	2	4	2	....	....	....
1971-72	Peterborough Petes	OMJHL	58	26	37	63	....	....	....	36	....	....	....	....	....	....	....	....	....	....	15	5	9	14	15	....	....	....
	Peterborough Petes	Mem-Cup	3	*3	0	3	....	....	....	2	....	....	....	....	....	....	....	....	....	....	....	....	....	....	....	....	....	....
1972-73	**Pittsburgh Penguins**	**NHL**	9	0	0	0	0	0	0	2	0	0	0	2	0.0	0	0	1	1	0	....	....	....	....	....	....	....	....
	Hershey Bears	AHL	60	16	26	42	....	....	....	34	....	....	....	....	....	....	....	....	....	....	7	1	1	2	0	....	....	....
1973-74	**Pittsburgh Penguins**	**NHL**	73	10	17	27	10	14	24	14	0	1	2	70	14.3	38	2	41	7	2	....	....	....	....	....	....	....	....
1974-75	**Pittsburgh Penguins**	**NHL**	24	0	3	3	0	2	2	0	0	0	0	12	0.0	7	2	10	6	1	....	....	....	....	....	....	....	....
	Washington Capitals	**NHL**	50	12	14	26	10	10	20	27	4	1	1	67	17.9	31	6	89	25	–39	....	....	....	....	....	....	....	....
1975-76	**Washington Capitals**	**NHL**	80	9	19	28	8	14	22	19	2	1	0	92	9.8	48	6	94	26	–26	....	....	....	....	....	....	....	....
1976-77	**Washington Capitals**	**NHL**	76	12	17	29	11	13	24	24	0	0	0	83	14.5	44	0	105	41	–20	....	....	....	....	....	....	....	....
1977-78	**Washington Capitals**	**NHL**	67	1	5	6	1	4	5	16	0	0	0	48	2.1	18	0	71	35	–18	....	....	....	....	....	....	....	....
1978-79	**Washington Capitals**	**NHL**	18	1	3	4	1	2	3	4	0	1	0	8	12.5	6	0	11	4	–1	....	....	....	....	....	....	....	....
	Binghamton Dusters	AHL	26	7	7	14	....	....	....	0	....	....	....	....	....	....	....	....	....	....	....	....	....	....	....	....	....	....
	Hershey Bears	AHL	27	6	6	12	....	....	....	0	....	....	....	....	....	....	....	....	....	....	4	1	0	1	2	....	....	....
1979-80	Hershey Bears	AHL	65	13	17	30	....	....	....	22	....	....	....	....	....	....	....	....	....	....	16	2	3	5	6	....	....	....
1980-81	HC Salzburg	Austria	28	11	9	20	....	....	....	38	....	....	....	....	....	....	....	....	....	....	....	....	....	....	....	....	....	....
	NHL Totals		397	45	78	123	41	59	100	106	6	4	3	382	11.8	192	16	422	145		....	....	....	....	....	....	....	....

Traded to **Washington** by **Pittsburgh** for Lew Morrison, December 14, 1974.

• LALOR, Mike

Michael John D – L. 6', 200 lbs. b: Buffalo, NY, 3/8/1963.

Season	Club	League	GP	G	A	Pts	AG	AA	APts	PIM	PP	SH	GW	S	%	TGF	PGF	TGA	PGA	+/–	GP	G	A	Pts	PIM	PP	SH	GW
1980-81	Hamilton Mountain A's	OJHL	44	5	28	33	....	....	....	83	....	....	....	....	....	....	....	....	....	....	....	....	....	....	....	....	....	....
1981-82	Brantford Alexanders	OHL	64	3	13	16	....	....	....	114	....	....	....	....	....	....	....	....	....	....	11	0	6	6	11	....	....	....
1982-83	Brantford Alexanders	OHL	65	10	30	40	....	....	....	113	....	....	....	....	....	....	....	....	....	....	8	1	3	4	20	....	....	....
1983-84	Nova Scotia Voyageurs	AHL	67	5	11	16	....	....	....	80	....	....	....	....	....	....	....	....	....	....	12	0	2	2	13	....	....	....
1984-85	Sherbrooke Canadiens	AHL	79	9	23	32	....	....	....	114	....	....	....	....	....	....	....	....	....	....	17	3	5	8	36	....	....	....
1985-86♦	**Montreal Canadiens**	**NHL**	62	3	5	8	2	3	5	56	0	0	0	44	6.8	41	0	61	16	–4	17	1	2	3	29	0	0	1
1986-87	**Montreal Canadiens**	**NHL**	57	0	10	10	0	7	7	47	0	0	0	58	0.0	37	0	48	16	5	13	2	1	3	29	0	0	0
1987-88	**Montreal Canadiens**	**NHL**	66	1	10	11	1	7	8	113	0	0	0	41	2.4	55	1	61	11	4	11	0	0	0	11	0	0	0
1988-89	**Montreal Canadiens**	**NHL**	12	1	4	5	1	3	4	15	0	0	1	12	8.3	8	0	9	0	–1	....	....	....	....	....	....	....	....
	St. Louis Blues	**NHL**	36	1	14	15	1	10	11	54	0	0	1	40	2.5	41	1	46	21	15	10	1	1	2	14	1	0	0
1989-90	**St. Louis Blues**	**NHL**	78	0	16	16	0	11	11	81	0	0	0	79	0.0	79	2	120	37	–6	12	0	2	2	31	0	0	0
1990-91	**Washington Capitals**	**NHL**	68	1	5	6	1	4	5	61	0	0	0	49	2.0	41	1	74	11	–23	10	1	2	3	22	0	0	0
1991-92	**Washington Capitals**	**NHL**	64	5	7	12	5	5	10	64	0	0	1	54	9.3	54	2	42	4	14	....	....	....	....	....	....	....	....
	Winnipeg Jets	**NHL**	15	2	3	5	2	2	4	14	0	0	0	20	10.0	16	1	12	8	11	7	0	0	0	19	0	0	0
1992-93	**Winnipeg Jets**	**NHL**	64	1	8	9	1	5	6	76	0	0	0	75	1.3	51	1	87	27	–10	4	0	2	2	4	0	0	0
1993-94	**San Jose Sharks**	**NHL**	23	0	2	2	0	2	2	8	0	0	0	19	0.0	10	0	20	5	–5	....	....	....	....	....	....	....	....
	Dallas Stars	**NHL**	12	0	1	1	0	1	1	6	0	0	0	3	0.0	3	0	10	2	–5	5	0	0	0	6	0	0	0
1994-95	**Dallas Stars**	**NHL**	12	0	0	0	0	0	0	9	0	0	0	6	0.0	4	0	4	0	0	3	0	0	0	2	0	0	0
	Kalamazoo Wings	IHL	5	0	1	1	....	....	....	11	....	....	....	....	....	....	....	....	....	....	....	....	....	....	....	....	....	....
1995-96	**Dallas Stars**	**NHL**	63	1	2	3	1	2	3	31	0	0	0	46	2.2	29	2	49	12	–10	....	....	....	....	....	....	....	....
	San Francisco Spiders	IHL	12	2	2	4	....	....	....	6	....	....	....	....	....	....	....	....	....	....	....	....	....	....	....	....	....	....
	United States	WC-A	8	0	0	0	....	....	....	4	....	....	....	....	....	....	....	....	....	....	....	....	....	....	....	....	....	....
1996-97	**Dallas Stars**	**NHL**	55	1	1	2	1	1	2	42	0	0	0	32	3.1	25	0	35	13	3	....	....	....	....	....	....	....	....
	NHL Totals		687	17	88	105	16	63	79	677	0	0	3	578	2.9	494	11	678	183		92	5	10	15	167	1	0	1

Signed as a free agent by **Montreal**, September, 1983. Traded to **St. Louis** by **Montreal** with Montreal's 1st round choice (later traded to Vancouver — Vancouver selected Shawn Antoski) in 1990 Entry Draft for St. Louis' 1st round choice (Turner Stevenson) in 1990 Entry Draft and St. Louis' 3rd round choice (later traded back to St. Louis, St. Louis selected Nathan Lafayette) in 1991 Entry Draft, January 16, 1989. Traded to **Washington** by **St. Louis** with Peter Zezel for Geoff Courtnall, July 13, 1990. Traded to **Winnipeg** by **Washington** for Paul MacDermid, March 2, 1992. Signed as a free agent by **San Jose**, August 13, 1993. Traded to **Dallas** by **San Jose** with Doug Zmolek for Ulf Dahlen and Dallas' 7th round choice (Brad Mehalko) in 1995 Entry Draft, March 19, 1994.

• LAMB, Mark

Mark W. C – L. 5'9", 180 lbs. b: Ponteix, Sask., 8/3/1964. Calgary's 5th, 72nd overall, in 1982.

Season	Club	League	GP	G	A	Pts	AG	AA	APts	PIM	PP	SH	GW	S	%	TGF	PGF	TGA	PGA	+/–	GP	G	A	Pts	PIM	PP	SH	GW
1980-81	Melville Millionaires	SJHL	STATISTICS NOT AVAILABLE																									
	Billings Bighorns	WHL	24	1	8	9	....	....	....	12	....	....	....	....	....	....	....	....	....	....	....	....	....	....	....	....	....	....
1981-82	Billings Bighorns	WHL	72	45	56	101	....	....	....	46	....	....	....	....	....	....	....	....	....	....	5	4	6	10	4	....	....	....
1982-83	Nanaimo Islanders	WHL	30	14	37	51	....	....	....	16	....	....	....	....	....	....	....	....	....	....	....	....	....	....	....	....	....	....
	Medicine Hat Tigers	WHL	46	22	43	65	....	....	....	33	....	....	....	....	....	....	....	....	....	....	5	3	2	5	4	....	....	....
	Colorado Flames	CHL	....	....	....	....	....	....	....	....	....	....	....	....	....	....	....	....	....	....	6	0	2	2	0	....	....	....
1983-84	Medicine Hat Tigers	WHL	72	59	77	136	....	....	....	30	....	....	....	....	....	....	....	....	....	....	14	12	11	23	6	....	....	....
1984-85	Moncton Golden Flames	AHL	80	23	49	72	....	....	....	53	....	....	....	....	....	....	....	....	....	....	....	....	....	....	....	....	....	....
1985-86	**Calgary Flames**	**NHL**	1	0	0	0	0	0	0	0	0	0	0	0	0.0	0	0	0	0	0	....	....	....	....	....	....	....	....
	Moncton Golden Flames	AHL	79	26	50	76	....	....	....	51	....	....	....	....	....	....	....	....	....	....	10	2	6	8	17	....	....	....

Season	Club	League	GP	G	A	Pts	AG	AA	APts	PIM	PP	SH	GW	S	%	TGF	PGF	TGA	PGA	+/–	GP	G	A	Pts	PIM	PP	SH	GW
			REGULAR SEASON																		PLAYOFFS							
1986-87	**Detroit Red Wings**	**NHL**	**22**	**2**	**1**	**3**	**2**	**1**	**3**	**8**	**0**	**0**	**0**	**8**	**25.0**	**5**	**0**	**5**	**0**	**0**	**11**	**0**	**0**	**0**	**11**	**0**	**0**	**0**
	Adirondack Red Wings	AHL	49	14	36	50	....	....	....	45	....	....	....	....	....	....	....	....	....	....	....	....	....	....	....	....	....	....
1987-88	**Edmonton Oilers**	**NHL**	**2**	**0**	**0**	**0**	**0**	**0**	**0**	**0**	**0**	**0**	**0**	**0**	**0.0**	**0**	**0**	**0**	**0**	**0**	....	....	....	....	....	....	....	....
	Nova Scotia Oilers	AHL	69	27	61	88	....	....	....	45	....	....	....	....	....	....	....	....	....	....	5	0	5	5	6	....	....	....
1988-89	**Edmonton Oilers**	**NHL**	**20**	**2**	**8**	**10**	**2**	**6**	**8**	**14**	**1**	**0**	**0**	**20**	**10.0**	**13**	**1**	**9**	**1**	**4**	**6**	**0**	**2**	**2**	**8**	**0**	**0**	**0**
	Cape Breton Oilers	AHL	54	33	49	82	....	....	....	29	....	....	....	....	....	....	....	....	....	....	....	....	....	....	....	....	....	....
1989-90♦	**Edmonton Oilers**	**NHL**	**58**	**12**	**16**	**28**	**10**	**11**	**21**	**42**	**2**	**0**	**2**	**81**	**14.8**	**35**	**4**	**31**	**10**	**10**	**22**	**6**	**11**	**17**	**2**	**1**	**0**	**2**
1990-91	**Edmonton Oilers**	**NHL**	**37**	**4**	**8**	**12**	**4**	**6**	**10**	**25**	**1**	**0**	**1**	**41**	**9.8**	**21**	**3**	**31**	**11**	**–2**	**15**	**0**	**5**	**5**	**20**	**0**	**0**	**0**
1991-92	**Edmonton Oilers**	**NHL**	**59**	**6**	**22**	**28**	**5**	**17**	**22**	**46**	**2**	**0**	**1**	**61**	**9.8**	**41**	**6**	**49**	**18**	**4**	**16**	**1**	**1**	**2**	**10**	**0**	**0**	**0**
1992-93	**Ottawa Senators**	**NHL**	**71**	**7**	**19**	**26**	**6**	**13**	**19**	**64**	**1**	**0**	**0**	**123**	**5.7**	**50**	**5**	**131**	**46**	**–40**	....	....	....	....	....	....	....	....
1993-94	**Ottawa Senators**	**NHL**	**66**	**11**	**18**	**29**	**10**	**14**	**24**	**56**	**4**	**1**	**1**	**105**	**10.5**	**38**	**11**	**112**	**44**	**–41**	....	....	....	....	....	....	....	....
	Philadelphia Flyers	**NHL**	**19**	**1**	**6**	**7**	**1**	**5**	**6**	**16**	**0**	**0**	**1**	**19**	**5.3**	**9**	**1**	**17**	**6**	**–3**	....	....	....	....	....	....	....	....
1994-95	**Philadelphia Flyers**	**NHL**	**8**	**0**	**2**	**2**	**0**	**3**	**3**	**2**	**0**	**0**	**0**	**7**	**0.0**	**3**	**0**	**4**	**2**	**1**	....	....	....	....	....	....	....	....
	Montreal Canadiens	**NHL**	**39**	**1**	**0**	**1**	**2**	**0**	**2**	**18**	**0**	**0**	**0**	**23**	**4.3**	**3**	**0**	**29**	**13**	**–13**	....	....	....	....	....	....	....	....
1995-96	**Montreal Canadiens**	**NHL**	**1**	**0**	**0**	**0**	**0**	**0**	**0**	**0**	**0**	**0**	**0**	**0**	**0.0**	**0**	**0**	**0**	**0**	**0**	....	....	....	....	....	....	....	....
	Houston Aeros	IHL	67	17	60	77	....	....	....	65	....	....	....	....	....	....	....	....	....	....	....	....	....	....	....	....	....	....
1996-97	Houston Aeros	IHL	81	25	53	78	....	....	....	83	....	....	....	....	....	....	....	....	....	....	13	3	12	15	10	....	....	....
1997-98	EV Landshut	Germany	46	7	21	28	....	....	....	36	....	....	....	....	....	....	....	....	....	....	6	3	1	4	8	....	....	....
1998-99	Houston Aeros	IHL	79	21	49	70	....	....	....	72	....	....	....	....	....	....	....	....	....	....	19	1	10	11	12	....	....	....
99-2000	Houston Aeros	IHL	79	15	46	61	....	....	....	58	....	....	....	....	....	....	....	....	....	....	11	2	7	9	6	....	....	....
	NHL Totals		**403**	**46**	**100**	**146**	**42**	**76**	**118**	**291**	**11**	**1**	**6**	**488**	**9.4**	**218**	**31**	**418**	**151**		**70**	**7**	**19**	**26**	**51**	**1**	**0**	**2**

WHL East First All-Star Team (1984)

Signed as a free agent by **Detroit**, July 28, 1986. Claimed by **Edmonton** from **Detroit** in Waiver Draft, October 5, 1987. Claimed by **Ottawa** from **Edmonton** in Expansion Draft, June 18, 1992. Traded to **Philadelphia** by **Ottawa** for Claude Boivin and Kirk Daubenspeck, March 5, 1994. Traded to **Montreal** by **Philadelphia** for cash, February 10, 1995. Loaned to **Houston** (IHL) by **Montreal**, November 1, 1995. Signed as a free agent by **Houston** (IHL), September 13, 1996.

• LAMBERT, Dan

Daniel R. D – L. 5'8", 177 lbs. b: St. Boniface, Man., 1/12/1970. Quebec's 7th, 106th overall, in 1989.

Season	Club	League	GP	G	A	Pts	AG	AA	APts	PIM	PP	SH	GW	S	%	TGF	PGF	TGA	PGA	+/–	GP	G	A	Pts	PIM	PP	SH	GW
1985-86	Warroad Warriors	Hi-School	21	14	22	36	....	....	....	10	....	....	....	....	....	....	....	....	....	....	....	....	....	....	....	....	....	....
1986-87	Swift Current Broncos	WHL	68	13	53	66	....	....	....	95	....	....	....	....	....	....	....	....	....	....	4	1	1	2	9	....	....	....
1987-88	Swift Current Broncos	WHL	69	20	63	83	....	....	....	120	....	....	....	....	....	....	....	....	....	....	10	2	10	12	45	....	....	....
1988-89	Swift Current Broncos	WHL	57	25	77	102	....	....	....	158	....	....	....	....	....	....	....	....	....	....	12	9	19	28	12	....	....	....
	Swift Current Broncos	Mem-Cup	5	2	*6	8	....	....	....	12	....	....	....	....	....	....	....	....	....	....	....	....	....	....	....	....	....	....
1989-90	Swift Current Broncos	WHL	50	17	51	68	....	....	....	119	....	....	....	....	....	....	....	....	....	....	4	2	3	5	12	....	....	....
1990-91	**Quebec Nordiques**	**NHL**	**1**	**0**	**0**	**0**	**0**	**0**	**0**	**0**	**0**	**0**	**0**	**0**	**0.0**	**0**	**0**	**0**	**0**	**0**	....	....	....	....	....	....	....	....
	Halifax Citadels	AHL	30	7	13	20	....	....	....	20	....	....	....	....	....	....	....	....	....	....	....	....	....	....	....	....	....	....
	Canada	WJC-A	7	1	2	3	....	....	....	4	....	....	....	....	....	....	....	....	....	....	....	....	....	....	....	....	....	....
	Fort Wayne Komets	IHL	49	10	27	37	....	....	....	65	....	....	....	....	....	....	....	....	....	....	19	4	10	14	20	....	....	....
1991-92	**Quebec Nordiques**	**NHL**	**28**	**6**	**9**	**15**	**5**	**7**	**12**	**22**	**2**	**0**	**0**	**42**	**14.3**	**29**	**13**	**22**	**1**	**–5**	....	....	....	....	....	....	....	....
	Halifax Citadels	AHL	47	3	28	31	....	....	....	33	....	....	....	....	....	....	....	....	....	....	....	....	....	....	....	....	....	....
1992-93	Moncton Hawks	AHL	73	11	30	41	....	....	....	100	....	....	....	....	....	....	....	....	....	....	5	1	2	3	2	....	....	....
1993-94	HIFK Helsinki	Finland	13	1	2	3	....	....	....	8	....	....	....	....	....	....	....	....	....	....	....	....	....	....	....	....	....	....
	Fort Wayne Komets	IHL	62	10	27	37	....	....	....	138	....	....	....	....	....	....	....	....	....	....	18	3	12	15	20	....	....	....
1994-95	San Diego Gulls	IHL	70	6	19	25	....	....	....	95	....	....	....	....	....	....	....	....	....	....	5	0	5	5	10	....	....	....
1995-96	Los Angeles Ice Dogs	IHL	81	22	65	87	....	....	....	121	....	....	....	....	....	....	....	....	....	....	....	....	....	....	....	....	....	....
1996-97	Long Beach Ice Dogs	IHL	71	15	50	65	....	....	....	70	....	....	....	....	....	....	....	....	....	....	18	2	8	10	8	....	....	....
1997-98	Long Beach Ice Dogs	IHL	81	19	59	78	....	....	....	112	....	....	....	....	....	....	....	....	....	....	17	3	14	17	16	....	....	....
1998-99	Long Beach Ice Dogs	IHL	50	17	36	53	....	....	....	91	....	....	....	....	....	....	....	....	....	....	8	0	6	6	12	....	....	....
99-2000	Kolner Haie	Germany	50	9	16	25	....	....	....	52	....	....	....	....	....	....	....	....	....	....	10	1	3	4	10	....	....	....
	NHL Totals		**29**	**6**	**9**	**15**	**5**	**7**	**12**	**22**	**2**	**0**	**0**	**42**	**14.3**	**29**	**13**	**22**	**1**		....	....	....	....	....	....	....	....

WHL East First All-Star Team (1989, 1990) • Memorial Cup All-Star Team (1989) • Won Stafford Smythe Memorial Trophy (Memorial Cup Tournament MVP) (1989) • IHL Second All-Star Team (1996) • IHL First All-Star Team (1998) • Won Governor's Trophy (Top Defenseman - IHL) (1998) • IHL Second All-Star Team (1999)

Traded to **Winnipeg** by **Quebec** for Shawn Cronin, August 25, 1992.

• LAMBERT, Denny

LW – L. 5'10", 215 lbs. b: Wawa, Ont., 1/7/1970.

Season	Club	League	GP	G	A	Pts	AG	AA	APts	PIM	PP	SH	GW	S	%	TGF	PGF	TGA	PGA	+/–	GP	G	A	Pts	PIM	PP	SH	GW
1986-87	Sault Ste. Marie Legionaires	OMHA	22	8	13	21	....	....	....	129	....	....	....	....	....	....	....	....	....	....	....	....	....	....	....	....	....	....
1987-88	Sault Ste. Marie Thunderbirds	NOJHA	32	25	27	52	....	....	....	184	....	....	....	....	....	....	....	....	....	....	....	....	....	....	....	....	....	....
1988-89	Sault Ste. Marie Greyhounds	OHL	61	14	15	29	....	....	....	203	....	....	....	....	....	....	....	....	....	....	....	....	....	....	....	....	....	....
1989-90	Sault Ste. Marie Greyhounds	OHL	61	23	29	52	....	....	....	276	....	....	....	....	....	....	....	....	....	....	....	....	....	....	....	....	....	....
1990-91	Sault Ste. Marie Greyhounds	OHL	59	28	39	67	....	....	....	169	....	....	....	....	....	....	....	....	....	....	14	7	9	16	48	....	....	....
	Sault Ste. Marie Greyhounds	Mem-Cup	3	1	0	1	....	....	....	8	....	....	....	....	....	....	....	....	....	....	....	....	....	....	....	....	....	....
1991-92	San Diego Gulls	IHL	71	17	14	31	....	....	....	229	....	....	....	....	....	....	....	....	....	....	3	0	0	0	10	....	....	....
	St. Thomas Wildcats	ColHL	5	2	6	8	....	....	....	9	....	....	....	....	....	....	....	....	....	....	....	....	....	....	....	....	....	....
1992-93	San Diego Gulls	IHL	56	18	12	30	....	....	....	277	....	....	....	....	....	....	....	....	....	....	14	1	1	2	44	....	....	....
1993-94	San Diego Gulls	IHL	79	13	14	27	....	....	....	314	....	....	....	....	....	....	....	....	....	....	6	1	0	1	55	....	....	....
1994-95	San Diego Gulls	IHL	75	25	35	60	....	....	....	222	....	....	....	....	....	....	....	....	....	....	....	....	....	....	....	....	....	....
	Mighty Ducks of Anaheim	**NHL**	**13**	**1**	**3**	**4**	**2**	**4**	**6**	**4**	**0**	**0**	**0**	**14**	**7.1**	**7**	**0**	**4**	**0**	**3**	....	....	....	....	....	....	....	....
1995-96	**Mighty Ducks of Anaheim**	**NHL**	**33**	**0**	**8**	**8**	**0**	**7**	**7**	**55**	**0**	**0**	**0**	**28**	**0.0**	**11**	**0**	**13**	**0**	**–2**	....	....	....	....	....	....	....	....
	Baltimore Bandits	AHL	44	14	28	42	....	....	....	126	....	....	....	....	....	....	....	....	....	....	12	3	9	12	39	....	....	....
1996-97	**Ottawa Senators**	**NHL**	**80**	**4**	**16**	**20**	**4**	**14**	**18**	**217**	**0**	**0**	**1**	**58**	**6.9**	**25**	**1**	**28**	**0**	**–4**	**6**	**0**	**1**	**1**	**9**	**0**	**0**	**0**
1997-98	**Ottawa Senators**	**NHL**	**72**	**9**	**10**	**19**	**11**	**10**	**21**	**250**	**0**	**0**	**1**	**76**	**11.8**	**28**	**0**	**24**	**0**	**4**	**11**	**0**	**0**	**0**	**19**	**0**	**0**	**0**
1998-99	**Nashville Predators**	**NHL**	**76**	**5**	**11**	**16**	**6**	**11**	**17**	**218**	**1**	**0**	**0**	**66**	**7.6**	**28**	**2**	**29**	**0**	**–3**	....	....	....	....	....	....	....	....
99-2000	**Atlanta Thrashers**	**NHL**	**73**	**5**	**6**	**11**	**6**	**6**	**12**	***219**	**2**	**0**	**0**	**83**	**6.0**	**25**	**6**	**36**	**0**	**–17**	....	....	....	....	....	....	....	....
	NHL Totals		**347**	**24**	**54**	**78**	**29**	**52**	**81**	**963**	**3**	**0**	**2**	**325**	**7.4**	**124**	**9**	**134**	**0**		**17**	**0**	**1**	**1**	**28**	**0**	**0**	**0**

Signed as a free agent by **Anaheim**, August 16, 1993. Signed as a free agent by **Ottawa**, July 29, 1996. Claimed by **Nashville** from **Ottawa** in Expansion Draft, June 26, 1998. Traded to **Atlanta** by **Nashville** for the rights to Randy Robitaille, August 16, 1999.

• LAMBERT, Lane

Lane Douglas RW – R. 6', 185 lbs. b: Melfort, Sask., 11/18/1964. Detroit's 2nd, 25th overall, in 1983.

Season	Club	League	GP	G	A	Pts	AG	AA	APts	PIM	PP	SH	GW	S	%	TGF	PGF	TGA	PGA	+/–	GP	G	A	Pts	PIM	PP	SH	GW
1979-80	Swift Current Legionaires	SAHA	STATISTICS NOT AVAILABLE																									
1980-81	Swift Current Broncos	SJHL	55	43	54	97	....	....	....	63	....	....	....	....	....	....	....	....	....	....	....	....	....	....	....	....	....	....
1981-82	Saskatoon Blades	WHL	72	45	69	114	....	....	....	111	....	....	....	....	....	....	....	....	....	....	5	1	1	2	25	....	....	....
1982-83	Saskatoon Blades	WHL	64	59	60	119	....	....	....	126	....	....	....	....	....	....	....	....	....	....	6	4	3	7	7	....	....	....
1983-84	**Detroit Red Wings**	**NHL**	**73**	**20**	**15**	**35**	**16**	**10**	**26**	**115**	**1**	**0**	**2**	**88**	**22.7**	**59**	**6**	**58**	**0**	**–5**	**4**	**0**	**0**	**0**	**10**	**0**	**0**	**0**
1984-85	**Detroit Red Wings**	**NHL**	**69**	**14**	**11**	**25**	**11**	**7**	**18**	**104**	**0**	**0**	**1**	**69**	**20.3**	**44**	**1**	**46**	**0**	**–3**	....	....	....	....	....	....	....	....
1985-86	**Detroit Red Wings**	**NHL**	**34**	**2**	**3**	**5**	**2**	**2**	**4**	**130**	**0**	**0**	**0**	**32**	**6.3**	**15**	**1**	**42**	**17**	**–11**	....	....	....	....	....	....	....	....
	Adirondack Red Wings	AHL	45	16	25	41	....	....	....	69	....	....	....	....	....	....	....	....	....	....	16	5	5	10	9	....	....	....
1986-87	**New York Rangers**	**NHL**	**18**	**2**	**2**	**4**	**2**	**1**	**3**	**33**	**0**	**0**	**1**	**14**	**14.3**	**7**	**0**	**5**	**0**	**2**	....	....	....	....	....	....	....	....
	New Haven Nighthawks	AHL	11	3	3	6	....	....	....	19	....	....	....	....	....	....	....	....	....	....	....	....	....	....	....	....	....	....
	Quebec Nordiques	**NHL**	**15**	**5**	**5**	**10**	**4**	**4**	**8**	**18**	**0**	**0**	**0**	**29**	**17.2**	**17**	**0**	**18**	**0**	**–1**	**13**	**2**	**4**	**6**	**30**	**0**	**0**	**0**
1987-88	**Quebec Nordiques**	**NHL**	**61**	**13**	**28**	**41**	**11**	**20**	**31**	**98**	**0**	**0**	**2**	**98**	**13.3**	**53**	**10**	**52**	**9**	**0**	....	....	....	....	....	....	....	....
1988-89	**Quebec Nordiques**	**NHL**	**13**	**2**	**2**	**4**	**2**	**1**	**3**	**23**	**0**	**0**	**0**	**19**	**10.5**	**4**	**1**	**9**	**4**	**–2**	....	....	....	....	....	....	....	....
	Halifax Citadels	AHL	59	25	35	60	....	....	....	162	....	....	....	....	....	....	....	....	....	....	4	0	2	2	2	....	....	....
1989-90	Canada	Nat-Team	54	28	36	64	....	....	....	48	....	....	....	....	....	....	....	....	....	....	....	....	....	....	....	....	....	....
	Dusseldorfer EG	Germany	6	2	6	8	....	....	....	4	....	....	....	....	....	....	....	....	....	....	....	....	....	....	....	....	....	....
1990-91	HC Ajoie	Switz-2	36	40	45	85	....	....	....	82	....	....	....	....	....	....	....	....	....	....	10	11	7	18	30	....	....	....
	Canada	Nat-Team	4	0	1	1	....	....	....	0	....	....	....	....	....	....	....	....	....	....	....	....	....	....	....	....	....	....
1991-92	HC Ajoie	Switz-2	35	50	38	88	....	....	....	123	....	....	....	....	....	....	....	....	....	....	9	10	5	15	14	....	....	....
	Canada	Nat-Team	4	4	2	6	....	....	....	0	....	....	....	....	....	....	....	....	....	....	....	....	....	....	....	....	....	....
1992-93	HC Ajoie	Switz.	25	22	16	38	....	....	....	28	....	....	....	....	....	....	....	....	....	....	4	3	1	4	8	....	....	....
1993-94	HC La Chaux-de-Fonds	Switz-2	36	*39	29	68	....	....	....	62	....	....	....	....	....	....	....	....	....	....	5	5	2	7	8	....	....	....

			REGULAR SEASON																		PLAYOFFS							
Season	Club	League	GP	G	A	Pts	AG	AA	APts	PIM	PP	SH	GW	S	%	TGF	PGF	TGA	PGA	+/–	GP	G	A	Pts	PIM	PP	SH	GW
1994-95	HC Langnau	Switz-2	36	37	44	81	....	....	....	60	....	....	....	....	....	....	....	....	....	....	7	5	4	9	33	....	....	....
1995-96	HC Langnau	Switz-2	33	*39	40	*79	....	....	....	64	....	....	....	....	....	....	....	....	....	....	8	7	4	11	14	....	....	....
1996-97	Cleveland Lumberjacks	IHL	75	24	20	44	....	....	....	94	....	....	....	....	....	....	....	....	....	....	13	4	5	9	21	....	....	....
1997-98	Cleveland Lumberjacks	IHL	39	4	10	14	....	....	....	60	....	....	....	....	....	....	....	....	....	....	3	0	0	0	0	....	....	....
1998-99	Cleveland Lumberjacks	IHL	36	8	10	18	....	....	....	61	....	....	....	....	....	....	....	....	....	....	....	....	....	....	....	....	....	....
	Houston Aeros	IHL	9	2	1	3	....	....	....	4	....	....	....	....	....	....	....	....	....	....	19	4	1	5	26	....	....	....
99-2000	Houston Aeros	IHL	77	21	9	30	....	....	....	88	....	....	....	....	....	....	....	....	....	....	7	2	1	3	10	....	....	....
	NHL Totals		**283**	**58**	**66**	**124**	**48**	**45**	**93**	**521**	**1**	**0**	**6**	**349**	**16.6**	**199**	**19**	**230**	**30**		**17**	**2**	**4**	**6**	**40**	**0**	**0**	**0**

WHL Second All-Star Team (1983)

Traded to **NY Rangers** by **Detroit** with Kelly Kisio, Jim Leavins and Detroit's 5th round choice (later traded to Winnipeg–Winnipeg selected Benoit LeBeau) in 1988 Entry Draft for Glen Hanlon and NY Rangers' 3rd round choices in 1987 (Dennis Holland) and 1998 (Guy Dupuis) Entry Drafts, July 29, 1986. Traded to **Quebec** by **NY Rangers** for Pat Price, March 5, 1987. Traded to **Houston** (IHL) by **Cleveland** (IHL) for cash, March 24, 1999.

• LAMBERT, Yvon

Yvon Pierre LW – L. 6'2", 200 lbs. b: Drummondville, Que., 5/20/1950. Detroit's 3rd, 40th overall, in 1970.

Season	Club	League	GP	G	A	Pts	AG	AA	APts	PIM	PP	SH	GW	S	%	TGF	PGF	TGA	PGA	+/–	GP	G	A	Pts	PIM	PP	SH	GW
1969-70	Drummondville Rangers	QJHL	52	50	51	101	....	....	....	89	....	....	....	....	....	....	....	....	....	....	6	7	4	11	6	....	....	....
1970-71	Port Huron Flags	IHL	65	23	18	41	....	....	....	81	....	....	....	....	....	....	....	....	....	....	14	8	1	9	32	....	....	....
1971-72	Nova Scotia Voyageurs	AHL	67	18	21	39	....	....	....	116	....	....	....	....	....	....	....	....	....	....	15	4	4	8	28	....	....	....
1972-73	**Montreal Canadiens**	**NHL**	**1**	**0**	**0**	**0**	**0**	**0**	**0**	**0**	**0**	**0**	**0**	**1**	**0.0**	**0**	**0**	**0**	**0**	**0**	....	....	....	....	....	....	....	....
	Nova Scotia Voyageurs	AHL	76	*52	52	*104	....	....	....	84	....	....	....	....	....	....	....	....	....	....	13	9	9	18	32	....	....	....
1973-74	**Montreal Canadiens**	**NHL**	**60**	**6**	**10**	**16**	**6**	**8**	**14**	**42**	**0**	**0**	**0**	**34**	**17.6**	**24**	**0**	**19**	**0**	**5**	**5**	**0**	**0**	**0**	**7**	**0**	**0**	**0**
1974-75	**Montreal Canadiens**	**NHL**	**80**	**32**	**35**	**67**	**28**	**26**	**54**	**74**	**10**	**0**	**3**	**150**	**21.3**	**122**	**47**	**49**	**0**	**26**	**11**	**4**	**2**	**6**	**0**	**2**	**0**	**0**
1975-76♦	**Montreal Canadiens**	**NHL**	**80**	**32**	**35**	**67**	**28**	**26**	**54**	**28**	**12**	**0**	**4**	**156**	**20.5**	**99**	**39**	**50**	**0**	**10**	**12**	**2**	**3**	**5**	**18**	**0**	**0**	**1**
1976-77♦	**Montreal Canadiens**	**NHL**	**79**	**24**	**28**	**52**	**22**	**22**	**44**	**50**	**2**	**0**	**5**	**128**	**18.8**	**91**	**19**	**42**	**0**	**30**	**14**	**3**	**3**	**6**	**12**	**1**	**0**	**0**
1977-78♦	**Montreal Canadiens**	**NHL**	**77**	**18**	**22**	**40**	**16**	**17**	**33**	**20**	**7**	**0**	**3**	**107**	**16.8**	**64**	**19**	**39**	**4**	**10**	**15**	**2**	**4**	**6**	**6**	**1**	**0**	**1**
1978-79♦	**Montreal Canadiens**	**NHL**	**79**	**26**	**40**	**66**	**22**	**29**	**51**	**26**	**5**	**1**	**7**	**133**	**19.5**	**111**	**30**	**55**	**4**	**30**	**16**	**5**	**6**	**11**	**16**	**2**	**0**	**1**
1979-80	**Montreal Canadiens**	**NHL**	**77**	**21**	**32**	**53**	**18**	**23**	**41**	**23**	**7**	**0**	**7**	**104**	**20.2**	**80**	**22**	**72**	**17**	**3**	**10**	**8**	**4**	**12**	**4**	**1**	**0**	**1**
1980-81	**Montreal Canadiens**	**NHL**	**73**	**22**	**32**	**54**	**17**	**21**	**38**	**39**	**4**	**0**	**3**	**117**	**18.8**	**85**	**24**	**61**	**7**	**7**	**3**	**0**	**0**	**0**	**2**	**0**	**0**	**0**
1981-82	**Buffalo Sabres**	**NHL**	**77**	**25**	**39**	**64**	**20**	**26**	**46**	**38**	**14**	**0**	**4**	**108**	**23.1**	**102**	**31**	**49**	**0**	**22**	**4**	**3**	**0**	**3**	**2**	**1**	**0**	**0**
1982-83	Rochester Americans	AHL	79	26	22	48	....	....	....	10	....	....	....	....	....	....	....	....	....	....	12	2	4	6	2	....	....	....
1983-84	Rochester Americans	AHL	79	27	43	70	....	....	....	14	....	....	....	....	....	....	....	....	....	....	18	8	11	19	2	....	....	....
1984-85	Verdun Jr. Canadiens	QMJHL	DID NOT PLAY – COACHING																									
	NHL Totals		**683**	**206**	**273**	**479**	**177**	**198**	**375**	**340**	**61**	**1**	**36**	**1038**	**19.8**	**778**	**231**	**436**	**32**		**90**	**27**	**22**	**49**	**67**	**8**	**0**	**4**

AHL First All-Star Team (1973) • Won John B. Sollenberger Trophy (Top Scorer - AHL) (1973)

Claimed by **Montreal** from **Detroit** (Port Huron-IHL) in Reverse Draft, June 9, 1971. Claimed by **Buffalo** from **Montreal** in Waiver Draft, October 5, 1981.

• LAMBY, Dick

Richard A. D – R. 6'1", 200 lbs. b: Auburn, MA, 5/3/1955. St. Louis' 7th, 135th overall, in 1975.

Season	Club	League	GP	G	A	Pts	AG	AA	APts	PIM	PP	SH	GW	S	%	TGF	PGF	TGA	PGA	+/–	GP	G	A	Pts	PIM	PP	SH	GW
1974-75	Salem State University	ECAC-2	26	25	32	57	....	....	....	54	....	....	....	....	....	....	....	....	....	....	....	....	....	....	....	....	....	....
1975-76	United States	Nat-Team	63	12	35	47	....	....	....	146	....	....	....	....	....	....	....	....	....	....	....	....	....	....	....	....	....	....
	United States	Olympics	6	0	2	2	....	....	....	12	....	....	....	....	....	....	....	....	....	....	....	....	....	....	....	....	....	....
1976-77	Boston University	ECAC	24	9	36	45	....	....	....	44	....	....	....	....	....	....	....	....	....	....	....	....	....	....	....	....	....	....
1977-78	Boston University	ECAC	30	15	44	59	....	....	....	64	....	....	....	....	....	....	....	....	....	....	....	....	....	....	....	....	....	....
	United States	WEC-A	7	0	2	2	....	....	....	20	....	....	....	....	....	....	....	....	....	....	....	....	....	....	....	....	....	....
1978-79	**St. Louis Blues**	**NHL**	**9**	**0**	**4**	**4**	**0**	**3**	**3**	**12**	**0**	**0**	**0**	**11**	**0.0**	**18**	**1**	**14**	**2**	**5**	....	....	....	....	....	....	....	....
	Salt Lake Golden Eagles	CHL	60	4	15	19	....	....	....	122	....	....	....	....	....	....	....	....	....	....	10	2	5	7	21	....	....	....
1979-80	**St. Louis Blues**	**NHL**	**12**	**0**	**1**	**1**	**0**	**1**	**1**	**10**	**0**	**0**	**0**	**12**	**0.0**	**9**	**0**	**17**	**1**	**–7**	....	....	....	....	....	....	....	....
	Salt Lake Golden Eagles	CHL	49	3	14	17	....	....	....	93	....	....	....	....	....	....	....	....	....	....	....	....	....	....	....	....	....	....
1980-81	**St. Louis Blues**	**NHL**	**1**	**0**	**0**	**0**	**0**	**0**	**0**	**0**	**0**	**0**	**0**	**2**	**0.0**	**1**	**0**	**2**	**0**	**–1**	....	....	....	....	....	....	....	....
	Salt Lake Golden Eagles	CHL	53	7	30	37	....	....	....	74	....	....	....	....	....	....	....	....	....	....	14	1	5	6	23	....	....	....
1981-82	Fort Worth Texans	CHL	31	4	6	10	....	....	....	41	....	....	....	....	....	....	....	....	....	....	....	....	....	....	....	....	....	....
	Dallas Black Hawks	CHL	22	0	7	7	....	....	....	53	....	....	....	....	....	....	....	....	....	....	....	....	....	....	....	....	....	....
	Muskegon Mohawks	IHL	16	2	5	7	....	....	....	25	....	....	....	....	....	....	....	....	....	....	....	....	....	....	....	....	....	....
	NHL Totals		**22**	**0**	**5**	**5**	**0**	**4**	**4**	**22**	**0**	**0**	**0**	**25**	**0.0**	**28**	**1**	**33**	**3**		....	....	....	....	....	....	....	....

NCAA (College Div.) East All-American Team (1974, 1975) • ECAC Second All-Star Team (1978) • NCAA Championship All-Tournament Team (1978)

Traded to **Colorado** by **St. Louis** with Joe Micheletti for Bill Baker, December 4, 1981.

• LAMMENS, Hank

Hank Jacob D – L. 6'2", 210 lbs. b: Brockville, Ont., 2/21/1966. NY Islanders' 10th, 160th overall, in 1985.

Season	Club	League	GP	G	A	Pts	AG	AA	APts	PIM	PP	SH	GW	S	%	TGF	PGF	TGA	PGA	+/–	GP	G	A	Pts	PIM	PP	SH	GW
1982-83	Brockville Braves	OJHL	48	2	15	17	....	....	....	28	....	....	....	....	....	....	....	....	....	....	....	....	....	....	....	....	....	....
1983-84	Brockville Braves	OJHL	46	7	11	18	....	....	....	106	....	....	....	....	....	....	....	....	....	....	....	....	....	....	....	....	....	....
1984-85	St. Lawrence University	ECAC	21	17	9	26	....	....	....	16	....	....	....	....	....	....	....	....	....	....	....	....	....	....	....	....	....	....
1985-86	St. Lawrence University	ECAC	30	3	14	17	....	....	....	60	....	....	....	....	....	....	....	....	....	....	....	....	....	....	....	....	....	....
1986-87	St. Lawrence University	ECAC	35	6	13	19	....	....	....	92	....	....	....	....	....	....	....	....	....	....	....	....	....	....	....	....	....	....
1987-88	St. Lawrence University	ECAC	32	3	6	9	....	....	....	64	....	....	....	....	....	....	....	....	....	....	....	....	....	....	....	....	....	....
1988-89	Springfield Indians	AHL	69	1	13	14	....	....	....	55	....	....	....	....	....	....	....	....	....	....	....	....	....	....	....	....	....	....
1989-90	Springfield Indians	AHL	43	0	6	6	....	....	....	27	....	....	....	....	....	....	....	....	....	....	....	....	....	....	....	....	....	....
1990-91	Capital District Islanders	AHL	32	0	5	5	....	....	....	14	....	....	....	....	....	....	....	....	....	....	....	....	....	....	....	....	....	....
	Kansas City Blades	IHL	17	0	1	1	....	....	....	27	....	....	....	....	....	....	....	....	....	....	....	....	....	....	....	....	....	....
1991-92			DID NOT PLAY																									
1992-93	Canada	Nat-Team	64	8	14	22	....	....	....	83	....	....	....	....	....	....	....	....	....	....	....	....	....	....	....	....	....	....
1993-94	**Ottawa Senators**	**NHL**	**27**	**1**	**2**	**3**	**1**	**2**	**3**	**22**	**0**	**0**	**0**	**6**	**16.7**	**10**	**0**	**50**	**20**	**–20**	....	....	....	....	....	....	....	....
	P.E.I. Senators	AHL	50	2	9	11	....	....	....	32	....	....	....	....	....	....	....	....	....	....	....	....	....	....	....	....	....	....
	NHL Totals		**27**	**1**	**2**	**3**	**1**	**2**	**3**	**22**	**0**	**0**	**0**	**6**	**16.7**	**10**	**0**	**50**	**20**		....	....	....	....	....	....	....	....

ECAC Second All-Star Team (1987, 1988)

• Missed entire 1991-92 season training for the 1992 Summer Olympic Games. Signed as a free agent by **Ottawa**, June 25, 1993.

• LAMOUREUX, Mitch

C – L. 5'6", 175 lbs. b: Ottawa, Ont., 8/22/1962. Pittsburgh's 7th, 154th overall, in 1981.

Season	Club	League	GP	G	A	Pts	AG	AA	APts	PIM	PP	SH	GW	S	%	TGF	PGF	TGA	PGA	+/–	GP	G	A	Pts	PIM	PP	SH	GW
1978-79	Gloucester Rangers	OJHL	21	21	16	37	....	....	....	....	....	....	....	....	....	....	....	....	....	....	....	....	....	....	....	....	....	....
1979-80	Oshawa Generals	OMJHL	67	28	48	76	....	....	....	63	....	....	....	....	....	....	....	....	....	....	7	2	1	3	16	....	....	....
1980-81	Oshawa Generals	OMJHL	63	50	69	119	....	....	....	256	....	....	....	....	....	....	....	....	....	....	11	11	13	24	57	....	....	....
1981-82	Oshawa Generals	OHL	66	43	78	121	....	....	....	275	....	....	....	....	....	....	....	....	....	....	12	4	17	21	68	....	....	....
1982-83	Baltimore Skipjacks	AHL	80	57	50	107	....	....	....	107	....	....	....	....	....	....	....	....	....	....	....	....	....	....	....	....	....	....
1983-84	**Pittsburgh Penguins**	**NHL**	**8**	**1**	**1**	**2**	**1**	**1**	**2**	**6**	**0**	**0**	**0**	**13**	**7.7**	**4**	**1**	**10**	**1**	**–6**	....	....	....	....	....	....	....	....
	Baltimore Skipjacks	AHL	68	30	38	68	....	....	....	136	....	....	....	....	....	....	....	....	....	....	9	1	3	4	2	....	....	....
1984-85	**Pittsburgh Penguins**	**NHL**	**62**	**10**	**8**	**18**	**8**	**5**	**13**	**53**	**0**	**2**	**0**	**81**	**12.3**	**21**	**0**	**50**	**20**	**–9**	....	....	....	....	....	....	....	....
	Baltimore Skipjacks	AHL	18	10	14	24	....	....	....	34	....	....	....	....	....	....	....	....	....	....	....	....	....	....	....	....	....	....
1985-86	Baltimore Skipjacks	AHL	75	22	31	53	....	....	....	129	....	....	....	....	....	....	....	....	....	....	....	....	....	....	....	....	....	....
1986-87	Hershey Bears	AHL	78	43	46	89	....	....	....	122	....	....	....	....	....	....	....	....	....	....	5	1	2	3	8	....	....	....
1987-88	**Philadelphia Flyers**	**NHL**	**3**	**0**	**0**	**0**	**0**	**0**	**0**	**0**	**0**	**0**	**0**	**1**	**0.0**	**0**	**0**	**1**	**0**	**–1**	....	....	....	....	....	....	....	....
	Hershey Bears	AHL	78	35	52	87	....	....	....	171	....	....	....	....	....	....	....	....	....	....	12	9	7	*16	48	....	....	....
1988-89	HC Asiago	Italy	8	9	8	17	....	....	....	16	....	....	....	....	....	....	....	....	....	....	....	....	....	....	....	....	....	....
	Hershey Bears	AHL	9	9	7	16	....	....	....	14	....	....	....	....	....	....	....	....	....	....	9	1	4	5	14	....	....	....
1989-90	Canada	Nat-Team	4	1	2	3	....	....	....	6	....	....	....	....	....	....	....	....	....	....	....	....	....	....	....	....	....	....
	Maine Mariners	AHL	10	4	7	11	....	....	....	10	....	....	....	....	....	....	....	....	....	....	....	....	....	....	....	....	....	....
1990-91	EK Zell-am-Zee	Alpenliga	18	20	17	37	....	....	....	45	....	....	....	....	....	....	....	....	....	....	....	....	....	....	....	....	....	....
	EK Zell-am-Zee	Austria	24	16	27	43	....	....	....	18	....	....	....	....	....	....	....	....	....	....	....	....	....	....	....	....	....	....
1991-92	EV Lyss	Switz-2	25	29	27	56	....	....	....	....	....	....	....	....	....	....	....	....	....	....	....	....	....	....	....	....	....	....
	HC Allegne	Italy	2	1	3	4	....	....	....	0	....	....	....	....	....	....	....	....	....	....	9	11	8	19	12	....	....	....
1992-93	San Diego Gulls	IHL	71	28	39	67	....	....	....	130	....	....	....	....	....	....	....	....	....	....	4	0	0	0	11	....	....	....

			REGULAR SEASON																		PLAYOFFS							
Season	Club	League	GP	G	A	Pts	AG	AA	APts	PIM	PP	SH	GW	S	%	TGF	PGF	TGA	PGA	+/–	GP	G	A	Pts	PIM	PP	SH	GW
1993-94	Hershey Bears	AHL	80	45	60	105				92											11	3	4	7	26			
1994-95	Hershey Bears	AHL	76	39	46	85				112											6	0	2	2	8			
1995-96	Providence Bruins	AHL	63	22	29	51				62											4	2	3	5	2			
1996-97	Providence Bruins	AHL	75	25	29	54				70											3	0	0	0	4			
1997-98	Binghamton Icemen	UHL	16	18	15	33				10																		
	Hershey Bears	AHL	22	4	9	13				22											7	2	4	6	12			
1998-99	Hershey Bears	AHL	70	19	34	53				58											4	1	2	3	4			
	NHL Totals		**73**	**11**	**9**	**20**	**9**	**6**	**15**	**59**	**0**	**2**	**0**	**95**	**11.6**	**25**	**1**	**61**	**21**									

AHL Second All-Star Team (1983) • Won Dudley "Red" Garrett Memorial Award (Top Rookie - AHL) (1983) • Won Fred Hunt Memorial Trophy (Sportsmanship - AHL) (1999)

Signed as a free agent by **Philadelphia**, June 30, 1986. Signed as a free agent by **Hershey** (AHL), January 7, 1998. • Officially announced retirement to become Director of Hockey Operations for the United Hockey League, August 2, 1999.

• LAMPMAN, Mike

Michael David LW – L. 6'2", 195 lbs. b: Lakewood, CA, 4/20/1950. St. Louis' 10th, 111th overall, in 1970.

Season	Club	League	GP	G	A	Pts	AG	AA	APts	PIM	PP	SH	GW	S	%	TGF	PGF	TGA	PGA	+/–	GP	G	A	Pts	PIM	PP	SH	GW
1967-68	Marquette Iron Rangers	USHL	25	5	5	10				20																		
1968-69	University of Denver	WCHA	DID NOT PLAY – FRESHMAN																									
1969-70	University of Denver	WCHA	28	12	5	17				32																		
1970-71	University of Denver	WCHA	36	24	18	42				77																		
1971-72	University of Denver	WCHA	36	30	13	43				38																		
1972-73	**St. Louis Blues**	**NHL**	**18**	**2**	**3**	**5**	**2**	**2**	**4**	**2**	**0**	**0**	**0**	**18**	**11.1**	**9**	**2**	**3**	**0**	**4**								
	Denver Spurs	WHL	49	34	19	53				88											5	0	3	3	0			
1973-74	**St. Louis Blues**	**NHL**	**15**	**1**	**0**	**1**	**1**	**0**	**1**	**0**	**1**	**0**	**0**	**19**	**5.3**	**5**	**1**	**3**	**0**	**1**								
	Denver Spurs	WHL	5	5	6	11				4																		
	Vancouver Canucks	**NHL**	**14**	**1**	**0**	**1**	**1**	**0**	**1**	**0**	**0**	**0**	**0**	**17**	**5.9**	**5**	**0**	**15**	**0**	**–10**								
	Seattle Totems	WHL	30	8	14	22				13																		
1974-75	Richmond Robins	AHL	36	4	5	9				35											6	1	2	3	8			
1975-76	**Washington Capitals**	**NHL**	**27**	**7**	**12**	**19**	**6**	**9**	**15**	**28**	**0**	**0**	**1**	**55**	**12.7**	**23**	**3**	**27**	**1**	**–6**								
	Baltimore Clippers	AHL	35	13	24	37				24																		
1976-77	**Washington Capitals**	**NHL**	**22**	**6**	**5**	**11**	**5**	**4**	**9**	**4**	**1**	**0**	**0**	**47**	**12.8**	**16**	**2**	**18**	**0**	**–4**								
	NHL Totals		**96**	**17**	**20**	**37**	**15**	**15**	**30**	**34**	**2**	**0**	**1**	**156**	**10.9**	**58**	**8**	**66**	**1**									

WHL Second All-Star Team (1973)

Traded to **Vancouver** by **St. Louis** for John Wright, December 10, 1973. Claimed by **Washington** from **Vancouver** in Expansion Draft, June 12, 1974. • Suffered career-ending head injury in game vs. Cleveland, December 30, 1976.

• LANDON, Larry

Larry James RW – R. 6', 191 lbs. b: Niagara Falls, Ont., 5/4/1958. Montreal's 10th, 137th overall, in 1978.

Season	Club	League	GP	G	A	Pts	AG	AA	APts	PIM	PP	SH	GW	S	%	TGF	PGF	TGA	PGA	+/–	GP	G	A	Pts	PIM	PP	SH	GW
1975-76	Niagara Falls Canucks	OHA-B	48	56	56	112																						
	St. Catharines Fincups	OMJHL	16	1	1	2				2																		
1976-77	Niagara Falls Canucks	OHA-B	32	20	28	48																						
1977-78	RPI Engineers	ECAC	29	13	22	35				18																		
1978-79	RPI Engineers	ECAC	28	18	27	45				12																		
1979-80	RPI Engineers	ECAC	28	20	27	47				14																		
1980-81	RPI Engineers	ECAC	28	13	17	30				27																		
	Nova Scotia Voyageurs	AHL	2	0	0	0				0											2	0	0	0	0			
1981-82	Nova Scotia Voyageurs	AHL	69	11	15	26				31											8	1	0	1	6			
1982-83	Nova Scotia Voyageurs	AHL	68	18	25	43				43											7	2	0	2	0			
1983-84	**Montreal Canadiens**	**NHL**	**2**	**0**	**0**	**0**	**0**	**0**	**0**	**0**	**0**	**0**	**0**	**5**	**0.0**	**2**	**0**	**0**	**0**	**2**								
	Nova Scotia Voyageurs	AHL	79	26	30	56				19											12	7	2	9	2			
1984-85	Sherbrooke Canadiens	AHL	21	7	9	16				2																		
	Toronto Maple Leafs	**NHL**	**7**	**0**	**0**	**0**	**0**	**0**	**0**	**2**	**0**	**0**	**0**	**5**	**0.0**	**2**	**0**	**7**	**1**	**–4**								
	St. Catharines Saints	AHL	44	21	36	57				8																		
	NHL Totals		**9**	**0**	**0**	**0**	**0**	**0**	**0**	**2**	**0**	**0**	**0**	**10**	**0.0**	**4**	**0**	**7**	**1**									

Traded to **Toronto** by **Montreal** for Gaston Gingras, February 14, 1985.

• LANDRY, Eric

C – L. 5'11", 185 lbs. b: Gatineau, Que., 1/20/1975.

Season	Club	League	GP	G	A	Pts	AG	AA	APts	PIM	PP	SH	GW	S	%	TGF	PGF	TGA	PGA	+/–	GP	G	A	Pts	PIM	PP	SH	GW
1993-94	St-Hyacinthe Laser	QMJHL	69	42	34	76				128											7	4	2	6	13			
1994-95	St-Hyacinthe Laser	QMJHL	68	38	36	74				249											5	2	1	3	10			
1995-96	Cape Breton Oilers	AHL	74	19	33	52				187																		
1996-97	Hamilton Bulldogs	AHL	74	15	17	32				139											22	6	7	13	43			
1997-98	**Calgary Flames**	**NHL**	**12**	**1**	**0**	**1**	**1**	**0**	**1**	**4**	**0**	**0**	**0**	**7**	**14.3**	**3**	**0**	**8**	**3**	**–2**								
	Saint John Flames	AHL	61	17	21	38				194											20	4	6	10	58			
	United States	WC-A	2	0	0	0				0																		
1998-99	**Calgary Flames**	**NHL**	**3**	**0**	**1**	**1**	**0**	**1**	**1**	**0**	**0**	**0**	**0**	**1**	**0.0**	**1**	**0**	**0**	**0**	**1**								
	Saint John Flames	AHL	56	19	22	41				158											7	2	5	7	12			
99-2000	Kentucky Thoroughblades	AHL	79	35	31	66				170											9	3	6	9	2			
	NHL Totals		**15**	**1**	**1**	**2**	**1**	**1**	**2**	**4**	**0**	**0**	**0**	**8**	**12.5**	**4**	**0**	**8**	**3**									

Signed as a free agent by **Calgary**, August 20, 1997. Traded to **San Jose** by **Calgary** for Fredrik Oduya, July 12, 1999. Signed as a free agent by **Montreal**, July 7, 2000.

• LANE, Gord

Gordon T. D – L. 6'1", 190 lbs. b: Brandon, Man., 3/31/1953. Pittsburgh's 9th, 134th overall, in 1973.

Season	Club	League	GP	G	A	Pts	AG	AA	APts	PIM	PP	SH	GW	S	%	TGF	PGF	TGA	PGA	+/–	GP	G	A	Pts	PIM	PP	SH	GW
1970-71	Brandon Wheat Kings	WCJHL	20	0	4	4				53																		
1971-72	Brandon Wheat Kings	WCJHL	63	7	16	23				106											11	1	2	3	19			
1972-73	New Westminster Bruins	WCJHL	36	2	13	15				115											5	0	0	0	29			
1973-74	Fort Wayne Komets	IHL	67	1	14	15				214											4	0	1	1	27			
1974-75	Dayton Gems	IHL	50	6	10	16				225											14	1	3	4	31			
1975-76	**Washington Capitals**	**NHL**	**3**	**1**	**0**	**1**	**1**	**0**	**1**	**12**	**1**	**0**	**0**	**2**	**50.0**	**2**	**1**	**6**	**0**	**–5**								
	Hampton Gulls	SHL	12	1	7	8				58																		
	Dayton Gems	IHL	55	12	22	34				227											15	0	11	11	85			
1976-77	**Washington Capitals**	**NHL**	**80**	**2**	**15**	**17**	**2**	**12**	**14**	**207**	**0**	**0**	**0**	**59**	**3.4**	**60**	**1**	**105**	**21**	**–25**								
1977-78	**Washington Capitals**	**NHL**	**69**	**2**	**9**	**11**	**2**	**7**	**9**	**195**	**0**	**0**	**0**	**68**	**2.9**	**40**	**0**	**80**	**21**	**–19**								
	Hershey Bears	AHL	4	0	1	1				8																		
1978-79	**Washington Capitals**	**NHL**	**64**	**3**	**15**	**18**	**3**	**11**	**14**	**147**	**0**	**0**	**0**	**69**	**4.3**	**54**	**1**	**91**	**23**	**–15**								
	Hershey Bears	AHL	5	0	1	1				48																		
1979-80	**Washington Capitals**	**NHL**	**19**	**2**	**4**	**6**	**2**	**3**	**5**	**53**	**0**	**0**	**0**	**16**	**12.5**	**15**	**0**	**21**	**7**	**1**								
♦	**New York Islanders**	**NHL**	**55**	**2**	**14**	**16**	**2**	**10**	**12**	**152**	**0**	**0**	**1**	**60**	**3.3**	**56**	**1**	**57**	**12**	**10**	**21**	**1**	**3**	**4**	***85**	**0**	**0**	**0**
1980-81 ♦	**New York Islanders**	**NHL**	**60**	**3**	**9**	**12**	**2**	**6**	**8**	**124**	**0**	**1**	**1**	**54**	**5.6**	**48**	**1**	**63**	**10**	**–6**	**12**	**1**	**5**	**6**	**32**	**0**	**0**	**0**
1981-82 ♦	**New York Islanders**	**NHL**	**51**	**0**	**13**	**13**	**0**	**9**	**9**	**98**	**0**	**0**	**0**	**46**	**0.0**	**55**	**0**	**34**	**5**	**26**	**19**	**0**	**4**	**4**	**61**	**0**	**0**	**0**
1982-83 ♦	**New York Islanders**	**NHL**	**44**	**3**	**4**	**7**	**2**	**3**	**5**	**87**	**0**	**0**	**0**	**44**	**6.8**	**25**	**0**	**31**	**7**	**1**	**18**	**1**	**2**	**3**	**32**	**0**	**0**	**1**
1983-84	**New York Islanders**	**NHL**	**37**	**0**	**3**	**3**	**0**	**2**	**2**	**70**	**0**	**0**	**0**	**16**	**0.0**	**33**	**0**	**31**	**4**	**6**	**4**	**0**	**0**	**0**	**2**	**0**	**0**	**0**
1984-85	**New York Islanders**	**NHL**	**57**	**1**	**8**	**9**	**1**	**5**	**6**	**83**	**0**	**0**	**0**	**21**	**4.8**	**45**	**0**	**44**	**9**	**10**	**1**	**0**	**0**	**0**	**2**	**0**	**0**	**0**
1985-86	Brandon Wheat Kings	WHL	DID NOT PLAY – COACHING																									
1986-87	Springfield Indians	AHL	62	2	6	8				117																		
1987-88	Springfield Indians	AHL	DID NOT PLAY – COACHING																									
	NHL Totals		**539**	**19**	**94**	**113**	**17**	**68**	**85**	**1228**	**1**	**1**	**2**	**455**	**4.2**	**433**	**5**	**563**	**119**		**75**	**3**	**14**	**17**	**214**	**0**	**0**	**1**

Signed as a free agent by **Washington**, October 5, 1976. Traded to **NY Islanders** by **Washington** for Mike Kaszycki, December 7, 1979.

• LANG, Robert

C – R. 6'2", 216 lbs. b: Teplice, Czech., 12/19/1970. Los Angeles' 6th, 133rd overall, in 1990.

Season	Club	League	GP	G	A	Pts	AG	AA	APts	PIM	PP	SH	GW	S	%	TGF	PGF	TGA	PGA	+/–	GP	G	A	Pts	PIM	PP	SH	GW
1988-89	CHZ Litvinov	Czech.	7	3	2	5				0																		
1989-90	CHZ Litvinov	Czech.	32	8	7	15															8	3	3	6				
1990-91	CHZ Litvinov	Czech.	56	26	26	52				38																		

			REGULAR SEASON																		PLAYOFFS							
Season	Club	League	GP	G	A	Pts	AG	AA	APts	PIM	PP	SH	GW	S	%	TGF	PGF	TGA	PGA	+/–	GP	G	A	Pts	PIM	PP	SH	GW
1991-92	CHZ Litvinov	Czech.	43	12	31	43	....	....	....	34	....	....	....	....	....	....	....	....	....	....	....	....	....	....	....	....	....	....
	Czechoslovakia	Olympics	8	5	8	13	....	....	....	8	....	....	....	....	....	....	....	....	....	....	....	....	....	....	....	....	....	....
	Czechoslovakia	WC-A	8	2	2	4	....	....	....	2	....	....	....	....	....	....	....	....	....	....	....	....	....	....	....	....	....	....
1992-93	**Los Angeles Kings**	**NHL**	**11**	**0**	**5**	**5**	**0**	**3**	**3**	**2**	**0**	**0**	**0**	**3**	**0.0**	**6**	**0**	**9**	**0**	**–3**	....	....	....	....	....	....	....	....
	Phoenix Roadrunners	IHL	38	9	21	30	....	....	....	20	....	....	....	....	....	....	....	....	....	....	....	....	....	....	....	....	....	....
1993-94	**Los Angeles Kings**	**NHL**	**32**	**9**	**10**	**19**	**8**	**8**	**16**	**10**	**0**	**0**	**0**	**41**	**22.0**	**29**	**4**	**20**	**2**	**7**	....	....	....	....	....	....	....	....
	Phoenix Roadrunners	IHL	44	11	24	35	....	....	....	34	....	....	....	....	....	....	....	....	....	....	....	....	....	....	....	....	....	....
1994-95	CHZ Chemopetrol Litvinov	Czech-Rep	16	4	19	23	....	....	....	28	....	....	....	....	....	....	....	....	....	....	....	....	....	....	....	....	....	....
	Los Angeles Kings	**NHL**	**36**	**4**	**8**	**12**	**7**	**12**	**19**	**4**	**0**	**0**	**0**	**38**	**10.5**	**19**	**2**	**27**	**3**	**–7**	....	....	....	....	....	....	....	....
1995-96	**Los Angeles Kings**	**NHL**	**68**	**6**	**16**	**22**	**6**	**13**	**19**	**10**	**0**	**2**	**0**	**71**	**8.5**	**28**	**2**	**54**	**13**	**–15**	....	....	....	....	....	....	....	....
	Czech-Republic	WC-A	8	5	4	9	....	....	....	2	....	....	....	....	....	....	....	....	....	....	....	....	....	....	....	....	....	....
1996-97	Czech-Republic	W-Cup	3	0	0	0	....	....	....	2	....	....	....	....	....	....	....	....	....	....	....	....	....	....	....	....	....	....
	HC Sparta Praha	Czech-Rep	38	14	27	41	....	....	....	30	....	....	....	....	....	....	....	....	....	....	5	1	2	3	4	....	....	....
	HC Sparta Praha	EuroHL	4	2	2	4	....	....	....	0	....	....	....	....	....	....	....	....	....	....	4	2	1	3	2	....	....	....
	Czech-Republic	WC-A	8	1	1	2	....	....	....	25	....	....	....	....	....	....	....	....	....	....	....	....	....	....	....	....	....	....
1997-98	**Boston Bruins**	**NHL**	**3**	**0**	**0**	**0**	**0**	**0**	**0**	**2**	**0**	**0**	**0**	**2**	**0.0**	**1**	**0**	**0**	**0**	**1**	....	....	....	....	....	....	....	....
	Czech-Republic	Olympics	6	0	3	3	....	....	....	0	....	....	....	....	....	....	....	....	....	....	....	....	....	....	....	....	....	....
	Pittsburgh Penguins	**NHL**	**51**	**9**	**13**	**22**	**11**	**13**	**24**	**14**	**1**	**1**	**2**	**64**	**14.1**	**32**	**7**	**29**	**10**	**6**	**6**	**0**	**3**	**3**	**2**	**0**	**0**	**0**
	Houston Aeros	IHL	9	1	7	8	....	....	....	4	....	....	....	....	....	....	....	....	....	....	....	....	....	....	....	....	....	....
1998-99	**Pittsburgh Penguins**	**NHL**	**72**	**21**	**23**	**44**	**25**	**22**	**47**	**24**	**7**	**0**	**3**	**137**	**15.3**	**63**	**18**	**57**	**2**	**–10**	**12**	**0**	**2**	**2**	**0**	**0**	**0**	**0**
99-2000	**Pittsburgh Penguins**	**NHL**	**78**	**23**	**42**	**65**	**26**	**39**	**65**	**14**	**13**	**0**	**5**	**142**	**16.2**	**100**	**40**	**71**	**2**	**–9**	**11**	**3**	**3**	**6**	**0**	**2**	**0**	**0**
	NHL Totals		**351**	**72**	**117**	**189**	**83**	**110**	**193**	**80**	**21**	**3**	**10**	**498**	**14.5**	**278**	**73**	**267**	**32**		**29**	**3**	**8**	**11**	**2**	**2**	**0**	**0**

Signed as a free agent by **Pittsburgh**, September 2, 1997. Claimed by **Boston** from **Pittsburgh** in NHL Waiver Draft, September 28, 1997. Claimed on waivers by **Pittsburgh** from **Boston**, October 25, 1997.

• LANGDON, Darren

LW – L. 6'1", 200 lbs. b: Deer Lake, Nfld., 1/8/1971.

Season	Club	League	GP	G	A	Pts	AG	AA	APts	PIM	PP	SH	GW	S	%	TGF	PGF	TGA	PGA	+/–	GP	G	A	Pts	PIM	PP	SH	GW
1991-92	Summerside Lightning	MJrHL	44	34	49	83	....	....	....	441	....	....	....	....	....	....	....	....	....	....	....	....	....	....	....	....	....	....
1992-93	Binghamton Rangers	AHL	18	3	4	7	....	....	....	115	....	....	....	....	....	....	....	....	....	....	8	0	1	1	14	....	....	....
	Dayton Bombers	ECHL	54	23	22	45	....	....	....	429	....	....	....	....	....	....	....	....	....	....	3	0	1	1	40	....	....	....
1993-94	Binghamton Rangers	AHL	54	2	7	9	....	....	....	327	....	....	....	....	....	....	....	....	....	....	....	....	....	....	....	....	....	....
1994-95	Binghamton Rangers	AHL	55	6	14	20	....	....	....	296	....	....	....	....	....	....	....	....	....	....	11	1	3	4	*84	....	....	....
	New York Rangers	**NHL**	**18**	**1**	**1**	**2**	**2**	**1**	**3**	**62**	**0**	**0**	**0**	**6**	**16.7**	**5**	**0**	**5**	**0**	**0**	....	....	....	....	....	....	....	....
1995-96	**New York Rangers**	**NHL**	**64**	**7**	**4**	**11**	**7**	**3**	**10**	**175**	**0**	**0**	**1**	**29**	**24.1**	**12**	**0**	**10**	**0**	**2**	**2**	**0**	**0**	**0**	**0**	**0**	**0**	**0**
	Binghamton Rangers	AHL	1	0	0	0	....	....	....	12	....	....	....	....	....	....	....	....	....	....	....	....	....	....	....	....	....	....
1996-97	**New York Rangers**	**NHL**	**60**	**3**	**6**	**9**	**3**	**5**	**8**	**195**	**0**	**0**	**1**	**24**	**12.5**	**10**	**0**	**11**	**0**	**–1**	**10**	**0**	**0**	**0**	**2**	**0**	**0**	**0**
1997-98	**New York Rangers**	**NHL**	**70**	**3**	**3**	**6**	**4**	**3**	**7**	**197**	**0**	**0**	**0**	**15**	**20.0**	**9**	**0**	**9**	**0**	**0**	....	....	....	....	....	....	....	....
1998-99	**New York Rangers**	**NHL**	**44**	**0**	**0**	**0**	**0**	**0**	**0**	**80**	**0**	**0**	**0**	**8**	**0.0**	**3**	**0**	**6**	**0**	**–3**	....	....	....	....	....	....	....	....
99-2000	**New York Rangers**	**NHL**	**21**	**0**	**1**	**1**	**0**	**1**	**1**	**26**	**0**	**0**	**0**	**13**	**0.0**	**2**	**0**	**4**	**0**	**–2**	....	....	....	....	....	....	....	....
	NHL Totals		**277**	**14**	**15**	**29**	**16**	**13**	**29**	**735**	**0**	**0**	**2**	**95**	**14.7**	**41**	**0**	**45**	**0**		**12**	**0**	**0**	**0**	**2**	**0**	**0**	**0**

Signed as a free agent by **NY Rangers**, August 16, 1993. • Missed remainder of 1999-2000 season recovering from hernia injury suffered in game vs. New Jersey, December 1, 1999. Played w/ RHI's Anaheim Bullfrogs in 1994 (21-3-23-26-119).

• LANGDON, Steve

Stephen Murray LW – L. 5'11", 175 lbs. b: Toronto, Ont., 12/23/1953. Boston's 5th, 63rd overall, in 1973.

Season	Club	League	GP	G	A	Pts	AG	AA	APts	PIM	PP	SH	GW	S	%	TGF	PGF	TGA	PGA	+/–	GP	G	A	Pts	PIM	PP	SH	GW
1971-72	Toronto Marlboros	OMJHL	14	1	3	4	....	....	....	2	....	....	....	....	....	....	....	....	....	....	....	....	....	....	....	....	....	....
1972-73	London Knights	OMJHL	72	31	47	78	....	....	....	93	....	....	....	....	....	....	....	....	....	....	....	....	....	....	....	....	....	....
1973-74	Albuquerque 6-Guns	CHL	67	21	13	34	....	....	....	16	....	....	....	....	....	....	....	....	....	....	....	....	....	....	....	....	....	....
1974-75	**Boston Bruins**	**NHL**	**1**	**0**	**1**	**1**	**0**	**1**	**1**	**0**	**0**	**0**	**0**	**0**	**0.0**	**1**	**0**	**0**	**0**	**1**	....	....	....	....	....	....	....	....
	Rochester Americans	AHL	56	8	11	19	....	....	....	8	....	....	....	....	....	....	....	....	....	....	12	0	2	2	5	....	....	....
	Binghamton Dusters	NAHL	1	3	1	4	....	....	....	0	....	....	....	....	....	....	....	....	....	....	....	....	....	....	....	....	....	....
1975-76	**Boston Bruins**	**NHL**	**4**	**0**	**0**	**0**	**0**	**0**	**0**	**2**	**0**	**0**	**0**	**2**	**0.0**	**0**	**0**	**1**	**0**	**–1**	**4**	**0**	**0**	**0**	**0**	**0**	**0**	**0**
	Binghamton Dusters	NAHL	2	0	1	1	....	....	....	2	....	....	....	....	....	....	....	....	....	....	....	....	....	....	....	....	....	....
	Rochester Americans	AHL	62	18	11	29	....	....	....	11	....	....	....	....	....	....	....	....	....	....	5	0	1	1	0	....	....	....
1976-77	Rochester Americans	AHL	43	16	15	31	....	....	....	4	....	....	....	....	....	....	....	....	....	....	12	2	5	7	2	....	....	....
1977-78	**Boston Bruins**	**NHL**	**2**	**0**	**0**	**0**	**0**	**0**	**0**	**0**	**0**	**0**	**0**	**1**	**0.0**	**0**	**0**	**1**	**0**	**–1**	....	....	....	....	....	....	....	....
	Rochester Americans	AHL	72	30	27	57	....	....	....	0	....	....	....	....	....	....	....	....	....	....	6	1	3	4	0	....	....	....
1978-79	Rochester Americans	AHL	80	25	23	48	....	....	....	14	....	....	....	....	....	....	....	....	....	....	....	....	....	....	....	....	....	....
	NHL Totals		**7**	**0**	**1**	**1**	**0**	**1**	**1**	**2**	**0**	**0**	**0**	**3**	**0.0**	**1**	**0**	**2**	**0**		**4**	**0**	**0**	**0**	**0**	**0**	**0**	**0**

• LANGENBRUNNER, Jamie

James C. C – R. 6'1", 200 lbs. b: Duluth, MN, 7/24/1975. Dallas' 2nd, 35th overall, in 1993.

Season	Club	League	GP	G	A	Pts	AG	AA	APts	PIM	PP	SH	GW	S	%	TGF	PGF	TGA	PGA	+/–	GP	G	A	Pts	PIM	PP	SH	GW
1990-91	Cloquet Lumberjacks	Hi-School	20	6	16	22	....	....	....	8	....	....	....	....	....	....	....	....	....	....	....	....	....	....	....	....	....	....
1991-92	Cloquet Lumberjacks	Hi-School	23	16	23	39	....	....	....	24	....	....	....	....	....	....	....	....	....	....	....	....	....	....	....	....	....	....
1992-93	Cloquet Lumberjacks	Hi-School	27	27	62	89	....	....	....	18	....	....	....	....	....	....	....	....	....	....	....	....	....	....	....	....	....	....
1993-94	Peterborough Petes	OHL	62	33	58	91	....	....	....	53	....	....	....	....	....	....	....	....	....	....	7	4	6	10	2	....	....	....
	United States	WJC-A	7	2	0	2	....	....	....	13	....	....	....	....	....	....	....	....	....	....	....	....	....	....	....	....	....	....
1994-95	Peterborough Petes	OHL	62	42	57	99	....	....	....	84	....	....	....	....	....	....	....	....	....	....	11	8	14	22	12	....	....	....
	United States	WJC-A	7	1	1	2	....	....	....	6	....	....	....	....	....	....	....	....	....	....	....	....	....	....	....	....	....	....
	Dallas Stars	**NHL**	**2**	**0**	**0**	**0**	**0**	**0**	**0**	**2**	**0**	**0**	**0**	**1**	**0.0**	**1**	**0**	**1**	**0**	**0**	....	....	....	....	....	....	....	....
	Kalamazoo Wings	IHL	....	....	....	....	....	....	....	....	....	....	....	....	....	....	....	....	....	....	11	1	3	4	2	....	....	....
1995-96	**Dallas Stars**	**NHL**	**12**	**2**	**2**	**4**	**2**	**2**	**4**	**6**	**1**	**0**	**0**	**15**	**13.3**	**7**	**3**	**6**	**0**	**–2**	....	....	....	....	....	....	....	....
	Michigan K-Wings	IHL	59	25	40	65	....	....	....	129	....	....	....	....	....	....	....	....	....	....	10	3	10	13	8	....	....	....
1996-97	**Dallas Stars**	**NHL**	**76**	**13**	**26**	**39**	**14**	**23**	**37**	**51**	**3**	**0**	**3**	**112**	**11.6**	**50**	**15**	**37**	**0**	**–2**	**5**	**1**	**1**	**2**	**14**	**0**	**0**	**1**
1997-98	**Dallas Stars**	**NHL**	**81**	**23**	**29**	**52**	**27**	**28**	**55**	**61**	**8**	**0**	**6**	**159**	**14.5**	**80**	**33**	**42**	**4**	**9**	**16**	**1**	**4**	**5**	**14**	**0**	**0**	**1**
	United States	Olympics	3	0	0	0	....	....	....	4	....	....	....	....	....	....	....	....	....	....	....	....	....	....	....	....	....	....
1998-99♦	**Dallas Stars**	**NHL**	**75**	**12**	**33**	**45**	**14**	**32**	**46**	**62**	**4**	**0**	**1**	**145**	**8.3**	**72**	**27**	**37**	**2**	**10**	**23**	**10**	**7**	**17**	**16**	**4**	**0**	**3**
99-2000	**Dallas Stars**	**NHL**	**65**	**18**	**21**	**39**	**20**	**19**	**39**	**68**	**4**	**2**	**6**	**153**	**11.8**	**65**	**16**	**36**	**3**	**16**	**15**	**1**	**7**	**8**	**18**	**1**	**0**	**0**
	NHL Totals		**311**	**68**	**111**	**179**	**77**	**104**	**181**	**250**	**20**	**2**	**16**	**585**	**11.6**	**275**	**94**	**159**	**9**		**59**	**13**	**19**	**32**	**62**	**5**	**0**	**5**

• LANGEVIN, Chris

Christopher LW – L. 6', 190 lbs. b: Montreal, Que., 11/27/1959.

Season	Club	League	GP	G	A	Pts	AG	AA	APts	PIM	PP	SH	GW	S	%	TGF	PGF	TGA	PGA	+/–	GP	G	A	Pts	PIM	PP	SH	GW
1977-78	Chicoutimi Sagueneens	QMJHL	67	8	20	28	....	....	....	183	....	....	....	....	....	....	....	....	....	....	....	....	....	....	....	....	....	....
1978-79	Chicoutimi Sagueneens	QMJHL	65	24	23	47	....	....	....	182	....	....	....	....	....	....	....	....	....	....	4	0	2	2	19	....	....	....
1979-80	Chicoutimi Sagueneens	QMJHL	46	22	30	52	....	....	....	97	....	....	....	....	....	....	....	....	....	....	2	0	3	3	14	....	....	....
1980-81	Saginaw Gears	IHL	75	35	48	83	....	....	....	179	....	....	....	....	....	....	....	....	....	....	13	2	5	7	24	....	....	....
1981-82	Rochester Americans	AHL	33	3	5	8	....	....	....	150	....	....	....	....	....	....	....	....	....	....	9	4	5	9	33	....	....	....
1982-83	Rochester Americans	AHL	71	18	25	43	....	....	....	255	....	....	....	....	....	....	....	....	....	....	11	0	3	3	34	....	....	....
1983-84	**Buffalo Sabres**	**NHL**	**6**	**1**	**0**	**1**	**1**	**0**	**1**	**2**	**0**	**0**	**0**	**4**	**25.0**	**1**	**0**	**3**	**0**	**–2**	....	....	....	....	....	....	....	....
	Rochester Americans	AHL	41	11	14	25	....	....	....	133	....	....	....	....	....	....	....	....	....	....	15	3	2	5	39	....	....	....
1984-85	Rochester Americans	AHL	63	19	21	40	....	....	....	212	....	....	....	....	....	....	....	....	....	....	5	2	1	3	16	....	....	....
1985-86	**Buffalo Sabres**	**NHL**	**16**	**2**	**1**	**3**	**2**	**1**	**3**	**20**	**0**	**0**	**0**	**10**	**20.0**	**7**	**0**	**4**	**0**	**3**	....	....	....	....	....	....	....	....
	NHL Totals		**22**	**3**	**1**	**4**	**3**	**1**	**4**	**22**	**0**	**0**	**0**	**14**	**21.4**	**8**	**0**	**7**	**0**		....	....	....	....	....	....	....	....

Signed as a free agent by **Buffalo**, October 14, 1983. • Suffered career-ending knee injury in game vs. Quebec, November 22, 1985.

• LANGEVIN, Dave

David "The Bammer" D – L. 6'2", 200 lbs. b: St. Paul, MN, 5/15/1954. NY Islanders' 6th, 112th overall, in 1974. **USHOF**

Season	Club	League	GP	G	A	Pts	AG	AA	APts	PIM	PP	SH	GW	S	%	TGF	PGF	TGA	PGA	+/–	GP	G	A	Pts	PIM	PP	SH	GW
1971-72	Hill-Murray Pioneers	Hi-School	STATISTICS NOT AVAILABLE																									
1972-73	University of Minnesota-Duluth	WCHA	36	6	11	17	....	....	....	74	....	....	....	....	....	....	....	....	....	....	....	....	....	....	....	....	....	....
1973-74	University of Minnesota-Duluth	WCHA	37	2	11	13	....	....	....	56	....	....	....	....	....	....	....	....	....	....	....	....	....	....	....	....	....	....
1974-75	University of Minnesota-Duluth	WCHA	35	8	24	32	....	....	....	91	....	....	....	....	....	....	....	....	....	....	....	....	....	....	....	....	....	....
1975-76	University of Minnesota-Duluth	WCHA	34	19	26	45	....	....	....	82	....	....	....	....	....	....	....	....	....	....	....	....	....	....	....	....	....	....
	United States	WEC-A	10	1	0	1	....	....	....	11	....	....	....	....	....	....	....	....	....	....	....	....	....	....	....	....	....	....

Season	Club	League	REGULAR SEASON																		PLAYOFFS							
			GP	G	A	Pts	AG	AA	APts	PIM	PP	SH	GW	S	%	TGF	PGF	TGA	PGA	+/–	GP	G	A	Pts	PIM	PP	SH	GW
1976-77	Edmonton Oilers	WHA	77	7	16	23	....	....	....	94	....	....	....	....	....	....	....	....	....	....	5	2	1	3	9	....	....	....
1977-78	Edmonton Oilers	WHA	62	6	22	28	....	....	....	90	....	....	....	....	....	....	....	....	....	....	5	0	2	2	10	....	....	....
1978-79	Edmonton Oilers	WHA	77	6	21	27	....	....	....	76	....	....	....	....	....	....	....	....	....	....	13	0	1	1	25	....	....	....
1979-80♦	**New York Islanders**	**NHL**	**76**	**3**	**13**	**16**	**3**	**9**	**12**	**109**	**0**	**1**	**0**	**82**	**3.7**	**74**	**1**	**77**	**15**	**11**	**21**	**0**	**3**	**3**	**32**	**0**	**0**	**0**
1980-81♦	**New York Islanders**	**NHL**	**75**	**1**	**16**	**17**	**1**	**11**	**12**	**122**	**0**	**0**	**0**	**68**	**1.5**	**87**	**3**	**66**	**22**	**40**	**18**	**0**	**3**	**3**	**25**	**0**	**0**	**0**
1981-82	United States	Can-Cup	6	0	1	1	....	....	....	8	....	....	....	....	....	....	....	....	....	....	....	....	....	....	....	....	....	....
♦	**New York Islanders**	**NHL**	**73**	**1**	**20**	**21**	**1**	**13**	**14**	**82**	**0**	**0**	**0**	**73**	**1.4**	**93**	**2**	**85**	**28**	**34**	**19**	**2**	**4**	**6**	**16**	**0**	**0**	**1**
1982-83♦	**New York Islanders**	**NHL**	**73**	**4**	**17**	**21**	**3**	**12**	**15**	**64**	**0**	**0**	**0**	**107**	**3.7**	**74**	**0**	**69**	**17**	**22**	**8**	**0**	**2**	**2**	**2**	**0**	**0**	**0**
1983-84	**New York Islanders**	**NHL**	**69**	**3**	**16**	**19**	**2**	**11**	**13**	**53**	**0**	**0**	**1**	**89**	**3.4**	**78**	**1**	**72**	**21**	**26**	**12**	**0**	**4**	**4**	**18**	**0**	**0**	**0**
1984-85	**New York Islanders**	**NHL**	**56**	**0**	**13**	**13**	**0**	**9**	**9**	**35**	**0**	**0**	**0**	**33**	**0.0**	**46**	**1**	**69**	**18**	**–6**	**4**	**0**	**0**	**0**	**4**	**0**	**0**	**0**
1985-86	**Minnesota North Stars**	**NHL**	**80**	**0**	**8**	**8**	**0**	**5**	**5**	**58**	**0**	**0**	**0**	**54**	**0.0**	**55**	**2**	**116**	**46**	**–17**	**5**	**0**	**1**	**1**	**9**	**0**	**0**	**0**
1986-87	**Los Angeles Kings**	**NHL**	**11**	**0**	**4**	**4**	**0**	**3**	**3**	**7**	**0**	**0**	**0**	**5**	**0.0**	**8**	**0**	**17**	**6**	**–3**	....	....	....	....	....	....	....	....
	New Haven Nighthawks	AHL	10	1	1	2	....	....	....	7	....	....	....	....	....	....	....	....	....	....	....	....	....	....	....	....	....	....
	NHL Totals		**513**	**12**	**107**	**119**	**10**	**73**	**83**	**530**	**0**	**1**	**1**	**511**	**2.3**	**515**	**10**	**571**	**173**		**87**	**2**	**17**	**19**	**106**	**0**	**0**	**1**
	Other Major League Totals		216	19	59	78	....	....	....	260	....	....	....	....	....	....	....	....	....	....	23	2	4	6	44	....	....	....

WCHA Second All-Star Team (1976) • WHA Second All-Star Team (1979) • Played in NHL All-Star Game (1983)

Selected by **Edmonton** (WHA) in 1974 WHA Amateur Draft, June, 1974. Reclaimed by **NY Islanders** from **Edmonton** prior to Expansion Draft, June 9, 1979. Claimed by **Minnesota** from **NY Islanders** in Waiver Draft, October 7, 1985. Signed as a free agent by **LA Kings**, February 4, 1987.

• LANGKOW, Daymond

C – L. 5'11", 175 lbs. b: Edmonton, Alta, 9/27/1976. Tampa Bay's 1st, 5th overall, in 1995.

Season	Club	League	GP	G	A	Pts	AG	AA	APts	PIM	PP	SH	GW	S	%	TGF	PGF	TGA	PGA	+/–	GP	G	A	Pts	PIM	PP	SH	GW
1991-92	Edmonton Pats	AMHL	35	36	45	81	....	....	....	100	....	....	....	....	....	....	....	....	....	....	....	....	....	....	....	....	....	....
	Tri-City Americans	WHL	1	0	0	0	....	....	....	0	....	....	....	....	....	....	....	....	....	....	....	....	....	....	....	....	....	....
1992-93	Tri-City Americans	WHL	64	22	42	64	....	....	....	100	....	....	....	....	....	....	....	....	....	....	4	1	0	1	4	....	....	....
1993-94	Tri-City Americans	WHL	61	40	43	83	....	....	....	174	....	....	....	....	....	....	....	....	....	....	4	2	2	4	15	....	....	....
1994-95	Tri-City Americans	WHL	72	*67	73	*140	....	....	....	142	....	....	....	....	....	....	....	....	....	....	17	12	15	27	52	....	....	....
1995-96	Tri-City Americans	WHL	48	30	61	91	....	....	....	103	....	....	....	....	....	....	....	....	....	....	11	14	13	27	20	....	....	....
	Canada	WJC-A	5	3	3	6	....	....	....	2	....	....	....	....	....	....	....	....	....	....	....	....	....	....	....	....	....	....
	Tampa Bay Lightning	**NHL**	**4**	**0**	**1**	**1**	**0**	**1**	**1**	**0**	**0**	**0**	**0**	**4**	**0.0**	**1**	**0**	**2**	**0**	**–1**	....	....	....	....	....	....	....	....
1996-97	**Tampa Bay Lightning**	**NHL**	**79**	**15**	**13**	**28**	**16**	**12**	**28**	**35**	**3**	**1**	**1**	**170**	**8.8**	**48**	**7**	**44**	**4**	**1**	....	....	....	....	....	....	....	....
	Adirondack Red Wings	AHL	2	1	1	2	....	....	....	0	....	....	....	....	....	....	....	....	....	....	....	....	....	....	....	....	....	....
1997-98	**Tampa Bay Lightning**	**NHL**	**68**	**8**	**14**	**22**	**9**	**14**	**23**	**62**	**2**	**0**	**1**	**156**	**5.1**	**36**	**7**	**63**	**25**	**–9**	....	....	....	....	....	....	....	....
1998-99	**Tampa Bay Lightning**	**NHL**	**22**	**4**	**6**	**10**	**5**	**6**	**11**	**15**	**1**	**0**	**1**	**40**	**10.0**	**16**	**3**	**19**	**6**	**0**	....	....	....	....	....	....	....	....
	Cleveland Lumberjacks	IHL	4	1	1	2	....	....	....	18	....	....	....	....	....	....	....	....	....	....	....	....	....	....	....	....	....	....
	Philadelphia Flyers	**NHL**	**56**	**10**	**13**	**23**	**12**	**13**	**25**	**24**	**3**	**1**	**1**	**109**	**9.2**	**36**	**11**	**38**	**5**	**–8**	**6**	**0**	**2**	**2**	**2**	**0**	**0**	**0**
99-2000	**Philadelphia Flyers**	**NHL**	**82**	**18**	**32**	**50**	**20**	**30**	**50**	**56**	**5**	**0**	**7**	**222**	**8.1**	**79**	**34**	**55**	**11**	**1**	**16**	**5**	**5**	**10**	**23**	**1**	**1**	**2**
	NHL Totals		**311**	**55**	**79**	**134**	**62**	**76**	**138**	**192**	**14**	**2**	**11**	**701**	**7.8**	**216**	**62**	**221**	**51**		**22**	**5**	**7**	**12**	**25**	**1**	**1**	**2**

• Brother of Scott • WHL West First All-Star Team (1995) • Canadian Major Junior First All-Star Team (1995) • WHL West Second All-Star Team (1996)

Traded to **Philadelphia** by **Tampa Bay** with Mikael Renberg for Chris Gratton and Mike Sillinger, December 12, 1998.

• LANGLAIS, Alain

Alain Joseph Alfred LW – L. 5'10", 175 lbs. b: Chicoutimi, Que., 10/9/1950.

Season	Club	League	GP	G	A	Pts	AG	AA	APts	PIM	PP	SH	GW	S	%	TGF	PGF	TGA	PGA	+/–	GP	G	A	Pts	PIM	PP	SH	GW
1968-69	Sorel Black Hawks	MMJHL	STATISTICS NOT AVAILABLE																									
	Sorel Black Hawks	Mem-Cup	4	0	0	0	....	....	....	10	....	....	....	....	....	....	....	....	....	....	....	....	....	....	....	....	....	....
1969-70	Sorel Eperviers	QJHL	49	60	51	111	....	....	....	105	....	....	....	....	....	....	....	....	....	....	10	7	6	13	22	....	....	....
1970-71	Toledo Hornets	IHL	31	8	8	16	....	....	....	50	....	....	....	....	....	....	....	....	....	....	....	....	....	....	....	....	....	....
	Jersey–Long Island Ducks	EHL	47	13	20	33	....	....	....	72	....	....	....	....	....	....	....	....	....	....	....	....	....	....	....	....	....	....
1971-72	Long Island Ducks	EHL	75	45	31	76	....	....	....	125	....	....	....	....	....	....	....	....	....	....	....	....	....	....	....	....	....	....
1972-73	Chicoutimi Sagueneens	QSHL	STATISTICS NOT AVAILABLE																									
1973-74	**Minnesota North Stars**	**NHL**	**14**	**3**	**3**	**6**	**3**	**2**	**5**	**8**	**0**	**0**	**0**	**45**	**6.7**	**8**	**0**	**15**	**1**	**–6**	....	....	....	....	....	....	....	....
	Saginaw Gears	IHL	11	3	3	6	....	....	....	14	....	....	....	....	....	....	....	....	....	....	....	....	....	....	....	....	....	....
	New Haven Nighthawks	AHL	45	21	16	37	....	....	....	73	....	....	....	....	....	....	....	....	....	....	10	6	3	9	9	....	....	....
1974-75	**Minnesota North Stars**	**NHL**	**11**	**1**	**1**	**2**	**1**	**1**	**2**	**2**	**0**	**0**	**0**	**15**	**6.7**	**4**	**0**	**7**	**0**	**–3**	....	....	....	....	....	....	....	....
	New Haven Nighthawks	AHL	66	41	29	70	....	....	....	109	....	....	....	....	....	....	....	....	....	....	12	7	6	13	23	....	....	....
1975-76	New Haven Nighthawks	AHL	53	14	17	31	....	....	....	34	....	....	....	....	....	....	....	....	....	....	....	....	....	....	....	....	....	....
	Richmond Robins	AHL	21	7	11	18	....	....	....	27	....	....	....	....	....	....	....	....	....	....	8	1	0	1	10	....	....	....
1976-77	New Haven Nighthawks	AHL	4	0	0	0	....	....	....	4	....	....	....	....	....	....	....	....	....	....	....	....	....	....	....	....	....	....
	Tulsa Oilers	CHL	68	13	22	35	....	....	....	71	....	....	....	....	....	....	....	....	....	....	9	4	4	8	9	....	....	....
1977-78	Chicoutimi Comets	QIPHL	STATISTICS NOT AVAILABLE																									
1978-79	Chicoutimi Comets	QIPHL	STATISTICS NOT AVAILABLE																									
1979-80	Flint Generals	IHL	17	4	2	6	....	....	....	21	....	....	....	....	....	....	....	....	....	....	....	....	....	....	....	....	....	....
	NHL Totals		**25**	**4**	**4**	**8**	**4**	**3**	**7**	**10**	**0**	**0**	**0**	**60**	**6.7**	**12**	**0**	**22**	**1**		....	....	....	....	....	....	....	....

EHL North First All-Star Team (1972) • AHL Second All-Star Team (1975)

Signed as a free agent by **Minnesota**, September, 1973. Traded to **Washington** by **New Haven** (AHL) with Rich Nantais for Ron H. Anderson and Bob Gryp, February 23, 1976.

• LANGWAY, Rod

Rod Corry D – L. 6'3", 218 lbs. b: Maag, Formosa, 5/3/1957. Montreal's 3rd, 36th overall, in 1977. **USHOF**

Season	Club	League	GP	G	A	Pts	AG	AA	APts	PIM	PP	SH	GW	S	%	TGF	PGF	TGA	PGA	+/–	GP	G	A	Pts	PIM	PP	SH	GW
1972-73	Randolph Rockets	Hi-School	16	20	19	39	....	....	....	....	....	....	....	....	....	....	....	....	....	....	....	....	....	....	....	....	....	....
1973-1975	Randolph Rockets	Hi-School	STATISTICS NOT AVAILABLE																									
1975-76	University of New Hampshire	ECAC	31	3	13	16	....	....	....	10	....	....	....	....	....	....	....	....	....	....	....	....	....	....	....	....	....	....
1976-77	University of New Hampshire	ECAC	34	10	43	53	....	....	....	52	....	....	....	....	....	....	....	....	....	....	....	....	....	....	....	....	....	....
1977-78	Birmingham Bulls	WHA	52	3	18	21	....	....	....	52	....	....	....	....	....	....	....	....	....	....	4	0	0	0	9	....	....	....
	Hampton Gulls	AHL	30	6	16	22	....	....	....	50	....	....	....	....	....	....	....	....	....	....	....	....	....	....	....	....	....	....
1978-79♦	**Montreal Canadiens**	**NHL**	**45**	**3**	**4**	**7**	**3**	**3**	**6**	**30**	**0**	**0**	**0**	**48**	**6.3**	**32**	**1**	**26**	**0**	**5**	**8**	**0**	**0**	**0**	**16**	**0**	**0**	**0**
	Nova Scotia Voyageurs	AHL	18	6	13	19	....	....	....	29	....	....	....	....	....	....	....	....	....	....	....	....	....	....	....	....	....	....
1979-80	**Montreal Canadiens**	**NHL**	**77**	**7**	**29**	**36**	**6**	**21**	**27**	**81**	**0**	**0**	**1**	**112**	**6.3**	**108**	**7**	**83**	**18**	**36**	**10**	**3**	**3**	**6**	**2**	**1**	**0**	**0**
1980-81	**Montreal Canadiens**	**NHL**	**80**	**11**	**34**	**45**	**9**	**23**	**32**	**120**	**5**	**1**	**2**	**165**	**6.7**	**136**	**21**	**85**	**23**	**53**	**3**	**0**	**0**	**0**	**6**	**0**	**0**	**0**
1981-82	United States	Can-Cup	6	0	1	1	....	....	....	8	....	....	....	....	....	....	....	....	....	....	....	....	....	....	....	....	....	....
	Montreal Canadiens	**NHL**	**66**	**5**	**34**	**39**	**4**	**23**	**27**	**116**	**1**	**0**	**1**	**139**	**3.6**	**133**	**16**	**73**	**22**	**66**	**5**	**0**	**3**	**3**	**18**	**0**	**0**	**0**
	United States	WEC-A	6	0	2	2	....	....	....	4	....	....	....	....	....	....	....	....	....	....	....	....	....	....	....	....	....	....
1982-83	**Washington Capitals**	**NHL**	**80**	**3**	**29**	**32**	**2**	**20**	**22**	**75**	**1**	**0**	**0**	**126**	**2.4**	**107**	**7**	**135**	**35**	**0**	**4**	**0**	**0**	**0**	**0**	**0**	**0**	**0**
1983-84	**Washington Capitals**	**NHL**	**80**	**9**	**24**	**33**	**7**	**16**	**23**	**61**	**1**	**2**	**2**	**168**	**5.4**	**112**	**18**	**106**	**26**	**14**	**8**	**0**	**5**	**5**	**7**	**0**	**0**	**0**
1984-85	United States	Can-Cup	6	1	1	2	....	....	....	8	....	....	....	....	....	....	....	....	....	....	....	....	....	....	....	....	....	....
	Washington Capitals	**NHL**	**79**	**4**	**22**	**26**	**3**	**15**	**18**	**54**	**0**	**0**	**1**	**102**	**3.9**	**99**	**9**	**94**	**39**	**35**	**5**	**0**	**1**	**1**	**6**	**0**	**0**	**0**
1985-86	**Washington Capitals**	**NHL**	**71**	**1**	**17**	**18**	**1**	**11**	**12**	**61**	**1**	**0**	**0**	**54**	**1.9**	**85**	**3**	**89**	**34**	**27**	**9**	**1**	**2**	**3**	**6**	**1**	**0**	**0**
1986-87	**Washington Capitals**	**NHL**	**78**	**2**	**25**	**27**	**2**	**18**	**20**	**53**	**0**	**0**	**1**	**76**	**2.6**	**83**	**8**	**95**	**31**	**11**	**7**	**0**	**1**	**1**	**2**	**0**	**0**	**0**
	NHL All-Stars	RV-87	2	0	0	0	....	....	....	0	....	....	....	....	....	....	....	....	....	....	....	....	....	....	....	....	....	....
1987-88	United States	Can-Cup	5	0	1	1	....	....	....	6	....	....	....	....	....	....	....	....	....	....	....	....	....	....	....	....	....	....
	Washington Capitals	**NHL**	**63**	**3**	**13**	**16**	**3**	**9**	**12**	**28**	**0**	**0**	**1**	**49**	**6.1**	**47**	**1**	**77**	**32**	**1**	**6**	**0**	**0**	**0**	**8**	**0**	**0**	**0**
1988-89	**Washington Capitals**	**NHL**	**76**	**2**	**19**	**21**	**2**	**13**	**15**	**65**	**0**	**0**	**0**	**80**	**2.5**	**74**	**4**	**98**	**40**	**12**	**6**	**0**	**0**	**0**	**6**	**0**	**0**	**0**
1989-90	Washington Capitals	Fr-Tour	4	0	0	0	....	....	....	2	....	....	....	....	....	....	....	....	....	....	....	....	....	....	....	....	....	....
	Washington Capitals	**NHL**	**58**	**0**	**8**	**8**	**0**	**6**	**6**	**39**	**0**	**0**	**0**	**46**	**0.0**	**40**	**1**	**62**	**30**	**7**	**15**	**1**	**4**	**5**	**12**	**0**	**0**	**1**
1990-91	**Washington Capitals**	**NHL**	**56**	**1**	**7**	**8**	**1**	**5**	**6**	**24**	**0**	**0**	**0**	**32**	**3.1**	**42**	**0**	**52**	**22**	**12**	**11**	**0**	**2**	**2**	**6**	**0**	**0**	**0**
1991-92	**Washington Capitals**	**NHL**	**64**	**0**	**13**	**13**	**0**	**10**	**10**	**22**	**0**	**0**	**0**	**32**	**0.0**	**55**	**1**	**72**	**29**	**11**	**7**	**0**	**1**	**1**	**2**	**0**	**0**	**0**
1992-93	**Washington Capitals**	**NHL**	**21**	**0**	**0**	**0**	**0**	**0**	**0**	**20**	**0**	**0**	**0**	**6**	**0.0**	**2**	**0**	**20**	**5**	**–13**	....	....	....	....	....	....	....	....
1993-94	Richmond Renegades	ECHL	DID NOT PLAY – ASSISTANT COACH																									
1994-95	Richmond Renegades	ECHL	6	0	0	0	....	....	....	2	....	....	....	....	....	....	....	....	....	....	9	1	1	2	4	....	....	....
1995-96	San Francisco Spiders	IHL	46	1	5	6	....	....	....	38	....	....	....	....	....	....	....	....	....	....	....	....	....	....	....	....	....	....

Season	Club	League	GP	G	A	Pts	AG	AA	APts	PIM	PP	SH	GW	S	%	TGF	PGF	TGA	PGA	+/–	GP	G	A	Pts	PIM	PP	SH	GW
			REGULAR SEASON																		PLAYOFFS							
1996-97	Richmond Renegades	ECHL	DID NOT PLAY – ASSISTANT COACH																									
1997-98	Providence Bruins	AHL	10	0	1	1	....	....	....	10	....	....	....	....	....	....	....	....	....	....	....	....	....	....	....	....	....	....
1998-2000	Richmond Renegades	ECHL	DID NOT PLAY – ASSISTANT COACH																									
	NHL Totals		**994**	**51**	**278**	**329**	**43**	**193**	**236**	**849**	**9**	**3**	**9**	**1235**	**4.1**	**1155**	**97**	**1167**	**386**		**104**	**5**	**22**	**27**	**97**	**2**	**0**	**1**
	Other Major League Totals		52	3	18	21	....	....	....	52	....	....	....	....	....	....	....	....	....	....	4	0	0	0	9	....	....	....

NHL First All-Star Team (1983, 1984) • Won James Norris Trophy (1983, 1984) • Canada Cup All-Star Team (1984) • NHL Second All-Star Team (1985)

Played in NHL All-Star Game (1981, 1982, 1983, 1984, 1985, 1986)

Selected by **Birmingham** (WHA) in 1977 WHA Amateur Draft, May, 1977. Claimed by **Montreal** as a fill-in during Expansion Draft, June 13, 1979. Traded to **Washington** by **Montreal** with Doug Jarvis, Craig Laughlin and Brian Engblom for Ryan Walter and Rick Green, September 9, 1982.

• LANK, Jeff

D – L. 6'3", 205 lbs. b: Indian Head, Sask., 3/1/1975. Philadelphia's 9th, 230th overall, in 1995.

Season	Club	League	GP	G	A	Pts	AG	AA	APts	PIM	PP	SH	GW	S	%	TGF	PGF	TGA	PGA	+/–	GP	G	A	Pts	PIM	PP	SH	GW
1990-91	Columbia Valley Rockies	KIJHL	54	6	28	34	....	....	....	33	....	....	....	....	....	....	....	....	....	....	....	....	....	....	....	....	....	....
1991-92	Prince Albert Raiders	WHL	56	2	8	10	....	....	....	26	....	....	....	....	....	....	....	....	....	....	9	0	0	0	2	....	....	....
1992-93	Prince Albert Raiders	WHL	63	1	11	12	....	....	....	60	....	....	....	....	....	....	....	....	....	....	....	....	....	....	....	....	....	....
1993-94	Prince Albert Raiders	WHL	72	9	38	47	....	....	....	62	....	....	....	....	....	....	....	....	....	....	....	....	....	....	....	....	....	....
1994-95	Prince Albert Raiders	WHL	68	12	25	37	....	....	....	60	....	....	....	....	....	....	....	....	....	....	13	2	10	12	8	....	....	....
1995-96	Hershey Bears	AHL	72	7	13	20	....	....	....	70	....	....	....	....	....	....	....	....	....	....	5	0	0	0	8	....	....	....
1996-97	Philadelphia Phantoms	AHL	44	2	12	14	....	....	....	49	....	....	....	....	....	....	....	....	....	....	7	2	1	3	4	....	....	....
1997-98	Philadelphia Phantoms	AHL	69	7	9	16	....	....	....	59	....	....	....	....	....	....	....	....	....	....	20	1	4	5	22	....	....	....
1998-99	Philadelphia Phantoms	AHL	51	5	10	15	....	....	....	36	....	....	....	....	....	....	....	....	....	....	2	0	0	0	2	....	....	....
99-2000	**Philadelphia Flyers**	**NHL**	**2**	**0**	**0**	**0**	**0**	**0**	**0**	**2**	**0**	**0**	**0**	**0**	**0.0**	**0**	**0**	**0**	**0**	**0**	....	....	....	....	....	....	....	....
	Philadelphia Phantoms	AHL	26	1	4	5	....	....	....	16	....	....	....	....	....	....	....	....	....	....	3	0	0	0	2	....	....	....
	NHL Totals		**2**	**0**	**0**	**0**	**0**	**0**	**0**	**2**	**0**	**0**	**0**	**0**	**0.0**	**0**	**0**	**0**	**0**		....	....	....	....	....	....	....	....

• Re-entered NHL draft. Originally Montreal's 6th choice, 113th overall in 1993 Entry Draft.

• LANTHIER, Jean-Marc

RW – R. 6'2", 195 lbs. b: Montreal, Que., 3/27/1963. Vancouver's 2nd, 52nd overall, in 1981.

Season	Club	League	GP	G	A	Pts	AG	AA	APts	PIM	PP	SH	GW	S	%	TGF	PGF	TGA	PGA	+/–	GP	G	A	Pts	PIM	PP	SH	GW
1978-79	Mercier Sportive	QAAA	STATISTICS NOT AVAILABLE																									
1979-80	Quebec Remparts	QMJHL	63	14	32	46	....	....	....	4	....	....	....	....	....	....	....	....	....	....	5	0	1	1	0	....	....	....
1980-81	Quebec Remparts	QMJHL	37	13	32	45	....	....	....	18	....	....	....	....	....	....	....	....	....	....	....	....	....	....	....	....	....	....
	Sorel Black Hawks	QMJHL	35	6	33	39	....	....	....	29	....	....	....	....	....	....	....	....	....	....	7	1	4	5	4	....	....	....
1981-82	Laval Voisins	QMJHL	60	44	34	78	....	....	....	48	....	....	....	....	....	....	....	....	....	....	18	8	11	19	8	....	....	....
1982-83	Laval Voisins	QMJHL	69	39	71	110	....	....	....	54	....	....	....	....	....	....	....	....	....	....	12	6	17	23	8	....	....	....
1983-84	**Vancouver Canucks**	**NHL**	**11**	**2**	**1**	**3**	**2**	**1**	**3**	**2**	**0**	**0**	**0**	**9**	**22.2**	**6**	**0**	**8**	**0**	**–2**	....	....	....	....	....	....	....	....
	Fredericton Express	AHL	60	25	17	42	....	....	....	29	....	....	....	....	....	....	....	....	....	....	7	4	6	10	0	....	....	....
1984-85	**Vancouver Canucks**	**NHL**	**27**	**6**	**4**	**10**	**5**	**3**	**8**	**13**	**2**	**0**	**1**	**23**	**26.1**	**16**	**3**	**30**	**1**	**–16**	....	....	....	....	....	....	....	....
	Fredericton Express	AHL	50	21	21	42	....	....	....	13	....	....	....	....	....	....	....	....	....	....	4	1	1	2	4	....	....	....
1985-86	**Vancouver Canucks**	**NHL**	**62**	**7**	**10**	**17**	**6**	**7**	**13**	**12**	**3**	**0**	**1**	**50**	**14.0**	**31**	**9**	**39**	**0**	**–17**	....	....	....	....	....	....	....	....
	Fredericton Express	AHL	7	5	5	10	....	....	....	2	....	....	....	....	....	....	....	....	....	....	....	....	....	....	....	....	....	....
1986-87	Fredericton Express	AHL	78	15	38	53	....	....	....	24	....	....	....	....	....	....	....	....	....	....	....	....	....	....	....	....	....	....
1987-88	**Vancouver Canucks**	**NHL**	**5**	**1**	**1**	**2**	**1**	**1**	**2**	**2**	**0**	**0**	**0**	**3**	**33.3**	**2**	**0**	**3**	**0**	**–1**	....	....	....	....	....	....	....	....
	Fredericton Express	AHL	74	35	71	106	....	....	....	37	....	....	....	....	....	....	....	....	....	....	15	3	8	11	14	....	....	....
1988-89	Maine Mariners	AHL	24	7	16	23	....	....	....	16	....	....	....	....	....	....	....	....	....	....	....	....	....	....	....	....	....	....
	Utica Devils	AHL	55	23	26	49	....	....	....	22	....	....	....	....	....	....	....	....	....	....	3	3	0	3	2	....	....	....
1989-90	Fort Wayne Komets	IHL	7	4	7	11	....	....	....	4	....	....	....	....	....	....	....	....	....	....	....	....	....	....	....	....	....	....
	Utica Devils	AHL	50	13	19	32	....	....	....	32	....	....	....	....	....	....	....	....	....	....	4	1	1	2	2	....	....	....
	NHL Totals		**105**	**16**	**16**	**32**	**14**	**12**	**26**	**29**	**5**	**0**	**2**	**85**	**18.8**	**55**	**12**	**80**	**1**		....	....	....	....	....	....	....	....

Signed as a free agent by **Boston**, July 1, 1988. Traded to **New Jersey** by **Boston** for Dan Dorion, December 9, 1988.

• LANYON, Ted

Edward George D – R. 5'11", 175 lbs. b: Winnipeg, Man., 6/11/1939.

Season	Club	League	GP	G	A	Pts	AG	AA	APts	PIM	PP	SH	GW	S	%	TGF	PGF	TGA	PGA	+/–	GP	G	A	Pts	PIM	PP	SH	GW
1957-58	St. Boniface Canadiens	MJHL	28	7	14	21	....	....	....	92	....	....	....	....	....	....	....	....	....	....	12	2	5	7	27	....	....	....
	St. Boniface Canadiens	Mem-Cup	11	3	2	5	....	....	....	35	....	....	....	....	....	....	....	....	....	....	....	....	....	....	....	....	....	....
1958-59	St. Boniface Canadiens	MJHL	28	8	12	20	....	....	....	67	....	....	....	....	....	....	....	....	....	....	9	0	1	1	18	....	....	....
1959-60	Johnstown Jets	EHL	14	4	3	7	....	....	....	25	....	....	....	....	....	....	....	....	....	....	13	0	0	0	12	....	....	....
	St. Paul Saints	IHL	54	4	9	13	....	....	....	50	....	....	....	....	....	....	....	....	....	....	....	....	....	....	....	....	....	....
1960-61	Milwaukee Falcons	IHL	15	7	2	9	....	....	....	28	....	....	....	....	....	....	....	....	....	....	....	....	....	....	....	....	....	....
1961-62	Minneapolis Millers	IHL	49	6	12	18	....	....	....	88	....	....	....	....	....	....	....	....	....	....	....	....	....	....	....	....	....	....
1962-63	Greensboro Generals	EHL	68	15	25	40	....	....	....	104	....	....	....	....	....	....	....	....	....	....	4	2	1	3	18	....	....	....
1963-64	Greensboro Generals	EHL	44	8	14	22	....	....	....	96	....	....	....	....	....	....	....	....	....	....	....	....	....	....	....	....	....	....
	Cleveland Barons	AHL	1	0	0	0	....	....	....	2	....	....	....	....	....	....	....	....	....	....	....	....	....	....	....	....	....	....
1964-65	Omaha Knights	CPHL	2	0	0	0	....	....	....	0	....	....	....	....	....	....	....	....	....	....	....	....	....	....	....	....	....	....
	Cleveland Barons	AHL	70	9	13	22	....	....	....	37	....	....	....	....	....	....	....	....	....	....	....	....	....	....	....	....	....	....
1965-66	Cleveland Barons	AHL	64	5	10	15	....	....	....	55	....	....	....	....	....	....	....	....	....	....	12	0	5	5	4	....	....	....
1966-67	Buffalo Bisons	AHL	69	9	13	22	....	....	....	110	....	....	....	....	....	....	....	....	....	....	....	....	....	....	....	....	....	....
1967-68	**Pittsburgh Penguins**	**NHL**	**5**	**0**	**0**	**0**	**0**	**0**	**0**	**4**	**0**	**0**	**0**	**1**	**0.0**	**1**	**0**	**0**	**0**	**1**	....	....	....	....	....	....	....	....
	Baltimore Clippers	AHL	34	1	9	10	....	....	....	22	....	....	....	....	....	....	....	....	....	....	....	....	....	....	....	....	....	....
1968-69	Amarillo Wranglers	CHL	58	6	26	32	....	....	....	168	....	....	....	....	....	....	....	....	....	....	....	....	....	....	....	....	....	....
1969-70	Baltimore Clippers	AHL	9	1	1	2	....	....	....	13	....	....	....	....	....	....	....	....	....	....	....	....	....	....	....	....	....	....
	Greensboro Generals	EHL	47	13	33	46	....	....	....	80	....	....	....	....	....	....	....	....	....	....	16	5	13	18	18	....	....	....
1970-71	Greensboro Generals	EHL	70	20	40	60	....	....	....	128	....	....	....	....	....	....	....	....	....	....	9	0	5	5	2	....	....	....
	Omaha Knights	CHL	....	....	....	....	....	....	....	....	....	....	....	....	....	....	....	....	....	....	6	1	0	1	2	....	....	....
1971-72	Greensboro Generals	EHL	35	8	27	35	....	....	....	39	....	....	....	....	....	....	....	....	....	....	11	2	2	4	27	....	....	....
1972-73	Johnstown Jets	EHL	54	7	30	37	....	....	....	69	....	....	....	....	....	....	....	....	....	....	12	3	6	9	0	....	....	....
	NHL Totals		**5**	**0**	**0**	**0**	**0**	**0**	**0**	**4**	**0**	**0**	**0**	**1**	**0.0**	**1**	**0**	**0**	**0**		....	....	....	....	....	....	....	....

EHL South First All-Star Team (1970, 1971, 1972, 1973)

Traded to **Pittsburgh** by **Cleveland** (AHL) for cash, August 11, 1966. Loaned to **Buffalo** by **Pittsburgh** for 1966-67 season, October, 1966.

• LANZ, Rick

Rick Roman D – R. 6'2", 203 lbs. b: Karlovy Vary, Czech., 9/16/1961. Vancouver's 1st, 7th overall, in 1980.

Season	Club	League	GP	G	A	Pts	AG	AA	APts	PIM	PP	SH	GW	S	%	TGF	PGF	TGA	PGA	+/–	GP	G	A	Pts	PIM	PP	SH	GW
1976-77	Burlington Cougars	OHA-B	45	10	25	35	....	....	....	28	....	....	....	....	....	....	....	....	....	....	....	....	....	....	....	....	....	....
1977-78	Oshawa Generals	OMJHL	65	1	41	42	....	....	....	51	....	....	....	....	....	....	....	....	....	....	6	0	2	2	4	....	....	....
1978-79	Oshawa Generals	OMJHL	65	12	47	59	....	....	....	88	....	....	....	....	....	....	....	....	....	....	5	1	3	4	14	....	....	....
1979-80	Oshawa Generals	OMJHL	52	18	38	56	....	....	....	51	....	....	....	....	....	....	....	....	....	....	7	2	3	5	6	....	....	....
	Canada	WJC-A	5	0	1	1	....	....	....	6	....	....	....	....	....	....	....	....	....	....	....	....	....	....	....	....	....	....
1980-81	**Vancouver Canucks**	**NHL**	**76**	**7**	**22**	**29**	**5**	**15**	**20**	**40**	**3**	**0**	**1**	**134**	**5.2**	**95**	**23**	**86**	**15**	**1**	**3**	**0**	**0**	**0**	**4**	**0**	**0**	**0**
1981-82	**Vancouver Canucks**	**NHL**	**39**	**3**	**11**	**14**	**2**	**7**	**9**	**48**	**2**	**0**	**0**	**94**	**3.2**	**42**	**15**	**50**	**10**	**–13**	....	....	....	....	....	....	....	....
1982-83	**Vancouver Canucks**	**NHL**	**74**	**10**	**38**	**48**	**8**	**26**	**34**	**46**	**4**	**0**	**2**	**180**	**5.6**	**104**	**44**	**69**	**4**	**–5**	**4**	**2**	**1**	**3**	**0**	**1**	**0**	**0**
	Canada	WEC-A	6	0	2	2	....	....	....	2	....	....	....	....	....	....	....	....	....	....	....	....	....	....	....	....	....	....
1983-84	**Vancouver Canucks**	**NHL**	**79**	**18**	**39**	**57**	**14**	**27**	**41**	**45**	**14**	**0**	**3**	**230**	**7.8**	**147**	**60**	**117**	**27**	**–3**	**4**	**0**	**4**	**4**	**2**	**0**	**0**	**0**
1984-85	**Vancouver Canucks**	**NHL**	**57**	**2**	**17**	**19**	**2**	**12**	**14**	**69**	**2**	**0**	**0**	**131**	**1.5**	**65**	**21**	**99**	**33**	**–22**	....	....	....	....	....	....	....	....
1985-86	**Vancouver Canucks**	**NHL**	**75**	**15**	**38**	**53**	**12**	**26**	**38**	**73**	**11**	**0**	**0**	**191**	**7.9**	**139**	**60**	**139**	**34**	**–26**	**3**	**0**	**0**	**0**	**0**	**0**	**0**	**0**
1986-87	**Vancouver Canucks**	**NHL**	**17**	**1**	**6**	**7**	**1**	**4**	**5**	**10**	**1**	**0**	**0**	**39**	**2.6**	**18**	**10**	**24**	**3**	**–13**	....	....	....	....	....	....	....	....
	Toronto Maple Leafs	**NHL**	**44**	**2**	**19**	**21**	**2**	**14**	**16**	**32**	**1**	**0**	**0**	**91**	**2.2**	**76**	**20**	**70**	**18**	**4**	**13**	**1**	**3**	**4**	**27**	**0**	**0**	**1**
1987-88	**Toronto Maple Leafs**	**NHL**	**75**	**6**	**22**	**28**	**5**	**16**	**21**	**65**	**3**	**0**	**0**	**145**	**4.1**	**100**	**17**	**137**	**42**	**–12**	**1**	**0**	**0**	**0**	**2**	**0**	**0**	**0**
1988-89	**Toronto Maple Leafs**	**NHL**	**32**	**1**	**9**	**10**	**1**	**6**	**7**	**18**	**0**	**0**	**1**	**56**	**1.8**	**35**	**13**	**54**	**15**	**–17**	....	....	....	....	....	....	....	....
1989-90	HC Ambri-Piotta	Switz.	36	4	14	18	....	....	....	....	....	....	....	....	....	....	....	....	....	....	....	....	....	....	....	....	....	....
1990-91	Indianapolis Ice	IHL	8	0	5	5	....	....	....	18	....	....	....	....	....	....	....	....	....	....	....	....	....	....	....	....	....	....
1991-92	**Chicago Blackhawks**	**NHL**	**1**	**0**	**0**	**0**	**0**	**0**	**0**	**2**	**0**	**0**	**0**	**0**	**0.0**	**1**	**0**	**1**	**0**	**0**	....	....	....	....	....	....	....	....
	Phoenix Roadrunners	IHL	38	7	14	21	....	....	....	21	....	....	....	....	....	....	....	....	....	....	....	....	....	....	....	....	....	....
	Canada	Nat-Team	4	0	1	1	....	....	....	2	....	....	....	....	....	....	....	....	....	....	....	....	....	....	....	....	....	....

Season	Club	League	REGULAR SEASON																		PLAYOFFS							
			GP	G	A	Pts	AG	AA	APts	PIM	PP	SH	GW	S	%	TGF	PGF	TGA	PGA	+/–	GP	G	A	Pts	PIM	PP	SH	GW
1992-93	Atlanta Knights	IHL	25	6	12	18	....	....	....	30	....	....	....	....	....	....	....	....	....	....	....	....	....	....	....	....	....	....
1993-1994			OUT OF HOCKEY – RETIRED																									
1994-1995	Penticton Panthers	BCJHL	DID NOT PLAY – ASSISTANT COACH																									
1995-1997	South Surrey Eagles	BCJHL	DID NOT PLAY – COACHING																									
1997-1998	Tri-City Americans	WHL	DID NOT PLAY – COACHING																									
1998-2000	Langley Hornets	BCJHL	DID NOT PLAY – COACHING																									
	NHL Totals		**569**	**65**	**221**	**286**	**52**	**153**	**205**	**448**	**41**	**0**	**7**	**1291**	**5.0**	**822**	**283**	**846**	**201**		**28**	**3**	**8**	**11**	**35**	**1**	**0**	**1**

Traded to **Toronto** by **Vancouver** for Jim Benning and Dan Hodgson, December 2, 1986. Signed as a free agent by **Chicago**, August 13, 1990. Traded to **LA Kings** by **Chicago** for cash, November 29, 1991.

• LAPERRIERE, Daniel

Daniel J. D – L. 6'1", 195 lbs. b: Laval, Que., 3/28/1969. St. Louis' 4th, 93rd overall, in 1989.

Season	Club	League	GP	G	A	Pts	AG	AA	APts	PIM	PP	SH	GW	S	%	TGF	PGF	TGA	PGA	+/–	GP	G	A	Pts	PIM	PP	SH	GW
1986-87	St-Sacrement High School	Hi-School	17	22	17	39	....	....	....	....	....	....	....	....	....	....	....	....	....	....	....	....	....	....	....	....	....	....
1987-88	Laval College-Francais	CEGEP	STATISTICS NOT AVAILABLE																									
1988-89	St. Lawrence University	ECAC	28	0	7	7	....	....	....	10	....	....	....	....	....	....	....	....	....	....	....	....	....	....	....	....	....	....
1989-90	St. Lawrence University	ECAC	31	6	19	25	....	....	....	16	....	....	....	....	....	....	....	....	....	....	....	....	....	....	....	....	....	....
1990-91	St. Lawrence University	ECAC	34	7	31	38	....	....	....	18	....	....	....	....	....	....	....	....	....	....	....	....	....	....	....	....	....	....
1991-92	St. Lawrence University	ECAC	32	8	*45	53	....	....	....	36	....	....	....	....	....	....	....	....	....	....	....	....	....	....	....	....	....	....
1992-93	**St. Louis Blues**	**NHL**	**5**	**0**	**1**	**1**	**0**	**1**	**1**	**0**	**0**	**0**	**0**	**7**	**0.0**	**2**	**1**	**4**	**0**	**-3**	....	....	....	....	....	....	....	....
	Peoria Rivermen	IHL	54	4	20	24	....	....	....	28	....	....	....	....	....	....	....	....	....	....	....	....	....	....	....	....	....	....
1993-94	**St. Louis Blues**	**NHL**	**20**	**1**	**3**	**4**	**1**	**2**	**3**	**8**	**1**	**0**	**0**	**20**	**5.0**	**14**	**7**	**8**	**0**	**-1**	....	....	....	....	....	....	....	....
	Peoria Rivermen	IHL	56	10	37	47	....	....	....	16	....	....	....	....	....	....	....	....	....	....	6	0	2	2	2	....	....	....
1994-95	Peoria Rivermen	IHL	65	19	33	52	....	....	....	42	....	....	....	....	....	....	....	....	....	....	....	....	....	....	....	....	....	....
	St. Louis Blues	**NHL**	**4**	**0**	**0**	**0**	**0**	**0**	**0**	**15**	**0**	**0**	**0**	**0**	**0.0**	**2**	**0**	**1**	**0**	**1**	....	....	....	....	....	....	....	....
	Ottawa Senators	**NHL**	**13**	**1**	**1**	**2**	**2**	**1**	**3**	**0**	**1**	**0**	**0**	**18**	**5.6**	**14**	**5**	**15**	**2**	**-4**	....	....	....	....	....	....	....	....
1995-96	**Ottawa Senators**	**NHL**	**6**	**0**	**0**	**0**	**0**	**0**	**0**	**4**	**0**	**0**	**0**	**12**	**0.0**	**6**	**2**	**2**	**0**	**2**	....	....	....	....	....	....	....	....
	P.E.I. Senators	AHL	15	2	7	9	....	....	....	4	....	....	....	....	....	....	....	....	....	....	....	....	....	....	....	....	....	....
	Atlanta Knights	IHL	15	4	9	13	....	....	....	4	....	....	....	....	....	....	....	....	....	....	....	....	....	....	....	....	....	....
	Kansas City Blades	IHL	23	2	6	8	....	....	....	11	....	....	....	....	....	....	....	....	....	....	5	0	1	1	0	....	....	....
1996-97	Portland Pirates	AHL	69	14	26	40	....	....	....	33	....	....	....	....	....	....	....	....	....	....	5	0	2	2	2	....	....	....
1997-98	Schwenningen Wild Wings	Germany	50	14	27	41	....	....	....	18	....	....	....	....	....	....	....	....	....	....	....	....	....	....	....	....	....	....
1998-99	Schwenningen Wild Wings	Germany	46	9	30	39	....	....	....	52	....	....	....	....	....	....	....	....	....	....	....	....	....	....	....	....	....	....
99-2000	Schwenningen Wild Wings	Germany	67	19	33	52	....	....	....	16	....	....	....	....	....	....	....	....	....	....	....	....	....	....	....	....	....	....
	NHL Totals		**48**	**2**	**5**	**7**	**3**	**4**	**7**	**27**	**2**	**0**	**0**	**57**	**3.5**	**38**	**15**	**30**	**2**		....	....	....	....	....	....	....	....

• Son of Jacques • ECAC Second All-Star Team (1991) • ECAC First All-Star Team (1992) • NCAA East First All-American Team (1992)

Traded to **Ottawa** by **St. Louis** with St. Louis' 9th round choice (Erik Kaminski) in 1995 Entry Draft for Ottawa's 9th round choice (Libor Zabransky) in 1995 Entry Draft, April 7, 1995. Signed as a free agent by **Washington**, July 12, 1996.

• LAPERRIERE, Ian

C – R. 6'1", 201 lbs. b: Montreal, Que., 1/19/1974. St. Louis' 6th, 158th overall, in 1992.

Season	Club	League	GP	G	A	Pts	AG	AA	APts	PIM	PP	SH	GW	S	%	TGF	PGF	TGA	PGA	+/–	GP	G	A	Pts	PIM	PP	SH	GW
1989-90	Montreal-Bourassa	QAAA	22	4	10	14	....	....	....	10	....	....	....	....	....	....	....	....	....	....	3	0	1	1	0	....	....	....
1990-91	Drummondville Voltigeurs	QMJHL	65	19	29	48	....	....	....	117	....	....	....	....	....	....	....	....	....	....	14	2	9	11	48	....	....	....
	Drummondville Voltigeurs	Mem-Cup	5	3	1	4	....	....	....	10	....	....	....	....	....	....	....	....	....	....	....	....	....	....	....	....	....	....
1991-92	Drummondville Voltigeurs	QMJHL	70	28	49	77	....	....	....	160	....	....	....	....	....	....	....	....	....	....	4	2	2	4	9	....	....	....
1992-93	Drummondville Voltigeurs	QMJHL	60	44	*96	140	....	....	....	188	....	....	....	....	....	....	....	....	....	....	10	6	13	19	20	....	....	....
1993-94	Drummondville Voltigeurs	QMJHL	62	41	72	113	....	....	....	150	....	....	....	....	....	....	....	....	....	....	9	4	6	10	35	....	....	....
	St. Louis Blues	**NHL**	**1**	**0**	**0**	**0**	**0**	**0**	**0**	**0**	**0**	**0**	**0**	**1**	**0.0**	**0**	**0**	**0**	**0**	**0**	....	....	....	....	....	....	....	....
	Peoria Rivermen	IHL	....	....	....	....	....	....	....	....	....	....	....	....	....	....	....	....	....	....	5	1	3	4	2	....	....	....
1994-95	Peoria Rivermen	IHL	51	16	32	48	....	....	....	111	....	....	....	....	....	....	....	....	....	....	....	....	....	....	....	....	....	....
	St. Louis Blues	**NHL**	**37**	**13**	**14**	**27**	**23**	**21**	**44**	**85**	**1**	**0**	**1**	**53**	**24.5**	**33**	**3**	**19**	**1**	**12**	**7**	**0**	**4**	**4**	**21**	**0**	**0**	**0**
1995-96	**St. Louis Blues**	**NHL**	**33**	**3**	**6**	**9**	**3**	**5**	**8**	**87**	**1**	**0**	**1**	**31**	**9.7**	**11**	**3**	**13**	**1**	**-4**	....	....	....	....	....	....	....	....
	Worcester IceCats	AHL	3	2	1	3	....	....	....	22	....	....	....	....	....	....	....	....	....	....	....	....	....	....	....	....	....	....
	New York Rangers	**NHL**	**28**	**1**	**2**	**3**	**1**	**2**	**3**	**53**	**0**	**0**	**0**	**21**	**4.8**	**3**	**0**	**8**	**0**	**-5**	....	....	....	....	....	....	....	....
	Los Angeles Kings	**NHL**	**10**	**2**	**3**	**5**	**2**	**2**	**4**	**15**	**0**	**0**	**0**	**18**	**11.1**	**7**	**2**	**7**	**0**	**-2**	....	....	....	....	....	....	....	....
1996-97	**Los Angeles Kings**	**NHL**	**62**	**8**	**15**	**23**	**8**	**13**	**21**	**102**	**0**	**1**	**2**	**84**	**9.5**	**25**	**1**	**67**	**18**	**-25**	....	....	....	....	....	....	....	....
1997-98	**Los Angeles Kings**	**NHL**	**77**	**6**	**15**	**21**	**7**	**15**	**22**	**131**	**0**	**1**	**1**	**74**	**8.1**	**32**	**4**	**58**	**30**	**0**	**4**	**1**	**0**	**1**	**6**	**0**	**0**	**0**
1998-99	**Los Angeles Kings**	**NHL**	**72**	**3**	**10**	**13**	**4**	**10**	**14**	**138**	**0**	**0**	**1**	**62**	**4.8**	**14**	**1**	**32**	**14**	**-5**	....	....	....	....	....	....	....	....
99-2000	**Los Angeles Kings**	**NHL**	**79**	**9**	**13**	**22**	**10**	**12**	**22**	**185**	**0**	**0**	**1**	**87**	**10.3**	**30**	**3**	**61**	**20**	**-14**	**4**	**0**	**0**	**0**	**2**	**0**	**0**	**0**
	NHL Totals		**399**	**45**	**78**	**123**	**58**	**80**	**138**	**796**	**2**	**2**	**7**	**431**	**10.4**	**155**	**17**	**265**	**84**		**15**	**1**	**4**	**5**	**29**	**0**	**0**	**0**

QMJHL Second All-Star Team (1993)

Traded to **NY Rangers** by **St. Louis** for Stephane Matteau, December 28, 1995. Traded to **LA Kings** by **NY Rangers** with Ray Ferraro, Mattias Norstrom, Nathan Lafayette and NY Rangers' 4th round choice (Sean Blanchard) in 1997 Entry Draft for Marty McSorley, Jari Kurri and Shane Churla, March 14, 1996.

• LAPERRIERE, Jacques

Joseph Jacques Hugues D – L. 6'2", 180 lbs. b: Rouyn, Que., 11/22/1941. **HHOF**

Season	Club	League	GP	G	A	Pts	AG	AA	APts	PIM	PP	SH	GW	S	%	TGF	PGF	TGA	PGA	+/–	GP	G	A	Pts	PIM	PP	SH	GW
1958-59	Hull-Ottawa Canadiens	X-Games	STATISTICS NOT AVAILABLE																									
	Hull-Ottawa Canadiens	EOHL	1	1	1	2	....	....	....	2	....	....	....	....	....	....	....	....	....	....	2	0	0	0	0	....	....	....
	Hull-Ottawa Canadiens	Mem-Cup	9	1	0	1	....	....	....	16	....	....	....	....	....	....	....	....	....	....	....	....	....	....	....	....	....	....
1959-60	Brockville Jr. Canadiens	OVJHL	STATISTICS NOT AVAILABLE																									
	Hull-Ottawa Canadiens	EPHL	5	0	2	2	....	....	....	0	....	....	....	....	....	....	....	....	....	....	....	....	....	....	....	....	....	....
	Brockville Jr. Canadiens	Mem-Cup	13	0	13	13	....	....	....	34	....	....	....	....	....	....	....	....	....	....	....	....	....	....	....	....	....	....
1960-61	Hull Canadiens	IPSHL	....	11	29	40	....	....	....	....	....	....	....	....	....	....	....	....	....	....	....	....	....	....	....	....	....	....
	Hull-Ottawa Canadiens	EPHL	5	0	0	0	....	....	....	2	....	....	....	....	....	....	....	....	....	....	3	0	2	2	4	....	....	....
	Hull Canadiens	Al-Cup	3	0	0	0	....	....	....	4	....	....	....	....	....	....	....	....	....	....	....	....	....	....	....	....	....	....
1961-62	Montreal Jr. Canadiens	OHA-Jr.	48	20	37	57	....	....	....	98	....	....	....	....	....	....	....	....	....	....	6	0	1	1	11	....	....	....
	Hull-Ottawa Canadiens	EPHL	1	0	0	0	....	....	....	4	....	....	....	....	....	....	....	....	....	....	7	1	4	5	6	....	....	....
1962-63	**Montreal Canadiens**	**NHL**	**6**	**0**	**2**	**2**	**0**	**2**	**2**	**2**	....	....	....	....	....	....	....	....	....	....	**5**	**0**	**1**	**1**	**4**	**0**	**0**	**0**
	Hull-Ottawa Canadiens	EPHL	40	8	19	27	....	....	....	51	....	....	....	....	....	....	....	....	....	....	2	0	0	0	0	....	....	....
1963-64	**Montreal Canadiens**	**NHL**	**65**	**2**	**28**	**30**	**2**	**29**	**31**	**102**	....	....	....	....	....	....	....	....	....	....	**7**	**1**	**1**	**2**	**8**	**0**	**1**	**0**
1964-65♦	**Montreal Canadiens**	**NHL**	**67**	**5**	**22**	**27**	**6**	**23**	**29**	**92**	....	....	....	....	....	....	....	....	....	....	**6**	**1**	**1**	**2**	**16**	**1**	**0**	**0**
1965-66♦	**Montreal Canadiens**	**NHL**	**57**	**6**	**25**	**31**	**7**	**24**	**31**	**85**	....	....	....	....	....	....	....	....	....	....	....	....	....	....	....	....	....	....
1966-67	**Montreal Canadiens**	**NHL**	**61**	**0**	**20**	**20**	**0**	**20**	**20**	**48**	....	....	....	....	....	....	....	....	....	....	**9**	**0**	**1**	**1**	**9**	**0**	**0**	**0**
1967-68♦	**Montreal Canadiens**	**NHL**	**72**	**4**	**21**	**25**	**5**	**21**	**26**	**84**	**1**	**0**	**0**	**122**	**3.3**	**110**	**23**	**88**	**24**	**23**	**13**	**1**	**3**	**4**	**20**	**0**	**0**	**0**
1968-69♦	**Montreal Canadiens**	**NHL**	**69**	**5**	**26**	**31**	**5**	**23**	**28**	**45**	**0**	**0**	**1**	**166**	**3.0**	**114**	**14**	**85**	**22**	**37**	**14**	**1**	**3**	**4**	**28**	**1**	**0**	**0**
1969-70	**Montreal Canadiens**	**NHL**	**73**	**6**	**31**	**37**	**6**	**29**	**35**	**98**	**2**	**1**	**1**	**169**	**3.6**	**126**	**34**	**96**	**32**	**28**	....	....	....	....	....	....	....	....
1970-71♦	**Montreal Canadiens**	**NHL**	**49**	**0**	**16**	**16**	**0**	**13**	**13**	**20**	**0**	**0**	**0**	**65**	**0.0**	**78**	**9**	**68**	**23**	**24**	**20**	**4**	**9**	**13**	**12**	**1**	**0**	**1**
1971-72	**Montreal Canadiens**	**NHL**	**73**	**3**	**25**	**28**	**3**	**22**	**25**	**50**	**2**	**0**	**0**	**97**	**3.1**	**116**	**9**	**104**	**33**	**36**	**4**	**0**	**0**	**0**	**2**	**0**	**0**	**0**
1972-73♦	**Montreal Canadiens**	**NHL**	**57**	**7**	**16**	**23**	**7**	**13**	**20**	**34**	**2**	**0**	**0**	**88**	**8.0**	**129**	**11**	**64**	**24**	**78**	**10**	**1**	**3**	**4**	**2**	**0**	**0**	**0**
1973-74	**Montreal Canadiens**	**NHL**	**42**	**2**	**10**	**12**	**2**	**8**	**10**	**14**	**0**	**1**	**0**	**60**	**3.3**	**66**	**7**	**59**	**15**	**15**	....	....	....	....	....	....	....	....
1975-1976	Montreal Red-White-Blue	QMJHL	DID NOT PLAY – COACHING																									
1976-1977	Montreal Juniors	QMJHL	DID NOT PLAY – COACHING																									
1977-1980			OUT OF HOCKEY – RETIRED																									
1980-1981	**Montreal Canadiens**	**NHL**	DID NOT PLAY – ASSISTANT GENERAL MANAGER																									
1981-1997	**Montreal Canadiens**	**NHL**	DID NOT PLAY – ASSISTANT COACH																									
1997-2000	**Boston Bruins**	**NHL**	DID NOT PLAY – ASSISTANT COACH																									
	NHL Totals		**691**	**40**	**242**	**282**	**43**	**227**	**270**	**674**	....	....	....	....	....	....	....	....	....	....	**88**	**9**	**22**	**31**	**101**	....	....	....

• Father of Daniel • NHL Second All-Star Team (1964, 1970) • Won Calder Memorial Trophy (1964) • NHL First All-Star Team (1965, 1966) • Won James Norris Trophy (1966) • NHL Plus/Minus Leader (1973) • Played in NHL All-Star Game (1964, 1965, 1967, 1968, 1970)

• Suffered career-ending knee injury in game vs. Boston, January 19, 1974.

• LAPLANTE, Darryl

C – L. 6'1", 185 lbs. b: Calgary, Alta., 3/28/1977. Detroit's 3rd, 58th overall, in 1995.

			REGULAR SEASON																			PLAYOFFS							
Season	Club	League	GP	G	A	Pts	AG	AA	APts	PIM	PP	SH	GW	S	%	TGF	PGF	TGA	PGA	+/–	GP	G	A	Pts	PIM	PP	SH	GW
1992-93	Calgary Bantam Royals	AAHA	32	20	26	46	....	....	....	60	....	....	....	....	....	....	....	....	....	....	....	....	....	....	....	....	....	....
1993-94	Calgary Royals	AAHA	35	24	27	51	....	....	....	50	....	....	....	....	....	....	....	....	....	....	....	....	....	....	....	....	....	....
1994-95	Moose Jaw Warriors	WHL	71	22	24	46	....	....	....	66	....	....	....	....	....	....	....	....	....	....	10	2	2	4	7	....	....	....
1995-96	Moose Jaw Warriors	WHL	72	42	40	82	....	....	....	76	....	....	....	....	....	....	....	....	....	....	....	....	....	....	....	....	....	....
1996-97	Moose Jaw Warriors	WHL	69	38	42	80	....	....	....	79	....	....	....	....	....	....	....	....	....	....	12	2	4	6	15	....	....	....
1997-98	**Detroit Red Wings**	**NHL**	**2**	**0**	**0**	**0**	**0**	**0**	**0**	**0**	**0**	**0**	**0**	**2**	**0.0**	**0**	**0**	**0**	**0**	**0**	....	....	....	....	....	....	....	....
	Adirondack Red Wings	AHL	77	15	10	25	....	....	....	51	....	....	....	....	....	....	....	....	....	....	3	0	1	1	4	....	....	....
1998-99	**Detroit Red Wings**	**NHL**	**3**	**0**	**0**	**0**	**0**	**0**	**0**	**0**	**0**	**0**	**0**	**0**	**0.0**	**0**	**0**	**0**	**0**	**0**	....	....	....	....	....	....	....	....
	Adirondack Red Wings	AHL	71	17	15	32	....	....	....	96	....	....	....	....	....	....	....	....	....	....	3	0	1	1	0	....	....	....
99-2000	**Detroit Red Wings**	**NHL**	**30**	**0**	**6**	**6**	**0**	**6**	**6**	**10**	**0**	**0**	**0**	**19**	**0.0**	**15**	**0**	**17**	**0**	**–2**	....	....	....	....	....	....	....	....
	Cincinnati Mighty Ducks	AHL	35	13	9	22	....	....	....	47	....	....	....	....	....	....	....	....	....	....	....	....	....	....	....	....	....	....
	NHL Totals		**35**	**0**	**6**	**6**	**0**	**6**	**6**	**10**	**0**	**0**	**0**	**21**	**0.0**	**15**	**0**	**17**	**0**		....	....	....	....	....	....	....	....

Selected by **Minnesota** from **Detroit** in Expansion Draft, June 23, 2000.

• LAPOINTE, Claude

C – L. 5'9", 181 lbs. b: Lachine, Que., 10/11/1968. Quebec's 12th, 234th overall, in 1988.

Season	Club	League	GP	G	A	Pts	AG	AA	APts	PIM	PP	SH	GW	S	%	TGF	PGF	TGA	PGA	+/–	GP	G	A	Pts	PIM	PP	SH	GW
1983-84	Lac St-Louis Lions	QAAA	42	28	29	57	....	....	....	....	....	....	....	....	....	....	....	....	....	....	....	....	....	....	....	....	....	....
1984-85	Lac St-Louis Lions	QAAA	42	20	32	52	....	....	....	....	....	....	....	....	....	....	....	....	....	....	....	....	....	....	....	....	....	....
1985-86	Trois-Rivieres Draveurs	QMJHL	63	14	32	46	....	....	....	70	....	....	....	....	....	....	....	....	....	....	9	5	6	11	4	....	....	....
1986-87	Trois-Rivieres Draveurs	QMJHL	70	47	57	104	....	....	....	123	....	....	....	....	....	....	....	....	....	....	....	....	....	....	....	....	....	....
1987-88	Laval Titan	QMJHL	69	37	83	120	....	....	....	143	....	....	....	....	....	....	....	....	....	....	13	2	17	19	53	....	....	....
1988-89	Laval Titan	QMJHL	63	32	72	104	....	....	....	158	....	....	....	....	....	....	....	....	....	....	17	5	14	19	66	....	....	....
	Laval Titan	Mem-Cup	4	2	2	4	....	....	....	4	....	....	....	....	....	....	....	....	....	....	....	....	....	....	....	....	....	....
1989-90	Halifax Citadels	AHL	63	18	19	37	....	....	....	51	....	....	....	....	....	....	....	....	....	....	6	1	1	2	34	....	....	....
1990-91	**Quebec Nordiques**	**NHL**	**13**	**2**	**2**	**4**	**2**	**2**	**4**	**4**	**0**	**0**	**0**	**7**	**28.6**	**6**	**0**	**6**	**3**	**3**	....	....	....	....	....	....	....	....
	Halifax Citadels	AHL	43	17	17	34	....	....	....	46	....	....	....	....	....	....	....	....	....	....	....	....	....	....	....	....	....	....
1991-92	**Quebec Nordiques**	**NHL**	**78**	**13**	**20**	**33**	**12**	**15**	**27**	**86**	**0**	**2**	**2**	**95**	**13.7**	**42**	**2**	**81**	**33**	**–8**	....	....	....	....	....	....	....	....
1992-93	**Quebec Nordiques**	**NHL**	**74**	**10**	**26**	**36**	**8**	**18**	**26**	**98**	**0**	**0**	**1**	**91**	**11.0**	**52**	**1**	**66**	**20**	**5**	**6**	**2**	**4**	**6**	**8**	**0**	**0**	**0**
1993-94	**Quebec Nordiques**	**NHL**	**59**	**11**	**17**	**28**	**10**	**13**	**23**	**70**	**1**	**1**	**1**	**73**	**15.1**	**47**	**3**	**59**	**17**	**2**	....	....	....	....	....	....	....	....
1994-95	**Quebec Nordiques**	**NHL**	**29**	**4**	**8**	**12**	**7**	**12**	**19**	**41**	**0**	**0**	**0**	**40**	**10.0**	**19**	**0**	**19**	**5**	**5**	**5**	**0**	**0**	**0**	**8**	**0**	**0**	**0**
1995-96	**Colorado Avalanche**	**NHL**	**3**	**0**	**0**	**0**	**0**	**0**	**0**	**0**	**0**	**0**	**0**	**0**	**0.0**	**0**	**0**	**1**	**0**	**–1**	....	....	....	....	....	....	....	....
	Calgary Flames	**NHL**	**32**	**4**	**5**	**9**	**4**	**4**	**8**	**20**	**0**	**2**	**1**	**44**	**9.1**	**15**	**0**	**23**	**10**	**2**	**2**	**0**	**0**	**0**	**0**	**0**	**0**	**0**
	Saint John Flames	AHL	12	5	3	8	....	....	....	10	....	....	....	....	....	....	....	....	....	....	....	....	....	....	....	....	....	....
1996-97	**New York Islanders**	**NHL**	**73**	**13**	**5**	**18**	**14**	**4**	**18**	**49**	**0**	**3**	**3**	**80**	**16.3**	**33**	**1**	**68**	**24**	**–12**	....	....	....	....	....	....	....	....
	Utah Grizzlies	IHL	9	7	6	13	....	....	....	14	....	....	....	....	....	....	....	....	....	....	....	....	....	....	....	....	....	....
1997-98	**New York Islanders**	**NHL**	**78**	**10**	**10**	**20**	**12**	**10**	**22**	**47**	**0**	**1**	**3**	**82**	**12.2**	**31**	**0**	**57**	**17**	**–9**	....	....	....	....	....	....	....	....
1998-99	**New York Islanders**	**NHL**	**82**	**14**	**23**	**37**	**16**	**22**	**38**	**62**	**2**	**2**	**1**	**134**	**10.4**	**48**	**6**	**90**	**29**	**–19**	....	....	....	....	....	....	....	....
	Canada	WC-A	10	1	3	4	....	....	....	10	....	....	....	....	....	....	....	....	....	....	....	....	....	....	....	....	....	....
99-2000	**New York Islanders**	**NHL**	**76**	**15**	**16**	**31**	**17**	**15**	**32**	**60**	**2**	**1**	**3**	**129**	**11.6**	**45**	**10**	**101**	**44**	**–22**	....	....	....	....	....	....	....	....
	NHL Totals		**597**	**96**	**132**	**228**	**102**	**115**	**217**	**537**	**5**	**12**	**15**	**775**	**12.4**	**338**	**23**	**571**	**202**		**13**	**2**	**4**	**6**	**16**	**0**	**0**	**0**

Transferred to **Colorado** after **Quebec** franchise relocated, June 21, 1995. Traded to **Calgary** by **Colorado** for Calgary's 7th round choice (Samuel Pahlsson) in 1996 Entry Draft, November 1, 1995. Signed as a free agent by **NY Islanders**, August 14, 1996.

• LAPOINTE, Guy

Guy Gerard D – L. 6', 205 lbs. b: Montreal, Que., 3/18/1948. **HHOF**

Season	Club	League	GP	G	A	Pts	AG	AA	APts	PIM	PP	SH	GW	S	%	TGF	PGF	TGA	PGA	+/–	GP	G	A	Pts	PIM	PP	SH	GW
1965-66	Verdun Jr. Maple Leafs	QJHL	37	7	13	20	....	....	....	96	....	....	....	....	....	....	....	....	....	....	....	....	....	....	....	....	....	....
1966-67	Verdun Jr. Maple Leafs	QJHL	....	....	....	....	....	....	....	....	....	....	....	....	....	....	....	....	....	....	12	1	1	2	14	....	....	....
1967-68	Montreal Jr. Canadiens	OHA-Jr.	51	11	27	38	....	....	....	147	....	....	....	....	....	....	....	....	....	....	11	1	6	7	40	....	....	....
1968-69	**Montreal Canadiens**	**NHL**	**1**	**0**	**0**	**0**	**0**	**0**	**0**	**2**	**0**	**0**	**0**	**0**	**0.0**	**0**	**0**	**0**	**0**	**0**	....	....	....	....	....	....	....	....
	Houston Apollos	CHL	65	3	15	18	....	....	....	120	....	....	....	....	....	....	....	....	....	....	3	1	0	1	6	....	....	....
1969-70	**Montreal Canadiens**	**NHL**	**5**	**0**	**0**	**0**	**0**	**0**	**0**	**4**	**0**	**0**	**0**	**0**	**0.0**	**0**	**0**	**0**	**0**	**0**	....	....	....	....	....	....	....	....
	Montreal Voyageurs	AHL	57	8	30	38	....	....	....	92	....	....	....	....	....	....	....	....	....	....	8	3	5	8	6	....	....	....
1970-71 ♦	**Montreal Canadiens**	**NHL**	**78**	**15**	**29**	**44**	**15**	**24**	**39**	**107**	**5**	**0**	**1**	**228**	**6.6**	**131**	**32**	**87**	**16**	**28**	**20**	**4**	**5**	**9**	**34**	**1**	**0**	**2**
1971-72	**Montreal Canadiens**	**NHL**	**69**	**11**	**38**	**49**	**11**	**33**	**44**	**58**	**4**	**0**	**4**	**227**	**4.8**	**123**	**38**	**78**	**8**	**15**	**6**	**0**	**1**	**1**	**0**	**0**	**0**	**0**
1972-73	Team Canada	Summit-72	7	0	1	1	....	....	....	6	....	....	....	....	....	....	....	....	....	....	....	....	....	....	....	....	....	....
♦	**Montreal Canadiens**	**NHL**	**76**	**19**	**35**	**54**	**18**	**28**	**46**	**117**	**3**	**0**	**2**	**196**	**9.7**	**164**	**37**	**92**	**16**	**51**	**17**	**6**	**7**	**13**	**20**	**2**	**0**	**1**
1973-74	**Montreal Canadiens**	**NHL**	**71**	**13**	**40**	**53**	**12**	**33**	**45**	**63**	**5**	**1**	**2**	**205**	**6.3**	**140**	**40**	**117**	**29**	**12**	**6**	**0**	**2**	**2**	**4**	**0**	**0**	**0**
1974-75	**Montreal Canadiens**	**NHL**	**80**	**28**	**47**	**75**	**24**	**35**	**59**	**88**	**11**	**1**	**0**	**219**	**12.8**	**186**	**65**	**116**	**41**	**46**	**11**	**6**	**4**	**10**	**4**	**3**	**1**	**0**
1975-76 ♦	**Montreal Canadiens**	**NHL**	**77**	**21**	**47**	**68**	**18**	**35**	**53**	**78**	**8**	**1**	**1**	**317**	**6.6**	**183**	**60**	**88**	**29**	**64**	**13**	**3**	**3**	**6**	**12**	**1**	**0**	**1**
1976-77	Canada	Can-Cup	7	0	4	4	....	....	....	2	....	....	....	....	....	....	....	....	....	....	....	....	....	....	....	....	....	....
♦	**Montreal Canadiens**	**NHL**	**77**	**25**	**51**	**76**	**23**	**39**	**62**	**53**	**10**	**0**	**6**	**289**	**8.7**	**177**	**41**	**91**	**24**	**69**	**12**	**3**	**9**	**12**	**4**	**1**	**0**	**0**
1977-78 ♦	**Montreal Canadiens**	**NHL**	**49**	**13**	**29**	**42**	**12**	**22**	**34**	**19**	**4**	**0**	**2**	**148**	**8.8**	**115**	**31**	**52**	**14**	**46**	**14**	**1**	**6**	**7**	**16**	**1**	**0**	**0**
1978-79 ♦	**Montreal Canadiens**	**NHL**	**69**	**13**	**42**	**55**	**11**	**30**	**41**	**43**	**6**	**0**	**1**	**209**	**6.2**	**145**	**42**	**98**	**22**	**27**	**10**	**2**	**6**	**8**	**10**	**1**	**0**	**0**
	NHL All-Stars	Chal-Cup	1	0	0	0	....	....	....	0	....	....	....	....	....	....	....	....	....	....	....	....	....	....	....	....	....	....
1979-80	**Montreal Canadiens**	**NHL**	**45**	**6**	**20**	**26**	**5**	**15**	**20**	**29**	**0**	**0**	**0**	**124**	**4.8**	**75**	**23**	**69**	**15**	**–2**	**2**	**0**	**0**	**0**	**0**	**0**	**0**	**0**
1980-81	**Montreal Canadiens**	**NHL**	**33**	**1**	**9**	**10**	**1**	**6**	**7**	**79**	**1**	**0**	**1**	**47**	**2.1**	**39**	**12**	**39**	**6**	**–6**	**1**	**0**	**0**	**0**	**17**	**0**	**0**	**0**
1981-82	**Montreal Canadiens**	**NHL**	**47**	**1**	**19**	**20**	**1**	**13**	**14**	**72**	**0**	**0**	**0**	**97**	**1.0**	**64**	**25**	**59**	**17**	**–3**	....	....	....	....	....	....	....	....
	St. Louis Blues	**NHL**	**8**	**0**	**6**	**6**	**0**	**4**	**4**	**4**	**0**	**0**	**0**	**15**	**0.0**	**15**	**7**	**15**	**4**	**–3**	**7**	**1**	**0**	**1**	**8**	**1**	**0**	**1**
1982-83	**St. Louis Blues**	**NHL**	**54**	**3**	**23**	**26**	**2**	**16**	**18**	**43**	**1**	**1**	**1**	**106**	**2.8**	**69**	**21**	**75**	**15**	**–12**	**4**	**0**	**1**	**1**	**9**	**0**	**0**	**0**
1983-84	**Boston Bruins**	**NHL**	**45**	**2**	**16**	**18**	**2**	**11**	**13**	**34**	**1**	**0**	**1**	**57**	**3.5**	**46**	**17**	**34**	**2**	**–3**	....	....	....	....	....	....	....	....
1984-85	**Quebec Nordiques**	**NHL**	DID NOT PLAY – ASSISTANT COACH																									
1985-1987	Longueuil Chevaliers	QMJHL	DID NOT PLAY – COACHING																									
	NHL Totals		**884**	**171**	**451**	**622**	**155**	**344**	**499**	**893**	**59**	**4**	**22**	**2484**	**6.9**	**1672**	**491**	**1110**	**258**		**123**	**26**	**44**	**70**	**138**	**11**	**1**	**5**

AHL First All-Star Team (1970) • NHL First All-Star Team (1973) • NHL Second All-Star Team (1975, 1976, 1977) • Played in NHL All-Star Game (1973, 1975, 1976, 1977)

Traded to **St. Louis** by **Montreal** for St. Louis' 2nd round choice (Sergio Momesso) in 1983 Entry Draft, March 9, 1982. Signed as a free agent by **Boston**, August 15, 1983.

• LAPOINTE, Martin

RW – R. 5'11", 200 lbs. b: Ville Ste. Pierre, Que., 9/12/1973. Detroit's 1st, 10th overall, in 1991.

Season	Club	League	GP	G	A	Pts	AG	AA	APts	PIM	PP	SH	GW	S	%	TGF	PGF	TGA	PGA	+/–	GP	G	A	Pts	PIM	PP	SH	GW
1988-89	Lac St-Louis Lions	QAAA	42	39	45	84	....	....	....	....	....	....	....	....	....	....	....	....	....	....	....	....	....	....	....	....	....	....
1989-90	Laval Titan	QMJHL	65	42	54	96	....	....	....	77	....	....	....	....	....	....	....	....	....	....	14	8	17	25	54	....	....	....
	Laval Titan	Mem-Cup	4	1	1	2	....	....	....	4	....	....	....	....	....	....	....	....	....	....	....	....	....	....	....	....	....	....
1990-91	Laval Titan	QMJHL	64	44	54	98	....	....	....	66	....	....	....	....	....	....	....	....	....	....	13	7	14	21	26	....	....	....
	Canada	WJC-A	7	0	3	3	....	....	....	2	....	....	....	....	....	....	....	....	....	....	....	....	....	....	....	....	....	....
1991-92	Laval Titan	QMJHL	31	25	30	55	....	....	....	84	....	....	....	....	....	....	....	....	....	....	10	4	10	14	32	....	....	....
	Canada	WJC-A	7	4	1	5	....	....	....	10	....	....	....	....	....	....	....	....	....	....	....	....	....	....	....	....	....	....
	Detroit Red Wings	**NHL**	**4**	**0**	**1**	**1**	**0**	**1**	**1**	**5**	**0**	**0**	**0**	**2**	**0.0**	**2**	**0**	**0**	**0**	**2**	**3**	**0**	**1**	**1**	**4**	**0**	**0**	**0**
	Adirondack Red Wings	AHL	....	....	....	....	....	....	....	....	....	....	....	....	....	....	....	....	....	....	8	2	2	4	4	....	....	....
1992-93	Laval Titan	QMJHL	35	38	51	89	....	....	....	41	....	....	....	....	....	....	....	....	....	....	13	*13	*17	*30	22	....	....	....
	Canada	WJC-A	7	5	4	9	....	....	....	6	....	....	....	....	....	....	....	....	....	....	....	....	....	....	....	....	....	....
	Detroit Red Wings	**NHL**	**3**	**0**	**0**	**0**	**0**	**0**	**0**	**0**	**0**	**0**	**0**	**2**	**0.0**	**0**	**0**	**2**	**0**	**–2**	....	....	....	....	....	....	....	....
	Adirondack Red Wings	AHL	8	1	2	3	....	....	....	9	....	....	....	....	....	....	....	....	....	....	....	....	....	....	....	....	....	....
	Laval Titan	Mem-Cup	5	1	8	9	....	....	....	11	....	....	....	....	....	....	....	....	....	....	....	....	....	....	....	....	....	....
1993-94	**Detroit Red Wings**	**NHL**	**50**	**8**	**8**	**16**	**7**	**6**	**13**	**55**	**2**	**0**	**0**	**45**	**17.8**	**34**	**4**	**23**	**0**	**7**	**4**	**0**	**0**	**0**	**6**	**0**	**0**	**0**
	Adirondack Red Wings	AHL	28	25	21	46	....	....	....	47	....	....	....	....	....	....	....	....	....	....	4	1	1	2	8	....	....	....
1994-95	Adirondack Red Wings	AHL	39	29	16	45	....	....	....	80	....	....	....	....	....	....	....	....	....	....	....	....	....	....	....	....	....	....
	Detroit Red Wings	**NHL**	**39**	**4**	**6**	**10**	**7**	**9**	**16**	**73**	**0**	**0**	**1**	**46**	**8.7**	**16**	**2**	**14**	**1**	**1**	**2**	**0**	**1**	**1**	**8**	**0**	**0**	**0**
1995-96	**Detroit Red Wings**	**NHL**	**58**	**6**	**3**	**9**	**6**	**2**	**8**	**93**	**1**	**0**	**0**	**76**	**7.9**	**22**	**5**	**17**	**0**	**0**	**11**	**1**	**2**	**3**	**12**	**0**	**0**	**0**
1996-97 ♦	**Detroit Red Wings**	**NHL**	**78**	**16**	**17**	**33**	**17**	**15**	**32**	**167**	**5**	**1**	**1**	**149**	**10.7**	**52**	**17**	**53**	**4**	**–14**	**20**	**4**	**8**	**12**	**60**	**1**	**0**	**1**
1997-98 ♦	**Detroit Red Wings**	**NHL**	**79**	**15**	**19**	**34**	**18**	**19**	**37**	**106**	**4**	**0**	**3**	**154**	**9.7**	**52**	**14**	**42**	**4**	**0**	**21**	**9**	**6**	**15**	**20**	**2**	**1**	**1**

			REGULAR SEASON																		PLAYOFFS							
Season	**Club**	**League**	**GP**	**G**	**A**	**Pts**	**AG**	**AA**	**APts**	**PIM**	**PP**	**SH**	**GW**	**S**	**%**	**TGF**	**PGF**	**TGA**	**PGA**	**+/–**	**GP**	**G**	**A**	**Pts**	**PIM**	**PP**	**SH**	**GW**
1998-99	**Detroit Red Wings**	**NHL**	**77**	**16**	**13**	**29**	**19**	**13**	**32**	**141**	**7**	**1**	**4**	**153**	**10.5**	**60**	**17**	**42**	**6**	**7**	**10**	**0**	**2**	**2**	**20**	**0**	**0**	**0**
99-2000	**Detroit Red Wings**	**NHL**	**82**	**16**	**25**	**41**	**18**	**23**	**41**	**121**	**1**	**1**	**2**	**127**	**12.6**	**63**	**13**	**42**	**9**	**17**	**9**	**3**	**1**	**4**	**20**	**2**	**0**	**1**
	Canada	WC-A	3	0	0	0	....	....	....	4	....	....	....	....	....	....	....	....	....	....	....	....	....	....	....	....	....	....
	NHL Totals		**470**	**81**	**92**	**173**	**92**	**88**	**180**	**761**	**20**	**3**	**11**	**754**	**10.7**	**301**	**72**	**235**	**24**		**80**	**17**	**21**	**38**	**150**	**5**	**1**	**3**

QMJHL First All-Star Team (1990, 1993) • QMJHL Second All-Star Team (1991) • Memorial Cup All-Star Team (1993)

• LAPOINTE, Rick

Richard Paul "Jumbo" D – L. 6'2", 200 lbs. b: Victoria, B.C., 8/2/1955 d: 10/17/1999. Detroit's 1st, 5th overall, in 1975.

Season	Club	League	GP	G	A	Pts	AG	AA	APts	PIM	PP	SH	GW	S	%	TGF	PGF	TGA	PGA	+/–	GP	G	A	Pts	PIM	PP	SH	GW
1971-72	Nanaimo Clippers	BCJHL	STATISTICS NOT AVAILABLE																									
	Victoria Cougars	WCJHL	4	0	0	0	....	....	....	0	....	....	....	....	....	....	....	....	....	....	....	....	....	....	....	....	....	....
1972-73	Victoria Cougars	WCJHL	39	3	12	15	....	....	....	31	....	....	....	....	....	....	....	....	....	....	....	....	....	....	....	....	....	....
1973-74	Victoria Cougars	WCJHL	66	8	18	26	....	....	....	207	....	....	....	....	....	....	....	....	....	....	....	....	....	....	....	....	....	....
1974-75	Victoria Cougars	WCJHL	67	19	51	70	....	....	....	177	....	....	....	....	....	....	....	....	....	....	12	1	12	13	26	....	....	....
	Canada	WJC-A	5	2	3	5	....	....	....	16	....	....	....	....	....	....	....	....	....	....	....	....	....	....	....	....	....	....
1975-76	**Detroit Red Wings**	**NHL**	**80**	**10**	**23**	**33**	**9**	**17**	**26**	**95**	**2**	**0**	**0**	**106**	**9.4**	**98**	**16**	**121**	**36**	**–3**	....	....	....	....	....	....	....	....
1976-77	**Detroit Red Wings**	**NHL**	**49**	**2**	**11**	**13**	**2**	**8**	**10**	**80**	**1**	**0**	**0**	**59**	**3.4**	**42**	**8**	**59**	**8**	**–17**	....	....	....	....	....	....	....	....
	Kansas City Blues	CHL	6	0	0	0	....	....	....	6	....	....	....	....	....	....	....	....	....	....	....	....	....	....	....	....	....	....
	Philadelphia Flyers	**NHL**	**22**	**1**	**8**	**9**	**1**	**6**	**7**	**39**	**0**	**0**	**1**	**27**	**3.7**	**30**	**2**	**11**	**3**	**20**	**10**	**0**	**0**	**0**	**7**	**0**	**0**	**0**
1977-78	**Philadelphia Flyers**	**NHL**	**47**	**4**	**16**	**20**	**4**	**12**	**16**	**91**	**1**	**0**	**0**	**56**	**7.1**	**64**	**6**	**32**	**9**	**35**	**12**	**0**	**3**	**3**	**19**	**0**	**0**	**0**
1978-79	**Philadelphia Flyers**	**NHL**	**77**	**3**	**18**	**21**	**3**	**13**	**16**	**53**	**1**	**1**	**0**	**75**	**4.0**	**81**	**6**	**80**	**20**	**15**	**7**	**0**	**1**	**1**	**14**	**0**	**0**	**0**
1979-80	**St. Louis Blues**	**NHL**	**80**	**6**	**19**	**25**	**5**	**14**	**19**	**87**	**0**	**0**	**1**	**113**	**5.3**	**108**	**6**	**150**	**24**	**–24**	**3**	**0**	**1**	**1**	**6**	**0**	**0**	**0**
1980-81	**St. Louis Blues**	**NHL**	**80**	**8**	**25**	**33**	**6**	**17**	**23**	**124**	**0**	**0**	**3**	**84**	**9.5**	**129**	**8**	**113**	**28**	**36**	**8**	**2**	**2**	**4**	**12**	**0**	**0**	**0**
1981-82	**St. Louis Blues**	**NHL**	**71**	**2**	**20**	**22**	**2**	**13**	**15**	**127**	**0**	**0**	**0**	**91**	**2.2**	**84**	**6**	**110**	**26**	**–6**	**3**	**0**	**0**	**0**	**6**	**0**	**0**	**0**
1982-83	**Quebec Nordiques**	**NHL**	**43**	**2**	**9**	**11**	**2**	**6**	**8**	**59**	**0**	**0**	**0**	**48**	**4.2**	**58**	**1**	**68**	**25**	**14**	....	....	....	....	....	....	....	....
	Fredericton Express	AHL	31	4	14	18	....	....	....	50	....	....	....	....	....	....	....	....	....	....	12	0	6	6	8	....	....	....
1983-84	**Quebec Nordiques**	**NHL**	**22**	**2**	**10**	**12**	**2**	**7**	**9**	**12**	**0**	**0**	**0**	**24**	**8.3**	**30**	**2**	**21**	**2**	**9**	**3**	**0**	**0**	**0**	**0**	**0**	**0**	**0**
	Fredericton Express	AHL	54	8	22	30	....	....	....	79	....	....	....	....	....	....	....	....	....	....	....	....	....	....	....	....	....	....
1984-85	**Los Angeles Kings**	**NHL**	**73**	**4**	**13**	**17**	**3**	**9**	**12**	**46**	**0**	**0**	**1**	**69**	**5.8**	**74**	**1**	**103**	**20**	**–10**	....	....	....	....	....	....	....	....
1985-86	**Los Angeles Kings**	**NHL**	**20**	**0**	**4**	**4**	**0**	**3**	**3**	**18**	**0**	**0**	**0**	**7**	**0.0**	**10**	**1**	**28**	**6**	**–13**	....	....	....	....	....	....	....	....
	NHL Totals		**664**	**44**	**176**	**220**	**39**	**125**	**164**	**831**	**5**	**1**	**6**	**759**	**5.8**	**808**	**63**	**896**	**207**		**46**	**2**	**7**	**9**	**64**	**0**	**0**	**0**

WJC-A All-Star Team (1975) • WCJHL First All-Star Team (1975) • AHL First All-Star Team (1984)

Traded to **Philadelphia** by **Detroit** with Mike Korney for Terry Murray, Bob Ritchie, Steve Coates and Dave Kelly, February 17, 1977. Traded to **St. Louis** by **Philadelphia** with Blake Dunlop for Phil Myre, June 7, 1979. Traded to **Quebec** by **St. Louis** for Pat Hickey, August 4, 1982. Signed as a free agent by **LA Kings**, October 10, 1984.

• LAPPIN, Peter

RW – R. 5'11", 180 lbs. b: St. Charles, IL, 12/31/1965. Calgary's 1st, 24th overall, in 1987 Supplemental Draft.

Season	Club	League	GP	G	A	Pts	AG	AA	APts	PIM	PP	SH	GW	S	%	TGF	PGF	TGA	PGA	+/–	GP	G	A	Pts	PIM	PP	SH	GW
1983-84	Canterbury High School	Hi-School	STATISTICS NOT AVAILABLE																									
1984-85	St. Lawrence University	ECAC	32	10	12	22	....	....	....	22	....	....	....	....	....	....	....	....	....	....	....	....	....	....	....	....	....	....
1985-86	St. Lawrence University	ECAC	30	20	26	46	....	....	....	64	....	....	....	....	....	....	....	....	....	....	....	....	....	....	....	....	....	....
1986-87	St. Lawrence University	ECAC	35	34	24	58	....	....	....	32	....	....	....	....	....	....	....	....	....	....	....	....	....	....	....	....	....	....
1987-88	St. Lawrence University	ECAC	30	16	36	52	....	....	....	26	....	....	....	....	....	....	....	....	....	....	....	....	....	....	....	....	....	....
	Salt Lake Golden Eagles	IHL	3	1	1	2	....	....	....	0	....	....	....	....	....	....	....	....	....	....	17	*16	12	*28	11	....	....	....
1988-89	Salt Lake Golden Eagles	IHL	81	48	42	90	....	....	....	50	....	....	....	....	....	....	....	....	....	....	14	*9	9	18	4	....	....	....
1989-90	**Minnesota North Stars**	**NHL**	**6**	**0**	**0**	**0**	**0**	**0**	**0**	**2**	**0**	**0**	**0**	**8**	**0.0**	**1**	**1**	**5**	**0**	**–5**	....	....	....	....	....	....	....	....
	Kalamazoo Wings	IHL	74	45	35	80	....	....	....	42	....	....	....	....	....	....	....	....	....	....	8	5	2	7	4	....	....	....
1990-91	Kalamazoo Wings	IHL	73	20	47	67	....	....	....	74	....	....	....	....	....	....	....	....	....	....	11	5	4	9	8	....	....	....
1991-92	**San Jose Sharks**	**NHL**	**1**	**0**	**0**	**0**	**0**	**0**	**0**	**0**	**0**	**0**	**0**	**2**	**0.0**	**0**	**0**	**0**	**0**	**0**	....	....	....	....	....	....	....	....
	Kansas City Blades	IHL	78	28	30	58	....	....	....	41	....	....	....	....	....	....	....	....	....	....	4	2	1	3	0	....	....	....
	NHL Totals		**7**	**0**	**0**	**0**	**0**	**0**	**0**	**2**	**0**	**0**	**0**	**10**	**0.0**	**1**	**1**	**5**	**0**		....	....	....	....	....	....	....	....

ECAC Second All-Star Team (1987) • ECAC First All-Star Team (1988) • NCAA Championship All-Tournament Team (1988) • IHL Second All-Star Team (1990)

Traded to **Minnesota** by **Calgary** for Minnesota's 2nd round choice (later traded to New Jersey — New Jersey selected Chris Gotziaman) in 1990 Entry Draft, September 5, 1989. Claimed by **San Jose** from **Minnesota** in Dispersal Draft, May 30, 1991.

• LARAQUE, Georges

RW – R. 6'3", 230 lbs. b: Montreal, Que., 12/7/1976. Edmonton's 2nd, 31st overall, in 1995.

Season	Club	League	GP	G	A	Pts	AG	AA	APts	PIM	PP	SH	GW	S	%	TGF	PGF	TGA	PGA	+/–	GP	G	A	Pts	PIM	PP	SH	GW
1991-92	Montreal-Bourassa	QAAA	28	20	20	40	....	....	....	30	....	....	....	....	....	....	....	....	....	....	....	....	....	....	....	....	....	....
1992-93	Montreal-Bourassa	QAAA	37	8	20	28	....	....	....	50	....	....	....	....	....	....	....	....	....	....	3	1	2	3	2	....	....	....
1993-94	St-Jean Lynx	QMJHL	70	11	11	22	....	....	....	142	....	....	....	....	....	....	....	....	....	....	4	0	0	0	7	....	....	....
1994-95	St-Jean Lynx	QMJHL	62	19	22	41	....	....	....	259	....	....	....	....	....	....	....	....	....	....	7	1	1	2	42	....	....	....
1995-96	Laval Titan	QMJHL	11	8	13	21	....	....	....	76	....	....	....	....	....	....	....	....	....	....	....	....	....	....	....	....	....	....
	St-Hyacinthe Laser	QMJHL	8	3	4	7	....	....	....	59	....	....	....	....	....	....	....	....	....	....	....	....	....	....	....	....	....	....
	Granby Bisons	QMJHL	22	9	7	16	....	....	....	125	....	....	....	....	....	....	....	....	....	....	18	7	6	13	104	....	....	....
	Granby Bisons	Mem-Cup	4	0	4	4	....	....	....	4	....	....	....	....	....	....	....	....	....	....	....	....	....	....	....	....	....	....
1996-97	Hamilton Bulldogs	AHL	73	14	20	34	....	....	....	179	....	....	....	....	....	....	....	....	....	....	15	1	3	4	12	....	....	....
1997-98	**Edmonton Oilers**	**NHL**	**11**	**0**	**0**	**0**	**0**	**0**	**0**	**59**	**0**	**0**	**0**	**4**	**0.0**	**2**	**1**	**6**	**1**	**–4**	....	....	....	....	....	....	....	....
	Hamilton Bulldogs	AHL	46	10	20	30	....	....	....	154	....	....	....	....	....	....	....	....	....	....	3	0	0	0	11	....	....	....
1998-99	**Edmonton Oilers**	**NHL**	**39**	**3**	**2**	**5**	**4**	**2**	**6**	**57**	**0**	**0**	**0**	**17**	**17.6**	**7**	**0**	**8**	**0**	**–1**	**4**	**0**	**0**	**0**	**2**	**0**	**0**	**0**
	Hamilton Bulldogs	AHL	25	6	8	14	....	....	....	93	....	....	....	....	....	....	....	....	....	....	....	....	....	....	....	....	....	....
99-2000	**Edmonton Oilers**	**NHL**	**76**	**8**	**8**	**16**	**9**	**7**	**16**	**123**	**0**	**0**	**0**	**56**	**14.3**	**21**	**0**	**16**	**0**	**5**	**5**	**0**	**1**	**1**	**6**	**0**	**0**	**0**
	NHL Totals		**126**	**11**	**10**	**21**	**13**	**9**	**22**	**239**	**0**	**0**	**0**	**77**	**14.3**	**30**	**1**	**30**	**1**		**9**	**0**	**1**	**1**	**8**	**0**	**0**	**0**

• LARIONOV, Igor

C – L. 5'9", 170 lbs. b: Voskresensk, USSR, 12/3/1960. Vancouver's 11th, 214th overall, in 1985.

Season	Club	League	GP	G	A	Pts	AG	AA	APts	PIM	PP	SH	GW	S	%	TGF	PGF	TGA	PGA	+/–	GP	G	A	Pts	PIM	PP	SH	GW
1977-78	Khimik Voskresensk	USSR	6	3	0	3	....	....	....	4	....	....	....	....	....	....	....	....	....	....	....	....	....	....	....	....	....	....
	Soviet Union	EJC-A	5	2	1	3	....	....	....	4	....	....	....	....	....	....	....	....	....	....	....	....	....	....	....	....	....	....
1978-79	Khimik Voskresensk	USSR	32	3	4	7	....	....	....	12	....	....	....	....	....	....	....	....	....	....	....	....	....	....	....	....	....	....
	Soviet Union	WJC-A	5	2	4	6	....	....	....	8	....	....	....	....	....	....	....	....	....	....	....	....	....	....	....	....	....	....
1979-80	Khimik Voskresensk	USSR	42	11	7	18	....	....	....	24	....	....	....	....	....	....	....	....	....	....	....	....	....	....	....	....	....	....
	Soviet Union	WJC-A	5	3	3	6	....	....	....	4	....	....	....	....	....	....	....	....	....	....	....	....	....	....	....	....	....	....
1980-81	Khimik Voskresensk	USSR	43	22	23	45	....	....	....	36	....	....	....	....	....	....	....	....	....	....	....	....	....	....	....	....	....	....
1981-82	Soviet Union	Can-Cup	7	4	1	5	....	....	....	8	....	....	....	....	....	....	....	....	....	....	....	....	....	....	....	....	....	....
	CSKA Moscow	USSR	46	31	22	53	....	....	....	6	....	....	....	....	....	....	....	....	....	....	....	....	....	....	....	....	....	....
	Soviet Union	WEC-A	10	4	6	10	....	....	....	2	....	....	....	....	....	....	....	....	....	....	....	....	....	....	....	....	....	....
1982-83	CSKA Moscow	USSR	44	20	19	39	....	....	....	20	....	....	....	....	....	....	....	....	....	....	....	....	....	....	....	....	....	....
	USSR	Super-S	6	4	2	6	....	....	....	0	....	....	....	....	....	....	....	....	....	....	....	....	....	....	....	....	....	....
	Soviet Union	WEC-A	9	5	7	12	....	....	....	4	....	....	....	....	....	....	....	....	....	....	....	....	....	....	....	....	....	....
1983-84	CSKA Moscow	USSR	43	15	26	41	....	....	....	30	....	....	....	....	....	....	....	....	....	....	....	....	....	....	....	....	....	....
	Soviet Union	Olympics	6	1	4	5	....	....	....	6	....	....	....	....	....	....	....	....	....	....	....	....	....	....	....	....	....	....
1984-85	Soviet Union	Can-Cup	5	1	2	3	....	....	....	6	....	....	....	....	....	....	....	....	....	....	....	....	....	....	....	....	....	....
	CSKA Moscow	USSR	40	18	28	46	....	....	....	20	....	....	....	....	....	....	....	....	....	....	....	....	....	....	....	....	....	....
	Soviet Union	WEC-A	10	2	4	6	....	....	....	8	....	....	....	....	....	....	....	....	....	....	....	....	....	....	....	....	....	....
1985-86	CSKA Moscow	USSR	40	21	31	52	....	....	....	33	....	....	....	....	....	....	....	....	....	....	....	....	....	....	....	....	....	....
	Soviet Union	WEC-A	10	7	1	8	....	....	....	4	....	....	....	....	....	....	....	....	....	....	....	....	....	....	....	....	....	....
1986-87	CSKA Moscow	USSR	39	20	26	46	....	....	....	34	....	....	....	....	....	....	....	....	....	....	....	....	....	....	....	....	....	....
	USSR	RV-87	2	0	2	2	....	....	....	0	....	....	....	....	....	....	....	....	....	....	....	....	....	....	....	....	....	....
	Soviet Union	WEC-A	10	4	8	12	....	....	....	2	....	....	....	....	....	....	....	....	....	....	....	....	....	....	....	....	....	....
1987-88	Soviet Union	Can-Cup	9	1	2	3	....	....	....	6	....	....	....	....	....	....	....	....	....	....	....	....	....	....	....	....	....	....
	CSKA Moscow	USSR	51	25	32	57	....	....	....	54	....	....	....	....	....	....	....	....	....	....	....	....	....	....	....	....	....	....
	Soviet Union	Olympics	8	4	*9	13	....	....	....	4	....	....	....	....	....	....	....	....	....	....	....	....	....	....	....	....	....	....
1988-89	CSKA Moscow	USSR	31	15	12	27	....	....	....	22	....	....	....	....	....	....	....	....	....	....	....	....	....	....	....	....	....	....
	CSKA Moscow	Super-S	7	0	7	7	....	....	....	6	....	....	....	....	....	....	....	....	....	....	....	....	....	....	....	....	....	....
	Soviet Union	WEC-A	8	3	0	3	....	....	....	11	....	....	....	....	....	....	....	....	....	....	....	....	....	....	....	....	....	....

			REGULAR SEASON																		PLAYOFFS							
Season	**Club**	**League**	**GP**	**G**	**A**	**Pts**	**AG**	**AA**	**APts**	**PIM**	**PP**	**SH**	**GW**	**S**	**%**	**TGF**	**PGF**	**TGA**	**PGA**	**+/–**	**GP**	**G**	**A**	**Pts**	**PIM**	**PP**	**SH**	**GW**
1989-90	**Vancouver Canucks**	**NHL**	**74**	**17**	**27**	**44**	**15**	**19**	**34**	**20**	**8**	**0**	**2**	**118**	**14.4**	**71**	**26**	**54**	**4**	**–5**	....	....	....	....	....	....	....	....
1990-91	**Vancouver Canucks**	**NHL**	**64**	**13**	**21**	**34**	**12**	**16**	**28**	**14**	**1**	**1**	**0**	**66**	**19.7**	**53**	**7**	**68**	**19**	**–3**	**6**	**1**	**0**	**1**	**6**	**0**	**0**	**0**
1991-92	**Vancouver Canucks**	**NHL**	**72**	**21**	**44**	**65**	**19**	**33**	**52**	**54**	**10**	**3**	**4**	**97**	**21.6**	**88**	**34**	**71**	**24**	**7**	**13**	**3**	**7**	**10**	**4**	**1**	**0**	**0**
1992-93	HC Lugano	Switz.	24	10	19	29	....	....	....	44	....	....	....	....	....	....	....	....	....	....	8	3	15	18	0	....	....	....
1993-94	**San Jose Sharks**	**NHL**	**60**	**18**	**38**	**56**	**17**	**30**	**47**	**40**	**3**	**2**	**2**	**72**	**25.0**	**85**	**23**	**51**	**9**	**20**	**14**	**5**	**13**	**18**	**10**	**0**	**0**	**0**
1994-95	**San Jose Sharks**	**NHL**	**33**	**4**	**20**	**24**	**7**	**30**	**37**	**14**	**0**	**0**	**1**	**69**	**5.8**	**36**	**8**	**37**	**6**	**–3**	**11**	**1**	**8**	**9**	**2**	**0**	**0**	**0**
1995-96	**San Jose Sharks**	**NHL**	**4**	**1**	**1**	**2**	**1**	**1**	**2**	**0**	**1**	**0**	**0**	**5**	**20.0**	**4**	**2**	**11**	**3**	**–6**	....	....	....	....	....	....	....	....
	Detroit Red Wings	**NHL**	**69**	**21**	**50**	**71**	**21**	**41**	**62**	**34**	**9**	**1**	**5**	**108**	**19.4**	**110**	**39**	**37**	**3**	**37**	**19**	**6**	**7**	**13**	**6**	**3**	**0**	**2**
1996-97	Russia	W-Cup	5	0	4	4	....	....	....	2	....	....	....	....	....	....	....	....	....	....	....	....	....	....	....	....	....	....
♦	**Detroit Red Wings**	**NHL**	**64**	**12**	**42**	**54**	**13**	**37**	**50**	**26**	**2**	**1**	**4**	**95**	**12.6**	**100**	**37**	**34**	**2**	**31**	**20**	**4**	**8**	**12**	**8**	**3**	**0**	**1**
1997-98♦	**Detroit Red Wings**	**NHL**	**69**	**8**	**39**	**47**	**9**	**38**	**47**	**40**	**3**	**0**	**2**	**93**	**8.6**	**68**	**24**	**33**	**3**	**14**	**22**	**3**	**10**	**13**	**12**	**0**	**0**	**0**
1998-99	**Detroit Red Wings**	**NHL**	**75**	**14**	**49**	**63**	**16**	**47**	**63**	**48**	**4**	**2**	**2**	**83**	**16.9**	**81**	**31**	**40**	**3**	**13**	**7**	**0**	**2**	**2**	**0**	**0**	**0**	**0**
99-2000	**Detroit Red Wings**	**NHL**	**79**	**9**	**38**	**47**	**10**	**35**	**45**	**28**	**3**	**0**	**4**	**69**	**13.0**	**71**	**22**	**41**	**5**	**13**	**9**	**1**	**2**	**3**	**6**	**1**	**0**	**0**
	NHL Totals		**663**	**138**	**369**	**507**	**140**	**327**	**467**	**318**	**44**	**10**	**26**	**875**	**15.8**	**767**	**253**	**477**	**81**		**121**	**24**	**57**	**81**	**54**	**8**	**0**	**3**

WJC-A All-Star Team (1980) • USSR First All-Star (1983, 1986, 1987, 1988) • WEC-A All-Star Team (1983, 1986) • USSR Player of the Year (1988) • Played in NHL All-Star Game (1998)

Claimed by **San Jose** from **Vancouver** in NHL Waiver Draft, October 4, 1992. Traded to **Detroit** by **San Jose** with future considerations for Ray Sheppard, October 24, 1995. Signed as a free agent by Florida, July 1, 2000.

• LARIVIERE, Garry

Garry Joseph D – R. 6', 190 lbs. b: St. Catharines, Ont., 12/6/1954. Buffalo's 5th, 83rd overall, in 1974.

Season	**Club**	**League**	**GP**	**G**	**A**	**Pts**	**AG**	**AA**	**APts**	**PIM**	**PP**	**SH**	**GW**	**S**	**%**	**TGF**	**PGF**	**TGA**	**PGA**	**+/–**	**GP**	**G**	**A**	**Pts**	**PIM**	**PP**	**SH**	**GW**
1971-72	St. Catharines Black Hawks	OMJHL	62	4	19	23	....	....	....	114	....	....	....	....	....	....	....	....	....	....	5	0	2	2	21	....	....	....
1972-73	St. Catharines Black Hawks	OMJHL	55	5	32	37	....	....	....	140	....	....	....	....	....	....	....	....	....	....	....	....	....	....	....	....	....	....
1973-74	St. Catharines Black Hawks	OMJHL	60	3	35	38	....	....	....	153	....	....	....	....	....	....	....	....	....	....	....	....	....	....	....	....	....	....
	St. Catharines Black Hawks	Mem-Cup	3	0	1	1	....	....	....	21	....	....	....	....	....	....	....	....	....	....	....	....	....	....	....	....	....	....
1974-75	Phoenix Roadrunners	WHA	4	0	1	1	....	....	....	28	....	....	....	....	....	....	....	....	....	....	1	0	0	0	0	....	....	....
	Tulsa Oilers	CHL	76	15	38	53	....	....	....	168	....	....	....	....	....	....	....	....	....	....	....	....	....	....	....	....	....	....
1975-76	Phoenix Roadrunners	WHA	79	7	17	24	....	....	....	100	....	....	....	....	....	....	....	....	....	....	5	0	2	2	2	....	....	....
1976-77	Phoenix Roadrunners	WHA	61	7	23	30	....	....	....	48	....	....	....	....	....	....	....	....	....	....	....	....	....	....	....	....	....	....
	Quebec Nordiques	WHA	15	0	3	3	....	....	....	8	....	....	....	....	....	....	....	....	....	....	17	0	10	10	10	....	....	....
1977-78	Quebec Nordiques	WHA	80	7	49	56	....	....	....	78	....	....	....	....	....	....	....	....	....	....	11	3	2	5	4	....	....	....
1978-79	Quebec Nordiques	WHA	50	5	33	38	....	....	....	54	....	....	....	....	....	....	....	....	....	....	4	0	1	1	2	....	....	....
1979-80	**Quebec Nordiques**	**NHL**	**75**	**2**	**19**	**21**	**2**	**14**	**16**	**56**	**1**	**0**	**0**	**73**	**2.7**	**67**	**4**	**117**	**44**	**–10**	....	....	....	....	....	....	....	....
1980-81	**Quebec Nordiques**	**NHL**	**52**	**3**	**13**	**16**	**2**	**9**	**11**	**50**	**1**	**0**	**0**	**58**	**5.2**	**62**	**7**	**81**	**24**	**–2**	....	....	....	....	....	....	....	....
	Edmonton Oilers	**NHL**	**13**	**0**	**2**	**2**	**0**	**1**	**1**	**6**	**0**	**0**	**0**	**8**	**0.0**	**18**	**0**	**12**	**3**	**9**	**9**	**0**	**3**	**3**	**8**	**0**	**0**	**0**
1981-82	**Edmonton Oilers**	**NHL**	**62**	**1**	**21**	**22**	**1**	**14**	**15**	**41**	**0**	**0**	**0**	**46**	**2.2**	**88**	**2**	**73**	**14**	**27**	**4**	**0**	**1**	**1**	**0**	**0**	**0**	**0**
1982-83	**Edmonton Oilers**	**NHL**	**17**	**0**	**2**	**2**	**0**	**1**	**1**	**14**	**0**	**0**	**0**	**15**	**0.0**	**22**	**0**	**15**	**6**	**13**	**1**	**0**	**1**	**1**	**0**	**0**	**0**	**0**
1983-84	St. Catharines Saints	AHL	65	7	35	42	....	....	....	41	....	....	....	....	....	....	....	....	....	....	7	0	3	3	2	....	....	....
1984-85	St. Catharines Saints	AHL	72	4	32	36	....	....	....	47	....	....	....	....	....	....	....	....	....	....	....	....	....	....	....	....	....	....
1985-86	St. Catharines Saints	AHL	52	0	9	9	....	....	....	10	....	....	....	....	....	....	....	....	....	....	6	0	1	1	6	....	....	....
	NHL Totals		**219**	**6**	**57**	**63**	**5**	**39**	**44**	**167**	**2**	**0**	**0**	**200**	**3.0**	**257**	**13**	**298**	**91**		**14**	**0**	**5**	**5**	**8**	**0**	**0**	**0**
	Other Major League Totals		289	26	126	152	....	....	....	316	....	....	....	....	....	....	....	....	....	....	38	3	15	18	18	....	....	....

CHL First All-Star Team (1975) • AHL First All-Star Team (1984) • Won Eddie Shore Award (Outstanding Defenseman - AHL) (1984) • Shared Les Cunningham Award (MVP - AHL) with Mal Davis (1984)

Selected by **Chicago** (WHA) in 1974 WHA Amateur Draft, May, 1974. Traded to **Phoenix** (WHA) by **Chicago** (WHA) for future considerations, September, 1974. Rights traded to **NY Islanders** by **Buffalo** for the rights to Gerry Desjardins, February 19, 1975. Traded to **Quebec** (WHA) by **Phoenix** (WHA) for cash, March, 1977. Reclaimed by **NY Islanders** from **Quebec** prior to Expansion Draft, June 9, 1979. Claimed as a priority selection by **Quebec**, June 9, 1979. Traded to **Vancouver** by **Quebec** for Mario Marois, March 10, 1981. Traded to **Edmonton** by **Vancouver** with Ken Berry for Blair MacDonald and the rights to Lars Gunnar Pettersson, March 10, 1981.

• LARMER, Jeff

LW – L. 5'10", 175 lbs. b: Peterborough, Ont., 11/10/1962. Colorado's 7th, 129th overall, in 1981.

Season	**Club**	**League**	**GP**	**G**	**A**	**Pts**	**AG**	**AA**	**APts**	**PIM**	**PP**	**SH**	**GW**	**S**	**%**	**TGF**	**PGF**	**TGA**	**PGA**	**+/–**	**GP**	**G**	**A**	**Pts**	**PIM**	**PP**	**SH**	**GW**
1978-79	Peterborough Jr. Bees	OHA-B	40	29	23	52	....	....	....	27	....	....	....	....	....	....	....	....	....	....	....	....	....	....	....	....	....	....
1979-80	Kitchener Rangers	OMJHL	61	19	27	46	....	....	....	80	....	....	....	....	....	....	....	....	....	....	....	....	....	....	....	....	....	....
1980-81	Kitchener Rangers	OMJHL	68	54	54	108	....	....	....	103	....	....	....	....	....	....	....	....	....	....	16	12	16	28	27	....	....	....
	Kitchener Rangers	Mem-Cup	5	2	4	6	....	....	....	2	....	....	....	....	....	....	....	....	....	....	....	....	....	....	....	....	....	....
1981-82	Kitchener Rangers	OHL	49	51	44	95	....	....	....	95	....	....	....	....	....	....	....	....	....	....	15	*21	14	*35	16	....	....	....
	Colorado Rockies	**NHL**	**8**	**1**	**1**	**2**	**1**	**1**	**2**	**8**	**0**	**0**	**0**	**9**	**11.1**	**6**	**0**	**9**	**0**	**–3**	....	....	....	....	....	....	....	....
	Kitchener Rangers	Mem-Cup	5	4	*9	*13	....	....	....	10	....	....	....	....	....	....	....	....	....	....	....	....	....	....	....	....	....	....
1982-83	**New Jersey Devils**	**NHL**	**65**	**21**	**24**	**45**	**17**	**17**	**34**	**21**	**5**	**0**	**0**	**123**	**17.1**	**57**	**14**	**49**	**0**	**–6**	....	....	....	....	....	....	....	....
	Wichita Wind	CHL	10	6	5	11	....	....	....	2	....	....	....	....	....	....	....	....	....	....	....	....	....	....	....	....	....	....
1983-84	**New Jersey Devils**	**NHL**	**40**	**6**	**13**	**19**	**5**	**9**	**14**	**8**	**0**	**0**	**0**	**57**	**10.5**	**27**	**6**	**38**	**0**	**–17**	....	....	....	....	....	....	....	....
	Chicago Black Hawks	**NHL**	**36**	**9**	**13**	**22**	**7**	**9**	**16**	**20**	**2**	**0**	**1**	**62**	**14.5**	**34**	**5**	**28**	**2**	**3**	**5**	**1**	**0**	**1**	**2**	**1**	**0**	**0**
1984-85	**Chicago Black Hawks**	**NHL**	**7**	**0**	**0**	**0**	**0**	**0**	**0**	**0**	**0**	**0**	**0**	**5**	**0.0**	**1**	**0**	**0**	**0**	**1**	....	....	....	....	....	....	....	....
	Milwaukee Admirals	IHL	61	24	37	61	....	....	....	30	....	....	....	....	....	....	....	....	....	....	....	....	....	....	....	....	....	....
1985-86	**Chicago Black Hawks**	**NHL**	**2**	**0**	**0**	**0**	**0**	**0**	**0**	**0**	**0**	**0**	**0**	**1**	**0.0**	**1**	**0**	**0**	**0**	**1**	....	....	....	....	....	....	....	....
	Nova Scotia Oilers	AHL	77	20	44	64	....	....	....	46	....	....	....	....	....	....	....	....	....	....	....	....	....	....	....	....	....	....
1986-87			OUT OF HOCKEY – RETIRED																									
1987-88			OUT OF HOCKEY – RETIRED																									
1988-89	HC Davos	Switz.	8	2	2	4	....	....	....	....	....	....	....	....	....	....	....	....	....	....	7	4	4	8	....	....	....	....
1989-90	Solihull Barons	Aut-Cup	8	14	11	25	....	....	....	16	....	....	....	....	....	....	....	....	....	....	....	....	....	....	....	....	....	....
	Solihull Barons	Britain	16	23	25	48	....	....	....	14	....	....	....	....	....	....	....	....	....	....	....	....	....	....	....	....	....	....
	EC Nordhorn	Germany-3	12	24	21	45	....	....	....	16	....	....	....	....	....	....	....	....	....	....	10	8	11	19	14	....	....	....
1990-91			OUT OF HOCKEY – RETIRED																									
1991-92	Milwaukee Admirals	IHL	76	27	35	62	....	....	....	22	....	....	....	....	....	....	....	....	....	....	5	1	4	5	4	....	....	....
1992-93	Milwaukee Admirals	IHL	78	31	34	65	....	....	....	46	....	....	....	....	....	....	....	....	....	....	6	0	2	2	2	....	....	....
1993-94	Milwaukee Admirals	IHL	25	2	9	11	....	....	....	14	....	....	....	....	....	....	....	....	....	....	1	0	0	0	0	....	....	....
	NHL Totals		**158**	**37**	**51**	**88**	**30**	**36**	**66**	**57**	**7**	**0**	**1**	**257**	**14.4**	**126**	**25**	**124**	**2**		**5**	**1**	**0**	**1**	**2**	**1**	**0**	**0**

• Brother of Steve • OHL Second All-Star Team (1982) • Memorial Cup All-Star Team (1982)

Transferred to **New Jersey** after **Colorado** franchise relocated, June 30, 1982. Traded to **Chicago** by **New Jersey** for Tim Higgins, January 11, 1984.

• LARMER, Steve

Stephen Donald RW – L. 5'11", 195 lbs. b: Peterborough, Ont., 6/16/1961. Chicago's 11th, 120th overall, in 1980.

Season	**Club**	**League**	**GP**	**G**	**A**	**Pts**	**AG**	**AA**	**APts**	**PIM**	**PP**	**SH**	**GW**	**S**	**%**	**TGF**	**PGF**	**TGA**	**PGA**	**+/–**	**GP**	**G**	**A**	**Pts**	**PIM**	**PP**	**SH**	**GW**
1976-77	Peterborough Voyageurs	OMHA	50	50	30	80	....	....	....	26	....	....	....	....	....	....	....	....	....	....	....	....	....	....	....	....	....	....
1977-78	Peterborough Petes	OMJHL	62	24	17	41	....	....	....	51	....	....	....	....	....	....	....	....	....	....	18	5	7	12	27	....	....	....
	Peterborough Petes	Mem-Cup	3	1	3	4	....	....	....	11	....	....	....	....	....	....	....	....	....	....	....	....	....	....	....	....	....	....
1978-79	Niagara Falls Flyers	OMJHL	66	37	47	84	....	....	....	108	....	....	....	....	....	....	....	....	....	....	20	11	13	24	43	....	....	....
1979-80	Niagara Falls Flyers	OMJHL	67	45	69	114	....	....	....	71	....	....	....	....	....	....	....	....	....	....	10	5	9	14	15	....	....	....
1980-81	Niagara Falls Flyers	OMJHL	61	55	78	133	....	....	....	73	....	....	....	....	....	....	....	....	....	....	12	13	8	21	24	....	....	....
	Chicago Black Hawks	**NHL**	**4**	**0**	**1**	**1**	**0**	**1**	**1**	**0**	**0**	**0**	**0**	**3**	**0.0**	**3**	**0**	**2**	**0**	**1**	....	....	....	....	....	....	....	....
1981-82	**Chicago Black Hawks**	**NHL**	**3**	**0**	**0**	**0**	**0**	**0**	**0**	**0**	**0**	**0**	**0**	**1**	**0.0**	**0**	**0**	**0**	**0**	**0**	....	....	....	....	....	....	....	....
	New Brunswick Hawks	AHL	74	38	44	82	....	....	....	46	....	....	....	....	....	....	....	....	....	....	15	6	6	12	0	....	....	....
1982-83	**Chicago Black Hawks**	**NHL**	**80**	**43**	**47**	**90**	**35**	**33**	**68**	**28**	**13**	**0**	**9**	**195**	**22.1**	**154**	**57**	**53**	**0**	**44**	**11**	**5**	**7**	**12**	**8**	**2**	**0**	**1**
1983-84	**Chicago Black Hawks**	**NHL**	**80**	**35**	**40**	**75**	**28**	**27**	**55**	**34**	**13**	**0**	**3**	**206**	**17.0**	**124**	**47**	**78**	**0**	**–1**	**5**	**2**	**2**	**4**	**7**	**1**	**0**	**0**
1984-85	**Chicago Black Hawks**	**NHL**	**80**	**46**	**40**	**86**	**38**	**27**	**65**	**16**	**14**	**0**	**6**	**206**	**22.3**	**127**	**43**	**68**	**1**	**17**	**15**	**9**	**13**	**22**	**14**	**5**	**0**	**1**
1985-86	**Chicago Black Hawks**	**NHL**	**80**	**31**	**45**	**76**	**25**	**30**	**55**	**47**	**13**	**1**	**3**	**184**	**16.8**	**132**	**45**	**95**	**17**	**9**	**3**	**0**	**3**	**3**	**4**	**0**	**0**	**0**
1986-87	**Chicago Blackhawks**	**NHL**	**80**	**28**	**56**	**84**	**24**	**41**	**65**	**22**	**10**	**0**	**4**	**216**	**13.0**	**124**	**38**	**75**	**9**	**20**	**4**	**0**	**0**	**0**	**2**	**0**	**0**	**0**
1987-88	**Chicago Blackhawks**	**NHL**	**80**	**41**	**48**	**89**	**35**	**34**	**69**	**42**	**21**	**7**	**0**	**245**	**16.7**	**139**	**69**	**111**	**36**	**–5**	**5**	**1**	**6**	**7**	**0**	**1**	**0**	**0**
1988-89	**Chicago Blackhawks**	**NHL**	**80**	**43**	**44**	**87**	**36**	**31**	**67**	**54**	**19**	**1**	**2**	**269**	**16.0**	**136**	**62**	**113**	**41**	**2**	**16**	**8**	**9**	**17**	**22**	**3**	**0**	**2**
1989-90	**Chicago Blackhawks**	**NHL**	**80**	**31**	**59**	**90**	**27**	**42**	**69**	**40**	**8**	**2**	**4**	**265**	**11.7**	**136**	**49**	**89**	**27**	**25**	**20**	**7**	**15**	**22**	**2**	**2**	**2**	**2**
1990-91	**Chicago Blackhawks**	**NHL**	**80**	**44**	**57**	**101**	**40**	**43**	**83**	**79**	**17**	**2**	**9**	**231**	**19.0**	**143**	**62**	**72**	**28**	**37**	**6**	**5**	**1**	**6**	**4**	**1**	**0**	**0**
	Canada	WEC-A	10	5	3	8	....	....	....	4	....	....	....	....	....	....	....	....	....	....	....	....	....	....	....	....	....	....
1991-92	Canada	Can-Cup	8	6	5	11	....	....	....	4	....	....	....	....	....	....	....	....	....	....	....	....	....	....	....	....	....	....
	Chicago Blackhawks	**NHL**	**80**	**29**	**45**	**74**	**26**	**34**	**60**	**65**	**11**	**2**	**3**	**292**	**9.9**	**113**	**49**	**88**	**34**	**10**	**18**	**8**	**7**	**15**	**6**	**3**	**0**	**0**

			REGULAR SEASON																		PLAYOFFS							
Season	Club	League	GP	G	A	Pts	AG	AA	APts	PIM	PP	SH	GW	S	%	TGF	PGF	TGA	PGA	+/–	GP	G	A	Pts	PIM	PP	SH	GW
1992-93	**Chicago Blackhawks**	**NHL**	84	35	35	70	29	24	53	48	14	4	6	228	15.4	123	56	75	31	23	4	0	3	3	0	0	0	0
1993-94♦	**New York Rangers**	**NHL**	68	21	39	60	20	30	50	41	6	4	7	146	14.4	87	38	43	8	14	23	9	7	16	14	3	0	0
1994-95	**New York Rangers**	**NHL**	47	14	15	29	25	22	47	16	3	1	4	116	12.1	42	12	37	15	8	10	2	2	4	6	0	1	1
	NHL Totals		1006	441	571	1012	388	419	807	532	162	24	60	2803	15.7	1583	627	999	247		140	56	75	131	89	21	3	7

• Brother of Jeff • OMJHL Second All-Star Team (1981) • AHL Second All-Star Team (1982) • NHL All-Rookie Team (1983) • Won Calder Memorial Trophy (1983) • Played in NHL All-Star Game (1990, 1991)

Traded to **Hartford** by **Chicago** with Bryan Marchment for Eric Weinrich and Patrick Poulin, November 2, 1993. Traded to **NY Rangers** by **Hartford** with Nick Kypreos, Barry Richter and Hartford's 6th round choice (Yuri Litvinov) in 1994 Entry Draft for Darren Turcotte and James Patrick, November 2, 1993.

• LAROCQUE, Denis

D – L. 6'1", 195 lbs. b: Hawkesbury, Ont., 10/5/1967. Los Angeles' 2nd, 44th overall, in 1986.

Season	Club	League	GP	G	A	Pts	AG	AA	APts	PIM	PP	SH	GW	S	%	TGF	PGF	TGA	PGA	+/–	GP	G	A	Pts	PIM	PP	SH	GW
1982-83	Hawkesbury Hawks	OJHL	31	0	13	13	....	....	....	83	....	....	....	....	....	....	....	....	....	....	....	....	....	....	....	....	....	....
1983-84	Guelph Platers	OHL	65	1	5	6	....	....	....	74	....	....	....	....	....	....	....	....	....	....	....	....	....	....	....	....	....	....
1984-85	Guelph Platers	OHL	62	1	15	16	....	....	....	67	....	....	....	....	....	....	....	....	....	....	....	....	....	....	....	....	....	....
1985-86	Guelph Platers	OHL	62	2	17	19	....	....	....	144	....	....	....	....	....	....	....	....	....	....	20	1	4	5	44	....	....	....
	Guelph Platers	Mem-Cup	4	0	2	2	....	....	....	0	....	....	....	....	....	....	....	....	....	....	....	....	....	....	....	....	....	....
1986-87	Guelph Platers	OHL	45	4	10	14	....	....	....	82	....	....	....	....	....	....	....	....	....	....	5	0	2	2	9	....	....	....
1987-88	**Los Angeles Kings**	**NHL**	8	0	1	1	0	1	1	18	0	0	0	2	0.0	3	0	10	3	–4	....	....	....	....	....	....	....	....
	New Haven Nighthawks	AHL	58	4	10	14	....	....	....	154	....	....	....	....	....	....	....	....	....	....	....	....	....	....	....	....	....	....
1988-89	New Haven Nighthawks	AHL	15	2	2	4	....	....	....	51	....	....	....	....	....	....	....	....	....	....	....	....	....	....	....	....	....	....
	Denver Rangers	IHL	30	2	8	10	....	....	....	39	....	....	....	....	....	....	....	....	....	....	4	0	2	2	10	....	....	....
1989-90	Flint Spirits	IHL	31	1	2	3	....	....	....	66	....	....	....	....	....	....	....	....	....	....	....	....	....	....	....	....	....	....
	Cape Breton Oilers	AHL	26	2	4	6	....	....	....	39	....	....	....	....	....	....	....	....	....	....	6	0	1	1	2	....	....	....
1990-91	Moncton Hawks	AHL	68	2	9	11	....	....	....	92	....	....	....	....	....	....	....	....	....	....	1	0	0	0	2	....	....	....
1991-92	St. Thomas Wildcats	ColHL	55	9	21	30	....	....	....	133	....	....	....	....	....	....	....	....	....	....	....	....	....	....	....	....	....	....
1992-93	Dayton Bombers	ECHL	5	0	0	0	....	....	....	17	....	....	....	....	....	....	....	....	....	....	....	....	....	....	....	....	....	....
	St. Thomas Wildcats	ColHL	18	1	4	5	....	....	....	17	....	....	....	....	....	....	....	....	....	....	13	1	3	4	24	....	....	....
	NHL Totals		8	0	1	1	0	1	1	18	0	0	0	2	0.0	3	0	10	3		....	....	....	....	....	....	....	....

Traded to **NY Rangers** by **LA Kings** with Dean Kennedy for Igor Liba, Michael Boyce, Todd Elik and future considerations, December 12, 1988.

• LAROCQUE, Mario

D – L. 6'2", 182 lbs. b: Montreal, Que., 4/24/1978. Tampa Bay's 1st, 16th overall, in 1996.

Season	Club	League	GP	G	A	Pts	AG	AA	APts	PIM	PP	SH	GW	S	%	TGF	PGF	TGA	PGA	+/–	GP	G	A	Pts	PIM	PP	SH	GW
1994-95	Montreal-Bourassa College	QAAA	43	0	6	6	....	....	....	153	....	....	....	....	....	....	....	....	....	....	....	....	....	....	....	....	....	....
1995-96	Hull Olympiques	QMJHL	68	7	19	26	....	....	....	196	....	....	....	....	....	....	....	....	....	....	14	2	5	7	16	....	....	....
1996-97	Hull Olympiques	QMJHL	64	14	36	50	....	....	....	155	....	....	....	....	....	....	....	....	....	....	14	2	6	8	36	....	....	....
	Hull Olympiques	Mem-Cup	4	2	2	4	....	....	....	2	....	....	....	....	....	....	....	....	....	....	....	....	....	....	....	....	....	....
1997-98	Sherbrooke Faucons	QMJHL	28	6	10	16	....	....	....	125	....	....	....	....	....	....	....	....	....	....	....	....	....	....	....	....	....	....
1998-99	**Tampa Bay Lightning**	**NHL**	5	0	0	0	0	0	0	16	0	0	0	3	0.0	0	0	4	0	–4	....	....	....	....	....	....	....	....
	Cleveland Lumberjacks	IHL	59	5	7	12	....	....	....	202	....	....	....	....	....	....	....	....	....	....	....	....	....	....	....	....	....	....
99-2000	Detroit Vipers	IHL	60	0	5	5	....	....	....	234	....	....	....	....	....	....	....	....	....	....	....	....	....	....	....	....	....	....
	NHL Totals		5	0	0	0	0	0	0	16	0	0	0	3	0.0	0	0	4	0		....	....	....	....	....	....	....	....

• LAROSE, Claude

Claude David RW – R. 6', 180 lbs. b: Hearst, Ont., 3/2/1942.

Season	Club	League	GP	G	A	Pts	AG	AA	APts	PIM	PP	SH	GW	S	%	TGF	PGF	TGA	PGA	+/–	GP	G	A	Pts	PIM	PP	SH	GW
1959-60	Peterborough Petes	OHA-Jr.	48	9	10	19	....	....	....	34	....	....	....	....	....	....	....	....	....	....	12	2	7	9	17	....	....	....
1960-61	Peterborough Petes	OHA-Jr.	46	36	27	63	....	....	....	108	....	....	....	....	....	....	....	....	....	....	5	5	0	5	31	....	....	....
1961-62	Peterborough Petes	OHA-Jr.	50	18	36	54	....	....	....	150	....	....	....	....	....	....	....	....	....	....	....	....	....	....	....	....	....	....
	Hull-Ottawa Canadiens	EPHL	1	0	1	1	....	....	....	2	....	....	....	....	....	....	....	....	....	....	6	3	1	4	6	....	....	....
1962-63	**Montreal Canadiens**	**NHL**	4	0	0	0	0	0	0	0	....	....	....	....	....	....	....	....	....	....	....	....	....	....	....	....	....	....
	Hull-Ottawa Canadiens	EPHL	49	19	24	43	....	....	....	42	....	....	....	....	....	....	....	....	....	....	3	1	0	1	2	....	....	....
1963-64	**Montreal Canadiens**	**NHL**	21	1	1	2	1	1	2	43	....	....	....	....	....	....	....	....	....	....	2	1	0	1	0	0	0	0
	Omaha Knights	CPHL	47	27	22	49	....	....	....	105	....	....	....	....	....	....	....	....	....	....	8	*8	6	14	17	....	....	....
1964-65♦	**Montreal Canadiens**	**NHL**	68	21	16	37	25	16	41	82	....	....	....	....	....	....	....	....	....	....	13	0	1	1	14	0	0	0
1965-66♦	**Montreal Canadiens**	**NHL**	64	15	18	33	17	17	34	67	....	....	....	....	....	....	....	....	....	....	6	0	1	1	31	0	0	0
1966-67	**Montreal Canadiens**	**NHL**	69	19	16	35	22	16	38	82	....	....	....	....	....	....	....	....	....	....	10	1	5	6	15	0	0	0
1967-68♦	**Montreal Canadiens**	**NHL**	42	2	9	11	2	9	11	28	0	0	0	70	2.9	19	1	18	0	0	12	3	2	5	8	0	0	0
	Houston Apollos	CPHL	10	6	7	13	....	....	....	32	....	....	....	....	....	....	....	....	....	....	....	....	....	....	....	....	....	....
1968-69	**Minnesota North Stars**	**NHL**	67	25	37	62	27	33	60	106	5	0	3	268	9.3	82	30	63	1	–10	....	....	....	....	....	....	....	....
1969-70	**Minnesota North Stars**	**NHL**	75	24	23	47	26	22	48	109	6	1	4	262	9.2	77	34	67	7	–17	6	1	1	2	25	0	0	0
1970-71♦	**Montreal Canadiens**	**NHL**	64	10	13	23	10	11	21	90	0	0	2	120	8.3	37	5	40	0	–8	11	1	0	1	10	0	0	0
1971-72	**Montreal Canadiens**	**NHL**	77	20	18	38	20	16	36	64	1	3	4	169	11.8	56	4	55	12	9	6	2	1	3	23	0	0	0
1972-73♦	**Montreal Canadiens**	**NHL**	73	11	23	34	10	18	28	30	0	0	0	132	8.3	62	1	41	9	29	17	3	4	7	6	0	0	0
1973-74	**Montreal Canadiens**	**NHL**	39	17	7	24	16	6	22	52	1	0	1	71	23.9	36	1	27	3	11	5	0	2	2	11	0	0	0
1974-75	**Montreal Canadiens**	**NHL**	8	1	2	3	1	1	2	6	0	0	0	8	12.5	2	0	5	0	–3	....	....	....	....	....	....	....	....
	St. Louis Blues	**NHL**	56	10	17	27	9	13	22	38	0	0	1	146	6.8	49	4	39	1	7	2	1	1	2	0	0	0	0
1975-76	**St. Louis Blues**	**NHL**	67	13	25	38	11	19	30	48	3	0	0	169	7.7	61	11	44	1	7	3	0	0	0	0	0	0	0
1976-77	**St. Louis Blues**	**NHL**	80	29	19	48	26	15	41	22	1	1	2	212	13.7	71	5	67	6	5	4	1	0	1	0	0	0	0
1977-78	**St. Louis Blues**	**NHL**	69	8	13	21	7	10	17	20	2	0	0	116	6.9	38	8	57	8	–19	....	....	....	....	....	....	....	....
	NHL Totals		943	226	257	483	230	223	453	887	....	....	....	....	....	....	....	....	....	....	97	14	18	32	143	....	....	....

• Father of Guy • Played in NHL All-Star Game (1965, 1967, 1969, 1970)

Traded to **Minnesota** by **Montreal** with Danny Grant and future considerations (Bob Murdoch, May 25, 1971) for Minnesota's 1st round choice (Dave Gardner) in 1972 Amateur Draft, cash, and future considerations (Marshall Johnston, May 25, 1971), June 10, 1968. Traded to **Montreal** by **Minnesota** for Bobby Rousseau, June 10, 1970. Traded to **St. Louis** by **Montreal** for cash, December 5, 1974.

• LAROSE, Claude

Claude Andre LW – L. 5'10", 175 lbs. b: St. Jean, Que., 5/17/1955. NY Rangers' 7th, 120th overall, in 1975.

Season	Club	League	GP	G	A	Pts	AG	AA	APts	PIM	PP	SH	GW	S	%	TGF	PGF	TGA	PGA	+/–	GP	G	A	Pts	PIM	PP	SH	GW
1971-72	Drummondville Rangers	QMJHL	61	9	10	19	....	....	....	2	....	....	....	....	....	....	....	....	....	....	9	0	2	2	0	....	....	....
1972-73	Drummondville Rangers	QMJHL	61	63	50	113	....	....	....	12	....	....	....	....	....	....	....	....	....	....	....	....	....	....	....	....	....	....
1973-74	Drummondville Rangers	QMJHL	68	56	77	133	....	....	....	16	....	....	....	....	....	....	....	....	....	....	....	....	....	....	....	....	....	....
1974-75	Shawinigan Bruins	QMJHL	29	40	45	85	....	....	....	6	....	....	....	....	....	....	....	....	....	....	....	....	....	....	....	....	....	....
	Sherbrooke Beavers	QMJHL	74	69	76	145	....	....	....	12	....	....	....	....	....	....	....	....	....	....	....	....	....	....	....	....	....	....
	Sherbrooke Beavers	Mem-Cup	3	5	3	8	....	....	....	2	....	....	....	....	....	....	....	....	....	....	....	....	....	....	....	....	....	....
1975-76	Cincinnati Stingers	WHA	79	28	24	52	....	....	....	19	....	....	....	....	....	....	....	....	....	....	....	....	....	....	....	....	....	....
1976-77	Cincinnati Stingers	WHA	81	30	46	76	....	....	....	8	....	....	....	....	....	....	....	....	....	....	4	2	1	3	0	....	....	....
1977-78	Cincinnati Stingers	WHA	51	11	20	31	....	....	....	6	....	....	....	....	....	....	....	....	....	....	....	....	....	....	....	....	....	....
	Indianapolis Racers	WHA	28	14	16	30	....	....	....	12	....	....	....	....	....	....	....	....	....	....	....	....	....	....	....	....	....	....
1978-79	Indianapolis Racers	WHA	13	5	8	13	....	....	....	0	....	....	....	....	....	....	....	....	....	....	....	....	....	....	....	....	....	....
	New Haven Nighthawks	AHL	42	25	25	50	....	....	....	7	....	....	....	....	....	....	....	....	....	....	10	7	5	12	2	....	....	....
1979-80	**New York Rangers**	**NHL**	25	4	7	11	3	5	8	2	0	0	0	50	8.0	19	5	19	0	–5	....	....	....	....	....	....	....	....
	New Haven Nighthawks	AHL	31	16	27	43	....	....	....	4	....	....	....	....	....	....	....	....	....	....	....	....	....	....	....	....	....	....
1980-81	New Haven Nighthawks	AHL	80	30	27	57	....	....	....	12	....	....	....	....	....	....	....	....	....	....	4	1	2	3	0	....	....	....
1981-82	Springfield Indians	AHL	76	30	36	66	....	....	....	12	....	....	....	....	....	....	....	....	....	....	....	....	....	....	....	....	....	....
	New York Rangers	**NHL**	....	....	....	....	....	....	....	....	....	....	....	....	....	....	....	....	....	....	2	0	0	0	0	0	0	0
1982-83			DID NOT PLAY																									

Season	Club	League	GP	G	A	Pts	AG	AA	APts	PIM	PP	SH	GW	S	%	TGF	PGF	TGA	PGA	+/–	GP	G	A	Pts	PIM	PP	SH	GW
			REGULAR SEASON																		PLAYOFFS							
1983-84	Sherbrooke Jets	AHL	80	53	67	120	....	....	....	6	....	....	....	....	....	....	....	....	....	....	....	....	....	....	....	....	....	....
1984-85	Sherbrooke Canadiens	AHL	77	36	43	79	....	....	....	4	....	....	....	....	....	....	....	....	....	....	17	*10	6	16	8	....	....	....
1985-86	Sherbrooke Canadiens	AHL	65	38	39	77	....	....	....	2	....	....	....	....	....	....	....	....	....	....	....	....	....	....	....	....	....	....
	NHL Totals		**25**	**4**	**7**	**11**	**3**	**5**	**8**	**2**	**0**	**0**	**0**	**50**	**8.0**	**19**	**5**	**19**	**0**		**2**	**0**	**0**	**0**	**0**	**0**	**0**	**0**
	Other Major League Totals		252	88	114	202	....	....	....	45	....	....	....	....	....	....	....	....	....	....	4	2	1	3	0	....	....	....

QMJHL Second All-Star Team (1973, 1974, 1975) • Memorial Cup All-Star Team (1975) • AHL First All-Star Team (1984) • Won Fred T. Hunt Memorial Trophy (Sportsmanship - AHL) (1984) • Won John B. Sollenberger Trophy (Top Scorer - AHL) (1984)

Selected by **Cincinnati** (WHA) in 1975 WHA Amateur Draft, May, 1975. Traded to **Indianapolis** (WHA) by **Cincinnati** (WHA) with Rich Leduc for Darryl Maggs and Reg Thomas, February, 1978. Rights reclaimed by **NY Rangers** after **Indianapolis** (WHA) franchise folded, December 15, 1978.

• LAROSE, Guy

C – L. 5'9", 180 lbs. b: Hull, Que., 8/31/1967. Buffalo's 11th, 224th overall, in 1985.

Season	Club	League	GP	G	A	Pts	AG	AA	APts	PIM	PP	SH	GW	S	%	TGF	PGF	TGA	PGA	+/–	GP	G	A	Pts	PIM	PP	SH	GW
1983-84	Ottawa Jr. Senators	OJHL	54	37	66	103	....	....	....	66	....	....	....	....	....	....	....	....	....	....	....	....	....	....	....	....	....	....
1984-85	Guelph Platers	OHL	58	30	30	60	....	....	....	63	....	....	....	....	....	....	....	....	....	....	....	....	....	....	....	....	....	....
1985-86	Guelph Platers	OHL	37	12	36	48	....	....	....	55	....	....	....	....	....	....	....	....	....	....	....	....	....	....	....	....	....	....
	Ottawa 67's	OHL	28	19	25	44	....	....	....	63	....	....	....	....	....	....	....	....	....	....	....	....	....	....	....	....	....	....
1986-87	Ottawa 67's	OHL	66	28	49	77	....	....	....	77	....	....	....	....	....	....	....	....	....	....	11	2	8	10	27	....	....	....
1987-88	Moncton Hawks	AHL	77	22	31	53	....	....	....	127	....	....	....	....	....	....	....	....	....	....	....	....	....	....	....	....	....	....
1988-89	**Winnipeg Jets**	**NHL**	**3**	**0**	**1**	**1**	**0**	**1**	**1**	**6**	**0**	**0**	**0**	**2**	**0.0**	**2**	**0**	**3**	**0**	**–1**	....	....	....	....	....	....	....	....
	Moncton Hawks	AHL	72	32	27	59	....	....	....	176	....	....	....	....	....	....	....	....	....	....	10	4	4	8	37	....	....	....
1989-90	Moncton Hawks	AHL	79	44	26	70	....	....	....	232	....	....	....	....	....	....	....	....	....	....	....	....	....	....	....	....	....	....
1990-91	**Winnipeg Jets**	**NHL**	**7**	**0**	**0**	**0**	**0**	**0**	**0**	**8**	**0**	**0**	**0**	**7**	**0.0**	**1**	**0**	**3**	**1**	**–1**	....	....	....	....	....	....	....	....
	Moncton Hawks	AHL	35	14	10	24	....	....	....	60	....	....	....	....	....	....	....	....	....	....	....	....	....	....	....	....	....	....
	Binghamton Rangers	AHL	34	21	15	36	....	....	....	48	....	....	....	....	....	....	....	....	....	....	10	8	5	13	37	....	....	....
1991-92	Binghamton Rangers	AHL	30	10	11	21	....	....	....	36	....	....	....	....	....	....	....	....	....	....	....	....	....	....	....	....	....	....
	Toronto Maple Leafs	**NHL**	**34**	**9**	**5**	**14**	**8**	**4**	**12**	**27**	**0**	**0**	**0**	**60**	**15.0**	**21**	**2**	**27**	**0**	**–8**	....	....	....	....	....	....	....	....
	St. John's Maple Leafs	AHL	15	7	7	14	....	....	....	26	....	....	....	....	....	....	....	....	....	....	....	....	....	....	....	....	....	....
1992-93	**Toronto Maple Leafs**	**NHL**	**9**	**0**	**0**	**0**	**0**	**0**	**0**	**8**	**0**	**0**	**0**	**8**	**0.0**	**0**	**0**	**3**	**0**	**–3**	....	....	....	....	....	....	....	....
	St. John's Maple Leafs	AHL	5	0	1	1	....	....	....	8	....	....	....	....	....	....	....	....	....	....	9	5	2	7	6	....	....	....
1993-94	**Toronto Maple Leafs**	**NHL**	**10**	**1**	**2**	**3**	**1**	**2**	**3**	**10**	**0**	**0**	**0**	**9**	**11.1**	**3**	**0**	**5**	**0**	**–2**	....	....	....	....	....	....	....	....
	St. John's Maple Leafs	AHL	23	13	16	29	....	....	....	41	....	....	....	....	....	....	....	....	....	....	....	....	....	....	....	....	....	....
	Calgary Flames	**NHL**	**7**	**0**	**1**	**1**	**0**	**1**	**1**	**4**	**0**	**0**	**0**	**3**	**0.0**	**3**	**0**	**6**	**0**	**–3**	....	....	....	....	....	....	....	....
	Saint John Flames	AHL	15	11	11	22	....	....	....	20	....	....	....	....	....	....	....	....	....	....	7	3	2	5	22	....	....	....
1994-95	Providence Bruins	AHL	68	25	33	58	....	....	....	93	....	....	....	....	....	....	....	....	....	....	12	4	6	10	22	....	....	....
	Boston Bruins	**NHL**	....	....	....	....	**-2**	**-1**	**-3**	....	....	....	....	....	....	....	....	....	....	....	**4**	**0**	**0**	**0**	**0**	**0**	**0**	**0**
1995-96	Detroit Vipers	IHL	50	28	15	43	....	....	....	53	....	....	....	....	....	....	....	....	....	....	....	....	....	....	....	....	....	....
	Las Vegas Thunder	IHL	25	10	22	32	....	....	....	54	....	....	....	....	....	....	....	....	....	....	15	3	6	9	14	....	....	....
1996-97	Houston Aeros	IHL	79	29	25	54	....	....	....	108	....	....	....	....	....	....	....	....	....	....	13	6	7	13	12	....	....	....
1997-98	Revier Lowen	Germany	45	11	17	28	....	....	....	73	....	....	....	....	....	....	....	....	....	....	....	....	....	....	....	....	....	....
1998-99	Chicago Wolves	IHL	80	19	22	41	....	....	....	117	....	....	....	....	....	....	....	....	....	....	10	1	3	4	14	....	....	....
99-2000	Chicago Wolves	IHL	79	9	24	33	....	....	....	100	....	....	....	....	....	....	....	....	....	....	16	1	4	5	14	....	....	....
	NHL Totals		**70**	**10**	**9**	**19**	**7**	**7**	**14**	**63**	**0**	**0**	**0**	**89**	**11.2**	**30**	**2**	**47**	**1**		**4**	**0**	**0**	**0**	**0**	**0**	**0**	**0**

• Son of Claude

Signed as a free agent by **Winnipeg**, July 16, 1987. Traded to **NY Rangers** by **Winnipeg** for Rudy Poeschek, January 22, 1991. Traded to **Toronto** by **NY Rangers** for Mike Stevens, December 26, 1991. Claimed on waivers by **Calgary** from **Toronto**, January 1, 1994. Signed as a free agent by **Boston**, July 11, 1994. Signed as a free agent by **Chicago Wolves** (IHL), September 14, 1998.

• LAROUCHE, Pierre

Pierre R. "Lucky Pierre" C – R. 5'11", 175 lbs. b: Taschereau, Que., 11/16/1955. Pittsburgh's 1st, 8th overall, in 1974.

Season	Club	League	GP	G	A	Pts	AG	AA	APts	PIM	PP	SH	GW	S	%	TGF	PGF	TGA	PGA	+/–	GP	G	A	Pts	PIM	PP	SH	GW
1972-73	Quebec Remparts	QMJHL	20	6	7	13	....	....	....	20	....	....	....	....	....	....	....	....	....	....	....	....	....	....	....	....	....	....
	Sorel Black Hawks	QMJHL	43	47	54	101	....	....	....	24	....	....	....	....	....	....	....	....	....	....	10	7	6	13	2	....	....	....
1973-74	Sorel Black Hawks	QMJHL	67	94	*157	*251	....	....	....	53	....	....	....	....	....	....	....	....	....	....	13	15	18	33	20	....	....	....
1974-75	**Pittsburgh Penguins**	**NHL**	**79**	**31**	**37**	**68**	**27**	**28**	**55**	**52**	**5**	**0**	**4**	**172**	**18.0**	**87**	**17**	**70**	**2**	**2**	**9**	**2**	**5**	**7**	**2**	**0**	**0**	**1**
1975-76	**Pittsburgh Penguins**	**NHL**	**76**	**53**	**58**	**111**	**47**	**43**	**90**	**33**	**18**	**0**	**3**	**319**	**16.6**	**136**	**43**	**90**	**1**	**4**	**3**	**0**	**1**	**1**	**0**	**0**	**0**	**0**
1976-77	**Pittsburgh Penguins**	**NHL**	**65**	**29**	**34**	**63**	**26**	**26**	**52**	**14**	**8**	**0**	**6**	**227**	**12.8**	**84**	**27**	**72**	**5**	**–10**	**3**	**0**	**3**	**3**	**0**	**0**	**0**	**0**
	Canada	WEC-A	10	7	8	15	....	....	....	16	....	....	....	....	....	....	....	....	....	....	....	....	....	....	....	....	....	....
1977-78	**Pittsburgh Penguins**	**NHL**	**20**	**6**	**5**	**11**	**5**	**4**	**9**	**0**	**0**	**0**	**0**	**50**	**12.0**	**14**	**2**	**25**	**0**	**–13**	....	....	....	....	....	....	....	....
♦	**Montreal Canadiens**	**NHL**	**44**	**17**	**32**	**49**	**15**	**25**	**40**	**11**	**3**	**0**	**1**	**87**	**19.5**	**70**	**17**	**21**	**0**	**32**	**5**	**2**	**1**	**3**	**4**	**1**	**0**	**1**
1978-79♦	**Montreal Canadiens**	**NHL**	**36**	**9**	**13**	**22**	**8**	**9**	**17**	**4**	**4**	**0**	**0**	**64**	**14.1**	**33**	**17**	**13**	**0**	**3**	**6**	**1**	**3**	**4**	**0**	**0**	**0**	**1**
1979-80	**Montreal Canadiens**	**NHL**	**73**	**50**	**41**	**91**	**43**	**30**	**73**	**16**	**12**	**0**	**7**	**220**	**22.7**	**130**	**39**	**55**	**0**	**36**	**9**	**1**	**7**	**8**	**2**	**0**	**0**	**0**
1980-81	**Montreal Canadiens**	**NHL**	**61**	**25**	**28**	**53**	**19**	**19**	**38**	**28**	**5**	**0**	**2**	**154**	**16.2**	**77**	**25**	**40**	**1**	**13**	**2**	**0**	**2**	**2**	**0**	**0**	**0**	**0**
1981-82	**Montreal Canadiens**	**NHL**	**22**	**9**	**12**	**21**	**7**	**8**	**15**	**0**	**3**	**0**	**0**	**40**	**22.5**	**24**	**9**	**18**	**0**	**–3**	....	....	....	....	....	....	....	....
	Hartford Whalers	**NHL**	**45**	**25**	**25**	**50**	**20**	**17**	**37**	**12**	**11**	**1**	**1**	**121**	**20.7**	**71**	**30**	**71**	**13**	**–17**	....	....	....	....	....	....	....	....
1982-83	**Hartford Whalers**	**NHL**	**38**	**18**	**22**	**40**	**15**	**15**	**30**	**8**	**4**	**0**	**0**	**114**	**15.8**	**60**	**20**	**67**	**3**	**–24**	....	....	....	....	....	....	....	....
1983-84	**New York Rangers**	**NHL**	**77**	**48**	**33**	**81**	**39**	**22**	**61**	**22**	**19**	**0**	**4**	**241**	**19.9**	**103**	**36**	**98**	**16**	**–15**	**5**	**3**	**1**	**4**	**2**	**2**	**0**	**0**
1984-85	**New York Rangers**	**NHL**	**65**	**24**	**36**	**60**	**20**	**24**	**44**	**8**	**5**	**0**	**3**	**171**	**14.0**	**82**	**26**	**78**	**5**	**–17**	....	....	....	....	....	....	....	....
1985-86	**New York Rangers**	**NHL**	**28**	**20**	**7**	**27**	**16**	**5**	**21**	**4**	**7**	**0**	**2**	**85**	**23.5**	**35**	**10**	**31**	**0**	**–6**	**16**	**8**	**9**	**17**	**2**	**4**	**0**	**1**
	Hershey Bears	AHL	32	22	17	39	....	....	....	16	....	....	....	....	....	....	....	....	....	....	....	....	....	....	....	....	....	....
1986-87	**New York Rangers**	**NHL**	**73**	**28**	**35**	**63**	**24**	**25**	**49**	**12**	**8**	**0**	**3**	**193**	**14.5**	**95**	**35**	**67**	**0**	**–7**	**6**	**3**	**2**	**5**	**4**	**0**	**0**	**1**
1987-88	**New York Rangers**	**NHL**	**10**	**3**	**9**	**12**	**3**	**6**	**9**	**13**	**2**	**0**	**0**	**30**	**10.0**	**14**	**8**	**9**	**0**	**–3**	....	....	....	....	....	....	....	....
	NHL Totals		**812**	**395**	**427**	**822**	**334**	**306**	**640**	**237**	**114**	**1**	**36**	**2288**	**17.3**	**1115**	**361**	**825**	**46**		**64**	**20**	**34**	**54**	**16**	**7**	**0**	**5**

QMJHL Second All-Star Team (1974) • Played in NHL All-Star Game (1976, 1984)

Traded to **Montreal** by **Pittsburgh** with future considerations (rights to Peter Marsh, December 15, 1977) for Pete Mahovlich and Peter Lee, November 29, 1977. Traded to **Hartford** by **Montreal** with Montreal's 1st round choice (Sylvain Cote) in 1984 Entry Draft and 3rd round choice (later traded to Pittsburgh — Pittsburgh selected Bruce Racine) in 1985 Entry Draft for Hartford's 1st (Petr Svoboda) and 2nd (later traded to St. Louis — St. Louis selected Brian Benning) round choices in 1984 Entry Draft and 3rd round choice (Rocky Dundas) in 1985 Entry Draft, December 21, 1981. Signed as a free agent by **NY Rangers**, September 12, 1983.

• LAROUCHE, Steve

C – R. 6', 180 lbs. b: Rouyn, Que., 4/14/1971. Montreal's 3rd, 41st overall, in 1989.

Season	Club	League	GP	G	A	Pts	AG	AA	APts	PIM	PP	SH	GW	S	%	TGF	PGF	TGA	PGA	+/–	GP	G	A	Pts	PIM	PP	SH	GW
1985-86	Rouyn Citadels	NOHA	9	4	5	9	....	....	....	15	....	....	....	....	....	....	....	....	....	....	....	....	....	....	....	....	....	....
1986-87	Richelieu Regents	QAAA	42	25	35	60	....	....	....	....	....	....	....	....	....	....	....	....	....	....	....	....	....	....	....	....	....	....
1987-88	Trois-Rivieres Draveurs	QMJHL	66	11	29	40	....	....	....	25	....	....	....	....	....	....	....	....	....	....	....	....	....	....	....	....	....	....
1988-89	Trois-Rivieres Draveurs	QMJHL	70	51	102	153	....	....	....	53	....	....	....	....	....	....	....	....	....	....	4	4	2	6	6	....	....	....
1989-90	Trois-Rivieres Draveurs	QMJHL	60	55	90	145	....	....	....	40	....	....	....	....	....	....	....	....	....	....	7	3	5	8	8	....	....	....
	Canada	Nat-Team	1	1	0	1	....	....	....	0	....	....	....	....	....	....	....	....	....	....	....	....	....	....	....	....	....	....
1990-91	Chicoutimi Sagueneens	QMJHL	45	35	41	76	....	....	....	64	....	....	....	....	....	....	....	....	....	....	17	*13	*20	*33	20	....	....	....
	Chicoutimi Sagueneens	Mem-Cup	4	2	3	5	....	....	....	10	....	....	....	....	....	....	....	....	....	....	....	....	....	....	....	....	....	....
1991-92	Fredericton Canadiens	AHL	74	21	35	56	....	....	....	41	....	....	....	....	....	....	....	....	....	....	7	1	0	1	0	....	....	....
1992-93	Fredericton Canadiens	AHL	77	27	65	92	....	....	....	52	....	....	....	....	....	....	....	....	....	....	5	2	5	7	6	....	....	....
1993-94	Atlanta Knights	IHL	80	43	53	96	....	....	....	73	....	....	....	....	....	....	....	....	....	....	14	*16	10	*26	16	....	....	....
1994-95	P.E.I. Senators	AHL	70	*53	48	101	....	....	....	54	....	....	....	....	....	....	....	....	....	....	2	1	0	1	0	....	....	....
	Ottawa Senators	**NHL**	**18**	**8**	**7**	**15**	**14**	**10**	**24**	**6**	**2**	**0**	**2**	**38**	**21.1**	**19**	**9**	**15**	**0**	**–5**	....	....	....	....	....	....	....	....
1995-96	**New York Rangers**	**NHL**	**1**	**0**	**0**	**0**	**0**	**0**	**0**	**0**	**0**	**0**	**0**	**1**	**0.0**	**1**	**1**	**0**	**0**	**0**	....	....	....	....	....	....	....	....
	Binghamton Rangers	AHL	39	20	46	66	....	....	....	47	....	....	....	....	....	....	....	....	....	....	....	....	....	....	....	....	....	....
	Los Angeles Kings	**NHL**	**7**	**1**	**2**	**3**	**1**	**2**	**3**	**4**	**1**	**0**	**0**	**13**	**7.7**	**5**	**2**	**3**	**0**	**0**	....	....	....	....	....	....	....	....
	Phoenix Roadrunners	IHL	33	19	17	36	....	....	....	14	....	....	....	....	....	....	....	....	....	....	4	0	1	1	8	....	....	....
1996-97	Quebec Rafales	IHL	79	49	53	102	....	....	....	78	....	....	....	....	....	....	....	....	....	....	9	3	10	13	18	....	....	....

Season	Club	League	REGULAR SEASON																		PLAYOFFS							
			GP	G	A	Pts	AG	AA	APts	PIM	PP	SH	GW	S	%	TGF	PGF	TGA	PGA	+/–	GP	G	A	Pts	PIM	PP	SH	GW
1997-98	Quebec Rafales	IHL	68	23	44	67	....	....	....	40	....	....	....	....	....	....	....	....	....	....	....	....	....	....	....	....	....	....
	Chicago Wolves	IHL	13	9	10	19	....	....	....	20	....	....	....	....	....	....	....	....	....	....	22	9	11	20	14	....	....	....
1998-99	Chicago Wolves	IHL	33	13	25	38	....	....	....	18	....	....	....	....	....	....	....	....	....	....	....	....	....	....	....	....	....	....
99-2000	Chicago Wolves	IHL	82	31	*57	88	....	....	....	52	....	....	....	....	....	....	....	....	....	....	16	6	8	14	22	....	....	....
	NHL Totals		**26**	**9**	**9**	**18**	**15**	**12**	**27**	**10**	**3**	**0**	**2**	**52**	**17.3**	**25**	**12**	**18**	**0**		....	....	....	....	....	....	....	....

QMJHL Second All-Star Team (1990) • AHL First All-Star Team (1995) • Won Fred Hunt Memorial Trophy (Sportsmanship - AHL) (1995) • Won Les Cunningham Award (MVP - AHL) (1995) • IHL First All-Star Team (1997, 2000)

Signed as a free agent by **Ottawa**, September 11, 1994. Traded to **NY Rangers** by **Ottawa** for Jean-Yves Roy, October 5, 1995. Traded to **LA Kings** by **NY Rangers** for Chris Snell, January 14, 1996. Traded to **Chicago Wolves** (IHL) by **Quebec** (IHL) for cash, March 19, 1998. • Suffered season-ending knee injury in game vs. Detroit (IHL), December 29, 1998.

• LARSEN, Brad

Bradley Alexander LW – L. 5'11", 212 lbs. b: Nakusp, B.C., 1/28/1977. Colorado's 5th, 87th overall, in 1997.

Season	Club	League	GP	G	A	Pts	AG	AA	APts	PIM	PP	SH	GW	S	%	TGF	PGF	TGA	PGA	+/–	GP	G	A	Pts	PIM	PP	SH	GW
1992-93	Nelson Maple Leafs	RMJHL	42	31	37	68	....	....	....	164	....	....	....	....	....	....	....	....	....	....	....	....	....	....	....	....	....	....
1993-94	Swift Current Broncos	WHL	64	15	18	33	....	....	....	32	....	....	....	....	....	....	....	....	....	....	7	1	2	3	4	....	....	....
1994-95	Swift Current Broncos	WHL	62	24	33	57	....	....	....	73	....	....	....	....	....	....	....	....	....	....	6	0	1	1	2	....	....	....
1995-96	Swift Current Bronocs	WHL	51	30	47	77	....	....	....	67	....	....	....	....	....	....	....	....	....	....	6	3	2	5	13	....	....	....
	Canada	WJC-A	6	1	1	2	....	....	....	4	....	....	....	....	....	....	....	....	....	....	....	....	....	....	....	....	....	....
1996-97	Swift Current Broncos	WHL	61	36	46	82	....	....	....	61	....	....	....	....	....	....	....	....	....	....	....	....	....	....	....	....	....	....
	Canada	WJC-A	7	0	1	1	....	....	....	6	....	....	....	....	....	....	....	....	....	....	....	....	....	....	....	....	....	....
1997-98	**Colorado Avalanche**	**NHL**	**1**	**0**	**0**	**0**	**0**	**0**	**0**	**0**	**0**	**0**	**0**	**0**	**0.0**	**0**	**0**	**0**	**0**	**0**	....	....	....	....	....	....	....	....
	Hershey Bears	AHL	65	12	10	22	....	....	....	80	....	....	....	....	....	....	....	....	....	....	7	3	2	5	2	....	....	....
1998-99	Hershey Bears	AHL	18	3	4	7	....	....	....	11	....	....	....	....	....	....	....	....	....	....	5	0	1	1	6	....	....	....
99-2000	Hershey Bears	AHL	52	13	26	39	....	....	....	66	....	....	....	....	....	....	....	....	....	....	14	5	2	7	29	....	....	....
	NHL Totals		**1**	**0**	**0**	**0**	**0**	**0**	**0**	**0**	**0**	**0**	**0**	**0**	**0.0**	**0**	**0**	**0**	**0**		....	....	....	....	....	....	....	....

WHL East Second All-Star Team (1997)

• Re-entered NHL draft. Originally Ottawa's 3rd choice, 53rd overall, in 1995 Entry Draft.

Rights traded to **Colorado** by **Ottawa** for Janne Laukkanen, January 26, 1996. • Missed majority of 1998-99 season recovering from abdominal injury suffered in game vs. Albany (AHL), November 20, 1998.

• LARSON, Reed

Reed David D – R. 6', 195 lbs. b: Minneapolis, MN, 7/30/1956. Detroit's 2nd, 22nd overall, in 1976. **USHOF**

Season	Club	League	GP	G	A	Pts	AG	AA	APts	PIM	PP	SH	GW	S	%	TGF	PGF	TGA	PGA	+/–	GP	G	A	Pts	PIM	PP	SH	GW
1973-74	Roosevelt High School	Hi-School	STATISTICS NOT AVAILABLE																									
1974-75	University of Minnesota	WCHA	41	11	17	28	....	....	....	37	....	....	....	....	....	....	....	....	....	....	....	....	....	....	....	....	....	....
1975-76	University of Minnesota	WCHA	42	13	29	42	....	....	....	94	....	....	....	....	....	....	....	....	....	....	....	....	....	....	....	....	....	....
1976-77	University of Minnesota	WCHA	21	10	15	25	....	....	....	30	....	....	....	....	....	....	....	....	....	....	....	....	....	....	....	....	....	....
	Detroit Red Wings	**NHL**	**14**	**0**	**1**	**1**	**0**	**1**	**1**	**23**	**0**	**0**	**0**	**23**	**0.0**	**6**	**0**	**8**	**0**	**–2**	....	....	....	....	....	....	....	....
1977-78	**Detroit Red Wings**	**NHL**	**75**	**19**	**41**	**60**	**17**	**32**	**49**	**95**	**7**	**1**	**4**	**240**	**7.9**	**132**	**45**	**131**	**36**	**–8**	**7**	**0**	**2**	**2**	**4**	**0**	**0**	**0**
1978-79	**Detroit Red Wings**	**NHL**	**79**	**18**	**49**	**67**	**15**	**36**	**51**	**169**	**6**	**2**	**0**	**271**	**6.6**	**124**	**51**	**125**	**32**	**–20**	....	....	....	....	....	....	....	....
1979-80	**Detroit Red Wings**	**NHL**	**80**	**22**	**44**	**66**	**19**	**32**	**51**	**101**	**7**	**0**	**2**	**293**	**7.5**	**149**	**44**	**145**	**33**	**–7**	....	....	....	....	....	....	....	....
1980-81	**Detroit Red Wings**	**NHL**	**78**	**27**	**31**	**58**	**21**	**21**	**42**	**153**	**8**	**0**	**0**	**297**	**9.1**	**122**	**32**	**177**	**52**	**–35**	....	....	....	....	....	....	....	....
	United States	WEC-A	8	5	1	6	....	....	....	6	....	....	....	....	....	....	....	....	....	....	....	....	....	....	....	....	....	....
1981-82	United States	Can-Cup	5	1	1	2	....	....	....	4	....	....	....	....	....	....	....	....	....	....	....	....	....	....	....	....	....	....
	Detroit Red Wings	**NHL**	**80**	**21**	**39**	**60**	**17**	**26**	**43**	**112**	**4**	**2**	**2**	**311**	**6.8**	**137**	**26**	**161**	**33**	**–17**	....	....	....	....	....	....	....	....
1982-83	**Detroit Red Wings**	**NHL**	**80**	**22**	**52**	**74**	**18**	**36**	**54**	**104**	**7**	**1**	**1**	**271**	**8.1**	**145**	**30**	**159**	**37**	**–7**	....	....	....	....	....	....	....	....
1983-84	**Detroit Red Wings**	**NHL**	**78**	**23**	**39**	**62**	**18**	**27**	**45**	**122**	**10**	**0**	**5**	**262**	**8.8**	**137**	**48**	**136**	**37**	**–10**	**4**	**2**	**0**	**2**	**21**	**2**	**0**	**0**
1984-85	**Detroit Red Wings**	**NHL**	**77**	**17**	**45**	**62**	**14**	**31**	**45**	**139**	**7**	**0**	**0**	**233**	**7.3**	**149**	**47**	**137**	**42**	**7**	**3**	**1**	**2**	**3**	**20**	**0**	**0**	**0**
1985-86	**Detroit Red Wings**	**NHL**	**67**	**19**	**41**	**60**	**15**	**28**	**43**	**109**	**11**	**0**	**0**	**205**	**9.3**	**131**	**57**	**151**	**41**	**–36**	....	....	....	....	....	....	....	....
	Boston Bruins	**NHL**	**13**	**3**	**4**	**7**	**2**	**3**	**5**	**8**	**1**	**0**	**0**	**41**	**7.3**	**18**	**4**	**12**	**3**	**5**	**3**	**1**	**0**	**1**	**6**	**1**	**0**	**0**
1986-87	**Boston Bruins**	**NHL**	**66**	**12**	**24**	**36**	**10**	**17**	**27**	**95**	**9**	**0**	**1**	**209**	**5.7**	**117**	**40**	**85**	**17**	**9**	**4**	**0**	**2**	**2**	**2**	**0**	**0**	**0**
1987-88	**Boston Bruins**	**NHL**	**62**	**10**	**24**	**34**	**9**	**17**	**26**	**93**	**5**	**1**	**1**	**151**	**6.6**	**81**	**23**	**71**	**16**	**3**	**8**	**0**	**1**	**1**	**6**	**0**	**0**	**0**
	Maine Mariners	AHL	2	2	0	2	....	....	....	4	....	....	....	....	....	....	....	....	....	....	....	....	....	....	....	....	....	....
1988-89	**Edmonton Oilers**	**NHL**	**10**	**2**	**7**	**9**	**2**	**5**	**7**	**15**	**0**	**1**	**0**	**19**	**10.5**	**15**	**3**	**13**	**2**	**1**	....	....	....	....	....	....	....	....
	New York Islanders	**NHL**	**33**	**7**	**13**	**20**	**6**	**9**	**15**	**35**	**6**	**0**	**1**	**77**	**9.1**	**56**	**28**	**47**	**11**	**–8**	....	....	....	....	....	....	....	....
	Minnesota North Stars	**NHL**	**11**	**0**	**9**	**9**	**0**	**6**	**6**	**18**	**0**	**0**	**0**	**19**	**0.0**	**15**	**7**	**12**	**1**	**–3**	**3**	**0**	**0**	**0**	**4**	**0**	**0**	**0**
1989-90	HC Alleghe	Italy	34	17	32	49	....	....	....	49	....	....	....	....	....	....	....	....	....	....	9	7	18	25	2	....	....	....
	Buffalo Sabres	**NHL**	**1**	**0**	**0**	**0**	**0**	**0**	**0**	**0**	**0**	**0**	**0**	**1**	**0.0**	**4**	**1**	**2**	**0**	**1**	....	....	....	....	....	....	....	....
1990-91	HC Alleghe	Italy	36	13	38	51	....	....	....	24	....	....	....	....	....	....	....	....	....	....	7	3	7	10	6	....	....	....
1991-92	HC Milano Saima	Alpenliga	5	2	2	4	....	....	....	6	....	....	....	....	....	....	....	....	....	....	....	....	....	....	....	....	....	....
	HC Milano Saima	Italy	17	5	11	16	....	....	....	6	....	....	....	....	....	....	....	....	....	....	12	4	10	14	8	....	....	....
1992-93	HC Courmaosta	Italy-2	32	30	48	78	....	....	....	83	....	....	....	....	....	....	....	....	....	....	....	....	....	....	....	....	....	....
1993-94	HC Courmaosta	Italy	19	6	20	26	....	....	....	18	....	....	....	....	....	....	....	....	....	....	12	5	7	12	7	....	....	....
1994-95	Minnesota Moose	IHL	9	2	2	4	....	....	....	11	....	....	....	....	....	....	....	....	....	....	....	....	....	....	....	....	....	....
	NHL Totals		**904**	**222**	**463**	**685**	**183**	**327**	**510**	**1391**	**88**	**8**	**17**	**2923**	**7.6**	**1538**	**486**	**1572**	**393**		**32**	**4**	**7**	**11**	**63**	**3**	**0**	**0**

NCAA Championship All-Tournament Team (1975) • WCHA First All-Star Team (1976) • Played in NHL All-Star Game (1978, 1980, 1981)

Traded to **Boston** by **Detroit** for Mike O'Connell, March 10, 1986. Signed as a free agent by **Edmonton**, September 30, 1988. Signed as a free agent by **NY Islanders**, December 5, 1988. Traded to **Minnesota** by **NY Islanders** for Minnesota's 7th round choice (Brett Harkins) in 1989 Entry Draft and future considerations (Mike Kelfer, May 12, 1989), March 7, 1989. Signed as a free agent by **Alleghe-Sile** (Italy), August, 1989. Signed as a free agent by **Buffalo**, March 6, 1990. • Played w/ RHI's Minnesota Artic Blast in 1994 (6-2-4-6-12).

• LARTER, Tyler

C – L. 5'10", 185 lbs. b: Charlottetown, P.E.I., 3/12/1968. Washington's 3rd, 78th overall, in 1987.

Season	Club	League	GP	G	A	Pts	AG	AA	APts	PIM	PP	SH	GW	S	%	TGF	PGF	TGA	PGA	+/–	GP	G	A	Pts	PIM	PP	SH	GW
1983-84	Charlottetown Tigers	MJrHL	26	24	32	56	....	....	....	....	....	....	....	....	....	....	....	....	....	....	....	....	....	....	....	....	....	....
1984-85	Sault Ste. Marie Greyhounds	OHL	64	14	26	40	....	....	....	48	....	....	....	....	....	....	....	....	....	....	16	3	9	12	12	....	....	....
1985-86	Sault Ste. Marie Greyhounds	OHL	60	15	40	55	....	....	....	137	....	....	....	....	....	....	....	....	....	....	....	....	....	....	....	....	....	....
1986-87	Sault Ste. Marie Greyhounds	OHL	59	34	59	93	....	....	....	122	....	....	....	....	....	....	....	....	....	....	4	0	2	2	8	....	....	....
1987-88	Sault Ste. Marie Greyhounds	OHL	65	44	65	109	....	....	....	155	....	....	....	....	....	....	....	....	....	....	4	3	9	12	8	....	....	....
1988-89	Baltimore Skipjacks	AHL	71	9	19	28	....	....	....	189	....	....	....	....	....	....	....	....	....	....	....	....	....	....	....	....	....	....
1989-90	**Washington Capitals**	**NHL**	**1**	**0**	**0**	**0**	**0**	**0**	**0**	**0**	**0**	**0**	**0**	**2**	**0.0**	**0**	**0**	**1**	**0**	**–1**	....	....	....	....	....	....	....	....
	Baltimore Skipjacks	AHL	79	31	36	67	....	....	....	104	....	....	....	....	....	....	....	....	....	....	12	5	6	11	57	....	....	....
1990-91	Baltimore Skipjacks	AHL	62	21	21	42	....	....	....	84	....	....	....	....	....	....	....	....	....	....	6	1	0	1	13	....	....	....
1991-92	Moncton Hawks	AHL	68	25	51	76	....	....	....	156	....	....	....	....	....	....	....	....	....	....	10	5	5	10	33	....	....	....
	Kalamazoo Wings	IHL	3	0	2	2	....	....	....	4	....	....	....	....	....	....	....	....	....	....	....	....	....	....	....	....	....	....
1992-93	VEU Feldkirch	Austria	39	16	25	41	....	....	....	....	....	....	....	....	....	....	....	....	....	....	....	....	....	....	....	....	....	....
	HC Gardena-Groden	Italy	3	2	2	4	....	....	....	2	....	....	....	....	....	....	....	....	....	....	....	....	....	....	....	....	....	....
1993-94	Durham Wasps	BH-Cup	5	8	14	22	....	....	....	10	....	....	....	....	....	....	....	....	....	....	....	....	....	....	....	....	....	....
	Durham Wasps	Britain	2	2	1	3	....	....	....	8	....	....	....	....	....	....	....	....	....	....	....	....	....	....	....	....	....	....
	Whitley Warriors	BH-Cup	3	6	6	12	....	....	....	10	....	....	....	....	....	....	....	....	....	....	....	....	....	....	....	....	....	....
	Whitley Warriors	Britain	32	32	30	62	....	....	....	38	....	....	....	....	....	....	....	....	....	....	5	9	3	12	8	....	....	....
	NHL Totals		**1**	**0**	**0**	**0**	**0**	**0**	**0**	**0**	**0**	**0**	**0**	**2**	**0.0**	**0**	**0**	**1**	**0**		....	....	....	....	....	....	....	....

Traded to **Winnipeg** by **Washington** with Bob Joyce and Kent Paynter for Craig Duncanson, Brent Hughes and Simon Wheeldon, May 21, 1991. Claimed by **Minnesota** from **Winnipeg** in Expansion Draft, May 30, 1991. Traded to **Winnipeg** by **Minnesota** for Tony Joseph, October 15, 1991.

• LATAL, Jiri

D – L. 6', 190 lbs. b: Olomouc, Czech., 2/2/1967. Toronto's 6th, 106th overall, in 1985.

Season	Club	League	GP	G	A	Pts	AG	AA	APts	PIM	PP	SH	GW	S	%	TGF	PGF	TGA	PGA	+/–	GP	G	A	Pts	PIM	PP	SH	GW
1983-84	HC Sparta Praha	Czech-Jr.	STATISTICS NOT AVAILABLE																									
	Czechoslovakia	EJC-A	5	0	0	0	....	....	....	6	....	....	....	....	....	....	....	....	....	....	....	....	....	....	....	....	....	....
1984-85	HC Sparta Praha	Czech.	28	2	2	4	....	....	....	10	....	....	....	....	....	....	....	....	....	....	....	....	....	....	....	....	....	....
	Czechoslovakia	WJC-A	7	0	4	4	....	....	....	2	....	....	....	....	....	....	....	....	....	....	....	....	....	....	....	....	....	....
1985-86	HC Sparta Praha	Czech.	27	3	2	5	....	....	....	....	....	....	....	....	....	....	....	....	....	....	....	....	....	....	....	....	....	....
	Czechoslovakia	WJC-A	7	0	2	2	....	....	....	2	....	....	....	....	....	....	....	....	....	....	....	....	....	....	....	....	....	....
1986-87	HC Sparta Praha	Czech.	12	1	2	3	....	....	....	....	....	....	....	....	....	....	....	....	....	....	....	....	....	....	....	....	....	....
	Czechoslovakia	WJC-A	7	4	2	6	....	....	....	0	....	....	....	....	....	....	....	....	....	....	....	....	....	....	....	....	....	....

			REGULAR SEASON																		PLAYOFFS							
Season	Club	League	GP	G	A	Pts	AG	AA	APts	PIM	PP	SH	GW	S	%	TGF	PGF	TGA	PGA	+/-	GP	G	A	Pts	PIM	PP	SH	GW
1987-88	Dukla Trencin	Czech.	46	8	15	23	....	....	....	27	....	....	....	....	....	....	....	....	....	....	....	....	....	....	....	....	....	....
1988-89	Dukla Trencin	Czech.	48	6	22	28	....	....	....	....	....	....	....	....	....	....	....	....	....	....	....	....	....	....	....	....	....	....
	Czechoslovakia	WEC-A	1	0	0	0	....	....	....	0	....	....	....	....	....	....	....	....	....	....	....	....	....	....	....	....	....	....
1989-90	**Philadelphia Flyers**	**NHL**	**32**	**6**	**13**	**19**	**5**	**9**	**14**	**6**	**3**	**0**	**0**	**59**	**10.2**	**49**	**12**	**33**	**0**	**4**	....	....	....	....	....	....	....	....
	Hershey Bears	AHL	22	10	18	28	....	....	....	10	....	....	....	....	....	....	....	....	....	....	....	....	....	....	....	....	....	....
1990-91	**Philadelphia Flyers**	**NHL**	**50**	**5**	**21**	**26**	**5**	**16**	**21**	**14**	**1**	**0**	**0**	**81**	**6.2**	**46**	**17**	**49**	**1**	**–19**	....	....	....	....	....	....	....	....
1991-92	**Philadelphia Flyers**	**NHL**	**10**	**1**	**2**	**3**	**1**	**2**	**3**	**4**	**0**	**0**	**1**	**22**	**4.5**	**10**	**2**	**7**	**0**	**1**	....	....	....	....	....	....	....	....
	Valerenga IF Oslo	Norway	32	7	16	23	....	....	....	18	....	....	....	....	....	....	....	....	....	....	....	....	....	....	....	....	....	....
1992-93	H-Reipas Lahti	Finland	41	5	20	25	....	....	....	18	....	....	....	....	....	....	....	....	....	....	....	....	....	....	....	....	....	....
1993-94	Valerenga IF Oslo	Norway	STATISTICS NOT AVAILABLE																									
	HC Olomouc	Czech-Rep	2	0	0	0	....	....	....	0	....	....	....	....	....	....	....	....	....	....	....	....	....	....	....	....	....	....
1994-95	HC Olomouc	Czech-Rep	27	5	8	13	....	....	....	18	....	....	....	....	....	....	....	....	....	....	4	2	2	4	0	....	....	....
1995-96	HC Olomouc	Czech-Rep	29	5	10	15	....	....	....	....	....	....	....	....	....	....	....	....	....	....	4	2	2	4	0	....	....	....
	NHL Totals		**92**	**12**	**36**	**48**	**11**	**27**	**38**	**24**	**4**	**0**	**1**	**162**	**7.4**	**105**	**31**	**89**	**1**		....	....	....	....	....	....	....	....

EJC-A All-Star Team (1984) • WJC-A All-Star Team (1987)

Rights traded to **Philadelphia** by **Toronto** for Philadelphia's 7th round choice (later traded back to Philadelphia — Philadelphia selected Andrei Lomakin) in 1991 Entry Draft, August 28, 1989.

• LATOS, James "Knuckles" RW – R. 6'1", 200 lbs. b: Wakaw, Sask., 1/4/1966.

Season	Club	League	GP	G	A	Pts	AG	AA	APts	PIM	PP	SH	GW	S	%	TGF	PGF	TGA	PGA	+/-	GP	G	A	Pts	PIM	PP	SH	GW
1982-83	Prince Albert Mintos	SAHA	28	11	18	29	....	....	....	20	....	....	....	....	....	....	....	....	....	....	....	....	....	....	....	....	....	....
1983-84	Humboldt Broncos	SJHL	53	12	15	27	....	....	....	131	....	....	....	....	....	....	....	....	....	....	....	....	....	....	....	....	....	....
1984-85	Saskatoon Blades	WHL	62	9	9	18	....	....	....	120	....	....	....	....	....	....	....	....	....	....	3	1	1	2	0	....	....	....
1985-86	Saskatoon Blades	WHL	40	4	7	11	....	....	....	111	....	....	....	....	....	....	....	....	....	....	....	....	....	....	....	....	....	....
	Portland Winter Hawks	WHL	21	6	7	13	....	....	....	80	....	....	....	....	....	....	....	....	....	....	9	1	1	2	32	....	....	....
1986-87	Portland Winter Hawks	WHL	69	27	18	45	....	....	....	210	....	....	....	....	....	....	....	....	....	....	20	5	3	8	56	....	....	....
1987-88	Colorado Rangers	IHL	38	11	12	23	....	....	....	98	....	....	....	....	....	....	....	....	....	....	....	....	....	....	....	....	....	....
1988-89	**New York Rangers**	**NHL**	**1**	**0**	**0**	**0**	**0**	**0**	**0**	**0**	**0**	**0**	**0**	**0**	**0.0**	**0**	**0**	**1**	**0**	**–1**	....	....	....	....	....	....	....	....
	Denver Rangers	IHL	37	7	5	12	....	....	....	157	....	....	....	....	....	....	....	....	....	....	4	0	0	0	17	....	....	....
1989-90	Flint Spirits	IHL	71	12	15	27	....	....	....	244	....	....	....	....	....	....	....	....	....	....	4	0	0	0	0	....	....	....
1990-91	Kansas City Blades	IHL	61	14	14	28	....	....	....	187	....	....	....	....	....	....	....	....	....	....	....	....	....	....	....	....	....	....
1991-92	Knoxville Cherokees	ECHL	10	5	2	7	....	....	....	24	....	....	....	....	....	....	....	....	....	....	....	....	....	....	....	....	....	....
	Muskegon Lumberjacks	IHL	27	4	4	8	....	....	....	54	....	....	....	....	....	....	....	....	....	....	6	0	1	1	10	....	....	....
	St. Thomas Wildcats	ColHL	27	7	13	20	....	....	....	62	....	....	....	....	....	....	....	....	....	....	....	....	....	....	....	....	....	....
1992-93	Muskegon Fury	ColHL	59	10	24	34	....	....	....	163	....	....	....	....	....	....	....	....	....	....	7	2	0	2	4	....	....	....
	Cleveland Lumberjacks	IHL	1	0	0	0	....	....	....	0	....	....	....	....	....	....	....	....	....	....	....	....	....	....	....	....	....	....
1993-94	Wichita Thunder	ColHL	63	19	34	53	....	....	....	227	....	....	....	....	....	....	....	....	....	....	11	4	5	9	27	....	....	....
1994-95	Lee Valley Lions	Aut-Cup	44	2	4	6	....	....	....	27	....	....	....	....	....	....	....	....	....	....	....	....	....	....	....	....	....	....
	Lee Valley Lions	Britain-2	12	11	5	16	....	....	....	32	....	....	....	....	....	....	....	....	....	....	....	....	....	....	....	....	....	....
	Wichita Thunder	CHL	55	13	23	36	....	....	....	167	....	....	....	....	....	....	....	....	....	....	11	2	5	7	44	....	....	....
1995-96	Louisiana Ice Gators	ECHL	8	2	1	3	....	....	....	30	....	....	....	....	....	....	....	....	....	....	....	....	....	....	....	....	....	....
1996-97	Louisiana Ice Gators	ECHL	32	4	7	11	....	....	....	150	....	....	....	....	....	....	....	....	....	....	....	....	....	....	....	....	....	....
	NHL Totals		**1**	**0**	**0**	**0**	**0**	**0**	**0**	**0**	**0**	**0**	**0**	**0**	**0.0**	**0**	**0**	**1**	**0**		....	....	....	....	....	....	....	....

Signed as a free agent by **NY Rangers**, June 5, 1987.

• LATTA, David LW – L. 6'1", 190 lbs. b: Thunder Bay, Ont., 1/3/1967. Quebec's 1st, 15th overall, in 1985.

Season	Club	League	GP	G	A	Pts	AG	AA	APts	PIM	PP	SH	GW	S	%	TGF	PGF	TGA	PGA	+/-	GP	G	A	Pts	PIM	PP	SH	GW
1981-82	Thunder Bay Kings	TBAHA	STATISTICS NOT AVAILABLE																									
1982-83	Orillia Travelways	OJHL	43	16	25	41	....	....	....	26	....	....	....	....	....	....	....	....	....	....	....	....	....	....	....	....	....	....
1983-84	Kitchener Rangers	OHL	66	17	26	43	....	....	....	54	....	....	....	....	....	....	....	....	....	....	16	3	6	9	9	....	....	....
	Kitchener Rangers	Mem-Cup	4	0	0	0	....	....	....	0	....	....	....	....	....	....	....	....	....	....	....	....	....	....	....	....	....	....
1984-85	Kitchener Rangers	OHL	52	38	27	65	....	....	....	26	....	....	....	....	....	....	....	....	....	....	4	2	4	6	4	....	....	....
1985-86	Kitchener Rangers	OHL	55	36	34	70	....	....	....	60	....	....	....	....	....	....	....	....	....	....	5	7	1	8	15	....	....	....
	Quebec Nordiques	**NHL**	**1**	**0**	**0**	**0**	**0**	**0**	**0**	**0**	**0**	**0**	**0**	**1**	**0.0**	**0**	**0**	**0**	**0**	**0**	....	....	....	....	....	....	....	....
	Fredericton Express	AHL	3	1	0	1	....	....	....	0	....	....	....	....	....	....	....	....	....	....	5	0	3	3	0	....	....	....
1986-87	Kitchener Rangers	OHL	50	32	46	78	....	....	....	46	....	....	....	....	....	....	....	....	....	....	4	0	3	3	2	....	....	....
	Canada	WJC-A	6	4	6	10	....	....	....	12	....	....	....	....	....	....	....	....	....	....	....	....	....	....	....	....	....	....
1987-88	**Quebec Nordiques**	**NHL**	**10**	**0**	**0**	**0**	**0**	**0**	**0**	**0**	**0**	**0**	**0**	**13**	**0.0**	**2**	**1**	**5**	**0**	**–4**	....	....	....	....	....	....	....	....
	Fredericton Express	AHL	34	11	21	32	....	....	....	28	....	....	....	....	....	....	....	....	....	....	15	9	4	13	24	....	....	....
1988-89	**Quebec Nordiques**	**NHL**	**24**	**4**	**8**	**12**	**3**	**6**	**9**	**4**	**1**	**0**	**1**	**30**	**13.3**	**16**	**4**	**20**	**0**	**–8**	....	....	....	....	....	....	....	....
	Halifax Citadels	AHL	42	20	26	46	....	....	....	36	....	....	....	....	....	....	....	....	....	....	4	0	2	2	2	....	....	....
1989-90	Halifax Citadels	AHL	34	11	5	16	....	....	....	45	....	....	....	....	....	....	....	....	....	....	....	....	....	....	....	....	....	....
1990-91	**Quebec Nordiques**	**NHL**	**1**	**0**	**0**	**0**	**0**	**0**	**0**	**0**	**0**	**0**	**0**	**1**	**0.0**	**0**	**0**	**0**	**0**	**0**	....	....	....	....	....	....	....	....
	Halifax Citadels	AHL	22	4	7	11	....	....	....	12	....	....	....	....	....	....	....	....	....	....	....	....	....	....	....	....	....	....
	Canada	Nat-Team	30	5	14	19	....	....	....	24	....	....	....	....	....	....	....	....	....	....	....	....	....	....	....	....	....	....
1991-92	New Haven Nighthawks	AHL	76	18	27	45	....	....	....	100	....	....	....	....	....	....	....	....	....	....	5	1	1	2	4	....	....	....
1992-93	EC Bad Nauheim	Germany-2	9	8	8	16	....	....	....	....	....	....	....	....	....	....	....	....	....	....	....	....	....	....	....	....	....	....
	Cincinnati Cyclones	IHL	13	4	7	11	....	....	....	26	....	....	....	....	....	....	....	....	....	....	....	....	....	....	....	....	....	....
1993-94	EC Bad Tolz	Germany-2	30	18	19	37	....	....	....	....	....	....	....	....	....	....	....	....	....	....	11	12	15	27	....	....	....	....
1994-95	EHC Zweibruken	Germany-3	30	67	147	214	....	....	....	252	....	....	....	....	....	....	....	....	....	....	....	....	....	....	....	....	....	....
	Adler Mannheim	Germany	2	1	1	2	....	....	....	2	....	....	....	....	....	....	....	....	....	....	....	....	....	....	....	....	....	....
1995-96	EC Bad Tolz	Germany-2	33	14	26	40	....	....	....	36	....	....	....	....	....	....	....	....	....	....	....	....	....	....	....	....	....	....
	EC Peiting	Germany-2	10	2	4	6	....	....	....	8	....	....	....	....	....	....	....	....	....	....	....	....	....	....	....	....	....	....
	Augsburger Panther	Germany	1	1	0	1	....	....	....	0	....	....	....	....	....	....	....	....	....	....	....	....	....	....	....	....	....	....
1996-97	EC Peiting	Germany-2	36	4	8	12	....	....	....	4	....	....	....	....	....	....	....	....	....	....	....	....	....	....	....	....	....	....
	Manchester Storm	Britain	21	1	3	4	....	....	....	10	....	....	....	....	....	....	....	....	....	....	....	....	....	....	....	....	....	....
1997-98	Anchorage Aces	WCHL	48	10	13	23	....	....	....	64	....	....	....	....	....	....	....	....	....	....	5	0	0	0	2	....	....	....
	NHL Totals		**36**	**4**	**8**	**12**	**3**	**6**	**9**	**4**	**1**	**0**	**1**	**45**	**8.9**	**18**	**5**	**25**	**0**		....	....	....	....	....	....	....	....

• LAUEN, Mike Michael Arthur RW – R. 6'1", 185 lbs. b: Edina, MN, 2/9/1961. Winnipeg's 8th, 135th overall, in 1980.

Season	Club	League	GP	G	A	Pts	AG	AA	APts	PIM	PP	SH	GW	S	%	TGF	PGF	TGA	PGA	+/-	GP	G	A	Pts	PIM	PP	SH	GW
1976-1979	Edina Hornets	Hi-School	STATISTICS NOT AVAILABLE																									
1979-80	Michigan Tech Huskies	CCHA	35	24	21	45	....	....	....	16	....	....	....	....	....	....	....	....	....	....	....	....	....	....	....	....	....	....
	United States	WJC-A	5	3	2	5	....	....	....	8	....	....	....	....	....	....	....	....	....	....	....	....	....	....	....	....	....	....
1980-81	Michigan Tech Huskies	CCHA	44	24	20	44	....	....	....	14	....	....	....	....	....	....	....	....	....	....	....	....	....	....	....	....	....	....
1981-82	Michigan Tech Huskies	CCHA	30	13	15	28	....	....	....	28	....	....	....	....	....	....	....	....	....	....	....	....	....	....	....	....	....	....
1982-83	Michigan Tech Huskies	CCHA	38	12	17	29	....	....	....	18	....	....	....	....	....	....	....	....	....	....	....	....	....	....	....	....	....	....
	Sherbrooke Jets	AHL	5	0	3	3	....	....	....	0	....	....	....	....	....	....	....	....	....	....	....	....	....	....	....	....	....	....
1983-84	**Winnipeg Jets**	**NHL**	**4**	**0**	**1**	**1**	**0**	**1**	**1**	**0**	**0**	**0**	**0**	**3**	**0.0**	**2**	**0**	**2**	**0**	**0**	....	....	....	....	....	....	....	....
	Sherbrooke Jets	AHL	62	23	29	52	....	....	....	13	....	....	....	....	....	....	....	....	....	....	....	....	....	....	....	....	....	....
1984-85	Sherbrooke Canadiens	AHL	25	6	10	16	....	....	....	2	....	....	....	....	....	....	....	....	....	....	....	....	....	....	....	....	....	....
1985-86	Toledo Goaldiggers	IHL	27	4	10	14	....	....	....	16	....	....	....	....	....	....	....	....	....	....	....	....	....	....	....	....	....	....
	NHL Totals		**4**	**0**	**1**	**1**	**0**	**1**	**1**	**0**	**0**	**0**	**0**	**3**	**0.0**	**2**	**0**	**2**	**0**		....	....	....	....	....	....	....	....

• LAUER, Brad Brad R. LW – L. 6', 195 lbs. b: Humboldt, Sask., 10/27/1966. NY Islanders' 3rd, 34th overall, in 1985.

Season	Club	League	GP	G	A	Pts	AG	AA	APts	PIM	PP	SH	GW	S	%	TGF	PGF	TGA	PGA	+/-	GP	G	A	Pts	PIM	PP	SH	GW
1982-83	Notre Dame Midget Hounds	SAHA	STATISTICS NOT AVAILABLE																									
1983-84	Regina Pats	WHL	60	5	7	12	....	....	....	51	....	....	....	....	....	....	....	....	....	....	16	0	1	1	24	....	....	....
1984-85	Regina Pats	WHL	72	33	46	79	....	....	....	57	....	....	....	....	....	....	....	....	....	....	8	6	6	12	9	....	....	....
1985-86	Regina Pats	WHL	57	36	38	74	....	....	....	69	....	....	....	....	....	....	....	....	....	....	10	4	5	9	2	....	....	....
1986-87	**New York Islanders**	**NHL**	**61**	**7**	**14**	**21**	**6**	**10**	**16**	**65**	**1**	**0**	**1**	**75**	**9.3**	**31**	**2**	**31**	**2**	**0**	**6**	**2**	**0**	**2**	**4**	**0**	**0**	**0**
1987-88	**New York Islanders**	**NHL**	**69**	**17**	**18**	**35**	**14**	**13**	**27**	**67**	**3**	**0**	**4**	**94**	**18.1**	**44**	**8**	**24**	**1**	**13**	**5**	**3**	**1**	**4**	**4**	**0**	**0**	**0**
1988-89	**New York Islanders**	**NHL**	**14**	**3**	**2**	**5**	**3**	**1**	**4**	**2**	**0**	**0**	**0**	**21**	**14.3**	**11**	**2**	**11**	**0**	**–2**	....	....	....	....	....	....	....	....
	Springfield Indians	AHL	8	1	5	6	....	....	....	0	....	....	....	....	....	....	....	....	....	....	....	....	....	....	....	....	....	....

			REGULAR SEASON																		PLAYOFFS							
Season	Club	League	GP	G	A	Pts	AG	AA	APts	PIM	PP	SH	GW	S	%	TGF	PGF	TGA	PGA	+/-	GP	G	A	Pts	PIM	PP	SH	GW
1989-90	**New York Islanders**	**NHL**	**63**	**6**	**18**	**24**	**5**	**13**	**18**	**19**	**0**	**0**	**2**	**86**	**7.0**	**41**	**2**	**53**	**19**	**5**	**4**	**0**	**2**	**2**	**10**	**0**	**0**	**0**
	Springfield Indians	AHL	7	4	2	6				0																		
1990-91	**New York Islanders**	**NHL**	**44**	**4**	**8**	**12**	**4**	**6**	**10**	**45**	**0**	**1**	**0**	**70**	**5.7**	**22**	**1**	**39**	**12**	**–6**								
	Capital District Islanders	AHL	11	5	11	16				14																		
1991-92	**New York Islanders**	**NHL**	**8**	**1**	**0**	**1**	**1**	**0**	**1**	**2**	**0**	**1**	**0**	**12**	**8.3**	**2**	**0**	**5**	**1**	**–2**								
	Chicago Blackhawks	**NHL**	**6**	**0**	**0**	**0**	**0**	**0**	**0**	**4**	**0**	**0**	**0**	**6**	**0.0**	**0**	**0**	**3**	**0**	**–3**	**7**	**1**	**1**	**2**	**2**	**0**	**0**	**0**
	Indianapolis Ice	IHL	57	24	30	54				46																		
1992-93	**Chicago Blackhawks**	**NHL**	**7**	**0**	**1**	**1**	**0**	**1**	**1**	**2**	**0**	**0**	**0**	**8**	**0.0**	**4**	**1**	**4**	**0**	**–1**								
	Indianapolis Ice	IHL	62	*50	41	91				80											5	3	1	4	6			
1993-94	**Ottawa Senators**	**NHL**	**30**	**2**	**5**	**7**	**2**	**4**	**6**	**6**	**0**	**1**	**0**	**45**	**4.4**	**11**	**2**	**37**	**13**	**–15**								
	Las Vegas Thunder	IHL	32	21	21	42				30											4	1	0	1	2			
1994-95	Cleveland Lumberjacks	IHL	51	32	27	59				48											4	4	2	6	6			
1995-96	**Pittsburgh Penguins**	**NHL**	**21**	**4**	**1**	**5**	**4**	**1**	**5**	**6**	**1**	**0**	**1**	**29**	**13.8**	**10**	**1**	**14**	**0**	**–5**	**12**	**1**	**1**	**2**	**4**	**0**	**0**	**0**
	Cleveland Lumberjacks	IHL	53	25	27	52				44																		
1996-97	Cleveland Lumberjacks	IHL	64	27	21	48				61											14	4	6	10	8			
1997-98	Cleveland Lumberjacks	IHL	68	22	33	55				74											10	0	3	3	12			
1998-99	Utah Grizzlies	IHL	78	31	30	61				68																		
99-2000	Utah Grizzlies	IHL	71	26	22	48				73											5	0	1	1	2			
	NHL Totals		**323**	**44**	**67**	**111**	**39**	**49**	**88**	**218**	**5**	**3**	**8**	**446**	**9.9**	**176**	**19**	**221**	**48**		**34**	**7**	**5**	**12**	**24**	**0**	**0**	**0**

IHL First All-Star Team (1993)

• Missed majority of 1988-89 season recovering from knee injury suffered in training camp, October, 1988. Traded to **Chicago** by **NY Islanders** with Brent Sutter for Adam Creighton and Steve Thomas, October 25, 1991. Signed as a free agent by **Ottawa**, January 3, 1994. Signed as a free agent by **Pittsburgh**, August 10, 1995.

• LAUGHLIN, Craig

Craig Alan RW – R. 6', 190 lbs. b: Toronto, Ont., 9/19/1957. Montreal's 17th, 162nd overall, in 1977.

Season	Club	League	GP	G	A	Pts	AG	AA	APts	PIM	PP	SH	GW	S	%	TGF	PGF	TGA	PGA	+/-	GP	G	A	Pts	PIM	PP	SH	GW
1976-77	Clarkson College	ECAC	33	12	13	25				44																		
1977-78	Clarkson College	ECAC	30	17	31	48				56																		
1978-79	Clarkson College	ECAC	30	18	29	47				22																		
1979-80	Clarkson College	ECAC	34	18	30	48				38																		
	Nova Scotia Voyageurs	AHL	2	0	0	0				2																		
1980-81	Nova Scotia Voyageurs	AHL	46	32	29	61				15											6	0	1	1	6			
1981-82	**Montreal Canadiens**	**NHL**	**36**	**12**	**11**	**23**	**9**	**7**	**16**	**33**	**2**	**0**	**1**	**52**	**23.1**	**36**	**6**	**20**	**0**	**10**	**3**	**0**	**1**	**1**	**0**	**0**	**0**	**0**
	Nova Scotia Voyageurs	AHL	26	14	15	29				16																		
1982-83	**Washington Capitals**	**NHL**	**75**	**17**	**27**	**44**	**14**	**19**	**33**	**41**	**5**	**0**	**3**	**128**	**13.3**	**73**	**25**	**57**	**2**	**–7**	**4**	**1**	**0**	**1**	**0**	**0**	**0**	**0**
1983-84	**Washington Capitals**	**NHL**	**80**	**20**	**32**	**52**	**16**	**22**	**38**	**69**	**7**	**0**	**3**	**111**	**18.0**	**77**	**33**	**40**	**0**	**4**	**8**	**4**	**2**	**6**	**6**	**1**	**0**	**3**
1984-85	**Washington Capitals**	**NHL**	**78**	**16**	**34**	**50**	**13**	**23**	**36**	**38**	**5**	**0**	**3**	**104**	**15.4**	**86**	**29**	**47**	**2**	**12**	**5**	**0**	**0**	**0**	**2**	**0**	**0**	**0**
1985-86	**Washington Capitals**	**NHL**	**75**	**30**	**45**	**75**	**24**	**30**	**54**	**43**	**10**	**0**	**4**	**114**	**26.3**	**126**	**51**	**53**	**2**	**24**	**9**	**1**	**2**	**3**	**10**	**0**	**0**	**1**
1986-87	**Washington Capitals**	**NHL**	**80**	**22**	**30**	**52**	**19**	**22**	**41**	**67**	**11**	**0**	**5**	**109**	**20.2**	**89**	**36**	**56**	**0**	**–3**	**1**	**0**	**0**	**0**	**0**	**0**	**0**	**0**
1987-88	**Washington Capitals**	**NHL**	**40**	**5**	**5**	**10**	**4**	**4**	**8**	**26**	**3**	**0**	**1**	**45**	**11.1**	**18**	**8**	**18**	**0**	**–8**								
	Los Angeles Kings	**NHL**	**19**	**4**	**8**	**12**	**3**	**6**	**9**	**6**	**2**	**0**	**0**	**29**	**13.8**	**17**	**7**	**19**	**1**	**–8**	**3**	**0**	**1**	**1**	**2**	**0**	**0**	**0**
1988-89	**Toronto Maple Leafs**	**NHL**	**66**	**10**	**13**	**23**	**8**	**9**	**17**	**41**	**0**	**0**	**0**	**87**	**11.5**	**33**	**4**	**56**	**5**	**–22**								
1989-90	EV Landshut	Germany	35	22	11	33				80											18	10	*37	*47	10			
	NHL Totals		**549**	**136**	**205**	**341**	**110**	**142**	**252**	**364**	**45**	**0**	**20**	**779**	**17.5**	**555**	**199**	**366**	**12**		**33**	**6**	**6**	**12**	**20**	**1**	**0**	**4**

Traded to **Washington** by **Montreal** with Doug Jarvis, Rod Langway and Brian Engblom for Ryan Walter and Rick Green, September 9, 1982. Traded to **LA Kings** by **Washington** for Grant Ledyard, February 9, 1988. Signed as a free agent by **Toronto**, June 10, 1988.

• LAUGHTON, Mike

Michael Frederick C – L. 6'2", 185 lbs. b: Nelson, B.C., 2/21/1944.

Season	Club	League	GP	G	A	Pts	AG	AA	APts	PIM	PP	SH	GW	S	%	TGF	PGF	TGA	PGA	+/-	GP	G	A	Pts	PIM	PP	SH	GW
1961-62	Nelson Knights	BCJHL	STATISTICS NOT AVAILABLE																									
	Nelson Maple Leafs	WIHL	1	0	0	0				2																		
1962-63	Nelson Knights	BCJHL	STATISTICS NOT AVAILABLE																									
1963-64	Nelson Maple Leafs	WIHL	48	19	27	46				24											3	1	0	1	0			
1964-65	Nelson Maple Leafs	WIHL	48	35	21	56				44											10	5	8	13	18			
	Nelson Maple Leafs	Al-Cup	16	*12	6	18				18																		
1965-66	Nelson Maple Leafs	WIHL	45	36	34	70				72																		
1966-67	Victoria Maple Leafs	WHL	62	16	11	27				37																		
1967-68	**Oakland Seals**	**NHL**	**35**	**2**	**6**	**8**	**2**	**6**	**8**	**38**	**2**	**0**	**0**	**53**	**3.8**	**13**	**5**	**27**	**2**	**–17**								
	Vancouver Canucks	WHL	23	8	5	13				10																		
1968-69	**Oakland Seals**	**NHL**	**53**	**20**	**23**	**43**	**21**	**20**	**41**	**22**	**3**	**0**	**5**	**103**	**19.4**	**55**	**8**	**47**	**0**	**0**	**7**	**2**	**3**	**5**	**0**	**0**	**0**	**0**
	Cleveland Barons	AHL	13	2	6	8				6																		
1969-70	**Oakland Seals**	**NHL**	**76**	**16**	**19**	**35**	**17**	**18**	**35**	**39**	**3**	**0**	**4**	**147**	**10.9**	**50**	**8**	**70**	**0**	**–28**	**4**	**0**	**1**	**1**	**0**	**0**	**0**	**0**
1970-71	**California Golden Seals**	**NHL**	**25**	**1**	**0**	**1**	**1**	**0**	**1**	**2**	**1**	**0**	**0**	**22**	**4.5**	**2**	**1**	**13**	**0**	**–12**								
1971-72	Nova Scotia Voyageurs	AHL	73	23	28	51				6											15	3	7	10	12			
1972-73	New York Raiders	WHA	67	16	20	36				44																		
1973-74	New York-Jersey Knights	WHA	71	20	18	38				34																		
1974-75	San Diego Mariners	WHA	65	7	9	16				22											10	4	1	5	0			
	Syracuse Blazers	NAHL	5	0	5	5				2																		
1975-76			DID NOT PLAY																									
1976-77	Nelson Maple Leafs	WIHL	48	31	47	78				25																		
1977-78	Nelson Maple Leafs	WIHL	22	4	5	9				2																		
	NHL Totals		**189**	**39**	**48**	**87**	**41**	**44**	**85**	**101**	**9**	**0**	**9**	**325**	**12.0**	**120**	**22**	**157**	**2**		**11**	**2**	**4**	**6**	**0**	**0**	**0**	**0**
	Other Major League Totals		203	43	47	90				100											10	4	1	5	0			

WIHL Second All-Star Team (1977)

Claimed by **Oakland** from **Toronto** in Expansion Draft, June 6, 1967. Traded to **Montreal** by **California** for cash, October, 1971. Selected by **NY Raiders** (WHA) in 1972 WHA General Player Draft, February 12, 1972. Transferred to **San Diego** (WHA) after **New York-Jersey** (WHA) franchise relocated, April 30, 1974. Claimed by **Calgary** (WHA) from **San Diego** (WHA) in WHA Intra-League Draft, May 19, 1975.

• LAUKKANEN, Janne

D – L. 6', 194 lbs. b: Lahti, Finland, 3/19/1970. Quebec's 8th, 156th overall, in 1991.

Season	Club	League	GP	G	A	Pts	AG	AA	APts	PIM	PP	SH	GW	S	%	TGF	PGF	TGA	PGA	+/-	GP	G	A	Pts	PIM	PP	SH	GW
1986-87	Kiekkoreipas Lahti	Finland-Jr.	1	0	0	0				0																		
1987-88	Kiekkoreipas Lahti-2	Finland-Jr.	20	5	5	10				48																		
	Finland	EJC-A	6	0	0	0				6																		
1988-89	Kiekkoreipas Lahti-2	Finland-2	33	1	7	8				24																		
	Army Sport Academy	Finland-Jr.	6	0	1	1				6																		
1989-90	Hockey-Reipas Lahti	Finland-Jr.	2	2	2	4				2																		
	Hockey-Reipas Lahti	Finland-2	44	8	22	30				60																		
	Finland	WJC-A	7	0	1	1				4																		
1990-91	Hockey-Reipas Lahti	Finland	44	8	14	22				56																		
1991-92	Finland	Can-Cup	6	1	2	3				2																		
	HPK Hameenlinna	Finland	43	5	14	19				62																		
	Finland	Olympics	8	0	1	1				6																		
	Finland	WC-A	8	2	2	4				12																		
1992-93	HPK Hameenlinna	Finland	47	8	21	29				76											12	1	4	5	10			
	Finland	WC-A	6	1	0	1				10																		
1993-94	HPK Hameenlinna	Finland	48	5	24	29				46																		
	Finland	Olympics	8	0	2	2				12																		
	Motor Ceske Budjovice	Czech-Rep	....	....	....	....				....											3	0	1	1	0			
	Finland	WC-A	8	0	3	3				6																		
1994-95	Cornwall Aces	AHL	55	8	26	34				41																		
	Quebec Nordiques	**NHL**	**11**	**0**	**3**	**3**	**0**	**4**	**4**	**4**	**0**	**0**	**0**	**12**	**0.0**	**10**	**4**	**3**	**0**	**3**	**6**	**1**	**0**	**1**	**2**	**0**	**0**	**0**

Season	Club	League	GP	G	A	Pts	AG	AA	APts	PIM	PP	SH	GW	S	%	TGF	PGF	TGA	PGA	+/–	GP	G	A	Pts	PIM	PP	SH	GW
			REGULAR SEASON																		PLAYOFFS							
1995-96	**Colorado Avalanche**	**NHL**	**3**	**1**	**0**	**1**	**1**	**0**	**1**	**0**	**1**	**0**	**0**	**4**	**25.0**	**3**	**2**	**2**	**0**	**–1**	....	....	....	....	....	....	....	....
	Cornwall Aces	AHL	35	7	20	27	....	....	....	60	....	....	....	....	....	....	....	....	....	....	....	....	....	....	....	....	....	....
	Ottawa Senators	**NHL**	**20**	**0**	**2**	**2**	**0**	**2**	**2**	**14**	**0**	**0**	**0**	**31**	**0.0**	**14**	**8**	**8**	**2**	**0**	....	....	....	....	....	....	....	....
1996-97	Finland	W-Cup	4	0	0	0	....	....	....	4	....	....	....	....	....	....	....	....	....	....	....	....	....	....	....	....	....	....
	Ottawa Senators	**NHL**	**76**	**3**	**18**	**21**	**3**	**16**	**19**	**76**	**2**	**0**	**0**	**109**	**2.8**	**83**	**24**	**85**	**12**	**–14**	**7**	**0**	**1**	**1**	**6**	**0**	**0**	**0**
1997-98	**Ottawa Senators**	**NHL**	**60**	**4**	**17**	**21**	**5**	**17**	**22**	**64**	**2**	**0**	**2**	**69**	**5.8**	**45**	**18**	**55**	**13**	**–15**	**11**	**2**	**2**	**4**	**8**	**1**	**0**	**1**
	Finland	Olympics	6	0	0	0	....	....	....	4	....	....	....	....	....	....	....	....	....	....	....	....	....	....	....	....	....	....
1998-99	**Ottawa Senators**	**NHL**	**50**	**1**	**11**	**12**	**1**	**11**	**12**	**40**	**0**	**0**	**0**	**46**	**2.2**	**41**	**1**	**34**	**12**	**18**	**4**	**0**	**0**	**0**	**4**	**0**	**0**	**0**
99-2000	**Ottawa Senators**	**NHL**	**60**	**1**	**11**	**12**	**1**	**10**	**11**	**55**	**0**	**0**	**0**	**62**	**1.6**	**56**	**3**	**56**	**17**	**14**	....	....	....	....	....	....	....	....
	Pittsburgh Penguins	**NHL**	**11**	**1**	**7**	**8**	**1**	**6**	**7**	**12**	**1**	**0**	**0**	**19**	**5.3**	**16**	**6**	**7**	**0**	**3**	**11**	**2**	**4**	**6**	**10**	**1**	**0**	**1**
	NHL Totals		**291**	**11**	**69**	**80**	**12**	**66**	**78**	**265**	**6**	**0**	**2**	**352**	**3.1**	**268**	**66**	**250**	**56**		**39**	**5**	**7**	**12**	**30**	**2**	**0**	**2**

Finnish First All-Star Team (1993)

Transferred to **Colorado** after **Quebec** franchise relocated, June 21, 1995. Traded to **Ottawa** by **Colorado** for the rights to Brad Larsen, January 26, 1996. Traded to **Pittsburgh** by **Ottawa** with Ron Tugnutt for Tom Barrasso, March 14, 2000.

• LAURENCE, Don

Donald Gray "Red" C – R. 5'9", 175 lbs. b: Galt, Ont., 6/27/1957. Atlanta's 2nd, 28th overall, in 1977.

Season	Club	League	GP	G	A	Pts	AG	AA	APts	PIM	PP	SH	GW	S	%	TGF	PGF	TGA	PGA	+/–	GP	G	A	Pts	PIM	PP	SH	GW
1973-74	Peterborough Petes	OMJHL	60	28	15	43	....	....	....	41	....	....	....	....	....	....	....	....	....	....	....	....	....	....	....	....	....	....
1974-75	Peterborough Petes	OMJHL	69	40	49	89	....	....	....	53	....	....	....	....	....	....	....	....	....	....	11	5	6	11	13	....	....	....
1975-76	Kitchener Rangers	OMJHL	59	50	36	86	....	....	....	75	....	....	....	....	....	....	....	....	....	....	8	5	3	8	15	....	....	....
1976-77	Kitchener Rangers	OMJHL	35	43	45	88	....	....	....	14	....	....	....	....	....	....	....	....	....	....	....	....	....	....	....	....	....	....
1977-78	Tulsa Oilers	CHL	39	15	11	26	....	....	....	10	....	....	....	....	....	....	....	....	....	....	7	3	2	5	4	....	....	....
1978-79	**Atlanta Flames**	**NHL**	**59**	**14**	**20**	**34**	**12**	**14**	**26**	**6**	**2**	**0**	**3**	**113**	**12.4**	**47**	**5**	**36**	**2**	**8**	....	....	....	....	....	....	....	....
	Nova Scotia Voyageurs	AHL	20	7	7	14	....	....	....	9	....	....	....	....	....	....	....	....	....	....	....	....	....	....	....	....	....	....
1979-80	**St. Louis Blues**	**NHL**	**20**	**1**	**2**	**3**	**1**	**1**	**2**	**8**	**0**	**0**	**1**	**35**	**2.9**	**7**	**0**	**14**	**0**	**–7**	....	....	....	....	....	....	....	....
	Salt Lake Golden Eagles	CHL	27	7	15	22	....	....	....	8	....	....	....	....	....	....	....	....	....	....	13	*9	3	12	2	....	....	....
1980-81	Salt Lake Golden Eagles	CHL	71	39	33	72	....	....	....	41	....	....	....	....	....	....	....	....	....	....	17	6	5	11	8	....	....	....
1981-82	Indianapolis Checkers	CHL	77	43	55	98	....	....	....	43	....	....	....	....	....	....	....	....	....	....	13	10	5	15	18	....	....	....
1982-83	Indianapolis Checkers	CHL	80	*43	55	98	....	....	....	33	....	....	....	....	....	....	....	....	....	....	13	11	11	22	2	....	....	....
1983-84	Indianapolis Checkers	CHL	69	41	37	78	....	....	....	42	....	....	....	....	....	....	....	....	....	....	10	*9	4	*13	0	....	....	....
1984-85	HC Ambri-Piotta	Switz-2	35	*58	20	*78	....	....	....	....	....	....	....	....	....	....	....	....	....	....	....	0	1	1	....	....	....	....
1985-86	HC Ambri-Piotta	Switz.	36	25	13	38	....	....	....	....	....	....	....	....	....	....	....	....	....	....	....	....	....	....	....	....	....	....
1986-87	EV Zug	Switz.	35	*57	21	78	....	....	....	....	....	....	....	....	....	....	....	....	....	....	....	....	....	....	....	....	....	....
1987-88	EV Zug	Switz.	30	27	11	38	....	....	....	....	....	....	....	....	....	....	....	....	....	....	....	....	....	....	....	....	....	....
1988-89	EV Zug	Switz.	36	46	27	*73	....	....	....	....	....	....	....	....	....	....	....	....	....	....	....	....	....	....	....	....	....	....
1989-90	EV Zug	Switz-2	35	32	31	63	....	....	....	....	....	....	....	....	....	....	....	....	....	....	2	2	0	2	....	....	....	....
1990-91	EV Zug	Switz-2	28	22	16	38	....	....	....	....	....	....	....	....	....	....	....	....	....	....	....	....	....	....	....	....	....	....
	NHL Totals		**79**	**15**	**22**	**37**	**13**	**15**	**28**	**14**	**2**	**0**	**4**	**148**	**10.1**	**54**	**5**	**50**	**2**		....	....	....	....	....	....	....	....

CHL Second All-Star Team (1983)

• Missed remainder of 1976-77 and majority of 1977-78 seasons recovering from leg injury suffered in game vs. Ottawa (OMJHL), December 12, 1976. Traded to **St. Louis** by **Atlanta** with Ed Kea and Atlanta's 2nd round choice (Hakan Nordin) in 1981 Entry Draft for Garry Unger, October 10, 1979. Signed as a free agent by **NY Islanders**, October 16, 1981.

• LAUS, Paul

RW – R. 6'1", 212 lbs. b: Beamsville, Ont., 9/26/1970. Pittsburgh's 2nd, 37th overall, in 1989.

Season	Club	League	GP	G	A	Pts	AG	AA	APts	PIM	PP	SH	GW	S	%	TGF	PGF	TGA	PGA	+/–	GP	G	A	Pts	PIM	PP	SH	GW
1986-87	St. Catharines Falcons	OJHL-B	40	1	8	9	....	....	....	56	....	....	....	....	....	....	....	....	....	....	....	....	....	....	....	....	....	....
1987-88	Hamilton Steelhawks	OHL	56	1	9	10	....	....	....	171	....	....	....	....	....	....	....	....	....	....	14	0	0	0	28	....	....	....
1988-89	Niagara Falls Thunder	OHL	49	1	10	11	....	....	....	225	....	....	....	....	....	....	....	....	....	....	15	0	5	5	56	....	....	....
1989-90	Niagara Falls Thunder	OHL	60	13	35	48	....	....	....	231	....	....	....	....	....	....	....	....	....	....	16	6	16	22	71	....	....	....
1990-91	Albany Choppers	IHL	7	0	0	0	....	....	....	7	....	....	....	....	....	....	....	....	....	....	....	....	....	....	....	....	....	....
	Knoxville Cherokees	ECHL	20	6	12	18	....	....	....	83	....	....	....	....	....	....	....	....	....	....	....	....	....	....	....	....	....	....
	Muskegon Lumberjacks	IHL	35	3	4	7	....	....	....	103	....	....	....	....	....	....	....	....	....	....	4	0	0	0	13	....	....	....
1991-92	Muskegon Lumberjacks	IHL	75	0	21	21	....	....	....	248	....	....	....	....	....	....	....	....	....	....	14	2	5	7	70	....	....	....
1992-93	Cleveland Lumberjacks	IHL	76	8	18	26	....	....	....	427	....	....	....	....	....	....	....	....	....	....	4	1	0	1	27	....	....	....
1993-94	**Florida Panthers**	**NHL**	**39**	**2**	**0**	**2**	**2**	**0**	**2**	**109**	**0**	**0**	**1**	**15**	**13.3**	**16**	**1**	**6**	**0**	**9**	....	....	....	....	....	....	....	....
1994-95	**Florida Panthers**	**NHL**	**37**	**0**	**7**	**7**	**0**	**10**	**10**	**138**	**0**	**0**	**0**	**18**	**0.0**	**29**	**1**	**17**	**1**	**12**	....	....	....	....	....	....	....	....
1995-96	**Florida Panthers**	**NHL**	**78**	**3**	**6**	**9**	**3**	**5**	**8**	**236**	**0**	**0**	**0**	**45**	**6.7**	**39**	**0**	**57**	**16**	**–2**	**21**	**2**	**6**	**8**	***62**	**0**	**0**	**0**
1996-97	**Florida Panthers**	**NHL**	**77**	**0**	**12**	**12**	**0**	**11**	**11**	**313**	**0**	**0**	**0**	**63**	**0.0**	**44**	**3**	**32**	**4**	**13**	**5**	**0**	**1**	**1**	**4**	**0**	**0**	**0**
1997-98	**Florida Panthers**	**NHL**	**77**	**0**	**11**	**11**	**0**	**11**	**11**	**293**	**0**	**0**	**0**	**64**	**0.0**	**34**	**4**	**45**	**10**	**–5**	....	....	....	....	....	....	....	....
1998-99	**Florida Panthers**	**NHL**	**75**	**1**	**9**	**10**	**1**	**9**	**10**	**218**	**0**	**0**	**0**	**54**	**1.9**	**26**	**0**	**29**	**2**	**–1**	....	....	....	....	....	....	....	....
99-2000	**Florida Panthers**	**NHL**	**77**	**3**	**8**	**11**	**3**	**7**	**10**	**172**	**0**	**0**	**0**	**44**	**6.8**	**20**	**1**	**25**	**5**	**–1**	**4**	**0**	**0**	**0**	**8**	**0**	**0**	**0**
	NHL Totals		**460**	**9**	**53**	**62**	**9**	**53**	**62**	**1479**	**0**	**0**	**1**	**303**	**3.0**	**208**	**10**	**211**	**38**		**30**	**2**	**7**	**9**	**74**	**0**	**0**	**0**

Claimed by **Florida** from **Pittsburgh** in Expansion Draft, June 24, 1993.

• LaVALLEE, Kevin

Kevin A. LW – L. 5'8", 180 lbs. b: Sudbury, Ont., 9/16/1961. Calgary's 3rd, 32nd overall, in 1980.

Season	Club	League	GP	G	A	Pts	AG	AA	APts	PIM	PP	SH	GW	S	%	TGF	PGF	TGA	PGA	+/–	GP	G	A	Pts	PIM	PP	SH	GW
1977-78	Sudbury MacIssacs	NOHA	30	45	48	93	....	....	....	....	....	....	....	....	....	....	....	....	....	....	....	....	....	....	....	....	....	....
1978-79	Brantford Alexanders	OMJHL	66	27	23	50	....	....	....	30	....	....	....	....	....	....	....	....	....	....	....	....	....	....	....	....	....	....
1979-80	Brantford Alexanders	OMJHL	65	65	70	135	....	....	....	50	....	....	....	....	....	....	....	....	....	....	10	10	4	14	7	....	....	....
1980-81	**Calgary Flames**	**NHL**	**77**	**15**	**20**	**35**	**12**	**13**	**25**	**16**	**3**	**0**	**2**	**131**	**11.5**	**69**	**25**	**48**	**0**	**–4**	**8**	**2**	**3**	**5**	**4**	**1**	**0**	**1**
1981-82	**Calgary Flames**	**NHL**	**75**	**32**	**29**	**61**	**25**	**19**	**44**	**30**	**6**	**0**	**3**	**169**	**18.9**	**84**	**15**	**78**	**0**	**–9**	**3**	**0**	**0**	**0**	**7**	**0**	**0**	**0**
1982-83	**Calgary Flames**	**NHL**	**60**	**19**	**16**	**35**	**16**	**11**	**27**	**17**	**1**	**0**	**2**	**139**	**13.7**	**50**	**3**	**53**	**0**	**–6**	**8**	**1**	**3**	**4**	**4**	**0**	**0**	**0**
	Colorado Flames	CHL	5	5	4	9	....	....	....	0	....	....	....	....	....	....	....	....	....	....	....	....	....	....	....	....	....	....
1983-84	**Los Angeles Kings**	**NHL**	**19**	**3**	**3**	**6**	**2**	**2**	**4**	**2**	**0**	**0**	**0**	**41**	**7.3**	**8**	**0**	**15**	**2**	**–5**	....	....	....	....	....	....	....	....
	New Haven Nighthawks	AHL	47	29	23	52	....	....	....	25	....	....	....	....	....	....	....	....	....	....	....	....	....	....	....	....	....	....
1984-85	**St. Louis Blues**	**NHL**	**38**	**15**	**17**	**32**	**12**	**12**	**24**	**8**	**2**	**0**	**1**	**68**	**22.1**	**44**	**9**	**33**	**0**	**2**	....	....	....	....	....	....	....	....
1985-86	**St. Louis Blues**	**NHL**	**64**	**18**	**20**	**38**	**14**	**13**	**27**	**8**	**7**	**0**	**2**	**129**	**14.0**	**59**	**20**	**31**	**0**	**8**	**13**	**2**	**2**	**4**	**6**	**0**	**0**	**0**
1986-87	**Pittsburgh Penguins**	**NHL**	**33**	**8**	**20**	**28**	**7**	**15**	**22**	**4**	**5**	**0**	**0**	**80**	**10.0**	**42**	**24**	**20**	**0**	**–2**	....	....	....	....	....	....	....	....
1987-88	IEV Innsbruck	Austria	34	39	33	72	....	....	....	....	....	....	....	....	....	....	....	....	....	....	....	....	....	....	....	....	....	....
	HC Ambri-Piotta	Switz.	5	4	1	5	....	....	....	....	....	....	....	....	....	....	....	....	....	....	....	....	....	....	....	....	....	....
1988-89	IEV Innsbruck	Austria	40	45	47	92	....	....	....	....	....	....	....	....	....	....	....	....	....	....	....	....	....	....	....	....	....	....
1989-90	IEV Innsbruck	Austria	33	43	42	85	....	....	....	34	....	....	....	....	....	....	....	....	....	....	....	....	....	....	....	....	....	....
1990-91	HC Milano Saima	Italy	36	33	50	83	....	....	....	16	....	....	....	....	....	....	....	....	....	....	10	12	9	21	0	....	....	....
1991-92	HC Milano Saima	Alpenliga	10	7	9	16	....	....	....	4	....	....	....	....	....	....	....	....	....	....	....	....	....	....	....	....	....	....
	HC Milano Saima	Italy	16	15	17	32	....	....	....	4	....	....	....	....	....	....	....	....	....	....	12	5	7	12	7	....	....	....
1992-93	Ayr Scottish Raiders	BH-Cup	8	20	11	31	....	....	....	8	....	....	....	....	....	....	....	....	....	....	....	....	....	....	....	....	....	....
	HC Ajoie	Switz.	9	3	7	10	....	....	....	27	....	....	....	....	....	....	....	....	....	....	....	....	....	....	....	....	....	....
	EC Ratinger-Lowen	Germany	10	6	12	18	....	....	....	2	....	....	....	....	....	....	....	....	....	....	....	....	....	....	....	....	....	....
1993-94	Dusseldorfer EG	Germany	44	19	19	38	....	....	....	33	....	....	....	....	....	....	....	....	....	....	....	....	....	....	....	....	....	....
1994-95	Dusseldorfer EG	Germany	39	14	14	28	....	....	....	26	....	....	....	....	....	....	....	....	....	....	10	8	4	12	4	....	....	....
1995-96	Hannover Scorpions	Germany	23	16	20	36	....	....	....	22	....	....	....	....	....	....	....	....	....	....	....	....	....	....	....	....	....	....
	HC Davos	Switz.	18	8	10	18	....	....	....	6	....	....	....	....	....	....	....	....	....	....	3	1	1	2	2	....	....	....
	NHL Totals		**366**	**110**	**125**	**235**	**88**	**85**	**173**	**85**	**24**	**0**	**10**	**757**	**14.5**	**356**	**96**	**278**	**2**		**32**	**5**	**8**	**13**	**21**	**1**	**0**	**1**

Traded to **LA Kings** by **Calgary** with Carl Mokosak for Steve Bozek, June 20, 1983. Signed as a free agent by **St. Louis**, September 13, 1984. Signed as a free agent by **Pittsburgh**, September 13, 1986.

• LaVARRE, Mark

Mark James RW – R. 5'11", 170 lbs. b: Evanston, IL, 2/21/1965. Chicago's 7th, 123rd overall, in 1983.

Season	Club	League	GP	G	A	Pts	AG	AA	APts	PIM	PP	SH	GW	S	%	TGF	PGF	TGA	PGA	+/–	GP	G	A	Pts	PIM	PP	SH	GW
1982-83	Stratford Cullitons	OJHL-B	40	33	62	95	....	....	....	88	....	....	....	....	....	....	....	....	....	....	....	....	....	....	....	....	....	....
1983-84	North Bay Centennials	OHL	41	19	22	41	....	....	....	15	....	....	....	....	....	....	....	....	....	....	....	....	....	....	....	....	....	....
1984-85	Windsor Spitfires	OHL	46	15	30	45	....	....	....	30	....	....	....	....	....	....	....	....	....	....	4	0	0	0	0	....	....	....
1985-86	**Chicago Black Hawks**	**NHL**	**2**	**0**	**0**	**0**	**0**	**0**	**0**	**0**	**0**	**0**	**0**	**2**	**0.0**	**0**	**0**	**2**	**0**	**–2**	....	....	....	....	....	....	....	....
	Nova Scotia Oilers	AHL	62	15	19	34	....	....	....	32	....	....	....	....	....	....	....	....	....	....	....	....	....	....	....	....	....	....

			REGULAR SEASON																		PLAYOFFS							
Season	Club	League	GP	G	A	Pts	AG	AA	APts	PIM	PP	SH	GW	S	%	TGF	PGF	TGA	PGA	+/–	GP	G	A	Pts	PIM	PP	SH	GW
1986-87	**Chicago Blackhawks**	**NHL**	**58**	**8**	**15**	**23**	**7**	**11**	**18**	**33**	**0**	**0**	**0**	**46**	**17.4**	**38**	**1**	**26**	**0**	**11**	....	....	....	....	....	....	....	....
	Nova Scotia Oilers	AHL	17	12	8	20	....	....	....	8	....	....	....	....	....	....	....	....	....	....	....	....	....	....	....	....	....	....
1987-88	**Chicago Blackhawks**	**NHL**	**18**	**1**	**1**	**2**	**1**	**1**	**2**	**25**	**0**	**0**	**0**	**17**	**5.9**	**2**	**0**	**11**	**1**	**–8**	**1**	**0**	**0**	**0**	**2**	**0**	**0**	**0**
	Saginaw Hawks	IHL	39	27	18	45	....	....	....	121	....	....	....	....	....	....	....	....	....	....	5	4	3	7	36	....	....	....
1988-89	Binghamton Whalers	AHL	37	20	21	41	....	....	....	70	....	....	....	....	....	....	....	....	....	....	....	....	....	....	....	....	....	....
1989-90	ZSC Zurich	Switz.	6	1	4	5	....	....	....	....	....	....	....	....	....	....	....	....	....	....	....	....	....	....	....	....	....	....
	NHL Totals		**78**	**9**	**16**	**25**	**8**	**12**	**20**	**58**	**0**	**0**	**0**	**65**	**13.8**	**40**	**1**	**39**	**1**		**1**	**0**	**0**	**0**	**2**	**0**	**0**	**0**

Traded to **Hartford** by **Chicago** for future considerations, October 6, 1988.

• LAVENDER, Brian

Brian James LW – L. 6', 174 lbs. b: Edmonton, Alta., 4/20/1947.

Season	Club	League	GP	G	A	Pts	AG	AA	APts	PIM	PP	SH	GW	S	%	TGF	PGF	TGA	PGA	+/–	GP	G	A	Pts	PIM	PP	SH	GW
1965-66	Regina Pats	SJHL	60	32	35	67	....	....	....	90	....	....	....	....	....	....	....	....	....	....	5	1	2	3	2	....	....	....
1966-67	Regina Pats	CMJHL	56	39	71	110	....	....	....	100	....	....	....	....	....	....	....	....	....	....	16	6	14	20	28	....	....	....
1967-68	Houston Apollos	CPHL	49	7	11	18	....	....	....	105	....	....	....	....	....	....	....	....	....	....	....	....	....	....	....	....	....	....
1968-69	Houston Apollos	CHL	71	14	29	43	....	....	....	113	....	....	....	....	....	....	....	....	....	....	3	0	0	0	6	....	....	....
1969-70	Cleveland Barons	AHL	67	8	13	21	....	....	....	89	....	....	....	....	....	....	....	....	....	....	....	....	....	....	....	....	....	....
1970-71	Montreal Voyageurs	AHL	59	7	9	16	....	....	....	38	....	....	....	....	....	....	....	....	....	....	3	0	0	0	0	....	....	....
1971-72	**St. Louis Blues**	**NHL**	**46**	**5**	**11**	**16**	**5**	**9**	**14**	**54**	**0**	**0**	**1**	**68**	**7.4**	**24**	**1**	**28**	**3**	**–2**	**3**	**0**	**0**	**0**	**2**	**0**	**0**	**0**
	Denver Spurs	WHL	27	14	16	30	....	....	....	73	....	....	....	....	....	....	....	....	....	....	....	....	....	....	....	....	....	....
1972-73	**New York Islanders**	**NHL**	**43**	**6**	**6**	**12**	**6**	**5**	**11**	**47**	**2**	**0**	**0**	**74**	**8.1**	**18**	**4**	**57**	**1**	**–42**	....	....	....	....	....	....	....	....
	Detroit Red Wings	**NHL**	**26**	**2**	**2**	**4**	**2**	**2**	**4**	**14**	**0**	**0**	**0**	**13**	**15.4**	**5**	**0**	**3**	**0**	**2**	....	....	....	....	....	....	....	....
1973-74	**Detroit Red Wings**	**NHL**	**4**	**0**	**0**	**0**	**0**	**0**	**0**	**11**	**0**	**0**	**0**	**2**	**0.0**	**0**	**0**	**4**	**0**	**–4**	....	....	....	....	....	....	....	....
	Virginia Wings	AHL	53	11	19	30	....	....	....	72	....	....	....	....	....	....	....	....	....	....	....	....	....	....	....	....	....	....
	Providence Reds	AHL	10	1	6	7	....	....	....	2	....	....	....	....	....	....	....	....	....	....	14	6	1	7	24	....	....	....
1974-75	**California Golden Seals**	**NHL**	**65**	**3**	**7**	**10**	**3**	**5**	**8**	**48**	**0**	**0**	**1**	**30**	**10.0**	**19**	**4**	**51**	**26**	**–10**	....	....	....	....	....	....	....	....
1975-76	Denver-Ottawa Civics	WHA	37	2	0	2	....	....	....	7	....	....	....	....	....	....	....	....	....	....	....	....	....	....	....	....	....	....
	NHL Totals		**184**	**16**	**26**	**42**	**16**	**21**	**37**	**174**	**2**	**0**	**2**	**187**	**8.6**	**66**	**9**	**143**	**30**		**3**	**0**	**0**	**0**	**2**	**0**	**0**	**0**
	Other Major League Totals		37	2	0	2	....	....	....	7	....	....	....	....	....	....	....	....	....	....	....	....	....	....	....	....	....	....

Claimed by **Minnesota** from **Montreal** in Intra-League Draft, June 8, 1971. Claimed by **St. Louis** (Denver-WHL) from **Minnesota** in Reverse Draft, June 8, 1971. Selected by **Edmonton** (WHA) in 1972 WHA General Player Draft, February 12, 1972. Traded to **NY Islanders** by **St. Louis** for cash, September 1, 1972. Traded to **Detroit** by **NY Islanders** with Ken Murray for Ralph Stewart and Bob Cook, January 17, 1973. Traded to **NY Rangers** by **Detroit** for Claude Houde, February 28, 1974. Traded to **California** by **NY Rangers** for Hartland Monahan, September 23, 1974. WHA rights traded to **Denver** (WHA) by **Edmonton** (WHA) for cash, September, 1975.

• LAVIGNE, Eric

D – L. 6'3", 195 lbs. b: Victoriaville, Que., 11/4/1972. Washington's 3rd, 25th overall, in 1991.

Season	Club	League	GP	G	A	Pts	AG	AA	APts	PIM	PP	SH	GW	S	%	TGF	PGF	TGA	PGA	+/–	GP	G	A	Pts	PIM	PP	SH	GW
1988-89	Ste-Foy Gouverneurs	QAAA	39	2	10	12	....	....	....	95	....	....	....	....	....	....	....	....	....	....	....	....	....	....	....	....	....	....
1989-90	Hull Olympiques	QMJHL	69	7	11	18	....	....	....	203	....	....	....	....	....	....	....	....	....	....	11	0	0	0	32	....	....	....
1990-91	Hull Olympiques	QMJHL	66	11	11	22	....	....	....	153	....	....	....	....	....	....	....	....	....	....	4	0	1	1	16	....	....	....
1991-92	Hull Olympiques	QMJHL	46	4	17	21	....	....	....	101	....	....	....	....	....	....	....	....	....	....	6	0	0	0	32	....	....	....
1992-93	Hull Olympiques	QMJHL	59	7	20	27	....	....	....	221	....	....	....	....	....	....	....	....	....	....	10	2	4	6	47	....	....	....
1993-94	Phoenix Roadrunners	IHL	62	3	11	14	....	....	....	168	....	....	....	....	....	....	....	....	....	....	....	....	....	....	....	....	....	....
1994-95	Phoenix Roadrunners	IHL	69	4	10	14	....	....	....	233	....	....	....	....	....	....	....	....	....	....	....	....	....	....	....	....	....	....
	Los Angeles Kings	**NHL**	**1**	**0**	**0**	**0**	**0**	**0**	**0**	**0**	**0**	**0**	**0**	**0**	**0.0**	**0**	**0**	**1**	**0**	**–1**	....	....	....	....	....	....	....	....
	Detroit Vipers	IHL	1	0	0	0	....	....	....	2	....	....	....	....	....	....	....	....	....	....	5	0	0	0	26	....	....	....
1995-96	P.E.I. Senators	AHL	72	5	13	18	....	....	....	154	....	....	....	....	....	....	....	....	....	....	2	0	0	0	6	....	....	....
1996-97	Rochester Americans	AHL	46	1	6	7	....	....	....	89	....	....	....	....	....	....	....	....	....	....	6	0	1	1	21	....	....	....
1997-98	Rochester Americans	AHL	28	0	1	1	....	....	....	118	....	....	....	....	....	....	....	....	....	....	....	....	....	....	....	....	....	....
	Grand Rapids Griffins	IHL	4	0	1	1	....	....	....	13	....	....	....	....	....	....	....	....	....	....	....	....	....	....	....	....	....	....
	Cleveland Lumberjacks	IHL	16	0	0	0	....	....	....	34	....	....	....	....	....	....	....	....	....	....	10	1	1	2	44	....	....	....
1998-99	Cleveland Lumberjacks	IHL	66	11	7	18	....	....	....	259	....	....	....	....	....	....	....	....	....	....	....	....	....	....	....	....	....	....
99-2000	Cleveland Lumberjacks	IHL	11	0	2	2	....	....	....	21	....	....	....	....	....	....	....	....	....	....	....	....	....	....	....	....	....	....
	Michigan K-Wings	IHL	22	0	2	2	....	....	....	70	....	....	....	....	....	....	....	....	....	....	....	....	....	....	....	....	....	....
	NHL Totals		**1**	**0**	**0**	**0**	**0**	**0**	**0**	**0**	**0**	**0**	**0**	**0**	**0.0**	**0**	**0**	**1**	**0**		....	....	....	....	....	....	....	....

Signed as a free agent by **LA Kings**, October 13, 1993. • Played w/ RHI's LA Blades in 1995 (13-5-3-8-50).

• LAVIOLETTE, Peter

D – L. 6'2", 200 lbs. b: Norwood, MA, 12/7/1964.

Season	Club	League	GP	G	A	Pts	AG	AA	APts	PIM	PP	SH	GW	S	%	TGF	PGF	TGA	PGA	+/–	GP	G	A	Pts	PIM	PP	SH	GW
1982-83	Westfield State College	NCAA-2	26	3	7	10	....	....	....	14	....	....	....	....	....	....	....	....	....	....	....	....	....	....	....	....	....	....
1983-84	Westfield State College	NCAA-2	25	15	14	29	....	....	....	52	....	....	....	....	....	....	....	....	....	....	....	....	....	....	....	....	....	....
1984-85	Westfield State College	NCAA-2	23	13	15	28	....	....	....	22	....	....	....	....	....	....	....	....	....	....	....	....	....	....	....	....	....	....
1985-86	Westfield State College	NCAA-2	19	12	8	20	....	....	....	44	....	....	....	....	....	....	....	....	....	....	....	....	....	....	....	....	....	....
1986-87	Indianapolis Checkers	IHL	72	10	20	30	....	....	....	146	....	....	....	....	....	....	....	....	....	....	5	0	1	1	12	....	....	....
1987-88	United States	Nat-Team	54	4	20	24	....	....	....	82	....	....	....	....	....	....	....	....	....	....	....	....	....	....	....	....	....	....
	United States	Olympics	5	0	2	2	....	....	....	4	....	....	....	....	....	....	....	....	....	....	....	....	....	....	....	....	....	....
	Colorado Rangers	IHL	19	2	5	7	....	....	....	27	....	....	....	....	....	....	....	....	....	....	9	3	5	8	7	....	....	....
1988-89	**New York Rangers**	**NHL**	**12**	**0**	**0**	**0**	**0**	**0**	**0**	**6**	**0**	**0**	**0**	**2**	**0.0**	**5**	**0**	**3**	**0**	**2**	....	....	....	....	....	....	....	....
	Denver Rangers	IHL	57	6	19	25	....	....	....	120	....	....	....	....	....	....	....	....	....	....	3	0	0	0	4	....	....	....
1989-90	Flint Spirits	IHL	62	6	18	24	....	....	....	82	....	....	....	....	....	....	....	....	....	....	4	0	0	0	4	....	....	....
1990-91	Binghamton Rangers	AHL	65	12	24	36	....	....	....	72	....	....	....	....	....	....	....	....	....	....	10	2	7	9	30	....	....	....
1991-92	Binghamton Rangers	AHL	50	4	10	14	....	....	....	50	....	....	....	....	....	....	....	....	....	....	11	2	7	9	9	....	....	....
1992-93	Providence Bruins	AHL	74	13	42	55	....	....	....	64	....	....	....	....	....	....	....	....	....	....	6	0	4	4	10	....	....	....
1993-94	United States	Nat-Team	56	10	25	35	....	....	....	63	....	....	....	....	....	....	....	....	....	....	....	....	....	....	....	....	....	....
	United States	Olympics	8	1	0	1	....	....	....	6	....	....	....	....	....	....	....	....	....	....	....	....	....	....	....	....	....	....
	San Diego Gulls	IHL	17	3	4	7	....	....	....	20	....	....	....	....	....	....	....	....	....	....	9	3	0	3	6	....	....	....
1994-95	Providence Bruins	AHL	65	7	23	30	....	....	....	84	....	....	....	....	....	....	....	....	....	....	13	2	8	10	17	....	....	....
1995-96	Providence Bruins	AHL	72	9	17	26	....	....	....	53	....	....	....	....	....	....	....	....	....	....	4	1	1	2	8	....	....	....
1996-97	Providence Bruins	AHL	41	6	8	14	....	....	....	40	....	....	....	....	....	....	....	....	....	....	....	....	....	....	....	....	....	....
1997-1998	Wheeling Nailers	ECHL	DID NOT PLAY – COACHING																									
1998-2000	Providence Bruins	AHL	DID NOT PLAY – COACHING																									
	NHL Totals		**12**	**0**	**0**	**0**	**0**	**0**	**0**	**6**	**0**	**0**	**0**	**2**	**0.0**	**5**	**0**	**3**	**0**		....	....	....	....	....	....	....	....

Signed as a free agent by **NY Rangers**, August 12, 1987. Signed as a free agent by **Boston**, September 8, 1992. • Named Assistant Coach of **Boston Bruins**, June 30, 2000.

• LAVOIE, Dominic

"The Hammer" D – R. 6'2", 205 lbs. b: Montreal, Que., 11/21/1967.

Season	Club	League	GP	G	A	Pts	AG	AA	APts	PIM	PP	SH	GW	S	%	TGF	PGF	TGA	PGA	+/–	GP	G	A	Pts	PIM	PP	SH	GW
1984-85	St-Jean Castors	QMJHL	30	1	1	2	....	....	....	10	....	....	....	....	....	....	....	....	....	....	....	....	....	....	....	....	....	....
1985-86	St-Jean Castors	QMJHL	70	12	37	49	....	....	....	99	....	....	....	....	....	....	....	....	....	....	10	2	3	5	20	....	....	....
1986-87	St-Jean Castors	QMJHL	64	12	42	54	....	....	....	97	....	....	....	....	....	....	....	....	....	....	8	2	7	9	2	....	....	....
1987-88	Peoria Rivermen	IHL	65	7	26	33	....	....	....	54	....	....	....	....	....	....	....	....	....	....	7	2	2	4	8	....	....	....
1988-89	**St. Louis Blues**	**NHL**	**1**	**0**	**0**	**0**	**0**	**0**	**0**	**0**	**0**	**0**	**0**	**1**	**0.0**	**2**	**0**	**0**	**0**	**2**	....	....	....	....	....	....	....	....
	Peoria Rivermen	IHL	69	11	31	42	....	....	....	98	....	....	....	....	....	....	....	....	....	....	4	0	0	0	4	....	....	....
1989-90	**St. Louis Blues**	**NHL**	**13**	**1**	**1**	**2**	**1**	**1**	**2**	**16**	**1**	**0**	**0**	**20**	**5.0**	**11**	**6**	**10**	**0**	**–5**	....	....	....	....	....	....	....	....
	Peoria Rivermen	IHL	58	19	23	42	....	....	....	32	....	....	....	....	....	....	....	....	....	....	5	2	2	4	16	....	....	....
1990-91	**St. Louis Blues**	**NHL**	**6**	**1**	**2**	**3**	**1**	**2**	**3**	**2**	**0**	**0**	**0**	**11**	**9.1**	**7**	**0**	**3**	**0**	**4**	....	....	....	....	....	....	....	....
	Peoria Rivermen	IHL	46	15	25	40	....	....	....	72	....	....	....	....	....	....	....	....	....	....	16	5	7	12	22	....	....	....
1991-92	**St. Louis Blues**	**NHL**	**6**	**0**	**1**	**1**	**0**	**1**	**1**	**10**	**0**	**0**	**0**	**11**	**0.0**	**4**	**1**	**6**	**0**	**–3**	....	....	....	....	....	....	....	....
	Peoria Rivermen	IHL	58	20	32	52	....	....	....	87	....	....	....	....	....	....	....	....	....	....	10	3	4	7	12	....	....	....
1992-93	**Ottawa Senators**	**NHL**	**2**	**0**	**1**	**1**	**0**	**1**	**1**	**0**	**0**	**0**	**0**	**8**	**0.0**	**2**	**1**	**1**	**0**	**0**	....	....	....	....	....	....	....	....
	New Haven Nighthawks	AHL	14	2	7	9	....	....	....	14	....	....	....	....	....	....	....	....	....	....	....	....	....	....	....	....	....	....
	Boston Bruins	**NHL**	**2**	**0**	**0**	**0**	**0**	**0**	**0**	**2**	**0**	**0**	**0**	**7**	**0.0**	**2**	**1**	**2**	**0**	**–1**	....	....	....	....	....	....	....	....
	Providence Bruins	AHL	53	16	27	43	....	....	....	62	....	....	....	....	....	....	....	....	....	....	6	1	2	3	24	....	....	....
1993-94	**Los Angeles Kings**	**NHL**	**8**	**3**	**3**	**6**	**3**	**2**	**5**	**2**	**2**	**0**	**1**	**21**	**14.3**	**15**	**12**	**5**	**0**	**–2**	....	....	....	....	....	....	....	....
	Phoenix Roadrunners	IHL	58	20	33	53	....	....	....	70	....	....	....	....	....	....	....	....	....	....	....	....	....	....	....	....	....	....
	San Diego Gulls	IHL	9	2	2	4	....	....	....	12	....	....	....	....	....	....	....	....	....	....	8	1	0	1	20	....	....	....

Season	Club	League	REGULAR SEASON GP	G	A	Pts	AG	AA	APts	PIM	PP	SH	GW	S	%	TGF	PGF	TGA	PGA	+/–	PLAYOFFS GP	G	A	Pts	PIM	PP	SH	GW
1994-95	VEU Feldkirch	Alpenliga	17	9	15	24	....	....	....	30	....	....	....	....	....	....	....	....	....	....	....	....	....	....	....	....	....	....
	VEU Feldkirch	Austria	28	12	13	25	....	....	....	79	....	....	....	....	....	....	....	....	....	....	13	4	8	12	22	....	....	....
1995-96	VEU Feldkirch	Alpenliga	8	5	7	12	....	....	....	14	....	....	....	....	....	....	....	....	....	....	....	....	....	....	....	....	....	....
	VEU Feldkirch	Austria	35	20	33	53	....	....	....	75	....	....	....	....	....	....	....	....	....	....	8	5	7	12	14	....	....	....
1996-97	VEU Feldkirch	Alpenliga	43	18	29	47	....	....	....	46	....	....	....	....	....	....	....	....	....	....	....	....	....	....	....	....	....	....
	VEU Feldkirch	Austria	11	2	4	6	....	....	....	29	....	....	....	....	....	....	....	....	....	....	....	....	....	....	....	....	....	....
1997-98	VEU Feldkirch	Alpenliga	21	8	8	16	....	....	....	12	....	....	....	....	....	....	....	....	....	....	....	....	....	....	....	....	....	....
	VEU Feldkirch	Austria	15	5	6	11	....	....	....	16	....	....	....	....	....	....	....	....	....	....	....	....	....	....	....	....	....	....
	VEU Feldkirch	EuroHL	6	1	5	6	....	....	....	10	....	....	....	....	....	....	....	....	....	....	4	2	2	4	8	....	....	....
	Austria	Olympics	4	5	1	6	....	....	....	8	....	....	....	....	....	....	....	....	....	....	....	....	....	....	....	....	....	....
1998-99	VEU Feldkirch	Alpenliga	32	14	14	28	....	....	....	18	....	....	....	....	....	....	....	....	....	....	....	....	....	....	....	....	....	....
	VEU Feldkirch	Austria	17	2	9	11	....	....	....	22	....	....	....	....	....	....	....	....	....	....	....	....	....	....	....	....	....	....
	VEU Feldkirch	EuroHL	6	3	2	5	....	....	....	22	....	....	....	....	....	....	....	....	....	....	....	....	....	....	....	....	....	....
	Austria	WC-A	6	2	0	2	....	....	....	8	....	....	....	....	....	....	....	....	....	....	....	....	....	....	....	....	....	....
99-2000	Hannover Scorpions	Germany	67	25	33	58	....	....	....	122	....	....	....	....	....	....	....	....	....	....	....	....	....	....	....	....	....	....
	Austria	WC-A	6	0	1	1	....	....	....	12	....	....	....	....	....	....	....	....	....	....	....	....	....	....	....	....	....	....
	NHL Totals		**38**	**5**	**8**	**13**	**5**	**7**	**12**	**32**	**3**	**0**	**1**	**79**	**6.3**	**43**	**21**	**27**	**0**		....	....	....	....	....	....	....	....

IHL First All-Star Team (1991) • IHL Second All-Star Team (1992)

Signed as a free agent by **St. Louis**, September 22, 1986. Claimed by **Ottawa** from **St. Louis** in Expansion Draft, June 18, 1992. Claimed on waivers by **Boston** from **Ottawa**, November 20, 1992. Signed as a free agent by **LA Kings**, July 16, 1993.

• LAWLESS, Paul

LW – L. 5'11", 185 lbs. b: Scarborough, Ont., 7/2/1964. Hartford's 1st, 14th overall, in 1982.

Season	Club	League	GP	G	A	Pts	AG	AA	APts	PIM	PP	SH	GW	S	%	TGF	PGF	TGA	PGA	+/–	GP	G	A	Pts	PIM	PP	SH	GW
1980-81	Wexford Raiders	MTHL	40	38	40	78	....	....	....	....	....	....	....	....	....	....	....	....	....	....	....	....	....	....	....	....	....	....
	Wexford Warriors	OHA-B	4	3	1	4	....	....	....	2	....	....	....	....	....	....	....	....	....	....	....	....	....	....	....	....	....	....
1981-82	Windsor Spitfires	OHL	68	24	25	49	....	....	....	47	....	....	....	....	....	....	....	....	....	....	9	1	1	2	4	....	....	....
1982-83	Windsor Spitfires	OHL	33	15	20	35	....	....	....	25	....	....	....	....	....	....	....	....	....	....	....	....	....	....	....	....	....	....
	Hartford Whalers	**NHL**	**47**	**6**	**9**	**15**	**5**	**6**	**11**	**4**	**1**	**0**	**0**	**84**	**7.1**	**27**	**3**	**55**	**0**	**–31**	....	....	....	....	....	....	....	....
1983-84	Windsor Spitfires	OHL	55	31	49	80	....	....	....	26	....	....	....	....	....	....	....	....	....	....	2	0	1	1	0	....	....	....
	Hartford Whalers	**NHL**	**6**	**0**	**3**	**3**	**0**	**2**	**2**	**0**	**0**	**0**	**0**	**7**	**0.0**	**3**	**1**	**7**	**0**	**–5**	....	....	....	....	....	....	....	....
1984-85	Binghamton Whalers	AHL	8	1	1	2	....	....	....	0	....	....	....	....	....	....	....	....	....	....	....	....	....	....	....	....	....	....
	Salt Lake Golden Eagles	IHL	72	49	48	97	....	....	....	14	....	....	....	....	....	....	....	....	....	....	7	5	3	8	20	....	....	....
1985-86	**Hartford Whalers**	**NHL**	**64**	**17**	**21**	**38**	**14**	**14**	**28**	**20**	**5**	**0**	**1**	**139**	**12.2**	**58**	**16**	**46**	**1**	**–3**	**1**	**0**	**0**	**0**	**0**	**0**	**0**	**0**
1986-87	**Hartford Whalers**	**NHL**	**60**	**22**	**32**	**54**	**19**	**23**	**42**	**14**	**4**	**0**	**2**	**161**	**13.7**	**68**	**11**	**33**	**0**	**24**	**2**	**0**	**2**	**2**	**2**	**0**	**0**	**0**
1987-88	**Hartford Whalers**	**NHL**	**28**	**4**	**5**	**9**	**3**	**4**	**7**	**16**	**0**	**0**	**1**	**71**	**5.6**	**20**	**6**	**16**	**0**	**–2**	....	....	....	....	....	....	....	....
	Philadelphia Flyers	**NHL**	**8**	**0**	**5**	**5**	**0**	**4**	**4**	**0**	**0**	**0**	**0**	**10**	**0.0**	**7**	**0**	**7**	**0**	**0**	....	....	....	....	....	....	....	....
	Vancouver Canucks	**NHL**	**13**	**0**	**1**	**1**	**0**	**1**	**1**	**0**	**0**	**0**	**0**	**15**	**0.0**	**5**	**2**	**12**	**0**	**–9**	....	....	....	....	....	....	....	....
1988-89	Milwaukee Admirals	IHL	53	30	35	65	....	....	....	58	....	....	....	....	....	....	....	....	....	....	....	....	....	....	....	....	....	....
	Toronto Maple Leafs	**NHL**	**7**	**0**	**0**	**0**	**0**	**0**	**0**	**0**	**0**	**0**	**0**	**11**	**0.0**	**2**	**0**	**4**	**0**	**–2**	....	....	....	....	....	....	....	....
1989-90	HC Davos	Switz-2	36	8	21	29	....	....	....	29	....	....	....	....	....	....	....	....	....	....	10	13	13	26	....	....	....	....
	Toronto Maple Leafs	**NHL**	**6**	**0**	**1**	**1**	**0**	**1**	**1**	**0**	**0**	**0**	**0**	**6**	**0.0**	**3**	**0**	**8**	**1**	**–4**	....	....	....	....	....	....	....	....
	Newmarket Saints	AHL	3	1	0	1	....	....	....	0	....	....	....	....	....	....	....	....	....	....	....	....	....	....	....	....	....	....
1990-91	HC Lausanne	Switz-2	36	26	29	55	....	....	....	....	....	....	....	....	....	....	....	....	....	....	10	10	15	25	....	....	....	....
1991-92	HC Lausanne	Switz-2	STATISTICS NOT AVAILABLE																									
	HC Bolzano	Italy	5	3	5	8	....	....	....	0	....	....	....	....	....	....	....	....	....	....	7	4	9	13	4	....	....	....
1992-93	EC Graz	Austria	29	21	27	48	....	....	....	....	....	....	....	....	....	....	....	....	....	....	....	....	....	....	....	....	....	....
	New Haven Senators	AHL	20	10	12	22	....	....	....	63	....	....	....	....	....	....	....	....	....	....	....	....	....	....	....	....	....	....
	Cincinnati Cyclones	IHL	29	29	25	54	....	....	....	64	....	....	....	....	....	....	....	....	....	....	....	....	....	....	....	....	....	....
1993-94	Cincinnati Cyclones	IHL	71	30	27	57	....	....	....	112	....	....	....	....	....	....	....	....	....	....	11	4	4	8	4	....	....	....
1994-95	Cincinnati Cyclones	IHL	64	44	52	96	....	....	....	119	....	....	....	....	....	....	....	....	....	....	10	9	9	18	8	....	....	....
1995-96	Cincinnati Cyclones	IHL	77	27	58	85	....	....	....	99	....	....	....	....	....	....	....	....	....	....	17	4	6	10	16	....	....	....
1996-97	Cincinnati Cyclones	IHL	14	2	10	12	....	....	....	14	....	....	....	....	....	....	....	....	....	....	....	....	....	....	....	....	....	....
	Austin Ice Bats	WPHL	30	11	35	46	....	....	....	54	....	....	....	....	....	....	....	....	....	....	6	2	4	6	26	....	....	....
1997-98	Austin Ice Bats	WPHL	1	1	0	1	....	....	....	14	....	....	....	....	....	....	....	....	....	....	....	....	....	....	....	....	....	....
1998-99	Austin Ice Bats	WPHL	2	2	1	3	....	....	....	2	....	....	....	....	....	....	....	....	....	....	....	....	....	....	....	....	....	....
	NHL Totals		**239**	**49**	**77**	**126**	**41**	**55**	**96**	**54**	**10**	**0**	**4**	**504**	**9.7**	**193**	**39**	**188**	**2**		**3**	**0**	**2**	**2**	**2**	**0**	**0**	**0**

OHL Second All-Star Team (1984) • IHL Second All-Star Team (1994)

Traded to **Philadelphia** by **Hartford** for Lindsay Carson, January 22, 1988. Traded to **Vancouver** by **Philadelphia** with Vancouver's 5th round choice (previously acquired, later traded to Edmonton — Edmonton selected Peter White) in 1989 Entry Draft for Willie Huber, March 1, 1988. Traded to **Toronto** by **Vancouver** for the rights to Peter Deboer, February 27, 1989. • Retired to become Assistant Coach/co-owner of **Austin** (WPHL), November 21, 1997. • Named Head Coach of **Austin** (WPHL), February 10, 1998.

• LAWRENCE, Mark

Mark J. RW – R. 6'4", 215 lbs. b: Burlington, Ont., 1/27/1972. Minnesota's 4th, 118th overall, in 1991.

Season	Club	League	GP	G	A	Pts	AG	AA	APts	PIM	PP	SH	GW	S	%	TGF	PGF	TGA	PGA	+/–	GP	G	A	Pts	PIM	PP	SH	GW
1987-88	Burlington Cougars	OJHL-B	40	11	12	23	....	....	....	90	....	....	....	....	....	....	....	....	....	....	....	....	....	....	....	....	....	....
1988-89	Niagara Falls Thunder	OHL	63	9	27	36	....	....	....	142	....	....	....	....	....	....	....	....	....	....	....	....	....	....	....	....	....	....
1989-90	Niagara Falls Thunder	OHL	54	15	18	33	....	....	....	123	....	....	....	....	....	....	....	....	....	....	16	2	5	7	42	....	....	....
1990-91	Detroit Ambassadors	OHL	66	27	38	65	....	....	....	53	....	....	....	....	....	....	....	....	....	....	....	....	....	....	....	....	....	....
1991-92	Detroit Ambassadors	OHL	28	19	26	45	....	....	....	54	....	....	....	....	....	....	....	....	....	....	....	....	....	....	....	....	....	....
	North Bay Centennials	OHL	24	13	14	27	....	....	....	21	....	....	....	....	....	....	....	....	....	....	21	*23	12	35	36	....	....	....
1992-93	Dayton Bombers	ECHL	20	8	14	22	....	....	....	46	....	....	....	....	....	....	....	....	....	....	....	....	....	....	....	....	....	....
	Kalamazoo Wings	IHL	57	22	13	35	....	....	....	47	....	....	....	....	....	....	....	....	....	....	....	....	....	....	....	....	....	....
1993-94	Kalamazoo Wings	IHL	64	17	20	37	....	....	....	90	....	....	....	....	....	....	....	....	....	....	....	....	....	....	....	....	....	....
1994-95	Kalamazoo Wings	IHL	77	21	29	50	....	....	....	92	....	....	....	....	....	....	....	....	....	....	16	3	7	10	28	....	....	....
	Dallas Stars	**NHL**	**2**	**0**	**0**	**0**	**0**	**0**	**0**	**0**	**0**	**0**	**0**	**3**	**0.0**	**0**	**0**	**0**	**0**	**0**	....	....	....	....	....	....	....	....
1995-96	**Dallas Stars**	**NHL**	**13**	**0**	**1**	**1**	**0**	**1**	**1**	**17**	**0**	**0**	**0**	**13**	**0.0**	**3**	**0**	**3**	**0**	**0**	....	....	....	....	....	....	....	....
	Michigan K-Wings	IHL	55	15	14	29	....	....	....	92	....	....	....	....	....	....	....	....	....	....	10	3	4	7	30	....	....	....
1996-97	Michigan K-Wings	IHL	68	15	21	36	....	....	....	141	....	....	....	....	....	....	....	....	....	....	4	0	0	0	18	....	....	....
1997-98	**New York Islanders**	**NHL**	**2**	**0**	**0**	**0**	**0**	**0**	**0**	**2**	**0**	**0**	**0**	**4**	**0.0**	**0**	**0**	**0**	**0**	**0**	....	....	....	....	....	....	....	....
	Utah Grizzlies	IHL	80	36	28	64	....	....	....	102	....	....	....	....	....	....	....	....	....	....	4	1	1	2	4	....	....	....
1998-99	**New York Islanders**	**NHL**	**60**	**14**	**16**	**30**	**16**	**15**	**31**	**38**	**4**	**0**	**2**	**88**	**15.9**	**40**	**16**	**32**	**0**	**–8**	....	....	....	....	....	....	....	....
	Lowell Lock Monsters	AHL	21	10	6	16	....	....	....	28	....	....	....	....	....	....	....	....	....	....	....	....	....	....	....	....	....	....
99-2000	**New York Islanders**	**NHL**	**29**	**1**	**5**	**6**	**1**	**5**	**6**	**26**	**0**	**0**	**0**	**33**	**3.0**	**7**	**4**	**16**	**0**	**–13**	....	....	....	....	....	....	....	....
	Chicago Wolves	IHL	16	4	6	10	....	....	....	32	....	....	....	....	....	....	....	....	....	....	....	....	....	....	....	....	....	....
	Lowell Lock Monsters	AHL	18	4	4	8	....	....	....	8	....	....	....	....	....	....	....	....	....	....	7	2	2	4	10	....	....	....
	NHL Totals		**106**	**15**	**22**	**37**	**17**	**21**	**38**	**83**	**4**	**0**	**2**	**141**	**10.6**	**50**	**20**	**51**	**0**		....	....	....	....	....	....	....	....

Rights transferred to **Dallas** after **Minnesota** franchise relocated, June 9, 1993. Signed as a free agent by **NY Islanders**, August 25, 1997.

• LAWSON, Danny

Daniel Michael RW – R. 5'11", 180 lbs. b: Toronto, Ont., 10/30/1947.

Season	Club	League	GP	G	A	Pts	AG	AA	APts	PIM	PP	SH	GW	S	%	TGF	PGF	TGA	PGA	+/–	GP	G	A	Pts	PIM	PP	SH	GW
1964-65	Hamilton Red Wings	OHA-Jr.	3	0	0	0	....	....	....	2	....	....	....	....	....	....	....	....	....	....	....	....	....	....	....	....	....	....
1965-66	Hamilton Red Wings	OHA-Jr.	30	7	9	16	....	....	....	4	....	....	....	....	....	....	....	....	....	....	5	1	1	2	2	....	....	....
1966-67	Hamilton Red Wings	OHA-Jr.	48	25	24	49	....	....	....	27	....	....	....	....	....	....	....	....	....	....	17	15	11	26	11	....	....	....
1967-68	Hamilton Red Wings	OHA-Jr.	54	52	38	90	....	....	....	26	....	....	....	....	....	....	....	....	....	....	11	8	7	15	11	....	....	....
	Detroit Red Wings	**NHL**	**1**	**0**	**0**	**0**	**0**	**0**	**0**	**0**	**0**	**0**	**0**	**1**	**0.0**	**0**	**0**	**0**	**0**	**0**	....	....	....	....	....	....	....	....
1968-69	**Detroit Red Wings**	**NHL**	**44**	**5**	**7**	**12**	**5**	**6**	**11**	**21**	**0**	**0**	**0**	**58**	**8.6**	**15**	**2**	**15**	**0**	**–2**	....	....	....	....	....	....	....	....
	Fort Worth Wings	CHL	8	4	5	9	....	....	....	0	....	....	....	....	....	....	....	....	....	....	....	....	....	....	....	....	....	....
	Minnesota North Stars	**NHL**	**18**	**3**	**3**	**6**	**3**	**3**	**6**	**4**	**0**	**0**	**0**	**13**	**23.1**	**7**	**1**	**14**	**1**	**–7**	....	....	....	....	....	....	....	....
1969-70	**Minnesota North Stars**	**NHL**	**45**	**9**	**8**	**17**	**10**	**7**	**17**	**19**	**0**	**0**	**0**	**58**	**15.5**	**22**	**1**	**24**	**0**	**–3**	**6**	**0**	**1**	**1**	**2**	**0**	**0**	**0**
	Iowa Stars	CHL	31	12	21	33	....	....	....	8	....	....	....	....	....	....	....	....	....	....	....	....	....	....	....	....	....	....
1970-71	**Minnesota North Stars**	**NHL**	**33**	**1**	**5**	**6**	**1**	**4**	**5**	**2**	**0**	**0**	**0**	**25**	**4.0**	**8**	**0**	**5**	**0**	**3**	**10**	**0**	**0**	**0**	**0**	**0**	**0**	**0**
	Cleveland Barons	AHL	10	3	4	7	....	....	....	14	....	....	....	....	....	....	....	....	....	....	....	....	....	....	....	....	....	....
1971-72	**Buffalo Sabres**	**NHL**	**78**	**10**	**6**	**16**	**10**	**5**	**15**	**15**	**0**	**1**	**0**	**176**	**5.7**	**29**	**2**	**90**	**40**	**–23**	....	....	....	....	....	....	....	....

Season	Club	League	GP	G	A	Pts	AG	AA	APts	PIM	PP	SH	GW	S	%	TGF	PGF	TGA	PGA	+/–	GP	G	A	Pts	PIM	PP	SH	GW
			REGULAR SEASON																		PLAYOFFS							
1972-73	Philadelphia Blazers	WHA	78	*61	45	106	....	....	....	35	....	....	....	....	....	....	....	....	....	....	4	0	1	1	0	....	....	....
1973-74	Vancouver Blazers	WHA	78	50	38	88	....	....	....	14	....	....	....	....	....	....	....	....	....	....	....	....	....	....	....	....	....	....
1974-75	Vancouver Blazers	WHA	78	33	43	76	....	....	....	19	....	....	....	....	....	....	....	....	....	....	....	....	....	....	....	....	....	....
1975-76	Calgary Cowboys	WHA	80	44	52	96	....	....	....	46	....	....	....	....	....	....	....	....	....	....	9	4	4	8	19	....	....	....
1976-77	Calgary Cowboys	WHA	64	24	19	43	....	....	....	26	....	....	....	....	....	....	....	....	....	....	....	....	....	....	....	....	....	....
	Winnipeg Jets	WHA	14	6	7	13	....	....	....	2	....	....	....	....	....	....	....	....	....	....	13	2	4	6	6	....	....	....
	NHL Totals		**219**	**28**	**29**	**57**	**29**	**25**	**54**	**61**	**0**	**1**	**0**	**331**	**8.5**	**81**	**6**	**148**	**41**		**16**	**0**	**1**	**1**	**2**	**0**	**0**	**0**
	Other Major League Totals		392	218	204	422	....	....	....	142	....	....	....	....	....	....	....	....	....	....	26	6	9	15	25	....	....	....

OHA-Jr. First All-Star Team (1968) • WHA First All-Star Team (1973)

Traded to **Minnesota** by **Detroit** with the rights to Brian Conacher for Wayne Connelly, February 15, 1969. Claimed by **Buffalo** from **Minnesota** in Intra-League Draft, June 8, 1971. Selected by **Miami-Philadelphia** (WHA) in 1972 WHA General Player Draft, February 12, 1972. Transferred to **Vancouver** (WHA) after **Philadelphia** (WHA) franchise relocated, May, 1973. Transferred to **Calgary** (WHA) after **Vancouver** (WHA) franchise relocated, May 7, 1975. Traded to **Winnipeg** (WHA) by **Calgary** (WHA) with Mike Ford and future considerations for Veli Pekka-Ketola, Heikki Riihiranta and Ron Ward, March, 1977.

• LAWTON, Brian

Brian R. LW – L. 6', 180 lbs. b: New Brunswick, NJ, 6/29/1965. Minnesota's 1st, 1st overall, in 1983.

Season	Club	League	GP	G	A	Pts	AG	AA	APts	PIM	PP	SH	GW	S	%	TGF	PGF	TGA	PGA	+/–	GP	G	A	Pts	PIM	PP	SH	GW
1981-82	Mount St. Charles Mounties	Hi-School	26	45	43	88	....	....	....	....	....	....	....	....	....	....	....	....	....	....	....	....	....	....	....	....	....	....
1982-83	Mount St. Charles Mounties	Hi-School	23	40	43	83	....	....	....	....	....	....	....	....	....	....	....	....	....	....	....	....	....	....	....	....	....	....
	United States	Nat-Team	7	3	2	5	....	....	....	6	....	....	....	....	....	....	....	....	....	....	....	....	....	....	....	....	....	....
	United States	WJC-A	7	3	1	4	....	....	....	6	....	....	....	....	....	....	....	....	....	....	....	....	....	....	....	....	....	....
1983-84	**Minnesota North Stars**	**NHL**	**58**	**10**	**21**	**31**	**8**	**14**	**22**	**33**	**0**	**0**	**4**	**74**	**13.5**	**48**	**7**	**42**	**1**	**0**	**5**	**0**	**0**	**0**	**10**	**0**	**0**	**0**
1984-85	United States	Can-Cup	6	5	0	5	....	....	....	4	....	....	....	....	....	....	....	....	....	....	....	....	....	....	....	....	....	....
	Minnesota North Stars	**NHL**	**40**	**5**	**6**	**11**	**4**	**4**	**8**	**24**	**1**	**0**	**1**	**40**	**12.5**	**21**	**3**	**22**	**2**	**–2**	....	....	....	....	....	....	....	....
	Springfield Indians	AHL	42	14	28	42	....	....	....	37	....	....	....	....	....	....	....	....	....	....	4	1	1	2	2	....	....	....
1985-86	**Minnesota North Stars**	**NHL**	**65**	**18**	**17**	**35**	**14**	**11**	**25**	**36**	**4**	**0**	**7**	**98**	**18.4**	**53**	**10**	**33**	**0**	**10**	**3**	**0**	**1**	**1**	**2**	**0**	**0**	**0**
1986-87	**Minnesota North Stars**	**NHL**	**66**	**21**	**23**	**44**	**18**	**17**	**35**	**86**	**2**	**0**	**2**	**125**	**16.8**	**66**	**6**	**41**	**1**	**20**	....	....	....	....	....	....	....	....
	United States	WEC-A	8	3	3	6	....	....	....	14	....	....	....	....	....	....	....	....	....	....	....	....	....	....	....	....	....	....
1987-88	**Minnesota North Stars**	**NHL**	**74**	**17**	**24**	**41**	**14**	**17**	**31**	**71**	**7**	**0**	**1**	**155**	**11.0**	**72**	**35**	**66**	**19**	**–10**	....	....	....	....	....	....	....	....
1988-89	**New York Rangers**	**NHL**	**30**	**7**	**10**	**17**	**6**	**7**	**13**	**39**	**3**	**0**	**0**	**58**	**12.1**	**24**	**6**	**21**	**1**	**–2**	....	....	....	....	....	....	....	....
	Hartford Whalers	**NHL**	**35**	**10**	**16**	**26**	**8**	**11**	**19**	**28**	**7**	**0**	**2**	**70**	**14.3**	**44**	**24**	**29**	**0**	**–9**	**3**	**1**	**0**	**1**	**0**	**0**	**0**	**0**
1989-90	**Hartford Whalers**	**NHL**	**13**	**2**	**1**	**3**	**2**	**1**	**3**	**6**	**1**	**0**	**0**	**17**	**11.8**	**4**	**2**	**4**	**0**	**–2**	....	....	....	....	....	....	....	....
	Quebec Nordiques	**NHL**	**14**	**5**	**6**	**11**	**4**	**4**	**8**	**10**	**3**	**0**	**0**	**25**	**20.0**	**19**	**6**	**22**	**0**	**–9**	....	....	....	....	....	....	....	....
	Boston Bruins	**NHL**	**8**	**0**	**0**	**0**	**0**	**0**	**0**	**14**	**0**	**0**	**0**	**10**	**0.0**	**1**	**1**	**4**	**0**	**–4**	....	....	....	....	....	....	....	....
	Maine Mariners	AHL	5	0	0	0	....	....	....	14	....	....	....	....	....	....	....	....	....	....	....	....	....	....	....	....	....	....
1990-91	Phoenix Roadrunners	IHL	63	26	40	66	....	....	....	108	....	....	....	....	....	....	....	....	....	....	11	4	9	13	40	....	....	....
1991-92	**San Jose Sharks**	**NHL**	**59**	**15**	**22**	**37**	**14**	**17**	**31**	**42**	**7**	**0**	**1**	**131**	**11.5**	**56**	**26**	**68**	**13**	**–25**	....	....	....	....	....	....	....	....
1992-93	**San Jose Sharks**	**NHL**	**21**	**2**	**8**	**10**	**2**	**5**	**7**	**12**	**0**	**0**	**0**	**29**	**6.9**	**19**	**6**	**26**	**4**	**–9**	....	....	....	....	....	....	....	....
	Kansas City Blades	IHL	9	6	4	10	....	....	....	10	....	....	....	....	....	....	....	....	....	....	....	....	....	....	....	....	....	....
	Cincinnati Cyclones	IHL	17	5	11	16	....	....	....	30	....	....	....	....	....	....	....	....	....	....	....	....	....	....	....	....	....	....
	NHL Totals		**483**	**112**	**154**	**266**	**94**	**108**	**202**	**401**	**35**	**0**	**18**	**832**	**13.5**	**427**	**132**	**378**	**41**		**11**	**1**	**1**	**2**	**12**	**0**	**0**	**0**

Traded to **NY Rangers** by **Minnesota** with Igor Liba and the rights to Rick Bennett for Paul Jerrard, Mark Tinordi, the rights to Bret Barnett and Mike Sullivan and LA Kings' 3rd round choice (previously acquired, Minnesota selected Murray Garbutt) in 1989 Entry Draft, October 11, 1988. Traded to **Hartford** by **NY Rangers** with Norm MacIver and Don Maloney for Carey Wilson and Hartford's 5th round choice (Lubos Rob) in 1990 Entry Draft, December 26, 1988. Claimed on waivers by **Quebec** from **Hartford**, December 1, 1989. Signed as a free agent by **Boston**, February 7, 1990. Signed as a free agent by **LA Kings**, July 27, 1990. Signed as a free agent by **San Jose**, August 9, 1991. Traded to **New Jersey** by **San Jose** for future considerations, January 22, 1993.

• LAXDAL, Derek

RW – R. 6'1", 175 lbs. b: St. Boniface, Man., 2/21/1966. Toronto's 7th, 151st overall, in 1984.

Season	Club	League	GP	G	A	Pts	AG	AA	APts	PIM	PP	SH	GW	S	%	TGF	PGF	TGA	PGA	+/–	GP	G	A	Pts	PIM	PP	SH	GW
1982-83	Red Deer Rebels	AJHL	STATISTICS NOT AVAILABLE																									
	Portland Winter Hawks	WHL	39	4	9	13	....	....	....	27	....	....	....	....	....	....	....	....	....	....	14	0	2	2	2	....	....	....
	Portland Winter Hawks	Mem-Cup	4	0	0	0	....	....	....	0	....	....	....	....	....	....	....	....	....	....	....	....	....	....	....	....	....	....
1983-84	Brandon Wheat Kings	WHL	70	23	20	43	....	....	....	86	....	....	....	....	....	....	....	....	....	....	12	0	4	4	10	....	....	....
1984-85	Brandon Wheat Kings	WHL	69	61	41	102	....	....	....	74	....	....	....	....	....	....	....	....	....	....	....	....	....	....	....	....	....	....
	Toronto Maple Leafs	**NHL**	**3**	**0**	**0**	**0**	**0**	**0**	**0**	**6**	**0**	**0**	**0**	**3**	**0.0**	**0**	**0**	**1**	**0**	**–1**	....	....	....	....	....	....	....	....
	St. Catharines Saints	AHL	5	3	2	5	....	....	....	2	....	....	....	....	....	....	....	....	....	....	....	....	....	....	....	....	....	....
1985-86	Brandon Wheat Kings	WHL	42	34	35	69	....	....	....	62	....	....	....	....	....	....	....	....	....	....	....	....	....	....	....	....	....	....
	Canada	WJC-A	7	1	4	5	....	....	....	6	....	....	....	....	....	....	....	....	....	....	....	....	....	....	....	....	....	....
	New Westminster Bruins	WHL	18	9	6	15	....	....	....	14	....	....	....	....	....	....	....	....	....	....	....	....	....	....	....	....	....	....
	St. Catharines Saints	AHL	7	0	1	1	....	....	....	15	....	....	....	....	....	....	....	....	....	....	12	1	1	2	24	....	....	....
1986-87	**Toronto Maple Leafs**	**NHL**	**2**	**0**	**0**	**0**	**0**	**0**	**0**	**7**	**0**	**0**	**0**	**0**	**0.0**	**0**	**0**	**1**	**0**	**–1**	....	....	....	....	....	....	....	....
	Newmarket Saints	AHL	78	24	20	44	....	....	....	69	....	....	....	....	....	....	....	....	....	....	....	....	....	....	....	....	....	....
1987-88	**Toronto Maple Leafs**	**NHL**	**5**	**0**	**0**	**0**	**0**	**0**	**0**	**6**	**0**	**0**	**0**	**2**	**0.0**	**1**	**0**	**1**	**0**	**0**	....	....	....	....	....	....	....	....
	Newmarket Saints	AHL	67	18	25	43	....	....	....	81	....	....	....	....	....	....	....	....	....	....	....	....	....	....	....	....	....	....
1988-89	**Toronto Maple Leafs**	**NHL**	**41**	**9**	**6**	**15**	**8**	**4**	**12**	**65**	**1**	**0**	**0**	**41**	**22.0**	**20**	**4**	**28**	**1**	**–11**	....	....	....	....	....	....	....	....
	Newmarket Saints	AHL	34	22	22	44	....	....	....	53	....	....	....	....	....	....	....	....	....	....	2	0	2	2	5	....	....	....
1989-90	Newmarket Saints	AHL	23	7	8	15	....	....	....	52	....	....	....	....	....	....	....	....	....	....	....	....	....	....	....	....	....	....
	New York Islanders	**NHL**	**12**	**3**	**1**	**4**	**3**	**1**	**4**	**4**	**0**	**0**	**0**	**20**	**15.0**	**4**	**0**	**8**	**0**	**–4**	**1**	**0**	**2**	**2**	**2**	**0**	**0**	**0**
	Springfield Indians	AHL	28	13	12	25	....	....	....	42	....	....	....	....	....	....	....	....	....	....	13	8	6	14	47	....	....	....
1990-91	**New York Islanders**	**NHL**	**4**	**0**	**0**	**0**	**0**	**0**	**0**	**0**	**0**	**0**	**0**	**3**	**0.0**	**0**	**0**	**1**	**0**	**–1**	....	....	....	....	....	....	....	....
	Capital District Islanders	AHL	65	14	25	39	....	....	....	75	....	....	....	....	....	....	....	....	....	....	....	....	....	....	....	....	....	....
1991-92	Capital District Islanders	AHL	49	7	7	14	....	....	....	61	....	....	....	....	....	....	....	....	....	....	4	1	1	2	10	....	....	....
1992-93	Canada	Nat-Team	51	13	27	40	....	....	....	71	....	....	....	....	....	....	....	....	....	....	....	....	....	....	....	....	....	....
1993-94	Herforder EG	Germany-3	STATISTICS NOT AVAILABLE																									
	Ilves Tampere	Finland	17	6	5	11	....	....	....	20	....	....	....	....	....	....	....	....	....	....	3	1	0	1	4	....	....	....
1994-95	Roanoke Express	ECHL	66	32	24	56	....	....	....	144	....	....	....	....	....	....	....	....	....	....	8	2	4	6	25	....	....	....
1995-96	Humberside Hawks	BH-Cup	8	10	15	25	....	....	....	33	....	....	....	....	....	....	....	....	....	....	....	....	....	....	....	....	....	....
	Humberside Hawks	Britain	33	29	29	58	....	....	....	163	....	....	....	....	....	....	....	....	....	....	7	9	4	13	16	....	....	....
1996-97	Nottingham Panthers	BH-Cup	11	8	1	9	....	....	....	37	....	....	....	....	....	....	....	....	....	....	....	....	....	....	....	....	....	....
	Nottingham Panthers	Britain	31	14	14	28	....	....	....	54	....	....	....	....	....	....	....	....	....	....	8	1	3	4	27	....	....	....
1997-98	Nottingham Panthers	BH-Cup	12	7	9	16	....	....	....	16	....	....	....	....	....	....	....	....	....	....	....	....	....	....	....	....	....	....
	Nottingham Panthers	Britain	44	24	23	47	....	....	....	103	....	....	....	....	....	....	....	....	....	....	6	1	3	4	10	....	....	....
1998-99	Sheffield Steelers	BH-Cup	10	0	6	6	....	....	....	6	....	....	....	....	....	....	....	....	....	....	....	....	....	....	....	....	....	....
	Sheffield Steelers	Britain	29	9	13	22	....	....	....	32	....	....	....	....	....	....	....	....	....	....	....	....	....	....	....	....	....	....
99-2000	Sheffield Steelers	BH-Cup	10	6	6	12	....	....	....	6	....	....	....	....	....	....	....	....	....	....	....	....	....	....	....	....	....	....
	Sheffield Steelers	Britain	18	3	3	6	....	....	....	20	....	....	....	....	....	....	....	....	....	....	....	....	....	....	....	....	....	....
	Odessa Jackalopes	WPHL	46	28	25	53	....	....	....	53	....	....	....	....	....	....	....	....	....	....	2	0	0	0	4	....	....	....
	NHL Totals		**67**	**12**	**7**	**19**	**11**	**5**	**16**	**88**	**1**	**0**	**0**	**69**	**17.4**	**25**	**4**	**40**	**1**		**1**	**0**	**2**	**2**	**2**	**0**	**0**	**0**

Traded to **NY Islanders** by **Toronto** with Jack Capuano and Paul Gagne for Mike Stevens and Gilles Thibaudeau, December 20, 1989. Signed as a free agent by **Odessa** (WPHL), December 9, 1999. • Played w/ RHI's Ottawa Loggers in 1995 (22-25-28-53-38) and Denver Dare Devils in 1996 (16-3-15-18-32).

• LAZARO, Jeff

Jeffrey Adam LW – L. 5'10", 180 lbs. b: Waltham, MA, 3/21/1968.

Season	Club	League	GP	G	A	Pts	AG	AA	APts	PIM	PP	SH	GW	S	%	TGF	PGF	TGA	PGA	+/–	GP	G	A	Pts	PIM	PP	SH	GW
1985-86	Waltham High School	Hi-School	STATISTICS NOT AVAILABLE																									
1986-87	University of New Hampshire	H-East	38	7	14	21	....	....	....	38	....	....	....	....	....	....	....	....	....	....	....	....	....	....	....	....	....	....
1987-88	University of New Hampshire	H-East	30	4	13	17	....	....	....	48	....	....	....	....	....	....	....	....	....	....	....	....	....	....	....	....	....	....
1988-89	University of New Hampshire	H-East	31	8	14	22	....	....	....	38	....	....	....	....	....	....	....	....	....	....	....	....	....	....	....	....	....	....
1989-90	University of New Hampshire	H-East	39	16	19	35	....	....	....	34	....	....	....	....	....	....	....	....	....	....	....	....	....	....	....	....	....	....
1990-91	**Boston Bruins**	**NHL**	**49**	**5**	**13**	**18**	**5**	**10**	**15**	**67**	**1**	**1**	**1**	**73**	**6.8**	**36**	**1**	**37**	**9**	**7**	**19**	**3**	**2**	**5**	**30**	**0**	**0**	**0**
	Maine Mariners	AHL	26	8	11	19	....	....	....	18	....	....	....	....	....	....	....	....	....	....	....	....	....	....	....	....	....	....
1991-92	**Boston Bruins**	**NHL**	**27**	**3**	**6**	**9**	**3**	**5**	**8**	**31**	**0**	**0**	**0**	**46**	**6.5**	**14**	**0**	**20**	**10**	**4**	**9**	**0**	**1**	**1**	**2**	**0**	**0**	**0**
	Maine Mariners	AHL	21	8	4	12	....	....	....	32	....	....	....	....	....	....	....	....	....	....	....	....	....	....	....	....	....	....

Season	Club	League	GP	G	A	Pts	AG	AA	APts	PIM	PP	SH	GW	S	%	TGF	PGF	TGA	PGA	+/–	GP	G	A	Pts	PIM	PP	SH	GW
			REGULAR SEASON																		PLAYOFFS							
1992-93	**Ottawa Senators**	**NHL**	**26**	**6**	**4**	**10**	**5**	**3**	**8**	**16**	**0**	**1**	**0**	**38**	**15.8**	**12**	**1**	**30**	**11**	**–8**	....	....	....	....	....	....	....	....
	New Haven Senators	AHL	27	12	13	25	....	....	....	49	....	....	....	....	....	....	....	....	....	....	....	....	....	....	....	....	....	....
	United States	WC-A	4	2	0	2	....	....	....	2	....	....	....	....	....	....	....	....	....	....	....	....	....	....	....	....	....	....
1993-94	Providence Bruins	AHL	16	3	4	7	....	....	....	26	....	....	....	....	....	....	....	....	....	....	....	....	....	....	....	....	....	....
	United States	Nat-Team	43	18	25	43	....	....	....	57	....	....	....	....	....	....	....	....	....	....	....	....	....	....	....	....	....	....
	United States	Olympics	8	2	2	4	....	....	....	4	....	....	....	....	....	....	....	....	....	....	....	....	....	....	....	....	....	....
	United States	WC-A	8	0	0	0	....	....	....	10	....	....	....	....	....	....	....	....	....	....	....	....	....	....	....	....	....	....
1994-95	EC Graz	Austria	23	23	23	46	....	....	....	84	....	....	....	....	....	....	....	....	....	....	8	5	6	11	6	....	....	....
1995-96	Ratinger Lowen	Germany	46	25	41	66	....	....	....	54	....	....	....	....	....	....	....	....	....	....	3	0	0	0	8	....	....	....
1996-97	Ratinger Lowen	Germany	44	13	23	36	....	....	....	69	....	....	....	....	....	....	....	....	....	....	7	5	3	8	8	....	....	....
1997-98	New Orleans Brass	ECHL	70	37	64	101	....	....	....	151	....	....	....	....	....	....	....	....	....	....	4	0	4	4	8	....	....	....
	Hamilton Bulldogs	AHL	2	2	0	2	....	....	....	0	....	....	....	....	....	....	....	....	....	....	8	2	3	5	2	....	....	....
1998-99	Adirondack Red Wings	AHL	16	2	8	10	....	....	....	10	....	....	....	....	....	....	....	....	....	....	....	....	....	....	....	....	....	....
	New Orleans Brass	ECHL	52	26	44	70	....	....	....	81	....	....	....	....	....	....	....	....	....	....	11	9	7	16	14	....	....	....
99-2000	New Orleans Brass	ECHL	70	24	56	80	....	....	....	109	....	....	....	....	....	....	....	....	....	....	3	1	0	1	4	....	....	....
	NHL Totals		**102**	**14**	**23**	**37**	**13**	**18**	**31**	**114**	**1**	**2**	**1**	**157**	**8.9**	**62**	**2**	**87**	**30**		**28**	**3**	**3**	**6**	**32**	**0**	**0**	**0**

ECHL First All-Star Team (1998)

Signed as a free agent by **Boston**, September 26, 1990. Claimed by **Ottawa** from **Boston** in Expansion Draft, June 18, 1992.

• LEACH, Jamie

RW – R. 6'1", 205 lbs. b: Winnipeg, Man., 8/25/1969. Pittsburgh's 3rd, 47th overall, in 1987.

Season	Club	League	GP	G	A	Pts	AG	AA	APts	PIM	PP	SH	GW	S	%	TGF	PGF	TGA	PGA	+/–	GP	G	A	Pts	PIM	PP	SH	GW
1983-84	Cherry Hill East High School	Hi-School	60	48	51	99	....	....	....	68	....	....	....	....	....	....	....	....	....	....	....	....	....	....	....	....	....	....
1984-85	Philadelphia Jr. Flyers	NAJHL	70	35	35	70	....	....	....	24	....	....	....	....	....	....	....	....	....	....	....	....	....	....	....	....	....	....
1985-86	New Westminster Bruins	WHL	58	8	7	15	....	....	....	20	....	....	....	....	....	....	....	....	....	....	....	....	....	....	....	....	....	....
1986-87	Hamilton Steelhawks	OHL	64	12	19	31	....	....	....	67	....	....	....	....	....	....	....	....	....	....	....	....	....	....	....	....	....	....
1987-88	Hamilton Steelhawks	OHL	64	24	19	43	....	....	....	79	....	....	....	....	....	....	....	....	....	....	14	6	7	13	12	....	....	....
1988-89	Niagara Falls Flyers	OHL	58	45	62	107	....	....	....	47	....	....	....	....	....	....	....	....	....	....	17	9	11	20	25	....	....	....
1989-90	**Pittsburgh Penguins**	**NHL**	**10**	**0**	**3**	**3**	**0**	**2**	**2**	**0**	**0**	**0**	**0**	**10**	**0.0**	**3**	**0**	**0**	**0**	**3**	....	....	....	....	....	....	....	....
	Muskegon Lumberjacks	IHL	72	22	36	58	....	....	....	39	....	....	....	....	....	....	....	....	....	....	15	9	4	13	14	....	....	....
1990-91	**Pittsburgh Penguins**	**NHL**	**7**	**2**	**0**	**2**	**2**	**0**	**2**	**0**	**0**	**0**	**0**	**8**	**25.0**	**3**	**1**	**3**	**0**	**–1**	....	....	....	....	....	....	....	....
	Muskegon Lumberjacks	IHL	43	33	22	55	....	....	....	26	....	....	....	....	....	....	....	....	....	....	....	....	....	....	....	....	....	....
1991-92	**Pittsburgh Penguins**	**NHL**	**38**	**5**	**4**	**9**	**5**	**3**	**8**	**8**	**1**	**0**	**0**	**32**	**15.6**	**14**	**2**	**14**	**0**	**–2**	....	....	....	....	....	....	....	....
	Muskegon Lumberjacks	IHL	3	1	1	2	....	....	....	2	....	....	....	....	....	....	....	....	....	....	....	....	....	....	....	....	....	....
1992-93	**Pittsburgh Penguins**	**NHL**	**5**	**0**	**0**	**0**	**0**	**0**	**0**	**2**	**0**	**0**	**0**	**2**	**0.0**	**0**	**0**	**2**	**0**	**–2**	....	....	....	....	....	....	....	....
	Cleveland Lumberjacks	IHL	9	5	3	8	....	....	....	2	....	....	....	....	....	....	....	....	....	....	4	1	2	3	0	....	....	....
	Hartford Whalers	**NHL**	**19**	**3**	**2**	**5**	**2**	**1**	**3**	**2**	**0**	**0**	**0**	**17**	**17.6**	**10**	**2**	**13**	**0**	**–5**	....	....	....	....	....	....	....	....
	Springfield Indians	AHL	29	13	15	28	....	....	....	33	....	....	....	....	....	....	....	....	....	....	....	....	....	....	....	....	....	....
1993-94	**Florida Panthers**	**NHL**	**2**	**1**	**0**	**1**	**1**	**0**	**1**	**0**	**0**	**0**	**0**	**2**	**50.0**	**1**	**0**	**3**	**0**	**–2**	....	....	....	....	....	....	....	....
	Cincinnati Cyclones	IHL	74	15	19	34	....	....	....	64	....	....	....	....	....	....	....	....	....	....	11	1	0	1	4	....	....	....
1994-95	Canada	Nat-Team	41	12	26	38	....	....	....	26	....	....	....	....	....	....	....	....	....	....	....	....	....	....	....	....	....	....
	Cincinnati Cyclones	IHL	11	0	2	2	....	....	....	9	....	....	....	....	....	....	....	....	....	....	....	....	....	....	....	....	....	....
	San Diego Gulls	IHL	....	....	....	....	....	....	....	....	....	....	....	....	....	....	....	....	....	....	4	0	0	0	0	....	....	....
1995-96	Rochester Americans	AHL	47	12	14	26	....	....	....	52	....	....	....	....	....	....	....	....	....	....	2	0	0	0	0	....	....	....
	South Carolina Stingrays	ECHL	5	6	1	7	....	....	....	4	....	....	....	....	....	....	....	....	....	....	....	....	....	....	....	....	....	....
1996-97	Sheffield Steelers	BH-Cup	10	13	4	17	....	....	....	2	....	....	....	....	....	....	....	....	....	....	....	....	....	....	....	....	....	....
	Sheffield Steelers	Britain	36	17	20	37	....	....	....	26	....	....	....	....	....	....	....	....	....	....	8	4	5	9	12	....	....	....
1997-98	Nottingham Panthers	BH-Cup	11	6	7	13	....	....	....	2	....	....	....	....	....	....	....	....	....	....	....	....	....	....	....	....	....	....
	Nottingham Panthers	Britain	39	20	25	45	....	....	....	36	....	....	....	....	....	....	....	....	....	....	5	1	1	2	2	....	....	....
1998-99	Nottingham Panthers	BH-Cup	12	8	9	17	....	....	....	10	....	....	....	....	....	....	....	....	....	....	....	....	....	....	....	....	....	....
	Nottingham Panthers	Britain	32	16	13	29	....	....	....	14	....	....	....	....	....	....	....	....	....	....	8	4	5	9	0	....	....	....
99-2000	Nottingham Panthers	BH-Cup	9	2	5	7	....	....	....	4	....	....	....	....	....	....	....	....	....	....	....	....	....	....	....	....	....	....
	Nottingham Panthers	Britain	42	17	29	46	....	....	....	18	....	....	....	....	....	....	....	....	....	....	6	2	3	5	12	....	....	....
	NHL Totals		**81**	**11**	**9**	**20**	**10**	**6**	**16**	**12**	**1**	**0**	**0**	**71**	**15.5**	**31**	**5**	**35**	**0**		....	....	....	....	....	....	....	....

• Son of Reggie

Claimed on waivers by **Hartford** from **Pittsburgh**, November 21, 1992. Signed as a free agent by **Florida**, August 31, 1993.

• LEACH, Reggie

Reginald Joseph "The Riverton Rifle" RW – R. 6', 180 lbs. b: Riverton, Man., 4/23/1950. Boston's 1st, 3rd overall, in 1970.

Season	Club	League	GP	G	A	Pts	AG	AA	APts	PIM	PP	SH	GW	S	%	TGF	PGF	TGA	PGA	+/–	GP	G	A	Pts	PIM	PP	SH	GW
1966-67	Flin Flon Bombers	MJHL	45	67	46	113	....	....	....	118	....	....	....	....	....	....	....	....	....	....	14	*18	12	*30	15	....	....	....
	Flin Flon Bombers	Mem-Cup	6	6	1	7	....	....	....	11	....	....	....	....	....	....	....	....	....	....	....	....	....	....	....	....	....	....
1967-68	Flin Flon Bombers	WCJHL	59	*87	44	131	....	....	....	208	....	....	....	....	....	....	....	....	....	....	15	12	3	15	48	....	....	....
1968-69	Flin Flon Bombers	WCJHL	22	36	10	46	....	....	....	49	....	....	....	....	....	....	....	....	....	....	18	*13	8	21	0	....	....	....
1969-70	Flin Flon Bombers	WCJHL	57	*65	46	*111	....	....	....	168	....	....	....	....	....	....	....	....	....	....	17	*16	11	27	50	....	....	....
1970-71	**Boston Bruins**	**NHL**	**23**	**2**	**4**	**6**	**2**	**3**	**5**	**0**	**0**	**0**	**0**	**30**	**6.7**	**8**	**0**	**1**	**0**	**7**	**3**	**0**	**0**	**0**	**0**	**0**	**0**	**0**
	Oklahoma City Blazers	CHL	41	24	18	42	....	....	....	32	....	....	....	....	....	....	....	....	....	....	....	....	....	....	....	....	....	....
1971-72	**Boston Bruins**	**NHL**	**56**	**7**	**13**	**20**	**7**	**11**	**18**	**12**	**0**	**0**	**2**	**66**	**10.6**	**25**	**1**	**19**	**0**	**5**	....	....	....	....	....	....	....	....
	California Golden Seals	**NHL**	**17**	**6**	**7**	**13**	**6**	**6**	**12**	**7**	**2**	**0**	**1**	**38**	**15.8**	**24**	**4**	**19**	**1**	**2**	....	....	....	....	....	....	....	....
1972-73	**California Golden Seals**	**NHL**	**76**	**23**	**12**	**35**	**22**	**9**	**31**	**45**	**3**	**0**	**4**	**184**	**12.5**	**63**	**14**	**92**	**2**	**–41**	....	....	....	....	....	....	....	....
1973-74	**California Golden Seals**	**NHL**	**78**	**22**	**24**	**46**	**21**	**20**	**41**	**34**	**2**	**0**	**3**	**214**	**10.3**	**67**	**17**	**113**	**2**	**–61**	....	....	....	....	....	....	....	....
1974-75♦	**Philadelphia Flyers**	**NHL**	**80**	**45**	**33**	**78**	**39**	**25**	**64**	**63**	**12**	**0**	**10**	**289**	**15.6**	**113**	**38**	**24**	**2**	**53**	**17**	**8**	**2**	**10**	**6**	**2**	**0**	**2**
1975-76	**Philadelphia Flyers**	**NHL**	**80**	***61**	**30**	**91**	**54**	**22**	**76**	**41**	**10**	**0**	**11**	**335**	**18.2**	**152**	**46**	**33**	**0**	**73**	**16**	***19**	**5**	***24**	**8**	**2**	**0**	**2**
1976-77	Canada	Can-Cup	6	1	1	2	....	....	....	4	....	....	....	....	....	....	....	....	....	....	....	....	....	....	....	....	....	....
	Philadelphia Flyers	**NHL**	**77**	**32**	**14**	**46**	**29**	**11**	**40**	**23**	**10**	**0**	**3**	**237**	**13.5**	**77**	**25**	**46**	**0**	**6**	**10**	**4**	**5**	**9**	**0**	**0**	**0**	**2**
1977-78	**Philadelphia Flyers**	**NHL**	**72**	**24**	**28**	**52**	**22**	**22**	**44**	**24**	**9**	**0**	**4**	**195**	**12.3**	**82**	**25**	**39**	**2**	**20**	**12**	**2**	**2**	**4**	**0**	**1**	**0**	**0**
1978-79	**Philadelphia Flyers**	**NHL**	**76**	**34**	**20**	**54**	**29**	**14**	**43**	**20**	**13**	**0**	**6**	**279**	**12.2**	**77**	**29**	**52**	**1**	**–3**	**8**	**5**	**1**	**6**	**0**	**3**	**0**	**2**
1979-80	**Philadelphia Flyers**	**NHL**	**76**	**50**	**26**	**76**	**43**	**19**	**62**	**28**	**5**	**4**	**7**	**328**	**15.2**	**99**	**14**	**69**	**24**	**40**	**19**	**9**	**7**	**16**	**6**	**2**	**1**	**0**
1980-81	**Philadelphia Flyers**	**NHL**	**79**	**34**	**36**	**70**	**26**	**24**	**50**	**59**	**15**	**1**	**2**	**321**	**10.6**	**105**	**39**	**64**	**19**	**21**	**9**	**0**	**0**	**0**	**2**	**0**	**0**	**0**
1981-82	**Philadelphia Flyers**	**NHL**	**66**	**26**	**21**	**47**	**21**	**14**	**35**	**18**	**5**	**0**	**5**	**211**	**12.3**	**71**	**22**	**51**	**4**	**2**	....	....	....	....	....	....	....	....
1982-83	**Detroit Red Wings**	**NHL**	**78**	**15**	**17**	**32**	**12**	**12**	**24**	**13**	**2**	**0**	**0**	**139**	**10.8**	**49**	**4**	**64**	**18**	**–1**	....	....	....	....	....	....	....	....
1983-84	Montana Magic	CHL	76	21	29	50	....	....	....	34	....	....	....	....	....	....	....	....	....	....	....	....	....	....	....	....	....	....
	NHL Totals		**934**	**381**	**285**	**666**	**333**	**212**	**545**	**387**	**88**	**5**	**58**	**2866**	**13.3**	**1012**	**278**	**686**	**75**		**94**	**47**	**22**	**69**	**22**	**10**	**1**	**8**

• Father of Jamie • WCJHL First All-Star Team (1968, 1969, 1970) • NHL Second All-Star Team (1976) • Won Conn Smythe Trophy (1976) • Played in NHL All-Star Game (1976, 1980)

• Missed majority of 1968-69 season recovering from seperated shoulder, December, 1968. Traded to **California** by **Boston** with Rick Smith and Bob Stewart for Carol Vadnais and Don O'Donoghue, February 23, 1972. Traded to **Philadelphia** by **California** for Larry Wright, Al MacAdam and Philadelphia's 1st round choice (Ron Chipperfield) in 1974 Amateur Draft, May 24, 1974. Signed as a free agent by **Detroit**, August 25, 1982.

• LEACH, Stephen

RW – R. 5'11", 197 lbs. b: Cambridge, MA, 1/16/1966. Washington's 2nd, 34th overall, in 1984.

Season	Club	League	GP	G	A	Pts	AG	AA	APts	PIM	PP	SH	GW	S	%	TGF	PGF	TGA	PGA	+/–	GP	G	A	Pts	PIM	PP	SH	GW
1982-83	Matignon Warriors	Hi-School	23	17	21	38	....	....	....		....	....	....	....	....	....	....	....	....	....	....	....	....	....	....	....	....	....
1983-84	Matignon Warriors	Hi-School	21	27	22	49	....	....	....	49	....	....	....	....	....	....	....	....	....	....	....	....	....	....	....	....	....	....
1984-85	University of New Hampshire	H-East	41	12	25	37	....	....	....	53	....	....	....	....	....	....	....	....	....	....	....	....	....	....	....	....	....	....
	United States	WJC-A	7	2	0	2	....	....	....	12	....	....	....	....	....	....	....	....	....	....	....	....	....	....	....	....	....	....
1985-86	University of New Hampshire	H-East	25	22	6	28	....	....	....	30	....	....	....	....	....	....	....	....	....	....	....	....	....	....	....	....	....	....
	United States	WJC-A	7	6	5	11	....	....	....	4	....	....	....	....	....	....	....	....	....	....	....	....	....	....	....	....	....	....
	Washington Capitals	**NHL**	**11**	**1**	**1**	**2**	**1**	**1**	**2**	**2**	**0**	**0**	**0**	**4**	**25.0**	**4**	**0**	**4**	**0**	**0**	**6**	**0**	**1**	**1**	**0**	**0**	**0**	**0**
1986-87	**Washington Capitals**	**NHL**	**15**	**1**	**0**	**1**	**1**	**0**	**1**	**6**	**0**	**0**	**0**	**17**	**5.9**	**4**	**0**	**9**	**1**	**–4**	....	....	....	....	....	....	....	....
	Binghamton Whalers	AHL	54	18	21	39	....	....	....	39	....	....	....	....	....	....	....	....	....	....	13	3	1	4	6	....	....	....
1987-88	United States	Nat-Team	49	26	20	46	....	....	....	30	....	....	....	....	....	....	....	....	....	....	....	....	....	....	....	....	....	....
	United States	Olympics	6	1	2	3	....	....	....	0	....	....	....	....	....	....	....	....	....	....	....	....	....	....	....	....	....	....
	Washington Capitals	**NHL**	**8**	**1**	**1**	**2**	**1**	**1**	**2**	**17**	**0**	**0**	**1**	**5**	**20.0**	**3**	**0**	**1**	**0**	**2**	**9**	**2**	**1**	**3**	**0**	**0**	**0**	**1**
1988-89	**Washington Capitals**	**NHL**	**74**	**11**	**19**	**30**	**9**	**13**	**22**	**94**	**4**	**0**	**0**	**145**	**7.6**	**45**	**8**	**43**	**2**	**–4**	**6**	**1**	**0**	**1**	**12**	**1**	**0**	**0**
1989-90	**Washington Capitals**	**NHL**	**70**	**18**	**14**	**32**	**15**	**10**	**25**	**104**	**0**	**0**	**2**	**122**	**14.8**	**47**	**1**	**38**	**2**	**10**	**14**	**2**	**2**	**4**	**8**	**0**	**0**	**0**

			REGULAR SEASON																		PLAYOFFS							
Season	Club	League	GP	G	A	Pts	AG	AA	APts	PIM	PP	SH	GW	S	%	TGF	PGF	TGA	PGA	+/–	GP	G	A	Pts	PIM	PP	SH	GW
1990-91	**Washington Capitals**	**NHL**	68	11	19	30	10	14	24	99	4	0	1	134	8.2	43	14	38	0	–9	9	1	2	3	8	0	0	0
1991-92	**Boston Bruins**	**NHL**	78	31	29	60	28	22	50	147	12	0	4	243	12.8	100	36	79	7	–8	15	4	0	4	10	0	0	1
1992-93	**Boston Bruins**	**NHL**	79	26	25	51	22	17	39	126	9	0	4	256	10.2	80	28	58	0	–6	4	1	1	2	2	0	0	0
1993-94	**Boston Bruins**	**NHL**	42	5	10	15	5	8	13	74	1	0	1	89	5.6	29	8	31	0	–10	5	0	1	1	2	0	0	0
1994-95	**Boston Bruins**	**NHL**	35	5	6	11	9	9	18	68	1	0	1	82	6.1	18	4	18	1	–3	....	....	....	....	....	....	....	....
1995-96	**Boston Bruins**	**NHL**	59	9	13	22	9	11	20	86	1	0	2	124	7.3	36	2	38	0	–4	....	....	....	....	....	....	....	....
	St. Louis Blues	**NHL**	14	2	4	6	2	3	5	22	0	0	0	33	6.1	10	3	11	1	–3	11	3	2	5	10	1	0	1
1996-97	**St. Louis Blues**	**NHL**	17	2	1	3	2	1	3	24	0	0	0	33	6.1	7	0	9	0	–2	6	0	0	0	33	0	0	0
1997-98	**Carolina Hurricanes**	**NHL**	45	4	5	9	5	5	10	42	1	1	2	60	6.7	11	1	36	7	–19	....	....	....	....	....	....	....	....
1998-99	**Ottawa Senators**	**NHL**	9	0	2	2	0	2	2	6	0	0	0	4	0.0	3	0	4	0	–1	....	....	....	....	....	....	....	....
	Detroit Vipers	IHL	4	0	0	0	....	....	....	2	....	....	....	....	....	....	....	....	....	....	....	....	....	....	....	....	....	....
	Phoenix Coyotes	**NHL**	22	1	1	2	1	1	2	37	0	0	0	23	4.3	2	0	8	0	–6	7	1	1	2	2	0	0	0
	Springfield Falcons	AHL	13	5	3	8	....	....	....	10	....	....	....	....	....	....	....	....	....	....	....	....	....	....	....	....	....	....
99-2000	**Pittsburgh Penguins**	**NHL**	56	2	3	5	2	3	5	24	0	0	1	41	4.9	7	2	18	2	–11	....	....	....	....	....	....	....	....
	Wilkes-Barre Penguins	AHL	4	2	3	5	....	....	....	4	....	....	....	....	....	....	....	....	....	....	....	....	....	....	....	....	....	....
	NHL Totals		**702**	**130**	**153**	**283**	**122**	**121**	**243**	**978**	**33**	**1**	**19**	**1415**	**9.2**	**449**	**107**	**443**	**23**		**92**	**15**	**11**	**26**	**87**	**2**	**0**	**3**

Traded to **Boston** by **Washington** for Randy Burridge, June 21, 1991. Traded to **St. Louis** by **Boston** for Kevin Sawyer and Steve Staios, March 8, 1996. Traded to **Carolina** by **St. Louis** for Alexander Godynyuk and Carolina's 6th round choice in 1998 Entry Draft, June 27, 1997. Signed as a free agent by **Ottawa**, October 4, 1998. Signed as a free agent by **Phoenix**, December 3, 1998. Signed as a free agent by **Pittsburgh**, October 19, 1999.

• LEAVINS, Jim

James T. D – L. 5'11", 185 lbs. b: Dinsmore, Sask., 7/28/1960.

Season	Club	League	GP	G	A	Pts	AG	AA	APts	PIM	PP	SH	GW	S	%	TGF	PGF	TGA	PGA	+/–	GP	G	A	Pts	PIM	PP	SH	GW
1978-79	Swift Current Broncos	SJHL	STATISTICS NOT AVAILABLE																									
	Regina Pats	WHL	9	1	1	2	....	....	....	0	....	....	....	....	....	....	....	....	....	....	....	....	....	....	....	....	....	....
1979-80	Swift Current Broncos	SJHL	STATISTICS NOT AVAILABLE																									
1980-81	University of Denver	WCHA	40	8	18	26	....	....	....	18	....	....	....	....	....	....	....	....	....	....	....	....	....	....	....	....	....	....
1981-82	University of Denver	WCHA	41	8	34	42	....	....	....	56	....	....	....	....	....	....	....	....	....	....	....	....	....	....	....	....	....	....
1982-83	University of Denver	WCHA	33	16	24	40	....	....	....	20	....	....	....	....	....	....	....	....	....	....	....	....	....	....	....	....	....	....
1983-84	University of Denver	WCHA	39	13	26	39	....	....	....	38	....	....	....	....	....	....	....	....	....	....	....	....	....	....	....	....	....	....
1984-85	Fort Wayne Komets	IHL	76	5	50	55	....	....	....	57	....	....	....	....	....	....	....	....	....	....	13	3	8	11	10	....	....	....
1985-86	**Detroit Red Wings**	**NHL**	37	2	11	13	2	7	9	26	1	0	0	63	3.2	46	14	69	14	–23	....	....	....	....	....	....	....	....
	Adirondack Red Wings	AHL	36	4	21	25	....	....	....	19	....	....	....	....	....	....	....	....	....	....	....	....	....	....	....	....	....	....
1986-87	**New York Rangers**	**NHL**	4	0	1	1	0	1	1	4	0	0	0	4	0.0	8	4	4	0	0	....	....	....	....	....	....	....	....
	New Haven Nighthawks	AHL	54	7	21	28	....	....	....	16	....	....	....	....	....	....	....	....	....	....	7	0	4	4	2	....	....	....
1987-88	New Haven Nighthawks	AHL	11	2	5	7	....	....	....	8	....	....	....	....	....	....	....	....	....	....	....	....	....	....	....	....	....	....
	Salt Lake Golden Eagles	IHL	68	12	45	57	....	....	....	45	....	....	....	....	....	....	....	....	....	....	16	5	5	10	8	....	....	....
1988-89	KooKoo Kouvola	Finland	42	12	11	23	....	....	....	39	....	....	....	....	....	....	....	....	....	....	....	....	....	....	....	....	....	....
	Salt Lake Golden Eagles	IHL	25	8	13	21	....	....	....	14	....	....	....	....	....	....	....	....	....	....	14	2	11	13	6	....	....	....
1989-90	KooKoo Kouvola	Finland	44	7	24	31	....	....	....	36	....	....	....	....	....	....	....	....	....	....	....	....	....	....	....	....	....	....
	Canada	Nat-Team	5	0	2	2	....	....	....	4	....	....	....	....	....	....	....	....	....	....	....	....	....	....	....	....	....	....
	Salt Lake Golden Eagles	IHL	11	0	6	6	....	....	....	2	....	....	....	....	....	....	....	....	....	....	11	0	8	8	2	....	....	....
1990-91	Farjestads BK Karlstad	Sweden	40	9	8	17	....	....	....	24	....	....	....	....	....	....	....	....	....	....	8	0	3	3	8	....	....	....
	Canada	Nat-Team	4	0	1	1	....	....	....	0	....	....	....	....	....	....	....	....	....	....	....	....	....	....	....	....	....	....
1991-92			STATISTICS NOT AVAILABLE																									
1992-93	HC Varese	Alpenliga	30	6	16	22	....	....	....	13	....	....	....	....	....	....	....	....	....	....	....	....	....	....	....	....	....	....
	HC Varese	Italy	15	3	12	15	....	....	....	12	....	....	....	....	....	....	....	....	....	....	2	0	0	0	0	....	....	....
1993-94			DID NOT PLAY																									
1994-95	Los Angeles Bandits	SCSHL	STATISTICS NOT AVAILABLE																									
	NHL Totals		**41**	**2**	**12**	**14**	**2**	**8**	**10**	**30**	**1**	**0**	**0**	**67**	**3.0**	**54**	**18**	**73**	**14**		....	....	....	....	....	....	....	....

WCHA First All-Star Team (1984) • IHL Second All-Star Team (1988)

Signed as a free agent by **Detroit**, November 9, 1985. Traded to **NY Rangers** by **Detroit** with Kelly Kisio, Lane Lambert and Detroit's 5th round choice (later traded to Winnipeg–Winnipeg selected Benoit LeBeau) in 1988 Entry Draft for Glen Hanlon and NY Rangers' 3rd round choices in 1987 (Dennis Holland) and 1988 (Guy Dupuis) Entry Drafts, July 29, 1986. Traded to **Calgary** by **NY Rangers** for Don Mercier, November 6, 1987.

• LEBEAU, Patrick

LW – L. 5'10", 172 lbs. b: St. Jerome, Que., 3/17/1970. Montreal's 9th, 167th overall, in 1989.

Season	Club	League	GP	G	A	Pts	AG	AA	APts	PIM	PP	SH	GW	S	%	TGF	PGF	TGA	PGA	+/–	GP	G	A	Pts	PIM	PP	SH	GW
1984-85	Montreal L'est Cantonniers	QAAA	38	16	19	35	....	....	....	....	....	....	....	....	....	....	....	....	....	....	....	....	....	....	....	....	....	....
1985-86	Montreal L'est Cantonniers	QAAA	42	43	47	90	....	....	....	....	....	....	....	....	....	....	....	....	....	....	....	....	....	....	....	....	....	....
1986-87	Shawinigan Cataractes	QMJHL	66	26	52	78	....	....	....	90	....	....	....	....	....	....	....	....	....	....	13	2	6	8	17	....	....	....
1987-88	Shawinigan Cataractes	QMJHL	53	43	56	99	....	....	....	116	....	....	....	....	....	....	....	....	....	....	11	3	9	12	16	....	....	....
1988-89	Shawinigan Cataractes	QMJHL	17	19	17	36	....	....	....	18	....	....	....	....	....	....	....	....	....	....	....	....	....	....	....	....	....	....
	St-Jean Lynx	QMJHL	49	43	70	113	....	....	....	71	....	....	....	....	....	....	....	....	....	....	4	4	3	7	6	....	....	....
1989-90	Victoriaville Tigres	QMJHL	72	68	*106	*174	....	....	....	109	....	....	....	....	....	....	....	....	....	....	16	7	15	22	12	....	....	....
1990-91	**Montreal Canadiens**	**NHL**	2	1	1	2	1	1	2	0	0	0	0	3	33.3	2	1	1	0	0	....	....	....	....	....	....	....	....
	Fredericton Canadiens	AHL	69	50	51	101	....	....	....	32	....	....	....	....	....	....	....	....	....	....	9	4	7	11	8	....	....	....
1991-92	Fredericton Canadiens	AHL	55	33	38	71	....	....	....	48	....	....	....	....	....	....	....	....	....	....	7	4	5	9	10	....	....	....
	Canada	Nat-Team	7	4	2	6	....	....	....	6	....	....	....	....	....	....	....	....	....	....	....	....	....	....	....	....	....	....
	Canada	Olympics	8	1	3	4	....	....	....	4	....	....	....	....	....	....	....	....	....	....	....	....	....	....	....	....	....	....
1992-93	**Calgary Flames**	**NHL**	1	0	0	0	0	0	0	0	0	0	0	0	0.0	0	0	0	0	0	....	....	....	....	....	....	....	....
	Salt Lake Golden Eagles	IHL	75	40	60	100	....	....	....	65	....	....	....	....	....	....	....	....	....	....	....	....	....	....	....	....	....	....
1993-94	**Florida Panthers**	**NHL**	4	1	1	2	1	1	2	4	1	0	0	4	25.0	2	2	0	0	0	....	....	....	....	....	....	....	....
	Cincinnati Cyclones	IHL	74	47	42	89	....	....	....	90	....	....	....	....	....	....	....	....	....	....	11	4	8	12	14	....	....	....
1994-95	ZSC Lions Zurich	Switz.	36	27	25	52	....	....	....	22	....	....	....	....	....	....	....	....	....	....	5	4	6	10	6	....	....	....
1995-96	ZSC Lions Zurich	Switz.	11	6	8	14	....	....	....	0	....	....	....	....	....	....	....	....	....	....	....	....	....	....	....	....	....	....
	Dusseldorfer EG	Germany	17	13	8	21	....	....	....	18	....	....	....	....	....	....	....	....	....	....	13	11	5	16	14	....	....	....
1996-97	ZSC Lions Zurich	Switz.	38	27	19	46	....	....	....	26	....	....	....	....	....	....	....	....	....	....	4	1	0	1	25	....	....	....
1997-98	HC La Chaux-de-Fonds	Switz.	40	17	45	62	....	....	....	32	....	....	....	....	....	....	....	....	....	....	....	....	....	....	....	....	....	....
1998-99	**Pittsburgh Penguins**	**NHL**	8	1	0	1	1	0	1	2	0	0	0	4	25.0	1	0	5	2	–2	....	....	....	....	....	....	....	....
99-2000	HC Ambri-Piotta	Switz.	44	*25	38	63	....	....	....	32	....	....	....	....	....	....	....	....	....	....	9	5	5	10	8	....	....	....
	NHL Totals		**15**	**3**	**2**	**5**	**3**	**2**	**5**	**6**	**1**	**0**	**0**	**11**	**27.3**	**5**	**3**	**6**	**2**		....	....	....	....	....	....	....	....

• Brother of Stephan • QMJHL First All-Star Team (1990) • AHL Second All-Star Team (1991) • Won Dudley "Red" Garrett Memorial Award (Top Rookie - AHL) (1991)

Traded to **Calgary** by **Montreal** for future considerations, September 27, 1986. Signed as a free agent by **Florida**, July 26, 1993. Signed as a free agent by **Pittsburgh**, October 18, 1998.

• LEBEAU, Stephan

C – R. 5'10", 173 lbs. b: St. Jerome, Que., 2/28/1968.

Season	Club	League	GP	G	A	Pts	AG	AA	APts	PIM	PP	SH	GW	S	%	TGF	PGF	TGA	PGA	+/–	GP	G	A	Pts	PIM	PP	SH	GW
1983-84	Montreal L'est Cantonniers	QAAA	25	15	35	50	....	....	....	....	....	....	....	....	....	....	....	....	....	....	....	....	....	....	....	....	....	....
1984-85	Shawinigan Cataractes	QMJHL	66	41	38	79	....	....	....	18	....	....	....	....	....	....	....	....	....	....	9	4	5	9	4	....	....	....
	Shawinigan Cataractes	Mem-Cup	2	0	0	0	....	....	....	2	....	....	....	....	....	....	....	....	....	....	....	....	....	....	....	....	....	....
1985-86	Shawinigan Cataractes	QMJHL	72	69	77	146	....	....	....	22	....	....	....	....	....	....	....	....	....	....	5	4	2	6	4	....	....	....
1986-87	Shawinigan Cataractes	QMJHL	65	77	90	167	....	....	....	60	....	....	....	....	....	....	....	....	....	....	14	9	20	29	20	....	....	....
1987-88	Shawinigan Cataractes	QMJHL	67	*94	94	188	....	....	....	66	....	....	....	....	....	....	....	....	....	....	11	17	9	26	10	....	....	....
	Sherbrooke Canadiens	AHL	....	....	....	....	....	....	....	....	....	....	....	....	....	....	....	....	....	....	1	0	1	1	0	....	....	....
1988-89	**Montreal Canadiens**	**NHL**	1	0	1	1	0	1	1	2	0	0	0	1	0.0	1	0	0	0	1	....	....	....	....	....	....	....	....
	Sherbrooke Canadiens	AHL	78	*70	64	*134	....	....	....	47	....	....	....	....	....	....	....	....	....	....	6	1	4	5	8	....	....	....
1989-90	**Montreal Canadiens**	**NHL**	57	15	20	35	13	14	27	11	5	0	3	79	19.0	56	18	25	0	13	2	3	0	3	0	0	0	1
1990-91	Montreal Canadiens	Fr-Tour	2	1	0	1	....	....	....	0	....	....	....	....	....	....	....	....	....	....	....	....	....	....	....	....	....	....
	Montreal Canadiens	**NHL**	73	22	31	53	20	24	44	24	8	0	2	108	20.4	70	32	34	0	4	7	2	1	3	2	0	0	0
1991-92	**Montreal Canadiens**	**NHL**	77	27	31	58	25	23	48	14	13	0	5	178	15.2	81	31	34	2	18	8	1	3	4	4	1	0	0
1992-93♦	**Montreal Canadiens**	**NHL**	71	31	49	80	26	34	60	20	8	0	7	150	20.7	109	29	57	0	23	13	3	3	6	6	1	0	1
1993-94	**Montreal Canadiens**	**NHL**	34	9	7	16	8	5	13	8	4	0	2	61	14.8	26	10	16	1	1	....	....	....	....	....	....	....	....
	Mighty Ducks of Anaheim	**NHL**	22	6	4	10	6	3	9	14	2	0	1	37	16.2	13	5	13	0	–5	....	....	....	....	....	....	....	....
1994-95	**Mighty Ducks of Anaheim**	**NHL**	38	8	16	24	14	24	38	12	1	0	2	70	11.4	33	8	19	0	6	....	....	....	....	....	....	....	....

			REGULAR SEASON																		PLAYOFFS							
Season	**Club**	**League**	**GP**	**G**	**A**	**Pts**	**AG**	**AA**	**APts**	**PIM**	**PP**	**SH**	**GW**	**S**	**%**	**TGF**	**PGF**	**TGA**	**PGA**	**+/–**	**GP**	**G**	**A**	**Pts**	**PIM**	**PP**	**SH**	**GW**
1995-96	HC Lugano	Switz.	36	25	28	53	....	....	....	10	....	....	....	....	....	....	....	....	....	....	4	2	2	4	0	....	....	....
1996-97	HC Lugano	Switz.	18	14	12	26	....	....	....	12	....	....	....	....	....	....	....	....	....	....	....	....	....	....	....	....	....	....
1997-98	HC La Chaux-de-Fonds	Switz.	40	31	39	70	....	....	....	14	....	....	....	....	....	....	....	....	....	....	....	....	....	....	....	....	....	....
1998-99	HC La Chaux-de-Fonds	Switz-2	40	32	48	80	....	....	....	....	....	....	....	....	....	....	....	....	....	....	11	9	10	19	....	....	....	....
99-2000	HC Ambri-Piotta	Switz.	45	20	*47	*67	....	....	....	39	....	....	....	....	....	....	....	....	....	....	9	0	7	7	6	....	....	....
	NHL Totals		**373**	**118**	**159**	**277**	**112**	**128**	**240**	**105**	**41**	**0**	**22**	**684**	**17.3**	**389**	**133**	**198**	**3**		**30**	**9**	**7**	**16**	**12**	**2**	**0**	**2**

• Brother of Patrick • QMJHL Second All-Star Team (1987, 1988) • AHL First All-Star Team (1989) • Won Dudley "Red" Garrett Memorial Trophy (Top Rookie - AHL) (1989) • Won John B. Sollenberger Trophy (Top Scorer - AHL) (1989) • Won Les Cunningham Award (MVP - AHL) (1989)

Signed as a free agent by **Montreal**, September 27, 1986. Traded to **Anaheim** by **Montreal** for Ron Tugnutt, February 20, 1994.

• LEBLANC, Fern

Fernand C – L. 5'9", 170 lbs. b: Gaspesie, Que., 1/12/1956. Detroit's 7th, 111th overall, in 1976.

Season	Club	League	GP	G	A	Pts	AG	AA	APts	PIM	PP	SH	GW	S	%	TGF	PGF	TGA	PGA	+/–	GP	G	A	Pts	PIM	PP	SH	GW
1973-74	Sherbrooke Beavers	QMJHL	70	37	30	67	....	....	....	46	....	....	....	....	....	....	....	....	....	....	....	....	....	....	....	....	....	....
1974-75	Sherbrooke Beavers	QMJHL	22	17	12	29	....	....	....	8	....	....	....	....	....	....	....	....	....	....	....	....	....	....	....	....	....	....
1975-76	Sherbrooke Beavers	QMJHL	71	63	71	134	....	....	....	31	....	....	....	....	....	....	....	....	....	....	....	....	....	....	....	....	....	....
1976-77	**Detroit Red Wings**	**NHL**	**3**	**0**	**0**	**0**	**0**	**0**	**0**	**0**	**0**	**0**	**0**	**1**	**0.0**	**0**	**0**	**3**	**0**	**–3**	....	....	....	....	....	....	....	....
	Kalamazoo Wings	IHL	77	39	32	71	....	....	....	57	....	....	....	....	....	....	....	....	....	....	10	9	8	17	4	....	....	....
1977-78	**Detroit Red Wings**	**NHL**	**2**	**0**	**0**	**0**	**0**	**0**	**0**	**0**	**0**	**0**	**0**	**0**	**0.0**	**2**	**0**	**4**	**0**	**–2**	....	....	....	....	....	....	....	....
	Kansas City Red Wings	CHL	69	29	21	50	....	....	....	39	....	....	....	....	....	....	....	....	....	....	....	....	....	....	....	....	....	....
1978-79	**Detroit Red Wings**	**NHL**	**29**	**5**	**6**	**11**	**4**	**4**	**8**	**0**	**1**	**0**	**0**	**27**	**18.5**	**17**	**4**	**12**	**0**	**1**	....	....	....	....	....	....	....	....
	Kansas City Red Wings	CHL	35	15	26	41	....	....	....	14	....	....	....	....	....	....	....	....	....	....	....	....	....	....	....	....	....	....
1979-1982			STATISTICS NOT AVAILABLE																									
1982-83	EHC Chur	Switz-2	38	*60	36	*96	....	....	....	....	....	....	....	....	....	....	....	....	....	....	....	....	....	....	....	....	....	....
1983-84	EHC Chur	Switz-2	38	61	29	90	....	....	....	....	....	....	....	....	....	....	....	....	....	....	....	....	....	....	....	....	....	....
1984-85	EHC Chur	Switz.	36	29	17	46	....	....	....	....	....	....	....	....	....	....	....	....	....	....	....	....	....	....	....	....	....	....
1985-86	SC Herisau	Switz-2	38	*39	*35	*74	....	....	....	....	....	....	....	....	....	....	....	....	....	....	....	....	....	....	....	....	....	....
1986-87	SC Herisau	Switz-2	38	*56	46	*102	....	....	....	....	....	....	....	....	....	....	....	....	....	....	....	....	....	....	....	....	....	....
1987-88	HC Ajoie	Switz-2	38	46	41	*87	....	....	....	....	....	....	....	....	....	....	....	....	....	....	6	3	3	6	....	....	....	....
1988-89	HC Ajoie	Switz-2	5	3	3	6	....	....	....	....	....	....	....	....	....	....	....	....	....	....	....	....	....	....	....	....	....	....
	NHL Totals		**34**	**5**	**6**	**11**	**4**	**4**	**8**	**0**	**1**	**0**	**0**	**28**	**17.9**	**19**	**4**	**19**	**0**		....	....	....	....	....	....	....	....

• LEBLANC, J.P.

Jean-Paul C – L. 5'10", 170 lbs. b: South Durham, Que., 10/20/1946.

Season	Club	League	GP	G	A	Pts	AG	AA	APts	PIM	PP	SH	GW	S	%	TGF	PGF	TGA	PGA	+/–	GP	G	A	Pts	PIM	PP	SH	GW
1965-66	St. Catharines Black Hawks	OHA-Jr.	22	9	15	24	....	....	....	6	....	....	....	....	....	....	....	....	....	....	....	....	....	....	....	....	....	....
1966-67	St. Catharines Black Hawks	OHA-Jr.	48	18	26	44	....	....	....	73	....	....	....	....	....	....	....	....	....	....	6	1	1	2	23	....	....	....
	Columbus Checkers	IHL	2	1	0	1	....	....	....	2	....	....	....	....	....	....	....	....	....	....	....	....	....	....	....	....	....	....
	St. Louis Braves	CPHL	1	0	0	0	....	....	....	0	....	....	....	....	....	....	....	....	....	....	....	....	....	....	....	....	....	....
1967-68	Dallas Black Hawks	CPHL	66	19	31	50	....	....	....	83	....	....	....	....	....	....	....	....	....	....	5	1	0	1	2	....	....	....
1968-69	**Chicago Black Hawks**	**NHL**	**6**	**1**	**2**	**3**	**1**	**2**	**3**	**0**	**0**	**0**	**0**	**9**	**11.1**	**3**	**0**	**3**	**1**	**1**	....	....	....	....	....	....	....	....
	Dallas Black Hawks	CHL	67	18	34	52	....	....	....	82	....	....	....	....	....	....	....	....	....	....	11	2	5	7	35	....	....	....
1969-70	Dallas Black Hawks	CHL	68	28	35	63	....	....	....	138	....	....	....	....	....	....	....	....	....	....	....	....	....	....	....	....	....	....
	Portland Buckaroos	WHL	....	....	....	....	....	....	....	....	....	....	....	....	....	....	....	....	....	....	11	0	4	4	22	....	....	....
1970-71	Dallas Black Hawks	CHL	57	13	31	44	....	....	....	61	....	....	....	....	....	....	....	....	....	....	9	3	5	8	7	....	....	....
1971-72	Dallas Black Hawks	CHL	70	22	*68	90	....	....	....	117	....	....	....	....	....	....	....	....	....	....	12	6	7	13	21	....	....	....
1972-73	Los Angeles Sharks	WHA	77	19	50	69	....	....	....	49	....	....	....	....	....	....	....	....	....	....	6	0	5	5	2	....	....	....
1973-74	Los Angeles Sharks	WHA	78	20	46	66	....	....	....	58	....	....	....	....	....	....	....	....	....	....	....	....	....	....	....	....	....	....
1974-75	Baltimore-Michigan Stags	WHA	78	16	33	49	....	....	....	100	....	....	....	....	....	....	....	....	....	....	....	....	....	....	....	....	....	....
1975-76	Denver Invaders	WHA	15	1	5	6	....	....	....	25	....	....	....	....	....	....	....	....	....	....	....	....	....	....	....	....	....	....
	Detroit Red Wings	**NHL**	**46**	**4**	**9**	**13**	**3**	**7**	**10**	**39**	**0**	**0**	**0**	**60**	**6.7**	**23**	**2**	**39**	**13**	**–5**	....	....	....	....	....	....	....	....
1976-77	**Detroit Red Wings**	**NHL**	**74**	**7**	**11**	**18**	**6**	**8**	**14**	**40**	**0**	**0**	**2**	**77**	**9.1**	**27**	**0**	**63**	**20**	**–16**	....	....	....	....	....	....	....	....
1977-78	**Detroit Red Wings**	**NHL**	**3**	**0**	**2**	**2**	**0**	**2**	**2**	**4**	**0**	**0**	**0**	**5**	**0.0**	**3**	**1**	**2**	**1**	**1**	**2**	**0**	**0**	**0**	**0**	**0**	**0**	**0**
	Kansas City Red Wings	CHL	65	20	35	55	....	....	....	42	....	....	....	....	....	....	....	....	....	....	....	....	....	....	....	....	....	....
1978-79	**Detroit Red Wings**	**NHL**	**24**	**2**	**6**	**8**	**2**	**4**	**6**	**4**	**2**	**0**	**0**	**27**	**7.4**	**10**	**4**	**19**	**6**	**–7**	....	....	....	....	....	....	....	....
	Kansas City Red Wings	CHL	53	20	33	53	....	....	....	72	....	....	....	....	....	....	....	....	....	....	4	0	0	0	0	....	....	....
1979-80	Adirondack Red Wings	AHL	75	16	42	58	....	....	....	69	....	....	....	....	....	....	....	....	....	....	4	1	1	2	2	....	....	....
1980-81	Adirondack Red Wings	AHL	77	12	36	48	....	....	....	106	....	....	....	....	....	....	....	....	....	....	17	5	7	12	27	....	....	....
1981-82	Kalamazoo Wings	IHL	DID NOT PLAY – COACHING																									
	NHL Totals		**153**	**14**	**30**	**44**	**12**	**23**	**35**	**87**	**2**	**0**	**2**	**178**	**7.9**	**66**	**7**	**126**	**41**		**2**	**0**	**0**	**0**	**0**	**0**	**0**	**0**
	Other Major League Totals		248	56	134	190	....	....	....	232	....	....	....	....	....	....	....	....	....	....	6	0	5	5	2	....	....	....

CHL Second All-Star Team (1972, 1979) • CHL First All-Star Team (1978)

Selected by **LA Sharks** in 1972 WHA General Player Draft, February 12, 1972. Signed as a free agent by **Michigan** (WHA) after **LA Sharks** (WHA) franchise folded, April 11, 1974. Traded to **Detroit** by **Chicago** for Detroit's 2nd round choice (Jean Savard) in 1977 Amateur Draft, November 20, 1975.

• LeBLANC, John

John Glenn RW – L. 6'1", 190 lbs. b: Campbellton, N.B., 1/21/1964.

Season	Club	League	GP	G	A	Pts	AG	AA	APts	PIM	PP	SH	GW	S	%	TGF	PGF	TGA	PGA	+/–	GP	G	A	Pts	PIM	PP	SH	GW
1982-83	Mount Allison University	AUAA	20	21	26	47	....	....	....	10	....	....	....	....	....	....	....	....	....	....	....	....	....	....	....	....	....	....
1983-84	Hull Olympiques	QMJHL	69	39	35	74	....	....	....	32	....	....	....	....	....	....	....	....	....	....	....	....	....	....	....	....	....	....
1984-85	University of New Brunswick	AUAA	24	25	32	57	....	....	....	24	....	....	....	....	....	....	....	....	....	....	....	....	....	....	....	....	....	....
1985-86	University of New Brunswick	AUAA	24	*38	26	*64	....	....	....	34	....	....	....	....	....	....	....	....	....	....	....	....	....	....	....	....	....	....
	Canada	Nat-Team	3	1	1	2	....	....	....	0	....	....	....	....	....	....	....	....	....	....	....	....	....	....	....	....	....	....
1986-87	**Vancouver Canucks**	**NHL**	**2**	**1**	**0**	**1**	**1**	**0**	**1**	**0**	**0**	**0**	**0**	**4**	**25.0**	**2**	**0**	**1**	**0**	**1**	....	....	....	....	....	....	....	....
	Fredericton Express	AHL	75	40	30	70	....	....	....	27	....	....	....	....	....	....	....	....	....	....	....	....	....	....	....	....	....	....
1987-88	**Vancouver Canucks**	**NHL**	**41**	**12**	**10**	**22**	**10**	**7**	**17**	**18**	**3**	**0**	**1**	**86**	**14.0**	**35**	**10**	**38**	**1**	**–12**	....	....	....	....	....	....	....	....
	Fredericton Express	AHL	35	26	25	51	....	....	....	54	....	....	....	....	....	....	....	....	....	....	15	6	7	13	34	....	....	....
1988-89	Milwaukee Admirals	IHL	61	39	31	70	....	....	....	42	....	....	....	....	....	....	....	....	....	....	....	....	....	....	....	....	....	....
	Edmonton Oilers	**NHL**	**2**	**1**	**0**	**1**	**1**	**0**	**1**	**0**	**0**	**0**	**0**	**5**	**20.0**	**1**	**0**	**1**	**0**	**0**	**1**	**0**	**0**	**0**	**0**	**0**	**0**	**0**
	Cape Breton Oilers	AHL	3	4	0	4	....	....	....	0	....	....	....	....	....	....	....	....	....	....	....	....	....	....	....	....	....	....
1989-90	Cape Breton Oilers	AHL	77	*54	34	88	....	....	....	50	....	....	....	....	....	....	....	....	....	....	6	4	0	4	4	....	....	....
1990-91	**Edmonton Oilers**	**NHL**	DID NOT PLAY – SUSPENDED																									
1991-92	**Winnipeg Jets**	**NHL**	**16**	**6**	**1**	**7**	**5**	**1**	**6**	**6**	**5**	**0**	**1**	**32**	**18.8**	**10**	**9**	**7**	**0**	**–6**	....	....	....	....	....	....	....	....
	Moncton Hawks	AHL	56	31	22	53	....	....	....	24	....	....	....	....	....	....	....	....	....	....	10	3	2	5	8	....	....	....
1992-93	**Winnipeg Jets**	**NHL**	**3**	**0**	**0**	**0**	**0**	**0**	**0**	**2**	**0**	**0**	**0**	**5**	**0.0**	**0**	**0**	**0**	**0**	**0**	....	....	....	....	....	....	....	....
	Moncton Hawks	AHL	77	48	40	88	....	....	....	29	....	....	....	....	....	....	....	....	....	....	5	2	1	3	6	....	....	....
1993-94	**Winnipeg Jets**	**NHL**	**17**	**6**	**2**	**8**	**6**	**2**	**8**	**2**	**1**	**1**	**1**	**29**	**20.7**	**9**	**3**	**8**	**0**	**–2**	....	....	....	....	....	....	....	....
	Moncton Hawks	AHL	41	25	26	51	....	....	....	38	....	....	....	....	....	....	....	....	....	....	20	3	6	9	6	....	....	....
1994-95	**Winnipeg Jets**	**NHL**	**2**	**0**	**0**	**0**	**0**	**0**	**0**	**0**	**0**	**0**	**0**	**0**	**0.0**	**0**	**0**	**0**	**0**	**0**	....	....	....	....	....	....	....	....
	Springfield Falcons	AHL	65	39	34	73	....	....	....	32	....	....	....	....	....	....	....	....	....	....	....	....	....	....	....	....	....	....
1995-96	Orlando Solar Bears	IHL	60	22	24	46	....	....	....	20	....	....	....	....	....	....	....	....	....	....	....	....	....	....	....	....	....	....
	Fort Wayne Komets	IHL	16	12	11	23	....	....	....	4	....	....	....	....	....	....	....	....	....	....	5	0	2	2	14	....	....	....
1996-97	Fort Wayne Komets	IHL	77	30	31	61	....	....	....	22	....	....	....	....	....	....	....	....	....	....	....	....	....	....	....	....	....	....
1997-98	Utah Grizzlies	IHL	69	25	17	42	....	....	....	16	....	....	....	....	....	....	....	....	....	....	2	0	0	0	2	....	....	....
1998-99			OUT OF HOCKEY – RETIRED																									
99-2000	Campbellton Tigers	MJrHL	DID NOT PLAY – COACHING																									
	Causapscal Forestiers	QPSHL	2	4	1	5	....	....	....	0	....	....	....	....	....	....	....	....	....	....	....	....	....	....	....	....	....	....
	NHL Totals		**83**	**26**	**13**	**39**	**23**	**10**	**33**	**28**	**9**	**1**	**3**	**161**	**16.1**	**57**	**22**	**55**	**1**		**1**	**0**	**0**	**0**	**0**	**0**	**0**	**0**

Canadian University Player of the Year (1986)

Signed as a free agent by **Vancouver**, April 12, 1986. Traded to **Edmonton** by **Vancouver** with Vancouver's 5th round choice (Peter White) in 1989 Entry Draft for Doug Smith and Greg C. Adams, March 7, 1989. • Sat out entire 1990-91 season after failing to come to contract terms with Edmonton. Traded to **Winnipeg** by **Edmonton** with Edmonton's 10th round choice (Teemu Numminen) in 1992 Entry Draft for Winnipeg's 5th round choice (Ryan Haggerty) in 1991 Entry Draft, June 12, 1991.

• LeBOUTILLIER, Peter

RW – R. 6'1", 205 lbs. b: Minnedosa, Man., 1/11/1975. Anaheim's 5th, 133rd overall, in 1995.

Season	Club	League	GP	G	A	Pts	AG	AA	APts	PIM	PP	SH	GW	S	%	TGF	PGF	TGA	PGA	+/–	Playoffs GP	G	A	Pts	PIM	PP	SH	GW
1989-90	Souris Southwest Bantams	MAHA	55	91	109	200	....	....	....	64	....	....	....	....	....	....	....	....	....	....	....	....	....	....	....	....	....	....
1990-91	Souris Southwest Cougars	MAHA	10	7	12	19	....	....	....	6	....	....	....	....	....	....	....	....	....	....	....	....	....	....	....	....	....	....
1991-92	Neepawa Natives	MJHL	35	11	14	25	....	....	....	99	....	....	....	....	....	....	....	....	....	....	....	....	....	....	....	....	....	....
	Brandon Wheat Kings	WHL	2	0	0	0	....	....	....	5	....	....	....	....	....	....	....	....	....	....	....	....	....	....	....	....	....	....
1992-93	Red Deer Rebels	WHL	67	8	26	34	....	....	....	284	....	....	....	....	....	....	....	....	....	....	2	0	1	1	5	....	....	....
1993-94	Red Deer Rebels	WHL	66	19	20	39	....	....	....	300	....	....	....	....	....	....	....	....	....	....	2	0	1	1	4	....	....	....
1994-95	Red Deer Rebels	WHL	59	27	16	43	....	....	....	159	....	....	....	....	....	....	....	....	....	....	....	....	....	....	....	....	....	....
1995-96	Baltimore Bandits	AHL	68	7	9	16	....	....	....	228	....	....	....	....	....	....	....	....	....	....	11	0	0	0	33	....	....	....
1996-97	**Mighty Ducks of Anaheim**	**NHL**	**23**	**1**	**0**	**1**	**1**	**0**	**1**	**121**	**0**	**0**	**0**	**5**	**20.0**	**2**	**0**	**2**	**0**	**0**	....	....	....	....	....	....	....	....
	Baltimore Bandits	AHL	47	6	12	18	....	....	....	175	....	....	....	....	....	....	....	....	....	....	....	....	....	....	....	....	....	....
1997-98	**Mighty Ducks of Anaheim**	**NHL**	**12**	**1**	**1**	**2**	**1**	**1**	**2**	**55**	**0**	**0**	**0**	**6**	**16.7**	**2**	**0**	**3**	**0**	**–1**	....	....	....	....	....	....	....	....
	Cincinnati Mighty Ducks	AHL	51	9	11	20	....	....	....	143	....	....	....	....	....	....	....	....	....	....	....	....	....	....	....	....	....	....
1998-99	Cincinnati Mighty Ducks	AHL	63	12	12	24	....	....	....	189	....	....	....	....	....	....	....	....	....	....	3	0	0	0	2	....	....	....
99-2000	Cincinnati Mighty Ducks	AHL	19	2	1	3	....	....	....	69	....	....	....	....	....	....	....	....	....	....	....	....	....	....	....	....	....	....
	NHL Totals		**35**	**2**	**1**	**3**	**2**	**1**	**3**	**176**	**0**	**0**	**0**	**11**	**18.2**	**4**	**0**	**5**	**0**		....	....	....	....	....	....	....	....

• Re-entered NHL draft. Originally NY Islanders' 6th choice, 144th overall, in 1993 Entry Draft.

• LECAINE, Bill

William Joseph LW – R. 6', 172 lbs. b: Moose Jaw, Sask., 3/11/1940.

Season	Club	League	GP	G	A	Pts	AG	AA	APts	PIM	PP	SH	GW	S	%	TGF	PGF	TGA	PGA	+/–	Playoffs GP	G	A	Pts	PIM	PP	SH	GW
1955-56	Regina Pats	SJHL	1	1	1	2	....	....	....	0	....	....	....	....	....	....	....	....	....	....	....	....	....	....	....	....	....	....
	Regina Pats	Mem-Cup	7	0	1	1	....	....	....	7	....	....	....	....	....	....	....	....	....	....	....	....	....	....	....	....	....	....
1956-57	Regina Pats	SJHL	48	20	22	42	....	....	....	21	....	....	....	....	....	....	....	....	....	....	7	2	0	2	2	....	....	....
1957-58	Regina Pats	SJHL	39	16	20	36	....	....	....	22	....	....	....	....	....	....	....	....	....	....	12	5	8	13	18	....	....	....
	Regina Pats	Mem-Cup	15	3	4	7	....	....	....	8	....	....	....	....	....	....	....	....	....	....	....	....	....	....	....	....	....	....
	Regina Pats	Mem-Cup	16	5	5	10	....	....	....	10	....	....	....	....	....	....	....	....	....	....	....	....	....	....	....	....	....	....
1958-59	University of North Dakota	WCHA	DID NOT PLAY – FRESHMAN																									
1959-60	Minneapolis Millers	IHL	56	25	32	57	....	....	....	62	....	....	....	....	....	....	....	....	....	....	6	1	2	3	0	....	....	....
1960-61	Minneapolis Millers	IHL	68	35	47	82	....	....	....	61	....	....	....	....	....	....	....	....	....	....	8	2	4	6	7	....	....	....
1961-62	Minneapolis–Indianapolis	IHL	54	24	39	63	....	....	....	77	....	....	....	....	....	....	....	....	....	....	....	....	....	....	....	....	....	....
	Portland Buckaroos	WHL	2	0	0	0	....	....	....	0	....	....	....	....	....	....	....	....	....	....	....	....	....	....	....	....	....	....
1962-63	Port Huron Flags	IHL	61	30	43	73	....	....	....	93	....	....	....	....	....	....	....	....	....	....	....	....	....	....	....	....	....	....
1963-64	Port Huron Flags	IHL	70	28	59	87	....	....	....	110	....	....	....	....	....	....	....	....	....	....	7	1	2	3	*42	....	....	....
1964-65	Port Huron Flags	IHL	66	42	59	101	....	....	....	151	....	....	....	....	....	....	....	....	....	....	7	5	4	9	11	....	....	....
1965-66	Port Huron Flags	IHL	65	41	75	116	....	....	....	178	....	....	....	....	....	....	....	....	....	....	7	5	8	13	29	....	....	....
1966-67	Port Huron Flags	IHL	39	26	38	64	....	....	....	160	....	....	....	....	....	....	....	....	....	....	....	....	....	....	....	....	....	....
1967-68	Baltimore Clippers	AHL	69	15	22	37	....	....	....	28	....	....	....	....	....	....	....	....	....	....	....	....	....	....	....	....	....	....
1968-69	**Pittsburgh Penguins**	**NHL**	**4**	**0**	**0**	**0**	**0**	**0**	**0**	**0**	**0**	**0**	**0**	**1**	**0.0**	**0**	**0**	**0**	**0**	**0**	....	....	....	....	....	....	....	....
	Amarillo Wranglers	CHL	51	17	22	39	....	....	....	60	....	....	....	....	....	....	....	....	....	....	....	....	....	....	....	....	....	....
1969-70	Port Huron Flags	IHL	47	25	29	54	....	....	....	100	....	....	....	....	....	....	....	....	....	....	14	5	8	13	8	....	....	....
1970-71	Port Huron Flags	IHL	68	26	30	56	....	....	....	74	....	....	....	....	....	....	....	....	....	....	14	2	13	15	56	....	....	....
1971-72	Port Huron Wings	IHL	39	15	29	44	....	....	....	52	....	....	....	....	....	....	....	....	....	....	14	2	5	7	38	....	....	....
1972-73	Port Huron Wings	IHL	60	28	38	66	....	....	....	63	....	....	....	....	....	....	....	....	....	....	11	3	3	6	18	....	....	....
1973-74			OUT OF HOCKEY – RETIRED																									
1974-75	Port Huron Flags	IHL	19	4	5	9	....	....	....	28	....	....	....	....	....	....	....	....	....	....	....	....	....	....	....	....	....	....
	NHL Totals		**4**	**0**	**0**	**0**	**0**	**0**	**0**	**0**	**0**	**0**	**0**	**1**	**0.0**	**0**	**0**	**0**	**0**		....	....	....	....	....	....	....	....

IHL First All-Star Team (1963, 1966) • IHL Second All-Star Team (1965, 1967, 1973)

Loaned to **Indianapolis** (IHL) by **Minneapolis** (IHL) for the loan of Dan Summers, January, 1962. Traded to **Port Huron** (IHL) by **Minneapolis** (IHL) for Larry Hale, October, 1962. Signed as a free agent by **Pittsburgh**, August, 1967.

• LECAVALIER, Vincent

C – L. 6'4", 180 lbs. b: Ile Bizard, Que., 4/21/1980. Tampa Bay's 1st, 1st overall, in 1998.

Season	Club	League	GP	G	A	Pts	AG	AA	APts	PIM	PP	SH	GW	S	%	TGF	PGF	TGA	PGA	+/–	Playoffs GP	G	A	Pts	PIM	PP	SH	GW
1995-96	Notre Dame Midget Hounds	SAHA	22	52	52	104	....	....	....	....	....	....	....	....	....	....	....	....	....	....	....	....	....	....	....	....	....	....
1996-97	Rimouski L'Oceanic	QMJHL	64	42	61	103	....	....	....	38	....	....	....	....	....	....	....	....	....	....	4	4	3	7	2	....	....	....
1997-98	Rimouski L'Oceanic	QMJHL	58	44	71	115	....	....	....	117	....	....	....	....	....	....	....	....	....	....	18	*15	*26	*41	46	....	....	....
1998-99	**Tampa Bay Lightning**	**NHL**	**82**	**13**	**15**	**28**	**15**	**14**	**29**	**23**	**2**	**0**	**2**	**125**	**10.4**	**44**	**12**	**51**	**0**	**–19**	....	....	....	....	....	....	....	....
99-2000	**Tampa Bay Lightning**	**NHL**	**80**	**25**	**42**	**67**	**28**	**39**	**67**	**43**	**6**	**0**	**3**	**166**	**15.1**	**90**	**39**	**79**	**3**	**–25**	....	....	....	....	....	....	....	....
	NHL Totals		**162**	**38**	**57**	**95**	**43**	**53**	**96**	**66**	**8**	**0**	**5**	**291**	**13.1**	**134**	**51**	**130**	**3**		....	....	....	....	....	....	....	....

QMJHL First All-Star Team (1998) • Canadian Major Junior First All-Star Team (1998) • Canadian Major Junior Rookie of the Year (1997)

• LeCLAIR, John

LW – L. 6'3", 226 lbs. b: St. Albans, VT, 7/5/1969. Montreal's 2nd, 33rd overall, in 1987.

Season	Club	League	GP	G	A	Pts	AG	AA	APts	PIM	PP	SH	GW	S	%	TGF	PGF	TGA	PGA	+/–	Playoffs GP	G	A	Pts	PIM	PP	SH	GW
1985-86	Bellows Free Academy	Hi-School	22	41	28	69	....	....	....	14	....	....	....	....	....	....	....	....	....	....	....	....	....	....	....	....	....	....
1986-87	Bellows Free Academy	Hi-School	23	44	40	84	....	....	....	14	....	....	....	....	....	....	....	....	....	....	....	....	....	....	....	....	....	....
1987-88	University of Vermont	ECAC	31	12	22	34	....	....	....	62	....	....	....	....	....	....	....	....	....	....	....	....	....	....	....	....	....	....
	United States	WJC-A	7	4	2	6	....	....	....	12	....	....	....	....	....	....	....	....	....	....	....	....	....	....	....	....	....	....
1988-89	University of Vermont	ECAC	18	9	12	21	....	....	....	40	....	....	....	....	....	....	....	....	....	....	....	....	....	....	....	....	....	....
	United States	WJC-A	7	6	4	10	....	....	....	12	....	....	....	....	....	....	....	....	....	....	....	....	....	....	....	....	....	....
1989-90	University of Vermont	ECAC	10	10	6	16	....	....	....	38	....	....	....	....	....	....	....	....	....	....	....	....	....	....	....	....	....	....
1990-91	University of Vermont	ECAC	33	25	20	45	....	....	....	58	....	....	....	....	....	....	....	....	....	....	....	....	....	....	....	....	....	....
	Montreal Canadiens	**NHL**	**10**	**2**	**5**	**7**	**2**	**4**	**6**	**2**	**0**	**0**	**1**	**12**	**16.7**	**8**	**0**	**7**	**0**	**1**	**3**	**0**	**0**	**0**	**0**	**0**	**0**	**0**
1991-92	**Montreal Canadiens**	**NHL**	**59**	**8**	**11**	**19**	**7**	**8**	**15**	**14**	**3**	**0**	**0**	**73**	**11.0**	**26**	**4**	**17**	**0**	**5**	**8**	**1**	**1**	**2**	**4**	**0**	**0**	**0**
	Fredericton Canadiens	AHL	8	7	7	14	....	....	....	10	....	....	....	....	....	....	....	....	....	....	2	0	0	0	4	....	....	....
1992-93♦	**Montreal Canadiens**	**NHL**	**72**	**19**	**25**	**44**	**16**	**17**	**33**	**33**	**2**	**0**	**2**	**139**	**13.7**	**61**	**6**	**45**	**1**	**11**	**20**	**4**	**6**	**10**	**14**	**0**	**0**	**3**
1993-94	**Montreal Canadiens**	**NHL**	**74**	**19**	**24**	**43**	**18**	**19**	**37**	**32**	**1**	**0**	**1**	**153**	**12.4**	**63**	**9**	**37**	**0**	**17**	**7**	**2**	**1**	**3**	**8**	**1**	**0**	**0**
1994-95	**Montreal Canadiens**	**NHL**	**9**	**1**	**4**	**5**	**2**	**6**	**8**	**10**	**1**	**0**	**0**	**18**	**5.6**	**8**	**3**	**8**	**2**	**–1**	....	....	....	....	....	....	....	....
	Philadelphia Flyers	**NHL**	**37**	**25**	**24**	**49**	**44**	**35**	**79**	**20**	**5**	**0**	**7**	**113**	**22.1**	**72**	**22**	**29**	**0**	**21**	**15**	**5**	**7**	**12**	**4**	**1**	**0**	**1**
1995-96	**Philadelphia Flyers**	**NHL**	**82**	**51**	**46**	**97**	**50**	**38**	**88**	**64**	**19**	**0**	**10**	**270**	**18.9**	**141**	**57**	**63**	**0**	**21**	**11**	**6**	**5**	**11**	**6**	**4**	**0**	**1**
1996-97	United States	W-Cup	7	6	4	10	....	....	....	6	....	....	....	....	....	....	....	....	....	....	....	....	....	....	....	....	....	....
	Philadelphia Flyers	**NHL**	**82**	**50**	**47**	**97**	**53**	**42**	**95**	**58**	**10**	**0**	**5**	**324**	**15.4**	**153**	**43**	**66**	**0**	**44**	**19**	**9**	**12**	**21**	**10**	**4**	**0**	**3**
1997-98	**Philadelphia Flyers**	**NHL**	**82**	**51**	**36**	**87**	**60**	**35**	**95**	**32**	**16**	**0**	**9**	**303**	**16.8**	**124**	**45**	**49**	**0**	**30**	**5**	**1**	**1**	**2**	**8**	**1**	**0**	**1**
	United States	Olympics	4	0	1	1	....	....	....	0	....	....	....	....	....	....	....	....	....	....	....	....	....	....	....	....	....	....
1998-99	**Philadelphia Flyers**	**NHL**	**76**	**43**	**47**	**90**	**51**	**45**	**96**	**30**	**16**	**0**	**7**	**246**	**17.5**	**131**	**48**	**47**	**0**	**36**	**6**	**3**	**0**	**3**	**12**	**2**	**0**	**0**
99-2000	**Philadelphia Flyers**	**NHL**	**82**	**40**	**37**	**77**	**45**	**34**	**79**	**36**	**13**	**0**	**7**	**249**	**16.1**	**114**	**47**	**60**	**1**	**8**	**18**	**6**	**7**	**13**	**6**	**4**	**0**	**2**
	NHL Totals		**665**	**309**	**306**	**615**	**348**	**283**	**631**	**331**	**86**	**0**	**49**	**1900**	**16.3**	**901**	**284**	**428**	**4**		**112**	**37**	**40**	**77**	**72**	**17**	**0**	**11**

ECAC Second All-Star Team (1991) • NHL First All-Star Team (1995, 1998) • NHL Second All-Star Team (1996, 1997, 1999) • World Cup All-Star Team (1996) • Won Bud Light Plus/Minus Award (1997) • Won Bud Ice Plus/Minus Award (1999) • Played in NHL All-Star Game (1996, 1997, 1998, 1999, 2000)

• Missed majority of 1989-90 and 1990-91 seasons recovering from knee surgery, January 20, 1990. Traded to **Philadelphia** by **Montreal** with Eric Desjardins and Gilbert Dionne for Mark Recchi and Philadelphia's 3rd round choice (Martin Hohenberger) in 1995 Entry Draft, February 9, 1995.

• LECLERC, Mike

LW – L. 6'1", 205 lbs. b: Winnipeg, Man., 11/10/1976. Anaheim's 3rd, 55th overall, in 1995.

Season	Club	League	GP	G	A	Pts	AG	AA	APts	PIM	PP	SH	GW	S	%	TGF	PGF	TGA	PGA	+/–	Playoffs GP	G	A	Pts	PIM	PP	SH	GW
1990-91	Winnipeg Hawks	MAHA	STATISTICS NOT AVAILABLE																									
1991-92	St. Boniface Saints	MJHL	43	16	12	28	....	....	....	25	....	....	....	....	....	....	....	....	....	....	....	....	....	....	....	....	....	....
	Victoria Cougars	WHL	2	0	0	0	....	....	....	0	....	....	....	....	....	....	....	....	....	....	....	....	....	....	....	....	....	....
1992-93	Victoria Cougars	WHL	70	4	11	15	....	....	....	118	....	....	....	....	....	....	....	....	....	....	....	....	....	....	....	....	....	....
1993-94	Victoria Cougars	WHL	68	29	11	40	....	....	....	112	....	....	....	....	....	....	....	....	....	....	....	....	....	....	....	....	....	....
1994-95	Prince George Cougars	WHL	43	20	36	56	....	....	....	78	....	....	....	....	....	....	....	....	....	....	....	....	....	....	....	....	....	....
	Brandon Wheat Kings	WHL	23	5	8	13	....	....	....	50	....	....	....	....	....	....	....	....	....	....	18	10	6	16	33	....	....	....
	Brandon Wheat Kings	Mem-Cup	4	0	1	1	....	....	....	2	....	....	....	....	....	....	....	....	....	....	....	....	....	....	....	....	....	....

Season	Club	League	GP	G	A	Pts	AG	AA	APts	PIM	PP	SH	GW	S	%	TGF	PGF	TGA	PGA	+/-	GP	G	A	Pts	PIM	PP	SH	GW
			REGULAR SEASON																		PLAYOFFS							
1995-96	Brandon Wheat Kings	WHL	71	58	53	111	....	....	....	161	....	....	....	....	....	....	....	....	....	....	19	6	19	25	25	....	....	....
	Brandon Wheat Kings	Mem-Cup	4	1	3	4	....	....	....	12	....	....	....	....	....	....	....	....	....	....	....	....	....	....	....	....	....	....
1996-97	**Mighty Ducks of Anaheim**	**NHL**	**5**	**1**	**1**	**2**	**1**	**1**	**2**	**0**	**0**	**0**	**1**	**3**	**33.3**	**2**	**0**	**0**	**0**	**2**	**1**	**0**	**0**	**0**	**0**	**0**	**0**	**0**
	Baltimore Bandits	AHL	71	29	27	56	....	....	....	134	....	....	....	....	....	....	....	....	....	....	....	....	....	....	....	....	....	....
1997-98	**Mighty Ducks of Anaheim**	**NHL**	**7**	**0**	**0**	**0**	**0**	**0**	**0**	**6**	**0**	**0**	**0**	**11**	**0.0**	**0**	**0**	**6**	**0**	**–6**	....	....	....	....	....	....	....	....
	Cincinnati Mighty Ducks	AHL	48	18	22	40	....	....	....	83	....	....	....	....	....	....	....	....	....	....	....	....	....	....	....	....	....	....
1998-99	**Mighty Ducks of Anaheim**	**NHL**	**7**	**0**	**0**	**0**	**0**	**0**	**0**	**4**	**0**	**0**	**0**	**1**	**0.0**	**0**	**0**	**2**	**0**	**–2**	**1**	**0**	**0**	**0**	**0**	**0**	**0**	**0**
	Cincinnati Mighty Ducks	AHL	65	25	28	53	....	....	....	153	....	....	....	....	....	....	....	....	....	....	3	0	1	1	19	....	....	....
99-2000	**Mighty Ducks of Anaheim**	**NHL**	**69**	**8**	**11**	**19**	**9**	**10**	**19**	**70**	**0**	**0**	**2**	**105**	**7.6**	**27**	**1**	**43**	**2**	**–15**	....	....	....	....	....	....	....	....
	NHL Totals		**88**	**9**	**12**	**21**	**10**	**11**	**21**	**80**	**0**	**0**	**3**	**120**	**7.5**	**29**	**1**	**51**	**2**		**2**	**0**	**0**	**0**	**0**	**0**	**0**	**0**

WHL East Second All-Star Team (1996)

• LeCLERC, Rene

Renald RW – R. 5'11", 165 lbs. b: Ville de Vanier, Que., 11/12/1947. Detroit's 4th, 19th overall, in 1964.

Season	Club	League	GP	G	A	Pts	AG	AA	APts	PIM	PP	SH	GW	S	%	TGF	PGF	TGA	PGA	+/-	GP	G	A	Pts	PIM	PP	SH	GW
1963-64	Hamilton Kilty B's	OHA-B	STATISTICS NOT AVAILABLE																									
	Hamilton Red Wings	OHA-Jr.	3	0	0	0	....	....	....	0	....	....	....	....	....	....	....	....	....	....	....	....	....	....	....	....	....	....
1964-65	Hamilton Red Wings	OHA-Jr.	5	0	0	0	....	....	....	8	....	....	....	....	....	....	....	....	....	....	....	....	....	....	....	....	....	....
1965-66	Hamilton Red Wings	OHA-Jr.	21	4	5	9	....	....	....	34	....	....	....	....	....	....	....	....	....	....	....	....	....	....	....	....	....	....
1966-67	Hamilton Red Wings	OHA-Jr.	48	17	27	44	....	....	....	89	....	....	....	....	....	....	....	....	....	....	17	10	12	22	43	....	....	....
1967-68	Hamilton Red Wings	OHA-Jr.	54	31	42	73	....	....	....	119	....	....	....	....	....	....	....	....	....	....	11	10	5	15	19	....	....	....
	Fort Worth Wings	CPHL	....	....	....	....	....	....	....	....	....	....	....	....	....	....	....	....	....	....	6	1	1	2	2	....	....	....
1968-69	**Detroit Red Wings**	**NHL**	**43**	**2**	**3**	**5**	**2**	**3**	**5**	**62**	**0**	**0**	**0**	**38**	**5.3**	**6**	**0**	**14**	**0**	**–8**	....	....	....	....	....	....	....	....
	Fort Worth Wings	CHL	22	4	5	9	....	....	....	32	....	....	....	....	....	....	....	....	....	....	....	....	....	....	....	....	....	....
1969-70	Fort Worth Wings	CHL	9	1	2	3	....	....	....	27	....	....	....	....	....	....	....	....	....	....	....	....	....	....	....	....	....	....
	Cleveland Barons	AHL	61	16	20	36	....	....	....	108	....	....	....	....	....	....	....	....	....	....	....	....	....	....	....	....	....	....
1970-71	**Detroit Red Wings**	**NHL**	**44**	**8**	**8**	**16**	**8**	**7**	**15**	**43**	**3**	**0**	**1**	**56**	**14.3**	**19**	**4**	**27**	**9**	**–3**	....	....	....	....	....	....	....	....
	Fort Worth Wings	CHL	23	8	14	22	....	....	....	28	....	....	....	....	....	....	....	....	....	....	....	....	....	....	....	....	....	....
1971-72	Fort Worth Wings	CHL	2	0	0	0	....	....	....	0	....	....	....	....	....	....	....	....	....	....	....	....	....	....	....	....	....	....
	San Diego Gulls	WHL	28	6	7	13	....	....	....	39	....	....	....	....	....	....	....	....	....	....	....	....	....	....	....	....	....	....
	Tidewater Red Wings	AHL	31	6	6	12	....	....	....	57	....	....	....	....	....	....	....	....	....	....	....	....	....	....	....	....	....	....
1972-73	Quebec Nordiques	WHA	67	24	28	52	....	....	....	111	....	....	....	....	....	....	....	....	....	....	....	....	....	....	....	....	....	....
1973-74	Quebec Nordiques	WHA	53	17	27	44	....	....	....	84	....	....	....	....	....	....	....	....	....	....	....	....	....	....	....	....	....	....
1974-75	Quebec Nordiques	WHA	73	18	32	50	....	....	....	85	....	....	....	....	....	....	....	....	....	....	14	7	7	14	41	....	....	....
1975-76	Quebec Nordiques	WHA	42	15	17	32	....	....	....	35	....	....	....	....	....	....	....	....	....	....	....	....	....	....	....	....	....	....
	Indianapolis Racers	WHA	40	18	21	39	....	....	....	52	....	....	....	....	....	....	....	....	....	....	7	2	3	5	7	....	....	....
1976-77	Indianapolis Racers	WHA	68	25	30	55	....	....	....	43	....	....	....	....	....	....	....	....	....	....	9	1	1	2	4	....	....	....
1977-78	Indianapolis Racers	WHA	60	12	15	27	....	....	....	31	....	....	....	....	....	....	....	....	....	....	....	....	....	....	....	....	....	....
1978-79	Indianapolis Racers	WHA	22	5	7	12	....	....	....	12	....	....	....	....	....	....	....	....	....	....	....	....	....	....	....	....	....	....
	Quebec Nordiques	WHA	23	0	0	0	....	....	....	8	....	....	....	....	....	....	....	....	....	....	4	0	0	0	0	....	....	....
	NHL Totals		**87**	**10**	**11**	**21**	**10**	**10**	**20**	**105**	**3**	**0**	**1**	**94**	**10.6**	**25**	**4**	**41**	**9**		....	....	....	....	....	....	....	....
	Other Major League Totals		448	134	177	311	....	....	....	461	....	....	....	....	....	....	....	....	....	....	34	10	11	21	52	....	....	....

Selected by **Quebec** (WHA) in 1972 WHA General Player Draft, February 12, 1972. Traded to **Indianapolis** (WHA) by **Quebec** (WHA) for Bill Prentice, January, 1976. Signed as a free agent by **Quebec** (WHA) after **Indianapolis** (WHA) franchise folded, December 18, 1978.

• LECUYER, Doug

Douglas J. LW – L. 5'9", 180 lbs. b: Wainwright, Alta., 3/10/1958. Chicago's 2nd, 29th overall, in 1978.

Season	Club	League	GP	G	A	Pts	AG	AA	APts	PIM	PP	SH	GW	S	%	TGF	PGF	TGA	PGA	+/-	GP	G	A	Pts	PIM	PP	SH	GW
1972-73	Edmonton Mets	AJHL	STATISTICS NOT AVAILABLE																									
1973-74	Edmonton Oil Kings	WCJHL	54	15	22	37	....	....	....	130	....	....	....	....	....	....	....	....	....	....	5	1	1	2	16	....	....	....
1974-75	Edmonton Oil Kings	WCJHL	67	33	39	72	....	....	....	284	....	....	....	....	....	....	....	....	....	....	....	....	....	....	....	....	....	....
1975-76	Edmonton Oil Kings	WCJHL	61	40	32	72	....	....	....	335	....	....	....	....	....	....	....	....	....	....	5	2	2	4	52	....	....	....
1976-77	Portland Winter Hawks	WCJHL	5	6	4	10	....	....	....	10	....	....	....	....	....	....	....	....	....	....	....	....	....	....	....	....	....	....
	Calgary Centennials	WCJHL	50	40	42	82	....	....	....	216	....	....	....	....	....	....	....	....	....	....	....	....	....	....	....	....	....	....
1977-78	Portland Winter Hawks	WCJHL	65	43	46	89	....	....	....	342	....	....	....	....	....	....	....	....	....	....	....	....	....	....	....	....	....	....
1978-79	**Chicago Black Hawks**	**NHL**	**2**	**1**	**0**	**1**	**1**	**0**	**1**	**0**	**0**	**0**	**0**	**9**	**11.1**	**1**	**0**	**2**	**0**	**–1**	....	....	....	....	....	....	....	....
	New Brunswick Hawks	AHL	43	18	29	47	....	....	....	125	....	....	....	....	....	....	....	....	....	....	....	....	....	....	....	....	....	....
1979-80	**Chicago Black Hawks**	**NHL**	**53**	**3**	**10**	**13**	**3**	**7**	**10**	**59**	**0**	**0**	**1**	**75**	**4.0**	**25**	**2**	**30**	**0**	**–7**	**7**	**4**	**0**	**4**	**15**	**0**	**0**	**1**
	New Brunswick Hawks	AHL	5	4	3	7	....	....	....	12	....	....	....	....	....	....	....	....	....	....	....	....	....	....	....	....	....	....
	Dallas Black Hawks	CHL	5	1	0	1	....	....	....	2	....	....	....	....	....	....	....	....	....	....	....	....	....	....	....	....	....	....
1980-81	**Chicago Black Hawks**	**NHL**	**14**	**0**	**0**	**0**	**0**	**0**	**0**	**41**	**0**	**0**	**0**	**10**	**0.0**	**3**	**0**	**7**	**2**	**–2**	....	....	....	....	....	....	....	....
	Winnipeg Jets	**NHL**	**45**	**6**	**17**	**23**	**5**	**11**	**16**	**66**	**0**	**0**	**1**	**61**	**9.8**	**34**	**1**	**74**	**14**	**–27**	....	....	....	....	....	....	....	....
1981-82	Tulsa Oilers	CHL	69	30	38	68	....	....	....	114	....	....	....	....	....	....	....	....	....	....	3	0	1	1	8	....	....	....
1982-83	**Pittsburgh Penguins**	**NHL**	**12**	**1**	**4**	**5**	**1**	**3**	**4**	**12**	**0**	**0**	**1**	**8**	**12.5**	**8**	**2**	**8**	**0**	**–2**	....	....	....	....	....	....	....	....
	Baltimore Skipjacks	AHL	63	17	33	50	....	....	....	56	....	....	....	....	....	....	....	....	....	....	....	....	....	....	....	....	....	....
	NHL Totals		**126**	**11**	**31**	**42**	**10**	**21**	**31**	**178**	**0**	**0**	**3**	**163**	**6.7**	**71**	**5**	**121**	**16**		**7**	**4**	**0**	**4**	**15**	**0**	**0**	**1**

Traded to **Winnipeg** by **Chicago** with Tim Trimper for Peter Marsh, December 1, 1980. Claimed by **Pittsburgh** from **Winnipeg** in Waiver Draft, October 4, 1982.

• LEDINGHAM, Walt

Walter Norman LW – L. 5'11", 180 lbs. b: Weyburn, Sask., 10/26/1950. Chicago's 4th, 56th overall, in 1970.

Season	Club	League	GP	G	A	Pts	AG	AA	APts	PIM	PP	SH	GW	S	%	TGF	PGF	TGA	PGA	+/-	GP	G	A	Pts	PIM	PP	SH	GW
1966-67	Weyburn Red Wings	SJHL	3	0	0	0	....	....	....	2	....	....	....	....	....	....	....	....	....	....	....	....	....	....	....	....	....	....
1967-68	Weyburn Red Wings	SJHL	60	22	28	50	....	....	....	30	....	....	....	....	....	....	....	....	....	....	....	....	....	....	....	....	....	....
1968-69	University of Minnesota	WCHA	DID NOT PLAY – FRESHMAN																									
1969-70	University of Minnesota	WCHA	27	16	11	27	....	....	....	4	....	....	....	....	....	....	....	....	....	....	....	....	....	....	....	....	....	....
1970-71	University of Minnesota	WCHA	33	26	28	54	....	....	....	38	....	....	....	....	....	....	....	....	....	....	....	....	....	....	....	....	....	....
1971-72	University of Minnesota	WCHA	35	24	29	53	....	....	....	18	....	....	....	....	....	....	....	....	....	....	....	....	....	....	....	....	....	....
1972-73	**Chicago Black Hawks**	**NHL**	**9**	**0**	**1**	**1**	**0**	**1**	**1**	**4**	**0**	**0**	**0**	**7**	**0.0**	**1**	**0**	**1**	**0**	**0**	....	....	....	....	....	....	....	....
	Dallas Black Hawks	CHL	62	22	31	53	....	....	....	55	....	....	....	....	....	....	....	....	....	....	7	4	3	7	4	....	....	....
1973-74	Dallas Black Hawks	CHL	59	13	22	35	....	....	....	17	....	....	....	....	....	....	....	....	....	....	10	5	6	*11	4	....	....	....
1974-75	**New York Islanders**	**NHL**	**2**	**0**	**1**	**1**	**0**	**1**	**1**	**0**	**0**	**0**	**0**	**2**	**0.0**	**1**	**0**	**4**	**0**	**–3**	....	....	....	....	....	....	....	....
	New Haven Nighthawks	AHL	76	30	36	66	....	....	....	44	....	....	....	....	....	....	....	....	....	....	16	4	10	14	4	....	....	....
1975-76	Fort Worth Texans	CHL	55	13	19	32	....	....	....	20	....	....	....	....	....	....	....	....	....	....	....	....	....	....	....	....	....	....
1976-77	**New York Islanders**	**NHL**	**4**	**0**	**0**	**0**	**0**	**0**	**0**	**0**	**0**	**0**	**0**	**5**	**0.0**	**0**	**0**	**1**	**0**	**–1**	....	....	....	....	....	....	....	....
	Rhode Island Reds	AHL	73	29	57	86	....	....	....	20	....	....	....	....	....	....	....	....	....	....	....	....	....	....	....	....	....	....
	NHL Totals		**15**	**0**	**2**	**2**	**0**	**2**	**2**	**4**	**0**	**0**	**0**	**14**	**0.0**	**2**	**0**	**6**	**0**		....	....	....	....	....	....	....	....

WCHA First All-Star Team (1971) • NCAA West First All-American Team (1971, 1972) • WCHA Second All-Star Team (1972) • AHL First All-Star Team (1977)

Traded to **NY Islanders** by **Chicago** to complete transaction that sent Germaine Gagnon to Chicago (March 7, 1974), May 24, 1974.

• LEDUC, Rich

Richard Henri C – L. 5'11", 170 lbs. b: Ile Perrot, Que., 8/24/1951. California's 2nd, 29th overall, in 1971.

Season	Club	League	GP	G	A	Pts	AG	AA	APts	PIM	PP	SH	GW	S	%	TGF	PGF	TGA	PGA	+/-	GP	G	A	Pts	PIM	PP	SH	GW
1968-69	Sorel Black Hawks	MMJHL	STATISTICS NOT AVAILABLE																									
	Sorel Black Hawks	Mem-Cup	....	....	....	....	....	....	....	....	....	....	....	....	....	....	....	....	....	....	....	....	....	....	....	....	....	....
1969-70	Trois-Rivieres Dukes	QJHL	55	61	90	151	....	....	....	253	....	....	....	....	....	....	....	....	....	....	....	....	....	....	....	....	....	....
1970-71	Trois-Rivieres Dukes	QJHL	59	56	76	132	....	....	....	195	....	....	....	....	....	....	....	....	....	....	11	9	10	19	59	....	....	....
1971-72	Cleveland Barons	AHL	14	1	4	5	....	....	....	27	....	....	....	....	....	....	....	....	....	....	....	....	....	....	....	....	....	....
	Boston Braves	AHL	61	26	27	53	....	....	....	92	....	....	....	....	....	....	....	....	....	....	9	3	3	6	34	....	....	....
1972-73	**Boston Bruins**	**NHL**	**5**	**1**	**1**	**2**	**1**	**1**	**2**	**2**	**0**	**0**	**0**	**12**	**8.3**	**3**	**0**	**4**	**0**	**–1**	....	....	....	....	....	....	....	....
	Boston Braves	AHL	65	31	42	73	....	....	....	75	....	....	....	....	....	....	....	....	....	....	10	9	5	14	4	....	....	....
1973-74	**Boston Bruins**	**NHL**	**28**	**3**	**3**	**6**	**3**	**2**	**5**	**12**	**0**	**0**	**0**	**23**	**13.0**	**8**	**0**	**5**	**0**	**3**	**5**	**0**	**0**	**0**	**9**	**0**	**0**	**0**
	Boston Braves	AHL	29	7	11	18	....	....	....	60	....	....	....	....	....	....	....	....	....	....	....	....	....	....	....	....	....	....
1974-75	Cleveland Crusaders	WHA	78	34	31	65	....	....	....	122	....	....	....	....	....	....	....	....	....	....	5	0	2	2	2	....	....	....
1975-76	Cleveland Crusaders	WHA	79	36	22	58	....	....	....	76	....	....	....	....	....	....	....	....	....	....	3	2	1	3	2	....	....	....
1976-77	Cincinnati Stingers	WHA	81	52	55	107	....	....	....	75	....	....	....	....	....	....	....	....	....	....	4	1	3	4	16	....	....	....

Season	Club	League	GP	G	A	Pts	AG	AA	APts	PIM	PP	SH	GW	S	%	TGF	PGF	TGA	PGA	+/-	GP	G	A	Pts	PIM	PP	SH	GW
			REGULAR SEASON																		PLAYOFFS							
1977-78	Cincinnati Stingers	WHA	54	27	31	58	....	....	....	44	....	....	....	....	....	....	....	....	....	....	4	1	3	4	16	....	....	....
	Indianapolis Racers	WHA	28	10	15	25	....	....	....	38	....	....	....	....	....	....	....	....	....	....	....	....	....	....	....	....	....	....
1978-79	Indianapolis Racers	WHA	13	5	9	14	....	....	....	14	....	....	....	....	....	....	....	....	....	....	....	....	....	....	....	....	....	....
	Quebec Nordiques	WHA	61	30	32	62	....	....	....	30	....	....	....	....	....	....	....	....	....	....	4	0	2	2	0	....	....	....
1979-80	**Quebec Nordiques**	**NHL**	**75**	**21**	**27**	**48**	**18**	**20**	**38**	**49**	**9**	**1**	**1**	**145**	**14.5**	**68**	**22**	**98**	**17**	**-35**	....	....	....	....	....	....	....	....
1980-81	**Quebec Nordiques**	**NHL**	**22**	**3**	**7**	**10**	**2**	**5**	**7**	**6**	**0**	**0**	**0**	**21**	**14.3**	**13**	**3**	**12**	**4**	**2**	....	....	....	....	....	....	....	....
	Rochester Americans	AHL	23	5	7	12	....	....	....	35	....	....	....	....	....	....	....	....	....	....	....	....	....	....	....	....	....	....
	Oklahoma City Stars	CHL	19	5	8	13	....	....	....	6	....	....	....	....	....	....	....	....	....	....	3	1	2	3	0	....	....	....
	NHL Totals		**130**	**28**	**38**	**66**	**24**	**28**	**52**	**69**	**9**	**1**	**1**	**201**	**13.9**	**92**	**25**	**119**	**21**		**5**	**0**	**0**	**0**	**9**	**0**	**0**	**0**
	Other Major League Totals		394	194	195	389	....	....	....	399	....	....	....	....	....	....	....	....	....	....	20	4	11	15	36	....	....	....

QJHL Second All-Star Team (1970) • QJHL First All-Star Team (1971)

Traded to **Boston** by **California** with Chris Oddleifson for Ivan Boldirev, November 17, 1971. Selected by **Cleveland** (WHA) in 1973 WHA Professional Player Draft, June, 1973. Traded to **Cincinnati** (WHA) by **Cleveland** (WHA) for cash, June, 1976. Traded to **Indianapolis** (WHA) by **Cincinnati** (WHA) with Claude Larose for Darryl Maggs and Reg Thomas, February, 1978. Traded to **Quebec** (WHA) by **Indianapolis** (WHA) with Kevin Morrison for future considerations, November, 1978. Rights retained by **Quebec** prior to Expansion Draft, June 9, 1979. Signed as a free agent by **Minnesota**, February, 1981.

• LEDYARD, Grant

Grant S. "Granville" D – L. 6'2", 195 lbs. b: Winnipeg, Man., 11/19/1961.

Season	Club	League	GP	G	A	Pts	AG	AA	APts	PIM	PP	SH	GW	S	%	TGF	PGF	TGA	PGA	+/-	GP	G	A	Pts	PIM	PP	SH	GW
1979-80	Fort Garry Blues	MJHL	49	13	24	37	....	....	....	90	....	....	....	....	....	....	....	....	....	....	....	....	....	....	....	....	....	....
1980-81	Saskatoon Blades	WHL	71	9	28	37	....	....	....	148	....	....	....	....	....	....	....	....	....	....	....	....	....	....	....	....	....	....
1981-82	Fort Garry Blues	MJHL	63	25	45	70	....	....	....	150	....	....	....	....	....	....	....	....	....	....	....	....	....	....	....	....	....	....
1982-83	Tulsa Oilers	CHL	80	13	29	42	....	....	....	115	....	....	....	....	....	....	....	....	....	....	....	....	....	....	....	....	....	....
1983-84	Tulsa Oilers	CHL	58	9	17	26	....	....	....	71	....	....	....	....	....	....	....	....	....	....	9	5	4	9	10	....	....	....
1984-85	**New York Rangers**	**NHL**	**42**	**8**	**12**	**20**	**6**	**8**	**14**	**53**	**1**	**0**	**1**	**91**	**8.8**	**63**	**16**	**50**	**11**	**8**	**3**	**0**	**2**	**2**	**4**	**0**	**0**	**0**
	New Haven Nighthawks	AHL	36	6	20	26	....	....	....	18	....	....	....	....	....	....	....	....	....	....	....	....	....	....	....	....	....	....
	Canada	WEC-A	3	0	1	1	....	....	....	0	....	....	....	....	....	....	....	....	....	....	....	....	....	....	....	....	....	....
1985-86	**New York Rangers**	**NHL**	**27**	**2**	**9**	**11**	**2**	**6**	**8**	**20**	**0**	**0**	**0**	**57**	**3.5**	**32**	**13**	**39**	**13**	**-7**	....	....	....	....	....	....	....	....
	Los Angeles Kings	**NHL**	**52**	**7**	**18**	**25**	**6**	**12**	**18**	**78**	**4**	**0**	**2**	**113**	**6.2**	**66**	**21**	**87**	**20**	**-22**	....	....	....	....	....	....	....	....
	Canada	WEC-A	10	0	2	2	....	....	....	10	....	....	....	....	....	....	....	....	....	....	....	....	....	....	....	....	....	....
1986-87	**Los Angeles Kings**	**NHL**	**67**	**14**	**23**	**37**	**12**	**17**	**29**	**93**	**5**	**0**	**1**	**144**	**9.7**	**88**	**38**	**120**	**30**	**-40**	**5**	**0**	**0**	**0**	**10**	**0**	**0**	**0**
1987-88	**Los Angeles Kings**	**NHL**	**23**	**1**	**7**	**8**	**1**	**5**	**6**	**52**	**1**	**0**	**0**	**40**	**2.5**	**16**	**7**	**17**	**1**	**-7**	....	....	....	....	....	....	....	....
	New Haven Nighthawks	AHL	3	2	1	3	....	....	....	4	....	....	....	....	....	....	....	....	....	....	....	....	....	....	....	....	....	....
	Washington Capitals	**NHL**	**21**	**4**	**3**	**7**	**3**	**2**	**5**	**14**	**1**	**0**	**1**	**41**	**9.8**	**13**	**3**	**17**	**3**	**-4**	**14**	**1**	**0**	**1**	**30**	**0**	**0**	**0**
1988-89	**Washington Capitals**	**NHL**	**61**	**3**	**11**	**14**	**3**	**8**	**11**	**43**	**1**	**0**	**1**	**81**	**3.7**	**49**	**16**	**37**	**5**	**1**	....	....	....	....	....	....	....	....
	Buffalo Sabres	**NHL**	**13**	**1**	**5**	**6**	**1**	**4**	**5**	**8**	**0**	**0**	**1**	**25**	**4.0**	**13**	**2**	**11**	**1**	**1**	**5**	**1**	**2**	**3**	**2**	**0**	**0**	**0**
1989-90	**Buffalo Sabres**	**NHL**	**67**	**2**	**13**	**15**	**2**	**9**	**11**	**37**	**0**	**0**	**1**	**91**	**2.2**	**65**	**14**	**53**	**4**	**2**	....	....	....	....	....	....	....	....
1990-91	**Buffalo Sabres**	**NHL**	**60**	**8**	**23**	**31**	**7**	**17**	**24**	**46**	**2**	**1**	**1**	**118**	**6.8**	**87**	**24**	**65**	**15**	**13**	**6**	**3**	**3**	**6**	**10**	**0**	**0**	**0**
1991-92	**Buffalo Sabres**	**NHL**	**50**	**5**	**16**	**21**	**5**	**12**	**17**	**45**	**0**	**0**	**0**	**87**	**5.7**	**54**	**10**	**72**	**24**	**-4**	....	....	....	....	....	....	....	....
1992-93	**Buffalo Sabres**	**NHL**	**50**	**2**	**14**	**16**	**2**	**10**	**12**	**45**	**1**	**0**	**0**	**79**	**2.5**	**53**	**4**	**62**	**11**	**-2**	**8**	**0**	**0**	**0**	**8**	**0**	**0**	**0**
	Rochester Americans	AHL	5	0	2	2	....	....	....	8	....	....	....	....	....	....	....	....	....	....	....	....	....	....	....	....	....	....
1993-94	**Dallas Stars**	**NHL**	**84**	**9**	**37**	**46**	**8**	**29**	**37**	**42**	**6**	**0**	**1**	**177**	**5.1**	**137**	**56**	**100**	**26**	**7**	**9**	**1**	**2**	**3**	**6**	**0**	**0**	**1**
1994-95	**Dallas Stars**	**NHL**	**38**	**5**	**13**	**18**	**9**	**19**	**28**	**20**	**4**	**0**	**0**	**79**	**6.3**	**45**	**22**	**22**	**5**	**6**	**3**	**0**	**0**	**0**	**2**	**0**	**0**	**0**
1995-96	**Dallas Stars**	**NHL**	**73**	**5**	**19**	**24**	**5**	**16**	**21**	**20**	**2**	**0**	**1**	**123**	**4.1**	**63**	**19**	**97**	**38**	**-15**	....	....	....	....	....	....	....	....
1996-97	**Dallas Stars**	**NHL**	**67**	**1**	**15**	**16**	**1**	**13**	**14**	**61**	**0**	**0**	**0**	**99**	**1.0**	**71**	**11**	**44**	**15**	**31**	**7**	**0**	**2**	**2**	**0**	**0**	**0**	**0**
1997-98	**Vancouver Canucks**	**NHL**	**49**	**2**	**13**	**15**	**2**	**13**	**15**	**14**	**1**	**0**	**0**	**57**	**3.5**	**35**	**7**	**38**	**8**	**-2**	....	....	....	....	....	....	....	....
	Boston Bruins	**NHL**	**22**	**2**	**7**	**9**	**2**	**7**	**9**	**6**	**1**	**0**	**0**	**33**	**6.1**	**19**	**9**	**17**	**5**	**-2**	**6**	**0**	**0**	**0**	**2**	**0**	**0**	**0**
1998-99	**Boston Bruins**	**NHL**	**47**	**4**	**8**	**12**	**5**	**8**	**13**	**33**	**1**	**0**	**2**	**47**	**8.5**	**30**	**7**	**37**	**6**	**-8**	**2**	**0**	**0**	**0**	**2**	**0**	**0**	**0**
99-2000	**Ottawa Senators**	**NHL**	**40**	**2**	**4**	**6**	**2**	**4**	**6**	**8**	**0**	**0**	**1**	**42**	**4.8**	**22**	**0**	**25**	**0**	**-3**	**6**	**0**	**0**	**0**	**16**	**0**	**0**	**0**
	NHL Totals		**953**	**87**	**270**	**357**	**84**	**219**	**303**	**738**	**31**	**1**	**14**	**1624**	**5.4**	**1021**	**299**	**1010**	**241**		**74**	**6**	**11**	**17**	**92**	**0**	**0**	**1**

Won Bob Gassoff Trophy (CHL's Most Improved Defenseman) (1984)

Signed as a free agent by **NY Rangers**, July 7, 1982. Traded to **LA Kings** by **NY Rangers** with Rollie Melanson for LA Kings' 4th round choice (Mike Sullivan) in 1987 Entry Draft and Brian MacLellan, December 9, 1985. Traded to **Washington** by **LA Kings** for Craig Laughlin, February 9, 1988. Traded to **Buffalo** by **Washington** with Clint Malarchuk and Washington's 6th round choice (Brian Holzinger) in 1991 Entry Draft for Calle Johansson and Buffalo's 2nd round choice (Byron Dafoe) in 1989 Entry Draft, March 7, 1989. Signed as a free agent by **Dallas**, August 12, 1993. Signed as a free agent by **Vancouver**, July 17, 1997. Traded to **Boston** by **Vancouver** for Boston's 8th round choice (Curtis Valentine) in 1998 Entry Draft, March 3, 1998. Signed as a free agent by **Ottawa**, November 16, 1999.

• LEE, Edward

Edward Hubert RW – R. 6'2", 180 lbs. b: Rochester, NY, 12/17/1961. Quebec's 4th, 95th overall, in 1981.

Season	Club	League	GP	G	A	Pts	AG	AA	APts	PIM	PP	SH	GW	S	%	TGF	PGF	TGA	PGA	+/-	GP	G	A	Pts	PIM	PP	SH	GW
1980-81	Princeton University	ECAC	21	6	8	14	....	....	....	34	....	....	....	....	....	....	....	....	....	....	....	....	....	....	....	....	....	....
	United States	WJC-A	5	2	2	4	....	....	....	8	....	....	....	....	....	....	....	....	....	....	....	....	....	....	....	....	....	....
1981-82	Princeton University	ECAC	26	12	21	33	....	....	....	46	....	....	....	....	....	....	....	....	....	....	....	....	....	....	....	....	....	....
1982-83	Princeton University	ECAC	25	19	25	44	....	....	....	51	....	....	....	....	....	....	....	....	....	....	....	....	....	....	....	....	....	....
	United States	Nat-Team	5	5	3	8	....	....	....	8	....	....	....	....	....	....	....	....	....	....	....	....	....	....	....	....	....	....
1983-84	Princeton University	ECAC	11	10	18	28	....	....	....	22	....	....	....	....	....	....	....	....	....	....	....	....	....	....	....	....	....	....
	Fredericton Express	AHL	6	0	4	4	....	....	....	4	....	....	....	....	....	....	....	....	....	....	....	....	....	....	....	....	....	....
1984-85	**Quebec Nordiques**	**NHL**	**2**	**0**	**0**	**0**	**0**	**0**	**0**	**5**	**0**	**0**	**0**	**2**	**0.0**	**0**	**0**	**4**	**0**	**-4**	....	....	....	....	....	....	....	....
	Fredericton Express	AHL	21	11	7	18	....	....	....	45	....	....	....	....	....	....	....	....	....	....	....	....	....	....	....	....	....	....
1985-86	Fredericton Express	AHL	6	3	1	4	....	....	....	2	....	....	....	....	....	....	....	....	....	....	....	....	....	....	....	....	....	....
	Springfield Indians	AHL	24	3	4	7	....	....	....	26	....	....	....	....	....	....	....	....	....	....	....	....	....	....	....	....	....	....
	Indianapolis Checkers	IHL	2	0	0	0	....	....	....	0	....	....	....	....	....	....	....	....	....	....	....	....	....	....	....	....	....	....
1986-87	ESC Ahaus	Germany-4	STATISTICS NOT AVAILABLE																									
1987-88	ESC Ahaus	Germany-3	36	71	56	127	....	....	....	....	....	....	....	....	....	....	....	....	....	....	....	....	....	....	....	....	....	....
	NHL Totals		**2**	**0**	**0**	**0**	**0**	**0**	**0**	**5**	**0**	**0**	**0**	**2**	**0.0**	**0**	**0**	**4**	**0**		....	....	....	....	....	....	....	....

Traded to **Minnesota** by **Quebec** for Minnesota's 6th round choice (Scott White) in 1986 Entry Draft, November 15, 1985.

• LEE, Peter

Peter John RW – R. 5'9", 180 lbs. b: Ellesmere, England, 1/2/1956. Montreal's 1st, 12th overall, in 1976.

Season	Club	League	GP	G	A	Pts	AG	AA	APts	PIM	PP	SH	GW	S	%	TGF	PGF	TGA	PGA	+/-	GP	G	A	Pts	PIM	PP	SH	GW
1971-72	Ottawa Jr. Senators	OJHL	STATISTICS NOT AVAILABLE																									
	Ottawa 67's	OMJHL	12	1	0	1	....	....	....	0	....	....	....	....	....	....	....	....	....	....	18	2	5	7	11	....	....	....
1972-73	Ottawa 67's	OMJHL	63	25	51	76	....	....	....	110	....	....	....	....	....	....	....	....	....	....	9	4	8	12	14	....	....	....
1973-74	Ottawa 67's	OMJHL	69	38	42	80	....	....	....	40	....	....	....	....	....	....	....	....	....	....	7	2	1	3	0	....	....	....
1974-75	Ottawa 67's	OMJHL	70	*68	58	126	....	....	....	82	....	....	....	....	....	....	....	....	....	....	7	6	5	11	6	....	....	....
1975-76	Ottawa 67's	OMJHL	66	*81	80	161	....	....	....	59	....	....	....	....	....	....	....	....	....	....	11	7	11	18	15	....	....	....
1976-77	Nova Scotia Voyageurs	AHL	76	33	27	60	....	....	....	88	....	....	....	....	....	....	....	....	....	....	12	5	3	8	6	....	....	....
1977-78	Nova Scotia Voyageurs	AHL	23	8	11	19	....	....	....	25	....	....	....	....	....	....	....	....	....	....	....	....	....	....	....	....	....	....
	Pittsburgh Penguins	**NHL**	**60**	**5**	**13**	**18**	**5**	**10**	**15**	**19**	**1**	**0**	**1**	**89**	**5.6**	**32**	**9**	**34**	**0**	**-11**	....	....	....	....	....	....	....	....
1978-79	**Pittsburgh Penguins**	**NHL**	**80**	**32**	**26**	**58**	**27**	**19**	**46**	**24**	**10**	**0**	**7**	**219**	**14.6**	**85**	**24**	**75**	**1**	**-13**	**7**	**0**	**3**	**3**	**0**	**0**	**0**	**0**
1979-80	**Pittsburgh Penguins**	**NHL**	**74**	**16**	**29**	**45**	**14**	**21**	**35**	**20**	**4**	**0**	**2**	**161**	**9.9**	**64**	**19**	**58**	**0**	**-13**	**4**	**0**	**1**	**1**	**0**	**0**	**0**	**0**
1980-81	**Pittsburgh Penguins**	**NHL**	**80**	**30**	**34**	**64**	**23**	**23**	**46**	**86**	**4**	**1**	**4**	**196**	**15.3**	**86**	**17**	**101**	**32**	**0**	**5**	**0**	**4**	**4**	**4**	**0**	**0**	**0**
1981-82	**Pittsburgh Penguins**	**NHL**	**74**	**18**	**16**	**34**	**14**	**11**	**25**	**98**	**2**	**0**	**3**	**183**	**9.8**	**56**	**8**	**58**	**2**	**-8**	**3**	**0**	**0**	**0**	**0**	**0**	**0**	**0**
1982-83	**Pittsburgh Penguins**	**NHL**	**63**	**13**	**13**	**26**	**11**	**9**	**20**	**10**	**1**	**0**	**1**	**113**	**11.5**	**40**	**5**	**44**	**0**	**-9**	....	....	....	....	....	....	....	....
	Baltimore Skipjacks	AHL	14	11	6	17	....	....	....	12	....	....	....	....	....	....	....	....	....	....	....	....	....	....	....	....	....	....
1983-84	Dusseldorfer EG	Germany	46	25	24	49	....	....	....	56	....	....	....	....	....	....	....	....	....	....	....	....	....	....	....	....	....	....
1984-85	Dusseldorfer EG	Germany	33	29	34	63	....	....	....	55	....	....	....	....	....	....	....	....	....	....	4	3	0	3	24	....	....	....
1985-86	Dusseldorfer EG	Germany	32	40	37	77	....	....	....	58	....	....	....	....	....	....	....	....	....	....	9	7	12	19	....	....	....	....
1986-87	Dusseldorfer EG	Germany	43	40	35	75	....	....	....	77	....	....	....	....	....	....	....	....	....	....	8	7	9	16	....	....	....	....
1987-88	Dusseldorfer EG	Germany	36	*31	31	62	....	....	....	42	....	....	....	....	....	....	....	....	....	....	8	4	5	9	....	....	....	....
1988-89	Dusseldorfer EG	Germany	36	31	34	65	....	....	....	46	....	....	....	....	....	....	....	....	....	....	11	*11	7	18	14	....	....	....

			REGULAR SEASON																		PLAYOFFS							
Season	Club	League	GP	G	A	Pts	AG	AA	APts	PIM	PP	SH	GW	S	%	TGF	PGF	TGA	PGA	+/–	GP	G	A	Pts	PIM	PP	SH	GW
1989-90	Dusseldorfer EG	Germany	20	17	18	35	....	....	....	28	....	....	....	....	....	....	....	....	....	....	11	8	8	16	....	....	....	....
1990-91	Dusseldorfer EG	Germany	37	23	26	49	....	....	....	26	....	....	....	....	....	....	....	....	....	....	13	10	5	15	2	....	....	....
1991-92	Dusseldorfer EG	Germany	44	24	20	44	....	....	....	24	....	....	....	....	....	....	....	....	....	....	9	4	6	10	6	....	....	....
1992-93	Dusseldorfer EG	Germany	44	29	26	55	....	....	....	28	....	....	....	....	....	....	....	....	....	....	11	4	6	10	....	....	....	....
1993-94	Ottawa 67's	OHL	DID NOT PLAY – COACHING																									
1994-95	Ottawa 67's	OHL	DID NOT PLAY – COACHING																									
1995-96	EC Wolfsburg	Germany-2	15	14	11	25	....	....	....	59	....	....	....	....	....	....	....	....	....	....	....	....	....	....	....	....	....	....
	Eisbaren Berlin	Germany	21	7	6	13	....	....	....	36	....	....	....	....	....	....	....	....	....	....	....	....	....	....	....	....	....	....
1996-97	Eisbaren Berlin	Germany	50	14	14	28	....	....	....	42	....	....	....	....	....	....	....	....	....	....	8	0	1	1	4	....	....	....
	NHL Totals		**431**	**114**	**131**	**245**	**94**	**93**	**187**	**257**	**22**	**1**	**18**	**961**	**11.9**	**363**	**82**	**370**	**35**		**19**	**0**	**8**	**8**	**4**	**0**	**0**	**0**

OMJHL Second All-Star Team (1975) • OMJHL First All-Star Team (1976) • Canadian Major Junior Player of the Year (1976)

Traded to **Pittsburgh** by **Montreal** with Pete Mahovlich for Pierre Larouche and future considerations (rights to Peter Marsh, December 15, 1977), November 29, 1977.

• LEEB, Brad

RW – R. 5'11", 180 lbs. b: Red Deer, Alta., 8/27/1979.

Season	Club	League	GP	G	A	Pts	AG	AA	APts	PIM	PP	SH	GW	S	%	TGF	PGF	TGA	PGA	+/–	GP	G	A	Pts	PIM	PP	SH	GW
1994-95	Red Deer Rebels	WHL	3	0	0	0	....	....	....	4	....	....	....	....	....	....	....	....	....	....	10	2	0	2	11	....	....	....
1995-96	Red Deer Rebels	WHL	38	3	6	9	....	....	....	30	....	....	....	....	....	....	....	....	....	....	16	3	3	6	6	....	....	....
1996-97	Red Deer Rebels	WHL	70	15	20	35	....	....	....	76	....	....	....	....	....	....	....	....	....	....	3	2	0	2	2	....	....	....
1997-98	Red Deer Rebels	WHL	63	23	23	46	....	....	....	88	....	....	....	....	....	....	....	....	....	....	9	5	9	14	10	....	....	....
1998-99	Red Deer Rebels	WHL	64	32	47	79	....	....	....	84	....	....	....	....	....	....	....	....	....	....	4	0	0	0	6	....	....	....
99-2000	Syracuse Crunch	AHL	61	19	18	37	....	....	....	50	....	....	....	....	....	....	....	....	....	....	....	....	....	....	....	....	....	....
	Vancouver Canucks	**NHL**	**2**	**0**	**0**	**0**	**0**	**0**	**0**	**2**	**0**	**0**	**0**	**3**	**0.0**	....	....	....	....	....	....	....	....	....	....	....	....	....
	NHL Totals		**2**	**0**	**0**	**0**	**0**	**0**	**0**	**2**	**0**	**0**	**0**	**3**	**0.0**	....	....	....	....		....	....	....	....	....	....	....	....

Signed as a free agent by **Vancouver**, October 8, 1999.

• LEEMAN, Gary

RW – R. 5'11", 175 lbs. b: Toronto, Ont., 2/19/1964. Toronto's 2nd, 24th overall, in 1982.

Season	Club	League	GP	G	A	Pts	AG	AA	APts	PIM	PP	SH	GW	S	%	TGF	PGF	TGA	PGA	+/–	GP	G	A	Pts	PIM	PP	SH	GW
1980-81	Notre Dame Midget Hounds	SAHA	24	15	23	38	....	....	....	28	....	....	....	....	....	....	....	....	....	....	....	....	....	....	....	....	....	....
1981-82	Regina Pats	WHL	72	19	41	60	....	....	....	112	....	....	....	....	....	....	....	....	....	....	3	2	2	4	0	....	....	....
1982-83	Regina Pats	WHL	63	24	62	86	....	....	....	88	....	....	....	....	....	....	....	....	....	....	5	1	5	6	4	....	....	....
	Canada	WJC-A	7	1	2	3	....	....	....	2	....	....	....	....	....	....	....	....	....	....	....	....	....	....	....	....	....	....
	Toronto Maple Leafs	**NHL**	....	....	....	....	....	....	....	....	....	....	....	....	....	....	....	....	....	....	**2**	**0**	**0**	**0**	**0**	**0**	**0**	**0**
1983-84	**Toronto Maple Leafs**	**NHL**	**52**	**4**	**8**	**12**	**3**	**5**	**8**	**31**	**1**	**0**	**0**	**41**	**9.8**	**29**	**6**	**38**	**1**	**–14**	....	....	....	....	....	....	....	....
	Canada	WJC-A	7	3	6	9	....	....	....	12	....	....	....	....	....	....	....	....	....	....	....	....	....	....	....	....	....	....
1984-85	**Toronto Maple Leafs**	**NHL**	**53**	**5**	**26**	**31**	**4**	**18**	**22**	**72**	**3**	**0**	**0**	**88**	**5.7**	**50**	**23**	**47**	**8**	**–12**	....	....	....	....	....	....	....	....
	St. Catharines Saints	AHL	7	2	2	4	....	....	....	11	....	....	....	....	....	....	....	....	....	....	....	....	....	....	....	....	....	....
1985-86	**Toronto Maple Leafs**	**NHL**	**53**	**9**	**23**	**32**	**7**	**15**	**22**	**20**	**1**	**1**	**0**	**123**	**7.3**	**47**	**11**	**49**	**12**	**–1**	**10**	**2**	**10**	**12**	**2**	**0**	**0**	**0**
	St. Catharines Saints	AHL	25	15	13	28	....	....	....	6	....	....	....	....	....	....	....	....	....	....	....	....	....	....	....	....	....	....
1986-87	**Toronto Maple Leafs**	**NHL**	**80**	**21**	**31**	**52**	**18**	**23**	**41**	**66**	**4**	**3**	**2**	**196**	**10.7**	**99**	**37**	**107**	**19**	**–26**	**5**	**0**	**1**	**1**	**14**	**0**	**0**	**0**
1987-88	**Toronto Maple Leafs**	**NHL**	**80**	**30**	**31**	**61**	**26**	**22**	**48**	**62**	**6**	**0**	**0**	**234**	**12.8**	**101**	**27**	**103**	**23**	**–6**	**2**	**2**	**0**	**2**	**2**	**2**	**0**	**0**
1988-89	**Toronto Maple Leafs**	**NHL**	**61**	**32**	**43**	**75**	**27**	**30**	**57**	**66**	**7**	**1**	**3**	**195**	**16.4**	**98**	**34**	**74**	**15**	**5**	....	....	....	....	....	....	....	....
1989-90	**Toronto Maple Leafs**	**NHL**	**80**	**51**	**44**	**95**	**44**	**32**	**76**	**63**	**14**	**1**	**5**	**256**	**19.9**	**144**	**45**	**109**	**14**	**4**	**5**	**3**	**3**	**6**	**16**	**2**	**0**	**0**
1990-91	**Toronto Maple Leafs**	**NHL**	**52**	**17**	**12**	**29**	**16**	**9**	**25**	**39**	**4**	**0**	**1**	**135**	**12.6**	**48**	**19**	**60**	**6**	**–25**	....	....	....	....	....	....	....	....
1991-92	**Toronto Maple Leafs**	**NHL**	**34**	**7**	**13**	**20**	**6**	**10**	**16**	**44**	**3**	**0**	**0**	**91**	**7.7**	**38**	**17**	**25**	**3**	**–1**	....	....	....	....	....	....	....	....
	Calgary Flames	**NHL**	**29**	**2**	**7**	**9**	**2**	**5**	**7**	**27**	**1**	**0**	**0**	**50**	**4.0**	**19**	**9**	**22**	**1**	**–11**	....	....	....	....	....	....	....	....
1992-93	**Calgary Flames**	**NHL**	**30**	**9**	**5**	**14**	**7**	**3**	**10**	**10**	**0**	**0**	**2**	**49**	**18.4**	**26**	**6**	**15**	**0**	**5**	....	....	....	....	....	....	....	....
♦	**Montreal Canadiens**	**NHL**	**20**	**6**	**12**	**18**	**5**	**8**	**13**	**14**	**1**	**0**	**1**	**36**	**16.7**	**28**	**10**	**10**	**1**	**9**	**11**	**1**	**2**	**3**	**2**	**0**	**0**	**0**
1993-94	**Montreal Canadiens**	**NHL**	**31**	**4**	**11**	**15**	**4**	**9**	**13**	**17**	**0**	**0**	**0**	**53**	**7.5**	**21**	**8**	**10**	**2**	**5**	**1**	**0**	**0**	**0**	**0**	**0**	**0**	**0**
	Fredericton Canadiens	AHL	23	18	8	26	....	....	....	16	....	....	....	....	....	....	....	....	....	....	....	....	....	....	....	....	....	....
1994-95	**Vancouver Canucks**	**NHL**	**10**	**2**	**0**	**2**	**4**	**0**	**4**	**0**	**0**	**0**	**1**	**14**	**14.3**	**4**	**0**	**7**	**0**	**–3**	....	....	....	....	....	....	....	....
1995-96	HC Gardena-Groden	Alpenliga	7	5	4	9	....	....	....	4	....	....	....	....	....	....	....	....	....	....	....	....	....	....	....	....	....	....
	HC Gardena-Groden	Italy	20	7	12	19	....	....	....	59	....	....	....	....	....	....	....	....	....	....	7	2	4	6	12	....	....	....
1996-97	**St. Louis Blues**	**NHL**	**2**	**0**	**1**	**1**	**0**	**1**	**1**	**0**	**0**	**0**	**0**	**3**	**0.0**	**1**	**1**	**0**	**0**	**0**	....	....	....	....	....	....	....	....
	Worcester IceCats	AHL	24	9	7	16	....	....	....	41	....	....	....	....	....	....	....	....	....	....	....	....	....	....	....	....	....	....
	Utah Grizzlies	IHL	15	6	1	7	....	....	....	20	....	....	....	....	....	....	....	....	....	....	4	0	3	3	4	....	....	....
1997-98	Hannover Scorpions	Germany	44	13	38	51	....	....	....	16	....	....	....	....	....	....	....	....	....	....	4	2	0	2	12	....	....	....
1998-99	Hannover Scorpions	Germany	10	2	3	5	....	....	....	31	....	....	....	....	....	....	....	....	....	....	....	....	....	....	....	....	....	....
	EHC Biel-Bienne	Switz-2	8	7	4	11	....	....	....	10	....	....	....	....	....	....	....	....	....	....	....	....	....	....	....	....	....	....
	HC Sierre	Switz-2	1	2	1	3	....	....	....	0	....	....	....	....	....	....	....	....	....	....	....	....	....	....	....	....	....	....
	NHL Totals		**667**	**199**	**267**	**466**	**173**	**190**	**363**	**531**	**45**	**6**	**15**	**1564**	**12.7**	**753**	**253**	**676**	**105**		**36**	**8**	**16**	**24**	**36**	**4**	**0**	**0**

WHL First All-Star Team (1983) • Played in NHL All-Star Game (1989)

Traded to **Calgary** by **Toronto** with Craig Berube, Alexander Godynyuk, Michel Petit and Jeff Reese for Doug Gilmour, Jamie Macoun, Ric Nattress, Rick Wamsley and Kent Manderville, January 2, 1992. Traded to **Montreal** by **Calgary** for Brian Skrudland, January 28, 1993. Signed as a free agent by **Vancouver**, January 18, 1995. Signed as a free agent by **St. Louis**, September 26, 1996.

• LEETCH, Brian

D – L. 6'1", 190 lbs. b: Corpus Christi, TX, 3/3/1968. NY Rangers' 1st, 9th overall, in 1986.

Season	Club	League	GP	G	A	Pts	AG	AA	APts	PIM	PP	SH	GW	S	%	TGF	PGF	TGA	PGA	+/–	GP	G	A	Pts	PIM	PP	SH	GW
1983-84	Avon Farms Winged Beavers	Hi-School	28	52	49	101	....	....	....	24	....	....	....	....	....	....	....	....	....	....	....	....	....	....	....	....	....	....
1984-85	Avon Farms Winged Beavers	Hi-School	26	30	46	76	....	....	....	15	....	....	....	....	....	....	....	....	....	....	....	....	....	....	....	....	....	....
	United States	WJC-A	7	0	0	0	....	....	....	2	....	....	....	....	....	....	....	....	....	....	....	....	....	....	....	....	....	....
1985-86	Avon Farms Winged Beavers	Hi-School	28	40	44	84	....	....	....	18	....	....	....	....	....	....	....	....	....	....	....	....	....	....	....	....	....	....
	United States	WJC-A	7	1	4	5	....	....	....	2	....	....	....	....	....	....	....	....	....	....	....	....	....	....	....	....	....	....
1986-87	Boston College	H-East	37	9	38	47	....	....	....	10	....	....	....	....	....	....	....	....	....	....	....	....	....	....	....	....	....	....
	United States	WEC-A	10	4	5	9	....	....	....	4	....	....	....	....	....	....	....	....	....	....	....	....	....	....	....	....	....	....
	United States	WJC-A	7	1	2	3	....	....	....	8	....	....	....	....	....	....	....	....	....	....	....	....	....	....	....	....	....	....
1987-88	United States	Nat-Team	50	13	61	74	....	....	....	38	....	....	....	....	....	....	....	....	....	....	....	....	....	....	....	....	....	....
	United States	Olympics	6	1	5	6	....	....	....	4	....	....	....	....	....	....	....	....	....	....	....	....	....	....	....	....	....	....
	New York Rangers	**NHL**	**17**	**2**	**12**	**14**	**2**	**9**	**11**	**0**	**1**	**0**	**1**	**40**	**5.0**	**35**	**16**	**14**	**0**	**5**	....	....	....	....	....	....	....	....
1988-89	**New York Rangers**	**NHL**	**68**	**23**	**48**	**71**	**19**	**34**	**53**	**50**	**8**	**3**	**1**	**268**	**8.6**	**155**	**62**	**110**	**25**	**8**	**4**	**3**	**2**	**5**	**2**	**2**	**0**	**0**
	United States	WEC-A	10	3	4	7	....	....	....	4	....	....	....	....	....	....	....	....	....	....	....	....	....	....	....	....	....	....
1989-90	**New York Rangers**	**NHL**	**72**	**11**	**45**	**56**	**9**	**32**	**41**	**26**	**5**	**0**	**2**	**222**	**5.0**	**128**	**65**	**104**	**23**	**–18**	....	....	....	....	....	....	....	....
1990-91	**New York Rangers**	**NHL**	**80**	**16**	**72**	**88**	**15**	**55**	**70**	**42**	**6**	**0**	**4**	**206**	**7.8**	**178**	**87**	**116**	**27**	**2**	**6**	**1**	**3**	**4**	**0**	**0**	**0**	**0**
1991-92	United States	Can-Cup	7	1	3	4	....	....	....	2	....	....	....	....	....	....	....	....	....	....	....	....	....	....	....	....	....	....
	New York Rangers	**NHL**	**80**	**22**	**80**	**102**	**20**	**61**	**81**	**26**	**10**	**1**	**3**	**245**	**9.0**	**193**	**79**	**114**	**25**	**25**	**13**	**4**	**11**	**15**	**4**	**1**	**1**	**0**
1992-93	**New York Rangers**	**NHL**	**36**	**6**	**30**	**36**	**5**	**21**	**26**	**26**	**2**	**1**	**1**	**150**	**4.0**	**84**	**40**	**58**	**16**	**2**	....	....	....	....	....	....	....	....
1993-94♦	**New York Rangers**	**NHL**	**84**	**23**	**56**	**79**	**21**	**44**	**65**	**67**	**17**	**1**	**4**	**328**	**7.0**	**187**	**86**	**118**	**45**	**28**	**23**	**11**	***23**	***34**	**6**	**4**	**0**	**4**
1994-95	**New York Rangers**	**NHL**	**48**	**9**	**32**	**41**	**16**	**47**	**63**	**18**	**3**	**0**	**2**	**182**	**4.9**	**84**	**38**	**71**	**25**	**0**	**10**	**6**	**8**	**14**	**8**	**3**	**0**	**1**
1995-96	**New York Rangers**	**NHL**	**82**	**15**	**70**	**85**	**15**	**58**	**73**	**30**	**7**	**0**	**3**	**276**	**5.4**	**158**	**78**	**125**	**57**	**12**	**11**	**1**	**6**	**7**	**4**	**1**	**0**	**0**
1996-97	United States	W-Cup	7	0	*7	7	....	....	....	4	....	....	....	....	....	....	....	....	....	....	....	....	....	....	....	....	....	....
	New York Rangers	**NHL**	**82**	**20**	**58**	**78**	**21**	**52**	**73**	**40**	**9**	**0**	**2**	**256**	**7.8**	**166**	**59**	**115**	**39**	**31**	**15**	**2**	**8**	**10**	**6**	**1**	**0**	**1**
1997-98	**New York Rangers**	**NHL**	**76**	**17**	**33**	**50**	**20**	**32**	**52**	**32**	**11**	**0**	**2**	**230**	**7.4**	**117**	**58**	**120**	**25**	**–36**	....	....	....	....	....	....	....	....
	United States	Olympics	4	1	1	2	....	....	....	0	....	....	....	....	....	....	....	....	....	....	....	....	....	....	....	....	....	....
1998-99	**New York Rangers**	**NHL**	**82**	**13**	**42**	**55**	**15**	**41**	**56**	**42**	**4**	**0**	**1**	**184**	**7.1**	**142**	**68**	**111**	**30**	**–7**	....	....	....	....	....	....	....	....
99-2000	**New York Rangers**	**NHL**	**50**	**7**	**19**	**26**	**8**	**18**	**26**	**20**	**3**	**0**	**2**	**124**	**5.6**	**70**	**23**	**77**	**14**	**–16**	....	....	....	....	....	....	....	....
	NHL Totals		**857**	**184**	**597**	**781**	**186**	**504**	**690**	**419**	**86**	**6**	**28**	**2711**	**6.8**	**1697**	**759**	**1253**	**351**		**82**	**28**	**61**	**89**	**30**	**12**	**1**	**6**

WJC-A All-Star Team (1987) • Hockey East First All-Star Team (1987) • NCAA East First All-American Team (1987) • NHL All-Rookie Team (1989) • Won Calder Memorial Trophy (1989) • NHL Second All-Star Team (1991, 1994, 1996) • Won James Norris Memorial Trophy (1992, 1997) • NHL First All-Star Team (1992, 1997) • Won Conn Smythe Trophy (1994) • Played in NHL All-Star Game (1990, 1991, 1992, 1994, 1996, 1997, 1998)

• LEFEBVRE, Patrice

RW – L. 5'6", 160 lbs. b: Montreal, Que., 6/28/1967.

			REGULAR SEASON																		PLAYOFFS							
Season	Club	League	GP	G	A	Pts	AG	AA	APts	PIM	PP	SH	GW	S	%	TGF	PGF	TGA	PGA	+/–	GP	G	A	Pts	PIM	PP	SH	GW
1983-84	Montreal Concordia	QAAA	42	36	45	81	....	....	....	....	....	....	....	....	....	....	....	....	....	....	....	....	....	....	....	....	....	....
1984-85	Shawinigan Cataractes	QMJHL	68	28	52	80	....	....	....	63	....	....	....	....	....	....	....	....	....	....	....	....	....	....	....	....	....	....
	Shawinigan Cataractes	Mem-Cup	4	2	1	3	....	....	....	2	....	....	....	....	....	....	....	....	....	....	....	....	....	....	....	....	....	....
1985-86	Shawinigan Cataractes	QMJHL	69	38	98	136	....	....	....	119	....	....	....	....	....	....	....	....	....	....	....	....	....	....	....	....	....	....
1986-87	Shawinigan Cataractes	QMJHL	69	57	122	179	....	....	....	144	....	....	....	....	....	....	....	....	....	....	12	9	16	25	19	....	....	....
1987-88	Shawinigan Cataractes	QMJHL	70	64	136	200	....	....	....	142	....	....	....	....	....	....	....	....	....	....	....	....	....	....	....	....	....	....
1988-89	Paris Francais Volants	France	38	32	36	68	....	....	....	46	....	....	....	....	....	....	....	....	....	....	....	....	....	....	....	....	....	....
1989-90	HC Ajoie	Switz	32	23	23	46	....	....	....	....	....	....	....	....	....	....	....	....	....	....	....	....	....	....	....	....	....	....
1990-91	HC Langnau	Switz-2	3	1	8	9	....	....	....	....	....	....	....	....	....	....	....	....	....	....	....	....	....	....	....	....	....	....
	Louisville Icehawks	ECHL	26	17	26	43	....	....	....	32	....	....	....	....	....	....	....	....	....	....	7	2	5	7	8	....	....	....
	Milwaukee Admirals	IHL	16	6	4	10	....	....	....	13	....	....	....	....	....	....	....	....	....	....	....	....	....	....	....	....	....	....
	Springfield Indians	AHL	1	0	0	0	....	....	....	2	....	....	....	....	....	....	....	....	....	....	....	....	....	....	....	....	....	....
1991-92	HC Kloten	Switz	10	4	12	16	....	....	....	....	....	....	....	....	....	....	....	....	....	....	....	....	....	....	....	....	....	....
	HC Sierre	Switz-2	3	3	2	5	....	....	....	....	....	....	....	....	....	....	....	....	....	....	....	....	....	....	....	....	....	....
1992-93	Billingham Bombers	Britain	36	56	109	165	....	....	....	75	....	....	....	....	....	....	....	....	....	....	6	5	13	18	26	....	....	....
1993-94	Las Vegas Thunder	IHL	76	31	67	98	....	....	....	71	....	....	....	....	....	....	....	....	....	....	5	3	4	7	4	....	....	....
1994-95	Las Vegas Thunder	IHL	75	32	62	94	....	....	....	74	....	....	....	....	....	....	....	....	....	....	10	2	3	5	2	....	....	....
1995-96	Las Vegas Thunder	IHL	77	36	78	114	....	....	....	85	....	....	....	....	....	....	....	....	....	....	15	9	11	20	12	....	....	....
1996-97	Las Vegas Thunder	IHL	82	21	73	94	....	....	....	94	....	....	....	....	....	....	....	....	....	....	3	0	2	2	2	....	....	....
1997-98	Las Vegas Thunder	IHL	77	27	*89	*116	....	....	....	113	....	....	....	....	....	....	....	....	....	....	4	2	0	2	2	....	....	....
1998-99	Las Vegas Thunder	IHL	42	11	26	37	....	....	....	40	....	....	....	....	....	....	....	....	....	....	....	....	....	....	....	....	....	....
	Washington Capitals	**NHL**	**3**	**0**	**0**	**0**	**0**	**0**	**0**	**2**	**0**	**0**	**0**	**2**	**0.0**	**1**	**1**	**2**	**0**	**–2**	....	....	....	....	....	....	....	....
	Long Beach Ice Dogs	IHL	14	1	12	13	....	....	....	8	....	....	....	....	....	....	....	....	....	....	8	0	3	3	2	....	....	....
99-2000	Adler Mannheim	Germany	54	20	31	51	....	....	....	148	....	....	....	....	....	....	....	....	....	....	5	1	2	3	4	....	....	....
	NHL Totals		**3**	**0**	**0**	**0**	**0**	**0**	**0**	**2**	**0**	**0**	**0**	**2**	**0.0**	**1**	**1**	**2**	**0**		....	....	....	....	....	....	....	....

QMJHL Second All-Star Team (1986) • QMJHL First All-Star Team (1987, 1988) • IHL First All-Star Team (1998) • Won Leo P. Lamoureux Memorial Trophy (Top Scorer - IHL) (1998) • Won James Gatschene Memorial Trophy (MVP - IHL) (1998)

Signed as a free agent by **Washington**, December 18, 1998. • Played w/ RHI's Montreal Roadrunners in 1994 (8-10-18-28-10) and 1997 (4-5-10-15-13).

• LEFEBVRE, Sylvain

D – L. 6'2", 205 lbs. b: Richmond, Que., 10/14/1967.

			REGULAR SEASON																		PLAYOFFS							
Season	Club	League	GP	G	A	Pts	AG	AA	APts	PIM	PP	SH	GW	S	%	TGF	PGF	TGA	PGA	+/–	GP	G	A	Pts	PIM	PP	SH	GW
1984-85	Laval Titan	QMJHL	66	7	5	12	....	....	....	31	....	....	....	....	....	....	....	....	....	....	....	....	....	....	....	....	....	....
1985-86	Laval Titan	QMJHL	71	8	17	25	....	....	....	48	....	....	....	....	....	....	....	....	....	....	14	1	0	1	25	....	....	....
1986-87	Laval Titan	QMJHL	70	10	36	46	....	....	....	44	....	....	....	....	....	....	....	....	....	....	15	1	6	7	12	....	....	....
1987-88	Sherbrooke Canadiens	AHL	79	3	24	27	....	....	....	73	....	....	....	....	....	....	....	....	....	....	6	2	3	5	4	....	....	....
1988-89	Sherbrooke Canadiens	AHL	77	15	32	47	....	....	....	119	....	....	....	....	....	....	....	....	....	....	6	1	3	4	4	....	....	....
1989-90	**Montreal Canadiens**	**NHL**	**68**	**3**	**10**	**13**	**3**	**7**	**10**	**61**	**0**	**0**	**0**	**89**	**3.4**	**82**	**10**	**68**	**14**	**18**	**6**	**0**	**0**	**0**	**2**	**0**	**0**	**0**
1990-91	Montreal Canadiens	Fr-Tour	4	1	0	1	....	....	....	6	....	....	....	....	....	....	....	....	....	....	....	....	....	....	....	....	....	....
	Montreal Canadiens	**NHL**	**63**	**5**	**18**	**23**	**5**	**14**	**19**	**30**	**1**	**0**	**1**	**76**	**6.6**	**62**	**14**	**73**	**14**	**–11**	**11**	**1**	**0**	**1**	**6**	**0**	**0**	**0**
1991-92	**Montreal Canadiens**	**NHL**	**69**	**3**	**14**	**17**	**3**	**11**	**14**	**91**	**0**	**0**	**0**	**85**	**3.5**	**65**	**9**	**64**	**17**	**9**	**2**	**0**	**0**	**0**	**2**	**0**	**0**	**0**
1992-93	**Toronto Maple Leafs**	**NHL**	**81**	**2**	**12**	**14**	**2**	**8**	**10**	**90**	**0**	**0**	**0**	**81**	**2.5**	**58**	**2**	**85**	**37**	**8**	**21**	**3**	**3**	**6**	**20**	**0**	**0**	**0**
1993-94	**Toronto Maple Leafs**	**NHL**	**84**	**2**	**9**	**11**	**2**	**7**	**9**	**79**	**0**	**0**	**0**	**96**	**2.1**	**88**	**1**	**100**	**46**	**33**	**18**	**0**	**3**	**3**	**16**	**0**	**0**	**0**
1994-95	**Quebec Nordiques**	**NHL**	**48**	**2**	**11**	**13**	**4**	**16**	**20**	**17**	**0**	**0**	**0**	**81**	**2.5**	**65**	**13**	**59**	**20**	**13**	**6**	**0**	**2**	**2**	**2**	**0**	**0**	**0**
1995-96♦	**Colorado Avalanche**	**NHL**	**75**	**5**	**11**	**16**	**5**	**9**	**14**	**49**	**2**	**0**	**0**	**115**	**4.3**	**81**	**8**	**75**	**28**	**26**	**22**	**0**	**5**	**5**	**12**	**0**	**0**	**0**
1996-97	**Colorado Avalanche**	**NHL**	**71**	**2**	**11**	**13**	**2**	**10**	**12**	**30**	**1**	**0**	**0**	**77**	**2.6**	**57**	**3**	**60**	**18**	**12**	**17**	**0**	**0**	**0**	**25**	**0**	**0**	**0**
1997-98	**Colorado Avalanche**	**NHL**	**81**	**0**	**10**	**10**	**0**	**10**	**10**	**48**	**0**	**0**	**0**	**66**	**0.0**	**44**	**2**	**64**	**24**	**2**	**7**	**0**	**0**	**0**	**4**	**0**	**0**	**0**
1998-99	**Colorado Avalanche**	**NHL**	**76**	**2**	**18**	**20**	**2**	**17**	**19**	**48**	**0**	**0**	**0**	**64**	**3.1**	**63**	**0**	**74**	**29**	**18**	**19**	**0**	**1**	**1**	**12**	**0**	**0**	**0**
99-2000	**New York Rangers**	**NHL**	**82**	**2**	**10**	**12**	**2**	**9**	**11**	**43**	**0**	**0**	**0**	**67**	**3.0**	**46**	**1**	**74**	**16**	**–13**	....	....	....	....	....	....	....	....
	NHL Totals		**798**	**28**	**134**	**162**	**30**	**118**	**148**	**586**	**4**	**0**	**1**	**897**	**3.1**	**711**	**63**	**796**	**263**		**129**	**4**	**14**	**18**	**101**	**0**	**0**	**0**

AHL Second All-Star Team (1989)

Signed as a free agent by **Montreal**, September 24, 1986. Traded to **Toronto** by **Montreal** for Toronto's 3rd round choice (Martin Belanger) in 1994 Entry Draft, August 20, 1992. Traded to **Quebec** by **Toronto** with Wendel Clark, Landon Wilson and Toronto's 1st round choice (Jeffrey Kealty) in 1994 Entry Draft for Mats Sundin, Garth Butcher, Todd Warriner and Philadelphia's 1st round choice (previously acquired by Quebec — later traded to Washington — Washington selected Nolan Baumgartner) in 1994 Entry Draft, June 28, 1994. Transferred to **Colorado** after **Quebec** franchise relocated, June 21, 1995. Signed as a free agent by **NY Rangers**, July 22, 1999.

• LEFLEY, Bryan

Bryan Andrew D/LW – L. 6', 195 lbs. b: Grosse Isle, Man., 10/18/1948 d: 10/28/1997.

			REGULAR SEASON																		PLAYOFFS							
Season	Club	League	GP	G	A	Pts	AG	AA	APts	PIM	PP	SH	GW	S	%	TGF	PGF	TGA	PGA	+/–	GP	G	A	Pts	PIM	PP	SH	GW
1964-65	Winnipeg Rangers	MJHL	24	3	2	5	....	....	....	8	....	....	....	....	....	....	....	....	....	....	4	0	0	0	0	....	....	....
1965-66	Winnipeg Rangers	MJHL	14	1	1	2	....	....	....	10	....	....	....	....	....	....	....	....	....	....	9	0	2	2	12	....	....	....
1966-67	Winnipeg Rangers	MJHL	36	5	15	20	....	....	....	26	....	....	....	....	....	....	....	....	....	....	7	1	1	2	16	....	....	....
1967-68	Winnipeg Rangers	MJHL	STATISTICS NOT AVAILABLE																									
1968-69	Nelson Maple Leafs	WIHL	STATISTICS NOT AVAILABLE																									
1969-70	Omaha Knights	CHL	63	7	9	16	....	....	....	42	....	....	....	....	....	....	....	....	....	....	12	7	3	10	9	....	....	....
1970-71	Omaha Knights	CHL	67	8	25	33	....	....	....	111	....	....	....	....	....	....	....	....	....	....	10	0	3	3	2	....	....	....
1971-72	Omaha Knights	CHL	71	10	20	30	....	....	....	109	....	....	....	....	....	....	....	....	....	....	....	....	....	....	....	....	....	....
1972-73	**New York Islanders**	**NHL**	**63**	**3**	**7**	**10**	**3**	**6**	**9**	**56**	**0**	**0**	**0**	**39**	**7.7**	**31**	**3**	**78**	**11**	**–39**	....	....	....	....	....	....	....	....
1973-74	**New York Islanders**	**NHL**	**7**	**0**	**0**	**0**	**0**	**0**	**0**	**0**	**0**	**0**	**0**	**1**	**0.0**	**1**	**0**	**1**	**0**	**0**	....	....	....	....	....	....	....	....
	Fort Worth Wings	CHL	58	8	36	44	....	....	....	88	....	....	....	....	....	....	....	....	....	....	5	0	1	1	6	....	....	....
1974-75	**Kansas City Scouts**	**NHL**	**29**	**0**	**3**	**3**	**0**	**2**	**2**	**6**	**0**	**0**	**0**	**12**	**0.0**	**13**	**0**	**43**	**7**	**–23**	....	....	....	....	....	....	....	....
	Baltimore Clippers	AHL	9	3	0	3	....	....	....	10	....	....	....	....	....	....	....	....	....	....	....	....	....	....	....	....	....	....
	Providence Reds	AHL	29	3	10	13	....	....	....	32	....	....	....	....	....	....	....	....	....	....	1	0	0	0	2	....	....	....
1975-76	Springfield Indians	AHL	71	4	25	29	....	....	....	48	....	....	....	....	....	....	....	....	....	....	....	....	....	....	....	....	....	....
1976-77	**Colorado Rockies**	**NHL**	**58**	**0**	**6**	**6**	**0**	**5**	**5**	**27**	**0**	**0**	**0**	**40**	**0.0**	**39**	**5**	**68**	**19**	**–15**	....	....	....	....	....	....	....	....
	Oklahoma City Blazers	CHL	8	2	3	5	....	....	....	4	....	....	....	....	....	....	....	....	....	....	....	....	....	....	....	....	....	....
1977-78	**Colorado Rockies**	**NHL**	**71**	**4**	**13**	**17**	**4**	**10**	**14**	**12**	**0**	**1**	**1**	**65**	**6.2**	**34**	**4**	**50**	**16**	**–4**	**2**	**0**	**0**	**0**	**0**	**0**	**0**	**0**
1978-79	Dusseldorfer EG	Germany	51	13	25	38	....	....	....	44	....	....	....	....	....	....	....	....	....	....	....	....	....	....	....	....	....	....
1979-80	Dusseldorfer EG	Germany	45	13	23	36	....	....	....	36	....	....	....	....	....	....	....	....	....	....	....	....	....	....	....	....	....	....
1980-81	Dusseldorfer EG	Germany	2	0	1	1	....	....	....	0	....	....	....	....	....	....	....	....	....	....	....	....	....	....	....	....	....	....
	SC Bern	Switz.	28	7	20	27	....	....	....	26	....	....	....	....	....	....	....	....	....	....	....	....	....	....	....	....	....	....
	NHL Totals		**228**	**7**	**29**	**36**	**7**	**23**	**30**	**101**	**0**	**1**	**1**	**157**	**4.5**	**118**	**12**	**240**	**53**		**2**	**0**	**0**	**0**	**0**	**0**	**0**	**0**

• Brother of Chuck • CHL First All-Star Team (1974)

Claimed by **NY Islanders** from **NY Rangers** in Expansion Draft, June 6, 1972. Claimed by **Kansas City** from **NY Islanders** in Expansion Draft, June 12, 1974. Transferred to **Colorado** after **Kansas City** franchise relocated, July 15, 1976. • Died of injuries suffered in automobile accident in Italy, October 28, 1997.

• LEFLEY, Chuck

Charles Thomas LW – L. 6'2", 185 lbs. b: Winnipeg, Man., 1/20/1950. Montreal's 2nd, 6th overall, in 1970.

			REGULAR SEASON																		PLAYOFFS							
Season	Club	League	GP	G	A	Pts	AG	AA	APts	PIM	PP	SH	GW	S	%	TGF	PGF	TGA	PGA	+/–	GP	G	A	Pts	PIM	PP	SH	GW
1965-66	Winnipeg Rangers	MJHL	46	19	20	39	....	....	....	10	....	....	....	....	....	....	....	....	....	....	9	4	5	9	2	....	....	....
1966-67	Winnipeg Rangers	MJHL	43	25	21	46	....	....	....	33	....	....	....	....	....	....	....	....	....	....	7	6	2	8	2	....	....	....
1967-68	Canada	Nat-Team	STATISTICS NOT AVAILABLE																									
1968-69	Canada	Nat-Team	STATISTICS NOT AVAILABLE																									
	Canada	WEC-A	7	0	1	1	....	....	....	10	....	....	....	....	....	....	....	....	....	....	....	....	....	....	....	....	....	....
1969-70	Canada	Nat-Team	STATISTICS NOT AVAILABLE																									
	Brandon Wheat Kings	WCJHL	7	6	6	12	....	....	....	0	....	....	....	....	....	....	....	....	....	....	....	....	....	....	....	....	....	....
1970-71♦	**Montreal Canadiens**	**NHL**	**1**	**0**	**0**	**0**	**0**	**0**	**0**	**0**	**0**	**0**	**0**	**1**	**0.0**	**0**	**0**	**1**	**0**	**–1**	**1**	**0**	**0**	**0**	**0**	**0**	**0**	**0**
	Montreal Voyageurs	AHL	48	16	19	35	....	....	....	53	....	....	....	....	....	....	....	....	....	....	3	1	1	2	2	....	....	....

			REGULAR SEASON																		PLAYOFFS							
Season	**Club**	**League**	**GP**	**G**	**A**	**Pts**	**AG**	**AA**	**APts**	**PIM**	**PP**	**SH**	**GW**	**S**	**%**	**TGF**	**PGF**	**TGA**	**PGA**	**+/–**	**GP**	**G**	**A**	**Pts**	**PIM**	**PP**	**SH**	**GW**
1971-72	**Montreal Canadiens**	**NHL**	**16**	**0**	**2**	**2**	**0**	**2**	**2**	**0**	**0**	**0**	**0**	**7**	**0.0**	**3**	**0**	**4**	**0**	**–1**	....	....	....	....	....	....	....	....
	Nova Scotia Voyageurs	AHL	45	15	30	45	....	....	....	18	....	....	....	....	....	....	....	....	....	....	15	7	7	14	0	....	....	....
1972-73♦	**Montreal Canadiens**	**NHL**	**65**	**21**	**25**	**46**	**20**	**20**	**40**	**22**	**1**	**1**	**7**	**99**	**21.2**	**73**	**3**	**35**	**0**	**35**	**17**	**3**	**5**	**8**	**6**	**0**	**0**	**0**
1973-74	**Montreal Canadiens**	**NHL**	**74**	**23**	**31**	**54**	**22**	**26**	**48**	**34**	**1**	**2**	**2**	**150**	**15.3**	**80**	**11**	**80**	**20**	**9**	**6**	**0**	**1**	**1**	**0**	**0**	**0**	**0**
1974-75	**Montreal Canadiens**	**NHL**	**18**	**1**	**2**	**3**	**1**	**1**	**2**	**4**	**0**	**0**	**0**	**29**	**3.4**	**10**	**2**	**10**	**2**	**0**	....	....	....	....	....	....	....	....
	St. Louis Blues	**NHL**	**57**	**23**	**26**	**49**	**20**	**19**	**39**	**24**	**5**	**2**	**3**	**151**	**15.2**	**76**	**19**	**65**	**14**	**6**	**2**	**0**	**0**	**0**	**2**	**0**	**0**	**0**
1975-76	**St. Louis Blues**	**NHL**	**75**	**43**	**42**	**85**	**38**	**31**	**69**	**41**	**4**	**8**	**9**	**207**	**20.8**	**112**	**36**	**99**	**38**	**15**	**2**	**2**	**1**	**3**	**0**	**0**	**1**	**0**
1976-77	**St. Louis Blues**	**NHL**	**71**	**11**	**30**	**41**	**10**	**23**	**33**	**12**	**3**	**0**	**1**	**156**	**7.1**	**64**	**21**	**60**	**2**	**–15**	**1**	**0**	**1**	**1**	**2**	**0**	**0**	**0**
1977-78	Jokerit Helsinki	Finland	24	11	12	23	....	....	....	12	....	....	....	....	....	....	....	....	....	....	....	....	....	....	....	....	....	....
1978-79	Dusseldorfer EG	Germany	26	17	5	22	....	....	....	2	....	....	....	....	....	....	....	....	....	....	....	....	....	....	....	....	....	....
1979-80	**St. Louis Blues**	**NHL**	**28**	**6**	**6**	**12**	**5**	**4**	**9**	**0**	**0**	**0**	**0**	**37**	**16.2**	**21**	**3**	**15**	**2**	**5**	....	....	....	....	....	....	....	....
1980-81	**St. Louis Blues**	**NHL**	**2**	**0**	**0**	**0**	**0**	**0**	**0**	**0**	**0**	**0**	**0**	**1**	**0.0**	**0**	**0**	**0**	**0**	**0**	....	....	....	....	....	....	....	....
	NHL Totals		**407**	**128**	**164**	**292**	**116**	**126**	**242**	**137**	**14**	**13**	**22**	**838**	**15.3**	**439**	**95**	**369**	**78**		**29**	**5**	**8**	**13**	**10**	**0**	**1**	**0**

Brother of Bryan

Traded to **St. Louis** by **Montreal** for Don Awrey, November 28, 1974.

• LEGGE, Barry

Barry Graham D – L. 6', 186 lbs. b: Winnipeg, Man., 10/22/1954. Montreal's 9th, 61st overall, in 1974.

Season	Club	League	GP	G	A	Pts	AG	AA	APts	PIM	PP	SH	GW	S	%	TGF	PGF	TGA	PGA	+/–	GP	G	A	Pts	PIM	PP	SH	GW
1970-71	St. James Canadians	MJHL	47	7	22	29	....	....	....	98	....	....	....	....	....	....	....	....	....	....	....	....	....	....	....	....	....	....
1971-72	Winnipeg Jets	WCJHL	61	1	16	17	....	....	....	138	....	....	....	....	....	....	....	....	....	....	....	....	....	....	....	....	....	....
1972-73	Winnipeg Jets	WCJHL	63	10	43	53	....	....	....	161	....	....	....	....	....	....	....	....	....	....	....	....	....	....	....	....	....	....
1973-74	Winnipeg Jets	WCJHL	66	13	34	47	....	....	....	198	....	....	....	....	....	....	....	....	....	....	....	....	....	....	....	....	....	....
1974-75	Michigan-Baltimore Blades	WHA	36	3	18	21	....	....	....	20	....	....	....	....	....	....	....	....	....	....	....	....	....	....	....	....	....	....
	Greensboro Generals	SHL	37	3	16	19	....	....	....	60	....	....	....	....	....	....	....	....	....	....	....	....	....	....	....	....	....	....
1975-76	Denver-Ottawa Civics	WHA	40	6	8	14	....	....	....	15	....	....	....	....	....	....	....	....	....	....	....	....	....	....	....	....	....	....
	Cleveland Crusaders	WHA	35	0	7	7	....	....	....	22	....	....	....	....	....	....	....	....	....	....	3	0	1	1	12	....	....	....
1976-77	Minnesota Fighting Saints	WHA	2	0	0	0	....	....	....	0	....	....	....	....	....	....	....	....	....	....	....	....	....	....	....	....	....	....
	Cincinnati Stingers	WHA	74	7	22	29	....	....	....	39	....	....	....	....	....	....	....	....	....	....	4	0	0	0	0	....	....	....
1977-78	Cincinnati Stingers	WHA	78	7	17	24	....	....	....	114	....	....	....	....	....	....	....	....	....	....	....	....	....	....	....	....	....	....
1978-79	Cincinnati Stingers	WHA	80	3	8	11	....	....	....	131	....	....	....	....	....	....	....	....	....	....	3	0	4	4	0	....	....	....
1979-80	**Quebec Nordiques**	**NHL**	**31**	**0**	**3**	**3**	**0**	**2**	**2**	**18**	**0**	**0**	**0**	**15**	**0.0**	**22**	**0**	**25**	**5**	**2**	....	....	....	....	....	....	....	....
	Syracuse Firebirds	AHL	5	0	1	1	....	....	....	4	....	....	....	....	....	....	....	....	....	....	....	....	....	....	....	....	....	....
1980-81	**Winnipeg Jets**	**NHL**	**38**	**0**	**6**	**6**	**0**	**4**	**4**	**69**	**0**	**0**	**0**	**14**	**0.0**	**26**	**1**	**68**	**10**	**–33**	....	....	....	....	....	....	....	....
	Tulsa Oilers	CHL	25	2	4	6	....	....	....	88	....	....	....	....	....	....	....	....	....	....	....	....	....	....	....	....	....	....
1981-82	**Winnipeg Jets**	**NHL**	**38**	**1**	**2**	**3**	**1**	**1**	**2**	**57**	**0**	**0**	**0**	**23**	**4.3**	**26**	**0**	**45**	**13**	**–6**	....	....	....	....	....	....	....	....
	Tulsa Oilers	CHL	1	0	1	1	....	....	....	0	....	....	....	....	....	....	....	....	....	....	....	....	....	....	....	....	....	....
	NHL Totals		**107**	**1**	**11**	**12**	**1**	**7**	**8**	**144**	**0**	**0**	**0**	**52**	**1.9**	**74**	**1**	**138**	**28**		....	....	....	....	....	....	....	....
	Other Major League Totals		345	26	80	106	....	....	....	341	....	....	....	....	....	....	....	....	....	....	10	0	5	5	12	....	....	....

Selected by **Michigan** (WHA) in 1974 WHA Amateur Draft, May, 1974. Claimed by **Denver** (WHA) from **Michigan-Baltimore** (WHA) in WHA Expansion Draft, June 19, 1975. Traded to **Cleveland** (WHA) by **Denver-Ottawa** (WHA) with Gary McFarlane for cash, January 20, 1976. Signed as a free agent by **Minnesota** (WHA) after **Cleveland** franchise folded, July, 1976. Traded to **Cincinnati** (WHA) by **Minnesota** (WHA) for cash, October, 1976. Claimed by **Winnipeg** from **Cincinnati** (WHA) in WHA Dispersal Draft, June 8, 1979. Traded to **Quebec** by **Winnipeg** with Jamie Hislop for Barry Melrose, June 28, 1979. Traded to **Winnipeg** by **Quebec** for cash, May 26, 1980.

• LEGGE, Randy

Norman Randall D – R. 5'11", 184 lbs. b: Newmarket, Ont., 12/16/1945.

Season	Club	League	GP	G	A	Pts	AG	AA	APts	PIM	PP	SH	GW	S	%	TGF	PGF	TGA	PGA	+/–	GP	G	A	Pts	PIM	PP	SH	GW
1962-63	Guelph Royals	OHA-Jr.	48	2	4	6	....	....	....	44	....	....	....	....	....	....	....	....	....	....	....	....	....	....	....	....	....	....
1963-64	Kitchener Rangers	OHA-Jr.	56	6	6	12	....	....	....	150	....	....	....	....	....	....	....	....	....	....	....	....	....	....	....	....	....	....
1964-65	Kitchener Rangers	OHA-Jr.	42	3	12	15	....	....	....	103	....	....	....	....	....	....	....	....	....	....	....	....	....	....	....	....	....	....
1965-66	Kitchener Rangers	OHA-Jr.	47	5	24	29	....	....	....	155	....	....	....	....	....	....	....	....	....	....	19	0	3	3	41	....	....	....
1966-67	Fort Wayne Komets	IHL	72	8	40	48	....	....	....	170	....	....	....	....	....	....	....	....	....	....	11	1	6	7	19	....	....	....
1967-68	Omaha Knights	CPHL	61	2	17	19	....	....	....	148	....	....	....	....	....	....	....	....	....	....	....	....	....	....	....	....	....	....
1968-69	Omaha Knights	CHL	8	1	3	4	....	....	....	22	....	....	....	....	....	....	....	....	....	....	....	....	....	....	....	....	....	....
	Buffalo Bisons	AHL	57	1	15	16	....	....	....	66	....	....	....	....	....	....	....	....	....	....	6	0	0	0	4	....	....	....
1969-70	Buffalo Bisons	AHL	72	0	18	18	....	....	....	161	....	....	....	....	....	....	....	....	....	....	14	0	3	3	30	....	....	....
1970-71	Seattle Totems	WHL	72	4	17	21	....	....	....	150	....	....	....	....	....	....	....	....	....	....	....	....	....	....	....	....	....	....
1971-72	Providence Reds	AHL	71	2	7	9	....	....	....	73	....	....	....	....	....	....	....	....	....	....	5	1	1	2	6	....	....	....
1972-73	**New York Rangers**	**NHL**	**12**	**0**	**2**	**2**	**0**	**2**	**2**	**2**	**0**	**0**	**0**	**10**	**0.0**	**5**	**0**	**6**	**1**	**0**	....	....	....	....	....	....	....	....
	Providence Reds	AHL	61	3	9	12	....	....	....	126	....	....	....	....	....	....	....	....	....	....	4	1	1	2	2	....	....	....
1973-74	Providence Reds	AHL	75	4	21	25	....	....	....	121	....	....	....	....	....	....	....	....	....	....	15	0	4	4	9	....	....	....
1974-75	Michigan-Baltimore Blades	WHA	78	1	14	15	....	....	....	69	....	....	....	....	....	....	....	....	....	....	....	....	....	....	....	....	....	....
1975-76	Winnipeg Jets	WHA	1	0	0	0	....	....	....	0	....	....	....	....	....	....	....	....	....	....	....	....	....	....	....	....	....	....
	Mohawk Valley Comets	NAHL	24	1	12	13	....	....	....	50	....	....	....	....	....	....	....	....	....	....	....	....	....	....	....	....	....	....
	Cleveland Crusaders	WHA	44	1	8	9	....	....	....	23	....	....	....	....	....	....	....	....	....	....	3	0	0	0	0	....	....	....
1976-77	San Diego Mariners	WHA	69	1	9	10	....	....	....	69	....	....	....	....	....	....	....	....	....	....	7	0	0	0	18	....	....	....
	NHL Totals		**12**	**0**	**2**	**2**	**0**	**2**	**2**	**2**	**0**	**0**	**0**	**10**	**0.0**	**5**	**0**	**6**	**1**		....	....	....	....	....	....	....	....
	Other Major League Totals		192	3	31	34	....	....	....	161	....	....	....	....	....	....	....	....	....	....	10	0	0	0	18	....	....	....

Selected by **Dayton-Houston** (WHA) in 1972 WHA General Player Draft, February 12, 1972. WHA rights traded to **Michigan** (WHA) by **Houston** (WHA) for cash, June, 1974. Selected by **Winnipeg** (WHA) from **Michigan-Baltimore** (WHA) in WHA Dispersal Draft, June 19, 1975. Traded to **Cleveland** (WHA) by **Winnipeg** (WHA) with future considerations for Lyle Moffat, January, 1976. Signed as a free agent by **San Diego** (WHA) after **Cleveland** (WHA) franchise folded, July, 1976.

• LEGWAND, David

C – L. 6'2", 180 lbs. b: Detroit, MI, 8/17/1980. Nashville's 1st, 2nd overall, in 1998.

Season	Club	League	GP	G	A	Pts	AG	AA	APts	PIM	PP	SH	GW	S	%	TGF	PGF	TGA	PGA	+/–	GP	G	A	Pts	PIM	PP	SH	GW
1996-97	Detroit Compuware	MNHL	44	21	41	62	....	....	....	58	....	....	....	....	....	....	....	....	....	....	....	....	....	....	....	....	....	....
1997-98	Plymouth Whalers	OHL	59	54	51	105	....	....	....	56	....	....	....	....	....	....	....	....	....	....	15	8	12	20	24	....	....	....
	United States	WJC-A	7	0	0	0	....	....	....	2	....	....	....	....	....	....	....	....	....	....	....	....	....	....	....	....	....	....
1998-99	Plymouth Whalers	OHL	55	31	49	80	....	....	....	65	....	....	....	....	....	....	....	....	....	....	11	3	8	11	8	....	....	....
	United States	WJC-A	6	1	3	4	....	....	....	31	....	....	....	....	....	....	....	....	....	....	....	....	....	....	....	....	....	....
	Nashville Predators	**NHL**	**1**	**0**	**0**	**0**	**0**	**0**	**0**	**0**	**0**	**0**	**0**	**2**	**0.0**	**0**	**0**	**0**	**0**	**0**	....	....	....	....	....	....	....	....
	United States	WC-A	6	0	2	2	....	....	....	4	....	....	....	....	....	....	....	....	....	....	....	....	....	....	....	....	....	....
99-2000	**Nashville Predators**	**NHL**	**71**	**13**	**15**	**28**	**15**	**14**	**29**	**30**	**4**	**0**	**2**	**111**	**11.7**	**46**	**15**	**37**	**0**	**–6**	....	....	....	....	....	....	....	....
	United States	WC-A	6	1	1	2	....	....	....	4	....	....	....	....	....	....	....	....	....	....	....	....	....	....	....	....	....	....
	NHL Totals		**72**	**13**	**15**	**28**	**15**	**14**	**29**	**30**	**4**	**0**	**2**	**113**	**11.5**	**46**	**15**	**37**	**0**		....	....	....	....	....	....	....	....

OHL First All-Star Team (1998) • Canadian Major Junior Rookie of the Year (1998)

• LEHMAN, Tommy

C – L. 6'1", 185 lbs. b: Stockholm, Sweden, 2/3/1964. Boston's 11th, 228th overall, in 1982.

Season	Club	League	GP	G	A	Pts	AG	AA	APts	PIM	PP	SH	GW	S	%	TGF	PGF	TGA	PGA	+/–	GP	G	A	Pts	PIM	PP	SH	GW
1980-81	Stocksunds IF	Sweden-3	12	0	6	6	....	....	....	....	....	....	....	....	....	....	....	....	....	....	....	....	....	....	....	....	....	....
1981-82	Stocksunds IF	Sweden-3	22	13	*20	33	....	....	....	....	....	....	....	....	....	....	....	....	....	....	....	....	....	....	....	....	....	....
	Sweden	WJC-A	5	1	3	4	....	....	....	0	....	....	....	....	....	....	....	....	....	....	....	....	....	....	....	....	....	....
1982-83	AIK Solna Stockholm	Sweden	28	1	5	6	....	....	....	2	....	....	....	....	....	....	....	....	....	....	3	0	0	0	0	....	....	....
1983-84	AIK Solna Stockholm	Sweden	22	4	5	9	....	....	....	6	....	....	....	....	....	....	....	....	....	....	6	2	2	4	2	....	....	....
1984-85	AIK Solna Stockholm	Sweden	34	13	13	26	....	....	....	6	....	....	....	....	....	....	....	....	....	....	....	....	....	....	....	....	....	....
1985-86	AIK Solna Stockholm	Sweden	35	11	13	24	....	....	....	12	....	....	....	....	....	....	....	....	....	....	....	....	....	....	....	....	....	....
1986-87	AIK Solna Stockholm	Sweden	32	25	15	40	....	....	....	12	....	....	....	....	....	....	....	....	....	....	....	....	....	....	....	....	....	....
1987-88	**Boston Bruins**	**NHL**	**9**	**1**	**3**	**4**	**1**	**2**	**3**	**6**	**0**	**0**	**0**	**5**	**20.0**	**5**	**1**	**4**	**0**	**0**	....	....	....	....	....	....	....	....
	Maine Mariners	AHL	11	3	5	8	....	....	....	2	....	....	....	....	....	....	....	....	....	....	....	....	....	....	....	....	....	....
1988-89	**Boston Bruins**	**NHL**	**26**	**4**	**2**	**6**	**3**	**1**	**4**	**10**	**1**	**1**	**1**	**26**	**15.4**	**13**	**3**	**17**	**0**	**–7**	....	....	....	....	....	....	....	....
	Maine Mariners	AHL	26	1	13	14	....	....	....	12	....	....	....	....	....	....	....	....	....	....	....	....	....	....	....	....	....	....

Season	Club	League	GP	G	A	Pts	AG	AA	APts	PIM	PP	SH	GW	S	%	TGF	PGF	TGA	PGA	+/–	GP	G	A	Pts	PIM	PP	SH	GW
			REGULAR SEASON																		PLAYOFFS							
1989-90	AIK Solna Stockholm	Sweden	22	7	9	16	....	....	....	12	....	....	....	....	....	....	....	....	....	....	3	1	1	2	0	....	....	....
	Edmonton Oilers	**NHL**	**1**	**0**	**0**	**0**	**0**	**0**	**0**	**0**	**0**	**0**	**0**	**0**	**0.0**	**1**	**0**	**0**	**0**	**1**	....	....	....	....	....	....	....	....
	Cape Breton Oilers	AHL	19	6	11	17	....	....	....	7	....	....	....	....	....	....	....	....	....	....	6	2	2	4	2	....	....	....
1990-91	AIK Solna Stockholm	Sweden	37	11	14	25	....	....	....	40	....	....	....	....	....	....	....	....	....	....	....	....	....	....	....	....	....	....
1991-92	AIK Solna Stockholm	Sweden	38	4	11	15	....	....	....	12	....	....	....	....	....	....	....	....	....	....	3	0	0	0	2	....	....	....
1992-93	MoDo AIK	Sweden	40	7	7	14	....	....	....	22	....	....	....	....	....	....	....	....	....	....	3	1	0	1	2	....	....	....
1993-94	AIK Solna Stockholm	Sweden-2	37	13	24	37	....	....	....	30	....	....	....	....	....	....	....	....	....	....	9	4	3	7	8	....	....	....
1994-95	AIK Solna Stockholm	Sweden	35	4	11	15	....	....	....	16	....	....	....	....	....	....	....	....	....	....	....	....	....	....	....	....	....	....
1995-96	AIK Solna Stockholm	Sweden	6	0	0	0	....	....	....	2	....	....	....	....	....	....	....	....	....	....	....	....	....	....	....	....	....	....
1996-97	Sodertalje SK	Sweden	2	0	0	0	....	....	....	2	....	....	....	....	....	....	....	....	....	....	....	....	....	....	....	....	....	....
	NHL Totals		**36**	**5**	**5**	**10**	**4**	**3**	**7**	**16**	**1**	**1**	**1**	**31**	**16.1**	**19**	**4**	**21**	**0**		....	....	....	....	....	....	....	....

Traded to **Edmonton** by **Boston** for Edmonton's 3rd round choice (Wes Walz) in 1989 Entry Draft, June 17, 1989.

• LEHTINEN, Jere

Jere K. RW – R. 6', 200 lbs. b: Espoo, Finland, 6/24/1973. Minnesota's 3rd, 88th overall, in 1992.

Season	Club	League	GP	G	A	Pts	AG	AA	APts	PIM	PP	SH	GW	S	%	TGF	PGF	TGA	PGA	+/–	GP	G	A	Pts	PIM	PP	SH	GW
1989-90	Kiekoo-67 Turku	Finland-Jr.	32	23	23	46	....	....	....	6	....	....	....	....	....	....	....	....	....	....	5	0	3	3	0	....	....	....
1990-91	Kiekko-Espoo	Finland-Jr.	3	3	1	4	....	....	....	0	....	....	....	....	....	....	....	....	....	....	....	....	....	....	....	....	....	....
	Kiekko-Espoo	Finland-2	32	15	9	24	....	....	....	12	....	....	....	....	....	....	....	....	....	....	....	....	....	....	....	....	....	....
	Finland	WJC-A	4	2	0	2	....	....	....	0	....	....	....	....	....	....	....	....	....	....	....	....	....	....	....	....	....	....
	Finland	EJC-A	5	5	4	9	....	....	....	6	....	....	....	....	....	....	....	....	....	....	....	....	....	....	....	....	....	....
1991-92	Kiekoo-67 Turku	Finland-Jr.	8	5	4	9	....	....	....	2	....	....	....	....	....	....	....	....	....	....	....	....	....	....	....	....	....	....
	Kiekko-Espoo	Finland-2	43	32	17	49	....	....	....	6	....	....	....	....	....	....	....	....	....	....	....	....	....	....	....	....	....	....
	Finland	WJC-A	7	0	2	2	....	....	....	2	....	....	....	....	....	....	....	....	....	....	....	....	....	....	....	....	....	....
	Finland	WC-A	7	1	1	2	....	....	....	0	....	....	....	....	....	....	....	....	....	....	....	....	....	....	....	....	....	....
1992-93	Kiekoo-67 Turku	Finland-Jr.	4	5	3	8	....	....	....	8	....	....	....	....	....	....	....	....	....	....	....	....	....	....	....	....	....	....
	Kiekko-Espoo	Finland	45	13	14	27	....	....	....	6	....	....	....	....	....	....	....	....	....	....	....	....	....	....	....	....	....	....
	Finland	WJC-A	7	6	8	14	....	....	....	10	....	....	....	....	....	....	....	....	....	....	....	....	....	....	....	....	....	....
1993-94	TPS Turku	Finland	42	19	20	39	....	....	....	6	....	....	....	....	....	....	....	....	....	....	11	*11	2	13	*2	....	....	....
	Finland	Olympics	8	3	0	3	....	....	....	0	....	....	....	....	....	....	....	....	....	....	....	....	....	....	....	....	....	....
	Finland	WC-A	8	3	5	8	....	....	....	4	....	....	....	....	....	....	....	....	....	....	....	....	....	....	....	....	....	....
1994-95	TPS Turku	Finland	39	19	23	42	....	....	....	33	....	....	....	....	....	....	....	....	....	....	13	*8	6	14	4	....	....	....
	Finland	WC-A	8	2	5	7	....	....	....	4	....	....	....	....	....	....	....	....	....	....	....	....	....	....	....	....	....	....
1995-96	**Dallas Stars**	**NHL**	**57**	**6**	**22**	**28**	**6**	**18**	**24**	**16**	**0**	**0**	**1**	**109**	**5.5**	**43**	**11**	**37**	**10**	**5**	....	....	....	....	....	....	....	....
	Michigan K-Wings	IHL	1	1	0	1	....	....	....	0	....	....	....	....	....	....	....	....	....	....	....	....	....	....	....	....	....	....
1996-97	Finland	W-Cup	4	2	2	4	....	....	....	0	....	....	....	....	....	....	....	....	....	....	....	....	....	....	....	....	....	....
	Dallas Stars	**NHL**	**63**	**16**	**27**	**43**	**17**	**24**	**41**	**2**	**3**	**1**	**2**	**134**	**11.9**	**57**	**7**	**40**	**16**	**26**	**7**	**2**	**2**	**4**	**0**	**0**	**0**	**0**
1997-98	**Dallas Stars**	**NHL**	**72**	**23**	**19**	**42**	**27**	**19**	**46**	**20**	**7**	**2**	**6**	**201**	**11.4**	**80**	**30**	**42**	**11**	**19**	**12**	**3**	**5**	**8**	**2**	**1**	**0**	**0**
	Finland	Olympics	6	4	2	6	....	....	....	2	....	....	....	....	....	....	....	....	....	....	....	....	....	....	....	....	....	....
1998-99♦	**Dallas Stars**	**NHL**	**74**	**20**	**32**	**52**	**23**	**31**	**54**	**18**	**7**	**1**	**2**	**173**	**11.6**	**96**	**34**	**45**	**12**	**29**	**23**	**10**	**3**	**13**	**2**	**1**	**1**	**0**
99-2000	**Dallas Stars**	**NHL**	**17**	**3**	**5**	**8**	**3**	**5**	**8**	**0**	**0**	**0**	**1**	**29**	**10.3**	**12**	**3**	**10**	**2**	**1**	**13**	**1**	**5**	**6**	**2**	**0**	**0**	**0**
	NHL Totals		**283**	**68**	**105**	**173**	**76**	**97**	**173**	**56**	**17**	**4**	**12**	**646**	**10.5**	**288**	**85**	**174**	**51**		**55**	**16**	**15**	**31**	**6**	**2**	**1**	**0**

Finnish First All-Star Team (1995) • WC-A All-Star Team (1995) • Won Frank J. Selke Trophy (1998, 1999) • Played in NHL All-Star Game (1998)

Rights transferred to **Dallas** after **Minnesota** franchise relocated, June 9, 1993. • Missed majority of 1999-2000 season recovering from broken leg suffered in game vs. Nashville, October 16, 1999.

• LEHTO, Petteri

D – L. 5'11", 195 lbs. b: Turku, Finland, 3/13/1961.

Season	Club	League	GP	G	A	Pts	AG	AA	APts	PIM	PP	SH	GW	S	%	TGF	PGF	TGA	PGA	+/–	GP	G	A	Pts	PIM	PP	SH	GW
1977-78	TPS Turku	Finland-Jr.	25	5	14	19	....	....	....	*92	....	....	....	....	....	....	....	....	....	....	....	....	....	....	....	....	....	....
1978-79	TPS Turku	Finland-Jr.	24	4	5	9	....	....	....	36	....	....	....	....	....	....	....	....	....	....	....	....	....	....	....	....	....	....
	TPS Turku	Finland	....	....	....	....	....	....	....	....	....	....	....	....	....	....	....	....	....	....	3	0	0	0	2	....	....	....
1979-80	TPS Turku	Finland-Jr.	15	7	6	13	....	....	....	36	....	....	....	....	....	....	....	....	....	....	....	....	....	....	....	....	....	....
	Melville Millionaires	SJHL	STATISTICS NOT AVAILABLE																									
1980-81	TPS Turku	Finland-Jr.	15	7	6	13	....	....	....	36	....	....	....	....	....	....	....	....	....	....	....	....	....	....	....	....	....	....
	TPS Turku	Finland	31	0	2	2	....	....	....	16	....	....	....	....	....	....	....	....	....	....	....	....	....	....	....	....	....	....
1981-82	Lukko Rauma	Finland	34	3	8	11	....	....	....	24	....	....	....	....	....	....	....	....	....	....	....	....	....	....	....	....	....	....
1982-83	TPS Turku	Finland	33	3	6	9	....	....	....	52	....	....	....	....	....	....	....	....	....	....	3	0	0	0	2	....	....	....
1983-84	TPS Turku	Finland	36	8	10	18	....	....	....	32	....	....	....	....	....	....	....	....	....	....	10	2	1	3	8	....	....	....
	Finland	Olympics	6	2	2	4	....	....	....	10	....	....	....	....	....	....	....	....	....	....	....	....	....	....	....	....	....	....
1984-85	**Pittsburgh Penguins**	**NHL**	**6**	**0**	**0**	**0**	**0**	**0**	**0**	**4**	**0**	**0**	**0**	**5**	**0.0**	**2**	**0**	**6**	**0**	**–4**	....	....	....	....	....	....	....	....
	Baltimore Skipjacks	AHL	52	3	18	21	....	....	....	55	....	....	....	....	....	....	....	....	....	....	....	....	....	....	....	....	....	....
1985-86	TPS Turku	Finland	33	3	10	13	....	....	....	62	....	....	....	....	....	....	....	....	....	....	7	0	2	2	10	....	....	....
1986-87	TPS Turku	Finland	22	1	5	6	....	....	....	30	....	....	....	....	....	....	....	....	....	....	....	....	....	....	....	....	....	....
1987-88	KalPa Kuopio	Finland	32	3	11	14	....	....	....	32	....	....	....	....	....	....	....	....	....	....	....	....	....	....	....	....	....	....
1988-89	TPS Turku	Finland	40	2	9	11	....	....	....	20	....	....	....	....	....	....	....	....	....	....	10	0	0	0	4	....	....	....
1989-90	TPS Turku	Finland	42	0	1	1	....	....	....	27	....	....	....	....	....	....	....	....	....	....	9	0	0	0	6	....	....	....
	NHL Totals		**6**	**0**	**0**	**0**	**0**	**0**	**0**	**4**	**0**	**0**	**0**	**5**	**0.0**	**2**	**0**	**6**	**0**		....	....	....	....	....	....	....	....

Signed as a free agent by **Pittsburgh**, July, 1984.

• LEHTONEN, Antero

LW – L. 6', 185 lbs. b: Tampere, Finland, 4/12/1954.

Season	Club	League	GP	G	A	Pts	AG	AA	APts	PIM	PP	SH	GW	S	%	TGF	PGF	TGA	PGA	+/–	GP	G	A	Pts	PIM	PP	SH	GW
1971-72	Tappara Tampere	Finland-Jr.	14	18	13	31	....	....	....	16	....	....	....	....	....	....	....	....	....	....	....	....	....	....	....	....	....	....
	Tappara Tampere	Finland	1	0	0	0	....	....	....	2	....	....	....	....	....	....	....	....	....	....	....	....	....	....	....	....	....	....
1972-73	Tappara Tampere	Finland	36	20	5	25	....	....	....	23	....	....	....	....	....	....	....	....	....	....	....	....	....	....	....	....	....	....
1973-74	Tappara Tampere	Finland	36	9	7	16	....	....	....	10	....	....	....	....	....	....	....	....	....	....	....	....	....	....	....	....	....	....
	Finland	WJC-A	5	1	2	3	....	....	....	6	....	....	....	....	....	....	....	....	....	....	....	....	....	....	....	....	....	....
1974-75	Tappara Tampere	Finland	36	26	7	33	....	....	....	26	....	....	....	....	....	....	....	....	....	....	....	....	....	....	....	....	....	....
1975-76	Tappara Tampere	Finland	36	19	11	30	....	....	....	21	....	....	....	....	....	....	....	....	....	....	4	0	2	2	8	....	....	....
1976-77	TPS Turku	Finland	36	26	12	38	....	....	....	12	....	....	....	....	....	....	....	....	....	....	8	4	1	5	4	....	....	....
	Finland	Nat-Team	14	2	2	4	....	....	....	0	....	....	....	....	....	....	....	....	....	....	....	....	....	....	....	....	....	....
	Finland	WEC-A	9	1	1	2	....	....	....	6	....	....	....	....	....	....	....	....	....	....	....	....	....	....	....	....	....	....
1977-78	TPS Turku	Finland	35	23	13	36	....	....	....	38	....	....	....	....	....	....	....	....	....	....	8	3	5	8	4	....	....	....
1978-79	Tappara Tampere	Finland	36	35	19	54	....	....	....	43	....	....	....	....	....	....	....	....	....	....	10	8	5	13	6	....	....	....
	Finland	Nat-Team	15	3	5	8	....	....	....	6	....	....	....	....	....	....	....	....	....	....	....	....	....	....	....	....	....	....
	Finland	WEC-A	8	3	3	6	....	....	....	0	....	....	....	....	....	....	....	....	....	....	....	....	....	....	....	....	....	....
1979-80	**Washington Capitals**	**NHL**	**65**	**9**	**12**	**21**	**8**	**9**	**17**	**14**	**2**	**0**	**1**	**101**	**8.9**	**30**	**3**	**31**	**0**	**–4**	....	....	....	....	....	....	....	....
	Hershey Bears	AHL	4	3	0	3	....	....	....	2	....	....	....	....	....	....	....	....	....	....	....	....	....	....	....	....	....	....
1980-81	Tappara Tampere	Finland	27	13	7	20	....	....	....	24	....	....	....	....	....	....	....	....	....	....	8	7	3	10	6	....	....	....
	Finland	Nat-Team	4	0	0	0	....	....	....	2	....	....	....	....	....	....	....	....	....	....	....	....	....	....	....	....	....	....
	Finland	WEC-A	8	0	3	3	....	....	....	0	....	....	....	....	....	....	....	....	....	....	....	....	....	....	....	....	....	....
1981-82	TPS Turku	Finland	36	14	8	22	....	....	....	35	....	....	....	....	....	....	....	....	....	....	7	2	1	3	6	....	....	....
1982-83	TPS Turku	Finland	36	11	10	21	....	....	....	16	....	....	....	....	....	....	....	....	....	....	3	4	0	4	0	....	....	....
1983-84	TPS Turku	Finland	30	8	13	21	....	....	....	14	....	....	....	....	....	....	....	....	....	....	9	1	1	2	4	....	....	....
1984-85	JyP-HT Jyvaskyla	Finland	35	35	25	60	....	....	....	16	....	....	....	....	....	....	....	....	....	....	....	....	....	....	....	....	....	....
1985-86	JyP-HT Jyvaskyla	Finland	36	24	12	36	....	....	....	18	....	....	....	....	....	....	....	....	....	....	....	....	....	....	....	....	....	....
1986-87	JyP-HT Jyvaskyla	Finland	39	10	8	18	....	....	....	20	....	....	....	....	....	....	....	....	....	....	....	....	....	....	....	....	....	....
	NHL Totals		**65**	**9**	**12**	**21**	**8**	**9**	**17**	**14**	**2**	**0**	**1**	**101**	**8.9**	**30**	**3**	**31**	**0**		....	....	....	....	....	....	....	....

Finnish First All-Star Team (1979)

Signed as a free agent by **Washington**, September 16, 1979.

• LEHVONEN, Henri

"Hank" D – L. 5'11", 200 lbs. b: Sarnia, Ont., 8/26/1950. Minnesota's 5th, 62nd overall, in 1970.

			REGULAR SEASON																		PLAYOFFS							
Season	Club	League	GP	G	A	Pts	AG	AA	APts	PIM	PP	SH	GW	S	%	TGF	PGF	TGA	PGA	+/–	GP	G	A	Pts	PIM	PP	SH	GW
1966-67	Sarnia Legionaires	OHA-B	STATISTICS NOT AVAILABLE																									
1967-68	Peterborough Petes	OHA-Jr.	12	0	3	3	....	....	....	6	....	....	....	....	....	....	....	....	....	....	....	....	....	....	....	....	....	....
	Kitchener Rangers	OHA-Jr.	24	2	11	13	....	....	....	8	....	....	....	....	....	....	....	....	....	....	17	3	12	15	12	....	....	....
1968-69	Kitchener Rangers	OHA-Jr.	51	12	21	33	....	....	....	20	....	....	....	....	....	....	....	....	....	....	....	....	....	....	....	....	....	....
1969-70	Kitchener Rangers	OHA-Jr.	29	2	9	11	....	....	....	25	....	....	....	....	....	....	....	....	....	....	6	0	1	1	4	....	....	....
1970-71	Clinton Comets	EHL	3	0	0	0	....	....	....	0	....	....	....	....	....	....	....	....	....	....	....	....	....	....	....	....	....	....
	Port Huron Flags	IHL	51	4	21	25	....	....	....	29	....	....	....	....	....	....	....	....	....	....	14	1	3	4	6	....	....	....
1971-72	Port Huron Wings	IHL	9	0	6	6	....	....	....	6	....	....	....	....	....	....	....	....	....	....	....	....	....	....	....	....	....	....
1972-73	Port Huron Wings	IHL	66	10	38	48	....	....	....	83	....	....	....	....	....	....	....	....	....	....	11	2	2	4	10	....	....	....
1973-74			OUT OF HOCKEY – RETIRED																									
1974-75	**Kansas City Scouts**	**NHL**	**4**	**0**	**0**	**0**	**0**	**0**	**0**	**0**	**0**	**0**	**0**	**2**	**0.0**	**5**	**0**	**1**	**0**	**4**	....	....	....	....	....	....	....	....
	Port Huron Flags	IHL	58	6	29	35	....	....	....	94	....	....	....	....	....	....	....	....	....	....	5	3	2	5	2	....	....	....
1975-76	Port Huron Flags	IHL	16	1	6	7	....	....	....	18	....	....	....	....	....	....	....	....	....	....	....	....	....	....	....	....	....	....
	Toledo Goaldiggers	IHL	35	3	10	13	....	....	....	22	....	....	....	....	....	....	....	....	....	....	4	2	3	5	6	....	....	....
1976-77	Port Huron Flags	IHL	41	0	12	12	....	....	....	18	....	....	....	....	....	....	....	....	....	....	....	....	....	....	....	....	....	....
1977-78			DID NOT PLAY																									
1978-79	Jokerit Helsinki	Finland	36	5	5	10	....	....	....	39	....	....	....	....	....	....	....	....	....	....	....	....	....	....	....	....	....	....
1979-80	Jokerit Helsinki	Finland	35	3	10	13	....	....	....	69	....	....	....	....	....	....	....	....	....	....	....	....	....	....	....	....	....	....
1980-81	Ilves Tampere	Finland	35	0	4	4	....	....	....	40	....	....	....	....	....	....	....	....	....	....	2	0	0	0	6	....	....	....
1981-82	Ilves Tampere	Finland	16	1	1	2	....	....	....	20	....	....	....	....	....	....	....	....	....	....	....	....	....	....	....	....	....	....
	NHL Totals		**4**	**0**	**0**	**0**	**0**	**0**	**0**	**0**	**0**	**0**	**0**	**2**	**0.0**	**5**	**0**	**1**	**0**		....	....	....	....	....	....	....	....

• Missed entire 1973-74 season after failing to come to contract terms with **Port Huron** (IHL). Signed as a free agent by **Kansas City** and assigned to **Port Huron** (IHL), November 15, 1974. Traded to **Detroit** (Kalamazoo-IHL) by **Kansas City** (IHL) for Frank Bathe, November, 1975. Traded to **Toledo** (IHL) by **Detroit** (Kalamazoo-IHL) for Reg Meserve, Jim Mitchell and Tony Piroski, November, 1975.

• LEINONEN, Mikko

Mikko Simo Yrjana "Breeze" C – L. 6', 175 lbs. b: Tampere, Finland, 7/15/1955.

Season	Club	League	GP	G	A	Pts	AG	AA	APts	PIM	PP	SH	GW	S	%	TGF	PGF	TGA	PGA	+/–	GP	G	A	Pts	PIM	PP	SH	GW
1973-74	Tappara Tampere	Finland	35	26	13	39	....	....	....	30	....	....	....	....	....	....	....	....	....	....	....	....	....	....	....	....	....	....
	Finland	WJC-A	5	4	1	5	....	....	....	2	....	....	....	....	....	....	....	....	....	....	....	....	....	....	....	....	....	....
1974-75	Tappara Tampere	Finland	34	17	11	28	....	....	....	14	....	....	....	....	....	....	....	....	....	....	....	....	....	....	....	....	....	....
	Finland	WJC-A	5	0	3	3	....	....	....	2	....	....	....	....	....	....	....	....	....	....	....	....	....	....	....	....	....	....
1975-76	Tappara Tampere	Finland	36	23	24	47	....	....	....	42	....	....	....	....	....	....	....	....	....	....	4	1	1	2	8	....	....	....
1976-77	Tappara Tampere	Finland	33	23	24	47	....	....	....	43	....	....	....	....	....	....	....	....	....	....	6	7	4	11	6	....	....	....
1977-78	MoDo AIK	Sweden	36	19	26	45	....	....	....	51	....	....	....	....	....	....	....	....	....	....	2	0	0	0	4	....	....	....
	Finland	WEC-A	8	0	1	1	....	....	....	4	....	....	....	....	....	....	....	....	....	....	....	....	....	....	....	....	....	....
1978-79	MoDo AIK	Sweden	34	10	19	29	....	....	....	32	....	....	....	....	....	....	....	....	....	....	6	2	*7	9	4	....	....	....
	Finland	WEC-A	8	1	1	2	....	....	....	4	....	....	....	....	....	....	....	....	....	....	....	....	....	....	....	....	....	....
1979-80	Karpat Oulu	Finland	36	32	20	52	....	....	....	40	....	....	....	....	....	....	....	....	....	....	6	2	2	4	4	....	....	....
	Finland	Olympics	7	6	4	10	....	....	....	0	....	....	....	....	....	....	....	....	....	....	....	....	....	....	....	....	....	....
1980-81	Karpat Oulu	Finland	36	16	36	52	....	....	....	43	....	....	....	....	....	....	....	....	....	....	12	3	7	10	14	....	....	....
	Finland	WEC-A	8	5	3	8	....	....	....	2	....	....	....	....	....	....	....	....	....	....	....	....	....	....	....	....	....	....
1981-82	Finland	Can-Cup	5	0	1	1	....	....	....	0	....	....	....	....	....	....	....	....	....	....	....	....	....	....	....	....	....	....
	New York Rangers	DN-Cup	4	2	1	3	....	....	....	....	....	....	....	....	....	....	....	....	....	....	....	....	....	....	....	....	....	....
	New York Rangers	**NHL**	**53**	**11**	**20**	**31**	**9**	**13**	**22**	**18**	**2**	**0**	**3**	**67**	**16.4**	**45**	**10**	**33**	**0**	**2**	**7**	**1**	**6**	**7**	**20**	**0**	**0**	**0**
	Springfield Indians	AHL	6	4	2	6	....	....	....	2	....	....	....	....	....	....	....	....	....	....	....	....	....	....	....	....	....	....
1982-83	**New York Rangers**	**NHL**	**78**	**17**	**34**	**51**	**14**	**24**	**38**	**23**	**3**	**0**	**0**	**135**	**12.6**	**87**	**34**	**48**	**7**	**12**	**7**	**1**	**3**	**4**	**4**	**1**	**0**	**0**
1983-84	**New York Rangers**	**NHL**	**28**	**3**	**23**	**26**	**2**	**16**	**18**	**28**	**0**	**0**	**1**	**39**	**7.7**	**35**	**13**	**26**	**8**	**4**	**5**	**0**	**2**	**2**	**4**	**0**	**0**	**0**
	Tulsa Oilers	CHL	33	15	23	38	....	....	....	38	....	....	....	....	....	....	....	....	....	....	....	....	....	....	....	....	....	....
1984-85	Karpat Oulu	Finland	35	19	15	34	....	....	....	*70	....	....	....	....	....	....	....	....	....	....	7	2	3	5	6	....	....	....
	Washington Capitals	**NHL**	**3**	**0**	**1**	**1**	**0**	**1**	**1**	**2**	**0**	**0**	**0**	**5**	**0.0**	**2**	**0**	**1**	**0**	**1**	**1**	**0**	**0**	**0**	**0**	**0**	**0**	**0**
1985-86	Karpat Oulu	Finland	36	6	17	23	....	....	....	40	....	....	....	....	....	....	....	....	....	....	5	1	1	2	0	....	....	....
1986-87	KaiPa Kuopio	Finland	5	4	0	4	....	....	....	31	....	....	....	....	....	....	....	....	....	....	....	....	....	....	....	....	....	....
	NHL Totals		**162**	**31**	**78**	**109**	**25**	**54**	**79**	**71**	**5**	**0**	**4**	**246**	**12.6**	**169**	**57**	**108**	**15**		**20**	**2**	**11**	**13**	**28**	**1**	**0**	**0**

Finnish First All-Star Team (1981)

Signed as a free agent by **NY Rangers**, September 8, 1981. Signed as a free agent by **Washington**, March 13, 1985.

• LEITER, Bobby

Robert Edward C – L. 5'9", 175 lbs. b: Winnipeg, Man., 3/22/1941.

Season	Club	League	GP	G	A	Pts	AG	AA	APts	PIM	PP	SH	GW	S	%	TGF	PGF	TGA	PGA	+/–	GP	G	A	Pts	PIM	PP	SH	GW
1958-59	Winnipeg Braves	MJHL	31	14	21	35	....	....	....	8	....	....	....	....	....	....	....	....	....	....	8	3	4	7	4	....	....	....
	Winnipeg Braves	Mem-Cup	16	3	*14	17	....	....	....	12	....	....	....	....	....	....	....	....	....	....	....	....	....	....	....	....	....	....
1959-60	Winnipeg Braves	MJHL	31	22	*31	53	....	....	....	48	....	....	....	....	....	....	....	....	....	....	4	1	2	3	2	....	....	....
	Winnipeg Warriors	WHL	1	0	0	0	....	....	....	0	....	....	....	....	....	....	....	....	....	....	....	....	....	....	....	....	....	....
1960-61	Winnipeg Braves	MJHL	30	20	14	34	....	....	....	31	....	....	....	....	....	....	....	....	....	....	3	0	3	3	0	....	....	....
	Winnipeg Warriors	WHL	5	1	3	4	....	....	....	0	....	....	....	....	....	....	....	....	....	....	....	....	....	....	....	....	....	....
	Winnipeg Maroons	Al-Cup	20	11	4	15	....	....	....	2	....	....	....	....	....	....	....	....	....	....	....	....	....	....	....	....	....	....
1961-62	Kingston Frontenacs	EPHL	69	24	32	56	....	....	....	61	....	....	....	....	....	....	....	....	....	....	11	8	8	*16	8	....	....	....
1962-63	**Boston Bruins**	**NHL**	**51**	**9**	**13**	**22**	**10**	**13**	**23**	**34**	....	....	....	....	....	....	....	....	....	....	....	....	....	....	....	....	....	....
	Kingston Frontenacs	EPHL	20	15	23	38	....	....	....	17	....	....	....	....	....	....	....	....	....	....	....	....	....	....	....	....	....	....
1963-64	**Boston Bruins**	**NHL**	**56**	**6**	**13**	**19**	**7**	**14**	**21**	**43**	....	....	....	....	....	....	....	....	....	....	....	....	....	....	....	....	....	....
	Hershey Bears	AHL	15	6	6	12	....	....	....	6	....	....	....	....	....	....	....	....	....	....	6	2	4	6	2	....	....	....
1964-65	**Boston Bruins**	**NHL**	**18**	**3**	**1**	**4**	**4**	**1**	**5**	**6**	....	....	....	....	....	....	....	....	....	....	....	....	....	....	....	....	....	....
1965-66	**Boston Bruins**	**NHL**	**9**	**2**	**1**	**3**	**2**	**1**	**3**	**2**	....	....	....	....	....	....	....	....	....	....	....	....	....	....	....	....	....	....
	Hershey Bears	AHL	45	9	23	32	....	....	....	16	....	....	....	....	....	....	....	....	....	....	3	1	2	3	2	....	....	....
1966-67	California Seals	WHL	20	2	8	10	....	....	....	10	....	....	....	....	....	....	....	....	....	....	1	0	0	0	0	....	....	....
1967-68	Hershey Bears	AHL	72	22	48	70	....	....	....	57	....	....	....	....	....	....	....	....	....	....	5	0	0	0	4	....	....	....
1968-69	**Boston Bruins**	**NHL**	**1**	**0**	**0**	**0**	**0**	**0**	**0**	**0**	**0**	**0**	**0**	**0**	**0.0**	**0**	**0**	**0**	**0**	**0**	....	....	....	....	....	....	....	....
	Hershey Bears	AHL	72	26	33	59	....	....	....	35	....	....	....	....	....	....	....	....	....	....	11	2	8	10	12	....	....	....
1969-70	Hershey Bears	AHL	72	21	41	62	....	....	....	51	....	....	....	....	....	....	....	....	....	....	7	3	2	5	4	....	....	....
1970-71	Hershey Bears	AHL	72	33	36	69	....	....	....	26	....	....	....	....	....	....	....	....	....	....	4	0	2	2	4	....	....	....
1971-72	**Pittsburgh Penguins**	**NHL**	**78**	**14**	**17**	**31**	**14**	**15**	**29**	**18**	**5**	**0**	**3**	**147**	**9.5**	**42**	**15**	**54**	**2**	**–25**	**4**	**3**	**0**	**3**	**0**	**1**	**0**	**0**
1972-73	**Atlanta Flames**	**NHL**	**78**	**26**	**34**	**60**	**24**	**27**	**51**	**19**	**5**	**0**	**3**	**174**	**14.9**	**72**	**14**	**71**	**1**	**–12**	....	....	....	....	....	....	....	....
1973-74	**Atlanta Flames**	**NHL**	**78**	**26**	**26**	**52**	**25**	**21**	**46**	**10**	**10**	**0**	**4**	**178**	**14.6**	**76**	**34**	**46**	**0**	**–4**	**4**	**0**	**0**	**0**	**2**	**0**	**0**	**0**
1974-75	**Atlanta Flames**	**NHL**	**52**	**10**	**18**	**28**	**9**	**13**	**22**	**8**	**6**	**0**	**1**	**96**	**10.4**	**42**	**22**	**35**	**0**	**–15**	....	....	....	....	....	....	....	....
1975-76	**Atlanta Flames**	**NHL**	**26**	**2**	**3**	**5**	**2**	**2**	**4**	**4**	**1**	**0**	**0**	**26**	**7.7**	**12**	**4**	**8**	**0**	**0**	....	....	....	....	....	....	....	....
	Calgary Cowboys	WHA	51	17	17	34	....	....	....	8	....	....	....	....	....	....	....	....	....	....	3	2	0	2	0	....	....	....
	NHL Totals		**447**	**98**	**126**	**224**	**97**	**107**	**204**	**144**	....	....	....	....	....	....	....	....	....	....	**8**	**3**	**0**	**3**	**2**	....	....	....
	Other Major League Totals		51	17	17	34	....	....	....	8	....	....	....	....	....	....	....	....	....	....	3	2	0	2	0	....	....	....

AHL Second All-Star Team (1971)

Traded to **Pittsburgh** by **Boston** for cash, May, 1971. Selected by **Winnipeg** (WHA) in 1972 WHA General Player Draft, February 12, 1972., 1975. Claimed by **Atlanta** from **Pittsburgh** in Expansion Draft, June 6, 1972. WHA rights traded to **Calgary** (WHA) by **Winnipeg** (WHA) for future considerations, June, 1975.

• LEITER, Ken

D – L. 6'1", 195 lbs. b: Detroit, MI, 4/19/1961. NY Islanders' 6th, 101st overall, in 1980.

Season	Club	League	GP	G	A	Pts	AG	AA	APts	PIM	PP	SH	GW	S	%	TGF	PGF	TGA	PGA	+/–	GP	G	A	Pts	PIM	PP	SH	GW
1978-79	Detroit-St. Mary's High	Hi-School	STATISTICS NOT AVAILABLE																									
1979-80	Michigan State Spartans	WCHA	38	0	10	10	....	....	....	96	....	....	....	....	....	....	....	....	....	....	....	....	....	....	....	....	....	....
1980-81	Michigan State Spartans	WCHA	31	2	12	14	....	....	....	48	....	....	....	....	....	....	....	....	....	....	....	....	....	....	....	....	....	....
1981-82	Michigan State Spartans	CCHA	31	7	13	20	....	....	....	50	....	....	....	....	....	....	....	....	....	....	....	....	....	....	....	....	....	....
1982-83	Michigan State Spartans	CCHA	40	3	28	31	....	....	....	47	....	....	....	....	....	....	....	....	....	....	....	....	....	....	....	....	....	....
1983-84	Indianapolis Checkers	CHL	68	10	26	36	....	....	....	46	....	....	....	....	....	....	....	....	....	....	10	3	4	7	0	....	....	....
1984-85	**New York Islanders**	**NHL**	**5**	**0**	**2**	**2**	**0**	**1**	**1**	**2**	**0**	**0**	**0**	**9**	**0.0**	**5**	**0**	**6**	**1**	**0**	....	....	....	....	....	....	....	....
	Springfield Indians	AHL	39	3	12	15	....	....	....	12	....	....	....	....	....	....	....	....	....	....	4	0	3	3	2	....	....	....

Season	Club	League	GP	G	A	Pts	AG	AA	APts	PIM	PP	SH	GW	S	%	TGF	PGF	TGA	PGA	+/–	GP	G	A	Pts	PIM	PP	SH	GW
			REGULAR SEASON																		PLAYOFFS							
1985-86	**New York Islanders**	**NHL**	**9**	**1**	**1**	**2**	**1**	**1**	**2**	**6**	**0**	**0**	**0**	**9**	**11.1**	**10**	**1**	**8**	**0**	**1**	....	....	....	....	....	....	....	....
	Springfield Indians	AHL	68	7	27	34	....	....	....	51	....	....	....	....	....	....	....	....	....	....	....	....	....	....	....	....	....	....
1986-87	**New York Islanders**	**NHL**	**74**	**9**	**20**	**29**	**8**	**15**	**23**	**30**	**4**	**0**	**0**	**159**	**5.7**	**85**	**30**	**64**	**11**	**2**	**11**	**0**	**5**	**5**	**6**	**0**	**0**	**0**
1987-88	**New York Islanders**	**NHL**	**51**	**4**	**13**	**17**	**3**	**9**	**12**	**24**	**1**	**0**	**1**	**104**	**3.8**	**62**	**19**	**40**	**15**	**18**	**4**	**0**	**1**	**1**	**2**	**0**	**0**	**0**
	Springfield Indians	AHL	2	0	4	4	....	....	....	0	....	....	....	....	....	....	....	....	....	....	....	....	....	....	....	....	....	....
1988-89			OUT OF HOCKEY – RETIRED																									
1989-90	**Minnesota North Stars**	**NHL**	**4**	**0**	**0**	**0**	**0**	**0**	**0**	**0**	**0**	**0**	**0**	**5**	**0.0**	**2**	**1**	**3**	**0**	**–2**	....	....	....	....	....	....	....	....
	Kalamazoo Wings	IHL	4	1	1	2	....	....	....	0	....	....	....	....	....	....	....	....	....	....	....	....	....	....	....	....	....	....
	NHL Totals		**143**	**14**	**36**	**50**	**12**	**26**	**38**	**62**	**5**	**0**	**1**	**286**	**4.9**	**164**	**51**	**121**	**27**		**15**	**0**	**6**	**6**	**8**	**0**	**0**	**0**

CCHA First All-Star Team (1983)

Claimed by **Minnesota** from **NY Islanders** in Waiver Draft, October 2, 1989.

• LEMAIRE, Jacques

Jacques Gerard C – L. 5′10″, 180 lbs. b: LaSalle, Que., 9/7/1945. **HHOF**

Season	Club	League	GP	G	A	Pts	AG	AA	APts	PIM	PP	SH	GW	S	%	TGF	PGF	TGA	PGA	+/–	GP	G	A	Pts	PIM	PP	SH	GW
1962-63	Lachine Maroons	QJHL	42	41	63	*104	....	....	....	....	....	....	....	....	....	....	....	....	....	....	....	....	....	....	....	....	....	....
1963-64	Montreal Jr. Canadiens	OHA-Jr.	42	25	30	55	....	....	....	17	....	....	....	....	....	....	....	....	....	....	17	10	6	16	4	....	....	....
1964-65	Montreal Jr. Canadiens	OHA-Jr.	56	25	47	72	....	....	....	52	....	....	....	....	....	....	....	....	....	....	7	1	5	6	0	....	....	....
	Quebec Aces	AHL	1	0	0	0	....	....	....	0	....	....	....	....	....	....	....	....	....	....	....	....	....	....	....	....	....	....
1965-66	Montreal Jr. Canadiens	OHA-Jr.	48	41	52	93	....	....	....	69	....	....	....	....	....	....	....	....	....	....	10	11	2	13	14	....	....	....
1966-67	Houston Apollos	CPHL	69	19	30	49	....	....	....	19	....	....	....	....	....	....	....	....	....	....	6	0	1	1	0	....	....	....
1967-68♦	**Montreal Canadiens**	**NHL**	**69**	**22**	**20**	**42**	**26**	**20**	**46**	**16**	**3**	**1**	**3**	**182**	**12.1**	**58**	**8**	**37**	**2**	**15**	**13**	**7**	**6**	**13**	**6**	**2**	**0**	**2**
1968-69♦	**Montreal Canadiens**	**NHL**	**75**	**29**	**34**	**63**	**31**	**30**	**61**	**29**	**5**	**0**	**4**	**330**	**8.8**	**102**	**27**	**51**	**7**	**31**	**14**	**4**	**2**	**6**	**6**	**1**	**0**	**0**
1969-70	**Montreal Canadiens**	**NHL**	**69**	**32**	**28**	**60**	**35**	**26**	**61**	**16**	**13**	**0**	**5**	**237**	**13.5**	**92**	**25**	**49**	**1**	**19**	....	....	....	....	....	....	....	....
1970-71♦	**Montreal Canadiens**	**NHL**	**78**	**28**	**28**	**56**	**28**	**23**	**51**	**18**	**6**	**0**	**3**	**252**	**11.1**	**85**	**22**	**63**	**0**	**0**	**20**	**9**	**10**	**19**	**17**	**4**	**0**	**1**
1971-72	**Montreal Canadiens**	**NHL**	**77**	**32**	**49**	**81**	**32**	**43**	**75**	**26**	**8**	**0**	**7**	**266**	**12.0**	**129**	**42**	**52**	**2**	**37**	**6**	**2**	**1**	**3**	**2**	**0**	**0**	**0**
1972-73♦	**Montreal Canadiens**	**NHL**	**77**	**44**	**51**	**95**	**41**	**41**	**82**	**16**	**9**	**0**	**5**	**294**	**15.0**	**145**	**37**	**50**	**1**	**59**	**17**	**7**	**13**	**20**	**2**	**3**	**0**	**1**
1973-74	**Montreal Canadiens**	**NHL**	**66**	**29**	**38**	**67**	**28**	**31**	**59**	**10**	**10**	**0**	**7**	**219**	**13.2**	**95**	**34**	**59**	**2**	**4**	**6**	**0**	**4**	**4**	**2**	**0**	**0**	**0**
1974-75	**Montreal Canadiens**	**NHL**	**80**	**36**	**56**	**92**	**32**	**42**	**74**	**20**	**12**	**0**	**8**	**260**	**13.8**	**138**	**63**	**53**	**3**	**25**	**11**	**5**	**7**	**12**	**4**	**1**	**0**	**0**
1975-76♦	**Montreal Canadiens**	**NHL**	**61**	**20**	**32**	**52**	**18**	**24**	**42**	**20**	**6**	**0**	**3**	**226**	**8.8**	**86**	**32**	**32**	**4**	**26**	**13**	**3**	**3**	**6**	**2**	**1**	**1**	**1**
1976-77♦	**Montreal Canadiens**	**NHL**	**75**	**34**	**41**	**75**	**31**	**32**	**63**	**22**	**5**	**2**	**4**	**272**	**12.5**	**138**	**31**	**48**	**11**	**70**	**14**	**7**	**12**	**19**	**6**	**1**	**0**	**3**
1977-78♦	**Montreal Canadiens**	**NHL**	**76**	**36**	**61**	**97**	**33**	**47**	**80**	**14**	**6**	**0**	**5**	**310**	**11.6**	**143**	**41**	**60**	**12**	**54**	**15**	**6**	**8**	**14**	**10**	**0**	**0**	**1**
1978-79♦	**Montreal Canadiens**	**NHL**	**50**	**24**	**31**	**55**	**21**	**22**	**43**	**10**	**6**	**1**	**4**	**203**	**11.8**	**82**	**26**	**53**	**6**	**9**	**16**	***11**	**12**	***23**	**6**	**6**	**0**	**2**
1979-80	HC Sierre	Switz-2	28	29	16	45	....	....	....	....	....	....	....	....	....	....	....	....	....	....	....	....	....	....	....	....	....	....
1980-81	HC Sierre	Switz-2	12	13	13	26	....	....	....	....	....	....	....	....	....	....	....	....	....	....	....	....	....	....	....	....	....	....
1981-1982	SUNY Plattsburgh	NCAA-2	DID NOT PLAY – ASSISTANT COACH																									
1982-1983	Longueuil Chevaliers	QMJHL	DID NOT PLAY – COACHING																									
1983-1985	**Montreal Canadiens**	**NHL**	DID NOT PLAY – COACHING																									
1985-1993	**Montreal Canadiens**	**NHL**	DID NOT PLAY – ASSISTANT GENERAL MANAGER																									
1993-1998	**New Jersey Devils**	**NHL**	DID NOT PLAY – COACHING																									
1998-2000	**Montreal Canadiens**	**NHL**	DID NOT PLAY – ASSISTANT GENERAL MANAGER																									
	NHL Totals		**853**	**366**	**469**	**835**	**356**	**381**	**737**	**217**	**89**	**4**	**58**	**3051**	**12.0**	**1293**	**388**	**607**	**51**		**145**	**61**	**78**	**139**	**63**	**19**	**1**	**11**

Won Jack Adams Award (1994) • Played in NHL All-Star Game (1970, 1973)

• Named as Head Coach of **Minnesota Wild**, June 11, 2000.

• LEMAY, Moe

Maurice LW – L. 5′11″, 185 lbs. b: Saskatoon, Sask., 2/18/1962. Vancouver's 4th, 105th overall, in 1981.

Season	Club	League	GP	G	A	Pts	AG	AA	APts	PIM	PP	SH	GW	S	%	TGF	PGF	TGA	PGA	+/–	GP	G	A	Pts	PIM	PP	SH	GW
1978-79	South Ottawa Canadians	OMHA	80	54	82	136	....	....	....	55	....	....	....	....	....	....	....	....	....	....	....	....	....	....	....	....	....	....
1979-80	Ottawa 67's	OMJHL	62	16	23	39	....	....	....	20	....	....	....	....	....	....	....	....	....	....	10	2	3	5	19	....	....	....
1980-81	Ottawa 67's	OMJHL	63	32	45	77	....	....	....	102	....	....	....	....	....	....	....	....	....	....	7	3	5	8	17	....	....	....
1981-82	Ottawa 67's	OHL	62	*68	70	138	....	....	....	48	....	....	....	....	....	....	....	....	....	....	17	9	*19	28	18	....	....	....
	Canada	WJC-A	7	2	0	2	....	....	....	4	....	....	....	....	....	....	....	....	....	....	....	....	....	....	....	....	....	....
	Vancouver Canucks	**NHL**	**5**	**1**	**2**	**3**	**1**	**1**	**2**	**0**	**1**	**0**	**0**	**14**	**7.1**	**7**	**3**	**3**	**0**	**1**	....	....	....	....	....	....	....	....
1982-83	**Vancouver Canucks**	**NHL**	**44**	**11**	**9**	**20**	**9**	**6**	**15**	**41**	**3**	**0**	**1**	**72**	**15.3**	**37**	**13**	**30**	**0**	**–6**	....	....	....	....	....	....	....	....
	Fredericton Express	AHL	26	7	8	15	....	....	....	6	....	....	....	....	....	....	....	....	....	....	9	0	2	2	10	....	....	....
1983-84	**Vancouver Canucks**	**NHL**	**56**	**12**	**18**	**30**	**10**	**12**	**22**	**38**	**1**	**0**	**1**	**109**	**11.0**	**48**	**7**	**38**	**1**	**4**	**4**	**0**	**0**	**0**	**12**	**0**	**0**	**0**
	Fredericton Express	AHL	23	9	7	16	....	....	....	32	....	....	....	....	....	....	....	....	....	....	....	....	....	....	....	....	....	....
1984-85	**Vancouver Canucks**	**NHL**	**74**	**21**	**31**	**52**	**17**	**21**	**38**	**68**	**4**	**1**	**2**	**162**	**13.0**	**72**	**18**	**69**	**4**	**–11**	....	....	....	....	....	....	....	....
1985-86	**Vancouver Canucks**	**NHL**	**48**	**16**	**15**	**31**	**13**	**10**	**23**	**92**	**6**	**0**	**1**	**112**	**14.3**	**42**	**17**	**39**	**0**	**–14**	....	....	....	....	....	....	....	....
1986-87	**Vancouver Canucks**	**NHL**	**52**	**9**	**17**	**26**	**8**	**12**	**20**	**128**	**2**	**0**	**0**	**86**	**10.5**	**38**	**7**	**34**	**1**	**–2**	....	....	....	....	....	....	....	....
♦	**Edmonton Oilers**	**NHL**	**10**	**1**	**2**	**3**	**1**	**1**	**2**	**36**	**0**	**0**	**0**	**7**	**14.3**	**6**	**0**	**4**	**0**	**2**	**9**	**2**	**1**	**3**	**11**	**0**	**0**	**1**
1987-88	**Edmonton Oilers**	**NHL**	**4**	**0**	**0**	**0**	**0**	**0**	**0**	**2**	**0**	**0**	**0**	**5**	**0.0**	**0**	**0**	**1**	**0**	**–1**	....	....	....	....	....	....	....	....
	Nova Scotia Oilers	AHL	39	14	25	39	....	....	....	89	....	....	....	....	....	....	....	....	....	....	....	....	....	....	....	....	....	....
	Boston Bruins	**NHL**	**2**	**0**	**0**	**0**	**0**	**0**	**0**	**0**	**0**	**0**	**0**	**2**	**0.0**	**0**	**0**	**2**	**0**	**–2**	**15**	**4**	**2**	**6**	**32**	**0**	**0**	**0**
	Maine Mariners	AHL	11	5	6	11	....	....	....	14	....	....	....	....	....	....	....	....	....	....	3	2	1	3	22	....	....	....
1988-89	**Boston Bruins**	**NHL**	**12**	**0**	**0**	**0**	**0**	**0**	**0**	**23**	**0**	**0**	**0**	**6**	**0.0**	**2**	**0**	**7**	**0**	**–5**	....	....	....	....	....	....	....	....
	Maine Mariners	AHL	13	6	2	8	....	....	....	32	....	....	....	....	....	....	....	....	....	....	....	....	....	....	....	....	....	....
	Winnipeg Jets	**NHL**	**10**	**1**	**0**	**1**	**1**	**0**	**1**	**14**	**0**	**0**	**0**	**15**	**6.7**	**2**	**0**	**6**	**1**	**–3**	....	....	....	....	....	....	....	....
	Moncton Hawks	AHL	16	9	11	20	....	....	....	21	....	....	....	....	....	....	....	....	....	....	10	3	6	9	25	....	....	....
1989-90	KAC Klagenfurt	Austria	16	9	5	14	....	....	....	26	....	....	....	....	....	....	....	....	....	....	....	....	....	....	....	....	....	....
	Canada	Nat-Team	4	0	3	3	....	....	....	0	....	....	....	....	....	....	....	....	....	....	....	....	....	....	....	....	....	....
	ZSC Zurich	Switz-2	25	19	20	39	....	....	....	34	....	....	....	....	....	....	....	....	....	....	10	9	8	17	....	....	....	....
1990-91	ECD Sauerland	Germany-2	47	42	73	115	....	....	....	74	....	....	....	....	....	....	....	....	....	....	....	....	....	....	....	....	....	....
1991-92	ECD Sauerland	Germany-2	37	30	47	77	....	....	....	72	....	....	....	....	....	....	....	....	....	....	8	5	11	16	9	....	....	....
1992-93	EHC Hannover	Germany-2	48	38	48	86	....	....	....	82	....	....	....	....	....	....	....	....	....	....	....	....	....	....	....	....	....	....
1993-94	EHC Hannover	Germany-2	30	14	15	29	....	....	....	95	....	....	....	....	....	....	....	....	....	....	....	....	....	....	....	....	....	....
1994-95	ETC Timmendorf	Germany-2	17	14	20	34	....	....	....	47	....	....	....	....	....	....	....	....	....	....	....	....	....	....	....	....	....	....
1995-96	EC Bad Nauheim	Germany-2	22	11	12	23	....	....	....	36	....	....	....	....	....	....	....	....	....	....	....	....	....	....	....	....	....	....
1996-97	ESC Wedemark	Germany	41	8	9	17	....	....	....	60	....	....	....	....	....	....	....	....	....	....	6	0	2	2	35	....	....	....
1997-98	EC Bad Nauheim	Germany-2	29	14	26	40	....	....	....	36	....	....	....	....	....	....	....	....	....	....	....	....	....	....	....	....	....	....
	Braunlager EHC	Germany-2	15	15	18	33	....	....	....	30	....	....	....	....	....	....	....	....	....	....	4	1	3	4	8	....	....	....
1998-99	Braunlager EHC	Germany-2	50	18	25	43	....	....	....	90	....	....	....	....	....	....	....	....	....	....	4	1	2	3	8	....	....	....
99-2000	EHC Hamburg	Germany-2	15	0	2	2	....	....	....	14	....	....	....	....	....	....	....	....	....	....	....	....	....	....	....	....	....	....
	NHL Totals		**317**	**72**	**94**	**166**	**60**	**63**	**123**	**442**	**17**	**1**	**5**	**590**	**12.2**	**254**	**65**	**233**	**7**		**28**	**6**	**3**	**9**	**55**	**0**	**0**	**1**

OHL First All-Star Team (1982)

Traded to **Edmonton** by **Vancouver** for Raimo Summanen, March 10, 1987. Traded to **Boston** by **Edmonton** for Alan May, March 8, 1988. Traded to **Winnipeg** by **Boston** for Ray Neufeld, December 30, 1988. • Played w/ RHI's Ottawa Loggers in 1995 (7-1-9-10-4).

• LEMELIN, Roger

Roger Marcel D – R. 6′3″, 215 lbs. b: Iroquois Falls, Ont., 2/6/1954. Kansas City's 4th, 56th overall, in 1974.

Season	Club	League	GP	G	A	Pts	AG	AA	APts	PIM	PP	SH	GW	S	%	TGF	PGF	TGA	PGA	+/–	GP	G	A	Pts	PIM	PP	SH	GW
1972-73	London Knights	OMJHL	62	6	12	18	....	....	....	92	....	....	....	....	....	....	....	....	....	....	....	....	....	....	....	....	....	....
1973-74	London Knights	OMJHL	48	10	30	40	....	....	....	100	....	....	....	....	....	....	....	....	....	....	....	....	....	....	....	....	....	....
1974-75	**Kansas City Scouts**	**NHL**	**8**	**0**	**1**	**1**	**0**	**1**	**1**	**6**	**0**	**0**	**0**	**4**	**0.0**	**3**	**1**	**13**	**2**	**–9**	....	....	....	....	....	....	....	....
	Baltimore Clippers	AHL	36	1	13	14	....	....	....	59	....	....	....	....	....	....	....	....	....	....	....	....	....	....	....	....	....	....
	Springfield Indians	AHL	23	1	3	4	....	....	....	24	....	....	....	....	....	....	....	....	....	....	17	2	2	4	36	....	....	....
1975-76	**Kansas City Scouts**	**NHL**	**11**	**0**	**0**	**0**	**0**	**0**	**0**	**0**	**0**	**0**	**0**	**1**	**0.0**	**2**	**0**	**5**	**2**	**–1**	....	....	....	....	....	....	....	....
	Springfield Indians	AHL	53	4	14	18	....	....	....	83	....	....	....	....	....	....	....	....	....	....	....	....	....	....	....	....	....	....
1976-77	**Colorado Rockies**	**NHL**	**14**	**1**	**1**	**2**	**1**	**1**	**2**	**21**	**0**	**0**	**0**	**25**	**4.0**	**10**	**0**	**21**	**5**	**–6**	....	....	....	....	....	....	....	....
	Rhode Island Reds	AHL	47	2	8	10	....	....	....	73	....	....	....	....	....	....	....	....	....	....	....	....	....	....	....	....	....	....
1977-78	**Colorado Rockies**	**NHL**	**3**	**0**	**0**	**0**	**0**	**0**	**0**	**0**	**0**	**0**	**0**	**0**	**0.0**	**0**	**0**	**0**	**0**	**0**	....	....	....	....	....	....	....	....
	Phoenix Roadrunners	CHL	27	1	5	6	....	....	....	72	....	....	....	....	....	....	....	....	....	....	....	....	....	....	....	....	....	....
	Hampton Gulls	AHL	16	1	4	5	....	....	....	22	....	....	....	....	....	....	....	....	....	....	....	....	....	....	....	....	....	....
	Philadelphia Firebirds	AHL	33	0	5	5	....	....	....	52	....	....	....	....	....	....	....	....	....	....	....	....	....	....	....	....	....	....

			REGULAR SEASON																		PLAYOFFS							
Season	Club	League	GP	G	A	Pts	AG	AA	APts	PIM	PP	SH	GW	S	%	TGF	PGF	TGA	PGA	+/–	GP	G	A	Pts	PIM	PP	SH	GW
1978-79	Hampton Aces	NEHL	38	4	12	16	....	....	....	109	....	....	....	....	....	....	....	....	....	....	....	....	....	....	....	....	....	....
1979-80	Hershey Bears	AHL	3	0	1	1	....	....	....	2	....	....	....	....	....	....	....	....	....	....	15	0	1	1	62	....	....	....
	Hampton Aces	EHL	5	0	1	1	....	....	....	20	....	....	....	....	....	....	....	....	....	....	....	....	....	....	....	....	....	....
1980-81	Hershey Bears	AHL	12	0	2	2	....	....	....	14	....	....	....	....	....	....	....	....	....	....	....	....	....	....	....	....	....	....
	Oklahoma City Stars	CHL	11	0	1	1	....	....	....	6	....	....	....	....	....	....	....	....	....	....	....	....	....	....	....	....	....	....
	Hampton Aces	EHL	21	0	6	6	....	....	....	24	....	....	....	....	....	....	....	....	....	....	....	....	....	....	....	....	....	....
1981-82			DID NOT PLAY																									
1982-83			DID NOT PLAY																									
1983-84	Muskegon Mohawks	IHL	57	3	13	16	....	....	....	65	....	....	....	....	....	....	....	....	....	....	....	....	....	....	....	....	....	....
	NHL Totals		**36**	**1**	**2**	**3**	**1**	**2**	**3**	**27**	**0**	**0**	**0**	**30**	**3.3**	**15**	**1**	**39**	**9**		....	....	....	....	....	....	....	....

Transferred to **Colorado** after **Kansas City** franchise relocated, July 15, 1976.

• LEMIEUX, Alain

C – L. 6', 185 lbs. b: Montreal, Que., 5/24/1961. St. Louis' 4th, 96th overall, in 1980.

Season	Club	League	GP	G	A	Pts	AG	AA	APts	PIM	PP	SH	GW	S	%	TGF	PGF	TGA	PGA	+/–	GP	G	A	Pts	PIM	PP	SH	GW
1978-79	Chicoutimi Sagueneens	QMJHL	31	15	27	42	....	....	....	5	....	....	....	....	....	....	....	....	....	....	....	....	....	....	....	....	....	....
	Montreal Jr. Canadiens	QMJHL	39	7	5	12	....	....	....	2	....	....	....	....	....	....	....	....	....	....	....	....	....	....	....	....	....	....
1979-80	Chicoutimi Sagueneens	QMJHL	72	47	95	142	....	....	....	36	....	....	....	....	....	....	....	....	....	....	12	8	12	20	8	....	....	....
1980-81	Chicoutimi Sagueneens	QMJHL	1	0	0	0	....	....	....	2	....	....	....	....	....	....	....	....	....	....	....	....	....	....	....	....	....	....
	Trois-Rivieres Draveurs	QMJHL	69	68	98	166	....	....	....	62	....	....	....	....	....	....	....	....	....	....	19	18	*31	*49	38	....	....	....
1981-82	**St. Louis Blues**	**NHL**	**3**	**0**	**1**	**1**	**0**	**1**	**1**	**0**	**0**	**0**	**0**	**7**	**0.0**	**2**	**0**	**3**	**0**	**–1**	....	....	....	....	....	....	....	....
	Salt Lake Golden Eagles	CHL	74	41	42	83	....	....	....	61	....	....	....	....	....	....	....	....	....	....	10	6	4	10	14	....	....	....
1982-83	**St. Louis Blues**	**NHL**	**42**	**9**	**25**	**34**	**7**	**17**	**24**	**18**	**1**	**0**	**0**	**71**	**12.7**	**42**	**6**	**46**	**0**	**–10**	**4**	**0**	**1**	**1**	**0**	**0**	**0**	**0**
	Salt Lake Golden Eagles	CHL	29	20	24	44	....	....	....	35	....	....	....	....	....	....	....	....	....	....	....	....	....	....	....	....	....	....
1983-84	**St. Louis Blues**	**NHL**	**17**	**4**	**5**	**9**	**3**	**3**	**6**	**6**	**1**	**0**	**0**	**14**	**28.6**	**10**	**2**	**8**	**0**	**0**	....	....	....	....	....	....	....	....
	Montana Magic	CHL	38	28	41	69	....	....	....	36	....	....	....	....	....	....	....	....	....	....	....	....	....	....	....	....	....	....
	Springfield Indians	AHL	14	11	14	25	....	....	....	18	....	....	....	....	....	....	....	....	....	....	4	0	3	3	2	....	....	....
1984-85	**St. Louis Blues**	**NHL**	**19**	**4**	**2**	**6**	**3**	**1**	**4**	**0**	**0**	**0**	**1**	**11**	**36.4**	**11**	**2**	**7**	**0**	**2**	....	....	....	....	....	....	....	....
	Peoria Rivermen	IHL	2	1	0	1	....	....	....	0	....	....	....	....	....	....	....	....	....	....	....	....	....	....	....	....	....	....
	Quebec Nordiques	**NHL**	**30**	**11**	**11**	**22**	**9**	**7**	**16**	**12**	**2**	**0**	**2**	**48**	**22.9**	**35**	**17**	**19**	**0**	**–1**	**14**	**3**	**3**	**6**	**0**	**2**	**0**	**0**
1985-86	**Quebec Nordiques**	**NHL**	**7**	**0**	**0**	**0**	**0**	**0**	**0**	**2**	**0**	**0**	**0**	**1**	**0.0**	**0**	**0**	**1**	**0**	**–1**	**1**	**1**	**2**	**3**	**0**	**1**	**0**	**0**
	Fredericton Express	AHL	64	29	45	74	....	....	....	54	....	....	....	....	....	....	....	....	....	....	5	5	2	7	5	....	....	....
1986-87	EHC Chur	Switz.	2	0	1	1	....	....	....	....	....	....	....	....	....	....	....	....	....	....	....	....	....	....	....	....	....	....
	Pittsburgh Penguins	**NHL**	**1**	**0**	**0**	**0**	**0**	**0**	**0**	**0**	**0**	**0**	**0**	**0**	**0.0**	**0**	**0**	**1**	**0**	**–1**	....	....	....	....	....	....	....	....
	Baltimore Skipjacks	AHL	72	41	56	97	....	....	....	62	....	....	....	....	....	....	....	....	....	....	....	....	....	....	....	....	....	....
1987-88	Hershey Bears	AHL	20	8	10	18	....	....	....	10	....	....	....	....	....	....	....	....	....	....	....	....	....	....	....	....	....	....
	Baltimore Skipjacks	AHL	16	2	14	16	....	....	....	4	....	....	....	....	....	....	....	....	....	....	....	....	....	....	....	....	....	....
	Springfield Indians	AHL	15	7	10	17	....	....	....	4	....	....	....	....	....	....	....	....	....	....	....	....	....	....	....	....	....	....
1988-89	SaiPa Lappeenranta	Finland	5	1	4	5	....	....	....	4	....	....	....	....	....	....	....	....	....	....	....	....	....	....	....	....	....	....
	Karpat Oulu	Finland	16	4	9	13	....	....	....	16	....	....	....	....	....	....	....	....	....	....	....	....	....	....	....	....	....	....
	Indianapolis Ice	IHL	29	18	26	44	....	....	....	90	....	....	....	....	....	....	....	....	....	....	....	....	....	....	....	....	....	....
1989-90			DID NOT PLAY																									
1990-91	Albany Choppers	IHL	33	5	36	41	....	....	....	24	....	....	....	....	....	....	....	....	....	....	....	....	....	....	....	....	....	....
	Milwaukee Admirals	IHL	30	8	21	29	....	....	....	30	....	....	....	....	....	....	....	....	....	....	6	2	5	7	12	....	....	....
1991-1997			OUT OF HOCKEY – RETIRED																									
1997-98	Tuscon Gila Monsters	WCHL	8	5	11	16	....	....	....	24	....	....	....	....	....	....	....	....	....	....	....	....	....	....	....	....	....	....
1998-99	LaRoche College	NCAA-3	DID NOT PLAY – GENERAL MANAGER																									
99-2000	Jacksonville Lizard Kings	ECHL	DID NOT PLAY – COACHING																									
	NHL Totals		**119**	**28**	**44**	**72**	**22**	**29**	**51**	**38**	**4**	**0**	**3**	**152**	**18.4**	**100**	**27**	**85**	**0**		**19**	**4**	**6**	**10**	**0**	**3**	**0**	**0**

• Brother of Mario • QMJHL Second All-Star Team (1981) • AHL Second All-Star Team (1987)

Traded to **Quebec** by **St. Louis** for Luc Dufour, January 29, 1985. Signed as a free agent by **Pittsburgh**, December, 1986. • Served as Assistant Coach for **Tuscon** (WCHL) during 1997-98 season. • Played w/ RHI's Pittsburgh Phantoms 1993-94 (12-12-16-28-32).

• LEMIEUX, Bob

Robert D – L. 6'1", 195 lbs. b: Montreal, Que., 12/16/1944.

Season	Club	League	GP	G	A	Pts	AG	AA	APts	PIM	PP	SH	GW	S	%	TGF	PGF	TGA	PGA	+/–	GP	G	A	Pts	PIM	PP	SH	GW
1962-63	Montreal Jr. Canadiens	OHA-Jr.	50	5	12	17	....	....	....	135	....	....	....	....	....	....	....	....	....	....	10	4	1	5	24	....	....	....
	Hull-Ottawa Canadiens	EPHL	1	0	0	0	....	....	....	0	....	....	....	....	....	....	....	....	....	....	....	....	....	....	....	....	....	....
1963-64	Montreal Jr. Canadiens	OHA-Jr.	56	7	33	40	....	....	....	*219	....	....	....	....	....	....	....	....	....	....	17	2	8	10	58	....	....	....
1964-65	Montreal Jr. Canadiens	OHA-Jr.	52	3	20	23	....	....	....	132	....	....	....	....	....	....	....	....	....	....	7	0	1	1	12	....	....	....
1965-66	Houston Apollos	CPHL	2	0	0	0	....	....	....	2	....	....	....	....	....	....	....	....	....	....	....	....	....	....	....	....	....	....
	Muskegon Zephyrs	IHL	70	14	44	58	....	....	....	199	....	....	....	....	....	....	....	....	....	....	4	0	2	2	24	....	....	....
1966-67	Seattle Totems	WHL	72	10	13	23	....	....	....	117	....	....	....	....	....	....	....	....	....	....	10	2	2	4	14	....	....	....
1967-68	**Oakland Seals**	**NHL**	**19**	**0**	**1**	**1**	**0**	**1**	**1**	**12**	....	....	....	....	....	....	....	....	....	....	....	....	....	....	....	....	....	....
	Vancouver Canucks	WHL	44	10	21	31	....	....	....	70	....	....	....	....	....	....	....	....	....	....	....	....	....	....	....	....	....	....
1968-69	Vancouver Canucks	WHL	65	3	12	15	....	....	....	115	....	....	....	....	....	....	....	....	....	....	7	0	2	2	4	....	....	....
1969-70	Vancouver Canucks	WHL	59	7	10	17	....	....	....	62	....	....	....	....	....	....	....	....	....	....	11	1	0	1	2	....	....	....
	NHL Totals		**19**	**0**	**1**	**1**	**0**	**1**	**1**	**12**	....	....	....	....	....	....	....	....	....	....	....	....	....	....	....	....	....	....

IHL First All-Star Team (1966) • Won Governors' Trophy (Top Defenseman - IHL) (1966)

Claimed by **Oakland** from **Montreal** in Expansion Draft, June 6, 1967.

• LEMIEUX, Claude

Claude Percy RW – R. 6'1", 215 lbs. b: Buckingham, Que., 7/16/1965. Montreal's 2nd, 26th overall, in 1983.

Season	Club	League	GP	G	A	Pts	AG	AA	APts	PIM	PP	SH	GW	S	%	TGF	PGF	TGA	PGA	+/–	GP	G	A	Pts	PIM	PP	SH	GW
1981-82	Richelieu Regents	QAAA	48	24	48	72	....	....	....	96	....	....	....	....	....	....	....	....	....	....	....	....	....	....	....	....	....	....
1982-83	Trois-Rivieres Draveurs	QMJHL	62	28	38	66	....	....	....	187	....	....	....	....	....	....	....	....	....	....	4	1	0	1	30	....	....	....
1983-84	Verdun Juniors	QMJHL	51	41	45	86	....	....	....	225	....	....	....	....	....	....	....	....	....	....	9	8	12	20	63	....	....	....
	Montreal Canadiens	**NHL**	**8**	**1**	**1**	**2**	**1**	**1**	**2**	**12**	**0**	**0**	**0**	**7**	**14.3**	**2**	**0**	**4**	**0**	**–2**	....	....	....	....	....	....	....	....
	Nova Scotia Voyageurs	AHL	....	....	....	....	....	....	....	....	....	....	....	....	....	....	....	....	....	....	2	1	0	1	0	....	....	....
	Verdun Juniors	Mem-Cup	3	1	3	4	....	....	....	2	....	....	....	....	....	....	....	....	....	....	....	....	....	....	....	....	....	....
1984-85	Verdun Jr. Canadiens	QMJHL	52	58	66	124	....	....	....	152	....	....	....	....	....	....	....	....	....	....	14	23	17	40	38	....	....	....
	Canada	WJC-A	6	3	2	5	....	....	....	6	....	....	....	....	....	....	....	....	....	....	....	....	....	....	....	....	....	....
	Montreal Canadiens	**NHL**	**1**	**0**	**1**	**1**	**0**	**1**	**1**	**7**	**0**	**0**	**0**	**0**	**0.0**	**1**	**0**	**0**	**0**	**1**	....	....	....	....	....	....	....	....
1985-86♦	**Montreal Canadiens**	**NHL**	**10**	**1**	**2**	**3**	**1**	**1**	**2**	**22**	**1**	**0**	**0**	**16**	**6.3**	**5**	**1**	**10**	**0**	**–6**	**20**	**10**	**6**	**16**	**68**	**4**	**0**	**4**
	Sherbrooke Canadiens	AHL	58	21	32	53	....	....	....	145	....	....	....	....	....	....	....	....	....	....	....	....	....	....	....	....	....	....
1986-87	**Montreal Canadiens**	**NHL**	**76**	**27**	**26**	**53**	**23**	**19**	**42**	**156**	**5**	**0**	**1**	**184**	**14.7**	**91**	**31**	**60**	**0**	**0**	**17**	**4**	**9**	**13**	**41**	**2**	**0**	**0**
	NHL All-Stars	RV-87	2	0	0	0	....	....	....	4	....	....	....	....	....	....	....	....	....	....	....	....	....	....	....	....	....	....
1987-88	Canada	Can-Cup	6	1	1	2	....	....	....	4	....	....	....	....	....	....	....	....	....	....	....	....	....	....	....	....	....	....
	Montreal Canadiens	**NHL**	**78**	**31**	**30**	**61**	**26**	**21**	**47**	**137**	**6**	**0**	**3**	**241**	**12.9**	**102**	**32**	**55**	**1**	**16**	**11**	**3**	**2**	**5**	**20**	**0**	**0**	**2**
1988-89	**Montreal Canadiens**	**NHL**	**69**	**29**	**22**	**51**	**25**	**16**	**41**	**136**	**7**	**0**	**3**	**220**	**13.2**	**73**	**26**	**33**	**0**	**14**	**18**	**4**	**3**	**7**	**58**	**0**	**0**	**0**
1989-90	**Montreal Canadiens**	**NHL**	**39**	**8**	**10**	**18**	**7**	**7**	**14**	**106**	**3**	**0**	**1**	**104**	**7.7**	**26**	**11**	**24**	**1**	**–8**	**11**	**1**	**3**	**4**	**38**	**0**	**0**	**1**
1990-91	**New Jersey Devils**	**NHL**	**78**	**30**	**17**	**47**	**28**	**13**	**41**	**105**	**10**	**0**	**2**	**271**	**11.1**	**71**	**24**	**57**	**2**	**–8**	**7**	**4**	**0**	**4**	**34**	**2**	**0**	**1**
1991-92	**New Jersey Devils**	**NHL**	**74**	**41**	**27**	**68**	**37**	**20**	**57**	**109**	**13**	**1**	**8**	**296**	**13.9**	**110**	**33**	**73**	**5**	**9**	**7**	**4**	**3**	**7**	**26**	**1**	**0**	**0**
1992-93	**New Jersey Devils**	**NHL**	**77**	**30**	**51**	**81**	**25**	**35**	**60**	**155**	**13**	**0**	**3**	**311**	**9.6**	**122**	**46**	**74**	**1**	**3**	**5**	**2**	**0**	**2**	**19**	**1**	**0**	**0**
1993-94	**New Jersey Devils**	**NHL**	**79**	**18**	**26**	**44**	**17**	**20**	**37**	**86**	**5**	**0**	**5**	**181**	**9.9**	**73**	**20**	**63**	**23**	**13**	**20**	**7**	**11**	**18**	**44**	**0**	**0**	**2**
1994-95♦	**New Jersey Devils**	**NHL**	**45**	**6**	**13**	**19**	**11**	**19**	**30**	**86**	**1**	**0**	**1**	**117**	**5.1**	**36**	**10**	**33**	**9**	**2**	**20**	***13**	**3**	**16**	**20**	**0**	**0**	**3**
1995-96♦	**Colorado Avalanche**	**NHL**	**79**	**39**	**32**	**71**	**38**	**26**	**64**	**117**	**9**	**2**	**10**	**315**	**12.4**	**117**	**39**	**78**	**14**	**14**	**19**	**5**	**7**	**12**	**55**	**3**	**0**	**0**
1996-97	Canada	W-Cup	8	1	1	2	....	....	....	19	....	....	....	....	....	....	....	....	....	....	....	....	....	....	....	....	....	....
	Colorado Avalanche	**NHL**	**45**	**11**	**17**	**28**	**12**	**15**	**27**	**43**	**5**	**0**	**4**	**168**	**6.5**	**51**	**20**	**35**	**0**	**–4**	**17**	***13**	**10**	**23**	**32**	**4**	**0**	**4**

Season	Club	League	GP	G	A	Pts	AG	AA	APts	PIM	PP	SH	GW	S	%	TGF	PGF	TGA	PGA	+/–	GP	G	A	Pts	PIM	PP	SH	GW
			REGULAR SEASON																		PLAYOFFS							
1997-98	**Colorado Avalanche**	**NHL**	**78**	**26**	**27**	**53**	**30**	**26**	**56**	**115**	**11**	**1**	**1**	**261**	**10.0**	**95**	**45**	**58**	**1**	**–7**	**7**	**3**	**3**	**6**	**8**	**1**	**0**	**1**
1998-99	**Colorado Avalanche**	**NHL**	**82**	**27**	**24**	**51**	**32**	**23**	**55**	**102**	**11**	**0**	**8**	**292**	**9.2**	**99**	**49**	**64**	**14**	**0**	**19**	**3**	**11**	**14**	**26**	**1**	**0**	**0**
99-2000	**Colorado Avalanche**	**NHL**	**13**	**3**	**6**	**9**	**3**	**6**	**9**	**4**	**0**	**0**	**0**	**36**	**8.3**	**13**	**2**	**12**	**1**	**0**	....	....	....	....	....	....	....	....
	♦ New Jersey Devils	**NHL**	**70**	**17**	**21**	**38**	**19**	**19**	**38**	**86**	**7**	**0**	**3**	**221**	**7.7**	**57**	**19**	**49**	**8**	**–3**	**23**	**4**	**6**	**10**	**28**	**1**	**0**	**0**
	NHL Totals		**1001**	**345**	**353**	**698**	**335**	**288**	**623**	**1584**	**107**	**4**	**53**	**3241**	**10.6**	**1144**	**408**	**782**	**80**		**221**	**80**	**77**	**157**	**517**	**20**	**0**	**18**

• Brother of Jocelyn • QMJHL Second All-Star Team (1984) • QMJHL First All-Star Team (1985) • Won Conn Smythe Trophy (1995)

• Missed majority of 1989-90 season recovering from abdominal injury suffered in game vs. Boston, October 9, 1989. Traded to **New Jersey** by **Montreal** for Sylvain Turgeon, September 4, 1990. Traded to **NY Islanders** by **New Jersey** for Steve Thomas, October 3, 1995. Traded to **Colorado** by **NY Islanders** for Wendel Clark, October 3, 1995. Traded to **New Jersey** by **Colorado** with Colorado's 1st (David Hale) and 2nd (Matt DeMarchi) round choices in 2000 Entry Draft for Brian Rolston, New Jersey's 1st round choice (later traded to Boston - Boston selected Martin Samuelsson) in 2000 Entry Draft and future considerations, November 3, 1999.

• LEMIEUX, Jacques

D – R. 6'2", 190 lbs. b: Matane, Que., 4/8/1943.

1963-64	Rouyn-Noranda Alouettes	NOHA	STATISTICS NOT AVAILABLE																									
	Omaha Knights	CPHL	2	0	0	0	....	....	....	0	....	....	....	....	....	....	....	....	....	....	....	....	....	....	....	....	....	....
1964-65	Rouyn-Noranda Alouettes	NOHA	STATISTICS NOT AVAILABLE																									
	Omaha Knights	CPHL	14	0	3	3	....	....	....	13	....	....	....	....	....	....	....	....	....	....	6	0	2	2	14	....	....	....
1965-66	Houston Apollos	CPHL	70	7	19	26	....	....	....	59	....	....	....	....	....	....	....	....	....	....	....	....	....	....	....	....	....	....
1966-67	Cleveland Barons	AHL	68	6	30	36	....	....	....	47	....	....	....	....	....	....	....	....	....	....	5	0	2	2	6	....	....	....
1967-68	**Los Angeles Kings**	**NHL**	**16**	**0**	**3**	**3**	**0**	**3**	**3**	**8**	**0**	**0**	**0**	**5**	**0.0**	**10**	**4**	**9**	**6**	**3**	....	....	....	....	....	....	....	....
1968-69	Denver Spurs	WHL	25	5	8	13	....	....	....	16	....	....	....	....	....	....	....	....	....	....	....	....	....	....	....	....	....	....
	Springfield Kings	AHL	51	4	31	35	....	....	....	6	....	....	....	....	....	....	....	....	....	....	....	....	....	....	....	....	....	....
	Los Angeles Kings	**NHL**	....	....	....	....	....	....	....	....	....	....	....	....	....	....	....	....	....	....	**1**	**0**	**0**	**0**	**0**	**0**	**0**	**0**
1969-70	**Los Angeles Kings**	**NHL**	**3**	**0**	**1**	**1**	**0**	**1**	**1**	**0**	**0**	**0**	**0**	**0**	**0.0**	**1**	**0**	**1**	**0**	**0**	....	....	....	....	....	....	....	....
	Springfield Kings	AHL	7	0	0	0	....	....	....	2	....	....	....	....	....	....	....	....	....	....	....	....	....	....	....	....	....	....
	Denver Spurs	WHL	7	1	0	1	....	....	....	4	....	....	....	....	....	....	....	....	....	....	....	....	....	....	....	....	....	....
	NHL Totals		**19**	**0**	**4**	**4**	**0**	**4**	**4**	**8**	**0**	**0**	**0**	**5**	**0.0**	**11**	**4**	**10**	**6**		**1**	**0**	**0**	**0**	**0**	**0**	**0**	**0**

Claimed by **LA Kings** from **Montreal** in Expansion Draft, June 6, 1967. Traded to **Toronto**by **LA Kings** and assigned to **Phoenix-** (WHL) for Gary Marsh, February, 1970. • Suspended for remainder of 1969-70 season by **Toronto** for refusing to report to **Phoenix**, February, 1970.

• LEMIEUX, Jean

Jean Louis D – R. 6'1", 180 lbs. b: Noranda, Que., 5/31/1952. Atlanta's 3rd, 34th overall, in 1972.

1969-70	Sherbrooke Castors	QJHL	54	7	23	30	....	....	....	32	....	....	....	....	....	....	....	....	....	....	....	....	....	....	....	....	....	....
1970-71	Sherbrooke Castors	QJHL	62	18	37	55	....	....	....	52	....	....	....	....	....	....	....	....	....	....	11	2	5	7	4	....	....	....
1971-72	Sherbrooke Castors	QMJHL	61	20	50	70	....	....	....	32	....	....	....	....	....	....	....	....	....	....	4	1	4	5	15	....	....	....
1972-73	Omaha Knights	CHL	64	10	32	42	....	....	....	35	....	....	....	....	....	....	....	....	....	....	11	4	5	9	0	....	....	....
1973-74	**Atlanta Flames**	**NHL**	**32**	**3**	**5**	**8**	**3**	**4**	**7**	**6**	**2**	**0**	**0**	**58**	**5.2**	**29**	**9**	**24**	**0**	**–4**	**3**	**1**	**1**	**2**	**0**	**1**	**0**	**0**
	Nova Scotia Voyageurs	AHL	24	3	7	10	....	....	....	6	....	....	....	....	....	....	....	....	....	....	....	....	....	....	....	....	....	....
1974-75	**Atlanta Flames**	**NHL**	**75**	**3**	**24**	**27**	**3**	**18**	**21**	**19**	**1**	**0**	**2**	**140**	**2.1**	**78**	**20**	**65**	**4**	**–3**	....	....	....	....	....	....	....	....
1975-76	**Atlanta Flames**	**NHL**	**33**	**4**	**9**	**13**	**3**	**7**	**10**	**10**	**1**	**0**	**0**	**51**	**7.8**	**36**	**15**	**17**	**0**	**4**	....	....	....	....	....	....	....	....
	Washington Capitals	**NHL**	**33**	**6**	**14**	**20**	**5**	**10**	**15**	**2**	**5**	**0**	**1**	**65**	**9.2**	**37**	**15**	**49**	**6**	**–21**	....	....	....	....	....	....	....	....
	Nova Scotia Voyageurs	AHL	11	1	9	10	....	....	....	2	....	....	....	....	....	....	....	....	....	....	....	....	....	....	....	....	....	....
1976-77	**Washington Capitals**	**NHL**	**15**	**4**	**4**	**8**	**4**	**3**	**7**	**2**	**2**	**0**	**0**	**19**	**21.1**	**17**	**10**	**17**	**1**	**–9**	....	....	....	....	....	....	....	....
	Springfield Indians	AHL	65	17	28	45	....	....	....	11	....	....	....	....	....	....	....	....	....	....	....	....	....	....	....	....	....	....
1977-78	**Washington Capitals**	**NHL**	**16**	**3**	**7**	**10**	**3**	**5**	**8**	**0**	**3**	**0**	**0**	**24**	**12.5**	**15**	**11**	**16**	**0**	**–12**	....	....	....	....	....	....	....	....
	Hershey Bears	AHL	55	7	25	32	....	....	....	12	....	....	....	....	....	....	....	....	....	....	....	....	....	....	....	....	....	....
1978-79	Nova Scotia Voyageurs	AHL	63	6	37	43	....	....	....	14	....	....	....	....	....	....	....	....	....	....	10	1	8	9	2	....	....	....
	NHL Totals		**204**	**23**	**63**	**86**	**21**	**47**	**68**	**39**	**14**	**0**	**3**	**357**	**6.4**	**212**	**80**	**188**	**11**		**3**	**1**	**1**	**2**	**0**	**1**	**0**	**0**

Traded to **Washington** by **Atlanta** with Gerry Meehan and Buffalo's 1st round choice (previously acquired, Washington selected Greg Carroll) in 1976 Amateur Draft for Bill Clement, January 22, 1976.

• LEMIEUX, Jocelyn

RW – L. 5'11", 220 lbs. b: Mont-Laurier, Que., 11/18/1967. St. Louis' 1st, 10th overall, in 1986.

1983-84	Montreal Concordia	QAAA	40	15	36	51	....	....	....	....	....	....	....	....	....	....	....	....	....	....	....	....	....	....	....	....	....	....
1984-85	Laval Titan	QMJHL	68	13	19	32	....	....	....	92	....	....	....	....	....	....	....	....	....	....	....	....	....	....	....	....	....	....
1985-86	Laval Titan	QMJHL	71	57	68	125	....	....	....	131	....	....	....	....	....	....	....	....	....	....	14	9	15	24	37	....	....	....
1986-87	**St. Louis Blues**	**NHL**	**53**	**10**	**8**	**18**	**9**	**6**	**15**	**94**	**1**	**0**	**1**	**48**	**20.8**	**32**	**1**	**31**	**1**	**1**	**5**	**0**	**1**	**1**	**6**	**0**	**0**	**0**
1987-88	**St. Louis Blues**	**NHL**	**23**	**1**	**0**	**1**	**1**	**0**	**1**	**42**	**0**	**0**	**0**	**19**	**5.3**	**5**	**0**	**10**	**0**	**–5**	**5**	**0**	**0**	**0**	**15**	**0**	**0**	**0**
	Peoria Rivermen	IHL	8	0	5	5	....	....	....	35	....	....	....	....	....	....	....	....	....	....	....	....	....	....	....	....	....	....
1988-89	**Montreal Canadiens**	**NHL**	**1**	**0**	**1**	**1**	**0**	**1**	**1**	**0**	**0**	**0**	**0**	**0**	**0.0**	**0**	**0**	**1**	**0**	**–1**	....	....	....	....	....	....	....	....
	Sherbrooke Canadiens	AHL	73	25	28	53	....	....	....	134	....	....	....	....	....	....	....	....	....	....	4	3	1	4	6	....	....	....
1989-90	**Montreal Canadiens**	**NHL**	**34**	**4**	**2**	**6**	**3**	**1**	**4**	**61**	**0**	**0**	**1**	**34**	**11.8**	**13**	**0**	**14**	**0**	**–1**	....	....	....	....	....	....	....	....
	Chicago Blackhawks	**NHL**	**39**	**10**	**11**	**21**	**9**	**8**	**17**	**47**	**1**	**0**	**1**	**78**	**12.8**	**28**	**3**	**29**	**4**	**0**	**18**	**1**	**8**	**9**	**28**	**0**	**0**	**0**
1990-91	**Chicago Blackhawks**	**NHL**	**67**	**6**	**7**	**13**	**5**	**5**	**10**	**119**	**1**	**1**	**2**	**89**	**6.7**	**24**	**5**	**34**	**8**	**–7**	**4**	**0**	**0**	**0**	**0**	**0**	**0**	**0**
1991-92	**Chicago Blackhawks**	**NHL**	**78**	**6**	**10**	**16**	**5**	**8**	**13**	**80**	**0**	**0**	**1**	**103**	**5.8**	**29**	**4**	**31**	**4**	**–2**	**18**	**3**	**1**	**4**	**33**	**0**	**0**	**2**
1992-93	**Chicago Blackhawks**	**NHL**	**81**	**10**	**21**	**31**	**8**	**14**	**22**	**111**	**1**	**0**	**2**	**117**	**8.5**	**37**	**3**	**29**	**0**	**5**	**4**	**1**	**0**	**1**	**2**	**0**	**0**	**0**
1993-94	**Chicago Blackhawks**	**NHL**	**66**	**12**	**8**	**20**	**11**	**6**	**17**	**63**	**0**	**0**	**0**	**129**	**9.3**	**35**	**1**	**29**	**0**	**5**	....	....	....	....	....	....	....	....
	Hartford Whalers	**NHL**	**16**	**6**	**1**	**7**	**6**	**1**	**7**	**19**	**0**	**0**	**2**	**22**	**27.3**	**8**	**0**	**20**	**4**	**–8**	....	....	....	....	....	....	....	....
1994-95	**Hartford Whalers**	**NHL**	**41**	**6**	**5**	**11**	**11**	**7**	**18**	**32**	**0**	**0**	**1**	**78**	**7.7**	**16**	**0**	**25**	**2**	**–7**	....	....	....	....	....	....	....	....
1995-96	**Hartford Whalers**	**NHL**	**29**	**1**	**2**	**3**	**1**	**2**	**3**	**31**	**0**	**0**	**0**	**43**	**2.3**	**7**	**0**	**18**	**0**	**–11**	....	....	....	....	....	....	....	....
	New Jersey Devils	**NHL**	**18**	**0**	**1**	**1**	**0**	**1**	**1**	**4**	**0**	**0**	**0**	**20**	**0.0**	**3**	**0**	**10**	**0**	**–7**	....	....	....	....	....	....	....	....
	Calgary Flames	**NHL**	**20**	**4**	**4**	**8**	**4**	**3**	**7**	**10**	**0**	**0**	**0**	**27**	**14.8**	**10**	**0**	**15**	**4**	**–1**	**4**	**0**	**0**	**0**	**0**	**0**	**0**	**0**
1996-97	Long Beach Ice Dogs	IHL	28	4	10	14	....	....	....	54	....	....	....	....	....	....	....	....	....	....	....	....	....	....	....	....	....	....
	Phoenix Coyotes	**NHL**	**2**	**1**	**0**	**1**	**1**	**0**	**1**	**0**	**0**	**0**	**1**	**4**	**25.0**	**1**	**0**	**1**	**0**	**0**	**2**	**0**	**0**	**0**	**4**	**0**	**0**	**0**
1997-98	**Phoenix Coyotes**	**NHL**	**30**	**3**	**3**	**6**	**4**	**3**	**7**	**27**	**1**	**0**	**0**	**32**	**9.4**	**9**	**1**	**8**	**0**	**0**	....	....	....	....	....	....	....	....
	Long Beach Ice Dogs	IHL	10	3	5	8	....	....	....	24	....	....	....	....	....	....	....	....	....	....	....	....	....	....	....	....	....	....
	Springfield Falcons	AHL	6	3	1	4	....	....	....	0	....	....	....	....	....	....	....	....	....	....	4	2	2	4	2	....	....	....
1998-99	Long Beach Ice Dogs	IHL	17	4	4	8	....	....	....	16	....	....	....	....	....	....	....	....	....	....	8	0	2	2	15	....	....	....
	NHL Totals		**598**	**80**	**84**	**164**	**78**	**66**	**144**	**740**	**5**	**1**	**12**	**843**	**9.5**	**257**	**18**	**305**	**27**		**60**	**5**	**10**	**15**	**88**	**0**	**0**	**2**

• Brother of Claude • QMJHL First All-Star Team (1986)

Traded to **Montreal** by **St. Louis** with Darrell May and St. Louis' 2nd round choice (Patrice Brisebois) in 1989 Entry Draft for Sergio Momesso and Vincent Riendeau, August 9, 1988. Traded to **Chicago** by **Montreal** for Chicago's 3rd round choice (Charles Poulin) in 1990 Entry Draft, January 5, 1990. Traded to **Hartford** by **Chicago** with Frantisek Kucera for Gary Suter, Randy Cunneyworth and Hartford's 3rd round choice (later traded to Vancouver — Vancouver selected Larry Courville) in 1995 Entry Draft, March 11, 1994. Traded to **New Jersey** by **Hartford** with Hartford's 2nd round choice in 1998 Entry Draft for Jim Dowd and New Jersey's 2nd round choice (later traded to Calgary — Calgary selected Dmitri Kokorev) in 1997 Entry Draft, December 19, 1995. Traded to **Calgary** by **New Jersey** with Tommy Albelin and Cale Hulse for Phil Housley and Dan Keczmer, February 26, 1996. Signed as a free agent by **Phoenix**, March 18, 1997.
• Missed majority of 1998-99 season recovering from shoulder injury suffered during summer training, July, 1998.

• LEMIEUX, Mario

"The Magnificent" C – R. 6'4", 225 lbs. b: Montreal, Que., 10/5/1965. Pittsburgh's 1st, 1st overall, in 1984. **HHOF**

1979-80	Montreal Hurricanes	QAAA	STATISTICS NOT AVAILABLE																									
1980-81	Montreal Concordia	QAAA	47	62	62	124	....	....	....	....	....	....	....	....	....	....	....	....	....	....	....	....	....	....	....	....	....	....
1981-82	Laval Titan	QMJHL	64	30	66	96	....	....	....	22	....	....	....	....	....	....	....	....	....	....	18	5	9	14	31	....	....	....
1982-83	Laval Titan	QMJHL	66	84	100	184	....	....	....	76	....	....	....	....	....	....	....	....	....	....	12	14	18	32	18	....	....	....
	Canada	WJC-A	7	5	5	10	....	....	....	12	....	....	....	....	....	....	....	....	....	....	....	....	....	....	....	....	....	....
1983-84	Laval Titan	QMJHL	70	*133	*149	*282	....	....	....	92	....	....	....	....	....	....	....	....	....	....	14	*29	*23	*52	29	....	....	....
	Laval Titan	Mem-Cup	3	1	2	3	....	....	....	0	....	....	....	....	....	....	....	....	....	....	....	....	....	....	....	....	....	....
1984-85	**Pittsburgh Penguins**	**NHL**	**73**	**43**	**57**	**100**	**35**	**39**	**74**	**54**	**11**	**0**	**2**	**209**	**20.6**	**125**	**46**	**114**	**0**	**–35**	....	....	....	....	....	....	....	....
	Canada	WEC-A	9	4	6	10	....	....	....	2	....	....	....	....	....	....	....	....	....	....	....	....	....	....	....	....	....	....
1985-86	**Pittsburgh Penguins**	**NHL**	**79**	**48**	**93**	**141**	**38**	**63**	**101**	**43**	**17**	**0**	**4**	**276**	**17.4**	**173**	**81**	**100**	**2**	**–6**	....	....	....	....	....	....	....	....
1986-87	**Pittsburgh Penguins**	**NHL**	**63**	**54**	**53**	**107**	**47**	**39**	**86**	**57**	**19**	**0**	**4**	**267**	**20.2**	**133**	**51**	**72**	**3**	**13**	....	....	....	....	....	....	....	....
	NHL All-Stars	RV-87	2	0	3	3	....	....	....	0	....	....	....	....	....	....	....	....	....	....	....	....	....	....	....	....	....	....

			REGULAR SEASON																		PLAYOFFS							
Season	Club	League	GP	G	A	Pts	AG	AA	APts	PIM	PP	SH	GW	S	%	TGF	PGF	TGA	PGA	+/–	GP	G	A	Pts	PIM	PP	SH	GW
1987-88	Canada	Can-Cup	9	*11	7	18	....	....	....	8	....	....	....	....	....	....	....	....	....	....	....	....	....	....	....	....	....	....
	Pittsburgh Penguins	**NHL**	77	*70	98	*168	60	71	131	92	22	10	7	382	18.3	211	106	121	39	23	....	....	....	....	....	....	....	....
1988-89	**Pittsburgh Penguins**	**NHL**	76	*85	*114	*199	73	81	154	100	31	13	8	313	27.2	254	110	163	60	41	11	12	7	19	16	7	1	0
1989-90	**Pittsburgh Penguins**	**NHL**	59	45	78	123	39	56	95	78	14	3	4	226	19.9	151	67	134	32	–18	....	....	....	....	....	....	....	....
1990-91♦	**Pittsburgh Penguins**	**NHL**	26	19	26	45	17	20	37	30	6	1	2	89	21.3	61	25	29	1	8	23	16	*28	*44	16	6	2	0
1991-92♦	**Pittsburgh Penguins**	**NHL**	64	44	87	*131	40	66	106	94	12	4	5	249	17.7	182	70	99	14	27	15	*16	18	*34	2	8	2	5
1992-93	**Pittsburgh Penguins**	**NHL**	60	69	91	*160	58	63	121	38	16	6	10	286	24.1	203	82	89	23	55	11	8	10	18	10	3	1	1
1993-94	**Pittsburgh Penguins** •	**NHL**	22	17	20	37	16	16	32	32	7	0	4	92	18.5	42	19	31	6	–2	6	4	3	7	2	1	0	0
1994-95	**Pittsburgh Penguins**	**NHL**	DID NOT PLAY																									
1995-96	**Pittsburgh Penguins**	**NHL**	70	*69	*92	*161	68	76	144	54	31	8	8	338	20.4	197	102	113	28	10	18	11	16	27	33	3	1	2
1996-97	**Pittsburgh Penguins**	**NHL**	76	50	*72	*122	53	64	117	65	15	3	7	327	15.3	156	54	102	27	27	5	3	3	6	4	0	0	0
	NHL Totals		745	613	881	1494	544	654	1198	737	201	48	65	3054	20.1	1888	813	1167	235		89	70	85	155	83	28	7	8

• Brother of Alain

QMJHL Second All-Star Team (1983) • QMJHL First All-Star Team (1984) • Canadian Major Junior Player of the Year (1984) • NHL All-Rookie Team (1985) • Won Calder Memorial Trophy (1985) • NHL Second All-Star Team (1986, 1987, 1992) • Won Lester B. Pearson Award (1986, 1988, 1993, 1996) • Canada Cup All-Star Team (1987) • NHL First All-Star Team (1988, 1989, 1993, 1996, 1997) • Won Dodge Performance of the Year Award (1988) • Won Dodge Performer of the Year Award (1988, 1989) • Won Art Ross Trophy (1988, 1989, 1992, 1993, 1996, 1997) • Won Hart Trophy (1988, 1993, 1996) • Won Dodge Ram Tough Award (1989) • Won Conn Smythe Trophy (1991, 1992) • Won ProSet/NHL Player of the Year Award (1992) • Won Alka-Seltzer Plus Award (1993) • Won Bill Masterton Memorial Trophy (1993) • Won Lester Patrick Trophy (2000) • Played in NHL All-Star Game (1985, 1986, 1988, 1989, 1990, 1992, 1996, 1997)

• LEMIEUX, Real

Real Gaston LW – L. 5'11", 180 lbs. b: Victoriaville, Que., 1/3/1945 d: 10/24/1975.

Season	Club	League	GP	G	A	Pts	AG	AA	APts	PIM	PP	SH	GW	S	%	TGF	PGF	TGA	PGA	+/–	GP	G	A	Pts	PIM	PP	SH	GW
1960-1963	Lachine Maroons	MMJHL	STATISTICS NOT AVAILABLE																									
1963-64	Hamilton Red Wings	OHA-Jr.	42	20	24	44	....	....	....	58	....	....	....	....	....	....	....	....	....	....	....	....	....	....	....	....	....	....
1964-65	Hamilton Red Wings	OHA-Jr.	48	48	40	88	....	....	....	64	....	....	....	....	....	....	....	....	....	....	....	....	....	....	....	....	....	....
	Memphis Wings	CPHL	8	5	7	12	....	....	....	0	....	....	....	....	....	....	....	....	....	....	....	....	....	....	....	....	....	....
1965-66	Memphis Wings	CPHL	53	11	15	26	....	....	....	68	....	....	....	....	....	....	....	....	....	....	....	....	....	....	....	....	....	....
1966-67	**Detroit Red Wings**	**NHL**	1	0	0	0	0	0	0	0	....	....	....	....	....	....	....	....	....	....	....	....	....	....	....	....	....	....
	Memphis Wings	CPHL	68	28	34	62	....	....	....	*211	....	....	....	....	....	....	....	....	....	....	7	4	0	4	7	....	....	....
1967-68	**Los Angeles Kings**	**NHL**	74	12	23	35	14	23	37	60	5	1	0	129	9.3	60	16	77	31	–2	7	1	1	2	0	0	0	0
1968-69	**Los Angeles Kings**	**NHL**	75	11	29	40	12	26	38	68	2	0	2	134	8.2	66	14	97	23	–22	11	1	3	4	10	1	0	0
1969-70	**New York Rangers**	**NHL**	55	4	6	10	4	6	10	51	0	0	0	49	8.2	19	1	24	7	1	....	....	....	....	....	....	....	....
	Los Angeles Kings	**NHL**	18	2	4	6	2	4	6	10	0	0	1	28	7.1	10	2	14	5	–1	....	....	....	....	....	....	....	....
1970-71	**Los Angeles Kings**	**NHL**	43	3	6	9	3	5	8	22	0	0	1	36	8.3	22	2	39	12	–7	....	....	....	....	....	....	....	....
	Springfield Kings	AHL	33	14	22	36	....	....	....	25	....	....	....	....	....	....	....	....	....	....	....	....	....	....	....	....	....	....
1971-72	**Los Angeles Kings**	**NHL**	78	13	25	38	13	22	35	28	2	0	0	102	12.7	56	12	103	19	–40	....	....	....	....	....	....	....	....
1972-73	**Los Angeles Kings**	**NHL**	74	5	10	15	5	8	13	19	1	1	0	43	11.6	29	3	45	18	–1	....	....	....	....	....	....	....	....
1973-74	**Los Angeles Kings**	**NHL**	20	0	0	0	0	0	0	0	0	0	0	2	0.0	2	0	13	11	0	....	....	....	....	....	....	....	....
	New York Rangers	**NHL**	7	0	0	0	0	0	0	0	0	0	0	0	0.0	0	0	1	0	–1	....	....	....	....	....	....	....	....
	Buffalo Sabres	**NHL**	11	1	1	2	1	1	2	4	0	0	0	4	25.0	3	0	4	1	0	....	....	....	....	....	....	....	....
	NHL Totals		456	51	104	155	54	95	149	262	....	....	....	....	....	....	....	....	....		18	2	4	6	10	....	....	....

Claimed by **LA Kings** from **Detroit** in Expansion Draft, June 6, 1967. Traded to **NY Rangers** by **LA Kings** for Leon Rochefort and Dennis Hextall, June 9, 1969. Traded to **LA Kings** by **NY Rangers** with Juha Widing for Ted Irvine, February 28, 1970. Traded to **NY Rangers** by **LA Kings** with Gilles Marotte for Sheldon Kannegiesser, Mike Murphy and Tom Williams, November 30, 1973. Traded to **Buffalo** by **NY Rangers** for Paul Curtis, January 21, 1974.

• LEMIEUX, Richard

Richard Bernard C – L. 5'8", 155 lbs. b: Temiscamingue, Que., 4/19/1951. Vancouver's 3rd, 39th overall, in 1971.

Season	Club	League	GP	G	A	Pts	AG	AA	APts	PIM	PP	SH	GW	S	%	TGF	PGF	TGA	PGA	+/–	GP	G	A	Pts	PIM	PP	SH	GW
1967-68	Thetford Mines Canadiens	QJHL	44	28	32	60	....	....	....	....	....	....	....	....	....	....	....	....	....	....	7	5	8	13	7	....	....	....
1968-69	Montreal Jr. Canadiens	OHA-Jr.	51	10	28	38	....	....	....	51	....	....	....	....	....	....	....	....	....	....	14	6	12	18	6	....	....	....
	Montreal Jr. Canadiens	Mem-Cup	8	2	7	9	....	....	....	17	....	....	....	....	....	....	....	....	....	....	....	....	....	....	....	....	....	....
1969-70	Montreal Jr. Canadiens	OHA-Jr.	50	29	43	72	....	....	....	75	....	....	....	....	....	....	....	....	....	....	16	10	16	26	6	....	....	....
	Montreal Jr. Canadiens	Mem-Cup	12	12	15	27	....	....	....	24	....	....	....	....	....	....	....	....	....	....	....	....	....	....	....	....	....	....
1970-71	Montreal Jr. Canadiens	OHA-Jr.	15	11	23	34	....	....	....	35	....	....	....	....	....	....	....	....	....	....	4	2	6	8	5	....	....	....
1971-72	**Vancouver Canucks**	**NHL**	42	7	9	16	7	8	15	4	0	0	0	82	8.5	23	0	36	0	–13	....	....	....	....	....	....	....	....
	Rochester Americans	AHL	34	12	12	24	....	....	....	30	....	....	....	....	....	....	....	....	....	....	....	....	....	....	....	....	....	....
1972-73	**Vancouver Canucks**	**NHL**	78	17	35	52	16	28	44	41	3	0	2	138	12.3	73	23	80	5	–25	....	....	....	....	....	....	....	....
1973-74	**Vancouver Canucks**	**NHL**	72	5	17	22	5	14	19	23	1	0	0	73	6.8	28	6	49	3	–24	....	....	....	....	....	....	....	....
1974-75	**Kansas City Scouts**	**NHL**	79	10	20	30	9	15	24	64	3	0	1	131	7.6	48	16	68	1	–35	....	....	....	....	....	....	....	....
1975-76	**Kansas City Scouts**	**NHL**	2	0	0	0	0	0	0	0	0	0	0	1	0.0	0	0	0	0	0	....	....	....	....	....	....	....	....
	Atlanta Flames	**NHL**	1	0	1	1	0	1	1	0	0	0	0	1	0.0	2	0	0	0	2	2	0	0	0	0	0	0	0
	Nova Scotia Voyageurs	AHL	60	25	23	48	....	....	....	37	....	....	....	....	....	....	....	....	....	....	9	*8	6	14	4	....	....	....
1976-77	Calgary Cowboys	WHA	33	6	11	17	....	....	....	9	....	....	....	....	....	....	....	....	....	....	....	....	....	....	....	....	....	....
	NHL Totals		274	39	82	121	37	66	103	132	7	0	3	426	9.2	174	45	233	9		2	0	0	0	0	0	0	0
	Other Major League Totals		33	6	11	17	....	....	....	9	....	....	....	....	....	....	....	....	....	....	....	....	....	....	....	....	....	....

Selected by **LA Sharks** (WHA) in 1972 WHA General Player Draft, February 12, 1972. WHA rights transferred to **Michigan** (WHA) after **LA Sharks** (WHA) franchise relocated, April 11, 1974. Claimed by **Kansas City** from **Vancouver** in Expansion Draft, June 12, 1974. Traded to **Atlanta** by **Kansas City** with Kansas City's 2nd round choice (Miles Zaharko) in 1977 Amateur Draft for Buster Harvey, October 13, 1975. Signed as a free agent by **Calgary** (WHA) after **Michigan-Baltimore** (WHA) franchise folded, June, 1976. Traded to **Minnesota** (WHA) by **Calgary** (WHA) for Butch Deadmarsh, January, 1977. •Transaction voided when Lemieux refused to report to team.

• LENARDON, Tim

Tim Norman C – L. 6'2", 185 lbs. b: Trail, B.C., 5/11/1962.

Season	Club	League	GP	G	A	Pts	AG	AA	APts	PIM	PP	SH	GW	S	%	TGF	PGF	TGA	PGA	+/–	GP	G	A	Pts	PIM	PP	SH	GW
1979-80	Trail Smoke Eaters	KIJHL	30	21	35	56	....	....	....	....	....	....	....	....	....	....	....	....	....	....	....	....	....	....	....	....	....	....
1980-81	Trail Smoke Eaters	KIJHL	40	49	60	109	....	....	....	....	....	....	....	....	....	....	....	....	....	....	....	....	....	....	....	....	....	....
1981-82	Trail Smoke Eaters	KIJHL	40	78	61	139	....	....	....	....	....	....	....	....	....	....	....	....	....	....	....	....	....	....	....	....	....	....
1982-83	Trail Smoke Eaters	KIJHL	38	86	86	172	....	....	....	....	....	....	....	....	....	....	....	....	....	....	....	....	....	....	....	....	....	....
1983-84	Brandon University	GPAC	24	22	21	43	....	....	....	36	....	....	....	....	....	....	....	....	....	....	....	....	....	....	....	....	....	....
1984-85	Brandon University	GPAC	24	20	39	59	....	....	....	42	....	....	....	....	....	....	....	....	....	....	....	....	....	....	....	....	....	....
1985-86	Brandon University	CWUAA	28	*27	*40	*67	....	....	....	54	....	....	....	....	....	....	....	....	....	....	....	....	....	....	....	....	....	....
1986-87	**New Jersey Devils**	**NHL**	7	1	1	2	1	1	2	0	0	0	0	13	7.7	3	0	5	0	–2	....	....	....	....	....	....	....	....
	Maine Mariners	AHL	61	28	35	63	....	....	....	30	....	....	....	....	....	....	....	....	....	....	....	....	....	....	....	....	....	....
1987-88	Utica Devils	AHL	79	38	53	91	....	....	....	72	....	....	....	....	....	....	....	....	....	....	....	....	....	....	....	....	....	....
1988-89	Utica Devils	AHL	63	28	27	55	....	....	....	48	....	....	....	....	....	....	....	....	....	....	....	....	....	....	....	....	....	....
	Milwaukee Admirals	IHL	15	6	5	11	....	....	....	27	....	....	....	....	....	....	....	....	....	....	10	2	3	5	25	....	....	....
1989-90	**Vancouver Canucks**	**NHL**	8	1	0	1	1	0	1	4	0	0	0	9	11.1	1	0	4	1	–2	....	....	....	....	....	....	....	....
	Milwaukee Admirals	IHL	66	32	36	68	....	....	....	134	....	....	....	....	....	....	....	....	....	....	6	1	1	2	4	....	....	....
1990-91	HC Fiemme	Italy	36	23	28	51	....	....	....	50	....	....	....	....	....	....	....	....	....	....	10	8	18	26	0	....	....	....
1991-92	Kalamazoo Wings	IHL	73	27	24	51	....	....	....	37	....	....	....	....	....	....	....	....	....	....	12	5	5	10	4	....	....	....
1992-93	Kalamazoo Wings	IHL	60	12	18	30	....	....	....	56	....	....	....	....	....	....	....	....	....	....	....	....	....	....	....	....	....	....
	NHL Totals		15	2	1	3	2	1	3	4	0	0	0	22	9.1	4	0	9	1		....	....	....	....	....	....	....	....

Signed as a free agent by **New Jersey**, August 6, 1986. Traded to **Vancouver** by **New Jersey** for Claude Vilgrain, March 7, 1989. Signed as a free agent by **Minnesota**, July 25, 1991.

• LEROUX, Francois

D – L. 6'6", 235 lbs. b: Ste.-Adele, Que., 4/18/1970. Edmonton's 1st, 19th overall, in 1988.

Season	Club	League	GP	G	A	Pts	AG	AA	APts	PIM	PP	SH	GW	S	%	TGF	PGF	TGA	PGA	+/–	GP	G	A	Pts	PIM	PP	SH	GW
1986-87	Laval-Laurentide	QAAA	42	5	11	16	....	....	....	76	....	....	....	....	....	....	....	....	....	....	....	....	....	....	....	....	....	....
1987-88	St-Jean Lynx	QMJHL	58	3	8	11	....	....	....	143	....	....	....	....	....	....	....	....	....	....	7	2	0	2	21	....	....	....
1988-89	St-Jean Lynx	QMJHL	57	8	34	42	....	....	....	185	....	....	....	....	....	....	....	....	....	....	....	....	....	....	....	....	....	....
	Edmonton Oilers	**NHL**	2	0	0	0	0	0	0	0	0	0	0	0	0.0	1	0	0	0	1	....	....	....	....	....	....	....	....
1989-90	Victoriaville Tigres	QMJHL	54	4	33	37	....	....	....	169	....	....	....	....	....	....	....	....	....	....	....	....	....	....	....	....	....	....
	Edmonton Oilers	**NHL**	3	0	1	1	0	1	1	0	0	0	0	0	0.0	1	0	3	0	–2	....	....	....	....	....	....	....	....
1990-91	**Edmonton Oilers**	**NHL**	1	0	2	2	0	2	2	0	0	0	0	1	0.0	2	0	1	0	1	....	....	....	....	....	....	....	....
	Cape Breton Oilers	AHL	71	2	7	9	....	....	....	124	....	....	....	....	....	....	....	....	....	....	4	0	1	1	19	....	....	....
1991-92	**Edmonton Oilers**	**NHL**	4	0	0	0	0	0	0	7	0	0	0	0	0.0	2	1	2	0	–1	....	....	....	....	....	....	....	....
	Cape Breton Oilers	AHL	61	7	22	29	....	....	....	114	....	....	....	....	....	....	....	....	....	....	5	0	0	0	8	....	....	....

			REGULAR SEASON																		PLAYOFFS							
Season	**Club**	**League**	**GP**	**G**	**A**	**Pts**	**AG**	**AA**	**APts**	**PIM**	**PP**	**SH**	**GW**	**S**	**%**	**TGF**	**PGF**	**TGA**	**PGA**	**+/-**	**GP**	**G**	**A**	**Pts**	**PIM**	**PP**	**SH**	**GW**
1992-93	**Edmonton Oilers**	**NHL**	**1**	**0**	**0**	**0**	**0**	**0**	**0**	**4**	**0**	**0**	**0**	**0**	**0.0**	**0**	**0**	**1**	**1**	**0**	....	....	....	....	....	....	....	....
	Cape Breton Oilers	AHL	55	10	24	34	....	....	....	139	....	....	....	....	....	....	....	....	....	....	16	0	5	5	29	....	....	....
1993-94	**Ottawa Senators**	**NHL**	**23**	**0**	**1**	**1**	**0**	**1**	**1**	**70**	**0**	**0**	**0**	**8**	**0.0**	**6**	**0**	**13**	**3**	**–4**	....	....	....	....	....	....	....	....
	P.E.I. Senators	AHL	25	4	6	10	....	....	....	52	....	....	....	....	....	....	....	....	....	....	....	....	....	....	....	....	....	....
1994-95	P.E.I. Senators	AHL	45	4	14	18	....	....	....	137	....	....	....	....	....	....	....	....	....	....	....	....	....	....	....	....	....	....
	Pittsburgh Penguins	**NHL**	**40**	**0**	**2**	**2**	**0**	**3**	**3**	**114**	**0**	**0**	**0**	**19**	**0.0**	**22**	**0**	**19**	**4**	**7**	**12**	**0**	**2**	**2**	**14**	**0**	**0**	**0**
1995-96	**Pittsburgh Penguins**	**NHL**	**66**	**2**	**9**	**11**	**2**	**7**	**9**	**161**	**0**	**0**	**0**	**43**	**4.7**	**45**	**0**	**65**	**22**	**2**	**18**	**1**	**1**	**2**	**20**	**0**	**0**	**1**
1996-97	**Pittsburgh Penguins**	**NHL**	**59**	**0**	**3**	**3**	**0**	**3**	**3**	**81**	**0**	**0**	**0**	**5**	**0.0**	**14**	**1**	**23**	**7**	**–3**	**3**	**0**	**0**	**0**	**0**	**0**	**0**	**0**
1997-98	**Colorado Avalanche**	**NHL**	**50**	**1**	**2**	**3**	**1**	**2**	**3**	**140**	**0**	**0**	**0**	**14**	**7.1**	**4**	**0**	**7**	**0**	**–3**	....	....	....	....	....	....	....	....
1998-99	Grand Rapids Griffins	IHL	13	1	1	2	....	....	....	22	....	....	....	....	....	....	....	....	....	....	....	....	....	....	....	....	....	....
99-2000	Springfield Falcons	AHL	64	3	6	9	....	....	....	162	....	....	....	....	....	....	....	....	....	....	5	0	0	0	2	....	....	....
	NHL Totals		**249**	**3**	**20**	**23**	**3**	**19**	**22**	**577**	**0**	**0**	**0**	**90**	**3.3**	**97**	**2**	**134**	**37**		**33**	**1**	**3**	**4**	**34**	**0**	**0**	**1**

Claimed on waivers by **Ottawa** from **Edmonton**, October 6, 1993. Claimed by **Pittsburgh** from **Ottawa** in Waiver Draft, January 18, 1995. Traded to **Colorado** by **Pittsburgh** for Colorado's 3rd round choice (David Cameron) in 1998 Entry Draft, September 28, 1997. Signed as a free agent by **Grand Rapids** (IHL), February 18, 1999. Signed as a free agent by **Phoenix**, July 20, 1999.

• LEROUX, Jean-Yves

LW – L. 6'2", 211 lbs. b: Montreal, Que., 6/24/1976. Chicago's 2nd, 40th overall, in 1994.

Season	Club	League	GP	G	A	Pts	AG	AA	APts	PIM	PP	SH	GW	S	%	TGF	PGF	TGA	PGA	+/-	GP	G	A	Pts	PIM	PP	SH	GW
1991-92	Montreal-Bourassa	QAAA	35	14	31	45	....	....	....	29	....	....	....	....	....	....	....	....	....	....	....	....	....	....	....	....	....	....
1992-93	Beauport Harfangs	QMJHL	62	20	25	45	....	....	....	33	....	....	....	....	....	....	....	....	....	....	....	....	....	....	....	....	....	....
1993-94	Beauport Harfangs	QMJHL	45	14	25	39	....	....	....	43	....	....	....	....	....	....	....	....	....	....	15	7	6	13	33	....	....	....
1994-95	Beauport Harfangs	QMJHL	59	19	33	52	....	....	....	125	....	....	....	....	....	....	....	....	....	....	17	4	6	10	39	....	....	....
1995-96	Beauport Harfangs	QMJHL	54	41	41	82	....	....	....	176	....	....	....	....	....	....	....	....	....	....	20	5	18	23	20	....	....	....
1996-97	**Chicago Blackhawks**	**NHL**	**1**	**0**	**1**	**1**	**0**	**1**	**1**	**5**	**0**	**0**	**0**	**0**	**0.0**	**1**	**0**	**0**	**0**	**1**	....	....	....	....	....	....	....	....
	Indianapolis Ice	IHL	69	14	17	31	....	....	....	112	....	....	....	....	....	....	....	....	....	....	4	1	0	1	2	....	....	....
1997-98	**Chicago Blackhawks**	**NHL**	**66**	**6**	**7**	**13**	**7**	**7**	**14**	**55**	**0**	**0**	**0**	**57**	**10.5**	**25**	**2**	**25**	**0**	**–2**	....	....	....	....	....	....	....	....
1998-99	**Chicago Blackhawks**	**NHL**	**40**	**3**	**5**	**8**	**4**	**5**	**9**	**21**	**0**	**0**	**0**	**47**	**6.4**	**12**	**1**	**21**	**3**	**–7**	....	....	....	....	....	....	....	....
	Chicago Wolves	IHL	....	....	....	....	....	....	....	....	....	....	....	....	....	....	....	....	....	....	10	1	1	2	18	....	....	....
99-2000	**Chicago Blackhawks**	**NHL**	**54**	**3**	**5**	**8**	**3**	**5**	**8**	**43**	**0**	**0**	**1**	**36**	**8.3**	**16**	**0**	**32**	**6**	**–10**	....	....	....	....	....	....	....	....
	NHL Totals		**161**	**12**	**18**	**30**	**14**	**18**	**32**	**124**	**0**	**0**	**1**	**140**	**8.6**	**54**	**3**	**78**	**9**		....	....	....	....	....	....	....	....

QMJHL Second All-Star Team (1994)

• LESCHYSHYN, Curtis

Curtis Michael D – L. 6'1", 205 lbs. b: Thompson, Man., 9/21/1969. Quebec's 1st, 3rd overall, in 1988.

Season	Club	League	GP	G	A	Pts	AG	AA	APts	PIM	PP	SH	GW	S	%	TGF	PGF	TGA	PGA	+/-	GP	G	A	Pts	PIM	PP	SH	GW
1985-86	Saskatoon Blazers	SAHA	34	9	34	43	....	....	....	52	....	....	....	....	....	....	....	....	....	....	....	....	....	....	....	....	....	....
	Saskatoon Blades	WHL	1	0	0	0	....	....	....	0	....	....	....	....	....	....	....	....	....	....	....	....	....	....	....	....	....	....
1986-87	Saskatoon Blades	WHL	70	14	26	40	....	....	....	107	....	....	....	....	....	....	....	....	....	....	11	1	5	6	14	....	....	....
1987-88	Saskatoon Blades	WHL	56	14	41	55	....	....	....	86	....	....	....	....	....	....	....	....	....	....	10	2	5	7	16	....	....	....
1988-89	**Quebec Nordiques**	**NHL**	**71**	**4**	**9**	**13**	**3**	**6**	**9**	**71**	**1**	**1**	**0**	**58**	**6.9**	**53**	**3**	**99**	**17**	**–32**	....	....	....	....	....	....	....	....
1989-90	**Quebec Nordiques**	**NHL**	**68**	**2**	**6**	**8**	**2**	**4**	**6**	**44**	**1**	**0**	**0**	**42**	**4.8**	**48**	**2**	**120**	**33**	**–41**	....	....	....	....	....	....	....	....
	Canada	WEC-A	9	0	0	0	....	....	....	4	....	....	....	....	....	....	....	....	....	....	....	....	....	....	....	....	....	....
1990-91	**Quebec Nordiques**	**NHL**	**55**	**3**	**7**	**10**	**3**	**5**	**8**	**49**	**2**	**0**	**1**	**57**	**5.3**	**41**	**6**	**70**	**16**	**–19**	....	....	....	....	....	....	....	....
1991-92	**Quebec Nordiques**	**NHL**	**42**	**5**	**12**	**17**	**5**	**9**	**14**	**42**	**3**	**0**	**1**	**61**	**8.2**	**43**	**22**	**61**	**12**	**–28**	....	....	....	....	....	....	....	....
	Halifax Citadels	AHL	6	0	2	2	....	....	....	4	....	....	....	....	....	....	....	....	....	....	....	....	....	....	....	....	....	....
1992-93	**Quebec Nordiques**	**NHL**	**82**	**9**	**23**	**32**	**7**	**16**	**23**	**61**	**4**	**0**	**2**	**73**	**12.3**	**110**	**23**	**100**	**38**	**25**	**6**	**1**	**1**	**2**	**6**	**1**	**0**	**0**
1993-94	**Quebec Nordiques**	**NHL**	**72**	**5**	**17**	**22**	**5**	**13**	**18**	**65**	**3**	**0**	**2**	**97**	**5.2**	**90**	**24**	**103**	**35**	**–2**	....	....	....	....	....	....	....	....
1994-95	**Quebec Nordiques**	**NHL**	**44**	**2**	**13**	**15**	**4**	**19**	**23**	**20**	**0**	**0**	**0**	**43**	**4.7**	**67**	**9**	**45**	**16**	**29**	**3**	**0**	**1**	**1**	**4**	**0**	**0**	**0**
1995-96♦	**Colorado Avalanche**	**NHL**	**77**	**4**	**15**	**19**	**4**	**12**	**16**	**73**	**0**	**0**	**1**	**76**	**5.3**	**86**	**9**	**62**	**17**	**32**	**17**	**1**	**2**	**3**	**8**	**0**	**0**	**0**
1996-97	**Colorado Avalanche**	**NHL**	**11**	**0**	**5**	**5**	**0**	**4**	**4**	**6**	**0**	**0**	**0**	**8**	**0.0**	**6**	**0**	**5**	**0**	**1**	....	....	....	....	....	....	....	....
	Washington Capitals	**NHL**	**2**	**0**	**0**	**0**	**0**	**0**	**0**	**2**	**0**	**0**	**0**	**0**	**0.0**	**1**	**0**	**1**	**0**	**0**	....	....	....	....	....	....	....	....
	Hartford Whalers	**NHL**	**64**	**4**	**13**	**17**	**4**	**12**	**16**	**30**	**1**	**1**	**1**	**94**	**4.3**	**49**	**13**	**74**	**19**	**–19**	....	....	....	....	....	....	....	....
1997-98	**Carolina Hurricanes**	**NHL**	**73**	**2**	**10**	**12**	**2**	**10**	**12**	**45**	**1**	**0**	**1**	**53**	**3.8**	**48**	**5**	**64**	**19**	**–2**	....	....	....	....	....	....	....	....
1998-99	**Carolina Hurricanes**	**NHL**	**65**	**2**	**7**	**9**	**2**	**7**	**9**	**50**	**0**	**0**	**0**	**35**	**5.7**	**44**	**2**	**62**	**19**	**–1**	**6**	**0**	**0**	**0**	**6**	**0**	**0**	**0**
99-2000	**Carolina Hurricanes**	**NHL**	**53**	**0**	**2**	**2**	**0**	**2**	**2**	**14**	**0**	**0**	**0**	**31**	**0.0**	**23**	**0**	**58**	**16**	**–19**	....	....	....	....	....	....	....	....
	NHL Totals		**779**	**42**	**139**	**181**	**41**	**119**	**160**	**572**	**16**	**2**	**9**	**728**	**5.8**	**709**	**118**	**924**	**257**		**32**	**2**	**4**	**6**	**24**	**1**	**0**	**0**

Transferred to **Colorado** after **Quebec** franchise relcoated, June 21, 1995. Traded to **Washington** by **Colorado** with Chris Simon for Keith Jones, Washington's 1st (Mathieu Biron) and 4th (Chris Corrinet) round choices in 1998 Entry Draft, November 2, 1996. Traded to **Hartford** by **Washington** for Andrei Nikolishin, November 9, 1996. Transferred to **Carolina** after **Hartford** franchise relocated, June 25, 1997. Selected by **Minnesota** from **Carolina** in Expansion Draft, June 23, 2000.

• LESSARD, Rick

D – L. 6'2", 206 lbs. b: Timmins, Ont., 1/9/1968. Calgary's 6th, 142nd overall, in 1986.

Season	Club	League	GP	G	A	Pts	AG	AA	APts	PIM	PP	SH	GW	S	%	TGF	PGF	TGA	PGA	+/-	GP	G	A	Pts	PIM	PP	SH	GW
1983-84	Timmins Bears	OMHA	60	13	41	54	....	....	....	78	....	....	....	....	....	....	....	....	....	....	....	....	....	....	....	....	....	....
1984-85	Ottawa 67's	OHL	60	2	13	15	....	....	....	128	....	....	....	....	....	....	....	....	....	....	5	1	4	5	10	....	....	....
1985-86	Ottawa 67's	OHL	64	1	20	21	....	....	....	231	....	....	....	....	....	....	....	....	....	....	....	....	....	....	....	....	....	....
1986-87	Ottawa 67's	OHL	66	5	36	41	....	....	....	188	....	....	....	....	....	....	....	....	....	....	11	1	7	8	30	....	....	....
1987-88	Ottawa 67's	OHL	58	5	34	39	....	....	....	210	....	....	....	....	....	....	....	....	....	....	16	1	0	1	31	....	....	....
1988-89	**Calgary Flames**	**NHL**	**6**	**0**	**1**	**1**	**0**	**1**	**1**	**2**	**0**	**0**	**0**	**0**	**0.0**	**2**	**0**	**4**	**0**	**–2**	....	....	....	....	....	....	....	....
	Salt Lake Golden Eagles	IHL	76	10	42	52	....	....	....	239	....	....	....	....	....	....	....	....	....	....	14	1	6	7	35	....	....	....
1989-90	Salt Lake Golden Eagles	IHL	66	3	18	21	....	....	....	169	....	....	....	....	....	....	....	....	....	....	10	1	2	3	64	....	....	....
1990-91	**Calgary Flames**	**NHL**	**1**	**0**	**1**	**1**	**0**	**1**	**1**	**0**	**0**	**0**	**0**	**0**	**0.0**	**1**	**0**	**2**	**0**	**–1**	....	....	....	....	....	....	....	....
	Salt Lake Golden Eagles	IHL	80	8	27	35	....	....	....	272	....	....	....	....	....	....	....	....	....	....	4	0	1	1	12	....	....	....
1991-92	**San Jose Sharks**	**NHL**	**8**	**0**	**2**	**2**	**0**	**2**	**2**	**16**	**0**	**0**	**0**	**4**	**0.0**	**4**	**0**	**10**	**2**	**–4**	....	....	....	....	....	....	....	....
	Kansas City Blades	IHL	46	3	16	19	....	....	....	117	....	....	....	....	....	....	....	....	....	....	3	0	0	0	2	....	....	....
1992-93	Kansas City Blades	IHL	1	0	0	0	....	....	....	0	....	....	....	....	....	....	....	....	....	....	....	....	....	....	....	....	....	....
	Providence Bruins	AHL	6	0	0	0	....	....	....	6	....	....	....	....	....	....	....	....	....	....	....	....	....	....	....	....	....	....
	Hamilton Canucks	AHL	52	0	17	17	....	....	....	151	....	....	....	....	....	....	....	....	....	....	....	....	....	....	....	....	....	....
1993-94	South Carolina Stingrays	ECHL	5	1	0	1	....	....	....	10	....	....	....	....	....	....	....	....	....	....	....	....	....	....	....	....	....	....
	Salt Lake Golden Eagles	IHL	31	1	2	3	....	....	....	110	....	....	....	....	....	....	....	....	....	....	....	....	....	....	....	....	....	....
	Rochester Americans	AHL	8	1	2	3	....	....	....	2	....	....	....	....	....	....	....	....	....	....	4	0	0	0	2	....	....	....
	NHL Totals		**15**	**0**	**4**	**4**	**0**	**4**	**4**	**18**	**0**	**0**	**0**	**4**	**0.0**	**7**	**0**	**16**	**2**		....	....	....	....	....	....	....	....

IHL First All-Star Team (1989)

Claimed by **San Jose** from **Calgary** in Expansion Draft, May 30, 1991. Traded to **Vancouver** by **San Jose** for Robin Bawa, December 15, 1992. • Played w/ RHI's Utah Rollerbees in 1994 (9-2-12-14-16).

• LESUK, Bill

William Anton LW – L. 5'9", 187 lbs. b: Moose Jaw, Sask., 11/1/1946.

Season	Club	League	GP	G	A	Pts	AG	AA	APts	PIM	PP	SH	GW	S	%	TGF	PGF	TGA	PGA	+/-	GP	G	A	Pts	PIM	PP	SH	GW
1963-64	Weyburn Red Wings	SJHL	62	12	18	30	....	....	....	78	....	....	....	....	....	....	....	....	....	....	8	4	2	6	18	....	....	....
1964-65	Weyburn Red Wings	SJHL	55	25	33	58	....	....	....	73	....	....	....	....	....	....	....	....	....	....	15	3	11	14	28	....	....	....
1965-66	Weyburn Red Wings	SJHL	60	36	40	76	....	....	....	111	....	....	....	....	....	....	....	....	....	....	18	6	10	16	40	....	....	....
	Estevan Bruins	Mem-Cup	4	1	0	1	....	....	....	4	....	....	....	....	....	....	....	....	....	....	....	....	....	....	....	....	....	....
1966-67	Weyburn Red Wings	SJHL	56	36	46	82	....	....	....	62	....	....	....	....	....	....	....	....	....	....	5	0	5	5	4	....	....	....
1967-68	Oklahoma City Blazers	CPHL	67	14	10	24	....	....	....	53	....	....	....	....	....	....	....	....	....	....	7	3	3	6	0	....	....	....
1968-69	**Boston Bruins**	**NHL**	**5**	**0**	**1**	**1**	**0**	**1**	**1**	**0**	**0**	**0**	**0**	**2**	**0.0**	**2**	**0**	**0**	**0**	**2**	**1**	**0**	**0**	**0**	**0**	**0**	**0**	**0**
	Oklahoma City Blazers	CHL	64	17	30	47	....	....	....	46	....	....	....	....	....	....	....	....	....	....	12	0	4	4	8	....	....	....
1969-70♦	**Boston Bruins**	**NHL**	**3**	**0**	**0**	**0**	**0**	**0**	**0**	**0**	**0**	**0**	**0**	**2**	**0.0**	**1**	**0**	**0**	**0**	**1**	**2**	**0**	**0**	**0**	**0**	**0**	**0**	**0**
	Hershey Bears	AHL	70	20	20	40	....	....	....	82	....	....	....	....	....	....	....	....	....	....	7	5	4	9	10	....	....	....
1970-71	**Philadelphia Flyers**	**NHL**	**78**	**17**	**19**	**36**	**17**	**16**	**33**	**81**	**2**	**0**	**2**	**149**	**11.4**	**67**	**9**	**74**	**11**	**–5**	**4**	**1**	**0**	**1**	**8**	**1**	**0**	**0**
1971-72	**Philadelphia Flyers**	**NHL**	**45**	**7**	**6**	**13**	**7**	**5**	**12**	**31**	**2**	**0**	**1**	**116**	**6.0**	**29**	**7**	**48**	**12**	**–14**	....	....	....	....	....	....	....	....
	Los Angeles Kings	**NHL**	**27**	**4**	**10**	**14**	**4**	**9**	**13**	**14**	**1**	**0**	**1**	**47**	**8.5**	**27**	**6**	**19**	**0**	**2**	....	....	....	....	....	....	....	....
1972-73	**Los Angeles Kings**	**NHL**	**67**	**6**	**14**	**20**	**6**	**11**	**17**	**90**	**0**	**0**	**0**	**129**	**4.7**	**35**	**4**	**35**	**2**	**–2**	....	....	....	....	....	....	....	....
1973-74	**Los Angeles Kings**	**NHL**	**35**	**2**	**1**	**3**	**2**	**1**	**3**	**32**	**0**	**0**	**0**	**25**	**8.0**	**7**	**0**	**12**	**1**	**–4**	**2**	**0**	**0**	**0**	**4**	**0**	**0**	**0**
1974-75	**Washington Capitals**	**NHL**	**79**	**8**	**11**	**19**	**7**	**8**	**15**	**77**	**1**	**2**	**0**	**119**	**6.7**	**34**	**6**	**107**	**45**	**–34**	....	....	....	....	....	....	....	....
1975-76	Winnipeg Jets	WHA	81	15	21	36	....	....	....	92	....	....	....	....	....	....	....	....	....	....	13	2	2	4	8	....	....	....

			REGULAR SEASON																		PLAYOFFS							
Season	Club	League	GP	G	A	Pts	AG	AA	APts	PIM	PP	SH	GW	S	%	TGF	PGF	TGA	PGA	+/–	GP	G	A	Pts	PIM	PP	SH	GW
1976-77	Winnipeg Jets	WHA	78	14	27	41	....	....	....	85	....	....	....	....	....	....	....	....	....	....	18	2	1	3	22	....	....	....
1977-78	Winnipeg Jets	WHA	80	9	18	27	....	....	....	48	....	....	....	....	....	....	....	....	....	....	9	2	5	7	12	....	....	....
1978-79	Winnipeg Jets	WHA	79	17	15	32	....	....	....	44	....	....	....	....	....	....	....	....	....	....	10	1	3	4	6	....	....	....
1979-80	**Winnipeg Jets**	**NHL**	**49**	**0**	**1**	**1**	**0**	**1**	**1**	**43**	**0**	**0**	**0**	**37**	**0.0**	**4**	**0**	**27**	**8**	**–15**	....	....	....	....	....	....	....	....
	Tulsa Oilers	CHL	9	1	2	3	....	....	....	0	....	....	....	....	....	....	....	....	....	....	....	....	....	....	....	....	....	....
	NHL Totals		**388**	**44**	**63**	**107**	**43**	**52**	**95**	**368**	**6**	**2**	**4**	**626**	**7.0**	**206**	**32**	**322**	**79**		**9**	**1**	**0**	**1**	**12**	**1**	**0**	**0**
	Other Major League Totals		318	55	81	136	....	....	....	269	....	....	....	....	....	....	....	....	....	....	50	7	11	18	48	....	....	....

SJHL Second All-Star Team (1966)

Traded to **Boston** by **Detroit** with Gary Doak, Ron Murphy and future considerations (Steve Atkinson, June 6, 1966) for Leo Boivin and Dean Prentice, February 16, 1966. Claimed by **Philadelphia** from **Boston** in Intra-League Draft, June 9, 1970. Traded to **LA Kings** by **Philadelphia** with Jim Johnson and Serge Bernier for Bill Flett, Eddie Joyal, Jean Potvin, and Ross Lonsberry, January 28, 1972. Selected by **Alberta** (WHA) in 1972 WHA General Player Draft, February 12, 1972. Traded to **Washington** by **LA Kings** for cash, July 28, 1974. WHA rights traded to **Winnipeg** (WHA) by **Edmonton** (WHA) for future considerations, June, 1975.

• LETANG, Alan

D – L. 6′, 205 lbs. b: Renfrew, Ont., 9/4/1975. Montreal's 10th, 203rd overall, in 1993.

Season	Club	League	GP	G	A	Pts	AG	AA	APts	PIM	PP	SH	GW	S	%	TGF	PGF	TGA	PGA	+/–	GP	G	A	Pts	PIM	PP	SH	GW
1990-91	Ottawa Valley Titans	OMHA	32	3	26	29	....	....	....	16	....	....	....	....	....	....	....	....	....	....	....	....	....	....	....	....	....	....
1991-92	Cornwall Royals	OHL	47	1	4	5	....	....	....	16	....	....	....	....	....	....	....	....	....	....	6	0	0	0	2	....	....	....
1992-93	Newmarket Royals	OHL	66	1	25	26	....	....	....	14	....	....	....	....	....	....	....	....	....	....	6	0	3	3	2	....	....	....
1993-94	Newmarket Royals	OHL	58	3	21	24	....	....	....	30	....	....	....	....	....	....	....	....	....	....	....	....	....	....	....	....	....	....
1994-95	Sarnia Sting	OHL	62	5	36	41	....	....	....	35	....	....	....	....	....	....	....	....	....	....	4	2	2	4	6	....	....	....
1995-96	Fredericton Canadiens	AHL	71	0	26	26	....	....	....	40	....	....	....	....	....	....	....	....	....	....	....	....	....	....	....	....	....	....
1996-97	Fredericton Canadiens	AHL	60	2	9	11	....	....	....	8	....	....	....	....	....	....	....	....	....	....	....	....	....	....	....	....	....	....
1997-98	ESV Kaufenbeuren	Germany	15	1	5	6	....	....	....	8	....	....	....	....	....	....	....	....	....	....	....	....	....	....	....	....	....	....
	SC Langnau	Switz-2	11	4	3	7	....	....	....	6	....	....	....	....	....	....	....	....	....	....	....	....	....	....	....	....	....	....
	Augsburger Panther	Germany	17	0	1	1	....	....	....	4	....	....	....	....	....	....	....	....	....	....	....	....	....	....	....	....	....	....
1998-99	Canada	Nat-Team	41	3	9	12	....	....	....	20	....	....	....	....	....	....	....	....	....	....	....	....	....	....	....	....	....	....
	Michigan K-Wings	IHL	12	3	3	6	....	....	....	0	....	....	....	....	....	....	....	....	....	....	5	0	2	2	0	....	....	....
99-2000	**Dallas Stars**	**NHL**	**8**	**0**	**0**	**0**	**0**	**0**	**0**	**2**	**0**	**0**	**0**	**1**	**0.0**	**2**	**0**	**7**	**0**	**–5**	....	....	....	....	....	....	....	....
	Michigan K-Wings	IHL	51	1	12	13	....	....	....	30	....	....	....	....	....	....	....	....	....	....	....	....	....	....	....	....	....	....
	NHL Totals		**8**	**0**	**0**	**0**	**0**	**0**	**0**	**2**	**0**	**0**	**0**	**1**	**0.0**	**2**	**0**	**7**	**0**		....	....	....	....	....	....	....	....

Signed as a free agent by **Dallas**, March 22, 1999.

• LETOWSKI, Trevor

Trevor Lindsay C – R. 5′10″, 173 lbs. b: Thunder Bay, Ont., 4/5/1977. Phoenix's 6th, 174th overall, in 1996.

Season	Club	League	GP	G	A	Pts	AG	AA	APts	PIM	PP	SH	GW	S	%	TGF	PGF	TGA	PGA	+/–	GP	G	A	Pts	PIM	PP	SH	GW
1993-94	Thunder Bay Kings	TBAHA	64	41	60	101	....	....	....	48	....	....	....	....	....	....	....	....	....	....	....	....	....	....	....	....	....	....
1994-95	Sarnia Sting	OHL	66	22	19	41	....	....	....	33	....	....	....	....	....	....	....	....	....	....	4	0	1	1	9	....	....	....
1995-96	Sarnia Sting	OHL	66	36	63	99	....	....	....	66	....	....	....	....	....	....	....	....	....	....	10	9	5	14	10	....	....	....
1996-97	Sarnia Sting	OHL	55	35	73	108	....	....	....	51	....	....	....	....	....	....	....	....	....	....	12	9	12	21	20	....	....	....
	Canada	WJC-A	7	2	1	3	....	....	....	4	....	....	....	....	....	....	....	....	....	....	....	....	....	....	....	....	....	....
1997-98	Springfield Falcons	AHL	75	11	20	31	....	....	....	26	....	....	....	....	....	....	....	....	....	....	4	1	0	1	2	....	....	....
1998-99	**Phoenix Coyotes**	**NHL**	**14**	**2**	**2**	**4**	**2**	**2**	**4**	**2**	**0**	**0**	**0**	**8**	**25.0**	**4**	**0**	**3**	**0**	**1**	....	....	....	....	....	....	....	....
	Springfield Falcons	AHL	67	32	35	67	....	....	....	46	....	....	....	....	....	....	....	....	....	....	3	1	0	1	2	....	....	....
99-2000	**Phoenix Coyotes**	**NHL**	**82**	**19**	**20**	**39**	**21**	**19**	**40**	**20**	**3**	**4**	**3**	**125**	**15.2**	**52**	**5**	**62**	**17**	**2**	**5**	**1**	**1**	**2**	**4**	**0**	**0**	**0**
	Canada	WC-A	9	0	2	2	....	....	....	6	....	....	....	....	....	....	....	....	....	....	....	....	....	....	....	....	....	....
	NHL Totals		**96**	**21**	**22**	**43**	**23**	**21**	**44**	**22**	**3**	**4**	**3**	**133**	**15.8**	**56**	**5**	**65**	**17**		**5**	**1**	**1**	**2**	**4**	**0**	**0**	**0**

• LEVEILLE, Normand

LW – L. 5′10″, 175 lbs. b: Montreal, Que., 1/10/1963. Boston's 1st, 14th overall, in 1981.

Season	Club	League	GP	G	A	Pts	AG	AA	APts	PIM	PP	SH	GW	S	%	TGF	PGF	TGA	PGA	+/–	GP	G	A	Pts	PIM	PP	SH	GW
1979-80	Chicoutimi Sagueneens	QMJHL	60	24	12	36	....	....	....	39	....	....	....	....	....	....	....	....	....	....	12	4	6	10	2	....	....	....
1980-81	Chicoutimi Sagueneens	QMJHL	72	55	46	101	....	....	....	46	....	....	....	....	....	....	....	....	....	....	12	11	15	26	8	....	....	....
1981-82	**Boston Bruins**	**NHL**	**66**	**14**	**19**	**33**	**11**	**13**	**24**	**49**	**1**	**0**	**4**	**148**	**9.5**	**58**	**4**	**38**	**0**	**16**	....	....	....	....	....	....	....	....
1982-83	**Boston Bruins**	**NHL**	**9**	**3**	**6**	**9**	**2**	**4**	**6**	**0**	**2**	**0**	**2**	**31**	**9.7**	**12**	**4**	**7**	**0**	**1**	....	....	....	....	....	....	....	....
	NHL Totals		**75**	**17**	**25**	**42**	**13**	**17**	**30**	**49**	**3**	**0**	**6**	**179**	**9.5**	**70**	**8**	**45**	**0**		....	....	....	....	....	....	....	....

QMJHL Second All-Star Team (1981) • Suffered career-ending brain aneurysm during game vs. Vancouver, October 23, 1982.

• LEVEQUE, Guy

C – R. 5′11″, 180 lbs. b: Kingston, Ont., 12/28/1972. Los Angeles' 1st, 42nd overall, in 1991.

Season	Club	League	GP	G	A	Pts	AG	AA	APts	PIM	PP	SH	GW	S	%	TGF	PGF	TGA	PGA	+/–	GP	G	A	Pts	PIM	PP	SH	GW
1988-89	Kingston Legionaires	OMHA	47	55	29	84	....	....	....	52	....	....	....	....	....	....	....	....	....	....	....	....	....	....	....	....	....	....
1989-90	Cornwall Royals	OHL	62	10	15	25	....	....	....	30	....	....	....	....	....	....	....	....	....	....	3	0	0	0	4	....	....	....
1990-91	Cornwall Royals	OHL	66	41	56	97	....	....	....	34	....	....	....	....	....	....	....	....	....	....	....	....	....	....	....	....	....	....
1991-92	Cornwall Royals	OHL	37	23	36	59	....	....	....	40	....	....	....	....	....	....	....	....	....	....	6	3	5	8	2	....	....	....
1992-93	**Los Angeles Kings**	**NHL**	**12**	**2**	**1**	**3**	**2**	**1**	**3**	**19**	**0**	**0**	**0**	**12**	**16.7**	**4**	**1**	**7**	**0**	**–4**	....	....	....	....	....	....	....	....
	Phoenix Roadrunners	IHL	56	27	30	57	....	....	....	71	....	....	....	....	....	....	....	....	....	....	....	....	....	....	....	....	....	....
1993-94	**Los Angeles Kings**	**NHL**	**5**	**0**	**1**	**1**	**0**	**1**	**1**	**2**	**0**	**0**	**0**	**3**	**0.0**	**1**	**0**	**0**	**0**	**1**	....	....	....	....	....	....	....	....
	Phoenix Roadrunners	IHL	39	10	16	26	....	....	....	47	....	....	....	....	....	....	....	....	....	....	....	....	....	....	....	....	....	....
1994-95	Canada	Nat-Team	31	17	17	34	....	....	....	14	....	....	....	....	....	....	....	....	....	....	....	....	....	....	....	....	....	....
	Phoenix Roadrunners	IHL	2	0	0	0	....	....	....	15	....	....	....	....	....	....	....	....	....	....	....	....	....	....	....	....	....	....
	St. John's Maple Leafs	AHL	37	8	14	22	....	....	....	31	....	....	....	....	....	....	....	....	....	....	3	0	0	0	0	....	....	....
1995-96	Minnesota Moose	IHL	12	1	4	5	....	....	....	2	....	....	....	....	....	....	....	....	....	....	....	....	....	....	....	....	....	....
1996-97	San Antonio Dragons	IHL	3	0	1	1	....	....	....	0	....	....	....	....	....	....	....	....	....	....	....	....	....	....	....	....	....	....
1997-98	Phoenix Mustangs	WCHL	48	24	32	56	....	....	....	41	....	....	....	....	....	....	....	....	....	....	6	2	3	5	2	....	....	....
1998-99			DID NOT PLAY – INJURED																									
99-2000	London Knights	BH-Cup	1	0	0	0	....	....	....	2	....	....	....	....	....	....	....	....	....	....	....	....	....	....	....	....	....	....
	NHL Totals		**17**	**2**	**2**	**4**	**2**	**2**	**4**	**21**	**0**	**0**	**0**	**15**	**13.3**	**5**	**1**	**7**	**0**		....	....	....	....	....	....	....	....

Traded to **Toronto** by **LA Kings** with Dixon Ward, Kelly Fairchild and Shayne Toporoswki for Eric Lacroix, Chris Snell and Toronto's 4th round choice (Eric Belanger) in 1996 Entry Draft, October 3, 1994. • Missed entire 1998-99 and majority of 1999-2000 seasons recovering from back surgery, June, 1998.

• LEVER, Don

Donald Richard "Cleaver" LW – L. 5′11″, 185 lbs. b: South Porcupine, Ont., 11/14/1952. Vancouver's 1st, 3rd overall, in 1972.

Season	Club	League	GP	G	A	Pts	AG	AA	APts	PIM	PP	SH	GW	S	%	TGF	PGF	TGA	PGA	+/–	GP	G	A	Pts	PIM	PP	SH	GW
1969-70	Niagara Falls Flyers	OHA-Jr.	2	0	1	1	....	....	....	4	....	....	....	....	....	....	....	....	....	....	....	....	....	....	....	....	....	....
1970-71	Niagara Falls Flyers	OHA-Jr.	59	35	36	71	....	....	....	112	....	....	....	....	....	....	....	....	....	....	....	....	....	....	....	....	....	....
1971-72	Niagara Falls Flyers	OMJHL	63	61	65	126	....	....	....	69	....	....	....	....	....	....	....	....	....	....	6	3	1	4	45	....	....	....
1972-73	**Vancouver Canucks**	**NHL**	**78**	**12**	**26**	**38**	**11**	**21**	**32**	**49**	**3**	**1**	**1**	**138**	**8.7**	**62**	**12**	**85**	**8**	**–27**	....	....	....	....	....	....	....	....
1973-74	**Vancouver Canucks**	**NHL**	**78**	**23**	**25**	**48**	**22**	**21**	**43**	**28**	**4**	**1**	**1**	**175**	**13.1**	**70**	**20**	**96**	**30**	**–16**	....	....	....	....	....	....	....	....
1974-75	**Vancouver Canucks**	**NHL**	**80**	**38**	**30**	**68**	**33**	**22**	**55**	**49**	**11**	**0**	**3**	**214**	**17.8**	**92**	**34**	**73**	**2**	**–13**	**5**	**0**	**1**	**1**	**4**	**0**	**0**	**0**
1975-76	**Vancouver Canucks**	**NHL**	**80**	**25**	**40**	**65**	**22**	**30**	**52**	**93**	**8**	**0**	**1**	**166**	**15.1**	**89**	**28**	**72**	**9**	**–2**	**2**	**0**	**0**	**0**	**0**	**0**	**0**	**0**
1976-77	**Vancouver Canucks**	**NHL**	**80**	**27**	**30**	**57**	**24**	**23**	**47**	**28**	**8**	**1**	**2**	**198**	**13.6**	**90**	**24**	**95**	**21**	**–8**	....	....	....	....	....	....	....	....
1977-78	**Vancouver Canucks**	**NHL**	**75**	**17**	**32**	**49**	**15**	**25**	**40**	**58**	**6**	**0**	**1**	**168**	**10.1**	**74**	**21**	**100**	**18**	**–29**	....	....	....	....	....	....	....	....
	Canada	WEC-A	10	4	3	7	....	....	....	4	....	....	....	....	....	....	....	....	....	....	....	....	....	....	....	....	....	....
1978-79	**Vancouver Canucks**	**NHL**	**71**	**23**	**21**	**44**	**20**	**15**	**35**	**17**	**8**	**0**	**2**	**170**	**13.5**	**64**	**23**	**104**	**22**	**–41**	**3**	**2**	**1**	**3**	**2**	**1**	**0**	**1**
1979-80	**Vancouver Canucks**	**NHL**	**51**	**21**	**17**	**38**	**18**	**12**	**30**	**32**	**5**	**0**	**0**	**134**	**15.7**	**55**	**17**	**65**	**14**	**–13**	....	....	....	....	....	....	....	....
	Atlanta Flames	**NHL**	**28**	**14**	**16**	**30**	**12**	**12**	**24**	**4**	**1**	**1**	**1**	**74**	**18.9**	**41**	**6**	**32**	**2**	**5**	**4**	**1**	**1**	**2**	**0**	**1**	**0**	**0**
1980-81	**Calgary Flames**	**NHL**	**62**	**26**	**31**	**57**	**20**	**21**	**41**	**56**	**4**	**1**	**4**	**157**	**16.6**	**99**	**24**	**74**	**20**	**21**	**16**	**4**	**7**	**11**	**20**	**0**	**0**	**0**
1981-82	**Calgary Flames**	**NHL**	**23**	**8**	**11**	**19**	**6**	**7**	**13**	**6**	**1**	**0**	**0**	**55**	**14.5**	**24**	**8**	**35**	**5**	**–14**	....	....	....	....	....	....	....	....
	Colorado Rockies	**NHL**	**59**	**22**	**28**	**50**	**17**	**19**	**36**	**20**	**3**	**0**	**1**	**136**	**16.2**	**68**	**16**	**78**	**16**	**–10**	....	....	....	....	....	....	....	....
1982-83	**New Jersey Devils**	**NHL**	**79**	**23**	**30**	**53**	**19**	**21**	**40**	**68**	**9**	**3**	**0**	**143**	**16.1**	**80**	**35**	**126**	**46**	**–35**	....	....	....	....	....	....	....	....
1983-84	**New Jersey Devils**	**NHL**	**70**	**14**	**19**	**33**	**11**	**13**	**24**	**44**	**3**	**0**	**2**	**111**	**12.6**	**54**	**12**	**82**	**19**	**–21**	....	....	....	....	....	....	....	....
1984-85	**New Jersey Devils**	**NHL**	**67**	**10**	**8**	**18**	**8**	**5**	**13**	**31**	**0**	**1**	**1**	**83**	**12.0**	**30**	**5**	**68**	**14**	**–29**	....	....	....	....	....	....	....	....
1985-86	**Buffalo Sabres**	**NHL**	**29**	**7**	**1**	**8**	**6**	**1**	**7**	**6**	**0**	**1**	**1**	**31**	**22.6**	**14**	**0**	**30**	**11**	**–5**	....	....	....	....	....	....	....	....
	Rochester Americans	AHL	29	6	11	17	....	....	....	16	....	....	....	....	....	....	....	....	....	....	....	....	....	....	....	....	....	....
1986-87	**Buffalo Sabres**	**NHL**	**10**	**3**	**2**	**5**	**3**	**1**	**4**	**4**	**3**	**0**	**1**	**8**	**37.5**	**8**	**4**	**8**	**1**	**–3**	....	....	....	....	....	....	....	....
	Rochester Americans	AHL	57	29	25	54	....	....	....	69	....	....	....	....	....	....	....	....	....	....	18	4	3	7	14	....	....	....

			REGULAR SEASON																		PLAYOFFS							
Season	Club	League	GP	G	A	Pts	AG	AA	APts	PIM	PP	SH	GW	S	%	TGF	PGF	TGA	PGA	+/–	GP	G	A	Pts	PIM	PP	SH	GW
1987-1990	**Buffalo Sabres**	**NHL**	DID NOT PLAY – ASSISTANT COACH																									
1990-1993	Rochester Americans	AHL	DID NOT PLAY – COACHING																									
1993-2000	**Buffalo Sabres**	**NHL**	DID NOT PLAY – ASSISTANT COACH																									
	NHL Totals		**1020**	**313**	**367**	**680**	**267**	**269**	**536**	**593**	**77**	**10**	**22**	**2161**	**14.5**	**1014**	**289**	**1223**	**258**		**30**	**7**	**10**	**17**	**26**	**2**	**0**	**1**

OMJHL First All-Star Team (1972) • Played in NHL All-Star Game (1982)

Traded to **Atlanta** by **Vancouver** with Brad Smith for Ivan Boldirev and Darcy Rota, February 8, 1980. Transferred to **Calgary** after **Colorado** franchise relocated, June 24, 1980. Traded to **Colorado** by **Calgary** with Bob MacMillan for Lanny McDonald and Colorado's 4th round choice (later traded to NY Islanders — NY Islanders selected Mikko Makela) in 1983 Entry Draft, November 25, 1981. Transferred to **New Jersey** after **Colorado** franchise relocated, June 30, 1982. Rights traded to **Buffalo** by **New Jersey** for cash, September 9, 1985.

• LEVIE, Craig

Craig Dean D – R. 5'11", 190 lbs. b: Calgary, Alta., 8/17/1959. Montreal's 3rd, 43rd overall, in 1979.

Season	Club	League	GP	G	A	Pts	AG	AA	APts	PIM	PP	SH	GW	S	%	TGF	PGF	TGA	PGA	+/–	GP	G	A	Pts	PIM	PP	SH	GW
1976-77	Pincher Creek Panthers	AJHL	27	8	10	18	....	....	....	32	....	....	....	....	....	....	....	....	....	....	....	....	....	....	....	....	....	....
	Calgary Wranglers	WCJHL	2	0	1	1	....	....	....	0	....	....	....	....	....	....	....	....	....	....	....	....	....	....	....	....	....	....
1977-78	Flin Flon Bombers	WCJHL	72	25	64	89	....	....	....	167	....	....	....	....	....	....	....	....	....	....	16	3	7	10	58	....	....	....
1978-79	Edmonton Oil Kings	WHL	69	29	63	92	....	....	....	200	....	....	....	....	....	....	....	....	....	....	7	4	6	10	11	....	....	....
1979-80	Nova Scotia Voyageurs	AHL	72	6	21	27	....	....	....	74	....	....	....	....	....	....	....	....	....	....	6	0	2	2	17	....	....	....
1980-81	Nova Scotia Voyageurs	AHL	80	20	*62	82	....	....	....	162	....	....	....	....	....	....	....	....	....	....	6	5	2	7	16	....	....	....
1981-82	**Winnipeg Jets**	**NHL**	**40**	**4**	**9**	**13**	**3**	**6**	**9**	**48**	**0**	**0**	**1**	**56**	**7.1**	**40**	**4**	**33**	**1**	**4**	....	....	....	....	....	....	....	....
	Tulsa Oilers	CHL	14	4	7	11	....	....	....	17	....	....	....	....	....	....	....	....	....	....	....	....	....	....	....	....	....	....
1982-83	**Winnipeg Jets**	**NHL**	**22**	**4**	**5**	**9**	**3**	**3**	**6**	**31**	**0**	**0**	**1**	**31**	**12.9**	**24**	**8**	**21**	**2**	**–3**	....	....	....	....	....	....	....	....
	Sherbrooke Jets	AHL	44	3	27	30	....	....	....	52	....	....	....	....	....	....	....	....	....	....	....	....	....	....	....	....	....	....
1983-84	**Minnesota North Stars**	**NHL**	**37**	**6**	**13**	**19**	**5**	**9**	**14**	**44**	**0**	**0**	**1**	**55**	**10.9**	**53**	**4**	**55**	**15**	**9**	**15**	**2**	**3**	**5**	**32**	**0**	**0**	**0**
	Salt Lake Golden Eagles	CHL	37	8	20	28	....	....	....	101	....	....	....	....	....	....	....	....	....	....	....	....	....	....	....	....	....	....
1984-85	**St. Louis Blues**	**NHL**	**61**	**6**	**23**	**29**	**5**	**16**	**21**	**33**	**2**	**0**	**1**	**94**	**6.4**	**72**	**33**	**41**	**4**	**2**	**1**	**0**	**0**	**0**	**0**	**0**	**0**	**0**
1985-86	**Minnesota North Stars**	**NHL**	**14**	**2**	**2**	**4**	**2**	**1**	**3**	**8**	**0**	**0**	**0**	**22**	**9.1**	**9**	**4**	**10**	**0**	**–5**	....	....	....	....	....	....	....	....
	Springfield Indians	AHL	36	5	23	28	....	....	....	82	....	....	....	....	....	....	....	....	....	....	....	....	....	....	....	....	....	....
1986-87	HC Davos	Switz.	6	7	4	11	....	....	....	....	....	....	....	....	....	....	....	....	....	....	....	....	....	....	....	....	....	....
	Vancouver Canucks	**NHL**	**9**	**0**	**1**	**1**	**0**	**1**	**1**	**13**	**0**	**0**	**0**	**8**	**0.0**	**10**	**1**	**6**	**0**	**3**	....	....	....	....	....	....	....	....
1987-88	HC Davos	Switz.	36	5	12	17	....	....	....	....	....	....	....	....	....	....	....	....	....	....	....	....	....	....	....	....	....	....
1988-89	HC Milano Saima	Italy	35	17	30	47	....	....	....	10	....	....	....	....	....	....	....	....	....	....	5	4	2	6	12	....	....	....
1989-90	HC Milano Saima	Italy	40	21	32	53	....	....	....	22	....	....	....	....	....	....	....	....	....	....	....	....	....	....	....	....	....	....
1990-91	HC Milano Saima	Italy	36	12	29	41	....	....	....	27	....	....	....	....	....	....	....	....	....	....	9	2	7	9	30	....	....	....
1991-92	Fort Wayne Komets	IHL	1	0	0	0	....	....	....	0	....	....	....	....	....	....	....	....	....	....	....	....	....	....	....	....	....	....
	NHL Totals		**183**	**22**	**53**	**75**	**18**	**36**	**54**	**177**	**2**	**0**	**4**	**266**	**8.3**	**208**	**54**	**166**	**22**		**16**	**2**	**3**	**5**	**32**	**0**	**0**	**0**

WHL Second All-Star Team (1979) • AHL First All-Star Team (1981) • Won Eddie Shore Award (Outstanding Defenseman - AHL) (1981)

Claimed by **Winnipeg** from **Montreal** in Waiver Draft, October 5, 1981. Traded to **Minnesota** by **Winnipeg** with the rights to Tom Ward for Tim Young, August 3, 1983. Claimed by **St. Louis** from **Minnesota** in Waiver Draft, October 9, 1984. Claimed by **Calgary** from **St. Louis** in Waiver Draft, October 7, 1985. Claimed on waivers by **Minnesota** from **Calgary**, October 7, 1985. Signed as a free agent by **Vancouver**, March 1, 1987.

• LEVINS, Scott

Scott M. C/RW – R. 6'4", 210 lbs. b: Spokane, WA, 1/30/1970. Winnipeg's 4th, 75th overall, in 1990.

Season	Club	League	GP	G	A	Pts	AG	AA	APts	PIM	PP	SH	GW	S	%	TGF	PGF	TGA	PGA	+/–	GP	G	A	Pts	PIM	PP	SH	GW
1987-88	Spokane Braves	KIJHL	42	49	59	108	....	....	....	180	....	....	....	....	....	....	....	....	....	....	....	....	....	....	....	....	....	....
1988-89	Penticton Knights	BCJHL	50	27	58	85	....	....	....	154	....	....	....	....	....	....	....	....	....	....	....	....	....	....	....	....	....	....
1989-90	Tri-City Americans	WHL	71	25	37	62	....	....	....	132	....	....	....	....	....	....	....	....	....	....	6	2	3	5	18	....	....	....
1990-91	Moncton Hawks	AHL	74	12	26	38	....	....	....	133	....	....	....	....	....	....	....	....	....	....	4	0	0	0	4	....	....	....
1991-92	Moncton Hawks	AHL	69	15	18	33	....	....	....	271	....	....	....	....	....	....	....	....	....	....	11	3	4	7	30	....	....	....
1992-93	**Winnipeg Jets**	**NHL**	**9**	**0**	**1**	**1**	**0**	**1**	**1**	**18**	**0**	**0**	**0**	**8**	**0.0**	**1**	**0**	**3**	**0**	**–2**	....	....	....	....	....	....	....	....
	Moncton Hawks	AHL	54	22	26	48	....	....	....	158	....	....	....	....	....	....	....	....	....	....	5	1	3	4	14	....	....	....
1993-94	**Florida Panthers**	**NHL**	**29**	**5**	**6**	**11**	**5**	**5**	**10**	**69**	**2**	**0**	**1**	**38**	**13.2**	**16**	**6**	**10**	**0**	**0**	....	....	....	....	....	....	....	....
	Ottawa Senators	**NHL**	**33**	**3**	**5**	**8**	**3**	**4**	**7**	**93**	**2**	**0**	**0**	**39**	**7.7**	**13**	**7**	**33**	**1**	**–26**	....	....	....	....	....	....	....	....
1994-95	**Ottawa Senators**	**NHL**	**24**	**5**	**6**	**11**	**9**	**9**	**18**	**51**	**0**	**0**	**0**	**34**	**14.7**	**16**	**2**	**10**	**0**	**4**	....	....	....	....	....	....	....	....
	P.E.I. Senators	AHL	6	0	4	4	....	....	....	14	....	....	....	....	....	....	....	....	....	....	....	....	....	....	....	....	....	....
1995-96	**Ottawa Senators**	**NHL**	**27**	**0**	**2**	**2**	**0**	**2**	**2**	**80**	**0**	**0**	**0**	**6**	**0.0**	**4**	**0**	**8**	**1**	**–3**	....	....	....	....	....	....	....	....
	Detroit Vipers	IHL	9	0	0	0	....	....	....	9	....	....	....	....	....	....	....	....	....	....	....	....	....	....	....	....	....	....
1996-97	Springfield Falcons	AHL	68	24	23	47	....	....	....	267	....	....	....	....	....	....	....	....	....	....	11	5	4	9	37	....	....	....
1997-98	**Phoenix Coyotes**	**NHL**	**2**	**0**	**0**	**0**	**0**	**0**	**0**	**5**	**0**	**0**	**0**	**2**	**0.0**	**0**	**0**	**1**	**0**	**–1**	....	....	....	....	....	....	....	....
	Springfield Falcons	AHL	79	28	39	67	....	....	....	177	....	....	....	....	....	....	....	....	....	....	4	2	0	2	24	....	....	....
1998-99	Beast of New Haven	AHL	80	32	26	58	....	....	....	189	....	....	....	....	....	....	....	....	....	....	....	....	....	....	....	....	....	....
99-2000	Revier Lowen	Germany	48	14	12	26	....	....	....	124	....	....	....	....	....	....	....	....	....	....	....	....	....	....	....	....	....	....
	Quad City Mallards	UHL	11	4	4	8	....	....	....	46	....	....	....	....	....	....	....	....	....	....	....	....	....	....	....	....	....	....
	NHL Totals		**124**	**13**	**20**	**33**	**17**	**21**	**38**	**316**	**4**	**0**	**1**	**127**	**10.2**	**50**	**15**	**65**	**2**		....	....	....	....	....	....	....	....

WHL West Second All-Star Team (1990)

Claimed by **Florida** from **Winnipeg** in Expansion Draft, June 24, 1993. Traded to **Ottawa** by **Florida** with Evgeny Davydov, Florida's 6th round choice (Mike Gaffney) in 1994 Entry Draft and Dallas' 4th round choice (previously acquired, Ottawa selected Kevin Bolibruck) in 1995 Entry Draft for Bob Kudelski, January 6, 1994. Signed as a free agent by **Phoenix**, October 3, 1996. Signed as a free agent by **Carolina**, August 18, 1998.

• LEVO, Tapio

D – L. 6'2", 200 lbs. b: Pori, Finland, 9/24/1955. Pittsburgh's 8th, 139th overall, in 1975.

Season	Club	League	GP	G	A	Pts	AG	AA	APts	PIM	PP	SH	GW	S	%	TGF	PGF	TGA	PGA	+/–	GP	G	A	Pts	PIM	PP	SH	GW
1972-73	Assat Pori	Finland	1	0	0	0	....	....	....	0	....	....	....	....	....	....	....	....	....	....	....	....	....	....	....	....	....	....
1973-74	Assat Pori	Finland	10	0	0	0	....	....	....	4	....	....	....	....	....	....	....	....	....	....	....	....	....	....	....	....	....	....
1974-75	Assat Pori	Finland	36	5	2	7	....	....	....	48	....	....	....	....	....	....	....	....	....	....	....	....	....	....	....	....	....	....
	Finland	WJC-A	5	1	2	3	....	....	....	7	....	....	....	....	....	....	....	....	....	....	....	....	....	....	....	....	....	....
1975-76	Assat Pori	Finland	36	12	8	20	....	....	....	47	....	....	....	....	....	....	....	....	....	....	4	0	1	1	6	....	....	....
	Finland	WEC-A	10	1	0	1	....	....	....	6	....	....	....	....	....	....	....	....	....	....	....	....	....	....	....	....	....	....
1976-77	Finland	Can-Cup	4	1	2	3	....	....	....	2	....	....	....	....	....	....	....	....	....	....	....	....	....	....	....	....	....	....
	Assat Pori	Finland	36	12	7	19	....	....	....	34	....	....	....	....	....	....	....	....	....	....	....	....	....	....	....	....	....	....
1977-78	Assat Pori	Finland	36	8	11	19	....	....	....	32	....	....	....	....	....	....	....	....	....	....	9	2	1	3	12	....	....	....
	Finland	WEC-A	10	2	0	2	....	....	....	2	....	....	....	....	....	....	....	....	....	....	....	....	....	....	....	....	....	....
1978-79	Assat Pori	Finland	36	15	6	21	....	....	....	34	....	....	....	....	....	....	....	....	....	....	8	7	2	9	20	....	....	....
1979-80	Assat Pori	Finland	30	11	8	19	....	....	....	55	....	....	....	....	....	....	....	....	....	....	7	6	3	9	4	....	....	....
	Finland	Olympics	4	1	4	5	....	....	....	2	....	....	....	....	....	....	....	....	....	....	....	....	....	....	....	....	....	....
1980-81	Assat Pori	Finland	36	16	7	23	....	....	....	38	....	....	....	....	....	....	....	....	....	....	2	1	1	2	4	....	....	....
	Finland	WEC-A	8	4	4	8	....	....	....	10	....	....	....	....	....	....	....	....	....	....	....	....	....	....	....	....	....	....
1981-82	Finland	Can-Cup	5	0	1	1	....	....	....	2	....	....	....	....	....	....	....	....	....	....	....	....	....	....	....	....	....	....
	Colorado Rockies	**NHL**	**34**	**9**	**13**	**22**	**7**	**9**	**16**	**14**	**3**	**0**	**0**	**70**	**12.9**	**47**	**14**	**55**	**9**	**–13**	....	....	....	....	....	....	....	....
	Finland	WEC-A	7	2	1	3	....	....	....	4	....	....	....	....	....	....	....	....	....	....	....	....	....	....	....	....	....	....
1982-83	**New Jersey Devils**	**NHL**	**73**	**7**	**40**	**47**	**6**	**28**	**34**	**22**	**5**	**0**	**0**	**187**	**3.7**	**102**	**56**	**89**	**2**	**–41**	....	....	....	....	....	....	....	....
	Finland	WEC-A	10	4	1	5	....	....	....	6	....	....	....	....	....	....	....	....	....	....	....	....	....	....	....	....	....	....
1983-84	Assat Pori	Finland	34	9	20	29	....	....	....	52	....	....	....	....	....	....	....	....	....	....	9	4	7	11	16	....	....	....
1984-85	Assat Pori	Finland	36	20	22	42	....	....	....	26	....	....	....	....	....	....	....	....	....	....	8	1	3	4	16	....	....	....
1985-86	Assat Pori	Finland	35	15	20	35	....	....	....	34	....	....	....	....	....	....	....	....	....	....	....	....	....	....	....	....	....	....
1986-87	Assat Pori	Finland	44	22	17	39	....	....	....	26	....	....	....	....	....	....	....	....	....	....	....	....	....	....	....	....	....	....
1987-88	Assat Pori	Finland	44	15	23	38	....	....	....	38	....	....	....	....	....	....	....	....	....	....	....	....	....	....	....	....	....	....
1988-89	Assat Pori	Finland	43	21	21	42	....	....	....	28	....	....	....	....	....	....	....	....	....	....	....	....	....	....	....	....	....	....
1989-90	Assat Pori	Finland-2	44	32	47	79	....	....	....	12	....	....	....	....	....	....	....	....	....	....	....	....	....	....	....	....	....	....
1990-91	Assat Pori	Finland	39	10	23	33	....	....	....	28	....	....	....	....	....	....	....	....	....	....	....	....	....	....	....	....	....	....

			REGULAR SEASON																		PLAYOFFS							
Season	Club	League	GP	G	A	Pts	AG	AA	APts	PIM	PP	SH	GW	S	%	TGF	PGF	TGA	PGA	+/–	GP	G	A	Pts	PIM	PP	SH	GW
1991-92	Assat Pori	Finland	44	9	16	25	....	....	....	36	....	....	....	....	....	....	....	....	....	....	8	1	3	4	8	....	....	....
1992-93	Junkkarit Kalajoki	Finland-2	26	11	22	33	....	....	....	41	....	....	....	....	....	....	....	....	....	....	....	....	....	....	....	....	....	....
	HPK Hameenlinna	Finland	17	1	3	4	....	....	....	2	....	....	....	....	....	....	....	....	....	....	5	0	1	1	0	....	....	....
	NHL Totals		**107**	**16**	**53**	**69**	**13**	**37**	**50**	**36**	**8**	**0**	**0**	**257**	**6.2**	**149**	**70**	**144**	**11**		....	....	....	....	....	....	....	....

Finnish First All-Star Team (1984, 1985)

Signed as a free agent by **New Jersey**, July 8, 1981. Transferred to **New Jersey** after **Colorado** franchise relocated, June 30, 1982.

• LEWIS, Dale

Robert Dale LW – L. 6', 190 lbs. b: Edmonton, Alta., 7/28/1952.

Season	Club	League	GP	G	A	Pts	AG	AA	APts	PIM	PP	SH	GW	S	%	TGF	PGF	TGA	PGA	+/–	GP	G	A	Pts	PIM	PP	SH	GW
1971-72	Red Deer Ramblers	AJHL	48	36	42	78	....	....	....	99	....	....	....	....	....	....	....	....	....	....	....	....	....	....	....	....	....	....
	Vancouver Nats	WCJHL	2	0	1	1	....	....	....	2	....	....	....	....	....	....	....	....	....	....	....	....	....	....	....	....	....	....
1972-73	Sun Coast Suns	EHL	76	32	43	75	....	....	....	51	....	....	....	....	....	....	....	....	....	....	5	4	3	7	2	....	....	....
1973-74	Portland Buckaroos	WHL	72	18	18	36	....	....	....	38	....	....	....	....	....	....	....	....	....	....	10	2	*7	9	8	....	....	....
1974-75	Springfield Indians	AHL	74	28	43	71	....	....	....	43	....	....	....	....	....	....	....	....	....	....	17	9	12	21	8	....	....	....
1975-76	**New York Rangers**	**NHL**	**8**	**0**	**0**	**0**	**0**	**0**	**0**	**0**	**0**	**0**	**0**	**3**	**0.0**	**0**	**0**	**2**	**0**	**–2**	....	....	....	....	....	....	....	....
	Providence Reds	AHL	65	14	27	41	....	....	....	37	....	....	....	....	....	....	....	....	....	....	3	1	1	2	0	....	....	....
1976-77	New Haven Nighthawks	AHL	80	25	45	70	....	....	....	10	....	....	....	....	....	....	....	....	....	....	6	4	1	5	2	....	....	....
1977-78	New Haven Nighthawks	AHL	80	19	29	48	....	....	....	20	....	....	....	....	....	....	....	....	....	....	15	6	4	10	2	....	....	....
1978-79	New Haven Nighthawks	AHL	76	29	51	80	....	....	....	20	....	....	....	....	....	....	....	....	....	....	10	2	2	4	2	....	....	....
1979-80	Birmingham Bulls	CHL	78	28	33	61	....	....	....	30	....	....	....	....	....	....	....	....	....	....	4	2	5	7	0	....	....	....
1980-81	Birmingham Bulls	CHL	12	5	9	14	....	....	....	13	....	....	....	....	....	....	....	....	....	....	....	....	....	....	....	....	....	....
	New Haven Nighthawks	AHL	63	13	26	39	....	....	....	14	....	....	....	....	....	....	....	....	....	....	4	2	1	3	0	....	....	....
	NHL Totals		**8**	**0**	**0**	**0**	**0**	**0**	**0**	**0**	**0**	**0**	**0**	**3**	**0.0**	**0**	**0**	**2**	**0**		....	....	....	....	....	....	....	....

Signed as a free agent by **LA Kings**, September, 1973. Claimed by **NY Rangers** from **LA Kings** (Springfield-AHL) in Intra-League Draft, June 17, 1975. Signed as a free agent by **Atlanta**, September 11, 1979. Transferred to **Calgary** after **Atlanta** franchise relocated, June 24, 1980. Traded to **NY Rangers** by **Calgary** for Frank Beaton, November 18, 1980.

• LEWIS, Dave

David Rodney D – L. 6'2", 205 lbs. b: Kindersley, Sask., 7/3/1953. NY Islanders' 2nd, 33rd overall, in 1973.

Season	Club	League	GP	G	A	Pts	AG	AA	APts	PIM	PP	SH	GW	S	%	TGF	PGF	TGA	PGA	+/–	GP	G	A	Pts	PIM	PP	SH	GW
1971-72	Saskatoon Blades	WCJHL	52	2	9	11	....	....	....	68	....	....	....	....	....	....	....	....	....	....	8	2	3	5	4	....	....	....
1972-73	Saskatoon Blades	WCJHL	67	10	35	45	....	....	....	89	....	....	....	....	....	....	....	....	....	....	16	3	12	15	44	....	....	....
1973-74	**New York Islanders**	**NHL**	**66**	**2**	**15**	**17**	**2**	**12**	**14**	**58**	**1**	**1**	**1**	**63**	**3.2**	**55**	**3**	**78**	**19**	**–7**	....	....	....	....	....	....	....	....
1974-75	**New York Islanders**	**NHL**	**78**	**5**	**14**	**19**	**4**	**10**	**14**	**98**	**0**	**0**	**1**	**95**	**5.3**	**64**	**2**	**69**	**15**	**8**	**17**	**0**	**1**	**1**	**28**	**0**	**0**	**0**
1975-76	**New York Islanders**	**NHL**	**73**	**0**	**19**	**19**	**0**	**14**	**14**	**54**	**0**	**0**	**0**	**91**	**0.0**	**75**	**1**	**58**	**13**	**29**	**13**	**0**	**1**	**1**	**44**	**0**	**0**	**0**
1976-77	**New York Islanders**	**NHL**	**79**	**4**	**24**	**28**	**4**	**18**	**22**	**44**	**0**	**1**	**1**	**102**	**3.9**	**77**	**0**	**72**	**24**	**29**	**12**	**1**	**6**	**7**	**4**	**0**	**0**	**0**
1977-78	**New York Islanders**	**NHL**	**77**	**3**	**11**	**14**	**3**	**8**	**11**	**58**	**0**	**1**	**1**	**111**	**2.7**	**93**	**0**	**82**	**21**	**32**	**7**	**0**	**1**	**1**	**11**	**0**	**0**	**0**
1978-79	**New York Islanders**	**NHL**	**79**	**5**	**18**	**23**	**4**	**13**	**17**	**43**	**0**	**0**	**0**	**95**	**5.3**	**98**	**0**	**83**	**28**	**43**	**10**	**0**	**0**	**0**	**4**	**0**	**0**	**0**
1979-80	**New York Islanders**	**NHL**	**62**	**5**	**16**	**21**	**4**	**12**	**16**	**54**	**0**	**0**	**0**	**66**	**7.6**	**65**	**2**	**90**	**37**	**10**	....	....	....	....	....	....	....	....
	Los Angeles Kings	**NHL**	**11**	**1**	**1**	**2**	**1**	**1**	**2**	**12**	**0**	**0**	**0**	**11**	**9.1**	**11**	**1**	**9**	**2**	**3**	**4**	**0**	**1**	**1**	**2**	**0**	**0**	**0**
1980-81	**Los Angeles Kings**	**NHL**	**67**	**1**	**12**	**13**	**1**	**8**	**9**	**98**	**0**	**0**	**0**	**46**	**2.2**	**73**	**1**	**73**	**26**	**25**	**4**	**0**	**2**	**2**	**4**	**0**	**0**	**0**
1981-82	**Los Angeles Kings**	**NHL**	**64**	**1**	**13**	**14**	**1**	**9**	**10**	**75**	**0**	**0**	**0**	**50**	**2.0**	**54**	**2**	**99**	**28**	**–19**	**10**	**0**	**4**	**4**	**36**	**0**	**0**	**0**
1982-83	**Los Angeles Kings**	**NHL**	**79**	**2**	**10**	**12**	**2**	**7**	**9**	**53**	**0**	**0**	**0**	**64**	**3.1**	**67**	**4**	**111**	**26**	**–22**	....	....	....	....	....	....	....	....
1983-84	**New Jersey Devils**	**NHL**	**66**	**2**	**5**	**7**	**2**	**3**	**5**	**63**	**0**	**0**	**0**	**38**	**5.3**	**49**	**0**	**94**	**26**	**–19**	....	....	....	....	....	....	....	....
1984-85	**New Jersey Devils**	**NHL**	**74**	**3**	**9**	**12**	**2**	**6**	**8**	**78**	**0**	**0**	**2**	**51**	**5.9**	**57**	**0**	**120**	**34**	**–29**	....	....	....	....	....	....	....	....
1985-86	**New Jersey Devils**	**NHL**	**69**	**0**	**15**	**15**	**0**	**10**	**10**	**81**	**0**	**0**	**0**	**38**	**0.0**	**69**	**3**	**109**	**43**	**0**	....	....	....	....	....	....	....	....
1986-87	**Detroit Red Wings**	**NHL**	**58**	**2**	**5**	**7**	**2**	**4**	**6**	**66**	**0**	**0**	**0**	**37**	**5.4**	**42**	**0**	**46**	**16**	**12**	**14**	**0**	**4**	**4**	**10**	**0**	**0**	**0**
1987-88	**Detroit Red Wings**	**NHL**	**6**	**0**	**0**	**0**	**0**	**0**	**0**	**18**	**0**	**0**	**0**	**3**	**0.0**	**2**	**1**	**7**	**3**	**–3**	....	....	....	....	....	....	....	....
1988-2000	**Detroit Red Wings**	**NHL**	DID NOT PLAY – ASSISTANT COACH																									
	NHL Totals		**1008**	**36**	**187**	**223**	**32**	**135**	**167**	**953**	**1**	**3**	**6**	**961**	**3.7**	**951**	**20**	**1200**	**361**		**91**	**1**	**20**	**21**	**143**	**0**	**0**	**0**

Traded to **LA Kings** by **NY Islanders** with Billy Harris for Butch Goring, March 10, 1980. Traded to **Minnesota** by **LA Kings** for Steve Christoff and Fred Barrett, October 3, 1983. Traded to **New Jersey** by **Minnesota** for Brent Ashton, October 3, 1983. Signed as a free agent by **Detroit**, July 27, 1986.

• LEY, Rick

Richard Norman D – L. 5'9", 190 lbs. b: Orillia, Ont., 11/2/1948. Toronto's 3rd, 16th overall, in 1966.

Season	Club	League	GP	G	A	Pts	AG	AA	APts	PIM	PP	SH	GW	S	%	TGF	PGF	TGA	PGA	+/–	GP	G	A	Pts	PIM	PP	SH	GW
1964-65	Niagara Falls Flyers	OHA-Jr.	50	0	11	11	....	....	....	58	....	....	....	....	....	....	....	....	....	....	11	0	3	3	28	....	....	....
	Niagara Falls Flyers	Mem-Cup	8	0	2	2	....	....	....	8	....	....	....	....	....	....	....	....	....	....	....	....	....	....	....	....	....	....
1965-66	Niagara Falls Flyers	OHA-Jr.	46	3	13	16	....	....	....	180	....	....	....	....	....	....	....	....	....	....	6	0	6	6	18	....	....	....
1966-67	Niagara Falls Flyers	OHA-Jr.	48	10	27	37	....	....	....	128	....	....	....	....	....	....	....	....	....	....	12	2	4	6	24	....	....	....
1967-68	Niagara Falls Flyers	OHA-Jr.	53	16	48	64	....	....	....	81	....	....	....	....	....	....	....	....	....	....	19	1	15	16	38	....	....	....
	Niagara Falls Flyers	Mem-Cup	10	1	6	7	....	....	....	15	....	....	....	....	....	....	....	....	....	....	....	....	....	....	....	....	....	....
1968-69	**Toronto Maple Leafs**	**NHL**	**38**	**1**	**11**	**12**	**1**	**10**	**11**	**39**	**0**	**0**	**0**	**37**	**2.7**	**38**	**10**	**34**	**8**	**2**	**3**	**0**	**0**	**0**	**9**	**0**	**0**	**0**
	Tulsa Oilers	CHL	19	0	5	5	....	....	....	23	....	....	....	....	....	....	....	....	....	....	....	....	....	....	....	....	....	....
1969-70	**Toronto Maple Leafs**	**NHL**	**48**	**2**	**13**	**15**	**2**	**12**	**14**	**102**	**1**	**0**	**0**	**52**	**3.8**	**52**	**10**	**78**	**20**	**–16**	....	....	....	....	....	....	....	....
1970-71	**Toronto Maple Leafs**	**NHL**	**76**	**4**	**16**	**20**	**4**	**13**	**17**	**151**	**0**	**0**	**0**	**78**	**5.1**	**90**	**13**	**87**	**21**	**11**	**6**	**0**	**2**	**2**	**4**	**0**	**0**	**0**
1971-72	**Toronto Maple Leafs**	**NHL**	**67**	**1**	**14**	**15**	**1**	**12**	**13**	**124**	**0**	**0**	**0**	**65**	**1.5**	**49**	**7**	**70**	**31**	**3**	**5**	**0**	**0**	**0**	**7**	**0**	**0**	**0**
1972-73	New England Whalers	WHA	76	3	27	30	....	....	....	108	....	....	....	....	....	....	....	....	....	....	15	3	7	10	24	....	....	....
1973-74	New England Whalers	WHA	72	6	35	41	....	....	....	148	....	....	....	....	....	....	....	....	....	....	7	1	5	6	18	....	....	....
1974-75	Team Canada	Summit-74	7	0	0	0	....	....	....	16	....	....	....	....	....	....	....	....	....	....	....	....	....	....	....	....	....	....
	New England Whalers	WHA	62	6	36	42	....	....	....	50	....	....	....	....	....	....	....	....	....	....	6	1	1	2	32	....	....	....
1975-76	New England Whalers	WHA	67	8	30	38	....	....	....	78	....	....	....	....	....	....	....	....	....	....	17	1	4	5	49	....	....	....
1976-77	New England Whalers	WHA	55	2	21	23	....	....	....	102	....	....	....	....	....	....	....	....	....	....	5	0	4	4	4	....	....	....
1977-78	New England Whalers	WHA	73	3	41	44	....	....	....	95	....	....	....	....	....	....	....	....	....	....	14	1	8	9	4	....	....	....
1978-79	New England Whalers	WHA	73	7	20	27	....	....	....	135	....	....	....	....	....	....	....	....	....	....	9	0	4	4	11	....	....	....
1979-80	**Hartford Whalers**	**NHL**	**65**	**4**	**16**	**20**	**3**	**12**	**15**	**92**	**0**	**0**	**1**	**78**	**5.1**	**104**	**13**	**120**	**31**	**2**	....	....	....	....	....	....	....	....
1980-81	**Hartford Whalers**	**NHL**	**16**	**0**	**2**	**2**	**0**	**1**	**1**	**20**	**0**	**0**	**0**	**19**	**0.0**	**14**	**1**	**33**	**7**	**–13**	....	....	....	....	....	....	....	....
1981-1983	**Hartford Whalers**	**NHL**	DID NOT PLAY – ASSISTANT COACH																									
1983-1984	Binghamton Whalers	AHL	DID NOT PLAY – COACHING																									
1984-1988	Muskegon Lumberjacks	IHL	DID NOT PLAY – COACHING																									
1988-1989	Milwaukee Admirals	IHL	DID NOT PLAY – COACHING																									
1989-1991	**Hartford Whalers**	**NHL**	DID NOT PLAY – COACHING																									
1991-1994	**Vancouver Canucks**	**NHL**	DID NOT PLAY – ASSISTANT COACH																									
1994-1996	**Vancouver Canucks**	**NHL**	DID NOT PLAY – COACHING																									
1996-1998	**Vancouver Canucks**	**NHL**	DID NOT PLAY – SCOUTING																									
1998-2000	**Toronto Maple Leafs**	**NHL**	DID NOT PLAY – ASSISTANT COACH																									
	NHL Totals		**310**	**12**	**72**	**84**	**11**	**60**	**71**	**528**	**1**	**0**	**1**	**329**	**3.6**	**347**	**54**	**422**	**118**		**14**	**0**	**2**	**2**	**20**	**0**	**0**	**0**
	Other Major League Totals		478	35	210	245				716											73	7	33	40	142			

OHA-Jr. First All-Star Team (1968) • WHA Second All-Star Team (1978) • WHA First All-Star Team (1979) • Won Dennis A. Murphy Trophy (WHA Top Defenseman) (1979)

Selected by **New England** (WHA) in 1972 WHA General Player Draft, February 12, 1972. Reclaimed by **Toronto** from **Hartford** prior to Expansion Draft, June 9, 1979. Claimed by **Hartford** from **Toronto** in Expansion Draft, June 13, 1979.

• LIBA, Igor

LW – R. 6', 192 lbs. b: Kosice, Czech., 11/4/1960. Calgary's 7th, 94th overall, in 1983.

Season	Club	League	GP	G	A	Pts	AG	AA	APts	PIM	PP	SH	GW	S	%	TGF	PGF	TGA	PGA	+/–	GP	G	A	Pts	PIM	PP	SH	GW
1970-1978	ZPA Presov	Czech-3	STATISTICS NOT AVAILABLE																									
1978-79	ZPA Presov	Czech-3	STATISTICS NOT AVAILABLE																									
	Czechoslovakia	WJC-A	5	0	0	0	....	....	....	0	....	....	....	....	....	....	....	....	....	....								
1979-80	VSZ Kosice	Czech.	42	16	10	26	....	....	....	16	....	....	....	....	....	....	....	....	....	....								
	Czechoslovakia	WJC-A	5	4	1	5	....	....	....	4	....	....	....	....	....	....	....	....	....	....								
1980-81	VSZ Kosice	Czech.	43	17	24	41	....	....	....	20	....	....	....	....	....	....	....	....	....	....								
1981-82	VSZ Kosice	Czech.	44	*35	18	53	....	....	....	34	....	....	....	....	....	....	....	....	....	....								
	Czechoslovakia	WEC-A	10	3	2	5	....	....	....	6	....	....	....	....	....	....	....	....	....	....								
1982-83	Dukla Jihlava	Czech.	43	27	18	45	....	....	....	24	....	....	....	....	....	....	....	....	....	....								
	Czechoslovakia	WEC-A	10	2	8	10	....	....	....	0	....	....	....	....	....	....	....	....	....	....								

			REGULAR SEASON																		PLAYOFFS							
Season	Club	League	GP	G	A	Pts	AG	AA	APts	PIM	PP	SH	GW	S	%	TGF	PGF	TGA	PGA	+/–	GP	G	A	Pts	PIM	PP	SH	GW
1983-84	Dukla Jihlava	Czech.	41	14	18	32	....	....	....	16	....	....	....	....	....	....	....	....	....	....	....	....	....	....	....	....	....	....
	Czechoslovakia	Olympics	7	4	3	7	....	....	....	6	....	....	....	....	....	....	....	....	....	....	....	....	....	....	....	....	....	....
1984-85	Czechoslovakia	Can-Cup	5	2	3	5	....	....	....	6	....	....	....	....	....	....	....	....	....	....	....	....	....	....	....	....	....	....
	VSZ Kosice	Czech.	44	28	26	54	....	....	....	22	....	....	....	....	....	....	....	....	....	....	....	....	....	....	....	....	....	....
	Czechoslovakia	WEC-A	10	2	5	7	....	....	....	16	....	....	....	....	....	....	....	....	....	....	....	....	....	....	....	....	....	....
1985-86	VSZ Kosice	Czech.	34	25	*29	54	....	....	....	32	....	....	....	....	....	....	....	....	....	....	14	7	6	13	....	....	....	....
	Czechoslovakia	WEC-A	10	2	4	6	....	....	....	18	....	....	....	....	....	....	....	....	....	....	....	....	....	....	....	....	....	....
1986-87	VSZ Kosice	Czech.	31	13	16	29	....	....	....	38	....	....	....	....	....	....	....	....	....	....	7	4	4	8	....	....	....	....
	Czechoslovakia	WEC-A	10	2	3	5	....	....	....	12	....	....	....	....	....	....	....	....	....	....	....	....	....	....	....	....	....	....
1987-88	Czechoslovakia	Can-Cup	6	0	4	4	....	....	....	6	....	....	....	....	....	....	....	....	....	....	....	....	....	....	....	....	....	....
	VSZ Kosice	Czech.	42	21	37	58	....	....	....	86	....	....	....	....	....	....	....	....	....	....	....	....	....	....	....	....	....	....
	Czechoslovakia	Olympics	8	4	6	10	....	....	....	8	....	....	....	....	....	....	....	....	....	....	....	....	....	....	....	....	....	....
1988-89	**New York Rangers**	**NHL**	**10**	**2**	**5**	**7**	**2**	**4**	**6**	**15**	**1**	**0**	**0**	**14**	**14.3**	**9**	**4**	**4**	**0**	**1**	....	....	....	....	....	....	....	....
	Los Angeles Kings	**NHL**	**27**	**5**	**13**	**18**	**4**	**9**	**13**	**21**	**1**	**0**	**0**	**28**	**17.9**	**25**	**9**	**20**	**0**	**–4**	**2**	**0**	**0**	**0**	**2**	**0**	**0**	**0**
1989-90	VSZ Kosice	Czech.	40	16	12	28	....	....	....	37	....	....	....	....	....	....	....	....	....	....	4	1	8	9	....	....	....	....
1990-91	VSZ Kosice	Czech.	2	0	1	1	....	....	....	0	....	....	....	....	....	....	....	....	....	....	....	....	....	....	....	....	....	....
	EHC Biel-Bienne	Switz.	27	5	13	18	....	....	....	2	....	....	....	....	....	....	....	....	....	....	2	0	0	0	2	....	....	....
1991-92	VSZ Kosice	Czech.	16	7	8	15	....	....	....	....	....	....	....	....	....	....	....	....	....	....	....	....	....	....	....	....	....	....
	HC Fiemme	Italy	18	11	34	45	....	....	....	2	....	....	....	....	....	....	....	....	....	....	4	2	7	9	6	....	....	....
	Czechoslovakia	Olympics	4	1	2	3	....	....	....	4	....	....	....	....	....	....	....	....	....	....	....	....	....	....	....	....	....	....
	Czechoslovakia	WC-A	8	2	1	3	....	....	....	10	....	....	....	....	....	....	....	....	....	....	....	....	....	....	....	....	....	....
1992-93	TuTo Turku	Finland-2	44	22	34	56	....	....	....	111	....	....	....	....	....	....	....	....	....	....	4	2	2	4	4	....	....	....
1993-94	EV Zeltweg	Austria-2	STATISTICS NOT AVAILABLE																									
1994-95	EV Zeltweg	Austria-2	26	27	19	46	....	....	....	44	....	....	....	....	....	....	....	....	....	....	4	3	4	7	0	....	....	....
1995-96	EV Zeltweg	Austria-2	33	15	19	34	....	....	....	34	....	....	....	....	....	....	....	....	....	....	....	....	....	....	....	....	....	....
1996-97	HK VTJ Spisska	Slovakia	32	19	17	36	....	....	....	....	....	....	....	....	....	....	....	....	....	....	....	....	....	....	....	....	....	....
	HK VTJ Spisska	Slovakia-Q	14	7	8	15	....	....	....	....	....	....	....	....	....	....	....	....	....	....	....	....	....	....	....	....	....	....
1997-98	VTJ Rebisov	Slovakia-2	4	1	4	5	....	....	....	2	....	....	....	....	....	....	....	....	....	....	....	....	....	....	....	....	....	....
	HC Kosice	Slovakia	32	10	24	34	....	....	....	36	....	....	....	....	....	....	....	....	....	....	10	3	4	7	24	....	....	....
1998-99	HC Kosice	Slovakia	41	13	21	34	....	....	....	12	....	....	....	....	....	....	....	....	....	....	11	2	4	6	12	....	....	....
99-2000	EV Zeltweg	Austria-2	30	24	36	60	....	....	....	18	....	....	....	....	....	....	....	....	....	....	....	....	....	....	....	....	....	....
	NHL Totals		**37**	**7**	**18**	**25**	**6**	**13**	**19**	**36**	**2**	**0**	**0**	**42**	**16.7**	**34**	**13**	**24**	**0**		**2**	**0**	**0**	**0**	**2**	**0**	**0**	**0**

Czechoslovakian Player of the Year (1984) • Czechoslovakian First All-Star Team (1988)

Rights traded to **Minnesota** by **Calgary** for Minnesota's 5th round choice (Thomas Forslund) in 1988 Entry Draft, May 20, 1988. Traded to **NY Rangers** by **Minnesota** with Brian Lawton and the rights to Rick Bennett for Paul Jerrard, Mark Tinordi the rights to Bret Barnett and Mike Sullivan and LA Kings' 3rd round choice (previously acquired, Minnesota selected Murray Garbutt) in 1989 Entry Draft, October 11, 1988. Traded to **LA Kings** by **NY Rangers** with Todd Elik, Michael Boyce and future considerations for Dean Kennedy and Denis Larocque, December 12, 1988.

• LIBBY, Jeff

D – L. 6'3", 215 lbs. b: Waterville, ME, 3/1/1974.

Season	Club	League	GP	G	A	Pts	AG	AA	APts	PIM	PP	SH	GW	S	%	TGF	PGF	TGA	PGA	+/–	GP	G	A	Pts	PIM	PP	SH	GW
1993-94	New Hampton Prep	Hi-School	STATISTICS NOT AVAILABLE																									
1994-95	University of Maine	H-East	22	2	4	6	....	....	....	6	....	....	....	....	....	....	....	....	....	....	....	....	....	....	....	....	....	....
1995-96	University of Maine	H-East	39	0	9	9	....	....	....	42	....	....	....	....	....	....	....	....	....	....	....	....	....	....	....	....	....	....
1996-97	University of Maine	H-East	34	6	25	31	....	....	....	41	....	....	....	....	....	....	....	....	....	....	....	....	....	....	....	....	....	....
1997-98	**New York Islanders**	**NHL**	**1**	**0**	**0**	**0**	**0**	**0**	**0**	**0**	**0**	**0**	**0**	**0**	**0.0**	**0**	**0**	**0**	**0**	**0**	....	....	....	....	....	....	....	....
	Kentucky Thoroughblades	AHL	8	0	3	3	....	....	....	4	....	....	....	....	....	....	....	....	....	....	3	0	0	0	4	....	....	....
	Utah Grizzlies	IHL	47	1	5	6	....	....	....	25	....	....	....	....	....	....	....	....	....	....	1	0	0	0	0	....	....	....
1998-99	Lowell Lock Monsters	AHL	5	0	0	0	....	....	....	2	....	....	....	....	....	....	....	....	....	....	....	....	....	....	....	....	....	....
	NHL Totals		**1**	**0**	**0**	**0**	**0**	**0**	**0**	**0**	**0**	**0**	**0**	**0**	**0.0**	**0**	**0**	**0**	**0**		....	....	....	....	....	....	....	....

Signed as a free agent by **NY Islanders**, May 12, 1997. • Suffered career-ending eye injury in game vs. St. John's (AHL), November 7, 1998.

• LIBETT, Nick

Lynn Nicholas LW – L. 6'1", 195 lbs. b: Stratford, Ont., 12/9/1945.

Season	Club	League	GP	G	A	Pts	AG	AA	APts	PIM	PP	SH	GW	S	%	TGF	PGF	TGA	PGA	+/–	GP	G	A	Pts	PIM	PP	SH	GW
1961-62	Stratford Cullitons	OHA-B	STATISTICS NOT AVAILABLE																									
1962-63	Hamilton Red Wings	OHA-Jr.	32	1	4	5	....	....	....	21	....	....	....	....	....	....	....	....	....	....	....	....	....	....	....	....	....	....
1963-64	Hamilton Red Wings	OHA-Jr.	49	23	19	42	....	....	....	58	....	....	....	....	....	....	....	....	....	....	....	....	....	....	....	....	....	....
	Cincinnati Wings	CPHL	3	0	2	2	....	....	....	0	....	....	....	....	....	....	....	....	....	....	....	....	....	....	....	....	....	....
1964-65	Hamilton Red Wings	OHA-Jr.	51	24	37	61	....	....	....	60	....	....	....	....	....	....	....	....	....	....	....	....	....	....	....	....	....	....
1965-66	Hamilton Red Wings	OHA-Jr.	42	22	22	44	....	....	....	39	....	....	....	....	....	....	....	....	....	....	5	2	1	3	6	....	....	....
	Memphis Wings	CPHL	4	1	0	1	....	....	....	2	....	....	....	....	....	....	....	....	....	....	....	....	....	....	....	....	....	....
1966-67	Memphis Wings	CPHL	62	12	18	30	....	....	....	30	....	....	....	....	....	....	....	....	....	....	7	2	2	4	4	....	....	....
1967-68	**Detroit Red Wings**	**NHL**	**22**	**2**	**1**	**3**	**2**	**1**	**3**	**12**	**1**	**0**	**0**	**29**	**6.9**	**10**	**3**	**20**	**0**	**–13**	....	....	....	....	....	....	....	....
	Fort Worth Wings	CPHL	40	11	28	39	....	....	....	22	....	....	....	....	....	....	....	....	....	....	....	....	....	....	....	....	....	....
	San Diego Gulls	WHL	10	4	2	6	....	....	....	0	....	....	....	....	....	....	....	....	....	....	....	....	....	....	....	....	....	....
1968-69	**Detroit Red Wings**	**NHL**	**75**	**10**	**14**	**24**	**11**	**12**	**23**	**34**	**1**	**0**	**2**	**98**	**10.2**	**33**	**3**	**64**	**18**	**–16**	....	....	....	....	....	....	....	....
1969-70	**Detroit Red Wings**	**NHL**	**76**	**20**	**20**	**40**	**22**	**19**	**41**	**39**	**3**	**1**	**2**	**148**	**13.5**	**65**	**10**	**57**	**11**	**9**	**4**	**2**	**0**	**2**	**2**	**1**	**0**	**0**
1970-71	**Detroit Red Wings**	**NHL**	**78**	**16**	**13**	**29**	**16**	**11**	**27**	**25**	**2**	**0**	**1**	**156**	**10.3**	**50**	**7**	**95**	**14**	**–38**	....	....	....	....	....	....	....	....
1971-72	**Detroit Red Wings**	**NHL**	**77**	**31**	**22**	**53**	**31**	**19**	**50**	**50**	**6**	**3**	**5**	**219**	**14.2**	**83**	**13**	**81**	**18**	**7**	....	....	....	....	....	....	....	....
1972-73	**Detroit Red Wings**	**NHL**	**78**	**19**	**34**	**53**	**18**	**27**	**45**	**56**	**4**	**1**	**3**	**202**	**9.4**	**84**	**22**	**72**	**11**	**1**	....	....	....	....	....	....	....	....
1973-74	**Detroit Red Wings**	**NHL**	**67**	**24**	**24**	**48**	**23**	**20**	**43**	**37**	**3**	**1**	**5**	**177**	**13.6**	**68**	**13**	**90**	**9**	**–26**	....	....	....	....	....	....	....	....
1974-75	**Detroit Red Wings**	**NHL**	**80**	**23**	**28**	**51**	**20**	**21**	**41**	**39**	**8**	**1**	**2**	**194**	**11.9**	**77**	**28**	**113**	**23**	**–41**	....	....	....	....	....	....	....	....
1975-76	**Detroit Red Wings**	**NHL**	**80**	**20**	**26**	**46**	**18**	**19**	**37**	**71**	**3**	**1**	**3**	**224**	**8.9**	**72**	**16**	**85**	**20**	**–9**	....	....	....	....	....	....	....	....
1976-77	**Detroit Red Wings**	**NHL**	**80**	**14**	**27**	**41**	**13**	**21**	**34**	**25**	**3**	**1**	**0**	**210**	**6.7**	**63**	**14**	**99**	**25**	**–25**	....	....	....	....	....	....	....	....
1977-78	**Detroit Red Wings**	**NHL**	**80**	**23**	**22**	**45**	**21**	**17**	**38**	**46**	**1**	**1**	**1**	**155**	**14.8**	**63**	**10**	**77**	**21**	**–3**	**7**	**3**	**1**	**4**	**0**	**1**	**0**	**0**
1978-79	**Detroit Red Wings**	**NHL**	**68**	**15**	**19**	**34**	**13**	**14**	**27**	**20**	**3**	**1**	**0**	**130**	**11.5**	**60**	**13**	**58**	**15**	**4**	....	....	....	....	....	....	....	....
	Canada	WEC-A	8	1	0	1	....	....	....	4	....	....	....	....	....	....	....	....	....	....	....	....	....	....	....	....	....	....
1979-80	**Pittsburgh Penguins**	**NHL**	**78**	**14**	**12**	**26**	**12**	**9**	**21**	**14**	**1**	**1**	**2**	**118**	**11.9**	**44**	**3**	**72**	**12**	**–19**	**5**	**1**	**1**	**2**	**0**	**1**	**0**	**0**
1980-81	**Pittsburgh Penguins**	**NHL**	**43**	**6**	**6**	**12**	**5**	**4**	**9**	**4**	**1**	**0**	**1**	**47**	**12.8**	**19**	**2**	**18**	**3**	**2**	....	....	....	....	....	....	....	....
	NHL Totals		**982**	**237**	**268**	**505**	**225**	**214**	**439**	**472**	**40**	**12**	**27**	**2107**	**11.2**	**791**	**157**	**1001**	**200**		**16**	**6**	**2**	**8**	**2**	**3**	**0**	**0**

Played in NHL All-Star Game (1977)

Traded to **Pittsburgh** by **Detroit** for Pete Mahovlich, August 3, 1979.

• LIDDINGTON, Bob

Robert Allen LW – L. 6', 175 lbs. b: Calgary, Alta., 9/15/1948.

Season	Club	League	GP	G	A	Pts	AG	AA	APts	PIM	PP	SH	GW	S	%	TGF	PGF	TGA	PGA	+/–	GP	G	A	Pts	PIM	PP	SH	GW
1966-67	Calgary Buffaloes	CMJHL	27	6	4	10	....	....	....	15	....	....	....	....	....	....	....	....	....	....	....	....	....	....	....	....	....	....
	Calgary Spurs	WCSHL	....	....	....	....	....	....	....	....	....	....	....	....	....	....	....	....	....	....	1	0	0	0	0	....	....	....
1967-68	Calgary Centennials	WCJHL	59	36	32	68	....	....	....	24	....	....	....	....	....	....	....	....	....	....	....	....	....	....	....	....	....	....
1968-69	Calgary Centennials	WCJHL	60	*58	33	91	....	....	....	26	....	....	....	....	....	....	....	....	....	....	11	7	3	10	0	....	....	....
1969-70	Tulsa Oilers	CHL	68	22	17	39	....	....	....	33	....	....	....	....	....	....	....	....	....	....	3	0	0	0	0	....	....	....
1970-71	**Toronto Maple Leafs**	**NHL**	**11**	**0**	**1**	**1**	**0**	**1**	**1**	**2**	**0**	**0**	**0**	**2**	**0.0**	**4**	**1**	**5**	**0**	**–2**	....	....	....	....	....	....	....	....
	Tulsa Oilers	CHL	61	18	21	39	....	....	....	55	....	....	....	....	....	....	....	....	....	....	....	....	....	....	....	....	....	....
1971-72	Phoenix Roadrunners	WHL	72	22	19	41	....	....	....	58	....	....	....	....	....	....	....	....	....	....	6	2	4	6	4	....	....	....
1972-73	Chicago Cougars	WHA	78	20	11	31	....	....	....	24	....	....	....	....	....	....	....	....	....	....	....	....	....	....	....	....	....	....
1973-74	Chicago Cougars	WHA	73	26	21	47	....	....	....	20	....	....	....	....	....	....	....	....	....	....	18	6	5	11	11	....	....	....
1974-75	Chicago Cougars	WHA	78	23	18	41	....	....	....	27	....	....	....	....	....	....	....	....	....	....	....	....	....	....	....	....	....	....
1975-76	Denver-Ottawa Civics	WHA	35	7	8	15	....	....	....	14	....	....	....	....	....	....	....	....	....	....	....	....	....	....	....	....	....	....
	Houston Aeros	WHA	2	0	0	0	....	....	....	2	....	....	....	....	....	....	....	....	....	....	....	....	....	....	....	....	....	....
	Tucson Mavericks	CHL	23	12	12	24	....	....	....	20	....	....	....	....	....	....	....	....	....	....	....	....	....	....	....	....	....	....
1976-77	Phoenix Roadrunners	WHA	80	20	24	44	....	....	....	28	....	....	....	....	....	....	....	....	....	....	....	....	....	....	....	....	....	....

Season	Club	League	REGULAR SEASON GP	G	A	Pts	AG	AA	APts	PIM	PP	SH	GW	S	%	TGF	PGF	TGA	PGA	+/–	PLAYOFFS GP	G	A	Pts	PIM	PP	SH	GW
1977-78	Binghamton Dusters	AHL	11	3	2	5				2																		
	Long Beach Sharks-Rockets	PHL	33	15	24	39				6																		
1978-79	Phoenix Roadrunners	PHL	60	34	20	54				16																		
	NHL Totals		**11**	**0**	**1**	**1**	**0**	**1**	**1**	**2**	**0**	**0**	**0**	**2**	**0.0**	**4**	**1**	**5**	**0**									
	Other Major League Totals		346	96	82	178				115											18	6	5	11	11			

Signed as a free agent by **Toronto**, October, 1969. Selected by **LA Sharks** (WHA) in 1972 WHA General Player Draft, February 12, 1972. Traded to **Chicago** (WHA) by **LA Sharks** (WHA) with Bob Whitlock and the rights to Larry Cahan for Bill Young and future considerations, July, 1972. Selected by **Denver** (WHA) from **Chicago** (WHA) in WHA Expansion Draft, May, 1975. Signed as a free agent by **Houston** (WHA) after **Denver-Ottawa** (WHA) franchise folded, February, 1976. Traded to **Phoenix** (WHA) by **Houston** (WHA) for Cam Connor, October, 1976.

• LIDSTER, Doug

Douglas D – R. 6'1", 190 lbs. b: Kamloops, B.C., 10/18/1960. Vancouver's 6th, 133rd overall, in 1980.

Season	Club	League	GP	G	A	Pts	AG	AA	APts	PIM	PP	SH	GW	S	%	TGF	PGF	TGA	PGA	+/–	GP	G	A	Pts	PIM	PP	SH	GW
1976-77	Kamloops Jardines	BCAHA	STATISTICS NOT AVAILABLE																									
1977-78	Kamloops Chiefs	BCJHL	64	24	39	63				46																		
	Seattle Breakers	WCJHL	2	0	0	0				0																		
1978-79	Kamloops Rockets	BCJHL	59	36	47	83				50																		
1979-80	Colorado College	WCHA	39	18	25	43				52																		
1980-81	Colorado College	WCHA	36	10	30	40				54																		
1981-82	Colorado College	WCHA	36	13	22	35				32																		
1982-83	Colorado College	WCHA	34	15	41	56				30																		
1983-84	Canada	Nat-Team	59	6	20	26				28																		
	Canada	Olympics	7	0	2	2				2																		
	Vancouver Canucks	**NHL**	**8**	**0**	**0**	**0**	**0**	**0**	**0**	**4**	**0**	**0**	**0**	**7**	**0.0**	**3**	**1**	**9**	**0**	**–7**	**2**	**0**	**1**	**1**	**0**	**0**	**0**	**0**
1984-85	**Vancouver Canucks**	**NHL**	**78**	**6**	**24**	**30**	**5**	**16**	**21**	**55**	**2**	**0**	**0**	**125**	**4.8**	**96**	**12**	**115**	**20**	**–11**								
	Canada	WEC-A	10	3	1	4				4																		
1985-86	**Vancouver Canucks**	**NHL**	**78**	**12**	**16**	**28**	**10**	**11**	**21**	**56**	**1**	**1**	**0**	**151**	**7.9**	**95**	**8**	**131**	**32**	**–12**	**3**	**0**	**1**	**1**	**2**	**0**	**0**	**0**
1986-87	**Vancouver Canucks**	**NHL**	**80**	**12**	**51**	**63**	**10**	**37**	**47**	**40**	**3**	**0**	**0**	**176**	**6.8**	**154**	**61**	**172**	**44**	**–35**								
1987-88	**Vancouver Canucks**	**NHL**	**64**	**4**	**32**	**36**	**3**	**23**	**26**	**105**	**2**	**1**	**0**	**133**	**3.0**	**97**	**42**	**110**	**36**	**–19**								
1988-89	**Vancouver Canucks**	**NHL**	**63**	**5**	**17**	**22**	**4**	**12**	**16**	**78**	**3**	**0**	**0**	**116**	**4.3**	**62**	**17**	**82**	**33**	**–4**	**7**	**1**	**1**	**2**	**9**	**0**	**0**	**0**
1989-90	**Vancouver Canucks**	**NHL**	**80**	**8**	**28**	**36**	**7**	**20**	**27**	**36**	**1**	**0**	**0**	**143**	**5.6**	**85**	**19**	**136**	**54**	**–16**								
	Canada	WEC-A	10	1	0	1				6																		
1990-91	**Vancouver Canucks**	**NHL**	**78**	**6**	**32**	**38**	**5**	**24**	**29**	**77**	**4**	**0**	**1**	**157**	**3.8**	**115**	**37**	**133**	**49**	**–6**	**6**	**0**	**2**	**2**	**6**	**0**	**0**	**0**
	Canada	WEC-A	10	1	4	5				8																		
1991-92	**Vancouver Canucks**	**NHL**	**66**	**6**	**23**	**29**	**5**	**17**	**22**	**39**	**3**	**0**	**2**	**89**	**6.7**	**77**	**20**	**79**	**31**	**9**	**11**	**1**	**2**	**3**	**11**	**0**	**0**	**0**
1992-93	**Vancouver Canucks**	**NHL**	**71**	**6**	**19**	**25**	**5**	**13**	**18**	**36**	**3**	**0**	**0**	**76**	**7.9**	**80**	**10**	**93**	**32**	**9**	**12**	**0**	**3**	**3**	**8**	**0**	**0**	**0**
1993-94♦	**New York Rangers**	**NHL**	**34**	**0**	**2**	**2**	**0**	**2**	**2**	**33**	**0**	**0**	**0**	**25**	**0.0**	**18**	**4**	**33**	**7**	**–12**	**9**	**2**	**0**	**2**	**10**	**0**	**0**	**0**
1994-95	**St. Louis Blues**	**NHL**	**37**	**2**	**7**	**9**	**4**	**10**	**14**	**12**	**1**	**0**	**0**	**37**	**5.4**	**33**	**3**	**30**	**9**	**9**	**4**	**0**	**0**	**0**	**2**	**0**	**0**	**0**
1995-96	**New York Rangers**	**NHL**	**59**	**5**	**9**	**14**	**5**	**7**	**12**	**50**	**0**	**0**	**0**	**73**	**6.8**	**50**	**7**	**48**	**16**	**11**	**7**	**1**	**0**	**1**	**6**	**1**	**0**	**0**
1996-97	**New York Rangers**	**NHL**	**48**	**3**	**4**	**7**	**3**	**4**	**7**	**24**	**0**	**0**	**0**	**42**	**7.1**	**31**	**0**	**27**	**6**	**10**	**15**	**1**	**5**	**6**	**8**	**0**	**0**	**0**
1997-98	**New York Rangers**	**NHL**	**36**	**0**	**4**	**4**	**0**	**4**	**4**	**24**	**0**	**0**	**0**	**25**	**0.0**	**19**	**0**	**22**	**5**	**2**								
1998-99	Canada	Nat-Team	38	4	15	19				64																		
♦	**Dallas Stars**	**NHL**	**17**	**0**	**0**	**0**	**0**	**0**	**0**	**10**	**0**	**0**	**0**	**7**	**0.0**	**4**	**0**	**4**	**0**	**0**	**4**	**0**	**0**	**0**	**2**	**0**	**0**	**0**
	NHL Totals		**897**	**75**	**268**	**343**	**66**	**200**	**266**	**679**	**23**	**2**	**3**	**1382**	**5.4**	**1019**	**241**	**1224**	**374**		**80**	**6**	**15**	**21**	**64**	**1**	**0**	**0**

WCHA First All-Star Team (1982, 1983) • NCAA West First All-American Team (1983)

Traded to **NY Rangers** by **Vancouver** to complete transaction that sent John Vanbiesbrouck to Vancouver (June 20, 1993), June 25, 1993. Traded to **St. Louis** by **NY Rangers** with Esa Tikkanen for Petr Nedved, July 24, 1994. Traded to **NY Rangers** by **St. Louis** for Jay Wells, July 28, 1995. Signed as a free agent by **Dallas**, February 26, 1999.

• LIDSTROM, Nicklas

Nicklas E. D – L. 6'2", 185 lbs. b: Vasteras, Sweden, 4/28/1970. Detroit's 3rd, 53rd overall, in 1989.

Season	Club	League	GP	G	A	Pts	AG	AA	APts	PIM	PP	SH	GW	S	%	TGF	PGF	TGA	PGA	+/–	GP	G	A	Pts	PIM	PP	SH	GW
1987-88	Vasteras IK	Sweden-2	3	0	0	0				0											5	0	0	0	6			
1988-89	Vasteras IK	Sweden	19	0	2	2				4																		
1989-90	Vasteras IK	Sweden	39	8	8	16				14											2	0	1	1	2			
	Sweden	WJC-A	7	3	3	6				2																		
1990-91	Vasteras IK	Sweden	38	4	19	23				2											4	0	0	0	4			
	Sweden	WEC-A	10	3	3	6				4																		
1991-92	Sweden	Can-Cup	6	1	1	2				4																		
	Detroit Red Wings	**NHL**	**80**	**11**	**49**	**60**	**10**	**37**	**47**	**22**	**5**	**0**	**1**	**168**	**6.5**	**141**	**50**	**80**	**25**	**36**	**11**	**1**	**2**	**3**	**0**	**1**	**0**	**0**
1992-93	**Detroit Red Wings**	**NHL**	**84**	**7**	**34**	**41**	**6**	**23**	**29**	**28**	**3**	**0**	**2**	**156**	**4.5**	**136**	**51**	**100**	**22**	**7**	**7**	**1**	**0**	**1**	**0**	**1**	**0**	**0**
1993-94	**Detroit Red Wings**	**NHL**	**84**	**10**	**46**	**56**	**9**	**36**	**45**	**26**	**4**	**0**	**3**	**200**	**5.0**	**174**	**45**	**111**	**25**	**43**	**7**	**3**	**2**	**5**	**0**	**1**	**1**	**0**
	Sweden	WC-A	4	1	0	1				2																		
1994-95	Vasteras IK	Sweden	13	2	10	12				4																		
	Detroit Red Wings	**NHL**	**43**	**10**	**16**	**26**	**18**	**24**	**42**	**6**	**7**	**0**	**0**	**90**	**11.1**	**73**	**26**	**41**	**9**	**15**	**18**	**4**	**12**	**16**	**8**	**3**	**0**	**2**
1995-96	**Detroit Red Wings**	**NHL**	**81**	**17**	**50**	**67**	**17**	**41**	**58**	**20**	**8**	**1**	**1**	**211**	**8.1**	**150**	**67**	**73**	**19**	**29**	**19**	**5**	**9**	**14**	**10**	**1**	**0**	**0**
1996-97	Sweden	W-Cup	4	2	1	3				0																		
♦	**Detroit Red Wings**	**NHL**	**79**	**15**	**42**	**57**	**16**	**37**	**53**	**30**	**8**	**0**	**1**	**214**	**7.0**	**117**	**48**	**87**	**29**	**11**	**20**	**2**	**6**	**8**	**2**	**0**	**0**	**0**
1997-98♦	**Detroit Red Wings**	**NHL**	**80**	**17**	**42**	**59**	**20**	**41**	**61**	**18**	**7**	**1**	**1**	**205**	**8.3**	**126**	**48**	**75**	**19**	**22**	**22**	**6**	**13**	**19**	**8**	**2**	**0**	**2**
	Sweden	Olympics	4	1	1	2				2																		
1998-99	**Detroit Red Wings**	**NHL**	**81**	**14**	**43**	**57**	**16**	**42**	**58**	**14**	**6**	**2**	**3**	**205**	**6.8**	**129**	**49**	**93**	**27**	**14**	**10**	**2**	**9**	**11**	**4**	**2**	**0**	**0**
99-2000	**Detroit Red Wings**	**NHL**	**81**	**20**	**53**	**73**	**22**	**49**	**71**	**18**	**9**	**4**	**3**	**218**	**9.2**	**148**	**54**	**103**	**28**	**19**	**9**	**2**	**4**	**6**	**4**	**1**	**0**	**0**
	NHL Totals		**693**	**121**	**375**	**496**	**134**	**330**	**464**	**182**	**57**	**8**	**15**	**1667**	**7.3**	**1194**	**438**	**763**	**203**		**123**	**26**	**57**	**83**	**36**	**12**	**1**	**4**

NHL All-Rookie Team (1992) • NHL First All-Star Team (1998, 1999, 2000) • Played in NHL All-Star Game (1996, 1998, 1999, 2000)

• LILLEY, John

John E. RW – R. 5'9", 170 lbs. b: Wakefield, MA, 8/3/1972. Winnipeg's 8th, 140th overall, in 1990.

Season	Club	League	GP	G	A	Pts	AG	AA	APts	PIM	PP	SH	GW	S	%	TGF	PGF	TGA	PGA	+/–	GP	G	A	Pts	PIM	PP	SH	GW
1989-90	Cushing Academy Penguins	Hi-School	20	22	30	52																						
1990-91	Cushing Academy Penguins	Hi-School	25	29	42	71																						
1991-92	Boston University	H-East	23	9	9	18				43																		
	United States	WJC-A	7	3	4	7				10																		
1992-93	Boston University	H-East	4	0	1	1				13																		
	Seattle Thunderbirds	WHL	45	22	28	50				55											5	1	3	4	9			
1993-94	United States	Nat-Team	58	27	23	50				117																		
	United States	Olympics	8	3	1	4				16																		
	Mighty Ducks of Anaheim	**NHL**	**13**	**1**	**6**	**7**	**1**	**5**	**6**	**8**	**0**	**0**	**1**	**20**	**5.0**	**7**	**0**	**6**	**0**	**1**								
	San Diego Gulls	IHL	2	2	1	3				0																		
	United States	WC-A	8	1	0	1				29																		
1994-95	San Diego Gulls	IHL	45	9	15	24				71											2	0	0	0	2			
	Mighty Ducks of Anaheim	**NHL**	**9**	**2**	**2**	**4**	**4**	**3**	**7**	**5**	**1**	**0**	**0**	**10**	**20.0**	**7**	**1**	**4**	**0**	**2**								
1995-96	**Mighty Ducks of Anaheim**	**NHL**	**1**	**0**	**0**	**0**	**0**	**0**	**0**	**0**	**0**	**0**	**0**	**0**	**0.0**	**0**	**0**	**1**	**0**	**–1**								
	Baltimore Bandits	AHL	12	2	4	6				34																		
	Los Angeles Ice Dogs	IHL	64	12	20	32				112																		
1996-97	Rochester Americans	AHL	1	0	2	2				15																		
	Providence Bruins	AHL	63	12	23	35				130											10	3	0	3	24			
	Detroit Vipers	IHL	1	0	0	0				2																		
1997-98	Dusseldorfer EG	Germany	44	9	14	23				120											3	0	0	0	4			
1998-99	Kassel Huskies	Germany	18	1	3	4				22																		
	Schwenningen Wild Wings	Germany	8	2	1	3				16																		
	United States	WC-Q	3	0	0	0				27																		
99-2000	Schwenningen Wild Wings	Germany	59	8	14	22				182																		
	NHL Totals		**23**	**3**	**8**	**11**	**5**	**8**	**13**	**13**	**1**	**0**	**1**	**30**	**10.0**	**14**	**1**	**11**	**0**									

Signed as a free agent by **Anaheim**, March 9, 1994.

• LIND, Juha

C – L. 5'11", 180 lbs. b: Helsinki, Finland, 1/2/1974. Minnesota's 6th, 178th overall, in 1992.

Season	Club	League	GP	G	A	Pts	AG	AA	APts	PIM	PP	SH	GW	S	%	TGF	PGF	TGA	PGA	+/-	PO GP	PO G	PO A	PO Pts	PO PIM	PO PP	PO SH	PO GW
							REGULAR SEASON														PLAYOFFS							
1990-91	Jokerit Helsinki	Finland-Jr.	8	1	1	2				0																		
1991-92	Jokerit Helsinki-2	Finland-Jr.	14	9	16	25				2											14	7	8	15	8			
	Finland	EJC-A	6	2	7	9				4																		
1992-93	Vantaa HT	Finland-2	25	8	12	20				8																		
	Jokerit Helsinki	Finland-2	3	2	4	6				2																		
	Jokerit Helsinki	Finland	6	0	0	0				2											1	0	0	0	0			
1993-94	Jokerit Helsinki	Finland-2	11	6	7	13				4																		
	Finland	WJC-A	7	5	2	7				2																		
	Jokerit Helsinki	Finland	47	17	11	28				37											11	2	5	7	4			
1994-95	Jokerit Helsinki	Finland-Jr.	3	2	1	3				2																		
	Jokerit Helsinki	Finland	50	10	8	18				12											11	1	2	3	6			
1995-96	Jokerit Helsinki	Finland	50	15	22	37				32											11	4	5	9	4			
1996-97	Jokerit Helsinki	Finland	50	16	22	38				28											9	5	3	8	0			
	Jokerit Helsinki	EuroHL	6	4	1	5				6											2	1	0	1	0			
	Finland	WC-A	8	1	0	1				8																		
1997-98	**Dallas Stars**	**NHL**	**39**	**2**	**3**	**5**	**2**	**3**	**5**	**6**	**0**	**0**	**0**	**27**	**7.4**	**9**	**0**	**7**	**2**	**4**	**15**	**2**	**2**	**4**	**8**	**0**	**0**	**1**
	Michigan K-Wings	IHL	8	2	2	4				2																		
	Finland	Olympics	6	0	1	1				6																		
1998-99	Jokerit Helsinki	Finland	50	20	19	39				22											3	3	1	4	2			
	Jokerit Helsinki	EuroHL	6	6	2	8				14											2	0	2	2	0			
	Finland	WC-A	12	3	2	5				2																		
99-2000	**Dallas Stars**	**NHL**	**34**	**3**	**4**	**7**	**3**	**4**	**7**	**6**	**0**	**0**	**0**	**36**	**8.3**	**10**	**0**	**12**	**1**	**–1**								
	Montreal Canadiens	**NHL**	**13**	**1**	**2**	**3**	**1**	**2**	**3**	**4**	**0**	**0**	**0**	**6**	**16.7**	**3**	**0**	**5**	**0**	**–2**								
	Finland	WC-A	9	3	4	7				4																		
	NHL Totals		**86**	**6**	**9**	**15**	**6**	**9**	**15**	**16**	**0**	**0**	**0**	**69**	**8.7**	**22**	**0**	**24**	**3**		**15**	**2**	**2**	**4**	**8**	**0**	**0**	**1**

Rights transferred to **Dallas** after **Minnesota** franchise relocated, June 9, 1993. Traded to **Montreal** by **Dallas** for Scott Thornton, January 22, 2000.

• LINDBERG, Chris

Christopher Lawrence LW – L. 6'1", 190 lbs. b: Fort Frances, Ont., 4/16/1967.

Season	Club	League	GP	G	A	Pts	AG	AA	APts	PIM	PP	SH	GW	S	%	TGF	PGF	TGA	PGA	+/-	PO GP	PO G	PO A	PO Pts	PO PIM	PO PP	PO SH	PO GW
1985-86	Estevan Bruins	SJHL	60	30	38	68				110											15	5	14	19	6			
1986-87	Estevan Bruins	SJHL	STATISTICS NOT AVAILABLE																									
1987-88	University of Minnesota-Duluth	WCHA	35	12	10	22				36																		
1988-89	University of Minnesota-Duluth	WCHA	36	15	18	33				51																		
1989-90	Binghamton Whalers	AHL	32	4	4	8				36																		
	Virginia Lancers	ECHL	26	11	23	34				27											4	0	3	3	2			
1990-91	Canada	Nat-Team	55	25	31	56				53																		
	Springfield Indians	AHL	1	0	0	0				2											1	0	0	0	0			
1991-92	Canada	Nat-Team	56	33	35	68				63																		
	Canada	Olympics	8	1	4	5				4																		
	Calgary Flames	**NHL**	**17**	**2**	**5**	**7**	**2**	**4**	**6**	**17**	**0**	**0**	**0**	**19**	**10.5**	**9**	**0**	**16**	**10**	**3**								
	Canada	WC-A	5	1	0	1				8																		
1992-93	**Calgary Flames**	**NHL**	**62**	**9**	**12**	**21**	**7**	**8**	**15**	**18**	**1**	**0**	**1**	**74**	**12.2**	**35**	**2**	**54**	**18**	**–3**	**2**	**0**	**1**	**1**	**2**	**0**	**0**	**0**
1993-94	**Quebec Nordiques**	**NHL**	**37**	**6**	**8**	**14**	**6**	**6**	**12**	**12**	**0**	**0**	**0**	**42**	**14.3**	**19**	**1**	**20**	**1**	**–1**								
	Cornwall Aces	AHL	23	14	13	27				28											13	11	3	14	10			
1994-95	Krefeld Pinguine	Germany	42	25	41	66				103											15	4	10	14	20			
1995-96	Krefeld Pinguine	Germany	49	21	35	56				96											6	4	7	11	8			
1996-97	Krefeld Pinguine	Germany	47	*37	35	72				129											3	0	1	1	6			
	SC Herisau	Switz-2																			1	0	0	0	0			
1997-98	Grand Rapids Griffins	IHL	18	8	14	22				25																		
	Krefeld Pinguine	Germany	15	2	7	9				33																		
	EV Zug	Switz.	2	1	1	2				0											17	6	*15	21	22			
1998-99	SC Rapperswil-Jona	Switz.	43	22	28	50				*114											5	1	2	3	4			
99-2000	ZSC Lions Zurich	Switz.	22	5	8	13				62																		
	Canada	Nat-Team	9	6	2	8				8																		
	NHL Totals		**116**	**17**	**25**	**42**	**15**	**18**	**33**	**47**	**1**	**0**	**1**	**135**	**12.6**	**63**	**3**	**90**	**29**		**2**	**0**	**1**	**1**	**2**	**0**	**0**	**0**

Signed as a free agent by **Hartford**, March 17, 1989. Signed as a free agent by **Calgary**, August 2, 1991. Claimed by **Ottawa** from **Calgary** in Expansion Draft, June 18, 1992. Traded to **Calgary** by **Ottawa** for Mark Osiecki, June 22, 1992. Signed as a free agent by **Quebec**, September 9, 1993.

• LINDBOM, Johan

LW – L. 6'2", 216 lbs. b: Alvesta, Sweden, 7/8/1971. NY Rangers' 6th, 134th overall, in 1997.

Season	Club	League	GP	G	A	Pts	AG	AA	APts	PIM	PP	SH	GW	S	%	TGF	PGF	TGA	PGA	+/-	PO GP	PO G	PO A	PO Pts	PO PIM	PO PP	PO SH	PO GW
1990-91	Tyringe SoSS	Sweden-2	25	9	6	15				26																		
1991-92	Tyringe SoSS	Sweden-2	30	10	11	21				68																		
1992-93	Troja-Ljungby	Sweden-2	30	10	16	26				20											10	6	3	9	18			
1993-94	Troja-Ljungby	Sweden-2	33	16	11	27				30											11	6	6	12	2			
1994-95	HV-71 Jonkoping	Sweden	39	9	7	16				30											13	2	5	7	12			
1995-96	HV-71 Jonkoping	Sweden	37	12	14	26				30											4	0	0	0	4			
1996-97	HV-71 Jonkoping	Sweden	49	20	14	34				26											5	1	0	1	6			
	Sweden	WC-A	8	0	1	1				6																		
1997-98	**New York Rangers**	**NHL**	**38**	**1**	**3**	**4**	**1**	**3**	**4**	**28**	**0**	**0**	**0**	**38**	**2.6**	**13**	**0**	**10**	**1**	**4**								
	Hartford Wolf Pack	AHL	7	1	5	6				6																		
1998-99	HV-71 Jonkoping	Sweden	49	9	17	26				40																		
99-2000	HV-71 Jonkoping	Sweden	31	4	5	9				28											4	1	1	2	2			
	NHL Totals		**38**	**1**	**3**	**4**	**1**	**3**	**4**	**28**	**0**	**0**	**0**	**38**	**2.6**	**13**	**0**	**10**	**1**									

• LINDEN, Jamie

Jamie Marion RW – R. 6'3", 185 lbs. b: Medicine Hat, Alta., 7/19/1972.

Season	Club	League	GP	G	A	Pts	AG	AA	APts	PIM	PP	SH	GW	S	%	TGF	PGF	TGA	PGA	+/-	PO GP	PO G	PO A	PO Pts	PO PIM	PO PP	PO SH	PO GW
1988-89	Medicine Hat Midget Tigers	AAHA	37	16	13	29				85																		
	Portland Winter Hawks	WHL	1	0	1	1				0																		
1989-90	Portland Winter Hawks	WHL	67	5	7	12				124																		
1990-91	Portland Winter Hawks	WHL	2	0	1	1				6																		
	Prince Albert Raiders	WHL	64	9	12	21				114											3	0	0	0	0			
1991-92	Prince Albert Raiders	WHL	4	2	1	3				8																		
	Spokane Chiefs	WHL	60	7	10	17				302											10	0	0	0	69			
1992-93	Spokane Chiefs	WHL	15	3	1	4				58																		
	Medicine Hat Tigers	WHL	50	9	9	18				147											10	1	6	7	15			
1993-94	Cincinnati Cyclones	IHL	47	1	5	6				55											2	0	0	0	2			
	Birmingham Bulls	ECHL	16	3	7	10				38																		
1994-95	**Florida Panthers**	**NHL**	**4**	**0**	**0**	**0**	**0**	**0**	**0**	**17**	**0**	**0**	**0**	**0**	**0.0**	**0**	**0**	**1**	**0**	**–1**								
	Cincinnati Cyclones	IHL	51	3	6	9				173																		
1995-96	Carolina Monarchs	AHL	50	4	8	12				92																		
1996-97	Carolina Monarchs	AHL	3	0	0	0				5																		
	Grand Rapids Griffins	IHL	48	8	8	16				138											5	1	1	2	4			
1997-98	Las Vegas Thunder	IHL	28	1	1	2				62																		
	Grand Rapids Griffins	IHL	2	0	1	1				5											1	0	0	0	0			
	NHL Totals		**4**	**0**	**0**	**0**	**0**	**0**	**0**	**17**	**0**	**0**	**0**	**0**	**0.0**	**0**	**0**	**1**	**0**									

• Family name was originally Van der Linden • Brother of Trevor • Signed as a free agent by **Florida**, October 4, 1993.

• LINDEN, Trevor

C/RW – R. 6'4", 220 lbs. b: Medicine Hat, Alta., 4/11/1970. Vancouver's 1st, 2nd overall, in 1988.

										REGULAR SEASON											PLAYOFFS							
Season	Club	League	GP	G	A	Pts	AG	AA	APts	PIM	PP	SH	GW	S	%	TGF	PGF	TGA	PGA	+/–	GP	G	A	Pts	PIM	PP	SH	GW
1985-86	Medicine Hat Midget Tigers	AAHA	40	14	22	36				14																		
	Medicine Hat Tigers	WHL	5	2	0	2				0																		
1986-87	Medicine Hat Tigers	WHL	72	14	22	36				59											20	5	4	9	17			
	Medicine Hat Tigers	Mem-Cup	5	2	1	3				6																		
1987-88	Medicine Hat Tigers	WHL	67	46	64	110				76											16	*13	12	25	19			
	Canada	WJC-A	7	1	0	1				0																		
	Medicine Hat Tigers	Mem-Cup	5	3	4	7				0																		
1988-89	**Vancouver Canucks**	**NHL**	**80**	**30**	**29**	**59**	**25**	**21**	**46**	**41**	**10**	**1**	**2**	**186**	**16.1**	**99**	**41**	**74**	**6**	**–10**	**7**	**3**	**4**	**7**	**8**	**2**	**1**	**0**
1989-90	**Vancouver Canucks**	**NHL**	**73**	**21**	**30**	**51**	**18**	**21**	**39**	**43**	**6**	**2**	**3**	**171**	**12.3**	**83**	**34**	**85**	**19**	**–17**								
1990-91	**Vancouver Canucks**	**NHL**	**80**	**33**	**37**	**70**	**30**	**28**	**58**	**65**	**16**	**2**	**4**	**229**	**14.4**	**103**	**47**	**109**	**28**	**–25**	**6**	**0**	**7**	**7**	**2**	**0**	**0**	**0**
	Canada	WEC-A	10	1	4	5				4																		
1991-92	**Vancouver Canucks**	**NHL**	**80**	**31**	**44**	**75**	**28**	**33**	**61**	**101**	**6**	**1**	**6**	**201**	**15.4**	**109**	**47**	**74**	**15**	**3**	**13**	**4**	**8**	**12**	**6**	**2**	**0**	**1**
1992-93	**Vancouver Canucks**	**NHL**	**84**	**33**	**39**	**72**	**27**	**27**	**54**	**64**	**8**	**0**	**3**	**209**	**15.8**	**112**	**33**	**93**	**33**	**19**	**12**	**5**	**8**	**13**	**16**	**2**	**0**	**1**
1993-94	**Vancouver Canucks**	**NHL**	**84**	**32**	**29**	**61**	**30**	**22**	**52**	**73**	**10**	**2**	**3**	**234**	**13.7**	**114**	**52**	**86**	**30**	**6**	**24**	**12**	**13**	**25**	**18**	**5**	**1**	**1**
1994-95	**Vancouver Canucks**	**NHL**	**48**	**18**	**22**	**40**	**32**	**33**	**65**	**40**	**9**	**0**	**1**	**129**	**14.0**	**58**	**31**	**39**	**7**	**–5**	**11**	**2**	**6**	**8**	**12**	**1**	**0**	**0**
1995-96	**Vancouver Canucks**	**NHL**	**82**	**33**	**47**	**80**	**32**	**39**	**71**	**42**	**12**	**1**	**2**	**202**	**16.3**	**125**	**48**	**99**	**28**	**6**	**6**	**4**	**4**	**8**	**6**	**2**	**0**	**0**
1996-97	Canada	W-Cup	8	1	1	2				0																		
	Vancouver Canucks	**NHL**	**49**	**9**	**31**	**40**	**10**	**28**	**38**	**27**	**2**	**2**	**2**	**84**	**10.7**	**62**	**14**	**57**	**14**	**5**								
1997-98	**Vancouver Canucks**	**NHL**	**42**	**7**	**14**	**21**	**8**	**14**	**22**	**49**	**2**	**0**	**1**	**74**	**9.5**	**40**	**15**	**57**	**19**	**–13**								
	New York Islanders	**NHL**	**25**	**10**	**7**	**17**	**12**	**7**	**19**	**33**	**3**	**2**	**1**	**59**	**16.9**	**34**	**14**	**27**	**6**	**–1**								
	Canada	Olympics	6	1	0	1				10																		
	Canada	WC-A	6	1	4	5				4																		
1998-99	**New York Islanders**	**NHL**	**82**	**18**	**29**	**47**	**21**	**28**	**49**	**32**	**8**	**1**	**1**	**167**	**10.8**	**72**	**28**	**88**	**30**	**–14**								
99-2000	**Montreal Canadiens**	**NHL**	**50**	**13**	**17**	**30**	**15**	**16**	**31**	**34**	**4**	**0**	**3**	**87**	**14.9**	**42**	**14**	**38**	**7**	**–3**								
	NHL Totals		**859**	**288**	**375**	**663**	**288**	**317**	**605**	**644**	**96**	**14**	**32**	**2032**	**14.2**	**1053**	**418**	**926**	**242**		**79**	**30**	**50**	**80**	**68**	**14**	**2**	**3**

• Brother of Jamie • WHL East Second All-Star Team (1988) • NHL All-Rookie Team (1989) • Won King Clancy Memorial Trophy (1997) • Played in NHL All-Star Game (1991, 1992)

Traded to **NY Islanders** by **Vancouver** for Todd Bertuzzi, Bryan McCabe and NY Islanders' 3rd round choice (Jarkko Ruutu) in 1998 Entry Draft, February 6, 1998. Traded to **Montreal** by **NY Islanders** for Montreal's 1st round choice (Branislav Mezel) in 1999 Entry Draft, May 29, 1999.

• LINDGREN, Lars

Lars Sune D – L. 6'1", 200 lbs. b: Pitea, Sweden, 10/12/1952.

Season	Club	League	GP	G	A	Pts	AG	AA	APts	PIM	PP	SH	GW	S	%	TGF	PGF	TGA	PGA	+/–	GP	G	A	Pts	PIM	PP	SH	GW
1970-71	Pitea IF	Sweden-2	18	3	3	6																						
1971-72	Pitea IF	Sweden-2	18	6	6	12																						
1972-73	Skelleftea AIK	Sweden	13	0	3	3				10											6	1	2	3	8			
1973-74	Skelleftea AIK	Sweden	13	0	3	3				10											6	1	2	3	8			
1974-75	MoDo AIK	Sweden	30	4	8	12				20																		
1975-76	MoDo AIK	Sweden	36	2	4	6				22																		
1976-77	MoDo AIK	Sweden	35	6	6	12				36											4	0	0	0	2			
	Sweden	WEC-A	10	1	1	2				8																		
1977-78	MoDo AIK	Sweden	33	3	12	15				55																		
	Sweden	WEC-A	10	2	3	5				8																		
1978-79	**Vancouver Canucks**	**NHL**	**64**	**2**	**19**	**21**	**2**	**14**	**16**	**68**	**1**	**0**	**0**	**109**	**1.8**	**72**	**20**	**108**	**24**	**–32**	**3**	**0**	**0**	**0**	**6**	**0**	**0**	**0**
1979-80	**Vancouver Canucks**	**NHL**	**73**	**5**	**30**	**35**	**4**	**22**	**26**	**66**	**2**	**0**	**0**	**181**	**2.8**	**99**	**29**	**109**	**31**	**–8**	**2**	**0**	**1**	**1**	**0**	**0**	**0**	**0**
1980-81	**Vancouver Canucks**	**NHL**	**52**	**4**	**18**	**22**	**3**	**12**	**15**	**32**	**1**	**0**	**0**	**76**	**5.3**	**65**	**7**	**60**	**18**	**16**								
1981-82	Sweden	Can-Cup	5	0	1	1				6																		
	Vancouver Canucks	**NHL**	**75**	**5**	**16**	**21**	**4**	**11**	**15**	**74**	**0**	**0**	**1**	**95**	**5.3**	**78**	**7**	**105**	**36**	**2**	**16**	**2**	**4**	**6**	**6**	**0**	**0**	**0**
1982-83	**Vancouver Canucks**	**NHL**	**64**	**6**	**14**	**20**	**5**	**10**	**15**	**48**	**1**	**0**	**1**	**72**	**8.3**	**68**	**4**	**97**	**36**	**3**	**4**	**1**	**1**	**2**	**2**	**0**	**0**	**0**
1983-84	**Vancouver Canucks**	**NHL**	**7**	**1**	**2**	**3**	**1**	**1**	**2**	**4**	**0**	**0**	**0**	**4**	**25.0**	**12**	**2**	**19**	**9**	**0**								
	Minnesota North Stars	**NHL**	**59**	**2**	**14**	**16**	**2**	**10**	**12**	**33**	**0**	**0**	**0**	**66**	**3.0**	**66**	**3**	**90**	**24**	**–3**	**15**	**2**	**0**	**2**	**6**	**0**	**0**	**0**
1984-85	Lulea HF	Sweden	33	8	3	11				46																		
1985-86	Lulea HF	Sweden	35	2	7	9				32																		
1986-87	Lulea HF	Sweden	35	4	9	13				42											3	0	0	0	2			
1987-88	Lulea HF	Sweden	40	2	7	9				52																		
1988-89	Pitea IF	Sweden-2	DID NOT PLAY – COACHING																									
1989-90	Pitea IF	Sweden-2	2	0	0	0				2																		
	NHL Totals		**394**	**25**	**113**	**138**	**21**	**80**	**101**	**325**	**5**	**0**	**2**	**603**	**4.1**	**460**	**72**	**588**	**178**		**40**	**5**	**6**	**11**	**20**	**0**	**0**	**0**

Played in NHL All-Star Game (1980)

Signed as a free agent by **Vancouver**, June 5, 1978. Traded to **Minnesota** by **Vancouver** for Minnesota's 3rd round choice (Landis Chaulk) in 1984 Entry Draft, October 20, 1983.

• LINDGREN, Mats

C – L. 6'2", 202 lbs. b: Skelleftea, Sweden, 10/1/1974. Winnipeg's 1st, 15th overall, in 1993.

Season	Club	League	GP	G	A	Pts	AG	AA	APts	PIM	PP	SH	GW	S	%	TGF	PGF	TGA	PGA	+/–	GP	G	A	Pts	PIM	PP	SH	GW
1990-91	Skelleftea AIK	Sweden-2	10	0	1	1				0																		
1991-92	Skelleftea AIK	Sweden-2	29	14	18	32				12											3	3	2	5	2			
	Sweden	EJC-A	6	2	2	4				10																		
1992-93	Skelleftea AIK	Sweden-2	32	20	18	38				18											3	0	0	0	2			
	Sweden	WJC-A	7	1	2	3				8																		
1993-94	Farjestads BK Stockholm	Sweden	22	11	6	17				26																		
	Sweden	WJC-A	7	5	4	9				2																		
1994-95	Farjestads BK Stockholm	Sweden	37	17	15	32				20											3	0	0	0	4			
1995-96	Cape Breton Oilers	AHL	13	7	5	12				6																		
1996-97	**Edmonton Oilers**	**NHL**	**69**	**11**	**14**	**25**	**12**	**12**	**24**	**12**	**2**	**3**	**1**	**71**	**15.5**	**35**	**4**	**52**	**14**	**–7**	**12**	**0**	**4**	**4**	**0**	**0**	**0**	**0**
	Hamilton Bulldogs	AHL	9	6	7	13				6																		
1997-98	**Edmonton Oilers**	**NHL**	**82**	**13**	**13**	**26**	**15**	**13**	**28**	**42**	**1**	**3**	**3**	**131**	**9.9**	**41**	**6**	**59**	**24**	**0**	**12**	**1**	**1**	**2**	**10**	**0**	**0**	**0**
	Sweden	Olympics	4	0	0	0				2																		
1998-99	**Edmonton Oilers**	**NHL**	**48**	**5**	**12**	**17**	**6**	**12**	**18**	**22**	**0**	**1**	**0**	**53**	**9.4**	**30**	**1**	**30**	**5**	**4**								
	New York Islanders	**NHL**	**12**	**5**	**3**	**8**	**6**	**3**	**9**	**2**	**3**	**0**	**1**	**30**	**16.7**	**18**	**5**	**13**	**2**	**2**								
99-2000	**New York Islanders**	**NHL**	**43**	**9**	**7**	**16**	**10**	**6**	**16**	**24**	**1**	**0**	**1**	**68**	**13.2**	**26**	**5**	**44**	**23**	**0**								
	NHL Totals		**254**	**43**	**49**	**92**	**49**	**46**	**95**	**102**	**7**	**7**	**6**	**353**	**12.2**	**150**	**21**	**198**	**68**		**24**	**1**	**5**	**6**	**10**	**0**	**0**	**0**

Swedish Rookie of the Year (1994)

Traded to **Edmonton** by **Winnipeg** with Boris Mironov, Winnipeg's 1st round choice (Jason Bonsignore) in 1994 Entry Draft and Florida's 4th round choice (previously acquired, Edmonton selected Adam Copeland) in 1994 Entry Draft for Dave Manson and St. Louis' 6th round choice (previously acquired, Winnipeg selected Chris Kibermanis) in 1994 Entry Draft, March 15, 1994. Traded to **NY Islanders** by **Edmonton** with Edmonton's 8th round choice (Radek Martinek) in 1999 Entry Draft for Tommy Salo, March 20, 1999.

• LINDHOLM, Mikael

C – L. 6'1", 194 lbs. b: Gavle, Sweden, 12/19/1964. Los Angeles' 10th, 237th overall, in 1987.

Season	Club	League	GP	G	A	Pts	AG	AA	APts	PIM	PP	SH	GW	S	%	TGF	PGF	TGA	PGA	+/–	GP	G	A	Pts	PIM	PP	SH	GW
1979-80	Gavle GIK	Sweden-3	11	0	1	1				0																		
1980-81	Gavle GIK	Sweden-3	20	20	4	24				8																		
1981-82	Gavle EIK	Sweden-2	18	3	3	6				8																		
	Sweden	EJC-A	5	1	3	4				6																		
1982-83	Gavle EIK	Sweden-2	27	6	7	13				44																		
1983-84	Stromsbro AIK	Sweden-2	20	9	10	19				4																		
1984-85	Stromsbro AIK	Sweden-2	30	14	17	31				29																		
1985-86	Stromsbro AIK	Sweden-2	32	15	20	35				26											5	2	4	6	6			
1986-87	Brynas IF Gavle	Sweden	36	8	9	17				46																		
1987-88	Brynas IF Gavle	Sweden	38	9	8	17				56																		
1988-89	Brynas IF Gavle	Sweden	40	9	17	26				*98											4	0	0	0	4			
1989-90	**Los Angeles Kings**	**NHL**	**18**	**2**	**2**	**4**	**2**	**1**	**3**	**2**	**0**	**0**	**0**	**10**	**20.0**	**8**	**0**	**6**	**0**	**2**								
	New Haven Nighthawks	AHL	28	4	6	10				24																		
1990-91	Phoenix Roadrunners	IHL	70	16	45	61				92											11	0	12	12	14			
1991-92	Brynas IF Gavle	Sweden	36	7	11	18				24											5	0	1	1	2			

			REGULAR SEASON																		PLAYOFFS							
Season	Club	League	GP	G	A	Pts	AG	AA	APts	PIM	PP	SH	GW	S	%	TGF	PGF	TGA	PGA	+/-	GP	G	A	Pts	PIM	PP	SH	GW
1992-93	Brynas IF Gavle	Sweden	15	2	3	5	....	....	....	16	....	....	....	....	....	....	....	....	....	....	....	....	....	....	....	....	....	....
1993-94	Boden HC	Sweden-2	36	19	22	41	....	....	....	44	....	....	....	....	....	....	....	....	....	....	9	0	7	7	20	....	....	....
1994-95	Boden HC	Sweden-2	36	10	19	29	....	....	....	48	....	....	....	....	....	....	....	....	....	....	10	5	6	11	10	....	....	....
1995-96	Lulea HF	Sweden	39	8	12	20	....	....	....	38	....	....	....	....	....	....	....	....	....	....	13	3	3	6	16	....	....	....
1996-97	Lulea HF	Sweden	46	6	14	20	....	....	....	75	....	....	....	....	....	....	....	....	....	....	10	1	4	5	31	....	....	....
	Lulea HF	EuroHL	6	2	3	5	....	....	....	6	....	....	....	....	....	....	....	....	....	....	....	....	....	....	....	....	....	....
1997-98	Hannover Scorpions	Germany	47	7	9	16	....	....	....	16	....	....	....	....	....	....	....	....	....	....	4	0	1	1	16	....	....	....
1998-99	Malmo IF	Sweden	46	6	12	18	....	....	....	60	....	....	....	....	....	....	....	....	....	....	8	2	1	3	18	....	....	....
99-2000	Malmo IF	Sweden	48	3	15	18	....	....	....	114	....	....	....	....	....	....	....	....	....	....	6	0	1	1	12	....	....	....
	NHL Totals		**18**	**2**	**2**	**4**	**2**	**1**	**3**	**2**	**0**	**0**	**0**	**10**	**20.0**	**8**	**0**	**6**	**0**		....	....	....	....	....	....	....	....

• LINDQUIST, Fredrik

C – L. 6', 190 lbs. b: Stockholm, Sweden, 6/21/1973. New Jersey's 4th, 55th overall, in 1991.

Season	Club	League	GP	G	A	Pts	AG	AA	APts	PIM	PP	SH	GW	S	%	TGF	PGF	TGA	PGA	+/-	GP	G	A	Pts	PIM	PP	SH	GW
1989-90	Huddinge IF	Sweden-2	2	0	0	0	....	....	....	0	....	....	....	....	....	....	....	....	....	....	....	....	....	....	....	....	....	....
1990-91	Djurgardens IF Stockholm	Sweden	28	6	4	10	....	....	....	0	....	....	....	....	....	....	....	....	....	....	7	1	0	1	2	....	....	....
1991-92	Djurgardens IF Stockholm	Sweden	39	9	6	15	....	....	....	14	....	....	....	....	....	....	....	....	....	....	10	1	1	2	2	....	....	....
1992-93	Djurgardens IF Stockholm	Sweden	39	9	11	20	....	....	....	8	....	....	....	....	....	....	....	....	....	....	4	1	2	3	2	....	....	....
	Sweden	WJC-A	7	5	3	8	....	....	....	2	....	....	....	....	....	....	....	....	....	....	....	....	....	....	....	....	....	....
1993-94	Djurgardens IF Stockholm	Sweden-Jr.	1	0	1	1	....	....	....	0	....	....	....	....	....	....	....	....	....	....	....	....	....	....	....	....	....	....
	Djurgardens IF Stockholm	Sweden	25	5	8	13	....	....	....	8	....	....	....	....	....	....	....	....	....	....	6	2	1	3	2	....	....	....
1994-95	Djurgardens IF Stockholm	Sweden	40	11	16	27	....	....	....	14	....	....	....	....	....	....	....	....	....	....	3	0	0	0	2	....	....	....
1995-96	Djurgardens IF Stockholm	Sweden	33	12	19	31	....	....	....	16	....	....	....	....	....	....	....	....	....	....	1	0	0	0	0	....	....	....
1996-97	Djurgardens IF Stockholm	Sweden	44	19	28	47	....	....	....	20	....	....	....	....	....	....	....	....	....	....	4	0	3	3	2	....	....	....
1997-98	Djurgardens IF Stockholm	Sweden	42	10	*32	42	....	....	....	30	....	....	....	....	....	....	....	....	....	....	13	3	6	9	4	....	....	....
1998-99	**Edmonton Oilers**	**NHL**	**8**	**0**	**0**	**0**	**0**	**0**	**0**	**2**	**0**	**0**	**0**	**6**	**0.0**	**1**	**1**	**2**	**0**	**–2**	....	....	....	....	....	....	....	....
	Hamilton Bulldogs	AHL	57	18	36	54	....	....	....	20	....	....	....	....	....	....	....	....	....	....	11	2	2	4	2	....	....	....
99-2000	HC Davos	Switz.	44	14	27	41	....	....	....	20	....	....	....	....	....	....	....	....	....	....	5	2	3	5	4	....	....	....
	Sweden	WC-A	6	1	1	2	....	....	....	0	....	....	....	....	....	....	....	....	....	....	....	....	....	....	....	....	....	....
	NHL Totals		**8**	**0**	**0**	**0**	**0**	**0**	**0**	**2**	**0**	**0**	**0**	**6**	**0.0**	**1**	**1**	**2**	**0**		....	....	....	....	....	....	....	....

Traded to **Edmonton** by **New Jersey** with New Jersey's 4th (Kristian Antila) and 5th (Oleg Smirnov) round choices in 1998 Entry Draft for Pittsburgh's 3rd round choice (previously acquired, New Jersey selected Brian Gionta) in 1998 Entry Draft, June 27, 1998.

• LINDROS, Brett

RW – R. 6'4", 215 lbs. b: London, Ont., 12/2/1975. NY Islanders' 1st, 9th overall, in 1994.

Season	Club	League	GP	G	A	Pts	AG	AA	APts	PIM	PP	SH	GW	S	%	TGF	PGF	TGA	PGA	+/-	GP	G	A	Pts	PIM	PP	SH	GW
1991-92	St. Michael's Buzzers	OJHL	34	21	21	42	....	....	....	210	....	....	....	....	....	....	....	....	....	....	6	5	5	10	63	....	....	....
1992-93	Kingston Frontenacs	OHL	31	11	11	22	....	....	....	162	....	....	....	....	....	....	....	....	....	....	....	....	....	....	....	....	....	....
	Canada	Nat-Team	11	1	6	7	....	....	....	33	....	....	....	....	....	....	....	....	....	....	....	....	....	....	....	....	....	....
1993-94	Canada	Nat-Team	44	7	7	14	....	....	....	118	....	....	....	....	....	....	....	....	....	....	....	....	....	....	....	....	....	....
	Kingston Frontenacs	OHL	15	4	6	10	....	....	....	94	....	....	....	....	....	....	....	....	....	....	3	0	0	0	18	....	....	....
1994-95	**New York Islanders**	**NHL**	**33**	**1**	**3**	**4**	**2**	**4**	**6**	**100**	**0**	**0**	**1**	**35**	**2.9**	**13**	**3**	**18**	**0**	**–8**	....	....	....	....	....	....	....	....
	Kingston Frontenacs	OHL	26	24	23	47	....	....	....	63	....	....	....	....	....	....	....	....	....	....	....	....	....	....	....	....	....	....
1995-96	**New York Islanders**	**NHL**	**18**	**1**	**2**	**3**	**1**	**2**	**3**	**47**	**0**	**0**	**0**	**10**	**10.0**	**5**	**0**	**11**	**0**	**–6**	....	....	....	....	....	....	....	....
	NHL Totals		**51**	**2**	**5**	**7**	**3**	**6**	**9**	**147**	**0**	**0**	**1**	**45**	**4.4**	**18**	**3**	**29**	**0**		....	....	....	....	....	....	....	....

• Brother of Eric • Suffered eventual career-ending head injury in game vs. LA Kings, November 2, 1995. • Officially announced retirement, May 1, 1996.

• LINDROS, Eric

Eric B. C – R. 6'4", 236 lbs. b: London, Ont., 2/28/1973. Quebec's 1st, 1st overall, in 1991.

Season	Club	League	GP	G	A	Pts	AG	AA	APts	PIM	PP	SH	GW	S	%	TGF	PGF	TGA	PGA	+/-	GP	G	A	Pts	PIM	PP	SH	GW
1988-89	St. Michael's Buzzers	OJHL-B	37	24	43	67	....	....	....	193	....	....	....	....	....	....	....	....	....	....	27	23	25	48	155	....	....	....
	Canada	Nat-Team	2	1	0	1	....	....	....	0	....	....	....	....	....	....	....	....	....	....	....	....	....	....	....	....	....	....
1989-90	Detroit Compuware	NAJHL	14	23	29	52	....	....	....	123	....	....	....	....	....	....	....	....	....	....	....	....	....	....	....	....	....	....
	Canada	Nat-Team	3	1	0	1	....	....	....	4	....	....	....	....	....	....	....	....	....	....	....	....	....	....	....	....	....	....
	Canada	WJC-A	7	4	0	4	....	....	....	14	....	....	....	....	....	....	....	....	....	....	....	....	....	....	....	....	....	....
	Oshawa Generals	OHL	25	17	19	36	....	....	....	61	....	....	....	....	....	....	....	....	....	....	17	18	18	36	76	....	....	....
	Oshawa Generals	Mem-Cup	4	0	*9	9	....	....	....	12	....	....	....	....	....	....	....	....	....	....	....	....	....	....	....	....	....	....
1990-91	Oshawa Generals	OHL	57	*71	78	*149	....	....	....	189	....	....	....	....	....	....	....	....	....	....	16	*18	20	*38	*93	....	....	....
	Canada	WJC-A	7	6	11	17	....	....	....	6	....	....	....	....	....	....	....	....	....	....	....	....	....	....	....	....	....	....
1991-92	Canada	Can-Cup	8	3	2	5	....	....	....	8	....	....	....	....	....	....	....	....	....	....	....	....	....	....	....	....	....	....
	Oshawa Generals	OHL	13	9	22	31	....	....	....	54	....	....	....	....	....	....	....	....	....	....	....	....	....	....	....	....	....	....
	Canada	Nat-Team	24	19	16	35	....	....	....	34	....	....	....	....	....	....	....	....	....	....	....	....	....	....	....	....	....	....
	Canada	WJC-A	7	2	8	10	....	....	....	12	....	....	....	....	....	....	....	....	....	....	....	....	....	....	....	....	....	....
	Canada	Olympics	8	5	6	11	....	....	....	5	....	....	....	....	....	....	....	....	....	....	....	....	....	....	....	....	....	....
1992-93	**Philadelphia Flyers**	**NHL**	**61**	**41**	**34**	**75**	**34**	**23**	**57**	**147**	**8**	**1**	**5**	**180**	**22.8**	**119**	**34**	**63**	**6**	**28**	....	....	....	....	....	....	....	....
	Canada	WC-A	8	11	6	17	....	....	....	10	....	....	....	....	....	....	....	....	....	....	....	....	....	....	....	....	....	....
1993-94	**Philadelphia Flyers**	**NHL**	**65**	**44**	**53**	**97**	**41**	**41**	**82**	**103**	**13**	**2**	**9**	**197**	**22.3**	**134**	**47**	**82**	**11**	**16**	....	....	....	....	....	....	....	....
1994-95	**Philadelphia Flyers**	**NHL**	**46**	**29**	**41**	***70**	**51**	**61**	**112**	**60**	**7**	**0**	**4**	**144**	**20.1**	**94**	**30**	**40**	**3**	**27**	**12**	**4**	**11**	**15**	**18**	**0**	**0**	**1**
1995-96	**Philadelphia Flyers**	**NHL**	**73**	**47**	**68**	**115**	**46**	**56**	**102**	**163**	**15**	**0**	**4**	**294**	**16.0**	**148**	**57**	**78**	**13**	**26**	**12**	**6**	**6**	**12**	**43**	**3**	**0**	**2**
1996-97	Canada	W-Cup	8	3	3	6	....	....	....	10	....	....	....	....	....	....	....	....	....	....	....	....	....	....	....	....	....	....
	Philadelphia Flyers	**NHL**	**52**	**32**	**47**	**79**	**34**	**42**	**76**	**136**	**9**	**0**	**7**	**198**	**16.2**	**105**	**29**	**49**	**4**	**31**	**19**	**12**	**14**	***26**	**40**	**4**	**0**	**1**
1997-98	**Philadelphia Flyers**	**NHL**	**63**	**30**	**41**	**71**	**35**	**40**	**75**	**134**	**10**	**1**	**4**	**202**	**14.9**	**92**	**35**	**47**	**4**	**14**	**5**	**1**	**2**	**3**	**17**	**0**	**0**	**0**
	Canada	Olympics	6	2	3	5	....	....	....	2	....	....	....	....	....	....	....	....	....	....	....	....	....	....	....	....	....	....
1998-99	**Philadelphia Flyers**	**NHL**	**71**	**40**	**53**	**93**	**47**	**51**	**98**	**120**	**10**	**1**	**2**	**242**	**16.5**	**122**	**45**	**53**	**11**	**35**	....	....	....	....	....	....	....	....
99-2000	**Philadelphia Flyers**	**NHL**	**55**	**27**	**32**	**59**	**30**	**30**	**60**	**83**	**10**	**1**	**2**	**187**	**14.4**	**80**	**33**	**41**	**5**	**11**	**2**	**1**	**0**	**1**	**0**	**0**	**0**	**0**
	NHL Totals		**486**	**290**	**369**	**659**	**318**	**344**	**662**	**946**	**82**	**6**	**37**	**1644**	**17.6**	**894**	**310**	**453**	**57**		**50**	**24**	**33**	**57**	**118**	**7**	**0**	**4**

• Brother of Brett • Memorial Cup All-Star Team (1990) • WJC-A All-Star Team (1991) • Named Best Forward at WJC-A (1991) • OHL First All-Star Team (1991) • Canadian Major Junior Player of the Year (1991) • NHL All-Rookie Team (1993) • WC-A All-Star Team (1993) • Named Best Forward at WC-A (1993) • NHL First All-Star Team (1995) • Won Lester B. Pearson Award (1995) • Won Hart Trophy (1995) • NHL Second All-Star Team (1996) • Played in NHL All-Star Game (1994, 1996, 1997, 1998, 1999, 2000)

Rights traded to **Oshawa** (OHL) by **Sault Ste. Marie** (OHL) for Mike DeCoff, Jason Denomme, Mike Lenarduzzi and Oshawa's 2nd round choice in 1991 and 4th round choice (Joe Vanvolsen) in 1992 OHL Priority Draft, December 17, 1989. Traded to **Philadelphia** by **Quebec** for Peter Forsberg, Steve Duchesne, Kerry Huffman, Mike Ricci, Ron Hextall, Philadelphia's 1st round choice (Jocelyn Thibault) in 1993 Entry Draft, $15,000,000 and future considerations (Chris Simon and Philadelphia's 1st round choice (later traded to Toronto — later traded to Washington — Washington selected Nolan Baumgartner) in 1994 Entry Draft, July 21, 1992), June 30, 1992.

• LINDSAY, Bill

William Hamilton LW – L. 6', 195 lbs. b: Big Fork, MT, 5/17/1971. Quebec's 6th, 103rd overall, in 1991.

Season	Club	League	GP	G	A	Pts	AG	AA	APts	PIM	PP	SH	GW	S	%	TGF	PGF	TGA	PGA	+/-	GP	G	A	Pts	PIM	PP	SH	GW
1988-89	Vernon Lakers	BCJHL	56	24	29	53	....	....	....	166	....	....	....	....	....	....	....	....	....	....	....	....	....	....	....	....	....	....
1989-90	Tri-City Americans	WHL	72	40	45	85	....	....	....	84	....	....	....	....	....	....	....	....	....	....	7	3	0	3	17	....	....	....
1990-91	Tri-City Americans	WHL	63	46	47	93	....	....	....	151	....	....	....	....	....	....	....	....	....	....	5	3	6	9	10	....	....	....
	United States	WJC-A	7	3	5	8	....	....	....	8	....	....	....	....	....	....	....	....	....	....	....	....	....	....	....	....	....	....
1991-92	Tri-City Americans	WHL	42	34	59	93	....	....	....	81	....	....	....	....	....	....	....	....	....	....	3	2	3	5	16	....	....	....
	Quebec Nordiques	**NHL**	**23**	**2**	**4**	**6**	**2**	**3**	**5**	**14**	**0**	**0**	**1**	**35**	**5.7**	**11**	**1**	**16**	**0**	**–6**	....	....	....	....	....	....	....	....
1992-93	**Quebec Nordiques**	**NHL**	**44**	**4**	**9**	**13**	**3**	**6**	**9**	**16**	**0**	**0**	**0**	**58**	**6.9**	**24**	**0**	**36**	**12**	**0**	....	....	....	....	....	....	....	....
	Halifax Citadels	AHL	20	11	13	24	....	....	....	18	....	....	....	....	....	....	....	....	....	....	....	....	....	....	....	....	....	....
1993-94	**Florida Panthers**	**NHL**	**84**	**6**	**6**	**12**	**6**	**5**	**11**	**97**	**0**	**0**	**0**	**90**	**6.7**	**26**	**0**	**38**	**10**	**–2**	....	....	....	....	....	....	....	....
	United States	WC-A	5	3	1	4	....	....	....	2	....	....	....	....	....	....	....	....	....	....	....	....	....	....	....	....	....	....
1994-95	**Florida Panthers**	**NHL**	**48**	**10**	**9**	**19**	**18**	**13**	**31**	**46**	**0**	**1**	**0**	**63**	**15.9**	**25**	**1**	**31**	**8**	**1**	....	....	....	....	....	....	....	....
1995-96	**Florida Panthers**	**NHL**	**73**	**12**	**22**	**34**	**12**	**18**	**30**	**57**	**0**	**3**	**2**	**118**	**10.2**	**46**	**3**	**48**	**18**	**13**	**22**	**5**	**5**	**10**	**18**	**0**	**1**	**1**
1996-97	**Florida Panthers**	**NHL**	**81**	**11**	**23**	**34**	**12**	**20**	**32**	**120**	**0**	**1**	**3**	**168**	**6.5**	**42**	**1**	**63**	**23**	**1**	**3**	**0**	**1**	**1**	**8**	**0**	**0**	**0**

			REGULAR SEASON																		PLAYOFFS							
Season	Club	League	GP	G	A	Pts	AG	AA	APts	PIM	PP	SH	GW	S	%	TGF	PGF	TGA	PGA	+/–	GP	G	A	Pts	PIM	PP	SH	GW
1997-98	**Florida Panthers**	**NHL**	**82**	**12**	**16**	**28**	**14**	**16**	**30**	**80**	**0**	**2**	**5**	**150**	**8.0**	**31**	**0**	**66**	**33**	**–2**	....	....	....	....	....	....	....	....
1998-99	**Florida Panthers**	**NHL**	**75**	**12**	**15**	**27**	**14**	**14**	**28**	**92**	**0**	**1**	**2**	**135**	**8.9**	**32**	**0**	**56**	**23**	**–1**	....	....	....	....	....	....	....	....
99-2000	**Calgary Flames**	**NHL**	**80**	**8**	**12**	**20**	**9**	**11**	**20**	**86**	**0**	**0**	**2**	**147**	**5.4**	**34**	**2**	**64**	**25**	**–7**	....	....	....	....	....	....	....	....
	NHL Totals		**590**	**77**	**116**	**193**	**90**	**106**	**196**	**608**	**0**	**8**	**15**	**964**	**8.0**	**271**	**8**	**418**	**152**		**25**	**5**	**6**	**11**	**26**	**0**	**1**	**1**

WHL West Second All-Star Team (1992)

Claimed by **Florida** from **Quebec** in Expansion Draft, June 24, 1993. Traded to **Calgary** by **Florida** for Todd Simpson, September 30, 1999.

• LINDSTROM, Willy

Morgan Willy Bo "The Wisp" RW – L. 6', 180 lbs. b: Grums, Sweden, 5/5/1951.

Season	Club	League	GP	G	A	Pts	AG	AA	APts	PIM	PP	SH	GW	S	%	TGF	PGF	TGA	PGA	+/–	GP	G	A	Pts	PIM	PP	SH	GW
1967-68	Grums IK	Sweden-2	22	11	6	17	....	....	....	....	....	....	....	....	....	....	....	....	....	....	....	....	....	....	....	....	....	....
1968-69	Grums IK	Sweden-2	21	11	10	21	....	....	....	....	....	....	....	....	....	....	....	....	....	....	....	....	....	....	....	....	....	....
1969-70	Grums IK	Sweden-2	19	*30	12	42	....	....	....	....	....	....	....	....	....	....	....	....	....	....	....	....	....	....	....	....	....	....
1970-71	Vastra Frolunda	Sweden	14	7	4	11	....	....	....	10	....	....	....	....	....	....	....	....	....	....	8	3	0	3	2	....	....	....
1971-72	Vastra Frolunda	Sweden	27	12	11	23	....	....	....	18	....	....	....	....	....	....	....	....	....	....	....	....	....	....	....	....	....	....
1972-73	Vastra Frolunda	Sweden	14	7	5	12	....	....	....	14	....	....	....	....	....	....	....	....	....	....	14	6	1	7	4	....	....	....
1973-74	Vastra Frolunda	Sweden	27	19	11	30	....	....	....	22	....	....	....	....	....	....	....	....	....	....	....	....	....	....	....	....	....	....
	Sweden	Nat-Team	15	8	6	14	....	....	....	8	....	....	....	....	....	....	....	....	....	....	....	....	....	....	....	....	....	....
	Sweden	WEC-A	9	7	5	12	....	....	....	6	....	....	....	....	....	....	....	....	....	....	....	....	....	....	....	....	....	....
1974-75	Vastra Frolunda	Sweden	29	18	15	33	....	....	....	24	....	....	....	....	....	....	....	....	....	....	....	....	....	....	....	....	....	....
	Sweden	Nat-Team	27	7	5	12	....	....	....	10	....	....	....	....	....	....	....	....	....	....	....	....	....	....	....	....	....	....
	Sweden	WEC-A	7	2	1	3	....	....	....	4	....	....	....	....	....	....	....	....	....	....	....	....	....	....	....	....	....	....
1975-76	Winnipeg Jets	WHA	81	23	36	59	....	....	....	32	....	....	....	....	....	....	....	....	....	....	13	4	7	11	2	....	....	....
1976-77	Sweden	Can-Cup	1	0	0	0	....	....	....	5	....	....	....	....	....	....	....	....	....	....	....	....	....	....	....	....	....	....
	Winnipeg Jets	WHA	79	44	36	80	....	....	....	37	....	....	....	....	....	....	....	....	....	....	20	9	6	15	22	....	....	....
1977-78	Winnipeg Jets	WHA	77	30	30	60	....	....	....	42	....	....	....	....	....	....	....	....	....	....	8	3	4	7	17	....	....	....
1978-79	Winnipeg Jets	WHA	79	26	36	62	....	....	....	22	....	....	....	....	....	....	....	....	....	....	10	*10	5	15	9	....	....	....
1979-80	**Winnipeg Jets**	**NHL**	**79**	**23**	**26**	**49**	**20**	**19**	**39**	**20**	**5**	**0**	**4**	**243**	**9.5**	**91**	**36**	**79**	**5**	**–19**	....	....	....	....	....	....	....	....
1980-81	**Winnipeg Jets**	**NHL**	**72**	**22**	**13**	**35**	**17**	**9**	**26**	**45**	**7**	**0**	**1**	**163**	**13.5**	**60**	**22**	**72**	**6**	**–28**	....	....	....	....	....	....	....	....
1981-82	**Winnipeg Jets**	**NHL**	**74**	**32**	**27**	**59**	**25**	**18**	**43**	**33**	**5**	**0**	**5**	**236**	**13.6**	**87**	**17**	**59**	**0**	**11**	**4**	**2**	**1**	**3**	**2**	**0**	**0**	**0**
1982-83	**Winnipeg Jets**	**NHL**	**63**	**20**	**25**	**45**	**16**	**17**	**33**	**8**	**5**	**0**	**3**	**204**	**9.8**	**67**	**14**	**58**	**0**	**–5**	....	....	....	....	....	....	....	....
	Edmonton Oilers	**NHL**	**10**	**6**	**5**	**11**	**5**	**3**	**8**	**2**	**0**	**0**	**0**	**21**	**28.6**	**14**	**1**	**8**	**0**	**5**	**16**	**2**	**11**	**13**	**4**	**1**	**0**	**0**
1983-84♦	**Edmonton Oilers**	**NHL**	**73**	**22**	**16**	**38**	**18**	**11**	**29**	**38**	**2**	**0**	**3**	**116**	**19.0**	**68**	**13**	**38**	**0**	**17**	**19**	**5**	**5**	**10**	**10**	**3**	**0**	**0**
1984-85♦	**Edmonton Oilers**	**NHL**	**80**	**12**	**20**	**32**	**10**	**14**	**24**	**18**	**1**	**0**	**1**	**98**	**12.2**	**53**	**11**	**38**	**1**	**5**	**18**	**5**	**1**	**6**	**8**	**0**	**0**	**1**
1985-86	**Pittsburgh Penguins**	**NHL**	**71**	**14**	**17**	**31**	**11**	**11**	**22**	**30**	**0**	**0**	**1**	**87**	**16.1**	**43**	**1**	**44**	**2**	**0**	....	....	....	....	....	....	....	....
1986-87	**Pittsburgh Penguins**	**NHL**	**60**	**10**	**13**	**23**	**9**	**9**	**18**	**6**	**1**	**0**	**1**	**93**	**10.8**	**38**	**2**	**30**	**3**	**9**	....	....	....	....	....	....	....	....
1987-88	Brynas IF	Sweden	35	14	9	23	....	....	....	38	....	....	....	....	....	....	....	....	....	....	....	....	....	....	....	....	....	....
1988-89	Brynas IF Gavle	Sweden	29	12	5	17	....	....	....	26	....	....	....	....	....	....	....	....	....	....	5	3	1	4	4	....	....	....
1989-90	Brynas IF Gavle	Sweden	29	8	5	13	....	....	....	12	....	....	....	....	....	....	....	....	....	....	3	0	0	0	0	....	....	....
	NHL Totals		**582**	**161**	**162**	**323**	**131**	**111**	**242**	**200**	**26**	**0**	**19**	**1261**	**12.8**	**521**	**117**	**426**	**17**		**57**	**14**	**18**	**32**	**24**	**4**	**0**	**1**
	Other Major League Totals		316	123	138	261	....	....	....	133	....	....	....	....	....	....	....	....	....	....	51	26	22	48	50	....	....	....

Signed as a free agent by **Winnipeg** (WHA), July, 1975. Signed as a free agent by **Winnipeg**, July 25, 1979. Traded to **Edmonton** by **Winnipeg** for Laurie Boschman, March 7, 1983. Claimed by **Pittsburgh** from **Edmonton** in Waiver Draft, October 7, 1985.

• LING, David

David G. RW – R. 5'9", 185 lbs. b: Halifax, N.S., 1/9/1975. Quebec's 9th, 179th overall, in 1993.

Season	Club	League	GP	G	A	Pts	AG	AA	APts	PIM	PP	SH	GW	S	%	TGF	PGF	TGA	PGA	+/–	GP	G	A	Pts	PIM	PP	SH	GW
1991-92	Charlottetown Jr. Abbies	MJrHL	30	33	42	75	....	....	....	270	....	....	....	....	....	....	....	....	....	....	....	....	....	....	....	....	....	....
	St. Michael's Buzzers	OJHL	8	5	14	19	....	....	....	25	....	....	....	....	....	....	....	....	....	....	....	....	....	....	....	....	....	....
1992-93	Kingston Frontenacs	OHL	64	17	46	63	....	....	....	275	....	....	....	....	....	....	....	....	....	....	16	3	12	15	*72	....	....	....
1993-94	Kingston Frontenacs	OHL	61	37	40	77	....	....	....	*254	....	....	....	....	....	....	....	....	....	....	6	4	2	6	16	....	....	....
1994-95	Kingston Frontenacs	OHL	62	*61	74	135	....	....	....	136	....	....	....	....	....	....	....	....	....	....	6	7	8	15	12	....	....	....
1995-96	Saint John Flames	AHL	75	24	32	56	....	....	....	179	....	....	....	....	....	....	....	....	....	....	9	0	5	5	12	....	....	....
1996-97	Saint John Flames	AHL	5	0	2	2	....	....	....	19	....	....	....	....	....	....	....	....	....	....	....	....	....	....	....	....	....	....
	Montreal Canadiens	**NHL**	**2**	**0**	**0**	**0**	**0**	**0**	**0**	**0**	**0**	**0**	**0**	**0**	**0.0**	**0**	**0**	**0**	**0**	**0**	....	....	....	....	....	....	....	....
	Fredericton Canadiens	AHL	48	22	36	58	....	....	....	229	....	....	....	....	....	....	....	....	....	....	....	....	....	....	....	....	....	....
1997-98	**Montreal Canadiens**	**NHL**	**1**	**0**	**0**	**0**	**0**	**0**	**0**	**0**	**0**	**0**	**0**	**1**	**0.0**	**0**	**0**	**1**	**0**	**–1**	....	....	....	....	....	....	....	....
	Fredericton Canadiens	AHL	67	25	41	66	....	....	....	148	....	....	....	....	....	....	....	....	....	....	....	....	....	....	....	....	....	....
	Indianapolis Ice	IHL	12	8	6	14	....	....	....	30	....	....	....	....	....	....	....	....	....	....	5	4	1	5	31	....	....	....
1998-99	Kansas City Blades	IHL	82	30	42	72	....	....	....	112	....	....	....	....	....	....	....	....	....	....	3	1	0	1	20	....	....	....
99-2000	Kansas City Blades	IHL	82	35	48	83	....	....	....	210	....	....	....	....	....	....	....	....	....	....	....	....	....	....	....	....	....	....
	NHL Totals		**3**	**0**	**0**	**0**	**0**	**0**	**0**	**0**	**0**	**0**	**0**	**1**	**0.0**	**0**	**0**	**1**	**0**		....	....	....	....	....	....	....	....

OHL First All-Star Team (1995) • Canadian Major Junior First All-Star Team (1995) • Canadian Junior Player of the Year (1995) • IHL First All-Star Team (2000)

Rights transferred to **Colorado** after **Quebec** franchise relocated, June 21, 1995. Traded to **Calgary** by **Colorado** with Colorado's 9th round choice (Steve Shirreffs) in 1995 Entry Draft for Calgary's 9th round choice (Chris George) in 1995 Entry Draft, July 7, 1995. Traded to **Montreal** by **Calgary** with Calgary's 6th round choice (Gordie Dwyer) in 1998 Entry Draft for Scott Fraser, October 24, 1996. Traded to **Chicago** by **Montreal** for Martin Gendron, March 14, 1998. Signed as a free agent by **Kansas City** (IHL), September 3, 1998.

• LINSEMAN, Ken

"The Rat" C – L. 5'11", 180 lbs. b: Kingston, Ont., 8/11/1958. Philadelphia's 2nd, 7th overall, in 1978.

Season	Club	League	GP	G	A	Pts	AG	AA	APts	PIM	PP	SH	GW	S	%	TGF	PGF	TGA	PGA	+/–	GP	G	A	Pts	PIM	PP	SH	GW
1974-75	Kingston Canadians	OMJHL	59	19	28	47	....	....	....	70	....	....	....	....	....	....	....	....	....	....	8	2	5	7	8	....	....	....
1975-76	Kingston Canadians	OMJHL	65	61	51	112	....	....	....	92	....	....	....	....	....	....	....	....	....	....	7	5	0	5	18	....	....	....
1976-77	Kingston Canadians	OMJHL	63	53	74	127	....	....	....	210	....	....	....	....	....	....	....	....	....	....	10	9	12	21	54	....	....	....
1977-78	Birmingham Bulls	WHA	71	38	38	76	....	....	....	126	....	....	....	....	....	....	....	....	....	....	5	2	2	4	15	....	....	....
1978-79	**Philadelphia Flyers**	**NHL**	**30**	**5**	**20**	**25**	**4**	**14**	**18**	**23**	**1**	**0**	**1**	**57**	**8.8**	**36**	**8**	**14**	**2**	**16**	**8**	**2**	**6**	**8**	**22**	**0**	**0**	**1**
	Maine Mariners	AHL	38	17	22	39	....	....	....	106	....	....	....	....	....	....	....	....	....	....	....	....	....	....	....	....	....	....
1979-80	**Philadelphia Flyers**	**NHL**	**80**	**22**	**57**	**79**	**19**	**42**	**61**	**107**	**2**	**0**	**4**	**168**	**13.1**	**100**	**20**	**56**	**2**	**26**	**17**	**4**	***18**	**22**	**40**	**0**	**0**	**1**
1980-81	**Philadelphia Flyers**	**NHL**	**51**	**17**	**30**	**47**	**13**	**20**	**33**	**150**	**1**	**1**	**1**	**126**	**13.5**	**61**	**15**	**45**	**8**	**9**	**12**	**4**	**16**	**20**	**67**	**0**	**0**	**3**
1981-82	Canada	Can-Cup	4	0	1	1	....	....	....	4	....	....	....	....	....	....	....	....	....	....	....	....	....	....	....	....	....	....
	Philadelphia Flyers	**NHL**	**79**	**24**	**68**	**92**	**19**	**45**	**64**	**275**	**2**	**3**	**0**	**212**	**11.3**	**109**	**29**	**95**	**21**	**6**	**4**	**1**	**2**	**3**	**6**	**1**	**0**	**0**
1982-83	**Edmonton Oilers**	**NHL**	**72**	**33**	**42**	**75**	**27**	**29**	**56**	**181**	**10**	**4**	**3**	**141**	**23.4**	**121**	**34**	**87**	**16**	**16**	**16**	**6**	**8**	**14**	**22**	**1**	**0**	**1**
1983-84♦	**Edmonton Oilers**	**NHL**	**72**	**18**	**49**	**67**	**14**	**33**	**47**	**119**	**5**	**1**	**2**	**105**	**17.1**	**101**	**22**	**62**	**13**	**30**	**19**	**10**	**4**	**14**	**65**	**3**	**1**	**4**
1984-85	**Boston Bruins**	**NHL**	**74**	**25**	**49**	**74**	**20**	**33**	**53**	**126**	**5**	**1**	**5**	**162**	**15.4**	**110**	**39**	**56**	**7**	**22**	**5**	**4**	**6**	**10**	**8**	**0**	**0**	**1**
1985-86	**Boston Bruins**	**NHL**	**64**	**23**	**58**	**81**	**18**	**39**	**57**	**97**	**8**	**0**	**3**	**132**	**17.4**	**119**	**54**	**62**	**12**	**15**	**3**	**0**	**1**	**1**	**17**	**0**	**0**	**0**
1986-87	**Boston Bruins**	**NHL**	**64**	**15**	**34**	**49**	**13**	**25**	**38**	**126**	**3**	**0**	**3**	**94**	**16.0**	**78**	**14**	**49**	**0**	**15**	**4**	**1**	**1**	**2**	**22**	**0**	**0**	**0**
1987-88	**Boston Bruins**	**NHL**	**77**	**29**	**45**	**74**	**25**	**32**	**57**	**167**	**7**	**0**	**5**	**150**	**19.3**	**120**	**36**	**65**	**17**	**36**	**23**	**11**	**14**	**25**	**56**	**4**	**1**	**0**
1988-89	**Boston Bruins**	**NHL**	**78**	**27**	**45**	**72**	**23**	**32**	**55**	**164**	**13**	**1**	**2**	**159**	**17.0**	**107**	**44**	**67**	**19**	**15**	....	....	....	....	....	....	....	....
1989-90	**Boston Bruins**	**NHL**	**32**	**6**	**16**	**22**	**5**	**11**	**16**	**66**	**1**	**0**	**0**	**47**	**12.8**	**40**	**11**	**20**	**3**	**12**	....	....	....	....	....	....	....	....
	Philadelphia Flyers	**NHL**	**29**	**5**	**9**	**14**	**4**	**6**	**10**	**30**	**1**	**0**	**0**	**32**	**15.6**	**22**	**8**	**26**	**5**	**–7**	....	....	....	....	....	....	....	....
1990-91	**Edmonton Oilers**	**NHL**	**56**	**7**	**29**	**36**	**6**	**22**	**28**	**94**	**2**	**1**	**0**	**49**	**14.3**	**53**	**7**	**36**	**5**	**15**	**2**	**0**	**1**	**1**	**0**	**0**	**0**	**0**
1991-92	**Toronto Maple Leafs**	**NHL**	**2**	**0**	**0**	**0**	**0**	**0**	**0**	**2**	**0**	**0**	**0**	**0**	**0.0**	**0**	**0**	**2**	**0**	**–2**	....	....	....	....	....	....	....	....
	HC Asiago	Italy	5	3	3	6	....	....	....	4	....	....	....	....	....	....	....	....	....	....	7	3	4	7	47	....	....	....
	NHL Totals		**860**	**256**	**551**	**807**	**210**	**383**	**593**	**1727**	**61**	**12**	**29**	**1634**	**15.7**	**1177**	**341**	**742**	**130**		**113**	**43**	**77**	**120**	**325**	**9**	**2**	**11**
	Other Major League Totals		71	38	38	76	....	....	....	126	....	....	....	....	....	....	....	....	....	....	5	2	2	4	15	....	....	....

OMJHL Second All-Star Team (1977)

Traded to **Hartford** by **Philadelphia** with Greg C. Adams and Philadelphia's 1st (David Jensen) and 3rd (Leif Karlsson) round choices in 1982 Entry Draft for Mark Howe and Hartford's 3rd round choice (Derrick Smith) in 1983 Entry Draft, August 19, 1982. Traded to **Edmonton** by **Harford** with Dan Nachbaur for Risto Siltanen and the rights to Brent Loney, August 19, 1982. Traded to **Boston** by **Edmonton** for Mike Krushelnyski, June 21, 1984. Traded to **Philadelphia** by **Boston** for Dave Poulin, January 16, 1990. Signed as a free agent by **Edmonton**, August 31, 1990. Traded to **Toronto** by **Edmonton** for cash, October 7, 1991.

Season	Club	League	GP	G	A	Pts	AG	AA	APts	PIM	PP	SH	GW	S	%	TGF	PGF	TGA	PGA	+/–	GP	G	A	Pts	PIM	PP	SH	GW
										REGULAR SEASON											PLAYOFFS							

• LINTNER, Richard

D – R. 6'3", 214 lbs. b: Trencin, Czech., 11/15/1977. Phoenix's 4th, 119th overall, in 1996.

Season	Club	League	GP	G	A	Pts	AG	AA	APts	PIM	PP	SH	GW	S	%	TGF	PGF	TGA	PGA	+/–	GP	G	A	Pts	PIM	PP	SH	GW
1994-95	Dukla Trencin	Slovakia-Jr.	42	12	13	25				20																		
1995-96	Dukla Trencin	Slovakia-Jr.	30	15	17	32				210																		
	Dukla Trencin	Slovakia	2	0	0	0				0																		
	Slovakia	WJC-A	6	0	1	1				12																		
1996-97	Spisska Nova Ves	Slovakia	35	2	1	3																						
	Slovakia	WJC-A	6	2	1	3				22																		
1997-98	Springfield Falcons	AHL	71	6	9	15				61											3	1	1	2	4			
1998-99	Springfield Falcons	AHL	8	0	1	1				16																		
	Milwaukee Admirals	IHL	66	9	16	25				75																		
99-2000	Milwaukee Admirals	IHL	31	13	8	21				37																		
	Nashville Predators	**NHL**	**33**	**1**	**5**	**6**	**1**	**5**	**6**	**22**	**0**	**0**	**0**	**58**	**1.7**	**17**	**4**	**19**	**0**	**–6**								
	NHL Totals		**33**	**1**	**5**	**6**	**1**	**5**	**6**	**22**	**0**	**0**	**0**	**58**	**1.7**	**17**	**4**	**19**	**0**									

Traded to **Nashville** by **Phoenix** with Cliff Ronning for future considerations, October 31, 1998.

• LIPUMA, Chris

Christopher Paul D – L. 6', 183 lbs. b: Bridgeview, IL, 3/23/1971.

Season	Club	League	GP	G	A	Pts	AG	AA	APts	PIM	PP	SH	GW	S	%	TGF	PGF	TGA	PGA	+/–	GP	G	A	Pts	PIM	PP	SH	GW
1987-88	Chicago Young Americans	USAHA	19	6	16	22				31																		
1988-89	Kitchener Dutchmen	OJHL	2	0	0	0				17																		
	Kitchener Rangers	OHL	59	7	13	20				101																		
1989-90	Kitchener Rangers	OHL	63	11	26	37				125											17	1	4	5	6			
	Kitchener Rangers	Mem-Cup	5	0	1	1				4																		
1990-91	Kitchener Rangers	OHL	61	6	30	36				145											4	0	1	1	4			
1991-92	Kitchener Rangers	OHL	61	13	59	72				115											14	4	9	13	34			
1992-93	**Tampa Bay Lightning**	**NHL**	**15**	**0**	**5**	**5**	**0**	**3**	**3**	**34**	**0**	**0**	**0**	**17**	**0.0**	**11**	**0**	**16**	**6**	**1**								
	Atlanta Knights	IHL	66	4	14	18				379											9	1	1	2	35			
1993-94	**Tampa Bay Lightning**	**NHL**	**27**	**0**	**4**	**4**	**0**	**3**	**3**	**77**	**0**	**0**	**0**	**20**	**0.0**	**21**	**0**	**22**	**2**	**1**								
	Atlanta Knights	IHL	42	2	10	12				254											11	1	1	2	28			
1994-95	Atlanta Knights	IHL	41	5	12	17				191																		
	Tampa Bay Lightning	**NHL**	**1**	**0**	**0**	**0**	**0**	**0**	**0**	**0**	**0**	**0**	**0**	**1**	**0.0**	**2**	**0**	**0**	**0**	**2**								
	Nashville Knights	ECHL	1	0	0	0				0																		
1995-96	**Tampa Bay Lightning**	**NHL**	**21**	**0**	**0**	**0**	**0**	**0**	**0**	**13**	**0**	**0**	**0**	**8**	**0.0**	**3**	**0**	**11**	**1**	**–7**								
	Atlanta Knights	IHL	48	5	11	16				146																		
1996-97	**San Jose Sharks**	**NHL**	**8**	**0**	**0**	**0**	**0**	**0**	**0**	**22**	**0**	**0**	**0**	**4**	**0.0**	**3**	**0**	**6**	**1**	**–2**								
	Kentucky Thoroughblades	AHL	48	6	17	23				93											4	0	3	3	6			
1997-98	Orlando Solar Bears	IHL	13	1	4	5				63																		
	San Antonio Dragons	IHL	60	1	10	11				116																		
1998-99	Chicago Wolves	IHL	34	0	10	10				186																		
99-2000	Chicago Wolves	IHL	42	0	4	4				98											5	0	0	0	8			
	NHL Totals		**72**	**0**	**9**	**9**	**0**	**6**	**6**	**146**	**0**	**0**	**0**	**50**	**0.0**	**40**	**0**	**55**	**10**									

Signed as a free agent by **Tampa Bay**, June 29, 1992. Signed as a free agent by **San Jose**, August 23, 1996. Claimed on waivers by **New Jersey** from **San Jose**, March 18, 1997. Signed as a free agent by **Chicago** (IHL), September 8, 1998.

• LOACH, Lonnie

LW – L. 5'10", 181 lbs. b: New Liskeard, Ont., 4/14/1968. Chicago's 4th, 98th overall, in 1986.

Season	Club	League	GP	G	A	Pts	AG	AA	APts	PIM	PP	SH	GW	S	%	TGF	PGF	TGA	PGA	+/–	GP	G	A	Pts	PIM	PP	SH	GW
1982-83	New Liskeard Cubs	NOHA	1	1	0	1				2																		
1983-84	New Liskeard Cubs	NOHA	30	17	26	43				39																		
1984-85	Haileybury 54's	NOHA	2	0	0	0				0																		
	St. Mary's Lincolns	OJHL-B	44	26	36	62				113																		
1985-86	Guelph Platers	OHL	65	41	42	83				63											20	7	8	15	16			
	Guelph Platers	Mem-Cup	4	1	3	4				0																		
1986-87	Guelph Platers	OHL	56	31	24	55				42											5	2	1	3	2			
1987-88	Guelph Platers	OHL	66	43	49	92				75																		
1988-89	Flint Spirits	IHL	41	22	26	48				30																		
	Saginaw Hawks	IHL	32	7	6	13				27																		
1989-90	Canada	Nat-Team	9	3	1	4				2																		
	Indianapolis Ice	IHL	3	0	0	0				0																		
	Fort Wayne Komets	IHL	54	15	33	48				40											5	4	2	6	15			
1990-91	Fort Wayne Komets	IHL	81	55	76	*131				45											19	5	11	16	13			
1991-92	Adirondack Red Wings	AHL	67	37	49	86				69											19	*13	4	17	10			
1992-93	**Ottawa Senators**	**NHL**	**3**	**0**	**0**	**0**	**0**	**0**	**0**	**0**	**0**	**0**	**0**	**3**	**0.0**	**1**	**1**	**0**	**0**	**0**								
	Los Angeles Kings	**NHL**	**50**	**10**	**13**	**23**	**8**	**9**	**17**	**27**	**1**	**0**	**0**	**55**	**18.2**	**31**	**7**	**21**	**0**	**3**	**1**	**0**	**0**	**0**	**0**	**0**	**0**	**0**
	Phoenix Roadrunners	IHL	4	2	3	5				10																		
1993-94	**Mighty Ducks of Anaheim**	**NHL**	**3**	**0**	**0**	**0**	**0**	**0**	**0**	**2**	**0**	**0**	**0**	**8**	**0.0**	**0**	**0**	**2**	**0**	**–2**								
	San Diego Gulls	IHL	74	42	49	91				65											9	4	10	14	6			
1994-95	San Diego Gulls	IHL	13	3	10	13				21																		
	Detroit Vipers	IHL	64	32	43	75				45											3	2	1	3	2			
1995-96	Detroit Vipers	IHL	79	35	51	86				75											11	1	5	6	8			
1996-97	San Antonio Dragons	IHL	70	24	37	61				45											9	1	3	4	10			
1997-98	ZSC Lions Zurich	Switz.	15	2	5	7				6																		
	San Antonio Dragons	IHL	52	7	29	36				22																		
1998-99	HK Olimpija Ljubjana	Alpenliga	11	4	10	14				12																		
	Long Beach Ice Dogs	IHL	30	12	9	21				18																		
	Kansas City Blades	IHL	22	9	5	14				6											3	1	0	1	0			
99-2000	Missouri River Otters	UHL	58	29	56	85				20											3	3	2	5	2			
	Chicago Wolves	IHL	1	0	0	0				0											8	0	3	3	0			
	NHL Totals		**56**	**10**	**13**	**23**	**8**	**9**	**17**	**29**	**1**	**0**	**0**	**66**	**15.2**	**32**	**8**	**23**	**0**		**1**	**0**	**0**	**0**	**0**	**0**	**0**	**0**

IHL Second All-Star Team (1991) • Won Leo P. Lamoureux Memorial Trophy (Leading Scorer - IHL) (1991)

Signed as a free agent by **Detroit**, June 7, 1991. Claimed by **Ottawa** from **Detroit** in Expansion Draft, June 18, 1992. Claimed on waivers by **LA Kings** from **Ottawa**, October 21, 1992. Claimed by **Anaheim** from **LA Kings** in Expansion Draft, June 24, 1993.

• LOCHEAD, Bill

William Alexander "Whip" LW – R. 6'1", 195 lbs. b: Forest, Ont., 10/13/1954. Detroit's 1st, 9th overall, in 1974.

Season	Club	League	GP	G	A	Pts	AG	AA	APts	PIM	PP	SH	GW	S	%	TGF	PGF	TGA	PGA	+/–	GP	G	A	Pts	PIM	PP	SH	GW
1971-72	Oshawa Generals	OMJHL	37	27	20	47				62											11	2	2	4	21			
1972-73	Oshawa Generals	OMJHL	59	56	54	110				89																		
1973-74	Oshawa Generals	OMJHL	62	57	64	121				108																		
1974-75	**Detroit Red Wings**	**NHL**	**65**	**16**	**12**	**28**	**14**	**9**	**23**	**34**	**3**	**0**	**2**	**116**	**13.8**	**46**	**16**	**60**	**0**	**–30**								
1975-76	**Detroit Red Wings**	**NHL**	**53**	**9**	**11**	**20**	**8**	**8**	**16**	**22**	**0**	**0**	**3**	**81**	**11.1**	**28**	**6**	**37**	**0**	**–15**								
	New Haven Nighthawks	AHL	24	17	13	30				24																		
1976-77	**Detroit Red Wings**	**NHL**	**61**	**16**	**14**	**30**	**14**	**11**	**25**	**39**	**4**	**0**	**3**	**127**	**12.6**	**46**	**12**	**45**	**0**	**–11**								
	Kansas City Blues	CHL	10	8	8	16				0																		
1977-78	**Detroit Red Wings**	**NHL**	**77**	**20**	**16**	**36**	**18**	**12**	**30**	**47**	**2**	**0**	**4**	**124**	**16.1**	**55**	**8**	**41**	**0**	**6**	**7**	**3**	**0**	**3**	**6**	**0**	**0**	**1**
1978-79	**Detroit Red Wings**	**NHL**	**40**	**4**	**7**	**11**	**3**	**5**	**8**	**20**	**0**	**0**	**0**	**33**	**12.1**	**16**	**1**	**19**	**0**	**–4**								
	Colorado Rockies	**NHL**	**27**	**4**	**2**	**6**	**3**	**1**	**4**	**14**	**1**	**1**	**0**	**64**	**6.3**	**12**	**6**	**21**	**0**	**–15**								
1979-80	**New York Rangers**	**NHL**	**7**	**0**	**0**	**0**	**0**	**0**	**0**	**4**	**0**	**0**	**0**	**3**	**0.0**	**0**	**0**	**5**	**0**	**–5**								
	New Haven Nighthawks	AHL	68	46	43	89				90											10	6	5	11	8			
1980-81	ESV Kaufbeuren	Germany	21	27	25	52				59																		
	EC Kolner	Germany	14	12	7	19				48											3	4	1	5	13			
1981-82	VfL Bad Nauheim	Germany	42	*66	34	100				*195																		
1982-83	Mannheimer ERC	Germany	34	36	24	60				117																		
1983-84	Mannheimer ERC	Germany	47	36	27	63				77																		

Season	Club	League	REGULAR SEASON																			PLAYOFFS							
			GP	G	A	Pts	AG	AA	APts	PIM	PP	SH	GW	S	%	TGF	PGF	TGA	PGA	+/–	GP	G	A	Pts	PIM	PP	SH	GW
1984-85	EHC Chur	Switz.	5	1	3	4	....	....	....	....	....	....	....	....	....	....	....	....	....	....	....	....	....	....	....	....	....	....
	EC Bad Nauheim	Germany	16	28	20	48	....	....	....	61	....	....	....	....	....	....	....	....	....	....	....	....	....	....	....	....	....	....
1985-86	EC Bad Nauheim	Germany-2	45	71	49	120	....	....	....	....	....	....	....	....	....	....	....	....	....	....	10	*37	16	53	....	....	....	....
1986-87	WEV Wein	Austria	19	12	8	20	....	....	....	24	....	....	....	....	....	....	....	....	....	....	....	....	....	....	....	....	....	....
1987-1988	EV Regensburg	Germany-2	DID NOT PLAY – COACHING																									
1987-1989	ESC Wolfsburg	Germany-2	DID NOT PLAY – COACHING																									
1989-1991	London Knights	OHL	DID NOT PLAY – COACHING																									
1991-1992	EHC Solohurn	Switz-2	DID NOT PLAY – COACHING																									
1992-1993	EHC Olten	Switz.	DID NOT PLAY – COACHING																									
1993-1994	ECD Sauerland	Germany-2	DID NOT PLAY – COACHING																									
1994-1997	Ratinger Lowen	Germany	DID NOT PLAY – COACHING																									
1997-2000	Kassel Huskies	Germany	DID NOT PLAY – COACHING																									
	NHL Totals		**330**	**69**	**62**	**131**	**60**	**46**	**106**	**180**	**10**	**1**	**12**	**548**	**12.6**	**203**	**49**	**228**	**0**		**7**	**3**	**0**	**3**	**6**	**0**	**0**	**1**

OMJHL Second All-Star Team (1973) • OMJHL First All-Star Team (1974) • AHL First All-Star Team (1980)

Claimed on waivers by **Colorado** from **Detroit**, February 9, 1979. Traded to **NY Rangers** by **Colorado** for the rights to Hardy Astrom, July 2, 1979.

• LOEWEN, Darcy

LW – L. 5'10", 185 lbs. b: Calgary, Alta., 2/26/1969. Buffalo's 2nd, 55th overall, in 1988.

Season	Club	League	GP	G	A	Pts	AG	AA	APts	PIM	PP	SH	GW	S	%	TGF	PGF	TGA	PGA	+/–	GP	G	A	Pts	PIM	PP	SH	GW
1985-86	Red Deer Chiefs	AAHA	41	19	33	52	....	....	....	240	....	....	....	....	....	....	....	....	....	....	....	....	....	....	....	....	....	....
	Spokane Chiefs	WHL	8	2	1	3	....	....	....	19	....	....	....	....	....	....	....	....	....	....	....	....	....	....	....	....	....	....
1986-87	Spokane Chiefs	WHL	68	15	25	40	....	....	....	129	....	....	....	....	....	....	....	....	....	....	5	0	0	0	16	....	....	....
1987-88	Spokane Chiefs	WHL	72	30	44	74	....	....	....	231	....	....	....	....	....	....	....	....	....	....	15	7	5	12	54	....	....	....
1988-89	Spokane Chiefs	WHL	60	31	27	58	....	....	....	194	....	....	....	....	....	....	....	....	....	....	....	....	....	....	....	....	....	....
	Canada	Nat-Team	2	0	0	0	....	....	....	0	....	....	....	....	....	....	....	....	....	....	....	....	....	....	....	....	....	....
	Canada	WJC-A	7	1	1	2	....	....	....	12	....	....	....	....	....	....	....	....	....	....	....	....	....	....	....	....	....	....
1989-90	**Buffalo Sabres**	**NHL**	**4**	**0**	**0**	**0**	**0**	**0**	**0**	**4**	**0**	**0**	**0**	**1**	**0.0**	**1**	**0**	**4**	**0**	**–3**	....	....	....	....	....	....	....	....
	Rochester Americans	AHL	50	7	11	18	....	....	....	193	....	....	....	....	....	....	....	....	....	....	5	1	0	1	6	....	....	....
1990-91	**Buffalo Sabres**	**NHL**	**6**	**0**	**0**	**0**	**0**	**0**	**0**	**8**	**0**	**0**	**0**	**2**	**0.0**	**2**	**0**	**7**	**1**	**–4**	....	....	....	....	....	....	....	....
	Rochester Americans	AHL	71	13	15	28	....	....	....	130	....	....	....	....	....	....	....	....	....	....	15	1	5	6	14	....	....	....
1991-92	**Buffalo Sabres**	**NHL**	**2**	**0**	**0**	**0**	**0**	**0**	**0**	**2**	**0**	**0**	**0**	**1**	**0.0**	**0**	**0**	**0**	**0**	**0**	....	....	....	....	....	....	....	....
	Rochester Americans	AHL	73	11	20	31	....	....	....	193	....	....	....	....	....	....	....	....	....	....	4	0	1	1	8	....	....	....
1992-93	**Ottawa Senators**	**NHL**	**79**	**4**	**5**	**9**	**3**	**3**	**6**	**145**	**0**	**0**	**0**	**42**	**9.5**	**17**	**0**	**65**	**22**	**–26**	....	....	....	....	....	....	....	....
1993-94	**Ottawa Senators**	**NHL**	**44**	**0**	**3**	**3**	**0**	**2**	**2**	**52**	**0**	**0**	**0**	**39**	**0.0**	**10**	**0**	**27**	**6**	**–11**	....	....	....	....	....	....	....	....
1994-95	Las Vegas Thunder	IHL	64	9	21	30	....	....	....	183	....	....	....	....	....	....	....	....	....	....	7	1	1	2	16	....	....	....
1995-96	Las Vegas Thunder	IHL	72	14	23	37	....	....	....	198	....	....	....	....	....	....	....	....	....	....	....	....	....	....	....	....	....	....
1996-97	Las Vegas Thunder	IHL	76	14	19	33	....	....	....	177	....	....	....	....	....	....	....	....	....	....	3	0	0	0	0	....	....	....
1997-98	Las Vegas Thunder	IHL	42	4	6	10	....	....	....	117	....	....	....	....	....	....	....	....	....	....	....	....	....	....	....	....	....	....
	Utah Grizzlies	IHL	34	1	7	8	....	....	....	99	....	....	....	....	....	....	....	....	....	....	4	0	1	1	15	....	....	....
1998-99	Nottingham Panthers	BH-Cup	4	0	2	2	....	....	....	0	....	....	....	....	....	....	....	....	....	....	....	....	....	....	....	....	....	....
	Nottingham Panthers	Britain	27	3	3	6	....	....	....	35	....	....	....	....	....	....	....	....	....	....	8	0	3	3	31	....	....	....
	Idaho Steelheads	WCHL	3	1	2	3	....	....	....	21	....	....	....	....	....	....	....	....	....	....	....	....	....	....	....	....	....	....
99-2000	Idaho Steelheads	WCHL	62	9	16	25	....	....	....	62	....	....	....	....	....	....	....	....	....	....	3	0	0	0	0	....	....	....
	NHL Totals		**135**	**4**	**8**	**12**	**3**	**5**	**8**	**211**	**0**	**0**	**0**	**85**	**4.7**	**30**	**0**	**103**	**29**		....	....	....	....	....	....	....	....

Claimed by **Ottawa** from **Buffalo** in Expansion Draft, June 18, 1992. • Offically announced retirement, June 2, 2000.

• LOFTHOUSE, Mark

Mark Allen RW/C – R. 6'2", 195 lbs. b: New Westminster, B.C., 4/21/1957. Washington's 2nd, 21st overall, in 1977.

Season	Club	League	GP	G	A	Pts	AG	AA	APts	PIM	PP	SH	GW	S	%	TGF	PGF	TGA	PGA	+/–	GP	G	A	Pts	PIM	PP	SH	GW
1973-74	Kelowna Buckaroos	BCJHL	62	44	42	86	....	....	....	59	....	....	....	....	....	....	....	....	....	....	17	5	5	10	26	....	....	....
1974-75	New Westminster Bruins	WCJHL	61	36	28	64	....	....	....	53	....	....	....	....	....	....	....	....	....	....	17	5	5	10	26	....	....	....
	New Westminster Bruins	Mem-Cup	3	1	3	4	....	....	....	2	....	....	....	....	....	....	....	....	....	....	....	....	....	....	....	....	....	....
1975-76	New Westminster Bruins	WCJHL	72	68	48	116	....	....	....	55	....	....	....	....	....	....	....	....	....	....	17	9	12	21	22	....	....	....
	New Westminster Bruins	Mem-Cup	4	4	2	6	....	....	....	2	....	....	....	....	....	....	....	....	....	....	....	....	....	....	....	....	....	....
1976-77	New Westminster Bruins	WCJHL	70	54	58	112	....	....	....	59	....	....	....	....	....	....	....	....	....	....	14	10	8	18	19	....	....	....
	New Westminster Bruins	Mem-Cup	6	*6	4	10	....	....	....	10	....	....	....	....	....	....	....	....	....	....	....	....	....	....	....	....	....	....
1977-78	**Washington Capitals**	**NHL**	**18**	**2**	**1**	**3**	**2**	**1**	**3**	**8**	**0**	**0**	**0**	**21**	**9.5**	**6**	**2**	**9**	**0**	**–5**	....	....	....	....	....	....	....	....
	Hershey Bears	AHL	35	8	6	14	....	....	....	39	....	....	....	....	....	....	....	....	....	....	....	....	....	....	....	....	....	....
	Salt Lake Golden Eagles	CHL	13	0	1	1	....	....	....	4	....	....	....	....	....	....	....	....	....	....	5	0	1	1	6	....	....	....
1978-79	**Washington Capitals**	**NHL**	**52**	**13**	**10**	**23**	**11**	**7**	**18**	**10**	**1**	**0**	**0**	**75**	**17.3**	**29**	**4**	**36**	**0**	**–11**	....	....	....	....	....	....	....	....
	Hershey Bears	AHL	16	7	7	14	....	....	....	6	....	....	....	....	....	....	....	....	....	....	4	0	1	1	2	....	....	....
1979-80	**Washington Capitals**	**NHL**	**68**	**15**	**18**	**33**	**13**	**13**	**26**	**20**	**1**	**0**	**1**	**138**	**10.9**	**51**	**8**	**56**	**4**	**–9**	....	....	....	....	....	....	....	....
	Hershey Bears	AHL	9	7	3	10	....	....	....	6	....	....	....	....	....	....	....	....	....	....	....	....	....	....	....	....	....	....
1980-81	**Washington Capitals**	**NHL**	**3**	**1**	**1**	**2**	**1**	**1**	**2**	**4**	**0**	**0**	**0**	**3**	**33.3**	**2**	**0**	**2**	**0**	**0**	....	....	....	....	....	....	....	....
	Hershey Bears	AHL	72	*48	55	*103	....	....	....	131	....	....	....	....	....	....	....	....	....	....	10	6	9	15	24	....	....	....
1981-82	**Detroit Red Wings**	**NHL**	**12**	**3**	**4**	**7**	**2**	**3**	**5**	**13**	**0**	**0**	**0**	**21**	**14.3**	**8**	**1**	**14**	**0**	**–7**	....	....	....	....	....	....	....	....
	Adirondack Red Wings	AHL	69	33	38	71	....	....	....	75	....	....	....	....	....	....	....	....	....	....	5	2	3	5	2	....	....	....
1982-83	**Detroit Red Wings**	**NHL**	**28**	**8**	**4**	**12**	**7**	**3**	**10**	**18**	**0**	**0**	**0**	**37**	**21.6**	**22**	**4**	**10**	**0**	**8**	....	....	....	....	....	....	....	....
	Adirondack Red Wings	AHL	39	27	18	45	....	....	....	20	....	....	....	....	....	....	....	....	....	....	....	....	....	....	....	....	....	....
1983-84	New Haven Nighthawks	AHL	79	37	64	101	....	....	....	45	....	....	....	....	....	....	....	....	....	....	....	....	....	....	....	....	....	....
1984-85	ZSC Zurich	Switz-2	30	24	24	48	....	....	....	....	....	....	....	....	....	....	....	....	....	....	....	....	....	....	....	....	....	....
	New Haven Nighthawks	AHL	12	11	4	15	....	....	....	4	....	....	....	....	....	....	....	....	....	....	....	....	....	....	....	....	....	....
1985-86	New Haven Nighthawks	AHL	70	32	35	67	....	....	....	56	....	....	....	....	....	....	....	....	....	....	5	2	1	3	0	....	....	....
1986-87	New Haven Nighthawks	AHL	47	18	27	45	....	....	....	34	....	....	....	....	....	....	....	....	....	....	4	0	1	1	2	....	....	....
1987-88	Hershey Bears	AHL	51	21	21	42	....	....	....	64	....	....	....	....	....	....	....	....	....	....	10	6	5	11	6	....	....	....
1988-89	Hershey Bears	AHL	74	32	47	79	....	....	....	71	....	....	....	....	....	....	....	....	....	....	12	3	4	7	20	....	....	....
	NHL Totals		**181**	**42**	**38**	**80**	**36**	**28**	**64**	**73**	**2**	**0**	**1**	**295**	**14.2**	**118**	**19**	**127**	**4**		....	....	....	....	....	....	....	....

WCJHL Second All-Star Team (1977) • Memorial Cup All-Star Team (1977) • AHL First All-Star Team (1981) • Won John B. Sollenberger Trophy (Top Scorer - AHL) (1981) • AHL Second All-Star Team (1984)

Traded to **Detroit** by **Washington** for Al Jensen, July 23, 1981. Signed as a free agent by **LA Kings**, August 10, 1983. Signed as a free agent by **Philadelphia**, August 15, 1987.

• LOGAN, Dave

David George D – L. 5'10", 190 lbs. b: Montreal, Que., 7/2/1954. Chicago's 5th, 88th overall, in 1974.

Season	Club	League	GP	G	A	Pts	AG	AA	APts	PIM	PP	SH	GW	S	%	TGF	PGF	TGA	PGA	+/–	GP	G	A	Pts	PIM	PP	SH	GW
1971-72	Montreal Jr. Canadiens	OMJHL	57	20	17	37	....	....	....	53	....	....	....	....	....	....	....	....	....	....	....	....	....	....	....	....	....	....
1972-73	Montreal Red-White-Blue	QMJHL	5	1	5	6	....	....	....	2	....	....	....	....	....	....	....	....	....	....	....	....	....	....	....	....	....	....
1973-74	Laval Nationale	QMJHL	65	21	41	62	....	....	....	156	....	....	....	....	....	....	....	....	....	....	11	2	2	4	36	....	....	....
1974-75	Dallas Black Hawks	CHL	74	7	18	25	....	....	....	239	....	....	....	....	....	....	....	....	....	....	10	0	3	3	48	....	....	....
1975-76	**Chicago Black Hawks**	**NHL**	**2**	**0**	**0**	**0**	**0**	**0**	**0**	**0**	**0**	**0**	**0**	**0**	**0.0**	**0**	**0**	**1**	**0**	**–1**	....	....	....	....	....	....	....	....
	Dallas Black Hawks	CHL	40	3	11	14	....	....	....	131	....	....	....	....	....	....	....	....	....	....	10	0	3	3	*68	....	....	....
1976-77	**Chicago Black Hawks**	**NHL**	**34**	**0**	**2**	**2**	**0**	**2**	**2**	**61**	**0**	**0**	**0**	**36**	**0.0**	**12**	**0**	**42**	**8**	**–22**	....	....	....	....	....	....	....	....
	Dallas Black Hawks	CHL	32	4	10	14	....	....	....	83	....	....	....	....	....	....	....	....	....	....	5	0	1	1	16	....	....	....
	Flint Generals	IHL	1	0	0	0	....	....	....	2	....	....	....	....	....	....	....	....	....	....	....	....	....	....	....	....	....	....
1977-78	**Chicago Black Hawks**	**NHL**	**54**	**1**	**5**	**6**	**1**	**4**	**5**	**77**	**1**	**0**	**0**	**51**	**2.0**	**30**	**2**	**51**	**9**	**–14**	**4**	**0**	**0**	**0**	**8**	**0**	**0**	**0**
1978-79	**Chicago Black Hawks**	**NHL**	**76**	**1**	**14**	**15**	**1**	**10**	**11**	**176**	**0**	**0**	**0**	**77**	**1.3**	**62**	**1**	**105**	**35**	**–9**	**4**	**0**	**0**	**0**	**2**	**0**	**0**	**0**
1979-80	**Chicago Black Hawks**	**NHL**	**12**	**2**	**3**	**5**	**2**	**2**	**4**	**34**	**0**	**0**	**1**	**13**	**15.4**	**10**	**0**	**6**	**1**	**5**	....	....	....	....	....	....	....	....
	Vancouver Canucks	**NHL**	**33**	**1**	**5**	**6**	**1**	**4**	**5**	**109**	**0**	**0**	**0**	**31**	**3.2**	**27**	**1**	**43**	**8**	**–9**	**4**	**0**	**0**	**0**	**0**	**0**	**0**	**0**
1980-81	**Vancouver Canucks**	**NHL**	**7**	**0**	**0**	**0**	**0**	**0**	**0**	**13**	**0**	**0**	**0**	**3**	**0.0**	**4**	**0**	**3**	**0**	**1**	....	....	....	....	....	....	....	....
	Dallas Black Hawks	CHL	23	1	8	9	....	....	....	28	....	....	....	....	....	....	....	....	....	....	....	....	....	....	....	....	....	....
	Maine Mariners	AHL	13	2	1	3	....	....	....	27	....	....	....	....	....	....	....	....	....	....	18	0	3	3	*129	....	....	....

Season	Club	League	GP	G	A	Pts	AG	AA	APts	PIM	PP	SH	GW	S	%	TGF	PGF	TGA	PGA	+/-	GP	G	A	Pts	PIM	PP	SH	GW
			REGULAR SEASON																		PLAYOFFS							
1981-82	Cincinnati Tigers	CHL	53	4	12	16	....	....	....	199	....	....	....	....	....	....	....	....	....	....	4	0	0	0	36	....	....	....
1982-83	St. Catharines Saints	AHL	12	2	2	4	....	....	....	2	....	....	....	....	....	....	....	....	....	....	....	....	....	....	....	....	....	....
	Birmingham South Stars	CHL	63	1	7	8	....	....	....	176	....	....	....	....	....	....	....	....	....	....	10	0	1	1	20	....	....	....
	NHL Totals		**218**	**5**	**29**	**34**	**5**	**22**	**27**	**470**	**1**	**0**	**1**	**211**	**2.4**	**145**	**4**	**251**	**61**		**12**	**0**	**0**	**0**	**10**	**0**	**0**	**0**

Traded to **Vancouver** by **Chicago** with Harold Phillipoff for Ron Sedlbauer, December 21, 1979. Signed as a free agent by **Philadelphia**, March 6, 1981. Signed as a free agent by **Toronto**, August 11, 1981. Traded to **Minnesota** by **Toronto** for cash, January 10, 1983.

• LOGAN, Robert

RW – L. 6', 190 lbs. b: Montreal, Que., 2/22/1964. Buffalo's 8th, 100th overall, in 1982.

Season	Club	League	GP	G	A	Pts	AG	AA	APts	PIM	PP	SH	GW	S	%	TGF	PGF	TGA	PGA	+/-	GP	G	A	Pts	PIM	PP	SH	GW
1980-81	Lac St-Louis Lions	QAAA	42	32	34	66	....	....	....	....	....	....	....	....	....	....	....	....	....	....	....	....	....	....	....	....	....	....
1981-82	Montreal West Island	QJHL	STATISTICS NOT AVAILABLE																									
1982-83	Yale University	ECAC	28	13	12	25	....	....	....	8	....	....	....	....	....	....	....	....	....	....	....	....	....	....	....	....	....	....
1983-84	Yale University	ECAC	22	9	13	22	....	....	....	25	....	....	....	....	....	....	....	....	....	....	....	....	....	....	....	....	....	....
1984-85	Yale University	ECAC	32	19	12	31	....	....	....	18	....	....	....	....	....	....	....	....	....	....	....	....	....	....	....	....	....	....
1985-86	Yale University	ECAC	27	19	21	40	....	....	....	22	....	....	....	....	....	....	....	....	....	....	....	....	....	....	....	....	....	....
1986-87	**Buffalo Sabres**	**NHL**	**22**	**7**	**3**	**10**	**6**	**2**	**8**	**0**	**1**	**0**	**0**	**22**	**31.8**	**13**	**1**	**7**	**0**	**5**	....	....	....	....	....	....	....	....
	Rochester Americans	AHL	56	30	14	44	....	....	....	27	....	....	....	....	....	....	....	....	....	....	18	5	10	15	4	....	....	....
1987-88	**Buffalo Sabres**	**NHL**	**16**	**3**	**2**	**5**	**3**	**1**	**4**	**0**	**1**	**0**	**1**	**15**	**20.0**	**8**	**2**	**5**	**0**	**1**	....	....	....	....	....	....	....	....
	Rochester Americans	AHL	45	23	15	38	....	....	....	35	....	....	....	....	....	....	....	....	....	....	....	....	....	....	....	....	....	....
1988-89	Rochester Americans	AHL	5	2	2	4	....	....	....	2	....	....	....	....	....	....	....	....	....	....	....	....	....	....	....	....	....	....
	Los Angeles Kings	**NHL**	**4**	**0**	**0**	**0**	**0**	**0**	**0**	**0**	**0**	**0**	**0**	**0**	**0.0**	**0**	**0**	**0**	**0**	**0**	....	....	....	....	....	....	....	....
	New Haven Nighthawks	AHL	66	21	32	53	....	....	....	27	....	....	....	....	....	....	....	....	....	....	13	2	3	5	9	....	....	....
1989-90	New Haven Nighthawks	AHL	11	2	4	6	....	....	....	4	....	....	....	....	....	....	....	....	....	....	....	....	....	....	....	....	....	....
	HC Ambri-Piotta	Switz-2	12	4	1	5	....	....	....	....	....	....	....	....	....	....	....	....	....	....	....	....	....	....	....	....	....	....
	NHL Totals		**42**	**10**	**5**	**15**	**9**	**3**	**12**	**0**	**2**	**0**	**1**	**37**	**27.0**	**21**	**3**	**12**	**0**		....	....	....	....	....	....	....	....

ECAC Second All-Star Team (1986)

Traded to **LA Kings** by **Buffalo** with Buffalo's 9th round choice (Jim Glacin) in 1989 Entry Draft, October 21, 1988.

• LOISELLE, Claude

Claude G. C – L. 5'11", 195 lbs. b: Ottawa, Ont., 5/29/1963. Detroit's 1st, 23rd overall, in 1981.

Season	Club	League	GP	G	A	Pts	AG	AA	APts	PIM	PP	SH	GW	S	%	TGF	PGF	TGA	PGA	+/-	GP	G	A	Pts	PIM	PP	SH	GW
1979-80	Gloucester Rangers	OJHL	50	21	38	59	....	....	....	26	....	....	....	....	....	....	....	....	....	....	....	....	....	....	....	....	....	....
1980-81	Windsor Spitfires	OMJHL	68	38	56	94	....	....	....	103	....	....	....	....	....	....	....	....	....	....	11	3	3	6	40	....	....	....
1981-82	Windsor Spitfires	OHL	68	36	73	109	....	....	....	192	....	....	....	....	....	....	....	....	....	....	9	2	10	12	42	....	....	....
	Detroit Red Wings	**NHL**	**4**	**1**	**0**	**1**	**1**	**0**	**1**	**2**	**1**	**0**	**0**	**2**	**50.0**	**2**	**2**	**2**	**0**	**–2**	....	....	....	....	....	....	....	....
1982-83	Windsor Spitfires	OHL	46	39	49	88	....	....	....	75	....	....	....	....	....	....	....	....	....	....	....	....	....	....	....	....	....	....
	Detroit Red Wings	**NHL**	**18**	**2**	**0**	**2**	**2**	**0**	**2**	**15**	**0**	**0**	**0**	**24**	**8.3**	**7**	**0**	**27**	**6**	**–14**	....	....	....	....	....	....	....	....
	Adirondack Red Wings	AHL	6	1	7	8	....	....	....	0	....	....	....	....	....	....	....	....	....	....	6	2	4	6	0	....	....	....
1983-84	**Detroit Red Wings**	**NHL**	**28**	**4**	**6**	**10**	**3**	**4**	**7**	**32**	**0**	**0**	**0**	**20**	**20.0**	**13**	**0**	**13**	**4**	**4**	....	....	....	....	....	....	....	....
	Adirondack Red Wings	AHL	29	13	16	29	....	....	....	59	....	....	....	....	....	....	....	....	....	....	....	....	....	....	....	....	....	....
1984-85	**Detroit Red Wings**	**NHL**	**30**	**8**	**1**	**9**	**6**	**1**	**7**	**45**	**0**	**0**	**0**	**30**	**26.7**	**15**	**0**	**22**	**2**	**–5**	**3**	**0**	**2**	**2**	**0**	**0**	**0**	**0**
	Adirondack Red Wings	AHL	47	22	29	51	....	....	....	24	....	....	....	....	....	....	....	....	....	....	....	....	....	....	....	....	....	....
1985-86	**Detroit Red Wings**	**NHL**	**48**	**7**	**15**	**22**	**6**	**10**	**16**	**142**	**2**	**0**	**1**	**83**	**8.4**	**29**	**8**	**71**	**23**	**–27**	....	....	....	....	....	....	....	....
	Adirondack Red Wings	AHL	21	15	11	26	....	....	....	32	....	....	....	....	....	....	....	....	....	....	16	5	10	15	38	....	....	....
1986-87	**New Jersey Devils**	**NHL**	**75**	**16**	**24**	**40**	**14**	**17**	**31**	**137**	**2**	**1**	**3**	**145**	**11.0**	**65**	**10**	**92**	**30**	**–7**	....	....	....	....	....	....	....	....
1987-88	**New Jersey Devils**	**NHL**	**68**	**17**	**18**	**35**	**14**	**13**	**27**	**121**	**3**	**2**	**2**	**117**	**14.5**	**47**	**8**	**67**	**35**	**7**	**20**	**4**	**6**	**10**	**50**	**0**	**2**	**0**
1988-89	**New Jersey Devils**	**NHL**	**74**	**7**	**14**	**21**	**6**	**10**	**16**	**209**	**0**	**1**	**1**	**92**	**7.6**	**34**	**0**	**91**	**47**	**–10**	....	....	....	....	....	....	....	....
1989-90	**Quebec Nordiques**	**NHL**	**72**	**11**	**14**	**25**	**9**	**10**	**19**	**104**	**0**	**3**	**0**	**128**	**8.6**	**34**	**3**	**100**	**42**	**–27**	....	....	....	....	....	....	....	....
1990-91	**Quebec Nordiques**	**NHL**	**59**	**5**	**10**	**15**	**5**	**8**	**13**	**86**	**0**	**2**	**0**	**79**	**6.3**	**21**	**1**	**68**	**28**	**–20**	....	....	....	....	....	....	....	....
	Toronto Maple Leafs	**NHL**	**7**	**1**	**1**	**2**	**1**	**1**	**2**	**2**	**0**	**0**	**0**	**10**	**10.0**	**5**	**0**	**7**	**2**	**0**	....	....	....	....	....	....	....	....
1991-92	**Toronto Maple Leafs**	**NHL**	**64**	**6**	**9**	**15**	**5**	**7**	**12**	**102**	**1**	**0**	**1**	**91**	**6.6**	**24**	**2**	**63**	**20**	**–21**	....	....	....	....	....	....	....	....
	New York Islanders	**NHL**	**11**	**1**	**1**	**2**	**1**	**1**	**2**	**13**	**0**	**0**	**0**	**10**	**10.0**	**3**	**0**	**12**	**6**	**–3**	....	....	....	....	....	....	....	....
1992-93	**New York Islanders**	**NHL**	**41**	**5**	**3**	**8**	**4**	**2**	**6**	**90**	**0**	**0**	**0**	**41**	**12.2**	**11**	**0**	**23**	**7**	**–5**	**18**	**0**	**3**	**3**	**10**	**0**	**0**	**0**
1993-94	**New York Islanders**	**NHL**	**17**	**1**	**1**	**2**	**1**	**1**	**2**	**49**	**0**	**0**	**0**	**14**	**7.1**	**6**	**0**	**15**	**7**	**–2**	....	....	....	....	....	....	....	....
	NHL Totals		**616**	**92**	**117**	**209**	**78**	**85**	**163**	**1149**	**9**	**9**	**8**	**886**	**10.4**	**316**	**34**	**673**	**259**		**41**	**4**	**11**	**15**	**60**	**0**	**2**	**0**

Traded to **New Jersey** by **Detroit** for Tim Higgins, June 25, 1986. Traded to **Quebec** by **New Jersey** with Joe Cirella and New Jersey's 8th round choice (Alexander Karpovtsev) in 1990 Entry Draft for Walt Poddubny and Quebec's 4th round choice (Mike Bodnarchuk) in 1990 Entry Draft, June 17, 1989. Claimed on waivers by **Toronto** from **Quebec**, March 5, 1991. Traded to **NY Islanders** by **Toronto** with Daniel Marois for Ken Baumgartner and Dave McLlwain, March 10, 1992. • Suffered career-ending knee injury in game vs. Dallas, November 24, 1993.

• LOMAKIN, Andrei

RW – L. 5'10", 175 lbs. b: Voskresensk, USSR, 4/3/1964. Philadelphia's 7th, 138th overall, in 1991.

Season	Club	League	GP	G	A	Pts	AG	AA	APts	PIM	PP	SH	GW	S	%	TGF	PGF	TGA	PGA	+/-	GP	G	A	Pts	PIM	PP	SH	GW
1981-82	Khimik Voskresensk	USSR	8	1	1	2	....	....	....	2	....	....	....	....	....	....	....	....	....	....	....	....	....	....	....	....	....	....
	Soviet Union	EJC-A	5	2	0	2	....	....	....	6	....	....	....	....	....	....	....	....	....	....	....	....	....	....	....	....	....	....
1982-83	Khimik Voskresensk	USSR	56	15	8	23	....	....	....	32	....	....	....	....	....	....	....	....	....	....	....	....	....	....	....	....	....	....
1983-84	Khimik Voskresensk	USSR	44	10	8	18	....	....	....	26	....	....	....	....	....	....	....	....	....	....	....	....	....	....	....	....	....	....
	Soviet Union	WJC-A	7	5	5	10	....	....	....	2	....	....	....	....	....	....	....	....	....	....	....	....	....	....	....	....	....	....
1984-85	Khimik Voskresensk	USSR	52	13	10	23	....	....	....	24	....	....	....	....	....	....	....	....	....	....	....	....	....	....	....	....	....	....
1985-86	Khimik Voskresensk	USSR	DID NOT PLAY																									
1986-87	Dynamo Moscow	USSR	40	15	14	29	....	....	....	30	....	....	....	....	....	....	....	....	....	....	....	....	....	....	....	....	....	....
1987-88	Soviet Union	Can-Cup	9	2	4	6	....	....	....	10	....	....	....	....	....	....	....	....	....	....	....	....	....	....	....	....	....	....
	Dynamo Moscow	USSR	45	10	15	25	....	....	....	24	....	....	....	....	....	....	....	....	....	....	....	....	....	....	....	....	....	....
	Soviet Union	Olympics	8	1	3	4	....	....	....	2	....	....	....	....	....	....	....	....	....	....	....	....	....	....	....	....	....	....
1988-89	Dynamo Moscow	USSR	44	9	16	25	....	....	....	22	....	....	....	....	....	....	....	....	....	....	....	....	....	....	....	....	....	....
	Dynamo Riga	Super-S	6	1	3	4	....	....	....	8	....	....	....	....	....	....	....	....	....	....	....	....	....	....	....	....	....	....
1989-90	Dynamo Moscow	Fr-Tour	1	1	1	2	....	....	....	4	....	....	....	....	....	....	....	....	....	....	....	....	....	....	....	....	....	....
	Dynamo Moscow	USSR	48	11	15	26	....	....	....	36	....	....	....	....	....	....	....	....	....	....	....	....	....	....	....	....	....	....
	Dynamo Moscow	Super-S	4	3	1	4	....	....	....	0	....	....	....	....	....	....	....	....	....	....	....	....	....	....	....	....	....	....
1990-91	Dynamo Moscow	Fr-Tour	1	0	0	0	....	....	....	0	....	....	....	....	....	....	....	....	....	....	....	....	....	....	....	....	....	....
	Dynamo Moscow	USSR	45	16	17	33	....	....	....	22	....	....	....	....	....	....	....	....	....	....	....	....	....	....	....	....	....	....
	Dynamo Moscow	Super-S	7	1	3	4	....	....	....	0	....	....	....	....	....	....	....	....	....	....	....	....	....	....	....	....	....	....
	Soviet Union	WEC-A	10	3	3	6	....	....	....	4	....	....	....	....	....	....	....	....	....	....	....	....	....	....	....	....	....	....
1991-92	Soviet Union	Can-Cup	5	0	2	2	....	....	....	0	....	....	....	....	....	....	....	....	....	....	....	....	....	....	....	....	....	....
	Dynamo Moscow	CIS	2	1	3	4	....	....	....	2	....	....	....	....	....	....	....	....	....	....	....	....	....	....	....	....	....	....
	Philadelphia Flyers	**NHL**	**57**	**14**	**16**	**30**	**13**	**12**	**25**	**26**	**2**	**0**	**0**	**82**	**17.1**	**43**	**8**	**51**	**10**	**–6**	....	....	....	....	....	....	....	....
1992-93	**Philadelphia Flyers**	**NHL**	**51**	**8**	**12**	**20**	**7**	**8**	**15**	**34**	**0**	**0**	**0**	**64**	**12.5**	**27**	**3**	**9**	**0**	**15**	....	....	....	....	....	....	....	....
1993-94	**Florida Panthers**	**NHL**	**76**	**19**	**28**	**47**	**18**	**22**	**40**	**26**	**3**	**0**	**2**	**139**	**13.7**	**71**	**26**	**44**	**0**	**1**	....	....	....	....	....	....	....	....
1994-95	**Florida Panthers**	**NHL**	**31**	**1**	**6**	**7**	**2**	**9**	**11**	**6**	**1**	**0**	**0**	**25**	**4.0**	**13**	**5**	**13**	**0**	**–5**	....	....	....	....	....	....	....	....
1995-96	HC Fribourg-Gotteron	Switz.	8	3	3	6	....	....	....	10	....	....	....	....	....	....	....	....	....	....	....	....	....	....	....	....	....	....
	Eisbaren Berlin	Germany	26	21	14	35	....	....	....	30	....	....	....	....	....	....	....	....	....	....	....	....	....	....	....	....	....	....
1996-97	Eisbaren Berlin	Germany	30	7	8	15	....	....	....	10	....	....	....	....	....	....	....	....	....	....	....	....	....	....	....	....	....	....
	Frankfurt Lions	Germany	12	3	4	7	....	....	....	10	....	....	....	....	....	....	....	....	....	....	2	0	0	0	0	....	....	....
	NHL Totals		**215**	**42**	**62**	**104**	**40**	**51**	**91**	**92**	**6**	**0**	**2**	**310**	**13.5**	**154**	**42**	**117**	**10**		....	....	....	....	....	....	....	....

Claimed by **Florida** from **Philadelphia** in Expansion Draft, June 24, 1993.

• LONEY, Brian

Brian D. RW – R. 6'2", 200 lbs. b: Winnipeg, Man., 8/9/1972. Vancouver's 6th, 110th overall, in 1992.

Season	Club	League	GP	G	A	Pts	AG	AA	APts	PIM	PP	SH	GW	S	%	TGF	PGF	TGA	PGA	+/-	GP	G	A	Pts	PIM	PP	SH	GW
1990-91	Notre Dame Hounds	SJHL	43	33	45	78	....	....	....	98	....	....	....	....	....	....	....	....	....	....	....	....	....	....	....	....	....	....
1991-92	Ohio State University	CCHA	37	21	34	55	....	....	....	109	....	....	....	....	....	....	....	....	....	....	....	....	....	....	....	....	....	....
1992-93	Red Deer Rebels	WHL	66	39	36	75	....	....	....	147	....	....	....	....	....	....	....	....	....	....	4	1	1	2	19	....	....	....
	Canada	Nat-Team	1	0	1	1	....	....	....	0	....	....	....	....	....	....	....	....	....	....	....	....	....	....	....	....	....	....
	Hamilton Canucks	AHL	3	0	2	2	....	....	....	0	....	....	....	....	....	....	....	....	....	....	....	....	....	....	....	....	....	....
1993-94	Hamilton Canucks	AHL	67	18	16	34	....	....	....	76	....	....	....	....	....	....	....	....	....	....	4	0	0	0	8	....	....	....
1994-95	Syracuse Crunch	AHL	67	23	17	40	....	....	....	98	....	....	....	....	....	....	....	....	....	....	....	....	....	....	....	....	....	....

Season	Club	League	GP	G	A	Pts	AG	AA	APts	PIM	PP	SH	GW	S	%	TGF	PGF	TGA	PGA	+/–	GP	G	A	Pts	PIM	PP	SH	GW
			REGULAR SEASON																		PLAYOFFS							
1995-96	Vancouver Canucks	NHL	12	2	3	5	2	2	4	6	0	0	0	19	10.5	5	0	3	0	2	....	....	....	....	....	....	....	....
	Syracuse Crunch	AHL	48	34	17	51	....	....	....	157	....	....	....	....	....	....	....	....	....	....	14	3	8	11	20	....	....	....
1996-97	Syracuse Crunch	AHL	76	19	39	58	....	....	....	123	....	....	....	....	....	....	....	....	....	....	3	0	0	0	0	....	....	....
1997-98	Kassel Huskies	Germany	19	6	7	13	....	....	....	24	....	....	....	....	....	....	....	....	....	....	....	....	....	....	....	....	....	....
	Kassel Huskies	EuroHL	2	0	1	1	....	....	....	0	....	....	....	....	....	....	....	....	....	....	....	....	....	....	....	....	....	....
	Lukko Rauma	Finland	12	5	2	7	....	....	....	45	....	....	....	....	....	....	....	....	....	....	....	....	....	....	....	....	....	....
1998-99	HC Bolzano-Bozen	Italy	19	12	12	24	....	....	....	40	....	....	....	....	....	....	....	....	....	....	....	....	....	....	....	....	....	....
	Central Texas Stampede	WPHL	25	18	33	51	....	....	....	43	....	....	....	....	....	....	....	....	....	....	....	....	....	....	....	....	....	....
99-2000	Augsburger Panther	Germany	33	5	9	14	....	....	....	44	....	....	....	....	....	....	....	....	....	....	....	....	....	....	....	....	....	....
	HC Bolzano-Bozen	Italy	15	15	21	36	....	....	....	45	....	....	....	....	....	....	....	....	....	....	12	11	7	18	44	....	....	....
	NHL Totals		12	2	3	5	2	2	4	6	0	0	0	19	10.5	5	0	3	0		....	....	....	....	....	....	....	....

• LONEY, Troy

Troy Ayne LW – L. 6'3", 209 lbs. b: Bow Island, Alta., 9/21/1963. Pittsburgh's 3rd, 52nd overall, in 1982.

Season	Club	League	GP	G	A	Pts	AG	AA	APts	PIM	PP	SH	GW	S	%	TGF	PGF	TGA	PGA	+/–	GP	G	A	Pts	PIM	PP	SH	GW
1979-80	Taber Midnight Sons	AAHA	STATISTICS NOT AVAILABLE																									
1980-81	Lethbridge Broncos	WHL	71	18	13	31	....	....	....	100	....	....	....	....	....	....	....	....	....	....	9	2	2	5	14	....	....	....
1981-82	Lethbridge Broncos	WHL	71	26	33	59	....	....	....	152	....	....	....	....	....	....	....	....	....	....	12	3	3	6	10	....	....	....
1982-83	Lethbridge Broncos	WHL	72	33	34	67	....	....	....	156	....	....	....	....	....	....	....	....	....	....	20	10	7	17	43	....	....	....
	Lethbridge Broncos	Mem-Cup	3	1	1	2	....	....	....	8	....	....	....	....	....	....	....	....	....	....	....	....	....	....	....	....	....	....
1983-84	Pittsburgh Penguins	NHL	13	0	0	0	0	0	0	9	0	0	0	5	0.0	0	0	7	0	–7	....	....	....	....	....	....	....	....
	Baltimore Skipjacks	AHL	63	18	13	31	....	....	....	147	....	....	....	....	....	....	....	....	....	....	10	0	2	2	19	....	....	....
1984-85	Pittsburgh Penguins	NHL	46	10	8	18	8	5	13	59	1	0	1	79	12.7	32	2	57	16	–11	....	....	....	....	....	....	....	....
	Baltimore Skipjacks	AHL	15	4	2	6	....	....	....	25	....	....	....	....	....	....	....	....	....	....	....	....	....	....	....	....	....	....
1985-86	Pittsburgh Penguins	NHL	47	3	9	12	2	6	8	95	0	0	1	50	6.0	24	1	37	6	–8	....	....	....	....	....	....	....	....
	Baltimore Skipjacks	AHL	33	12	11	23	....	....	....	84	....	....	....	....	....	....	....	....	....	....	....	....	....	....	....	....	....	....
1986-87	Pittsburgh Penguins	NHL	23	8	7	15	7	5	12	22	1	0	1	48	16.7	19	3	17	1	0	....	....	....	....	....	....	....	....
	Baltimore Skipjacks	AHL	40	13	14	27	....	....	....	134	....	....	....	....	....	....	....	....	....	....	....	....	....	....	....	....	....	....
1987-88	Pittsburgh Penguins	NHL	65	5	13	18	4	9	13	151	1	0	0	87	5.7	38	4	56	19	–3	....	....	....	....	....	....	....	....
1988-89	Pittsburgh Penguins	NHL	69	10	6	16	8	4	12	165	0	0	1	90	11.1	38	0	73	30	–5	11	1	3	4	24	0	0	0
1989-90	Pittsburgh Penguins	NHL	67	11	16	27	9	11	20	168	0	0	1	78	14.1	37	0	52	6	–9	....	....	....	....	....	....	....	....
1990-91 ♦	Pittsburgh Penguins	NHL	44	7	9	16	6	7	13	85	0	0	2	51	13.7	27	0	17	0	10	24	2	2	4	41	0	0	0
	Muskegon Lumberjacks	IHL	2	0	0	0	....	....	....	5	....	....	....	....	....	....	....	....	....	....	....	....	....	....	....	....	....	....
1991-92 ♦	Pittsburgh Penguins	NHL	76	10	16	26	9	12	21	127	0	0	1	94	10.6	32	0	44	7	–5	21	4	5	9	32	0	0	0
1992-93	Pittsburgh Penguins	NHL	82	5	16	21	4	11	15	99	0	0	1	83	6.0	32	2	34	5	1	10	1	4	5	0	0	0	0
1993-94	Mighty Ducks of Anaheim	NHL	62	13	6	19	12	5	17	88	6	0	1	93	14.0	45	13	38	1	–5	....	....	....	....	....	....	....	....
1994-95	New York Islanders	NHL	26	5	4	9	9	6	15	23	2	0	1	45	11.1	12	3	9	0	0	....	....	....	....	....	....	....	....
	New York Rangers	NHL	4	0	0	0	0	0	0	0	0	0	0	2	0.0	0	0	2	0	–2	1	0	0	0	0	0	0	0
	NHL Totals		624	87	110	197	78	81	159	1091	11	0	11	805	10.8	336	28	443	91		67	8	14	22	97	0	0	0

Claimed by **Anaheim** from **Pittsburgh** in Expansion Draft, June 24, 1993. Traded to **NY Islanders** by **Anaheim** for Tom Kurvers, June 29, 1994. Claimed on waivers by **NY Rangers** from **NY Islanders**, April 10, 1995.

• LONG, Barry

Barry Kenneth "Marathon Man" D – L. 6'2", 210 lbs. b: Brantford, Ont., 1/3/1949.

Season	Club	League	GP	G	A	Pts	AG	AA	APts	PIM	PP	SH	GW	S	%	TGF	PGF	TGA	PGA	+/–	GP	G	A	Pts	PIM	PP	SH	GW
1966-67	Moose Jaw Canucks	CMJHL	56	8	11	19	....	....	....	148	....	....	....	....	....	....	....	....	....	....	14	3	9	12	16	....	....	....
1967-68	Moose Jaw Canucks	WCJHL	52	11	33	44	....	....	....	202	....	....	....	....	....	....	....	....	....	....	13	4	2	6	19	....	....	....
1968-69	Dallas Black Hawks	CHL	46	4	11	15	....	....	....	85	....	....	....	....	....	....	....	....	....	....	....	....	....	....	....	....	....	....
1969-70	Dallas Black Hawks	CHL	71	11	22	33	....	....	....	127	....	....	....	....	....	....	....	....	....	....	....	....	....	....	....	....	....	....
1970-71	Dallas Black Hawks	CHL	72	9	24	33	....	....	....	90	....	....	....	....	....	....	....	....	....	....	10	1	0	1	10	....	....	....
1971-72	Portland Buckaroos	WHL	66	14	33	47	....	....	....	52	....	....	....	....	....	....	....	....	....	....	11	3	7	10	8	....	....	....
1972-73	Los Angeles Kings	NHL	70	2	13	15	2	10	12	48	0	0	0	110	1.8	57	2	65	3	–7	....	....	....	....	....	....	....	....
1973-74	Los Angeles Kings	NHL	60	3	19	22	3	16	19	118	1	0	0	111	2.7	84	7	70	18	25	5	0	1	1	18	0	0	0
1974-75	Team Canada	Summit-74	DID NOT PLAY																									
	Edmonton Oilers	WHA	78	20	40	60	....	....	....	116	....	....	....	....	....	....	....	....	....	....	....	....	....	....	....	....	....	....
1975-76	Edmonton Oilers	WHA	78	10	32	42	....	....	....	66	....	....	....	....	....	....	....	....	....	....	4	0	0	0	4	....	....	....
1976-77	Edmonton Oilers	WHA	2	0	1	1	....	....	....	2	....	....	....	....	....	....	....	....	....	....	....	....	....	....	....	....	....	....
	Winnipeg Jets	WHA	71	9	38	47	....	....	....	54	....	....	....	....	....	....	....	....	....	....	20	1	5	6	10	....	....	....
1977-78	Winnipeg Jets	WHA	78	7	24	31	....	....	....	42	....	....	....	....	....	....	....	....	....	....	9	0	5	5	6	....	....	....
1978-79	Winnipeg Jets	WHA	79	5	36	41	....	....	....	42	....	....	....	....	....	....	....	....	....	....	10	2	3	5	0	....	....	....
1979-80	Detroit Red Wings	NHL	80	0	17	17	0	12	12	38	0	0	0	87	0.0	74	0	157	55	–28	....	....	....	....	....	....	....	....
1980-81	Winnipeg Jets	NHL	65	6	17	23	5	11	16	42	0	0	0	88	6.8	71	4	142	28	–47	....	....	....	....	....	....	....	....
	Canada	WEC-A	7	1	0	1	....	....	....	8	....	....	....	....	....	....	....	....	....	....	....	....	....	....	....	....	....	....
1981-82	Winnipeg Jets	NHL	5	0	2	2	0	1	1	4	0	0	0	8	0.0	9	1	11	2	–1	....	....	....	....	....	....	....	....
	NHL Totals		280	11	68	79	10	50	60	250	1	0	0	404	2.7	295	14	445	106		5	0	1	1	18	0	0	0
	Other Major League Totals		386	51	171	222	....	....	....	322	....	....	....	....	....	....	....	....	....	....	43	3	13	16	20	....	....	....

WHA Second All-Star Team (1975, 1978)

Selected by **Edmonton** (WHA) in 1972 WHA General Player Draft, February 12, 1972. Claimed by **LA Kings** from **Chicago** in Intra-League Draft, June 5, 1972. Traded to **Winnipeg** (WHA) by **Edmonton** (WHA) for future considerations, October, 1976. Rights traded to **Detroit** by **LA Kings** with Montreal's 3rd round choice (previously acquired, Detroit selected Doug Derkson) in 1978 Amateur Draft for Danny Grant, January 9, 1978. Reclaimed by **Detroit** from **Winnipeg** prior to Expansion Draft, June 9, 1979. Traded to **Winnipeg** by **Detroit** for cash, October 31, 1980.

• LONSBERRY, Ross

David Ross LW – L. 5'11", 195 lbs. b: Humboldt, Sask., 2/7/1947.

Season	Club	League	GP	G	A	Pts	AG	AA	APts	PIM	PP	SH	GW	S	%	TGF	PGF	TGA	PGA	+/–	GP	G	A	Pts	PIM	PP	SH	GW
1962-63	Humboldt Indians	SAHA-I	STATISTICS NOT AVAILABLE																									
	Estevan Bruins	SJHL	1	0	1	1	....	....	....	0	....	....	....	....	....	....	....	....	....	....	....	....	....	....	....	....	....	....
1963-64	Estevan Bruins	SJHL	61	18	26	44	....	....	....	55	....	....	....	....	....	....	....	....	....	....	11	6	9	15	23	....	....	....
	Estevan Bruins	Mem-Cup	5	1	1	2	....	....	....	8	....	....	....	....	....	....	....	....	....	....	....	....	....	....	....	....	....	....
1964-65	Estevan Bruins	SJHL	56	40	56	96	....	....	....	130	....	....	....	....	....	....	....	....	....	....	6	3	5	8	18	....	....	....
	Minneapolis Bruins	CPHL	2	0	0	0	....	....	....	0	....	....	....	....	....	....	....	....	....	....	5	1	0	1	4	....	....	....
	Estevan Bruins	Mem-Cup	19	20	10	30	....	....	....	23	....	....	....	....	....	....	....	....	....	....	....	....	....	....	....	....	....	....
1965-66	Estevan Bruins	SJHL	60	*67	77	*144	....	....	....	109	....	....	....	....	....	....	....	....	....	....	12	*13	6	19	26	....	....	....
	Estevan Bruins	Mem-Cup	13	*10	9	*19	....	....	....	17	....	....	....	....	....	....	....	....	....	....	....	....	....	....	....	....	....	....
	Edmonton Oil Kings	Mem-Cup	6	2	1	3	....	....	....	6	....	....	....	....	....	....	....	....	....	....	....	....	....	....	....	....	....	....
1966-67	Boston Bruins	NHL	8	0	1	1	0	1	1	2	....	....	....	....	....	....	....	....	....	....	....	....	....	....	....	....	....	....
	Buffalo Bisons	AHL	7	1	1	2	....	....	....	4	....	....	....	....	....	....	....	....	....	....	....	....	....	....	....	....	....	....
	Oklahoma City Blazers	CPHL	46	12	10	22	....	....	....	83	....	....	....	....	....	....	....	....	....	....	11	3	2	5	31	....	....	....
1967-68	Boston Bruins	NHL	19	2	2	4	2	2	4	12	0	0	0	39	5.1	13	2	9	0	2	....	....	....	....	....	....	....	....
	Oklahoma City Blazers	CPHL	41	16	18	34	....	....	....	116	....	....	....	....	....	....	....	....	....	....	7	3	3	6	22	....	....	....
1968-69	Boston Bruins	NHL	6	0	0	0	0	0	0	2	0	0	0	4	0.0	0	0	0	0	0	....	....	....	....	....	....	....	....
	Oklahoma City Blazers	CHL	65	28	39	67	....	....	....	169	....	....	....	....	....	....	....	....	....	....	12	4	8	12	21	....	....	....
1969-70	Los Angeles Kings	NHL	76	20	22	42	22	21	43	118	3	1	4	226	8.8	66	21	84	21	–18	....	....	....	....	....	....	....	....
1970-71	Los Angeles Kings	NHL	76	25	28	53	25	23	48	80	5	2	0	238	10.5	81	22	118	24	–35	....	....	....	....	....	....	....	....
1971-72	Los Angeles Kings	NHL	50	9	14	23	9	12	21	39	1	0	0	112	8.0	33	3	52	4	–18	....	....	....	....	....	....	....	....
	Philadelphia Flyers	NHL	32	7	7	14	7	6	13	22	0	0	0	88	8.0	25	5	30	1	–9	....	....	....	....	....	....	....	....
1972-73	Philadelphia Flyers	NHL	77	21	29	50	20	23	43	59	6	0	3	205	10.2	94	28	74	14	6	11	4	3	7	9	0	0	1
1973-74 ♦	Philadelphia Flyers	NHL	75	32	19	51	31	16	47	48	6	1	5	213	15.0	75	22	49	12	16	17	4	9	13	18	1	1	1
1974-75 ♦	Philadelphia Flyers	NHL	80	24	25	49	21	19	40	99	9	0	3	180	13.3	77	19	43	13	28	17	4	3	7	10	1	0	1
1975-76	Philadelphia Flyers	NHL	80	19	28	47	17	21	38	87	4	0	0	209	9.1	88	26	56	23	29	16	4	3	7	2	1	0	1
1976-77	Philadelphia Flyers	NHL	75	23	32	55	21	25	46	43	3	1	3	173	13.3	91	12	49	12	42	10	1	2	3	29	0	0	0
1977-78	Philadelphia Flyers	NHL	78	18	30	48	16	23	39	45	2	1	5	172	10.5	82	11	47	17	41	12	2	2	4	6	1	0	1

Season	Club	League	REGULAR SEASON GP	G	A	Pts	AG	AA	APts	PIM	PP	SH	GW	S	%	TGF	PGF	TGA	PGA	+/-	PLAYOFFS GP	G	A	Pts	PIM	PP	SH	GW
1978-79	**Pittsburgh Penguins**	**NHL**	**80**	**24**	**22**	**46**	**21**	**16**	**37**	**38**	**4**	**0**	**1**	**179**	**13.4**	**86**	**20**	**72**	**13**	**7**	**7**	**0**	**2**	**2**	**9**	**0**	**0**	**0**
1979-80	**Pittsburgh Penguins**	**NHL**	**76**	**15**	**18**	**33**	**13**	**13**	**26**	**36**	**2**	**0**	**0**	**135**	**11.1**	**71**	**10**	**81**	**16**	**–4**	**5**	**2**	**1**	**3**	**2**	**0**	**0**	**1**
1980-81	**Pittsburgh Penguins**	**NHL**	**80**	**17**	**33**	**50**	**13**	**22**	**35**	**76**	**7**	**1**	**2**	**161**	**10.6**	**111**	**45**	**92**	**23**	**–3**	**5**	**0**	**0**	**0**	**2**	**0**	**0**	**0**
	NHL Totals		**968**	**256**	**310**	**566**	**238**	**243**	**481**	**806**											**100**	**21**	**25**	**46**	**87**			

• SJHL Second All-Star Team (1965) • SJHL First All-Star Team (1966) • CHL Second All-Star Team (1969) • Played in NHL All-Star Game (1972)

Traded to **LA Kings** by **Boston** with Eddie Shack for Ken Turlik, LA Kings' 1st round choice in the 1971 (Ron Jones) and 1973 (Andre Savard) Amateur Drafts, May 14, 1969. Traded to **Philadelphia** by **LA Kings** with Bill Flett, Eddie Joyal and Jean Potvin for Bill Lesuk, Jim Johnson and Serge Bernier, January 28, 1972. Traded to **Pittsburgh** by **Philadelphia** with Tom Bladon and Orest Kindrachuk for Pittsburgh's 1st round choice (Behn Wilson) in 1978 Amateur Draft, June 14, 1978.

• LOOB, Hakan

Hakan P. RW – R. 5'9", 170 lbs. b: Karlstad, Sweden, 7/3/1960. Calgary's 10th, 181st overall, in 1980.

Season	Club	League	GP	G	A	Pts	AG	AA	APts	PIM	PP	SH	GW	S	%	TGF	PGF	TGA	PGA	+/-	GP	G	A	Pts	PIM	PP	SH	GW
1975-76	IK Graip Slite	Sweden-3	22	12	2	14																						
1976-77	Roma IF Romakloster	Sweden-3	20	19	12	31																						
1977-78	Karlskrona IK	Sweden-2	25	15	4	19				37																		
	Sweden	EJC-A	5	3	1	4				2																		
1978-79	Karlskrona IK	Sweden-2	23	23	9	32				8											5	3	2	5	0			
	Sweden	WJC-A	6	0	2	2				0																		
1979-80	Farjestads BK Karlstad	Sweden	36	15	4	19				20																		
	Sweden	WJC-A	5	7	2	9				2																		
1980-81	Farjestads BK Karlstad	Sweden	36	23	6	29				14											7	*5	3	*8	6			
1981-82	Farjestads BK Karlstad	Sweden	36	26	15	41				28											2	1	0	1	0			
	Sweden	Nat-Team	21	8	3	11				8																		
	Sweden	WEC-A	8	3	1	4				6																		
1982-83	Farjestads BK Karlstad	Sweden	36	*42	*34	*76				29											8	*10	4	*14	6			
	Sweden	Nat-Team	11	2	2	4				8																		
1983-84	**Calgary Flames**	**NHL**	**77**	**30**	**25**	**55**	**24**	**17**	**41**	**22**	**3**	**0**	**2**	**178**	**16.9**	**88**	**16**	**65**	**4**	**11**	**11**	**2**	**3**	**5**	**2**	**1**	**0**	**2**
1984-85	Sweden	Can-Cup	8	6	4	10				2																		
	Calgary Flames	**NHL**	**78**	**37**	**35**	**72**	**30**	**24**	**54**	**14**	**8**	**1**	**5**	**224**	**16.5**	**110**	**37**	**70**	**11**	**14**	**4**	**3**	**3**	**6**	**0**	**0**	**1**	**0**
1985-86	**Calgary Flames**	**NHL**	**68**	**31**	**36**	**67**	**25**	**24**	**49**	**36**	**10**	**0**	**1**	**174**	**17.8**	**95**	**30**	**58**	**15**	**22**	**22**	**4**	**10**	**14**	**6**	**1**	**2**	**0**
1986-87	**Calgary Flames**	**NHL**	**68**	**18**	**26**	**44**	**16**	**19**	**35**	**26**	**7**	**0**	**1**	**129**	**14.0**	**62**	**25**	**66**	**16**	**–13**	**5**	**1**	**2**	**3**	**0**	**0**	**1**	**0**
	Sweden	WEC-A	8	5	4	9				4																		
1987-88	**Calgary Flames**	**NHL**	**80**	**50**	**56**	**106**	**43**	**40**	**83**	**47**	**9**	**8**	**4**	**198**	**25.3**	**158**	**63**	**93**	**39**	**41**	**9**	**8**	**1**	**9**	**4**	**2**	**2**	**0**
1988-89♦	**Calgary Flames**	**NHL**	**79**	**27**	**58**	**85**	**23**	**41**	**64**	**44**	**5**	**0**	**4**	**223**	**12.1**	**113**	**40**	**56**	**11**	**28**	**22**	**8**	**9**	**17**	**4**	**2**	**2**	**1**
1989-90	Farjestads BK Karlstad	Sweden	40	22	*31	53				24											10	*9	5	*14	2			
	Sweden	WEC-A	10	4	7	11				10																		
1990-91	Farjestads BK Karlstad	Sweden	40	*33	25	*58				16											8	*6	4	10	8			
	Sweden	WEC-A	10	2	7	9				6																		
1991-92	Farjestads BK Karlstad	Sweden	40	*37	29	*66				14											6	2	2	4	2			
	Sweden	Olympics	8	4	4	8				0																		
1992-93	Farjestads BK Karlstad	Sweden	40	*25	26	*51				28											3	4	1	5	0			
1993-94	Farjestads BK Karlstad	Sweden	22	9	11	20				12																		
	Sweden	Olympics	8	4	5	9				2																		
1994-95	Farjestads BK Karlstad	Sweden	39	13	25	38				58											4	2	0	2	2			
1995-96	Farjestads BK Karlstad	Sweden	40	17	31	48				37																		
	NHL Totals		**450**	**193**	**236**	**429**	**161**	**165**	**326**	**189**	**42**	**9**	**17**	**1126**	**17.1**	**626**	**211**	**408**	**96**		**73**	**26**	**28**	**54**	**16**	**6**	**8**	**3**

• Brother of Peter • WJC-A All-Star Team (1980) • Swedish World All-Star Team (1983, 1985, 1990, 1991, 1992) • Swedish Player of the Year (1983) • NHL All-Rookie Team (1984) • NHL First All-Star Team (1988)

• LOOB, Peter

D – R. 6'3", 190 lbs. b: Karlstad, Sweden, 7/23/1957. Quebec's 10th, 244th overall, in 1984.

Season	Club	League	GP	G	A	Pts	AG	AA	APts	PIM	PP	SH	GW	S	%	TGF	PGF	TGA	PGA	+/-	GP	G	A	Pts	PIM	PP	SH	GW
1972-73	IK Graip	Sweden-3	3	0	0	0				0																		
1973-74	IK Graip	Sweden-3	14	16	....	16																						
1974-75	IK Graip	Sweden-3	19	25	....	25																						
1975-76	IK Graip	Sweden-3	STATISTICS NOT AVAILABLE																									
1976-77	Karlskrona AIK	Sweden-2	33	11	5	16																						
1977-78	Karlskrona AIK	Sweden-2	15	3	5	8				26																		
1978-79	Karlskrona AIK	Sweden-2	25	12	14	26				36																		
1979-80	Karlskrona AIK	Sweden-2	27	19	9	28				*60											6	3	5	8	14			
1980-81	Farjestads BK Karlstad	Sweden	16	1	3	4				15																		
1981-82	Farjestads BK Karlstad	Sweden	25	8	8	16				24											2	0	0	0	0			
1982-83	Farjestads BK Karlstad	Sweden	36	16	23	39				32											8	0	7	7	18			
	Sweden	WEC-A	3	1	2	3				8																		
1983-84	Sodertalje SK	Sweden	36	12	15	27				36																		
1984-85	**Quebec Nordiques**	**NHL**	**8**	**1**	**2**	**3**	**1**	**1**	**2**	**0**	**0**	**0**	**0**	**10**	**10.0**	**10**	**1**	**5**	**1**	**5**								
	Fredericton Express	AHL	35	4	10	14				12																		
	Muskegon Mohawks	IHL	10	0	4	4				0																		
1985-86	Sodertalje SK	Sweden	34	15	5	20				20											7	4	2	6	4			
1986-87	Sodertalje SK	Sweden	33	6	11	17				22																		
1987-88	Nykopings BIS	Sweden-3	27	17	35	52																						
1988-89	IK Talje	Sweden-2	26	6	13	19				48																		
1989-1991			OUT OF HOCKEY – RETIRED																									
1991-92	Follingbro IF	Sweden-3	2	0	1	1				2																		
	NHL Totals		**8**	**1**	**2**	**3**	**1**	**1**	**2**	**0**	**0**	**0**	**0**	**10**	**10.0**	**10**	**1**	**5**	**1**									

• Brother of Hakan. • Only games played and goals scored totals available for IK Graip during 1973-74 and 1974-75 seasons.

• LORENTZ, Jim

James Peter "Batman" C/RW – L. 6', 190 lbs. b: Waterloo, Ont., 5/1/1947.

Season	Club	League	GP	G	A	Pts	AG	AA	APts	PIM	PP	SH	GW	S	%	TGF	PGF	TGA	PGA	+/-	GP	G	A	Pts	PIM	PP	SH	GW
1963-64	Waterloo Siskins	OHA-B	STATISTICS NOT AVAILABLE																									
1964-65	Niagara Falls Flyers	OHA-Jr.	43	7	14	21				20											11	5	6	11	16			
1965-66	Niagara Falls Flyers	OHA-Jr.	38	11	22	33				47											4	1	2	3	4			
	Niagara Falls Flyers	Mem-Cup	13	5	8	13				14																		
1966-67	Niagara Falls Flyers	OHA-Jr.	48	33	59	92				79											13	4	*17	21	10			
1967-68	Oklahoma City Blazers	CPHL	70	33	50	83				105											7	1	1	2	10			
1968-69	**Boston Bruins**	**NHL**	**11**	**1**	**3**	**4**	**1**	**3**	**4**	**6**	**0**	**0**	**1**	**16**	**6.3**	**5**	**0**	**8**	**0**	**–3**								
	Oklahoma City Blazers	CHL	56	33	*68	*101				67											12	9	*16	*25	17			
1969-70♦	**Boston Bruins**	**NHL**	**68**	**7**	**16**	**23**	**8**	**15**	**23**	**30**	**2**	**0**	**0**	**92**	**7.6**	**42**	**7**	**21**	**0**	**14**	**11**	**1**	**0**	**1**	**4**	**0**	**0**	**0**
1970-71	**St. Louis Blues**	**NHL**	**76**	**19**	**21**	**40**	**19**	**18**	**37**	**34**	**6**	**0**	**2**	**160**	**11.9**	**72**	**21**	**49**	**0**	**2**	**6**	**0**	**1**	**1**	**4**	**0**	**0**	**0**
1971-72	**St. Louis Blues**	**NHL**	**12**	**0**	**1**	**1**	**0**	**1**	**1**	**12**	**0**	**0**	**0**	**16**	**0.0**	**2**	**0**	**10**	**0**	**–8**								
	New York Rangers	**NHL**	**7**	**0**	**0**	**0**	**0**	**0**	**0**	**0**	**0**	**0**	**0**	**1**	**0.0**	**0**	**0**	**2**	**1**	**–1**								
	Buffalo Sabres	**NHL**	**33**	**10**	**14**	**24**	**10**	**12**	**22**	**12**	**2**	**0**	**1**	**85**	**11.8**	**36**	**11**	**38**	**2**	**–11**								
1972-73	**Buffalo Sabres**	**NHL**	**78**	**27**	**35**	**62**	**25**	**28**	**53**	**30**	**11**	**0**	**5**	**175**	**15.4**	**105**	**35**	**68**	**4**	**6**	**6**	**0**	**3**	**3**	**2**	**0**	**0**	**0**
1973-74	**Buffalo Sabres**	**NHL**	**78**	**23**	**31**	**54**	**22**	**26**	**48**	**28**	**12**	**0**	**4**	**145**	**15.9**	**83**	**40**	**63**	**1**	**–19**								
1974-75	**Buffalo Sabres**	**NHL**	**72**	**25**	**45**	**70**	**22**	**34**	**56**	**18**	**6**	**0**	**6**	**140**	**17.9**	**114**	**44**	**59**	**6**	**17**	**16**	**6**	**4**	**10**	**6**	**0**	**0**	**2**
1975-76	**Buffalo Sabres**	**NHL**	**75**	**17**	**24**	**41**	**15**	**18**	**33**	**18**	**2**	**1**	**4**	**116**	**14.7**	**63**	**14**	**54**	**8**	**3**	**9**	**1**	**2**	**3**	**6**	**0**	**0**	**0**
1976-77	**Buffalo Sabres**	**NHL**	**79**	**23**	**33**	**56**	**21**	**25**	**46**	**8**	**7**	**0**	**3**	**156**	**14.7**	**81**	**16**	**62**	**0**	**3**	**6**	**4**	**0**	**4**	**8**	**0**	**0**	**0**
1977-78	**Buffalo Sabres**	**NHL**	**70**	**9**	**15**	**24**	**8**	**12**	**20**	**12**	**6**	**0**	**2**	**85**	**10.6**	**40**	**14**	**34**	**4**	**–4**								
	NHL Totals		**659**	**161**	**238**	**399**	**151**	**192**	**343**	**208**	**54**	**1**	**28**	**1187**	**13.6**	**643**	**202**	**468**	**26**		**54**	**12**	**10**	**22**	**30**	**0**	**0**	**2**

CPHL First All-Star Team (1968) • CHL First All-Star Team (1969) • Won Ken McKenzie Trophy (Rookie of the Year - CPHL) (1968) • Won Tommy Ivan Trophy (MVP - CHL) (1969)

Traded to **St. Louis** by **Boston** for St. Louis' 1st round choice (Ron Plumb) in 1970 Amateur Draft, May 26, 1970. Traded to **NY Rangers** by **St. Louis** with Gene Carr and Wayne Connelly for Jack Egers, Andre Dupont and Mike Murphy, November 15, 1971. Traded to **Buffalo** by **NY Rangers** for Buffalo's 2nd round choice (Lawrence Sacharuk) in 1972 Amateur Draft, January 14, 1972.

• LORIMER, Bob

Robert Roy D – R. 6'1", 200 lbs. b: Toronto, Ont., 8/25/1953. NY Islanders' 10th, 129th overall, in 1973.

			REGULAR SEASON																		PLAYOFFS							
Season	Club	League	GP	G	A	Pts	AG	AA	APts	PIM	PP	SH	GW	S	%	TGF	PGF	TGA	PGA	+/–	GP	G	A	Pts	PIM	PP	SH	GW
1970-71	Aurora Tigers	OHA-B	STATISTICS NOT AVAILABLE																									
1971-72	Michigan Tech Huskies	WCHA	32	1	7	8	....	....	....	63	....	....	....	....	....	....	....	....	....	....	....	....	....	....	....	....	....	....
1972-73	Michigan Tech Huskies	WCHA	38	2	9	11	....	....	....	74	....	....	....	....	....	....	....	....	....	....	....	....	....	....	....	....	....	....
1973-74	Michigan Tech Huskies	CCHA	39	3	18	21	....	....	....	46	....	....	....	....	....	....	....	....	....	....	....	....	....	....	....	....	....	....
1974-75	Michigan Tech Huskies	WCHA	38	10	21	31	....	....	....	68	....	....	....	....	....	....	....	....	....	....	....	....	....	....	....	....	....	....
1975-76	Fort Worth Texans	CHL	2	0	0	0	....	....	....	2	....	....	....	....	....	....	....	....	....	....	3	0	0	0	2	....	....	....
	Muskegon Mohawks	IHL	78	6	21	27	....	....	....	94	....	....	....	....	....	....	....	....	....	....	....	....	....	....	....	....	....	....
1976-77	**New York Islanders**	**NHL**	**1**	**0**	**1**	**1**	**0**	**1**	**1**	**0**	**0**	**0**	**0**	**0**	**0.0**	**1**	**0**	**0**	**0**	**1**	....	....	....	....	....	....	....	....
	Fort Worth Texans	CHL	28	4	6	10	....	....	....	38	....	....	....	....	....	....	....	....	....	....	6	0	0	0	17	....	....	....
1977-78	**New York Islanders**	**NHL**	**5**	**1**	**0**	**1**	**1**	**0**	**1**	**0**	**0**	**0**	**0**	**3**	**33.3**	**5**	**0**	**5**	**0**	**0**	....	....	....	....	....	....	....	....
	Fort Worth Texans	CHL	71	6	13	19	....	....	....	81	....	....	....	....	....	....	....	....	....	....	14	1	7	8	25	....	....	....
1978-79	**New York Islanders**	**NHL**	**67**	**3**	**18**	**21**	**3**	**13**	**16**	**42**	**0**	**0**	**0**	**64**	**4.7**	**78**	**1**	**68**	**18**	**27**	**10**	**1**	**3**	**4**	**15**	**0**	**0**	**0**
1979-80♦	**New York Islanders**	**NHL**	**74**	**3**	**16**	**19**	**3**	**12**	**15**	**53**	**0**	**0**	**1**	**98**	**3.1**	**91**	**3**	**92**	**36**	**32**	**21**	**1**	**3**	**4**	**41**	**0**	**0**	**1**
1980-81♦	**New York Islanders**	**NHL**	**73**	**1**	**12**	**13**	**1**	**8**	**9**	**77**	**0**	**0**	**0**	**65**	**1.5**	**98**	**1**	**81**	**29**	**45**	**18**	**1**	**4**	**5**	**27**	**0**	**0**	**0**
1981-82	**Colorado Rockies**	**NHL**	**79**	**5**	**15**	**20**	**4**	**10**	**14**	**68**	**1**	**0**	**0**	**69**	**7.2**	**74**	**2**	**128**	**37**	**–19**	....	....	....	....	....	....	....	....
1982-83	**New Jersey Devils**	**NHL**	**66**	**3**	**10**	**13**	**2**	**7**	**9**	**42**	**0**	**0**	**0**	**53**	**5.7**	**49**	**0**	**104**	**35**	**–20**	....	....	....	....	....	....	....	....
1983-84	**New Jersey Devils**	**NHL**	**72**	**2**	**10**	**12**	**2**	**7**	**9**	**62**	**1**	**0**	**0**	**65**	**3.1**	**51**	**6**	**99**	**26**	**–28**	....	....	....	....	....	....	....	....
1984-85	**New Jersey Devils**	**NHL**	**46**	**2**	**6**	**8**	**2**	**4**	**6**	**35**	**0**	**0**	**0**	**40**	**5.0**	**47**	**1**	**56**	**16**	**6**	....	....	....	....	....	....	....	....
1985-86	**New Jersey Devils**	**NHL**	**46**	**2**	**2**	**4**	**2**	**1**	**3**	**52**	**0**	**0**	**0**	**28**	**7.1**	**37**	**2**	**77**	**29**	**–13**	....	....	....	....	....	....	....	....
	NHL Totals		**529**	**22**	**90**	**112**	**20**	**63**	**83**	**431**	**2**	**0**	**1**	**485**	**4.5**	**531**	**16**	**710**	**226**		**49**	**3**	**10**	**13**	**83**	**0**	**0**	**1**

WCHA Second All-Star Team (1975) • NCAA Championship All-Tournament Team (1975)

Traded to **Colorado** by **NY Islanders** with Dave Cameron for Colorado's 1st round choice (Pat LaFontaine) in 1983 Entry Draft, October 1, 1981. Transferred to **New Jersey** after **Colorado** franchise relocated, June 30, 1982.

• LOVSIN, Ken

Kenneth D – R. 6', 195 lbs. b: Peace River, Alta., 12/3/1966. Hartford's 1st, 22nd overall, in 1987 Supplemental Draft.

Season	Club	League	GP	G	A	Pts	AG	AA	APts	PIM	PP	SH	GW	S	%	TGF	PGF	TGA	PGA	+/–	GP	G	A	Pts	PIM	PP	SH	GW
1985-86	Camrose Lutheran College	ACAC	25	2	19	21	....	....	....	18	....	....	....	....	....	....	....	....	....	....	....	....	....	....	....	....	....	....
1986-87	University of Saskatchewan	CWUAA	28	3	13	16	....	....	....	14	....	....	....	....	....	....	....	....	....	....	9	3	1	4	6	....	....	....
1987-88	University of Saskatchewan	CWUAA	26	10	28	38	....	....	....	27	....	....	....	....	....	....	....	....	....	....	3	1	3	4	2	....	....	....
1988-89	Canada	Nat-Team	59	0	10	10	....	....	....	59	....	....	....	....	....	....	....	....	....	....	....	....	....	....	....	....	....	....
1989-90	Canada	Nat-Team	66	7	15	22	....	....	....	80	....	....	....	....	....	....	....	....	....	....	....	....	....	....	....	....	....	....
1990-91	**Washington Capitals**	**NHL**	**1**	**0**	**0**	**0**	**0**	**0**	**0**	**0**	**0**	**0**	**0**	**2**	**0.0**	**1**	**1**	**2**	**0**	**–2**	....	....	....	....	....	....	....	....
	Baltimore Skipjacks	AHL	79	8	28	36	....	....	....	54	....	....	....	....	....	....	....	....	....	....	6	1	1	2	2	....	....	....
1991-92	Baltimore Skipjacks	AHL	77	11	24	35	....	....	....	60	....	....	....	....	....	....	....	....	....	....	....	....	....	....	....	....	....	....
1992-93	Mora IF	Sweden-2	36	7	13	20	....	....	....	50	....	....	....	....	....	....	....	....	....	....	5	0	2	2	12	....	....	....
	Canada	Nat-Team	9	0	3	3	....	....	....	0	....	....	....	....	....	....	....	....	....	....	....	....	....	....	....	....	....	....
1993-94	Canada	Nat-Team	62	3	11	14	....	....	....	22	....	....	....	....	....	....	....	....	....	....	....	....	....	....	....	....	....	....
	Canada	Olympics	8	0	0	0	....	....	....	8	....	....	....	....	....	....	....	....	....	....	....	....	....	....	....	....	....	....
	NHL Totals		**1**	**0**	**0**	**0**	**0**	**0**	**0**	**0**	**0**	**0**	**0**	**2**	**0.0**	**1**	**1**	**2**	**0**		....	....	....	....	....	....	....	....

Signed as a free agent by **Washington**, July 3, 1990.

• LOWDERMILK, Dwayne

Dwayne Kenneth D – R. 6', 201 lbs. b: Burnaby, B.C., 1/9/1958. NY Islanders' 3rd, 51st overall, in 1978.

Season	Club	League	GP	G	A	Pts	AG	AA	APts	PIM	PP	SH	GW	S	%	TGF	PGF	TGA	PGA	+/–	GP	G	A	Pts	PIM	PP	SH	GW
1975-76	Langley Lords	BCJHL	STATISTICS NOT AVAILABLE																									
	Kamloops Chiefs	WCJHL	35	5	7	12	....	....	....	10	....	....	....	....	....	....	....	....	....	....	12	0	2	2	2	....	....	....
1976-77	Kamloops Chiefs	WCJHL	72	13	46	59	....	....	....	79	....	....	....	....	....	....	....	....	....	....	5	1	1	2	0	....	....	....
1977-78	Seattle Breakers	WCJHL	71	28	58	86	....	....	....	108	....	....	....	....	....	....	....	....	....	....	....	....	....	....	....	....	....	....
1978-79	Fort Worth Texans	CHL	75	13	37	50	....	....	....	63	....	....	....	....	....	....	....	....	....	....	4	0	0	0	2	....	....	....
1979-80	Indianapolis Checkers	CHL	79	7	29	36	....	....	....	38	....	....	....	....	....	....	....	....	....	....	7	2	2	4	0	....	....	....
1980-81	Indianapolis Checkers	CHL	5	0	4	4	....	....	....	8	....	....	....	....	....	....	....	....	....	....	....	....	....	....	....	....	....	....
	Washington Capitals	**NHL**	**2**	**0**	**1**	**1**	**0**	**1**	**1**	**2**	**0**	**0**	**0**	**2**	**0.0**	**3**	**2**	**2**	**0**	**–1**	....	....	....	....	....	....	....	....
	Hershey Bears	AHL	46	6	17	23	....	....	....	28	....	....	....	....	....	....	....	....	....	....	5	2	1	3	2	....	....	....
	Fort Wayne Komets	IHL	21	7	10	17	....	....	....	19	....	....	....	....	....	....	....	....	....	....	....	....	....	....	....	....	....	....
1981-82	Hershey Bears	AHL	70	4	34	38	....	....	....	44	....	....	....	....	....	....	....	....	....	....	5	1	3	4	2	....	....	....
	NHL Totals		**2**	**0**	**1**	**1**	**0**	**1**	**1**	**2**	**0**	**0**	**0**	**2**	**0.0**	**3**	**2**	**2**	**0**		....	....	....	....	....	....	....	....

WCJHL Second All-Star Team (1978)

Traded to **Washington** by **NY Islanders** for future considerations, December 26, 1980.

• LOWE, Darren

Darren Craig RW – R. 5'10", 185 lbs. b: Toronto, Ont., 10/13/1960.

Season	Club	League	GP	G	A	Pts	AG	AA	APts	PIM	PP	SH	GW	S	%	TGF	PGF	TGA	PGA	+/–	GP	G	A	Pts	PIM	PP	SH	GW
1976-77	Don Valley Kings	MTHL	STATISTICS NOT AVAILABLE																									
1977-78	North York Rangers	OJHL	STATISTICS NOT AVAILABLE																									
	Kingston Canadians	OMJHL	1	0	0	0	....	....	....	2	....	....	....	....	....	....	....	....	....	....	....	....	....	....	....	....	....	....
1978-79	Richmond Hill Rams	OHA-B	STATISTICS NOT AVAILABLE																									
1979-80	University of Toronto	OUAA	STATISTICS NOT AVAILABLE																									
1980-81	University of Toronto	OUAA	28	28	23	51	....	....	....	26	....	....	....	....	....	....	....	....	....	....	....	....	....	....	....	....	....	....
1981-82	University of Toronto	OUAA	29	36	26	62	....	....	....	....	....	....	....	....	....	....	....	....	....	....	....	....	....	....	....	....	....	....
1982-83	University of Toronto	OUAA	24	23	32	55	....	....	....	....	....	....	....	....	....	....	....	....	....	....	....	....	....	....	....	....	....	....
1983-84	Canada	Nat-Team	60	16	13	29	....	....	....	22	....	....	....	....	....	....	....	....	....	....	....	....	....	....	....	....	....	....
	Canada	Olympics	7	2	1	3	....	....	....	0	....	....	....	....	....	....	....	....	....	....	....	....	....	....	....	....	....	....
	Pittsburgh Penguins	**NHL**	**8**	**1**	**2**	**3**	**1**	**1**	**2**	**0**	**0**	**0**	**0**	**14**	**7.1**	**4**	**0**	**9**	**0**	**–5**	....	....	....	....	....	....	....	....
1984-85	University of Toronto	OUAA	DID NOT PLAY – ACADEMICALLY INELIGIBLE																									
1985-86	University of Toronto	OUAA	STATISTICS NOT AVAILABLE																									
	Georgetown Raiders	OHA-Sr.	STATISTICS NOT AVAILABLE																									
1986-87	WEV Wien	Austria	22	18	11	29	....	....	....	6	....	....	....	....	....	....	....	....	....	....	....	....	....	....	....	....	....	....
	Jokerit Helsinki	Finland	18	7	2	9	....	....	....	16	....	....	....	....	....	....	....	....	....	....	....	....	....	....	....	....	....	....
1987-88	Flint Spirits	IHL	82	53	64	117	....	....	....	24	....	....	....	....	....	....	....	....	....	....	16	10	*15	25	34	....	....	....
1988-89	Maine Mariners	AHL	78	29	24	53	....	....	....	36	....	....	....	....	....	....	....	....	....	....	....	....	....	....	....	....	....	....
1989-90	Flint Spirits	IHL	67	31	35	66	....	....	....	44	....	....	....	....	....	....	....	....	....	....	4	1	4	5	2	....	....	....
1990-91	San Diego Gulls	IHL	79	21	37	58	....	....	....	60	....	....	....	....	....	....	....	....	....	....	....	....	....	....	....	....	....	....
1991-1992	Ryerson Tech Rams	OUAA	DID NOT PLAY – ASSISTANT COACH																									
1992-1995	University of Toronto	OUAA	DID NOT PLAY – ASSISTANT COACH																									
1995-2000	University of Toronto	OUAA	DID NOT PLAY – COACHING																									
	NHL Totals		**8**	**1**	**2**	**3**	**1**	**1**	**2**	**0**	**0**	**0**	**0**	**14**	**7.1**	**4**	**0**	**9**	**0**		....	....	....	....	....	....	....	....

OUAA Second All-Star Team (1982) • OUAA First All-Star Team (1983)

Signed as a free agent by **Pittsburgh**, February, 1984.

• LOWE, Kevin

Kevin Hugh D – L. 6'2", 200 lbs. b: Lachute, Que., 4/15/1959. Edmonton's 1st, 21st overall, in 1979.

Season	Club	League	GP	G	A	Pts	AG	AA	APts	PIM	PP	SH	GW	S	%	TGF	PGF	TGA	PGA	+/–	GP	G	A	Pts	PIM	PP	SH	GW
1976-77	Quebec Remparts	QMJHL	69	3	19	22	....	....	....	39	....	....	....	....	....	....	....	....	....	....	....	....	....	....	....	....	....	....
1977-78	Quebec Remparts	QMJHL	64	13	52	65	....	....	....	86	....	....	....	....	....	....	....	....	....	....	4	1	2	3	6	....	....	....
1978-79	Quebec Remparts	QMJHL	68	26	60	86	....	....	....	120	....	....	....	....	....	....	....	....	....	....	6	1	7	8	36	....	....	....
1979-80	**Edmonton Oilers**	**NHL**	**64**	**2**	**19**	**21**	**2**	**14**	**16**	**70**	**2**	**0**	**0**	**86**	**2.3**	**73**	**13**	**64**	**5**	**1**	**3**	**0**	**1**	**1**	**0**	**0**	**0**	**0**
1980-81	**Edmonton Oilers**	**NHL**	**79**	**10**	**24**	**34**	**8**	**16**	**24**	**94**	**4**	**0**	**2**	**115**	**8.7**	**90**	**15**	**109**	**24**	**–10**	**9**	**0**	**2**	**2**	**11**	**0**	**0**	**0**
1981-82	**Edmonton Oilers**	**NHL**	**80**	**9**	**31**	**40**	**7**	**21**	**28**	**63**	**1**	**1**	**2**	**110**	**8.2**	**129**	**16**	**104**	**37**	**46**	**5**	**0**	**3**	**3**	**0**	**0**	**0**	**0**
	Canada	WEC-A	9	1	1	2	....	....	....	2	....	....	....	....	....	....	....	....	....	....	....	....	....	....	....	....	....	....
1982-83	**Edmonton Oilers**	**NHL**	**80**	**6**	**34**	**40**	**5**	**24**	**29**	**43**	**1**	**0**	**0**	**92**	**6.5**	**122**	**15**	**111**	**43**	**39**	**16**	**1**	**8**	**9**	**10**	**0**	**0**	**0**
1983-84♦	**Edmonton Oilers**	**NHL**	**80**	**4**	**42**	**46**	**3**	**29**	**32**	**59**	**1**	**0**	**1**	**81**	**4.9**	**122**	**15**	**106**	**36**	**37**	**19**	**3**	**7**	**10**	**16**	**0**	**0**	**0**
1984-85	Canada	Can-Cup	7	0	4	4	....	....	....	8	....	....	....	....	....	....	....	....	....	....	....	....	....	....	....	....	....	....
♦	**Edmonton Oilers**	**NHL**	**80**	**4**	**21**	**25**	**3**	**14**	**17**	**104**	**1**	**0**	**1**	**83**	**4.8**	**93**	**15**	**106**	**37**	**9**	**16**	**0**	**5**	**5**	**8**	**0**	**0**	**0**

			REGULAR SEASON																		PLAYOFFS							
Season	Club	League	GP	G	A	Pts	AG	AA	APts	PIM	PP	SH	GW	S	%	TGF	PGF	TGA	PGA	+/–	GP	G	A	Pts	PIM	PP	SH	GW
1985-86	Edmonton Oilers	NHL	74	2	16	18	2	11	13	90	0	0	0	57	3.5	88	8	77	21	24	10	1	3	4	15	0	0	0
1986-87♦	Edmonton Oilers	NHL	77	8	29	37	7	21	28	94	2	2	1	99	8.1	112	11	85	25	41	21	2	4	6	22	0	2	1
1987-88♦	Edmonton Oilers	NHL	70	9	15	24	8	11	19	89	2	1	2	82	11.0	104	19	102	35	18	19	0	2	2	26	0	0	0
1988-89	Edmonton Oilers	NHL	76	7	18	25	6	13	19	98	0	0	1	85	8.2	113	12	112	37	26	7	1	2	3	4	0	0	0
1989-90♦	Edmonton Oilers	NHL	78	7	26	33	6	19	25	140	2	1	0	74	9.5	98	9	108	37	18	20	0	2	2	10	0	0	0
1990-91	Edmonton Oilers	NHL	73	3	13	16	3	10	13	113	0	0	0	51	5.9	51	2	81	23	–9	14	1	1	2	14	0	0	0
1991-92	Edmonton Oilers	NHL	55	2	8	10	2	6	8	107	0	0	0	33	6.1	38	0	64	22	–4	11	0	3	3	16	0	0	0
1992-93	New York Rangers	NHL	49	3	12	15	2	8	10	58	0	0	0	52	5.8	43	1	66	22	–2	....	....	....	....	....	....	....	....
1993-94♦	New York Rangers	NHL	71	5	14	19	5	11	16	70	0	0	1	50	10.0	59	3	64	12	4	22	1	0	1	20	0	0	0
1994-95	New York Rangers	NHL	44	1	7	8	2	10	12	58	1	0	0	35	2.9	26	1	30	3	–2	10	0	1	1	12	0	0	0
1995-96	New York Rangers	NHL	53	1	5	6	1	4	5	76	0	0	0	30	3.3	37	0	31	14	20	10	0	4	4	4	0	0	0
1996-97	Edmonton Oilers	NHL	64	1	13	14	1	12	13	50	0	0	0	46	2.2	43	3	59	18	–1	1	0	0	0	0	0	0	0
1997-98	Edmonton Oilers	NHL	7	0	0	0	0	0	0	22	0	0	0	5	0.0	2	0	5	0	–3	1	0	0	0	4	0	0	0
1998-99	Edmonton Oilers	NHL	DID NOT PLAY – ASSISTANT COACH																									
99-2000	Edmonton Oilers	NHL	DID NOT PLAY – COACHING																									
	NHL Totals		1254	84	347	431	73	254	327	1498	17	5	11	1266	6.6	1443	158	1484	451		214	10	48	58	192	0	2	1

QMJHL Second All-Star Team (1978, 1979) • Won Bud Man of the Year Award (1990) • Won King Clancy Memorial Trophy (1990) • Played in NHL All-Star Game (1984, 1985, 1986, 1988, 1989, 1990, 1993)

Traded to **NY Rangers** by **Edmonton** for Roman Oksiuta and NY Rangers' 3rd round choice (Alexander Kerch) in 1993 Entry Draft, December 11, 1992. Signed as a free agent by **Edmonton**, September 28, 1996. • Named General Manager of **Edmonton Oilers**, June 9, 2000.

• LOWRY, Dave

Dave John "Pie" LW – L. 6'1", 200 lbs. b: Sudbury, Ont., 2/14/1965. Vancouver's 6th, 114th overall, in 1983.

Season	Club	League	GP	G	A	Pts	AG	AA	APts	PIM	PP	SH	GW	S	%	TGF	PGF	TGA	PGA	+/–	GP	G	A	Pts	PIM	PP	SH	GW
1981-82	Nepean Midget Raiders	OMHA	60	50	64	114	....	....	....	46	....	....	....	....	....	....	....	....	....	....	....	....	....	....	....	....	....	....
1982-83	London Knights	OHL	42	11	16	27	....	....	....	48	....	....	....	....	....	....	....	....	....	....	3	0	0	0	14	....	....	....
1983-84	London Knights	OHL	66	29	47	76	....	....	....	125	....	....	....	....	....	....	....	....	....	....	8	6	6	12	41	....	....	....
1984-85	London Knights	OHL	61	60	60	120	....	....	....	94	....	....	....	....	....	....	....	....	....	....	8	6	5	11	10	....	....	....
1985-86	Vancouver Canucks	NHL	73	10	8	18	8	5	13	143	1	0	1	66	15.2	25	3	43	0	–21	3	0	0	0	0	0	0	0
1986-87	Vancouver Canucks	NHL	70	8	10	18	7	7	14	176	0	0	1	74	10.8	25	0	48	0	–23	....	....	....	....	....	....	....	....
1987-88	Vancouver Canucks	NHL	22	1	3	4	1	2	3	38	0	0	0	14	7.1	12	6	9	1	–2	....	....	....	....	....	....	....	....
	Fredericton Express	AHL	46	18	27	45	....	....	....	59	....	....	....	....	....	....	....	....	....	....	14	7	3	10	72	....	....	....
1988-89	St. Louis Blues	NHL	21	3	3	6	3	2	5	11	0	1	0	22	13.6	13	0	21	9	1	10	0	5	5	4	0	0	0
	Peoria Rivermen	IHL	58	31	35	66	....	....	....	45	....	....	....	....	....	....	....	....	....	....	....	....	....	....	....	....	....	....
1989-90	St. Louis Blues	NHL	78	19	6	25	16	4	20	75	0	2	1	98	19.4	35	0	73	39	1	12	2	1	3	39	0	0	0
1990-91	St. Louis Blues	NHL	79	19	21	40	17	16	33	168	0	2	5	123	15.4	64	2	66	23	19	13	1	4	5	35	0	0	0
1991-92	St. Louis Blues	NHL	75	7	13	20	6	10	16	77	0	0	1	85	8.2	27	0	56	18	–11	6	0	1	1	20	0	0	0
1992-93	St. Louis Blues	NHL	58	5	8	13	4	5	9	101	0	0	0	59	8.5	16	0	44	10	–18	11	2	0	2	14	0	1	0
1993-94	Florida Panthers	NHL	80	15	22	37	14	17	31	64	3	0	3	122	12.3	67	27	50	6	–4	....	....	....	....	....	....	....	....
1994-95	Florida Panthers	NHL	45	10	10	20	18	15	33	25	2	0	3	70	14.3	33	11	25	0	–3	....	....	....	....	....	....	....	....
1995-96	Florida Panthers	NHL	63	10	14	24	10	11	21	36	0	0	1	83	12.0	41	13	31	1	–2	22	10	7	17	39	4	0	2
1996-97	Florida Panthers	NHL	77	15	14	29	16	12	28	51	2	0	2	96	15.6	48	11	39	4	2	5	0	0	0	0	0	0	0
1997-98	Florida Panthers	NHL	7	0	0	0	0	0	0	2	0	0	0	4	0.0	4	0	6	1	–1	....	....	....	....	....	....	....	....
	San Jose Sharks	NHL	50	4	4	8	5	4	9	51	0	0	1	47	8.5	12	0	13	1	0	6	0	0	0	18	0	0	0
1998-99	San Jose Sharks	NHL	61	6	9	15	7	9	16	24	2	0	0	58	10.3	17	3	21	2	–5	1	0	0	0	0	0	0	0
99-2000	San Jose Sharks	NHL	32	1	4	5	1	4	5	18	0	0	0	25	4.0	8	0	7	0	1	12	1	2	3	6	0	0	0
	NHL Totals		891	133	149	282	133	123	256	1060	10	5	19	1046	12.7	447	76	552	115		101	16	20	36	175	4	1	2

OHL First All-Star Team (1985)

Traded to **St. Louis** by **Vancouver** for Ernie Vargas, September 29, 1988. Claimed by **Florida** from **St. Louis** in Expansion Draft, June 24, 1993. Traded to **San Jose** by **Florida** with Florida's 1st round choice (later traded to Tampa Bay - Tampa Bay selected Vincent Lecavalier) for Viktor Kozlov and Florida's 5th round choice (previously acquired, Florida selected Jaroslav Spacek) in 1998 Entry Draft, November 13, 1997. • Missed majority of 1999-2000 season recovering from shoulder injury suffered in game vs. Montreal, November 23, 1999.

• LUCAS, Danny

Daniel Kenneth RW – L. 6'1", 197 lbs. b: Powell River, B.C., 2/28/1958. Philadelphia's 3rd, 14th overall, in 1978.

Season	Club	League	GP	G	A	Pts	AG	AA	APts	PIM	PP	SH	GW	S	%	TGF	PGF	TGA	PGA	+/–	GP	G	A	Pts	PIM	PP	SH	GW
1973-74	Humboldt Indians	SJHL	18	11	11	22	....	....	....	14	....	....	....	....	....	....	....	....	....	....	....	....	....	....	....	....	....	....
	Victoria Cougars	WCJHL	29	6	10	16	....	....	....	38	....	....	....	....	....	....	....	....	....	....	....	....	....	....	....	....	....	....
1974-75	Victoria Cougars	WCJHL	70	57	56	113	....	....	....	74	....	....	....	....	....	....	....	....	....	....	12	3	2	5	22	....	....	....
1975-76	Victoria Cougars	WCJHL	32	20	24	44	....	....	....	63-	....	....	....	....	....	....	....	....	....	....	....	....	....	....	....	....	....	....
1976-77	University of British Columbia	CWUAA	26	12	17	29	....	....	....	44	....	....	....	....	....	....	....	....	....	....	....	....	....	....	....	....	....	....
1977-78	Sault Ste. Marie Greyhounds	OMJHL	61	50	67	117	....	....	....	90	....	....	....	....	....	....	....	....	....	....	13	5	10	15	10	....	....	....
1978-79	Philadelphia Flyers	NHL	6	1	0	1	1	0	1	0	0	0	0	8	12.5	2	1	3	0	–2	....	....	....	....	....	....	....	....
	Maine Mariners	AHL	70	21	19	40	....	....	....	54	....	....	....	....	....	....	....	....	....	....	10	3	6	9	4	....	....	....
1979-80	Maine Mariners	AHL	80	25	27	52	....	....	....	33	....	....	....	....	....	....	....	....	....	....	12	2	9	11	6	....	....	....
1980-81	Fort Worth Texans	CHL	38	5	8	13	....	....	....	23	....	....	....	....	....	....	....	....	....	....	....	....	....	....	....	....	....	....
	Maine Mariners	AHL	2	0	0	0	....	....	....	2	....	....	....	....	....	....	....	....	....	....	....	....	....	....	....	....	....	....
	NHL Totals		6	1	0	1	1	0	1	0	0	0	0	8	12.5	2	1	3	0		....	....	....	....	....	....	....	....

Signed as a free agent by **Colorado**, October, 1980.

• LUCE, Don

Donald Harold C – L. 6'2", 185 lbs. b: London, Ont., 10/2/1948. NY Rangers' 3rd, 14th overall, in 1966.

Season	Club	League	GP	G	A	Pts	AG	AA	APts	PIM	PP	SH	GW	S	%	TGF	PGF	TGA	PGA	+/–	GP	G	A	Pts	PIM	PP	SH	GW
1965-66	Kitchener Rangers	OHA-Jr.	47	16	19	35	....	....	....	71	....	....	....	....	....	....	....	....	....	....	19	4	12	16	20	....	....	....
1966-67	Kitchener Rangers	OHA-Jr.	48	19	42	61	....	....	....	94	....	....	....	....	....	....	....	....	....	....	13	7	9	16	35	....	....	....
1967-68	Kitchener Rangers	OHA-Jr.	54	24	*70	94	....	....	....	88	....	....	....	....	....	....	....	....	....	....	19	4	8	12	42	....	....	....
1968-69	Omaha Knights	CHL	72	22	34	56	....	....	....	56	....	....	....	....	....	....	....	....	....	....	7	3	4	7	11	....	....	....
1969-70	Omaha Knights	CHL	64	22	35	57	....	....	....	82	....	....	....	....	....	....	....	....	....	....	2	1	2	3	4	....	....	....
	New York Rangers	NHL	12	1	2	3	1	2	3	8	0	0	0	20	5.0	3	0	5	0	–2	5	0	1	1	4	0	0	0
1970-71	New York Rangers	NHL	9	0	1	1	0	1	1	0	0	0	0	3	0.0	1	0	1	0	0	....	....	....	....	....	....	....	....
	Detroit Red Wings	NHL	58	3	11	14	3	9	12	18	0	0	0	71	4.2	25	1	39	9	–6	....	....	....	....	....	....	....	....
1971-72	Buffalo Sabres	NHL	78	11	8	19	11	7	18	38	0	0	1	126	8.7	26	0	84	40	–18	....	....	....	....	....	....	....	....
1972-73	Buffalo Sabres	NHL	78	18	25	43	17	20	37	32	0	3	2	198	9.1	51	0	69	25	7	6	1	1	2	2	0	0	0
1973-74	Buffalo Sabres	NHL	75	26	31	57	25	26	51	44	2	3	1	237	11.0	67	4	93	33	3	....	....	....	....	....	....	....	....
1974-75	Buffalo Sabres	NHL	80	33	43	76	29	32	61	45	1	8	6	245	13.5	105	7	79	42	61	16	5	8	13	19	0	1	0
1975-76	Buffalo Sabres	NHL	77	21	49	70	18	37	55	42	2	2	2	214	9.8	95	8	85	35	37	9	4	3	7	6	0	0	1
1976-77	Buffalo Sabres	NHL	80	26	43	69	23	33	56	16	6	1	6	206	12.6	97	14	69	24	38	6	3	1	4	2	2	0	0
1977-78	Buffalo Sabres	NHL	78	26	35	61	24	27	51	24	5	2	3	170	15.3	103	17	79	25	32	8	0	2	2	6	0	0	0
1978-79	Buffalo Sabres	NHL	79	26	35	61	22	25	47	14	6	2	7	149	17.4	86	18	87	39	20	3	1	1	2	0	0	0	0
1979-80	Buffalo Sabres	NHL	80	14	29	43	12	21	33	30	0	0	0	137	10.2	65	4	69	30	22	14	3	3	6	11	0	1	1
1980-81	Buffalo Sabres	NHL	61	15	13	28	12	9	21	19	0	4	2	94	16.0	38	0	47	23	14	....	....	....	....	....	....	....	....
	Los Angeles Kings	NHL	10	1	0	1	1	0	1	2	0	0	0	8	12.5	1	0	10	5	–4	4	0	2	2	2	0	0	0
1981-82	Toronto Maple Leafs	NHL	39	4	4	8	3	3	6	32	0	1	0	36	11.1	12	0	37	18	–7	....	....	....	....	....	....	....	....
	Salt Lake Golden Eagles	CHL	2	1	0	1	....	....	....	4	....	....	....	....	....	....	....	....	....	....	10	2	5	7	8	....	....	....
	NHL Totals		894	225	329	554	201	252	453	364	22	26	30	1914	11.8	775	73	853	348		71	17	22	39	52	2	2	2

CHL First All-Star Team (1970) • Won Bill Masterton Trophy (1975) • Played in NHL All-Star Game (1975)

Traded to **Detroit** by **NY Rangers** for Steve Andrascik, November 2, 1970. Traded to **Buffalo** by **Detroit** with Mike Robitaille for Joe Daley, May 25, 1971. Traded to **LA Kings** by **Buffalo** for LA Kings' 6th round choice (Jacob Gustavsson) in 1982 Entry Draft, March 10, 1981. Traded to **Toronto** by **LA Kings** for Bob Gladney and Toronto's 6th round choice (Kevin Stevens) in 1983 Entry Draft, August 10, 1981.

• LUDVIG, Jan

RW – R. 5'10", 190 lbs. b: Liberec, Czech., 9/17/1961.

Season	Club	League	GP	G	A	Pts	AG	AA	APts	PIM	PP	SH	GW	S	%	TGF	PGF	TGA	PGA	+/–	GP	G	A	Pts	PIM	PP	SH	GW
			REGULAR SEASON																		PLAYOFFS							
1978-79	Czechoslovakia	EJC-A	5	5	0	5	....	....	....	8	....	....	....	....	....	....	....	....	....	....	....	....	....	....	....	....	....	....
1980-81	CHZ Litvinov	Czech.	3	0	0	0	....	....	....	0	....	....	....	....	....	....	....	....	....	....	....	....	....	....	....	....	....	....
1981-82	St. Albert Saints	AJHL	4	2	4	6	....	....	....	20	....	....	....	....	....	....	....	....	....	....	....	....	....	....	....	....	....	....
	Kamloops Jr. Oilers	WHL	37	31	34	65	....	....	....	136	....	....	....	....	....	....	....	....	....	....	4	2	0	2	7	....	....	....
	Wichita Wind	CHL	....	....	....	....	....	....	....	....	....	....	....	....	....	....	....	....	....	....	3	2	0	2	0	....	....	....
1982-83	**New Jersey Devils**	**NHL**	**51**	**7**	**10**	**17**	**6**	**7**	**13**	**30**	**2**	**0**	**0**	**103**	**6.8**	**33**	**11**	**49**	**0**	**–27**	....	....	....	....	....	....	....	....
	Wichita Wind	CHL	9	3	0	3	....	....	....	19	....	....	....	....	....	....	....	....	....	....	....	....	....	....	....	....	....	....
1983-84	**New Jersey Devils**	**NHL**	**74**	**22**	**32**	**54**	**18**	**22**	**40**	**70**	**7**	**0**	**2**	**176**	**12.5**	**76**	**31**	**65**	**2**	**–18**	....	....	....	....	....	....	....	....
1984-85	**New Jersey Devils**	**NHL**	**74**	**12**	**19**	**31**	**10**	**13**	**23**	**53**	**3**	**0**	**1**	**134**	**9.0**	**63**	**20**	**62**	**0**	**–19**	....	....	....	....	....	....	....	....
1985-86	**New Jersey Devils**	**NHL**	**42**	**5**	**9**	**14**	**4**	**6**	**10**	**63**	**0**	**0**	**0**	**72**	**6.9**	**22**	**7**	**31**	**0**	**–16**	....	....	....	....	....	....	....	....
1986-87	**New Jersey Devils**	**NHL**	**47**	**7**	**9**	**16**	**6**	**7**	**13**	**98**	**1**	**0**	**0**	**56**	**12.5**	**29**	**4**	**30**	**0**	**–5**	....	....	....	....	....	....	....	....
	Maine Mariners	AHL	14	6	4	10	....	....	....	46	....	....	....	....	....	....	....	....	....	....	....	....	....	....	....	....	....	....
1987-88	**Buffalo Sabres**	**NHL**	**13**	**1**	**6**	**7**	**1**	**4**	**5**	**65**	**0**	**0**	**0**	**13**	**7.7**	**11**	**2**	**8**	**0**	**1**	....	....	....	....	....	....	....	....
1988-89	**Buffalo Sabres**	**NHL**	**13**	**0**	**2**	**2**	**0**	**1**	**1**	**39**	**0**	**0**	**0**	**11**	**0.0**	**6**	**0**	**7**	**0**	**–1**	....	....	....	....	....	....	....	....
	NHL Totals		**314**	**54**	**87**	**141**	**45**	**60**	**105**	**418**	**13**	**0**	**3**	**565**	**9.6**	**240**	**75**	**252**	**2**		....	....	....	....	....	....	....	....

EJC-A All-Star Team (1979) • Named Best Forward at EJC-A (1979)

Signed as a free agent by **New Jersey**, October 28, 1982. Traded to **Buffalo** by **New Jersey** for Jim Korn, May 22, 1987.

• LUDWIG, Craig

Craig Lee D – L. 6'3", 220 lbs. b: Rhinelander, WI, 3/15/1961. Montreal's 5th, 61st overall, in 1980.

Season	Club	League	GP	G	A	Pts	AG	AA	APts	PIM	PP	SH	GW	S	%	TGF	PGF	TGA	PGA	+/–	GP	G	A	Pts	PIM	PP	SH	GW
1979-80	University of North Dakota	WCHA	33	1	8	9	....	....	....	32	....	....	....	....	....	....	....	....	....	....	....	....	....	....	....	....	....	....
1980-81	University of North Dakota	WCHA	34	4	8	12	....	....	....	48	....	....	....	....	....	....	....	....	....	....	....	....	....	....	....	....	....	....
	United States	WJC-A	5	0	0	0	....	....	....	12	....	....	....	....	....	....	....	....	....	....	....	....	....	....	....	....	....	....
1981-82	University of North Dakota	WCHA	37	4	17	21	....	....	....	42	....	....	....	....	....	....	....	....	....	....	....	....	....	....	....	....	....	....
1982-83	**Montreal Canadiens**	**NHL**	**80**	**0**	**25**	**25**	**0**	**17**	**17**	**59**	**0**	**0**	**0**	**81**	**0.0**	**92**	**8**	**105**	**25**	**4**	**3**	**0**	**0**	**0**	**2**	**0**	**0**	**0**
1983-84	**Montreal Canadiens**	**NHL**	**80**	**7**	**18**	**25**	**6**	**12**	**18**	**52**	**0**	**0**	**1**	**116**	**6.0**	**103**	**6**	**147**	**40**	**–10**	**15**	**0**	**3**	**3**	**23**	**0**	**0**	**0**
1984-85	**Montreal Canadiens**	**NHL**	**72**	**5**	**14**	**19**	**4**	**10**	**14**	**90**	**1**	**0**	**0**	**73**	**6.8**	**76**	**3**	**101**	**33**	**5**	**12**	**0**	**2**	**2**	**6**	**0**	**0**	**0**
1985-86♦	**Montreal Canadiens**	**NHL**	**69**	**2**	**4**	**6**	**2**	**3**	**5**	**63**	**0**	**0**	**0**	**58**	**3.4**	**67**	**0**	**103**	**43**	**7**	**20**	**0**	**1**	**1**	**48**	**0**	**0**	**0**
1986-87	**Montreal Canadiens**	**NHL**	**75**	**4**	**12**	**16**	**3**	**9**	**12**	**105**	**0**	**0**	**0**	**55**	**7.3**	**63**	**0**	**72**	**12**	**3**	**17**	**2**	**3**	**5**	**30**	**0**	**0**	**1**
1987-88	**Montreal Canadiens**	**NHL**	**74**	**4**	**10**	**14**	**3**	**7**	**10**	**69**	**0**	**0**	**0**	**82**	**4.9**	**66**	**1**	**83**	**35**	**17**	**11**	**1**	**1**	**2**	**6**	**0**	**0**	**0**
1988-89	**Montreal Canadiens**	**NHL**	**74**	**3**	**13**	**16**	**3**	**9**	**12**	**73**	**0**	**1**	**1**	**83**	**3.6**	**94**	**3**	**97**	**39**	**33**	**21**	**0**	**2**	**2**	**24**	**0**	**0**	**0**
1989-90	**Montreal Canadiens**	**NHL**	**73**	**1**	**15**	**16**	**1**	**11**	**12**	**108**	**0**	**0**	**0**	**49**	**2.0**	**73**	**0**	**81**	**32**	**24**	**11**	**0**	**1**	**1**	**16**	**0**	**0**	**0**
1990-91	**New York Islanders**	**NHL**	**75**	**1**	**8**	**9**	**1**	**6**	**7**	**77**	**0**	**0**	**0**	**46**	**2.2**	**46**	**0**	**108**	**38**	**–24**	....	....	....	....	....	....	....	....
1991-92	**Minnesota North Stars**	**NHL**	**73**	**2**	**9**	**11**	**2**	**7**	**9**	**54**	**0**	**0**	**0**	**51**	**3.9**	**45**	**0**	**85**	**40**	**0**	**7**	**0**	**1**	**1**	**19**	**0**	**0**	**0**
1992-93	**Minnesota North Stars**	**NHL**	**78**	**1**	**10**	**11**	**1**	**7**	**8**	**153**	**0**	**0**	**0**	**66**	**1.5**	**68**	**1**	**95**	**29**	**1**	....	....	....	....	....	....	....	....
1993-94	**Dallas Stars**	**NHL**	**84**	**1**	**13**	**14**	**1**	**10**	**11**	**123**	**1**	**0**	**0**	**65**	**1.5**	**65**	**1**	**100**	**35**	**–1**	**9**	**0**	**3**	**3**	**8**	**0**	**0**	**0**
1994-95	**Dallas Stars**	**NHL**	**47**	**2**	**7**	**9**	**4**	**10**	**14**	**61**	**0**	**0**	**0**	**55**	**3.6**	**34**	**0**	**60**	**20**	**–6**	**4**	**0**	**1**	**1**	**2**	**0**	**0**	**0**
1995-96	**Dallas Stars**	**NHL**	**65**	**1**	**2**	**3**	**1**	**2**	**3**	**70**	**0**	**0**	**0**	**47**	**2.1**	**28**	**0**	**72**	**27**	**–17**	....	....	....	....	....	....	....	....
1996-97	**Dallas Stars**	**NHL**	**77**	**2**	**11**	**13**	**2**	**10**	**12**	**62**	**0**	**0**	**1**	**59**	**3.4**	**60**	**0**	**60**	**17**	**17**	**7**	**0**	**2**	**2**	**18**	**0**	**0**	**0**
1997-98	**Dallas Stars**	**NHL**	**80**	**0**	**7**	**7**	**0**	**7**	**7**	**131**	**0**	**0**	**0**	**46**	**0.0**	**45**	**0**	**39**	**15**	**21**	**17**	**0**	**1**	**1**	**22**	**0**	**0**	**0**
1998-99♦	**Dallas Stars**	**NHL**	**80**	**2**	**6**	**8**	**2**	**6**	**8**	**87**	**0**	**0**	**0**	**39**	**5.1**	**36**	**0**	**48**	**17**	**5**	**23**	**1**	**4**	**5**	**20**	**0**	**0**	**0**
1999-2000	**Dallas Stars**	**NHL**	DID NOT PLAY – SCOUTING																									
	Michigan K-Wings	IHL	DID NOT PLAY – ASSISTANT COACH																									
	NHL Totals		**1256**	**38**	**184**	**222**	**36**	**143**	**179**	**1437**	**2**	**1**	**3**	**1071**	**3.5**	**1061**	**23**	**1456**	**497**		**177**	**4**	**25**	**29**	**244**	**0**	**0**	**1**

WCHA Second All-Star Team (1982)

Traded to **NY Islanders** by **Montreal** for Gerald Diduck, September 4, 1990. Traded to **Minnesota** by **NY Islanders** for Tom Kurvers, June 22, 1991. Transferred to **Dallas** after **Minnesota** franchise relocated, June 9, 1993. • Named Assistant Coach of **Michigan** (IHL), January 27, 2000.

• LUDZIK, Steve

Stephen Paul C – L. 5'11", 185 lbs. b: Toronto, Ont., 4/3/1962. Chicago's 3rd, 28th overall, in 1980.

Season	Club	League	GP	G	A	Pts	AG	AA	APts	PIM	PP	SH	GW	S	%	TGF	PGF	TGA	PGA	+/–	GP	G	A	Pts	PIM	PP	SH	GW
1977-78	Markham Waxers	OHA-B	31	30	20	50	....	....	....	15	....	....	....	....	....	....	....	....	....	....	....	....	....	....	....	....	....	....
1978-79	Niagara Falls Flyers	OMJHL	68	32	65	97	....	....	....	138	....	....	....	....	....	....	....	....	....	....	20	7	17	24	48	....	....	....
1979-80	Niagara Falls Flyers	OMJHL	67	43	76	119	....	....	....	102	....	....	....	....	....	....	....	....	....	....	10	6	6	12	16	....	....	....
1980-81	Niagara Falls Flyers	OMJHL	58	50	92	142	....	....	....	108	....	....	....	....	....	....	....	....	....	....	12	5	9	14	40	....	....	....
1981-82	**Chicago Black Hawks**	**NHL**	**8**	**2**	**1**	**3**	**2**	**1**	**3**	**2**	**0**	**0**	**0**	**9**	**22.2**	**4**	**0**	**3**	**0**	**1**	....	....	....	....	....	....	....	....
	New Brunswick Hawks	AHL	73	21	41	62	....	....	....	142	....	....	....	....	....	....	....	....	....	....	15	3	7	10	6	....	....	....
1982-83	**Chicago Black Hawks**	**NHL**	**66**	**6**	**19**	**25**	**5**	**13**	**18**	**63**	**0**	**0**	**0**	**56**	**10.7**	**34**	**1**	**27**	**1**	**7**	**13**	**3**	**5**	**8**	**20**	**0**	**0**	**0**
1983-84	**Chicago Black Hawks**	**NHL**	**80**	**9**	**20**	**29**	**7**	**14**	**21**	**73**	**0**	**0**	**0**	**102**	**8.8**	**44**	**4**	**49**	**4**	**–5**	**4**	**0**	**1**	**1**	**9**	**0**	**0**	**0**
1984-85	**Chicago Black Hawks**	**NHL**	**79**	**11**	**20**	**31**	**9**	**14**	**23**	**86**	**0**	**1**	**1**	**100**	**11.0**	**44**	**0**	**63**	**24**	**5**	**15**	**1**	**1**	**2**	**16**	**0**	**0**	**0**
1985-86	**Chicago Black Hawks**	**NHL**	**49**	**6**	**5**	**11**	**5**	**3**	**8**	**21**	**0**	**1**	**0**	**41**	**14.6**	**19**	**0**	**39**	**18**	**–2**	**3**	**0**	**0**	**0**	**12**	**0**	**0**	**0**
1986-87	**Chicago Blackhawks**	**NHL**	**52**	**5**	**12**	**17**	**4**	**9**	**13**	**34**	**0**	**0**	**1**	**56**	**8.9**	**23**	**0**	**51**	**25**	**–3**	**4**	**0**	**0**	**0**	**0**	**0**	**0**	**0**
1987-88	**Chicago Blackhawks**	**NHL**	**73**	**6**	**15**	**21**	**5**	**11**	**16**	**40**	**1**	**0**	**1**	**55**	**10.9**	**28**	**4**	**58**	**20**	**–14**	**5**	**0**	**1**	**1**	**13**	**0**	**0**	**0**
1988-89	**Chicago Blackhawks**	**NHL**	**6**	**1**	**0**	**1**	**1**	**0**	**1**	**8**	**0**	**0**	**0**	**7**	**14.3**	**2**	**0**	**3**	**1**	**0**	....	....	....	....	....	....	....	....
	Saginaw Hawks	IHL	65	21	57	78	....	....	....	129	....	....	....	....	....	....	....	....	....	....	6	0	1	1	17	....	....	....
1989-90	**Buffalo Sabres**	**NHL**	**11**	**0**	**1**	**1**	**0**	**1**	**1**	**6**	**0**	**0**	**0**	**15**	**0.0**	**1**	**0**	**3**	**0**	**–2**	....	....	....	....	....	....	....	....
	Rochester Americans	AHL	54	25	29	54	....	....	....	71	....	....	....	....	....	....	....	....	....	....	16	5	6	11	57	....	....	....
1990-91	Rochester Americans	AHL	65	22	29	51	....	....	....	137	....	....	....	....	....	....	....	....	....	....	8	3	5	8	6	....	....	....
1991-92	Rochester Americans	AHL	45	6	22	28	....	....	....	88	....	....	....	....	....	....	....	....	....	....	14	2	1	3	8	....	....	....
1992-93	EK Zell-am-Zee	Austria	51	18	35	53	....	....	....	....	....	....	....	....	....	....	....	....	....	....	....	....	....	....	....	....	....	....
1993-1995	Muskegon Fury	ColHL	DID NOT PLAY – COACHING																									
1995-1996	Detroit Vipers	IHL	DID NOT PLAY – ASSISTANT COACH																									
1996-1999	Detroit Vipers	IHL	DID NOT PLAY – COACHING																									
1999-2000	**Tampa Bay Lightning**	**NHL**	DID NOT PLAY – COACHING																									
	NHL Totals		**424**	**46**	**93**	**139**	**38**	**66**	**104**	**333**	**1**	**2**	**3**	**441**	**10.4**	**199**	**9**	**296**	**93**		**44**	**4**	**8**	**12**	**70**	**0**	**0**	**0**

Traded to **Buffalo** by **Chicago** with Buffalo's 6th round choice (Derek Edgerly) in 1990 Entry Draft for Jacques Cloutier and Chicago's 5th round choice (Todd Bojcun) in 1990 Entry Draft, September 28, 1989.

• LUHNING, Warren

Warren A. RW – R. 6'2", 185 lbs. b: Edmonton, Alta., 7/3/1975. NY Islanders' 4th, 92nd overall, in 1993.

Season	Club	League	GP	G	A	Pts	AG	AA	APts	PIM	PP	SH	GW	S	%	TGF	PGF	TGA	PGA	+/–	GP	G	A	Pts	PIM	PP	SH	GW
1992-93	Calgary Royals	AJHL	46	18	25	43	....	....	....	287	....	....	....	....	....	....	....	....	....	....	....	....	....	....	....	....	....	....
1993-94	University of Michigan	CCHA	38	13	6	19	....	....	....	83	....	....	....	....	....	....	....	....	....	....	....	....	....	....	....	....	....	....
1994-95	University of Michigan	CCHA	36	17	23	40	....	....	....	80	....	....	....	....	....	....	....	....	....	....	....	....	....	....	....	....	....	....
1995-96	University of Michigan	CCHA	40	20	32	52	....	....	....	123	....	....	....	....	....	....	....	....	....	....	....	....	....	....	....	....	....	....
1996-97	University of Michigan	CCHA	43	22	23	45	....	....	....	106	....	....	....	....	....	....	....	....	....	....	....	....	....	....	....	....	....	....
1997-98	**New York Islanders**	**NHL**	**8**	**0**	**0**	**0**	**0**	**0**	**0**	**0**	**0**	**0**	**0**	**6**	**0.0**	**0**	**0**	**4**	**0**	**–4**	....	....	....	....	....	....	....	....
	Kentucky Thoroughblades	AHL	51	6	7	13	....	....	....	82	....	....	....	....	....	....	....	....	....	....	....	....	....	....	....	....	....	....
1998-99	**New York Islanders**	**NHL**	**11**	**0**	**0**	**0**	**0**	**0**	**0**	**8**	**0**	**0**	**0**	**11**	**0.0**	**1**	**0**	**5**	**0**	**–4**	....	....	....	....	....	....	....	....
	Lowell Lock Monsters	AHL	56	20	20	40	....	....	....	67	....	....	....	....	....	....	....	....	....	....	3	0	3	3	16	....	....	....
99-2000	**Dallas Stars**	**NHL**	**10**	**0**	**1**	**1**	**0**	**1**	**1**	**13**	**0**	**0**	**0**	**7**	**0.0**	**2**	**0**	**4**	**0**	**–2**	....	....	....	....	....	....	....	....
	Michigan K-Wings	IHL	3	1	1	2	....	....	....	4	....	....	....	....	....	....	....	....	....	....	....	....	....	....	....	....	....	....
	NHL Totals		**29**	**0**	**1**	**1**	**0**	**1**	**1**	**21**	**0**	**0**	**0**	**24**	**0.0**	**3**	**0**	**13**	**0**		....	....	....	....	....	....	....	....

Traded to **Dallas** by **NY Islanders** for Dallas' 3rd round choice (previously acquired, Dallas selected Mathias Tjarnqvist) in 1999 Entry Draft, June 25, 1999.

• LUKOWICH, Bernie

Bernard Joseph RW – R. 6', 190 lbs. b: North Battleford, Sask., 3/18/1952. Pittsburgh's 2nd, 30th overall, in 1972.

Season	Club	League	GP	G	A	Pts	AG	AA	APts	PIM	PP	SH	GW	S	%	TGF	PGF	TGA	PGA	+/–	GP	G	A	Pts	PIM	PP	SH	GW
1968-69	North Battleford North Stars	AAHA	STATISTICS NOT AVAILABLE																									
	Estevan Bruins	WCJHL	3	0	0	0	....	....	....	0	....	....	....	....	....	....	....	....	....	....	....	....	....	....	....	....	....	....
1969-70	Estevan Bruins	WCJHL	60	23	31	54	....	....	....	47	....	....	....	....	....	....	....	....	....	....	5	0	0	0	6	....	....	....
1970-71	Estevan Bruins	WCJHL	65	36	38	74	....	....	....	75	....	....	....	....	....	....	....	....	....	....	7	5	3	8	2	....	....	....
1971-72	New Westminster Bruins	WCJHL	68	37	39	76	....	....	....	107	....	....	....	....	....	....	....	....	....	....	5	3	0	3	4	....	....	....

Season	Club	League	GP	G	A	Pts	AG	AA	APts	PIM	PP	SH	GW	S	%	TGF	PGF	TGA	PGA	+/-	GP	G	A	Pts	PIM	PP	SH	GW
			REGULAR SEASON																		PLAYOFFS							
1972-73	Hershey Bears	AHL	69	22	23	45				64											7	0	2	2	26			
1973-74	**Pittsburgh Penguins**	**NHL**	**53**	**9**	**10**	**19**	**9**	**8**	**17**	**32**	**1**	**0**	**2**	**60**	**15.0**	**26**	**2**	**28**	**0**	**–4**								
	Hershey Bears	AHL	17	4	5	9				12																		
1974-75	Hershey Bears	AHL	27	9	14	23				53																		
	St. Louis Blues	**NHL**	**26**	**4**	**5**	**9**	**3**	**4**	**7**	**2**	**2**	**0**	**2**	**19**	**21.1**	**14**	**3**	**8**	**1**	**4**	**2**	**0**	**0**	**0**	**0**	**0**	**0**	**0**
	Denver Spurs	CHL	7	6	6	12				8																		
1975-76	Providence Reds	AHL	64	21	17	38				62																		
	Calgary Cowboys	WHA	15	5	2	7				18											10	3	4	7	8			
1976-77	Hershey Bears	AHL	37	15	18	33				19											6	1	1	2	4			
	Tidewater Sharks	SHL	29	13	15	28				4																		
	Calgary Cowboys	WHA	6	0	1	1				0																		
1977-78	Cranbrook Royals	WIHL	32	10	25	35				30																		
1978-79			OUT OF HOCKEY – RETIRED																									
1979-80			OUT OF HOCKEY – RETIRED																									
1980-81	Cranbrook Royals	WIHL	34	15	12	27				29																		
1981-82	Cranbrook Royals	WIHL	32	10	22	32				35																		
	NHL Totals		**79**	**13**	**15**	**28**	**12**	**12**	**24**	**34**	**3**	**0**	**4**	**79**	**16.5**	**40**	**5**	**36**	**1**		**2**	**0**	**0**	**0**	**0**	**0**	**0**	**0**
	Other Major League Totals		21	5	3	8				18											10	3	4	7	8			

Selected by **Calgary-Cleveland** (WHA) in 1972 WHA General Player Draft, February 12, 1972. Traded to **St. Louis** by **Pittsburgh** for Bob Stumpf, January 20, 1975. Signed as a free agent by **Calgary** (WHA), March, 1977.

• LUKOWICH, Brad

D – L. 6'1", 200 lbs. b: Cranbrook, B.C., 8/12/1976. NY Islanders' 4th, 90th overall, in 1994.

Season	Club	League	GP	G	A	Pts	AG	AA	APts	PIM	PP	SH	GW	S	%	TGF	PGF	TGA	PGA	+/-	GP	G	A	Pts	PIM	PP	SH	GW
1992-93	Cranbrook Colts	KIJHL	54	21	41	62				162																		
	Kamloops Blazers	WHL	1	0	0	0				0																		
1993-94	Kamloops Blazers	WHL	42	5	11	16				166											16	0	1	1	35			
	Kamloops Blazers	Mem-Cup	3	0	2	2				0																		
1994-95	Kamloops Blazers	WHL	63	10	35	45				125											18	0	7	7	21			
	Kamloops Blazers	Mem-Cup	4	1	3	4				0																		
1995-96	Kamloops Blazers	WHL	65	14	55	69				114											13	2	10	12	29			
1996-97	Michigan K-Wings	IHL	69	2	6	8				77											4	0	1	1	2			
1997-98	**Dallas Stars**	**NHL**	**4**	**0**	**1**	**1**	**0**	**1**	**1**	**2**	**0**	**0**	**0**	**2**	**0.0**	**1**	**0**	**3**	**0**	**–2**								
	Michigan K-Wings	IHL	60	6	27	33				104											4	0	4	4	14			
1998-99♦	**Dallas Stars**	**NHL**	**14**	**1**	**2**	**3**	**1**	**2**	**3**	**19**	**0**	**0**	**0**	**8**	**12.5**	**8**	**0**	**5**	**0**	**3**	**8**	**0**	**1**	**1**	**4**	**0**	**0**	**0**
	Michigan K-Wings	IHL	67	8	21	29				95																		
99-2000	**Dallas Stars**	**NHL**	**60**	**3**	**1**	**4**	**3**	**1**	**4**	**50**	**0**	**0**	**1**	**33**	**9.1**	**20**	**0**	**37**	**3**	**–14**								
	NHL Totals		**78**	**4**	**4**	**8**	**4**	**4**	**8**	**71**	**0**	**0**	**1**	**43**	**9.3**	**29**	**0**	**45**	**3**		**8**	**0**	**1**	**1**	**4**	**0**	**0**	**0**

Traded to **Dallas** by **NY Islanders** for Dallas' 3rd round choice (Robert Schnabel) in 1997 Entry Draft, June 1, 1996. Traded to **Minnesota** by **Dallas** with Manny Fernandez for Minnesota's 3rd round choice (Joel Lundqvist) in 2000 Entry Draft and 4th round choice in 2001 Entry Draft, June 12, 2000. Traded to **Dallas** by **Minnesota** with Minnesota's 3rd and 9th round choices in 2001 Entry Draft for Aaron Gavey, Pavel Patera, Dallas' 8th round choice (Eric Johansson) in 2000 Entry Draft and Minnesota's 4th round choice (previously acquired) in 2002 Entry Draft, June 25, 2000.

• LUKOWICH, Morris

Morris Eugene LW – L. 5'9", 170 lbs. b: Speers, Sask., 6/1/1956. Pittsburgh's 4th, 47th overall, in 1976.

Season	Club	League	GP	G	A	Pts	AG	AA	APts	PIM	PP	SH	GW	S	%	TGF	PGF	TGA	PGA	+/-	GP	G	A	Pts	PIM	PP	SH	GW
1972-73	Saskatoon Blazers	SAHA	STATISTICS NOT AVAILABLE																									
1973-74	Medicine Hat Tigers	WCJHL	65	13	14	27				55											6	1	1	2	21			
1974-75	Medicine Hat Tigers	WCJHL	70	40	54	94				111											5	4	1	5	2			
1975-76	Medicine Hat Tigers	WCJHL	72	65	77	142				195											9	5	8	13	20			
1976-77	Houston Aeros	WHA	62	27	18	45				67											11	6	4	10	19			
1977-78	Houston Aeros	WHA	80	40	35	75				131											6	1	2	3	17			
1978-79	Winnipeg Jets	WHA	80	65	34	99				119											10	8	7	15	21			
1979-80	**Winnipeg Jets**	**NHL**	**78**	**35**	**39**	**74**	**30**	**28**	**58**	**77**	**13**	**1**	**2**	**201**	**17.4**	**105**	**42**	**93**	**14**	**–16**								
1980-81	**Winnipeg Jets**	**NHL**	**80**	**33**	**34**	**67**	**26**	**23**	**49**	**90**	**9**	**2**	**2**	**175**	**18.9**	**104**	**35**	**136**	**28**	**–39**								
	Canada	WEC-A	8	2	1	3				4																		
1981-82	**Winnipeg Jets**	**NHL**	**77**	**43**	**49**	**92**	**34**	**33**	**67**	**102**	**13**	**0**	**6**	**229**	**18.8**	**121**	**39**	**94**	**8**	**–4**	**4**	**0**	**2**	**2**	**16**	**0**	**0**	**0**
1982-83	**Winnipeg Jets**	**NHL**	**69**	**22**	**21**	**43**	**18**	**15**	**33**	**67**	**6**	**0**	**2**	**162**	**13.6**	**62**	**23**	**67**	**0**	**–28**								
1983-84	**Winnipeg Jets**	**NHL**	**80**	**30**	**25**	**55**	**24**	**17**	**41**	**71**	**4**	**0**	**1**	**155**	**19.4**	**94**	**23**	**61**	**0**	**10**	**3**	**0**	**0**	**0**	**0**	**0**	**0**	**0**
1984-85	**Winnipeg Jets**	**NHL**	**47**	**5**	**9**	**14**	**4**	**6**	**10**	**31**	**1**	**0**	**2**	**37**	**13.5**	**25**	**8**	**32**	**2**	**–13**								
	Boston Bruins	**NHL**	**22**	**5**	**8**	**13**	**4**	**5**	**9**	**21**	**0**	**0**	**1**	**29**	**17.2**	**20**	**2**	**12**	**1**	**7**	**1**	**0**	**0**	**0**	**0**	**0**	**0**	**0**
1985-86	**Boston Bruins**	**NHL**	**14**	**1**	**4**	**5**	**1**	**3**	**4**	**10**	**0**	**0**	**0**	**25**	**4.0**	**10**	**1**	**7**	**0**	**2**								
	Los Angeles Kings	**NHL**	**55**	**11**	**9**	**20**	**9**	**6**	**15**	**51**	**0**	**0**	**0**	**85**	**12.9**	**41**	**10**	**51**	**1**	**–19**								
1986-87	**Los Angeles Kings**	**NHL**	**60**	**14**	**21**	**35**	**12**	**15**	**27**	**64**	**4**	**0**	**2**	**105**	**13.3**	**69**	**32**	**37**	**0**	**0**	**3**	**0**	**0**	**0**	**8**	**0**	**0**	**0**
1987-88	HC Merano	Italy	23	16	31	47				46																		
1988-89			STATISTICS NOT AVAILABLE																									
1989-90	SC Rapperswil-Jona	Switz-2	36	30	35	65																						
	NHL Totals		**582**	**199**	**219**	**418**	**162**	**151**	**313**	**584**	**50**	**3**	**18**	**1203**	**16.5**	**651**	**215**	**590**	**54**		**11**	**0**	**2**	**2**	**24**	**0**	**0**	**0**
	Other Major League Totals		222	132	87	219				317											27	15	13	28	57			

WCJHL All-Star Team (1976) • WHA Second All-Star Team (1979) • Played in NHL All-Star Game (1980, 1981)

Selected by **Houston** (WHA) in 1976 WHA Amateur Draft, May, 1976. Traded to **Winnipeg** (WHA) by **Houston** (WHA) for cash, July, 1978. Reclaimed by **Pittsburgh** from **Winnipeg** prior to Expansion Draft, June 9, 1979. Claimed as a priority selection by **Winnipeg**, June 9, 1979. Traded to **Boston** by **Winnipeg** for Jim Nill, February 4, 1985. Claimed on waivers by **LA Kings** from **Boston**, November 15, 1985. • Played w/ RHI's Calgary Radz in 1993 (3-1-5-6-10).

• LUKSA, Charlie

Charles "Chuck" D – L. 6'1", 190 lbs. b: Toronto, Ont., 2/19/1954. Montreal's 15th, 172nd overall, in 1974.

Season	Club	League	GP	G	A	Pts	AG	AA	APts	PIM	PP	SH	GW	S	%	TGF	PGF	TGA	PGA	+/-	GP	G	A	Pts	PIM	PP	SH	GW
1971-72	Ottawa Jr. Senators	OCJHL	STATISTICS NOT AVAILABLE																									
	Oshawa Generals	OMJHL	1	0	0	0				0																		
1972-73	Kenora Huskies	MJHL	47	7	37	44				119																		
1973-74	University of Toronto	OUAA	22	3	19	22				50																		
	Kitchener Rangers	OMJHL	10	2	7	9																						
1974-75	Nova Scotia Voyageurs	AHL	32	0	4	4				54											6	1	0	1	5			
1975-76	Nova Scotia Voyageurs	AHL	73	5	13	18				75											9	0	2	2	6			
1976-77	Nova Scotia Voyageurs	AHL	80	9	31	40				72											12	1	5	6	7			
1977-78	Nova Scotia Voyageurs	AHL	66	3	23	26				89											11	1	4	5	25			
1978-79	Cincinnati Stingers	WHA	78	8	12	20				116											3	0	0	0	7			
1979-80	**Hartford Whalers**	**NHL**	**8**	**0**	**1**	**1**	**0**	**1**	**1**	**4**	**0**	**0**	**0**	**3**	**0.0**	**6**	**0**	**8**	**2**	**0**								
	Springfield Indians	AHL	72	10	39	49				83																		
1980-81	Binghamton Whalers	AHL	63	3	18	21				104											6	0	2	2	12			
1981-82	Jokerit Helsinki	Finland	21	1	2	3				58																		
	Rochester Americans	AHL	33	2	8	10				33											6	0	2	2	4			
	NHL Totals		**8**	**0**	**1**	**1**	**0**	**1**	**1**	**4**	**0**	**0**	**0**	**3**	**0.0**	**6**	**0**	**8**	**2**									
	Other Major League Totals		78	8	12	20				116											3	0	0	0	7			

AHL Second All-Star Team (1978)

Selected by **Phoenix** (WHA) in 1974 WHA Amateur Draft, May, 1974. Signed as a free agent by **Cincinnati** (WHA) after **Phoenix** (WHA) franchise folded, July, 1978. Claimed by **Hartford** from **Cincinnati** (WHA) in WHA Dispersal Draft, June 9, 1979.

• LUMLEY, Dave

David E. "Lummer" RW – R. 6', 185 lbs. b: Toronto, Ont., 9/1/1954. Montreal's 17th, 199th overall, in 1974.

Season	Club	League	GP	G	A	Pts	AG	AA	APts	PIM	PP	SH	GW	S	%	TGF	PGF	TGA	PGA	+/-	GP	G	A	Pts	PIM	PP	SH	GW
1972-73	Scarborough Sabres	OHA-B	STATISTICS NOT AVAILABLE																									
	Richmond Hill Rams	OHA-B	STATISTICS NOT AVAILABLE																									
1973-74	University of New Hampshire	ECAC	31	12	19	31				38																		
1974-75	University of New Hampshire	ECAC	26	12	26	38				56																		
1975-76	University of New Hampshire	ECAC	30	9	32	41				55																		
1976-77	University of New Hampshire	ECAC	39	22	38	60				42																		

Season	Club	League	GP	G	A	Pts	AG	AA	APts	PIM	PP	SH	GW	S	%	TGF	PGF	TGA	PGA	+/–	Playoffs GP	G	A	Pts	PIM	PP	SH	GW
			REGULAR SEASON																		**PLAYOFFS**							
1977-78	Nova Scotia Voyageurs	AHL	58	22	21	43	....	....	....	58	....	....	....	....	....	....	....	....	....	....	2	0	1	1	5	....	....	....
1978-79	**Montreal Canadiens**	**NHL**	**3**	**0**	**0**	**0**	**0**	**0**	**0**	**0**	**0**	**0**	**0**	**2**	**0.0**	**0**	**0**	**0**	**0**	**0**								
	Nova Scotia Voyageurs	AHL	61	22	58	80	....	....	....	160	....	....	....	....	....	....	....	....	....	....	10	6	8	14	35	....	....	....
1979-80	**Edmonton Oilers**	**NHL**	**80**	**20**	**38**	**58**	**17**	**28**	**45**	**138**	**1**	**0**	**6**	**145**	**13.8**	**88**	**13**	**62**	**2**	**15**	**3**	**1**	**0**	**1**	**12**	**1**	**0**	**0**
1980-81	**Edmonton Oilers**	**NHL**	**53**	**7**	**9**	**16**	**5**	**6**	**11**	**74**	**0**	**0**	**1**	**54**	**13.0**	**30**	**4**	**43**	**2**	**–15**	**7**	**1**	**0**	**1**	**4**	**0**	**0**	**0**
1981-82	**Edmonton Oilers**	**NHL**	**66**	**32**	**42**	**74**	**25**	**28**	**53**	**96**	**4**	**1**	**6**	**148**	**21.6**	**109**	**21**	**87**	**11**	**12**	**5**	**2**	**1**	**3**	**21**	**0**	**0**	**0**
1982-83	**Edmonton Oilers**	**NHL**	**72**	**13**	**24**	**37**	**11**	**17**	**28**	**158**	**2**	**0**	**1**	**96**	**13.5**	**68**	**8**	**41**	**0**	**19**	**16**	**0**	**0**	**0**	**19**	**0**	**0**	**0**
1983-84♦	**Edmonton Oilers**	**NHL**	**56**	**6**	**15**	**21**	**5**	**10**	**15**	**68**	**0**	**0**	**0**	**44**	**13.6**	**47**	**2**	**31**	**0**	**14**	**19**	**2**	**5**	**7**	**44**	**0**	**0**	**0**
1984-85	**Hartford Whalers**	**NHL**	**48**	**8**	**20**	**28**	**6**	**14**	**20**	**98**	**1**	**0**	**0**	**77**	**10.4**	**41**	**6**	**62**	**10**	**–17**	....	....	....	....	....	....	....	....
♦	**Edmonton Oilers**	**NHL**	**12**	**1**	**3**	**4**	**1**	**2**	**3**	**13**	**0**	**0**	**0**	**10**	**10.0**	**5**	**2**	**4**	**0**	**–1**	**8**	**0**	**0**	**0**	**29**	**0**	**0**	**0**
1985-86	**Edmonton Oilers**	**NHL**	**46**	**11**	**9**	**20**	**9**	**6**	**15**	**35**	**1**	**0**	**1**	**33**	**33.3**	**31**	**1**	**17**	**0**	**13**	**3**	**0**	**2**	**2**	**2**	**0**	**0**	**0**
1986-87	**Edmonton Oilers**	**NHL**	**1**	**0**	**0**	**0**	**0**	**0**	**0**	**0**	**0**	**0**	**0**	**0**	**0.0**	**1**	**0**	**1**	**0**	**0**	....	....	....	....	....	....	....	....
	NHL Totals		**437**	**98**	**160**	**258**	**79**	**111**	**190**	**680**	**9**	**1**	**15**	**609**	**16.1**	**420**	**57**	**348**	**25**		**61**	**6**	**8**	**14**	**131**	**1**	**0**	**0**

AHL Second All-Star Team (1979)

Traded to **Edmonton** by **Montreal** with Dan Newman for Edmonton's 2nd round choice (Ric Nattress) in 1980 Entry Draft, June 13, 1979. Claimed by **Hartford** from **Edmonton** in Waiver Draft, October 9, 1984. Claimed on waivers by **Edmonton** from **Hartford**, February 6, 1985. • Officially announced retirement, November 5, 1986.

• LUMME, Jyrki

Jyrki Olavi D – L. 6'1", 205 lbs. b: Tampere, Finland, 7/16/1966. Montreal's 3rd, 57th overall, in 1986.

Season	Club	League	GP	G	A	Pts	AG	AA	APts	PIM	PP	SH	GW	S	%	TGF	PGF	TGA	PGA	+/–	Playoffs GP	G	A	Pts	PIM	PP	SH	GW
1983-84	KooVee Tampere	Finland-Jr.	28	5	4	9	....	....	....	61	....	....	....	....	....	....	....	....	....	....	....	....	....	....	....	....	....	....
1984-85	KooVee Tampere	Finland-3	30	6	4	10	....	....	....	44	....	....	....	....	....	....	....	....	....	....	....	....	....	....	....	....	....	....
1985-86	Ilves Tampere	Finland-Jr.	6	3	3	6	....	....	....	6	....	....	....	....	....	....	....	....	....	....	4	0	0	0	8	....	....	....
	Ilves Tampere	Finland	31	1	4	5	....	....	....	4	....	....	....	....	....	....	....	....	....	....	....	....	....	....	....	....	....	....
	Finland	WJC-A	7	1	4	5	....	....	....	2	....	....	....	....	....	....	....	....	....	....	....	....	....	....	....	....	....	....
1986-87	Ilves Tampere	Finland-Jr.	1	0	1	1	....	....	....	6	....	....	....	....	....	....	....	....	....	....	1	1	0	1	6	....	....	....
	Ilves Tampere	Finland	43	12	12	24	....	....	....	52	....	....	....	....	....	....	....	....	....	....	4	0	1	1	2	....	....	....
1987-88	Ilves Tampere	Finland	43	8	22	30	....	....	....	75	....	....	....	....	....	....	....	....	....	....	....	....	....	....	....	....	....	....
	Finland	Olympics	6	0	1	1	....	....	....	2	....	....	....	....	....	....	....	....	....	....	....	....	....	....	....	....	....	....
1988-89	**Montreal Canadiens**	**NHL**	**21**	**1**	**3**	**4**	**1**	**2**	**3**	**10**	**1**	**0**	**0**	**18**	**5.6**	**21**	**8**	**12**	**2**	**3**	....	....	....	....	....	....	....	....
	Sherbrooke Canadiens	AHL	26	4	11	15	....	....	....	10	....	....	....	....	....	....	....	....	....	....	6	1	3	4	4	....	....	....
1989-90	**Montreal Canadiens**	**NHL**	**54**	**1**	**19**	**20**	**1**	**14**	**15**	**41**	**0**	**0**	**0**	**79**	**1.3**	**64**	**13**	**39**	**5**	**17**	....	....	....	....	....	....	....	....
	Vancouver Canucks	**NHL**	**11**	**3**	**7**	**10**	**3**	**5**	**8**	**8**	**0**	**0**	**1**	**30**	**10.0**	**21**	**10**	**11**	**0**	**0**	....	....	....	....	....	....	....	....
	Finland	WEC-A	10	3	4	7	....	....	....	6	....	....	....	....	....	....	....	....	....	....	....	....	....	....	....	....	....	....
1990-91	**Vancouver Canucks**	**NHL**	**80**	**5**	**27**	**32**	**5**	**21**	**26**	**59**	**1**	**0**	**0**	**157**	**3.2**	**91**	**25**	**96**	**15**	**–15**	**6**	**2**	**3**	**5**	**0**	**1**	**1**	**0**
	Finland	WEC-A	10	0	7	7	....	....	....	12	....	....	....	....	....	....	....	....	....	....	....	....	....	....	....	....	....	....
1991-92	Finland	Can-Cup	6	0	2	2	....	....	....	8	....	....	....	....	....	....	....	....	....	....	....	....	....	....	....	....	....	....
	Vancouver Canucks	**NHL**	**75**	**12**	**32**	**44**	**11**	**24**	**35**	**65**	**3**	**1**	**1**	**106**	**11.3**	**125**	**45**	**77**	**22**	**25**	**13**	**2**	**3**	**5**	**4**	**1**	**0**	**1**
1992-93	**Vancouver Canucks**	**NHL**	**74**	**8**	**36**	**44**	**7**	**25**	**32**	**55**	**3**	**2**	**1**	**123**	**6.5**	**110**	**29**	**80**	**29**	**30**	**12**	**0**	**5**	**5**	**6**	**0**	**0**	**0**
1993-94	**Vancouver Canucks**	**NHL**	**83**	**13**	**42**	**55**	**12**	**33**	**45**	**50**	**1**	**3**	**3**	**161**	**8.1**	**107**	**34**	**117**	**47**	**3**	**24**	**2**	**11**	**13**	**16**	**2**	**0**	**1**
1994-95	Ilves Tampere	Finland	12	4	4	8	....	....	....	24	....	....	....	....	....	....	....	....	....	....	....	....	....	....	....	....	....	....
	Vancouver Canucks	**NHL**	**36**	**5**	**12**	**17**	**9**	**18**	**27**	**26**	**3**	**0**	**1**	**78**	**6.4**	**47**	**13**	**41**	**11**	**4**	**11**	**2**	**6**	**8**	**8**	**1**	**0**	**0**
1995-96	**Vancouver Canucks**	**NHL**	**80**	**17**	**37**	**54**	**17**	**30**	**47**	**50**	**8**	**0**	**2**	**192**	**8.9**	**109**	**43**	**119**	**44**	**–9**	**6**	**1**	**3**	**4**	**2**	**1**	**0**	**0**
	Finland	WC-A	1	0	0	0	....	....	....	0	....	....	....	....	....	....	....	....	....	....	....	....	....	....	....	....	....	....
1996-97	Finland	W-Cup	4	2	1	3	....	....	....	4	....	....	....	....	....	....	....	....	....	....	....	....	....	....	....	....	....	....
	Vancouver Canucks	**NHL**	**66**	**11**	**24**	**35**	**12**	**21**	**33**	**32**	**5**	**0**	**2**	**107**	**10.3**	**82**	**25**	**75**	**26**	**8**	....	....	....	....	....	....	....	....
	Finland	WC-A	8	0	3	3	....	....	....	4	....	....	....	....	....	....	....	....	....	....	....	....	....	....	....	....	....	....
1997-98	**Vancouver Canucks**	**NHL**	**74**	**9**	**21**	**30**	**11**	**21**	**32**	**34**	**4**	**0**	**1**	**117**	**7.7**	**86**	**28**	**117**	**34**	**–25**	....	....	....	....	....	....	....	....
	Finland	Olympics	6	1	0	1	....	....	....	16	....	....	....	....	....	....	....	....	....	....	....	....	....	....	....	....	....	....
1998-99	**Phoenix Coyotes**	**NHL**	**60**	**7**	**21**	**28**	**8**	**20**	**28**	**34**	**1**	**0**	**4**	**121**	**5.8**	**58**	**16**	**50**	**13**	**5**	**7**	**0**	**1**	**1**	**6**	**0**	**0**	**0**
99-2000	**Phoenix Coyotes**	**NHL**	**74**	**8**	**32**	**40**	**9**	**30**	**39**	**44**	**4**	**0**	**3**	**142**	**5.6**	**104**	**29**	**88**	**22**	**9**	**5**	**0**	**1**	**1**	**2**	**0**	**0**	**0**
	Finland	WC-A	9	2	3	5	....	....	....	4	....	....	....	....	....	....	....	....	....	....	....	....	....	....	....	....	....	....
	NHL Totals		**788**	**100**	**313**	**413**	**106**	**264**	**370**	**508**	**34**	**6**	**19**	**1431**	**7.0**	**1025**	**318**	**922**	**270**		**84**	**9**	**33**	**42**	**44**	**6**	**1**	**2**

Traded to **Vancouver** by **Montreal** for St. Louis' 2nd round choice (previously acquired, Montreal selected Craig Darby) in 1991 Entry Draft, March 6, 1990. Signed as a free agent by **Phoenix**, July 3, 1998.

• LUNDBERG, Brian

Brian Frederick D – R. 5'10", 190 lbs. b: Burnaby, B.C., 6/5/1960. Pittsburgh's 7th, 177th overall, in 1980.

Season	Club	League	GP	G	A	Pts	AG	AA	APts	PIM	PP	SH	GW	S	%	TGF	PGF	TGA	PGA	+/–	Playoffs GP	G	A	Pts	PIM	PP	SH	GW
1977-78	Bellingham Blazers	BCJHL	STATISTICS NOT AVAILABLE																									
	Seattle Breakers	WCJHL	1	0	0	0	....	....	....	0	....	....	....	....	....	....	....	....	....	....	....	....	....	....	....	....	....	....
1978-79	University of Michigan	CCHA	DID NOT PLAY – FRESHMAN																									
1979-80	University of Michigan	CCHA	37	2	14	16	....	....	....	94	....	....	....	....	....	....	....	....	....	....	....	....	....	....	....	....	....	....
1980-81	University of Michigan	CCHA	40	1	6	7	....	....	....	42	....	....	....	....	....	....	....	....	....	....	....	....	....	....	....	....	....	....
1981-82	University of Michigan	CCHA	32	3	16	19	....	....	....	42	....	....	....	....	....	....	....	....	....	....	....	....	....	....	....	....	....	....
	Erie Blades	AHL	10	0	4	4	....	....	....	6	....	....	....	....	....	....	....	....	....	....	....	....	....	....	....	....	....	....
1982-83	**Pittsburgh Penguins**	**NHL**	**1**	**0**	**0**	**0**	**0**	**0**	**0**	**2**	**0**	**0**	**0**	**0**	**0.0**	**0**	**0**	**1**	**0**	**–1**	....	....	....	....	....	....	....	....
	Baltimore Skipjacks	AHL	79	4	15	19	....	....	....	103	....	....	....	....	....	....	....	....	....	....	....	....	....	....	....	....	....	....
1983-84	Muskegon Mohawks	IHL	34	3	12	15	....	....	....	46	....	....	....	....	....	....	....	....	....	....	....	....	....	....	....	....	....	....
	Baltimore Skipjacks	AHL	47	1	5	6	....	....	....	97	....	....	....	....	....	....	....	....	....	....	10	0	3	3	8	....	....	....
	NHL Totals		**1**	**0**	**0**	**0**	**0**	**0**	**0**	**2**	**0**	**0**	**0**	**0**	**0.0**	**0**	**0**	**1**	**0**									

• LUNDE, Len

Leonard Melvin C – R. 6'1", 194 lbs. b: Campbell River, B.C., 11/13/1936.

Season	Club	League	GP	G	A	Pts	AG	AA	APts	PIM	PP	SH	GW	S	%	TGF	PGF	TGA	PGA	+/–	Playoffs GP	G	A	Pts	PIM	PP	SH	GW
1953-54	Edmonton Oil Kings	WCJHL	3	0	0	0	....	....	....	0	....	....	....	....	....	....	....	....	....	....	....	....	....	....	....	....	....	....
1954-55	Edmonton Oil Kings	WCJHL	35	28	18	46	....	....	....	37	....	....	....	....	....	....	....	....	....	....	4	3	2	5	0	....	....	....
1955-56	Edmonton Oil Kings	WCJHL	35	37	30	67	....	....	....	27	....	....	....	....	....	....	....	....	....	....	6	2	2	4	2	....	....	....
	Edmonton Flyers	WHL	4	0	2	2	....	....	....	2	....	....	....	....	....	....	....	....	....	....	2	0	1	1	0	....	....	....
	Regina Pats	Mem-Cup	5	0	2	2	....	....	....	2	....	....	....	....	....	....	....	....	....	....	....	....	....	....	....	....	....	....
1956-57	Edmonton Flyers	WHL	70	20	41	61	....	....	....	22	....	....	....	....	....	....	....	....	....	....	8	3	5	8	2	....	....	....
1957-58	Edmonton Flyers	WHL	67	39	43	82	....	....	....	17	....	....	....	....	....	....	....	....	....	....	5	1	4	5	2	....	....	....
1958-59	**Detroit Red Wings**	**NHL**	**68**	**14**	**12**	**26**	**17**	**12**	**29**	**15**																		
1959-60	**Detroit Red Wings**	**NHL**	**66**	**6**	**17**	**23**	**7**	**16**	**23**	**10**											**6**	**1**	**2**	**3**	**0**	**1**	**0**	**0**
1960-61	**Detroit Red Wings**	**NHL**	**53**	**6**	**12**	**18**	**7**	**12**	**19**	**10**											**10**	**2**	**0**	**2**	**0**	**2**	**0**	**0**
1961-62	**Detroit Red Wings**	**NHL**	**23**	**2**	**9**	**11**	**2**	**9**	**11**	**4**																		
	Edmonton Flyers	WHL	41	26	37	63	....	....	....	21	....	....	....	....	....	....	....	....	....	....	12	9	9	18	2	....	....	....
1962-63	**Chicago Black Hawks**	**NHL**	**60**	**6**	**22**	**28**	**7**	**22**	**29**	**30**											**4**	**0**	**0**	**0**	**2**	**0**	**0**	**0**
1963-64	Buffalo Bisons	AHL	72	30	43	73	....	....	....	38	....	....	....	....	....	....	....	....	....	....	....	....	....	....	....	....	....	....
1964-65	Buffalo Bisons	AHL	72	*50	46	96	....	....	....	40	....	....	....	....	....	....	....	....	....	....	9	4	4	8	4	....	....	....
1965-66	**Chicago Black Hawks**	**NHL**	**24**	**4**	**7**	**11**	**4**	**7**	**11**	**4**																		
	St. Louis Braves	CPHL	11	3	5	8	....	....	....	6	....	....	....	....	....	....	....	....	....	....	....	....	....	....	....	....	....	....
1966-67	Portland Buckaroos	WHL	72	26	33	59	....	....	....	16	....	....	....	....	....	....	....	....	....	....	4	0	0	0	7	....	....	....
1967-68	**Minnesota North Stars**	**NHL**	**7**	**0**	**1**	**1**	**0**	**1**	**1**	**0**	**0**	**0**	**0**	**21**	**0.0**	**2**	**0**	**9**	**0**	**–7**	....	....	....	....	....	....	....	....
	Rochester Americans	AHL	37	19	33	52	....	....	....	13	....	....	....	....	....	....	....	....	....	....	11	2	4	6	0	....	....	....
1968-69	Vancouver Canucks	WHL	65	26	27	53	....	....	....	8	....	....	....	....	....	....	....	....	....	....	8	3	3	6	0	....	....	....
1969-70	Vancouver Canucks	WHL	68	29	34	63	....	....	....	4	....	....	....	....	....	....	....	....	....	....	11	*10	5	15	8	....	....	....
1970-71	**Vancouver Canucks**	**NHL**	**20**	**1**	**3**	**4**	**1**	**2**	**3**	**2**	**0**	**1**	**0**	**20**	**5.0**	**5**	**1**	**17**	**10**	**–3**	....	....	....	....	....	....	....	....
1971-72	Ilves Tampere	Finland	31	28	21	49	....	....	....	40	....	....	....	....	....	....	....	....	....	....	....	....	....	....	....	....	....	....
1972-73	Ilves Tampere	Finland	DID NOT PLAY – COACHING																									

			REGULAR SEASON																		PLAYOFFS							
Season	Club	League	GP	G	A	Pts	AG	AA	APts	PIM	PP	SH	GW	S	%	TGF	PGF	TGA	PGA	+/-	GP	G	A	Pts	PIM	PP	SH	GW
1973-74	Edmonton Oilers	WHA	71	26	22	48	....	....	....	8	....	....	....	....	....	....	....	....	....	....	5	0	1	1	0	....	....	....
1974-1979			OUT OF HOCKEY – RETIRED																									
1979-80	Mora IK	Sweden-2	1	2	0	2	....	....	....	4	....	....	....	....	....	....	....	....	....	....	....	....	....	....	....	....	....	....
	NHL Totals		**321**	**39**	**83**	**122**	**45**	**81**	**126**	**75**	....	....	....	....	....	....	....	....	....		**20**	**3**	**2**	**5**	**2**	....	....	....
	Other Major League Totals		71	26	22	48	....	....	....	8	....	....	....	....	....	....	....	....	....	....	5	0	1	1	0	....	....	....

AHL First All-Star Team (1965)

Traded to **Chicago** by **Detroit** with John McKenzie for Doug Barkley, June 5, 1962. Claimed by **Minnesota** from **Chicago** in Expansion Draft, June 6, 1967. Traded to **Toronto** (Rochester-AHL) by **Minnesota** with Duke Harris, Don Johns, Ted Taylor, Murray Hall and the loan of Carl Wetzel for Jean-Paul Parise and Milan Marcetta, December 23, 1967. Rights transferred to **Vancouver** (WHL) after WHL club purchased **Rochester** (AHL) franchise, August 13, 1968. NHL rights transferred to **Vancouver** after NHL club purchased **Vancouver** (WHL) franchise, December 13, 1969. Selected by **Edmonton** (WHA) in 1972 WHA General Player Draft, February 12, 1972.

• LUNDHOLM, Bengt

LW – L. 6′, 180 lbs. b: Falun, Sweden, 8/4/1955.

Season	Club	League	GP	G	A	Pts	AG	AA	APts	PIM	PP	SH	GW	S	%	TGF	PGF	TGA	PGA	+/-	GP	G	A	Pts	PIM	PP	SH	GW
1971-72	Falu IF	Sweden-2	11	2	....	2	....	....	....	....	....	....	....	....	....	....	....	....	....	....	....	....	....	....	....	....	....	....
1972-73	Falu IF	Sweden-2	16	11	....	11	....	....	....	....	....	....	....	....	....	....	....	....	....	....	....	....	....	....	....	....	....	....
1973-74	Leksands IF	Sweden-Jr.	....	....	....	....	....	....	....	....	....	....	....	....	....	....	....	....	....	....	....	....	....	....	....	....	....	....
	Leksands IF	Sweden	3	0	0	0	....	....	....	0	....	....	....	....	....	....	....	....	....	....	6	0	1	1	4	....	....	....
	Sweden	WJC-A	1	0	1	1	....	....	....	0	....	....	....	....	....	....	....	....	....	....	....	....	....	....	....	....	....	....
	Sweden	EJC-A	5	6	2	8	....	....	....	4	....	....	....	....	....	....	....	....	....	....	....	....	....	....	....	....	....	....
1974-75	Leksands IF	Sweden	18	4	7	11	....	....	....	6	....	....	....	....	....	....	....	....	....	....	4	1	3	4	4	....	....	....
	Sweden	WJC-A	....	0	3	3	....	....	....	....	....	....	....	....	....	....	....	....	....	....	....	....	....	....	....	....	....	....
1975-76	Leksands IF	Sweden	36	15	22	37	....	....	....	23	....	....	....	....	....	....	....	....	....	....	7	3	4	7	2	....	....	....
	Sweden	WEC-A	8	0	2	2	....	....	....	6	....	....	....	....	....	....	....	....	....	....	....	....	....	....	....	....	....	....
1976-77	Leksands IF	Sweden	34	8	23	31	....	....	....	28	....	....	....	....	....	....	....	....	....	....	5	4	3	7	*16	....	....	....
	Sweden	WEC-A	8	5	3	8	....	....	....	4	....	....	....	....	....	....	....	....	....	....	....	....	....	....	....	....	....	....
1977-78	AIK Solna Stockholm	Sweden	36	16	15	31	....	....	....	22	....	....	....	....	....	....	....	....	....	....	6	1	*4	5	4	....	....	....
	Sweden	WEC-A	10	6	5	11	....	....	....	4	....	....	....	....	....	....	....	....	....	....	....	....	....	....	....	....	....	....
1978-79	AIK Solna Stockholm	Sweden	34	10	10	20	....	....	....	24	....	....	....	....	....	....	....	....	....	....	....	....	....	....	....	....	....	....
	Sweden	Nat-Team	17	2	6	8	....	....	....	8	....	....	....	....	....	....	....	....	....	....	....	....	....	....	....	....	....	....
	Sweden	WEC-A	7	1	3	4	....	....	....	4	....	....	....	....	....	....	....	....	....	....	....	....	....	....	....	....	....	....
1979-80	AIK Solna Stockholm	Sweden	36	16	16	32	....	....	....	34	....	....	....	....	....	....	....	....	....	....	....	....	....	....	....	....	....	....
	Sweden	Nat-Team	6	1	0	1	....	....	....	0	....	....	....	....	....	....	....	....	....	....	....	....	....	....	....	....	....	....
	Sweden	Olympics	7	1	0	1	....	....	....	2	....	....	....	....	....	....	....	....	....	....	....	....	....	....	....	....	....	....
1980-81	AIK Solna Stockholm	DN-Cup	3	0	0	0	....	....	....	2	....	....	....	....	....	....	....	....	....	....	....	....	....	....	....	....	....	....
	AIK Solna Stockholm	Sweden	24	6	8	14	....	....	....	40	....	....	....	....	....	....	....	....	....	....	5	1	0	1	2	....	....	....
	Sweden	Nat-Team	4	1	1	2	....	....	....	0	....	....	....	....	....	....	....	....	....	....	....	....	....	....	....	....	....	....
1981-82	Sweden	Can-Cup	5	1	0	1	....	....	....	2	....	....	....	....	....	....	....	....	....	....	....	....	....	....	....	....	....	....
	Winnipeg Jets	**NHL**	**66**	**14**	**30**	**44**	**11**	**20**	**31**	**10**	**3**	**0**	**3**	**99**	**14.1**	**57**	**11**	**41**	**0**	**5**	**4**	**1**	**1**	**2**	**2**	**0**	**0**	**0**
1982-83	**Winnipeg Jets**	**NHL**	**58**	**14**	**28**	**42**	**11**	**19**	**30**	**16**	**1**	**0**	**0**	**66**	**21.2**	**68**	**9**	**50**	**1**	**10**	**3**	**0**	**1**	**1**	**2**	**0**	**0**	**0**
1983-84	**Winnipeg Jets**	**NHL**	**57**	**5**	**14**	**19**	**4**	**10**	**14**	**20**	**1**	**0**	**0**	**48**	**10.4**	**31**	**5**	**36**	**3**	**–7**	....	....	....	....	....	....	....	....
1984-85	**Winnipeg Jets**	**NHL**	**78**	**12**	**18**	**30**	**10**	**12**	**22**	**20**	**1**	**0**	**1**	**58**	**20.7**	**50**	**3**	**45**	**6**	**8**	**5**	**2**	**2**	**4**	**8**	**0**	**2**	**0**
1985-86	**Winnipeg Jets**	**NHL**	**16**	**3**	**5**	**8**	**2**	**3**	**5**	**6**	**0**	**1**	**0**	**14**	**21.4**	**11**	**1**	**16**	**2**	**–4**	**2**	**0**	**0**	**0**	**2**	**0**	**0**	**0**
	Djurgardens IF Stockholm	Sweden	13	1	1	2	....	....	....	4	....	....	....	....	....	....	....	....	....	....	....	....	....	....	....	....	....	....
1986-87	AIK Solna Stockholm	Sweden-2	26	13	14	27	....	....	....	16	....	....	....	....	....	....	....	....	....	....	....	....	....	....	....	....	....	....
	NHL Totals		**275**	**48**	**95**	**143**	**38**	**64**	**102**	**72**	**6**	**1**	**4**	**285**	**16.8**	**217**	**29**	**188**	**12**		**14**	**3**	**4**	**7**	**14**	**0**	**2**	**0**

Signed as a free agent by **Winnipeg**, June 19, 1981. • Only games played and goals scored totals available for Falu IF during 1971-72 and 1972-73 seasons.

• LUNDRIGAN, Joe

Joseph Roche D – L. 5′11″, 180 lbs. b: Corner Brook, Nfld., 9/12/1948.

Season	Club	League	GP	G	A	Pts	AG	AA	APts	PIM	PP	SH	GW	S	%	TGF	PGF	TGA	PGA	+/-	GP	G	A	Pts	PIM	PP	SH	GW
1967-68	Corner Brook Royals	Nfld-Sr.	28	1	10	11	....	....	....	33	....	....	....	....	....	....	....	....	....	....	12	1	1	2	14	....	....	....
	Corner Brook Royals	Al-Cup	8	0	1	1	....	....	....	6	....	....	....	....	....	....	....	....	....	....	....	....	....	....	....	....	....	....
1968-69	St. Francis Xavier X-Men	AUAA	20	14	11	25	....	....	....	50	....	....	....	....	....	....	....	....	....	....	....	....	....	....	....	....	....	....
1969-70	St. Francis Xavier X-Men	AUAA	20	10	6	16	....	....	....	73	....	....	....	....	....	....	....	....	....	....	....	....	....	....	....	....	....	....
1970-71	St. Francis Xavier X-Men	AUAA	10	6	13	19	....	....	....	56	....	....	....	....	....	....	....	....	....	....	....	....	....	....	....	....	....	....
1971-72	Tulsa Oilers	CHL	67	3	34	37	....	....	....	110	....	....	....	....	....	....	....	....	....	....	13	2	9	11	24	....	....	....
1972-73	**Toronto Maple Leafs**	**NHL**	**49**	**2**	**8**	**10**	**2**	**6**	**8**	**20**	**1**	**0**	**1**	**53**	**3.8**	**44**	**3**	**47**	**10**	**4**	....	....	....	....	....	....	....	....
	Tulsa Oilers	CHL	8	3	2	5	....	....	....	10	....	....	....	....	....	....	....	....	....	....	....	....	....	....	....	....	....	....
1973-74	Oklahoma City Blazers	CHL	62	7	34	41	....	....	....	143	....	....	....	....	....	....	....	....	....	....	10	0	3	3	10	....	....	....
1974-75	**Washington Capitals**	**NHL**	**3**	**0**	**0**	**0**	**0**	**0**	**0**	**2**	**0**	**0**	**0**	**2**	**0.0**	**1**	**1**	**3**	**0**	**–3**	....	....	....	....	....	....	....	....
	Richmond Robins	AHL	28	3	3	6	....	....	....	49	....	....	....	....	....	....	....	....	....	....	....	....	....	....	....	....	....	....
	Hershey Bears	AHL	33	6	13	19	....	....	....	60	....	....	....	....	....	....	....	....	....	....	12	2	4	6	8	....	....	....
1975-76			REINSTATED AS AN AMATEUR																									
1976-77	Corner Brook Royals	Nfld-Sr.	32	13	34	47	....	....	....	43	....	....	....	....	....	....	....	....	....	....	10	4	10	14	4	....	....	....
	NHL Totals		**52**	**2**	**8**	**10**	**2**	**6**	**8**	**22**	**1**	**0**	**1**	**55**	**3.6**	**45**	**4**	**50**	**10**		....	....	....	....	....	....	....	....

CHL Second All-Star Team (1972)

Signed as a free agent by **Toronto**, October 1, 1971. Claimed by **Washington** from **Toronto** in Expansion Draft, June 12, 1974.

• LUNDSTROM, Tord

LW – L. 5′11″, 176 lbs. b: Kiruna, Sweden, 3/4/1945.

Season	Club	League	GP	G	A	Pts	AG	AA	APts	PIM	PP	SH	GW	S	%	TGF	PGF	TGA	PGA	+/-	GP	G	A	Pts	PIM	PP	SH	GW
1960-61	Kiruna AIF	Sweden-2	STATISTICS NOT AVAILABLE																									
1961-62	Kiruna AIF	Sweden-2	16	15	6	21	....	....	....	4	....	....	....	....	....	....	....	....	....	....	....	....	....	....	....	....	....	....
1962-63	Kiruna AIF	Sweden-2	20	32	12	44	....	....	....	8	....	....	....	....	....	....	....	....	....	....	....	....	....	....	....	....	....	....
1963-64	Brynas IF Gavle	Sweden	14	10	6	16	....	....	....	8	....	....	....	....	....	....	....	....	....	....	7	7	7	14	11	....	....	....
1964-65	Brynas IF Gavle	Sweden	14	14	10	24	....	....	....	4	....	....	....	....	....	....	....	....	....	....	14	*17	12	29	4	....	....	....
	Sweden	WEC-A	7	6	3	9	....	....	....	4	....	....	....	....	....	....	....	....	....	....	....	....	....	....	....	....	....	....
1965-66	Brynas IF Gavle	Sweden	14	10	9	19	....	....	....	4	....	....	....	....	....	....	....	....	....	....	7	7	5	12	6	....	....	....
	Sweden	WEC-A	7	0	1	1	....	....	....	4	....	....	....	....	....	....	....	....	....	....	....	....	....	....	....	....	....	....
1966-67	Brynas IF Gavle	Sweden	14	18	6	24	....	....	....	12	....	....	....	....	....	....	....	....	....	....	6	5	6	11	0	....	....	....
1967-68	Brynas IF Gavle	Sweden	14	15	14	29	....	....	....	4	....	....	....	....	....	....	....	....	....	....	7	6	7	13	2	....	....	....
	Sweden	Olympics	7	2	3	5	....	....	....	6	....	....	....	....	....	....	....	....	....	....	....	....	....	....	....	....	....	....
1968-69	Brynas IF Gavle	Sweden	14	7	8	15	....	....	....	2	....	....	....	....	....	....	....	....	....	....	7	6	6	12	6	....	....	....
	Sweden	WEC-A	10	5	2	7	....	....	....	12	....	....	....	....	....	....	....	....	....	....	....	....	....	....	....	....	....	....
1969-70	Brynas IF Gavle	Sweden	14	*17	10	*27	....	....	....	8	....	....	....	....	....	....	....	....	....	....	14	10	6	16	6	....	....	....
	Sweden	WEC-A	10	5	5	10	....	....	....	0	....	....	....	....	....	....	....	....	....	....	....	....	....	....	....	....	....	....
1970-71	Brynas IF Gavle	Sweden	14	17	13	30	....	....	....	2	....	....	....	....	....	....	....	....	....	....	14	9	*16	*25	14	....	....	....
	Sweden	WEC-A	10	6	4	10	....	....	....	4	....	....	....	....	....	....	....	....	....	....	....	....	....	....	....	....	....	....
1971-72	Brynas IF Gavle	Sweden	14	8	6	14	....	....	....	4	....	....	....	....	....	....	....	....	....	....	14	9	10	19	4	....	....	....
	Sweden	Olympics	6	3	2	5	....	....	....	2	....	....	....	....	....	....	....	....	....	....	....	....	....	....	....	....	....	....
	Sweden	WEC-A	10	4	5	9	....	....	....	8	....	....	....	....	....	....	....	....	....	....	....	....	....	....	....	....	....	....
1972-73	Brynas IF Gavle	Sweden	14	16	11	27	....	....	....	4	....	....	....	....	....	....	....	....	....	....	14	10	4	14	6	....	....	....
	Sweden	WEC-A	10	3	2	5	....	....	....	0	....	....	....	....	....	....	....	....	....	....	....	....	....	....	....	....	....	....
1973-74	**Detroit Red Wings**	**NHL**	**11**	**1**	**1**	**2**	**1**	**1**	**2**	**0**	**0**	**0**	**0**	**7**	**14.3**	**2**	**0**	**4**	**0**	**–2**	....	....	....	....	....	....	....	....
	London Lions	Britain	45	38	31	69	....	....	....	24	....	....	....	....	....	....	....	....	....	....	....	....	....	....	....	....	....	....
1974-75	Brynas IF Gavle	Sweden	21	15	17	32	....	....	....	32	....	....	....	....	....	....	....	....	....	....	6	0	3	3	2	....	....	....
	Sweden	WEC-A	10	11	4	15	....	....	....	2	....	....	....	....	....	....	....	....	....	....	....	....	....	....	....	....	....	....
1975-76	Brynas IF Gavle	Sweden	35	21	*27	48	....	....	....	16	....	....	....	....	....	....	....	....	....	....	7	4	1	5	0	....	....	....
1976-77	Sweden	Can-Cup	5	1	3	4	....	....	....	6	....	....	....	....	....	....	....	....	....	....	....	....	....	....	....	....	....	....
	Brynas IF Gavle	Sweden	36	16	19	35	....	....	....	37	....	....	....	....	....	....	....	....	....	....	4	1	*7	8	0	....	....	....

			REGULAR SEASON																		PLAYOFFS							
Season	Club	League	GP	G	A	Pts	AG	AA	APts	PIM	PP	SH	GW	S	%	TGF	PGF	TGA	PGA	+/–	GP	G	A	Pts	PIM	PP	SH	GW
1977-78	Brynas IF Gavle	Sweden	36	20	15	35	....	....	....	28	....	....	....	....	....	....	....	....	....	....	3	0	1	1	0	....	....	....
1978-79	Brynas IF Gavle	Sweden	36	12	13	25	....	....	....	29	....	....	....	....	....	....	....	....	....	....	....	....	....	....	....	....	....	....
1979-80	Morrums GOIS	Sweden-2	4	1	1	2	....	....	....	2	....	....	....	....	....	....	....	....	....	....	....	....	....	....	....	....	....	....
	NHL Totals		11	1	1	2	1	1	2	0	0	0	0	7	14.3	2	0	4	0		....	....	....	....	....	....	....	....

Signed as a free agent by **Detroit**, June, 1973.

• LUONGO, Chris

D – R. 5'10", 206 lbs. b: Detroit, MI, 3/17/1967. Detroit's 5th, 92nd overall, in 1985.

Season	Club	League	GP	G	A	Pts	AG	AA	APts	PIM	PP	SH	GW	S	%	TGF	PGF	TGA	PGA	+/–	GP	G	A	Pts	PIM	PP	SH	GW
1984-85	St. Clair Shores Falcons	NAJHL	41	2	27	29	....	....	....	....	....	....	....	....	....	....	....	....	....	....	....	....	....	....	....	....	....	....
1985-86	Michigan State Spartans	CCHA	38	1	5	6	....	....	....	29	....	....	....	....	....	....	....	....	....	....	....	....	....	....	....	....	....	....
1986-87	Michigan State Spartans	CCHA	27	4	16	20	....	....	....	38	....	....	....	....	....	....	....	....	....	....	....	....	....	....	....	....	....	....
1987-88	Michigan State Spartans	CCHA	45	3	15	18	....	....	....	49	....	....	....	....	....	....	....	....	....	....	....	....	....	....	....	....	....	....
1988-89	Michigan State Spartans	CCHA	47	4	21	25	....	....	....	42	....	....	....	....	....	....	....	....	....	....	....	....	....	....	....	....	....	....
1989-90	Adirondack Red Wings	AHL	53	9	14	23	....	....	....	37	....	....	....	....	....	....	....	....	....	....	3	0	0	0	0	....	....	....
	Phoenix Roadrunners	IHL	23	5	9	14	....	....	....	41	....	....	....	....	....	....	....	....	....	....	....	....	....	....	....	....	....	....
1990-91	Detroit Red Wings	NHL	4	0	1	1	0	1	1	4	0	0	0	4	0.0	2	0	4	2	0	....	....	....	....	....	....	....	....
	Adirondack Red Wings	AHL	76	14	25	39	....	....	....	71	....	....	....	....	....	....	....	....	....	....	2	0	0	0	7	....	....	....
1991-92	Adirondack Red Wings	AHL	80	6	20	26	....	....	....	60	....	....	....	....	....	....	....	....	....	....	19	3	5	8	10	....	....	....
1992-93	Ottawa Senators	NHL	76	3	9	12	2	6	8	68	1	0	0	76	3.9	37	5	109	30	–47	....	....	....	....	....	....	....	....
	New Haven Senators	AHL	7	0	2	2	....	....	....	2	....	....	....	....	....	....	....	....	....	....	....	....	....	....	....	....	....	....
1993-94	New York Islanders	NHL	17	1	3	4	1	2	3	13	0	0	0	16	6.3	11	0	19	7	–1	....	....	....	....	....	....	....	....
	Salt Lake Golden Eagles	IHL	51	9	31	40	....	....	....	54	....	....	....	....	....	....	....	....	....	....	....	....	....	....	....	....	....	....
1994-95	Denver Grizzlies	IHL	41	1	14	15	....	....	....	26	....	....	....	....	....	....	....	....	....	....	....	....	....	....	....	....	....	....
	New York Islanders	NHL	47	1	3	4	2	4	6	36	0	0	0	44	2.3	34	0	53	17	–2	....	....	....	....	....	....	....	....
1995-96	New York Islanders	NHL	74	3	7	10	3	6	9	55	1	0	0	46	6.5	42	4	83	22	–23	....	....	....	....	....	....	....	....
	United States	WC-A	8	1	0	1	....	....	....	6	....	....	....	....	....	....	....	....	....	....	....	....	....	....	....	....	....	....
1996-97	Milwaukee Admirals	IHL	81	10	35	45	....	....	....	69	....	....	....	....	....	....	....	....	....	....	2	0	0	0	0	....	....	....
1997-98	EV Landshut	Germany	48	5	13	18	....	....	....	54	....	....	....	....	....	....	....	....	....	....	6	0	2	2	18	....	....	....
	United States	WC-A	6	0	0	0	....	....	....	2	....	....	....	....	....	....	....	....	....	....	....	....	....	....	....	....	....	....
1998-99	EV Landshut	Germany	51	1	14	15	....	....	....	115	....	....	....	....	....	....	....	....	....	....	3	1	0	1	0	....	....	....
	United States	WC-Q	3	1	0	1	....	....	....	2	....	....	....	....	....	....	....	....	....	....	....	....	....	....	....	....	....	....
	Detroit Vipers	IHL	11	0	1	1	....	....	....	4	....	....	....	....	....	....	....	....	....	....	11	0	4	4	16	....	....	....
99-2000	Munich Barons	Germany	56	6	11	17	....	....	....	50	....	....	....	....	....	....	....	....	....	....	12	0	0	0	18	....	....	....
	United States	WC-A	5	1	0	1	....	....	....	0	....	....	....	....	....	....	....	....	....	....	....	....	....	....	....	....	....	....
	NHL Totals		218	8	23	31	8	19	27	176	2	0	0	186	4.3	126	9	268	78		....	....	....	....	....	....	....	....

NCAA Championship All-Tournament Team (1987) • CCHA Second All-Star Team (1989)

Signed as a free agent by **Ottawa**, September 9, 1992. Traded to **NY Islanders** by **Ottawa** for Jeff Finley, June 30, 1993. Traded to **Ottawa** by **NY Islanders** for cash, March 19, 1999.

• LUPIEN, Gilles

"Loopy" D – L. 6'6", 210 lbs. b: Lachute, Que., 4/20/1954. Montreal's 7th, 33rd overall, in 1974.

Season	Club	League	GP	G	A	Pts	AG	AA	APts	PIM	PP	SH	GW	S	%	TGF	PGF	TGA	PGA	+/–	GP	G	A	Pts	PIM	PP	SH	GW
1971-72	Quebec Remparts	QMJHL	36	0	5	5	....	....	....	54	....	....	....	....	....	....	....	....	....	....	15	0	3	3	17	....	....	....
1972-73	Montreal Red-White-Blue	QMJHL	26	4	4	8	....	....	....	66	....	....	....	....	....	....	....	....	....	....	....	....	....	....	....	....	....	....
	Sherbrooke Castors	QMJHL	26	0	5	5	....	....	....	71	....	....	....	....	....	....	....	....	....	....	....	....	....	....	....	....	....	....
1973-74	Montreal Jr. Canadiens	QMJHL	44	3	29	32	....	....	....	168	....	....	....	....	....	....	....	....	....	....	....	....	....	....	....	....	....	....
1974-75	Nova Scotia Voyageurs	AHL	73	6	9	15	....	....	....	*316	....	....	....	....	....	....	....	....	....	....	6	0	0	0	61	....	....	....
1975-76	Nova Scotia Voyageurs	AHL	56	2	6	8	....	....	....	134	....	....	....	....	....	....	....	....	....	....	9	0	4	4	29	....	....	....
1976-77	Nova Scotia Voyageurs	AHL	69	6	16	22	....	....	....	*215	....	....	....	....	....	....	....	....	....	....	12	0	2	2	*35	....	....	....
1977-78♦	Montreal Canadiens	NHL	46	1	3	4	1	2	3	108	0	0	0	20	5.0	28	1	8	0	19	8	0	0	0	17	0	0	0
	Nova Scotia Voyageurs	AHL	7	1	2	3	....	....	....	10	....	....	....	....	....	....	....	....	....	....	....	....	....	....	....	....	....	....
1978-79♦	Montreal Canadiens	NHL	72	1	9	10	1	7	8	124	0	0	0	58	1.7	57	0	26	2	33	13	0	0	0	2	0	0	0
1979-80	Montreal Canadiens	NHL	56	1	7	8	1	5	6	109	0	0	1	42	2.4	46	0	33	0	13	4	0	0	0	2	0	0	0
1980-81	Pittsburgh Penguins	NHL	31	0	1	1	0	1	1	34	0	0	0	11	0.0	7	0	27	5	–15	....	....	....	....	....	....	....	....
	Hartford Whalers	NHL	20	2	4	6	2	3	5	39	0	0	0	16	12.5	16	1	22	1	–6	....	....	....	....	....	....	....	....
	Binghamton Whalers	AHL	11	1	4	5	....	....	....	71	....	....	....	....	....	....	....	....	....	....	....	....	....	....	....	....	....	....
1981-82	Hartford Whalers	NHL	1	0	1	1	0	1	1	2	0	0	0	0	0.0	1	0	2	1	0	....	....	....	....	....	....	....	....
	Binghamton Whalers	AHL	53	8	12	20	....	....	....	280	....	....	....	....	....	....	....	....	....	....	13	2	5	7	58	....	....	....
	NHL Totals		226	5	25	30	5	19	24	416	0	0	1	147	3.4	155	2	118	9		25	0	0	0	21	0	0	0

Claimed by **Montreal** as a fill-in during Expansion Draft, June 13, 1979. Traded to **Pittsburgh** by **Montreal** for Pittsburgh's 3rd round choice (later traded to Winnipeg — Winnipeg selected Peter Taglianetti) in 1983 Entry Draft, September 26, 1980. Traded to **Hartford** by **Pittsburgh** for Hartford's 6th round choice (Paul Edwards) in 1981 Entry Draft, February 20, 1981.

• LUPUL, Gary

Gary John C/LW – L. 5'9", 172 lbs. b: Powell River, B.C., 4/4/1959.

Season	Club	League	GP	G	A	Pts	AG	AA	APts	PIM	PP	SH	GW	S	%	TGF	PGF	TGA	PGA	+/–	GP	G	A	Pts	PIM	PP	SH	GW
1975-76	Nanaimo Clippers	BCJHL	66	49	68	117	....	....	....	....	....	....	....	....	....	....	....	....	....	....	....	....	....	....	....	....	....	....
	Victoria Cougars	WCJHL	4	1	1	2	....	....	....	2	....	....	....	....	....	....	....	....	....	....	1	0	0	0	0	....	....	....
1976-77	Victoria Cougars	WCJHL	71	38	63	101	....	....	....	116	....	....	....	....	....	....	....	....	....	....	4	1	0	1	2	....	....	....
1977-78	Victoria Cougars	WCJHL	59	37	49	86	....	....	....	79	....	....	....	....	....	....	....	....	....	....	13	6	15	21	2	....	....	....
1978-79	Victoria Cougars	WHL	71	53	54	107	....	....	....	85	....	....	....	....	....	....	....	....	....	....	15	10	14	24	19	....	....	....
	Canada	WJC-A	5	2	1	3	....	....	....	0	....	....	....	....	....	....	....	....	....	....	....	....	....	....	....	....	....	....
1979-80	Vancouver Canucks	NHL	51	9	11	20	8	8	16	24	3	0	0	71	12.7	29	5	39	3	–12	4	1	0	1	0	1	0	0
	Dallas Black Hawks	CHL	26	9	15	24	....	....	....	4	....	....	....	....	....	....	....	....	....	....	....	....	....	....	....	....	....	....
1980-81	Vancouver Canucks	NHL	7	0	2	2	0	1	1	2	0	0	0	5	0.0	2	0	3	0	–1	....	....	....	....	....	....	....	....
	Dallas Black Hawks	CHL	53	25	32	57	....	....	....	27	....	....	....	....	....	....	....	....	....	....	6	4	1	5	5	....	....	....
1981-82	Vancouver Canucks	NHL	41	10	7	17	8	5	13	26	0	1	0	45	22.2	23	1	30	6	–2	10	2	3	5	4	0	0	1
	Dallas Black Hawks	CHL	31	22	17	39	....	....	....	76	....	....	....	....	....	....	....	....	....	....	....	....	....	....	....	....	....	....
1982-83	Vancouver Canucks	NHL	40	18	10	28	15	7	22	46	3	0	2	64	28.1	35	7	32	5	1	4	1	3	4	0	0	0	0
	Fredericton Express	AHL	35	16	26	42	....	....	....	48	....	....	....	....	....	....	....	....	....	....	....	....	....	....	....	....	....	....
1983-84	Vancouver Canucks	NHL	69	17	27	44	14	18	32	51	6	0	2	128	13.3	62	21	72	15	–16	4	0	1	1	7	0	0	0
1984-85	Vancouver Canucks	NHL	66	12	17	29	10	12	22	82	2	0	2	107	11.2	45	6	65	11	–15	....	....	....	....	....	....	....	....
1985-86	Vancouver Canucks	NHL	19	4	1	5	3	1	4	12	0	0	0	17	23.5	10	2	9	1	0	3	0	0	0	0	0	0	0
	Fredericton Express	AHL	43	13	22	35	....	....	....	76	....	....	....	....	....	....	....	....	....	....	3	2	0	2	4	....	....	....
1986-87	SG Brunico	Italy	42	28	38	66	....	....	....	24	....	....	....	....	....	....	....	....	....	....	....	....	....	....	....	....	....	....
1987-88	BSC Preussen Berlin	Germany	11	1	2	3	....	....	....	6	....	....	....	....	....	....	....	....	....	....	16	16	20	26	14	....	....	....
	NHL Totals		293	70	75	145	58	52	110	243	14	1	6	437	16.0	206	42	250	41		25	4	7	11	11	1	0	1

Signed as a free agent by **Vancouver**, September 14, 1979.

• LYASHENKO, Roman

C – R. 6', 189 lbs. b: Murmansk, Russia, 5/2/1979. Dallas' 2nd, 52nd overall, in 1997.

Season	Club	League	GP	G	A	Pts	AG	AA	APts	PIM	PP	SH	GW	S	%	TGF	PGF	TGA	PGA	+/–	GP	G	A	Pts	PIM	PP	SH	GW
1995-96	Torpedo Yaroslavl-2	CIS-2	60	7	10	17	....	....	....	12	....	....	....	....	....	....	....	....	....	....	....	....	....	....	....	....	....	....
1996-97	Torpedo Yaroslavl-2	Russia-3	2	1	1	2	....	....	....	8	....	....	....	....	....	....	....	....	....	....	....	....	....	....	....	....	....	....
	Torpedo Yaroslavl	Russia	42	5	7	12	....	....	....	16	....	....	....	....	....	....	....	....	....	....	9	3	0	3	6	....	....	....
	Russia	WJC-A	6	1	2	3	....	....	....	4	....	....	....	....	....	....	....	....	....	....	....	....	....	....	....	....	....	....
	Russia	EJC-A	6	4	2	6	....	....	....	8	....	....	....	....	....	....	....	....	....	....	....	....	....	....	....	....	....	....
1997-98	Torpedo Yaroslavl	Russia	46	7	6	13	....	....	....	28	....	....	....	....	....	....	....	....	....	....	....	....	....	....	....	....	....	....
	Torpedo Yaroslavl	EuroHL	10	1	1	2	....	....	....	2	....	....	....	....	....	....	....	....	....	....	....	....	....	....	....	....	....	....
	Russia	WJC-A	7	0	3	3	....	....	....	6	....	....	....	....	....	....	....	....	....	....	....	....	....	....	....	....	....	....
1998-99	Torpedo Yaroslavl	Russia	42	10	9	19	....	....	....	51	....	....	....	....	....	....	....	....	....	....	9	0	4	4	8	....	....	....
	Russia	WJC-A	7	3	2	5	....	....	....	0	....	....	....	....	....	....	....	....	....	....	....	....	....	....	....	....	....	....
99-2000	Dallas Stars	NHL	58	6	6	12	7	6	13	10	0	0	1	51	11.8	21	2	21	0	–2	16	2	1	3	0	0	0	2
	Michigan K-Wings	IHL	9	3	2	5	....	....	....	8	....	....	....	....	....	....	....	....	....	....	....	....	....	....	....	....	....	....
	NHL Totals		58	6	6	12	7	6	13	10	0	0	1	51	11.8	21	2	21	0		16	2	1	3	0	0	0	2

			REGULAR SEASON																		PLAYOFFS							
Season	**Club**	**League**	**GP**	**G**	**A**	**Pts**	**AG**	**AA**	**APts**	**PIM**	**PP**	**SH**	**GW**	**S**	**%**	**TGF**	**PGF**	**TGA**	**PGA**	**+/–**	**GP**	**G**	**A**	**Pts**	**PIM**	**PP**	**SH**	**GW**

• LYLE, George

George Wallace "Sparky" LW – L. 6'2", 205 lbs. b: North Vancouver, B.C., 11/24/1953. Detroit's 9th, 123rd overall, in 1973.

Season	Club	League	GP	G	A	Pts	AG	AA	APts	PIM	PP	SH	GW	S	%	TGF	PGF	TGA	PGA	+/–	GP	G	A	Pts	PIM	PP	SH	GW
1970-71	Norwest Caps	BCJHL	STATISTICS NOT AVAILABLE																									
1972-73	Calumet Chiefs	USHL	33	23	16	39	....	....	....	42	....	....	....	....	....	....	....	....	....	....	....	....	....	....	....	....	....	....
1973-74	Michigan Tech Huskies	WCHA	19	9	13	22	....	....	....	20	....	....	....	....	....	....	....	....	....	....	....	....	....	....	....	....	....	....
1974-75	Michigan Tech Huskies	WCHA	38	37	19	56	....	....	....	76	....	....	....	....	....	....	....	....	....	....	....	....	....	....	....	....	....	....
1975-76	Michigan Tech Huskies	WCHA	43	47	41	88	....	....	....	42	....	....	....	....	....	....	....	....	....	....	....	....	....	....	....	....	....	....
1976-77	New England Whalers	WHA	75	39	33	72	....	....	....	62	....	....	....	....	....	....	....	....	....	....	5	1	0	1	4	....	....	....
1977-78	New England Whalers	WHA	68	30	24	54	....	....	....	74	....	....	....	....	....	....	....	....	....	....	12	2	1	3	13	....	....	....
1978-79	Springfield Indians	AHL	4	2	4	6	....	....	....	6	....	....	....	....	....	....	....	....	....	....	....	....	....	....	....	....	....	....
	New England Whalers	WHA	59	17	18	35	....	....	....	54	....	....	....	....	....	....	....	....	....	....	9	3	5	8	25	....	....	....
1979-80	**Detroit Red Wings**	**NHL**	**27**	**7**	**4**	**11**	**6**	**3**	**9**	**2**	**0**	**0**	**2**	**41**	**17.1**	**20**	**1**	**21**	**0**	**–2**	....	....	....	....	....	....	....	....
	Adirondack Red Wings	AHL	33	23	9	32	....	....	....	40	....	....	....	....	....	....	....	....	....	....	....	....	....	....	....	....	....	....
1980-81	**Detroit Red Wings**	**NHL**	**31**	**10**	**14**	**24**	**8**	**9**	**17**	**28**	**3**	**0**	**0**	**49**	**20.4**	**35**	**10**	**28**	**3**	**0**	....	....	....	....	....	....	....	....
	Adirondack Red Wings	AHL	40	20	16	36	....	....	....	84	....	....	....	....	....	....	....	....	....	....	18	9	9	18	34	....	....	....
1981-82	**Detroit Red Wings**	**NHL**	**11**	**1**	**2**	**3**	**1**	**1**	**2**	**4**	**0**	**0**	**0**	**9**	**11.1**	**4**	**1**	**5**	**0**	**–2**	....	....	....	....	....	....	....	....
	Hartford Whalers	**NHL**	**14**	**2**	**12**	**14**	**2**	**8**	**10**	**9**	**1**	**0**	**0**	**33**	**6.1**	**21**	**9**	**15**	**0**	**–3**	....	....	....	....	....	....	....	....
1982-83	**Hartford Whalers**	**NHL**	**16**	**4**	**6**	**10**	**3**	**4**	**7**	**8**	**0**	**1**	**0**	**33**	**12.1**	**18**	**2**	**11**	**0**	**5**	....	....	....	....	....	....	....	....
	Binghamton Whalers	AHL	56	19	24	43	....	....	....	63	....	....	....	....	....	....	....	....	....	....	4	1	2	3	8	....	....	....
	NHL Totals		**99**	**24**	**38**	**62**	**20**	**25**	**45**	**51**	**4**	**1**	**2**	**165**	**14.5**	**98**	**23**	**80**	**3**		....	....	....	....	....	....	....	....
	Other Major League Totals		202	86	75	161	....	....	....	190	....	....	....	....	....	....	....	....	....	....	26	6	6	12	42	....	....	....

WCHA First All-Star Team (1976) • NCAA West First All-American Team (1976) • Won Lou Kaplan Trophy (WHA Rookie of the Year) (1977)

Signed as a free agent by **New England** (WHA), July, 1976. Reclaimed by **Detroit** from **Hartford** prior to Expansion Draft, June 9, 1979. Claimed on waivers by **Hartford** from **Detroit**, November 13, 1981.

• LYNCH, Jack

John Alan D – R. 6'2", 180 lbs. b: Toronto, Ont., 5/28/1952. Pittsburgh's 1st, 24th overall, in 1972.

Season	Club	League	GP	G	A	Pts	AG	AA	APts	PIM	PP	SH	GW	S	%	TGF	PGF	TGA	PGA	+/–	GP	G	A	Pts	PIM	PP	SH	GW
1969-70	Oshawa Legionaires	OHA-B	STATISTICS NOT AVAILABLE																									
1970-71	Oshawa Generals	OHA-Jr.	60	18	29	47	....	....	....	86	....	....	....	....	....	....	....	....	....	....	....	....	....	....	....	....	....	....
1971-72	Oshawa Generals	OMJHL	59	18	38	56	....	....	....	55	....	....	....	....	....	....	....	....	....	....	12	2	3	5	54	....	....	....
1972-73	**Pittsburgh Penguins**	**NHL**	**47**	**1**	**18**	**19**	**1**	**14**	**15**	**40**	**0**	**0**	**0**	**78**	**1.3**	**53**	**21**	**63**	**10**	**–21**	....	....	....	....	....	....	....	....
	Hershey Bears	AHL	26	4	17	21	....	....	....	26	....	....	....	....	....	....	....	....	....	....	7	0	1	1	28	....	....	....
1973-74	**Pittsburgh Penguins**	**NHL**	**17**	**0**	**7**	**7**	**0**	**6**	**6**	**21**	**0**	**0**	**0**	**23**	**0.0**	**17**	**10**	**26**	**4**	**–15**	....	....	....	....	....	....	....	....
	Hershey Bears	AHL	20	3	10	13	....	....	....	24	....	....	....	....	....	....	....	....	....	....	....	....	....	....	....	....	....	....
	Detroit Red Wings	**NHL**	**35**	**3**	**9**	**12**	**3**	**7**	**10**	**27**	**1**	**0**	**1**	**64**	**4.7**	**49**	**8**	**64**	**9**	**–14**	....	....	....	....	....	....	....	....
1974-75	**Detroit Red Wings**	**NHL**	**50**	**2**	**15**	**17**	**2**	**11**	**13**	**46**	**0**	**0**	**0**	**52**	**3.8**	**51**	**8**	**74**	**16**	**–15**	....	....	....	....	....	....	....	....
	Washington Capitals	**NHL**	**20**	**1**	**5**	**6**	**1**	**4**	**5**	**16**	**0**	**0**	**0**	**28**	**3.6**	**18**	**12**	**78**	**18**	**–54**	....	....	....	....	....	....	....	....
1975-76	**Washington Capitals**	**NHL**	**79**	**9**	**13**	**22**	**8**	**10**	**18**	**78**	**5**	**0**	**1**	**126**	**7.1**	**90**	**24**	**151**	**33**	**–52**	....	....	....	....	....	....	....	....
1976-77	**Washington Capitals**	**NHL**	**75**	**5**	**25**	**30**	**4**	**19**	**23**	**90**	**0**	**0**	**0**	**132**	**3.8**	**87**	**19**	**99**	**16**	**–15**	....	....	....	....	....	....	....	....
1977-78	**Washington Capitals**	**NHL**	**29**	**1**	**8**	**9**	**1**	**6**	**7**	**4**	**0**	**0**	**0**	**58**	**1.7**	**25**	**5**	**39**	**6**	**–13**	....	....	....	....	....	....	....	....
1978-79	**Washington Capitals**	**NHL**	**30**	**2**	**6**	**8**	**2**	**4**	**6**	**14**	**1**	**0**	**0**	**37**	**5.4**	**26**	**6**	**21**	**3**	**2**	....	....	....	....	....	....	....	....
	Hershey Bears	AHL	20	7	6	13	....	....	....	8	....	....	....	....	....	....	....	....	....	....	....	....	....	....	....	....	....	....
	NHL Totals		**382**	**24**	**106**	**130**	**22**	**81**	**103**	**336**	**7**	**0**	**2**	**598**	**4.0**	**416**	**113**	**615**	**115**		....	....	....	....	....	....	....	....

Traded to **Detroit** by **Pittsburgh** with Jim Rutherford for Ron Stackhouse, January 17, 1974. Traded to **Washington** by **Detroit** for Dave Kryskow, February 8, 1975.

• LYON, Steve

D/RW – R. 5'10", 169 lbs. b: Toronto, Ont., 5/16/1952. Minnesota's 10th, 145th overall, in 1972.

Season	Club	League	GP	G	A	Pts	AG	AA	APts	PIM	PP	SH	GW	S	%	TGF	PGF	TGA	PGA	+/–	GP	G	A	Pts	PIM	PP	SH	GW
1971-72	Peterborough Petes	OMJHL	36	7	21	28	....	....	....	118	....	....	....	....	....	....	....	....	....	....	15	1	12	13	4	....	....	....
1972-73	Saginaw Gears	IHL	65	3	30	33	....	....	....	105	....	....	....	....	....	....	....	....	....	....	....	....	....	....	....	....	....	....
1973-74	Columbus Owls	IHL	76	10	60	70	....	....	....	169	....	....	....	....	....	....	....	....	....	....	6	4	2	6	4	....	....	....
1974-75	Columbus Owls	IHL	76	15	51	66	....	....	....	130	....	....	....	....	....	....	....	....	....	....	5	0	1	1	22	....	....	....
	Rochester Americans	AHL	....	....	....	....	....	....	....	....	....	....	....	....	....	....	....	....	....	....	3	0	0	0	5	....	....	....
1975-76	Columbus Owls	IHL	76	25	43	68	....	....	....	165	....	....	....	....	....	....	....	....	....	....	....	....	....	....	....	....	....	....
1976-77	**Pittsburgh Penguins**	**NHL**	**3**	**0**	**0**	**0**	**0**	**0**	**0**	**2**	**0**	**0**	**0**	**2**	**0.0**	**0**	**0**	**0**	**0**	**0**	....	....	....	....	....	....	....	....
	Columbus Owls	IHL	77	33	58	91	....	....	....	123	....	....	....	....	....	....	....	....	....	....	7	1	1	2	17	....	....	....
1977-78	Grand Rapids Owls	IHL	3	0	3	3	....	....	....	2	....	....	....	....	....	....	....	....	....	....	....	....	....	....	....	....	....	....
	Whitby Warriors	OHA-Sr.	28	2	21	23	....	....	....	20	....	....	....	....	....	....	....	....	....	....	....	....	....	....	....	....	....	....
1978-79	Whitby Warriors	OHA-Sr.	40	13	52	65	....	....	....	....	....	....	....	....	....	....	....	....	....	....	....	....	....	....	....	....	....	....
1979-80			DID NOT PLAY																									
1980-81	Georgetown Aces	OHA-Sr.	36	9	50	59	....	....	....	....	....	....	....	....	....	....	....	....	....	....	....	....	....	....	....	....	....	....
1981-82	Georgetown Aces	OHA-Sr.	36	11	*60	71	....	....	....	....	....	....	....	....	....	....	....	....	....	....	....	....	....	....	....	....	....	....
1982-83	Georgetown Aces	OHA-Sr.	STATISTICS NOT AVAILABLE																									
	NHL Totals		**3**	**0**	**0**	**0**	**0**	**0**	**0**	**2**	**0**	**0**	**0**	**2**	**0.0**	**0**	**0**	**0**	**0**		....	....	....	....	....	....	....	....

IHL First All-Star Team (1974, 1975)

Signed as a free agent by **Pittsburgh**, November, 1976.

• LYSIAK, Tom

Thomas James "The Bomb" C – L. 6'1", 185 lbs. b: High Prairie, Alta., 4/22/1953. Atlanta's 1st, 2nd overall, in 1973.

Season	Club	League	GP	G	A	Pts	AG	AA	APts	PIM	PP	SH	GW	S	%	TGF	PGF	TGA	PGA	+/–	GP	G	A	Pts	PIM	PP	SH	GW
1970-71	Medicine Hat Tigers	WCJHL	60	14	16	30	....	....	....	112	....	....	....	....	....	....	....	....	....	....	....	....	....	....	....	....	....	....
1971-72	Medicine Hat Tigers	WCJHL	68	46	*97	*143	....	....	....	96	....	....	....	....	....	....	....	....	....	....	7	7	5	12	18	....	....	....
1972-73	Medicine Hat Tigers	WCJHL	67	58	*96	*154	....	....	....	104	....	....	....	....	....	....	....	....	....	....	17	12	*27	*39	48	....	....	....
	Medicine Hat Tigers	Mem-Cup	2	1	1	2	....	....	....	4	....	....	....	....	....	....	....	....	....	....	....	....	....	....	....	....	....	....
1973-74	**Atlanta Flames**	**NHL**	**77**	**19**	**45**	**64**	**18**	**37**	**55**	**54**	**4**	**0**	**2**	**216**	**8.8**	**96**	**42**	**70**	**1**	**–15**	**4**	**0**	**2**	**2**	**0**	**0**	**0**	**0**
1974-75	**Atlanta Flames**	**NHL**	**77**	**25**	**52**	**77**	**22**	**39**	**61**	**73**	**9**	**0**	**2**	**206**	**12.1**	**122**	**49**	**68**	**18**	**23**	....	....	....	....	....	....	....	....
1975-76	**Atlanta Flames**	**NHL**	**80**	**31**	**51**	**82**	**27**	**38**	**65**	**60**	**9**	**1**	**5**	**233**	**13.3**	**108**	**44**	**74**	**12**	**2**	**2**	**0**	**0**	**0**	**2**	**0**	**0**	**0**
1976-77	**Atlanta Flames**	**NHL**	**79**	**30**	**51**	**81**	**27**	**39**	**66**	**52**	**5**	**1**	**3**	**277**	**10.8**	**120**	**30**	**93**	**6**	**3**	**3**	**1**	**3**	**4**	**8**	**1**	**0**	**0**
1977-78	**Atlanta Flames**	**NHL**	**80**	**27**	**42**	**69**	**25**	**33**	**58**	**54**	**3**	**0**	**5**	**215**	**12.6**	**93**	**19**	**81**	**4**	**–3**	**2**	**1**	**0**	**1**	**2**	**0**	**0**	**0**
	Canada	WEC-A	7	1	1	2	....	....	....	4	....	....	....	....	....	....	....	....	....	....	....	....	....	....	....	....	....	....
1978-79	**Atlanta Flames**	**NHL**	**52**	**23**	**35**	**58**	**20**	**25**	**45**	**36**	**7**	**1**	**2**	**137**	**16.8**	**86**	**25**	**52**	**7**	**16**	....	....	....	....	....	....	....	....
	Chicago Black Hawks	**NHL**	**14**	**0**	**10**	**10**	**0**	**7**	**7**	**14**	**0**	**0**	**0**	**27**	**0.0**	**18**	**4**	**11**	**0**	**3**	**4**	**0**	**0**	**0**	**2**	**0**	**0**	**0**
1979-80	**Chicago Black Hawks**	**NHL**	**77**	**26**	**43**	**69**	**22**	**31**	**53**	**31**	**10**	**0**	**7**	**160**	**16.3**	**93**	**36**	**75**	**11**	**–7**	**7**	**4**	**4**	**8**	**0**	**4**	**0**	**0**
1980-81	**Chicago Black Hawks**	**NHL**	**72**	**21**	**55**	**76**	**16**	**37**	**53**	**20**	**5**	**2**	**3**	**167**	**12.6**	**105**	**31**	**103**	**36**	**7**	**3**	**0**	**3**	**3**	**0**	**0**	**0**	**0**
1981-82	**Chicago Black Hawks**	**NHL**	**71**	**32**	**50**	**82**	**25**	**33**	**58**	**84**	**10**	**2**	**4**	**170**	**18.8**	**108**	**34**	**105**	**23**	**–8**	**15**	**6**	**9**	**15**	**13**	**3**	**0**	**0**
1982-83	**Chicago Black Hawks**	**NHL**	**61**	**23**	**38**	**61**	**19**	**26**	**45**	**27**	**6**	**0**	**4**	**122**	**18.9**	**82**	**25**	**52**	**8**	**13**	**13**	**6**	**7**	**13**	**8**	**2**	**0**	**2**
1983-84	**Chicago Black Hawks**	**NHL**	**54**	**17**	**30**	**47**	**14**	**20**	**34**	**35**	**5**	**1**	**2**	**103**	**16.5**	**65**	**17**	**68**	**7**	**–13**	**5**	**1**	**1**	**2**	**2**	**0**	**0**	**0**
1984-85	**Chicago Black Hawks**	**NHL**	**74**	**16**	**30**	**46**	**13**	**20**	**33**	**13**	**2**	**0**	**4**	**100**	**16.0**	**72**	**20**	**76**	**8**	**–16**	**15**	**4**	**8**	**12**	**10**	**0**	**0**	**0**
1985-86	**Chicago Black Hawks**	**NHL**	**51**	**2**	**19**	**21**	**2**	**13**	**15**	**14**	**0**	**0**	**0**	**77**	**2.6**	**33**	**4**	**50**	**2**	**–19**	**3**	**2**	**1**	**3**	**2**	**0**	**0**	**0**
	NHL Totals		**919**	**292**	**551**	**843**	**250**	**398**	**648**	**567**	**75**	**8**	**43**	**2210**	**13.2**	**1201**	**380**	**978**	**143**		**76**	**25**	**38**	**63**	**49**	**10**	**0**	**2**

WCJHL All-Star Team (1972, 1973) • Played in NHL All-Star Game (1975, 1976, 1977)

Traded to **Chicago** by **Atlanta** with Pat Ribble, Greg Fox, Harold Phillipoff and Miles Zaharko for Ivan Boldirev, Phil Russell and Darcy Rota, March 13, 1979. • Suspended for 20 games for abusing linesman Ron Foyt, October 30, 1983.

• MacADAM, Al

Reginald Allan RW – L. 6', 180 lbs. b: Charlottetown, P.E.I., 3/16/1952. Philadelphia's 4th, 55th overall, in 1972.

Season	Club	League	GP	G	A	Pts	AG	AA	APts	PIM	PP	SH	GW	S	%	TGF	PGF	TGA	PGA	+/–	GP	G	A	Pts	PIM	PP	SH	GW
1969-70	Charlottetown Islanders	MJrHL	41	23	38	61	....	....	....	55	....	....	....	....	....	....	....	....	....	....	11	4	7	11	2	....	....	....
	Charlottetown Islanders	Mem-Cup	14	5	6	11	....	....	....	6	....	....	....	....	....	....	....	....	....	....	....	....	....	....	....	....	....	....
1970-71	Charlottetown Islanders	MJrHL	35	19	37	56	....	....	....	22	....	....	....	....	....	....	....	....	....	....	7	2	3	5	7	....	....	....
	Charlottetown Islanders	Cen-Cup	21	23	19	42	....	....	....	31	....	....	....	....	....	....	....	....	....	....	....	....	....	....	....	....	....	....
1971-72	University of P.E.I.	AUAA	26	32	21	53	....	....	....	8	....	....	....	....	....	....	....	....	....	....	....	....	....	....	....	....	....	....
	Charlottetown Islanders	MJrHL	11	15	21	36	....	....	....		....	....	....	....	....	....	....	....	....	....	....	....	....	....	....	....	....	....
1972-73	Richmond Robins	AHL	68	19	32	51	....	....	....	42	....	....	....	....	....	....	....	....	....	....	4	0	2	2	0	....	....	....

			REGULAR SEASON																		PLAYOFFS							
Season	Club	League	GP	G	A	Pts	AG	AA	APts	PIM	PP	SH	GW	S	%	TGF	PGF	TGA	PGA	+/–	GP	G	A	Pts	PIM	PP	SH	GW
1973-74♦	**Philadelphia Flyers**	**NHL**	5	0	0	0	0	0	0	0	0	0	0	2	0.0	0	0	2	0	–2	1	0	0	0	0	0	0	0
	Richmond Robins	AHL	62	23	22	45	....	....	....	36	....	....	....	....	....	....	....	....	....	....	5	1	4	5	4	....	....	....
1974-75	**California Golden Seals**	**NHL**	80	18	25	43	16	19	35	55	2	0	1	160	11.3	70	14	85	6	–23	....	....	....	....	....	....	....	....
1975-76	**California Golden Seals**	**NHL**	80	32	31	63	28	23	51	49	8	4	5	177	18.1	89	27	89	18	–9	....	....	....	....	....	....	....	....
1976-77	**Cleveland Barons**	**NHL**	80	22	41	63	20	32	52	68	6	0	3	194	11.3	97	27	85	13	–2	....	....	....	....	....	....	....	....
	Canada	WEC-A	10	4	4	8	....	....	....	0	....	....	....	....	....	....	....	....	....	....	....	....	....	....	....	....	....	....
1977-78	**Cleveland Barons**	**NHL**	80	16	32	48	15	25	40	42	3	0	1	149	10.7	76	17	110	32	–19	....	....	....	....	....	....	....	....
1978-79	**Minnesota North Stars**	**NHL**	69	24	34	58	21	25	46	30	6	0	4	135	17.8	89	27	66	4	0	....	....	....	....	....	....	....	....
	Canada	WEC-A	8	4	4	8	....	....	....	0	....	....	....	....	....	....	....	....	....	....	....	....	....	....	....	....	....	....
1979-80	**Minnesota North Stars**	**NHL**	80	42	51	93	36	37	73	24	13	0	2	170	24.7	139	47	60	4	36	15	7	9	16	4	1	0	2
1980-81	Minnesota North Stars	DN-Cup	2	0	0	0	....	....	....	0	....	....	....	....	....	....	....	....	....	....	....	....	....	....	....	....	....	....
	Minnesota North Stars	**NHL**	78	21	39	60	16	26	42	94	6	0	7	145	14.5	103	47	64	2	–6	19	9	10	19	4	1	1	1
1981-82	**Minnesota North Stars**	**NHL**	79	18	43	61	14	29	43	37	5	2	4	141	12.8	100	28	82	19	9	4	1	0	1	4	0	0	0
1982-83	**Minnesota North Stars**	**NHL**	73	11	22	33	9	15	24	60	0	3	2	93	11.8	51	5	68	25	3	9	2	1	3	2	0	0	0
1983-84	**Minnesota North Stars**	**NHL**	80	22	13	35	18	9	27	23	1	4	1	104	21.2	52	1	92	36	–5	16	1	4	5	7	0	0	0
1984-85	**Vancouver Canucks**	**NHL**	80	14	20	34	11	14	25	27	0	2	2	80	17.5	48	4	108	35	–29	....	....	....	....	....	....	....	....
1985-86	Fredericton Express	AHL	11	0	4	4	....	....	....	5	....	....	....	....	....	....	....	....	....	....	....	....	....	....	....	....	....	....
1986-87	Charlottetown Islanders	NBSHL	11	11	11	22	....	....	....	2	....	....	....	....	....	....	....	....	....	....	....	....	....	....	....	....	....	....
1987-1997	St. Thomas University	AUAA	DID NOT PLAY – COACHING																									
1997-2000	St. John's Maple Leafs	AHL	DID NOT PLAY – COACHING																									
	NHL Totals		864	240	351	591	204	254	458	509	50	15	32	1550	15.5	914	244	911	194		64	20	24	44	21	2	1	3

Won Bill Masterton Trophy (1980) • Played in NHL All-Star Game (1976, 1977)

Traded to **California** by **Philadelphia** with Larry Wright and Philadelphia's 1st round choice (Rob Chipperfield) in 1974 Amateur Draft for Reggie Leach, May 24, 1974. Transferred to **Cleveland** after **California** franchise relocated, August 26, 1976. Protected by **Minnesota** prior to **Minnesota-Cleveland** Dispersal Draft, June 15, 1978. Traded to **Vancouver** by **Minnesota** for Harold Snepsts, June 21, 1984.

• MacDERMID, Paul

RW – R. 6'1", 205 lbs. b: Chesley, Ont., 4/14/1963. Hartford's 2nd, 61st overall, in 1981.

Season	Club	League	GP	G	A	Pts	AG	AA	APts	PIM	PP	SH	GW	S	%	TGF	PGF	TGA	PGA	+/–	GP	G	A	Pts	PIM	PP	SH	GW
1979-80	Port Elgin Bears	OHA-C	30	23	20	43	....	....	....	87	....	....	....	....	....	....	....	....	....	....	....	....	....	....	....	....	....	....
1980-81	Windsor Spitfires	OMJHL	68	15	17	32	....	....	....	106	....	....	....	....	....	....	....	....	....	....	....	....	....	....	....	....	....	....
1981-82	Windsor Spitfires	OHL	65	26	45	71	....	....	....	179	....	....	....	....	....	....	....	....	....	....	9	6	4	10	17	....	....	....
	Hartford Whalers	**NHL**	3	1	0	1	1	0	1	2	0	0	0	4	25.0	2	0	2	0	0	....	....	....	....	....	....	....	....
1982-83	Windsor Spitfires	OHL	42	35	45	80	....	....	....	9	....	....	....	....	....	....	....	....	....	....	....	....	....	....	....	....	....	....
	Hartford Whalers	**NHL**	7	0	0	0	0	0	0	2	0	0	0	7	0.0	0	0	6	0	–6	....	....	....	....	....	....	....	....
1983-84	**Hartford Whalers**	**NHL**	3	0	1	1	0	1	1	0	0	0	0	2	0.0	1	0	0	0	1	....	....	....	....	....	....	....	....
	Binghamton Whalers	AHL	70	31	30	61	....	....	....	130	....	....	....	....	....	....	....	....	....	....	....	....	....	....	....	....	....	....
1984-85	**Hartford Whalers**	**NHL**	31	4	7	11	3	5	8	29	0	0	0	27	14.8	18	0	15	0	3	....	....	....	....	....	....	....	....
	Binghamton Whalers	AHL	48	9	31	40	....	....	....	87	....	....	....	....	....	....	....	....	....	....	....	....	....	....	....	....	....	....
1985-86	**Hartford Whalers**	**NHL**	74	13	10	23	10	7	17	160	0	0	2	88	14.8	32	0	33	2	1	10	2	1	3	20	0	0	1
1986-87	**Hartford Whalers**	**NHL**	72	7	11	18	6	8	14	202	0	0	1	72	9.7	28	1	24	0	3	6	2	1	3	34	0	0	1
1987-88	**Hartford Whalers**	**NHL**	80	20	15	35	17	11	28	139	4	0	2	96	20.8	63	15	45	0	3	6	0	5	5	14	0	0	0
1988-89	**Hartford Whalers**	**NHL**	74	17	27	44	14	19	33	141	5	0	3	113	15.0	83	28	54	0	1	4	1	1	2	16	0	0	0
1989-90	**Hartford Whalers**	**NHL**	29	6	12	18	5	9	14	69	3	0	2	37	16.2	22	8	13	0	1	....	....	....	....	....	....	....	....
	Winnipeg Jets	**NHL**	44	7	10	17	6	7	13	100	1	0	1	48	14.6	36	6	26	0	4	7	0	2	2	8	0	0	0
1990-91	**Winnipeg Jets**	**NHL**	69	15	21	36	14	16	30	128	3	0	1	94	16.0	63	16	53	0	–6	....	....	....	....	....	....	....	....
1991-92	**Winnipeg Jets**	**NHL**	59	10	11	21	9	8	17	151	2	0	2	71	14.1	36	10	34	0	–8	....	....	....	....	....	....	....	....
	Washington Capitals	**NHL**	15	2	5	7	2	4	6	43	0	0	0	21	9.5	11	0	9	0	2	7	0	1	1	22	0	0	0
1992-93	**Washington Capitals**	**NHL**	72	9	8	17	7	5	12	80	1	0	3	45	20.0	22	4	31	0	–13	....	....	....	....	....	....	....	....
1993-94	**Quebec Nordiques**	**NHL**	44	2	3	5	2	2	4	35	0	0	0	16	12.5	12	0	15	0	–3	....	....	....	....	....	....	....	....
1994-95	**Quebec Nordiques**	**NHL**	14	3	1	4	5	1	6	22	0	0	1	13	23.1	8	0	5	0	3	3	0	0	0	2	0	0	0
	NHL Totals		690	116	142	258	101	103	204	1303	19	0	18	754	15.4	437	88	365	2		43	5	11	16	116	0	0	2

Traded to **Winnipeg** by **Hartford** for Randy Cunneyworth, December 13, 1989. Traded to **Washington** by **Winnipeg** for Mike Lalor, March 2, 1992. Traded to **Quebec** by **Washington** with Reggie Savage for Mike Hough, June 20, 1993. • Suffered eventual career-ending back injury in game vs. Vancouver, November 23, 1993.

• MacDONALD, Blair

Blair Neil Joseph "B.J." RW – R. 5'10", 180 lbs. b: Cornwall, Ont., 11/17/1953. Los Angeles' 4th, 86th overall, in 1973.

Season	Club	League	GP	G	A	Pts	AG	AA	APts	PIM	PP	SH	GW	S	%	TGF	PGF	TGA	PGA	+/–	GP	G	A	Pts	PIM	PP	SH	GW
1970-71	Cornwall Royals	QMJHL	51	24	14	38	....	....	....	6	....	....	....	....	....	....	....	....	....	....	....	....	....	....	....	....	....	....
1971-72	Cornwall Royals	QMJHL	61	45	45	90	....	....	....	36	....	....	....	....	....	....	....	....	....	....	16	10	5	15	10	....	....	....
	Cornwall Royals	Mem-Cup	3	0	1	1	....	....	....	4	....	....	....	....	....	....	....	....	....	....	....	....	....	....	....	....	....	....
1972-73	Cornwall Royals	QMJHL	64	63	39	102	....	....	....	44	....	....	....	....	....	....	....	....	....	....	16	14	14	28	10	....	....	....
1973-74	Edmonton Oilers	WHA	78	21	24	45	....	....	....	34	....	....	....	....	....	....	....	....	....	....	5	4	2	6	2	....	....	....
1974-75	Edmonton Oilers	WHA	72	22	24	46	....	....	....	14	....	....	....	....	....	....	....	....	....	....	....	....	....	....	....	....	....	....
1975-76	Edmonton Oilers	WHA	29	7	5	12	....	....	....	8	....	....	....	....	....	....	....	....	....	....	....	....	....	....	....	....	....	....
	Indianapolis Racers	WHA	56	19	11	30	....	....	....	14	....	....	....	....	....	....	....	....	....	....	7	0	0	0	0	....	....	....
1976-77	Indianapolis Racers	WHA	81	34	30	64	....	....	....	28	....	....	....	....	....	....	....	....	....	....	13	7	8	15	4	....	....	....
1977-78	Edmonton Oilers	WHA	80	34	34	68	....	....	....	11	....	....	....	....	....	....	....	....	....	....	5	1	1	2	0	....	....	....
1978-79	Edmonton Oilers	WHA	80	34	37	71	....	....	....	44	....	....	....	....	....	....	....	....	....	....	13	8	10	18	6	....	....	....
1979-80	**Edmonton Oilers**	**NHL**	80	46	48	94	39	35	74	6	13	2	6	266	17.3	144	45	139	41	1	3	0	3	3	0	0	0	0
1980-81	**Edmonton Oilers**	**NHL**	51	19	24	43	15	16	31	27	5	0	1	134	14.2	67	23	70	18	–8	....	....	....	....	....	....	....	....
	Vancouver Canucks	**NHL**	12	5	9	14	4	6	10	10	2	0	2	38	13.2	19	4	14	0	1	3	0	1	1	2	0	0	0
1981-82	Dallas Black Hawks	CHL	3	1	1	2	....	....	....	0	....	....	....	....	....	....	....	....	....	....	....	....	....	....	....	....	....	....
	Vancouver Canucks	**NHL**	59	18	15	33	14	10	24	20	4	0	2	116	15.5	54	18	37	1	0	3	0	0	0	0	0	0	0
1982-83	**Vancouver Canucks**	**NHL**	17	3	4	7	2	3	5	2	2	0	0	29	10.3	15	6	11	1	–1	2	0	2	2	0	0	0	0
	Fredericton Express	AHL	60	29	37	66	....	....	....	20	....	....	....	....	....	....	....	....	....	....	7	2	3	5	2	....	....	....
1983-84	WAT Stadlau	Austria	26	30	32	62	....	....	....	....	....	....	....	....	....	....	....	....	....	....	....	....	....	....	....	....	....	....
	Montana Magic	CHL	4	1	0	1	....	....	....	0	....	....	....	....	....	....	....	....	....	....	....	....	....	....	....	....	....	....
1984-85	WAT Stadlau	Austria	34	37	29	66	....	....	....	30	....	....	....	....	....	....	....	....	....	....	....	....	....	....	....	....	....	....
1985-86	IEV Innsbruck	Austria	23	20	18	38	....	....	....	8	....	....	....	....	....	....	....	....	....	....	10	9	11	20	....	....	....	....
1986-1987	IEV Innsbruck	Austria	DID NOT PLAY – COACHING																									
1987-1988	Fredericton Canadiens	AHL	DID NOT PLAY – COACHING																									
1988-1991	Cleveland Lumberjacks	IHL	DID NOT PLAY – COACHING																									
1991-1999			OUT OF HOCKEY – RETIRED																									
1999-2000	Cleveland Lumberjacks	IHL	DID NOT PLAY – COACHING																									
	NHL Totals		219	91	100	191	74	70	144	65	26	2	11	583	15.6	299	96	271	61		11	0	6	6	2	0	0	0
	Other Major League Totals		476	171	165	336	....	....	....	153	....	....	....	....	....	....	....	....	....	....	43	20	21	41	12	....	....	....

QMJHL Second All-Star Team (1973) • WHA Second All-Star Team (1979) • Played in NHL All-Star Game (1980)

Selected by **Edmonton** (WHA) in 1972 WHA General Player Draft, February 12, 1972. Traded to **Indianapolis** (WHA) by **Edmonton** (WHA) for future considerations, December, 1976. Traded to **Edmonton** (WHA) by **Indianapolis** (WHA) with Dave Inkpen and Mike Zuke for Kevin Devine, Barry Wilkins, Rusty Patenaude and Claude St. Sauveur, September, 1977. Rights retained by **Edmonton** prior to Expansion Draft, June 9, 1979. Traded to **Vancouver** by **Edmonton** with the rights to Lars Gunnar Petterson for Garry Lariviere and Ken Berry, March 10, 1981.

• MacDONALD, Brett

D – L. 6'1", 205 lbs. b: Bothwell, Ont., 1/5/1966. Vancouver's 7th, 94th overall, in 1984.

Season	Club	League	GP	G	A	Pts	AG	AA	APts	PIM	PP	SH	GW	S	%	TGF	PGF	TGA	PGA	+/–	GP	G	A	Pts	PIM	PP	SH	GW
1982-83	Dixie Beehives	OJHL	44	5	18	23	....	....	....	28	....	....	....	....	....	....	....	....	....	....	....	....	....	....	....	....	....	....
1983-84	North Bay Centennials	OHL	70	8	18	26	....	....	....	83	....	....	....	....	....	....	....	....	....	....	4	0	1	1	0	....	....	....
1984-85	North Bay Centennials	OHL	58	6	27	33	....	....	....	72	....	....	....	....	....	....	....	....	....	....	8	1	1	2	11	....	....	....
1985-86	North Bay Centennials	OHL	15	0	6	6	....	....	....	42	....	....	....	....	....	....	....	....	....	....	....	....	....	....	....	....	....	....
	Kitchener Rangers	OHL	53	10	27	37	....	....	....	52	....	....	....	....	....	....	....	....	....	....	5	3	7	10	6	....	....	....
1986-87	Fredericton Express	AHL	49	0	9	9	....	....	....	29	....	....	....	....	....	....	....	....	....	....	....	....	....	....	....	....	....	....
1987-88	**Vancouver Canucks**	**NHL**	1	0	0	0	0	0	0	0	0	0	0	0	0.0	1	0	2	0	–1	....	....	....	....	....	....	....	....
	Fredericton Express	AHL	15	1	5	6	....	....	....	23	....	....	....	....	....	....	....	....	....	....	....	....	....	....	....	....	....	....
	Flint Spirits	IHL	49	2	21	23	....	....	....	43	....	....	....	....	....	....	....	....	....	....	15	2	2	4	12	....	....	....

			REGULAR SEASON																		PLAYOFFS							
Season	Club	League	GP	G	A	Pts	AG	AA	APts	PIM	PP	SH	GW	S	%	TGF	PGF	TGA	PGA	+/–	GP	G	A	Pts	PIM	PP	SH	GW
1988-89	New Haven Nighthawks	AHL	15	2	4	6	....	....	....	6	....	....	....	....	....	....	....	....	....	....	....	....	....	....	....	....	....	....
	Flint Spirits	IHL	57	3	24	27	....	....	....	53	....	....	....	....	....	....	....	....	....	....	....	....	....	....	....	....	....	....
1989-90	Krefelder EV	Germany-2	26	6	22	28	....	....	....	32	....	....	....	....	....	....	....	....	....	....	....	....	....	....	....	....	....	....
1990-91	Nashville Knights	ECHL	64	19	62	81	....	....	....	56	....	....	....	....	....	....	....	....	....	....	....	....	....	....	....	....	....	....
	San Diego Gulls	IHL	3	0	1	1	....	....	....	0	....	....	....	....	....	....	....	....	....	....	....	....	....	....	....	....	....	....
	Moncton Hawks	AHL	2	0	0	0	....	....	....	0	....	....	....	....	....	....	....	....	....	....	7	1	3	4	4	....	....	....
1991-92	Flint Bulldogs	ColHL	46	12	33	45	....	....	....	23	....	....	....	....	....	....	....	....	....	....	....	....	....	....	....	....	....	....
	Moncton Hawks	AHL	3	0	0	0	....	....	....	2	....	....	....	....	....	....	....	....	....	....	....	....	....	....	....	....	....	....
1992-93	Flint Bulldogs	ColHL	60	12	39	51	....	....	....	60	....	....	....	....	....	....	....	....	....	....	6	0	5	5	21	....	....	....
1993-94	Chatham Wheels	ColHL	42	8	31	39	....	....	....	29	....	....	....	....	....	....	....	....	....	....	14	6	9	15	4	....	....	....
1994-95	Saginaw Wheels	ColHL	62	17	42	59	....	....	....	42	....	....	....	....	....	....	....	....	....	....	....	....	....	....	....	....	....	....
	Muskegon Fury	ColHL	11	3	8	11	....	....	....	14	....	....	....	....	....	....	....	....	....	....	16	2	5	7	12	....	....	....
1995-96	Orlando Solar Bears	IHL	1	0	0	0	....	....	....	2	....	....	....	....	....	....	....	....	....	....	....	....	....	....	....	....	....	....
	Flint Generals	ColHL	62	16	39	55	....	....	....	55	....	....	....	....	....	....	....	....	....	....	15	1	8	9	2	....	....	....
1996-97	Flint Generals	ColHL	74	8	64	72	....	....	....	44	....	....	....	....	....	....	....	....	....	....	14	1	11	12	12	....	....	....
1997-98	Flint Generals	UHL	56	7	37	44	....	....	....	32	....	....	....	....	....	....	....	....	....	....	17	1	6	7	14	....	....	....
1998-99	Flint Generals	UHL	23	2	9	11	....	....	....	16	....	....	....	....	....	....	....	....	....	....	12	1	3	4	12	....	....	....
	NHL Totals		**1**	**0**	**0**	**0**	**0**	**0**	**0**	**0**	**0**	**0**	**0**	**0**	**0.0**	**1**	**0**	**2**	**0**		....	....	....	....	....	....	....	....

ECHL First All-Star Team (1991) • Defenseman of the Year - ECHL (1991) • ColHL First All-Star Team (1993)

• MacDONALD, Craig

C – L. 6'2", 195 lbs. b: Antigonish, N.S., 4/7/1977. Hartford's 3rd, 88th overall, in 1996.

Season	Club	League	GP	G	A	Pts	AG	AA	APts	PIM	PP	SH	GW	S	%	TGF	PGF	TGA	PGA	+/–	GP	G	A	Pts	PIM	PP	SH	GW
1994-95	Lawrence Academy	Hi-School	30	25	52	77	....	....	....	10	....	....	....	....	....	....	....	....	....	....	....	....	....	....	....	....	....	....
1995-96	Harvard University	ECAC	34	7	10	17	....	....	....	10	....	....	....	....	....	....	....	....	....	....	....	....	....	....	....	....	....	....
1996-97	Harvard University	ECAC	32	6	10	16	....	....	....	20	....	....	....	....	....	....	....	....	....	....	....	....	....	....	....	....	....	....
1997-98	Canada	Nat-Team	58	18	29	47	....	....	....	38	....	....	....	....	....	....	....	....	....	....	....	....	....	....	....	....	....	....
1998-99	**Carolina Hurricanes**	**NHL**	**11**	**0**	**0**	**0**	**0**	**0**	**0**	**0**	**0**	**0**	**0**	**5**	**0.0**	**0**	**0**	**0**	**0**	**0**	**1**	**0**	**0**	**0**	**0**	**0**	**0**	**0**
	Beast of New Haven	AHL	62	17	31	48	....	....	....	77	....	....	....	....	....	....	....	....	....	....	....	....	....	....	....	....	....	....
99-2000	Cincinnati Cyclones	IHL	78	12	24	36	....	....	....	76	....	....	....	....	....	....	....	....	....	....	11	4	1	5	8	....	....	....
	NHL Totals		**11**	**0**	**0**	**0**	**0**	**0**	**0**	**0**	**0**	**0**	**0**	**5**	**0.0**	**0**	**0**	**0**	**0**		**1**	**0**	**0**	**0**	**0**	**0**	**0**	**0**

Rights transferred to **Carolina** after **Hartford** franchise relocated, June 25, 1997

• MacDONALD, Doug

Douglas B. LW – L. 6', 192 lbs. b: Assiniboia, Sask., 2/8/1969. Buffalo's 3rd, 77th overall, in 1989.

Season	Club	League	GP	G	A	Pts	AG	AA	APts	PIM	PP	SH	GW	S	%	TGF	PGF	TGA	PGA	+/–	GP	G	A	Pts	PIM	PP	SH	GW
1984-85	Burnaby Midget AAA	BCAHA	50	53	105	158	....	....	....	....	....	....	....	....	....	....	....	....	....	....	....	....	....	....	....	....	....	....
1985-86	Langley Eagles	BCJHL	45	21	33	54	....	....	....	8	....	....	....	....	....	....	....	....	....	....	....	....	....	....	....	....	....	....
1986-87	Delta Flyers	BCJHL	51	28	49	77	....	....	....	61	....	....	....	....	....	....	....	....	....	....	....	....	....	....	....	....	....	....
1987-88	Delta Flyers	BCJHL	51	50	54	104	....	....	....	72	....	....	....	....	....	....	....	....	....	....	9	5	9	14	16	....	....	....
1988-89	University of Wisconsin	WCHA	44	23	25	48	....	....	....	50	....	....	....	....	....	....	....	....	....	....	....	....	....	....	....	....	....	....
1989-90	University of Wisconsin	WCHA	44	16	35	51	....	....	....	52	....	....	....	....	....	....	....	....	....	....	....	....	....	....	....	....	....	....
1990-91	University of Wisconsin	WCHA	31	20	26	46	....	....	....	50	....	....	....	....	....	....	....	....	....	....	....	....	....	....	....	....	....	....
1991-92	University of Wisconsin	WCHA	29	14	25	39	....	....	....	58	....	....	....	....	....	....	....	....	....	....	....	....	....	....	....	....	....	....
1992-93	**Buffalo Sabres**	**NHL**	**5**	**1**	**0**	**1**	**1**	**0**	**1**	**2**	**0**	**0**	**0**	**1**	**100.0**	**3**	**0**	**3**	**0**	**0**	....	....	....	....	....	....	....	....
	Rochester Americans	AHL	64	25	33	58	....	....	....	58	....	....	....	....	....	....	....	....	....	....	7	0	2	2	4	....	....	....
1993-94	**Buffalo Sabres**	**NHL**	**4**	**0**	**0**	**0**	**0**	**0**	**0**	**0**	**0**	**0**	**0**	**3**	**0.0**	**1**	**0**	**3**	**0**	**–2**	....	....	....	....	....	....	....	....
	Rochester Americans	AHL	63	25	19	44	....	....	....	46	....	....	....	....	....	....	....	....	....	....	4	1	1	2	8	....	....	....
1994-95	Rochester Americans	AHL	58	21	25	46	....	....	....	73	....	....	....	....	....	....	....	....	....	....	5	0	1	1	0	....	....	....
	Buffalo Sabres	**NHL**	**2**	**0**	**0**	**0**	**0**	**0**	**0**	**0**	**0**	**0**	**0**	**0**	**0.0**	**0**	**0**	**1**	**0**	**–1**	....	....	....	....	....	....	....	....
1995-96	Cincinnati Cyclones	IHL	71	19	40	59	....	....	....	66	....	....	....	....	....	....	....	....	....	....	15	1	3	4	14	....	....	....
1996-97	Cincinnati Cyclones	IHL	65	20	34	54	....	....	....	36	....	....	....	....	....	....	....	....	....	....	3	0	0	0	0	....	....	....
1997-98	Cincinnati Cyclones	IHL	70	17	19	36	....	....	....	64	....	....	....	....	....	....	....	....	....	....	4	0	4	4	0	....	....	....
1998-99	Cincinnati Cyclones	IHL	33	7	11	18	....	....	....	22	....	....	....	....	....	....	....	....	....	....	....	....	....	....	....	....	....	....
99-2000	Cincinnati Cyclones	IHL	7	0	1	1	....	....	....	2	....	....	....	....	....	....	....	....	....	....	....	....	....	....	....	....	....	....
	Kolner Haie	Germany	26	6	10	16	....	....	....	12	....	....	....	....	....	....	....	....	....	....	10	4	1	5	12	....	....	....
	NHL Totals		**11**	**1**	**0**	**1**	**1**	**0**	**1**	**2**	**0**	**0**	**0**	**4**	**25.0**	**4**	**0**	**7**	**0**		....	....	....	....	....	....	....	....

Signed as a free agent by **Cincinnati** (IHL), July 26, 1998.

• MacDONALD, Kevin

Kevin Scott D – R. 6', 200 lbs. b: Prescott, Ont., 2/24/1966.

Season	Club	League	GP	G	A	Pts	AG	AA	APts	PIM	PP	SH	GW	S	%	TGF	PGF	TGA	PGA	+/–	GP	G	A	Pts	PIM	PP	SH	GW
1982-83	Brockville Braves	OJHL	45	1	4	5	....	....	....	154	....	....	....	....	....	....	....	....	....	....	....	....	....	....	....	....	....	....
1983-84	Belleville Bulls	OHL	4	0	0	0	....	....	....	4	....	....	....	....	....	....	....	....	....	....	....	....	....	....	....	....	....	....
	Sudbury Wolves	OHL	1	0	0	0	....	....	....	0	....	....	....	....	....	....	....	....	....	....	....	....	....	....	....	....	....	....
	Peterborough Petes	OHL	32	3	3	6	....	....	....	78	....	....	....	....	....	....	....	....	....	....	8	0	1	1	16	....	....	....
1984-85	Peterborough Petes	OHL	63	3	13	16	....	....	....	162	....	....	....	....	....	....	....	....	....	....	15	1	1	2	6	....	....	....
1985-86	Peterborough Petes	OHL	51	4	15	19	....	....	....	132	....	....	....	....	....	....	....	....	....	....	16	0	5	5	24	....	....	....
1986-87	Peterborough Petes	OHL	48	4	4	8	....	....	....	183	....	....	....	....	....	....	....	....	....	....	10	0	1	1	16	....	....	....
1987-88	St. Thomas University	AUAA	24	7	14	21	....	....	....	140	....	....	....	....	....	....	....	....	....	....	....	....	....	....	....	....	....	....
1988-89	Muskegon Lumberjacks	IHL	64	2	13	15	....	....	....	190	....	....	....	....	....	....	....	....	....	....	11	2	3	5	22	....	....	....
1989-90	New Haven Nighthawks	AHL	27	0	1	1	....	....	....	111	....	....	....	....	....	....	....	....	....	....	....	....	....	....	....	....	....	....
	Phoenix Roadrunners	IHL	30	1	5	6	....	....	....	201	....	....	....	....	....	....	....	....	....	....	....	....	....	....	....	....	....	....
1990-91	Phoenix Roadrunners	IHL	74	1	9	10	....	....	....	327	....	....	....	....	....	....	....	....	....	....	11	0	1	1	22	....	....	....
1991-92	Phoenix Roadrunners	IHL	76	7	14	21	....	....	....	304	....	....	....	....	....	....	....	....	....	....	....	....	....	....	....	....	....	....
1992-93	Phoenix Roadrunners	IHL	6	0	1	1	....	....	....	23	....	....	....	....	....	....	....	....	....	....	....	....	....	....	....	....	....	....
	Fort Wayne Komets	IHL	65	4	9	13	....	....	....	283	....	....	....	....	....	....	....	....	....	....	11	0	0	0	21	....	....	....
1993-94	Fort Wayne Komets	IHL	29	0	3	3	....	....	....	140	....	....	....	....	....	....	....	....	....	....	15	0	4	4	76	....	....	....
	Ottawa Senators	**NHL**	**1**	**0**	**0**	**0**	**0**	**0**	**0**	**2**	**0**	**0**	**0**	**0**	**0.0**	**0**	**0**	**0**	**0**	**0**	....	....	....	....	....	....	....	....
	P.E.I. Senators	AHL	40	2	4	6	....	....	....	245	....	....	....	....	....	....	....	....	....	....	....	....	....	....	....	....	....	....
1994-95	Chicago Wolves	IHL	75	1	12	13	....	....	....	*390	....	....	....	....	....	....	....	....	....	....	3	0	0	0	17	....	....	....
1995-96	Chicago Wolves	IHL	75	2	6	8	....	....	....	274	....	....	....	....	....	....	....	....	....	....	9	0	3	3	23	....	....	....
1996-97	Fort Wayne Komets	IHL	53	1	2	3	....	....	....	251	....	....	....	....	....	....	....	....	....	....	....	....	....	....	....	....	....	....
	Hershey Bears	AHL	16	1	1	2	....	....	....	74	....	....	....	....	....	....	....	....	....	....	12	1	0	1	13	....	....	....
1997-98	Hershey Bears	AHL	5	0	0	0	....	....	....	37	....	....	....	....	....	....	....	....	....	....	....	....	....	....	....	....	....	....
	Baton Rouge Kingfish	ECHL	58	2	17	19	....	....	....	222	....	....	....	....	....	....	....	....	....	....	....	....	....	....	....	....	....	....
	Hershey Bears	AHL	DID NOT PLAY – ASSISTANT COACH																									
1998-2000	Bakersfield Condors	WCHL	DID NOT PLAY – COACHING																									
	NHL Totals		**1**	**0**	**0**	**0**	**0**	**0**	**0**	**2**	**0**	**0**	**0**	**0**	**0.0**	**0**	**0**	**0**	**0**		....	....	....	....	....	....	....	....

Signed as a free agent by **Edmonton**, July, 1990. Signed as a free agent by **Ottawa**, December 22, 1993. • Served as playing coach with **Baton Rouge** (WCHL) during 1997-98 season. • Served as Assistant Coach with **Hershey** (AHL) during 1997-98 playoffs. • Played w/ RHI's Ottawa Loggers 1996 (1-0-0-0-0).

• MacDONALD, Lowell

Lowell Wilson LW – R. 5'11", 185 lbs. b: New Glasgow, N.S., 8/30/1941.

Season	Club	League	GP	G	A	Pts	AG	AA	APts	PIM	PP	SH	GW	S	%	TGF	PGF	TGA	PGA	+/–	GP	G	A	Pts	PIM	PP	SH	GW
1959-60	Hamilton Tiger Cubs	OHA-Jr.	48	17	19	36	....	....	....	7	....	....	....	....	....	....	....	....	....	....	....	....	....	....	....	....	....	....
1960-61	Hamilton Red Wings	OHA-Jr.	48	26	28	54	....	....	....	15	....	....	....	....	....	....	....	....	....	....	11	6	9	15	4	....	....	....
1961-62	Hamilton Red Wings	OHA-Jr.	50	*46	39	85	....	....	....	10	....	....	....	....	....	....	....	....	....	....	10	*7	5	*12	8	....	....	....
	Detroit Red Wings	**NHL**	**1**	**0**	**0**	**0**	**0**	**0**	**0**	**2**	....	....	....	....	....	....	....	....	....	....	....	....	....	....	....	....	....	....
	Hamilton Red Wings	Mem-Cup	14	*17	7	*24	....	....	....	14	....	....	....	....	....	....	....	....	....	....	....	....	....	....	....	....	....	....
1962-63	**Detroit Red Wings**	**NHL**	**26**	**2**	**1**	**3**	**2**	**1**	**3**	**8**	....	....	....	....	....	....	....	....	....	....	**1**	**0**	**0**	**0**	**2**	**0**	**0**	**0**
	Pittsburgh Hornets	AHL	41	20	19	39	....	....	....	4	....	....	....	....	....	....	....	....	....	....	....	....	....	....	....	....	....	....
1963-64	**Detroit Red Wings**	**NHL**	**10**	**1**	**4**	**5**	**1**	**4**	**5**	**0**	....	....	....	....	....	....	....	....	....	....	....	....	....	....	....	....	....	....
	Pittsburgh Hornets	AHL	59	31	29	60	....	....	....	6	....	....	....	....	....	....	....	....	....	....	5	3	1	4	2	....	....	....
1964-65	**Detroit Red Wings**	**NHL**	**9**	**2**	**1**	**3**	**2**	**1**	**3**	**0**	....	....	....	....	....	....	....	....	....	....	....	....	....	....	....	....	....	....
	Pittsburgh Hornets	AHL	59	16	20	36	....	....	....	10	....	....	....	....	....	....	....	....	....	....	2	0	0	0	0	....	....	....

			REGULAR SEASON																		PLAYOFFS							
Season	Club	League	GP	G	A	Pts	AG	AA	APts	PIM	PP	SH	GW	S	%	TGF	PGF	TGA	PGA	+/-	GP	G	A	Pts	PIM	PP	SH	GW
1965-66	Rochester Americans	AHL	1	0	0	0	....	....	....	0	....	....	....	....	....	....	....	....	....	....	....	....	....	....	....	....	....	....
	Tulsa Oilers	CPHL	57	33	25	58	....	....	....	4	....	....	....	....	....	....	....	....	....	....	11	5	4	9	0	....	....	....
1966-67	Tulsa Oilers	CPHL	33	14	17	31	....	....	....	8	....	....	....	....	....	....	....	....	....	....	....	....	....	....	....	....	....	....
1967-68	**Los Angeles Kings**	**NHL**	**74**	**21**	**24**	**45**	**24**	**24**	**48**	**12**	**2**	**1**	**2**	**232**	**9.1**	**63**	**6**	**75**	**7**	**–11**	**7**	**3**	**4**	**7**	**2**	**1**	**0**	**1**
1968-69	**Los Angeles Kings**	**NHL**	**58**	**14**	**14**	**28**	**15**	**12**	**27**	**10**	**1**	**1**	**0**	**181**	**7.7**	**43**	**4**	**53**	**3**	**–11**	**7**	**2**	**3**	**5**	**0**	**0**	**1**	**0**
	Springfield Kings	AHL	9	6	9	15	....	....	....	0	....	....	....	....	....	....	....	....	....	....	....	....	....	....	....	....	....	....
1969-70	Springfield Kings	AHL	14	4	3	7	....	....	....	0	....	....	....	....	....	....	....	....	....	....	3	0	0	0	0	....	....	....
1970-71	**Pittsburgh Penguins**	**NHL**	**10**	**0**	**1**	**1**	**0**	**1**	**1**	**0**	**0**	**0**	**0**	**11**	**0.0**	**2**	**0**	**8**	**0**	**–6**	....	....	....	....	....	....	....	....
1971-72	**Pittsburgh Penguins**	**NHL**	DID NOT PLAY – INJURED																									
1972-73	**Pittsburgh Penguins**	**NHL**	**78**	**34**	**41**	**75**	**32**	**33**	**65**	**8**	**6**	**0**	**3**	**244**	**13.9**	**115**	**22**	**68**	**12**	**37**	....	....	....	....	....	....	....	....
1973-74	**Pittsburgh Penguins**	**NHL**	**78**	**43**	**39**	**82**	**42**	**32**	**74**	**14**	**9**	**0**	**2**	**260**	**16.5**	**120**	**36**	**75**	**8**	**17**	....	....	....	....	....	....	....	....
1974-75	**Pittsburgh Penguins**	**NHL**	**71**	**27**	**33**	**60**	**24**	**25**	**49**	**24**	**6**	**0**	**5**	**220**	**12.3**	**101**	**26**	**59**	**0**	**16**	**9**	**4**	**2**	**6**	**4**	**1**	**0**	**1**
1975-76	**Pittsburgh Penguins**	**NHL**	**69**	**30**	**43**	**73**	**26**	**32**	**58**	**12**	**12**	**0**	**3**	**181**	**16.6**	**106**	**40**	**56**	**4**	**14**	**3**	**1**	**0**	**1**	**0**	**1**	**0**	**1**
1976-77	**Pittsburgh Penguins**	**NHL**	**3**	**1**	**1**	**2**	**1**	**1**	**2**	**0**	**1**	**0**	**0**	**9**	**11.1**	**2**	**1**	**2**	**0**	**–1**	**3**	**1**	**2**	**3**	**4**	**0**	**0**	**0**
1977-78	**Pittsburgh Penguins**	**NHL**	**19**	**5**	**8**	**13**	**5**	**6**	**11**	**2**	**2**	**0**	**0**	**31**	**16.1**	**18**	**8**	**10**	**0**	**0**	....	....	....	....	....	....	....	....
	NHL Totals		**506**	**180**	**210**	**390**	**174**	**172**	**346**	**92**	....	....	....	....	....	....	....	....	....	....	**30**	**11**	**11**	**22**	**12**	....	....	....

OHA-Jr. First All-Star Team (1962) • Won Bill Masterton Trophy (1973) • Played in NHL All-Star Game (1973, 1974)

Traded to **Toronto** by **Detroit** with Marcel Pronovost, Eddie Joyal, Larry Jeffrey and Aut Erickson for Andy Bathgate, Billy Harris and Gary Jarrett, May 20, 1965. Claimed by **LA Kings** from **Toronto** in Expansion Draft, June 6, 1967. • Missed majority of 1969-70 season in retirement. Claimed by **Pittsburgh** from **LA Kings** in Intra-League Draft, June 9, 1970. • Missed majority of 1970-71 and entire 1971-72 seasons recovering from knee injury suffered in game vs. LA Kings, October 21, 1970. • Missed majority of 1976-77 and 1977-78 seasons recovering from shoulder injury originally suffered in game vs. Pittsburgh, December 10, 1975.

• MacDONALD, Parker

Calvin Parker C – L. 5'11", 160 lbs. b: Sydney, N.S., 6/14/1933.

Season	Club	League	GP	G	A	Pts	AG	AA	APts	PIM	PP	SH	GW	S	%	TGF	PGF	TGA	PGA	+/-	GP	G	A	Pts	PIM	PP	SH	GW
1949-50	Sydney Millionaires	CBSHL	1	1	0	1	....	....	....	0	....	....	....	....	....	....	....	....	....	....	1	1	0	1	0	....	....	....
1950-51	Toronto Marlboros	OHA-Jr.	51	31	22	53	....	....	....	50	....	....	....	....	....	....	....	....	....	....	13	9	5	14	6	....	....	....
1951-52	Toronto Marlboros	OHA-Jr.	52	39	51	90	....	....	....	58	....	....	....	....	....	....	....	....	....	....	6	2	3	5	4	....	....	....
1952-53	Toronto Marlboros	OHA-Jr.	55	39	20	59	....	....	....	48	....	....	....	....	....	....	....	....	....	....	7	3	2	5	4	....	....	....
	Toronto Maple Leafs	**NHL**	**1**	**0**	**0**	**0**	**0**	**0**	**0**	**0**	....	....	....	....	....	....	....	....	....	....	....	....	....	....	....	....	....	....
	Pittsburgh Hornets	AHL	....	....	....	....	....	....	....	....	....	....	....	....	....	....	....	....	....	....	1	0	0	0	0	....	....	....
1953-54	Pittsburgh Hornets	AHL	70	29	24	53	....	....	....	22	....	....	....	....	....	....	....	....	....	....	5	0	2	2	0	....	....	....
1954-55	**Toronto Maple Leafs**	**NHL**	**62**	**8**	**3**	**11**	**10**	**3**	**13**	**36**	....	....	....	....	....	....	....	....	....	....	**4**	**0**	**0**	**0**	**4**	....	....	....
	Pittsburgh Hornets	AHL	8	3	4	7	....	....	....	2	....	....	....	....	....	....	....	....	....	....	....	....	....	....	....	....	....	....
1955-56	Pittsburgh Hornets	AHL	58	35	32	67	....	....	....	60	....	....	....	....	....	....	....	....	....	....	3	0	3	3	2	....	....	....
1956-57	**New York Rangers**	**NHL**	**45**	**7**	**8**	**15**	**9**	**9**	**18**	**24**	....	....	....	....	....	....	....	....	....	....	**1**	**1**	**1**	**2**	**0**	....	....	....
	Providence Reds	AHL	2	4	1	5	....	....	....	0	....	....	....	....	....	....	....	....	....	....	....	....	....	....	....	....	....	....
1957-58	**New York Rangers**	**NHL**	**70**	**8**	**10**	**18**	**10**	**10**	**20**	**30**	....	....	....	....	....	....	....	....	....	....	**6**	**1**	**2**	**3**	**2**	....	....	....
1958-59	Buffalo Bisons	AHL	67	17	21	38	....	....	....	58	....	....	....	....	....	....	....	....	....	....	11	2	7	9	8	....	....	....
1959-60	**New York Rangers**	**NHL**	**4**	**0**	**0**	**0**	**0**	**0**	**0**	**0**	....	....	....	....	....	....	....	....	....	....	....	....	....	....	....	....	....	....
	Springfield Indians	AHL	65	37	36	73	....	....	....	16	....	....	....	....	....	....	....	....	....	....	10	3	7	10	4	....	....	....
1960-61	**Detroit Red Wings**	**NHL**	**70**	**14**	**12**	**26**	**16**	**12**	**28**	**6**	....	....	....	....	....	....	....	....	....	....	**9**	**1**	**0**	**1**	**0**	....	....	....
1961-62	**Detroit Red Wings**	**NHL**	**32**	**5**	**7**	**12**	**6**	**7**	**13**	**8**	....	....	....	....	....	....	....	....	....	....	....	....	....	....	....	....	....	....
	Hershey Bears	AHL	20	10	4	14	....	....	....	8	....	....	....	....	....	....	....	....	....	....	....	....	....	....	....	....	....	....
1962-63	**Detroit Red Wings**	**NHL**	**69**	**33**	**28**	**61**	**39**	**28**	**67**	**32**	....	....	....	....	....	....	....	....	....	....	**11**	**3**	**2**	**5**	**2**	....	....	....
1963-64	**Detroit Red Wings**	**NHL**	**68**	**21**	**25**	**46**	**26**	**26**	**52**	**25**	....	....	....	....	....	....	....	....	....	....	**14**	**3**	**3**	**6**	**2**	....	....	....
1964-65	**Detroit Red Wings**	**NHL**	**69**	**13**	**33**	**46**	**16**	**34**	**50**	**38**	....	....	....	....	....	....	....	....	....	....	**7**	**1**	**1**	**2**	**6**	....	....	....
1965-66	**Boston Bruins**	**NHL**	**29**	**6**	**4**	**10**	**7**	**4**	**11**	**6**	....	....	....	....	....	....	....	....	....	....	....	....	....	....	....	....	....	....
	Detroit Red Wings	**NHL**	**37**	**5**	**12**	**17**	**6**	**11**	**17**	**24**	....	....	....	....	....	....	....	....	....	....	**9**	**0**	**0**	**0**	**2**	....	....	....
1966-67	**Detroit Red Wings**	**NHL**	**16**	**3**	**5**	**8**	**3**	**5**	**8**	**2**	....	....	....	....	....	....	....	....	....	....	....	....	....	....	....	....	....	....
	Pittsburgh Hornets	AHL	59	16	30	46	....	....	....	18	....	....	....	....	....	....	....	....	....	....	9	1	3	4	4	....	....	....
1967-68	**Minnesota North Stars**	**NHL**	**69**	**19**	**23**	**42**	**22**	**23**	**45**	**22**	**9**	**0**	**3**	**183**	**10.4**	**67**	**28**	**57**	**0**	**–18**	**14**	**4**	**5**	**9**	**2**	**0**	**0**	**2**
	Memphis South Stars	CPHL	5	2	3	5	....	....	....	2	....	....	....	....	....	....	....	....	....	....	....	....	....	....	....	....	....	....
1968-69	**Minnesota North Stars**	**NHL**	**35**	**2**	**9**	**11**	**2**	**8**	**10**	**0**	**0**	**0**	**0**	**50**	**4.0**	**20**	**9**	**25**	**0**	**–14**	....	....	....	....	....	....	....	....
	Memphis South Stars	CHL	28	6	11	17	....	....	....	0	....	....	....	....	....	....	....	....	....	....	....	....	....	....	....	....	....	....
1969-70	Iowa Stars	CHL	DID NOT PLAY – COACHING																									
	NHL Totals		**676**	**144**	**179**	**323**	**172**	**180**	**352**	**253**	....	....	....	....	....	....	....	....	....	....	**75**	**14**	**14**	**28**	**20**	....	....	....

AHL Second All-Star Team (1956, 1960)

Signed as a free agent by **Toronto** (Pittsburgh-AHL), September 28, 1953. Claimed by **NY Rangers** from **Toronto** in Intra-League Draft, June 5, 1956. Claimed by **Detroit** from **NY Rangers** in Intra-League Draft, June 8, 1960. Traded to **Boston** by **Detroit** with Albert Langlois, Ron Harris and Bob Dillabough for Ab McDonald, Bob McCord and Ken Stephanson, May 31, 1965. Traded to **Detroit** by **Boston** for Pit Martin, December 30, 1965. Claimed by **Minnesota** from **Detroit** in Expansion Draft, June 6, 1967. • Named playing-coach of Memphis (CHL), February, 1969.

• MacDOUGALL, Kim

D – L. 5'11", 180 lbs. b: Regina, Sask., 8/29/1954. Minnesota's 4th, 60th overall, in 1974.

Season	Club	League	GP	G	A	Pts	AG	AA	APts	PIM	PP	SH	GW	S	%	TGF	PGF	TGA	PGA	+/-	GP	G	A	Pts	PIM	PP	SH	GW
1971-72	Regina Pat Canadians	SAHA	STATISTICS NOT AVAILABLE																									
	Regina Pats	WCJHL	1	0	0	0	....	....	....	0	....	....	....	....	....	....	....	....	....	....	4	0	0	0	2	....	....	....
1972-73	Regina Pats	WJCHL	68	3	15	18	....	....	....	37	....	....	....	....	....	....	....	....	....	....	4	0	0	0	2	....	....	....
1973-74	Regina Pats	WCJHL	68	5	51	56	....	....	....	96	....	....	....	....	....	....	....	....	....	....	16	2	4	6	17	....	....	....
1974-75	**Minnesota North Stars**	**NHL**	**1**	**0**	**0**	**0**	**0**	**0**	**0**	**0**	**0**	**0**	**0**	**0**	**0.0**	**0**	**0**	**1**	**0**	**–1**	....	....	....	....	....	....	....	....
	New Haven Nighthawks	AHL	57	3	12	15	....	....	....	24	....	....	....	....	....	....	....	....	....	....	16	0	2	2	21	....	....	....
1975-76	Fort Wayne Komets	IHL	52	8	16	24	....	....	....	38	....	....	....	....	....	....	....	....	....	....	....	....	....	....	....	....	....	....
	Columbus Owls	IHL	8	0	2	2	....	....	....	2	....	....	....	....	....	....	....	....	....	....	....	....	....	....	....	....	....	....
1976-77			OUT OF HOCKEY – RETIRED																									
1977-78	Lumsden Lords	AIHA	STATISTICS NOT AVAILABLE																									
	NHL Totals		**1**	**0**	**0**	**0**	**0**	**0**	**0**	**0**	**0**	**0**	**0**	**0**	**0.0**	**0**	**0**	**1**	**0**		....	....	....	....	....	....	....	....

• MacEACHERN, Shane

C – L. 5'11", 180 lbs. b: Charlottetown, P.E.I., 12/14/1967.

Season	Club	League	GP	G	A	Pts	AG	AA	APts	PIM	PP	SH	GW	S	%	TGF	PGF	TGA	PGA	+/-	GP	G	A	Pts	PIM	PP	SH	GW
1983-84	Verdun Juniors	QMJHL	65	13	27	40	....	....	....	62	....	....	....	....	....	....	....	....	....	....	10	3	5	8	30	....	....	....
1984-85	Verdun Jr. Canadiens	QMJHL	57	14	21	35	....	....	....	109	....	....	....	....	....	....	....	....	....	....	13	1	3	4	27	....	....	....
	Verdun Jr. Canadiens	Mem-Cup	3	0	0	0	....	....	....	10	....	....	....	....	....	....	....	....	....	....	....	....	....	....	....	....	....	....
1985-86	Hull Olympiques	QMJHL	70	20	45	65	....	....	....	128	....	....	....	....	....	....	....	....	....	....	15	11	11	22	17	....	....	....
	Hull Olympiques	Mem-Cup	5	0	2	2	....	....	....	12	....	....	....	....	....	....	....	....	....	....	....	....	....	....	....	....	....	....
1986-87	Hull Olympiques	QMJHL	69	44	58	102	....	....	....	126	....	....	....	....	....	....	....	....	....	....	8	6	7	13	8	....	....	....
1987-88	**St. Louis Blues**	**NHL**	**1**	**0**	**0**	**0**	**0**	**0**	**0**	**0**	**0**	**0**	**0**	**0**	**0.0**	**0**	**0**	**0**	**0**	**0**	....	....	....	....	....	....	....	....
	Peoria Rivermen	IHL	68	18	30	48	....	....	....	67	....	....	....	....	....	....	....	....	....	....	7	1	6	7	8	....	....	....
1988-89	Peoria Rivermen	IHL	73	17	37	54	....	....	....	83	....	....	....	....	....	....	....	....	....	....	4	0	1	1	2	....	....	....
1989-90	Swindon Wildcats	Britain	9	17	17	34	....	....	....	10	....	....	....	....	....	....	....	....	....	....	....	....	....	....	....	....	....	....
	Charlottetown Wildcats	NBSHL	11	7	12	19	....	....	....	10	....	....	....	....	....	....	....	....	....	....	....	....	....	....	....	....	....	....
1990-91	Charlottetown Wildcats	NBSHL	10	8	7	15	....	....	....	2	....	....	....	....	....	....	....	....	....	....	....	....	....	....	....	....	....	....
1991-92	HC Lyss	Switz-2	STATISTICS NOT AVAILABLE																									
1992-93	Norwich-Peterborough Pirates	Britain	29	33	44	77	....	....	....	48	....	....	....	....	....	....	....	....	....	....	6	9	5	14	8	....	....	....
1993-94	SIJ Geleen	Holland	40	35	49	84	....	....	....	....	....	....	....	....	....	....	....	....	....	....	....	....	....	....	....	....	....	....
1994-95	Brantford Smoke	ColHL	71	30	52	82	....	....	....	58	....	....	....	....	....	....	....	....	....	....	....	....	....	....	....	....	....	....
	NHL Totals		**1**	**0**	**0**	**0**	**0**	**0**	**0**	**0**	**0**	**0**	**0**	**0**	**0.0**	**0**	**0**	**0**	**0**		....	....	....	....	....	....	....	....

Signed as a free agent by **St. Louis**, September 22, 1986.

• MacGREGOR, Bruce

Bruce Cameron "The Redheaded Rocket" C – R. 5'10", 180 lbs. b: Edmonton, Alta., 4/26/1941.

Season	Club	League	GP	G	A	Pts	AG	AA	APts	PIM	PP	SH	GW	S	%	TGF	PGF	TGA	PGA	+/-	GP	G	A	Pts	PIM	PP	SH	GW
1958-59	Edmonton Oil Kings	CAHL	37	33	39	72	....	....	....	22	....	....	....	....	....	....	....	....	....	....	....	....	....	....	....	....	....	....
	Edmonton Oil Kings	Mem-Cup	4	1	4	5	....	....	....	6	....	....	....	....	....	....	....	....	....	....	....	....	....	....	....	....	....	....
1959-60	Edmonton Oil Kings	CAHL	24	24	18	42	....	....	....	15	....	....	....	....	....	....	....	....	....	....	....	....	....	....	....	....	....	....
	Edmonton Oil Kings	Mem-Cup	22	22	17	39	....	....	....	33	....	....	....	....	....	....	....	....	....	....	....	....	....	....	....	....	....	....

			REGULAR SEASON																		PLAYOFFS							
Season	Club	League	GP	G	A	Pts	AG	AA	APts	PIM	PP	SH	GW	S	%	TGF	PGF	TGA	PGA	+/–	GP	G	A	Pts	PIM	PP	SH	GW
1960-61	Edmonton Flyers	WHL	54	20	26	46	....	....	....	33	....	....	....	....	....	....	....	....	....	....	....	....	....	....	....	....	....	....
	Detroit Red Wings	**NHL**	**12**	**0**	**1**	**1**	**0**	**1**	**1**	**0**	....	....	....	....	....	....	....	....	....	....	**8**	**1**	**2**	**3**	**6**	....	....	....
1961-62	**Detroit Red Wings**	**NHL**	**65**	**6**	**12**	**18**	**7**	**11**	**18**	**16**	....	....	....	....	....	....	....	....	....	....	....	....	....	....	....	....	....	....
1962-63	**Detroit Red Wings**	**NHL**	**67**	**11**	**11**	**22**	**13**	**11**	**24**	**12**	....	....	....	....	....	....	....	....	....	....	**10**	**1**	**4**	**5**	**10**	....	....	....
1963-64	**Detroit Red Wings**	**NHL**	**63**	**11**	**21**	**32**	**14**	**22**	**36**	**15**	....	....	....	....	....	....	....	....	....	....	**14**	**5**	**2**	**7**	**12**	....	....	....
1964-65	**Detroit Red Wings**	**NHL**	**66**	**21**	**20**	**41**	**25**	**20**	**45**	**19**	....	....	....	....	....	....	....	....	....	....	**7**	**0**	**2**	**2**	**2**	....	....	....
1965-66	**Detroit Red Wings**	**NHL**	**70**	**20**	**14**	**34**	**23**	**13**	**36**	**28**	....	....	....	....	....	....	....	....	....	....	**12**	**1**	**4**	**5**	**2**	....	....	....
1966-67	**Detroit Red Wings**	**NHL**	**70**	**28**	**19**	**47**	**33**	**19**	**52**	**14**	....	....	....	....	....	....	....	....	....	....	....	....	....	....	....	....	....	....
1967-68	**Detroit Red Wings**	**NHL**	**71**	**15**	**24**	**39**	**17**	**24**	**41**	**13**	**1**	**0**	**0**	**165**	**9.1**	**67**	**12**	**95**	**21**	**–19**	....	....	....	....	....	....	....	....
1968-69	**Detroit Red Wings**	**NHL**	**69**	**18**	**23**	**41**	**19**	**20**	**39**	**14**	**2**	**3**	**3**	**168**	**10.7**	**60**	**5**	**63**	**14**	**6**	....	....	....	....	....	....	....	....
1969-70	**Detroit Red Wings**	**NHL**	**73**	**15**	**23**	**38**	**16**	**22**	**38**	**24**	**3**	**1**	**4**	**153**	**9.8**	**55**	**12**	**60**	**16**	**–1**	**4**	**1**	**0**	**1**	**2**	**0**	**0**	**0**
1970-71	**Detroit Red Wings**	**NHL**	**47**	**6**	**16**	**22**	**6**	**13**	**19**	**18**	**0**	**0**	**0**	**68**	**8.8**	**34**	**3**	**55**	**13**	**–11**	....	....	....	....	....	....	....	....
	New York Rangers	**NHL**	**27**	**12**	**13**	**25**	**12**	**11**	**23**	**4**	**2**	**1**	**3**	**60**	**20.0**	**30**	**6**	**16**	**4**	**12**	**13**	**0**	**4**	**4**	**2**	**0**	**0**	**0**
1971-72	**New York Rangers**	**NHL**	**75**	**19**	**21**	**40**	**19**	**18**	**37**	**22**	**1**	**3**	**5**	**137**	**13.9**	**64**	**4**	**53**	**16**	**23**	**16**	**2**	**6**	**8**	**4**	**0**	**1**	**0**
1972-73	**New York Rangers**	**NHL**	**52**	**14**	**12**	**26**	**13**	**9**	**22**	**12**	**0**	**0**	**4**	**85**	**16.5**	**44**	**3**	**34**	**7**	**14**	**10**	**2**	**2**	**4**	**2**	**0**	**0**	**0**
1973-74	**New York Rangers**	**NHL**	**66**	**17**	**27**	**44**	**16**	**22**	**38**	**6**	**0**	**2**	**1**	**91**	**18.7**	**56**	**2**	**67**	**12**	**–1**	**13**	**6**	**2**	**8**	**2**	**0**	**0**	**2**
1974-75	Team Canada	Summit-74	5	0	1	1	....	....	....	5	....	....	....	....	....	....	....	....	....	....	....	....	....	....	....	....	....	....
	Edmonton Oilers	WHA	72	24	28	52	....	....	....	10	....	....	....	....	....	....	....	....	....	....	....	....	....	....	....	....	....	....
1975-76	Edmonton Oilers	WHA	63	13	10	23	....	....	....	13	....	....	....	....	....	....	....	....	....	....	4	0	1	1	0	....	....	....
	NHL Totals		**893**	**213**	**257**	**470**	**233**	**236**	**469**	**217**	....	....	....	....	....	....	....	....	....	....	**107**	**19**	**28**	**47**	**44**	....	....	....
	Other Major League Totals		135	37	38	75	....	....	....	23	....	....	....	....	....	....	....	....	....	....	4	0	1	1	0	....	....	....

Traded to **NY Rangers** by **Detroit** with Larry Brown for Arnie Brown, Mike Robitaille and Tom Miller, February 2, 1971. Selected by **Edmonton** (WHA) in 1973 WHA Professional Player Draft, June, 1973.

• MacGREGOR, Randy

Randy Kenneth RW – L. 5'9", 175 lbs. b: Cobourg, Ont., 7/9/1953.

Season	Club	League	GP	G	A	Pts	AG	AA	APts	PIM	PP	SH	GW	S	%	TGF	PGF	TGA	PGA	+/–	GP	G	A	Pts	PIM	PP	SH	GW
1971-72	Chatham Maroons	OHA-B	56	18	25	43	....	....	....	*216	....	....	....	....	....	....	....	....	....	....	....	....	....	....	....	....	....	....
1972-73	Chatham Maroons	OHA-B	58	36	20	56	....	....	....	176	....	....	....	....	....	....	....	....	....	....	....	....	....	....	....	....	....	....
1973-74	Broome Dusters	NAHL	71	17	28	45	....	....	....	139	....	....	....	....	....	....	....	....	....	....	....	....	....	....	....	....	....	....
1974-75	Binghamton Dusters	NAHL	73	23	48	71	....	....	....	154	....	....	....	....	....	....	....	....	....	....	....	....	....	....	....	....	....	....
1975-76	Binghamton Dusters	NAHL	43	9	10	19	....	....	....	84	....	....	....	....	....	....	....	....	....	....	....	....	....	....	....	....	....	....
1976-77	Binghamton Dusters	NAHL	71	21	26	47	....	....	....	128	....	....	....	....	....	....	....	....	....	....	6	2	4	6	31	....	....	....
	Muskegon Mohawks	IHL	....	....	....	....	....	....	....	....	....	....	....	....	....	....	....	....	....	....	3	0	0	0	5	....	....	....
1977-78	Binghamton Dusters	AHL	78	20	29	49	....	....	....	117	....	....	....	....	....	....	....	....	....	....	....	....	....	....	....	....	....	....
1978-79	Binghamton Dusters	AHL	64	29	46	75	....	....	....	113	....	....	....	....	....	....	....	....	....	....	....	....	....	....	....	....	....	....
1979-80	Binghamton Dusters	AHL	71	21	23	44	....	....	....	164	....	....	....	....	....	....	....	....	....	....	....	....	....	....	....	....	....	....
1980-81	VSV Villach	Austria	23	8	11	19	....	....	....	66	....	....	....	....	....	....	....	....	....	....	....	....	....	....	....	....	....	....
	Binghamton Whalers	AHL	28	14	9	23	....	....	....	49	....	....	....	....	....	....	....	....	....	....	5	2	0	2	20	....	....	....
1981-82	**Hartford Whalers**	**NHL**	**2**	**1**	**1**	**2**	**1**	**1**	**2**	**2**	**0**	**0**	**0**	**1**	**100.0**	**2**	**0**	**0**	**0**	**2**	....	....	....	....	....	....	....	....
	Binghamton Whalers	AHL	71	23	50	73	....	....	....	115	....	....	....	....	....	....	....	....	....	....	15	6	7	13	49	....	....	....
1982-83	Binghamton Whalers	AHL	62	13	17	30	....	....	....	112	....	....	....	....	....	....	....	....	....	....	5	1	1	2	29	....	....	....
1983-84	Adirondack Red Wings	AHL	45	6	15	21	....	....	....	60	....	....	....	....	....	....	....	....	....	....	2	0	0	0	2	....	....	....
	NHL Totals		**2**	**1**	**1**	**2**	**1**	**1**	**2**	**2**	**0**	**0**	**0**	**1**	**100.0**	**2**	**0**	**0**	**0**		....	....	....	....	....	....	....	....

Signed as a free agent by **Hartford**, February, 1981.

• MacGUIGAN, Garth

Garth Leslie C – L. 6', 190 lbs. b: Charlottetown, P.E.I., 2/16/1956. NY Islanders' 3rd, 50th overall, in 1976.

Season	Club	League	GP	G	A	Pts	AG	AA	APts	PIM	PP	SH	GW	S	%	TGF	PGF	TGA	PGA	+/–	GP	G	A	Pts	PIM	PP	SH	GW
1974-75	Montreal Red-White-Blue	QMJHL	63	30	38	68	....	....	....	97	....	....	....	....	....	....	....	....	....	....	9	2	4	6	14	....	....	....
1975-76	Montreal Juniors	QMJHL	69	47	46	93	....	....	....	94	....	....	....	....	....	....	....	....	....	....	6	5	2	7	33	....	....	....
1976-77	Muskegon Mohawks	IHL	78	54	40	94	....	....	....	156	....	....	....	....	....	....	....	....	....	....	7	5	3	8	0	....	....	....
	Fort Worth Texans	CHL	1	0	0	0	....	....	....	0	....	....	....	....	....	....	....	....	....	....	2	0	0	0	0	....	....	....
1977-78	Fort Worth Texans	CHL	70	17	24	41	....	....	....	54	....	....	....	....	....	....	....	....	....	....	14	3	4	7	18	....	....	....
1978-79	Fort Worth Texans	CHL	75	28	21	49	....	....	....	120	....	....	....	....	....	....	....	....	....	....	5	1	2	3	9	....	....	....
1979-80	**New York Islanders**	**NHL**	**2**	**0**	**0**	**0**	**0**	**0**	**0**	**2**	**0**	**0**	**0**	**1**	**0.0**	**1**	**0**	**0**	**0**	**1**	....	....	....	....	....	....	....	....
	Indianapolis Checkers	CHL	77	28	34	62	....	....	....	94	....	....	....	....	....	....	....	....	....	....	7	2	3	5	14	....	....	....
1980-81	Indianapolis Checkers	CHL	38	37	38	75	....	....	....	96	....	....	....	....	....	....	....	....	....	....	5	1	2	3	20	....	....	....
1981-82	Indianapolis Checkers	CHL	80	24	51	75	....	....	....	112	....	....	....	....	....	....	....	....	....	....	13	4	7	11	54	....	....	....
1982-83	Indianapolis Checkers	CHL	80	37	35	72	....	....	....	70	....	....	....	....	....	....	....	....	....	....	13	4	7	11	21	....	....	....
1983-84	**New York Islanders**	**NHL**	**3**	**0**	**1**	**1**	**0**	**1**	**1**	**0**	**0**	**0**	**0**	**2**	**0.0**	**2**	**0**	**2**	**0**	**0**	....	....	....	....	....	....	....	....
	Indianapolis Checkers	CHL	68	25	41	66	....	....	....	109	....	....	....	....	....	....	....	....	....	....	10	3	3	6	2	....	....	....
1984-85	Indianapolis Checkers	IHL	67	24	32	56	....	....	....	52	....	....	....	....	....	....	....	....	....	....	7	0	5	5	4	....	....	....
	NHL Totals		**5**	**0**	**1**	**1**	**0**	**1**	**1**	**2**	**0**	**0**	**0**	**3**	**0.0**	**3**	**0**	**2**	**0**		....	....	....	....	....	....	....	....

QMJHL West Division Second All-Star Team (1976) • Won Garry F. Longman Memorial Trophy (Top Rookie - IHL) (1977) • CHL Second All-Star Team (1981)

• MacINNIS, Al

Allan "Chopper" D – R. 6'2", 209 lbs. b: Inverness, N.S., 7/11/1963. Calgary's 1st, 15th overall, in 1981.

Season	Club	League	GP	G	A	Pts	AG	AA	APts	PIM	PP	SH	GW	S	%	TGF	PGF	TGA	PGA	+/–	GP	G	A	Pts	PIM	PP	SH	GW
1978-79	Cole Harbour Wings	NSAHA	STATISTICS NOT AVAILABLE																									
1979-80	Regina Blues	SJHL	59	20	28	48	....	....	....	110	....	....	....	....	....	....	....	....	....	....	....	....	....	....	....	....	....	....
1980-81	Kitchener Rangers	OMJHL	47	11	28	39	....	....	....	59	....	....	....	....	....	....	....	....	....	....	18	4	12	16	20	....	....	....
	Kitchener Rangers	Mem-Cup	5	0	1	1	....	....	....	10	....	....	....	....	....	....	....	....	....	....	....	....	....	....	....	....	....	....
1981-82	Kitchener Rangers	OHL	59	25	50	75	....	....	....	145	....	....	....	....	....	....	....	....	....	....	15	5	10	15	44	....	....	....
	Calgary Flames	**NHL**	**2**	**0**	**0**	**0**	**0**	**0**	**0**	**0**	**0**	**0**	**0**	**2**	**0.0**	**1**	**0**	**1**	**0**	**0**	....	....	....	....	....	....	....	....
	Kitchener Rangers	Mem-Cup	5	3	6	9	....	....	....	11	....	....	....	....	....	....	....	....	....	....	....	....	....	....	....	....	....	....
1982-83	Kitchener Rangers	OHL	51	38	46	84	....	....	....	67	....	....	....	....	....	....	....	....	....	....	8	3	8	11	9	....	....	....
	Calgary Flames	**NHL**	**14**	**1**	**3**	**4**	**1**	**2**	**3**	**9**	**0**	**0**	**0**	**7**	**14.3**	**13**	**0**	**14**	**1**	**0**	....	....	....	....	....	....	....	....
1983-84	**Calgary Flames**	**NHL**	**51**	**11**	**34**	**45**	**9**	**23**	**32**	**42**	**7**	**0**	**2**	**160**	**6.9**	**84**	**47**	**38**	**1**	**0**	**11**	**2**	**12**	**14**	**13**	**2**	**0**	**1**
	Colorado Flames	CHL	19	5	14	19	....	....	....	22	....	....	....	....	....	....	....	....	....	....	....	....	....	....	....	....	....	....
1984-85	**Calgary Flames**	**NHL**	**67**	**14**	**52**	**66**	**11**	**35**	**46**	**75**	**8**	**0**	**0**	**259**	**5.4**	**137**	**61**	**70**	**1**	**7**	**4**	**1**	**2**	**3**	**8**	**1**	**0**	**0**
1985-86	**Calgary Flames**	**NHL**	**77**	**11**	**57**	**68**	**9**	**38**	**47**	**76**	**4**	**0**	**0**	**241**	**4.6**	**165**	**76**	**80**	**29**	**38**	**21**	**4**	***15**	**19**	**30**	**2**	**0**	**0**
1986-87	**Calgary Flames**	**NHL**	**79**	**20**	**56**	**76**	**17**	**41**	**58**	**97**	**7**	**0**	**2**	**262**	**7.6**	**154**	**59**	**116**	**41**	**20**	**4**	**1**	**0**	**1**	**0**	**1**	**0**	**0**
1987-88	**Calgary Flames**	**NHL**	**80**	**25**	**58**	**83**	**21**	**42**	**63**	**114**	**7**	**2**	**2**	**245**	**10.2**	**166**	**76**	**108**	**31**	**13**	**7**	**3**	**6**	**9**	**18**	**2**	**0**	**0**
1988-89◆	**Calgary Flames**	**NHL**	**79**	**16**	**58**	**74**	**14**	**41**	**55**	**126**	**8**	**0**	**3**	**277**	**5.8**	**189**	**84**	**102**	**35**	**38**	**22**	**7**	***24**	***31**	**46**	**5**	**0**	**4**
1989-90	Calgary Flames	Fr-Tour	4	1	1	2	....	....	....	2	....	....	....	....	....	....	....	....	....	....	....	....	....	....	....	....	....	....
	Calgary Flames	**NHL**	**79**	**28**	**62**	**90**	**24**	**45**	**69**	**82**	**14**	**1**	**3**	**304**	**9.2**	**192**	**94**	**102**	**24**	**20**	**6**	**2**	**3**	**5**	**8**	**1**	**0**	**0**
	Canada	WEC-A	9	1	3	4	....	....	....	10	....	....	....	....	....	....	....	....	....	....	....	....	....	....	....	....	....	....
1990-91	**Calgary Flames**	**NHL**	**78**	**28**	**75**	**103**	**26**	**57**	**83**	**90**	**17**	**0**	**1**	**305**	**9.2**	**185**	**83**	**90**	**30**	**42**	**7**	**2**	**3**	**5**	**8**	**2**	**0**	**0**
1991-92	Canada	Can-Cup	8	2	4	6	....	....	....	23	....	....	....	....	....	....	....	....	....	....	....	....	....	....	....	....	....	....
	Calgary Flames	**NHL**	**72**	**20**	**57**	**77**	**18**	**43**	**61**	**83**	**11**	**0**	**0**	**304**	**6.6**	**146**	**71**	**112**	**50**	**13**	....	....	....	....	....	....	....	....
1992-93	**Calgary Flames**	**NHL**	**50**	**11**	**43**	**54**	**9**	**30**	**39**	**61**	**7**	**0**	**4**	**201**	**5.5**	**106**	**49**	**57**	**15**	**15**	**6**	**1**	**6**	**7**	**10**	**1**	**0**	**0**
1993-94	**Calgary Flames**	**NHL**	**75**	**28**	**54**	**82**	**26**	**42**	**68**	**95**	**12**	**1**	**5**	**324**	**8.6**	**154**	**67**	**77**	**25**	**35**	**7**	**2**	**6**	**8**	**12**	**1**	**0**	**0**
1994-95	**St. Louis Blues**	**NHL**	**32**	**8**	**20**	**28**	**14**	**30**	**44**	**43**	**2**	**0**	**0**	**110**	**7.3**	**59**	**20**	**33**	**13**	**19**	**7**	**1**	**5**	**6**	**10**	**0**	**0**	**0**
1995-96	**St. Louis Blues**	**NHL**	**82**	**17**	**44**	**61**	**17**	**36**	**53**	**88**	**9**	**1**	**1**	**317**	**5.4**	**128**	**60**	**105**	**42**	**5**	**13**	**3**	**4**	**7**	**20**	**1**	**0**	**0**
1996-97	**St. Louis Blues**	**NHL**	**72**	**13**	**30**	**43**	**14**	**27**	**41**	**65**	**6**	**1**	**1**	**296**	**4.4**	**116**	**36**	**96**	**18**	**2**	**6**	**1**	**2**	**3**	**4**	**1**	**0**	**0**

Season	Club	League	REGULAR SEASON GP	G	A	Pts	AG	AA	APts	PIM	PP	SH	GW	S	%	TGF	PGF	TGA	PGA	+/–	PLAYOFFS GP	G	A	Pts	PIM	PP	SH	GW
1997-98	**St. Louis Blues**	**NHL**	**71**	**19**	**30**	**49**	**22**	**29**	**51**	**80**	**9**	**1**	**2**	**227**	**8.4**	**113**	**46**	**78**	**17**	**6**	**8**	**2**	**6**	**8**	**12**	**1**	**0**	**0**
	Canada	Olympics	6	2	0	2	....	....	....	2	....	....	....	....	....	....	....	....	....	....	....	....	....	....	....	....	....	....
1998-99	**St. Louis Blues**	**NHL**	**82**	**20**	**42**	**62**	**23**	**41**	**64**	**70**	**11**	**1**	**2**	**314**	**6.4**	**150**	**60**	**79**	**22**	**33**	**13**	**4**	**8**	**12**	**20**	**2**	**0**	**0**
99-2000	**St. Louis Blues**	**NHL**	**61**	**11**	**28**	**39**	**12**	**26**	**38**	**34**	**6**	**0**	**7**	**245**	**4.5**	**93**	**41**	**44**	**12**	**20**	**7**	**1**	**3**	**4**	**14**	**1**	**0**	**0**
	NHL Totals		**1203**	**301**	**803**	**1104**	**287**	**628**	**915**	**1330**	**145**	**8**	**35**	**4400**	**6.8**	**2351**	**1030**	**1402**	**407**		**149**	**37**	**105**	**142**	**233**	**24**	**0**	**5**

OHL First All-Star Team (1982, 1983) • NHL Second All-Star Team (1987, 1989, 1994) • Won Conn Smythe Trophy (1989) • NHL First All-Star Team (1990, 1991, 1999) • Canada Cup All-Star Team (1991) • Won James Norris Memorial Trophy (1999) • Played in NHL All-Star Game (1985, 1988, 1990, 1991, 1992, 1994, 1996, 1997, 1998, 1999, 2000)

Traded to **St. Louis** by **Calgary** with Calgary's 4th round choice (Didier Tremblay) in 1997 Entry Draft for Phil Housley and St. Louis' 2nd round choices in 1996 (Steve Begin) and 1997 (John Tripp) Entry Drafts, July 4, 1994.

• MacIVER, Don

D – L. 6', 200 lbs. b: Montreal, Que., 5/3/1955.

Season	Club	League	GP	G	A	Pts	AG	AA	APts	PIM	PP	SH	GW	S	%	TGF	PGF	TGA	PGA	+/–	GP	G	A	Pts	PIM	PP	SH	GW
1976-77	St. Mary's University	AUAA	7	0	3	3	....	....	....	6	....	....	....	....	....	....	....	....	....	....	....	....	....	....	....	....	....	....
1977-78	St. Mary's University	AUAA	16	1	9	10	....	....	....	19	....	....	....	....	....	....	....	....	....	....	....	....	....	....	....	....	....	....
1978-79	St. Mary's University	AUAA	20	3	11	14	....	....	....	43	....	....	....	....	....	....	....	....	....	....	....	....	....	....	....	....	....	....
1979-80	**Winnipeg Jets**	**NHL**	**6**	**0**	**0**	**0**	**0**	**0**	**0**	**2**	**0**	**0**	**0**	**2**	**0.0**	**0**	**0**	**5**	**0**	**–5**	....	....	....	....	....	....	....	....
	Tulsa Oilers	CHL	56	3	12	15	....	....	....	98	....	....	....	....	....	....	....	....	....	....	3	0	0	0	6	....	....	....
1980-81	Tulsa Oilers	CHL	72	3	9	12	....	....	....	155	....	....	....	....	....	....	....	....	....	....	8	0	1	1	16	....	....	....
1981-82	Tulsa Oilers	CHL	66	2	22	24	....	....	....	166	....	....	....	....	....	....	....	....	....	....	2	0	0	0	0	....	....	....
1982-83	Tulsa Oilers	CHL	77	3	9	12	....	....	....	113	....	....	....	....	....	....	....	....	....	....	....	....	....	....	....	....	....	....
	NHL Totals		**6**	**0**	**0**	**0**	**0**	**0**	**0**	**2**	**0**	**0**	**0**	**2**	**0.0**	**0**	**0**	**5**	**0**		....	....	....	....	....	....	....	....

Signed as a free agent by **Winnipeg**, October 16, 1979.

• MACIVER, Norm

D – L. 5'11", 180 lbs. b: Thunder Bay, Ont., 9/8/1964.

Season	Club	League	GP	G	A	Pts	AG	AA	APts	PIM	PP	SH	GW	S	%	TGF	PGF	TGA	PGA	+/–	GP	G	A	Pts	PIM	PP	SH	GW
1982-83	University of Minnesota-Duluth	WCHA	45	1	26	27	....	....	....	40	....	....	....	....	....	....	....	....	....	....	6	0	2	2	2	....	....	....
1983-84	University of Minnesota-Duluth	WCHA	31	13	28	41	....	....	....	28	....	....	....	....	....	....	....	....	....	....	8	1	10	11	8	....	....	....
1984-85	University of Minnesota-Duluth	WCHA	47	14	47	61	....	....	....	63	....	....	....	....	....	....	....	....	....	....	10	3	3	6	6	....	....	....
1985-86	University of Minnesota-Duluth	WCHA	42	11	51	62	....	....	....	36	....	....	....	....	....	....	....	....	....	....	4	2	3	5	2	....	....	....
1986-87	**New York Rangers**	**NHL**	**3**	**0**	**1**	**1**	**0**	**1**	**1**	**0**	**0**	**0**	**0**	**2**	**0.0**	**1**	**1**	**5**	**0**	**–5**	....	....	....	....	....	....	....	....
	New Haven Nighthawks	AHL	71	6	30	36	....	....	....	73	....	....	....	....	....	....	....	....	....	....	7	0	0	0	9	....	....	....
1987-88	**New York Rangers**	**NHL**	**37**	**9**	**15**	**24**	**8**	**11**	**19**	**14**	**1**	**0**	**2**	**65**	**13.8**	**66**	**30**	**26**	**0**	**10**	....	....	....	....	....	....	....	....
	Colorado Rangers	IHL	27	6	20	26	....	....	....	22	....	....	....	....	....	....	....	....	....	....	....	....	....	....	....	....	....	....
1988-89	**New York Rangers**	**NHL**	**26**	**0**	**10**	**10**	**0**	**7**	**7**	**14**	**0**	**0**	**0**	**36**	**0.0**	**27**	**9**	**22**	**1**	**–3**	....	....	....	....	....	....	....	....
	Hartford Whalers	**NHL**	**37**	**1**	**22**	**23**	**1**	**16**	**17**	**24**	**1**	**0**	**0**	**51**	**2.0**	**51**	**25**	**26**	**0**	**0**	**1**	**0**	**0**	**0**	**2**	**0**	**0**	**0**
1989-90	Binghamton Whalers	AHL	2	0	0	0	....	....	....	0	....	....	....	....	....	....	....	....	....	....	....	....	....	....	....	....	....	....
	Edmonton Oilers	**NHL**	**1**	**0**	**0**	**0**	**0**	**0**	**0**	**0**	**0**	**0**	**0**	**0**	**0.0**	**1**	**0**	**2**	**0**	**–1**	....	....	....	....	....	....	....	....
	Cape Breton Oilers	AHL	68	13	37	50	....	....	....	55	....	....	....	....	....	....	....	....	....	....	6	0	7	7	10	....	....	....
1990-91	**Edmonton Oilers**	**NHL**	**21**	**2**	**5**	**7**	**2**	**4**	**6**	**14**	**1**	**0**	**0**	**25**	**8.0**	**21**	**6**	**21**	**7**	**1**	**18**	**0**	**4**	**4**	**8**	**0**	**0**	**0**
	Cape Breton Oilers	AHL	56	13	46	59	....	....	....	60	....	....	....	....	....	....	....	....	....	....	....	....	....	....	....	....	....	....
1991-92	**Edmonton Oilers**	**NHL**	**57**	**6**	**34**	**40**	**5**	**26**	**31**	**38**	**2**	**0**	**3**	**69**	**8.7**	**98**	**27**	**63**	**12**	**20**	**13**	**1**	**2**	**3**	**10**	**0**	**0**	**0**
1992-93	**Ottawa Senators**	**NHL**	**80**	**17**	**46**	**63**	**14**	**32**	**46**	**84**	**7**	**1**	**2**	**184**	**9.2**	**121**	**60**	**146**	**39**	**–46**	....	....	....	....	....	....	....	....
	Canada	WC-A	8	0	5	5	....	....	....	4	....	....	....	....	....	....	....	....	....	....	....	....	....	....	....	....	....	....
1993-94	**Ottawa Senators**	**NHL**	**53**	**3**	**20**	**23**	**3**	**16**	**19**	**26**	**0**	**0**	**0**	**88**	**3.4**	**60**	**27**	**66**	**7**	**–26**	....	....	....	....	....	....	....	....
1994-95	**Ottawa Senators**	**NHL**	**28**	**4**	**7**	**11**	**7**	**10**	**17**	**10**	**0**	**0**	**0**	**30**	**13.3**	**35**	**14**	**31**	**1**	**–9**	....	....	....	....	....	....	....	....
	Pittsburgh Penguins	**NHL**	**13**	**0**	**9**	**9**	**0**	**13**	**13**	**6**	**2**	**0**	**0**	**20**	**0.0**	**21**	**5**	**10**	**1**	**7**	**12**	**1**	**4**	**5**	**8**	**0**	**0**	**1**
1995-96	**Pittsburgh Penguins**	**NHL**	**32**	**2**	**21**	**23**	**2**	**17**	**19**	**32**	**1**	**0**	**0**	**30**	**6.7**	**68**	**29**	**36**	**9**	**12**	....	....	....	....	....	....	....	....
	Winnipeg Jets	**NHL**	**39**	**5**	**25**	**30**	**5**	**20**	**25**	**26**	**2**	**0**	**0**	**49**	**10.2**	**62**	**30**	**41**	**3**	**–6**	**6**	**1**	**0**	**1**	**2**	**0**	**0**	**0**
1996-97	**Phoenix Coyotes**	**NHL**	**32**	**4**	**9**	**13**	**4**	**8**	**12**	**24**	**1**	**0**	**1**	**40**	**10.0**	**36**	**21**	**27**	**1**	**–11**	....	....	....	....	....	....	....	....
1997-98	**Phoenix Coyotes**	**NHL**	**41**	**2**	**6**	**8**	**2**	**6**	**8**	**38**	**0**	**1**	**0**	**37**	**5.4**	**24**	**6**	**34**	**5**	**–11**	**6**	**0**	**1**	**1**	**2**	**0**	**0**	**0**
1998-99	Houston Aeros	IHL	49	6	25	31	....	....	....	48	....	....	....	....	....	....	....	....	....	....	10	0	5	5	14	....	....	....
	NHL Totals		**500**	**55**	**230**	**285**	**53**	**187**	**240**	**350**	**18**	**2**	**8**	**726**	**7.6**	**692**	**290**	**556**	**86**		**56**	**3**	**11**	**14**	**32**	**0**	**0**	**1**

WCHA First All-Star Team (1985, 1986) • NCAA West First All-American Team (1985, 1986) • AHL First All-Star Team (1991) • Won Eddie Shore Award (Top Defenseman - AHL) (1991)

Signed as a free agent by **NY Rangers**, September 8, 1986. Traded to **Hartford** by **NY Rangers** with Brian Lawton and Don Maloney for Carey Wilson and Hartford's 5th round choice (Lubos Rob) in 1990 Entry Draft, December 26, 1988. Traded to **Edmonton** by **Hartford** for Jim Ennis, October 10, 1989. Claimed by **Ottawa** from **Edmonton** in NHL Waiver Draft, October 4, 1992. Traded to **Pittsburgh** by **Ottawa** with Troy Murray for Martin Straka, April 7, 1995. Traded to **Winnipeg** by **Pittsburgh** for Neil Wilkinson, December 28, 1995. Transferred to **Phoenix** after **Winnipeg** franchise relocated, July 1, 1996.

• MacKASEY, Blair

Blair David D – R. 6'2", 200 lbs. b: Hamilton, Ont., 12/13/1955. Washington's 3rd, 55th overall, in 1975.

Season	Club	League	GP	G	A	Pts	AG	AA	APts	PIM	PP	SH	GW	S	%	TGF	PGF	TGA	PGA	+/–	GP	G	A	Pts	PIM	PP	SH	GW
1969-70	Verdun Catholic High	Hi-School	STATISTICS NOT AVAILABLE																									
1970-71	Montreal Jr. Canadiens	OHA-Jr.	57	1	5	6	....	....	....	38	....	....	....	....	....	....	....	....	....	....	....	....	....	....	....	....	....	....
1971-72	Montreal Jr. Canadiens	OMJHL	59	2	25	27	....	....	....	85	....	....	....	....	....	....	....	....	....	....	....	....	....	....	....	....	....	....
1972-73	Montreal Red-White-Blue	QMJHL	52	1	23	24	....	....	....	108	....	....	....	....	....	....	....	....	....	....	....	....	....	....	....	....	....	....
1973-74	Montreal Red-White-Blue	QMJHL	60	13	41	54	....	....	....	70	....	....	....	....	....	....	....	....	....	....	....	....	....	....	....	....	....	....
1974-75	Montreal Red-White-Blue	QMJHL	62	12	40	52	....	....	....	100	....	....	....	....	....	....	....	....	....	....	....	....	....	....	....	....	....	....
1975-76	Richmond Robins	AHL	9	1	0	1	....	....	....	4	....	....	....	....	....	....	....	....	....	....	....	....	....	....	....	....	....	....
	Dayton Gems	IHL	50	6	21	27	....	....	....	69	....	....	....	....	....	....	....	....	....	....	12	1	2	3	9	....	....	....
1976-77	**Toronto Maple Leafs**	**NHL**	**1**	**0**	**0**	**0**	**0**	**0**	**0**	**2**	....	....	....	....	....	....	....	....	....	....	....	....	....	....	....	....	....	....
	Dallas Black Hawks	CHL	24	1	11	12	....	....	....	51	....	....	....	....	....	....	....	....	....	....	....	....	....	....	....	....	....	....
1977-78	Dallas Black Hawks	CHL	54	1	8	9	....	....	....	58	....	....	....	....	....	....	....	....	....	....	11	0	0	0	8	....	....	....
	NHL Totals		**1**	**0**	**0**	**0**	**0**	**0**	**0**	**2**	....	....	....	....	....	....	....	....	....	....	....	....	....	....	....	....	....	....

Traded to **Toronto** by **Washington**, September 27, 1976.

• MacKENZIE, Barry

Barry John Barry D – L. 6', 190 lbs. b: Toronto, Ont., 8/16/1941.

Season	Club	League	GP	G	A	Pts	AG	AA	APts	PIM	PP	SH	GW	S	%	TGF	PGF	TGA	PGA	+/–	GP	G	A	Pts	PIM	PP	SH	GW
1960-61	St. Michael's Majors	OHA-Jr.	9	1	4	5	....	....	....	8	....	....	....	....	....	....	....	....	....	....	14	0	4	4	8	....	....	....
	St. Michael's Majors	Mem-Cup	9	1	1	2	....	....	....	16	....	....	....	....	....	....	....	....	....	....	....	....	....	....	....	....	....	....
1961-62	St. Michael's Majors	MTJHL	18	5	9	14	....	....	....	58	....	....	....	....	....	....	....	....	....	....	11	0	4	4	14	....	....	....
	St. Michael's Majors	Mem-Cup	5	0	1	1	....	....	....	20	....	....	....	....	....	....	....	....	....	....	....	....	....	....	....	....	....	....
1962-63	University of British Columbia	WUAA	STATISTICS NOT AVAILABLE																									
1963-64	Canada	Nat-Team	....	....	....	....	....	....	....	....	....	....	....	....	....	....	....	....	....	....	....	....	....	....	....	....	....	....
	Canada	Olympics	7	0	2	2	....	....	....	4	....	....	....	....	....	....	....	....	....	....	....	....	....	....	....	....	....	....
1964-65	Canada	Nat-Team	STATISTICS NOT AVAILABLE																									
	Canada	WEC-A	7	2	1	3	....	....	....	8	....	....	....	....	....	....	....	....	....	....	....	....	....	....	....	....	....	....
1965-66	Canada	Nat-Team	STATISTICS NOT AVAILABLE																									
	Canada	WEC-A	7	0	4	4	....	....	....	6	....	....	....	....	....	....	....	....	....	....	....	....	....	....	....	....	....	....
1966-67	Canada	Nat-Team	STATISTICS NOT AVAILABLE																									
	Canada	WEC-A	7	0	0	0	....	....	....	12	....	....	....	....	....	....	....	....	....	....	....	....	....	....	....	....	....	....
1967-68	Ottawa Nats	OHA-Sr.	23	2	9	11	....	....	....	40	....	....	....	....	....	....	....	....	....	....	....	....	....	....	....	....	....	....
	Canada	Olympics	7	0	2	2	....	....	....	8	....	....	....	....	....	....	....	....	....	....	....	....	....	....	....	....	....	....
1968-69	**Minnesota North Stars**	**NHL**	**6**	**0**	**1**	**1**	**0**	**1**	**1**	**6**	**0**	**0**	**0**	**3**	**0.0**	**2**	**0**	**4**	**0**	**–2**	....	....	....	....	....	....	....	....
	Memphis South Stars	CHL	57	5	16	21	....	....	....	54	....	....	....	....	....	....	....	....	....	....	....	....	....	....	....	....	....	....
1969-70	IHC Seibu-Tetusdo	Japan	PLAYER/COACH – STATISTICS UNAVAILABLE																									
	NHL Totals		**6**	**0**	**1**	**1**	**0**	**1**	**1**	**6**	**0**	**0**	**0**	**3**	**0.0**	**2**	**0**	**4**	**0**		....	....	....	....	....	....	....	....

Traded to **Minnesota** by **Toronto** for cash, June 6, 1967.

• MACKEY, David

David R. LW – L. 6'4", 205 lbs. b: Richmond, B.C., 7/24/1966. Chicago's 12th, 224th overall, in 1984.

Season	Club	League	GP	G	A	Pts	AG	AA	APts	PIM	PP	SH	GW	S	%	TGF	PGF	TGA	PGA	+/–	GP	G	A	Pts	PIM	PP	SH	GW
1981-82	Seafair Islanders	BCAHA	60	48	62	110	....	....	....	99	....	....	....	....	....	....	....	....	....	....	....	....	....	....	....	....	....	....
1982-83	Victoria Cougars	WHL	69	16	16	32	....	....	....	53	....	....	....	....	....	....	....	....	....	....	12	11	1	2	4	....	....	....
1983-84	Victoria Cougars	WHL	69	15	15	30	....	....	....	97	....	....	....	....	....	....	....	....	....	....	....	....	....	....	....	....	....	....

			REGULAR SEASON																		PLAYOFFS							
Season	Club	League	GP	G	A	Pts	AG	AA	APts	PIM	PP	SH	GW	S	%	TGF	PGF	TGA	PGA	+/–	GP	G	A	Pts	PIM	PP	SH	GW
1984-85	Victoria Cougars	WHL	16	5	6	11	....	....	....	45	....	....	....	....	....	....	....	....	....	....	....	....	....	....	....	....	....	....
	Portland Winter Hawks	WHL	56	28	32	60	....	....	....	122	....	....	....	....	....	....	....	....	....	....	6	2	1	3	13	....	....	....
1985-86	Kamloops Blazers	WHL	9	3	4	7	....	....	....	13	....	....	....	....	....	....	....	....	....	....	....	....	....	....	....	....	....	....
	Medicine Hat Tigers	WHL	60	25	32	57	....	....	....	167	....	....	....	....	....	....	....	....	....	....	25	6	3	9	72	....	....	....
1986-87	Saginaw Generals	IHL	81	26	49	75	....	....	....	173	....	....	....	....	....	....	....	....	....	....	10	5	6	11	22	....	....	....
1987-88	**Chicago Blackhawks**	**NHL**	**23**	**1**	**3**	**4**	**1**	**2**	**3**	**71**	**0**	**0**	**1**	**23**	**4.3**	**7**	**0**	**22**	**1**	**–14**	....	....	....	....	....	....	....	....
	Saginaw Hawks	IHL	62	29	22	51	....	....	....	211	....	....	....	....	....	....	....	....	....	....	10	3	7	10	44	....	....	....
1988-89	**Chicago Blackhawks**	**NHL**	**23**	**1**	**2**	**3**	**1**	**1**	**2**	**78**	**0**	**0**	**0**	**15**	**6.7**	**7**	**0**	**8**	**0**	**–1**	....	....	....	....	....	....	....	....
	Saginaw Hawks	IHL	57	22	23	45	....	....	....	223	....	....	....	....	....	....	....	....	....	....	....	....	....	....	....	....	....	....
1989-90	**Minnesota North Stars**	**NHL**	**16**	**2**	**0**	**2**	**2**	**0**	**2**	**28**	**0**	**0**	**1**	**8**	**25.0**	**2**	**0**	**5**	**0**	**–3**	....	....	....	....	....	....	....	....
1990-91	Milwaukee Admirals	IHL	82	28	30	58	....	....	....	226	....	....	....	....	....	....	....	....	....	....	6	7	2	9	6	....	....	....
1991-92	**St. Louis Blues**	**NHL**	**19**	**1**	**0**	**1**	**1**	**0**	**1**	**49**	**0**	**0**	**1**	**12**	**8.3**	**3**	**0**	**7**	**0**	**–4**	**1**	**0**	**0**	**0**	**0**	**0**	**0**	**0**
	Peoria Rivermen	IHL	35	20	17	37	....	....	....	90	....	....	....	....	....	....	....	....	....	....	....	....	....	....	....	....	....	....
1992-93	**St. Louis Blues**	**NHL**	**15**	**1**	**4**	**5**	**1**	**3**	**4**	**23**	**0**	**0**	**0**	**17**	**5.9**	**6**	**0**	**9**	**0**	**–3**	....	....	....	....	....	....	....	....
	Peoria Rivermen	IHL	42	24	22	46	....	....	....	112	....	....	....	....	....	....	....	....	....	....	4	1	0	1	22	....	....	....
1993-94	**St. Louis Blues**	**NHL**	**30**	**2**	**3**	**5**	**2**	**2**	**4**	**56**	**0**	**0**	**0**	**21**	**9.5**	**7**	**0**	**11**	**0**	**–4**	**2**	**0**	**0**	**0**	**2**	**0**	**0**	**0**
	Peoria Rivermen	IHL	49	14	21	35	....	....	....	132	....	....	....	....	....	....	....	....	....	....	....	....	....	....	....	....	....	....
1994-95	Milwaukee Admirals	IHL	74	19	18	37	....	....	....	261	....	....	....	....	....	....	....	....	....	....	15	6	4	10	34	....	....	....
1995-96	Milwaukee Admirals	IHL	77	15	16	31	....	....	....	235	....	....	....	....	....	....	....	....	....	....	4	2	1	3	10	....	....	....
1996-97	Milwaukee Admirals	IHL	79	15	15	30	....	....	....	223	....	....	....	....	....	....	....	....	....	....	3	0	0	0	19	....	....	....
1997-98	Milwaukee Admirals	IHL	36	3	6	9	....	....	....	134	....	....	....	....	....	....	....	....	....	....	....	....	....	....	....	....	....	....
	Orlando Solar Bears	IHL	31	5	6	11	....	....	....	68	....	....	....	....	....	....	....	....	....	....	14	4	3	7	92	....	....	....
1998-99	Orlando Solar Bears	IHL	78	21	20	41	....	....	....	192	....	....	....	....	....	....	....	....	....	....	17	3	0	3	38	....	....	....
99-2000	Chicago Wolves	IHL	45	5	2	7	....	....	....	54	....	....	....	....	....	....	....	....	....	....	....	....	....	....	....	....	....	....
	NHL Totals		**126**	**8**	**12**	**20**	**8**	**8**	**16**	**305**	**0**	**0**	**3**	**96**	**8.3**	**32**	**0**	**62**	**1**		**3**	**0**	**0**	**0**	**2**	**0**	**0**	**0**

Claimed by **Minnesota** from **Chicago** in Waiver Draft, October 2, 1989. Traded to **Vancouver** by **Minnesota** for future considerations, September 7, 1990. Signed as a free agent by **St. Louis**, August 7, 1991. Traded to **Orlando** (IHL) by **Milwaukee** (IHL) with Sean McCann for Kelly Fairchild and Dave McIntyre, January 11, 1998. Signed as a free agent by **Chicago Wolves** (IHL), September 29, 1999.

• MacKINNON, Paul

Paul Gregory D – R. 6', 195 lbs. b: Brantford, Ont., 11/6/1958. Washington's 4th, 23rd overall, in 1978.

Season	Club	League	GP	G	A	Pts	AG	AA	APts	PIM	PP	SH	GW	S	%	TGF	PGF	TGA	PGA	+/–	GP	G	A	Pts	PIM	PP	SH	GW
1975-76	Peterborough Petes	OMJHL	48	1	10	11	....	....	....	42	....	....	....	....	....	....	....	....	....	....	....	....	....	....	....	....	....	....
1976-77	Peterborough Petes	OMJHL	65	2	38	40	....	....	....	96	....	....	....	....	....	....	....	....	....	....	4	0	2	2	2	....	....	....
1977-78	Peterborough Petes	OMJHL	60	1	25	26	....	....	....	77	....	....	....	....	....	....	....	....	....	....	21	0	7	7	28	....	....	....
	Peterborough Petes	Mem-Cup	5	0	3	3	....	....	....	4	....	....	....	....	....	....	....	....	....	....	....	....	....	....	....	....	....	....
1978-79	Winnipeg Jets	WHA	73	2	15	17	....	....	....	70	....	....	....	....	....	....	....	....	....	....	10	2	5	7	4	....	....	....
1979-80	**Washington Capitals**	**NHL**	**63**	**1**	**11**	**12**	**1**	**8**	**9**	**22**	**0**	**0**	**0**	**68**	**1.5**	**67**	**0**	**91**	**23**	**–1**	....	....	....	....	....	....	....	....
1980-81	**Washington Capitals**	**NHL**	**14**	**0**	**0**	**0**	**0**	**0**	**0**	**22**	**0**	**0**	**0**	**7**	**0.0**	**12**	**0**	**12**	**5**	**5**	....	....	....	....	....	....	....	....
1981-82	**Washington Capitals**	**NHL**	**39**	**2**	**9**	**11**	**2**	**6**	**8**	**35**	**0**	**0**	**0**	**28**	**7.1**	**34**	**2**	**61**	**19**	**–10**	....	....	....	....	....	....	....	....
	Hershey Bears	AHL	26	4	17	21	....	....	....	30	....	....	....	....	....	....	....	....	....	....	5	0	0	0	2	....	....	....
1982-83	**Washington Capitals**	**NHL**	**19**	**2**	**2**	**4**	**2**	**1**	**3**	**8**	**1**	**0**	**0**	**10**	**20.0**	**17**	**6**	**10**	**0**	**1**	....	....	....	....	....	....	....	....
	Hershey Bears	AHL	59	2	14	16	....	....	....	32	....	....	....	....	....	....	....	....	....	....	5	1	0	1	0	....	....	....
1983-84	**Washington Capitals**	**NHL**	**12**	**0**	**1**	**1**	**0**	**1**	**1**	**4**	**0**	**0**	**0**	**3**	**0.0**	**3**	**0**	**11**	**1**	**–7**	....	....	....	....	....	....	....	....
	Hershey Bears	AHL	63	3	19	22	....	....	....	29	....	....	....	....	....	....	....	....	....	....	....	....	....	....	....	....	....	....
	NHL Totals		**147**	**5**	**23**	**28**	**5**	**16**	**21**	**91**	**1**	**0**	**0**	**116**	**4.3**	**133**	**8**	**185**	**48**		....	....	....	....	....	....	....	....
	Other Major League Totals		73	2	15	17	....	....	....	70	....	....	....	....	....	....	....	....	....	....	10	2	5	7	4	....	....	....

Memorial Cup All-Star Team (1978)

Signed as an underage free agent by **Winnipeg** (WHA), June, 1978. Reclaimed by **Washington** from **Winnipeg** prior to Expansion Draft, June 9, 1979.

• MacLEAN, Donald

Donald S. C – L. 6'2", 205 lbs. b: Sydney, N.S., 1/14/1977. Los Angeles' 2nd, 33rd overall, in 1995.

Season	Club	League	GP	G	A	Pts	AG	AA	APts	PIM	PP	SH	GW	S	%	TGF	PGF	TGA	PGA	+/–	GP	G	A	Pts	PIM	PP	SH	GW
1992-93	Halifax Hawks	NSAHA	27	15	25	40	....	....	....	34	....	....	....	....	....	....	....	....	....	....	....	....	....	....	....	....	....	....
1993-94	Halifax Hawks	NSAHA	25	35	35	70	....	....	....	151	....	....	....	....	....	....	....	....	....	....	....	....	....	....	....	....	....	....
1994-95	Beauport Harfangs	QMJHL	64	15	27	42	....	....	....	37	....	....	....	....	....	....	....	....	....	....	17	4	4	8	6	....	....	....
1995-96	Beauport Harfangs	QMJHL	1	0	1	1	....	....	....	0	....	....	....	....	....	....	....	....	....	....	....	....	....	....	....	....	....	....
	Laval Titan	QMJHL	21	17	11	28	....	....	....	29	....	....	....	....	....	....	....	....	....	....	....	....	....	....	....	....	....	....
	Hull Olympiques	QMJHL	39	26	34	60	....	....	....	44	....	....	....	....	....	....	....	....	....	....	17	6	7	13	14	....	....	....
1996-97	Hull Olympiques	QMJHL	69	34	47	81	....	....	....	67	....	....	....	....	....	....	....	....	....	....	14	11	10	21	39	....	....	....
	Hull	Mem-Cup	4	4	6	10	....	....	....	6	....	....	....	....	....	....	....	....	....	....	....	....	....	....	....	....	....	....
1997-98	**Los Angeles Kings**	**NHL**	**22**	**5**	**2**	**7**	**6**	**2**	**8**	**4**	**2**	**0**	**0**	**25**	**20.0**	**9**	**2**	**8**	**0**	**–1**	....	....	....	....	....	....	....	....
	Fredericton Canadiens	AHL	39	9	5	14	....	....	....	32	....	....	....	....	....	....	....	....	....	....	4	1	3	4	2	....	....	....
1998-99	Springfield Falcons	AHL	41	5	14	19	....	....	....	31	....	....	....	....	....	....	....	....	....	....	....	....	....	....	....	....	....	....
	Grand Rapids Griffins	IHL	28	6	13	19	....	....	....	8	....	....	....	....	....	....	....	....	....	....	....	....	....	....	....	....	....	....
99-2000	Lowell Lock Monsters	AHL	40	11	17	28	....	....	....	18	....	....	....	....	....	....	....	....	....	....	....	....	....	....	....	....	....	....
	St. John's Maple Leafs	AHL	21	14	12	26	....	....	....	8	....	....	....	....	....	....	....	....	....	....	....	....	....	....	....	....	....	....
	NHL Totals		**22**	**5**	**2**	**7**	**6**	**2**	**8**	**4**	**2**	**0**	**0**	**25**	**20.0**	**9**	**2**	**8**	**0**		....	....	....	....	....	....	....	....

Traded to **Toronto** by **Los Angeles** for Craig Charron, February 23, 2000.

• MacLEAN, John

John Harold RW – R. 6', 200 lbs. b: Oshawa, Ont., 11/20/1964. New Jersey's 1st, 6th overall, in 1983.

Season	Club	League	GP	G	A	Pts	AG	AA	APts	PIM	PP	SH	GW	S	%	TGF	PGF	TGA	PGA	+/–	GP	G	A	Pts	PIM	PP	SH	GW
1980-81	Oshawa Legionaires	OJHL	41	35	35	70	....	....	....	151	....	....	....	....	....	....	....	....	....	....	....	....	....	....	....	....	....	....
1981-82	Oshawa Generals	OHL	67	17	22	39	....	....	....	197	....	....	....	....	....	....	....	....	....	....	12	3	6	9	63	....	....	....
1982-83	Oshawa Generals	OHL	66	47	51	98	....	....	....	138	....	....	....	....	....	....	....	....	....	....	17	*18	20	*38	35	....	....	....
	Oshawa Generals	Mem-Cup	5	3	4	7	....	....	....	14	....	....	....	....	....	....	....	....	....	....	....	....	....	....	....	....	....	....
1983-84	Oshawa Generals	OHL	30	23	36	59	....	....	....	58	....	....	....	....	....	....	....	....	....	....	7	2	5	7	18	....	....	....
	Canada	WJC-A	7	7	1	8	....	....	....	4	....	....	....	....	....	....	....	....	....	....	....	....	....	....	....	....	....	....
	New Jersey Devils	**NHL**	**23**	**1**	**0**	**1**	**1**	**0**	**1**	**10**	**0**	**0**	**0**	**22**	**4.5**	**12**	**3**	**18**	**2**	**–7**	....	....	....	....	....	....	....	....
1984-85	**New Jersey Devils**	**NHL**	**61**	**13**	**20**	**33**	**11**	**14**	**25**	**44**	**1**	**0**	**4**	**92**	**14.1**	**58**	**19**	**51**	**1**	**–11**	....	....	....	....	....	....	....	....
1985-86	**New Jersey Devils**	**NHL**	**74**	**21**	**36**	**57**	**17**	**24**	**41**	**112**	**1**	**0**	**4**	**139**	**15.1**	**77**	**14**	**66**	**0**	**–3**	....	....	....	....	....	....	....	....
1986-87	**New Jersey Devils**	**NHL**	**80**	**31**	**36**	**67**	**27**	**26**	**53**	**120**	**9**	**0**	**4**	**197**	**15.7**	**85**	**26**	**83**	**1**	**–23**	....	....	....	....	....	....	....	....
1987-88	**New Jersey Devils**	**NHL**	**76**	**23**	**16**	**39**	**20**	**11**	**31**	**147**	**12**	**0**	**4**	**204**	**11.3**	**67**	**32**	**46**	**1**	**–10**	**20**	**7**	**11**	**18**	**60**	**2**	**0**	**2**
1988-89	**New Jersey Devils**	**NHL**	**74**	**42**	**45**	**87**	**36**	**32**	**68**	**122**	**14**	**0**	**4**	**266**	**15.8**	**125**	**47**	**57**	**5**	**26**	....	....	....	....	....	....	....	....
	Canada	WEC-A	10	3	6	9	....	....	....	4	....	....	....	....	....	....	....	....	....	....	....	....	....	....	....	....	....	....
1989-90	**New Jersey Devils**	**NHL**	**80**	**41**	**38**	**79**	**35**	**27**	**62**	**80**	**10**	**3**	**11**	**322**	**12.7**	**122**	**33**	**93**	**21**	**17**	**6**	**4**	**1**	**5**	**12**	**2**	**1**	**0**
1990-91	**New Jersey Devils**	**NHL**	**78**	**45**	**33**	**78**	**41**	**25**	**66**	**150**	**19**	**2**	**7**	**292**	**15.4**	**108**	**37**	**79**	**16**	**8**	**7**	**5**	**3**	**8**	**20**	**1**	**0**	**0**
1991-92	**New Jersey Devils**	**NHL**	DID NOT PLAY – INJURED																									
1992-93	**New Jersey Devils**	**NHL**	**80**	**24**	**24**	**48**	**20**	**17**	**37**	**102**	**7**	**1**	**3**	**195**	**12.3**	**75**	**23**	**75**	**17**	**–6**	**5**	**0**	**1**	**1**	**10**	**0**	**0**	**0**
1993-94	**New Jersey Devils**	**NHL**	**80**	**37**	**33**	**70**	**34**	**26**	**60**	**95**	**8**	**0**	**4**	**277**	**13.4**	**105**	**29**	**69**	**23**	**30**	**20**	**6**	**10**	**16**	**22**	**2**	**0**	**1**
1994-95♦	**New Jersey Devils**	**NHL**	**46**	**17**	**12**	**29**	**30**	**18**	**48**	**32**	**2**	**1**	**0**	**139**	**12.2**	**46**	**11**	**29**	**7**	**13**	**20**	**5**	**13**	**18**	**14**	**2**	**0**	**0**
1995-96	**New Jersey Devils**	**NHL**	**76**	**20**	**28**	**48**	**20**	**23**	**43**	**91**	**3**	**3**	**3**	**237**	**8.4**	**58**	**19**	**57**	**21**	**3**	....	....	....	....	....	....	....	....
1996-97	**New Jersey Devils**	**NHL**	**80**	**29**	**25**	**54**	**31**	**22**	**53**	**49**	**5**	**0**	**6**	**254**	**11.4**	**71**	**13**	**65**	**18**	**11**	**10**	**4**	**5**	**9**	**4**	**2**	**1**	**1**
1997-98	**New Jersey Devils**	**NHL**	**26**	**3**	**8**	**11**	**4**	**8**	**12**	**14**	**1**	**0**	**1**	**74**	**4.1**	**15**	**7**	**19**	**5**	**–6**	....	....	....	....	....	....	....	....
	San Jose Sharks	**NHL**	**51**	**13**	**19**	**32**	**15**	**19**	**34**	**28**	**5**	**0**	**2**	**139**	**9.4**	**46**	**19**	**34**	**7**	**0**	**6**	**2**	**3**	**5**	**4**	**1**	**0**	**0**
1998-99	**New York Rangers**	**NHL**	**82**	**28**	**27**	**55**	**33**	**26**	**59**	**46**	**11**	**1**	**2**	**231**	**12.1**	**84**	**31**	**63**	**15**	**5**	....	....	....	....	....	....	....	....
99-2000	**New York Rangers**	**NHL**	**77**	**18**	**24**	**42**	**20**	**22**	**42**	**52**	**6**	**2**	**3**	**158**	**11.4**	**52**	**11**	**59**	**16**	**–2**	....	....	....	....	....	....	....	....
	NHL Totals		**1144**	**406**	**424**	**830**	**395**	**340**	**735**	**1294**	**114**	**13**	**62**	**3238**	**12.5**	**1206**	**374**	**963**	**176**		**94**	**33**	**47**	**80**	**146**	**12**	**2**	**4**

Memorial Cup All-Star Team (1983) • Played in NHL All-Star Game (1989, 1991)

• Missed entire 1991-92 season recovering from knee surgery, June, 1991. Traded to **San Jose** by **New Jersey** with Ken Sutton for Doug Bodger and Dody Wood, December 7, 1997. Signed as a free agent by **NY Rangers**, July 22, 1998.

• MacLEAN, Paul

Paul A. RW – R. 6'2", 218 lbs. b: Grostenquin, France, 3/9/1958. St. Louis' 6th, 109th overall, in 1978.

			REGULAR SEASON																		PLAYOFFS							
Season	Club	League	GP	G	A	Pts	AG	AA	APts	PIM	PP	SH	GW	S	%	TGF	PGF	TGA	PGA	+/-	GP	G	A	Pts	PIM	PP	SH	GW
1974-75	Antigonish Bulldogs	MJrHL	STATISTICS NOT AVAILABLE																									
1975-76	Brockville Braves	OHA-B	44	35	25	60	....	....	....	70	....	....	....	....	....	....	....	....	....	....	....	....	....	....	....	....	....	....
1976-77	Brockville Braves	OHA-B	52	37	29	66	....	....	....	63	....	....	....	....	....	....	....	....	....	....	....	....	....	....	....	....	....	....
1977-78	Hull Festivals	QMJHL	66	38	33	71	....	....	....	125	....	....	....	....	....	....	....	....	....	....	....	....	....	....	....	....	....	....
1978-79	Dalhousie University	AUAA	18	12	17	29	....	....	....	71	....	....	....	....	....	....	....	....	....	....	....	....	....	....	....	....	....	....
1979-80	Canada	Nat-Team	50	21	11	32	....	....	....	90	....	....	....	....	....	....	....	....	....	....	....	....	....	....	....	....	....	....
	Canada	Olympics	6	2	3	5	....	....	....	6	....	....	....	....	....	....	....	....	....	....	....	....	....	....	....	....	....	....
1980-81	St. Louis Blues	NHL	1	0	0	0	0	0	0	0	0	0	0	1	0.0	1	0	1	1	1	1	0	0	0	0	0	0	0
	Salt Lake Golden Eagles	CHL	80	36	42	78	....	....	....	160	....	....	....	....	....	....	....	....	....	....	17	11	5	16	47	....	....	....
1981-82	Winnipeg Jets	NHL	74	36	25	61	28	17	45	106	12	0	1	164	22.0	100	39	71	1	–9	4	3	2	5	26	2	0	1
1982-83	Winnipeg Jets	NHL	80	32	44	76	26	31	57	121	15	0	2	163	19.6	114	53	66	0	–5	3	1	2	3	6	1	0	0
1983-84	Winnipeg Jets	NHL	76	40	31	71	32	21	53	155	13	0	5	158	25.3	103	31	87	0	–15	3	1	0	1	0	0	0	0
1984-85	Winnipeg Jets	NHL	79	41	60	101	33	41	74	119	4	0	6	186	22.0	142	47	91	1	5	8	3	4	7	4	2	0	0
1985-86	Winnipeg Jets	NHL	69	27	29	56	22	19	41	74	11	0	2	168	16.1	85	31	68	0	–14	2	1	0	1	7	0	0	0
1986-87	Winnipeg Jets	NHL	72	32	42	74	28	31	59	75	10	0	6	155	20.6	115	32	71	0	12	10	5	2	7	16	2	0	0
1987-88	Winnipeg Jets	NHL	77	40	39	79	34	28	62	76	22	0	2	176	22.7	132	70	79	0	–17	5	2	0	2	23	2	0	0
1988-89	Detroit Red Wings	NHL	76	36	35	71	31	25	56	118	16	0	5	148	24.3	125	46	73	1	7	5	1	1	2	8	0	0	0
1989-90	St. Louis Blues	NHL	78	34	33	67	29	24	53	100	12	0	6	141	24.1	85	25	58	0	2	12	4	3	7	20	3	0	0
1990-91	St. Louis Blues	NHL	37	6	11	17	5	8	13	24	0	0	2	53	11.3	26	6	22	0	–2	....	....	....	....	....	....	....	....
1991-1993			OUT OF HOCKEY – RETIRED																									
1993-1996	Peoria Rivermen	IHL	DID NOT PLAY – COACHING																									
1996-1997	Phoenix Coyotes	NHL	DID NOT PLAY – ASSISTANT COACH																									
1997-2000	Kansas City Blades	IHL	DID NOT PLAY – COACHING																									
	NHL Totals		719	324	349	673	268	245	513	968	115	0	37	1513	21.4	1028	380	687	4		53	21	14	35	110	12	0	1

Played in NHL All-Star Game (1985)

Traded to **Winnipeg** by **St. Louis** with Bryan Maxwell and Ed Staniowski for Scott Campbell and John Markell, July 3, 1981. Traded to **Detroit** by **Winnipeg** for Brent Ashton, June 13, 1988. Traded to **St. Louis** by **Detroit** with Adam Oates for Bernie Federko and Tony McKegney, June 15, 1989.

• MacLEISH, Rick

Richard George C – L. 5'11", 185 lbs. b: Lindsay, Ont., 1/3/1950. Boston's 2nd, 4th overall, in 1970.

Season	Club	League	GP	G	A	Pts	AG	AA	APts	PIM	PP	SH	GW	S	%	TGF	PGF	TGA	PGA	+/-	GP	G	A	Pts	PIM	PP	SH	GW
1966-67	Cannington Cougars	OMHA	STATISTICS NOT AVAILABLE																									
	London Knights	OHA-Jr.	2	0	0	0	....	....	....	0	....	....	....	....	....	....	....	....	....	....	....	....	....	....	....	....	....	....
	Peterborough Petes	OHA-Jr.	8	0	0	0	....	....	....	0	....	....	....	....	....	....	....	....	....	....	....	....	....	....	....	....	....	....
1967-68	Peterborough Petes	OHA-Jr.	54	24	25	49	....	....	....	16	....	....	....	....	....	....	....	....	....	....	5	2	1	3	0	....	....	....
1968-69	Peterborough Petes	OHA-Jr.	54	50	42	92	....	....	....	29	....	....	....	....	....	....	....	....	....	....	10	7	14	21	8	....	....	....
1969-70	Peterborough Petes	OHA-Jr.	54	45	56	101	....	....	....	135	....	....	....	....	....	....	....	....	....	....	6	4	4	8	10	....	....	....
1970-71	Oklahoma City Blazers	CHL	46	13	15	28	....	....	....	93	....	....	....	....	....	....	....	....	....	....	....	....	....	....	....	....	....	....
	Philadelphia Flyers	NHL	26	2	4	6	2	3	5	19	0	0	0	54	3.7	13	2	18	3	–4	4	1	0	1	0	0	0	0
1971-72	Philadelphia Flyers	NHL	17	1	2	3	1	2	3	9	0	0	0	37	2.7	5	2	13	1	–9	....	....	....	....	....	....	....	....
	Richmond Robins	AHL	42	24	11	35	....	....	....	33	....	....	....	....	....	....	....	....	....	....	....	....	....	....	....	....	....	....
1972-73	Philadelphia Flyers	NHL	78	50	50	100	47	40	87	69	21	2	6	279	17.9	124	46	83	20	15	10	3	4	7	2	2	0	1
1973-74♦	Philadelphia Flyers	NHL	78	32	45	77	31	37	68	42	13	4	5	270	11.9	101	37	54	11	21	17	*13	9	*22	20	5	0	4
1974-75♦	Philadelphia Flyers	NHL	80	38	41	79	33	31	64	50	11	3	8	309	12.3	110	44	52	15	29	17	11	9	*20	8	4	0	1
1975-76	Philadelphia Flyers	NHL	51	22	23	45	19	17	36	16	6	1	4	222	9.9	70	27	49	12	6	....	....	....	....	....	....	....	....
1976-77	Philadelphia Flyers	NHL	79	49	48	97	44	37	81	42	10	1	8	252	19.4	126	33	58	11	46	10	4	9	13	2	2	0	1
1977-78	Philadelphia Flyers	NHL	76	31	39	70	28	30	58	33	7	2	7	253	12.3	98	29	54	9	24	12	7	9	16	4	3	0	3
1978-79	Philadelphia Flyers	NHL	71	26	32	58	22	23	45	47	7	5	4	211	12.3	83	26	73	20	4	7	0	1	1	0	0	0	0
1979-80	Philadelphia Flyers	NHL	78	31	35	66	26	26	52	28	6	3	4	234	13.2	91	18	74	24	23	19	9	6	15	2	1	0	1
1980-81	Philadelphia Flyers	NHL	78	38	36	74	30	24	54	25	14	0	3	214	17.8	102	33	60	13	22	12	5	5	10	0	4	0	0
1981-82	Hartford Whalers	NHL	34	6	16	22	5	11	16	16	4	0	0	68	8.8	30	13	31	1	–13	....	....	....	....	....	....	....	....
	Pittsburgh Penguins	NHL	40	13	12	25	10	8	18	28	2	2	1	101	12.9	43	15	45	10	–7	5	1	1	2	0	0	0	0
1982-83	Pittsburgh Penguins	NHL	6	0	5	5	0	3	3	2	0	0	0	8	0.0	5	3	10	3	–5	....	....	....	....	....	....	....	....
1983-84	Philadelphia Flyers	NHL	29	8	14	22	6	10	16	4	3	0	2	70	11.4	31	11	18	2	4	....	....	....	....	....	....	....	....
	Detroit Red Wings	NHL	25	2	8	10	2	5	7	4	0	0	0	26	7.7	16	1	19	0	–4	1	0	0	0	0	0	0	0
	NHL Totals		846	349	410	759	306	307	613	434	104	23	52	2608	13.4	1048	340	711	155		114	54	53	107	38	21	0	11

OHA-Jr. First All-Star Team (1970) • Played in NHL All-Star Game (1976, 1977, 1980)

Traded to **Philadelphia** by **Boston** with Danny Schock for Mike Walton, February 1, 1971. Traded to **Hartford** by **Philadelphia** with Blake Wesley, Don Gillen and Philadelphia's 1st (Paul Lawless), 2nd (Mark Patterson) and 3rd (Kevin Dineen) round choices in 1982 Entry Draft for Ray Allison, Fred Arthur and Hartford's 1st (Ron Sutter), and 3rd (Miroslav Dvorak) round choices in 1983 Entry Draft, July 3, 1981. Traded to **Pittsburgh** by **Hartford** for Pittsburgh's 8th round choice (Chris Duperron) in 1983 Entry Draft and Russ Anderson, December 29, 1981. Signed as a free agent by **Philadelphia**, October 6, 1983. Traded to **Detroit** by **Philadelphia** for future considerations, January 8, 1984.

• MacLELLAN, Brian

Brian J. LW – L. 6'3", 220 lbs. b: Guelph, Ont., 10/27/1958.

Season	Club	League	GP	G	A	Pts	AG	AA	APts	PIM	PP	SH	GW	S	%	TGF	PGF	TGA	PGA	+/-	GP	G	A	Pts	PIM	PP	SH	GW
1978-79	Bowling Green University	CCHA	44	34	29	63	....	....	....	94	....	....	....	....	....	....	....	....	....	....	....	....	....	....	....	....	....	....
1979-80	Bowling Green University	CCHA	38	8	15	23	....	....	....	46	....	....	....	....	....	....	....	....	....	....	....	....	....	....	....	....	....	....
1980-81	Bowling Green University	CCHA	37	11	14	25	....	....	....	96	....	....	....	....	....	....	....	....	....	....	....	....	....	....	....	....	....	....
1981-82	Bowling Green University	CCHA	41	11	21	32	....	....	....	109	....	....	....	....	....	....	....	....	....	....	....	....	....	....	....	....	....	....
1982-83	Los Angeles Kings	NHL	8	0	3	3	0	2	2	7	0	0	0	5	0.0	3	0	8	0	–5	....	....	....	....	....	....	....	....
	New Haven Nighthawks	AHL	71	11	15	26	....	....	....	40	....	....	....	....	....	....	....	....	....	....	12	5	3	8	4	....	....	....
1983-84	Los Angeles Kings	NHL	72	25	29	54	20	20	40	45	3	1	1	106	23.6	91	25	109	22	–21	....	....	....	....	....	....	....	....
	New Haven Nighthawks	AHL	2	0	2	2	....	....	....	0	....	....	....	....	....	....	....	....	....	....	....	....	....	....	....	....	....	....
1984-85	Los Angeles Kings	NHL	80	31	54	85	25	37	62	53	14	0	3	170	18.2	133	56	75	0	2	3	0	1	1	0	0	0	0
	Canada	WEC-A	4	0	0	0	....	....	....	0	....	....	....	....	....	....	....	....	....	....	....	....	....	....	....	....	....	....
1985-86	Los Angeles Kings	NHL	27	5	8	13	4	5	9	19	4	0	0	53	9.4	28	9	32	0	–13	....	....	....	....	....	....	....	....
	New York Rangers	NHL	51	11	21	32	9	14	23	47	8	0	1	112	9.8	46	22	44	0	–20	16	2	4	6	15	0	0	1
1986-87	Minnesota North Stars	NHL	76	32	31	63	28	23	51	69	13	0	5	146	21.9	93	42	64	1	–12	....	....	....	....	....	....	....	....
1987-88	Minnesota North Stars	NHL	75	16	32	48	14	23	37	74	7	0	4	194	8.2	78	42	86	6	–44	....	....	....	....	....	....	....	....
1988-89	Minnesota North Stars	NHL	60	16	23	39	14	16	30	104	7	0	0	114	14.0	51	17	34	0	0	....	....	....	....	....	....	....	....
♦	Calgary Flames	NHL	12	2	3	5	2	2	4	14	0	0	0	23	8.7	12	3	6	0	3	21	3	2	5	19	0	0	1
1989-90	Calgary Flames	Fr-Tour	3	0	1	1	....	....	....	6	....	....	....	....	....	....	....	....	....	....	....	....	....	....	....	....	....	....
	Calgary Flames	NHL	65	20	18	38	17	13	30	26	10	0	3	127	15.7	57	20	40	0	–3	6	0	2	2	8	0	0	0
1990-91	Calgary Flames	NHL	57	13	14	27	12	11	23	55	5	0	2	74	17.6	50	9	27	1	15	1	0	0	0	0	0	0	0
1991-92	Detroit Red Wings	NHL	23	1	5	6	1	4	5	38	0	0	0	17	5.9	10	2	4	0	4	....	....	....	....	....	....	....	....
	NHL Totals		606	172	241	413	146	170	316	551	71	1	19	1141	15.1	652	247	529	30		47	5	9	14	42	0	0	2

CCHA First All-Star Team (1982) • NCAA West First All-American Team (1982)

Signed as a free agent by **LA Kings**, May 12, 1982. Traded to **NY Rangers** by **LA Kings** with LA Kings' 4th round choice (Mike Sullivan) in 1987 Entry Draft for Rollie Melanson and Grant Ledyard, December 9, 1985. Traded to **Minnesota** by **NY Rangers** for Minnesota's 3rd round choice (Simon Gagne) in 1987 Entry Draft, September 8, 1986. Traded to **Calgary** by **Minnesota** with Minnesota's 4th round choice (Robert Reichel) in 1989 Entry Draft for Shane Churla and Perry Berezan, March 4, 1989. Traded to **Detroit** by **Calgary** for Marc Habscheid, June 11, 1991.

• MacLEOD, Pat

Patrick L. D – L. 5'11", 190 lbs. b: Melfort, Sask., 6/15/1969. Minnesota's 5th, 87th overall, in 1989.

Season	Club	League	GP	G	A	Pts	AG	AA	APts	PIM	PP	SH	GW	S	%	TGF	PGF	TGA	PGA	+/-	GP	G	A	Pts	PIM	PP	SH	GW
1986-87	Fort Saskatchewan Traders	SJHL	59	12	40	52	....	....	....	29	....	....	....	....	....	....	....	....	....	....	....	....	....	....	....	....	....	....
1987-88	Kamloops Blazers	WHL	50	13	33	46	....	....	....	27	....	....	....	....	....	....	....	....	....	....	18	2	7	9	6	....	....	....
1988-89	Kamloops Blazers	WHL	37	11	34	45	....	....	....	14	....	....	....	....	....	....	....	....	....	....	15	7	18	25	24	....	....	....
1989-90	Kalamazoo Wings	IHL	82	9	38	47	....	....	....	27	....	....	....	....	....	....	....	....	....	....	10	1	6	7	2	....	....	....
1990-91	Minnesota North Stars	NHL	1	0	1	1	0	1	1	0	0	0	0	1	0.0	2	1	0	0	1	....	....	....	....	....	....	....	....
	Kalamazoo Wings	IHL	59	10	30	40	....	....	....	16	....	....	....	....	....	....	....	....	....	....	11	1	2	3	5	....	....	....
1991-92	San Jose Sharks	NHL	37	5	11	16	5	8	13	4	3	0	0	77	6.5	34	19	59	12	–32	....	....	....	....	....	....	....	....
	Kansas City Blades	IHL	45	9	21	30	....	....	....	19	....	....	....	....	....	....	....	....	....	....	11	1	4	5	4	....	....	....

Season	Club	League	REGULAR SEASON																		PLAYOFFS							
			GP	G	A	Pts	AG	AA	APts	PIM	PP	SH	GW	S	%	TGF	PGF	TGA	PGA	+/–	GP	G	A	Pts	PIM	PP	SH	GW
1992-93	**San Jose Sharks**	**NHL**	**13**	**0**	**1**	**1**	**0**	**1**	**1**	**10**	**0**	**0**	**0**	**20**	**0.0**	**6**	**1**	**31**	**7**	**–19**								
	Kansas City Blades	IHL	18	8	8	16				14											10	2	4	6	7			
1993-94	Milwaukee Admirals	IHL	73	21	52	73				18											3	1	2	3	0			
1994-95	Milwaukee Admirals	IHL	69	11	36	47				16											15	3	6	9	8			
1995-96	**Dallas Stars**	**NHL**	**2**	**0**	**0**	**0**	**0**	**0**	**0**	**0**	**0**	**0**	**0**	**2**	**0.0**	**1**	**1**	**0**	**0**	**0**								
	Michigan K-Wings	IHL	50	3	23	26				18											7	0	3	3	0			
1996-97	Farjestads BK Karlstad	Sweden	12	1	2	3				4																		
	Farjestads BK Karlstad	EuroHL	4	2	0	2				2																		
	Cincinnati Cyclones	IHL	41	5	8	13				8											3	2	0	2	0			
1997-98	Cincinnati Cyclones	IHL	78	16	39	55				51											9	0	6	6	8			
1998-99	Cincinnati Cyclones	IHL	18	5	5	10				4											3	0	2	2	4			
99-2000	Cincinnati Cyclones	IHL	62	1	18	19				29											7	0	1	1	0			
	Florida Everblades	ECHL	3	0	2	2				4																		
	NHL Totals		**53**	**5**	**13**	**18**	**5**	**10**	**15**	**14**	**3**	**0**	**0**	**100**	**5.0**	**43**	**22**	**90**	**19**									

WHL West Second All-Star Team (1989) • IHL Second All-Star Team (1992) • IHL First All-Star Team (1994)

Claimed by **San Jose** from **Minnesota** in Dispersal Draft, May 30, 1991. Signed as a free agent by **Dallas**, July 31, 1995. Signed as a free agent by **Cincnnati** (IHL), December 23, 1996. • Missed majority of 1998-99 season recovering from knee injury suffered in game vs. Chicago (IHL), November 25, 1998.

• MacMILLAN, Billy

William Stewart RW – L. 5'10", 185 lbs. b: Charlottetown, P.E.I., 3/7/1943.

Season	Club	League	GP	G	A	Pts	AG	AA	APts	PIM	PP	SH	GW	S	%	TGF	PGF	TGA	PGA	+/–	GP	G	A	Pts	PIM	PP	SH	GW
1959-60	St. Michael's Buzzers	OHA-B	STATISTICS NOT AVAILABLE																									
	St. Michael's Majors	OHA-Jr.	2	0	0	0				0											5	0	1	1	0			
1960-61	St. Michael's Majors	OHA-Jr.	46	7	12	19				31											7	1	1	2	4			
	St. Michael's Majors	Mem-Cup	4	2	1	3				0																		
1961-62	St. Michael's Majors	MTJHL	32	14	15	29				11											9	12	2	14	*41			
	St. Michael's Majors	Mem-Cup	5	1	0	1				7																		
1962-63	Neil McNeil Maroons	MTJHL	32	25	12	37				11											10	9	11	20	9			
	Sudbury Wolves	EPHL	1	0	0	0				0																		
	Neil McNeil Maroons	Mem-Cup	6	1	4	5				18																		
1963-64	St. Dunstan's University	MIAU	11	*25	11	*36				17																		
1964-65	St. Dunstan's University	AUAA	20	25	....	*25				12																		
1965-66	Canada	Nat-Team	STATISTICS NOT AVAILABLE																									
	Canada	WEC-A	7	2	2	4				6																		
1966-67	Canada	Nat-Team	STATISTICS NOT AVAILABLE																									
1967-68	Ottawa Nationals	OHA-Sr.	20	13	8	21				20																		
1968-69	Canada	Nat-Team	STATISTICS NOT AVAILABLE																									
1969-70	Canada	Nat-Team	STATISTICS NOT AVAILABLE																									
	Tulsa Oilers	CHL	3	1	6	7				0																		
1970-71	**Toronto Maple Leafs**	**NHL**	**76**	**22**	**19**	**41**	**22**	**16**	**38**	**42**	**3**	**1**	**4**	**156**	**14.1**	**67**	**9**	**61**	**13**	**10**	**6**	**0**	**3**	**3**	**2**	**0**	**0**	**0**
1971-72	**Toronto Maple Leafs**	**NHL**	**61**	**10**	**7**	**17**	**10**	**6**	**16**	**39**	**2**	**0**	**2**	**95**	**10.5**	**30**	**5**	**26**	**0**	**–1**	**5**	**0**	**0**	**0**	**0**	**0**	**0**	**0**
1972-73	**Atlanta Flames**	**NHL**	**78**	**10**	**15**	**25**	**9**	**12**	**21**	**52**	**3**	**0**	**2**	**101**	**9.9**	**54**	**8**	**61**	**5**	**–10**								
1973-74	**New York Islanders**	**NHL**	**55**	**4**	**9**	**13**	**4**	**7**	**11**	**16**	**0**	**0**	**0**	**65**	**6.2**	**23**	**0**	**34**	**5**	**–6**								
1974-75	**New York Islanders**	**NHL**	**69**	**13**	**12**	**25**	**11**	**9**	**20**	**12**	**2**	**1**	**1**	**74**	**17.6**	**41**	**5**	**55**	**19**	**0**	**17**	**0**	**1**	**1**	**23**	**0**	**0**	**0**
1975-76	**New York Islanders**	**NHL**	**64**	**9**	**7**	**16**	**8**	**5**	**13**	**10**	**0**	**0**	**2**	**75**	**12.0**	**27**	**0**	**25**	**3**	**5**	**13**	**4**	**2**	**6**	**8**	**0**	**0**	**2**
1976-77	**New York Islanders**	**NHL**	**43**	**6**	**8**	**14**	**5**	**6**	**11**	**13**	**0**	**1**	**1**	**34**	**17.6**	**21**	**0**	**22**	**5**	**4**	**12**	**2**	**0**	**2**	**7**	**0**	**0**	**2**
	Rhode Island Reds	AHL	2	1	1	2				4																		
	Fort Worth Texans	CHL	12	1	7	8				2																		
1977-78	Fort Worth Texans	CHL	59	5	13	18				26											14	2	2	4	2			
	NHL Totals		**446**	**74**	**77**	**151**	**69**	**61**	**130**	**184**	**10**	**3**	**12**	**600**	**12.3**	**263**	**27**	**284**	**50**		**53**	**6**	**6**	**12**	**40**	**0**	**0**	**4**

• Brother of Bob

Claimed by **Atlanta** from **Toronto** in Expansion Draft, June 6, 1972. Traded to **NY Islanders** by **Atlanta** to complete transaction that sent Arnie Brown to Atlanta (February 13, 1973), May 29, 1973.

• MacMILLAN, Bob

Robert Lea "Mack the Knife" RW – L. 5'11", 185 lbs. b: Charlottetown, P.E.I., 12/3/1952. NY Rangers' 2nd, 15th overall, in 1972.

Season	Club	League	GP	G	A	Pts	AG	AA	APts	PIM	PP	SH	GW	S	%	TGF	PGF	TGA	PGA	+/–	GP	G	A	Pts	PIM	PP	SH	GW
1969-70	Charlottetown Islanders	MJrHL	40	33	35	68				38											15	*12	8	20	13			
	Charlottetown Islanders	Mem-Cup	15	7	14	21				11																		
1970-71	St. Catharines Black Hawks	OHA-Jr.	59	41	62	103				93											15	9	14	23	24			
1971-72	St. Catharines Black Hawks	OHA-Jr.	39	12	41	53				41											5	1	1	2	15			
1972-73	Minnesota Fighting Saints	WHA	75	13	27	40				48											5	0	3	3	0			
1973-74	Minnesota Fighting Saints	WHA	78	14	34	48				81											11	2	3	5	4			
1974-75	**New York Rangers**	**NHL**	**22**	**1**	**2**	**3**	**1**	**1**	**2**	**4**	**0**	**0**	**0**	**16**	**6.3**	**7**	**0**	**5**	**1**	**3**								
	Providence Reds	AHL	46	18	29	47				58											6	3	2	5	17			
1975-76	**St. Louis Blues**	**NHL**	**80**	**20**	**32**	**52**	**18**	**24**	**42**	**41**	**2**	**1**	**2**	**151**	**13.2**	**88**	**20**	**83**	**28**	**13**	**3**	**0**	**1**	**1**	**0**	**0**	**0**	**0**
1976-77	**St. Louis Blues**	**NHL**	**80**	**19**	**39**	**58**	**17**	**30**	**47**	**11**	**10**	**0**	**1**	**168**	**11.3**	**86**	**31**	**57**	**3**	**1**	**4**	**0**	**1**	**1**	**0**	**0**	**0**	**0**
1977-78	**St. Louis Blues**	**NHL**	**28**	**7**	**12**	**19**	**6**	**9**	**15**	**23**	**3**	**0**	**0**	**77**	**9.1**	**26**	**9**	**34**	**6**	**–11**								
	Atlanta Flames	**NHL**	**52**	**31**	**21**	**52**	**28**	**16**	**44**	**26**	**5**	**0**	**3**	**148**	**20.9**	**84**	**22**	**40**	**6**	**28**	**2**	**0**	**2**	**2**	**0**	**0**	**0**	**0**
	Canada	WEC-A	10	0	3	3				6																		
1978-79	**Atlanta Flames**	**NHL**	**79**	**37**	**71**	**108**	**32**	**52**	**84**	**14**	**8**	**1**	**4**	**194**	**19.1**	**143**	**35**	**78**	**4**	**34**	**2**	**0**	**1**	**1**	**0**	**0**	**0**	**0**
1979-80	**Atlanta Flames**	**NHL**	**77**	**22**	**39**	**61**	**19**	**28**	**47**	**10**	**2**	**3**	**4**	**164**	**13.4**	**92**	**23**	**81**	**15**	**3**	**4**	**0**	**0**	**0**	**9**	**0**	**0**	**0**
1980-81	**Calgary Flames**	**NHL**	**77**	**28**	**35**	**63**	**22**	**23**	**45**	**47**	**2**	**4**	**2**	**162**	**17.3**	**97**	**17**	**95**	**33**	**18**	**16**	**8**	**6**	**14**	**7**	**2**	**0**	**1**
1981-82	**Calgary Flames**	**NHL**	**23**	**4**	**7**	**11**	**3**	**5**	**8**	**14**	**1**	**0**	**0**	**26**	**15.4**	**16**	**4**	**28**	**5**	**–11**								
	Colorado Rockies	**NHL**	**57**	**18**	**32**	**50**	**14**	**21**	**35**	**27**	**3**	**0**	**1**	**106**	**17.0**	**69**	**18**	**74**	**14**	**–9**								
1982-83	**New Jersey Devils**	**NHL**	**71**	**19**	**29**	**48**	**16**	**20**	**36**	**8**	**6**	**0**	**3**	**120**	**15.8**	**71**	**28**	**113**	**35**	**–35**								
1983-84	**New Jersey Devils**	**NHL**	**71**	**17**	**23**	**40**	**14**	**16**	**30**	**23**	**2**	**0**	**2**	**114**	**14.9**	**58**	**13**	**83**	**17**	**–21**								
1984-85	**Chicago Black Hawks**	**NHL**	**36**	**5**	**7**	**12**	**4**	**5**	**9**	**12**	**0**	**0**	**1**	**39**	**12.8**	**22**	**0**	**38**	**0**	**–16**								
	Milwaukee Admirals	IHL	8	2	2	4				2																		
1985-86	Charlottetown Islanders	NBSHL	PLAYER/COACH – STATISTICS UNAVAILABLE																									
1986-87	Charlottetown Islanders	NBSHL	PLAYER/COACH – STATISTICS UNAVAILABLE																									
1987-88	Charlottetown Islanders	NBSHL	2	2	2	4				0																		
	NHL Totals		**753**	**228**	**349**	**577**	**194**	**250**	**444**	**260**	**44**	**9**	**23**	**1485**	**15.4**	**859**	**220**	**809**	**167**		**31**	**8**	**11**	**19**	**16**	**2**	**0**	**1**
	Other Major League Totals		153	27	61	88				129											16	2	6	8	4			

• Brother of Billy • Won Lady Byng Trophy (1979)

Selected by **Minnesota** (WHA) in 1972 WHA General Player Draft, February 12, 1972. Traded to **St. Louis** by **NY Rangers** for Larry Sacharuk, September 20, 1975. Traded to **Atlanta** by **St. Louis** with Yves Belanger, Dick Redmond and St. Louis' 2nd round choice (Mike Perovich) in 1979 Entry Draft for Phil Myre, Barry Gibbs and Curt Bennett, December 12, 1977. Transferred to **Calgary** after **Atlanta** franchise relocated, June 24, 1980. Traded to **Colorado** by **Calgary** with Don Lever for Lanny McDonald and Colorado's 4th round choice (later traded to NY Islanders — NY Islanders selected Mikko Makela) in 1983 Entry Draft, November 25, 1981. Transferred to **New Jersey** after **Colorado** franchise relocated, June 30, 1982. Traded to **Chicago** by **New Jersey** with New Jersey's 5th round choice (Rick Herbert) in 1985 Entry Draft for Don Dietrich, Rich Preston and Chicago's 2nd round choice (Eric Weinrich) in 1985 Entry Draft, June 19, 1984.

• MacNEIL, Al

Allister Wences D – L. 5'10", 183 lbs. b: Sydney, N.S., 9/27/1935.

Season	Club	League	GP	G	A	Pts	AG	AA	APts	PIM	PP	SH	GW	S	%	TGF	PGF	TGA	PGA	+/–	GP	G	A	Pts	PIM	PP	SH	GW
1951-52	Sydney Academy	Hi-School	STATISTICS NOT AVAILABLE																									
1952-53	Weston Dukes	OHA-B	STATISTICS NOT AVAILABLE																									
1953-54	Toronto Marlboros	OHA-Jr.	59	3	12	15				112											15	2	3	5	18			
1954-55	Toronto Marlboros	OHA-Jr.	47	3	16	19				141											13	0	4	4	*37			
	Toronto Marlboros	Mem-Cup	11	2	3	5				17																		
1955-56	Toronto Marlboros	OHA-Jr.	48	9	12	21				58											11	0	5	5	*63			
	Toronto Maple Leafs	**NHL**	**1**	**0**	**0**	**0**	**0**	**0**	**0**	**2**																		
	Toronto Marlboros	Mem-Cup	13	3	6	9				28																		
1956-57	**Toronto Maple Leafs**	**NHL**	**53**	**4**	**8**	**12**	**5**	**9**	**14**	**84**																		
	Rochester Americans	AHL	13	0	4	4				35																		

			REGULAR SEASON																		PLAYOFFS							
Season	Club	League	GP	G	A	Pts	AG	AA	APts	PIM	PP	SH	GW	S	%	TGF	PGF	TGA	PGA	+/–	GP	G	A	Pts	PIM	PP	SH	GW
1957-58	**Toronto Maple Leafs**	**NHL**	**13**	**0**	**0**	**0**	**0**	**0**	**0**	**9**	....	....	....	....	....	....	....	....	....	....	....	....	....	....	....	....	....	....
	Rochester Americans	AHL	54	3	18	21	....	....	....	91	....	....	....	....	....	....	....	....	....	....	....	....	....	....	....	....	....	....
1958-59	Rochester Americans	AHL	69	4	13	17	....	....	....	119	....	....	....	....	....	....	....	....	....	....	5	1	1	2	17	....	....	....
1959-60	**Toronto Maple Leafs**	**NHL**	**4**	**0**	**0**	**0**	**0**	**0**	**0**	**2**	....	....	....	....	....	....	....	....	....	....	....	....	....	....	....	....	....	....
	Rochester Americans	AHL	49	4	16	20	....	....	....	44	....	....	....	....	....	....	....	....	....	....	12	1	2	3	12	....	....	....
1960-61	Hull-Ottawa Canadiens	EPHL	60	6	20	26	....	....	....	101	....	....	....	....	....	....	....	....	....	....	14	2	4	6	21	....	....	....
1961-62	**Montreal Canadiens**	**NHL**	**61**	**1**	**7**	**8**	**1**	**7**	**8**	**74**	....	....	....	....	....	....	....	....	....	....	**5**	**0**	**0**	**0**	**2**	**0**	**0**	**0**
1962-63	**Chicago Black Hawks**	**NHL**	**70**	**2**	**19**	**21**	**2**	**19**	**21**	**100**	....	....	....	....	....	....	....	....	....	....	**4**	**0**	**1**	**1**	**4**	**0**	**0**	**0**
1963-64	**Chicago Black Hawks**	**NHL**	**70**	**5**	**19**	**24**	**6**	**20**	**26**	**91**	....	....	....	....	....	....	....	....	....	....	**7**	**0**	**2**	**2**	**25**	**0**	**0**	**0**
1964-65	**Chicago Black Hawks**	**NHL**	**69**	**3**	**7**	**10**	**4**	**7**	**11**	**119**	....	....	....	....	....	....	....	....	....	....	**14**	**0**	**1**	**1**	**34**	**0**	**0**	**0**
1965-66	**Chicago Black Hawks**	**NHL**	**51**	**0**	**1**	**1**	**0**	**1**	**1**	**34**	....	....	....	....	....	....	....	....	....	....	**3**	**0**	**0**	**0**	**0**	**0**	**0**	**0**
1966-67	**New York Rangers**	**NHL**	**58**	**0**	**4**	**4**	**0**	**4**	**4**	**44**	....	....	....	....	....	....	....	....	....	....	**4**	**0**	**0**	**0**	**2**	**0**	**0**	**0**
1967-68	**Pittsburgh Penguins**	**NHL**	**74**	**2**	**10**	**12**	**2**	**10**	**12**	**58**	**0**	**0**	**0**	**76**	**2.6**	**61**	**1**	**75**	**9**	**–6**	....	....	....	....	....	....	....	....
1968-69	Houston Apollos	CHL	70	1	11	12	....	....	....	79	....	....	....	....	....	....	....	....	....	....	3	0	1	1	0	....	....	....
1969-70	Montreal Voyageurs	AHL	66	0	10	10	....	....	....	14	....	....	....	....	....	....	....	....	....	....	8	0	1	1	0	....	....	....
1970-71	**Montreal Canadiens**	**NHL**	DID NOT PLAY – COACHING																									
	NHL Totals		**524**	**17**	**75**	**92**	**20**	**77**	**97**	**617**	....	....	....	....	....	....	....	....	....	....	**37**	**0**	**4**	**4**	**67**	....	....	....

EPHL First All-Star Team (1961)

Traded to **Montreal** by **Toronto** for Stan Smrke, June 7, 1960. Traded to **Chicago** by **Montreal** for Wayne Hicks, May 30, 1962. Claimed by **Montreal** from **Chicago** in Intra-League Draft, June 15, 1966. Claimed by **NY Rangers** from **Montreal** in Intra-League Draft, June 15, 1966. Claimed by **Pittsburgh** from **NY Rangers** in Expansion Draft, June 6, 1967. Traded to **Montreal** by **Pittsburgh** for Wally Boyer, June 12, 1968. • Named Player/Coach of **Houston** (CHL), September, 1968.

• MacNEIL, Bernie

Stephan Bernard LW – L. 5'11", 190 lbs. b: Sudbury, Ont., 3/7/1950. Detroit's 6th, 82nd overall, in 1970.

Season	Club	League	GP	G	A	Pts	AG	AA	APts	PIM	PP	SH	GW	S	%	TGF	PGF	TGA	PGA	+/–	GP	G	A	Pts	PIM	PP	SH	GW
1968-69	Espanola Miners	NOJHA	STATISTICS NOT AVAILABLE																									
1969-70	Espanola Miners	NOJHA	40	34	47	81	....	....	....	276	....	....	....	....	....	....	....	....	....	....	....	....	....	....	....	....	....	....
1970-71	Fort Wayne Komets	IHL	69	24	21	45	....	....	....	121	....	....	....	....	....	....	....	....	....	....	5	2	0	2	18	....	....	....
1971-72	Fort Wayne Komets	IHL	67	19	13	32	....	....	....	140	....	....	....	....	....	....	....	....	....	....	8	0	0	0	2	....	....	....
1972-73	Greensboro Generals	EHL	10	6	12	18	....	....	....	72	....	....	....	....	....	....	....	....	....	....	....	....	....	....	....	....	....	....
	Los Angeles Sharks	WHA	42	4	7	11	....	....	....	48	....	....	....	....	....	....	....	....	....	....	3	0	0	0	4	....	....	....
1973-74	**St. Louis Blues**	**NHL**	**4**	**0**	**0**	**0**	**0**	**0**	**0**	**0**	**0**	**0**	**0**	**5**	**0.0**	**1**	**0**	**0**	**0**	**1**	....	....	....	....	....	....	....	....
	Denver Spurs	WHL	33	8	15	23	....	....	....	151	....	....	....	....	....	....	....	....	....	....	....	....	....	....	....	....	....	....
	San Diego Gulls	WHL	35	5	10	15	....	....	....	86	....	....	....	....	....	....	....	....	....	....	4	0	3	3	10	....	....	....
1974-75	Rochester Americans	AHL	9	0	1	1	....	....	....	12	....	....	....	....	....	....	....	....	....	....	....	....	....	....	....	....	....	....
	Binghamton Dusters	NAHL	53	12	20	32	....	....	....	145	....	....	....	....	....	....	....	....	....	....	14	5	4	9	*55	....	....	....
1975-76	Cincinnati Stingers	WHA	77	15	12	27	....	....	....	83	....	....	....	....	....	....	....	....	....	....	....	....	....	....	....	....	....	....
	NHL Totals		**4**	**0**	**0**	**0**	**0**	**0**	**0**	**0**	**0**	**0**	**0**	**5**	**0.0**	**1**	**0**	**0**	**0**		....	....	....	....	....	....	....	....
	Other Major League Totals		119	19	19	38	....	....	....	131	....	....	....	....	....	....	....	....	....	....	3	0	0	0	4	....	....	....

NOJHA Second All-Star Team (1970)

Selected by **LA Sharks** (WHA) in 1972 WHA General Player Draft, February 12, 1972. Traded to **San Diego** (WHL) by **St. Louis** (Denver-WHL) for Jim Stanfield, January 16, 1974. Signed as a free agent by **St. Louis**, September, 1975. Signed as a free agent by **Cincinnati** (WHA), May, 1975.

• MACOUN, Jamie

James Neil D – L. 6'2", 200 lbs. b: Newmarket, Ont., 8/17/1961.

Season	Club	League	GP	G	A	Pts	AG	AA	APts	PIM	PP	SH	GW	S	%	TGF	PGF	TGA	PGA	+/–	GP	G	A	Pts	PIM	PP	SH	GW
1978-79	Newmarket Flyers	OJHL	49	9	14	23	....	....	....	33	....	....	....	....	....	....	....	....	....	....	....	....	....	....	....	....	....	....
1979-80	Aurora Tigers	OJHL	13	1	11	12	....	....	....	26	....	....	....	....	....	....	....	....	....	....	....	....	....	....	....	....	....	....
	Newmarket Flyers	OJHL	30	9	19	28	....	....	....	30	....	....	....	....	....	....	....	....	....	....	....	....	....	....	....	....	....	....
1980-81	Newmarket Flyers	OJHL	4	0	0	0	....	....	....	5	....	....	....	....	....	....	....	....	....	....	....	....	....	....	....	....	....	....
	Ohio State University	CCHA	38	9	20	29	....	....	....	83	....	....	....	....	....	....	....	....	....	....	....	....	....	....	....	....	....	....
1981-82	Ohio State University	CCHA	25	2	18	20	....	....	....	89	....	....	....	....	....	....	....	....	....	....	....	....	....	....	....	....	....	....
1982-83	Ohio State University	CCHA	19	6	21	27	....	....	....	54	....	....	....	....	....	....	....	....	....	....	....	....	....	....	....	....	....	....
	Calgary Flames	**NHL**	**22**	**1**	**4**	**5**	**1**	**3**	**4**	**25**	**0**	**0**	**0**	**18**	**5.6**	**16**	**0**	**13**	**0**	**3**	**9**	**0**	**2**	**2**	**8**	**0**	**0**	**0**
1983-84	**Calgary Flames**	**NHL**	**72**	**9**	**23**	**32**	**7**	**16**	**23**	**97**	**0**	**1**	**0**	**165**	**5.5**	**95**	**2**	**121**	**31**	**3**	**11**	**1**	**0**	**1**	**0**	**1**	**0**	**0**
1984-85	**Calgary Flames**	**NHL**	**70**	**9**	**30**	**39**	**7**	**20**	**27**	**67**	**0**	**0**	**2**	**129**	**7.0**	**110**	**1**	**105**	**40**	**44**	**4**	**1**	**0**	**1**	**4**	**0**	**0**	**0**
	Canada	WEC-A	9	0	0	0	....	....	....	10	....	....	....	....	....	....	....	....	....	....	....	....	....	....	....	....	....	....
1985-86	**Calgary Flames**	**NHL**	**77**	**11**	**21**	**32**	**9**	**14**	**23**	**81**	**0**	**2**	**1**	**133**	**8.3**	**91**	**2**	**120**	**45**	**14**	**22**	**1**	**6**	**7**	**23**	**0**	**0**	**0**
1986-87	**Calgary Flames**	**NHL**	**79**	**7**	**33**	**40**	**6**	**24**	**30**	**111**	**1**	**0**	**0**	**137**	**5.1**	**118**	**14**	**114**	**43**	**33**	**3**	**0**	**1**	**1**	**8**	**0**	**0**	**0**
1987-88	**Calgary Flames**	**NHL**	DID NOT PLAY – INJURED																									
1988-89♦	**Calgary Flames**	**NHL**	**72**	**8**	**19**	**27**	**7**	**13**	**20**	**76**	**0**	**0**	**2**	**89**	**9.0**	**92**	**3**	**73**	**24**	**40**	**22**	**3**	**6**	**9**	**30**	**0**	**0**	**1**
1989-90	Calgary Flames	Fr-Tour	1	0	0	0	....	....	....	0	....	....	....	....	....	....	....	....	....	....	....	....	....	....	....	....	....	....
	Calgary Flames	**NHL**	**78**	**8**	**27**	**35**	**7**	**19**	**26**	**70**	**1**	**0**	**1**	**120**	**6.7**	**97**	**10**	**95**	**42**	**34**	**6**	**0**	**3**	**3**	**10**	**0**	**0**	**0**
	Canada	WEC-A	8	1	1	2	....	....	....	6	....	....	....	....	....	....	....	....	....	....	....	....	....	....	....	....	....	....
1990-91	**Calgary Flames**	**NHL**	**79**	**7**	**15**	**22**	**6**	**11**	**17**	**84**	**1**	**1**	**0**	**117**	**6.0**	**111**	**7**	**112**	**37**	**29**	**7**	**0**	**1**	**1**	**4**	**0**	**0**	**0**
	Canada	WEC-A	8	4	1	5	....	....	....	10	....	....	....	....	....	....	....	....	....	....	....	....	....	....	....	....	....	....
1991-92	**Calgary Flames**	**NHL**	**37**	**2**	**12**	**14**	**2**	**9**	**11**	**53**	**1**	**0**	**0**	**58**	**3.4**	**45**	**4**	**45**	**14**	**10**	....	....	....	....	....	....	....	....
	Toronto Maple Leafs	**NHL**	**39**	**3**	**13**	**16**	**3**	**10**	**13**	**18**	**2**	**0**	**0**	**71**	**4.2**	**70**	**24**	**65**	**19**	**0**	....	....	....	....	....	....	....	....
1992-93	**Toronto Maple Leafs**	**NHL**	**77**	**4**	**15**	**19**	**3**	**10**	**13**	**55**	**2**	**0**	**1**	**114**	**3.5**	**86**	**16**	**105**	**38**	**3**	**21**	**0**	**6**	**6**	**36**	**0**	**0**	**0**
1993-94	**Toronto Maple Leafs**	**NHL**	**82**	**3**	**27**	**30**	**3**	**21**	**24**	**115**	**1**	**0**	**1**	**122**	**2.5**	**83**	**14**	**114**	**40**	**–5**	**18**	**1**	**1**	**2**	**12**	**0**	**0**	**0**
1994-95	**Toronto Maple Leafs**	**NHL**	**46**	**2**	**8**	**10**	**4**	**12**	**16**	**75**	**1**	**0**	**0**	**84**	**2.4**	**43**	**4**	**60**	**15**	**–6**	**7**	**1**	**2**	**3**	**8**	**0**	**0**	**0**
1995-96	**Toronto Maple Leafs**	**NHL**	**82**	**0**	**8**	**8**	**0**	**7**	**7**	**87**	**0**	**0**	**0**	**74**	**0.0**	**62**	**1**	**105**	**46**	**2**	**6**	**0**	**2**	**2**	**8**	**0**	**0**	**0**
1996-97	**Toronto Maple Leafs**	**NHL**	**73**	**1**	**10**	**11**	**1**	**9**	**10**	**93**	**0**	**0**	**1**	**64**	**1.6**	**61**	**0**	**103**	**28**	**–14**	....	....	....	....	....	....	....	....
1997-98	**Toronto Maple Leafs**	**NHL**	**67**	**0**	**7**	**7**	**0**	**7**	**7**	**63**	**0**	**0**	**0**	**67**	**0.0**	**45**	**0**	**83**	**21**	**–17**	....	....	....	....	....	....	....	....
♦	**Detroit Red Wings**	**NHL**	**7**	**0**	**0**	**0**	**0**	**0**	**0**	**2**	**0**	**0**	**0**	**11**	**0.0**	**4**	**0**	**7**	**3**	**0**	**22**	**2**	**2**	**4**	**18**	**0**	**0**	**2**
1998-99	**Detroit Red Wings**	**NHL**	**69**	**1**	**10**	**11**	**1**	**10**	**11**	**36**	**0**	**0**	**0**	**62**	**1.6**	**44**	**0**	**56**	**11**	**–1**	**1**	**0**	**0**	**0**	**0**	**0**	**0**	**0**
	NHL Totals		**1128**	**76**	**282**	**358**	**67**	**215**	**282**	**1208**	**10**	**4**	**9**	**1635**	**4.6**	**1273**	**102**	**1496**	**497**		**159**	**10**	**32**	**42**	**169**	**1**	**0**	**3**

NHL All-Rookie Team (1984) • Named Best Defenseman at WEC-A (1991)

Signed as a free agent by **Calgary**, January 30, 1983. • Missed entire 1987-88 season recovering from arm injury suffered in automobile accident, May, 1987. Traded to **Toronto** by **Calgary** with Doug Gilmour, Ric Natress, Kent Manderville and Rick Wamsley for Gary Leeman, Alexander Godynyuk, Jeff Reese, Michel Petit and Craig Berube, January 2, 1992. Traded to **Detroit** by **Toronto** for Tampa Bay's 4th round choice (previously acquired, Toronto selected Alexei Ponikarovsky) in 1998 Entry Draft, March 24, 1998.

• MacSWEYN, Ralph

Donald Ralph D – R. 5'11", 190 lbs. b: Hawkesbury, Ont., 9/8/1942.

Season	Club	League	GP	G	A	Pts	AG	AA	APts	PIM	PP	SH	GW	S	%	TGF	PGF	TGA	PGA	+/–	GP	G	A	Pts	PIM	PP	SH	GW
1963-64	Lancaster Dodgers	SLSHL	STATISTICS NOT AVAILABLE																									
1964-65	Johnstown Jets	EHL	51	2	17	19	....	....	....	19	....	....	....	....	....	....	....	....	....	....	5	0	1	1	6	....	....	....
1965-66	Johnstown Jets	EHL	71	6	26	32	....	....	....	38	....	....	....	....	....	....	....	....	....	....	3	0	0	0	0	....	....	....
1966-67	Portland Buckaroos	WHL	1	0	0	0	....	....	....	0	....	....	....	....	....	....	....	....	....	....	....	....	....	....	....	....	....	....
	Johnstown Jets	EHL	72	6	28	34	....	....	....	82	....	....	....	....	....	....	....	....	....	....	5	0	3	3	6	....	....	....
1967-68	**Philadelphia Flyers**	**NHL**	**4**	**0**	**0**	**0**	**0**	**0**	**0**	**0**	**0**	**0**	**0**	**2**	**0.0**	**2**	**0**	**1**	**0**	**1**	....	....	....	....	....	....	....	....
	Quebec Aces	AHL	51	2	11	13	....	....	....	56	....	....	....	....	....	....	....	....	....	....	15	0	8	8	37	....	....	....
1968-69	**Philadelphia Flyers**	**NHL**	**24**	**0**	**4**	**4**	**0**	**4**	**4**	**6**	**0**	**0**	**0**	**12**	**0.0**	**26**	**0**	**31**	**9**	**4**	**4**	**0**	**0**	**0**	**4**	**0**	**0**	**0**
	Quebec Aces	AHL	41	1	12	13	....	....	....	30	....	....	....	....	....	....	....	....	....	....	....	....	....	....	....	....	....	....
1969-70	**Philadelphia Flyers**	**NHL**	**17**	**0**	**0**	**0**	**0**	**0**	**0**	**4**	**0**	**0**	**0**	**8**	**0.0**	**9**	**0**	**19**	**3**	**–7**	....	....	....	....	....	....	....	....
	Quebec Aces	AHL	54	2	19	21	....	....	....	31	....	....	....	....	....	....	....	....	....	....	6	0	3	3	9	....	....	....
1970-71	Quebec Aces	AHL	72	2	24	26	....	....	....	50	....	....	....	....	....	....	....	....	....	....	1	0	0	0	2	....	....	....
	Philadelphia Flyers	**NHL**	....	....	....	....	....	....	....	....	....	....	....	....	....	....	....	....	....	....	**4**	**0**	**0**	**0**	**2**	**0**	**0**	**0**
1971-72	**Philadelphia Flyers**	**NHL**	**2**	**0**	**1**	**1**	**0**	**1**	**1**	**0**	**0**	**0**	**0**	**2**	**0.0**	**3**	**1**	**2**	**0**	**0**	....	....	....	....	....	....	....	....
	Richmond Robins	AHL	60	0	15	15	....	....	....	52	....	....	....	....	....	....	....	....	....	....	....	....	....	....	....	....	....	....
1972-73	Los Angeles Sharks	WHA	78	0	23	23	....	....	....	39	....	....	....	....	....	....	....	....	....	....	6	1	2	3	4	....	....	....
1973-74	Los Angeles Sharks	WHA	13	0	3	3	....	....	....	6	....	....	....	....	....	....	....	....	....	....	....	....	....	....	....	....	....	....
	Vancouver Blazers	WHA	56	2	18	20	....	....	....	52	....	....	....	....	....	....	....	....	....	....	....	....	....	....	....	....	....	....
1974-75	Richmond Robins	AHL	54	1	6	7	....	....	....	32	....	....	....	....	....	....	....	....	....	....	6	0	3	3	6	....	....	....
1975-76	Baltimore Clippers	AHL	74	4	8	12	....	....	....	42	....	....	....	....	....	....	....	....	....	....	....	....	....	....	....	....	....	....

			REGULAR SEASON																		PLAYOFFS							
Season	Club	League	GP	G	A	Pts	AG	AA	APts	PIM	PP	SH	GW	S	%	TGF	PGF	TGA	PGA	+/–	GP	G	A	Pts	PIM	PP	SH	GW
1976-77	Richmond Wildcats	SHL	37	1	6	7	....	....	....	10	....	....	....	....	....	....	....	....	....	....	....	....	....	....	....	....	....	....
	Johnstown Jets	NAHL	26	0	7	7	....	....	....	8	....	....	....	....	....	....	....	....	....	....	3	0	2	2	0	....	....	....
1977-78	Embrum Panthers	PIHA	STATISTICS NOT AVAILABLE																									
	NHL Totals		**47**	**0**	**5**	**5**	**0**	**5**	**5**	**10**	**0**	**0**	**0**	**24**	**0.0**	**40**	**1**	**53**	**12**		**8**	**0**	**0**	**0**	**6**	**0**	**0**	**0**
	Other Major League Totals		147	2	44	46	....	....	....	97	....	....	....	....	....	....	....	....	....	....	6	1	2	3	4	....	....	....

EHL North First All-Star Team (1967) • AHL First All-Star Team (1971) • AHL Second All-Star Team (1972)

NHL rights transferred to **Philadelphia** after NHL club purchased **Quebec** (AHL) franchise, May 8, 1967. Selected by **LA Sharks** (WHA) in 1972 WHA General Player Draft, February 12, 1972. Traded to **Vancouver** (WHA) by **LA Sharks** (WHA) to complete transaction that sent Ron Ward to LA Sharks (October, 1973), November 5, 1973.

• MacTAVISH, Craig

C – L. 6'1", 195 lbs. b: London, Ont., 8/15/1958. Boston's 8th, 153rd overall, in 1978.

Season	Club	League	GP	G	A	Pts	AG	AA	APts	PIM	PP	SH	GW	S	%	TGF	PGF	TGA	PGA	+/–	GP	G	A	Pts	PIM	PP	SH	GW
1977-78	U. of Massachusetts-Lowell	ECAC 2	21	26	19	45	....	....	....	....	....	....	....	....	....	....	....	....	....	....	....	....	....	....	....	....	....	....
1978-79	U. of Massachusetts-Lowell	ECAC 2	31	36	52	*88	....	....	....	....	....	....	....	....	....	....	....	....	....	....	....	....	....	....	....	....	....	....
1979-80	**Boston Bruins**	**NHL**	**46**	**11**	**17**	**28**	**9**	**12**	**21**	**8**	**0**	**0**	**2**	**61**	**18.0**	**44**	**6**	**22**	**0**	**16**	**10**	**2**	**3**	**5**	**7**	**0**	**0**	**0**
	Binghamton Dusters	AHL	34	17	15	32	....	....	....	29	....	....	....	....	....	....	....	....	....	....	....	....	....	....	....	....	....	....
1980-81	**Boston Bruins**	**NHL**	**24**	**3**	**5**	**8**	**2**	**3**	**5**	**13**	**0**	**0**	**0**	**44**	**6.8**	**16**	**5**	**12**	**0**	**–1**	....	....	....	....	....	....	....	....
	Springfield Indians	AHL	53	19	24	43	....	....	....	81	....	....	....	....	....	....	....	....	....	....	7	5	4	9	8	....	....	....
1981-82	**Boston Bruins**	**NHL**	**2**	**0**	**1**	**1**	**0**	**1**	**1**	**0**	**0**	**0**	**0**	**1**	**0.0**	**1**	**0**	**1**	**0**	**0**	....	....	....	....	....	....	....	....
	Erie Blades	AHL	72	23	32	55	....	....	....	37	....	....	....	....	....	....	....	....	....	....	....	....	....	....	....	....	....	....
1982-83	**Boston Bruins**	**NHL**	**75**	**10**	**20**	**30**	**8**	**14**	**22**	**18**	**0**	**0**	**1**	**120**	**8.3**	**51**	**2**	**34**	**0**	**15**	**17**	**3**	**1**	**4**	**18**	**0**	**0**	**0**
1983-84	**Boston Bruins**	**NHL**	**70**	**20**	**23**	**43**	**16**	**16**	**32**	**35**	**7**	**0**	**4**	**135**	**14.8**	**61**	**11**	**42**	**1**	**9**	**1**	**0**	**0**	**0**	**0**	**0**	**0**	**0**
1984-85	**Boston Bruins**	**NHL**	DID NOT PLAY – SUSPENDED																									
1985-86	**Edmonton Oilers**	**NHL**	**74**	**23**	**24**	**47**	**18**	**16**	**34**	**70**	**4**	**1**	**5**	**121**	**19.0**	**70**	**8**	**63**	**18**	**17**	**10**	**4**	**4**	**8**	**11**	**1**	**0**	**0**
1986-87♦	**Edmonton Oilers**	**NHL**	**79**	**20**	**19**	**39**	**17**	**14**	**31**	**55**	**1**	**4**	**2**	**140**	**14.3**	**57**	**4**	**70**	**26**	**9**	**21**	**1**	**9**	**10**	**16**	**0**	**0**	**0**
1987-88♦	**Edmonton Oilers**	**NHL**	**80**	**15**	**17**	**32**	**13**	**12**	**25**	**47**	**0**	**3**	**5**	**90**	**16.7**	**51**	**6**	**75**	**27**	**–3**	**19**	**0**	**1**	**1**	**31**	**0**	**0**	**0**
1988-89	**Edmonton Oilers**	**NHL**	**80**	**21**	**31**	**52**	**18**	**22**	**40**	**55**	**2**	**4**	**2**	**120**	**17.5**	**64**	**4**	**84**	**34**	**10**	**7**	**0**	**1**	**1**	**8**	**0**	**0**	**0**
1989-90♦	**Edmonton Oilers**	**NHL**	**80**	**21**	**22**	**43**	**18**	**16**	**34**	**89**	**1**	**6**	**5**	**109**	**19.3**	**62**	**2**	**87**	**40**	**13**	**22**	**2**	**6**	**8**	**29**	**0**	**0**	**0**
1990-91	**Edmonton Oilers**	**NHL**	**80**	**17**	**15**	**32**	**16**	**11**	**27**	**76**	**2**	**6**	**1**	**113**	**15.0**	**44**	**4**	**82**	**41**	**–1**	**18**	**3**	**3**	**6**	**20**	**0**	**0**	**1**
1991-92	**Edmonton Oilers**	**NHL**	**80**	**12**	**18**	**30**	**11**	**14**	**25**	**98**	**0**	**2**	**1**	**86**	**14.0**	**46**	**2**	**93**	**48**	**–1**	**16**	**3**	**0**	**3**	**28**	**0**	**1**	**1**
1992-93	**Edmonton Oilers**	**NHL**	**82**	**10**	**20**	**30**	**8**	**14**	**22**	**110**	**0**	**3**	**3**	**101**	**9.9**	**40**	**2**	**102**	**48**	**–16**	....	....	....	....	....	....	....	....
1993-94	**Edmonton Oilers**	**NHL**	**66**	**16**	**10**	**26**	**15**	**8**	**23**	**80**	**0**	**0**	**1**	**97**	**16.5**	**27**	**2**	**72**	**27**	**–20**	....	....	....	....	....	....	....	....
♦	**New York Rangers**	**NHL**	**12**	**4**	**2**	**6**	**4**	**2**	**6**	**11**	**1**	**0**	**1**	**25**	**16.0**	**10**	**1**	**5**	**2**	**6**	**23**	**1**	**4**	**5**	**22**	**0**	**0**	**0**
1994-95	**Philadelphia Flyers**	**NHL**	**45**	**3**	**9**	**12**	**5**	**13**	**18**	**23**	**0**	**0**	**0**	**38**	**7.9**	**19**	**0**	**47**	**30**	**2**	**15**	**1**	**4**	**5**	**20**	**0**	**0**	**0**
1995-96	**Philadelphia Flyers**	**NHL**	**55**	**5**	**8**	**13**	**5**	**7**	**12**	**62**	**0**	**0**	**1**	**42**	**11.9**	**18**	**0**	**32**	**11**	**–3**	....	....	....	....	....	....	....	....
	St. Louis Blues	**NHL**	**13**	**0**	**1**	**1**	**0**	**1**	**1**	**8**	**0**	**0**	**0**	**16**	**0.0**	**3**	**0**	**13**	**4**	**–6**	**13**	**0**	**2**	**2**	**6**	**0**	**0**	**0**
1996-97	**St. Louis Blues**	**NHL**	**50**	**2**	**5**	**7**	**2**	**4**	**6**	**33**	**0**	**0**	**0**	**26**	**7.7**	**10**	**0**	**31**	**9**	**–12**	**1**	**0**	**0**	**0**	**2**	**0**	**0**	**0**
1997-1999	**New York Rangers**	**NHL**	DID NOT PLAY – ASSISTANT COACH																									
99-2000	**Edmonton Oilers**	**NHL**	DID NOT PLAY – ASSISTANT COACH																									
	NHL Totals		**1093**	**213**	**267**	**480**	**185**	**200**	**385**	**891**	**18**	**29**	**34**	**1485**	**14.3**	**694**	**59**	**967**	**366**		**193**	**20**	**38**	**58**	**218**	**1**	**1**	**2**

NCAA (College Div.) East All-American Team (1979) • Played in NHL All-Star Game (1996) • Suspended for entire 1984-85 season after being convicted of vehicular homicide, May, 1984. Signed as a free agent by **Edmonton,** February 1, 1985. Traded to **NY Rangers** by **Edmonton** for Todd Marchant, March 21, 1994. Signed as a free agent by **Philadelphia**, July 6, 1994. Traded to **St. Louis** by **Philadelphia** for Dale Hawerchuk, March 15, 1996. • Named Head Coach of Edmonton Oilers, June 22, 2000.

• MacWilliam, Mike

Michael Kristen LW – L. 6'4", 230 lbs. b: Burnaby, B.C., 2/14/1967.

Season	Club	League	GP	G	A	Pts	AG	AA	APts	PIM	PP	SH	GW	S	%	TGF	PGF	TGA	PGA	+/–	GP	G	A	Pts	PIM	PP	SH	GW
1984-85	Langley Eagles	BCJHL	13	2	1	3	....	....	....	63	....	....	....	....	....	....	....	....	....	....	....	....	....	....	....	....	....	....
	Kamloops Blazers	WHL	3	0	0	0	....	....	....	4	....	....	....	....	....	....	....	....	....	....	....	....	....	....	....	....	....	....
	New Westminster Bruins	WHL	5	0	0	0	....	....	....	5	....	....	....	....	....	....	....	....	....	....	....	....	....	....	....	....	....	....
1985-86	New Westminster Bruins	WHL	52	8	6	14	....	....	....	98	....	....	....	....	....	....	....	....	....	....	....	....	....	....	....	....	....	....
1986-87	Medicine Hat Tigers	WHL	44	7	17	24	....	....	....	134	....	....	....	....	....	....	....	....	....	....	19	1	0	1	35	....	....	....
	Medicine Hat Tigers	Mem-Cup	1	0	0	0	....	....	....	10	....	....	....	....	....	....	....	....	....	....	....	....	....	....	....	....	....	....
1987-88			DID NOT PLAY – INJURED																									
1988-89	Milwaukee Admirals	IHL	6	1	1	2	....	....	....	28	....	....	....	....	....	....	....	....	....	....	1	0	0	0	0	....	....	....
	Flint Spirits	IHL	18	0	0	0	....	....	....	92	....	....	....	....	....	....	....	....	....	....	....	....	....	....	....	....	....	....
1989-90			DID NOT PLAY – INJURED																									
1990-91	Adirondack Red Wings	AHL	8	0	0	0	....	....	....	32	....	....	....	....	....	....	....	....	....	....	....	....	....	....	....	....	....	....
	Greensboro Monarchs	ECHL	15	2	7	9	....	....	....	94	....	....	....	....	....	....	....	....	....	....	9	3	1	4	*118	....	....	....
1991-92	St. John's Maple Leafs	AHL	44	7	8	15	....	....	....	301	....	....	....	....	....	....	....	....	....	....	2	0	0	0	8	....	....	....
1992-93	Greensboro Monarchs	ECHL	12	5	5	10	....	....	....	137	....	....	....	....	....	....	....	....	....	....	....	....	....	....	....	....	....	....
1993-94	Tulsa Oilers	CHL	39	16	12	28	....	....	....	*326	....	....	....	....	....	....	....	....	....	....	8	4	0	4	88	....	....	....
1994-95	Denver Grizzlies	IHL	30	5	6	11	....	....	....	218	....	....	....	....	....	....	....	....	....	....	12	2	2	4	56	....	....	....
1995-96	**New York Islanders**	**NHL**	**6**	**0**	**0**	**0**	**0**	**0**	**0**	**14**	**0**	**0**	**0**	**4**	**0.0**	**0**	**0**	**1**	**0**	**–1**	....	....	....	....	....	....	....	....
	Utah Grizzlies	IHL	53	8	16	24	....	....	....	317	....	....	....	....	....	....	....	....	....	....	6	0	2	2	53	....	....	....
1996-97	Phoenix Roadrunners	IHL	29	1	3	4	....	....	....	169	....	....	....	....	....	....	....	....	....	....	....	....	....	....	....	....	....	....
1997-98	Cardiff Devils	BH-Cup	4	0	0	0	....	....	....	14	....	....	....	....	....	....	....	....	....	....	....	....	....	....	....	....	....	....
	Cardiff Devils	Britain	27	4	0	4	....	....	....	82	....	....	....	....	....	....	....	....	....	....	9	3	1	4	16	....	....	....
1998-99	Cardiff Devils	BH-Cup	10	3	1	4	....	....	....	*101	....	....	....	....	....	....	....	....	....	....	....	....	....	....	....	....	....	....
	Cardiff Devils	Britain	32	7	10	17	....	....	....	141	....	....	....	....	....	....	....	....	....	....	8	0	0	0	51	....	....	....
	NHL Totals		**6**	**0**	**0**	**0**	**0**	**0**	**0**	**14**	**0**	**0**	**0**	**4**	**0.0**	**0**	**0**	**1**	**0**									

Signed as a free agent by **Philadelphia**, October 7, 1986. Signed as a free agent by **Toronto**, July 30, 1991. Signed as a free agent by **NY Islanders**, July 25, 1995. • Played w/ RHI's Sacremento River Rats (7-5-5-10-59) and Vancouver Voodoo (11-3-6-9-74) in 1994.

• MADDEN, John

John Joseph LW – L. 5'11", 195 lbs. b: Barrie, Ont., 5/4/1975.

Season	Club	League	GP	G	A	Pts	AG	AA	APts	PIM	PP	SH	GW	S	%	TGF	PGF	TGA	PGA	+/–	GP	G	A	Pts	PIM	PP	SH	GW
1989-90	Alliston Hornets	OJHL-C	31	24	25	49	....	....	....	26	....	....	....	....	....	....	....	....	....	....	....	....	....	....	....	....	....	....
1990-91	Alliston Hornets	OJHL-C	14	15	21	36	....	....	....	10	....	....	....	....	....	....	....	....	....	....	....	....	....	....	....	....	....	....
	Barrie Colts	OJHL-B	1	0	0	0	....	....	....	0	....	....	....	....	....	....	....	....	....	....	....	....	....	....	....	....	....	....
1991-92	Barrie Colts	OJHL-B	42	50	54	104	....	....	....	46	....	....	....	....	....	....	....	....	....	....	13	10	9	19	14	....	....	....
1992-93	Barrie Colts	OJHL	43	49	75	124	....	....	....	62	....	....	....	....	....	....	....	....	....	....	....	....	....	....	....	....	....	....
1993-94	University of Michigan	CCHA	36	6	11	17	....	....	....	14	....	....	....	....	....	....	....	....	....	....	....	....	....	....	....	....	....	....
1994-95	University of Michigan	CCHA	39	21	22	43	....	....	....	8	....	....	....	....	....	....	....	....	....	....	....	....	....	....	....	....	....	....
1995-96	University of Michigan	CCHA	43	27	30	57	....	....	....	45	....	....	....	....	....	....	....	....	....	....	....	....	....	....	....	....	....	....
1996-97	University of Michigan	CCHA	42	26	37	63	....	....	....	56	....	....	....	....	....	....	....	....	....	....	....	....	....	....	....	....	....	....
1997-98	Albany River Rats	AHL	74	20	36	56	....	....	....	40	....	....	....	....	....	....	....	....	....	....	13	3	13	16	14	....	....	....
1998-99	**New Jersey Devils**	**NHL**	**4**	**0**	**1**	**1**	**0**	**1**	**1**	**0**	**0**	**0**	**0**	**4**	**0.0**	**1**	**1**	**3**	**1**	**–2**	....	....	....	....	....	....	....	....
	Albany River Rats	AHL	75	38	60	98	....	....	....	44	....	....	....	....	....	....	....	....	....	....	5	2	2	4	6	....	....	....
99-2000♦	**New Jersey Devils**	**NHL**	**74**	**16**	**9**	**25**	**18**	**8**	**26**	**6**	**0**	**6**	**3**	**115**	**13.9**	**33**	**0**	**44**	**18**	**7**	**20**	**3**	**4**	**7**	**0**	**0**	**1**	**2**
	NHL Totals		**78**	**16**	**10**	**26**	**18**	**9**	**27**	**6**	**0**	**6**	**3**	**119**	**13.4**	**34**	**1**	**47**	**19**		**20**	**3**	**4**	**7**	**0**	**0**	**1**	**2**

CCHA First All-Star Team (1997) • NCAA West First All-American Team (1997)

Signed as a free agent by **New Jersey**, June 26, 1997.

• MADIGAN, Connie

Cornelius Dennis "Mad Dog" D – L. 5'10", 185 lbs. b: Port Arthur, Ont., 10/4/1934.

Season	Club	League	GP	G	A	Pts	AG	AA	APts	PIM	PP	SH	GW	S	%	TGF	PGF	TGA	PGA	+/–	GP	G	A	Pts	PIM	PP	SH	GW
1952-53	Port Arthur Bruins	TBJHL	27	4	3	7	....	....	....	67	....	....	....	....	....	....	....	....	....	....	....	....	....	....	....	....	....	....
1953-54	Port Arthur Bruins	TBJHL	26	2	11	13	....	....	....	124	....	....	....	....	....	....	....	....	....	....	9	1	2	3	*18	....	....	....
1954-55	Port Arthur Bruins	TBJHL	34	7	11	18	....	....	....	*168	....	....	....	....	....	....	....	....	....	....	....	....	....	....	....	....	....	....
	Humboldt Indians	AJHL	5	0	0	0	....	....	....	0	....	....	....	....	....	....	....	....	....	....	....	....	....	....	....	....	....	....
1955-56	Penticton Vees	OSHL	54	4	18	22	....	....	....	231	....	....	....	....	....	....	....	....	....	....	....	....	....	....	....	....	....	....
1956-57	Penticton Vees	OSHL	STATISTICS NOT AVAILABLE																									
1957-58	Vernon Canadians	OSHL	8	0	3	3	....	....	....	34	....	....	....	....	....	....	....	....	....	....	....	....	....	....	....	....	....	....

			REGULAR SEASON																		PLAYOFFS							
Season	Club	League	GP	G	A	Pts	AG	AA	APts	PIM	PP	SH	GW	S	%	TGF	PGF	TGA	PGA	+/–	GP	G	A	Pts	PIM	PP	SH	GW
1958-59	Nelson Maple Leafs	WIHL	50	4	24	28				*145											11	2	4	6	*24			
	Spokane Comets	WHL	3	1	1	2				2																		
	Nelson Maple Leafs	Al-Cup	7	0	3	3				12																		
1959-60	Fort Wayne Komets	IHL	66	7	50	57				*272											13	0	3	3	44			
1960-61	Cleveland Barons	AHL	8	0	2	2				13																		
	Fort Wayne Komets	IHL	57	9	28	37				231											8	2	3	5	26			
1961-62	Fort Wayne Komets	IHL	2	0	0	0				9																		
	Spokane Comets	WHL	63	9	28	37				*171											16	0	4	4	28			
1962-63	Spokane Comets	WHL	48	7	15	22				115																		
1963-64	Los Angeles Blades	WHL	68	10	27	37				120											12	2	4	6	*49			
1964-65	Providence Reds	AHL	10	1	2	3				34																		
	Portland Buckaroos	WHL	60	11	20	31				158											10	1	4	5	18			
1965-66	Portland Buckaroos	WHL	72	13	31	44				159											14	1	6	7	15			
1966-67	Portland Buckaroos	WHL	72	9	42	51				147											4	2	1	3	6			
1967-68	Portland Buckaroos	WHL	59	7	25	32				105											12	1	5	6	16			
1968-69	Portland Buckaroos	WHL	71	3	25	28				175											10	1	8	9	22			
1969-70	Dallas Black Hawks	CHL	10	1	4	5				26																		
	Portland Buckaroos	WHL	60	5	28	33				101											11	0	6	6	59			
1970-71	Portland Buckaroos	WHL	72	8	59	67				175											3	0	3	3	38			
1971-72	Portland Buckaroos	WHL	61	8	48	56				170											11	0	7	7	*44			
1972-73	Portland Buckaroos	WHL	42	3	26	29				146																		
	St. Louis Blues	**NHL**	**20**	**0**	**3**	**3**	**0**	**2**	**2**	**25**	**0**	**0**	**0**	**11**	**0.0**	**16**	**0**	**16**	**1**	**1**	**5**	**0**	**0**	**0**	**4**	**0**	**0**	**0**
1973-74	San Diego Gulls	WHL	39	3	19	22				80																		
	Portland Buckaroos	WHL	16	0	12	12				22											9	0	2	2	*40			
1974-75	Portland Buckaroos	WIHL	10	2	11	13				20																		
	NHL Totals		**20**	**0**	**3**	**3**	**0**	**2**	**2**	**25**	**0**	**0**	**0**	**11**	**0.0**	**16**	**0**	**16**	**1**		**5**	**0**	**0**	**0**	**4**	**0**	**0**	**0**

WIHL First All-Star Team (1959) • IHL Second All-Star Team (1960) • WHL Second All-Star Team (1965, 1971, 1972) • WHL First All-Star Team (1966, 1967, 1968, 1969) • Won Hal Laycoe Cup (WHL Top Defenseman) (1966)

Rights transferred to **Toronto** after NHL club purchased **Spokane** (WHL) franchise, June 4, 1963. Transferred to **Denver** (WHL) after **Spokane** (WHL) franchise relocated, September, 1963. Traded to **LA Blades** (WHL) by **Toronto** (Denver-WHL) for cash, October, 1963. Traded to **Providence** (AHL) by **LA Blades** (WHL) for cash, September, 1964. Traded to **Portland** (WHL) by **Providence** (AHL) for cash, October, 1964. Traded to **St. Louis** by **Portland** (WHL) for cash and the loan of Andre Aubry for the remainder of the 1972-73 season, January 31, 1973. • Oldest rookie in NHL history. Traded to **San Diego** (WHL) by **St. Louis** for cash, September, 1973. Traded to **Portland** (WHL) by **San Diego** (WHL) for cash, February, 1974.

• MADILL, Jeff

Jeffrey G. "Mad Dog" RW – L. 5'11", 195 lbs. b: Oshawa, Ont., 6/21/1965. New Jersey's 2nd, 7th overall, in 1987 Supplemental Draft.

Season	Club	League	GP	G	A	Pts	AG	AA	APts	PIM	PP	SH	GW	S	%	TGF	PGF	TGA	PGA	+/–	GP	G	A	Pts	PIM	PP	SH	GW
1982-83	North York Rangers	OJHL	31	3	18	21				94																		
	North York Rangers	Cen-Cup																										
1983-84	North York Rangers	OJHL	40	44	41	85				94																		
1984-85	Ohio State University	CCHA	12	5	6	11				18																		
1985-86	Ohio State University	CCHA	41	32	25	57				65																		
1986-87	Ohio State University	CCHA	43	38	32	70				139																		
1987-88	Utica Devils	AHL	58	18	15	33				127																		
1988-89	Utica Devils	AHL	69	23	25	48				225											4	1	0	1	35			
1989-90	Utica Devils	AHL	74	43	26	69				233											4	1	2	3	33			
1990-91	**New Jersey Devils**	**NHL**	**14**	**4**	**0**	**4**	**4**	**0**	**4**	**46**	**0**	**0**	**0**	**24**	**16.7**	**6**	**2**	**7**	**2**	**–1**	**7**	**0**	**2**	**2**	**8**	**0**	**0**	**0**
	Utica Devils	AHL	54	42	35	77				151																		
1991-92	Kansas City Blades	IHL	62	32	20	52				167											6	2	2	4	30			
1992-93	Cincinnati Cyclones	IHL	58	36	17	53				175																		
	Milwaukee Admirals	IHL	23	13	6	19				53											4	3	0	3	9			
1993-94	Atlanta Knights	IHL	80	42	44	86				186											14	4	2	6	33			
1994-95	Denver Grizzlies	IHL	73	35	30	65				207											17	8	6	14	53			
1995-96	San Francisco Spiders	IHL	27	16	13	29				73																		
	Kansas City Blades	IHL	41	17	16	33				169											5	4	2	6	21			
1996-97	Kansas City Blades	IHL	59	18	18	36				42																		
	Phoenix Roadrunners	IHL	9	5	2	7				22																		
	NHL Totals		**14**	**4**	**0**	**4**	**4**	**0**	**4**	**46**	**0**	**0**	**0**	**24**	**16.7**	**6**	**2**	**7**	**2**		**7**	**0**	**2**	**2**	**8**	**0**	**0**	**0**

AHL Second All-Star Team (1991) • IHL Second All-Star Team (1993)

Claimed by **San Jose** from **New Jersey** in Expansion Draft, May 30, 1991. Traded to **Milwaukee** (IHL) by **Cincinnati** (IHL) for Ian Kidd, February 25, 1993. • Played w/ RHI's Atlanta Fire Ants in 1994 (12-12-18-30-30).

• MAGEE, Dean

Dean James LW – L. 6'2", 210 lbs. b: Rockey Mountain House, Alta., 4/29/1955. Minnesota's 8th, 130th overall, in 1975.

Season	Club	League	GP	G	A	Pts	AG	AA	APts	PIM	PP	SH	GW	S	%	TGF	PGF	TGA	PGA	+/–	GP	G	A	Pts	PIM	PP	SH	GW
1972-73	Calgary Canucks	AJHL	56	22	51	73				127																		
1973-74	Calgary Canucks	AJHL	56	36	30	66				142																		
1974-75	Colorado College	WCHA	36	15	13	28				130																		
1975-76	Colorado College	WCHA	33	9	7	16				104																		
1976-77	Colorado College	WCHA	39	23	18	41				144																		
1977-78	Colorado College	WCHA	25	13	15	28				60																		
	Minnesota North Stars	**NHL**	**7**	**0**	**0**	**0**	**0**	**0**	**0**	**4**	**0**	**0**	**0**	**4**	**0.0**	**0**	**0**	**3**	**0**	**–3**								
	Fort Worth Texans	CHL	3	0	0	0				0																		
1978-79	Indianapolis Racers	WHA	5	0	1	1				10																		
	Grand Rapids Owls	IHL	68	35	37	72				148											21	*15	11	26	45			
1979-80	Houston Apollos	CHL	70	24	34	58				73											6	2	4	6	6			
	NHL Totals		**7**	**0**	**0**	**0**	**0**	**0**	**0**	**4**	**0**	**0**	**0**	**4**	**0.0**	**0**	**0**	**3**	**0**									
	Other Major League Totals		5	0	1	1				10																		

Signed as a free agent by **Indianapolis** (WHA), November 15, 1978.

• MAGGS, Daryl

Daryl John D – R. 6'2", 195 lbs. b: Victoria, B.C., 4/6/1949. Chicago's 4th, 48th overall, in 1969.

Season	Club	League	GP	G	A	Pts	AG	AA	APts	PIM	PP	SH	GW	S	%	TGF	PGF	TGA	PGA	+/–	GP	G	A	Pts	PIM	PP	SH	GW
1967-68	Red Deer Rustlers	AJHL	60	6	20	26				50											11	2	3	5				
1968-69	Calgary Centennials	WCJHL	35	9	20	29				55																		
1969-70	University of Calgary	CWUAA	14	10	15	25				43											4	3	3	6	13			
1970-71	Dallas Black Hawks	CHL	71	14	36	50				144											10	5	1	6	23			
1971-72	**Chicago Black Hawks**	**NHL**	**59**	**7**	**4**	**11**	**7**	**3**	**10**	**4**	**0**	**0**	**0**	**47**	**14.9**	**17**	**0**	**18**	**0**	**–1**	**4**	**0**	**0**	**0**	**0**	**0**	**0**	**0**
1972-73	**Chicago Black Hawks**	**NHL**	**17**	**0**	**0**	**0**	**0**	**0**	**0**	**4**	**0**	**0**	**0**	**10**	**0.0**	**3**	**0**	**5**	**1**	**–1**								
	California Golden Seals	**NHL**	**54**	**7**	**15**	**22**	**7**	**12**	**19**	**46**	**0**	**0**	**1**	**95**	**7.4**	**65**	**8**	**90**	**11**	**–22**								
1973-74	Chicago Cougars	WHA	78	8	22	30				148											18	3	5	8	*71			
1974-75	Chicago Cougars	WHA	77	6	27	33				137																		
1975-76	Denver-Ottawa Civics	WHA	41	4	23	27				42																		
	Indianapolis Racers	WHA	36	5	16	21				40											7	1	0	1	20			
1976-77	Indianapolis Racers	WHA	81	16	55	71				114											9	1	4	5	4			
1977-78	Indianapolis Racers	WHA	51	6	15	21				30																		
	Cincinnati Stingers	WHA	11	2	5	7				7																		

			REGULAR SEASON																		PLAYOFFS							
Season	**Club**	**League**	**GP**	**G**	**A**	**Pts**	**AG**	**AA**	**APts**	**PIM**	**PP**	**SH**	**GW**	**S**	**%**	**TGF**	**PGF**	**TGA**	**PGA**	**+/–**	**GP**	**G**	**A**	**Pts**	**PIM**	**PP**	**SH**	**GW**
1978-79	Cincinnati Stingers	WHA	27	4	14	18	....	....	....	63	....	....	....	....	....	....	....	....	....	....	....	....	....	....	....	....	....	....
	Mannheimer ERC	Germany	11	6	4	10	....	....	....	34	....	....	....	....	....	....	....	....	....	....	....	....	....	....	....	....	....	....
1979-80	**Toronto Maple Leafs**	**NHL**	**5**	**0**	**0**	**0**	**0**	**0**	**0**	**0**	**0**	**0**	**0**	**7**	**0.0**	**2**	**0**	**6**	**0**	**–4**	....	....	....	....	....	....	....	....
	NHL Totals		**135**	**14**	**19**	**33**	**14**	**15**	**29**	**54**	**0**	**0**	**1**	**159**	**8.8**	**87**	**8**	**119**	**12**		**4**	**0**	**0**	**0**	**0**	**0**	**0**	**0**
	Other Major League Totals		402	51	177	228	....	....	....	581	....	....	....	....	....	....	....	....	....	....	34	5	9	14	95	....	....	....

CWUAA First All-Star Team (1970) • CHL Second All-Star Team (1971) • WHA First All-Star Team (1977)

Selected by **Chicago** (WHA) in 1972 WHA General Player Draft, February 12, 1972. Traded to **California** by **Chicago** for Dick Redmond and the rights to Bobby Sheehan, December 5, 1972. Selected by **Denver** (WHA) from **Chicago** (WHA) in WHA Expansion Draft, May, 1975. Traded to **Indianapolis** (WHA) by **Denver-Ottawa** (WHA) with Bryon Baltimore, Francois Rochon and Mark Lomenda for cash, January 20, 1976. Traded to **Cincinnati** (WHA) by **Indianapolis** (WHA) with Reg Thomas for Claude Larose and Rich Leduc, February, 1978. Signed to 5-game free agent try-out contract by **Toronto**, December, 1979.

• MAGNAN, Marc

LW – L. 5'11", 195 lbs. b: Beaumont, Alta., 2/17/1962. Toronto's 9th, 195th overall, in 1981.

Season	**Club**	**League**	**GP**	**G**	**A**	**Pts**	**AG**	**AA**	**APts**	**PIM**	**PP**	**SH**	**GW**	**S**	**%**	**TGF**	**PGF**	**TGA**	**PGA**	**+/–**	**GP**	**G**	**A**	**Pts**	**PIM**	**PP**	**SH**	**GW**
1979-80	St. Albert Saints	AJHL	42	14	23	37	....	....	....	178	....	....	....	....	....	....	....	....	....	....	....	....	....	....	....	....	....	....
	Lethbridge Broncos	WHL	1	0	1	1	....	....	....	0	....	....	....	....	....	....	....	....	....	....	....	....	....	....	....	....	....	....
1980-81	Lethbridge Broncos	WHL	66	16	30	46	....	....	....	284	....	....	....	....	....	....	....	....	....	....	9	4	1	5	78	....	....	....
1981-82	Lethbridge Broncos	WHL	64	33	38	71	....	....	....	406	....	....	....	....	....	....	....	....	....	....	12	10	5	15	60	....	....	....
1982-83	St. Catharines Saints	AHL	67	6	10	16	....	....	....	229	....	....	....	....	....	....	....	....	....	....	....	....	....	....	....	....	....	....
	Toronto Maple Leafs	**NHL**	**4**	**0**	**1**	**1**	**0**	**1**	**1**	**5**	**0**	**0**	**0**	**1**	**0.0**	**1**	**1**	**0**	**0**	**0**	....	....	....	....	....	....	....	....
1983-84	St. Catharines Saints	AHL	54	3	6	9	....	....	....	170	....	....	....	....	....	....	....	....	....	....	....	....	....	....	....	....	....	....
	Muskegon Mohawks	IHL	19	3	10	13	....	....	....	30	....	....	....	....	....	....	....	....	....	....	....	....	....	....	....	....	....	....
1984-85	Indianapolis Checkers	IHL	72	9	24	33	....	....	....	244	....	....	....	....	....	....	....	....	....	....	7	1	3	4	13	....	....	....
1985-86	Indianapolis Checkers	IHL	69	15	22	37	....	....	....	279	....	....	....	....	....	....	....	....	....	....	5	0	1	1	48	....	....	....
1986-87	Indianapolis Checkers	IHL	77	11	21	32	....	....	....	353	....	....	....	....	....	....	....	....	....	....	6	0	0	0	22	....	....	....
1987-88	Flint Spirits	IHL	11	0	2	2	....	....	....	50	....	....	....	....	....	....	....	....	....	....	....	....	....	....	....	....	....	....
	NHL Totals		**4**	**0**	**1**	**1**	**0**	**1**	**1**	**5**	**0**	**0**	**0**	**1**	**0.0**	**1**	**1**	**0**	**0**		....	....	....	....	....	....	....	....

• MAGNUSON, Keith

Keith Arlen D – R. 6', 185 lbs. b: Saskatoon, Sask., 4/27/1947.

Season	**Club**	**League**	**GP**	**G**	**A**	**Pts**	**AG**	**AA**	**APts**	**PIM**	**PP**	**SH**	**GW**	**S**	**%**	**TGF**	**PGF**	**TGA**	**PGA**	**+/–**	**GP**	**G**	**A**	**Pts**	**PIM**	**PP**	**SH**	**GW**
1963-64	Saskatoon Midwest Litho	SAHA	STATISTICS NOT AVAILABLE																									
1964-65	Saskatoon Blades	SJHL	54	2	9	11	....	....	....	77	....	....	....	....	....	....	....	....	....	....	5	0	2	2	6	....	....	....
1965-66	University of Denver	WCHA	DID NOT PLAY – FRESHMAN																									
1966-67	University of Denver	WCHA	30	4	17	21	....	....	....	56	....	....	....	....	....	....	....	....	....	....	....	....	....	....	....	....	....	....
1967-68	University of Denver	WCHA	34	5	15	20	....	....	....	59	....	....	....	....	....	....	....	....	....	....	....	....	....	....	....	....	....	....
1968-69	University of Denver	WCHA	32	7	27	34	....	....	....	48	....	....	....	....	....	....	....	....	....	....	....	....	....	....	....	....	....	....
1969-70	**Chicago Black Hawks**	**NHL**	**76**	**0**	**24**	**24**	**0**	**22**	**22**	***213**	**0**	**0**	**0**	**77**	**0.0**	**92**	**2**	**65**	**13**	**38**	**8**	**1**	**2**	**3**	**17**	**0**	**0**	**0**
1970-71	**Chicago Black Hawks**	**NHL**	**76**	**3**	**20**	**23**	**3**	**17**	**20**	***291**	**0**	**0**	**1**	**66**	**4.5**	**91**	**1**	**85**	**27**	**32**	**18**	**0**	**2**	**2**	***63**	**0**	**0**	**0**
1971-72	**Chicago Black Hawks**	**NHL**	**74**	**2**	**19**	**21**	**2**	**16**	**18**	**201**	**0**	**0**	**0**	**83**	**2.4**	**101**	**3**	**53**	**7**	**52**	**8**	**0**	**1**	**1**	**29**	**0**	**0**	**0**
1972-73	**Chicago Black Hawks**	**NHL**	**77**	**0**	**19**	**19**	**0**	**15**	**15**	**140**	**0**	**0**	**0**	**64**	**0.0**	**94**	**1**	**88**	**19**	**24**	**7**	**0**	**2**	**2**	**4**	**0**	**0**	**0**
1973-74	**Chicago Black Hawks**	**NHL**	**57**	**2**	**11**	**13**	**2**	**9**	**11**	**105**	**0**	**0**	**0**	**29**	**6.9**	**61**	**1**	**56**	**12**	**16**	**11**	**1**	**0**	**1**	**17**	**0**	**0**	**0**
1974-75	**Chicago Black Hawks**	**NHL**	**48**	**2**	**12**	**14**	**2**	**9**	**11**	**117**	**0**	**0**	**0**	**31**	**6.5**	**43**	**1**	**45**	**13**	**10**	**8**	**1**	**2**	**3**	**15**	**0**	**0**	**0**
1975-76	**Chicago Black Hawks**	**NHL**	**48**	**1**	**6**	**7**	**1**	**4**	**5**	**99**	**0**	**0**	**0**	**27**	**3.7**	**49**	**0**	**52**	**16**	**13**	**4**	**0**	**0**	**0**	**12**	**0**	**0**	**0**
1976-77	**Chicago Black Hawks**	**NHL**	**37**	**1**	**6**	**7**	**1**	**5**	**6**	**86**	**0**	**0**	**0**	**30**	**3.3**	**25**	**0**	**48**	**12**	**–11**	....	....	....	....	....	....	....	....
1977-78	**Chicago Black Hawks**	**NHL**	**67**	**2**	**4**	**6**	**2**	**3**	**5**	**145**	**0**	**0**	**0**	**46**	**4.3**	**46**	**1**	**61**	**16**	**0**	**4**	**0**	**0**	**0**	**7**	**0**	**0**	**0**
1978-79	**Chicago Black Hawks**	**NHL**	**26**	**1**	**4**	**5**	**1**	**3**	**4**	**41**	**0**	**0**	**0**	**8**	**12.5**	**10**	**0**	**21**	**7**	**–4**	....	....	....	....	....	....	....	....
1979-80	**Chicago Black Hawks**	**NHL**	**3**	**0**	**0**	**0**	**0**	**0**	**0**	**4**	**0**	**0**	**0**	**0**	**0.0**	**2**	**0**	**2**	**0**	**0**	....	....	....	....	....	....	....	....
	Chicago Black Hawks	**NHL**	DID NOT PLAY – ASSISTANT COACH																									
1980-1982	**Chicago Black Hawks**	**NHL**	DID NOT PLAY – COACHING																									
	NHL Totals		**589**	**14**	**125**	**139**	**14**	**103**	**117**	**1442**	**0**	**0**	**1**	**461**	**3.0**	**614**	**10**	**576**	**142**		**68**	**3**	**9**	**12**	**164**	**0**	**0**	**0**

WCHA First All-Star Team (1967, 1968, 1969) • NCAA West First All-American Team (1968, 1969) • NCAA Championship All-Tournament Team (1968, 1969) • NCAA Championship Tournament MVP (1969) • Played in NHL All-Star Game (1971, 1972)

Signed as a free agent by **Chicago**, September, 1969. • Missed majority of 1978-79 season recovering from knee injury suffered in game vs. St. Louis, December 27, 1978. Claimed by **Chicago** as a fill-in during Expansion Draft, June 13, 1979. • Officially announced retirement and named Assistant Coach with **Chicago**, October 30, 1979.

• MAGUIRE, Kevin

RW – R. 6'2", 200 lbs. b: Toronto, Ont., 1/5/1963.

Season	**Club**	**League**	**GP**	**G**	**A**	**Pts**	**AG**	**AA**	**APts**	**PIM**	**PP**	**SH**	**GW**	**S**	**%**	**TGF**	**PGF**	**TGA**	**PGA**	**+/–**	**GP**	**G**	**A**	**Pts**	**PIM**	**PP**	**SH**	**GW**
1982-83	Orillia Travelways	OJHL	41	18	28	46	....	....	....	139	....	....	....	....	....	....	....	....	....	....	....	....	....	....	....	....	....	....
1983-84	Orillia Travelways	OJHL	35	42	77	119	....	....	....	....	....	....	....	....	....	....	....	....	....	....	....	....	....	....	....	....	....	....
1984-85	St. Catharines Saints	AHL	76	10	15	25	....	....	....	112	....	....	....	....	....	....	....	....	....	....	....	....	....	....	....	....	....	....
1985-86	St. Catharines Saints	AHL	61	6	9	15	....	....	....	161	....	....	....	....	....	....	....	....	....	....	1	0	0	0	0	....	....	....
1986-87	**Toronto Maple Leafs**	**NHL**	**17**	**0**	**0**	**0**	**0**	**0**	**0**	**74**	**0**	**0**	**0**	**2**	**0.0**	**0**	**0**	**6**	**0**	**–6**	**1**	**0**	**0**	**0**	**0**	**0**	**0**	**0**
	Newmarket Saints	AHL	51	4	2	6	....	....	....	131	....	....	....	....	....	....	....	....	....	....	....	....	....	....	....	....	....	....
1987-88	**Buffalo Sabres**	**NHL**	**46**	**4**	**6**	**10**	**3**	**4**	**7**	**162**	**0**	**0**	**0**	**25**	**16.0**	**17**	**0**	**18**	**0**	**–1**	**5**	**0**	**0**	**0**	**50**	**0**	**0**	**0**
1988-89	**Buffalo Sabres**	**NHL**	**60**	**8**	**10**	**18**	**7**	**7**	**14**	**241**	**0**	**0**	**2**	**35**	**22.9**	**29**	**1**	**20**	**1**	**9**	**5**	**0**	**0**	**0**	**36**	**0**	**0**	**0**
1989-90	**Buffalo Sabres**	**NHL**	**61**	**6**	**9**	**15**	**5**	**6**	**11**	**115**	**0**	**0**	**1**	**62**	**9.7**	**24**	**0**	**27**	**0**	**–3**	....	....	....	....	....	....	....	....
	Philadelphia Flyers	**NHL**	**5**	**1**	**0**	**1**	**1**	**0**	**1**	**6**	**0**	**0**	**0**	**7**	**14.3**	**1**	**0**	**2**	**0**	**–1**	....	....	....	....	....	....	....	....
1990-91	**Toronto Maple Leafs**	**NHL**	**63**	**9**	**5**	**14**	**8**	**4**	**12**	**180**	**1**	**0**	**0**	**52**	**17.3**	**24**	**2**	**32**	**0**	**–10**	....	....	....	....	....	....	....	....
1991-92	**Toronto Maple Leafs**	**NHL**	**8**	**1**	**0**	**1**	**1**	**0**	**1**	**4**	**0**	**0**	**0**	**8**	**12.5**	**2**	**1**	**5**	**0**	**–4**	....	....	....	....	....	....	....	....
	St. John's Maple Leafs	AHL	30	11	15	26	....	....	....	112	....	....	....	....	....	....	....	....	....	....	11	3	7	10	43	....	....	....
1992-2000			DID NOT PLAY – REFEREE																									
	NHL Totals		**260**	**29**	**30**	**59**	**25**	**21**	**46**	**782**	**1**	**0**	**3**	**191**	**15.2**	**97**	**4**	**110**	**1**		**11**	**0**	**0**	**0**	**86**	**0**	**0**	**0**

Signed as a free agent by **Toronto**, October 10, 1984. Claimed by **Buffalo** from **Toronto** in Waiver Draft, October 5, 1987. Traded to **Philadelphia** by **Buffalo** with Buffalo's 2nd round choice (Mikael Renberg) in 1990 Entry Draft for Jay Wells and Philadelphia's 4th round choice (Peter Ambroziak) in 1991 Entry Draft, March 5, 1990. Traded to **Toronto** by **Philadelphia** with Philadelphia's 8th round choice (Dimitri Mironov) in 1991 Entry Draft for Toronto's 3rd round choice (Al Kinsky) in 1990 Entry Draft, June 16, 1990.

• MAHOVLICH, Frank

Francis William "The Big M" LW – L. 6', 205 lbs. b: Timmins, Ont., 1/10/1938. **HHOF**

Season	**Club**	**League**	**GP**	**G**	**A**	**Pts**	**AG**	**AA**	**APts**	**PIM**	**PP**	**SH**	**GW**	**S**	**%**	**TGF**	**PGF**	**TGA**	**PGA**	**+/–**	**GP**	**G**	**A**	**Pts**	**PIM**	**PP**	**SH**	**GW**
1953-54	Schmaucher Lions	NOJHA	STATISTICS NOT AVAILABLE																									
	St. Michael's Majors	OHA-Jr.	1	0	1	1	....	....	....	2	....	....	....	....	....	....	....	....	....	....	....	....	....	....	....	....	....	....
1954-55	St. Michael's Majors	OHA-Jr.	25	12	11	23	....	....	....	18	....	....	....	....	....	....	....	....	....	....	....	....	....	....	....	....	....	....
1955-56	St. Michael's Majors	OHA-Jr.	30	24	26	50	....	....	....	55	....	....	....	....	....	....	....	....	....	....	8	5	5	10	24	....	....	....
1956-57	St. Michael's Majors	OHA-Jr.	49	*52	36	88	....	....	....	122	....	....	....	....	....	....	....	....	....	....	4	2	7	9	14	....	....	....
	Toronto Maple Leafs	**NHL**	**3**	**1**	**0**	**1**	**1**	**0**	**1**	**2**																		
1957-58	**Toronto Maple Leafs**	**NHL**	**67**	**20**	**16**	**36**	**25**	**16**	**41**	**67**																		
1958-59	**Toronto Maple Leafs**	**NHL**	**63**	**22**	**27**	**49**	**26**	**27**	**53**	**94**											**12**	**6**	**5**	**11**	**18**			
1959-60	**Toronto Maple Leafs**	**NHL**	**70**	**18**	**21**	**39**	**21**	**20**	**41**	**61**											**10**	**3**	**1**	**4**	**27**			
1960-61	**Toronto Maple Leafs**	**NHL**	**70**	**48**	**36**	**84**	**57**	**35**	**92**	**131**											**5**	**1**	**1**	**2**	**6**			
1961-62♦	**Toronto Maple Leafs**	**NHL**	**70**	**33**	**38**	**71**	**38**	**37**	**75**	**87**											**12**	**6**	**6**	**12**	***29**			
1962-63♦	**Toronto Maple Leafs**	**NHL**	**67**	**36**	**37**	**73**	**42**	**37**	**79**	**56**											**9**	**0**	**2**	**2**	**8**			
1963-64♦	**Toronto Maple Leafs**	**NHL**	**70**	**26**	**29**	**55**	**33**	**31**	**64**	**66**											**14**	**4**	***11**	**15**	**20**			
1964-65	**Toronto Maple Leafs**	**NHL**	**59**	**23**	**28**	**51**	**28**	**29**	**57**	**76**											**6**	**0**	**3**	**3**	**9**			
1965-66	**Toronto Maple Leafs**	**NHL**	**68**	**32**	**24**	**56**	**37**	**23**	**60**	**68**											**4**	**1**	**0**	**1**	**10**			
1966-67♦	**Toronto Maple Leafs**	**NHL**	**63**	**18**	**28**	**46**	**21**	**27**	**48**	**44**											**12**	**3**	**7**	**10**	**8**			
1967-68	**Toronto Maple Leafs**	**NHL**	**50**	**19**	**17**	**36**	**22**	**17**	**39**	**30**	**2**	**0**	**4**	**151**	**12.6**	**48**	**11**	**36**	**0**	**1**	....	....	....	....	....	....	....	....
	Detroit Red Wings	**NHL**	**13**	**7**	**9**	**16**	**8**	**9**	**17**	**2**	**0**	**0**	**1**	**39**	**17.9**	**25**	**5**	**19**	**2**	**3**	....	....	....	....	....	....	....	....
1968-69	**Detroit Red Wings**	**NHL**	**76**	**49**	**29**	**78**	**52**	**26**	**78**	**38**	**7**	**0**	**5**	**293**	**16.7**	**124**	**27**	**53**	**2**	**46**	....	....	....	....	....	....	....	....
1969-70	**Detroit Red Wings**	**NHL**	**74**	**38**	**32**	**70**	**42**	**30**	**72**	**59**	**15**	**1**	**5**	**251**	**15.1**	**98**	**35**	**55**	**8**	**16**	**4**	**0**	**0**	**0**	**2**	**0**	**0**	**0**
1970-71	**Detroit Red Wings**	**NHL**	**35**	**14**	**18**	**32**	**14**	**15**	**29**	**30**	**6**	**1**	**2**	**104**	**13.5**	**51**	**19**	**35**	**6**	**3**	....	....	....	....	....	....	....	....
♦	**Montreal Canadiens**	**NHL**	**38**	**17**	**24**	**41**	**17**	**20**	**37**	**11**	**4**	**1**	**2**	**100**	**17.0**	**59**	**22**	**42**	**9**	**4**	**20**	***14**	**13**	***27**	**18**	**1**	**0**	**0**
1971-72	**Montreal Canadiens**	**NHL**	**76**	**43**	**53**	**96**	**43**	**46**	**89**	**36**	**14**	**4**	**4**	**261**	**16.5**	**149**	**54**	**70**	**17**	**42**	**6**	**3**	**2**	**5**	**2**	**0**	**0**	**1**
1972-73	Canada	Summit	6	1	1	2	....	....	....	0	....	....	....	....	....	....	....	....	....	....	....	....	....	....	....	....	....	....
♦	**Montreal Canadiens**	**NHL**	**78**	**38**	**55**	**93**	**36**	**44**	**80**	**51**	**8**	**2**	**5**	**242**	**15.7**	**134**	**39**	**72**	**19**	**42**	**17**	**9**	**14**	**23**	**6**	**1**	**0**	**0**

Season	Club	League	GP	G	A	Pts	AG	AA	APts	PIM	PP	SH	GW	S	%	TGF	PGF	TGA	PGA	+/–	GP	G	A	Pts	PIM	PP	SH	GW
			REGULAR SEASON																		PLAYOFFS							
1973-74	**Montreal Canadiens**	**NHL**	**71**	**31**	**49**	**80**	**30**	**41**	**71**	**47**	**8**	**2**	**3**	**221**	**14.0**	**116**	**36**	**79**	**15**	**16**	**6**	**1**	**2**	**3**	**0**	**0**	**0**	**0**
1974-75	Canada	Summit	6	1	1	2	....	....	....	6	....	....	....	....	....	....	....	....	....	....	....	....	....	....	....	....	....	....
	Toronto Toros	WHA	73	38	44	82	....	....	....	27	....	....	....	....	....	....	....	....	....	....	6	3	0	3	2	....	....	....
1975-76	Toronto Toros	WHA	75	34	55	89	....	....	....	14	....	....	....	....	....	....	....	....	....	....	....	....	....	....	....	....	....	....
1976-77	Birmingham Bulls	WHA	17	3	20	23	....	....	....	12	....	....	....	....	....	....	....	....	....	....	....	....	....	....	....	....	....	....
1977-78	Birmingham Bulls	WHA	72	14	24	38	....	....	....	22	....	....	....	....	....	....	....	....	....	....	3	1	1	2	0	....	....	....
	NHL Totals		**1181**	**533**	**570**	**1103**	**593**	**530**	**1123**	**1056**	....	....	....	....	....	....	....	....	....		**137**	**51**	**67**	**118**	**163**	....	....	....
	Other Major League Totals		237	89	143	232	....	....	....	75	....	....	....	....	....	....	....	....	....	....	9	4	1	5	2	....	....	....

• Brother of Peter • Won Calder Memorial Trophy (1958) • NHL First All-Star Team (1961, 1963, 1973) • NHL Second All-Star Team (1962, 1964, 1965, 1966, 1969, 1970) • Played in NHL All-Star Game (1959, 1960, 1961, 1962, 1963, 1964, 1965, 1967, 1968, 1969, 1970, 1971, 1972, 1973, 1974)

Traded to **Detroit** by **Toronto** with Pete Stemkowski, Garry Unger and the rights to Carl Brewer for Norm Ullman, Paul Henderson, Floyd Smith and Doug Barrie, March 3, 1968. Traded to **Montreal** by **Detroit** for Guy Charron, Bill Collins and Mickey Redmond, January 13, 1971. Selected by **Dayton-Houston** (WHA) in 1972 WHA General Player Draft, February 12, 1972. WHA rights traded to **Toronto** (WHA) by **Houston** (WHA) for future considerations, June, 1974. Transferred to **Birmingham** (WHA) after **Toronto** (WHA) franchise relocated, June 30, 1976. • Missed remainder of 1976-77 season recovering from knee injury suffered in game vs. San Diego (WHA), November 10, 1976. • Officially announced retirement after comeback attempt with Detroit failed, October 7, 1979.

• MAHOVLICH, Pete

Peter Joseph "The Little M" C – L. 6'5", 210 lbs. b: Timmins, Ont., 10/10/1946. Detroit's 1st, 2nd overall, in 1963.

Season	Club	League	GP	G	A	Pts	AG	AA	APts	PIM	PP	SH	GW	S	%	TGF	PGF	TGA	PGA	+/–	GP	G	A	Pts	PIM	PP	SH	GW
1962-63	St. Michael's JV Buzzers	OHA-B	STATISTICS NOT AVAILABLE																									
1963-64	Hamilton Red Wings	OHA-Jr.	54	20	27	47	....	....	....	67	....	....	....	....	....	....	....	....	....	....	....	....	....	....	....	....	....	....
1964-65	Hamilton Red Wings	OHA-Jr.	55	20	35	55	....	....	....	88	....	....	....	....	....	....	....	....	....	....	....	....	....	....	....	....	....	....
1965-66	Hamilton Red Wings	OHA-Jr.	46	14	22	36	....	....	....	121	....	....	....	....	....	....	....	....	....	....	4	0	0	0	2	....	....	....
	Detroit Red Wings	**NHL**	**3**	**0**	**1**	**1**	**0**	**1**	**1**	**0**	....	....	....	....	....	....	....	....	....	....	....	....	....	....	....	....	....	....
1966-67	**Detroit Red Wings**	**NHL**	**34**	**1**	**3**	**4**	**1**	**3**	**4**	**16**	....	....	....	....	....	....	....	....	....	....	....	....	....	....	....	....	....	....
	Pittsburgh Hornets	AHL	18	4	7	11	....	....	....	37	....	....	....	....	....	....	....	....	....	....	9	0	0	0	2	....	....	....
1967-68	**Detroit Red Wings**	**NHL**	**15**	**6**	**4**	**10**	**7**	**4**	**11**	**13**	**0**	**0**	**0**	**35**	**17.1**	**17**	**4**	**19**	**0**	**–6**	....	....	....	....	....	....	....	....
	Fort Worth Wings	CPHL	42	20	14	34	....	....	....	103	....	....	....	....	....	....	....	....	....	....	....	....	....	....	....	....	....	....
1968-69	**Detroit Red Wings**	**NHL**	**30**	**2**	**2**	**4**	**2**	**2**	**4**	**21**	**0**	**0**	**0**	**37**	**5.4**	**6**	**0**	**24**	**3**	**–15**	....	....	....	....	....	....	....	....
	Fort Worth Wings	CHL	34	19	17	36	....	....	....	54	....	....	....	....	....	....	....	....	....	....	....	....	....	....	....	....	....	....
1969-70	**Montreal Canadiens**	**NHL**	**36**	**9**	**8**	**17**	**10**	**7**	**17**	**51**	**0**	**0**	**2**	**75**	**12.0**	**29**	**6**	**14**	**0**	**9**	....	....	....	....	....	....	....	....
	Montreal Voyageurs	AHL	31	21	19	40	....	....	....	77	....	....	....	....	....	....	....	....	....	....	....	....	....	....	....	....	....	....
1970-71 ♦	**Montreal Canadiens**	**NHL**	**78**	**35**	**26**	**61**	**35**	**22**	**57**	**181**	**12**	**3**	**5**	**189**	**18.5**	**108**	**41**	**55**	**13**	**25**	**20**	**10**	**6**	**16**	**43**	**1**	**1**	**1**
1971-72	**Montreal Canadiens**	**NHL**	**75**	**35**	**32**	**67**	**35**	**28**	**63**	**103**	**7**	**4**	**6**	**207**	**16.9**	**107**	**31**	**80**	**20**	**16**	**6**	**0**	**2**	**2**	**12**	**0**	**0**	**0**
1972-73	Canada	Summit	7	1	1	2	....	....	....	4	....	....	....	....	....	....	....	....	....	....	....	....	....	....	....	....	....	....
♦	**Montreal Canadiens**	**NHL**	**61**	**21**	**38**	**59**	**20**	**30**	**50**	**49**	**3**	**4**	**3**	**173**	**12.1**	**82**	**21**	**58**	**18**	**21**	**17**	**4**	**9**	**13**	**22**	**2**	**1**	**0**
1973-74	**Montreal Canadiens**	**NHL**	**78**	**36**	**37**	**73**	**35**	**31**	**66**	**122**	**7**	**4**	**7**	**178**	**20.2**	**115**	**27**	**77**	**31**	**42**	**6**	**2**	**1**	**3**	**4**	**1**	**0**	**0**
1974-75	**Montreal Canadiens**	**NHL**	**80**	**35**	**82**	**117**	**31**	**62**	**93**	**64**	**13**	**1**	**3**	**240**	**14.6**	**163**	**62**	**85**	**25**	**41**	**11**	**6**	**10**	**16**	**10**	**1**	**0**	**1**
1975-76 ♦	**Montreal Canadiens**	**NHL**	**80**	**34**	**71**	**105**	**30**	**53**	**83**	**76**	**8**	**1**	**7**	**200**	**17.0**	**149**	**40**	**42**	**4**	**71**	**13**	**4**	**8**	**12**	**24**	**2**	**0**	**1**
1976-77 ♦	**Montreal Canadiens**	**NHL**	**76**	**15**	**47**	**62**	**13**	**36**	**49**	**45**	**3**	**0**	**1**	**161**	**9.3**	**106**	**24**	**47**	**1**	**36**	**13**	**4**	**5**	**9**	**19**	**2**	**0**	**1**
1977-78	**Montreal Canadiens**	**NHL**	**17**	**3**	**5**	**8**	**3**	**4**	**7**	**4**	**0**	**0**	**1**	**28**	**10.7**	**15**	**3**	**7**	**1**	**6**	....	....	....	....	....	....	....	....
	Pittsburgh Penguins	**NHL**	**57**	**25**	**36**	**61**	**23**	**28**	**51**	**37**	**9**	**2**	**1**	**201**	**12.4**	**91**	**34**	**82**	**29**	**4**	....	....	....	....	....	....	....	....
1978-79	**Pittsburgh Penguins**	**NHL**	**60**	**14**	**39**	**53**	**12**	**28**	**40**	**39**	**5**	**0**	**0**	**153**	**9.2**	**69**	**17**	**65**	**2**	**–11**	**2**	**0**	**1**	**1**	**0**	**0**	**0**	**0**
1979-80	**Detroit Red Wings**	**NHL**	**80**	**16**	**50**	**66**	**14**	**36**	**50**	**69**	**3**	**0**	**1**	**143**	**11.2**	**109**	**40**	**88**	**22**	**3**	....	....	....	....	....	....	....	....
1980-81	**Detroit Red Wings**	**NHL**	**24**	**1**	**4**	**5**	**1**	**3**	**4**	**26**	**0**	**0**	**1**	**25**	**4.0**	**7**	**1**	**22**	**8**	**–8**	....	....	....	....	....	....	....	....
	Adirondack Red Wings	AHL	37	18	18	36	....	....	....	49	....	....	....	....	....	....	....	....	....	....	18	1	*18	19	23	....	....	....
1981-82	Adirondack Red Wings	AHL	80	22	45	67	....	....	....	71	....	....	....	....	....	....	....	....	....	....	4	2	1	3	2	....	....	....
1982-1985			DID NOT PLAY																									
1985-86	Toledo Goaldiggers	IHL	DID NOT PLAY – COACHING																									
	Toledo Goaldiggers	IHL	23	4	10	14	....	....	....	50	....	....	....	....	....	....	....	....	....	....	....	....	....	....	....	....	....	....
	NHL Totals		**884**	**288**	**485**	**773**	**272**	**378**	**650**	**916**	....	....	....	....	....	....	....	....	....		**88**	**30**	**42**	**72**	**134**	....	....	....

• Brother of Frank • Played in NHL All-Star Game (1971, 1976)

Traded to **Montreal** by **Detroit** with Bart Crashley for Garry Monahan and Doug Piper, June 6, 1969. Traded to **Pittsburgh** by **Montreal** with Peter Lee for Pierre Larouche and future considerations (rights to Peter Marsh, December 15, 1977), November 29, 1977. Traded to **Detroit** by **Pittsburgh** for Nick Libett, August 3, 1979. • Came out of retirement as emergency injury replacement, November 6, 1985.

• MAILHOT, Jacques

LW – L. 6'2", 208 lbs. b: Shawinigan, Que., 12/5/1961.

Season	Club	League	GP	G	A	Pts	AG	AA	APts	PIM	PP	SH	GW	S	%	TGF	PGF	TGA	PGA	+/–	GP	G	A	Pts	PIM	PP	SH	GW
1981-82	Limoilou Titans	QAAA	STATISTICS NOT AVAILABLE																									
1982-83	Louisville Jets	QPHL	STATISTICS NOT AVAILABLE																									
1983-84	Joliette Cyclones	QPHL	STATISTICS NOT AVAILABLE																									
1984-85	Rimouski Mariners	RHL	STATISTICS NOT AVAILABLE																									
1985-86	Rimouski Mariners	RHL	36	13	17	30	....	....	....	*262	....	....	....	....	....	....	....	....	....	....	....	....	....	....	....	....	....	....
1986-87	Rimouski Mariners	RHL	19	9	12	21	....	....	....	164	....	....	....	....	....	....	....	....	....	....	7	1	2	3		....	....	....
1987-88	Baltimore Skipjacks	AHL	15	2	0	2	....	....	....	167	....	....	....	....	....	....	....	....	....	....	....	....	....	....	....	....	....	....
	Fredericton Express	AHL	28	2	6	8	....	....	....	137	....	....	....	....	....	....	....	....	....	....	8	0	0	0	18	....	....	....
1988-89	**Quebec Nordiques**	**NHL**	**5**	**0**	**0**	**0**	**0**	**0**	**0**	**33**	**0**	**0**	**0**	**0**	**0.0**	**0**	**0**	**0**	**0**	**0**	....	....	....	....	....	....	....	....
	Halifax Citadels	AHL	35	4	1	5	....	....	....	259	....	....	....	....	....	....	....	....	....	....	1	0	0	0	5	....	....	....
1989-90	Moncton Hawks	AHL	6	0	0	0	....	....	....	20	....	....	....	....	....	....	....	....	....	....	....	....	....	....	....	....	....	....
	Cape Breton Oilers	AHL	6	0	1	1	....	....	....	12	....	....	....	....	....	....	....	....	....	....	....	....	....	....	....	....	....	....
	Hampton Roads Admirals	ECHL	5	0	2	2	....	....	....	62	....	....	....	....	....	....	....	....	....	....	....	....	....	....	....	....	....	....
	Phoenix Roadrunners	IHL	5	0	2	2	....	....	....	70	....	....	....	....	....	....	....	....	....	....	....	....	....	....	....	....	....	....
1990-91	Moncton Hawks	AHL	13	0	0	0	....	....	....	43	....	....	....	....	....	....	....	....	....	....	....	....	....	....	....	....	....	....
	San Diego Gulls	IHL	1	0	0	0	....	....	....	2	....	....	....	....	....	....	....	....	....	....	....	....	....	....	....	....	....	....
	Johnstown Chiefs	ECHL	2	0	0	0	....	....	....	21	....	....	....	....	....	....	....	....	....	....	9	1	3	4	46	....	....	....
	Miramichi Packers	NBSHL	20	10	6	16	....	....	....	117	....	....	....	....	....	....	....	....	....	....	....	....	....	....	....	....	....	....
1991-92	Flint Bulldogs	ColHL	21	15	12	27	....	....	....	237	....	....	....	....	....	....	....	....	....	....	....	....	....	....	....	....	....	....
	Detroit Falcons	ColHL	5	2	2	4	....	....	....	44	....	....	....	....	....	....	....	....	....	....	....	....	....	....	....	....	....	....
1992-93	Detroit Falcons	ColHL	48	14	21	35	....	....	....	273	....	....	....	....	....	....	....	....	....	....	4	2	4	6	12	....	....	....
1993-94	Detroit Falcons	ColHL	29	1	9	10	....	....	....	122	....	....	....	....	....	....	....	....	....	....	3	0	1	1	49	....	....	....
1994-95	Rochester Americans	AHL	15	0	1	1	....	....	....	52	....	....	....	....	....	....	....	....	....	....	....	....	....	....	....	....	....	....
	Utica Blizzard	ColHL	59	11	17	28	....	....	....	302	....	....	....	....	....	....	....	....	....	....	....	....	....	....	....	....	....	....
1995-96	Utica Blizzard	ColHL	8	1	0	1	....	....	....	71	....	....	....	....	....	....	....	....	....	....	....	....	....	....	....	....	....	....
	Quad City Mallards	ColHL	50	14	8	22	....	....	....	253	....	....	....	....	....	....	....	....	....	....	3	0	0	0	52	....	....	....
1996-97	Louiseville Jets	QSPHL	2	1	1	2	....	....	....	2	....	....	....	....	....	....	....	....	....	....	....	....	....	....	....	....	....	....
	Utah Grizzlies	IHL	4	0	1	1	....	....	....	32	....	....	....	....	....	....	....	....	....	....	....	....	....	....	....	....	....	....
	Central Texas Stampede	WPHL	34	5	8	13	....	....	....	247	....	....	....	....	....	....	....	....	....	....	8	0	3	3	24	....	....	....
1997-98	Central Texas Stampede	WPHL	50	14	18	32	....	....	....	277	....	....	....	....	....	....	....	....	....	....	4	2	1	3	44	....	....	....
1998-99	Fresno Fighting Falcons	WCHL	50	7	22	29	....	....	....	289	....	....	....	....	....	....	....	....	....	....	3	1	0	1	10	....	....	....
99-2000	Central Texas Stampede	WPHL	10	0	1	1	....	....	....	51	....	....	....	....	....	....	....	....	....	....	....	....	....	....	....	....	....	....
	NHL Totals		**5**	**0**	**0**	**0**	**0**	**0**	**0**	**33**	**0**	**0**	**0**	**0**	**0.0**	**0**	**0**	**0**	**0**		....	....	....	....	....	....	....	....

Signed as a free agent by **Quebec**, August 15, 1988. • Played w/ RHI's Portland Rage in 1994 (4-0-1-1-4).

• MAIR, Adam

C – R. 6'1", 195 lbs. b: Hamilton, Ont., 2/15/1979. Toronto's 2nd, 84th overall, in 1997.

Season	Club	League	GP	G	A	Pts	AG	AA	APts	PIM	PP	SH	GW	S	%	TGF	PGF	TGA	PGA	+/–	GP	G	A	Pts	PIM	PP	SH	GW
1994-95	Ohsweken Golden Eagles	OJHL-B	39	21	23	44	....	....	....	91	....	....	....	....	....	....	....	....	....	....	....	....	....	....	....	....	....	....
1995-96	Owen Sound Platers	OHL	62	12	15	27	....	....	....	63	....	....	....	....	....	....	....	....	....	....	6	0	0	0	2	....	....	....
1996-97	Owen Sound Platers	OHL	65	16	35	51	....	....	....	113	....	....	....	....	....	....	....	....	....	....	4	1	0	1	2	....	....	....
1997-98	Owen Sound Platers	OHL	56	25	27	52	....	....	....	179	....	....	....	....	....	....	....	....	....	....	11	6	3	9	31	....	....	....

			REGULAR SEASON																		PLAYOFFS							
Season	**Club**	**League**	**GP**	**G**	**A**	**Pts**	**AG**	**AA**	**APts**	**PIM**	**PP**	**SH**	**GW**	**S**	**%**	**TGF**	**PGF**	**TGA**	**PGA**	**+/–**	**GP**	**G**	**A**	**Pts**	**PIM**	**PP**	**SH**	**GW**
1998-99	Owen Sound Platers	OHL	43	23	41	64	....	....	....	109	....	....	....	....	....	....	....	....	....	....	16	10	10	20	*47	....	....	....
	St. John's Maple Leafs	AHL	....	....	....	....	....	....	....	....	....	....	....	....	....	....	....	....	....	....	3	1	0	1	6	....	....	....
	Toronto Maple Leafs	**NHL**	....	....	....	....	....	....	....	....	....	....	....	....	....	....	....	....	....	....	**5**	**1**	**0**	**1**	**14**	**0**	**0**	**0**
	Canada	WJC-A	7	1	1	2	....	....	....	29	....	....	....	....	....	....	....	....	....	....	....	....	....	....	....	....	....	....
99-2000	**Toronto Maple Leafs**	**NHL**	**8**	**1**	**0**	**1**	**1**	**0**	**1**	**6**	**0**	**0**	**0**	**7**	**14.3**	**1**	**0**	**2**	**0**	**–1**	**5**	**0**	**0**	**0**	**8**	**0**	**0**	**0**
	St. John's Maple Leafs	AHL	66	22	27	49	....	....	....	124	....	....	....	....	....	....	....	....	....	....	....	....	....	....	....	....	....	....
	NHL Totals		**8**	**1**	**0**	**1**	**1**	**0**	**1**	**6**	**0**	**0**	**0**	**7**	**14.3**	**1**	**0**	**2**	**0**		**10**	**1**	**0**	**1**	**22**	**0**	**0**	**0**

• MAIR, Jim

James McKay D – R. 5'9", 170 lbs. b: Schumacher, Ont., 5/15/1946.

Season	**Club**	**League**	**GP**	**G**	**A**	**Pts**	**AG**	**AA**	**APts**	**PIM**	**PP**	**SH**	**GW**	**S**	**%**	**TGF**	**PGF**	**TGA**	**PGA**	**+/–**	**GP**	**G**	**A**	**Pts**	**PIM**	**PP**	**SH**	**GW**
1963-64	Hamilton Red Wings	OHA-Jr.	4	2	1	3	....	....	....	2	....	....	....	....	....	....	....	....	....	....	....	....	....	....	....	....	....	....
1964-65	Hamilton Red Wings	OHA-Jr.	39	7	14	21	....	....	....	76	....	....	....	....	....	....	....	....	....	....	....	....	....	....	....	....	....	....
1965-66	St-Jerome Alouettes	QJHL	47	11	26	37	....	....	....	145	....	....	....	....	....	....	....	....	....	....	5	1	0	1	6	....	....	....
1966-67	Johnstown Jets	EHL	62	10	25	35	....	....	....	247	....	....	....	....	....	....	....	....	....	....	5	2	3	5	0	....	....	....
1967-68	Johnstown Jets	EHL	71	20	45	65	....	....	....	247	....	....	....	....	....	....	....	....	....	....	3	0	0	0	0	....	....	....
1968-69	Johnstown Jets	EHL	61	27	31	58	....	....	....	158	....	....	....	....	....	....	....	....	....	....	3	0	2	2	0	....	....	....
1969-70	Quebec Aces	AHL	47	5	7	12	....	....	....	58	....	....	....	....	....	....	....	....	....	....	6	2	0	2	12	....	....	....
1970-71	**Philadelphia Flyers**	**NHL**	**2**	**0**	**0**	**0**	**0**	**0**	**0**	**0**	**0**	**0**	**0**	**6**	**0.0**	**2**	**2**	**1**	**0**	**–1**	**3**	**1**	**2**	**3**	**4**	**1**	**0**	**0**
	Quebec Aces	AHL	62	11	16	27	....	....	....	52	....	....	....	....	....	....	....	....	....	....	1	0	0	0	4	....	....	....
1971-72	**Philadelphia Flyers**	**NHL**	**2**	**0**	**0**	**0**	**0**	**0**	**0**	**0**	**0**	**0**	**0**	**3**	**0.0**	**2**	**2**	**2**	**0**	**–2**	....	....	....	....	....	....	....	....
	Richmond Robins	AHL	69	10	25	35	....	....	....	75	....	....	....	....	....	....	....	....	....	....	....	....	....	....	....	....	....	....
1972-73	**New York Islanders**	**NHL**	**49**	**2**	**11**	**13**	**2**	**9**	**11**	**41**	**0**	**0**	**0**	**134**	**1.5**	**43**	**9**	**88**	**16**	**–38**	....	....	....	....	....	....	....	....
	Vancouver Canucks	**NHL**	**15**	**1**	**0**	**1**	**1**	**0**	**1**	**8**	**0**	**0**	**0**	**23**	**4.3**	**8**	**0**	**12**	**0**	**–4**	....	....	....	....	....	....	....	....
1973-74	**Vancouver Canucks**	**NHL**	**6**	**1**	**3**	**4**	**1**	**2**	**3**	**0**	**1**	**0**	**1**	**32**	**3.1**	**15**	**6**	**7**	**1**	**3**	....	....	....	....	....	....	....	....
	Seattle Totems	WHL	65	8	30	38	....	....	....	115	....	....	....	....	....	....	....	....	....	....	....	....	....	....	....	....	....	....
1974-75	**Vancouver Canucks**	**NHL**	**2**	**0**	**1**	**1**	**0**	**1**	**1**	**0**	**0**	**0**	**0**	**8**	**0.0**	**1**	**1**	**2**	**0**	**–2**	....	....	....	....	....	....	....	....
	Seattle Totems	CHL	63	12	17	29	....	....	....	96	....	....	....	....	....	....	....	....	....	....	....	....	....	....	....	....	....	....
	NHL Totals		**76**	**4**	**15**	**19**	**4**	**12**	**16**	**49**	**1**	**0**	**1**	**206**	**1.9**	**71**	**20**	**112**	**17**		**3**	**1**	**2**	**3**	**4**	**1**	**0**	**0**

Signed as a free agent by **Philadelphia**, September 29, 1969. Claimed by **NY Islanders** from **Philadelphia** in Expansion Draft, June 6, 1972. Claimed by **Vancouver** from **NY Islanders** in Waiver Draft, February 19, 1973.

• MAJOR, Bruce

Bruce A. C – L. 6'3", 180 lbs. b: Vernon, B.C., 1/3/1967. Quebec's 6th, 99th overall, in 1985.

Season	**Club**	**League**	**GP**	**G**	**A**	**Pts**	**AG**	**AA**	**APts**	**PIM**	**PP**	**SH**	**GW**	**S**	**%**	**TGF**	**PGF**	**TGA**	**PGA**	**+/–**	**GP**	**G**	**A**	**Pts**	**PIM**	**PP**	**SH**	**GW**
1984-85	Richmond Sockeyes	BCJHL	48	43	56	99	....	....	....	56	....	....	....	....	....	....	....	....	....	....	....	....	....	....	....	....	....	....
1985-86	University of Maine	H-East	38	14	14	28	....	....	....	39	....	....	....	....	....	....	....	....	....	....	....	....	....	....	....	....	....	....
1986-87	University of Maine	H-East	37	14	10	24	....	....	....	12	....	....	....	....	....	....	....	....	....	....	....	....	....	....	....	....	....	....
1987-88	University of Maine	H-East	26	0	5	5	....	....	....	14	....	....	....	....	....	....	....	....	....	....	....	....	....	....	....	....	....	....
1988-89	University of Maine	H-East	42	13	11	24	....	....	....	22	....	....	....	....	....	....	....	....	....	....	....	....	....	....	....	....	....	....
1989-90	Halifax Citadels	AHL	32	5	6	11	....	....	....	23	....	....	....	....	....	....	....	....	....	....	....	....	....	....	....	....	....	....
	Greensboro Monarchs	ECHL	12	4	3	7	....	....	....	6	....	....	....	....	....	....	....	....	....	....	10	2	2	4	12	....	....	....
1990-91	**Quebec Nordiques**	**NHL**	**4**	**0**	**0**	**0**	**0**	**0**	**0**	**0**	**0**	**0**	**0**	**0**	**0.0**	**0**	**0**	**1**	**0**	**–1**	....	....	....	....	....	....	....	....
	Halifax Citadels	AHL	9	2	0	2	....	....	....	9	....	....	....	....	....	....	....	....	....	....	....	....	....	....	....	....	....	....
	Fort Wayne Komets	IHL	62	11	25	36	....	....	....	48	....	....	....	....	....	....	....	....	....	....	18	1	3	4	6	....	....	....
1991-92	Halifax Citadels	AHL	16	1	3	4	....	....	....	11	....	....	....	....	....	....	....	....	....	....	....	....	....	....	....	....	....	....
	NHL Totals		**4**	**0**	**0**	**0**	**0**	**0**	**0**	**0**	**0**	**0**	**0**	**0**	**0.0**	**0**	**0**	**1**	**0**		....	....	....	....	....	....	....	....

• MAJOR, Mark

Mark O. LW – L. 6'3", 223 lbs. b: Toronto, Ont., 3/20/1970. Pittsburgh's 2nd, 25th overall, in 1988.

Season	**Club**	**League**	**GP**	**G**	**A**	**Pts**	**AG**	**AA**	**APts**	**PIM**	**PP**	**SH**	**GW**	**S**	**%**	**TGF**	**PGF**	**TGA**	**PGA**	**+/–**	**GP**	**G**	**A**	**Pts**	**PIM**	**PP**	**SH**	**GW**
1986-87	Don Mills Flyers	MTHL	36	12	14	26	....	....	....	81	....	....	....	....	....	....	....	....	....	....	....	....	....	....	....	....	....	....
1987-88	North Bay Centennials	OHL	57	16	17	33	....	....	....	272	....	....	....	....	....	....	....	....	....	....	4	0	2	2	8	....	....	....
1988-89	North Bay Centennials	OHL	11	3	2	5	....	....	....	58	....	....	....	....	....	....	....	....	....	....	....	....	....	....	....	....	....	....
	Kingston Raiders	OHL	53	22	29	51	....	....	....	193	....	....	....	....	....	....	....	....	....	....	....	....	....	....	....	....	....	....
1989-90	Kingston Frontenacs	OHL	62	29	32	61	....	....	....	168	....	....	....	....	....	....	....	....	....	....	6	3	3	6	12	....	....	....
1990-91	Muskegon Lumberjacks	IHL	60	8	10	18	....	....	....	160	....	....	....	....	....	....	....	....	....	....	5	0	0	0	0	....	....	....
1991-92	Muskegon Lumberjacks	IHL	80	13	18	31	....	....	....	302	....	....	....	....	....	....	....	....	....	....	12	1	3	4	29	....	....	....
1992-93	Cleveland Lumberjacks	IHL	82	13	15	28	....	....	....	155	....	....	....	....	....	....	....	....	....	....	3	0	0	0	0	....	....	....
1993-94	Providence Bruins	AHL	61	17	9	26	....	....	....	176	....	....	....	....	....	....	....	....	....	....	....	....	....	....	....	....	....	....
1994-95	Detroit Vipers	IHL	78	17	19	36	....	....	....	229	....	....	....	....	....	....	....	....	....	....	5	0	1	1	23	....	....	....
1995-96	Adirondack Red Wings	AHL	78	10	19	29	....	....	....	234	....	....	....	....	....	....	....	....	....	....	3	0	0	0	21	....	....	....
1996-97	**Detroit Red Wings**	**NHL**	**2**	**0**	**0**	**0**	**0**	**0**	**0**	**5**	**0**	**0**	**0**	**0**	**0.0**	**0**	**0**	**0**	**0**	**0**	....	....	....	....	....	....	....	....
	Adirondack Red Wings	AHL	78	17	18	35	....	....	....	213	....	....	....	....	....	....	....	....	....	....	4	0	0	0	13	....	....	....
1997-98	Portland Pirates	AHL	79	13	2	15	....	....	....	355	....	....	....	....	....	....	....	....	....	....	10	2	1	3	52	....	....	....
1998-99	Portland Pirates	AHL	66	5	4	9	....	....	....	250	....	....	....	....	....	....	....	....	....	....	....	....	....	....	....	....	....	....
99-2000	Houston Aeros	IHL	20	1	0	1	....	....	....	81	....	....	....	....	....	....	....	....	....	....	....	....	....	....	....	....	....	....
	Flint Generals	UHL	36	23	18	41	....	....	....	135	....	....	....	....	....	....	....	....	....	....	15	8	3	11	67	....	....	....
	NHL Totals		**2**	**0**	**0**	**0**	**0**	**0**	**0**	**5**	**0**	**0**	**0**	**0**	**0.0**	**0**	**0**	**0**	**0**		....	....	....	....	....	....	....	....

Signed as a free agent by **Boston**, July 22, 1993. Signed as a free agent by **Detroit**, June 26, 1995. Signed as a free agent by **Washington**, August 20, 1997. • Played w/ RHI's Buffalo Stampede in 1994 (21-18-14-32-63) and 1995 (23-17-20-37-97); Empire State Cobras in 1996 (23-11-19-30-98); New Jersey R&R in 1997 (10-8-8-16-73); Buffalo Wings in 1998 (13-21-10-31-85) and 1999 (23-24-34-58-111).

• MAKAROV, Sergei

RW – L. 5'11", 185 lbs. b: Chelyabinsk, USSR, 6/19/1958. Calgary's 14th, 241st overall, in 1983.

Season	**Club**	**League**	**GP**	**G**	**A**	**Pts**	**AG**	**AA**	**APts**	**PIM**	**PP**	**SH**	**GW**	**S**	**%**	**TGF**	**PGF**	**TGA**	**PGA**	**+/–**	**GP**	**G**	**A**	**Pts**	**PIM**	**PP**	**SH**	**GW**
1976-77	Traktor Chelyabinsk	USSR	11	1	0	1	....	....	....	4	....	....	....	....	....	....	....	....	....	....	....	....	....	....	....	....	....	....
	Soviet Union	WJC-A	7	4	4	8	....	....	....	4	....	....	....	....	....	....	....	....	....	....	....	....	....	....	....	....	....	....
1977-78	Traktor Chelyabinsk	USSR	36	18	13	31	....	....	....	10	....	....	....	....	....	....	....	....	....	....	....	....	....	....	....	....	....	....
	Soviet Union	WJC-A	7	8	7	15	....	....	....	4	....	....	....	....	....	....	....	....	....	....	....	....	....	....	....	....	....	....
	Soviet Union	WEC-A	10	3	2	5	....	....	....	5	....	....	....	....	....	....	....	....	....	....	....	....	....	....	....	....	....	....
1978-79	CSKA Moscow	USSR	44	18	21	39	....	....	....	12	....	....	....	....	....	....	....	....	....	....	....	....	....	....	....	....	....	....
	USSR	Chal-Cup	3	1	2	3	....	....	....	0	....	....	....	....	....	....	....	....	....	....	....	....	....	....	....	....	....	....
	Soviet Union	WEC-A	8	8	4	12	....	....	....	6	....	....	....	....	....	....	....	....	....	....	....	....	....	....	....	....	....	....
1979-80	CSKA Moscow	USSR	44	29	39	68	....	....	....	16	....	....	....	....	....	....	....	....	....	....	....	....	....	....	....	....	....	....
	CSKA Moscow	Super-S	5	1	3	4	....	....	....	0	....	....	....	....	....	....	....	....	....	....	....	....	....	....	....	....	....	....
	Soviet Union	Olympics	7	5	6	11	....	....	....	2	....	....	....	....	....	....	....	....	....	....	....	....	....	....	....	....	....	....
1980-81	CSKA Moscow	USSR	49	42	37	79	....	....	....	22	....	....	....	....	....	....	....	....	....	....	....	....	....	....	....	....	....	....
	Soviet Union	WEC-A	8	3	5	8	....	....	....	12	....	....	....	....	....	....	....	....	....	....	....	....	....	....	....	....	....	....
1981-82	Soviet Union	Can-Cup	7	3	6	9	....	....	....	0	....	....	....	....	....	....	....	....	....	....	....	....	....	....	....	....	....	....
	CSKA Moscow	USSR	46	32	43	75	....	....	....	18	....	....	....	....	....	....	....	....	....	....	....	....	....	....	....	....	....	....
	Soviet Union	WEC-A	10	6	7	13	....	....	....	8	....	....	....	....	....	....	....	....	....	....	....	....	....	....	....	....	....	....
1982-83	CSKA Moscow	USSR	30	25	17	42	....	....	....	6	....	....	....	....	....	....	....	....	....	....	....	....	....	....	....	....	....	....
	Soviet Union	WEC-A	10	9	9	18	....	....	....	4	....	....	....	....	....	....	....	....	....	....	....	....	....	....	....	....	....	....
1983-84	CSKA Moscow	USSR	44	36	37	73	....	....	....	28	....	....	....	....	....	....	....	....	....	....	....	....	....	....	....	....	....	....
	Soviet Union	Olympics	7	3	3	6	....	....	....	6	....	....	....	....	....	....	....	....	....	....	....	....	....	....	....	....	....	....
1984-85	Soviet Union	Can-Cup	6	6	1	7	....	....	....	4	....	....	....	....	....	....	....	....	....	....	....	....	....	....	....	....	....	....
	CSKA Moscow	USSR	40	26	39	65	....	....	....	28	....	....	....	....	....	....	....	....	....	....	....	....	....	....	....	....	....	....
	Soviet Union	WEC-A	10	9	5	14	....	....	....	8	....	....	....	....	....	....	....	....	....	....	....	....	....	....	....	....	....	....
1985-86	CSKA Moscow	USSR	40	30	32	62	....	....	....	28	....	....	....	....	....	....	....	....	....	....	....	....	....	....	....	....	....	....
	CSKA Moscow	Super-S	6	5	1	6	....	....	....	0	....	....	....	....	....	....	....	....	....	....	....	....	....	....	....	....	....	....
	Soviet Union	WEC-A	10	4	14	18	....	....	....	12	....	....	....	....	....	....	....	....	....	....	....	....	....	....	....	....	....	....
1986-87	CSKA Moscow	USSR	40	21	32	53	....	....	....	26	....	....	....	....	....	....	....	....	....	....	....	....	....	....	....	....	....	....
	USSR	RV-87	2	0	1	1	....	....	....	0	....	....	....	....	....	....	....	....	....	....	....	....	....	....	....	....	....	....
	Soviet Union	WEC-A	10	4	10	14	....	....	....	8	....	....	....	....	....	....	....	....	....	....	....	....	....	....	....	....	....	....

			REGULAR SEASON																		PLAYOFFS							
Season	Club	League	GP	G	A	Pts	AG	AA	APts	PIM	PP	SH	GW	S	%	TGF	PGF	TGA	PGA	+/–	GP	G	A	Pts	PIM	PP	SH	GW
1987-88	CSKA Moscow	USSR	51	23	45	68	....	....	....	50	....	....	....	....	....	....	....	....	....	....	....	....	....	....	....	....	....	....
	Soviet Union	Can-Cup	9	7	8	15	....	....	....	8	....	....	....	....	....	....	....	....	....	....	....	....	....	....	....	....	....	....
	Soviet Union	Olympics	8	3	8	11	....	....	....	10	....	....	....	....	....	....	....	....	....	....	....	....	....	....	....	....	....	....
1988-89	CSKA Moscow	USSR	44	21	33	54	....	....	....	42	....	....	....	....	....	....	....	....	....	....	....	....	....	....	....	....	....	....
	CSKA Moscow	Super-S	7	3	6	9	....	....	....	0	....	....	....	....	....	....	....	....	....	....	....	....	....	....	....	....	....	....
	Soviet Union	WEC-A	10	5	3	8	....	....	....	8	....	....	....	....	....	....	....	....	....	....	....	....	....	....	....	....	....	....
1989-90	Calgary Flames	Fr-Tour	4	0	1	1	....	....	....	0	....	....	....	....	....	....	....	....	....	....	....	....	....	....	....	....	....	....
	Calgary Flames	**NHL**	**80**	**24**	**62**	**86**	**21**	**45**	**66**	**55**	**6**	**0**	**4**	**118**	**20.3**	**144**	**53**	**58**	**0**	**33**	**6**	**0**	**6**	**6**	**0**	**0**	**0**	**0**
	Soviet Union	WEC-A	7	2	1	3	....	....	....	8	....	....	....	....	....	....	....	....	....	....	....	....	....	....	....	....	....	....
1990-91	**Calgary Flames**	**NHL**	**78**	**30**	**49**	**79**	**28**	**37**	**65**	**44**	**9**	**0**	**5**	**93**	**32.3**	**122**	**51**	**58**	**2**	**15**	**3**	**1**	**0**	**1**	**0**	**0**	**0**	**0**
	Soviet Union	WEC-A	8	3	7	10	....	....	....	6	....	....	....	....	....	....	....	....	....	....	....	....	....	....	....	....	....	....
1991-92	**Calgary Flames**	**NHL**	**68**	**22**	**48**	**70**	**20**	**36**	**56**	**60**	**6**	**0**	**2**	**83**	**26.5**	**95**	**31**	**51**	**1**	**14**	....	....	....	....	....	....	....	....
1992-93	**Calgary Flames**	**NHL**	**71**	**18**	**39**	**57**	**15**	**27**	**42**	**40**	**5**	**0**	**3**	**105**	**17.1**	**95**	**32**	**64**	**1**	**0**	....	....	....	....	....	....	....	....
1993-94	**San Jose Sharks**	**NHL**	**80**	**30**	**38**	**68**	**28**	**30**	**58**	**78**	**10**	**0**	**5**	**155**	**19.4**	**103**	**31**	**61**	**0**	**11**	**14**	**8**	**2**	**10**	**4**	**3**	**0**	**2**
1994-95	**San Jose Sharks**	**NHL**	**43**	**10**	**14**	**24**	**18**	**21**	**39**	**40**	**1**	**0**	**1**	**56**	**17.9**	**33**	**5**	**32**	**0**	**–4**	**11**	**3**	**3**	**6**	**4**	**0**	**0**	**0**
1995-96			DID NOT PLAY																									
1996-97	HC Fribourg-Gotteron	Switz.	6	3	2	5	....	....	....	2	....	....	....	....	....	....	....	....	....	....	....	....	....	....	....	....	....	....
	Dallas Stars	**NHL**	**4**	**0**	**0**	**0**	**0**	**0**	**0**	**0**	**0**	**0**	**0**	**0**	**0.0**	**2**	**2**	**2**	**0**	**–2**	....	....	....	....	....	....	....	....
	NHL Totals		**424**	**134**	**250**	**384**	**130**	**196**	**326**	**317**	**37**	**0**	**20**	**610**	**22.0**	**594**	**205**	**326**	**4**		**34**	**12**	**11**	**23**	**8**	**3**	**0**	**2**

USSR First All-Star Team (1981, 1982, 1983, 1984, 1985, 1986, 1987, 1988) • Won Izvestia Trophy (USSR's leading scorer (1980, 1981, 1982, 1984, 1985, 1986, 1987, 1988, 1989) • USSR Player of the Year (1980, 1985, 1989) • Canada Cup All-Star Team (1984) • Named Best Forward at WEC-A (1985) • NHL All-Rookie Team (1990) • Won Calder Memorial Trophy (1990)

Traded to **Hartford** by **Calgary** for future considerations (Washington's 4th round choice — previously acquired, Calgary selected Jason Smith — in 1993 Entry Draft, June 26, 1993), June 20, 1993. Traded to **San Jose** by **Hartford** with Hartford's 1st (Viktor Kozlov) and 3rd (Ville Peltonen) round choices in 1993 Entry Draft and Toronto's 2nd round choice (previously acquired, San Jose selected Vlastimil Kroupa) in 1993 Entry Draft for San Jose's 1st round choice (Chris Pronger) in 1993 Entry Draft, June 26, 1993. Signed as a free agent by **Dallas**, November 1, 1996.

• MAKELA, Mikko

Mikko Matti LW – L. 6'1", 194 lbs. b: Tampere, Finland, 2/28/1965. NY Islanders' 5th, 66th overall, in 1983.

Season	Club	League	GP	G	A	Pts	AG	AA	APts	PIM	PP	SH	GW	S	%	TGF	PGF	TGA	PGA	+/–	GP	G	A	Pts	PIM	PP	SH	GW
1982-83	Ilves Tampere	Finland-Jr.	23	29	11	40	....	....	....	26	....	....	....	....	....	....	....	....	....	....	4	2	5	7	2	....	....	....
	Finland	EJC-A	5	1	3	4	....	....	....	8	....	....	....	....	....	....	....	....	....	....	....	....	....	....	....	....	....	....
1983-84	Ilves Tampere	Finland	35	17	11	28	....	....	....	26	....	....	....	....	....	....	....	....	....	....	2	0	1	1	0	....	....	....
	Finland	WJC-A	5	1	0	1	....	....	....	0	....	....	....	....	....	....	....	....	....	....	....	....	....	....	....	....	....	....
1984-85	Ilves Tampere	Finland	36	*34	25	59	....	....	....	24	....	....	....	....	....	....	....	....	....	....	9	4	7	11	10	....	....	....
	Finland	WJC-A	7	11	2	13	....	....	....	6	....	....	....	....	....	....	....	....	....	....	....	....	....	....	....	....	....	....
	Finland	WEC-A	8	2	2	4	....	....	....	2	....	....	....	....	....	....	....	....	....	....	....	....	....	....	....	....	....	....
1985-86	**New York Islanders**	**NHL**	**58**	**16**	**20**	**36**	**13**	**13**	**26**	**28**	**2**	**0**	**3**	**68**	**23.5**	**61**	**16**	**34**	**1**	**12**	....	....	....	....	....	....	....	....
	Springfield Indians	AHL	2	1	1	2	....	....	....	0	....	....	....	....	....	....	....	....	....	....	....	....	....	....	....	....	....	....
1986-87	**New York Islanders**	**NHL**	**80**	**24**	**33**	**57**	**21**	**24**	**45**	**24**	**11**	**0**	**3**	**142**	**16.9**	**89**	**29**	**57**	**0**	**3**	**11**	**2**	**4**	**6**	**8**	**1**	**0**	**1**
1987-88	Finland	Can-Cup	5	1	1	2	....	....	....	12	....	....	....	....	....	....	....	....	....	....	....	....	....	....	....	....	....	....
	New York Islanders	**NHL**	**73**	**36**	**40**	**76**	**31**	**29**	**60**	**22**	**13**	**2**	**4**	**142**	**25.4**	**109**	**50**	**51**	**6**	**14**	**6**	**1**	**4**	**5**	**6**	**1**	**0**	**0**
1988-89	**New York Islanders**	**NHL**	**76**	**17**	**28**	**45**	**14**	**20**	**34**	**22**	**4**	**0**	**0**	**123**	**13.8**	**72**	**24**	**68**	**4**	**–16**	....	....	....	....	....	....	....	....
1989-90	**New York Islanders**	**NHL**	**20**	**2**	**3**	**5**	**2**	**2**	**4**	**2**	**1**	**0**	**0**	**24**	**8.3**	**11**	**4**	**17**	**0**	**–10**	....	....	....	....	....	....	....	....
	Los Angeles Kings	**NHL**	**45**	**7**	**14**	**21**	**6**	**10**	**16**	**16**	**0**	**0**	**0**	**58**	**12.1**	**27**	**0**	**31**	**0**	**–4**	**1**	**0**	**0**	**0**	**0**	**0**	**0**	**0**
1990-91	**Buffalo Sabres**	**NHL**	**60**	**15**	**7**	**22**	**14**	**5**	**19**	**25**	**2**	**2**	**1**	**62**	**24.2**	**37**	**3**	**48**	**12**	**–2**	....	....	....	....	....	....	....	....
1991-92	TPS Turku	Finland	44	25	45	*70	....	....	....	38	....	....	....	....	....	....	....	....	....	....	3	2	3	5	0	....	....	....
	Finland	Olympics	5	3	3	6	....	....	....	0	....	....	....	....	....	....	....	....	....	....	....	....	....	....	....	....	....	....
	Finland	WC-A	8	2	8	10	....	....	....	0	....	....	....	....	....	....	....	....	....	....	....	....	....	....	....	....	....	....
1992-93	TPS Turku	Finland	38	17	27	44	....	....	....	22	....	....	....	....	....	....	....	....	....	....	11	4	8	12	0	....	....	....
1993-94	Malmo IF	Sweden	37	15	21	36	....	....	....	20	....	....	....	....	....	....	....	....	....	....	11	4	7	11	2	....	....	....
	Finland	Olympics	8	2	3	5	....	....	....	4	....	....	....	....	....	....	....	....	....	....	....	....	....	....	....	....	....	....
	Finland	WC-A	8	5	4	9	....	....	....	6	....	....	....	....	....	....	....	....	....	....	....	....	....	....	....	....	....	....
1994-95	Ilves Tampere	Finland	18	3	11	14	....	....	....	4	....	....	....	....	....	....	....	....	....	....	....	....	....	....	....	....	....	....
	Boston Bruins	**NHL**	**11**	**1**	**2**	**3**	**2**	**3**	**5**	**0**	**1**	**0**	**0**	**10**	**10.0**	**4**	**3**	**1**	**0**	**0**	....	....	....	....	....	....	....	....
	Providence Bruins	AHL	....	....	....	....	....	....	....	....	....	....	....	....	....	....	....	....	....	....	7	2	4	6	2	....	....	....
1995-96	Dusseldorfer EG	Germany	47	16	37	53	....	....	....	16	....	....	....	....	....	....	....	....	....	....	13	0	14	*14	12	....	....	....
1996-97	Dusseldorfer EG	Germany	39	4	14	18	....	....	....	0	....	....	....	....	....	....	....	....	....	....	4	1	1	2	0	....	....	....
1997-98	Sodertalje SK	Sweden	25	2	11	13	....	....	....	14	....	....	....	....	....	....	....	....	....	....	....	....	....	....	....	....	....	....
1998-99	Tappara Tampere	Finland	41	4	6	10	....	....	....	14	....	....	....	....	....	....	....	....	....	....	....	....	....	....	....	....	....	....
	NHL Totals		**423**	**118**	**147**	**265**	**103**	**106**	**209**	**139**	**34**	**4**	**11**	**629**	**18.8**	**410**	**129**	**307**	**23**		**18**	**3**	**8**	**11**	**14**	**2**	**0**	**1**

WJC-A All-Star Team (1985) • Finnish First All-Star Team (1985, 1992) • Finnish Player of the Year (1992)

Traded to **LA Kings** by **NY Islanders** for Ken Baumgartner and Hubie McDonough, November 29, 1989. Traded to **Buffalo** by **LA Kings** for Mike Donnelly, September 30, 1990. Signed as a free agent by **Boston**, July 18, 1994.

• MAKI, Chico

Ronald Patrick RW – R. 5'10", 170 lbs. b: Sault Ste. Marie, Ont., 8/17/1939.

Season	Club	League	GP	G	A	Pts	AG	AA	APts	PIM	PP	SH	GW	S	%	TGF	PGF	TGA	PGA	+/–	GP	G	A	Pts	PIM	PP	SH	GW
1955-56	Sault Ste. Marie North Stars	NOJHA	....	12	9	21	....	....	....	14	....	....	....	....	....	....	....	....	....	....	....	....	....	....	....	....	....	....
1956-57	St. Catharines Teepees	OHA-Jr.	47	6	6	12	....	....	....	32	....	....	....	....	....	....	....	....	....	....	14	2	1	3	32	....	....	....
1957-58	St. Catharines Teepees	OHA-Jr.	49	21	19	40	....	....	....	72	....	....	....	....	....	....	....	....	....	....	8	3	5	8	10	....	....	....
1958-59	St. Catharines Teepees	OHA-Jr.	54	*41	53	94	....	....	....	64	....	....	....	....	....	....	....	....	....	....	7	2	1	3	10	....	....	....
	Buffalo Bisons	AHL	1	0	0	0	....	....	....	2	....	....	....	....	....	....	....	....	....	....	....	....	....	....	....	....	....	....
	Trois-Rivieres Lions	QHL	....	....	....	....	....	....	....	....	....	....	....	....	....	....	....	....	....	....	1	0	0	0	0	....	....	....
1959-60	St. Catharines Teepees	OHA-Jr.	47	39	*53	*92	....	....	....	75	....	....	....	....	....	....	....	....	....	....	17	11	*18	29	40	....	....	....
	Sault Ste. Marie Thunderbirds	EPHL	1	0	1	1	....	....	....	0	....	....	....	....	....	....	....	....	....	....	....	....	....	....	....	....	....	....
	Buffalo Bisons	AHL	3	1	4	5	....	....	....	0	....	....	....	....	....	....	....	....	....	....	....	....	....	....	....	....	....	....
	St. Catharines Teepees	Mem-Cup	14	8	*19	*27	....	....	....	41	....	....	....	....	....	....	....	....	....	....	....	....	....	....	....	....	....	....
1960-61	Buffalo Bisons	AHL	69	30	42	72	....	....	....	20	....	....	....	....	....	....	....	....	....	....	4	0	0	0	2	....	....	....
	♦ **Chicago Black Hawks**	**NHL**	....	....	....	....	....	....	....	....	....	....	....	....	....	....	....	....	....	....	**1**	**0**	**0**	**0**	**0**	**0**	**0**	**0**
1961-62	**Chicago Black Hawks**	**NHL**	**16**	**4**	**6**	**10**	**5**	**6**	**11**	**2**	....	....	....	....	....	....	....	....	....	....	....	....	....	....	....	....	....	....
	Buffalo Bisons	AHL	51	21	28	49	....	....	....	65	....	....	....	....	....	....	....	....	....	....	11	3	5	8	15	....	....	....
1962-63	**Chicago Black Hawks**	**NHL**	**65**	**7**	**17**	**24**	**8**	**17**	**25**	**35**	....	....	....	....	....	....	....	....	....	....	**6**	**0**	**1**	**1**	**2**	**0**	**0**	**0**
1963-64	**Chicago Black Hawks**	**NHL**	**68**	**8**	**14**	**22**	**10**	**15**	**25**	**70**	....	....	....	....	....	....	....	....	....	....	**7**	**0**	**0**	**0**	**15**	**0**	**0**	**0**
1964-65	**Chicago Black Hawks**	**NHL**	**65**	**16**	**24**	**40**	**19**	**25**	**44**	**58**	....	....	....	....	....	....	....	....	....	....	**14**	**3**	**9**	**12**	**8**	**1**	**0**	**0**
1965-66	**Chicago Black Hawks**	**NHL**	**68**	**17**	**31**	**48**	**19**	**30**	**49**	**41**	....	....	....	....	....	....	....	....	....	....	**3**	**1**	**1**	**2**	**0**	**1**	**0**	**0**
1966-67	**Chicago Black Hawks**	**NHL**	**56**	**9**	**29**	**38**	**10**	**28**	**38**	**14**	....	....	....	....	....	....	....	....	....	....	**6**	**0**	**0**	**0**	**0**	**0**	**0**	**0**
1967-68	**Chicago Black Hawks**	**NHL**	**60**	**8**	**16**	**24**	**9**	**16**	**25**	**4**	**0**	**0**	**1**	**102**	**7.8**	**42**	**3**	**52**	**3**	**–10**	**11**	**2**	**5**	**7**	**4**	**0**	**0**	**1**
1968-69	**Chicago Black Hawks**	**NHL**	**66**	**7**	**21**	**28**	**7**	**19**	**26**	**30**	**0**	**1**	**0**	**127**	**5.5**	**40**	**1**	**57**	**17**	**–1**	....	....	....	....	....	....	....	....
1969-70	**Chicago Black Hawks**	**NHL**	**75**	**10**	**24**	**34**	**11**	**22**	**33**	**27**	**0**	**1**	**2**	**93**	**10.8**	**51**	**9**	**45**	**12**	**9**	**8**	**2**	**2**	**4**	**2**	**1**	**1**	**0**
1970-71	**Chicago Black Hawks**	**NHL**	**72**	**22**	**26**	**48**	**22**	**22**	**44**	**18**	**2**	**2**	**3**	**110**	**20.0**	**74**	**12**	**40**	**9**	**31**	**18**	**6**	**5**	**11**	**6**	**1**	**0**	**0**
1971-72	**Chicago Black Hawks**	**NHL**	**62**	**13**	**34**	**47**	**13**	**29**	**42**	**22**	**3**	**1**	**2**	**136**	**9.6**	**81**	**17**	**25**	**5**	**44**	**8**	**1**	**4**	**5**	**4**	**0**	**0**	**1**
1972-73	**Chicago Black Hawks**	**NHL**	**77**	**13**	**19**	**32**	**12**	**15**	**27**	**10**	**1**	**2**	**1**	**118**	**11.0**	**58**	**10**	**62**	**19**	**5**	**16**	**2**	**8**	**10**	**0**	**0**	**0**	**0**
1973-74	**Chicago Black Hawks**	**NHL**	**69**	**9**	**25**	**34**	**9**	**21**	**30**	**12**	**2**	**0**	**0**	**89**	**10.1**	**51**	**6**	**42**	**10**	**13**	**11**	**0**	**1**	**1**	**2**	**0**	**0**	**0**
1974-75			OUT OF HOCKEY – RETIRED																									
1975-76	**Chicago Black Hawks**	**NHL**	**22**	**0**	**6**	**6**	**0**	**4**	**4**	**2**	**0**	**0**	**0**	**13**	**0.0**	**11**	**6**	**15**	**1**	**–9**	**4**	**0**	**0**	**0**	**0**	**0**	**0**	**0**
	NHL Totals		**841**	**143**	**292**	**435**	**154**	**269**	**423**	**345**	....	....	....	....	....	....	....	....	....	....	**113**	**17**	**36**	**53**	**43**	....	....	....

• Brother of Wayne • OHA-Jr. First All-Star Team (1960) • Won Dudley "Red" Garrett Memorial Award (Top Rookie - AHL) (1961) • Played in NHL All-Star Game (1961, 1971, 1972)

• MAKI, Wayne

LW – L. 6', 185 lbs. b: Sault Ste. Marie, Ont., 11/10/1944 d: 5/1/1974.

Season	Club	League	GP	G	A	Pts	AG	AA	APts	PIM	PP	SH	GW	S	%	TGF	PGF	TGA	PGA	+/–	GP	G	A	Pts	PIM	PP	SH	GW
1963-64	Sault Ste. Marie Greyhounds	NOJHA	36	43	31	74	....	....	....	44	....	....	....	....	....	....	....	....	....	....	....	....	....	....	....	....	....	....
1964-65	St. Catharines Black Hawks	OHA-Jr.	56	29	48	77	....	....	....	43	....	....	....	....	....	....	....	....	....	....	4	3	4	7	10	....	....	....
	St. Louis Braves	CPHL	3	0	0	0	....	....	....	4	....	....	....	....	....	....	....	....	....	....	....	....	....	....	....	....	....	....
1965-66	St. Louis Braves	CPHL	69	25	26	51	....	....	....	46	....	....	....	....	....	....	....	....	....	....	2	0	1	1	13	....	....	....
1966-67	St. Louis Braves	CPHL	67	31	28	59	....	....	....	69	....	....	....	....	....	....	....	....	....	....	....	....	....	....	....	....	....	....

Season	Club	League	GP	G	A	Pts	AG	AA	APts	PIM	PP	SH	GW	S	%	TGF	PGF	TGA	PGA	+/–	GP	G	A	Pts	PIM	PP	SH	GW
			REGULAR SEASON																		PLAYOFFS							
1967-68	Dallas Black Hawks	CPHL	12	5	7	12	....	....	....	14	....	....	....	....	....	....	....	....	....	....	5	2	1	3	17	....	....	....
	Chicago Black Hawks	**NHL**	**49**	**5**	**5**	**10**	**6**	**5**	**11**	**32**	**1**	**0**	**1**	**54**	**9.3**	**22**	**5**	**23**	**2**	**–4**	**2**	**1**	**0**	**1**	**2**	**0**	**0**	**0**
1968-69	**Chicago Black Hawks**	**NHL**	**1**	**0**	**0**	**0**	**0**	**0**	**0**	**0**	**0**	**0**	**0**	**1**	**0.0**	**0**	**0**	**0**	**0**	**0**	....	....	....	....	....	....	....	....
	Dallas Black Hawks	CHL	50	25	24	49	....	....	....	74	....	....	....	....	....	....	....	....	....	....	11	7	7	14	37	....	....	....
1969-70	**St. Louis Blues**	**NHL**	**16**	**2**	**1**	**3**	**2**	**1**	**3**	**4**	**0**	**0**	**1**	**35**	**5.7**	**6**	**0**	**10**	**0**	**–4**	....	....	....	....	....	....	....	....
	Buffalo Bisons	AHL	40	13	20	33	....	....	....	72	....	....	....	....	....	....	....	....	....	....	14	4	4	8	*61	....	....	....
1970-71	**Vancouver Canucks**	**NHL**	**78**	**25**	**38**	**63**	**25**	**32**	**57**	**99**	**8**	**0**	**2**	**184**	**13.6**	**86**	**27**	**72**	**0**	**–13**	....	....	....	....	....	....	....	....
1971-72	**Vancouver Canucks**	**NHL**	**76**	**22**	**25**	**47**	**22**	**22**	**44**	**43**	**5**	**0**	**3**	**160**	**13.8**	**67**	**17**	**55**	**1**	**–4**	....	....	....	....	....	....	....	....
1972-73	**Vancouver Canucks**	**NHL**	**26**	**3**	**10**	**13**	**3**	**8**	**11**	**6**	**0**	**0**	**0**	**56**	**5.4**	**17**	**1**	**27**	**0**	**–11**	....	....	....	....	....	....	....	....
	NHL Totals		**246**	**57**	**79**	**136**	**58**	**68**	**126**	**184**	**14**	**0**	**7**	**490**	**11.6**	**198**	**50**	**187**	**3**		**2**	**1**	**0**	**1**	**2**	**0**	**0**	**0**

• Brother of Chico • CPHL Second All-Star Team (1967)

Claimed by **St. Louis** from **Chicago** in Intra-League Draft, June 11, 1969. Claimed by **Vancouver** from **St. Louis** in Expansion Draft, June 10, 1970. • Missed remainder of 1972-73 season after being diagnosed with brain cancer, December 14, 1972.

• MAKKONEN, Kari

RW – R. 6', 190 lbs. b: Pori, Finland, 1/20/1955. NY Islanders' 12th, 194th overall, in 1975.

Season	Club	League	GP	G	A	Pts	AG	AA	APts	PIM	PP	SH	GW	S	%	TGF	PGF	TGA	PGA	+/–	GP	G	A	Pts	PIM	PP	SH	GW
1974-75	Assat Pori	Finland	36	5	5	10	....	....	....	8	....	....	....	....	....	....	....	....	....	....	....	....	....	....	....	....	....	....
	Finland	WJC-A	5	2	2	4	....	....	....	4	....	....	....	....	....	....	....	....	....	....	....	....	....	....	....	....	....	....
1975-76	Assat Pori	Finland	36	24	15	39	....	....	....	25	....	....	....	....	....	....	....	....	....	....	4	1	2	3	2	....	....	....
	Finland	WEC-A	10	3	3	6	....	....	....	6	....	....	....	....	....	....	....	....	....	....	....	....	....	....	....	....	....	....
1976-77	Finland	Can-Cup	5	3	1	4	....	....	....	2	....	....	....	....	....	....	....	....	....	....	....	....	....	....	....	....	....	....
	Assat Pori	Finland	36	17	20	37	....	....	....	18	....	....	....	....	....	....	....	....	....	....	....	....	....	....	....	....	....	....
	Finland	WEC-A	10	4	4	8	....	....	....	2	....	....	....	....	....	....	....	....	....	....	....	....	....	....	....	....	....	....
1977-78	Assat Pori	Finland	39	19	25	44	....	....	....	28	....	....	....	....	....	....	....	....	....	....	9	4	5	9	9	....	....	....
	Finland	WEC-A	10	1	0	1	....	....	....	4	....	....	....	....	....	....	....	....	....	....	....	....	....	....	....	....	....	....
1978-79	Assat Pori	Finland	36	*36	18	54	....	....	....	55	....	....	....	....	....	....	....	....	....	....	1	0	0	0	0	....	....	....
1979-80	**Edmonton Oilers**	**NHL**	**9**	**2**	**2**	**4**	**2**	**1**	**3**	**0**	**0**	**0**	**0**	**11**	**18.2**	**8**	**2**	**8**	**0**	**–2**	....	....	....	....	....	....	....	....
	Houston Apollos	CHL	16	5	5	10	....	....	....	2	....	....	....	....	....	....	....	....	....	....	....	....	....	....	....	....	....	....
1980-81	Assat Pori	Finland	36	19	21	40	....	....	....	20	....	....	....	....	....	....	....	....	....	....	1	0	0	0	0	....	....	....
	Finland	Nat-Team	18	3	3	6	....	....	....	14	....	....	....	....	....	....	....	....	....	....	....	....	....	....	....	....	....	....
1981-82	Finland	Can-Cup	3	0	0	0	....	....	....	0	....	....	....	....	....	....	....	....	....	....	....	....	....	....	....	....	....	....
	Assat Pori	Finland	36	24	20	44	....	....	....	12	....	....	....	....	....	....	....	....	....	....	9	5	4	9	0	....	....	....
	Finland	WEC-A	7	2	2	4	....	....	....	2	....	....	....	....	....	....	....	....	....	....	....	....	....	....	....	....	....	....
1982-83	Assat Pori	Finland	35	14	18	32	....	....	....	22	....	....	....	....	....	....	....	....	....	....	....	....	....	....	....	....	....	....
	Finland	WEC-A	10	1	1	2	....	....	....	8	....	....	....	....	....	....	....	....	....	....	....	....	....	....	....	....	....	....
1983-84	Assat Pori	Finland	37	27	15	42	....	....	....	28	....	....	....	....	....	....	....	....	....	....	9	3	4	7	19	....	....	....
1984-85	Assat Pori	Finland	36	18	20	38	....	....	....	32	....	....	....	....	....	....	....	....	....	....	8	6	4	10	6	....	....	....
	Finland	WEC-A	10	1	0	1	....	....	....	4	....	....	....	....	....	....	....	....	....	....	....	....	....	....	....	....	....	....
1985-86	Assat Pori	Finland	34	23	26	49	....	....	....	24	....	....	....	....	....	....	....	....	....	....	....	....	....	....	....	....	....	....
	Finland	WEC-A	10	4	2	6	....	....	....	10	....	....	....	....	....	....	....	....	....	....	....	....	....	....	....	....	....	....
1986-87	Assat Pori	Finland	43	14	22	36	....	....	....	20	....	....	....	....	....	....	....	....	....	....	....	....	....	....	....	....	....	....
1987-88	Assat Pori	Finland	43	21	16	37	....	....	....	36	....	....	....	....	....	....	....	....	....	....	....	....	....	....	....	....	....	....
1988-89	Assat Pori	Finland	42	16	24	40	....	....	....	20	....	....	....	....	....	....	....	....	....	....	....	....	....	....	....	....	....	....
1989-90	Assat Pori	Finland-2	44	31	52	83	....	....	....	18	....	....	....	....	....	....	....	....	....	....	3	3	3	6	2	....	....	....
1990-91	Assat Pori	Finland	43	9	24	33	....	....	....	20	....	....	....	....	....	....	....	....	....	....	....	....	....	....	....	....	....	....
	NHL Totals		**9**	**2**	**2**	**4**	**2**	**1**	**3**	**0**	**0**	**0**	**0**	**11**	**18.2**	**8**	**2**	**8**	**0**		....	....	....	....	....	....	....	....

Finnish Rookie of the Year (1976) • Finnish First All-Star Team (1978, 1979)

Signed as a free agent by **Edmonton**, July 22, 1979.

• MALAKHOV, Vladimir

Vladimir I. D – L. 6'4", 230 lbs. b: Ekaterinburg, USSR, 8/30/1968. NY Islanders' 12th, 191st overall, in 1989.

Season	Club	League	GP	G	A	Pts	AG	AA	APts	PIM	PP	SH	GW	S	%	TGF	PGF	TGA	PGA	+/–	GP	G	A	Pts	PIM	PP	SH	GW
1986-87	Spartak Moscow	USSR	22	0	1	1	....	....	....	12	....	....	....	....	....	....	....	....	....	....	....	....	....	....	....	....	....	....
1987-88	Spartak Moscow	USSR	28	2	2	4	....	....	....	26	....	....	....	....	....	....	....	....	....	....	....	....	....	....	....	....	....	....
1988-89	CSKA Moscow	USSR	34	6	2	8	....	....	....	16	....	....	....	....	....	....	....	....	....	....	....	....	....	....	....	....	....	....
	CSKA Moscow	Super-S	7	0	1	1	....	....	....	6	....	....	....	....	....	....	....	....	....	....	....	....	....	....	....	....	....	....
1989-90	CSKA Moscow	Fr-Tour	1	0	0	0	....	....	....	0	....	....	....	....	....	....	....	....	....	....	....	....	....	....	....	....	....	....
	CSKA Moscow	USSR	48	2	10	12	....	....	....	34	....	....	....	....	....	....	....	....	....	....	....	....	....	....	....	....	....	....
	CSKA Moscow	Super-S	5	0	1	1	....	....	....	8	....	....	....	....	....	....	....	....	....	....	....	....	....	....	....	....	....	....
	Soviet Union	WEC-A	10	0	1	1	....	....	....	10	....	....	....	....	....	....	....	....	....	....	....	....	....	....	....	....	....	....
1990-91	CSKA Moscow	Fr-Tour	1	0	0	0	....	....	....	25	....	....	....	....	....	....	....	....	....	....	....	....	....	....	....	....	....	....
	CSKA Moscow	USSR	46	5	13	18	....	....	....	22	....	....	....	....	....	....	....	....	....	....	....	....	....	....	....	....	....	....
	CSKA Moscow	Super-S	3	1	0	1	....	....	....	0	....	....	....	....	....	....	....	....	....	....	....	....	....	....	....	....	....	....
	Soviet Union	WEC-A	10	0	0	0	....	....	....	4	....	....	....	....	....	....	....	....	....	....	....	....	....	....	....	....	....	....
1991-92	Soviet Union	Can-Cup	5	0	0	0	....	....	....	4	....	....	....	....	....	....	....	....	....	....	....	....	....	....	....	....	....	....
	CSKA Moscow	CIS	40	1	9	10	....	....	....	12	....	....	....	....	....	....	....	....	....	....	....	....	....	....	....	....	....	....
	Russia	Olympics	8	3	0	3	....	....	....	4	....	....	....	....	....	....	....	....	....	....	....	....	....	....	....	....	....	....
	Russia	WC-A	6	2	1	3	....	....	....	4	....	....	....	....	....	....	....	....	....	....	....	....	....	....	....	....	....	....
1992-93	**New York Islanders**	**NHL**	**64**	**14**	**38**	**52**	**12**	**26**	**38**	**59**	**7**	**0**	**0**	**178**	**7.9**	**117**	**44**	**72**	**13**	**14**	**17**	**3**	**6**	**9**	**12**	**0**	**0**	**0**
	Capital District Islanders	AHL	3	2	1	3	....	....	....	11	....	....	....	....	....	....	....	....	....	....	....	....	....	....	....	....	....	....
1993-94	**New York Islanders**	**NHL**	**76**	**10**	**47**	**57**	**9**	**37**	**46**	**80**	**4**	**0**	**2**	**235**	**4.3**	**139**	**54**	**83**	**27**	**29**	**4**	**0**	**0**	**0**	**6**	**0**	**0**	**0**
1994-95	**New York Islanders**	**NHL**	**26**	**3**	**13**	**16**	**5**	**19**	**24**	**32**	**1**	**0**	**0**	**61**	**4.9**	**31**	**12**	**27**	**7**	**–1**	....	....	....	....	....	....	....	....
	Montreal Canadiens	**NHL**	**14**	**1**	**4**	**5**	**2**	**6**	**8**	**14**	**0**	**0**	**0**	**30**	**3.3**	**14**	**4**	**19**	**7**	**–2**	....	....	....	....	....	....	....	....
1995-96	**Montreal Canadiens**	**NHL**	**61**	**5**	**23**	**28**	**5**	**19**	**24**	**79**	**2**	**0**	**0**	**122**	**4.1**	**82**	**30**	**57**	**12**	**7**	....	....	....	....	....	....	....	....
1996-97	Russia	W-Cup	4	1	0	1	....	....	....	8	....	....	....	....	....	....	....	....	....	....	....	....	....	....	....	....	....	....
	Montreal Canadiens	**NHL**	**65**	**10**	**20**	**30**	**11**	**18**	**29**	**43**	**5**	**0**	**1**	**177**	**5.6**	**81**	**29**	**71**	**22**	**3**	**5**	**0**	**0**	**0**	**6**	**0**	**0**	**0**
1997-98	**Montreal Canadiens**	**NHL**	**74**	**13**	**31**	**44**	**15**	**30**	**45**	**70**	**8**	**0**	**2**	**166**	**7.8**	**110**	**47**	**68**	**21**	**16**	**9**	**3**	**4**	**7**	**10**	**2**	**0**	**0**
1998-99	**Montreal Canadiens**	**NHL**	**62**	**13**	**21**	**34**	**15**	**20**	**35**	**77**	**8**	**0**	**3**	**143**	**9.1**	**77**	**33**	**66**	**15**	**–7**	....	....	....	....	....	....	....	....
99-2000	**Montreal Canadiens**	**NHL**	**7**	**0**	**0**	**0**	**0**	**0**	**0**	**4**	**0**	**0**	**0**	**7**	**0.0**	**3**	**0**	**7**	**4**	**0**	....	....	....	....	....	....	....	....
♦	**New Jersey Devils**	**NHL**	**17**	**1**	**4**	**5**	**1**	**4**	**5**	**19**	**1**	**0**	**1**	**11**	**9.1**	**20**	**5**	**16**	**2**	**1**	**23**	**1**	**4**	**5**	**18**	**1**	**0**	**0**
	NHL Totals		**466**	**70**	**201**	**271**	**75**	**179**	**254**	**477**	**36**	**0**	**9**	**1130**	**6.2**	**674**	**258**	**486**	**130**		**58**	**7**	**14**	**21**	**52**	**3**	**0**	**0**

NHL All-Rookie Team (1993)

Traded to **Montreal** by **NY Islanders** with Pierre Turgeon for Kirk Muller, Mathieu Schneider and Craig Darby, April 5, 1995. • Missed majority of 1999-2000 season recovering from knee injury suffered in exhibition game vs. Boston, September 27, 1999. Traded to **New Jersey** by **Montreal** for Sheldon Souray, Josh DeWolf and New Jersey's 2nd round choice in 2001 Entry Draft, March 1, 2000. Signed as a free agent by **NY Rangers**, July 10, 2000.

• MALEY, David

David Joseph LW – L. 6'2", 195 lbs. b: Beaver Dam, WI, 4/24/1963. Montreal's 4th, 33rd overall, in 1982.

Season	Club	League	GP	G	A	Pts	AG	AA	APts	PIM	PP	SH	GW	S	%	TGF	PGF	TGA	PGA	+/–	GP	G	A	Pts	PIM	PP	SH	GW
1979-1981	Edina-West Cougars	Hi-School	STATISTICS NOT AVAILABLE																									
1981-82	Edina Hornets	Hi-School	26	22	28	50	....	....	....	26	....	....	....	....	....	....	....	....	....	....	....	....	....	....	....	....	....	....
1982-83	University of Wisconsin	WCHA	47	17	23	40	....	....	....	24	....	....	....	....	....	....	....	....	....	....	....	....	....	....	....	....	....	....
1983-84	University of Wisconsin	WCHA	38	10	28	38	....	....	....	56	....	....	....	....	....	....	....	....	....	....	....	....	....	....	....	....	....	....
1984-85	University of Wisconsin	WCHA	38	19	9	28	....	....	....	86	....	....	....	....	....	....	....	....	....	....	....	....	....	....	....	....	....	....
1985-86	University of Wisconsin	WCHA	42	20	40	60	....	....	....	135	....	....	....	....	....	....	....	....	....	....	....	....	....	....	....	....	....	....
♦	**Montreal Canadiens**	**NHL**	**3**	**0**	**0**	**0**	**0**	**0**	**0**	**0**	**0**	**0**	**0**	**0**	**0.0**	**1**	**0**	**1**	**0**	**0**	**7**	**1**	**3**	**4**	**2**	**0**	**0**	**0**
1986-87	**Montreal Canadiens**	**NHL**	**48**	**6**	**12**	**18**	**5**	**9**	**14**	**55**	**0**	**0**	**0**	**45**	**13.3**	**20**	**3**	**18**	**0**	**–1**	....	....	....	....	....	....	....	....
	Sherbrooke Canadiens	AHL	11	1	5	6	....	....	....	25	....	....	....	....	....	....	....	....	....	....	12	7	7	14	10	....	....	....
1987-88	**New Jersey Devils**	**NHL**	**44**	**4**	**2**	**6**	**3**	**1**	**4**	**65**	**1**	**0**	**1**	**44**	**9.1**	**20**	**9**	**24**	**0**	**–13**	**20**	**3**	**1**	**4**	**80**	**0**	**0**	**0**
	Utica Devils	AHL	9	5	3	8	....	....	....	40	....	....	....	....	....	....	....	....	....	....	....	....	....	....	....	....	....	....
1988-89	**New Jersey Devils**	**NHL**	**68**	**5**	**6**	**11**	**4**	**4**	**8**	**249**	**0**	**0**	**0**	**63**	**7.9**	**23**	**7**	**43**	**0**	**–27**	....	....	....	....	....	....	....	....
1989-90	**New Jersey Devils**	**NHL**	**67**	**8**	**17**	**25**	**7**	**12**	**19**	**160**	**0**	**0**	**2**	**82**	**9.8**	**37**	**1**	**39**	**1**	**–2**	**6**	**0**	**0**	**0**	**25**	**0**	**0**	**0**
1990-91	**New Jersey Devils**	**NHL**	**64**	**8**	**14**	**22**	**7**	**11**	**18**	**151**	**1**	**0**	**3**	**67**	**11.9**	**34**	**3**	**25**	**3**	**9**	....	....	....	....	....	....	....	....
	United States	WEC-A	8	0	1	1	....	....	....	2	....	....	....	....	....	....	....	....	....	....	....	....	....	....	....	....	....	....

			REGULAR SEASON																		PLAYOFFS							
Season	Club	League	GP	G	A	Pts	AG	AA	APts	PIM	PP	SH	GW	S	%	TGF	PGF	TGA	PGA	+/–	GP	G	A	Pts	PIM	PP	SH	GW
1991-92	**New Jersey Devils**	**NHL**	**37**	**7**	**11**	**18**	**6**	**8**	**14**	**58**	**1**	**0**	**0**	**42**	**16.7**	**29**	**6**	**24**	**1**	**0**	....	....	....	....	....	....	....	....
	Edmonton Oilers	**NHL**	**23**	**3**	**6**	**9**	**3**	**5**	**8**	**46**	**0**	**0**	**1**	**31**	**9.7**	**20**	**1**	**12**	**1**	**8**	**10**	**1**	**1**	**2**	**4**	**0**	**0**	**0**
1992-93	**Edmonton Oilers**	**NHL**	**13**	**1**	**1**	**2**	**1**	**1**	**2**	**29**	**0**	**0**	**0**	**9**	**11.1**	**3**	**0**	**6**	**0**	**–3**	....	....	....	....	....	....	....	....
	San Jose Sharks	**NHL**	**43**	**1**	**6**	**7**	**1**	**4**	**5**	**126**	**1**	**0**	**0**	**48**	**2.1**	**11**	**3**	**38**	**5**	**–25**	....	....	....	....	....	....	....	....
1993-94	**San Jose Sharks**	**NHL**	**19**	**0**	**0**	**0**	**0**	**0**	**0**	**30**	**0**	**0**	**0**	**4**	**0.0**	**2**	**0**	**3**	**0**	**–1**	....	....	....	....	....	....	....	....
	New York Islanders	**NHL**	**37**	**0**	**6**	**6**	**0**	**5**	**5**	**74**	**0**	**0**	**0**	**19**	**0.0**	**10**	**4**	**12**	**0**	**–6**	**3**	**0**	**0**	**0**	**0**	**0**	**0**	**0**
1994-95			DID NOT PLAY																									
1995-96	San Francisco Spiders	IHL	71	16	13	29	....	....	....	248	....	....	....	....	....	....	....	....	....	....	4	0	0	0	2	....	....	....
1996-1999			OUT OF HOCKEY – RETIRED																									
99-2000	Albany River Rats	AHL	60	5	10	15	....	....	....	52	....	....	....	....	....	....	....	....	....	....	5	0	1	1	4	....	....	....
	NHL Totals		**466**	**43**	**81**	**124**	**37**	**60**	**97**	**1043**	**4**	**0**	**7**	**454**	**9.5**	**210**	**37**	**245**	**11**		**46**	**5**	**5**	**10**	**111**	**0**	**0**	**0**

Traded to **New Jersey** by **Montreal** for New Jersey's 3rd round choice (Mathieu Schneider) in 1987 Entry Draft, June 13, 1987. Traded to **Edmonton** by **New Jersey** for Troy Mallette, January 12, 1992. Claimed on waivers by **San Jose** from **Edmonton**, January 1, 1993. Traded to **NY Islanders** by **San Jose** for cash, January 23, 1994. • Retired from hockey to serve as President of Rollin' Ice, a roller rink complex in California. Signed as a free agent by **New Jersey**, October 1, 1999.

• MALGUNAS, Stewart

Stewart J. D – L. 6', 200 lbs. b: Prince George, B.C., 4/21/1970. Detroit's 3rd, 66th overall, in 1990.

Season	Club	League	GP	G	A	Pts	AG	AA	APts	PIM	PP	SH	GW	S	%	TGF	PGF	TGA	PGA	+/–	GP	G	A	Pts	PIM	PP	SH	GW
1985-86	Prince George Bantam Kings	BCAHA	49	10	25	35	....	....	....	85	....	....	....	....	....	....	....	....	....	....	....	....	....	....	....	....	....	....
1986-87	Prince George Midget Kings	BCAHA	50	11	31	42	....	....	....	102	....	....	....	....	....	....	....	....	....	....	....	....	....	....	....	....	....	....
1987-88	Prince George Spruce Kings	BCJHL	48	12	34	46	....	....	....	99	....	....	....	....	....	....	....	....	....	....	....	....	....	....	....	....	....	....
	New Westminster Bruins	WHL	6	0	0	0	....	....	....	0	....	....	....	....	....	....	....	....	....	....	....	....	....	....	....	....	....	....
1988-89	Seattle Thunderbirds	WHL	72	11	41	52	....	....	....	51	....	....	....	....	....	....	....	....	....	....	....	....	....	....	....	....	....	....
1989-90	Seattle Thunderbirds	WHL	63	15	48	63	....	....	....	116	....	....	....	....	....	....	....	....	....	....	13	2	9	11	32	....	....	....
	Canada	WJC-A	7	0	1	1	....	....	....	0	....	....	....	....	....	....	....	....	....	....	....	....	....	....	....	....	....	....
1990-91	Adirondack Red Wings	AHL	78	5	19	24	....	....	....	70	....	....	....	....	....	....	....	....	....	....	2	0	0	0	4	....	....	....
1991-92	Adirondack Red Wings	AHL	69	4	28	32	....	....	....	82	....	....	....	....	....	....	....	....	....	....	18	2	6	8	28	....	....	....
1992-93	Adirondack Red Wings	AHL	45	3	12	15	....	....	....	39	....	....	....	....	....	....	....	....	....	....	11	3	3	6	8	....	....	....
1993-94	**Philadelphia Flyers**	**NHL**	**67**	**1**	**3**	**4**	**1**	**2**	**3**	**86**	**0**	**0**	**0**	**54**	**1.9**	**55**	**2**	**65**	**14**	**2**	....	....	....	....	....	....	....	....
1994-95	**Philadelphia Flyers**	**NHL**	**4**	**0**	**0**	**0**	**0**	**0**	**0**	**4**	**0**	**0**	**0**	**1**	**0.0**	**3**	**0**	**4**	**0**	**–1**	....	....	....	....	....	....	....	....
	Hershey Bears	AHL	32	3	5	8	....	....	....	28	....	....	....	....	....	....	....	....	....	....	6	2	1	3	31	....	....	....
1995-96	**Winnipeg Jets**	**NHL**	**29**	**0**	**1**	**1**	**0**	**1**	**1**	**32**	**0**	**0**	**0**	**13**	**0.0**	**8**	**0**	**25**	**7**	**–10**	....	....	....	....	....	....	....	....
	Washington Capitals	**NHL**	**1**	**0**	**0**	**0**	**0**	**0**	**0**	**0**	**0**	**0**	**0**	**0**	**0.0**	**0**	**0**	**0**	**0**	**0**	....	....	....	....	....	....	....	....
	Portland Pirates	AHL	16	2	5	7	....	....	....	18	....	....	....	....	....	....	....	....	....	....	13	1	3	4	19	....	....	....
1996-97	**Washington Capitals**	**NHL**	**6**	**0**	**0**	**0**	**0**	**0**	**0**	**2**	**0**	**0**	**0**	**3**	**0.0**	**2**	**0**	**0**	**0**	**2**	....	....	....	....	....	....	....	....
	Portland Pirates	AHL	68	6	12	18	....	....	....	59	....	....	....	....	....	....	....	....	....	....	5	0	0	0	8	....	....	....
1997-98	**Washington Capitals**	**NHL**	**8**	**0**	**0**	**0**	**0**	**0**	**0**	**12**	**0**	**0**	**0**	**5**	**0.0**	**6**	**0**	**6**	**1**	**1**	....	....	....	....	....	....	....	....
	Portland Pirates	AHL	69	14	25	39	....	....	....	73	....	....	....	....	....	....	....	....	....	....	9	1	1	2	19	....	....	....
1998-99	**Washington Capitals**	**NHL**	**10**	**0**	**0**	**0**	**0**	**0**	**0**	**6**	**0**	**0**	**0**	**2**	**0.0**	**1**	**0**	**6**	**0**	**–5**	....	....	....	....	....	....	....	....
	Portland Pirates	AHL	33	2	10	12	....	....	....	49	....	....	....	....	....	....	....	....	....	....	....	....	....	....	....	....	....	....
	Detroit Vipers	IHL	9	0	2	2	....	....	....	10	....	....	....	....	....	....	....	....	....	....	11	0	1	1	21	....	....	....
99-2000	Utah Grizzlies	IHL	34	4	9	13	....	....	....	55	....	....	....	....	....	....	....	....	....	....	....	....	....	....	....	....	....	....
	Calgary Flames	**NHL**	**4**	**0**	**1**	**1**	**0**	**1**	**1**	**2**	**0**	**0**	**0**	**0**	**0.0**	**2**	**0**	**4**	**3**	**1**	....	....	....	....	....	....	....	....
	NHL Totals		**129**	**1**	**5**	**6**	**1**	**4**	**5**	**144**	**0**	**0**	**0**	**78**	**1.3**	**77**	**2**	**110**	**25**		....	....	....	....	....	....	....	....

WHL West First All-Star Team (1990)

Traded to **Philadelphia** by **Detroit** for Philadelphia's 5th round choice (David Arsenault) in 1995 Entry Draft, September 9, 1993. Signed as a free agent by **Winnipeg**, August 9, 1995. Traded to **Washington** by **Winnipeg** for Denis Chasse, February 15, 1996. Traded to **Nashville** by **Washington** for future considerations, February 2, 2000. Claimed on waivers by **Calgary** from **Nashville**, February 3, 2000. • Missed remainder of 1999-2000 season recovering from head injury suffered in game vs. Los Angeles, February 14, 2000.

• MALHOTRA, Manny

C – L. 6'2", 210 lbs. b: Mississauga, Ont., 5/18/1980. NY Rangers' 1st, 7th overall, in 1998.

Season	Club	League	GP	G	A	Pts	AG	AA	APts	PIM	PP	SH	GW	S	%	TGF	PGF	TGA	PGA	+/–	GP	G	A	Pts	PIM	PP	SH	GW
1995-96	Mississauga Reps	MTHL	54	27	44	71	....	....	....	62	....	....	....	....	....	....	....	....	....	....	....	....	....	....	....	....	....	....
1996-97	Guelph Storm	OHL	61	16	28	44	....	....	....	26	....	....	....	....	....	....	....	....	....	....	18	7	7	14	11	....	....	....
1997-98	Guelph Storm	OHL	57	16	35	51	....	....	....	29	....	....	....	....	....	....	....	....	....	....	12	7	6	13	8	....	....	....
	Guelph Storm	Mem-Cup	5	1	6	7	....	....	....	2	....	....	....	....	....	....	....	....	....	....	....	....	....	....	....	....	....	....
1998-99	**New York Rangers**	**NHL**	**73**	**8**	**8**	**16**	**9**	**8**	**17**	**13**	**1**	**0**	**2**	**61**	**13.1**	**23**	**1**	**26**	**2**	**–2**	....	....	....	....	....	....	....	....
99-2000	**New York Rangers**	**NHL**	**27**	**0**	**0**	**0**	**0**	**0**	**0**	**4**	**0**	**0**	**0**	**18**	**0.0**	**2**	**0**	**8**	**0**	**–6**	....	....	....	....	....	....	....	....
	Canada	WJC-A	7	0	2	2	....	....	....	8	....	....	....	....	....	....	....	....	....	....	....	....	....	....	....	....	....	....
	Guelph Storm	OHL	5	2	2	4	....	....	....	4	....	....	....	....	....	....	....	....	....	....	6	0	2	2	4	....	....	....
	Hartford Wolf Pack	AHL	12	1	5	6	....	....	....	2	....	....	....	....	....	....	....	....	....	....	23	1	2	3	10	....	....	....
	NHL Totals		**100**	**8**	**8**	**16**	**9**	**8**	**17**	**17**	**1**	**0**	**2**	**79**	**10.1**	**25**	**1**	**34**	**2**		....	....	....	....	....	....	....	....

Memorial Cup All-Star Team (1998) • Won George Parsons Trophy (Memorial Cup Tournament Most Sportsmanlike Player) (1998) .

• MALIK, Marek

D – L. 6'5", 190 lbs. b: Ostrava, Czech., 6/24/1975. Hartford's 2nd, 72nd overall, in 1993.

Season	Club	League	GP	G	A	Pts	AG	AA	APts	PIM	PP	SH	GW	S	%	TGF	PGF	TGA	PGA	+/–	GP	G	A	Pts	PIM	PP	SH	GW
1992-93	TJ Vitkovice	Czech-Jr.	20	5	10	15	....	....	....	16	....	....	....	....	....	....	....	....	....	....	....	....	....	....	....	....	....	....
	Czech-Republic	EJC-A	2	0	2	2	....	....	....	0	....	....	....	....	....	....	....	....	....	....	....	....	....	....	....	....	....	....
1993-94	HC Vitkovice	Czech-Rep	38	3	3	6	....	....	....	0	....	....	....	....	....	....	....	....	....	....	3	0	1	1	0	....	....	....
	Czech-Republic	WJC-A	7	2	4	6	....	....	....	20	....	....	....	....	....	....	....	....	....	....	....	....	....	....	....	....	....	....
1994-95	Springfield Falcons	AHL	58	11	30	41	....	....	....	91	....	....	....	....	....	....	....	....	....	....	....	....	....	....	....	....	....	....
	Czech-Republic	WJC-A	7	2	5	7	....	....	....	12	....	....	....	....	....	....	....	....	....	....	....	....	....	....	....	....	....	....
	Hartford Whalers	**NHL**	**1**	**0**	**1**	**1**	**0**	**1**	**1**	**0**	**0**	**0**	**0**	**0**	**0.0**	**1**	**0**	**0**	**0**	**1**	....	....	....	....	....	....	....	....
1995-96	**Hartford Whalers**	**NHL**	**7**	**0**	**0**	**0**	**0**	**0**	**0**	**4**	**0**	**0**	**0**	**2**	**0.0**	**4**	**0**	**9**	**2**	**–3**	....	....	....	....	....	....	....	....
	Springfield Falcons	AHL	68	8	14	22	....	....	....	135	....	....	....	....	....	....	....	....	....	....	8	1	3	4	20	....	....	....
1996-97	**Hartford Whalers**	**NHL**	**47**	**1**	**5**	**6**	**1**	**4**	**5**	**50**	**0**	**0**	**1**	**33**	**3.0**	**37**	**2**	**31**	**1**	**5**	....	....	....	....	....	....	....	....
	Springfield Falcons	AHL	3	0	3	3	....	....	....	4	....	....	....	....	....	....	....	....	....	....	....	....	....	....	....	....	....	....
1997-98	Malmo IF	Sweden	37	1	5	6	....	....	....	21	....	....	....	....	....	....	....	....	....	....	....	....	....	....	....	....	....	....
1998-99	HC Vitkovice	Czech-Rep	1	1	0	1	....	....	....	6	....	....	....	....	....	....	....	....	....	....	....	....	....	....	....	....	....	....
	Carolina Hurricanes	**NHL**	**52**	**2**	**9**	**11**	**2**	**9**	**11**	**36**	**1**	**0**	**0**	**36**	**5.6**	**36**	**2**	**56**	**16**	**–6**	**4**	**0**	**0**	**0**	**4**	**0**	**0**	**0**
	Beast of New Haven	AHL	21	2	8	10	....	....	....	28	....	....	....	....	....	....	....	....	....	....	....	....	....	....	....	....	....	....
99-2000	**Carolina Hurricanes**	**NHL**	**57**	**4**	**10**	**14**	**4**	**9**	**13**	**63**	**0**	**0**	**1**	**57**	**7.0**	**48**	**6**	**37**	**8**	**13**	....	....	....	....	....	....	....	....
	NHL Totals		**164**	**7**	**25**	**32**	**7**	**23**	**30**	**153**	**1**	**0**	**2**	**128**	**5.5**	**126**	**10**	**133**	**27**		**4**	**0**	**0**	**0**	**4**	**0**	**0**	**0**

Transferred to **Carolina** after **Hartford** franchise relocated, June 25, 1997.

• MALINOWSKI, Merlin

Merlin Travis "The Magician" C – L. 6', 190 lbs. b: North Battleford, Sask., 9/27/1958. Colorado's 2nd, 27th overall, in 1978.

Season	Club	League	GP	G	A	Pts	AG	AA	APts	PIM	PP	SH	GW	S	%	TGF	PGF	TGA	PGA	+/–	GP	G	A	Pts	PIM	PP	SH	GW
1973-74	Drumheller Falcons	AJHL	2	0	0	0	....	....	....	0	....	....	....	....	....	....	....	....	....	....	....	....	....	....	....	....	....	....
1974-75	Drumheller Falcons	AJHL	59	23	44	67	....	....	....	58	....	....	....	....	....	....	....	....	....	....	....	....	....	....	....	....	....	....
1975-76	Drumheller Falcons	AJHL	59	60	86	146	....	....	....	79	....	....	....	....	....	....	....	....	....	....	....	....	....	....	....	....	....	....
1976-77	Medicine Hat Tigers	WCJHL	70	22	48	70	....	....	....	40	....	....	....	....	....	....	....	....	....	....	4	1	5	6	4	....	....	....
1977-78	Medicine Hat Tigers	WCJHL	72	48	78	126	....	....	....	131	....	....	....	....	....	....	....	....	....	....	11	9	11	20	16	....	....	....
1978-79	Philadelphia Firebirds	AHL	25	3	9	12	....	....	....	12	....	....	....	....	....	....	....	....	....	....	....	....	....	....	....	....	....	....
	Colorado Rockies	**NHL**	**54**	**6**	**17**	**23**	**5**	**12**	**17**	**10**	**0**	**0**	**1**	**76**	**7.9**	**33**	**3**	**50**	**3**	**–17**	....	....	....	....	....	....	....	....
1979-80	**Colorado Rockies**	**NHL**	**10**	**2**	**4**	**6**	**2**	**3**	**5**	**2**	**0**	**0**	**0**	**16**	**12.5**	**8**	**2**	**8**	**1**	**–1**	....	....	....	....	....	....	....	....
	Fort Worth Texans	CHL	66	34	42	76	....	....	....	58	....	....	....	....	....	....	....	....	....	....	15	8	*16	*24	34	....	....	....
1980-81	**Colorado Rockies**	**NHL**	**69**	**25**	**37**	**62**	**19**	**25**	**44**	**61**	**4**	**0**	**1**	**152**	**16.4**	**84**	**33**	**77**	**2**	**–24**	....	....	....	....	....	....	....	....
1981-82	**Colorado Rockies**	**NHL**	**69**	**13**	**28**	**41**	**10**	**19**	**29**	**32**	**0**	**1**	**0**	**95**	**13.7**	**60**	**8**	**80**	**6**	**–22**	....	....	....	....	....	....	....	....
1982-83	**New Jersey Devils**	**NHL**	**5**	**3**	**2**	**5**	**2**	**1**	**3**	**0**	**1**	**0**	**1**	**8**	**37.5**	**6**	**3**	**2**	**0**	**1**	....	....	....	....	....	....	....	....
	Hartford Whalers	**NHL**	**75**	**5**	**23**	**28**	**4**	**16**	**20**	**16**	**1**	**0**	**0**	**94**	**5.3**	**34**	**6**	**71**	**2**	**–41**	....	....	....	....	....	....	....	....
1983-84	EC Arosa	Switz.	32	37	26	63	....	....	....	....	....	....	....	....	....	....	....	....	....	....	....	....	....	....	....	....	....	....
1984-85	EC Arosa	Switz.	38	48	36	84	....	....	....	35	....	....	....	....	....	....	....	....	....	....	....	....	....	....	....	....	....	....
1985-86	EC Arosa	Switz.	36	26	28	54	....	....	....	30	....	....	....	....	....	....	....	....	....	....	....	....	....	....	....	....	....	....
1986-87	SC Langnau	Switz.	36	32	*45	77	....	....	....	42	....	....	....	....	....	....	....	....	....	....	5	8	9	17	....	....	....	....

Season	Club	League	GP	G	A	Pts	AG	AA	APts	PIM	PP	SH	GW	S	%	TGF	PGF	TGA	PGA	+/-	GP	G	A	Pts	PIM	PP	SH	GW
			REGULAR SEASON																		PLAYOFFS							
1987-88	SC Langnau	Switz.	30	23	22	45	....	....	....	26	....	....	....	....	....	....	....	....	....	....	8	6	8	14	....	....	....	....
	Canada	Nat-Team	2	0	0	0	....	....	....	0	....	....	....	....	....	....	....	....	....	....	....	....	....	....	....	....	....	....
	Canada	Olympics	8	3	2	5	....	....	....	0	....	....	....	....	....	....	....	....	....	....	....	....	....	....	....	....	....	....
1988-89	SC Langnau	Switz.	32	28	34	62	....	....	....	....	....	....	....	....	....	....	....	....	....	....	8	7	8	15	....	....	....	....
1989-90	SC Langnau	Switz-2	36	31	30	61	....	....	....	....	....	....	....	....	....	....	....	....	....	....	....	....	....	....	....	....	....	....
	NHL Totals		**282**	**54**	**111**	**165**	**42**	**76**	**118**	**121**	**6**	**1**	**3**	**441**	**12.2**	**225**	**55**	**288**	**14**		....	....	....	....	....	....	....	....

CHL Second All-Star Team (1980)

Transferred to **New Jersey** after **Colorado** franchise relocated, June 30, 1982. Traded to **Hartford** by **New Jersey** with the rights to Scott Fusco for Garry Howatt and Rick Meagher, October 15, 1982.

• MALKOC, Dean

D – L. 6'3", 215 lbs. b: Vancouver, B.C., 1/26/1970. New Jersey's 7th, 95th overall, in 1990.

Season	Club	League	GP	G	A	Pts	AG	AA	APts	PIM	PP	SH	GW	S	%	TGF	PGF	TGA	PGA	+/-	GP	G	A	Pts	PIM	PP	SH	GW
1987-88	Williams Lake Mustangs	PCJHL	55	6	32	38	....	....	....	215	....	....	....	....	....	....	....	....	....	....	....	....	....	....	....	....	....	....
1988-89	Powell River Paper Kings	BCJHL	55	10	32	42	....	....	....	370	....	....	....	....	....	....	....	....	....	....	....	....	....	....	....	....	....	....
1989-90	Kamloops Blazers	WHL	48	3	18	21	....	....	....	209	....	....	....	....	....	....	....	....	....	....	17	0	3	3	56	....	....	....
	Kamloops Blazers	Mem-Cup	2	0	0	0	....	....	....	2	....	....	....	....	....	....	....	....	....	....	....	....	....	....	....	....	....	....
1990-91	Kamloops Blazers	WHL	8	1	4	5	....	....	....	47	....	....	....	....	....	....	....	....	....	....	....	....	....	....	....	....	....	....
	Swift Current Broncos	WHL	56	10	23	33	....	....	....	248	....	....	....	....	....	....	....	....	....	....	3	0	2	2	5	....	....	....
	Utica Devils	AHL	1	0	0	0	....	....	....	0	....	....	....	....	....	....	....	....	....	....	....	....	....	....	....	....	....	....
1991-92	Utica Devils	AHL	66	1	11	12	....	....	....	274	....	....	....	....	....	....	....	....	....	....	4	0	2	2	6	....	....	....
1992-93	Utica Devils	AHL	73	5	19	24	....	....	....	255	....	....	....	....	....	....	....	....	....	....	5	0	1	1	8	....	....	....
1993-94	Albany River Rats	AHL	79	0	9	9	....	....	....	296	....	....	....	....	....	....	....	....	....	....	5	0	0	0	21	....	....	....
1994-95	Albany River Rats	AHL	9	0	1	1	....	....	....	52	....	....	....	....	....	....	....	....	....	....	....	....	....	....	....	....	....	....
	Indianapolis Ice	IHL	62	1	3	4	....	....	....	193	....	....	....	....	....	....	....	....	....	....	....	....	....	....	....	....	....	....
1995-96	**Vancouver Canucks**	**NHL**	**41**	**0**	**2**	**2**	**0**	**2**	**2**	**136**	**0**	**0**	**0**	**8**	**0.0**	**17**	**0**	**33**	**6**	**-10**	....	....	....	....	....	....	....	....
1996-97	**Boston Bruins**	**NHL**	**33**	**0**	**0**	**0**	**0**	**0**	**0**	**70**	**0**	**0**	**0**	**7**	**0.0**	**7**	**0**	**23**	**2**	**-14**	....	....	....	....	....	....	....	....
	Providence Bruins	AHL	4	0	2	2	....	....	....	28	....	....	....	....	....	....	....	....	....	....	....	....	....	....	....	....	....	....
1997-98	**Boston Bruins**	**NHL**	**40**	**1**	**0**	**1**	**1**	**0**	**1**	**86**	**0**	**0**	**0**	**15**	**6.7**	**7**	**0**	**19**	**0**	**-12**	....	....	....	....	....	....	....	....
1998-99	**New York Islanders**	**NHL**	**2**	**0**	**1**	**1**	**0**	**1**	**1**	**7**	**0**	**0**	**0**	**1**	**0.0**	**5**	**0**	**2**	**0**	**3**	....	....	....	....	....	....	....	....
	Lowell Lock Monsters	AHL	61	2	8	10	....	....	....	193	....	....	....	....	....	....	....	....	....	....	3	0	0	0	8	....	....	....
99-2000	Chicago Wolves	IHL	62	2	8	10	....	....	....	130	....	....	....	....	....	....	....	....	....	....	1	0	0	0	0	....	....	....
	NHL Totals		**116**	**1**	**3**	**4**	**1**	**3**	**4**	**299**	**0**	**0**	**0**	**31**	**3.2**	**36**	**0**	**77**	**8**		....	....	....	....	....	....	....	....

Traded to **Chicago** by **New Jersey** for Rob Conn, January 30, 1995. Signed as a free agent by **Vancouver**, September 8, 1995. Claimed by **Boston** from **Vancouver** in NHL Waiver Draft, September 30, 1996. Signed as a free agent by **NY Islanders**, August 19, 1998. Traded to **Anaheim** by **NY Islanders** with Tony Hrkac for Ted Drury, October 29, 1999.

• MALLETTE, Troy

Troy Matthew LW – L. 6'2", 210 lbs. b: Sudbury, Ont., 2/25/1970. NY Rangers' 1st, 22nd overall, in 1988.

Season	Club	League	GP	G	A	Pts	AG	AA	APts	PIM	PP	SH	GW	S	%	TGF	PGF	TGA	PGA	+/-	GP	G	A	Pts	PIM	PP	SH	GW
1985-86	Rayside-Belfour Selects	OMHA	27	24	26	50	....	....	....	75	....	....	....	....	....	....	....	....	....	....	....	....	....	....	....	....	....	....
	Chelmsford Canadiens	NOJHA	STATISTICS NOT AVAILABLE																		....	....	....	....	....	....	....	....
1986-87	Sault Ste. Marie Greyhounds	OHL	65	20	25	45	....	....	....	157	....	....	....	....	....	....	....	....	....	....	4	0	2	2	12	....	....	....
1987-88	Sault Ste. Marie Greyhounds	OHL	62	18	30	48	....	....	....	186	....	....	....	....	....	....	....	....	....	....	6	1	3	4	12	....	....	....
1988-89	Sault Ste. Marie Greyhounds	OHL	64	39	37	76	....	....	....	172	....	....	....	....	....	....	....	....	....	....	....	....	....	....	....	....	....	....
1989-90	**New York Rangers**	**NHL**	**79**	**13**	**16**	**29**	**11**	**11**	**22**	**305**	**4**	**0**	**1**	**107**	**12.1**	**54**	**16**	**46**	**0**	**-8**	**10**	**2**	**2**	**4**	**81**	**0**	**0**	**0**
1990-91	**New York Rangers**	**NHL**	**71**	**12**	**10**	**22**	**11**	**8**	**19**	**252**	**0**	**0**	**2**	**91**	**13.2**	**33**	**1**	**41**	**1**	**-8**	**5**	**0**	**0**	**0**	**18**	**0**	**0**	**0**
1991-92	**Edmonton Oilers**	**NHL**	**15**	**1**	**3**	**4**	**1**	**2**	**3**	**36**	**0**	**0**	**0**	**9**	**11.1**	**7**	**0**	**8**	**0**	**-1**	....	....	....	....	....	....	....	....
	New Jersey Devils	**NHL**	**17**	**3**	**4**	**7**	**3**	**3**	**6**	**43**	**0**	**0**	**0**	**19**	**15.8**	**9**	**0**	**2**	**0**	**7**	....	....	....	....	....	....	....	....
1992-93	**New Jersey Devils**	**NHL**	**34**	**4**	**3**	**7**	**3**	**2**	**5**	**56**	**0**	**0**	**0**	**19**	**21.1**	**14**	**0**	**11**	**0**	**3**	....	....	....	....	....	....	....	....
	Utica Devils	AHL	5	3	3	6	....	....	....	17	....	....	....	....	....	....	....	....	....	....	....	....	....	....	....	....	....	....
1993-94	**Ottawa Senators**	**NHL**	**82**	**7**	**16**	**23**	**6**	**12**	**18**	**166**	**0**	**0**	**0**	**100**	**7.0**	**32**	**4**	**72**	**11**	**-33**	....	....	....	....	....	....	....	....
1994-95	**Ottawa Senators**	**NHL**	**23**	**3**	**5**	**8**	**5**	**7**	**12**	**35**	**0**	**0**	**1**	**21**	**14.3**	**16**	**0**	**10**	**0**	**6**	....	....	....	....	....	....	....	....
	P.E.I. Senators	AHL	5	1	5	6	....	....	....	9	....	....	....	....	....	....	....	....	....	....	....	....	....	....	....	....	....	....
1995-96	**Ottawa Senators**	**NHL**	**64**	**2**	**3**	**5**	**2**	**2**	**4**	**171**	**0**	**0**	**0**	**51**	**3.9**	**11**	**0**	**18**	**0**	**-7**	....	....	....	....	....	....	....	....
1996-97	**Boston Bruins**	**NHL**	**68**	**6**	**8**	**14**	**6**	**7**	**13**	**155**	**0**	**0**	**2**	**61**	**9.8**	**25**	**1**	**32**	**0**	**-8**	....	....	....	....	....	....	....	....
1997-98	**Tampa Bay Lightning**	**NHL**	**3**	**0**	**0**	**0**	**0**	**0**	**0**	**7**	**0**	**0**	**0**	**0**	**0.0**	**0**	**0**	**0**	**0**	**0**	....	....	....	....	....	....	....	....
	NHL Totals		**456**	**51**	**68**	**119**	**48**	**54**	**102**	**1226**	**4**	**0**	**6**	**478**	**10.7**	**201**	**22**	**240**	**12**		**15**	**2**	**2**	**4**	**99**	**0**	**0**	**0**

Transferred to **Edmonton** by **NY Rangers** as compensation for NY Rangers' signing of free agent Adam Graves, September 12, 1991. Traded to **New Jersey** by **Edmonton** for David Maley, January 12, 1992. Traded to **Ottawa** by **New Jersey** with Craig Billington and New Jersey's 4th round choice (Cosmo Dupaul) in 1993 Entry Draft for Peter Sidorkiewicz and future considerations (Mike Peluso, June 26, 1993), June 20, 1993. Signed as a free agent by **Boston**, July 24, 1996. Signed as a free agent by **Tampa Bay**, October 2, 1997. • Suffered eventual career-ending back injury in game vs. Chicago, October 25, 1997.

• MALONE, Greg

William Gregory C – L. 6', 190 lbs. b: Fredericton, N.B., 3/8/1956. Pittsburgh's 2nd, 19th overall, in 1976.

Season	Club	League	GP	G	A	Pts	AG	AA	APts	PIM	PP	SH	GW	S	%	TGF	PGF	TGA	PGA	+/-	GP	G	A	Pts	PIM	PP	SH	GW
1971-72	Fredericton Black Kats	Hi-School	21	26	21	47	....	....	....	28	....	....	....	....	....	....	....	....	....	....	4	6	7	13	4	....	....	....
1972-73	Fredericton Black Kats	Hi-School	23	*35	*41	*76	....	....	....	79	....	....	....	....	....	....	....	....	....	....	8	*17	*10	*27	*37	....	....	....
1973-74	Oshawa Generals	OMJHL	62	11	45	56	....	....	....	63	....	....	....	....	....	....	....	....	....	....	....	....	....	....	....	....	....	....
1974-75	Oshawa Generals	OMJHL	68	37	41	78	....	....	....	86	....	....	....	....	....	....	....	....	....	....	5	1	3	4	9	....	....	....
1975-76	Oshawa Generals	OMJHL	61	36	36	72	....	....	....	75	....	....	....	....	....	....	....	....	....	....	5	3	2	5	2	....	....	....
1976-77	**Pittsburgh Penguins**	**NHL**	**66**	**18**	**19**	**37**	**16**	**15**	**31**	**43**	**4**	**0**	**1**	**121**	**14.9**	**46**	**7**	**40**	**4**	**3**	**3**	**1**	**1**	**2**	**2**	**0**	**0**	**1**
1977-78	**Pittsburgh Penguins**	**NHL**	**78**	**18**	**43**	**61**	**16**	**33**	**49**	**80**	**2**	**0**	**1**	**179**	**10.1**	**88**	**13**	**118**	**27**	**-16**	....	....	....	....	....	....	....	....
1978-79	**Pittsburgh Penguins**	**NHL**	**80**	**35**	**30**	**65**	**30**	**22**	**52**	**52**	**8**	**0**	**5**	**198**	**17.7**	**94**	**13**	**87**	**12**	**6**	**7**	**0**	**1**	**1**	**10**	**0**	**0**	**0**
1979-80	**Pittsburgh Penguins**	**NHL**	**51**	**19**	**32**	**51**	**16**	**23**	**39**	**46**	**5**	**0**	**2**	**103**	**18.4**	**71**	**16**	**65**	**14**	**4**	....	....	....	....	....	....	....	....
1980-81	**Pittsburgh Penguins**	**NHL**	**62**	**21**	**29**	**50**	**16**	**19**	**35**	**68**	**5**	**0**	**2**	**144**	**14.6**	**77**	**22**	**76**	**7**	**-14**	**5**	**2**	**3**	**5**	**16**	**0**	**0**	**0**
1981-82	**Pittsburgh Penguins**	**NHL**	**78**	**15**	**24**	**39**	**12**	**16**	**28**	**125**	**3**	**0**	**2**	**120**	**12.5**	**62**	**13**	**79**	**6**	**-24**	**3**	**0**	**0**	**0**	**4**	**0**	**0**	**0**
1982-83	**Pittsburgh Penguins**	**NHL**	**80**	**17**	**44**	**61**	**14**	**31**	**45**	**82**	**3**	**0**	**0**	**158**	**10.8**	**91**	**26**	**145**	**51**	**-29**	....	....	....	....	....	....	....	....
1983-84	**Hartford Whalers**	**NHL**	**78**	**17**	**37**	**54**	**14**	**25**	**39**	**56**	**3**	**0**	**2**	**124**	**13.7**	**74**	**19**	**80**	**15**	**-10**	....	....	....	....	....	....	....	....
1984-85	**Hartford Whalers**	**NHL**	**76**	**22**	**39**	**61**	**18**	**27**	**45**	**67**	**6**	**0**	**4**	**131**	**16.8**	**73**	**18**	**75**	**4**	**-16**	....	....	....	....	....	....	....	....
1985-86	**Hartford Whalers**	**NHL**	**22**	**6**	**7**	**13**	**5**	**5**	**10**	**24**	**1**	**0**	**0**	**35**	**17.1**	**19**	**6**	**19**	**1**	**-5**	....	....	....	....	....	....	....	....
	Quebec Nordiques	**NHL**	**27**	**3**	**5**	**8**	**2**	**3**	**5**	**18**	**0**	**0**	**0**	**26**	**11.5**	**10**	**0**	**15**	**2**	**-3**	**1**	**0**	**0**	**0**	**0**	**0**	**0**	**0**
1986-87	**Quebec Nordiques**	**NHL**	**6**	**0**	**1**	**1**	**0**	**1**	**1**	**0**	**0**	**0**	**0**	**6**	**0.0**	**1**	**0**	**1**	**0**	**0**	**1**	**0**	**0**	**0**	**0**	**0**	**0**	**0**
	Fredericton Express	AHL	49	13	22	35	....	....	....	50	....	....	....	....	....	....	....	....	....	....	....	....	....	....	....	....	....	....
	NHL Totals		**704**	**191**	**310**	**501**	**159**	**220**	**379**	**661**	**40**	**0**	**19**	**1345**	**14.2**	**706**	**153**	**800**	**143**		**20**	**3**	**5**	**8**	**32**	**0**	**0**	**1**

Traded to **Hartford** by **Pittsburgh** for Hartford's 5th round choice (Bruce Racine) in 1985 Entry Draft, September 30, 1983. Traded to **Quebec** by **Hartford** for Wayne Babych, January 17, 1986.

• MALONEY, Dan

Daniel Charles LW – L. 6'2", 195 lbs. b: Barrie, Ont., 9/24/1950. Chicago's 1st, 14th overall, in 1970.

Season	Club	League	GP	G	A	Pts	AG	AA	APts	PIM	PP	SH	GW	S	%	TGF	PGF	TGA	PGA	+/-	GP	G	A	Pts	PIM	PP	SH	GW
1967-68	Markham Waxers	OHA-B	STATISTICS NOT AVAILABLE																									
1968-69	London Knights	OHA-Jr.	53	12	28	40	....	....	....	62	....	....	....	....	....	....	....	....	....	....	6	2	1	3	16	....	....	....
1969-70	London Knights	OHA-Jr.	54	31	35	66	....	....	....	232	....	....	....	....	....	....	....	....	....	....	11	1	3	4	66	....	....	....
1970-71	**Chicago Black Hawks**	**NHL**	**74**	**12**	**14**	**26**	**12**	**12**	**24**	**174**	**2**	**0**	**1**	**98**	**12.2**	**39**	**5**	**27**	**0**	**7**	**10**	**0**	**1**	**1**	**8**	**0**	**0**	**0**
1971-72	Dallas Black Hawks	CHL	72	25	45	70	....	....	....	161	....	....	....	....	....	....	....	....	....	....	12	4	5	9	44	....	....	....
1972-73	**Chicago Black Hawks**	**NHL**	**57**	**13**	**17**	**30**	**12**	**13**	**25**	**63**	**5**	**0**	**4**	**104**	**12.5**	**45**	**10**	**25**	**1**	**11**	....	....	....	....	....	....	....	....
	Los Angeles Kings	**NHL**	**14**	**4**	**7**	**11**	**4**	**6**	**10**	**18**	**0**	**0**	**1**	**35**	**11.4**	**18**	**4**	**8**	**0**	**6**	....	....	....	....	....	....	....	....
1973-74	**Los Angeles Kings**	**NHL**	**65**	**15**	**17**	**32**	**14**	**14**	**28**	**113**	**5**	**0**	**5**	**157**	**9.6**	**55**	**11**	**38**	**0**	**6**	**5**	**0**	**0**	**0**	**2**	**0**	**0**	**0**
1974-75	**Los Angeles Kings**	**NHL**	**80**	**27**	**39**	**66**	**24**	**29**	**53**	**165**	**3**	**0**	**2**	**227**	**11.9**	**91**	**11**	**53**	**2**	**29**	**3**	**0**	**0**	**0**	**2**	**0**	**0**	**0**
1975-76	**Detroit Red Wings**	**NHL**	**77**	**27**	**39**	**66**	**24**	**29**	**53**	**203**	**6**	**2**	**3**	**254**	**10.6**	**94**	**28**	**84**	**18**	**0**	....	....	....	....	....	....	....	....
1976-77	**Detroit Red Wings**	**NHL**	**34**	**13**	**13**	**26**	**12**	**10**	**22**	**64**	**3**	**1**	**0**	**107**	**12.1**	**43**	**14**	**36**	**10**	**3**	....	....	....	....	....	....	....	....
1977-78	**Detroit Red Wings**	**NHL**	**66**	**16**	**29**	**45**	**15**	**22**	**37**	**151**	**3**	**0**	**1**	**165**	**9.7**	**74**	**23**	**48**	**1**	**4**	....	....	....	....	....	....	....	....
	Toronto Maple Leafs	**NHL**	**13**	**3**	**4**	**7**	**3**	**3**	**6**	**25**	**0**	**0**	**1**	**27**	**11.1**	**15**	**4**	**16**	**0**	**-5**	**13**	**1**	**3**	**4**	**17**	**1**	**0**	**0**
1978-79	**Toronto Maple Leafs**	**NHL**	**77**	**17**	**36**	**53**	**15**	**26**	**41**	**157**	**0**	**0**	**5**	**141**	**12.1**	**82**	**17**	**47**	**1**	**19**	**6**	**3**	**3**	**6**	**2**	**1**	**0**	**1**

			REGULAR SEASON																		PLAYOFFS							
Season	Club	League	GP	G	A	Pts	AG	AA	APts	PIM	PP	SH	GW	S	%	TGF	PGF	TGA	PGA	+/–	GP	G	A	Pts	PIM	PP	SH	GW
1979-80	**Toronto Maple Leafs**	**NHL**	**71**	**17**	**16**	**33**	**14**	**12**	**26**	**102**	**1**	**0**	**1**	**108**	**15.7**	**50**	**5**	**58**	**0**	**–13**	....	....	....	....	....	....	....	....
1980-81	**Toronto Maple Leafs**	**NHL**	**65**	**20**	**21**	**41**	**16**	**14**	**30**	**183**	**13**	**0**	**2**	**80**	**25.0**	**70**	**41**	**39**	**0**	**–10**	**3**	**0**	**0**	**0**	**4**	**0**	**0**	**0**
1981-82	**Toronto Maple Leafs**	**NHL**	**44**	**8**	**7**	**15**	**6**	**5**	**11**	**71**	**1**	**0**	**0**	**60**	**13.3**	**35**	**5**	**41**	**0**	**–11**	....	....	....	....	....	....	....	....
	NHL Totals		**737**	**192**	**259**	**451**	**171**	**195**	**366**	**1489**	**42**	**3**	**26**	**1563**	**12.3**	**711**	**178**	**520**	**33**		**40**	**4**	**7**	**11**	**35**	**2**	**0**	**1**

CHL First All-Star Team (1972) • Played in NHL All-Star Game (1976)

Traded to **LA Kings** by **Chicago** for Ralph Backstrom, February 26, 1973. Traded to **Detroit** by **LA Kings** with Terry Harper and LA Kings' 2nd round choice (later traded to Minnesota — Minnesota selected Jim Roberts) in 1976 Amateur Draft for Bart Crashley and the rights to Marcel Dionne, June 23, 1975. Traded to **Toronto** by **Detroit** with Detroit's 2nd round choice (Craig Muni) in 1980 Entry Draft for Errol Thompson and Toronto's 1st (Brent Peterson) and 2nd (Al Jenson) round choices in 1978 Amateur Draft and Toronto's 1st round choice (Mike Blaisdell) in 1980 Entry Draft, March 13, 1978.

• MALONEY, Dave

David Wilfred D – L. 6'1", 195 lbs. b: Kitchener, Ont., 7/31/1956. NY Rangers' 1st, 14th overall, in 1974.

Season	Club	League	GP	G	A	Pts	AG	AA	APts	PIM	PP	SH	GW	S	%	TGF	PGF	TGA	PGA	+/–	GP	G	A	Pts	PIM	PP	SH	GW
1971-72	St. Michael's Buzzers	OHA-B	STATISTICS NOT AVAILABLE																									
	Kitchener Rangers	OMJHL	1	0	0	0	....	....	....	0	....	....	....	....	....	....	....	....	....	....	2	0	0	0	2	....	....	....
1972-73	Kitchener Rangers	OMJHL	49	8	21	29	....	....	....	101	....	....	....	....	....	....	....	....	....	....	....	....	....	....	....	....	....	....
1973-74	Kitchener Rangers	OMJHL	69	15	53	68	....	....	....	109	....	....	....	....	....	....	....	....	....	....	....	....	....	....	....	....	....	....
1974-75	**New York Rangers**	**NHL**	**4**	**0**	**2**	**2**	**0**	**1**	**1**	**0**	**0**	**0**	**0**	**2**	**0.0**	**5**	**0**	**3**	**0**	**2**	....	....	....	....	....	....	....	....
	Providence Reds	AHL	58	5	28	33	....	....	....	122	....	....	....	....	....	....	....	....	....	....	6	0	6	6	6	....	....	....
1975-76	**New York Rangers**	**NHL**	**21**	**1**	**3**	**4**	**1**	**2**	**3**	**66**	**0**	**0**	**0**	**40**	**2.5**	**18**	**3**	**29**	**7**	**–7**	....	....	....	....	....	....	....	....
	Providence Reds	AHL	26	5	17	22	....	....	....	81	....	....	....	....	....	....	....	....	....	....	....	....	....	....	....	....	....	....
1976-77	**New York Rangers**	**NHL**	**66**	**3**	**18**	**21**	**3**	**14**	**17**	**100**	**0**	**0**	**1**	**126**	**2.4**	**79**	**3**	**108**	**24**	**–8**	....	....	....	....	....	....	....	....
1977-78	**New York Rangers**	**NHL**	**56**	**2**	**19**	**21**	**2**	**15**	**17**	**63**	**0**	**0**	**0**	**71**	**2.8**	**68**	**3**	**65**	**18**	**18**	**3**	**0**	**0**	**0**	**11**	**0**	**0**	**0**
1978-79	**New York Rangers**	**NHL**	**76**	**11**	**17**	**28**	**9**	**12**	**21**	**151**	**1**	**2**	**1**	**83**	**13.3**	**83**	**1**	**108**	**43**	**17**	**17**	**3**	**4**	**7**	**45**	**0**	**1**	**0**
1979-80	**New York Rangers**	**NHL**	**77**	**12**	**25**	**37**	**10**	**18**	**28**	**186**	**3**	**0**	**0**	**102**	**11.8**	**97**	**15**	**91**	**19**	**10**	**8**	**2**	**1**	**3**	**8**	**0**	**1**	**0**
1980-81	**New York Rangers**	**NHL**	**79**	**11**	**36**	**47**	**9**	**24**	**33**	**132**	**3**	**0**	**1**	**140**	**7.9**	**121**	**26**	**101**	**30**	**24**	**2**	**0**	**2**	**2**	**9**	**0**	**0**	**0**
1981-82	New York Rangers	DN-Cup	4	1	1	2	....	....	....	....	....	....	....	....	....	....	....	....	....	....	....	....	....	....	....	....	....	....
	New York Rangers	**NHL**	**64**	**13**	**36**	**49**	**10**	**24**	**34**	**105**	**6**	**1**	**3**	**107**	**12.1**	**101**	**22**	**106**	**29**	**2**	**10**	**1**	**4**	**5**	**6**	**1**	**0**	**1**
1982-83	**New York Rangers**	**NHL**	**78**	**8**	**42**	**50**	**7**	**29**	**36**	**132**	**3**	**1**	**0**	**136**	**5.9**	**107**	**31**	**117**	**38**	**–3**	**7**	**1**	**6**	**7**	**10**	**0**	**0**	**0**
1983-84	**New York Rangers**	**NHL**	**68**	**7**	**26**	**33**	**6**	**18**	**24**	**168**	**2**	**0**	**1**	**76**	**9.2**	**90**	**20**	**75**	**16**	**11**	**1**	**0**	**0**	**0**	**2**	**0**	**0**	**0**
1984-85	**New York Rangers**	**NHL**	**16**	**2**	**1**	**3**	**2**	**1**	**3**	**10**	**0**	**0**	**0**	**16**	**12.5**	**14**	**0**	**12**	**1**	**3**	....	....	....	....	....	....	....	....
	Buffalo Sabres	**NHL**	**52**	**1**	**21**	**22**	**1**	**14**	**15**	**41**	**0**	**0**	**0**	**37**	**2.7**	**56**	**4**	**37**	**5**	**20**	**1**	**0**	**0**	**0**	**0**	**0**	**0**	**0**
	NHL Totals		**657**	**71**	**246**	**317**	**60**	**172**	**232**	**1154**	**18**	**4**	**7**	**936**	**7.6**	**839**	**128**	**852**	**230**		**49**	**7**	**17**	**24**	**91**	**1**	**2**	**1**

• Brother of Don • OMJHL Second All-Star Team (1974)

Traded to **Buffalo** by **NY Rangers** with Chris Renaud for Steve Patrick and Jim Wiemer, December 6, 1984.

• MALONEY, Don

Donald Michael "Big Frame" LW – L. 6'1", 190 lbs. b: Lindsay, Ont., 9/5/1958. NY Rangers' 1st, 26th overall, in 1978.

Season	Club	League	GP	G	A	Pts	AG	AA	APts	PIM	PP	SH	GW	S	%	TGF	PGF	TGA	PGA	+/–	GP	G	A	Pts	PIM	PP	SH	GW
1974-75	Kitchener Greenshirts	OHA-B	STATISTICS NOT AVAILABLE																									
	Kitchener Rangers	OMJHL	5	1	3	4	....	....	....	0	....	....	....	....	....	....	....	....	....	....	....	....	....	....	....	....	....	....
1975-76	Kitchener Rangers	OMJHL	61	27	41	68	....	....	....	132	....	....	....	....	....	....	....	....	....	....	5	3	1	4	9	....	....	....
1976-77	Kitchener Rangers	OMJHL	38	22	34	56	....	....	....	126	....	....	....	....	....	....	....	....	....	....	....	....	....	....	....	....	....	....
1977-78	Kitchener Rangers	OMJHL	62	30	74	104	....	....	....	143	....	....	....	....	....	....	....	....	....	....	9	4	9	13	40	....	....	....
1978-79	**New York Rangers**	**NHL**	**28**	**9**	**17**	**26**	**8**	**12**	**20**	**39**	**3**	**0**	**0**	**39**	**23.1**	**36**	**11**	**22**	**1**	**4**	**18**	**7**	***13**	**20**	**19**	**0**	**0**	**1**
	New Haven Nighthawks	AHL	38	18	26	44	....	....	....	62	....	....	....	....	....	....	....	....	....	....	....	....	....	....	....	....	....	....
1979-80	**New York Rangers**	**NHL**	**79**	**25**	**48**	**73**	**21**	**35**	**56**	**97**	**6**	**1**	**3**	**123**	**20.3**	**97**	**33**	**84**	**5**	**–15**	**9**	**0**	**4**	**4**	**10**	**0**	**0**	**0**
1980-81	**New York Rangers**	**NHL**	**61**	**29**	**23**	**52**	**23**	**15**	**38**	**99**	**7**	**5**	**9**	**124**	**23.4**	**89**	**23**	**60**	**11**	**17**	**13**	**1**	**6**	**7**	**13**	**1**	**0**	**0**
1981-82	New York Rangers	DN-Cup	4	0	2	2	....	....	....	....	....	....	....	....	....	....	....	....	....	....	....	....	....	....	....	....	....	....
	New York Rangers	**NHL**	**54**	**22**	**36**	**58**	**17**	**24**	**41**	**73**	**6**	**1**	**5**	**99**	**22.2**	**88**	**20**	**71**	**12**	**9**	**10**	**5**	**5**	**10**	**10**	**2**	**0**	**0**
1982-83	**New York Rangers**	**NHL**	**78**	**29**	**40**	**69**	**24**	**28**	**52**	**88**	**14**	**1**	**2**	**133**	**21.8**	**105**	**39**	**83**	**12**	**–5**	**5**	**0**	**1**	**1**	**0**	**0**	**0**	**0**
1983-84	**New York Rangers**	**NHL**	**79**	**24**	**42**	**66**	**19**	**29**	**48**	**62**	**5**	**3**	**5**	**129**	**18.6**	**90**	**30**	**87**	**22**	**–5**	**5**	**1**	**4**	**5**	**0**	**0**	**0**	**0**
1984-85	**New York Rangers**	**NHL**	**37**	**11**	**16**	**27**	**9**	**11**	**20**	**32**	**5**	**0**	**0**	**56**	**19.6**	**41**	**13**	**45**	**8**	**–9**	**3**	**4**	**0**	**4**	**2**	**2**	**0**	**0**
	Canada	WEC-A	8	1	1	2	....	....	....	....	....	....	....	....	....	....	....	....	....	....	....	....	....	....	....	....	....	....
1985-86	**New York Rangers**	**NHL**	**68**	**11**	**17**	**28**	**9**	**11**	**20**	**56**	**0**	**0**	**1**	**89**	**12.4**	**55**	**10**	**50**	**23**	**18**	**16**	**2**	**1**	**3**	**31**	**0**	**0**	**0**
1986-87	**New York Rangers**	**NHL**	**72**	**19**	**38**	**57**	**16**	**28**	**44**	**117**	**3**	**3**	**0**	**130**	**14.6**	**83**	**13**	**88**	**25**	**7**	**6**	**2**	**1**	**3**	**6**	**0**	**0**	**0**
1987-88	**New York Rangers**	**NHL**	**66**	**12**	**21**	**33**	**10**	**15**	**25**	**60**	**1**	**0**	**2**	**88**	**13.6**	**46**	**1**	**59**	**26**	**12**	....	....	....	....	....	....	....	....
1988-89	**New York Rangers**	**NHL**	**31**	**4**	**9**	**13**	**3**	**6**	**9**	**16**	**0**	**0**	**0**	**38**	**10.5**	**22**	**0**	**36**	**16**	**2**	....	....	....	....	....	....	....	....
	Hartford Whalers	**NHL**	**21**	**3**	**11**	**14**	**3**	**8**	**11**	**23**	**1**	**0**	**1**	**34**	**8.8**	**18**	**5**	**13**	**1**	**1**	**4**	**0**	**0**	**0**	**8**	**0**	**0**	**0**
1989-90	**New York Islanders**	**NHL**	**79**	**16**	**27**	**43**	**14**	**19**	**33**	**47**	**0**	**1**	**2**	**113**	**14.2**	**61**	**4**	**73**	**22**	**6**	**5**	**0**	**0**	**0**	**2**	**0**	**0**	**0**
1990-91	**New York Islanders**	**NHL**	**12**	**0**	**5**	**5**	**0**	**4**	**4**	**6**	**0**	**0**	**0**	**10**	**0.0**	**5**	**0**	**10**	**2**	**–3**	....	....	....	....	....	....	....	....
1991-1992	**New York Islanders**	**NHL**	DID NOT PLAY – ASSISTANT GENERAL MANAGER																									
1992-1995	**New York Islanders**	**NHL**	DID NOT PLAY – GENERAL MANAGER																									
1995-1996			OUT OF HOCKEY – RETIRED																									
1996-1997	**San Jose Sharks**	**NHL**	DID NOT PLAY – SCOUTING																									
1997-2000	**New York Rangers**	**NHL**	DID NOT PLAY – ASSISTANT GENERAL MANAGER																									
	NHL Totals		**765**	**214**	**350**	**564**	**176**	**245**	**421**	**815**	**51**	**15**	**30**	**1205**	**17.8**	**836**	**202**	**781**	**186**		**94**	**22**	**35**	**57**	**101**	**5**	**0**	**1**

• Brother of Dave • Played in NHL All-Star Game (1983, 1984)

• Missed majority of 1984-85 season recovering from leg injury suffered in game vs. New Jersey, November 18, 1984. Traded to **Hartford** by **NY Rangers** with Brian Lawton and Norm MacIver for Carey Wilson and Hartford's 5th round choice (Lubos Rob) in 1990 Entry Draft, December 26, 1988. Signed as a free agent by **NY Islanders**, August 25, 1989.

• MALTAIS, Steve

Steve G. LW – L. 6'2", 205 lbs. b: Arvida, Que., 1/25/1969. Washington's 2nd, 57th overall, in 1987.

Season	Club	League	GP	G	A	Pts	AG	AA	APts	PIM	PP	SH	GW	S	%	TGF	PGF	TGA	PGA	+/–	GP	G	A	Pts	PIM	PP	SH	GW
1985-86	Wexford Midget Raiders	MTHL	33	35	19	54	....	....	....	38	....	....	....	....	....	....	....	....	....	....	....	....	....	....	....	....	....	....
	Wexford Raiders	OJHL-B	1	1	0	1	....	....	....	0	....	....	....	....	....	....	....	....	....	....	....	....	....	....	....	....	....	....
1986-87	Cornwall Royals	OHL	65	32	12	44	....	....	....	29	....	....	....	....	....	....	....	....	....	....	5	0	0	0	2	....	....	....
1987-88	Cornwall Royals	OHL	59	39	46	85	....	....	....	30	....	....	....	....	....	....	....	....	....	....	11	9	6	15	33	....	....	....
1988-89	Cornwall Royals	OHL	58	53	70	123	....	....	....	67	....	....	....	....	....	....	....	....	....	....	18	14	16	30	16	....	....	....
	Fort Wayne Komets	IHL	....	....	....	....	....	....	....	....	....	....	....	....	....	....	....	....	....	....	4	2	1	3	0	....	....	....
1989-90	**Washington Capitals**	**NHL**	**8**	**0**	**0**	**0**	**0**	**0**	**0**	**2**	**0**	**0**	**0**	**11**	**0.0**	**3**	**0**	**5**	**0**	**–2**	**1**	**0**	**0**	**0**	**0**	**0**	**0**	**0**
	Baltimore Skipjacks	AHL	67	29	37	66	....	....	....	54	....	....	....	....	....	....	....	....	....	....	12	6	10	16	6	....	....	....
1990-91	**Washington Capitals**	**NHL**	**7**	**0**	**0**	**0**	**0**	**0**	**0**	**2**	**0**	**0**	**0**	**3**	**0.0**	**1**	**0**	**2**	**0**	**–1**	....	....	....	....	....	....	....	....
	Baltimore Skipjacks	AHL	73	36	43	79	....	....	....	97	....	....	....	....	....	....	....	....	....	....	6	1	4	5	10	....	....	....
1991-92	**Minnesota North Stars**	**NHL**	**12**	**2**	**1**	**3**	**2**	**1**	**3**	**2**	**0**	**0**	**0**	**6**	**33.3**	**5**	**0**	**7**	**1**	**–1**	....	....	....	....	....	....	....	....
	Kalamazoo Wings	IHL	48	25	31	56	....	....	....	51	....	....	....	....	....	....	....	....	....	....	....	....	....	....	....	....	....	....
	Halifax Citadels	AHL	10	3	3	6	....	....	....	0	....	....	....	....	....	....	....	....	....	....	....	....	....	....	....	....	....	....
1992-93	**Tampa Bay Lightning**	**NHL**	**63**	**7**	**13**	**20**	**6**	**9**	**15**	**35**	**4**	**0**	**1**	**96**	**7.3**	**46**	**14**	**59**	**7**	**–20**	....	....	....	....	....	....	....	....
	Atlanta Knights	IHL	16	14	10	24	....	....	....	22	....	....	....	....	....	....	....	....	....	....	....	....	....	....	....	....	....	....
1993-94	**Detroit Red Wings**	**NHL**	**4**	**0**	**1**	**1**	**0**	**1**	**1**	**0**	**0**	**0**	**0**	**2**	**0.0**	**1**	**0**	**2**	**0**	**–1**	....	....	....	....	....	....	....	....
	Adirondack Red Wings	AHL	73	35	49	84	....	....	....	79	....	....	....	....	....	....	....	....	....	....	12	5	11	16	14	....	....	....
1994-95	Chicago Wolves	IHL	79	*57	40	97	....	....	....	145	....	....	....	....	....	....	....	....	....	....	3	1	1	2	0	....	....	....
1995-96	Chicago Wolves	IHL	81	56	66	122	....	....	....	161	....	....	....	....	....	....	....	....	....	....	9	7	7	14	20	....	....	....
1996-97	Chicago Wolves	IHL	81	*60	54	114	....	....	....	62	....	....	....	....	....	....	....	....	....	....	4	2	0	2	4	....	....	....
1997-98	Chicago Wolves	IHL	82	*46	57	103	....	....	....	120	....	....	....	....	....	....	....	....	....	....	22	8	11	19	28	....	....	....
1998-99	Chicago Wolves	IHL	82	*56	44	100	....	....	....	164	....	....	....	....	....	....	....	....	....	....	10	4	6	10	2	....	....	....
99-2000	Chicago Wolves	IHL	82	*44	46	*90	....	....	....	78	....	....	....	....	....	....	....	....	....	....	16	9	4	13	14	....	....	....
	NHL Totals		**94**	**9**	**15**	**24**	**8**	**11**	**19**	**41**	**4**	**0**	**1**	**118**	**7.6**	**56**	**14**	**75**	**8**		**1**	**0**	**0**	**0**	**0**	**0**	**0**	**0**

OHL Second All-Star Team (1989) • IHL First All-Star Team (1995, 1999, 2000) • IHL Second All-Star Team (1996, 1997) • Won Leo P. Lamoureux Memorial Trophy (Top Scorer - IHL) (2000)

Traded to **Minnesota** by **Washington** with Trent Klatt for Shawn Chambers, June 21, 1991. Traded to **Quebec** by **Minnesota** for Kip Miller, March 8, 1992. Claimed by **Tampa Bay** from **Quebec** in Expansion Draft, June 18, 1992. Traded to **Detroit** by **Tampa Bay** for Dennis Vial, June 8, 1993. Signed as a free agent by **Chicago Wolves** (IHL), August 25, 1998.

• MALTBY, Kirk

RW – R. 6', 180 lbs. b: Guelph, Ont., 12/22/1972. Edmonton's 4th, 65th overall, in 1992.

			REGULAR SEASON																		PLAYOFFS							
Season	Club	League	GP	G	A	Pts	AG	AA	APts	PIM	PP	SH	GW	S	%	TGF	PGF	TGA	PGA	+/–	GP	G	A	Pts	PIM	PP	SH	GW
1988-89	Cambridge Winter Hawks	OJHL-B	48	28	18	46	....	....	....	138	....	....	....	....	....	....	....	....	....	....	....	....	....	....	....	....	....	....
1989-90	Owen Sound Platers	OHL	61	12	15	27	....	....	....	90	....	....	....	....	....	....	....	....	....	....	12	1	6	7	15	....	....	....
1990-91	Owen Sound Platers	OHL	66	34	32	66	....	....	....	100	....	....	....	....	....	....	....	....	....	....	....	....	....	....	....	....	....	....
1991-92	Owen Sound Platers	OHL	66	50	41	91	....	....	....	99	....	....	....	....	....	....	....	....	....	....	5	3	3	6	18	....	....	....
1992-93	Cape Breton Oilers	AHL	73	22	23	45	....	....	....	130	....	....	....	....	....	....	....	....	....	....	16	3	3	6	45	....	....	....
1993-94	**Edmonton Oilers**	**NHL**	68	11	8	19	10	6	16	74	0	1	1	89	12.4	37	2	55	18	–2	....	....	....	....	....	....	....	....
1994-95	**Edmonton Oilers**	**NHL**	47	8	3	11	14	4	18	49	0	2	1	73	11.0	24	6	44	15	–11	....	....	....	....	....	....	....	....
1995-96	**Edmonton Oilers**	**NHL**	49	2	6	8	2	5	7	61	0	0	1	51	3.9	14	4	43	17	–16	....	....	....	....	....	....	....	....
	Cape Breton Oilers	AHL	4	1	2	3	....	....	....	6	....	....	....	....	....	....	....	....	....	....	....	....	....	....	....	....	....	....
	Detroit Red Wings	**NHL**	6	1	0	1	1	0	1	6	0	0	0	4	25.0	4	1	3	0	0	8	0	1	1	4	0	0	0
1996-97♦	**Detroit Red Wings**	**NHL**	66	3	5	8	3	4	7	75	0	0	0	62	4.8	18	2	21	8	3	20	5	2	7	24	0	1	1
1997-98♦	**Detroit Red Wings**	**NHL**	65	14	9	23	16	9	25	89	2	1	3	106	13.2	37	2	37	13	11	22	3	1	4	30	0	1	0
1998-99	**Detroit Red Wings**	**NHL**	53	8	6	14	9	6	15	34	0	1	2	76	10.5	17	1	30	8	–6	10	1	0	1	8	0	0	1
99-2000	**Detroit Red Wings**	**NHL**	41	6	8	14	7	7	14	24	0	2	1	71	8.5	19	0	28	10	1	8	0	1	1	4	0	0	0
	NHL Totals		395	53	45	98	62	41	103	412	2	7	9	532	10.0	170	18	261	89		68	9	5	14	70	0	2	2

Traded to **Detroit** by **Edmonton** for Dan McGillis, March 20, 1996. • Missed majority of 1999-2000 season recovering from hernia injury suffered in game vs. Dallas, October 5, 1999.

• MALUTA, Ray

Raymond William D – R. 5'8", 173 lbs. b: Flin Flon, Man., 7/24/1954. Boston's 8th, 126th overall, in 1974.

Season	Club	League	GP	G	A	Pts	AG	AA	APts	PIM	PP	SH	GW	S	%	TGF	PGF	TGA	PGA	+/–	GP	G	A	Pts	PIM	PP	SH	GW
1970-71	Flin Flon Bombers	WCJHL	9	0	2	2	....	....	....	6	....	....	....	....	....	....	....	....	....	....	1	0	0	0	0	....	....	....
1971-72	Flin Flon Bombers	WCJHL	64	8	32	40	....	....	....	142	....	....	....	....	....	....	....	....	....	....	5	1	4	5	18	....	....	....
1972-73	Flin Flon Bombers	WCJHL	65	11	40	51	....	....	....	116	....	....	....	....	....	....	....	....	....	....	9	3	8	11	21	....	....	....
1973-74	Flin Flon Bombers	WCJHL	68	40	57	97	....	....	....	151	....	....	....	....	....	....	....	....	....	....	7	0	4	4	23	....	....	....
1974-75	Rochester Americans	AHL	75	7	12	19	....	....	....	117	....	....	....	....	....	....	....	....	....	....	12	3	0	3	42	....	....	....
1975-76	**Boston Bruins**	**NHL**	2	0	0	0	0	0	0	2	0	0	0	2	0.0	1	0	4	0	–3	2	0	0	0	0	0	0	0
	Rochester Americans	AHL	74	3	43	46	....	....	....	170	....	....	....	....	....	....	....	....	....	....	7	0	2	2	6	....	....	....
1976-77	**Boston Bruins**	**NHL**	23	2	3	5	2	2	4	4	0	0	0	24	8.3	17	3	10	0	4	....	....	....	....	....	....	....	....
	Rochester Americans	AHL	51	2	24	26	....	....	....	138	....	....	....	....	....	....	....	....	....	....	12	0	5	5	16	....	....	....
1977-78	Rochester Americans	AHL	79	9	32	41	....	....	....	125	....	....	....	....	....	....	....	....	....	....	6	1	3	4	16	....	....	....
1978-79	Rochester Americans	AHL	35	4	14	18	....	....	....	58	....	....	....	....	....	....	....	....	....	....	....	....	....	....	....	....	....	....
1979-80	HC Salzburg	Austria	33	15	45	60	....	....	....	70	....	....	....	....	....	....	....	....	....	....	....	....	....	....	....	....	....	....
	NHL Totals		25	2	3	5	2	2	4	6	0	0	0	26	7.7	18	3	14	0		2	0	0	0	0	0	0	0

• MANDERVILLE, Kent

Kent S. LW – L. 6'3", 210 lbs. b: Edmonton, Alta., 4/12/1971. Calgary's 1st, 24th overall, in 1989.

Season	Club	League	GP	G	A	Pts	AG	AA	APts	PIM	PP	SH	GW	S	%	TGF	PGF	TGA	PGA	+/–	GP	G	A	Pts	PIM	PP	SH	GW
1986-87	Victoria Racquet Club	BCAHA	STATISTICS NOT AVAILABLE																									
1987-88	Notre Dame Midget Hounds	SAHA	32	22	18	40	....	....	....	42	....	....	....	....	....	....	....	....	....	....	....	....	....	....	....	....	....	....
1988-89	Notre Dame Hounds	SJHL	58	39	36	75	....	....	....	165	....	....	....	....	....	....	....	....	....	....	....	....	....	....	....	....	....	....
1989-90	Cornell University	ECAC	26	11	15	26	....	....	....	28	....	....	....	....	....	....	....	....	....	....	....	....	....	....	....	....	....	....
	Canada	WJC-A	7	1	2	3	....	....	....	0	....	....	....	....	....	....	....	....	....	....	....	....	....	....	....	....	....	....
1990-91	Cornell University	ECAC	28	17	14	31	....	....	....	60	....	....	....	....	....	....	....	....	....	....	....	....	....	....	....	....	....	....
	Canada	Nat-Team	3	1	2	3	....	....	....	0	....	....	....	....	....	....	....	....	....	....	....	....	....	....	....	....	....	....
	Canada	WJC-A	7	1	6	7	....	....	....	0	....	....	....	....	....	....	....	....	....	....	....	....	....	....	....	....	....	....
1991-92	Canada	Nat-Team	63	16	24	40	....	....	....	78	....	....	....	....	....	....	....	....	....	....	....	....	....	....	....	....	....	....
	Canada	Olympics	8	1	2	3	....	....	....	0	....	....	....	....	....	....	....	....	....	....	....	....	....	....	....	....	....	....
	Toronto Maple Leafs	**NHL**	15	0	4	4	0	3	3	0	0	0	0	14	0.0	5	0	5	1	1	....	....	....	....	....	....	....	....
	St. John's Maple Leafs	AHL	....	....	....	....	....	....	....	....	....	....	....	....	....	....	....	....	....	....	12	5	9	14	14	....	....	....
1992-93	**Toronto Maple Leafs**	**NHL**	18	1	1	2	1	1	2	17	0	0	1	15	6.7	2	0	19	8	–9	18	1	0	1	8	0	0	0
	St. John's Maple Leafs	AHL	56	19	28	47	....	....	....	86	....	....	....	....	....	....	....	....	....	....	2	0	2	2	0	....	....	....
1993-94	**Toronto Maple Leafs**	**NHL**	67	7	9	16	6	7	13	63	0	0	1	81	8.6	20	0	29	14	5	12	1	0	1	4	0	1	0
1994-95	**Toronto Maple Leafs**	**NHL**	36	0	1	1	0	1	1	22	0	0	0	43	0.0	7	0	15	6	–2	7	0	0	0	6	0	0	0
1995-96	**Edmonton Oilers**	**NHL**	37	3	5	8	3	4	7	38	0	2	0	63	4.8	11	1	22	7	–5	....	....	....	....	....	....	....	....
	St. John's Maple Leafs	AHL	27	16	12	28	....	....	....	26	....	....	....	....	....	....	....	....	....	....	....	....	....	....	....	....	....	....
1996-97	**Hartford Whalers**	**NHL**	44	6	5	11	6	4	10	18	0	0	1	51	11.8	19	1	21	6	3	....	....	....	....	....	....	....	....
	Springfield Falcons	AHL	23	5	20	25	....	....	....	18	....	....	....	....	....	....	....	....	....	....	....	....	....	....	....	....	....	....
1997-98	**Carolina Hurricanes**	**NHL**	77	4	4	8	5	4	9	31	0	0	0	80	5.0	13	0	35	16	–6	....	....	....	....	....	....	....	....
1998-99	**Carolina Hurricanes**	**NHL**	81	5	11	16	6	11	17	38	0	0	0	71	7.0	25	1	33	18	9	6	0	0	0	2	0	0	0
99-2000	**Carolina Hurricanes**	**NHL**	56	1	4	5	1	4	5	12	0	0	1	45	2.2	6	0	24	10	–8	....	....	....	....	....	....	....	....
	Philadelphia Flyers	**NHL**	13	0	3	3	0	3	3	4	0	0	0	17	0.0	4	0	2	0	2	18	0	1	1	22	0	0	0
	NHL Totals		444	27	47	74	28	42	70	243	0	2	4	480	5.6	112	3	205	86		61	2	1	3	42	0	1	0

Traded to **Toronto** by **Calgary** with Doug Gilmour, Jamie Macoun, Rick Wamsley and Ric Nattress for Gary Leeman, Alexander Godynyuk, Jeff Reese, Michel Petit and Craig Berube, January 2, 1992. Traded to **Edmonton** by **Toronto** for Peter White and Edmonton's 4th round choice (Jason Sessa) in 1996 Entry Draft, December 4, 1995. Signed as a free agent by **Hartford**, October 2, 1996. Transferred to **Carolina** after **Hartford** franchise relocated, June 25, 1997. Traded to **Philadelphia** by **Carolina** for Sandy McCarthy, March 14, 2000.

• MANDICH, Dan

Daniel G. D – R. 6'3", 205 lbs. b: Brantford, Ont., 6/12/1960.

Season	Club	League	GP	G	A	Pts	AG	AA	APts	PIM	PP	SH	GW	S	%	TGF	PGF	TGA	PGA	+/–	GP	G	A	Pts	PIM	PP	SH	GW
1977-78	Chatham Maroons	OHA-B	STATISTICS NOT AVAILABLE																									
	Windsor Spitfires	OMJHL	15	0	1	1	....	....	....	20	....	....	....	....	....	....	....	....	....	....	....	....	....	....	....	....	....	....
1978-79	Ohio State University	CCHA	38	7	18	25	....	....	....	126	....	....	....	....	....	....	....	....	....	....	....	....	....	....	....	....	....	....
1979-80	Ohio State University	CCHA	35	10	17	27	....	....	....	146	....	....	....	....	....	....	....	....	....	....	....	....	....	....	....	....	....	....
1980-81	Ohio State University	CCHA	39	20	26	46	....	....	....	188	....	....	....	....	....	....	....	....	....	....	....	....	....	....	....	....	....	....
1981-82	Ohio State University	CCHA	33	14	26	40	....	....	....	157	....	....	....	....	....	....	....	....	....	....	....	....	....	....	....	....	....	....
	Nashville South Stars	CHL	16	2	5	7	....	....	....	24	....	....	....	....	....	....	....	....	....	....	3	0	0	0	26	....	....	....
1982-83	**Minnesota North Stars**	**NHL**	67	3	4	7	2	3	5	169	0	0	1	49	6.1	48	1	57	10	0	7	0	0	0	2	0	0	0
	Birmingham South Stars	CHL	6	0	4	4	....	....	....	18	....	....	....	....	....	....	....	....	....	....	....	....	....	....	....	....	....	....
1983-84	**Minnesota North Stars**	**NHL**	31	2	7	9	2	5	7	77	0	0	0	29	6.9	23	1	33	5	–6	....	....	....	....	....	....	....	....
	Salt Lake Golden Eagles	CHL	3	2	2	4	....	....	....	13	....	....	....	....	....	....	....	....	....	....	....	....	....	....	....	....	....	....
1984-85	**Minnesota North Stars**	**NHL**	10	0	0	0	0	0	0	32	0	0	0	4	0.0	1	0	7	3	–3	....	....	....	....	....	....	....	....
1985-86	**Minnesota North Stars**	**NHL**	3	0	0	0	0	0	0	25	0	0	0	0	0.0	0	0	0	0	0	....	....	....	....	....	....	....	....
	Springfield Indians	AHL	3	0	0	0	....	....	....	4	....	....	....	....	....	....	....	....	....	....	....	....	....	....	....	....	....	....
	NHL Totals		111	5	11	16	4	8	12	303	0	0	1	82	6.1	72	2	97	18		7	0	0	0	2	0	0	0

CCHA First All-Star Team (1981)

Signed as a free agent by **Minnesota**, July 19, 1982.

• MANELUK, Mike

LW – R. 5'11", 190 lbs. b: Winnipeg, Man., 10/1/1973.

Season	Club	League	GP	G	A	Pts	AG	AA	APts	PIM	PP	SH	GW	S	%	TGF	PGF	TGA	PGA	+/–	GP	G	A	Pts	PIM	PP	SH	GW
1989-90	Winnipeg Hawks	MAHA	40	49	38	87	....	....	....	92	....	....	....	....	....	....	....	....	....	....	....	....	....	....	....	....	....	....
1990-91	St. Boniface Saints	MJHL	45	29	41	70	....	....	....	199	....	....	....	....	....	....	....	....	....	....	....	....	....	....	....	....	....	....
1991-92	Brandon Wheat Kings	WHL	68	23	30	53	....	....	....	102	....	....	....	....	....	....	....	....	....	....	....	....	....	....	....	....	....	....
1992-93	Brandon Wheat Kings	WHL	72	36	51	87	....	....	....	75	....	....	....	....	....	....	....	....	....	....	4	2	1	3	2	....	....	....
1993-94	Brandon Wheat Kings	WHL	63	50	47	97	....	....	....	112	....	....	....	....	....	....	....	....	....	....	13	11	3	14	23	....	....	....
	San Diego Gulls	IHL	....	....	....	....	....	....	....	....	....	....	....	....	....	....	....	....	....	....	1	0	0	0	0	....	....	....
1994-95	Canada	Nat-Team	44	36	24	60	....	....	....	34	....	....	....	....	....	....	....	....	....	....	....	....	....	....	....	....	....	....
	San Diego Gulls	IHL	10	0	1	1	....	....	....	4	....	....	....	....	....	....	....	....	....	....	....	....	....	....	....	....	....	....
	Canada	WC-A	8	0	2	2	....	....	....	0	....	....	....	....	....	....	....	....	....	....	....	....	....	....	....	....	....	....
1995-96	Baltimore Bandits	AHL	74	33	38	71	....	....	....	73	....	....	....	....	....	....	....	....	....	....	6	4	3	7	14	....	....	....
1996-97	Worcester IceCats	AHL	70	27	27	54	....	....	....	89	....	....	....	....	....	....	....	....	....	....	5	1	2	3	14	....	....	....
1997-98	Worcester IceCats	AHL	5	3	3	6	....	....	....	4	....	....	....	....	....	....	....	....	....	....	....	....	....	....	....	....	....	....
	Philadelphia Phantoms	AHL	66	27	35	62	....	....	....	62	....	....	....	....	....	....	....	....	....	....	20	*13	*21	*34	30	....	....	....

Season	Club	League	REGULAR SEASON GP	G	A	Pts	AG	AA	APts	PIM	PP	SH	GW	S	%	TGF	PGF	TGA	PGA	+/–	PLAYOFFS GP	G	A	Pts	PIM	PP	SH	GW
1998-99	**Philadelphia Flyers**	**NHL**	**13**	**2**	**6**	**8**	**2**	**6**	**8**	**8**	**0**	**0**	**0**	**23**	**8.7**	**12**	**1**	**7**	**0**	**4**	....	....	....	....	....	....	....	....
	Chicago Blackhawks	**NHL**	**28**	**4**	**3**	**7**	**5**	**3**	**8**	**8**	**1**	**0**	**0**	**3**	**13.8**	**11**	**1**	**9**	**1**	**2**	....	....	....	....	....	....	....	....
	New York Rangers	**NHL**	**4**	**0**	**0**	**0**	**0**	**0**	**0**	**4**	**0**	**0**	**0**	**3**	**0.0**	**0**	**0**	**1**	**0**	**–1**	....	....	....	....	....	....	....	....
99-2000	**Philadelphia Flyers**	**NHL**	**1**	**0**	**0**	**0**	**0**	**0**	**0**	**4**	**0**	**0**	**0**	**2**	**0.0**	**0**	**0**	**0**	**0**	**0**	....	....	....	....	....	....	....	....
	Philadelphia Phantoms	AHL	73	*47	40	87	....	....	....	158	....	....	....	....	....	....	....	....	....	....	4	1	2	3	4	....	....	....
	NHL Totals		**46**	**6**	**9**	**15**	**7**	**9**	**16**	**24**	**1**	**0**	**0**	**31**	**19.4**	**23**	**2**	**17**	**1**		....	....	....	....	....	....	....	....

Won Jack A. Butterfield Trophy (Playoff MVP - AHL) (1998) • AHL First All-Star Team (2000)

Signed as a free agent by **Anaheim**, January 28, 1994. Traded to **Ottawa** by **Anaheim** for Kevin Brown, July 1, 1996. Traded to **Philadelphia** by **Ottawa** for future considerations, October 21, 1997. Traded to **Chicago** by **Philadelphia** for Roman Vopat, November 17, 1998. Claimed on waivers by **NY Rangers** from **Chicago**, March 4, 1999. Signed as a free agent by **Philadelphia**, August 2, 1999.

• MANERY, Kris

Kris Franklin C/RW – R. 6', 185 lbs. b: Leamington, Ont., 9/24/1954.

Season	Club	League	GP	G	A	Pts	AG	AA	APts	PIM	PP	SH	GW	S	%	TGF	PGF	TGA	PGA	+/–	GP	G	A	Pts	PIM	PP	SH	GW
1972-73	Leamington Flyers	OHA-C	STATISTICS NOT AVAILABLE																									
1973-74	University of Michigan	WCHA	36	14	14	28	....	....	....	36	....	....	....	....	....	....	....	....	....	....	....	....	....	....	....	....	....	....
1974-75	University of Michigan	WCHA	40	22	24	46	....	....	....	44	....	....	....	....	....	....	....	....	....	....	....	....	....	....	....	....	....	....
1975-76	University of Michigan	WCHA	42	37	24	61	....	....	....	42	....	....	....	....	....	....	....	....	....	....	....	....	....	....	....	....	....	....
1976-77	University of Michigan	WCHA	45	38	35	73	....	....	....	51	....	....	....	....	....	....	....	....	....	....	....	....	....	....	....	....	....	....
1977-78	**Cleveland Barons**	**NHL**	**78**	**22**	**27**	**49**	**20**	**21**	**41**	**14**	**7**	**0**	**1**	**188**	**11.7**	**80**	**16**	**87**	**8**	**–15**	....	....	....	....	....	....	....	....
1978-79	**Minnesota North Stars**	**NHL**	**60**	**17**	**19**	**36**	**15**	**14**	**29**	**16**	**3**	**0**	**1**	**126**	**13.5**	**58**	**17**	**59**	**5**	**–13**	....	....	....	....	....	....	....	....
	Oklahoma City Stars	CHL	13	4	4	8	....	....	....	6	....	....	....	....	....	....	....	....	....	....	....	....	....	....	....	....	....	....
1979-80	**Minnesota North Stars**	**NHL**	**28**	**3**	**4**	**7**	**3**	**3**	**6**	**16**	**0**	**0**	**0**	**40**	**7.5**	**17**	**1**	**22**	**1**	**–5**	....	....	....	....	....	....	....	....
	Vancouver Canucks	**NHL**	**21**	**2**	**1**	**3**	**2**	**1**	**3**	**15**	**0**	**0**	**0**	**34**	**5.9**	**8**	**0**	**16**	**2**	**–6**	....	....	....	....	....	....	....	....
	Winnipeg Jets	**NHL**	**16**	**6**	**4**	**10**	**5**	**3**	**8**	**6**	**4**	**0**	**0**	**36**	**16.7**	**18**	**10**	**16**	**0**	**–8**	....	....	....	....	....	....	....	....
1980-81	**Winnipeg Jets**	**NHL**	**47**	**13**	**9**	**22**	**10**	**6**	**16**	**24**	**4**	**1**	**0**	**82**	**15.9**	**35**	**13**	**41**	**4**	**–15**	....	....	....	....	....	....	....	....
	Tulsa Oilers	CHL	22	19	13	32	....	....	....	12	....	....	....	....	....	....	....	....	....	....	8	5	3	8	14	....	....	....
1981-82	Tulsa Oilers	CHL	80	54	35	89	....	....	....	60	....	....	....	....	....	....	....	....	....	....	3	0	0	0	2	....	....	....
1982-83	WEV Wein	Austria	31	26	31	57	....	....	....	36	....	....	....	....	....	....	....	....	....	....	....	....	....	....	....	....	....	....
1983-84	SC Rapperswil-Jona	Switz-2	STATISTICS NOT AVAILABLE																									
1984-85	SC Rapperswil-Jona	Switz-2	48	36	18	54	....	....	....												....	....	....	....	....	....	....	....
	Binghamton Whalers	AHL	6	1	7	8	....	....	....	2	....	....	....	....	....	....	....	....	....	....	8	2	2	4	0	....	....	....
	NHL Totals		**250**	**63**	**64**	**127**	**55**	**48**	**103**	**91**	**18**	**1**	**2**	**506**	**12.5**	**216**	**57**	**241**	**20**		....	....	....	....	....	....	....	....

• Brother of Randy • WCHA First All-Star Team (1977) • CHL Second All-Star Team (1982)

Signed as a free agent by **Cleveland**, October, 1977. Placed on **Minnesota** Reserve List after **Minnesota-Cleveland** Dispersal Draft, June 15, 1978. Traded to **Vancouver** by **Minnesota** for Vancouver's 2nd round choice (later traded to Montreal — Montreal selected Kent Carlson) in 1982 Entry Draft, January 4, 1980. Claimed on waivers by **Winnipeg** from **Vancouver**, February 27, 1980.

• MANERY, Randy

Randy Neal D – R. 6', 185 lbs. b: Leamington, Ont., 1/10/1949.

Season	Club	League	GP	G	A	Pts	AG	AA	APts	PIM	PP	SH	GW	S	%	TGF	PGF	TGA	PGA	+/–	GP	G	A	Pts	PIM	PP	SH	GW
1966-67	Hamilton Red Wings	OHA-Jr.	47	2	3	5	....	....	....	28	....	....	....	....	....	....	....	....	....	....	17	2	2	4	18	....	....	....
1967-68	Hamilton Red Wings	OHA-Jr.	53	3	20	23	....	....	....	65	....	....	....	....	....	....	....	....	....	....	11	0	7	7	28	....	....	....
1968-69	Hamilton Red Wings	OHA-Jr.	54	4	25	29	....	....	....	100	....	....	....	....	....	....	....	....	....	....	5	1	1	2	6	....	....	....
1969-70	Fort Worth Wings	CHL	67	1	15	16	....	....	....	46	....	....	....	....	....	....	....	....	....	....	7	0	0	0	2	....	....	....
1970-71	**Detroit Red Wings**	**NHL**	**2**	**0**	**0**	**0**	**0**	**0**	**0**	**0**	**0**	**0**	**0**	**3**	**0.0**	**0**	**0**	**1**	**0**	**–1**	....	....	....	....	....	....	....	....
	Fort Worth Wings	CHL	72	16	32	48	....	....	....	53	....	....	....	....	....	....	....	....	....	....	4	0	1	1	4	....	....	....
1971-72	**Detroit Red Wings**	**NHL**	**1**	**0**	**0**	**0**	**0**	**0**	**0**	**0**	**0**	**0**	**0**	**0**	**0.0**	**0**	**0**	**0**	**0**	**0**	....	....	....	....	....	....	....	....
	Fort Worth Wings	CHL	72	6	35	41	....	....	....	89	....	....	....	....	....	....	....	....	....	....	7	1	3	4	6	....	....	....
1972-73	**Atlanta Flames**	**NHL**	**78**	**5**	**30**	**35**	**5**	**24**	**29**	**44**	**2**	**1**	**0**	**159**	**3.1**	**95**	**30**	**96**	**29**	**–2**	....	....	....	....	....	....	....	....
1973-74	**Atlanta Flames**	**NHL**	**78**	**8**	**29**	**37**	**8**	**24**	**32**	**75**	**2**	**0**	**1**	**189**	**4.2**	**121**	**30**	**105**	**29**	**15**	**4**	**0**	**2**	**2**	**4**	**0**	**0**	**0**
1974-75	**Atlanta Flames**	**NHL**	**68**	**5**	**27**	**32**	**4**	**20**	**24**	**48**	**3**	**0**	**0**	**118**	**4.2**	**80**	**17**	**66**	**21**	**18**	....	....	....	....	....	....	....	....
1975-76	**Atlanta Flames**	**NHL**	**80**	**7**	**32**	**39**	**6**	**24**	**30**	**42**	**3**	**0**	**3**	**139**	**5.0**	**95**	**27**	**71**	**5**	**2**	**2**	**0**	**0**	**0**	**0**	**0**	**0**	**0**
1976-77	**Atlanta Flames**	**NHL**	**73**	**5**	**24**	**29**	**4**	**18**	**22**	**33**	**0**	**0**	**2**	**108**	**4.6**	**84**	**14**	**82**	**10**	**–2**	**3**	**0**	**0**	**0**	**0**	**0**	**0**	**0**
1977-78	**Los Angeles Kings**	**NHL**	**79**	**6**	**27**	**33**	**5**	**21**	**26**	**61**	**3**	**0**	**0**	**173**	**3.5**	**100**	**21**	**107**	**16**	**–12**	**2**	**0**	**0**	**0**	**2**	**0**	**0**	**0**
1978-79	**Los Angeles Kings**	**NHL**	**71**	**8**	**27**	**35**	**7**	**20**	**27**	**64**	**2**	**0**	**2**	**116**	**6.9**	**118**	**36**	**100**	**24**	**6**	**2**	**0**	**0**	**0**	**6**	**0**	**0**	**0**
1979-80	**Los Angeles Kings**	**NHL**	**52**	**6**	**10**	**16**	**5**	**7**	**12**	**48**	**3**	**0**	**0**	**73**	**8.2**	**54**	**20**	**62**	**15**	**–13**	....	....	....	....	....	....	....	....
	NHL Totals		**582**	**50**	**206**	**256**	**44**	**158**	**202**	**415**	**18**	**1**	**8**	**1078**	**4.6**	**747**	**195**	**690**	**149**		**13**	**0**	**2**	**2**	**12**	**0**	**0**	**0**

• Brother of Kris • OHA-Jr. First All-Star Team (1969) • CHL Second All-Star Team (1972) • Played in NHL All-Star Game (1973)

Claimed by **Atlanta** from **Detroit** in Expansion Draft, June 6, 1972. Traded to **LA Kings** by **Atlanta** for Ab DeMarco Jr., May 23, 1977.

• MANN, Cameron

Cameron Douglas RW – R. 6', 194 lbs. b: Thompson, Man., 4/20/1977. Boston's 5th, 99th overall, in 1995.

Season	Club	League	GP	G	A	Pts	AG	AA	APts	PIM	PP	SH	GW	S	%	TGF	PGF	TGA	PGA	+/–	GP	G	A	Pts	PIM	PP	SH	GW
1992-93	Kenora Thistles	NOJHA	35	23	24	47	....	....	....	49	....	....	....	....	....	....	....	....	....	....	....	....	....	....	....	....	....	....
1993-94	Peterborough Petes	OJHL	16	3	14	17	....	....	....	23	....	....	....	....	....	....	....	....	....	....	....	....	....	....	....	....	....	....
	Peterborough Petes	OHL	49	8	17	25	....	....	....	18	....	....	....	....	....	....	....	....	....	....	7	1	1	2	2	....	....	....
1994-95	Peterborough Petes	OHL	64	19	24	43	....	....	....	40	....	....	....	....	....	....	....	....	....	....	11	3	8	11	4	....	....	....
1995-96	Peterborough Petes	OHL	66	42	60	102	....	....	....	108	....	....	....	....	....	....	....	....	....	....	24	*27	16	*43	33	....	....	....
	Peterborough Petes	Mem-Cup	5	*4	2	6	....	....	....	4	....	....	....	....	....	....	....	....	....	....	....	....	....	....	....	....	....	....
1996-97	Peterborough Petes	OHL	51	33	50	83	....	....	....	91	....	....	....	....	....	....	....	....	....	....	11	10	18	28	16	....	....	....
	Canada	WJC-A	7	3	4	7	....	....	....	10	....	....	....	....	....	....	....	....	....	....	....	....	....	....	....	....	....	....
1997-98	**Boston Bruins**	**NHL**	**9**	**0**	**1**	**1**	**0**	**1**	**1**	**4**	**0**	**0**	**0**	**6**	**0.0**	**3**	**1**	**1**	**0**	**1**	....	....	....	....	....	....	....	....
	Providence Bruins	AHL	71	21	26	47	....	....	....	99	....	....	....	....	....	....	....	....	....	....	....	....	....	....	....	....	....	....
1998-99	**Boston Bruins**	**NHL**	**33**	**5**	**2**	**7**	**6**	**2**	**8**	**17**	**1**	**0**	**1**	**42**	**11.9**	**15**	**3**	**13**	**1**	**0**	**1**	**0**	**0**	**0**	**0**	**0**	**0**	**0**
	Providence Bruins	AHL	43	21	25	46	....	....	....	65	....	....	....	....	....	....	....	....	....	....	11	7	7	14	4	....	....	....
99-2000	**Boston Bruins**	**NHL**	**32**	**8**	**4**	**12**	**9**	**4**	**13**	**13**	**1**	**0**	**0**	**48**	**16.7**	**19**	**1**	**27**	**3**	**–6**	....	....	....	....	....	....	....	....
	Providence Bruins	AHL	29	7	12	19	....	....	....	45	....	....	....	....	....	....	....	....	....	....	11	6	7	13	0	....	....	....
	NHL Totals		**74**	**13**	**7**	**20**	**15**	**7**	**22**	**34**	**2**	**0**	**1**	**96**	**13.5**	**37**	**5**	**41**	**4**		**1**	**0**	**0**	**0**	**0**	**0**	**0**	**0**

OHL First All-Star Team (1996, 1997) • Memorial Cup All-Star Team (1996) • Won Stafford Smythe Memorial Trophy (Memorial Cup Tournament MVP) (1996)

• MANN, Jimmy

James Edward RW – R. 6', 205 lbs. b: Montreal, Que., 4/17/1959. Winnipeg's 1st, 19th overall, in 1979.

Season	Club	League	GP	G	A	Pts	AG	AA	APts	PIM	PP	SH	GW	S	%	TGF	PGF	TGA	PGA	+/–	GP	G	A	Pts	PIM	PP	SH	GW
1975-76	Laval National	QMJHL	65	8	9	17	....	....	....	107	....	....	....	....	....	....	....	....	....	....	....	....	....	....	....	....	....	....
1976-77	Sherbrooke Beavers	QMJHL	69	12	14	26	....	....	....	200	....	....	....	....	....	....	....	....	....	....	....	....	....	....	....	....	....	....
	Sherbrooke Beavers	Mem-Cup	4	0	0	0	....	....	....	21	....	....	....	....	....	....	....	....	....	....	....	....	....	....	....	....	....	....
1977-78	Sherbrooke Beavers	QMJHL	67	27	54	81	....	....	....	277	....	....	....	....	....	....	....	....	....	....	7	3	9	12	14	....	....	....
1978-79	Sherbrooke Beavers	QMJHL	65	35	47	82	....	....	....	260	....	....	....	....	....	....	....	....	....	....	12	14	12	26	83	....	....	....
1979-80	**Winnipeg Jets**	**NHL**	**72**	**3**	**5**	**8**	**3**	**4**	**7**	***287**	**1**	**0**	**1**	**60**	**5.0**	**15**	**4**	**31**	**0**	**–20**	....	....	....	....	....	....	....	....
1980-81	**Winnipeg Jets**	**NHL**	**37**	**3**	**3**	**6**	**2**	**2**	**4**	**105**	**0**	**0**	**0**	**30**	**10.0**	**9**	**0**	**27**	**0**	**–18**	....	....	....	....	....	....	....	....
	Tulsa Oilers	CHL	26	4	7	11	....	....	....	175	....	....	....	....	....	....	....	....	....	....	5	0	0	0	21	....	....	....
1981-82	**Winnipeg Jets**	**NHL**	**37**	**3**	**2**	**5**	**2**	**1**	**3**	**79**	**0**	**0**	**0**	**22**	**13.6**	**9**	**0**	**17**	**0**	**–8**	**3**	**0**	**0**	**0**	**7**	**0**	**0**	**0**
1982-83	**Winnipeg Jets**	**NHL**	**40**	**0**	**1**	**1**	**0**	**1**	**1**	**73**	**0**	**0**	**0**	**20**	**0.0**	**2**	**0**	**9**	**0**	**–7**	**1**	**0**	**0**	**0**	**0**	**0**	**0**	**0**
1983-84	**Winnipeg Jets**	**NHL**	**16**	**0**	**1**	**1**	**0**	**1**	**1**	**54**	**0**	**0**	**0**	**5**	**0.0**	**2**	**0**	**2**	**0**	**0**	....	....	....	....	....	....	....	....
	Sherbrooke Jets	AHL	20	6	3	9	....	....	....	94	....	....	....	....	....	....	....	....	....	....	....	....	....	....	....	....	....	....
	Quebec Nordiques	**NHL**	**22**	**1**	**1**	**2**	**1**	**1**	**2**	**42**	**0**	**0**	**0**	**15**	**6.7**	**4**	**0**	**7**	**0**	**–3**	**3**	**0**	**0**	**0**	**22**	**0**	**0**	**0**
1984-85	**Quebec Nordiques**	**NHL**	**25**	**0**	**4**	**4**	**0**	**3**	**3**	**54**	**0**	**0**	**0**	**12**	**0.0**	**6**	**0**	**3**	**0**	**3**	**13**	**0**	**0**	**0**	**41**	**0**	**0**	**0**
	Fredericton Express	AHL	13	4	4	8	....	....	....	97	....	....	....	....	....	....	....	....	....	....	....	....	....	....	....	....	....	....
1985-86	**Quebec Nordiques**	**NHL**	**35**	**0**	**3**	**3**	**0**	**2**	**2**	**148**	**0**	**0**	**0**	**4**	**0.0**	**2**	**0**	**4**	**0**	**–2**	**2**	**0**	**0**	**0**	**19**	**0**	**0**	**0**
1986-87	**Quebec Nordiques**	**NHL**	DID NOT PLAY – INJURED																									

			REGULAR SEASON																	PLAYOFFS							
Season	Club	League	GP	G	A	Pts	AG	AA	APts	PIM	PP	SH	GW	S	%	TGF	PGF	TGA	PGA	+/–	GP	G	A	Pts	PIM	PP	SH	GW
1987-88	**Pittsburgh Penguins**	**NHL**	**9**	**0**	**0**	**0**	**0**	**0**	**0**	**53**	**0**	**0**	**0**	**1**	**0.0**	**0**	**0**	**0**	**0**	**0**	....	....	....	....	....	....	....	....
	Muskegon Lumberjacks	IHL	10	0	2	2	....	....	....	61	....	....	....	....	....	....	....	....	....	....	....	....	....	....	....	....	....	....
1988-89	Indianapolis Ice	IHL	38	5	10	15	....	....	....	275	....	....	....	....	....	....	....	....	....	....	....	....	....	....	....	....	....	....
	NHL Totals		**293**	**10**	**20**	**30**	**8**	**15**	**23**	**895**	**1**	**0**	**1**	**169**	**5.9**	**49**	**4**	**100**	**0**		**22**	**0**	**0**	**0**	**89**	**0**	**0**	**0**

QMJHL First All-Star Team (1979)

Traded to **Quebec** by **Winnipeg** for Quebec's 5th round choice (Brent Severyn) in 1984 Entry Draft, February 6, 1984. • Missed entire 1986-87 season recovering from abdominal injury origianlly suffered in December, 1984. Signed as a free agent by **Pittsburgh**, June 16, 1987.

• MANN, Ken

Kenneth Ross RW – R. 5'11", 200 lbs. b: Hamilton, Ont., 9/5/1953.

Season	Club	League	GP	G	A	Pts	AG	AA	APts	PIM	PP	SH	GW	S	%	TGF	PGF	TGA	PGA	+/–	GP	G	A	Pts	PIM	PP	SH	GW
1971-72	Hamilton Red Wings	OMJHL	36	1	11	12	....	....	....	40	....	....	....	....	....	....	....	....	....	....	....	....	....	....	....	....	....	....
1972-73	Windsor Spitfires	OJHL	58	44	35	79	....	....	....	214	....	....	....	....	....	....	....	....	....	....	....	....	....	....	....	....	....	....
1973-74	Flint-Port Huron Flags	IHL	68	32	26	58	....	....	....	46	....	....	....	....	....	....	....	....	....	....	....	....	....	....	....	....	....	....
1974-75	Virginia Wings	AHL	68	14	19	33	....	....	....	82	....	....	....	....	....	....	....	....	....	....	5	1	1	2	28	....	....	....
1975-76	**Detroit Red Wings**	**NHL**	**1**	**0**	**0**	**0**	**0**	**0**	**0**	**0**	**0**	**0**	**0**	**1**	**0.0**	**0**	**0**	**1**	**0**	**–1**	....	....	....	....	....	....	....	....
	Kalamazoo Wings	IHL	75	39	35	74	....	....	....	100	....	....	....	....	....	....	....	....	....	....	6	3	2	5	4	....	....	....
1976-77	Kalamazoo Wings	IHL	45	23	23	46	....	....	....	46	....	....	....	....	....	....	....	....	....	....	....	....	....	....	....	....	....	....
	Kansas City Blues	CHL	31	7	9	16	....	....	....	14	....	....	....	....	....	....	....	....	....	....	....	....	....	....	....	....	....	....
1977-78	Brantford Alexanders	OHA-Sr.	34	6	10	16	....	....	....	49	....	....	....	....	....	....	....	....	....	....	....	....	....	....	....	....	....	....
	NHL Totals		**1**	**0**	**0**	**0**	**0**	**0**	**0**	**0**	**0**	**0**	**0**	**1**	**0.0**	**0**	**0**	**1**	**0**		....	....	....	....	....	....	....	....

Signed as a free agent by **Detroit**, October 2, 1974.

• MANNO, Bob

Robert John D – L. 6', 185 lbs. b: Niagara Falls, Ont., 10/31/1956. Vancouver's 1st, 26th overall, in 1976.

Season	Club	League	GP	G	A	Pts	AG	AA	APts	PIM	PP	SH	GW	S	%	TGF	PGF	TGA	PGA	+/–	GP	G	A	Pts	PIM	PP	SH	GW
1972-73	Niagara Falls Flyers	OJHL	36	1	14	15	....	....	....	78	....	....	....	....	....	....	....	....	....	....	....	....	....	....	....	....	....	....
1973-74	Hamilton Red Wings	OMJHL	63	3	19	22	....	....	....	105	....	....	....	....	....	....	....	....	....	....	....	....	....	....	....	....	....	....
1974-75	St. Catharines Black Hawks	OMJHL	70	9	38	47	....	....	....	171	....	....	....	....	....	....	....	....	....	....	4	0	1	1	23	....	....	....
1975-76	St. Catharines Black Hawks	OMJHL	55	9	54	63	....	....	....	187	....	....	....	....	....	....	....	....	....	....	4	1	4	5	14	....	....	....
1976-77	**Vancouver Canucks**	**NHL**	**2**	**0**	**0**	**0**	**0**	**0**	**0**	**0**	**0**	**0**	**0**	**0**	**0.0**	**0**	**0**	**3**	**1**	**–2**	....	....	....	....	....	....	....	....
	Tulsa Oilers	CHL	73	18	36	54	....	....	....	109	....	....	....	....	....	....	....	....	....	....	9	1	7	8	19	....	....	....
1977-78	**Vancouver Canucks**	**NHL**	**49**	**5**	**14**	**19**	**5**	**11**	**16**	**29**	**4**	**0**	**1**	**50**	**10.0**	**47**	**13**	**62**	**5**	**–23**	....	....	....	....	....	....	....	....
	Tulsa Oilers	CHL	20	5	15	20	....	....	....	21	....	....	....	....	....	....	....	....	....	....	....	....	....	....	....	....	....	....
1978-79	**Vancouver Canucks**	**NHL**	**52**	**5**	**16**	**21**	**4**	**12**	**16**	**42**	**0**	**0**	**1**	**71**	**7.0**	**52**	**14**	**62**	**7**	**–17**	**3**	**0**	**1**	**1**	**4**	**0**	**0**	**0**
	Dallas Black Hawks	CHL	23	8	9	17	....	....	....	18	....	....	....	....	....	....	....	....	....	....	....	....	....	....	....	....	....	....
1979-80	**Vancouver Canucks**	**NHL**	**40**	**3**	**14**	**17**	**3**	**10**	**13**	**14**	**1**	**0**	**0**	**73**	**4.1**	**46**	**11**	**45**	**15**	**5**	**4**	**1**	**0**	**1**	**6**	**0**	**0**	**0**
1980-81	Dallas Black Hawks	CHL	40	7	36	43	....	....	....	65	....	....	....	....	....	....	....	....	....	....	....	....	....	....	....	....	....	....
	Vancouver Canucks	**NHL**	**20**	**0**	**11**	**11**	**0**	**7**	**7**	**30**	**0**	**0**	**0**	**29**	**0.0**	**23**	**4**	**33**	**8**	**–6**	**3**	**0**	**0**	**0**	**2**	**0**	**0**	**0**
1981-82	**Toronto Maple Leafs**	**NHL**	**72**	**9**	**41**	**50**	**7**	**27**	**34**	**67**	**3**	**1**	**0**	**108**	**8.3**	**129**	**28**	**142**	**46**	**5**	....	....	....	....	....	....	....	....
	Italy	WEC-A	7	1	1	2	....	....	....	12	....	....	....	....	....	....	....	....	....	....	....	....	....	....	....	....	....	....
1982-83	HC Merano	Italy	28	15	32	47	....	....	....	40	....	....	....	....	....	....	....	....	....	....	10	4	12	16	17	....	....	....
	Italy	WEC-A	10	0	4	4	....	....	....	16	....	....	....	....	....	....	....	....	....	....	....	....	....	....	....	....	....	....
1983-84	**Detroit Red Wings**	**NHL**	**62**	**9**	**13**	**22**	**7**	**9**	**16**	**60**	**0**	**1**	**4**	**70**	**12.9**	**42**	**4**	**60**	**21**	**–1**	**4**	**0**	**3**	**3**	**0**	**0**	**0**	**0**
	Adirondack Red Wings	AHL	12	5	11	16	....	....	....	18	....	....	....	....	....	....	....	....	....	....	....	....	....	....	....	....	....	....
1984-85	**Detroit Red Wings**	**NHL**	**74**	**10**	**22**	**32**	**8**	**15**	**23**	**32**	**0**	**3**	**1**	**62**	**16.1**	**45**	**3**	**97**	**55**	**0**	**3**	**1**	**0**	**1**	**0**	**0**	**0**	**0**
1985-86	HC Merano	Italy	36	28	78	106	....	....	....	68	....	....	....	....	....	....	....	....	....	....	6	1	8	9	12	....	....	....
	Italy	WEC-B	7	2	1	3	....	....	....	10	....	....	....	....	....	....	....	....	....	....	....	....	....	....	....	....	....	....
1986-87	HC Merano	Italy	28	14	42	56	....	....	....	54	....	....	....	....	....	....	....	....	....	....	....	....	....	....	....	....	....	....
	Italy	WEC-B	4	0	2	2	....	....	....	8	....	....	....	....	....	....	....	....	....	....	....	....	....	....	....	....	....	....
1987-88	HC Fassa	Italy	43	14	61	75	....	....	....	97	....	....	....	....	....	....	....	....	....	....	....	....	....	....	....	....	....	....
1988-89	HC Fassa	Italy	38	12	52	64	....	....	....	61	....	....	....	....	....	....	....	....	....	....	....	....	....	....	....	....	....	....
	Italy	WEC-B	7	0	5	5	....	....	....	5	....	....	....	....	....	....	....	....	....	....	....	....	....	....	....	....	....	....
1989-90	HC Milano Saima	Italy	34	13	39	52	....	....	....	61	....	....	....	....	....	....	....	....	....	....	6	1	3	4	13	....	....	....
	Italy	WEC-B	7	1	4	5	....	....	....	10	....	....	....	....	....	....	....	....	....	....	....	....	....	....	....	....	....	....
1990-91	HC Milano Saima	Italy	32	7	43	50	....	....	....	61	....	....	....	....	....	....	....	....	....	....	6	1	12	13	4	....	....	....
	Italy	WEC-B	7	0	7	7	....	....	....	4	....	....	....	....	....	....	....	....	....	....	....	....	....	....	....	....	....	....
1991-92	HC Milano Saima	Italy	11	3	13	16	....	....	....	13	....	....	....	....	....	....	....	....	....	....	12	4	6	10	10	....	....	....
	Italy	Olympics	7	1	2	3	....	....	....	22	....	....	....	....	....	....	....	....	....	....	....	....	....	....	....	....	....	....
1992-93	HC Bolzano	Italy	15	3	16	19	....	....	....	9	....	....	....	....	....	....	....	....	....	....	11	1	8	9	20	....	....	....
1993-94	HC Bolzano	Alpenliga	24	5	29	34	....	....	....	69	....	....	....	....	....	....	....	....	....	....	....	....	....	....	....	....	....	....
	HC Bolzano	Italy	10	1	12	13	....	....	....	22	....	....	....	....	....	....	....	....	....	....	9	3	2	5	22	....	....	....
	NHL Totals		**371**	**41**	**131**	**172**	**34**	**91**	**125**	**274**	**8**	**5**	**7**	**463**	**8.9**	**384**	**77**	**504**	**158**		**17**	**2**	**4**	**6**	**12**	**0**	**0**	**0**

WEC-B All-Star Team (1986, 1989, 1991) • Named Best Defenseman at WEC-B (1989) • Played in NHL All-Star Game (1982)

Signed as a free agent by **Toronto**, September 30, 1981. Signed as a free agent by **Detroit**, August 2, 1983.

• MANSON, Dave

David "Charlie" D – L. 6'2", 220 lbs. b: Prince Albert, Sask., 1/27/1967. Chicago's 1st, 11th overall, in 1985.

Season	Club	League	GP	G	A	Pts	AG	AA	APts	PIM	PP	SH	GW	S	%	TGF	PGF	TGA	PGA	+/–	GP	G	A	Pts	PIM	PP	SH	GW
1982-83	Prince Albert Midget Raiders	SAHA	28	11	11	22	....	....	....	170	....	....	....	....	....	....	....	....	....	....	....	....	....	....	....	....	....	....
	Prince Albert Raiders	WHL	6	0	1	1	....	....	....	9	....	....	....	....	....	....	....	....	....	....	....	....	....	....	....	....	....	....
1983-84	Prince Albert Raiders	WHL	70	2	7	9	....	....	....	233	....	....	....	....	....	....	....	....	....	....	5	0	0	0	4	....	....	....
1984-85	Prince Albert Raiders	WHL	72	8	30	38	....	....	....	247	....	....	....	....	....	....	....	....	....	....	13	1	0	1	34	....	....	....
	Prince Albert Raiders	Mem-Cup	5	0	1	1	....	....	....	10	....	....	....	....	....	....	....	....	....	....	....	....	....	....	....	....	....	....
1985-86	Prince Albert Raiders	WHL	70	14	34	48	....	....	....	177	....	....	....	....	....	....	....	....	....	....	20	1	8	9	63	....	....	....
1986-87	**Chicago Blackhawks**	**NHL**	**63**	**1**	**8**	**9**	**1**	**6**	**7**	**146**	**0**	**0**	**0**	**42**	**2.4**	**49**	**0**	**57**	**6**	**–2**	**3**	**0**	**0**	**0**	**10**	**0**	**0**	**0**
1987-88	**Chicago Blackhawks**	**NHL**	**54**	**1**	**6**	**7**	**1**	**4**	**5**	**185**	**0**	**0**	**0**	**47**	**2.1**	**38**	**1**	**62**	**13**	**–12**	**5**	**0**	**0**	**0**	**27**	**0**	**0**	**0**
	Saginaw Hawks	IHL	6	0	3	3	....	....	....	37	....	....	....	....	....	....	....	....	....	....	....	....	....	....	....	....	....	....
1988-89	**Chicago Blackhawks**	**NHL**	**79**	**18**	**36**	**54**	**15**	**25**	**40**	**352**	**8**	**1**	**0**	**224**	**8.0**	**151**	**50**	**159**	**63**	**5**	**16**	**0**	**8**	**8**	**84**	**0**	**0**	**0**
1989-90	**Chicago Blackhawks**	**NHL**	**59**	**5**	**23**	**28**	**4**	**16**	**20**	**301**	**1**	**0**	**1**	**126**	**4.0**	**88**	**20**	**85**	**21**	**4**	**20**	**2**	**4**	**6**	**46**	**1**	**0**	**0**
1990-91	**Chicago Blackhawks**	**NHL**	**75**	**14**	**15**	**29**	**13**	**11**	**24**	**191**	**6**	**1**	**2**	**154**	**9.1**	**93**	**18**	**77**	**22**	**20**	**6**	**0**	**1**	**1**	**36**	**0**	**0**	**0**
1991-92	**Edmonton Oilers**	**NHL**	**79**	**15**	**32**	**47**	**14**	**24**	**38**	**220**	**7**	**0**	**2**	**206**	**7.3**	**130**	**39**	**110**	**28**	**9**	**16**	**3**	**9**	**12**	**44**	**1**	**0**	**0**
1992-93	**Edmonton Oilers**	**NHL**	**83**	**15**	**30**	**45**	**12**	**21**	**33**	**210**	**9**	**1**	**1**	**244**	**6.1**	**118**	**46**	**137**	**37**	**–28**	....	....	....	....	....	....	....	....
	Canada	WC-A	8	3	7	10	....	....	....	22	....	....	....	....	....	....	....	....	....	....	....	....	....	....	....	....	....	....
1993-94	**Edmonton Oilers**	**NHL**	**57**	**3**	**13**	**16**	**3**	**10**	**13**	**140**	**0**	**0**	**0**	**144**	**2.1**	**67**	**18**	**75**	**22**	**–4**	....	....	....	....	....	....	....	....
	Winnipeg Jets	**NHL**	**13**	**1**	**4**	**5**	**1**	**3**	**4**	**51**	**1**	**0**	**0**	**36**	**2.8**	**18**	**7**	**29**	**8**	**–10**	....	....	....	....	....	....	....	....
1994-95	**Winnipeg Jets**	**NHL**	**44**	**3**	**15**	**18**	**5**	**22**	**27**	**139**	**2**	**0**	**1**	**104**	**2.9**	**48**	**13**	**79**	**24**	**–20**	....	....	....	....	....	....	....	....
1995-96	**Winnipeg Jets**	**NHL**	**82**	**7**	**23**	**30**	**7**	**19**	**26**	**205**	**3**	**0**	**0**	**189**	**3.7**	**112**	**18**	**130**	**44**	**8**	**6**	**2**	**1**	**3**	**30**	**0**	**0**	**1**
1996-97	**Phoenix Coyotes**	**NHL**	**66**	**3**	**17**	**20**	**3**	**15**	**18**	**164**	**2**	**0**	**0**	**153**	**2.0**	**50**	**13**	**75**	**13**	**–25**	....	....	....	....	....	....	....	....
	Montreal Canadiens	**NHL**	**9**	**1**	**1**	**2**	**1**	**1**	**2**	**23**	**0**	**0**	**0**	**22**	**4.5**	**9**	**2**	**8**	**0**	**–1**	**5**	**0**	**0**	**0**	**17**	**0**	**0**	**0**
1997-98	**Montreal Canadiens**	**NHL**	**81**	**4**	**30**	**34**	**5**	**29**	**34**	**122**	**2**	**0**	**0**	**148**	**2.7**	**88**	**21**	**65**	**20**	**22**	**10**	**0**	**1**	**1**	**14**	**0**	**0**	**0**
1998-99	**Montreal Canadiens**	**NHL**	**11**	**0**	**2**	**2**	**0**	**2**	**2**	**48**	**0**	**0**	**0**	**11**	**0.0**	**6**	**2**	**8**	**1**	**–3**	....	....	....	....	....	....	....	....
	Chicago Blackhwaks	**NHL**	**64**	**6**	**15**	**21**	**7**	**14**	**21**	**107**	**2**	**0**	**0**	**134**	**4.5**	**60**	**14**	**67**	**25**	**4**	....	....	....	....	....	....	....	....
99-2000	**Chicago Blackhawks**	**NHL**	**37**	**0**	**7**	**7**	**0**	**6**	**6**	**40**	**0**	**0**	**0**	**45**	**0.0**	**,30**	**5**	**28**	**5**	**2**	....	....	....	....	....	....	....	....
	Dallas Stars	**NHL**	**26**	**1**	**2**	**3**	**1**	**2**	**3**	**22**	**0**	**0**	**0**	**21**	**4.8**	**19**	**2**	**7**	**0**	**10**	**23**	**0**	**0**	**0**	**33**	**0**	**0**	**0**
	NHL Totals		**982**	**98**	**279**	**377**	**93**	**230**	**323**	**2666**	**43**	**3**	**7**	**2050**	**4.8**	**1174**	**289**	**1258**	**352**		**110**	**7**	**24**	**31**	**341**	**2**	**0**	**1**

WHL East Second All-Star Team (1986) • WC-A All-Star Team (1993) • Played in NHL All-Star Game (1989, 1993)

Traded to **Edmonton** by **Chicago** with Chicago's 3rd round choice (Kirk Maltby) in 1992 Entry Draft for Steve Smith, October 2, 1991. Traded to **Winnipeg** by **Edmonton** with St. Louis' 6th round choice (previously acquired, Winnipeg selected Chris Kibermanis) in 1994 Entry Draft for Boris Mironov, Mats Lindgren, Winnipeg's 1st round choice (Jason Bonsignore) in 1994 Entry Draft and Florida's 4th round choice (previously acquired, Edmonton selected Adam Copeland) in 1994 Entry Draft, March 15, 1994. Transferred to **Phoenix** after **Winnipeg** franchise relocated, July 1, 1996. Traded to **Montreal** by **Phoenix** for Murray Baron and Chris Murray, March 18, 1997. Traded to **Chicago** by **Montreal** with Jocelyn Thibault and Brad Brown for Jeff Hackett, Eric Weinrich, Alain Nasreddine and Tampa Bay's 4th round choice (previously acquired, Montreal selected Chris Dyment) in 1999 Entry Draft, November 16, 1998. Traded to **Dallas** by **Chicago** with Sylvain Cote for Kevin Dean, Derek Plante and Dallas' 2nd round choice in 2001 Entry Draft, February 8, 2000.

• MANTHA, Moe

Maurice William D – R. 6'2", 210 lbs. b: Lakewood, OH, 1/21/1961. Winnipeg's 2nd, 23rd overall, in 1980.

			REGULAR SEASON																		PLAYOFFS							
Season	Club	League	GP	G	A	Pts	AG	AA	APts	PIM	PP	SH	GW	S	%	TGF	PGF	TGA	PGA	+/–	GP	G	A	Pts	PIM	PP	SH	GW
1976-77	Streetsville Derbys	OHA-B	63	35	70	105				75																		
1978-79	Toronto Marlboros	OMJHL	68	10	38	48				57											3	0	0	0	0			
1979-80	Toronto Marlboros	OMJHL	58	8	38	46				86											4	0	2	2	11			
1980-81	**Winnipeg Jets**	**NHL**	58	2	23	25	2	15	17	35	1	0	0	94	2.1	65	22	79	3	–33								
1981-82	**Winnipeg Jets**	**NHL**	25	0	12	12	0	8	8	28	0	0	0	39	0.0	23	4	31	2	–10	4	1	3	4	16	0	0	0
	Tulsa Oilers	CHL	33	8	15	23				56																		
	United States	WEC-A	7	1	1	2				6																		
1982-83	**Winnipeg Jets**	**NHL**	21	2	7	9	2	5	7	6	1	0	1	27	7.4	17	9	8	0	0	2	2	2	4	0	2	0	0
	Sherbrooke Jets	AHL	13	1	4	5				13																		
1983-84	**Winnipeg Jets**	**NHL**	72	16	38	54	13	26	39	67	3	0	1	228	7.0	128	42	120	20	–14	3	1	0	1	0	0	1	0
	Sherbrooke Jets	AHL	7	1	1	2				10																		
1984-85	**Pittsburgh Penguins**	**NHL**	71	11	40	51	9	27	36	54	3	0	1	204	5.4	117	40	148	36	–35								
	United States	WEC-A	10	2	1	3				10																		
1985-86	**Pittsburgh Penguins**	**NHL**	78	15	52	67	12	35	47	102	11	2	0	224	6.7	152	63	127	34	–4								
1986-87	**Pittsburgh Penguins**	**NHL**	62	9	31	40	8	23	31	44	8	0	0	167	5.4	102	44	96	32	–6								
1987-88	**Pittsburgh Penguins**	**NHL**	21	2	8	10	2	6	8	23	1	0	1	66	3.0	31	8	26	9	6								
	Edmonton Oilers	**NHL**	25	0	6	6	0	4	4	26	0	0	0	50	0.0	36	11	27	9	7								
	Minnesota North Stars	**NHL**	30	9	13	22	8	9	17	4	2	0	0	107	8.4	45	16	56	13	–14								
1988-89	**Minnesota North Stars**	**NHL**	16	1	6	7	1	4	5	10	1	0	0	32	3.1	17	7	13	4	1								
	Philadelphia Flyers	**NHL**	30	3	8	11	3	6	9	33	2	0	0	71	4.2	35	14	28	2	–5	1	0	0	0	0	0	0	0
1989-90	**Winnipeg Jets**	**NHL**	73	2	26	28	2	19	21	28	0	1	0	114	1.8	91	10	82	9	8	7	1	5	6	2	0	0	0
1990-91	**Winnipeg Jets**	**NHL**	57	9	15	24	8	11	19	33	4	1	2	102	8.8	53	11	76	14	–20								
	United States	WEC-A	9	0	0	0				2																		
1991-92	**Winnipeg Jets**	**NHL**	12	0	4	4	0	3	3	6	0	0	0	10	0.0	8	1	9	2	0								
	United States	Nat-Team	13	0	2	2				29																		
	United States	Olympics	8	1	1	2				4																		
	Philadelphia Flyers	**NHL**	5	0	0	0	0	0	0	2	0	0	0	7	0.0	1	0	3	2	0								
1992-93	Hershey Bears	AHL	1	0	0	0				0																		
1993-1994	Hershey Bears	AHL	DID NOT PLAY – ASSISTANT COACH																									
1994-1996	Columbus Chill	ECHL	DID NOT PLAY – COACHING																									
1996-1997	Baltimore Blades	AHL	DID NOT PLAY – COACHING																									
1997-2000	Cincinnati Mighty Ducks	AHL	DID NOT PLAY – COACHING																									
	NHL Totals		**656**	**81**	**289**	**370**	**70**	**201**	**271**	**501**	**37**	**4**	**6**	**1542**	**5.3**	**921**	**302**	**929**	**191**		**17**	**5**	**10**	**15**	**18**	**2**	**1**	**0**

Traded to **Pittsburgh** by **Winnipeg** to complete transaction that sent Randy Carlyle to Winnipeg (March 5, 1984), May 1, 1984. Traded to **Edmonton** by **Pittsburgh** with Craig Simpson, Dave Hanna and Chris Joseph for Paul Coffey, Dave Hunter and Wayne Van Dorp, November 24, 1987. Traded to **Minnesota** by **Edmonton** for Keith Acton, January 22, 1988. Traded to **Philadelphia** by **Minnesota** for Toronto's 5th round choice (previously acquired, Philadelphia selected Pat McLeod) in 1989 Entry Draft, December 8, 1988. Claimed by **Winnipeg** from **Philadelphia** in Waiver Draft, October 2, 1989. Traded to **Philadelphia** by **Winnipeg** for future considerations, February 27, 1992.

• MARA, Paul

D – L. 6'4", 202 lbs. b: Ridgewood, NJ, 9/7/1979. Tampa Bay's 1st, 7th overall, in 1997.

Season	Club	League	GP	G	A	Pts	AG	AA	APts	PIM	PP	SH	GW	S	%	TGF	PGF	TGA	PGA	+/–	GP	G	A	Pts	PIM	PP	SH	GW
1994-95	Belmont Hill Hillies	Hi-School	28	5	17	22				28																		
1995-96	Belmont Hill Hillies	Hi-School	28	18	20	38				40																		
1996-97	Sudbury Wolves	OHL	44	9	34	43				61																		
	United States	WJC-A	6	0	0	0				0																		
1997-98	Sudbury Wolves	OHL	25	8	18	26				79																		
	United States	WJC-A	7	1	1	2				6																		
	Plymouth Whalers	OHL	25	8	15	23				30											15	3	14	17	30			
1998-99	Plymouth Whalers	OHL	52	13	41	54				95											11	5	7	12	28			
	Tampa Bay Lighning	**NHL**	1	1	1	2	1	1	2	0	1	0	0	1	100.0	2	2	3	0	–3								
	United States	WJC-A	6	1	4	5				22																		
99-2000	**Tampa Bay Lightning**	**NHL**	54	7	11	18	8	10	18	73	4	0	1	78	9.0	49	17	70	11	–27								
	Detroit Vipers	IHL	15	3	5	8				22																		
	NHL Totals		**55**	**8**	**12**	**20**	**9**	**11**	**20**	**73**	**5**	**0**	**1**	**79**	**10.1**	**51**	**19**	**73**	**11**									

• MARCETTA, Milan

"Millie" C – L. 6', 195 lbs. b: Cadomin, Alta., 9/19/1936.

Season	Club	League	GP	G	A	Pts	AG	AA	APts	PIM	PP	SH	GW	S	%	TGF	PGF	TGA	PGA	+/–	GP	G	A	Pts	PIM	PP	SH	GW
1953-54	Medicine Hat Tigers	WCJHL	13	5	3	8				2											10	2	3	5	0			
1954-55	Medicine Hat Tigers	WCJHL	40	23	23	46				4											8	7	4	11	2			
1955-56	Yorkton Terriers	SJHL	47	34	38	72				37											3	0	0	0	2			
1956-57	Calgary Stampeders	WHL	67	27	22	49				20											1	0	0	0	0			
1957-58	Buffalo Bisons	AHL	17	1	0	1				8																		
	Calgary Stampeders	WHL	41	11	6	17				14											14	4	0	4	2			
1958-59	Springfield Indians	AHL	28	3	6	9				10																		
	Saskatoon Quakers	WHL	20	4	5	9				2																		
1959-60	Sault Ste. Marie Thunderbirds	EPHL	70	28	55	83				19																		
	Buffalo Bisons	AHL	1	0	1	1				0																		
1960-61	Sault Ste. Marie Thunderbirds	EPHL	50	8	18	26				59											6	0	0	0	0			
1961-62	Sault Ste. Marie Thunderbirds	EPHL	69	32	45	77				11																		
1962-63	St. Louis Braves	EPHL	20	9	4	13				27																		
	Calgary Stampeders	WHL	44	18	23	41				40																		
1963-64	Denver Invaders	WHL	58	23	23	46				19											6	5	1	6	12			
1964-65	Victoria Maple Leafs	WHL	70	34	46	80				21											10	2	2	4	6			
1965-66	Tulsa Oilers	CHL	8	8	7	15				2																		
	Victoria Maple Leafs	WHL	61	28	54	82				22											14	7	*13	*20	6			
1966-67	Victoria Maple Leafs	WHL	70	40	35	75				2																		
	♦ **Toronto Maple Leafs**	**NHL**																			3	0	0	0	0	0	0	0
1967-68	Rochester Americans	AHL	29	18	21	39				4																		
	Minnesota North Stars	**NHL**	36	4	13	17	5	13	18	6	0	0	0	41	9.8	20	4	26	0	–10	14	7	7	14	4	1	0	1
1968-69	**Minnesota North Stars**	**NHL**	18	3	2	5	3	2	5	4	2	0	0	18	16.7	5	3	6	0	–4								
	Memphis South Stars	CHL	22	6	9	15				22																		
	Phoenix Roadrunners	WHL	20	6	8	14				6																		
1969-70	Phoenix Roadrunners	WHL	73	34	32	66				14																		
1970-71	Phoenix Roadrunners	WHL	12	2	4	6				0																		
	Denver Spurs	WHL	30	6	17	23				2											5	2	6	8	0			
1971-72	Denver Spurs	WHL	72	22	45	67				19											9	2	2	4	6			
1972-73	Denver Spurs	WHL	52	18	22	40				14											5	2	2	4	2			
	NHL Totals		**54**	**7**	**15**	**22**	**8**	**15**	**23**	**10**											**17**	**7**	**7**	**14**	**4**			

Signed as a free agent by **NY Rangers**, September, 1958. Loaned to **Springfield** (AHL) by **NY Rangers**, October, 1958. Loaned to **Vancouver** (WHL) by **NY Rangers** (Springfield-AHL) for the loan of Larry Cahan, January 10, 1959. Traded to **Saskatoon** (WHL) by **NY Rangers** with Alex Kuzma for Bob Robinson and Les Lilley, February 3, 1959. Signed as a free agent by **Chicago**, September, 1959. Traded to **Calgary** (WHL) by **Chicago** for Jack Turner and cash, December, 1962. Signed as a free agent by **Toronto** (Denver-WHL), August, 1963. Traded to **Minnesota** by **Toronto** (Rochester-AHL) with Jean-Paul Parise for Murray Hall, Ted Taylor, Duke Harris, Len Lunde, Don Johns and the loan of Carl Wetzel, December 23, 1967. • Assigned to **Memphis** (CHL) and named Player/Coach, December, 1968. Traded to **Phoenix** (WHL) by **Minnesota** with Brian D. Smith for Tom Polanic, February 11, 1969. Claimed on waivers by **Denver** (WHL) from **Phoenix** (WHL), November 24, 1970.

• MARCHANT, Todd

Todd Michael C – L. 5'10", 178 lbs. b: Buffalo, NY, 8/12/1973. NY Rangers' 8th, 164th overall, in 1993.

Season	Club	League	GP	G	A	Pts	AG	AA	APts	PIM	PP	SH	GW	S	%	TGF	PGF	TGA	PGA	+/–	GP	G	A	Pts	PIM	PP	SH	GW
1990-91	Niagara Scenics	NAJHL	37	31	47	78																						
1991-92	Clarkson University	ECAC	32	20	12	32				32																		
1992-93	Clarkson University	ECAC	33	18	28	46				38																		
	United States	WJC-A	7	2	3	5				2																		

			REGULAR SEASON																		PLAYOFFS							
Season	Club	League	GP	G	A	Pts	AG	AA	APts	PIM	PP	SH	GW	S	%	TGF	PGF	TGA	PGA	+/–	GP	G	A	Pts	PIM	PP	SH	GW
1993-94	United States	Nat-Team	59	28	39	67	....	....	....	48	....	....	....	....	....	....	....	....	....	....	....	....	....	....	....	....	....	....
	United States	Olympics	8	1	1	2	....	....	....	6	....	....	....	....	....	....	....	....	....	....	....	....	....	....	....	....	....	....
	New York Rangers	**NHL**	**1**	**0**	**0**	**0**	**0**	**0**	**0**	**0**	**0**	**0**	**0**	**1**	**0.0**	**1**	**0**	**2**	**0**	**–1**	....	....	....	....	....	....	....	....
	Binghamton Rangers	AHL	8	2	7	9	....	....	....	6	....	....	....	....	....	....	....	....	....	....	....	....	....	....	....	....	....	....
	Edmonton Oilers	**NHL**	**3**	**0**	**1**	**1**	**0**	**1**	**1**	**2**	**0**	**0**	**0**	**5**	**0.0**	**1**	**0**	**3**	**1**	**–1**	....	....	....	....	....	....	....	....
	Cape Breton Oilers	AHL	3	1	4	5	....	....	....	2	....	....	....	....	....	....	....	....	....	....	5	1	1	2	0	....	....	....
1994-95	Cape Breton Oilers	AHL	38	22	25	47	....	....	....	25	....	....	....	....	....	....	....	....	....	....	....	....	....	....	....	....	....	....
	Edmonton Oilers	**NHL**	**45**	**13**	**14**	**27**	**23**	**21**	**44**	**32**	**3**	**2**	**2**	**95**	**13.7**	**38**	**10**	**53**	**22**	**–3**	....	....	....	....	....	....	....	....
1995-96	**Edmonton Oilers**	**NHL**	**81**	**19**	**19**	**38**	**19**	**16**	**35**	**66**	**2**	**3**	**2**	**221**	**8.6**	**46**	**4**	**92**	**31**	**–19**	....	....	....	....	....	....	....	....
1996-97	**Edmonton Oilers**	**NHL**	**79**	**14**	**19**	**33**	**15**	**17**	**32**	**44**	**0**	**4**	**3**	**202**	**6.9**	**44**	**3**	**60**	**30**	**11**	**12**	**4**	**2**	**6**	**12**	**0**	**3**	**1**
1997-98	**Edmonton Oilers**	**NHL**	**76**	**14**	**21**	**35**	**16**	**21**	**37**	**71**	**2**	**1**	**3**	**194**	**7.2**	**56**	**10**	**57**	**20**	**9**	**12**	**1**	**1**	**2**	**10**	**0**	**0**	**0**
1998-99	**Edmonton Oilers**	**NHL**	**82**	**14**	**22**	**36**	**16**	**21**	**37**	**65**	**3**	**1**	**2**	**183**	**7.7**	**49**	**6**	**77**	**37**	**3**	**4**	**1**	**1**	**2**	**12**	**0**	**0**	**0**
99-2000	**Edmonton Oilers**	**NHL**	**82**	**17**	**23**	**40**	**19**	**21**	**40**	**70**	**0**	**1**	**0**	**170**	**10.0**	**57**	**7**	**68**	**25**	**7**	**3**	**1**	**0**	**1**	**2**	**0**	**0**	**0**
	NHL Totals		**449**	**91**	**119**	**210**	**108**	**118**	**226**	**350**	**10**	**12**	**12**	**1071**	**8.5**	**292**	**40**	**412**	**166**		**31**	**7**	**4**	**11**	**36**	**0**	**3**	**1**

ECAC Second All-Star Team (1993)

Traded to **Edmonton** by **NY Rangers** for Craig MacTavish, March 21, 1994.

• MARCHINKO, Brian

Brian Nicholas Wayne C – R. 6', 180 lbs. b: Weyburn, Sask., 8/2/1948.

Season	Club	League	GP	G	A	Pts	AG	AA	APts	PIM	PP	SH	GW	S	%	TGF	PGF	TGA	PGA	+/–	GP	G	A	Pts	PIM	PP	SH	GW
1966-67	Melfort Millionaires	SJHL	STATISTICS NOT AVAILABLE																									
1967-68	London Nationals/Knights	OHA-Jr.	25	0	1	1	....	....	....	0	....	....	....	....	....	....	....	....	....	....	....	....	....	....	....	....	....	....
	Flin Flon Bombers	WCJHL	43	9	16	25	....	....	....	13	....	....	....	....	....	....	....	....	....	....	15	5	9	14	4	....	....	....
1968-69	Flin Flon Bombers	WCJHL	60	41	45	86	....	....	....	96	....	....	....	....	....	....	....	....	....	....	18	6	9	15	4	....	....	....
1969-70	Tulsa Oilers	CHL	59	8	14	22	....	....	....	30	....	....	....	....	....	....	....	....	....	....	6	1	0	1	0	....	....	....
1970-71	**Toronto Maple Leafs**	**NHL**	**2**	**0**	**0**	**0**	**0**	**0**	**0**	**0**	**0**	**0**	**0**	**0**	**0.0**	**0**	**0**	**0**	**0**	**0**	....	....	....	....	....	....	....	....
	Tulsa Oilers	CHL	67	15	24	39	....	....	....	47	....	....	....	....	....	....	....	....	....	....	....	....	....	....	....	....	....	....
1971-72	**Toronto Maple Leafs**	**NHL**	**3**	**0**	**0**	**0**	**0**	**0**	**0**	**0**	**0**	**0**	**0**	**1**	**0.0**	**0**	**0**	**0**	**0**	**0**	....	....	....	....	....	....	....	....
	Tulsa Oilers	CHL	68	10	24	34	....	....	....	29	....	....	....	....	....	....	....	....	....	....	13	3	3	6	7	....	....	....
1972-73	**New York Islanders**	**NHL**	**36**	**2**	**6**	**8**	**2**	**5**	**7**	**0**	**0**	**0**	**1**	**19**	**10.5**	**10**	**0**	**25**	**5**	**–10**	....	....	....	....	....	....	....	....
	New Haven Nighthawks	AHL	7	0	0	0	....	....	....	0	....	....	....	....	....	....	....	....	....	....	....	....	....	....	....	....	....	....
1973-74	**New York Islanders**	**NHL**	**6**	**0**	**0**	**0**	**0**	**0**	**0**	**0**	**0**	**0**	**0**	**7**	**0.0**	**0**	**0**	**0**	**0**	**0**	....	....	....	....	....	....	....	....
	Fort Worth Wings	CHL	54	7	19	26	....	....	....	24	....	....	....	....	....	....	....	....	....	....	....	....	....	....	....	....	....	....
	Providence Reds	AHL	10	3	0	3	....	....	....	8	....	....	....	....	....	....	....	....	....	....	15	7	2	9	9	....	....	....
1974-75	Fort Worth Texans	CHL	78	23	20	43	....	....	....	32	....	....	....	....	....	....	....	....	....	....	....	....	....	....	....	....	....	....
1975-76	Erie Blades	NAHL	63	27	34	61	....	....	....	29	....	....	....	....	....	....	....	....	....	....	5	1	2	3	0	....	....	....
1976-77	Erie Blades	NAHL	47	16	21	37	....	....	....	4	....	....	....	....	....	....	....	....	....	....	....	....	....	....	....	....	....	....
	Johnstown Jets	NAHL	21	8	9	17	....	....	....	4	....	....	....	....	....	....	....	....	....	....	3	2	0	2	0	....	....	....
	NHL Totals		**47**	**2**	**6**	**8**	**2**	**5**	**7**	**0**	**0**	**0**	**1**	**27**	**7.4**	**10**	**0**	**25**	**5**		....	....	....	....	....	....	....	....

Signed as a free agent by **Toronto**, October 1, 1969. Claimed by **NY Islanders** from **Toronto** in Expansion Draft, June 6, 1972.

• MARCHMENT, Bryan

Bryan William D – L. 6'1", 200 lbs. b: Scarborough, Ont., 5/1/1969. Winnipeg's 1st, 16th overall, in 1987.

Season	Club	League	GP	G	A	Pts	AG	AA	APts	PIM	PP	SH	GW	S	%	TGF	PGF	TGA	PGA	+/–	GP	G	A	Pts	PIM	PP	SH	GW
1984-85	Toronto Young Nationals	MTHL	69	14	35	49	....	....	....	229	....	....	....	....	....	....	....	....	....	....	....	....	....	....	....	....	....	....
1985-86	Belleville Bulls	OHL	57	5	15	20	....	....	....	225	....	....	....	....	....	....	....	....	....	....	21	0	7	7	83	....	....	....
1986-87	Belleville Bulls	OHL	52	6	38	44	....	....	....	238	....	....	....	....	....	....	....	....	....	....	6	0	4	4	17	....	....	....
1987-88	Belleville Bulls	OHL	56	7	51	58	....	....	....	200	....	....	....	....	....	....	....	....	....	....	6	1	3	4	19	....	....	....
1988-89	Belleville Bulls	OHL	43	14	36	50	....	....	....	118	....	....	....	....	....	....	....	....	....	....	5	0	1	1	12	....	....	....
	Winnipeg Jets	**NHL**	**2**	**0**	**0**	**0**	**0**	**0**	**0**	**2**	**0**	**0**	**0**	**1**	**0.0**	**0**	**0**	**0**	**0**	**0**	....	....	....	....	....	....	....	....
1989-90	**Winnipeg Jets**	**NHL**	**7**	**0**	**2**	**2**	**0**	**1**	**1**	**28**	**0**	**0**	**0**	**5**	**0.0**	**6**	**0**	**6**	**0**	**0**	....	....	....	....	....	....	....	....
	Moncton Hawks	AHL	56	4	19	23	....	....	....	217	....	....	....	....	....	....	....	....	....	....	....	....	....	....	....	....	....	....
1990-91	**Winnipeg Jets**	**NHL**	**28**	**2**	**2**	**4**	**2**	**2**	**4**	**91**	**0**	**0**	**0**	**24**	**8.3**	**24**	**3**	**30**	**4**	**–5**	....	....	....	....	....	....	....	....
	Moncton Hawks	AHL	33	2	11	13	....	....	....	101	....	....	....	....	....	....	....	....	....	....	....	....	....	....	....	....	....	....
1991-92	**Chicago Blackhawks**	**NHL**	**58**	**5**	**10**	**15**	**5**	**8**	**13**	**168**	**2**	**0**	**0**	**55**	**9.1**	**38**	**6**	**42**	**6**	**–4**	**16**	**1**	**0**	**1**	**36**	**0**	**0**	**0**
1992-93	**Chicago Blackhawks**	**NHL**	**78**	**5**	**15**	**20**	**4**	**10**	**14**	**313**	**1**	**0**	**1**	**75**	**6.7**	**61**	**5**	**51**	**10**	**15**	**4**	**0**	**0**	**0**	**12**	**0**	**0**	**0**
1993-94	**Chicago Blackhawks**	**NHL**	**13**	**1**	**4**	**5**	**1**	**3**	**4**	**42**	**0**	**0**	**0**	**18**	**5.6**	**9**	**0**	**15**	**4**	**–2**	....	....	....	....	....	....	....	....
	Hartford Whalers	**NHL**	**42**	**3**	**7**	**10**	**3**	**5**	**8**	**124**	**0**	**1**	**1**	**74**	**4.1**	**30**	**1**	**55**	**14**	**–12**	....	....	....	....	....	....	....	....
1994-95	**Edmonton Oilers**	**NHL**	**40**	**1**	**5**	**6**	**2**	**7**	**9**	**184**	**0**	**0**	**0**	**57**	**1.8**	**25**	**1**	**47**	**12**	**–11**	....	....	....	....	....	....	....	....
1995-96	**Edmonton Oilers**	**NHL**	**78**	**3**	**15**	**18**	**3**	**12**	**15**	**202**	**0**	**0**	**0**	**96**	**3.1**	**82**	**9**	**121**	**41**	**–7**	....	....	....	....	....	....	....	....
1996-97	**Edmonton Oilers**	**NHL**	**71**	**3**	**13**	**16**	**3**	**12**	**15**	**132**	**1**	**0**	**0**	**89**	**3.4**	**64**	**2**	**67**	**18**	**13**	**3**	**0**	**0**	**0**	**4**	**0**	**0**	**0**
1997-98	**Edmonton Oilers**	**NHL**	**27**	**0**	**4**	**4**	**0**	**4**	**4**	**58**	**0**	**0**	**0**	**23**	**0.0**	**17**	**2**	**26**	**9**	**–2**	....	....	....	....	....	....	....	....
	Tampa Bay Lightning	**NHL**	**22**	**2**	**4**	**6**	**2**	**4**	**6**	**43**	**0**	**0**	**0**	**20**	**10.0**	**20**	**1**	**30**	**8**	**–3**	....	....	....	....	....	....	....	....
	San Jose Sharks	**NHL**	**12**	**0**	**3**	**3**	**0**	**3**	**3**	**43**	**0**	**0**	**0**	**13**	**0.0**	**12**	**1**	**10**	**1**	**2**	**6**	**0**	**0**	**0**	**10**	**0**	**0**	**0**
1998-99	**San Jose Sharks**	**NHL**	**59**	**2**	**6**	**8**	**2**	**6**	**8**	**101**	**0**	**0**	**0**	**49**	**4.1**	**29**	**2**	**45**	**11**	**–7**	**6**	**0**	**0**	**0**	**4**	**0**	**0**	**0**
99-2000	**San Jose Sharks**	**NHL**	**49**	**0**	**4**	**4**	**0**	**4**	**4**	**72**	**0**	**0**	**0**	**51**	**0.0**	**33**	**1**	**40**	**11**	**3**	**11**	**2**	**1**	**3**	**12**	**0**	**0**	**0**
	NHL Totals		**586**	**27**	**94**	**121**	**27**	**81**	**108**	**1603**	**4**	**1**	**2**	**650**	**4.2**	**450**	**34**	**585**	**149**		**46**	**3**	**1**	**4**	**78**	**0**	**0**	**0**

OHL Second All-Star Team (1989)

Traded to **Chicago** by **Winnipeg** with Chris Norton for Troy Murray and Warren Rychel, July 22, 1991. Traded to **Hartford** by **Chicago** with Steve Larmer for Eric Weinrich and Patrick Poulin, November 2, 1993. Transferred to **Edmonton** from **Hartford** as compensation for Hartford's signing of free agent Steven Rice, August 30, 1994. Traded to **Tampa Bay** by **Edmonton** with Steve Kelly and Jason Bonsignore for Roman Hamrlik and Paul Comrie, December 30, 1997. Traded to **San Jose** by **Tampa Bay** with David Shaw and Tampa Bay's 1st round choice (later traded to Nashville - Nashville selected David Legwand) in 1998 Entry Draft for Andrei Nazarov and Florida's 1st round choice (previously acquired, Tampa Bay selected Vincent Lecavallier) in 1998 Entry Draft, March 24, 1998.

• MARCINYSHYN, Dave

David Joseph D – L. 6'3", 210 lbs. b: Edmonton, Alta., 2/4/1967.

Season	Club	League	GP	G	A	Pts	AG	AA	APts	PIM	PP	SH	GW	S	%	TGF	PGF	TGA	PGA	+/–	GP	G	A	Pts	PIM	PP	SH	GW
1984-85	Fort Saskatchewan Traders	AJHL	55	11	41	52	....	....	....	311	....	....	....	....	....	....	....	....	....	....	....	....	....	....	....	....	....	....
1985-86	Kamloops Blazers	WHL	57	2	7	9	....	....	....	111	....	....	....	....	....	....	....	....	....	....	16	1	3	4	12	....	....	....
	Kamloops Blazers	Mem-Cup	5	0	2	2	....	....	....	22	....	....	....	....	....	....	....	....	....	....	....	....	....	....	....	....	....	....
1986-87	Kamloops Blazers	WHL	68	5	27	32	....	....	....	106	....	....	....	....	....	....	....	....	....	....	13	0	3	3	35	....	....	....
1987-88	Utica Devils	AHL	73	2	7	9	....	....	....	179	....	....	....	....	....	....	....	....	....	....	....	....	....	....	....	....	....	....
	Flint Spirits	IHL	3	0	0	0	....	....	....	4	....	....	....	....	....	....	....	....	....	....	16	0	2	2	31	....	....	....
1988-89	Utica Devils	AHL	74	4	14	18	....	....	....	101	....	....	....	....	....	....	....	....	....	....	5	0	0	0	13	....	....	....
1989-90	Utica Devils	AHL	74	6	18	24	....	....	....	164	....	....	....	....	....	....	....	....	....	....	5	0	2	2	21	....	....	....
1990-91	**New Jersey Devils**	**NHL**	**9**	**0**	**1**	**1**	**0**	**1**	**1**	**21**	**0**	**0**	**0**	**4**	**0.0**	**5**	**0**	**7**	**1**	**–1**	....	....	....	....	....	....	....	....
	Utica Devils	AHL	52	4	9	13	....	....	....	81	....	....	....	....	....	....	....	....	....	....	....	....	....	....	....	....	....	....
1991-92	**Quebec Nordiques**	**NHL**	**5**	**0**	**0**	**0**	**0**	**0**	**0**	**26**	**0**	**0**	**0**	**3**	**0.0**	**2**	**0**	**3**	**0**	**–1**	....	....	....	....	....	....	....	....
	Halifax Citadels	AHL	74	10	42	52	....	....	....	138	....	....	....	....	....	....	....	....	....	....	....	....	....	....	....	....	....	....
1992-93	**New York Rangers**	**NHL**	**2**	**0**	**0**	**0**	**0**	**0**	**0**	**2**	**0**	**0**	**0**	**1**	**0.0**	**0**	**0**	**1**	**0**	**–1**	....	....	....	....	....	....	....	....
	Binghamton Rangers	AHL	67	5	25	30	....	....	....	184	....	....	....	....	....	....	....	....	....	....	6	0	3	3	14	....	....	....
1993-94	Milwaukee Admirals	IHL	1	0	0	0	....	....	....	0	....	....	....	....	....	....	....	....	....	....	....	....	....	....	....	....	....	....
1994-95	Milwaukee Admirals	IHL	63	2	14	16	....	....	....	176	....	....	....	....	....	....	....	....	....	....	....	....	....	....	....	....	....	....
	Kalamazoo K-Wings	IHL	3	0	0	0	....	....	....	6	....	....	....	....	....	....	....	....	....	....	16	0	1	1	16	....	....	....
1995-96	Cincinnati Cyclones	IHL	65	6	16	22	....	....	....	99	....	....	....	....	....	....	....	....	....	....	3	0	0	0	4	....	....	....
1996-97	Cincinnati Cyclones	IHL	74	1	9	10	....	....	....	141	....	....	....	....	....	....	....	....	....	....	....	....	....	....	....	....	....	....
1997-98	Dusseldorfer EG	Germany	47	6	16	22	....	....	....	99	....	....	....	....	....	....	....	....	....	....	3	0	0	0	4	....	....	....
1998-99	Schwenningen Wild Wings	Germany	43	5	9	14	....	....	....	101	....	....	....	....	....	....	....	....	....	....	....	....	....	....	....	....	....	....
	NHL Totals		**16**	**0**	**1**	**1**	**0**	**1**	**1**	**49**	**0**	**0**	**0**	**8**	**0.0**	**7**	**0**	**11**	**1**		....	....	....	....	....	....	....	....

Signed as a free agent by **New Jersey**, September 26, 1986. Traded to **Quebec** by **New Jersey** for Brent Severyn, June 3, 1991. Signed as a free agent by **NY Rangers**, August 5, 1992. Signed as a free agent by **Cincinnati** (IHL), August 30, 1995.

● MARCOTTE, Don

Donald Michel LW – L. 5'11", 183 lbs. b: Asbestos, Que., 4/15/1947.

			REGULAR SEASON																		PLAYOFFS							
Season	Club	League	GP	G	A	Pts	AG	AA	APts	PIM	PP	SH	GW	S	%	TGF	PGF	TGA	PGA	+/–	GP	G	A	Pts	PIM	PP	SH	GW
1963-64	Victoriaville Bruins	QJHL	....	....	....	....	....	....	....	....	....	....	....	....	....	....	....	....	....	....	9	14	2	16	33	....	....	....
1964-65	Niagara Falls Flyers	OHA-Jr.	56	28	23	51	....	....	....	94	....	....	....	....	....	....	....	....	....	....	11	7	5	12	30	....	....	....
	Niagara Falls Flyers	Mem-Cup	13	9	6	15	....	....	....	22	....	....	....	....	....	....	....	....	....	....	....	....	....	....	....	....	....	....
1965-66	Niagara Falls Flyers	OHA-Jr.	45	28	22	50	....	....	....	76	....	....	....	....	....	....	....	....	....	....	6	3	3	6	11	....	....	....
	Boston Bruins	**NHL**	**1**	**0**	**0**	**0**	**0**	**0**	**0**	**0**	....	....	....	....	....	....	....	....	....	....	....	....	....	....	....	....	....	....
	Oklahoma City Blazers	CPHL	2	1	0	1	....	....	....	2	....	....	....	....	....	....	....	....	....	....	5	2	0	2	0	....	....	....
1966-67	Niagara Falls Flyers	OHA-Jr.	35	21	21	42	....	....	....	38	....	....	....	....	....	....	....	....	....	....	13	8	8	16	28	....	....	....
1967-68	Hershey Bears	AHL	72	31	22	53	....	....	....	35	....	....	....	....	....	....	....	....	....	....	5	0	1	1	16	....	....	....
1968-69	**Boston Bruins**	**NHL**	**7**	**1**	**0**	**1**	**1**	**0**	**1**	**2**	**0**	**0**	**0**	**7**	**14.3**	**3**	**0**	**4**	**1**	**0**	....	....	....	....	....	....	....	....
	Hershey Bears	AHL	67	35	21	56	....	....	....	65	....	....	....	....	....	....	....	....	....	....	11	7	2	9	25	....	....	....
1969-70♦	**Boston Bruins**	**NHL**	**35**	**9**	**3**	**12**	**10**	**3**	**13**	**14**	**0**	**0**	**1**	**73**	**12.3**	**17**	**0**	**29**	**9**	**–3**	**14**	**2**	**0**	**2**	**11**	**0**	**0**	**1**
	Hershey Bears	AHL	35	28	15	43	....	....	....	23	....	....	....	....	....	....	....	....	....	....	....	....	....	....	....	....	....	....
1970-71	**Boston Bruins**	**NHL**	**75**	**15**	**13**	**28**	**15**	**11**	**26**	**30**	**0**	**6**	**2**	**87**	**17.2**	**40**	**0**	**46**	**26**	**20**	**4**	**0**	**0**	**0**	**0**	**0**	**0**	**0**
1971-72♦	**Boston Bruins**	**NHL**	**47**	**6**	**4**	**10**	**6**	**3**	**9**	**12**	**0**	**0**	**1**	**51**	**11.8**	**16**	**0**	**26**	**10**	**0**	**14**	**3**	**0**	**3**	**6**	**0**	**1**	**1**
	Boston Braves	AHL	8	4	7	11	....	....	....	2	....	....	....	....	....	....	....	....	....	....	....	....	....	....	....	....	....	....
1972-73	**Boston Bruins**	**NHL**	**78**	**24**	**31**	**55**	**23**	**25**	**48**	**49**	**1**	**2**	**3**	**175**	**13.7**	**82**	**1**	**68**	**19**	**32**	**5**	**1**	**1**	**2**	**0**	**0**	**0**	**0**
1973-74	**Boston Bruins**	**NHL**	**78**	**24**	**26**	**50**	**23**	**21**	**44**	**18**	**0**	**3**	**3**	**150**	**16.0**	**81**	**1**	**62**	**26**	**44**	**16**	**4**	**2**	**6**	**8**	**0**	**0**	**1**
1974-75	**Boston Bruins**	**NHL**	**80**	**31**	**33**	**64**	**27**	**25**	**52**	**76**	**1**	**0**	**2**	**165**	**18.8**	**99**	**6**	**92**	**23**	**24**	**3**	**1**	**0**	**1**	**0**	**0**	**0**	**0**
1975-76	**Boston Bruins**	**NHL**	**58**	**16**	**20**	**36**	**14**	**15**	**29**	**24**	**1**	**0**	**2**	**96**	**16.7**	**58**	**6**	**49**	**12**	**15**	**12**	**4**	**2**	**6**	**8**	**1**	**0**	**0**
1976-77	**Boston Bruins**	**NHL**	**80**	**27**	**18**	**45**	**24**	**14**	**38**	**20**	**3**	**1**	**5**	**176**	**15.3**	**89**	**9**	**67**	**15**	**28**	**14**	**5**	**6**	**11**	**10**	**0**	**1**	**0**
1977-78	**Boston Bruins**	**NHL**	**77**	**20**	**34**	**54**	**18**	**26**	**44**	**16**	**4**	**2**	**0**	**159**	**12.6**	**96**	**14**	**94**	**44**	**32**	**15**	**5**	**4**	**9**	**8**	**1**	**0**	**1**
1978-79	**Boston Bruins**	**NHL**	**79**	**20**	**27**	**47**	**17**	**20**	**37**	**10**	**2**	**4**	**5**	**156**	**12.8**	**71**	**4**	**113**	**52**	**6**	**11**	**5**	**3**	**8**	**10**	**0**	**0**	**0**
	NHL All-Stars	Chal-Cup	1	0	0	0	....	....	....	2	....	....	....	....	....	....	....	....	....	....	....	....	....	....	....	....	....	....
1979-80	**Boston Bruins**	**NHL**	**32**	**4**	**11**	**15**	**3**	**8**	**11**	**0**	**0**	**1**	**1**	**39**	**10.3**	**22**	**0**	**29**	**11**	**4**	**10**	**2**	**3**	**5**	**4**	**0**	**0**	**1**
1980-81	**Boston Bruins**	**NHL**	**72**	**20**	**13**	**33**	**16**	**9**	**25**	**32**	**4**	**1**	**2**	**128**	**15.6**	**58**	**5**	**87**	**37**	**3**	**3**	**2**	**2**	**4**	**6**	**0**	**0**	**0**
1981-82	**Boston Bruins**	**NHL**	**69**	**13**	**21**	**34**	**10**	**14**	**24**	**14**	**0**	**0**	**3**	**86**	**15.1**	**62**	**2**	**84**	**22**	**–2**	**11**	**0**	**4**	**4**	**10**	**0**	**0**	**0**
	NHL Totals		**868**	**230**	**254**	**484**	**207**	**194**	**401**	**317**	....	....	....	....	....	....	....	....	....		**132**	**34**	**27**	**61**	**81**	....	....	....

● MARHA, Josef

C – L. 6', 176 lbs. b: Havlickuv, Czech., 6/2/1976. Quebec's 3rd, 35th overall, in 1994.

Season	Club	League	GP	G	A	Pts	AG	AA	APts	PIM	PP	SH	GW	S	%	TGF	PGF	TGA	PGA	+/–	GP	G	A	Pts	PIM	PP	SH	GW
1991-92	Dukla Jihlava	Czech-Jr.	25	12	13	25	....	....	....	0	....	....	....	....	....	....	....	....	....	....	....	....	....	....	....	....	....	....
1992-93	Dukla Jihlava	Czech.	7	2	2	4	....	....	....	....	....	....	....	....	....	....	....	....	....	....	....	....	....	....	....	....	....	....
1993-94	Dukla Jihlava	Czech-Rep	41	7	2	9	....	....	....	....	....	....	....	....	....	....	....	....	....	....	3	0	1	1	....	....	....	....
	Czech-Republic	WJC-A	5	4	0	4	....	....	....	2	....	....	....	....	....	....	....	....	....	....	....	....	....	....	....	....	....	....
	Czech-Republic	EJC-A	5	4	5	9	....	....	....	4	....	....	....	....	....	....	....	....	....	....	....	....	....	....	....	....	....	....
1994-95	Dukla Jihlava	Czech-Rep	35	3	7	10	....	....	....	6	....	....	....	....	....	....	....	....	....	....	....	....	....	....	....	....	....	....
	Czech-Republic	WJC-A	7	5	5	10	....	....	....	0	....	....	....	....	....	....	....	....	....	....	....	....	....	....	....	....	....	....
1995-96	**Colorado Avalanche**	**NHL**	**2**	**0**	**1**	**1**	**0**	**1**	**1**	**0**	**0**	**0**	**0**	**2**	**0.0**	**1**	**0**	**0**	**0**	**1**	....	....	....	....	....	....	....	....
	Cornwall Aces	AHL	74	18	30	48	....	....	....	30	....	....	....	....	....	....	....	....	....	....	8	1	2	3	10	....	....	....
1996-97	**Colorado Avalanche**	**NHL**	**6**	**0**	**1**	**1**	**0**	**1**	**1**	**0**	**0**	**0**	**0**	**6**	**0.0**	**2**	**0**	**2**	**0**	**0**	....	....	....	....	....	....	....	....
	Hershey Bears	AHL	67	23	49	72	....	....	....	44	....	....	....	....	....	....	....	....	....	....	19	6	*16	*22	10	....	....	....
1997-98	**Colorado Avalanche**	**NHL**	**11**	**2**	**5**	**7**	**2**	**5**	**7**	**4**	**0**	**0**	**0**	**10**	**20.0**	**8**	**4**	**4**	**0**	**0**	....	....	....	....	....	....	....	....
	Hershey Bears	AHL	55	6	46	52	....	....	....	30	....	....	....	....	....	....	....	....	....	....	....	....	....	....	....	....	....	....
	Mighty Ducks of Anaheim	**NHL**	**12**	**7**	**4**	**11**	**8**	**4**	**12**	**0**	**3**	**0**	**0**	**21**	**33.3**	**13**	**6**	**6**	**3**	**4**	....	....	....	....	....	....	....	....
1998-99	**Mighty Ducks of Anaheim**	**NHL**	**10**	**0**	**1**	**1**	**0**	**1**	**1**	**0**	**0**	**0**	**0**	**13**	**0.0**	**1**	**0**	**5**	**0**	**–4**	....	....	....	....	....	....	....	....
	Cincinnati Mighty Ducks	AHL	3	1	0	1	....	....	....	4	....	....	....	....	....	....	....	....	....	....	....	....	....	....	....	....	....	....
	Chicago Blackhawks	**NHL**	**22**	**2**	**5**	**7**	**2**	**5**	**7**	**4**	**1**	**0**	**1**	**32**	**6.3**	**20**	**3**	**13**	**1**	**5**	....	....	....	....	....	....	....	....
	Portland Pirates	AHL	8	0	8	8	....	....	....	2	....	....	....	....	....	....	....	....	....	....	....	....	....	....	....	....	....	....
99-2000	**Chicago Blackhawks**	**NHL**	**81**	**10**	**12**	**22**	**11**	**11**	**22**	**18**	**2**	**1**	**3**	**91**	**11.0**	**38**	**5**	**62**	**19**	**–10**	....	....	....	....	....	....	....	....
	NHL Totals		**144**	**21**	**29**	**50**	**23**	**28**	**51**	**26**	**6**	**1**	**4**	**175**	**12.0**	**83**	**18**	**92**	**23**		....	....	....	....	....	....	....	....

Rights transferred to **Colorado** after **Quebec** franchise relocated, June 21, 1995. Traded to **Anaheim** by **Colorado** for Warren Rychel and Anaheim's 4th round choice (Sanny Lindstrom) in 1999 Entry Draft, March 24, 1998. Traded to **Chicago** by **Anaheim** for Chicago's 4th round choice (Alexandr Chagodayev) in 1999 Entry Draft, January 28, 1999.

● MARINI, Hector

Joseph Hector "The Wreaker" RW – R. 6'1", 204 lbs. b: Timmins, Ont., 1/27/1957. NY Islanders' 3rd, 50th overall, in 1977.

Season	Club	League	GP	G	A	Pts	AG	AA	APts	PIM	PP	SH	GW	S	%	TGF	PGF	TGA	PGA	+/–	GP	G	A	Pts	PIM	PP	SH	GW
1974-75	Sudbury Wolves	OMJHL	69	12	19	31	....	....	....	70	....	....	....	....	....	....	....	....	....	....	15	2	6	8	9	....	....	....
1975-76	Sudbury Wolves	OMJHL	66	32	45	77	....	....	....	102	....	....	....	....	....	....	....	....	....	....	17	7	5	12	32	....	....	....
1976-77	Sudbury Wolves	OMJHL	64	32	58	90	....	....	....	89	....	....	....	....	....	....	....	....	....	....	6	1	3	4	9	....	....	....
1977-78	Fort Worth Texans	CHL	2	0	0	0	....	....	....	4	....	....	....	....	....	....	....	....	....	....	....	....	....	....	....	....	....	....
	Muskegon Mohawks	IHL	80	33	60	93	....	....	....	127	....	....	....	....	....	....	....	....	....	....	6	7	4	11	5	....	....	....
1978-79	**New York Islanders**	**NHL**	**1**	**0**	**0**	**0**	**0**	**0**	**0**	**2**	**0**	**0**	**0**	**1**	**0.0**	**0**	**0**	**2**	**0**	**–2**	**1**	**0**	**0**	**0**	**0**	**0**	**0**	**0**
	Fort Worth Texans	CHL	74	21	27	48	....	....	....	172	....	....	....	....	....	....	....	....	....	....	5	1	4	5	7	....	....	....
1979-80	Indianapolis Checkers	CHL	76	29	34	63	....	....	....	144	....	....	....	....	....	....	....	....	....	....	7	1	4	5	20	....	....	....
1980-81♦	**New York Islanders**	**NHL**	**14**	**4**	**7**	**11**	**3**	**5**	**8**	**39**	**1**	**0**	**0**	**9**	**44.4**	**16**	**2**	**5**	**0**	**9**	**9**	**3**	**6**	**9**	**14**	**0**	**0**	**0**
	Indianapolis Checkers	CHL	54	15	37	52	....	....	....	85	....	....	....	....	....	....	....	....	....	....	....	....	....	....	....	....	....	....
1981-82	**New York Islanders**	**NHL**	**30**	**4**	**9**	**13**	**3**	**6**	**9**	**53**	**1**	**0**	**1**	**14**	**28.6**	**16**	**2**	**11**	**0**	**3**	....	....	....	....	....	....	....	....
1982-83	**New Jersey Devils**	**NHL**	**77**	**17**	**28**	**45**	**14**	**19**	**33**	**105**	**5**	**0**	**3**	**109**	**15.6**	**70**	**24**	**62**	**1**	**–15**	....	....	....	....	....	....	....	....
1983-84	**New Jersey Devils**	**NHL**	**32**	**2**	**2**	**4**	**2**	**1**	**3**	**47**	**0**	**0**	**0**	**33**	**6.1**	**14**	**2**	**14**	**0**	**–2**	....	....	....	....	....	....	....	....
	Maine Mariners	AHL	17	7	4	11	....	....	....	23	....	....	....	....	....	....	....	....	....	....	....	....	....	....	....	....	....	....
1984-85	Maine Mariners	AHL	30	1	5	6	....	....	....	67	....	....	....	....	....	....	....	....	....	....	....	....	....	....	....	....	....	....
1985-86	Maine Mariners	AHL	6	0	5	5	....	....	....	17	....	....	....	....	....	....	....	....	....	....	....	....	....	....	....	....	....	....
	Fort Wayne Komets	IHL	7	1	1	2	....	....	....	5	....	....	....	....	....	....	....	....	....	....	....	....	....	....	....	....	....	....
	NHL Totals		**154**	**27**	**46**	**73**	**22**	**31**	**53**	**246**	**7**	**0**	**4**	**166**	**16.3**	**116**	**30**	**94**	**1**		**10**	**3**	**6**	**9**	**14**	**0**	**0**	**0**

Played in NHL All-Star Game (1983)

Traded to **New Jersey** by **NY Islanders** with NY Islanders' 4th round choice (later traded to Calgary — Calgary selected Bill Claviter) in 1983 Entry Draft for New Jersey's 4th round choice (Mikko Makela) in 1983 Entry Draft, October 1, 1982. • Suffered career-ending eye injury in game vs. Indianapolis (IHL), December 5, 1985.

● MARINUCCI, Chris

C – L. 6', 188 lbs. b: Grand Rapids, MN, 12/29/1971. NY Islanders' 4th, 90th overall, in 1990.

Season	Club	League	GP	G	A	Pts	AG	AA	APts	PIM	PP	SH	GW	S	%	TGF	PGF	TGA	PGA	+/–	GP	G	A	Pts	PIM	PP	SH	GW
1988-89	Grand Rapids Thunderhawk	Hi-School	25	24	18	42	....	....	....	....	....	....	....	....	....	....	....	....	....	....	....	....	....	....	....	....	....	....
1989-90	Grand Rapids Thunderhawk	Hi-School	28	24	39	63	....	....	....	12	....	....	....	....	....	....	....	....	....	....	....	....	....	....	....	....	....	....
1990-91	University of Minnesota-Duluth	WCHA	36	6	10	16	....	....	....	20	....	....	....	....	....	....	....	....	....	....	....	....	....	....	....	....	....	....
1991-92	University of Minnesota-Duluth	WCHA	37	6	13	19	....	....	....	41	....	....	....	....	....	....	....	....	....	....	....	....	....	....	....	....	....	....
1992-93	University of Minnesota-Duluth	WCHA	40	35	42	77	....	....	....	52	....	....	....	....	....	....	....	....	....	....	....	....	....	....	....	....	....	....
1993-94	University of Minnesota-Duluth	WCHA	38	*30	31	61	....	....	....	65	....	....	....	....	....	....	....	....	....	....	....	....	....	....	....	....	....	....
1994-95	**New York Islanders**	**NHL**	**12**	**1**	**4**	**5**	**2**	**6**	**8**	**2**	**0**	**0**	**0**	**11**	**9.1**	**7**	**1**	**7**	**0**	**–1**	....	....	....	....	....	....	....	....
	Denver Grizzlies	IHL	74	29	40	69	....	....	....	42	....	....	....	....	....	....	....	....	....	....	14	3	4	7	12	....	....	....
1995-96	Utah Grizzlies	IHL	8	3	5	8	....	....	....	8	....	....	....	....	....	....	....	....	....	....	....	....	....	....	....	....	....	....
1996-97	Utah Grizzlies	IHL	21	3	13	16	....	....	....	6	....	....	....	....	....	....	....	....	....	....	....	....	....	....	....	....	....	....
	Los Angeles Kings	**NHL**	**1**	**0**	**0**	**0**	**0**	**0**	**0**	**0**	**0**	**0**	**0**	**1**	**0.0**	**0**	**0**	**2**	**0**	**–2**	....	....	....	....	....	....	....	....
	Phoenix Roadrunners	IHL	62	23	29	52	....	....	....	26	....	....	....	....	....	....	....	....	....	....	....	....	....	....	....	....	....	....
	United States	WC-A	8	1	0	1	....	....	....	2	....	....	....	....	....	....	....	....	....	....	....	....	....	....	....	....	....	....
1997-98	Chicago Wolves	IHL	78	27	48	75	....	....	....	35	....	....	....	....	....	....	....	....	....	....	22	7	6	13	12	....	....	....
1998-99	Chicago Wolves	IHL	82	41	40	81	....	....	....	24	....	....	....	....	....	....	....	....	....	....	10	3	5	8	10	....	....	....
99-2000	Chicago Wolves	IHL	80	31	33	64	....	....	....	18	....	....	....	....	....	....	....	....	....	....	16	5	4	9	10	....	....	....
	NHL Totals		**13**	**1**	**4**	**5**	**2**	**6**	**8**	**2**	**0**	**0**	**0**	**12**	**8.3**	**7**	**1**	**9**	**0**		....	....	....	....	....	....	....	....

WCHA Second All-Star Team (1993) • WCHA First All-Star Team (1994) • NCAA West First All-American Team (1994) • Won Hobey Baker Memorial Award (Top U.S. Collegiate Player) (1994) • IHL Second All-Star Team (1999)

Traded to **LA Kings** by **NY Islanders** for Nick Vachon, November 19, 1996.

• MARK, Gordon

Gordon F. D – R. 6'4", 218 lbs. b: Edmonton, Alta., 9/10/1964. New Jersey's 4th, 108th overall, in 1983.

			REGULAR SEASON																		PLAYOFFS							
Season	Club	League	GP	G	A	Pts	AG	AA	APts	PIM	PP	SH	GW	S	%	TGF	PGF	TGA	PGA	+/-	GP	G	A	Pts	PIM	PP	SH	GW
1981-82	Wainwright Rangers	CVJHL	STATISTICS NOT AVAILABLE																									
1982-83	Kamloops Jr. Oilers	WHL	71	12	20	32	....	....	....	135	....	....	....	....	....	....	....	....	....	....	7	1	1	2	8	....	....	....
1983-84	Kamloops Jr. Oilers	WHL	67	12	30	42	....	....	....	202	....	....	....	....	....	....	....	....	....	....	17	2	6	8	27	....	....	....
	Kamloops	Mem-Cup	4	0	1	1	....	....	....	6	....	....	....	....	....	....	....	....	....	....	....	....	....	....	....	....	....	....
1984-85	Kamloops Blazers	WHL	32	11	23	34	....	....	....	68	....	....	....	....	....	....	....	....	....	....	7	1	2	3	10	....	....	....
1985-86	Maine Mariners	AHL	77	9	13	22	....	....	....	134	....	....	....	....	....	....	....	....	....	....	5	0	1	1	9	....	....	....
1986-87	**New Jersey Devils**	**NHL**	**36**	**3**	**5**	**8**	**3**	**4**	**7**	**82**	**0**	**0**	**0**	**31**	**9.7**	**30**	**1**	**43**	**10**	**–4**	....	....	....	....	....	....	....	....
	Maine Mariners	AHL	29	4	10	14	....	....	....	66	....	....	....	....	....	....	....	....	....	....	....	....	....	....	....	....	....	....
1987-88	**New Jersey Devils**	**NHL**	**19**	**0**	**2**	**2**	**0**	**1**	**1**	**27**	**0**	**0**	**0**	**11**	**0.0**	**4**	**0**	**20**	**3**	**–13**	....	....	....	....	....	....	....	....
	Utica Devils	AHL	50	5	21	26	....	....	....	96	....	....	....	....	....	....	....	....	....	....	....	....	....	....	....	....	....	....
1988-1992	Stony Plain Eagles	ASHL	STATISTICS NOT AVAILABLE																									
1992-93	Cape Breton Oilers	AHL	60	3	21	24	....	....	....	78	....	....	....	....	....	....	....	....	....	....	16	1	7	8	20	....	....	....
1993-94	**Edmonton Oilers**	**NHL**	**12**	**0**	**1**	**1**	**0**	**1**	**1**	**43**	**0**	**0**	**0**	**8**	**0.0**	**8**	**0**	**11**	**1**	**–2**	....	....	....	....	....	....	....	....
	Cape Breton Oilers	AHL	49	11	20	31	....	....	....	116	....	....	....	....	....	....	....	....	....	....	5	0	2	2	26	....	....	....
1994-95	**Edmonton Oilers**	**NHL**	**18**	**0**	**2**	**2**	**0**	**3**	**3**	**35**	**0**	**0**	**0**	**21**	**0.0**	**8**	**0**	**20**	**3**	**–9**	....	....	....	....	....	....	....	....
1995-96	Las Vegas Thunder	IHL	60	2	7	9	....	....	....	98	....	....	....	....	....	....	....	....	....	....	1	0	0	0	0	....	....	....
1996-97	Providence Bruins	AHL	7	0	1	1	....	....	....	36	....	....	....	....	....	....	....	....	....	....	....	....	....	....	....	....	....	....
	Utah Grizzlies	IHL	12	1	2	3	....	....	....	11	....	....	....	....	....	....	....	....	....	....	....	....	....	....	....	....	....	....
1997-2000	Stony Plains Eagles	AIHA	STATISTICS NOT AVAILABLE																									
	NHL Totals		**85**	**3**	**10**	**13**	**3**	**9**	**12**	**187**	**0**	**0**	**0**	**71**	**4.2**	**50**	**1**	**94**	**17**		....	....	....	....	....	....	....	....

Signed as a free agent by **Edmonton**, February 1, 1994.

• MARKELL, John

John Richard LW – L. 5'11", 185 lbs. b: Cornwall, Ont., 3/10/1956.

			REGULAR SEASON																		PLAYOFFS							
Season	Club	League	GP	G	A	Pts	AG	AA	APts	PIM	PP	SH	GW	S	%	TGF	PGF	TGA	PGA	+/-	GP	G	A	Pts	PIM	PP	SH	GW
1973-74	Cornwall Royals	QMJHL	18	4	1	5	....	....	....	0	....	....	....	....	....	....	....	....	....	....	....	....	....	....	....	....	....	....
1974-75	Cornwall Royals	QMJHL	42	9	19	28	....	....	....	22	....	....	....	....	....	....	....	....	....	....	....	....	....	....	....	....	....	....
1975-76	Bowling Green University	CCHA	30	12	25	37	....	....	....	24	....	....	....	....	....	....	....	....	....	....	....	....	....	....	....	....	....	....
1976-77	Bowling Green University	CCHA	39	26	32	58	....	....	....	48	....	....	....	....	....	....	....	....	....	....	....	....	....	....	....	....	....	....
1977-78	Bowling Green University	CCHA	39	33	28	61	....	....	....	81	....	....	....	....	....	....	....	....	....	....	....	....	....	....	....	....	....	....
1978-79	Bowling Green University	CCHA	42	31	49	80	....	....	....	96	....	....	....	....	....	....	....	....	....	....	....	....	....	....	....	....	....	....
1979-80	**Winnipeg Jets**	**NHL**	**38**	**10**	**7**	**17**	**8**	**5**	**13**	**21**	**2**	**0**	**1**	**46**	**21.7**	**27**	**9**	**31**	**1**	**–12**	....	....	....	....	....	....	....	....
	Tulsa Oilers	CHL	35	15	14	29	....	....	....	45	....	....	....	....	....	....	....	....	....	....	....	....	....	....	....	....	....	....
1980-81	**Winnipeg Jets**	**NHL**	**14**	**1**	**3**	**4**	**1**	**2**	**3**	**15**	**1**	**0**	**0**	**11**	**9.1**	**7**	**4**	**15**	**1**	**–11**	....	....	....	....	....	....	....	....
	Tulsa Oilers	CHL	48	24	18	42	....	....	....	34	....	....	....	....	....	....	....	....	....	....	8	5	1	6	28	....	....	....
1981-82	Salt Lake Golden Eagles	CHL	69	19	53	72	....	....	....	33	....	....	....	....	....	....	....	....	....	....	10	4	11	15	2	....	....	....
1982-83	Salt Lake Golden Eagles	CHL	77	33	27	60	....	....	....	35	....	....	....	....	....	....	....	....	....	....	6	3	2	5	6	....	....	....
1983-84	**St. Louis Blues**	**NHL**	**2**	**0**	**0**	**0**	**0**	**0**	**0**	**0**	**0**	**0**	**0**	**0**	**0.0**	**0**	**0**	**4**	**0**	**–4**	....	....	....	....	....	....	....	....
	Montana Magic	CHL	69	*44	40	84	....	....	....	61	....	....	....	....	....	....	....	....	....	....	....	....	....	....	....	....	....	....
1984-85	Schwenninger ERC	Germany	23	13	15	28	....	....	....	65	....	....	....	....	....	....	....	....	....	....	....	....	....	....	....	....	....	....
	Minnesota North Stars	**NHL**	**1**	**0**	**0**	**0**	**0**	**0**	**0**	....	**0**	**0**	**0**	**0**	**0.0**	**0**	**0**	**0**	**0**	**0**	....	....	....	....	....	....	....	....
	Springfield Indians	AHL	46	16	25	41	....	....	....	23	....	....	....	....	....	....	....	....	....	....	....	....	....	....	....	....	....	....
1985-86	EC Bad Nauheim	Germany-2	48	37	*74	111	....	....	....	....	....	....	....	....	....	....	....	....	....	....	10	12	30	42	28	....	....	....
1986-87	EC Bad Nauheim	Germany-2	48	52	58	110	....	....	....	....	....	....	....	....	....	....	....	....	....	....	18	*24	*33	*57	....	....	....	....
1987-88	ESC Wolfsburg	Germany-2	36	36	62	98	....	....	....	100	....	....	....	....	....	....	....	....	....	....	20	26	*52	78	59	....	....	....
1988-89	ESC Wolfsburg	Germany-2	34	28	52	80	....	....	....	62	....	....	....	....	....	....	....	....	....	....	18	21	24	45	41	....	....	....
1989-90	ESC Wolfsburg	Germany-2	32	39	43	82	....	....	....	70	....	....	....	....	....	....	....	....	....	....	19	8	16	24	....	....	....	....
1990-91	ESC Wolfsburg	Germany-2	47	45	71	116	....	....	....	109	....	....	....	....	....	....	....	....	....	....	....	....	....	....	....	....	....	....
1991-92	ESC Wolfsburg	Germany-2	45	41	94	135	....	....	....	64	....	....	....	....	....	....	....	....	....	....	....	....	....	....	....	....	....	....
1992-1993	ESC Wolfsburg	Germany-2	DID NOT PLAY – COACHING																									
1993-1995	Ohio State University	CCHA	DID NOT PLAY – ASSISTANT COACH																									
1995-2000	Ohio State University	CCHA	DID NOT PLAY – COACHING																									
	NHL Totals		**55**	**11**	**10**	**21**	**9**	**7**	**16**	**36**	**3**	**0**	**1**	**57**	**19.3**	**34**	**13**	**50**	**2**		....	....	....	....	....	....	....	....

CCHA First All-Star Team (1977, 1978, 1979) • CHL First All-Star Team (1984)

Signed as a free agent by **Winnipeg**, April 16, 1979. Traded to **St. Louis** by **Winnipeg** with Scott Campbell for Ed Staniowski, Bryan Maxwell and Paul MacLean, July 3, 1981. Signed as a free agent by **Minnesota**, December 17, 1984.

• MARKHAM, Ray

Ray Joseph C – R. 6'3", 220 lbs. b: Windsor, Ont., 1/23/1958. NY Rangers' 2nd, 43rd overall, in 1978.

			REGULAR SEASON																		PLAYOFFS							
Season	Club	League	GP	G	A	Pts	AG	AA	APts	PIM	PP	SH	GW	S	%	TGF	PGF	TGA	PGA	+/-	GP	G	A	Pts	PIM	PP	SH	GW
1975-76	Notre Dame Hounds	Hi-School	45	15	19	34	....	....	....	245	....	....	....	....	....	....	....	....	....	....	....	....	....	....	....	....	....	....
1976-77	Flin Flon Bombers	WCJHL	68	33	41	74	....	....	....	318	....	....	....	....	....	....	....	....	....	....	....	....	....	....	....	....	....	....
1977-78	Flin Flon Bombers	WCJHL	68	35	65	100	....	....	....	323	....	....	....	....	....	....	....	....	....	....	17	10	13	23	96	....	....	....
1978-79	New Haven Nighthawks	AHL	77	13	15	28	....	....	....	151	....	....	....	....	....	....	....	....	....	....	8	2	3	5	10	....	....	....
1979-80	**New York Rangers**	**NHL**	**14**	**1**	**1**	**2**	**1**	**1**	**2**	**21**	**0**	**0**	**0**	**6**	**16.7**	**3**	**0**	**6**	**0**	**–3**	**7**	**1**	**0**	**1**	**24**	**0**	**0**	**0**
	New Haven Nighthawks	AHL	57	9	20	29	....	....	....	198	....	....	....	....	....	....	....	....	....	....	....	....	....	....	....	....	....	....
1980-81	New Haven Nighthawks	AHL	42	10	9	19	....	....	....	122	....	....	....	....	....	....	....	....	....	....	....	....	....	....	....	....	....	....
	Wichita Wind	CHL	7	1	1	2	....	....	....	18	....	....	....	....	....	....	....	....	....	....	....	....	....	....	....	....	....	....
1981-82	Wichita Wind	CHL	48	15	12	27	....	....	....	110	....	....	....	....	....	....	....	....	....	....	....	....	....	....	....	....	....	....
1982-83	Flint Generals	IHL	42	16	30	46	....	....	....	176	....	....	....	....	....	....	....	....	....	....	5	2	4	6	52	....	....	....
1983-84	Flint Generals	IHL	12	2	3	5	....	....	....	39	....	....	....	....	....	....	....	....	....	....	....	....	....	....	....	....	....	....
	Kalamazoo Wings	IHL	69	23	28	51	....	....	....	172	....	....	....	....	....	....	....	....	....	....	3	1	2	3	9	....	....	....
	NHL Totals		**14**	**1**	**1**	**2**	**1**	**1**	**2**	**21**	**0**	**0**	**0**	**6**	**16.7**	**3**	**0**	**6**	**0**		**7**	**1**	**0**	**1**	**24**	**0**	**0**	**0**

Traded to **Edmonton** by **NY Rangers** for John Hughes, March 10, 1981.

• MARKOV, Danny

Danny Daniil D – L. 6'1", 196 lbs. b: Moscow, USSR, 7/11/1976. Toronto's 7th, 223rd overall, in 1995.

			REGULAR SEASON																		PLAYOFFS							
Season	Club	League	GP	G	A	Pts	AG	AA	APts	PIM	PP	SH	GW	S	%	TGF	PGF	TGA	PGA	+/-	GP	G	A	Pts	PIM	PP	SH	GW
1993-94	Spartak Moscow	CIS	13	1	0	1	....	....	....	6	....	....	....	....	....	....	....	....	....	....	1	0	0	0	0	....	....	....
1994-95	Spartak Moscow	CIS	39	0	1	1	....	....	....	36	....	....	....	....	....	....	....	....	....	....	....	....	....	....	....	....	....	....
1995-96	Spartak Moscow	CIS	38	2	0	2	....	....	....	12	....	....	....	....	....	....	....	....	....	....	2	0	0	0	2	....	....	....
1996-97	Spartak Moscow	Russia	39	3	6	9	....	....	....	41	....	....	....	....	....	....	....	....	....	....	....	....	....	....	....	....	....	....
	St. John's Maple Leafs	AHL	10	2	4	6	....	....	....	18	....	....	....	....	....	....	....	....	....	....	11	2	6	8	14	....	....	....
1997-98	**Toronto Maple Leafs**	**NHL**	**25**	**2**	**5**	**7**	**2**	**5**	**7**	**28**	**1**	**0**	**0**	**15**	**13.3**	**18**	**3**	**16**	**1**	**0**	....	....	....	....	....	....	....	....
	St. John's Maple Leafs	AHL	52	3	23	26	....	....	....	124	....	....	....	....	....	....	....	....	....	....	2	0	1	1	0	....	....	....
	Russia	WC-A	4	0	0	0	....	....	....	0	....	....	....	....	....	....	....	....	....	....	....	....	....	....	....	....	....	....
1998-99	**Toronto Maple Leafs**	**NHL**	**57**	**4**	**8**	**12**	**5**	**8**	**13**	**47**	**0**	**0**	**0**	**34**	**11.8**	**42**	**5**	**43**	**11**	**5**	**17**	**0**	**6**	**6**	**18**	**0**	**0**	**0**
99-2000	**Toronto Maple Leafs**	**NHL**	**59**	**0**	**10**	**10**	**0**	**9**	**9**	**28**	**0**	**0**	**0**	**38**	**0.0**	**50**	**7**	**49**	**19**	**13**	**12**	**0**	**3**	**3**	**10**	**0**	**0**	**0**
	NHL Totals		**141**	**6**	**23**	**29**	**7**	**22**	**29**	**103**	**1**	**0**	**0**	**87**	**6.9**	**110**	**15**	**108**	**31**		**29**	**0**	**9**	**9**	**28**	**0**	**0**	**0**

• MARKS, John

John Garrison LW – L. 6'2", 200 lbs. b: Hamiota, Man., 3/22/1948. Chicago's 1st, 9th overall, in 1968.

			REGULAR SEASON																		PLAYOFFS							
Season	Club	League	GP	G	A	Pts	AG	AA	APts	PIM	PP	SH	GW	S	%	TGF	PGF	TGA	PGA	+/-	GP	G	A	Pts	PIM	PP	SH	GW
1966-67	St. James Braves	MJHL	6	1	3	4	....	....	....	0	....	....	....	....	....	....	....	....	....	....	....	....	....	....	....	....	....	....
1967-68	University of North Dakota	WCHA	33	3	6	9	....	....	....	16	....	....	....	....	....	....	....	....	....	....	....	....	....	....	....	....	....	....
1968-69	University of North Dakota	WCHA	29	6	26	32	....	....	....	38	....	....	....	....	....	....	....	....	....	....	....	....	....	....	....	....	....	....
1969-70	University of North Dakota	WCHA	30	5	14	19	....	....	....	34	....	....	....	....	....	....	....	....	....	....	....	....	....	....	....	....	....	....
1970-71	Dallas Black Hawks	CHL	66	3	16	19	....	....	....	49	....	....	....	....	....	....	....	....	....	....	10	0	4	4	14	....	....	....
1971-72	Dallas Black Hawks	CHL	72	8	35	43	....	....	....	105	....	....	....	....	....	....	....	....	....	....	12	1	2	3	8	....	....	....
1972-73	**Chicago Black Hawks**	**NHL**	**55**	**3**	**10**	**13**	**3**	**8**	**11**	**21**	**1**	**0**	**0**	**45**	**6.7**	**33**	**4**	**28**	**4**	**5**	**16**	**1**	**2**	**3**	**2**	**1**	**0**	**1**
1973-74	**Chicago Black Hawks**	**NHL**	**76**	**13**	**18**	**31**	**12**	**15**	**27**	**22**	**3**	**0**	**1**	**139**	**9.4**	**62**	**16**	**25**	**1**	**22**	**11**	**2**	**0**	**2**	**8**	**0**	**0**	**1**
1974-75	**Chicago Black Hawks**	**NHL**	**80**	**17**	**30**	**47**	**15**	**22**	**37**	**56**	**4**	**0**	**3**	**163**	**10.4**	**86**	**19**	**49**	**9**	**27**	**8**	**2**	**6**	**8**	**34**	**0**	**0**	**1**
1975-76	**Chicago Black Hawks**	**NHL**	**80**	**21**	**23**	**44**	**18**	**17**	**35**	**43**	**6**	**1**	**4**	**152**	**13.8**	**79**	**29**	**68**	**14**	**–4**	**4**	**0**	**0**	**0**	**10**	**0**	**0**	**0**
1976-77	**Chicago Black Hawks**	**NHL**	**80**	**7**	**15**	**22**	**6**	**12**	**18**	**41**	**0**	**0**	**0**	**156**	**4.5**	**54**	**7**	**84**	**16**	**–21**	**2**	**0**	**0**	**0**	**4**	**0**	**0**	**0**
1977-78	**Chicago Black Hawks**	**NHL**	**80**	**15**	**22**	**37**	**14**	**17**	**31**	**26**	**0**	**0**	**1**	**118**	**12.7**	**71**	**1**	**72**	**29**	**27**	**4**	**0**	**1**	**1**	**0**	**0**	**0**	**0**

			REGULAR SEASON																		PLAYOFFS							
Season	Club	League	GP	G	A	Pts	AG	AA	APts	PIM	PP	SH	GW	S	%	TGF	PGF	TGA	PGA	+/–	GP	G	A	Pts	PIM	PP	SH	GW
1978-79	**Chicago Black Hawks**	**NHL**	**80**	**21**	**24**	**45**	**18**	**17**	**35**	**35**	**4**	**0**	**2**	**152**	**13.8**	**69**	**11**	**91**	**35**	**2**	**4**	**0**	**0**	**0**	**2**	**0**	**0**	**0**
1979-80	**Chicago Black Hawks**	**NHL**	**74**	**6**	**15**	**21**	**5**	**11**	**16**	**51**	**1**	**0**	**1**	**111**	**5.4**	**30**	**5**	**56**	**15**	**–16**	**4**	**0**	**0**	**0**	**0**	**0**	**0**	**0**
1980-81	**Chicago Black Hawks**	**NHL**	**39**	**8**	**6**	**14**	**6**	**4**	**10**	**28**	**1**	**1**	**0**	**41**	**19.5**	**21**	**1**	**36**	**13**	**–3**	**3**	**0**	**0**	**0**	**0**	**0**	**0**	**0**
1981-82	**Chicago Black Hawks**	**NHL**	**13**	**1**	**0**	**1**	**1**	**0**	**1**	**7**	**0**	**0**	**0**	**8**	**12.5**	**8**	**0**	**11**	**3**	**0**	**1**	**0**	**0**	**0**	**0**	**0**	**0**	**0**
	Indianapolis Checkers	CHL	53	6	20	26	....	....	....	73	....	....	....	....	....	....	....	....	....	....	....	....	....	....	....	....	....	....
1982-83			OUT OF HOCKEY – RETIRED																									
1983-1987	University of Notre Dame	NCAA-1	DID NOT PLAY – ASSISTANT COACH																									
1987-1990	Indianapolis Ice	IHL	DID NOT PLAY – COACHING																									
1990-1993	Kansas City Blades	IHL	DID NOT PLAY – COACHING																									
1993-1998	Charolotte Checkers	ECHL	DID NOT PLAY – COACHING																									
1998-2000	Grenville Growl	ECHL	DID NOT PLAY – COACHING																									
	NHL Totals		**657**	**112**	**163**	**275**	**98**	**123**	**221**	**330**	**20**	**2**	**12**	**1085**	**10.3**	**513**	**93**	**520**	**139**		**57**	**5**	**9**	**14**	**60**	**1**	**0**	**3**

WCHA Second All-Star Team (1969) • NCAA West First All-American Team (1969, 1970) • WCHA First All-Star Team (1970) • Played in NHL All-Star Game (1976)

• MARKWART, Nevin

Nevin G. LW – L. 5'10", 180 lbs. b: Toronto, Ont., 12/9/1964. Boston's 1st, 21st overall, in 1983.

Season	Club	League	GP	G	A	Pts	AG	AA	APts	PIM	PP	SH	GW	S	%	TGF	PGF	TGA	PGA	+/–	GP	G	A	Pts	PIM	PP	SH	GW
1980-81	Regina Pat Canadians	AAHA	65	43	78	121	....	....	....	193	....	....	....	....	....	....	....	....	....	....	....	....	....	....	....	....	....	....
1981-82	Regina Blues	SJHL	45	18	36	54	....	....	....	185	....	....	....	....	....	....	....	....	....	....	....	....	....	....	....	....	....	....
	Regina Pats	WHL	25	2	12	14	....	....	....	56	....	....	....	....	....	....	....	....	....	....	20	2	2	4	82	....	....	....
1982-83	Regina Pats	WHL	43	27	39	66	....	....	....	91	....	....	....	....	....	....	....	....	....	....	1	0	0	0	0	....	....	....
1983-84	**Boston Bruins**	**NHL**	**70**	**14**	**16**	**30**	**11**	**11**	**22**	**121**	**0**	**0**	**3**	**66**	**21.2**	**57**	**2**	**63**	**10**	**2**	....	....	....	....	....	....	....	....
1984-85	**Boston Bruins**	**NHL**	**26**	**0**	**4**	**4**	**0**	**3**	**3**	**36**	**0**	**0**	**0**	**5**	**0.0**	**5**	**0**	**7**	**1**	**–1**	**1**	**0**	**0**	**0**	**0**	**0**	**0**	**0**
	Hershey Bears	AHL	38	13	18	31	....	....	....	79	....	....	....	....	....	....	....	....	....	....	....	....	....	....	....	....	....	....
1985-86	**Boston Bruins**	**NHL**	**65**	**7**	**15**	**22**	**6**	**10**	**16**	**207**	**0**	**0**	**1**	**42**	**16.7**	**34**	**1**	**54**	**19**	**–2**	....	....	....	....	....	....	....	....
1986-87	**Boston Bruins**	**NHL**	**64**	**10**	**9**	**19**	**9**	**7**	**16**	**225**	**0**	**0**	**2**	**65**	**15.4**	**33**	**0**	**39**	**0**	**–6**	**4**	**0**	**0**	**0**	**9**	**0**	**0**	**0**
	Moncton Golden Flames	AHL	3	3	3	6	....	....	....	11	....	....	....	....	....	....	....	....	....	....	....	....	....	....	....	....	....	....
1987-88	**Boston Bruins**	**NHL**	**25**	**1**	**12**	**13**	**1**	**9**	**10**	**85**	**0**	**0**	**0**	**24**	**4.2**	**19**	**1**	**17**	**3**	**4**	**2**	**0**	**0**	**0**	**2**	**0**	**0**	**0**
1988-89	Maine Mariners	AHL	1	0	1	1	....	....	....	0	....	....	....	....	....	....	....	....	....	....	....	....	....	....	....	....	....	....
1989-90	**Boston Bruins**	**NHL**	**8**	**1**	**2**	**3**	**1**	**1**	**2**	**15**	**1**	**0**	**0**	**6**	**16.7**	**3**	**1**	**6**	**2**	**–2**	....	....	....	....	....	....	....	....
1990-91	**Boston Bruins**	**NHL**	**23**	**3**	**3**	**6**	**3**	**2**	**5**	**36**	**0**	**0**	**0**	**13**	**23.1**	**13**	**1**	**15**	**3**	**0**	**12**	**1**	**0**	**1**	**22**	**0**	**0**	**0**
	Maine Mariners	AHL	21	5	5	10	....	....	....	22	....	....	....	....	....	....	....	....	....	....	....	....	....	....	....	....	....	....
1991-92	EHC Biel-Bienne	Switz.	4	2	2	4	....	....	....	2	....	....	....	....	....	....	....	....	....	....	....	....	....	....	....	....	....	....
	Boston Bruins	**NHL**	**18**	**3**	**6**	**9**	**3**	**5**	**8**	**44**	**0**	**0**	**0**	**12**	**25.0**	**14**	**0**	**16**	**4**	**2**	....	....	....	....	....	....	....	....
	Maine Mariners	AHL	17	4	7	11	....	....	....	32	....	....	....	....	....	....	....	....	....	....	....	....	....	....	....	....	....	....
	Calgary Flames	**NHL**	**10**	**2**	**1**	**3**	**2**	**1**	**3**	**25**	**0**	**0**	**0**	**4**	**50.0**	**5**	**0**	**10**	**3**	**–2**	....	....	....	....	....	....	....	....
1992-93	Springfield Indians	AHL	7	2	0	2	....	....	....	24	....	....	....	....	....	....	....	....	....	....	....	....	....	....	....	....	....	....
	NHL Totals		**309**	**41**	**68**	**109**	**36**	**49**	**85**	**794**	**1**	**0**	**6**	**237**	**17.3**	**183**	**6**	**227**	**45**		**19**	**1**	**0**	**1**	**33**	**0**	**0**	**0**

Missed majority of 1988-89 and 1989-90 seasons recovering from abdominal injury that required surgery, July, 1989. Claimed on waivers by **Calgary** from **Boston**, February 14, 1992.

• MARLEAU, Patrick

Patrick Denis C – L. 6'2", 205 lbs. b: Swift Current, Sask., 9/15/1979. San Jose's 1st, 2nd overall, in 1997.

Season	Club	League	GP	G	A	Pts	AG	AA	APts	PIM	PP	SH	GW	S	%	TGF	PGF	TGA	PGA	+/–	GP	G	A	Pts	PIM	PP	SH	GW
1993-94	Swift Current Bantam A's	SAHA	53	72	95	167	....	....	....	....	....	....	....	....	....	....	....	....	....	....	....	....	....	....	....	....	....	....
1994-95	Swift Current Midget Broncos	SAHA	31	30	22	52	....	....	....	18	....	....	....	....	....	....	....	....	....	....	....	....	....	....	....	....	....	....
1995-96	Seattle Thunderbirds	WHL	72	32	42	74	....	....	....	22	....	....	....	....	....	....	....	....	....	....	5	3	4	7	4	....	....	....
1996-97	Seattle Thunderbirds	WHL	71	51	74	125	....	....	....	37	....	....	....	....	....	....	....	....	....	....	15	7	16	23	12	....	....	....
1997-98	**San Jose Sharks**	**NHL**	**74**	**13**	**19**	**32**	**15**	**19**	**34**	**14**	**1**	**0**	**2**	**90**	**14.4**	**50**	**13**	**32**	**0**	**5**	**5**	**0**	**1**	**1**	**0**	**0**	**0**	**0**
1998-99	**San Jose Sharks**	**NHL**	**81**	**21**	**24**	**45**	**25**	**23**	**48**	**24**	**4**	**0**	**4**	**134**	**15.7**	**65**	**19**	**37**	**1**	**10**	**6**	**2**	**1**	**3**	**4**	**2**	**0**	**0**
	Canada	WC-A	7	1	2	3	....	....	....	0	....	....	....	....	....	....	....	....	....	....	....	....	....	....	....	....	....	....
99-2000	**San Jose Sharks**	**NHL**	**81**	**17**	**23**	**40**	**19**	**21**	**40**	**36**	**3**	**0**	**3**	**161**	**10.6**	**56**	**17**	**48**	**0**	**–9**	**5**	**1**	**1**	**2**	**2**	**1**	**0**	**0**
	NHL Totals		**236**	**51**	**66**	**117**	**59**	**63**	**122**	**74**	**8**	**0**	**9**	**385**	**13.2**	**171**	**49**	**117**	**1**		**16**	**3**	**3**	**6**	**6**	**3**	**0**	**0**

WHL West First All-Star Team (1997)

• MAROIS, Daniel

RW – R. 6', 190 lbs. b: Montreal, Que., 10/3/1968. Toronto's 2nd, 28th overall, in 1987.

Season	Club	League	GP	G	A	Pts	AG	AA	APts	PIM	PP	SH	GW	S	%	TGF	PGF	TGA	PGA	+/–	GP	G	A	Pts	PIM	PP	SH	GW
1984-85	Montreal L'est Cantonniers	QAAA	40	37	29	66	....	....	....	....	....	....	....	....	....	....	....	....	....	....	....	....	....	....	....	....	....	....
1985-86	Verdun Jr. Canadiens	QMJHL	58	42	35	77	....	....	....	110	....	....	....	....	....	....	....	....	....	....	5	4	2	6	6	....	....	....
1986-87	Verdun Jr. Canadiens	QMJHL	32	16	21	37	....	....	....	132	....	....	....	....	....	....	....	....	....	....	....	....	....	....	....	....	....	....
	Chicoutimi Sagueneens	QMJHL	8	6	5	11	....	....	....	11	....	....	....	....	....	....	....	....	....	....	16	7	14	21	25	....	....	....
1987-88	Verdun Jr. Canadiens	QMJHL	67	52	36	88	....	....	....	153	....	....	....	....	....	....	....	....	....	....	....	....	....	....	....	....	....	....
	Newmarket Saints	AHL	8	4	4	8	....	....	....	4	....	....	....	....	....	....	....	....	....	....	....	....	....	....	....	....	....	....
	Toronto Maple Leafs	**NHL**	....	....	....	....	....	....	....	....	....	....	....	....	....	....	....	....	....	....	**3**	**1**	**0**	**1**	**0**	**0**	**0**	**0**
1988-89	**Toronto Maple Leafs**	**NHL**	**76**	**31**	**23**	**54**	**26**	**16**	**42**	**76**	**7**	**0**	**4**	**146**	**21.2**	**77**	**17**	**64**	**0**	**–4**	....	....	....	....	....	....	....	....
1989-90	**Toronto Maple Leafs**	**NHL**	**68**	**39**	**37**	**76**	**34**	**27**	**61**	**82**	**14**	**0**	**3**	**183**	**21.3**	**111**	**40**	**70**	**0**	**1**	**5**	**2**	**2**	**4**	**12**	**2**	**0**	**0**
1990-91	**Toronto Maple Leafs**	**NHL**	**78**	**21**	**9**	**30**	**19**	**7**	**26**	**112**	**6**	**0**	**1**	**152**	**13.8**	**70**	**25**	**61**	**0**	**–16**	....	....	....	....	....	....	....	....
1991-92	**Toronto Maple Leafs**	**NHL**	**63**	**15**	**11**	**26**	**14**	**8**	**22**	**76**	**4**	**0**	**0**	**140**	**10.7**	**51**	**18**	**69**	**0**	**–36**	....	....	....	....	....	....	....	....
	New York Islanders	**NHL**	**12**	**2**	**5**	**7**	**2**	**4**	**6**	**18**	**0**	**0**	**0**	**19**	**10.5**	**10**	**0**	**8**	**0**	**2**	....	....	....	....	....	....	....	....
1992-93	**New York Islanders**	**NHL**	**28**	**2**	**5**	**7**	**2**	**3**	**5**	**35**	**0**	**0**	**0**	**41**	**4.9**	**14**	**1**	**18**	**2**	**–3**	....	....	....	....	....	....	....	....
	Capital District Islanders	AHL	4	2	0	2	....	....	....	0	....	....	....	....	....	....	....	....	....	....	....	....	....	....	....	....	....	....
1993-94	**Boston Bruins**	**NHL**	**22**	**7**	**3**	**10**	**6**	**2**	**8**	**18**	**3**	**0**	**0**	**32**	**21.9**	**18**	**8**	**15**	**1**	**–4**	**11**	**0**	**1**	**1**	**16**	**0**	**0**	**0**
	Providence Bruins	AHL	6	1	2	3	....	....	....	6	....	....	....	....	....	....	....	....	....	....	....	....	....	....	....	....	....	....
1994-95	**Boston Bruins**	**NHL**	DID NOT PLAY – INJURED																									
1995-96	Michigan K-Wings	IHL	61	28	28	56	....	....	....	105	....	....	....	....	....	....	....	....	....	....	....	....	....	....	....	....	....	....
	Dallas Stars	**NHL**	**3**	**0**	**0**	**0**	**0**	**0**	**0**	**2**	**0**	**0**	**0**	**1**	**0.0**	**2**	**2**	**0**	**0**	**0**	....	....	....	....	....	....	....	....
	Minnesota Moose	IHL	13	4	3	7	....	....	....	20	....	....	....	....	....	....	....	....	....	....	....	....	....	....	....	....	....	....
1996-97	Quebec Rafales	IHL	7	1	1	2	....	....	....	12	....	....	....	....	....	....	....	....	....	....	....	....	....	....	....	....	....	....
	Utah Grizzlies	IHL	29	7	9	16	....	....	....	58	....	....	....	....	....	....	....	....	....	....	....	....	....	....	....	....	....	....
	SC Bern	Switz.	8	7	7	14	....	....	....	10	....	....	....	....	....	....	....	....	....	....	11	4	8	12	26	....	....	....
1997-98	Adler Mannheim	EuroHL	4	1	1	2	....	....	....	52	....	....	....	....	....	....	....	....	....	....	....	....	....	....	....	....	....	....
	Adler Mannheim	Germany	19	3	6	9	....	....	....	38	....	....	....	....	....	....	....	....	....	....	....	....	....	....	....	....	....	....
	SC Bern	EuroHL	1	1	0	1	....	....	....	0	....	....	....	....	....	....	....	....	....	....	....	....	....	....	....	....	....	....
	SC Bern	Switz.	21	16	4	20	....	....	....	72	....	....	....	....	....	....	....	....	....	....	7	1	5	6	16	....	....	....
1998-99	SC Bern	Switz.	45	27	31	58	....	....	....	93	....	....	....	....	....	....	....	....	....	....	6	3	2	5	18	....	....	....
99-2000	HC Lausanne	Switz-2	18	17	10	27	....	....	....	40	....	....	....	....	....	....	....	....	....	....	....	....	....	....	....	....	....	....
	Ilves Tampere	Finland	13	4	2	6	....	....	....	16	....	....	....	....	....	....	....	....	....	....	....	....	....	....	....	....	....	....
	NHL Totals		**350**	**117**	**93**	**210**	**103**	**67**	**170**	**419**	**34**	**0**	**8**	**714**	**16.4**	**353**	**111**	**305**	**3**		**19**	**3**	**3**	**6**	**28**	**2**	**0**	**0**

Traded to **NY Islanders** by **Toronto** with Claude Loiselle for Ken Baumgartner and Dave McLlwain, March 10, 1992. Traded to **Boston** by **NY Islanders** for Boston's 8th round choice (Peter Hogardh) in 1994 Entry Draft, March 18, 1993. • Missed entire 1994-95 season recovering from back surgery. Signed as a free agent by **Dallas**, January 26, 1995. Signed as a free agent by **Toronto**, August 22, 1996.

• MAROIS, Mario

Mario Joseph D – R. 5'11", 190 lbs. b: Quebec City, Que., 12/15/1957. NY Rangers' 5th, 62nd overall, in 1977.

Season	Club	League	GP	G	A	Pts	AG	AA	APts	PIM	PP	SH	GW	S	%	TGF	PGF	TGA	PGA	+/–	GP	G	A	Pts	PIM	PP	SH	GW
1975-76	Quebec Remparts	QMJHL	67	11	42	53	....	....	....	270	....	....	....	....	....	....	....	....	....	....	15	2	3	5	86	....	....	....
	Quebec Remparts	Mem-Cup	3	0	0	0	....	....	....	7	....	....	....	....	....	....	....	....	....	....	....	....	....	....	....	....	....	....
1976-77	Quebec Remparts	QMJHL	72	17	67	84	....	....	....	239	....	....	....	....	....	....	....	....	....	....	14	1	17	18	75	....	....	....
1977-78	**New York Rangers**	**NHL**	**8**	**1**	**1**	**2**	**1**	**1**	**2**	**15**	**0**	**0**	**0**	**13**	**7.7**	**6**	**2**	**7**	**0**	**–3**	**1**	**0**	**0**	**0**	**5**	**0**	**0**	**0**
	New Haven Nighthawks	AHL	52	8	23	31	....	....	....	147	....	....	....	....	....	....	....	....	....	....	12	5	3	8	31	....	....	....
1978-79	**New York Rangers**	**NHL**	**71**	**5**	**26**	**31**	**4**	**19**	**23**	**153**	**1**	**0**	**0**	**115**	**4.3**	**106**	**25**	**72**	**9**	**18**	**18**	**0**	**6**	**6**	**29**	**0**	**0**	**0**
1979-80	**New York Rangers**	**NHL**	**79**	**8**	**23**	**31**	**7**	**17**	**24**	**142**	**1**	**0**	**1**	**158**	**5.1**	**96**	**13**	**102**	**19**	**0**	**9**	**0**	**2**	**2**	**8**	**0**	**0**	**0**
1980-81	**New York Rangers**	**NHL**	**8**	**1**	**2**	**3**	**1**	**1**	**2**	**46**	**0**	**0**	**0**	**11**	**9.1**	**8**	**2**	**12**	**1**	**–5**	....	....	....	....	....	....	....	....
	Vancouver Canucks	**NHL**	**50**	**4**	**12**	**16**	**3**	**8**	**11**	**115**	**1**	**0**	**0**	**79**	**5.1**	**50**	**3**	**52**	**5**	**0**	....	....	....	....	....	....	....	....
	Quebec Nordiques	**NHL**	**11**	**0**	**7**	**7**	**0**	**5**	**5**	**20**	**0**	**0**	**0**	**17**	**0.0**	**23**	**1**	**13**	**2**	**11**	**5**	**0**	**1**	**1**	**6**	**0**	**0**	**0**
1981-82	**Quebec Nordiques**	**NHL**	**71**	**11**	**32**	**43**	**9**	**21**	**30**	**161**	**2**	**0**	**0**	**124**	**8.9**	**122**	**9**	**136**	**42**	**19**	**13**	**1**	**2**	**3**	**44**	**0**	**0**	**0**
1982-83	**Quebec Nordiques**	**NHL**	**36**	**2**	**12**	**14**	**2**	**8**	**10**	**108**	**0**	**0**	**0**	**83**	**2.4**	**57**	**5**	**74**	**27**	**5**	....	....	....	....	....	....	....	....

Season	Club	League	GP	G	A	Pts	AG	AA	APts	PIM	PP	SH	GW	S	%	TGF	PGF	TGA	PGA	+/–	GP	G	A	Pts	PIM	PP	SH	GW
			REGULAR SEASON																		PLAYOFFS							
1983-84	**Quebec Nordiques**	**NHL**	**80**	**13**	**36**	**49**	**10**	**25**	**35**	**151**	**4**	**0**	**0**	**186**	**7.0**	**154**	**28**	**118**	**43**	**51**	**9**	**1**	**4**	**5**	**6**	**0**	**0**	**0**
1984-85	**Quebec Nordiques**	**NHL**	**76**	**6**	**37**	**43**	**5**	**25**	**30**	**91**	**2**	**0**	**0**	**152**	**3.9**	**109**	**28**	**117**	**38**	**2**	**18**	**0**	**8**	**8**	**12**	**0**	**0**	**0**
1985-86	**Quebec Nordiques**	**NHL**	**20**	**1**	**12**	**13**	**1**	**8**	**9**	**42**	**1**	**0**	**1**	**52**	**1.9**	**24**	**9**	**33**	**8**	**–10**	....	....	....	....	....	....	....	....
	Winnipeg Jets	**NHL**	**56**	**4**	**28**	**32**	**3**	**19**	**22**	**110**	**0**	**0**	**0**	**121**	**3.3**	**89**	**28**	**108**	**25**	**–22**	**3**	**1**	**4**	**5**	**6**	**1**	**0**	**0**
1986-87	**Winnipeg Jets**	**NHL**	**79**	**4**	**40**	**44**	**3**	**29**	**32**	**106**	**1**	**0**	**0**	**193**	**2.1**	**100**	**26**	**103**	**28**	**–1**	**10**	**1**	**3**	**4**	**23**	**0**	**0**	**1**
1987-88	**Winnipeg Jets**	**NHL**	**79**	**7**	**44**	**51**	**6**	**32**	**38**	**111**	**3**	**0**	**1**	**170**	**4.1**	**106**	**30**	**129**	**58**	**5**	**5**	**0**	**4**	**4**	**6**	**0**	**0**	**0**
1988-89	**Winnipeg Jets**	**NHL**	**7**	**1**	**1**	**2**	**1**	**1**	**2**	**17**	**1**	**0**	**0**	**10**	**10.0**	**5**	**3**	**16**	**8**	**–6**	....	....	....	....	....	....	....	....
	Quebec Nordiques	**NHL**	**42**	**2**	**11**	**13**	**2**	**8**	**10**	**101**	**0**	**0**	**0**	**61**	**3.3**	**38**	**7**	**66**	**20**	**–15**	....	....	....	....	....	....	....	....
	Canada	WEC-A	10	0	4	4	....	....	....	6	....	....	....	....	....	....	....	....	....	....	....	....	....	....	....	....	....	....
1989-90	**Quebec Nordiques**	**NHL**	**67**	**3**	**15**	**18**	**3**	**11**	**14**	**104**	**2**	**0**	**0**	**108**	**2.8**	**54**	**10**	**124**	**35**	**–45**	....	....	....	....	....	....	....	....
1990-91	**St. Louis Blues**	**NHL**	**64**	**2**	**14**	**16**	**2**	**11**	**13**	**81**	**0**	**0**	**0**	**59**	**3.4**	**62**	**3**	**61**	**19**	**17**	**9**	**0**	**0**	**0**	**37**	**0**	**0**	**0**
1991-92	**St. Louis Blues**	**NHL**	**17**	**0**	**1**	**1**	**0**	**1**	**1**	**38**	**0**	**0**	**0**	**11**	**0.0**	**6**	**0**	**12**	**3**	**–3**	....	....	....	....	....	....	....	....
	Winnipeg Jets	**NHL**	**34**	**1**	**3**	**4**	**1**	**2**	**3**	**34**	**0**	**1**	**0**	**32**	**3.1**	**15**	**0**	**32**	**9**	**–8**	....	....	....	....	....	....	....	....
1992-93	Hamilton Canucks	AHL	68	5	27	32	....	....	....	86	....	....	....	....	....	....	....	....	....	....	....	....	....	....	....	....	....	....
	NHL Totals		**955**	**76**	**357**	**433**	**64**	**252**	**316**	**1746**	**19**	**1**	**3**	**1755**	**4.3**	**1230**	**232**	**1387**	**399**		**100**	**4**	**34**	**38**	**182**	**1**	**0**	**1**

QMJHL Second All-Star Team (1977)

Traded to **Vancouver** by **NY Rangers** with Jim Mayer for Jere Gillis and Jeff Bandura, November 11, 1980. Traded to **Quebec** by **Vancouver** for Garry Lariviere, March 10, 1981. • Missed majority of 1982-83 season recovering from leg injury suffered in exhibition game vs. USSR, December 30, 1982. Traded to **Winnipeg** by **Quebec** for Robert Picard, November 27, 1985. Traded to **Quebec** by **Winnipeg** for Gord Donnelly, December 6, 1988. Claimed by **St. Louis** from **Winnipeg** in Waiver Draft, October 1, 1990. Traded to **Winnipeg** by **Quebec** for future considerations, November 26, 1991.

• MAROTTE, Gilles

Jean Gilles "Captain Crunch" D – L. 5'9", 205 lbs. b: Montreal, Que., 6/7/1945.

Season	Club	League	GP	G	A	Pts	AG	AA	APts	PIM	PP	SH	GW	S	%	TGF	PGF	TGA	PGA	+/–	GP	G	A	Pts	PIM	PP	SH	GW
1961-62	Victoriaville Bruins	QJHL	43	15	28	43	....	....	....	....	....	....	....	....	....	....	....	....	....	....	10	1	3	4	6	....	....	....
1962-63	Victoriaville Bruins	QJHL	52	12	25	37	....	....	....	....	....	....	....	....	....	....	....	....	....	....	10	1	7	8	20	....	....	....
1963-64	Niagara Falls Flyers	OHA-Jr.	56	12	34	46	....	....	....	160	....	....	....	....	....	....	....	....	....	....	4	0	0	0	9	....	....	....
	Niagara Falls Flyers	Mem-Cup	13	4	9	13	....	....	....	30	....	....	....	....	....	....	....	....	....	....	....	....	....	....	....	....	....	....
1964-65	Niagara Falls Flyers	OHA-Jr.	52	12	25	37	....	....	....	122	....	....	....	....	....	....	....	....	....	....	11	2	0	2	50	....	....	....
1965-66	Niagara Falls Flyers	OHA-Jr.	13	2	20	22	....	....	....	52	....	....	....	....	....	....	....	....	....	....	....	....	....	....	....	....	....	....
	Boston Bruins	**NHL**	**51**	**3**	**17**	**20**	**3**	**16**	**19**	**52**	....	....	....	....	....	....	....	....	....	....	....	....	....	....	....	....	....	....
1966-67	**Boston Bruins**	**NHL**	**67**	**7**	**8**	**15**	**8**	**8**	**16**	**112**	....	....	....	....	....	....	....	....	....	....	....	....	....	....	....	....	....	....
1967-68	**Chicago Black Hawks**	**NHL**	**73**	**0**	**21**	**21**	**0**	**21**	**21**	**122**	**0**	**0**	**0**	**153**	**0.0**	**92**	**2**	**97**	**11**	**4**	**11**	**3**	**1**	**4**	**14**	**0**	**0**	**1**
1968-69	**Chicago Black Hawks**	**NHL**	**68**	**5**	**29**	**34**	**5**	**26**	**31**	**120**	**1**	**0**	**1**	**131**	**3.8**	**105**	**5**	**95**	**18**	**23**	....	....	....	....	....	....	....	....
1969-70	**Chicago Black Hawks**	**NHL**	**51**	**5**	**13**	**18**	**5**	**12**	**17**	**52**	**0**	**0**	**1**	**101**	**5.0**	**57**	**7**	**58**	**5**	**–3**	....	....	....	....	....	....	....	....
	Los Angeles Kings	**NHL**	**21**	**0**	**6**	**6**	**0**	**6**	**6**	**32**	**0**	**0**	**0**	**57**	**0.0**	**24**	**2**	**40**	**10**	**–8**	....	....	....	....	....	....	....	....
1970-71	**Los Angeles Kings**	**NHL**	**78**	**6**	**27**	**33**	**6**	**23**	**29**	**96**	**0**	**0**	**0**	**218**	**2.8**	**116**	**24**	**131**	**30**	**–9**	....	....	....	....	....	....	....	....
1971-72	**Los Angeles Kings**	**NHL**	**72**	**10**	**24**	**34**	**10**	**21**	**31**	**83**	**4**	**0**	**1**	**203**	**4.9**	**111**	**26**	**152**	**34**	**–33**	....	....	....	....	....	....	....	....
1972-73	**Los Angeles Kings**	**NHL**	**78**	**6**	**39**	**45**	**6**	**31**	**37**	**70**	**3**	**0**	**0**	**207**	**2.9**	**126**	**50**	**121**	**24**	**–21**	....	....	....	....	....	....	....	....
1973-74	**Los Angeles Kings**	**NHL**	**22**	**1**	**11**	**12**	**1**	**9**	**10**	**23**	**1**	**0**	**0**	**48**	**2.1**	**24**	**11**	**39**	**7**	**–19**	....	....	....	....	....	....	....	....
	New York Rangers	**NHL**	**46**	**2**	**17**	**19**	**2**	**14**	**16**	**28**	**0**	**0**	**1**	**87**	**2.3**	**68**	**3**	**69**	**11**	**7**	**12**	**0**	**1**	**1**	**6**	**0**	**0**	**0**
1974-75	**New York Rangers**	**NHL**	**77**	**4**	**32**	**36**	**3**	**24**	**27**	**69**	**0**	**0**	**1**	**148**	**2.7**	**117**	**7**	**140**	**30**	**0**	**3**	**0**	**1**	**1**	**4**	**0**	**0**	**0**
1975-76	**New York Rangers**	**NHL**	**57**	**4**	**17**	**21**	**3**	**13**	**16**	**34**	**1**	**0**	**0**	**113**	**3.5**	**75**	**8**	**98**	**28**	**–3**	....	....	....	....	....	....	....	....
1976-77	**St. Louis Blues**	**NHL**	**47**	**3**	**4**	**7**	**3**	**3**	**6**	**26**	**0**	**0**	**1**	**59**	**5.1**	**46**	**2**	**73**	**16**	**–13**	**3**	**0**	**0**	**0**	**2**	**0**	**0**	**0**
	Kansas City Blues	CHL	26	1	10	11	....	....	....	46	....	....	....	....	....	....	....	....	....	....	7	2	0	2	2	....	....	....
1977-78	Cincinnati Stingers	WHA	29	1	7	8	....	....	....	58	....	....	....	....	....	....	....	....	....	....	....	....	....	....	....	....	....	....
	Indianapolis Racers	WHA	44	2	13	15	....	....	....	18	....	....	....	....	....	....	....	....	....	....	....	....	....	....	....	....	....	....
	NHL Totals		**808**	**56**	**265**	**321**	**55**	**227**	**282**	**919**	....	....	....	....	....	....	....	....	....	....	**29**	**3**	**3**	**6**	**26**	....	....	....
	Other Major League Totals		73	3	20	23	....	....	....	76	....	....	....	....	....	....	....	....	....	....	....	....	....	....	....	....	....	....

QJHL First All-Star Team (1963) • OHA-Jr. First All-Star Team (1965) • Played in NHL All-Star Game (1973)

Traded to **Chicago** by **Boston** with Jack Norris and Pit Martin for Phil Esposito, Ken Hodge and Fred Stanfield, May 15, 1967. Traded to **LA Kings** by **Chicago** with Jim Stanfield and Denis DeJordy for Bryan Campbell, Bill White and Gerry Desjardins, February 20, 1970. Selected by **Edmonton** (WHA) in 1972 WHA General Player Draft, February 12, 1972. Traded to **NY Rangers** by **LA Kings** with Real Lemieux for Sheldon Kannegiesser, Mike Murphy and Tom Williams, November 30, 1973. Claimed on waivers by **St. Louis** from **NY Rangers**, October 12, 1976. WHA rights traded to **Cincinnati** (WHA) by **Edmonton** (WHA) for cash, July, 1976. Traded to **Indianapolis** (WHA) by **Cincinnati** (WHA) with Blaine Stoughton for Bryon Baltimore and Hugh Harris, January, 1978.

• MARSH, Brad

Charles Bradley D – L. 6'3", 220 lbs. b: London, Ont., 3/31/1958. Atlanta's 1st, 11th overall, in 1978.

Season	Club	League	GP	G	A	Pts	AG	AA	APts	PIM	PP	SH	GW	S	%	TGF	PGF	TGA	PGA	+/–	GP	G	A	Pts	PIM	PP	SH	GW
1972-73	London Legionaires	OMHA	STATISTICS NOT AVAILABLE																									
	London Knights	OMJHL	13	0	0	0	....	....	....	2	....	....	....	....	....	....	....	....	....	....	....	....	....	....	....	....	....	....
1974-75	London Knights	OMJHL	70	4	17	21	....	....	....	160	....	....	....	....	....	....	....	....	....	....	....	....	....	....	....	....	....	....
1975-76	London Knights	OMJHL	61	3	26	29	....	....	....	184	....	....	....	....	....	....	....	....	....	....	5	1	2	3	18	....	....	....
1976-77	London Knights	OMJHL	63	7	33	40	....	....	....	121	....	....	....	....	....	....	....	....	....	....	20	3	5	8	47	....	....	....
	Canada	WJC-A	7	1	3	4	....	....	....	14	....	....	....	....	....	....	....	....	....	....	....	....	....	....	....	....	....	....
1977-78	London Knights	OMJHL	62	8	55	63	....	....	....	192	....	....	....	....	....	....	....	....	....	....	11	2	10	12	21	....	....	....
	Canada	WJC-A	6	0	4	4	....	....	....	2	....	....	....	....	....	....	....	....	....	....	....	....	....	....	....	....	....	....
1978-79	**Atlanta Flames**	**NHL**	**80**	**0**	**19**	**19**	**0**	**14**	**14**	**101**	**0**	**0**	**0**	**80**	**0.0**	**98**	**2**	**97**	**24**	**23**	**2**	**0**	**0**	**0**	**17**	**0**	**0**	**0**
	Canada	WEC-A	6	1	0	1	....	....	....	4	....	....	....	....	....	....	....	....	....	....	....	....	....	....	....	....	....	....
1979-80	**Atlanta Flames**	**NHL**	**80**	**2**	**9**	**11**	**2**	**7**	**9**	**119**	**0**	**0**	**0**	**73**	**2.7**	**66**	**1**	**120**	**40**	**–15**	**4**	**0**	**1**	**1**	**2**	**0**	**0**	**0**
1980-81	**Calgary Flames**	**NHL**	**80**	**1**	**12**	**13**	**1**	**8**	**9**	**87**	**0**	**0**	**0**	**58**	**1.7**	**79**	**0**	**135**	**54**	**–2**	**16**	**0**	**5**	**5**	**8**	**0**	**0**	**0**
1981-82	**Calgary Flames**	**NHL**	**17**	**0**	**1**	**1**	**0**	**1**	**1**	**10**	**0**	**0**	**0**	**17**	**0.0**	**11**	**0**	**43**	**16**	**–16**	....	....	....	....	....	....	....	....
	Philadelphia Flyers	**NHL**	**66**	**2**	**22**	**24**	**2**	**15**	**17**	**106**	**0**	**0**	**1**	**58**	**3.4**	**81**	**0**	**98**	**34**	**17**	**4**	**0**	**0**	**0**	**2**	**0**	**0**	**0**
1982-83	**Philadelphia Flyers**	**NHL**	**68**	**2**	**11**	**13**	**2**	**8**	**10**	**52**	**0**	**0**	**0**	**76**	**2.6**	**66**	**0**	**72**	**26**	**20**	**2**	**0**	**1**	**1**	**0**	**0**	**0**	**0**
1983-84	**Philadelphia Flyers**	**NHL**	**77**	**3**	**14**	**17**	**2**	**10**	**12**	**83**	**0**	**0**	**0**	**90**	**3.3**	**89**	**1**	**95**	**31**	**24**	**3**	**1**	**1**	**2**	**2**	**0**	**0**	**0**
1984-85	**Philadelphia Flyers**	**NHL**	**77**	**2**	**18**	**20**	**2**	**12**	**14**	**91**	**0**	**0**	**0**	**65**	**3.1**	**100**	**0**	**87**	**29**	**42**	**19**	**0**	**6**	**6**	**65**	**0**	**0**	**0**
1985-86	**Philadelphia Flyers**	**NHL**	**79**	**0**	**13**	**13**	**0**	**9**	**9**	**123**	**0**	**0**	**0**	**104**	**0.0**	**77**	**2**	**108**	**33**	**0**	**5**	**0**	**0**	**0**	**2**	**0**	**0**	**0**
1986-87	**Philadelphia Flyers**	**NHL**	**77**	**2**	**9**	**11**	**2**	**7**	**9**	**124**	**0**	**0**	**1**	**81**	**2.5**	**62**	**1**	**81**	**29**	**9**	**26**	**3**	**4**	**7**	**16**	**0**	**1**	**0**
1987-88	**Philadelphia Flyers**	**NHL**	**70**	**3**	**9**	**12**	**3**	**6**	**9**	**57**	**0**	**1**	**1**	**57**	**5.3**	**47**	**1**	**87**	**28**	**–13**	**7**	**1**	**0**	**1**	**8**	**0**	**0**	**0**
1988-89	**Toronto Maple Leafs**	**NHL**	**80**	**1**	**15**	**16**	**1**	**11**	**12**	**79**	**0**	**0**	**0**	**69**	**1.4**	**79**	**1**	**147**	**53**	**–16**	....	....	....	....	....	....	....	....
1989-90	**Toronto Maple Leafs**	**NHL**	**79**	**1**	**13**	**14**	**1**	**9**	**10**	**95**	**0**	**0**	**0**	**50**	**2.0**	**100**	**1**	**125**	**40**	**14**	**5**	**1**	**0**	**1**	**2**	**0**	**0**	**0**
1990-91	**Toronto Maple Leafs**	**NHL**	**22**	**0**	**0**	**0**	**0**	**0**	**0**	**15**	**0**	**0**	**0**	**18**	**0.0**	**13**	**0**	**32**	**13**	**–6**	....	....	....	....	....	....	....	....
	Detroit Red Wings	**NHL**	**20**	**1**	**3**	**4**	**1**	**2**	**3**	**16**	**0**	**0**	**0**	**16**	**6.3**	**17**	**0**	**33**	**13**	**–3**	**1**	**0**	**0**	**0**	**0**	**0**	**0**	**0**
1991-92	**Detroit Red Wings**	**NHL**	**55**	**3**	**4**	**7**	**3**	**3**	**6**	**53**	**0**	**0**	**1**	**29**	**10.3**	**47**	**0**	**55**	**16**	**8**	**3**	**0**	**0**	**0**	**0**	**0**	**0**	**0**
1992-93	**Ottawa Senators**	**NHL**	**59**	**0**	**3**	**3**	**0**	**2**	**2**	**30**	**0**	**0**	**0**	**35**	**0.0**	**16**	**0**	**66**	**21**	**–29**	....	....	....	....	....	....	....	....
	NHL Totals		**1086**	**23**	**175**	**198**	**22**	**124**	**146**	**1241**	**0**	**1**	**4**	**976**	**2.4**	**1048**	**10**	**1481**	**500**		**97**	**6**	**18**	**24**	**124**	**0**	**1**	**0**

OMJHL First All-Star Team (1978) • Played in NHL All-Star Game (1993)

Claimed by **Atlanta** as a fill-in during Expansion Draft, June 13, 1979. Transferred to **Calgary** after **Atlanta** franchise relocated, June 21, 1982. Traded to **Philadelphia** by **Calgary** for Mel Bridgman, November 11, 1981. Claimed by **Toronto** from **Philadelphia** in Waiver Draft, October 3, 1988. Traded to **Detroit** by **Toronto** for Detroit's 8th round choice (Robb McIntyre) in 1991 Entry Draft, February 4, 1991. Traded to **Toronto** by **Detroit** for cash, June 10, 1992. Traded to **Ottawa** by **Toronto** for future considerations, July 20, 1992.

• MARSH, Gary

Gary Arthur LW – L. 5'10", 172 lbs. b: Toronto, Ont., 3/9/1946.

Season	Club	League	GP	G	A	Pts	AG	AA	APts	PIM	PP	SH	GW	S	%	TGF	PGF	TGA	PGA	+/–	GP	G	A	Pts	PIM	PP	SH	GW
1962-63	Hamilton Red Wings	OHA-Jr.	50	4	4	8	....	....	....	43	....	....	....	....	....	....	....	....	....	....	5	0	0	0	15	....	....	....
1963-64	Hamilton Red Wings	OHA-Jr.	56	17	25	42	....	....	....	76	....	....	....	....	....	....	....	....	....	....	....	....	....	....	....	....	....	....
1964-65	Hamilton Red Wings	OHA-Jr.	14	3	2	5	....	....	....	26	....	....	....	....	....	....	....	....	....	....	....	....	....	....	....	....	....	....
	Etobicoke Indians	OHA-B	STATISTICS NOT AVAILABLE																									
1965-66	Hamilton Red Wings	OHA-Jr.	42	25	25	50	....	....	....	60	....	....	....	....	....	....	....	....	....	....	5	3	3	6	6	....	....	....
	Memphis Wings	CPHL	4	1	1	2	....	....	....	4	....	....	....	....	....	....	....	....	....	....	....	....	....	....	....	....	....	....
1966-67	Memphis Wings	CPHL	63	16	15	31	....	....	....	85	....	....	....	....	....	....	....	....	....	....	7	2	3	5	2	....	....	....
1967-68	**Detroit Red Wings**	**NHL**	**6**	**1**	**3**	**4**	**1**	**3**	**4**	**4**	**0**	**0**	**1**	**7**	**14.3**	**6**	**0**	**4**	**0**	**2**	....	....	....	....	....	....	....	....
	Fort Worth Wings	CPHL	64	25	28	53	....	....	....	77	....	....	....	....	....	....	....	....	....	....	13	*6	4	10	6	....	....	....

			REGULAR SEASON																		PLAYOFFS							
Season	Club	League	GP	G	A	Pts	AG	AA	APts	PIM	PP	SH	GW	S	%	TGF	PGF	TGA	PGA	+/–	GP	G	A	Pts	PIM	PP	SH	GW
1968-69	**Toronto Maple Leafs**	**NHL**	1	0	0	0	0	0	0	0	0	0	0	0	0.0	0	0	0	0	0	....	....	....	....	....	....	....	....
	Phoenix Roadrunners	WHL	2	0	0	0	....	....	....	0	....	....	....	....	....	....	....	....	....	....	....	....	....	....	....	....	....	....
	Rochester Americans	AHL	7	1	2	3	....	....	....	4	....	....	....	....	....	....	....	....	....	....	....	....	....	....	....	....	....	....
	Tulsa Oilers	CHL	51	22	37	59	....	....	....	65	....	....	....	....	....	....	....	....	....	....	7	2	2	4	22	....	....	....
1969-70	Phoenix Roadrunners	WHL	45	8	16	24	....	....	....	17	....	....	....	....	....	....	....	....	....	....	....	....	....	....	....	....	....	....
	Springfield Kings	AHL	22	2	1	3	....	....	....	0	....	....	....	....	....	....	....	....	....	....	14	0	0	0	2	....	....	....
1970-71	Springfield Kings	AHL	26	2	4	6	....	....	....	6	....	....	....	....	....	....	....	....	....	....	....	....	....	....	....	....	....	....
	Kansas City Blues	CHL	19	2	8	10	....	....	....	4	....	....	....	....	....	....	....	....	....	....	....	....	....	....	....	....	....	....
1971-72	Orillia Terriers	OHA-Sr.	38	15	26	41	....	....	....	37	....	....	....	....	....	....	....	....	....	....	....	....	....	....	....	....	....	....
1972-73	Orillia Terriers	OHA-Sr.	39	12	15	27	....	....	....	33	....	....	....	....	....	....	....	....	....	....	....	....	....	....	....	....	....	....
1973-74	Orillia Terriers	OHA-Sr.	34	11	35	46	....	....	....	32	....	....	....	....	....	....	....	....	....	....	....	....	....	....	....	....	....	....
	NHL Totals		7	1	3	4	1	3	4	4	0	0	1	7	14.3	6	0	4	0		....	....	....	....	....	....	....	....

Claimed by **Toronto** from **Detroit** in Intra-League Draft, June 12, 1968. Traded to **LA Kings** by **Toronto** (Phoenix-WHL) for Jacques Lemieux, February, 1970.

• MARSH, Peter

Peter William RW – L. 6'1", 180 lbs. b: Halifax, N.S., 12/21/1956. Pittsburgh's 3rd, 29th overall, in 1976.

Season	Club	League	GP	G	A	Pts	AG	AA	APts	PIM	PP	SH	GW	S	%	TGF	PGF	TGA	PGA	+/–	GP	G	A	Pts	PIM	PP	SH	GW
1973-74	Sherbrooke Castors	QMJHL	43	7	9	16	....	....	....	45	....	....	....	....	....	....	....	....	....	....	....	....	....	....	....	....	....	....
1974-75	Sherbrooke Castors	QMJHL	65	36	34	70	....	....	....	133	....	....	....	....	....	....	....	....	....	....	12	10	10	20	32	....	....	....
	Sherbrooke Castors	Mem-Cup	3	0	2	2	....	....	....	0	....	....	....	....	....	....	....	....	....	....	....	....	....	....	....	....	....	....
1975-76	Sherbrooke Castors	QMJHL	70	75	81	156	....	....	....	103	....	....	....	....	....	....	....	....	....	....	16	9	10	19	19	....	....	....
	Canada	WJC-A	4	4	0	4	....	....	....	8	....	....	....	....	....	....	....	....	....	....	....	....	....	....	....	....	....	....
1976-77	Cincinnati Stingers	WHA	76	23	28	51	....	....	....	52	....	....	....	....	....	....	....	....	....	....	4	2	0	2	0	....	....	....
1977-78	Cincinnati Stingers	WHA	74	25	25	50	....	....	....	123	....	....	....	....	....	....	....	....	....	....	....	....	....	....	....	....	....	....
1978-79	Cincinnati Stingers	WHA	80	43	23	66	....	....	....	95	....	....	....	....	....	....	....	....	....	....	3	1	0	1	0	....	....	....
1979-80	**Winnipeg Jets**	**NHL**	57	18	20	38	15	15	30	59	9	0	0	187	9.6	55	22	72	1	–38	....	....	....	....	....	....	....	....
1980-81	**Winnipeg Jets**	**NHL**	24	6	7	13	5	5	10	9	3	0	0	63	9.5	15	6	28	2	–17	....	....	....	....	....	....	....	....
	Chicago Black Hawks	**NHL**	29	4	6	10	3	4	7	10	0	0	0	48	8.3	16	2	15	1	0	2	1	1	2	2	0	0	0
1981-82	**Chicago Black Hawks**	**NHL**	57	10	18	28	8	12	20	47	0	0	0	122	8.2	45	2	49	9	3	12	0	2	2	31	0	0	0
1982-83	**Chicago Black Hawks**	**NHL**	68	6	14	20	5	10	15	55	0	0	2	121	5.0	32	0	61	21	–8	12	0	2	2	0	0	0	0
1983-84	**Chicago Black Hawks**	**NHL**	43	4	6	10	3	4	7	44	0	0	0	86	4.7	18	0	40	11	–11	....	....	....	....	....	....	....	....
	Springfield Indians	AHL	23	8	13	21	....	....	....	32	....	....	....	....	....	....	....	....	....	....	4	2	0	2	0	....	....	....
	NHL Totals		278	48	71	119	39	50	89	224	12	0	2	627	7.7	181	32	265	45		26	1	5	6	33	0	0	0
	Other Major League Totals		230	91	76	167	....	....	....	270	....	....	....	....	....	....	....	....	....	....	7	3	0	3	0	....	....	....

WJC-A All-Star Team (1976) • QMJHL West Division First All-Star Team (1976)

Selected by **Cincinnati** (WHA) in 1976 WHA Amateur Draft, May, 1976. Rights traded to **Montreal** by **Pittsburgh** to complete transaction that sent Peter Mahovlich to Pittsburgh (November 29, 1977), December 15, 1977. Reclaimed by **Montreal** from **Cincinnati** (WHA) prior to Expansion Draft, June 9, 1979. Claimed by **Winnipeg** from **Montreal** in Expansion Draft, June 13, 1979. Traded to **Chicago** by **Winnipeg** for Doug Lecuyer and Tim Trimper, December 1, 1980.

• MARSHALL, Bert

Albert Leroy D – L. 6'3", 205 lbs. b: Kamloops, B.C., 11/22/1943.

Season	Club	League	GP	G	A	Pts	AG	AA	APts	PIM	PP	SH	GW	S	%	TGF	PGF	TGA	PGA	+/–	GP	G	A	Pts	PIM	PP	SH	GW
1962-63	Edmonton Oil Kings	CAHL	STATISTICS NOT AVAILABLE																									
	Edmonton Oil Kings	Mem-Cup	17	0	2	2	....	....	....	10	....	....	....	....	....	....	....	....	....	....	....	....	....	....	....	....	....	....
1963-64	Edmonton Oil Kings	CAHL	30	28	35	63	....	....	....	78	....	....	....	....	....	....	....	....	....	....	5	1	3	4	6	....	....	....
	Cincinnati Wings	CPHL	1	0	0	0	....	....	....	0	....	....	....	....	....	....	....	....	....	....	....	....	....	....	....	....	....	....
	Edmonton Oil Kings	Mem-Cup	19	8	21	29	....	....	....	10	....	....	....	....	....	....	....	....	....	....	....	....	....	....	....	....	....	....
1964-65	Memphis Wings	CPHL	51	3	11	14	....	....	....	43	....	....	....	....	....	....	....	....	....	....	....	....	....	....	....	....	....	....
1965-66	**Detroit Red Wings**	**NHL**	61	0	19	19	0	18	18	45	....	....	....	....	....	....	....	....	....	....	12	1	3	4	16	0	0	0
	Pittsburgh Hornets	AHL	12	2	0	2	....	....	....	8	....	....	....	....	....	....	....	....	....	....	....	....	....	....	....	....	....	....
1966-67	**Detroit Red Wings**	**NHL**	57	0	10	10	0	10	10	68	....	....	....	....	....	....	....	....	....	....	....	....	....	....	....	....	....	....
1967-68	**Detroit Red Wings**	**NHL**	37	1	5	6	1	5	6	56	0	0	0	50	2.0	44	2	53	17	6	....	....	....	....	....	....	....	....
	Oakland Seals	**NHL**	20	0	4	4	0	4	4	18	0	0	0	44	0.0	26	8	30	10	–2	....	....	....	....	....	....	....	....
1968-69	**Oakland Seals**	**NHL**	68	3	15	18	3	13	16	81	0	0	0	118	2.5	81	19	105	19	–24	7	0	7	7	20	0	0	0
1969-70	**Oakland Seals**	**NHL**	72	1	15	16	1	14	15	109	0	0	0	130	0.8	64	16	92	23	–21	4	0	1	1	12	0	0	0
1970-71	**California Golden Seals**	**NHL**	32	2	6	8	2	5	7	48	1	0	0	54	3.7	34	6	63	15	–20	....	....	....	....	....	....	....	....
1971-72	**California Golden Seals**	**NHL**	66	0	14	14	0	12	12	68	0	0	0	35	0.0	54	0	81	22	–5	....	....	....	....	....	....	....	....
1972-73	**California Golden Seals**	**NHL**	55	2	6	8	2	5	7	71	1	0	0	55	3.6	46	3	98	19	–36	....	....	....	....	....	....	....	....
	New York Rangers	**NHL**	8	0	0	0	0	0	0	14	0	0	0	4	0.0	1	0	4	0	–3	6	0	1	1	8	0	0	0
1973-74	**New York Islanders**	**NHL**	69	1	7	8	1	6	7	84	0	0	0	51	2.0	66	1	103	43	5	....	....	....	....	....	....	....	....
1974-75	**New York Islanders**	**NHL**	77	2	28	30	2	21	23	58	0	0	0	69	2.9	80	1	95	34	18	17	2	5	7	16	0	0	0
1975-76	**New York Islanders**	**NHL**	71	0	16	16	0	12	12	72	0	0	0	70	0.0	82	2	72	29	37	13	1	3	4	12	0	0	1
1976-77	**New York Islanders**	**NHL**	72	4	21	25	4	16	20	61	0	0	1	62	6.5	93	0	74	29	48	6	0	0	0	6	0	0	0
1977-78	**New York Islanders**	**NHL**	58	0	7	7	0	5	5	44	0	0	0	32	0.0	43	0	38	5	10	7	0	2	2	9	0	0	0
1978-79	**New York Islanders**	**NHL**	45	1	8	9	1	6	7	29	0	0	0	26	3.8	43	0	42	8	9	....	....	....	....	....	....	....	....
1979-80	Indianapolis Checkers	CHL	6	0	0	0	....	....	....	6	....	....	....	....	....	....	....	....	....	....	....	....	....	....	....	....	....	....
	NHL Totals		868	17	181	198	17	152	169	926	....	....	....	....	....	....	....	....	....	....	72	4	22	26	99	....	....	....

CAHL Second All-Star Team (1964)

Traded to **Oakland** by **Detroit** with John Brenneman and Ted Hampson for Kent Douglas, January 9, 1968. Traded to **NY Rangers** by **California** for cash and future considerations (Dave Hrechkosy and Gary Coalter, May 17, 1973), March 4, 1973. Claimed by **NY Islanders** from **NY Rangers** in Intra-League Draft, June 12, 1973.

• MARSHALL, Don

Donald Robert LW – L. 5'10", 160 lbs. b: Montreal, Que., 3/23/1932.

Season	Club	League	GP	G	A	Pts	AG	AA	APts	PIM	PP	SH	GW	S	%	TGF	PGF	TGA	PGA	+/–	GP	G	A	Pts	PIM	PP	SH	GW
1949-50	Montreal Jr. Canadiens	QJHL	35	8	7	15	....	....	....	10	....	....	....	....	....	....	....	....	....	....	16	1	4	5	4	....	....	....
	Montreal Jr. Canadiens	Mem-Cup	13	8	6	14	....	....	....	2	....	....	....	....	....	....	....	....	....	....	....	....	....	....	....	....	....	....
1950-51	Montreal Jr. Canadiens	QJHL	37	19	32	51	....	....	....	6	....	....	....	....	....	....	....	....	....	....	9	5	8	13	0	....	....	....
1951-52	Montreal Jr. Canadiens	QJHL	43	32	46	78	....	....	....	6	....	....	....	....	....	....	....	....	....	....	11	4	5	9	6	....	....	....
	Montreal Canadiens	**NHL**	1	0	0	0	0	0	0	0	....	....	....	....	....	....	....	....	....	....	....	....	....	....	....	....	....	....
	Montreal Jr. Canadiens	Mem-Cup	8	6	5	11	....	....	....	8	....	....	....	....	....	....	....	....	....	....	....	....	....	....	....	....	....	....
1952-53	Cincinnati Mohawks	IHL	60	46	51	97	....	....	....	24	....	....	....	....	....	....	....	....	....	....	9	5	5	10	0	....	....	....
	Montreal Royals	QSHL	2	0	0	0	....	....	....	2	....	....	....	....	....	....	....	....	....	....	....	....	....	....	....	....	....	....
1953-54	Buffalo Bisons	AHL	70	39	55	94	....	....	....	8	....	....	....	....	....	....	....	....	....	....	3	1	4	5	0	....	....	....
1954-55	**Montreal Canadiens**	**NHL**	39	5	3	8	6	3	9	9	....	....	....	....	....	....	....	....	....	....	12	1	1	2	2	0	0	1
	Montreal Royals	QHL	10	5	3	8	....	....	....	2	....	....	....	....	....	....	....	....	....	....	....	....	....	....	....	....	....	....
1955-56♦	**Montreal Canadiens**	**NHL**	66	4	1	5	5	1	6	10	....	....	....	....	....	....	....	....	....	....	10	1	0	1	0	0	1	0
1956-57♦	**Montreal Canadiens**	**NHL**	70	12	8	20	15	9	24	6	....	....	....	....	....	....	....	....	....	....	10	1	3	4	2	0	0	0
1957-58♦	**Montreal Canadiens**	**NHL**	68	22	19	41	27	20	47	14	....	....	....	....	....	....	....	....	....	....	10	0	2	2	4	0	0	0
1958-59♦	**Montreal Canadiens**	**NHL**	70	10	22	32	12	22	34	12	....	....	....	....	....	....	....	....	....	....	11	0	2	2	2	0	0	0
1959-60♦	**Montreal Canadiens**	**NHL**	70	16	22	38	19	21	40	4	....	....	....	....	....	....	....	....	....	....	8	2	2	4	0	0	0	0
1960-61	**Montreal Canadiens**	**NHL**	70	14	17	31	16	16	32	8	....	....	....	....	....	....	....	....	....	....	6	0	2	2	0	0	0	0
1961-62	**Montreal Canadiens**	**NHL**	66	18	28	46	21	27	48	12	....	....	....	....	....	....	....	....	....	....	6	0	1	1	2	0	0	0
1962-63	**Montreal Canadiens**	**NHL**	65	13	20	33	15	20	35	6	....	....	....	....	....	....	....	....	....	....	5	0	0	0	0	0	0	0
1963-64	**New York Rangers**	**NHL**	70	11	12	23	14	13	27	8	....	....	....	....	....	....	....	....	....	....	....	....	....	....	....	....	....	....
1964-65	**New York Rangers**	**NHL**	69	20	15	35	24	15	39	2	....	....	....	....	....	....	....	....	....	....	....	....	....	....	....	....	....	....
1965-66	**New York Rangers**	**NHL**	69	26	28	54	30	27	57	6	....	....	....	....	....	....	....	....	....	....	....	....	....	....	....	....	....	....
1966-67	**New York Rangers**	**NHL**	70	24	22	46	28	21	49	4	....	....	....	....	....	....	....	....	....	....	4	0	1	1	2	0	0	0
1967-68	**New York Rangers**	**NHL**	70	19	30	49	22	30	52	2	4	0	3	146	13.0	81	19	61	18	19	6	2	1	3	0	0	0	1
1968-69	**New York Rangers**	**NHL**	74	20	19	39	21	17	38	12	7	0	4	149	13.4	68	14	41	2	15	4	1	0	1	0	0	0	0

Season	Club	League	GP	G	A	Pts	AG	AA	APts	PIM	PP	SH	GW	S	%	TGF	PGF	TGA	PGA	+/–	GP	G	A	Pts	PIM	PP	SH	GW
			REGULAR SEASON																		PLAYOFFS							
1969-70	**New York Rangers**	**NHL**	**57**	**9**	**15**	**24**	**10**	**14**	**24**	**6**	**2**	**0**	**3**	**81**	**11.1**	**32**	**4**	**38**	**16**	**6**	**1**	**0**	**0**	**0**	**0**	**0**	**0**	**0**
1970-71	**Buffalo Sabres**	**NHL**	**62**	**20**	**29**	**49**	**20**	**24**	**44**	**6**	**9**	**0**	**1**	**112**	**17.9**	**77**	**39**	**53**	**2**	**–13**	....	....	....	....	....	....	....	....
1971-72	**Toronto Maple Leafs**	**NHL**	**50**	**2**	**14**	**16**	**2**	**12**	**14**	**0**	**1**	**0**	**0**	**48**	**4.2**	**26**	**8**	**30**	**14**	**2**	**1**	**0**	**0**	**0**	**0**	**0**	**0**	**0**
	NHL Totals		**1176**	**265**	**324**	**589**	**307**	**312**	**619**	**127**	....	....	....	....	....	....	....	....	....	....	**94**	**8**	**15**	**23**	**14**	....	....	....

QJHL First All-Star Team (1952) • IHL First All-Star Team (1953) • Won James Gatschene Memorial Trophy (MVP - IHL) (1953) • Won Dudley "Red" Garrett Memorial Award (Top Rookie - AHL) (1954) • NHL Second All-Star Team (1967) • Played in NHL All-Star Game (1956, 1957, 1958, 1959, 1960, 1961, 1968)

Traded to **NY Rangers** by **Montreal** with Jacques Plante and Phil Goyette for Dave Balon, Leon Rochefort, Len Ronson and Gump Worsley, June 4, 1963. Claimed by **Buffalo** from **NY Rangers** in Expansion Draft, June 10, 1970. Claimed by **Toronto** from **Buffalo** in Intra-League Draft, June 8, 1971.

• MARSHALL, Grant

RW – R. 6'1", 200 lbs. b: Mississauga, Ont., 6/9/1973. Toronto's 2nd, 23rd overall, in 1992.

Season	Club	League	GP	G	A	Pts	AG	AA	APts	PIM	PP	SH	GW	S	%	TGF	PGF	TGA	PGA	+/–	GP	G	A	Pts	PIM	PP	SH	GW
1989-90	Toronto Young Nationals	MTHL	39	15	28	43	....	....	....	56	....	....	....	....	....	....	....	....	....	....	....	....	....	....	....	....	....	....
1990-91	Ottawa 67's	OHL	26	6	11	17	....	....	....	25	....	....	....	....	....	....	....	....	....	....	1	0	0	0	0	....	....	....
1991-92	Ottawa 67's	OHL	61	32	51	83	....	....	....	132	....	....	....	....	....	....	....	....	....	....	11	6	11	17	11	....	....	....
1992-93	Ottawa 67's	OHL	30	14	29	43	....	....	....	83	....	....	....	....	....	....	....	....	....	....	....	....	....	....	....	....	....	....
	Newmarket Royals	OHL	31	11	25	36	....	....	....	89	....	....	....	....	....	....	....	....	....	....	7	4	7	11	20	....	....	....
	St. John's Maple Leafs	AHL	2	0	0	0	....	....	....	0	....	....	....	....	....	....	....	....	....	....	2	0	0	0	2	....	....	....
1993-94	St. John's Maple Leafs	AHL	67	11	29	40	....	....	....	155	....	....	....	....	....	....	....	....	....	....	11	1	5	6	17	....	....	....
1994-95	**Dallas Stars**	**NHL**	**2**	**0**	**1**	**1**	**0**	**1**	**1**	**0**	**0**	**0**	**0**	**0**	**0.0**	**1**	**0**	**0**	**0**	**1**	....	....	....	....	....	....	....	....
	Kalamazoo Wings	IHL	61	17	29	46	....	....	....	96	....	....	....	....	....	....	....	....	....	....	16	9	3	12	27	....	....	....
1995-96	**Dallas Stars**	**NHL**	**70**	**9**	**19**	**28**	**9**	**16**	**25**	**111**	**0**	**0**	**0**	**62**	**14.5**	**33**	**2**	**31**	**0**	**0**	....	....	....	....	....	....	....	....
1996-97	**Dallas Stars**	**NHL**	**56**	**6**	**4**	**10**	**6**	**4**	**10**	**98**	**0**	**0**	**0**	**0**	**0.0**	**23**	**1**	**17**	**0**	**5**	**5**	**0**	**2**	**2**	**8**	**0**	**0**	**0**
1997-98	**Dallas Stars**	**NHL**	**72**	**9**	**10**	**19**	**11**	**10**	**21**	**96**	**3**	**0**	**1**	**91**	**9.9**	**23**	**7**	**18**	**0**	**–2**	**17**	**0**	**2**	**2**	***47**	**0**	**0**	**0**
1998-99♦	**Dallas Stars**	**NHL**	**82**	**13**	**18**	**31**	**15**	**17**	**32**	**85**	**2**	**0**	**4**	**112**	**11.6**	**51**	**15**	**35**	**0**	**1**	**14**	**0**	**3**	**3**	**20**	**0**	**0**	**0**
99-2000	**Dallas Stars**	**NHL**	**45**	**2**	**6**	**8**	**2**	**6**	**8**	**38**	**1**	**0**	**0**	**43**	**4.7**	**16**	**6**	**15**	**0**	**–5**	**14**	**0**	**1**	**1**	**4**	**0**	**0**	**0**
	NHL Totals		**327**	**39**	**58**	**97**	**43**	**54**	**97**	**428**	**6**	**0**	**5**	**308**	**12.7**	**147**	**31**	**116**	**0**		**50**	**0**	**8**	**8**	**79**	**0**	**0**	**0**

• Missed majority of 1990-91 season recovering from neck injury suffered in game vs. Sudbury (OHL), December 4, 1990. Transferred to **Dallas** from **Toronto** with Peter Zezel as compensation for Toronto's signing of free agent Mike Craig, August 10, 1994.

• MARSHALL, Jason

D – R. 6'2", 200 lbs. b: Cranbrook, B.C., 2/22/1971. St. Louis' 1st, 9th overall, in 1989.

Season	Club	League	GP	G	A	Pts	AG	AA	APts	PIM	PP	SH	GW	S	%	TGF	PGF	TGA	PGA	+/–	GP	G	A	Pts	PIM	PP	SH	GW
1987-88	Columbia Valley Rockies	RMJHL	40	4	28	32	....	....	....	150	....	....	....	....	....	....	....	....	....	....	....	....	....	....	....	....	....	....
1988-89	Vernon Lakers	BCJHL	48	10	30	40	....	....	....	197	....	....	....	....	....	....	....	....	....	....	31	6	6	12	14	....	....	....
	Canada	Nat-Team	2	0	1	1	....	....	....	0	....	....	....	....	....	....	....	....	....	....	....	....	....	....	....	....	....	....
1989-90	Canada	Nat-Team	73	1	11	12	....	....	....	57	....	....	....	....	....	....	....	....	....	....	....	....	....	....	....	....	....	....
1990-91	Tri-City Americans	WHL	59	10	34	44	....	....	....	236	....	....	....	....	....	....	....	....	....	....	7	1	2	3	20	....	....	....
	Canada	WJC-A	7	0	4	4	....	....	....	6	....	....	....	....	....	....	....	....	....	....	....	....	....	....	....	....	....	....
	Peoria Rivermen	IHL	....	....	....	....	....	....	....	....	....	....	....	....	....	....	....	....	....	....	18	0	1	1	48	....	....	....
1991-92	**St. Louis Blues**	**NHL**	**2**	**1**	**0**	**1**	**1**	**0**	**1**	**4**	**0**	**0**	**0**	**2**	**50.0**	**1**	**0**	**1**	**0**	**0**	....	....	....	....	....	....	....	....
	Peoria Rivermen	IHL	78	4	18	22	....	....	....	178	....	....	....	....	....	....	....	....	....	....	10	0	1	1	16	....	....	....
1992-93	Peoria Rivermen	IHL	77	4	16	20	....	....	....	229	....	....	....	....	....	....	....	....	....	....	4	0	0	0	20	....	....	....
1993-94	Canada	Nat-Team	41	3	10	13	....	....	....	60	....	....	....	....	....	....	....	....	....	....	....	....	....	....	....	....	....	....
	Peoria Rivermen	IHL	20	1	1	2	....	....	....	72	....	....	....	....	....	....	....	....	....	....	3	2	0	2	2	....	....	....
1994-95	**Mighty Ducks of Anaheim**	**NHL**	**1**	**0**	**0**	**0**	**0**	**0**	**0**	**0**	**0**	**0**	**0**	**1**	**0.0**	**1**	**0**	**3**	**0**	**–2**	....	....	....	....	....	....	....	....
	San Diego Gulls	IHL	80	7	18	25	....	....	....	218	....	....	....	....	....	....	....	....	....	....	5	0	1	1	8	....	....	....
1995-96	**Mighty Ducks of Anaheim**	**NHL**	**24**	**0**	**1**	**1**	**0**	**1**	**1**	**42**	**0**	**0**	**0**	**9**	**0.0**	**11**	**0**	**14**	**6**	**3**	....	....	....	....	....	....	....	....
	Baltimore Bandits	AHL	57	1	13	14	....	....	....	150	....	....	....	....	....	....	....	....	....	....	....	....	....	....	....	....	....	....
1996-97	**Mighty Ducks of Anaheim**	**NHL**	**73**	**1**	**9**	**10**	**1**	**8**	**9**	**140**	**0**	**0**	**0**	**34**	**2.9**	**44**	**1**	**60**	**23**	**6**	**7**	**0**	**1**	**1**	**4**	**0**	**0**	**0**
1997-98	**Mighty Ducks of Anaheim**	**NHL**	**72**	**3**	**6**	**9**	**4**	**6**	**10**	**189**	**1**	**0**	**0**	**68**	**4.4**	**47**	**7**	**71**	**23**	**–8**	....	....	....	....	....	....	....	....
1998-99	**Mighty Ducks of Anaheim**	**NHL**	**72**	**1**	**7**	**8**	**1**	**7**	**8**	**142**	**0**	**0**	**0**	**63**	**1.6**	**38**	**0**	**66**	**23**	**–5**	**4**	**1**	**0**	**1**	**10**	**1**	**0**	**0**
99-2000	**Mighty Ducks of Anaheim**	**NHL**	**55**	**0**	**3**	**3**	**0**	**3**	**3**	**88**	**0**	**0**	**0**	**41**	**0.0**	**23**	**0**	**51**	**18**	**–10**	....	....	....	....	....	....	....	....
	NHL Totals		**299**	**6**	**26**	**32**	**7**	**25**	**32**	**605**	**1**	**0**	**0**	**218**	**2.8**	**165**	**8**	**266**	**93**		**11**	**1**	**1**	**2**	**14**	**1**	**0**	**0**

Traded to **Anaheim** by **St. Louis** for Bill Houlder, August 29, 1994.

• MARSHALL, Paul

LW – L. 6'2", 180 lbs. b: Toronto, Ont., 9/7/1960. Pittsburgh's 1st, 31st overall, in 1979.

Season	Club	League	GP	G	A	Pts	AG	AA	APts	PIM	PP	SH	GW	S	%	TGF	PGF	TGA	PGA	+/–	GP	G	A	Pts	PIM	PP	SH	GW
1976-77	Don Mills Flyers	MTHL	58	42	56	98	....	....	....	....	....	....	....	....	....	....	....	....	....	....	....	....	....	....	....	....	....	....
1977-78	Hamilton Fincups	OMJHL	58	36	34	70	....	....	....	54	....	....	....	....	....	....	....	....	....	....	20	5	2	7	34	....	....	....
1978-79	Brantford Alexanders	OMJHL	67	42	72	114	....	....	....	59	....	....	....	....	....	....	....	....	....	....	....	....	....	....	....	....	....	....
1979-80	Brantford Alexanders	OMJHL	4	2	2	4	....	....	....	0	....	....	....	....	....	....	....	....	....	....	....	....	....	....	....	....	....	....
	Pittsburgh Penguins	**NHL**	**46**	**9**	**12**	**21**	**8**	**9**	**17**	**9**	**1**	**0**	**5**	**68**	**13.2**	**35**	**13**	**24**	**0**	**–2**	**1**	**0**	**0**	**0**	**0**	**0**	**0**	**0**
1980-81	**Pittsburgh Penguins**	**NHL**	**13**	**3**	**0**	**3**	**2**	**0**	**2**	**4**	**1**	**0**	**0**	**8**	**37.5**	**4**	**2**	**9**	**0**	**–7**	....	....	....	....	....	....	....	....
	Binghamton Whalers	AHL	2	2	1	3	....	....	....	0	....	....	....	....	....	....	....	....	....	....	....	....	....	....	....	....	....	....
	Toronto Maple Leafs	**NHL**	**13**	**0**	**2**	**2**	**0**	**1**	**1**	**2**	**0**	**0**	**0**	**8**	**0.0**	**4**	**2**	**4**	**0**	**–2**	....	....	....	....	....	....	....	....
	New Brunswick Hawks	AHL	47	25	28	53	....	....	....	41	....	....	....	....	....	....	....	....	....	....	13	6	7	13	10	....	....	....
1981-82	**Toronto Maple Leafs**	**NHL**	**10**	**2**	**2**	**4**	**2**	**1**	**3**	**2**	**1**	**0**	**0**	**14**	**14.3**	**7**	**2**	**9**	**0**	**–4**	....	....	....	....	....	....	....	....
	Cincinnati Tigers	CHL	54	23	29	52	....	....	....	61	....	....	....	....	....	....	....	....	....	....	4	2	1	3	0	....	....	....
1982-83	**Hartford Whalers**	**NHL**	**13**	**1**	**2**	**3**	**1**	**1**	**2**	**0**	**0**	**0**	**0**	**10**	**10.0**	**9**	**1**	**10**	**0**	**–2**	....	....	....	....	....	....	....	....
	Binghamton Whalers	AHL	61	25	26	51	....	....	....	21	....	....	....	....	....	....	....	....	....	....	5	3	2	5	0	....	....	....
	NHL Totals		**95**	**15**	**18**	**33**	**13**	**12**	**25**	**17**	**3**	**0**	**5**	**108**	**13.9**	**59**	**20**	**56**	**0**		**1**	**0**	**0**	**0**	**0**	**0**	**0**	**0**

Traded to **Toronto** by **Pittsburgh** with Kim Davis for Dave Burrows and Paul Gardner, November 18, 1980. Traded to **Hartford** by **Toronto** for Hartford's 10th round choice (Greg Rolston) in 1983 Entry Draft, October 5, 1982.

• MARSON, Mike

Michael Robert LW – L. 5'9", 200 lbs. b: Scarborough, Ont., 7/24/1955. Washington's 2nd, 19th overall, in 1974.

Season	Club	League	GP	G	A	Pts	AG	AA	APts	PIM	PP	SH	GW	S	%	TGF	PGF	TGA	PGA	+/–	GP	G	A	Pts	PIM	PP	SH	GW
1972-73	Sudbury Wolves	OMJHL	57	12	21	33	....	....	....	117	....	....	....	....	....	....	....	....	....	....	4	1	0	1	2	....	....	....
1973-74	Sudbury Wolves	OMJHL	69	35	59	94	....	....	....	146	....	....	....	....	....	....	....	....	....	....	4	1	0	1	0	....	....	....
1974-75	**Washington Capitals**	**NHL**	**76**	**16**	**12**	**28**	**14**	**9**	**23**	**59**	**5**	**0**	**2**	**89**	**18.0**	**44**	**9**	**100**	**0**	**–65**	....	....	....	....	....	....	....	....
1975-76	**Washington Capitals**	**NHL**	**57**	**4**	**7**	**11**	**3**	**5**	**8**	**50**	**0**	**0**	**0**	**35**	**11.4**	**16**	**2**	**34**	**1**	**–19**	....	....	....	....	....	....	....	....
	Baltimore Clippers	AHL	12	1	3	4	....	....	....	16	....	....	....	....	....	....	....	....	....	....	....	....	....	....	....	....	....	....
1976-77	**Washington Capitals**	**NHL**	**10**	**0**	**1**	**1**	**0**	**1**	**1**	**18**	**0**	**0**	**0**	**5**	**0.0**	**1**	**0**	**2**	**0**	**–1**	....	....	....	....	....	....	....	....
	Springfield Indians	AHL	66	15	17	32	....	....	....	81	....	....	....	....	....	....	....	....	....	....	....	....	....	....	....	....	....	....
1977-78	**Washington Capitals**	**NHL**	**46**	**4**	**4**	**8**	**4**	**3**	**7**	**101**	**0**	**0**	**0**	**30**	**13.3**	**16**	**0**	**15**	**0**	**1**	....	....	....	....	....	....	....	....
	Hershey Bears	AHL	20	5	3	8	....	....	....	35	....	....	....	....	....	....	....	....	....	....	....	....	....	....	....	....	....	....
1978-79	**Washington Capitals**	**NHL**	**4**	**0**	**0**	**0**	**0**	**0**	**0**	**0**	**0**	**0**	**0**	**1**	**0.0**	**0**	**0**	**3**	**0**	**–3**	....	....	....	....	....	....	....	....
	Philadelphia Firebirds	AHL	6	3	2	5	....	....	....	19	....	....	....	....	....	....	....	....	....	....	....	....	....	....	....	....	....	....
	Binghamton Dusters	AHL	68	12	11	23	....	....	....	132	....	....	....	....	....	....	....	....	....	....	10	4	3	7	20	....	....	....
1979-80	**Los Angeles Kings**	**NHL**	**3**	**0**	**0**	**0**	**0**	**0**	**0**	**5**	**0**	**0**	**0**	**1**	**0.0**	**0**	**0**	**2**	**0**	**–2**	....	....	....	....	....	....	....	....
	Binghamton Dusters	AHL	58	7	8	15	....	....	....	85	....	....	....	....	....	....	....	....	....	....	....	....	....	....	....	....	....	....
	NHL Totals		**196**	**24**	**24**	**48**	**21**	**18**	**39**	**233**	**5**	**0**	**2**	**161**	**14.9**	**77**	**11**	**156**	**1**		....	....	....	....	....	....	....	....

OMJHL Second All-Star Team (1974)

Traded to **LA Kings** by **Washington** for Steve Clippingdale, June 11, 1979.

• MARTIN, Craig

Craig D. RW – R. 6'2", 215 lbs. b: Amherst, N.S., 1/21/1971. Winnipeg's 6th, 98th overall, in 1990.

Season	Club	League	GP	G	A	Pts	AG	AA	APts	PIM	PP	SH	GW	S	%	TGF	PGF	TGA	PGA	+/–	GP	G	A	Pts	PIM	PP	SH	GW
1985-86	Pictou Pipers	NSAHA	STATISTICS NOT AVAILABLE																									
1986-87	Pictou County Subways	MJrHL	38	19	15	34	....	....	....	90	....	....	....	....	....	....	....	....	....	....	....	....	....	....	....	....	....	....
1987-88	Hull Olympiques	QMJHL	66	5	5	10	....	....	....	137	....	....	....	....	....	....	....	....	....	....	....	....	....	....	....	....	....	....
	Hull Olympiques	Mem-Cup	4	0	0	0	....	....	....	8	....	....	....	....	....	....	....	....	....	....	....	....	....	....	....	....	....	....
1988-89	Hull Olympiques	QMJHL	70	14	29	43	....	....	....	260	....	....	....	....	....	....	....	....	....	....	....	....	....	....	....	....	....	....
1989-90	Hull Olympiques	QMJHL	66	14	31	45	....	....	....	299	....	....	....	....	....	....	....	....	....	....	11	2	1	3	65	....	....	....

			REGULAR SEASON																		PLAYOFFS							
Season	Club	League	GP	G	A	Pts	AG	AA	APts	PIM	PP	SH	GW	S	%	TGF	PGF	TGA	PGA	+/–	GP	G	A	Pts	PIM	PP	SH	GW
1990-91	Hull Olympiques	QMJHL	18	5	6	11	....	....	....	87	....	....	....	....	....	....	....	....	....	....	....	....	....	....	....	....	....	....
	St-Hyacinthe Laser	QMJHL	36	8	9	17	....	....	....	166	....	....	....	....	....	....	....	....	....	....	....	....	....	....	....	....	....	....
1991-92	Moncton Hawks	AHL	11	1	1	2	....	....	....	70	....	....	....	....	....	....	....	....	....	....	....	....	....	....	....	....	....	....
	Fort Wayne Komets	IHL	24	0	0	0	....	....	....	115	....	....	....	....	....	....	....	....	....	....	....	....	....	....	....	....	....	....
1992-93	Moncton Hawks	AHL	64	5	13	18	....	....	....	198	....	....	....	....	....	....	....	....	....	....	5	0	1	1	22	....	....	....
1993-94	Adirondack Red Wings	AHL	76	15	24	39	....	....	....	297	....	....	....	....	....	....	....	....	....	....	12	2	2	4	63	....	....	....
1994-95	**Winnipeg Jets**	**NHL**	**20**	**0**	**1**	**1**	**0**	**1**	**1**	**19**	**0**	**0**	**0**	**3**	**0.0**	**3**	**0**	**7**	**0**	**–4**	....	....	....	....	....	....	....	....
	Springfield Falcons	AHL	6	0	1	1	....	....	....	21	....	....	....	....	....	....	....	....	....	....	....	....	....	....	....	....	....	....
1995-96	Springfield Falcons	AHL	48	6	5	11	....	....	....	245	....	....	....	....	....	....	....	....	....	....	8	0	1	1	34	....	....	....
1996-97	**Florida Panthers**	**NHL**	**1**	**0**	**0**	**0**	**0**	**0**	**0**	**5**	**0**	**0**	**0**	**1**	**0.0**	**0**	**0**	**0**	**0**	**0**	....	....	....	....	....	....	....	....
	Carolina Monarchs	AHL	44	1	2	3	....	....	....	239	....	....	....	....	....	....	....	....	....	....	....	....	....	....	....	....	....	....
	San Antonio Dragons	IHL	15	3	3	6	....	....	....	99	....	....	....	....	....	....	....	....	....	....	6	0	1	1	25	....	....	....
1997-98	Quebec Rafales	IHL	24	1	3	4	....	....	....	115	....	....	....	....	....	....	....	....	....	....	....	....	....	....	....	....	....	....
	San Antonio Dragons	IHL	6	1	1	2	....	....	....	21	....	....	....	....	....	....	....	....	....	....	....	....	....	....	....	....	....	....
	Manitoba Moose	IHL	30	4	3	7	....	....	....	202	....	....	....	....	....	....	....	....	....	....	1	0	0	0	10	....	....	....
1998-99	Berlin Capitals	Germany	45	0	1	1	....	....	....	183	....	....	....	....	....	....	....	....	....	....	....	....	....	....	....	....	....	....
99-2000	Adirondack IceHawks	UHL	7	0	1	1	....	....	....	26	....	....	....	....	....	....	....	....	....	....	....	....	....	....	....	....	....	....
	Phoenix Mustangs	WCHL	50	12	10	22	....	....	....	286	....	....	....	....	....	....	....	....	....	....	10	4	2	6	28	....	....	....
	NHL Totals		**21**	**0**	**1**	**1**	**0**	**1**	**1**	**24**	**0**	**0**	**0**	**4**	**0.0**	**3**	**0**	**7**	**0**		....	....	....	....	....	....	....	....

Signed as a free agent by **Detroit**, July 28, 1993. Claimed on waivers by **Winnipeg** from **Detroit**, January 20, 1995. Signed as a free agent by **Florida**, August 1, 1996. Signed as a free agent by **Phoenix Mustangs** (WCHL), November 9, 1999. • Played w/ RHI's Buffalo Stampede in 1994 (19-6-8-14-83).

• MARTIN, Grant

Grant Michael LW – L. 5'10", 190 lbs. b: Smooth Rock Falls, Ont., 3/13/1962. Vancouver's 9th, 196th overall, in 1980.

Season	Club	League	GP	G	A	Pts	AG	AA	APts	PIM	PP	SH	GW	S	%	TGF	PGF	TGA	PGA	+/–	GP	G	A	Pts	PIM	PP	SH	GW
1977-78	Hespeler Shamrocks	OHA-B	40	18	25	43	....	....	....	32	....	....	....	....	....	....	....	....	....	....	....	....	....	....	....	....	....	....
1978-79	Guelph Platers	OJHL	49	21	29	50	....	....	....	70	....	....	....	....	....	....	....	....	....	....	....	....	....	....	....	....	....	....
1979-80	Kitchener Rangers	OMJHL	65	31	21	52	....	....	....	62	....	....	....	....	....	....	....	....	....	....	....	....	....	....	....	....	....	....
1980-81	Kitchener Rangers	OMJHL	66	41	57	98	....	....	....	77	....	....	....	....	....	....	....	....	....	....	18	9	20	29	42	....	....	....
	Kitchener Rangers	Mem-Cup	1	0	0	0	....	....	....	0	....	....	....	....	....	....	....	....	....	....	....	....	....	....	....	....	....	....
1981-82	Kitchener Rangers	OHL	54	33	63	96	....	....	....	97	....	....	....	....	....	....	....	....	....	....	12	3	15	18	33	....	....	....
	Kitchener Rangers	Mem-Cup	5	5	3	8	....	....	....	2	....	....	....	....	....	....	....	....	....	....	....	....	....	....	....	....	....	....
1982-83	Fredericton Express	AHL	80	19	27	46	....	....	....	73	....	....	....	....	....	....	....	....	....	....	12	4	1	5	14	....	....	....
1983-84	**Vancouver Canucks**	**NHL**	**12**	**0**	**2**	**2**	**0**	**1**	**1**	**6**	**0**	**0**	**0**	**7**	**0.0**	**4**	**0**	**6**	**0**	**–2**	....	....	....	....	....	....	....	....
	Fredericton Express	AHL	57	36	24	60	....	....	....	46	....	....	....	....	....	....	....	....	....	....	7	4	5	9	16	....	....	....
1984-85	**Vancouver Canucks**	**NHL**	**12**	**0**	**1**	**1**	**0**	**1**	**1**	**39**	**0**	**0**	**0**	**1**	**0.0**	**3**	**0**	**14**	**3**	**–8**	....	....	....	....	....	....	....	....
	Fredericton Express	AHL	65	31	47	78	....	....	....	78	....	....	....	....	....	....	....	....	....	....	6	1	4	5	8	....	....	....
	Salt Lake Golden Eagles	IHL	2	0	0	0	....	....	....	0	....	....	....	....	....	....	....	....	....	....	....	....	....	....	....	....	....	....
1985-86	**Washington Capitals**	**NHL**	**11**	**0**	**1**	**1**	**0**	**1**	**1**	**6**	**0**	**0**	**0**	**5**	**0.0**	**2**	**0**	**7**	**0**	**–5**	....	....	....	....	....	....	....	....
	Baltimore Skipjacks	AHL	54	27	49	76	....	....	....	97	....	....	....	....	....	....	....	....	....	....	6	1	3	4	14	....	....	....
1986-87	**Washington Capitals**	**NHL**	**9**	**0**	**0**	**0**	**0**	**0**	**0**	**4**	**0**	**0**	**0**	**5**	**0.0**	**1**	**0**	**3**	**1**	**–1**	**1**	**1**	**0**	**1**	**2**	**0**	**0**	**0**
	Binghamton Whalers	AHL	63	30	23	53	....	....	....	86	....	....	....	....	....	....	....	....	....	....	12	3	1	4	16	....	....	....
1987-88	VSV Villach	Austria	34	29	31	60	....	....	....	40	....	....	....	....	....	....	....	....	....	....	....	....	....	....	....	....	....	....
	Rochester Americans	AHL	22	11	15	26	....	....	....	18	....	....	....	....	....	....	....	....	....	....	7	4	5	9	17	....	....	....
1988-89	JyP-HT Jyvaskyla	Finland	43	20	29	49	....	....	....	48	....	....	....	....	....	....	....	....	....	....	11	1	5	6	11	....	....	....
	Rochester Americans	AHL	6	7	5	12	....	....	....	6	....	....	....	....	....	....	....	....	....	....	....	....	....	....	....	....	....	....
1989-90	Schwenninger ERC	Germany	31	16	19	35	....	....	....	53	....	....	....	....	....	....	....	....	....	....	10	11	10	21	14	....	....	....
	Canada	Nat-Team	5	1	0	1	....	....	....	8	....	....	....	....	....	....	....	....	....	....	....	....	....	....	....	....	....	....
1990-91	Schwenninger ERC	Germany	44	30	28	58	....	....	....	71	....	....	....	....	....	....	....	....	....	....	4	3	5	8	22	....	....	....
	VSV Villach	Austria	1	1	1	2	....	....	....	....	....	....	....	....	....	....	....	....	....	....	....	....	....	....	....	....	....	....
1991-92	Schwenninger ERC	Germany	43	26	35	61	....	....	....	32	....	....	....	....	....	....	....	....	....	....	3	0	0	0	6	....	....	....
1992-93	Schwenninger ERC	Germany	41	21	30	51	....	....	....	52	....	....	....	....	....	....	....	....	....	....	....	....	....	....	....	....	....	....
1993-94	Schwenninger ERC	Germany	41	14	27	41	....	....	....	52	....	....	....	....	....	....	....	....	....	....	....	....	....	....	....	....	....	....
1994-95	Schwenningen Wild Wings	Germany	1	0	0	0	....	....	....	0	....	....	....	....	....	....	....	....	....	....	....	....	....	....	....	....	....	....
1995-96	Schwenningen Wild Wings	Germany	48	19	19	38	....	....	....	91	....	....	....	....	....	....	....	....	....	....	4	2	0	2	8	....	....	....
1996-97	Schwenningen Wild Wings	Germany	48	16	23	39	....	....	....	42	....	....	....	....	....	....	....	....	....	....	5	3	4	7	10	....	....	....
1997-98	Schwenningen Wild Wings	Germany	22	7	13	20	....	....	....	22	....	....	....	....	....	....	....	....	....	....	....	....	....	....	....	....	....	....
	NHL Totals		**44**	**0**	**4**	**4**	**0**	**3**	**3**	**55**	**0**	**0**	**0**	**18**	**0.0**	**10**	**0**	**30**	**4**		**1**	**1**	**0**	**1**	**2**	**0**	**0**	**0**

Signed as a free agent by **Washington**, August 6, 1985.

• MARTIN, Matt

Matthew S. D – L. 6'3", 230 lbs. b: Hamden, CT, 4/30/1971. Toronto's 4th, 66th overall, in 1989.

Season	Club	League	GP	G	A	Pts	AG	AA	APts	PIM	PP	SH	GW	S	%	TGF	PGF	TGA	PGA	+/–	GP	G	A	Pts	PIM	PP	SH	GW
1987-88	South Connecticut Selects	MBAHL	23	3	7	10	....	....	....	....	....	....	....	....	....	....	....	....	....	....	....	....	....	....	....	....	....	....
1988-89	Avon Farms Winged Beavers	Hi-School	25	9	23	32	....	....	....	....	....	....	....	....	....	....	....	....	....	....	....	....	....	....	....	....	....	....
1989-90	Avon Farms Winged Beavers	Hi-School	STATISTICS NOT AVAILABLE																									
1990-91	University of Maine	H-East	35	3	12	15	....	....	....	48	....	....	....	....	....	....	....	....	....	....	....	....	....	....	....	....	....	....
1991-92	University of Maine	H-East	30	4	14	18	....	....	....	46	....	....	....	....	....	....	....	....	....	....	....	....	....	....	....	....	....	....
1992-93	University of Maine	H-East	44	6	26	32	....	....	....	88	....	....	....	....	....	....	....	....	....	....	....	....	....	....	....	....	....	....
	St. John's Maple Leafs	AHL	2	0	0	0	....	....	....	2	....	....	....	....	....	....	....	....	....	....	9	1	5	6	4	....	....	....
1993-94	United States	Nat-Team	39	7	8	15	....	....	....	127	....	....	....	....	....	....	....	....	....	....	....	....	....	....	....	....	....	....
	United States	Olympics	8	0	2	2	....	....	....	8	....	....	....	....	....	....	....	....	....	....	....	....	....	....	....	....	....	....
	Toronto Maple Leafs	**NHL**	**12**	**0**	**1**	**1**	**0**	**1**	**1**	**6**	**0**	**0**	**0**	**6**	**0.0**	**4**	**0**	**5**	**1**	**0**	....	....	....	....	....	....	....	....
	St. John's Maple Leafs	AHL	12	1	5	6	....	....	....	9	....	....	....	....	....	....	....	....	....	....	11	1	5	6	33	....	....	....
1994-95	**Toronto Maple Leafs**	**NHL**	**15**	**0**	**0**	**0**	**0**	**0**	**0**	**13**	**0**	**0**	**0**	**14**	**0.0**	**10**	**0**	**9**	**1**	**2**	....	....	....	....	....	....	....	....
	St. John's Maple Leafs	AHL	49	2	16	18	....	....	....	54	....	....	....	....	....	....	....	....	....	....	....	....	....	....	....	....	....	....
1995-96	**Toronto Maple Leafs**	**NHL**	**13**	**0**	**0**	**0**	**0**	**0**	**0**	**14**	**0**	**0**	**0**	**3**	**0.0**	**5**	**0**	**6**	**0**	**–1**	....	....	....	....	....	....	....	....
1996-97	**Toronto Maple Leafs**	**NHL**	**36**	**0**	**4**	**4**	**0**	**4**	**4**	**38**	**0**	**0**	**0**	**30**	**0.0**	**19**	**0**	**38**	**7**	**–12**	....	....	....	....	....	....	....	....
	St. John's Maple Leafs	AHL	12	1	3	4	....	....	....	4	....	....	....	....	....	....	....	....	....	....	....	....	....	....	....	....	....	....
	United States	WC-A	8	0	0	0	....	....	....	0	....	....	....	....	....	....	....	....	....	....	....	....	....	....	....	....	....	....
1997-98	Chicago Wolves	IHL	78	7	22	29	....	....	....	95	....	....	....	....	....	....	....	....	....	....	19	0	5	5	24	....	....	....
1998-99	Michigan K-Wings	IHL	76	3	12	15	....	....	....	114	....	....	....	....	....	....	....	....	....	....	5	0	0	0	10	....	....	....
99-2000	Michigan K-Wings	IHL	76	0	11	11	....	....	....	66	....	....	....	....	....	....	....	....	....	....	....	....	....	....	....	....	....	....
	NHL Totals		**76**	**0**	**5**	**5**	**0**	**5**	**5**	**71**	**0**	**0**	**0**	**53**	**0.0**	**38**	**0**	**58**	**9**		....	....	....	....	....	....	....	....

Signed as a free agent by **Dallas**, July 24, 1998.

• MARTIN, Pit

Hubert Jacques C – R. 5'9", 170 lbs. b: Noranda, Que., 12/9/1943.

Season	Club	League	GP	G	A	Pts	AG	AA	APts	PIM	PP	SH	GW	S	%	TGF	PGF	TGA	PGA	+/–	GP	G	A	Pts	PIM	PP	SH	GW
1959-60	Hamilton Tiger-Cubs	OHA-Jr.	29	13	12	25	....	....	....	14	....	....	....	....	....	....	....	....	....	....	....	....	....	....	....	....	....	....
1960-61	Hamilton Red Wings	OHA-Jr.	48	20	21	41	....	....	....	17	....	....	....	....	....	....	....	....	....	....	10	7	2	9	8	....	....	....
1961-62	Hamilton Red Wings	OHA-Jr.	48	42	46	88	....	....	....	46	....	....	....	....	....	....	....	....	....	....	10	3	*9	*12	0	....	....	....
	Detroit Red Wings	**NHL**	**1**	**0**	**1**	**1**	**0**	**1**	**1**	**0**	....	....	....	....	....	....	....	....	....	....	....	....	....	....	....	....	....	....
	Hamilton Red Wings	Mem-Cup	14	12	11	23	....	....	....	22	....	....	....	....	....	....	....	....	....	....	....	....	....	....	....	....	....	....
1962-63	Hamilton Red Wings	OHA-Jr.	49	36	49	85	....	....	....	67	....	....	....	....	....	....	....	....	....	....	5	1	1	2	10	....	....	....
	Pittsburgh Hornets	AHL	5	1	2	3	....	....	....	0	....	....	....	....	....	....	....	....	....	....	....	....	....	....	....	....	....	....
1963-64	**Detroit Red Wings**	**NHL**	**50**	**9**	**12**	**21**	**11**	**13**	**24**	**28**	....	....	....	....	....	....	....	....	....	....	**14**	**1**	**4**	**5**	**14**	**1**	**0**	**0**
	Pittsburgh Hornets	AHL	21	3	7	10	....	....	....	2	....	....	....	....	....	....	....	....	....	....	....	....	....	....	....	....	....	....
1964-65	**Detroit Red Wings**	**NHL**	**58**	**8**	**9**	**17**	**10**	**9**	**19**	**32**	....	....	....	....	....	....	....	....	....	....	**3**	**0**	**1**	**1**	**2**	**0**	**0**	**0**
1965-66	Pittsburgh Hornets	AHL	16	6	6	12	....	....	....	26	....	....	....	....	....	....	....	....	....	....	....	....	....	....	....	....	....	....
	Detroit Red Wings	**NHL**	**10**	**1**	**1**	**2**	**1**	**1**	**2**	**0**	....	....	....	....	....	....	....	....	....	....	....	....	....	....	....	....	....	....
	Boston Bruins	**NHL**	**41**	**16**	**11**	**27**	**18**	**10**	**28**	**10**	....	....	....	....	....	....	....	....	....	....	....	....	....	....	....	....	....	....
1966-67	**Boston Bruins**	**NHL**	**70**	**20**	**22**	**42**	**23**	**21**	**44**	**40**	....	....	....	....	....	....	....	....	....	....	....	....	....	....	....	....	....	....
1967-68	**Chicago Black Hawks**	**NHL**	**63**	**16**	**19**	**35**	**19**	**19**	**38**	**36**	**0**	**0**	**2**	**118**	**13.6**	**57**	**6**	**42**	**0**	**9**	**11**	**3**	**6**	**9**	**2**	**0**	**0**	**0**
1968-69	**Chicago Black Hawks**	**NHL**	**76**	**23**	**38**	**61**	**24**	**34**	**58**	**73**	**5**	**0**	**4**	**173**	**13.3**	**92**	**20**	**63**	**0**	**9**	....	....	....	....	....	....	....	....
1969-70	**Chicago Black Hawks**	**NHL**	**73**	**30**	**33**	**63**	**33**	**31**	**64**	**61**	**5**	**0**	**1**	**160**	**18.8**	**86**	**26**	**38**	**0**	**22**	**8**	**3**	**3**	**6**	**4**	**2**	**1**	**0**

Season	Club	League	REGULAR SEASON GP	G	A	Pts	AG	AA	APts	PIM	PP	SH	GW	S	%	TGF	PGF	TGA	PGA	+/–	PLAYOFFS GP	G	A	Pts	PIM	PP	SH	GW
1970-71	**Chicago Black Hawks**	**NHL**	**62**	**22**	**33**	**55**	**22**	**28**	**50**	**40**	**6**	**0**	**5**	**126**	**17.5**	**69**	**18**	**34**	**1**	**18**	**17**	**2**	**7**	**9**	**12**	**0**	**0**	**1**
1971-72	**Chicago Black Hawks**	**NHL**	**78**	**24**	**51**	**75**	**24**	**44**	**68**	**56**	**5**	**1**	**7**	**170**	**14.1**	**101**	**16**	**42**	**1**	**44**	**8**	**4**	**2**	**6**	**4**	**0**	**0**	**1**
1972-73	**Chicago Black Hawks**	**NHL**	**78**	**29**	**61**	**90**	**27**	**49**	**76**	**30**	**4**	**0**	**3**	**185**	**15.7**	**118**	**21**	**77**	**7**	**27**	**15**	**10**	**6**	**16**	**6**	**4**	**0**	**1**
1973-74	**Chicago Black Hawks**	**NHL**	**78**	**30**	**47**	**77**	**29**	**39**	**68**	**43**	**8**	**2**	**4**	**175**	**17.1**	**103**	**27**	**62**	**15**	**29**	**7**	**2**	**0**	**2**	**4**	**1**	**0**	**0**
1974-75	**Chicago Black Hawks**	**NHL**	**70**	**19**	**26**	**45**	**17**	**19**	**36**	**34**	**4**	**1**	**2**	**136**	**14.0**	**70**	**22**	**73**	**22**	**–3**	**8**	**1**	**1**	**2**	**2**	**0**	**0**	**0**
1975-76	**Chicago Black Hawks**	**NHL**	**80**	**32**	**39**	**71**	**28**	**29**	**57**	**44**	**8**	**2**	**4**	**188**	**17.0**	**109**	**43**	**95**	**35**	**6**	**4**	**1**	**0**	**1**	**4**	**0**	**0**	**0**
1976-77	**Chicago Black Hawks**	**NHL**	**75**	**17**	**36**	**53**	**15**	**28**	**43**	**22**	**6**	**1**	**2**	**117**	**14.5**	**78**	**24**	**82**	**24**	**–4**	**2**	**0**	**0**	**0**	**0**	**0**	**0**	**0**
1977-78	**Chicago Black Hawks**	**NHL**	**7**	**1**	**1**	**2**	**1**	**1**	**2**	**0**	**0**	**0**	**0**	**7**	**14.3**	**2**	**0**	**3**	**0**	**–1**	....	....	....	....	....	....	....	....
	Vancouver Canucks	**NHL**	**67**	**15**	**31**	**46**	**14**	**24**	**38**	**36**	**4**	**0**	**0**	**104**	**14.4**	**70**	**25**	**80**	**9**	**–26**	....	....	....	....	....	....	....	....
1978-79	**Vancouver Canucks**	**NHL**	**64**	**12**	**14**	**26**	**10**	**10**	**20**	**24**	**1**	**0**	**1**	**80**	**15.0**	**37**	**6**	**43**	**9**	**–3**	**3**	**0**	**1**	**1**	**2**	**0**	**0**	**0**
	NHL Totals		**1101**	**324**	**485**	**809**	**326**	**410**	**736**	**609**	....	....	....	....	....	....	....	....	....	....	**100**	**27**	**31**	**58**	**56**	....	....	....

OHA-Jr. First All-Star Team (1962) • Won Bill Masterton Trophy (1970) • Played in NHL All-Star Game (1971, 1972, 1973, 1974)

Traded to **Boston** by **Detroit** for Parker MacDonald, December 30, 1965. Traded to **Chicago** by **Boston** with Jack Norris and Gilles Marotte for Phil Esposito, Ken Hodge and Fred Stanfield, May 15, 1967. Traded to **Vancouver** by **Chicago** for future considerations (Murray Bannerman, May 27, 1978), November 4, 1977.

• MARTIN, Rick

Richard Lionel LW – L. 5'11", 179 lbs. b: Verdun, Que., 7/26/1951. Buffalo's 1st, 5th overall, in 1971.

Season	Club	League	GP	G	A	Pts	AG	AA	APts	PIM	PP	SH	GW	S	%	TGF	PGF	TGA	PGA	+/–	GP	G	A	Pts	PIM	PP	SH	GW
1967-68	Thetford Mines Canadiens	QJHL	40	38	35	73	....	....	....	....	....	....	....	....	....	....	....	....	....	....	7	2	0	2	4	....	....	....
1968-69	Montreal Jr. Canadiens	OHA-Jr.	52	22	21	43	....	....	....	27	....	....	....	....	....	....	....	....	....	....	14	3	0	3	2	....	....	....
	Montreal Jr. Canadiens	Mem-Cup	6	2	1	3	....	....	....	12	....	....	....	....	....	....	....	....	....	....	....	....	....	....	....	....	....	....
1969-70	Montreal Jr. Canadiens	OHA-Jr.	34	23	32	55	....	....	....	10	....	....	....	....	....	....	....	....	....	....	16	14	20	34	12	....	....	....
	Montreal Jr. Canadiens	Mem-Cup	12	14	13	27	....	....	....	8	....	....	....	....	....	....	....	....	....	....	....	....	....	....	....	....	....	....
1970-71	Montreal Jr. Canadiens	OHA-Jr.	60	*71	50	121	....	....	....	106	....	....	....	....	....	....	....	....	....	....	11	17	7	24	10	....	....	....
1971-72	**Buffalo Sabres**	**NHL**	**73**	**44**	**30**	**74**	**44**	**26**	**70**	**36**	**19**	**0**	**5**	**266**	**16.5**	**109**	**49**	**98**	**0**	**–38**	....	....	....	....	....	....	....	....
1972-73	Team Canada	Summit-72	DID NOT PLAY																									
	Buffalo Sabres	**NHL**	**75**	**37**	**36**	**73**	**35**	**29**	**64**	**79**	**11**	**0**	**4**	**299**	**12.4**	**120**	**45**	**72**	**1**	**4**	**6**	**3**	**2**	**5**	**12**	**2**	**0**	**0**
1973-74	**Buffalo Sabres**	**NHL**	**78**	**52**	**34**	**86**	**50**	**28**	**78**	**38**	**8**	**0**	**6**	**320**	**16.3**	**121**	**41**	**102**	**0**	**–22**	....	....	....	....	....	....	....	....
1974-75	**Buffalo Sabres**	**NHL**	**68**	**52**	**43**	**95**	**46**	**32**	**78**	**72**	**21**	**0**	**6**	**301**	**17.3**	**143**	**61**	**77**	**0**	**5**	**17**	**7**	**8**	**15**	**20**	**5**	**0**	**1**
1975-76	**Buffalo Sabres**	**NHL**	**80**	**49**	**37**	**86**	**43**	**28**	**71**	**67**	**18**	**0**	**7**	**327**	**15.0**	**147**	**56**	**68**	**0**	**23**	**9**	**4**	**7**	**11**	**12**	**2**	**0**	**1**
1976-77	Canada	Can-Cup	4	3	2	5	....	....	....	0	....	....	....	....	....	....	....	....	....	....	....	....	....	....	....	....	....	....
	Buffalo Sabres	**NHL**	**66**	**36**	**29**	**65**	**33**	**22**	**55**	**58**	**12**	**0**	**6**	**221**	**16.3**	**99**	**32**	**57**	**0**	**10**	**6**	**2**	**1**	**3**	**9**	**1**	**0**	**1**
1977-78	**Buffalo Sabres**	**NHL**	**65**	**28**	**35**	**63**	**25**	**27**	**52**	**16**	**7**	**0**	**6**	**221**	**12.7**	**87**	**21**	**50**	**0**	**16**	**7**	**2**	**4**	**6**	**13**	**1**	**0**	**1**
1978-79	**Buffalo Sabres**	**NHL**	**73**	**32**	**21**	**53**	**27**	**15**	**42**	**35**	**8**	**0**	**3**	**250**	**12.8**	**85**	**26**	**66**	**0**	**–7**	**3**	**0**	**3**	**3**	**0**	**0**	**0**	**0**
1979-80	**Buffalo Sabres**	**NHL**	**80**	**45**	**34**	**79**	**38**	**25**	**63**	**54**	**8**	**0**	**3**	**257**	**17.5**	**115**	**30**	**67**	**0**	**18**	**14**	**6**	**4**	**10**	**8**	**1**	**0**	**0**
1980-81	**Buffalo Sabres**	**NHL**	**23**	**7**	**14**	**21**	**5**	**9**	**14**	**20**	**2**	**0**	**1**	**57**	**12.3**	**29**	**7**	**18**	**0**	**4**	....	....	....	....	....	....	....	....
	Los Angeles Kings	**NHL**	**1**	**1**	**1**	**2**	**1**	**1**	**2**	**0**	**0**	**0**	**0**	**2**	**50.0**	**4**	**2**	**1**	**0**	**1**	**1**	**0**	**0**	**0**	**0**	**0**	**0**	**0**
1981-82	**Los Angeles Kings**	**NHL**	**3**	**1**	**3**	**4**	**1**	**2**	**3**	**2**	**1**	**0**	**0**	**9**	**11.1**	**4**	**2**	**1**	**0**	**1**	....	....	....	....	....	....	....	....
	NHL Totals		**685**	**384**	**317**	**701**	**348**	**244**	**592**	**477**	**115**	**0**	**47**	**2530**	**15.2**	**1063**	**372**	**677**	**1**		**63**	**24**	**29**	**53**	**74**	**12**	**0**	**4**

QJHL First All-Star Team (1968) • OHA-Jr. First All-Star Team (1971) • NHL First All-Star Team (1974, 1975) • NHL Second All-Star Team (1976, 1977) • Played in NHL All-Star Game (1972, 1973, 1974, 1975, 1976, 1977, 1978)

• Suffered eventual career-ending knee injury in game vs. Washington, November 8, 1980. Traded to **LA Kings** by **Buffalo** for LA Kings' 3rd round choice (Colin Chisholm) in 1981 Entry Draft and 1st round choice (Tom Barrasso) in 1983 Entry Draft, March 10, 1981.

• MARTIN, Terry

Terry George LW – L. 5'11", 195 lbs. b: Barrie, Ont., 10/25/1955. Buffalo's 3rd, 44th overall, in 1975.

Season	Club	League	GP	G	A	Pts	AG	AA	APts	PIM	PP	SH	GW	S	%	TGF	PGF	TGA	PGA	+/–	GP	G	A	Pts	PIM	PP	SH	GW
1972-73	London Knights	OMJHL	59	17	22	39	....	....	....	25	....	....	....	....	....	....	....	....	....	....	....	....	....	....	....	....	....	....
1973-74	London Knights	OMJHL	63	33	24	57	....	....	....	38	....	....	....	....	....	....	....	....	....	....	....	....	....	....	....	....	....	....
1974-75	London Knights	OMJHL	70	43	57	100	....	....	....	118	....	....	....	....	....	....	....	....	....	....	....	....	....	....	....	....	....	....
1975-76	**Buffalo Sabres**	**NHL**	**1**	**0**	**0**	**0**	**0**	**0**	**0**	**0**	**0**	**0**	**0**	**0**	**0.0**	**0**	**0**	**0**	**0**	**0**	....	....	....	....	....	....	....	....
	Charlotte Checkers	SHL	25	12	10	22	....	....	....	30	....	....	....	....	....	....	....	....	....	....	9	2	3	5	2	....	....	....
	Hershey Bears	AHL	19	3	6	9	....	....	....	18	....	....	....	....	....	....	....	....	....	....	....	....	....	....	....	....	....	....
1976-77	**Buffalo Sabres**	**NHL**	**62**	**11**	**12**	**23**	**10**	**9**	**19**	**8**	**1**	**0**	**0**	**72**	**15.3**	**40**	**1**	**33**	**0**	**6**	**3**	**0**	**2**	**2**	**5**	**0**	**0**	**0**
	Hershey Bears	AHL	12	1	4	5	....	....	....	12	....	....	....	....	....	....	....	....	....	....	....	....	....	....	....	....	....	....
1977-78	**Buffalo Sabres**	**NHL**	**21**	**3**	**2**	**5**	**3**	**2**	**5**	**9**	**0**	**0**	**2**	**17**	**17.6**	**6**	**0**	**7**	**0**	**–1**	**8**	**2**	**0**	**2**	**5**	**0**	**0**	**0**
	Hershey Bears	AHL	4	2	1	3	....	....	....	2	....	....	....	....	....	....	....	....	....	....	....	....	....	....	....	....	....	....
1978-79	**Buffalo Sabres**	**NHL**	**64**	**6**	**8**	**14**	**5**	**6**	**11**	**33**	**1**	**0**	**0**	**38**	**15.8**	**29**	**4**	**50**	**8**	**–17**	....	....	....	....	....	....	....	....
1979-80	**Quebec Nordiques**	**NHL**	**3**	**0**	**0**	**0**	**0**	**0**	**0**	**0**	**0**	**0**	**0**	**4**	**0.0**	**0**	**0**	**5**	**0**	**–5**	....	....	....	....	....	....	....	....
	Syracuse Firebirds	AHL	18	9	9	18	....	....	....	6	....	....	....	....	....	....	....	....	....	....	....	....	....	....	....	....	....	....
	Toronto Maple Leafs	**NHL**	**37**	**6**	**15**	**21**	**5**	**11**	**16**	**2**	**1**	**0**	**2**	**40**	**15.0**	**41**	**2**	**34**	**1**	**6**	**3**	**2**	**0**	**2**	**7**	**0**	**0**	**0**
	New Brunswick Hawks	AHL	3	0	1	1	....	....	....	0	....	....	....	....	....	....	....	....	....	....	....	....	....	....	....	....	....	....
1980-81	**Toronto Maple Leafs**	**NHL**	**69**	**23**	**14**	**37**	**18**	**9**	**27**	**32**	**1**	**0**	**4**	**111**	**20.7**	**71**	**3**	**69**	**16**	**15**	**3**	**0**	**0**	**0**	**0**	**0**	**0**	**0**
1981-82	**Toronto Maple Leafs**	**NHL**	**72**	**25**	**24**	**49**	**20**	**16**	**36**	**39**	**4**	**0**	**1**	**133**	**18.8**	**74**	**17**	**89**	**14**	**–18**	....	....	....	....	....	....	....	....
1982-83	**Toronto Maple Leafs**	**NHL**	**76**	**14**	**13**	**27**	**11**	**9**	**20**	**28**	**3**	**1**	**0**	**95**	**14.7**	**48**	**9**	**92**	**24**	**–29**	**4**	**0**	**0**	**0**	**9**	**0**	**0**	**0**
1983-84	**Toronto Maple Leafs**	**NHL**	**63**	**15**	**10**	**25**	**12**	**7**	**19**	**51**	**2**	**2**	**1**	**62**	**24.2**	**43**	**8**	**66**	**23**	**–8**	....	....	....	....	....	....	....	....
1984-85	**Edmonton Oilers**	**NHL**	**4**	**0**	**2**	**2**	**0**	**1**	**1**	**0**	**0**	**0**	**0**	**6**	**0.0**	**3**	**0**	**0**	**0**	**3**	....	....	....	....	....	....	....	....
	Nova Scotia Oilers	AHL	28	17	11	28	....	....	....	4	....	....	....	....	....	....	....	....	....	....	....	....	....	....	....	....	....	....
	Minnesota North Stars	**NHL**	**7**	**1**	**1**	**2**	**1**	**1**	**2**	**0**	**0**	**0**	**0**	**5**	**20.0**	**3**	**1**	**2**	**0**	**0**	....	....	....	....	....	....	....	....
1985-86	Springfield Indians	AHL	72	19	22	41	....	....	....	17	....	....	....	....	....	....	....	....	....	....	....	....	....	....	....	....	....	....
1986-87	Newmarket Saints	AHL	72	8	7	15	....	....	....	8	....	....	....	....	....	....	....	....	....	....	....	....	....	....	....	....	....	....
1987-88	Toronto Marlboros	OHL	DID NOT PLAY – COACHING																									
	NHL Totals		**479**	**104**	**101**	**205**	**85**	**71**	**156**	**202**	**13**	**3**	**10**	**583**	**17.8**	**358**	**45**	**447**	**86**		**21**	**4**	**2**	**6**	**26**	**0**	**0**	**0**

Claimed by **Quebec** from **Buffalo** in Expansion Draft, June 13, 1979. Traded to **Toronto** by **Quebec** with Dave Farrish for Reg Thomas, December 13, 1979. Claimed by **Edmonton** from **Toronto** in Waiver Draft, October 9, 1984. Traded to **Minnesota** by **Edmonton** with Gord Sherven for Mark Napier, January 24, 1985.

• MARTIN, Tom

Thomas Raymond RW – R. 5'9", 170 lbs. b: Toronto, Ont., 10/16/1947. Toronto's 1st, 5th overall, in 1964.

Season	Club	League	GP	G	A	Pts	AG	AA	APts	PIM	PP	SH	GW	S	%	TGF	PGF	TGA	PGA	+/–	GP	G	A	Pts	PIM	PP	SH	GW
1965-66	Toronto Marlboros	OHA-Jr.	48	19	21	40	....	....	....	23	....	....	....	....	....	....	....	....	....	....	11	2	2	4	2	....	....	....
1966-67	Toronto Marlboros	OHA-Jr.	42	18	28	46	....	....	....	29	....	....	....	....	....	....	....	....	....	....	17	12	12	24	4	....	....	....
	Toronto Marlboros	Mem-Cup	9	9	6	15	....	....	....	9	....	....	....	....	....	....	....	....	....	....	....	....	....	....	....	....	....	....
1967-68	Toronto Marlboros	OHA-Jr.	54	37	48	85	....	....	....	43	....	....	....	....	....	....	....	....	....	....	5	3	3	6	16	....	....	....
	Toronto Maple Leafs	**NHL**	**3**	**1**	**0**	**1**	**1**	**0**	**1**	**0**	**1**	**0**	**0**	**2**	**50.0**	**1**	**1**	**0**	**0**	**0**	....	....	....	....	....	....	....	....
	Tulsa Oilers	CPHL	....	....	....	....	....	....	....	....	....	....	....	....	....	....	....	....	....	....	1	0	0	0	0	....	....	....
1968-69	Tulsa Oilers	CHL	4	2	0	2	....	....	....	4	....	....	....	....	....	....	....	....	....	....	....	....	....	....	....	....	....	....
	Ottawa Nationals	OHA-Sr.	6	3	8	11	....	....	....	8	....	....	....	....	....	....	....	....	....	....	....	....	....	....	....	....	....	....
1969-70	Tulsa Oilers	CHL	65	21	35	56	....	....	....	26	....	....	....	....	....	....	....	....	....	....	6	5	3	8	4	....	....	....
1970-71	Fort Worth Wings	CHL	59	23	33	56	....	....	....	31	....	....	....	....	....	....	....	....	....	....	....	....	....	....	....	....	....	....
1971-72	Fort Worth Wings	CHL	31	14	21	35	....	....	....	17	....	....	....	....	....	....	....	....	....	....	....	....	....	....	....	....	....	....
	Tidewater Red Wings	AHL	42	16	13	29	....	....	....	23	....	....	....	....	....	....	....	....	....	....	....	....	....	....	....	....	....	....
1972-73	Ottawa Nationals	WHA	75	19	27	46	....	....	....	27	....	....	....	....	....	....	....	....	....	....	5	0	5	5	2	....	....	....
1973-74	Toronto Toros	WHA	74	25	32	57	....	....	....	14	....	....	....	....	....	....	....	....	....	....	12	7	3	10	2	....	....	....
1974-75	Toronto Toros	WHA	64	15	17	32	....	....	....	18	....	....	....	....	....	....	....	....	....	....	5	1	5	6	0	....	....	....
1975-76	Lulea HF	Sweden-2	20	23	19	*42	....	....	....	....	....	....	....	....	....	....	....	....	....	....	....	....	....	....	....	....	....	....
1976-77	MoDo AIK	Sweden	33	9	8	17	....	....	....	46	....	....	....	....	....	....	....	....	....	....	2	0	1	1	4	....	....	....
1977-78	IK Viking	Sweden-3	18	21	14	35	....	....	....	....	....	....	....	....	....	....	....	....	....	....	....	....	....	....	....	....	....	....
1978-79	IK Viking	Sweden-2	23	11	17	28	....	....	....	*91	....	....	....	....	....	....	....	....	....	....	....	....	....	....	....	....	....	....
	NHL Totals		**3**	**1**	**0**	**1**	**1**	**0**	**1**	**0**	**1**	**0**	**0**	**2**	**50.0**	**1**	**1**	**0**	**0**		....	....	....	....	....	....	....	....
	Other Major League Totals		213	59	76	135	....	....	....	59	....	....	....	....	....	....	....	....	....	....	22	8	13	21	4	....	....	....

Traded to **Phoenix** (WHL) by **Toronto** for cash, May 22, 1970. Claimed by **Detroit** from **Phoenix** (WHL) in Intra-League Draft, June 9, 1970. Selected by **Ontario-Ottawa** (WHA) in 1972 WHA General Player Draft, February 12, 1972. Transferred to **Toronto** (WHA) after **Ottawa** (WHA) franchise relocated, May, 1973. Traded to **San Diego** (WHA) by **Toronto** (WHA) for the rights to Angelo Moretto, June 20, 1975.

• MARTIN, Tom

LW – L. 6'2", 200 lbs. b: Kelowna, B.C., 5/11/1965. Winnipeg's 2nd, 74th overall, in 1982.

Season	Club	League	GP	G	A	Pts	AG	AA	APts	PIM	PP	SH	GW	S	%	TGF	PGF	TGA	PGA	+/–	Playoffs GP	G	A	Pts	PIM	PP	SH	GW
1979-80	Victoria Kings	BCAHA	STATISTICS NOT AVAILABLE																									
1980-81	Kelowna Buckaroos	BCJHL	43	17	34	51				143																		
1981-82	Kelowna Buckaroos	BCJHL	43	32	34	66				194																		
1982-83	University of Denver	WCHA	37	8	18	26				128																		
1983-84	Victoria Cougars	WHL	60	30	45	75				261																		
	Sherbrooke Jets	AHL	5	0	0	0				16																		
1984-85	**Winnipeg Jets**	**NHL**	**8**	**1**	**0**	**1**	**1**	**0**	**1**	**42**	**0**	**0**	**0**	**5**	**20.0**	**1**	**0**	**0**	**0**	**1**	**3**	**0**	**0**	**0**	**2**	**0**	**0**	**0**
	Sherbrooke Canadiens	AHL	58	4	15	19				212												12	1	1	2	72			
1985-86	**Winnipeg Jets**	**NHL**	**5**	**0**	**0**	**0**	**0**	**0**	**0**	**0**	**0**	**0**	**0**	**1**	**0.0**	**0**	**0**	**0**	**0**	**0**								
	Sherbrooke Canadiens	AHL	69	11	18	29				227																		
1986-87	**Winnipeg Jets**	**NHL**	**11**	**1**	**0**	**1**	**1**	**0**	**1**	**49**	**0**	**0**	**0**	**2**	**50.0**	**1**	**0**	**0**	**0**	**1**								
	Adirondack Red Wings	AHL	18	5	6	11				57																		
1987-88	**Hartford Whalers**	**NHL**	**5**	**1**	**2**	**3**	**1**	**1**	**2**	**14**	**0**	**0**	**0**	**8**	**12.5**	**3**	**0**	**4**	**0**	**–1**								
	Binghamton Whalers	AHL	71	28	61	89				344												3	0	0	0	18			
1988-89	**Minnesota North Stars**	**NHL**	**4**	**1**	**1**	**2**	**1**	**1**	**2**	**4**	**0**	**0**	**0**	**6**	**16.7**	**2**	**0**	**1**	**0**	**1**								
	Hartford Whalers	**NHL**	**38**	**7**	**6**	**13**	**6**	**4**	**10**	**113**	**0**	**0**	**1**	**40**	**17.5**	**21**	**0**	**13**	**0**	**8**	**1**	**0**	**0**	**0**	**4**	**0**	**0**	**0**
1989-90	**Hartford Whalers**	**NHL**	**21**	**1**	**2**	**3**	**1**	**1**	**2**	**27**	**0**	**0**	**0**	**13**	**7.7**	**6**	**0**	**6**	**0**	**0**								
	Binghamton Whalers	AHL	24	4	10	14				113																		
1990-91	New Haven Nighthawks	AHL	22	11	7	18				88																		
	NHL Totals		**92**	**12**	**11**	**23**	**11**	**7**	**18**	**249**	**0**	**0**	**1**	**75**	**16.0**	**34**	**0**	**24**	**0**		**4**	**0**	**0**	**0**	**6**	**0**	**0**	**0**

AHL First All-Star Team (1988)

Rights traded to **Victoria** (WHL) by **Seattle** (WHL) for used bus and future considerations, January, 1983. Signed as a free agent by **Hartford**, July 29, 1987. Claimed by **Minnesota** from **Hartford** in Waiver Draft, October 3, 1988. Claimed on waivers by **Hartford** from **Minnesota**, December, 1988. Signed as a free agent by **LA Kings**, July, 1990.

• MARTINEAU, Don

Donald Jean RW – R. 6', 190 lbs. b: Kimberley, B.C., 4/25/1952. Atlanta's 4th, 50th overall, in 1972.

Season	Club	League	GP	G	A	Pts	AG	AA	APts	PIM	PP	SH	GW	S	%	TGF	PGF	TGA	PGA	+/–	Playoffs GP	G	A	Pts	PIM	PP	SH	GW
1969-70	Estevan Bruins	WCJHL	56	4	3	7				106											3	0	0	0	14			
1970-71	Estevan Bruins	WCJHL	66	18	32	50				126											7	0	3	3	8			
1971-72	New Westminster Bruins	WCJHL	67	25	35	60				221											5	1	2	3	15			
1972-73	Omaha Knights	CHL	72	22	28	50				170											11	1	2	3	*36			
1973-74	**Atlanta Flames**	**NHL**	**4**	**0**	**0**	**0**	**0**	**0**	**0**	**2**	**0**	**0**	**0**	**3**	**0.0**	**0**	**0**	**3**	**0**	**–3**								
	Omaha Knights	CHL	48	12	26	38				122											5	2	2	4	18			
1974-75	**Minnesota North Stars**	**NHL**	**76**	**6**	**9**	**15**	**5**	**7**	**12**	**61**	**0**	**0**	**0**	**54**	**11.1**	**21**	**0**	**34**	**0**	**–13**								
1975-76	**Detroit Red Wings**	**NHL**	**9**	**0**	**1**	**1**	**0**	**1**	**1**	**0**	**0**	**0**	**0**	**1**	**0.0**	**1**	**0**	**2**	**0**	**–1**								
	New Haven Nighthawks	AHL	64	15	20	35				129											3	0	1	1	2			
1976-77	**Detroit Red Wings**	**NHL**	**1**	**0**	**0**	**0**	**0**	**0**	**0**	**0**	**0**	**0**	**0**	**0**	**0.0**	**0**	**0**	**0**	**0**	**0**								
	Kansas City Blues	CHL	76	27	38	65				57											10	2	1	3	2			
1977-78	Kansas City Red Wings	CHL	61	16	15	31				31																		
	NHL Totals		**90**	**6**	**10**	**16**	**5**	**8**	**13**	**63**	**0**	**0**	**0**	**58**	**10.3**	**22**	**0**	**39**	**0**									

CHL First All-Star Team (1977)

Traded to **Minnesota** by **Atlanta** with John Flesch for Buster Harvey and Jerry Byers, May 27, 1974. Traded to **Detroit** by **Minnesota** for Pierre Jarry, November 25, 1975.

• MARTINI, Darcy

Darcy R. D – L. 6'4", 220 lbs. b: Castlegar, B.C., 1/30/1969. Edmonton's 8th, 162nd overall, in 1989.

Season	Club	League	GP	G	A	Pts	AG	AA	APts	PIM	PP	SH	GW	S	%	TGF	PGF	TGA	PGA	+/–	Playoffs GP	G	A	Pts	PIM	PP	SH	GW
1984-85	Castlegar Rebels	KIJHL	38	4	17	21				58																		
1985-86	Castlegar Rebels	KIJHL	38	8	28	36				180																		
1986-87	Castlegar Rebels	KIJHL	40	12	53	65				260																		
1987-88	Vernon Lakers	BCJHL	48	9	26	35				193											12	2	9	11	28			
1988-89	Michigan Tech Huskies	WCHA	35	1	2	3				103																		
1989-90	Michigan Tech Huskies	WCHA	36	3	6	9				151																		
1990-91	Michigan Tech Huskies	WCHA	34	10	13	23				*184																		
1991-92	Michigan Tech Huskies	WCHA	17	5	13	18				58																		
1992-93	Cape Breton Oilers	AHL	47	1	6	7				36											2	0	1	1	0			
	Wheeling Thunderbirds	ECHL	6	0	2	2				2																		
1993-94	**Edmonton Oilers**	**NHL**	**2**	**0**	**0**	**0**	**0**	**0**	**0**	**0**	**0**	**0**	**0**	**0**	**0.0**	**0**	**0**	**1**	**0**	**–1**								
	Cape Breton Oilers	AHL	65	18	38	56				131											5	1	3	4	26			
1994-95	Cape Breton Oilers	AHL	31	2	13	15				75																		
	Portland Pirates	AHL	22	3	6	9				28																		
	Minnesota Moose	IHL	10	3	1	4				10											1	0	0	0	2			
1995-96	Los Angeles Ice Dogs	IHL	49	15	31	46				50																		
	San Francisco Spiders	IHL	17	3	4	7				10											4	0	2	2	2			
1996-97	KAC Klagenfurt	Austria	54	22	22	44				129																		
1997-98	KAC Klagenfurt	Austria	45	11	16	27				94																		
1998-99	Hannover Scorpions	Germany	49	12	17	29				202																		
99-2000	KAC Klagenfurt	IEL	29	9	6	15				50																		
	KAC Klagenfurt	Austria	15	1	9	10				62																		
	NHL Totals		**2**	**0**	**0**	**0**	**0**	**0**	**0**	**0**	**0**	**0**	**0**	**0**	**0.0**	**0**	**0**	**1**	**0**									

• MARTINS, Steve

C – L. 5'9", 175 lbs. b: Gatineau, Que., 4/13/1972. Hartford's 1st, 5th overall, in 1994 Supplemental Draft.

Season	Club	League	GP	G	A	Pts	AG	AA	APts	PIM	PP	SH	GW	S	%	TGF	PGF	TGA	PGA	+/–	Playoffs GP	G	A	Pts	PIM	PP	SH	GW
1988-89	L'Outaouais Frontaliers	QAAA	38	18	33	51																						
1989-90	Choate-Rosemary Wild Boars	Hi-School	STATISTICS NOT AVAILABLE																									
1990-91	Choate-Rosemary Wild Boars	Hi-School	STATISTICS NOT AVAILABLE																									
1991-92	Harvard University	ECAC	20	13	14	27				26																		
1992-93	Harvard University	ECAC	18	6	8	14				40																		
1993-94	Harvard University	ECAC	32	25	35	60				*93																		
1994-95	Harvard University	ECAC	28	15	23	38				93																		
1995-96	**Hartford Whalers**	**NHL**	**23**	**1**	**3**	**4**	**1**	**2**	**3**	**8**	**0**	**0**	**0**	**27**	**3.7**	**7**	**0**	**12**	**2**	**–3**								
	Springfield Falcons	AHL	30	9	20	29				10																		
1996-97	**Hartford Whalers**	**NHL**	**2**	**0**	**1**	**1**	**0**	**1**	**1**	**0**	**0**	**0**	**0**	**2**	**0.0**	**1**	**0**	**1**	**0**	**0**								
	Springfield Falcons	AHL	63	12	31	43				78											17	1	3	4	26			
1997-98	**Carolina Hurricanes**	**NHL**	**3**	**0**	**0**	**0**	**0**	**0**	**0**	**0**	**0**	**0**	**0**	**0**	**0.0**	**0**	**0**	**0**	**0**	**0**								
	Chicago Wolves	IHL	78	20	41	61				122											21	6	14	20	28			
1998-99	**Ottawa Senators**	**NHL**	**36**	**4**	**3**	**7**	**5**	**3**	**8**	**10**	**1**	**0**	**1**	**27**	**14.8**	**9**	**2**	**5**	**2**	**4**								
	Detroit Vipers	IHL	4	1	6	7				16																		
99-2000	**Ottawa Senators**	**NHL**	**2**	**1**	**0**	**1**	**1**	**0**	**1**	**0**	**0**	**0**	**0**	**3**	**33.3**	**1**	**0**	**2**	**0**	**–1**								
	Tampa Bay Lightning	**NHL**	**57**	**5**	**7**	**12**	**6**	**6**	**12**	**37**	**0**	**1**	**1**	**62**	**8.1**	**20**	**1**	**45**	**15**	**–11**								
	NHL Totals		**123**	**11**	**14**	**25**	**13**	**12**	**25**	**55**	**1**	**1**	**2**	**121**	**9.1**	**38**	**3**	**65**	**19**									

ECAC First All-Star Team (1994) • NCAA East First All-American Team (1994) • NCAA Final Four All-Tournament Team (1994)

Transferred to **Carolina** after **Hartford** franchise relocated, June 25, 1997. Signed as a free agent by **Ottawa**, July 20, 1998. Claimed on waivers by **Tampa Bay** from **Ottawa**, October 29, 1999.

• MARTINSON, Steve

LW – L. 6'1", 205 lbs. b: Minnetonka, MN, 6/21/1959.

Season	Club	League	GP	G	A	Pts	AG	AA	APts	PIM	PP	SH	GW	S	%	TGF	PGF	TGA	PGA	+/–	Playoffs GP	G	A	Pts	PIM	PP	SH	GW
1980-81	St. Cloud State Huskies	NCAA-2	31	19	21	40				57																		
1981-82	Toledo Goaldiggers	IHL	35	12	18	30				128																		
1982-83	Toledo Goaldiggers	IHL	32	9	10	19				111																		
	Birmingham South Stars	CHL	43	4	5	9				184											13	1	2	3	*80			
1983-84	Tulsa Oilers	CHL	42	3	6	9				240											6	0	0	0	43			
1984-85	Toledo Goaldiggers	IHL	54	4	10	14				300											2	0	0	0	21			
1985-86	Hershey Bears	AHL	69	3	6	9				*432											3	0	0	0	56			

Season	Club	League	GP	G	A	Pts	AG	AA	APts	PIM	PP	SH	GW	S	%	TGF	PGF	TGA	PGA	+/-	GP	G	A	Pts	PIM	PP	SH	GW
			REGULAR SEASON																		PLAYOFFS							
1986-87	Hershey Bears	AHL	17	0	3	3	....	....	....	85	....	....	....	....	....	....	....	....	....	....	....	....	....	....	....	....	....	....
	Adirondack Red Wings	AHL	14	1	1	2	....	....	....	78	....	....	....	....	....	....	....	....	....	....	11	2	0	2	108	....	....	....
1987-88	**Detroit Red Wings**	**NHL**	**10**	**1**	**1**	**2**	**1**	**1**	**2**	**84**	**0**	**0**	**1**	**3**	**33.3**	**3**	**0**	**0**	**0**	**3**	....	....	....	....	....	....	....	....
	Adirondack Red Wings	AHL	32	6	8	14	....	....	....	146	....	....	....	....	....	....	....	....	....	....	6	1	2	3	66	....	....	....
1988-89	**Montreal Canadiens**	**NHL**	**25**	**1**	**0**	**1**	**1**	**0**	**1**	**87**	**0**	**0**	**1**	**8**	**12.5**	**1**	**0**	**2**	**0**	**–1**	**1**	**0**	**0**	**0**	**10**	**0**	**0**	**0**
	Sherbrooke Canadiens	AHL	10	5	7	12	....	....	....	61	....	....	....	....	....	....	....	....	....	....	....	....	....	....	....	....	....	....
1989-90	**Montreal Canadiens**	**NHL**	**13**	**0**	**0**	**0**	**0**	**0**	**0**	**64**	**0**	**0**	**0**	**2**	**0.0**	**0**	**0**	**2**	**0**	**–2**	....	....	....	....	....	....	....	....
	Sherbrooke Canadiens	AHL	37	6	20	26	....	....	....	113	....	....	....	....	....	....	....	....	....	....	....	....	....	....	....	....	....	....
1990-91	San Diego Gulls	IHL	53	16	24	40	....	....	....	268	....	....	....	....	....	....	....	....	....	....	....	....	....	....	....	....	....	....
1991-92	**Minnesota North Stars**	**NHL**	**1**	**0**	**0**	**0**	**0**	**0**	**0**	**9**	**0**	**0**	**0**	**0**	**0.0**	**0**	**0**	**0**	**0**	**0**	....	....	....	....	....	....	....	....
	San Diego Gulls	IHL	70	18	15	33	....	....	....	279	....	....	....	....	....	....	....	....	....	....	4	1	1	2	15	....	....	....
1992-93	San Diego Gulls	IHL	10	0	4	4	....	....	....	55	....	....	....	....	....	....	....	....	....	....	....	....	....	....	....	....	....	....
1993-94			DID NOT PLAY																									
1994-95	Houston Aeros	IHL	6	0	1	1	....	....	....	30	....	....	....	....	....	....	....	....	....	....	....	....	....	....	....	....	....	....
	Fresno Falcons	SunHL	1	0	0	0	....	....	....	2	....	....	....	....	....	....	....	....	....	....	....	....	....	....	....	....	....	....
1995-96	San Diego Gulls	WCHL	1	0	0	0	....	....	....	0	....	....	....	....	....	....	....	....	....	....	....	....	....	....	....	....	....	....
1996-2000	San Diego Gulls	WCHL	DID NOT PLAY – COACHING																									
	NHL Totals		**49**	**2**	**1**	**3**	**2**	**1**	**3**	**244**	**0**	**0**	**2**	**13**	**15.4**	**4**	**0**	**4**	**0**		**1**	**0**	**0**	**0**	**10**	**0**	**0**	**0**

Signed as a free agent by **Philadelphia**, September 30, 1985. Signed as a free agent by **Detroit**, October 3, 1987. Signed as a free agent by **Montreal**, August 2, 1988. Signed as a free agent by **Winnipeg**, August 28, 1990. Signed as a free agent by **Minnesota**, October 1, 1991.

• MARUK, Dennis

Dennis John C – L. 5'8", 175 lbs. b: Toronto, Ont., 11/17/1955. California's 2nd, 21st overall, in 1975.

Season	Club	League	GP	G	A	Pts	AG	AA	APts	PIM	PP	SH	GW	S	%	TGF	PGF	TGA	PGA	+/-	GP	G	A	Pts	PIM	PP	SH	GW
1970-1972	Markham Waxers	OHA-B	STATISTICS NOT AVAILABLE																									
1971-72	Toronto Marlboros	OMJHL	8	2	1	3	....	....	....	4	....	....	....	....	....	....	....	....	....	....	....	....	....	....	....	....	....	....
1972-73	London Knights	OMJHL	59	46	67	113	....	....	....	54	....	....	....	....	....	....	....	....	....	....	....	....	....	....	....	....	....	....
1973-74	London Knights	OMJHL	67	47	65	112	....	....	....	61	....	....	....	....	....	....	....	....	....	....	....	....	....	....	....	....	....	....
1974-75	London Knights	OMJHL	65	66	79	145	....	....	....	53	....	....	....	....	....	....	....	....	....	....	....	....	....	....	....	....	....	....
1975-76	**California Golden Seals**	**NHL**	**80**	**30**	**32**	**62**	**26**	**24**	**50**	**44**	**7**	**5**	**3**	**233**	**12.9**	**88**	**26**	**93**	**25**	**–6**	....	....	....	....	....	....	....	....
1976-77	**Cleveland Barons**	**NHL**	**80**	**28**	**50**	**78**	**25**	**39**	**64**	**68**	**4**	**0**	**1**	**268**	**10.4**	**104**	**27**	**87**	**14**	**4**	....	....	....	....	....	....	....	....
1977-78	**Cleveland Barons**	**NHL**	**76**	**36**	**35**	**71**	**33**	**27**	**60**	**50**	**4**	**2**	**4**	**198**	**18.2**	**85**	**17**	**107**	**13**	**–26**	....	....	....	....	....	....	....	....
	Canada	WEC-A	10	6	1	7	....	....	....	2	....	....	....	....	....	....	....	....	....	....	....	....	....	....	....	....	....	....
1978-79	**Minnesota North Stars**	**NHL**	**2**	**0**	**0**	**0**	**0**	**0**	**0**	**0**	**0**	**0**	**0**	**2**	**0.0**	**0**	**0**	**1**	**0**	**–1**	....	....	....	....	....	....	....	....
	Washington Capitals	**NHL**	**76**	**31**	**59**	**90**	**27**	**43**	**70**	**71**	**6**	**2**	**3**	**189**	**16.4**	**115**	**38**	**136**	**45**	**–14**	....	....	....	....	....	....	....	....
	Canada	WEC-A	7	1	1	2	....	....	....	2	....	....	....	....	....	....	....	....	....	....	....	....	....	....	....	....	....	....
1979-80	**Washington Capitals**	**NHL**	**27**	**10**	**17**	**27**	**8**	**12**	**20**	**8**	**1**	**1**	**0**	**58**	**17.2**	**35**	**12**	**27**	**4**	**0**	....	....	....	....	....	....	....	....
1980-81	**Washington Capitals**	**NHL**	**80**	**50**	**47**	**97**	**39**	**31**	**70**	**87**	**16**	**2**	**5**	**242**	**20.7**	**119**	**42**	**93**	**9**	**–7**	....	....	....	....	....	....	....	....
	Canada	WEC-A	8	5	3	8	....	....	....	6	....	....	....	....	....	....	....	....	....	....	....	....	....	....	....	....	....	....
1981-82	Washington Capitals	DN-Cup	4	2	2	4	....	....	....	....	....	....	....	....	....	....	....	....	....	....	....	....	....	....	....	....	....	....
	Washington Capitals	**NHL**	**80**	**60**	**76**	**136**	**48**	**51**	**99**	**128**	**20**	**2**	**1**	**268**	**22.4**	**168**	**73**	**104**	**5**	**–4**	....	....	....	....	....	....	....	....
1982-83	**Washington Capitals**	**NHL**	**80**	**31**	**50**	**81**	**25**	**35**	**60**	**71**	**12**	**0**	**2**	**185**	**16.8**	**113**	**43**	**91**	**0**	**–21**	**4**	**1**	**1**	**2**	**2**	**0**	**0**	**0**
	Canada	WEC-A	10	4	3	7	....	....	....	4	....	....	....	....	....	....	....	....	....	....	....	....	....	....	....	....	....	....
1983-84	**Minnesota North Stars**	**NHL**	**71**	**17**	**43**	**60**	**14**	**29**	**43**	**42**	**7**	**0**	**2**	**130**	**13.1**	**82**	**30**	**74**	**5**	**–17**	**16**	**5**	**5**	**10**	**8**	**1**	**1**	**0**
1984-85	**Minnesota North Stars**	**NHL**	**71**	**19**	**41**	**60**	**15**	**28**	**43**	**56**	**5**	**0**	**3**	**126**	**15.1**	**86**	**31**	**68**	**11**	**–2**	**9**	**4**	**7**	**11**	**12**	**3**	**0**	**1**
1985-86	**Minnesota North Stars**	**NHL**	**70**	**21**	**37**	**58**	**17**	**25**	**42**	**67**	**1**	**0**	**2**	**135**	**15.6**	**76**	**12**	**51**	**0**	**13**	**5**	**4**	**9**	**13**	**4**	**1**	**0**	**0**
1986-87	**Minnesota North Stars**	**NHL**	**67**	**16**	**30**	**46**	**14**	**22**	**36**	**52**	**4**	**0**	**0**	**144**	**11.1**	**71**	**17**	**54**	**5**	**5**	....	....	....	....	....	....	....	....
1987-88	**Minnesota North Stars**	**NHL**	**22**	**7**	**4**	**11**	**6**	**3**	**9**	**15**	**2**	**0**	**0**	**45**	**15.6**	**18**	**5**	**22**	**10**	**1**	....	....	....	....	....	....	....	....
1988-89	**Minnesota North Stars**	**NHL**	**6**	**0**	**1**	**1**	**0**	**1**	**1**	**2**	**0**	**0**	**0**	**6**	**0.0**	**3**	**0**	**3**	**0**	**0**	....	....	....	....	....	....	....	....
	Kalamazoo Wings	IHL	5	1	5	6	....	....	....	4	....	....	....	....	....	....	....	....	....	....	....	....	....	....	....	....	....	....
1989-1998			OUT OF HOCKEY – RETIRED																									
1998-99	Lake Charles Ice Pirates	WPHL	6	0	2	2	....	....	....	4	....	....	....	....	....	....	....	....	....	....	3	0	0	0	2	....	....	....
	NHL Totals		**888**	**356**	**522**	**878**	**297**	**370**	**667**	**761**	**89**	**14**	**26**	**2229**	**16.0**	**1163**	**373**	**1011**	**146**		**34**	**14**	**22**	**36**	**26**	**5**	**1**	**1**

Won Metro OHA-B Rookie-of-the-Year Award (1971) • Played in NHL All-Star Game (1978, 1982)

Transferred to **Cleveland** after **California** franchise relocated, August 26, 1976. Protected by **Minnesota** prior to **Minnesota-Cleveland** Dispersal Draft, June 15, 1978. Traded to **Washington** by **Minnesota** for Pittsburgh's 1st round choice (previously acquired, Minnesota selected Tom McCarthy) in 1979 Entry Draft, October 18, 1978. Traded to **Minnesota** by **Washington** for Minnesota's 2nd round choice (Stephen Leach) in 1984 Entry Draft, July 5, 1983. Signed as a free agent by **Lake Charles** (WPHL), March 3, 1999. • Played w/ RHI's Minnesota Blue Ox in 1995 (2-0-0-0-11).

• MASTERS, Jamie

James Edward D – R. 6'1", 190 lbs. b: Toronto, Ont., 4/14/1955. St. Louis' 2nd, 36th overall, in 1975.

Season	Club	League	GP	G	A	Pts	AG	AA	APts	PIM	PP	SH	GW	S	%	TGF	PGF	TGA	PGA	+/-	GP	G	A	Pts	PIM	PP	SH	GW
1972-73	Ottawa 67's	OMJHL	59	9	19	28	....	....	....	44	....	....	....	....	....	....	....	....	....	....	9	1	4	5	10	....	....	....
1973-74	Ottawa 67's	OMJHL	61	6	29	35	....	....	....	28	....	....	....	....	....	....	....	....	....	....	6	1	0	1	14	....	....	....
1974-75	Ottawa 67's	OMJHL	69	26	69	95	....	....	....	80	....	....	....	....	....	....	....	....	....	....	7	0	8	8	14	....	....	....
1975-76	**St. Louis Blues**	**NHL**	**7**	**0**	**0**	**0**	**0**	**0**	**0**	**0**	**0**	**0**	**0**	**1**	**0.0**	**4**	**0**	**1**	**1**	**4**	**1**	**0**	**0**	**0**	**0**	**0**	**0**	**0**
	Providence Reds	AHL	62	7	27	34	....	....	....	86	....	....	....	....	....	....	....	....	....	....	1	1	0	1	2	....	....	....
1976-77	**St. Louis Blues**	**NHL**	**16**	**1**	**7**	**8**	**1**	**5**	**6**	**2**	**1**	**0**	**0**	**22**	**4.5**	**11**	**8**	**12**	**2**	**–7**	**1**	**0**	**0**	**0**	**0**	**0**	**0**	**0**
	Kansas City Blues	CHL	58	7	21	28	....	....	....	46	....	....	....	....	....	....	....	....	....	....	....	....	....	....	....	....	....	....
1977-78	Salt Lake Golden Eagles	CHL	76	4	20	24	....	....	....	73	....	....	....	....	....	....	....	....	....	....	6	0	3	3	0	....	....	....
1978-79	**St. Louis Blues**	**NHL**	**10**	**0**	**6**	**6**	**0**	**4**	**4**	**0**	**0**	**0**	**0**	**10**	**0.0**	**14**	**4**	**17**	**1**	**–6**	....	....	....	....	....	....	....	....
	Salt Lake Golden Eagles	CHL	62	2	24	26	....	....	....	98	....	....	....	....	....	....	....	....	....	....	10	0	1	1	13	....	....	....
1979-80	Cincinnati Stingers	CHL	33	9	13	22	....	....	....	24	....	....	....	....	....	....	....	....	....	....	....	....	....	....	....	....	....	....
	Syracuse Firebirds	AHL	46	6	17	23	....	....	....	26	....	....	....	....	....	....	....	....	....	....	4	0	3	3	0	....	....	....
1980-81	SB Rosenheim	Germany-2	44	15	14	29	....	....	....	61	....	....	....	....	....	....	....	....	....	....	6	2	1	3	20	....	....	....
1981-82	SB Rosenheim	Germany-2	44	11	29	40	....	....	....	51	....	....	....	....	....	....	....	....	....	....	....	....	....	....	....	....	....	....
1982-83	SB Rosenheim	Germany-2	35	5	16	21	....	....	....	22	....	....	....	....	....	....	....	....	....	....	....	....	....	....	....	....	....	....
1983-84	SB Rosenheim	Germany-2	36	11	20	31	....	....	....	38	....	....	....	....	....	....	....	....	....	....	....	....	....	....	....	....	....	....
1984-85	SB Rosenheim	Germany-2	36	7	13	20	....	....	....	21	....	....	....	....	....	....	....	....	....	....	9	0	5	5	10	....	....	....
1985-86	VSV Villach	Austria	40	19	46	65	....	....	....	66	....	....	....	....	....	....	....	....	....	....	....	....	....	....	....	....	....	....
1986-87	VSV Villach	Austria	23	8	31	39	....	....	....	12	....	....	....	....	....	....	....	....	....	....	....	....	....	....	....	....	....	....
	NHL Totals		**33**	**1**	**13**	**14**	**1**	**9**	**10**	**2**	**1**	**0**	**0**	**33**	**3.0**	**29**	**12**	**30**	**4**		**2**	**0**	**0**	**0**	**0**	**0**	**0**	**0**

Claimed by **Quebec** from **St. Louis** in Expansion Draft, June 13, 1979.

• MASTERTON, Bill

William "Bat" C – R. 6', 189 lbs. b: Winnipeg, Man., 8/13/1938 d: 1/15/1968.

Season	Club	League	GP	G	A	Pts	AG	AA	APts	PIM	PP	SH	GW	S	%	TGF	PGF	TGA	PGA	+/-	GP	G	A	Pts	PIM	PP	SH	GW
1955-56	St. Boniface Canadiens	MJHL	22	23	26	49	....	....	....	16	....	....	....	....	....	....	....	....	....	....	4	4	2	6	2	....	....	....
	St. Boniface Canadiens	Mem-Cup	6	3	5	8	....	....	....	2	....	....	....	....	....	....	....	....	....	....	....	....	....	....	....	....	....	....
1956-57	St. Boniface Canadiens	MJHL	30	23	30	53	....	....	....	16	....	....	....	....	....	....	....	....	....	....	7	8	*10	18	2	....	....	....
1957-58	University of Denver	WCHA	DID NOT PLAY – FRESHMAN																									
1958-59	University of Denver	WCHA	23	21	28	49	....	....	....	6	....	....	....	....	....	....	....	....	....	....	....	....	....	....	....	....	....	....
1959-60	University of Denver	WCHA	34	21	46	67	....	....	....	2	....	....	....	....	....	....	....	....	....	....	....	....	....	....	....	....	....	....
1960-61	University of Denver	WCHA	32	24	56	80	....	....	....	4	....	....	....	....	....	....	....	....	....	....	....	....	....	....	....	....	....	....
1961-62	Hull-Ottawa Canadiens	EPHL	65	31	35	66	....	....	....	18	....	....	....	....	....	....	....	....	....	....	12	0	4	4	0	....	....	....
1962-63	Cleveland Barons	AHL	72	27	55	82	....	....	....	12	....	....	....	....	....	....	....	....	....	....	7	4	5	9	2	....	....	....
1963-64			REINSTATED AS AN AMATEUR																									
1964-65	Rochester Mustangs	USHL	STATISTICS NOT AVAILABLE																									
1965-66	St. Paul Steers	USHL	30	27	*40	67	....	....	....	6	....	....	....	....	....	....	....	....	....	....	....	....	....	....	....	....	....	....
1966-67	United States	Nat-Team	21	10	*29	39	....	....	....	4	....	....	....	....	....	....	....	....	....	....	....	....	....	....	....	....	....	....
1967-68	**Minnesota North Stars**	**NHL**	**38**	**4**	**8**	**12**	**5**	**8**	**13**	**4**	**2**	**0**	**0**	**83**	**4.8**	**21**	**8**	**20**	**3**	**–4**	....	....	....	....	....	....	....	....
	NHL Totals		**38**	**4**	**8**	**12**	**5**	**8**	**13**	**4**	**2**	**0**	**0**	**83**	**4.8**	**21**	**8**	**20**	**3**		....	....	....	....	....	....	....	....

WCHA First All-Star Team (1960, 1961) • NCAA West First All-American Team (1960, 1961) • NCAA Championship All-Tournament Team (1961) • NCAA Championship Tournament MVP (1961)

Rights traded to **Minnesota** by **Montreal** for cash, June 14, 1967. • Died of head injury suffered in game vs. California, (January 13, 1968), January 15, 1968.

• MATHIASEN, Dwight Dwight Wayne RW – R. 6'1", 190 lbs. b: Brandon, Man., 5/12/1963.

Season	Club	League	GP	G	A	Pts	AG	AA	APts	PIM	PP	SH	GW	S	%	TGF	PGF	TGA	PGA	+/–	GP	G	A	Pts	PIM	PP	SH	GW
			REGULAR SEASON																		PLAYOFFS							
1982-83	Abbotsford Flyers	BCJHL	48	50	73	123	....	....	....	113	....	....	....	....	....	....	....	....	....	....	....	....	....	....	....	....	....	....
1983-84	University of Denver	CCHA	36	24	27	51	....	....	....	48	....	....	....	....	....	....	....	....	....	....	....	....	....	....	....	....	....	....
1984-85	University of Denver	CCHA	39	26	32	58	....	....	....	64	....	....	....	....	....	....	....	....	....	....	....	....	....	....	....	....	....	....
1985-86	University of Denver	CCHA	48	40	49	89	....	....	....	48	....	....	....	....	....	....	....	....	....	....	....	....	....	....	....	....	....	....
	Pittsburgh Penguins	**NHL**	**4**	**1**	**0**	**1**	**1**	**0**	**1**	**2**	**0**	**0**	**0**	**4**	**25.0**	**2**	**1**	**5**	**0**	**–4**	....	....	....	....	....	....	....	....
1986-87	**Pittsburgh Penguins**	**NHL**	**6**	**0**	**1**	**1**	**0**	**1**	**1**	**2**	**0**	**0**	**0**	**4**	**0.0**	**1**	**0**	**2**	**0**	**–1**	....	....	....	....	....	....	....	....
	Baltimore Skipjacks	AHL	61	23	22	45	....	....	....	49	....	....	....	....	....	....	....	....	....	....	....	....	....	....	....	....	....	....
1987-88	**Pittsburgh Penguins**	**NHL**	**23**	**0**	**6**	**6**	**0**	**4**	**4**	**14**	**0**	**0**	**0**	**29**	**0.0**	**13**	**1**	**19**	**0**	**–7**	....	....	....	....	....	....	....	....
	Muskegon Lumberjacks	IHL	46	19	42	61	....	....	....	35	....	....	....	....	....	....	....	....	....	....	4	1	2	3	9	....	....	....
1988-1994			OUT OF HOCKEY – RETIRED																									
1994-95	Fresno Falcons	SunHL	12	8	10	18	....	....	....	14	....	....	....	....	....	....	....	....	....	....	....	....	....	....	....	....	....	....
1995-96	Fresno Falcons	WCHL	2	0	0	0	....	....	....	2	....	....	....	....	....	....	....	....	....	....	....	....	....	....	....	....	....	....
	NHL Totals		**33**	**1**	**7**	**8**	**1**	**5**	**6**	**18**	**0**	**0**	**0**	**37**	**2.7**	**16**	**2**	**26**	**0**		....	....	....	....	....	....	....	....

Signed as a free agent by **Pittsburgh**, March 31, 1986.

• MATHIESON, Jim James John D – L. 6'1", 209 lbs. b: Kindersley, Sask., 1/24/1970. Washington's 3rd, 59th overall, in 1989.

Season	Club	League	GP	G	A	Pts	AG	AA	APts	PIM	PP	SH	GW	S	%	TGF	PGF	TGA	PGA	+/–	GP	G	A	Pts	PIM	PP	SH	GW
1985-86	Regina Canadians	SJHL	STATISTICS NOT AVAILABLE																									
1986-87	Regina Pats	WHL	40	0	9	9	....	....	....	40	....	....	....	....	....	....	....	....	....	....	3	0	1	1	2	....	....	....
1987-88	Regina Pats	WHL	72	3	12	15	....	....	....	115	....	....	....	....	....	....	....	....	....	....	4	0	2	2	4	....	....	....
1988-89	Regina Pats	WHL	62	5	22	27	....	....	....	151	....	....	....	....	....	....	....	....	....	....	....	....	....	....	....	....	....	....
1989-90	Regina Pats	WHL	67	1	26	27	....	....	....	158	....	....	....	....	....	....	....	....	....	....	11	0	7	7	16	....	....	....
	Washington Capitals	**NHL**	**2**	**0**	**0**	**0**	**0**	**0**	**0**	**4**	**0**	**0**	**0**	**0**	**0.0**	**0**	**0**	**0**	**0**	**0**	....	....	....	....	....	....	....	....
	Baltimore Skipjacks	AHL	....	....	....	....	....	....	....	....	....	....	....	....	....	....	....	....	....	....	3	0	0	0	4	....	....	....
1990-91	Baltimore Skipjacks	AHL	65	3	5	8	....	....	....	168	....	....	....	....	....	....	....	....	....	....	4	1	0	1	6	....	....	....
1991-92	Baltimore Skipjacks	AHL	74	2	9	11	....	....	....	206	....	....	....	....	....	....	....	....	....	....	....	....	....	....	....	....	....	....
1992-93	Baltimore Skipjacks	AHL	46	3	5	8	....	....	....	88	....	....	....	....	....	....	....	....	....	....	3	0	1	1	23	....	....	....
1993-94	Portland Pirates	AHL	43	0	7	7	....	....	....	89	....	....	....	....	....	....	....	....	....	....	12	0	1	1	36	....	....	....
1994-95	Portland Pirates	AHL	35	5	5	10	....	....	....	119	....	....	....	....	....	....	....	....	....	....	7	1	0	1	4	....	....	....
1995-96	Portland Pirates	AHL	35	3	4	7	....	....	....	110	....	....	....	....	....	....	....	....	....	....	....	....	....	....	....	....	....	....
1996-97	Newcastle Cobras	BH-Cup	2	0	1	1	....	....	....	25	....	....	....	....	....	....	....	....	....	....	....	....	....	....	....	....	....	....
	Newcastle Cobras	Britain	35	1	0	1	....	....	....	36	....	....	....	....	....	....	....	....	....	....	5	0	0	0	29	....	....	....
1997-98	Nottingham Panthers	BH-Cup	11	0	4	4	....	....	....	8	....	....	....	....	....	....	....	....	....	....	....	....	....	....	....	....	....	....
	Nottingham Panthers	Britain	40	2	7	9	....	....	....	64	....	....	....	....	....	....	....	....	....	....	6	0	0	0	4	....	....	....
1998-99	Newcastle Riverkings	BH-Cup	8	1	2	3	....	....	....	10	....	....	....	....	....	....	....	....	....	....	....	....	....	....	....	....	....	....
	Newcastle Riverkings	Britain	42	2	7	9	....	....	....	57	....	....	....	....	....	....	....	....	....	....	6	0	1	1	6	....	....	....
99-2000	Ayr Scottish Eagles	BH-Cup	7	0	1	1	....	....	....	2	....	....	....	....	....	....	....	....	....	....	....	....	....	....	....	....	....	....
	Ayr Scottish Eagles	Britain	34	1	3	4	....	....	....	59	....	....	....	....	....	....	....	....	....	....	6	0	1	1	8	....	....	....
	NHL Totals		**2**	**0**	**0**	**0**	**0**	**0**	**0**	**4**	**0**	**0**	**0**	**0**	**0.0**	**0**	**0**	**0**	**0**		....	....	....	....	....	....	....	....

• Played w/ RHI's New England Stingers in 1994 (9-1-4-5-32).

• MATHIEU, Marquis Marquis Jean C – R. 5'11", 190 lbs. b: Hartford, CT, 5/31/1973.

Season	Club	League	GP	G	A	Pts	AG	AA	APts	PIM	PP	SH	GW	S	%	TGF	PGF	TGA	PGA	+/–	GP	G	A	Pts	PIM	PP	SH	GW
1990-91	Hawkesbury Hawks	OJHL	20	6	8	14	....	....	....	62	....	....	....	....	....	....	....	....	....	....	....	....	....	....	....	....	....	....
	Beauport Harfangs	QMJHL	26	4	13	17	....	....	....	73	....	....	....	....	....	....	....	....	....	....	....	....	....	....	....	....	....	....
1991-92	St-Jean Lynx	QMJHL	70	20	36	56	....	....	....	166	....	....	....	....	....	....	....	....	....	....	....	....	....	....	....	....	....	....
1992-93	St-Jean Lynx	QMJHL	61	31	36	67	....	....	....	115	....	....	....	....	....	....	....	....	....	....	2	1	0	1	33	....	....	....
1993-94	Wheeling Thunderbirds	ECHL	42	12	11	23	....	....	....	75	....	....	....	....	....	....	....	....	....	....	9	1	3	4	23	....	....	....
	Fredericton Canadiens	AHL	22	4	6	10	....	....	....	28	....	....	....	....	....	....	....	....	....	....	....	....	....	....	....	....	....	....
1994-95	Toledo Storm	ECHL	33	13	22	35	....	....	....	168	....	....	....	....	....	....	....	....	....	....	....	....	....	....	....	....	....	....
	Raleigh Icecaps	ECHL	33	15	17	32	....	....	....	181	....	....	....	....	....	....	....	....	....	....	....	....	....	....	....	....	....	....
	Worcester IceCats	AHL	2	0	0	0	....	....	....	0	....	....	....	....	....	....	....	....	....	....	....	....	....	....	....	....	....	....
1995-96	Johnstown Chiefs	ECHL	25	4	17	21	....	....	....	89	....	....	....	....	....	....	....	....	....	....	....	....	....	....	....	....	....	....
	Worcester IceCats	AHL	17	3	10	13	....	....	....	26	....	....	....	....	....	....	....	....	....	....	....	....	....	....	....	....	....	....
	Houston Aeros	IHL	2	1	0	1	....	....	....	9	....	....	....	....	....	....	....	....	....	....	....	....	....	....	....	....	....	....
	Birmingham Bulls	ECHL	18	5	7	12	....	....	....	87	....	....	....	....	....	....	....	....	....	....	....	....	....	....	....	....	....	....
1996-97	Worcester IceCats	AHL	30	8	16	24	....	....	....	88	....	....	....	....	....	....	....	....	....	....	1	0	0	0	0	....	....	....
1997-98	Wheeling Nailers	ECHL	58	26	29	55	....	....	....	276	....	....	....	....	....	....	....	....	....	....	15	1	10	11	38	....	....	....
1998-99	**Boston Bruins**	**NHL**	**9**	**0**	**0**	**0**	**0**	**0**	**0**	**8**	**0**	**0**	**0**	**4**	**0.0**	**1**	**0**	**2**	**0**	**–1**	....	....	....	....	....	....	....	....
	Providence Bruins	AHL	64	15	15	30	....	....	....	166	....	....	....	....	....	....	....	....	....	....	19	4	7	11	30	....	....	....
99-2000	**Boston Bruins**	**NHL**	**6**	**0**	**2**	**2**	**0**	**2**	**2**	**4**	**0**	**0**	**0**	**3**	**0.0**	**2**	**0**	**6**	**2**	**–2**	....	....	....	....	....	....	....	....
	Providence Bruins	AHL	18	3	3	6	....	....	....	45	....	....	....	....	....	....	....	....	....	....	....	....	....	....	....	....	....	....
	NHL Totals		**15**	**0**	**2**	**2**	**0**	**2**	**2**	**12**	**0**	**0**	**0**	**7**	**0.0**	**3**	**0**	**8**	**2**		....	....	....	....	....	....	....	....

Signed as a free agent by **Boston**, October 26, 1998. • Missed majority of 1999-2000 season recovering from hip injury that resulted in surgery, June 1999.

• MATTE, Christian RW – R. 5'11", 170 lbs. b: Hull, Que., 1/20/1975. Quebec's 8th, 153rd overall, in 1993.

Season	Club	League	GP	G	A	Pts	AG	AA	APts	PIM	PP	SH	GW	S	%	TGF	PGF	TGA	PGA	+/–	GP	G	A	Pts	PIM	PP	SH	GW
1991-92	Timiscaminque Forestiers	QAAA	42	18	27	45	....	....	....	30	....	....	....	....	....	....	....	....	....	....	....	....	....	....	....	....	....	....
1992-93	Granby Bisons	QMJHL	68	17	36	53	....	....	....	59	....	....	....	....	....	....	....	....	....	....	....	....	....	....	....	....	....	....
1993-94	Granby Bisons	QMJHL	59	50	47	97	....	....	....	103	....	....	....	....	....	....	....	....	....	....	7	5	5	10	12	....	....	....
	Cornwall Aces	AHL	1	0	0	0	....	....	....	0	....	....	....	....	....	....	....	....	....	....	....	....	....	....	....	....	....	....
1994-95	Granby Bisons	QMJHL	66	50	66	116	....	....	....	86	....	....	....	....	....	....	....	....	....	....	13	11	7	18	12	....	....	....
	Cornwall Aces	AHL	....	....	....	....	....	....	....	....	....	....	....	....	....	....	....	....	....	....	3	0	1	1	2	....	....	....
1995-96	Cornwall Aces	AHL	64	20	32	52	....	....	....	51	....	....	....	....	....	....	....	....	....	....	7	1	1	2	6	....	....	....
1996-97	**Colorado Avalanche**	**NHL**	**5**	**1**	**1**	**2**	**1**	**1**	**2**	**0**	**0**	**0**	**0**	**6**	**16.7**	**2**	**0**	**1**	**0**	**1**	....	....	....	....	....	....	....	....
	Hershey Bears	AHL	49	18	18	36	....	....	....	78	....	....	....	....	....	....	....	....	....	....	22	8	3	11	25	....	....	....
1997-98	**Colorado Avalanche**	**NHL**	**5**	**0**	**0**	**0**	**0**	**0**	**0**	**6**	**0**	**0**	**0**	**5**	**0.0**	**1**	**0**	**1**	**0**	**0**	....	....	....	....	....	....	....	....
	Hershey Bears	AHL	71	33	40	73	....	....	....	109	....	....	....	....	....	....	....	....	....	....	7	3	2	5	4	....	....	....
1998-99	**Colorado Avalanche**	**NHL**	**7**	**1**	**1**	**2**	**1**	**1**	**2**	**0**	**0**	**0**	**0**	**9**	**11.1**	**2**	**0**	**4**	**0**	**–2**	....	....	....	....	....	....	....	....
	Hershey Bears	AHL	60	31	47	78	....	....	....	48	....	....	....	....	....	....	....	....	....	....	5	2	1	3	8	....	....	....
99-2000	**Colorado Avalanche**	**NHL**	**5**	**0**	**1**	**1**	**0**	**1**	**1**	**4**	**0**	**0**	**0**	**1**	**0.0**	**1**	**1**	**2**	**0**	**–2**	....	....	....	....	....	....	....	....
	Hershey Bears	AHL	73	43	*61	*104	....	....	....	85	....	....	....	....	....	....	....	....	....	....	14	8	6	14	10	....	....	....
	NHL Totals		**22**	**2**	**3**	**5**	**2**	**3**	**5**	**10**	**0**	**0**	**0**	**21**	**9.5**	**6**	**1**	**8**	**0**		....	....	....	....	....	....	....	....

QMJHL Second All-Star Team (1994) • AHL First All-Star Team (2000) • Won John P. Sollenberger Trophy (Top Scorer - AHL) (2000)
Rights transferred to **Colorado** after **Quebec** franchise relocated, June 21, 1995. Signed as a free agent by **Minnesota**, July 11, 2000.

• MATTEAU, Stephane LW – L. 6'4", 220 lbs. b: Rouyn-Noranda, Que., 9/2/1969. Calgary's 2nd, 25th overall, in 1987.

Season	Club	League	GP	G	A	Pts	AG	AA	APts	PIM	PP	SH	GW	S	%	TGF	PGF	TGA	PGA	+/–	GP	G	A	Pts	PIM	PP	SH	GW
1985-86	Hull Olympiques	QMJHL	60	6	8	14	....	....	....	19	....	....	....	....	....	....	....	....	....	....	4	0	0	0	0	....	....	....
	Hull Olympiques	Mem-Cup	5	0	0	0	....	....	....	5	....	....	....	....	....	....	....	....	....	....	....	....	....	....	....	....	....	....
1986-87	Hull Olympiques	QMJHL	69	27	48	75	....	....	....	113	....	....	....	....	....	....	....	....	....	....	8	3	7	10	8	....	....	....
1987-88	Hull Olympiques	QMJHL	57	17	40	57	....	....	....	179	....	....	....	....	....	....	....	....	....	....	18	5	14	19	94	....	....	....
	Hull Olympiques	Mem-Cup	4	1	2	3	....	....	....	4	....	....	....	....	....	....	....	....	....	....	....	....	....	....	....	....	....	....
1988-89	Hull Olympiques	QMJHL	59	44	45	89	....	....	....	202	....	....	....	....	....	....	....	....	....	....	9	8	6	14	30	....	....	....
	Salt Lake Golden Eagles	IHL	....	....	....	....	....	....	....	....	....	....	....	....	....	....	....	....	....	....	9	0	4	4	13	....	....	....
1989-90	Salt Lake Golden Eagles	IHL	81	23	35	58	....	....	....	130	....	....	....	....	....	....	....	....	....	....	10	6	3	9	38	....	....	....
1990-91	**Calgary Flames**	**NHL**	**78**	**15**	**19**	**34**	**14**	**14**	**28**	**93**	**0**	**1**	**1**	**114**	**13.2**	**61**	**1**	**53**	**10**	**17**	**5**	**0**	**1**	**1**	**0**	**0**	**0**	**0**
1991-92	**Calgary Flames**	**NHL**	**4**	**1**	**0**	**1**	**1**	**0**	**1**	**19**	**0**	**0**	**0**	**7**	**14.3**	**2**	**0**	**2**	**2**	**2**	....	....	....	....	....	....	....	....
	Chicago Blackhawks	**NHL**	**20**	**5**	**8**	**13**	**5**	**6**	**11**	**45**	**1**	**0**	**0**	**31**	**16.1**	**15**	**2**	**10**	**0**	**3**	**18**	**4**	**6**	**10**	**24**	**1**	**1**	**0**
1992-93	**Chicago Blackhawks**	**NHL**	**79**	**15**	**18**	**33**	**12**	**12**	**24**	**98**	**2**	**0**	**4**	**95**	**15.8**	**55**	**11**	**43**	**5**	**6**	**3**	**0**	**1**	**1**	**2**	**0**	**0**	**0**

Season	Club	League	GP	G	A	Pts	AG	AA	APts	PIM	PP	SH	GW	S	%	TGF	PGF	TGA	PGA	+/-	GP	G	A	Pts	PIM	PP	SH	GW
			REGULAR SEASON																		PLAYOFFS							
1993-94	**Chicago Blackhawks**	**NHL**	**65**	**15**	**16**	**31**	**14**	**12**	**26**	**55**	**2**	**0**	**2**	**113**	**13.3**	**47**	**6**	**45**	**14**	**10**	....	....	....	....	....	....	....	....
◆	**New York Rangers**	**NHL**	**12**	**4**	**3**	**7**	**4**	**2**	**6**	**2**	**1**	**0**	**0**	**22**	**18.2**	**15**	**5**	**6**	**1**	**5**	**23**	**6**	**3**	**9**	**20**	**1**	**0**	**2**
1994-95	**New York Rangers**	**NHL**	**41**	**3**	**5**	**8**	**5**	**7**	**12**	**25**	**0**	**0**	**0**	**37**	**8.1**	**13**	**0**	**21**	**0**	**-8**	**9**	**0**	**1**	**1**	**10**	**0**	**0**	**0**
1995-96	**New York Rangers**	**NHL**	**32**	**4**	**2**	**6**	**4**	**2**	**6**	**22**	**1**	**0**	**0**	**39**	**10.3**	**8**	**1**	**12**	**1**	**-4**	....	....	....	....	....	....	....	....
	St. Louis Blues	**NHL**	**46**	**7**	**13**	**20**	**7**	**11**	**18**	**65**	**3**	**0**	**2**	**70**	**10.0**	**33**	**8**	**36**	**7**	**-4**	**11**	**0**	**2**	**2**	**8**	**0**	**0**	**0**
1996-97	**St. Louis Blues**	**NHL**	**74**	**16**	**20**	**36**	**17**	**18**	**35**	**50**	**1**	**2**	**2**	**98**	**16.3**	**56**	**2**	**49**	**6**	**11**	**5**	**0**	**0**	**0**	**0**	**0**	**0**	**0**
1997-98	**San Jose Sharks**	**NHL**	**73**	**15**	**14**	**29**	**18**	**14**	**32**	**60**	**1**	**0**	**2**	**79**	**19.0**	**45**	**3**	**46**	**8**	**4**	**4**	**0**	**1**	**1**	**0**	**0**	**0**	**0**
1998-99	**San Jose Sharks**	**NHL**	**68**	**8**	**15**	**23**	**9**	**14**	**23**	**73**	**0**	**0**	**0**	**72**	**11.1**	**34**	**2**	**43**	**13**	**2**	**5**	**0**	**0**	**0**	**6**	**0**	**0**	**0**
99-2000	**San Jose Sharks**	**NHL**	**69**	**12**	**12**	**24**	**13**	**11**	**24**	**61**	**0**	**0**	**3**	**73**	**16.4**	**30**	**1**	**36**	**4**	**-3**	**10**	**0**	**2**	**2**	**8**	**0**	**0**	**0**
	NHL Totals		**661**	**120**	**145**	**265**	**123**	**123**	**246**	**668**	**12**	**3**	**16**	**850**	**14.1**	**414**	**42**	**402**	**71**		**93**	**10**	**17**	**27**	**78**	**2**	**1**	**2**

• Missed majority of 1991-92 season recovering from thigh injury suffered in game vs. LA Kings, October 10, 1991. Traded to **Chicago** by **Calgary** for Trent Yawney, December 16, 1991. Traded to **NY Rangers** by **Chicago** with Brian Noonan for Tony Amonte and the rights to Matt Oates, March 21, 1994. Traded to **St. Louis** by **NY Rangers** for Ian Laperriere, December 28, 1995. Traded to **San Jose** by **St. Louis** for Darren Turcotte, July 24, 1997.

• MATTIUSSI, Dick

Richard Arthur LW – L. 5'10", 185 lbs. b: Smooth Rock Falls, Ont., 5/1/1938.

Season	Club	League	GP	G	A	Pts	AG	AA	APts	PIM	PP	SH	GW	S	%	TGF	PGF	TGA	PGA	+/-	GP	G	A	Pts	PIM	PP	SH	GW
1955-56	St. Michael's Majors	OHA-Jr.	48	10	7	17	....	....	....	68	....	....	....	....	....	....	....	....	....	....	8	0	2	2	11	....	....	....
1956-57	St. Michael's Majors	OHA-Jr.	52	12	18	30	....	....	....	80	....	....	....	....	....	....	....	....	....	....	4	0	0	0	19	....	....	....
1957-58	St. Michael's Majors	OHA-Jr.	51	9	15	24	....	....	....	98	....	....	....	....	....	....	....	....	....	....	9	0	6	6	26	....	....	....
1958-59	Kitchener-Waterloo Dutchmen	OHA-Sr.	51	6	21	27	....	....	....	89	....	....	....	....	....	....	....	....	....	....	11	1	4	5	21	....	....	....
1959-60	Rochester Americans	AHL	72	2	20	22	....	....	....	76	....	....	....	....	....	....	....	....	....	....	12	0	0	0	14	....	....	....
1960-61	Rochester Americans	AHL	61	3	23	26	....	....	....	141	....	....	....	....	....	....	....	....	....	....	....	....	....	....	....	....	....	....
1961-62	Pittsburgh Hornets	AHL	65	9	19	28	....	....	....	164	....	....	....	....	....	....	....	....	....	....	....	....	....	....	....	....	....	....
1962-63	Cleveland Barons	AHL	70	6	28	34	....	....	....	124	....	....	....	....	....	....	....	....	....	....	4	2	2	4	6	....	....	....
1963-64	Cleveland Barons	AHL	72	6	17	23	....	....	....	110	....	....	....	....	....	....	....	....	....	....	9	1	5	6	20	....	....	....
1964-65	Cleveland Barons	AHL	67	8	18	26	....	....	....	98	....	....	....	....	....	....	....	....	....	....	....	....	....	....	....	....	....	....
1965-66	Cleveland Barons	AHL	72	8	35	43	....	....	....	138	....	....	....	....	....	....	....	....	....	....	12	0	5	5	10	....	....	....
1966-67	Cleveland Barons	AHL	71	10	44	54	....	....	....	78	....	....	....	....	....	....	....	....	....	....	5	1	2	3	2	....	....	....
1967-68	**Pittsburgh Penguins**	**NHL**	**32**	**0**	**2**	**2**	**0**	**2**	**2**	**18**	**0**	**0**	**0**	**31**	**0.0**	**15**	**1**	**26**	**3**	**-9**	....	....	....	....	....	....	....	....
	Baltimore Clippers	AHL	3	0	0	0	....	....	....	0	....	....	....	....	....	....	....	....	....	....	....	....	....	....	....	....	....	....
1968-69	**Pittsburgh Penguins**	**NHL**	**12**	**0**	**2**	**2**	**0**	**2**	**2**	**14**	**0**	**0**	**0**	**10**	**0.0**	**11**	**2**	**11**	**0**	**-2**	....	....	....	....	....	....	....	....
	Amarillo Wranglers	CHL	8	0	2	2	....	....	....	8	....	....	....	....	....	....	....	....	....	....	....	....	....	....	....	....	....	....
	Oakland Seals	**NHL**	**24**	**1**	**9**	**10**	**1**	**8**	**9**	**16**	**0**	**0**	**0**	**17**	**5.9**	**34**	**5**	**31**	**5**	**3**	**7**	**0**	**1**	**1**	**6**	**0**	**0**	**0**
1969-70	**Oakland Seals**	**NHL**	**65**	**4**	**10**	**14**	**4**	**9**	**13**	**38**	**0**	**0**	**0**	**55**	**7.3**	**34**	**8**	**49**	**2**	**-21**	**1**	**0**	**0**	**0**	**0**	**0**	**0**	**0**
1970-71	**California Golden Seals**	**NHL**	**67**	**3**	**8**	**11**	**3**	**7**	**10**	**38**	**1**	**0**	**1**	**72**	**4.2**	**38**	**7**	**70**	**5**	**-34**	....	....	....	....	....	....	....	....
1971-72	Baltimore Clippers	AHL	67	3	8	11	....	....	....	103	....	....	....	....	....	....	....	....	....	....	18	0	0	0	10	....	....	....
1972-73	Providence Reds	AHL	23	2	6	8	....	....	....	30	....	....	....	....	....	....	....	....	....	....	....	....	....	....	....	....	....	....
1973-74	Rochester Americans	AHL	76	12	26	38	....	....	....	84	....	....	....	....	....	....	....	....	....	....	5	0	2	2	8	....	....	....
1974-75	Rochester Americans	AHL	DID NOT PLAY – COACHING																									
1975-76	Rochester Americans	AHL	3	0	0	0	....	....	....	0	....	....	....	....	....	....	....	....	....	....	....	....	....	....	....	....	....	....
	NHL Totals		**200**	**8**	**31**	**39**	**8**	**28**	**36**	**124**	**1**	**0**	**1**	**185**	**4.3**	**132**	**23**	**187**	**15**		**8**	**0**	**1**	**1**	**6**	**0**	**0**	**0**

Traded to **Springfield** (AHL) by **Toronto** with Jim Wilcox, Wally Boyer, Bill White and Roger Cote for Kent Douglas, June 7, 1962. Traded to **Cleveland** (AHL) by **Springfield** (AHL) for Wayne Larkin and Murray Davison, October 16, 1962. Traded to **Pittsburgh** by **Cleveland** (AHL) for cash, August 11, 1966. Loaned to **Cleveland** (AHL) by **Pittsburgh** for 1966-67 season for cash, October, 1966. Traded to **Oakland** by **Pittsburgh** with Earl Ingarfield and Gene Ubriaco for Bryan Watson, George Swarbrick and Tracy Pratt, January 30, 1969.

• MATVICHUK, Richard

D – L. 6'2", 215 lbs. b: Edmonton, Alta., 2/5/1973. Minnesota's 1st, 8th overall, in 1991.

Season	Club	League	GP	G	A	Pts	AG	AA	APts	PIM	PP	SH	GW	S	%	TGF	PGF	TGA	PGA	+/-	GP	G	A	Pts	PIM	PP	SH	GW
1988-89	Fort Saskatchewan Traders	AJHL	58	7	36	43	....	....	....	147	....	....	....	....	....	....	....	....	....	....	....	....	....	....	....	....	....	....
1989-90	Saskatoon Blades	WHL	56	8	24	32	....	....	....	126	....	....	....	....	....	....	....	....	....	....	10	2	8	10	16	....	....	....
1990-91	Saskatoon Blades	WHL	68	13	36	49	....	....	....	117	....	....	....	....	....	....	....	....	....	....	....	....	....	....	....	....	....	....
1991-92	Saskatoon Blades	WHL	58	14	40	54	....	....	....	126	....	....	....	....	....	....	....	....	....	....	22	1	9	10	61	....	....	....
	Canada	WJC-A	4	0	0	0	....	....	....	2	....	....	....	....	....	....	....	....	....	....	....	....	....	....	....	....	....	....
1992-93	**Minnesota North Stars**	**NHL**	**53**	**2**	**3**	**5**	**2**	**2**	**4**	**26**	**1**	**0**	**0**	**51**	**3.9**	**33**	**6**	**39**	**4**	**-8**	....	....	....	....	....	....	....	....
	Kalamazoo Wings	IHL	3	0	1	1	....	....	....	6	....	....	....	....	....	....	....	....	....	....	....	....	....	....	....	....	....	....
1993-94	**Dallas Stars**	**NHL**	**25**	**0**	**3**	**3**	**0**	**2**	**2**	**22**	**0**	**0**	**0**	**18**	**0.0**	**15**	**5**	**11**	**2**	**1**	**7**	**1**	**1**	**2**	**12**	**1**	**0**	**0**
	Kalamazoo Wings	IHL	43	8	17	25	....	....	....	84	....	....	....	....	....	....	....	....	....	....	....	....	....	....	....	....	....	....
1994-95	**Dallas Stars**	**NHL**	**14**	**0**	**2**	**2**	**0**	**3**	**3**	**14**	**0**	**0**	**0**	**21**	**0.0**	**10**	**3**	**14**	**0**	**-7**	**5**	**0**	**2**	**2**	**4**	**0**	**0**	**0**
	Kalamazoo Wings	IHL	17	0	6	6	....	....	....	16	....	....	....	....	....	....	....	....	....	....	....	....	....	....	....	....	....	....
1995-96	**Dallas Stars**	**NHL**	**73**	**6**	**16**	**22**	**6**	**13**	**19**	**71**	**0**	**0**	**1**	**81**	**7.4**	**54**	**9**	**50**	**9**	**4**	....	....	....	....	....	....	....	....
1996-97	**Dallas Stars**	**NHL**	**57**	**5**	**7**	**12**	**5**	**6**	**11**	**87**	**0**	**2**	**0**	**83**	**6.0**	**49**	**1**	**67**	**20**	**1**	**7**	**0**	**1**	**1**	**20**	**0**	**0**	**0**
1997-98	**Dallas Stars**	**NHL**	**74**	**3**	**15**	**18**	**4**	**15**	**19**	**63**	**0**	**0**	**0**	**71**	**4.2**	**58**	**6**	**69**	**24**	**7**	**16**	**1**	**1**	**2**	**14**	**0**	**0**	**0**
1998-99◆	**Dallas Stars**	**NHL**	**64**	**3**	**9**	**12**	**4**	**9**	**13**	**51**	**1**	**0**	**0**	**54**	**5.6**	**66**	**2**	**59**	**18**	**23**	**22**	**1**	**5**	**6**	**20**	**0**	**0**	**0**
99-2000	**Dallas Stars**	**NHL**	**70**	**4**	**21**	**25**	**4**	**19**	**23**	**42**	**0**	**0**	**1**	**73**	**5.5**	**60**	**8**	**70**	**25**	**7**	**23**	**2**	**5**	**7**	**14**	**0**	**0**	**0**
	NHL Totals		**430**	**23**	**76**	**99**	**25**	**69**	**94**	**376**	**2**	**2**	**2**	**452**	**5.1**	**345**	**40**	**379**	**102**		**80**	**5**	**15**	**20**	**84**	**1**	**0**	**0**

WHL East First All-Star Team (1992)

Transferred to **Dallas** after **Minnesota** franchise relocated, June 9, 1993.

• MAXWELL, Brad

Bradley Robert D – R. 6'2", 195 lbs. b: Brandon, Man., 7/8/1957. Minnesota's 1st, 7th overall, in 1977.

Season	Club	League	GP	G	A	Pts	AG	AA	APts	PIM	PP	SH	GW	S	%	TGF	PGF	TGA	PGA	+/-	GP	G	A	Pts	PIM	PP	SH	GW
1973-74	Bellingham Blazers	BCJHL	61	20	37	57	....	....	....	132	....	....	....	....	....	....	....	....	....	....	....	....	....	....	....	....	....	....
1974-75	New Westminster Bruins	WCJHL	69	13	47	60	....	....	....	124	....	....	....	....	....	....	....	....	....	....	18	7	13	20	33	....	....	....
	New Westminster Bruins	Mem-Cup	3	0	5	5	....	....	....	8	....	....	....	....	....	....	....	....	....	....	....	....	....	....	....	....	....	....
1975-76	New Westminster Bruins	WCJHL	72	19	80	99	....	....	....	239	....	....	....	....	....	....	....	....	....	....	17	3	12	15	86	....	....	....
	New Westminster Bruins	Mem-Cup	4	1	3	4	....	....	....	*29	....	....	....	....	....	....	....	....	....	....	....	....	....	....	....	....	....	....
1976-77	New Westminster Bruins	WCJHL	70	21	58	79	....	....	....	205	....	....	....	....	....	....	....	....	....	....	14	7	15	22	39	....	....	....
	New Westminster Bruins	Mem-Cup	5	2	4	6	....	....	....	6	....	....	....	....	....	....	....	....	....	....	....	....	....	....	....	....	....	....
1977-78	**Minnesota North Stars**	**NHL**	**75**	**18**	**29**	**47**	**16**	**22**	**38**	**100**	**12**	**0**	**0**	**209**	**8.6**	**110**	**42**	**131**	**6**	**-57**	....	....	....	....	....	....	....	....
	Canada	WEC-A	10	2	1	3	....	....	....	12	....	....	....	....	....	....	....	....	....	....	....	....	....	....	....	....	....	....
1978-79	**Minnesota North Stars**	**NHL**	**70**	**9**	**28**	**37**	**8**	**20**	**28**	**145**	**5**	**0**	**0**	**200**	**4.5**	**88**	**25**	**89**	**13**	**-13**	....	....	....	....	....	....	....	....
	Oklahoma City Stars	CHL	2	0	1	1	....	....	....	21	....	....	....	....	....	....	....	....	....	....	....	....	....	....	....	....	....	....
	Canada	WEC-A	4	1	0	1	....	....	....	8	....	....	....	....	....	....	....	....	....	....	....	....	....	....	....	....	....	....
1979-80	**Minnesota North Stars**	**NHL**	**58**	**7**	**30**	**37**	**6**	**22**	**28**	**126**	**0**	**0**	**0**	**135**	**5.2**	**109**	**27**	**82**	**9**	**9**	**11**	**0**	**8**	**8**	**20**	**0**	**0**	**0**
1980-81	Minnesota North Stars	DN-Cup	3	0	1	1	....	....	....	2	....	....	....	....	....	....	....	....	....	....	....	....	....	....	....	....	....	....
	Minnesota North Stars	**NHL**	**27**	**3**	**13**	**16**	**2**	**9**	**11**	**98**	**3**	**0**	**1**	**71**	**4.2**	**43**	**15**	**35**	**6**	**-1**	**18**	**3**	**11**	**14**	**35**	**1**	**0**	**0**
1981-82	**Minnesota North Stars**	**NHL**	**51**	**10**	**21**	**31**	**8**	**14**	**22**	**96**	**0**	**1**	**1**	**109**	**9.2**	**85**	**30**	**57**	**8**	**6**	**4**	**0**	**3**	**3**	**13**	**0**	**0**	**0**
	Canada	WEC-A	7	0	0	0	....	....	....	10	....	....	....	....	....	....	....	....	....	....	....	....	....	....	....	....	....	....
1982-83	**Minnesota North Stars**	**NHL**	**77**	**11**	**28**	**39**	**9**	**19**	**28**	**157**	**2**	**0**	**3**	**162**	**6.8**	**113**	**31**	**108**	**25**	**-1**	**9**	**5**	**6**	**11**	**23**	**2**	**0**	**0**
1983-84	**Minnesota North Stars**	**NHL**	**78**	**19**	**54**	**73**	**15**	**37**	**52**	**225**	**8**	**0**	**2**	**228**	**8.3**	**179**	**72**	**142**	**28**	**-7**	**16**	**2**	**11**	**13**	**40**	**1**	**0**	**0**
1984-85	**Minnesota North Stars**	**NHL**	**18**	**3**	**7**	**10**	**2**	**5**	**7**	**53**	**1**	**0**	**0**	**29**	**10.3**	**19**	**8**	**25**	**6**	**-8**	....	....	....	....	....	....	....	....
	Quebec Nordiques	**NHL**	**50**	**7**	**24**	**31**	**6**	**16**	**22**	**119**	**1**	**0**	**1**	**109**	**6.4**	**87**	**24**	**45**	**4**	**22**	**18**	**2**	**9**	**11**	**35**	**1**	**0**	**0**
1985-86	**Toronto Maple Leafs**	**NHL**	**52**	**8**	**18**	**26**	**6**	**12**	**18**	**108**	**4**	**0**	**0**	**93**	**8.6**	**79**	**29**	**87**	**10**	**-27**	**3**	**0**	**1**	**1**	**12**	**0**	**0**	**0**
1986-87	**Vancouver Canucks**	**NHL**	**30**	**1**	**7**	**8**	**1**	**5**	**6**	**28**	**1**	**0**	**0**	**43**	**2.3**	**25**	**11**	**26**	**3**	**-9**	....	....	....	....	....	....	....	....
	New York Rangers	**NHL**	**9**	**0**	**4**	**4**	**0**	**3**	**3**	**6**	**0**	**0**	**0**	**10**	**0.0**	**11**	**3**	**9**	**0**	**-1**	....	....	....	....	....	....	....	....
	Minnesota North Stars	**NHL**	**17**	**2**	**7**	**9**	**2**	**5**	**7**	**31**	**0**	**0**	**1**	**33**	**6.1**	**30**	**7**	**24**	**4**	**3**	....	....	....	....	....	....	....	....
	NHL Totals		**612**	**98**	**270**	**368**	**81**	**189**	**270**	**1292**	**37**	**1**	**9**	**1431**	**6.8**	**978**	**324**	**860**	**122**		**79**	**12**	**49**	**61**	**178**	**5**	**0**	**0**

Memorial Cup All-Star Team (1975, 1977) • Played in NHL All-Star Game (1984)

Traded to **Quebec** by **Minnesota** with Brent Ashton for Tony McKegney and Bo Berglund, December 14, 1984. Traded to **Toronto** by **Quebec** for John Anderson, August 21, 1985. Traded to **Vancouver** by **Toronto** for Vancouver's 5th round choice (Len Esau) in 1988 Entry Draft, October 3, 1986. Claimed on waivers by **NY Rangers** from **Vancouver**, January 20, 1987. Traded to **Minnesota** by **NY Rangers** for future considerations, February 21, 1987.

• MAXWELL, Bryan Bryan Clifford D – L. 6'2", 200 lbs. b: North Bay, Ont., 9/7/1955. Minnesota's 1st, 4th overall, in 1975.

			REGULAR SEASON																		PLAYOFFS							
Season	Club	League	GP	G	A	Pts	AG	AA	APts	PIM	PP	SH	GW	S	%	TGF	PGF	TGA	PGA	+/–	GP	G	A	Pts	PIM	PP	SH	GW
1972-73	Drumheller Falcons	AJHL	STATISTICS NOT AVAILABLE																									
	Medicine Hat Tigers	WCJHL	37	1	11	12				25											16	0	1	1	29			
1973-74	Medicine Hat Tigers	WCJHL	63	11	56	67				229											6	0	4	4	18			
1974-75	Medicine Hat Tigers	WCJHL	63	14	50	64				288											5	3	4	7	19			
	Canada	WJC-A	5	0	0	0				10																		
1975-76	Cleveland Crusaders	WHA	73	3	14	17				177											2	0	1	1	4			
1976-77	Cincinnati Stingers	WHA	34	1	8	9				29											4	0	0	0	29			
	Springfield Indians	AHL	13	2	3	5				67																		
1977-78	New England Whalers	WHA	17	2	1	3				11																		
	Binghamton Dusters	AHL	24	2	8	10				69																		
	Minnesota North Stars	**NHL**	**18**	**2**	**5**	**7**	**2**	**4**	**6**	**41**	**1**	**0**	**0**	**33**	**6.1**	**20**	**1**	**23**	**6**	**2**								
1978-79	**Minnesota North Stars**	**NHL**	**25**	**1**	**6**	**7**	**1**	**4**	**5**	**46**	**0**	**0**	**0**	**32**	**3.1**	**15**	**0**	**32**	**4**	**–13**								
	Oklahoma City Stars	CHL	15	1	4	5				35																		
1979-80	**St. Louis Blues**	**NHL**	**57**	**1**	**11**	**12**	**1**	**8**	**9**	**112**	**0**	**0**	**0**	**34**	**2.9**	**39**	**1**	**53**	**2**	**–13**	**1**	**0**	**0**	**0**	**9**	**0**	**0**	**0**
	Salt Lake Golden Eagles	CHL	3	0	1	1				10																		
1980-81	**St. Louis Blues**	**NHL**	**40**	**3**	**10**	**13**	**2**	**7**	**9**	**137**	**0**	**0**	**0**	**35**	**8.6**	**39**	**0**	**34**	**2**	**7**	**11**	**0**	**1**	**1**	**54**	**0**	**0**	**0**
	Salt Lake Golden Eagles	CHL	5	0	1	1				7																		
1981-82	**Winnipeg Jets**	**NHL**	**45**	**1**	**9**	**10**	**1**	**6**	**7**	**110**	**0**	**0**	**0**	**45**	**2.2**	**50**	**4**	**73**	**16**	**–11**								
1982-83	**Winnipeg Jets**	**NHL**	**54**	**7**	**13**	**20**	**6**	**9**	**15**	**131**	**1**	**0**	**0**	**78**	**9.0**	**65**	**12**	**55**	**8**	**6**	**3**	**1**	**0**	**1**	**23**	**1**	**0**	**0**
1983-84	**Winnipeg Jets**	**NHL**	**3**	**0**	**3**	**3**	**0**	**2**	**2**	**27**	**0**	**0**	**0**	**6**	**0.0**	**5**	**0**	**4**	**0**	**1**								
	Pittsburgh Penguins	**NHL**	**45**	**3**	**12**	**15**	**2**	**8**	**10**	**84**	**0**	**0**	**0**	**55**	**5.5**	**58**	**10**	**64**	**18**	**2**								
1984-85	**Pittsburgh Penguins**	**NHL**	**44**	**0**	**8**	**8**	**0**	**5**	**5**	**57**	**0**	**0**	**0**	**27**	**0.0**	**30**	**1**	**73**	**21**	**–23**								
	Baltimore Skipjacks	AHL	4	0	0	0				2											14	3	2	5	40			
1985-86			OUT OF HOCKEY – RETIRED																									
1987-1988	Medicine Hat Tigers	WHL	DID NOT PLAY – COACHING																									
1988-1989	**Los Angeles Kings**	**NHL**	DID NOT PLAY – ASSISTANT COACH																									
1989-1994	Spokane Chiefs	WHL	DID NOT PLAY – COACHING																									
1994-1996			OUT OF HOCKEY – RETIRED																									
1996-2000	Lethbridge Hurricanes	WHL	DID NOT PLAY – COACHING																									
	NHL Totals		**331**	**18**	**77**	**95**	**15**	**53**	**68**	**745**	**2**	**0**	**0**	**345**	**5.2**	**321**	**29**	**411**	**77**		**15**	**1**	**1**	**2**	**86**	**1**	**0**	**0**
	Other Major League Totals		124	6	23	29				217											6	0	1	1	33			

Selected by **Cleveland** (WHA) in 1975 WHA Amateur Draft, June, 1975. Transferred to **Minnesota** (WHA) after **Cleveland** (WHA) franchise relocated, June, 1976. Traded to **Cincinnati** (WHA) by **Minnesota** (WHA) for John McKenzie and the rights to Ivan Hlinka, September, 1976. Traded to **New England** (WHA) by **Cincinnati** (WHA) with Greg Carroll for the rights to Mike Liut and future considerations, May, 1977. Signed as a free agent by **Minnesota** after securing release from **New England** (WHA), February, 1978. Traded to **St. Louis** by **Minnesota** with Ritchie Hansen for St. Louis' 2nd round choice (later traded to Calgary — Calgary selected Dave Reierson) in 1982 Entry Draft, June 10, 1979. Traded to **Winnipeg** by **St. Louis** with Paul MacLean and Ed Staniowski for Scott Campbell and John Markell, July 3, 1981. Claimed on waivers by **Pittsburgh** from **Winnipeg**, October 13, 1983.

• MAXWELL, Kevin Kevin Preston C – R. 5'9", 165 lbs. b: Edmonton, Alta., 3/30/1960. Minnesota's 4th, 63rd overall, in 1979.

Season	Club	League	GP	G	A	Pts	AG	AA	APts	PIM	PP	SH	GW	S	%	TGF	PGF	TGA	PGA	+/–	GP	G	A	Pts	PIM	PP	SH	GW
1976-77	Penticton Vees	BCJHL	67	63	82	*145				135																		
1977-78	Penticton Vees	BCJHL	43	53	65	118				101																		
1978-79	University of North Dakota	WCHA	42	31	51	82				79																		
1979-80	Canada	Nat-Team	57	25	46	71				28																		
	Canada	Olympics	6	0	5	5				4																		
1980-81	Minnesota North Stars	DN-Cup	2	0	2	2				*8																		
	Minnesota North Stars	**NHL**	**6**	**0**	**3**	**3**	**0**	**2**	**2**	**7**	**0**	**0**	**0**	**9**	**0.0**	**4**	**0**	**5**	**0**	**–1**	**16**	**3**	**4**	**7**	**24**	**0**	**1**	**0**
	Oklahoma City Stars	CHL	31	8	13	21				38																		
1981-82	**Minnesota North Stars**	**NHL**	**12**	**1**	**4**	**5**	**1**	**3**	**4**	**8**	**0**	**0**	**0**	**20**	**5.0**	**9**	**1**	**9**	**0**	**–1**								
	Nashville South Stars	CHL	5	4	2	6				6																		
	Colorado Rockies	**NHL**	**34**	**5**	**5**	**10**	**4**	**3**	**7**	**44**	**0**	**0**	**1**	**52**	**9.6**	**19**	**0**	**38**	**3**	**–16**								
1982-83	Wichita Wind	CHL	68	24	41	65				47																		
1983-84	**New Jersey Devils**	**NHL**	**14**	**0**	**3**	**3**	**0**	**2**	**2**	**2**	**0**	**0**	**0**	**8**	**0.0**	**3**	**0**	**13**	**1**	**–9**								
	Maine Mariners	AHL	56	21	27	48				59											17	5	11	16	36			
1984-85	Maine Mariners	AHL	52	25	21	46				70											11	7	7	14	4			
1985-86	Maine Mariners	AHL	49	14	17	31				77											5	2	1	3	9			
1986-87	Hershey Bears	AHL	56	12	20	32				139											3	1	0	1	30			
1987-88	Hershey Bears	AHL	77	36	49	85				55											12	3	5	8	20			
	NHL Totals		**66**	**6**	**15**	**21**	**5**	**10**	**15**	**61**	**0**	**0**	**1**	**89**	**6.7**	**35**	**1**	**65**	**4**		**16**	**3**	**4**	**7**	**24**	**0**	**1**	**0**

WCHA First All-Star Team (1979) • NCAA West First All-American Team (1979)

Traded to **Colorado** by **Minnesota** with the rights to Jim Dobson for cash, December 31, 1981. Transferred to **New Jersey** after **Colorado** franchise relocated, June 30, 1982.

• MAY, Alan Alan Randy RW – R. 6'1", 200 lbs. b: Swan Hills, Alta., 1/14/1965.

Season	Club	League	GP	G	A	Pts	AG	AA	APts	PIM	PP	SH	GW	S	%	TGF	PGF	TGA	PGA	+/–	GP	G	A	Pts	PIM	PP	SH	GW
1984-85	Estevan Bruins	SJHL	64	51	47	98				409																		
1985-86	Medicine Hat Tigers	WHL	6	1	0	1				25																		
	New Westminster Bruins	WHL	32	8	9	17				81																		
1986-87	Springfield Indians	AHL	4	0	2	2				11																		
	Carolina Thunderbirds	ACHL	42	23	14	37				310											5	2	2	4	57			
1987-88	**Boston Bruins**	**NHL**	**3**	**0**	**0**	**0**	**0**	**0**	**0**	**15**	**0**	**0**	**0**	**3**	**0.0**	**0**	**0**	**1**	**0**	**–1**								
	Maine Mariners	AHL	61	14	11	25				257																		
	Nova Scotia Oilers	AHL	13	4	1	5				54											4	0	0	0	51			
1988-89	**Edmonton Oilers**	**NHL**	**3**	**1**	**0**	**1**	**1**	**0**	**1**	**7**	**0**	**0**	**1**	**3**	**33.3**	**1**	**0**	**1**	**0**	**0**								
	Cape Breton Oilers	AHL	50	12	13	25				214																		
	New Haven Nighthawks	AHL	12	2	8	10				99											16	6	3	9	*105			
1989-90	Washington Capitals	Fr-Tour	3	1	0	1				4																		
	Washington Capitals	**NHL**	**77**	**7**	**10**	**17**	**6**	**7**	**13**	**339**	**1**	**0**	**2**	**67**	**10.4**	**32**	**5**	**29**	**1**	**–1**	**15**	**0**	**0**	**0**	**37**	**0**	**0**	**0**
1990-91	**Washington Capitals**	**NHL**	**67**	**4**	**6**	**10**	**4**	**5**	**9**	**264**	**0**	**0**	**0**	**66**	**6.1**	**19**	**0**	**29**	**0**	**–10**	**11**	**1**	**1**	**2**	**37**	**0**	**0**	**1**
1991-92	**Washington Capitals**	**NHL**	**75**	**6**	**9**	**15**	**5**	**7**	**12**	**221**	**0**	**0**	**1**	**43**	**14.0**	**22**	**1**	**28**	**0**	**–7**	**7**	**0**	**0**	**0**	**0**	**0**	**0**	**0**
1992-93	**Washington Capitals**	**NHL**	**83**	**6**	**10**	**16**	**5**	**7**	**12**	**268**	**0**	**0**	**1**	**75**	**8.0**	**26**	**0**	**25**	**0**	**1**	**6**	**0**	**1**	**1**	**6**	**0**	**0**	**0**
1993-94	**Washington Capitals**	**NHL**	**43**	**4**	**7**	**11**	**4**	**5**	**9**	**97**	**0**	**0**	**0**	**33**	**12.1**	**15**	**0**	**17**	**0**	**–2**								
	Dallas Stars	**NHL**	**8**	**1**	**0**	**1**	**1**	**0**	**1**	**18**	**0**	**0**	**1**	**7**	**14.3**	**1**	**0**	**3**	**1**	**–1**	**1**	**0**	**0**	**0**	**0**	**0**	**0**	**0**
1994-95	**Dallas Stars**	**NHL**	**27**	**1**	**1**	**2**	**2**	**1**	**3**	**106**	**0**	**0**	**0**	**23**	**4.3**	**8**	**0**	**7**	**0**	**1**								
	Calgary Flames	**NHL**	**7**	**1**	**2**	**3**	**2**	**3**	**5**	**13**	**0**	**0**	**0**	**5**	**20.0**	**5**	**0**	**3**	**0**	**2**								
1995-96	Orlando Solar Bears	IHL	4	0	0	0				11																		
	Detroit Vipers	IHL	17	2	5	7				49																		
	Utah Grizzlies	IHL	53	13	12	25				108											14	1	2	3	14			
1996-97	Houston Aeros	IHL	82	7	11	18				270											13	1	2	3	28			
1997-98	Fayetteville Force	CHL	DID NOT PLAY – COACHING																									
1998-99	Abilene Aviators	WPHL	22	6	10	16				48											3	1	0	1	9			
99-2000	Lubbock Cottonkings	WPHL	DID NOT PLAY – COACHING																									
	NHL Totals		**393**	**31**	**45**	**76**	**30**	**35**	**65**	**1348**	**1**	**0**	**6**	**325**	**9.5**	**129**	**6**	**143**	**2**		**40**	**1**	**2**	**3**	**80**	**0**	**0**	**1**

Signed as a free agent by **Boston**, October 30, 1987. Traded to **Edmonton** by **Boston** for Moe Lemay, March 8, 1988. Traded to **LA Kings** by **Edmonton** with Jim Wiemer for Brian Wilks and John English, March 7, 1989. Traded to **Washington** by **LA Kings** for Washington's 5th round choice (Thomas Newman) in 1989 Entry Draft, June 17, 1989. Traded to **Dallas** by **Washington** with Washington's 7th round choice (Jeff Dewar) in 1995 Entry Draft for Jim Johnson, March 21, 1994. Traded to **Calgary** by **Dallas** for Calgary's 8th round choice (Sergei Luchinkin) in 1995 Entry Draft, April 7, 1995.

• MAY, Brad Bradley S. LW – L. 6'1", 210 lbs. b: Toronto, Ont., 11/29/1971. Buffalo's 1st, 14th overall, in 1990.

Season	Club	League	GP	G	A	Pts	AG	AA	APts	PIM	PP	SH	GW	S	%	TGF	PGF	TGA	PGA	+/–	GP	G	A	Pts	PIM	PP	SH	GW
1987-88	Markham Majors	OMHA	31	22	37	59				58																		
	Markham Travelways	OJHL	6	1	1	2				21																		
1988-89	Niagara Falls Thunder	OHL	65	8	14	22				304											17	0	1	1	55			

Season	Club	League	GP	G	A	Pts	AG	AA	APts	PIM	PP	SH	GW	S	%	TGF	PGF	TGA	PGA	+/–	GP	G	A	Pts	PIM	PP	SH	GW
			REGULAR SEASON																		PLAYOFFS							
1989-90	Niagara Falls Thunder	OHL	61	32	58	90	....	....	....	223	....	....	....	....	....	....	....	....	....	....	16	9	13	22	64	....	....	....
1990-91	Niagara Falls Thunder	OHL	34	37	32	69	....	....	....	93	....	....	....	....	....	....	....	....	....	....	14	11	14	25	53	....	....	....
	Canada	WJC-A	7	1	0	1	....	....	....	2	....	....	....	....	....	....	....	....	....	....	....	....	....	....	....	....	....	....
1991-92	**Buffalo Sabres**	**NHL**	**69**	**11**	**6**	**17**	**10**	**5**	**15**	**309**	**1**	**0**	**3**	**82**	**13.4**	**25**	**1**	**36**	**0**	**–12**	**7**	**1**	**4**	**5**	**2**	**0**	**0**	**1**
1992-93	**Buffalo Sabres**	**NHL**	**82**	**13**	**13**	**26**	**11**	**9**	**20**	**242**	**0**	**0**	**1**	**114**	**11.4**	**55**	**2**	**50**	**0**	**3**	**8**	**1**	**1**	**2**	**14**	**0**	**0**	**1**
1993-94	**Buffalo Sabres**	**NHL**	**84**	**18**	**27**	**45**	**17**	**21**	**38**	**171**	**3**	**0**	**3**	**166**	**10.8**	**72**	**24**	**54**	**0**	**–6**	**7**	**0**	**2**	**2**	**9**	**0**	**0**	**0**
1994-95	**Buffalo Sabres**	**NHL**	**33**	**3**	**3**	**6**	**5**	**4**	**9**	**87**	**1**	**0**	**0**	**42**	**7.1**	**16**	**1**	**10**	**0**	**5**	**4**	**0**	**0**	**0**	**2**	**0**	**0**	**0**
1995-96	**Buffalo Sabres**	**NHL**	**79**	**15**	**29**	**44**	**15**	**24**	**39**	**295**	**3**	**0**	**4**	**168**	**8.9**	**70**	**17**	**48**	**1**	**6**	....	....	....	....	....	....	....	....
	Canada	WC-A	8	0	0	0	....	....	....	6	....	....	....	....	....	....	....	....	....	....	....	....	....	....	....	....	....	....
1996-97	**Buffalo Sabres**	**NHL**	**42**	**3**	**4**	**7**	**3**	**4**	**7**	**106**	**1**	**0**	**1**	**75**	**4.0**	**14**	**6**	**16**	**0**	**–8**	**10**	**1**	**1**	**2**	**32**	**0**	**0**	**0**
1997-98	**Buffalo Sabres**	**NHL**	**36**	**4**	**7**	**11**	**5**	**7**	**12**	**113**	**0**	**0**	**0**	**41**	**9.8**	**12**	**0**	**10**	**0**	**2**	....	....	....	....	....	....	....	....
	Vancouver Canucks	**NHL**	**27**	**9**	**3**	**12**	**11**	**3**	**14**	**41**	**4**	**0**	**2**	**56**	**16.1**	**23**	**8**	**16**	**1**	**0**	....	....	....	....	....	....	....	....
1998-99	**Vancouver Canucks**	**NHL**	**66**	**6**	**11**	**17**	**7**	**11**	**18**	**102**	**1**	**0**	**1**	**91**	**6.6**	**30**	**8**	**39**	**3**	**–14**	....	....	....	....	....	....	....	....
99-2000	**Vancouver Canucks**	**NHL**	**59**	**9**	**7**	**16**	**10**	**6**	**16**	**90**	**0**	**0**	**3**	**66**	**13.6**	**22**	**0**	**24**	**0**	**–2**	....	....	....	....	....	....	....	....
	NHL Totals		**577**	**91**	**110**	**201**	**94**	**94**	**188**	**1556**	**14**	**0**	**18**	**901**	**10.1**	**339**	**67**	**303**	**5**		**36**	**3**	**8**	**11**	**59**	**0**	**0**	**2**

OHL Second All-Star Team (1990, 1991)

• Missed majority of 1990-91 season recovering from knee injury suffered at Team Canada Juniors evaluation camp, August 21, 1990. Traded to **Vancouver** by **Buffalo** with Buffalo's 3rd round choice (later traded to Tampa Bay - Tampa Bay selected Jimmie Olvestad) in 1999 Entry Draft for Geoff Sanderson, February 4, 1998. Traded to **Phoenix** by **Vancouver** for future considerations, June 24, 2000.

• MAYER, Derek

D – R. 6', 200 lbs. b: Rossland, B.C., 5/21/1967. Detroit's 3rd, 43rd overall, in 1986.

Season	Club	League	GP	G	A	Pts	AG	AA	APts	PIM	PP	SH	GW	S	%	TGF	PGF	TGA	PGA	+/–	GP	G	A	Pts	PIM	PP	SH	GW
1984-85	Penticton Knights	BCJHL	42	6	30	36	....	....	....	137	....	....	....	....	....	....	....	....	....	....	....	....	....	....	....	....	....	....
	Penticton Knights	Cen-Cup	5	0	3	3	....	....	....	4	....	....	....	....	....	....	....	....	....	....	....	....	....	....	....	....	....	....
1985-86	University of Denver	WCHA	44	2	7	9	....	....	....	42	....	....	....	....	....	....	....	....	....	....	....	....	....	....	....	....	....	....
1986-87	University of Denver	WCHA	38	5	17	22	....	....	....	87	....	....	....	....	....	....	....	....	....	....	....	....	....	....	....	....	....	....
1987-88	University of Denver	WCHA	34	5	16	21	....	....	....	82	....	....	....	....	....	....	....	....	....	....	....	....	....	....	....	....	....	....
1988-89	Canada	Nat-Team	58	3	13	16	....	....	....	81	....	....	....	....	....	....	....	....	....	....	....	....	....	....	....	....	....	....
1989-90	Adirondack Red Wings	AHL	62	4	26	30	....	....	....	56	....	....	....	....	....	....	....	....	....	....	5	0	6	6	4	....	....	....
1990-91	San Diego Gulls	IHL	31	9	24	33	....	....	....	31	....	....	....	....	....	....	....	....	....	....	....	....	....	....	....	....	....	....
	Adirondack Red Wings	AHL	21	4	9	13	....	....	....	20	....	....	....	....	....	....	....	....	....	....	2	0	1	1	0	....	....	....
1991-92	Adirondack Red Wings	AHL	25	4	11	15	....	....	....	31	....	....	....	....	....	....	....	....	....	....	....	....	....	....	....	....	....	....
	San Diego Gulls	IHL	30	7	16	23	....	....	....	47	....	....	....	....	....	....	....	....	....	....	4	0	0	0	20	....	....	....
1992-93	Canada	Nat-Team	64	12	28	40	....	....	....	108	....	....	....	....	....	....	....	....	....	....	....	....	....	....	....	....	....	....
	Canada	WC-A	8	0	0	0	....	....	....	2	....	....	....	....	....	....	....	....	....	....	....	....	....	....	....	....	....	....
1993-94	Canada	Nat-Team	49	4	15	19	....	....	....	61	....	....	....	....	....	....	....	....	....	....	....	....	....	....	....	....	....	....
	Canada	Olympics	8	1	2	3	....	....	....	18	....	....	....	....	....	....	....	....	....	....	....	....	....	....	....	....	....	....
	Ottawa Senators	**NHL**	**17**	**2**	**2**	**4**	**2**	**2**	**4**	**8**	**1**	**0**	**0**	**29**	**6.9**	**14**	**8**	**27**	**5**	**–16**	....	....	....	....	....	....	....	....
1994-95	Atlanta Knights	IHL	55	7	17	24	....	....	....	77	....	....	....	....	....	....	....	....	....	....	5	1	1	2	10	....	....	....
1995-96	Tappara Tampere	Finland	50	17	8	25	....	....	....	96	....	....	....	....	....	....	....	....	....	....	4	3	4	7	18	....	....	....
	Canada	Nat-Team	12	1	4	5	....	....	....	25	....	....	....	....	....	....	....	....	....	....	....	....	....	....	....	....	....	....
	Canada	WC-A	8	1	1	2	....	....	....	2	....	....	....	....	....	....	....	....	....	....	....	....	....	....	....	....	....	....
1996-97	Eisbaren Berlin	Germany	47	7	14	21	....	....	....	134	....	....	....	....	....	....	....	....	....	....	8	0	3	3	16	....	....	....
1997-98	Eisbaren Berlin	Germany	47	7	11	18	....	....	....	77	....	....	....	....	....	....	....	....	....	....	10	2	2	4	2	....	....	....
1998-99	Eisbaren Berlin	Germany	41	6	12	18	....	....	....	34	....	....	....	....	....	....	....	....	....	....	8	0	0	0	6	....	....	....
	Eisbaren Berlin	EuroHL	2	0	0	0	....	....	....	0	....	....	....	....	....	....	....	....	....	....	6	0	1	1	29	....	....	....
99-2000	Eisbaren Berlin	Germany	50	3	11	14	....	....	....	81	....	....	....	....	....	....	....	....	....	....	....	....	....	....	....	....	....	....
	NHL Totals		**17**	**2**	**2**	**4**	**2**	**2**	**4**	**8**	**1**	**0**	**0**	**29**	**6.9**	**14**	**8**	**27**	**5**		....	....	....	....	....	....	....	....

Signed as a free agent by **Ottawa**, March 4, 1994.

• MAYER, Jim

James Patrick RW – R. 6', 190 lbs. b: Capreol, Ont., 10/30/1954. NY Rangers' 20th, 239th overall, in 1974.

Season	Club	League	GP	G	A	Pts	AG	AA	APts	PIM	PP	SH	GW	S	%	TGF	PGF	TGA	PGA	+/–	GP	G	A	Pts	PIM	PP	SH	GW
1971-72	Chelmsford Cougars	NOHA	52	31	42	73	....	....	....	39	....	....	....	....	....	....	....	....	....	....	....	....	....	....	....	....	....	....
1972-73	Michigan Tech Huskies	WCHA	32	6	10	16	....	....	....	10	....	....	....	....	....	....	....	....	....	....	....	....	....	....	....	....	....	....
1973-74	Michigan Tech Huskies	WCHA	30	3	9	12	....	....	....	24	....	....	....	....	....	....	....	....	....	....	....	....	....	....	....	....	....	....
1974-75	Michigan Tech Huskies	WCHA	26	9	7	16	....	....	....	12	....	....	....	....	....	....	....	....	....	....	....	....	....	....	....	....	....	....
1975-76	Michigan Tech Huskies	WCHA	43	29	42	71	....	....	....	58	....	....	....	....	....	....	....	....	....	....	....	....	....	....	....	....	....	....
1976-77	Calgary Cowboys	WHA	21	2	3	5	....	....	....	0	....	....	....	....	....	....	....	....	....	....	....	....	....	....	....	....	....	....
	Erie Blades	NAHL	14	5	4	9	....	....	....	15	....	....	....	....	....	....	....	....	....	....	....	....	....	....	....	....	....	....
	Tidewater Sharks	SHL	23	11	12	23	....	....	....	8	....	....	....	....	....	....	....	....	....	....	....	....	....	....	....	....	....	....
1977-78	New England Whalers	WHA	51	11	9	20	....	....	....	21	....	....	....	....	....	....	....	....	....	....	....	....	....	....	....	....	....	....
	Springfield Indians	AHL	19	6	7	13	....	....	....	31	....	....	....	....	....	....	....	....	....	....	4	0	2	2	6	....	....	....
1978-79	Edmonton Oilers	WHA	2	0	0	0	....	....	....	0	....	....	....	....	....	....	....	....	....	....	....	....	....	....	....	....	....	....
	Dallas Black Hawks	CHL	64	33	43	76	....	....	....	78	....	....	....	....	....	....	....	....	....	....	9	4	6	10	14	....	....	....
1979-80	**New York Rangers**	**NHL**	**4**	**0**	**0**	**0**	**0**	**0**	**0**	**0**	**0**	**0**	**0**	**2**	**0.0**	**2**	**1**	**0**	**0**	**1**	....	....	....	....	....	....	....	....
	New Haven Nighthawks	AHL	62	32	35	67	....	....	....	91	....	....	....	....	....	....	....	....	....	....	10	7	2	9	25	....	....	....
1980-81	New Haven Nighthawks	AHL	10	1	4	5	....	....	....	6	....	....	....	....	....	....	....	....	....	....	....	....	....	....	....	....	....	....
	Dallas Black Hawks	CHL	13	1	5	6	....	....	....	2	....	....	....	....	....	....	....	....	....	....	....	....	....	....	....	....	....	....
	Fort Worth Texans	CHL	50	13	9	22	....	....	....	36	....	....	....	....	....	....	....	....	....	....	5	0	2	2	2	....	....	....
1981-82	New Haven Nighthawks	AHL	75	11	23	34	....	....	....	33	....	....	....	....	....	....	....	....	....	....	4	2	3	5	0	....	....	....
	NHL Totals		**4**	**0**	**0**	**0**	**0**	**0**	**0**	**0**	**0**	**0**	**0**	**2**	**0.0**	**2**	**1**	**0**	**0**		....	....	....	....	....	....	....	....
	Other Major League Totals		74	13	12	25	....	....	....	21	....	....	....	....	....	....	....	....	....	....	....	....	....	....	....	....	....	....

CHL Second All-Star Team (1979)

Signed as a free agent by **Calgary** (WHA), September, 1976. Signed as a free agent by **New England** (WHA) after **Calgary** (WHA) franchise folded, July 11, 1977. Claimed on waivers by **Edmonton** (WHA) from **New England** (WHA), May, 1978. Reclaimed by **NY Rangers** from **Edmonton** prior to Expansion Draft, June 9, 1979. Traded to **Vancouver** by **NY Rangers** with Mario Marois for Jeff Bandura and Jere Gillis, November 11, 1980. Traded to **Colorado** by **Vancouver** for Mike Christie, December, 1980.

• MAYER, Pat

Patrick D – L. 6'3", 225 lbs. b: Royal Oak, MI, 7/24/1961.

Season	Club	League	GP	G	A	Pts	AG	AA	APts	PIM	PP	SH	GW	S	%	TGF	PGF	TGA	PGA	+/–	GP	G	A	Pts	PIM	PP	SH	GW
1982-83	USA International University	GWHC	30	3	6	9	....	....	....	68	....	....	....	....	....	....	....	....	....	....	....	....	....	....	....	....	....	....
1983-84	USA International University	GWHC	35	1	15	16	....	....	....	89	....	....	....	....	....	....	....	....	....	....	....	....	....	....	....	....	....	....
1984-85	USA International University	GWHC	28	3	14	17	....	....	....	94	....	....	....	....	....	....	....	....	....	....	....	....	....	....	....	....	....	....
1985-86	Toledo Goaldiggers	IHL	61	1	13	14	....	....	....	216	....	....	....	....	....	....	....	....	....	....	....	....	....	....	....	....	....	....
	Muskegon Lumberjacks	IHL	13	1	2	3	....	....	....	17	....	....	....	....	....	....	....	....	....	....	13	0	2	2	37	....	....	....
1986-87	Muskegon Lumberjacks	IHL	71	4	14	18	....	....	....	387	....	....	....	....	....	....	....	....	....	....	13	1	0	1	53	....	....	....
1987-88	**Pittsburgh Penguins**	**NHL**	**1**	**0**	**0**	**0**	**0**	**0**	**0**	**4**	**0**	**0**	**0**	**0**	**0.0**	**0**	**0**	**0**	**0**	**0**	....	....	....	....	....	....	....	....
	Muskegon Lumberjacks	IHL	73	3	10	13	....	....	....	*450	....	....	....	....	....	....	....	....	....	....	5	0	0	0	47	....	....	....
1988-89	Muskegon Lumberjacks	IHL	56	0	13	13	....	....	....	314	....	....	....	....	....	....	....	....	....	....	....	....	....	....	....	....	....	....
	New Haven Nighthawks	AHL	6	0	0	0	....	....	....	35	....	....	....	....	....	....	....	....	....	....	....	....	....	....	....	....	....	....
	NHL Totals		**1**	**0**	**0**	**0**	**0**	**0**	**0**	**4**	**0**	**0**	**0**	**0**	**0.0**	**0**	**0**	**0**	**0**		....	....	....	....	....	....	....	....

Signed as a free agent by **Pittsburgh**, July 10, 1987. Traded to **LA Kings** by **Pittsburgh** for Tim Tookey, March 7, 1989.

• MAYERS, Jamal

Jamal David "Jammer" C – R. 6'1", 212 lbs. b: Toronto, Ont., 10/24/1974. St. Louis' 3rd, 89th overall, in 1993.

Season	Club	League	GP	G	A	Pts	AG	AA	APts	PIM	PP	SH	GW	S	%	TGF	PGF	TGA	PGA	+/–	GP	G	A	Pts	PIM	PP	SH	GW
1990-91	Thornhill Rattlers	OJHL	44	12	24	36	....	....	....	78	....	....	....	....	....	....	....	....	....	....	....	....	....	....	....	....	....	....
1991-92	Thornhill Rattlers	OJHL	56	38	69	107	....	....	....	36	....	....	....	....	....	....	....	....	....	....	....	....	....	....	....	....	....	....
1992-93	Western Michigan University	CCHA	38	8	17	25	....	....	....	26	....	....	....	....	....	....	....	....	....	....	....	....	....	....	....	....	....	....
1993-94	Western Michigan University	CCHA	40	17	32	49	....	....	....	40	....	....	....	....	....	....	....	....	....	....	....	....	....	....	....	....	....	....
1994-95	Western Michigan University	CCHA	39	13	32	45	....	....	....	40	....	....	....	....	....	....	....	....	....	....	....	....	....	....	....	....	....	....
1995-96	Western Michigan University	CCHA	38	17	22	39	....	....	....	75	....	....	....	....	....	....	....	....	....	....	....	....	....	....	....	....	....	....
1996-97	**St. Louis Blues**	**NHL**	**6**	**0**	**1**	**1**	**0**	**1**	**1**	**2**	**0**	**0**	**0**	**7**	**0.0**	**1**	**1**	**4**	**1**	**–3**	....	....	....	....	....	....	....	....
	Worcester IceCats	AHL	62	12	14	26	....	....	....	104	....	....	....	....	....	....	....	....	....	....	5	4	5	9	4	....	....	....

Season	Club	League	GP	G	A	Pts	AG	AA	APts	PIM	PP	SH	GW	S	%	TGF	PGF	TGA	PGA	+/–	GP	G	A	Pts	PIM	PP	SH	GW
			REGULAR SEASON																		PLAYOFFS							
1997-98	Worcester IceCats	AHL	61	19	24	43	....	....	....	117	....	....	....	....	....	....	....	....	....	....	11	3	4	7	10	....	....	....
1998-99	**St. Louis Blues**	**NHL**	**34**	**4**	**5**	**9**	**5**	**5**	**10**	**40**	**0**	**0**	**0**	**48**	**8.3**	**11**	**0**	**14**	**0**	**–3**	**11**	**0**	**1**	**1**	**8**	**0**	**0**	**0**
	Worcester IceCats	AHL	20	9	7	16	....	....	....	34	....	....	....	....	....	....	....	....	....	....	....	....	....	....	....	....	....	....
99-2000	**St. Louis Blues**	**NHL**	**79**	**7**	**10**	**17**	**8**	**9**	**17**	**90**	**0**	**0**	**0**	**99**	**7.1**	**26**	**0**	**26**	**0**	**0**	**7**	**0**	**4**	**4**	**2**	**0**	**0**	**0**
	Canada	WC-A	7	1	0	1	....	....	....	2	....	....	....	....	....	....	....	....	....	....	....	....	....	....	....	....	....	....
	NHL Totals		**119**	**11**	**16**	**27**	**13**	**15**	**28**	**132**	**0**	**0**	**0**	**154**	**7.1**	**38**	**1**	**44**	**1**		**18**	**0**	**5**	**5**	**10**	**0**	**0**	**0**

• MAZUR, Jay

John A. C/RW – R. 6'2", 205 lbs. b: Hamilton, Ont., 1/22/1965. Vancouver's 12th, 240th overall, in 1983.

Season	Club	League	GP	G	A	Pts	AG	AA	APts	PIM	PP	SH	GW	S	%	TGF	PGF	TGA	PGA	+/–	GP	G	A	Pts	PIM	PP	SH	GW
1982-83	Breck Mustangs	Hi-School	STATISTICS NOT AVAILABLE																									
1983-84	University of Maine	H-East	34	14	9	23	....	....	....	14	....	....	....	....	....	....	....	....	....	....	....	....	....	....	....	....	....	....
1984-85	University of Maine	H-East	31	0	6	6	....	....	....	20	....	....	....	....	....	....	....	....	....	....	....	....	....	....	....	....	....	....
1985-86	University of Maine	H-East	34	5	7	12	....	....	....	18	....	....	....	....	....	....	....	....	....	....	....	....	....	....	....	....	....	....
1986-87	University of Maine	H-East	39	16	10	26	....	....	....	61	....	....	....	....	....	....	....	....	....	....	....	....	....	....	....	....	....	....
1987-88	Flint Spirits	IHL	39	17	11	28	....	....	....	28	....	....	....	....	....	....	....	....	....	....	....	....	....	....	....	....	....	....
	Fredericton Express	AHL	31	14	6	20	....	....	....	28	....	....	....	....	....	....	....	....	....	....	15	4	2	6	38	....	....	....
1988-89	**Vancouver Canucks**	**NHL**	**1**	**0**	**0**	**0**	**0**	**0**	**0**	**0**	**0**	**0**	**0**	**0**	**0.0**	**0**	**0**	**0**	**0**	**0**	....	....	....	....	....	....	....	....
	Milwaukee Admirals	IHL	73	33	31	64	....	....	....	86	....	....	....	....	....	....	....	....	....	....	11	6	5	11	2	....	....	....
1989-90	**Vancouver Canucks**	**NHL**	**5**	**0**	**0**	**0**	**0**	**0**	**0**	**4**	**0**	**0**	**0**	**4**	**0.0**	**0**	**0**	**3**	**1**	**–2**	....	....	....	....	....	....	....	....
	Milwaukee Admirals	IHL	70	20	27	47	....	....	....	63	....	....	....	....	....	....	....	....	....	....	6	3	0	3	6	....	....	....
1990-91	**Vancouver Canucks**	**NHL**	**36**	**11**	**7**	**18**	**10**	**5**	**15**	**14**	**1**	**1**	**2**	**59**	**18.6**	**29**	**2**	**40**	**16**	**3**	**6**	**0**	**1**	**1**	**8**	**0**	**0**	**0**
	Milwaukee Admirals	IHL	7	2	3	5	....	....	....	21	....	....	....	....	....	....	....	....	....	....	....	....	....	....	....	....	....	....
1991-92	**Vancouver Canucks**	**NHL**	**5**	**0**	**0**	**0**	**0**	**0**	**0**	**2**	**0**	**0**	**0**	**3**	**0.0**	**1**	**0**	**6**	**3**	**–2**	....	....	....	....	....	....	....	....
	Milwaukee Admirals	IHL	56	17	20	37	....	....	....	49	....	....	....	....	....	....	....	....	....	....	5	2	3	5	0	....	....	....
1992-93	Hamilton Canucks	AHL	59	21	17	38	....	....	....	30	....	....	....	....	....	....	....	....	....	....	....	....	....	....	....	....	....	....
1993-94	Hamilton Canucks	AHL	78	40	55	95	....	....	....	40	....	....	....	....	....	....	....	....	....	....	4	2	2	4	4	....	....	....
1994-95	Detroit Vipers	IHL	64	23	27	50	....	....	....	64	....	....	....	....	....	....	....	....	....	....	1	0	1	1	2	....	....	....
1995-96	Tallahassee Tiger Sharks	ECHL	10	7	8	15	....	....	....	6	....	....	....	....	....	....	....	....	....	....	....	....	....	....	....	....	....	....
	Portland Pirates	AHL	38	11	7	18	....	....	....	39	....	....	....	....	....	....	....	....	....	....	....	....	....	....	....	....	....	....
	Rochester Americans	AHL	16	5	2	7	....	....	....	16	....	....	....	....	....	....	....	....	....	....	19	3	7	10	19	....	....	....
1996-97	HC Milano	Alpenliga	13	2	4	6	....	....	....	23	....	....	....	....	....	....	....	....	....	....	....	....	....	....	....	....	....	....
	HC Milano	EuroHL	3	0	0	0	....	....	....	14	....	....	....	....	....	....	....	....	....	....	....	....	....	....	....	....	....	....
	EV Duisburg	Germany-2	38	28	26	54	....	....	....	34	....	....	....	....	....	....	....	....	....	....	....	....	....	....	....	....	....	....
1997-98	Pee Dee Pride	ECHL	69	25	33	58	....	....	....	55	....	....	....	....	....	....	....	....	....	....	8	2	6	8	2	....	....	....
1998-99	Alexandria Warthogs	WPHL	61	22	53	75	....	....	....	12	....	....	....	....	....	....	....	....	....	....	....	....	....	....	....	....	....	....
99-2000	Alexandria Warthogs	WPHL	47	21	34	55	....	....	....	27	....	....	....	....	....	....	....	....	....	....	....	....	....	....	....	....	....	....
	NHL Totals		**47**	**11**	**7**	**18**	**10**	**5**	**15**	**20**	**1**	**1**	**2**	**66**	**16.7**	**30**	**2**	**49**	**20**		**6**	**0**	**1**	**1**	**8**	**0**	**0**	**0**

• Played w/ RHI's Detroit Mustangs in 1995 (9-2-3-5-4); Pennsylvania Posse in 1998 (13-7-16-23-3) and Chicago Bluesmen in 1999 (1-0-0-0-0).

• McADAM, Gary

Gary F. LW – L. 5'11", 175 lbs. b: Smiths Falls, Ont., 12/31/1955. Buffalo's 4th, 53rd overall, in 1975.

Season	Club	League	GP	G	A	Pts	AG	AA	APts	PIM	PP	SH	GW	S	%	TGF	PGF	TGA	PGA	+/–	GP	G	A	Pts	PIM	PP	SH	GW
1972-73	Ottawa 67's	OMJHL	61	14	8	22	....	....	....	23	....	....	....	....	....	....	....	....	....	....	9	2	1	3	4	....	....	....
1973-74	St. Catharines Black Hawks	OMJHL	67	30	37	67	....	....	....	41	....	....	....	....	....	....	....	....	....	....	....	....	....	....	....	....	....	....
	St. Catharines Black Hawks	Mem-Cup	3	0	2	2	....	....	....	7	....	....	....	....	....	....	....	....	....	....	....	....	....	....	....	....	....	....
1974-75	St. Catharines Black Hawks	OMJHL	65	24	53	77	....	....	....	111	....	....	....	....	....	....	....	....	....	....	4	4	0	4	4	....	....	....
1975-76	**Buffalo Sabres**	**NHL**	**31**	**1**	**2**	**3**	**1**	**1**	**2**	**2**	**0**	**0**	**0**	**12**	**8.3**	**3**	**0**	**4**	**1**	**0**	**1**	**0**	**0**	**0**	**0**	**0**	**0**	**0**
	Hershey Bears	AHL	24	14	13	27	....	....	....	45	....	....	....	....	....	....	....	....	....	....	10	3	2	5	9	....	....	....
1976-77	**Buffalo Sabres**	**NHL**	**73**	**13**	**16**	**29**	**12**	**12**	**24**	**17**	**1**	**0**	**2**	**86**	**15.1**	**42**	**1**	**24**	**0**	**17**	**6**	**1**	**0**	**1**	**0**	**0**	**0**	**0**
1977-78	**Buffalo Sabres**	**NHL**	**79**	**19**	**22**	**41**	**17**	**17**	**34**	**44**	**2**	**0**	**5**	**160**	**11.9**	**62**	**8**	**51**	**0**	**3**	**8**	**2**	**2**	**4**	**7**	**0**	**0**	**0**
1978-79	**Buffalo Sabres**	**NHL**	**40**	**6**	**5**	**11**	**5**	**4**	**9**	**13**	**1**	**0**	**1**	**39**	**15.4**	**17**	**3**	**21**	**1**	**–6**	....	....	....	....	....	....	....	....
	Pittsburgh Penguins	**NHL**	**28**	**5**	**9**	**14**	**4**	**7**	**11**	**2**	**0**	**0**	**1**	**52**	**9.6**	**28**	**1**	**23**	**0**	**4**	**7**	**2**	**1**	**3**	**0**	**0**	**0**	**0**
1979-80	**Pittsburgh Penguins**	**NHL**	**78**	**19**	**22**	**41**	**16**	**16**	**32**	**63**	**3**	**0**	**2**	**195**	**9.7**	**61**	**11**	**69**	**2**	**–17**	**5**	**1**	**2**	**3**	**9**	**0**	**0**	**0**
1980-81	**Pittsburgh Penguins**	**NHL**	**34**	**3**	**9**	**12**	**2**	**6**	**8**	**30**	**0**	**0**	**0**	**52**	**5.8**	**15**	**0**	**41**	**10**	**–16**	....	....	....	....	....	....	....	....
	Detroit Red Wings	**NHL**	**40**	**5**	**14**	**19**	**4**	**9**	**13**	**27**	**1**	**0**	**0**	**92**	**5.4**	**28**	**5**	**39**	**2**	**–14**	....	....	....	....	....	....	....	....
1981-82	**Calgary Flames**	**NHL**	**46**	**12**	**15**	**27**	**9**	**10**	**19**	**18**	**0**	**0**	**1**	**72**	**16.7**	**39**	**1**	**52**	**8**	**–6**	**3**	**0**	**0**	**0**	**0**	**0**	**0**	**0**
	Dallas Black Hawks	CHL	12	10	10	20	....	....	....	14	....	....	....	....	....	....	....	....	....	....	....	....	....	....	....	....	....	....
1982-83	**Buffalo Sabres**	**NHL**	**4**	**1**	**0**	**1**	**1**	**0**	**1**	**0**	**0**	**0**	**0**	**3**	**33.3**	**2**	**0**	**9**	**3**	**–4**	....	....	....	....	....	....	....	....
	Rochester Americans	AHL	73	40	29	69	....	....	....	58	....	....	....	....	....	....	....	....	....	....	16	3	4	7	4	....	....	....
1983-84	Maine Mariners	AHL	10	3	4	7	....	....	....	18	....	....	....	....	....	....	....	....	....	....	....	....	....	....	....	....	....	....
	Washington Capitals	**NHL**	**24**	**1**	**5**	**6**	**1**	**3**	**4**	**12**	**0**	**0**	**1**	**23**	**4.3**	**9**	**0**	**9**	**0**	**0**	....	....	....	....	....	....	....	....
	New Jersey Devils	**NHL**	**38**	**9**	**6**	**15**	**7**	**4**	**11**	**15**	**0**	**2**	**1**	**60**	**15.0**	**19**	**0**	**32**	**9**	**–4**	....	....	....	....	....	....	....	....
1984-85	**New Jersey Devils**	**NHL**	**4**	**1**	**1**	**2**	**1**	**1**	**2**	**0**	**0**	**0**	**0**	**1**	**100.0**	**2**	**0**	**4**	**2**	**0**	....	....	....	....	....	....	....	....
	Maine Mariners	AHL	70	32	20	52	....	....	....	39	....	....	....	....	....	....	....	....	....	....	10	4	6	10	0	....	....	....
1985-86	**Toronto Maple Leafs**	**NHL**	**15**	**1**	**6**	**7**	**1**	**4**	**5**	**0**	**0**	**0**	**0**	**9**	**11.1**	**9**	**0**	**25**	**5**	**–11**	....	....	....	....	....	....	....	....
	St. Catharines Saints	AHL	27	15	18	33	....	....	....	16	....	....	....	....	....	....	....	....	....	....	....	....	....	....	....	....	....	....
	NHL Totals		**534**	**96**	**132**	**228**	**81**	**94**	**175**	**243**	**8**	**2**	**14**	**856**	**11.2**	**336**	**30**	**403**	**43**		**30**	**6**	**5**	**11**	**16**	**0**	**0**	**0**

Traded to **Pittsburgh** by **Buffalo** for Dave Schultz, February 6, 1979. Traded to **Detroit** by **Pittsburgh** for Errol Thompson, January 8, 1981. Traded to **Calgary** by **Detroit** with Detroit's 4th round choice (John Bekkers) in 1983 Entry Draft for Eric Vail, November 10, 1981. Signed as a free agent by **Buffalo**, September 17, 1982. Signed as a free agent by **New Jersey**, August 4, 1983. Claimed on waivers by **Washington** from **New Jersey**, November 17, 1983. Rights traded to **New Jersey** by **Washington** for cash, January 18, 1984. Signed as a free agent by **Toronto**, July 31, 1985.

• McALLISTER, Chris

Chris J. D – L. 6'7", 235 lbs. b: Saskatoon, Sask., 6/16/1975. Vancouver's 1st, 40th overall, in 1995.

Season	Club	League	GP	G	A	Pts	AG	AA	APts	PIM	PP	SH	GW	S	%	TGF	PGF	TGA	PGA	+/–	GP	G	A	Pts	PIM	PP	SH	GW
1992-93	Saskatoon Royals	SJHL-B	40	14	14	28	....	....	....	224	....	....	....	....	....	....	....	....	....	....	....	....	....	....	....	....	....	....
	Saskatoon Blades	WHL	4	0	0	0	....	....	....	2	....	....	....	....	....	....	....	....	....	....	....	....	....	....	....	....	....	....
1993-94	Humboldt Broncos	SJHL	50	3	5	8	....	....	....	150	....	....	....	....	....	....	....	....	....	....	....	....	....	....	....	....	....	....
	Saskatoon Blades	WHL	2	0	0	0	....	....	....	5	....	....	....	....	....	....	....	....	....	....	....	....	....	....	....	....	....	....
1994-95	Saskatoon Blades	WHL	65	2	8	10	....	....	....	134	....	....	....	....	....	....	....	....	....	....	10	0	0	0	28	....	....	....
1995-96	Syracuse Crunch	AHL	68	0	2	2	....	....	....	142	....	....	....	....	....	....	....	....	....	....	16	0	0	0	34	....	....	....
1996-97	Syracuse Crunch	AHL	43	3	1	4	....	....	....	108	....	....	....	....	....	....	....	....	....	....	3	0	0	0	6	....	....	....
1997-98	**Vancouver Canucks**	**NHL**	**36**	**1**	**2**	**3**	**1**	**2**	**3**	**106**	**0**	**0**	**0**	**15**	**6.7**	**10**	**0**	**24**	**2**	**–12**	....	....	....	....	....	....	....	....
	Syracuse Crunch	AHL	23	0	1	1	....	....	....	71	....	....	....	....	....	....	....	....	....	....	5	0	0	0	21	....	....	....
1998-99	**Vancouver Canucks**	**NHL**	**28**	**1**	**1**	**2**	**1**	**1**	**2**	**63**	**0**	**0**	**0**	**6**	**16.7**	**3**	**0**	**10**	**0**	**–7**	....	....	....	....	....	....	....	....
	Syracuse Crunch	AHL	5	0	0	0	....	....	....	24	....	....	....	....	....	....	....	....	....	....	....	....	....	....	....	....	....	....
	Toronto Maple Leafs	**NHL**	**20**	**0**	**2**	**2**	**0**	**2**	**2**	**39**	**0**	**0**	**0**	**12**	**0.0**	**12**	**0**	**15**	**7**	**4**	**6**	**0**	**1**	**1**	**4**	**0**	**0**	**0**
99-2000	**Toronto Maple Leafs**	**NHL**	**36**	**0**	**3**	**3**	**0**	**3**	**3**	**68**	**0**	**0**	**0**	**12**	**0.0**	**13**	**0**	**18**	**1**	**–4**	....	....	....	....	....	....	....	....
	NHL Totals		**120**	**2**	**8**	**10**	**2**	**8**	**10**	**276**	**0**	**0**	**0**	**45**	**4.4**	**38**	**0**	**67**	**10**		**6**	**0**	**1**	**1**	**4**	**0**	**0**	**0**

Traded to **Toronto** by **Vancouver** for Darby Hendrickson, February 16, 1999.

• McALPINE, Chris

Christopher Walter "Mule" D – R. 6', 210 lbs. b: Roseville, MN, 12/1/1971. New Jersey's 10th, 137th overall, in 1990.

Season	Club	League	GP	G	A	Pts	AG	AA	APts	PIM	PP	SH	GW	S	%	TGF	PGF	TGA	PGA	+/–	GP	G	A	Pts	PIM	PP	SH	GW
1988-89	St. Paul Vulcans	USHL	STATISTICS NOT AVAILABLE																									
1989-90	Roseville High School	Hi-School	25	15	13	28	....	....	....	....	....	....	....	....	....	....	....	....	....	....	....	....	....	....	....	....	....	....
1990-91	University of Minnesota	WCHA	38	7	9	16	....	....	....	112	....	....	....	....	....	....	....	....	....	....	....	....	....	....	....	....	....	....
1991-92	University of Minnesota	WCHA	39	3	9	12	....	....	....	126	....	....	....	....	....	....	....	....	....	....	....	....	....	....	....	....	....	....
1992-93	University of Minnesota	WCHA	41	14	9	23	....	....	....	82	....	....	....	....	....	....	....	....	....	....	....	....	....	....	....	....	....	....
1993-94	University of Minnesota	WCHA	36	12	18	30	....	....	....	121	....	....	....	....	....	....	....	....	....	....	....	....	....	....	....	....	....	....
1994-95	Albany River Rats	AHL	48	4	18	22	....	....	....	49	....	....	....	....	....	....	....	....	....	....	....	....	....	....	....	....	....	....
♦	**New Jersey Devils**	**NHL**	**24**	**0**	**3**	**3**	**0**	**4**	**4**	**17**	**0**	**0**	**0**	**19**	**0.0**	**21**	**1**	**18**	**2**	**4**	....	....	....	....	....	....	....	....
1995-96	Albany River Rats	AHL	57	5	14	19	....	....	....	72	....	....	....	....	....	....	....	....	....	....	4	0	0	0	13	....	....	....
1996-97	Albany River Rats	AHL	44	1	9	10	....	....	....	48	....	....	....	....	....	....	....	....	....	....	....	....	....	....	....	....	....	....
	St. Louis Blues	**NHL**	**15**	**0**	**0**	**0**	**0**	**0**	**0**	**24**	**0**	**0**	**0**	**3**	**0.0**	**4**	**0**	**6**	**0**	**–2**	**4**	**0**	**1**	**1**	**0**	**0**	**0**	**0**
1997-98	**St. Louis Blues**	**NHL**	**54**	**3**	**7**	**10**	**4**	**7**	**11**	**36**	**0**	**0**	**0**	**35**	**8.6**	**29**	**0**	**17**	**2**	**14**	**10**	**0**	**0**	**0**	**16**	**0**	**0**	**0**

			REGULAR SEASON																		PLAYOFFS							
Season	Club	League	GP	G	A	Pts	AG	AA	APts	PIM	PP	SH	GW	S	%	TGF	PGF	TGA	PGA	+/–	GP	G	A	Pts	PIM	PP	SH	GW
1998-99	**St. Louis Blues**	**NHL**	51	1	1	2	1	1	2	50	0	0	0	56	1.8	19	0	35	6	–10	13	0	0	0	2	0	0	0
99-2000	**St. Louis Blues**	**NHL**	21	1	1	2	1	1	2	14	0	0	0	25	4.0	7	0	6	0	1	....	....	....	....	....	....	....	....
	Worcester IceCats	AHL	10	1	4	5	....	....	....	4	....	....	....	....	....	....	....	....	....	....	....	....	....	....	....	....	....	....
	Tampa Bay Lightning	**NHL**	10	1	1	2	1	1	2	10	0	0	0	5	20.0	3	0	12	4	–5	....	....	....	....	....	....	....	....
	Atlanta Thrashers	**NHL**	3	0	0	0	0	0	0	2	0	0	0	4	0.0	1	0	6	1	–4	....	....	....	....	....	....	....	....
	Detroit Vipers	IHL	8	0	0	0	....	....	....	6	....	....	....	....	....	....	....	....	....	....	....	....	....	....	....	....	....	....
	NHL Totals		**178**	**6**	**13**	**19**	**7**	**14**	**21**	**153**	**0**	**0**	**0**	**147**	**4.1**	**84**	**1**	**100**	**15**		**27**	**0**	**1**	**1**	**18**	**0**	**0**	**0**

WCHA First All-Star Team (1994) • NCAA West Second All-American Team (1994)

Traded to **St. Louis** by **New Jersey** with New Jersey's 9th round choice (James Desmarais) in 1999 Entry Draft for Peter Zezel, February 11, 1997. Traded to **Tampa Bay** by **St. Louis** with Rich Parent for Stephane Richer, January 13, 2000. Traded to **Atlanta** by **Tampa Bay** for Mikko Kuparinen, March 11, 2000.

• McAMMOND, Dean

C – L. 5′11″, 200 lbs. b: Grand Cache, Alta., 6/15/1973. Chicago's 1st, 22nd overall, in 1991.

Season	Club	League	GP	G	A	Pts	AG	AA	APts	PIM	PP	SH	GW	S	%	TGF	PGF	TGA	PGA	+/–	GP	G	A	Pts	PIM	PP	SH	GW
1988-89	St. Albert Raiders	AAHA	36	33	44	77	....	....	....	132	....	....	....	....	....	....	....	....	....	....	....	....	....	....	....	....	....	....
1989-90	Prince Albert Raiders	WHL	53	11	11	22	....	....	....	49	....	....	....	....	....	....	....	....	....	....	14	2	3	5	18	....	....	....
1990-91	Prince Albert Raiders	WHL	71	33	35	68	....	....	....	108	....	....	....	....	....	....	....	....	....	....	2	0	1	1	6	....	....	....
1991-92	Prince Albert Raiders	WHL	63	37	54	91	....	....	....	189	....	....	....	....	....	....	....	....	....	....	10	12	11	23	26	....	....	....
	Chicago Blackhawks	**NHL**	5	0	2	2	0	2	2	0	0	0	0	4	0.0	2	2	2	0	–2	3	0	0	0	2	0	0	0
1992-93	Prince Albert Raiders	WHL	30	19	29	48	....	....	....	44	....	....	....	....	....	....	....	....	....	....	....	....	....	....	....	....	....	....
	Canada	WJC-A	7	0	1	1	....	....	....	12	....	....	....	....	....	....	....	....	....	....	....	....	....	....	....	....	....	....
	Swift Current Broncos	WHL	18	10	13	23	....	....	....	24	....	....	....	....	....	....	....	....	....	....	17	*16	19	35	20	....	....	....
	Swift Current Broncos	Mem-Cup	4	0	3	3	....	....	....	10	....	....	....	....	....	....	....	....	....	....	....	....	....	....	....	....	....	....
1993-94	**Edmonton Oilers**	**NHL**	45	6	21	27	6	16	22	16	2	0	0	52	11.5	42	9	26	5	12	....	....	....	....	....	....	....	....
	Cape Breton Oilers	AHL	28	9	12	21	....	....	....	38	....	....	....	....	....	....	....	....	....	....	....	....	....	....	....	....	....	....
1994-95	**Edmonton Oilers**	**NHL**	6	0	0	0	0	0	0	0	0	0	0	3	0.0	0	0	2	1	–1	....	....	....	....	....	....	....	....
1995-96	**Edmonton Oilers**	**NHL**	53	15	15	30	15	12	27	23	4	0	0	79	19.0	42	12	28	4	6	....	....	....	....	....	....	....	....
	Cape Breton Oilers	AHL	22	9	15	24	....	....	....	55	....	....	....	....	....	....	....	....	....	....	....	....	....	....	....	....	....	....
	Canada	WC-A	8	0	2	2	....	....	....	2	....	....	....	....	....	....	....	....	....	....	....	....	....	....	....	....	....	....
1996-97	**Edmonton Oilers**	**NHL**	57	12	17	29	13	15	28	28	4	0	6	106	11.3	40	13	47	5	–15	....	....	....	....	....	....	....	....
1997-98	**Edmonton Oilers**	**NHL**	77	19	31	50	22	30	52	46	8	0	3	128	14.8	78	36	33	0	9	12	1	4	5	12	0	0	0
1998-99	**Edmonton Oilers**	**NHL**	65	9	16	25	11	15	26	36	1	0	0	122	7.4	44	7	35	3	5	....	....	....	....	....	....	....	....
	Chicago Blackhawks	**NHL**	12	1	4	5	1	4	5	2	0	0	1	16	6.3	9	1	6	1	3	....	....	....	....	....	....	....	....
99-2000	**Chicago Blackhawks**	**NHL**	76	14	18	32	16	17	33	72	1	0	1	118	11.9	49	4	47	13	11	....	....	....	....	....	....	....	....
	Canada	WC-A	8	0	0	0	....	....	....	0	....	....	....	....	....	....	....	....	....	....	....	....	....	....	....	....	....	....
	NHL Totals		**396**	**76**	**124**	**200**	**84**	**111**	**195**	**223**	**20**	**0**	**11**	**628**	**12.1**	**306**	**84**	**226**	**32**		**15**	**1**	**4**	**5**	**14**	**0**	**0**	**0**

Traded to **Edmonton** by **Chicago** with Igor Kravchuk for Joe Murphy, February 24, 1993. Traded to **Chicago** by **Edmonton** with Boris Mironov and Jonas Elofsson for Chad Kilger, Daniel Cleary, Ethan Moreau and Christian Laflamme, March 20, 1999.

• McANEELEY, Ted

Edward Joseph D – L. 5′9″, 185 lbs. b: Cranbrook, B.C., 11/7/1950. California's 4th, 47th overall, in 1970.

Season	Club	League	GP	G	A	Pts	AG	AA	APts	PIM	PP	SH	GW	S	%	TGF	PGF	TGA	PGA	+/–	GP	G	A	Pts	PIM	PP	SH	GW
1966-67	Calgary Buffalos	CMJHL	53	3	10	13	....	....	....	102	....	....	....	....	....	....	....	....	....	....	....	....	....	....	....	....	....	....
1967-68	Edmonton Oil Kings	WCJHL	46	2	5	7	....	....	....	114	....	....	....	....	....	....	....	....	....	....	10	0	0	0	0	....	....	....
1968-69	Edmonton Oil Kings	WCJHL	52	8	19	27	....	....	....	171	....	....	....	....	....	....	....	....	....	....	17	1	7	8	10	....	....	....
1969-70	Edmonton Oil Kings	WCJHL	60	29	25	54	....	....	....	92	....	....	....	....	....	....	....	....	....	....	16	3	9	12	79	....	....	....
1970-71	Providence Reds	AHL	60	4	3	7	....	....	....	71	....	....	....	....	....	....	....	....	....	....	10	0	0	0	2	....	....	....
1971-72	Baltimore Clippers	AHL	61	3	14	17	....	....	....	61	....	....	....	....	....	....	....	....	....	....	18	1	1	2	61	....	....	....
1972-73	**California Golden Seals**	**NHL**	77	4	13	17	4	10	14	75	1	0	0	74	5.4	57	5	85	4	–29	....	....	....	....	....	....	....	....
1973-74	**California Golden Seals**	**NHL**	72	4	20	24	4	16	20	62	0	1	0	80	5.0	78	11	105	14	–24	....	....	....	....	....	....	....	....
1974-75	**California Golden Seals**	**NHL**	9	0	2	2	0	1	1	4	0	0	0	7	0.0	2	0	10	2	–6	....	....	....	....	....	....	....	....
	Salt Lake Golden Eagles	CHL	63	9	41	50	....	....	....	147	....	....	....	....	....	....	....	....	....	....	11	1	4	5	18	....	....	....
1975-76	Edmonton Oilers	WHA	79	2	17	19	....	....	....	71	....	....	....	....	....	....	....	....	....	....	4	0	0	0	4	....	....	....
1976-77	Spokane Flyers	WIHL	56	4	21	25	....	....	....	42	....	....	....	....	....	....	....	....	....	....	....	....	....	....	....	....	....	....
1977-78	Spokane Flyers	WIHL	56	6	17	23	....	....	....	160	....	....	....	....	....	....	....	....	....	....	....	....	....	....	....	....	....	....
1978-79	Spokane Flyers	PHL	55	10	28	38	....	....	....	95	....	....	....	....	....	....	....	....	....	....	....	....	....	....	....	....	....	....
	NHL Totals		**158**	**8**	**35**	**43**	**8**	**27**	**35**	**141**	**1**	**1**	**0**	**161**	**5.0**	**137**	**16**	**200**	**20**		....	....	....	....	....	....	....	....
	Other Major League Totals		79	2	17	19	....	....	....	71	....	....	....	....	....	....	....	....	....	....	4	0	0	0	4	....	....	....

CHL Second All-Star Team (1975) • WIHL Second All-Star Team (1977) • WIHL First All-Star Team (1978) • PHL First All-Star Team (1979)

Selected by **Dayton-Houston** (WHA) in 1972 WHA General Player Draft, February 12, 1972. WHA rights traded to **Edmonton** (WHA) by **Houston** (WHA) for future considerations, June, 1975.

• McBAIN, Andrew

Andrew Burton RW – R. 6′1″, 205 lbs. b: Scarborough, Ont., 1/18/1965. Winnipeg's 1st, 8th overall, in 1983.

Season	Club	League	GP	G	A	Pts	AG	AA	APts	PIM	PP	SH	GW	S	%	TGF	PGF	TGA	PGA	+/–	GP	G	A	Pts	PIM	PP	SH	GW
1980-81	Aurora Eagles	OJHL	43	16	21	37	....	....	....	21	....	....	....	....	....	....	....	....	....	....	....	....	....	....	....	....	....	....
1981-82	Niagara Falls Flyers	OHL	68	19	25	44	....	....	....	35	....	....	....	....	....	....	....	....	....	....	5	0	3	3	4	....	....	....
1982-83	North Bay Centennials	OHL	67	33	87	120	....	....	....	61	....	....	....	....	....	....	....	....	....	....	8	2	6	8	17	....	....	....
1983-84	**Winnipeg Jets**	**NHL**	78	11	19	30	9	13	22	37	0	0	0	93	11.8	41	1	46	0	–6	3	2	0	2	0	0	0	0
1984-85	**Winnipeg Jets**	**NHL**	77	7	15	22	6	10	16	45	0	0	0	63	11.1	39	3	39	1	–2	7	1	0	1	0	0	0	0
1985-86	**Winnipeg Jets**	**NHL**	28	3	3	6	2	2	4	17	0	0	0	24	12.5	8	0	19	0	–11	....	....	....	....	....	....	....	....
1986-87	**Winnipeg Jets**	**NHL**	71	11	21	32	9	15	24	106	1	1	0	85	12.9	53	5	51	9	6	9	0	2	2	10	0	0	0
1987-88	**Winnipeg Jets**	**NHL**	74	32	31	63	27	22	49	145	20	0	5	146	21.9	102	60	72	20	–10	5	2	5	7	29	0	1	0
1988-89	**Winnipeg Jets**	**NHL**	80	37	40	77	31	28	59	71	20	1	3	180	20.6	113	52	120	24	–35	....	....	....	....	....	....	....	....
	Canada	WEC-A	10	6	2	8	....	....	....	8	....	....	....	....	....	....	....	....	....	....	....	....	....	....	....	....	....	....
1989-90	**Pittsburgh Penguins**	**NHL**	41	5	9	14	4	6	10	51	1	0	0	56	8.9	25	4	48	19	–8	....	....	....	....	....	....	....	....
	Vancouver Canucks	**NHL**	26	4	5	9	3	4	7	22	3	0	0	50	8.0	22	7	28	10	–3	....	....	....	....	....	....	....	....
1990-91	**Vancouver Canucks**	**NHL**	13	0	5	5	0	4	4	32	0	0	0	8	0.0	9	2	10	0	–3	....	....	....	....	....	....	....	....
	Milwaukee Admirals	IHL	47	27	24	51	....	....	....	69	....	....	....	....	....	....	....	....	....	....	6	2	5	7	12	....	....	....
1991-92	**Vancouver Canucks**	**NHL**	6	1	0	1	1	0	1	0	0	0	0	11	9.1	4	3	2	0	–1	....	....	....	....	....	....	....	....
	Milwaukee Admirals	IHL	65	24	54	78	....	....	....	132	....	....	....	....	....	....	....	....	....	....	5	1	2	3	10	....	....	....
1992-93	**Ottawa Senators**	**NHL**	59	7	16	23	6	11	17	43	1	0	0	71	9.9	29	7	63	4	–37	....	....	....	....	....	....	....	....
	New Haven Senators	AHL	1	0	1	1	....	....	....	4	....	....	....	....	....	....	....	....	....	....	....	....	....	....	....	....	....	....
1993-94	**Ottawa Senators**	**NHL**	55	11	8	19	10	6	16	64	8	0	0	91	12.1	33	19	69	14	–41	....	....	....	....	....	....	....	....
	P.E.I. Senators	AHL	26	6	10	16	....	....	....	102	....	....	....	....	....	....	....	....	....	....	....	....	....	....	....	....	....	....
1994-95	Las Vegas Thunder	IHL	62	15	27	42	....	....	....	111	....	....	....	....	....	....	....	....	....	....	8	0	3	3	33	....	....	....
1995-96	Fort Wayne Komets	IHL	77	15	15	30	....	....	....	85	....	....	....	....	....	....	....	....	....	....	5	0	2	2	10	....	....	....
	NHL Totals		**608**	**129**	**172**	**301**	**108**	**121**	**229**	**633**	**54**	**2**	**8**	**878**	**14.7**	**478**	**163**	**567**	**101**		**24**	**5**	**7**	**12**	**39**	**0**	**1**	**0**

OHL Second All-Star Team (1983)

• Missed majority of 1985-86 season recovering from knee injury suffered in game vs. LA Kings, December 8, 1985. Traded to **Pittsburgh** by **Winnipeg** with Jim Kyte and Randy Gilhen for Randy Cunneyworth, Rick Tabaracci and Dave McLlwain, June 17, 1989. Traded to **Vancouver** by **Pittsburgh** with Dave Capuano and Dan Quinn for Rod Buskas, Barry Pederson and Tony Tanti, January 8, 1990. Signed as a free agent by **Ottawa**, July 30, 1992.

• McBAIN, Jason

Jason D. D – L. 6′2″, 180 lbs. b: Ilion, NY, 4/12/1974. Hartford's 5th, 81st overall, in 1992.

Season	Club	League	GP	G	A	Pts	AG	AA	APts	PIM	PP	SH	GW	S	%	TGF	PGF	TGA	PGA	+/–	GP	G	A	Pts	PIM	PP	SH	GW
1989-90	Kimberley Bantam Dynamiters	BCAHA	37	20	38	58	....	....	....	77	....	....	....	....	....	....	....	....	....	....	....	....	....	....	....	....	....	....
1990-91	Lethbridge Hurricanes	WHL	52	2	7	9	....	....	....	39	....	....	....	....	....	....	....	....	....	....	1	0	0	0	0	....	....	....
1991-92	Lethbridge Hurricanes	WHL	13	0	1	1	....	....	....	12	....	....	....	....	....	....	....	....	....	....	....	....	....	....	....	....	....	....
	Portland Winter Hawks	WHL	54	9	23	32	....	....	....	95	....	....	....	....	....	....	....	....	....	....	6	1	0	1	13	....	....	....
1992-93	Portland Winter Hawks	WHL	71	9	35	44	....	....	....	76	....	....	....	....	....	....	....	....	....	....	16	2	12	14	14	....	....	....
1993-94	Portland Winter Hawks	WHL	63	15	51	66	....	....	....	86	....	....	....	....	....	....	....	....	....	....	10	2	7	9	14	....	....	....
	United States	WJC-A	7	1	1	2	....	....	....	10	....	....	....	....	....	....	....	....	....	....	....	....	....	....	....	....	....	....
1994-95	Springfield Falcons	AHL	77	16	28	44	....	....	....	92	....	....	....	....	....	....	....	....	....	....	....	....	....	....	....	....	....	....
	United States	WC-A	6	0	1	1	....	....	....	4	....	....	....	....	....	....	....	....	....	....	....	....	....	....	....	....	....	....
1995-96	**Hartford Whalers**	**NHL**	3	0	0	0	0	0	0	0	0	0	0	0	0.0	1	0	2	0	–1	....	....	....	....	....	....	....	....
	Springfield Falcons	AHL	73	11	33	44	....	....	....	43	....	....	....	....	....	....	....	....	....	....	8	1	1	2	2	....	....	....

			REGULAR SEASON																		PLAYOFFS							
Season	Club	League	GP	G	A	Pts	AG	AA	APts	PIM	PP	SH	GW	S	%	TGF	PGF	TGA	PGA	+/–	GP	G	A	Pts	PIM	PP	SH	GW
1996-97	**Hartford Whalers**	**NHL**	**6**	**0**	**0**	**0**	**0**	**0**	**0**	**0**	**0**	**0**	**0**	**1**	**0.0**	**0**	**0**	**4**	**0**	**–4**	....	....	....	....	....	....	....	....
	Springfield Falcons	AHL	58	8	26	34	....	....	....	40	....	....	....	....	....	....	....	....	....	....	16	0	8	8	12	....	....	....
1997-98	Cleveland Lumberjacks	IHL	65	8	22	30	....	....	....	62	....	....	....	....	....	....	....	....	....	....	3	0	2	2	2	....	....	....
1998-99	Las Vegas Thunder	IHL	65	9	37	46	....	....	....	54	....	....	....	....	....	....	....	....	....	....	....	....	....	....	....	....	....	....
	Providence Bruins	AHL	9	1	7	8	....	....	....	10	....	....	....	....	....	....	....	....	....	....	19	1	8	9	16	....	....	....
99-2000	Quebec Citadelles	AHL	51	8	16	24	....	....	....	29	....	....	....	....	....	....	....	....	....	....	....	....	....	....	....	....	....	....
	Grand Rapids Griffins	IHL	16	1	6	7	....	....	....	23	....	....	....	....	....	....	....	....	....	....	15	2	5	7	12	....	....	....
	NHL Totals		**9**	**0**	**0**	**0**	**0**	**0**	**0**	**0**	**0**	**0**	**0**	**1**	**0.0**	**1**	**0**	**6**	**0**		....	....	....	....	....	....	....	....

Transferred to **Carolina** after **Hartford** franchise relocated, June 25, 1997. Signed as a free agent by **Montreal**, August 23, 1999. Loaned to **Grand Rapids** (IHL) by **Montreal**, March 16, 2000.

• McBAIN, Mike

D – L. 6'2", 195 lbs. b: Kimberley, B.C., 1/12/1977. Tampa Bay's 2nd, 30th overall, in 1995.

Season	Club	League	GP	G	A	Pts	AG	AA	APts	PIM	PP	SH	GW	S	%	TGF	PGF	TGA	PGA	+/–	GP	G	A	Pts	PIM	PP	SH	GW
1991-92	Kimberley Bantam Dynamiters	BCAHA	35	25	62	87	....	....	....	39	....	....	....	....	....	....	....	....	....	....	....	....	....	....	....	....	....	....
1992-93	Kimberley Dynamiters	RMJHL	35	0	4	4	....	....	....	48	....	....	....	....	....	....	....	....	....	....	....	....	....	....	....	....	....	....
1993-94	Red Deer Rebels	WHL	58	4	13	17	....	....	....	41	....	....	....	....	....	....	....	....	....	....	4	0	0	0	0	....	....	....
1994-95	Red Deer Rebels	WHL	68	6	28	34	....	....	....	55	....	....	....	....	....	....	....	....	....	....	....	....	....	....	....	....	....	....
1995-96	Red Deer Rebels	WHL	68	7	34	41	....	....	....	68	....	....	....	....	....	....	....	....	....	....	10	1	7	8	10	....	....	....
1996-97	Red Deer Rebels	WHL	59	14	35	49	....	....	....	55	....	....	....	....	....	....	....	....	....	....	15	1	6	7	9	....	....	....
1997-98	**Tampa Bay Lightning**	**NHL**	**27**	**0**	**1**	**1**	**0**	**1**	**1**	**8**	**0**	**0**	**0**	**17**	**0.0**	**8**	**0**	**28**	**10**	**–10**	....	....	....	....	....	....	....	....
	Adirondack Red Wings	AHL	42	2	13	15	....	....	....	28	....	....	....	....	....	....	....	....	....	....	....	....	....	....	....	....	....	....
1998-99	**Tampa Bay Lighning**	**NHL**	**37**	**0**	**6**	**6**	**0**	**6**	**6**	**14**	**0**	**0**	**0**	**22**	**0.0**	**17**	**0**	**35**	**7**	**–11**	....	....	....	....	....	....	....	....
	Cleveland Lumberjacks	IHL	28	2	4	6	....	....	....	15	....	....	....	....	....	....	....	....	....	....	....	....	....	....	....	....	....	....
99-2000	Detroit Vipers	IHL	16	0	3	3	....	....	....	4	....	....	....	....	....	....	....	....	....	....	....	....	....	....	....	....	....	....
	Quebec Citadelles	AHL	53	5	7	12	....	....	....	34	....	....	....	....	....	....	....	....	....	....	3	0	0	0	2	....	....	....
	NHL Totals		**64**	**0**	**7**	**7**	**0**	**7**	**7**	**22**	**0**	**0**	**0**	**39**	**0.0**	**25**	**0**	**63**	**17**		....	....	....	....	....	....	....	....

Traded to **Montreal** by **Tampa Bay** for Gordie Dwyer, November 26, 1999.

• McBEAN, Wayne

Wayne A. D – L. 6'2", 185 lbs. b: Calgary, Alta., 2/21/1969. Los Angeles' 1st, 4th overall, in 1987.

Season	Club	League	GP	G	A	Pts	AG	AA	APts	PIM	PP	SH	GW	S	%	TGF	PGF	TGA	PGA	+/–	GP	G	A	Pts	PIM	PP	SH	GW
1984-85	Calgary North Stars	AAHA	38	8	34	42	....	....	....	46	....	....	....	....	....	....	....	....	....	....	....	....	....	....	....	....	....	....
1985-86	Medicine Hat Tigers	WHL	67	1	14	15	....	....	....	73	....	....	....	....	....	....	....	....	....	....	25	1	5	6	36	....	....	....
1986-87	Medicine Hat Tigers	WHL	71	12	41	53	....	....	....	163	....	....	....	....	....	....	....	....	....	....	20	2	8	10	40	....	....	....
	Medicine Hat Tigers	Mem-Cup	5	1	1	2	....	....	....	4	....	....	....	....	....	....	....	....	....	....	....	....	....	....	....	....	....	....
1987-88	Medicine Hat Tigers	WHL	30	15	30	45	....	....	....	48	....	....	....	....	....	....	....	....	....	....	16	6	17	23	50	....	....	....
	Canada	WJC-A	7	1	0	1	....	....	....	2	....	....	....	....	....	....	....	....	....	....	....	....	....	....	....	....	....	....
	Los Angeles Kings	**NHL**	**27**	**0**	**1**	**1**	**0**	**1**	**1**	**26**	**0**	**0**	**0**	**21**	**0.0**	**17**	**2**	**46**	**17**	**–14**	....	....	....	....	....	....	....	....
	Medicine Hat Tigers	Mem-Cup	5	1	4	5	....	....	....	8	....	....	....	....	....	....	....	....	....	....	....	....	....	....	....	....	....	....
1988-89	**Los Angeles Kings**	**NHL**	**33**	**0**	**5**	**5**	**0**	**4**	**4**	**23**	**0**	**0**	**0**	**19**	**0.0**	**12**	**0**	**22**	**1**	**–9**	....	....	....	....	....	....	....	....
	New Haven Nighthawks	AHL	7	1	1	2	....	....	....	2	....	....	....	....	....	....	....	....	....	....	....	....	....	....	....	....	....	....
	New York Islanders	**NHL**	**19**	**0**	**1**	**1**	**0**	**1**	**1**	**12**	**0**	**0**	**0**	**17**	**0.0**	**12**	**1**	**19**	**4**	**–4**	....	....	....	....	....	....	....	....
1989-90	**New York Islanders**	**NHL**	**5**	**0**	**1**	**1**	**0**	**1**	**1**	**2**	**0**	**0**	**0**	**3**	**0.0**	**4**	**1**	**4**	**0**	**–1**	**2**	**1**	**1**	**2**	**0**	**0**	**0**	**0**
	Springfield Indians	AHL	58	6	33	39	....	....	....	48	....	....	....	....	....	....	....	....	....	....	17	4	11	15	31	....	....	....
1990-91	**New York Islanders**	**NHL**	**52**	**5**	**14**	**19**	**5**	**11**	**16**	**47**	**2**	**0**	**0**	**93**	**5.4**	**43**	**16**	**62**	**14**	**–21**	....	....	....	....	....	....	....	....
	Capital District Islanders	AHL	22	9	9	18	....	....	....	19	....	....	....	....	....	....	....	....	....	....	....	....	....	....	....	....	....	....
1991-92	**New York Islanders**	**NHL**	**25**	**2**	**4**	**6**	**2**	**3**	**5**	**18**	**0**	**1**	**1**	**51**	**3.9**	**36**	**4**	**27**	**6**	**11**	....	....	....	....	....	....	....	....
1992-93	Capital District Islanders	AHL	20	1	9	10	....	....	....	35	....	....	....	....	....	....	....	....	....	....	3	0	1	1	9	....	....	....
1993-94	**New York Islanders**	**NHL**	**19**	**1**	**4**	**5**	**1**	**3**	**4**	**16**	**0**	**0**	**0**	**33**	**3.0**	**13**	**5**	**22**	**1**	**–13**	....	....	....	....	....	....	....	....
	Salt Lake Golden Eagles	IHL	5	0	6	6	....	....	....	2	....	....	....	....	....	....	....	....	....	....	....	....	....	....	....	....	....	....
	Winnipeg Jets	**NHL**	**31**	**2**	**9**	**11**	**2**	**7**	**9**	**24**	**2**	**0**	**0**	**81**	**2.5**	**30**	**18**	**34**	**1**	**–21**	....	....	....	....	....	....	....	....
1994-95	**Pittsburgh Penguins**	**NHL**	DID NOT PLAY – INJURED																									
	NHL Totals		**211**	**10**	**39**	**49**	**10**	**31**	**41**	**168**	**4**	**1**	**1**	**318**	**3.1**	**167**	**47**	**236**	**44**		**2**	**1**	**1**	**2**	**0**	**0**	**0**	**0**

WHL East First All-Star Team (1987) • Memorial Cup All-Star Team (1987) • Won Stafford Smythe Memorial Trophy (Memorial Cup Tournament MVP) (1987)

Traded to **NY Islanders** by **LA Kings** with Mark Fitzpatrick and future considerations (Doug Crossman, May 23, 1989) for Kelly Hrudey, February 22, 1989. • Missed remainder of 1991-92 season recovering from knee injury suffered in game vs. Pittsburgh, December 23, 1991. Traded to **Winnipeg** by **NY Islanders** for Yan Kaminsky, February 1, 1994. Claimed by **Pittsburgh** from **Winnipeg** in Waiver Draft, January 18, 1995. • Missed entire 1994-95 season recovering from eventual career-ending wrist surgery, October, 1994.

• McCABE, Bryan

Bryan T. D – L. 6'1", 210 lbs. b: St. Catharines, Ont., 6/8/1975. NY Islanders' 2nd, 40th overall, in 1993.

Season	Club	League	GP	G	A	Pts	AG	AA	APts	PIM	PP	SH	GW	S	%	TGF	PGF	TGA	PGA	+/–	GP	G	A	Pts	PIM	PP	SH	GW
1990-91	Calgary Canucks	AAHA	33	14	34	48	....	....	....	55	....	....	....	....	....	....	....	....	....	....	....	....	....	....	....	....	....	....
1991-92	Medicine Hat Tigers	WHL	68	6	24	30	....	....	....	157	....	....	....	....	....	....	....	....	....	....	4	0	0	0	6	....	....	....
1992-93	Medicine Hat Tigers	WHL	14	0	13	13	....	....	....	83	....	....	....	....	....	....	....	....	....	....	....	....	....	....	....	....	....	....
	Spokane Chiefs	WHL	46	3	44	47	....	....	....	134	....	....	....	....	....	....	....	....	....	....	6	1	5	6	28	....	....	....
1993-94	Spokane Chiefs	WHL	64	22	62	84	....	....	....	218	....	....	....	....	....	....	....	....	....	....	3	0	4	4	4	....	....	....
	Canada	WJC-A	7	0	0	0	....	....	....	6	....	....	....	....	....	....	....	....	....	....	....	....	....	....	....	....	....	....
1994-95	Spokane Chiefs	WHL	42	14	39	53	....	....	....	115	....	....	....	....	....	....	....	....	....	....	....	....	....	....	....	....	....	....
	Canada	WJC-A	7	3	9	12	....	....	....	4	....	....	....	....	....	....	....	....	....	....	....	....	....	....	....	....	....	....
	Brandon Wheat Kings	WHL	20	6	10	16	....	....	....	38	....	....	....	....	....	....	....	....	....	....	18	4	13	17	59	....	....	....
	Brandon Wheat Kings	Mem-Cup	4	3	4	7	....	....	....	6	....	....	....	....	....	....	....	....	....	....	....	....	....	....	....	....	....	....
1995-96	**New York Islanders**	**NHL**	**82**	**7**	**16**	**23**	**7**	**13**	**20**	**156**	**3**	**0**	**1**	**130**	**5.4**	**82**	**22**	**121**	**37**	**–24**	....	....	....	....	....	....	....	....
1996-97	**New York Islanders**	**NHL**	**82**	**8**	**20**	**28**	**8**	**18**	**26**	**165**	**2**	**1**	**2**	**117**	**6.8**	**89**	**17**	**99**	**25**	**–2**	....	....	....	....	....	....	....	....
	Canada	WC-A	11	0	2	2	....	....	....	10	....	....	....	....	....	....	....	....	....	....	....	....	....	....	....	....	....	....
1997-98	**New York Islanders**	**NHL**	**56**	**3**	**9**	**12**	**4**	**9**	**13**	**145**	**1**	**0**	**0**	**81**	**3.7**	**57**	**7**	**57**	**16**	**9**	....	....	....	....	....	....	....	....
	Vancouver Canucks	**NHL**	**26**	**1**	**11**	**12**	**1**	**11**	**12**	**64**	**0**	**1**	**0**	**42**	**2.4**	**32**	**7**	**26**	**11**	**10**	....	....	....	....	....	....	....	....
	Canada	WC-A	6	1	2	3	....	....	....	4	....	....	....	....	....	....	....	....	....	....	....	....	....	....	....	....	....	....
1998-99	**Vancouver Canucks**	**NHL**	**69**	**7**	**14**	**21**	**8**	**13**	**21**	**120**	**1**	**2**	**0**	**98**	**7.1**	**52**	**10**	**93**	**40**	**–11**	....	....	....	....	....	....	....	....
	Canada	WC-A	10	1	3	4	....	....	....	10	....	....	....	....	....	....	....	....	....	....	....	....	....	....	....	....	....	....
99-2000	**Chicago Blackhawks**	**NHL**	**79**	**6**	**19**	**25**	**7**	**18**	**25**	**139**	**2**	**0**	**2**	**119**	**5.0**	**88**	**17**	**103**	**24**	**–8**	....	....	....	....	....	....	....	....
	NHL Totals		**394**	**32**	**89**	**121**	**35**	**82**	**117**	**789**	**9**	**4**	**5**	**587**	**5.5**	**400**	**80**	**499**	**153**		....	....	....	....	....	....	....	....

WHL West Second All-Star Team (1993) • WHL West First All-Star Team (1994) • WJC-A All-Star Team (1995) • Named Best Defenseman at WJC-A (1995) • WHL East First All-Star Team (1995) • Memorial Cup All-Star Team (1995)

Traded to **Vancouver** by **NY Islanders** with Todd Bertuzzi and NY Islanders' 3rd round choice (Jarkko Ruutu) in 1998 Entry Draft for Trevor Linden, February 6, 1998. Traded to **Chicago** by **Vancouver** with Vancouver's 1st round choice (Pavel Vorobiev) in 2000 Entry Draft for Chicago's 1st round choice (later traded to Tampa Bay - later traded to NY Rangers - NY Rangers selected Pavel Brendl) in 1999 Entry Draft, June 25, 1999.

• McCAHILL, John

John Walter D – R. 6'1", 215 lbs. b: Sarnia, Ont., 12/2/1955.

Season	Club	League	GP	G	A	Pts	AG	AA	APts	PIM	PP	SH	GW	S	%	TGF	PGF	TGA	PGA	+/–	GP	G	A	Pts	PIM	PP	SH	GW
1974-75	University of Michigan	WCHA	21	0	7	7	....	....	....	18	....	....	....	....	....	....	....	....	....	....	....	....	....	....	....	....	....	....
1975-76	University of Michigan	WCHA	42	3	23	26	....	....	....	28	....	....	....	....	....	....	....	....	....	....	....	....	....	....	....	....	....	....
1976-77	University of Michigan	CCHA	45	0	27	27	....	....	....	54	....	....	....	....	....	....	....	....	....	....	....	....	....	....	....	....	....	....
1977-78	University of Michigan	CCHA	35	5	23	28	....	....	....	32	....	....	....	....	....	....	....	....	....	....	....	....	....	....	....	....	....	....
	Colorado Rockies	**NHL**	**1**	**0**	**0**	**0**	**0**	**0**	**0**	**0**	**0**	**0**	**0**	**0**	**0.0**	**0**	**0**	**0**	**0**	**0**	....	....	....	....	....	....	....	....
	Tulsa Oilers	CHL	9	1	0	1	....	....	....	0	....	....	....	....	....	....	....	....	....	....	7	0	0	0	7	....	....	....
1978-79	Philadelphia Firebirds	AHL	77	5	12	17	....	....	....	36	....	....	....	....	....	....	....	....	....	....	....	....	....	....	....	....	....	....
1979-80	Fort Worth Texans	CHL	31	4	14	18	....	....	....	10	....	....	....	....	....	....	....	....	....	....	....	....	....	....	....	....	....	....
	Oklahoma City Stars	CHL	51	4	19	23	....	....	....	14	....	....	....	....	....	....	....	....	....	....	....	....	....	....	....	....	....	....
1980-81	Fort Worth Texans	CHL	8	1	2	3	....	....	....	11	....	....	....	....	....	....	....	....	....	....	....	....	....	....	....	....	....	....
	Muskegon Mohawks	IHL	48	7	20	27	....	....	....	29	....	....	....	....	....	....	....	....	....	....	....	....	....	....	....	....	....	....
	NHL Totals		**1**	**0**	**0**	**0**	**0**	**0**	**0**	**0**	**0**	**0**	**0**	**0**	**0.0**	**0**	**0**	**0**	**0**		....	....	....	....	....	....	....	....

Signed as a free agent by **Colorado**, March 17, 1978.

Season	Club	League	REGULAR SEASON GP	G	A	Pts	AG	AA	APts	PIM	PP	SH	GW	S	%	TGF	PGF	TGA	PGA	+/-	PLAYOFFS GP	G	A	Pts	PIM	PP	SH	GW

• McCALLUM, Dunc

Duncan Selby D – R. 6'1", 193 lbs. b: Flin Flon, Man., 3/29/1940 d: 3/31/1983.

Season	Club	League	GP	G	A	Pts	AG	AA	APts	PIM	PP	SH	GW	S	%	TGF	PGF	TGA	PGA	+/-	GP	G	A	Pts	PIM	PP	SH	GW
1958-59	Brandon Wheat Kings	MJHL	28	10	11	21				48																		
1959-60	Brandon Wheat Kings	MJHL	32	8	9	17				84											11	4	3	7	10			
	Brandon Wheat Kings	Mem-Cup	11	4	3	7				21																		
	Edmonton Oil Kings	Mem-Cup	6	0	1	1				8																		
1960-61	Fort Wayne Komets	IHL	65	6	18	24				74											8	0	3	3	6			
1961-62	Seattle Totems	WHL	69	1	12	13				82											2	1	0	1	2			
1962-63	Sudbury Wolves	EPHL	62	5	20	25				*153											8	1	2	3	8			
1963-64	Vancouver Canucks	WHL	62	6	13	19				78																		
1964-65	Vancouver Canucks	WHL	68	8	11	19				104											5	1	0	1	10			
1965-66	**New York Rangers**	**NHL**	**2**	**0**	**0**	**0**	**0**	**0**	**0**	**2**																		
	Vancouver Canucks	WHL	68	5	19	24				104											7	1	1	2	16			
1966-67	Omaha Knights	CPHL	38	3	16	19				91											10	0	3	3	23			
1967-68	**Pittsburgh Penguins**	**NHL**	**32**	**0**	**2**	**2**	**0**	**2**	**2**	**36**	**0**	**0**	**0**	**34**	**0.0**	**28**	**2**	**29**	**1**	**–2**								
	Baltimore Clippers	AHL	19	3	7	10				37																		
1968-69	**Pittsburgh Penguins**	**NHL**	**62**	**5**	**13**	**18**	**5**	**12**	**17**	**81**	**2**	**1**	**1**	**99**	**5.1**	**59**	**12**	**95**	**13**	**–35**								
1969-70	**Pittsburgh Penguins**	**NHL**	**14**	**0**	**0**	**0**	**0**	**0**	**0**	**16**	**0**	**0**	**0**	**11**	**0.0**	**6**	**2**	**11**	**3**	**–4**	**10**	**1**	**2**	**3**	**12**	**0**	**0**	**0**
	Baltimore Clippers	AHL	4	2	0	2				6																		
1970-71	**Pittsburgh Penguins**	**NHL**	**77**	**9**	**20**	**29**	**9**	**17**	**26**	**95**	**1**	**0**	**1**	**104**	**8.7**	**70**	**4**	**93**	**14**	**–13**								
1971-72	San Diego Gulls	WHL	61	10	30	40				99											4	1	1	2	2			
1972-73	Houston Aeros	WHA	69	9	20	29				112											10	2	3	5	6			
1973-74	Houston Aeros	WHA	DID NOT PLAY – INJURED																									
1974-75	Chicago Cougars	WHA	31	0	10	10				24																		
	Long Island Cougars	NAHL	10	1	6	7				30																		
	NHL Totals		**187**	**14**	**35**	**49**	**14**	**31**	**45**	**230**											**10**	**1**	**2**	**3**	**12**			
	Other Major League Totals		100	9	30	39				136											10	2	3	5	6			

• Loaned to **Edmonton** (CAHL) by **Brandon** (MJHL) for Memorial Cup playoffs, March, 1960. Claimed by **Detroit** from **Vancouver** (WHL) in Inter-League Draft, June 8, 1965. Traded to **NY Rangers** by **Detroit** (Pittsburgh-AHL) for Bob Cunningham, June, 1965. Traded to **Pittsburgh** by **NY Rangers** with George Konik, Paul Andrea and Frank Francis for Larry Jeffrey, June 6, 1967. Selected by **Providence** (AHL) from **Pittsburgh** in 1969 NHL Reverse Draft, June 12, 1969. Suspened by **Providence** (AHL) for refusing to report to club, October, 1969. Traded to **Pittsburgh** by **Providence** (AHL) for cash, January, 1970. Selected by **Dayton-Houston** (WHA) in 1972 WHA General Player Draft, February 12, 1972. • Missed entire 1973-74 season recovering from broken leg suffered in exhibition game vs. LA Sharks (WHA), September 27, 1973. Signed as a free agent by **Chicago** (WHA) November 4, 1974.

• McCANN, Rick

Richard Leo C – L. 5'9", 178 lbs. b: Hamilton, Ont., 5/27/1944.

Season	Club	League	GP	G	A	Pts	AG	AA	APts	PIM	PP	SH	GW	S	%	TGF	PGF	TGA	PGA	+/-	GP	G	A	Pts	PIM	PP	SH	GW
1963-64	St. Mary's Lincolns	OHA-B	STATISTICS NOT AVAILABLE																									
1964-65	Michigan Tech Huskies	WCHA	DID NOT PLAY – FRESHMAN																									
1965-66	Canada	Nat-Team	STATISTICS NOT AVAILABLE																									
	Canada	WEC-A	1	0	0	0				2																		
1966-67	Memphis Wings	CPHL	61	15	26	41				23											1	0	0	0	0			
1967-68	**Detroit Red Wings**	**NHL**	**3**	**0**	**0**	**0**	**0**	**0**	**0**	**0**	**0**	**0**	**0**	**0**	**0.0**	**0**	**0**	**0**	**0**	**0**								
	Fort Worth Wings	CPHL	68	20	51	71				98											13	5	*11	*16	13			
1968-69	**Detroit Red Wings**	**NHL**	**3**	**0**	**0**	**0**	**0**	**0**	**0**	**0**	**0**	**0**	**0**	**2**	**0.0**	**0**	**0**	**2**	**1**	**–1**								
	Fort Worth Wings	CHL	67	22	49	71				63																		
1969-70	**Detroit Red Wings**	**NHL**	**18**	**0**	**1**	**1**	**0**	**1**	**1**	**4**	**0**	**0**	**0**	**10**	**0.0**	**2**	**0**	**6**	**2**	**–2**								
	Fort Worth Wings	CHL	47	15	24	39				29											7	2	4	6	4			
1970-71	**Detroit Red Wings**	**NHL**	**5**	**0**	**0**	**0**	**0**	**0**	**0**	**0**	**0**	**0**	**0**	**8**	**0.0**	**1**	**1**	**3**	**1**	**–2**								
	Baltimore Clippers	AHL	62	18	20	38				21											6	3	1	4	13			
1971-72	**Detroit Red Wings**	**NHL**	**1**	**0**	**0**	**0**	**0**	**0**	**0**	**0**	**0**	**0**	**0**	**0**	**0.0**	**0**	**0**	**0**	**0**	**0**								
	Tidewater Red Wings	AHL	69	13	38	51				39																		
1972-73	Virginia Wings	AHL	66	12	44	56				75											11	1	9	10	4			
1973-74	London Lions	Britain	70	25	55	80				28																		
1974-75	**Detroit Red Wings**	**NHL**	**13**	**1**	**3**	**4**	**1**	**2**	**3**	**2**	**0**	**0**	**0**	**10**	**10.0**	**5**	**0**	**12**	**3**	**–4**								
	Virginia Wings	AHL	65	19	48	67				60											5	1	4	5	0			
1975-76	New Haven Nighthawks	AHL	73	15	42	57				47											3	0	0	0	0			
	NHL Totals		**43**	**1**	**4**	**5**	**1**	**3**	**4**	**6**	**0**	**0**	**0**	**30**	**3.3**	**8**	**1**	**23**	**7**									

Signed as a free agent by **Detroit** (Memphis-CPHL), September, 1967.

• McCARTHY, Dan

Daniel Michael C – L. 5'9", 185 lbs. b: St. Marys, Ont., 4/7/1958. NY Rangers' 16th, 223rd overall, in 1978.

Season	Club	League	GP	G	A	Pts	AG	AA	APts	PIM	PP	SH	GW	S	%	TGF	PGF	TGA	PGA	+/-	GP	G	A	Pts	PIM	PP	SH	GW
1974-75	Stratford Cullitons	OHA-B	36	23	37	60				73																		
1975-76	Sudbury Wolves	OMJHL	65	17	30	47				23											17	1	7	8	8			
1976-77	Sudbury Wolves	OMJHL	54	23	32	55				76											6	0	3	3	12			
1977-78	Sudbury Wolves	OMJHL	68	30	51	81				96																		
	Toledo Goaldiggers	IHL	9	2	4	6				9																		
1978-79	Flint Generals	IHL	75	38	42	80				80																		
1979-80	New Haven Nighthawks	AHL	26	6	3	9				8																		
	Richmond Rifles	EHL	8	6	4	10				7											5	3	1	4	22			
1980-81	**New York Rangers**	**NHL**	**5**	**4**	**0**	**4**	**3**	**0**	**3**	**4**	**2**	**0**	**0**	**7**	**57.1**	**7**	**2**	**2**	**0**	**3**								
	New Haven Nighthawks	AHL	71	28	17	45				54											4	0	0	0	4			
1981-82	Springfield Indians	AHL	78	26	32	58				57																		
1982-83	Birmingham South Stars	CHL	76	30	35	65				67											13	4	5	9	15			
1983-84	Baltimore Skipjacks	AHL	27	8	11	19				8																		
1984-85	Baltimore Skipjacks	AHL	32	3	11	14				15											15	3	4	7	18			
1985-86	Springfield Indians	AHL	33	7	9	16				46																		
	NHL Totals		**5**	**4**	**0**	**4**	**3**	**0**	**3**	**4**	**2**	**0**	**0**	**7**	**57.1**	**7**	**2**	**2**	**0**									

Traded to **Minnesota** by **NY Rangers** for Shawn Dineen, August 23, 1982.

• McCARTHY, Kevin

D – R. 5'11", 195 lbs. b: Winnipeg, Man., 7/14/1957. Philadelphia's 1st, 17th overall, in 1977.

Season	Club	League	GP	G	A	Pts	AG	AA	APts	PIM	PP	SH	GW	S	%	TGF	PGF	TGA	PGA	+/-	GP	G	A	Pts	PIM	PP	SH	GW
1973-74	Winnipeg Clubs	WCJHL	66	5	22	27				65																		
1974-75	Winnipeg Clubs	WCJHL	66	20	61	81				102																		
	Canada	WJC-A	5	1	4	5				6																		
1975-76	Winnipeg Clubs	WCJHL	72	33	88	121				160											6	2	9	11	8			
1976-77	Winnipeg Monarchs	WCJHL	72	22	*105	127				110											7	0	4	4	27			
1977-78	**Philadelphia Flyers**	**NHL**	**62**	**2**	**15**	**17**	**2**	**12**	**14**	**32**	**0**	**0**	**0**	**91**	**2.2**	**56**	**0**	**35**	**8**	**29**	**10**	**0**	**1**	**1**	**8**	**0**	**0**	**0**
1978-79	**Philadelphia Flyers**	**NHL**	**22**	**1**	**2**	**3**	**1**	**1**	**2**	**21**	**0**	**0**	**0**	**16**	**6.3**	**14**	**2**	**16**	**6**	**2**								
	Vancouver Canucks	**NHL**	**1**	**0**	**0**	**0**	**0**	**0**	**0**	**0**	**0**	**0**	**0**	**0**	**0.0**	**0**	**0**	**2**	**0**	**–2**								
1979-80	**Vancouver Canucks**	**NHL**	**79**	**15**	**30**	**45**	**13**	**22**	**35**	**70**	**4**	**0**	**3**	**161**	**9.3**	**106**	**28**	**113**	**30**	**–5**	**4**	**1**	**0**	**1**	**0**	**0**	**0**	**0**
1980-81	**Vancouver Canucks**	**NHL**	**80**	**16**	**37**	**53**	**12**	**25**	**37**	**85**	**4**	**1**	**1**	**140**	**11.4**	**119**	**42**	**145**	**57**	**–11**	**3**	**0**	**1**	**1**	**0**	**0**	**0**	**0**
1981-82	**Vancouver Canucks**	**NHL**	**71**	**6**	**39**	**45**	**5**	**26**	**31**	**84**	**1**	**0**	**0**	**152**	**3.9**	**119**	**34**	**104**	**31**	**12**								
1982-83	**Vancouver Canucks**	**NHL**	**74**	**12**	**28**	**40**	**10**	**19**	**29**	**88**	**3**	**0**	**0**	**99**	**12.1**	**85**	**13**	**94**	**21**	**–1**	**4**	**1**	**1**	**2**	**12**	**0**	**0**	**0**
1983-84	**Vancouver Canucks**	**NHL**	**47**	**2**	**14**	**16**	**2**	**10**	**12**	**61**	**0**	**0**	**0**	**44**	**4.5**	**42**	**9**	**52**	**11**	**–8**								
	Pittsburgh Penguins	**NHL**	**31**	**4**	**16**	**20**	**3**	**11**	**14**	**52**	**1**	**0**	**0**	**57**	**7.0**	**36**	**11**	**76**	**19**	**–32**								
1984-85	**Pittsburgh Penguins**	**NHL**	**64**	**9**	**10**	**19**	**7**	**7**	**14**	**30**	**0**	**1**	**0**	**46**	**19.6**	**35**	**3**	**74**	**22**	**–20**								
1985-86	**Philadelphia Flyers**	**NHL**	**4**	**0**	**0**	**0**	**0**	**0**	**0**	**4**	**0**	**0**	**0**	**0**	**0.0**	**1**	**0**	**1**	**0**	**0**								
	Hershey Bears	AHL	64	15	40	55				157											17	1	10	11	12			

Season	Club	League	REGULAR SEASON																		PLAYOFFS							
			GP	G	A	Pts	AG	AA	APts	PIM	PP	SH	GW	S	%	TGF	PGF	TGA	PGA	+/–	GP	G	A	Pts	PIM	PP	SH	GW
1986-87	**Philadelphia Flyers**	**NHL**	2	0	0	0	0	0	0	0	0	0	0	0	0.0	0	0	1	0	–1								
	Hershey Bears	AHL	74	6	44	50				86											5	0	4	4	4			
1987-88	Hershey Bears	AHL	61	9	30	39				83											12	2	6	8	17			
	NHL Totals		**537**	**67**	**191**	**258**	**55**	**133**	**188**	**527**	**13**	**2**	**4**	**806**	**8.3**	**613**	**142**	**713**	**205**		**21**	**2**	**3**	**5**	**20**	**0**	**0**	**0**

WCJHL All-Star Team (1976, 1977) • AHL First All-Star Team (1986) • Played in NHL All-Star Game (1981)

Traded to **Vancouver** by **Philadelphia** with Drew Callander for Dennis Ververgaert, December 29, 1978. Traded to **Pittsburgh** by **Vancouver** for Philadelphia's 3rd round choice (previously acquired, later traded back to Philadelphia — Philadelphia selected David McClay) in 1985 Entry Draft, January 26, 1984. Signed as a free agent by **Philadelphia**, July 19, 1985.

• McCARTHY, Sandy

Alexander RW – R. 6'3", 225 lbs. b: Toronto, Ont., 6/15/1972. Calgary's 3rd, 52nd overall, in 1991.

Season	Club	League	GP	G	A	Pts	AG	AA	APts	PIM	PP	SH	GW	S	%	TGF	PGF	TGA	PGA	+/–	GP	G	A	Pts	PIM	PP	SH	GW
1987-88	Midland Centennials	OJHL-C	18	2	1	3				70																		
1988-89	Hawkesbury Hawks	OJHL	42	4	11	15				139																		
1989-90	Laval Titan	QMJHL	65	10	11	21				269											14	3	3	6	60			
	Laval Titan	Mem-Cup	4	0	0	0				2																		
1990-91	Laval Titan	QMJHL	68	21	19	40				297											13	6	5	11	67			
1991-92	Laval Titan	QMJHL	62	39	51	90				326											8	4	5	9	81			
1992-93	Salt Lake Golden Eagles	IHL	77	18	20	38				220																		
1993-94	**Calgary Flames**	**NHL**	79	5	5	10	5	4	9	173	0	0	0	39	12.8	18	0	22	1	–3	7	0	0	0	34	0	0	0
1994-95	**Calgary Flames**	**NHL**	37	5	3	8	9	4	13	101	0	0	2	29	17.2	21	6	14	0	1	6	0	1	1	17	0	0	0
1995-96	**Calgary Flames**	**NHL**	75	9	7	16	9	6	15	173	3	0	1	98	9.2	36	16	28	0	–8	4	0	0	0	10	0	0	0
1996-97	**Calgary Flames**	**NHL**	33	3	5	8	3	4	7	113	1	0	1	38	7.9	12	4	16	0	–8								
1997-98	**Calgary Flames**	**NHL**	52	8	5	13	9	5	14	170	1	0	1	68	11.8	19	7	30	0	–18								
	Tampa Bay Lightning	**NHL**	14	0	5	5	0	5	5	71	0	0	0	26	0.0	6	1	6	0	–1								
1998-99	**Tampa Bay Lightning**	**NHL**	67	5	7	12	6	7	13	135	1	0	0	89	5.6	19	2	39	0	–22								
	Philadelphia Flyers	**NHL**	13	0	1	1	0	1	1	25	0	0	0	18	0.0	3	0	5	0	–2	6	0	1	1	0	0	0	0
99-2000	**Philadelphia Flyers**	**NHL**	58	6	5	11	7	5	12	111	1	0	0	68	8.8	20	4	21	0	–5								
	Carolina Hurricanes	**NHL**	13	0	0	0	0	0	0	9	0	0	0	12	0.0	4	1	1	0	2								
	NHL Totals		**441**	**41**	**43**	**84**	**48**	**41**	**89**	**1081**	**7**	**0**	**5**	**485**	**8.5**	**158**	**41**	**182**	**1**		**23**	**0**	**2**	**2**	**61**	**0**	**0**	**0**

Traded to **Tampa Bay** by **Calgary** with Calgary's 3rd (Brad Richards) and 5th (Curtis Rich) round choices in 1998 Entry Draft for Jason Wiemer, March 24, 1998. Traded to **Philadelphia** by **Tampa Bay** with Mikael Andersson for Colin Forbes and Philadelphia's 4th round choice (Michal Lanisak) in 1999 Entry Draft, March 20, 1999. Traded to **Carolina** by **Philadelphia** for Kent Manderville, March 14, 2000.

• McCARTHY, Steve

D – L. 6', 197 lbs. b: Trail, B.C., 2/3/1981. Chicago's 1st, 23rd overall, in 1999.

Season	Club	League	GP	G	A	Pts	AG	AA	APts	PIM	PP	SH	GW	S	%	TGF	PGF	TGA	PGA	+/–	GP	G	A	Pts	PIM	PP	SH	GW
1996-97	B.C. River Rats	BCAHA	57	25	52	77				81																		
	Edmonton Ice	WHL	2	0	0	0				0																		
1997-98	Edmonton Ice	WHL	58	11	29	40				59																		
1998-99	Kootenay Ice	WHL	57	19	33	52				79											6	0	5	5	8			
99-2000	**Chicago Blackhawks**	**NHL**	5	1	1	2	1	1	2	4	1	0	0	4	25.0	4	2	2	0	0								
	Kootenay Ice	WHL	37	13	23	36				36																		
	Canada	WJC-A	7	0	2	2				0																		
	Kootenay Ice	Mem-Cup	DID NOT PLAY – INJURED																									
	NHL Totals		**5**	**1**	**1**	**2**	**1**	**1**	**2**	**4**	**1**	**0**	**0**	**4**	**25.0**	**4**	**2**	**2**	**0**									

Returned to **Kootenay** (WHL) by **Chicago**, October 22, 1999. • Missed remainder of 1999-2000 season recovering from shoulder injury suffered in game vs. Swift Current, March 3, 2000.

• McCARTHY, Tom

Tom Joseph "Jug" LW – L. 6'2", 200 lbs. b: Toronto, Ont., 7/31/1960. Minnesota's 2nd, 10th overall, in 1979.

Season	Club	League	GP	G	A	Pts	AG	AA	APts	PIM	PP	SH	GW	S	%	TGF	PGF	TGA	PGA	+/–	GP	G	A	Pts	PIM	PP	SH	GW
1976-77	North York Rangers	MTHL	43	49	47	96				12																		
	Kingston Canadians	OMJHL	2	1	0	1				0																		
1977-78	Oshawa Generals	OMJHL	62	47	46	93				72											6	3	5	8	4			
1978-79	Oshawa Generals	OMJHL	63	69	75	144				98											3	1	0	1	9			
1979-80	**Minnesota North Stars**	**NHL**	68	16	20	36	14	15	29	39	1	0	5	101	15.8	64	15	56	0	–7	15	5	6	11	20	3	0	0
1980-81	Minnesota North Stars	DN-Cup	3	3	1	*4				2																		
	Minnesota North Stars	**NHL**	62	23	25	48	18	17	35	62	4	0	2	147	15.6	75	24	51	3	3	8	0	3	3	6	0	0	0
1981-82	**Minnesota North Stars**	**NHL**	40	12	30	42	9	20	29	36	3	0	1	89	13.5	68	17	45	4	10	4	0	2	2	4	0	0	0
1982-83	**Minnesota North Stars**	**NHL**	80	28	48	76	23	33	56	59	4	1	4	171	16.4	109	37	60	6	18	9	2	4	6	9	0	0	0
1983-84	**Minnesota North Stars**	**NHL**	66	39	31	70	31	21	52	49	16	2	7	165	23.6	109	42	62	12	17	8	1	4	5	6	1	0	1
1984-85	**Minnesota North Stars**	**NHL**	44	16	21	37	13	14	27	36	6	0	1	80	20.0	48	14	41	10	3	7	0	2	2	0	0	0	0
1985-86	**Minnesota North Stars**	**NHL**	25	12	12	24	10	8	18	12	4	0	2	45	26.7	35	16	22	0	–3								
1986-87	**Boston Bruins**	**NHL**	68	30	29	59	26	21	47	31	7	0	6	121	24.8	84	35	39	0	10	4	1	1	2	4	1	0	0
	Moncton Golden Flames	AHL	2	1	0	1				0																		
1987-88	Maine Mariners	AHL	17	7	6	13				14																		
	Boston Bruins	**NHL**	7	2	5	7	2	4	6	6	1	0	0	10	20.0	7	2	2	0	3	13	3	4	7	18	0	0	0
1988-89	HC Asiago	Italy	19	9	26	35				8																		
	NHL Totals		**460**	**178**	**221**	**399**	**146**	**153**	**299**	**330**	**46**	**3**	**28**	**929**	**19.2**	**599**	**202**	**378**	**35**		**68**	**12**	**26**	**38**	**67**	**5**	**0**	**1**

OMJHL First All-Star Team (1979) • Played in NHL All-Star Game (1983)

• Missed majority of 1985-86 season recovering from Bells Palsy, November 23, 1985. Traded to **Boston** by **Minnesota** for Boston's 3rd round choice (Rob Zettler) in 1986 Entry Draft and 2nd round choice (Scott McGrady) in 1987 Entry Draft, May 16, 1986.

• McCARTY, Darren

RW – R. 6'1", 210 lbs. b: Burnaby, B.C., 4/1/1972. Detroit's 2nd, 46th overall, in 1992.

Season	Club	League	GP	G	A	Pts	AG	AA	APts	PIM	PP	SH	GW	S	%	TGF	PGF	TGA	PGA	+/–	GP	G	A	Pts	PIM	PP	SH	GW
1988-89	Peterborough Roadrunners	OJHL-B	34	18	17	35				135																		
1989-90	Belleville Bulls	OHL	63	12	15	27				142											11	1	1	2	21			
1990-91	Belleville Bulls	OHL	60	30	37	67				151											6	2	2	4	13			
1991-92	Belleville Bulls	OHL	65	*55	72	127				177											5	1	4	5	13			
1992-93	Adirondack Red Wings	AHL	73	17	19	36				278											11	0	1	1	33			
1993-94	**Detroit Red Wings**	**NHL**	67	9	17	26	8	13	21	181	0	0	2	81	11.1	47	3	32	0	12	7	2	2	4	8	0	0	0
1994-95	**Detroit Red Wings**	**NHL**	31	5	8	13	9	12	21	88	1	0	2	27	18.5	19	3	12	1	5	18	3	2	5	14	0	0	0
1995-96	**Detroit Red Wings**	**NHL**	63	15	14	29	15	11	26	158	8	0	1	102	14.7	56	16	27	1	14	19	3	2	5	20	0	0	1
1996-97♦	**Detroit Red Wings**	**NHL**	68	19	30	49	20	27	47	126	5	0	6	171	11.1	77	26	37	0	14	20	3	4	7	34	0	0	2
1997-98♦	**Detroit Red Wings**	**NHL**	71	15	22	37	18	22	40	157	5	1	2	166	9.0	66	27	47	8	0	22	3	8	11	34	0	0	1
1998-99	**Detroit Red Wings**	**NHL**	69	14	26	40	16	25	41	108	6	0	1	140	10.0	60	10	50	10	10	10	1	1	2	23	0	0	0
99-2000	**Detroit Red Wings**	**NHL**	24	6	6	12	7	6	13	48	0	0	1	40	15.0	17	0	16	0	1	9	0	1	1	12	0	0	0
	NHL Totals		**393**	**83**	**123**	**206**	**93**	**116**	**209**	**866**	**25**	**1**	**15**	**727**	**11.4**	**342**	**85**	**221**	**20**		**105**	**15**	**20**	**35**	**145**	**0**	**0**	**4**

OHL First All-Star Team (1992)

• Missed majority of 1999-2000 season recovering from hernia injury suffered in game vs. Dallas, November 10, 1999.

• McCASKILL, Ted

Edward Joel C – L. 6'1", 195 lbs. b: Kapuskasing, Ont., 10/29/1936.

Season	Club	League	GP	G	A	Pts	AG	AA	APts	PIM	PP	SH	GW	S	%	TGF	PGF	TGA	PGA	+/–	GP	G	A	Pts	PIM	PP	SH	GW
1954-55	Kitchener Canucks	OHA-Jr.	39	7	7	14				59																		
1955-56	Kitchener Canucks	OHA-Jr.	16	2	2	4				8																		
1956-57	Kapuskasing Huskies	NOHA	PLAYER/COACH – STATISTICS UNAVAILABLE																									
1957-58	Kapuskasing Huskies	NOHA	PLAYER/COACH – STATISTICS UNAVAILABLE																									
1958-59	Edinborough Royals	Britain	25	27	18	45				21																		
1959-60	Paisley Pirates	A-Cup	28	27	17	44				52																		
	Paisley Pirates	Britain	28	27	17	44				52																		
1960-61	Kapuskasing GM's	NOHA	40	32	32	64																						
1961-62	Kapuskasing GM's	NOHA	PLAYER/COACH – STATISTICS UNAVAILABLE																									
1962-63	Nashville Dixie Flyers	EHL	65	21	43	64				62											3	1	1	2	6			
1963-64	Nashville Dixie Flyers	EHL	70	36	50	86				107											3	1	1	2	2			
1964-65	Nashville Dixie Flyers	EHL	72	60	65	125															13	8	14	22	26			

			REGULAR SEASON																		PLAYOFFS							
Season	Club	League	GP	G	A	Pts	AG	AA	APts	PIM	PP	SH	GW	S	%	TGF	PGF	TGA	PGA	+/-	GP	G	A	Pts	PIM	PP	SH	GW
1965-66	Nashville Dixie Flyers	EHL	70	39	61	100	....	....	....	151	....	....	....	....	....	....	....	....	....	....	11	3	*13	*16	18	....	....	....
1966-67	Nashville Dixie Flyers	EHL	72	53	65	118	....	....	....	188	....	....	....	....	....	....	....	....	....	....	14	8	13	21	46	....	....	....
1967-68	**Minnesota North Stars**	**NHL**	**4**	**0**	**2**	**2**	**0**	**2**	**2**	**0**	**0**	**0**	**0**	**2**	**0.0**	**3**	**1**	**4**	**0**	**−2**	....	....	....	....	....	....	....	....
	Memphis South Stars	CPHL	62	17	29	46	....	....	....	136	....	....	....	....	....	....	....	....	....	....	3	2	0	2	0	....	....	....
1968-69	Memphis South Stars	CHL	5	0	0	0	....	....	....	6	....	....	....	....	....	....	....	....	....	....	....	....	....	....	....	....	....	....
	Vancouver Canucks	WHL	45	11	13	24	....	....	....	83	....	....	....	....	....	....	....	....	....	....	8	0	6	6	6	....	....	....
1969-70	Vancouver Canucks	WHL	72	24	18	42	....	....	....	110	....	....	....	....	....	....	....	....	....	....	11	0	2	2	47	....	....	....
1970-71	Phoenix Roadrunners	WHL	70	23	24	47	....	....	....	169	....	....	....	....	....	....	....	....	....	....	10	3	4	7	8	....	....	....
1971-72	Phoenix Roadrunners	WHL	71	18	37	55	....	....	....	*237	....	....	....	....	....	....	....	....	....	....	6	1	2	3	18	....	....	....
1972-73	Los Angeles Sharks	WHA	73	11	11	22	....	....	....	150	....	....	....	....	....	....	....	....	....	....	6	2	3	5	12	....	....	....
1973-74	Los Angeles Sharks	WHA	18	2	2	4	....	....	....	63	....	....	....	....	....	....	....	....	....	....	....	....	....	....	....	....	....	....
1974-75	Binghamton Dusters	NAHL	40	14	20	34	....	....	....	77	....	....	....	....	....	....	....	....	....	....	15	3	10	13	....	....	....	....
	NHL Totals		**4**	**0**	**2**	**2**	**0**	**2**	**2**	**0**	**0**	**0**	**0**	**2**	**0.0**	**3**	**1**	**4**	**0**		....	....	....	....	....	....	....	....
	Other Major League Totals		91	13	13	26	....	....	....	213	....	....	....	....	....	....	....	....	....	....	6	2	3	5	12	....	....	....

EHL South First All-Star Team (1965, 1966, 1967)

Signed as a free agent by **Minnesota** (Memphis-CPHL), September, 1967. Claimed on waivers by **Vancouver** (WHL) from **Minnesota**, November, 1968. NHL rights transferred to **Vancouver** after NHL club purchased **Vancouver** (WHL) franchise, December 19, 1969. Traded to **Toronto** (Phoenix-WHL) by **Vancouver** with Pat Hannigan for Andre Hinse, August, 1970. Selected by **LA Sharks** (WHA) in 1972 WHA General Player Draft, February 12, 1972. • Named interim coach of the **LA Sharks**, December, 1973. • Father of major league pitcher Kirk McCaskill.

• McCAULEY, Alyn

Alyn D. C – L. 5'11", 191 lbs. b: Brockville, Ont., 5/29/1977. New Jersey's 5th, 79th overall, in 1995.

Season	Club	League	GP	G	A	Pts	AG	AA	APts	PIM	PP	SH	GW	S	%	TGF	PGF	TGA	PGA	+/-	GP	G	A	Pts	PIM	PP	SH	GW
1991-92	Kingston Voyageurs	OJHL	37	5	17	22	....	....	....	6	....	....	....	....	....	....	....	....	....	....	....	....	....	....	....	....	....	....
1992-93	Kingston Voyageurs	OJHL	38	31	29	60	....	....	....	18	....	....	....	....	....	....	....	....	....	....	....	....	....	....	....	....	....	....
1993-94	Ottawa 67's	OHL	38	13	23	36	....	....	....	10	....	....	....	....	....	....	....	....	....	....	13	5	14	19	4	....	....	....
1994-95	Ottawa 67's	OHL	65	16	38	54	....	....	....	20	....	....	....	....	....	....	....	....	....	....	....	....	....	....	....	....	....	....
1995-96	Ottawa 67's	OHL	55	34	48	82	....	....	....	24	....	....	....	....	....	....	....	....	....	....	2	0	0	0	0	....	....	....
	Canada	WJC-A	6	2	3	5	....	....	....	2	....	....	....	....	....	....	....	....	....	....	....	....	....	....	....	....	....	....
1996-97	Ottawa 67's	OHL	50	*56	56	112	....	....	....	16	....	....	....	....	....	....	....	....	....	....	22	14	22	36	14	....	....	....
	Canada	WJC-A	7	0	5	5	....	....	....	2	....	....	....	....	....	....	....	....	....	....	....	....	....	....	....	....	....	....
	St. John's Maple Leafs	AHL	....	....	....	....	....	....	....	....	....	....	....	....	....	....	....	....	....	....	3	0	1	1	0	....	....	....
1997-98	**Toronto Maple Leafs**	**NHL**	**60**	**6**	**10**	**16**	**7**	**10**	**17**	**6**	**0**	**0**	**1**	**77**	**7.8**	**23**	**2**	**34**	**6**	**−7**	....	....	....	....	....	....	....	....
1998-99	**Toronto Maple Leafs**	**NHL**	**39**	**9**	**15**	**24**	**11**	**14**	**25**	**2**	**1**	**0**	**1**	**76**	**11.8**	**33**	**6**	**23**	**3**	**7**	....	....	....	....	....	....	....	....
99-2000	**Toronto Maple Leafs**	**NHL**	**45**	**5**	**5**	**10**	**6**	**5**	**11**	**10**	**1**	**0**	**0**	**41**	**12.2**	**15**	**2**	**22**	**3**	**−6**	**5**	**0**	**0**	**0**	**6**	**0**	**0**	**0**
	St. John's Maple Leafs	AHL	5	1	1	2	....	....	....	0	....	....	....	....	....	....	....	....	....	....	....	....	....	....	....	....	....	....
	NHL Totals		**144**	**20**	**30**	**50**	**24**	**29**	**53**	**18**	**2**	**0**	**2**	**194**	**10.3**	**71**	**10**	**79**	**12**		**5**	**0**	**0**	**0**	**6**	**0**	**0**	**0**

OHL First All-Star Team (1996, 1997) • Canadian Major Junior First All-Star Team (1997) • Canadian Major Junior Player of the Year (1997)

Rights traded to **Toronto** by **New Jersey** with Jason Smith and Steve Sullivan for Doug Gilmour, Dave Ellett and New Jersey's 3rd round choice (previously acquired, New Jersey selected Andre Lakos) in 1999 Entry Draft, February 25, 1997.

• McCLANAHAN, Rob

Robert Bruce C – R. 5'10", 180 lbs. b: St. Paul, MN, 1/9/1958. Buffalo's 3rd, 49th overall, in 1978.

Season	Club	League	GP	G	A	Pts	AG	AA	APts	PIM	PP	SH	GW	S	%	TGF	PGF	TGA	PGA	+/-	GP	G	A	Pts	PIM	PP	SH	GW
1975-76	St. Paul-Moundsview High	Hi-School	STATISTICS NOT AVAILABLE																									
1976-77	University of Minnesota	WCHA	40	11	6	17	....	....	....	24	....	....	....	....	....	....	....	....	....	....	....	....	....	....	....	....	....	....
1977-78	University of Minnesota	WCHA	38	17	25	42	....	....	....	10	....	....	....	....	....	....	....	....	....	....	....	....	....	....	....	....	....	....
1978-79	University of Minnesota	WCHA	43	17	32	49	....	....	....	34	....	....	....	....	....	....	....	....	....	....	....	....	....	....	....	....	....	....
	United States	WEC-A	8	1	3	4	....	....	....	6	....	....	....	....	....	....	....	....	....	....	....	....	....	....	....	....	....	....
1979-80	United States	Nat-Team	63	34	36	70	....	....	....	38	....	....	....	....	....	....	....	....	....	....	....	....	....	....	....	....	....	....
	United States	Olympics	7	5	3	8	....	....	....	2	....	....	....	....	....	....	....	....	....	....	....	....	....	....	....	....	....	....
	Buffalo Sabres	**NHL**	**13**	**2**	**5**	**7**	**2**	**4**	**6**	**0**	**0**	**0**	**0**	**13**	**15.4**	**12**	**1**	**4**	**1**	**8**	**10**	**0**	**1**	**1**	**4**	**0**	**0**	**0**
1980-81	**Buffalo Sabres**	**NHL**	**53**	**3**	**12**	**15**	**2**	**8**	**10**	**38**	**1**	**0**	**1**	**67**	**4.5**	**26**	**7**	**42**	**4**	**−19**	**5**	**0**	**1**	**1**	**13**	**0**	**0**	**0**
	Rochester Americans	AHL	18	9	13	22	....	....	....	10	....	....	....	....	....	....	....	....	....	....	....	....	....	....	....	....	....	....
1981-82	United States	Can-Cup	6	0	0	0	....	....	....	2	....	....	....	....	....	....	....	....	....	....	....	....	....	....	....	....	....	....
	Hartford Whalers	**NHL**	**17**	**0**	**3**	**3**	**0**	**2**	**2**	**11**	**0**	**0**	**0**	**9**	**0.0**	**4**	**0**	**15**	**4**	**−7**	....	....	....	....	....	....	....	....
	Binghamton Whalers	AHL	27	11	18	29	....	....	....	21	....	....	....	....	....	....	....	....	....	....	....	....	....	....	....	....	....	....
	New York Rangers	**NHL**	**22**	**5**	**9**	**14**	**4**	**6**	**10**	**10**	**0**	**0**	**1**	**36**	**13.9**	**23**	**1**	**20**	**5**	**7**	**10**	**2**	**5**	**7**	**2**	**0**	**0**	**0**
	Springfield Indians	AHL	7	4	5	9	....	....	....	0	....	....	....	....	....	....	....	....	....	....	....	....	....	....	....	....	....	....
1982-83	**New York Rangers**	**NHL**	**78**	**22**	**26**	**48**	**18**	**18**	**36**	**46**	**0**	**2**	**0**	**118**	**18.6**	**61**	**0**	**64**	**15**	**12**	**9**	**2**	**5**	**7**	**12**	**0**	**0**	**1**
1983-84	**New York Rangers**	**NHL**	**41**	**6**	**8**	**14**	**5**	**5**	**10**	**21**	**0**	**0**	**2**	**52**	**11.5**	**21**	**0**	**24**	**3**	**0**	....	....	....	....	....	....	....	....
	Tulsa Oilers	CHL	10	4	10	14	....	....	....	10	....	....	....	....	....	....	....	....	....	....	....	....	....	....	....	....	....	....
	NHL Totals		**224**	**38**	**63**	**101**	**31**	**43**	**74**	**126**	**1**	**2**	**4**	**295**	**12.9**	**147**	**9**	**169**	**32**		**34**	**4**	**12**	**16**	**31**	**0**	**0**	**1**

Claimed by **Hartford** from **Buffalo** in Waiver Draft, October 6, 1981. Traded to **NY Rangers** by **Hartford** for NY Rangers' 10th round choice (Reine Karlsson) in 1983 Entry Draft, February 2, 1982. Traded to **Detroit** by **NY Rangers** for future considerations, May 23, 1984. Traded to **Vancouver** by **Detroit** for Tiger Williams, August 8, 1984.

• McCLEARY, Trent

Trent Kenneth RW – R. 6', 180 lbs. b: Swift Current, Sask., 9/8/1972.

Season	Club	League	GP	G	A	Pts	AG	AA	APts	PIM	PP	SH	GW	S	%	TGF	PGF	TGA	PGA	+/-	GP	G	A	Pts	PIM	PP	SH	GW
1988-89	Swift Current Legionaires	SAHA	34	12	12	24	....	....	....	85	....	....	....	....	....	....	....	....	....	....	....	....	....	....	....	....	....	....
	Swift Current Broncos	WHL	3	0	0	0	....	....	....	0	....	....	....	....	....	....	....	....	....	....	....	....	....	....	....	....	....	....
1989-90	Swift Current Broncos	WHL	70	3	15	18	....	....	....	43	....	....	....	....	....	....	....	....	....	....	4	1	0	1	0	....	....	....
1990-91	Swift Current Broncos	WHL	70	16	24	40	....	....	....	53	....	....	....	....	....	....	....	....	....	....	3	0	0	0	2	....	....	....
1991-92	Swift Current Broncos	WHL	72	23	22	45	....	....	....	190	....	....	....	....	....	....	....	....	....	....	8	1	2	3	16	....	....	....
1992-93	Swift Current Broncos	WHL	63	17	33	50	....	....	....	138	....	....	....	....	....	....	....	....	....	....	17	5	4	9	16	....	....	....
	New Haven Senators	AHL	2	1	0	1	....	....	....	6	....	....	....	....	....	....	....	....	....	....	....	....	....	....	....	....	....	....
	Swift Current Broncos	Mem-Cup	4	0	0	0	....	....	....	2	....	....	....	....	....	....	....	....	....	....	....	....	....	....	....	....	....	....
1993-94	P.E.I. Senators	AHL	4	0	0	0	....	....	....	6	....	....	....	....	....	....	....	....	....	....	....	....	....	....	....	....	....	....
	Thunder Bay Senators	ColHL	51	23	17	40	....	....	....	123	....	....	....	....	....	....	....	....	....	....	9	2	11	13	15	....	....	....
1994-95	P.E.I. Senators	AHL	51	9	20	29	....	....	....	60	....	....	....	....	....	....	....	....	....	....	9	2	3	5	26	....	....	....
1995-96	**Ottawa Senators**	**NHL**	**75**	**4**	**10**	**14**	**4**	**8**	**12**	**68**	**0**	**1**	**0**	**58**	**6.9**	**23**	**0**	**55**	**17**	**−15**	....	....	....	....	....	....	....	....
1996-97	**Boston Bruins**	**NHL**	**59**	**3**	**5**	**8**	**3**	**4**	**7**	**33**	**0**	**0**	**1**	**41**	**7.3**	**12**	**0**	**34**	**6**	**−16**	....	....	....	....	....	....	....	....
1997-98	Detroit Vipers	IHL	21	1	1	2	....	....	....	45	....	....	....	....	....	....	....	....	....	....	....	....	....	....	....	....	....	....
	Las Vegas Thunder	IHL	54	7	6	13	....	....	....	120	....	....	....	....	....	....	....	....	....	....	3	1	0	1	2	....	....	....
1998-99	**Montreal Canadiens**	**NHL**	**46**	**0**	**0**	**0**	**0**	**0**	**0**	**29**	**0**	**0**	**0**	**18**	**0.0**	**5**	**0**	**7**	**1**	**−1**	....	....	....	....	....	....	....	....
99-2000	**Montreal Canadiens**	**NHL**	**12**	**1**	**0**	**1**	**1**	**0**	**1**	**4**	**0**	**0**	**0**	**4**	**25.0**	**2**	**0**	**0**	**0**	**2**	....	....	....	....	....	....	....	....
	NHL Totals		**192**	**8**	**15**	**23**	**8**	**12**	**20**	**134**	**0**	**1**	**1**	**121**	**6.6**	**42**	**0**	**96**	**24**		....	....	....	....	....	....	....	....

Signed as a free agent by **Ottawa**, October 9, 1992. Traded to **Boston** by **Ottawa** with Ottawa's 3rd round choice (Eric Naud) in 1996 Entry Draft for Shawn McEachern, June 22, 1996. Signed as a free agent by **Montreal**, October 9, 1998. • Missed remainder of 1999-2000 season recovering from throat injury suffered in game vs. Philadelphia, January 29, 2000.

• McCLELLAND, Kevin

Kevin William RW – R. 6'2", 205 lbs. b: Oshawa, Ont., 7/4/1962. Hartford's 4th, 71st overall, in 1980.

Season	Club	League	GP	G	A	Pts	AG	AA	APts	PIM	PP	SH	GW	S	%	TGF	PGF	TGA	PGA	+/-	GP	G	A	Pts	PIM	PP	SH	GW
1978-79	Oshawa Legionaires	OMHA	64	50	74	124	....	....	....	....	....	....	....	....	....	....	....	....	....	....	....	....	....	....	....	....	....	....
1979-80	Niagara Falls Flyers	OMJHL	67	14	14	28	....	....	....	71	....	....	....	....	....	....	....	....	....	....	10	6	3	9	49	....	....	....
1980-81	Niagara Falls Flyers	OMJHL	68	36	72	108	....	....	....	186	....	....	....	....	....	....	....	....	....	....	12	8	13	21	42	....	....	....
1981-82	Niagara Falls Flyers	OHL	46	36	47	83	....	....	....	184	....	....	....	....	....	....	....	....	....	....	....	....	....	....	....	....	....	....
	Pittsburgh Penguins	**NHL**	**10**	**1**	**4**	**5**	**1**	**3**	**4**	**4**	**0**	**0**	**0**	**18**	**5.6**	**9**	**1**	**4**	**2**	**6**	**5**	**1**	**1**	**2**	**5**	**0**	**0**	**0**
1982-83	**Pittsburgh Penguins**	**NHL**	**38**	**5**	**4**	**9**	**4**	**3**	**7**	**73**	**0**	**0**	**0**	**70**	**7.1**	**11**	**0**	**31**	**2**	**−18**	....	....	....	....	....	....	....	....
1983-84	**Pittsburgh Penguins**	**NHL**	**24**	**2**	**4**	**6**	**2**	**3**	**5**	**62**	**0**	**2**	**0**	**40**	**5.0**	**9**	**0**	**24**	**8**	**−7**	....	....	....	....	....	....	....	....
	Baltimore Skipjacks	AHL	3	1	1	2	....	....	....	0	....	....	....	....	....	....	....	....	....	....	....	....	....	....	....	....	....	....
♦	**Edmonton Oilers**	**NHL**	**52**	**8**	**20**	**28**	**6**	**14**	**20**	**127**	**0**	**2**	**2**	**65**	**12.3**	**43**	**1**	**33**	**0**	**9**	**18**	**4**	**6**	**10**	**42**	**0**	**0**	**1**
1984-85 ♦	**Edmonton Oilers**	**NHL**	**62**	**8**	**15**	**23**	**6**	**10**	**16**	**205**	**0**	**0**	**3**	**96**	**8.3**	**36**	**1**	**49**	**3**	**−11**	**18**	**1**	**3**	**4**	**75**	**0**	**0**	**0**
1985-86	**Edmonton Oilers**	**NHL**	**79**	**11**	**25**	**36**	**9**	**17**	**26**	**266**	**0**	**0**	**1**	**104**	**10.6**	**45**	**1**	**37**	**2**	**9**	**10**	**1**	**0**	**1**	**32**	**0**	**0**	**0**
1986-87 ♦	**Edmonton Oilers**	**NHL**	**72**	**12**	**13**	**25**	**10**	**9**	**19**	**238**	**0**	**0**	**1**	**76**	**15.8**	**38**	**0**	**42**	**0**	**−4**	**21**	**2**	**3**	**5**	**43**	**0**	**0**	**0**
1987-88 ♦	**Edmonton Oilers**	**NHL**	**74**	**10**	**6**	**16**	**9**	**4**	**13**	**281**	**0**	**0**	**0**	**61**	**16.4**	**28**	**0**	**28**	**1**	**1**	**19**	**2**	**3**	**5**	**68**	**0**	**0**	**0**
1988-89	**Edmonton Oilers**	**NHL**	**79**	**6**	**14**	**20**	**5**	**10**	**15**	**161**	**0**	**0**	**0**	**43**	**14.0**	**25**	**2**	**33**	**0**	**−10**	**7**	**0**	**2**	**2**	**16**	**0**	**0**	**0**

			REGULAR SEASON																		PLAYOFFS							
Season	Club	League	GP	G	A	Pts	AG	AA	APts	PIM	PP	SH	GW	S	%	TGF	PGF	TGA	PGA	+/-	GP	G	A	Pts	PIM	PP	SH	GW
1989-90	**Edmonton Oilers**	**NHL**	10	1	1	2	1	1	2	13	0	0	0	7	14.3	3	0	4	0	–1	....	....	....	....	....	....	....	....
	Detroit Red Wings	**NHL**	61	4	5	9	3	4	7	183	0	0	0	24	16.7	13	0	19	1	–5	....	....	....	....	....	....	....	....
1990-91	**Detroit Red Wings**	**NHL**	3	0	0	0	0	0	0	7	0	0	0	1	0.0	0	0	4	0	–4	....	....	....	....	....	....	....	....
	Adirondack Red Wings	AHL	27	5	14	19	....	....	....	125	....	....	....	....	....	....	....	....	....	....	....	....	....	....	....	....	....	....
1991-92	**Toronto Maple Leafs**	**NHL**	18	0	1	1	0	1	1	33	0	0	0	5	0.0	1	0	4	0	–3	....	....	....	....	....	....	....	....
	St. John's Maple Leafs	AHL	34	7	15	22	....	....	....	199	....	....	....	....	....	....	....	....	....	....	5	0	1	1	9	....	....	....
1992-93	St. John's Maple Leafs	AHL	55	7	20	27	....	....	....	221	....	....	....	....	....	....	....	....	....	....	1	0	0	0	7	....	....	....
1993-94	**Winnipeg Jets**	**NHL**	6	0	0	0	0	0	0	19	0	0	0	1	0.0	0	0	0	0	0	....	....	....	....	....	....	....	....
	Moncton Hawks	AHL	39	3	5	8	....	....	....	233	....	....	....	....	....	....	....	....	....	....	1	0	0	0	2	....	....	....
1994-95	Rochester Americans	AHL	22	0	2	2	....	....	....	93	....	....	....	....	....	....	....	....	....	....	....	....	....	....	....	....	....	....
1995-1996	Bowmanville Eagles	OJHL	DID NOT PLAY – COACHING																									
1996-1998	Barrie Colts	OHL	DID NOT PLAY – ASSISTANT COACH																									
1998-2000	Prince Albert Raiders	WHL	DID NOT PLAY – COACHING																									
	NHL Totals		**588**	**68**	**112**	**180**	**56**	**79**	**135**	**1672**	**0**	**4**	**7**	**611**	**11.1**	**261**	**6**	**312**	**19**		**98**	**11**	**18**	**29**	**281**	**0**	**0**	**1**

Transferred to **Pittsburgh** by **Hartford** with Pat Boutette as compensation for Hartford's signing of free agent Greg Millen, June 29, 1981. • Missed majority of 1982-83 season recovering from a shoulder injury suffered in a game vs. Toronto, January 24, 1983. Traded to **Edmonton** by **Pittsburgh** with Pittsburgh's 6th round choice (Emanuel Viveiros) in 1984 Entry Draft for Tom Roulston, December 5, 1983. Traded to **Detroit** by **Edmonton** with Jimmy Carson and Edmonton's 5th round choice (later traded to Montreal — Montreal selected Brad Layzell) in 1991 Entry Draft for Petr Klima, Joe Murphy, Adam Graves and Jeff Sharples, November 2, 1989. Signed as a free agent by **Toronto**, September 2, 1991. Traded to **Winnipeg** by **Toronto** for cash, August 12, 1993. Traded to **Buffalo** by **Winnipeg** for future considerations, July 8, 1994.

• McCORD, Bob

Robert Lomer D – R. 6'1", 202 lbs. b: Matheson, Ont., 3/30/1934.

Season	Club	League	GP	G	A	Pts	AG	AA	APts	PIM	PP	SH	GW	S	%	TGF	PGF	TGA	PGA	+/-	GP	G	A	Pts	PIM	PP	SH	GW
1951-52	South Porcupine Combines	NOJHA	STATISTICS NOT AVAILABLE																									
	South Porcupine Combines	Mem-Cup	7	3	5	8	....	....	....	4	....	....	....	....	....	....	....	....	....	....	....	....	....	....	....	....	....	....
1952-53	Kitchener Greenshirts	OHA-Jr.	23	3	7	10	....	....	....	14	....	....	....	....	....	....	....	....	....	....	....	....	....	....	....	....	....	....
	Montreal Jr. Canadiens	QJHL	21	0	4	4	....	....	....	10	....	....	....	....	....	....	....	....	....	....	7	2	3	5	6	....	....	....
1953-54	Montreal Jr. Canadiens	QJHL	49	11	20	31	....	....	....	84	....	....	....	....	....	....	....	....	....	....	8	5	4	9	20	....	....	....
	Montreal Royals	QHL	3	0	0	0	....	....	....	2	....	....	....	....	....	....	....	....	....	....	....	....	....	....	....	....	....	....
1954-55	Springfield Indians	AHL	52	5	18	23	....	....	....	32	....	....	....	....	....	....	....	....	....	....	4	1	1	2	4	....	....	....
1955-56	Springfield Indians	AHL	57	6	21	27	....	....	....	45	....	....	....	....	....	....	....	....	....	....	....	....	....	....	....	....	....	....
1956-57	Springfield Indians	AHL	59	10	21	31	....	....	....	53	....	....	....	....	....	....	....	....	....	....	....	....	....	....	....	....	....	....
1957-58	Trois-Rivieres Lions	QHL	19	2	4	6	....	....	....	19	....	....	....	....	....	....	....	....	....	....	....	....	....	....	....	....	....	....
	Springfield Indians	AHL	41	0	5	5	....	....	....	38	....	....	....	....	....	....	....	....	....	....	....	....	....	....	....	....	....	....
1958-59	Springfield Indians	AHL	5	0	0	0	....	....	....	4	....	....	....	....	....	....	....	....	....	....	....	....	....	....	....	....	....	....
	Trois-Rivieres Lions	QHL	56	8	21	29	....	....	....	75	....	....	....	....	....	....	....	....	....	....	8	2	2	4	4	....	....	....
1959-60	Springfield Indians	AHL	70	11	28	39	....	....	....	114	....	....	....	....	....	....	....	....	....	....	9	0	2	2	8	....	....	....
1960-61	Springfield Indians	AHL	69	12	36	48	....	....	....	51	....	....	....	....	....	....	....	....	....	....	8	0	4	4	8	....	....	....
1961-62	Springfield Indians	AHL	66	8	29	37	....	....	....	62	....	....	....	....	....	....	....	....	....	....	11	0	5	5	16	....	....	....
1962-63	Springfield Indians	AHL	69	11	35	46	....	....	....	42	....	....	....	....	....	....	....	....	....	....	....	....	....	....	....	....	....	....
1963-64	**Boston Bruins**	**NHL**	65	1	9	10	1	9	10	49	....	....	....	....	....	....	....	....	....	....	....	....	....	....	....	....	....	....
1964-65	**Boston Bruins**	**NHL**	43	0	6	6	0	6	6	26	....	....	....	....	....	....	....	....	....	....	....	....	....	....	....	....	....	....
	Hershey Bears	AHL	24	3	7	10	....	....	....	16	....	....	....	....	....	....	....	....	....	....	15	1	6	7	*44	....	....	....
1965-66	**Detroit Red Wings**	**NHL**	9	0	2	2	0	2	2	16	....	....	....	....	....	....	....	....	....	....	....	....	....	....	....	....	....	....
	Pittsburgh Hornets	AHL	62	7	26	33	....	....	....	54	....	....	....	....	....	....	....	....	....	....	3	0	0	0	7	....	....	....
1966-67	**Detroit Red Wings**	**NHL**	14	1	2	3	1	2	3	27	....	....	....	....	....	....	....	....	....	....	....	....	....	....	....	....	....	....
	Pittsburgh Hornets	AHL	61	8	26	34	....	....	....	40	....	....	....	....	....	....	....	....	....	....	9	2	4	6	2	....	....	....
1967-68	**Detroit Red Wings**	**NHL**	3	0	0	0	0	0	0	2	0	0	0	1	0.0	2	0	6	1	–3	....	....	....	....	....	....	....	....
	Minnesota North Stars	**NHL**	70	3	9	12	3	9	12	39	0	0	0	97	3.1	68	1	98	21	–10	14	2	5	7	10	0	0	0
1968-69	**Minnesota North Stars**	**NHL**	69	4	17	21	4	15	19	70	1	0	0	85	4.7	55	4	99	15	–33	....	....	....	....	....	....	....	....
1969-70	Phoenix Roadrunners	WHL	63	11	23	34	....	....	....	41	....	....	....	....	....	....	....	....	....	....	....	....	....	....	....	....	....	....
1970-71	Denver Spurs	WHL	71	7	38	45	....	....	....	54	....	....	....	....	....	....	....	....	....	....	5	1	1	2	2	....	....	....
1971-72	Denver Spurs	WHL	69	4	29	33	....	....	....	33	....	....	....	....	....	....	....	....	....	....	9	3	3	6	6	....	....	....
1972-73	**St. Louis Blues**	**NHL**	43	1	13	14	1	10	11	33	0	0	0	41	2.4	41	2	51	7	–5	....	....	....	....	....	....	....	....
	Denver Spurs	WHL	6	0	1	1	....	....	....	2	....	....	....	....	....	....	....	....	....	....	....	....	....	....	....	....	....	....
1973-74	Denver Spurs	WHL	32	6	12	18	....	....	....	8	....	....	....	....	....	....	....	....	....	....	....	....	....	....	....	....	....	....
1974-75	Denver Spurs	CHL	70	8	24	32	....	....	....	39	....	....	....	....	....	....	....	....	....	....	2	0	0	0	0	....	....	....
	NHL Totals		**316**	**10**	**58**	**68**	**10**	**53**	**63**	**262**	....	....	....	....	....	....	....	....	....	....	**14**	**2**	**5**	**7**	**10**	....	....	....

QHL Second All-Star Team (1959) • AHL Second All-Star Team (1960, 1962, 1963) • AHL First All-Star Team (1961, 1967) • Won Eddie Shore Award (Outstanding Defenseman - AHL) (1961, 1967) • WHL First All-Star Team (1972)

Traded to **Springfield** (AHL) by **Montreal** for Kelly Burnett, September 12, 1954. Traded to **Boston** by **Springfield** (AHL) for Bruce Gamble, Dale Rolfe, Terry Gray and Randy Miller, June, 1963. Traded to **Detroit** by **Boston** with Ab McDonald and Ken Stephanson for Albert Langlois, Ron Harris, Parker MacDonald and Bob Dillabough, May 31, 1965. Traded to **Minnesota** by **Detroit** with Duke Harris for Jean-Guy Talbot and Dave Richardson, October 19, 1967. Claimed by **Montreal** from **Minnesota** in Intra-League Draft, June 9, 1970. Traded to **Minnesota** by **Montreal** for cash, August, 1970. Traded to **St. Louis** (Denver-WHL) by **Minnesota** for cash, August, 1970.

• McCORD, Dennis

Dennis Frederick D – L. 5'10", 190 lbs. b: Chatham, Ont., 7/28/1951. Vancouver's 8th, 115th overall, in 1972.

Season	Club	League	GP	G	A	Pts	AG	AA	APts	PIM	PP	SH	GW	S	%	TGF	PGF	TGA	PGA	+/-	GP	G	A	Pts	PIM	PP	SH	GW
1969-70	Kitchener Rangers	OHA-Jr.	23	1	1	2	....	....	....	50	....	....	....	....	....	....	....	....	....	....	....	....	....	....	....	....	....	....
	Toronto Marlboros	OHA-Jr.	14	1	2	3	....	....	....	34	....	....	....	....	....	....	....	....	....	....	....	....	....	....	....	....	....	....
1970-71	Chatham Maroons	OHA-B	STATISTICS NOT AVAILABLE																									
1971-72	London Knights	OMJHL	59	9	31	40	....	....	....	123	....	....	....	....	....	....	....	....	....	....	....	....	....	....	....	....	....	....
1972-73	Seattle Totems	WHL	71	5	23	28	....	....	....	100	....	....	....	....	....	....	....	....	....	....	....	....	....	....	....	....	....	....
1973-74	**Vancouver Canucks**	**NHL**	3	0	0	0	0	0	0	6	0	0	0	2	0.0	1	0	1	0	0	....	....	....	....	....	....	....	....
	Seattle Totems	WHL	74	4	33	37	....	....	....	57	....	....	....	....	....	....	....	....	....	....	....	....	....	....	....	....	....	....
1974-75	Seattle Totems	CHL	26	0	8	8	....	....	....	38	....	....	....	....	....	....	....	....	....	....	....	....	....	....	....	....	....	....
1975-76	Tulsa Oilers	CHL	9	2	5	7	....	....	....	6	....	....	....	....	....	....	....	....	....	....	....	....	....	....	....	....	....	....
	Fort Wayne Komets	IHL	59	6	17	23	....	....	....	57	....	....	....	....	....	....	....	....	....	....	9	1	4	5	26	....	....	....
	NHL Totals		**3**	**0**	**0**	**0**	**0**	**0**	**0**	**6**	**0**	**0**	**0**	**2**	**0.0**	**1**	**0**	**1**	**0**		....	....	....	....	....	....	....	....

• McCOSH, Shawn

Shawn M. C – R. 6', 197 lbs. b: Oshawa, Ont., 6/5/1969. Detroit's 5th, 95th overall, in 1989.

Season	Club	League	GP	G	A	Pts	AG	AA	APts	PIM	PP	SH	GW	S	%	TGF	PGF	TGA	PGA	+/-	GP	G	A	Pts	PIM	PP	SH	GW
1985-86	Oshawa Legionaires	OMHA	68	67	81	148	....	....	....	145	....	....	....	....	....	....	....	....	....	....	....	....	....	....	....	....	....	....
1986-87	Hamilton Steelhawks	OHL	50	11	17	28	....	....	....	49	....	....	....	....	....	....	....	....	....	....	6	1	0	1	2	....	....	....
1987-88	Hamilton Steelhawks	OHL	64	17	36	53	....	....	....	96	....	....	....	....	....	....	....	....	....	....	14	6	8	14	14	....	....	....
1988-89	Niagara Falls Thunder	OHL	56	41	62	103	....	....	....	75	....	....	....	....	....	....	....	....	....	....	14	4	13	17	23	....	....	....
1989-90	Niagara Falls Thunder	OHL	9	6	10	16	....	....	....	24	....	....	....	....	....	....	....	....	....	....	....	....	....	....	....	....	....	....
	Hamilton Steelhawks	OHL	39	24	28	52	....	....	....	65	....	....	....	....	....	....	....	....	....	....	....	....	....	....	....	....	....	....
	Canada	Nat-Team	3	0	0	0	....	....	....	0	....	....	....	....	....	....	....	....	....	....	....	....	....	....	....	....	....	....
1990-91	New Haven Nighthawks	AHL	66	16	21	37	....	....	....	104	....	....	....	....	....	....	....	....	....	....	....	....	....	....	....	....	....	....
1991-92	**Los Angeles Kings**	**NHL**	4	0	0	0	0	0	0	4	0	0	0	2	0.0	0	0	0	0	0	....	....	....	....	....	....	....	....
	Phoenix Roadrunners	IHL	71	21	32	53	....	....	....	118	....	....	....	....	....	....	....	....	....	....	....	....	....	....	....	....	....	....
	New Haven Nighthawks	AHL	....	....	....	....	....	....	....	....	....	....	....	....	....	....	....	....	....	....	5	0	1	1	0	....	....	....
1992-93	Phoenix Roadrunners	IHL	22	9	8	17	....	....	....	36	....	....	....	....	....	....	....	....	....	....	....	....	....	....	....	....	....	....
	New Haven Senators	AHL	46	22	32	54	....	....	....	54	....	....	....	....	....	....	....	....	....	....	....	....	....	....	....	....	....	....
1993-94	Binghamton Rangers	AHL	75	31	44	75	....	....	....	68	....	....	....	....	....	....	....	....	....	....	....	....	....	....	....	....	....	....
1994-95	**New York Rangers**	**NHL**	5	1	0	1	2	0	2	2	0	0	0	2	50.0	1	0	0	0	1	....	....	....	....	....	....	....	....
	Binghamton Rangers	AHL	67	23	60	83	....	....	....	73	....	....	....	....	....	....	....	....	....	....	8	3	9	12	6	....	....	....
1995-96	Hershey Bears	AHL	71	31	52	83	....	....	....	82	....	....	....	....	....	....	....	....	....	....	5	1	5	6	8	....	....	....
1996-97	Philadelphia Phantoms	AHL	79	30	51	81	....	....	....	110	....	....	....	....	....	....	....	....	....	....	10	3	9	12	23	....	....	....
1997-98	Philadelphia Phantoms	AHL	80	24	54	78	....	....	....	102	....	....	....	....	....	....	....	....	....	....	20	6	13	19	14	....	....	....

Season	Club	League	REGULAR SEASON																		PLAYOFFS							
			GP	G	A	Pts	AG	AA	APts	PIM	PP	SH	GW	S	%	TGF	PGF	TGA	PGA	+/–	GP	G	A	Pts	PIM	PP	SH	GW
1998-99	Philadelphia Phantoms	AHL	38	12	25	37	....	....	....	43	....	....	....	....	....	....	....	....	....	....	....	....	....	....	....	....	....	....
	Michigan K-Wings	IHL	12	4	9	13	....	....	....	18	....	....	....	....	....	....	....	....	....	....	5	1	2	3	6	....	....	....
99-2000	Adler Mannheim	Germany	53	11	11	22	....	....	....	93	....	....	....	....	....	....	....	....	....	....	5	0	0	0	4	....	....	....
	Adler Mannheim	EuroHL	6	1	1	2	....	....	....	4	....	....	....	....	....	....	....	....	....	....	....	....	....	....	....	....	....	....
	NHL Totals		9	1	0	1	2	0	2	6	0	0	0	4	25.0	1	0	0	0		....	....	....	....	....	....	....	....

Traded to **LA Kings** by **Detroit** for LA Kings' 8th round choice (Justin Krall) in 1992 Entry Draft, August 15, 1990. Traded to **Ottawa** by **LA Kings** with Bob Kudelski for Marc Fortier and Jim Thomson, December 19, 1992. Signed as a free agent by **NY Rangers**, July 30, 1993. Signed as a free agent by **Philadelphia**, July 31, 1995.

• McCOURT, Dale

Dale Allen "Chief" C – R. 5'10", 180 lbs. b: Falconbridge, Ont., 1/26/1957. Detroit's 1st, 1st overall, in 1977.

Season	Club	League	GP	G	A	Pts	AG	AA	APts	PIM	PP	SH	GW	S	%	TGF	PGF	TGA	PGA	+/–	GP	G	A	Pts	PIM	PP	SH	GW
1972-73	Welland Cougars	OHA-B	34	35	28	63	....	....	....	39	....	....	....	....	....	....	....	....	....	....	....	....	....	....	....	....	....	....
	Sudbury Wolves	OMJHL	26	6	11	17	....	....	....	0	....	....	....	....	....	....	....	....	....	....	4	0	1	1	0	....	....	....
1973-74	Hamilton Red Wings	OMJHL	69	20	38	58	....	....	....	45	....	....	....	....	....	....	....	....	....	....	....	....	....	....	....	....	....	....
1974-75	Hamilton Fincups	OMJHL	69	52	74	126	....	....	....	57	....	....	....	....	....	....	....	....	....	....	17	10	17	27	0	....	....	....
1975-76	Hamilton Fincups	OMJHL	66	55	84	139	....	....	....	19	....	....	....	....	....	....	....	....	....	....	14	*20	8	28	12	....	....	....
	Hamilton Fincups	Mem-Cup	3	0	4	4	....	....	....	2	....	....	....	....	....	....	....	....	....	....	....	....	....	....	....	....	....	....
1976-77	St. Catharines Fincups	OMJHL	66	60	79	139	....	....	....	26	....	....	....	....	....	....	....	....	....	....	14	7	13	20	6	....	....	....
	Canada	WJC-A	7	10	8	*18	....	....	....	14	....	....	....	....	....	....	....	....	....	....	....	....	....	....	....	....	....	....
1977-78	**Detroit Red Wings**	**NHL**	76	33	39	72	30	30	60	10	10	3	5	219	15.1	108	42	71	15	10	7	4	2	6	2	2	0	0
1978-79	**Detroit Red Wings**	**NHL**	79	28	43	71	24	31	55	14	14	2	3	222	12.6	119	59	123	36	–27	....	....	....	....	....	....	....	....
	Canada	WEC-A	7	0	1	1	....	....	....	6	....	....	....	....	....	....	....	....	....	....	....	....	....	....	....	....	....	....
1979-80	**Detroit Red Wings**	**NHL**	80	30	51	81	26	37	63	12	7	2	3	200	15.0	122	34	120	33	1	....	....	....	....	....	....	....	....
1980-81	**Detroit Red Wings**	**NHL**	80	30	56	86	23	37	60	50	11	2	2	286	10.5	128	46	140	41	–17	....	....	....	....	....	....	....	....
	Canada	WEC-A	4	1	0	1	....	....	....	2	....	....	....	....	....	....	....	....	....	....	....	....	....	....	....	....	....	....
1981-82	**Detroit Red Wings**	**NHL**	26	13	14	27	10	9	19	6	6	0	0	84	15.5	40	12	50	19	–3	....	....	....	....	....	....	....	....
	Buffalo Sabres	**NHL**	52	20	22	42	16	15	31	12	4	1	2	122	16.4	71	19	62	9	–1	4	2	3	5	0	1	0	0
1982-83	**Buffalo Sabres**	**NHL**	62	20	32	52	16	22	38	10	3	1	3	117	17.1	70	18	70	6	–12	10	3	2	5	4	2	0	1
1983-84	**Buffalo Sabres**	**NHL**	5	1	3	4	1	2	3	0	0	0	0	5	20.0	5	1	7	1	–2	....	....	....	....	....	....	....	....
	Toronto Maple Leafs	**NHL**	72	19	24	43	15	16	31	10	8	2	1	98	19.4	69	28	83	26	–16	....	....	....	....	....	....	....	....
1984-85	HC Ambri-Piotta	Switz-2	26	22	14	36	....	....	....	....	....	....	....	....	....	....	....	....	....	....	14	12	11	23	....	....	....	....
1985-86	HC Ambri-Piotta	Switz-2	35	41	15	56	....	....	....	....	....	....	....	....	....	....	....	....	....	....	....	....	....	....	....	....	....	....
1986-87	HC Ambri-Piotta	Switz.	35	25	28	53	....	....	....	....	....	....	....	....	....	....	....	....	....	....	3	5	2	7	....	....	....	....
1987-88	HC Ambri-Piotta	Switz.	35	33	22	55	....	....	....	....	....	....	....	....	....	....	....	....	....	....	4	6	6	12	....	....	....	....
1988-89	HC Ambri-Piotta	Switz.	38	42	24	66	....	....	....	....	....	....	....	....	....	....	....	....	....	....	6	1	4	5	....	....	....	....
1989-90	HC Ambri-Piotta	Switz.	38	18	26	44	....	....	....	....	....	....	....	....	....	....	....	....	....	....	2	0	0	0	0	....	....	....
1990-91	HC Ambri-Piotta	Switz.	35	10	12	22	....	....	....	....	....	....	....	....	....	....	....	....	....	....	....	....	....	....	....	....	....	....
1991-92	HC Ambri-Piotta	Switz.	5	4	1	5	....	....	....	2	....	....	....	....	....	....	....	....	....	....	....	....	....	....	....	....	....	....
	NHL Totals		532	194	284	478	161	199	360	124	63	13	19	1353	14.3	732	259	726	186		21	9	7	16	6	5	0	1

OMJHL First All-Star Team (1976, 1977) • Memorial Cup All-Star Team (1976) • Won Stafford Smythe Memorial Trophy (Memorial Cup Tournament MVP) (1976) • WJC-A All-Star Team (1977) • Canadian Major Junior Player of the Year (1977)

Rights transferred to **LA Kings** by **Detroit** as compensation for Detroit's signing of free agent Rogie Vachon, August 8, 1978. McCourt remained property of Detroit pending result of litigation hearing. Rights traded to **Detroit** by **LA Kings** for Andre St. Laurent and Detroit's 1st round choices in 1980 (Larry Murphy) and 1981 (Doug Smith) Entry Drafts, August 22, 1979. Traded to **Buffalo** by **Detroit** with Mike Foligno and Brent Peterson for Danny Gare, Jim Schoenfeld and Derek Smith, December 2, 1981. Signed as a free agent by **Toronto**, October 22, 1983.

• McCREARY, Bill Jr.

William Edward RW – R. 6', 190 lbs. b: Springfield, MA, 4/15/1960. Toronto's 5th, 114th overall, in 1979.

Season	Club	League	GP	G	A	Pts	AG	AA	APts	PIM	PP	SH	GW	S	%	TGF	PGF	TGA	PGA	+/–	GP	G	A	Pts	PIM	PP	SH	GW
1976-77	Cleveland Jr. Barons	GLJHL	40	26	24	50	....	....	....	....	....	....	....	....	....	....	....	....	....	....	....	....	....	....	....	....	....	....
1977-78	Cleveland Jr. Barons	GLJHL	40	51	72	123	....	....	....	....	....	....	....	....	....	....	....	....	....	....	....	....	....	....	....	....	....	....
1978-79	Colgate University	ECAC	24	19	25	44	....	....	....	70	....	....	....	....	....	....	....	....	....	....	....	....	....	....	....	....	....	....
1979-80	Colgate University	ECAC	12	7	13	20	....	....	....	44	....	....	....	....	....	....	....	....	....	....	....	....	....	....	....	....	....	....
1980-81	**Toronto Maple Leafs**	**NHL**	12	1	0	1	1	0	1	4	0	0	0	7	14.3	3	0	9	0	–6	....	....	....	....	....	....	....	....
	New Brunswick Hawks	AHL	61	19	24	43	....	....	....	120	....	....	....	....	....	....	....	....	....	....	12	2	0	2	13	....	....	....
1981-82	Cincinnati Tigers	CHL	69	8	27	35	....	....	....	61	....	....	....	....	....	....	....	....	....	....	4	0	4	4	2	....	....	....
1982-83	Saginaw Gears	IHL	60	19	28	47	....	....	....	17	....	....	....	....	....	....	....	....	....	....	....	....	....	....	....	....	....	....
	Peoria Prancers	IHL	16	4	6	10	....	....	....	11	....	....	....	....	....	....	....	....	....	....	....	....	....	....	....	....	....	....
	St. Catharines Saints	AHL	4	0	1	1	....	....	....	2	....	....	....	....	....	....	....	....	....	....	....	....	....	....	....	....	....	....
1983-84	Milwaukee Admirals	IHL	81	28	35	63	....	....	....	44	....	....	....	....	....	....	....	....	....	....	4	0	2	2	2	....	....	....
1984-85	Milwaukee Admirals	IHL	10	1	0	1	....	....	....	4	....	....	....	....	....	....	....	....	....	....	....	....	....	....	....	....	....	....
1985-86	Milwaukee Admirals	IHL	80	30	31	61	....	....	....	83	....	....	....	....	....	....	....	....	....	....	5	3	0	3	6	....	....	....
1986-87	Milwaukee Admirals	IHL	74	30	35	65	....	....	....	64	....	....	....	....	....	....	....	....	....	....	6	2	2	4	10	....	....	....
1987-88	Milwaukee Admirals	IHL	67	23	30	53	....	....	....	51	....	....	....	....	....	....	....	....	....	....	....	....	....	....	....	....	....	....
	NHL Totals		12	1	0	1	1	0	1	4	0	0	0	7	14.3	3	0	9	0		....	....	....	....	....	....	....	....

• Son of Bill Sr.

• McCREARY, Bill Sr.

William Edward LW – L. 5'10", 172 lbs. b: Sundridge, Ont., 12/2/1934.

Season	Club	League	GP	G	A	Pts	AG	AA	APts	PIM	PP	SH	GW	S	%	TGF	PGF	TGA	PGA	+/–	GP	G	A	Pts	PIM	PP	SH	GW
1951-52	Guelph Biltmores	OHA-Jr.	52	30	28	58	....	....	....	12	....	....	....	....	....	....	....	....	....	....	11	4	4	8	6	....	....	....
	Guelph Biltmores	Mem-Cup	12	5	10	15	....	....	....	4	....	....	....	....	....	....	....	....	....	....	....	....	....	....	....	....	....	....
1952-53	Guelph Biltmores	OHA-Jr.	50	32	25	57	....	....	....	31	....	....	....	....	....	....	....	....	....	....	....	....	....	....	....	....	....	....
	Toronto Marlboros	Mem-Cup	7	2	3	5	....	....	....	2	....	....	....	....	....	....	....	....	....	....	....	....	....	....	....	....	....	....
1953-54	Guelph Biltmores	OHA-Jr.	59	35	49	84	....	....	....	57	....	....	....	....	....	....	....	....	....	....	3	0	3	3	4	....	....	....
	New York Rangers	**NHL**	2	0	0	0	0	0	0	2	....	....	....	....	....	....	....	....	....	....	....	....	....	....	....	....	....	....
1954-55	Guelph Biltmores	OHA-Jr.	48	46	37	83	....	....	....	38	....	....	....	....	....	....	....	....	....	....	6	4	3	7	2	....	....	....
	New York Rangers	**NHL**	8	0	2	2	0	2	2	0	....	....	....	....	....	....	....	....	....	....	....	....	....	....	....	....	....	....
1955-56	Providence Reds	AHL	37	8	13	21	....	....	....	18	....	....	....	....	....	....	....	....	....	....	....	....	....	....	....	....	....	....
	Saskatoon Quakers	WHL	25	12	20	32	....	....	....	45	....	....	....	....	....	....	....	....	....	....	3	0	0	0	0	....	....	....
1956-57	Edmonton Flyers	WHL	69	33	26	59	....	....	....	37	....	....	....	....	....	....	....	....	....	....	8	2	7	9	4	....	....	....
1957-58	**Detroit Red Wings**	**NHL**	3	1	0	1	1	0	1	2	....	....	....	....	....	....	....	....	....	....	....	....	....	....	....	....	....	....
	Edmonton Flyers	WHL	21	7	7	14	....	....	....	10	....	....	....	....	....	....	....	....	....	....	5	2	1	3	2	....	....	....
	Hershey Bears	AHL	31	4	9	13	....	....	....	6	....	....	....	....	....	....	....	....	....	....	....	....	....	....	....	....	....	....
1958-59	Springfield Indians	AHL	65	14	34	48	....	....	....	22	....	....	....	....	....	....	....	....	....	....	....	....	....	....	....	....	....	....
1959-60	Springfield Indians	AHL	69	19	31	50	....	....	....	16	....	....	....	....	....	....	....	....	....	....	10	6	4	10	6	....	....	....
1960-61	Springfield Indians	AHL	72	33	54	87	....	....	....	26	....	....	....	....	....	....	....	....	....	....	8	*5	4	9	6	....	....	....
1961-62	Springfield Indians	AHL	69	27	49	76	....	....	....	49	....	....	....	....	....	....	....	....	....	....	2	0	2	2	0	....	....	....
1962-63	**Montreal Canadiens**	**NHL**	14	2	3	5	2	3	5	0	....	....	....	....	....	....	....	....	....	....	....	....	....	....	....	....	....	....
	Hull-Ottawa Canadiens	EPHL	46	15	32	47	....	....	....	22	....	....	....	....	....	....	....	....	....	....	....	....	....	....	....	....	....	....
1963-64	Omaha Knights	CPHL	72	24	51	75	....	....	....	56	....	....	....	....	....	....	....	....	....	....	3	1	0	1	2	....	....	....
1964-65	Omaha Knights	CPHL	70	24	44	68	....	....	....	48	....	....	....	....	....	....	....	....	....	....	6	0	3	3	0	....	....	....
1965-66	Houston Apollos	CPHL	70	26	26	52	....	....	....	44	....	....	....	....	....	....	....	....	....	....	....	....	....	....	....	....	....	....
1966-67	Houston Apollos	CPHL	56	22	34	56	....	....	....	34	....	....	....	....	....	....	....	....	....	....	6	1	2	3	0	....	....	....
1967-68	**St. Louis Blues**	**NHL**	70	13	13	26	15	13	28	22	2	4	2	154	8.4	42	9	41	10	2	15	3	2	5	0	0	2	2
1968-69	**St. Louis Blues**	**NHL**	71	13	17	30	14	15	29	50	3	1	4	130	10.0	41	6	46	15	4	12	1	5	6	14	1	1	0
1969-70	**St. Louis Blues**	**NHL**	73	15	17	32	16	16	32	16	2	1	1	174	8.6	5	15	56	23	–43	15	1	7	8	0	0	0	0
1970-71	**St. Louis Blues**	**NHL**	68	9	10	19	9	8	17	16	0	3	0	90	10.0	30	4	39	20	7	6	1	2	3	0	0	0	0
	NHL Totals		309	53	62	115	57	57	114	108	....	....	....	....	....	....	....	....	....		48	6	16	22	14	....	....	....

• Brother of Keith • Father of Bill Jr. • WHL Prairie Division Second All-Star Team (1957) • CPHL First All-Star Team (1964, 1966)

Loaned to **Toronto** (OHA-Jr.) by **Guelph** (OHA-Jr.) for Memorial Cup playoffs, April, 1953. Claimed by **Detroit** from **NY Rangers** in Intra-League Draft, June 5, 1956. Traded to **Springfield** (AHL) by **Detroit** with Dennis Olson and Hank Bassen for Gerry Ehman, May 1, 1958. Traded to **Montreal** by **Springfield** (AHL) for Bob McCammon, Andre Tardiff and Norm Waslowski, October 25, 1962. Traded to **St. Louis** by **Montreal** for Claude Cardin and Phil Obendorf, June 14, 1967.

• McCREARY, Keith

Vernon Keith RW – L. 5'10", 180 lbs. b: Sundridge, Ont., 6/19/1940.

Season	Club	League	REGULAR SEASON																		PLAYOFFS							
			GP	G	A	Pts	AG	AA	APts	PIM	PP	SH	GW	S	%	TGF	PGF	TGA	PGA	+/–	GP	G	A	Pts	PIM	PP	SH	GW
1956-57	Peterborough Petes	OHA-Jr.	22	0	1	1	....	....	....	0	....	....	....	....	....	....	....	....	....	....	....	....	....	....	....	....	....	....
1957-58	Sundridge Beavers	OHA-B	STATISTICS NOT AVAILABLE																									
1958-59	Hull-Ottawa Canadiens	X-Games	STATISTICS NOT AVAILABLE																									
	Hull-Ottawa Canadiens	EOHL	3	1	0	1	....	....	....	0	....	....	....	....	....	....	....	....	....	....	....	....	....	....	....	....	....	....
	Hull-Ottawa Canadiens	Mem-Cup	7	1	4	5	....	....	....	2	....	....	....	....	....	....	....	....	....	....	....	....	....	....	....	....	....	....
1959-60	Hull-Ottawa Canadiens	X-Games	STATISTICS NOT AVAILABLE																									
	Hull-Ottawa Canadiens	EPHL	5	0	0	0	....	....	....	0	....	....	....	....	....	....	....	....	....	....	....	....	....	....	....	....	....	....
	Brockville Jr. Canadiens	Mem-Cup	13	5	9	14	....	....	....	23	....	....	....	....	....	....	....	....	....	....	....	....	....	....	....	....	....	....
1960-61	Hull-Ottawa Canadiens	EPHL	61	19	21	40	....	....	....	35	....	....	....	....	....	....	....	....	....	....	14	4	2	6	15	....	....	....
1961-62	Hull-Ottawa Canadiens	EPHL	64	30	36	66	....	....	....	48	....	....	....	....	....	....	....	....	....	....	12	5	8	13	2	....	....	....
	Montreal Canadiens	**NHL**	....	....	....	....	....	....	....	....	....	....	....	....	....	....	....	....	....	....	**1**	**0**	**0**	**0**	**0**	**0**	**0**	**0**
1962-63	Hull-Ottawa Canadiens	EPHL	69	27	34	61	....	....	....	44	....	....	....	....	....	....	....	....	....	....	3	1	1	2	0	....	....	....
1963-64	Hershey Bears	AHL	66	25	19	44	....	....	....	21	....	....	....	....	....	....	....	....	....	....	6	2	4	6	2	....	....	....
1964-65	**Montreal Canadiens**	**NHL**	**9**	**0**	**3**	**3**	**0**	**3**	**3**	**4**	....	....	....	....	....	....	....	....	....	....	....	....	....	....	....	....	....	....
	Hershey Bears	AHL	46	16	18	34	....	....	....	36	....	....	....	....	....	....	....	....	....	....	14	0	7	7	24	....	....	....
1965-66	Cleveland Barons	AHL	66	18	24	42	....	....	....	42	....	....	....	....	....	....	....	....	....	....	12	5	4	9	8	....	....	....
1966-67	Cleveland Barons	AHL	70	28	29	57	....	....	....	50	....	....	....	....	....	....	....	....	....	....	5	1	2	3	0	....	....	....
1967-68	**Pittsburgh Penguins**	**NHL**	**70**	**14**	**12**	**26**	**16**	**12**	**28**	**44**	**0**	**0**	**1**	**133**	**10.5**	**45**	**3**	**50**	**5**	**–3**	....	....	....	....	....	....	....	....
1968-69	**Pittsburgh Penguins**	**NHL**	**70**	**25**	**23**	**48**	**27**	**20**	**47**	**42**	**7**	**0**	**4**	**208**	**12.0**	**67**	**23**	**68**	**1**	**–23**	....	....	....	....	....	....	....	....
1969-70	**Pittsburgh Penguins**	**NHL**	**60**	**18**	**8**	**26**	**20**	**7**	**27**	**67**	**4**	**0**	**2**	**134**	**13.4**	**35**	**8**	**33**	**0**	**–6**	**10**	**0**	**4**	**4**	**4**	**0**	**0**	**0**
1970-71	**Pittsburgh Penguins**	**NHL**	**59**	**21**	**12**	**33**	**21**	**10**	**31**	**24**	**3**	**0**	**3**	**116**	**18.1**	**56**	**9**	**41**	**1**	**7**	....	....	....	....	....	....	....	....
1971-72	**Pittsburgh Penguins**	**NHL**	**33**	**4**	**4**	**8**	**4**	**3**	**7**	**22**	**0**	**0**	**0**	**68**	**5.9**	**13**	**2**	**21**	**0**	**–10**	**1**	**0**	**0**	**0**	**2**	**0**	**0**	**0**
1972-73	**Atlanta Flames**	**NHL**	**77**	**20**	**21**	**41**	**19**	**17**	**36**	**21**	**9**	**0**	**3**	**157**	**12.7**	**53**	**13**	**69**	**7**	**–22**	....	....	....	....	....	....	....	....
1973-74	**Atlanta Flames**	**NHL**	**76**	**18**	**19**	**37**	**17**	**16**	**33**	**62**	**2**	**0**	**4**	**109**	**16.5**	**53**	**3**	**58**	**2**	**–6**	**4**	**0**	**0**	**0**	**0**	**0**	**0**	**0**
1974-75	**Atlanta Flames**	**NHL**	**78**	**11**	**10**	**21**	**10**	**7**	**17**	**8**	**2**	**2**	**2**	**79**	**13.9**	**43**	**5**	**55**	**29**	**12**	....	....	....	....	....	....	....	....
	NHL Totals		**532**	**131**	**112**	**243**	**134**	**95**	**229**	**294**	....	....	....	....	....	....	....	....	....		**16**	**0**	**4**	**4**	**6**	....	....	....

• Brother of Bill Jr. • EPHL First All-Star Team (1962) • EPHL Second All-Star Team (1963)

Claimed by **Pittsburgh** from **Montreal** in Expansion Draft, June 6, 1967. Claimed by **Atlanta** from **Pittsburgh** in Expansion Draft, June 6, 1972.

• McCRIMMON, Brad

Brad Byron D – L. 5'11", 197 lbs. b: Dodsland, Sask., 3/29/1959. Boston's 2nd, 15th overall, in 1979.

Season	Club	League	GP	G	A	Pts	AG	AA	APts	PIM	PP	SH	GW	S	%	TGF	PGF	TGA	PGA	+/–	GP	G	A	Pts	PIM	PP	SH	GW
1974-75	Prince Albert Raiders	SJHL	38	4	22	26	....	....	....	....	....	....	....	....	....	....	....	....	....	....	....	....	....	....	....	....	....	....
1975-76	Prince Albert Raiders	SJHL	46	19	39	58	....	....	....	126	....	....	....	....	....	....	....	....	....	....	....	....	....	....	....	....	....	....
1976-77	Brandon Wheat Kings	WCJHL	72	18	66	84	....	....	....	96	....	....	....	....	....	....	....	....	....	....	15	3	10	13	16	....	....	....
1977-78	Brandon Wheat Kings	WCJHL	65	19	78	97	....	....	....	245	....	....	....	....	....	....	....	....	....	....	8	2	11	13	20	....	....	....
	Canada	WJC-A	6	0	2	2	....	....	....	4	....	....	....	....	....	....	....	....	....	....	....	....	....	....	....	....	....	....
1978-79	Brandon Wheat Kings	WHL	66	24	74	98	....	....	....	139	....	....	....	....	....	....	....	....	....	....	22	9	19	28	34	....	....	....
	Canada	WJC-A	5	1	2	3	....	....	....	2	....	....	....	....	....	....	....	....	....	....	....	....	....	....	....	....	....	....
	Brandon Wheat Kings	Mem-Cup	5	0	5	5	....	....	....	10	....	....	....	....	....	....	....	....	....	....	....	....	....	....	....	....	....	....
1979-80	**Boston Bruins**	**NHL**	**72**	**5**	**11**	**16**	**4**	**8**	**12**	**94**	**1**	**0**	**1**	**89**	**5.6**	**67**	**1**	**80**	**11**	**–3**	**10**	**1**	**1**	**2**	**28**	**0**	**0**	**0**
1980-81	**Boston Bruins**	**NHL**	**78**	**11**	**18**	**29**	**9**	**12**	**21**	**148**	**1**	**0**	**1**	**113**	**9.7**	**91**	**4**	**94**	**34**	**27**	**3**	**0**	**1**	**1**	**2**	**0**	**0**	**0**
1981-82	**Boston Bruins**	**NHL**	**78**	**1**	**8**	**9**	**1**	**5**	**6**	**83**	**0**	**0**	**0**	**136**	**0.7**	**89**	**1**	**95**	**11**	**4**	**2**	**0**	**0**	**0**	**2**	**0**	**0**	**0**
1982-83	**Philadelphia Flyers**	**NHL**	**79**	**4**	**21**	**25**	**3**	**15**	**18**	**61**	**1**	**0**	**1**	**107**	**3.7**	**86**	**9**	**77**	**24**	**24**	**3**	**0**	**0**	**0**	**4**	**0**	**0**	**0**
1983-84	**Philadelphia Flyers**	**NHL**	**71**	**0**	**24**	**24**	**0**	**16**	**16**	**76**	**0**	**0**	**0**	**106**	**0.0**	**89**	**10**	**93**	**33**	**19**	**1**	**0**	**0**	**0**	**4**	**0**	**0**	**0**
1984-85	**Philadelphia Flyers**	**NHL**	**66**	**8**	**35**	**43**	**6**	**24**	**30**	**81**	**1**	**0**	**1**	**141**	**5.7**	**137**	**27**	**84**	**26**	**52**	**11**	**2**	**1**	**3**	**15**	**0**	**0**	**0**
1985-86	**Philadelphia Flyers**	**NHL**	**80**	**13**	**43**	**56**	**10**	**29**	**39**	**85**	**2**	**0**	**2**	**162**	**8.0**	**176**	**34**	**93**	**34**	**83**	**5**	**2**	**0**	**2**	**2**	**0**	**0**	**1**
1986-87	**Philadelphia Flyers**	**NHL**	**71**	**10**	**29**	**39**	**9**	**21**	**30**	**52**	**3**	**2**	**4**	**110**	**9.1**	**123**	**25**	**82**	**29**	**45**	**26**	**3**	**5**	**8**	**30**	**1**	**0**	**1**
1987-88	**Calgary Flames**	**NHL**	**80**	**7**	**35**	**42**	**6**	**25**	**31**	**98**	**1**	**3**	**2**	**102**	**6.9**	**130**	**16**	**100**	**34**	**48**	**9**	**2**	**3**	**5**	**22**	**2**	**0**	**0**
1988-89♦	**Calgary Flames**	**NHL**	**72**	**5**	**17**	**22**	**4**	**12**	**16**	**96**	**2**	**1**	**2**	**78**	**6.4**	**88**	**8**	**68**	**31**	**43**	**22**	**0**	**3**	**3**	**30**	**0**	**0**	**0**
1989-90	Calgary Flames	Fr-Tour	4	0	1	1	....	....	....	2	....	....	....	....	....	....	....	....	....	....	....	....	....	....	....	....	....	....
	Calgary Flames	**NHL**	**79**	**4**	**15**	**19**	**3**	**11**	**14**	**78**	**0**	**0**	**0**	**97**	**4.1**	**83**	**4**	**75**	**14**	**18**	**6**	**0**	**2**	**2**	**8**	**0**	**0**	**0**
1990-91	**Detroit Red Wings**	**NHL**	**64**	**0**	**13**	**13**	**0**	**10**	**10**	**81**	**0**	**0**	**0**	**43**	**0.0**	**62**	**4**	**81**	**30**	**7**	**7**	**1**	**1**	**2**	**21**	**0**	**0**	**0**
1991-92	**Detroit Red Wings**	**NHL**	**79**	**7**	**22**	**29**	**6**	**17**	**23**	**118**	**2**	**1**	**1**	**94**	**7.4**	**97**	**15**	**78**	**35**	**39**	**11**	**0**	**1**	**1**	**8**	**0**	**0**	**0**
1992-93	**Detroit Red Wings**	**NHL**	**60**	**1**	**14**	**15**	**1**	**10**	**11**	**71**	**1**	**0**	**0**	**53**	**1.9**	**65**	**11**	**50**	**17**	**21**	....	....	....	....	....	....	....	....
1993-94	**Hartford Whalers**	**NHL**	**65**	**1**	**5**	**6**	**1**	**4**	**5**	**72**	**0**	**0**	**0**	**39**	**2.6**	**30**	**2**	**60**	**25**	**–7**	....	....	....	....	....	....	....	....
1994-95	**Hartford Whalers**	**NHL**	**33**	**0**	**1**	**1**	**0**	**1**	**1**	**42**	**0**	**0**	**0**	**13**	**0.0**	**17**	**1**	**18**	**9**	**7**	....	....	....	....	....	....	....	....
1995-96	**Hartford Whalers**	**NHL**	**58**	**3**	**6**	**9**	**3**	**5**	**8**	**62**	**0**	**1**	**0**	**39**	**7.7**	**45**	**1**	**43**	**14**	**15**	....	....	....	....	....	....	....	....
1996-97	**Phoenix Coyotes**	**NHL**	**37**	**1**	**5**	**6**	**1**	**4**	**5**	**18**	**0**	**0**	**0**	**28**	**3.6**	**21**	**0**	**23**	**4**	**2**	....	....	....	....	....	....	....	....
1997-1999	**New York Islanders**	**NHL**	DID NOT PLAY – ASSISTANT COACH																									
1999-2000	Saskatoon Blades	WHL	DID NOT PLAY – COACHING																									
	NHL Totals		**1222**	**81**	**322**	**403**	**67**	**229**	**296**	**1416**	**15**	**8**	**15**	**1550**	**5.2**	**1496**	**173**	**1294**	**415**		**116**	**11**	**18**	**29**	**176**	**3**	**0**	**2**

WHL First All-Star Team (1978, 1979) • NHL Second All-Star Team (1988) • NHL Plus/Minus Leader (1988) • Played in NHL All-Star Game (1988)

Traded to **Philadelphia** by **Boston** for Pete Peeters, June 9, 1982. Traded to **Calgary** by **Philadelphia** for Calgary's 3rd round choice (Dominic Roussel) in 1988 Entry Draft and 1st round choice (later traded to Toronto — Toronto selected Steve Bancroft) in 1989 Entry Draft, August 26, 1987. Traded to **Detroit** by **Calgary** for Detroit's 2nd round choice (later traded to New Jersey — New Jersey selected David Harlock) in 1990 Entry Draft, June 15, 1990. Traded to **Hartford** by **Detroit** for Detroit's 6th round choice (previously acquired, Detroit selected Tim Spitzig) in 1993 Entry Draft, June 1, 1993. Signed as a free agent by **Phoenix**, July 16, 1996.

• McCRIMMON, Jim

John James D – R. 6'1", 210 lbs. b: Ponoka, AB, 5/29/1953. Los Angeles' 2nd, 54th overall, in 1973.

Season	Club	League	GP	G	A	Pts	AG	AA	APts	PIM	PP	SH	GW	S	%	TGF	PGF	TGA	PGA	+/–	GP	G	A	Pts	PIM	PP	SH	GW
1969-70	Ponoka Stampeders	AJHL	41	3	12	15	....	....	....	91	....	....	....	....	....	....	....	....	....	....	....	....	....	....	....	....	....	....
1970-71	Ponoka Stampeders	AJHL	10	0	3	3	....	....	....	8	....	....	....	....	....	....	....	....	....	....	....	....	....	....	....	....	....	....
	Medicine Hat Tigers	WCJHL	52	1	4	5	....	....	....	89	....	....	....	....	....	....	....	....	....	....	....	....	....	....	....	....	....	....
1971-72	Medicine Hat Tigers	WCJHL	53	3	20	23	....	....	....	270	....	....	....	....	....	....	....	....	....	....	....	....	....	....	....	....	....	....
1972-73	Medicine Hat Tigers	WCJHL	54	7	30	37	....	....	....	179	....	....	....	....	....	....	....	....	....	....	17	3	5	8	76	....	....	....
	Medicine Hat Tigers	Mem-Cup	2	0	0	0	....	....	....	4	....	....	....	....	....	....	....	....	....	....	....	....	....	....	....	....	....	....
1973-74	Edmonton Oilers	WHA	75	2	3	5	....	....	....	106	....	....	....	....	....	....	....	....	....	....	....	....	....	....	....	....	....	....
1974-75	Edmonton Oilers	WHA	34	1	5	6	....	....	....	50	....	....	....	....	....	....	....	....	....	....	....	....	....	....	....	....	....	....
	Winston-Salem Polar Bears	SHL	21	8	13	21	....	....	....	64	....	....	....	....	....	....	....	....	....	....	....	....	....	....	....	....	....	....
	St. Louis Blues	**NHL**	**2**	**0**	**0**	**0**	**0**	**0**	**0**	**0**	**0**	**0**	**0**	**0**	**0.0**	**0**	**0**	**0**	**0**	**0**	....	....	....	....	....	....	....	....
1975-76	Providence Reds	AHL	47	1	9	10	....	....	....	94	....	....	....	....	....	....	....	....	....	....	....	....	....	....	....	....	....	....
	Calgary Cowboys	WHA	5	0	0	0	....	....	....	2	....	....	....	....	....	....	....	....	....	....	....	....	....	....	....	....	....	....
	Baltimore Clippers	AHL	9	1	0	1	....	....	....	6	....	....	....	....	....	....	....	....	....	....	....	....	....	....	....	....	....	....
1976-77	Richmond Wildcats	SHL	33	6	18	24	....	....	....	58	....	....	....	....	....	....	....	....	....	....	....	....	....	....	....	....	....	....
	Mohawk Valley Comets	NAHL	13	0	5	5	....	....	....	14	....	....	....	....	....	....	....	....	....	....	....	....	....	....	....	....	....	....
1977-78	Kimberley Dynamiters	WIHL	40	9	28	37	....	....	....	68	....	....	....	....	....	....	....	....	....	....	....	....	....	....	....	....	....	....
	NHL Totals		**2**	**0**	**0**	**0**	**0**	**0**	**0**	**0**	**0**	**0**	**0**	**0**	**0.0**	**0**	**0**	**0**	**0**		....	....	....	....	....	....	....	....
	Other Major League Totals		114	3	8	11	....	....	....	158	....	....	....	....	....	....	....	....	....	....	....	....	....	....	....	....	....	....

Selected by **Edmonton** (WHA) in 1973 WHA Amateur Draft, May, 1973. Traded to **St. Louis** by **LA Kings** for cash, March 10, 1975. Signed as a free agent by **Calgary** (WHA) after being released by **St. Louis**, March, 1975.

• McCUTCHEON, Brian

Brian Kenneth "Boom-Boom" LW – L. 5'10", 180 lbs. b: Toronto, Ont., 8/3/1949.

Season	Club	League	GP	G	A	Pts	AG	AA	APts	PIM	PP	SH	GW	S	%	TGF	PGF	TGA	PGA	+/–	GP	G	A	Pts	PIM	PP	SH	GW
1968-69	Cornell University	ECAC	28	17	22	39	....	....	....	28	....	....	....	....	....	....	....	....	....	....	....	....	....	....	....	....	....	....
1969-70	Cornell University	ECAC	29	25	21	46	....	....	....	44	....	....	....	....	....	....	....	....	....	....	....	....	....	....	....	....	....	....
1970-71	Cornell University	ECAC	27	17	24	41	....	....	....	48	....	....	....	....	....	....	....	....	....	....	....	....	....	....	....	....	....	....
1971-72	Fort Worth Wings	CHL	13	0	1	1	....	....	....	9	....	....	....	....	....	....	....	....	....	....	....	....	....	....	....	....	....	....
	Tidewater Red Wings	AHL	18	1	1	2	....	....	....	2	....	....	....	....	....	....	....	....	....	....	....	....	....	....	....	....	....	....
	Port Huron Wings	IHL	14	2	2	4	....	....	....	0	....	....	....	....	....	....	....	....	....	....	....	....	....	....	....	....	....	....
1972-73	Tidewater Red Wings	AHL	68	23	19	42	....	....	....	64	....	....	....	....	....	....	....	....	....	....	13	3	1	4	7	....	....	....
1973-74	London Lions	Britain	71	47	28	75	....	....	....	75	....	....	....	....	....	....	....	....	....	....	....	....	....	....	....	....	....	....

			REGULAR SEASON																		PLAYOFFS							
Season	Club	League	GP	G	A	Pts	AG	AA	APts	PIM	PP	SH	GW	S	%	TGF	PGF	TGA	PGA	+/–	GP	G	A	Pts	PIM	PP	SH	GW
1974-75	Virginia Wings	AHL	30	12	9	21	....	....	....	24	....	....	....	....	....	....	....	....	....	....	....	....	....	....	....	....	....	....
	Detroit Red Wings	**NHL**	**17**	**3**	**1**	**4**	**3**	**1**	**4**	**2**	**0**	**0**	**0**	**15**	**20.0**	**5**	**0**	**8**	**0**	**–3**	....	....	....	....	....	....	....	....
1975-76	**Detroit Red Wings**	**NHL**	**8**	**0**	**0**	**0**	**0**	**0**	**0**	**5**	**0**	**0**	**0**	**4**	**0.0**	**0**	**0**	**5**	**3**	**–2**	....	....	....	....	....	....	....	....
	New Haven Nighthawks	AHL	58	27	19	46	....	....	....	22	....	....	....	....	....	....	....	....	....	....	....	....	....	....	....	....	....	....
1976-77	**Detroit Red Wings**	**NHL**	**12**	**0**	**0**	**0**	**0**	**0**	**0**	**0**	**0**	**0**	**0**	**1**	**0.0**	**0**	**0**	**1**	**1**	**0**	....	....	....	....	....	....	....	....
	Kansas City Blues	CHL	27	11	8	19	....	....	....	12	....	....	....	....	....	....	....	....	....	....	....	....	....	....	....	....	....	....
1977-78	Kansas City Red Wings	CHL	60	17	16	33	....	....	....	27	....	....	....	....	....	....	....	....	....	....	....	....	....	....	....	....	....	....
1978-1980	EC Graz	Austria	PLAYER/COACH – STATISTICS UNAVAILABLE																									
1980-1981	Elmira College	ECAC-3	DID NOT PLAY – ASSISTANT COACH																									
1981-1987	Elmira College	ECAC-3	DID NOT PLAY – COACHING																									
1987-1995	Cornell University	ECAC	DID NOT PLAY – COACHING																									
1995-1996	Long Beach Ice Dogs	IHL	DID NOT PLAY – ASSISTANT COACH																									
1996-1997	Columbus Chill	ECHL	DID NOT PLAY – COACHING																									
1997-2000	Rochester Americans	AHL	DID NOT PLAY – COACHING																									
	NHL Totals		**37**	**3**	**1**	**4**	**3**	**1**	**4**	**7**	**0**	**0**	**0**	**20**	**15.0**	**5**	**0**	**14**	**4**		....	....	....	....	....	....	....	....

ECAC Second All-Star Team (1971)

Signed as a free agent by **Detroit**, September 29, 1971. • Named Assistant Coach of **Buffalo**, July 6, 2000.

• McCUTCHEON, Darwin

D – L. 6'4", 190 lbs. b: Listowel, Ont., 4/19/1962. Toronto's 9th, 179th overall, in 1980.

Season	Club	League	GP	G	A	Pts	AG	AA	APts	PIM	PP	SH	GW	S	%	TGF	PGF	TGA	PGA	+/–	GP	G	A	Pts	PIM	PP	SH	GW
1979-80	Kitchener Rangers	OMJHL	28	0	3	3	....	....	....	30	....	....	....	....	....	....	....	....	....	....	....	....	....	....	....	....	....	....
	Toronto Marlboros	OMJHL	18	0	1	1	....	....	....	2	....	....	....	....	....	....	....	....	....	....	1	0	0	0	0	....	....	....
1980-81	Windsor Spitfires	OMJHL	26	1	7	8	....	....	....	36	....	....	....	....	....	....	....	....	....	....	....	....	....	....	....	....	....	....
	Toronto Marlboros	OMJHL	38	1	3	4	....	....	....	50	....	....	....	....	....	....	....	....	....	....	....	....	....	....	....	....	....	....
1981-82	Windsor Spitfires	OHL	67	5	24	29	....	....	....	141	....	....	....	....	....	....	....	....	....	....	9	1	3	4	24	....	....	....
	Toronto Maple Leafs	**NHL**	**1**	**0**	**0**	**0**	**0**	**0**	**0**	**2**	**0**	**0**	**0**	**0**	**0.0**	**0**	**0**	**1**	**0**	**–1**	....	....	....	....	....	....	....	....
1982-83	Kitchener Rangers	OHL	11	4	7	11	....	....	....	25	....	....	....	....	....	....	....	....	....	....	....	....	....	....	....	....	....	....
	University of P.E.I.	AUAA	9	1	6	7	....	....	....	26	....	....	....	....	....	....	....	....	....	....	....	....	....	....	....	....	....	....
1983-84	University of P.E.I.	AUAA	24	4	13	17	....	....	....	25	....	....	....	....	....	....	....	....	....	....	....	....	....	....	....	....	....	....
1984-85	University of P.E.I.	AUAA	24	5	30	35	....	....	....	73	....	....	....	....	....	....	....	....	....	....	7	0	0	0	4	....	....	....
1985-86	University of P.E.I.	AUAA	24	4	21	25	....	....	....	55	....	....	....	....	....	....	....	....	....	....	....	....	....	....	....	....	....	....
	Moncton Golden Flames	AHL	12	0	2	2	....	....	....	30	....	....	....	....	....	....	....	....	....	....	9	0	0	0	9	....	....	....
1986-87	Moncton Golden Flames	AHL	69	1	10	11	....	....	....	187	....	....	....	....	....	....	....	....	....	....	4	0	1	1	51	....	....	....
1987-88	Salt Lake Golden Eagles	IHL	64	2	8	10	....	....	....	150	....	....	....	....	....	....	....	....	....	....	13	0	2	2	94	....	....	....
1988-89	Flint Spirits	IHL	37	2	4	6	....	....	....	89	....	....	....	....	....	....	....	....	....	....	....	....	....	....	....	....	....	....
	Indianapolis Ice	IHL	34	2	6	8	....	....	....	99	....	....	....	....	....	....	....	....	....	....	....	....	....	....	....	....	....	....
1989-90	Charlottetown Islanders	NBSHL	10	0	1	1	....	....	....	4	....	....	....	....	....	....	....	....	....	....	....	....	....	....	....	....	....	....
1990-91	Charlottetown Islanders	NBSHL	20	5	20	25	....	....	....	85	....	....	....	....	....	....	....	....	....	....	....	....	....	....	....	....	....	....
	NHL Totals		**1**	**0**	**0**	**0**	**0**	**0**	**0**	**2**	**0**	**0**	**0**	**0**	**0.0**	**0**	**0**	**1**	**0**		....	....	....	....	....	....	....	....

Signed as a free agent by **Calgary**, March 10, 1986.

• McDILL, Jeff

Jeffrey Donald RW – R. 5'11", 190 lbs. b: Thunder Bay, Ont., 3/16/1956. Chicago's 2nd, 27th overall, in 1976.

Season	Club	League	GP	G	A	Pts	AG	AA	APts	PIM	PP	SH	GW	S	%	TGF	PGF	TGA	PGA	+/–	GP	G	A	Pts	PIM	PP	SH	GW
1972-73	Dauphin Kings	MJHL	48	16	17	33	....	....	....	143	....	....	....	....	....	....	....	....	....	....	....	....	....	....	....	....	....	....
1973-74	Flin Flon Bombers	WCJHL	66	22	14	36	....	....	....	86	....	....	....	....	....	....	....	....	....	....	7	3	3	6	13	....	....	....
1974-75	Flin Flon Bombers	WCJHL	46	24	44	68	....	....	....	75	....	....	....	....	....	....	....	....	....	....	....	....	....	....	....	....	....	....
1975-76	Victoria Cougars	WCJHL	72	55	66	121	....	....	....	197	....	....	....	....	....	....	....	....	....	....	15	8	9	17	42	....	....	....
1976-77	**Chicago Black Hawks**	**NHL**	**1**	**0**	**0**	**0**	**0**	**0**	**0**	**0**	**0**	**0**	**0**	**0**	**0.0**	**0**	**0**	**0**	**0**	**0**	....	....	....	....	....	....	....	....
	Flint Generals	IHL	74	31	39	70	....	....	....	42	....	....	....	....	....	....	....	....	....	....	5	0	1	1	5	....	....	....
	Dallas Black Hawks	CHL	1	0	0	0	....	....	....	0	....	....	....	....	....	....	....	....	....	....	....	....	....	....	....	....	....	....
1977-78	Kalamazoo Wings	IHL	14	1	5	6	....	....	....	20	....	....	....	....	....	....	....	....	....	....	....	....	....	....	....	....	....	....
	Muskegon Mohawks	IHL	47	18	25	43	....	....	....	28	....	....	....	....	....	....	....	....	....	....	6	1	4	5	0	....	....	....
	Maine Mariners	AHL	4	1	1	2	....	....	....	5	....	....	....	....	....	....	....	....	....	....	....	....	....	....	....	....	....	....
1978-79	New Haven Nighthawks	AHL	71	24	26	50	....	....	....	75	....	....	....	....	....	....	....	....	....	....	10	5	7	12	12	....	....	....
1979-80	New Haven Nighthawks	AHL	75	27	36	63	....	....	....	61	....	....	....	....	....	....	....	....	....	....	10	5	0	5	20	....	....	....
	NHL Totals		**1**	**0**	**0**	**0**	**0**	**0**	**0**	**0**	**0**	**0**	**0**	**0**	**0.0**	**0**	**0**	**0**	**0**		....	....	....	....	....	....	....	....

Signed as a free agent by **NY Rangers**, October 13, 1978.

• McDONALD, Ab

Alvin Brian LW – L. 6'3", 192 lbs. b: Winnipeg, Man., 2/18/1936.

Season	Club	League	GP	G	A	Pts	AG	AA	APts	PIM	PP	SH	GW	S	%	TGF	PGF	TGA	PGA	+/–	GP	G	A	Pts	PIM	PP	SH	GW
1951-52	St. Boniface Canadiens	MJHL	20	*20	15	*35	....	....	....	....	....	....	....	....	....	....	....	....	....	....	17	11	12	23	6	....	....	....
1952-53	St. Boniface Canadiens	MJHL	35	26	24	50	....	....	....	0	....	....	....	....	....	....	....	....	....	....	8	5	*7	*12	0	....	....	....
	St. Boniface Canadiens	Mem-Cup	17	11	12	23	....	....	....	6	....	....	....	....	....	....	....	....	....	....	....	....	....	....	....	....	....	....
1953-54	St. Boniface Canadiens	MJHL	35	33	25	*58	....	....	....	14	....	....	....	....	....	....	....	....	....	....	10	7	6	13	4	....	....	....
	St. Boniface Canadiens	Mem-Cup	8	2	2	4	....	....	....	6	....	....	....	....	....	....	....	....	....	....	....	....	....	....	....	....	....	....
1954-55	St. Catharines Teepees	OHA-Jr.	49	33	37	70	....	....	....	20	....	....	....	....	....	....	....	....	....	....	10	2	6	8	25	....	....	....
1955-56	St. Catharines Teepees	OHA-Jr.	48	49	34	83	....	....	....	24	....	....	....	....	....	....	....	....	....	....	6	4	2	6	9	....	....	....
1956-57	Rochester Americans	AHL	64	21	31	52	....	....	....	8	....	....	....	....	....	....	....	....	....	....	9	3	1	4	0	....	....	....
1957-58	Rochester Americans	AHL	70	30	33	63	....	....	....	18	....	....	....	....	....	....	....	....	....	....	....	....	....	....	....	....	....	....
♦	**Montreal Canadiens**	**NHL**	....	....	....	....	....	....	....	....	....	....	....	....	....	....	....	....	....	....	**2**	**0**	**0**	**0**	**2**	....	....	....
1958-59♦	**Montreal Canadiens**	**NHL**	**69**	**13**	**23**	**36**	**15**	**23**	**38**	**35**	....	....	....	....	....	....	....	....	....	....	**11**	**1**	**1**	**2**	**6**	....	....	....
1959-60♦	**Montreal Canadiens**	**NHL**	**68**	**9**	**13**	**22**	**10**	**13**	**23**	**26**	....	....	....	....	....	....	....	....	....	....	....	....	....	....	....	....	....	....
1960-61♦	**Chicago Black Hawks**	**NHL**	**61**	**17**	**16**	**33**	**20**	**15**	**35**	**22**	....	....	....	....	....	....	....	....	....	....	**8**	**2**	**2**	**4**	**0**	....	....	....
1961-62	**Chicago Black Hawks**	**NHL**	**65**	**22**	**18**	**40**	**25**	**17**	**42**	**8**	....	....	....	....	....	....	....	....	....	....	**12**	**6**	**6**	**12**	**0**	....	....	....
1962-63	**Chicago Black Hawks**	**NHL**	**69**	**20**	**41**	**61**	**23**	**41**	**64**	**12**	....	....	....	....	....	....	....	....	....	....	**6**	**2**	**3**	**5**	**9**	....	....	....
1963-64	**Chicago Black Hawks**	**NHL**	**70**	**14**	**32**	**46**	**17**	**34**	**51**	**19**	....	....	....	....	....	....	....	....	....	....	**7**	**2**	**2**	**4**	**0**	....	....	....
1964-65	**Boston Bruins**	**NHL**	**60**	**9**	**9**	**18**	**11**	**9**	**20**	**6**	....	....	....	....	....	....	....	....	....	....	....	....	....	....	....	....	....	....
	Providence Reds	AHL	6	2	1	3	....	....	....	2	....	....	....	....	....	....	....	....	....	....	....	....	....	....	....	....	....	....
1965-66	**Detroit Red Wings**	**NHL**	**43**	**6**	**16**	**22**	**7**	**15**	**22**	**6**	....	....	....	....	....	....	....	....	....	....	**10**	**1**	**4**	**5**	**2**	....	....	....
	Memphis Wings	CPHL	20	9	6	15	....	....	....	4	....	....	....	....	....	....	....	....	....	....	....	....	....	....	....	....	....	....
1966-67	**Detroit Red Wings**	**NHL**	**12**	**2**	**0**	**2**	**2**	**0**	**2**	**2**	....	....	....	....	....	....	....	....	....	....	....	....	....	....	....	....	....	....
	Pittsburgh Hornets	AHL	61	25	31	56	....	....	....	22	....	....	....	....	....	....	....	....	....	....	9	5	2	7	4	....	....	....
1967-68	**Pittsburgh Penguins**	**NHL**	**74**	**22**	**21**	**43**	**26**	**21**	**47**	**38**	**6**	**1**	**2**	**185**	**11.9**	**68**	**14**	**64**	**6**	**–4**	....	....	....	....	....	....	....	....
1968-69	**St. Louis Blues**	**NHL**	**68**	**21**	**21**	**42**	**22**	**19**	**41**	**12**	**2**	**0**	**4**	**138**	**15.2**	**76**	**19**	**38**	**0**	**19**	**12**	**2**	**1**	**3**	**10**	**0**	**0**	**0**
1969-70	**St. Louis Blues**	**NHL**	**64**	**25**	**30**	**55**	**27**	**28**	**55**	**8**	**11**	**0**	**4**	**170**	**14.7**	**88**	**42**	**35**	**0**	**11**	**16**	**5**	**10**	**15**	**13**	**3**	**0**	**0**
1970-71	**St. Louis Blues**	**NHL**	**20**	**0**	**5**	**5**	**0**	**4**	**4**	**6**	**0**	**0**	**0**	**31**	**0.0**	**9**	**4**	**8**	**0**	**–3**	....	....	....	....	....	....	....	....
1971-72	**Detroit Red Wings**	**NHL**	**19**	**2**	**3**	**5**	**2**	**3**	**5**	**0**	**1**	**0**	**0**	**29**	**6.9**	**7**	**1**	**14**	**0**	**–8**	....	....	....	....	....	....	....	....
	Tidewater Red Wings	AHL	41	5	7	12	....	....	....	4	....	....	....	....	....	....	....	....	....	....	....	....	....	....	....	....	....	....
1972-73	Winnipeg Jets	WHA	77	17	24	41	....	....	....	16	....	....	....	....	....	....	....	....	....	....	14	2	5	7	2	....	....	....
1973-74	Winnipeg Jets	WHA	70	12	17	29	....	....	....	8	....	....	....	....	....	....	....	....	....	....	4	0	1	1	2	....	....	....
	NHL Totals		**762**	**182**	**248**	**430**	**207**	**242**	**449**	**200**	....	....	....	....	....	....	....	....	....		**84**	**21**	**29**	**50**	**42**	....	....	....
	Other Major League Totals		147	29	41	70	....	....	....	24	....	....	....	....	....	....	....	....	....	....	18	2	6	8	4	....	....	....

MJHL Second All-Star Team (1953) • Played in NHL All-Star Game (1958, 1959, 1961, 1969, 1970)

Traded to **Chicago** by **Montreal** with Reggie Fleming, Bob Courcy and Cec Hoekstra for Terry Gray, Glen Skov, the rights to Danny Lewicki, Lorne Ferguson and Bob Bailey, June 7, 1960. Traded to **Boston** by **Chicago** with Reggie Fleming for Doug Mohns, June 8, 1964. Traded to **Detroit** by **Boston** with Bob McCord and Ken Stephanson for Albert Langlois, Ron Harris, Parker MacDonald and Bob Dillabaugh, May 31, 1965. Claimed by **Pittsburgh** from **Detroit** in Expansion Draft, June 6, 1967. Traded to **St. Louis** by **Pittsburgh** for Lou Angotti, June 11, 1968. Traded to **Detroit** by **St. Louis** with Bob Wall and Mike Lowe to complete transaction that sent Carl Brewer to St. Louis (February 22, 1971), May 12, 1971. Selected by **Winnipeg** (WHA) in 1972 WHA General Player Draft, February 12, 1972.

• McDONALD, Brian

Brian Harold "Butch" C – R. 5'11", 190 lbs. b: Toronto, Ont., 3/23/1945.

			REGULAR SEASON																		PLAYOFFS							
Season	Club	League	GP	G	A	Pts	AG	AA	APts	PIM	PP	SH	GW	S	%	TGF	PGF	TGA	PGA	+/-	GP	G	A	Pts	PIM	PP	SH	GW
1963-64	St. Catharines Black Hawks	OHA-Jr.	56	31	44	75	....	....	....	98	....	....	....	....	....	....	....	....	....	....	13	7	11	18	24	....	....	....
1964-65	St. Catharines Black Hawks	OHA-Jr.	56	47	61	108	....	....	....	100	....	....	....	....	....	....	....	....	....	....	5	4	2	6	34	....	....	....
	St. Louis Braves	CPHL	3	0	1	1	....	....	....	0	....	....	....	....	....	....	....	....	....	....	....	....	....	....	....	....	....	....
1965-66	St. Louis Braves	CPHL	70	13	33	46	....	....	....	45	....	....	....	....	....	....	....	....	....	....	5	1	2	3	2	....	....	....
1966-67	St. Louis Braves	CPHL	67	10	33	43	....	....	....	59	....	....	....	....	....	....	....	....	....	....	....	....	....	....	....	....	....	....
1967-68	Dallas Black Hawks	CPHL	67	24	45	69	....	....	....	104	....	....	....	....	....	....	....	....	....	....	5	0	4	4	21	....	....	....
	Chicago Black Hawks	**NHL**	....	....	....	....	....	....	....	....	....	....	....	....	....	....	....	....	....	....	**8**	**0**	**0**	**0**	**2**	**0**	**0**	**0**
1968-69	Dallas Black Hawks	CHL	67	19	41	60	....	....	....	65	....	....	....	....	....	....	....	....	....	....	11	7	6	13	28	....	....	....
1969-70	Denver Spurs	WHL	70	34	34	68	....	....	....	54	....	....	....	....	....	....	....	....	....	....	....	....	....	....	....	....	....	....
1970-71	**Buffalo Sabres**	**NHL**	**12**	**0**	**0**	**0**	**0**	**0**	**0**	**29**	**0**	**0**	**0**	**15**	**0.0**	**0**	**0**	**8**	**0**	**–8**	....	....	....	....	....	....	....	....
	Salt Lake Golden Eagles	WHL	56	29	18	47	....	....	....	70	....	....	....	....	....	....	....	....	....	....	....	....	....	....	....	....	....	....
1971-72	San Diego Gulls	WHL	63	24	22	46	....	....	....	88	....	....	....	....	....	....	....	....	....	....	4	0	1	1	24	....	....	....
1972-73	Houston Aeros	WHA	71	20	20	40	....	....	....	78	....	....	....	....	....	....	....	....	....	....	10	3	0	3	16	....	....	....
1973-74	Los Angeles Sharks	WHA	56	22	30	52	....	....	....	54	....	....	....	....	....	....	....	....	....	....	....	....	....	....	....	....	....	....
1974-75	Michigan Stags	WHA	18	3	5	8	....	....	....	15	....	....	....	....	....	....	....	....	....	....	....	....	....	....	....	....	....	....
	Indianapolis Racers	WHA	47	14	15	29	....	....	....	19	....	....	....	....	....	....	....	....	....	....	....	....	....	....	....	....	....	....
	Mohawk Valley Comets	NAHL	10	5	9	14	....	....	....	17	....	....	....	....	....	....	....	....	....	....	....	....	....	....	....	....	....	....
1975-76	Indianapolis Racers	WHA	62	16	17	33	....	....	....	54	....	....	....	....	....	....	....	....	....	....	7	0	1	1	12	....	....	....
1976-77	Indianapolis Racers	WHA	50	15	13	28	....	....	....	48	....	....	....	....	....	....	....	....	....	....	9	3	4	7	33	....	....	....
	NHL Totals		**12**	**0**	**0**	**0**	**0**	**0**	**0**	**29**	**0**	**0**	**0**	**15**	**0.0**	**0**	**0**	**8**	**0**		**8**	**0**	**0**	**0**	**2**	**0**	**0**	**0**
	Other Major League Totals		304	90	100	190	....	....	....	268	....	....	....	....	....	....	....	....	....	....	26	6	5	11	61	....	....	....

Traded to **Denver** (WHL) by **Chicago** for cash, September, 1970. Claimed by **Buffalo** from **Denver** (WHL) in Inter-League Draft, June 9, 1970. Claimed by **San Diego** (WHL) from **Buffalo** (Salt Lake-CHL) in Reverse Draft, June, 1971. Selected by **Dayton-Houston** (WHA) in 1972 WHA General Player Draft, February 12, 1972. Traded to **LA Sharks** (WHA) by **Houston** (WHA) for Joe Szura, September, 1973. Transferred to **Michigan** (WHA) after **LA Sharks** (WHA) franchise relocated, April 11, 1974. Traded to **Indianapolis** (WHA) by **Michigan** (WHA) with Jacques Locas for Steve Andrascik and Steve Richardson, November, 1974.

• McDONALD, Gerry

Girard J. D – R. 6'3", 190 lbs. b: Weymouth, MA, 3/18/1958.

Season	Club	League	GP	G	A	Pts	AG	AA	APts	PIM	PP	SH	GW	S	%	TGF	PGF	TGA	PGA	+/-	GP	G	A	Pts	PIM	PP	SH	GW
1977-1980	North Adams State College	ECAC-3	STATISTICS NOT AVAILABLE																									
1980-81	Tulsa Oilers	CHL	5	0	1	1	....	....	....	2	....	....	....	....	....	....	....	....	....	....	....	....	....	....	....	....	....	....
	New Haven Nighthawks	AHL	70	6	23	29	....	....	....	67	....	....	....	....	....	....	....	....	....	....	4	0	0	0	0	....	....	....
1981-82	**Hartford Whalers**	**NHL**	**3**	**0**	**0**	**0**	**0**	**0**	**0**	**0**	**0**	**0**	**0**	**1**	**0.0**	**2**	**0**	**4**	**0**	**–2**	....	....	....	....	....	....	....	....
	Binghamton Whalers	AHL	57	3	11	14	....	....	....	42	....	....	....	....	....	....	....	....	....	....	....	....	....	....	....	....	....	....
1982-83	Binghamton Whalers	AHL	74	8	33	41	....	....	....	62	....	....	....	....	....	....	....	....	....	....	5	0	4	4	23	....	....	....
1983-84	**Hartford Whalers**	**NHL**	**5**	**0**	**0**	**0**	**0**	**0**	**0**	**4**	**0**	**0**	**0**	**7**	**0.0**	**4**	**1**	**7**	**1**	**–3**	....	....	....	....	....	....	....	....
	Binghamton Whalers	AHL	72	4	39	43	....	....	....	34	....	....	....	....	....	....	....	....	....	....	....	....	....	....	....	....	....	....
	NHL Totals		**8**	**0**	**0**	**0**	**0**	**0**	**0**	**4**	**0**	**0**	**0**	**8**	**0.0**	**6**	**1**	**11**	**1**		....	....	....	....	....	....	....	....

Signed as a free agent by **NY Rangers**, December 12, 1980. Traded to **Hartford** by **NY Rangers** with Doug Sulliman and Chris Kotsopoulos for Mike Rogers and Hartford's 10th round choice (Simo Saarinen) in 1982 Entry Draft, October 2, 1981.

• McDONALD, Lanny

Lanny King RW – R. 6', 185 lbs. b: Hanna, Alta., 2/16/1953. Toronto's 1st, 4th overall, in 1973. **HHOF**

Season	Club	League	GP	G	A	Pts	AG	AA	APts	PIM	PP	SH	GW	S	%	TGF	PGF	TGA	PGA	+/-	GP	G	A	Pts	PIM	PP	SH	GW
1969-70	Lethbridge Sugar Kings	AJHL	34	2	9	11	....	....	....	19	....	....	....	....	....	....	....	....	....	....	....	....	....	....	....	....	....	....
1970-71	Lethbridge Sugar Kings	AJHL	45	37	45	82	....	....	....	56	....	....	....	....	....	....	....	....	....	....	....	....	....	....	....	....	....	....
	Calgary Centennials	WCJHL	6	0	2	2	....	....	....	6	....	....	....	....	....	....	....	....	....	....	....	....	....	....	....	....	....	....
1971-72	Medicine Hat Tigers	WCJHL	68	50	64	114	....	....	....	54	....	....	....	....	....	....	....	....	....	....	7	2	2	4	6	....	....	....
1972-73	Medicine Hat Tigers	WCJHL	68	62	77	139	....	....	....	84	....	....	....	....	....	....	....	....	....	....	17	*18	19	37	6	....	....	....
	Medicine Hat Tigers	Mem-Cup	2	0	0	0	....	....	....	2	....	....	....	....	....	....	....	....	....	....	....	....	....	....	....	....	....	....
1973-74	**Toronto Maple Leafs**	**NHL**	**70**	**14**	**16**	**30**	**13**	**13**	**26**	**43**	**2**	**0**	**3**	**142**	**9.9**	**58**	**12**	**47**	**4**	**3**	....	....	....	....	....	....	....	....
1974-75	**Toronto Maple Leafs**	**NHL**	**64**	**17**	**27**	**44**	**15**	**20**	**35**	**86**	**2**	**1**	**1**	**168**	**10.1**	**70**	**12**	**69**	**16**	**5**	**7**	**0**	**0**	**0**	**2**	**0**	**0**	**0**
1975-76	**Toronto Maple Leafs**	**NHL**	**75**	**37**	**56**	**93**	**33**	**42**	**75**	**70**	**6**	**5**	**4**	**270**	**13.7**	**126**	**37**	**95**	**30**	**24**	**10**	**4**	**4**	**8**	**4**	**2**	**0**	**1**
1976-77	Canada	Can-Cup	5	0	2	2	....	....	....	0	....	....	....	....	....	....	....	....	....	....	....	....	....	....	....	....	....	....
	Toronto Maple Leafs	**NHL**	**80**	**46**	**44**	**90**	**42**	**34**	**76**	**77**	**16**	**4**	**5**	**293**	**15.7**	**136**	**44**	**105**	**25**	**12**	**9**	**10**	**7**	**17**	**6**	**3**	**0**	**1**
1977-78	**Toronto Maple Leafs**	**NHL**	**74**	**47**	**40**	**87**	**43**	**31**	**74**	**54**	**11**	**0**	**5**	**243**	**19.3**	**126**	**39**	**54**	**1**	**34**	**13**	**3**	**4**	**7**	**10**	**1**	**0**	**2**
1978-79	**Toronto Maple Leafs**	**NHL**	**79**	**43**	**42**	**85**	**37**	**30**	**67**	**32**	**16**	**0**	**2**	**314**	**13.7**	**130**	**46**	**72**	**0**	**12**	**6**	**3**	**2**	**5**	**0**	**0**	**0**	**0**
	NHL All-Stars	Chal-Cup	3	0	0	0	....	....	....	2	....	....	....	....	....	....	....	....	....	....	....	....	....	....	....	....	....	....
1979-80	**Toronto Maple Leafs**	**NHL**	**35**	**15**	**15**	**30**	**13**	**11**	**24**	**10**	**6**	**0**	**2**	**140**	**10.7**	**51**	**17**	**36**	**1**	**–1**	....	....	....	....	....	....	....	....
	Colorado Rockies	**NHL**	**46**	**25**	**20**	**45**	**21**	**15**	**36**	**43**	**8**	**0**	**3**	**194**	**12.9**	**64**	**25**	**64**	**10**	**–15**	....	....	....	....	....	....	....	....
1980-81	**Colorado Rockies**	**NHL**	**80**	**35**	**46**	**81**	**27**	**31**	**58**	**56**	**11**	**0**	**2**	**298**	**11.7**	**116**	**45**	**117**	**19**	**–27**	....	....	....	....	....	....	....	....
	Canada	WEC-A	8	3	0	3	....	....	....	4	....	....	....	....	....	....	....	....	....	....	....	....	....	....	....	....	....	....
1981-82	**Colorado Rockies**	**NHL**	**16**	**6**	**9**	**15**	**5**	**6**	**11**	**20**	**0**	**0**	**1**	**65**	**9.2**	**25**	**8**	**20**	**0**	**–3**	....	....	....	....	....	....	....	....
	Calgary Flames	**NHL**	**55**	**34**	**33**	**67**	**27**	**22**	**49**	**37**	**10**	**1**	**3**	**178**	**19.1**	**99**	**34**	**57**	**14**	**22**	**3**	**0**	**1**	**1**	**6**	**0**	**0**	**0**
1982-83	**Calgary Flames**	**NHL**	**80**	**66**	**32**	**98**	**54**	**22**	**76**	**90**	**17**	**0**	**8**	**272**	**24.3**	**151**	**61**	**98**	**6**	**–2**	**7**	**3**	**4**	**7**	**19**	**1**	**0**	**0**
1983-84	**Calgary Flames**	**NHL**	**65**	**33**	**33**	**66**	**27**	**22**	**49**	**64**	**10**	**0**	**1**	**245**	**13.5**	**101**	**41**	**76**	**1**	**–15**	**11**	**6**	**7**	**13**	**6**	**3**	**0**	**1**
1984-85	**Calgary Flames**	**NHL**	**43**	**19**	**18**	**37**	**15**	**12**	**27**	**36**	**9**	**0**	**2**	**117**	**16.2**	**60**	**21**	**43**	**0**	**–4**	**1**	**0**	**0**	**0**	**0**	**0**	**0**	**0**
1985-86	**Calgary Flames**	**NHL**	**80**	**28**	**43**	**71**	**22**	**29**	**51**	**44**	**11**	**0**	**3**	**227**	**12.3**	**102**	**42**	**64**	**2**	**–2**	**22**	**11**	**7**	**18**	**30**	**4**	**0**	**2**
1986-87	**Calgary Flames**	**NHL**	**58**	**14**	**12**	**26**	**12**	**9**	**21**	**54**	**4**	**0**	**3**	**127**	**11.0**	**49**	**12**	**44**	**4**	**–3**	**5**	**0**	**0**	**0**	**2**	**0**	**0**	**0**
1987-88	**Calgary Flames**	**NHL**	**60**	**10**	**13**	**23**	**9**	**9**	**18**	**57**	**0**	**0**	**2**	**79**	**12.7**	**34**	**2**	**31**	**1**	**2**	**9**	**3**	**1**	**4**	**6**	**0**	**0**	**0**
1988-89♦	**Calgary Flames**	**NHL**	**51**	**11**	**7**	**18**	**9**	**5**	**14**	**26**	**0**	**0**	**3**	**72**	**15.3**	**23**	**2**	**22**	**0**	**–1**	**14**	**1**	**3**	**4**	**29**	**0**	**0**	**0**
	NHL Totals		**1111**	**500**	**506**	**1006**	**424**	**363**	**787**	**899**	**139**	**11**	**53**	**3444**	**14.5**	**1521**	**500**	**1114**	**134**		**117**	**44**	**40**	**84**	**120**	**14**	**0**	**7**

AJHL Second All-Star Team (1971) • WCJHL First All-Star Team (1973) • NHL Second All-Star Team (1977, 1983) • Won Bill Masterton Trophy (1983) • Won King Clancy Memorial Trophy (1988) • Won Bud Man of the Year Award (1989) • Played in NHL All-Star Game (1977, 1978, 1983, 1984)

Traded to **Colorado** by **Toronto** with Joel Quenneville for Pat Hickey and Wilf Paiement, December 29, 1979. Traded to **Calgary** by **Colorado** with Colorado's 4th round choice (later traded to NY Islanders — NY Islanders selected Mikko Makela) in 1983 Entry Draft for Bob MacMillan and Don Lever, November 25, 1981.

• McDONALD, Terry

Terry Grant D – L. 6'1", 180 lbs. b: Coquitlam, B.C., 1/1/1956. Kansas City's 5th, 74th overall, in 1975.

Season	Club	League	GP	G	A	Pts	AG	AA	APts	PIM	PP	SH	GW	S	%	TGF	PGF	TGA	PGA	+/-	GP	G	A	Pts	PIM	PP	SH	GW
1971-72	Coquitlam Selects	BCJHL	STATISTICS NOT AVAILABLE																									
1972-73	Vancouver Nats	WCJHL	49	9	18	27	....	....	....	81	....	....	....	....	....	....	....	....	....	....	....	....	....	....	....	....	....	....
1973-74	Kamloops Chiefs	WCJHL	68	10	22	32	....	....	....	102	....	....	....	....	....	....	....	....	....	....	....	....	....	....	....	....	....	....
1974-75	Kamloops Chiefs	WCJHL	66	32	37	69	....	....	....	89	....	....	....	....	....	....	....	....	....	....	6	3	1	4	2	....	....	....
1975-76	**Kansas City Scouts**	**NHL**	**8**	**0**	**1**	**1**	**0**	**1**	**1**	**6**	**0**	**0**	**0**	**4**	**0.0**	**4**	**1**	**9**	**1**	**–5**	....	....	....	....	....	....	....	....
	Springfield Indians	AHL	24	0	0	0	....	....	....	13	....	....	....	....	....	....	....	....	....	....	....	....	....	....	....	....	....	....
	Port Huron Flags	IHL	43	6	25	31	....	....	....	75	....	....	....	....	....	....	....	....	....	....	15	5	2	7	23	....	....	....
1976-77	Rhode Island Reds	AHL	76	20	18	38	....	....	....	18	....	....	....	....	....	....	....	....	....	....	....	....	....	....	....	....	....	....
	Flint Generals	IHL	2	0	0	0	....	....	....	0	....	....	....	....	....	....	....	....	....	....	....	....	....	....	....	....	....	....
1977-78	Phoenix Roadrunners	CHL	27	12	10	22	....	....	....	11	....	....	....	....	....	....	....	....	....	....	....	....	....	....	....	....	....	....
	Flint Generals	IHL	42	19	32	51	....	....	....	29	....	....	....	....	....	....	....	....	....	....	5	3	0	3	0	....	....	....
1978-79	Phoenix Roadrunners	PHL	60	26	31	57	....	....	....	20	....	....	....	....	....	....	....	....	....	....	....	....	....	....	....	....	....	....
	NHL Totals		**8**	**0**	**1**	**1**	**0**	**1**	**1**	**6**	**0**	**0**	**0**	**4**	**0.0**	**4**	**1**	**9**	**1**		....	....	....	....	....	....	....	....

• McDONNELL, Joe

Joseph Michael Patrick D – R. 6'2", 200 lbs. b: Kitchener, Ont., 5/11/1961.

Season	Club	League	GP	G	A	Pts	AG	AA	APts	PIM	PP	SH	GW	S	%	TGF	PGF	TGA	PGA	+/-	GP	G	A	Pts	PIM	PP	SH	GW
1976-77	Kitchener Ranger B's	OHA-B	21	8	20	28	....	....	....	28	....	....	....	....	....	....	....	....	....	....	....	....	....	....	....	....	....	....
	Kitchener Rangers	OMJHL	29	0	4	4	....	....	....	8	....	....	....	....	....	....	....	....	....	....	....	....	....	....	....	....	....	....
1977-78	Kitchener Rangers	OMJHL	55	0	4	4	....	....	....	14	....	....	....	....	....	....	....	....	....	....	3	0	0	0	0	....	....	....
1978-79	Kitchener Rangers	OMJHL	60	1	6	7	....	....	....	43	....	....	....	....	....	....	....	....	....	....	10	0	1	0	33	....	....	....
1979-80	Kitchener Rangers	OMJHL	62	6	21	27	....	....	....	81	....	....	....	....	....	....	....	....	....	....	....	....	....	....	....	....	....	....
1980-81	Kitchener Rangers	OMJHL	66	15	50	65	....	....	....	103	....	....	....	....	....	....	....	....	....	....	16	4	9	13	8	....	....	....
	Kitchener Rangers	Mem-Cup	5	1	2	3	....	....	....	0	....	....	....	....	....	....	....	....	....	....	....	....	....	....	....	....	....	....

Season	Club	League	GP	G	A	Pts	AG	AA	APts	PIM	PP	SH	GW	S	%	TGF	PGF	TGA	PGA	+/–	GP	G	A	Pts	PIM	PP	SH	GW
			REGULAR SEASON																		PLAYOFFS							
1981-82	**Vancouver Canucks**	**NHL**	**7**	**0**	**1**	**1**	**0**	**1**	**1**	**12**	**0**	**0**	**0**	**6**	**0.0**	**4**	**0**	**6**	**0**	**–2**	....	....	....	....	....	....	....	....
	Dallas Black Hawks	CHL	60	13	24	37	....	....	....	46	....	....	....	....	....	....	....	....	....	....	9	2	1	3	12	....	....	....
1982-83	Moncton Alpines	AHL	79	14	21	35	....	....	....	44	....	....	....	....	....	....	....	....	....	....	....	....	....	....	....	....	....	....
1983-84	Moncton Alpines	AHL	78	12	33	45	....	....	....	44	....	....	....	....	....	....	....	....	....	....	....	....	....	....	....	....	....	....
1984-85	**Pittsburgh Penguins**	**NHL**	**40**	**2**	**9**	**11**	**2**	**6**	**8**	**20**	**2**	**0**	**0**	**75**	**2.7**	**46**	**10**	**64**	**9**	**–19**	....	....	....	....	....	....	....	....
	Baltimore Skipjacks	AHL	41	7	27	34	....	....	....	22	....	....	....	....	....	....	....	....	....	....	....	....	....	....	....	....	....	....
1985-86	**Pittsburgh Penguins**	**NHL**	**3**	**0**	**0**	**0**	**0**	**0**	**0**	**2**	**0**	**0**	**0**	**1**	**0.0**	**1**	**0**	**4**	**0**	**–3**	....	....	....	....	....	....	....	....
	Baltimore Skipjacks	AHL	31	1	13	14	....	....	....	20	....	....	....	....	....	....	....	....	....	....	....	....	....	....	....	....	....	....
	NHL Totals		**50**	**2**	**10**	**12**	**2**	**7**	**9**	**34**	**2**	**0**	**0**	**82**	**2.4**	**51**	**10**	**74**	**9**		....	....	....	....	....	....	....	....

Memorial Cup All-Star Team (1981)

Signed as a free agent by **Vancouver**, September 22, 1980. Signed as a free agent by **Edmonton**, August 16, 1982. Signed as a free agent by **Pittsburgh**, December 30, 1984.

• McDONOUGH, Al

James Allison RW – R. 6'1", 175 lbs. b: Hamilton, Ont., 6/6/1950. Los Angeles' 1st, 24th overall, in 1970.

Season	Club	League	GP	G	A	Pts	AG	AA	APts	PIM	PP	SH	GW	S	%	TGF	PGF	TGA	PGA	+/–	GP	G	A	Pts	PIM	PP	SH	GW
1967-68	St. Catharines Black Hawks	OHA-Jr.	49	12	8	20	....	....	....	13	....	....	....	....	....	....	....	....	....	....	4	1	0	1	0	....	....	....
1968-69	St. Catharines Black Hawks	OHA-Jr.	54	26	20	46	....	....	....	34	....	....	....	....	....	....	....	....	....	....	17	5	7	12	12	....	....	....
1969-70	St. Catharines Black Hawks	OHA-Jr.	53	47	56	103	....	....	....	57	....	....	....	....	....	....	....	....	....	....	10	4	8	12	15	....	....	....
1970-71	**Los Angeles Kings**	**NHL**	**6**	**2**	**1**	**3**	**2**	**1**	**3**	**0**	**0**	**0**	**1**	**13**	**15.4**	**7**	**0**	**5**	**0**	**2**	....	....	....	....	....	....	....	....
	Springfield Kings	AHL	65	33	16	49	....	....	....	27	....	....	....	....	....	....	....	....	....	....	12	1	2	3	9	....	....	....
1971-72	**Los Angeles Kings**	**NHL**	**31**	**3**	**2**	**5**	**3**	**2**	**5**	**8**	**1**	**0**	**0**	**28**	**10.7**	**9**	**5**	**12**	**0**	**–8**	....	....	....	....	....	....	....	....
	Pittsburgh Penguins	**NHL**	**37**	**7**	**11**	**18**	**7**	**9**	**16**	**8**	**1**	**0**	**1**	**113**	**6.2**	**35**	**17**	**24**	**0**	**–6**	**4**	**0**	**1**	**1**	**0**	**0**	**0**	**0**
1972-73	**Pittsburgh Penguins**	**NHL**	**78**	**35**	**41**	**76**	**33**	**33**	**66**	**26**	**7**	**0**	**4**	**285**	**12.3**	**118**	**38**	**60**	**0**	**20**	....	....	....	....	....	....	....	....
1973-74	**Pittsburgh Penguins**	**NHL**	**37**	**14**	**22**	**36**	**13**	**18**	**31**	**12**	**3**	**0**	**4**	**142**	**9.9**	**50**	**18**	**35**	**0**	**–3**	....	....	....	....	....	....	....	....
	Atlanta Flames	**NHL**	**35**	**10**	**9**	**19**	**10**	**7**	**17**	**15**	**3**	**0**	**1**	**108**	**9.3**	**37**	**13**	**29**	**1**	**–4**	**4**	**0**	**0**	**0**	**2**	**0**	**0**	**0**
1974-75	Cleveland Crusaders	WHA	78	34	30	64	....	....	....	27	....	....	....	....	....	....	....	....	....	....	5	2	1	3	2	....	....	....
1975-76	Cleveland Crusaders	WHA	80	23	22	45	....	....	....	19	....	....	....	....	....	....	....	....	....	....	3	1	0	1	0	....	....	....
1976-77	Minnesota Fighting Saints	WHA	42	9	21	30	....	....	....	6	....	....	....	....	....	....	....	....	....	....	....	....	....	....	....	....	....	....
1977-78	**Detroit Red Wings**	**NHL**	**13**	**2**	**2**	**4**	**2**	**2**	**4**	**4**	**0**	**0**	**0**	**18**	**11.1**	**6**	**1**	**3**	**0**	**2**	....	....	....	....	....	....	....	....
	Kansas City Red Wings	CHL	52	18	24	42	....	....	....	14	....	....	....	....	....	....	....	....	....	....	....	....	....	....	....	....	....	....
	NHL Totals		**237**	**73**	**88**	**161**	**70**	**72**	**142**	**73**	**15**	**0**	**11**	**707**	**10.3**	**262**	**92**	**168**	**1**		**8**	**0**	**1**	**1**	**2**	**0**	**0**	**0**
	Other Major League Totals		200	66	73	139	....	....	....	52	....	....	....	....	....	....	....	....	....	....	8	3	1	4	2	....	....	....

OHA-Jr. First All-Star Team (1970) • Played in NHL All-Star Game (1974)

Traded to **Pittsburgh** by **LA Kings** for Bob Woytowich, January 11, 1972. Selected by **Calgary-Cleveland** (WHA) in 1972 WHA General Player Draft, February 12, 1972. Traded to **Atlanta** by **Pittsburgh** for Chuck Arnason and Bob Paradise, January 4, 1974. Transferred to **Minnesota** (WHA) after **Cleveland** (WHA) franchise relocated, July, 1976. Traded to **Detroit** by **Atlanta** for future considerations, August, 1977.

• McDONOUGH, Hubie

Hubert Brian C – L. 5'9", 180 lbs. b: Manchester, NH, 7/8/1963.

Season	Club	League	GP	G	A	Pts	AG	AA	APts	PIM	PP	SH	GW	S	%	TGF	PGF	TGA	PGA	+/–	GP	G	A	Pts	PIM	PP	SH	GW
1982-83	St. Anselm College	ECAC-2	27	24	21	45	....	....	....	12	....	....	....	....	....	....	....	....	....	....	....	....	....	....	....	....	....	....
1983-84	St. Anselm College	ECAC-2	26	37	15	52	....	....	....	20	....	....	....	....	....	....	....	....	....	....	....	....	....	....	....	....	....	....
1984-85	St. Anselm College	ECAC-2	26	41	30	71	....	....	....	48	....	....	....	....	....	....	....	....	....	....	....	....	....	....	....	....	....	....
1985-86	St. Anselm College	ECAC-2	25	22	20	42	....	....	....	16	....	....	....	....	....	....	....	....	....	....	....	....	....	....	....	....	....	....
1986-87	Flint Spirits	IHL	82	27	52	79	....	....	....	59	....	....	....	....	....	....	....	....	....	....	6	3	2	5	0	....	....	....
1987-88	New Haven Nighthawks	AHL	78	30	29	59	....	....	....	43	....	....	....	....	....	....	....	....	....	....	....	....	....	....	....	....	....	....
1988-89	**Los Angeles Kings**	**NHL**	**4**	**0**	**1**	**1**	**0**	**1**	**1**	**0**	**0**	**0**	**0**	**3**	**0.0**	**2**	**0**	**0**	**0**	**2**	....	....	....	....	....	....	....	....
	New Haven Nighthawks	AHL	74	37	55	92	....	....	....	41	....	....	....	....	....	....	....	....	....	....	17	10	*21	*31	6	....	....	....
1989-90	**Los Angeles Kings**	**NHL**	**22**	**3**	**4**	**7**	**3**	**3**	**6**	**10**	**0**	**0**	**1**	**13**	**23.1**	**11**	**0**	**20**	**13**	**4**	....	....	....	....	....	....	....	....
	New York Islanders	**NHL**	**54**	**18**	**11**	**29**	**15**	**8**	**23**	**26**	**0**	**3**	**3**	**92**	**19.6**	**36**	**1**	**44**	**19**	**10**	**5**	**1**	**0**	**1**	**4**	**0**	**0**	**0**
1990-91	**New York Islanders**	**NHL**	**52**	**6**	**6**	**12**	**5**	**5**	**10**	**10**	**0**	**1**	**0**	**47**	**12.8**	**13**	**1**	**49**	**23**	**–14**	....	....	....	....	....	....	....	....
	Capital District Islanders	AHL	17	9	9	18	....	....	....	4	....	....	....	....	....	....	....	....	....	....	....	....	....	....	....	....	....	....
1991-92	**New York Islanders**	**NHL**	**33**	**7**	**2**	**9**	**6**	**2**	**8**	**15**	**1**	**1**	**0**	**31**	**22.6**	**11**	**1**	**26**	**12**	**–4**	....	....	....	....	....	....	....	....
	Capital District Islanders	AHL	21	11	18	29	....	....	....	14	....	....	....	....	....	....	....	....	....	....	....	....	....	....	....	....	....	....
1992-93	**San Jose Sharks**	**NHL**	**30**	**6**	**2**	**8**	**5**	**1**	**6**	**6**	**2**	**0**	**0**	**41**	**14.6**	**14**	**5**	**36**	**6**	**–21**	....	....	....	....	....	....	....	....
	San Diego Gulls	IHL	48	26	49	75	....	....	....	26	....	....	....	....	....	....	....	....	....	....	14	4	7	11	6	....	....	....
1993-94	San Diego Gulls	IHL	69	31	48	79	....	....	....	61	....	....	....	....	....	....	....	....	....	....	8	0	7	7	6	....	....	....
1994-95	San Diego Gulls	IHL	80	43	55	98	....	....	....	10	....	....	....	....	....	....	....	....	....	....	5	0	1	1	4	....	....	....
1995-96	Los Angeles Ice Dogs	IHL	11	11	9	20	....	....	....	10	....	....	....	....	....	....	....	....	....	....	....	....	....	....	....	....	....	....
	Orlando Solar Bears	IHL	58	26	32	58	....	....	....	40	....	....	....	....	....	....	....	....	....	....	23	7	11	18	10	....	....	....
1996-97	Orlando Solar Bears	IHL	68	30	25	55	....	....	....	60	....	....	....	....	....	....	....	....	....	....	10	5	8	13	6	....	....	....
1997-98	Orlando Solar Bears	IHL	80	32	33	65	....	....	....	62	....	....	....	....	....	....	....	....	....	....	17	11	10	21	2	....	....	....
1998-99	Orlando Solar Bears	IHL	74	20	33	53	....	....	....	52	....	....	....	....	....	....	....	....	....	....	17	2	*12	14	14	....	....	....
99-2000	Orlando Solar Bears	IHL	DID NOT PLAY – ASSISTANT COACH																									
	NHL Totals		**195**	**40**	**26**	**66**	**34**	**20**	**54**	**67**	**3**	**5**	**4**	**227**	**17.6**	**87**	**8**	**175**	**73**		**5**	**1**	**0**	**1**	**4**	**0**	**0**	**0**

NCAA (College Div.) East All-American Team (1986) • IHL Second All-Star Team (1993, 1995)

Signed as a free agent by **LA Kings**, April 18, 1988. Traded to **NY Islanders** by **LA Kings** with Ken Baumgartner for Mikko Makela, November 29, 1989. Traded to **San Jose** by **NY Islanders** for cash, August 28, 1992. Traded to **Orlando** (IHL) by **LA Ice Dogs** (IHL) for cash, October 28, 1995. • Officially announced retirement, July 26, 1999.

• McDOUGAL, Mike

Michael George RW – L. 6'2", 200 lbs. b: Port Huron, MI, 4/30/1958. NY Rangers' 6th, 76th overall, in 1978.

Season	Club	League	GP	G	A	Pts	AG	AA	APts	PIM	PP	SH	GW	S	%	TGF	PGF	TGA	PGA	+/–	GP	G	A	Pts	PIM	PP	SH	GW
1973-74	Port Huron Jr. Flags	MWJHL	40	27	33	60	....	....	....	....	....	....	....	....	....	....	....	....	....	....	....	....	....	....	....	....	....	....
1974-75	Montreal Red-White-Blue	QMJHL	70	21	27	48	....	....	....	121	....	....	....	....	....	....	....	....	....	....	....	....	....	....	....	....	....	....
1975-76	Montreal Juniors	QMJHL	71	31	44	75	....	....	....	71	....	....	....	....	....	....	....	....	....	....	....	....	....	....	....	....	....	....
1976-77	Port Huron Flags	IHL	59	25	29	54	....	....	....	46	....	....	....	....	....	....	....	....	....	....	....	....	....	....	....	....	....	....
	United States	WJC-A	....	....	....	....	....	....	....	....	....	....	....	....	....	....	....	....	....	....	....	....	....	....	....	....	....	....
1977-78	Port Huron Flags	IHL	44	15	16	31	....	....	....	65	....	....	....	....	....	....	....	....	....	....	....	....	....	....	....	....	....	....
	United States	WJC-A	6	3	5	8	....	....	....	10	....	....	....	....	....	....	....	....	....	....	....	....	....	....	....	....	....	....
1978-79	**New York Rangers**	**NHL**	**1**	**0**	**0**	**0**	**0**	**0**	**0**	**0**	**0**	**0**	**0**	**0**	**0.0**	**0**	**0**	**0**	**0**	**0**	....	....	....	....	....	....	....	....
	New Haven Nighthawks	AHL	78	24	26	50	....	....	....	60	....	....	....	....	....	....	....	....	....	....	10	1	5	6	8	....	....	....
1979-80	New Haven Nighthawks	AHL	68	17	25	42	....	....	....	43	....	....	....	....	....	....	....	....	....	....	3	0	3	3	0	....	....	....
1980-81	**New York Rangers**	**NHL**	**2**	**0**	**0**	**0**	**0**	**0**	**0**	**0**	**0**	**0**	**0**	**1**	**0.0**	**1**	**0**	**0**	**0**	**1**	....	....	....	....	....	....	....	....
	New Haven Nighthawks	AHL	66	21	23	44	....	....	....	20	....	....	....	....	....	....	....	....	....	....	4	0	0	0	2	....	....	....
1981-82	**Hartford Whalers**	**NHL**	**3**	**0**	**0**	**0**	**0**	**0**	**0**	**0**	**0**	**0**	**0**	**2**	**0.0**	**1**	**0**	**1**	**0**	**0**	....	....	....	....	....	....	....	....
	Binghamton Whalers	AHL	58	10	18	28	....	....	....	56	....	....	....	....	....	....	....	....	....	....	14	1	8	9	12	....	....	....
1982-83	**Hartford Whalers**	**NHL**	**55**	**8**	**10**	**18**	**7**	**7**	**14**	**43**	**0**	**0**	**0**	**61**	**13.1**	**32**	**1**	**68**	**4**	**–33**	....	....	....	....	....	....	....	....
	Binghamton Whalers	AHL	14	7	5	12	....	....	....	20	....	....	....	....	....	....	....	....	....	....	....	....	....	....	....	....	....	....
1983-84	Binghamton Whalers	AHL	59	11	14	25	....	....	....	56	....	....	....	....	....	....	....	....	....	....	....	....	....	....	....	....	....	....
	NHL Totals		**61**	**8**	**10**	**18**	**7**	**7**	**14**	**43**	**0**	**0**	**0**	**64**	**12.5**	**34**	**1**	**69**	**4**		....	....	....	....	....	....	....	....

Claimed by **Hartford** from **NY Rangers** in Waiver Draft, October 6, 1981.

• McDOUGALL, Bill

William Henry C – R. 6', 185 lbs. b: Mississauga, Ont., 8/10/1966.

Season	Club	League	GP	G	A	Pts	AG	AA	APts	PIM	PP	SH	GW	S	%	TGF	PGF	TGA	PGA	+/–	GP	G	A	Pts	PIM	PP	SH	GW
1984-85	Streetsville Derbys	OJHL-B	9	4	7	11	....	....	....	32	....	....	....	....	....	....	....	....	....	....	....	....	....	....	....	....	....	....
	Dixie Beehives	OJHL	27	16	32	48	....	....	....	104	....	....	....	....	....	....	....	....	....	....	....	....	....	....	....	....	....	....
1985-86	Streetsville Derbys	OJHL-B	42	45	*87	*132	....	....	....	*262	....	....	....	....	....	....	....	....	....	....	....	....	....	....	....	....	....	....
1986-87	Humboldt Broncos	SJHL	60	*83	*104	*187	....	....	....	....	....	....	....	....	....	....	....	....	....	....	....	....	....	....	....	....	....	....
	Humboldt Broncos	Cen-Cup	4	4	3	7	....	....	....	6	....	....	....	....	....	....	....	....	....	....	....	....	....	....	....	....	....	....
1987-88	St. John's Capitals	Nfld-Sr.	42	66	71	137	....	....	....	47	....	....	....	....	....	....	....	....	....	....	....	....	....	....	....	....	....	....
1988-89	Port-aux-Basques Mariners	Nfld-Sr.	26	20	41	61	....	....	....	129	....	....	....	....	....	....	....	....	....	....	....	....	....	....	....	....	....	....
1989-90	Erie Panthers	ECHL	57	*80	*68	*148	....	....	....	226	....	....	....	....	....	....	....	....	....	....	7	5	5	10	20	....	....	....
	Adirondack Red Wings	AHL	11	10	7	17	....	....	....	4	....	....	....	....	....	....	....	....	....	....	2	1	1	2	2	....	....	....

			REGULAR SEASON																		PLAYOFFS							
Season	Club	League	GP	G	A	Pts	AG	AA	APts	PIM	PP	SH	GW	S	%	TGF	PGF	TGA	PGA	+/–	GP	G	A	Pts	PIM	PP	SH	GW
1990-91	**Detroit Red Wings**	**NHL**	**2**	**0**	**1**	**1**	**0**	**1**	**1**	**0**	**0**	**0**	**0**	**3**	**0.0**	**2**	**0**	**2**	**0**	**0**	**1**	**0**	**0**	**0**	**0**	**0**	**0**	**0**
	Adirondack Red Wings	AHL	71	47	52	99	....	....	....	192	....	....	....	....	....	....	....	....	....	....	2	1	2	3	2	....	....	....
1991-92	Adirondack Red Wings	AHL	45	28	24	52	....	....	....	112	....	....	....	....	....	....	....	....	....	....	....	....	....	....	....	....	....	....
	Cape Breton Oilers	AHL	22	8	18	26	....	....	....	36	....	....	....	....	....	....	....	....	....	....	4	0	1	1	8	....	....	....
1992-93	**Edmonton Oilers**	**NHL**	**4**	**2**	**1**	**3**	**2**	**1**	**3**	**4**	**0**	**0**	**0**	**8**	**25.0**	**6**	**2**	**2**	**0**	**2**	....	....	....	....	....	....	....	....
	Cape Breton Oilers	AHL	71	42	46	88	....	....	....	16	....	....	....	....	....	....	....	....	....	....	16	*26	*26	*52	30	....	....	....
1993-94	**Tampa Bay Lightning**	**NHL**	**22**	**3**	**3**	**6**	**3**	**2**	**5**	**8**	**1**	**0**	**0**	**26**	**11.5**	**10**	**3**	**11**	**0**	**–4**	....	....	....	....	....	....	....	....
	Atlanta Knights	IHL	48	17	30	47	....	....	....	141	....	....	....	....	....	....	....	....	....	....	14	12	7	19	30	....	....	....
1994-95	HC Courmaosta	Italy	30	30	34	64	....	....	....	*107	....	....	....	....	....	....	....	....	....	....	....	....	....	....	....	....	....	....
	HC Courmaosta	EuroHL	17	24	17	41	....	....	....	44	....	....	....	....	....	....	....	....	....	....	....	....	....	....	....	....	....	....
1995-96	HK Olimpija Ljubljana	Alpenliga	36	14	17	31	....	....	....	....	....	....	....	....	....	....	....	....	....	....	....	....	....	....	....	....	....	....
	EV Zug	Switz.	15	15	14	29	....	....	....	69	....	....	....	....	....	....	....	....	....	....	9	7	4	11	37	....	....	....
1996-97	EV Zug	Switz.	45	*41	30	71	....	....	....	110	....	....	....	....	....	....	....	....	....	....	6	1	2	3	6	....	....	....
1997-98	EV Zug	Switz.	40	25	25	50	....	....	....	50	....	....	....	....	....	....	....	....	....	....	19	*16	11	27	51	....	....	....
	EV Zug	EuroHL	5	2	6	8	....	....	....	20	....	....	....	....	....	....	....	....	....	....	....	....	....	....	....	....	....	....
1998-99	EHC Kloten	Switz.	22	13	10	23	....	....	....	101	....	....	....	....	....	....	....	....	....	....	....	....	....	....	....	....	....	....
	HC Lugano	Switz.	10	6	2	8	....	....	....	10	....	....	....	....	....	....	....	....	....	....	6	0	5	5	10	....	....	....
99-2000	Munich Barons	Germany	39	16	22	38	....	....	....	64	....	....	....	....	....	....	....	....	....	....	....	....	....	....	....	....	....	....
	NHL Totals		**28**	**5**	**5**	**10**	**5**	**4**	**9**	**12**	**1**	**0**	**0**	**37**	**13.5**	**18**	**5**	**15**	**0**		**1**	**0**	**0**	**0**	**0**	**0**	**0**	**0**

Centennial Cup All-Star Team (1987)

ECHL First All-Star Team (1990) • Rookie of the Year - ECHL (1990) • MVP - ECHL (1990) • Won Jack A. Butterfield Trophy (Playoff MVP - AHL) (1993)

Signed as a free agent by **Detroit**, January 9, 1990. Traded to **Edmonton** by **Detroit** for Max Middendorf, February 22, 1992. Signed as a free agent by **Tampa Bay**, August 13, 1993.

• McEACHERN, Shawn

Shawn K. LW – L. 5'11", 193 lbs. b: Waltham, MA, 2/28/1969. Pittsburgh's 6th, 110th overall, in 1987.

Season	Club	League	GP	G	A	Pts	AG	AA	APts	PIM	PP	SH	GW	S	%	TGF	PGF	TGA	PGA	+/–	GP	G	A	Pts	PIM	PP	SH	GW
1985-86	Matignon Warriors	Hi-School	20	32	20	52	....	....	....	....	....	....	....	....	....	....	....	....	....	....	....	....	....	....	....	....	....	....
1986-87	Matignon Warriors	Hi-School	16	29	28	57	....	....	....	....	....	....	....	....	....	....	....	....	....	....	....	....	....	....	....	....	....	....
1987-88	Matignon Warriors	Hi-School	22	52	40	92	....	....	....	....	....	....	....	....	....	....	....	....	....	....	....	....	....	....	....	....	....	....
1988-89	Boston University	H-East	36	20	28	48	....	....	....	32	....	....	....	....	....	....	....	....	....	....	....	....	....	....	....	....	....	....
1989-90	Boston University	H-East	43	25	31	56	....	....	....	78	....	....	....	....	....	....	....	....	....	....	....	....	....	....	....	....	....	....
1990-91	Boston University	H-East	41	34	48	82	....	....	....	43	....	....	....	....	....	....	....	....	....	....	....	....	....	....	....	....	....	....
	United States	WEC-A	10	3	2	5	....	....	....	6	....	....	....	....	....	....	....	....	....	....	....	....	....	....	....	....	....	....
1991-92	United States	Nat-Team	57	26	23	49	....	....	....	38	....	....	....	....	....	....	....	....	....	....	....	....	....	....	....	....	....	....
	United States	Olympics	8	1	0	1	....	....	....	10	....	....	....	....	....	....	....	....	....	....	....	....	....	....	....	....	....	....
♦	**Pittsburgh Penguins**	**NHL**	**15**	**0**	**4**	**4**	**0**	**3**	**3**	**0**	**0**	**0**	**0**	**14**	**0.0**	**6**	**1**	**4**	**0**	**1**	**19**	**2**	**7**	**9**	**4**	**0**	**0**	**0**
1992-93	**Pittsburgh Penguins**	**NHL**	**84**	**28**	**33**	**61**	**23**	**23**	**46**	**46**	**7**	**0**	**6**	**196**	**14.3**	**82**	**17**	**54**	**10**	**21**	**12**	**3**	**2**	**5**	**10**	**0**	**0**	**1**
1993-94	**Los Angeles Kings**	**NHL**	**49**	**8**	**13**	**21**	**7**	**10**	**17**	**24**	**0**	**3**	**0**	**81**	**9.9**	**30**	**2**	**35**	**8**	**1**	....	....	....	....	....	....	....	....
	Pittsburgh Penguins	**NHL**	**27**	**12**	**9**	**21**	**11**	**7**	**18**	**10**	**0**	**2**	**1**	**78**	**15.4**	**27**	**2**	**22**	**10**	**13**	**6**	**1**	**0**	**1**	**2**	**0**	**0**	**0**
1994-95	Kiekko-Espoo	Finland	8	1	3	4	....	....	....	6	....	....	....	....	....	....	....	....	....	....	....	....	....	....	....	....	....	....
	Pittsburgh Penguins	**NHL**	**44**	**13**	**13**	**26**	**23**	**19**	**42**	**22**	**1**	**2**	**1**	**97**	**13.4**	**37**	**4**	**46**	**17**	**4**	**11**	**0**	**2**	**2**	**8**	**0**	**0**	**0**
1995-96	**Boston Bruins**	**NHL**	**82**	**24**	**29**	**53**	**24**	**24**	**48**	**34**	**3**	**2**	**3**	**238**	**10.1**	**84**	**18**	**82**	**11**	**–5**	**5**	**2**	**1**	**3**	**8**	**0**	**0**	**0**
1996-97	United States	W-Cup	1	0	1	1	....	....	....	0	....	....	....	....	....	....	....	....	....	....	....	....	....	....	....	....	....	....
	Ottawa Senators	**NHL**	**65**	**11**	**20**	**31**	**12**	**18**	**30**	**18**	**0**	**1**	**2**	**150**	**7.3**	**56**	**12**	**61**	**12**	**–5**	**7**	**2**	**0**	**2**	**8**	**1**	**0**	**0**
1997-98	**Ottawa Senators**	**NHL**	**81**	**24**	**24**	**48**	**28**	**24**	**52**	**42**	**8**	**2**	**4**	**229**	**10.5**	**74**	**22**	**65**	**14**	**1**	**11**	**0**	**4**	**4**	**8**	**0**	**0**	**0**
1998-99	**Ottawa Senators**	**NHL**	**77**	**31**	**25**	**56**	**36**	**24**	**60**	**46**	**7**	**0**	**4**	**223**	**13.9**	**86**	**31**	**53**	**6**	**8**	**4**	**2**	**0**	**2**	**6**	**1**	**0**	**0**
99-2000	**Ottawa Senators**	**NHL**	**69**	**29**	**22**	**51**	**33**	**20**	**53**	**24**	**10**	**0**	**4**	**219**	**13.2**	**76**	**25**	**51**	**2**	**2**	**6**	**0**	**3**	**3**	**4**	**0**	**0**	**0**
	NHL Totals		**593**	**180**	**192**	**372**	**197**	**172**	**369**	**266**	**36**	**12**	**25**	**1525**	**11.8**	**558**	**134**	**473**	**90**		**81**	**12**	**19**	**31**	**58**	**2**	**0**	**1**

Hockey East Second All-Star Team (1990) • Hockey East First All-Star Team (1991) • NCAA East First All-American Team (1991)

Traded to **LA Kings** by **Pittsburgh** for Marty McSorley, August 27, 1993. Traded to **Pittsburgh** by **LA Kings** with Tomas Sandstrom for Marty McSorley and Jim Paek, February 16, 1994. Traded to **Boston** by **Pittsburgh** with Kevin Stevens for Glen Murray, Bryan Smolinski and Boston's 3rd round choice (Boyd Kane) in 1996 Entry Draft, August 2, 1995. Traded to **Ottawa** by **Boston** for Trent McCleary and Ottawa's 3rd round choice (Eric Naud) in 1996 Entry Draft, June 22, 1996.

• McELMURY, Jim

James Donald D – L. 6'1", 190 lbs. b: St. Paul, MN, 10/3/1949.

Season	Club	League	GP	G	A	Pts	AG	AA	APts	PIM	PP	SH	GW	S	%	TGF	PGF	TGA	PGA	+/–	GP	G	A	Pts	PIM	PP	SH	GW
1967-1970	Bemidji State Beavers	NAIA	STATISTICS NOT AVAILABLE																									
1970-71	Bemidji State Beavers	NAIA	12	5	5	10	....	....	....	20	....	....	....	....	....	....	....	....	....	....	....	....	....	....	....	....	....	....
	United States	WEC-A	10	2	0	2	....	....	....	2	....	....	....	....	....	....	....	....	....	....	....	....	....	....	....	....	....	....
1971-72	United States	Nat-Team	10	2	0	2	....	....	....	2	....	....	....	....	....	....	....	....	....	....	....	....	....	....	....	....	....	....
	United States	Olympics	6	0	1	1	....	....	....	6	....	....	....	....	....	....	....	....	....	....	....	....	....	....	....	....	....	....
	Cleveland Barons	AHL	15	2	2	4	....	....	....	4	....	....	....	....	....	....	....	....	....	....	6	0	3	3	10	....	....	....
1972-73	**Minnesota North Stars**	**NHL**	**7**	**0**	**1**	**1**	**0**	**1**	**1**	**2**	**0**	**0**	**0**	**0**	**0.0**	**2**	**0**	**2**	**1**	**1**	....	....	....	....	....	....	....	....
	Cleveland-Jacksonville Barons	AHL	69	4	23	27	....	....	....	20	....	....	....	....	....	....	....	....	....	....	....	....	....	....	....	....	....	....
1973-74	Portland Buckaroos	WHL	76	8	23	31	....	....	....	46	....	....	....	....	....	....	....	....	....	....	10	1	6	7	2	....	....	....
1974-75	**Kansas City Scouts**	**NHL**	**78**	**5**	**17**	**22**	**4**	**13**	**17**	**25**	**1**	**0**	**1**	**137**	**3.6**	**64**	**24**	**110**	**22**	**–48**	....	....	....	....	....	....	....	....
1975-76	**Kansas City Scouts**	**NHL**	**38**	**2**	**6**	**8**	**2**	**4**	**6**	**6**	**1**	**0**	**0**	**43**	**4.7**	**28**	**4**	**49**	**12**	**–13**	....	....	....	....	....	....	....	....
	Springfield Indians	AHL	36	4	12	16	....	....	....	10	....	....	....	....	....	....	....	....	....	....	....	....	....	....	....	....	....	....
1976-77	**Colorado Rockies**	**NHL**	**55**	**7**	**23**	**30**	**6**	**18**	**24**	**16**	**1**	**0**	**1**	**81**	**8.6**	**75**	**26**	**77**	**13**	**–15**	....	....	....	....	....	....	....	....
	Rhode Island Reds	AHL	24	3	13	16	....	....	....	16	....	....	....	....	....	....	....	....	....	....	....	....	....	....	....	....	....	....
	United States	WEC-A	10	2	3	5	....	....	....	10	....	....	....	....	....	....	....	....	....	....	....	....	....	....	....	....	....	....
1977-78	**Colorado Rockies**	**NHL**	**2**	**0**	**0**	**0**	**0**	**0**	**0**	**0**	**0**	**0**	**0**	**0**	**0.0**	**1**	**0**	**0**	**0**	**1**	....	....	....	....	....	....	....	....
	Phoenix Roadrunners	CHL	12	0	3	3	....	....	....	8	....	....	....	....	....	....	....	....	....	....	....	....	....	....	....	....	....	....
	Hampton Gulls	AHL	11	1	7	8	....	....	....	4	....	....	....	....	....	....	....	....	....	....	....	....	....	....	....	....	....	....
	NHL Totals		**180**	**14**	**47**	**61**	**12**	**36**	**48**	**49**	**3**	**0**	**2**	**261**	**5.4**	**170**	**54**	**238**	**48**		....	....	....	....	....	....	....	....

First Team NAIA All-American (1968, 1969, 1970, 1971)

Signed as a free agent by **Minnesota**, February 29, 1972. Traded to **LA Kings** by **Minnesota** for cash, March 1, 1974. Signed as a free agent by **Kansas City**, June 27, 1974. Transferred to **Colorado** after **Kansas City** franchise relocated, July 15, 1976.

• McEWEN, Mike

Michael Todd "Q" D – L. 6'1", 185 lbs. b: Hornepayne, Ont., 8/10/1956. NY Rangers' 3rd, 42nd overall, in 1976.

Season	Club	League	GP	G	A	Pts	AG	AA	APts	PIM	PP	SH	GW	S	%	TGF	PGF	TGA	PGA	+/–	GP	G	A	Pts	PIM	PP	SH	GW
1973-74	Toronto Marlboros	OMJHL	68	5	32	37	....	....	....	81	....	....	....	....	....	....	....	....	....	....	....	....	....	....	....	....	....	....
1974-75	Toronto Marlboros	OMJHL	68	18	63	81	....	....	....	52	....	....	....	....	....	....	....	....	....	....	23	5	14	19	33	....	....	....
	Toronto Marlboros	Mem-Cup	4	1	3	4	....	....	....	4	....	....	....	....	....	....	....	....	....	....	....	....	....	....	....	....	....	....
1975-76	Toronto Marlboros	OMJHL	65	23	40	63	....	....	....	63	....	....	....	....	....	....	....	....	....	....	10	3	9	12	20	....	....	....
1976-77	**New York Rangers**	**NHL**	**80**	**14**	**29**	**43**	**13**	**22**	**35**	**38**	**5**	**0**	**0**	**204**	**6.9**	**107**	**35**	**102**	**6**	**–24**	....	....	....	....	....	....	....	....
1977-78	**New York Rangers**	**NHL**	**57**	**5**	**13**	**18**	**5**	**10**	**15**	**52**	**2**	**0**	**0**	**65**	**7.7**	**43**	**19**	**35**	**0**	**–11**	....	....	....	....	....	....	....	....
1978-79	**New York Rangers**	**NHL**	**80**	**20**	**38**	**58**	**17**	**28**	**45**	**35**	**7**	**0**	**4**	**204**	**9.8**	**121**	**38**	**91**	**18**	**10**	**18**	**2**	**11**	**13**	**8**	**2**	**0**	**1**
1979-80	**New York Rangers**	**NHL**	**9**	**1**	**7**	**8**	**1**	**5**	**6**	**8**	**1**	**0**	**0**	**16**	**6.3**	**19**	**4**	**14**	**2**	**3**	....	....	....	....	....	....	....	....
	Colorado Rockies	**NHL**	**67**	**11**	**40**	**51**	**9**	**29**	**38**	**33**	**5**	**1**	**1**	**178**	**6.2**	**99**	**31**	**86**	**5**	**–13**	....	....	....	....	....	....	....	....
1980-81	**Colorado Rockies**	**NHL**	**65**	**11**	**35**	**46**	**9**	**23**	**32**	**84**	**5**	**0**	**1**	**229**	**4.8**	**105**	**35**	**128**	**25**	**–33**	....	....	....	....	....	....	....	....
♦	**New York Islanders**	**NHL**	**13**	**0**	**3**	**3**	**0**	**2**	**2**	**10**	**0**	**0**	**0**	**27**	**0.0**	**15**	**2**	**10**	**0**	**3**	**17**	**6**	**8**	**14**	**6**	**4**	**0**	**0**
1981-82♦	**New York Islanders**	**NHL**	**73**	**10**	**39**	**49**	**8**	**26**	**34**	**50**	**1**	**0**	**1**	**161**	**6.2**	**114**	**22**	**77**	**15**	**30**	**15**	**3**	**7**	**10**	**18**	**2**	**0**	**0**
1982-83♦	**New York Islanders**	**NHL**	**42**	**2**	**11**	**13**	**2**	**8**	**10**	**16**	**1**	**0**	**0**	**82**	**2.4**	**51**	**13**	**34**	**7**	**11**	**12**	**0**	**2**	**2**	**4**	**0**	**0**	**0**
1983-84	**New York Islanders**	**NHL**	**15**	**0**	**2**	**2**	**0**	**1**	**1**	**6**	**0**	**0**	**0**	**27**	**0.0**	**12**	**0**	**18**	**1**	**–5**	....	....	....	....	....	....	....	....
	Los Angeles Kings	**NHL**	**47**	**10**	**24**	**34**	**8**	**16**	**24**	**14**	**7**	**0**	**0**	**133**	**7.5**	**74**	**35**	**54**	**3**	**–12**	....	....	....	....	....	....	....	....
	New Haven Nighthawks	AHL	9	3	7	10	....	....	....	26	....	....	....	....	....	....	....	....	....	....	....	....	....	....	....	....	....	....
1984-85	**Washington Capitals**	**NHL**	**56**	**11**	**27**	**38**	**9**	**18**	**27**	**42**	**4**	**0**	**3**	**151**	**7.3**	**97**	**40**	**37**	**2**	**22**	**5**	**0**	**1**	**1**	**4**	**0**	**0**	**0**
	Binghamton Whalers	AHL	14	2	10	12	....	....	....	14	....	....	....	....	....	....	....	....	....	....	....	....	....	....	....	....	....	....
1985-86	**Detroit Red Wings**	**NHL**	**29**	**0**	**10**	**10**	**0**	**7**	**7**	**16**	**0**	**0**	**0**	**82**	**0.0**	**36**	**15**	**36**	**7**	**–8**	....	....	....	....	....	....	....	....
	New York Rangers	**NHL**	**16**	**2**	**5**	**7**	**2**	**3**	**5**	**8**	**0**	**0**	**1**	**36**	**5.6**	**17**	**4**	**17**	**0**	**–4**	....	....	....	....	....	....	....	....
	New Haven Nighthawks	AHL	2	0	3	3	....	....	....	2	....	....	....	....	....	....	....	....	....	....	....	....	....	....	....	....	....	....
	Hartford Whalers	**NHL**	**10**	**3**	**2**	**5**	**2**	**1**	**3**	**6**	**0**	**0**	**0**	**18**	**16.7**	**13**	**2**	**6**	**0**	**5**	**8**	**0**	**4**	**4**	**6**	**0**	**0**	**0**
1986-87	**Hartford Whalers**	**NHL**	**48**	**8**	**8**	**16**	**7**	**6**	**13**	**32**	**5**	**0**	**2**	**86**	**9.3**	**40**	**19**	**30**	**0**	**–9**	**1**	**1**	**1**	**2**	**0**	**1**	**0**	**0**

Season	Club	League	GP	G	A	Pts	AG	AA	APts	PIM	PP	SH	GW	S	%	TGF	PGF	TGA	PGA	+/–	GP	G	A	Pts	PIM	PP	SH	GW
			REGULAR SEASON																		PLAYOFFS							
1987-88	HC Sierre	Switz.	32	18	31	49	....	....	....	....	....	....	....	....	....	....	....	....	....	....	....	....	....	....	....	....	....	....
	Hartford Whalers	**NHL**	**9**	**0**	**3**	**3**	**0**	**2**	**2**	**10**	**0**	**0**	**0**	**22**	**0.0**	**11**	**2**	**10**	**0**	**–1**	**2**	**0**	**2**	**2**	**2**	**0**	**0**	**0**
1988-89	EHC Olten	Switz.	36	20	21	41	....	....	....	....	....	....	....	....	....	....	....	....	....	....	2	2	0	2	....	....	....	....
1989-90	EHC Olten	Switz.	36	10	15	25	....	....	....	....	....	....	....	....	....	....	....	....	....	....	....	....	....	....	....	....	....	....
1990-91	EHC Olten	Switz.	33	7	21	28	....	....	....	....	....	....	....	....	....	....	....	....	....	....	....	....	....	....	....	....	....	....
1991-92	New Haven Nighthawks	AHL	51	4	19	23	....	....	....	32	....	....	....	....	....	....	....	....	....	....	....	....	....	....	....	....	....	....
1992-93	Oklahoma City Blazers	CHL	DID NOT PLAY – COACHING																									
	NHL Totals		**716**	**108**	**296**	**404**	**92**	**207**	**299**	**460**	**43**	**1**	**13**	**1721**	**6.3**	**974**	**316**	**785**	**91**		**78**	**12**	**36**	**48**	**48**	**9**	**0**	**1**

Played in NHL All-Star Game (1980)

Traded to **Colorado** by **NY Rangers** with Lucien DeBlois, Pat Hickey, Dean Turner and future considerations (Bobby Crawford, January 15, 1980) for Barry Beck, November 2, 1979. Traded to **NY Islanders** by **Colorado** with Jari Kaarela for Glenn Resch and Steve Tambellini, March 10, 1981. Traded to **LA Kings** by **NY Islanders** for Detroit's 4th round choice (previously acquired, NY Islanders selected Doug Wieck) in 1984 Entry Draft, November 17, 1983. Signed as a free agent by **Washington**, August 7, 1984. Signed as a free agent by **Detroit**, August 12, 1985. Traded to **NY Rangers** by **Detroit** for Steve Richmond, December 26, 1985. Traded to **Hartford** by **NY Rangers** for Bob Crawford, March 11, 1986.

• McFALL, Dan

D – R. 6', 180 lbs. b: Kenmore, NY, 4/8/1963. Winnipeg's 8th, 148th overall, in 1981.

Season	Club	League	GP	G	A	Pts	AG	AA	APts	PIM	PP	SH	GW	S	%	TGF	PGF	TGA	PGA	+/–	GP	G	A	Pts	PIM	PP	SH	GW
1979-80	Buffalo Jr. Sabres	NAJHL	36	25	58	83	....	....	....	....	....	....	....	....	....	....	....	....	....	....	16	19	20	39	....	....	....	....
1980-81	Buffalo Jr. Sabres	NAJHL	STATISTICS NOT AVAILABLE																									
1981-82	Michigan State Spartans	CCHA	42	3	17	20	....	....	....	28	....	....	....	....	....	....	....	....	....	....	....	....	....	....	....	....	....	....
	United States	WJC-A	7	2	0	2	....	....	....	4	....	....	....	....	....	....	....	....	....	....	....	....	....	....	....	....	....	....
1982-83	Michigan State Spartans	CCHA	36	12	14	26	....	....	....	22	....	....	....	....	....	....	....	....	....	....	....	....	....	....	....	....	....	....
	United States	WJC-A	7	0	0	0	....	....	....	6	....	....	....	....	....	....	....	....	....	....	....	....	....	....	....	....	....	....
1983-84	Michigan State Spartans	CCHA	46	14	20	34	....	....	....	56	....	....	....	....	....	....	....	....	....	....	....	....	....	....	....	....	....	....
1984-85	Michigan State Spartans	CCHA	44	7	25	32	....	....	....	32	....	....	....	....	....	....	....	....	....	....	....	....	....	....	....	....	....	....
	Winnipeg Jets	**NHL**	**2**	**0**	**0**	**0**	**0**	**0**	**0**	**0**	**0**	**0**	**0**	**2**	**0.0**	**1**	**0**	**4**	**0**	**–3**	....	....	....	....	....	....	....	....
1985-86	**Winnipeg Jets**	**NHL**	**7**	**0**	**1**	**1**	**0**	**1**	**1**	**0**	**0**	**0**	**0**	**2**	**0.0**	**3**	**0**	**7**	**1**	**–3**	....	....	....	....	....	....	....	....
	Sherbrooke Canadiens	AHL	50	2	10	12	....	....	....	16	....	....	....	....	....	....	....	....	....	....	....	....	....	....	....	....	....	....
1986-87	Fort Wayne Komets	IHL	11	0	5	5	....	....	....	0	....	....	....	....	....	....	....	....	....	....	....	....	....	....	....	....	....	....
	NHL Totals		**9**	**0**	**1**	**1**	**0**	**1**	**1**	**0**	**0**	**0**	**0**	**4**	**0.0**	**4**	**0**	**11**	**1**		....	....	....	....	....	....	....	....

CCHA First All-Star Team (1984) • NCAA West Second All-American Team (1984) • CCHA Second All-Star Team (1985) • NCAA West First All-American Team (1985)

• McGEOUGH, Jim

C – L. 5'8", 170 lbs. b: Regina, Sask., 4/13/1963. Washington's 6th, 110th overall, in 1981.

Season	Club	League	GP	G	A	Pts	AG	AA	APts	PIM	PP	SH	GW	S	%	TGF	PGF	TGA	PGA	+/–	GP	G	A	Pts	PIM	PP	SH	GW
1979-80	Regina Capitals	SJHL	57	56	77	133	....	....	....	94	....	....	....	....	....	....	....	....	....	....	....	....	....	....	....	....	....	....
	Regina Pats	WHL	10	1	4	5	....	....	....	2	....	....	....	....	....	....	....	....	....	....	6	2	0	2	0	....	....	....
	Regina Pats	Mem-Cup	3	0	1	1	....	....	....	6	....	....	....	....	....	....	....	....	....	....	....	....	....	....	....	....	....	....
1980-81	Regina Pats	WHL	4	1	2	3	....	....	....	2	....	....	....	....	....	....	....	....	....	....	....	....	....	....	....	....	....	....
	Billings Bighorns	WHL	67	49	42	91	....	....	....	139	....	....	....	....	....	....	....	....	....	....	5	2	5	7	15	....	....	....
1981-82	Billings Bighorns	WHL	71	93	66	159	....	....	....	142	....	....	....	....	....	....	....	....	....	....	5	2	1	3	4	....	....	....
	Washington Capitals	**NHL**	**4**	**0**	**0**	**0**	**0**	**0**	**0**	**0**	**0**	**0**	**0**	**7**	**0.0**	**0**	**0**	**2**	**0**	**–2**	....	....	....	....	....	....	....	....
1982-83	Nanaimo Islanders	WHL	72	76	56	132	....	....	....	126	....	....	....	....	....	....	....	....	....	....	....	....	....	....	....	....	....	....
	Hershey Bears	AHL	5	1	1	2	....	....	....	10	....	....	....	....	....	....	....	....	....	....	5	0	2	2	25	....	....	....
1983-84	Hershey Bears	AHL	79	40	36	76	....	....	....	108	....	....	....	....	....	....	....	....	....	....	....	....	....	....	....	....	....	....
1984-85	**Washington Capitals**	**NHL**	**11**	**3**	**0**	**3**	**2**	**0**	**2**	**12**	**0**	**0**	**0**	**22**	**13.6**	**4**	**0**	**4**	**0**	**0**	....	....	....	....	....	....	....	....
	Pittsburgh Penguins	**NHL**	**14**	**0**	**4**	**4**	**0**	**3**	**3**	**4**	**0**	**0**	**0**	**34**	**0.0**	**8**	**0**	**12**	**0**	**–4**	....	....	....	....	....	....	....	....
	Binghamton Whalers	AHL	57	32	21	53	....	....	....	26	....	....	....	....	....	....	....	....	....	....	....	....	....	....	....	....	....	....
1985-86	**Pittsburgh Penguins**	**NHL**	**17**	**3**	**2**	**5**	**2**	**1**	**3**	**8**	**0**	**0**	**1**	**29**	**10.3**	**8**	**0**	**18**	**6**	**–4**	....	....	....	....	....	....	....	....
	Baltimore Skipjacks	AHL	38	14	13	27	....	....	....	20	....	....	....	....	....	....	....	....	....	....	....	....	....	....	....	....	....	....
1986-87	**Pittsburgh Penguins**	**NHL**	**11**	**1**	**4**	**5**	**1**	**3**	**4**	**8**	**0**	**0**	**0**	**24**	**4.2**	**8**	**0**	**13**	**0**	**–5**	....	....	....	....	....	....	....	....
	Baltimore Skipjacks	AHL	45	18	19	37	....	....	....	37	....	....	....	....	....	....	....	....	....	....	....	....	....	....	....	....	....	....
	Muskegon Lumberjacks	IHL	18	13	15	28	....	....	....	6	....	....	....	....	....	....	....	....	....	....	15	*14	8	22	10	....	....	....
1987-88	KAC Klagenfurt	Austria	34	34	18	52	....	....	....	52	....	....	....	....	....	....	....	....	....	....	....	....	....	....	....	....	....	....
	Springfield Indians	AHL	30	11	13	24	....	....	....	28	....	....	....	....	....	....	....	....	....	....	....	....	....	....	....	....	....	....
1988-89	KAC Klagenfurt	Austria	44	28	24	52	....	....	....	....	....	....	....	....	....	....	....	....	....	....	....	....	....	....	....	....	....	....
1989-90	Phoenix Roadrunners	IHL	77	35	46	81	....	....	....	90	....	....	....	....	....	....	....	....	....	....	....	....	....	....	....	....	....	....
1990-91	Albany Choppers	IHL	12	9	3	12	....	....	....	4	....	....	....	....	....	....	....	....	....	....	....	....	....	....	....	....	....	....
	Kalamazoo Wings	IHL	7	0	0	0	....	....	....	2	....	....	....	....	....	....	....	....	....	....	....	....	....	....	....	....	....	....
	San Diego Gulls	IHL	10	2	4	6	....	....	....	4	....	....	....	....	....	....	....	....	....	....	....	....	....	....	....	....	....	....
	Nashville Knights	ECHL	4	2	1	3	....	....	....	0	....	....	....	....	....	....	....	....	....	....	....	....	....	....	....	....	....	....
1991-92	Bracknell Bees	Britain	12	15	9	24	....	....	....	20	....	....	....	....	....	....	....	....	....	....	....	....	....	....	....	....	....	....
	Thunder Bay Thunder Cats	ColHL	2	0	1	1	....	....	....	0	....	....	....	....	....	....	....	....	....	....	....	....	....	....	....	....	....	....
	Richmond Renegades	ECHL	24	16	12	28	....	....	....	34	....	....	....	....	....	....	....	....	....	....	7	0	2	2	8	....	....	....
1992-93	St. Petersburg Renegades	SunHL	19	17	14	31	....	....	....	36	....	....	....	....	....	....	....	....	....	....	....	....	....	....	....	....	....	....
	Richmond Renegades	ECHL	39	14	27	41	....	....	....	66	....	....	....	....	....	....	....	....	....	....	....	....	....	....	....	....	....	....
1993-94	Richmond Renegades	ECHL	26	10	8	18	....	....	....	10	....	....	....	....	....	....	....	....	....	....	....	....	....	....	....	....	....	....
	Dallas Freeze	CHL	28	21	16	37	....	....	....	24	....	....	....	....	....	....	....	....	....	....	7	3	5	8	8	....	....	....
1994-95	Dallas Freeze	CHL	66	50	50	100	....	....	....	38	....	....	....	....	....	....	....	....	....	....	....	....	....	....	....	....	....	....
1995-96	Reno Rage	WCHL	15	4	10	14	....	....	....	4	....	....	....	....	....	....	....	....	....	....	....	....	....	....	....	....	....	....
	Wichita Thunder	CHL	31	11	20	31	....	....	....	16	....	....	....	....	....	....	....	....	....	....	....	....	....	....	....	....	....	....
1996-97	Wichita Thunder	CHL	21	6	20	26	....	....	....	4	....	....	....	....	....	....	....	....	....	....	9	9	2	11	8	....	....	....
1997-98	Wichita Thunder	CHL	68	38	39	77	....	....	....	78	....	....	....	....	....	....	....	....	....	....	15	10	9	19	10	....	....	....
1998-99	Wichita Thunder	CHL	27	18	22	40	....	....	....	24	....	....	....	....	....	....	....	....	....	....	4	1	3	4	6	....	....	....
99-2000	Wichita Thunder	CHL	37	12	13	25	....	....	....	30	....	....	....	....	....	....	....	....	....	....	5	1	1	2	4	....	....	....
	NHL Totals		**57**	**7**	**10**	**17**	**5**	**7**	**12**	**32**	**0**	**0**	**1**	**116**	**6.0**	**28**	**0**	**49**	**6**		....	....	....	....	....	....	....	....

Traded to **Pittsburgh** by **Washington** for Mark Taylor, March 12, 1985.

• McGILL, Bob

Robert Paul "Big Daddy" D – R. 6'1", 193 lbs. b: Edmonton, Alta., 4/27/1962. Toronto's 2nd, 26th overall, in 1980.

Season	Club	League	GP	G	A	Pts	AG	AA	APts	PIM	PP	SH	GW	S	%	TGF	PGF	TGA	PGA	+/–	GP	G	A	Pts	PIM	PP	SH	GW
1978-79	Abbotsford Flyers	BCJHL	46	3	20	23	....	....	....	242	....	....	....	....	....	....	....	....	....	....	....	....	....	....	....	....	....	....
1979-80	Victoria Cougars	WHL	70	3	18	21	....	....	....	230	....	....	....	....	....	....	....	....	....	....	15	0	5	5	64	....	....	....
1980-81	Victoria Cougars	WHL	66	5	36	41	....	....	....	295	....	....	....	....	....	....	....	....	....	....	11	1	5	6	67	....	....	....
	Victoria Cougars	Mem-Cup	3	0	1	1	....	....	....	5	....	....	....	....	....	....	....	....	....	....	....	....	....	....	....	....	....	....
1981-82	**Toronto Maple Leafs**	**NHL**	**68**	**1**	**10**	**11**	**1**	**7**	**8**	**263**	**0**	**0**	**0**	**34**	**2.9**	**59**	**1**	**83**	**16**	**–9**	....	....	....	....	....	....	....	....
1982-83	**Toronto Maple Leafs**	**NHL**	**30**	**0**	**0**	**0**	**0**	**0**	**0**	**146**	**0**	**0**	**0**	**13**	**0.0**	**11**	**1**	**37**	**3**	**–24**	....	....	....	....	....	....	....	....
	St. Catharines Saints	AHL	32	2	5	7	....	....	....	95	....	....	....	....	....	....	....	....	....	....	....	....	....	....	....	....	....	....
1983-84	**Toronto Maple Leafs**	**NHL**	**11**	**0**	**2**	**2**	**0**	**1**	**1**	**51**	**0**	**0**	**0**	**3**	**0.0**	**5**	**0**	**5**	**1**	**1**	....	....	....	....	....	....	....	....
	St. Catharines Saints	AHL	55	1	15	16	....	....	....	217	....	....	....	....	....	....	....	....	....	....	6	0	0	0	26	....	....	....
1984-85	**Toronto Maple Leafs**	**NHL**	**72**	**0**	**5**	**5**	**0**	**3**	**3**	**250**	**0**	**0**	**0**	**22**	**0.0**	**31**	**0**	**54**	**23**	**0**	....	....	....	....	....	....	....	....
1985-86	**Toronto Maple Leafs**	**NHL**	**61**	**1**	**4**	**5**	**1**	**3**	**4**	**141**	**0**	**0**	**0**	**28**	**3.6**	**45**	**0**	**82**	**20**	**–17**	**9**	**0**	**0**	**0**	**35**	**0**	**0**	**0**
1986-87	**Toronto Maple Leafs**	**NHL**	**56**	**1**	**4**	**5**	**1**	**3**	**4**	**103**	**0**	**0**	**0**	**27**	**3.7**	**33**	**0**	**40**	**5**	**–2**	**3**	**0**	**0**	**0**	**0**	**0**	**0**	**0**
1987-88	**Chicago Blackhawks**	**NHL**	**67**	**4**	**7**	**11**	**3**	**5**	**8**	**131**	**0**	**0**	**1**	**56**	**7.1**	**45**	**1**	**100**	**37**	**–19**	**3**	**0**	**0**	**0**	**2**	**0**	**0**	**0**
1988-89	**Chicago Blackhawks**	**NHL**	**68**	**0**	**4**	**4**	**0**	**3**	**3**	**155**	**0**	**0**	**0**	**38**	**0.0**	**30**	**0**	**26**	**5**	**9**	**16**	**0**	**0**	**0**	**33**	**0**	**0**	**0**
1989-90	**Chicago Blackhawks**	**NHL**	**69**	**2**	**10**	**12**	**2**	**7**	**9**	**204**	**0**	**1**	**0**	**53**	**3.8**	**42**	**0**	**55**	**6**	**–7**	**5**	**0**	**0**	**0**	**2**	**0**	**0**	**0**
1990-91	**Chicago Blackhawks**	**NHL**	**77**	**4**	**5**	**9**	**4**	**4**	**8**	**151**	**0**	**0**	**0**	**69**	**5.8**	**40**	**2**	**32**	**2**	**8**	**5**	**0**	**0**	**0**	**2**	**0**	**0**	**0**
1991-92	**San Jose Sharks**	**NHL**	**62**	**3**	**1**	**4**	**3**	**1**	**4**	**70**	**0**	**1**	**1**	**56**	**5.4**	**35**	**2**	**96**	**29**	**–34**	....	....	....	....	....	....	....	....
	Detroit Red Wings	**NHL**	**12**	**0**	**0**	**0**	**0**	**0**	**0**	**21**	**0**	**0**	**0**	**6**	**0.0**	**5**	**0**	**9**	**1**	**–3**	**8**	**0**	**0**	**0**	**14**	**0**	**0**	**0**
1992-93	**Toronto Maple Leafs**	**NHL**	**19**	**1**	**0**	**1**	**1**	**0**	**1**	**34**	**0**	**0**	**0**	**8**	**12.5**	**10**	**0**	**6**	**1**	**5**	....	....	....	....	....	....	....	....
1993-94	**New York Islanders**	**NHL**	**3**	**0**	**0**	**0**	**0**	**0**	**0**	**5**	**0**	**0**	**0**	**0**	**0.0**	**2**	**0**	**2**	**0**	**0**	....	....	....	....	....	....	....	....
	Hartford Whalers	**NHL**	**30**	**0**	**3**	**3**	**0**	**2**	**2**	**41**	**0**	**0**	**0**	**14**	**0.0**	**16**	**0**	**30**	**7**	**–7**	....	....	....	....	....	....	....	....
	Springfield Indians	AHL	5	0	0	0	....	....	....	24	....	....	....	....	....	....	....	....	....	....	....	....	....	....	....	....	....	....
1994-95			OUT OF HOCKEY – RETIRED																									

			REGULAR SEASON																		PLAYOFFS							
Season	Club	League	GP	G	A	Pts	AG	AA	APts	PIM	PP	SH	GW	S	%	TGF	PGF	TGA	PGA	+/–	GP	G	A	Pts	PIM	PP	SH	GW
1995-96	Chicago Wolves	IHL	8	0	0	0	....	....	....	6	....	....	....	....	....	....	....	....	....	....	....	....	....	....	....	....	....	....
1996-1998	Hershey Bears	AHL	DID NOT PLAY – ASSISTANT COACH																									
1998-2000	Adirondack IceHawks	UHL	DID NOT PLAY – COACHING																									
	NHL Totals		**705**	**17**	**55**	**72**	**16**	**39**	**55**	**1766**	**0**	**2**	**2**	**427**	**4.0**	**409**	**7**	**657**	**156**		**49**	**0**	**0**	**0**	**88**	**0**	**0**	**0**

Traded to **Chicago** by **Toronto** with Steve Thomas and Rick Vaive for Ed Olczyk and Al Secord, September 3, 1987. Claimed by **San Jose** from **Chicago** in Expansion Draft, May 30, 1991. Traded to **Detroit** by **San Jose** with Vancouver's 8th round choice (previously acquired, Detroit selected C.J. Denomme) in 1992 Entry Draft for Johan Garpenlov, March 9, 1992. Claimed by **Tampa Bay** from **Detroit** in Expansion Draft, June 18, 1992. Claimed on waivers by **Toronto** from **Tampa Bay**, September 9, 1992. Signed as a free agent by **NY Islanders**, September 7, 1993. Claimed on waivers by **Hartford** from **NY Islanders**, November 3, 1993.

• McGILL, Ryan

Ryan Clifford D – R. 6'2", 210 lbs. b: Prince Albert, Sask., 2/28/1969. Chicago's 2nd, 29th overall, in 1987.

Season	Club	League	GP	G	A	Pts	AG	AA	APts	PIM	PP	SH	GW	S	%	TGF	PGF	TGA	PGA	+/–	GP	G	A	Pts	PIM	PP	SH	GW
1984-85	Sherwood Park Crusaders	AAHA	STATISTICS NOT AVAILABLE																									
1985-86	Lethbridge Broncos	WHL	64	5	10	15	....	....	....	171	....	....	....	....	....	....	....	....	....	....	10	0	1	1	9	....	....	....
1986-87	Swift Current Broncos	WHL	72	12	36	48	....	....	....	226	....	....	....	....	....	....	....	....	....	....	4	1	0	1	9	....	....	....
1987-88	Medicine Hat Tigers	WHL	67	5	30	35	....	....	....	224	....	....	....	....	....	....	....	....	....	....	15	7	3	10	47	....	....	....
	Medicine Hat Tigers	Mem-Cup	5	1	0	1	....	....	....	13	....	....	....	....	....	....	....	....	....	....	....	....	....	....	....	....	....	....
1988-89	Medicine Hat Tigers	WHL	57	26	45	71	....	....	....	172	....	....	....	....	....	....	....	....	....	....	3	0	2	2	15	....	....	....
	Saginaw Hawks	IHL	8	2	0	2	....	....	....	12	....	....	....	....	....	....	....	....	....	....	6	0	0	0	42	....	....	....
1989-90	Indianapolis Ice	IHL	77	11	17	28	....	....	....	215	....	....	....	....	....	....	....	....	....	....	14	2	2	4	29	....	....	....
1990-91	Indianapolis Ice	IHL	63	11	40	51	....	....	....	200	....	....	....	....	....	....	....	....	....	....	....	....	....	....	....	....	....	....
	Halifax Citadels	AHL	7	0	4	4	....	....	....	6	....	....	....	....	....	....	....	....	....	....	....	....	....	....	....	....	....	....
1991-92	**Chicago Blackhawks**	**NHL**	**9**	**0**	**2**	**2**	**0**	**2**	**2**	**20**	**0**	**0**	**0**	**15**	**0.0**	**8**	**0**	**9**	**2**	**1**	....	....	....	....	....	....	....	....
	Indianapolis Ice	IHL	40	7	19	26	....	....	....	170	....	....	....	....	....	....	....	....	....	....	....	....	....	....	....	....	....	....
	Hershey Bears	AHL	17	3	5	8	....	....	....	67	....	....	....	....	....	....	....	....	....	....	6	1	1	2	4	....	....	....
1992-93	**Philadelphia Flyers**	**NHL**	**72**	**3**	**10**	**13**	**2**	**7**	**9**	**238**	**0**	**0**	**0**	**68**	**4.4**	**57**	**0**	**56**	**8**	**9**	....	....	....	....	....	....	....	....
	Hershey Bears	AHL	4	0	2	2	....	....	....	26	....	....	....	....	....	....	....	....	....	....	....	....	....	....	....	....	....	....
1993-94	**Philadelphia Flyers**	**NHL**	**50**	**1**	**3**	**4**	**1**	**2**	**3**	**112**	**0**	**0**	**0**	**53**	**1.9**	**34**	**0**	**54**	**15**	**–5**	....	....	....	....	....	....	....	....
1994-95	**Philadelphia Flyers**	**NHL**	**12**	**0**	**0**	**0**	**0**	**0**	**0**	**13**	**0**	**0**	**0**	**2**	**0.0**	**3**	**0**	**3**	**0**	**0**	....	....	....	....	....	....	....	....
	Edmonton Oilers	**NHL**	**8**	**0**	**0**	**0**	**0**	**0**	**0**	**8**	**0**	**0**	**0**	**6**	**0.0**	**5**	**0**	**10**	**1**	**–4**	....	....	....	....	....	....	....	....
1995-1996			OUT OF HOCKEY – RETIRED																									
1996-1997	Edmonton Ice	WHL	DID NOT PLAY – ASSISTANT COACH																									
1997-1998	Edmonton Ice	WHL	DID NOT PLAY – COACHING																									
1998-2000	Kootenay Ice	WHL	DID NOT PLAY – COACHING																									
	NHL Totals		**151**	**4**	**15**	**19**	**3**	**11**	**14**	**391**	**0**	**0**	**0**	**144**	**2.8**	**107**	**0**	**132**	**26**		....	....	....	....	....	....	....	....

IHL Second All-Star Team (1991)

Traded to **Quebec** by **Chicago** with Mike McNeill for Paul Gillis and Dan Vincelette, March 5, 1991. Traded to **Chicago** by **Quebec** for Mike Dagenais, September 27, 1991. Traded to **Philadelphia** by **Chicago** for Tony Horacek, February 7, 1992. Traded to **Edmonton** by **Philadelphia** for Brad Zavisha and Edmonton's 6th round choice (Jamie Sokolosky) in 1995 Entry Draft, March 13, 1995. • Suffered career-ending eye injury in game vs. Anaheim, April 5, 1995.

• McGILLIS, Dan

D – L. 6'2", 225 lbs. b: Hawkesbury, Ont., 7/1/1972. Detroit's 10th, 238th overall, in 1992.

Season	Club	League	GP	G	A	Pts	AG	AA	APts	PIM	PP	SH	GW	S	%	TGF	PGF	TGA	PGA	+/–	GP	G	A	Pts	PIM	PP	SH	GW
1989-90	Hawkesbury Hawks	OJHL	55	2	1	3	....	....	....	52	....	....	....	....	....	....	....	....	....	....	....	....	....	....	....	....	....	....
1990-91	Hawkesbury Hawks	OJHL	56	8	22	30	....	....	....	92	....	....	....	....	....	....	....	....	....	....	....	....	....	....	....	....	....	....
1991-92	Hawkesbury Hawks	OJHL	36	5	19	24	....	....	....	106	....	....	....	....	....	....	....	....	....	....	....	....	....	....	....	....	....	....
1992-93	Northeastern University	H-East	35	5	12	17	....	....	....	42	....	....	....	....	....	....	....	....	....	....	....	....	....	....	....	....	....	....
1993-94	Northeastern University	H-East	38	4	25	29	....	....	....	82	....	....	....	....	....	....	....	....	....	....	....	....	....	....	....	....	....	....
1994-95	Northeastern University	H-East	34	9	22	31	....	....	....	70	....	....	....	....	....	....	....	....	....	....	....	....	....	....	....	....	....	....
1995-96	Northeastern University	H-East	34	12	24	36	....	....	....	50	....	....	....	....	....	....	....	....	....	....	....	....	....	....	....	....	....	....
1996-97	**Edmonton Oilers**	**NHL**	**73**	**6**	**16**	**22**	**6**	**14**	**20**	**52**	**2**	**1**	**2**	**139**	**4.3**	**85**	**27**	**69**	**13**	**2**	**12**	**0**	**5**	**5**	**24**	**0**	**0**	**0**
1997-98	**Edmonton Oilers**	**NHL**	**67**	**10**	**15**	**25**	**12**	**15**	**27**	**74**	**5**	**0**	**3**	**119**	**8.4**	**58**	**23**	**75**	**23**	**–17**	....	....	....	....	....	....	....	....
	Philadelphia Flyers	**NHL**	**13**	**1**	**5**	**6**	**1**	**5**	**6**	**35**	**1**	**0**	**0**	**18**	**5.6**	**15**	**7**	**15**	**3**	**–4**	**5**	**1**	**2**	**3**	**10**	**1**	**0**	**0**
1998-99	**Philadelphia Flyers**	**NHL**	**78**	**8**	**37**	**45**	**9**	**36**	**45**	**61**	**6**	**0**	**4**	**164**	**4.9**	**100**	**41**	**58**	**15**	**16**	**6**	**0**	**1**	**1**	**12**	**0**	**0**	**0**
99-2000	**Philadelphia Flyers**	**NHL**	**68**	**4**	**14**	**18**	**4**	**13**	**17**	**55**	**3**	**0**	**1**	**128**	**3.1**	**63**	**16**	**44**	**13**	**16**	**18**	**2**	**6**	**8**	**12**	**0**	**0**	**0**
	NHL Totals		**299**	**29**	**87**	**116**	**32**	**83**	**115**	**277**	**17**	**1**	**10**	**568**	**5.1**	**321**	**114**	**261**	**67**		**41**	**3**	**14**	**17**	**58**	**1**	**0**	**0**

Hockey East First All-Star Team (1995, 1996) • NCAA East First All-American Team (1996)

Traded to **Edmonton** by **Detroit** for Kirk Maltby, March 20, 1996. Traded to **Philadelphia** by **Edmonton** with Edmonton's 2nd round choice (Jason Beckett) in 1998 Entry Draft for Janne Niinimaa, March 24, 1998.

• McHUGH, Mike

Michael LW – L. 5'10", 190 lbs. b: Bowdoin, MA, 8/16/1965. Minnesota's 1st, 1st overall, in 1988 Supplemental Draft.

Season	Club	League	GP	G	A	Pts	AG	AA	APts	PIM	PP	SH	GW	S	%	TGF	PGF	TGA	PGA	+/–	GP	G	A	Pts	PIM	PP	SH	GW
1983-84	New Hampton Prep School	Hi-School	21	24	22	46	....	....	....	....	....	....	....	....	....	....	....	....	....	....	....	....	....	....	....	....	....	....
1984-85	University of Maine	H-East	25	9	8	17	....	....	....	9	....	....	....	....	....	....	....	....	....	....	....	....	....	....	....	....	....	....
1985-86	University of Maine	H-East	38	9	10	19	....	....	....	24	....	....	....	....	....	....	....	....	....	....	....	....	....	....	....	....	....	....
1986-87	University of Maine	H-East	42	21	29	50	....	....	....	40	....	....	....	....	....	....	....	....	....	....	....	....	....	....	....	....	....	....
1987-88	University of Maine	H-East	44	29	37	66	....	....	....	90	....	....	....	....	....	....	....	....	....	....	....	....	....	....	....	....	....	....
1988-89	**Minnesota North Stars**	**NHL**	**3**	**0**	**0**	**0**	**0**	**0**	**0**	**2**	**0**	**0**	**0**	**1**	**0.0**	**0**	**0**	**2**	**1**	**–1**	....	....	....	....	....	....	....	....
	Kalamazoo Wings	IHL	70	17	29	46	....	....	....	89	....	....	....	....	....	....	....	....	....	....	6	3	1	4	17	....	....	....
1989-90	**Minnesota North Stars**	**NHL**	**3**	**0**	**0**	**0**	**0**	**0**	**0**	**0**	**0**	**0**	**0**	**2**	**0.0**	**0**	**0**	**1**	**0**	**–1**	....	....	....	....	....	....	....	....
	Kalamazoo Wings	IHL	73	14	17	31	....	....	....	96	....	....	....	....	....	....	....	....	....	....	10	0	6	6	16	....	....	....
1990-91	**Minnesota North Stars**	**NHL**	**6**	**0**	**0**	**0**	**0**	**0**	**0**	**0**	**0**	**0**	**0**	**4**	**0.0**	**0**	**0**	**3**	**0**	**–3**	....	....	....	....	....	....	....	....
	Kalamazoo Wings	IHL	69	27	38	65	....	....	....	82	....	....	....	....	....	....	....	....	....	....	11	3	8	11	6	....	....	....
1991-92	**San Jose Sharks**	**NHL**	**8**	**1**	**0**	**1**	**1**	**0**	**1**	**14**	**0**	**0**	**0**	**5**	**20.0**	**4**	**0**	**8**	**1**	**–3**	....	....	....	....	....	....	....	....
	Springfield Indians	AHL	70	23	31	54	....	....	....	51	....	....	....	....	....	....	....	....	....	....	11	4	7	11	25	....	....	....
1992-93	Springfield Indians	AHL	67	19	27	46	....	....	....	111	....	....	....	....	....	....	....	....	....	....	11	5	2	7	12	....	....	....
1993-94	Hershey Bears	AHL	80	27	43	70	....	....	....	58	....	....	....	....	....	....	....	....	....	....	11	9	3	12	14	....	....	....
1994-95	Hershey Bears	AHL	68	24	26	50	....	....	....	102	....	....	....	....	....	....	....	....	....	....	6	3	2	5	6	....	....	....
1995-96	Hershey Bears	AHL	75	15	42	57	....	....	....	118	....	....	....	....	....	....	....	....	....	....	5	2	2	4	2	....	....	....
1996-97	Hershey Bears	AHL	77	23	45	68	....	....	....	135	....	....	....	....	....	....	....	....	....	....	23	9	7	16	33	....	....	....
1997-98	Hershey Bears	AHL	66	12	25	37	....	....	....	143	....	....	....	....	....	....	....	....	....	....	7	1	1	2	16	....	....	....
	NHL Totals		**20**	**1**	**0**	**1**	**1**	**0**	**1**	**16**	**0**	**0**	**0**	**12**	**8.3**	**4**	**0**	**14**	**2**		....	....	....	....	....	....	....	....

Hockey East First All-Star Team (1988) • Won Jack A. Butterfield Trophy (Playoff MVP - AHL) (1997)

Claimed by **San Jose** from **Minnesota** in Dispersal Draft, May 30, 1991. Traded to **Hartford** by **San Jose** for Paul Fenton, October 18, 1991.

• McILHARGEY, Jack

John Cecil D – L. 6', 190 lbs. b: Edmonton, Alta., 3/7/1952.

Season	Club	League	GP	G	A	Pts	AG	AA	APts	PIM	PP	SH	GW	S	%	TGF	PGF	TGA	PGA	+/–	GP	G	A	Pts	PIM	PP	SH	GW
1970-71	New Westminster Royals	BCJHL	STATISTICS NOT AVAILABLE																									
1971-72	Victoria Cougars	WCJHL	24	1	1	2	....	....	....	137	....	....	....	....	....	....	....	....	....	....	....	....	....	....	....	....	....	....
	Flin Flon Bombers	WCJHL	33	1	4	5	....	....	....	142	....	....	....	....	....	....	....	....	....	....	7	0	1	1	39	....	....	....
1972-73	Jersey Devils	EHL	72	2	7	9	....	....	....	229	....	....	....	....	....	....	....	....	....	....	....	....	....	....	....	....	....	....
	Richmond Robins	AHL	9	0	1	1	....	....	....	4	....	....	....	....	....	....	....	....	....	....	4	0	0	0	7	....	....	....
1973-74	Des Moines Capitals	IHL	16	1	2	3	....	....	....	52	....	....	....	....	....	....	....	....	....	....	....	....	....	....	....	....	....	....
	Richmond Robins	AHL	54	2	10	12	....	....	....	163	....	....	....	....	....	....	....	....	....	....	5	0	0	0	12	....	....	....
1974-75	**Philadelphia Flyers**	**NHL**	**2**	**0**	**0**	**0**	**0**	**0**	**0**	**11**	**0**	**0**	**0**	**1**	**0.0**	**0**	**0**	**1**	**0**	**–1**	....	....	....	....	....	....	....	....
	Richmond Robins	AHL	72	4	3	7	....	....	....	*316	....	....	....	....	....	....	....	....	....	....	7	0	3	3	45	....	....	....
1975-76	**Philadelphia Flyers**	**NHL**	**57**	**1**	**2**	**3**	**1**	**1**	**2**	**205**	**0**	**0**	**0**	**23**	**4.3**	**31**	**1**	**20**	**1**	**11**	**15**	**0**	**3**	**3**	**41**	**0**	**0**	**0**
	Richmond Robins	AHL	4	0	0	0	....	....	....	17	....	....	....	....	....	....	....	....	....	....	....	....	....	....	....	....	....	....
1976-77	**Philadelphia Flyers**	**NHL**	**40**	**2**	**1**	**3**	**2**	**1**	**3**	**164**	**0**	**0**	**0**	**27**	**7.4**	**26**	**0**	**21**	**1**	**6**	....	....	....	....	....	....	....	....
	Vancouver Canucks	**NHL**	**21**	**1**	**7**	**8**	**1**	**5**	**6**	**61**	**0**	**0**	**0**	**18**	**5.6**	**25**	**1**	**29**	**8**	**3**	....	....	....	....	....	....	....	....
1977-78	**Vancouver Canucks**	**NHL**	**69**	**3**	**5**	**8**	**3**	**4**	**7**	**172**	**0**	**0**	**0**	**36**	**8.3**	**42**	**1**	**103**	**17**	**–45**	....	....	....	....	....	....	....	....
1978-79	**Vancouver Canucks**	**NHL**	**53**	**2**	**4**	**6**	**2**	**3**	**5**	**129**	**0**	**0**	**0**	**26**	**7.7**	**41**	**1**	**66**	**10**	**–16**	**3**	**0**	**0**	**0**	**2**	**0**	**0**	**0**
1979-80	**Vancouver Canucks**	**NHL**	**24**	**0**	**2**	**2**	**0**	**1**	**1**	**41**	**0**	**0**	**0**	**6**	**0.0**	**9**	**0**	**14**	**0**	**–5**	....	....	....	....	....	....	....	....
	Philadelphia Flyers	**NHL**	**26**	**0**	**4**	**4**	**0**	**3**	**3**	**95**	**0**	**0**	**0**	**15**	**0.0**	**22**	**0**	**26**	**11**	**7**	**9**	**0**	**0**	**0**	**25**	**0**	**0**	**0**

Season	Club	League	GP	G	A	Pts	AG	AA	APts	PIM	PP	SH	GW	S	%	TGF	PGF	TGA	PGA	+/-	GP	G	A	Pts	PIM	PP	SH	GW
			REGULAR SEASON																		PLAYOFFS							
1980-81	**Philadelphia Flyers**	**NHL**	**3**	**0**	**0**	**0**	**0**	**0**	**0**	**22**	**0**	**0**	**0**	**0**	**0.0**	**3**	**0**	**1**	**0**	**2**	....	....	....	....	....	....	....	....
	Maine Mariners	AHL	3	0	1	1	....	....	....	7	....	....	....	....	....	....	....	....	....	....	....	....	....	....	....	....	....	....
	Hartford Whalers	**NHL**	**48**	**1**	**6**	**7**	**1**	**4**	**5**	**142**	**0**	**0**	**0**	**14**	**7.1**	**37**	**0**	**53**	**13**	**–3**	....	....	....	....	....	....	....	....
1981-82	**Hartford Whalers**	**NHL**	**50**	**1**	**5**	**6**	**1**	**3**	**4**	**60**	**0**	**0**	**0**	**23**	**4.3**	**21**	**0**	**33**	**4**	**–8**	....	....	....	....	....	....	....	....
1982-1984			OUT OF HOCKEY – RETIRED																									
1984-1985	**Vancouver Canucks**	**NHL**	DID NOT PLAY – ASSISTANT GENERAL MANAGER																									
	Vancouver Canucks	**NHL**	DID NOT PLAY – ASSISTANT COACH																									
1985-1991	**Vancouver Canucks**	**NHL**	DID NOT PLAY – ASSISTANT COACH																									
1991-1992	Milwaukee Admirals	IHL	DID NOT PLAY – COACHING																									
1992-1993	Hamilton Canucks	AHL	DID NOT PLAY – COACHING																									
1993-1999	Syracuse Crunch	AHL	DID NOT PLAY – COACHING																									
1999-2000	**Vancouver Canucks**	**NHL**	DID NOT PLAY – ASSISTANT COACH																									
	NHL Totals		**393**	**11**	**36**	**47**	**11**	**25**	**36**	**1102**	**0**	**0**	**0**	**189**	**5.8**	**257**	**4**	**367**	**65**		**27**	**0**	**3**	**3**	**68**	**0**	**0**	**0**

Signed as a free agent by **Philadelphia** (Jersey-EHL), September, 1972. Traded to **Vancouver** by **Philadelphia** with Larry Goodenough for Bob Dailey, January 20, 1977. Traded to **Philadelphia** by **Vancouver** for cash, January 2, 1980. Traded to **Hartford** by **Philadelphia** with Norm Barnes for Hartford's 2nd round choice (later traded to Toronto — Toronto selected Peter Ihnacak) in 1982 Entry Draft, November 21, 1980.

• McINNIS, Marty

Marty Edward LW – R. 5'11", 190 lbs. b: Weymouth, MA., 6/2/1970. NY Islanders' 10th, 163rd overall, in 1988.

Season	Club	League	GP	G	A	Pts	AG	AA	APts	PIM	PP	SH	GW	S	%	TGF	PGF	TGA	PGA	+/-	GP	G	A	Pts	PIM	PP	SH	GW
1986-87	Milton Academy	Hi-School	25	21	19	40	....	....	....	....	....	....	....	....	....	....	....	....	....	....	....	....	....	....	....	....	....	....
1987-88	Milton Academy	Hi-School	25	26	25	51	....	....	....	....	....	....	....	....	....	....	....	....	....	....	....	....	....	....	....	....	....	....
1988-89	Boston College	H-East	39	13	19	32	....	....	....	8	....	....	....	....	....	....	....	....	....	....	....	....	....	....	....	....	....	....
1989-90	Boston College	H-East	41	24	29	53	....	....	....	43	....	....	....	....	....	....	....	....	....	....	....	....	....	....	....	....	....	....
1990-91	Boston College	H-East	38	21	36	57	....	....	....	40	....	....	....	....	....	....	....	....	....	....	....	....	....	....	....	....	....	....
1991-92	United States	Nat-Team	54	15	19	34	....	....	....	20	....	....	....	....	....	....	....	....	....	....	....	....	....	....	....	....	....	....
	United States	Olympics	8	5	2	7	....	....	....	4	....	....	....	....	....	....	....	....	....	....	....	....	....	....	....	....	....	....
	New York Islanders	**NHL**	**15**	**3**	**5**	**8**	**3**	**4**	**7**	**0**	**0**	**0**	**0**	**24**	**12.5**	**14**	**3**	**8**	**3**	**6**	....	....	....	....	....	....	....	....
1992-93	**New York Islanders**	**NHL**	**56**	**10**	**20**	**30**	**8**	**14**	**22**	**24**	**0**	**1**	**0**	**60**	**16.7**	**46**	**4**	**47**	**12**	**7**	**3**	**0**	**1**	**1**	**0**	**0**	**0**	**0**
	Capital District Islanders	AHL	10	4	12	16	....	....	....	2	....	....	....	....	....	....	....	....	....	....	....	....	....	....	....	....	....	....
1993-94	**New York Islanders**	**NHL**	**81**	**25**	**31**	**56**	**23**	**24**	**47**	**24**	**3**	**5**	**3**	**136**	**18.4**	**78**	**10**	**71**	**34**	**31**	**4**	**0**	**0**	**0**	**0**	**0**	**0**	**0**
1994-95	**New York Islanders**	**NHL**	**41**	**9**	**7**	**16**	**16**	**10**	**26**	**8**	**0**	**0**	**1**	**68**	**13.2**	**23**	**4**	**33**	**13**	**–1**	....	....	....	....	....	....	....	....
1995-96	**New York Islanders**	**NHL**	**74**	**12**	**34**	**46**	**12**	**28**	**40**	**39**	**2**	**0**	**1**	**167**	**7.2**	**72**	**23**	**92**	**32**	**–11**	....	....	....	....	....	....	....	....
	United States	WC-A	7	0	2	2	....	....	....	4	....	....	....	....	....	....	....	....	....	....	....	....	....	....	....	....	....	....
1996-97	**New York Islanders**	**NHL**	**70**	**20**	**22**	**42**	**21**	**20**	**41**	**20**	**4**	**1**	**4**	**163**	**12.3**	**71**	**19**	**78**	**19**	**–7**	....	....	....	....	....	....	....	....
	Calgary Flames	**NHL**	**10**	**3**	**4**	**7**	**3**	**4**	**7**	**2**	**1**	**0**	**0**	**19**	**15.8**	**7**	**2**	**9**	**3**	**–1**	....	....	....	....	....	....	....	....
	United States	WC-A	8	2	2	4	....	....	....	2	....	....	....	....	....	....	....	....	....	....	....	....	....	....	....	....	....	....
1997-98	**Calgary Flames**	**NHL**	**75**	**19**	**25**	**44**	**22**	**24**	**46**	**34**	**5**	**4**	**0**	**128**	**14.8**	**63**	**14**	**74**	**26**	**1**	....	....	....	....	....	....	....	....
1998-99	**Calgary Flames**	**NHL**	**6**	**1**	**1**	**2**	**1**	**1**	**2**	**6**	**0**	**0**	**0**	**7**	**14.3**	**3**	**0**	**7**	**3**	**–1**	....	....	....	....	....	....	....	....
	Mighty Ducks of Anaheim	**NHL**	**75**	**18**	**34**	**52**	**21**	**33**	**54**	**36**	**11**	**1**	**5**	**139**	**12.9**	**88**	**55**	**59**	**12**	**–14**	**4**	**2**	**0**	**2**	**2**	**2**	**0**	**0**
99-2000	**Mighty Ducks of Anaheim**	**NHL**	**62**	**10**	**18**	**28**	**11**	**17**	**28**	**26**	**2**	**1**	**2**	**129**	**7.8**	**49**	**21**	**50**	**18**	**–4**	....	....	....	....	....	....	....	....
	NHL Totals		**565**	**130**	**201**	**331**	**141**	**179**	**320**	**219**	**28**	**13**	**16**	**1040**	**12.5**	**514**	**155**	**528**	**175**		**11**	**2**	**1**	**3**	**2**	**2**	**0**	**0**

Traded to **Calgary** by **NY Islanders** with Tyrone Garner and Calgary's 6th round choice (previously acquired, Calgary selected Ilja Demidov) in 1997 Entry Draft for Robert Reichel, March 18, 1997. Traded to **Chicago** by **Calgary** with Eric Andersson and Jamie Allison for Jeff Shantz and Steve Dubinsky, October 27, 1998. Traded to **Anaheim** by **Chicago** for Toronto's 4th round choice (previously acquired, later traded to Washington - Washington selected Ryan Vanbuskirk) in 2000 Entry Draft, October 27, 1998.

• McINTOSH, Bruce

D – L. 6', 178 lbs. b: Minneapolis, MN, 3/17/1949.

Season	Club	League	GP	G	A	Pts	AG	AA	APts	PIM	PP	SH	GW	S	%	TGF	PGF	TGA	PGA	+/-	GP	G	A	Pts	PIM	PP	SH	GW
1965-1967	Edina Hornets	Hi-School	STATISTICS NOT AVAILABLE																									
1967-68	University of Minnesota	WCHA	DID NOT PLAY – FRESHMAN																									
1968-69	University of Minnesota	WCHA	7	0	0	0	....	....	....	0	....	....	....	....	....	....	....	....	....	....	....	....	....	....	....	....	....	....
1969-70	University of Minnesota	WCHA	33	3	12	15	....	....	....	26	....	....	....	....	....	....	....	....	....	....	....	....	....	....	....	....	....	....
1970-71	University of Minnesota	WCHA	33	8	13	21	....	....	....	29	....	....	....	....	....	....	....	....	....	....	....	....	....	....	....	....	....	....
1971-72	United States	Nat-Team	STATISTICS NOT AVAILABLE																									
1972-73	**Minnesota North Stars**	**NHL**	**2**	**0**	**0**	**0**	**0**	**0**	**0**	**0**	**0**	**0**	**0**	**0**	**0.0**	**0**	**0**	**0**	**0**	**0**	....	....	....	....	....	....	....	....
	Cleveland-Jacksonville Barons	AHL	23	1	5	6	....	....	....	4	....	....	....	....	....	....	....	....	....	....	....	....	....	....	....	....	....	....
	Saginaw Gears	IHL	30	5	16	21	....	....	....	23	....	....	....	....	....	....	....	....	....	....	....	....	....	....	....	....	....	....
	NHL Totals		**2**	**0**	**0**	**0**	**0**	**0**	**0**	**0**	**0**	**0**	**0**	**0**	**0.0**	**0**	**0**	**0**	**0**		....	....	....	....	....	....	....	....

NCAA Championship All-Tournament Team (1971)

Signed as a free agent by **Minnesota**, September 30, 1972.

• McINTOSH, Paul

Paul Hugh D – R. 5'10", 177 lbs. b: Listowel, Ont., 3/13/1954. Buffalo's 4th, 65th overall, in 1974.

Season	Club	League	GP	G	A	Pts	AG	AA	APts	PIM	PP	SH	GW	S	%	TGF	PGF	TGA	PGA	+/-	GP	G	A	Pts	PIM	PP	SH	GW
1971-72	Peterborough Jr. Bees	OHA-B	STATISTICS NOT AVAILABLE																									
	Peterborough Petes	OMJHL	29	2	2	4	....	....	....	39	....	....	....	....	....	....	....	....	....	....	4	0	1	1	0	....	....	....
1972-73	Peterborough Petes	OMJHL	63	7	32	39	....	....	....	67	....	....	....	....	....	....	....	....	....	....	....	....	....	....	....	....	....	....
1973-74	Peterborough Petes	OMJHL	62	16	34	50	....	....	....	153	....	....	....	....	....	....	....	....	....	....	15	0	13	13	....	....	....	....
	Canada	WJC-A	5	3	2	5	....	....	....	6	....	....	....	....	....	....	....	....	....	....	....	....	....	....	....	....	....	....
1974-75	**Buffalo Sabres**	**NHL**	**6**	**0**	**1**	**1**	**0**	**1**	**1**	**5**	**0**	**0**	**0**	**1**	**0.0**	**4**	**0**	**3**	**1**	**2**	**1**	**0**	**0**	**0**	**0**	**0**	**0**	**0**
	Hershey Bears	AHL	68	2	11	13	....	....	....	195	....	....	....	....	....	....	....	....	....	....	12	1	1	2	43	....	....	....
1975-76	**Buffalo Sabres**	**NHL**	**42**	**0**	**1**	**1**	**0**	**1**	**1**	**61**	**0**	**0**	**0**	**9**	**0.0**	**13**	**0**	**19**	**1**	**–5**	**1**	**0**	**0**	**0**	**7**	**0**	**0**	**0**
	Hershey Bears	AHL	12	0	2	2	....	....	....	63	....	....	....	....	....	....	....	....	....	....	....	....	....	....	....	....	....	....
1976-77	Hershey Bears	AHL	62	6	10	16	....	....	....	171	....	....	....	....	....	....	....	....	....	....	3	0	0	0	6	....	....	....
1977-78	Springfield Indians	AHL	77	5	22	27	....	....	....	189	....	....	....	....	....	....	....	....	....	....	4	0	0	0	18	....	....	....
1978-79	Saginaw Gears	IHL	78	11	34	45	....	....	....	147	....	....	....	....	....	....	....	....	....	....	4	0	1	1	6	....	....	....
1979-80	Saginaw Gears	IHL	10	0	3	3	....	....	....	62	....	....	....	....	....	....	....	....	....	....	....	....	....	....	....	....	....	....
	NHL Totals		**48**	**0**	**2**	**2**	**0**	**2**	**2**	**66**	**0**	**0**	**0**	**10**	**0.0**	**17**	**0**	**22**	**2**		**2**	**0**	**0**	**0**	**7**	**0**	**0**	**0**

WJC-A All-Star Team (1974) • OMJHL Second All-Star Team (1974)

• McINTYRE, John

"Jack" C – L. 6'1", 190 lbs. b: Ravenswood, Ont., 4/29/1969. Toronto's 3rd, 49th overall, in 1987.

Season	Club	League	GP	G	A	Pts	AG	AA	APts	PIM	PP	SH	GW	S	%	TGF	PGF	TGA	PGA	+/-	GP	G	A	Pts	PIM	PP	SH	GW
1983-84	Thedford Browns	OJHL-D	34	18	29	47	....	....	....	36	....	....	....	....	....	....	....	....	....	....	....	....	....	....	....	....	....	....
1984-85	Strathroy Rockets	OJHL-B	48	21	23	44	....	....	....	49	....	....	....	....	....	....	....	....	....	....	....	....	....	....	....	....	....	....
1985-86	Guelph Platers	OHL	30	4	6	10	....	....	....	25	....	....	....	....	....	....	....	....	....	....	20	1	5	6	31	....	....	....
	Guelph Platers	Mem-Cup	4	0	1	1	....	....	....	4	....	....	....	....	....	....	....	....	....	....	....	....	....	....	....	....	....	....
1986-87	Guelph Platers	OHL	47	8	22	30	....	....	....	95	....	....	....	....	....	....	....	....	....	....	....	....	....	....	....	....	....	....
1987-88	Guelph Platers	OHL	39	24	18	42	....	....	....	109	....	....	....	....	....	....	....	....	....	....	....	....	....	....	....	....	....	....
1988-89	Guelph Platers	OHL	52	30	26	56	....	....	....	129	....	....	....	....	....	....	....	....	....	....	7	5	4	9	25	....	....	....
	Canada	WJC-A	7	1	0	1	....	....	....	4	....	....	....	....	....	....	....	....	....	....	....	....	....	....	....	....	....	....
	Newmarket Saints	AHL	3	0	2	2	....	....	....	7	....	....	....	....	....	....	....	....	....	....	5	1	1	2	20	....	....	....
1989-90	**Toronto Maple Leafs**	**NHL**	**59**	**5**	**12**	**17**	**4**	**9**	**13**	**117**	**0**	**1**	**1**	**44**	**11.4**	**26**	**5**	**46**	**13**	**–12**	**2**	**0**	**0**	**0**	**2**	**0**	**0**	**0**
	Newmarket Saints	AHL	6	2	2	4	....	....	....	12	....	....	....	....	....	....	....	....	....	....	....	....	....	....	....	....	....	....
1990-91	**Toronto Maple Leafs**	**NHL**	**13**	**0**	**3**	**3**	**0**	**2**	**2**	**25**	**0**	**0**	**0**	**7**	**0.0**	**4**	**0**	**11**	**7**	**0**	....	....	....	....	....	....	....	....
	Los Angeles Kings	**NHL**	**56**	**8**	**5**	**13**	**7**	**4**	**11**	**115**	**0**	**1**	**0**	**26**	**30.8**	**18**	**0**	**21**	**9**	**6**	**12**	**0**	**1**	**1**	**24**	**0**	**0**	**0**
1991-92	**Los Angeles Kings**	**NHL**	**73**	**5**	**19**	**24**	**5**	**14**	**19**	**100**	**0**	**0**	**1**	**40**	**12.5**	**31**	**0**	**51**	**20**	**0**	**6**	**0**	**4**	**4**	**12**	**0**	**0**	**0**
1992-93	**Los Angeles Kings**	**NHL**	**49**	**2**	**5**	**7**	**2**	**3**	**5**	**80**	**0**	**0**	**0**	**31**	**6.5**	**16**	**0**	**39**	**10**	**–13**	....	....	....	....	....	....	....	....
	New York Rangers	**NHL**	**11**	**1**	**0**	**1**	**1**	**0**	**1**	**4**	**0**	**0**	**0**	**5**	**20.0**	**2**	**0**	**4**	**1**	**–1**	....	....	....	....	....	....	....	....

			REGULAR SEASON																		PLAYOFFS							
Season	Club	League	GP	G	A	Pts	AG	AA	APts	PIM	PP	SH	GW	S	%	TGF	PGF	TGA	PGA	+/–	GP	G	A	Pts	PIM	PP	SH	GW
1993-94	**Vancouver Canucks**	**NHL**	62	3	6	9	3	5	8	38	0	0	0	30	10.0	15	0	49	25	–9	24	0	1	1	16	0	0	0
1994-95	**Vancouver Canucks**	**NHL**	28	0	4	4	0	6	6	37	0	0	0	6	0.0	5	0	13	5	–3	....	....	....	....	....	....	....	....
1995-96	Syracuse Crunch	AHL	53	13	14	27	....	....	....	78	....	....	....	....	....	....	....	....	....	....	....	....	....	....	....	....	....	....
	NHL Totals		351	24	54	78	22	43	65	516	0	2	2	189	12.7	117	5	234	90		44	0	6	6	54	0	0	0

Traded to **LA Kings** by **Toronto** for Mike Krushelnyski, November 9, 1990. Traded to **NY Rangers** by **LA Kings** for Mark Hardy and Ottawa's 5th round choice (previously acquired, LA Kings selected Frederick Beaubien) in 1993 Entry Draft, March 22, 1993. Claimed by **Vancouver** from **NY Rangers** in Waiver Draft, October 3, 1993.

• McINTYRE, Larry

Lawrence Albert D – L. 6'1", 190 lbs. b: Moose Jaw, Sask., 7/13/1949. Toronto's 3rd, 31st overall, in 1969.

Season	Club	League	GP	G	A	Pts	AG	AA	APts	PIM	PP	SH	GW	S	%	TGF	PGF	TGA	PGA	+/–	GP	G	A	Pts	PIM	PP	SH	GW
1966-67	Moose Jaw Canucks	CMJHL	32	0	3	3	....	....	....	9	....	....	....	....	....	....	....	....	....	....	10	0	0	0	2	....	....	....
1967-68	Moose Jaw Canucks	WCJHL	60	7	13	20	....	....	....	66	....	....	....	....	....	....	....	....	....	....	10	0	3	3	4	....	....	....
1968-69	Moose Jaw Canucks	WCJHL	4	1	6	7	....	....	....	4	....	....	....	....	....	....	....	....	....	....	....	....	....	....	....	....	....	....
1969-70	Tulsa Oilers	CHL	60	2	12	14	....	....	....	41	....	....	....	....	....	....	....	....	....	....	6	0	0	0	4	....	....	....
	Toronto Maple Leafs	**NHL**	1	0	0	0	0	0	0	0	0	0	0	1	0.0	3	0	0	0	3	....	....	....	....	....	....	....	....
	Buffalo Bisons	AHL	....	....	....	....	....	....	....	....	....	....	....	....	....	....	....	....	....	....	1	0	0	0	0	....	....	....
1970-71	Tulsa Oilers	CHL	41	0	4	4	....	....	....	18	....	....	....	....	....	....	....	....	....	....	....	....	....	....	....	....	....	....
1971-72	Tulsa Oilers	CHL	72	1	11	12	....	....	....	55	....	....	....	....	....	....	....	....	....	....	13	0	9	9	10	....	....	....
1972-73	**Toronto Maple Leafs**	**NHL**	40	0	3	3	0	2	2	26	0	0	0	22	0.0	31	0	32	7	6	....	....	....	....	....	....	....	....
	Tulsa Oilers	CHL	14	0	8	8	....	....	....	20	....	....	....	....	....	....	....	....	....	....	....	....	....	....	....	....	....	....
1973-74	Seattle Totems	WHL	52	2	14	16	....	....	....	32	....	....	....	....	....	....	....	....	....	....	....	....	....	....	....	....	....	....
1974-75	Seattle Totems	CHL	68	2	13	15	....	....	....	50	....	....	....	....	....	....	....	....	....	....	....	....	....	....	....	....	....	....
1975-76	Tulsa Oilers	CHL	76	7	29	36	....	....	....	36	....	....	....	....	....	....	....	....	....	....	9	1	3	4	6	....	....	....
	NHL Totals		41	0	3	3	0	2	2	26	0	0	0	23	0.0	34	0	32	7		....	....	....	....	....	....	....	....

CHL Second All-Star Team (1976)

Traded to **Vancouver** by **Toronto** with Murray Heatley for Dunc Wilson, May 29, 1973.

• McKAY, Randy

Hugh Randall RW – R. 6'2", 210 lbs. b: Montreal, Que., 1/25/1967. Detroit's 6th, 113th overall, in 1985.

Season	Club	League	GP	G	A	Pts	AG	AA	APts	PIM	PP	SH	GW	S	%	TGF	PGF	TGA	PGA	+/–	GP	G	A	Pts	PIM	PP	SH	GW
1983-84	Lac St-Louis Lions	QAAA	38	18	28	46	....	....	....	62	....	....	....	....	....	....	....	....	....	....	....	....	....	....	....	....	....	....
1984-85	Michigan Tech Huskies	WCHA	25	4	5	9	....	....	....	32	....	....	....	....	....	....	....	....	....	....	....	....	....	....	....	....	....	....
1985-86	Michigan Tech Huskies	WCHA	40	12	22	34	....	....	....	46	....	....	....	....	....	....	....	....	....	....	....	....	....	....	....	....	....	....
1986-87	Michigan Tech Huskies	WCHA	39	5	11	16	....	....	....	46	....	....	....	....	....	....	....	....	....	....	....	....	....	....	....	....	....	....
1987-88	Michigan Tech Huskies	WCHA	41	17	24	41	....	....	....	70	....	....	....	....	....	....	....	....	....	....	....	....	....	....	....	....	....	....
	Adirondack Red Wings	AHL	10	0	3	3	....	....	....	12	....	....	....	....	....	....	....	....	....	....	6	0	4	4	0	....	....	....
1988-89	**Detroit Red Wings**	**NHL**	3	0	0	0	0	0	0	0	0	0	0	2	0.0	1	0	2	0	–1	2	0	0	0	2	0	0	0
	Adirondack Red Wings	AHL	58	29	34	63	....	....	....	170	....	....	....	....	....	....	....	....	....	....	14	4	7	11	60	....	....	....
1989-90	**Detroit Red Wings**	**NHL**	33	3	6	9	3	4	7	51	0	0	0	33	9.1	17	0	16	0	1	....	....	....	....	....	....	....	....
	Adirondack Red Wings	AHL	36	16	23	39	....	....	....	99	....	....	....	....	....	....	....	....	....	....	6	3	0	3	35	....	....	....
1990-91	**Detroit Red Wings**	**NHL**	47	1	7	8	1	5	6	183	0	0	0	22	4.5	12	0	27	0	–15	5	0	1	1	41	0	0	0
1991-92	**New Jersey Devils**	**NHL**	80	17	16	33	15	12	27	246	2	0	1	111	15.3	47	4	43	6	6	7	1	3	4	10	1	0	0
1992-93	**New Jersey Devils**	**NHL**	73	11	11	22	9	8	17	206	1	0	2	94	11.7	31	1	40	10	0	5	0	0	0	16	0	0	0
1993-94	**New Jersey Devils**	**NHL**	78	12	15	27	11	12	23	244	0	0	1	77	15.6	41	0	17	0	24	20	1	2	3	24	0	0	0
1994-95♦	**New Jersey Devils**	**NHL**	33	5	7	12	9	10	19	44	0	0	0	44	11.4	20	3	7	0	10	19	8	4	12	11	2	0	2
1995-96	**New Jersey Devils**	**NHL**	76	11	10	21	11	8	19	145	3	0	3	97	11.3	39	9	23	0	7	....	....	....	....	....	....	....	....
1996-97	**New Jersey Devils**	**NHL**	77	9	18	27	10	16	26	109	0	0	2	92	9.8	42	5	22	0	15	10	1	1	2	0	0	0	0
1997-98	**New Jersey Devils**	**NHL**	74	24	24	48	28	24	52	86	8	0	5	141	17.0	70	19	21	0	30	6	0	1	1	0	0	0	0
1998-99	**New Jersey Devils**	**NHL**	70	17	20	37	20	19	39	143	3	0	5	136	12.5	63	19	34	0	10	7	3	2	5	2	0	0	1
99-2000♦	**New Jersey Devils**	**NHL**	67	16	23	39	18	21	39	80	3	0	4	116	13.8	66	17	41	0	8	23	0	6	6	9	0	0	0
	NHL Totals		711	126	157	283	135	139	274	1537	20	0	23	965	13.1	449	77	293	16		104	14	20	34	115	3	0	3

Transferred to **New Jersey** by **Detroit** with Dave Barr as compensation for Detroit's signing of free agent Troy Crowder, September 9, 1991.

• McKAY, Ray

Ray Owen D – L. 6'4", 183 lbs. b: Edmonton, Alta., 8/22/1946.

Season	Club	League	GP	G	A	Pts	AG	AA	APts	PIM	PP	SH	GW	S	%	TGF	PGF	TGA	PGA	+/–	GP	G	A	Pts	PIM	PP	SH	GW
1965-66	Moose Jaw Canucks	SJHL	57	3	20	23	....	....	....	103	....	....	....	....	....	....	....	....	....	....	5	0	2	2	8	....	....	....
1966-67	Moose Jaw Canucks	CMJHL	56	6	22	28	....	....	....	104	....	....	....	....	....	....	....	....	....	....	14	0	6	6	34	....	....	....
1967-68	Dallas Black Hawks	CPHL	58	2	5	7	....	....	....	68	....	....	....	....	....	....	....	....	....	....	5	0	0	0	9	....	....	....
1968-69	**Chicago Black Hawks**	**NHL**	9	0	1	1	0	1	1	12	0	0	0	4	0.0	8	0	5	0	3	....	....	....	....	....	....	....	....
	Dallas Black Hawks	CHL	61	4	13	17	....	....	....	164	....	....	....	....	....	....	....	....	....	....	....	....	....	....	....	....	....	....
1969-70	**Chicago Black Hawks**	**NHL**	17	0	0	0	0	0	0	23	0	0	0	7	0.0	2	0	12	2	–8	....	....	....	....	....	....	....	....
	Dallas Black Hawks	CHL	12	0	3	3	....	....	....	18	....	....	....	....	....	....	....	....	....	....	....	....	....	....	....	....	....	....
	Portland Buckaroos	WHL	....	....	....	....	....	....	....	....	....	....	....	....	....	....	....	....	....	....	2	0	0	0	25	....	....	....
1970-71	**Chicago Black Hawks**	**NHL**	2	0	0	0	0	0	0	0	0	0	0	1	0.0	0	0	0	0	0	....	....	....	....	....	....	....	....
	Portland Buckaroos	WHL	55	1	25	26	....	....	....	111	....	....	....	....	....	....	....	....	....	....	11	0	7	7	10	....	....	....
1971-72	**Buffalo Sabres**	**NHL**	39	0	3	3	0	3	3	18	0	0	0	18	0.0	9	0	32	11	–12	....	....	....	....	....	....	....	....
	Cincinnati Swords	AHL	14	1	4	5	....	....	....	39	....	....	....	....	....	....	....	....	....	....	10	0	4	4	36	....	....	....
1972-73	**Buffalo Sabres**	**NHL**	1	0	0	0	0	0	0	0	0	0	0	0	0.0	0	0	0	0	0	....	....	....	....	....	....	....	....
	Cincinnati Swords	AHL	70	5	32	37	....	....	....	123	....	....	....	....	....	....	....	....	....	....	15	0	8	8	49	....	....	....
1973-74	**California Golden Seals**	**NHL**	72	2	12	14	2	10	12	49	1	0	0	101	2.0	71	7	106	11	–31	....	....	....	....	....	....	....	....
1974-75	Edmonton Oilers	WHA	69	8	20	28	....	....	....	47	....	....	....	....	....	....	....	....	....	....	....	....	....	....	....	....	....	....
1975-76	Cleveland Crusaders	WHA	68	3	10	13	....	....	....	44	....	....	....	....	....	....	....	....	....	....	3	0	0	0	4	....	....	....
	Syracuse Blazers	NAHL	3	1	1	2	....	....	....	0	....	....	....	....	....	....	....	....	....	....	....	....	....	....	....	....	....	....
1976-77	Minnesota Fighting Saints	WHA	42	2	9	11	....	....	....	28	....	....	....	....	....	....	....	....	....	....	....	....	....	....	....	....	....	....
	Birmingham Bulls	WHA	19	0	1	1	....	....	....	11	....	....	....	....	....	....	....	....	....	....	....	....	....	....	....	....	....	....
1977-78	Edmonton Oilers	WHA	14	1	4	5	....	....	....	4	....	....	....	....	....	....	....	....	....	....	4	0	1	1	4	....	....	....
1978-79	Springfield Indians	AHL	69	2	27	29	....	....	....	42	....	....	....	....	....	....	....	....	....	....	....	....	....	....	....	....	....	....
1979-80	Adirondack Red Wings	AHL	5	0	0	0	....	....	....	27	....	....	....	....	....	....	....	....	....	....	....	....	....	....	....	....	....	....
	Hershey Bears	AHL	67	2	28	30	....	....	....	37	....	....	....	....	....	....	....	....	....	....	16	4	10	14	11	....	....	....
	NHL Totals		140	2	16	18	2	14	16	102	1	0	0	131	1.5	90	7	155	24		....	....	....	....	....	....	....	....
	Other Major League Totals		212	14	44	58	....	....	....	134	....	....	....	....	....	....	....	....	....	....	7	0	1	1	8	....	....	....

AHL First All-Star Team (1973) • Won Eddie Shore Award (Outstanding Defenseman - AHL) (1973)

Claimed by **Buffalo** from **Chicago** in Intra-League Draft, June 8, 1971. Selected by **Calgary-Cleveland** (WHA) in 1972 WHA General Player Draft, February 12, 1972. Claimed by **California** from **Buffalo** in Intra-League Draft, June 12, 1973. WHA rights traded to **Edmonton** (WHA) by **Cleveland** (WHA) for future considerations, June, 1974. Traded to **Cleveland** (WHA) by **Edmonton** (WHA) for Skip Krake, August, 1975. Transferred to **Minnesota** (WHA) after **Cleveland** (WHA) franchise relocated, July, 1976. Signed as a free agent by **Birmingham** (WHA) after **Minnesota** (WHA) franchise folded, January 27, 1977. Signed as a free agent by **Edmonton** (WHA), March, 1978.

• McKAY, Scott

Scott Gordon C – R. 5'11", 200 lbs. b: Burlington, Ont., 1/26/1972.

Season	Club	League	GP	G	A	Pts	AG	AA	APts	PIM	PP	SH	GW	S	%	TGF	PGF	TGA	PGA	+/–	GP	G	A	Pts	PIM	PP	SH	GW
1988-89	Burlington Comets	OJHL-B	25	19	25	44	....	....	....	40	....	....	....	....	....	....	....	....	....	....	....	....	....	....	....	....	....	....
1989-90	London Knights	OHL	59	20	29	49	....	....	....	37	....	....	....	....	....	....	....	....	....	....	5	1	1	2	12	....	....	....
1990-91	London Knights	OHL	62	29	40	69	....	....	....	29	....	....	....	....	....	....	....	....	....	....	7	4	2	6	6	....	....	....
1991-92	London Knights	OHL	64	30	45	75	....	....	....	97	....	....	....	....	....	....	....	....	....	....	10	3	8	11	8	....	....	....
1992-93	London Knights	OHL	63	38	57	95	....	....	....	49	....	....	....	....	....	....	....	....	....	....	12	1	14	15	6	....	....	....
1993-94	**Mighty Ducks of Anaheim**	**NHL**	1	0	0	0	0	0	0	0	0	0	0	1	0.0	0	0	0	0	0	....	....	....	....	....	....	....	....
	San Diego Gulls	IHL	58	10	6	16	....	....	....	35	....	....	....	....	....	....	....	....	....	....	9	2	5	7	6	....	....	....
1994-95	Greensboro Monarchs	ECHL	17	7	7	14	....	....	....	54	....	....	....	....	....	....	....	....	....	....	....	....	....	....	....	....	....	....
	San Diego Gulls	IHL	1	0	0	0	....	....	....	2	....	....	....	....	....	....	....	....	....	....	....	....	....	....	....	....	....	....
1995-96	Baltimore Bandits	AHL	16	1	0	1	....	....	....	6	....	....	....	....	....	....	....	....	....	....	....	....	....	....	....	....	....	....
	Raleigh IceCaps	ECHL	2	1	0	1	....	....	....	0	....	....	....	....	....	....	....	....	....	....	....	....	....	....	....	....	....	....

Season	Club	League	Regular Season GP	G	A	Pts	AG	AA	APts	PIM	PP	SH	GW	S	%	TGF	PGF	TGA	PGA	+/-	Playoffs GP	G	A	Pts	PIM	PP	SH	GW
1996-97	EC Graz	Alpenliga	17	6	7	13				16																		
	Port Huron Border Cats	ColHL	20	9	12	21				28																		
	Carolina Monarchs	AHL	30	1	9	10				2																		
1997-98	Louisiana IceGators	ECHL	48	20	16	36				55											9	2	3	5	4			
	NHL Totals		**1**	**0**	**0**	**0**	**0**	**0**	**0**	**0**	**0**	**0**	**0**	**1**	**0.0**	**0**	**0**	**0**	**0**									

Signed as a free agent by **Anaheim**, August 2, 1993.

• McKECHNIE, Walt

Walter Thomas John "McKetch" C – L. 6'2", 195 lbs. b: London, Ont., 6/19/1947. Toronto's 1st, 6th overall, in 1963.

Season	Club	League	GP	G	A	Pts	AG	AA	APts	PIM	PP	SH	GW	S	%	TGF	PGF	TGA	PGA	+/-	GP	G	A	Pts	PIM	PP	SH	GW
1964-65	London Diamonds	OHA-B	STATISTICS NOT AVAILABLE																									
1965-66	London Nationals	OHA-Jr.	46	13	28	41				68																		
1966-67	London Nationals	OHA-Jr.	48	13	46	59				125											6	7	10	17	2			
1967-68	London Nationals	OHA-Jr.	1	0	0	0				2																		
	Phoenix Roadrunners	WHL	67	24	30	54				24											4	1	1	2	2			
	Minnesota North Stars	**NHL**	**4**	**0**	**0**	**0**	**0**	**0**	**0**	**0**	**0**	**0**	**0**	**9**	**0.0**	**1**	**1**	**3**	**0**	**–3**	**9**	**3**	**2**	**5**	**0**	**0**	**0**	**0**
1968-69	**Minnesota North Stars**	**NHL**	**58**	**5**	**9**	**14**	**5**	**8**	**13**	**22**	**1**	**0**	**1**	**81**	**6.2**	**19**	**3**	**27**	**1**	**–10**								
	Phoenix Roadrunners	WHL	10	3	11	14				6																		
1969-70	**Minnesota North Stars**	**NHL**	**20**	**1**	**3**	**4**	**1**	**3**	**4**	**21**	**0**	**0**	**0**	**16**	**6.3**	**4**	**0**	**10**	**1**	**–5**								
	Iowa Stars	CHL	42	17	24	41				82											11	1	9	10	18			
1970-71	**Minnesota North Stars**	**NHL**	**30**	**3**	**1**	**4**	**3**	**1**	**4**	**34**	**0**	**0**	**0**	**39**	**7.7**	**7**	**2**	**13**	**1**	**–7**								
	Cleveland Barons	AHL	35	16	31	47				28											8	2	4	6	10			
1971-72	**California Golden Seals**	**NHL**	**56**	**11**	**20**	**31**	**11**	**17**	**28**	**40**	**2**	**1**	**1**	**111**	**9.9**	**50**	**11**	**44**	**7**	**2**								
1972-73	**California Golden Seals**	**NHL**	**78**	**16**	**38**	**54**	**15**	**30**	**45**	**58**	**4**	**1**	**0**	**182**	**8.8**	**86**	**20**	**123**	**31**	**–26**								
1973-74	**California Golden Seals**	**NHL**	**63**	**23**	**29**	**52**	**22**	**24**	**46**	**14**	**4**	**2**	**1**	**135**	**17.0**	**65**	**18**	**69**	**8**	**–14**								
1974-75	**Boston Bruins**	**NHL**	**53**	**3**	**3**	**6**	**3**	**2**	**5**	**8**	**0**	**1**	**0**	**36**	**8.3**	**15**	**2**	**33**	**14**	**–6**								
	Detroit Red Wings	**NHL**	**23**	**6**	**11**	**17**	**5**	**8**	**13**	**6**	**1**	**0**	**2**	**41**	**14.6**	**26**	**6**	**24**	**1**	**–3**								
1975-76	**Detroit Red Wings**	**NHL**	**80**	**26**	**56**	**82**	**23**	**42**	**65**	**85**	**2**	**3**	**7**	**186**	**14.0**	**110**	**30**	**112**	**41**	**9**								
1976-77	**Detroit Red Wings**	**NHL**	**80**	**25**	**34**	**59**	**23**	**26**	**49**	**50**	**3**	**3**	**1**	**189**	**13.2**	**78**	**24**	**110**	**32**	**–24**								
	Canada	WEC-A	10	1	6	7				28																		
1977-78	**Washington Capitals**	**NHL**	**16**	**4**	**1**	**5**	**4**	**1**	**5**	**0**	**1**	**0**	**0**	**24**	**16.7**	**7**	**2**	**20**	**1**	**–14**								
	Cleveland Barons	**NHL**	**53**	**12**	**22**	**34**	**11**	**17**	**28**	**12**	**2**	**0**	**0**	**97**	**12.4**	**45**	**11**	**67**	**25**	**–8**								
1978-79	**Toronto Maple Leafs**	**NHL**	**79**	**25**	**36**	**61**	**21**	**26**	**47**	**18**	**7**	**1**	**6**	**123**	**20.3**	**80**	**14**	**49**	**4**	**21**	**6**	**4**	**3**	**7**	**7**	**0**	**1**	**1**
1979-80	**Toronto Maple Leafs**	**NHL**	**54**	**7**	**36**	**43**	**6**	**26**	**32**	**4**	**1**	**0**	**0**	**77**	**9.1**	**71**	**32**	**73**	**28**	**–6**								
	Colorado Rockies	**NHL**	**17**	**0**	**4**	**4**	**0**	**3**	**3**	**2**	**0**	**0**	**0**	**35**	**0.0**	**7**	**4**	**23**	**6**	**–14**								
1980-81	**Colorado Rockies**	**NHL**	**53**	**15**	**23**	**38**	**12**	**15**	**27**	**18**	**2**	**2**	**2**	**92**	**16.3**	**68**	**22**	**82**	**29**	**–7**								
1981-82	**Detroit Red Wings**	**NHL**	**74**	**18**	**37**	**55**	**14**	**25**	**39**	**35**	**2**	**0**	**3**	**87**	**20.7**	**86**	**16**	**80**	**9**	**–1**								
1982-83	**Detroit Red Wings**	**NHL**	**64**	**14**	**29**	**43**	**11**	**20**	**31**	**42**	**3**	**3**	**0**	**73**	**19.2**	**57**	**12**	**80**	**36**	**1**								
1983-84	Salt Lake Golden Eagles	CHL	69	9	32	41				36																		
	NHL Totals		**955**	**214**	**392**	**606**	**190**	**294**	**484**	**469**	**35**	**17**	**24**	**1633**	**13.1**	**882**	**230**	**1042**	**275**		**15**	**7**	**5**	**12**	**7**	**0**	**1**	**1**

Won WHL Rookie of the Year Award (1968)

Traded to **Phoenix** (WHL) by **Toronto** for Steve Witiuk, October 15, 1967. Traded to **Minnesota** by **Phoenix** (WHL) for Leo Thiffault and Bob Charlebois, February 17, 1968. Traded to **California** by **Minnesota** with Joey Johnson for Dennis Hextall, May 20, 1971. Claimed by **NY Rangers** from **California** in Intra-League Draft, June 10, 1974. Traded to **Boston** by **NY Rangers** for Derek Sanderson, June 12, 1974. Traded to **Detroit** by **Boston** with Boston's 3rd round choice (Clarke Hamilton) in 1975 Amateur Draft for Hank Nowak and Earl Anderson, February 18, 1975. Traded to **Washington** by **Detroit** with Detroit's 3rd round choice (Jay Johnston) in 1978 Amateur Draft and 2nd round choice (Errol Rousse) in 1979 Amateur Draft for the rights to Ron Low and Washington's 3rd round choice (Borris Fistric) in 1979 Amateur Draft, August 17, 1977. Traded to **Cleveland** by **Washington** for Bob Girard and Cleveland's 2nd round choice (Paul McKinnon) in 1978 Amateur Draft, December 9, 1977. Placed on **Minnesota** Reserve List after **Cleveland-Minnesota** Dispersal Draft, June 15, 1978. Traded to **Toronto** by **Minnesota** for Toronto's 3rd round choice (Randy Velischek) in 1980 Entry Draft, October 5, 1978. Traded to **Colorado** by **Toronto** for Colorado's 3rd round choice (Fred Boimistruck) in 1980 Entry Draft, March 3, 1980. Signed as a free agent by **Detroit**, October 1, 1981.

• McKEE, Jay

D – L. 6'3", 195 lbs. b: Kingston, Ont., 9/8/1977. Buffalo's 1st, 14th overall, in 1995.

Season	Club	League	GP	G	A	Pts	AG	AA	APts	PIM	PP	SH	GW	S	%	TGF	PGF	TGA	PGA	+/-	GP	G	A	Pts	PIM	PP	SH	GW
1991-92	Kingston Voyageurs	OJHL	1	0	0	0				0																		
	Mimico Monarchs	OJHL	39	7	9	16				67																		
1992-93	Ernestown Jets	OJHL-C	36	0	17	17				37																		
	Kingston Voyageurs	OJHL	2	0	0	0				0																		
1993-94	Sudbury Wolves	OHL	51	0	1	1				51											3	0	0	0	0			
1994-95	Sudbury Wolves	OHL	39	6	6	12				91																		
	Niagara Falls Thunder	OHL	26	3	13	16				60											6	2	3	5	10			
1995-96	Niagara Falls Thunder	OHL	64	5	41	46				129											10	1	5	6	16			
	Buffalo Sabres	**NHL**	**1**	**0**	**1**	**1**	**0**	**1**	**1**	**2**	**0**	**0**	**0**	**2**	**0.0**	**2**	**0**	**1**	**0**	**1**								
	Rochester Americans	AHL	4	0	1	1				15																		
1996-97	**Buffalo Sabres**	**NHL**	**43**	**1**	**9**	**10**	**1**	**8**	**9**	**35**	**0**	**0**	**0**	**29**	**3.4**	**35**	**7**	**28**	**3**	**3**	**3**	**0**	**0**	**0**	**0**	**0**	**0**	**0**
	Rochester Americans	AHL	7	2	5	7				4																		
1997-98	**Buffalo Sabres**	**NHL**	**56**	**1**	**13**	**14**	**1**	**13**	**14**	**42**	**0**	**0**	**0**	**55**	**1.8**	**38**	**8**	**46**	**15**	**–1**	**1**	**0**	**0**	**0**	**0**	**0**	**0**	**0**
	Rochester Americans	AHL	13	1	7	8				11																		
1998-99	**Buffalo Sabres**	**NHL**	**72**	**0**	**6**	**6**	**0**	**6**	**6**	**75**	**0**	**0**	**0**	**57**	**0.0**	**52**	**4**	**45**	**17**	**20**	**21**	**0**	**3**	**3**	**24**	**0**	**0**	**0**
99-2000	**Buffalo Sabres**	**NHL**	**78**	**5**	**12**	**17**	**6**	**11**	**17**	**50**	**1**	**0**	**1**	**84**	**6.0**	**57**	**1**	**83**	**32**	**5**	**1**	**0**	**0**	**0**	**0**	**0**	**0**	**0**
	NHL Totals		**250**	**7**	**41**	**48**	**8**	**39**	**47**	**204**	**1**	**0**	**1**	**227**	**3.1**	**184**	**20**	**203**	**67**		**26**	**0**	**3**	**3**	**24**	**0**	**0**	**0**

OHL Second All-Star Team (1996)

• McKEE, Mike

LW – R. 6'3", 203 lbs. b: Toronto, Ont., 6/18/1969. Quebec's 1st, 1st overall, in 1990 Supplemental Draft.

Season	Club	League	GP	G	A	Pts	AG	AA	APts	PIM	PP	SH	GW	S	%	TGF	PGF	TGA	PGA	+/-	GP	G	A	Pts	PIM	PP	SH	GW
1987-88	Upper Canada College	Hi-School	STATISTICS NOT AVAILABLE																									
1988-89	Princeton University	ECAC	16	2	1	3				14																		
1989-90	Princeton University	ECAC	26	7	18	25				18																		
1990-91	Princeton University	ECAC	15	1	4	5				16																		
1991-92	Princeton University	ECAC	27	12	17	29				34																		
1992-93	Halifax Citadels	AHL	32	6	7	13				25																		
	Greensboro Monarchs	ECHL	7	1	3	4				6																		
1993-94	**Quebec Nordiques**	**NHL**	**48**	**3**	**12**	**15**	**3**	**9**	**12**	**41**	**2**	**0**	**0**	**60**	**5.0**	**50**	**13**	**35**	**3**	**5**								
	Cornwall Aces	AHL	24	6	14	20				18											10	0	3	3	4			
1994-95	Cornwall Aces	AHL	36	2	11	13				24																		
	NHL Totals		**48**	**3**	**12**	**15**	**3**	**9**	**12**	**41**	**2**	**0**	**0**	**60**	**5.0**	**50**	**13**	**35**	**3**									

ECAC Second All-Star Team (1990)

• McKEGNEY, Ian

Ian Robert D – L. 5'11", 165 lbs. b: Sarnia, Ont., 5/7/1947.

Season	Club	League	GP	G	A	Pts	AG	AA	APts	PIM	PP	SH	GW	S	%	TGF	PGF	TGA	PGA	+/-	GP	G	A	Pts	PIM	PP	SH	GW
1965-1967	Sarnia Legionaires	OHA-B	STATISTICS NOT AVAILABLE																									
1967-1970	University of Waterloo	OQAA	STATISTICS NOT AVAILABLE																									
1970-71	University of Waterloo	OUAA	15	2	12	14				15																		
1971-72	Lulea IF	Sweden-2	18	5	13	18																						
1972-73	Dallas Black Hawks	CHL	72	10	24	34				20											7	1	2	3	0			
1973-74	Dallas Black Hawks	CHL	65	1	27	28				18											10	2	4	6	4			
1974-75	Dallas Black Hawks	CHL	76	10	31	41				21											10	2	5	7	2			
1975-76	Dallas Black Hawks	CHL	76	3	29	32				20											10	3	2	5	0			

			REGULAR SEASON																		PLAYOFFS							
Season	Club	League	GP	G	A	Pts	AG	AA	APts	PIM	PP	SH	GW	S	%	TGF	PGF	TGA	PGA	+/–	GP	G	A	Pts	PIM	PP	SH	GW
1976-77	**Chicago Black Hawks**	**NHL**	**3**	**0**	**0**	**0**	**0**	**0**	**0**	**2**	**0**	**0**	**0**	**1**	**0.0**	**5**	**0**	**13**	**0**	**–8**								
	Dallas Black Hawks	CHL	61	6	22	28				18											5	1	1	2	0			
1977-78	Nova Scotia Voyageurs	AHL	12	0	5	5				0											11	1	4	5	7			
1978-79	IEV Innsbruck	Austria	33	13	19	32				27																		
	NHL Totals		**3**	**0**	**0**	**0**	**0**	**0**	**0**	**2**	**0**	**0**	**0**	**1**	**0.0**	**5**	**0**	**13**	**0**									

CHL Second All-Star Team (1973) • CHL First All-Star Team (1975, 1976) • Named CHL's Top Defenseman (1975, 1976) • Won Tommy Ivan Trophy (MVP - CHL) (1976)

Signed as a free agent by **Chicago**, September 30, 1972.

• McKEGNEY, Tony

Anthony Syiid LW – L. 6'th", 200 lbs. b: Montreal, Que., 2/15/1958. Buffalo's 2nd, 32nd overall, in 1978.

Season	Club	League	GP	G	A	Pts	AG	AA	APts	PIM	PP	SH	GW	S	%	TGF	PGF	TGA	PGA	+/–	GP	G	A	Pts	PIM	PP	SH	GW
1972-73	Sarnia Black Hawks	OMHA	STATISTICS NOT AVAILABLE																									
1973-74	Sarnia Jr. Bees	OHA-B	40	40	55	95																						
1974-75	Kingston Canadians	OMJHL	52	27	48	75				36											8	5	7	12	0			
1975-76	Kingston Canadians	OMJHL	65	24	56	80				20											7	5	6	11	2			
1976-77	Kingston Canadians	OMJHL	66	58	77	135				30											14	13	10	23	14			
1977-78	Kingston Canadians	OMJHL	55	43	49	92				19											5	3	3	6	0			
	Canada	WJC-A	6	2	6	8				0																		
1978-79	**Buffalo Sabres**	**NHL**	**52**	**8**	**14**	**22**	**7**	**10**	**17**	**10**	**0**	**0**	**1**	**67**	**11.9**	**32**	**4**	**30**	**0**	**–2**	**2**	**0**	**1**	**1**	**0**	**0**	**0**	**0**
	Hershey Bears	AHL	24	21	18	39				4											1	0	0	0	0			
1979-80	**Buffalo Sabres**	**NHL**	**80**	**23**	**29**	**52**	**20**	**21**	**41**	**24**	**1**	**0**	**6**	**140**	**16.4**	**77**	**4**	**33**	**0**	**40**	**14**	**3**	**4**	**7**	**2**	**0**	**0**	**0**
1980-81	**Buffalo Sabres**	**NHL**	**80**	**37**	**32**	**69**	**29**	**21**	**50**	**24**	**9**	**0**	**4**	**236**	**15.7**	**97**	**24**	**63**	**1**	**11**	**8**	**5**	**3**	**8**	**2**	**1**	**0**	**0**
1981-82	**Buffalo Sabres**	**NHL**	**73**	**23**	**29**	**52**	**18**	**19**	**37**	**41**	**8**	**0**	**0**	**187**	**12.3**	**71**	**21**	**62**	**0**	**–12**	**4**	**0**	**0**	**0**	**2**	**0**	**0**	**0**
1982-83	**Buffalo Sabres**	**NHL**	**78**	**36**	**37**	**73**	**30**	**26**	**56**	**18**	**10**	**0**	**2**	**180**	**20.0**	**96**	**23**	**76**	**5**	**2**	**10**	**3**	**1**	**4**	**4**	**1**	**0**	**2**
1983-84	**Quebec Nordiques**	**NHL**	**75**	**24**	**27**	**51**	**19**	**18**	**37**	**23**	**4**	**0**	**2**	**171**	**14.0**	**85**	**21**	**63**	**3**	**4**	**7**	**0**	**0**	**0**	**0**	**0**	**0**	**0**
1984-85	**Quebec Nordiques**	**NHL**	**30**	**12**	**9**	**21**	**10**	**6**	**16**	**12**	**1**	**3**	**1**	**85**	**14.1**	**30**	**4**	**33**	**9**	**2**								
	Minnesota North Stars	**NHL**	**27**	**11**	**13**	**24**	**9**	**9**	**18**	**4**	**2**	**0**	**1**	**81**	**13.6**	**36**	**8**	**29**	**10**	**9**	**9**	**8**	**6**	**14**	**0**	**2**	**0**	**1**
1985-86	**Minnesota North Stars**	**NHL**	**70**	**15**	**25**	**40**	**12**	**17**	**29**	**48**	**3**	**1**	**0**	**141**	**10.6**	**57**	**11**	**71**	**20**	**–5**	**5**	**2**	**1**	**3**	**22**	**0**	**0**	**0**
1986-87	**Minnesota North Stars**	**NHL**	**11**	**2**	**3**	**5**	**2**	**2**	**4**	**16**	**0**	**0**	**0**	**15**	**13.3**	**7**	**1**	**4**	**0**	**2**								
	New York Rangers	**NHL**	**64**	**29**	**17**	**46**	**25**	**12**	**37**	**56**	**7**	**2**	**6**	**166**	**17.5**	**68**	**16**	**55**	**2**	**–1**	**6**	**0**	**0**	**0**	**12**	**0**	**0**	**0**
1987-88	**St. Louis Blues**	**NHL**	**80**	**40**	**38**	**78**	**34**	**27**	**61**	**82**	**13**	**3**	**1**	**241**	**16.6**	**111**	**39**	**84**	**22**	**10**	**9**	**3**	**6**	**9**	**8**	**1**	**0**	**1**
1988-89	**St. Louis Blues**	**NHL**	**71**	**25**	**17**	**42**	**21**	**12**	**33**	**58**	**7**	**0**	**2**	**154**	**16.2**	**71**	**25**	**52**	**5**	**–1**	**3**	**0**	**1**	**1**	**0**	**0**	**0**	**0**
1989-90	**Detroit Red Wings**	**NHL**	**14**	**2**	**1**	**3**	**2**	**1**	**3**	**8**	**0**	**0**	**0**	**18**	**11.1**	**10**	**1**	**7**	**0**	**2**								
	Quebec Nordiques	**NHL**	**48**	**16**	**11**	**27**	**14**	**8**	**22**	**45**	**5**	**0**	**0**	**89**	**18.0**	**39**	**16**	**63**	**9**	**–31**								
1990-91	**Quebec Nordiques**	**NHL**	**50**	**17**	**16**	**33**	**16**	**12**	**28**	**44**	**7**	**0**	**2**	**111**	**15.3**	**58**	**28**	**55**	**0**	**–25**								
	Chicago Blackhawks	**NHL**	**9**	**0**	**1**	**1**	**0**	**1**	**1**	**4**	**0**	**0**	**0**	**10**	**0.0**	**3**	**1**	**5**	**1**	**–2**	**2**	**0**	**0**	**0**	**4**	**0**	**0**	**0**
1991-92	HC Varese	Alpenliga	17	18	14	32				55																		
	HC Varese	Italy	16	15	13	28				70											6	8	2	10	12			
	Canada	Nat-Team	3	2	2	4				6																		
1992-93	San Diego Gulls	IHL	23	8	5	13				38											3	0	1	1	4			
	NHL Totals		**912**	**320**	**319**	**639**	**268**	**222**	**490**	**517**	**77**	**9**	**28**	**2092**	**15.3**	**948**	**247**	**785**	**87**		**79**	**24**	**23**	**47**	**56**	**5**	**0**	**4**

OMJHL First All-Star Team (1977) • OMJHL Second All-Star Team (1978)

Traded to **Quebec** by **Buffalo** with Andre Savard, Jean Sauve and Buffalo's 3rd round choice (Iiro Jarvi) in 1983 Entry Draft for Real Cloutier and Quebec's 1st round choice (Adam Creighton) in 1983 Entry Draft, June 8, 1983. Traded to **Minnesota** by **Quebec** with Bo Berglund for Brad Maxwell and Brent Ashton, December 14, 1984. Traded to **NY Rangers** by **Minnesota** with Curt Giles and Minnesota's 2nd round choice (Troy Mallette) in 1988 Entry Draft for Bob Brooke and Minnesota's 4th round choice (previously acquired, Minnesota selected Jeffrey Stolp) in 1988 Entry Draft, November 13, 1986. Traded to **St. Louis** by **NY Rangers** with Rob Whistle for Bruce Bell and future considerations, May 28, 1987. Traded to **Detroit** by **St. Louis** with Bernie Federko for Adam Oates and Paul MacLean, June 15, 1989. Traded to **Quebec** by **Detroit** for Robert Picard and Greg C. Adams, December 4, 1989. Traded to **Chicago** by **Quebec** for Jacques Cloutier, January 29, 1991.

• McKENDRY, Alex

W – L. 6'4", 200 lbs. b: Midland, Ont., 11/21/1956. NY Islanders' 1st, 14th overall, in 1976.

Season	Club	League	GP	G	A	Pts	AG	AA	APts	PIM	PP	SH	GW	S	%	TGF	PGF	TGA	PGA	+/–	GP	G	A	Pts	PIM	PP	SH	GW
1973-74	Sudbury Wolves	OMJHL	61	4	8	12				173											4	0	1	1	0			
1974-75	Sudbury Wolves	OMJHL	57	19	34	53				181											15	5	8	13	29			
1975-76	Sudbury Wolves	OMJHL	65	43	59	102				121											16	4	8	12	15			
1976-77	Fort Worth Texans	CHL	65	7	14	21				80											6	0	2	2	4			
1977-78	**New York Islanders**	**NHL**	**4**	**0**	**0**	**0**	**0**	**0**	**0**	**2**	**0**	**0**	**0**	**7**	**0.0**	**1**	**0**	**1**	**0**	**0**								
	Fort Worth Texans	CHL	72	22	22	44				148											10	1	3	4	30			
1978-79	**New York Islanders**	**NHL**	**4**	**0**	**0**	**0**	**0**	**0**	**0**	**0**	**0**	**0**	**0**	**0**	**0.0**	**0**	**0**	**1**	**0**	**–1**								
	Fort Worth Texans	CHL	59	12	26	38				202											5	0	2	2	4			
1979-80♦	**New York Islanders**	**NHL**	**2**	**0**	**0**	**0**	**0**	**0**	**0**	**0**	**0**	**0**	**0**	**0**	**0.0**	**0**	**0**	**1**	**0**	**–1**	**6**	**2**	**2**	**4**	**0**	**0**	**0**	**0**
	Indianapolis Checkers	CHL	76	40	37	77				64											4	2	4	6	7			
1980-81	**Calgary Flames**	**NHL**	**36**	**3**	**6**	**9**	**2**	**4**	**6**	**19**	**0**	**0**	**0**	**30**	**10.0**	**17**	**1**	**22**	**0**	**–6**								
	Birmingham Bulls	CHL	10	1	5	6				23																		
	Fort Worth Texans	CHL	19	3	3	6				25											5	0	0	0	13			
1981-82	Oklahoma City Stars	CHL	80	27	57	86				163											4	1	1	2	9			
1982-83	Colorado Flames	CHL	72	25	42	67				44											5	0	2	2	4			
	NHL Totals		**46**	**3**	**6**	**9**	**2**	**4**	**6**	**21**	**0**	**0**	**0**	**37**	**8.1**	**18**	**1**	**25**	**0**		**6**	**2**	**2**	**4**	**0**	**0**	**0**	**0**

CHL First All-Star Team (1980)

Traded to **Calgary** by **NY Islanders** for Calgary's 3rd round choice (Ron Handy) in 1981 Entry Draft, October 9, 1980.

• McKENNA, Sean

Sean Michael RW – R. 6', 190 lbs. b: Asbestos, Que., 3/7/1962. Buffalo's 3rd, 56th overall, in 1980.

Season	Club	League	GP	G	A	Pts	AG	AA	APts	PIM	PP	SH	GW	S	%	TGF	PGF	TGA	PGA	+/–	GP	G	A	Pts	PIM	PP	SH	GW
1977-78	Asbestos Midget AAA	QAAA	STATISTICS NOT AVAILABLE																									
1978-79	Montreal Juniors	QMJHL	66	9	14	23				14																		
1979-80	Montreal Juniors	QMJHL	16	1	3	4				5																		
	Sherbrooke Beavers	QMJHL	43	19	16	35				19											15	7	7	14	9			
1980-81	Sherbrooke Beavers	QMJHL	71	57	47	104				122											14	9	9	18	12			
1981-82	Sherbrooke Beavers	QMJHL	59	57	33	90				29											22	*26	18	44	28			
	Buffalo Sabres	**NHL**	**3**	**0**	**1**	**1**	**0**	**1**	**1**	**2**	**0**	**0**	**0**	**6**	**0.0**	**4**	**0**	**1**	**0**	**3**								
	Sherbrooke Beavers	Mem-Cup	4	6	5	11				7																		
1982-83	**Buffalo Sabres**	**NHL**	**46**	**10**	**14**	**24**	**8**	**10**	**18**	**4**	**1**	**0**	**1**	**69**	**14.5**	**35**	**4**	**35**	**0**	**–4**								
	Rochester Americans	AHL	26	16	10	26				14											16	*14	8	22	18			
1983-84	**Buffalo Sabres**	**NHL**	**78**	**20**	**10**	**30**	**16**	**7**	**23**	**45**	**0**	**0**	**2**	**107**	**18.7**	**47**	**0**	**49**	**2**	**0**	**3**	**1**	**0**	**1**	**2**	**0**	**0**	**0**
1984-85	**Buffalo Sabres**	**NHL**	**65**	**20**	**16**	**36**	**16**	**11**	**27**	**41**	**2**	**0**	**0**	**109**	**18.3**	**49**	**6**	**49**	**0**	**–6**	**5**	**0**	**1**	**1**	**0**	**0**	**0**	**0**
1985-86	**Buffalo Sabres**	**NHL**	**45**	**6**	**12**	**18**	**5**	**8**	**13**	**28**	**1**	**0**	**2**	**83**	**7.2**	**32**	**5**	**41**	**6**	**–8**								
	Los Angeles Kings	**NHL**	**30**	**4**	**0**	**4**	**3**	**0**	**3**	**7**	**0**	**1**	**0**	**47**	**8.5**	**10**	**0**	**35**	**10**	**–15**								
1986-87	**Los Angeles Kings**	**NHL**	**69**	**14**	**19**	**33**	**12**	**14**	**26**	**10**	**0**	**1**	**0**	**102**	**13.7**	**52**	**3**	**69**	**31**	**11**	**5**	**0**	**1**	**1**	**0**	**0**	**0**	**0**
1987-88	**Los Angeles Kings**	**NHL**	**30**	**3**	**2**	**5**	**3**	**1**	**4**	**12**	**0**	**0**	**0**	**34**	**8.8**	**9**	**1**	**26**	**4**	**–14**								
	Toronto Maple Leafs	**NHL**	**40**	**5**	**5**	**10**	**4**	**4**	**8**	**12**	**0**	**0**	**1**	**46**	**10.9**	**18**	**0**	**30**	**1**	**–11**	**2**	**0**	**0**	**0**	**0**	**0**	**0**	**0**
1988-89	**Toronto Maple Leafs**	**NHL**	**3**	**0**	**1**	**1**	**0**	**1**	**1**	**0**	**0**	**0**	**0**	**1**	**0.0**	**1**	**0**	**3**	**1**	**–1**								
	Newmarket Saints	AHL	61	14	27	41				35											5	1	1	2	4			
1989-90	**Toronto Maple Leafs**	**NHL**	**5**	**0**	**0**	**0**	**0**	**0**	**0**	**20**	**0**	**0**	**0**	**6**	**0.0**	**0**	**0**	**3**	**0**	**–3**								
	Newmarket Saints	AHL	73	17	17	34				30																		
1990-91	SC Rapperswil-Jona	Switz-2	STATISTICS NOT AVAILABLE																									
1991-1996			OUT OF HOCKEY – RETIRED																									
1996-97	Windsor Papetiers	QSPHL	4	0	1	1				17																		
	NHL Totals		**414**	**82**	**80**	**162**	**67**	**57**	**124**	**181**	**4**	**2**	**6**	**610**	**13.4**	**257**	**19**	**341**	**55**		**15**	**1**	**2**	**3**	**2**	**0**	**0**	**0**

QMJHL First All-Star Team (1981) • QMJHL Second All-Star Team (1982) • Memorial Cup All-Star Team (1982) • Won Stafford Smythe Memorial Trophy (Memorial Cup Tournament MVP) (1982)

Traded to **LA Kings** by **Buffalo** with Larry Playfair and Ken Baumgartner for Brian Engblom and Doug Smith, Januray 30, 1986. Traded to **Toronto** by **LA Kings** for Mike Allison, December 14, 1987.

Season	Club	League	REGULAR SEASON																		PLAYOFFS							
Season	Club	League	GP	G	A	Pts	AG	AA	APts	PIM	PP	SH	GW	S	%	TGF	PGF	TGA	PGA	+/-	GP	G	A	Pts	PIM	PP	SH	GW

• McKENNA, Steve "Stretch" LW – L. 6'8", 255 lbs. b: Toronto, Ont., 8/21/1973.

Season	Club	League	GP	G	A	Pts	AG	AA	APts	PIM	PP	SH	GW	S	%	TGF	PGF	TGA	PGA	+/-	GP	G	A	Pts	PIM	PP	SH	GW
1990-91	Mass-Central Outlaws	MBHL	STATISTICS NOT AVAILABLE																									
1991-92	Cambridge Winterhawks	OJHL-B	48	21	23	44	....	....	....	173	....	....	....	....	....	....	....	....	....	....	....	....	....	....	....	....	....	....
1992-93	Notre Dame Hounds	SJHL	STATISTICS NOT AVAILABLE																									
1993-94	Merrimack College	H-East	37	1	2	3	....	....	....	74	....	....	....	....	....	....	....	....	....	....	....	....	....	....	....	....	....	....
1994-95	Merrimack College	H-East	37	1	9	10	....	....	....	74	....	....	....	....	....	....	....	....	....	....	....	....	....	....	....	....	....	....
1995-96	Merrimack College	H-East	33	3	11	14	....	....	....	67	....	....	....	....	....	....	....	....	....	....	....	....	....	....	....	....	....	....
1996-97	**Los Angeles Kings**	**NHL**	**9**	**0**	**0**	**0**	**0**	**0**	**0**	**37**	**0**	**0**	**0**	**6**	**0.0**	**2**	**0**	**1**	**0**	**1**	....	....	....	....	....	....	....	....
	Phoenix Roadrunners	IHL	66	6	5	11	....	....	....	187	....	....	....	....	....	....	....	....	....	....	....	....	....	....	....	....	....	....
1997-98	**Los Angeles Kings**	**NHL**	**62**	**4**	**4**	**8**	**5**	**4**	**9**	**150**	**1**	**0**	**0**	**42**	**9.5**	**14**	**1**	**25**	**3**	**-9**	**3**	**0**	**1**	**1**	**8**	**0**	**0**	**0**
	Fredericton Canadiens	AHL	6	2	1	3	....	....	....	48	....	....	....	....	....	....	....	....	....	....	....	....	....	....	....	....	....	....
1998-99	**Los Angeles Kings**	**NHL**	**20**	**1**	**0**	**1**	**1**	**0**	**1**	**36**	**0**	**0**	**0**	**12**	**8.3**	**4**	**0**	**7**	**0**	**-3**	....	....	....	....	....	....	....	....
99-2000	**Los Angeles Kings**	**NHL**	**46**	**0**	**5**	**5**	**0**	**5**	**5**	**125**	**0**	**0**	**0**	**14**	**0.0**	**9**	**0**	**6**	**0**	**3**	....	....	....	....	....	....	....	....
	NHL Totals		**137**	**5**	**9**	**14**	**6**	**9**	**15**	**348**	**1**	**0**	**0**	**74**	**6.8**	**29**	**1**	**39**	**3**		**3**	**0**	**1**	**1**	**8**	**0**	**0**	**0**

Signed as a free agent by **LA Kings**, May 23, 1996. Selected by **Minnesota** from **LA Kings** in Expansion Draft, June 23, 2000.

• McKENNEY, Don Donald Hamilton "Slip" C – L. 5'11", 160 lbs. b: Smiths Falls, Ont., 4/30/1934.

Season	Club	League	GP	G	A	Pts	AG	AA	APts	PIM	PP	SH	GW	S	%	TGF	PGF	TGA	PGA	+/-	GP	G	A	Pts	PIM	PP	SH	GW
1950-51	Barrie Flyers	OHA-Jr.	4	0	2	2	....	....	....	6	....	....	....	....	....	....	....	....	....	....	....	....	....	....	....	....	....	....
1951-52	Barrie Flyers	OHA-Jr.	52	32	39	71	....	....	....	24	....	....	....	....	....	....	....	....	....	....	....	....	....	....	....	....	....	....
1952-53	Barrie Flyers	OHA-Jr.	50	33	33	66	....	....	....	24	....	....	....	....	....	....	....	....	....	....	15	6	8	14	2	....	....	....
	Barrie Flyers	Mem-Cup	10	9	12	21	....	....	....	4	....	....	....	....	....	....	....	....	....	....	....	....	....	....	....	....	....	....
1953-54	Hershey Bears	AHL	54	13	21	34	....	....	....	4	....	....	....	....	....	....	....	....	....	....	11	3	5	8	4	....	....	....
1954-55	**Boston Bruins**	**NHL**	**69**	**22**	**20**	**42**	**29**	**23**	**52**	**34**	....	....	....	....	....	....	....	....	....	....	**5**	**1**	**2**	**3**	**4**	....	....	....
1955-56	**Boston Bruins**	**NHL**	**65**	**10**	**24**	**34**	**14**	**29**	**43**	**20**	....	....	....	....	....	....	....	....	....	....	....	....	....	....	....	....	....	....
1956-57	**Boston Bruins**	**NHL**	**69**	**21**	**39**	**60**	**27**	**43**	**70**	**31**	....	....	....	....	....	....	....	....	....	....	**10**	**1**	**5**	**6**	**4**	....	....	....
1957-58	**Boston Bruins**	**NHL**	**70**	**28**	**30**	**58**	**35**	**31**	**66**	**22**	....	....	....	....	....	....	....	....	....	....	**12**	**9**	**8**	**17**	**0**	....	....	....
1958-59	**Boston Bruins**	**NHL**	**70**	**32**	**30**	**62**	**39**	**30**	**69**	**20**	....	....	....	....	....	....	....	....	....	....	**7**	**2**	**5**	**7**	**0**	....	....	....
1959-60	**Boston Bruins**	**NHL**	**70**	**20**	***49**	**69**	**23**	**48**	**71**	**28**	....	....	....	....	....	....	....	....	....	....	....	....	....	....	....	....	....	....
1960-61	**Boston Bruins**	**NHL**	**68**	**26**	**23**	**49**	**30**	**22**	**52**	**22**	....	....	....	....	....	....	....	....	....	....	....	....	....	....	....	....	....	....
1961-62	**Boston Bruins**	**NHL**	**70**	**22**	**33**	**55**	**25**	**32**	**57**	**10**	....	....	....	....	....	....	....	....	....	....	....	....	....	....	....	....	....	....
1962-63	**Boston Bruins**	**NHL**	**41**	**14**	**19**	**33**	**16**	**19**	**35**	**2**	....	....	....	....	....	....	....	....	....	....	....	....	....	....	....	....	....	....
	New York Rangers	**NHL**	**21**	**8**	**16**	**24**	**9**	**16**	**25**	**4**	....	....	....	....	....	....	....	....	....	....	....	....	....	....	....	....	....	....
1963-64	**New York Rangers**	**NHL**	**55**	**9**	**17**	**26**	**11**	**18**	**29**	**6**	....	....	....	....	....	....	....	....	....	....	....	....	....	....	....	....	....	....
♦	**Toronto Maple Leafs**	**NHL**	**15**	**9**	**6**	**15**	**11**	**6**	**17**	**2**	....	....	....	....	....	....	....	....	....	....	**12**	**4**	**8**	**12**	**0**	....	....	....
1964-65	**Toronto Maple Leafs**	**NHL**	**52**	**6**	**13**	**19**	**7**	**13**	**20**	**6**	....	....	....	....	....	....	....	....	....	....	**6**	**0**	**0**	**0**	**0**	....	....	....
	Rochester Americans	AHL	18	7	9	16	....	....	....	4	....	....	....	....	....	....	....	....	....	....	....	....	....	....	....	....	....	....
1965-66	**Detroit Red Wings**	**NHL**	**24**	**1**	**6**	**7**	**1**	**6**	**7**	**0**	....	....	....	....	....	....	....	....	....	....	....	....	....	....	....	....	....	....
	Pittsburgh Hornets	AHL	37	11	19	30	....	....	....	8	....	....	....	....	....	....	....	....	....	....	3	0	1	1	0	....	....	....
1966-67	Pittsburgh Hornets	AHL	67	26	36	62	....	....	....	16	....	....	....	....	....	....	....	....	....	....	9	2	7	9	2	....	....	....
1967-68	**St. Louis Blues**	**NHL**	**39**	**9**	**20**	**29**	**10**	**20**	**30**	**4**	**1**	**0**	**1**	**93**	**9.7**	**45**	**15**	**29**	**0**	**1**	**6**	**1**	**1**	**2**	**2**	**0**	**0**	**0**
	Kansas City Blues	CPHL	11	9	6	15	....	....	....	5	....	....	....	....	....	....	....	....	....	....	1	0	0	0	0	....	....	....
1968-69	Providence Reds	AHL	74	26	48	74	....	....	....	12	....	....	....	....	....	....	....	....	....	....	9	4	7	11	0	....	....	....
1969-70	Providence Reds	AHL	31	3	12	15	....	....	....	2	....	....	....	....	....	....	....	....	....	....	....	....	....	....	....	....	....	....
	NHL Totals		**798**	**237**	**345**	**582**	**287**	**356**	**643**	**211**	....	....	....	....	....	....	....	....	....	....	**58**	**18**	**29**	**47**	**10**	....	....	....

Won Lady Byng Trophy (1960) • Played in NHL All-Star Game (1957, 1958, 1959, 1960, 1961, 1962, 1964)

Traded to **NY Rangers** by **Boston** with Dick Meissner for Dean Prentice, February 4, 1963. • Terms of transaction stipulated that Meissner would report to the NY Rangers following the 1962-63 season. Traded to **Toronto** by **NY Rangers** with Andy Bathgate for Dick Duff, Rod Seiling, Bill Collins, Bob Nevin and Arnie Brown, February 22, 1964. Claimed on waivers by **Detroit** from **Toronto**, June 8, 1965. Claimed by **St. Louis** from **Detroit** in Expansion Draft, June 6, 1967.

• McKENNY, Jim James Claude "Howie" D – R. 5'11", 192 lbs. b: Ottawa, Ont., 12/1/1946. Toronto's 3rd, 17th overall, in 1963.

Season	Club	League	GP	G	A	Pts	AG	AA	APts	PIM	PP	SH	GW	S	%	TGF	PGF	TGA	PGA	+/-	GP	G	A	Pts	PIM	PP	SH	GW
1962-63	Neil McNeil Maroons	MTJHL	37	5	12	17	....	....	....	43	....	....	....	....	....	....	....	....	....	....	10	3	3	6	10	....	....	....
	Neil McNeil Maroons	Mem-Cup	6	1	1	2	....	....	....	8	....	....	....	....	....	....	....	....	....	....	....	....	....	....	....	....	....	....
1963-64	Toronto Marlboros	OHA-Jr.	56	7	31	38	....	....	....	102	....	....	....	....	....	....	....	....	....	....	9	2	0	2	22	....	....	....
	Toronto Marlboros	Mem-Cup	12	1	7	8	....	....	....	22	....	....	....	....	....	....	....	....	....	....	....	....	....	....	....	....	....	....
1964-65	Toronto Marlboros	OHA-Jr.	52	7	41	48	....	....	....	117	....	....	....	....	....	....	....	....	....	....	19	4	15	19	43	....	....	....
1965-66	Toronto Marlboros	OHA-Jr.	42	14	26	40	....	....	....	78	....	....	....	....	....	....	....	....	....	....	14	3	10	13	38	....	....	....
	Toronto Maple Leafs	**NHL**	**2**	**0**	**0**	**0**	**0**	**0**	**0**	**2**	....	....	....	....	....	....	....	....	....	....	....	....	....	....	....	....	....	....
	Rochester Americans	AHL	1	0	1	1	....	....	....	0	....	....	....	....	....	....	....	....	....	....	....	....	....	....	....	....	....	....
	Tulsa Oilers	CPHL	....	....	....	....	....	....	....	....	....	....	....	....	....	....	....	....	....	....	4	2	2	4	2	....	....	....
1966-67	**Toronto Maple Leafs**	**NHL**	**6**	**1**	**0**	**1**	**1**	**0**	**1**	**0**	....	....	....	....	....	....	....	....	....	....	....	....	....	....	....	....	....	....
	Tulsa Oilers	CPHL	45	9	19	28	....	....	....	29	....	....	....	....	....	....	....	....	....	....	....	....	....	....	....	....	....	....
	Rochester Americans	AHL	19	3	6	9	....	....	....	10	....	....	....	....	....	....	....	....	....	....	7	0	0	0	2	....	....	....
1967-68	**Toronto Maple Leafs**	**NHL**	**5**	**1**	**0**	**1**	**1**	**0**	**1**	**0**	**1**	**0**	**1**	**2**	**50.0**	**1**	**1**	**2**	**0**	**-2**	....	....	....	....	....	....	....	....
	Rochester Americans	AHL	46	10	22	32	....	....	....	33	....	....	....	....	....	....	....	....	....	....	11	2	2	4	4	....	....	....
1968-69	**Toronto Maple Leafs**	**NHL**	**7**	**0**	**0**	**0**	**0**	**0**	**0**	**2**	**0**	**0**	**0**	**5**	**0.0**	**5**	**2**	**3**	**1**	**1**	....	....	....	....	....	....	....	....
	Rochester Americans	AHL	47	19	31	50	....	....	....	22	....	....	....	....	....	....	....	....	....	....	....	....	....	....	....	....	....	....
	Vancouver Canucks	WHL	18	7	14	21	....	....	....	4	....	....	....	....	....	....	....	....	....	....	8	5	5	10	6	....	....	....
1969-70	**Toronto Maple Leafs**	**NHL**	**73**	**11**	**33**	**44**	**12**	**31**	**43**	**34**	**3**	**0**	**0**	**170**	**6.5**	**104**	**29**	**95**	**18**	**-2**	....	....	....	....	....	....	....	....
1970-71	**Toronto Maple Leafs**	**NHL**	**68**	**4**	**26**	**30**	**4**	**22**	**26**	**42**	**2**	**1**	**1**	**131**	**3.1**	**85**	**21**	**68**	**15**	**11**	**6**	**2**	**1**	**3**	**2**	**1**	**0**	**0**
1971-72	**Toronto Maple Leafs**	**NHL**	**76**	**5**	**31**	**36**	**5**	**27**	**32**	**27**	**2**	**0**	**0**	**156**	**3.2**	**86**	**27**	**73**	**15**	**1**	**5**	**3**	**0**	**3**	**2**	**2**	**1**	**0**
1972-73	**Toronto Maple Leafs**	**NHL**	**77**	**11**	**41**	**52**	**10**	**33**	**43**	**55**	**5**	**0**	**0**	**208**	**5.3**	**148**	**31**	**145**	**34**	**6**	....	....	....	....	....	....	....	....
1973-74	**Toronto Maple Leafs**	**NHL**	**77**	**14**	**28**	**42**	**13**	**23**	**36**	**36**	**3**	**0**	**1**	**129**	**10.9**	**111**	**21**	**99**	**25**	**16**	**4**	**0**	**2**	**2**	**0**	**0**	**0**	**0**
1974-75	**Toronto Maple Leafs**	**NHL**	**66**	**8**	**35**	**43**	**7**	**26**	**33**	**31**	**0**	**1**	**1**	**105**	**7.6**	**106**	**30**	**98**	**18**	**-4**	**7**	**0**	**1**	**1**	**2**	**0**	**0**	**0**
1975-76	**Toronto Maple Leafs**	**NHL**	**46**	**10**	**19**	**29**	**9**	**14**	**23**	**19**	**4**	**0**	**0**	**76**	**13.2**	**44**	**14**	**42**	**5**	**-7**	**6**	**2**	**3**	**5**	**2**	**1**	**0**	**1**
1976-77	**Toronto Maple Leafs**	**NHL**	**76**	**14**	**31**	**45**	**13**	**24**	**37**	**36**	**3**	**0**	**3**	**115**	**12.2**	**80**	**13**	**111**	**18**	**-26**	**9**	**0**	**2**	**2**	**2**	**0**	**0**	**0**
1977-78	**Toronto Maple Leafs**	**NHL**	**15**	**2**	**2**	**4**	**2**	**2**	**4**	**8**	**0**	**0**	**0**	**12**	**16.7**	**9**	**2**	**3**	**0**	**4**	....	....	....	....	....	....	....	....
	Dallas Black Hawks	CHL	55	21	31	52	....	....	....	45	....	....	....	....	....	....	....	....	....	....	13	1	6	7	8	....	....	....
1978-79	**Minnesota North Stars**	**NHL**	**10**	**1**	**1**	**2**	**1**	**1**	**2**	**2**	**1**	**0**	**0**	**8**	**12.5**	**5**	**2**	**7**	**1**	**-3**	....	....	....	....	....	....	....	....
	Oklahoma City Stars	CHL	33	11	23	34	....	....	....	10	....	....	....	....	....	....	....	....	....	....	....	....	....	....	....	....	....	....
1979-80	SC Rapperswil-Jona	Switz-2	STATISTICS NOT AVAILABLE																									
	HC Lyon	France	STATISTICS NOT AVAILABLE																									
	NHL Totals		**604**	**82**	**247**	**329**	**78**	**203**	**281**	**294**	....	....	....	....	....	....	....	....	....	....	**37**	**7**	**9**	**16**	**10**	....	....	....

CHL Second All-Star Team (1978) • Played in NHL All-Star Game (1974)

Traded to **Minnesota** by **Toronto** for cash and future considerations (the rights to Owen Lloyd, October 25, 1978), May 15, 1978.

• McKENZIE, Brian Brian Stewart LW – L. 5'10", 165 lbs. b: St. Catharines, Ont., 3/16/1951. Pittsburgh's 1st, 18th overall, in 1971.

Season	Club	League	GP	G	A	Pts	AG	AA	APts	PIM	PP	SH	GW	S	%	TGF	PGF	TGA	PGA	+/-	GP	G	A	Pts	PIM	PP	SH	GW
1967-68	Stamford Steamers	OHA-B	STATISTICS NOT AVAILABLE																									
1968-69	St. Catharines Black Hawks	OHA-Jr.	54	10	21	31	....	....	....	70	....	....	....	....	....	....	....	....	....	....	18	5	5	10	29	....	....	....
1969-70	St. Catharines Black Hawks	OHA-Jr.	53	17	41	58	....	....	....	128	....	....	....	....	....	....	....	....	....	....	10	3	4	7	20	....	....	....
1970-71	St. Catharines Black Hawks	OHA-Jr.	60	39	*85	124	....	....	....	108	....	....	....	....	....	....	....	....	....	....	15	3	17	20	10	....	....	....
1971-72	**Pittsburgh Penguins**	**NHL**	**6**	**1**	**1**	**2**	**1**	**1**	**2**	**4**	**0**	**0**	**0**	**8**	**12.5**	**3**	**1**	**4**	**0**	**-2**	....	....	....	....	....	....	....	....
	Hershey Bears	AHL	66	15	13	28	....	....	....	92	....	....	....	....	....	....	....	....	....	....	4	0	0	0	0	....	....	....
1972-73	Hershey Bears	AHL	3	0	2	2	....	....	....	16	....	....	....	....	....	....	....	....	....	....	....	....	....	....	....	....	....	....
	Omaha Knights	CHL	64	16	36	52	....	....	....	71	....	....	....	....	....	....	....	....	....	....	9	5	4	9	28	....	....	....
1973-74	Edmonton Oilers	WHA	78	18	20	38	....	....	....	66	....	....	....	....	....	....	....	....	....	....	5	0	1	1	0	....	....	....
1974-75	Mohawk Valley Comets	NAHL	55	28	37	65	....	....	....	37	....	....	....	....	....	....	....	....	....	....	....	....	....	....	....	....	....	....
	Indianapolis Racers	WHA	9	1	0	1	....	....	....	6	....	....	....	....	....	....	....	....	....	....	....	....	....	....	....	....	....	....
1975-76	Mohawk Valley Comets	NAHL	20	10	14	24	....	....	....	24	....	....	....	....	....	....	....	....	....	....	....	....	....	....	....	....	....	....
	Toledo Goaldiggers	IHL	42	12	19	31	....	....	....	64	....	....	....	....	....	....	....	....	....	....	4	2	3	5	2	....	....	....

			REGULAR SEASON																		PLAYOFFS							
Season	Club	League	GP	G	A	Pts	AG	AA	APts	PIM	PP	SH	GW	S	%	TGF	PGF	TGA	PGA	+/-	GP	G	A	Pts	PIM	PP	SH	GW
1976-77	Toledo Goaldiggers	IHL	77	32	58	90				85											15	9	5	14	10			
1977-78	Toledo Goaldiggers	IHL	2	0	0	0				0																		
	Milwaukee Admirals	IHL	15	2	9	11				18																		
	NHL Totals		**6**	**1**	**1**	**2**	**1**	**1**	**2**	**4**	**0**	**0**	**0**	**8**	**12.5**	**3**	**1**	**4**	**0**									
	Other Major League Totals		87	19	20	39				72											5	0	1	1	0			

Selected by **Ontario-Ottawa** (WHA) in 1972 WHA General Player Draft, February 12, 1972. Traded to **Atlanta** by **Pittsburgh** for cash, October, 1972. Selected by **Edmonton** (WHA) in 1973 WHA Professional Player Draft, May, 1973. Claimed by **Indianapolis** (WHA) from **Edmonton** (WHA) in 1974 WHA Expansion Draft, May, 1974. Signed as a free agent by **Toledo** (IHL), December, 1975.

• McKENZIE, Jim

LW – L. 6'3", 229 lbs. b: Gull Lake, Sask., 11/3/1969. Hartford's 3rd, 73rd overall, in 1989.

Season	Club	League	GP	G	A	Pts	AG	AA	APts	PIM	PP	SH	GW	S	%	TGF	PGF	TGA	PGA	+/-	GP	G	A	Pts	PIM	PP	SH	GW
1985-86	Moose Jaw Midget Warriors	SAHA	36	18	26	44				89																		
	Moose Jaw Warriors	WHL	3	0	2	2				0																		
1986-87	Moose Jaw Warriors	WHL	65	5	3	8				125											9	0	0	0	7			
1987-88	Moose Jaw Warriors	WHL	62	1	17	18				134																		
1988-89	Victoria Cougars	WHL	67	15	27	42				176											8	1	4	5	30			
1989-90	**Hartford Whalers**	**NHL**	**5**	**0**	**0**	**0**	**0**	**0**	**0**	**4**	**0**	**0**	**0**	**0**	**0.0**	**0**	**0**	**0**	**0**	**0**								
	Binghamton Whalers	AHL	56	4	12	16				149																		
1990-91	**Hartford Whalers**	**NHL**	**41**	**4**	**3**	**7**	**4**	**2**	**6**	**108**	**0**	**0**	**0**	**16**	**25.0**	**9**	**0**	**16**	**0**	**–7**	**6**	**0**	**0**	**0**	**8**	**0**	**0**	**0**
	Springfield Indians	AHL	24	3	4	7				102																		
1991-92	**Hartford Whalers**	**NHL**	**67**	**5**	**1**	**6**	**5**	**1**	**6**	**87**	**0**	**0**	**0**	**34**	**14.7**	**11**	**0**	**17**	**0**	**–6**								
1992-93	**Hartford Whalers**	**NHL**	**64**	**3**	**6**	**9**	**2**	**4**	**6**	**202**	**0**	**0**	**0**	**36**	**8.3**	**19**	**0**	**29**	**0**	**–10**								
1993-94	**Hartford Whalers**	**NHL**	**26**	**1**	**2**	**3**	**1**	**2**	**3**	**67**	**0**	**0**	**0**	**9**	**11.1**	**5**	**2**	**10**	**1**	**–6**								
	Dallas Stars	**NHL**	**34**	**2**	**3**	**5**	**2**	**2**	**4**	**63**	**0**	**0**	**1**	**18**	**11.1**	**10**	**0**	**6**	**0**	**4**								
	Pittsburgh Penguins	**NHL**	**11**	**0**	**0**	**0**	**0**	**0**	**0**	**16**	**0**	**0**	**0**	**6**	**0.0**	**0**	**0**	**5**	**0**	**–5**	**3**	**0**	**0**	**0**	**0**	**0**	**0**	**0**
1994-95	**Pittsburgh Penguins**	**NHL**	**39**	**2**	**1**	**3**	**4**	**1**	**5**	**63**	**0**	**0**	**1**	**16**	**12.5**	**8**	**1**	**14**	**0**	**–7**	**5**	**0**	**0**	**0**	**4**	**0**	**0**	**0**
1995-96	**Winnipeg Jets**	**NHL**	**73**	**4**	**2**	**6**	**4**	**2**	**6**	**202**	**0**	**0**	**0**	**28**	**14.3**	**9**	**0**	**13**	**0**	**–4**	**1**	**0**	**0**	**0**	**2**	**0**	**0**	**0**
1996-97	**Phoenix Coyotes**	**NHL**	**65**	**5**	**3**	**8**	**5**	**3**	**8**	**200**	**0**	**0**	**1**	**38**	**13.2**	**12**	**0**	**17**	**0**	**–5**	**7**	**0**	**0**	**0**	**2**	**0**	**0**	**0**
1997-98	**Phoenix Coyotes**	**NHL**	**64**	**3**	**4**	**7**	**4**	**4**	**8**	**146**	**0**	**0**	**0**	**35**	**8.6**	**17**	**0**	**24**	**0**	**–7**	**1**	**0**	**0**	**0**	**0**	**0**	**0**	**0**
1998-99	**Mighty Ducks of Anaheim**	**NHL**	**73**	**5**	**4**	**9**	**6**	**4**	**10**	**99**	**1**	**0**	**1**	**59**	**8.5**	**15**	**4**	**29**	**0**	**–18**	**4**	**0**	**0**	**0**	**4**	**0**	**0**	**0**
99-2000	**Mighty Ducks of Anaheim**	**NHL**	**31**	**3**	**3**	**6**	**3**	**3**	**6**	**48**	**0**	**0**	**0**	**22**	**13.6**	**9**	**0**	**14**	**0**	**–5**								
	Washington Capitals	**NHL**	**30**	**1**	**2**	**3**	**1**	**2**	**3**	**16**	**0**	**0**	**0**	**10**	**10.0**	**5**	**0**	**5**	**0**	**0**	**1**	**0**	**0**	**0**	**0**	**0**	**0**	**0**
	NHL Totals		**623**	**38**	**34**	**72**	**41**	**30**	**71**	**1321**	**1**	**0**	**4**	**327**	**11.6**	**129**	**7**	**199**	**1**		**28**	**0**	**0**	**0**	**20**	**0**	**0**	**0**

Traded to **Florida** by **Hartford** for Alexander Godynyuk, December 16, 1993. Traded to **Dallas** by **Florida** for Dallas' 4th round choice (later traded to Ottawa — Ottawa selected Kevin Bolibruck) in 1995 Entry Draft, December 16, 1993. Traded to **Pittsburgh** by **Dallas** for Mike Needham, March 21, 1994. Signed as a free agent by **NY Islanders**, August 2, 1995. Claimed by **Winnipeg** from **NY Islanders** in NHL Waiver Draft, October 2, 1995. Transferred to **Phoenix** after **Winnipeg** franchise relocated, July 1, 1996. Traded to **Anaheim** by **Phoenix** for J.F. Jomphe, June 18, 1998. Claimed on waivers by **Washington** from **Anaheim**, January 20, 2000. Signed as a free agent by **New Jersey**, July 3, 2000.

• McKENZIE, John

John Albert "Pie" RW – R. 5'9", 175 lbs. b: High River, Alta., 12/12/1937.

Season	Club	League	GP	G	A	Pts	AG	AA	APts	PIM	PP	SH	GW	S	%	TGF	PGF	TGA	PGA	+/-	GP	G	A	Pts	PIM	PP	SH	GW
1953-54	Calgary Buffalos	WCJHL	34	6	8	14				12											5	0	0	0	2			
1954-55	Medicine Hat Tigers	WCJHL	39	14	4	18				33											5	0	0	0	4			
1955-56	Nanton Palaminos	FHHL	STATISTICS NOT AVAILABLE																									
	Calgary Stampeders	WHL	1	0	0	0				0											2	0	1	1	2			
1956-57	St. Catharines Teepees	OHA-Jr.	52	32	38	70				143											14	9	11	20	50			
1957-58	St. Catharines Teepees	OHA-Jr.	52	*48	51	*99				*227											8	8	4	12	19			
1958-59	**Chicago Black Hawks**	**NHL**	**32**	**3**	**4**	**7**	**4**	**4**	**8**	**22**											**2**	**0**	**0**	**0**	**2**	**0**	**0**	**0**
	Calgary Stampeders	WHL	13	2	5	7				18																		
1959-60	**Detroit Red Wings**	**NHL**	**59**	**8**	**12**	**20**	**9**	**12**	**21**	**50**											**2**	**0**	**0**	**0**	**0**	**0**	**0**	**0**
1960-61	**Detroit Red Wings**	**NHL**	**16**	**3**	**1**	**4**	**3**	**1**	**4**	**13**																		
	Hershey Bears	AHL	47	19	23	42				84											8	3	6	9	10			
1961-62	Hershey Bears	AHL	58	30	29	59				149											7	1	2	3	19			
1962-63	Buffalo Bisons	AHL	71	35	46	81				122											13	8	12	*20	28			
1963-64	**Chicago Black Hawks**	**NHL**	**45**	**9**	**9**	**18**	**11**	**9**	**20**	**50**											**4**	**0**	**1**	**1**	**6**	**0**	**0**	**0**
1964-65	**Chicago Black Hawks**	**NHL**	**51**	**8**	**10**	**18**	**10**	**10**	**20**	**46**											**11**	**0**	**1**	**1**	**6**	**0**	**0**	**0**
	St. Louis Braves	CPHL	5	5	4	9				17																		
1965-66	**New York Rangers**	**NHL**	**35**	**6**	**5**	**11**	**7**	**5**	**12**	**36**																		
	Boston Bruins	**NHL**	**36**	**13**	**9**	**22**	**15**	**9**	**24**	**36**																		
1966-67	**Boston Bruins**	**NHL**	**69**	**17**	**19**	**36**	**20**	**19**	**39**	**98**																		
1967-68	**Boston Bruins**	**NHL**	**74**	**28**	**38**	**66**	**33**	**38**	**71**	**107**	**7**	**0**	**4**	**184**	**15.2**	**93**	**21**	**62**	**4**	**14**	**4**	**1**	**1**	**2**	**8**	**0**	**0**	**0**
1968-69	**Boston Bruins**	**NHL**	**60**	**29**	**27**	**56**	**31**	**24**	**55**	**99**	**8**	**1**	**7**	**123**	**23.6**	**82**	**27**	**48**	**6**	**13**	**10**	**2**	**2**	**4**	**17**	**1**	**0**	**0**
1969-70♦	**Boston Bruins**	**NHL**	**72**	**29**	**41**	**70**	**32**	**39**	**71**	**114**	**9**	**1**	**6**	**196**	**14.8**	**109**	**55**	**48**	**14**	**20**	**14**	**5**	**12**	**17**	**35**	**0**	**3**	**0**
1970-71	**Boston Bruins**	**NHL**	**65**	**31**	**46**	**77**	**31**	**39**	**70**	**120**	**11**	**0**	**3**	**151**	**20.5**	**120**	**52**	**42**	**1**	**27**	**7**	**2**	**3**	**5**	**22**	**1**	**0**	**1**
1971-72♦	**Boston Bruins**	**NHL**	**77**	**22**	**47**	**69**	**22**	**41**	**63**	**126**	**10**	**0**	**3**	**133**	**16.5**	**121**	**61**	**41**	**0**	**19**	**15**	**5**	**12**	**17**	**37**	**3**	**0**	**0**
1972-73	Philadelphia Blazers	WHA	60	28	50	78				157											4	3	1	4	8			
1973-74	Vancouver Blazers	WHA	45	14	38	52				71																		
1974-75	Team Canada	Summit-74	7	2	3	5				14																		
	Vancouver Blazers	WHA	74	23	37	60				84																		
1975-76	Minnesota Fighting Saints	WHA	57	21	26	47				52																		
	Cincinnati Stingers	WHA	12	3	10	13				6																		
1976-77	Minnesota Fighting Saints	WHA	40	17	13	30				77																		
	New England Whalers	WHA	34	11	19	30				25											5	2	1	3	8			
1977-78	New England Whalers	WHA	79	27	29	56				61											14	6	6	12	16			
1978-79	New England Whalers	WHA	76	19	28	47				115											10	3	7	10	10			
	NHL Totals		**691**	**206**	**268**	**474**	**228**	**250**	**478**	**917**											**69**	**15**	**32**	**47**	**133**			
	Other Major League Totals		477	163	250	413				648											33	14	15	29	42			

AHL First All-Star Team (1963) • NHL Second All-Star Team (1970) • Played in NHL All-Star Game (1970, 1972)

Claimed by **Detroit** from **Chicago** in Intra-League Draft, June 10, 1959. Traded to **Chicago** by **Detroit** with Len Lunde for Doug Barkley, June 5, 1962. Traded to **NY Rangers** by **Chicago** with Ray Cullen for Tracy Pratt, Dick Meissner, Dave Richardson and Mel Pearson, June 4, 1965. Traded to **Boston** by **NY Rangers** for Reggie Fleming, January 10, 1966. Selected by **Quebec** (WHA) in 1972 WHA General Player Draft, February 12, 1972. WHA rights traded to **Philadelphia** (WHA) by **Quebec** (WHA) for future considerations, May, 1972. Traded to **Philadelphia** by **Boston** for cash, August 3, 1972. Transferred to **Vancouver** (WHA) after **Philadelphia** (WHA) franchise relocated, May, 1973. Transferred to **Calgary** (WHA) after **Vancouver** (WHA) franchise relocated, May 7, 1975. Traded to **Minnesota** (WHA) by **Calgary** (WHA) with cash for George Morrison, Don Tannahill and the rights to Joe Micheletti and Wally Olds, September, 1975. Signed as a free agent by **Cincinnati** (WHA) after **Minnesota** (WHA) franchise folded, February 27, 1976. Traded to **Minnesota** (WHA) by **Cincinnati** (WHA) with the rights to Ivan Hlinka for Bryan Maxwell, September, 1976. Traded to **Edmonton** (WHA) by **Minnesota** (WHA) with Jean-Louis Lavasseur, Bill Butters, Mike Antonovich, Dave Keon, Steve Carlson and Jack Carlson for cash, January, 1977. Traded to **New England** (WHA) by **Edmonton** (WHA) with Dave Keon, Steve Carlson, Dave Dryden and Jack Carlson for future considerations (Dave Debol, June, 1977), Dan Arndt and cash, January, 1977.

• McKIM, Andrew

Andrew Harry C – R. 5'8", 175 lbs. b: St. John, N.B., 7/6/1970.

Season	Club	League	GP	G	A	Pts	AG	AA	APts	PIM	PP	SH	GW	S	%	TGF	PGF	TGA	PGA	+/-	GP	G	A	Pts	PIM	PP	SH	GW
1985-86	Moncton Flyers	NBAHA	12	6	8	14																						
1986-87	Verdun Jr. Canadiens	QMJHL	70	28	59	87				12																		
1987-88	Verdun Jr. Canadiens	QMJHL	62	27	32	59				27																		
1988-89	Verdun Jr. Canadiens	QMJHL	68	50	56	106				36																		
1989-90	Hull Olympiques	QMJHL	70	66	64	130				44											11	8	10	18	8			
1990-91	Salt Lake Golden Eagles	IHL	74	30	30	60				48											4	0	2	2	6			
1991-92	St. John's Maple Leafs	AHL	79	43	50	93				79											16	11	12	23	4			
1992-93	**Boston Bruins**	**NHL**	**7**	**1**	**3**	**4**	**1**	**2**	**3**	**0**	**0**	**0**	**0**	**12**	**8.3**	**7**	**2**	**3**	**0**	**2**								
	Providence Bruins	AHL	61	23	46	69				64											6	2	2	4	0			
1993-94	**Boston Bruins**	**NHL**	**29**	**0**	**1**	**1**	**0**	**1**	**1**	**4**	**0**	**0**	**0**	**22**	**0.0**	**2**	**0**	**12**	**0**	**–10**								
	Providence Bruins	AHL	46	13	24	37				49																		
1994-95	**Detroit Red Wings**	**NHL**	**2**	**0**	**0**	**0**	**0**	**0**	**0**	**2**	**0**	**0**	**0**	**0**	**0.0**	**0**	**0**	**0**	**0**	**0**								
	Adirondack Red Wings	AHL	77	39	55	94				22											4	3	3	6	0			
	Canada	WC-A	8	6	7	13				4																		

Season	Club	League	REGULAR SEASON																		PLAYOFFS							
Season	Club	League	GP	G	A	Pts	AG	AA	APts	PIM	PP	SH	GW	S	%	TGF	PGF	TGA	PGA	+/–	GP	G	A	Pts	PIM	PP	SH	GW
1995-96	HC Geneve-Servette	Switz-2	35	20	25	45	....	....	....	14	....	....	....	....	....	....	....	....	....	....	1	0	0	0	4	....	....	....
	Canada	Nat-Team	10	7	7	14	....	....	....	6	....	....	....	....	....	....	....	....	....	....	....	....	....	....	....	....	....	....
1996-97	Eisbaren Berlin	Germany	47	23	22	45	....	....	....	12	....	....	....	....	....	....	....	....	....	....	8	3	7	10	29	....	....	....
1997-98	Eisbaren Berlin	Germany	48	16	29	45	....	....	....	10	....	....	....	....	....	....	....	....	....	....	10	6	5	11	6	....	....	....
	Eisbaren Berlin	EuroHL	10	0	4	4	....	....	....	2	....	....	....	....	....	....	....	....	....	....	6	0	1	1	2	....	....	....
1998-99	Eisbaren Berlin	Germany	42	19	18	37	....	....	....	22	....	....	....	....	....	....	....	....	....	....	7	1	1	2	4	....	....	....
	Eisbaren Berlin	EuroHL	4	0	3	3	....	....	....	0	....	....	....	....	....	....	....	....	....	....	6	0	1	1	2	....	....	....
99-2000	EHC Kloten	Switz.	44	*25	20	45	....	....	....	20	....	....	....	....	....	....	....	....	....	....	7	4	3	7	12	....	....	....
	Canada	Nat-Team	4	0	1	1	....	....	....	17	....	....	....	....	....	....	....	....	....	....	....	....	....	....	....	....	....	....
	NHL Totals		**38**	**1**	**4**	**5**	**1**	**3**	**4**	**6**	**0**	**0**	**0**	**34**	**2.9**	**9**	**2**	**15**	**0**		....	....	....	....	....	....	....	....

QMJHL First All-Star Team (1990) • Canadian Major Junior Most Sportsmanlike Player of the Year (1990)

Signed as a free agent by **Calgary**, October 5, 1990. Signed as a free agent by **Toronto**, October, 1991. Signed as a free agent by **Boston**, July 23, 1992. Signed as a free agent by **Detroit**, August 31, 1994.

• McLAREN, Kyle

D – L. 6'4", 219 lbs. b: Humboldt, Sask., 6/18/1977. Boston's 1st, 9th overall, in 1995.

Season	Club	League	GP	G	A	Pts	AG	AA	APts	PIM	PP	SH	GW	S	%	TGF	PGF	TGA	PGA	+/–	GP	G	A	Pts	PIM	PP	SH	GW
1992-93	Lethbridge Golden Hawks	AAHA	60	28	28	56	....	....	....	84	....	....	....	....	....	....	....	....	....	....	....	....	....	....	....	....	....	....
1993-94	Tacoma Rockets	WHL	62	1	9	10	....	....	....	53	....	....	....	....	....	....	....	....	....	....	6	1	4	5	6	....	....	....
1994-95	Tacoma Rockets	WHL	47	13	19	32	....	....	....	68	....	....	....	....	....	....	....	....	....	....	4	1	1	2	4	....	....	....
1995-96	**Boston Bruins**	**NHL**	**74**	**5**	**12**	**17**	**5**	**10**	**15**	**73**	**0**	**0**	**0**	**74**	**6.8**	**83**	**3**	**93**	**29**	**16**	**5**	**0**	**0**	**0**	**14**	**0**	**0**	**0**
1996-97	**Boston Bruins**	**NHL**	**58**	**5**	**9**	**14**	**5**	**8**	**13**	**54**	**0**	**0**	**1**	**68**	**7.4**	**53**	**2**	**80**	**20**	**–9**	....	....	....	....	....	....	....	....
1997-98	**Boston Bruins**	**NHL**	**66**	**5**	**20**	**25**	**6**	**20**	**26**	**56**	**2**	**0**	**0**	**101**	**5.0**	**78**	**23**	**54**	**12**	**13**	**6**	**1**	**0**	**1**	**4**	**1**	**0**	**0**
1998-99	**Boston Bruins**	**NHL**	**52**	**6**	**18**	**24**	**7**	**17**	**24**	**48**	**3**	**0**	**0**	**97**	**6.2**	**56**	**23**	**37**	**5**	**1**	**12**	**0**	**3**	**3**	**10**	**0**	**0**	**0**
99-2000	**Boston Bruins**	**NHL**	**71**	**8**	**11**	**19**	**9**	**10**	**19**	**67**	**2**	**0**	**3**	**142**	**5.6**	**68**	**14**	**78**	**20**	**–4**	....	....	....	....	....	....	....	....
	NHL Totals		**321**	**29**	**70**	**99**	**32**	**65**	**97**	**298**	**7**	**0**	**4**	**482**	**6.0**	**338**	**65**	**342**	**86**		**23**	**1**	**3**	**4**	**28**	**1**	**0**	**0**

NHL All-Rookie Team (1996)

• McLEAN, Don

Robert Donald D – R. 6'1", 200 lbs. b: Niagara Falls, Ont., 1/19/1954. Philadelphia's 1st, 35th overall, in 1974.

Season	Club	League	GP	G	A	Pts	AG	AA	APts	PIM	PP	SH	GW	S	%	TGF	PGF	TGA	PGA	+/–	GP	G	A	Pts	PIM	PP	SH	GW
1968-69	Niagara Falls Canucks	OHA-B	STATISTICS NOT AVAILABLE																									
	Niagara Falls Flyers	OHA-Jr.	1	0	1	1	....	....	....	2	....	....	....	....	....	....	....	....	....	....	....	....	....	....	....	....	....	....
1969-70	Niagara Falls Canucks	OHA-B	STATISTICS NOT AVAILABLE																									
	Niagara Falls Flyers	OHA-Jr.	29	0	0	0	....	....	....	58	....	....	....	....	....	....	....	....	....	....	....	....	....	....	....	....	....	....
1970-71	Niagara Falls Flyers	OMJHL	54	1	6	7	....	....	....	72	....	....	....	....	....	....	....	....	....	....	....	....	....	....	....	....	....	....
1971-72	Niagara Falls Flyers	OMJHL	34	0	5	5	....	....	....	10	....	....	....	....	....	....	....	....	....	....	....	....	....	....	....	....	....	....
1972-73	Sudbury Wolves	OMJHL	46	5	12	17	....	....	....	124	....	....	....	....	....	....	....	....	....	....	....	....	....	....	....	....	....	....
1973-74	Sudbury Wolves	OMJHL	57	6	17	23	....	....	....	*305	....	....	....	....	....	....	....	....	....	....	....	....	....	....	....	....	....	....
1974-75	Richmond Robins	AHL	58	1	8	9	....	....	....	188	....	....	....	....	....	....	....	....	....	....	4	0	1	1	2	....	....	....
1975-76	**Washington Capitals**	**NHL**	**9**	**0**	**0**	**0**	**0**	**0**	**0**	**6**	**0**	**0**	**0**	**4**	**0.0**	**5**	**0**	**10**	**2**	**–3**	....	....	....	....	....	....	....	....
	Richmond Robins	AHL	20	0	0	0	....	....	....	16	....	....	....	....	....	....	....	....	....	....	....	....	....	....	....	....	....	....
	Salt Lake Golden Eagles	CHL	34	1	12	13	....	....	....	77	....	....	....	....	....	....	....	....	....	....	3	0	0	0	2	....	....	....
1976-77	Johnstown Jets	NAHL	5	0	3	3	....	....	....	4	....	....	....	....	....	....	....	....	....	....	....	....	....	....	....	....	....	....
	NHL Totals		**9**	**0**	**0**	**0**	**0**	**0**	**0**	**6**	**0**	**0**	**0**	**4**	**0.0**	**5**	**0**	**10**	**2**		....	....	....	....	....	....	....	....

Traded to **Washington** by **Philadelphia** with Bill Clement and Philadelphia's 1st round choice (Alex Forsythe) in 1975 Amateur Draft for Washington's 1st round choice (Mel Bridgman) in 1975 Amateur Draft, June 4, 1975.

• McLEAN, Jeff

C – L. 5'10", 190 lbs. b: Port Moody, B.C., 10/6/1969. San Jose's 1st, 1st overall, in 1991 Supplemental Draft.

Season	Club	League	GP	G	A	Pts	AG	AA	APts	PIM	PP	SH	GW	S	%	TGF	PGF	TGA	PGA	+/–	GP	G	A	Pts	PIM	PP	SH	GW
1986-87	Langley Eagles	BCJHL	43	17	20	37	....	....	....	8	....	....	....	....	....	....	....	....	....	....	....	....	....	....	....	....	....	....
1987-88	University of North Dakota	WCHA	37	0	3	3	....	....	....	14	....	....	....	....	....	....	....	....	....	....	....	....	....	....	....	....	....	....
1988-89	New Westminster Bruins	BCJHL	60	*70	*91	*161	....	....	....	128	....	....	....	....	....	....	....	....	....	....	....	....	....	....	....	....	....	....
1989-90	University of North Dakota	WCHA	45	10	16	26	....	....	....	42	....	....	....	....	....	....	....	....	....	....	....	....	....	....	....	....	....	....
1990-91	University of North Dakota	WCHA	42	19	26	45	....	....	....	22	....	....	....	....	....	....	....	....	....	....	....	....	....	....	....	....	....	....
1991-92	University of North Dakota	WCHA	38	27	43	70	....	....	....	40	....	....	....	....	....	....	....	....	....	....	....	....	....	....	....	....	....	....
1992-93	Kansas City Blades	IHL	60	21	23	44	....	....	....	45	....	....	....	....	....	....	....	....	....	....	10	3	1	4	2	....	....	....
1993-94	**San Jose Sharks**	**NHL**	**6**	**1**	**0**	**1**	**1**	**0**	**1**	**0**	**0**	**0**	**0**	**5**	**20.0**	**2**	**0**	**1**	**0**	**1**	....	....	....	....	....	....	....	....
	Kansas City Blades	IHL	69	27	30	57	....	....	....	44	....	....	....	....	....	....	....	....	....	....	....	....	....	....	....	....	....	....
1994-95	Kalamazoo Wings	IHL	41	16	18	34	....	....	....	22	....	....	....	....	....	....	....	....	....	....	4	1	4	5	0	....	....	....
1995-96	Kansas City Blades	IHL	71	17	27	44	....	....	....	34	....	....	....	....	....	....	....	....	....	....	3	0	3	3	2	....	....	....
1996-97	Kansas City Blades	IHL	39	8	15	23	....	....	....	14	....	....	....	....	....	....	....	....	....	....	....	....	....	....	....	....	....	....
	Cincinnati Cyclones	IHL	9	1	3	4	....	....	....	2	....	....	....	....	....	....	....	....	....	....	....	....	....	....	....	....	....	....
	Fort Wayne Komets	IHL	6	1	1	2	....	....	....	2	....	....	....	....	....	....	....	....	....	....	....	....	....	....	....	....	....	....
1997-98	Kassel Huskies	Germany	12	3	5	8	....	....	....	12	....	....	....	....	....	....	....	....	....	....	....	....	....	....	....	....	....	....
	Kassel Huskies	EuroHL	2	1	0	1	....	....	....	0	....	....	....	....	....	....	....	....	....	....	....	....	....	....	....	....	....	....
1998-99	South Carolina Stingrays	ECHL	28	8	11	19	....	....	....	17	....	....	....	....	....	....	....	....	....	....	....	....	....	....	....	....	....	....
	Tallahassee Tiger Sharks	ECHL	21	16	15	31	....	....	....	12	....	....	....	....	....	....	....	....	....	....	....	....	....	....	....	....	....	....
99-2000	Tallahassee Tiger Sharks	ECHL	16	3	15	18	....	....	....	2	....	....	....	....	....	....	....	....	....	....	....	....	....	....	....	....	....	....
	Quebec Citadelles	AHL	2	0	1	1	....	....	....	0	....	....	....	....	....	....	....	....	....	....	....	....	....	....	....	....	....	....
	NHL Totals		**6**	**1**	**0**	**1**	**1**	**0**	**1**	**0**	**0**	**0**	**0**	**5**	**20.0**	**2**	**0**	**1**	**0**		....	....	....	....	....	....	....	....

Named BCJHL MVP (1989)

• McLELLAN, Scott

Daniel Scott RW – R. 6'1", 175 lbs. b: Toronto, Ont., 2/10/1963. Boston's 3rd, 77th overall, in 1981.

Season	Club	League	GP	G	A	Pts	AG	AA	APts	PIM	PP	SH	GW	S	%	TGF	PGF	TGA	PGA	+/–	GP	G	A	Pts	PIM	PP	SH	GW
1979-80	St. Michael's Buzzers	OHA-B	41	43	48	91	....	....	....	....	....	....	....	....	....	....	....	....	....	....	....	....	....	....	....	....	....	....
1980-81	Niagara Falls Flyers	OMJHL	33	7	4	11	....	....	....	39	....	....	....	....	....	....	....	....	....	....	12	1	0	1	2	....	....	....
1981-82	Niagara Falls Flyers	OHL	12	1	6	7	....	....	....	33	....	....	....	....	....	....	....	....	....	....	....	....	....	....	....	....	....	....
	Peterborough Petes	OHL	46	20	31	51	....	....	....	42	....	....	....	....	....	....	....	....	....	....	6	1	2	3	10	....	....	....
1982-83	Peterborough Petes	OHL	65	43	58	101	....	....	....	38	....	....	....	....	....	....	....	....	....	....	4	2	2	4	2	....	....	....
	Boston Bruins	**NHL**	**2**	**0**	**0**	**0**	**0**	**0**	**0**	**0**	**0**	**0**	**0**	**0**	**0.0**	**0**	**0**	**0**	**0**	**0**	....	....	....	....	....	....	....	....
1983-84	Toledo Goaldiggers	IHL	5	1	2	3	....	....	....	0	....	....	....	....	....	....	....	....	....	....	....	....	....	....	....	....	....	....
	Hershey Bears	AHL	73	9	12	21	....	....	....	14	....	....	....	....	....	....	....	....	....	....	....	....	....	....	....	....	....	....
1984-85	Hershey Bears	AHL	47	12	12	24	....	....	....	32	....	....	....	....	....	....	....	....	....	....	....	....	....	....	....	....	....	....
	NHL Totals		**2**	**0**	**0**	**0**	**0**	**0**	**0**	**0**	**0**	**0**	**0**	**0**	**0.0**	**0**	**0**	**0**	**0**		....	....	....	....	....	....	....	....

• McLELLAN, Todd

C – L. 5'11", 185 lbs. b: Melville, Sask., 10/3/1967. NY Islanders' 6th, 104th overall, in 1986.

Season	Club	League	GP	G	A	Pts	AG	AA	APts	PIM	PP	SH	GW	S	%	TGF	PGF	TGA	PGA	+/–	GP	G	A	Pts	PIM	PP	SH	GW
1982-83	Saskatoon Blazers	SAHA	25	6	9	15	....	....	....	6	....	....	....	....	....	....	....	....	....	....	....	....	....	....	....	....	....	....
1983-84	Saskatoon Blades	WHL	50	8	14	22	....	....	....	15	....	....	....	....	....	....	....	....	....	....	....	....	....	....	....	....	....	....
1984-85	Saskatoon Blades	WHL	41	15	35	50	....	....	....	33	....	....	....	....	....	....	....	....	....	....	3	1	0	1	0	....	....	....
1985-86	Saskatoon Blades	WHL	27	9	10	19	....	....	....	13	....	....	....	....	....	....	....	....	....	....	13	9	3	12	8	....	....	....
1986-87	Saskatoon Blades	WHL	60	34	39	73	....	....	....	66	....	....	....	....	....	....	....	....	....	....	6	1	1	2	2	....	....	....
1987-88	**New York Islanders**	**NHL**	**5**	**1**	**1**	**2**	**1**	**1**	**2**	**0**	**0**	**0**	**0**	**4**	**25.0**	**2**	**0**	**4**	**1**	**–1**	....	....	....	....	....	....	....	....
	Springfield Indians	AHL	70	18	26	44	....	....	....	32	....	....	....	....	....	....	....	....	....	....	....	....	....	....	....	....	....	....
1988-89	Springfield Indians	AHL	37	7	19	26	....	....	....	17	....	....	....	....	....	....	....	....	....	....	....	....	....	....	....	....	....	....
1989-1992	SIJ Utrecht	Holland	PLAYER/COACH – STATISTICS UNAVAILABLE																									
1993-1994	Swift Current Broncos	WHL	DID NOT PLAY – ASSISTANT COACH																									
1994-2000	Swift Current Broncos	WHL	DID NOT PLAY – COACHING																									
	NHL Totals		**5**	**1**	**1**	**2**	**1**	**1**	**2**	**0**	**0**	**0**	**0**	**4**	**25.0**	**2**	**0**	**4**	**1**		....	....	....	....	....	....	....	....

• McCLEOD, Al
Allan Sidney "Moose" D – L. 5'11", 200 lbs. b: Medicine Hat, Alta., 6/17/1949.

			REGULAR SEASON																		PLAYOFFS							
Season	Club	League	GP	G	A	Pts	AG	AA	APts	PIM	PP	SH	GW	S	%	TGF	PGF	TGA	PGA	+/–	GP	G	A	Pts	PIM	PP	SH	GW
1966-67	Calgary Buffaloes	AJHL	STATISTICS NOT AVAILABLE																									
1967-68	Michigan Tech Huskies	WCHA	DID NOT PLAY – FRESHMAN																									
1968-69	Michigan Tech Huskies	WCHA	23	2	3	5	....	....	....	10	....	....	....	....	....	....	....	....	....	....	....	....	....	....	....	....	....	....
1969-70	Michigan Tech Huskies	WCHA	34	14	17	31	....	....	....	32	....	....	....	....	....	....	....	....	....	....	....	....	....	....	....	....	....	....
1970-71	Michigan Tech Huskies	WCHA	32	13	26	39	....	....	....	14	....	....	....	....	....	....	....	....	....	....	....	....	....	....	....	....	....	....
1971-72	Fort Worth Wings	CHL	22	1	6	7	....	....	....	4	....	....	....	....	....	....	....	....	....	....	....	....	....	....	....	....	....	....
	Port Huron Wings	IHL	35	1	12	13	....	....	....	15	....	....	....	....	....	....	....	....	....	....	15	0	3	3	13	....	....	....
1972-73	Virginia Wings	AHL	76	4	15	19	....	....	....	105	....	....	....	....	....	....	....	....	....	....	13	0	1	1	22	....	....	....
1973-74	**Detroit Red Wings**	**NHL**	**26**	**2**	**2**	**4**	**2**	**2**	**4**	**24**	**0**	**0**	**0**	**23**	**8.7**	**24**	**2**	**35**	**6**	**–7**	....	....	....	....	....	....	....	....
	Virginia Wings	AHL	54	1	13	14	....	....	....	52	....	....	....	....	....	....	....	....	....	....	....	....	....	....	....	....	....	....
1974-75	Phoenix Roadrunners	WHA	77	3	16	19	....	....	....	98	....	....	....	....	....	....	....	....	....	....	5	0	4	4	4	....	....	....
1975-76	Phoenix Roadrunners	WHA	80	2	18	20	....	....	....	82	....	....	....	....	....	....	....	....	....	....	5	0	2	2	4	....	....	....
1976-77	Phoenix Roadrunners	WHA	29	1	5	6	....	....	....	35	....	....	....	....	....	....	....	....	....	....	....	....	....	....	....	....	....	....
	Houston Aeros	WHA	51	7	21	28	....	....	....	20	....	....	....	....	....	....	....	....	....	....	10	1	3	4	9	....	....	....
1977-78	Houston Aeros	WHA	80	2	22	24	....	....	....	54	....	....	....	....	....	....	....	....	....	....	6	1	0	1	2	....	....	....
1978-79	Indianapolis Racers	WHA	25	0	11	11	....	....	....	22	....	....	....	....	....	....	....	....	....	....	....	....	....	....	....	....	....	....
	NHL Totals		**26**	**2**	**2**	**4**	**2**	**2**	**4**	**24**	**0**	**0**	**0**	**23**	**8.7**	**24**	**2**	**35**	**6**		....	....	....	....	....	....	....	....
	Other Major League Totals		342	15	93	108	....	....	....	311	....	....	....	....	....	....	....	....	....	....	26	2	9	11	19	....	....	....

Signed as a free agent by **Detroit** (Fort Worth-CHL), October 1, 1971. Signed as a free agent by **Phoenix** (WHA), August, 1974. Traded to **Houston** (WHA) by **Phoenix** (WHA) with John Gray and Neil Lyseng for Andre Hinse and Frank Hughes, Decemeber, 1976. Traded to **Winnipeg** (WHA) by **Houston** (WHA) for cash, July 6, 1978. Traded to **Indianapolis** (WHA) by **Winnipeg** (WHA) for cash, July 15, 1978.

• McLLWAIN, Dave
David Allan C/RW – L. 6', 185 lbs. b: Seaforth, Ont., 1/9/1967. Pittsburgh's 9th, 172nd overall, in 1986.

			REGULAR SEASON																		PLAYOFFS							
Season	Club	League	GP	G	A	Pts	AG	AA	APts	PIM	PP	SH	GW	S	%	TGF	PGF	TGA	PGA	+/–	GP	G	A	Pts	PIM	PP	SH	GW
1982-83	Seaforth Centennaires	OJHL-D	34	25	20	45	....	....	....	26	....	....	....	....	....	....	....	....	....	....	....	....	....	....	....	....	....	....
1983-84	Seaforth Centennaires	OJHL-D	33	42	36	78	....	....	....	30	....	....	....	....	....	....	....	....	....	....	....	....	....	....	....	....	....	....
1984-85	Dixie Beehives	OJHL	1	1	1	2	....	....	....	0	....	....	....	....	....	....	....	....	....	....	....	....	....	....	....	....	....	....
	Kitchener Rangers	OHL	61	13	21	34	....	....	....	29	....	....	....	....	....	....	....	....	....	....	....	....	....	....	....	....	....	....
1985-86	Kitchener Rangers	OHL	13	7	7	14	....	....	....	12	....	....	....	....	....	....	....	....	....	....	....	....	....	....	....	....	....	....
	North Bay Centennials	OHL	51	30	28	58	....	....	....	25	....	....	....	....	....	....	....	....	....	....	10	4	4	8	2	....	....	....
1986-87	North Bay Centennials	OHL	60	46	73	119	....	....	....	35	....	....	....	....	....	....	....	....	....	....	24	7	18	25	40	....	....	....
	Canada	WJC-A	6	4	3	7	....	....	....	2	....	....	....	....	....	....	....	....	....	....	....	....	....	....	....	....	....	....
1987-88	**Pittsburgh Penguins**	**NHL**	**66**	**11**	**8**	**19**	**9**	**6**	**15**	**40**	**1**	**0**	**0**	**65**	**16.9**	**28**	**2**	**35**	**8**	**–1**	....	....	....	....	....	....	....	....
	Muskegon Lumberjacks	IHL	9	4	6	10	....	....	....	23	....	....	....	....	....	....	....	....	....	....	6	2	3	5	8	....	....	....
1988-89	**Pittsburgh Penguins**	**NHL**	**24**	**1**	**2**	**3**	**1**	**1**	**2**	**4**	**0**	**0**	**0**	**14**	**7.1**	**5**	**1**	**15**	**0**	**–11**	**3**	**0**	**1**	**1**	**0**	**0**	**0**	**0**
	Muskegon Lumberjacks	IHL	46	37	35	72	....	....	....	51	....	....	....	....	....	....	....	....	....	....	7	8	2	10	6	....	....	....
1989-90	**Winnipeg Jets**	**NHL**	**80**	**25**	**26**	**51**	**21**	**19**	**40**	**60**	**1**	**7**	**2**	**180**	**13.9**	**64**	**9**	**70**	**14**	**–1**	**7**	**0**	**1**	**1**	**2**	**0**	**0**	**0**
1990-91	**Winnipeg Jets**	**NHL**	**60**	**14**	**11**	**25**	**13**	**8**	**21**	**46**	**2**	**2**	**2**	**104**	**13.5**	**40**	**2**	**75**	**24**	**–13**	....	....	....	....	....	....	....	....
1991-92	**Winnipeg Jets**	**NHL**	**3**	**1**	**1**	**2**	**1**	**1**	**2**	**2**	**0**	**0**	**0**	**3**	**33.3**	**2**	**0**	**3**	**2**	**1**	....	....	....	....	....	....	....	....
	Buffalo Sabres	**NHL**	**5**	**0**	**0**	**0**	**0**	**0**	**0**	**2**	**0**	**0**	**0**	**5**	**0.0**	**1**	**0**	**8**	**4**	**–3**	....	....	....	....	....	....	....	....
	New York Islanders	**NHL**	**54**	**8**	**15**	**23**	**7**	**11**	**18**	**28**	**1**	**1**	**1**	**71**	**11.3**	**30**	**2**	**65**	**29**	**–8**	....	....	....	....	....	....	....	....
	Toronto Maple Leafs	**NHL**	**11**	**1**	**2**	**3**	**1**	**2**	**3**	**4**	**0**	**0**	**1**	**12**	**8.3**	**5**	**0**	**8**	**4**	**1**	....	....	....	....	....	....	....	....
1992-93	**Toronto Maple Leafs**	**NHL**	**66**	**14**	**4**	**18**	**12**	**3**	**15**	**30**	**1**	**1**	**3**	**85**	**16.5**	**23**	**3**	**63**	**25**	**–18**	**4**	**0**	**0**	**0**	**0**	**0**	**0**	**0**
1993-94	**Ottawa Senators**	**NHL**	**66**	**17**	**26**	**43**	**16**	**20**	**36**	**48**	**1**	**1**	**1**	**115**	**14.8**	**62**	**13**	**123**	**34**	**–40**	....	....	....	....	....	....	....	....
1994-95	**Ottawa Senators**	**NHL**	**43**	**5**	**6**	**11**	**9**	**9**	**18**	**22**	**1**	**0**	**0**	**48**	**10.4**	**17**	**3**	**59**	**19**	**–26**	....	....	....	....	....	....	....	....
1995-96	**Ottawa Senators**	**NHL**	**1**	**0**	**1**	**1**	**0**	**1**	**1**	**2**	**0**	**0**	**0**	**1**	**0.0**	**1**	**1**	**0**	**0**	**0**	....	....	....	....	....	....	....	....
	Cleveland Lumberjacks	IHL	60	30	45	75	....	....	....	80	....	....	....	....	....	....	....	....	....	....	....	....	....	....	....	....	....	....
	Pittsburgh Penguins	**NHL**	**18**	**2**	**4**	**6**	**2**	**3**	**5**	**4**	**0**	**0**	**1**	**19**	**10.5**	**8**	**0**	**15**	**2**	**–5**	**6**	**0**	**0**	**0**	**0**	**0**	**0**	**0**
1996-97	**New York Islanders**	**NHL**	**4**	**1**	**1**	**2**	**1**	**1**	**2**	**0**	**1**	**0**	**0**	**3**	**33.3**	**3**	**1**	**4**	**0**	**–2**	....	....	....	....	....	....	....	....
	Cleveland Lumberjacks	IHL	63	29	46	75	....	....	....	85	....	....	....	....	....	....	....	....	....	....	14	8	15	23	6	....	....	....
1997-98	EV Landshut	Germany	47	21	13	34	....	....	....	34	....	....	....	....	....	....	....	....	....	....	3	0	0	0	4	....	....	....
1998-99	SC Bern	Switz.	39	20	34	54	....	....	....	30	....	....	....	....	....	....	....	....	....	....	6	2	2	4	6	....	....	....
99-2000	SC Bern	Switz.	45	16	33	49	....	....	....	51	....	....	....	....	....	....	....	....	....	....	5	1	1	2	6	....	....	....
	Canada	Nat-Team	3	0	0	0	....	....	....	0	....	....	....	....	....	....	....	....	....	....	....	....	....	....	....	....	....	....
	NHL Totals		**501**	**100**	**107**	**207**	**93**	**85**	**178**	**292**	**9**	**12**	**11**	**725**	**13.8**	**289**	**37**	**543**	**165**		**20**	**0**	**2**	**2**	**2**	**0**	**0**	**0**

OHL Second All-Star Team (1987)

Traded to **Winnipeg** by **Pittsburgh** with Randy Cunneyworth and Rick Tabaracci for Jim Kyte, Andrew McBain and Randy Gilhen, June 17, 1989. Traded to **Buffalo** by **Winnipeg** with Gord Donnelly, Winnipeg's 5th round choice (Yuri Khmylev) in 1992 Entry Draft and cash for Darrin Shannon, Mike Hartman and Dean Kennedy, October 11, 1991. Traded to **NY Islanders** by **Buffalo** with Pierre Turgeon, Uwe Krupp and Benoit Hogue for Pat LaFontaine, Randy Hillier, Randy Wood and NY Islanders' 4th round choice (Dean Melanson) in 1992 Entry Draft, October 25, 1991. Traded to **Toronto** by **NY Islanders** with Ken Baumgartner for Daniel Marois and Claude Loiselle, March 10, 1992. Claimed by **Ottawa** from **Toronto** in NHL Waiver Draft, October 3, 1993. Traded to **Pittsburgh** by **Ottawa** for Pittsburgh's 8th round choice (Erich Goldmann) in 1996 Entry Draft, March 1, 1996. Signed as a free agent by **NY Islanders**, July 29, 1996.

• McMAHON, Mike
Michael William D – L. 5'11", 180 lbs. b: Quebec City, Que., 8/30/1941.

			REGULAR SEASON																		PLAYOFFS							
Season	Club	League	GP	G	A	Pts	AG	AA	APts	PIM	PP	SH	GW	S	%	TGF	PGF	TGA	PGA	+/–	GP	G	A	Pts	PIM	PP	SH	GW
1958-59	Fort Erie Meteors	OHA-C	STATISTICS NOT AVAILABLE																									
1959-60	Guelph Biltmores	OHA-Jr.	48	7	16	23	....	....	....	94	....	....	....	....	....	....	....	....	....	....	5	0	0	0	15	....	....	....
1960-61	Guelph Biltmores	OHA-Jr.	46	10	36	46	....	....	....	114	....	....	....	....	....	....	....	....	....	....	9	3	6	9	8	....	....	....
1961-62	Guelph Biltmores	OHA-Jr.	45	9	28	37	....	....	....	94	....	....	....	....	....	....	....	....	....	....	....	....	....	....	....	....	....	....
	Kitchener-Waterloo Beavers	EPHL	5	0	1	1	....	....	....	0	....	....	....	....	....	....	....	....	....	....	3	0	0	0	0	....	....	....
1962-63	Sudbury Wolves	EPHL	71	12	39	51	....	....	....	107	....	....	....	....	....	....	....	....	....	....	8	3	3	6	8	....	....	....
1963-64	**New York Rangers**	**NHL**	**18**	**0**	**1**	**1**	**0**	**1**	**1**	**16**	....	....	....	....	....	....	....	....	....	....	....	....	....	....	....	....	....	....
	Baltimore Clippers	AHL	40	7	10	17	....	....	....	66	....	....	....	....	....	....	....	....	....	....	....	....	....	....	....	....	....	....
	St. Paul Rangers	CPHL	13	3	9	12	....	....	....	30	....	....	....	....	....	....	....	....	....	....	....	....	....	....	....	....	....	....
1964-65	**New York Rangers**	**NHL**	**1**	**0**	**0**	**0**	**0**	**0**	**0**	**0**	....	....	....	....	....	....	....	....	....	....	....	....	....	....	....	....	....	....
	Baltimore Clippers	AHL	8	0	0	0	....	....	....	6	....	....	....	....	....	....	....	....	....	....	....	....	....	....	....	....	....	....
	St. Paul Rangers	CPHL	63	20	41	61	....	....	....	204	....	....	....	....	....	....	....	....	....	....	11	4	5	9	23	....	....	....
1965-66	**New York Rangers**	**NHL**	**41**	**0**	**12**	**12**	**0**	**11**	**11**	**34**	....	....	....	....	....	....	....	....	....	....	....	....	....	....	....	....	....	....
	Minnesota Rangers	CPHL	25	3	13	16	....	....	....	45	....	....	....	....	....	....	....	....	....	....	4	1	3	4	0	....	....	....
1966-67	Houston Apollos	CPHL	64	13	37	50	....	....	....	129	....	....	....	....	....	....	....	....	....	....	6	0	3	3	6	....	....	....
	Quebec Aces	AHL	....	....	....	....	....	....	....	....	....	....	....	....	....	....	....	....	....	....	1	0	1	1	2	....	....	....
1967-68	**Minnesota North Stars**	**NHL**	**74**	**14**	**33**	**47**	**16**	**33**	**49**	**71**	**4**	**0**	**1**	**150**	**9.3**	**119**	**48**	**98**	**14**	**–13**	**14**	**3**	**7**	**10**	**4**	**0**	**2**	**0**
1968-69	**Minnesota North Stars**	**NHL**	**43**	**0**	**11**	**11**	**0**	**10**	**10**	**21**	**0**	**0**	**0**	**113**	**0.0**	**52**	**25**	**55**	**2**	**–26**	....	....	....	....	....	....	....	....
	Cleveland Barons	AHL	6	1	4	5	....	....	....	4	....	....	....	....	....	....	....	....	....	....	....	....	....	....	....	....	....	....
	Chicago Black Hawks	**NHL**	**20**	**0**	**8**	**8**	**0**	**7**	**7**	**6**	**0**	**0**	**0**	**31**	**0.0**	**29**	**2**	**18**	**6**	**15**	....	....	....	....	....	....	....	....
1969-70	**Detroit Red Wings**	**NHL**	**2**	**0**	**0**	**0**	**0**	**0**	**0**	**0**	**0**	**0**	**0**	**0**	**0.0**	**1**	**0**	**2**	**1**	**0**	....	....	....	....	....	....	....	....
	Pittsburgh Penguins	**NHL**	**12**	**1**	**3**	**4**	**1**	**3**	**4**	**19**	**0**	**0**	**0**	**12**	**8.3**	**11**	**6**	**9**	**6**	**2**	....	....	....	....	....	....	....	....
	Baltimore Clippers	AHL	48	13	25	38	....	....	....	29	....	....	....	....	....	....	....	....	....	....	5	0	0	0	2	....	....	....
1970-71	**Buffalo Sabres**	**NHL**	**12**	**0**	**0**	**0**	**0**	**0**	**0**	**4**	**0**	**0**	**0**	**20**	**0.0**	**5**	**3**	**14**	**4**	**–8**	....	....	....	....	....	....	....	....
	Springfield Kings	AHL	36	5	14	19	....	....	....	43	....	....	....	....	....	....	....	....	....	....	12	3	10	13	57	....	....	....
1971-72	**New York Rangers**	**NHL**	**1**	**0**	**0**	**0**	**0**	**0**	**0**	**0**	**0**	**0**	**0**	**0**	**0.0**	**1**	**0**	**0**	**0**	**1**	....	....	....	....	....	....	....	....
	Providence Reds	AHL	39	3	19	22	....	....	....	74	....	....	....	....	....	....	....	....	....	....	....	....	....	....	....	....	....	....
	Rochester Americans	AHL	9	0	10	10	....	....	....	4	....	....	....	....	....	....	....	....	....	....	....	....	....	....	....	....	....	....
1972-73	Minnesota Fighting Saints	WHA	75	12	39	51	....	....	....	87	....	....	....	....	....	....	....	....	....	....	5	0	5	5	2	....	....	....
1973-74	Minnesota Fighting Saints	WHA	71	10	35	45	....	....	....	82	....	....	....	....	....	....	....	....	....	....	11	1	7	8	9	....	....	....

Season	Club	League	GP	G	A	Pts	AG	AA	APts	PIM	PP	SH	GW	S	%	TGF	PGF	TGA	PGA	+/–	GP	G	A	Pts	PIM	PP	SH	GW
			REGULAR SEASON																		PLAYOFFS							
1974-75	Minnesota Fighting Saints	WHA	64	5	15	20				42											7	0	1	1	0			
1975-76	San Diego Mariners	WHA	69	2	12	14				38											9	0	1	1	2			
1976-77	Springfield Indians	AHL	59	6	25	31				64																		
	NHL Totals		**224**	**15**	**68**	**83**	**17**	**65**	**82**	**171**											**14**	**3**	**7**	**10**	**4**			
	Other Major League Totals		279	29	101	130				249											32	1	14	15	13			

• Son of Mike Sr. • OHA-Jr. Second All-Star Team (1961) • OHA-Jr. First All-Star Team (1962) • CPHL First All-Star Team (1965) • Named Top Defenseman - CPHL (1965, 1967) • CPHL First All-Star Team (1967) • AHL Second All-Star Team (1970)

Claimed by **Montreal** from **NY Rangers** in Intra-League Draft, June 15, 1966. Traded to **Minnesota** by **Montreal** for cash, June 14, 1967. Traded to **Chicago** by **Minnesota** with Andre Boudrias for Tom Reid and Bill Orban, February 14, 1969. Claimed on waivers by **Detroit** from **Chicago**, October 14, 1969. Traded to **Pittsburgh** by **Detroit** for Billy Dea, October 28, 1969. Claimed by **Buffalo** from **Pittsburgh** in Expansion Draft, June 10, 1970. Traded to **LA Kings** by **Buffalo** with future considerations for Eddie Shack and Dick Duff, November 25, 1970. Traded to **NY Rangers** (Baltimore-AHL) by **LA Kings** (Springfield-AHL) for Wayne Rivers, October, 1971. Selected by **Minnesota** (WHA) in 1972 WHA General Player Draft, February 12, 1972. Loaned to **Vancouver** (Rochester-AHL) by **NY Rangers** (Providence-AHL) for the remainder of the 1971-72 season for Ron Stewart, March 5, 1972. Claimed by **San Diego** (WHA) from **Minnesota** (WHA) in WHA Intra-League Draft, June 19, 1975.

• McMANAMA, Bob

Robert Samuel C – L. 6′, 180 lbs. b: Belmont, MA, 10/7/1951.

Season	Club	League	GP	G	A	Pts	AG	AA	APts	PIM	PP	SH	GW	S	%	TGF	PGF	TGA	PGA	+/–	GP	G	A	Pts	PIM	PP	SH	GW
1966-1969	Belmont Hill Hillies	Hi-School	STATISTICS NOT AVAILABLE																									
1969-70	Harvard University	ECAC	DID NOT PLAY – FRESHMAN																									
1970-71	Harvard University	ECAC	27	13	32	45				36																		
1971-72	Harvard University	ECAC	26	24	30	54				34																		
1972-73	Harvard University	ECAC	22	27	25	52				33																		
	United States	WEC-B	7	4	10	14																						
1973-74	**Pittsburgh Penguins**	**NHL**	**47**	**5**	**14**	**19**	**5**	**12**	**17**	**18**	**0**	**0**	**1**	**70**	**7.1**	**27**	**2**	**38**	**1**	**–12**								
	Hershey Bears	AHL	26	10	18	28				12																		
1974-75	**Pittsburgh Penguins**	**NHL**	**40**	**5**	**9**	**14**	**4**	**7**	**11**	**6**	**0**	**0**	**0**	**33**	**15.2**	**17**	**1**	**17**	**7**	**6**	**8**	**0**	**1**	**1**	**6**	**0**	**0**	**0**
	Hershey Bears	AHL	21	9	13	22				19																		
1975-76	**Pittsburgh Penguins**	**NHL**	**12**	**1**	**2**	**3**	**1**	**1**	**2**	**4**	**0**	**1**	**0**	**4**	**25.0**	**3**	**0**	**11**	**8**	**0**								
	Hershey Bears	AHL	8	3	3	6				6																		
	New England Whalers	WHA	37	3	10	13				28											12	4	3	7	4			
	Binghamton Dusters	NAHL	5	3	5	8				0																		
	NHL Totals		**99**	**11**	**25**	**36**	**10**	**20**	**30**	**28**	**0**	**1**	**1**	**107**	**10.3**	**47**	**3**	**66**	**16**		**8**	**0**	**1**	**1**	**6**	**0**	**0**	**0**
	Other Major League Totals		37	3	10	13				28											12	4	3	7	4			

ECAC Second All-Star Team (1972) • ECAC First All-Star Team (1973) • NCAA East First All-American Team (1973)

Selected by **New England** (WHA) in 1972 WHA General Player Draft, February 12, 1972. Signed as a free agent by **Pittsburgh**, August, 1973. Traded to **Minnesota** (WHA) by **New England** (WHA) with Fred O'Donnell for Wayne Connelly, June, 1976.

• McMURCHY, Tom

RW – L. 5′9″, 165 lbs. b: New Westminster, B.C., 12/2/1963. Chicago's 3rd, 49th overall, in 1982.

Season	Club	League	GP	G	A	Pts	AG	AA	APts	PIM	PP	SH	GW	S	%	TGF	PGF	TGA	PGA	+/–	GP	G	A	Pts	PIM	PP	SH	GW
1979-80	Bellingham Blazers	BCJHL	61	72	66	138				70																		
1980-81	Medicine Hat Tigers	WHL	14	5	0	5				46																		
	Brandon Wheat Kings	WHL	46	20	33	53				101											5	2	2	4	4			
1981-82	Brandon Wheat Kings	WHL	68	59	63	122				179											4	7	3	10	4			
1982-83	Brandon Wheat Kings	WHL	42	43	38	81				48																		
	Springfield Indians	AHL	8	2	2	4				0																		
1983-84	**Chicago Black Hawks**	**NHL**	**27**	**3**	**1**	**4**	**2**	**1**	**3**	**42**	**0**	**0**	**0**	**21**	**14.3**	**7**	**0**	**15**	**1**	**–7**								
	Springfield Indians	AHL	43	16	14	30				54											4	4	0	4	0			
1984-85	**Chicago Black Hawks**	**NHL**	**15**	**1**	**2**	**3**	**1**	**1**	**2**	**13**	**0**	**0**	**0**	**8**	**12.5**	**4**	**0**	**5**	**0**	**–1**								
	Milwaukee Admirals	IHL	69	30	26	56				61																		
1985-86	**Chicago Black Hawks**	**NHL**	**4**	**0**	**0**	**0**	**0**	**0**	**0**	**2**	**0**	**0**	**0**	**2**	**0.0**	**2**	**0**	**3**	**0**	**–1**								
	Nova Scotia Oilers	AHL	49	26	21	47				73																		
	Moncton Golden Flames	AHL	16	7	3	10				27											2	0	1	1	6			
1986-87	Nova Scotia Oilers	AHL	67	21	35	56				99											4	3	2	5	4			
1987-88	**Edmonton Oilers**	**NHL**	**9**	**4**	**1**	**5**	**3**	**1**	**4**	**8**	**0**	**0**	**1**	**11**	**36.4**	**6**	**0**	**4**	**0**	**2**								
	Nova Scotia Oilers	AHL	61	40	21	61				132											3	2	1	3	4			
1988-89	EHC Bulach	Switz-2	STATISTICS NOT AVAILABLE																									
	Halifax Citadels	AHL	11	10	3	13				18											3	0	2	2	2			
1989-90	HC Fiemme	Italy	33	54	46	100				62											10	18	30	48	18			
1990-91	HC Fiemme	Italy	29	22	26	48				56											6	8	8	16	10			
1991-92	HC Cortina	Italy-2	31	53	26	79				79																		
	NHL Totals		**55**	**8**	**4**	**12**	**6**	**3**	**9**	**65**	**0**	**0**	**1**	**42**	**19.0**	**19**	**0**	**27**	**1**									

Traded to **Calgary** by **Chicago** for Rik Wilson, March 11, 1986. Signed as a free agent by **Edmonton**, August 18, 1986.

• McNAB, Peter

Peter Maxwell C – L. 6′3″, 210 lbs. b: Vancouver, B.C., 5/8/1952. Buffalo's 6th, 85th overall, in 1972.

Season	Club	League	GP	G	A	Pts	AG	AA	APts	PIM	PP	SH	GW	S	%	TGF	PGF	TGA	PGA	+/–	GP	G	A	Pts	PIM	PP	SH	GW
1970-71	University of Denver	WCHA	28	19	14	33				6																		
1971-72	University of Denver	WCHA	38	27	38	65				16																		
1972-73	University of Denver	WCHA	28	23	29	52				12																		
1973-74	**Buffalo Sabres**	**NHL**	**22**	**3**	**6**	**9**	**3**	**5**	**8**	**2**	**0**	**0**	**0**	**24**	**12.5**	**14**	**1**	**16**	**0**	**–3**								
	Cincinnati Swords	AHL	49	34	39	73				16											5	2	6	8	0			
1974-75	**Buffalo Sabres**	**NHL**	**53**	**22**	**21**	**43**	**19**	**16**	**35**	**8**	**1**	**0**	**1**	**90**	**24.4**	**48**	**5**	**30**	**0**	**13**	**17**	**2**	**6**	**8**	**4**	**0**	**0**	**0**
1975-76	**Buffalo Sabres**	**NHL**	**79**	**24**	**32**	**56**	**21**	**24**	**45**	**16**	**3**	**0**	**3**	**125**	**19.2**	**69**	**8**	**43**	**0**	**18**	**8**	**0**	**0**	**0**	**0**	**0**	**0**	**0**
1976-77	**Boston Bruins**	**NHL**	**80**	**38**	**48**	**86**	**34**	**37**	**71**	**11**	**6**	**0**	**8**	**207**	**18.4**	**101**	**17**	**58**	**0**	**26**	**14**	**5**	**3**	**8**	**2**	**2**	**0**	**0**
1977-78	**Boston Bruins**	**NHL**	**79**	**41**	**39**	**80**	**37**	**30**	**67**	**4**	**5**	**0**	**5**	**227**	**18.1**	**104**	**16**	**53**	**0**	**35**	**15**	**8**	**11**	**19**	**2**	**0**	**0**	**2**
1978-79	**Boston Bruins**	**NHL**	**76**	**35**	**45**	**80**	**30**	**33**	**63**	**10**	**4**	**0**	**4**	**200**	**17.5**	**119**	**20**	**71**	**1**	**29**	**11**	**5**	**3**	**8**	**0**	**0**	**0**	**0**
1979-80	**Boston Bruins**	**NHL**	**74**	**40**	**38**	**78**	**34**	**28**	**62**	**10**	**11**	**0**	**9**	**193**	**20.7**	**100**	**19**	**59**	**2**	**24**	**10**	**8**	**6**	**14**	**2**	**3**	**0**	**1**
1980-81	**Boston Bruins**	**NHL**	**80**	**37**	**46**	**83**	**29**	**31**	**60**	**24**	**16**	**0**	**4**	**201**	**18.4**	**113**	**50**	**52**	**1**	**12**	**3**	**3**	**0**	**3**	**0**	**1**	**0**	**0**
1981-82	**Boston Bruins**	**NHL**	**80**	**36**	**40**	**76**	**28**	**27**	**55**	**19**	**11**	**1**	**5**	**172**	**20.9**	**105**	**41**	**72**	**8**	**0**	**11**	**6**	**8**	**14**	**6**	**2**	**0**	**1**
1982-83	**Boston Bruins**	**NHL**	**74**	**22**	**52**	**74**	**18**	**36**	**54**	**23**	**5**	**0**	**2**	**160**	**13.8**	**97**	**40**	**42**	**1**	**16**	**15**	**3**	**5**	**8**	**4**	**0**	**0**	**0**
1983-84	**Boston Bruins**	**NHL**	**52**	**14**	**16**	**30**	**11**	**11**	**22**	**10**	**2**	**0**	**3**	**81**	**17.3**	**53**	**15**	**31**	**0**	**7**								
	Vancouver Canucks	**NHL**	**13**	**1**	**6**	**7**	**1**	**4**	**5**	**10**	**1**	**0**	**0**	**20**	**5.0**	**11**	**6**	**7**	**0**	**–2**	**3**	**0**	**0**	**0**	**0**	**0**	**0**	**0**
1984-85	**Vancouver Canucks**	**NHL**	**75**	**23**	**25**	**48**	**19**	**17**	**36**	**10**	**9**	**0**	**1**	**114**	**20.2**	**63**	**17**	**67**	**1**	**–20**								
1985-86	**New Jersey Devils**	**NHL**	**71**	**19**	**24**	**43**	**15**	**16**	**31**	**14**	**6**	**0**	**0**	**93**	**20.4**	**57**	**15**	**54**	**1**	**–11**								
	United States	WEC-A	10	0	1	1				4																		
1986-87	**New Jersey Devils**	**NHL**	**46**	**8**	**12**	**20**	**7**	**9**	**16**	**8**	**2**	**0**	**2**	**49**	**16.3**	**24**	**3**	**35**	**0**	**–14**								
	NHL Totals		**954**	**363**	**450**	**813**	**306**	**324**	**630**	**179**	**82**	**1**	**47**	**1956**	**18.6**	**1078**	**273**	**690**	**15**		**107**	**40**	**42**	**82**	**20**	**8**	**0**	**4**

• Son of Max • WCHA First All-Star Team (1973) • NCAA Championship All-Tournament Team (1973) • Played in NHL All-Star Game (1977)

Transferred to **Boston** by **Buffalo** as compensation for Buffalo's signing of free agent Andre Savard, June 11, 1976. Traded to **Vancouver** by **Boston** for Jim Nill, February 3, 1984. Signed as a free agent by **New Jersey**, August 20, 1985.

• McNEILL, Mike

RW – L. 6′1″, 195 lbs. b: Winona, MN, 7/22/1966. St. Louis' 1st, 14th overall, in 1988 Supplemental Draft.

Season	Club	League	GP	G	A	Pts	AG	AA	APts	PIM	PP	SH	GW	S	%	TGF	PGF	TGA	PGA	+/–	GP	G	A	Pts	PIM	PP	SH	GW
1983-84	St. Joseph's High School	Hi-School	STATISTICS NOT AVAILABLE																									
1984-85	University of Notre Dame	NCAA	28	16	26	42				12																		
1985-86	University of Notre Dame	NCAA	34	18	29	47				32																		
1986-87	University of Notre Dame	NCAA	30	21	16	37				24																		
1987-88	University of Notre Dame	NCAA	32	28	44	72				12																		
1988-89	Moncton Hawks	AHL	1	0	0	0				0																		
	Fort Wayne Komets	IHL	75	27	35	62				12											11	1	5	6	2			
1989-90	Indianapolis Ice	IHL	74	17	24	41				10											14	6	4	10	21			

			REGULAR SEASON																		PLAYOFFS							
Season	Club	League	GP	G	A	Pts	AG	AA	APts	PIM	PP	SH	GW	S	%	TGF	PGF	TGA	PGA	+/–	GP	G	A	Pts	PIM	PP	SH	GW
1990-91	**Chicago Blackhawks**	NHL	23	2	2	4	2	2	4	6	0	1	0	20	10.0	6	0	11	4	–1	....	....	....	....	....	....	....	....
	Indianapolis Ice	IHL	33	16	9	25	....	....	....	19	....	....	....	....	....	....	....	....	....	....	....	....	....	....	....	....	....	....
	Quebec Nordiques	NHL	14	2	5	7	2	4	6	4	1	0	0	11	18.2	9	1	10	7	5	....	....	....	....	....	....	....	....
	United States	WEC-A	10	1	0	1	....	....	....	4	....	....	....	....	....	....	....	....	....	....	....	....	....	....	....	....	....	....
1991-92	**Quebec Nordiques**	NHL	26	1	4	5	1	3	4	8	1	0	0	15	6.7	10	6	23	11	–8	....	....	....	....	....	....	....	....
	Halifax Citadels	AHL	30	10	8	18	....	....	....	20	....	....	....	....	....	....	....	....	....	....	....	....	....	....	....	....	....	....
1992-93	Milwaukee Admirals	IHL	75	17	17	34	....	....	....	34	....	....	....	....	....	....	....	....	....	....	6	2	0	2	0	....	....	....
1993-94	Milwaukee Admirals	IHL	78	21	25	46	....	....	....	40	....	....	....	....	....	....	....	....	....	....	4	0	1	1	6	....	....	....
1994-95	Milwaukee Admirals	IHL	80	23	15	38	....	....	....	30	....	....	....	....	....	....	....	....	....	....	15	2	2	4	14	....	....	....
1995-96	Milwaukee Admirals	IHL	64	8	9	17	....	....	....	32	....	....	....	....	....	....	....	....	....	....	5	2	0	2	2	....	....	....
1996-97	Milwaukee Admirals	IHL	74	18	26	44	....	....	....	24	....	....	....	....	....	....	....	....	....	....	3	0	1	1	0	....	....	....
1997-98	Milwaukee Admirals	IHL	81	10	18	28	....	....	....	58	....	....	....	....	....	....	....	....	....	....	10	2	1	3	12	....	....	....
1998-99	Revier Lowen	Germany	47	8	16	24	....	....	....	10	....	....	....	....	....	....	....	....	....	....	....	....	....	....	....	....	....	....
99-2000	Revier Lowen	Germany	22	1	7	8	....	....	....	6	....	....	....	....	....	....	....	....	....	....	....	....	....	....	....	....	....	....
	NHL Totals		63	5	11	16	5	9	14	18	2	1	0	46	10.9	25	7	44	22		....	....	....	....	....	....	....	....

Won "Bud" Poile Trophy (Playoff MVP - IHL) (1990)

Signed as a free agent by **Chicago**, September, 1989. Traded to **Quebec** by **Chicago** with Ryan McGill for Paul Gillis and Dan Vincelette, March 5, 1991.

• McPHEE, George

"Fenster" LW – L. 5'9", 170 lbs. b: Guelph, Ont., 7/2/1958.

Season	Club	League	GP	G	A	Pts	AG	AA	APts	PIM	PP	SH	GW	S	%	TGF	PGF	TGA	PGA	+/–	GP	G	A	Pts	PIM	PP	SH	GW
1977-78	Guelph Platers	OJHL	48	53	57	110	....	....	....	150	....	....	....	....	....	....	....	....	....	....	....	....	....	....	....	....	....	....
	Guelph Platers	Cen-Cup	STATISTICS NOT AVAILABLE																									
1978-79	Bowling Green University	CCHA	43	*40	48	*88	....	....	....	58	....	....	....	....	....	....	....	....	....	....	....	....	....	....	....	....	....	....
1979-80	Bowling Green University	CCHA	34	21	24	45	....	....	....	51	....	....	....	....	....	....	....	....	....	....	....	....	....	....	....	....	....	....
1980-81	Bowling Green University	CCHA	36	25	29	54	....	....	....	68	....	....	....	....	....	....	....	....	....	....	....	....	....	....	....	....	....	....
1981-82	Bowling Green University	CCHA	40	28	52	80	....	....	....	57	....	....	....	....	....	....	....	....	....	....	....	....	....	....	....	....	....	....
1982-83	Tulsa Oilers	CHL	61	17	43	60	....	....	....	145	....	....	....	....	....	....	....	....	....	....	7	1	1	2	14	....	....	....
	New York Rangers	NHL	....	....	....	....	....	....	....	....	....	....	....	....	....	....	0	0	0	0	9	3	3	6	2	1	0	0
1983-84	**New York Rangers**	NHL	9	1	1	2	1	1	2	11	0	0	0	1	100.0	2	0	2	0	0	....	....	....	....	....	....	....	....
	Tulsa Oilers	CHL	49	20	28	48	....	....	....	133	....	....	....	....	....	....	....	....	....	....	....	....	....	....	....	....	....	....
1984-85	**New York Rangers**	NHL	49	12	15	27	10	10	20	139	1	0	1	54	22.2	36	2	43	0	–9	3	1	0	1	7	0	0	0
	New Haven Nighthawks	AHL	3	2	2	4	....	....	....	13	....	....	....	....	....	....	....	....	....	....	....	....	....	....	....	....	....	....
1985-86	**New York Rangers**	NHL	30	4	4	8	3	3	6	63	0	0	1	31	12.9	15	0	10	0	5	11	0	0	0	32	0	0	0
1986-87	**New York Rangers**	NHL	21	4	4	8	3	3	6	34	0	0	2	31	12.9	14	0	16	0	–2	6	1	0	1	28	1	0	0
1987-88	**New Jersey Devils**	NHL	5	3	0	3	3	0	3	8	0	0	1	5	60.0	4	0	2	0	2	....	....	....	....	....	....	....	....
1988-89	**New Jersey Devils**	NHL	1	0	1	1	0	1	1	2	0	0	0	0	0.0	1	0	0	0	1	....	....	....	....	....	....	....	....
	Utica Devils	AHL	8	3	2	5	....	....	....	31	....	....	....	....	....	....	....	....	....	....	3	1	0	1	26	....	....	....
1989-1992			OUT OF HOCKEY – RETIRED																									
1992-1997	**Vancouver Canucks**	NHL	DID NOT PLAY – ASSISTANT GENERAL MANAGER																									
1997-2000	**Washington Capitals**	NHL	DID NOT PLAY – GENERAL MANAGER																									
	NHL Totals		115	24	25	49	20	18	38	257	1	0	5	122	19.7	72	2	73	0		29	5	3	8	69	2	0	0

Centennial Cup All-Star Team • CCHA Second All-Star Team (1979, 1981) • CCHA First All-Star Team (1982) • NCAA West First All-American Team (1982) • Won Hobey Baker Memorial Award (Top U.S. Collegiate Player) (1982)

Signed as a free agent by **NY Rangers**, July 1, 1982. • Suffered eventual career-ending back injury in game vs. Pittsburgh, November 4, 1985. Traded to **Winnipeg** by **NY Rangers** for Winnipeg's 4th round choice (Jim Cummins) in 1989 Entry Draft, September 30, 1987. • Missed majority of 1986-87 season recovering from shoulder injury suffered in exhibition game vs. Pittsburgh, October 5, 1986. Traded to **New Jersey** by **Winnipeg** for New Jersey's 7th round choice (Doug Evans) in 1989 Entry Draft, October 7, 1987. • Attended Rutgers University and earned Law Degree, 1989-1992.

• McPHEE, Mike

Michael Joseph LW – L. 6'1", 203 lbs. b: Sydney, N.S., 7/14/1960. Montreal's 8th, 124th overall, in 1980.

Season	Club	League	GP	G	A	Pts	AG	AA	APts	PIM	PP	SH	GW	S	%	TGF	PGF	TGA	PGA	+/–	GP	G	A	Pts	PIM	PP	SH	GW
1977-78	Port Hawksbury Pirates	MJrHL	32	50	37	87	....	....	....		....	....	....	....	....	....	....	....	....	....	....	....	....	....	....	....	....	....
1978-79	RPI Engineers	ECAC	26	14	19	33	....	....	....	16	....	....	....	....	....	....	....	....	....	....	....	....	....	....	....	....	....	....
1979-80	RPI Engineers	ECAC	27	15	21	36	....	....	....	22	....	....	....	....	....	....	....	....	....	....	....	....	....	....	....	....	....	....
1980-81	RPI Engineers	ECAC	29	28	18	46	....	....	....	22	....	....	....	....	....	....	....	....	....	....	....	....	....	....	....	....	....	....
1981-82	RPI Engineers	ECAC	6	0	3	3	....	....	....	4	....	....	....	....	....	....	....	....	....	....	....	....	....	....	....	....	....	....
1982-83	Nova Scotia Voyageurs	AHL	42	10	15	25	....	....	....	29	....	....	....	....	....	....	....	....	....	....	7	1	1	2	14	....	....	....
1983-84	**Montreal Canadiens**	NHL	14	5	2	7	4	1	5	41	0	0	0	22	22.7	10	0	6	0	4	15	1	0	1	31	0	0	0
	Nova Scotia Voyageurs	AHL	67	22	33	55	....	....	....	101	....	....	....	....	....	....	....	....	....	....	....	....	....	....	....	....	....	....
1984-85	**Montreal Canadiens**	NHL	70	17	22	39	14	15	29	120	0	0	2	135	12.6	54	3	59	9	1	12	4	1	5	32	0	0	0
1985-86♦	**Montreal Canadiens**	NHL	70	19	21	40	15	14	29	69	0	2	3	103	18.4	53	1	54	10	8	20	3	4	7	45	0	1	1
1986-87	**Montreal Canadiens**	NHL	79	18	21	39	16	15	31	58	0	2	2	150	12.0	53	2	57	13	7	17	7	2	9	13	1	0	2
1987-88	**Montreal Canadiens**	NHL	77	23	20	43	20	14	34	53	0	2	4	151	15.2	61	2	58	18	19	11	4	3	7	8	0	1	0
1988-89	**Montreal Canadiens**	NHL	73	19	22	41	16	16	32	74	1	1	1	154	12.3	59	7	52	14	14	20	4	7	11	30	0	0	1
1989-90	**Montreal Canadiens**	NHL	56	23	18	41	20	13	33	47	-3	1	1	118	19.5	63	2	42	9	28	9	1	1	2	16	0	0	0
1990-91	Montreal Canadiens	Fr-Tour	2	0	0	0	....	....	....	27	....	....	....	....	....	....	....	....	....	....	....	....	....	....	....	....	....	....
	Montreal Canadiens	NHL	64	22	21	43	20	16	36	56	2	0	4	123	17.9	66	12	53	5	6	13	1	7	8	12	1	0	0
1991-92	**Montreal Canadiens**	NHL	78	16	15	31	15	11	26	63	0	0	1	146	11.0	47	1	47	7	6	8	1	1	2	4	0	0	0
1992-93	**Minnesota North Stars**	NHL	84	18	22	40	15	15	30	44	1	2	2	161	11.2	59	6	72	17	–2	....	....	....	....	....	....	....	....
1993-94	**Dallas Stars**	NHL	79	20	15	35	19	12	31	36	1	3	1	115	17.4	56	1	65	18	8	9	2	1	3	2	0	0	0
	NHL Totals		744	200	199	399	174	142	316	661	2	13	21	1378	14.5	581	37	565	120		134	28	27	55	193	2	2	4

Played in NHL All-Star Game (1989)

Traded to **Minnesota** by **Montreal** for Minnesota/Dallas' 5th round choice (Jeff Lank) in 1993 Entry Draft, August 14, 1992. Transferred to **Dallas** after **Minnesota** franchise relocated, June 9, 1993.

• McRAE, Basil

Basil Paul LW – L. 6'2", 210 lbs. b: Beaverton, Ont., 1/5/1961. Quebec's 3rd, 87th overall, in 1980.

Season	Club	League	GP	G	A	Pts	AG	AA	APts	PIM	PP	SH	GW	S	%	TGF	PGF	TGA	PGA	+/–	GP	G	A	Pts	PIM	PP	SH	GW
1977-78	Seneca Nats	OHA-B	36	21	38	59	....	....	....	80	....	....	....	....	....	....	....	....	....	....	....	....	....	....	....	....	....	....
1978-79	London Knights	OMJHL	66	13	28	41	....	....	....	79	....	....	....	....	....	....	....	....	....	....	7	0	0	0	0	....	....	....
1979-80	London Knights	OMJHL	67	24	36	60	....	....	....	116	....	....	....	....	....	....	....	....	....	....	5	0	0	0	18	....	....	....
1980-81	London Knights	OMJHL	65	29	23	52	....	....	....	266	....	....	....	....	....	....	....	....	....	....	....	....	....	....	....	....	....	....
1981-82	**Quebec Nordiques**	NHL	20	4	3	7	3	2	5	69	0	0	0	20	20.0	10	1	12	0	–3	9	1	0	1	34	0	0	0
	Fredericton Express	AHL	47	11	15	26	....	....	....	175	....	....	....	....	....	....	....	....	....	....	....	....	....	....	....	....	....	....
1982-83	**Quebec Nordiques**	NHL	22	1	1	2	1	1	2	59	0	0	0	6	16.7	4	0	5	0	–1	....	....	....	....	....	....	....	....
	Fredericton Express	AHL	53	22	19	41	....	....	....	146	....	....	....	....	....	....	....	....	....	....	12	1	5	6	75	....	....	....
1983-84	**Toronto Maple Leafs**	NHL	3	0	0	0	0	0	0	19	0	0	0	7	0.0	0	0	3	0	–3	....	....	....	....	....	....	....	....
	St. Catharines Saints	AHL	78	14	25	39	....	....	....	187	....	....	....	....	....	....	....	....	....	....	6	0	0	0	40	....	....	....
1984-85	**Toronto Maple Leafs**	NHL	1	0	0	0	0	0	0	0	0	0	0	0	0.0	0	0	0	0	0	....	....	....	....	....	....	....	....
	St. Catharines Saints	AHL	72	30	25	55	....	....	....	186	....	....	....	....	....	....	....	....	....	....	....	....	....	....	....	....	....	....
1985-86	**Detroit Red Wings**	NHL	4	0	0	0	0	0	0	5	0	0	0	3	0.0	0	0	4	0	–4	....	....	....	....	....	....	....	....
	Adirondack Red Wings	AHL	69	22	30	52	....	....	....	259	....	....	....	....	....	....	....	....	....	....	17	5	4	9	101	....	....	....
1986-87	**Detroit Red Wings**	NHL	36	2	2	4	2	1	3	193	1	0	1	21	9.5	12	2	13	0	–3	....	....	....	....	....	....	....	....
	Quebec Nordiques	NHL	33	9	5	14	8	4	12	149	3	0	1	36	25.0	21	5	15	0	1	13	3	1	4	*99	0	0	1
1987-88	**Minnesota North Stars**	NHL	80	5	11	16	4	8	12	382	0	0	0	107	4.7	26	1	53	0	–28	....	....	....	....	....	....	....	....
1988-89	**Minnesota North Stars**	NHL	78	12	19	31	10	13	23	365	4	0	0	122	9.8	54	15	47	0	–8	5	0	0	0	58	0	0	0
1989-90	**Minnesota North Stars**	NHL	66	9	17	26	8	12	20	*351	2	0	2	95	9.5	36	8	33	0	–5	7	1	0	1	24	0	0	0
1990-91	Minnesota North Stars	Fr-Tour	3	1	0	1	....	....	....	26	....	....	....	....	....	....	....	....	....	....	....	....	....	....	....	....	....	....
	Minnesota North Stars	NHL	40	1	3	4	1	2	3	224	0	0	0	44	2.3	9	2	15	0	–8	22	1	1	2	*94	0	0	0
1991-92	**Minnesota North Stars**	NHL	59	5	8	13	5	6	11	245	0	0	0	64	7.8	17	1	30	0	–14	....	....	....	....	....	....	....	....
1992-93	**Tampa Bay Lightning**	NHL	14	2	3	5	2	2	4	71	1	0	0	23	8.7	11	5	9	0	–3	....	....	....	....	....	....	....	....
	St. Louis Blues	NHL	33	1	3	4	1	2	3	98	1	0	0	22	4.5	6	1	18	0	–13	11	0	1	1	24	0	0	0
1993-94	**St. Louis Blues**	NHL	40	1	2	3	1	2	3	103	0	0	0	23	4.3	8	0	16	1	–7	2	0	0	0	12	0	0	0

			REGULAR SEASON																		PLAYOFFS							
Season	Club	League	GP	G	A	Pts	AG	AA	APts	PIM	PP	SH	GW	S	%	TGF	PGF	TGA	PGA	+/–	GP	G	A	Pts	PIM	PP	SH	GW
1994-95	**St. Louis Blues**	**NHL**	**21**	**0**	**5**	**5**	**0**	**7**	**7**	**72**	**0**	**0**	**0**	**14**	**0.0**	**7**	**0**	**3**	**0**	**4**	**7**	**2**	**1**	**3**	**4**	**0**	**0**	**0**
	Peoria Rivermen	IHL	2	0	0	0	....	....	....	12	....	....	....	....	....	....	....	....	....	....	....	....	....	....	....	....	....	....
1995-96	**St. Louis Blues**	**NHL**	**18**	**1**	**1**	**2**	**1**	**1**	**2**	**40**	**0**	**0**	**0**	**5**	**20.0**	**2**	**0**	**7**	**0**	**–5**	**2**	**0**	**0**	**0**	**0**	**0**	**0**	**0**
1996-97	**Chicago Blackhawks**	**NHL**	**8**	**0**	**0**	**0**	**0**	**0**	**0**	**12**	**0**	**0**	**0**	**1**	**0.0**	**1**	**0**	**3**	**0**	**–2**	....	....	....	....	....	....	....	....
	NHL Totals		**576**	**53**	**83**	**136**	**47**	**63**	**110**	**2457**	**12**	**0**	**4**	**613**	**8.6**	**224**	**41**	**286**	**1**		**78**	**8**	**4**	**12**	**349**	**0**	**0**	**1**

• Brother of Chris

Traded to **Toronto** by **Quebec** for Richard Turmel, August 12, 1983. Signed as a free agent by **Detroit**, July 17, 1985. Traded to **Quebec** by **Detroit** with John Ogrodnick and Doug Shedden for Brent Ashton, Gilbert Delorme and Mark Kumpel, January 17, 1987. Signed as a free agent by **Minnesota**, June 29, 1987. Claimed by **Tampa Bay** from **Minnesota** in Expansion Draft, June 18, 1992. Traded to **St. Louis** by **Tampa Bay** with Doug Crossman and Tampa Bay's 4th round choice (Andrei Petrakov) in 1996 Entry Draft for Jason Ruff, January 28, 1993. Signed as a free agent by **Chicago**, October 9, 1996.

• McRAE, Chris

LW – L. 6', 200 lbs. b: Beaverton, Ont., 8/26/1965.

Season	Club	League	GP	G	A	Pts	AG	AA	APts	PIM	PP	SH	GW	S	%	TGF	PGF	TGA	PGA	+/–	GP	G	A	Pts	PIM	PP	SH	GW
1982-83	Newmarket Saints	OJHL	42	11	22	33	....	....	....	207	....	....	....	....	....	....	....	....	....	....	....	....	....	....	....	....	....	....
1983-84	Belleville Bulls	OHL	9	0	0	0	....	....	....	19	....	....	....	....	....	....	....	....	....	....	....	....	....	....	....	....	....	....
	Sudbury Wolves	OHL	53	14	31	45	....	....	....	120	....	....	....	....	....	....	....	....	....	....	....	....	....	....	....	....	....	....
1984-85	Sudbury Wolves	OHL	6	0	2	2	....	....	....	10	....	....	....	....	....	....	....	....	....	....	....	....	....	....	....	....	....	....
	Oshawa Generals	OHL	43	8	7	15	....	....	....	118	....	....	....	....	....	....	....	....	....	....	5	0	1	1	2	....	....	....
	St. Catharines Saints	AHL	6	4	3	7	....	....	....	24	....	....	....	....	....	....	....	....	....	....	....	....	....	....	....	....	....	....
1985-86	St. Catharines Saints	AHL	59	1	1	2	....	....	....	233	....	....	....	....	....	....	....	....	....	....	11	0	1	1	65	....	....	....
1986-87	Newmarket Saints	AHL	51	3	6	9	....	....	....	193	....	....	....	....	....	....	....	....	....	....	....	....	....	....	....	....	....	....
1987-88	**Toronto Maple Leafs**	**NHL**	**11**	**0**	**0**	**0**	**0**	**0**	**0**	**65**	**0**	**0**	**0**	**0**	**0.0**	**0**	**0**	**0**	**0**	**0**	....	....	....	....	....	....	....	....
	Newmarket Saints	AHL	34	7	6	13	....	....	....	165	....	....	....	....	....	....	....	....	....	....	....	....	....	....	....	....	....	....
1988-89	**Toronto Maple Leafs**	**NHL**	**3**	**0**	**0**	**0**	**0**	**0**	**0**	**12**	**0**	**0**	**0**	**0**	**0.0**	**0**	**0**	**0**	**0**	**0**	....	....	....	....	....	....	....	....
	Newmarket Saints	AHL	18	3	1	4	....	....	....	85	....	....	....	....	....	....	....	....	....	....	....	....	....	....	....	....	....	....
	Denver Rangers	IHL	23	1	4	5	....	....	....	121	....	....	....	....	....	....	....	....	....	....	2	0	0	0	20	....	....	....
1989-90	**Detroit Red Wings**	**NHL**	**7**	**1**	**0**	**1**	**1**	**0**	**1**	**45**	**0**	**0**	**0**	**1**	**100.0**	**1**	**0**	**1**	**0**	**0**	....	....	....	....	....	....	....	....
	Adirondack Red Wings	AHL	46	9	10	19	....	....	....	290	....	....	....	....	....	....	....	....	....	....	....	....	....	....	....	....	....	....
1990-91	Adirondack Red Wings	AHL	23	2	3	5	....	....	....	109	....	....	....	....	....	....	....	....	....	....	2	0	0	0	11	....	....	....
1991-92	Fort Wayne Komets	IHL	60	20	14	34	....	....	....	*413	....	....	....	....	....	....	....	....	....	....	5	1	0	1	44	....	....	....
	NHL Totals		**21**	**1**	**0**	**1**	**1**	**0**	**1**	**122**	**0**	**0**	**0**	**1**	**100.0**	**1**	**0**	**1**	**0**		....	....	....	....	....	....	....	....

• Brother of Basil

Signed as a free agent by **Toronto**, October 16, 1985. Traded to **NY Rangers** by **Toronto** for Ken Hammond, February 21, 1989. Traded to **Detroit** by **NY Rangers** with Detroit's 5th round choice (previously acquired, Detroit selected Tony Burns) in 1990 Entry Draft for Kris King, September 7, 1989. • Missed remainder of 1989-90 and majority of 1990-91 seasons recovering from eye injury suffered in game vs. NY Islanders, February 28, 1990.

• McRAE, Ken

C – R. 6'1", 195 lbs. b: Winchester, Ont., 4/23/1968. Quebec's 1st, 18th overall, in 1986.

Season	Club	League	GP	G	A	Pts	AG	AA	APts	PIM	PP	SH	GW	S	%	TGF	PGF	TGA	PGA	+/–	GP	G	A	Pts	PIM	PP	SH	GW
1984-85	Hawkesbury Hawks	OJHL	51	38	50	88	....	....	....	77	....	....	....	....	....	....	....	....	....	....	....	....	....	....	....	....	....	....
1985-86	Sudbury Wolves	OHL	66	25	49	74	....	....	....	127	....	....	....	....	....	....	....	....	....	....	4	2	1	3	12	....	....	....
1986-87	Sudbury Wolves	OHL	21	12	15	27	....	....	....	40	....	....	....	....	....	....	....	....	....	....	....	....	....	....	....	....	....	....
	Hamilton Steelhawks	OHL	20	7	12	19	....	....	....	25	....	....	....	....	....	....	....	....	....	....	7	1	1	2	12	....	....	....
1987-88	Hamilton Steelhawks	OHL	62	30	55	85	....	....	....	158	....	....	....	....	....	....	....	....	....	....	14	13	9	22	35	....	....	....
	Quebec Nordiques	**NHL**	**1**	**0**	**0**	**0**	**0**	**0**	**0**	**0**	**0**	**0**	**0**	**1**	**0.0**	**0**	**0**	**0**	**0**	**0**	....	....	....	....	....	....	....	....
	Fredericton Express	AHL	....	....	....	....	....	....	....	....	....	....	....	....	....	....	....	....	....	....	3	0	0	0	8	....	....	....
1988-89	**Quebec Nordiques**	**NHL**	**37**	**6**	**11**	**17**	**5**	**8**	**13**	**68**	**1**	**0**	**2**	**47**	**12.8**	**22**	**4**	**31**	**4**	**–9**	....	....	....	....	....	....	....	....
	Halifax Citadels	AHL	41	20	21	41	....	....	....	87	....	....	....	....	....	....	....	....	....	....	....	....	....	....	....	....	....	....
1989-90	**Quebec Nordiques**	**NHL**	**66**	**7**	**8**	**15**	**6**	**6**	**12**	**191**	**0**	**0**	**1**	**83**	**8.4**	**28**	**0**	**76**	**10**	**–38**	....	....	....	....	....	....	....	....
1990-91	**Quebec Nordiques**	**NHL**	**12**	**0**	**0**	**0**	**0**	**0**	**0**	**36**	**0**	**0**	**0**	**6**	**0.0**	**0**	**0**	**7**	**0**	**–7**	....	....	....	....	....	....	....	....
	Halifax Citadels	AHL	60	10	36	46	....	....	....	193	....	....	....	....	....	....	....	....	....	....	....	....	....	....	....	....	....	....
1991-92	**Quebec Nordiques**	**NHL**	**10**	**0**	**1**	**1**	**0**	**1**	**1**	**31**	**0**	**0**	**0**	**10**	**0.0**	**1**	**0**	**6**	**0**	**–5**	....	....	....	....	....	....	....	....
	Halifax Citadels	AHL	52	30	41	71	....	....	....	184	....	....	....	....	....	....	....	....	....	....	....	....	....	....	....	....	....	....
1992-93	**Toronto Maple Leafs**	**NHL**	**2**	**0**	**0**	**0**	**0**	**0**	**0**	**2**	**0**	**0**	**0**	**3**	**0.0**	**0**	**0**	**1**	**0**	**–1**	....	....	....	....	....	....	....	....
	St. John's Maple Leafs	AHL	64	30	44	74	....	....	....	135	....	....	....	....	....	....	....	....	....	....	9	6	6	12	27	....	....	....
1993-94	**Toronto Maple Leafs**	**NHL**	**9**	**1**	**1**	**2**	**1**	**1**	**2**	**36**	**0**	**0**	**0**	**11**	**9.1**	**5**	**0**	**4**	**0**	**1**	**6**	**0**	**0**	**0**	**4**	**0**	**0**	**0**
	St. John's Maple Leafs	AHL	65	23	41	64	....	....	....	200	....	....	....	....	....	....	....	....	....	....	....	....	....	....	....	....	....	....
1994-95	Detroit Vipers	IHL	24	4	9	13	....	....	....	38	....	....	....	....	....	....	....	....	....	....	....	....	....	....	....	....	....	....
	Phoenix Roadrunners	IHL	2	2	0	2	....	....	....	0	....	....	....	....	....	....	....	....	....	....	9	3	8	11	21	....	....	....
1995-96	Phoenix Roadrunners	IHL	45	11	14	25	....	....	....	102	....	....	....	....	....	....	....	....	....	....	4	1	1	2	24	....	....	....
1996-97	Phoenix Roadrunners	IHL	72	25	28	53	....	....	....	190	....	....	....	....	....	....	....	....	....	....	....	....	....	....	....	....	....	....
	Providence Bruins	AHL	9	5	5	10	....	....	....	26	....	....	....	....	....	....	....	....	....	....	10	1	3	4	17	....	....	....
1997-98	Houston Aeros	IHL	78	22	32	54	....	....	....	192	....	....	....	....	....	....	....	....	....	....	1	0	0	0	0	....	....	....
1998-1999	Houston Aeros	IHL	DID NOT PLAY – ASSISTANT COACH																									
1999-2000	Austin Ice Bats	WPHL	DID NOT PLAY – ASSISTANT COACH																									
	NHL Totals		**137**	**14**	**21**	**35**	**12**	**16**	**28**	**364**	**1**	**0**	**3**	**161**	**8.7**	**56**	**4**	**125**	**14**		**6**	**0**	**0**	**0**	**4**	**0**	**0**	**0**

Traded to **Toronto** by **Quebec** for Len Esau, July 21, 1992.

• McREYNOLDS, Brian

C – L. 6'1", 192 lbs. b: Penetanguishene, Ont., 1/5/1965. NY Rangers' 6th, 112th overall, in 1985.

Season	Club	League	GP	G	A	Pts	AG	AA	APts	PIM	PP	SH	GW	S	%	TGF	PGF	TGA	PGA	+/–	GP	G	A	Pts	PIM	PP	SH	GW
1982-83	Penetang Kings	OJHL-C	34	36	34	70	....	....	....	62	....	....	....	....	....	....	....	....	....	....	....	....	....	....	....	....	....	....
1983-84	Penetang Kings	OJHL-C	28	31	42	73	....	....	....	75	....	....	....	....	....	....	....	....	....	....	....	....	....	....	....	....	....	....
1984-85	Orillia Travelways	OJHL	48	40	54	94	....	....	....	....	....	....	....	....	....	....	....	....	....	....	....	....	....	....	....	....	....	....
	Orillia Travelways	Cen-Cup	4	4	5	9	....	....	....	8	....	....	....	....	....	....	....	....	....	....	....	....	....	....	....	....	....	....
1985-86	Michigan State Spartans	CCHA	45	14	24	38	....	....	....	78	....	....	....	....	....	....	....	....	....	....	....	....	....	....	....	....	....	....
1986-87	Michigan State Spartans	CCHA	45	16	24	40	....	....	....	68	....	....	....	....	....	....	....	....	....	....	....	....	....	....	....	....	....	....
1987-88	Michigan State Spartans	CCHA	43	10	24	34	....	....	....	50	....	....	....	....	....	....	....	....	....	....	....	....	....	....	....	....	....	....
1988-89	Canada	Nat-Team	58	5	25	30	....	....	....	59	....	....	....	....	....	....	....	....	....	....	....	....	....	....	....	....	....	....
1989-90	**Winnipeg Jets**	**NHL**	**9**	**0**	**2**	**2**	**0**	**1**	**1**	**4**	**0**	**0**	**0**	**11**	**0.0**	**3**	**0**	**8**	**1**	**–4**	....	....	....	....	....	....	....	....
	Moncton Hawks	AHL	72	18	41	59	....	....	....	87	....	....	....	....	....	....	....	....	....	....	....	....	....	....	....	....	....	....
1990-91	**New York Rangers**	**NHL**	**1**	**0**	**0**	**0**	**0**	**0**	**0**	**0**	**0**	**0**	**0**	**0**	**0.0**	**0**	**0**	**1**	**0**	**–1**	....	....	....	....	....	....	....	....
	Binghamton Rangers	AHL	77	30	42	72	....	....	....	74	....	....	....	....	....	....	....	....	....	....	10	0	4	4	6	....	....	....
1991-92	Binghamton Rangers	AHL	48	19	28	47	....	....	....	22	....	....	....	....	....	....	....	....	....	....	7	2	2	4	12	....	....	....
1992-93	Binghamton Rangers	AHL	79	30	70	100	....	....	....	88	....	....	....	....	....	....	....	....	....	....	14	3	10	13	18	....	....	....
1993-94	**Los Angeles Kings**	**NHL**	**20**	**1**	**3**	**4**	**1**	**2**	**3**	**4**	**0**	**0**	**0**	**10**	**10.0**	**6**	**0**	**14**	**6**	**–2**	....	....	....	....	....	....	....	....
	Phoenix Roadrunners	IHL	51	14	33	47	....	....	....	65	....	....	....	....	....	....	....	....	....	....	....	....	....	....	....	....	....	....
1994-95	Phoenix Roadrunners	IHL	55	5	27	32	....	....	....	60	....	....	....	....	....	....	....	....	....	....	....	....	....	....	....	....	....	....
	Atlanta Knights	IHL	11	5	7	12	....	....	....	14	....	....	....	....	....	....	....	....	....	....	5	4	5	9	4	....	....	....
1995-96	Ratingen Lowen	Germany	6	2	4	6	....	....	....	29	....	....	....	....	....	....	....	....	....	....	....	....	....	....	....	....	....	....
	Malmo IF	Sweden	16	1	4	5	....	....	....	12	....	....	....	....	....	....	....	....	....	....	....	....	....	....	....	....	....	....
1996-97	Ratingen Lowen	Germany	35	9	20	29	....	....	....	53	....	....	....	....	....	....	....	....	....	....	7	1	2	3	20	....	....	....
1997-98	Star Bulls Rosenheim	Germany	31	2	12	14	....	....	....	28	....	....	....	....	....	....	....	....	....	....	....	....	....	....	....	....	....	....
	Kolner Haie	Germany	16	2	6	8	....	....	....	10	....	....	....	....	....	....	....	....	....	....	3	0	0	0	4	....	....	....
1998-99	Kolner Haie	Germany	36	4	3	7	....	....	....	26	....	....	....	....	....	....	....	....	....	....	....	....	....	....	....	....	....	....
	NHL Totals		**30**	**1**	**5**	**6**	**1**	**3**	**4**	**8**	**0**	**0**	**0**	**21**	**4.8**	**9**	**0**	**23**	**7**		....	....	....	....	....	....	....	....

Signed as a free agent by **Winnipeg**, June 20, 1989. Traded to **NY Rangers** by **Winnipeg** for Simon Wheeldon, July 9, 1990. Signed as a free agent by **LA Kings**, July 29, 1993.

• McSHEFFREY, Bryan

Bryan Gerald RW – R. 6'2", 205 lbs. b: Ottawa, Ont., 9/25/1952. Vancouver's 2nd, 19th overall, in 1972.

Season	Club	League	GP	G	A	Pts	AG	AA	APts	PIM	PP	SH	GW	S	%	TGF	PGF	TGA	PGA	+/–	GP	G	A	Pts	PIM	PP	SH	GW
1967-68	Ottawa South Canadians	OMHA	STATISTICS NOT AVAILABLE																									
	Oshawa Generals	OHA-Jr.	1	0	1	1	....	....	....	0	....	....	....	....	....	....	....	....	....	....	....	....	....	....	....	....	....	....
1968-69	Ottawa 67's	OHA-Jr.	53	10	7	17	....	....	....	12	....	....	....	....	....	....	....	....	....	....	7	1	1	2	2	....	....	....
1969-70	Ottawa 67's	OHA-Jr.	54	35	32	67	....	....	....	51	....	....	....	....	....	....	....	....	....	....	5	0	1	1	6	....	....	....

			REGULAR SEASON																		PLAYOFFS							
Season	Club	League	GP	G	A	Pts	AG	AA	APts	PIM	PP	SH	GW	S	%	TGF	PGF	TGA	PGA	+/–	GP	G	A	Pts	PIM	PP	SH	GW
1970-71	Ottawa 67's	OHA-Jr.	57	38	41	79	....	....	....	86	....	....	....	....	....	....	....	....	....	....	11	7	7	14	27	....	....	....
1971-72	Ottawa 67's	OMJHL	61	52	44	96	....	....	....	63	....	....	....	....	....	....	....	....	....	....	13	4	9	13	20	....	....	....
1972-73	**Vancouver Canucks**	**NHL**	**33**	**4**	**4**	**8**	**4**	**3**	**7**	**10**	**0**	**0**	**0**	**45**	**8.9**	**10**	**2**	**41**	**1**	**–32**	....	....	....	....	....	....	....	....
	Seattle Totems	WHL	39	27	22	49	....	....	....	24	....	....	....	....	....	....	....	....	....	....	....	....	....	....	....	....	....	....
1973-74	**Vancouver Canucks**	**NHL**	**54**	**9**	**3**	**12**	**9**	**2**	**11**	**34**	**3**	**0**	**0**	**71**	**12.7**	**17**	**5**	**26**	**0**	**–14**	....	....	....	....	....	....	....	....
1974-75	**Buffalo Sabres**	**NHL**	**3**	**0**	**0**	**0**	**0**	**0**	**0**	**0**	**0**	**0**	**0**	**1**	**0.0**	**2**	**1**	**0**	**0**	**1**	....	....	....	....	....	....	....	....
	Hershey Bears	AHL	47	12	8	20	....	....	....	20	....	....	....	....	....	....	....	....	....	....	11	1	0	1	0	....	....	....
1975-76	Mohawk Valley Comets	NAHL	12	4	3	7	....	....	....	0	....	....	....	....	....	....	....	....	....	....	4	0	2	2	6	....	....	....
	Cape Cod Codders	NAHL	3	1	0	1	....	....	....	0	....	....	....	....	....	....	....	....	....	....	....	....	....	....	....	....	....	....
	Buffalo Norsemen	NAHL	46	27	31	58	....	....	....	26	....	....	....	....	....	....	....	....	....	....	....	....	....	....	....	....	....	....
1976-77	Mohawk Valley Comets	NAHL	63	29	43	72	....	....	....	28	....	....	....	....	....	....	....	....	....	....	3	0	1	1	0	....	....	....
1977-78	Long Beach Sharks-Rockets	PHL	18	7	8	15	....	....	....	11	....	....	....	....	....	....	....	....	....	....	....	....	....	....	....	....	....	....
1978-79	HYS-Intervam	Holland	18	*32	32	*64	....	....	....	18	....	....	....	....	....	....	....	....	....	....	18	*29	22	51	19	....	....	....
1979-80	HYS-Intervam	Holland	22	26	34	60	....	....	....	....	....	....	....	....	....	....	....	....	....	....	....	....	....	....	....	....	....	....
	NHL Totals		**90**	**13**	**7**	**20**	**13**	**5**	**18**	**44**	**3**	**0**	**0**	**117**	**11.1**	**29**	**8**	**67**	**1**		....	....	....	....	....	....	....	....

Traded to **Buffalo** by **Vancouver** with Jocelyn Guevremont for Gerry Meehan and Mike Robitaille, October 14, 1974. Traded to **Cape Cod** (NAHL) by **Buffalo** (NAHL) for cash, January 23, 1976.

• McSORLEY, Marty

Martin James D – R. 6'1", 235 lbs. b: Hamilton, Ont., 5/18/1963.

Season	Club	League	GP	G	A	Pts	AG	AA	APts	PIM	PP	SH	GW	S	%	TGF	PGF	TGA	PGA	+/–	GP	G	A	Pts	PIM	PP	SH	GW
1979-80	Cayuga Red Wings	OHA-D	27	8	18	26	....	....	....	92	....	....	....	....	....	....	....	....	....	....	....	....	....	....	....	....	....	....
1980-81	Hamilton Kilty B's	OHA-B	40	16	17	33	....	....	....	72	....	....	....	....	....	....	....	....	....	....	....	....	....	....	....	....	....	....
1981-82	Belleville Bulls	OHL	58	6	13	19	....	....	....	234	....	....	....	....	....	....	....	....	....	....	....	....	....	....	....	....	....	....
1982-83	Belleville Bulls	OHL	70	10	41	51	....	....	....	183	....	....	....	....	....	....	....	....	....	....	4	0	0	0	7	....	....	....
	Baltimore Skipjacks	AHL	2	0	0	0	....	....	....	22	....	....	....	....	....	....	....	....	....	....	....	....	....	....	....	....	....	....
1983-84	**Pittsburgh Penguins**	**NHL**	**72**	**2**	**7**	**9**	**2**	**5**	**7**	**224**	**0**	**0**	**0**	**75**	**2.7**	**39**	**0**	**83**	**5**	**–39**	....	....	....	....	....	....	....	....
1984-85	**Pittsburgh Penguins**	**NHL**	**15**	**0**	**0**	**0**	**0**	**0**	**0**	**15**	**0**	**0**	**0**	**11**	**0.0**	**1**	**0**	**4**	**0**	**–3**	....	....	....	....	....	....	....	....
	Baltimore Skipjacks	AHL	58	6	24	30	....	....	....	154	....	....	....	....	....	....	....	....	....	....	14	0	7	7	47	....	....	....
1985-86	**Edmonton Oilers**	**NHL**	**59**	**11**	**12**	**23**	**9**	**8**	**17**	**265**	**0**	**0**	**2**	**72**	**15.3**	**39**	**1**	**30**	**1**	**9**	**8**	**0**	**2**	**2**	**50**	**0**	**0**	**0**
	Nova Scotia Oilers	AHL	9	2	4	6	....	....	....	34	....	....	....	....	....	....	....	....	....	....	....	....	....	....	....	....	....	....
1986-87♦	**Edmonton Oilers**	**NHL**	**41**	**2**	**4**	**6**	**2**	**3**	**5**	**159**	**0**	**0**	**0**	**32**	**6.3**	**14**	**0**	**18**	**0**	**–4**	**21**	**4**	**3**	**7**	**65**	**0**	**0**	**1**
	Nova Scotia Oilers	AHL	7	2	2	4	....	....	....	48	....	....	....	....	....	....	....	....	....	....	....	....	....	....	....	....	....	....
1987-88♦	**Edmonton Oilers**	**NHL**	**60**	**9**	**17**	**26**	**8**	**12**	**20**	**223**	**0**	**0**	**1**	**66**	**13.6**	**40**	**1**	**17**	**1**	**23**	**16**	**0**	**3**	**3**	**67**	**0**	**0**	**0**
1988-89	**Los Angeles Kings**	**NHL**	**66**	**10**	**17**	**27**	**8**	**12**	**20**	**350**	**2**	**0**	**1**	**87**	**11.5**	**56**	**5**	**49**	**1**	**3**	**11**	**0**	**2**	**2**	**33**	**0**	**0**	**0**
1989-90	**Los Angeles Kings**	**NHL**	**75**	**15**	**21**	**36**	**13**	**15**	**28**	**322**	**2**	**1**	**0**	**127**	**11.8**	**98**	**15**	**98**	**17**	**2**	**10**	**1**	**3**	**4**	**18**	**1**	**0**	**0**
1990-91	**Los Angeles Kings**	**NHL**	**61**	**7**	**32**	**39**	**6**	**24**	**30**	**221**	**1**	**1**	**1**	**100**	**7.0**	**106**	**15**	**64**	**21**	**48**	**12**	**0**	**0**	**0**	**58**	**0**	**0**	**0**
1991-92	**Los Angeles Kings**	**NHL**	**71**	**7**	**22**	**29**	**6**	**17**	**23**	**268**	**2**	**1**	**0**	**119**	**5.9**	**80**	**24**	**93**	**24**	**–13**	**6**	**1**	**0**	**1**	**21**	**0**	**0**	**0**
1992-93	**Los Angeles Kings**	**NHL**	**81**	**15**	**26**	**41**	**12**	**18**	**30**	***399**	**3**	**3**	**0**	**197**	**7.6**	**101**	**26**	**127**	**53**	**1**	**24**	**4**	**6**	**10**	***60**	**2**	**0**	**1**
1993-94	**Pittsburgh Penguins**	**NHL**	**47**	**3**	**18**	**21**	**3**	**14**	**17**	**139**	**0**	**0**	**0**	**122**	**2.5**	**53**	**15**	**61**	**14**	**–9**	....	....	....	....	....	....	....	....
	Los Angeles Kings	**NHL**	**18**	**4**	**6**	**10**	**4**	**5**	**9**	**55**	**1**	**0**	**1**	**38**	**10.5**	**20**	**7**	**31**	**15**	**–3**	....	....	....	....	....	....	....	....
1994-95	**Los Angeles Kings**	**NHL**	**41**	**3**	**18**	**21**	**5**	**27**	**32**	**83**	**1**	**0**	**0**	**75**	**4.0**	**51**	**19**	**59**	**13**	**–14**	....	....	....	....	....	....	....	....
1995-96	**Los Angeles Kings**	**NHL**	**59**	**10**	**21**	**31**	**10**	**17**	**27**	**148**	**1**	**1**	**1**	**118**	**8.5**	**68**	**20**	**91**	**29**	**–14**	....	....	....	....	....	....	....	....
	New York Rangers	**NHL**	**9**	**0**	**2**	**2**	**0**	**2**	**2**	**21**	**0**	**0**	**0**	**12**	**0.0**	**3**	**1**	**10**	**2**	**–6**	**4**	**0**	**0**	**0**	**0**	**0**	**0**	**0**
1996-97	**San Jose Sharks**	**NHL**	**57**	**4**	**12**	**16**	**4**	**11**	**15**	**186**	**0**	**1**	**1**	**74**	**5.4**	**62**	**13**	**65**	**10**	**–6**	....	....	....	....	....	....	....	....
1997-98	**San Jose Sharks**	**NHL**	**56**	**2**	**10**	**12**	**2**	**10**	**12**	**140**	**0**	**0**	**0**	**46**	**4.3**	**33**	**2**	**23**	**2**	**10**	....	....	....	....	....	....	....	....
1998-99	**Edmonton Oilers**	**NHL**	**46**	**2**	**3**	**5**	**2**	**3**	**5**	**101**	**0**	**0**	**0**	**29**	**6.9**	**26**	**1**	**42**	**12**	**–5**	**3**	**0**	**0**	**0**	**2**	**0**	**0**	**0**
99-2000	**Boston Bruins**	**NHL**	**27**	**2**	**3**	**5**	**2**	**3**	**5**	**62**	**0**	**0**	**0**	**24**	**8.3**	**16**	**2**	**16**	**4**	**2**	....	....	....	....	....	....	....	....
	NHL Totals		**961**	**108**	**251**	**359**	**98**	**206**	**304**	**3381**	**13**	**8**	**8**	**1424**	**7.6**	**906**	**167**	**981**	**224**		**115**	**10**	**19**	**29**	**374**	**3**	**0**	**2**

Co-winner of Alka-Seltzer Plus Award with Theoren Fleury (1991)

Signed as a free agent by **Pittsburgh**, July 30, 1982. Traded to **Edmonton** by **Pittsburgh** with Tim Hrynewich and future considerations (Craig Muni, October 6, 1986) for Gilles Meloche, September 11, 1985. Traded to **LA Kings** by **Edmonton** with Wayne Gretzky and Mike Krushelnyski for Jimmy Carson, Martin Gelinas, LA Kings' 1st round choices in 1989 (later traded to New Jersey — New Jersey selected Jason Miller), 1991 (Martin Rucinsky) and 1993 (Nick Stajduhar) Entry Drafts and cash, August 9, 1988. Traded to **Pittsburgh** by **LA Kings**, for Shawn McEachern, August 27, 1993. Traded to **LA Kings** by **Pittsburgh** with Jim Paek for Tomas Sandstrom and Shawn McEachern, February 16, 1994. Traded to **NY Rangers** by **LA Kings** with Jari Kurri and Shane Churla for Ray Ferraro, Ian Laperriere, Mattias Norstrom, Nathan Lafayette and NY Rangers' 4th round choice (Sean Blanchard) in 1997 Entry Draft, March 14, 1996. Traded to **San Jose** by **NY Rangers** for Jayson More, Brian Swanson and San Jose's 4th round choice (later traded back to San Jose - San Jose selected Adam Colagiacomo) in 1997 Entry Draft(, August 20, 1996. Signed as a free agent by **Edmonton**, October 1, 1998. Signed as a free agent by **Boston**, December 9, 1999. • Suspended by NHL for remainder of 1999-2000 season for stick assault on Donald Brashear in game vs. Vancouver, February 21, 2000.

• McSWEEN, Don

Donald K. D – L. 5'11", 197 lbs. b: Detroit, MI, 6/9/1964. Buffalo's 10th, 160th overall, in 1983.

Season	Club	League	GP	G	A	Pts	AG	AA	APts	PIM	PP	SH	GW	S	%	TGF	PGF	TGA	PGA	+/–	GP	G	A	Pts	PIM	PP	SH	GW
1982-83	Redford Royals	NAJHL	37	9	33	42	....	....	....	....	....	....	....	....	....	....	....	....	....	....	....	....	....	....	....	....	....	....
1983-84	Michigan State Spartans	CCHA	46	10	26	36	....	....	....	30	....	....	....	....	....	....	....	....	....	....	....	....	....	....	....	....	....	....
1984-85	Michigan State Spartans	CCHA	44	2	23	25	....	....	....	52	....	....	....	....	....	....	....	....	....	....	....	....	....	....	....	....	....	....
1985-86	Michigan State Spartans	CCHA	45	9	29	38	....	....	....	18	....	....	....	....	....	....	....	....	....	....	....	....	....	....	....	....	....	....
1986-87	Michigan State Spartans	CCHA	45	7	23	30	....	....	....	34	....	....	....	....	....	....	....	....	....	....	....	....	....	....	....	....	....	....
1987-88	**Buffalo Sabres**	**NHL**	**5**	**0**	**1**	**1**	**0**	**1**	**1**	**6**	**0**	**0**	**0**	**4**	**0.0**	**4**	**0**	**3**	**0**	**1**	....	....	....	....	....	....	....	....
	Rochester Americans	AHL	63	9	29	38	....	....	....	108	....	....	....	....	....	....	....	....	....	....	6	0	1	1	15	....	....	....
1988-89	Rochester Americans	AHL	66	7	22	29	....	....	....	45	....	....	....	....	....	....	....	....	....	....	....	....	....	....	....	....	....	....
1989-90	**Buffalo Sabres**	**NHL**	**4**	**0**	**0**	**0**	**0**	**0**	**0**	**6**	**0**	**0**	**0**	**4**	**0.0**	**2**	**1**	**4**	**0**	**–3**	....	....	....	....	....	....	....	....
	Rochester Americans	AHL	70	16	43	59	....	....	....	43	....	....	....	....	....	....	....	....	....	....	17	3	10	13	12	....	....	....
1990-91	Rochester Americans	AHL	74	7	44	51	....	....	....	57	....	....	....	....	....	....	....	....	....	....	15	2	5	7	8	....	....	....
1991-92	Rochester Americans	AHL	75	6	32	38	....	....	....	60	....	....	....	....	....	....	....	....	....	....	16	5	6	11	18	....	....	....
1992-93	San Diego Gulls	IHL	80	15	40	55	....	....	....	85	....	....	....	....	....	....	....	....	....	....	14	1	2	3	10	....	....	....
1993-94	San Diego Gulls	IHL	38	5	13	18	....	....	....	36	....	....	....	....	....	....	....	....	....	....	....	....	....	....	....	....	....	....
	Mighty Ducks of Anaheim	**NHL**	**32**	**3**	**9**	**12**	**3**	**7**	**10**	**39**	**1**	**0**	**2**	**43**	**7.0**	**30**	**8**	**24**	**6**	**4**	....	....	....	....	....	....	....	....
	United States	WC-A	8	1	1	2	....	....	....	0	....	....	....	....	....	....	....	....	....	....	....	....	....	....	....	....	....	....
1994-95	**Mighty Ducks of Anaheim**	**NHL**	**2**	**0**	**0**	**0**	**0**	**0**	**0**	**0**	**0**	**0**	**0**	**1**	**0.0**	**0**	**0**	**1**	**1**	**0**	....	....	....	....	....	....	....	....
1995-96	**Mighty Ducks of Anaheim**	**NHL**	**4**	**0**	**0**	**0**	**0**	**0**	**0**	**4**	**0**	**0**	**0**	**1**	**0.0**	**2**	**0**	**3**	**1**	**0**	....	....	....	....	....	....	....	....
	Baltimore Bandits	AHL	12	1	9	10	....	....	....	2	....	....	....	....	....	....	....	....	....	....	....	....	....	....	....	....	....	....
1996-97	Grand Rapids Griffins	IHL	75	7	20	27	....	....	....	66	....	....	....	....	....	....	....	....	....	....	3	0	1	1	8	....	....	....
1997-98	Grand Rapids Griffins	IHL	2	0	0	0	....	....	....	4	....	....	....	....	....	....	....	....	....	....	....	....	....	....	....	....	....	....
	Milwaukee Admirals	IHL	76	4	21	25	....	....	....	128	....	....	....	....	....	....	....	....	....	....	10	0	0	0	14	....	....	....
1998-99	Muskegon Fury	UHL	6	0	3	3	....	....	....	4	....	....	....	....	....	....	....	....	....	....	8	2	2	4	10	....	....	....
99-2000	Muskegon Fury	UHL	6	1	3	4	....	....	....	5	....	....	....	....	....	....	....	....	....	....	....	....	....	....	....	....	....	....
	NHL Totals		**47**	**3**	**10**	**13**	**3**	**8**	**11**	**55**	**1**	**0**	**2**	**53**	**5.7**	**38**	**9**	**35**	**8**		....	....	....	....	....	....	....	....

CCHA First All-Star Team (1985, 1986, 1987) • NCAA West Second All-American Team (1986, 1987) • NCAA Championship All-Tournament Team (1986, 1987) • AHL First All-Star Team (1990)

Signed as a free agent by **Anaheim**, January 12, 1994. • Missed majority of 1994-95 season recovering from arm injury suffered in game vs. Winnipeg, January 21, 1995.

• McTAGGART, Jim

James Robert D – L. 5'11", 200 lbs. b: Weyburn, Sask., 3/31/1960.

Season	Club	League	GP	G	A	Pts	AG	AA	APts	PIM	PP	SH	GW	S	%	TGF	PGF	TGA	PGA	+/–	GP	G	A	Pts	PIM	PP	SH	GW
1976-77	Swift Current Broncos	SJHL	47	5	29	34	....	....	....	97	....	....	....	....	....	....	....	....	....	....	....	....	....	....	....	....	....	....
1977-78	Saskatoon Blades	WCJHL	65	7	20	27	....	....	....	221	....	....	....	....	....	....	....	....	....	....	....	....	....	....	....	....	....	....
1978-79	Saskatoon Blades	WHL	37	6	19	25	....	....	....	86	....	....	....	....	....	....	....	....	....	....	....	....	....	....	....	....	....	....
	Billings Bighorns	WHL	30	1	12	13	....	....	....	93	....	....	....	....	....	....	....	....	....	....	....	....	....	....	....	....	....	....
1979-80	Billings Bighorns	WHL	65	16	37	53	....	....	....	204	....	....	....	....	....	....	....	....	....	....	....	....	....	....	....	....	....	....
	Hershey Bears	AHL	....	....	....	....	....	....	....	....	....	....	....	....	....	....	....	....	....	....	9	0	0	0	23	....	....	....
1980-81	**Washington Capitals**	**NHL**	**52**	**1**	**6**	**7**	**1**	**4**	**5**	**185**	**0**	**0**	**0**	**40**	**2.5**	**42**	**2**	**65**	**20**	**–5**	....	....	....	....	....	....	....	....
	Hershey Bears	AHL	23	2	1	3	....	....	....	81	....	....	....	....	....	....	....	....	....	....	....	....	....	....	....	....	....	....
1981-82	Washington Capitals	DN-Cup	4	1	0	1	....	....	....	....	....	....	....	....	....	....	....	....	....	....	....	....	....	....	....	....	....	....
	Washington Capitals	**NHL**	**19**	**2**	**4**	**6**	**2**	**3**	**5**	**20**	**0**	**1**	**1**	**24**	**8.3**	**17**	**1**	**25**	**7**	**–2**	....	....	....	....	....	....	....	....
	Hershey Bears	AHL	57	3	12	15	....	....	....	190	....	....	....	....	....	....	....	....	....	....	5	0	3	3	2	....	....	....
1982-83	Wichita Wind	CHL	21	3	9	12	....	....	....	38	....	....	....	....	....	....	....	....	....	....	....	....	....	....	....	....	....	....
	Moncton Alpines	AHL	49	0	7	7	....	....	....	63	....	....	....	....	....	....	....	....	....	....	....	....	....	....	....	....	....	....

Season	Club	League	REGULAR SEASON																		PLAYOFFS							
			GP	G	A	Pts	AG	AA	APts	PIM	PP	SH	GW	S	%	TGF	PGF	TGA	PGA	+/-	GP	G	A	Pts	PIM	PP	SH	GW
1983-84	Montana Magic	CHL	70	5	13	18				104																		
1984-1987			OUT OF HOCKEY – RETIRED																									
1987-88	Peterborough Pirates	Britain	28	9	24	33				92											2	0	5	5	6			
	NHL Totals		**71**	**3**	**10**	**13**	**3**	**7**	**10**	**205**	**0**	**1**	**1**	**64**	**4.7**	**59**	**3**	**90**	**27**									

Signed as a free agent by **Washington**, November 9, 1979. Signed as a free agent by **Edmonton**, October 27, 1982. Traded to **New Jersey** by **Edmonton** with Ron Low for Lindsay Middlebrook and Paul Miller, February 19, 1983.

• McTAVISH, Dale

Dale Neil Bradley C – L. 6'1", 200 lbs. b: Eganville, Ont., 2/28/1972.

Season	Club	League	GP	G	A	Pts	AG	AA	APts	PIM	PP	SH	GW	S	%	TGF	PGF	TGA	PGA	+/-	GP	G	A	Pts	PIM	PP	SH	GW
1988-89	Pembroke Lumber Kings	OJHL	56	26	24	50				58																		
1989-90	Peterborough Petes	OHL	66	26	35	61				34											12	1	5	6	2			
1990-91	Peterborough Petes	OHL	66	21	27	48				44											4	1	0	1	0			
1991-92	Peterborough Petes	OHL	60	25	31	56				59											10	2	5	7	11			
1992-93	Peterborough Petes	OHL	66	31	50	81				98											21	9	8	17	22			
	Peterborough Petes	Mem-Cup	5	2	1	3				16																		
1993-94	St. Francis Xavier X-Men	AUAA	27	30	24	54				71																		
1994-95	St. Francis Xavier X-Men	AUAA	27	25	27	52				59																		
1995-96	Canada	Nat-Team	53	24	32	56				91																		
	Saint John Flames	AHL	4	2	3	5				5											15	5	4	9	15			
1996-97	**Calgary Flames**	**NHL**	**9**	**1**	**2**	**3**	**1**	**2**	**3**	**2**	**0**	**0**	**0**	**14**	**7.1**	**3**	**0**	**7**	**0**	**–4**								
	Saint John Flames	AHL	53	16	21	37				65											3	0	1	1	0			
1997-98	SaiPa Lappeenranta	Finland	47	*25	18	43				73											3	0	3	3	4			
1998-99	SaiPa Lappeenranta	Finland	44	22	17	39				117											7	4	5	9	2			
	Canada	Nat-Team	4	1	1	2				2																		
99-2000	Blues Espoo	Finland	53	32	19	51				87											4	1	0	1	12			
	Canada	Nat-Team	4	0	3	3				2																		
	NHL Totals		**9**	**1**	**2**	**3**	**1**	**2**	**3**	**2**	**0**	**0**	**0**	**14**	**7.1**	**3**	**0**	**7**	**0**									

Signed as a free agent by **Calgary**, August 1, 1996. • Played w/ RHI's New Jersey R&R in 1995 (6-2-3-5-20).

• McTAVISH, Gord

Gordon C – R. 6'4", 200 lbs. b: Guelph, Ont., 6/3/1954. Montreal's 5th, 15th overall, in 1974.

Season	Club	League	GP	G	A	Pts	AG	AA	APts	PIM	PP	SH	GW	S	%	TGF	PGF	TGA	PGA	+/-	GP	G	A	Pts	PIM	PP	SH	GW
1973-74	Sudbury Wolves	OMJHL	68	34	49	83				155											3	0	0	0	2			
1974-75	Nova Scotia Voyageurs	AHL	63	14	19	33				125											4	0	1	1	5			
1975-76	Nova Scotia Voyageurs	AHL	44	12	17	29				69											9	3	2	5	18			
1976-77	Nova Scotia Voyageurs	AHL	78	30	28	58				84											12	4	8	12	12			
1977-78	Nova Scotia Voyageurs	AHL	76	26	41	67				108											11	4	5	9	6			
1978-79	**St. Louis Blues**	**NHL**	**1**	**0**	**0**	**0**	**0**	**0**	**0**	**0**	**0**	**0**	**0**	**1**	**0.0**	**0**	**0**	**2**	**0**	**–2**								
	Salt Lake Golden Eagles	CHL	68	36	22	58				64											10	*6	6	12	27			
1979-80	**Winnipeg Jets**	**NHL**	**10**	**1**	**3**	**4**	**1**	**2**	**3**	**2**	**0**	**0**	**0**	**9**	**11.1**	**8**	**0**	**4**	**0**	**4**								
	Tulsa Oilers	CHL	26	6	12	18				6																		
1980-81	SC Rapperswil-Jona	Switz-2	STATISTICS NOT AVAILABLE																									
	NHL Totals		**11**	**1**	**3**	**4**	**1**	**2**	**3**	**2**	**0**	**0**	**0**	**10**	**10.0**	**8**	**0**	**6**	**0**									

Traded to **St. Louis** by **Montreal** for Mike Korney, October 7, 1978. Selected by **Winnipeg** from **St. Louis** in Expansion Draft, June 13, 1979.

• MEAGHER, Rick

Richard Joseph C – L. 5'9", 192 lbs. b: Belleville, Ont., 11/2/1953.

Season	Club	League	GP	G	A	Pts	AG	AA	APts	PIM	PP	SH	GW	S	%	TGF	PGF	TGA	PGA	+/-	GP	G	A	Pts	PIM	PP	SH	GW
1971-1973	Belleville Bobcats	OHA-B	STATISTICS NOT AVAILABLE																									
1973-74	Boston University	ECAC	30	19	21	40				26																		
1974-75	Boston University	ECAC	32	25	28	53				80																		
1975-76	Boston University	ECAC	28	12	25	37				22																		
1976-77	Boston University	ECAC	34	34	46	80				42																		
1977-78	Nova Scotia Voyageurs	AHL	57	20	27	47				33											11	5	3	8	11			
1978-79	Nova Scotia Voyageurs	AHL	79	35	46	81				57											10	1	6	7	11			
1979-80	**Montreal Canadiens**	**NHL**	**2**	**0**	**0**	**0**	**0**	**0**	**0**	**0**	**0**	**0**	**0**	**0**	**0.0**	**0**	**0**	**0**	**0**	**0**								
	Nova Scotia Voyageurs	AHL	64	32	44	76				53											6	3	4	7	2			
1980-81	**Hartford Whalers**	**NHL**	**27**	**7**	**10**	**17**	**5**	**7**	**12**	**19**	**0**	**0**	**0**	**73**	**9.6**	**25**	**3**	**25**	**5**	**2**								
	Binghamton Whalers	AHL	50	23	35	58				54																		
1981-82	**Hartford Whalers**	**NHL**	**65**	**24**	**19**	**43**	**19**	**13**	**32**	**51**	**2**	**1**	**2**	**171**	**14.0**	**63**	**9**	**75**	**17**	**–4**								
1982-83	**Hartford Whalers**	**NHL**	**4**	**0**	**0**	**0**	**0**	**0**	**0**	**0**	**0**	**0**	**0**	**3**	**0.0**	**0**	**0**	**3**	**0**	**–3**								
	New Jersey Devils	**NHL**	**57**	**15**	**14**	**29**	**12**	**10**	**22**	**11**	**7**	**0**	**1**	**135**	**11.1**	**41**	**18**	**54**	**10**	**–21**								
1983-84	**New Jersey Devils**	**NHL**	**52**	**14**	**14**	**28**	**11**	**10**	**21**	**16**	**2**	**0**	**2**	**125**	**11.2**	**39**	**10**	**41**	**3**	**–9**								
	Maine Mariners	AHL	10	6	4	10				2																		
1984-85	**New Jersey Devils**	**NHL**	**71**	**11**	**20**	**31**	**9**	**14**	**23**	**22**	**1**	**1**	**1**	**139**	**7.9**	**43**	**3**	**76**	**23**	**–13**								
1985-86	**St. Louis Blues**	**NHL**	**79**	**11**	**19**	**30**	**9**	**13**	**22**	**28**	**0**	**3**	**3**	**109**	**10.1**	**37**	**1**	**78**	**41**	**–1**	**19**	**4**	**4**	**8**	**12**	**0**	**1**	**0**
1986-87	**St. Louis Blues**	**NHL**	**80**	**18**	**21**	**39**	**16**	**15**	**31**	**54**	**2**	**2**	**1**	**170**	**10.6**	**50**	**5**	**80**	**26**	**–9**	**6**	**0**	**0**	**0**	**11**	**0**	**0**	**0**
1987-88	**St. Louis Blues**	**NHL**	**76**	**18**	**16**	**34**	**15**	**11**	**26**	**76**	**0**	**5**	**3**	**113**	**15.9**	**47**	**2**	**79**	**34**	**0**	**10**	**0**	**0**	**0**	**8**	**0**	**0**	**0**
1988-89	**St. Louis Blues**	**NHL**	**78**	**15**	**14**	**29**	**13**	**10**	**23**	**53**	**0**	**1**	**1**	**109**	**13.8**	**45**	**0**	**74**	**38**	**9**	**10**	**3**	**2**	**5**	**6**	**0**	**0**	**1**
1989-90	**St. Louis Blues**	**NHL**	**76**	**8**	**17**	**25**	**7**	**12**	**19**	**47**	**0**	**2**	**1**	**99**	**8.1**	**36**	**0**	**68**	**36**	**4**	**8**	**1**	**0**	**1**	**2**	**0**	**0**	**0**
1990-91	**St. Louis Blues**	**NHL**	**24**	**3**	**1**	**4**	**3**	**1**	**4**	**6**	**0**	**0**	**0**	**21**	**14.3**	**10**	**1**	**11**	**2**	**0**	**9**	**0**	**1**	**1**	**2**	**0**	**0**	**0**
	NHL Totals		**691**	**144**	**165**	**309**	**119**	**116**	**235**	**383**	**14**	**15**	**15**	**1267**	**11.4**	**436**	**52**	**664**	**235**		**62**	**8**	**7**	**15**	**41**	**0**	**1**	**1**

Won Metro OHA-B Rookie-of-the-Year Award (1972) • ECAC Second All-Star Team (1974, 1975) • NCAA East First All-American Team (1975, 1976, 1977) • ECAC First All-Star Team (1976, 1977) • NCAA Championship All-Tournament Team (1977) • Won Frank J. Selke Trophy (1990)

Signed as a free agent by **Montreal**, June 27, 1977. Traded to **Hartford** by **Montreal** with Montreal's 3rd (Paul MacDermid) and 5th (Dan Bourbonnais) round choices in 1981 Entry Draft for Hartford's 3rd (Dieter Hegen) and 5th (Steve Rooney) round choices in 1981 Entry Draft, June 5, 1980. Traded to **New Jersey** by **Hartford** with Garry Howatt for Merlin Malinowski and the rights to Scott Fusco, October 15, 1982. Traded to **St. Louis** by **New Jersey** with New Jersey's 12th round choice (Bill Butler) in 1986 Entry Draft for Perry Anderson, August 29, 1985.

• MEEHAN, Gerry

Gerard Marcus C – L. 6'2", 200 lbs. b: Toronto, Ont., 9/3/1946. Toronto's 4th, 21st overall, in 1963.

Season	Club	League	GP	G	A	Pts	AG	AA	APts	PIM	PP	SH	GW	S	%	TGF	PGF	TGA	PGA	+/-	GP	G	A	Pts	PIM	PP	SH	GW
1962-63	Neil McNeil Maroons	MTJHL	7	1	0	1				0											5	0	0	0	0			
	Neil McNeil Maroons	Mem-Cup	5	0	0	0				0																		
1963-64	Toronto Marlboros	OHA-Jr.	12	2	3	5				0																		
1964-65	Toronto Marlboros	OHA-Jr.	56	14	30	44				24											19	7	4	11	12			
1965-66	Toronto Marlboros	OHA-Jr.	47	25	26	51				47											14	6	10	16	9			
	Rochester Americans	AHL	1	0	0	0				0																		
1966-67	Toronto Marlboros	OHA-Jr.	48	26	42	68				27											17	8	8	16	8			
	Toronto Marlboros	Mem-Cup	9	6	8	14				2																		
1967-68	Tulsa Oilers	CPHL	70	31	41	72				17											11	3	8	11	0			
1968-69	**Toronto Maple Leafs**	**NHL**	**25**	**0**	**2**	**2**	**0**	**2**	**2**	**2**	**0**	**0**	**0**	**28**	**0.0**	**7**	**2**	**6**	**0**	**–1**								
	Phoenix Roadrunners	WHL	17	6	6	12				2																		
	Philadelphia Flyers	**NHL**	**12**	**0**	**3**	**3**	**0**	**3**	**3**	**4**	**0**	**0**	**0**	**25**	**0.0**	**6**	**1**	**6**	**0**	**–1**	**4**	**0**	**0**	**0**	**0**	**0**	**0**	**0**
1969-70	Seattle Totems	WHL	67	23	30	53				23											4	0	1	1	0			
1970-71	**Buffalo Sabres**	**NHL**	**77**	**24**	**31**	**55**	**24**	**26**	**50**	**8**	**5**	**0**	**1**	**163**	**14.7**	**67**	**12**	**67**	**0**	**–12**								
1971-72	**Buffalo Sabres**	**NHL**	**77**	**19**	**27**	**46**	**19**	**23**	**42**	**12**	**4**	**0**	**2**	**164**	**11.6**	**56**	**12**	**72**	**0**	**–28**								
1972-73	**Buffalo Sabres**	**NHL**	**77**	**31**	**29**	**60**	**29**	**23**	**52**	**21**	**3**	**1**	**6**	**208**	**14.9**	**70**	**8**	**61**	**3**	**4**	**6**	**0**	**1**	**1**	**0**	**0**	**0**	**0**
1973-74	**Buffalo Sabres**	**NHL**	**72**	**20**	**26**	**46**	**19**	**21**	**40**	**17**	**6**	**0**	**1**	**160**	**12.5**	**57**	**20**	**44**	**0**	**–7**								
1974-75	**Buffalo Sabres**	**NHL**	**3**	**0**	**1**	**1**	**0**	**1**	**1**	**2**	**0**	**0**	**0**	**4**	**0.0**	**1**	**0**	**4**	**0**	**–3**								
	Vancouver Canucks	**NHL**	**57**	**10**	**15**	**25**	**9**	**11**	**20**	**4**	**0**	**0**	**2**	**121**	**8.3**	**33**	**3**	**37**	**0**	**–7**								
	Atlanta Flames	**NHL**	**14**	**4**	**10**	**14**	**3**	**7**	**10**	**0**	**2**	**0**	**1**	**29**	**13.8**	**20**	**7**	**13**	**2**	**2**								
1975-76	**Atlanta Flames**	**NHL**	**48**	**7**	**20**	**27**	**6**	**15**	**21**	**8**	**2**	**0**	**1**	**71**	**9.9**	**37**	**9**	**30**	**1**	**–1**								
	Washington Capitals	**NHL**	**32**	**16**	**15**	**31**	**14**	**11**	**25**	**10**	**3**	**0**	**0**	**80**	**20.0**	**42**	**12**	**47**	**10**	**–7**								
1976-77	**Washington Capitals**	**NHL**	**80**	**28**	**36**	**64**	**25**	**28**	**53**	**13**	**9**	**1**	**6**	**193**	**14.5**	**83**	**31**	**70**	**7**	**–11**								

			REGULAR SEASON																		PLAYOFFS							
Season	Club	League	GP	G	A	Pts	AG	AA	APts	PIM	PP	SH	GW	S	%	TGF	PGF	TGA	PGA	+/-	GP	G	A	Pts	PIM	PP	SH	GW
1977-78	**Washington Capitals**	**NHL**	**78**	**19**	**24**	**43**	**17**	**19**	**36**	**10**	**7**	**0**	**2**	**172**	**11.0**	**60**	**20**	**87**	**6**	**–41**								
1978-79	**Washington Capitals**	**NHL**	**18**	**2**	**4**	**6**	**2**	**3**	**5**	**0**	**1**	**0**	**1**	**32**	**6.3**	**8**	**2**	**13**	**4**	**–3**								
	Cincinnati Stingers	WHA	2	0	0	0				0																		
	NHL Totals		**670**	**180**	**243**	**423**	**167**	**193**	**360**	**111**	**42**	**2**	**23**	**1450**	**12.4**	**547**	**139**	**557**	**33**		**10**	**0**	**1**	**1**	**0**	**0**	**0**	**0**
	Other Major League Totals		2	0	0	0				0																		

Traded to **Philadelphia** by **Toronto** with Mike Byers and Bill Sutherland for Brit Selby and Forbes Kennedy, March 2, 1969. Claimed by **Buffalo** from **Philadelphia** in Expansion Draft, June 10, 1970. Selected by **LA Sharks** (WHA) in 1972 WHA General Player Draft, February 12, 1972. Traded to **Vancouver** by **Buffalo** with Mike Robitaille for Jocelyn Guevremont and Bryan McSheffrey, October 14, 1974. Traded to **Atlanta** by **Vancouver** for Bob J. Murray, March 9, 1975. Traded to **Washington** by **Atlanta** with Jean Lemieux and Buffalo's 1st round choice (previously acquired, Washington selected Greg Carroll) in 1976 Amateur Draft for Bill Clement, January 22, 1976. Signed as a free agent **Cincinnati** (WHA) following release by **Washington**, December 4, 1978.

• MEEKE, Brent

Brent Alan D – L. 5'11", 175 lbs. b: Toronto, Ont., 4/10/1952. California's 8th, 118th overall, in 1972.

Season	Club	League	GP	G	A	Pts	AG	AA	APts	PIM	PP	SH	GW	S	%	TGF	PGF	TGA	PGA	+/-	GP	G	A	Pts	PIM	PP	SH	GW
1968-69	Humber Valley Packers	MTHL	STATISTICS NOT AVAILABLE																									
1969-70	Niagara Falls Flyers	OHA-Jr.	53	5	11	16				26																		
1970-71	Niagara Falls Flyers	OHA-Jr.	59	3	27	30				69																		
1971-72	Niagara Falls Flyers	OMJHL	30	2	12	14				35											6	1	1	2	9			
1972-73	**California Golden Seals**	**NHL**	**3**	**0**	**0**	**0**	**0**	**0**	**0**	**0**	**0**	**0**	**0**	**1**	**0.0**	**1**	**1**	**0**	**0**	**0**								
	Phoenix Roadrunners	WHL	62	14	22	36				36											6	1	1	2	4			
1973-74	**California Golden Seals**	**NHL**	**18**	**1**	**9**	**10**	**1**	**7**	**8**	**4**	**0**	**0**	**0**	**40**	**2.5**	**26**	**4**	**34**	**1**	**–11**								
	Salt Lake Golden Eagles	WHL	65	15	37	52				44											5	1	0	1	4			
1974-75	**California Golden Seals**	**NHL**	**4**	**0**	**0**	**0**	**0**	**0**	**0**	**0**	**0**	**0**	**0**	**6**	**0.0**	**3**	**0**	**2**	**0**	**1**								
	Salt Lake Golden Eagles	CHL	75	18	39	57				72											11	1	8	9	14			
1975-76	**California Golden Seals**	**NHL**	**1**	**0**	**0**	**0**	**0**	**0**	**0**	**0**	**0**	**0**	**0**	**2**	**0.0**	**0**	**0**	**0**	**0**	**0**								
	Salt Lake Golden Eagles	CHL	76	23	39	62				71											5	1	3	4	0			
1976-77	**Cleveland Barons**	**NHL**	**49**	**8**	**13**	**21**	**7**	**10**	**17**	**4**	**1**	**0**	**0**	**74**	**10.8**	**47**	**19**	**43**	**0**	**–15**								
	Salt Lake Golden Eagles	CHL	26	5	16	21				24																		
1977-78			STATISTICS NOT AVAILABLE																									
1978-79	Mannheimer ERC	Germany	51	18	23	41				118																		
1979-80	Mannheimer ERC	Germany	48	13	31	44				135																		
1980-81	Mannheimer ERC	Germany	53	11	35	46				122											10	0	4	4	12			
	NHL Totals		**75**	**9**	**22**	**31**	**8**	**17**	**25**	**8**	**1**	**0**	**0**	**123**	**7.3**	**77**	**24**	**79**	**1**									

CHL Second All-Star Team (1975, 1976)

Transferred to **Cleveland** after **California** franchise relocated, August 26, 1976.

• MEEKER, Mike

Michael Thomas RW – R. 5'11", 195 lbs. b: Kingston, Ont., 2/23/1958. Pittsburgh's 1st, 25th overall, in 1978.

Season	Club	League	GP	G	A	Pts	AG	AA	APts	PIM	PP	SH	GW	S	%	TGF	PGF	TGA	PGA	+/-	GP	G	A	Pts	PIM	PP	SH	GW
1974-75	Nepean Raiders	OJHL	STATISTICS NOT AVAILABLE																									
1975-76	University of Wisconsin	WCHA	31	12	9	21				21																		
1976-77	University of Wisconsin	WCHA	41	26	27	53				50																		
1977-78	University of Wisconsin	WCHA	4	6	2	8				4																		
	Peterborough Petes	OMJHL	44	33	36	69				21											16	6	7	13	17			
	Peterborough Petes	Mem-Cup	5	2	4	6				0																		
1978-79	**Pittsburgh Penguins**	**NHL**	**4**	**0**	**0**	**0**	**0**	**0**	**0**	**5**	**0**	**0**	**0**	**2**	**0.0**	**0**	**0**	**1**	**0**	**–1**								
	Binghamton Dusters	AHL	75	30	35	65				70																		
1979-1981			STATISTICS NOT AVAILABLE																									
1981-82	Karlskrona IK	Sweden-2	20	17	9	26				32																		
1982-83	Karlskrona IK	Sweden-2	17	19	7	26				17																		
	NHL Totals		**4**	**0**	**0**	**0**	**0**	**0**	**0**	**5**	**0**	**0**	**0**	**2**	**0.0**	**0**	**0**	**1**	**0**									

Won Dudley "Red" Garrett Memorial Award (Top Rookie - AHL) (1979)

• MEIGHAN, Ron

Ron James D – R. 6'3", 195 lbs. b: Montreal, Que., 5/26/1963. Minnesota's 1st, 13th overall, in 1981.

Season	Club	League	GP	G	A	Pts	AG	AA	APts	PIM	PP	SH	GW	S	%	TGF	PGF	TGA	PGA	+/-	GP	G	A	Pts	PIM	PP	SH	GW
1978-79	South Ottawa Canadians	OMHA	55	16	34	50																						
1979-80	Niagara Falls Flyers	OMJHL	61	3	10	13				20											10	0	0	0	6			
1980-81	Niagara Falls Flyers	OMJHL	63	8	27	35				92											12	0	0	0	14			
1981-82	Niagara Falls Flyers	OHL	58	27	41	68				85											4	0	4	4	9			
	Minnesota North Stars	**NHL**	**7**	**1**	**1**	**2**	**1**	**1**	**2**	**2**	**0**	**0**	**0**	**4**	**25.0**	**8**	**0**	**11**	**1**	**–2**								
1982-83	North Bay Centennials	OHL	29	19	22	41				30																		
	Pittsburgh Penguins	**NHL**	**41**	**2**	**6**	**8**	**2**	**4**	**6**	**16**	**1**	**0**	**0**	**48**	**4.2**	**36**	**5**	**47**	**6**	**–10**								
1983-84	Baltimore Skipjacks	AHL	75	4	16	20				36																		
	NHL Totals		**48**	**3**	**7**	**10**	**3**	**5**	**8**	**18**	**1**	**0**	**0**	**52**	**5.8**	**44**	**5**	**58**	**7**									

Won Max Kaminsky Trophy (Top Defenseman - OHL) (1982) • OHL First All-Star Team (1982)

Traded to **Pittsburgh** by **Minnesota** with Anders Hakansson and Minnesota's 1st round choice (Bob Errey) in 1983 Entry Draft for George Ferguson and Pittsburgh's 1st round choice (Brian Lawton) in 1983 Entry Draft, October 28, 1982.

• MEISSNER, Barrie

Barrie Michael LW – L. 5'9", 165 lbs. b: Kindersley, Sask., 7/26/1946.

Season	Club	League	GP	G	A	Pts	AG	AA	APts	PIM	PP	SH	GW	S	%	TGF	PGF	TGA	PGA	+/-	GP	G	A	Pts	PIM	PP	SH	GW
1963-64	Regina Pats	SJHL	6	0	0	0				4											1	0	0	0	2			
1964-65	Regina Pats	SJHL	52	27	31	58				91											12	4	4	8	32			
	Regina Pats	Mem-Cup	10	5	9	14				11																		
1965-66	Regina Pats	SJHL	60	47	56	103				148											5	1	5	6	8			
1966-67	Regina Pats	CMJHL	53	35	44	79				78											15	12	17	29	34			
1967-68	**Minnesota North Stars**	**NHL**	**1**	**0**	**0**	**0**	**0**	**0**	**0**	**2**	**0**	**0**	**0**	**2**	**0.0**	**1**	**1**	**1**	**0**	**–1**								
	Memphis South Stars	CPHL	64	15	24	39				66																		
1968-69	**Minnesota North Stars**	**NHL**	**5**	**0**	**1**	**1**	**0**	**1**	**1**	**2**	**0**	**0**	**0**	**1**	**0.0**	**1**	**0**	**0**	**0**	**1**								
	Memphis South Stars	CHL	67	27	26	53				80																		
1969-70	Iowa Stars	CHL	49	7	10	17				62											11	0	2	2	4			
1970-71	Cleveland Barons	AHL	61	22	16	38				39											4	1	4	5	14			
1971-72	Cleveland Barons	AHL	9	2	1	3				6																		
	Seattle Totems	WHL	7	0	2	2				6																		
	Omaha Knights	CHL	37	6	9	15				18																		
1972-73	Cleveland-Jacksonville Barons	AHL	68	20	25	45				71																		
	NHL Totals		**6**	**0**	**1**	**1**	**0**	**1**	**1**	**4**	**0**	**0**	**0**	**3**	**0.0**	**2**	**1**	**1**	**0**									

• Brother of Dick

Rights traded to **Minnesota** by **Montreal** with Bill Plager and the rights to Leo Thiffault for Bryan Watson, June 6, 1967.

• MELAMETSA, Anssi

LW – L. 6', 190 lbs. b: Jyvaskyla, Fin., 6/21/1961. Winnipeg's 12th, 249th overall, in 1985.

Season	Club	League	GP	G	A	Pts	AG	AA	APts	PIM	PP	SH	GW	S	%	TGF	PGF	TGA	PGA	+/-	GP	G	A	Pts	PIM	PP	SH	GW
1977-78	Jokerit Helsinki	Finland-Jr.	20	14	2	16				8																		
1978-79	Peterborough Petes	OMJHL	64	9	21	30				27																		
	Peterborough Petes	Mem-Cup	4	0	0	0				4																		
1979-80	Jokerit Helsinki	Finland	36	6	13	19				55																		
	Finland	WJC-A	5	0	4	4				4																		
1980-81	Jokerit Helsinki	Finland	36	14	22	36				46																		
	Finland	WJC-A	5	1	3	4				2																		
1981-82	HIFK Helsinki	Finland	28	17	12	29				30											7	2	5	7	8			
1982-83	HIFK Helsinki	Finland	36	13	20	33				59											9	2	6	8	6			
	Finland	WEC-A	10	6	3	9				20																		

			REGULAR SEASON																		PLAYOFFS							
Season	Club	League	GP	G	A	Pts	AG	AA	APts	PIM	PP	SH	GW	S	%	TGF	PGF	TGA	PGA	+/–	GP	G	A	Pts	PIM	PP	SH	GW
1983-84	HIFK Helsinki	Finland	37	16	17	33	....	....	....	44	....	....	....	....	....	....	....	....	....	....	2	0	0	0	0	....	....	....
	Finland	Nat-Team	10	2	2	4	....	....	....	10	....	....	....	....	....	....	....	....	....	....	....	....	....	....	....	....	....	....
	Finland	Olympics	6	4	3	7	....	....	....	10	....	....	....	....	....	....	....	....	....	....	....	....	....	....	....	....	....	....
1984-85	HIFK Helsinki	Finland	36	16	15	31	....	....	....	18	....	....	....	....	....	....	....	....	....	....	....	....	....	....	....	....	....	....
	Finland	WEC-A	10	2	2	4	....	....	....	10	....	....	....	....	....	....	....	....	....	....	....	....	....	....	....	....	....	....
1985-86	**Winnipeg Jets**	**NHL**	**27**	**0**	**3**	**3**	**0**	**2**	**2**	**2**	**0**	**0**	**0**	**20**	**0.0**	**5**	**0**	**10**	**0**	**–5**	....	....	....	....	....	....	....	....
	Sherbrooke Canadiens	AHL	14	7	5	12	....	....	....	6	....	....	....	....	....	....	....	....	....	....	....	....	....	....	....	....	....	....
1986-87	HIFK Helsinki	Finland	35	13	12	25	....	....	....	44	....	....	....	....	....	....	....	....	....	....	4	0	0	0	6	....	....	....
1987-88	HIFK Helsinki	Finland	41	8	8	16	....	....	....	42	....	....	....	....	....	....	....	....	....	....	6	2	0	2	12	....	....	....
1988-89	Jokerit Helsinki	Finland-2	STATISTICS NOT AVAILABLE																		....	....	....	....	....	....	....	....
1989-90	Jokerit Helsinki	Finland	44	24	27	51	....	....	....	28	....	....	....	....	....	....	....	....	....	....	....	....	....	....	....	....	....	....
1990-91	Jokerit Helsinki	Finland	44	10	21	31	....	....	....	20	....	....	....	....	....	....	....	....	....	....	....	....	....	....	....	....	....	....
1991-92	HC Boro	Sweden-2	31	5	23	28	....	....	....	16	....	....	....	....	....	....	....	....	....	....	9	1	4	5	6	....	....	....
	NHL Totals		**27**	**0**	**3**	**3**	**0**	**2**	**2**	**2**	**0**	**0**	**0**	**20**	**0.0**	**5**	**0**	**10**	**0**		....	....	....	....	....	....	....	....

• MELANSON, Dean

Dean C. D – R. 5'11", 190 lbs. b: Antigonish, N.S., 11/19/1973. Buffalo's 4th, 80th overall, in 1992.

Season	Club	League	GP	G	A	Pts	AG	AA	APts	PIM	PP	SH	GW	S	%	TGF	PGF	TGA	PGA	+/–	GP	G	A	Pts	PIM	PP	SH	GW
1989-90	Antigonish Bulldogs	MJrHL	STATISTICS NOT AVAILABLE																									
1990-91	St-Hyacinthe Laser	QMJHL	69	10	17	27	....	....	....	110	....	....	....	....	....	....	....	....	....	....	4	0	1	1	2	....	....	....
1991-92	St-Hyacinthe Laser	QMJHL	42	8	19	27	....	....	....	158	....	....	....	....	....	....	....	....	....	....	6	1	2	3	25	....	....	....
1992-93	St-Hyacinthe Laser	QMJHL	57	13	29	42	....	....	....	253	....	....	....	....	....	....	....	....	....	....	....	....	....	....	....	....	....	....
	Rochester Americans	AHL	8	0	1	1	....	....	....	6	....	....	....	....	....	....	....	....	....	....	14	1	6	7	18	....	....	....
1993-94	Rochester Americans	AHL	80	1	21	22	....	....	....	138	....	....	....	....	....	....	....	....	....	....	4	0	1	1	2	....	....	....
1994-95	**Buffalo Sabres**	**NHL**	**5**	**0**	**0**	**0**	**0**	**0**	**0**	**4**	**0**	**0**	**0**	**1**	**0.0**	**1**	**0**	**2**	**0**	**–1**	....	....	....	....	....	....	....	....
	Rochester Americans	AHL	43	4	7	11	....	....	....	84	....	....	....	....	....	....	....	....	....	....	....	....	....	....	....	....	....	....
1995-96	Rochester Americans	AHL	70	3	13	16	....	....	....	204	....	....	....	....	....	....	....	....	....	....	14	3	3	6	22	....	....	....
1996-97	Quebec Rafales	IHL	72	3	21	24	....	....	....	95	....	....	....	....	....	....	....	....	....	....	7	0	2	2	12	....	....	....
1997-98	Rochester Americans	AHL	73	7	9	16	....	....	....	228	....	....	....	....	....	....	....	....	....	....	4	0	2	2	0	....	....	....
1998-99	Rochester Americans	AHL	79	7	27	34	....	....	....	192	....	....	....	....	....	....	....	....	....	....	17	3	2	5	32	....	....	....
99-2000	Philadelphia Phantoms	AHL	58	11	25	36	....	....	....	178	....	....	....	....	....	....	....	....	....	....	4	2	3	5	10	....	....	....
	NHL Totals		**5**	**0**	**0**	**0**	**0**	**0**	**0**	**4**	**0**	**0**	**0**	**1**	**0.0**	**1**	**0**	**2**	**0**		....	....	....	....	....	....	....	....

Signed as a free agent by **Philadelphia**, July 22, 1999.

• MELIN, Roger

Roger Alf LW – L. 6'4", 195 lbs. b: Enkoping, Sweden, 4/25/1956.

Season	Club	League	GP	G	A	Pts	AG	AA	APts	PIM	PP	SH	GW	S	%	TGF	PGF	TGA	PGA	+/–	GP	G	A	Pts	PIM	PP	SH	GW
1972-73	Vasby IK	Sweden-2	16	2	8	10	....	....	....	....	....	....	....	....	....	....	....	....	....	....	....	....	....	....	....	....	....	....
1973-74	Vasby IK	Sweden-2	18	4	5	9	....	....	....	....	....	....	....	....	....	....	....	....	....	....	....	....	....	....	....	....	....	....
1974-75	Vasby IK	Sweden-2	22	11	12	23	....	....	....	....	....	....	....	....	....	....	....	....	....	....	....	....	....	....	....	....	....	....
1976-77	Orebro IK	Sweden	21	3	4	7	....	....	....	2	....	....	....	....	....	....	....	....	....	....	....	....	....	....	....	....	....	....
1977-78	Orebro IK	Sweden-2	21	6	18	24	....	....	....	2	....	....	....	....	....	....	....	....	....	....	....	....	....	....	....	....	....	....
1978-79	Orebro IK	Sweden-2	23	2	1	3	....	....	....	6	....	....	....	....	....	....	....	....	....	....	....	....	....	....	....	....	....	....
1979-80	Vasby AIK	Sweden-2	36	28	17	45	....	....	....	12	....	....	....	....	....	....	....	....	....	....	....	....	....	....	....	....	....	....
1980-81	**Minnesota North Stars**	**NHL**	**1**	**0**	**0**	**0**	**0**	**0**	**0**	**0**	**0**	**0**	**0**	**1**	**0.0**	**0**	**0**	**1**	**0**	**–1**	....	....	....	....	....	....	....	....
	Oklahoma City Stars	CHL	9	1	1	2	....	....	....	4	....	....	....	....	....	....	....	....	....	....	....	....	....	....	....	....	....	....
1981-82	**Minnesota North Stars**	**NHL**	**2**	**0**	**0**	**0**	**0**	**0**	**0**	**0**	**0**	**0**	**0**	**0**	**0.0**	**0**	**0**	**0**	**0**	**0**	....	....	....	....	....	....	....	....
	Nashville South Stars	CHL	77	18	27	45	....	....	....	7	....	....	....	....	....	....	....	....	....	....	3	0	2	2	0	....	....	....
1982-83	Hammarby IF	Sweden	26	9	8	17	....	....	....	14	....	....	....	....	....	....	....	....	....	....	....	....	....	....	....	....	....	....
1983-84	Hammarby IF	Sweden	30	16	19	35	....	....	....	20	....	....	....	....	....	....	....	....	....	....	....	....	....	....	....	....	....	....
1984-85	Hammarby IF	Sweden	32	6	9	15	....	....	....	8	....	....	....	....	....	....	....	....	....	....	....	....	....	....	....	....	....	....
1985-1987			OUT OF HOCKEY – RETIRED																									
1987-88	Enkopings SK	Sweden-3	9	4	7	11	....	....	....	....	....	....	....	....	....	....	....	....	....	....	....	....	....	....	....	....	....	....
	NHL Totals		**3**	**0**	**0**	**0**	**0**	**0**	**0**	**0**	**0**	**0**	**0**	**1**	**0.0**	**0**	**0**	**1**	**0**		....	....	....	....	....	....	....	....

Signed as a free agent by **Minnesota**, March 23, 1981. • Activated as an emergency injury replacement while serving as Coach of **Enkopings SK** (Sweden-3) during 1987-88 season.

• MELLANBY, Scott

Scott E. RW – R. 6'1", 205 lbs. b: Montreal, Que., 6/11/1966. Philadelphia's 2nd, 27th overall, in 1984.

Season	Club	League	GP	G	A	Pts	AG	AA	APts	PIM	PP	SH	GW	S	%	TGF	PGF	TGA	PGA	+/–	GP	G	A	Pts	PIM	PP	SH	GW
1982-83	Don Mills Flyers	MTHL	72	66	52	118	....	....	....	38	....	....	....	....	....	....	....	....	....	....	....	....	....	....	....	....	....	....
1983-84	Henry Carr Crusaders	OJHL-B	39	37	37	74	....	....	....	97	....	....	....	....	....	....	....	....	....	....	....	....	....	....	....	....	....	....
1984-85	University of Wisconsin	WCHA	40	14	24	38	....	....	....	60	....	....	....	....	....	....	....	....	....	....	....	....	....	....	....	....	....	....
1985-86	University of Wisconsin	WCHA	32	21	23	44	....	....	....	89	....	....	....	....	....	....	....	....	....	....	....	....	....	....	....	....	....	....
	Canada	WJC-A	7	5	4	9	....	....	....	6	....	....	....	....	....	....	....	....	....	....	....	....	....	....	....	....	....	....
	Philadelphia Flyers	**NHL**	**2**	**0**	**0**	**0**	**0**	**0**	**0**	**0**	**0**	**0**	**0**	**0**	**0.0**	**0**	**0**	**1**	**0**	**–1**	....	....	....	....	....	....	....	....
1986-87	**Philadelphia Flyers**	**NHL**	**71**	**11**	**21**	**32**	**9**	**15**	**24**	**94**	**1**	**0**	**0**	**118**	**9.3**	**54**	**10**	**38**	**2**	**8**	**24**	**5**	**5**	**10**	**46**	**0**	**0**	**1**
1987-88	**Philadelphia Flyers**	**NHL**	**75**	**25**	**26**	**51**	**21**	**19**	**40**	**185**	**7**	**0**	**2**	**190**	**13.2**	**81**	**31**	**65**	**8**	**–7**	**7**	**0**	**1**	**1**	**16**	**0**	**0**	**0**
1988-89	**Philadelphia Flyers**	**NHL**	**76**	**21**	**29**	**50**	**18**	**21**	**39**	**183**	**11**	**0**	**3**	**202**	**10.4**	**73**	**31**	**56**	**1**	**–13**	**19**	**4**	**5**	**9**	**28**	**0**	**0**	**0**
1989-90	**Philadelphia Flyers**	**NHL**	**57**	**6**	**17**	**23**	**5**	**12**	**17**	**77**	**0**	**0**	**1**	**104**	**5.8**	**41**	**6**	**39**	**0**	**–4**	....	....	....	....	....	....	....	....
1990-91	**Philadelphia Flyers**	**NHL**	**74**	**20**	**21**	**41**	**18**	**16**	**34**	**155**	**5**	**0**	**6**	**165**	**12.1**	**62**	**15**	**39**	**0**	**8**	....	....	....	....	....	....	....	....
1991-92	**Edmonton Oilers**	**NHL**	**80**	**23**	**27**	**50**	**21**	**20**	**41**	**197**	**7**	**0**	**5**	**159**	**14.5**	**79**	**23**	**51**	**0**	**5**	**16**	**2**	**1**	**3**	**29**	**1**	**0**	**1**
1992-93	**Edmonton Oilers**	**NHL**	**69**	**15**	**17**	**32**	**12**	**12**	**24**	**147**	**6**	**0**	**3**	**114**	**13.2**	**55**	**16**	**43**	**0**	**–4**	....	....	....	....	....	....	....	....
1993-94	**Florida Panthers**	**NHL**	**80**	**30**	**30**	**60**	**28**	**23**	**51**	**149**	**17**	**0**	**4**	**204**	**14.7**	**87**	**40**	**47**	**0**	**0**	....	....	....	....	....	....	....	....
1994-95	**Florida Panthers**	**NHL**	**48**	**13**	**12**	**25**	**23**	**18**	**41**	**90**	**4**	**0**	**5**	**130**	**10.0**	**40**	**16**	**40**	**0**	**–16**	....	....	....	....	....	....	....	....
1995-96	**Florida Panthers**	**NHL**	**79**	**32**	**38**	**70**	**31**	**31**	**62**	**160**	**19**	**0**	**3**	**225**	**14.2**	**106**	**55**	**47**	**0**	**4**	**22**	**3**	**6**	**9**	**44**	**2**	**0**	**0**
1996-97	**Florida Panthers**	**NHL**	**82**	**27**	**29**	**56**	**29**	**26**	**55**	**170**	**9**	**1**	**4**	**221**	**12.2**	**81**	**28**	**46**	**0**	**7**	**5**	**0**	**2**	**2**	**4**	**0**	**0**	**0**
1997-98	**Florida Panthers**	**NHL**	**79**	**15**	**24**	**39**	**18**	**24**	**42**	**127**	**6**	**0**	**1**	**188**	**8.0**	**67**	**29**	**54**	**2**	**–14**	....	....	....	....	....	....	....	....
1998-99	**Florida Panthers**	**NHL**	**67**	**18**	**27**	**45**	**21**	**26**	**47**	**85**	**4**	**0**	**3**	**136**	**13.2**	**62**	**20**	**37**	**0**	**5**	....	....	....	....	....	....	....	....
99-2000	**Florida Panthers**	**NHL**	**77**	**18**	**28**	**46**	**20**	**26**	**46**	**126**	**6**	**0**	**2**	**134**	**13.4**	**67**	**19**	**41**	**7**	**14**	**4**	**0**	**1**	**1**	**2**	**0**	**0**	**0**
	NHL Totals		**1016**	**274**	**346**	**620**	**274**	**289**	**563**	**1945**	**102**	**1**	**42**	**2290**	**12.0**	**955**	**339**	**644**	**20**		**97**	**14**	**21**	**35**	**169**	**3**	**0**	**2**

Played in NHL All-Star Game (1996)

Traded to **Edmonton** by **Philadelphia** with Craig Fisher and Craig Berube for Dave Brown, Corey Foster and Jari Kurri, May 30, 1991. Claimed by **Florida** from **Edmonton** in Expansion Draft, June 24, 1993.

• MELLOR, Tom

Thomas Robert D – R. 6'1", 185 lbs. b: Cranston, RI, 1/27/1950. Detroit's 5th, 68th overall, in 1970.

Season	Club	League	GP	G	A	Pts	AG	AA	APts	PIM	PP	SH	GW	S	%	TGF	PGF	TGA	PGA	+/–	GP	G	A	Pts	PIM	PP	SH	GW
1967-68	Cranston High School	Hi-School	STATISTICS NOT AVAILABLE																									
1968-69	Boston College	ECAC	17	9	10	19	....	....	....	12	....	....	....	....	....	....	....	....	....	....	....	....	....	....	....	....	....	....
1969-70	Boston College	ECAC	26	21	23	44	....	....	....	40	....	....	....	....	....	....	....	....	....	....	....	....	....	....	....	....	....	....
1970-71	Boston College	ECAC	25	10	30	40	....	....	....	43	....	....	....	....	....	....	....	....	....	....	....	....	....	....	....	....	....	....
1971-72	United States	Nat-Team	7	4	8	12	....	....	....	6	....	....	....	....	....	....	....	....	....	....	....	....	....	....	....	....	....	....
	United States	Olympics	6	0	0	0	....	....	....	4	....	....	....	....	....	....	....	....	....	....	....	....	....	....	....	....	....	....
	United States	WEC-A	10	1	3	4	....	....	....	2	....	....	....	....	....	....	....	....	....	....	....	....	....	....	....	....	....	....
1972-73	Boston College	ECAC	30	6	*45	51	....	....	....	50	....	....	....	....	....	....	....	....	....	....	....	....	....	....	....	....	....	....
	United States	WEC-B	7	4	8	12	....	....	....	....	....	....	....	....	....	....	....	....	....	....	....	....	....	....	....	....	....	....
1973-74	**Detroit Red Wings**	**NHL**	**25**	**2**	**4**	**6**	**2**	**3**	**5**	**25**	**0**	**0**	**0**	**24**	**8.3**	**18**	**1**	**30**	**4**	**–9**	....	....	....	....	....	....	....	....
	Virginia Wings	AHL	23	5	18	23	....	....	....	40	....	....	....	....	....	....	....	....	....	....	....	....	....	....	....	....	....	....
	London Lions	Britain	6	2	5	7	....	....	....	20	....	....	....	....	....	....	....	....	....	....	....	....	....	....	....	....	....	....
1974-75	**Detroit Red Wings**	**NHL**	**1**	**0**	**0**	**0**	**0**	**0**	**0**	**0**	**0**	**0**	**0**	**1**	**0.0**	**0**	**0**	**0**	**0**	**0**	....	....	....	....	....	....	....	....
	Virginia Wings	AHL	73	17	35	52	....	....	....	147	....	....	....	....	....	....	....	....	....	....	5	0	2	2	17	....	....	....

			REGULAR SEASON																		PLAYOFFS							
Season	Club	League	GP	G	A	Pts	AG	AA	APts	PIM	PP	SH	GW	S	%	TGF	PGF	TGA	PGA	+/–	GP	G	A	Pts	PIM	PP	SH	GW
1975-76	Vastra Frolunda	Sweden	34	8	8	16	....	....	....	41	....	....	....	....	....	....	....	....	....	....	....	....	....	....	....	....	....	....
	Toledo Goaldiggers	IHL	13	3	12	15	....	....	....	19	....	....	....	....	....	....	....	....	....	....	4	0	2	2	7	....	....	....
1976-77	Toledo Goaldiggers	IHL	75	13	62	75	....	....	....	118	....	....	....	....	....	....	....	....	....	....	19	4	*17	21	16	....	....	....
	NHL Totals		**26**	**2**	**4**	**6**	**2**	**3**	**5**	**25**	**0**	**0**	**0**	**25**	**8.0**	**18**	**1**	**30**	**4**		....	....	....	....	....	....	....	....

ECAC Second All-Star Team (1970, 1971) • ECAC First All-Star Team (1973) • NCAA East First All-American Team (1973) • IHL First All-Star Team (1977) • Won Governors' Trophy (Top Defenseman - IHL) (1977) • Won James Gatschene Memorial Trophy (MVP - IHL) (1977)

• MELNYK, Gerry

Michael Gerald C – R. 5'10", 165 lbs. b: Edmonton, Alta., 9/16/1934.

Season	Club	League	GP	G	A	Pts	AG	AA	APts	PIM	PP	SH	GW	S	%	TGF	PGF	TGA	PGA	+/–	GP	G	A	Pts	PIM	PP	SH	GW
1951-52	Edmonton Oil Kings	WCJHL	42	29	29	58	....	....	....	24	....	....	....	....	....	....	....	....	....	....	9	*9	4	13	2	....	....	....
1952-53	Edmonton Oil Kings	WCJHL	36	27	28	55	....	....	....	22	....	....	....	....	....	....	....	....	....	....	9	5	8	13	6	....	....	....
	Edmonton Flyers	WHL	....	....	....	....	....	....	....	....	....	....	....	....	....	....	....	....	....	....	2	0	1	1	0	....	....	....
1953-54	Edmonton Oil Kings	WCJHL	36	39	*49	88	....	....	....	25	....	....	....	....	....	....	....	....	....	....	10	10	15	25	10	....	....	....
	Edmonton Flyers	WHL	3	1	1	2	....	....	....	0	....	....	....	....	....	....	....	....	....	....	....	....	....	....	....	....	....	....
	Edmonton Oil Kings	Mem-Cup	14	7	17	24	....	....	....	10	....	....	....	....	....	....	....	....	....	....	....	....	....	....	....	....	....	....
1954-55	Edmonton Flyers	WHL	69	14	29	43	....	....	....	24	....	....	....	....	....	....	....	....	....	....	9	2	*8	10	0	....	....	....
1955-56	Edmonton Flyers	WHL	70	37	50	87	....	....	....	37	....	....	....	....	....	....	....	....	....	....	3	1	3	4	2	....	....	....
	Detroit Red Wings	**NHL**	....	....	....	....	....	....	....	....	....	....	....	....	....	....	....	....	....	....	**6**	**0**	**0**	**0**	**0**	**0**	**0**	**0**
1956-57	Edmonton Flyers	WHL	60	21	44	65	....	....	....	26	....	....	....	....	....	....	....	....	....	....	8	5	3	8	2	....	....	....
1957-58	Edmonton Flyers	WHL	50	22	40	62	....	....	....	19	....	....	....	....	....	....	....	....	....	....	....	....	....	....	....	....	....	....
1958-59	Edmonton Flyers	WHL	64	30	37	67	....	....	....	8	....	....	....	....	....	....	....	....	....	....	3	0	1	1	2	....	....	....
1959-60	**Detroit Red Wings**	**NHL**	**63**	**10**	**10**	**20**	**12**	**10**	**22**	**12**	....	....	....	....	....	....	....	....	....	....	**6**	**3**	**0**	**3**	**0**	**0**	**0**	**1**
1960-61	**Detroit Red Wings**	**NHL**	**70**	**9**	**16**	**25**	**10**	**15**	**25**	**2**	....	....	....	....	....	....	....	....	....	....	**11**	**1**	**0**	**1**	**2**	**0**	**0**	**1**
1961-62	**Chicago Black Hawks**	**NHL**	**63**	**5**	**16**	**21**	**6**	**15**	**21**	**6**	....	....	....	....	....	....	....	....	....	....	**7**	**0**	**0**	**0**	**2**	**0**	**0**	**0**
1962-63	Buffalo Bisons	AHL	72	14	36	50	....	....	....	20	....	....	....	....	....	....	....	....	....	....	13	6	7	13	4	....	....	....
1963-64	Buffalo Bisons	AHL	70	11	34	45	....	....	....	0	....	....	....	....	....	....	....	....	....	....	....	....	....	....	....	....	....	....
	St. Louis Braves	CPHL	....	....	....	....	....	....	....	....	....	....	....	....	....	....	....	....	....	....	6	1	4	5	2	....	....	....
1964-65	Buffalo Bisons	AHL	72	22	47	69	....	....	....	12	....	....	....	....	....	....	....	....	....	....	9	1	4	5	2	....	....	....
	Chicago Black Hawks	**NHL**	....	....	....	....	....	....	....	....	....	....	....	....	....	....	....	....	....	....	**6**	**0**	**0**	**0**	**0**	**0**	**0**	**0**
1965-66	Buffalo Bisons	AHL	69	18	61	79	....	....	....	10	....	....	....	....	....	....	....	....	....	....	....	....	....	....	....	....	....	....
1966-67	St. Louis Braves	CPHL	67	24	47	71	....	....	....	12	....	....	....	....	....	....	....	....	....	....	....	....	....	....	....	....	....	....
1967-68	**St. Louis Blues**	**NHL**	**73**	**15**	**35**	**50**	**17**	**35**	**52**	**14**	**3**	**1**	**3**	**144**	**10.4**	**71**	**26**	**71**	**15**	**–11**	**17**	**2**	**6**	**8**	**2**	**1**	**1**	**0**
	NHL Totals		**269**	**39**	**77**	**116**	**45**	**75**	**120**	**34**	....	....	....	....	....	....	....	....	....	....	**53**	**6**	**6**	**12**	**6**	....	....	....

WCJHL Second All-Star Team (1954) • CPHL Second All-Star Team (1967) • Played in NHL All-Star Game (1961)

Traded to **Chicago** by **Detroit** with Brian Smith for Eddie Litzenberger, June 12, 1961. Claimed by **St. Louis** from **Chicago** in Expansion Draft, June 6, 1967. Traded to **Philadelphia** by **St. Louis** with Darryl Edestrand for Lou Angotti and Ian Campbell, June 11, 1968.

• MELNYK, Larry

Larry Joseph D – L. 6', 195 lbs. b: Saskatoon, Sask., 2/21/1960. Boston's 5th, 78th overall, in 1979.

Season	Club	League	GP	G	A	Pts	AG	AA	APts	PIM	PP	SH	GW	S	%	TGF	PGF	TGA	PGA	+/–	GP	G	A	Pts	PIM	PP	SH	GW
1977-78	Abbotsford Flyers	BCJHL	39	10	9	19	....	....	....	100	....	....	....	....	....	....	....	....	....	....	....	....	....	....	....	....	....	....
	New Westminster Bruins	WCJHL	44	3	22	25	....	....	....	71	....	....	....	....	....	....	....	....	....	....	....	....	....	....	....	....	....	....
	New Westminster Bruins	Mem-Cup	5	1	3	4	....	....	....	7	....	....	....	....	....	....	....	....	....	....	....	....	....	....	....	....	....	....
1978-79	New Westminster Bruins	WHL	71	7	33	40	....	....	....	142	....	....	....	....	....	....	....	....	....	....	8	1	4	5	14	....	....	....
	Canada	WJC-A	5	1	1	2	....	....	....	2	....	....	....	....	....	....	....	....	....	....	....	....	....	....	....	....	....	....
1979-80	New Westminster Bruins	WHL	67	13	38	51	....	....	....	236	....	....	....	....	....	....	....	....	....	....	....	....	....	....	....	....	....	....
	Binghamton Dusters	AHL	6	0	3	3	....	....	....	20	....	....	....	....	....	....	....	....	....	....	....	....	....	....	....	....	....	....
1980-81	**Boston Bruins**	**NHL**	**26**	**0**	**4**	**4**	**0**	**3**	**3**	**39**	**0**	**0**	**0**	**30**	**0.0**	**13**	**1**	**21**	**2**	**–7**	....	....	....	....	....	....	....	....
	Springfield Indians	AHL	47	1	10	11	....	....	....	109	....	....	....	....	....	....	....	....	....	....	1	0	0	0	0	....	....	....
1981-82	**Boston Bruins**	**NHL**	**48**	**0**	**8**	**8**	**0**	**5**	**5**	**84**	**0**	**0**	**0**	**40**	**0.0**	**37**	**2**	**32**	**0**	**3**	**11**	**0**	**3**	**3**	**40**	**0**	**0**	**0**
	Erie Blades	AHL	10	0	3	3	....	....	....	36	....	....	....	....	....	....	....	....	....	....	....	....	....	....	....	....	....	....
1982-83	**Boston Bruins**	**NHL**	**1**	**0**	**0**	**0**	**0**	**0**	**0**	**0**	**0**	**0**	**0**	**2**	**0.0**	**0**	**0**	**2**	**0**	**–2**	**11**	**0**	**0**	**0**	**9**	**0**	**0**	**0**
	Baltimore Skipjacks	AHL	72	2	24	26	....	....	....	215	....	....	....	....	....	....	....	....	....	....	....	....	....	....	....	....	....	....
1983-84	Hershey Bears	AHL	50	0	18	18	....	....	....	156	....	....	....	....	....	....	....	....	....	....	....	....	....	....	....	....	....	....
	Moncton Alpines	AHL	14	0	3	3	....	....	....	17	....	....	....	....	....	....	....	....	....	....	....	....	....	....	....	....	....	....
♦	**Edmonton Oilers**	**NHL**	....	....	....	....	....	....	....	....	....	....	....	....	....	....	....	....	....	....	**6**	**0**	**1**	**1**	**0**	**0**	**0**	**0**
1984-85♦	**Edmonton Oilers**	**NHL**	**28**	**0**	**11**	**11**	**0**	**7**	**7**	**25**	**0**	**0**	**0**	**8**	**0.0**	**33**	**3**	**21**	**3**	**12**	**12**	**1**	**3**	**4**	**26**	**0**	**0**	**0**
	Nova Scotia Voyageurs	AHL	37	2	10	12	....	....	....	97	....	....	....	....	....	....	....	....	....	....	....	....	....	....	....	....	....	....
1985-86	**Edmonton Oilers**	**NHL**	**6**	**2**	**3**	**5**	**2**	**2**	**4**	**11**	**0**	**0**	**0**	**4**	**50.0**	**11**	**0**	**5**	**2**	**8**	....	....	....	....	....	....	....	....
	Nova Scotia Oilers	AHL	19	2	8	10	....	....	....	72	....	....	....	....	....	....	....	....	....	....	....	....	....	....	....	....	....	....
	New York Rangers	**NHL**	**46**	**1**	**8**	**9**	**1**	**5**	**6**	**65**	**0**	**0**	**0**	**33**	**3.0**	**45**	**1**	**58**	**16**	**2**	**16**	**1**	**2**	**3**	**46**	**0**	**0**	**0**
1986-87	**New York Rangers**	**NHL**	**73**	**3**	**12**	**15**	**3**	**9**	**12**	**182**	**0**	**0**	**1**	**53**	**5.7**	**62**	**3**	**110**	**38**	**–13**	**6**	**0**	**0**	**0**	**4**	**0**	**0**	**0**
1987-88	**New York Rangers**	**NHL**	**14**	**0**	**1**	**1**	**0**	**1**	**1**	**34**	**0**	**0**	**0**	**8**	**0.0**	**9**	**0**	**21**	**5**	**–7**	....	....	....	....	....	....	....	....
	Vancouver Canucks	**NHL**	**49**	**2**	**3**	**5**	**2**	**2**	**4**	**73**	**0**	**0**	**0**	**32**	**6.3**	**41**	**0**	**73**	**20**	**–12**	....	....	....	....	....	....	....	....
1988-89	**Vancouver Canucks**	**NHL**	**74**	**3**	**11**	**14**	**3**	**8**	**11**	**82**	**0**	**1**	**1**	**59**	**5.1**	**50**	**1**	**62**	**16**	**3**	**4**	**0**	**0**	**0**	**2**	**0**	**0**	**0**
1989-90	**Vancouver Canucks**	**NHL**	**67**	**0**	**2**	**2**	**0**	**1**	**1**	**91**	**0**	**0**	**0**	**45**	**0.0**	**37**	**0**	**84**	**20**	**–27**	....	....	....	....	....	....	....	....
	NHL Totals		**432**	**11**	**63**	**74**	**11**	**43**	**54**	**686**	**0**	**1**	**2**	**314**	**3.5**	**338**	**11**	**489**	**122**		**66**	**2**	**9**	**11**	**127**	**0**	**0**	**0**

Traded to **Edmonton** by **Boston** for John Blum, March 6, 1984. Traded to **NY Rangers** by **Edmonton** with Todd Strueby for Mike Rogers, December 20, 1985. Traded to **Vancouver** by **NY Rangers** with Willie Huber for Michel Petit, November 4, 1987.

• MELROSE, Barry

Barry James D – R. 6', 205 lbs. b: Kelvington, Sask., 7/15/1956. Montreal's 4th, 36th overall, in 1976.

Season	Club	League	GP	G	A	Pts	AG	AA	APts	PIM	PP	SH	GW	S	%	TGF	PGF	TGA	PGA	+/–	GP	G	A	Pts	PIM	PP	SH	GW
1972-73	Weyburn Red Wings	SJHL	STATISTICS NOT AVAILABLE																									
1973-74	Weyburn Red Wings	SJHL	50	2	19	21	....	....	....	162	....	....	....	....	....	....	....	....	....	....	....	....	....	....	....	....	....	....
1974-75	Kamloops Chiefs	WCJHL	70	6	18	24	....	....	....	95	....	....	....	....	....	....	....	....	....	....	6	1	1	2	21	....	....	....
1975-76	Kamloops Chiefs	WCJHL	72	12	49	61	....	....	....	112	....	....	....	....	....	....	....	....	....	....	12	4	6	10	14	....	....	....
1976-77	Cincinnati Stingers	WHA	29	1	4	5	....	....	....	8	....	....	....	....	....	....	....	....	....	....	2	0	0	0	0	....	....	....
	Springfield Indians	AHL	23	0	3	3	....	....	....	17	....	....	....	....	....	....	....	....	....	....	....	....	....	....	....	....	....	....
1977-78	Cincinnati Stingers	WHA	69	2	9	11	....	....	....	113	....	....	....	....	....	....	....	....	....	....	....	....	....	....	....	....	....	....
1978-79	Cincinnati Stingers	WHA	80	2	14	16	....	....	....	222	....	....	....	....	....	....	....	....	....	....	3	0	1	1	8	....	....	....
1979-80	**Winnipeg Jets**	**NHL**	**74**	**4**	**6**	**10**	**3**	**4**	**7**	**124**	**0**	**0**	**1**	**101**	**4.0**	**42**	**3**	**109**	**29**	**–41**	....	....	....	....	....	....	....	....
1980-81	**Winnipeg Jets**	**NHL**	**18**	**1**	**1**	**2**	**1**	**1**	**2**	**40**	**0**	**0**	**0**	**16**	**6.3**	**9**	**0**	**28**	**7**	**–12**	....	....	....	....	....	....	....	....
	Toronto Maple Leafs	**NHL**	**57**	**2**	**5**	**7**	**2**	**3**	**5**	**166**	**0**	**1**	**0**	**39**	**5.1**	**58**	**1**	**104**	**29**	**–18**	**3**	**0**	**1**	**1**	**15**	**0**	**0**	**0**
1981-82	**Toronto Maple Leafs**	**NHL**	**64**	**1**	**5**	**6**	**1**	**3**	**4**	**186**	**0**	**0**	**0**	**45**	**2.2**	**34**	**0**	**78**	**18**	**–26**	....	....	....	....	....	....	....	....
1982-83	**Toronto Maple Leafs**	**NHL**	**52**	**2**	**5**	**7**	**2**	**3**	**5**	**68**	**0**	**0**	**0**	**25**	**8.0**	**36**	**0**	**68**	**16**	**–16**	**4**	**0**	**1**	**1**	**23**	**0**	**0**	**0**
	St. Catharines Saints	AHL	25	1	10	11	....	....	....	106	....	....	....	....	....	....	....	....	....	....	....	....	....	....	....	....	....	....
1983-84	**Detroit Red Wings**	**NHL**	**21**	**0**	**1**	**1**	**0**	**1**	**1**	**74**	**0**	**0**	**0**	**8**	**0.0**	**6**	**0**	**10**	**4**	**0**	....	....	....	....	....	....	....	....
	Adirondack Red Wings	AHL	16	2	1	3	....	....	....	37	....	....	....	....	....	....	....	....	....	....	....	....	....	....	....	....	....	....
1984-85	Adirondack Red Wings	AHL	72	3	13	16	....	....	....	226	....	....	....	....	....	....	....	....	....	....	....	....	....	....	....	....	....	....
1985-86	**Detroit Red Wings**	**NHL**	**14**	**0**	**0**	**0**	**0**	**0**	**0**	**70**	**0**	**0**	**0**	**2**	**0.0**	**6**	**0**	**13**	**1**	**–6**	....	....	....	....	....	....	....	....
	Adirondack Red Wings	AHL	57	4	4	8	....	....	....	204	....	....	....	....	....	....	....	....	....	....	....	....	....	....	....	....	....	....
1986-87	Adirondack Red Wings	AHL	55	4	9	13	....	....	....	170	....	....	....	....	....	....	....	....	....	....	11	1	2	3	107	....	....	....
	NHL Totals		**300**	**10**	**23**	**33**	**9**	**15**	**24**	**728**	**0**	**1**	**1**	**236**	**4.2**	**191**	**4**	**410**	**104**		**7**	**0**	**2**	**2**	**38**	**0**	**0**	**0**
	Other Major League Totals		178	5	27	32	....	....	....	343	....	....	....	....	....	....	....	....	....	....	5	0	1	1	8	....	....	....

Selected by **Cincinnati** (WHA) in 1976 WHA Amateur Draft, May, 1976. Claimed by **Quebec** from **Cincinnati** (WHA) in WHA Dispersal Draft, June 8, 1979. Traded to **Winnipeg** by **Quebec** for Jamie Hislop and Barry Legge, June 28, 1979. Claimed on waivers by **Toronto** from **Winnipeg**, November 30, 1980. Signed as a free agent by **Detroit**, July 5, 1983.

• MENARD, Howie

Howard Hubert C – R. 5'8", 160 lbs. b: Timmins, Ont., 4/28/1942.

Season	Club	League	GP	G	A	Pts	AG	AA	APts	PIM	PP	SH	GW	S	%	TGF	PGF	TGA	PGA	+/–	GP	G	A	Pts	PIM	PP	SH	GW
1959-60	Toronto Marlboros	OHA-Jr.	48	21	29	50	....	....	....	63	....	....	....	....	....	....	....	....	....	....	4	1	1	2	2	....	....	....
1960-61	Toronto Marlboros	OHA-Jr.	21	11	9	20	....	....	....	34	....	....	....	....	....	....	....	....	....	....	....	....	....	....	....	....	....	....
	Hamilton Red Wings	OHA-Jr.	24	7	7	14	....	....	....	29	....	....	....	....	....	....	....	....	....	....	12	4	6	10	35	....	....	....

			REGULAR SEASON																		PLAYOFFS							
Season	Club	League	GP	G	A	Pts	AG	AA	APts	PIM	PP	SH	GW	S	%	TGF	PGF	TGA	PGA	+/-	GP	G	A	Pts	PIM	PP	SH	GW
1961-62	Hamilton Red Wings	OHA-Jr.	48	12	32	44	....	....	....	87	....	....	....	....	....	....	....	....	....	....	10	6	4	10	*30	....	....	....
	Hamilton Red Wings	Mem-Cup	14	9	*13	22	....	....	....	18	....	....	....	....	....	....	....	....	....	....	....	....	....	....	....	....	....	....
1962-63	Pittsburgh Hornets	AHL	69	16	29	45	....	....	....	62	....	....	....	....	....	....	....	....	....	....	....	....	....	....	....	....	....	....
1963-64	**Detroit Red Wings**	**NHL**	**3**	**0**	**0**	**0**	**0**	**0**	**0**	**0**	....	....	....	....	....	....	....	....	....	....	....	....	....	....	....	....	....	....
	Cincinnati Wings	CPHL	69	25	37	62	....	....	....	75	....	....	....	....	....	....	....	....	....	....	....	....	....	....	....	....	....	....
1964-65	Memphis Wings	CPHL	61	9	33	42	....	....	....	66	....	....	....	....	....	....	....	....	....	....	....	....	....	....	....	....	....	....
1965-66	Springfield Indians	AHL	71	15	42	57	....	....	....	42	....	....	....	....	....	....	....	....	....	....	6	3	2	5	10	....	....	....
1966-67	Springfield Indians	AHL	68	25	39	64	....	....	....	52	....	....	....	....	....	....	....	....	....	....	....	....	....	....	....	....	....	....
1967-68	**Los Angeles Kings**	**NHL**	**35**	**9**	**15**	**24**	**10**	**15**	**25**	**32**	**1**	**0**	**5**	**86**	**10.5**	**28**	**3**	**21**	**0**	**4**	**7**	**0**	**5**	**5**	**24**	**0**	**0**	**0**
	Springfield Kings	AHL	37	18	33	51	....	....	....	33	....	....	....	....	....	....	....	....	....	....	....	....	....	....	....	....	....	....
1968-69	**Los Angeles Kings**	**NHL**	**56**	**10**	**17**	**27**	**11**	**15**	**26**	**31**	**1**	**0**	**1**	**94**	**10.6**	**38**	**3**	**35**	**0**	**0**	**11**	**3**	**2**	**5**	**12**	**1**	**0**	**0**
	Springfield Kings	AHL	20	3	15	18	....	....	....	18	....	....	....	....	....	....	....	....	....	....	....	....	....	....	....	....	....	....
1969-70	**Chicago Black Hawks**	**NHL**	**19**	**2**	**3**	**5**	**2**	**3**	**5**	**8**	**1**	**0**	**0**	**10**	**20.0**	**7**	**1**	**1**	**0**	**5**	....	....	....	....	....	....	....	....
	Oakland Seals	**NHL**	**38**	**2**	**7**	**9**	**2**	**7**	**9**	**16**	**0**	**0**	**0**	**52**	**3.8**	**14**	**2**	**31**	**14**	**–5**	**1**	**0**	**0**	**0**	**0**	**0**	**0**	**0**
1970-71	Providence Reds	AHL	59	10	21	31	....	....	....	75	....	....	....	....	....	....	....	....	....	....	1	0	0	0	2	....	....	....
1971-72	Baltimore Clippers	AHL	73	26	30	56	....	....	....	79	....	....	....	....	....	....	....	....	....	....	18	5	13	18	28	....	....	....
1972-73	Salt Lake Golden Eagles	WHL	59	12	38	50	....	....	....	46	....	....	....	....	....	....	....	....	....	....	9	4	3	7	12	....	....	....
1973-74	Baltimore Clippers	AHL	73	42	39	81	....	....	....	66	....	....	....	....	....	....	....	....	....	....	9	3	3	6	13	....	....	....
1974-75	Baltimore Clippers	AHL	43	14	18	32	....	....	....	44	....	....	....	....	....	....	....	....	....	....	....	....	....	....	....	....	....	....
	Providence Reds	AHL	10	1	2	3	....	....	....	20	....	....	....	....	....	....	....	....	....	....	3	0	0	0	0	....	....	....
1975-76	Baltimore Clippers	AHL	38	7	11	18	....	....	....	30	....	....	....	....	....	....	....	....	....	....	....	....	....	....	....	....	....	....
	Whitby Warriors	OHA-Sr.	23	11	8	19	....	....	....	14	....	....	....	....	....	....	....	....	....	....	....	....	....	....	....	....	....	....
1976-77	Whitby Warriors	OHA-Sr.	2	0	1	1	....	....	....	0	....	....	....	....	....	....	....	....	....	....	....	....	....	....	....	....	....	....
	NHL Totals		**151**	**23**	**42**	**65**	**25**	**40**	**65**	**87**	....	....	....	....	....	....	....	....	....	....	**19**	**3**	**7**	**10**	**36**	....	....	....

• Brother of Hillary

Claimed by **Springfield** (AHL) from **Detroit** in Reverse Draft, June, 1965. NHL rights transferred to **LA Kings** after NHL club purchased **Springfield** (AHL) franchise, May, 1967. Claimed by **Chicago** from **LA Kings** in Intra-League Draft, June 11, 1969. Traded to **Oakland** by **Chicago** for Gene Ubriaco, December 15, 1969. Claimed by **Buffalo** from **Oakland** in Expansion Draft, June 10, 1970. Traded to **California** by **Buffalo** for cash, October, 1970.

• MERCREDI, Vic

Victor Dennis C – R. 5'11", 185 lbs. b: Yellowknife, NWT, 3/31/1953. Atlanta's 2nd, 16th overall, in 1973.

Season	Club	League	GP	G	A	Pts	AG	AA	APts	PIM	PP	SH	GW	S	%	TGF	PGF	TGA	PGA	+/-	GP	G	A	Pts	PIM	PP	SH	GW
1969-70	Penticton Broncos	BCJHL	48	16	18	34	....	....	....	....	....	....	....	....	....	....	....	....	....	....	....	....	....	....	....	....	....	....
1970-71	Penticton Broncos	BCJHL	51	50	56	106	....	....	....	38	....	....	....	....	....	....	....	....	....	....	....	....	....	....	....	....	....	....
1971-72	New Westminster Bruins	WCJHL	68	24	30	54	....	....	....	87	....	....	....	....	....	....	....	....	....	....	5	1	1	2	2	....	....	....
1972-73	New Westminster Bruins	WCJHL	67	52	61	113	....	....	....	135	....	....	....	....	....	....	....	....	....	....	5	8	4	12	14	....	....	....
1973-74	Omaha Knights	CHL	68	21	36	57	....	....	....	34	....	....	....	....	....	....	....	....	....	....	5	1	2	3	2	....	....	....
1974-75	**Atlanta Flames**	**NHL**	**2**	**0**	**0**	**0**	**0**	**0**	**0**	**0**	**0**	**0**	**0**	**0**	**0.0**	**0**	**0**	**0**	**0**	**0**	....	....	....	....	....	....	....	....
	Omaha Knights	CHL	64	10	16	26	....	....	....	16	....	....	....	....	....	....	....	....	....	....	6	0	0	0	0	....	....	....
1975-76	Calgary Cowboys	WHA	3	0	0	0	....	....	....	29	....	....	....	....	....	....	....	....	....	....	....	....	....	....	....	....	....	....
	Baltimore Clippers	AHL	52	6	9	15	....	....	....	15	....	....	....	....	....	....	....	....	....	....	....	....	....	....	....	....	....	....
1976-77	Hammarby IF	Sweden-2	18	5	9	14	....	....	....	67	....	....	....	....	....	....	....	....	....	....	....	....	....	....	....	....	....	....
1977-78	Springfield Indians	AHL	1	0	0	0	....	....	....	0	....	....	....	....	....	....	....	....	....	....	....	....	....	....	....	....	....	....
	Phoenix Roadrunners	PHL	42	16	24	40	....	....	....	48	....	....	....	....	....	....	....	....	....	....	....	....	....	....	....	....	....	....
1978-79	Tucson Rustlers	PHL	29	8	20	28	....	....	....	4	....	....	....	....	....	....	....	....	....	....	....	....	....	....	....	....	....	....
1979-80	Delta Hurry Kings	BCSHL	STATISTICS NOT AVAILABLE																									
	NHL Totals		**2**	**0**	**0**	**0**	**0**	**0**	**0**	**0**	**0**	**0**	**0**	**0**	**0.0**	**0**	**0**	**0**	**0**		....	....	....	....	....	....	....	....
	Other Major League Totals		3	0	0	0	....	....	....	29	....	....	....	....	....	....	....	....	....	....	....	....	....	....	....	....	....	....

Named BCJHL Most Valuable Player (1971) • BCJHL First All-Star Team (1971)

Selected by **Houston** (WHA) in 1973 WHA Amateur Player Draft, May, 1973. WHA rights traded to **Calgary** (WHA) by **Houston** (WHA) for future considerations, March, 1976.

• MEREDITH, Greg

Gregory Paul RW – R. 6'1", 210 lbs. b: Toronto, Ont., 2/23/1958. Atlanta's 5th, 97th overall, in 1978.

Season	Club	League	GP	G	A	Pts	AG	AA	APts	PIM	PP	SH	GW	S	%	TGF	PGF	TGA	PGA	+/-	GP	G	A	Pts	PIM	PP	SH	GW
1975-76	Upper Canada College	Hi-School	STATISTICS NOT AVAILABLE																									
	Toronto Marlboros	OMJHL	5	0	0	0	....	....	....	0	....	....	....	....	....	....	....	....	....	....	....	....	....	....	....	....	....	....
1976-77	University of Notre Dame	WCHA	34	21	20	41	....	....	....	18	....	....	....	....	....	....	....	....	....	....	....	....	....	....	....	....	....	....
1977-78	University of Notre Dame	WCHA	38	13	13	26	....	....	....	24	....	....	....	....	....	....	....	....	....	....	....	....	....	....	....	....	....	....
1978-79	University of Notre Dame	WCHA	35	28	22	50	....	....	....	14	....	....	....	....	....	....	....	....	....	....	....	....	....	....	....	....	....	....
1979-80	University of Notre Dame	WCHA	40	40	31	71	....	....	....	80	....	....	....	....	....	....	....	....	....	....	....	....	....	....	....	....	....	....
1980-81	**Calgary Flames**	**NHL**	**3**	**1**	**0**	**1**	**1**	**0**	**1**	**0**	**0**	**0**	**0**	**5**	**20.0**	**1**	**0**	**0**	**0**	**1**	....	....	....	....	....	....	....	....
	Birmingham Bulls	CHL	39	17	10	27	....	....	....	36	....	....	....	....	....	....	....	....	....	....	....	....	....	....	....	....	....	....
	Tulsa Oilers	CHL	10	6	4	10	....	....	....	12	....	....	....	....	....	....	....	....	....	....	....	....	....	....	....	....	....	....
1981-82	Oklahoma City Stars	CHL	80	10	23	33	....	....	....	64	....	....	....	....	....	....	....	....	....	....	4	2	0	2	6	....	....	....
1982-83	**Calgary Flames**	**NHL**	**35**	**5**	**4**	**9**	**4**	**3**	**7**	**8**	**2**	**1**	**0**	**39**	**12.8**	**24**	**8**	**23**	**2**	**–5**	**5**	**3**	**1**	**4**	**4**	**0**	**1**	**2**
	Colorado Flames	CHL	36	16	10	26	....	....	....	14	....	....	....	....	....	....	....	....	....	....	....	....	....	....	....	....	....	....
1983-84	Colorado Flames	CHL	54	23	20	43	....	....	....	39	....	....	....	....	....	....	....	....	....	....	6	1	2	3	9	....	....	....
	NHL Totals		**38**	**6**	**4**	**10**	**5**	**3**	**8**	**8**	**2**	**1**	**0**	**44**	**13.6**	**25**	**8**	**23**	**2**		**5**	**3**	**1**	**4**	**4**	**0**	**1**	**2**

WCHA First All-Star Team (1980) • NCAA West First All-American Team (1980)

Transferred to **Calgary** after **Atlanta** franchise relocated, June 24, 1980.

• MERKOSKY, Glenn

C – L. 5'10", 185 lbs. b: Edmonton, Alta., 4/8/1959.

Season	Club	League	GP	G	A	Pts	AG	AA	APts	PIM	PP	SH	GW	S	%	TGF	PGF	TGA	PGA	+/-	GP	G	A	Pts	PIM	PP	SH	GW
1977-78	Kelowna Buckaroos	BCJHL	61	55	91	146	....	....	....	66	....	....	....	....	....	....	....	....	....	....	....	....	....	....	....	....	....	....
	Seattle Breakers	WCJHL	6	5	2	7	....	....	....	2	....	....	....	....	....	....	....	....	....	....	....	....	....	....	....	....	....	....
1978-79	Michigan Tech Huskies	WCHA	38	14	29	43	....	....	....	22	....	....	....	....	....	....	....	....	....	....	....	....	....	....	....	....	....	....
1979-80	Calgary Wranglers	WHL	72	49	40	89	....	....	....	95	....	....	....	....	....	....	....	....	....	....	7	4	6	10	14	....	....	....
1980-81	Binghamton Whalers	AHL	80	26	35	61	....	....	....	61	....	....	....	....	....	....	....	....	....	....	5	0	2	2	2	....	....	....
1981-82	**Hartford Whalers**	**NHL**	**7**	**0**	**0**	**0**	**0**	**0**	**0**	**2**	**0**	**0**	**0**	**2**	**0.0**	**2**	**0**	**3**	**0**	**–1**	....	....	....	....	....	....	....	....
	Binghamton Whalers	AHL	72	29	40	69	....	....	....	83	....	....	....	....	....	....	....	....	....	....	10	0	2	2	2	....	....	....
1982-83	**New Jersey Devils**	**NHL**	**34**	**4**	**10**	**14**	**3**	**7**	**10**	**20**	**1**	**0**	**0**	**43**	**9.3**	**17**	**1**	**42**	**16**	**–10**	....	....	....	....	....	....	....	....
	Wichita Wind	CHL	45	26	23	49	....	....	....	15	....	....	....	....	....	....	....	....	....	....	....	....	....	....	....	....	....	....
1983-84	**New Jersey Devils**	**NHL**	**5**	**1**	**0**	**1**	**1**	**0**	**1**	**0**	**0**	**0**	**0**	**6**	**16.7**	**1**	**0**	**2**	**1**	**0**	....	....	....	....	....	....	....	....
	Maine Mariners	AHL	75	28	28	56	....	....	....	56	....	....	....	....	....	....	....	....	....	....	17	11	10	21	20	....	....	....
1984-85	Maine Mariners	AHL	80	38	38	76	....	....	....	19	....	....	....	....	....	....	....	....	....	....	11	2	3	5	13	....	....	....
1985-86	**Detroit Red Wings**	**NHL**	**17**	**0**	**2**	**2**	**0**	**1**	**1**	**0**	**0**	**0**	**0**	**18**	**0.0**	**5**	**0**	**28**	**11**	**–12**	....	....	....	....	....	....	....	....
	Adirondack Red Wings	AHL	59	24	33	57	....	....	....	22	....	....	....	....	....	....	....	....	....	....	17	5	7	12	15	....	....	....
1986-87	Adirondack Red Wings	AHL	77	*54	31	85	....	....	....	66	....	....	....	....	....	....	....	....	....	....	11	6	8	14	7	....	....	....
1987-88	Adirondack Red Wings	AHL	66	34	42	76	....	....	....	34	....	....	....	....	....	....	....	....	....	....	11	4	6	10	4	....	....	....
	SB Rosenheim	Germany	16	2	3	5	....	....	....	17	....	....	....	....	....	....	....	....	....	....	....	....	....	....	....	....	....	....
1988-89	Adirondack Red Wings	AHL	76	31	46	77	....	....	....	13	....	....	....	....	....	....	....	....	....	....	17	8	11	19	10	....	....	....
1989-90	**Detroit Red Wings**	**NHL**	**3**	**0**	**0**	**0**	**0**	**0**	**0**	**0**	**0**	**0**	**0**	**0**	**0.0**	**0**	**0**	**0**	**0**	**0**	....	....	....	....	....	....	....	....
	Adirondack Red Wings	AHL	75	33	31	64	....	....	....	29	....	....	....	....	....	....	....	....	....	....	6	2	1	3	6	....	....	....
1990-91	Adirondack Red Wings	AHL	77	28	29	57	....	....	....	37	....	....	....	....	....	....	....	....	....	....	2	1	1	2	0	....	....	....
1991-1992	Adirondack Red Wings	AHL	DID NOT PLAY – ASSISTANT COACH																									
1992-1996	Sudbury Wolves	OHL	DID NOT PLAY – COACHING																									
1995-1996	Flint Generals	ColHL	DID NOT PLAY – ASSISTANT COACH																									
1996-1999	Adirondack Red Wings	AHL	DID NOT PLAY – COACHING																									
	NHL Totals		**66**	**5**	**12**	**17**	**4**	**8**	**12**	**22**	**1**	**0**	**0**	**69**	**7.2**	**25**	**1**	**75**	**28**		....	....	....	....	....	....	....	....

AHL Second All-Star Team (1985) • AHL First All-Star Team (1987) • Won Fred T. Hunt Memorial Trophy (Sportsmanship - AHL) (1987, 1991)

Signed as a free agent by **Hartford**, August 10, 1980. Signed as a free agent by **New Jersey**, September 14, 1982. Signed as a free agent by **Detroit**, July 15, 1985.

• MERRICK, Wayne

Leonard Wayne "Bones" C – L. 6'1", 195 lbs. b: Sarnia, Ont., 4/23/1952. St. Louis' 1st, 9th overall, in 1972.

Season	Club	League	GP	G	A	Pts	AG	AA	APts	PIM	PP	SH	GW	S	%	TGF	PGF	TGA	PGA	+/-	GP	G	A	Pts	PIM	PP	SH	GW
			REGULAR SEASON																		PLAYOFFS							
1968-69	Sarnia Black Hawks	OMHA	STATISTICS NOT AVAILABLE																									
1969-70	Ottawa 67's	OHA-Jr.	51	10	17	27	....	....	....	10	....	....	....	....	....	....	....	....	....	....	5	0	2	2	0	....	....	....
1970-71	Ottawa 67's	OHA-Jr.	62	34	42	76	....	....	....	41	....	....	....	....	....	....	....	....	....	....	11	6	8	14	4	....	....	....
1971-72	Ottawa 67's	OHA-Jr.	62	39	56	95	....	....	....	21	....	....	....	....	....	....	....	....	....	....	18	13	6	19	0	....	....	....
1972-73	**St. Louis Blues**	**NHL**	**50**	**10**	**11**	**21**	**9**	**9**	**18**	**10**	**3**	**0**	**0**	**81**	**12.3**	**26**	**3**	**27**	**2**	**−2**	**5**	**0**	**1**	**1**	**2**	**0**	**0**	**0**
	Denver Spurs	WHL	22	6	13	19	....	....	....	6	....	....	....	....	....	....	....	....	....	....	....	....	....	....	....	....	....	....
1973-74	**St. Louis Blues**	**NHL**	**64**	**20**	**23**	**43**	**19**	**19**	**38**	**32**	**2**	**0**	**4**	**147**	**13.6**	**55**	**7**	**73**	**14**	**−11**	....	....	....	....	....	....	....	....
1974-75	**St. Louis Blues**	**NHL**	**76**	**28**	**37**	**65**	**24**	**28**	**52**	**57**	**2**	**0**	**3**	**205**	**13.7**	**95**	**20**	**48**	**2**	**29**	**2**	**1**	**1**	**2**	**0**	**1**	**0**	**0**
1975-76	**St. Louis Blues**	**NHL**	**19**	**7**	**8**	**15**	**6**	**6**	**12**	**0**	**1**	**0**	**0**	**56**	**12.5**	**17**	**4**	**15**	**2**	**0**	....	....	....	....	....	....	....	....
	California Golden Seals	**NHL**	**56**	**25**	**27**	**52**	**22**	**20**	**42**	**36**	**7**	**0**	**4**	**190**	**13.2**	**66**	**25**	**44**	**0**	**−3**	....	....	....	....	....	....	....	....
1976-77	**Cleveland Barons**	**NHL**	**80**	**18**	**38**	**56**	**16**	**29**	**45**	**25**	**4**	**0**	**2**	**201**	**9.0**	**76**	**26**	**71**	**0**	**−21**	....	....	....	....	....	....	....	....
	Canada	WEC-A	10	4	3	7	....	....	....	10	....	....	....	....	....	....	....	....	....	....	....	....	....	....	....	....	....	....
1977-78	**Cleveland Barons**	**NHL**	**18**	**2**	**5**	**7**	**2**	**4**	**6**	**8**	**0**	**0**	**0**	**42**	**4.8**	**13**	**7**	**17**	**1**	**−10**	....	....	....	....	....	....	....	....
	New York Islanders	**NHL**	**37**	**10**	**14**	**24**	**9**	**11**	**20**	**8**	**2**	**0**	**2**	**60**	**16.7**	**31**	**5**	**24**	**0**	**2**	**7**	**1**	**0**	**1**	**0**	**0**	**0**	**0**
1978-79	**New York Islanders**	**NHL**	**75**	**20**	**21**	**41**	**17**	**15**	**32**	**24**	**2**	**0**	**0**	**128**	**15.6**	**58**	**4**	**41**	**0**	**13**	**10**	**2**	**3**	**5**	**2**	**0**	**0**	**0**
1979-80♦	**New York Islanders**	**NHL**	**70**	**13**	**22**	**35**	**11**	**16**	**27**	**16**	**2**	**0**	**4**	**111**	**11.7**	**49**	**5**	**32**	**0**	**12**	**21**	**2**	**4**	**6**	**2**	**0**	**0**	**1**
1980-81♦	**New York Islanders**	**NHL**	**71**	**16**	**15**	**31**	**12**	**10**	**22**	**30**	**1**	**0**	**2**	**89**	**18.0**	**43**	**5**	**28**	**2**	**12**	**18**	**6**	**12**	**18**	**8**	**0**	**0**	**1**
1981-82♦	**New York Islanders**	**NHL**	**68**	**12**	**27**	**39**	**9**	**18**	**27**	**20**	**1**	**0**	**3**	**112**	**10.7**	**56**	**5**	**47**	**0**	**4**	**19**	**6**	**6**	**12**	**6**	**0**	**0**	**1**
1982-83♦	**New York Islanders**	**NHL**	**59**	**4**	**12**	**16**	**3**	**8**	**11**	**27**	**1**	**0**	**2**	**46**	**8.7**	**20**	**3**	**20**	**0**	**−3**	**19**	**1**	**3**	**4**	**10**	**0**	**0**	**0**
1983-84	**New York Islanders**	**NHL**	**31**	**6**	**5**	**11**	**5**	**3**	**8**	**10**	**0**	**0**	**0**	**32**	**18.8**	**14**	**0**	**12**	**0**	**2**	**1**	**0**	**0**	**0**	**0**	**0**	**0**	**0**
	NHL Totals		**774**	**191**	**265**	**456**	**164**	**196**	**360**	**303**	**28**	**0**	**26**	**1500**	**12.7**	**619**	**119**	**499**	**23**		**102**	**19**	**30**	**49**	**30**	**1**	**0**	**3**

Traded to **California** by **St. Louis** for Larry Patey and California's 3rd round choice (later traded back to California — California/Cleveland selected Reg Kerr) in 1977 Amateur Draft, November 24, 1975. Transferred to **Cleveland** after **California** franchise relocated, August 26, 1976. Traded to **NY Islanders** by **Cleveland** with Darcy Regier and Cleveland's 4th round choice (draft choice cancelled by the Cleveland-Minnesota merger) in 1978 Amateur Draft for Jean-Paul Parise and Jean Potvin, January 10, 1978.

• MERTZIG, Jan

D – L. 6'4", 218 lbs. b: Huddinge, Sweden, 7/18/1970. NY Rangers' 9th, 235th overall, in 1998.

Season	Club	League	GP	G	A	Pts	AG	AA	APts	PIM	PP	SH	GW	S	%	TGF	PGF	TGA	PGA	+/-	GP	G	A	Pts	PIM	PP	SH	GW
1989-90	Huddinge IF	Sweden-2	11	0	1	1	....	....	....	6	....	....	....	....	....	....	....	....	....	....	2	0	0	0	0	....	....	....
1990-91	Huddinge IF	Sweden-2	33	5	9	14	....	....	....	14	....	....	....	....	....	....	....	....	....	....	....	....	....	....	....	....	....	....
1991-92	Huddinge IF	Sweden-2	28	1	6	7	....	....	....	10	....	....	....	....	....	....	....	....	....	....	4	2	0	2	4	....	....	....
1992-93	Huddinge IF	Sweden-2	35	3	7	10	....	....	....	18	....	....	....	....	....	....	....	....	....	....	9	1	0	1	10	....	....	....
1993-94	Huddinge IF	Sweden-2	35	5	7	12	....	....	....	26	....	....	....	....	....	....	....	....	....	....	2	1	0	1	4	....	....	....
1994-95	Huddinge IF	Sweden-2	34	10	8	18	....	....	....	16	....	....	....	....	....	....	....	....	....	....	2	0	1	1	0	....	....	....
1995-96	Lulea HF	Sweden	38	8	9	17	....	....	....	14	....	....	....	....	....	....	....	....	....	....	13	3	3	6	6	....	....	....
1996-97	Lulea HF	Sweden	47	15	10	25	....	....	....	30	....	....	....	....	....	....	....	....	....	....	9	0	2	2	4	....	....	....
1997-98	Lulea HF	Sweden	45	7	8	15	....	....	....	27	....	....	....	....	....	....	....	....	....	....	3	1	0	1	4	....	....	....
1998-99	**New York Rangers**	**NHL**	**23**	**0**	**2**	**2**	**0**	**2**	**2**	**8**	**0**	**0**	**0**	**10**	**0.0**	**8**	**2**	**11**	**0**	**−5**	....	....	....	....	....	....	....	....
	Hartford Wolf Pack	AHL	35	3	2	5	....	....	....	14	....	....	....	....	....	....	....	....	....	....	....	....	....	....	....	....	....	....
	Utah Grizzlies	IHL	5	0	1	1	....	....	....	6	....	....	....	....	....	....	....	....	....	....	....	....	....	....	....	....	....	....
99-2000	KAC Klagenfurt	IEL	34	8	21	29	....	....	....	38	....	....	....	....	....	....	....	....	....	....	....	....	....	....	....	....	....	....
	KAC Klagenfurt	Austria	16	8	5	13	....	....	....	14	....	....	....	....	....	....	....	....	....	....	....	....	....	....	....	....	....	....
	NHL Totals		**23**	**0**	**2**	**2**	**0**	**2**	**2**	**8**	**0**	**0**	**0**	**10**	**0.0**	**8**	**2**	**11**	**0**		....	....	....	....	....	....	....	....

• MESSIER, Eric

D – L. 6'2", 200 lbs. b: Drummondville, Que., 10/29/1973.

Season	Club	League	GP	G	A	Pts	AG	AA	APts	PIM	PP	SH	GW	S	%	TGF	PGF	TGA	PGA	+/-	GP	G	A	Pts	PIM	PP	SH	GW
1990-91	Swift Textile Midgets	QAAA	STATISTICS NOT AVAILABLE																									
1991-92	Trois-Rivieres Draveurs	QMJHL	58	2	10	12	....	....	....	28	....	....	....	....	....	....	....	....	....	....	15	2	2	4	13	....	....	....
1992-93	Sherbrooke Faucons	QMJHL	51	4	17	21	....	....	....	82	....	....	....	....	....	....	....	....	....	....	15	0	4	4	18	....	....	....
1993-94	Sherbrooke Faucons	QMJHL	67	4	24	28	....	....	....	69	....	....	....	....	....	....	....	....	....	....	12	1	7	8	14	....	....	....
1994-95	U. of Quebec at Trois-Rivieres	OUAA	13	8	5	13	....	....	....	20	....	....	....	....	....	....	....	....	....	....	4	0	3	3	8	....	....	....
1995-96	Cornwall Aces	AHL	72	5	9	14	....	....	....	111	....	....	....	....	....	....	....	....	....	....	8	1	1	2	20	....	....	....
1996-97	**Colorado Avalanche**	**NHL**	**21**	**0**	**0**	**0**	**0**	**0**	**0**	**4**	**0**	**0**	**0**	**11**	**0.0**	**17**	**0**	**13**	**3**	**7**	**6**	**0**	**0**	**0**	**4**	**0**	**0**	**0**
	Hershey Bears	AHL	55	16	26	42	....	....	....	69	....	....	....	....	....	....	....	....	....	....	9	3	8	11	14	....	....	....
1997-98	**Colorado Avalanche**	**NHL**	**62**	**4**	**12**	**16**	**5**	**12**	**17**	**20**	**0**	**0**	**0**	**66**	**6.1**	**56**	**16**	**43**	**7**	**4**	....	....	....	....	....	....	....	....
1998-99	**Colorado Avalanche**	**NHL**	**31**	**4**	**2**	**6**	**5**	**2**	**7**	**14**	**1**	**0**	**1**	**30**	**13.3**	**19**	**2**	**17**	**0**	**0**	**3**	**0**	**0**	**0**	**0**	**0**	**0**	**0**
	Hershey Bears	AHL	6	1	3	4	....	....	....	4	....	....	....	....	....	....	....	....	....	....	....	....	....	....	....	....	....	....
99-2000	**Colorado Avalanche**	**NHL**	**61**	**3**	**6**	**9**	**3**	**6**	**9**	**24**	**1**	**0**	**0**	**28**	**10.7**	**25**	**5**	**30**	**10**	**0**	**14**	**0**	**1**	**1**	**4**	**0**	**0**	**0**
	NHL Totals		**175**	**11**	**20**	**31**	**13**	**20**	**33**	**62**	**2**	**0**	**1**	**135**	**8.1**	**117**	**23**	**103**	**20**		**23**	**0**	**1**	**1**	**8**	**0**	**0**	**0**

QMJHL Second All-Star Team (1994)

Signed as a free agent by **Colorado**, June 14, 1995. • Missed majority of 1998-99 season recovering from elbow injury suffered in game vs. Ottawa, October 10, 1998. • Played w/ RHI's Montreal Roadrunners in 1995 (22-0-11-11-46).

• MESSIER, Joby

D – R. 6', 200 lbs. b: Regina, Sask., 3/2/1970. NY Rangers' 7th, 118th overall, in 1989.

Season	Club	League	GP	G	A	Pts	AG	AA	APts	PIM	PP	SH	GW	S	%	TGF	PGF	TGA	PGA	+/-	GP	G	A	Pts	PIM	PP	SH	GW
1987-88	Notre Dame Hounds	SJHL	53	9	22	31	....	....	....	208	....	....	....	....	....	....	....	....	....	....	....	....	....	....	....	....	....	....
	Notre Dame Hounds	Cen-Cup	5	2	3	5	....	....	....	....	....	....	....	....	....	....	....	....	....	....	....	....	....	....	....	....	....	....
1988-89	Michigan State Spartans	CCHA	39	2	10	12	....	....	....	66	....	....	....	....	....	....	....	....	....	....	....	....	....	....	....	....	....	....
1989-90	Michigan State Spartans	CCHA	42	1	11	12	....	....	....	58	....	....	....	....	....	....	....	....	....	....	....	....	....	....	....	....	....	....
1990-91	Michigan State Spartans	CCHA	39	5	11	16	....	....	....	71	....	....	....	....	....	....	....	....	....	....	....	....	....	....	....	....	....	....
1991-92	Michigan State Spartans	CCHA	41	13	15	28	....	....	....	81	....	....	....	....	....	....	....	....	....	....	....	....	....	....	....	....	....	....
1992-93	**New York Rangers**	**NHL**	**11**	**0**	**0**	**0**	**0**	**0**	**0**	**6**	**0**	**0**	**0**	**11**	**0.0**	**5**	**0**	**7**	**2**	**0**	....	....	....	....	....	....	....	....
	Binghamton Rangers	AHL	60	5	16	21	....	....	....	63	....	....	....	....	....	....	....	....	....	....	14	1	1	2	6	....	....	....
1993-94	**New York Rangers**	**NHL**	**4**	**0**	**2**	**2**	**0**	**2**	**2**	**0**	**0**	**0**	**0**	**7**	**0.0**	**3**	**1**	**4**	**1**	**−1**	....	....	....	....	....	....	....	....
	Binghamton Rangers	AHL	42	6	14	20	....	....	....	58	....	....	....	....	....	....	....	....	....	....	....	....	....	....	....	....	....	....
1994-95	**New York Rangers**	**NHL**	**10**	**0**	**2**	**2**	**0**	**3**	**3**	**18**	**0**	**0**	**0**	**4**	**0.0**	**5**	**0**	**4**	**1**	**2**	....	....	....	....	....	....	....	....
	Binghamton Rangers	AHL	25	2	9	11	....	....	....	36	....	....	....	....	....	....	....	....	....	....	1	0	0	0	0	....	....	....
1995-96	**New York Islanders**	**NHL**	DID NOT PLAY – INJURED																									
1996-97	Utah Grizzlies	IHL	44	6	20	26	....	....	....	41	....	....	....	....	....	....	....	....	....	....	7	0	1	1	10	....	....	....
1997-98	Long Beach Ice Dogs	IHL	24	0	3	3	....	....	....	45	....	....	....	....	....	....	....	....	....	....	....	....	....	....	....	....	....	....
	NHL Totals		**25**	**0**	**4**	**4**	**0**	**5**	**5**	**24**	**0**	**0**	**0**	**22**	**0.0**	**13**	**1**	**15**	**4**		....	....	....	....	....	....	....	....

• Brother of Mitch • Centennial Cup All-Star Team (1988) • CCHA First All-Star Team (1992) • NCAA West First All-American Team (1992)

Signed as a free agent by **NY Islanders**, September 5, 1995. • Missed entire 1995-96 recovering from knee injury suffered in training camp, September 26, 1995. • Missed majority of 1996-97 season recovering from injuries suffered in automobile accident, August 23, 1996. • Suffered eventual career-ending head injury in game vs. Las Vegas (IHL), November 8, 1997.

• MESSIER, Mark

Mark John Douglas "Moose" LW/C – L. 6'1", 205 lbs. b: Edmonton, Alta., 1/18/1961. Edmonton's 2nd, 48th overall, in 1979.

Season	Club	League	GP	G	A	Pts	AG	AA	APts	PIM	PP	SH	GW	S	%	TGF	PGF	TGA	PGA	+/-	GP	G	A	Pts	PIM	PP	SH	GW
1976-77	Spruce Grove Mets	AJHL	57	27	39	66	....	....	....	91	....	....	....	....	....	....	....	....	....	....	....	....	....	....	....	....	....	....
1977-78	St. Albert Saints	AJHL	54	25	49	74	....	....	....	194	....	....	....	....	....	....	....	....	....	....	....	....	....	....	....	....	....	....
	Portland Winter Hawks	WHL	....	....	....	....	....	....	....	....	....	....	....	....	....	....	....	....	....	....	7	4	1	5	2	....	....	....
1978-79	St. Albert Saints	AJHL	17	15	18	33	....	....	....	64	....	....	....	....	....	....	....	....	....	....	....	....	....	....	....	....	....	....
	Indianapolis Racers	WHA	5	0	0	0	....	....	....	0	....	....	....	....	....	....	....	....	....	....	....	....	....	....	....	....	....	....
	Cincinnati Stingers	WHA	47	1	10	11	....	....	....	58	....	....	....	....	....	....	....	....	....	....	....	....	....	....	....	....	....	....
1979-80	**Edmonton Oilers**	**NHL**	**75**	**12**	**21**	**33**	**10**	**15**	**25**	**120**	**1**	**1**	**1**	**113**	**10.6**	**50**	**6**	**62**	**8**	**−10**	**3**	**1**	**2**	**3**	**2**	**0**	**1**	**0**
	Houston Apollos	CHL	4	0	3	3	....	....	....	4	....	....	....	....	....	....	....	....	....	....	....	....	....	....	....	....	....	....
1980-81	**Edmonton Oilers**	**NHL**	**72**	**23**	**40**	**63**	**18**	**27**	**45**	**102**	**4**	**0**	**1**	**179**	**12.8**	**82**	**17**	**107**	**30**	**−12**	**9**	**2**	**5**	**7**	**13**	**0**	**0**	**0**
1981-82	**Edmonton Oilers**	**NHL**	**78**	**50**	**38**	**88**	**40**	**25**	**65**	**119**	**10**	**0**	**3**	**235**	**21.3**	**135**	**32**	**95**	**13**	**21**	**5**	**1**	**2**	**3**	**8**	**0**	**0**	**0**
1982-83	**Edmonton Oilers**	**NHL**	**77**	**48**	**58**	**106**	**39**	**40**	**79**	**72**	**12**	**1**	**2**	**237**	**20.3**	**150**	**47**	**118**	**34**	**19**	**15**	**15**	**6**	**21**	**14**	**4**	**2**	**0**
1983-84♦	**Edmonton Oilers**	**NHL**	**73**	**37**	**64**	**101**	**30**	**44**	**74**	**165**	**7**	**4**	**7**	**219**	**16.9**	**140**	**40**	**85**	**25**	**40**	**19**	**8**	**18**	**26**	**19**	**1**	**1**	**2**
1984-85	Canada	Can-Cup	8	2	4	6	....	....	....	8	....	....	....	....	....	....	....	....	....	....	....	....	....	....	....	....	....	....
♦	**Edmonton Oilers**	**NHL**	**55**	**23**	**31**	**54**	**19**	**21**	**40**	**57**	**4**	**5**	**1**	**136**	**16.9**	**74**	**20**	**71**	**25**	**8**	**18**	**12**	**13**	**25**	**12**	**1**	**1**	**1**

			REGULAR SEASON																		PLAYOFFS							
Season	**Club**	**League**	**GP**	**G**	**A**	**Pts**	**AG**	**AA**	**APts**	**PIM**	**PP**	**SH**	**GW**	**S**	**%**	**TGF**	**PGF**	**TGA**	**PGA**	**+/–**	**GP**	**G**	**A**	**Pts**	**PIM**	**PP**	**SH**	**GW**
1985-86	**Edmonton Oilers**	**NHL**	**63**	**35**	**49**	**84**	**28**	**33**	**61**	**68**	**10**	**5**	**7**	**201**	**17.4**	**116**	**33**	**71**	**24**	**36**	**10**	**4**	**6**	**10**	**18**	**0**	**2**	**0**
1986-87♦	**Edmonton Oilers**	**NHL**	**77**	**37**	**70**	**107**	**32**	**51**	**83**	**73**	**7**	**4**	**5**	**208**	**17.8**	**130**	**39**	**108**	**38**	**21**	**21**	**12**	**16**	**28**	**16**	**1**	**2**	**1**
	NHL All-Stars	RV-87	2	1	0	1	....	....	....	0	....	....	....	....	....	....	....	....	....	....	....	....	....	....	....	....	....	....
1987-88	Canada	Can-Cup	9	1	6	7	....	....	....	6	....	....	....	....	....	....	....	....	....	....	....	....	....	....	....	....	....	....
♦	**Edmonton Oilers**	**NHL**	**77**	**37**	**74**	**111**	**32**	**53**	**85**	**103**	**12**	**3**	**7**	**182**	**20.3**	**149**	**54**	**114**	**40**	**21**	**19**	**11**	**23**	**34**	**29**	**7**	**1**	**0**
1988-89	**Edmonton Oilers**	**NHL**	**72**	**33**	**61**	**94**	**28**	**43**	**71**	**130**	**6**	**6**	**4**	**164**	**20.1**	**117**	**46**	**107**	**31**	**–5**	**7**	**1**	**11**	**12**	**8**	**0**	**0**	**0**
	Canada	WEC-A	6	3	3	6	....	....	....	8	....	....	....	....	....	....	....	....	....	....	....	....	....	....	....	....	....	....
1989-90♦	**Edmonton Oilers**	**NHL**	**79**	**45**	**84**	**129**	**39**	**60**	**99**	**79**	**13**	**6**	**3**	**211**	**21.3**	**159**	**60**	**117**	**37**	**19**	**22**	**9**	***22**	***31**	**20**	**1**	**1**	**1**
1990-91	**Edmonton Oilers**	**NHL**	**53**	**12**	**52**	**64**	**11**	**40**	**51**	**34**	**3**	**1**	**2**	**109**	**11.0**	**86**	**30**	**63**	**22**	**15**	**18**	**4**	**11**	**15**	**16**	**1**	**0**	**0**
1991-92	Canada	Can-Cup	8	2	6	8	....	....	....	10	....	....	....	....	....	....	....	....	....	....	....	....	....	....	....	....	....	....
	New York Rangers	**NHL**	**79**	**35**	**72**	**107**	**32**	**55**	**87**	**76**	**12**	**4**	**6**	**212**	**16.5**	**150**	**48**	**92**	**21**	**31**	**11**	**7**	**7**	**14**	**6**	**2**	**2**	**0**
1992-93	**New York Rangers**	**NHL**	**75**	**25**	**66**	**91**	**21**	**46**	**67**	**72**	**7**	**2**	**2**	**215**	**11.6**	**118**	**44**	**106**	**26**	**–6**	....	....	....	....	....	....	....	....
1993-94♦	**New York Rangers**	**NHL**	**76**	**26**	**58**	**84**	**24**	**45**	**69**	**76**	**6**	**2**	**5**	**216**	**12.0**	**127**	**56**	**81**	**35**	**25**	**23**	**12**	**18**	**30**	**33**	**2**	**1**	**4**
1994-95	**New York Rangers**	**NHL**	**46**	**14**	**39**	**53**	**25**	**58**	**83**	**40**	**3**	**3**	**2**	**126**	**11.1**	**71**	**30**	**50**	**17**	**8**	**10**	**3**	**10**	**13**	**8**	**2**	**0**	**1**
1995-96	**New York Rangers**	**NHL**	**74**	**47**	**52**	**99**	**46**	**43**	**89**	**122**	**14**	**1**	**5**	**241**	**19.5**	**129**	**48**	**98**	**46**	**29**	**11**	**4**	**7**	**11**	**16**	**2**	**0**	**1**
1996-97	Canada	W-Cup	7	1	4	5	....	....	....	12	....	....	....	....	....	....	....	....	....	....	....	....	....	....	....	....	....	....
	New York Rangers	**NHL**	**71**	**36**	**48**	**84**	**38**	**43**	**81**	**88**	**7**	**5**	**9**	**227**	**15.9**	**105**	**30**	**95**	**32**	**12**	**15**	**3**	**9**	**12**	**6**	**0**	**0**	**1**
1997-98	**Vancouver Canucks**	**NHL**	**82**	**22**	**38**	**60**	**26**	**37**	**63**	**58**	**8**	**2**	**2**	**139**	**15.8**	**100**	**36**	**113**	**39**	**–10**	....	....	....	....	....	....	....	....
1998-99	**Vancouver Canucks**	**NHL**	**59**	**13**	**35**	**48**	**15**	**34**	**49**	**33**	**4**	**2**	**2**	**97**	**13.4**	**68**	**33**	**73**	**26**	**–12**	....	....	....	....	....	....	....	....
99-2000	**Vancouver Canucks**	**NHL**	**66**	**17**	**37**	**54**	**19**	**34**	**53**	**30**	**6**	**0**	**4**	**131**	**13.0**	**71**	**30**	**73**	**17**	**–15**	....	....	....	....	....	....	....	....
	NHL Totals		**1479**	**627**	**1087**	**1714**	**572**	**847**	**1419**	**1717**	**156**	**57**	**80**	**3798**	**16.5**	**2327**	**779**	**1899**	**586**		**236**	**109**	**186**	**295**	**244**	**24**	**14**	**12**
	Other Major League Totals		52	1	10	11	....	....	....	58	....	....	....	....	....	....	....	....	....	....	....	....	....	....	....	....	....	....

• Brother of Paul • NHL First All-Star Team (1982, 1983, 1990, 1992) • NHL Second All-Star Team (1984) • Won Conn Smythe Trophy (1984) • Won Lester B. Pearson Award (1990, 1992) • Won Hart Trophy (1990, 1992) • Played in NHL All-Star Game (1982, 1983, 1984, 1986, 1988, 1989, 1990, 1991, 1992, 1994, 1996, 1997, 1998, 2000)

Signed as an underage free agent by **Indianapolis** (WHA) to a 10-game tryout contract, November 5, 1978. Signed as a free agent by **Cincinnati** (WHA) after **Indianapolis** (WHA) franchise folded, December, 1978. Traded to **NY Rangers** by **Edmonton** with future considerations (Jeff Beukeboom for David Shaw, November 12, 1991) for Bernie Nicholls, Steven Rice and Louie DeBrusk, October 4, 1991. Signed as a free agent by **Vancouver**, July 30, 1997. Signed as a free agent by **NY Rangers**, July 13, 2000.

• MESSIER, Mitch

Mitchell Ronald C – R. 6'2", 200 lbs. b: Regina, Sask., 8/21/1965. Minnesota's 4th, 57th overall, in 1983.

Season	Club	League	GP	G	A	Pts	AG	AA	APts	PIM	PP	SH	GW	S	%	TGF	PGF	TGA	PGA	+/–	GP	G	A	Pts	PIM	PP	SH	GW
1980-81	Notre Dame Midget Hounds	SAHA	71	118	145	263	....	....	....	....	....	....	....	....	....	....	....	....	....	....	....	....	....	....	....	....	....	....
1981-82	Notre Dame Hounds	Hi-School	26	8	20	28	....	....	....	....	....	....	....	....	....	....	....	....	....	....	....	....	....	....	....	....	....	....
1982-83	Notre Dame Hounds	Hi-School	60	*108	73	*181	....	....	....	160	....	....	....	....	....	....	....	....	....	....	....	....	....	....	....	....	....	....
1983-84	Michigan State Spartans	CCHA	37	6	15	21	....	....	....	22	....	....	....	....	....	....	....	....	....	....	....	....	....	....	....	....	....	....
1984-85	Michigan State Spartans	CCHA	42	12	21	33	....	....	....	46	....	....	....	....	....	....	....	....	....	....	....	....	....	....	....	....	....	....
1985-86	Michigan State Spartans	CCHA	38	24	40	64	....	....	....	36	....	....	....	....	....	....	....	....	....	....	....	....	....	....	....	....	....	....
1986-87	Michigan State Spartans	CCHA	45	44	48	92	....	....	....	89	....	....	....	....	....	....	....	....	....	....	....	....	....	....	....	....	....	....
1987-88	**Minnesota North Stars**	**NHL**	**13**	**0**	**1**	**1**	**0**	**1**	**1**	**11**	**0**	**0**	**0**	**5**	**0.0**	**2**	**0**	**7**	**0**	**–5**	....	....	....	....	....	....	....	....
	Kalamazoo Wings	IHL	69	29	37	66	....	....	....	42	....	....	....	....	....	....	....	....	....	....	4	2	1	3	0	....	....	....
1988-89	**Minnesota North Stars**	**NHL**	**3**	**0**	**1**	**1**	**0**	**1**	**1**	**0**	**0**	**0**	**0**	**3**	**0.0**	**3**	**0**	**4**	**0**	**–1**	....	....	....	....	....	....	....	....
	Kalamazoo Wings	IHL	67	34	46	80	....	....	....	71	....	....	....	....	....	....	....	....	....	....	6	4	3	7	0	....	....	....
1989-90	**Minnesota North Stars**	**NHL**	**2**	**0**	**0**	**0**	**0**	**0**	**0**	**0**	**0**	**0**	**0**	**1**	**0.0**	**0**	**0**	**2**	**0**	**–2**	....	....	....	....	....	....	....	....
	Kalamazoo Wings	IHL	65	26	58	84	....	....	....	56	....	....	....	....	....	....	....	....	....	....	8	4	3	7	25	....	....	....
1990-91	**Minnesota North Stars**	**NHL**	**2**	**0**	**0**	**0**	**0**	**0**	**0**	**0**	**0**	**0**	**0**	**0**	**0.0**	**0**	**0**	**2**	**0**	**–2**	....	....	....	....	....	....	....	....
	Kalamazoo Wings	IHL	73	30	46	76	....	....	....	34	....	....	....	....	....	....	....	....	....	....	11	4	8	12	2	....	....	....
1991-92	Kalamazoo Wings	IHL	77	43	33	76	....	....	....	42	....	....	....	....	....	....	....	....	....	....	12	3	3	6	25	....	....	....
1992-93	Milwaukee Admirals	IHL	62	18	23	41	....	....	....	84	....	....	....	....	....	....	....	....	....	....	6	0	1	1	0	....	....	....
1993-94	Fort Wayne Komets	IHL	69	33	27	60	....	....	....	77	....	....	....	....	....	....	....	....	....	....	14	8	6	14	14	....	....	....
1994-95	KAC Klagenfurt	Austria	28	17	15	32	....	....	....	51	....	....	....	....	....	....	....	....	....	....	7	4	8	12	6	....	....	....
1995-96	Fort Wayne Komets	IHL	59	15	21	36	....	....	....	55	....	....	....	....	....	....	....	....	....	....	3	0	1	1	4	....	....	....
	NHL Totals		**20**	**0**	**2**	**2**	**0**	**2**	**2**	**11**	**0**	**0**	**0**	**9**	**0.0**	**5**	**0**	**15**	**0**		....	....	....	....	....	....	....	....

• Brother of Joby • CCHA First All-Star Team (1987) • NCAA West First All-American Team (1987)

• Suffered career-ending head and neck injuries in automobile accident, August 23, 1996.

• MESSIER, Paul

Paul Edmond C – R. 6'1", 185 lbs. b: Nottingham, England, 1/27/1958. Colorado's 3rd, 41st overall, in 1978.

Season	Club	League	GP	G	A	Pts	AG	AA	APts	PIM	PP	SH	GW	S	%	TGF	PGF	TGA	PGA	+/–	GP	G	A	Pts	PIM	PP	SH	GW
1973-74	Edmonton Mets	AJHL	59	37	39	76	....	....	....	43	....	....	....	....	....	....	....	....	....	....	....	....	....	....	....	....	....	....
1974-75	Spruce Grove Mets	AJHL	57	45	56	101	....	....	....	48	....	....	....	....	....	....	....	....	....	....	11	7	*13	20	10	....	....	....
	Edmonton Oil Kings	WCJHL	1	2	0	2	....	....	....	0	....	....	....	....	....	....	....	....	....	....	....	....	....	....	....	....	....	....
	Spruce Grove Mets	Cen-Cup	....	....	....	....	....	....	....	....	....	....	....	....	....	....	....	....	....	....	....	....	....	....	....	....	....	....
1975-76	Spruce Grove Mets	AJHL	44	32	45	77	....	....	....	46	....	....	....	....	....	....	....	....	....	....	10	4	12	16	11	....	....	....
	Edmonton Oil Kings	WCJHL	11	1	12	13	....	....	....	2	....	....	....	....	....	....	....	....	....	....	....	....	....	....	....	....	....	....
1976-77	University of Denver	WCHA	30	15	12	27	....	....	....	47	....	....	....	....	....	....	....	....	....	....	....	....	....	....	....	....	....	....
1977-78	University of Denver	WCHA	38	20	31	51	....	....	....	53	....	....	....	....	....	....	....	....	....	....	....	....	....	....	....	....	....	....
1978-79	**Colorado Rockies**	**NHL**	**9**	**0**	**0**	**0**	**0**	**0**	**0**	**4**	**0**	**0**	**0**	**9**	**0.0**	**2**	**0**	**8**	**0**	**–6**	....	....	....	....	....	....	....	....
	Philadelphia Firebirds	AHL	16	2	3	5	....	....	....	18	....	....	....	....	....	....	....	....	....	....	....	....	....	....	....	....	....	....
	Tulsa Oilers	CHL	27	3	4	7	....	....	....	11	....	....	....	....	....	....	....	....	....	....	....	....	....	....	....	....	....	....
1979-80	Fort Worth Texans	CHL	7	0	1	1	....	....	....	2	....	....	....	....	....	....	....	....	....	....	....	....	....	....	....	....	....	....
	Birmingham Bulls	CHL	50	6	14	20	....	....	....	14	....	....	....	....	....	....	....	....	....	....	2	2	1	3	0	....	....	....
1980-81	Wichita Wind	CHL	45	13	13	26	....	....	....	26	....	....	....	....	....	....	....	....	....	....	....	....	....	....	....	....	....	....
1981-82	Binghamton Whalers	AHL	62	26	37	63	....	....	....	74	....	....	....	....	....	....	....	....	....	....	15	5	6	11	2	....	....	....
1982-83	Moncton Alpines	AHL	77	27	50	77	....	....	....	30	....	....	....	....	....	....	....	....	....	....	....	....	....	....	....	....	....	....
1983-84	EHC Iserlohn	Germany	46	24	26	50	....	....	....	40	....	....	....	....	....	....	....	....	....	....	....	....	....	....	....	....	....	....
1984-85	Mannheimer ERC	Germany	36	32	31	63	....	....	....	35	....	....	....	....	....	....	....	....	....	....	9	5	8	13	14	....	....	....
1985-86	Mannheimer ERC	Germany	35	32	33	65	....	....	....	66	....	....	....	....	....	....	....	....	....	....	3	0	2	2	0	....	....	....
1986-87	Mannheimer ERC	Germany	36	32	33	59	....	....	....	60	....	....	....	....	....	....	....	....	....	....	10	*10	2	12	0	....	....	....
1987-88	Mannheimer ERC	Germany	36	21	29	50	....	....	....	40	....	....	....	....	....	....	....	....	....	....	8	4	9	13	8	....	....	....
1988-89	Mannheimer ERC	Germany	36	32	17	49	....	....	....	30	....	....	....	....	....	....	....	....	....	....	9	3	11	14	6	....	....	....
1989-90	Mannheimer ERC	Germany	36	11	23	34	....	....	....	22	....	....	....	....	....	....	....	....	....	....	3	2	2	4	2	....	....	....
1990-91	HC Bolzano	Italy	2	1	1	2	....	....	....	0	....	....	....	....	....	....	....	....	....	....	....	....	....	....	....	....	....	....
	NHL Totals		**9**	**0**	**0**	**0**	**0**	**0**	**0**	**4**	**0**	**0**	**0**	**9**	**0.0**	**2**	**0**	**8**	**0**		....	....	....	....	....	....	....	....

• Brother of Mark • Centennial Cup All-Star Team (1975)

• METCALFE, Scott

"Metal" LW – L. 6', 195 lbs. b: Toronto, Ont., 1/6/1967. Edmonton's 1st, 20th overall, in 1985.

Season	Club	League	GP	G	A	Pts	AG	AA	APts	PIM	PP	SH	GW	S	%	TGF	PGF	TGA	PGA	+/–	GP	G	A	Pts	PIM	PP	SH	GW
1982-83	Toronto Young Nationals	MTHL	39	22	43	65	....	....	....	74	....	....	....	....	....	....	....	....	....	....	....	....	....	....	....	....	....	....
1983-84	Kingston Canadians	OHL	68	25	49	74	....	....	....	154	....	....	....	....	....	....	....	....	....	....	....	....	....	....	....	....	....	....
1984-85	Kingston Canadians	OHL	58	27	33	60	....	....	....	100	....	....	....	....	....	....	....	....	....	....	....	....	....	....	....	....	....	....
1985-86	Kingston Canadians	OHL	66	36	43	79	....	....	....	213	....	....	....	....	....	....	....	....	....	....	10	3	6	9	21	....	....	....
1986-87	Windsor Spitfires	OHL	57	25	57	82	....	....	....	156	....	....	....	....	....	....	....	....	....	....	13	5	5	10	27	....	....	....
	Canada	WJC-A	6	2	5	7	....	....	....	12	....	....	....	....	....	....	....	....	....	....	....	....	....	....	....	....	....	....
1987-88	**Edmonton Oilers**	**NHL**	**2**	**0**	**0**	**0**	**0**	**0**	**0**	**0**	**0**	**0**	**0**	**0**	**0.0**	**0**	**0**	**1**	**0**	**–1**	....	....	....	....	....	....	....	....
	Nova Scotia Oilers	AHL	43	9	19	28	....	....	....	87	....	....	....	....	....	....	....	....	....	....	....	....	....	....	....	....	....	....
	Buffalo Sabres	**NHL**	**1**	**0**	**1**	**1**	**0**	**1**	**1**	**0**	**0**	**0**	**0**	**1**	**0.0**	**1**	**0**	**2**	**0**	**–1**	....	....	....	....	....	....	....	....
	Rochester Americans	AHL	22	2	13	15	....	....	....	56	....	....	....	....	....	....	....	....	....	....	7	1	3	4	24	....	....	....
1988-89	**Buffalo Sabres**	**NHL**	**9**	**1**	**1**	**2**	**1**	**1**	**2**	**13**	**0**	**0**	**0**	**11**	**9.1**	**3**	**0**	**4**	**0**	**–1**	....	....	....	....	....	....	....	....
	Rochester Americans	AHL	60	20	31	51	....	....	....	241	....	....	....	....	....	....	....	....	....	....	....	....	....	....	....	....	....	....
1989-90	**Buffalo Sabres**	**NHL**	**7**	**0**	**0**	**0**	**0**	**0**	**0**	**5**	**0**	**0**	**0**	**5**	**0.0**	**2**	**0**	**2**	**0**	**0**	....	....	....	....	....	....	....	....
	Rochester Americans	AHL	43	12	17	29	....	....	....	93	....	....	....	....	....	....	....	....	....	....	2	0	1	1	0	....	....	....
1990-91	Rochester Americans	AHL	69	17	22	39	....	....	....	177	....	....	....	....	....	....	....	....	....	....	14	4	1	5	27	....	....	....
1991-92	EHC Eisbaren Berlin	Germany-2	25	19	16	35	....	....	....	83	....	....	....	....	....	....	....	....	....	....	....	....	....	....	....	....	....	....

			REGULAR SEASON																		PLAYOFFS							
Season	**Club**	**League**	**GP**	**G**	**A**	**Pts**	**AG**	**AA**	**APts**	**PIM**	**PP**	**SH**	**GW**	**S**	**%**	**TGF**	**PGF**	**TGA**	**PGA**	**+/–**	**GP**	**G**	**A**	**Pts**	**PIM**	**PP**	**SH**	**GW**
1992-93	ES Weiswasser	Germany-2	8	4	3	7	....	....	....	4	....	....	....	....	....	....	....	....	....	....	....	....	....	....	....	....	....	....
	EHC Eisbaren Berlin	Germany	27	8	17	25	....	....	....	45	....	....	....	....	....	....	....	....	....	....	4	2	2	4	8	....	....	....
1993-94	Knoxville Cherokees	ECHL	56	25	56	81	....	....	....	136	....	....	....	....	....	....	....	....	....	....	3	0	1	1	2	....	....	....
	Rochester Americans	AHL	16	5	7	12	....	....	....	16	....	....	....	....	....	....	....	....	....	....	4	1	0	1	31	....	....	....
1994-95	Rochester Americans	AHL	63	19	36	55	....	....	....	216	....	....	....	....	....	....	....	....	....	....	5	1	1	2	4	....	....	....
1995-96	Rochester Americans	AHL	71	21	24	45	....	....	....	228	....	....	....	....	....	....	....	....	....	....	19	6	8	14	23	....	....	....
1996-97	Rochester Americans	AHL	80	32	38	70	....	....	....	205	....	....	....	....	....	....	....	....	....	....	10	1	3	4	18	....	....	....
1997-98	Rochester Americans	AHL	75	9	24	33	....	....	....	192	....	....	....	....	....	....	....	....	....	....	4	0	0	0	0	....	....	....
1998-99	Hannover Scorpions	Germany	50	11	21	32	....	....	....	126	....	....	....	....	....	....	....	....	....	....	....	....	....	....	....	....	....	....
99-2000	Hannover Scorpions	Germany	61	10	18	28	....	....	....	85	....	....	....	....	....	....	....	....	....	....	....	....	....	....	....	....	....	....
	NHL Totals		**19**	**1**	**2**	**3**	**1**	**2**	**3**	**18**	**0**	**0**	**0**	**17**	**5.9**	**6**	**0**	**9**	**0**		....	....	....	....	....	....	....	....

Traded to **Buffalo** by **Edmonton** with Edmonton's 9th round choice (Donald Audette) in 1989 Entry Draft for Steve Dykstra and Buffalo's 7th round choice (David Payne) in 1989 Entry Draft, February 11, 1988.

• METROPOLIT, Glen

RW – R. 5'11", 185 lbs. b: Toronto, Ont., 6/25/1974.

Season	**Club**	**League**	**GP**	**G**	**A**	**Pts**	**AG**	**AA**	**APts**	**PIM**	**PP**	**SH**	**GW**	**S**	**%**	**TGF**	**PGF**	**TGA**	**PGA**	**+/–**	**GP**	**G**	**A**	**Pts**	**PIM**	**PP**	**SH**	**GW**
1992-93	Richmond Hill Riot	OJHL	43	27	36	63	....	....	....	36	....	....	....	....	....	....	....	....	....	....	....	....	....	....	....	....	....	....
1993-94	Richmond Hill Riot	OJHL	49	38	62	100	....	....	....	83	....	....	....	....	....	....	....	....	....	....	....	....	....	....	....	....	....	....
1994-95	Vernon Lakers	BCJHL	60	43	74	117	....	....	....	92	....	....	....	....	....	....	....	....	....	....	....	....	....	....	....	....	....	....
1995-96	Nashville Knights	ECHL	58	30	31	61	....	....	....	62	....	....	....	....	....	....	....	....	....	....	5	3	8	11	2	....	....	....
	Atlanta Knights	IHL	1	0	0	0	....	....	....	0	....	....	....	....	....	....	....	....	....	....	....	....	....	....	....	....	....	....
1996-97	Pensacola Ice Pilots	ECHL	54	35	47	82	....	....	....	45	....	....	....	....	....	....	....	....	....	....	12	9	16	25	28	....	....	....
	Quebec Rafales	IHL	22	5	4	9	....	....	....	14	....	....	....	....	....	....	....	....	....	....	5	0	0	0	2	....	....	....
1997-98	Grand Rapids Griffins	IHL	79	20	35	55	....	....	....	90	....	....	....	....	....	....	....	....	....	....	3	1	1	2	0	....	....	....
1998-99	Grand Rapids Griffins	IHL	77	28	53	81	....	....	....	92	....	....	....	....	....	....	....	....	....	....	....	....	....	....	....	....	....	....
99-2000	**Washington Capitals**	**NHL**	**30**	**6**	**13**	**19**	**7**	**12**	**19**	**4**	**1**	**0**	**1**	**57**	**10.5**	**27**	**6**	**16**	**0**	**5**	**2**	**0**	**0**	**0**	**2**	**0**	**0**	**0**
	Portland Pirates	AHL	48	18	42	60	....	....	....	73	....	....	....	....	....	....	....	....	....	....	1	1	0	1	0	....	....	....
	NHL Totals		**30**	**6**	**13**	**19**	**7**	**12**	**19**	**4**	**1**	**0**	**1**	**57**	**10.5**	**27**	**6**	**16**	**0**		**2**	**0**	**0**	**0**	**2**	**0**	**0**	**0**

Signed as a free agent by **Washington**, July 19, 1999. • Played w/ RHI's Long Island Jawz in 1996 (28-32-39-71-29), Anaheim Bulldogs (4-5-2-7-4) and New Jersey (2-1-1-2-0) in 1997.

• MICHAYLUK, Dave

David LW – L. 5'10", 189 lbs. b: Wakaw, Sask., 5/18/1962. Philadelphia's 5th, 65th overall, in 1981.

Season	**Club**	**League**	**GP**	**G**	**A**	**Pts**	**AG**	**AA**	**APts**	**PIM**	**PP**	**SH**	**GW**	**S**	**%**	**TGF**	**PGF**	**TGA**	**PGA**	**+/–**	**GP**	**G**	**A**	**Pts**	**PIM**	**PP**	**SH**	**GW**
1979-80	Prince Albert Raiders	SJHL	60	46	67	113	....	....	....	49	....	....	....	....	....	....	....	....	....	....	....	....	....	....	....	....	....	....
	Regina Pats	WHL	1	0	1	1	....	....	....	0	....	....	....	....	....	....	....	....	....	....	....	....	....	....	....	....	....	....
1980-81	Regina Pats	WHL	72	62	71	133	....	....	....	39	....	....	....	....	....	....	....	....	....	....	11	5	12	17	8	....	....	....
1981-82	Regina Pats	WHL	72	62	111	173	....	....	....	128	....	....	....	....	....	....	....	....	....	....	12	16	24	*40	23	....	....	....
	Philadelphia Flyers	**NHL**	**1**	**0**	**0**	**0**	**0**	**0**	**0**	**0**	**0**	**0**	**0**	**0**	**0.0**	**0**	**0**	**2**	**0**	**–2**	....	....	....	....	....	....	....	....
1982-83	**Philadelphia Flyers**	**NHL**	**13**	**2**	**6**	**8**	**2**	**4**	**6**	**8**	**0**	**0**	**0**	**18**	**11.1**	**12**	**3**	**12**	**4**	**1**	....	....	....	....	....	....	....	....
	Maine Mariners	AHL	69	32	40	72	....	....	....	16	....	....	....	....	....	....	....	....	....	....	8	0	2	2	0	....	....	....
1983-84	Springfield Indians	AHL	79	18	44	62	....	....	....	37	....	....	....	....	....	....	....	....	....	....	4	0	0	0	2	....	....	....
1984-85	Hershey Bears	AHL	3	0	2	2	....	....	....	2	....	....	....	....	....	....	....	....	....	....	....	....	....	....	....	....	....	....
	Kalamazoo Wings	IHL	82	*66	33	99	....	....	....	49	....	....	....	....	....	....	....	....	....	....	11	7	7	14	0	....	....	....
1985-86	Nova Scotia Oilers	AHL	3	0	1	1	....	....	....	0	....	....	....	....	....	....	....	....	....	....	....	....	....	....	....	....	....	....
	Muskegon Lumberjacks	IHL	77	52	52	104	....	....	....	73	....	....	....	....	....	....	....	....	....	....	14	6	9	15	12	....	....	....
1986-87	Muskegon Lumberjacks	IHL	82	47	53	100	....	....	....	29	....	....	....	....	....	....	....	....	....	....	15	2	14	16	8	....	....	....
1987-88	Muskegon Lumberjacks	IHL	81	*56	81	137	....	....	....	46	....	....	....	....	....	....	....	....	....	....	6	2	0	2	18	....	....	....
1988-89	Muskegon Lumberjacks	IHL	80	50	72	*122	....	....	....	84	....	....	....	....	....	....	....	....	....	....	13	*9	12	*21	24	....	....	....
1989-90	Muskegon Lumberjacks	IHL	79	*51	51	102	....	....	....	80	....	....	....	....	....	....	....	....	....	....	15	8	*14	*22	10	....	....	....
1990-91	Muskegon Lumberjacks	IHL	83	40	62	102	....	....	....	16	....	....	....	....	....	....	....	....	....	....	5	2	2	4	4	....	....	....
1991-92	Muskegon Lumberjacks	IHL	82	39	63	102	....	....	....	154	....	....	....	....	....	....	....	....	....	....	13	9	8	17	4	....	....	....
	♦ **Pittsburgh Penguins**	**NHL**	....	....	....	....	....	....	....	....	....	....	....	....	....	....	....	....	....	....	**7**	**1**	**1**	**2**	**0**	**0**	**0**	**0**
1992-93	Cleveland Lumberjacks	IHL	82	47	65	112	....	....	....	104	....	....	....	....	....	....	....	....	....	....	4	1	2	3	4	....	....	....
1993-94	Cleveland Lumberjacks	IHL	81	48	51	99	....	....	....	92	....	....	....	....	....	....	....	....	....	....	....	....	....	....	....	....	....	....
1994-95	Cleveland Lumberjacks	IHL	60	19	17	36	....	....	....	22	....	....	....	....	....	....	....	....	....	....	1	0	0	0	0	....	....	....
1995-96	Cleveland Lumberjacks	IHL	53	22	21	43	....	....	....	27	....	....	....	....	....	....	....	....	....	....	3	1	0	1	4	....	....	....
1996-97	Cleveland Lumberjacks	IHL	46	10	15	25	....	....	....	18	....	....	....	....	....	....	....	....	....	....	....	....	....	....	....	....	....	....
	NHL Totals		**14**	**2**	**6**	**8**	**2**	**4**	**6**	**8**	**0**	**0**	**0**	**18**	**11.1**	**12**	**3**	**14**	**4**		**7**	**1**	**1**	**2**	**0**	**0**	**0**	**0**

WHL Second All-Star Team (1982) • IHL Second All-Star Team (1985, 1992, 1993) • IHL First All-Star Team (1987, 1988, 1989, 1990) • Won Leo P. Lamoureux Memorial Trophy (Top Scorer - IHL) (1989) • Won James Gatschene Memorial Trophy (MVP - IHL) (1989) • Won "Bud" Poile Trophy (Playoff MVP - IHL) (1989)

Signed as a free agent by **Pittsburgh**, May 24, 1989.

• MICHELETTI, Joe

Joseph Robert D – L. 6', 185 lbs. b: Hibbing, MN, 10/24/1954. Montreal's 12th, 123rd overall, in 1974.

Season	**Club**	**League**	**GP**	**G**	**A**	**Pts**	**AG**	**AA**	**APts**	**PIM**	**PP**	**SH**	**GW**	**S**	**%**	**TGF**	**PGF**	**TGA**	**PGA**	**+/–**	**GP**	**G**	**A**	**Pts**	**PIM**	**PP**	**SH**	**GW**
1972-73	Hibbing Blue Jackets	Hi-School	STATISTICS NOT AVAILABLE																									
1973-74	University of Minnesota	WCHA	21	2	5	7	....	....	....	10	....	....	....	....	....	....	....	....	....	....	....	....	....	....	....	....	....	....
1974-75	University of Minnesota	WCHA	42	7	13	20	....	....	....	44	....	....	....	....	....	....	....	....	....	....	....	....	....	....	....	....	....	....
1975-76	University of Minnesota	WCHA	33	7	24	31	....	....	....	46	....	....	....	....	....	....	....	....	....	....	....	....	....	....	....	....	....	....
1976-77	University of Minnesota	WCHA	39	9	39	48	....	....	....	53	....	....	....	....	....	....	....	....	....	....	....	....	....	....	....	....	....	....
	Calgary Cowboys	WHA	14	3	3	6	....	....	....	10	....	....	....	....	....	....	....	....	....	....	....	....	....	....	....	....	....	....
	United States	WEC-A	10	0	5	5	....	....	....	8	....	....	....	....	....	....	....	....	....	....	....	....	....	....	....	....	....	....
1977-78	Edmonton Oilers	WHA	56	14	34	48	....	....	....	56	....	....	....	....	....	....	....	....	....	....	5	0	2	2	4	....	....	....
1978-79	Edmonton Oilers	WHA	72	14	33	47	....	....	....	85	....	....	....	....	....	....	....	....	....	....	13	0	9	9	2	....	....	....
1979-80	**St. Louis Blues**	**NHL**	**54**	**2**	**16**	**18**	**2**	**12**	**14**	**29**	**2**	**0**	**0**	**68**	**2.9**	**72**	**12**	**74**	**9**	**–5**	....	....	....	....	....	....	....	....
1980-81	**St. Louis Blues**	**NHL**	**63**	**4**	**27**	**31**	**3**	**18**	**21**	**53**	**3**	**0**	**1**	**102**	**3.9**	**95**	**42**	**50**	**9**	**12**	**11**	**1**	**11**	**12**	**10**	**1**	**0**	**0**
1981-82	**St. Louis Blues**	**NHL**	**20**	**3**	**11**	**14**	**2**	**7**	**9**	**28**	**2**	**0**	**0**	**30**	**10.0**	**33**	**12**	**27**	**4**	**–2**	....	....	....	....	....	....	....	....
	Colorado Rockies	**NHL**	**21**	**2**	**6**	**8**	**2**	**4**	**6**	**4**	**0**	**0**	**0**	**41**	**4.9**	**27**	**7**	**26**	**2**	**–4**	....	....	....	....	....	....	....	....
	Fort Worth Texans	CHL	17	3	14	17	....	....	....	26	....	....	....	....	....	....	....	....	....	....	....	....	....	....	....	....	....	....
	United States	WEC-A	5	0	0	0	....	....	....	2	....	....	....	....	....	....	....	....	....	....	....	....	....	....	....	....	....	....
	NHL Totals		**158**	**11**	**60**	**71**	**9**	**41**	**50**	**114**	**7**	**0**	**1**	**241**	**4.6**	**227**	**73**	**177**	**24**		**11**	**1**	**11**	**12**	**10**	**1**	**0**	**0**
	Other Major League Totals		142	31	70	101	....	....	....	151	....	....	....	....	....	....	....	....	....	....	18	0	11	11	6	....	....	....

• Brother of Pat

Selected by **Cincinnati** (WHA) in 1974 WHA Amateur Draft, May, 1974. WHA rights traded to **Minnesota** (WHA) by **Cincinnati** (WHA) for future considerations, July, 1975. WHA rights traded to **Calgary** (WHA) by **Minnesota** (WHA) with Don Tannahill, George Morrison and the rights to Wally Olds for John McKenzie and cash, September, 1975. Traded to **Winnipeg** (WHA) by **Calgary** (WHA) for future considerations, August, 1977. Traded to **Edmonton** (WHA) by **Winnipeg** (WHA) for future considerations, September, 1977. Rights retained by **Edmonton** prior to Expansion Draft, June 9, 1979. Traded to **St. Louis** by **Edmonton** for Tom Roulston and Risto Siltanen, August 7, 1979. Traded to **Colorado** by **St. Louis** with Dick Lamby for Bill Baker, December 4, 1981.

• MICHELETTI, Pat

Patrick J. C – L. 5'10", 175 lbs. b: Hibbing, MN, 12/11/1963. Minnesota's 9th, 185th overall, in 1982.

Season	**Club**	**League**	**GP**	**G**	**A**	**Pts**	**AG**	**AA**	**APts**	**PIM**	**PP**	**SH**	**GW**	**S**	**%**	**TGF**	**PGF**	**TGA**	**PGA**	**+/–**	**GP**	**G**	**A**	**Pts**	**PIM**	**PP**	**SH**	**GW**
1981-82	Hibbing Blue Jackets	Hi-School	22	26	39	65	....	....	....	50	....	....	....	....	....	....	....	....	....	....	....	....	....	....	....	....	....	....
1982-83	University of Minnesota	WCHA	20	11	11	22	....	....	....	52	....	....	....	....	....	....	....	....	....	....	....	....	....	....	....	....	....	....
1983-84	University of Minnesota	WCHA	39	26	34	60	....	....	....	62	....	....	....	....	....	....	....	....	....	....	....	....	....	....	....	....	....	....
1984-85	University of Minnesota	WCHA	44	48	48	96	....	....	....	154	....	....	....	....	....	....	....	....	....	....	....	....	....	....	....	....	....	....
1985-86	University of Minnesota	WCHA	48	32	48	80	....	....	....	113	....	....	....	....	....	....	....	....	....	....	....	....	....	....	....	....	....	....
	Springfield Indians	AHL	2	1	0	1	....	....	....	0	....	....	....	....	....	....	....	....	....	....	....	....	....	....	....	....	....	....
1986-87	Springfield Indians	AHL	67	17	26	43	....	....	....	39	....	....	....	....	....	....	....	....	....	....	....	....	....	....	....	....	....	....
1987-88	**Minnesota North Stars**	**NHL**	**12**	**2**	**0**	**2**	**2**	**0**	**2**	**8**	**0**	**0**	**0**	**18**	**11.1**	**4**	**0**	**2**	**0**	**2**	....	....	....	....	....	....	....	....
	Kalamazoo Wings	IHL	19	12	6	18	....	....	....	12	....	....	....	....	....	....	....	....	....	....	7	2	2	4	0	....	....	....
1988-89	HC Varese	Italy	46	48	50	98	....	....	....	105	....	....	....	....	....	....	....	....	....	....	....	....	....	....	....	....	....	....
1989-90	HC Varese	Italy-2	33	43	32	75	....	....	....	54	....	....	....	....	....	....	....	....	....	....	6	3	3	6	18	....	....	....

Season	Club	League	GP	G	A	Pts	AG	AA	APts	PIM	PP	SH	GW	S	%	TGF	PGF	TGA	PGA	+/–	GP	G	A	Pts	PIM	PP	SH	GW
			REGULAR SEASON																		PLAYOFFS							
1990-91	HC Varese	Italy	36	34	58	92	....	....	....	22	....	....	....	....	....	....	....	....	....	....	9	8	7	15	26	....	....	....
1991-92	HC Asagio	Alpenliga	18	23	23	46	....	....	....	67	....	....	....	....	....	....	....	....	....	....	....	....	....	....	....	....	....	....
	HC Asagio	Italy	9	4	12	16	....	....	....	16	....	....	....	....	....	....	....	....	....	....	10	2	3	5	26	....	....	....
	NHL Totals		**12**	**2**	**0**	**2**	**2**	**0**	**2**	**8**	**0**	**0**	**0**	**18**	**11.1**	**4**	**.0**	**2**	**0**		....	....	....	....	....	....	....	....

• Brother of Joe • WCHA First All-Star Team (1985) • NCAA West First All-American Team (1985) • WCHA Second All-Star Team (1986)

• MICKEY, Larry

Robert Larry RW – R. 5'11", 175 lbs. b: Lacombe, Alta., 10/21/1943 d: 7/23/1982.

Season	Club	League	GP	G	A	Pts	AG	AA	APts	PIM	PP	SH	GW	S	%	TGF	PGF	TGA	PGA	+/–	GP	G	A	Pts	PIM	PP	SH	GW
1961-62	Moose Jaw Canucks	SJHL	STATISTICS NOT AVAILABLE																									
	Moose Jaw Canucks	Mem-Cup	4	2	1	3	....	....	....	10	....	....	....	....	....	....	....	....	....	....	....	....	....	....	....	....	....	....
1962-63	Moose Jaw Canucks	SJHL	54	32	38	70	....	....	....	85	....	....	....	....	....	....	....	....	....	....	6	1	5	6	23	....	....	....
	Calgary Stampeders	WHL	2	0	1	1	....	....	....	0	....	....	....	....	....	....	....	....	....	....	....	....	....	....	....	....	....	....
1963-64	Moose Jaw Canucks	SJHL	62	69	73	142	....	....	....	139	....	....	....	....	....	....	....	....	....	....	5	7	2	9	6	....	....	....
	St. Louis Braves	CPHL	1	0	0	0	....	....	....	0	....	....	....	....	....	....	....	....	....	....	5	1	2	3	2	....	....	....
	Estevan Bruins	Mem-Cup	5	1	1	2	....	....	....	8	....	....	....	....	....	....	....	....	....	....	....	....	....	....	....	....	....	....
	Edmonton Oil Kings	Mem-Cup	4	0	0	0	....	....	....	2	....	....	....	....	....	....	....	....	....	....	....	....	....	....	....	....	....	....
1964-65	**Chicago Black Hawks**	**NHL**	**1**	**0**	**0**	**0**	**0**	**0**	**0**	**0**	....	....	....	....	....	....	....	....	....	....	....	....	....	....	....	....	....	....
	St. Louis Braves	CPHL	52	16	21	37	....	....	....	85	....	....	....	....	....	....	....	....	....	....	....	....	....	....	....	....	....	....
	Buffalo Bisons	AHL	1	0	1	1	....	....	....	2	....	....	....	....	....	....	....	....	....	....	....	....	....	....	....	....	....	....
1965-66	**New York Rangers**	**NHL**	**7**	**0**	**0**	**0**	**0**	**0**	**0**	**2**	....	....	....	....	....	....	....	....	....	....	....	....	....	....	....	....	....	....
	Minnesota Rangers	CPHL	38	14	25	39	....	....	....	50	....	....	....	....	....	....	....	....	....	....	7	5	5	10	2	....	....	....
1966-67	**New York Rangers**	**NHL**	**8**	**0**	**0**	**0**	**0**	**0**	**0**	**0**	....	....	....	....	....	....	....	....	....	....	....	....	....	....	....	....	....	....
	Omaha Knights	CPHL	63	33	41	74	....	....	....	86	....	....	....	....	....	....	....	....	....	....	9	5	*10	*15	4	....	....	....
1967-68	**New York Rangers**	**NHL**	**4**	**0**	**2**	**2**	**0**	**2**	**2**	**0**	**0**	**0**	**0**	**2**	**0.0**	**2**	**0**	**0**	**0**	**2**	....	....	....	....	....	....	....	....
	Buffalo Bisons	AHL	30	9	17	26	....	....	....	48	....	....	....	....	....	....	....	....	....	....	....	....	....	....	....	....	....	....
1968-69	**Toronto Maple Leafs**	**NHL**	**55**	**8**	**19**	**27**	**8**	**17**	**25**	**43**	**0**	**0**	**3**	**80**	**10.0**	**36**	**10**	**28**	**2**	**0**	**3**	**0**	**0**	**0**	**5**	**0**	**0**	**0**
1969-70	**Montreal Canadiens**	**NHL**	**21**	**4**	**4**	**8**	**4**	**4**	**8**	**4**	**3**	**0**	**2**	**38**	**10.5**	**15**	**9**	**16**	**0**	**–10**	....	....	....	....	....	....	....	....
	Montreal Voyageurs	AHL	50	24	38	62	....	....	....	90	....	....	....	....	....	....	....	....	....	....	....	....	....	....	....	....	....	....
1970-71	**Los Angeles Kings**	**NHL**	**65**	**6**	**12**	**18**	**6**	**10**	**16**	**46**	**0**	**1**	**2**	**101**	**5.9**	**37**	**13**	**49**	**10**	**–15**	....	....	....	....	....	....	....	....
1971-72	**Philadelphia Flyers**	**NHL**	**14**	**1**	**2**	**3**	**1**	**2**	**3**	**8**	**1**	**0**	**0**	**22**	**4.5**	**8**	**4**	**9**	**0**	**–5**	....	....	....	....	....	....	....	....
	Buffalo Sabres	**NHL**	**4**	**0**	**1**	**1**	**0**	**1**	**1**	**0**	**0**	**0**	**0**	**5**	**0.0**	**5**	**4**	**3**	**1**	**–1**	....	....	....	....	....	....	....	....
	Salt Lake Golden Eagles	WHL	53	19	30	49	....	....	....	92	....	....	....	....	....	....	....	....	....	....	....	....	....	....	....	....	....	....
1972-73	**Buffalo Sabres**	**NHL**	**77**	**15**	**9**	**24**	**14**	**7**	**21**	**47**	**1**	**0**	**2**	**160**	**9.4**	**40**	**1**	**47**	**2**	**–6**	**6**	**1**	**0**	**1**	**5**	**0**	**0**	**0**
1973-74	**Buffalo Sabres**	**NHL**	**13**	**3**	**4**	**7**	**3**	**3**	**6**	**8**	**0**	**0**	**0**	**18**	**16.7**	**10**	**0**	**6**	**1**	**5**	....	....	....	....	....	....	....	....
	Cincinnati Swords	AHL	9	2	3	5	....	....	....	5	....	....	....	....	....	....	....	....	....	....	....	....	....	....	....	....	....	....
1974-75	**Buffalo Sabres**	**NHL**	**23**	**2**	**0**	**2**	**2**	**0**	**2**	**2**	**0**	**0**	**0**	**6**	**33.3**	**2**	**0**	**2**	**1**	**1**	....	....	....	....	....	....	....	....
1975-76			DID NOT PLAY																									
1976-77	Dayton Gems	IHL	DID NOT PLAY – COACHING																									
1977-78	Dayton Gems	IHL	DID NOT PLAY – COACHING																									
1978-79	Utica Mohawks	NEHL	12	5	4	9	....	....	....	21	....	....	....	....	....	....	....	....	....	....	....	....	....	....	....	....	....	....
1979-80	Utica Mohawks	EHL	4	0	4	4	....	....	....	14	....	....	....	....	....	....	....	....	....	....	....	....	....	....	....	....	....	....
1980-81	Hampton Aces	EHL	38	5	14	19	....	....	....	50	....	....	....	....	....	....	....	....	....	....	....	....	....	....	....	....	....	....
	NHL Totals		**292**	**39**	**53**	**92**	**38**	**46**	**84**	**160**	....	....	....	....	....	....	....	....	....	....	**9**	**1**	**0**	**1**	**10**	....	....	....

SJHL First All-Star Team (1964) • CPHL First All-Star Team (1967)

• Loaned to **Estevan** (SJHL) and **Edmonton** (CAHL) by **Moose Jaw** (SJHL) for Memorial Cup playoffs, March, 1964. Claimed by **NY Rangers** from **Chicago** (St. Louis-CHL) in Inter-League Draft, June 8, 1965. • Missed majority of 1967-68 season recovering from arm injury suffered in game vs. Quebec (AHL), January 12, 1968. Claimed by **Toronto** from **NY Rangers** in Intra-League Draft, June 12, 1968. Claimed by **Montreal** from **Toronto** in Intra-League Draft, June 11, 1969. Traded to **LA Kings** by **Montreal** with Lucien Grenier and Jack Norris for Leon Rochefort, Wayne Thomas and Gregg Boddy, May 22, 1970. Traded to **Philadelphia** by **LA Kings** for Larry Hillman, June 13, 1971. Traded to **Buffalo** by **Philadelphia** for Larry Keenan, November 16, 1971.

• MIDDENDORF, Max

RW – R. 6'4", 210 lbs. b: Syracuse, NY, 8/18/1967. Quebec's 3rd, 57th overall, in 1985.

Season	Club	League	GP	G	A	Pts	AG	AA	APts	PIM	PP	SH	GW	S	%	TGF	PGF	TGA	PGA	+/–	GP	G	A	Pts	PIM	PP	SH	GW
1983-84	New Jersey Rockets	USAHA	58	94	74	168	....	....	....	....	....	....	....	....	....	....	....	....	....	....	....	....	....	....	....	....	....	....
1984-85	Sudbury Wolves	OHL	63	16	28	44	....	....	....	106	....	....	....	....	....	....	....	....	....	....	....	....	....	....	....	....	....	....
1985-86	Sudbury Wolves	OHL	61	40	42	82	....	....	....	71	....	....	....	....	....	....	....	....	....	....	4	4	2	6	11	....	....	....
	United States	WJC-A	7	2	2	4	....	....	....	4	....	....	....	....	....	....	....	....	....	....	....	....	....	....	....	....	....	....
1986-87	Sudbury Wolves	OHL	31	31	29	60	....	....	....	7	....	....	....	....	....	....	....	....	....	....	....	....	....	....	....	....	....	....
	Kitchener Rangers	OHL	17	7	15	22	....	....	....	6	....	....	....	....	....	....	....	....	....	....	4	2	5	7	5	....	....	....
	Quebec Nordiques	**NHL**	**6**	**1**	**4**	**5**	**1**	**3**	**4**	**4**	**0**	**0**	**0**	**4**	**25.0**	**7**	**4**	**5**	**0**	**–2**	....	....	....	....	....	....	....	....
1987-88	**Quebec Nordiques**	**NHL**	**1**	**0**	**0**	**0**	**0**	**0**	**0**	**0**	**0**	**0**	**0**	**0**	**0.0**	**0**	**0**	**0**	**0**	**0**	....	....	....	....	....	....	....	....
	Fredericton Express	AHL	38	11	13	24	....	....	....	57	....	....	....	....	....	....	....	....	....	....	12	4	4	8	18	....	....	....
1988-89	Halifax Citadels	AHL	72	41	39	80	....	....	....	85	....	....	....	....	....	....	....	....	....	....	4	1	2	3	6	....	....	....
1989-90	**Quebec Nordiques**	**NHL**	**3**	**0**	**0**	**0**	**0**	**0**	**0**	**0**	**0**	**0**	**0**	**5**	**0.0**	**0**	**0**	**9**	**0**	**–9**	....	....	....	....	....	....	....	....
	Halifax Citadels	AHL	48	20	17	37	....	....	....	60	....	....	....	....	....	....	....	....	....	....	....	....	....	....	....	....	....	....
1990-91	**Edmonton Oilers**	**NHL**	**3**	**1**	**0**	**1**	**1**	**0**	**1**	**2**	**0**	**0**	**0**	**1**	**100.0**	**1**	**0**	**1**	**0**	**0**	....	....	....	....	....	....	....	....
	Fort Wayne Komets	IHL	15	9	11	20	....	....	....	12	....	....	....	....	....	....	....	....	....	....	....	....	....	....	....	....	....	....
	Cape Breton Oilers	AHL	44	14	21	35	....	....	....	82	....	....	....	....	....	....	....	....	....	....	4	0	1	1	6	....	....	....
1991-92	Cape Breton Oilers	AHL	51	20	19	39	....	....	....	108	....	....	....	....	....	....	....	....	....	....	....	....	....	....	....	....	....	....
	Adirondack Red Wings	AHL	6	3	5	8	....	....	....	12	....	....	....	....	....	....	....	....	....	....	5	0	1	1	16	....	....	....
1992-93	Fort Wayne Komets	IHL	24	9	13	22	....	....	....	58	....	....	....	....	....	....	....	....	....	....	....	....	....	....	....	....	....	....
	San Diego Gulls	IHL	30	15	11	26	....	....	....	25	....	....	....	....	....	....	....	....	....	....	8	1	2	3	8	....	....	....
1993-94	Fort Wayne Komets	IHL	36	16	20	36	....	....	....	43	....	....	....	....	....	....	....	....	....	....	9	1	2	3	24	....	....	....
1994-95	Fort Wayne Komets	IHL	15	1	4	5	....	....	....	34	....	....	....	....	....	....	....	....	....	....	....	....	....	....	....	....	....	....
1995-96	KAC Klagenfurt	Austria	9	1	6	7	....	....	....	86	....	....	....	....	....	....	....	....	....	....	....	....	....	....	....	....	....	....
	Winston-Salem Mammoths	SHL	4	1	5	6	....	....	....	27	....	....	....	....	....	....	....	....	....	....	....	....	....	....	....	....	....	....
	Bakersfield Fog	WCHL	23	4	12	16	....	....	....	80	....	....	....	....	....	....	....	....	....	....	....	....	....	....	....	....	....	....
1996-97	Huntsville Channel Cats	CHL	42	14	32	46	....	....	....	79	....	....	....	....	....	....	....	....	....	....	....	....	....	....	....	....	....	....
1997-98	Fort Worth Brahmas	WPHL	18	4	10	14	....	....	....	56	....	....	....	....	....	....	....	....	....	....	....	....	....	....	....	....	....	....
	NHL Totals		**13**	**2**	**4**	**6**	**2**	**3**	**5**	**6**	**0**	**0**	**0**	**10**	**20.0**	**8**	**4**	**15**	**0**		....	....	....	....	....	....	....	....

Traded to **Edmonton** by **Quebec** for Edmonton's 9th round choice (Brent Brekke) in 1991 Entry Draft, November 10, 1990. Traded to **Detroit** by **Edmonton** for Bill McDougall, February 22, 1992. • Played w/ RHI's San Diego Barracudas in 1993 (14-29-28-47-60) and 1996 (6-1-2-3-47).

• MIDDLETON, Rick

Richard David "Niftie" RW – R. 5'11", 170 lbs. b: Toronto, Ont., 12/4/1953. NY Rangers' 1st, 14th overall, in 1973.

Season	Club	League	GP	G	A	Pts	AG	AA	APts	PIM	PP	SH	GW	S	%	TGF	PGF	TGA	PGA	+/–	GP	G	A	Pts	PIM	PP	SH	GW
1970-71	Toronto Young Nationals	OHA-B	STATISTICS NOT AVAILABLE																									
1971-72	Oshawa Generals	OMJHL	53	36	34	70	....	....	....	24	....	....	....	....	....	....	....	....	....	....	12	5	5	10	2	....	....	....
1972-73	Oshawa Generals	OMJHL	62	*67	70	137	....	....	....	14	....	....	....	....	....	....	....	....	....	....	....	....	....	....	....	....	....	....
1973-74	Providence Reds	AHL	63	36	48	84	....	....	....	14	....	....	....	....	....	....	....	....	....	....	15	9	6	15	2	....	....	....
1974-75	**New York Rangers**	**NHL**	**47**	**22**	**18**	**40**	**19**	**13**	**32**	**19**	**6**	**0**	**2**	**106**	**20.8**	**57**	**24**	**39**	**0**	**–6**	**3**	**0**	**0**	**0**	**2**	**0**	**0**	**0**
1975-76	**New York Rangers**	**NHL**	**77**	**24**	**26**	**50**	**21**	**19**	**40**	**14**	**7**	**0**	**5**	**159**	**15.1**	**85**	**38**	**86**	**1**	**–38**	....	....	....	....	....	....	....	....
1976-77	**Boston Bruins**	**NHL**	**72**	**20**	**22**	**42**	**18**	**17**	**35**	**2**	**0**	**0**	**1**	**128**	**15.6**	**70**	**8**	**60**	**0**	**2**	**13**	**5**	**4**	**9**	**0**	**0**	**0**	**1**
1977-78	**Boston Bruins**	**NHL**	**79**	**25**	**35**	**60**	**23**	**27**	**50**	**8**	**2**	**0**	**6**	**171**	**14.6**	**101**	**10**	**52**	**1**	**40**	**15**	**5**	**2**	**7**	**0**	**0**	**0**	**2**
1978-79	**Boston Bruins**	**NHL**	**71**	**38**	**48**	**86**	**33**	**35**	**68**	**7**	**12**	**1**	**5**	**152**	**25.0**	**117**	**29**	**69**	**14**	**33**	**11**	**4**	**8**	**12**	**0**	**2**	**0**	**1**
1979-80	**Boston Bruins**	**NHL**	**80**	**40**	**52**	**92**	**34**	**38**	**72**	**24**	**9**	**0**	**4**	**223**	**17.9**	**135**	**50**	**56**	**2**	**31**	**10**	**4**	**2**	**6**	**5**	**0**	**0**	**0**
1980-81	**Boston Bruins**	**NHL**	**80**	**44**	**59**	**103**	**34**	**39**	**73**	**16**	**16**	**4**	**7**	**222**	**19.8**	**138**	**64**	**68**	**9**	**15**	**3**	**0**	**1**	**1**	**2**	**0**	**0**	**0**
1981-82	Canada	Can-Cup	7	1	2	3	....	....	....	0	....	....	....	....	....	....	....	....	....	....	....	....	....	....	....	....	....	....
	Boston Bruins	**NHL**	**75**	**51**	**43**	**94**	**40**	**29**	**69**	**12**	**19**	**1**	**9**	**202**	**25.2**	**140**	**52**	**92**	**19**	**15**	**11**	**6**	**9**	**15**	**0**	**2**	**0**	**0**
1982-83	**Boston Bruins**	**NHL**	**80**	**49**	**47**	**96**	**40**	**33**	**73**	**8**	**6**	**3**	**7**	**214**	**22.9**	**134**	**29**	**102**	**30**	**33**	**17**	**11**	**22**	**33**	**6**	**4**	**1**	**1**
1983-84	**Boston Bruins**	**NHL**	**80**	**47**	**58**	**105**	**38**	**40**	**78**	**14**	**16**	**4**	**6**	**209**	**22.5**	**155**	**56**	**91**	**18**	**26**	**3**	**0**	**0**	**0**	**0**	**0**	**0**	**0**
1984-85	Canada	Can-Cup	7	4	4	8	....	....	....	0	....	....	....	....	....	....	....	....	....	....	....	....	....	....	....	....	....	....
	Boston Bruins	**NHL**	**80**	**30**	**46**	**76**	**24**	**31**	**55**	**6**	**12**	**3**	**3**	**169**	**17.8**	**107**	**32**	**102**	**29**	**2**	**5**	**3**	**0**	**3**	**0**	**0**	**0**	**0**
1985-86	**Boston Bruins**	**NHL**	**49**	**14**	**30**	**44**	**11**	**20**	**31**	**10**	**4**	**2**	**0**	**100**	**14.0**	**68**	**18**	**60**	**27**	**17**								

			REGULAR SEASON																		PLAYOFFS							
Season	Club	League	GP	G	A	Pts	AG	AA	APts	PIM	PP	SH	GW	S	%	TGF	PGF	TGA	PGA	+/–	GP	G	A	Pts	PIM	PP	SH	GW
1986-87	**Boston Bruins**	**NHL**	76	31	37	68	27	27	54	6	4	4	3	141	22.0	105	32	89	23	7	4	2	2	4	0	1	1	0
1987-88	**Boston Bruins**	**NHL**	59	13	19	32	11	14	25	11	2	3	1	79	16.5	49	11	62	27	3	19	5	5	10	4	0	1	3
1988-89	EHC Bulach	Switz-2	STATISTICS NOT AVAILABLE																									
	NHL Totals		1005	448	540	988	373	382	755	157	115	25	59	2275	19.7	1461	453	1028	200		114	45	55	100	19	9	3	8

OMJHL Second All-Star Team (1973) • AHL First All-Star Team (1974) • Won Dudley "Red" Garrett Memorial Award (Top Rookie - AHL) (1974) • NHL Second All-Star Team (1982) • Won Lady Byng Trophy (1982) • Played in NHL All-Star Game (1981, 1982, 1984)

Traded to **Boston** by **NY Rangers** for Ken Hodge, May 26, 1976. • Played w/ MRHL's Toronto Tornados in 1998 (3-0-2-2-1).

• MIEHM, Kevin

Kevin J. C – L. 6'2", 200 lbs. b: Kitchener, Ont., 9/10/1969. St. Louis' 2nd, 54th overall, in 1987.

Season	Club	League	GP	G	A	Pts	AG	AA	APts	PIM	PP	SH	GW	S	%	TGF	PGF	TGA	PGA	+/–	GP	G	A	Pts	PIM	PP	SH	GW
1985-86	Kitchener Greenshirts	OMHA	20	20	37	57	....	....	....	65	....	....	....	....	....	....	....	....	....	....	....	....	....	....	....	....	....	....
1986-87	Oshawa Generals	OHL	61	12	27	39	....	....	....	19	....	....	....	....	....	....	....	....	....	....	26	1	8	9	12	....	....	....
	Oshawa Generals	Mem-Cup	4	0	2	2	....	....	....	12	....	....	....	....	....	....	....	....	....	....	....	....	....	....	....	....	....	....
1987-88	Oshawa Generals	OHL	52	16	36	52	....	....	....	30	....	....	....	....	....	....	....	....	....	....	7	2	5	7	0	....	....	....
1988-89	Oshawa Generals	OHL	63	43	79	122	....	....	....	19	....	....	....	....	....	....	....	....	....	....	6	6	6	12	0	....	....	....
	Peoria Rivermen	IHL	3	1	1	2	....	....	....	0	....	....	....	....	....	....	....	....	....	....	4	0	2	2	0	....	....	....
1989-90	Peoria Rivermen	IHL	76	23	38	61	....	....	....	20	....	....	....	....	....	....	....	....	....	....	3	0	0	0	4	....	....	....
1990-91	Peoria Rivermen	IHL	73	25	39	64	....	....	....	14	....	....	....	....	....	....	....	....	....	....	16	5	7	12	2	....	....	....
1991-92	Peoria Rivermen	IHL	66	21	53	74	....	....	....	22	....	....	....	....	....	....	....	....	....	....	10	3	4	7	2	....	....	....
1992-93	**St. Louis Blues**	**NHL**	8	1	3	4	1	2	3	4	0	0	0	5	20.0	4	0	3	0	1	2	0	1	1	0	0	0	0
	Peoria Rivermen	IHL	30	12	33	45	....	....	....	13	....	....	....	....	....	....	....	....	....	....	4	0	1	1	2	....	....	....
1993-94	**St. Louis Blues**	**NHL**	14	0	1	1	0	1	1	4	0	0	0	5	0.0	1	0	4	0	–3	....	....	....	....	....	....	....	....
	Peoria Rivermen	IHL	11	2	3	5	....	....	....	0	....	....	....	....	....	....	....	....	....	....	4	1	0	1	0	....	....	....
1994-95	Peoria Rivermen	IHL	5	1	5	6	....	....	....	2	....	....	....	....	....	....	....	....	....	....	....	....	....	....	....	....	....	....
	Fort Wayne Komets	IHL	30	10	25	35	....	....	....	18	....	....	....	....	....	....	....	....	....	....	4	1	4	5	0	....	....	....
1995-96	Fort Wayne Komets	IHL	12	2	5	7	....	....	....	2	....	....	....	....	....	....	....	....	....	....	....	....	....	....	....	....	....	....
	Michigan K-Wings	IHL	44	13	20	33	....	....	....	12	....	....	....	....	....	....	....	....	....	....	10	1	1	2	4	....	....	....
1996-97	VSV Villach	Alpenliga	39	29	*60	*89	....	....	....	10	....	....	....	....	....	....	....	....	....	....	....	....	....	....	....	....	....	....
	VSV Villach	Austria	....	....	....	....	....	....	....	....	....	....	....	....	....	....	....	....	....	....	6	3	8	11	....	....	....	....
1997-98	VSV Villach	Alpenliga	10	5	7	12	....	....	....	20	....	....	....	....	....	....	....	....	....	....	....	....	....	....	....	....	....	....
	HC Asiago	Italy	11	6	11	17	....	....	....	8	....	....	....	....	....	....	....	....	....	....	....	....	....	....	....	....	....	....
1998-99	HC Thurgau	Switz-2	16	13	15	28	....	....	....	....	....	....	....	....	....	....	....	....	....	....	....	....	....	....	....	....	....	....
	Adler Mannheim	Germany	20	4	8	12	....	....	....	8	....	....	....	....	....	....	....	....	....	....	12	2	4	6	6	....	....	....
99-2000	VEU Feldkirch	IEL	25	20	39	59	....	....	....	42	....	....	....	....	....	....	....	....	....	....	....	....	....	....	....	....	....	....
	Nurnberg Ice Tigers	Germany	29	5	24	29	....	....	....	16	....	....	....	....	....	....	....	....	....	....	....	....	....	....	....	....	....	....
	NHL Totals		22	1	4	5	1	3	4	8	0	0	0	10	10.0	5	0	7	0		2	0	1	1	0	0	0	0

• MIKA, Petr

LW – R. 6'4", 194 lbs. b: Prague, Czech., 2/12/1979. NY Islanders' 6th, 85th overall, in 1997.

Season	Club	League	GP	G	A	Pts	AG	AA	APts	PIM	PP	SH	GW	S	%	TGF	PGF	TGA	PGA	+/–	GP	G	A	Pts	PIM	PP	SH	GW
1996-97	Slavia Praha	Czech-Rep	15	8	0	8	....	....	....	....	....	....	....	....	....	....	....	....	....	....	....	....	....	....	....	....	....	....
	HC Beroun-2	Czech-Rep	9	1	0	1	....	....	....	....	....	....	....	....	....	....	....	....	....	....	....	....	....	....	....	....	....	....
	Slavia Praha	Czech-Rep	20	1	2	3	....	....	....	6	....	....	....	....	....	....	....	....	....	....	....	....	....	....	....	....	....	....
1997-98	Ottawa 67's	OHL	41	10	8	18	....	....	....	28	....	....	....	....	....	....	....	....	....	....	....	....	....	....	....	....	....	....
1998-99	Slavia Praha	Czech-Rep	49	6	5	11	....	....	....	57	....	....	....	....	....	....	....	....	....	....	....	....	....	....	....	....	....	....
99-2000	**New York Islanders**	**NHL**	3	0	0	0	0	0	0	0	0	0	0	1	0.0	0	0	1	0	–1	....	....	....	....	....	....	....	....
	Lowell Lock Monsters	AHL	50	8	9	17	....	....	....	20	....	....	....	....	....	....	....	....	....	....	6	0	0	0	0	....	....	....
	NHL Totals		3	0	0	0	0	0	0	0	0	0	0	1	0.0	0	0	1	0		....	....	....	....	....	....	....	....

• MIKITA, Stan

Stanley Guoth "Stosh" C/RW – R. 5'9", 169 lbs. b: Sokolce, Czech., 5/20/1940. **HHOF**

Season	Club	League	GP	G	A	Pts	AG	AA	APts	PIM	PP	SH	GW	S	%	TGF	PGF	TGA	PGA	+/–	GP	G	A	Pts	PIM	PP	SH	GW
1956-57	St. Catharines Teepees	OHA-Jr.	52	16	31	47	....	....	....	129	....	....	....	....	....	....	....	....	....	....	14	8	9	17	44	....	....	....
1957-58	St. Catharines Teepees	OHA-Jr.	52	31	47	78	....	....	....	146	....	....	....	....	....	....	....	....	....	....	8	4	5	9	46	....	....	....
1958-59	St. Catharines Teepees	OHA-Jr.	45	38	*59	*97	....	....	....	197	....	....	....	....	....	....	....	....	....	....	....	....	....	....	....	....	....	....
	Chicago Black Hawks	**NHL**	3	0	1	1	0	1	1	4	....	....	....	....	....	....	....	....	....	....	....	....	....	....	....	....	....	....
1959-60	**Chicago Black Hawks**	**NHL**	67	8	18	26	9	17	26	119	....	....	....	....	....	....	....	....	....	....	3	0	1	1	2	....	....	....
1960-61 ♦	**Chicago Black Hawks**	**NHL**	66	19	34	53	22	33	55	100	....	....	....	....	....	....	....	....	....	....	12	*6	5	11	21	....	....	....
1961-62	**Chicago Black Hawks**	**NHL**	70	25	52	77	29	51	80	97	....	....	....	....	....	....	....	....	....	....	12	6	*15	*21	19	....	....	....
1962-63	**Chicago Black Hawks**	**NHL**	65	31	45	76	36	45	81	69	....	....	....	....	....	....	....	....	....	....	6	3	2	5	2	....	....	....
1963-64	**Chicago Black Hawks**	**NHL**	70	39	50	*89	49	53	102	146	....	....	....	....	....	....	....	....	....	....	7	3	6	9	8	....	....	....
1964-65	**Chicago Black Hawks**	**NHL**	70	28	*59	*87	34	62	96	154	....	....	....	....	....	....	....	....	....	....	14	3	7	10	*53	....	....	....
1965-66	**Chicago Black Hawks**	**NHL**	68	30	*48	78	34	46	80	58	....	....	....	....	....	....	....	....	....	....	6	1	2	3	2	....	....	....
1966-67	**Chicago Black Hawks**	**NHL**	70	35	*62	*97	41	62	103	12	....	....	....	....	....	....	....	....	....	....	6	2	2	4	2	....	....	....
1967-68	**Chicago Black Hawks**	**NHL**	72	40	47	*87	47	47	94	14	13	2	8	303	13.2	110	37	86	10	–3	11	5	7	12	6	2	1	0
1968-69	**Chicago Black Hawks**	**NHL**	74	30	67	97	32	60	92	52	7	3	2	299	10.0	126	39	83	13	17	....	....	....	....	....	....	....	....
1969-70	**Chicago Black Hawks**	**NHL**	76	39	47	86	43	44	87	50	7	0	8	352	11.1	120	44	60	13	29	8	4	6	10	2	3	1	0
1970-71	**Chicago Black Hawks**	**NHL**	74	24	48	72	24	40	64	85	7	0	4	220	10.9	103	43	46	7	21	18	5	13	18	16	1	0	1
1971-72	**Chicago Black Hawks**	**NHL**	74	26	39	65	26	34	60	46	5	0	6	185	14.1	86	24	55	9	16	8	3	1	4	4	0	0	0
1972-73	Team Canada	Summit-72	2	0	1	1	....	....	....	0	....	....	....	....	....	....	....	....	....	....	....	....	....	....	....	....	....	....
	Chicago Black Hawks	**NHL**	57	27	56	83	25	45	70	32	7	1	5	177	15.3	90	24	45	10	31	15	7	13	20	8	1	0	2
1973-74	**Chicago Black Hawks**	**NHL**	76	30	50	80	29	41	70	46	6	2	1	171	17.5	105	35	49	3	24	11	5	6	11	8	1	0	1
1974-75	**Chicago Black Hawks**	**NHL**	79	36	50	86	32	37	69	48	12	0	6	253	14.2	113	49	77	27	14	8	3	4	7	12	1	0	1
1975-76	**Chicago Black Hawks**	**NHL**	48	16	41	57	14	31	45	37	6	0	1	159	10.1	72	37	47	8	–4	4	0	0	0	4	0	0	0
1976-77	**Chicago Black Hawks**	**NHL**	57	19	30	49	17	23	40	20	6	1	4	128	14.8	64	25	62	14	–9	2	0	1	1	0	0	0	0
1977-78	**Chicago Black Hawks**	**NHL**	76	18	41	59	16	32	48	35	6	0	2	202	8.9	92	31	51	8	18	4	3	0	3	0	2	0	0
1978-79	**Chicago Black Hawks**	**NHL**	65	19	36	55	16	26	42	34	4	0	1	147	12.9	70	18	57	8	3	....	....	....	....	....	....	....	....
1979-80	**Chicago Black Hawks**	**NHL**	17	2	5	7	2	4	6	12	0	0	0	28	7.1	12	2	8	0	2	....	....	....	....	....	....	....	....
	NHL Totals		1394	541	926	1467	577	834	1411	1270											155	59	91	150	169	....	....	....

NHL First All-Star Team (1962, 1963, 1964, 1966, 1967, 1968) • Won Art Ross Trophy (1964, 1965, 1967, 1968) • NHL Second All-Star Team (1965, 1970) • Won Lady Byng Trophy (1967, 1968) • Won Hart Trophy (1967, 1968) • Won Lester Patrick Trophy (1976) • Played in NHL All-Star Game (1964, 1967, 1968, 1969, 1971, 1972, 1973, 1974, 1975)

• Missed remainder of 1979-80 season recovering from back surgery, November, 1979.

• MIKKELSON, Bill

William Robert D – L. 6', 185 lbs. b: Neepouna, Man., 5/21/1948.

Season	Club	League	GP	G	A	Pts	AG	AA	APts	PIM	PP	SH	GW	S	%	TGF	PGF	TGA	PGA	+/–	GP	G	A	Pts	PIM	PP	SH	GW
1964-65	Brandon Wheat Kings	SJHL	3	0	1	1	....	....	....	0	....	....	....	....	....	....	....	....	....	....	5	0	1	1	0	....	....	....
1965-66	Brandon Wheat Kings	SJHL	60	9	14	23	....	....	....	92	....	....	....	....	....	....	....	....	....	....	11	1	3	4	12	....	....	....
1966-67	Brandon Wheat Kings	MJHL	60	9	14	23	....	....	....	92	....	....	....	....	....	....	....	....	....	....	11	1	3	4	12	....	....	....
1967-68	Brandon Wheat Kings	WCJHL	56	14	27	41	....	....	....	119	....	....	....	....	....	....	....	....	....	....	8	0	1	1	4	....	....	....
1968-69	Winnipeg Jets	WCJHL	53	5	26	31	....	....	....	43	....	....	....	....	....	....	....	....	....	....	7	0	1	1	0	....	....	....
1969-70	Winnipeg Jets	WCJHL	59	5	34	39	....	....	....	76	....	....	....	....	....	....	....	....	....	....	14	1	5	6	16	....	....	....
1970-71	Springfield Kings	AHL	69	2	9	11	....	....	....	50	....	....	....	....	....	....	....	....	....	....	12	1	2	3	14	....	....	....
1971-72	**Los Angeles Kings**	**NHL**	15	0	1	1	0	1	1	6	0	0	0	8	0.0	3	0	15	1	–11	....	....	....	....	....	....	....	....
	Springfield Kings	AHL	32	2	3	5	....	....	....	36	....	....	....	....	....	....	....	....	....	....	....	....	....	....	....	....	....	....
1972-73	**New York Islanders**	**NHL**	72	1	10	11	1	8	9	45	0	0	0	39	2.6	55	0	137	28	–54	....	....	....	....	....	....	....	....
1973-74	Baltimore Clippers	AHL	75	1	21	22	....	....	....	77	....	....	....	....	....	....	....	....	....	....	7	0	1	1	6	....	....	....
1974-75	**Washington Capitals**	**NHL**	59	3	7	10	3	5	8	52	3	0	0	49	6.1	45	11	156	40	–82	....	....	....	....	....	....	....	....
	Richmond Robins	AHL	10	0	0	0	....	....	....	16	....	....	....	....	....	....	....	....	....	....	3	0	0	0	4	....	....	....
1975-76	Baltimore Clippers	AHL	76	3	18	21	....	....	....	52	....	....	....	....	....	....	....	....	....	....	....	....	....	....	....	....	....	....

			REGULAR SEASON																		PLAYOFFS							
Season	**Club**	**League**	**GP**	**G**	**A**	**Pts**	**AG**	**AA**	**APts**	**PIM**	**PP**	**SH**	**GW**	**S**	**%**	**TGF**	**PGF**	**TGA**	**PGA**	**+/–**	**GP**	**G**	**A**	**Pts**	**PIM**	**PP**	**SH**	**GW**
1976-77	**Washington Capitals**	**NHL**	**1**	**0**	**0**	**0**	**0**	**0**	**0**	**2**	**0**	**0**	**0**	**0**	**0.0**	**1**	**0**	**1**	**0**	**0**								
	Hershey Bears	AHL	22	1	2	3				18											6	0	1	1	4			
	Rhode Island Reds	AHL	51	3	7	10				28																		
	NHL Totals		**147**	**4**	**18**	**22**	**4**	**14**	**18**	**105**	**3**	**0**	**0**	**96**	**4.2**	**104**	**11**	**309**	**69**									

Signed as a free agent by **LA Kings** (Springfield-AHL), September, 1970. Claimed by **NY Islanders** from **LA Kings** in Expansion Draft, June 6, 1972. Claimed by **Washington** from **NY Islanders** in Expansion Draft, June 12, 1974.

• MIKULCHIK, Oleg

Oleg A. D – R. 6′2″, 200 lbs. b: Minsk, USSR, 6/27/1964.

Season	Club	League	GP	G	A	Pts	AG	AA	APts	PIM	PP	SH	GW	S	%	TGF	PGF	TGA	PGA	+/–	GP	G	A	Pts	PIM	PP	SH	GW
1981-82	Junostj Moscow	USSR-Jr.	STATISTICS NOT AVAILABLE																									
	Soviet Union	EJC-A	5	0	0	0				2																		
1982-83	Junostj Moscow	USSR-Jr.	STATISTICS NOT AVAILABLE																									
1983-84	Dynamo Moscow	USSR	17	0	0	0				6																		
	Soviet Union	WJC-A	7	0	3	3				2																		
1984-85	Dynamo Moscow	USSR	30	1	3	4				26																		
1985-86	Dynamo Moscow	USSR	40	0	1	1				36																		
	Dynamo Moscow	Super-S	2	0	0	0				2																		
1986-87	Dynamo Moscow	USSR	39	5	3	8				34																		
1987-88	Dynamo Moscow	USSR	48	7	8	15				63																		
1988-89	Dynamo Moscow	USSR	43	4	7	11				52																		
1989-90	Dynamo Moscow	Fr-Tour	1	0	0	0				15																		
	Dynamo Moscow	USSR	32	1	3	4				31																		
	Dynamo Moscow	Super-S	5	0	2	2				0																		
1990-91	Dynamo Moscow	Fr-Tour	1	0	0	0				20																		
	Dynamo Moscow	USSR	36	2	6	8				40																		
1991-92	Khimik Voskresensk	CIS	15	3	2	5				20																		
	New Haven Nighthawks	AHL	30	3	3	6				63											4	1	3	4	6			
1992-93	Moncton Hawks	AHL	75	6	20	26				159											5	0	0	0	4			
1993-94	**Winnipeg Jets**	**NHL**	**4**	**0**	**1**	**1**	**0**	**1**	**1**	**17**	**0**	**0**	**0**	**3**	**0.0**	**2**	**0**	**4**	**0**	**–2**								
	Moncton Hawks	AHL	67	9	38	47				121											21	2	10	12	18			
1994-95	**Winnipeg Jets**	**NHL**	**25**	**0**	**2**	**2**	**0**	**3**	**3**	**12**	**0**	**0**	**0**	**5**	**0.0**	**28**	**0**	**19**	**1**	**10**								
	Springfield Falcons	AHL	50	5	16	21				59																		
1995-96	**Mighty Ducks of Anaheim**	**NHL**	**8**	**0**	**0**	**0**	**0**	**0**	**0**	**4**	**0**	**0**	**0**	**0**	**0.0**	**3**	**1**	**5**	**1**	**–2**								
	Baltimore Bandits	AHL	19	1	7	8				46											12	2	3	5	22			
1996-97	Long Beach Ice Dogs	IHL	16	0	5	5				29																		
	Fort Wayne Komets	IHL	51	5	13	18				75																		
1997-98	Nurnberg Ice Tigers	Germany	41	4	15	19				174																		
	Belarus	WC-A	6	0	1	1				12																		
1998-99	Metallurg Magnotogorsk	Russia	38	1	3	4				108											16	2	2	4	48			
	Metallurg Magnotogorsk	EuroHL	3	1	0	1				26											5	0	0	0	10			
	Belarus	WC-A	6	0	0	0				0																		
99-2000	Metallurg Magnitogorsk	Russia	22	1	8	9				57											11	2	1	3	12			
	Metallurg Magnotogorsk	EuroHL	4	1	1	2				31											3	1	0	1	6			
	NHL Totals		**37**	**0**	**3**	**3**	**0**	**4**	**4**	**33**	**0**	**0**	**0**	**8**	**0.0**	**33**	**1**	**28**	**2**									

Signed as a free agent by **Winnipeg**, July 26, 1993. Signed as a free agent by **Anaheim**, August 8, 1995.

• MILBURY, Mike

Michael James D – L. 6′1″, 200 lbs. b: Brighton, MA, 6/17/1952.

Season	Club	League	GP	G	A	Pts	AG	AA	APts	PIM	PP	SH	GW	S	%	TGF	PGF	TGA	PGA	+/–	GP	G	A	Pts	PIM	PP	SH	GW
1970-1972	Walpole Rebels	Hi-School	STATISTICS NOT AVAILABLE																									
1972-73	Colgate University	ECAC	27	4	25	29				81																		
1973-74	Colgate University	ECAC	23	2	19	21				68																		
	Boston Braves	AHL	5	0	0	0				7																		
1974-75	Rochester Americans	AHL	71	2	15	17				246											8	0	3	3	24			
1975-76	**Boston Bruins**	**NHL**	**3**	**0**	**0**	**0**	**0**	**0**	**0**	**9**	**0**	**0**	**0**	**2**	**0.0**	**2**	**0**	**2**	**1**	**1**	**11**	**0**	**0**	**0**	**29**	**0**	**0**	**0**
	Rochester Americans	AHL	73	3	15	18				199											3	0	1	1	13			
1976-77	United States	Can-Cup	5	1	3	4				16																		
	Boston Bruins	**NHL**	**77**	**6**	**18**	**24**	**5**	**14**	**19**	**166**	**0**	**0**	**2**	**89**	**6.7**	**102**	**4**	**89**	**16**	**25**	**13**	**2**	**2**	**4**	***47**	**0**	**0**	**1**
1977-78	**Boston Bruins**	**NHL**	**80**	**8**	**30**	**38**	**7**	**23**	**30**	**151**	**0**	**0**	**0**	**82**	**9.8**	**135**	**4**	**106**	**27**	**52**	**15**	**1**	**8**	**9**	**27**	**0**	**0**	**0**
1978-79	**Boston Bruins**	**NHL**	**74**	**1**	**34**	**35**	**1**	**25**	**26**	**149**	**0**	**0**	**0**	**76**	**1.3**	**113**	**9**	**120**	**39**	**23**	**11**	**1**	**7**	**8**	**7**	**0**	**0**	**1**
1979-80	**Boston Bruins**	**NHL**	**72**	**10**	**13**	**23**	**8**	**9**	**17**	**59**	**1**	**0**	**0**	**101**	**9.9**	**79**	**4**	**94**	**26**	**7**	**10**	**0**	**2**	**2**	**50**	**0**	**0**	**0**
1980-81	**Boston Bruins**	**NHL**	**77**	**0**	**18**	**18**	**0**	**12**	**12**	**222**	**0**	**0**	**0**	**77**	**0.0**	**78**	**3**	**86**	**25**	**14**	**2**	**0**	**1**	**1**	**10**	**0**	**0**	**0**
1981-82	**Boston Bruins**	**NHL**	**51**	**2**	**10**	**12**	**2**	**7**	**9**	**71**	**0**	**0**	**1**	**42**	**4.8**	**66**	**1**	**64**	**9**	**10**	**11**	**0**	**4**	**4**	**6**	**0**	**0**	**0**
1982-83	**Boston Bruins**	**NHL**	**78**	**9**	**15**	**24**	**7**	**10**	**17**	**216**	**1**	**0**	**2**	**95**	**9.5**	**88**	**2**	**91**	**27**	**22**								
1983-84	**Boston Bruins**	**NHL**	**74**	**2**	**17**	**19**	**2**	**12**	**14**	**159**	**0**	**0**	**1**	**66**	**3.0**	**85**	**4**	**109**	**30**	**2**	**3**	**0**	**0**	**0**	**12**	**0**	**0**	**0**
1984-85	**Boston Bruins**	**NHL**	**78**	**3**	**13**	**16**	**2**	**9**	**11**	**152**	**0**	**1**	**0**	**84**	**3.6**	**81**	**3**	**119**	**35**	**–6**	**5**	**0**	**0**	**0**	**10**	**0**	**0**	**0**
1985-86	**Boston Bruins**	**NHL**	**22**	**2**	**5**	**7**	**2**	**3**	**5**	**102**	**0**	**0**	**0**	**12**	**16.7**	**20**	**1**	**27**	**9**	**1**	**1**	**0**	**0**	**0**	**17**	**0**	**0**	**0**
1986-87	**Boston Bruins**	**NHL**	**68**	**6**	**16**	**22**	**5**	**12**	**17**	**96**	**0**	**1**	**1**	**59**	**10.2**	**86**	**4**	**93**	**33**	**22**	**4**	**0**	**0**	**0**	**4**	**0**	**0**	**0**
1987-1989	Maine Mariners	AHL	DID NOT PLAY – COACHING																									
1989-1991	**Boston Bruins**	**NHL**	DID NOT PLAY – COACHING																									
1991-1995			OUT OF HOCKEY – RETIRED																									
1995-1996	**New York Islanders**	**NHL**	DID NOT PLAY – COACHING																									
1996-2000	**New York Islanders**	**NHL**	DID NOT PLAY – GENERAL MANAGER																									
	NHL Totals		**754**	**49**	**189**	**238**	**41**	**136**	**177**	**1552**	**2**	**2**	**7**	**785**	**6.2**	**935**	**39**	**1000**	**277**		**86**	**4**	**24**	**28**	**219**	**0**	**0**	**2**

Signed as a free agent by **Boston**, November 5, 1974. • Officially announced retirement and named Assistant Coach of **Maine** (AHL), May 6, 1985. • Came out of retirement due to injuries to Maine roster, January, 1986. • Named Player/Assistant Coach of **Maine** (AHL), November 8, 1986. • Named General Manager of **NY Islanders**, December 12, 1995. • Served as interim coach of **NY Islanders**, March 11, 1998 to January 21, 1999.

• MILLAR, Craig

D – L. 6′2″, 205 lbs. b: Winnipeg, Man., 7/12/1976. Buffalo's 10th, 225th overall, in 1994.

Season	Club	League	GP	G	A	Pts	AG	AA	APts	PIM	PP	SH	GW	S	%	TGF	PGF	TGA	PGA	+/–	GP	G	A	Pts	PIM	PP	SH	GW
1991-92	Winnipeg Hawks	MAHA	STATISTICS NOT AVAILABLE																									
1992-93	Swift Current Broncos	WHL	43	2	1	3				8																		
1993-94	Swift Current Broncos	WHL	66	2	9	11				53											7	0	3	3	4			
1994-95	Swift Current Broncos	WHL	72	8	42	50				80											6	1	1	2	10			
1995-96	Swift Current Broncos	WHL	72	31	46	77				151											6	1	0	1	22			
1996-97	Rochester Americans	AHL	64	7	18	25				65																		
	Edmonton Oilers	**NHL**	**1**	**0**	**0**	**0**	**0**	**0**	**0**	**2**	**0**	**0**	**0**	**1**	**0.0**	**0**	**0**	**0**	**0**	**0**								
	Hamilton Bulldogs	AHL	10	1	3	4				10											22	4	4	8	21			
1997-98	**Edmonton Oilers**	**NHL**	**11**	**4**	**0**	**4**	**5**	**0**	**5**	**8**	**1**	**0**	**0**	**10**	**40.0**	**10**	**3**	**14**	**4**	**–3**								
	Hamilton Bulldogs	AHL	60	10	22	32				113											9	3	1	4	22			
1998-99	**Edmonton Oilers**	**NHL**	**24**	**0**	**2**	**2**	**0**	**2**	**2**	**19**	**0**	**0**	**0**	**18**	**0.0**	**12**	**4**	**19**	**5**	**–6**								
	Hamilton Bulldogs	AHL	43	3	17	20				38											11	1	5	6	18			
99-2000	**Nashville Predators**	**NHL**	**57**	**3**	**11**	**14**	**3**	**10**	**13**	**28**	**0**	**0**	**1**	**50**	**6.0**	**39**	**3**	**49**	**7**	**–6**								
	Milwaukee Admirals	IHL	8	1	5	6				6																		
	NHL Totals		**93**	**7**	**13**	**20**	**8**	**12**	**20**	**57**	**1**	**0**	**1**	**79**	**8.9**	**61**	**10**	**82**	**16**									

WHL East First All-Star Team (1996)

Traded to **Edmonton** by **Buffalo** with Barrie Moore for Miroslav Satan, March 18, 1997. Traded to **Nashville** by **Edmonton** for Detroit's 3rd round choice (previously acquired, Edmonton selected Mike Comrie) in 1999 Entry Draft, June 26, 1999.

• MILLAR, Mike

RW – L. 5'10", 170 lbs. b: St. Catharines, Ont., 4/28/1965. Hartford's 2nd, 110th overall, in 1984.

			REGULAR SEASON																		PLAYOFFS							
Season	Club	League	GP	G	A	Pts	AG	AA	APts	PIM	PP	SH	GW	S	%	TGF	PGF	TGA	PGA	+/–	GP	G	A	Pts	PIM	PP	SH	GW
1981-82	St. Catharines Legionnaires	OMHA	30	32	32	64				24																		
1982-83	Brantford Alexanders	OHL	53	20	29	49				10											8	0	5	5	2			
1983-84	Brantford Alexanders	OHL	69	50	45	95				48											6	4	0	4	2			
1984-85	Hamilton Steelhawks	OHL	63	*66	60	126				54											17	9	10	19	14			
1985-86	Canada	Nat-Team	69	50	38	88				74																		
1986-87	**Hartford Whalers**	**NHL**	**10**	**2**	**2**	**4**	**2**	**1**	**3**	**0**	**1**	**0**	**0**	**13**	**15.4**	**6**	**2**	**1**	**0**	**3**								
	Binghamton Whalers	AHL	61	45	32	77				38											13	7	4	11	27			
1987-88	**Hartford Whalers**	**NHL**	**28**	**7**	**7**	**14**	**6**	**5**	**11**	**6**	**4**	**0**	**2**	**58**	**12.1**	**24**	**15**	**14**	**0**	**–5**								
	Binghamton Whalers	AHL	31	32	17	49				42																		
1988-89	**Washington Capitals**	**NHL**	**18**	**6**	**3**	**9**	**5**	**2**	**7**	**4**	**3**	**0**	**1**	**37**	**16.2**	**11**	**6**	**9**	**0**	**–4**								
	Baltimore Skipjacks	AHL	53	47	35	82				58																		
1989-90	Washington Capitals	Fr-Tour	1	0	0	0				2																		
	Boston Bruins	**NHL**	**15**	**1**	**4**	**5**	**1**	**3**	**4**	**0**	**0**	**0**	**0**	**18**	**5.6**	**6**	**1**	**7**	**0**	**–2**								
	Maine Mariners	AHL	60	40	33	73				77																		
1990-91	**Toronto Maple Leafs**	**NHL**	**7**	**2**	**2**	**4**	**2**	**2**	**4**	**2**	**0**	**0**	**0**	**11**	**18.2**	**8**	**2**	**7**	**0**	**–1**								
	Newmarket Saints	AHL	62	33	29	62				63																		
1991-92	ESV Kaufbeuren	Germany	42	34	21	55				86											5	4	9	13	4			
1992-93	EHC Chur	Switz.	35	31	21	52				70											7	3	5	8	48			
	Canada	Nat-Team	3	0	0	0				2																		
1993-94	Kassel Huskies	Germany-2	62	66	44	110				170																		
1994-95	Kassel Huskies	Germany	43	39	21	60				76											9	6	5	11	24			
1995-96	Kassel Huskies	Germany	50	31	23	54				96											8	3	5	8	8			
1996-97	Kassel Huskies	Germany	42	23	35	58				48											10	2	1	3	6			
1997-98	Kassel Huskies	Germany	6	1	3	4				6																		
	Kassel Huskies	EuroHL	2	1	0	1				0																		
	Frankfurt Lions	Germany	39	13	21	34				20											7	2	3	5	2			
1998-99	GEC Nordhorn	Germany-2	53	45	51	96				120											4	0	1	1	6			
99-2000	EHC Hamburg	Germany-2	29	22	14	36				64											23	23	16	39	56			
	NHL Totals		**78**	**18**	**18**	**36**	**16**	**13**	**29**	**12**	**8**	**0**	**3**	**137**	**13.1**	**55**	**26**	**38**	**0**									

AHL Second All-Star Team (1989)

Traded to **Washington** by **Hartford** with Neil Sheehy for Grant Jennings and Ed Kastelic, July 6, 1988. Traded to **Boston** by **Washington** for Alfie Turcotte, October 2, 1989. Signed as a free agent by **Toronto**, July 19, 1990.

• MILLEN, Corey

Corey Eugene C – R. 5'7", 170 lbs. b: Cloquet, MN, 3/30/1964. NY Rangers' 3rd, 57th overall, in 1982.

Season	Club	League	GP	G	A	Pts	AG	AA	APts	PIM	PP	SH	GW	S	%	TGF	PGF	TGA	PGA	+/–	GP	G	A	Pts	PIM	PP	SH	GW
1981-82	Cloquet Lumberjacks	Hi-School	18	46	35	81																						
	United States	WJC-A	7	2	4	6				4																		
1982-83	University of Minnesota	WCHA	21	14	15	29				18																		
1983-84	United States	Nat-Team	45	15	11	26				10																		
	United States	Olympics	6	0	0	0				2																		
1984-85	University of Minnesota	WCHA	38	28	36	64				60																		
	United States	WEC-A	10	3	1	4				10																		
1985-86	University of Minnesota	WCHA	48	41	42	83				64																		
1986-87	University of Minnesota	WCHA	42	36	29	65				62																		
1987-88	United States	Can-Cup	1	1	0	1				0																		
	United States	Nat-Team	47	41	43	84				26																		
	United States	Olympics	6	6	5	11				4																		
	HC Ambri-Piotta	Switz.	5	4	3	7															6	*8	5	13				
1988-89	HC Ambri-Piotta	Switz.	36	32	22	54				18											6	4	3	7	0			
	United States	WEC-A	4	0	1	1				0																		
1989-90	**New York Rangers**	**NHL**	**4**	**0**	**0**	**0**	**0**	**0**	**0**	**2**	**0**	**0**	**0**	**4**	**0.0**	**1**	**1**	**2**	**0**	**–2**								
	Flint Spirits	IHL	11	4	5	9				2																		
1990-91	**New York Rangers**	**NHL**	**4**	**3**	**1**	**4**	**3**	**1**	**4**	**0**	**2**	**0**	**0**	**8**	**37.5**	**4**	**2**	**1**	**0**	**1**	**6**	**1**	**2**	**3**	**0**	**1**	**0**	**0**
	Binghamton Rangers	AHL	40	19	37	56				68											6	0	7	7	6			
1991-92	**New York Rangers**	**NHL**	**11**	**1**	**4**	**5**	**1**	**3**	**4**	**10**	**0**	**0**	**0**	**20**	**5.0**	**7**	**4**	**4**	**0**	**–1**								
	Binghamton Rangers	AHL	15	8	7	15				44																		
	Los Angeles Kings	**NHL**	**46**	**20**	**21**	**41**	**18**	**16**	**34**	**44**	**8**	**1**	**3**	**89**	**22.5**	**61**	**27**	**41**	**10**	**3**	**6**	**0**	**1**	**1**	**6**	**0**	**0**	**0**
1992-93	**Los Angeles Kings**	**NHL**	**42**	**23**	**16**	**39**	**19**	**11**	**30**	**42**	**9**	**2**	**1**	**100**	**23.0**	**58**	**20**	**32**	**10**	**16**	**23**	**2**	**4**	**6**	**12**	**0**	**0**	**0**
1993-94	**New Jersey Devils**	**NHL**	**78**	**20**	**30**	**50**	**19**	**23**	**42**	**52**	**4**	**0**	**3**	**132**	**15.2**	**80**	**17**	**40**	**1**	**24**	**7**	**1**	**0**	**1**	**2**	**0**	**0**	**1**
1994-95	**New Jersey Devils**	**NHL**	**17**	**2**	**3**	**5**	**4**	**4**	**8**	**8**	**0**	**0**	**0**	**30**	**6.7**	**7**	**0**	**6**	**1**	**2**								
	Dallas Stars	**NHL**	**28**	**3**	**15**	**18**	**5**	**22**	**27**	**28**	**1**	**0**	**0**	**44**	**6.8**	**25**	**7**	**14**	**0**	**4**	**5**	**1**	**0**	**1**	**2**	**0**	**0**	**0**
1995-96	**Dallas Stars**	**NHL**	**13**	**3**	**4**	**7**	**3**	**3**	**6**	**8**	**1**	**0**	**0**	**25**	**12.0**	**8**	**2**	**6**	**0**	**0**								
	Michigan K-Wings	IHL	11	8	11	19				14																		
	Calgary Flames	**NHL**	**31**	**4**	**10**	**14**	**4**	**8**	**12**	**10**	**1**	**0**	**1**	**48**	**8.3**	**26**	**7**	**21**	**10**	**8**								
1996-97	**Calgary Flames**	**NHL**	**61**	**11**	**15**	**26**	**12**	**13**	**25**	**32**	**1**	**0**	**0**	**82**	**13.4**	**33**	**11**	**44**	**3**	**–19**								
1997-98	Kolner Haie	Germany	30	17	17	34				52											3	2	1	3	6			
	Kolner Haie	EuroHL	5	1	5	6				10																		
1998-99	Kolner Haie	Germany	48	26	39	65				143											5	2	2	4	37			
	United States	WC-Q	3	3	0	3				4																		
99-2000	Kolner Haie	Germany	38	17	32	49				52											10	4	3	7	16			
	NHL Totals		**335**	**90**	**119**	**209**	**88**	**104**	**192**	**236**	**27**	**3**	**8**	**582**	**15.5**	**310**	**98**	**211**	**35**		**47**	**5**	**7**	**12**	**22**	**1**	**0**	**1**

WCHA Second All-Star Team (1985, 1986, 1987) • NCAA West Second All-American Team (1986) • NCAA Championship All-Tournament Team (1987)

• Missed majority of 1989-90 season recovering from knee injury suffered in training camp, September 18, 1989. Traded to **LA Kings** by **NY Rangers** for Randy Gilhen, December 23, 1991. Traded to **New Jersey** by **LA Kings** for New Jersey's 5th round choice (Jason Saal) in 1993 Entry Draft, June 26, 1993. Traded to **Dallas** by **New Jersey** for Neal Broten, February 27, 1995. Traded to **Calgary** by **Dallas** with Jarome Iginla for Joe Nieuwendyk, December 19, 1995.

• MILLER, Aaron

Aaron M. D – R. 6'3", 200 lbs. b: Buffalo, NY, 8/11/1971. NY Rangers' 6th, 88th overall, in 1989.

Season	Club	League	GP	G	A	Pts	AG	AA	APts	PIM	PP	SH	GW	S	%	TGF	PGF	TGA	PGA	+/–	GP	G	A	Pts	PIM	PP	SH	GW
1987-88	Niagara Scenics	NAJHL	30	4	9	13				2																		
1988-89	Niagara Scenics	NAJHL	59	24	38	62				60																		
1989-90	University of Vermont	ECAC	31	1	15	16				24																		
1990-91	University of Vermont	ECAC	30	3	7	10				22																		
	United States	WJC-A	8	1	1	2				0																		
1991-92	University of Vermont	ECAC	31	3	16	19				28																		
1992-93	University of Vermont	ECAC	30	4	13	17				16																		
1993-94	**Quebec Nordiques**	**NHL**	**1**	**0**	**0**	**0**	**0**	**0**	**0**	**0**	**0**	**0**	**0**	**0**	**0.0**	**0**	**0**	**1**	**0**	**–1**								
	Cornwall Aces	AHL	64	4	10	14				49											13	0	2	2	10			
1994-95	**Quebec Nordiques**	**NHL**	**9**	**0**	**3**	**3**	**0**	**4**	**4**	**6**	**0**	**0**	**0**	**12**	**0.0**	**9**	**1**	**6**	**0**	**2**								
	Cornwall Aces	AHL	76	4	18	22				69																		
1995-96	**Colorado Avalanche**	**NHL**	**5**	**0**	**0**	**0**	**0**	**0**	**0**	**0**	**0**	**0**	**0**	**2**	**0.0**	**1**	**0**	**1**	**0**	**0**								
	Cornwall Aces	AHL	62	4	23	27				77											8	0	1	1	6			
1996-97	**Colorado Avalanche**	**NHL**	**56**	**5**	**12**	**17**	**5**	**11**	**16**	**15**	**0**	**0**	**3**	**47**	**10.6**	**38**	**2**	**22**	**1**	**15**	**17**	**1**	**2**	**3**	**10**	**0**	**0**	**0**
1997-98	**Colorado Avalanche**	**NHL**	**55**	**2**	**2**	**4**	**2**	**2**	**4**	**51**	**0**	**0**	**0**	**29**	**6.9**	**19**	**1**	**22**	**4**	**0**	**7**	**0**	**0**	**0**	**8**	**0**	**0**	**0**
1998-99	**Colorado Avalanche**	**NHL**	**76**	**5**	**13**	**18**	**6**	**13**	**19**	**42**	**1**	**0**	**2**	**87**	**5.7**	**61**	**7**	**85**	**34**	**3**	**19**	**1**	**5**	**6**	**10**	**0**	**0**	**0**
99-2000	**Colorado Avalanche**	**NHL**	**53**	**1**	**7**	**8**	**1**	**6**	**7**	**36**	**0**	**0**	**0**	**44**	**2.3**	**36**	**1**	**50**	**18**	**3**	**17**	**1**	**1**	**2**	**6**	**0**	**0**	**0**
	NHL Totals		**255**	**13**	**37**	**50**	**14**	**36**	**50**	**150**	**1**	**0**	**5**	**221**	**5.9**	**164**	**12**	**187**	**57**		**60**	**3**	**8**	**11**	**34**	**0**	**0**	**0**

ECAC First All-Star Team (1993) • NCAA East Second All-American Team (1993)

Traded to **Quebec** by **NY Rangers** with NY Rangers' 5th round choice (Bill Lindsay) in 1991 Entry Draft for Joe Cirella, January 17, 1991. Transferred to **Colorado** after **Quebec** franchise relocated, June 21, 1995.

			REGULAR SEASON																		PLAYOFFS							
Season	Club	League	GP	G	A	Pts	AG	AA	APts	PIM	PP	SH	GW	S	%	TGF	PGF	TGA	PGA	+/–	GP	G	A	Pts	PIM	PP	SH	GW

• MILLER, Bob

C – L. 5'11", 180 lbs. b: Medford, MA, 9/28/1956. Boston's 3rd, 70th overall, in 1976.

Season	Club	League	GP	G	A	Pts	AG	AA	APts	PIM	PP	SH	GW	S	%	TGF	PGF	TGA	PGA	+/–	GP	G	A	Pts	PIM	PP	SH	GW
1973-74	Billerica High School	Hi-School	STATISTICS NOT AVAILABLE																									
1974-75	University of New Hampshire	ECAC	27	21	38	59	....	....	....	26	....	....	....	....	....	....	....	....	....	....	....	....	....	....	....	....	....	....
1975-76	United States	Nat-Team	63	33	61	94	....	....	....	83	....	....	....	....	....	....	....	....	....	....	....	....	....	....	....	....	....	....
	United States	Olympics	6	0	3	3	....	....	....	0	....	....	....	....	....	....	....	....	....	....	....	....	....	....	....	....	....	....
	Ottawa 67's	OMJHL	6	5	5	10	....	....	....	5	....	....	....	....	....	....	....	....	....	....	12	2	4	6	9	....	....	....
1976-77	University of New Hampshire	ECAC	38	30	59	89	....	....	....	45	....	....	....	....	....	....	....	....	....	....	....	....	....	....	....	....	....	....
	United States	WEC-A	10	5	3	8	....	....	....	4	....	....	....	....	....	....	....	....	....	....	....	....	....	....	....	....	....	....
1977-78	**Boston Bruins**	**NHL**	**76**	**20**	**20**	**40**	**18**	**15**	**33**	**41**	**1**	**1**	**4**	**134**	**14.9**	**52**	**2**	**38**	**4**	**16**	**13**	**0**	**3**	**3**	**15**	**0**	**0**	**0**
	Rochester Americans	AHL	3	1	3	4	....	....	....	7	....	....	....	....	....	....	....	....	....	....	....	....	....	....	....	....	....	....
1978-79	**Boston Bruins**	**NHL**	**77**	**15**	**33**	**48**	**13**	**24**	**37**	**30**	**0**	**0**	**1**	**149**	**10.1**	**67**	**2**	**51**	**6**	**20**	**11**	**1**	**1**	**2**	**8**	**0**	**0**	**0**
1979-80	**Boston Bruins**	**NHL**	**80**	**16**	**25**	**41**	**14**	**18**	**32**	**53**	**0**	**1**	**2**	**137**	**11.7**	**57**	**1**	**86**	**39**	**9**	**10**	**3**	**2**	**5**	**4**	**0**	**1**	**0**
1980-81	**Boston Bruins**	**NHL**	**30**	**4**	**4**	**8**	**3**	**3**	**6**	**19**	**0**	**1**	**1**	**23**	**17.4**	**9**	**0**	**31**	**17**	**–5**	....	....	....	....	....	....	....	....
	Springfield Indians	AHL	3	1	2	3	....	....	....	0	....	....	....	....	....	....	....	....	....	....	....	....	....	....	....	....	....	....
	Colorado Rockies	**NHL**	**22**	**5**	**1**	**6**	**4**	**1**	**5**	**15**	**2**	**0**	**0**	**41**	**12.2**	**13**	**8**	**40**	**16**	**–19**	....	....	....	....	....	....	....	....
	United States	WEC-A	8	5	4	9	....	....	....	4	....	....	....	....	....	....	....	....	....	....	....	....	....	....	....	....	....	....
1981-82	United States	Can-Cup	6	0	1	1	....	....	....	6	....	....	....	....	....	....	....	....	....	....	....	....	....	....	....	....	....	....
	Colorado Rockies	**NHL**	**56**	**11**	**20**	**31**	**9**	**13**	**22**	**27**	**1**	**0**	**2**	**94**	**11.7**	**43**	**4**	**87**	**24**	**–24**	....	....	....	....	....	....	....	....
	United States	WEC-A	7	3	1	4	....	....	....	4	....	....	....	....	....	....	....	....	....	....	....	....	....	....	....	....	....	....
1982-83	Springfield Indians	AHL	59	17	31	48	....	....	....	60	....	....	....	....	....	....	....	....	....	....	....	....	....	....	....	....	....	....
1983-84	Karpat Oulu	Finland	37	17	31	48	....	....	....	66	....	....	....	....	....	....	....	....	....	....	9	5	4	9	20	....	....	....
1984-85	**Los Angeles Kings**	**NHL**	**63**	**4**	**16**	**20**	**3**	**11**	**14**	**35**	**0**	**0**	**0**	**64**	**6.3**	**24**	**0**	**59**	**18**	**–17**	**2**	**0**	**1**	**1**	**0**	**0**	**0**	**0**
	United States	WEC-A	10	1	6	7	....	....	....	2	....	....	....	....	....	....	....	....	....	....	....	....	....	....	....	....	....	....
1985-86	HC Sierre	Switz.	34	36	26	62	....	....	....	....	....	....	....	....	....	....	....	....	....	....	4	3	0	3	0	....	....	....
1986-87	HC Sierre	Switz.	....	2	6	8	....	....	....	....	....	....	....	....	....	....	....	....	....	....	....	....	....	....	....	....	....	....
	NHL Totals		**404**	**75**	**119**	**194**	**64**	**85**	**149**	**220**	**4**	**3**	**10**	**642**	**11.7**	**265**	**17**	**392**	**124**		**36**	**4**	**7**	**11**	**27**	**0**	**1**	**0**

• Brother of Paul • ECAC First All-Star Team (1977) • NCAA East First All-American Team (1977)

Traded to **Colorado** by **Boston** for Mike Gillis, February 18, 1981. Signed as a free agent by **LA Kings**, October 9, 1984.

• MILLER, Brad

D – L. 6'4", 220 lbs. b: Edmonton, Alta., 7/23/1969. Buffalo's 2nd, 22nd overall, in 1987.

Season	Club	League	GP	G	A	Pts	AG	AA	APts	PIM	PP	SH	GW	S	%	TGF	PGF	TGA	PGA	+/–	GP	G	A	Pts	PIM	PP	SH	GW
1984-85	Edmonton K of C Pats	AAHA	42	7	26	33	....	....	....	154	....	....	....	....	....	....	....	....	....	....	....	....	....	....	....	....	....	....
1985-86	Regina Pats	WHL	71	2	14	16	....	....	....	99	....	....	....	....	....	....	....	....	....	....	10	1	1	2	4	....	....	....
1986-87	Regina Pats	WHL	67	10	38	48	....	....	....	154	....	....	....	....	....	....	....	....	....	....	3	0	0	0	6	....	....	....
1987-88	Regina Pats	WHL	61	9	34	43	....	....	....	148	....	....	....	....	....	....	....	....	....	....	4	1	1	2	12	....	....	....
	Rochester Americans	AHL	3	0	0	0	....	....	....	4	....	....	....	....	....	....	....	....	....	....	2	0	0	0	2	....	....	....
1988-89	Regina Pats	WHL	34	8	18	26	....	....	....	95	....	....	....	....	....	....	....	....	....	....	....	....	....	....	....	....	....	....
	Buffalo Sabres	**NHL**	**7**	**0**	**0**	**0**	**0**	**0**	**0**	**6**	**0**	**0**	**0**	**0**	**0.0**	**5**	**0**	**6**	**0**	**–1**	....	....	....	....	....	....	....	....
	Rochester Americans	AHL	3	0	0	0	....	....	....	4	....	....	....	....	....	....	....	....	....	....	....	....	....	....	....	....	....	....
1989-90	**Buffalo Sabres**	**NHL**	**1**	**0**	**0**	**0**	**0**	**0**	**0**	**0**	**0**	**0**	**0**	**0**	**0.0**	**1**	**0**	**0**	**0**	**1**	....	....	....	....	....	....	....	....
	Rochester Americans	AHL	60	2	10	12	....	....	....	273	....	....	....	....	....	....	....	....	....	....	8	1	0	1	52	....	....	....
1990-91	**Buffalo Sabres**	**NHL**	**13**	**0**	**0**	**0**	**0**	**0**	**0**	**67**	**0**	**0**	**0**	**4**	**0.0**	**1**	**0**	**2**	**0**	**–1**	....	....	....	....	....	....	....	....
	Rochester Americans	AHL	49	0	9	9	....	....	....	248	....	....	....	....	....	....	....	....	....	....	12	0	4	4	*67	....	....	....
1991-92	**Buffalo Sabres**	**NHL**	**42**	**1**	**4**	**5**	**1**	**3**	**4**	**192**	**0**	**0**	**0**	**30**	**3.3**	**26**	**0**	**32**	**1**	**–5**	....	....	....	....	....	....	....	....
	Rochester Americans	AHL	27	0	4	4	....	....	....	113	....	....	....	....	....	....	....	....	....	....	11	0	0	0	61	....	....	....
1992-93	**Ottawa Senators**	**NHL**	**11**	**0**	**0**	**0**	**0**	**0**	**0**	**42**	**0**	**0**	**0**	**2**	**0.0**	**1**	**0**	**6**	**0**	**–5**	....	....	....	....	....	....	....	....
	New Haven Senators	AHL	41	1	9	10	....	....	....	138	....	....	....	....	....	....	....	....	....	....	....	....	....	....	....	....	....	....
	St. John's Maple Leafs	AHL	20	0	3	3	....	....	....	61	....	....	....	....	....	....	....	....	....	....	8	0	2	2	10	....	....	....
1993-94	**Calgary Flames**	**NHL**	**8**	**0**	**1**	**1**	**0**	**1**	**1**	**14**	**0**	**0**	**0**	**2**	**0.0**	**3**	**0**	**5**	**0**	**–2**	....	....	....	....	....	....	....	....
	Saint John Flames	AHL	36	3	12	15	....	....	....	174	....	....	....	....	....	....	....	....	....	....	6	1	0	1	21	....	....	....
1994-95	Minnesota Moose	IHL	55	1	13	14	....	....	....	181	....	....	....	....	....	....	....	....	....	....	3	0	0	0	12	....	....	....
1995-96	Minnesota Moose	IHL	33	0	5	5	....	....	....	170	....	....	....	....	....	....	....	....	....	....	....	....	....	....	....	....	....	....
	Atlanta Knights	IHL	5	0	0	0	....	....	....	8	....	....	....	....	....	....	....	....	....	....	....	....	....	....	....	....	....	....
	Utah Grizzlies	IHL	1	0	0	0	....	....	....	0	....	....	....	....	....	....	....	....	....	....	....	....	....	....	....	....	....	....
1996-97	Quebec Rafales	IHL	57	1	7	8	....	....	....	132	....	....	....	....	....	....	....	....	....	....	4	0	0	0	2	....	....	....
1997-98	San Antonio Dragons	IHL	58	3	6	9	....	....	....	228	....	....	....	....	....	....	....	....	....	....	....	....	....	....	....	....	....	....
	Utah Grizzlies	IHL	9	0	1	1	....	....	....	46	....	....	....	....	....	....	....	....	....	....	4	0	0	0	8	....	....	....
1998-99	Las Vegas Thunder	IHL	73	5	16	21	....	....	....	264	....	....	....	....	....	....	....	....	....	....	....	....	....	....	....	....	....	....
99-2000	Utah Grizzlies	IHL	49	0	4	4	....	....	....	118	....	....	....	....	....	....	....	....	....	....	1	0	0	0	4	....	....	....
	NHL Totals		**82**	**1**	**5**	**6**	**1**	**4**	**5**	**321**	**0**	**0**	**0**	**38**	**2.6**	**37**	**0**	**51**	**1**		....	....	....	....	....	....	....	....

Claimed by **Ottawa** from **Buffalo** in Expansion Draft, June 18, 1992. Traded to **Toronto** by **Ottawa** for Toronto's 9th round choice (Pavol Demitra) in 1993 Entry Draft, February 25, 1993. Traded to **Calgary** by **Toronto** with Jeff Perry for Todd Gillingham and Paul Holden, September 2, 1993. IHL rights acquired by **Utah** (IHL) from **Las Vegas** (IHL) with Russ Romaniuk, Scott Hollis and Kevin Kaminski after Las Vegas franchise folded, July 6, 1999.

• MILLER, Jason

LW – L. 6'1", 190 lbs. b: Edmonton, Alta., 3/1/1971. New Jersey's 2nd, 18th overall, in 1989.

Season	Club	League	GP	G	A	Pts	AG	AA	APts	PIM	PP	SH	GW	S	%	TGF	PGF	TGA	PGA	+/–	GP	G	A	Pts	PIM	PP	SH	GW
1986-87	Edmonton K of C Pats	AAHA	40	38	31	69	....	....	....	76	....	....	....	....	....	....	....	....	....	....	....	....	....	....	....	....	....	....
1987-88	Medicine Hat Tigers	WHL	71	11	18	29	....	....	....	28	....	....	....	....	....	....	....	....	....	....	15	0	1	1	2	....	....	....
1988-89	Medicine Hat Tigers	WHL	72	51	55	106	....	....	....	44	....	....	....	....	....	....	....	....	....	....	3	1	2	3	2	....	....	....
1989-90	Medicine Hat Tigers	WHL	66	43	56	99	....	....	....	40	....	....	....	....	....	....	....	....	....	....	3	3	2	5	0	....	....	....
1990-91	Medicine Hat Tigers	WHL	66	60	76	136	....	....	....	31	....	....	....	....	....	....	....	....	....	....	12	9	10	19	8	....	....	....
	New Jersey Devils	**NHL**	**1**	**0**	**0**	**0**	**0**	**0**	**0**	**0**	**0**	**0**	**0**	**0**	**0.0**	**1**	**0**	**0**	**0**	**1**	....	....	....	....	....	....	....	....
1991-92	**New Jersey Devils**	**NHL**	**3**	**0**	**0**	**0**	**0**	**0**	**0**	**0**	**0**	**0**	**0**	**1**	**0.0**	**1**	**0**	**1**	**0**	**0**	....	....	....	....	....	....	....	....
	Utica Devils	AHL	71	23	32	55	....	....	....	31	....	....	....	....	....	....	....	....	....	....	4	1	3	4	0	....	....	....
1992-93	**New Jersey Devils**	**NHL**	**2**	**0**	**0**	**0**	**0**	**0**	**0**	**0**	**0**	**0**	**0**	**1**	**0.0**	**0**	**0**	**1**	**0**	**–1**	....	....	....	....	....	....	....	....
	Utica Devils	AHL	72	28	42	70	....	....	....	43	....	....	....	....	....	....	....	....	....	....	5	4	4	8	2	....	....	....
1993-94	Albany River Rats	AHL	77	22	53	75	....	....	....	65	....	....	....	....	....	....	....	....	....	....	5	1	1	2	4	....	....	....
1994-95	Adirondack Red Wings	AHL	77	32	33	65	....	....	....	39	....	....	....	....	....	....	....	....	....	....	4	1	0	1	0	....	....	....
1995-96	HPK Hameenlinna	Finland	22	4	6	10	....	....	....	10	....	....	....	....	....	....	....	....	....	....	....	....	....	....	....	....	....	....
	ESV Kaufbeuren	Germany	3	1	1	2	....	....	....	0	....	....	....	....	....	....	....	....	....	....	....	....	....	....	....	....	....	....
	Peoria Rivermen	IHL	39	16	22	38	....	....	....	6	....	....	....	....	....	....	....	....	....	....	11	1	2	3	4	....	....	....
1996-97	San Antonio Dragons	IHL	76	26	43	69	....	....	....	43	....	....	....	....	....	....	....	....	....	....	9	1	4	5	6	....	....	....
1997-98	Dusseldorfer EG	Germany	46	15	19	34	....	....	....	26	....	....	....	....	....	....	....	....	....	....	3	1	2	3	0	....	....	....
1998-99	Nurnberg Ice Tigers	Germany	50	*30	31	61	....	....	....	56	....	....	....	....	....	....	....	....	....	....	13	5	6	11	8	....	....	....
99-2000	Nurnberg Ice Tigers	Germany	65	26	29	55	....	....	....	61	....	....	....	....	....	....	....	....	....	....	....	....	....	....	....	....	....	....
	Nurnberg Ice Tigers	EuroHL	6	3	3	6	....	....	....	4	....	....	....	....	....	....	....	....	....	....	2	2	0	2	2	....	....	....
	NHL Totals		**6**	**0**	**0**	**0**	**0**	**0**	**0**	**0**	**0**	**0**	**0**	**2**	**0.0**	**2**	**0**	**2**	**0**		....	....	....	....	....	....	....	....

WHL East Second All-Star Team (1991)

Signed as a free agent by **Detroit**, August 26, 1994.

• MILLER, Jay

LW – L. 6'2", 210 lbs. b: Wellesley, MA, 7/16/1960. Quebec's 2nd, 66th overall, in 1980.

Season	Club	League	GP	G	A	Pts	AG	AA	APts	PIM	PP	SH	GW	S	%	TGF	PGF	TGA	PGA	+/–	GP	G	A	Pts	PIM	PP	SH	GW
1978-79	Northwood Prep School	Hi-School	STATISTICS NOT AVAILABLE																									
1979-80	University of New Hampshire	ECAC	28	7	12	19	....	....	....	53	....	....	....	....	....	....	....	....	....	....	....	....	....	....	....	....	....	....
1980-81	University of New Hampshire	ECAC	10	4	8	12	....	....	....	14	....	....	....	....	....	....	....	....	....	....	....	....	....	....	....	....	....	....
1981-82	University of New Hampshire	ECAC	24	6	4	10	....	....	....	34	....	....	....	....	....	....	....	....	....	....	....	....	....	....	....	....	....	....
1982-83	University of New Hampshire	ECAC	28	5	5	10	....	....	....	28	....	....	....	....	....	....	....	....	....	....	....	....	....	....	....	....	....	....
	Fredericton Express	AHL	3	1	2	3	....	....	....	0	....	....	....	....	....	....	....	....	....	....	....	....	....	....	....	....	....	....
1983-84	Toledo Goaldiggers	IHL	2	0	0	0	....	....	....	2	....	....	....	....	....	....	....	....	....	....	....	....	....	....	....	....	....	....
	Maine Mariners	AHL	15	1	1	2	....	....	....	27	....	....	....	....	....	....	....	....	....	....	....	....	....	....	....	....	....	....
	Mohawk Valley Suns	ACHL	48	15	36	51	....	....	....	167	....	....	....	....	....	....	....	....	....	....	....	....	....	....	....	....	....	....
1984-85	Muskegon Mohawks	IHL	56	5	29	34	....	....	....	177	....	....	....	....	....	....	....	....	....	....	17	1	1	2	56	....	....	....

Season	Club	League	REGULAR SEASON GP	G	A	Pts	AG	AA	APts	PIM	PP	SH	GW	S	%	TGF	PGF	TGA	PGA	+/–	PLAYOFFS GP	G	A	Pts	PIM	PP	SH	GW
1985-86	**Boston Bruins**	**NHL**	**46**	**3**	**0**	**3**	**2**	**0**	**2**	**178**	**0**	**0**	**0**	**21**	**14.3**	**6**	**0**	**9**	**0**	**–3**	**2**	**0**	**0**	**0**	**17**	**0**	**0**	**0**
	Moncton Golden Flames	AHL	18	4	6	10	....	....	....	113	....	....	....	....	....	....	....	....	....	....	....	....	....	....	....	....	....	....
1986-87	**Boston Bruins**	**NHL**	**55**	**1**	**4**	**5**	**1**	**3**	**4**	**208**	**0**	**0**	**0**	**27**	**3.7**	**13**	**0**	**24**	**0**	**–11**	....	....	....	....	....	....	....	....
1987-88	**Boston Bruins**	**NHL**	**78**	**7**	**12**	**19**	**6**	**9**	**15**	**304**	**0**	**0**	**1**	**44**	**15.9**	**24**	**0**	**29**	**0**	**–5**	**12**	**0**	**0**	**0**	***124**	**0**	**0**	**0**
1988-89	**Boston Bruins**	**NHL**	**37**	**2**	**4**	**6**	**2**	**3**	**5**	**168**	**0**	**0**	**0**	**14**	**14.3**	**8**	**0**	**14**	**0**	**–6**	....	....	....	....	....	....	....	....
	Los Angeles Kings	**NHL**	**29**	**5**	**3**	**8**	**4**	**2**	**6**	**133**	**0**	**0**	**0**	**16**	**31.3**	**11**	**0**	**14**	**0**	**–3**	**11**	**0**	**1**	**1**	**63**	**0**	**0**	**0**
1989-90	**Los Angeles Kings**	**NHL**	**68**	**10**	**2**	**12**	**9**	**1**	**10**	**224**	**0**	**0**	**1**	**44**	**22.7**	**19**	**0**	**25**	**0**	**–6**	**10**	**1**	**1**	**2**	**10**	**0**	**0**	**0**
1990-91	**Los Angeles Kings**	**NHL**	**66**	**8**	**12**	**20**	**7**	**9**	**16**	**259**	**1**	**0**	**0**	**35**	**22.9**	**34**	**7**	**19**	**1**	**9**	**8**	**0**	**0**	**0**	**17**	**0**	**0**	**0**
1991-92	**Los Angeles Kings**	**NHL**	**67**	**4**	**7**	**11**	**4**	**5**	**9**	**249**	**0**	**0**	**0**	**32**	**12.5**	**17**	**2**	**23**	**0**	**–8**	**5**	**1**	**1**	**2**	**12**	**0**	**0**	**0**
	NHL Totals		**446**	**40**	**44**	**84**	**35**	**32**	**67**	**1723**	**1**	**0**	**2**	**233**	**17.2**	**132**	**9**	**157**	**1**		**48**	**2**	**3**	**5**	**243**	**0**	**0**	**0**

Traded to **Minnesota** by **Quebec** for Jim Dobson, June 29, 1983. Signed as a free agent by **Boston**, October 1, 1985. Traded to **LA Kings** by **Boston** for future considerations (Steve Kasper traded to Los Angeles by Boston for Bob Carpenter, January 23, 1989), January 22, 1989.

• MILLER, Kelly

Kelly D. LW – L. 5'11", 197 lbs. b: Lansing, MI, 3/3/1963. NY Rangers' 9th, 183rd overall, in 1982.

Season	Club	League	GP	G	A	Pts	AG	AA	APts	PIM	PP	SH	GW	S	%	TGF	PGF	TGA	PGA	+/–	GP	G	A	Pts	PIM	PP	SH	GW
1978-79	Detroit Adrays	MNHL	STATISTICS NOT AVAILABLE																									
1979-80	Redford Royals	GLJHL	45	31	37	68	....	....	....	6	....	....	....	....	....	....	....	....	....	....	....	....	....	....	....	....	....	....
1980-81	Redford Royals	GLJHL	48	39	51	90	....	....	....	8	....	....	....	....	....	....	....	....	....	....	....	....	....	....	....	....	....	....
	United States	WJC-A	5	0	0	0	....	....	....	0	....	....	....	....	....	....	....	....	....	....	....	....	....	....	....	....	....	....
1981-82	Michigan State Spartans	CCHA	38	11	18	29	....	....	....	17	....	....	....	....	....	....	....	....	....	....	....	....	....	....	....	....	....	....
	United States	WJC-A	7	2	4	6	....	....	....	0	....	....	....	....	....	....	....	....	....	....	....	....	....	....	....	....	....	....
1982-83	Michigan State Spartans	CCHA	36	16	19	35	....	....	....	12	....	....	....	....	....	....	....	....	....	....	....	....	....	....	....	....	....	....
	United States	WJC-A	7	0	1	1	....	....	....	0	....	....	....	....	....	....	....	....	....	....	....	....	....	....	....	....	....	....
1983-84	Michigan State Spartans	CCHA	46	28	21	49	....	....	....	12	....	....	....	....	....	....	....	....	....	....	....	....	....	....	....	....	....	....
1984-85	Michigan State Spartans	CCHA	43	27	23	50	....	....	....	21	....	....	....	....	....	....	....	....	....	....	....	....	....	....	....	....	....	....
	New York Rangers	**NHL**	**5**	**0**	**2**	**2**	**0**	**1**	**1**	**2**	**0**	**0**	**0**	**5**	**0.0**	**3**	**1**	**5**	**1**	**–2**	**3**	**0**	**0**	**0**	**2**	**0**	**0**	**0**
	United States	WEC-A	10	2	3	5	....	....	....	2	....	....	....	....	....	....	....	....	....	....	....	....	....	....	....	....	....	....
1985-86	**New York Rangers**	**NHL**	**74**	**13**	**20**	**33**	**10**	**13**	**23**	**52**	**0**	**1**	**3**	**112**	**11.6**	**53**	**1**	**75**	**26**	**3**	**16**	**3**	**4**	**7**	**4**	**0**	**1**	**0**
1986-87	**New York Rangers**	**NHL**	**38**	**6**	**14**	**20**	**5**	**10**	**15**	**22**	**2**	**0**	**1**	**58**	**10.3**	**30**	**8**	**39**	**12**	**–5**	....	....	....	....	....	....	....	....
	Washington Capitals	**NHL**	**39**	**10**	**12**	**22**	**9**	**9**	**18**	**26**	**3**	**1**	**0**	**50**	**20.0**	**38**	**9**	**23**	**4**	**10**	**7**	**2**	**2**	**4**	**0**	**0**	**0**	**0**
1987-88	United States	Can-Cup	5	0	0	0	....	....	....	0	....	....	....	....	....	....	....	....	....	....	....	....	....	....	....	....	....	....
	Washington Capitals	**NHL**	**80**	**9**	**23**	**32**	**8**	**16**	**24**	**35**	**0**	**1**	**3**	**96**	**9.4**	**52**	**1**	**65**	**23**	**9**	**14**	**4**	**4**	**8**	**10**	**0**	**1**	**1**
1988-89	**Washington Capitals**	**NHL**	**78**	**19**	**21**	**40**	**16**	**15**	**31**	**45**	**2**	**1**	**3**	**121**	**15.7**	**62**	**6**	**74**	**31**	**13**	**6**	**1**	**0**	**1**	**2**	**0**	**0**	**1**
	United States	WEC-A	9	2	4	6	....	....	....	2	....	....	....	....	....	....	....	....	....	....	....	....	....	....	....	....	....	....
1989-90	**Washington Capitals**	**NHL**	**80**	**18**	**22**	**40**	**15**	**16**	**31**	**49**	**3**	**2**	**2**	**107**	**16.8**	**67**	**12**	**98**	**41**	**–2**	**15**	**3**	**5**	**8**	**23**	**0**	**1**	**0**
1990-91	**Washington Capitals**	**NHL**	**80**	**24**	**26**	**50**	**22**	**20**	**42**	**29**	**4**	**2**	**3**	**155**	**15.5**	**79**	**13**	**84**	**28**	**10**	**11**	**4**	**2**	**6**	**6**	**0**	**1**	**0**
1991-92	**Washington Capitals**	**NHL**	**78**	**14**	**38**	**52**	**13**	**29**	**42**	**49**	**0**	**1**	**3**	**144**	**9.7**	**78**	**6**	**88**	**36**	**20**	**7**	**1**	**2**	**3**	**4**	**0**	**0**	**0**
1992-93	**Washington Capitals**	**NHL**	**84**	**18**	**27**	**45**	**15**	**19**	**34**	**32**	**3**	**0**	**3**	**144**	**12.5**	**63**	**6**	**110**	**51**	**–2**	**6**	**0**	**3**	**3**	**2**	**0**	**0**	**0**
1993-94	**Washington Capitals**	**NHL**	**84**	**14**	**25**	**39**	**13**	**19**	**32**	**32**	**0**	**1**	**3**	**138**	**10.1**	**59**	**2**	**79**	**30**	**8**	**11**	**2**	**7**	**9**	**0**	**1**	**1**	**0**
1994-95	**Washington Capitals**	**NHL**	**48**	**10**	**13**	**23**	**18**	**19**	**37**	**6**	**2**	**0**	**1**	**70**	**14.3**	**32**	**6**	**36**	**15**	**5**	**7**	**0**	**3**	**3**	**4**	**0**	**0**	**0**
1995-96	**Washington Capitals**	**NHL**	**74**	**7**	**13**	**20**	**7**	**11**	**18**	**30**	**0**	**2**	**1**	**93**	**7.5**	**33**	**4**	**57**	**35**	**7**	**6**	**0**	**1**	**1**	**4**	**0**	**0**	**0**
1996-97	**Washington Capitals**	**NHL**	**77**	**10**	**14**	**24**	**11**	**12**	**23**	**33**	**0**	**1**	**3**	**95**	**10.5**	**39**	**2**	**60**	**27**	**4**	....	....	....	....	....	....	....	....
1997-98	**Washington Capitals**	**NHL**	**76**	**7**	**7**	**14**	**8**	**7**	**15**	**41**	**0**	**3**	**3**	**68**	**10.3**	**22**	**0**	**35**	**11**	**–2**	**10**	**0**	**1**	**1**	**4**	**0**	**0**	**0**
1998-99	**Washington Capitals**	**NHL**	**62**	**2**	**5**	**7**	**2**	**5**	**7**	**29**	**0**	**0**	**1**	**49**	**4.1**	**11**	**1**	**26**	**11**	**–5**	....	....	....	....	....	....	....	....
	United States	WC-A	6	0	1	1	....	....	....	2	....	....	....	....	....	....	....	....	....	....	....	....	....	....	....	....	....	....
99-2000	Grand Rapids Griffins	IHL	DID NOT PLAY – ASSISTANT COACH																									
	Grand Rapids Griffins	IHL	26	4	4	8	....	....	....	8	....	....	....	....	....	....	....	....	....	....	7	0	1	1	2	....	....	....
	NHL Totals		**1057**	**181**	**282**	**463**	**172**	**221**	**393**	**512**	**19**	**16**	**33**	**1505**	**12.0**	**721**	**78**	**954**	**382**		**119**	**20**	**34**	**54**	**65**	**1**	**5**	**2**

• Brother of Kevin and Kip • CCHA First All-Star Team (1985) • NCAA West First All-American Team (1985)

Traded to **Washington** by **NY Rangers** with Bob Crawford and Mike Ridley for Bob Carpenter and Washington's 2nd round choice (Jason Prosofsky) in 1989 Entry Draft, January 1, 1987. Signed as a free agent by **Grand Rapids** (IHL), February 14, 2000.

• MILLER, Kevin

Kevin Bradley C – R. 5'11", 184 lbs. b: Lansing, MI, 9/2/1965. NY Rangers' 10th, 202nd overall, in 1984.

Season	Club	League	GP	G	A	Pts	AG	AA	APts	PIM	PP	SH	GW	S	%	TGF	PGF	TGA	PGA	+/–	GP	G	A	Pts	PIM	PP	SH	GW
1983-84	Redford Royals	GLJHL	44	28	57	85	....	....	....	....	....	....	....	....	....	....	....	....	....	....	....	....	....	....	....	....	....	....
1984-85	Michigan State Spartans	CCHA	44	11	29	40	....	....	....	84	....	....	....	....	....	....	....	....	....	....	....	....	....	....	....	....	....	....
1985-86	Michigan State Spartans	CCHA	45	19	52	71	....	....	....	112	....	....	....	....	....	....	....	....	....	....	....	....	....	....	....	....	....	....
1986-87	Michigan State Spartans	CCHA	42	25	56	81	....	....	....	63	....	....	....	....	....	....	....	....	....	....	....	....	....	....	....	....	....	....
1987-88	Michigan State Spartans	CCHA	9	6	3	9	....	....	....	18	....	....	....	....	....	....	....	....	....	....	....	....	....	....	....	....	....	....
	United States	Nat-Team	48	31	32	63	....	....	....	33	....	....	....	....	....	....	....	....	....	....	....	....	....	....	....	....	....	....
	United States	Olympics	5	1	3	4	....	....	....	4	....	....	....	....	....	....	....	....	....	....	....	....	....	....	....	....	....	....
1988-89	**New York Rangers**	**NHL**	**24**	**3**	**5**	**8**	**3**	**4**	**7**	**2**	**0**	**0**	**1**	**40**	**7.5**	**12**	**0**	**13**	**0**	**–1**	....	....	....	....	....	....	....	....
	Denver Rangers	IHL	55	29	47	76	....	....	....	19	....	....	....	....	....	....	....	....	....	....	4	2	1	3	2	....	....	....
1989-90	**New York Rangers**	**NHL**	**16**	**0**	**5**	**5**	**0**	**4**	**4**	**2**	**0**	**0**	**0**	**9**	**0.0**	**6**	**1**	**6**	**0**	**–1**	**1**	**0**	**0**	**0**	**0**	**0**	**0**	**0**
	Flint Spirits	IHL	48	19	23	42	....	....	....	41	....	....	....	....	....	....	....	....	....	....	....	....	....	....	....	....	....	....
1990-91	**New York Rangers**	**NHL**	**63**	**17**	**27**	**44**	**16**	**21**	**37**	**63**	**1**	**2**	**3**	**113**	**15.0**	**56**	**7**	**60**	**12**	**1**	....	....	....	....	....	....	....	....
	Detroit Red Wings	**NHL**	**11**	**5**	**2**	**7**	**5**	**2**	**7**	**4**	**0**	**1**	**0**	**23**	**21.7**	**9**	**2**	**15**	**4**	**–4**	**7**	**3**	**2**	**5**	**20**	**0**	**1**	**0**
	United States	WEC-A	9	3	5	8	....	....	....	10	....	....	....	....	....	....	....	....	....	....	....	....	....	....	....	....	....	....
1991-92	United States	Can-Cup	8	2	3	5	....	....	....	16	....	....	....	....	....	....	....	....	....	....	....	....	....	....	....	....	....	....
	Detroit Red Wings	**NHL**	**80**	**20**	**26**	**46**	**18**	**20**	**38**	**53**	**3**	**1**	**4**	**130**	**15.4**	**73**	**13**	**91**	**37**	**6**	**9**	**0**	**2**	**2**	**4**	**0**	**0**	**0**
1992-93	**Washington Capitals**	**NHL**	**10**	**0**	**3**	**3**	**0**	**2**	**2**	**35**	**0**	**0**	**0**	**10**	**0.0**	**3**	**0**	**7**	**0**	**–4**	....	....	....	....	....	....	....	....
	St. Louis Blues	**NHL**	**72**	**24**	**22**	**46**	**20**	**15**	**35**	**65**	**8**	**3**	**4**	**153**	**15.7**	**75**	**24**	**56**	**11**	**6**	**10**	**0**	**3**	**3**	**11**	**0**	**0**	**0**
1993-94	**St. Louis Blues**	**NHL**	**75**	**23**	**25**	**48**	**21**	**19**	**40**	**83**	**6**	**3**	**5**	**154**	**14.9**	**84**	**30**	**72**	**24**	**6**	**3**	**1**	**0**	**1**	**4**	**0**	**1**	**0**
1994-95	**St. Louis Blues**	**NHL**	**15**	**2**	**5**	**7**	**4**	**7**	**11**	**0**	**0**	**0**	**0**	**19**	**10.5**	**10**	**0**	**8**	**2**	**4**	....	....	....	....	....	....	....	....
	San Jose Sharks	**NHL**	**21**	**6**	**7**	**13**	**11**	**10**	**21**	**13**	**1**	**1**	**2**	**41**	**14.6**	**16**	**2**	**20**	**6**	**0**	**6**	**0**	**0**	**0**	**2**	**0**	**0**	**0**
1995-96	**San Jose Sharks**	**NHL**	**68**	**22**	**20**	**42**	**22**	**16**	**38**	**41**	**2**	**2**	**2**	**146**	**15.1**	**75**	**25**	**89**	**31**	**–8**	....	....	....	....	....	....	....	....
	Pittsburgh Penguins	**NHL**	**13**	**6**	**5**	**11**	**6**	**4**	**10**	**4**	**1**	**0**	**0**	**33**	**18.2**	**16**	**3**	**14**	**5**	**4**	**18**	**3**	**2**	**5**	**8**	**0**	**0**	**0**
1996-97	**Chicago Blackhawks**	**NHL**	**69**	**14**	**17**	**31**	**15**	**15**	**30**	**41**	**5**	**1**	**2**	**139**	**10.1**	**40**	**11**	**57**	**18**	**–10**	**6**	**0**	**1**	**1**	**0**	**0**	**0**	**0**
1997-98	**Chicago Blackhawks**	**NHL**	**37**	**4**	**7**	**11**	**5**	**7**	**12**	**8**	**0**	**0**	**1**	**37**	**10.8**	**15**	**0**	**22**	**3**	**–4**	....	....	....	....	....	....	....	....
	Indianapolis Ice	IHL	26	11	11	22	....	....	....	41	....	....	....	....	....	....	....	....	....	....	2	1	1	2	0	....	....	....
	United States	WC-A	5	0	1	1	....	....	....	29	....	....	....	....	....	....	....	....	....	....	....	....	....	....	....	....	....	....
1998-99	**New York Islanders**	**NHL**	**33**	**1**	**5**	**6**	**1**	**5**	**6**	**13**	**0**	**0**	**0**	**37**	**2.7**	**10**	**1**	**17**	**3**	**–5**	....	....	....	....	....	....	....	....
	Chicago Wolves	IHL	30	11	20	31	....	....	....	8	....	....	....	....	....	....	....	....	....	....	10	2	7	9	22	....	....	....
99-2000	**Ottawa Senators**	**NHL**	**9**	**3**	**2**	**5**	**3**	**2**	**5**	**2**	**1**	**0**	**2**	**11**	**27.3**	**11**	**2**	**8**	**0**	**1**	**1**	**0**	**0**	**0**	**0**	**0**	**0**	**0**
	Grand Rapids Griffins	IHL	63	20	34	54	....	....	....	51	....	....	....	....	....	....	....	....	....	....	17	*11	7	*18	30	....	....	....
	NHL Totals		**616**	**150**	**183**	**333**	**150**	**153**	**303**	**429**	**28**	**14**	**26**	**1095**	**13.7**	**511**	**121**	**555**	**156**		**61**	**7**	**10**	**17**	**49**	**0**	**2**	**0**

• Brother of Kelly and Kip

Traded to **Detroit** by **NY Rangers** with Jim Cummins and Dennis Vial for Joey Kocur and Per Djoos, March 5, 1991. Traded to **Washington** by **Detroit** for Dino Ciccarelli, June 20, 1992. Traded to **St. Louis** by **Washington** for Paul Cavallini, November 2, 1992. Traded to **San Jose** by **St. Louis** for Todd Elik, March 23, 1995. Traded to **Pittsburgh** by **San Jose** for Pittsburgh's 5th round choice (later traded to Boston — Boston selected Elias Abrahamsson) in 1996 Entry Draft , March 20, 1996. Signed as a free agent by **Chicago**, July 18, 1996. Signed as a free agent by **NY Islanders**, October 9, 1998. Signed as a free agent by **Ottawa**, August 24, 1999.

• MILLER, Kip

C – L. 5'10", 190 lbs. b: Lansing, MI, 6/11/1969. Quebec's 4th, 72nd overall, in 1987.

Season	Club	League	GP	G	A	Pts	AG	AA	APts	PIM	PP	SH	GW	S	%	TGF	PGF	TGA	PGA	+/–	GP	G	A	Pts	PIM	PP	SH	GW
1984-85	Detroit Midget Compuware	MNHL	65	69	63	132	....	....	....	....	....	....	....	....	....	....	....	....	....	....	....	....	....	....	....	....	....	....
1985-86	Detroit Compuware	GLJHL	30	25	28	53	....	....	....	....	....	....	....	....	....	....	....	....	....	....	....	....	....	....	....	....	....	....
1986-87	Michigan State Spartans	CCHA	41	20	19	39	....	....	....	92	....	....	....	....	....	....	....	....	....	....	....	....	....	....	....	....	....	....
1987-88	Michigan State Spartans	CCHA	39	16	25	41	....	....	....	51	....	....	....	....	....	....	....	....	....	....	....	....	....	....	....	....	....	....
	United States	WJC-A	7	2	2	4	....	....	....	2	....	....	....	....	....	....	....	....	....	....	....	....	....	....	....	....	....	....
1988-89	Michigan State Spartans	CCHA	47	32	45	77	....	....	....	94	....	....	....	....	....	....	....	....	....	....	....	....	....	....	....	....	....	....
1989-90	Michigan State Spartans	CCHA	45	*48	53	*101	....	....	....	60	....	....	....	....	....	....	....	....	....	....	....	....	....	....	....	....	....	....
	United States	WEC-A	9	1	1	2	....	....	....	10	....	....	....	....	....	....	....	....	....	....	....	....	....	....	....	....	....	....

Season	Club	League	REGULAR SEASON																		PLAYOFFS							
			GP	G	A	Pts	AG	AA	APts	PIM	PP	SH	GW	S	%	TGF	PGF	TGA	PGA	+/–	GP	G	A	Pts	PIM	PP	SH	GW
1990-91	**Quebec Nordiques**	**NHL**	**13**	**4**	**3**	**7**	**4**	**2**	**6**	**7**	**0**	**0**	**0**	**16**	**25.0**	**10**	**0**	**11**	**0**	**–1**								
	Halifax Citadels	AHL	66	36	33	69				40																		
1991-92	**Quebec Nordiques**	**NHL**	**36**	**5**	**10**	**15**	**5**	**8**	**13**	**12**	**1**	**0**	**2**	**46**	**10.9**	**19**	**3**	**38**	**1**	**–21**								
	Halifax Citadels	AHL	24	9	17	26				8																		
	Minnesota North Stars	**NHL**	**3**	**1**	**2**	**3**	**1**	**2**	**3**	**2**	**1**	**0**	**0**	**3**	**33.3**	**3**	**2**	**2**	**0**	**–1**								
	Kalamazoo Wings	IHL	6	1	8	9				4											12	3	9	12	12			
1992-93	Kalamazoo Wings	IHL	61	17	39	56				59																		
1993-94	**San Jose Sharks**	**NHL**	**11**	**2**	**2**	**4**	**2**	**2**	**4**	**6**	**0**	**0**	**0**	**21**	**9.5**	**9**	**2**	**8**	**0**	**–1**								
	Kansas City Blades	IHL	71	38	54	92				51																		
1994-95	Denver Grizzlies	IHL	71	46	60	106				54											17	*15	14	29	8			
	New York Islanders	**NHL**	**8**	**0**	**1**	**1**	**0**	**1**	**1**	**0**	**0**	**0**	**0**	**11**	**0.0**	**3**	**1**	**1**	**0**	**1**								
1995-96	**Chicago Blackhawks**	**NHL**	**10**	**1**	**4**	**5**	**1**	**3**	**4**	**2**	**0**	**0**	**0**	**12**	**8.3**	**8**	**3**	**4**	**0**	**1**								
	Indianapolis Ice	IHL	73	32	59	91				46											5	2	6	8	2			
1996-97	Chicago Wolves	IHL	43	11	41	52				32																		
	Indianapolis Ice	IHL	37	17	24	41				18											4	2	2	4	2			
1997-98	Utah Grizzlies	IHL	72	38	59	97				30											4	3	2	5	10			
	New York Islanders	**NHL**	**9**	**1**	**3**	**4**	**1**	**3**	**4**	**2**	**0**	**0**	**0**	**11**	**9.1**	**6**	**1**	**7**	**0**	**–2**								
1998-99	**Pittsburgh Penguins**	**NHL**	**77**	**19**	**23**	**42**	**22**	**22**	**44**	**22**	**1**	**0**	**4**	**125**	**15.2**	**59**	**12**	**52**	**6**	**1**	**13**	**2**	**7**	**9**	**19**	**1**	**0**	**0**
99-2000	**Pittsburgh Penguins**	**NHL**	**44**	**4**	**15**	**19**	**4**	**14**	**18**	**10**	**0**	**0**	**1**	**50**	**8.0**	**35**	**2**	**39**	**5**	**–1**								
	Mighty Ducks of Anaheim	**NHL**	**30**	**6**	**17**	**23**	**7**	**16**	**23**	**4**	**2**	**0**	**1**	**32**	**18.8**	**23**	**7**	**15**	**0**	**1**								
	NHL Totals		**241**	**43**	**80**	**123**	**47**	**73**	**120**	**67**	**5**	**0**	**8**	**327**	**13.1**	**175**	**33**	**177**	**12**		**13**	**2**	**7**	**9**	**19**	**1**	**0**	**0**

• Brother of Kelly and Kevin • CCHA First All-Star Team (1989, 1990) • NCAA West First All-American Team (1989, 1990) • Won Hobey Baker Memorial Award (Top U.S. Collegiate Player) (1990)

Traded to **Minnesota** by **Quebec** for Steve Maltais, March 8, 1992. Signed as a free agent by **San Jose**, August 10, 1993. Signed as a free agent by **NY Islanders**, July 7, 1994. Signed as a free agent by **Chicago**, July 21, 1995. Signed as a free agent by **NY Islanders**, November 26, 1997. Claimed by **Pittsburgh** from **NY Islanders** in NHL Waiver Draft, October 5, 1998. Traded to **Anaheim** by **Pittsburgh** for Anaheim's 9th round choice (Roman Simicek) in 2000 Entry Draft, January 29, 2000.

• MILLER, Paul

Paul Edward C – L. 5'10", 170 lbs. b: Billerica, MA, 8/21/1959.

Season	Club	League	GP	G	A	Pts	AG	AA	APts	PIM	PP	SH	GW	S	%	TGF	PGF	TGA	PGA	+/–	GP	G	A	Pts	PIM	PP	SH	GW
1976-77	Billerica High School	Hi-School	STATISTICS NOT AVAILABLE																									
1977-78	Boston University	ECAC	31	10	14	24				28																		
1978-79	Boston University	ECAC	29	15	20	35				10																		
1979-80	Boston University	ECAC	20	4	10	14				13																		
	Flint Generals	IHL	13	3	2	5				31											5	1	1	2	6			
1980-81	Syracuse Hornets	EHL	10	3	5	8				9																		
	Richmond Rifles	EHL	21	9	16	25				20											10	1	2	3	19			
1981-82	**Colorado Rockies**	**NHL**	**3**	**0**	**3**	**3**	**0**	**2**	**2**	**0**	**0**	**0**	**0**	**0**	**0.0**	**3**	**0**	**2**	**1**	**2**								
	Fort Worth Texans	CHL	65	25	38	63				44																		
	United States	WEC-A	4	0	0	0				0																		
1982-83	Wichita Wind	CHL	55	17	18	35				44																		
	Moncton Alpines	AHL	19	2	8	10				7																		
1983-84	Muskegon Mohawks	IHL	4	0	1	1				0																		
	Moncton Alpines	AHL	46	9	2	11				68																		
	Milwaukee Admirals	IHL	3	1	3	4				2																		
	NHL Totals		**3**	**0**	**3**	**3**	**0**	**2**	**2**	**0**	**0**	**0**	**0**	**0**	**0.0**	**3**	**0**	**2**	**1**									

• Brother of Bob

Signed as a free agent by **Richmond** (EHL) after **Syracuse** (EHL) franchise folded, November 13, 1980. Signed as a free agent by **Colorado**, November 20, 1981. Transfrerred to **New Jersey** after **Colorado** franchise relocated, June 30, 1982. Traded to **Edmonton** by **New Jersey** with Lindsay Middlebrook for Ron Low and Jim McTaggart, February 19, 1983.

• MILLER, Perry

Perry Elvin D – L. 6'1", 194 lbs. b: Winnipeg, Man., 6/24/1952.

Season	Club	League	GP	G	A	Pts	AG	AA	APts	PIM	PP	SH	GW	S	%	TGF	PGF	TGA	PGA	+/–	GP	G	A	Pts	PIM	PP	SH	GW
1970-71	West Kildonan North Stars	MJHL	40	3	11	14				179																		
1971-72	West Kildanan North Stars	MJHL	39	15	23	38				187																		
1972-73	Charlotte Checkers	EHL	65	3	20	23				126																		
1973-74	Charlotte Checkers	SHL	66	12	31	43				203																		
1974-75	Winnipeg Jets	WHA	67	9	19	28				133																		
1975-76	Winnipeg Jets	WHA	47	7	6	13				41																		
	Minnesota Fighting Saints	WHA	13	1	4	5				11																		
1976-77	Winnipeg Jets	WHA	74	14	30	44				124											20	4	6	10	27			
1977-78	**Detroit Red Wings**	**NHL**	**62**	**4**	**17**	**21**	**4**	**13**	**17**	**120**	**0**	**1**	**1**	**122**	**3.3**	**77**	**11**	**95**	**24**	**–5**								
1978-79	**Detroit Red Wings**	**NHL**	**75**	**5**	**23**	**28**	**4**	**17**	**21**	**156**	**3**	**0**	**1**	**122**	**4.1**	**81**	**18**	**110**	**34**	**–13**								
1979-80	**Detroit Red Wings**	**NHL**	**16**	**0**	**3**	**3**	**0**	**2**	**2**	**41**	**0**	**0**	**0**	**13**	**0.0**	**14**	**1**	**17**	**0**	**–4**								
	Adirondack Red Wings	AHL	55	9	27	36				155											5	3	0	3	6			
1980-81	**Detroit Red Wings**	**NHL**	**64**	**1**	**8**	**9**	**1**	**5**	**6**	**70**	**0**	**0**	**0**	**54**	**1.9**	**36**	**2**	**54**	**2**	**–18**								
	Adirondack Red Wings	AHL	4	1	1	2				47																		
1981-82	Adirondack Red Wings	AHL	58	12	31	43				118											2	0	0	0	10			
	NHL Totals		**217**	**10**	**51**	**61**	**9**	**37**	**46**	**387**	**3**	**1**	**2**	**311**	**3.2**	**208**	**32**	**276**	**60**									
	Other Major League Totals		201	31	59	90				309											20	4	6	10	27			

SHL Second All-Star Team (1974)

Signed as a free agent by **Winnipeg** (WHA), September, 1974. Traded to **Minnesota** (WHA) by **Winnipeg** (WHA) for Gerry Odrowski, January, 1976. Signed as a free agent by **Winnipeg** (WHA) after **Minnesota** (WHA) franchise folded, March, 1976. Signed as a free agent by **Detroit**, July 8, 1977.

• MILLER, Tom

Thomas William C – L. 6', 187 lbs. b: Kitchener, Ont., 3/31/1947.

Season	Club	League	GP	G	A	Pts	AG	AA	APts	PIM	PP	SH	GW	S	%	TGF	PGF	TGA	PGA	+/–	GP	G	A	Pts	PIM	PP	SH	GW
1962-63	Kitchener Legionaires	OMHA	STATISTICS NOT AVAILABLE																									
	Guelph Royals	OHA-B	1	0	0	0				0																		
1963-64	Kitchener Rangers	OHA-Jr.	56	9	18	27				21																		
1964-65	Kitchener Rangers	OHA-Jr.	55	14	13	27				23																		
1965-66	University of Denver	WCHA	DID NOT PLAY – FRESHMAN																									
1966-67	University of Denver	WCHA	30	24	17	41				16																		
1967-68	University of Denver	WCHA	34	20	27	47				16																		
1968-69	University of Denver	WCHA	24	7	16	23				14																		
1969-70	Omaha Knights	CHL	63	19	20	39				23											12	3	5	8	4			
1970-71	**Detroit Red Wings**	**NHL**	**29**	**1**	**7**	**8**	**1**	**6**	**7**	**9**	**1**	**0**	**0**	**30**	**3.3**	**14**	**1**	**31**	**0**	**–18**								
	Omaha Knights	CHL	47	19	33	52				7																		
1971-72	Cincinnati Swords	AHL	62	18	27	45				41											3	0	0	0	0			
1972-73	**New York Islanders**	**NHL**	**69**	**13**	**17**	**30**	**12**	**13**	**25**	**21**	**2**	**0**	**1**	**92**	**14.1**	**43**	**10**	**86**	**24**	**–29**								
1973-74	**New York Islanders**	**NHL**	**19**	**2**	**1**	**3**	**2**	**1**	**3**	**4**	**0**	**1**	**0**	**19**	**10.5**	**4**	**0**	**14**	**7**	**–3**								
	Fort Worth Wings	CHL	11	3	7	10				0																		
1974-75	**New York Islanders**	**NHL**	**1**	**0**	**0**	**0**	**0**	**0**	**0**	**0**	**0**	**0**	**0**	**1**	**0.0**	**0**	**0**	**0**	**0**	**0**								
	New Haven Nighthawks	AHL	73	13	30	43				28											16	1	7	8	19			
	NHL Totals		**118**	**16**	**25**	**41**	**15**	**20**	**35**	**34**	**3**	**1**	**1**	**142**	**11.3**	**61**	**11**	**131**	**31**									

WCHA Second All-Star Team (1969) • NCAA Championship All-Tournament Team (1969)

Traded to **Detroit** by **NY Rangers** with Arnie Brown and Mike Robitaille for Bruce MacGregor and Larry Brown, February 2, 1971. Claimed by **Buffalo** from **Detroit** in Intra-League Draft, June 8, 1971. Claimed by **NY Islanders** from **Buffalo** in Expansion Draft, June 6, 1972.

• MILLER, Warren

Warren Fredrick RW – R. 6', 180 lbs. b: South St. Paul, MN, 1/1/1954. NY Rangers' 21st, 241st overall, in 1974.

Season	Club	League	GP	G	A	Pts	AG	AA	APts	PIM	PP	SH	GW	S	%	TGF	PGF	TGA	PGA	+/–	GP	G	A	Pts	PIM	PP	SH	GW
1971-72	South St. Paul High School	Hi-School	STATISTICS NOT AVAILABLE																									
1972-73	University of Minnesota	WCHA	32	5	3	8				22																		
1973-74	University of Minnesota	WCHA	40	11	16	27				34																		
1974-75	University of Minnesota	WCHA	41	16	21	37				40																		

			REGULAR SEASON																		PLAYOFFS							
Season	Club	League	GP	G	A	Pts	AG	AA	APts	PIM	PP	SH	GW	S	%	TGF	PGF	TGA	PGA	+/–	GP	G	A	Pts	PIM	PP	SH	GW
1975-76	University of Minnesota	WCHA	44	26	31	57	....	....	....	50	....	....	....	....	....	....	....	....	....	....	....	....	....	....	....	....	....	....
	Calgary Cowboys	WHA	3	0	0	0	....	....	....	0	....	....	....	....	....	....	....	....	....	....	10	1	0	1	28	....	....	....
1976-77	Calgary Cowboys	WHA	80	23	32	55	....	....	....	51	....	....	....	....	....	....	....	....	....	....	3	0	0	0	0	....	....	....
	United States	WEC-A	10	2	2	4	....	....	....	4	....	....	....	....	....	....	....	....	....	....	....	....	....	....	....	....	....	....
1977-78	Edmonton Oilers	WHA	18	2	4	6	....	....	....	18	....	....	....	....	....	....	....	....	....	....	....	....	....	....	....	....	....	....
	Quebec Nordiques	WHA	60	14	24	38	....	....	....	50	....	....	....	....	....	....	....	....	....	....	11	0	2	2	0	....	....	....
1978-79	New England Whalers	WHA	77	26	23	49	....	....	....	44	....	....	....	....	....	....	....	....	....	....	10	0	8	8	28	....	....	....
1979-80	**New York Rangers**	**NHL**	**55**	**7**	**6**	**13**	**6**	**4**	**10**	**17**	**0**	**0**	**3**	**51**	**13.7**	**32**	**1**	**53**	**16**	**–6**	**6**	**1**	**0**	**1**	**0**	**0**	**0**	**0**
1980-81	**Hartford Whalers**	**NHL**	**77**	**22**	**22**	**44**	**17**	**15**	**32**	**37**	**3**	**3**	**1**	**160**	**13.8**	**64**	**15**	**107**	**27**	**–31**	....	....	....	....	....	....	....	....
	United States	WEC-A	7	3	2	5	....	....	....	4	....	....	....	....	....	....	....	....	....	....	....	....	....	....	....	....	....	....
1981-82	United States	Can-Cup	6	2	0	2	....	....	....	2	....	....	....	....	....	....	....	....	....	....	....	....	....	....	....	....	....	....
	Hartford Whalers	**NHL**	**74**	**10**	**12**	**22**	**8**	**8**	**16**	**68**	**1**	**1**	**0**	**152**	**6.6**	**41**	**6**	**67**	**18**	**–14**	....	....	....	....	....	....	....	....
1982-83	**Hartford Whalers**	**NHL**	**56**	**1**	**10**	**11**	**1**	**7**	**8**	**15**	**0**	**0**	**0**	**75**	**1.3**	**18**	**1**	**41**	**11**	**–13**	....	....	....	....	....	....	....	....
	NHL Totals		**262**	**40**	**50**	**90**	**32**	**34**	**66**	**137**	**4**	**4**	**4**	**438**	**9.1**	**155**	**23**	**268**	**72**		**6**	**1**	**0**	**1**	**0**	**0**	**0**	**0**
	Other Major League Totals		238	65	83	148	....	....	....	163	....	....	....	....	....	....	....	....	....	....	34	1	10	11	56	....	....	....

NCAA Championship All-Tournament Team (1975)

Selected by **Vancouver** (WHA) in 1974 WHA Amateur Draft, May, 1974. WHA rights transferred to **Calagry** (WHA) after **Vancouver** (WHA) franchise relocated, May 7, 1975. Signed as a free agent by **Edmonton** (WHA) after **Calgary** (WHA) franchise folded, May 31, 1977. Traded to **Quebec** (WHA) by **Edmonton** (WHA) with Rick Morris, Ken Broderick and Dave Inkpen for Don McLeod and Pierre Guite, November, 1977. Traded to **New England** (WHA) by **Quebec** (WHA) for Jean-Louis Levasseur, September, 1978. Reclaimed by **NY Rangers** from **Hartford** prior to Expansion Draft, June 9, 1979. Traded to **Hartford** by **NY Rangers** for cash, August 7, 1980.

• MILLS, Craig

Craig A. RW – R. 6', 190 lbs. b: Toronto, Ont., 8/27/1976. Winnipeg's 5th, 108th overall, in 1994.

Season	Club	League	GP	G	A	Pts	AG	AA	APts	PIM	PP	SH	GW	S	%	TGF	PGF	TGA	PGA	+/–	GP	G	A	Pts	PIM	PP	SH	GW
1992-93	St. Michael's Buzzers	OJHL-B	44	9	21	30	....	....	....	42	....	....	....	....	....	....	....	....	....	....	15	1	6	7	8	....	....	....
1993-94	Belleville Bulls	OHL	63	15	18	33	....	....	....	88	....	....	....	....	....	....	....	....	....	....	12	2	1	3	11	....	....	....
1994-95	Belleville Bulls	OHL	62	39	41	80	....	....	....	104	....	....	....	....	....	....	....	....	....	....	13	7	9	16	8	....	....	....
1995-96	Belleville Bulls	OHL	48	10	19	29	....	....	....	113	....	....	....	....	....	....	....	....	....	....	14	4	5	9	32	....	....	....
	Canada	WJC-A	6	0	0	0	....	....	....	4	....	....	....	....	....	....	....	....	....	....	....	....	....	....	....	....	....	....
	Winnipeg Jets	**NHL**	**4**	**0**	**2**	**2**	**0**	**2**	**2**	**0**	**0**	**0**	**0**	**0**	**0.0**	**3**	**0**	**3**	**0**	**0**	**1**	**0**	**0**	**0**	**0**	**0**	**0**	**0**
	Springfield Falcons	AHL	....	....	....	....	....	....	....	....	....	....	....	....	....	....	....	....	....	....	2	0	0	0	0	....	....	....
1996-97	Indianapolis Ice	IHL	80	12	7	19	....	....	....	199	....	....	....	....	....	....	....	....	....	....	4	0	0	0	4	....	....	....
1997-98	**Chicago Blackhawks**	**NHL**	**20**	**0**	**3**	**3**	**0**	**3**	**3**	**34**	**0**	**0**	**0**	**5**	**0.0**	**4**	**0**	**3**	**0**	**1**	....	....	....	....	....	....	....	....
	Indianapolis Ice	IHL	42	8	11	19	....	....	....	119	....	....	....	....	....	....	....	....	....	....	5	0	0	0	27	....	....	....
1998-99	**Chicago Blackhawks**	**NHL**	**7**	**0**	**0**	**0**	**0**	**0**	**0**	**2**	**0**	**0**	**0**	**1**	**0.0**	**0**	**0**	**2**	**0**	**–2**	....	....	....	....	....	....	....	....
	Chicago Wolves	IHL	5	0	0	0	....	....	....	14	....	....	....	....	....	....	....	....	....	....	....	....	....	....	....	....	....	....
	Portland Pirates	AHL	48	7	11	18	....	....	....	59	....	....	....	....	....	....	....	....	....	....	....	....	....	....	....	....	....	....
	Indianapolis Ice	IHL	12	2	3	5	....	....	....	14	....	....	....	....	....	....	....	....	....	....	6	1	0	1	5	....	....	....
99-2000	Springfield Falcons	AHL	78	10	13	23	....	....	....	151	....	....	....	....	....	....	....	....	....	....	5	2	1	3	6	....	....	....
	NHL Totals		**31**	**0**	**5**	**5**	**0**	**5**	**5**	**36**	**0**	**0**	**0**	**6**	**0.0**	**7**	**0**	**8**	**0**		**1**	**0**	**0**	**0**	**0**	**0**	**0**	**0**

Canadian Major Junior Humanitarian Player of the Year (1996)

Rights transferred to **Phoenix** after **Winnipeg** franchise relocated, July 1, 1996. Traded to **Chicago** by **Phoenix** with Alexei Zhamnov and Phoenix's 1st round choice (Ty Jones) in 1997 Entry Draft for Jeremy Roenick, August 16, 1996. Traded to **Phoenix** by **Chicago** for cash, September 11, 1999.

• MINER, John

D – R. 5'10", 180 lbs. b: Moose Jaw, Sask., 8/28/1965. Edmonton's 10th, 229th overall, in 1983.

Season	Club	League	GP	G	A	Pts	AG	AA	APts	PIM	PP	SH	GW	S	%	TGF	PGF	TGA	PGA	+/–	GP	G	A	Pts	PIM	PP	SH	GW
1980-81	Regina Pat Canadians	AAHA	26	4	10	14	....	....	....	57	....	....	....	....	....	....	....	....	....	....	....	....	....	....	....	....	....	....
1981-82	Regina Blues	SJHL	56	12	29	41	....	....	....	347	....	....	....	....	....	....	....	....	....	....	....	....	....	....	....	....	....	....
	Regina Pats	WHL	10	0	1	1	....	....	....	11	....	....	....	....	....	....	....	....	....	....	17	0	0	0	25	....	....	....
1982-83	Regina Pats	WHL	71	11	23	34	....	....	....	126	....	....	....	....	....	....	....	....	....	....	5	1	1	2	20	....	....	....
1983-84	Regina Pats	WHL	70	27	42	69	....	....	....	132	....	....	....	....	....	....	....	....	....	....	23	9	25	34	54	....	....	....
1984-85	Regina Pats	WHL	66	30	54	84	....	....	....	128	....	....	....	....	....	....	....	....	....	....	8	4	10	14	12	....	....	....
	Canada	WJC-A	7	0	2	2	....	....	....	12	....	....	....	....	....	....	....	....	....	....	....	....	....	....	....	....	....	....
	Nova Scotia Oilers	AHL	....	....	....	....	....	....	....	....	....	....	....	....	....	....	....	....	....	....	3	2	2	4	2	....	....	....
1985-86	Nova Scotia Oilers	AHL	79	10	33	43	....	....	....	90	....	....	....	....	....	....	....	....	....	....	....	....	....	....	....	....	....	....
1986-87	Nova Scotia Oilers	AHL	45	5	28	33	....	....	....	38	....	....	....	....	....	....	....	....	....	....	5	0	3	3	4	....	....	....
1987-88	**Edmonton Oilers**	**NHL**	**14**	**2**	**3**	**5**	**2**	**2**	**4**	**16**	**0**	**0**	**0**	**16**	**12.5**	**21**	**4**	**21**	**0**	**–4**	....	....	....	....	....	....	....	....
	Nova Scotia Oilers	AHL	61	8	26	34	....	....	....	61	....	....	....	....	....	....	....	....	....	....	....	....	....	....	....	....	....	....
1988-89	WEV Wien	Austria	37	19	33	52	....	....	....	....	....	....	....	....	....	....	....	....	....	....	....	....	....	....	....	....	....	....
	New Haven Nighthawks	AHL	7	2	3	5	....	....	....	4	....	....	....	....	....	....	....	....	....	....	17	3	12	15	40	....	....	....
1989-90	HC Lausanne	Switz-2	35	19	32	51	....	....	....	80	....	....	....	....	....	....	....	....	....	....	10	7	10	17	8	....	....	....
	New Haven Nighthawks	AHL	7	1	6	7	....	....	....	2	....	....	....	....	....	....	....	....	....	....	....	....	....	....	....	....	....	....
1990-91	HC Lausanne	Switz-2	36	17	40	57	....	....	....	60	....	....	....	....	....	....	....	....	....	....	9	6	10	16	10	....	....	....
1991-92	EK Zell-am-Zee	Austria	42	16	37	53	....	....	....	....	....	....	....	....	....	....	....	....	....	....	....	....	....	....	....	....	....	....
1992-93	EK Zell-am-Zee	Austria	52	19	52	71	....	....	....	....	....	....	....	....	....	....	....	....	....	....	....	....	....	....	....	....	....	....
1993-94	HC Ajoie	Switz-2	34	16	22	38	....	....	....	42	....	....	....	....	....	....	....	....	....	....	4	3	3	6	18	....	....	....
1994-95	HC Martigny	Switz-2	36	15	28	43	....	....	....	67	....	....	....	....	....	....	....	....	....	....	4	1	2	3	2	....	....	....
1995-96	EV Zug	Switz.	29	12	20	32	....	....	....	36	....	....	....	....	....	....	....	....	....	....	4	0	5	5	4	....	....	....
1996-97	EV Zug	Switz.	45	15	32	47	....	....	....	50	....	....	....	....	....	....	....	....	....	....	10	2	7	9	4	....	....	....
1997-98	EV Zug	Switz.	35	5	17	22	....	....	....	28	....	....	....	....	....	....	....	....	....	....	4	0	2	2	0	....	....	....
	EV Zug	EuroHL	4	2	1	3	....	....	....	4	....	....	....	....	....	....	....	....	....	....	....	....	....	....	....	....	....	....
1998-99	Kolner Haie	Germany	52	5	26	31	....	....	....	77	....	....	....	....	....	....	....	....	....	....	5	1	1	2	0	....	....	....
99-2000	Kolner Haie	Germany	56	7	27	34	....	....	....	50	....	....	....	....	....	....	....	....	....	....	10	2	*8	10	10	....	....	....
	NHL Totals		**14**	**2**	**3**	**5**	**2**	**2**	**4**	**16**	**0**	**0**	**0**	**16**	**12.5**	**21**	**4**	**21**	**0**		....	....	....	....	....	....	....	....

WHL East First All-Star Team (1985)

Traded to **LA Kings** by **Edmonton** for Craig Redmond, August 10, 1988.

• MINOR, Gerry

Gerald Robert "Bucky" C – L. 5'8", 178 lbs. b: Regina, Sask., 10/27/1958. Vancouver's 6th, 90th overall, in 1978.

Season	Club	League	GP	G	A	Pts	AG	AA	APts	PIM	PP	SH	GW	S	%	TGF	PGF	TGA	PGA	+/–	GP	G	A	Pts	PIM	PP	SH	GW
1974-75	Regina Pat Blues	SJHL	38	28	19	47	....	....	....	56	....	....	....	....	....	....	....	....	....	....	....	....	....	....	....	....	....	....
	Regina Pats	WCJHL	16	2	6	8	....	....	....	6	....	....	....	....	....	....	....	....	....	....	11	0	1	1	6	....	....	....
1975-76	Regina Pats	WHL	71	24	41	65	....	....	....	124	....	....	....	....	....	....	....	....	....	....	6	0	8	8	14	....	....	....
1976-77	Regina Pats	WCJHL	48	22	32	54	....	....	....	120	....	....	....	....	....	....	....	....	....	....	6	0	8	8	14	....	....	....
1977-78	Regina Pats	WCJHL	66	54	75	129	....	....	....	238	....	....	....	....	....	....	....	....	....	....	13	5	22	*37	31	....	....	....
1978-79	Fort Wayne Komets	IHL	42	18	28	46	....	....	....	67	....	....	....	....	....	....	....	....	....	....	....	....	....	....	....	....	....	....
	Dallas Black Hawks	CHL	37	14	25	39	....	....	....	76	....	....	....	....	....	....	....	....	....	....	9	3	4	7	31	....	....	....
1979-80	**Vancouver Canucks**	**NHL**	**5**	**0**	**1**	**1**	**0**	**1**	**1**	**2**	**0**	**0**	**0**	**4**	**0.0**	**1**	**0**	**2**	**1**	**0**	....	....	....	....	....	....	....	....
	Dallas Black Hawks	CHL	73	31	52	83	....	....	....	162	....	....	....	....	....	....	....	....	....	....	....	....	....	....	....	....	....	....
1980-81	**Vancouver Canucks**	**NHL**	**74**	**10**	**14**	**24**	**8**	**9**	**17**	**108**	**1**	**6**	**0**	**93**	**10.8**	**35**	**4**	**69**	**42**	**4**	**3**	**0**	**0**	**0**	**8**	**0**	**0**	**0**
1981-82	**Vancouver Canucks**	**NHL**	**13**	**0**	**1**	**1**	**0**	**1**	**1**	**6**	**0**	**0**	**0**	**18**	**0.0**	**1**	**0**	**18**	**11**	**–6**	**9**	**1**	**3**	**4**	**17**	**0**	**0**	**0**
	Dallas Black Hawks	CHL	12	5	8	13	....	....	....	92	....	....	....	....	....	....	....	....	....	....	....	....	....	....	....	....	....	....
1982-83	**Vancouver Canucks**	**NHL**	**39**	**1**	**5**	**6**	**1**	**3**	**4**	**57**	**0**	**0**	**0**	**24**	**4.2**	**8**	**0**	**35**	**21**	**–6**	....	....	....	....	....	....	....	....
	Fredericton Express	AHL	17	4	17	21	....	....	....	14	....	....	....	....	....	....	....	....	....	....	....	....	....	....	....	....	....	....
1983-84	**Vancouver Canucks**	**NHL**	**9**	**0**	**0**	**0**	**0**	**0**	**0**	**0**	**0**	**0**	**0**	**2**	**0.0**	**0**	**0**	**5**	**5**	**0**	....	....	....	....	....	....	....	....
	Fredericton Express	AHL	66	16	42	58	....	....	....	85	....	....	....	....	....	....	....	....	....	....	7	1	4	5	20	....	....	....
1984-85	Nova Scotia Voyageurs	AHL	21	4	10	14	....	....	....	8	....	....	....	....	....	....	....	....	....	....	....	....	....	....	....	....	....	....
	New Haven Nighthawks	AHL	52	11	29	40	....	....	....	65	....	....	....	....	....	....	....	....	....	....	....	....	....	....	....	....	....	....
1985-86	Indianapolis Checkers	IHL	72	28	46	74	....	....	....	108	....	....	....	....	....	....	....	....	....	....	5	3	4	7	8	....	....	....
1986-87	Muskegon Lumberjacks	IHL	68	17	22	39	....	....	....	93	....	....	....	....	....	....	....	....	....	....	15	3	9	12	32	....	....	....
	NHL Totals		**140**	**11**	**21**	**32**	**9**	**14**	**23**	**173**	**1**	**6**	**0**	**141**	**7.8**	**45**	**4**	**129**	**80**		**12**	**1**	**3**	**4**	**25**	**0**	**0**	**0**

• MIRONOV, Boris

D – R. 6'3", 223 lbs. b: Moscow, USSR, 3/21/1972. Winnipeg's 2nd, 27th overall, in 1992.

Season	Club	League	GP	G	A	Pts	AG	AA	APts	PIM	PP	SH	GW	S	%	TGF	PGF	TGA	PGA	+/–	GP	G	A	Pts	PIM	PP	SH	GW
			REGULAR SEASON																		PLAYOFFS							
1988-89	CSKA Moscow	USSR	1	0	0	0				0																		
	Soviet Union	EJC-A	5	3	2	5				2																		
1989-90	CSKA Moscow	USSR	7	0	0	0				0																		
	Soviet Union	EJC-A	6	1	0	1				0																		
1990-91	CSKA Moscow	USSR	36	1	5	6				16																		
1991-92	CSKA Moscow	CIS	36	2	1	3				22																		
	Russia	WJC-A	7	2	2	4				29																		
1992-93	CSKA Moscow	CIS	19	0	5	5				20																		
1993-94	**Winnipeg Jets**	**NHL**	**65**	**7**	**22**	**29**	**6**	**17**	**23**	**96**	**5**	**0**	**0**	**122**	**5.7**	**70**	**29**	**76**	**6**	**–29**								
	Edmonton Oilers	**NHL**	**14**	**0**	**2**	**2**	**0**	**2**	**2**	**14**	**0**	**0**	**0**	**23**	**0.0**	**11**	**2**	**15**	**2**	**–4**								
1994-95	**Edmonton Oilers**	**NHL**	**29**	**1**	**7**	**8**	**2**	**10**	**12**	**40**	**0**	**0**	**0**	**48**	**2.1**	**22**	**8**	**27**	**4**	**–9**								
	Cape Breton Oilers	AHL	4	2	5	7				23																		
1995-96	**Edmonton Oilers**	**NHL**	**78**	**8**	**24**	**32**	**8**	**20**	**28**	**101**	**7**	**0**	**1**	**158**	**5.1**	**72**	**30**	**81**	**16**	**–23**								
	Russia	WC-A	8	0	3	3				12																		
1996-97	**Edmonton Oilers**	**NHL**	**55**	**6**	**26**	**32**	**6**	**23**	**29**	**85**	**2**	**0**	**1**	**147**	**4.1**	**79**	**33**	**60**	**16**	**2**	**12**	**2**	**8**	**10**	**16**	**2**	**0**	**0**
1997-98	**Edmonton Oilers**	**NHL**	**81**	**16**	**30**	**46**	**19**	**29**	**48**	**100**	**10**	**1**	**1**	**203**	**7.9**	**108**	**51**	**93**	**28**	**–8**	**12**	**3**	**3**	**6**	**27**	**1**	**0**	**1**
	Russia	Olympics	6	0	2	2				2																		
1998-99	**Edmonton Oilers**	**NHL**	**63**	**11**	**29**	**40**	**13**	**28**	**41**	**104**	**5**	**0**	**4**	**138**	**8.0**	**85**	**29**	**74**	**24**	**6**								
	Chicago Blackhawks	**NHL**	**12**	**0**	**9**	**9**	**0**	**9**	**9**	**27**	**0**	**0**	**0**	**35**	**0.0**	**21**	**7**	**10**	**3**	**7**								
99-2000	**Chicago Blackhawks**	**NHL**	**58**	**9**	**28**	**37**	**10**	**26**	**36**	**72**	**4**	**2**	**1**	**144**	**6.3**	**81**	**20**	**74**	**10**	**–3**								
	Russia	WC-A	6	0	0	0				4																		
	NHL Totals		**455**	**58**	**177**	**235**	**64**	**164**	**228**	**639**	**33**	**3**	**8**	**1018**	**5.7**	**549**	**209**	**510**	**109**		**24**	**5**	**11**	**16**	**43**	**3**	**0**	**1**

• Brother of Dmitri • NHL All-Rookie Team (1994)

Traded to **Edmonton** by **Winnipeg** with Mats Lindgren, Winnipeg's 1st round choice (Jason Bonsignore) in 1994 Entry Draft and Florida's 4th round choice (previously acquired, Edmonton selected Adam Copeland) in 1994 Entry Draft for Dave Manson and St. Louis' 6th round choice (previously acquired, Winnipeg selected Chris Kibermanis) in 1994 Entry Draft, March 15, 1994. Traded to **Chicago** by **Edmonton** with Dean McAmmond and Jonas Elofsson for Chad Kilger, Daniel Cleary, Ethan Moreau and Christian Laflamme, March 20, 1999.

• MIRONOV, Dmitri

"Tree" D – R. 6'4", 224 lbs. b: Moscow, USSR, 12/25/1965. Toronto's 7th, 160th overall, in 1991.

Season	Club	League	GP	G	A	Pts	AG	AA	APts	PIM	PP	SH	GW	S	%	TGF	PGF	TGA	PGA	+/–	GP	G	A	Pts	PIM	PP	SH	GW
1985-86	CSKA Moscow	USSR	9	0	1	1				8																		
1986-87	CSKA Moscow	USSR	20	1	3	4				10																		
1987-88	Krylja Sovetov Moscow	USSR	44	12	6	18				30																		
1988-89	Krylja Sovetov Moscow	USSR	44	5	6	11				44																		
1989-90	Krylja Sovetov Moscow	Fr-Tour	1	0	0	0				0																		
	Krylja Sovetov Moscow	USSR	45	4	11	15				34																		
	Krylja Sovetov Moscow	Super-S	5	0	1	1				4																		
1990-91	Krylja Sovetov Moscow	Fr-Tour	1	0	1	1				0																		
	Krylja Sovetov Moscow	USSR	45	16	12	28				22																		
	CSKA Moscow	Super-S	6	0	1	1				6																		
	Soviet Union	WEC-A	10	4	2	6				6																		
1991-92	Soviet Union	Can-Cup	5	0	1	1				4																		
	Krylja Sovetov Moscow	CIS	35	15	16	31				62																		
	Toronto Maple Leafs	**NHL**	**7**	**1**	**0**	**1**	**1**	**0**	**1**	**0**	**0**	**0**	**1**	**7**	**14.3**	**3**	**0**	**8**	**1**	**–4**								
	Russia	Olympics	8	3	1	4				6																		
	Russia	WC-A	6	1	1	2				2																		
1992-93	**Toronto Maple Leafs**	**NHL**	**59**	**7**	**24**	**31**	**6**	**17**	**23**	**40**	**4**	**0**	**1**	**105**	**6.7**	**73**	**32**	**44**	**2**	**–1**	**14**	**1**	**2**	**3**	**2**	**1**	**0**	**0**
1993-94	**Toronto Maple Leafs**	**NHL**	**76**	**9**	**27**	**36**	**8**	**21**	**29**	**78**	**3**	**0**	**0**	**147**	**6.1**	**94**	**44**	**55**	**10**	**5**	**18**	**6**	**9**	**15**	**6**	**6**	**0**	**0**
1994-95	**Toronto Maple Leafs**	**NHL**	**33**	**5**	**12**	**17**	**9**	**18**	**27**	**28**	**2**	**0**	**0**	**68**	**7.4**	**44**	**20**	**20**	**2**	**6**	**6**	**2**	**1**	**3**	**2**	**1**	**0**	**0**
1995-96	**Pittsburgh Penguins**	**NHL**	**72**	**3**	**31**	**34**	**3**	**25**	**28**	**88**	**1**	**0**	**1**	**86**	**3.5**	**110**	**21**	**98**	**28**	**19**	**15**	**0**	**1**	**1**	**10**	**0**	**0**	**0**
1996-97	**Pittsburgh Penguins**	**NHL**	**15**	**1**	**5**	**6**	**1**	**4**	**5**	**24**	**0**	**0**	**1**	**19**	**5.3**	**12**	**3**	**14**	**1**	**–4**								
	Mighty Ducks of Anaheim	**NHL**	**62**	**12**	**34**	**46**	**13**	**30**	**43**	**77**	**3**	**1**	**1**	**158**	**7.6**	**116**	**39**	**76**	**19**	**20**	**11**	**1**	**10**	**11**	**10**	**1**	**0**	**0**
1997-98	**Mighty Ducks of Anaheim**	**NHL**	**66**	**6**	**30**	**36**	**7**	**29**	**36**	**115**	**2**	**0**	**1**	**142**	**4.2**	**82**	**24**	**93**	**28**	**–7**								
	Russia	Olympics	6	0	3	3				0																		
♦	**Detroit Red Wings**	**NHL**	**11**	**2**	**5**	**7**	**2**	**5**	**7**	**4**	**1**	**0**	**0**	**28**	**7.1**	**15**	**7**	**12**	**4**	**0**	**7**	**0**	**3**	**3**	**14**	**0**	**0**	**0**
1998-99	**Washington Capitals**	**NHL**	**46**	**2**	**14**	**16**	**2**	**13**	**15**	**80**	**2**	**0**	**0**	**86**	**2.3**	**42**	**16**	**43**	**12**	**–5**								
99-2000	**Washington Capitals**	**NHL**	**73**	**3**	**19**	**22**	**3**	**18**	**21**	**28**	**1**	**0**	**0**	**99**	**3.0**	**75**	**19**	**53**	**4**	**7**	**4**	**0**	**0**	**0**	**4**	**0**	**0**	**0**
	Russia	WC-A	6	0	0	0				4																		
	NHL Totals		**520**	**51**	**201**	**252**	**55**	**180**	**235**	**562**	**19**	**1**	**6**	**945**	**5.4**	**666**	**225**	**516**	**111**		**75**	**10**	**26**	**36**	**48**	**9**	**0**	**0**

• Brother of Boris • Played in NHL All-Star Game (1998)

Traded to **Pittsburgh** by **Toronto** with Toronto's 2nd round choice (later traded to New Jersey — New Jersey selected Joshua Dewolf) in 1996 Entry Draft for Larry Murphy, July 8, 1995. Traded to **Anaheim** by **Pittsburgh** with Shawn Antoski for Alex Hicks and Fredrik Olausson, November 19, 1996. Traded to **Detroit** by **Anaheim** for Jamie Pushor and Detroit's 4th round choice (Viktor Wallin) in 1998 Entry Draft, March 24, 1998. Signed as a free agent by **Washington**, July 29, 1998.

• MISZUK, John

John Stanley D – L. 6'1", 192 lbs. b: Naliboki, Poland, 9/29/1940.

Season	Club	League	GP	G	A	Pts	AG	AA	APts	PIM	PP	SH	GW	S	%	TGF	PGF	TGA	PGA	+/–	GP	G	A	Pts	PIM	PP	SH	GW
1957-58	Hamilton Kilty B's	OHA-B	STATISTICS NOT AVAILABLE																									
	Hamilton Tiger Cubs	OHA-Jr.																			1	0	0	0	0			
1958-59	Hamilton Kilty B's	OHA-B	STATISTICS NOT AVAILABLE																									
	Hamilton Tiger Cubs	OHA-Jr.	2	0	0	0				0																		
1959-60	Hamilton Tiger Cubs	OHA-Jr.	6	1	3	4				0																		
1960-61	Hamilton Tiger Cubs	OHA-Jr.	48	6	19	25				89											12	1	8	9	28			
1961-62	Edmonton Flyers	WHL	65	4	30	34				88											12	1	6	7	20			
1962-63	Edmonton Flyers	WHL	59	8	25	33				99											3	0	0	0	8			
	Pittsburgh Hornets	AHL	10	0	3	3				16																		
1963-64	**Detroit Red Wings**	**NHL**	**42**	**0**	**2**	**2**	**0**	**2**	**2**	**30**											**3**	**0**	**0**	**0**	**2**	**0**	**0**	**0**
	Pittsburgh Hornets	AHL	25	1	7	8				34																		
1964-65	Buffalo Bisons	AHL	71	9	46	55				100											9	0	3	3	12			
1965-66	**Chicago Black Hawks**	**NHL**	**2**	**1**	**1**	**2**	**1**	**1**	**2**	**2**											**3**	**0**	**0**	**0**	**4**	**0**	**0**	**0**
	St. Louis Braves	CPHL	69	7	29	36				116											5	0	2	2	4			
1966-67	**Chicago Black Hawks**	**NHL**	**3**	**0**	**0**	**0**	**0**	**0**	**0**	**0**											**2**	**0**	**0**	**0**	**2**	**0**	**0**	**0**
	St. Louis Braves	CPHL	68	3	28	31				104																		
1967-68	**Philadelphia Flyers**	**NHL**	**74**	**5**	**17**	**22**	**6**	**17**	**23**	**79**	**1**	**1**	**1**	**78**	**6.4**	**77**	**13**	**80**	**17**	**1**	**7**	**0**	**3**	**3**	**11**	**0**	**0**	**0**
1968-69	**Philadelphia Flyers**	**NHL**	**66**	**1**	**13**	**14**	**1**	**12**	**13**	**70**	**1**	**0**	**0**	**70**	**1.4**	**50**	**3**	**69**	**16**	**–6**	**4**	**0**	**0**	**0**	**0**	**0**	**0**	**0**
1969-70	**Minnesota North Stars**	**NHL**	**50**	**0**	**6**	**6**	**0**	**6**	**6**	**51**	**0**	**0**	**0**	**34**	**0.0**	**37**	**3**	**62**	**25**	**–3**								
	Iowa Stars	CHL	16	1	6	7				37											9	0	3	3	10			
1970-71	San Diego Gulls	WHL	72	5	30	35				98											6	0	1	1	4			
1971-72	San Diego Gulls	WHL	72	5	33	38				118											4	0	1	1	6			
1972-73	San Diego Gulls	WHL	72	2	39	41				85											6	0	4	4	13			
1973-74	San Diego Gulls	WHL	77	8	49	57				103											4	0	0	0	2			
1974-75	Michigan-Baltimore Stags	WHA	66	2	19	21				56																		
1975-76	Calgary Cowboys	WHA	69	2	21	23				66											10	1	0	1	28			

			REGULAR SEASON																		PLAYOFFS							
Season	Club	League	GP	G	A	Pts	AG	AA	APts	PIM	PP	SH	GW	S	%	TGF	PGF	TGA	PGA	+/–	GP	G	A	Pts	PIM	PP	SH	GW
1976-77	Calgary Cowboys	WHA	79	2	26	28	....	....	....	57	....	....	....	....	....	....	....	....	....	....	....	....	....	....	....	....	....	....
1977-78	San Francisco Shamrocks	PHL	10	0	15	15	....	....	....	12	....	....	....	....	....	....	....	....	....	....	....	....	....	....	....	....	....	....
1978-79	San Diego Hawks	PHL	25	2	11	13	....	....	....	24	....	....	....	....	....	....	....	....	....	....	....	....	....	....	....	....	....	....
	NHL Totals		**237**	**7**	**39**	**46**	**8**	**38**	**46**	**232**	....	....	....	....	....	....	....	....	....		**19**	**0**	**3**	**3**	**19**	....	....	....
	Other Major League Totals		214	6	66	72	....	....	....	179	....	....	....	....	....	....	....	....	....	....	10	1	0	1	28	....	....	....

AHL Second All-Star Team (1965) • CPHL First All-Star Team (1967) • WHL First All-Star Team (1973, 1974)

Traded to **Chicago** by **Detroit** with Art Stratton and Ian Cushenan for Ron Murphy and Aut Erickson, June 9, 1964. Claimed by **Philadelphia** from **Chicago** in Expansion Draft, June 6, 1967. Traded to **Minnesota** by **Philadelphia** for Wayne Hillman, May 14, 1969. Traded to **San Diego** (WHL) by **Minnesota** for cash, July, 1970. Selected by **LA Sharks** (WHA) in 1972 WHA General Player Draft, February 12, 1972. WHA rights transferred to **Michigan** (WHA) after **LA Sharks** (WHA) franchise relocated, April 30, 1974. Claimed by **Calgary** (WHA) from **Michigan-Baltimore** (WHA) in WHA Dispersal Draft, May 19, 1975.

• MITCHELL, Jeff

Jeffrey C/RW – R. 6'1", 190 lbs. b: Wayne, MI, 5/16/1975. Los Angeles' 2nd, 68th overall, in 1993.

Season	Club	League	GP	G	A	Pts	AG	AA	APts	PIM	PP	SH	GW	S	%	TGF	PGF	TGA	PGA	+/–	GP	G	A	Pts	PIM	PP	SH	GW
1990-91	Fruehauf Flyers	MNHL	62	52	63	115	....	....	....	196	....	....	....	....	....	....	....	....	....	....	....	....	....	....	....	....	....	....
1991-92	Fraser Falcons	MNHL	65	65	52	117	....	....	....	114	....	....	....	....	....	....	....	....	....	....	....	....	....	....	....	....	....	....
1992-93	Detroit Jr. Red Wings	OHL	62	10	15	25	....	....	....	100	....	....	....	....	....	....	....	....	....	....	15	3	3	6	16	....	....	....
1993-94	Detroit Jr. Red Wings	OHL	59	25	18	43	....	....	....	99	....	....	....	....	....	....	....	....	....	....	17	3	5	8	22	....	....	....
1994-95	Detroit Jr. Red Wings	OHL	61	30	30	60	....	....	....	121	....	....	....	....	....	....	....	....	....	....	21	9	12	21	48	....	....	....
	Detroit Jr. Red Wings	Mem-Cup	5	2	1	3	....	....	....	12	....	....	....	....	....	....	....	....	....	....	....	....	....	....	....	....	....	....
1995-96	Michigan K-Wings	IHL	50	5	4	9	....	....	....	119	....	....	....	....	....	....	....	....	....	....	....	....	....	....	....	....	....	....
1996-97	Michigan K-Wings	IHL	24	0	3	3	....	....	....	40	....	....	....	....	....	....	....	....	....	....	....	....	....	....	....	....	....	....
	Philadelphia Phantoms	AHL	31	7	5	12	....	....	....	103	....	....	....	....	....	....	....	....	....	....	10	1	1	2	20	....	....	....
1997-98	**Dallas Stars**	**NHL**	**7**	**0**	**0**	**0**	**0**	**0**	**0**	**7**	**0**	**0**	**0**	**3**	**0.0**	**0**	**0**	**0**	**0**	**0**	....	....	....	....	....	....	....	....
	Michigan K-Wings	IHL	62	9	8	17	....	....	....	206	....	....	....	....	....	....	....	....	....	....	4	0	0	0	30	....	....	....
1998-99	Michigan K-Wings	IHL	50	4	4	8	....	....	....	122	....	....	....	....	....	....	....	....	....	....	2	0	0	0	0	....	....	....
99-2000	Cincinnati Mighty Ducks	AHL	20	0	3	3	....	....	....	16	....	....	....	....	....	....	....	....	....	....	....	....	....	....	....	....	....	....
	Cincinnati Cyclones	IHL	1	0	0	0	....	....	....	0	....	....	....	....	....	....	....	....	....	....	....	....	....	....	....	....	....	....
	Dayton Bombers	ECHL	36	23	17	40	....	....	....	186	....	....	....	....	....	....	....	....	....	....	....	....	....	....	....	....	....	....
	NHL Totals		**7**	**0**	**0**	**0**	**0**	**0**	**0**	**7**	**0**	**0**	**0**	**3**	**0.0**	**0**	**0**	**0**	**0**		....	....	....	....	....	....	....	....

Rights traded to **Dallas** by **LA Kings** for Vancouver's 5th round choice (previously acquired, LA Kings selected Jason Morgan) in 1995 Entry Draft, June 7, 1995.

• MITCHELL, Roy

Roy A. D – R. 6'1", 199 lbs. b: Edmonton, Alta., 3/14/1969. Montreal's 10th, 188th overall, in 1989.

Season	Club	League	GP	G	A	Pts	AG	AA	APts	PIM	PP	SH	GW	S	%	TGF	PGF	TGA	PGA	+/–	GP	G	A	Pts	PIM	PP	SH	GW
1985-86	St. Albert Saints	AJHL	39	2	18	20	....	....	....	32	....	....	....	....	....	....	....	....	....	....	....	....	....	....	....	....	....	....
	Portland Winter Hawks	Mem-Cup	1	0	0	0	....	....	....	0	....	....	....	....	....	....	....	....	....	....	....	....	....	....	....	....	....	....
1986-87	Portland Winter Hawks	WHL	68	7	32	39	....	....	....	103	....	....	....	....	....	....	....	....	....	....	20	0	3	3	23	....	....	....
1987-88	Portland Winter Hawks	WHL	72	5	42	47	....	....	....	219	....	....	....	....	....	....	....	....	....	....	....	....	....	....	....	....	....	....
1988-89	Portland Winter Hawks	WHL	72	9	34	43	....	....	....	177	....	....	....	....	....	....	....	....	....	....	19	1	8	9	38	....	....	....
1989-90	Sherbrooke Canadiens	AHL	77	5	12	17	....	....	....	98	....	....	....	....	....	....	....	....	....	....	12	0	2	2	31	....	....	....
1990-91	Fredericton Canadiens	AHL	71	2	15	17	....	....	....	137	....	....	....	....	....	....	....	....	....	....	9	0	1	1	11	....	....	....
1991-92	Kalamazoo Wings	IHL	69	3	26	29	....	....	....	102	....	....	....	....	....	....	....	....	....	....	11	1	4	5	18	....	....	....
1992-93	**Minnesota North Stars**	**NHL**	**3**	**0**	**0**	**0**	**0**	**0**	**0**	**0**	**0**	**0**	**0**	**0**	**0.0**	**0**	**0**	**0**	**0**	**0**	....	....	....	....	....	....	....	....
	Kalamazoo Wings	IHL	79	7	25	32	....	....	....	119	....	....	....	....	....	....	....	....	....	....	....	....	....	....	....	....	....	....
1993-94	Kalamazoo Wings	IHL	13	0	4	4	....	....	....	21	....	....	....	....	....	....	....	....	....	....	....	....	....	....	....	....	....	....
	Binghamton Rangers	AHL	11	1	3	4	....	....	....	18	....	....	....	....	....	....	....	....	....	....	....	....	....	....	....	....	....	....
	Albany River Rats	AHL	42	3	12	15	....	....	....	43	....	....	....	....	....	....	....	....	....	....	3	0	0	0	0	....	....	....
1994-95	Worcester IceCats	AHL	80	5	25	30	....	....	....	97	....	....	....	....	....	....	....	....	....	....	....	....	....	....	....	....	....	....
1995-96	Worcester IceCats	AHL	52	1	3	4	....	....	....	62	....	....	....	....	....	....	....	....	....	....	4	0	0	0	2	....	....	....
1996-97	Central Texas Stampede	WPHL	20	1	8	9	....	....	....	12	....	....	....	....	....	....	....	....	....	....	11	2	7	9	10	....	....	....
1997-98	Newcastle Cobras	BH-Cup	14	2	6	8	....	....	....	14	....	....	....	....	....	....	....	....	....	....	....	....	....	....	....	....	....	....
	Newcastle Cobras	Britain	41	3	13	16	....	....	....	32	....	....	....	....	....	....	....	....	....	....	6	0	0	0	0	....	....	....
1998-99	Nottingham Panthers	BH-Cup	13	3	5	8	....	....	....	22	....	....	....	....	....	....	....	....	....	....	....	....	....	....	....	....	....	....
	Nottingham Panthers	Britain	42	3	4	7	....	....	....	28	....	....	....	....	....	....	....	....	....	....	8	0	1	1	8	....	....	....
99-2000	Idaho Steelheads	WCHL	47	1	17	18	....	....	....	47	....	....	....	....	....	....	....	....	....	....	3	0	1	1	8	....	....	....
	NHL Totals		**3**	**0**	**0**	**0**	**0**	**0**	**0**	**0**	**0**	**0**	**0**	**0**	**0.0**	**0**	**0**	**0**	**0**		....	....	....	....	....	....	....	....

Named Top Defenseman in British Elite League (1999)

Signed as a free agent by **Minnesota**, July 25, 1991. Transferred to **Dallas** after **Minnesota** franchise relocated, June 9, 1993. Traded to **New Jersey** by **Dallas** with Reid Simpson for future considerations, March 21, 1994. • Played w/ RHI's Edmonton Sled Dogs in 1994 (22-3-10-13-26).

• MITCHELL, Willie

Willie Reid D – L. 6'3", 205 lbs. b: Pt. McNeill, B.C., 4/23/1977. New Jersey's 12th, 199th overall, in 1996.

Season	Club	League	GP	G	A	Pts	AG	AA	APts	PIM	PP	SH	GW	S	%	TGF	PGF	TGA	PGA	+/–	GP	G	A	Pts	PIM	PP	SH	GW
1995-96	Melfort Mustangs	SJHL	19	2	6	8	....	....	....		....	....	....	....	....	....	....	....	....	....	14	0	2	2	12	....	....	....
1996-97	Melfort Mustangs	SJHL	64	14	42	56	....	....	....	227	....	....	....	....	....	....	....	....	....	....	4	0	1	1	23	....	....	....
1997-98	Clarkson University	ECAC	34	9	17	26	....	....	....	105	....	....	....	....	....	....	....	....	....	....	....	....	....	....	....	....	....	....
1998-99	Clarkson University	ECAC	34	10	19	29	....	....	....	40	....	....	....	....	....	....	....	....	....	....	....	....	....	....	....	....	....	....
	Albany River Rats	AHL	6	1	3	4	....	....	....	29	....	....	....	....	....	....	....	....	....	....	....	....	....	....	....	....	....	....
99-2000	**New Jersey Devils**	**NHL**	**2**	**0**	**0**	**0**	**0**	**0**	**0**	**0**	**0**	**0**	**0**	**2**	**0.0**	**1**	**0**	**0**	**0**	**1**	....	....	....	....	....	....	....	....
	Albany River Rats	AHL	63	5	14	19	....	....	....	71	....	....	....	....	....	....	....	....	....	....	5	1	2	3	4	....	....	....
	NHL Totals		**2**	**0**	**0**	**0**	**0**	**0**	**0**	**0**	**0**	**0**	**0**	**2**	**0.0**	**1**	**0**	**0**	**0**		....	....	....	....	....	....	....	....

ECAC Second All-Star Team (1998) • ECAC First All-Star Team (1999) • NCAA East Second All-American Team (1999)

• MODANO, Mike

C – L. 6'3", 205 lbs. b: Livonia, MI, 6/7/1970. Minnesota's 1st, 1st overall, in 1988.

Season	Club	League	GP	G	A	Pts	AG	AA	APts	PIM	PP	SH	GW	S	%	TGF	PGF	TGA	PGA	+/–	GP	G	A	Pts	PIM	PP	SH	GW
1985-86	Detroit Compuware	MNHL	69	66	65	131	....	....	....	32	....	....	....	....	....	....	....	....	....	....	....	....	....	....	....	....	....	....
1986-87	Prince Albert Raiders	WHL	70	32	30	62	....	....	....	96	....	....	....	....	....	....	....	....	....	....	8	1	4	5	4	....	....	....
1987-88	Prince Albert Raiders	WHL	65	47	80	127	....	....	....	80	....	....	....	....	....	....	....	....	....	....	9	7	11	18	18	....	....	....
	United States	WJC-A	7	4	1	5	....	....	....	8	....	....	....	....	....	....	....	....	....	....	....	....	....	....	....	....	....	....
1988-89	Prince Albert Raiders	WHL	41	39	66	105	....	....	....	74	....	....	....	....	....	....	....	....	....	....	....	....	....	....	....	....	....	....
	United States	WJC-A	7	6	9	15	....	....	....	12	....	....	....	....	....	....	....	....	....	....	....	....	....	....	....	....	....	....
	Minnesota North Stars	**NHL**	....	....	....	....	....	....	....	....	....	....	....	....	....	....	....	....	....	....	**2**	**0**	**0**	**0**	**0**	**0**	**0**	**0**
1989-90	**Minnesota North Stars**	**NHL**	**80**	**29**	**46**	**75**	**25**	**33**	**58**	**63**	**12**	**0**	**2**	**172**	**16.9**	**109**	**49**	**67**	**0**	**–7**	**7**	**1**	**1**	**2**	**12**	**0**	**0**	**0**
	United States	WEC-A	8	3	3	6	....	....	....	2	....	....	....	....	....	....	....	....	....	....	....	....	....	....	....	....	....	....
1990-91	Minnesota North Stars	Fr-Tour	4	3	0	3	....	....	....	2	....	....	....	....	....	....	....	....	....	....	....	....	....	....	....	....	....	....
	Minnesota North Stars	**NHL**	**79**	**28**	**36**	**64**	**26**	**27**	**53**	**65**	**9**	**0**	**2**	**232**	**12.1**	**95**	**38**	**59**	**4**	**2**	**23**	**8**	**12**	**20**	**16**	**3**	**0**	**1**
1991-92	United States	Can-Cup	8	2	7	9	....	....	....	2	....	....	....	....	....	....	....	....	....	....	....	....	....	....	....	....	....	....
	Minnesota North Stars	**NHL**	**76**	**33**	**44**	**77**	**30**	**33**	**63**	**46**	**5**	**0**	**8**	**256**	**12.9**	**102**	**38**	**75**	**2**	**–9**	**7**	**3**	**2**	**5**	**4**	**1**	**0**	**0**
1992-93	**Minnesota North Stars**	**NHL**	**82**	**33**	**60**	**93**	**27**	**41**	**68**	**83**	**9**	**0**	**7**	**307**	**10.7**	**130**	**59**	**90**	**12**	**–7**	....	....	....	....	....	....	....	....
	United States	WC-A	6	0	0	0	....	....	....	2	....	....	....	....	....	....	....	....	....	....	....	....	....	....	....	....	....	....
1993-94	**Dallas Stars**	**NHL**	**76**	**50**	**43**	**93**	**47**	**33**	**80**	**54**	**18**	**0**	**4**	**281**	**17.8**	**111**	**53**	**69**	**3**	**–8**	**9**	**7**	**3**	**10**	**16**	**2**	**0**	**2**
1994-95	**Dallas Stars**	**NHL**	**30**	**12**	**17**	**29**	**21**	**25**	**46**	**8**	**4**	**1**	**0**	**100**	**12.0**	**38**	**16**	**19**	**4**	**7**	....	....	....	....	....	....	....	....
1995-96	**Dallas Stars**	**NHL**	**78**	**36**	**45**	**81**	**35**	**37**	**72**	**63**	**8**	**4**	**4**	**320**	**11.3**	**112**	**49**	**99**	**24**	**–12**	....	....	....	....	....	....	....	....
1996-97	United States	W-Cup	7	2	4	6	....	....	....	4	....	....	....	....	....	....	....	....	....	....	....	....	....	....	....	....	....	....
	Dallas Stars	**NHL**	**80**	**35**	**48**	**83**	**37**	**43**	**80**	**42**	**9**	**5**	**9**	**291**	**12.0**	**113**	**31**	**65**	**26**	**43**	**7**	**4**	**1**	**5**	**0**	**1**	**1**	**2**
1997-98	**Dallas Stars**	**NHL**	**52**	**21**	**38**	**59**	**25**	**37**	**62**	**32**	**7**	**5**	**2**	**191**	**11.0**	**76**	**28**	**30**	**7**	**25**	**17**	**4**	**10**	**14**	**12**	**1**	**0**	**1**
	United States	Olympics	4	2	0	2	....	....	....	0	....	....	....	....	....	....	....	....	....	....	....	....	....	....	....	....	....	....
1998-99♦	**Dallas Stars**	**NHL**	**77**	**34**	**47**	**81**	**40**	**45**	**85**	**44**	**6**	**4**	**7**	**224**	**15.2**	**114**	**47**	**54**	**16**	**29**	**23**	**5**	***18**	**23**	**16**	**1**	**1**	**1**
99-2000	**Dallas Stars**	**NHL**	**77**	**38**	**43**	**81**	**43**	**40**	**83**	**48**	**11**	**1**	**8**	**188**	**20.2**	**101**	**39**	**77**	**15**	**0**	**23**	**10**	***13**	**23**	**10**	**4**	**0**	**2**
	NHL Totals		**787**	**349**	**467**	**816**	**356**	**394**	**750**	**548**	**98**	**20**	**53**	**2562**	**13.6**	**1101**	**447**	**704**	**113**		**118**	**42**	**60**	**102**	**86**	**13**	**2**	**9**

WHL East All-Star Team (1989) • NHL All-Rookie Team (1990) • NHL Second All-Star Team (2000) • Played in NHL All-Star Game (1993, 1998, 1999, 2000)

Transferred to **Dallas** after **Minnesota** franchise relocated, June 9, 1993.

Season	Club	League	GP	G	A	Pts	AG	AA	APts	PIM	PP	SH	GW	S	%	TGF	PGF	TGA	PGA	+/–	GP	G	A	Pts	PIM	PP	SH	GW
			REGULAR SEASON																		PLAYOFFS							

• MODIN, Fredrik

LW – L. 6'4", 220 lbs. b: Sundsvall, Sweden, 10/8/1974. Toronto's 3rd, 64th overall, in 1994.

Season	Club	League	GP	G	A	Pts	AG	AA	APts	PIM	PP	SH	GW	S	%	TGF	PGF	TGA	PGA	+/–	GP	G	A	Pts	PIM	PP	SH	GW
1991-92	Timra IF	Sweden 2	11	1	0	1				0																		
1992-93	Timra IF	Sweden 2	30	5	7	12				12											5	1	0	1	0			
1993-94	Timra IF	Sweden 2	30	16	15	31				36											2	0	1	1	6			
	Sweden	WJC-A	7	2	2	4				2																		
1994-95	Brynas IF Gavle	Sweden	38	9	10	19				33											14	4	4	8	6			
1995-96	Brynas IF Gavle	Sweden	22	4	8	12				22																		
	Sweden	WC-A	6	1	1	2				4																		
1996-97	**Toronto Maple Leafs**	**NHL**	**76**	**6**	**7**	**13**	**6**	**6**	**12**	**24**	**0**	**0**	**0**	**85**	**7.1**	**32**	**6**	**40**	**0**	**–14**								
1997-98	**Toronto Maple Leafs**	**NHL**	**74**	**16**	**16**	**32**	**19**	**16**	**35**	**32**	**1**	**0**	**4**	**137**	**11.7**	**44**	**5**	**44**	**0**	**–5**								
	Sweden	WC-A	5	3	3	6				2																		
1998-99	**Toronto Maple Leafs**	**NHL**	**67**	**16**	**15**	**31**	**19**	**14**	**33**	**35**	**1**	**0**	**3**	**108**	**14.8**	**52**	**2**	**36**	**0**	**14**	**8**	**0**	**0**	**0**	**6**	**0**	**0**	**0**
99-2000	**Tampa Bay Lightning**	**NHL**	**80**	**22**	**26**	**48**	**25**	**24**	**49**	**18**	**3**	**0**	**5**	**167**	**13.2**	**63**	**16**	**73**	**0**	**–26**								
	Sweden	WC-A	7	3	1	4				4																		
	NHL Totals		**297**	**60**	**64**	**124**	**69**	**60**	**129**	**109**	**5**	**0**	**12**	**497**	**12.1**	**191**	**29**	**193**	**0**		**8**	**0**	**0**	**0**	**6**	**0**	**0**	**0**

Traded to **Tampa Bay** by **Toronto** for Cory Cross and Tampa Bay's 7th round choice in 2001 Entry Draft, October 1, 1999.

• MODRY, Jaroslav

D – L. 6'2", 215 lbs. b: Ceske-Budejovice, Czech., 2/27/1971. New Jersey's 11th, 179th overall, in 1990.

Season	Club	League	GP	G	A	Pts	AG	AA	APts	PIM	PP	SH	GW	S	%	TGF	PGF	TGA	PGA	+/–	GP	G	A	Pts	PIM	PP	SH	GW
1987-88	Motor Ceske Budejovice	Czech.	3	0	0	0				0																		
1988-89	Motor Ceske Budejovice	Czech.	28	0	1	1				8																		
	Czechoslovakia	EJC-A	6	2	2	4				12																		
1989-90	Motor Ceske Budejovice	Czech.	41	2	2	4																						
1990-91	Dukla Trencin	Czech.	33	1	9	10				6																		
	Czechoslovakia	WJC-A	6	0	1	1				2																		
1991-92	Dukla Trencin	Czech.	18	0	4	4				6																		
	Motor Ceske Budejovice	Czech-2	14	4	10	14																						
1992-93	Utica Devils	AHL	80	7	35	42				62											5	0	2	2	2			
1993-94	**New Jersey Devils**	**NHL**	**41**	**2**	**15**	**17**	**2**	**12**	**14**	**18**	**2**	**0**	**0**	**35**	**5.7**	**48**	**8**	**35**	**5**	**10**								
	Albany River Rats	AHL	19	1	5	6				25																		
1994-95	HC Ceske Budejovice	Czech-Rep	19	1	3	4				30																		
	New Jersey Devils	**NHL**	**11**	**0**	**0**	**0**	**0**	**0**	**0**	**0**	**0**	**0**	**0**	**10**	**0.0**	**3**	**0**	**4**	**0**	**–1**								
	Albany River Rats	AHL	18	5	6	11				14											14	3	3	6	4			
1995-96	**Ottawa Senators**	**NHL**	**64**	**4**	**14**	**18**	**4**	**11**	**15**	**38**	**1**	**0**	**1**	**89**	**4.5**	**48**	**11**	**67**	**13**	**–17**								
	Los Angeles Kings	**NHL**	**9**	**0**	**3**	**3**	**0**	**2**	**2**	**6**	**0**	**0**	**0**	**17**	**0.0**	**12**	**1**	**18**	**3**	**–4**								
1996-97	**Los Angeles Kings**	**NHL**	**30**	**3**	**3**	**6**	**3**	**3**	**6**	**25**	**1**	**1**	**0**	**32**	**9.4**	**16**	**2**	**31**	**4**	**–13**								
	Phoenix Roadrunners	IHL	23	3	12	15				17																		
	Utah Grizzlies	IHL	11	1	4	5				20											7	0	1	1	6			
1997-98	Utah Grizzlies	IHL	74	12	21	33				72											4	0	2	2	6			
1998-99	**Los Angeles Kings**	**NHL**	**5**	**0**	**1**	**1**	**0**	**1**	**1**	**0**	**0**	**0**	**0**	**11**	**0.0**	**8**	**4**	**6**	**3**	**1**								
	Long Beach Ice Dogs	IHL	64	6	29	35				44											8	4	2	6	4			
99-2000	**Los Angeles Kings**	**NHL**	**26**	**5**	**4**	**9**	**6**	**4**	**10**	**18**	**5**	**0**	**1**	**32**	**15.6**	**22**	**11**	**19**	**6**	**–2**	**2**	**0**	**0**	**0**	**2**	**0**	**0**	**0**
	Long Beach Ice Dogs	IHL	11	2	4	6				8																		
	NHL Totals		**186**	**14**	**40**	**54**	**15**	**33**	**48**	**105**	**9**	**1**	**2**	**226**	**6.2**	**157**	**37**	**180**	**34**		**2**	**0**	**0**	**0**	**2**	**0**	**0**	**0**

Traded to **Ottawa** by **New Jersey** for Ottawa's 4th round choice (Alyn McCauley) in 1995 Entry Draft, July 8, 1995. Traded to **LA Kings** by **Ottawa** with Ottawa's 8th round choice (Stephen Valiquette) in 1996 Entry Draft for Kevin Brown, March 20, 1996.

• MOFFAT, Lyle

Lyle Gordon LW – . 5'10", 180 lbs. b: Calgary, Alta., 3/19/1948.

Season	Club	League	GP	G	A	Pts	AG	AA	APts	PIM	PP	SH	GW	S	%	TGF	PGF	TGA	PGA	+/–	GP	G	A	Pts	PIM	PP	SH	GW
1966-67	Calgary Buffalos	CMJHL	56	30	33	63				64																		
1967-68	Michigan Tech Huskies	WCHA	DID NOT PLAY – FRESHMAN																									
1968-69	Michigan Tech Huskies	WCHA	28	10	19	29				36																		
1969-70	Michigan Tech Huskies	WCHA	29	12	11	23				44																		
1970-71	Michigan Tech Huskies	WCHA	DID NOT PLAY – INJURED																									
1971-72	Tulsa Oilers	CHL	70	15	16	31				82											13	2	4	6	25			
1972-73	**Toronto Maple Leafs**	**NHL**	**1**	**0**	**0**	**0**	**0**	**0**	**0**	**0**	**0**	**0**	**0**	**0**	**0.0**	**0**	**0**	**1**	**0**	**–1**								
	Tulsa Oilers	CHL	71	*40	40	*80				108																		
1973-74	Oklahoma City Blazers	CHL	50	19	30	49				70																		
1974-75	**Toronto Maple Leafs**	**NHL**	**22**	**2**	**7**	**9**	**2**	**5**	**7**	**13**	**0**	**0**	**0**	**18**	**11.1**	**15**	**3**	**14**	**0**	**–2**								
	Oklahoma City Blazers	CHL	39	17	19	36				87											5	3	3	6	18			
1975-76	Cleveland Crusaders	WHA	33	4	7	11				33																		
	Winnipeg Jets	WHA	42	13	9	22				44											13	3	3	6	9			
1976-77	Winnipeg Jets	WHA	74	13	11	24				90											17	2	0	2	6			
1977-78	Winnipeg Jets	WHA	57	9	16	25				39											9	5	7	12	9			
1978-79	Winnipeg Jets	WHA	70	14	18	32				38											10	3	1	4	22			
1979-80	**Winnipeg Jets**	**NHL**	**74**	**10**	**9**	**19**	**8**	**7**	**15**	**38**	**0**	**0**	**1**	**86**	**11.6**	**25**	**1**	**71**	**23**	**–24**								
1980-81	Tulsa Oilers	CHL	66	17	31	48				58											8	4	8	12	8			
	NHL Totals		**97**	**12**	**16**	**28**	**10**	**12**	**22**	**51**	**0**	**0**	**1**	**104**	**11.5**	**40**	**4**	**86**	**23**									
	Other Major League Totals		276	53	61	114				244											49	13	11	24	46			

• Missed entire 1970-71 season recovering from back surgery, June, 1970. Signed as a free agent by **Toronto**, September, 1971. Signed as a free agent by **Cleveland** (WHA), June 3, 1975. Traded to **Winnipeg** (WHA) by **Cleveland** (WHA) for Randy Legge and future considerations, January, 1976. Rights retained by **Winnipeg** prior to Expansion Draft, June 9, 1979.

• MOGER, Sandy

C – R. 6'4", 220 lbs. b: 100 Mile House, B.C., 3/21/1969. Vancouver's 7th, 176th overall, in 1989.

Season	Club	League	GP	G	A	Pts	AG	AA	APts	PIM	PP	SH	GW	S	%	TGF	PGF	TGA	PGA	+/–	GP	G	A	Pts	PIM	PP	SH	GW
1986-87	Vernon Lakers	BCJHL	13	5	4	9				10																		
1987-88	Yorkton Terriers	SJHL	60	39	41	80				144											16	7	6	13				
1988-89	Lake Superior State	CCHA	21	3	5	8				26																		
1989-90	Lake Superior State	CCHA	46	17	15	32				76																		
1990-91	Lake Superior State	CCHA	45	27	21	48				*172																		
1991-92	Lake Superior State	CCHA	38	24	24	48				93																		
1992-93	Hamilton Canucks	AHL	78	23	26	49				57																		
1993-94	Hamilton Canucks	AHL	29	9	8	17				41																		
1994-95	**Boston Bruins**	**NHL**	**18**	**2**	**6**	**8**	**4**	**9**	**13**	**6**	**2**	**0**	**0**	**32**	**6.3**	**19**	**11**	**9**	**0**	**–1**								
	Providence Bruins	AHL	63	32	29	61				105																		
1995-96	**Boston Bruins**	**NHL**	**80**	**15**	**14**	**29**	**15**	**11**	**26**	**65**	**4**	**0**	**6**	**103**	**14.6**	**42**	**7**	**44**	**0**	**–9**	**5**	**2**	**2**	**4**	**12**	**1**	**0**	**0**
1996-97	**Boston Bruins**	**NHL**	**34**	**10**	**3**	**13**	**11**	**3**	**14**	**45**	**3**	**0**	**0**	**54**	**18.5**	**21**	**5**	**29**	**1**	**–12**								
	Providence Bruins	AHL	3	0	2	2				19																		
1997-98	**Los Angeles Kings**	**NHL**	**62**	**11**	**13**	**24**	**13**	**13**	**26**	**70**	**1**	**0**	**2**	**89**	**12.4**	**43**	**11**	**28**	**0**	**4**								
1998-99	**Los Angeles Kings**	**NHL**	**42**	**3**	**2**	**5**	**4**	**2**	**6**	**26**	**0**	**0**	**2**	**28**	**10.7**	**11**	**4**	**16**	**0**	**–9**								
99-2000	Houston Aeros	IHL	45	13	10	23				43											2	1	1	2	4			
	NHL Totals		**236**	**41**	**38**	**79**	**47**	**38**	**85**	**212**	**10**	**0**	**10**	**306**	**13.4**	**136**	**38**	**126**	**1**		**5**	**2**	**2**	**4**	**12**	**1**	**0**	**0**

CCHA Second All-Star Team (1992)

Signed as a free agent by **Boston**, June 22, 1994. • Missed majority of 1996-97 season recovering from elbow injury suffered in game vs. Buffalo, December 14, 1996. Traded to **LA Kings** by **Boston** with Jozef Stumpel and Boston's 4th round choice (later traded to New Jersey — New Jersey selected Pierre Dagenais) in 1998 Entry Draft for Dimitri Khristich and Byron Dafoe, August 29, 1997. Signed as a free agent by **Houston** (IHL), September 6, 1999.

• MOGILNY, Alexander

Alexander Gennadevitch RW – L. 5'11", 200 lbs. b: Khabarovsk, USSR, 2/18/1969. Buffalo's 4th, 89th overall, in 1988.

Season	Club	League	GP	G	A	Pts	AG	AA	APts	PIM	PP	SH	GW	S	%	TGF	PGF	TGA	PGA	+/–	GP	G	A	Pts	PIM	PP	SH	GW
1986-87	CSKA Moscow	USSR	28	15	1	16				4																		
1987-88	CSKA Moscow	USSR	39	12	8	20				14																		
	Soviet Union	WJC-A	7	8	*10	*18				2																		
	Soviet Union	Olympics	6	3	2	5				2																		

			REGULAR SEASON																		PLAYOFFS							
Season	Club	League	GP	G	A	Pts	AG	AA	APts	PIM	PP	SH	GW	S	%	TGF	PGF	TGA	PGA	+/–	GP	G	A	Pts	PIM	PP	SH	GW
1988-89	CSKA Moscow	USSR	31	11	11	22	....	....	....	24	....	....	....	....	....	....	....	....	....	....	....	....	....	....	....	....	....	....
	Soviet Union	WJC-A	7	7	5	12	....	....	....	4	....	....	....	....	....	....	....	....	....	....	....	....	....	....	....	....	....	....
	Soviet Union	WEC-A	10	0	3	3	....	....	....	2	....	....	....	....	....	....	....	....	....	....	....	....	....	....	....	....	....	....
1989-90	**Buffalo Sabres**	**NHL**	**65**	**15**	**28**	**43**	**13**	**20**	**33**	**16**	**4**	**0**	**2**	**130**	**11.5**	**57**	**14**	**35**	**0**	**8**	**4**	**0**	**1**	**1**	**2**	**0**	**0**	**0**
1990-91	**Buffalo Sabres**	**NHL**	**62**	**30**	**34**	**64**	**28**	**26**	**54**	**16**	**3**	**3**	**5**	**201**	**14.9**	**81**	**14**	**63**	**10**	**14**	**6**	**0**	**6**	**6**	**2**	**0**	**0**	**0**
1991-92	**Buffalo Sabres**	**NHL**	**67**	**39**	**45**	**84**	**36**	**34**	**70**	**73**	**15**	**0**	**2**	**236**	**16.5**	**133**	**67**	**71**	**12**	**7**	**2**	**0**	**2**	**2**	**0**	**0**	**0**	**0**
1992-93	**Buffalo Sabres**	**NHL**	**77**	***76**	**51**	**127**	**64**	**35**	**99**	**40**	**27**	**0**	**11**	**360**	**21.1**	**172**	**77**	**89**	**1**	**7**	**7**	**7**	**3**	**10**	**6**	**2**	**0**	**0**
1993-94	**Buffalo Sabres**	**NHL**	**66**	**32**	**47**	**79**	**30**	**37**	**67**	**22**	**17**	**0**	**7**	**258**	**12.4**	**106**	**56**	**42**	**0**	**8**	**7**	**4**	**2**	**6**	**6**	**1**	**0**	**0**
1994-95	Spartak	CIS	1	0	1	1	....	....	....	0	....	....	....	....	....	....	....	....	....	....	....	....	....	....	....	....	....	....
	Buffalo Sabres	**NHL**	**44**	**19**	**28**	**47**	**34**	**41**	**75**	**36**	**12**	**0**	**2**	**148**	**12.8**	**62**	**35**	**27**	**0**	**0**	**5**	**3**	**2**	**5**	**2**	**0**	**0**	**0**
1995-96	**Vancouver Canucks**	**NHL**	**79**	**55**	**52**	**107**	**54**	**43**	**97**	**16**	**10**	**5**	**6**	**292**	**18.8**	**135**	**44**	**101**	**24**	**14**	**6**	**1**	**8**	**9**	**8**	**0**	**0**	**0**
1996-97	Russia	W-Cup	5	2	4	6	....	....	....	0	....	....	....	....	....	....	....	....	....	....	....	....	....	....	....	....	....	....
	Vancouver Canucks	**NHL**	**76**	**31**	**42**	**73**	**33**	**37**	**70**	**18**	**7**	**1**	**4**	**174**	**17.8**	**97**	**22**	**73**	**7**	**9**	....	....	....	....	....	....	....	....
1997-98	**Vancouver Canucks**	**NHL**	**51**	**18**	**27**	**45**	**21**	**26**	**47**	**36**	**5**	**4**	**1**	**118**	**15.3**	**62**	**23**	**55**	**10**	**–6**	....	....	....	....	....	....	....	....
1998-99	**Vancouver Canucks**	**NHL**	**59**	**14**	**31**	**45**	**16**	**30**	**46**	**58**	**3**	**2**	**1**	**110**	**12.7**	**65**	**24**	**59**	**18**	**0**	....	....	....	....	....	....	....	....
99-2000	**Vancouver Canucks**	**NHL**	**47**	**21**	**17**	**38**	**24**	**16**	**40**	**16**	**3**	**1**	**1**	**126**	**16.7**	**50**	**9**	**39**	**5**	**7**	....	....	....	....	....	....	....	....
♦	**New Jersey Devils**	**NHL**	**12**	**3**	**3**	**6**	**3**	**3**	**6**	**4**	**2**	**0**	**0**	**35**	**8.6**	**10**	**5**	**10**	**1**	**–4**	**23**	**4**	**3**	**7**	**4**	**2**	**0**	**1**
	NHL Totals		**705**	**353**	**405**	**758**	**356**	**348**	**704**	**351**	**108**	**16**	**42**	**2188**	**16.1**	**1030**	**390**	**664**	**88**		**60**	**19**	**27**	**46**	**30**	**5**	**0**	**1**

WJC-A All-Star Team (1988) • Named Best Forward at WJC-A (1988) • NHL Second All-Star Team (1993, 1996) • Played in NHL All-Star Game (1992, 1993, 1994, 1996)

Traded to **Vancouver** by **Buffalo** with Buffalo's 5th round choice (Todd Norman) in 1995 Entry Draft for Mike Peca, Mike Wilson and Vancouver's 1st round choice (Jay McKee) in 1995 Entry Draft, July 8, 1995. Traded to **New Jersey** by **Vancouver** for Brendan Morrison and Denis Pederson, March 14, 2000.

• MOHER, Mike

RW – R. 5'10", 180 lbs. b: Manitouwadge, Ont., 3/26/1962. New Jersey's 6th, 106th overall, in 1982.

Season	Club	League	GP	G	A	Pts	AG	AA	APts	PIM	PP	SH	GW	S	%	TGF	PGF	TGA	PGA	+/–	GP	G	A	Pts	PIM	PP	SH	GW
1977-78	Schreiber North Stars	NOJHA	20	35	30	65	....	....	....	121	....	....	....	....	....	....	....	....	....	....	....	....	....	....	....	....	....	....
1978-79	Garson Native Sons	NOJHA	40	28	35	63	....	....	....	*248	....	....	....	....	....	....	....	....	....	....	....	....	....	....	....	....	....	....
1979-80	Sudbury Wolves	OMJHL	23	2	5	7	....	....	....	87	....	....	....	....	....	....	....	....	....	....	....	....	....	....	....	....	....	....
	Kitchener Rangers	OMJHL	45	11	21	32	....	....	....	271	....	....	....	....	....	....	....	....	....	....	....	....	....	....	....	....	....	....
1980-81	Kitchener Rangers	OMJHL	51	8	14	22	....	....	....	*372	....	....	....	....	....	....	....	....	....	....	18	3	3	6	*112	....	....	....
	Kitchener Rangers	Mem-Cup	5	2	4	6	....	....	....	*22	....	....	....	....	....	....	....	....	....	....	....	....	....	....	....	....	....	....
1981-82	Kitchener Rangers	OHL	43	13	14	27	....	....	....	*384	....	....	....	....	....	....	....	....	....	....	13	1	4	5	*120	....	....	....
	Kitchener	Mem-Cup	5	1	1	2	....	....	....	*35	....	....	....	....	....	....	....	....	....	....	....	....	....	....	....	....	....	....
1982-83	**New Jersey Devils**	**NHL**	**9**	**0**	**1**	**1**	**0**	**1**	**1**	**28**	**0**	**0**	**0**	**8**	**0.0**	**2**	**0**	**5**	**0**	**–3**	....	....	....	....	....	....	....	....
	Wichita Wind	CHL	48	19	7	26	....	....	....	238	....	....	....	....	....	....	....	....	....	....	....	....	....	....	....	....	....	....
1983-84	Maine Mariners	AHL	25	5	6	11	....	....	....	119	....	....	....	....	....	....	....	....	....	....	....	....	....	....	....	....	....	....
	NHL Totals		**9**	**0**	**1**	**1**	**0**	**1**	**1**	**28**	**0**	**0**	**0**	**8**	**0.0**	**2**	**0**	**5**	**0**		....	....	....	....	....	....	....	....

• MOHNS, Doug

Douglas Allen "Diesel" LW/D – L. 6', 185 lbs. b: Capreol, Ont., 12/13/1933.

Season	Club	League	GP	G	A	Pts	AG	AA	APts	PIM	PP	SH	GW	S	%	TGF	PGF	TGA	PGA	+/–	GP	G	A	Pts	PIM	PP	SH	GW
1950-51	Caperol Caps	NOJHA	STATISTICS NOT AVAILABLE																									
	Barrie Flyers	OHA-Jr.	....	....	....	....	....	....	....	....	....	....	....	....	....	....	....	....	....	....	1	0	0	0	0	....	....	....
	Barrie Flyers	Mem-Cup	4	1	0	1	....	....	....	4	....	....	....	....	....	....	....	....	....	....	....	....	....	....	....	....	....	....
1951-52	Barrie Flyers	OHA-Jr.	53	40	36	76	....	....	....	46	....	....	....	....	....	....	....	....	....	....	....	....	....	....	....	....	....	....
1952-53	Barrie Flyers	OHA-Jr.	56	34	42	76	....	....	....	28	....	....	....	....	....	....	....	....	....	....	15	5	4	9	8	....	....	....
	Barrie Flyers	Mem-Cup	10	6	12	18	....	....	....	14	....	....	....	....	....	....	....	....	....	....	....	....	....	....	....	....	....	....
1953-54	**Boston Bruins**	**NHL**	**70**	**13**	**14**	**27**	**18**	**17**	**35**	**27**											**4**	**1**	**0**	**1**	**4**			
1954-55	**Boston Bruins**	**NHL**	**70**	**14**	**18**	**32**	**18**	**21**	**39**	**82**											**5**	**0**	**0**	**0**	**4**			
1955-56	**Boston Bruins**	**NHL**	**64**	**10**	**8**	**18**	**14**	**9**	**23**	**48**																		
1956-57	**Boston Bruins**	**NHL**	**68**	**6**	**34**	**40**	**8**	**38**	**46**	**89**											**10**	**2**	**3**	**5**	**2**			
1957-58	**Boston Bruins**	**NHL**	**54**	**5**	**16**	**21**	**6**	**16**	**22**	**28**											**12**	**3**	**10**	**13**	**18**			
1958-59	**Boston Bruins**	**NHL**	**47**	**6**	**24**	**30**	**7**	**24**	**31**	**40**											**4**	**0**	**2**	**2**	**12**			
1959-60	**Boston Bruins**	**NHL**	**65**	**20**	**25**	**45**	**23**	**24**	**47**	**62**																		
1960-61	**Boston Bruins**	**NHL**	**65**	**12**	**21**	**33**	**14**	**20**	**34**	**63**																		
1961-62	**Boston Bruins**	**NHL**	**69**	**16**	**29**	**45**	**18**	**28**	**46**	**74**																		
1962-63	**Boston Bruins**	**NHL**	**68**	**7**	**23**	**30**	**8**	**23**	**31**	**63**																		
1963-64	**Boston Bruins**	**NHL**	**70**	**9**	**17**	**26**	**11**	**18**	**29**	**95**																		
1964-65	**Chicago Black Hawks**	**NHL**	**49**	**13**	**20**	**33**	**16**	**20**	**36**	**84**											**14**	**3**	**4**	**7**	**21**			
1965-66	**Chicago Black Hawks**	**NHL**	**70**	**22**	**27**	**49**	**25**	**26**	**51**	**63**											**5**	**1**	**0**	**1**	**4**			
1966-67	**Chicago Black Hawks**	**NHL**	**61**	**25**	**35**	**60**	**29**	**34**	**63**	**58**											**5**	**0**	**5**	**5**	**8**			
1967-68	**Chicago Black Hawks**	**NHL**	**65**	**24**	**29**	**53**	**28**	**29**	**57**	**53**	**5**	**1**	**4**	**161**	**14.9**	**90**	**29**	**61**	**7**	**7**	**11**	**1**	**5**	**6**	**12**	**0**	**0**	**0**
1968-69	**Chicago Black Hawks**	**NHL**	**65**	**22**	**19**	**41**	**23**	**17**	**40**	**47**	**7**	**0**	**2**	**149**	**14.8**	**84**	**19**	**67**	**10**	**8**								
1969-70	**Chicago Black Hawks**	**NHL**	**66**	**6**	**27**	**33**	**6**	**25**	**31**	**46**	**3**	**1**	**1**	**118**	**5.1**	**100**	**22**	**61**	**12**	**29**	**8**	**0**	**2**	**2**	**15**	**0**	**0**	**0**
1970-71	**Chicago Black Hawks**	**NHL**	**39**	**4**	**6**	**10**	**4**	**5**	**9**	**16**	**0**	**1**	**1**	**31**	**12.9**	**27**	**4**	**21**	**3**	**5**								
	Minnesota North Stars	**NHL**	**17**	**2**	**5**	**7**	**2**	**4**	**6**	**14**	**1**	**0**	**0**	**39**	**5.1**	**20**	**6**	**16**	**5**	**3**	**6**	**2**	**2**	**4**	**10**	**1**	**0**	**0**
1971-72	**Minnesota North Stars**	**NHL**	**78**	**6**	**30**	**36**	**6**	**26**	**32**	**82**	**4**	**0**	**3**	**143**	**4.2**	**96**	**34**	**77**	**21**	**6**	**4**	**1**	**2**	**3**	**10**	**1**	**0**	**0**
1972-73	**Minnesota North Stars**	**NHL**	**67**	**4**	**13**	**17**	**4**	**10**	**14**	**52**	**0**	**0**	**1**	**104**	**3.8**	**67**	**16**	**55**	**15**	**11**	**6**	**0**	**1**	**1**	**2**	**0**	**0**	**0**
1973-74	**Atlanta Flames**	**NHL**	**28**	**0**	**3**	**3**	**0**	**2**	**2**	**10**	**0**	**0**	**0**	**25**	**0.0**	**12**	**2**	**24**	**7**	**–7**	....	....	....	....	....	....	....	....
1974-75	**Washington Capitals**	**NHL**	**75**	**2**	**19**	**21**	**2**	**14**	**16**	**54**	**1**	**0**	**0**	**83**	**2.4**	**74**	**17**	**146**	**37**	**–52**	....	....	....	....	....	....	....	....
	NHL Totals		**1390**	**248**	**462**	**710**	**290**	**450**	**740**	**1250**	....	....	....	....	....	....	....	....	....	....	**94**	**14**	**36**	**50**	**122**	....	....	....

Played in NHL All-Star Game (1954, 1958, 1959, 1961, 1962, 1965, 1972)

Traded to **Chicago** by **Boston** for Reggie Fleming and Ab McDonald, June 8, 1964. Traded to **Minnesota** by **Chicago** with Terry Caffery for Danny O'Shea, February 22, 1971. Claimed by **Atlanta** from **Minnesota** in Intra-League Draft, June 12, 1973. Traded to **Washington** by **Atlanta** for cash, June 20, 1974.

• MOKOSAK, Carl

LW – L. 6'1", 180 lbs. b: Fort Saskatchewan, Alta., 9/22/1962.

Season	Club	League	GP	G	A	Pts	AG	AA	APts	PIM	PP	SH	GW	S	%	TGF	PGF	TGA	PGA	+/–	GP	G	A	Pts	PIM	PP	SH	GW
1978-79	Brandon Bobcats	MJHL	44	12	11	23	....	....	....	146	....	....	....	....	....	....	....	....	....	....	....	....	....	....	....	....	....	....
1979-80	Brandon Wheat Kings	WHL	61	12	21	33	....	....	....	226	....	....	....	....	....	....	....	....	....	....	11	0	4	4	66	....	....	....
1980-81	Brandon Wheat Kings	WHL	70	28	44	72	....	....	....	116	....	....	....	....	....	....	....	....	....	....	5	1	3	4	12	....	....	....
1981-82	Brandon Wheat Kings	WHL	69	46	61	107	....	....	....	363	....	....	....	....	....	....	....	....	....	....	4	0	1	1	11	....	....	....
	Calgary Flames	**NHL**	**1**	**0**	**1**	**1**	**0**	**1**	**1**	**0**	**0**	**0**	**0**	**0**	**0.0**	**1**	**0**	**0**	**0**	**1**	....	....	....	....	....	....	....	....
	Oklahoma City Stars	CHL	2	1	1	2	....	....	....	2	....	....	....	....	....	....	....	....	....	....	4	1	1	2	0	....	....	....
1982-83	**Calgary Flames**	**NHL**	**41**	**7**	**6**	**13**	**6**	**4**	**10**	**87**	**0**	**0**	**0**	**38**	**18.4**	**19**	**0**	**24**	**0**	**–5**	....	....	....	....	....	....	....	....
	Colorado Flames	CHL	28	10	12	22	....	....	....	106	....	....	....	....	....	....	....	....	....	....	5	1	0	1	12	....	....	....
1983-84	New Haven Nighthawks	AHL	80	18	21	39	....	....	....	206	....	....	....	....	....	....	....	....	....	....	....	....	....	....	....	....	....	....
1984-85	**Los Angeles Kings**	**NHL**	**30**	**4**	**8**	**12**	**3**	**5**	**8**	**43**	**0**	**0**	**0**	**29**	**13.8**	**14**	**0**	**23**	**1**	**–8**	....	....	....	....	....	....	....	....
	New Haven Nighthawks	AHL	11	6	6	12	....	....	....	26	....	....	....	....	....	....	....	....	....	....	....	....	....	....	....	....	....	....
1985-86	**Philadelphia Flyers**	**NHL**	**1**	**0**	**0**	**0**	**0**	**0**	**0**	**5**	**0**	**0**	**0**	**0**	**0.0**	**0**	**0**	**0**	**0**	**0**	....	....	....	....	....	....	....	....
	Hershey Bears	AHL	79	30	42	72	....	....	....	312	....	....	....	....	....	....	....	....	....	....	16	0	4	4	111	....	....	....
1986-87	**Pittsburgh Penguins**	**NHL**	**3**	**0**	**0**	**0**	**0**	**0**	**0**	**4**	**0**	**0**	**0**	**3**	**0.0**	**0**	**0**	**4**	**0**	**–4**	....	....	....	....	....	....	....	....
	Baltimore Skipjacks	AHL	67	23	27	50	....	....	....	228	....	....	....	....	....	....	....	....	....	....	....	....	....	....	....	....	....	....
1987-88	Muskegon Lumberjacks	IHL	81	29	37	66	....	....	....	308	....	....	....	....	....	....	....	....	....	....	6	3	2	5	60	....	....	....
1988-89	**Boston Bruins**	**NHL**	**7**	**0**	**0**	**0**	**0**	**0**	**0**	**31**	**0**	**0**	**0**	**3**	**0.0**	**0**	**0**	**2**	**0**	**–2**	**1**	**0**	**0**	**0**	**0**	**0**	**0**	**0**
	Maine Mariners	AHL	53	20	18	38	....	....	....	337	....	....	....	....	....	....	....	....	....	....	....	....	....	....	....	....	....	....
1989-90	Fort Wayne Komets	IHL	55	12	21	33	....	....	....	315	....	....	....	....	....	....	....	....	....	....	....	....	....	....	....	....	....	....
	Phoenix Roadrunners	IHL	15	6	6	12	....	....	....	48	....	....	....	....	....	....	....	....	....	....	....	....	....	....	....	....	....	....
1990-91	Indianapolis Ice	IHL	70	12	26	38	....	....	....	205	....	....	....	....	....	....	....	....	....	....	5	0	0	0	2	....	....	....
	San Diego Gulls	IHL	5	0	0	0	....	....	....	30	....	....	....	....	....	....	....	....	....	....	....	....	....	....	....	....	....	....
	NHL Totals		**83**	**11**	**15**	**26**	**9**	**10**	**19**	**170**	**0**	**0**	**0**	**73**	**15.1**	**34**	**0**	**53**	**1**		**1**	**0**	**0**	**0**	**0**	**0**	**0**	**0**

• Brother of John

Signed as a free agent by **Calgary**, July 21, 1981. Traded to **LA Kings** by **Calgary** with Kevin LaVallee for Steve Bozek, June 20, 1983. Signed as a free agent by **Philadelphia**, July 23, 1985. Signed as a free agent by **Pittsburgh**, July 23, 1986. Signed as a free agent by **Boston**, October 4, 1988.

• MOKOSAK, John

John W. D – L. 5'11", 200 lbs. b: Edmonton, Alta., 9/7/1963. Hartford's 6th, 130th overall, in 1981.

			REGULAR SEASON																		PLAYOFFS							
Season	Club	League	GP	G	A	Pts	AG	AA	APts	PIM	PP	SH	GW	S	%	TGF	PGF	TGA	PGA	+/–	GP	G	A	Pts	PIM	PP	SH	GW
1979-80	Fort Saskatchewan Traders	AJHL	58	5	13	18	....	....	....	57	....	....	....	....	....	....	....	....	....	....	....	....	....	....	....	....	....	....
1980-81	Victoria Cougars	WHL	71	2	18	20	....	....	....	59	....	....	....	....	....	....	....	....	....	....	15	0	3	3	53	....	....	....
	Victoria Cougars	Mem-Cup	4	0	0	0	....	....	....	2	....	....	....	....	....	....	....	....	....	....	....	....	....	....	....	....	....	....
1981-82	Victoria Cougars	WHL	69	6	45	51	....	....	....	102	....	....	....	....	....	....	....	....	....	....	4	1	1	2	0	....	....	....
1982-83	Victoria Cougars	WHL	70	10	33	43	....	....	....	102	....	....	....	....	....	....	....	....	....	....	12	0	0	0	8	....	....	....
1983-84	Binghamton Whalers	AHL	79	3	21	24	....	....	....	80	....	....	....	....	....	....	....	....	....	....	....	....	....	....	....	....	....	....
1984-85	Binghamton Whalers	AHL	54	1	13	14	....	....	....	109	....	....	....	....	....	....	....	....	....	....	7	0	0	0	12	....	....	....
	Salt Lake Golden Eagles	IHL	22	1	10	11	....	....	....	41	....	....	....	....	....	....	....	....	....	....	....	....	....	....	....	....	....	....
1985-86	Binghamton Whalers	AHL	64	0	9	9	....	....	....	196	....	....	....	....	....	....	....	....	....	....	6	0	0	0	6	....	....	....
1986-87	Binghamton Whalers	AHL	72	2	15	17	....	....	....	187	....	....	....	....	....	....	....	....	....	....	9	0	2	2	42	....	....	....
1987-88	Springfield Indians	AHL	77	1	16	17	....	....	....	178	....	....	....	....	....	....	....	....	....	....	....	....	....	....	....	....	....	....
1988-89	**Detroit Red Wings**	**NHL**	**8**	**0**	**1**	**1**	**0**	**1**	**1**	**14**	**0**	**0**	**0**	**0**	**0.0**	**6**	**0**	**6**	**0**	**0**	....	....	....	....	....	....	....	....
	Adirondack Red Wings	AHL	65	4	31	35	....	....	....	195	....	....	....	....	....	....	....	....	....	....	17	0	5	5	49	....	....	....
1989-90	**Detroit Red Wings**	**NHL**	**33**	**0**	**1**	**1**	**0**	**1**	**1**	**82**	**0**	**0**	**0**	**15**	**0.0**	**16**	**0**	**28**	**3**	**–9**	....	....	....	....	....	....	....	....
	Adirondack Red Wings	AHL	29	2	6	8	....	....	....	80	....	....	....	....	....	....	....	....	....	....	6	1	3	4	13	....	....	....
1990-91	Maine Mariners	AHL	68	1	12	13	....	....	....	194	....	....	....	....	....	....	....	....	....	....	2	0	1	1	4	....	....	....
1991-92	Binghamton Rangers	AHL	28	0	2	2	....	....	....	123	....	....	....	....	....	....	....	....	....	....	9	0	1	1	14	....	....	....
1992-93	Phoenix Roadrunners	IHL	46	4	9	13	....	....	....	169	....	....	....	....	....	....	....	....	....	....	....	....	....	....	....	....	....	....
	NHL Totals		**41**	**0**	**2**	**2**	**0**	**2**	**2**	**96**	**0**	**0**	**0**	**15**	**0.0**	**22**	**0**	**34**	**3**		....	....	....	....	....	....	....	....

• Brother of Carl

Signed as a free agent by **Detroit**, August 29, 1988. Signed as a free agent by **Boston**, July 16, 1990. Signed as a free agent by **NY Rangers**, August 28, 1991.

• MOLIN, Lars

LW – L. 6', 180 lbs. b: Ornskoldsvik, Sweden, 5/7/1956.

Season	Club	League	GP	G	A	Pts	AG	AA	APts	PIM	PP	SH	GW	S	%	TGF	PGF	TGA	PGA	+/–	GP	G	A	Pts	PIM	PP	SH	GW
1973-74	MoDo AIK	Sweden-Jr.	STATISTICS NOT AVAILABLE																									
	MoDo AIK	Sweden	....	....	....	....	....	....	....	....	....	....	....	....	....	....	....	....	....	....	4	0	0	0	0	....	....	....
1974-75	MoDo AIK	Sweden-Jr.	12	12	*33	*45	....	....	....	....	....	....	....	....	....	....	....	....	....	....	2	1	1	2	0	....	....	....
	MoDo AIK	Sweden	5	0	0	0	....	....	....	0	....	....	....	....	....	....	....	....	....	....	....	....	....	....	....	....	....	....
1975-76	MoDo AIK	Sweden	33	12	7	19	....	....	....	22	....	....	....	....	....	....	....	....	....	....	....	....	....	....	....	....	....	....
	Sweden	WJC-A	4	2	0	2	....	....	....	2	....	....	....	....	....	....	....	....	....	....	....	....	....	....	....	....	....	....
1976-77	MoDo AIK	Sweden	36	18	11	29	....	....	....	20	....	....	....	....	....	....	....	....	....	....	4	1	1	2	2	....	....	....
1977-78	MoDo AIK	Sweden	36	15	10	25	....	....	....	24	....	....	....	....	....	....	....	....	....	....	2	1	0	1	0	....	....	....
1978-79	MoDo AIK	Sweden	35	13	15	28	....	....	....	18	....	....	....	....	....	....	....	....	....	....	6	3	1	4	4	....	....	....
	Sweden	Nat-Team	11	4	11	15	....	....	....	14	....	....	....	....	....	....	....	....	....	....	....	....	....	....	....	....	....	....
1979-80	MoDo AIK	Sweden	36	12	8	20	....	....	....	34	....	....	....	....	....	....	....	....	....	....	....	....	....	....	....	....	....	....
	Sweden	Olympics	7	2	5	7	....	....	....	2	....	....	....	....	....	....	....	....	....	....	....	....	....	....	....	....	....	....
1980-81	MoDo AIK	Sweden	30	17	13	30	....	....	....	30	....	....	....	....	....	....	....	....	....	....	....	....	....	....	....	....	....	....
	Sweden	WEC-A	8	2	2	4	....	....	....	4	....	....	....	....	....	....	....	....	....	....	....	....	....	....	....	....	....	....
1981-82	Sweden	Can-Cup	5	2	2	4	....	....	....	0	....	....	....	....	....	....	....	....	....	....	....	....	....	....	....	....	....	....
	Vancouver Canucks	**NHL**	**72**	**15**	**31**	**46**	**12**	**21**	**33**	**10**	**1**	**1**	**4**	**150**	**10.0**	**63**	**16**	**64**	**17**	**0**	**17**	**2**	**9**	**11**	**7**	**0**	**0**	**2**
1982-83	**Vancouver Canucks**	**NHL**	**58**	**12**	**27**	**39**	**10**	**19**	**29**	**23**	**2**	**0**	**1**	**128**	**9.4**	**66**	**29**	**79**	**22**	**–20**	....	....	....	....	....	....	....	....
1983-84	**Vancouver Canucks**	**NHL**	**42**	**6**	**7**	**13**	**5**	**5**	**10**	**4**	**0**	**1**	**0**	**47**	**12.8**	**19**	**2**	**38**	**12**	**–9**	**2**	**0**	**0**	**0**	**0**	**0**	**0**	**0**
1984-85	MoDo AIK	Sweden-2	32	21	*36	57	....	....	....	22	....	....	....	....	....	....	....	....	....	....	....	....	....	....	....	....	....	....
	Sweden	WEC-A	5	1	2	3	....	....	....	2	....	....	....	....	....	....	....	....	....	....	....	....	....	....	....	....	....	....
1985-86	MoDo AIK	Sweden	34	19	19	38	....	....	....	24	....	....	....	....	....	....	....	....	....	....	....	....	....	....	....	....	....	....
1986-87	MoDo AIK	Sweden	34	8	16	24	....	....	....	42	....	....	....	....	....	....	....	....	....	....	....	....	....	....	....	....	....	....
	Sweden	WEC-A	9	1	1	2	....	....	....	8	....	....	....	....	....	....	....	....	....	....	....	....	....	....	....	....	....	....
1987-88	MoDo AIK	Sweden	24	7	7	14	....	....	....	54	....	....	....	....	....	....	....	....	....	....	4	1	0	1	2	....	....	....
	Sweden	Olympics	7	0	2	2	....	....	....	2	....	....	....	....	....	....	....	....	....	....	....	....	....	....	....	....	....	....
1988-89	Orebro IK	Sweden-2	33	11	26	37	....	....	....	68	....	....	....	....	....	....	....	....	....	....	10	3	7	10	2	....	....	....
1989-90	Orebro IK	Sweden-2	30	23	*42	65	....	....	....	30	....	....	....	....	....	....	....	....	....	....	6	2	6	8	4	....	....	....
1990-91	Orebro IK	Sweden-2	30	16	24	40	....	....	....	28	....	....	....	....	....	....	....	....	....	....	2	0	0	0	2	....	....	....
	NHL Totals		**172**	**33**	**65**	**98**	**27**	**45**	**72**	**37**	**3**	**2**	**5**	**325**	**10.2**	**148**	**47**	**181**	**51**		**19**	**2**	**9**	**11**	**7**	**0**	**0**	**2**

Swedish World All-Star Team (1980)

Signed as a free agent by **Vancouver**, May 18, 1981.

• MOLLER, Mike

Michael John RW – R. 6', 194 lbs. b: Calgary, Alta., 6/16/1962. Buffalo's 2nd, 41st overall, in 1980.

Season	Club	League	GP	G	A	Pts	AG	AA	APts	PIM	PP	SH	GW	S	%	TGF	PGF	TGA	PGA	+/–	GP	G	A	Pts	PIM	PP	SH	GW
1978-79	Red Deer Optomist Chiefs	AAHA	STATISTICS NOT AVAILABLE																									
1979-80	Lethbridge Broncos	WHL	72	30	41	71	....	....	....	55	....	....	....	....	....	....	....	....	....	....	4	0	6	6	0	....	....	....
1980-81	Lethbridge Broncos	WHL	70	39	69	108	....	....	....	71	....	....	....	....	....	....	....	....	....	....	9	6	10	16	12	....	....	....
	Buffalo Sabres	**NHL**	**5**	**2**	**2**	**4**	**2**	**1**	**3**	**0**	**0**	**0**	**0**	**7**	**28.6**	**6**	**0**	**3**	**0**	**3**	**3**	**0**	**1**	**1**	**0**	**0**	**0**	**0**
1981-82	Lethbridge Broncos	WHL	49	41	81	122	....	....	....	38	....	....	....	....	....	....	....	....	....	....	12	5	12	17	9	....	....	....
	Canada	WJC-A	7	5	9	14	....	....	....	4	....	....	....	....	....	....	....	....	....	....	....	....	....	....	....	....	....	....
	Buffalo Sabres	**NHL**	**9**	**0**	**0**	**0**	**0**	**0**	**0**	**0**	**0**	**0**	**0**	**2**	**0.0**	**2**	**0**	**9**	**0**	**–7**	....	....	....	....	....	....	....	....
1982-83	**Buffalo Sabres**	**NHL**	**49**	**6**	**12**	**18**	**5**	**8**	**13**	**14**	**1**	**0**	**3**	**43**	**14.0**	**28**	**1**	**25**	**0**	**2**	....	....	....	....	....	....	....	....
	Rochester Americans	AHL	10	1	6	7	....	....	....	2	....	....	....	....	....	....	....	....	....	....	11	2	4	6	4	....	....	....
1983-84	**Buffalo Sabres**	**NHL**	**59**	**5**	**11**	**16**	**4**	**7**	**11**	**27**	**0**	**0**	**1**	**43**	**11.6**	**31**	**3**	**29**	**3**	**2**	....	....	....	....	....	....	....	....
1984-85	**Buffalo Sabres**	**NHL**	**5**	**0**	**2**	**2**	**0**	**1**	**1**	**0**	**0**	**0**	**0**	**5**	**0.0**	**2**	**0**	**3**	**1**	**0**	....	....	....	....	....	....	....	....
	Rochester Americans	AHL	73	19	46	65	....	....	....	27	....	....	....	....	....	....	....	....	....	....	5	1	1	2	0	....	....	....
1985-86	**Edmonton Oilers**	**NHL**	**1**	**0**	**0**	**0**	**0**	**0**	**0**	**0**	**0**	**0**	**0**	**2**	**0.0**	**0**	**0**	**0**	**0**	**0**	....	....	....	....	....	....	....	....
	Nova Scotia Oilers	AHL	62	16	15	31	....	....	....	24	....	....	....	....	....	....	....	....	....	....	....	....	....	....	....	....	....	....
1986-87	**Edmonton Oilers**	**NHL**	**6**	**2**	**1**	**3**	**2**	**1**	**3**	**0**	**0**	**0**	**0**	**10**	**20.0**	**3**	**0**	**2**	**1**	**2**	....	....	....	....	....	....	....	....
	Nova Scotia Oilers	AHL	70	14	33	47	....	....	....	28	....	....	....	....	....	....	....	....	....	....	1	0	0	0	0	....	....	....
1987-88	Nova Scotia Oilers	AHL	60	12	31	43	....	....	....	14	....	....	....	....	....	....	....	....	....	....	5	3	0	3	0	....	....	....
1988-89	Canada	Nat-Team	58	18	16	34	....	....	....	18	....	....	....	....	....	....	....	....	....	....	....	....	....	....	....	....	....	....
1989-90	Binghamton Whalers	AHL	12	1	2	3	....	....	....	6	....	....	....	....	....	....	....	....	....	....	....	....	....	....	....	....	....	....
	NHL Totals		**134**	**15**	**28**	**43**	**13**	**18**	**31**	**41**	**1**	**0**	**4**	**112**	**13.4**	**72**	**4**	**71**	**5**		**3**	**0**	**1**	**1**	**0**	**0**	**0**	**0**

• Brother of Randy • WHL All-Star Team (1981) • WJC-A All-Star Team (1982) • WHL First All-Star Team (1982)

Traded to **Pittsburgh** by **Buffalo** with Randy Cunneyworth for Pat Hughes, October 4, 1985. Traded to **Edmonton** by **Pittsburgh** for Pat Hughes, October 4, 1985.

• MOLLER, Randy

Randy W. D – R. 6'2", 210 lbs. b: Red Deer, Alta., 8/23/1963. Quebec's 1st, 11th overall, in 1981.

Season	Club	League	GP	G	A	Pts	AG	AA	APts	PIM	PP	SH	GW	S	%	TGF	PGF	TGA	PGA	+/–	GP	G	A	Pts	PIM	PP	SH	GW
1978-79	Red Deer Optomist Chiefs	AAHA	STATISTICS NOT AVAILABLE																									
1979-80	Red Deer Rustlers	AJHL	56	3	34	37	....	....	....	253	....	....	....	....	....	....	....	....	....	....	....	....	....	....	....	....	....	....
	Billings Bighorns	WHL	2	0	0	0	....	....	....	4	....	....	....	....	....	....	....	....	....	....	....	....	....	....	....	....	....	....
	Red Deer Rustlers	Cen-Cup	STATISTICS NOT AVAILABLE																									
1980-81	Lethbridge Broncos	WHL	46	4	21	25	....	....	....	176	....	....	....	....	....	....	....	....	....	....	9	0	4	4	24	....	....	....
1981-82	Lethbridge Broncos	WHL	60	20	55	75	....	....	....	249	....	....	....	....	....	....	....	....	....	....	12	4	6	10	65	....	....	....
	Canada	WJC-A	7	0	3	3	....	....	....	4	....	....	....	....	....	....	....	....	....	....	....	....	....	....	....	....	....	....
	Quebec Nordiques	**NHL**	....	....	....	....	....	....	....	....	....	....	....	....	....	....	....	....	....	....	**1**	**0**	**0**	**0**	**0**	**0**	**0**	**0**
1982-83	**Quebec Nordiques**	**NHL**	**75**	**2**	**12**	**14**	**2**	**8**	**10**	**145**	**0**	**0**	**1**	**72**	**2.8**	**74**	**1**	**88**	**26**	**11**	**4**	**1**	**0**	**1**	**4**	**1**	**0**	**1**
1983-84	**Quebec Nordiques**	**NHL**	**74**	**4**	**14**	**18**	**3**	**10**	**13**	**147**	**0**	**0**	**1**	**78**	**5.1**	**93**	**3**	**82**	**18**	**26**	**9**	**1**	**0**	**1**	**45**	**0**	**0**	**0**
1984-85	**Quebec Nordiques**	**NHL**	**79**	**7**	**22**	**29**	**6**	**15**	**21**	**120**	**0**	**0**	**0**	**126**	**5.6**	**101**	**5**	**94**	**27**	**29**	**18**	**2**	**2**	**4**	**40**	**1**	**0**	**0**
1985-86	**Quebec Nordiques**	**NHL**	**69**	**5**	**18**	**23**	**4**	**12**	**16**	**141**	**0**	**0**	**1**	**105**	**4.8**	**78**	**7**	**98**	**36**	**9**	**3**	**0**	**0**	**0**	**26**	**0**	**0**	**0**
1986-87	**Quebec Nordiques**	**NHL**	**71**	**5**	**9**	**14**	**4**	**7**	**11**	**144**	**1**	**0**	**1**	**106**	**4.7**	**70**	**1**	**102**	**22**	**–11**	**13**	**1**	**4**	**5**	**23**	**0**	**0**	**0**
1987-88	**Quebec Nordiques**	**NHL**	**66**	**3**	**22**	**25**	**3**	**16**	**19**	**169**	**0**	**0**	**2**	**116**	**2.6**	**66**	**8**	**106**	**37**	**–11**	....	....	....	....	....	....	....	....
1988-89	**Quebec Nordiques**	**NHL**	**74**	**7**	**22**	**29**	**6**	**16**	**22**	**136**	**2**	**0**	**0**	**117**	**6.0**	**85**	**15**	**98**	**30**	**2**	....	....	....	....	....	....	....	....
1989-90	**New York Rangers**	**NHL**	**60**	**1**	**12**	**13**	**1**	**9**	**10**	**139**	**0**	**0**	**0**	**47**	**2.1**	**46**	**1**	**63**	**17**	**–1**	**10**	**1**	**6**	**7**	**32**	**0**	**0**	**0**
1990-91	**New York Rangers**	**NHL**	**61**	**4**	**19**	**23**	**4**	**14**	**18**	**161**	**1**	**0**	**0**	**75**	**5.3**	**85**	**21**	**64**	**13**	**13**	**6**	**0**	**2**	**2**	**11**	**0**	**0**	**0**

			REGULAR SEASON																		PLAYOFFS							
Season	**Club**	**League**	**GP**	**G**	**A**	**Pts**	**AG**	**AA**	**APts**	**PIM**	**PP**	**SH**	**GW**	**S**	**%**	**TGF**	**PGF**	**TGA**	**PGA**	**+/–**	**GP**	**G**	**A**	**Pts**	**PIM**	**PP**	**SH**	**GW**
1991-92	**New York Rangers**	**NHL**	**43**	**2**	**7**	**9**	**2**	**5**	**7**	**78**	**0**	**0**	**1**	**44**	**4.5**	**33**	**3**	**55**	**10**	**–15**	....	....	....	....	....	....	....	....
	Binghamton Rangers	AHL	3	0	1	1	....	....	....	0	....	....	....	....	....	....	....	....	....	....	....	....	....	....	....	....	....	....
	Buffalo Sabres	**NHL**	**13**	**1**	**2**	**3**	**1**	**2**	**3**	**59**	**0**	**0**	**0**	**19**	**5.3**	**6**	**0**	**11**	**6**	**1**	**7**	**0**	**0**	**0**	**8**	**0**	**0**	**0**
1992-93	**Buffalo Sabres**	**NHL**	**35**	**2**	**7**	**9**	**2**	**5**	**7**	**83**	**0**	**0**	**0**	**25**	**8.0**	**30**	**1**	**33**	**10**	**6**	....	....	....	....	....	....	....	....
	Rochester Americans	AHL	3	1	0	1	....	....	....	10	....	....	....	....	....	....	....	....	....	....	....	....	....	....	....	....	....	....
1993-94	**Buffalo Sabres**	**NHL**	**78**	**2**	**11**	**13**	**2**	**9**	**11**	**154**	**0**	**0**	**0**	**77**	**2.6**	**56**	**4**	**68**	**11**	**–5**	**7**	**0**	**2**	**2**	**8**	**0**	**0**	**0**
1994-95	**Florida Panthers**	**NHL**	**17**	**0**	**3**	**3**	**0**	**4**	**4**	**16**	**0**	**0**	**0**	**12**	**0.0**	**7**	**0**	**14**	**2**	**–5**	....	....	....	....	....	....	....	....
	NHL Totals		**815**	**45**	**180**	**225**	**40**	**132**	**172**	**1692**	**4**	**0**	**7**	**1019**	**4.4**	**830**	**70**	**976**	**265**		**78**	**6**	**16**	**22**	**197**	**2**	**0**	**1**

• Brother of Mike • WHL Second All-Star Team (1982)

Traded to **NY Rangers** by **Quebec** for Michel Petit, October 5, 1989. Traded to **Buffalo** by **NY Rangers** for Jay Wells, March 9, 1992. Signed as a free agent by **Florida**, July 11, 1994.

• MOLLOY, Mitch

Mitchell Dennis LW – L. 6'3", 212 lbs. b: Red Lake, Ont., 10/10/1966.

Season	Club	League	GP	G	A	Pts	AG	AA	APts	PIM	PP	SH	GW	S	%	TGF	PGF	TGA	PGA	+/–	GP	G	A	Pts	PIM	PP	SH	GW
1986-87	Camrose Lutheran College	CCAA	23	9	4	13	....	....	....	70	....	....	....	....	....	....	....	....	....	....	....	....	....	....	....	....	....	....
1987-88	Virginia Lancers	AAHL	43	26	45	71	....	....	....	196	....	....	....	....	....	....	....	....	....	....	8	5	4	9	63	....	....	....
1988-89	Maine Mariners	AHL	47	1	8	9	....	....	....	177	....	....	....	....	....	....	....	....	....	....	....	....	....	....	....	....	....	....
	Flint Spirits	IHL	5	1	1	2	....	....	....	21	....	....	....	....	....	....	....	....	....	....	....	....	....	....	....	....	....	....
1989-90	Johnstown Chiefs	ECHL	18	10	10	20	....	....	....	102	....	....	....	....	....	....	....	....	....	....	....	....	....	....	....	....	....	....
	Buffalo Sabres	**NHL**	**2**	**0**	**0**	**0**	**0**	**0**	**0**	**10**	**0**	**0**	**0**	**0**	**0.0**	**0**	**0**	**0**	**0**	**0**	....	....	....	....	....	....	....	....
	Rochester Americans	AHL	15	1	1	2	....	....	....	43	....	....	....	....	....	....	....	....	....	....	....	....	....	....	....	....	....	....
1990-91	Rochester Americans	AHL	25	1	0	1	....	....	....	127	....	....	....	....	....	....	....	....	....	....	....	....	....	....	....	....	....	....
1991-92	St. Thomas Wildcats	ColHL	52	26	33	59	....	....	....	149	....	....	....	....	....	....	....	....	....	....	10	9	5	14	30	....	....	....
1992-93	San Diego Gulls	IHL	8	0	0	0	....	....	....	8	....	....	....	....	....	....	....	....	....	....	....	....	....	....	....	....	....	....
	St. Thomas Wildcats	ColHL	9	2	6	8	....	....	....	14	....	....	....	....	....	....	....	....	....	....	12	6	3	9	39	....	....	....
	NHL Totals		**2**	**0**	**0**	**0**	**0**	**0**	**0**	**10**	**0**	**0**	**0**	**0**	**0.0**	**0**	**0**	**0**	**0**		....	....	....	....	....	....	....	....

Signed as a free agent by **Buffalo**, Februrary, 1990.

• MOMESSO, Sergio

Sergio F. LW – L. 6'3", 215 lbs. b: Montreal, Que., 9/4/1965. Montreal's 3rd, 27th overall, in 1983.

Season	Club	League	GP	G	A	Pts	AG	AA	APts	PIM	PP	SH	GW	S	%	TGF	PGF	TGA	PGA	+/–	GP	G	A	Pts	PIM	PP	SH	GW
1980-81	Montreal Concordia	QAAA	46	18	17	35	....	....	....	....	....	....	....	....	....	....	....	....	....	....	....	....	....	....	....	....	....	....
1981-82	Montreal Concordia	QAAA	45	30	38	68	....	....	....	....	....	....	....	....	....	....	....	....	....	....	....	....	....	....	....	....	....	....
1982-83	Shawinigan Cataractes	QMJHL	70	27	42	69	....	....	....	93	....	....	....	....	....	....	....	....	....	....	10	5	4	9	55	....	....	....
1983-84	Shawinigan Cataractes	QMJHL	68	42	88	130	....	....	....	235	....	....	....	....	....	....	....	....	....	....	6	4	4	8	13	....	....	....
	Montreal Canadiens	**NHL**	**1**	**0**	**0**	**0**	**0**	**0**	**0**	**0**	**0**	**0**	**0**	**0**	**0.0**	**1**	**0**	**0**	**0**	**1**	....	....	....	....	....	....	....	....
	Nova Scotia Voyageurs	AHL	....	....	....	....	....	....	....	....	....	....	....	....	....	....	....	....	....	....	8	0	2	2	4	....	....	....
1984-85	Shawinigan Cataractes	QMJHL	64	56	90	146	....	....	....	216	....	....	....	....	....	....	....	....	....	....	8	7	8	15	17	....	....	....
	Shawinigan Cataractes	Mem-Cup	4	1	4	5	....	....	....	18	....	....	....	....	....	....	....	....	....	....	....	....	....	....	....	....	....	....
1985-86	**Montreal Canadiens**	**NHL**	**24**	**8**	**7**	**15**	**6**	**5**	**11**	**46**	**3**	**0**	**3**	**37**	**21.6**	**25**	**10**	**19**	**0**	**–4**	....	....	....	....	....	....	....	....
1986-87	**Montreal Canadiens**	**NHL**	**59**	**14**	**17**	**31**	**12**	**12**	**24**	**96**	**3**	**0**	**4**	**95**	**14.7**	**18**	**3**	**14**	**0**	**1**	**11**	**1**	**3**	**4**	**31**	**0**	**0**	**0**
	Sherbrooke Canadiens	AHL	6	1	6	7	....	....	....	10	....	....	....	....	....	....	....	....	....	....	....	....	....	....	....	....	....	....
1987-88	**Montreal Canadiens**	**NHL**	**53**	**7**	**14**	**21**	**6**	**10**	**16**	**101**	**1**	**0**	**0**	**72**	**9.7**	**33**	**4**	**20**	**0**	**9**	**6**	**0**	**2**	**2**	**16**	**0**	**0**	**0**
1988-89	**St. Louis Blues**	**NHL**	**53**	**9**	**17**	**26**	**8**	**12**	**20**	**139**	**0**	**0**	**0**	**81**	**11.1**	**41**	**3**	**39**	**0**	**–1**	**10**	**2**	**5**	**7**	**24**	**0**	**0**	**0**
1989-90	**St. Louis Blues**	**NHL**	**79**	**24**	**32**	**56**	**21**	**23**	**44**	**199**	**4**	**0**	**4**	**182**	**13.2**	**94**	**31**	**79**	**1**	**–15**	**12**	**3**	**2**	**5**	**63**	**0**	**0**	**1**
1990-91	**St. Louis Blues**	**NHL**	**59**	**10**	**18**	**28**	**9**	**14**	**23**	**131**	**0**	**0**	**1**	**86**	**11.6**	**42**	**2**	**28**	**0**	**12**	....	....	....	....	....	....	....	....
	Vancouver Canucks	**NHL**	**11**	**6**	**2**	**8**	**5**	**2**	**7**	**43**	**3**	**0**	**2**	**33**	**18.2**	**9**	**3**	**5**	**0**	**1**	**6**	**0**	**3**	**3**	**25**	**0**	**0**	**0**
1991-92	**Vancouver Canucks**	**NHL**	**58**	**20**	**23**	**43**	**18**	**17**	**35**	**198**	**2**	**0**	**3**	**153**	**13.1**	**62**	**15**	**32**	**1**	**16**	**13**	**0**	**5**	**5**	**30**	**0**	**0**	**0**
1992-93	**Vancouver Canucks**	**NHL**	**84**	**18**	**20**	**38**	**15**	**14**	**29**	**200**	**4**	**0**	**1**	**146**	**12.3**	**70**	**16**	**44**	**1**	**11**	**12**	**3**	**0**	**3**	**30**	**0**	**0**	**1**
1993-94	**Vancouver Canucks**	**NHL**	**68**	**14**	**13**	**27**	**13**	**10**	**23**	**149**	**4**	**0**	**1**	**112**	**12.5**	**51**	**11**	**42**	**0**	**–2**	**24**	**3**	**4**	**7**	**56**	**0**	**0**	**1**
1994-95	HC Milano	Italy	2	1	4	5	....	....	....	2	....	....	....	....	....	....	....	....	....	....	....	....	....	....	....	....	....	....
	Vancouver Canucks	**NHL**	**48**	**10**	**15**	**25**	**18**	**22**	**40**	**65**	**6**	**0**	**1**	**82**	**12.2**	**40**	**13**	**29**	**0**	**–2**	**11**	**3**	**1**	**4**	**16**	**1**	**0**	**0**
1995-96	**Toronto Maple Leafs**	**NHL**	**54**	**7**	**8**	**15**	**7**	**7**	**14**	**112**	**4**	**0**	**1**	**91**	**7.7**	**30**	**12**	**29**	**0**	**–11**	....	....	....	....	....	....	....	....
	New York Rangers	**NHL**	**19**	**4**	**4**	**8**	**4**	**3**	**7**	**30**	**2**	**0**	**0**	**35**	**11.4**	**12**	**6**	**8**	**0**	**–2**	**11**	**3**	**1**	**4**	**14**	**0**	**0**	**0**
1996-97	**New York Rangers**	**NHL**	**9**	**0**	**0**	**0**	**0**	**0**	**0**	**11**	**0**	**0**	**0**	**11**	**0.0**	**0**	**0**	**2**	**0**	**–2**	....	....	....	....	....	....	....	....
	St. Louis Blues	**NHL**	**31**	**1**	**3**	**4**	**1**	**3**	**4**	**37**	**0**	**0**	**0**	**32**	**3.1**	**8**	**0**	**12**	**0**	**–4**	**3**	**0**	**0**	**0**	**6**	**0**	**0**	**0**
1997-98	Kolner Haie	Germany	42	14	18	32	....	....	....	*193	....	....	....	....	....	....	....	....	....	....	3	1	2	3	4	....	....	....
	Kolner Haie	EuroHL	6	4	4	8	....	....	....	29	....	....	....	....	....	....	....	....	....	....	....	....	....	....	....	....	....	....
1998-99	Nurnberg Ice Tigers	Germany	47	26	33	59	....	....	....	212	....	....	....	....	....	....	....	....	....	....	13	4	7	11	24	....	....	....
99-2000	Kolner Haie	Germany	51	16	21	37	....	....	....	165	....	....	....	....	....	....	....	....	....	....	10	4	1	5	6	....	....	....
	NHL Totals		**710**	**152**	**193**	**345**	**143**	**154**	**297**	**1557**	**36**	**0**	**21**	**1248**	**12.2**	**536**	**129**	**402**	**3**		**119**	**18**	**26**	**44**	**311**	**1**	**0**	**3**

QMJHL First All-Star Team (1985)

• Missed remainder of 1985-86 season recovering from knee injury, suffered in game vs. Boston, December 5, 1985. Traded to **St. Louis** by **Montreal** with Vincent Riendeau for Jocelyn Lemieux, Darrell May and St. Louis' 2nd round choice (Patrice Brisebois) in 1989 Entry Draft, August 9, 1988. Traded to **Vancouver** by **St. Louis** with Geoff Courtnall, Robert Dirk, Cliff Ronning and St. Louis' 5th round choice (Brian Loney) in 1992 Entry Draft for Dan Quinn and Garth Butcher, March 5, 1991. Traded to **Toronto** by **Vancouver** for Mike Ridley, July 8, 1995. Traded to **NY Rangers** by **Toronto** for Wayne Presley, February 29, 1996. Traded to **St. Louis** by **NY Rangers** for Brian Noonan, November 13, 1996.

• MONAHAN, Garry

Garry Michael LW – L. 6', 199 lbs. b: Barrie, Ont., 10/20/1946. Montreal's 1st, 1st overall, in 1963.

Season	Club	League	GP	G	A	Pts	AG	AA	APts	PIM	PP	SH	GW	S	%	TGF	PGF	TGA	PGA	+/–	GP	G	A	Pts	PIM	PP	SH	GW
1963-64	St. Michael's Buzzers	OHA-B	STATISTICS NOT AVAILABLE																									
1964-65	Peterborough Petes	OHA-Jr.	55	12	16	28	....	....	....	28	....	....	....	....	....	....	....	....	....	....	12	1	2	3	11	....	....	....
1965-66	Peterborough Petes	OHA-Jr.	46	6	10	16	....	....	....	43	....	....	....	....	....	....	....	....	....	....	6	0	3	3	9	....	....	....
1966-67	Peterborough Petes	OHA-Jr.	47	30	54	84	....	....	....	79	....	....	....	....	....	....	....	....	....	....	6	2	2	4	20	....	....	....
	Houston Apollos	CPHL	....	....	....	....	....	....	....	....	....	....	....	....	....	....	....	....	....	....	3	1	0	1	0	....	....	....
1967-68	**Montreal Canadiens**	**NHL**	**11**	**0**	**0**	**0**	**0**	**0**	**0**	**8**	**0**	**0**	**0**	**3**	**0.0**	**1**	**0**	**3**	**0**	**–2**	....	....	....	....	....	....	....	....
	Houston Apollos	CPHL	56	17	31	48	....	....	....	86	....	....	....	....	....	....	....	....	....	....	....	....	....	....	....	....	....	....
1968-69	**Montreal Canadiens**	**NHL**	**3**	**0**	**0**	**0**	**0**	**0**	**0**	**0**	**0**	**0**	**0**	**0**	**0.0**	**0**	**0**	**0**	**0**	**0**	....	....	....	....	....	....	....	....
	Cleveland Barons	AHL	70	18	26	44	....	....	....	81	....	....	....	....	....	....	....	....	....	....	5	2	0	2	10	....	....	....
1969-70	**Detroit Red Wings**	**NHL**	**51**	**3**	**4**	**7**	**3**	**4**	**7**	**24**	**0**	**0**	**1**	**44**	**6.8**	**13**	**2**	**18**	**1**	**–6**	....	....	....	....	....	....	....	....
	Los Angeles Kings	**NHL**	**21**	**0**	**3**	**3**	**0**	**3**	**3**	**12**	**0**	**0**	**0**	**15**	**0.0**	**6**	**1**	**15**	**4**	**–6**	....	....	....	....	....	....	....	....
1970-71	**Toronto Maple Leafs**	**NHL**	**78**	**15**	**22**	**37**	**15**	**18**	**33**	**79**	**4**	**1**	**4**	**173**	**8.7**	**75**	**11**	**60**	**7**	**11**	**6**	**2**	**0**	**2**	**2**	**0**	**0**	**0**
1971-72	**Toronto Maple Leafs**	**NHL**	**78**	**14**	**17**	**31**	**14**	**15**	**29**	**47**	**2**	**1**	**2**	**186**	**7.5**	**48**	**6**	**57**	**17**	**2**	**5**	**0**	**0**	**0**	**0**	**0**	**0**	**0**
1972-73	**Toronto Maple Leafs**	**NHL**	**78**	**13**	**18**	**31**	**12**	**14**	**26**	**53**	**0**	**0**	**3**	**135**	**9.6**	**56**	**3**	**72**	**16**	**–3**	....	....	....	....	....	....	....	....
1973-74	**Toronto Maple Leafs**	**NHL**	**78**	**9**	**16**	**25**	**9**	**13**	**22**	**70**	**0**	**0**	**1**	**139**	**6.5**	**37**	**3**	**58**	**28**	**4**	**4**	**0**	**1**	**1**	**7**	**0**	**0**	**0**
1974-75	**Toronto Maple Leafs**	**NHL**	**1**	**0**	**0**	**0**	**0**	**0**	**0**	**0**	**0**	**0**	**0**	**0**	**0.0**	**0**	**0**	**0**	**0**	**0**	....	....	....	....	....	....	....	....
	Vancouver Canucks	**NHL**	**78**	**14**	**20**	**34**	**12**	**15**	**27**	**51**	**3**	**1**	**2**	**154**	**9.1**	**55**	**6**	**82**	**23**	**–10**	**5**	**1**	**0**	**1**	**2**	**0**	**0**	**1**
1975-76	**Vancouver Canucks**	**NHL**	**66**	**16**	**17**	**33**	**14**	**13**	**27**	**39**	**3**	**1**	**2**	**126**	**12.7**	**51**	**6**	**69**	**25**	**1**	**2**	**0**	**0**	**0**	**2**	**0**	**0**	**0**
1976-77	**Vancouver Canucks**	**NHL**	**76**	**18**	**26**	**44**	**16**	**20**	**36**	**48**	**3**	**0**	**1**	**169**	**10.7**	**62**	**10**	**75**	**22**	**–1**	....	....	....	....	....	....	....	....
1977-78	**Vancouver Canucks**	**NHL**	**67**	**10**	**19**	**29**	**9**	**15**	**24**	**28**	**0**	**0**	**1**	**105**	**9.5**	**40**	**5**	**56**	**23**	**2**	....	....	....	....	....	....	....	....
	Tulsa Oilers	CHL	7	3	2	5	....	....	....	0	....	....	....	....	....	....	....	....	....	....	....	....	....	....	....	....	....	....
1978-79	**Toronto Maple Leafs**	**NHL**	**62**	**4**	**7**	**11**	**3**	**5**	**8**	**25**	**0**	**2**	**0**	**55**	**7.3**	**25**	**3**	**41**	**23**	**4**	....	....	....	....	....	....	....	....
1979-80	Seibu-Tetsudo Tokyo	Japan	20	13	17	30	....	....	....	....	....	....	....	....	....	....	....	....	....	....	....	....	....	....	....	....	....	....
1980-81	Seibu-Tetsudo Tokyo	Japan	20	12	14	26	....	....	....	....	....	....	....	....	....	....	....	....	....	....	....	....	....	....	....	....	....	....
1981-82	Seibu-Tetsudo Tokyo	Japan	20	17	19	36	....	....	....	....	....	....	....	....	....	....	....	....	....	....	....	....	....	....	....	....	....	....
	NHL Totals		**748**	**116**	**169**	**285**	**107**	**135**	**242**	**484**	**15**	**6**	**17**	**1304**	**8.9**	**469**	**56**	**606**	**189**		**22**	**3**	**1**	**4**	**13**	**0**	**0**	**1**

Traded to **Detroit** by **Montreal** with Doug Piper for Pete Mahovlich and Bart Crashley, June 6, 1969. Traded to **LA Kings** by **Detroit** with Matt Ravlich and Brian Gibbons for Dale Rolfe, Gary Croteau and Larry Johnston, February 20, 1970. Traded to **Toronto** by **LA Kings** with Brian Murphy for Bob Pulford, September 3, 1970. Traded to **Vancouver** by **Toronto** with John Grisdale for Dave Dunn, October 16, 1974. Traded to **Toronto** by **Vancouver** for cash, September 13, 1978.

• MONAHAN, Hartland

Hartland Patrick RW – R. 5'11", 197 lbs. b: Montreal, Que., 3/29/1951. California's 3rd, 43rd overall, in 1971.

Season	Club	League	GP	G	A	Pts	AG	AA	APts	PIM	PP	SH	GW	S	%	TGF	PGF	TGA	PGA	+/–	GP	G	A	Pts	PIM	PP	SH	GW
1968-69	Laval Saints	MMJHL	STATISTICS NOT AVAILABLE																									
1969-70	Montreal Jr. Canadiens	OHA-Jr.	54	10	14	24	....	....	....	72	....	....	....	....	....	....	....	....	....	....	16	5	4	9	24	....	....	....
	Montreal Jr. Canadiens	Mem-Cup	8	4	1	5	....	....	....	15	....	....	....	....	....	....	....	....	....	....	....	....	....	....	....	....	....	....

			REGULAR SEASON																		PLAYOFFS							
Season	Club	League	GP	G	A	Pts	AG	AA	APts	PIM	PP	SH	GW	S	%	TGF	PGF	TGA	PGA	+/–	GP	G	A	Pts	PIM	PP	SH	GW
1970-71	Montreal Jr. Canadiens	OHA-Jr.	43	14	29	43	....	....	....	135	....	....	....	....	....	....	....	....	....	....	11	9	10	19	25	....	....	....
1971-72	Baltimore Clippers	AHL	20	1	1	2	....	....	....	4	....	....	....	....	....	....	....	....	....	....	....	....	....	....	....	....	....	....
	Columbus Seals	IHL	36	8	19	27	....	....	....	55	....	....	....	....	....	....	....	....	....	....	....	....	....	....	....	....	....	....
1972-73	Salt Lake Golden Eagles	WHL	61	18	34	52	....	....	....	60	....	....	....	....	....	....	....	....	....	....	9	5	2	7	6	....	....	....
1973-74	**California Golden Seals**	**NHL**	**1**	**0**	**0**	**0**	**0**	**0**	**0**	**0**	**0**	**0**	**0**	**1**	**0.0**	**0**	**0**	**0**	**0**	**0**	....	....	....	....	....	....	....	....
	Salt Lake Golden Eagles	WHL	66	14	28	42	....	....	....	76	....	....	....	....	....	....	....	....	....	....	5	1	2	3	2	....	....	....
1974-75	**New York Rangers**	**NHL**	**6**	**0**	**1**	**1**	**0**	**1**	**1**	**4**	**0**	**0**	**0**	**5**	**0.0**	**2**	**0**	**4**	**0**	**–2**	....	....	....	....	....	....	....	....
	Providence Reds	AHL	70	28	42	70	....	....	....	96	....	....	....	....	....	....	....	....	....	....	6	2	2	4	14	....	....	....
1975-76	**Washington Capitals**	**NHL**	**80**	**17**	**29**	**46**	**15**	**22**	**37**	**35**	**2**	**0**	**2**	**142**	**12.0**	**76**	**17**	**122**	**14**	**–49**	....	....	....	....	....	....	....	....
1976-77	**Washington Capitals**	**NHL**	**79**	**23**	**27**	**50**	**21**	**21**	**42**	**37**	**7**	**1**	**4**	**137**	**16.8**	**80**	**20**	**92**	**4**	**–28**	....	....	....	....	....	....	....	....
1977-78	**Pittsburgh Penguins**	**NHL**	**7**	**2**	**0**	**2**	**2**	**0**	**2**	**2**	**1**	**0**	**0**	**13**	**15.4**	**5**	**2**	**10**	**0**	**–7**	....	....	....	....	....	....	....	....
	Los Angeles Kings	**NHL**	**64**	**10**	**9**	**19**	**9**	**7**	**16**	**45**	**0**	**0**	**1**	**97**	**10.3**	**35**	**2**	**46**	**0**	**–13**	**2**	**0**	**0**	**0**	**0**	**0**	**0**	**0**
1978-79	Springfield Indians	AHL	76	30	36	66	....	....	....	71	....	....	....	....	....	....	....	....	....	....	....	....	....	....	....	....	....	....
1979-80	**St. Louis Blues**	**NHL**	**72**	**5**	**12**	**17**	**4**	**9**	**13**	**36**	**1**	**1**	**0**	**93**	**5.4**	**32**	**1**	**67**	**14**	**–22**	**3**	**0**	**0**	**0**	**0**	**0**	**0**	**0**
1980-81	**St. Louis Blues**	**NHL**	**25**	**4**	**2**	**6**	**3**	**1**	**4**	**4**	**0**	**2**	**0**	**32**	**12.5**	**15**	**0**	**19**	**6**	**2**	**1**	**0**	**0**	**0**	**4**	**0**	**0**	**0**
	NHL Totals		**334**	**61**	**80**	**141**	**54**	**61**	**115**	**163**	**11**	**4**	**7**	**520**	**11.7**	**245**	**42**	**360**	**38**		**6**	**0**	**0**	**0**	**4**	**0**	**0**	**0**

AHL Second All-Star Team (1975)

Traded to **NY Rangers** by **California** for Brian Lavender, September 23, 1974. Claimed by **Washington** from **NY Rangers** in Intra-League Draft, June 17, 1975. Traded to **Pittsburgh** by **Washington** for Pittsburgh's 1st round choice (later traded to Minnesota — Minnesota selected Tom McCarthy) in 1979 Entry Draft, October 17, 1977. Traded to **LA Kings** by **Pittsburgh** with Syl Apps Jr. for Dave Schultz, Gene Carr and LA Kings' 4th round choice (Shane Pearsall) in 1978 Amateur Draft, November 2, 1977. Claimed by **Quebec** from **LA Kings** in Expansion Draft, June 13, 1979. Traded to **St. Louis** by **Quebec** for cash, June 13, 1979.

• MONDOU, Pierre

C – R. 5'10", 185 lbs. b: Sorel, Que., 11/27/1955. Montreal's 2nd, 15th overall, in 1975.

Season	Club	League	GP	G	A	Pts	AG	AA	APts	PIM	PP	SH	GW	S	%	TGF	PGF	TGA	PGA	+/–	GP	G	A	Pts	PIM	PP	SH	GW
1972-73	Sorel Eperviers	QMJHL	64	37	43	80	....	....	....	57	....	....	....	....	....	....	....	....	....	....	10	6	4	10	12	....	....	....
1973-74	Sorel Eperviers	QMJHL	60	62	57	119	....	....	....	104	....	....	....	....	....	....	....	....	....	....	2	0	0	0	0	....	....	....
1974-75	Sorel Eperviers	QMJHL	28	16	23	39	....	....	....	13	....	....	....	....	....	....	....	....	....	....	....	....	....	....	....	....	....	....
	Montreal Red-White-Blue	QMJHL	40	40	47	87	....	....	....	23	....	....	....	....	....	....	....	....	....	....	9	8	7	15	13	....	....	....
1975-76	Nova Scotia Voyageurs	AHL	74	34	43	77	....	....	....	30	....	....	....	....	....	....	....	....	....	....	9	1	5	6	4	....	....	....
1976-77	Nova Scotia Voyageurs	AHL	71	*44	45	89	....	....	....	21	....	....	....	....	....	....	....	....	....	....	12	*8	*11	*19	6	....	....	....
◆	**Montreal Canadiens**	**NHL**	....	....	....	....	....	....	....	....	....	....	....	....	....	....	....	....	....	....	**4**	**0**	**0**	**0**	**0**	**0**	**0**	**0**
1977-78◆	**Montreal Canadiens**	**NHL**	**71**	**19**	**30**	**49**	**17**	**23**	**40**	**8**	**4**	**0**	**3**	**132**	**14.4**	**71**	**15**	**24**	**0**	**32**	**15**	**3**	**7**	**10**	**4**	**2**	**0**	**1**
1978-79◆	**Montreal Canadiens**	**NHL**	**77**	**31**	**41**	**72**	**27**	**30**	**57**	**26**	**6**	**1**	**7**	**163**	**19.0**	**114**	**26**	**29**	**0**	**59**	**16**	**3**	**6**	**9**	**4**	**1**	**0**	**0**
1979-80	**Montreal Canadiens**	**NHL**	**75**	**30**	**36**	**66**	**26**	**26**	**52**	**12**	**8**	**0**	**3**	**152**	**19.7**	**92**	**28**	**38**	**0**	**26**	**4**	**1**	**4**	**5**	**4**	**0**	**0**	**0**
1980-81	**Montreal Canadiens**	**NHL**	**57**	**17**	**24**	**41**	**13**	**16**	**29**	**16**	**5**	**0**	**2**	**106**	**16.0**	**70**	**22**	**24**	**0**	**24**	**3**	**0**	**1**	**1**	**0**	**0**	**0**	**0**
1981-82	**Montreal Canadiens**	**NHL**	**73**	**35**	**33**	**68**	**28**	**22**	**50**	**57**	**8**	**2**	**4**	**146**	**24.0**	**92**	**20**	**69**	**15**	**18**	**5**	**2**	**5**	**7**	**8**	**1**	**1**	**0**
1982-83	**Montreal Canadiens**	**NHL**	**76**	**29**	**37**	**66**	**24**	**26**	**50**	**31**	**8**	**1**	**3**	**178**	**16.3**	**100**	**20**	**77**	**29**	**32**	**3**	**0**	**1**	**1**	**2**	**0**	**0**	**0**
1983-84	**Montreal Canadiens**	**NHL**	**52**	**15**	**22**	**37**	**12**	**15**	**27**	**8**	**3**	**1**	**1**	**105**	**14.3**	**51**	**7**	**46**	**11**	**9**	**14**	**6**	**3**	**9**	**2**	**1**	**0**	**1**
1984-85	**Montreal Canadiens**	**NHL**	**67**	**18**	**39**	**57**	**15**	**27**	**42**	**21**	**2**	**0**	**2**	**128**	**14.1**	**81**	**23**	**57**	**14**	**15**	**5**	**2**	**1**	**3**	**2**	**0**	**0**	**0**
	NHL Totals		**548**	**194**	**262**	**456**	**162**	**185**	**347**	**179**	**44**	**5**	**25**	**1110**	**17.5**	**671**	**161**	**364**	**69**		**69**	**17**	**28**	**45**	**26**	**5**	**1**	**2**

QMJHL Second All-Star Team (1975) • Won Dudley "Red" Garrett Memorial Award (Top Rookie - AHL) (1976) • AHL Second All-Star Team (1977)

• Suffered eventual career-ending eye injury in game vs. Hartford, March 9, 1985.

• MONGEAU, Michel

C – L. 5'9", 190 lbs. b: Montreal, Que., 2/9/1965.

Season	Club	League	GP	G	A	Pts	AG	AA	APts	PIM	PP	SH	GW	S	%	TGF	PGF	TGA	PGA	+/–	GP	G	A	Pts	PIM	PP	SH	GW
1981-82	Lac St-Louis Lions	QAAA	48	45	57	102	....	....	....	....	....	....	....	....	....	....	....	....	....	....	....	....	....	....	....	....	....	....
1982-83	Laval Titan	QMJHL	24	4	6	10	....	....	....	2	....	....	....	....	....	....	....	....	....	....	....	....	....	....	....	....	....	....
1983-84	Laval Titan	QMJHL	60	45	49	94	....	....	....	30	....	....	....	....	....	....	....	....	....	....	....	....	....	....	....	....	....	....
	Laval Titan	Mem-Cup	3	3	2	5	....	....	....	0	....	....	....	....	....	....	....	....	....	....	....	....	....	....	....	....	....	....
1984-85	Laval Titan	QMJHL	67	60	84	144	....	....	....	56	....	....	....	....	....	....	....	....	....	....	....	....	....	....	....	....	....	....
1985-86	Laval Titan	QMJHL	72	71	109	180	....	....	....	45	....	....	....	....	....	....	....	....	....	....	....	....	....	....	....	....	....	....
1986-87	Saginaw Generals	IHL	76	42	53	95	....	....	....	34	....	....	....	....	....	....	....	....	....	....	10	3	6	9	6	....	....	....
1987-88	ASG Tours	France	30	31	21	52	....	....	....	....	....	....	....	....	....	....	....	....	....	....	....	....	....	....	....	....	....	....
1988-89	Flint Spirits	IHL	82	41	*76	117	....	....	....	57	....	....	....	....	....	....	....	....	....	....	....	....	....	....	....	....	....	....
1989-90	**St. Louis Blues**	**NHL**	**7**	**1**	**5**	**6**	**1**	**4**	**5**	**2**	**0**	**0**	**0**	**2**	**50.0**	**8**	**3**	**1**	**0**	**4**	**2**	**0**	**1**	**1**	**0**	**0**	**0**	**0**
	Peoria Rivermen	IHL	73	39	*78	*117	....	....	....	53	....	....	....	....	....	....	....	....	....	....	5	3	4	7	6	....	....	....
1990-91	**St. Louis Blues**	**NHL**	**7**	**1**	**1**	**2**	**1**	**1**	**2**	**0**	**1**	**0**	**0**	**13**	**7.7**	**4**	**2**	**1**	**0**	**1**	....	....	....	....	....	....	....	....
	Peoria Rivermen	IHL	73	41	65	106	....	....	....	114	....	....	....	....	....	....	....	....	....	....	19	10	*16	26	32	....	....	....
1991-92	**St. Louis Blues**	**NHL**	**36**	**3**	**12**	**15**	**3**	**9**	**12**	**6**	**2**	**0**	**0**	**23**	**13.0**	**25**	**17**	**10**	**0**	**–2**	....	....	....	....	....	....	....	....
	Peoria Rivermen	IHL	32	21	34	55	....	....	....	77	....	....	....	....	....	....	....	....	....	....	10	5	14	19	8	....	....	....
1992-93	**Tampa Bay Lightning**	**NHL**	**4**	**1**	**1**	**2**	**1**	**1**	**2**	**2**	**0**	**0**	**0**	**2**	**50.0**	**3**	**2**	**3**	**0**	**–2**	....	....	....	....	....	....	....	....
	Milwaukee Admirals	IHL	45	24	41	65	....	....	....	69	....	....	....	....	....	....	....	....	....	....	4	1	4	5	4	....	....	....
	Halifax Citadels	AHL	22	13	18	31	....	....	....	10	....	....	....	....	....	....	....	....	....	....	....	....	....	....	....	....	....	....
1993-94	Cornwall Aces	AHL	7	3	11	14	....	....	....	4	....	....	....	....	....	....	....	....	....	....	....	....	....	....	....	....	....	....
	Peoria Rivermen	IHL	52	29	36	65	....	....	....	50	....	....	....	....	....	....	....	....	....	....	....	....	....	....	....	....	....	....
1994-95	Peoria Rivermen	IHL	74	30	52	82	....	....	....	72	....	....	....	....	....	....	....	....	....	....	....	....	....	....	....	....	....	....
1995-96	Peoria Rivermen	IHL	24	5	17	22	....	....	....	24	....	....	....	....	....	....	....	....	....	....	12	4	11	15	8	....	....	....
1996-97	Detroit Vipers	IHL	31	12	11	23	....	....	....	30	....	....	....	....	....	....	....	....	....	....	....	....	....	....	....	....	....	....
	Phoenix Roadrunners	IHL	16	4	10	14	....	....	....	8	....	....	....	....	....	....	....	....	....	....	....	....	....	....	....	....	....	....
	Milwaukee Admirals	IHL	31	6	19	25	....	....	....	29	....	....	....	....	....	....	....	....	....	....	2	0	1	1	2	....	....	....
1997-98	Quebec Rafales	IHL	34	5	12	17	....	....	....	18	....	....	....	....	....	....	....	....	....	....	....	....	....	....	....	....	....	....
	Manitoba Moose	IHL	43	12	22	34	....	....	....	24	....	....	....	....	....	....	....	....	....	....	3	0	1	1	6	....	....	....
1998-99	HC Asiago	Italy	9	9	4	13	....	....	....	38	....	....	....	....	....	....	....	....	....	....	1	0	1	1	2	....	....	....
	Joliette Blizzard	QSPHL	23	25	26	51	....	....	....	6	....	....	....	....	....	....	....	....	....	....	....	....	....	....	....	....	....	....
99-2000	EHC Biel-Bienne	Switz-2	28	12	25	37	....	....	....	54	....	....	....	....	....	....	....	....	....	....	....	....	....	....	....	....	....	....
	NHL Totals		**54**	**6**	**19**	**25**	**6**	**15**	**21**	**10**	**3**	**0**	**0**	**40**	**15.0**	**40**	**24**	**15**	**0**		**2**	**0**	**1**	**1**	**0**	**0**	**0**	**0**

QMJHL Second All-Star Team (1986) • Won Garry F. Longman Memorial Trophy (Top Rookie - IHL) (1987) • IHL First All-Star Team (1990) • Won Leo P. Lamoureux Memorial Trophy (Top Scorer - IHL) (1990) • Won James Gatschene Memorial Trophy (MVP - IHL) (1990) • IHL Second All-Star Team (1991) • Won "Bud" Poile Trophy (Playoff MVP - IHL) (1991)

Signed as a free agent by **St. Louis**, August 21, 1989. Claimed by **Tampa Bay** from **St. Louis** in Expansion Draft, June 18, 1992. Traded to **Quebec** by **Tampa Bay** with Martin Simard and Steve Tuttle for Herb Raglan, February 12, 1993. • Missed remainder of 1993-94 and majority of 1994-95 seasons recovering from facial lacerations suffered in game vs. Cleveland (IHL), February 27, 1994.

• MONGRAIN, Bob

Robert Julien C – L. 5'10", 165 lbs. b: La Sarre, Que., 8/31/1959.

Season	Club	League	GP	G	A	Pts	AG	AA	APts	PIM	PP	SH	GW	S	%	TGF	PGF	TGA	PGA	+/–	GP	G	A	Pts	PIM	PP	SH	GW
1975-76	Cap-de-Madelaine Barons	QJHL	STATISTICS NOT AVAILABLE																									
	Trois-Rivieres Draveurs	QMJHL	1	0	0	0	....	....	....	0	....	....	....	....	....	....	....	....	....	....	....	....	....	....	....	....	....	....
1976-77	Cap-de-Madelaine Barons	QJHL	60	53	79	132	....	....	....	....	....	....	....	....	....	....	....	....	....	....	....	....	....	....	....	....	....	....
	Trois-Rivieres Draveurs	QMJHL	12	0	2	2	....	....	....	0	....	....	....	....	....	....	....	....	....	....	....	....	....	....	....	....	....	....
1977-78	Trois-Rivieres Draveurs	QMJHL	72	35	43	78	....	....	....	77	....	....	....	....	....	....	....	....	....	....	13	2	4	6	7	....	....	....
	Trois-Rivieres Draveurs	Mem-Cup	4	1	2	3	....	....	....	0	....	....	....	....	....	....	....	....	....	....	....	....	....	....	....	....	....	....
1978-79	Trois-Rivieres Draveurs	QMJHL	72	66	76	142	....	....	....	55	....	....	....	....	....	....	....	....	....	....	13	4	14	18	13	....	....	....
	Trois-Rivieres Draveurs	Mem-Cup	4	3	0	3	....	....	....	2	....	....	....	....	....	....	....	....	....	....	....	....	....	....	....	....	....	....
1979-80	**Buffalo Sabres**	**NHL**	**34**	**4**	**6**	**10**	**3**	**4**	**7**	**4**	**0**	**0**	**1**	**33**	**12.1**	**14**	**0**	**11**	**3**	**6**	**9**	**1**	**2**	**3**	**2**	**0**	**0**	**0**
	Rochester Americans	AHL	39	25	24	49	....	....	....	58	....	....	....	....	....	....	....	....	....	....	....	....	....	....	....	....	....	....
1980-81	**Buffalo Sabres**	**NHL**	**4**	**0**	**0**	**0**	**0**	**0**	**0**	**2**	**0**	**0**	**0**	**2**	**0.0**	**1**	**1**	**3**	**1**	**–2**	....	....	....	....	....	....	....	....
	Rochester Americans	AHL	69	21	29	50	....	....	....	101	....	....	....	....	....	....	....	....	....	....	....	....	....	....	....	....	....	....
1981-82	**Buffalo Sabres**	**NHL**	**24**	**6**	**4**	**10**	**5**	**3**	**8**	**6**	**0**	**0**	**2**	**29**	**20.7**	**16**	**2**	**23**	**6**	**–3**	**1**	**0**	**0**	**0**	**0**	**0**	**0**	**0**
	Rochester Americans	AHL	56	37	37	74	....	....	....	45	....	....	....	....	....	....	....	....	....	....	....	....	....	....	....	....	....	....
1982-83	Rochester Americans	AHL	80	29	52	81	....	....	....	72	....	....	....	....	....	....	....	....	....	....	16	3	5	8	24	....	....	....
1983-84	Rochester Americans	AHL	78	41	44	85	....	....	....	154	....	....	....	....	....	....	....	....	....	....	18	11	9	20	46	....	....	....
	Buffalo Sabres	**NHL**	....	....	....	....	....	....	....	....	....	....	....	....	....	....	....	....	....	....	**1**	**0**	**0**	**0**	**0**	**0**	**0**	**0**

Season	Club	League	GP	G	A	Pts	AG	AA	APts	PIM	PP	SH	GW	S	%	TGF	PGF	TGA	PGA	+/–	GP	G	A	Pts	PIM	PP	SH	GW
			REGULAR SEASON																		PLAYOFFS							
1984-85	**Buffalo Sabres**	**NHL**	**8**	**1**	**1**	**2**	**1**	**1**	**2**	**0**	**0**	**0**	**0**	**10**	**10.0**	**3**	**0**	**5**	**3**	**1**	....	....	....	....	....	....	....	....
	EHC Kloten	Switz.	36	42	30	72	....	....	....	....	....	....	....	....	....	....	....	....	....	....	....	....	....	....	....	....	....	....
1985-86	EHC Kloten	Switz.	36	*46	32	78	....	....	....	....	....	....	....	....	....	....	....	....	....	....	5	*9	1	10	....	....	....	....
	Los Angeles Kings	**NHL**	**11**	**2**	**3**	**5**	**2**	**2**	**4**	**2**	**0**	**0**	**0**	**10**	**20.0**	**6**	**0**	**20**	**11**	**–3**	....	....	....	....	....	....	....	....
1986-87	EHC Kloten	Switz.	36	24	17	41	....	....	....	....	....	....	....	....	....	....	....	....	....	....	3	0	0	0	0	....	....	....
1987-88	EHC Kloten	Switz-2	36	28	16	44	....	....	....	....	....	....	....	....	....	....	....	....	....	....	7	8	4	12	....	....	....	....
1988-89	HC Martigny	Switz-2	36	36	31	67	....	....	....	....	....	....	....	....	....	....	....	....	....	....	7	6	4	10	....	....	....	....
1989-90	HC Sierre	Switz-2	36	27	39	66	....	....	....	....	....	....	....	....	....	....	....	....	....	....	10	8	7	15	....	....	....	....
1990-91	HC Sierre	Switz.	29	19	24	43	....	....	....	....	....	....	....	....	....	....	....	....	....	....	10	11	11	22	....	....	....	....
1991-92	HC Martigny	Switz-2	STATISTICS NOT AVAILABLE																									
1992-93	HC Martigny	Switz-2	DID NOT PLAY – COACHING																									
	NHL Totals		**81**	**13**	**14**	**27**	**11**	**10**	**21**	**14**	**0**	**0**	**3**	**84**	**15.5**	**40**	**3**	**62**	**24**		**11**	**1**	**2**	**3**	**2**	**0**	**0**	**0**

Signed as a free agent by **Buffalo**, September 16, 1979. Signed as a free agent by **LA Kings**, Macrch 6, 1986.

• MONTEITH, Hank

Henry George LW – L. 5'10", 170 lbs. b: Stratford, Ont., 10/2/1945.

Season	Club	League	GP	G	A	Pts	AG	AA	APts	PIM	PP	SH	GW	S	%	TGF	PGF	TGA	PGA	+/–	GP	G	A	Pts	PIM	PP	SH	GW
1961-62	Stratford Cullitons	OHA-B	STATISTICS NOT AVAILABLE																									
1962-83	University of Toronto	OQAA	16	10	30	40	....	....	....	....	....	....	....	....	....	....	....	....	....	....	....	....	....	....	....	....	....	....
1963-64	University of Toronto	OQAA	20	25	39	64	....	....	....	....	....	....	....	....	....	....	....	....	....	....	....	....	....	....	....	....	....	....
1964-65	University of Toronto	OQAA	13	23	*34	57	....	....	....	31	....	....	....	....	....	....	....	....	....	....	....	....	....	....	....	....	....	....
1965-66	University of Toronto	OQAA	16	*23	20	*43	....	....	....	30	....	....	....	....	....	....	....	....	....	....	....	....	....	....	....	....	....	....
1966-67	University of Toronto	OQAA	16	21	24	45	....	....	....	....	....	....	....	....	....	....	....	....	....	....	....	....	....	....	....	....	....	....
1967-68	Fort Worth Wings	CPHL	66	19	31	50	....	....	....	36	....	....	....	....	....	....	....	....	....	....	11	1	3	4	0	....	....	....
1968-69	**Detroit Red Wings**	**NHL**	**34**	**1**	**9**	**10**	**1**	**8**	**9**	**6**	**0**	**0**	**0**	**20**	**5.0**	**14**	**3**	**7**	**0**	**4**	....	....	....	....	....	....	....	....
	Fort Worth Wings	CHL	33	17	13	30	....	....	....	14	....	....	....	....	....	....	....	....	....	....	....	....	....	....	....	....	....	....
1969-70	**Detroit Red Wings**	**NHL**	**9**	**0**	**0**	**0**	**0**	**0**	**0**	**0**	**0**	**0**	**0**	**4**	**0.0**	**0**	**0**	**1**	**0**	**–1**	**4**	**0**	**0**	**0**	**0**	**0**	**0**	**0**
	Fort Worth Wings	CHL	52	20	28	48	....	....	....	38	....	....	....	....	....	....	....	....	....	....	....	....	....	....	....	....	....	....
1970-71	**Detroit Red Wings**	**NHL**	**34**	**4**	**3**	**7**	**4**	**2**	**6**	**0**	**0**	**0**	**0**	**37**	**10.8**	**14**	**0**	**19**	**0**	**–5**	....	....	....	....	....	....	....	....
	Fort Worth Wings	CHL	21	11	15	26	....	....	....	4	....	....	....	....	....	....	....	....	....	....	4	1	2	3	4	....	....	....
1971-72	Oakville Oaks	OHA-Sr.	27	16	24	40	....	....	....	14	....	....	....	....	....	....	....	....	....	....	....	....	....	....	....	....	....	....
1972-73	Oakville Oaks	OHA-Sr.	20	17	26	43	....	....	....	10	....	....	....	....	....	....	....	....	....	....	....	....	....	....	....	....	....	....
	Orillia Terriers	OHA-Sr.	16	4	15	19	....	....	....	4	....	....	....	....	....	....	....	....	....	....	....	....	....	....	....	....	....	....
1973-74	Orillia Terriers	OHA-Sr.	31	15	34	49	....	....	....	19	....	....	....	....	....	....	....	....	....	....	....	....	....	....	....	....	....	....
1974-75	Orillia Terriers	OHA-Sr.	29	20	14	34	....	....	....	6	....	....	....	....	....	....	....	....	....	....	....	....	....	....	....	....	....	....
	NHL Totals		**77**	**5**	**12**	**17**	**5**	**10**	**15**	**6**	**0**	**0**	**0**	**61**	**8.2**	**28**	**3**	**27**	**0**		**4**	**0**	**0**	**0**	**0**	**0**	**0**	**0**

Signed as a free agent by **Detroit**, September, 1967.

• MONTGOMERY, Jim

C – R. 5'10", 185 lbs. b: Montreal, Que., 6/30/1969.

Season	Club	League	GP	G	A	Pts	AG	AA	APts	PIM	PP	SH	GW	S	%	TGF	PGF	TGA	PGA	+/–	GP	G	A	Pts	PIM	PP	SH	GW
1988-89	Pembroke Lumber Kings	OJHL	50	53	*101	154	....	....	....	112	....	....	....	....	....	....	....	....	....	....	....	....	....	....	....	....	....	....
1989-90	University of Maine	H-East	45	26	34	60	....	....	....	35	....	....	....	....	....	....	....	....	....	....	....	....	....	....	....	....	....	....
1990-91	University of Maine	H-East	43	24	*57	81	....	....	....	44	....	....	....	....	....	....	....	....	....	....	....	....	....	....	....	....	....	....
1991-92	University of Maine	H-East	37	21	44	65	....	....	....	46	....	....	....	....	....	....	....	....	....	....	....	....	....	....	....	....	....	....
1992-93	University of Maine	H-East	45	32	63	95	....	....	....	40	....	....	....	....	....	....	....	....	....	....	....	....	....	....	....	....	....	....
1993-94	**St. Louis Blues**	**NHL**	**67**	**6**	**14**	**20**	**6**	**11**	**17**	**44**	**0**	**0**	**1**	**67**	**9.0**	**34**	**2**	**48**	**15**	**–1**	....	....	....	....	....	....	....	....
	Peoria Rivermen	IHL	12	7	8	15	....	....	....	10	....	....	....	....	....	....	....	....	....	....	....	....	....	....	....	....	....	....
1994-95	**Montreal Canadiens**	**NHL**	**5**	**0**	**0**	**0**	**0**	**0**	**0**	**2**	**0**	**0**	**0**	**3**	**0.0**	**0**	**0**	**2**	**0**	**–2**	....	....	....	....	....	....	....	....
	Philadelphia Flyers	**NHL**	**8**	**1**	**1**	**2**	**2**	**1**	**3**	**6**	**0**	**0**	**0**	**10**	**10.0**	**2**	**1**	**4**	**1**	**–2**	**7**	**1**	**0**	**1**	**2**	**0**	**0**	**0**
	Hershey Bears	AHL	16	8	6	14	....	....	....	14	....	....	....	....	....	....	....	....	....	....	6	3	2	5	25	....	....	....
1995-96	**Philadelphia Flyers**	**NHL**	**5**	**1**	**2**	**3**	**1**	**2**	**3**	**9**	**0**	**0**	**0**	**4**	**25.0**	**4**	**0**	**3**	**0**	**1**	**1**	**0**	**0**	**0**	**0**	**0**	**0**	**0**
	Hershey Bears	AHL	78	34	*71	105	....	....	....	95	....	....	....	....	....	....	....	....	....	....	4	3	2	5	6	....	....	....
1996-97	Kolner Haie	Germany	50	12	35	47	....	....	....	111	....	....	....	....	....	....	....	....	....	....	4	0	1	1	6	....	....	....
	Kolner Haie	EuroHL	6	0	1	1	....	....	....	16	....	....	....	....	....	....	....	....	....	....	....	....	....	....	....	....	....	....
1997-98	Philadelphia Phantoms	AHL	68	19	43	62	....	....	....	75	....	....	....	....	....	....	....	....	....	....	20	*13	16	29	55	....	....	....
1998-99	Philadelphia Phantoms	AHL	78	29	58	87	....	....	....	89	....	....	....	....	....	....	....	....	....	....	16	4	11	15	20	....	....	....
99-2000	Philadelphia Phantoms	AHL	13	3	9	12	....	....	....	22	....	....	....	....	....	....	....	....	....	....	....	....	....	....	....	....	....	....
	Manitoba Moose	IHL	67	18	28	46	....	....	....	111	....	....	....	....	....	....	....	....	....	....	....	....	....	....	....	....	....	....
	NHL Totals		**85**	**8**	**17**	**25**	**9**	**14**	**23**	**61**	**0**	**0**	**1**	**84**	**9.5**	**40**	**3**	**57**	**16**		**8**	**1**	**0**	**1**	**2**	**0**	**0**	**0**

Hockey East Second All-Star Team (1991, 1992) • Hockey East First All-Star Team (1993) • NCAA East Second All-American Team (1993) • NCAA Championship All-Tournament Team (1993) • NCAA Championship Tournament MVP (1993) • AHL Second All-Star Team (1996)

Signed as a free agent by **St. Louis**, June 2, 1993. Traded to **Montreal** by **St. Louis** for Guy Carbonneau, August 19, 1994. Claimed on waivers by **Philadelphia** from **Montreal**, February 10, 1995.

• MOORE, Barrie

LW – L. 5'11", 198 lbs. b: London, Ont., 5/22/1975. Buffalo's 7th, 220th overall, in 1993.

Season	Club	League	GP	G	A	Pts	AG	AA	APts	PIM	PP	SH	GW	S	%	TGF	PGF	TGA	PGA	+/–	GP	G	A	Pts	PIM	PP	SH	GW
1990-91	Strathroy Rockets	OJHL-B	24	9	10	19	....	....	....	14	....	....	....	....	....	....	....	....	....	....	....	....	....	....	....	....	....	....
1991-92	Sudbury Wolves	OHL	62	15	38	53	....	....	....	57	....	....	....	....	....	....	....	....	....	....	11	0	7	7	12	....	....	....
1992-93	Sudbury Wolves	OHL	57	13	26	39	....	....	....	71	....	....	....	....	....	....	....	....	....	....	14	4	3	7	19	....	....	....
1993-94	Sudbury Wolves	OHL	65	36	49	85	....	....	....	69	....	....	....	....	....	....	....	....	....	....	10	3	5	8	14	....	....	....
1994-95	Sudbury Wolves	OHL	60	47	42	89	....	....	....	67	....	....	....	....	....	....	....	....	....	....	18	*15	14	29	24	....	....	....
1995-96	**Buffalo Sabres**	**NHL**	**3**	**0**	**0**	**0**	**0**	**0**	**0**	**0**	**0**	**0**	**0**	**3**	**0.0**	**1**	**0**	**1**	**0**	**0**	....	....	....	....	....	....	....	....
	Rochester Americans	AHL	64	26	30	56	....	....	....	40	....	....	....	....	....	....	....	....	....	....	18	3	6	9	18	....	....	....
1996-97	**Buffalo Sabres**	**NHL**	**31**	**2**	**6**	**8**	**2**	**5**	**7**	**18**	**1**	**0**	**0**	**42**	**4.8**	**11**	**1**	**12**	**3**	**1**	....	....	....	....	....	....	....	....
	Rochester Americans	AHL	32	14	15	29	....	....	....	14	....	....	....	....	....	....	....	....	....	....	....	....	....	....	....	....	....	....
	Edmonton Oilers	**NHL**	**4**	**0**	**0**	**0**	**0**	**0**	**0**	**0**	**0**	**0**	**0**	**1**	**0.0**	**0**	**0**	**0**	**0**	**0**	....	....	....	....	....	....	....	....
	Hamilton Bulldogs	AHL	9	5	2	7	....	....	....	0	....	....	....	....	....	....	....	....	....	....	22	2	6	8	15	....	....	....
1997-98	Hamilton Bulldogs	AHL	70	22	29	51	....	....	....	64	....	....	....	....	....	....	....	....	....	....	8	0	1	1	4	....	....	....
1998-99	Indianapolis Ice	IHL	43	9	10	19	....	....	....	18	....	....	....	....	....	....	....	....	....	....	....	....	....	....	....	....	....	....
	Portland Pirates	AHL	23	3	7	10	....	....	....	4	....	....	....	....	....	....	....	....	....	....	....	....	....	....	....	....	....	....
99-2000	**Washington Capitals**	**NHL**	**1**	**0**	**0**	**0**	**0**	**0**	**0**	**0**	**0**	**0**	**0**	**2**	**0.0**	**1**	**0**	**1**	**0**	**0**	....	....	....	....	....	....	....	....
	Portland Pirates	AHL	80	18	33	51	....	....	....	50	....	....	....	....	....	....	....	....	....	....	4	0	0	0	6	....	....	....
	NHL Totals		**39**	**2**	**6**	**8**	**2**	**5**	**7**	**18**	**1**	**0**	**0**	**48**	**4.2**	**13**	**1**	**14**	**3**		....	....	....	....	....	....	....	....

Traded to **Edmonton** by **Buffalo** with Craig Millar for Miroslav Satan, March 18, 1997. Rights traded to **Washington** by **Edmonton** for Brad Church, February 3, 1999. Selected by **Columbus** from **Washington** in Expansion Draft, June 23, 2000.

• MOORE, Dickie

Richard Winston "Digger" LW – L. 5'10", 168 lbs. b: Montreal, Que., 1/6/1931. **HHOF**

Season	Club	League	GP	G	A	Pts	AG	AA	APts	PIM	PP	SH	GW	S	%	TGF	PGF	TGA	PGA	+/–	GP	G	A	Pts	PIM	PP	SH	GW
1947-48	Montreal Jr. Royals	QJHL	29	10	11	21	....	....	....	20	....	....	....	....	....	....	....	....	....	....	13	6	5	11	14	....	....	....
1948-49	Montreal Jr. Royals	QJHL	47	22	34	56	....	....	....	71	....	....	....	....	....	....	....	....	....	....	10	4	8	12	6	....	....	....
	Montreal Royals	QSHL	2	0	0	0	....	....	....	0	....	....	....	....	....	....	....	....	....	....	....	....	....	....	....	....	....	....
	Montreal Jr. Royals	Mem-Cup	15	8	5	13	....	....	....	31	....	....	....	....	....	....	....	....	....	....	....	....	....	....	....	....	....	....
1949-50	Montreal Jr. Royals	QJHL	1	0	1	1	....	....	....	5	....	....	....	....	....	....	....	....	....	....	....	....	....	....	....	....	....	....
	Montreal Jr. Canadiens	QJHL	35	24	19	43	....	....	....	110	....	....	....	....	....	....	....	....	....	....	16	8	*13	21	*51	....	....	....
	Montreal Jr. Canadiens	Mem-Cup	13	10	14	24	....	....	....	*41	....	....	....	....	....	....	....	....	....	....	....	....	....	....	....	....	....	....
1950-51	Montreal Jr. Canadiens	QJHL	33	12	22	34	....	....	....	58	....	....	....	....	....	....	....	....	....	....	9	5	4	9	34	....	....	....
1951-52	**Montreal Canadiens**	**NHL**	**33**	**18**	**15**	**33**	**24**	**18**	**42**	**44**	....	....	....	....	....	....	....	....	....	....	**11**	**1**	**1**	**2**	**12**	....	....	....
	Montreal Royals	QMHL	26	15	20	35	....	....	....	32	....	....	....	....	....	....	....	....	....	....	....	....	....	....	....	....	....	....
1952-53♦	**Montreal Canadiens**	**NHL**	**18**	**2**	**6**	**8**	**3**	**7**	**10**	**19**	....	....	....	....	....	....	....	....	....	....	**12**	**3**	**2**	**5**	**13**	....	....	....
	Buffalo Bisons	AHL	6	2	3	5	....	....	....	10	....	....	....	....	....	....	....	....	....	....	....	....	....	....	....	....	....	....
1953-54	**Montreal Canadiens**	**NHL**	**13**	**1**	**4**	**5**	**1**	**5**	**6**	**12**	....	....	....	....	....	....	....	....	....	....	**11**	**5**	***8**	***13**	**8**	....	....	....
	Montreal Royals	QHL	2	0	1	1	....	....	....	4	....	....	....	....	....	....	....	....	....	....	....	....	....	....	....	....	....	....
1954-55	**Montreal Canadiens**	**NHL**	**67**	**16**	**20**	**36**	**21**	**23**	**44**	**32**	....	....	....	....	....	....	....	....	....	....	**12**	**1**	**5**	**6**	**22**	....	....	....

			REGULAR SEASON																		PLAYOFFS							
Season	**Club**	**League**	**GP**	**G**	**A**	**Pts**	**AG**	**AA**	**APts**	**PIM**	**PP**	**SH**	**GW**	**S**	**%**	**TGF**	**PGF**	**TGA**	**PGA**	**+/–**	**GP**	**G**	**A**	**Pts**	**PIM**	**PP**	**SH**	**GW**
1955-56♦	**Montreal Canadiens**	**NHL**	70	11	39	50	15	47	62	55	....	....	....	....	....	....	....	....	....	....	10	3	6	9	12	....	....	....
1956-57♦	**Montreal Canadiens**	**NHL**	70	29	29	58	38	32	70	56	....	....	....	....	....	....	....	....	....	....	10	3	7	10	4	....	....	....
1957-58♦	**Montreal Canadiens**	**NHL**	70	*36	48	*84	45	50	95	65	....	....	....	....	....	....	....	....	....	....	10	4	7	11	4	....	....	....
1958-59♦	**Montreal Canadiens**	**NHL**	70	41	*55	*96	50	56	106	61	....	....	....	....	....	....	....	....	....	....	11	5	*12	*17	8	....	....	....
1959-60♦	**Montreal Canadiens**	**NHL**	62	22	42	64	26	41	67	54	....	....	....	....	....	....	....	....	....	....	8	*6	4	10	4	....	....	....
1960-61	**Montreal Canadiens**	**NHL**	57	35	34	69	41	33	74	62	....	....	....	....	....	....	....	....	....	....	6	3	1	4	4	....	....	....
1961-62	**Montreal Canadiens**	**NHL**	57	19	22	41	22	21	43	54	....	....	....	....	....	....	....	....	....	....	6	4	2	6	8	....	....	....
1962-63	**Montreal Canadiens**	**NHL**	67	24	26	50	28	26	54	61	....	....	....	....	....	....	....	....	....	....	5	0	1	1	2	....	....	....
1963-64			OUT OF HOCKEY – RETIRED																									
1964-65	**Toronto Maple Leafs**	**NHL**	38	2	4	6	2	4	6	68	....	....	....	....	....	....	....	....	....	....	5	1	1	2	6	....	....	....
1965-66			OUT OF HOCKEY – RETIRED																									
1966-67			OUT OF HOCKEY – RETIRED																									
1967-68	**St. Louis Blues**	**NHL**	27	5	3	8	6	3	9	9	1	0	1	37	13.5	13	4	17	0	–8	18	7	7	14	15	2	0	1
	NHL Totals		**719**	**261**	**347**	**608**	**322**	**366**	**688**	**652**	....	....	....	....	....	....	....	....	....		**135**	**46**	**64**	**110**	**122**	....	....	....

QJHL Second All-Star Team (1950 • QJHL First All-Star Team (1951) • NHL First All-Star Team (1958, 1959) • Won Art Ross Trophy (1958, 1959) • NHL Second All-Star Team (1961) • Played in NHL All-Star Game (1953, 1956, 1957, 1958, 1959, 1960)

• Missed majority of 1953-54 season recovering from collarbone injury suffered in game vs. Boston, October 10, 1953. Claimed by **Toronto** from **Montreal** in Intra-League Draft, June 10, 1964. Signed as a free agent by **St. Louis**, December 3, 1967.

• MORAN, Ian

RW – R. 6′, 206 lbs. b: Cleveland, OH, 8/24/1972. Pittsburgh's 5th, 107th overall, in 1990.

Season	Club	League	GP	G	A	Pts	AG	AA	APts	PIM	PP	SH	GW	S	%	TGF	PGF	TGA	PGA	+/–	GP	G	A	Pts	PIM	PP	SH	GW
1987-88	Belmont Hill Hillies	Hi-School	25	3	13	16	....	....	....	15	....	....	....	....	....	....	....	....	....	....	....	....	....	....	....	....	....	....
1988-89	Belmont Hill Hillies	Hi-School	23	7	25	32	....	....	....	8	....	....	....	....	....	....	....	....	....	....	....	....	....	....	....	....	....	....
1989-90	Belmont Hill Hillies	Hi-School	23	10	36	46	....	....	....	....	....	....	....	....	....	....	....	....	....	....	....	....	....	....	....	....	....	....
1990-91	Belmont Hill Hillies	Hi-School	23	7	44	51	....	....	....	12	....	....	....	....	....	....	....	....	....	....	....	....	....	....	....	....	....	....
	United States	WJC-A	6	0	2	2	....	....	....	2	....	....	....	....	....	....	....	....	....	....	....	....	....	....	....	....	....	....
1991-92	Boston College	H-East	30	2	16	18	....	....	....	44	....	....	....	....	....	....	....	....	....	....	....	....	....	....	....	....	....	....
1992-93	Boston College	H-East	31	8	12	20	....	....	....	32	....	....	....	....	....	....	....	....	....	....	....	....	....	....	....	....	....	....
	United States	WC-A	6	0	0	0	....	....	....	0	....	....	....	....	....	....	....	....	....	....	....	....	....	....	....	....	....	....
1993-94	United States	Nat-Team	50	8	15	23	....	....	....	69	....	....	....	....	....	....	....	....	....	....	....	....	....	....	....	....	....	....
	Cleveland Lumberjacks	IHL	33	5	13	18	....	....	....	39	....	....	....	....	....	....	....	....	....	....	....	....	....	....	....	....	....	....
1994-95	Cleveland Lumberjacks	IHL	64	7	31	38	....	....	....	94	....	....	....	....	....	....	....	....	....	....	4	0	1	1	2	....	....	....
	Pittsburgh Penguins	**NHL**	....	....	....	....	-2	-1	-3	....	....	....	....	....	....	....	....	....	....	....	**8**	**0**	**0**	**0**	**0**	**0**	**0**	**0**
1995-96	**Pittsburgh Penguins**	**NHL**	**51**	**1**	**1**	**2**	**1**	**1**	**2**	**47**	**0**	**0**	**0**	**44**	**2.3**	**28**	**0**	**43**	**14**	**–1**	....	....	....	....	....	....	....	....
1996-97	**Pittsburgh Penguins**	**NHL**	**36**	**4**	**5**	**9**	**4**	**4**	**8**	**22**	**0**	**0**	**0**	**50**	**8.0**	**33**	**7**	**47**	**10**	**–11**	**5**	**1**	**2**	**3**	**4**	**0**	**0**	**0**
	Cleveland Lumberjacks	IHL	36	6	23	29	....	....	....	26	....	....	....	....	....	....	....	....	....	....	....	....	....	....	....	....	....	....
1997-98	**Pittsburgh Penguins**	**NHL**	**37**	**1**	**6**	**7**	**1**	**6**	**7**	**19**	**0**	**0**	**1**	**33**	**3.0**	**12**	**2**	**14**	**4**	**0**	**6**	**0**	**0**	**0**	**2**	**0**	**0**	**0**
1998-99	**Pittsburgh Penguins**	**NHL**	**62**	**4**	**5**	**9**	**5**	**5**	**10**	**37**	**0**	**1**	**0**	**65**	**6.2**	**32**	**0**	**49**	**18**	**1**	**13**	**0**	**2**	**2**	**8**	**0**	**0**	**0**
99-2000	**Pittsburgh Penguins**	**NHL**	**73**	**4**	**8**	**12**	**4**	**7**	**11**	**28**	**0**	**0**	**0**	**58**	**6.9**	**27**	**1**	**45**	**9**	**–10**	**11**	**0**	**1**	**1**	**2**	**0**	**0**	**0**
	NHL Totals		**259**	**14**	**25**	**39**	**13**	**22**	**35**	**153**	**0**	**1**	**1**	**250**	**5.6**	**132**	**10**	**198**	**55**		**43**	**1**	**5**	**6**	**16**	**0**	**0**	**0**

• Missed majority of 1997-98 season recovering from kneecap injury suffered in training camp, September 30, 1997.

• MORAVEC, David

RW – L. 6′, 180 lbs. b: Vitkovice, Czech., 3/24/1973. Buffalo's 9th, 218th overall, in 1998.

Season	Club	League	GP	G	A	Pts	AG	AA	APts	PIM	PP	SH	GW	S	%	TGF	PGF	TGA	PGA	+/–	GP	G	A	Pts	PIM	PP	SH	GW
1994-95	HC Vitkovice	Czech-Rep	38	4	13	17	....	....	....	12	....	....	....	....	....	....	....	....	....	....	6	1	7	8	0	....	....	....
1995-96	HC Vitkovice	Czech-Rep	37	6	5	11	....	....	....	14	....	....	....	....	....	....	....	....	....	....	4	0	0	0	4	....	....	....
1996-97	HC Vitkovice	Czech-Rep	52	18	22	40	....	....	....	30	....	....	....	....	....	....	....	....	....	....	9	6	3	9	0	....	....	....
1997-98	HC Vitkovice	Czech-Rep	51	*38	26	64	....	....	....	28	....	....	....	....	....	....	....	....	....	....	11	6	9	15	8	....	....	....
1998-99	HC Vitkovice	Czech-Rep	50	21	22	43	....	....	....	44	....	....	....	....	....	....	....	....	....	....	4	1	1	2	....	....	....	....
99-2000	HC Vitkovice	Czech-Rep	38	11	18	29	....	....	....	34	....	....	....	....	....	....	....	....	....	....	....	....	....	....	....	....	....	....
	Buffalo Sabres	**NHL**	**1**	**0**	**0**	**0**	**0**	**0**	**0**	**0**	**0**	**0**	**0**	**2**	**0.0**	**0**	**0**	**1**	**0**	**–1**	....	....	....	....	....	....	....	....
	NHL Totals		**1**	**0**	**0**	**0**	**0**	**0**	**0**	**0**	**0**	**0**	**0**	**2**	**0.0**	**0**	**0**	**1**	**0**		....	....	....	....	....	....	....	....

• MORE, Jay

Jayson W. D – R. 6′1″, 210 lbs. b: Souris, Man., 1/12/1969. NY Rangers' 1st, 10th overall, in 1987.

Season	Club	League	GP	G	A	Pts	AG	AA	APts	PIM	PP	SH	GW	S	%	TGF	PGF	TGA	PGA	+/–	GP	G	A	Pts	PIM	PP	SH	GW
1984-85	Lethbridge Broncos	WHL	71	3	9	12	....	....	....	101	....	....	....	....	....	....	....	....	....	....	4	1	0	1	7	....	....	....
1985-86	Lethbridge Broncos	WHL	61	7	18	25	....	....	....	155	....	....	....	....	....	....	....	....	....	....	9	0	2	2	36	....	....	....
1986-87	Brandon Wheat Kings	WHL	21	4	6	10	....	....	....	62	....	....	....	....	....	....	....	....	....	....	....	....	....	....	....	....	....	....
	New Westminster Bruins	WHL	43	4	23	27	....	....	....	155	....	....	....	....	....	....	....	....	....	....	....	....	....	....	....	....	....	....
1987-88	New Westminster Bruins	WHL	70	13	47	60	....	....	....	270	....	....	....	....	....	....	....	....	....	....	5	0	2	2	26	....	....	....
1988-89	**New York Rangers**	**NHL**	**1**	**0**	**0**	**0**	**0**	**0**	**0**	**0**	**0**	**0**	**0**	**0**	**0.0**	**1**	**0**	**2**	**0**	**–1**	....	....	....	....	....	....	....	....
	Denver Rangers	IHL	62	7	15	22	....	....	....	138	....	....	....	....	....	....	....	....	....	....	3	0	1	1	26	....	....	....
1989-90	Flint Spirits	IHL	9	1	5	6	....	....	....	41	....	....	....	....	....	....	....	....	....	....	....	....	....	....	....	....	....	....
	Minnesota North Stars	**NHL**	**5**	**0**	**0**	**0**	**0**	**0**	**0**	**16**	**0**	**0**	**0**	**4**	**0.0**	**2**	**0**	**1**	**0**	**1**	....	....	....	....	....	....	....	....
	Kalamazoo Wings	IHL	64	9	25	34	....	....	....	316	....	....	....	....	....	....	....	....	....	....	10	0	3	3	13	....	....	....
1990-91	Kalamazoo Wings	IHL	10	0	5	5	....	....	....	46	....	....	....	....	....	....	....	....	....	....	....	....	....	....	....	....	....	....
	Fredericton Canadiens	AHL	57	7	17	24	....	....	....	152	....	....	....	....	....	....	....	....	....	....	9	1	1	2	34	....	....	....
1991-92	**San Jose Sharks**	**NHL**	**46**	**4**	**13**	**17**	**4**	**10**	**14**	**85**	**1**	**0**	**1**	**60**	**6.7**	**41**	**14**	**79**	**20**	**–32**	....	....	....	....	....	....	....	....
	Kansas City Blades	IHL	2	0	2	2	....	....	....	4	....	....	....	....	....	....	....	....	....	....	....	....	....	....	....	....	....	....
1992-93	**San Jose Sharks**	**NHL**	**73**	**5**	**6**	**11**	**4**	**4**	**8**	**179**	**0**	**1**	**0**	**107**	**4.7**	**51**	**2**	**129**	**45**	**–35**	....	....	....	....	....	....	....	....
1993-94	**San Jose Sharks**	**NHL**	**49**	**1**	**6**	**7**	**1**	**5**	**6**	**63**	**0**	**0**	**0**	**38**	**2.6**	**32**	**2**	**56**	**21**	**–5**	**13**	**0**	**2**	**2**	**32**	**0**	**0**	**0**
	Kansas City Blades	IHL	2	1	0	1	....	....	....	25	....	....	....	....	....	....	....	....	....	....	....	....	....	....	....	....	....	....
1994-95	**San Jose Sharks**	**NHL**	**45**	**0**	**6**	**6**	**0**	**9**	**9**	**71**	**0**	**0**	**0**	**25**	**0.0**	**32**	**2**	**36**	**13**	**7**	**11**	**0**	**4**	**4**	**6**	**0**	**0**	**0**
1995-96	**San Jose Sharks**	**NHL**	**74**	**2**	**7**	**9**	**2**	**6**	**8**	**147**	**0**	**0**	**0**	**67**	**3.0**	**51**	**1**	**122**	**40**	**–32**	....	....	....	....	....	....	....	....
1996-97	**New York Rangers**	**NHL**	**14**	**0**	**1**	**1**	**0**	**1**	**1**	**25**	**0**	**0**	**0**	**10**	**0.0**	**4**	**0**	**6**	**2**	**0**	....	....	....	....	....	....	....	....
	Phoenix Coyotes	**NHL**	**23**	**1**	**6**	**7**	**1**	**5**	**6**	**37**	**0**	**0**	**1**	**18**	**5.6**	**22**	**0**	**15**	**3**	**10**	**7**	**0**	**0**	**0**	**7**	**0**	**0**	**0**
1997-98	**Phoenix Coyotes**	**NHL**	**41**	**5**	**5**	**10**	**6**	**5**	**11**	**53**	**0**	**1**	**0**	**40**	**12.5**	**27**	**2**	**34**	**9**	**0**	....	....	....	....	....	....	....	....
	Chicago Blackhawks	**NHL**	**17**	**0**	**2**	**2**	**0**	**2**	**2**	**8**	**0**	**0**	**0**	**17**	**0.0**	**10**	**0**	**3**	**0**	**7**	....	....	....	....	....	....	....	....
1998-99	**Nashville Predators**	**NHL**	**18**	**0**	**2**	**2**	**0**	**2**	**2**	**18**	**0**	**0**	**0**	**24**	**0.0**	**13**	**2**	**15**	**6**	**2**	....	....	....	....	....	....	....	....
99-2000	**Nashville Predators**	**NHL**	DID NOT PLAY – INJURED																									
	NHL Totals		**406**	**18**	**54**	**72**	**18**	**49**	**67**	**702**	**1**	**2**	**2**	**410**	**4.4**	**286**	**25**	**498**	**159**		**31**	**0**	**6**	**6**	**45**	**0**	**0**	**0**

WHL All-Star Team (1988)

Traded to **Minnesota** by **NY Rangers** for Dave Archibald, November 1, 1989. Traded to **Montreal** by **Minnesota** for Brian Hayward, November 7, 1990. Claimed by **San Jose** from **Montreal** in Expansion Draft, May 30, 1991. Traded to **NY Rangers** by **San Jose** with Brian Swanson and San Jose's 4th round choice (later traded back to San Jose - San Jose selected Adam Colagiacomo) in 1997 Entry Draft for Marty McSorley, August 20, 1996. Traded to **Phoenix** by **NY Rangers** for Mike Eastwood and Dallas Eakins, February 6, 1997. Traded to **Chicago** by **Phoenix** with Chad Kilger for Keith Carney and Jim Cummins, March 4, 1998. Signed as a free agent by **Nashville**, June 4, 1998. • Missed majority of 1998-99 and entire 1999-2000 season recovering from head injury suffered in game vs. Florida, December 10, 1998.

• MOREAU, Ethan

Ethan Byron LW – L. 6′2″, 211 lbs. b: Huntsville, Ont., 9/22/1975. Chicago's 1st, 14th overall, in 1994.

Season	Club	League	GP	G	A	Pts	AG	AA	APts	PIM	PP	SH	GW	S	%	TGF	PGF	TGA	PGA	+/–	GP	G	A	Pts	PIM	PP	SH	GW
1990-91	Orillia Terriers	OJHL-B	42	17	22	39	....	....	....	26	....	....	....	....	....	....	....	....	....	....	12	6	6	12	18	....	....	....
1991-92	Niagara Falls Thunder	OHL	62	20	35	55	....	....	....	39	....	....	....	....	....	....	....	....	....	....	17	4	6	10	4	....	....	....
1992-93	Niagara Falls Thunder	OHL	65	32	41	73	....	....	....	69	....	....	....	....	....	....	....	....	....	....	4	0	3	3	4	....	....	....
1993-94	Niagara Falls Thunder	OHL	59	44	54	98	....	....	....	100	....	....	....	....	....	....	....	....	....	....	....	....	....	....	....	....	....	....
1994-95	Niagara Falls Thunder	OHL	39	25	41	66	....	....	....	69	....	....	....	....	....	....	....	....	....	....	....	....	....	....	....	....	....	....
	Sudbury Wolves	OHL	23	13	17	30	....	....	....	22	....	....	....	....	....	....	....	....	....	....	18	6	12	18	26	....	....	....
1995-96	**Chicago Blackhawks**	**NHL**	**8**	**0**	**1**	**1**	**0**	**1**	**1**	**4**	**0**	**0**	**0**	**1**	**0.0**	**1**	**0**	**0**	**0**	**1**	....	....	....	....	....	....	....	....
	Indianapolis Ice	IHL	71	21	20	41	....	....	....	126	....	....	....	....	....	....	....	....	....	....	5	4	0	4	8	....	....	....
1996-97	**Chicago Blackhawks**	**NHL**	**82**	**15**	**16**	**31**	**16**	**14**	**30**	**123**	**0**	**0**	**1**	**114**	**13.2**	**52**	**1**	**39**	**1**	**13**	**6**	**1**	**0**	**1**	**9**	**0**	**0**	**0**
1997-98	**Chicago Blackhawks**	**NHL**	**54**	**9**	**9**	**18**	**11**	**9**	**20**	**73**	**2**	**0**	**0**	**87**	**10.3**	**32**	**7**	**30**	**5**	**0**	....	....	....	....	....	....	....	....

			REGULAR SEASON																	PLAYOFFS							
Season	**Club**	**League**	**GP**	**G**	**A**	**Pts**	**AG**	**AA**	**APts**	**PIM**	**PP**	**SH**	**GW**	**S**	**%**	**TGF**	**PGF**	**TGA**	**PGA**	**+/–**	**GP**	**G**	**A**	**Pts**	**PIM**	**PP**	**SH**	**GW**
1998-99	**Chicago Blackhawks**	**NHL**	**66**	**9**	**6**	**15**	**11**	**6**	**17**	**84**	**0**	**0**	**1**	**80**	**11.3**	**27**	**1**	**39**	**8**	**–5**	....	....	....	....	....	....	....	....
	Edmonton Oilers	**NHL**	**14**	**1**	**5**	**6**	**1**	**5**	**6**	**8**	**0**	**0**	**1**	**16**	**6.3**	**7**	**1**	**4**	**0**	**2**	**4**	**0**	**3**	**3**	**6**	**0**	**0**	**0**
99-2000	**Edmonton Oilers**	**NHL**	**73**	**17**	**10**	**27**	**19**	**9**	**28**	**62**	**1**	**0**	**3**	**106**	**16.0**	**46**	**2**	**45**	**9**	**8**	**5**	**0**	**1**	**1**	**0**	**0**	**0**	**0**
	NHL Totals		**297**	**51**	**47**	**98**	**58**	**44**	**102**	**354**	**3**	**0**	**6**	**404**	**12.6**	**165**	**12**	**157**	**23**		**15**	**1**	**4**	**5**	**15**	**0**	**0**	**0**

Traded to **Edmonton** by **Chicago** with Daniel Cleary, Chad Kilger and Christian Laflamme for Boris Mironov, Dean McAmmond and Jonas Elofsson, March 20, 1999.

• MORETTO, Angelo

Angelo Joseph C – L. 6'3", 212 lbs. b: Toronto, Ont., 9/18/1953. California's 9th, 160th overall, in 1973.

Season	Club	League	GP	G	A	Pts	AG	AA	APts	PIM	PP	SH	GW	S	%	TGF	PGF	TGA	PGA	+/–	GP	G	A	Pts	PIM	PP	SH	GW
1972-73	University of Michigan	WCHA	30	10	17	27	....	....	....	36	....	....	....	....	....	....	....	....	....	....	....	....	....	....	....	....	....	....
1973-74	University of Michigan	WCHA	34	25	22	47	....	....	....	28	....	....	....	....	....	....	....	....	....	....	....	....	....	....	....	....	....	....
1974-75	University of Michigan	WCHA	38	39	28	67	....	....	....	43	....	....	....	....	....	....	....	....	....	....	....	....	....	....	....	....	....	....
1975-76	University of Michigan	CCHA	27	24	18	42	....	....	....	50	....	....	....	....	....	....	....	....	....	....	....	....	....	....	....	....	....	....
1976-77	**Cleveland Barons**	**NHL**	**5**	**1**	**2**	**3**	**1**	**2**	**3**	**2**	**0**	**0**	**0**	**13**	**7.7**	**5**	**1**	**4**	**0**	**0**	....	....	....	....	....	....	....	....
	Salt Lake Golden Eagles	CHL	71	19	13	32	....	....	....	19	....	....	....	....	....	....	....	....	....	....	....	....	....	....	....	....	....	....
1977-78	Phoenix Roadrunners	CHL	14	1	6	7	....	....	....	22	....	....	....	....	....	....	....	....	....	....	....	....	....	....	....	....	....	....
1978-79	Oklahoma City Stars	CHL	47	17	21	38	....	....	....	28	....	....	....	....	....	....	....	....	....	....	....	....	....	....	....	....	....	....
	Indianapolis Racers	WHA	18	3	1	4	....	....	....	2	....	....	....	....	....	....	....	....	....	....	....	....	....	....	....	....	....	....
	NHL Totals		**5**	**1**	**2**	**3**	**1**	**2**	**3**	**2**	**0**	**0**	**0**	**13**	**7.7**	**5**	**1**	**4**	**0**		....	....	....	....	....	....	....	....
	Other Major League Totals		18	3	1	4	....	....	....	2	....	....	....	....	....	....	....	....	....	....	....	....	....	....	....	....	....	....

Rights traded to **Toronto** (WHA) by **San Diego** (WHA) for Tom Martin, June 20, 1975. Transferred to **Cleveland** after **California** franchise relocated, August 26, 1976. Signed as a free agent by **Indianapolis** (WHA), September 30, 1978.

• MORGAN, Jason

C – L. 6'1", 200 lbs. b: St. John's, Nfld., 10/9/1976. Los Angeles' 5th, 118th overall, in 1995.

Season	Club	League	GP	G	A	Pts	AG	AA	APts	PIM	PP	SH	GW	S	%	TGF	PGF	TGA	PGA	+/–	GP	G	A	Pts	PIM	PP	SH	GW
1992-93	Kitchener Midget Rangers	OMHA	69	44	40	84	....	....	....	85	....	....	....	....	....	....	....	....	....	....	....	....	....	....	....	....	....	....
1993-94	Kitchener Rangers	OHL	65	6	15	21	....	....	....	16	....	....	....	....	....	....	....	....	....	....	5	1	0	1	0	....	....	....
1994-95	Kitchener Rangers	OHL	35	3	15	18	....	....	....	25	....	....	....	....	....	....	....	....	....	....	....	....	....	....	....	....	....	....
	Kingston Frontenacs	OHL	20	0	3	3	....	....	....	14	....	....	....	....	....	....	....	....	....	....	6	0	2	2	0	....	....	....
1995-96	Kingston Frontenacs	OHL	66	16	38	54	....	....	....	50	....	....	....	....	....	....	....	....	....	....	6	1	2	3	0	....	....	....
1996-97	**Los Angeles Kings**	**NHL**	**3**	**0**	**0**	**0**	**0**	**0**	**0**	**0**	**0**	**0**	**0**	**4**	**0.0**	**0**	**0**	**3**	**0**	**–3**	....	....	....	....	....	....	....	....
	Phoenix Roadrunners	IHL	57	3	6	9	....	....	....	29	....	....	....	....	....	....	....	....	....	....	....	....	....	....	....	....	....	....
	Mississippi Sea Wolves	ECHL	6	3	0	3	....	....	....	0	....	....	....	....	....	....	....	....	....	....	3	1	1	2	6	....	....	....
1997-98	**Los Angeles Kings**	**NHL**	**11**	**1**	**0**	**1**	**1**	**0**	**1**	**4**	**0**	**0**	**0**	**5**	**20.0**	**1**	**0**	**9**	**1**	**–7**	....	....	....	....	....	....	....	....
	Springfield Falcons	AHL	58	13	22	35	....	....	....	66	....	....	....	....	....	....	....	....	....	....	3	1	0	1	18	....	....	....
1998-99	Long Beach Ice Dogs	IHL	13	4	6	10	....	....	....	18	....	....	....	....	....	....	....	....	....	....	....	....	....	....	....	....	....	....
	Springfield Falcons	AHL	46	6	16	22	....	....	....	51	....	....	....	....	....	....	....	....	....	....	3	0	0	0	6	....	....	....
99-2000	Cincinnati Cyclones	IHL	15	1	3	4	....	....	....	14	....	....	....	....	....	....	....	....	....	....	....	....	....	....	....	....	....	....
	Florida Everblades	ECHL	48	14	25	39	....	....	....	79	....	....	....	....	....	....	....	....	....	....	5	2	2	4	16	....	....	....
	NHL Totals		**14**	**1**	**0**	**1**	**1**	**0**	**1**	**4**	**0**	**0**	**0**	**9**	**11.1**	**1**	**0**	**12**	**1**		....	....	....	....	....	....	....	....

• MORIN, Stephane

C – L. 6', 174 lbs. b: Montreal, Que., 3/27/1969 d: 10/6/1998. Quebec's 3rd, 43rd overall, in 1989.

Season	Club	League	GP	G	A	Pts	AG	AA	APts	PIM	PP	SH	GW	S	%	TGF	PGF	TGA	PGA	+/–	GP	G	A	Pts	PIM	PP	SH	GW
1984-85	Bourassa Angevins	QAAA	41	16	22	38	....	....	....	....	....	....	....	....	....	....	....	....	....	....	....	....	....	....	....	....	....	....
1985-86	Montreal-Bourassa	QAAA	42	26	37	63	....	....	....	....	....	....	....	....	....	....	....	....	....	....	....	....	....	....	....	....	....	....
1986-87	Shawinigan Cataractes	QMJHL	65	9	14	23	....	....	....	28	....	....	....	....	....	....	....	....	....	....	....	....	....	....	....	....	....	....
1987-88	Chicoutimi Sagueneens	QMJHL	68	38	45	83	....	....	....	18	....	....	....	....	....	....	....	....	....	....	6	3	8	11	2	....	....	....
1988-89	Chicoutimi Sagueneens	QMJHL	70	77	*109	*186	....	....	....	71	....	....	....	....	....	....	....	....	....	....	....	....	....	....	....	....	....	....
1989-90	**Quebec Nordiques**	**NHL**	**6**	**0**	**2**	**2**	**0**	**1**	**1**	**2**	**0**	**0**	**0**	**11**	**0.0**	**2**	**0**	**1**	**0**	**1**	....	....	....	....	....	....	....	....
	Halifax Citadels	AHL	65	28	32	60	....	....	....	60	....	....	....	....	....	....	....	....	....	....	6	3	4	7	6	....	....	....
1990-91	**Quebec Nordiques**	**NHL**	**48**	**13**	**27**	**40**	**12**	**21**	**33**	**30**	**3**	**1**	**2**	**63**	**20.6**	**53**	**11**	**42**	**6**	**6**	....	....	....	....	....	....	....	....
	Halifax Citadels	AHL	17	8	14	22	....	....	....	18	....	....	....	....	....	....	....	....	....	....	....	....	....	....	....	....	....	....
1991-92	**Quebec Nordiques**	**NHL**	**30**	**2**	**8**	**10**	**2**	**6**	**8**	**14**	**0**	**0**	**0**	**41**	**4.9**	**19**	**4**	**17**	**0**	**–2**	....	....	....	....	....	....	....	....
	Halifax Citadels	AHL	30	17	13	30	....	....	....	29	....	....	....	....	....	....	....	....	....	....	....	....	....	....	....	....	....	....
1992-93	**Vancouver Canucks**	**NHL**	**1**	**0**	**1**	**1**	**0**	**1**	**1**	**0**	**0**	**0**	**0**	**3**	**0.0**	**1**	**0**	**2**	**0**	**–1**	....	....	....	....	....	....	....	....
	Hamilton Canucks	AHL	70	31	54	85	....	....	....	49	....	....	....	....	....	....	....	....	....	....	....	....	....	....	....	....	....	....
1993-94	**Vancouver Canucks**	**NHL**	**5**	**1**	**1**	**2**	**1**	**1**	**2**	**6**	**0**	**0**	**0**	**6**	**16.7**	**2**	**0**	**2**	**0**	**0**	....	....	....	....	....	....	....	....
	Hamilton Canucks	AHL	69	38	71	109	....	....	....	48	....	....	....	....	....	....	....	....	....	....	4	3	2	5	4	....	....	....
1994-95	Minnesota Moose	IHL	81	33	*81	*114	....	....	....	53	....	....	....	....	....	....	....	....	....	....	2	0	1	1	0	....	....	....
1995-96	Minnesota Moose	IHL	80	27	51	78	....	....	....	75	....	....	....	....	....	....	....	....	....	....	....	....	....	....	....	....	....	....
1996-97	Manitoba Moose	IHL	12	3	6	9	....	....	....	4	....	....	....	....	....	....	....	....	....	....	....	....	....	....	....	....	....	....
	Long Beach Ice Dogs	IHL	65	25	57	82	....	....	....	73	....	....	....	....	....	....	....	....	....	....	18	6	13	19	14	....	....	....
1997-98	Long Beach Ice Dogs	IHL	27	10	17	27	....	....	....	30	....	....	....	....	....	....	....	....	....	....	13	1	10	11	18	....	....	....
1998-99	Berlin Capitals	Germany	7	2	6	8	....	....	....	6	....	....	....	....	....	....	....	....	....	....	....	....	....	....	....	....	....	....
	NHL Totals		**90**	**16**	**39**	**55**	**15**	**30**	**45**	**52**	**3**	**1**	**2**	**124**	**12.9**	**77**	**15**	**64**	**6**		....	....	....	....	....	....	....	....

QMJHL First All-Star Team (1989) • IHL First All-Star Team (1995) • Won Leo P. Lamoureux Memorial Trophy (Top Scorer - IHL) (1995)

Signed as a free agent by **Vancouver**, October 5, 1992. • Suffered fatal heart attack during game vs. Revier Lowen, October 6, 1998.

• MORISSETTE, Dave

LW – L. 6'1", 224 lbs. b: Baie Comeau, Que., 12/24/1971. Washington's 7th, 146th overall, in 1991.

Season	Club	League	GP	G	A	Pts	AG	AA	APts	PIM	PP	SH	GW	S	%	TGF	PGF	TGA	PGA	+/–	GP	G	A	Pts	PIM	PP	SH	GW
1987-88	Lac St-Jean Cascades	QAAA	41	11	25	36	....	....	....	....	....	....	....	....	....	....	....	....	....	....	....	....	....	....	....	....	....	....
1988-89	Shawinigan Cataractes	QMJHL	66	4	11	15	....	....	....	298	....	....	....	....	....	....	....	....	....	....	....	....	....	....	....	....	....	....
1989-90	Shawinigan Cataractes	QMJHL	66	2	9	11	....	....	....	269	....	....	....	....	....	....	....	....	....	....	....	....	....	....	....	....	....	....
1990-91	Shawinigan Cataractes	QMJHL	64	20	26	46	....	....	....	224	....	....	....	....	....	....	....	....	....	....	6	1	1	2	17	....	....	....
1991-92	Hampton Roads Admirals	ECHL	47	6	10	16	....	....	....	293	....	....	....	....	....	....	....	....	....	....	13	1	3	4	74	....	....	....
	Baltimore Skipjacks	AHL	2	0	0	0	....	....	....	6	....	....	....	....	....	....	....	....	....	....	....	....	....	....	....	....	....	....
1992-93	Hampton Roads Admirals	ECHL	54	9	13	22	....	....	....	226	....	....	....	....	....	....	....	....	....	....	2	0	0	0	2	....	....	....
1993-94	Roanoke Express	ECHL	45	8	10	18	....	....	....	278	....	....	....	....	....	....	....	....	....	....	2	0	1	1	4	....	....	....
1994-95	Minnesota Moose	IHL	50	1	4	5	....	....	....	174	....	....	....	....	....	....	....	....	....	....	....	....	....	....	....	....	....	....
1995-96	Minnesota Moose	IHL	33	3	2	5	....	....	....	104	....	....	....	....	....	....	....	....	....	....	....	....	....	....	....	....	....	....
1996-97	Houston Aeros	IHL	59	2	1	3	....	....	....	214	....	....	....	....	....	....	....	....	....	....	2	0	0	0	0	....	....	....
	Austin Ice Bats	WPHL	5	2	3	5	....	....	....	10	....	....	....	....	....	....	....	....	....	....	....	....	....	....	....	....	....	....
1997-98	Houston Aeros	IHL	67	4	4	8	....	....	....	254	....	....	....	....	....	....	....	....	....	....	2	0	0	0	2	....	....	....
1998-99	**Montreal Canadiens**	**NHL**	**10**	**0**	**0**	**0**	**0**	**0**	**0**	**52**	**0**	**0**	**0**	**2**	**0.0**	**1**	**0**	**0**	**0**	**1**	....	....	....	....	....	....	....	....
	Fredericton Canadiens	AHL	39	4	4	8	....	....	....	152	....	....	....	....	....	....	....	....	....	....	12	0	1	1	31	....	....	....
99-2000	**Montreal Canadiens**	**NHL**	**1**	**0**	**0**	**0**	**0**	**0**	**0**	**5**	**0**	**0**	**0**	**0**	**0.0**	**0**	**0**	**0**	**0**	**0**	....	....	....	....	....	....	....	....
	Quebec Citadelles	AHL	47	2	4	6	....	....	....	231	....	....	....	....	....	....	....	....	....	....	2	0	0	0	0	....	....	....
	NHL Totals		**11**	**0**	**0**	**0**	**0**	**0**	**0**	**57**	**0**	**0**	**0**	**2**	**0.0**	**1**	**0**	**0**	**0**		....	....	....	....	....	....	....	....

Signed as a free agent by **Montreal**, June 10, 1998.

• MORO, Marc

"Mad-Dog" D – L. 6'1", 225 lbs. b: Toronto, Ont., 7/17/1977. Ottawa's 2nd, 27th overall, in 1995.

Season	Club	League	GP	G	A	Pts	AG	AA	APts	PIM	PP	SH	GW	S	%	TGF	PGF	TGA	PGA	+/–	GP	G	A	Pts	PIM	PP	SH	GW
1992-93	Mississauga Reps	MTHL	42	9	18	27	....	....	....	56	....	....	....	....	....	....	....	....	....	....	....	....	....	....	....	....	....	....
	Mississauga Senators	OJHL	2	0	0	0	....	....	....	0	....	....	....	....	....	....	....	....	....	....	....	....	....	....	....	....	....	....
1993-94	Kingston Voyageurs	OJHL	12	0	2	2	....	....	....	10	....	....	....	....	....	....	....	....	....	....	....	....	....	....	....	....	....	....
	Kingston Frontenacs	OHL	43	0	3	3	....	....	....	81	....	....	....	....	....	....	....	....	....	....	....	....	....	....	....	....	....	....
1994-95	Kingston Frontenacs	OHL	64	4	12	16	....	....	....	255	....	....	....	....	....	....	....	....	....	....	6	0	0	0	23	....	....	....
1995-96	Kingston Frontenacs	OHL	66	4	17	21	....	....	....	261	....	....	....	....	....	....	....	....	....	....	6	0	0	0	12	....	....	....
	P.E.I. Senators	AHL	2	0	0	0	....	....	....	7	....	....	....	....	....	....	....	....	....	....	2	0	0	0	4	....	....	....
1996-97	Kingston Frontenacs	OHL	37	4	8	12	....	....	....	97	....	....	....	....	....	....	....	....	....	....	....	....	....	....	....	....	....	....
	Sault Ste. Marie Greyhounds	OHL	26	0	5	5	....	....	....	74	....	....	....	....	....	....	....	....	....	....	11	1	6	7	38	....	....	....
1997-98	**Mighty Ducks of Anaheim**	**NHL**	**1**	**0**	**0**	**0**	**0**	**0**	**0**	**0**	**0**	**0**	**0**	**0**	**0.0**	**0**	**0**	**0**	**0**	**0**	....	....	....	....	....	....	....	....
	Cincinnati Mighty Ducks	AHL	74	1	6	7	....	....	....	181	....	....	....	....	....	....	....	....	....	....	....	....	....	....	....	....	....	....

			REGULAR SEASON																		PLAYOFFS							
Season	Club	League	GP	G	A	Pts	AG	AA	APts	PIM	PP	SH	GW	S	%	TGF	PGF	TGA	PGA	+/–	GP	G	A	Pts	PIM	PP	SH	GW
1998-99	Milwaukee Admirals	IHL	80	0	5	5	....	....	....	264	....	....	....	....	....	....	....	....	....	....	2	0	0	0	4	....	....	....
99-2000	**Nashville Predators**	**NHL**	8	0	0	0	0	0	0	40	0	0	0	3	0.0	0	0	4	1	–3	....	....	....	....	....	....	....	....
	Milwaukee Admirals	IHL	64	5	5	10	....	....	....	203	....	....	....	....	....	....	....	....	....	....	....	....	....	....	....	....	....	....
	NHL Totals		9	0	0	0	0	0	0	40	0	0	0	3	0.0	0	0	4	1		....	....	....	....	....	....	....	....

Rights traded to **Anaheim** by **Ottawa** with Ted Drury for Jason York and Shaun Van Allen, October 1, 1996. Traded to **Nashville** by **Anaheim** with Chris Mason for Dominic Roussel, October 5, 1998.

• MOROZOV, Aleksey

RW – L. 6'1", 198 lbs. b: Moscow, USSR, 2/16/1977. Pittsburgh's 1st, 24th overall, in 1995.

Season	Club	League	GP	G	A	Pts	AG	AA	APts	PIM	PP	SH	GW	S	%	TGF	PGF	TGA	PGA	+/–	GP	G	A	Pts	PIM	PP	SH	GW
1993-94	Krylja Sovetov Moscow	CIS	7	0	0	0	....	....	....	0	....	....	....	....	....	....	....	....	....	....	3	0	0	0	2	....	....	....
1994-95	Krylja Sovetov Moscow	CIS	48	15	12	27	....	....	....	53	....	....	....	....	....	....	....	....	....	....	4	0	3	3	0	....	....	....
1995-96	Krylja Sovetov Moscow	CIS	47	13	9	22	....	....	....	26	....	....	....	....	....	....	....	....	....	....	....	....	....	....	....	....	....	....
	Russia	WJC-A	7	5	3	8	....	....	....	2	....	....	....	....	....	....	....	....	....	....	....	....	....	....	....	....	....	....
1996-97	Krylja Sovetov Moscow	Russia	44	21	11	32	....	....	....	32	....	....	....	....	....	....	....	....	....	....	2	0	1	1	2	....	....	....
	Russia	WJC-A	6	5	3	8	....	....	....	6	....	....	....	....	....	....	....	....	....	....	....	....	....	....	....	....	....	....
	Russia	WC-A	9	3	3	6	....	....	....	2	....	....	....	....	....	....	....	....	....	....	....	....	....	....	....	....	....	....
1997-98	Krylja Sovetov Moscow	Russia	6	2	1	3	....	....	....	4	....	....	....	....	....	....	....	....	....	....	....	....	....	....	....	....	....	....
	Pittsburgh Penguins	**NHL**	76	13	13	26	15	13	28	8	2	0	3	80	16.3	32	4	32	0	–4	6	0	1	1	2	0	0	0
	Russia	Olympics	6	2	2	4	....	....	....	0	....	....	....	....	....	....	....	....	....	....	....	....	....	....	....	....	....	....
	Russia	WC-A	4	0	3	3	....	....	....	2	....	....	....	....	....	....	....	....	....	....	....	....	....	....	....	....	....	....
1998-99	**Pittsburgh Penguins**	**NHL**	67	9	10	19	11	10	21	14	0	0	0	75	12.0	27	1	27	6	5	10	1	1	2	0	0	0	0
99-2000	**Pittsburgh Penguins**	**NHL**	68	12	19	31	13	18	31	14	0	1	0	101	11.9	40	2	31	5	12	5	0	0	0	0	0	0	0
	NHL Totals		211	34	42	76	39	41	80	36	2	1	3	256	13.3	99	7	90	11		21	1	2	3	2	0	0	0

EJC-A All-Star Team (1995) • CIS Rookie of the Year (1995) • WJC-A All-Star Team (1996) • Named Best Forward at WJC-A (1997)

• MORRIS, Derek

D – R. 5'11", 200 lbs. b: Edmonton, Alta., 8/24/1978. Calgary's 1st, 13th overall, in 1996.

Season	Club	League	GP	G	A	Pts	AG	AA	APts	PIM	PP	SH	GW	S	%	TGF	PGF	TGA	PGA	+/–	GP	G	A	Pts	PIM	PP	SH	GW
1994-95	Red Deer Optomist Chiefs	AAHA	31	6	35	41	....	....	....	74	....	....	....	....	....	....	....	....	....	....	....	....	....	....	....	....	....	....
1995-96	Regina Pats	WHL	67	8	44	52	....	....	....	70	....	....	....	....	....	....	....	....	....	....	11	1	7	8	26	....	....	....
1996-97	Regina Pats	WHL	67	18	57	75	....	....	....	180	....	....	....	....	....	....	....	....	....	....	5	0	3	3	9	....	....	....
	Saint John Flames	AHL	7	0	3	3	....	....	....	7	....	....	....	....	....	....	....	....	....	....	5	0	3	3	7	....	....	....
1997-98	**Calgary Flames**	**NHL**	82	9	20	29	11	20	31	88	5	1	1	120	7.5	80	18	76	15	1	....	....	....	....	....	....	....	....
1998-99	**Calgary Flames**	**NHL**	71	7	27	34	8	26	34	73	3	0	2	150	4.7	72	21	57	10	4	....	....	....	....	....	....	....	....
	Canada	WC-A	10	0	4	4	....	....	....	6	....	....	....	....	....	....	....	....	....	....	....	....	....	....	....	....	....	....
99-2000	**Calgary Flames**	**NHL**	78	9	29	38	10	27	37	80	3	0	2	193	4.7	95	31	94	32	2	....	....	....	....	....	....	....	....
	NHL Totals		231	25	76	101	29	73	102	241	11	1	5	463	5.4	247	70	227	57		....	....	....	....	....	....	....	....

WHL East First All-Star Team (1997) • NHL All-Rookie Team (1998)

• MORRIS, Jon

C – R. 6', 175 lbs. b: Lowell, MA, 5/6/1966. New Jersey's 5th, 86th overall, in 1984.

Season	Club	League	GP	G	A	Pts	AG	AA	APts	PIM	PP	SH	GW	S	%	TGF	PGF	TGA	PGA	+/–	GP	G	A	Pts	PIM	PP	SH	GW
1983-84	Chelmsford High School	Hi-School	24	31	50	81	....	....	....	....	....	....	....	....	....	....	....	....	....	....	....	....	....	....	....	....	....	....
1984-85	U. of Massachussetts-Lowell	H-East	42	29	31	60	....	....	....	16	....	....	....	....	....	....	....	....	....	....	....	....	....	....	....	....	....	....
1985-86	U. of Massachussetts-Lowell	H-East	39	25	31	56	....	....	....	52	....	....	....	....	....	....	....	....	....	....	....	....	....	....	....	....	....	....
1986-87	U. of Massachussetts-Lowell	H-East	35	28	33	61	....	....	....	48	....	....	....	....	....	....	....	....	....	....	....	....	....	....	....	....	....	....
1987-88	U. of Massachussetts-Lowell	H-East	37	15	39	54	....	....	....	39	....	....	....	....	....	....	....	....	....	....	....	....	....	....	....	....	....	....
1988-89	U. of Massachussetts-Lowell	H-East	DID NOT PLAY																									
	New Jersey Devils	**NHL**	4	0	2	2	0	1	1	0	0	0	0	1	0.0	4	2	2	0	0	....	....	....	....	....	....	....	....
1989-90	**New Jersey Devils**	**NHL**	20	6	7	13	5	5	10	8	2	0	1	17	35.3	23	5	6	0	12	6	1	3	4	23	1	0	0
	Utica Devils	AHL	49	27	37	64	....	....	....	6	....	....	....	....	....	....	....	....	....	....	....	....	....	....	....	....	....	....
1990-91	**New Jersey Devils**	**NHL**	53	9	19	28	8	14	22	27	1	0	1	44	20.5	47	6	34	2	9	5	0	4	4	2	0	0	0
	Utica Devils	AHL	6	4	2	6	....	....	....	5	....	....	....	....	....	....	....	....	....	....	....	....	....	....	....	....	....	....
1991-92	**New Jersey Devils**	**NHL**	7	1	2	3	1	2	3	6	1	0	0	5	20.0	4	4	6	0	–6	....	....	....	....	....	....	....	....
	Utica Devils	AHL	7	1	4	5	....	....	....	0	....	....	....	....	....	....	....	....	....	....	....	....	....	....	....	....	....	....
1992-93	**New Jersey Devils**	**NHL**	2	0	0	0	0	0	0	0	0	0	0	1	0.0	0	0	1	0	–1	....	....	....	....	....	....	....	....
	Utica Devils	AHL	31	16	24	40	....	....	....	28	....	....	....	....	....	....	....	....	....	....	....	....	....	....	....	....	....	....
	Cincinnati Cyclones	IHL	18	7	19	26	....	....	....	24	....	....	....	....	....	....	....	....	....	....	....	....	....	....	....	....	....	....
	San Jose Sharks	**NHL**	13	0	3	3	0	2	2	6	0	0	0	11	0.0	3	1	12	0	–10	....	....	....	....	....	....	....	....
1993-94	Kansas City Blades	IHL	3	0	3	3	....	....	....	2	....	....	....	....	....	....	....	....	....	....	....	....	....	....	....	....	....	....
	Boston Bruins	**NHL**	4	0	0	0	0	0	0	0	0	0	0	3	0.0	0	0	2	0	–2	....	....	....	....	....	....	....	....
	Providence Bruins	AHL	67	22	44	66	....	....	....	20	....	....	....	....	....	....	....	....	....	....	....	....	....	....	....	....	....	....
1994-95	HC Gardena-Groden	Alpenliga	13	10	15	25	....	....	....	8	....	....	....	....	....	....	....	....	....	....	....	....	....	....	....	....	....	....
	HC Gardena-Groden	Italy	35	28	41	69	....	....	....	36	....	....	....	....	....	....	....	....	....	....	3	1	3	4	0	....	....	....
	United States	WC-A	6	3	5	8	....	....	....	4	....	....	....	....	....	....	....	....	....	....	....	....	....	....	....	....	....	....
1995-96	Ratinger Lowen	Germany	4	2	4	6	....	....	....	4	....	....	....	....	....	....	....	....	....	....	....	....	....	....	....	....	....	....
	NHL Totals		103	16	33	49	14	24	38	47	4	0	2	82	19.5	81	18	63	2		11	1	7	8	25	1	0	0

Hockey East First All-Star Team (1987)

• Missed majority of 1988-89 season completing college degree at the U. of Massachusetts-Amherst. Claimed on waivers by **San Jose** from **New Jersey**, March 13, 1993. Traded to **Boston** by **San Jose** for cash, October 28, 1993.

• MORRISON, Brendan

C – L. 5'11", 190 lbs. b: Pitt Meadows, B.C., 8/15/1975. New Jersey's 3rd, 39th overall, in 1993.

Season	Club	League	GP	G	A	Pts	AG	AA	APts	PIM	PP	SH	GW	S	%	TGF	PGF	TGA	PGA	+/–	GP	G	A	Pts	PIM	PP	SH	GW
1990-91	Ridge Meadows Knights	BCAHA	77	126	127	253	....	....	....	88	....	....	....	....	....	....	....	....	....	....	....	....	....	....	....	....	....	....
1991-92	Ridge Meadows Lightning	BCAHA	55	56	111	167	....	....	....	56	....	....	....	....	....	....	....	....	....	....	....	....	....	....	....	....	....	....
1992-93	Penticton Panthers	BCJHL	56	35	*59	94	....	....	....	45	....	....	....	....	....	....	....	....	....	....	....	....	....	....	....	....	....	....
1993-94	University of Michigan	CCHA	38	20	28	48	....	....	....	24	....	....	....	....	....	....	....	....	....	....	5	2	7	9	2	....	....	....
1994-95	University of Michigan	CCHA	39	23	*53	*76	....	....	....	42	....	....	....	....	....	....	....	....	....	....	5	1	11	12	6	....	....	....
1995-96	University of Michigan	CCHA	35	28	44	*72	....	....	....	41	....	....	....	....	....	....	....	....	....	....	7	6	9	15	4	....	....	....
1996-97	University of Michigan	CCHA	43	31	*57	*88	....	....	....	52	....	....	....	....	....	....	....	....	....	....	6	6	8	14	8	....	....	....
1997-98	**New Jersey Devils**	**NHL**	11	5	4	9	6	4	10	0	0	0	1	19	26.3	13	4	6	0	3	3	0	1	1	0	0	0	0
	Albany River Rats	AHL	72	35	49	84	....	....	....	44	....	....	....	....	....	....	....	....	....	....	8	3	4	7	19	....	....	....
1998-99	**New Jersey Devils**	**NHL**	76	13	33	46	15	32	47	18	5	0	2	111	11.7	62	29	40	3	–4	7	0	2	2	0	0	0	0
99-2000	SK Slavia Trebic-2	Czech-Rep	2	0	0	0	....	....	....	0	....	....	....	....	....	....	....	....	....	....	....	....	....	....	....	....	....	....
	HC Pardubice	Czech-Rep	6	5	2	7	....	....	....	2	....	....	....	....	....	....	....	....	....	....	....	....	....	....	....	....	....	....
	New Jersey Devils	**NHL**	44	5	21	26	6	19	25	8	2	0	1	79	6.3	36	10	24	6	8	....	....	....	....	....	....	....	....
	Vancouver Canucks	**NHL**	12	2	7	9	2	6	8	10	0	0	0	17	11.8	14	3	8	1	4	....	....	....	....	....	....	....	....
	Canada	WC-A	7	1	3	4	....	....	....	2	....	....	....	....	....	....	....	....	....	....	....	....	....	....	....	....	....	....
	NHL Totals		143	25	65	90	29	61	90	36	7	0	4	226	11.1	125	46	78	10		10	0	3	3	0	0	0	0

CCHA First All-Star Team (1995, 1996, 1997) • NCAA West First All-American Team (1995, 1996, 1997) • NCAA Championship All-Tournament Team (1996) • NCAA Championship Tournament MVP (1996) • Won Hobey Baker Memorial Award (Top U.S. Collegiate Player) (1997)

Traded to **Vancouver** by **New Jersey** with Denis Pederson for Alexander Mogilny, March 14, 2000.

• MORRISON, Dave

David Stuart RW – R. 6', 190 lbs. b: Toronto, Ont., 6/12/1962. Los Angeles' 4th, 34th overall, in 1980.

Season	Club	League	GP	G	A	Pts	AG	AA	APts	PIM	PP	SH	GW	S	%	TGF	PGF	TGA	PGA	+/–	GP	G	A	Pts	PIM	PP	SH	GW
1977-78	Mississauga Reps	MTHL	STATISTICS NOT AVAILABLE																									
1978-79	Markham Waxers	OJHL	48	13	25	38	....	....	....	27	....	....	....	....	....	....	....	....	....	....	....	....	....	....	....	....	....	....
1979-80	Peterborough Petes	OMJHL	48	18	19	37	....	....	....	35	....	....	....	....	....	....	....	....	....	....	....	....	....	....	....	....	....	....
1980-81	Peterborough Petes	OMJHL	62	44	53	97	....	....	....	71	....	....	....	....	....	....	....	....	....	....	5	0	3	3	11	....	....	....
	Los Angeles Kings	**NHL**	3	0	0	0	0	0	0	0	0	0	0	2	0.0	0	0	1	0	–1	....	....	....	....	....	....	....	....
1981-82	Peterborough Petes	OHL	53	33	31	64	....	....	....	38	....	....	....	....	....	....	....	....	....	....	9	6	6	12	27	....	....	....
	Canada	WJC-A	7	1	2	3	....	....	....	0	....	....	....	....	....	....	....	....	....	....	....	....	....	....	....	....	....	....
	Los Angeles Kings	**NHL**	4	0	0	0	0	0	0	0	0	0	0	6	0.0	1	0	2	0	–1	....	....	....	....	....	....	....	....
	New Haven Nighthawks	AHL	2	0	0	0	....	....	....	2	....	....	....	....	....	....	....	....	....	....	3	1	1	2	0	....	....	....

			REGULAR SEASON																		PLAYOFFS							
Season	Club	League	GP	G	A	Pts	AG	AA	APts	PIM	PP	SH	GW	S	%	TGF	PGF	TGA	PGA	+/-	GP	G	A	Pts	PIM	PP	SH	GW
1982-83	**Los Angeles Kings**	**NHL**	**24**	**3**	**3**	**6**	**2**	**2**	**4**	**4**	**0**	**0**	**1**	**16**	**18.8**	**13**	**2**	**19**	**1**	**–7**	....	....	....	....	....	....	....	....
	New Haven Nighthawks	AHL	59	23	17	40	....	....	....	36	....	....	....	....	....	....	....	....	....	....	11	3	1	4	23	....	....	....
1983-84	New Haven Nighthawks	AHL	8	0	4	4	....	....	....	2	....	....	....	....	....	....	....	....	....	....	....	....	....	....	....	....	....	....
	Fredericton Express	AHL	68	14	19	33	....	....	....	51	....	....	....	....	....	....	....	....	....	....	7	2	4	6	0	....	....	....
1984-85	**Vancouver Canucks**	**NHL**	**8**	**0**	**0**	**0**	**0**	**0**	**0**	**0**	**0**	**0**	**0**	**8**	**0.0**	**0**	**0**	**12**	**6**	**–6**	....	....	....	....	....	....	....	....
1985-86	EC Stuttgart	Germany-3	26	38	28	66	....	....	....	18	....	....	....	....	....	....	....	....	....	....	14	22	23	45	10	....	....	....
1986-87	EC Stuttgart	Germany-3	28	*95	85	180	....	....	....	....	....	....	....	....	....	....	....	....	....	....	14	*32	27	59	....	....	....	....
1987-88	EC Stuttgart	Germany-2	28	62	61	123	....	....	....	....	....	....	....	....	....	....	....	....	....	....	12	*21	12	33	....	....	....	....
1988-89	SC Herisau	Switz-2	45	35	34	69	....	....	....	37	....	....	....	....	....	....	....	....	....	....	....	....	....	....	....	....	....	....
1989-90	EC Ratingen-Lowen	Germany-2	32	38	56	94	....	....	....	37	....	....	....	....	....	....	....	....	....	....	18	29	42	71	....	....	....	....
	Holland	WEC-B	7	1	3	4	....	....	....	0	....	....	....	....	....	....	....	....	....	....	....	....	....	....	....	....	....	....
1990-91	IJHC Rotterdam	Holland	40	12	21	33	....	....	....	8	....	....	....	....	....	....	....	....	....	....	....	....	....	....	....	....	....	....
	Holland	WEC-B	7	0	0	0	....	....	....	2	....	....	....	....	....	....	....	....	....	....	....	....	....	....	....	....	....	....
1991-92	EC Kassel	Germany-2	43	59	45	104	....	....	....	48	....	....	....	....	....	....	....	....	....	....	....	....	....	....	....	....	....	....
1992-93	Eisbaren Berlin	Germany	13	8	9	17	....	....	....	6	....	....	....	....	....	....	....	....	....	....	4	0	6	6	2	....	....	....
1993-94	Eisbaren Berlin	Germany	44	13	15	28	....	....	....	32	....	....	....	....	....	....	....	....	....	....	....	....	....	....	....	....	....	....
1994-95	Kassel Huskies	Germany	29	4	13	17	....	....	....	14	....	....	....	....	....	....	....	....	....	....	9	1	6	7	4	....	....	....
1995-96	Kassel Huskies	Germany	50	9	26	35	....	....	....	16	....	....	....	....	....	....	....	....	....	....	8	1	4	5	0	....	....	....
1996-97	Kassel Huskies	Germany	49	6	21	27	....	....	....	32	....	....	....	....	....	....	....	....	....	....	10	0	5	5	2	....	....	....
1997-98	Manchester Storm	BH-Cup	14	4	8	12	....	....	....	6	....	....	....	....	....	....	....	....	....	....	....	....	....	....	....	....	....	....
	Manchester Storm	Britain	36	5	26	31	....	....	....	10	....	....	....	....	....	....	....	....	....	....	9	4	2	6	0	....	....	....
	Manchester Storm	EuroHL	6	0	4	4	....	....	....	2	....	....	....	....	....	....	....	....	....	....	....	....	....	....	....	....	....	....
1998-99	Manchester Storm	BH-Cup	12	1	6	7	....	....	....	4	....	....	....	....	....	....	....	....	....	....	....	....	....	....	....	....	....	....
	Manchester Storm	Britain	36	5	16	21	....	....	....	8	....	....	....	....	....	....	....	....	....	....	5	0	1	1	12	....	....	....
	Manchester Storm	EuroHL	6	2	1	3	....	....	....	0	....	....	....	....	....	....	....	....	....	....	....	....	....	....	....	....	....	....
99-2000	**Vancouver Canucks**	**NHL**	DID NOT PLAY – SCOUTING																									
	NHL Totals		**39**	**3**	**3**	**6**	**2**	**2**	**4**	**4**	**0**	**0**	**1**	**32**	**9.4**	**14**	**2**	**34**	**7**		....	....	....	....	....	....	....	....

• Son of Jim

Signed as a free agent by **Vancouver**, October 28, 1983. • Announced retirement to become scout with Vancouver Canucks, April 15, 1999.

• MORRISON, Doug

Douglas RW – R. 5'11", 184 lbs. b: Vancouver, B.C., 2/1/1960. Boston's 3rd, 36th overall, in 1979.

Season	Club	League	GP	G	A	Pts	AG	AA	APts	PIM	PP	SH	GW	S	%	TGF	PGF	TGA	PGA	+/-	GP	G	A	Pts	PIM	PP	SH	GW
1975-76	Richmond Sockeyes	PCJHL	40	37	47	84	....	....	....	82	....	....	....	....	....	....	....	....	....	....	....	....	....	....	....	....	....	....
1976-77	Lethbridge Broncos	WCJHL	70	24	35	59	....	....	....	80	....	....	....	....	....	....	....	....	....	....	....	....	....	....	....	....	....	....
1977-78	Lethbridge Broncos	WCJHL	66	25	45	70	....	....	....	116	....	....	....	....	....	....	....	....	....	....	....	....	....	....	....	....	....	....
1978-79	Lethbridge Broncos	WHL	64	56	67	123	....	....	....	159	....	....	....	....	....	....	....	....	....	....	19	20	15	35	7	....	....	....
1979-80	Lethbridge Broncos	WHL	68	58	59	117	....	....	....	188	....	....	....	....	....	....	....	....	....	....	4	5	3	8	15	....	....	....
	Boston Bruins	**NHL**	**1**	**0**	**0**	**0**	**0**	**0**	**0**	**0**	**0**	**0**	**0**	**1**	**0.0**	**0**	**0**	**0**	**0**	**0**	....	....	....	....	....	....	....	....
1980-81	**Boston Bruins**	**NHL**	**18**	**7**	**3**	**10**	**5**	**2**	**7**	**13**	**2**	**0**	**0**	**30**	**23.3**	**17**	**5**	**7**	**0**	**5**	....	....	....	....	....	....	....	....
	Springfield Indians	AHL	42	19	30	49	....	....	....	28	....	....	....	....	....	....	....	....	....	....	7	4	5	9	2	....	....	....
1981-82	**Boston Bruins**	**NHL**	**3**	**0**	**0**	**0**	**0**	**0**	**0**	**0**	**0**	**0**	**0**	**1**	**0.0**	**1**	**0**	**3**	**0**	**–2**	....	....	....	....	....	....	....	....
	Erie Blades	AHL	75	23	35	58	....	....	....	31	....	....	....	....	....	....	....	....	....	....	....	....	....	....	....	....	....	....
1982-83	Maine Mariners	AHL	61	38	29	67	....	....	....	44	....	....	....	....	....	....	....	....	....	....	14	5	1	6	4	....	....	....
1983-84	Hershey Bears	AHL	72	38	40	78	....	....	....	42	....	....	....	....	....	....	....	....	....	....	....	....	....	....	....	....	....	....
1984-85	**Boston Bruins**	**NHL**	**1**	**0**	**0**	**0**	**0**	**0**	**0**	**2**	**0**	**0**	**0**	**1**	**0.0**	**0**	**0**	**0**	**0**	**0**	....	....	....	....	....	....	....	....
	Hershey Bears	AHL	65	28	25	53	....	....	....	25	....	....	....	....	....	....	....	....	....	....	....	....	....	....	....	....	....	....
1985-86	Salt Lake Golden Eagles	IHL	80	27	34	61	....	....	....	30	....	....	....	....	....	....	....	....	....	....	5	7	3	10	14	....	....	....
1986-87	Salt Lake Golden Eagles	IHL	73	48	39	87	....	....	....	24	....	....	....	....	....	....	....	....	....	....	17	9	8	17	26	....	....	....
1987-88	ECH Munich	Germany	28	*64	55	119	....	....	....	71	....	....	....	....	....	....	....	....	....	....	18	20	16	36	25	....	....	....
1988-89	ECH Munich	Germany-2	28	50	42	92	....	....	....	88	....	....	....	....	....	....	....	....	....	....	18	23	21	44	*55	....	....	....
1989-90	HC Merano	Italy-2	25	25	23	48	....	....	....	18	....	....	....	....	....	....	....	....	....	....	....	....	....	....	....	....	....	....
1990-91	EC Bad Tolz	Germany-2	1	0	1	1	....	....	....	2	....	....	....	....	....	....	....	....	....	....	....	....	....	....	....	....	....	....
1991-92	EC Peiting	Germany-3	14	11	17	28	....	....	....	10	....	....	....	....	....	....	....	....	....	....	12	13	18	31	11	....	....	....
	NHL Totals		**23**	**7**	**3**	**10**	**5**	**2**	**7**	**15**	**2**	**0**	**0**	**33**	**21.2**	**18**	**5**	**10**	**0**		....	....	....	....	....	....	....	....

• Brother of Mark

• MORRISON, Gary

RW – R. 6'2", 200 lbs. b: Detroit, MI, 11/8/1955. Philadelphia's 4th, 90th overall, in 1975.

Season	Club	League	GP	G	A	Pts	AG	AA	APts	PIM	PP	SH	GW	S	%	TGF	PGF	TGA	PGA	+/-	GP	G	A	Pts	PIM	PP	SH	GW
1972-73	Ecorse East Miners	MNHL	STATISTICS NOT AVAILABLE																		....	....	....	....	....	....	....	....
1973-74	University of Michigan	WCHA	15	7	0	7	....	....	....	25	....	....	....	....	....	....	....	....	....	....	....	....	....	....	....	....	....	....
1974-75	University of Michigan	WCHA	34	8	6	14	....	....	....	31	....	....	....	....	....	....	....	....	....	....	....	....	....	....	....	....	....	....
1975-76	University of Michigan	WCHA	25	5	5	10	....	....	....	27	....	....	....	....	....	....	....	....	....	....	....	....	....	....	....	....	....	....
1976-77	University of Michigan	WCHA	38	6	5	11	....	....	....	25	....	....	....	....	....	....	....	....	....	....	....	....	....	....	....	....	....	....
1977-78	Milwaukee Admirals	IHL	76	21	21	42	....	....	....	203	....	....	....	....	....	....	....	....	....	....	4	0	3	3	7	....	....	....
1978-79	Maine Mariners	AHL	62	14	15	29	....	....	....	73	....	....	....	....	....	....	....	....	....	....	10	0	8	8	35	....	....	....
1979-80	**Philadelphia Flyers**	**NHL**	**3**	**0**	**2**	**2**	**0**	**1**	**1**	**0**	**0**	**0**	**0**	**1**	**0.0**	**3**	**0**	**3**	**0**	**0**	**5**	**0**	**1**	**1**	**2**	**0**	**0**	**0**
	Maine Mariners	AHL	75	29	23	52	....	....	....	151	....	....	....	....	....	....	....	....	....	....	2	1	0	1	4	....	....	....
1980-81	**Philadelphia Flyers**	**NHL**	**33**	**1**	**13**	**14**	**1**	**9**	**10**	**68**	**0**	**0**	**1**	**21**	**4.8**	**24**	**2**	**12**	**0**	**10**	....	....	....	....	....	....	....	....
	Maine Mariners	AHL	34	9	6	15	....	....	....	53	....	....	....	....	....	....	....	....	....	....	17	4	5	9	80	....	....	....
1981-82	**Philadelphia Flyers**	**NHL**	**7**	**0**	**0**	**0**	**0**	**0**	**0**	**2**	**0**	**0**	**0**	**5**	**0.0**	**1**	**0**	**7**	**0**	**–6**	....	....	....	....	....	....	....	....
	Maine Mariners	AHL	46	13	10	23	....	....	....	52	....	....	....	....	....	....	....	....	....	....	3	1	0	1	4	....	....	....
	NHL Totals		**43**	**1**	**15**	**16**	**1**	**10**	**11**	**70**	**0**	**0**	**1**	**27**	**3.7**	**28**	**2**	**22**	**0**		**5**	**0**	**1**	**1**	**2**	**0**	**0**	**0**

• MORRISON, George

George Harold LW – L. 6'1", 170 lbs. b: Toronto, Ont., 12/24/1948.

Season	Club	League	GP	G	A	Pts	AG	AA	APts	PIM	PP	SH	GW	S	%	TGF	PGF	TGA	PGA	+/-	GP	G	A	Pts	PIM	PP	SH	GW
1968-69	University of Denver	WCHA	32	40	18	58	....	....	....	12	....	....	....	....	....	....	....	....	....	....	....	....	....	....	....	....	....	....
1969-70	University of Denver	WCHA	32	30	27	57	....	....	....	12	....	....	....	....	....	....	....	....	....	....	....	....	....	....	....	....	....	....
1970-71	**St. Louis Blues**	**NHL**	**73**	**15**	**10**	**25**	**15**	**8**	**23**	**6**	**3**	**0**	**1**	**122**	**12.3**	**42**	**12**	**32**	**0**	**–2**	**3**	**0**	**0**	**0**	**0**	**0**	**0**	**0**
1971-72	**St. Louis Blues**	**NHL**	**42**	**2**	**11**	**13**	**2**	**9**	**11**	**7**	**2**	**0**	**1**	**34**	**5.9**	**21**	**9**	**23**	**0**	**–11**	....	....	....	....	....	....	....	....
1972-73	Minnesota Fighting Saints	WHA	70	16	24	40	....	....	....	20	....	....	....	....	....	....	....	....	....	....	5	1	1	2	2	....	....	....
1973-74	Minnesota Fighting Saints	WHA	73	40	38	78	....	....	....	37	....	....	....	....	....	....	....	....	....	....	11	5	5	10	12	....	....	....
1974-75	Minnesota Fighting Saints	WHA	76	31	29	60	....	....	....	30	....	....	....	....	....	....	....	....	....	....	12	5	9	14	0	....	....	....
1975-76	Calgary Cowboys	WHA	79	25	32	57	....	....	....	13	....	....	....	....	....	....	....	....	....	....	10	3	2	5	0	....	....	....
1976-77	Calgary Cowboys	WHA	63	11	19	30	....	....	....	10	....	....	....	....	....	....	....	....	....	....	....	....	....	....	....	....	....	....
	NHL Totals		**115**	**17**	**21**	**38**	**17**	**17**	**34**	**13**	**5**	**0**	**2**	**156**	**10.9**	**63**	**21**	**55**	**0**		**3**	**0**	**0**	**0**	**0**	**0**	**0**	**0**
	Other Major League Totals		361	123	142	265	....	....	....	110	....	....	....	....	....	....	....	....	....	....	38	14	17	31	14	....	....	....

WCHA First All-Star Team (1969, 1970) • NCAA West First All-American Team (1969, 1970)

Signed as a free agent by **St. Louis**, September 30, 1970. Selected by **Minnesota** (WHA) in 1972 WHA General Player Draft, February 12, 1972. Traded to **Buffalo** by **St. Louis** with St. Louis' 2nd round choice (Larry Carriere) in 1972 Amateur Draft for Chris Evans, March 5, 1972. • Suspended by **Buffalo** for refusing to report to **Rochester** (AHL), March 8, 1972. Traded to **Calgary** (WHA) by **Minnesota** (WHA) with Don Tannahill and the rights to Joe Micheletti and Wally Olds for John McKenzie and cash, September, 1975.

• MORRISON, Jim

James Stewart Hunter D – L. 5'10", 183 lbs. b: Montreal, Que., 10/11/1931.

Season	Club	League	GP	G	A	Pts	AG	AA	APts	PIM	PP	SH	GW	S	%	TGF	PGF	TGA	PGA	+/-	GP	G	A	Pts	PIM	PP	SH	GW
1949-50	Verdun Jr. Maple Leafs	QJHL	36	15	15	30	....	....	....	16	....	....	....	....	....	....	....	....	....	....	4	3	1	4	0	....	....	....
1950-51	Barrie Flyers	OHA-Jr.	53	19	42	61	....	....	....	63	....	....	....	....	....	....	....	....	....	....	12	3	10	13	14	....	....	....
	Barrie Flyers	Mem-Cup	11	5	7	12	....	....	....	20	....	....	....	....	....	....	....	....	....	....	....	....	....	....	....	....	....	....
1951-52	**Boston Bruins**	**NHL**	**14**	**0**	**2**	**2**	**0**	**2**	**2**	**2**	....	....	....	....	....	....	....	....	....	....	....	....	....	....	....	....	....	....
	Hershey Bears	AHL	24	3	18	21	....	....	....	16	....	....	....	....	....	....	....	....	....	....	....	....	....	....	....	....	....	....
	Toronto Maple Leafs	**NHL**	**17**	**0**	**1**	**1**	**0**	**1**	**1**	**4**	....	....	....	....	....	....	....	....	....	....	**2**	**0**	**0**	**0**	**0**	**0**	**0**	**0**
	Pittsburgh Hornets	AHL	15	5	7	12	....	....	....	2	....	....	....	....	....	....	....	....	....	....	....	....	....	....	....	....	....	....
1952-53	**Toronto Maple Leafs**	**NHL**	**56**	**1**	**8**	**9**	**1**	**10**	**11**	**36**	....	....	....	....	....	....	....	....	....	....	....	....	....	....	....	....	....	....
1953-54	**Toronto Maple Leafs**	**NHL**	**60**	**9**	**11**	**20**	**12**	**13**	**25**	**51**	....	....	....	....	....	....	....	....	....	....	**5**	**0**	**0**	**0**	**4**	**0**	**0**	**0**

Season	Club	League	REGULAR SEASON																		PLAYOFFS							
			GP	G	A	Pts	AG	AA	APts	PIM	PP	SH	GW	S	%	TGF	PGF	TGA	PGA	+/–	GP	G	A	Pts	PIM	PP	SH	GW
1954-55	**Toronto Maple Leafs**	**NHL**	**70**	**5**	**12**	**17**	**6**	**14**	**20**	**84**	....	....	....	....	....	....	....	....	....	....	**4**	**0**	**1**	**1**	**4**	**0**	**0**	**0**
1955-56	**Toronto Maple Leafs**	**NHL**	**63**	**2**	**17**	**19**	**3**	**20**	**23**	**77**	....	....	....	....	....	....	....	....	....	....	**5**	**0**	**0**	**0**	**4**	**0**	**0**	**0**
1956-57	**Toronto Maple Leafs**	**NHL**	**63**	**3**	**17**	**20**	**4**	**19**	**23**	**44**	....	....	....	....	....	....	....	....	....	....	....	....	....	....	....	....	....	....
1957-58	**Toronto Maple Leafs**	**NHL**	**70**	**3**	**21**	**24**	**4**	**22**	**26**	**62**	....	....	....	....	....	....	....	....	....	....	....	....	....	....	....	....	....	....
1958-59	**Boston Bruins**	**NHL**	**70**	**8**	**17**	**25**	**9**	**17**	**26**	**42**	....	....	....	....	....	....	....	....	....	....	**6**	**0**	**6**	**6**	**16**	**0**	**0**	**0**
1959-60	**Detroit Red Wings**	**NHL**	**70**	**3**	**23**	**26**	**3**	**22**	**25**	**62**	....	....	....	....	....	....	....	....	....	....	**6**	**0**	**2**	**2**	**0**	**0**	**0**	**0**
1960-61	**New York Rangers**	**NHL**	**19**	**1**	**6**	**7**	**1**	**6**	**7**	**6**	....	....	....	....	....	....	....	....	....	....	....	....	....	....	....	....	....	....
	Quebec Aces	AHL	45	9	24	33	....	....	....	61	....	....	....	....	....	....	....	....	....	....	....	....	....	....	....	....	....	....
1961-62	Quebec Aces	AHL	68	8	28	36	....	....	....	55	....	....	....	....	....	....	....	....	....	....	....	....	....	....	....	....	....	....
1962-63	Quebec Aces	AHL	51	5	22	27	....	....	....	26	....	....	....	....	....	....	....	....	....	....	....	....	....	....	....	....	....	....
1963-64	Quebec Aces	AHL	69	11	28	39	....	....	....	42	....	....	....	....	....	....	....	....	....	....	9	1	0	1	8	....	....	....
1964-65	Quebec Aces	AHL	52	6	21	27	....	....	....	66	....	....	....	....	....	....	....	....	....	....	4	0	0	0	0	....	....	....
1965-66	Quebec Aces	AHL	71	11	48	59	....	....	....	78	....	....	....	....	....	....	....	....	....	....	6	2	3	5	8	....	....	....
1966-67	Quebec Aces	AHL	70	5	45	50	....	....	....	37	....	....	....	....	....	....	....	....	....	....	5	1	4	5	12	....	....	....
1967-68	Quebec Aces	AHL	58	4	35	39	....	....	....	30	....	....	....	....	....	....	....	....	....	....	15	4	12	16	14	....	....	....
1968-69	Baltimore Clippers	AHL	65	5	32	37	....	....	....	35	....	....	....	....	....	....	....	....	....	....	4	2	1	3	10	....	....	....
1969-70	**Pittsburgh Penguins**	**NHL**	**59**	**5**	**15**	**20**	**5**	**14**	**19**	**40**	**2**	**0**	**0**	**135**	**3.7**	**64**	**28**	**78**	**22**	**–20**	**8**	**0**	**3**	**3**	**10**	**0**	**0**	**0**
1970-71	**Pittsburgh Penguins**	**NHL**	**73**	**0**	**10**	**10**	**0**	**8**	**8**	**32**	**0**	**0**	**0**	**134**	**0.0**	**52**	**4**	**82**	**22**	**–12**	....	....	....	....	....	....	....	....
1971-72	Baltimore Clippers	AHL	68	8	22	30	....	....	....	62	....	....	....	....	....	....	....	....	....	....	18	2	7	9	14	....	....	....
1972-73	Baltimore Clippers	AHL	65	5	11	16	....	....	....	46	....	....	....	....	....	....	....	....	....	....	....	....	....	....	....	....	....	....
	NHL Totals		**704**	**40**	**160**	**200**	**48**	**168**	**216**	**542**	....	....	....	....	....	....	....	....	....		**36**	**0**	**12**	**12**	**38**	....	....	....

• Father of Dave • AHL Second All-Star Team (1962, 1964, 1965, 1967, 1968, 1969, 1972) • AHL First All-Star Team (1966) • Won Eddie Shore Award (Outstanding Defenseman - AHL) (1966)

Played in NHL All-Star Game (1955, 1956, 1957)

Traded to **Toronto** by **Boston** for Fleming Mackell, January 9, 1952. Traded to **Boston** by **Toronto** for Allan Stanley, October 8, 1958. Traded to **Detroit** by **Boston** for Nick Mickoski, August 25, 1959. Traded to **Chicago** by **Detroit** for Howie Glover, June 5, 1960. Claimed by **NY Rangers** from **Chicago** in Intra-League Draft, June 8, 1960. Traded to **Quebec** (AHL) by **NY Rangers** for cash, November 28, 1960. NHL rights transferred to **Philadelphia** after NHL club purchased **Quebec** (AHL) franchise, May 8, 1967. Claimed by **Baltimore** (AHL) from **Philadelphia** (Quebec-AHL) in Reverse Draft, June 13, 1968. Traded to **Pittsburgh** by **Baltimore** (AHL) for cash and future considerations (Bob Rivard, November, 1969), October, 1969.

• MORRISON, Kevin

Kevin Gregory Joseph D – L. 6′, 202 lbs. b: Sydney, N.S., 10/28/1949. NY Rangers' 4th, 35th overall, in 1969.

Season	Club	League	GP	G	A	Pts	AG	AA	APts	PIM	PP	SH	GW	S	%	TGF	PGF	TGA	PGA	+/–	GP	G	A	Pts	PIM	PP	SH	GW
1966-67	Drummonville Rangers	QJHL	3	0	0	0	....	....	....	4	....	....	....	....	....	....	....	....	....	....	....	....	....	....	....	....	....	....
1967-68	Drummondville Rangers	QJHL	10	1	1	2	....	....	....	21	....	....	....	....	....	....	....	....	....	....	....	....	....	....	....	....	....	....
	Drummondville Rangers	Mem-Cup	4	0	1	1	....	....	....	6	....	....	....	....	....	....	....	....	....	....	....	....	....	....	....	....	....	....
1968-69	St-Jerome Alouettes	QJHL	STATISTICS NOT AVAILABLE																									
1969-70	New Haven Blades	EHL	48	24	18	42	....	....	....	136	....	....	....	....	....	....	....	....	....	....	11	4	7	11	53	....	....	....
	Omaha Knights	CHL	....	....	....	....	....	....	....	....	....	....	....	....	....	....	....	....	....	....	5	2	0	2	20	....	....	....
1970-71	New Haven Blades	EHL	64	11	44	55	....	....	....	*348	....	....	....	....	....	....	....	....	....	....	14	3	6	9	67	....	....	....
	Fort Worth Wings	CHL	3	0	0	0	....	....	....	0	....	....	....	....	....	....	....	....	....	....	....	....	....	....	....	....	....	....
1971-72	Tidewater Red Wings	AHL	11	0	2	2	....	....	....	18	....	....	....	....	....	....	....	....	....	....	....	....	....	....	....	....	....	....
	Fort Worth Wings	CHL	26	2	1	3	....	....	....	56	....	....	....	....	....	....	....	....	....	....	....	....	....	....	....	....	....	....
	Rochester Americans	AHL	29	2	0	2	....	....	....	49	....	....	....	....	....	....	....	....	....	....	....	....	....	....	....	....	....	....
1972-73	New Haven Nighthawks	AHL	74	7	28	35	....	....	....	154	....	....	....	....	....	....	....	....	....	....	....	....	....	....	....	....	....	....
1973-74	New York-Jersey Knights	WHA	78	24	43	67	....	....	....	132	....	....	....	....	....	....	....	....	....	....	....	....	....	....	....	....	....	....
1974-75	San Diego Mariners	WHA	78	20	61	81	....	....	....	143	....	....	....	....	....	....	....	....	....	....	10	0	7	7	2	....	....	....
1975-76	San Diego Mariners	WHA	80	22	43	65	....	....	....	56	....	....	....	....	....	....	....	....	....	....	11	1	5	6	12	....	....	....
1976-77	San Diego Mariners	WHA	75	8	30	38	....	....	....	68	....	....	....	....	....	....	....	....	....	....	7	1	3	4	8	....	....	....
1977-78	Indianapolis Racers	WHA	75	17	40	57	....	....	....	49	....	....	....	....	....	....	....	....	....	....	....	....	....	....	....	....	....	....
1978-79	Indianapolis Racers	WHA	5	0	2	2	....	....	....	0	....	....	....	....	....	....	....	....	....	....	....	....	....	....	....	....	....	....
	Quebec Nordiques	WHA	27	2	5	7	....	....	....	14	....	....	....	....	....	....	....	....	....	....	....	....	....	....	....	....	....	....
	Philadelphia Firebirds	AHL	23	1	13	14	....	....	....	15	....	....	....	....	....	....	....	....	....	....	....	....	....	....	....	....	....	....
1979-80	**Colorado Rockies**	**NHL**	**41**	**4**	**11**	**15**	**3**	**8**	**11**	**23**	**2**	**0**	**1**	**64**	**6.3**	**40**	**11**	**39**	**4**	**–6**	....	....	....	....	....	....	....	....
	Fort Worth Texans	CHL	33	5	16	21	....	....	....	45	....	....	....	....	....	....	....	....	....	....	....	....	....	....	....	....	....	....
1980-81			REINSTATED AS AN AMATEUR																									
1981-1985	Stephenville Jets	Nfld-Sr.	STATISTICS NOT AVAILABLE																									
1985-86	Stephenville Jets	Nfld-Sr.	39	18	25	43	....	....	....	110	....	....	....	....	....	....	....	....	....	....	....	....	....	....	....	....	....	....
	NHL Totals		**41**	**4**	**11**	**15**	**3**	**8**	**11**	**23**	**2**	**0**	**1**	**64**	**6.3**	**40**	**11**	**39**	**4**		....	....	....	....	....	....	....	....
	Other Major League Totals		418	93	224	317	....	....	....	462	....	....	....	....	....	....	....	....	....	....	28	2	15	17	22	....	....	....

QJHL First All-Star Team (1968) • EHL North First All-Star Team (1971) • WHA First All-Star Team (1975) • WHA Second All-Star Team (1976)

• 1966-67 and 1967-68 Drummondville (QJHL) statistics are playoff totals only. Regular season totals unavailable. Claimed by **Detroit** from **NY Rangers** in Intra-League Draft, June, 1970. Selected by **LA Sharks** (WHA) in 1972 WHA General Player Draft, February 12, 1972. WHA rights traded to **NY Raiders** by **LA Sharks** for future considerations, June, 1973. Transferred to **San Diego** (WHA) after **New York-Jersey** (WHA) franchise relocated, April 30, 1974. Signed as a free agent by **Indianapolis** (WHA) after **San Diego** (WHA) franchise folded, July, 1977. Traded to **Quebec** (WHA) by **Indianapolis** (WHA) with Rich LeDuc for future considerations, November, 1978. Signed as a free agent by **Colorado**, June, 1979.

• MORRISON, Lew

Henry Lewis RW – R. 6′, 185 lbs. b: Gainsborough, Sask., 2/11/1948. Philadelphia's 1st, 8th overall, in 1968.

Season	Club	League	GP	G	A	Pts	AG	AA	APts	PIM	PP	SH	GW	S	%	TGF	PGF	TGA	PGA	+/–	GP	G	A	Pts	PIM	PP	SH	GW
1967-68	Flin Flon Bombers	WCJHL	56	26	23	49	....	....	....	31	....	....	....	....	....	....	....	....	....	....	15	7	1	8	15	....	....	....
1968-69	Quebec Aces	AHL	70	12	13	25	....	....	....	24	....	....	....	....	....	....	....	....	....	....	15	4	5	9	6	....	....	....
1969-70	**Philadelphia Flyers**	**NHL**	**66**	**9**	**10**	**19**	**10**	**9**	**19**	**19**	**3**	**0**	**3**	**130**	**6.9**	**41**	**8**	**52**	**16**	**–3**	....	....	....	....	....	....	....	....
1970-71	**Philadelphia Flyers**	**NHL**	**78**	**5**	**7**	**12**	**5**	**6**	**11**	**25**	**0**	**0**	**0**	**129**	**3.9**	**30**	**1**	**69**	**28**	**–12**	**4**	**0**	**0**	**0**	**2**	**0**	**0**	**0**
1971-72	**Philadelphia Flyers**	**NHL**	**58**	**5**	**5**	**10**	**5**	**4**	**9**	**26**	**1**	**0**	**0**	**57**	**8.8**	**15**	**1**	**49**	**17**	**–18**	....	....	....	....	....	....	....	....
	Richmond Robins	AHL	12	4	5	9	....	....	....	2	....	....	....	....	....	....	....	....	....	....	....	....	....	....	....	....	....	....
1972-73	**Atlanta Flames**	**NHL**	**78**	**6**	**9**	**15**	**6**	**7**	**13**	**19**	**0**	**1**	**2**	**52**	**11.5**	**23**	**5**	**70**	**41**	**–11**	....	....	....	....	....	....	....	....
1973-74	**Atlanta Flames**	**NHL**	**52**	**1**	**4**	**5**	**1**	**3**	**4**	**0**	**0**	**0**	**0**	**31**	**3.2**	**10**	**0**	**32**	**21**	**–1**	....	....	....	....	....	....	....	....
1974-75	Richmond Robins	AHL	9	7	4	11	....	....	....	8	....	....	....	....	....	....	....	....	....	....	....	....	....	....	....	....	....	....
	Washington Capitals	**NHL**	**18**	**0**	**4**	**4**	**0**	**3**	**3**	**6**	**0**	**0**	**0**	**21**	**0.0**	**9**	**2**	**30**	**9**	**–14**	....	....	....	....	....	....	....	....
	Pittsburgh Penguins	**NHL**	**52**	**7**	**5**	**12**	**6**	**4**	**10**	**4**	**1**	**1**	**1**	**41**	**17.1**	**19**	**2**	**40**	**18**	**–5**	**9**	**0**	**0**	**0**	**0**	**0**	**0**	**0**
1975-76	**Pittsburgh Penguins**	**NHL**	**78**	**4**	**5**	**9**	**3**	**4**	**7**	**8**	**0**	**2**	**0**	**24**	**16.7**	**15**	**0**	**51**	**43**	**7**	**3**	**0**	**0**	**0**	**0**	**0**	**0**	**0**
1976-77	**Pittsburgh Penguins**	**NHL**	**76**	**2**	**1**	**3**	**2**	**1**	**3**	**0**	**0**	**0**	**0**	**25**	**8.0**	**4**	**0**	**31**	**21**	**–6**	**1**	**0**	**0**	**0**	**0**	**0**	**0**	**0**
1977-78	**Pittsburgh Penguins**	**NHL**	**8**	**0**	**2**	**2**	**0**	**2**	**2**	**0**	**0**	**0**	**0**	**3**	**0.0**	**3**	**0**	**0**	**0**	**3**	....	....	....	....	....	....	....	....
	Binghamton Dusters	AHL	65	6	14	20	....	....	....	6	....	....	....	....	....	....	....	....	....	....	....	....	....	....	....	....	....	....
	NHL Totals		**564**	**39**	**52**	**91**	**38**	**43**	**81**	**107**	**5**	**4**	**6**	**513**	**7.6**	**169**	**19**	**424**	**214**		**17**	**0**	**0**	**0**	**2**	**0**	**0**	**0**

Claimed by **Atlanta** from **Philadelphia** in Expansion Draft, June 6, 1972. Claimed by **Washington** from **Atlanta** in Expansion Draft, June 12, 1974. Traded to **Pittsburgh** by **Washington** for Ron Lalonde, December 14, 1974.

• MORRISON, Mark

C – R. 5′8″, 150 lbs. b: Prince George, B.C., 3/11/1963. NY Rangers' 4th, 51st overall, in 1981.

Season	Club	League	GP	G	A	Pts	AG	AA	APts	PIM	PP	SH	GW	S	%	TGF	PGF	TGA	PGA	+/–	GP	G	A	Pts	PIM	PP	SH	GW
1978-79	Kerrisdale Kolts	BCAHA	STATISTICS NOT AVAILABLE																									
1979-80	Victoria Cougars	WHL	72	25	33	58	....	....	....	26	....	....	....	....	....	....	....	....	....	....	16	3	5	8	20	....	....	....
1980-81	Victoria Cougars	WHL	58	31	61	92	....	....	....	66	....	....	....	....	....	....	....	....	....	....	15	6	13	19	9	....	....	....
	Victoria Cougars	Mem-Cup	4	3	3	6	....	....	....	2	....	....	....	....	....	....	....	....	....	....	....	....	....	....	....	....	....	....
1981-82	Victoria Cougars	WHL	56	48	66	114	....	....	....	83	....	....	....	....	....	....	....	....	....	....	4	0	0	0	12	....	....	....
	Canada	WJC-A	7	3	7	10	....	....	....	0	....	....	....	....	....	....	....	....	....	....	....	....	....	....	....	....	....	....
	New York Rangers	**NHL**	**9**	**1**	**1**	**2**	**1**	**1**	**2**	**0**	**0**	**0**	**1**	**6**	**16.7**	**2**	**0**	**7**	**0**	**–5**	....	....	....	....	....	....	....	....
1982-83	Victoria Cougars	WHL	58	55	75	130	....	....	....	54	....	....	....	....	....	....	....	....	....	....	12	10	17	27	8	....	....	....
	Canada	WJC-A	7	3	2	5	....	....	....	0	....	....	....	....	....	....	....	....	....	....	....	....	....	....	....	....	....	....
1983-84	Canada	Nat-Team	43	15	22	37	....	....	....	34	....	....	....	....	....	....	....	....	....	....	....	....	....	....	....	....	....	....
	New York Rangers	**NHL**	**1**	**0**	**0**	**0**	**0**	**0**	**0**	**0**	**0**	**0**	**0**	**5**	**0.0**	**0**	**0**	**0**	**0**	**0**	....	....	....	....	....	....	....	....
	Tulsa Oilers	CHL	11	4	4	8	....	....	....	2	....	....	....	....	....	....	....	....	....	....	7	4	4	8	2	....	....	....
1984-85	New Haven Nighthawks	AHL	20	5	4	9	....	....	....	0	....	....	....	....	....	....	....	....	....	....	....	....	....	....	....	....	....	....
	Nova Scotia Voyageurs	AHL	11	0	1	1	....	....	....	4	....	....	....	....	....	....	....	....	....	....	....	....	....	....	....	....	....	....
1985-86	HC Meran	Italy	36	59	*88	*147	....	....	....	30	....	....	....	....	....	....	....	....	....	....	6	8	10	18	6	....	....	....
1986-87	SC Fribourg	Switz.	37	18	19	37	....	....	....	....	....	....	....	....	....	....	....	....	....	....	....	....	....	....	....	....	....	....

			REGULAR SEASON																		PLAYOFFS							
Season	Club	League	GP	G	A	Pts	AG	AA	APts	PIM	PP	SH	GW	S	%	TGF	PGF	TGA	PGA	+/-	GP	G	A	Pts	PIM	PP	SH	GW
1987-88	EHC Olten	Switz-2	STATISTICS NOT AVAILABLE																									
1988-89	Canada	Nat-Team	4	1	2	3				0																		
	HC Meran	Italy	41	38	76	114				25																		
1989-90	HC Milano Devils	Italy	36	39	42	81				30																		
1990-91	HC Milano Devils	Italy	33	29	41	70				18											10	7	9	16	2			
1991-92	HC Meran	Italy-2	26	44	44	88				45																		
1992-93	HC Meran	Italy-2	32	58	34	92				38																		
1993-94	Fife Flyers	BH-Cup	6	7	7	14				10																		
	Fife Flyers	Britain	44	78	77	155				73											9	7	11	18	20			
1994-95	Fife Flyers	BH-Cup	10	15	16	31				18																		
	Fife Flyers	Britain	36	52	63	115				24											2	2	4	6	2			
1995-96	Fife Flyers	BH-Cup	11	19	28	47				8																		
	Fife Flyers	Britain	31	34	36	70				64											1	1	0	1	2			
1996-97	Fife Flyers	Britain-2	35	68	58	126				60											12	11	22	33	22			
1997-98	Fife Flyers	Britain-2	40	49	54	103				74											9	7	11	18	2			
1998-99	Fife Flyers	Britain-2	38	22	25	47				40																		
99-2000	Fife Flyers	BH-Cup	10	10	5	15				22																		
	Fife Flyers	Britain-2	40	29	30	59				6											11	5	5	10	18			
	NHL Totals		**10**	**1**	**1**	**2**	**1**	**1**	**2**	**0**	**0**	**0**	**1**	**11**	**9.1**	**2**	**0**	**7**	**0**									

• Brother of Doug • Won George Parsons Trophy (Memorial Cup Tournament Most Sportsmanlike Player) (1981)

Traded to **Edmonton** by **NY Rangers** for cash, November 27, 1984.

• MORROW, Brenden

LW – L. 5'11", 200 lbs. b: Carlyle, Sask., 1/16/1979. Dallas' 1st, 25th overall, in 1997.

Season	Club	League	GP	G	A	Pts	AG	AA	APts	PIM	PP	SH	GW	S	%	TGF	PGF	TGA	PGA	+/-	GP	G	A	Pts	PIM	PP	SH	GW
1994-95	Estevan Bantam Bruins	SAHA	60	117	72	189				45																		
1995-96	Portland Winter Hawks	WHL	65	13	12	25				61											7	0	0	0	8			
1996-97	Portland Winter Hawks	WHL	71	39	49	88				178											6	2	1	3	4			
1997-98	Portland Winter Hawks	WHL	68	34	52	86				184											16	10	8	18	65			
	Portland	Mem-Cup	4	1	2	3				*20																		
1998-99	Portland Winter Hawks	WHL	61	41	44	85				248											4	0	4	4	18			
	Canada	WJC-A	7	1	7	8				4																		
99-2000	**Dallas Stars**	**NHL**	**64**	**14**	**19**	**33**	**16**	**18**	**34**	**81**	**3**	**0**	**3**	**113**	**12.4**	**54**	**15**	**31**	**0**	**8**	**21**	**2**	**4**	**6**	**22**	**1**	**0**	**0**
	Michigan K-Wings	IHL	9	2	0	2				18																		
	NHL Totals		**64**	**14**	**19**	**33**	**16**	**18**	**34**	**81**	**3**	**0**	**3**	**113**	**12.4**	**54**	**15**	**31**	**0**		**21**	**2**	**4**	**6**	**22**	**1**	**0**	**0**

WHL West First All-Star Team (1999)

• MORROW, Ken

D – R. 6'4", 210 lbs. b: Flint, MI, 10/17/1956. NY Islanders' 4th, 68th overall, in 1976. USHOF

Season	Club	League	GP	G	A	Pts	AG	AA	APts	PIM	PP	SH	GW	S	%	TGF	PGF	TGA	PGA	+/-	GP	G	A	Pts	PIM	PP	SH	GW
1975-76	Bowling Green University	CCHA	31	4	15	19				34																		
1976-77	Bowling Green University	CCHA	39	7	22	29				22																		
1977-78	Bowling Green University	CCHA	39	8	18	26				26																		
	United States	WEC-A	6	0	0	0				0																		
1978-79	Bowling Green University	CCHA	45	15	37	52				22																		
1979-80	United States	Nat-Team	56	4	18	22				6																		
	United States	Olympics	7	1	2	3				6																		
♦	**New York Islanders**	**NHL**	**18**	**0**	**3**	**3**	**0**	**2**	**2**	**4**	**0**	**0**	**0**	**19**	**0.0**	**20**	**0**	**22**	**6**	**4**	**20**	**1**	**2**	**3**	**12**	**0**	**0**	**1**
1980-81♦	**New York Islanders**	**NHL**	**80**	**2**	**11**	**13**	**2**	**7**	**9**	**20**	**0**	**0**	**0**	**69**	**2.9**	**89**	**1**	**98**	**29**	**19**	**18**	**3**	**4**	**7**	**8**	**0**	**0**	**1**
1981-82	United States	Can-Cup	6	0	0	0				6																		
♦	**New York Islanders**	**NHL**	**75**	**1**	**18**	**19**	**1**	**12**	**13**	**56**	**0**	**0**	**0**	**91**	**1.1**	**116**	**1**	**92**	**30**	**53**	**19**	**0**	**4**	**4**	**8**	**0**	**0**	**0**
1982-83♦	**New York Islanders**	**NHL**	**79**	**5**	**11**	**16**	**4**	**8**	**12**	**44**	**0**	**0**	**1**	**135**	**3.7**	**79**	**1**	**92**	**32**	**18**	**19**	**5**	**7**	**12**	**18**	**0**	**0**	**0**
1983-84	**New York Islanders**	**NHL**	**63**	**3**	**11**	**14**	**2**	**7**	**9**	**45**	**0**	**0**	**1**	**71**	**4.2**	**85**	**0**	**88**	**29**	**26**	**20**	**1**	**2**	**3**	**20**	**0**	**0**	**1**
1984-85	**New York Islanders**	**NHL**	**15**	**1**	**7**	**8**	**1**	**5**	**6**	**14**	**0**	**0**	**0**	**14**	**7.1**	**19**	**0**	**21**	**7**	**5**	**10**	**0**	**0**	**0**	**17**	**0**	**0**	**0**
1985-86	**New York Islanders**	**NHL**	**69**	**0**	**12**	**12**	**0**	**8**	**8**	**22**	**0**	**0**	**0**	**55**	**0.0**	**78**	**1**	**87**	**34**	**24**	**2**	**0**	**0**	**0**	**4**	**0**	**0**	**0**
1986-87	**New York Islanders**	**NHL**	**64**	**3**	**8**	**11**	**3**	**6**	**9**	**32**	**0**	**0**	**0**	**52**	**5.8**	**44**	**0**	**63**	**26**	**7**	**13**	**1**	**3**	**4**	**2**	**0**	**0**	**0**
1987-88	**New York Islanders**	**NHL**	**53**	**1**	**4**	**5**	**1**	**3**	**4**	**40**	**0**	**0**	**0**	**50**	**2.0**	**41**	**1**	**64**	**24**	**0**	**6**	**0**	**0**	**0**	**8**	**0**	**0**	**0**
1988-89	**New York Islanders**	**NHL**	**34**	**1**	**3**	**4**	**1**	**2**	**3**	**32**	**0**	**0**	**0**	**27**	**3.7**	**25**	**0**	**56**	**24**	**–7**								
	NHL Totals		**550**	**17**	**88**	**105**	**15**	**60**	**75**	**309**	**0**	**0**	**2**	**583**	**2.9**	**596**	**5**	**683**	**241**		**127**	**11**	**22**	**33**	**97**	**0**	**0**	**3**

CCHA First All-Star Team (1976, 1978, 1979) • CCHA Second All-Star Team (1977) • NCAA West First All-American Team (1978) • Won Lester Patrick Trophy (1996)

• MORROW, Scott

LW – L. 6'1", 185 lbs. b: Chicago, IL, 6/18/1969. Hartford's 4th, 95th overall, in 1988.

Season	Club	League	GP	G	A	Pts	AG	AA	APts	PIM	PP	SH	GW	S	%	TGF	PGF	TGA	PGA	+/-	GP	G	A	Pts	PIM	PP	SH	GW
1987-88	Northwood Prep School	Hi-School	24	10	18	28				30																		
1988-89	University of New Hampshire	H-East	19	6	7	13				14																		
1989-90	University of New Hampshire	H-East	29	10	11	21				35																		
1990-91	University of New Hampshire	H-East	31	11	11	22				52																		
1991-92	University of New Hampshire	H-East	35	30	23	53				65																		
	Springfield Indians	AHL	2	0	1	1				0											5	0	0	0	9			
1992-93	Springfield Indians	AHL	70	22	29	51				80											15	6	9	15	21			
1993-94	Springfield Indians	AHL	30	12	15	27				28																		
	Saint John Flames	AHL	8	2	2	4				0											7	2	1	3	10			
1994-95	**Calgary Flames**	**NHL**	**4**	**0**	**0**	**0**	**0**	**0**	**0**	**0**	**0**	**0**	**0**	**1**	**0.0**	**1**	**0**	**1**	**0**	**0**								
	Saint John Flames	AHL	64	18	21	39				105											5	2	0	2	4			
1995-96	Hershey Bears	AHL	79	48	45	93				110											5	2	2	4	6			
1996-97	Cincinnati Cyclones	IHL	67	14	23	37				50																		
	Providence Bruins	AHL	11	3	4	7				15											7	2	1	3	0			
1997-98	Binghamton Icemen	UHL	8	3	2	5				14																		
	Providence Bruins	AHL	5	1	4	5				7																		
	Cincinnati Cyclones	IHL	55	15	12	27				44											9	3	1	4	23			
1998-99	Cincinnati Cyclones	IHL	80	29	22	51				116											3	0	2	2	2			
99-2000	Boston Lagers	X-Games	2	2	3	5				0																		
	NHL Totals		**4**	**0**	**0**	**0**	**0**	**0**	**0**	**0**	**0**	**0**	**0**	**1**	**0.0**	**1**	**0**	**1**	**0**									

Hockey East Second All-Star Team (1992)

Traded to **Calgary** by **Hartford** for Todd Harkins, January 24, 1994. Signed as a free agent by **Philadelphia**, July 31, 1995.

• MORTON, Dean

D – R. 6'1", 196 lbs. b: Peterborough, Ont., 2/27/1968. Detroit's 8th, 148th overall, in 1986.

Season	Club	League	GP	G	A	Pts	AG	AA	APts	PIM	PP	SH	GW	S	%	TGF	PGF	TGA	PGA	+/-	GP	G	A	Pts	PIM	PP	SH	GW
1984-85	Peterborough Voyageurs	OMHA	47	9	38	47				158																		
1985-86	Ottawa 67's	OHL	16	3	1	4				32																		
	Oshawa Generals	OHL	48	2	6	8				92											5	0	0	0	9			
1986-87	Oshawa Generals	OHL	62	1	11	12				165											23	3	6	9	112			
	Oshawa Generals	Mem-Cup	4	0	0	0				19																		
1987-88	Oshawa Generals	OHL	57	6	19	25				187											7	0	0	0	18			
1988-89	Adirondack Red Wings	AHL	66	2	15	17				186											8	0	1	1	13			
1989-90	**Detroit Red Wings**	**NHL**	**1**	**1**	**0**	**1**	**1**	**0**	**1**	**2**	**0**	**0**	**0**	**2**	**50.0**	**1**	**0**	**2**	**0**	**–1**								
	Adirondack Red Wings	AHL	75	1	15	16				183											6	0	0	0	30			
1990-91	Adirondack Red Wings	AHL	1	0	0	0				0																		
	San Diego Gulls	IHL	47	0	6	6				124																		
	Hampton Roads Admirals	ECHL	2	1	1	2				0											14	3	10	13	58			

			REGULAR SEASON																		PLAYOFFS							
Season	Club	League	GP	G	A	Pts	AG	AA	APts	PIM	PP	SH	GW	S	%	TGF	PGF	TGA	PGA	+/–	GP	G	A	Pts	PIM	PP	SH	GW
1991-92	Moncton Hawks	AHL	6	1	1	2	....	....	....	15	....	....	....	....	....	....	....	....	....	....	....	....	....	....	....	....	....	....
	Michigan Falcons	ColHL	38	4	19	23	....	....	....	96	....	....	....	....	....	....	....	....	....	....	....	....	....	....	....	....	....	....
1992-93	Cincinnati Cyclones	IHL	7	0	0	0	....	....	....	44	....	....	....	....	....	....	....	....	....	....	....	....	....	....	....	....	....	....
	Brantford Smoke	ColHL	37	2	17	19	....	....	....	217	....	....	....	....	....	....	....	....	....	....	15	1	3	4	38	....	....	....
	NHL Totals		**1**	**1**	**0**	**1**	**1**	**0**	**1**	**2**	**0**	**0**	**0**	**2**	**50.0**	**1**	**0**	**2**	**0**		....	....	....	....	....	....	....	....

• One of only two players (Rolly Huard) to score a goal in only NHL game.

• MOTT, Morris

Morris Kenneth RW – L. 5'8", 165 lbs. b: Creelman, Sask., 5/25/1946.

Season	Club	League	GP	G	A	Pts	AG	AA	APts	PIM	PP	SH	GW	S	%	TGF	PGF	TGA	PGA	+/–	GP	G	A	Pts	PIM	PP	SH	GW
1963-64	Weyburn Red Wings	SJHL	62	19	30	49	....	....	....	16	....	....	....	....	....	....	....	....	....	....	8	0	7	7	0	....	....	....
1964-65	Weyburn Red Wings	SJHL	34	21	*52	*73	....	....	....	12	....	....	....	....	....	....	....	....	....	....	15	11	21	33	10	....	....	....
1965-66	Canada	Nat-Team	STATISTICS NOT AVAILABLE																									
	Canada	WEC-A	7	3	0	3	....	....	....	0	....	....	....	....	....	....	....	....	....	....	....	....	....	....	....	....	....	....
1966-67	Canada	Nat-Team	STATISTICS NOT AVAILABLE																									
	Canada	WEC-A	7	4	1	5	....	....	....	4	....	....	....	....	....	....	....	....	....	....	....	....	....	....	....	....	....	....
1967-68	Winnipeg Nats	WCSHL	15	13	9	22	....	....	....	14	....	....	....	....	....	....	....	....	....	....	....	....	....	....	....	....	....	....
	Canada	Olympics	7	5	1	6	....	....	....	2	....	....	....	....	....	....	....	....	....	....	....	....	....	....	....	....	....	....
1968-69	Canada	Nat-Team	STATISTICS NOT AVAILABLE																									
	Canada	WEC-A	10	2	2	4	....	....	....	4	....	....	....	....	....	....	....	....	....	....	....	....	....	....	....	....	....	....
1969-70	Canada	Nat-Team	STATISTICS NOT AVAILABLE																									
1970-71	Queens University	OUAA	20	14	*30	*44	....	....	....	6	....	....	....	....	....	....	....	....	....	....	....	....	....	....	....	....	....	....
1971-72	Queens University	OUAA	20	12	22	34	....	....	....	6	....	....	....	....	....	....	....	....	....	....	....	....	....	....	....	....	....	....
1972-73	**California Golden Seals**	**NHL**	**70**	**6**	**7**	**13**	**6**	**6**	**12**	**8**	**1**	**0**	**1**	**71**	**8.5**	**27**	**4**	**55**	**15**	**–17**	....	....	....	....	....	....	....	....
	Salt Lake Golden Eagles	WHL	6	8	5	13	....	....	....	0	....	....	....	....	....	....	....	....	....	....	....	....	....	....	....	....	....	....
1973-74	**California Golden Seals**	**NHL**	**77**	**9**	**17**	**26**	**9**	**14**	**23**	**33**	**1**	**1**	**0**	**90**	**10.0**	**35**	**7**	**70**	**23**	**–19**	....	....	....	....	....	....	....	....
1974-75	**California Golden Seals**	**NHL**	**52**	**3**	**8**	**11**	**3**	**6**	**9**	**8**	**0**	**0**	**1**	**31**	**9.7**	**16**	**2**	**46**	**22**	**–10**	....	....	....	....	....	....	....	....
	Salt Lake Golden Eagles	CHL	11	6	2	8	....	....	....	12	....	....	....	....	....	....	....	....	....	....	11	2	7	9	8	....	....	....
1975-76	Vastra Frolunda	Sweden	36	16	14	30	....	....	....	62	....	....	....	....	....	....	....	....	....	....	....	....	....	....	....	....	....	....
1976-77	Transcona Chargers	CASH	STATISTICS NOT AVAILABLE																									
	Winnipeg Jets	WHA	2	0	1	1	....	....	....	5	....	....	....	....	....	....	....	....	....	....	....	....	....	....	....	....	....	....
1977-78	University of Manitiba	GPAC	DID NOT PLAY – COACHING																									
	NHL Totals		**199**	**18**	**32**	**50**	**18**	**26**	**44**	**49**	**2**	**1**	**2**	**192**	**9.4**	**78**	**13**	**171**	**60**		....	....	....	....	....	....	....	....
	Other Major League Totals		2	0	1	1	....	....	....	5	....	....	....	....	....	....	....	....	....	....	....	....	....	....	....	....	....	....

Selected by **Calgary-Cleveland** (WHA) in 1972 WHA General Player Draft, February 12, 1972. Signed as a free agent by **California**, October 1, 1972. Signed as a free agent by **Winnipeg** (WHA), March, 1976.

• MOWERS, Mark

RW – R. 5'11", 188 lbs. b: Whitesboro, NY, 2/16/1974.

Season	Club	League	GP	G	A	Pts	AG	AA	APts	PIM	PP	SH	GW	S	%	TGF	PGF	TGA	PGA	+/–	GP	G	A	Pts	PIM	PP	SH	GW
1992-93	Saginaw Gears	NAJHL	39	31	39	70	....	....	....	....	....	....	....	....	....	....	....	....	....	....	....	....	....	....	....	....	....	....
1993-94	Dubuque Fighting Saints	USHL	47	51	31	82	....	....	....	80	....	....	....	....	....	....	....	....	....	....	....	....	....	....	....	....	....	....
1994-95	University of New Hampshire	H-East	36	13	23	36	....	....	....	16	....	....	....	....	....	....	....	....	....	....	....	....	....	....	....	....	....	....
1995-96	University of New Hampshire	H-East	34	21	26	47	....	....	....	18	....	....	....	....	....	....	....	....	....	....	....	....	....	....	....	....	....	....
1996-97	University of New Hampshire	H-East	39	26	32	58	....	....	....	52	....	....	....	....	....	....	....	....	....	....	....	....	....	....	....	....	....	....
1997-98	University of New Hampshire	H-East	35	25	31	56	....	....	....	32	....	....	....	....	....	....	....	....	....	....	....	....	....	....	....	....	....	....
1998-99	**Nashville Predators**	**NHL**	**30**	**0**	**6**	**6**	**0**	**6**	**6**	**4**	**0**	**0**	**0**	**24**	**0.0**	**5**	**0**	**9**	**0**	**–4**	....	....	....	....	....	....	....	....
	Milwaukee Admirals	IHL	51	14	22	36	....	....	....	24	....	....	....	....	....	....	....	....	....	....	1	0	0	0	0	....	....	....
99-2000	**Nashville Predators**	**NHL**	**41**	**4**	**5**	**9**	**4**	**5**	**9**	**10**	**0**	**0**	**0**	**50**	**8.0**	**10**	**0**	**10**	**0**	**0**	....	....	....	....	....	....	....	....
	Milwaukee Admirals	IHL	23	11	15	26	....	....	....	34	....	....	....	....	....	....	....	....	....	....	....	....	....	....	....	....	....	....
	NHL Totals		**71**	**4**	**11**	**15**	**4**	**11**	**15**	**14**	**0**	**0**	**0**	**74**	**5.4**	**15**	**0**	**19**	**0**		....	....	....	....	....	....	....	....

Hockey East Second All-Star Team (1998) • NCAA East First All-American Team (1998)

Signed as a free agent by **Nashville**, June 8, 1998.

• MOXEY, Jim

James George RW – L. 6'1", 190 lbs. b: Toronto, Ont., 5/28/1953. California's 3rd, 66th overall, in 1973.

Season	Club	League	GP	G	A	Pts	AG	AA	APts	PIM	PP	SH	GW	S	%	TGF	PGF	TGA	PGA	+/–	GP	G	A	Pts	PIM	PP	SH	GW
1970-71	Hamilton Red Wings	OMJHL	43	10	5	15	....	....	....	46	....	....	....	....	....	....	....	....	....	....	....	....	....	....	....	....	....	....
1971-72	Hamilton Red Wings	OMJHL	62	20	35	55	....	....	....	71	....	....	....	....	....	....	....	....	....	....	....	....	....	....	....	....	....	....
1972-73	Hamilton Red Wings	OMJHL	59	40	40	80	....	....	....	85	....	....	....	....	....	....	....	....	....	....	....	....	....	....	....	....	....	....
1973-74	Salt Lake Golden Eagles	WHL	76	26	23	49	....	....	....	83	....	....	....	....	....	....	....	....	....	....	5	0	0	0	0	....	....	....
1974-75	**California Golden Seals**	**NHL**	**47**	**5**	**4**	**9**	**4**	**3**	**7**	**4**	**1**	**0**	**0**	**77**	**6.5**	**18**	**4**	**33**	**15**	**–4**	....	....	....	....	....	....	....	....
	Salt Lake Golden Eagles	CHL	11	3	11	14	....	....	....	7	....	....	....	....	....	....	....	....	....	....	....	....	....	....	....	....	....	....
1975-76	**California Golden Seals**	**NHL**	**44**	**10**	**16**	**26**	**9**	**12**	**21**	**33**	**2**	**0**	**0**	**106**	**9.4**	**42**	**10**	**50**	**8**	**–10**	....	....	....	....	....	....	....	....
	Salt Lake Golden Eagles	CHL	30	11	17	28	....	....	....	31	....	....	....	....	....	....	....	....	....	....	....	....	....	....	....	....	....	....
1976-77	**Cleveland Barons**	**NHL**	**35**	**7**	**7**	**14**	**6**	**5**	**11**	**20**	**1**	**0**	**0**	**62**	**11.3**	**25**	**5**	**49**	**14**	**–15**	....	....	....	....	....	....	....	....
	Salt Lake Golden Eagles	CHL	4	6	3	9	....	....	....	4	....	....	....	....	....	....	....	....	....	....	....	....	....	....	....	....	....	....
	Los Angeles Kings	**NHL**	**1**	**0**	**0**	**0**	**0**	**0**	**0**	**2**	**0**	**0**	**0**	**0**	**0.0**	**0**	**0**	**0**	**0**	**0**	....	....	....	....	....	....	....	....
	Fort Worth Texans	CHL	29	9	9	18	....	....	....	27	....	....	....	....	....	....	....	....	....	....	6	1	1	2	2	....	....	....
1977-78	Springfield Indians	AHL	71	22	34	56	....	....	....	24	....	....	....	....	....	....	....	....	....	....	4	0	0	0	5	....	....	....
	NHL Totals		**127**	**22**	**27**	**49**	**19**	**20**	**39**	**59**	**4**	**0**	**0**	**245**	**9.0**	**85**	**19**	**132**	**37**		....	....	....	....	....	....	....	....

Transferred to **Cleveland** after **California** franchise relocated, August 26, 1976. Traded to **LA Kings** by **Cleveland** with Gary Simmons for Juha Widing and Gary Edwards, January 22, 1977.

• MUCKALT, Bill

RW – R. 6', 190 lbs. b: Surrey, B.C., 7/15/1974. Vancouver's 9th, 221st overall, in 1994.

Season	Club	League	GP	G	A	Pts	AG	AA	APts	PIM	PP	SH	GW	S	%	TGF	PGF	TGA	PGA	+/–	GP	G	A	Pts	PIM	PP	SH	GW
1991-92	Merritt Centennials	BCJHL	55	14	11	25	....	....	....	75	....	....	....	....	....	....	....	....	....	....	....	....	....	....	....	....	....	....
1992-93	Merritt Centennials	BCJHL	59	31	43	74	....	....	....	80	....	....	....	....	....	....	....	....	....	....	....	....	....	....	....	....	....	....
1993-94	Merritt Centennials	BCJHL	43	58	51	109	....	....	....	99	....	....	....	....	....	....	....	....	....	....	....	....	....	....	....	....	....	....
	Kelowna Spartans	BCJHL	15	12	10	22	....	....	....	20	....	....	....	....	....	....	....	....	....	....	....	....	....	....	....	....	....	....
1994-95	University of Michigan	CCHA	39	19	18	37	....	....	....	42	....	....	....	....	....	....	....	....	....	....	5	1	1	2	6	....	....	....
1995-96	University of Michigan	CCHA	41	28	30	58	....	....	....	34	....	....	....	....	....	....	....	....	....	....	7	5	6	11	6	....	....	....
1996-97	University of Michigan	CCHA	36	26	38	64	....	....	....	69	....	....	....	....	....	....	....	....	....	....	6	5	9	14	2	....	....	....
1997-98	University of Michigan	CCHA	46	32	*35	*67	....	....	....	94	....	....	....	....	....	....	....	....	....	....	....	....	....	....	....	....	....	....
1998-99	**Vancouver Canucks**	**NHL**	**73**	**16**	**20**	**36**	**19**	**19**	**38**	**98**	**4**	**2**	**1**	**119**	**13.4**	**57**	**24**	**48**	**6**	**–9**	....	....	....	....	....	....	....	....
99-2000	**Vancouver Canucks**	**NHL**	**33**	**4**	**8**	**12**	**4**	**7**	**11**	**17**	**1**	**0**	**1**	**53**	**7.5**	**22**	**6**	**10**	**0**	**6**	....	....	....	....	....	....	....	....
	New York Islanders	**NHL**	**12**	**4**	**3**	**7**	**4**	**3**	**7**	**4**	**0**	**0**	**0**	**26**	**15.4**	**8**	**0**	**3**	**0**	**5**	....	....	....	....	....	....	....	....
	NHL Totals		**118**	**24**	**31**	**55**	**27**	**29**	**56**	**119**	**5**	**2**	**2**	**198**	**12.1**	**87**	**30**	**61**	**6**		....	....	....	....	....	....	....	....

CCHA First All-Star Team (1998) • NCAA West First All-American Team (1998)

Traded to **NY Islanders** by **Vancouver** with Kevin Weekes and Dave Scatchard for Felix Potvin and NY Islanders' compensatory 2nd (later traded to New Jersey - New Jersey selected Teemu Laine) and 3rd (Thatcher Bell) round choices in 2000 Entry Draft, December 19, 1999. • Missed remainder of 1999-2000 season recovering from shoulder injury suffered in game vs. Tampa Bay, January 13, 2000.

• MUIR, Bryan

D – L. 6'4", 220 lbs. b: Winnipeg, Man., 6/8/1973.

Season	Club	League	GP	G	A	Pts	AG	AA	APts	PIM	PP	SH	GW	S	%	TGF	PGF	TGA	PGA	+/–	GP	G	A	Pts	PIM	PP	SH	GW
1991-92	Wexford Raiders	OJHL	44	3	19	22	....	....	....	35	....	....	....	....	....	....	....	....	....	....	....	....	....	....	....	....	....	....
1992-93	University of New Hampshire	H-East	26	1	2	3	....	....	....	24	....	....	....	....	....	....	....	....	....	....	....	....	....	....	....	....	....	....
1993-94	University of New Hampshire	H-East	40	0	4	4	....	....	....	48	....	....	....	....	....	....	....	....	....	....	....	....	....	....	....	....	....	....
1994-95	University of New Hampshire	H-East	28	9	9	18	....	....	....	46	....	....	....	....	....	....	....	....	....	....	....	....	....	....	....	....	....	....
1995-96	Canada	Nat-Team	42	6	12	18	....	....	....	38	....	....	....	....	....	....	....	....	....	....	....	....	....	....	....	....	....	....
	Edmonton Oilers	**NHL**	**5**	**0**	**0**	**0**	**0**	**0**	**0**	**6**	**0**	**0**	**0**	**4**	**0.0**	**1**	**0**	**5**	**0**	**–4**	....	....	....	....	....	....	....	....
1996-97	Hamilton Bulldogs	AHL	75	8	16	24	....	....	....	80	....	....	....	....	....	....	....	....	....	....	14	0	5	5	12	....	....	....
	Edmonton Oilers	**NHL**	....	....	....	....	....	....	....	....	....	....	....	....	....	....	....	....	....	....	**5**	**0**	**0**	**0**	**4**	**0**	**0**	**0**
1997-98	**Edmonton Oilers**	**NHL**	**7**	**0**	**0**	**0**	**0**	**0**	**0**	**17**	**0**	**0**	**0**	**6**	**0.0**	**2**	**0**	**3**	**1**	**0**	....	....	....	....	....	....	....	....
	Hamilton Bulldogs	AHL	28	3	10	13	....	....	....	62	....	....	....	....	....	....	....	....	....	....	....	....	....	....	....	....	....	....
	Albany River Rats	AHL	41	3	10	13	....	....	....	67	....	....	....	....	....	....	....	....	....	....	13	3	0	3	12	....	....	....

Season	Club	League	GP	G	A	Pts	AG	AA	APts	PIM	PP	SH	GW	S	%	TGF	PGF	TGA	PGA	+/–	GP	G	A	Pts	PIM	PP	SH	GW
			REGULAR SEASON																		PLAYOFFS							
1998-99	**New Jersey Devils**	**NHL**	**1**	**0**	**0**	**0**	**0**	**0**	**0**	**0**	**0**	**0**	**0**	**4**	**0.0**	**0**	**0**	**0**	**0**	**0**	....	....	....	....	....	....	....	....
	Albany River Rats	AHL	10	0	0	0	....	....	....	29	....	....	....	....	....	....	....	....	....	....	....	....	....	....	....	....	....	....
	Chicago Blackhawks	**NHL**	**53**	**1**	**4**	**5**	**1**	**4**	**5**	**50**	**0**	**0**	**0**	**78**	**1.3**	**32**	**1**	**43**	**13**	**1**	....	....	....	....	....	....	....	....
	Portland Pirates	AHL	2	1	1	2	....	....	....	2	....	....	....	....	....	....	....	....	....	....	....	....	....	....	....	....	....	....
99-2000	**Chicago Blackhawks**	**NHL**	**11**	**2**	**3**	**5**	**2**	**3**	**5**	**13**	**0**	**1**	**0**	**19**	**10.5**	**10**	**2**	**11**	**2**	**–1**	....	....	....	....	....	....	....	....
	Tampa Bay Lightning	**NHL**	**30**	**1**	**1**	**2**	**1**	**1**	**2**	**32**	**0**	**0**	**0**	**32**	**3.1**	**15**	**0**	**30**	**7**	**–8**	....	....	....	....	....	....	....	....
	NHL Totals		**107**	**4**	**8**	**12**	**4**	**8**	**12**	**118**	**0**	**1**	**0**	**143**	**2.8**	**60**	**3**	**92**	**23**		**5**	**0**	**0**	**0**	**4**	**0**	**0**	**0**

Signed to five-game Amateur try-out contract by **Edmonton**, February 29, 1996. Signed as a free agent by **Edmonton**, April 30, 1996. Traded to **New Jersey** by **Edmonton** with Jason Arnott for Valeri Zelepukin and Bill Guerin, January 4, 1998. Traded to **Chicago** by **New Jersey** for Chicago's 3rd round choice (Michael Rupp) in the 2000 Entry Draft, November 13, 1998. Traded to **Tampa Bay** by **Chicago** with Reid Simpson for Michael Nylander, November 12, 1999. • Missed majority of 1999-2000 season recovering from leg injury suffered in game vs. Atlanta, November 17, 1999.

• MULHERN, Richard

Richard Sidney D – L. 6'1", 188 lbs. b: Edmonton, Alta., 3/1/1955. Atlanta's 1st, 8th overall, in 1975.

Season	Club	League	GP	G	A	Pts	AG	AA	APts	PIM	PP	SH	GW	S	%	TGF	PGF	TGA	PGA	+/–	GP	G	A	Pts	PIM	PP	SH	GW
1973-74	Sherbrooke Beavers	QMJHL	40	8	37	45	....	....	....	96	....	....	....	....	....	....	....	....	....	....	....	....	....	....	....	....	....	....
1974-75	Sherbrooke Beavers	QMJHL	70	26	64	90	....	....	....	152	....	....	....	....	....	....	....	....	....	....	....	....	....	....	....	....	....	....
	Sherbrooke Beavers	Mem-Cup	3	1	2	3	....	....	....	16	....	....	....	....	....	....	....	....	....	....	....	....	....	....	....	....	....	....
1975-76	**Atlanta Flames**	**NHL**	**12**	**1**	**0**	**1**	**1**	**0**	**1**	**4**	**1**	**0**	**0**	**17**	**5.9**	**3**	**2**	**9**	**0**	**–8**	....	....	....	....	....	....	....	....
	Tulsa Oilers	CHL	56	7	26	33	....	....	....	84	....	....	....	....	....	....	....	....	....	....	9	1	6	7	6	....	....	....
1976-77	**Atlanta Flames**	**NHL**	**79**	**12**	**32**	**44**	**11**	**25**	**36**	**80**	**2**	**1**	**1**	**156**	**7.7**	**104**	**19**	**93**	**14**	**6**	**3**	**0**	**2**	**2**	**5**	**0**	**0**	**0**
1977-78	**Atlanta Flames**	**NHL**	**79**	**9**	**23**	**32**	**8**	**18**	**26**	**47**	**0**	**0**	**1**	**125**	**7.2**	**88**	**6**	**82**	**11**	**11**	**2**	**0**	**1**	**1**	**0**	**0**	**0**	**0**
1978-79	**Atlanta Flames**	**NHL**	**37**	**3**	**12**	**15**	**3**	**9**	**12**	**22**	**0**	**0**	**0**	**58**	**5.2**	**50**	**2**	**43**	**1**	**6**	....	....	....	....	....	....	....	....
	Los Angeles Kings	**NHL**	**36**	**2**	**9**	**11**	**2**	**7**	**9**	**23**	**1**	**0**	**0**	**57**	**3.5**	**48**	**2**	**63**	**14**	**–3**	**1**	**0**	**0**	**0**	**0**	**0**	**0**	**0**
1979-80	**Los Angeles Kings**	**NHL**	**15**	**0**	**3**	**3**	**0**	**2**	**2**	**16**	**0**	**0**	**0**	**8**	**0.0**	**16**	**1**	**22**	**8**	**1**	....	....	....	....	....	....	....	....
	Toronto Maple Leafs	**NHL**	**26**	**0**	**10**	**10**	**0**	**7**	**7**	**11**	**0**	**0**	**0**	**30**	**0.0**	**31**	**5**	**30**	**3**	**–1**	**1**	**0**	**0**	**0**	**0**	**0**	**0**	**0**
1980-81	**Winnipeg Jets**	**NHL**	**19**	**0**	**4**	**4**	**0**	**3**	**3**	**14**	**0**	**0**	**0**	**24**	**0.0**	**19**	**2**	**27**	**1**	**–9**	....	....	....	....	....	....	....	....
	Tulsa Oilers	CHL	5	2	3	5	....	....	....	0	....	....	....	....	....	....	....	....	....	....	....	....	....	....	....	....	....	....
	Dallas Black Hawks	CHL	20	7	11	18	....	....	....	16	....	....	....	....	....	....	....	....	....	....	....	....	....	....	....	....	....	....
	NHL Totals		**303**	**27**	**93**	**120**	**25**	**71**	**96**	**217**	**4**	**1**	**2**	**475**	**5.7**	**359**	**39**	**369**	**52**		**7**	**0**	**3**	**3**	**5**	**0**	**0**	**0**

QMJHL Second All-Star Team (1974) • QMJHL First All-Star Team (1975)

Traded to **LA Kings** by **Atlanta** with Atlanta's 2nd round choice (Dave Morrison) in 1980 Entry Draft for Bob Murdoch and LA Kings' 2nd round choice (Tony Curtale) in 1980 Entry Draft, January 16, 1979. Claimed on waivers by **Toronto** from **LA Kings**, February 10, 1980. Traded to **Winnipeg** by **Toronto** for cash, December 2, 1980.

• MULHERN, Ryan

C – R. 6'1", 202 lbs. b: Philadelphia, PA, 1/11/1973. Calgary's 9th, 174th overall, in 1992.

Season	Club	League	GP	G	A	Pts	AG	AA	APts	PIM	PP	SH	GW	S	%	TGF	PGF	TGA	PGA	+/–	GP	G	A	Pts	PIM	PP	SH	GW
1991-92	Canterbury High School	Hi-School	37	51	27	78	....	....	....	50	....	....	....	....	....	....	....	....	....	....	....	....	....	....	....	....	....	....
1992-93	Brown University	ECAC	31	15	9	24	....	....	....	46	....	....	....	....	....	....	....	....	....	....	....	....	....	....	....	....	....	....
1993-94	Brown University	ECAC	27	18	17	35	....	....	....	48	....	....	....	....	....	....	....	....	....	....	....	....	....	....	....	....	....	....
1994-95	Brown University	ECAC	30	18	16	34	....	....	....	*108	....	....	....	....	....	....	....	....	....	....	....	....	....	....	....	....	....	....
1995-96	Brown University	ECAC	32	10	16	26	....	....	....	78	....	....	....	....	....	....	....	....	....	....	....	....	....	....	....	....	....	....
1996-97	Hampton Roads Admirals	ECHL	40	22	16	38	....	....	....	52	....	....	....	....	....	....	....	....	....	....	....	....	....	....	....	....	....	....
	Portland Pirates	AHL	38	19	15	34	....	....	....	16	....	....	....	....	....	....	....	....	....	....	5	1	1	2	2	....	....	....
1997-98	**Washington Capitals**	**NHL**	**3**	**0**	**0**	**0**	**0**	**0**	**0**	**0**	**0**	**0**	**0**	**1**	**0.0**	**1**	**0**	**1**	**0**	**0**	....	....	....	....	....	....	....	....
	Portland Pirates	AHL	71	25	40	65	....	....	....	85	....	....	....	....	....	....	....	....	....	....	6	1	0	1	12	....	....	....
1998-99	Kansas City Blades	IHL	59	7	11	18	....	....	....	82	....	....	....	....	....	....	....	....	....	....	....	....	....	....	....	....	....	....
	Las Vegas Thunder	IHL	23	9	6	15	....	....	....	8	....	....	....	....	....	....	....	....	....	....	....	....	....	....	....	....	....	....
99-2000	Portland Pirates	AHL	73	20	16	36	....	....	....	61	....	....	....	....	....	....	....	....	....	....	3	0	0	0	6	....	....	....
	NHL Totals		**3**	**0**	**0**	**0**	**0**	**0**	**0**	**0**	**0**	**0**	**0**	**1**	**0.0**	**1**	**0**	**1**	**0**		....	....	....	....	....	....	....	....

AHL First All-Star Team (1998)

Signed as a free agent by **Washington**, March 17, 1997. • Played w/ RHI's New Jersey in 1997 (22-21-9-30-29) and Philadelphia Sting 1998 (1-1-1-2-1).

• MULLEN, Brian

Brian Patrick RW – L. 5'10", 180 lbs. b: New York, NY, 3/16/1962. Winnipeg's 7th, 128th overall, in 1980.

Season	Club	League	GP	G	A	Pts	AG	AA	APts	PIM	PP	SH	GW	S	%	TGF	PGF	TGA	PGA	+/–	GP	G	A	Pts	PIM	PP	SH	GW
1977-78	New York Westsiders	NYJHL	33	21	36	57	....	....	....	38	....	....	....	....	....	....	....	....	....	....	....	....	....	....	....	....	....	....
1978-79	New York Jr. Rangers	NYJHL	36	47	45	92	....	....	....	....	....	....	....	....	....	....	....	....	....	....	....	....	....	....	....	....	....	....
1979-80	New York Jr. Rangers	NYJHL	STATISTICS NOT AVAILABLE																									
	United States	WJC-A	5	2	3	5	....	....	....	0	....	....	....	....	....	....	....	....	....	....	....	....	....	....	....	....	....	....
1980-81	University of Wisconsin	WCHA	38	11	13	24	....	....	....	28	....	....	....	....	....	....	....	....	....	....	....	....	....	....	....	....	....	....
	United States	WJC-A	5	0	2	2	....	....	....	6	....	....	....	....	....	....	....	....	....	....	....	....	....	....	....	....	....	....
1981-82	University of Wisconsin	WCHA	33	20	17	37	....	....	....	10	....	....	....	....	....	....	....	....	....	....	....	....	....	....	....	....	....	....
1982-83	**Winnipeg Jets**	**NHL**	**80**	**24**	**26**	**50**	**20**	**18**	**38**	**14**	**7**	**0**	**1**	**194**	**12.4**	**90**	**27**	**52**	**0**	**11**	**3**	**1**	**0**	**1**	**0**	**0**	**0**	**0**
1983-84	**Winnipeg Jets**	**NHL**	**75**	**21**	**41**	**62**	**17**	**28**	**45**	**28**	**4**	**4**	**1**	**164**	**12.8**	**91**	**27**	**101**	**25**	**–12**	**3**	**0**	**3**	**3**	**6**	**0**	**0**	**0**
1984-85	United States	Can-Cup	4	0	0	0	....	....	....	0	....	....	....	....	....	....	....	....	....	....	....	....	....	....	....	....	....	....
	Winnipeg Jets	**NHL**	**69**	**32**	**39**	**71**	**26**	**27**	**53**	**32**	**8**	**0**	**4**	**191**	**16.8**	**123**	**40**	**72**	**4**	**15**	**8**	**1**	**2**	**3**	**4**	**0**	**0**	**1**
1985-86	**Winnipeg Jets**	**NHL**	**79**	**28**	**34**	**62**	**22**	**23**	**45**	**38**	**13**	**0**	**3**	**211**	**13.3**	**100**	**42**	**76**	**1**	**–17**	**3**	**1**	**2**	**3**	**6**	**1**	**0**	**0**
1986-87	**Winnipeg Jets**	**NHL**	**69**	**19**	**32**	**51**	**16**	**23**	**39**	**20**	**7**	**0**	**4**	**185**	**10.3**	**82**	**26**	**58**	**0**	**–2**	**9**	**4**	**2**	**6**	**0**	**2**	**0**	**0**
1987-88	**New York Rangers**	**NHL**	**74**	**25**	**29**	**54**	**21**	**21**	**42**	**42**	**10**	**0**	**4**	**147**	**17.0**	**75**	**25**	**55**	**3**	**–2**	....	....	....	....	....	....	....	....
1988-89	**New York Rangers**	**NHL**	**78**	**29**	**35**	**64**	**25**	**25**	**50**	**60**	**8**	**3**	**5**	**217**	**13.4**	**93**	**30**	**76**	**20**	**7**	**3**	**0**	**1**	**1**	**4**	**0**	**0**	**0**
	United States	WEC-A	10	2	3	5	....	....	....	4	....	....	....	....	....	....	....	....	....	....	....	....	....	....	....	....	....	....
1989-90	**New York Rangers**	**NHL**	**76**	**27**	**41**	**68**	**23**	**29**	**52**	**42**	**7**	**3**	**3**	**186**	**14.5**	**102**	**38**	**86**	**29**	**7**	**10**	**2**	**2**	**4**	**8**	**2**	**0**	**0**
1990-91	**New York Rangers**	**NHL**	**79**	**19**	**43**	**62**	**17**	**33**	**50**	**44**	**4**	**0**	**3**	**188**	**10.1**	**98**	**35**	**69**	**18**	**12**	**5**	**0**	**2**	**2**	**0**	**0**	**0**	**0**
	United States	WEC-A	10	4	4	8	....	....	....	6	....	....	....	....	....	....	....	....	....	....	....	....	....	....	....	....	....	....
1991-92	**San Jose Sharks**	**NHL**	**72**	**18**	**28**	**46**	**16**	**21**	**37**	**66**	**5**	**3**	**1**	**168**	**10.7**	**70**	**22**	**79**	**17**	**–14**	....	....	....	....	....	....	....	....
1992-93	**New York Islanders**	**NHL**	**81**	**18**	**14**	**32**	**15**	**10**	**25**	**28**	**1**	**0**	**1**	**126**	**14.3**	**49**	**3**	**62**	**21**	**5**	**18**	**3**	**4**	**7**	**2**	**0**	**0**	**0**
	NHL Totals		**832**	**260**	**362**	**622**	**218**	**258**	**476**	**414**	**74**	**13**	**30**	**1977**	**13.2**	**973**	**315**	**786**	**138**		**62**	**12**	**18**	**30**	**30**	**5**	**0**	**1**

• Brother of Joe • Won Lester Patrick Trophy (1995) • Played in NHL All-Star Game (1989)

Traded to **NY Rangers** by **Winnipeg** with Winnipeg's 10th round choice (Brett Barnett) in 1987 Entry Draft for Detroit's 5th round choice (previously acquired, Winnipeg selected Benoit Lebeau) in 1988 Entry Draft and NY Rangers' 3rd round choice (later traded to St. Louis — St. Louis selected Denny Felsner) in 1989 Entry Draft, June 8, 1987. Traded to **San Jose** by **NY Rangers** for Tim Kerr, May 30, 1991. Traded to **NY Islanders** by **San Jose** for the rights to Marcus Thuresson, August 24, 1992. • Suffered career-ending stroke during training, August 8, 1993.

• MULLEN, Joe

Joseph P. RW – R. 5'9", 180 lbs. b: New York, NY, 2/26/1957. **USHOF HHOF**

Season	Club	League	GP	G	A	Pts	AG	AA	APts	PIM	PP	SH	GW	S	%	TGF	PGF	TGA	PGA	+/–	GP	G	A	Pts	PIM	PP	SH	GW
1971-72	New York 14th Precinct	NYJHL	30	13	11	24	....	....	....	2	....	....	....	....	....	....	....	....	....	....	....	....	....	....	....	....	....	....
1972-73	New York Westsiders	NYJHL	40	14	28	42	....	....	....	8	....	....	....	....	....	....	....	....	....	....	....	....	....	....	....	....	....	....
1973-74	New York Westsiders	NYJHL	42	71	49	120	....	....	....	41	....	....	....	....	....	....	....	....	....	....	7	9	9	18	0	....	....	....
1974-75	New York Westsiders	NYJHL	40	*110	72	*182	....	....	....	20	....	....	....	....	....	....	....	....	....	....	13	*24	13	*37	2	....	....	....
1975-76	Boston College	ECAC	24	16	18	34	....	....	....	4	....	....	....	....	....	....	....	....	....	....	....	....	....	....	....	....	....	....
1976-77	Boston College	ECAC	28	28	26	54	....	....	....	8	....	....	....	....	....	....	....	....	....	....	....	....	....	....	....	....	....	....
1977-78	Boston College	ECAC	34	34	34	68	....	....	....	12	....	....	....	....	....	....	....	....	....	....	....	....	....	....	....	....	....	....
1978-79	Boston College	ECAC	25	32	24	56	....	....	....	8	....	....	....	....	....	....	....	....	....	....	....	....	....	....	....	....	....	....
	United States	WEC-A	8	7	1	8	....	....	....	2	....	....	....	....	....	....	....	....	....	....	....	....	....	....	....	....	....	....
1979-80	Salt Lake Golden Eagles	CHL	75	40	32	72	....	....	....	21	....	....	....	....	....	....	....	....	....	....	13	*9	11	20	0	....	....	....
	St. Louis Blues	**NHL**	....	....	....	....	....	....	....	....	....	....	....	....	....	....	....	....	....	....	**1**	**0**	**0**	**0**	**0**	**0**	**0**	**0**
1980-81	Salt Lake Golden Eagles	CHL	80	59	58	*117	....	....	....	8	....	....	....	....	....	....	....	....	....	....	17	11	9	20	0	....	....	....
1981-82	**St. Louis Blues**	**NHL**	**45**	**25**	**34**	**59**	**20**	**23**	**43**	**4**	**10**	**0**	**3**	**141**	**17.7**	**82**	**27**	**44**	**0**	**11**	**10**	**7**	**11**	**18**	**4**	**1**	**0**	**0**
	Salt Lake Golden Eagles	CHL	27	21	27	48	....	....	....	12	....	....	....	....	....	....	....	....	....	....	....	....	....	....	....	....	....	....
1982-83	**St. Louis Blues**	**NHL**	**49**	**17**	**30**	**47**	**14**	**21**	**35**	**6**	**5**	**0**	**0**	**128**	**13.3**	**63**	**21**	**48**	**1**	**–5**	....	....	....	....	....	....	....	....
1983-84	**St. Louis Blues**	**NHL**	**80**	**41**	**44**	**85**	**33**	**30**	**63**	**19**	**13**	**0**	**6**	**228**	**18.0**	**124**	**51**	**81**	**0**	**–8**	**6**	**2**	**0**	**2**	**0**	**0**	**0**	**0**
1984-85	United States	Can-Cup	6	1	3	4	....	....	....	2	....	....	....	....	....	....	....	....	....	....	....	....	....	....	....	....	....	....
	St. Louis Blues	**NHL**	**79**	**40**	**52**	**92**	**33**	**35**	**68**	**6**	**13**	**0**	**4**	**252**	**15.9**	**123**	**43**	**75**	**0**	**5**	**3**	**0**	**0**	**0**	**0**	**0**	**0**	**0**
1985-86	**St. Louis Blues**	**NHL**	**48**	**28**	**24**	**52**	**22**	**16**	**38**	**10**	**9**	**0**	**4**	**142**	**19.7**	**71**	**32**	**46**	**0**	**–7**	....	....	....	....	....	....	....	....
	Calgary Flames	**NHL**	**29**	**16**	**22**	**38**	**13**	**15**	**28**	**11**	**5**	**0**	**4**	**61**	**26.2**	**58**	**28**	**28**	**0**	**2**	**21**	***12**	**7**	**19**	**4**	**4**	**0**	**2**

			REGULAR SEASON																		PLAYOFFS							
Season	Club	League	GP	G	A	Pts	AG	AA	APts	PIM	PP	SH	GW	S	%	TGF	PGF	TGA	PGA	+/–	GP	G	A	Pts	PIM	PP	SH	GW
1986-87	**Calgary Flames**	**NHL**	**79**	**47**	**40**	**87**	**41**	**29**	**70**	**14**	**15**	**0**	**12**	**206**	**22.8**	**123**	**45**	**60**	**0**	**18**	**6**	**2**	**1**	**3**	**0**	**1**	**0**	**1**
1987-88	United States	Can-Cup	4	3	0	3	....	....	....	0	....	....	....	....	....	....	....	....	....	....	....	....	....	....	....	....	....	....
	Calgary Flames	**NHL**	**80**	**40**	**44**	**84**	**34**	**32**	**66**	**30**	**12**	**0**	**5**	**205**	**19.5**	**133**	**42**	**63**	**0**	**28**	**7**	**2**	**4**	**6**	**10**	**0**	**0**	**0**
1988-89♦	**Calgary Flames**	**NHL**	**79**	**51**	**59**	**110**	**43**	**42**	**85**	**16**	**13**	**1**	**7**	**270**	**18.9**	**155**	**62**	**57**	**15**	**51**	**21**	***16**	**8**	**24**	**4**	**6**	**0**	**1**
1989-90	**Calgary Flames**	**NHL**	**78**	**36**	**33**	**69**	**31**	**24**	**55**	**24**	**8**	**3**	**5**	**236**	**15.3**	**118**	**47**	**83**	**18**	**6**	**6**	**3**	**0**	**3**	**0**	**0**	**1**	**0**
1990-91♦	**Pittsburgh Penguins**	**NHL**	**47**	**17**	**22**	**39**	**16**	**17**	**33**	**6**	**8**	**0**	**2**	**85**	**20.0**	**63**	**24**	**35**	**5**	**9**	**22**	**8**	**9**	**17**	**4**	**1**	**0**	**1**
1991-92	United States	Can-Cup	8	2	3	5	....	....	....	0	....	....	....	....	....	....	....	....	....	....	....	....	....	....	....	....	....	....
♦	**Pittsburgh Penguins**	**NHL**	**77**	**42**	**45**	**87**	**38**	**34**	**72**	**30**	**14**	**0**	**4**	**226**	**18.6**	**119**	**40**	**86**	**19**	**12**	**9**	**3**	**1**	**4**	**4**	**1**	**0**	**0**
1992-93	**Pittsburgh Penguins**	**NHL**	**72**	**33**	**37**	**70**	**27**	**25**	**52**	**14**	**9**	**3**	**3**	**175**	**18.9**	**97**	**26**	**64**	**12**	**19**	**12**	**4**	**2**	**6**	**6**	**0**	**1**	**1**
1993-94	**Pittsburgh Penguins**	**NHL**	**84**	**38**	**32**	**70**	**35**	**25**	**60**	**41**	**6**	**2**	**9**	**231**	**16.5**	**96**	**19**	**91**	**23**	**9**	**6**	**1**	**0**	**1**	**2**	**0**	**0**	**0**
1994-95	**Pittsburgh Penguins**	**NHL**	**45**	**16**	**21**	**37**	**28**	**31**	**59**	**6**	**5**	**2**	**3**	**78**	**20.5**	**56**	**14**	**33**	**6**	**15**	**12**	**0**	**3**	**3**	**4**	**0**	**0**	**0**
1995-96	**Boston Bruins**	**NHL**	**37**	**8**	**7**	**15**	**8**	**6**	**14**	**0**	**4**	**0**	**1**	**60**	**13.3**	**23**	**8**	**17**	**0**	**–2**	....	....	....	....	....	....	....	....
1996-97	**Pittsburgh Penguins**	**NHL**	**54**	**7**	**15**	**22**	**7**	**13**	**20**	**4**	**1**	**0**	**1**	**63**	**11.1**	**30**	**6**	**24**	**0**	**0**	**1**	**0**	**0**	**0**	**0**	**0**	**0**	**0**
1997-1998			OUT OF HOCKEY – RETIRED																									
1998-99	United States	WC-Q	3	0	3	3	....	....	....	0	....	....	....	....	....	....	....	....	....	....	....	....	....	....	....	....	....	....
	NHL Totals		**1062**	**502**	**561**	**1063**	**443**	**418**	**861**	**241**	**150**	**11**	**73**	**2787**	**18.0**	**1534**	**535**	**935**	**99**		**143**	**60**	**46**	**106**	**42**	**14**	**2**	**6**

• Brother of Brian • ECAC First All-Star Team (1978, 1979) • NCAA East First All-American Team (1978, 1979) • CHL Second All-Star Team (1980) • Won Ken McKenzie Trophy (Rookie of the Year - CHL) (1980) • CHL First All-Star Team (1981) • Won Tommy Ivan Trophy (MVP - CHL) (1981) • Won Lady Byng Trophy (1987, 1989) • NHL First All-Star Team (1989) • NHL Plus/Minus Leader (1989) • Won Lester Patrick Trophy (1995) • Played in NHL All-Star Game (1989, 1990, 1994)

Signed as a free agent by **St. Louis,** August 16, 1979. Traded to **Calgary** by **St. Louis** with Terry Johnson and Rik Wilson for Eddy Beers, Charles Bourgeois and Gino Cavallini, February 1, 1986. Traded to **Pittsburgh** by **Calgary** for Pittsburgh's 2nd round choice (Nicolas Perreault) in 1990 Entry Draft, June 16, 1990. Signed as a free agent by **Boston**, September 13, 1995. Signed as a free agent by **Pittsburgh**, September 5, 1996.

• MULLER, Kirk

Kirk C. "Captain Kirk" LW – L. 6', 205 lbs. b: Kingston, Ont., 2/8/1966. New Jersey's 1st, 2nd overall, in 1984.

Season	Club	League	GP	G	A	Pts	AG	AA	APts	PIM	PP	SH	GW	S	%	TGF	PGF	TGA	PGA	+/–	GP	G	A	Pts	PIM	PP	SH	GW
1980-81	Kingston Voyageurs	OHA-B	42	17	37	54	....	....	....	5	....	....	....	....	....	....	....	....	....	....	....	....	....	....	....	....	....	....
	Kingston Canadians	OMJHL	2	0	0	0	....	....	....	0	....	....	....	....	....	....	....	....	....	....	....	....	....	....	....	....	....	....
1981-82	Kingston Canadians	OHL	67	12	39	51	....	....	....	27	....	....	....	....	....	....	....	....	....	....	4	5	1	6	4	....	....	....
1982-83	Guelph Platers	OHL	66	52	60	112	....	....	....	41	....	....	....	....	....	....	....	....	....	....	....	....	....	....	....	....	....	....
1983-84	Guelph Platers	OHL	49	31	63	94	....	....	....	27	....	....	....	....	....	....	....	....	....	....	....	....	....	....	....	....	....	....
	Canada	WJC-A	7	2	1	3	....	....	....	16	....	....	....	....	....	....	....	....	....	....	....	....	....	....	....	....	....	....
	Canada	Nat-Team	15	2	2	4	....	....	....	16	....	....	....	....	....	....	....	....	....	....	....	....	....	....	....	....	....	....
	Canada	Olympics	6	2	1	3	....	....	....	0	....	....	....	....	....	....	....	....	....	....	....	....	....	....	....	....	....	....
1984-85	**New Jersey Devils**	**NHL**	**80**	**17**	**37**	**54**	**14**	**25**	**39**	**69**	**9**	**1**	**0**	**157**	**10.8**	**79**	**29**	**109**	**28**	**–31**	....	....	....	....	....	....	....	....
	Canada	WEC-A	10	2	2	4	....	....	....	12	....	....	....	....	....	....	....	....	....	....	....	....	....	....	....	....	....	....
1985-86	**New Jersey Devils**	**NHL**	**77**	**25**	**41**	**66**	**20**	**28**	**48**	**45**	**5**	**1**	**1**	**168**	**14.9**	**90**	**23**	**122**	**35**	**–20**	....	....	....	....	....	....	....	....
	Canada	WEC-A	9	4	3	7	....	....	....	12	....	....	....	....	....	....	....	....	....	....	....	....	....	....	....	....	....	....
1986-87	**New Jersey Devils**	**NHL**	**79**	**26**	**50**	**76**	**22**	**36**	**58**	**75**	**10**	**1**	**4**	**193**	**13.5**	**110**	**48**	**96**	**27**	**–7**	....	....	....	....	....	....	....	....
	NHL All-Stars	RV-87	2	0	0	0	....	....	....	0	....	....	....	....	....	....	....	....	....	....	....	....	....	....	....	....	....	....
	Canada	WEC-A	10	2	0	2	....	....	....	8	....	....	....	....	....	....	....	....	....	....	....	....	....	....	....	....	....	....
1987-88	**New Jersey Devils**	**NHL**	**80**	**37**	**57**	**94**	**32**	**41**	**73**	**114**	**17**	**2**	**1**	**215**	**17.2**	**134**	**52**	**82**	**19**	**19**	**20**	**4**	**8**	**12**	**37**	**0**	**0**	**0**
1988-89	**New Jersey Devils**	**NHL**	**80**	**31**	**43**	**74**	**26**	**30**	**56**	**119**	**12**	**1**	**4**	**182**	**17.0**	**97**	**33**	**101**	**14**	**–23**	....	....	....	....	....	....	....	....
	Canada	WEC-A	9	6	4	10	....	....	....	6	....	....	....	....	....	....	....	....	....	....	....	....	....	....	....	....	....	....
1989-90	**New Jersey Devils**	**NHL**	**80**	**30**	**56**	**86**	**26**	**40**	**66**	**74**	**9**	**0**	**6**	**200**	**15.0**	**109**	**31**	**92**	**13**	**–1**	**6**	**1**	**3**	**4**	**11**	**0**	**0**	**0**
1990-91	**New Jersey Devils**	**NHL**	**80**	**19**	**51**	**70**	**17**	**39**	**56**	**76**	**7**	**0**	**3**	**221**	**8.6**	**110**	**43**	**88**	**22**	**1**	**7**	**0**	**2**	**2**	**10**	**0**	**0**	**0**
1991-92	**Montreal Canadiens**	**NHL**	**78**	**36**	**41**	**77**	**33**	**31**	**64**	**86**	**15**	**1**	**7**	**191**	**18.8**	**101**	**43**	**59**	**16**	**15**	**11**	**4**	**3**	**7**	**31**	**2**	**1**	**1**
1992-93♦	**Montreal Canadiens**	**NHL**	**80**	**37**	**57**	**94**	**31**	**39**	**70**	**77**	**12**	**0**	**4**	**231**	**16.0**	**131**	**47**	**103**	**27**	**8**	**20**	**10**	**7**	**17**	**18**	**3**	**0**	**3**
1993-94	**Montreal Canadiens**	**NHL**	**76**	**23**	**34**	**57**	**21**	**26**	**47**	**96**	**9**	**2**	**3**	**168**	**13.7**	**95**	**45**	**79**	**28**	**–1**	**7**	**6**	**2**	**8**	**4**	**3**	**0**	**2**
1994-95	**Montreal Canadiens**	**NHL**	**33**	**8**	**11**	**19**	**14**	**16**	**30**	**33**	**3**	**0**	**1**	**81**	**9.9**	**32**	**14**	**54**	**15**	**–21**	....	....	....	....	....	....	....	....
	New York Islanders	**NHL**	**12**	**3**	**5**	**8**	**5**	**7**	**12**	**14**	**1**	**1**	**1**	**16**	**18.8**	**15**	**4**	**14**	**6**	**3**	....	....	....	....	....	....	....	....
1995-96	**New York Islanders**	**NHL**	**15**	**4**	**3**	**7**	**4**	**2**	**6**	**15**	**0**	**0**	**0**	**23**	**17.4**	**10**	**2**	**28**	**10**	**–10**	....	....	....	....	....	....	....	....
	Toronto Maple Leafs	**NHL**	**36**	**9**	**16**	**25**	**9**	**13**	**22**	**42**	**7**	**0**	**1**	**79**	**11.4**	**39**	**15**	**46**	**19**	**–3**	**6**	**3**	**2**	**5**	**0**	**2**	**0**	**0**
1996-97	**Toronto Maple Leafs**	**NHL**	**66**	**20**	**17**	**37**	**21**	**15**	**36**	**85**	**9**	**1**	**3**	**153**	**13.1**	**57**	**19**	**80**	**19**	**–23**	....	....	....	....	....	....	....	....
	Florida Panthers	**NHL**	**10**	**1**	**2**	**3**	**1**	**2**	**3**	**4**	**1**	**0**	**1**	**21**	**4.8**	**8**	**4**	**8**	**2**	**–2**	**5**	**1**	**2**	**3**	**4**	**1**	**0**	**0**
1997-98	**Florida Panthers**	**NHL**	**70**	**8**	**21**	**29**	**9**	**21**	**30**	**54**	**1**	**0**	**3**	**115**	**7.0**	**44**	**13**	**61**	**16**	**–14**	....	....	....	....	....	....	....	....
1998-99	**Florida Panthers**	**NHL**	**82**	**4**	**11**	**15**	**5**	**11**	**16**	**49**	**0**	**0**	**1**	**107**	**3.7**	**28**	**1**	**62**	**24**	**–11**	....	....	....	....	....	....	....	....
99-2000	**Dallas Stars**	**NHL**	**47**	**7**	**15**	**22**	**8**	**14**	**22**	**24**	**3**	**0**	**2**	**57**	**12.3**	**35**	**14**	**27**	**3**	**–3**	**23**	**2**	**3**	**5**	**18**	**0**	**0**	**1**
	NHL Totals		**1161**	**345**	**568**	**913**	**318**	**436**	**754**	**1151**	**130**	**11**	**46**	**2578**	**13.4**	**1324**	**480**	**1311**	**343**		**105**	**31**	**32**	**63**	**133**	**11**	**1**	**7**

Played in NHL All-Star Game (1985, 1986, 1988, 1990, 1992, 1993)

Traded to **Montreal** by **New Jersey** with Rollie Melanson for Stephane Richer and Tom Chorske, September 20, 1991. Traded to **NY Islanders** by **Montreal** with Mathieu Schneider and Craig Darby for Pierre Turgeon and Vladimir Malakhov, April 5, 1995. Traded to **Toronto** by **NY Islanders** with Don Beaupre to complete transaction that sent Damian Rhodes and Ken Belanger to NY Islanders (January 23, 1996), January 23, 1996. Traded to **Florida** by **Toronto** for Jason Podollan, March 18, 1997. Signed as a free agent by **Dalls** December 15, 1999.

• MULOIN, Wayne

John Wayne D – L. 5'8", 175 lbs. b: Dryden, Ont., 12/24/1941.

Season	Club	League	GP	G	A	Pts	AG	AA	APts	PIM	PP	SH	GW	S	%	TGF	PGF	TGA	PGA	+/–	GP	G	A	Pts	PIM	PP	SH	GW
1959-60	Edmonton Oil Kings	CAHL	STATISTICS NOT AVAILABLE																									
	Edmonton Oil Kings	Mem-Cup	19	2	3	5	....	....	....	26	....	....	....	....	....	....	....	....	....	....	....	....	....	....	....	....	....	....
1960-61	Edmonton Oil Kings	CAHL	STATISTICS NOT AVAILABLE																									
	Edmonton Oil Kings	Mem-Cup	13	0	4	4	....	....	....	35	....	....	....	....	....	....	....	....	....	....	....	....	....	....	....	....	....	....
1961-62	Edmonton Oil Kings	CAHL	STATISTICS NOT AVAILABLE																									
	Edmonton Flyers	WHL	4	0	0	0	....	....	....	0	....	....	....	....	....	....	....	....	....	....	....	....	....	....	....	....	....	....
	Edmonton Oil Kings	Mem-Cup	21	1	11	12	....	....	....	50	....	....	....	....	....	....	....	....	....	....	....	....	....	....	....	....	....	....
1962-63	Edmonton Flyers	WHL	61	2	6	8	....	....	....	52	....	....	....	....	....	....	....	....	....	....	3	0	2	2	2	....	....	....
1963-64	**Detroit Red Wings**	**NHL**	**3**	**0**	**1**	**1**	**0**	**1**	**1**	**2**	....	....	....	....	....	....	....	....	....	....	....	....	....	....	....	....	....	....
	Cincinnati Wings	CPHL	69	4	11	15	....	....	....	169	....	....	....	....	....	....	....	....	....	....	....	....	....	....	....	....	....	....
1964-65	St. Paul Rangers	CPHL	67	0	10	10	....	....	....	95	....	....	....	....	....	....	....	....	....	....	5	0	2	2	6	....	....	....
1965-66	Vancouver Canucks	WHL	15	1	0	1	....	....	....	8	....	....	....	....	....	....	....	....	....	....	....	....	....	....	....	....	....	....
	Providence Reds	AHL	45	3	11	14	....	....	....	70	....	....	....	....	....	....	....	....	....	....	....	....	....	....	....	....	....	....
1966-67	Providence Reds	AHL	68	0	10	10	....	....	....	99	....	....	....	....	....	....	....	....	....	....	....	....	....	....	....	....	....	....
1967-68	Providence Reds	AHL	66	1	16	17	....	....	....	78	....	....	....	....	....	....	....	....	....	....	8	0	3	3	10	....	....	....
1968-69	Providence Reds	AHL	72	6	18	24	....	....	....	77	....	....	....	....	....	....	....	....	....	....	9	0	2	2	10	....	....	....
1969-70	**Oakland Seals**	**NHL**	**71**	**3**	**6**	**9**	**3**	**6**	**9**	**53**	**0**	**1**	**0**	**64**	**4.7**	**54**	**12**	**72**	**9**	**–21**	**4**	**0**	**0**	**0**	**0**	**0**	**0**	**0**
1970-71	**California Golden Seals**	**NHL**	**66**	**0**	**14**	**14**	**0**	**12**	**12**	**32**	**0**	**0**	**0**	**68**	**0.0**	**47**	**3**	**96**	**18**	**–34**	....	....	....	....	....	....	....	....
	Minnesota North Stars	**NHL**	**7**	**0**	**0**	**0**	**0**	**0**	**0**	**6**	**0**	**0**	**0**	**4**	**0.0**	**2**	**0**	**4**	**0**	**–2**	**7**	**0**	**0**	**0**	**2**	**0**	**0**	**0**
1971-72	Cleveland Barons	AHL	71	1	14	15	....	....	....	82	....	....	....	....	....	....	....	....	....	....	3	0	0	0	6	....	....	....
1972-73	Cleveland Crusaders	WHA	67	2	13	15	....	....	....	64	....	....	....	....	....	....	....	....	....	....	9	1	3	4	14	....	....	....
1973-74	Cleveland Crusaders	WHA	76	3	7	10	....	....	....	39	....	....	....	....	....	....	....	....	....	....	5	1	0	1	0	....	....	....
1974-75	Cleveland Crusaders	WHA	78	4	17	21	....	....	....	65	....	....	....	....	....	....	....	....	....	....	5	0	1	1	4	....	....	....
1975-76	Cleveland Crusaders	WHA	27	0	5	5	....	....	....	12	....	....	....	....	....	....	....	....	....	....	....	....	....	....	....	....	....	....
	Syracuse Blazers	NAHL	3	0	0	0	....	....	....	4	....	....	....	....	....	....	....	....	....	....	....	....	....	....	....	....	....	....
	Edmonton Oilers	WHA	10	1	1	2	....	....	....	0	....	....	....	....	....	....	....	....	....	....	1	0	0	0	0	....	....	....
1976-77	Rhode Island Reds	AHL	52	1	3	4	....	....	....	20	....	....	....	....	....	....	....	....	....	....	....	....	....	....	....	....	....	....
	NHL Totals		**147**	**3**	**21**	**24**	**3**	**19**	**22**	**93**	....	....	....	....	....	....	....	....	....	....	**11**	**0**	**0**	**0**	**2**	....	....	....
	Other Major League Totals		258	10	43	53	....	....	....	180	....	....	....	....	....	....	....	....	....	....	20	2	4	6	18	....	....	....

CAHL Second All-Star Team (1962)

Claimed by **NY Rangers** from **Detroit** in Intra-League Draft, June, 1964. Traded to **Providence** (AHL) by **Vancouver** (WHL) with Ron Hutchinson for Bob Blackburn, February 3, 1966. • Hutchinson failed to report to Providence (AHL). NHL rights transferred to **Oakland** when NHL club signed affiliation agreement with **Providence** (AHL), June, 1968. Traded to **Minnesota** by **California** with Ted Hampson for Tommy Williams and Dick Redmond, March 7, 1971. Selected by **Calgary-Cleveland** (WHA) in 1972 WHA General Player Draft, February 12, 1972. Traded to **Edmonton** (WHA) by **Cleveland** (WHA) for Bill Evo, January, 1976.

• MULVENNA, Glenn

C – L. 5'11", 187 lbs. b: Calgary, Alta., 2/18/1967.

Season	Club	League	GP	G	A	Pts	AG	AA	APts	PIM	PP	SH	GW	S	%	TGF	PGF	TGA	PGA	+/–	GP	G	A	Pts	PIM	PP	SH	GW
			REGULAR SEASON																		PLAYOFFS							
1983-84	Calgary Royals	AAHA	STATISTICS NOT AVAILABLE																									
1984-85	New Westminster Bruins	WHL	66	16	15	31	....	....	....	34	....	....	....	....	....	....	....	....	....	....	11	2	3	5	2	....	....	....
1985-86	New Westminster Bruins	WHL	65	24	31	55	....	....	....	55	....	....	....	....	....	....	....	....	....	....	....	....	....	....	....	....	....	....
1986-87	New Westminster Bruins	WHL	53	24	44	68	....	....	....	43	....	....	....	....	....	....	....	....	....	....	....	....	....	....	....	....	....	....
	Kamloops Chiefs	WHL	18	13	8	21	....	....	....	18	....	....	....	....	....	....	....	....	....	....	13	4	6	10	10	....	....	....
1987-88	Kamloops Chiefs	WHL	38	21	38	59	....	....	....	35	....	....	....	....	....	....	....	....	....	....	15	6	11	17	14	....	....	....
1988-89	Flint Spirits	IHL	32	9	14	23	....	....	....	12	....	....	....	....	....	....	....	....	....	....	....	....	....	....	....	....	....	....
	Muskegon Lumberjacks	IHL	11	3	2	5	....	....	....	0	....	....	....	....	....	....	....	....	....	....	....	....	....	....	....	....	....	....
	Knoxville Cherokees	ECHL	2	0	0	0	....	....	....	0	....	....	....	....	....	....	....	....	....	....	....	....	....	....	....	....	....	....
1989-90	Muskegon Lumberjacks	IHL	52	14	21	35	....	....	....	17	....	....	....	....	....	....	....	....	....	....	11	2	3	5	0	....	....	....
	Fort Wayne Komets	IHL	6	2	5	7	....	....	....	2	....	....	....	....	....	....	....	....	....	....	....	....	....	....	....	....	....	....
1990-91	Muskegon Lumberjacks	IHL	48	9	27	36	....	....	....	25	....	....	....	....	....	....	....	....	....	....	5	1	1	2	0	....	....	....
1991-92	Pittsburgh Penguins	NHL	1	0	0	0	0	0	0	2	0	0	0	0	0.0	0	0	1	0	–1	....	....	....	....	....	....	....	....
	Muskegon Lumberjacks	IHL	70	15	27	42	....	....	....	24	....	....	....	....	....	....	....	....	....	....	14	5	6	11	11	....	....	....
1992-93	Philadelphia Flyers	NHL	1	0	0	0	0	0	0	2	0	0	0	1	0.0	0	0	0	0	0	....	....	....	....	....	....	....	....
	Hershey Bears	AHL	35	5	17	22	....	....	....	8	....	....	....	....	....	....	....	....	....	....	....	....	....	....	....	....	....	....
1993-94	Kalamazoo Wings	IHL	55	13	9	22	....	....	....	18	....	....	....	....	....	....	....	....	....	....	4	0	0	0	0	....	....	....
1994-95	Peoria Rivermen	IHL	48	7	9	16	....	....	....	20	....	....	....	....	....	....	....	....	....	....	7	3	0	3	2	....	....	....
1995-96	Peoria Rivermen	IHL	42	2	5	7	....	....	....	16	....	....	....	....	....	....	....	....	....	....	5	0	0	0	0	....	....	....
1996-97	Sheffield Steelers	Britain	36	7	16	23	....	....	....	28	....	....	....	....	....	....	....	....	....	....	8	1	5	6	6	....	....	....
1997-98	VEU Feldkirch	Austria	3	0	0	0	....	....	....	8	....	....	....	....	....	....	....	....	....	....	....	....	....	....	....	....	....	....
	VEU Feldkirch	EuroHL	1	0	0	0	....	....	....	0	....	....	....	....	....	....	....	....	....	....	....	....	....	....	....	....	....	....
	Newcastle Cobras	Britain	28	4	9	13	....	....	....	2	....	....	....	....	....	....	....	....	....	....	5	0	1	1	0	....	....	....
	Peoria Rivermen	ECHL	4	0	1	1	....	....	....	14	....	....	....	....	....	....	....	....	....	....	....	....	....	....	....	....	....	....
1998-99	Newcastle Riverkings	BH-Cup	8	1	4	5	....	....	....	10	....	....	....	....	....	....	....	....	....	....	....	....	....	....	....	....	....	....
	Newcastle Riverkings	Britain	30	7	9	16	....	....	....	8	....	....	....	....	....	....	....	....	....	....	5	1	2	3	0	....	....	....
99-2000	Newcastle Riverkings	BH-Cup	5	0	4	4	....	....	....	2	....	....	....	....	....	....	....	....	....	....	....	....	....	....	....	....	....	....
	Newcastle Riverkings	Britain	36	8	6	14	....	....	....	8	....	....	....	....	....	....	....	....	....	....	8	2	1	3	0	....	....	....
	NHL Totals		2	0	0	0	0	0	0	4	0	0	0	1	0.0	0	0	1	0		....	....	....	....	....	....	....	....

Signed as a free agent by **Pittsburgh**, December 3, 1987. Signed as a free agent by **Philadelphia**, July 11, 1992.

• MULVEY, Grant

Grant Michael "Granny" RW – R. 6'4", 200 lbs. b: Sudbury, Ont., 9/17/1956. Chicago's 1st, 16th overall, in 1974.

Season	Club	League	GP	G	A	Pts	AG	AA	APts	PIM	PP	SH	GW	S	%	TGF	PGF	TGA	PGA	+/–	GP	G	A	Pts	PIM	PP	SH	GW
1972-73	Penticton Panthers	BCJHL	55	42	43	85	....	....	....	120	....	....	....	....	....	....	....	....	....	....	....	....	....	....	....	....	....	....
1973-74	Calgary Centennials	WCJHL	68	31	31	62	....	....	....	192	....	....	....	....	....	....	....	....	....	....	14	4	6	10	55	....	....	....
1974-75	Chicago Black Hawks	NHL	74	7	4	11	6	3	9	36	0	0	2	59	11.9	20	2	22	1	–3	6	2	0	2	6	0	0	0
1975-76	Chicago Black Hawks	NHL	64	11	17	28	10	13	23	72	1	0	1	90	12.2	48	4	50	1	–5	4	0	0	0	2	0	0	0
1976-77	Chicago Black Hawks	NHL	80	10	14	24	9	11	20	111	0	0	1	90	11.1	52	9	61	1	–17	2	1	0	1	2	1	0	0
1977-78	Chicago Black Hawks	NHL	78	14	24	38	13	19	32	135	3	0	0	157	8.9	66	20	48	1	–1	4	2	2	4	0	1	0	0
1978-79	Chicago Black Hawks	NHL	80	19	15	34	16	11	27	99	5	0	1	136	14.0	53	7	60	0	–14	1	0	0	0	2	0	0	0
1979-80	Chicago Black Hawks	NHL	80	39	26	65	33	19	52	122	14	0	7	228	17.1	94	28	63	0	3	7	1	1	2	8	0	0	0
1980-81	Chicago Black Hawks	NHL	42	18	14	32	14	9	23	81	6	1	4	168	10.7	49	13	56	2	–18	3	0	0	0	0	0	0	0
1981-82	Chicago Black Hawks	NHL	73	30	19	49	24	13	37	141	3	0	3	184	16.3	75	15	69	0	–9	15	4	2	6	50	1	0	0
1982-83	Chicago Black Hawks	NHL	3	0	0	0	0	0	0	0	0	0	0	4	0.0	2	0	2	0	0	....	....	....	....	....	....	....	....
	Springfield Indians	AHL	5	0	2	2	....	....	....	4	....	....	....	....	....	....	....	....	....	....	....	....	....	....	....	....	....	....
1983-84	New Jersey Devils	NHL	12	1	2	3	1	1	2	19	0	0	0	15	6.7	4	1	8	0	–5	....	....	....	....	....	....	....	....
	Maine Mariners	AHL	29	6	8	14	....	....	....	49	....	....	....	....	....	....	....	....	....	....	16	5	2	7	39	....	....	....
	NHL Totals		586	149	135	284	126	99	225	816	32	1	19	1131	13.2	463	99	439	6		42	10	5	15	70	3	0	0

• Brother of Paul

• Missed majority of 1982-83 season recovering from knee inury suffered in game vs. Detroit, October 18, 1982. Claimed by **Pittsburgh** from **Chicago** in Waiver Draft, October 3, 1983. Claimed on waivers by **New Jersey** from **Pittsburgh**, October 8, 1983.

• MULVEY, Paul

Joseph Paul LW – L. 6'4", 220 lbs. b: Sudbury, Ont., 9/27/1958. Washington's 3rd, 20th overall, in 1978.

Season	Club	League	GP	G	A	Pts	AG	AA	APts	PIM	PP	SH	GW	S	%	TGF	PGF	TGA	PGA	+/–	GP	G	A	Pts	PIM	PP	SH	GW
1973-74	Merritt Centennials	BCJHL	60	27	31	58	....	....	....	200	....	....	....	....	....	....	....	....	....	....	....	....	....	....	....	....	....	....
1974-75	Edmonton Oil Kings	WCJHL	49	18	19	37	....	....	....	179	....	....	....	....	....	....	....	....	....	....	....	....	....	....	....	....	....	....
1975-76	Edmonton Oil Kings	WCJHL	69	29	38	67	....	....	....	331	....	....	....	....	....	....	....	....	....	....	5	1	3	4	13	....	....	....
1976-77	Portland Winter Hawks	WCJHL	63	43	25	68	....	....	....	251	....	....	....	....	....	....	....	....	....	....	3	2	1	3	11	....	....	....
1977-78	Portland Winter Hawks	WCJHL	64	43	33	76	....	....	....	262	....	....	....	....	....	....	....	....	....	....	8	0	3	3	60	....	....	....
1978-79	Washington Capitals	NHL	55	7	4	11	6	3	9	81	1	0	1	60	11.7	22	2	39	1	–18	....	....	....	....	....	....	....	....
	Hershey Bears	AHL	24	10	3	13	....	....	....	113	....	....	....	....	....	....	....	....	....	....	....	....	....	....	....	....	....	....
1979-80	Washington Capitals	NHL	77	15	19	34	13	14	27	240	2	0	3	140	10.7	57	5	60	0	–8	....	....	....	....	....	....	....	....
1980-81	Washington Capitals	NHL	55	7	14	21	5	9	14	166	1	0	0	96	7.3	33	4	38	0	–9	....	....	....	....	....	....	....	....
	Hershey Bears	AHL	19	4	8	12	....	....	....	21	....	....	....	....	....	....	....	....	....	....	10	2	3	5	54	....	....	....
1981-82	Pittsburgh Penguins	NHL	27	1	7	8	1	5	6	76	0	0	0	44	2.3	16	3	20	0	–7	....	....	....	....	....	....	....	....
	Los Angeles Kings	NHL	11	0	7	7	0	5	5	50	0	0	0	8	0.0	10	0	10	0	0	....	....	....	....	....	....	....	....
	New Haven Nighthawks	AHL	19	3	3	6	....	....	....	65	....	....	....	....	....	....	....	....	....	....	3	0	0	0	14	....	....	....
1982-83	Moncton Alpines	AHL	58	11	11	22	....	....	....	270	....	....	....	....	....	....	....	....	....	....	....	....	....	....	....	....	....	....
	NHL Totals		225	30	51	81	25	36	61	613	4	0	4	348	8.6	138	14	167	1		....	....	....	....	....	....	....	....

• Brother of Grant

Transferred to **Pittsburgh** by **Washington** as compensation for Washington's signing of free agent Orest Kindrachuk, September 4, 1981. Claimed on waivers by **LA Kings** from **Pittsburgh**, December 30, 1981. Traded to **Edmonton** by **LA Kings** for Blair Barnes, June 22, 1982.

• MUNI, Craig

Craig Douglas D – L. 6'3", 208 lbs. b: Toronto, Ont., 7/19/1962. Toronto's 1st, 25th overall, in 1980.

Season	Club	League	GP	G	A	Pts	AG	AA	APts	PIM	PP	SH	GW	S	%	TGF	PGF	TGA	PGA	+/–	GP	G	A	Pts	PIM	PP	SH	GW
1978-79	Mississagua Reps	MTHL	35	8	16	24	....	....	....	....	....	....	....	....	....	....	....	....	....	....	....	....	....	....	....	....	....	....
	St. Michael's Buzzers	OHA-B	2	2	3	5	....	....	....	23	....	....	....	....	....	....	....	....	....	....	....	....	....	....	....	....	....	....
1979-80	Kingston Canadians	OMJHL	66	6	28	34	....	....	....	114	....	....	....	....	....	....	....	....	....	....	3	0	1	1	9	....	....	....
1980-81	Kingston Canadians	OMJHL	38	2	14	16	....	....	....	65	....	....	....	....	....	....	....	....	....	....	....	....	....	....	....	....	....	....
	Windsor Spitfires	OMJHL	25	5	11	16	....	....	....	41	....	....	....	....	....	....	....	....	....	....	11	1	4	5	14	....	....	....
	New Brunswick Hawks	AHL	....	....	....	....	....	....	....	....	....	....	....	....	....	....	....	....	....	....	2	0	1	1	10	....	....	....
1981-82	Windsor Spitfires	OHL	49	5	32	37	....	....	....	92	....	....	....	....	....	....	....	....	....	....	9	2	3	5	16	....	....	....
	Toronto Maple Leafs	NHL	3	0	0	0	0	0	0	2	0	0	0	0	0.0	0	0	5	1	–4	....	....	....	....	....	....	....	....
	Cincinnati Tigers	CHL	....	....	....	....	....	....	....	....	....	....	....	....	....	....	....	....	....	....	3	0	2	2	2	....	....	....
1982-83	Toronto Maple Leafs	NHL	2	0	1	1	0	1	1	0	0	0	0	2	0.0	0	0	3	0	–3	....	....	....	....	....	....	....	....
	St. Catharines Saints	AHL	64	6	32	38	....	....	....	52	....	....	....	....	....	....	....	....	....	....	....	....	....	....	....	....	....	....
1983-84	St. Catharines Saints	AHL	64	4	16	20	....	....	....	79	....	....	....	....	....	....	....	....	....	....	7	0	1	1	0	....	....	....
1984-85	Toronto Maple Leafs	NHL	8	0	0	0	0	0	0	0	0	0	0	1	0.0	2	0	5	3	0	....	....	....	....	....	....	....	....
	St. Catharines Saints	AHL	68	7	17	24	....	....	....	54	....	....	....	....	....	....	....	....	....	....	....	....	....	....	....	....	....	....
1985-86	Toronto Maple Leafs	NHL	6	0	1	1	0	1	1	4	0	0	0	2	0.0	5	0	15	7	–3	....	....	....	....	....	....	....	....
	St. Catharines Saints	AHL	73	3	34	37	....	....	....	91	....	....	....	....	....	....	....	....	....	....	13	0	5	5	16	....	....	....
1986-87♦	Edmonton Oilers	NHL	79	7	22	29	6	16	22	85	0	0	2	69	10.1	110	3	87	25	45	14	0	2	2	17	0	0	0
1987-88♦	Edmonton Oilers	NHL	72	4	15	19	3	11	14	77	0	1	0	56	7.1	90	1	86	29	32	19	0	4	4	31	0	0	0
1988-89	Edmonton Oilers	NHL	69	5	13	18	4	9	13	71	0	0	1	40	12.5	92	1	84	36	43	7	0	3	3	8	0	0	0
1989-90♦	Edmonton Oilers	NHL	71	5	12	17	4	9	13	81	0	2	0	42	11.9	77	0	83	28	22	22	0	3	3	16	0	0	0
1990-91	Edmonton Oilers	NHL	76	1	9	10	1	7	8	77	0	0	0	47	2.1	64	1	87	34	10	18	0	3	3	20	0	0	0
1991-92	Edmonton Oilers	NHL	54	2	5	7	2	4	6	34	0	0	0	38	5.3	52	1	59	19	11	3	0	0	0	2	0	0	0
1992-93	Edmonton Oilers	NHL	72	0	11	11	0	8	8	67	0	0	0	51	0.0	48	0	104	41	–15	....	....	....	....	....	....	....	....
	Chicago Blackhawks	NHL	9	0	0	0	0	0	0	8	0	0	0	9	0.0	5	1	5	2	1	4	0	0	0	2	0	0	0
1993-94	Chicago Blackhawks	NHL	9	0	4	4	0	3	3	4	0	0	0	6	0.0	6	0	5	2	3	....	....	....	....	....	....	....	....
	Buffalo Sabres	NHL	73	2	8	10	2	6	8	62	0	1	2	39	5.1	59	0	63	32	28	7	0	0	0	4	0	0	0

			REGULAR SEASON																		PLAYOFFS							
Season	Club	League	GP	G	A	Pts	AG	AA	APts	PIM	PP	SH	GW	S	%	TGF	PGF	TGA	PGA	+/–	GP	G	A	Pts	PIM	PP	SH	GW
1994-95	**Buffalo Sabres**	**NHL**	**40**	**0**	**6**	**6**	**0**	**9**	**9**	**36**	**0**	**0**	**0**	**32**	**0.0**	**25**	**1**	**39**	**11**	**–4**	**5**	**0**	**1**	**1**	**2**	**0**	**0**	**0**
1995-96	**Buffalo Sabres**	**NHL**	**47**	**0**	**4**	**4**	**0**	**3**	**3**	**69**	**0**	**0**	**0**	**25**	**0.0**	**22**	**0**	**61**	**27**	**–12**	....	....	....	....	....	....	....	....
	Winnipeg Jets	**NHL**	**25**	**1**	**3**	**4**	**1**	**2**	**3**	**37**	**0**	**0**	**0**	**16**	**6.3**	**19**	**0**	**21**	**8**	**6**	**6**	**0**	**1**	**1**	**2**	**0**	**0**	**0**
1996-97	**Pittsburgh Penguins**	**NHL**	**64**	**0**	**4**	**4**	**0**	**4**	**4**	**36**	**0**	**0**	**0**	**19**	**0.0**	**32**	**0**	**59**	**21**	**–6**	**3**	**0**	**0**	**0**	**0**	**0**	**0**	**0**
1997-98	**Dallas Stars**	**NHL**	**40**	**1**	**1**	**2**	**1**	**1**	**2**	**25**	**0**	**0**	**1**	**12**	**8.3**	**15**	**0**	**21**	**6**	**0**	**5**	**0**	**0**	**0**	**4**	**0**	**0**	**0**
	NHL Totals		**819**	**28**	**119**	**147**	**24**	**94**	**118**	**775**	**0**	**4**	**6**	**506**	**5.5**	**723**	**9**	**892**	**332**		**113**	**0**	**17**	**17**	**108**	**0**	**0**	**0**

Signed as a free agent by **Edmonton,** August 18, 1986. Traded to **Buffalo** by **Edmonton** for cash, October 2, 1986. Traded to **Pittsburgh** by **Buffalo** for cash, October 3, 1986. Traded to **Edmonton** by **Pittsburgh** to complete September 11, 1985 transaction which sent Gilles Meloche to Pittsburgh, October 6, 1986. Traded to **Chicago** by **Edmonton** for Mike Hudson, March 22, 1993. Traded to **Buffalo** by **Chicago** with Chicago's 5th round choice (Daniel Bienvenue) in 1995 Entry Draft for Keith Carney and Buffalo's 6th round choice (Marc Magliarditi) in 1995 Entry Draft, October 26, 1993. Traded to **Winnipeg** by **Buffalo** for Darryl Shannon and Michael Grosek, February 15, 1996. Signed as a free agent by **Pittsburgh**, October 2, 1996. Signed as a free agent by **Dallas**, October 2, 1997.

• MURDOCH, Bob

Robert Lovell RW – R. 5'11", 191 lbs. b: Cranbrook, B.C., 1/29/1954.

1972-73	Cranbrook Colts	KIJHL	STATISTICS NOT AVAILABLE																									
	Edmonton Oil Kings	WCJHL	1	0	0	0	....	....	....	0	....	....	....	....	....	....	....	....	....	....	....	....	....	....	....	....	....	....
1973-74	Cranbrook Royals	WIHL	48	37	24	61	....	....	....	....	....	....	....	....	....	....	....	....	....	....	....	....	....	....	....	....	....	....
1974-75	Salt Lake Golden Eagles	CHL	76	33	30	63	....	....	....	66	....	....	....	....	....	....	....	....	....	....	11	6	6	12	8	....	....	....
1975-76	**California Golden Seals**	**NHL**	**78**	**22**	**27**	**49**	**19**	**20**	**39**	**53**	**9**	**0**	**3**	**166**	**13.3**	**75**	**26**	**63**	**1**	**–13**	....	....	....	....	....	....	....	....
1976-77	**Cleveland Barons**	**NHL**	**57**	**23**	**19**	**42**	**21**	**15**	**36**	**30**	**6**	**0**	**3**	**141**	**16.3**	**60**	**18**	**47**	**0**	**–5**	....	....	....	....	....	....	....	....
1977-78	**Cleveland Barons**	**NHL**	**71**	**14**	**26**	**40**	**13**	**20**	**33**	**27**	**5**	**0**	**4**	**131**	**10.7**	**57**	**16**	**59**	**0**	**–18**	....	....	....	....	....	....	....	....
1978-79	**St. Louis Blues**	**NHL**	**54**	**13**	**13**	**26**	**11**	**9**	**20**	**17**	**1**	**0**	**3**	**92**	**14.1**	**43**	**8**	**41**	**0**	**–6**	....	....	....	....	....	....	....	....
	Salt Lake Golden Eagles	CHL	6	1	1	2	....	....	....	9	....	....	....	....	....	....	....	....	....	....	....	....	....	....	....	....	....	....
1979-80	Salt Lake Golden Eagles	CHL	29	8	14	22	....	....	....	23	....	....	....	....	....	....	....	....	....	....	....	....	....	....	....	....	....	....
	Adirondack Red Wings	AHL	21	5	9	14	....	....	....	19	....	....	....	....	....	....	....	....	....	....	....	....	....	....	....	....	....	....
1980-81			REINSTATED AS AN AMATEUR																									
1981-82	Cranbrook Royals	WIHL	PLAYER/COACH – STATISTICS UNAVAILABLE																									
	Cranbrook Royals	Al-Cup	5	8	2	10	....	....	....	0	....	....	....	....	....	....	....	....	....	....	....	....	....	....	....	....	....	....
	NHL Totals		**260**	**72**	**85**	**157**	**64**	**64**	**128**	**127**	**21**	**0**	**13**	**530**	**13.6**	**235**	**68**	**210**	**1**		....	....	....	....	....	....	....	....

• Brother of Don • CHL Second All-Star Team (1975) • Played in NHL All-Star Game (1975)

Signed as a free agent by **California**, October, 1974. Transferred to **Cleveland** after **California** franchise relocated, August 26, 1976. Placed on **Minnesota** Reserve List after **Cleveland-Minnesota** Dispersal Draft, June 15, 1978. Traded to **St. Louis** by **Minnesota** for cash, August 8, 1978. Claimed by **St. Louis** as a fill-in during Expansion Draft, June 13, 1979.

• MURDOCH, Bob

Robert John D – R. 6', 200 lbs. b: Kirkland Lake, Ont., 11/20/1946.

1968-69	Winnipeg Nationals	WCSHL	6	0	1	1	....	....	....	2	....	....	....	....	....	....	....	....	....	....	....	....	....	....	....	....	....	....
	Canada	Nat-Team	STATISTICS NOT AVAILABLE																									
	Canada	WEC-A	5	0	0	0	....	....	....	2	....	....	....	....	....	....	....	....	....	....	....	....	....	....	....	....	....	....
1969-70	Canada	Nat-Team	STATISTICS NOT AVAILABLE																									
	Montreal Voyageurs	AHL	6	0	2	2	....	....	....	6	....	....	....	....	....	....	....	....	....	....	....	....	....	....	....	....	....	....
1970-71♦	**Montreal Canadiens**	**NHL**	**1**	**0**	**2**	**2**	**0**	**2**	**2**	**2**	**0**	**0**	**0**	**2**	**0.0**	**2**	**1**	**1**	**0**	**0**	**2**	**0**	**0**	**0**	**0**	**0**	**0**	**0**
	Montreal Voyageurs	AHL	66	8	20	28	....	....	....	69	....	....	....	....	....	....	....	....	....	....	3	1	2	3	4	....	....	....
1971-72	**Montreal Canadiens**	**NHL**	**11**	**1**	**1**	**2**	**1**	**1**	**2**	**8**	**0**	**0**	**0**	**16**	**6.3**	**15**	**0**	**10**	**3**	**8**	**1**	**0**	**0**	**0**	**0**	**0**	**0**	**0**
	Nova Scotia Voyageurs	AHL	53	7	32	39	....	....	....	53	....	....	....	....	....	....	....	....	....	....	....	....	....	....	....	....	....	....
1972-73♦	**Montreal Canadiens**	**NHL**	**69**	**2**	**22**	**24**	**2**	**17**	**19**	**55**	**0**	**0**	**2**	**54**	**3.7**	**77**	**2**	**54**	**18**	**39**	**13**	**0**	**3**	**3**	**10**	**0**	**0**	**0**
1973-74	**Los Angeles Kings**	**NHL**	**76**	**8**	**20**	**28**	**8**	**16**	**24**	**85**	**1**	**0**	**1**	**160**	**5.0**	**87**	**11**	**107**	**20**	**–11**	**5**	**0**	**0**	**0**	**2**	**0**	**0**	**0**
1974-75	**Los Angeles Kings**	**NHL**	**80**	**13**	**29**	**42**	**11**	**22**	**33**	**116**	**2**	**1**	**0**	**201**	**6.5**	**126**	**26**	**80**	**19**	**39**	**3**	**0**	**1**	**1**	**4**	**0**	**0**	**0**
1975-76	**Los Angeles Kings**	**NHL**	**80**	**6**	**29**	**35**	**5**	**22**	**27**	**103**	**2**	**0**	**1**	**172**	**3.5**	**128**	**35**	**113**	**33**	**13**	**9**	**0**	**5**	**5**	**15**	**0**	**0**	**0**
1976-77	**Los Angeles Kings**	**NHL**	**70**	**9**	**23**	**32**	**8**	**18**	**26**	**79**	**0**	**0**	**1**	**125**	**7.2**	**113**	**9**	**91**	**23**	**36**	**9**	**2**	**3**	**5**	**14**	**1**	**0**	**1**
1977-78	**Los Angeles Kings**	**NHL**	**76**	**2**	**17**	**19**	**2**	**13**	**15**	**68**	**0**	**0**	**0**	**144**	**1.4**	**80**	**2**	**101**	**25**	**2**	**2**	**0**	**1**	**1**	**5**	**0**	**0**	**0**
1978-79	**Los Angeles Kings**	**NHL**	**32**	**3**	**12**	**15**	**3**	**9**	**12**	**46**	**0**	**0**	**1**	**63**	**4.8**	**52**	**11**	**49**	**8**	**0**								
	Atlanta Flames	**NHL**	**35**	**5**	**11**	**16**	**4**	**8**	**12**	**24**	**2**	**0**	**0**	**53**	**9.4**	**51**	**8**	**53**	**12**	**2**	**2**	**0**	**0**	**0**	**4**	**0**	**0**	**0**
1979-80	**Atlanta Flames**	**NHL**	**80**	**5**	**16**	**21**	**4**	**12**	**16**	**48**	**0**	**0**	**1**	**68**	**7.4**	**75**	**0**	**105**	**32**	**2**	**4**	**1**	**1**	**2**	**2**	**0**	**0**	**0**
1980-81	**Calgary Flames**	**NHL**	**74**	**3**	**19**	**22**	**2**	**13**	**15**	**54**	**0**	**0**	**0**	**90**	**3.3**	**100**	**4**	**91**	**17**	**22**	**16**	**1**	**4**	**5**	**36**	**0**	**0**	**0**
1981-82	**Calgary Flames**	**NHL**	**73**	**3**	**17**	**20**	**2**	**11**	**13**	**76**	**0**	**0**	**0**	**81**	**3.7**	**86**	**0**	**108**	**27**	**5**	**3**	**0**	**0**	**0**	**0**	**0**	**0**	**0**
1982-1987	**Calgary Flames**	**NHL**	DID NOT PLAY – ASSISTANT COACH																									
1987-1988	**Chicago Blackhawks**	**NHL**	DID NOT PLAY – COACHING																									
1988-1989	**Winnipeg Jets**	**NHL**	DID NOT PLAY – COACHING																									
1989-1991	**Winnipeg Jets**	**NHL**	DID NOT PLAY – ASSISTANT COACH																									
1991-1993			OUT OF HOCKEY – RETIRED																									
1993-1994	Team Canada	Nat-Team	DID NOT PLAY – COACHING																									
1994-1995	Munich Mad Dogs	Germany	DID NOT PLAY – COACHING																									
1995-1997	Cranbrook Colts	RMJHL	DID NOT PLAY – COACHING																									
1997-1999	Kolner Haie	Germany	DID NOT PLAY – COACHING																									
1999-2000	Nurnberg Ice Tigers	Germany	DID NOT PLAY – COACHING																									
	NHL Totals		**757**	**60**	**218**	**278**	**52**	**164**	**216**	**764**	**7**	**1**	**7**	**1229**	**4.9**	**992**	**109**	**963**	**237**		**69**	**4**	**18**	**22**	**92**	**1**	**0**	**1**

Won Jack Adams Award (1990)

Signed as a free agent by **Montreal**, March 2, 1970. Traded to **Minnesota** by **Montreal** with Marshall Johnston to complete transaction that sent Danny Grant and Claude Larose to Montreal (June 10, 1968), May 25, 1971. Claimed by **Montreal** from **Minnesota** in Intra-League Draft, June 8, 1971. Traded to **LA Kings** by **Montreal** with Randy Rota for LA Kings' 1st round choice (Mario Tremblay) in 1974 Amateur Draft and cash, May 29, 1973. Traded to **Atlanta** by **LA Kings** with LA Kings' 2nd round choice (Tony Curtale) in 1980 Entry Draft for Richard Mulhern and Atlanta's 2nd round choice (Dave Morrison) in 1980 Entry Draft, January 16, 1979. Transferred to **Calgary** after **Atlanta** franchise relocated, June 24, 1980.

• MURDOCH, Don

Donald Walter RW – R. 5'11", 180 lbs. b: Cranbrook, B.C., 10/25/1956. NY Rangers' 1st, 6th overall, in 1976.

1973-74	Vernon Vikings	BCJHL	45	50	32	82	....	....	....	69	....	....	....	....	....	....	....	....	....	....	....	....	....	....	....	....	....	....
	Kamloops Chiefs	WCJHL	4	1	0	1	....	....	....	9	....	....	....	....	....	....	....	....	....	....	....	....	....	....	....	....	....	....
1974-75	Medicine Hat Tigers	WCJHL	70	*82	59	141	....	....	....	83	....	....	....	....	....	....	....	....	....	....	5	1	5	6	15	....	....	....
1975-76	Medicine Hat Tigers	WCJHL	70	*88	77	165	....	....	....	202	....	....	....	....	....	....	....	....	....	....	7	4	3	7	23	....	....	....
1976-77	**New York Rangers**	**NHL**	**59**	**32**	**24**	**56**	**29**	**18**	**47**	**47**	**11**	**0**	**6**	**223**	**14.3**	**79**	**25**	**58**	**9**	**5**	....	....	....	....	....	....	....	....
1977-78	**New York Rangers**	**NHL**	**66**	**27**	**28**	**55**	**25**	**22**	**47**	**41**	**10**	**0**	**1**	**188**	**14.4**	**89**	**37**	**57**	**0**	**–5**	**3**	**1**	**3**	**4**	**4**	**0**	**0**	**1**
1978-79	**New York Rangers**	**NHL**	**40**	**15**	**22**	**37**	**13**	**16**	**29**	**6**	**4**	**0**	**2**	**133**	**11.3**	**54**	**19**	**41**	**0**	**–6**	**18**	**7**	**5**	**12**	**12**	**3**	**0**	**1**
1979-80	**New York Rangers**	**NHL**	**56**	**23**	**19**	**42**	**20**	**14**	**34**	**16**	**5**	**1**	**2**	**143**	**16.1**	**68**	**23**	**56**	**0**	**–11**	....	....	....	....	....	....	....	....
	Edmonton Oilers	**NHL**	**10**	**5**	**2**	**7**	**4**	**1**	**5**	**4**	**1**	**0**	**0**	**35**	**14.3**	**12**	**2**	**10**	**0**	**0**	**3**	**2**	**0**	**2**	**0**	**0**	**0**	**0**
1980-81	**Edmonton Oilers**	**NHL**	**40**	**10**	**9**	**19**	**8**	**6**	**14**	**18**	**4**	**0**	**2**	**102**	**9.8**	**33**	**11**	**38**	**0**	**–16**	....	....	....	....	....	....	....	....
	Wichita Wind	CHL	22	15	10	25	....	....	....	48	....	....	....	....	....	....	....	....	....	....	18	*17	7	24	24	....	....	....
1981-82	**Detroit Red Wings**	**NHL**	**49**	**9**	**13**	**22**	**7**	**9**	**16**	**23**	**1**	**0**	**1**	**97**	**9.3**	**38**	**8**	**29**	**0**	**1**	....	....	....	....	....	....	....	....
	Adirondack Red Wings	AHL	24	11	13	24	....	....	....	24	....	....	....	....	....	....	....	....	....	....	4	5	0	5	14	....	....	....
1982-83	Adirondack Red Wings	AHL	35	10	12	22	....	....	....	19	....	....	....	....	....	....	....	....	....	....	....	....	....	....	....	....	....	....
1983-84	Adirondack Red Wings	AHL	59	26	20	46	....	....	....	19	....	....	....	....	....	....	....	....	....	....	....	....	....	....	....	....	....	....
	Montana Magic	CHL	17	10	10	20	....	....	....	2	....	....	....	....	....	....	....	....	....	....	....	....	....	....	....	....	....	....
1984-85	Muskegon Mohawks	IHL	32	18	13	31	....	....	....	4	....	....	....	....	....	....	....	....	....	....	16	6	3	9	26	....	....	....
1985-86	Indianapolis Checkers	IHL	11	4	3	7	....	....	....	4	....	....	....	....	....	....	....	....	....	....	....	....	....	....	....	....	....	....
	Toledo Goaldiggers	IHL	37	15	23	38	....	....	....	8	....	....	....	....	....	....	....	....	....	....	....	....	....	....	....	....	....	....
	Muskegon Lumberjacks	IHL	12	4	4	8	....	....	....	0	....	....	....	....	....	....	....	....	....	....	....	....	....	....	....	....	....	....
1986-1987			OUT OF HOCKEY – RETIRED																									
1987-1989	**New York Rangers**	**NHL**	DID NOT PLAY – SCOUTING																									

			REGULAR SEASON																		PLAYOFFS							
Season	**Club**	**League**	**GP**	**G**	**A**	**Pts**	**AG**	**AA**	**APts**	**PIM**	**PP**	**SH**	**GW**	**S**	**%**	**TGF**	**PGF**	**TGA**	**PGA**	**+/–**	**GP**	**G**	**A**	**Pts**	**PIM**	**PP**	**SH**	**GW**
1989-1992			OUT OF HOCKEY – RETIRED																									
1992-1999	**Tampa Bay Lightning**	**NHL**	DID NOT PLAY – SCOUTING																									
1999-2000	Louisiana IceGators	ECHL	DID NOT PLAY – COACHING																									
	NHL Totals		**320**	**121**	**117**	**238**	**106**	**86**	**192**	**155**	**36**	**1**	**14**	**921**	**13.1**	**373**	**125**	**289**	**9**		**24**	**10**	**8**	**18**	**16**	**3**	**0**	**2**

• Brother of Bob • WCJHL First All-Star Team (1975, 1976) • Played in NHL All-Star Game (1977)

• Suspended for entire 1978-79 season by NHL for substance abuse violation, July 6, 1978. • Suspension lifted by NHL after 40 games, January 3, 1979. Traded to **Edmonton** by **NY Rangers** for Cam Connor and Edmonton's 3rd round choice (Peter Sundstrom) in 1981 Entry Draft, March 11, 1980. Rights traded to **Minnesota** by **Edmonton** for Don Jackson and Edmonton's 3rd round choice (previously acquired, Edmonton selected Wally Chapman) in 1982 Entry Draft, August 21, 1981. Rights traded to **Detroit** by **Minnesota** with Greg Smith and Minnesota's 1st round choice (Murray Craven) in 1982 Entry Draft for Detroit's 1st round choice (Brian Bellows) in 1982 Entry Draft, August 21, 1981.

• MURPHY, Brian

C/LW – L. 6'3", 200 lbs. b: Toronto, Ont., 8/20/1947.

Season	Club	League	GP	G	A	Pts	AG	AA	APts	PIM	PP	SH	GW	S	%	TGF	PGF	TGA	PGA	+/–	GP	G	A	Pts	PIM	PP	SH	GW
1964-65	Markham Waxers	OHA-B	STATISTICS NOT AVAILABLE																									
	Toronto Marlboros	OHA-Jr.	4	0	0	0	....	....	....	0	....	....	....	....	....	....	....	....	....	....	....	....	....	....	....	....	....	....
1965-66	Markham Waxers	OHA-B	40	24	16	40	....	....	....	....	....	....	....	....	....	....	....	....	....	....	....	....	....	....	....	....	....	....
	London Knights	OHA-Jr.	2	0	1	1	....	....	....	2	....	....	....	....	....	....	....	....	....	....	....	....	....	....	....	....	....	....
1966-67	London Knights	OHA-Jr.	42	16	23	39	....	....	....	9	....	....	....	....	....	....	....	....	....	....	6	1	3	4	2	....	....	....
1967-68	London Knights/Nationals	OHA-Jr.	54	25	31	56	....	....	....	41	....	....	....	....	....	....	....	....	....	....	5	5	2	7	0	....	....	....
1968-69	Springfield Kings	AHL	72	7	8	15	....	....	....	15	....	....	....	....	....	....	....	....	....	....	....	....	....	....	....	....	....	....
1969-70	Springfield Kings	AHL	72	8	23	31	....	....	....	31	....	....	....	....	....	....	....	....	....	....	14	4	3	7	16	....	....	....
1970-71	Springfield Kings	AHL	51	11	8	19	....	....	....	27	....	....	....	....	....	....	....	....	....	....	8	2	0	2	0	....	....	....
1971-72	Baltimore Clippers	AHL	57	7	16	23	....	....	....	22	....	....	....	....	....	....	....	....	....	....	18	2	8	10	20	....	....	....
1972-73	Baltimore Clippers	AHL	73	23	36	59	....	....	....	53	....	....	....	....	....	....	....	....	....	....	....	....	....	....	....	....	....	....
1973-74	Baltimore Clippers	AHL	76	30	48	78	....	....	....	74	....	....	....	....	....	....	....	....	....	....	9	1	3	4	6	....	....	....
1974-75	Baltimore Clippers	AHL	16	1	2	3	....	....	....	13	....	....	....	....	....	....	....	....	....	....	....	....	....	....	....	....	....	....
	Detroit Red Wings	**NHL**	**1**	**0**	**0**	**0**	**0**	**0**	**0**	**0**	**0**	**0**	**0**	**1**	**0.0**	**1**	**0**	**1**	**0**	**0**	....	....	....	....	....	....	....	....
	Virginia Wings	AHL	45	10	20	30	....	....	....	33	....	....	....	....	....	....	....	....	....	....	5	2	1	3	14	....	....	....
1975-76	Rochester Americans	AHL	66	14	22	36	....	....	....	37	....	....	....	....	....	....	....	....	....	....	2	0	0	0	0	....	....	....
1976-77			REINSTATED AS AN AMATEUR																									
1977-78	Lancaster Lancers	OHA-Sr.	21	14	19	33	....	....	....	31	....	....	....	....	....	....	....	....	....	....	....	....	....	....	....	....	....	....
	NHL Totals		**1**	**0**	**0**	**0**	**0**	**0**	**0**	**0**	**0**	**0**	**0**	**1**	**0.0**	**1**	**0**	**1**	**0**		....	....	....	....	....	....	....	....

Traded to **LA Kings** by **Toronto** with Gary Croteau and Wayne Thomas for Grant Moore and Lou Deveault, October 15, 1968. Traded to **Toronto** by **LA Kings** with Garry Monahan for Bob Pulford, September 3, 1970. Signed as a free agent by **Springfield** (AHL), November, 1970. Traded to **Baltimore** (AHL) by **Springfield** (AHL) for cash, June, 1971. Traded to **Detroit** by **Baltimore** (AHL) for cash, November, 1974.

• MURPHY, Gord

Gordon J. D – R. 6'2", 195 lbs. b: Willowdale, Ont., 3/23/1967. Philadelphia's 10th, 189th overall, in 1985.

Season	Club	League	GP	G	A	Pts	AG	AA	APts	PIM	PP	SH	GW	S	%	TGF	PGF	TGA	PGA	+/–	GP	G	A	Pts	PIM	PP	SH	GW
1983-84	Don Mills Flyers	MTHL	65	24	42	66	....	....	....	130	....	....	....	....	....	....	....	....	....	....	....	....	....	....	....	....	....	....
1984-85	Oshawa Generals	OHL	59	3	12	15	....	....	....	25	....	....	....	....	....	....	....	....	....	....	....	....	....	....	....	....	....	....
1985-86	Oshawa Generals	OHL	64	7	15	22	....	....	....	56	....	....	....	....	....	....	....	....	....	....	6	1	1	2	6	....	....	....
1986-87	Oshawa Generals	OHL	56	7	30	37	....	....	....	95	....	....	....	....	....	....	....	....	....	....	24	6	16	22	22	....	....	....
	Oshawa Generals	Mem-Cup	3	0	3	3	....	....	....	9	....	....	....	....	....	....	....	....	....	....	....	....	....	....	....	....	....	....
1987-88	Hershey Bears	AHL	62	8	20	28	....	....	....	44	....	....	....	....	....	....	....	....	....	....	12	0	8	8	12	....	....	....
1988-89	**Philadelphia Flyers**	**NHL**	**75**	**4**	**31**	**35**	**3**	**22**	**25**	**68**	**3**	**0**	**1**	**116**	**3.4**	**122**	**50**	**86**	**11**	**–3**	**19**	**2**	**7**	**9**	**13**	**1**	**0**	**1**
1989-90	**Philadelphia Flyers**	**NHL**	**75**	**14**	**27**	**41**	**12**	**19**	**31**	**95**	**4**	**0**	**1**	**160**	**8.8**	**106**	**37**	**100**	**24**	**–7**	....	....	....	....	....	....	....	....
1990-91	**Philadelphia Flyers**	**NHL**	**80**	**11**	**31**	**42**	**10**	**24**	**34**	**58**	**6**	**0**	**2**	**203**	**5.4**	**111**	**45**	**98**	**25**	**–7**	....	....	....	....	....	....	....	....
1991-92	**Philadelphia Flyers**	**NHL**	**31**	**2**	**8**	**10**	**2**	**6**	**8**	**33**	**0**	**0**	**0**	**50**	**4.0**	**32**	**10**	**32**	**6**	**–4**	....	....	....	....	....	....	....	....
	Boston Bruins	**NHL**	**42**	**3**	**6**	**9**	**3**	**5**	**8**	**51**	**0**	**0**	**0**	**82**	**3.7**	**41**	**5**	**48**	**14**	**2**	**15**	**1**	**0**	**1**	**12**	**0**	**0**	**0**
1992-93	**Boston Bruins**	**NHL**	**49**	**5**	**12**	**17**	**4**	**8**	**12**	**62**	**3**	**0**	**2**	**68**	**7.4**	**39**	**13**	**42**	**3**	**–13**	....	....	....	....	....	....	....	....
	Providence Bruins	AHL	2	1	3	4	....	....	....	2	....	....	....	....	....	....	....	....	....	....	....	....	....	....	....	....	....	....
1993-94	**Florida Panthers**	**NHL**	**84**	**14**	**29**	**43**	**13**	**22**	**35**	**71**	**9**	**0**	**2**	**172**	**8.1**	**106**	**44**	**101**	**28**	**–11**	....	....	....	....	....	....	....	....
1994-95	**Florida Panthers**	**NHL**	**46**	**6**	**16**	**22**	**11**	**24**	**35**	**24**	**5**	**0**	**0**	**94**	**6.4**	**50**	**20**	**63**	**19**	**–14**	....	....	....	....	....	....	....	....
1995-96	**Florida Panthers**	**NHL**	**70**	**8**	**22**	**30**	**8**	**18**	**26**	**30**	**4**	**0**	**0**	**125**	**6.4**	**82**	**28**	**90**	**41**	**5**	**14**	**0**	**4**	**4**	**6**	**0**	**0**	**0**
1996-97	**Florida Panthers**	**NHL**	**80**	**8**	**15**	**23**	**8**	**13**	**21**	**51**	**2**	**0**	**0**	**137**	**5.8**	**73**	**15**	**86**	**31**	**3**	**5**	**0**	**5**	**5**	**4**	**0**	**0**	**0**
1997-98	**Florida Panthers**	**NHL**	**79**	**6**	**11**	**17**	**7**	**11**	**18**	**46**	**3**	**0**	**0**	**123**	**4.9**	**65**	**8**	**102**	**42**	**–3**	....	....	....	....	....	....	....	....
	Canada	WC-A	6	1	0	1	....	....	....	2	....	....	....	....	....	....	....	....	....	....	....	....	....	....	....	....	....	....
1998-99	**Florida Panthers**	**NHL**	**51**	**0**	**7**	**7**	**0**	**7**	**7**	**16**	**0**	**0**	**0**	**56**	**0.0**	**35**	**4**	**42**	**15**	**4**	....	....	....	....	....	....	....	....
99-2000	**Atlanta Thrashers**	**NHL**	**58**	**1**	**10**	**11**	**1**	**9**	**10**	**38**	**0**	**0**	**0**	**74**	**1.4**	**44**	**8**	**88**	**26**	**–26**	....	....	....	....	....	....	....	....
	NHL Totals		**820**	**82**	**225**	**307**	**82**	**188**	**270**	**643**	**39**	**0**	**8**	**1460**	**5.6**	**906**	**287**	**978**	**285**		**53**	**3**	**16**	**19**	**35**	**1**	**0**	**1**

Traded to **Boston** by **Philadelphia** with Brian Dobbin, Philadelphia's 3rd round choice (Sergei Zholtok) in 1992 Entry Draft and 4th round choice (Charles Paquette) in 1993 Entry Draft, for Garry Galley, Wes Walz and Boston's 3rd round choice (Milos Holan) in 1993 Entry Draft, January 2, 1992. Traded to **Dallas** by **Boston** for future considerations (Jon Casey to Boston for Andy Moog, June 25, 1993), June 20, 1993. Claimed by **Florida** from **Dallas** in Expansion Draft, June 24, 1993. Traded to **Atlanta** by **Florida** with Herbert Vasiljevs, Daniel Tjarnqvist and Ottawa's 6th round choice (previously acquired, later traded to Dallas - Dallas selected Justin Cox) in 1999 Entry Draft for Trevor Kidd, June 25, 1999.

• MURPHY, Joe

Joseph Patrick RW – L. 6', 190 lbs. b: London, Ont., 10/16/1967. Detroit's 1st, 1st overall, in 1986.

Season	Club	League	GP	G	A	Pts	AG	AA	APts	PIM	PP	SH	GW	S	%	TGF	PGF	TGA	PGA	+/–	GP	G	A	Pts	PIM	PP	SH	GW
1984-85	Penticton Knights	BCJHL	51	68	84	*152	....	....	....	92	....	....	....	....	....	....	....	....	....	....	....	....	....	....	....	....	....	....
	Penticton Knights	Cen-Cup	5	5	*9	*14	....	....	....	12	....	....	....	....	....	....	....	....	....	....	....	....	....	....	....	....	....	....
1985-86	Michigan State Spartans	CCHA	35	24	37	61	....	....	....	50	....	....	....	....	....	....	....	....	....	....	....	....	....	....	....	....	....	....
	Canada	Nat-Team	8	3	3	6	....	....	....	2	....	....	....	....	....	....	....	....	....	....	....	....	....	....	....	....	....	....
	Canada	WJC-A	7	4	10	*14	....	....	....	2	....	....	....	....	....	....	....	....	....	....	....	....	....	....	....	....	....	....
1986-87	**Detroit Red Wings**	**NHL**	**5**	**0**	**1**	**1**	**0**	**1**	**1**	**2**	**0**	**0**	**0**	**3**	**0.0**	**1**	**0**	**1**	**0**	**0**	....	....	....	....	....	....	....	....
	Adirondack Red Wings	AHL	71	21	38	59	....	....	....	61	....	....	....	....	....	....	....	....	....	....	10	2	1	3	33	....	....	....
1987-88	**Detroit Red Wings**	**NHL**	**50**	**10**	**9**	**19**	**9**	**6**	**15**	**37**	**1**	**0**	**2**	**82**	**12.2**	**28**	**6**	**26**	**0**	**–4**	**8**	**0**	**1**	**1**	**6**	**0**	**0**	**0**
	Adirondack Red Wings	AHL	6	5	6	11	....	....	....	4	....	....	....	....	....	....	....	....	....	....	....	....	....	....	....	....	....	....
1988-89	**Detroit Red Wings**	**NHL**	**26**	**1**	**7**	**8**	**1**	**5**	**6**	**28**	**0**	**0**	**0**	**29**	**3.4**	**14**	**5**	**16**	**0**	**–7**	....	....	....	....	....	....	....	....
	Adirondack Red Wings	AHL	47	31	35	66	....	....	....	66	....	....	....	....	....	....	....	....	....	....	16	6	11	17	17	....	....	....
1989-90	**Detroit Red Wings**	**NHL**	**9**	**3**	**1**	**4**	**3**	**1**	**4**	**4**	**0**	**0**	**1**	**16**	**18.8**	**8**	**1**	**3**	**0**	**4**	....	....	....	....	....	....	....	....
♦	**Edmonton Oilers**	**NHL**	**62**	**7**	**18**	**25**	**6**	**13**	**19**	**56**	**2**	**0**	**0**	**101**	**6.9**	**43**	**4**	**38**	**0**	**1**	**22**	**6**	**8**	**14**	**16**	**0**	**0**	**2**
1990-91	**Edmonton Oilers**	**NHL**	**80**	**27**	**35**	**62**	**25**	**27**	**52**	**35**	**4**	**1**	**4**	**141**	**19.1**	**82**	**21**	**69**	**10**	**2**	**15**	**2**	**5**	**7**	**14**	**1**	**0**	**1**
1991-92	**Edmonton Oilers**	**NHL**	**80**	**35**	**47**	**82**	**32**	**36**	**68**	**52**	**10**	**2**	**2**	**193**	**18.1**	**122**	**36**	**86**	**17**	**17**	**16**	**8**	**16**	**24**	**12**	**4**	**0**	**2**
1992-93	**Chicago Blackhawks**	**NHL**	**19**	**7**	**10**	**17**	**6**	**7**	**13**	**18**	**5**	**0**	**1**	**43**	**16.3**	**27**	**18**	**12**	**0**	**–3**	**4**	**0**	**0**	**0**	**8**	**0**	**0**	**0**
1993-94	**Chicago Blackhawks**	**NHL**	**81**	**31**	**39**	**70**	**29**	**30**	**59**	**111**	**7**	**4**	**4**	**222**	**14.0**	**100**	**42**	**69**	**12**	**1**	**6**	**1**	**3**	**4**	**25**	**0**	**0**	**0**
1994-95	**Chicago Blackhawks**	**NHL**	**40**	**23**	**18**	**41**	**41**	**27**	**68**	**89**	**7**	**0**	**3**	**120**	**19.2**	**50**	**21**	**28**	**6**	**7**	**16**	**9**	**3**	**12**	**29**	**3**	**0**	**3**
1995-96	**Chicago Blackhawks**	**NHL**	**70**	**22**	**29**	**51**	**22**	**24**	**46**	**86**	**8**	**0**	**3**	**212**	**10.4**	**72**	**26**	**52**	**3**	**–3**	**10**	**6**	**2**	**8**	**33**	**0**	**0**	**2**
1996-97	**St. Louis Blues**	**NHL**	**75**	**20**	**25**	**45**	**21**	**22**	**43**	**69**	**4**	**1**	**2**	**151**	**13.2**	**65**	**18**	**56**	**8**	**–1**	**6**	**1**	**1**	**2**	**10**	**1**	**0**	**0**
1997-98	**St. Louis Blues**	**NHL**	**27**	**4**	**9**	**13**	**5**	**9**	**14**	**22**	**2**	**0**	**0**	**52**	**7.7**	**25**	**8**	**9**	**0**	**8**	....	....	....	....	....	....	....	....
	San Jose Sharks	**NHL**	**10**	**5**	**4**	**9**	**6**	**4**	**10**	**14**	**2**	**0**	**0**	**29**	**17.2**	**12**	**6**	**5**	**0**	**1**	**6**	**1**	**1**	**2**	**20**	**1**	**0**	**0**
1998-99	**San Jose Sharks**	**NHL**	**76**	**25**	**23**	**48**	**29**	**22**	**51**	**73**	**7**	**0**	**2**	**176**	**14.2**	**63**	**22**	**31**	**0**	**10**	**6**	**0**	**3**	**3**	**4**	**0**	**0**	**0**
99-2000	**Boston Bruins**	**NHL**	**26**	**7**	**7**	**14**	**8**	**6**	**14**	**41**	**3**	**0**	**0**	**68**	**10.3**	**17**	**7**	**19**	**2**	**–7**	....	....	....	....	....	....	....	....
	Washington Capitals	**NHL**	**29**	**5**	**8**	**13**	**6**	**7**	**13**	**53**	**1**	**0**	**2**	**50**	**10.0**	**19**	**3**	**8**	**0**	**8**	**5**	**0**	**0**	**0**	**8**	**0**	**0**	**0**
	NHL Totals		**765**	**232**	**290**	**522**	**249**	**247**	**496**	**790**	**63**	**8**	**26**	**1688**	**13.7**	**748**	**244**	**528**	**58**		**120**	**34**	**43**	**77**	**185**	**10**	**0**	**10**

Centennial Cup All-Star Team (1985)

Traded to **Edmonton** by **Detroit** with Petr Klima, Adam Graves and Jeff Sharples for Jimmy Carson, Kevin McClelland and Edmonton's 5th round choice (later traded to Montreal — Montreal selected Brad Layzell) in 1991 Entry Draft, November 2, 1989. • Missed majority of 1991-92 season after failing to come to contract terms with Edmonton Oilers. Traded to **Chicago** by **Edmonton** for Igor Kravchuk and Dean McAmmond, February 24, 1993. Signed as a free agent by **St. Louis**, July 8, 1996. Traded to **San Jose** by **St. Louis** for Todd Gill, March 24, 1998. Signed as a free agent by **Boston**, November 12, 1999. Claimed on waivers by **Washington** from **Boston**, February 10, 2000.

● **MURPHY, Larry** Lawrence Thomas D – R. 6'2", 210 lbs. b: Scarborough, Ont., 3/8/1961. Los Angeles' 1st, 4th overall, in 1980.

Season	Club	League	GP	G	A	Pts	AG	AA	APts	PIM	PP	SH	GW	S	%	TGF	PGF	TGA	PGA	+/-	GP	G	A	Pts	PIM	PP	SH	GW
			REGULAR SEASON																		PLAYOFFS							
1977-78	Don Mills Flyers	MTHL	STATISTICS NOT AVAILABLE																									
	Toronto Young Nationals	OHA-B	36	10	20	30	....	....	....	25	....	....	....	....	....	....	....	....	....	....	....	....	....	....	....	....	....	....
1978-79	Peterborough Petes	OMJHL	66	6	21	27	....	....	....	82	....	....	....	....	....	....	....	....	....	....	19	1	9	10	42	....	....	....
	Peterborough Petes	Mem-Cup	5	0	2	2	....	....	....	8	....	....	....	....	....	....	....	....	....	....	....	....	....	....	....	....	....	....
1979-80	Peterborough Petes	OMJHL	68	21	68	89	....	....	....	88	....	....	....	....	....	....	....	....	....	....	14	4	13	17	20	....	....	....
	Canada	WJC-A	5	1	0	1	....	....	....	4	....	....	....	....	....	....	....	....	....	....	....	....	....	....	....	....	....	....
	Peterborough Petes	Mem-Cup	5	1	*6	7	....	....	....	4	....	....	....	....	....	....	....	....	....	....	....	....	....	....	....	....	....	....
1980-81	**Los Angeles Kings**	**NHL**	**80**	**16**	**60**	**76**	**12**	**40**	**52**	**79**	**5**	**1**	**1**	**153**	**10.5**	**161**	**63**	**115**	**34**	**17**	**4**	**3**	**0**	**3**	**2**	**1**	**0**	**0**
1981-82	**Los Angeles Kings**	**NHL**	**79**	**22**	**44**	**66**	**17**	**29**	**46**	**95**	**8**	**1**	**2**	**191**	**11.5**	**134**	**43**	**133**	**29**	**–13**	**10**	**2**	**8**	**10**	**12**	**1**	**0**	**0**
1982-83	**Los Angeles Kings**	**NHL**	**77**	**14**	**48**	**62**	**11**	**33**	**44**	**81**	**9**	**0**	**2**	**172**	**8.1**	**133**	**51**	**108**	**28**	**2**	....	....	....	....	....	....	....	....
1983-84	**Los Angeles Kings**	**NHL**	**6**	**0**	**3**	**3**	**0**	**2**	**2**	**0**	**0**	**0**	**0**	**11**	**0.0**	**9**	**4**	**11**	**2**	**–4**	....	....	....	....	....	....	....	....
	Washington Capitals	**NHL**	**72**	**13**	**33**	**46**	**10**	**22**	**32**	**50**	**2**	**0**	**2**	**138**	**9.4**	**115**	**41**	**75**	**13**	**12**	**8**	**0**	**3**	**3**	**6**	**0**	**0**	**0**
1984-85	**Washington Capitals**	**NHL**	**79**	**13**	**42**	**55**	**11**	**29**	**40**	**51**	**3**	**0**	**0**	**153**	**8.5**	**125**	**43**	**79**	**18**	**21**	**5**	**2**	**3**	**5**	**0**	**2**	**0**	**0**
	Canada	WEC-A	8	2	6	8	....	....	....	4	....	....	....	....	....	....	....	....	....	....	....	....	....	....	....	....	....	....
1985-86	**Washington Capitals**	**NHL**	**78**	**21**	**44**	**65**	**17**	**30**	**47**	**50**	**8**	**1**	**2**	**180**	**11.7**	**131**	**50**	**100**	**21**	**2**	**9**	**1**	**5**	**6**	**6**	**1**	**0**	**0**
1986-87	**Washington Capitals**	**NHL**	**80**	**23**	**58**	**81**	**20**	**42**	**62**	**39**	**8**	**0**	**4**	**226**	**10.2**	**163**	**48**	**104**	**14**	**25**	**7**	**2**	**2**	**4**	**6**	**0**	**0**	**1**
	Canada	WEC-A	6	0	3	3	....	....	....	4	....	....	....	....	....	....	....	....	....	....	....	....	....	....	....	....	....	....
1987-88	Canada	Can-Cup	8	1	6	7	....	....	....	4	....	....	....	....	....	....	....	....	....	....	....	....	....	....	....	....	....	....
	Washington Capitals	**NHL**	**79**	**8**	**53**	**61**	**7**	**38**	**45**	**72**	**7**	**0**	**1**	**201**	**4.0**	**132**	**58**	**89**	**17**	**2**	**13**	**4**	**4**	**8**	**33**	**2**	**0**	**1**
1988-89	**Washington Capitals**	**NHL**	**65**	**7**	**29**	**36**	**6**	**21**	**27**	**70**	**3**	**0**	**0**	**129**	**5.4**	**95**	**39**	**67**	**6**	**–5**	....	....	....	....	....	....	....	....
	Minnesota North Stars	**NHL**	**13**	**4**	**6**	**10**	**3**	**4**	**7**	**12**	**3**	**0**	**1**	**31**	**12.9**	**20**	**11**	**5**	**1**	**5**	**5**	**0**	**2**	**2**	**8**	**0**	**0**	**0**
1989-90	**Minnesota North Stars**	**NHL**	**77**	**10**	**58**	**68**	**9**	**42**	**51**	**44**	**4**	**0**	**1**	**173**	**5.8**	**141**	**66**	**89**	**1**	**–13**	**7**	**1**	**2**	**3**	**31**	**0**	**0**	**1**
1990-91	Minnesota North Stars	Fr-Tour	3	0	0	0	....	....	....	0	....	....	....	....	....	....	....	....	....	....	....	....	....	....	....	....	....	....
	Minnesota North Stars	**NHL**	**31**	**4**	**11**	**15**	**4**	**8**	**12**	**38**	**1**	**0**	**2**	**103**	**3.9**	**39**	**17**	**39**	**9**	**–8**	....	....	....	....	....	....	....	....
♦	**Pittsburgh Penguins**	**NHL**	**44**	**5**	**23**	**28**	**5**	**17**	**22**	**30**	**2**	**0**	**0**	**85**	**5.9**	**86**	**36**	**53**	**5**	**2**	**23**	**5**	**18**	**23**	**44**	**4**	**0**	**0**
1991-92	Canada	Can-Cup	8	0	1	1	....	....	....	0	....	....	....	....	....	....	....	....	....	....	....	....	....	....	....	....	....	....
♦	**Pittsburgh Penguins**	**NHL**	**77**	**21**	**56**	**77**	**19**	**42**	**61**	**48**	**7**	**2**	**3**	**206**	**10.2**	**180**	**67**	**110**	**30**	**33**	**21**	**6**	**10**	**16**	**19**	**3**	**0**	**1**
1992-93	**Pittsburgh Penguins**	**NHL**	**83**	**22**	**63**	**85**	**18**	**43**	**61**	**73**	**6**	**2**	**2**	**230**	**9.6**	**225**	**82**	**137**	**39**	**45**	**12**	**2**	**11**	**13**	**10**	**2**	**0**	**1**
1993-94	**Pittsburgh Penguins**	**NHL**	**84**	**17**	**56**	**73**	**16**	**44**	**60**	**44**	**7**	**0**	**4**	**236**	**7.2**	**165**	**65**	**122**	**32**	**10**	**6**	**0**	**5**	**5**	**0**	**0**	**0**	**0**
1994-95	**Pittsburgh Penguins**	**NHL**	**48**	**13**	**25**	**38**	**23**	**37**	**60**	**18**	**4**	**0**	**3**	**124**	**10.5**	**97**	**33**	**71**	**19**	**12**	**12**	**2**	**13**	**15**	**0**	**1**	**0**	**0**
1995-96	**Toronto Maple Leafs**	**NHL**	**82**	**12**	**49**	**61**	**12**	**40**	**52**	**34**	**8**	**0**	**1**	**182**	**6.6**	**129**	**67**	**75**	**11**	**–2**	**6**	**0**	**2**	**2**	**4**	**0**	**0**	**0**
1996-97	**Toronto Maple Leafs**	**NHL**	**69**	**7**	**32**	**39**	**7**	**28**	**35**	**20**	**4**	**0**	**0**	**137**	**5.1**	**99**	**37**	**77**	**16**	**1**	....	....	....	....	....	....	....	....
♦	**Detroit Red Wings**	**NHL**	**12**	**2**	**4**	**6**	**2**	**4**	**6**	**0**	**1**	**0**	**1**	**21**	**9.5**	**12**	**3**	**8**	**1**	**2**	**20**	**2**	**9**	**11**	**8**	**1**	**0**	**1**
1997-98♦	**Detroit Red Wings**	**NHL**	**82**	**11**	**41**	**52**	**13**	**40**	**53**	**37**	**2**	**1**	**2**	**129**	**8.5**	**121**	**37**	**73**	**24**	**35**	**22**	**3**	**12**	**15**	**2**	**1**	**2**	**1**
1998-99	**Detroit Red Wings**	**NHL**	**80**	**10**	**42**	**52**	**12**	**41**	**53**	**42**	**5**	**1**	**2**	**168**	**6.0**	**121**	**34**	**88**	**22**	**21**	**10**	**0**	**2**	**2**	**8**	**0**	**0**	**0**
99-2000	**Detroit Red Wings**	**NHL**	**81**	**10**	**30**	**40**	**11**	**28**	**39**	**45**	**7**	**0**	**0**	**146**	**6.8**	**92**	**24**	**81**	**17**	**4**	**9**	**2**	**3**	**5**	**2**	**1**	**1**	**0**
	Canada	WC-A	3	0	0	0	....	....	....	0	....	....	....	....	....	....	....	....	....	....	....	....	....	....	....	....	....	....
	NHL Totals		**1558**	**285**	**910**	**1195**	**265**	**704**	**969**	**1072**	**114**	**9**	**36**	**3525**	**8.1**	**2725**	**1019**	**1909**	**409**		**209**	**37**	**114**	**151**	**201**	**20**	**3**	**7**

OMJHL First All-Star Team (1980) • NHL Second All-Star Team (1987, 1993, 1995) • Played in NHL All-Star Game (1994, 1996, 1999)

Traded to **Washington** by **LA Kings** for Ken Houston and Brian Engblom, October 18, 1983. Traded to **Minnesota** by **Washington** with Mike Gartner for Dino Ciccarelli and Bob Rouse, March 7, 1989. Traded to **Pittsburgh** by **Minnesota** with Peter Taglianetti for Chris Dahlquist and Jim Johnson, December 11, 1990. Traded to **Toronto** by **Pittsburgh** for Dmitri Mironov and Toronto's 2nd round choice (later traded to New Jersey — New Jersey selected Joshua Dewolf) in 1996 Entry Draft, July 8, 1995. Traded to **Detroit** by **Toronto** for future considerations, March 18, 1997.

● **MURPHY, Mike** Michael John "Murph" RW – R. 6', 190 lbs. b: Toronto, Ont., 9/12/1950. NY Rangers' 2nd, 25th overall, in 1970.

Season	Club	League	GP	G	A	Pts	AG	AA	APts	PIM	PP	SH	GW	S	%	TGF	PGF	TGA	PGA	+/-	GP	G	A	Pts	PIM	PP	SH	GW
1967-68	York Steel	OHA-B	30	19	19	38	....	....	....	....	....	....	....	....	....	....	....	....	....	....	....	....	....	....	....	....	....	....
1968-69	Toronto Marlboros	OHA-Jr.	44	16	23	39	....	....	....	53	....	....	....	....	....	....	....	....	....	....	6	1	4	5	6	....	....	....
1969-70	Toronto Marlboros	OHA-Jr.	54	23	27	50	....	....	....	68	....	....	....	....	....	....	....	....	....	....	6	7	6	13	16	....	....	....
1970-71	Omaha Knights	CHL	59	24	47	71	....	....	....	37	....	....	....	....	....	....	....	....	....	....	11	4	8	12	17	....	....	....
1971-72	Omaha Knights	CHL	8	1	4	5	....	....	....	12	....	....	....	....	....	....	....	....	....	....	....	....	....	....	....	....	....	....
	St. Louis Blues	**NHL**	**63**	**20**	**23**	**43**	**20**	**20**	**40**	**19**	**5**	**0**	**3**	**176**	**11.4**	**74**	**20**	**59**	**1**	**–4**	**11**	**2**	**3**	**5**	**6**	**1**	**0**	**0**
1972-73	**St. Louis Blues**	**NHL**	**64**	**18**	**27**	**45**	**17**	**21**	**38**	**48**	**3**	**0**	**3**	**182**	**9.9**	**72**	**12**	**48**	**1**	**13**	....	....	....	....	....	....	....	....
	New York Rangers	**NHL**	**15**	**4**	**4**	**8**	**4**	**3**	**7**	**5**	**0**	**0**	**1**	**35**	**11.4**	**9**	**0**	**15**	**1**	**–5**	**10**	**0**	**0**	**0**	**0**	**0**	**0**	**0**
1973-74	**New York Rangers**	**NHL**	**16**	**2**	**1**	**3**	**2**	**1**	**3**	**0**	**0**	**0**	**0**	**28**	**7.1**	**7**	**1**	**8**	**0**	**–2**	....	....	....	....	....	....	....	....
	Los Angeles Kings	**NHL**	**53**	**13**	**16**	**29**	**12**	**13**	**25**	**38**	**1**	**0**	**2**	**142**	**9.2**	**45**	**9**	**39**	**5**	**2**	**5**	**0**	**4**	**4**	**0**	**0**	**0**	**0**
1974-75	**Los Angeles Kings**	**NHL**	**78**	**30**	**38**	**68**	**26**	**28**	**54**	**44**	**3**	**3**	**6**	**175**	**17.1**	**98**	**23**	**57**	**14**	**32**	**3**	**3**	**0**	**3**	**4**	**2**	**0**	**1**
1975-76	**Los Angeles Kings**	**NHL**	**80**	**26**	**42**	**68**	**23**	**31**	**54**	**61**	**7**	**1**	**5**	**205**	**12.7**	**99**	**28**	**90**	**16**	**–3**	**9**	**1**	**4**	**5**	**6**	**1**	**0**	**0**
1976-77	**Los Angeles Kings**	**NHL**	**76**	**25**	**36**	**61**	**23**	**28**	**51**	**58**	**9**	**3**	**3**	**165**	**15.2**	**121**	**51**	**82**	**27**	**15**	**9**	**4**	**9**	**13**	**4**	**1**	**0**	**0**
1977-78	**Los Angeles Kings**	**NHL**	**72**	**20**	**36**	**56**	**18**	**28**	**46**	**48**	**7**	**0**	**6**	**207**	**9.7**	**83**	**28**	**79**	**23**	**–1**	**2**	**0**	**0**	**0**	**0**	**0**	**0**	**0**
	Canada	WEC-A	10	1	4	5	....	....	....	16	....	....	....	....	....	....	....	....	....	....	....	....	....	....	....	....	....	....
1978-79	**Los Angeles Kings**	**NHL**	**64**	**16**	**29**	**45**	**14**	**21**	**35**	**38**	**4**	**1**	**2**	**150**	**10.7**	**74**	**20**	**93**	**27**	**–12**	**2**	**0**	**1**	**1**	**0**	**0**	**0**	**0**
1979-80	**Los Angeles Kings**	**NHL**	**80**	**27**	**22**	**49**	**23**	**16**	**39**	**29**	**7**	**3**	**1**	**176**	**15.3**	**83**	**24**	**131**	**60**	**–12**	**4**	**1**	**0**	**1**	**2**	**0**	**1**	**0**
1980-81	**Los Angeles Kings**	**NHL**	**68**	**16**	**23**	**39**	**12**	**15**	**27**	**54**	**2**	**1**	**1**	**131**	**12.2**	**51**	**7**	**88**	**37**	**–7**	**1**	**0**	**1**	**1**	**0**	**0**	**0**	**0**
1981-82	**Los Angeles Kings**	**NHL**	**28**	**5**	**10**	**15**	**4**	**7**	**11**	**20**	**0**	**2**	**0**	**36**	**13.9**	**21**	**1**	**30**	**10**	**0**	**10**	**2**	**1**	**3**	**32**	**0**	**0**	**0**
1982-83	**Los Angeles Kings**	**NHL**	**74**	**16**	**11**	**27**	**13**	**8**	**21**	**52**	**0**	**5**	**2**	**135**	**11.9**	**42**	**3**	**79**	**29**	**–11**	....	....	....	....	....	....	....	....
	NHL Totals		**831**	**238**	**318**	**556**	**211**	**240**	**451**	**514**	**48**	**19**	**35**	**1943**	**12.2**	**879**	**227**	**898**	**251**		**66**	**13**	**23**	**36**	**54**	**5**	**1**	**1**

CHL Second All-Star Team (1971) • Won Ken McKenzie Trophy (CHL's Rookie of the Year) (1971) • Played in NHL All-Star Game (1980)

Traded to **St. Louis** by **NY Rangers** with Jack Egers and Andre Dupont for Gene Carr, Jim Lorentz and Wayne Connelly, November 15, 1971. Traded to **NY Rangers** by **St. Louis** for Ab DeMarco Jr., March 2, 1973. Traded to **LA Kings** by **NY Rangers** with Sheldon Kannegiesser and Tom Williams for Gilles Marcotte and Real Lemieux, November 30, 1973.

● **MURPHY, Rob** C – L. 6'3", 205 lbs. b: Hull, Que., 4/7/1969. Vancouver's 1st, 24th overall, in 1987.

Season	Club	League	GP	G	A	Pts	AG	AA	APts	PIM	PP	SH	GW	S	%	TGF	PGF	TGA	PGA	+/-	GP	G	A	Pts	PIM	PP	SH	GW
1985-86	Outaouais Selects	QAAA	41	17	33	50	....	....	....	47	....	....	....	....	....	....	....	....	....	....	....	....	....	....	....	....	....	....
1986-87	Laval Titan	QMJHL	70	35	54	89	....	....	....	86	....	....	....	....	....	....	....	....	....	....	14	3	4	7	15	....	....	....
1987-88	Laval Titan	QMJHL	26	11	25	36	....	....	....	82	....	....	....	....	....	....	....	....	....	....	....	....	....	....	....	....	....	....
	Drummondville Voltigeurs	QMJHL	33	16	28	44	....	....	....	41	....	....	....	....	....	....	....	....	....	....	17	4	15	19	45	....	....	....
	Vancouver Canucks	**NHL**	**5**	**0**	**0**	**0**	**0**	**0**	**0**	**2**	**0**	**0**	**0**	**4**	**0.0**	**1**	**0**	**2**	**0**	**–1**	....	....	....	....	....	....	....	....
	Drummondville Voltigeurs	Mem-Cup	3	2	0	2	....	....	....	0	....	....	....	....	....	....	....	....	....	....	....	....	....	....	....	....	....	....
1988-89	Drummondville Voltigeurs	QMJHL	26	13	25	38	....	....	....	16	....	....	....	....	....	....	....	....	....	....	4	1	3	4	20	....	....	....
	Canada	WJC-A	7	1	0	1	....	....	....	8	....	....	....	....	....	....	....	....	....	....	....	....	....	....	....	....	....	....
	Vancouver Canucks	**NHL**	**8**	**0**	**1**	**1**	**0**	**1**	**1**	**2**	**0**	**0**	**0**	**10**	**0.0**	**3**	**0**	**4**	**0**	**–1**	....	....	....	....	....	....	....	....
	Milwaukee Admirals	IHL	8	4	2	6	....	....	....	4	....	....	....	....	....	....	....	....	....	....	11	3	5	8	34	....	....	....
1989-90	**Vancouver Canucks**	**NHL**	**12**	**1**	**1**	**2**	**1**	**1**	**2**	**0**	**0**	**0**	**1**	**6**	**16.7**	**6**	**0**	**19**	**0**	**–13**	....	....	....	....	....	....	....	....
	Milwaukee Admirals	IHL	64	24	47	71	....	....	....	87	....	....	....	....	....	....	....	....	....	....	6	2	6	8	12	....	....	....
1990-91	**Vancouver Canucks**	**NHL**	**42**	**5**	**1**	**6**	**5**	**1**	**6**	**90**	**0**	**0**	**0**	**19**	**26.3**	**7**	**0**	**19**	**1**	**–11**	**4**	**0**	**0**	**0**	**2**	**0**	**0**	**0**
	Milwaukee Admirals	IHL	23	1	7	8	....	....	....	48	....	....	....	....	....	....	....	....	....	....	....	....	....	....	....	....	....	....
1991-92	**Vancouver Canucks**	**NHL**	**6**	**0**	**1**	**1**	**0**	**1**	**1**	**6**	**0**	**0**	**0**	**2**	**0.0**	**1**	**0**	**3**	**0**	**–2**	....	....	....	....	....	....	....	....
	Milwaukee Admirals	IHL	73	26	38	64	....	....	....	141	....	....	....	....	....	....	....	....	....	....	5	0	3	3	2	....	....	....
1992-93	**Ottawa Senators**	**NHL**	**44**	**3**	**7**	**10**	**2**	**5**	**7**	**30**	**0**	**0**	**0**	**55**	**5.5**	**13**	**0**	**36**	**0**	**–23**	....	....	....	....	....	....	....	....
	New Haven Senators	AHL	26	8	12	20	....	....	....	28	....	....	....	....	....	....	....	....	....	....	....	....	....	....	....	....	....	....
1993-94	**Los Angeles Kings**	**NHL**	**8**	**0**	**1**	**1**	**0**	**1**	**1**	**22**	**0**	**0**	**0**	**4**	**0.0**	**2**	**0**	**5**	**0**	**–3**	....	....	....	....	....	....	....	....
	Phoenix Roadrunners	IHL	72	23	34	57	....	....	....	101	....	....	....	....	....	....	....	....	....	....	....	....	....	....	....	....	....	....
1994-95	Phoenix Roadrunners	IHL	2	0	0	0	....	....	....	10	....	....	....	....	....	....	....	....	....	....	2	0	1	1	0	....	....	....
1995-96	Fort Wayne Komets	IHL	82	24	52	76	....	....	....	107	....	....	....	....	....	....	....	....	....	....	5	1	2	3	8	....	....	....
1996-97	Fort Wayne Komets	IHL	35	9	16	25	....	....	....	40	....	....	....	....	....	....	....	....	....	....	....	....	....	....	....	....	....	....

			REGULAR SEASON																		PLAYOFFS							
Season	Club	League	GP	G	A	Pts	AG	AA	APts	PIM	PP	SH	GW	S	%	TGF	PGF	TGA	PGA	+/–	GP	G	A	Pts	PIM	PP	SH	GW
1997-98	Star Bulls Rosenheim	Germany	44	9	24	33	....	....	....	68	....	....	....	....	....	....	....	....	....	....	....	....	....	....	....	....	....	....
1998-99	EV Landshut	Germany	52	14	30	44	....	....	....	77	....	....	....	....	....	....	....	....	....	....	3	0	1	1	8	....	....	....
99-2000	Eisbaren Berlin	Germany	58	10	24	34	....	....	....	95	....	....	....	....	....	....	....	....	....	....	....	....	....	....	....	....	....	....
	NHL Totals		**125**	**9**	**12**	**21**	**8**	**10**	**18**	**152**	**0**	**0**	**1**	**100**	**9.0**	**33**	**0**	**88**	**1**		**4**	**0**	**0**	**0**	**2**	**0**	**0**	**0**

Won Garry F. Longman Memorial Trophy (Top Rookie - IHL) (1990)

Claimed by **Ottawa** from **Vancouver** in Expansion Draft, June 18, 1992. Signed as a free agent by **LA Kings**, August 2, 1993.

• MURPHY, Ron

Ron Robert Ronald LW – L. 5'11", 185 lbs. b: Hamilton, Ont., 4/10/1933.

Season	Club	League	GP	G	A	Pts	AG	AA	APts	PIM	PP	SH	GW	S	%	TGF	PGF	TGA	PGA	+/–	GP	G	A	Pts	PIM	PP	SH	GW
1949-50	Guelph Biltmores	OHA-Jr.	1	0	0	0	....	....	....	2	....	....	....	....	....	....	....	....	....	....	....	....	....	....	....	....	....	....
1950-51	Guelph Biltmores	OHA-Jr.	54	44	44	88	....	....	....	38	....	....	....	....	....	....	....	....	....	....	4	2	1	3	2	....	....	....
1951-52	Guelph Biltmores	OHA-Jr.	51	58	58	116	....	....	....	36	....	....	....	....	....	....	....	....	....	....	10	*8	7	15	2	....	....	....
	Cincinnati Mohawks	AHL	1	0	0	0	....	....	....	0	....	....	....	....	....	....	....	....	....	....	....	....	....	....	....	....	....	....
	Guelph Biltmores	Mem-Cup	12	*13	7	20	....	....	....	4	....	....	....	....	....	....	....	....	....	....	....	....	....	....	....	....	....	....
1952-53	Guelph Biltmores	OHA-Jr.	45	39	42	81	....	....	....	52	....	....	....	....	....	....	....	....	....	....	....	....	....	....	....	....	....	....
	New York Rangers	**NHL**	**15**	**3**	**1**	**4**	**4**	**1**	**5**	**0**	....	....	....	....	....	....	....	....	....	....	....	....	....	....	....	....	....	....
1953-54	**New York Rangers**	**NHL**	**27**	**1**	**3**	**4**	**1**	**4**	**5**	**20**	....	....	....	....	....	....	....	....	....	....	....	....	....	....	....	....	....	....
	Saskatoon Quakers	WHL	24	7	5	12	....	....	....	2	....	....	....	....	....	....	....	....	....	....	6	1	2	3	2	....	....	....
1954-55	**New York Rangers**	**NHL**	**66**	**14**	**16**	**30**	**18**	**18**	**36**	**36**	....	....	....	....	....	....	....	....	....	....	....	....	....	....	....	....	....	....
1955-56	**New York Rangers**	**NHL**	**66**	**16**	**28**	**44**	**22**	**33**	**55**	**71**	....	....	....	....	....	....	....	....	....	....	**5**	**0**	**1**	**1**	**2**	**0**	**0**	**0**
1956-57	**New York Rangers**	**NHL**	**33**	**7**	**12**	**19**	**9**	**13**	**22**	**14**	....	....	....	....	....	....	....	....	....	....	**5**	**0**	**0**	**0**	**0**	**0**	**0**	**0**
	Providence Reds	AHL	21	12	11	23	....	....	....	14	....	....	....	....	....	....	....	....	....	....	....	....	....	....	....	....	....	....
1957-58	**Chicago Black Hawks**	**NHL**	**69**	**11**	**17**	**28**	**14**	**17**	**31**	**32**	....	....	....	....	....	....	....	....	....	....	....	....	....	....	....	....	....	....
1958-59	**Chicago Black Hawks**	**NHL**	**59**	**17**	**30**	**47**	**20**	**30**	**50**	**52**	....	....	....	....	....	....	....	....	....	....	....	....	....	....	....	....	....	....
1959-60	**Chicago Black Hawks**	**NHL**	**63**	**15**	**21**	**36**	**18**	**20**	**38**	**18**	....	....	....	....	....	....	....	....	....	....	**4**	**1**	**0**	**1**	**0**	**0**	**0**	**1**
1960-61 ♦	**Chicago Black Hawks**	**NHL**	**70**	**21**	**19**	**40**	**24**	**18**	**42**	**30**	....	....	....	....	....	....	....	....	....	....	**12**	**2**	**1**	**3**	**0**	**0**	**0**	**1**
1961-62	**Chicago Black Hawks**	**NHL**	**60**	**12**	**16**	**28**	**14**	**15**	**29**	**41**	....	....	....	....	....	....	....	....	....	....	....	....	....	....	....	....	....	....
1962-63	**Chicago Black Hawks**	**NHL**	**68**	**18**	**16**	**34**	**21**	**16**	**37**	**28**	....	....	....	....	....	....	....	....	....	....	**1**	**0**	**0**	**0**	**0**	**0**	**0**	**0**
1963-64	**Chicago Black Hawks**	**NHL**	**70**	**11**	**8**	**19**	**14**	**8**	**22**	**32**	....	....	....	....	....	....	....	....	....	....	**7**	**0**	**1**	**1**	**8**	**0**	**0**	**0**
1964-65	**Detroit Red Wings**	**NHL**	**58**	**20**	**19**	**39**	**24**	**19**	**43**	**32**	....	....	....	....	....	....	....	....	....	....	**5**	**0**	**1**	**1**	**4**	**0**	**0**	**0**
1965-66	**Detroit Red Wings**	**NHL**	**32**	**10**	**7**	**17**	**11**	**7**	**18**	**10**	....	....	....	....	....	....	....	....	....	....	....	....	....	....	....	....	....	....
	Boston Bruins	**NHL**	**2**	**0**	**1**	**1**	**0**	**1**	**1**	**0**	....	....	....	....	....	....	....	....	....	....	....	....	....	....	....	....	....	....
1966-67	**Boston Bruins**	**NHL**	**39**	**11**	**16**	**27**	**13**	**16**	**29**	**6**	....	....	....	....	....	....	....	....	....	....	....	....	....	....	....	....	....	....
1967-68	**Boston Bruins**	**NHL**	**12**	**0**	**1**	**1**	**0**	**1**	**1**	**4**	**0**	**0**	**0**	**17**	**0.0**	**2**	**1**	**3**	**0**	**–2**	**4**	**0**	**0**	**0**	**0**	**0**	**0**	**0**
	Oklahoma City Blazers	CPHL	6	2	2	4	....	....	....	2	....	....	....	....	....	....	....	....	....	....	....	....	....	....	....	....	....	....
1968-69	**Boston Bruins**	**NHL**	**60**	**16**	**38**	**54**	**17**	**34**	**51**	**26**	**5**	**0**	**0**	**113**	**14.2**	**76**	**15**	**38**	**0**	**23**	**10**	**4**	**4**	**8**	**12**	**0**	**0**	**0**
1969-70	**Boston Bruins**	**NHL**	**20**	**2**	**5**	**7**	**2**	**5**	**7**	**8**	**0**	**0**	**2**	**35**	**5.7**	**11**	**1**	**12**	**3**	**1**	....	....	....	....	....	....	....	....
	NHL Totals		**889**	**205**	**274**	**479**	**246**	**276**	**522**	**460**	....	....	....	....	....	....	....	....	....	....	**53**	**7**	**8**	**15**	**26**	....	....	....

Played in NHL All-Star Game (1961)

Traded to **Chicago** by **NY Rangers** for Hank Ciesla, June, 1957. Traded to **Detroit** by **Chicago** with Aut Erickson for Art Stratton, John Miszuk and Ian Cushenan, June 9, 1964. Traded to **Boston** by **Detroit** with Bill Lesuk, Gary Doak and future considerations (Steve Atkinson, June 6, 1966) for Dean Prentice and Leo Boivin, February 16, 1966. • Missed majority of 1966-67 recovering from shoulder (December, 1966) and foot injury suffered in game vs. Chicago, February 28, 1967.

• MURRAY, Bob

Robert John D – R. 6'1", 195 lbs. b: Peterborough, Ont., 7/16/1948.

Season	Club	League	GP	G	A	Pts	AG	AA	APts	PIM	PP	SH	GW	S	%	TGF	PGF	TGA	PGA	+/–	GP	G	A	Pts	PIM	PP	SH	GW
1966-67	Peterborough Petes	OHA-Jr.	48	3	9	12	....	....	....	32	....	....	....	....	....	....	....	....	....	....	6	0	0	0	0	....	....	....
1967-68	Michigan Tech Huskies	WCHA	DID NOT PLAY – FRESHMAN																									
1968-69	Michigan Tech Huskies	WCHA	31	2	13	15	....	....	....	43	....	....	....	....	....	....	....	....	....	....	....	....	....	....	....	....	....	....
1969-70	Michigan Tech Huskies	WCHA	32	3	12	15	....	....	....	61	....	....	....	....	....	....	....	....	....	....	....	....	....	....	....	....	....	....
1970-71	Michigan Tech Huskies	WCHA	32	6	19	25	....	....	....	67	....	....	....	....	....	....	....	....	....	....	....	....	....	....	....	....	....	....
1971-72	Nova Scotia Voyageurs	AHL	73	1	12	13	....	....	....	62	....	....	....	....	....	....	....	....	....	....	15	3	0	3	10	....	....	....
1972-73	Nova Scotia Voyageurs	AHL	60	4	22	26	....	....	....	61	....	....	....	....	....	....	....	....	....	....	13	1	5	6	29	....	....	....
1973-74	**Atlanta Flames**	**NHL**	**62**	**0**	**3**	**3**	**0**	**2**	**2**	**34**	**0**	**0**	**0**	**67**	**0.0**	**31**	**1**	**57**	**7**	**–20**	**4**	**1**	**0**	**1**	**2**	**0**	**0**	**0**
1974-75	**Atlanta Flames**	**NHL**	**42**	**3**	**3**	**6**	**3**	**2**	**5**	**22**	**0**	**0**	**1**	**34**	**8.8**	**24**	**0**	**28**	**9**	**5**	....	....	....	....	....	....	....	....
	Vancouver Canucks	**NHL**	**13**	**1**	**5**	**6**	**1**	**4**	**5**	**8**	**0**	**0**	**0**	**13**	**7.7**	**13**	**0**	**9**	**2**	**6**	**5**	**0**	**1**	**1**	**13**	**0**	**0**	**0**
1975-76	**Vancouver Canucks**	**NHL**	**65**	**2**	**5**	**7**	**2**	**4**	**6**	**28**	**0**	**1**	**0**	**48**	**4.2**	**30**	**0**	**45**	**18**	**3**	**1**	**0**	**0**	**0**	**0**	**0**	**0**	**0**
1976-77	**Vancouver Canucks**	**NHL**	**12**	**0**	**0**	**0**	**0**	**0**	**0**	**6**	**0**	**0**	**0**	**10**	**0.0**	**2**	**0**	**4**	**1**	**–1**	....	....	....	....	....	....	....	....
	Tulsa Oilers	CHL	58	5	16	21	....	....	....	49	....	....	....	....	....	....	....	....	....	....	9	1	0	1	14	....	....	....
	NHL Totals		**194**	**6**	**16**	**22**	**6**	**12**	**18**	**98**	**0**	**1**	**1**	**172**	**3.5**	**100**	**1**	**143**	**37**		**10**	**1**	**1**	**2**	**15**	**0**	**0**	**0**

WCHA First All-Star Team (1971) • NCAA West First All-American Team (1971) • AHL First All-Star Team (1973)

Signed as a territoral exemption by **Montreal** from **Peterborough** (OHA), September, 1971. Traded to **Atlanta** by **Montreal** for Atlanta's 3rd round choice (Pierre Lagace) in 1977 Amateur Draft, May 29, 1973. Traded to **Vancouver** by **Atlanta** for Gerry Meehan, March 9, 1975.

• MURRAY, Bob

Robert Frederick D – . 5'10", 183 lbs. b: Kingston, Ont., 11/26/1954. Chicago's 3rd, 52nd overall, in 1974.

Season	Club	League	GP	G	A	Pts	AG	AA	APts	PIM	PP	SH	GW	S	%	TGF	PGF	TGA	PGA	+/–	GP	G	A	Pts	PIM	PP	SH	GW
1971-72	Cornwall Royals	QMJHL	62	14	49	63	....	....	....	88	....	....	....	....	....	....	....	....	....	....	16	2	6	8	18	....	....	....
1972-73	Cornwall Royals	QMJHL	32	9	26	35	....	....	....	34	....	....	....	....	....	....	....	....	....	....	12	1	21	22	43	....	....	....
1973-74	Cornwall Royals	QMJHL	63	23	76	99	....	....	....	88	....	....	....	....	....	....	....	....	....	....	5	0	6	6	6	....	....	....
1974-75	Dallas Black Hawks	CHL	75	14	43	57	....	....	....	130	....	....	....	....	....	....	....	....	....	....	10	2	6	8	13	....	....	....
1975-76	**Chicago Black Hawks**	**NHL**	**64**	**1**	**2**	**3**	**1**	**1**	**2**	**44**	**0**	**0**	**0**	**61**	**1.6**	**34**	**2**	**41**	**3**	**–6**	....	....	....	....	....	....	....	....
1976-77	**Chicago Black Hawks**	**NHL**	**77**	**10**	**11**	**21**	**9**	**8**	**17**	**71**	**0**	**0**	**0**	**84**	**11.9**	**70**	**9**	**87**	**19**	**–7**	**2**	**0**	**1**	**1**	**2**	**0**	**0**	**0**
1977-78	**Chicago Black Hawks**	**NHL**	**70**	**14**	**17**	**31**	**13**	**13**	**26**	**41**	**2**	**0**	**3**	**124**	**11.3**	**87**	**9**	**81**	**14**	**11**	**4**	**1**	**4**	**5**	**2**	**0**	**0**	**0**
1978-79	**Chicago Black Hawks**	**NHL**	**79**	**19**	**32**	**51**	**16**	**23**	**39**	**38**	**4**	**1**	**0**	**220**	**8.6**	**125**	**23**	**134**	**36**	**4**	**4**	**1**	**0**	**1**	**6**	**0**	**0**	**0**
1979-80	**Chicago Black Hawks**	**NHL**	**74**	**16**	**34**	**50**	**14**	**25**	**39**	**60**	**8**	**0**	**1**	**224**	**7.1**	**116**	**56**	**96**	**20**	**–16**	**7**	**2**	**4**	**6**	**6**	**0**	**0**	**0**
1980-81	**Chicago Black Hawks**	**NHL**	**77**	**13**	**47**	**60**	**10**	**31**	**41**	**93**	**6**	**0**	**1**	**206**	**6.3**	**128**	**46**	**114**	**38**	**6**	**3**	**0**	**0**	**0**	**2**	**0**	**0**	**0**
1981-82	**Chicago Black Hawks**	**NHL**	**45**	**8**	**22**	**30**	**6**	**15**	**21**	**48**	**3**	**1**	**0**	**109**	**7.3**	**76**	**26**	**76**	**27**	**1**	**15**	**1**	**6**	**7**	**16**	**0**	**0**	**0**
1982-83	**Chicago Black Hawks**	**NHL**	**79**	**7**	**32**	**39**	**6**	**22**	**28**	**73**	**5**	**0**	**1**	**186**	**3.8**	**128**	**37**	**98**	**31**	**24**	**13**	**2**	**3**	**5**	**10**	**1**	**0**	**0**
1983-84	**Chicago Black Hawks**	**NHL**	**78**	**11**	**37**	**48**	**9**	**25**	**34**	**78**	**3**	**1**	**1**	**190**	**5.8**	**134**	**45**	**129**	**41**	**1**	**5**	**3**	**1**	**4**	**6**	**1**	**0**	**0**
1984-85	**Chicago Black Hawks**	**NHL**	**80**	**5**	**38**	**43**	**4**	**26**	**30**	**56**	**4**	**0**	**1**	**156**	**3.2**	**132**	**35**	**119**	**35**	**13**	**15**	**3**	**6**	**9**	**20**	**1**	**0**	**0**
1985-86	**Chicago Black Hawks**	**NHL**	**80**	**9**	**29**	**38**	**7**	**19**	**26**	**75**	**3**	**0**	**1**	**139**	**6.5**	**131**	**42**	**116**	**33**	**6**	**3**	**0**	**2**	**2**	**0**	**0**	**0**	**0**
1986-87	**Chicago Blackhawks**	**NHL**	**79**	**6**	**38**	**44**	**5**	**28**	**33**	**80**	**4**	**0**	**1**	**177**	**3.4**	**110**	**41**	**113**	**35**	**–9**	**4**	**1**	**0**	**1**	**4**	**0**	**0**	**0**
1987-88	**Chicago Blackhawks**	**NHL**	**62**	**6**	**20**	**26**	**5**	**14**	**19**	**44**	**1**	**0**	**0**	**97**	**6.2**	**72**	**29**	**71**	**21**	**–7**	**5**	**1**	**3**	**4**	**2**	**1**	**0**	**0**
1988-89	**Chicago Blackhawks**	**NHL**	**15**	**2**	**4**	**6**	**2**	**3**	**5**	**27**	**2**	**0**	**0**	**19**	**10.5**	**11**	**7**	**9**	**1**	**–4**	**16**	**2**	**3**	**5**	**22**	**1**	**0**	**0**
	Saginaw Hawks	IHL	18	3	7	10	....	....	....	14	....	....	....	....	....	....	....	....	....	....	....	....	....	....	....	....	....	....
1989-90	**Chicago Blackhawks**	**NHL**	**49**	**5**	**19**	**24**	**4**	**14**	**18**	**45**	**3**	**0**	**1**	**84**	**6.0**	**76**	**37**	**50**	**14**	**3**	**16**	**2**	**4**	**6**	**8**	**0**	**0**	**0**
	NHL Totals		**1008**	**132**	**382**	**514**	**111**	**267**	**378**	**873**	**48**	**3**	**11**	**2076**	**6.4**	**1430**	**444**	**1334**	**368**		**112**	**19**	**37**	**56**	**106**	**5**	**0**	**0**

Won Bergeron Trophy (QMJHL Rookie-of-the-Year) (1972) • QMJHL First All-Star Team (1974) • Played in NHL All-Star Game (1981, 1983)

• MURRAY, Chris

RW – R. 6'2", 209 lbs. b: Port Hardy, B.C., 10/25/1974. Montreal's 3rd, 54th overall, in 1994.

Season	Club	League	GP	G	A	Pts	AG	AA	APts	PIM	PP	SH	GW	S	%	TGF	PGF	TGA	PGA	+/–	GP	G	A	Pts	PIM	PP	SH	GW
1990-91	Bellingham Ice Hawks	BCJHL	54	5	8	13	....	....	....	150	....	....	....	....	....	....	....	....	....	....	....	....	....	....	....	....	....	....
1991-92	Kamloops Blazers	WHL	33	1	1	2	....	....	....	218	....	....	....	....	....	....	....	....	....	....	5	0	0	0	10	....	....	....
1992-93	Kamloops Blazers	WHL	62	6	10	16	....	....	....	217	....	....	....	....	....	....	....	....	....	....	13	0	4	4	34	....	....	....
1993-94	Kamloops Blazers	WHL	59	14	16	30	....	....	....	260	....	....	....	....	....	....	....	....	....	....	15	4	2	6	*107	....	....	....
	Kamloops Blazers	Mem-Cup	4	2	2	4	....	....	....	24	....	....	....	....	....	....	....	....	....	....	....	....	....	....	....	....	....	....
1994-95	**Montreal Canadiens**	**NHL**	**3**	**0**	**0**	**0**	**0**	**0**	**0**	**4**	**0**	**0**	**0**	**0**	**0.0**	**0**	**0**	**0**	**0**	**0**	....	....	....	....	....	....	....	....
	Fredericton Canadiens	AHL	55	6	12	18	....	....	....	234	....	....	....	....	....	....	....	....	....	....	12	1	1	2	50	....	....	....
1995-96	**Montreal Canadiens**	**NHL**	**48**	**3**	**4**	**7**	**3**	**3**	**6**	**163**	**0**	**0**	**1**	**32**	**9.4**	**13**	**0**	**9**	**1**	**5**	**4**	**0**	**0**	**0**	**4**	**0**	**0**	**0**
	Fredericton Canadiens	AHL	30	13	13	26	....	....	....	217	....	....	....	....	....	....	....	....	....	....	....	....	....	....	....	....	....	....
1996-97	**Montreal Canadiens**	**NHL**	**56**	**4**	**2**	**6**	**4**	**2**	**6**	**114**	**0**	**0**	**0**	**32**	**12.5**	**8**	**0**	**16**	**0**	**–8**	....	....	....	....	....	....	....	....
	Hartford Whalers	**NHL**	**8**	**1**	**1**	**2**	**1**	**1**	**2**	**10**	**0**	**0**	**0**	**9**	**11.1**	**3**	**0**	**2**	**0**	**1**	....	....	....	....	....	....	....	....

Season	Club	League	REGULAR SEASON GP	G	A	Pts	AG	AA	APts	PIM	PP	SH	GW	S	%	TGF	PGF	TGA	PGA	+/–	PLAYOFFS GP	G	A	Pts	PIM	PP	SH	GW
1997-98	Carolina Hurricanes	NHL	7	0	1	1	0	1	1	22	0	0	0	3	0.0	2	0	0	0	2	....	....	....	....	....	....	....	....
	Ottawa Senators	NHL	46	5	3	8	6	3	9	96	0	0	2	48	10.4	12	0	11	0	1	11	1	0	1	8	0	0	0
1998-99	Ottawa Senators	NHL	38	1	6	7	1	6	7	65	0	0	0	33	3.0	11	1	12	0	–2	....	....	....	....	....	....	....	....
	Chicago Blackhawks	NHL	4	0	0	0	0	0	0	14	0	0	0	4	0.0	0	0	0	0	0	....	....	....	....	....	....	....	....
99-2000	Dallas Stars	NHL	32	2	1	3	2	1	3	62	0	0	0	25	8.0	4	0	11	0	–7	....	....	....	....	....	....	....	....
	Michigan K-Wings	IHL	31	5	2	7	....	....	....	78	....	....	....	....	....	....	....	....	....	....	....	....	....	....	....	....	....	....
	NHL Totals		242	16	18	34	17	17	34	550	0	0	3	186	8.6	53	1	61	1		15	1	0	1	12	0	0	0

Traded to **Phoenix** by **Montreal** with Murray Baron for Dave Manson, March 18, 1997. Traded to **Hartford** by **Phoenix** for Gerald Diduck, March 18, 1997. Transferred to **Carolina** after **Hartford** franchise relocated, June 25, 1997. Traded to **Ottawa** by **Carolina** for Sean Hill, November 18, 1997. Traded to **Chicago** by **Ottawa** for Nelson Emerson, March 23, 1999. Claimed by **Dallas** from **Chicago** in Waiver Draft, September 30, 1999.

• MURRAY, Glen

"Muzz" RW – R. 6'3", 225 lbs. b: Halifax, N.S., 11/1/1972. Boston's 1st, 18th overall, in 1991.

Season	Club	League	GP	G	A	Pts	AG	AA	APts	PIM	PP	SH	GW	S	%	TGF	PGF	TGA	PGA	+/–	GP	G	A	Pts	PIM	PP	SH	GW
1988-89	Bridgewater Mustangs	NSAHA	45	50	56	106	....	....	....	62	....	....	....	....	....	....	....	....	....	....	....	....	....	....	....	....	....	....
1989-90	Sudbury Wolves	OHL	62	8	28	36	....	....	....	17	....	....	....	....	....	....	....	....	....	....	7	0	0	0	4	....	....	....
1990-91	Sudbury Wolves	OHL	66	27	38	65	....	....	....	82	....	....	....	....	....	....	....	....	....	....	5	8	4	12	10	....	....	....
1991-92	Sudbury Wolves	OHL	54	37	47	84	....	....	....	93	....	....	....	....	....	....	....	....	....	....	11	7	4	11	18	....	....	....
	Boston Bruins	NHL	5	3	1	4	3	1	4	0	1	0	0	20	15.0	8	3	3	0	2	15	4	2	6	10	1	0	0
1992-93	Boston Bruins	NHL	27	3	4	7	2	3	5	8	2	0	1	28	10.7	13	3	16	0	–6	....	....	....	....	....	....	....	....
	Providence Bruins	AHL	48	30	26	56	....	....	....	42	....	....	....	....	....	....	....	....	....	....	6	1	4	5	4	....	....	....
1993-94	Boston Bruins	NHL	81	18	13	31	17	10	27	48	0	0	4	114	15.8	42	1	43	1	–1	13	4	5	9	14	0	0	0
1994-95	Boston Bruins	NHL	35	5	2	7	9	3	12	46	0	0	2	64	7.8	18	1	28	0	–11	2	0	0	0	2	0	0	0
1995-96	Pittsburgh Penguins	NHL	69	14	15	29	14	12	26	57	0	0	2	100	14.0	40	0	37	1	4	18	2	6	8	10	0	0	1
1996-97	Pittsburgh Penguins	NHL	66	11	11	22	12	10	22	24	3	0	1	127	8.7	33	5	47	0	–19	....	....	....	....	....	....	....	....
	Los Angeles Kings	NHL	11	5	3	8	5	3	8	8	0	0	0	26	19.2	11	3	10	0	–2	....	....	....	....	....	....	....	....
1997-98	Los Angeles Kings	NHL	81	29	31	60	34	30	64	54	7	3	7	193	15.0	95	25	73	9	6	4	2	0	2	6	0	0	0
	Canada	WC-A	5	1	2	3	....	....	....	4	....	....	....	....	....	....	....	....	....	....	....	....	....	....	....	....	....	....
1998-99	Los Angeles Kings	NHL	61	16	15	31	19	14	33	36	3	3	3	173	9.2	52	14	64	12	–14	....	....	....	....	....	....	....	....
99-2000	Los Angeles Kings	NHL	78	29	33	62	33	31	64	60	10	1	2	202	14.4	86	25	60	12	13	4	0	0	0	2	0	0	0
	NHL Totals		514	133	128	261	148	117	265	341	26	7	22	1047	12.7	398	80	381	35		56	12	13	25	44	1	0	1

Traded to **Pittsburgh** by **Boston** with Bryan Smolinski and Boston's 3rd round choice (Boyd Kane) in 1996 Entry Draft for Kevin Stevens and Shawn McEachern, August 2, 1995. Traded to **LA Kings** by **Pittsburgh** for Ed Olczyk, March 18, 1997.

• MURRAY, Jim

Jim Arnold D – L. 6'1", 165 lbs. b: Virden, Man., 11/25/1943.

Season	Club	League	GP	G	A	Pts	AG	AA	APts	PIM	PP	SH	GW	S	%	TGF	PGF	TGA	PGA	+/–	GP	G	A	Pts	PIM	PP	SH	GW
1961-62	Brandon Wheat Kings	MJHL	37	6	8	14	....	....	....	32	....	....	....	....	....	....	....	....	....	....	8	0	1	1	16	....	....	....
	Brandon Wheat Kings	Mem-Cup	11	0	3	3	....	....	....	9	....	....	....	....	....	....	....	....	....	....	....	....	....	....	....	....	....	....
1962-63	Brandon Wheat Kings	MJHL	39	11	21	32	....	....	....	51	....	....	....	....	....	....	....	....	....	....	10	4	6	10	12	....	....	....
	Brandon Wheat Kings	Mem-Cup	9	2	4	6	....	....	....	6	....	....	....	....	....	....	....	....	....	....	....	....	....	....	....	....	....	....
1963-64	Brandon Wheat Kings	MJHL	30	11	23	34	....	....	....	38	....	....	....	....	....	....	....	....	....	....	10	1	*8	9	24	....	....	....
	Brandon Wheat Kings	Mem-Cup	11	2	4	6	....	....	....	14	....	....	....	....	....	....	....	....	....	....	....	....	....	....	....	....	....	....
1964-65	New York Rovers	EHL	72	10	29	39	....	....	....	113	....	....	....	....	....	....	....	....	....	....	....	....	....	....	....	....	....	....
1965-66	Knoxville Knights	EHL	70	9	42	51	....	....	....	50	....	....	....	....	....	....	....	....	....	....	3	0	2	2	2	....	....	....
1966-67	Knoxville Knights	EHL	72	17	35	52	....	....	....	79	....	....	....	....	....	....	....	....	....	....	4	0	1	1	4	....	....	....
1967-68	Los Angeles Kings	NHL	30	0	2	2	0	2	2	14	0	0	0	24	0.0	23	4	30	7	–4	....	....	....	....	....	....	....	....
	Springfield Kings	AHL	30	2	8	10	....	....	....	33	....	....	....	....	....	....	....	....	....	....	....	....	....	....	....	....	....	....
1968-69	Springfield Kings	AHL	72	7	26	33	....	....	....	83	....	....	....	....	....	....	....	....	....	....	....	....	....	....	....	....	....	....
1969-70	Phoenix Roadrunners	WHL	72	2	28	30	....	....	....	93	....	....	....	....	....	....	....	....	....	....	....	....	....	....	....	....	....	....
1970-71	Phoenix Roadrunners	WHL	72	4	18	22	....	....	....	58	....	....	....	....	....	....	....	....	....	....	10	0	1	1	14	....	....	....
1971-72	Phoenix Roadrunners	WHL	72	7	30	37	....	....	....	136	....	....	....	....	....	....	....	....	....	....	6	0	4	4	10	....	....	....
1972-73	Phoenix Roadrunners	WHL	72	10	53	63	....	....	....	138	....	....	....	....	....	....	....	....	....	....	10	1	6	7	8	....	....	....
1973-74	Phoenix Roadrunners	WHL	76	10	39	49	....	....	....	113	....	....	....	....	....	....	....	....	....	....	....	....	....	....	....	....	....	....
1974-75	Johnstown Jets	NAHL	5	0	2	2	....	....	....	2	....	....	....	....	....	....	....	....	....	....	....	....	....	....	....	....	....	....
	Winston-Salem Polar Bears	SHL	37	7	33	40	....	....	....	74	....	....	....	....	....	....	....	....	....	....	7	1	5	6	6	....	....	....
1975-76			OUT OF HOCKEY – RETIRED																									
1976-77			OUT OF HOCKEY – RETIRED																									
1977-78	Brandon Olympics	CCSHL	30	5	17	22	....	....	....	32	....	....	....	....	....	....	....	....	....	....	....	....	....	....	....	....	....	....
	NHL Totals		30	0	2	2	0	2	2	14	0	0	0	24	0.0	23	4	30	7		....	....	....	....	....	....	....	....

WHL Second All-Star Team (1973) • SHL Second All-Star Team (1975) • CCSHL First All-Star Team (1978)

Traded to **LA Kings** by **NY Rangers** with Trevor Fahey and Ken Turlik for Barclay Plager, June 16, 1967. Traded to **Phoenix** (WHL) by **LA Kings** for Roger Cote, September, 1969.

• MURRAY, Ken

Kenneth Richard D – R. 6', 180 lbs. b: Toronto, Ont., 1/22/1948.

Season	Club	League	GP	G	A	Pts	AG	AA	APts	PIM	PP	SH	GW	S	%	TGF	PGF	TGA	PGA	+/–	GP	G	A	Pts	PIM	PP	SH	GW
1968-69	St. Thomas Barons	OHA-B	STATISTICS NOT AVAILABLE																									
1969-70	Tulsa Oilers	CHL	62	3	13	16	....	....	....	136	....	....	....	....	....	....	....	....	....	....	6	0	0	0	6	....	....	....
	Toronto Maple Leafs	NHL	1	0	1	1	0	1	1	2	0	0	0	1	0.0	1	0	0	0	1	....	....	....	....	....	....	....	....
1970-71	Toronto Maple Leafs	NHL	4	0	0	0	0	0	0	0	0	0	0	1	0.0	1	0	0	0	1	....	....	....	....	....	....	....	....
	Tulsa Oilers	CHL	62	3	13	16	....	....	....	143	....	....	....	....	....	....	....	....	....	....	....	....	....	....	....	....	....	....
1971-72	Cincinnati Swords	AHL	68	0	7	7	....	....	....	167	....	....	....	....	....	....	....	....	....	....	10	0	0	0	14	....	....	....
1972-73	New York Islanders	NHL	39	0	4	4	0	3	3	59	0	0	0	20	0.0	22	0	53	10	–21	....	....	....	....	....	....	....	....
	Detroit Red Wings	NHL	31	1	1	2	1	1	2	36	0	0	0	18	5.6	14	0	18	3	–1	....	....	....	....	....	....	....	....
1973-74	Virginia Wings	AHL	54	3	6	9	....	....	....	159	....	....	....	....	....	....	....	....	....	....	....	....	....	....	....	....	....	....
	Seattle Totems	WHL	18	0	9	9	....	....	....	34	....	....	....	....	....	....	....	....	....	....	....	....	....	....	....	....	....	....
1974-75	Kansas City Scouts	NHL	8	0	2	2	0	1	1	14	0	0	0	5	0.0	9	0	6	0	3	....	....	....	....	....	....	....	....
	Baltimore Clippers	AHL	31	2	3	5	....	....	....	52	....	....	....	....	....	....	....	....	....	....	....	....	....	....	....	....	....	....
	Springfield Indians	AHL	29	1	9	10	....	....	....	91	....	....	....	....	....	....	....	....	....	....	15	3	5	8	30	....	....	....
1975-76	Kansas City Scouts	NHL	23	0	2	2	0	1	1	24	0	0	0	12	0.0	9	0	16	6	–1	....	....	....	....	....	....	....	....
	Springfield Indians	AHL	42	5	16	21	....	....	....	72	....	....	....	....	....	....	....	....	....	....	....	....	....	....	....	....	....	....
1976-77	Rhode Island Reds	AHL	59	1	9	10	....	....	....	107	....	....	....	....	....	....	....	....	....	....	....	....	....	....	....	....	....	....
1977-78	New Haven Nighthawks	AHL	68	2	12	14	....	....	....	84	....	....	....	....	....	....	....	....	....	....	15	0	1	1	22	....	....	....
1978-79	Philadelphia Firebirds	AHL	3	0	0	0	....	....	....	2	....	....	....	....	....	....	....	....	....	....	....	....	....	....	....	....	....	....
	NHL Totals		106	1	10	11	1	7	8	135	0	0	0	57	1.8	56	0	93	19		....	....	....	....	....	....	....	....

Signed as a free agent by **Toronto**, April 5, 1970. Claimed by **Buffalo** from **Toronto** in Intra-League Draft, June 8, 1971. Claimed by **NY Islanders** from **Buffalo** in Expansion Draft, June 6, 1972. Traded to **Detroit** by **NY Islanders** with Brian Lavender for Ralph Stewart and Bob Cook, January 17, 1973. Traded to **Seattle** (WHL) by **Detroit** (Virginia-AHL) for Gene Sobchuk, February 18, 1974. Claimed by **Kansas City** from **Detroit** in Expansion Draft, June 12, 1974. Traded to **LA Kings** by **Kansas City** for cash, February 10, 1975.

• MURRAY, Marty

C – L. 5'9", 178 lbs. b: Deloraine, Man., 2/16/1975. Calgary's 5th, 96th overall, in 1993.

Season	Club	League	GP	G	A	Pts	AG	AA	APts	PIM	PP	SH	GW	S	%	TGF	PGF	TGA	PGA	+/–	GP	G	A	Pts	PIM	PP	SH	GW
1990-91	Manitoba Southwest Cougars	MAHA	36	46	47	93	....	....	....	50	....	....	....	....	....	....	....	....	....	....	....	....	....	....	....	....	....	....
1991-92	Brandon Wheat Kings	WHL	68	20	36	56	....	....	....	22	....	....	....	....	....	....	....	....	....	....	....	....	....	....	....	....	....	....
1992-93	Brandon Wheat Kings	WHL	67	29	65	94	....	....	....	50	....	....	....	....	....	....	....	....	....	....	4	1	3	4	0	....	....	....
1993-94	Brandon Wheat Kings	WHL	64	43	71	114	....	....	....	33	....	....	....	....	....	....	....	....	....	....	14	6	14	20	14	....	....	....
	Canada	WJC-A	7	1	3	4	....	....	....	4	....	....	....	....	....	....	....	....	....	....	....	....	....	....	....	....	....	....
1994-95	Brandon Wheat Kings	WHL	65	40	*88	128	....	....	....	53	....	....	....	....	....	....	....	....	....	....	18	9	*20	29	16	....	....	....
	Canada	WJC-A	7	6	9	*15	....	....	....	0	....	....	....	....	....	....	....	....	....	....	....	....	....	....	....	....	....	....
	Brandon Wheat Kings	Mem-Cup	4	0	3	3	....	....	....	2	....	....	....	....	....	....	....	....	....	....	....	....	....	....	....	....	....	....
1995-96	Calgary Flames	NHL	15	3	3	6	3	2	5	0	2	0	0	22	13.6	9	5	12	4	–4	....	....	....	....	....	....	....	....
	Saint John Flames	AHL	58	25	31	56	....	....	....	20	....	....	....	....	....	....	....	....	....	....	14	2	4	6	4	....	....	....
1996-97	Calgary Flames	NHL	2	0	0	0	0	0	0	4	0	0	0	2	0.0	0	0	1	1	0	....	....	....	....	....	....	....	....
	Saint John Flames	AHL	67	19	39	58	....	....	....	40	....	....	....	....	....	....	....	....	....	....	5	2	3	5	4	....	....	....
1997-98	Calgary Flames	NHL	2	0	0	0	0	0	0	2	0	0	0	2	0.0	1	0	0	0	1	....	....	....	....	....	....	....	....
	Saint John Flames	AHL	41	10	30	40	....	....	....	16	....	....	....	....	....	....	....	....	....	....	21	10	10	20	12	....	....	....

			REGULAR SEASON																		PLAYOFFS							
Season	**Club**	**League**	**GP**	**G**	**A**	**Pts**	**AG**	**AA**	**APts**	**PIM**	**PP**	**SH**	**GW**	**S**	**%**	**TGF**	**PGF**	**TGA**	**PGA**	**+/–**	**GP**	**G**	**A**	**Pts**	**PIM**	**PP**	**SH**	**GW**
1998-99	VSV Villach	Alpenliga	33	26	41	67	....	....	....	12	....	....	....	....	....	....	....	....	....	....	....	....	....	....	....	....	....	....
	VSV Villach	Austria	17	13	17	30	....	....	....	6	....	....	....	....	....	....	....	....	....	....	6	1	4	5	0	....	....	....
	Canada	Nat-Team	5	1	3	4	....	....	....	2	....	....	....	....	....	....	....	....	....	....	....	....	....	....	....	....	....	....
99-2000	Kolner Haie	Germany	56	12	47	59	....	....	....	28	....	....	....	....	....	....	....	....	....	....	10	4	3	7	2	....	....	....
	NHL Totals		**19**	**3**	**3**	**6**	**3**	**2**	**5**	**6**	**2**	**0**	**0**	**26**	**11.5**	**10**	**5**	**13**	**5**		....	....	....	....	....	....	....	....

WHL East First All-Star Team (1994, 1995) • Canadian Major Junior Second All-Star Team (1994) • WJC-A All-Star Team (1995) • Named Best Forward at WJC-A (1995)

• MURRAY, Mike

C – L. 6', 195 lbs. b: Kingston, Ont., 8/29/1966. NY Islanders' 6th, 104th overall, in 1984.

Season	Club	League	GP	G	A	Pts	AG	AA	APts	PIM	PP	SH	GW	S	%	TGF	PGF	TGA	PGA	+/–	GP	G	A	Pts	PIM	PP	SH	GW
1982-83	Sarnia Bees	OJHL-B	57	61	39	100	....	....	....	48	....	....	....	....	....	....	....	....	....	....	....	....	....	....	....	....	....	....
1983-84	London Knights	OHL	70	8	24	32	....	....	....	14	....	....	....	....	....	....	....	....	....	....	8	1	4	5	2	....	....	....
1984-85	London Knights	OHL	43	21	35	56	....	....	....	19	....	....	....	....	....	....	....	....	....	....	....	....	....	....	....	....	....	....
	Guelph Platers	OHL	23	10	9	19	....	....	....	8	....	....	....	....	....	....	....	....	....	....	....	....	....	....	....	....	....	....
1985-86	Guelph Platers	OHL	56	27	38	65	....	....	....	19	....	....	....	....	....	....	....	....	....	....	20	7	13	20	0	....	....	....
1986-87	Hershey Bears	AHL	70	8	16	24	....	....	....	10	....	....	....	....	....	....	....	....	....	....	2	0	0	0	0	....	....	....
1987-88	**Philadelphia Flyers**	**NHL**	**1**	**0**	**0**	**0**	**0**	**0**	**0**	**0**	**0**	**0**	**0**	**1**	**0.0**	**0**	**0**	**0**	**0**	**0**	....	....	....	....	....	....	....	....
	Hershey Bears	AHL	57	14	14	28	....	....	....	34	....	....	....	....	....	....	....	....	....	....	2	0	0	0	0	....	....	....
1988-89	Hershey Bears	AHL	19	1	2	3	....	....	....	8	....	....	....	....	....	....	....	....	....	....	....	....	....	....	....	....	....	....
	Indianapolis Ice	IHL	17	5	11	16	....	....	....	2	....	....	....	....	....	....	....	....	....	....	....	....	....	....	....	....	....	....
1989-90	EHC Hannover	Germany	7	5	6	11	....	....	....	18	....	....	....	....	....	....	....	....	....	....	....	....	....	....	....	....	....	....
	Knoxville Cherokees	ECHL	21	11	17	28	....	....	....	4	....	....	....	....	....	....	....	....	....	....	....	....	....	....	....	....	....	....
1990-91	Kansas City Blades	IHL	2	0	0	0	....	....	....	0	....	....	....	....	....	....	....	....	....	....	....	....	....	....	....	....	....	....
	Knoxville Cherokees	ECHL	56	33	37	70	....	....	....	18	....	....	....	....	....	....	....	....	....	....	3	10	1	4	....	....	....	....
1991-92	EC Harz	Germany-3	41	*73	62	*135	....	....	....	39	....	....	....	....	....	....	....	....	....	....	12	*27	17	*44	10	....	....	....
1992-93	Svegs IK	Sweden-3	10	1	2	3	....	....	....	16	....	....	....	....	....	....	....	....	....	....	....	....	....	....	....	....	....	....
	Knoxville Cherokees	ECHL	64	23	42	65	....	....	....	40	....	....	....	....	....	....	....	....	....	....	....	....	....	....	....	....	....	....
1993-94	Knoxville Cherokees	ECHL	68	32	45	77	....	....	....	36	....	....	....	....	....	....	....	....	....	....	3	1	3	4	2	....	....	....
1994-95	Knoxville Cherokees	ECHL	53	24	23	47	....	....	....	56	....	....	....	....	....	....	....	....	....	....	....	....	....	....	....	....	....	....
1995-96	Dayton Bombers	ECHL	21	17	10	27	....	....	....	28	....	....	....	....	....	....	....	....	....	....	....	....	....	....	....	....	....	....
	Cornwall Aces	AHL	1	2	0	2	....	....	....	0	....	....	....	....	....	....	....	....	....	....	....	....	....	....	....	....	....	....
1996-1999			OUT OF HOCKEY – RETIRED																									
99-2000	Knoxville Speed	UHL	22	6	4	10	....	....	....	6	....	....	....	....	....	....	....	....	....	....	....	....	....	....	....	....	....	....
	NHL Totals		**1**	**0**	**0**	**0**	**0**	**0**	**0**	**0**	**0**	**0**	**0**	**1**	**0.0**	**0**	**0**	**0**	**0**		....	....	....	....	....	....	....	....

Traded to **Philadelphia** by **NY Islanders** for Philadelphia's 5th round choice (Todd McLellan) in 1986 Entry Draft, June 21, 1986. Signed as a free agent by **Knoxville** (UHL), November 26, 1999.

• MURRAY, Pat

Patrick E. LW – L. 6'2", 185 lbs. b: Stratford, Ont., 8/20/1969. Philadelphia's 2nd, 35th overall, in 1988.

Season	Club	League	GP	G	A	Pts	AG	AA	APts	PIM	PP	SH	GW	S	%	TGF	PGF	TGA	PGA	+/–	GP	G	A	Pts	PIM	PP	SH	GW
1984-85	Seaforth Centenaires	OJHL-D	31	29	19	48	....	....	....	16	....	....	....	....	....	....	....	....	....	....	....	....	....	....	....	....	....	....
1985-86	Stratford Cullitons	OJHL-B	36	13	27	40	....	....	....	10	....	....	....	....	....	....	....	....	....	....	....	....	....	....	....	....	....	....
1986-87	Stratford Cullitons	OJHL-B	42	34	*75	109	....	....	....	38	....	....	....	....	....	....	....	....	....	....	....	....	....	....	....	....	....	....
	Stratford Cullitons	OJHL-B	36	13	27	40	....	....	....	10	....	....	....	....	....	....	....	....	....	....	....	....	....	....	....	....	....	....
1987-88	Michigan State Spartans	CCHA	42	14	21	35	....	....	....	26	....	....	....	....	....	....	....	....	....	....	....	....	....	....	....	....	....	....
1988-89	Michigan State Spartans	CCHA	46	21	41	62	....	....	....	65	....	....	....	....	....	....	....	....	....	....	....	....	....	....	....	....	....	....
1989-90	Michigan State Spartans	CCHA	45	24	60	84	....	....	....	36	....	....	....	....	....	....	....	....	....	....	....	....	....	....	....	....	....	....
1990-91	**Philadelphia Flyers**	**NHL**	**16**	**2**	**1**	**3**	**2**	**1**	**3**	**15**	**1**	**0**	**0**	**16**	**12.5**	**5**	**2**	**8**	**0**	**–5**	....	....	....	....	....	....	....	....
	Hershey Bears	AHL	57	15	38	53	....	....	....	8	....	....	....	....	....	....	....	....	....	....	7	5	2	7	0	....	....	....
1991-92	**Philadelphia Flyers**	**NHL**	**9**	**1**	**0**	**1**	**1**	**0**	**1**	**0**	**0**	**0**	**0**	**8**	**12.5**	**4**	**0**	**1**	**0**	**3**	....	....	....	....	....	....	....	....
	Hershey Bears	AHL	69	19	43	62	....	....	....	25	....	....	....	....	....	....	....	....	....	....	6	1	2	3	0	....	....	....
1992-93	Hershey Bears	AHL	69	21	32	53	....	....	....	63	....	....	....	....	....	....	....	....	....	....	....	....	....	....	....	....	....	....
1993-94	Kalamazoo Wings	IHL	17	2	3	5	....	....	....	6	....	....	....	....	....	....	....	....	....	....	....	....	....	....	....	....	....	....
	Phoenix Roadrunners	IHL	25	6	8	14	....	....	....	44	....	....	....	....	....	....	....	....	....	....	....	....	....	....	....	....	....	....
1994-95	Knoxville Cherokees	ECHL	11	7	9	16	....	....	....	4	....	....	....	....	....	....	....	....	....	....	....	....	....	....	....	....	....	....
	Canada	Nat-Team	3	3	0	3	....	....	....	0	....	....	....	....	....	....	....	....	....	....	....	....	....	....	....	....	....	....
	Kalamazoo Wings	IHL	33	11	10	21	....	....	....	16	....	....	....	....	....	....	....	....	....	....	6	3	0	3	2	....	....	....
1995-96	ESC Essen-West	Germany-2	39	24	60	84	....	....	....	130	....	....	....	....	....	....	....	....	....	....	....	....	....	....	....	....	....	....
1996-97	ESC Essen-West	Germany-2	43	23	37	60	....	....	....	72	....	....	....	....	....	....	....	....	....	....	....	....	....	....	....	....	....	....
	Sorel Dinosaures	QSPHL	7	1	0	1	....	....	....	0	....	....	....	....	....	....	....	....	....	....	....	....	....	....	....	....	....	....
1997-98	ERC Sonthofen	Germany-2	28	17	20	37	....	....	....	....	....	....	....	....	....	....	....	....	....	....	....	....	....	....	....	....	....	....
	NHL Totals		**25**	**3**	**1**	**4**	**3**	**1**	**4**	**15**	**1**	**0**	**0**	**24**	**12.5**	**9**	**2**	**9**	**0**		....	....	....	....	....	....	....	....

CCHA Second All-Star Team (1990)

• MURRAY, Randy

Randall Charles D – R. 6'1", 195 lbs. b: Chatham, Ont., 8/24/1945.

Season	Club	League	GP	G	A	Pts	AG	AA	APts	PIM	PP	SH	GW	S	%	TGF	PGF	TGA	PGA	+/–	GP	G	A	Pts	PIM	PP	SH	GW
1964-65	Calgary Buffaloes	AJHL	STATISTICS NOT AVAILABLE																									
1965-66	London Nationals	OHA-Jr.	38	11	13	24	....	....	....	120	....	....	....	....	....	....	....	....	....	....	....	....	....	....	....	....	....	....
1966-67	Charlotte Checkers	EHL	65	10	25	35	....	....	....	148	....	....	....	....	....	....	....	....	....	....	8	1	4	5	19	....	....	....
	Tulsa Oilers	CPHL	5	0	0	0	....	....	....	17	....	....	....	....	....	....	....	....	....	....	....	....	....	....	....	....	....	....
1967-68	Tulsa Oilers	CPHL	61	3	14	17	....	....	....	108	....	....	....	....	....	....	....	....	....	....	6	1	0	1	12	....	....	....
1968-69	Tulsa Oilers	CHL	64	7	14	21	....	....	....	97	....	....	....	....	....	....	....	....	....	....	7	2	4	6	16	....	....	....
1969-70	**Toronto Maple Leafs**	**NHL**	**3**	**0**	**0**	**0**	**0**	**0**	**0**	**2**	**0**	**0**	**0**	**3**	**0.0**	**2**	**0**	**2**	**0**	**0**	....	....	....	....	....	....	....	....
	Tulsa Oilers	CHL	55	5	14	19	....	....	....	90	....	....	....	....	....	....	....	....	....	....	6	0	0	0	13	....	....	....
1970-71	Tulsa Oilers	CHL	68	2	27	29	....	....	....	143	....	....	....	....	....	....	....	....	....	....	....	....	....	....	....	....	....	....
1971-72	Calgary Stampeders	PrSHL	24	6	5	11	....	....	....	47	....	....	....	....	....	....	....	....	....	....	....	....	....	....	....	....	....	....
1972-73	Tulsa Oilers	CHL	38	0	10	10	....	....	....	59	....	....	....	....	....	....	....	....	....	....	....	....	....	....	....	....	....	....
1973-74	Calgary Trojans	AAHA-I	STATISTICS NOT AVAILABLE																									
	NHL Totals		**3**	**0**	**0**	**0**	**0**	**0**	**0**	**2**	**0**	**0**	**0**	**3**	**0.0**	**2**	**0**	**2**	**0**		....	....	....	....	....	....	....	....

• MURRAY, Rem

Raymond Joseph C/LW – L. 6'2", 195 lbs. b: Stratford, Ont., 10/9/1972. Los Angeles' 5th, 135th overall, in 1992.

Season	Club	League	GP	G	A	Pts	AG	AA	APts	PIM	PP	SH	GW	S	%	TGF	PGF	TGA	PGA	+/–	GP	G	A	Pts	PIM	PP	SH	GW
1989-90	Stratford Cullitons	OJHL-B	46	19	32	51	....	....	....	48	....	....	....	....	....	....	....	....	....	....	....	....	....	....	....	....	....	....
1990-91	Stratford Cullitons	OJHL-B	48	39	59	98	....	....	....	39	....	....	....	....	....	....	....	....	....	....	....	....	....	....	....	....	....	....
1991-92	Michigan State Spartans	CCHA	41	12	36	48	....	....	....	16	....	....	....	....	....	....	....	....	....	....	....	....	....	....	....	....	....	....
1992-93	Michigan State Spartans	CCHA	40	22	35	57	....	....	....	24	....	....	....	....	....	....	....	....	....	....	....	....	....	....	....	....	....	....
1993-94	Michigan State Spartans	CCHA	41	16	38	54	....	....	....	18	....	....	....	....	....	....	....	....	....	....	....	....	....	....	....	....	....	....
1994-95	Michigan State Spartans	CCHA	40	20	36	56	....	....	....	21	....	....	....	....	....	....	....	....	....	....	....	....	....	....	....	....	....	....
1995-96	Cape Breton Oilers	AHL	79	31	59	90	....	....	....	40	....	....	....	....	....	....	....	....	....	....	....	....	....	....	....	....	....	....
1996-97	**Edmonton Oilers**	**NHL**	**82**	**11**	**20**	**31**	**12**	**18**	**30**	**16**	**1**	**0**	**2**	**85**	**12.9**	**51**	**8**	**50**	**16**	**9**	**12**	**1**	**2**	**3**	**4**	**0**	**0**	**0**
1997-98	**Edmonton Oilers**	**NHL**	**61**	**9**	**9**	**18**	**11**	**9**	**20**	**39**	**2**	**2**	**0**	**59**	**15.3**	**27**	**7**	**46**	**17**	**–9**	**11**	**1**	**4**	**5**	**2**	**0**	**0**	**0**
1998-99	**Edmonton Oilers**	**NHL**	**78**	**21**	**18**	**39**	**25**	**17**	**42**	**20**	**4**	**1**	**4**	**116**	**18.1**	**57**	**18**	**53**	**18**	**4**	**4**	**1**	**1**	**2**	**2**	**0**	**0**	**0**
99-2000	**Edmonton Oilers**	**NHL**	**44**	**9**	**5**	**14**	**10**	**5**	**15**	**8**	**2**	**0**	**3**	**65**	**13.8**	**25**	**5**	**27**	**5**	**–2**	**5**	**0**	**1**	**1**	**2**	**0**	**0**	**0**
	NHL Totals		**265**	**50**	**52**	**102**	**58**	**49**	**107**	**83**	**9**	**3**	**9**	**325**	**15.4**	**160**	**38**	**176**	**56**		**32**	**3**	**8**	**11**	**10**	**0**	**0**	**0**

CCHA Second All-Star Team (1995)

Signed as a free agent by **Edmonton**, September 19, 1995.

• MURRAY, Rob

Robert Fredrick C – R. 6'1", 180 lbs. b: Toronto, Ont., 4/4/1967. Washington's 3rd, 61st overall, in 1985.

Season	Club	League	GP	G	A	Pts	AG	AA	APts	PIM	PP	SH	GW	S	%	TGF	PGF	TGA	PGA	+/–	GP	G	A	Pts	PIM	PP	SH	GW
1983-84	Mississauga Reps	MTHL	35	18	36	54	....	....	....	32	....	....	....	....	....	....	....	....	....	....	....	....	....	....	....	....	....	....
1984-85	Peterborough Petes	OHL	63	12	9	21	....	....	....	155	....	....	....	....	....	....	....	....	....	....	17	2	7	9	45	....	....	....
1985-86	Peterborough Petes	OHL	52	14	18	32	....	....	....	125	....	....	....	....	....	....	....	....	....	....	16	1	2	3	50	....	....	....
1986-87	Peterborough Petes	OHL	62	17	37	54	....	....	....	204	....	....	....	....	....	....	....	....	....	....	3	1	4	5	8	....	....	....
1987-88	Fort Wayne Komets	IHL	80	12	21	33	....	....	....	139	....	....	....	....	....	....	....	....	....	....	6	0	2	2	16	....	....	....
1988-89	Baltimore Skipjacks	AHL	80	11	23	34	....	....	....	235	....	....	....	....	....	....	....	....	....	....	....	....	....	....	....	....	....	....

			REGULAR SEASON																		PLAYOFFS							
Season	Club	League	GP	G	A	Pts	AG	AA	APts	PIM	PP	SH	GW	S	%	TGF	PGF	TGA	PGA	+/–	GP	G	A	Pts	PIM	PP	SH	GW
1989-90	**Washington Capitals**	**NHL**	41	2	7	9	2	5	7	58	0	0	0	29	6.9	13	0	35	12	–10	9	0	0	0	18	0	0	0
	Baltimore Skipjacks	AHL	23	5	4	9	....	....	....	63	....	....	....	....	....	....	....	....	....	....	....	....	....	....	....	....	....	....
1990-91	**Washington Capitals**	**NHL**	17	0	3	3	0	2	2	19	0	0	0	8	0.0	6	0	6	0	0	....	....	....	....	....	....	....	....
	Baltimore Skipjacks	AHL	48	6	20	26	....	....	....	177	....	....	....	....	....	....	....	....	....	....	4	0	0	0	12	....	....	....
1991-92	**Winnipeg Jets**	**NHL**	9	0	1	1	0	1	1	18	0	0	0	2	0.0	1	0	4	1	–2	....	....	....	....	....	....	....	....
	Moncton Hawks	AHL	60	16	15	31	....	....	....	247	....	....	....	....	....	....	....	....	....	....	8	0	1	1	56	....	....	....
1992-93	**Winnipeg Jets**	**NHL**	10	1	0	1	1	0	1	6	0	0	1	4	25.0	1	0	8	7	0	....	....	....	....	....	....	....	....
	Moncton Hawks	AHL	56	16	21	37	....	....	....	147	....	....	....	....	....	....	....	....	....	....	3	0	0	0	6	....	....	....
1993-94	**Winnipeg Jets**	**NHL**	6	0	0	0	0	0	0	2	0	0	0	1	0.0	1	0	1	0	0	....	....	....	....	....	....	....	....
	Moncton Hawks	AHL	69	25	32	57	....	....	....	280	....	....	....	....	....	....	....	....	....	....	21	2	3	5	60	....	....	....
1994-95	Springfield Falcons	AHL	78	16	38	54	....	....	....	373	....	....	....	....	....	....	....	....	....	....	....	....	....	....	....	....	....	....
	Winnipeg Jets	**NHL**	10	0	2	2	0	3	3	2	0	0	0	5	0.0	2	0	1	0	1	....	....	....	....	....	....	....	....
1995-96	**Winnipeg Jets**	**NHL**	1	0	0	0	0	0	0	2	0	0	0	1	0.0	0	0	1	0	–1	....	....	....	....	....	....	....	....
	Springfield Falcons	AHL	74	10	28	38	....	....	....	263	....	....	....	....	....	....	....	....	....	....	10	1	6	7	32	....	....	....
1996-97	Springfield Falcons	AHL	78	16	27	43	....	....	....	234	....	....	....	....	....	....	....	....	....	....	17	2	3	5	66	....	....	....
1997-98	Springfield Falcons	AHL	80	7	30	37	....	....	....	255	....	....	....	....	....	....	....	....	....	....	4	0	2	2	2	....	....	....
1998-99	**Phoenix Coyotes**	**NHL**	13	1	2	3	1	2	3	4	0	0	0	11	9.1	4	0	5	3	2	....	....	....	....	....	....	....	....
	Springfield Falcons	AHL	68	6	19	25	....	....	....	197	....	....	....	....	....	....	....	....	....	....	3	0	0	0	4	....	....	....
99-2000	Springfield Falcons	AHL	22	1	3	4	....	....	....	70	....	....	....	....	....	....	....	....	....	....	....	....	....	....	....	....	....	....
	Hamilton Bulldogs	AHL	55	11	20	31	....	....	....	100	....	....	....	....	....	....	....	....	....	....	10	2	3	5	4	....	....	....
	NHL Totals		**107**	**4**	**15**	**19**	**4**	**13**	**17**	**111**	**0**	**0**	**1**	**61**	**6.6**	**28**	**0**	**61**	**23**		**9**	**0**	**0**	**0**	**18**	**0**	**0**	**0**

Claimed by **Minnesota** from **Washington** in Expansion Draft, May 30, 1991. Traded to **Winnipeg** by **Minnesota** with future considerations for Winnipeg's 7th round choice (Geoff Finch) in 1991 Entry Draft and future considerations, May 31, 1991. Transferred to **Phoenix** after **Winnipeg** franchise relocated, July 1, 1996. Traded to **Edmonton** by **Phoenix** for Eric Houde, November 30, 1999.

• MURRAY, Terry

Terry Rodney D – R. 6'2", 190 lbs. b: Shawville, Que., 7/20/1950. Oakland's 3rd, 88th overall, in 1970.

Season	Club	League	GP	G	A	Pts	AG	AA	APts	PIM	PP	SH	GW	S	%	TGF	PGF	TGA	PGA	+/–	GP	G	A	Pts	PIM	PP	SH	GW
1967-68	Ottawa 67's	OHA-Jr.	53	0	4	4	....	....	....	59	....	....	....	....	....	....	....	....	....	....	....	....	....	....	....	....	....	....
1968-69	Ottawa 67's	OHA-Jr.	50	1	16	17	....	....	....	39	....	....	....	....	....	....	....	....	....	....	7	0	1	1	4	....	....	....
1969-70	Ottawa 67's	OHA-Jr.	50	4	24	28	....	....	....	43	....	....	....	....	....	....	....	....	....	....	5	0	0	0	2	....	....	....
1970-71	Providence Reds	AHL	57	1	22	23	....	....	....	47	....	....	....	....	....	....	....	....	....	....	10	0	1	1	5	....	....	....
1971-72	Baltimore Clippers	AHL	30	0	5	5	....	....	....	13	....	....	....	....	....	....	....	....	....	....	....	....	....	....	....	....	....	....
	Boston Braves	AHL	9	0	0	0	....	....	....	0	....	....	....	....	....	....	....	....	....	....	....	....	....	....	....	....	....	....
	Oklahoma City Blazers	CHL	17	1	1	2	....	....	....	19	....	....	....	....	....	....	....	....	....	....	6	0	0	0	2	....	....	....
1972-73	**California Golden Seals**	**NHL**	23	0	3	3	0	2	2	4	0	0	0	9	0.0	12	0	34	8	–14	....	....	....	....	....	....	....	....
	Salt Lake Golden Eagles	WHL	39	3	8	11	....	....	....	30	....	....	....	....	....	....	....	....	....	....	9	0	6	6	14	....	....	....
1973-74	**California Golden Seals**	**NHL**	58	0	12	12	0	10	10	48	0	0	0	55	0.0	55	9	103	14	–43	....	....	....	....	....	....	....	....
1974-75	**California Golden Seals**	**NHL**	9	0	2	2	0	1	1	8	0	0	0	8	0.0	8	0	7	1	2	....	....	....	....	....	....	....	....
	Salt Lake Golden Eagles	CHL	62	5	30	35	....	....	....	122	....	....	....	....	....	....	....	....	....	....	11	2	2	4	30	....	....	....
1975-76	**Philadelphia Flyers**	**NHL**	3	0	0	0	0	0	0	2	0	0	0	3	0.0	1	0	1	0	0	6	0	1	1	0	0	0	0
	Richmond Robins	AHL	67	8	48	56	....	....	....	95	....	....	....	....	....	....	....	....	....	....	6	1	4	5	2	....	....	....
1976-77	**Philadelphia Flyers**	**NHL**	36	0	13	13	0	10	10	14	0	0	0	32	0.0	46	5	24	4	21	....	....	....	....	....	....	....	....
	Detroit Red Wings	**NHL**	23	0	7	7	0	5	5	10	0	0	0	24	0.0	16	3	46	15	–18	....	....	....	....	....	....	....	....
1977-78	Philadelphia Firebirds	AHL	7	2	1	3	....	....	....	13	....	....	....	....	....	....	....	....	....	....	....	....	....	....	....	....	....	....
	Maine Mariners	AHL	68	9	40	49	....	....	....	53	....	....	....	....	....	....	....	....	....	....	12	1	7	8	28	....	....	....
1978-79	**Philadelphia Flyers**	**NHL**	5	0	0	0	0	0	0	0	0	0	0	3	0.0	2	1	1	0	0	....	....	....	....	....	....	....	....
	Maine Mariners	AHL	55	14	23	37	....	....	....	14	....	....	....	....	....	....	....	....	....	....	10	1	5	6	6	....	....	....
1979-80	Maine Mariners	AHL	68	3	19	22	....	....	....	26	....	....	....	....	....	....	....	....	....	....	12	2	2	4	10	....	....	....
1980-81	**Philadelphia Flyers**	**NHL**	71	1	17	18	1	11	12	53	0	0	0	65	1.5	96	2	72	24	46	12	2	1	3	10	0	0	0
	Maine Mariners	AHL	2	0	1	1	....	....	....	0	....	....	....	....	....	....	....	....	....	....	....	....	....	....	....	....	....	....
1981-82	**Washington Capitals**	**NHL**	74	3	22	25	2	15	17	60	0	0	0	75	4.0	85	6	126	33	–14	....	....	....	....	....	....	....	....
1982-1988	**Washington Capitals**	**NHL**	DID NOT PLAY – ASSISTANT COACH																									
1988-1989	Baltimore Skipjacks	AHL	DID NOT PLAY – COACHING																									
1989-1990	Baltimore Skipjacks	AHL	DID NOT PLAY – COACHING																									
	Washington Capitals	**NHL**	DID NOT PLAY – COACHING																									
1990-1993	**Washington Capitals**	**NHL**	DID NOT PLAY – COACHING																									
1993-1994	**Washington Capitals**	**NHL**	DID NOT PLAY – COACHING																									
	Cincinnati Cyclones	IHL	DID NOT PLAY – COACHING																									
1994-1997	**Philadelphia Flyers**	**NHL**	DID NOT PLAY – COACHING																									
1997-1998	**Philadelphia Flyers**	**NHL**	DID NOT PLAY – SCOUTING																									
1998-2000	**Florida Panthers**	**NHL**	DID NOT PLAY – COACHING																									
	NHL Totals		**302**	**4**	**76**	**80**	**3**	**54**	**57**	**199**	**0**	**0**	**0**	**274**	**1.5**	**321**	**26**	**414**	**99**		**18**	**2**	**2**	**4**	**10**	**0**	**0**	**0**

AHL First All-Star Team (1976, 1978, 1979) • Won Eddie Shore Award (Outstanding Defenseman - AHL) (1978, 1979)

Signed as a free agent by **Philadelphia**, September 23, 1975. Traded to **Detroit** by **Philadelphia** with Steve Coates, Bob Ritchie and Dave Kelly for Rick Lapointe and Mike Korney, February 17, 1977. Traded to **Philadelphia** by **Detroit** for cash, November 1, 1977. Claimed by **Washington** from **Philadelphia** in Waiver Draft, October 5, 1981.

• MURRAY, Troy

Troy Norman C – R. 6'1", 195 lbs. b: Calgary, Alta., 7/31/1962. Chicago's 6th, 57th overall, in 1980.

Season	Club	League	GP	G	A	Pts	AG	AA	APts	PIM	PP	SH	GW	S	%	TGF	PGF	TGA	PGA	+/–	GP	G	A	Pts	PIM	PP	SH	GW
1977-78	Calgary North Stars	AAHA	STATISTICS NOT AVAILABLE																									
	St. Albert Saints	AJHL	5	0	2	2	....	....	....	0	....	....	....	....	....	....	....	....	....	....	....	....	....	....	....	....	....	....
1978-79	St. Albert Saints	AJHL	58	33	47	80	....	....	....	92	....	....	....	....	....	....	....	....	....	....	....	....	....	....	....	....	....	....
1979-80	St. Albert Saints	AJHL	60	53	47	100	....	....	....	101	....	....	....	....	....	....	....	....	....	....	....	....	....	....	....	....	....	....
	Lethbridge Broncos	WHL	2	1	1	2	....	....	....	2	....	....	....	....	....	....	....	....	....	....	....	....	....	....	....	....	....	....
1980-81	University of North Dakota	WCHA	38	33	45	78	....	....	....	28	....	....	....	....	....	....	....	....	....	....	....	....	....	....	....	....	....	....
1981-82	University of North Dakota	WCHA	26	13	17	30	....	....	....	62	....	....	....	....	....	....	....	....	....	....	....	....	....	....	....	....	....	....
	Canada	WJC-A	7	4	4	8	....	....	....	6	....	....	....	....	....	....	....	....	....	....	....	....	....	....	....	....	....	....
	Chicago Black Hawks	**NHL**	1	0	0	0	0	0	0	0	0	0	0	2	0.0	0	0	0	0	0	7	1	0	1	5	0	0	0
1982-83	**Chicago Black Hawks**	**NHL**	54	8	8	16	7	6	13	27	1	0	2	53	15.1	26	2	31	3	–4	2	0	0	0	0	0	0	0
1983-84	**Chicago Black Hawks**	**NHL**	61	15	15	30	12	10	22	45	0	1	2	119	12.6	45	3	42	10	10	5	1	0	1	7	0	0	1
1984-85	**Chicago Black Hawks**	**NHL**	80	26	40	66	21	27	48	82	6	4	5	157	16.6	100	22	91	29	16	15	5	14	19	24	1	0	0
1985-86	**Chicago Black Hawks**	**NHL**	80	45	54	99	36	36	72	94	9	5	7	197	22.8	139	38	109	40	32	2	0	0	0	2	0	0	0
1986-87	**Chicago Blackhawks**	**NHL**	77	28	43	71	24	31	55	59	4	2	3	127	22.0	99	20	106	41	14	4	0	0	0	5	0	0	0
	Canada	WEC-A	10	2	2	4	....	....	....	14	....	....	....	....	....	....	....	....	....	....	....	....	....	....	....	....	....	....
1987-88	**Chicago Blackhawks**	**NHL**	79	22	36	58	19	26	45	96	3	2	2	148	14.9	97	36	109	31	–17	5	1	0	1	8	1	0	0
1988-89	**Chicago Blackhawks**	**NHL**	79	21	30	51	18	21	39	113	5	2	2	156	13.5	89	31	98	40	0	16	3	6	9	25	1	0	0
1989-90	**Chicago Blackhawks**	**NHL**	68	17	38	55	15	27	42	86	3	1	4	111	15.3	89	31	86	26	–2	20	4	4	8	22	1	0	0
1990-91	**Chicago Blackhawks**	**NHL**	75	14	23	37	13	17	30	74	4	0	2	130	10.8	56	16	46	19	13	6	0	1	1	12	0	0	0
1991-92	**Winnipeg Jets**	**NHL**	74	17	30	47	15	23	38	69	5	2	1	156	10.9	83	35	98	37	–13	7	0	0	0	2	0	0	0
1992-93	**Winnipeg Jets**	**NHL**	29	3	4	7	2	3	5	34	1	0	0	45	6.7	15	4	40	14	–15	....	....	....	....	....	....	....	....
	Chicago Blackhawks	**NHL**	22	1	3	4	1	2	3	25	1	0	0	32	3.1	6	1	9	4	0	4	0	0	0	2	0	0	0
1993-94	**Chicago Blackhawks**	**NHL**	12	0	1	1	0	1	1	6	0	0	0	7	0.0	2	0	2	1	1	....	....	....	....	....	....	....	....
	Indianapolis Ice	IHL	8	3	3	6	....	....	....	12	....	....	....	....	....	....	....	....	....	....	....	....	....	....	....	....	....	....
	Ottawa Senators	**NHL**	15	2	3	5	2	2	4	4	0	1	0	14	14.3	8	0	13	6	1	....	....	....	....	....	....	....	....

Season	Club	League	GP	G	A	Pts	AG	AA	APts	PIM	PP	SH	GW	S	%	TGF	PGF	TGA	PGA	+/–	GP	G	A	Pts	PIM	PP	SH	GW
			REGULAR SEASON																		PLAYOFFS							
1994-95	**Ottawa Senators**	**NHL**	**33**	**4**	**10**	**14**	**7**	**15**	**22**	**16**	**0**	**0**	**1**	**38**	**10.5**	**15**	**1**	**29**	**14**	**–1**	....	....	....	....	....	....	....	....
	Pittsburgh Penguins	**NHL**	**13**	**0**	**2**	**2**	**0**	**3**	**3**	**23**	**0**	**0**	**0**	**7**	**0.0**	**5**	**0**	**12**	**6**	**–1**	**12**	**2**	**1**	**3**	**12**	**0**	**0**	**0**
1995-96♦	**Colorado Avalanche**	**NHL**	**63**	**7**	**14**	**21**	**7**	**11**	**18**	**22**	**0**	**0**	**1**	**36**	**19.4**	**27**	**0**	**28**	**16**	**15**	**8**	**0**	**0**	**0**	**19**	**0**	**0**	**0**
1996-97	Chicago Wolves	IHL	81	21	29	50	....	....	....	63	....	....	....	....	....	....	....	....	....	....	4	0	2	2	2	....	....	....
	NHL Totals		**915**	**230**	**354**	**584**	**199**	**261**	**460**	**875**	**42**	**20**	**32**	**1535**	**15.0**	**901**	**240**	**949**	**337**		**113**	**17**	**26**	**43**	**145**	**4**	**0**	**1**

Won Frank J. Selke Trophy (1986)

WCHA Second All-Star Team (1981, 1982) • Won Frank J. Selke Memorial Trophy (1986)

Traded to **Winnipeg** by **Chicago** with Warren Rychel for Bryan Marchment and Chris Norton, July 22, 1991. Traded to **Chicago** by **Winnipeg** for Steve Bancroft and future considerations, February 21, 1993. Traded to **Ottawa** by **Chicago** with Chicago's 11th round choice (Antti Tormanen) in 1994 Entry Draft for Ottawa's 11th round choice (Rob Mara) in 1994 Entry Draft, March 11, 1994. Traded to **Pittsburgh** by **Ottawa** with Norm Maciver for Martin Straka, April 7, 1995. Signed as a free agent by **Colorado**, August 7, 1995.

• MURZYN, Dana

Dana Trevor D – L. 6'2", 200 lbs. b: Calgary, Alta., 12/9/1966. Hartford's 1st, 5th overall, in 1985.

Season	Club	League	GP	G	A	Pts	AG	AA	APts	PIM	PP	SH	GW	S	%	TGF	PGF	TGA	PGA	+/–	GP	G	A	Pts	PIM	PP	SH	GW
1981-82	Calgary Royals	AAHA	STATISTICS NOT AVAILABLE																									
1982-83	Calgary Spurs	AJHL	STATISTICS NOT AVAILABLE																									
1983-84	Calgary Wranglers	WHL	65	11	20	31	....	....	....	135	....	....	....	....	....	....	....	....	....	....	2	0	0	0	10	....	....	....
1984-85	Calgary Wranglers	WHL	72	32	60	92	....	....	....	233	....	....	....	....	....	....	....	....	....	....	8	1	11	12	16	....	....	....
1985-86	**Hartford Whalers**	**NHL**	**78**	**3**	**23**	**26**	**2**	**15**	**17**	**125**	**0**	**0**	**1**	**79**	**3.8**	**80**	**8**	**76**	**5**	**1**	**4**	**0**	**0**	**0**	**10**	**0**	**0**	**0**
1986-87	**Hartford Whalers**	**NHL**	**74**	**9**	**19**	**28**	**8**	**14**	**22**	**95**	**1**	**0**	**0**	**135**	**6.7**	**88**	**4**	**70**	**3**	**17**	**6**	**2**	**1**	**3**	**29**	**1**	**0**	**1**
1987-88	**Hartford Whalers**	**NHL**	**33**	**1**	**6**	**7**	**1**	**4**	**5**	**45**	**1**	**0**	**0**	**49**	**2.0**	**23**	**3**	**28**	**0**	**–8**	....	....	....	....	....	....	....	....
	Calgary Flames	**NHL**	**41**	**6**	**5**	**11**	**5**	**4**	**9**	**94**	**0**	**0**	**1**	**58**	**10.3**	**49**	**0**	**50**	**10**	**9**	**5**	**2**	**0**	**2**	**13**	**0**	**0**	**0**
1988-89♦	**Calgary Flames**	**NHL**	**63**	**3**	**19**	**22**	**3**	**13**	**16**	**142**	**0**	**1**	**1**	**91**	**3.3**	**60**	**6**	**43**	**15**	**26**	**21**	**0**	**3**	**3**	**20**	**0**	**0**	**0**
1989-90	Calgary Flames	Fr-Tour	4	1	0	1	....	....	....	6	....	....	....	....	....	....	....	....	....	....	....	....	....	....	....	....	....	....
	Calgary Flames	**NHL**	**78**	**7**	**13**	**20**	**6**	**9**	**15**	**140**	**1**	**0**	**0**	**97**	**7.2**	**80**	**1**	**82**	**22**	**19**	**6**	**2**	**2**	**4**	**2**	**0**	**0**	**0**
1990-91	**Calgary Flames**	**NHL**	**19**	**0**	**2**	**2**	**0**	**2**	**2**	**30**	**0**	**0**	**0**	**25**	**0.0**	**13**	**0**	**19**	**2**	**–4**	....	....	....	....	....	....	....	....
	Vancouver Canucks	**NHL**	**10**	**1**	**0**	**1**	**1**	**0**	**1**	**8**	**0**	**0**	**0**	**15**	**6.7**	**8**	**0**	**14**	**3**	**–3**	**6**	**0**	**1**	**1**	**8**	**0**	**0**	**0**
1991-92	**Vancouver Canucks**	**NHL**	**70**	**3**	**11**	**14**	**3**	**8**	**11**	**147**	**0**	**1**	**0**	**99**	**3.0**	**67**	**3**	**68**	**19**	**15**	**1**	**0**	**0**	**0**	**15**	**0**	**0**	**0**
1992-93	**Vancouver Canucks**	**NHL**	**79**	**5**	**11**	**16**	**4**	**8**	**12**	**196**	**0**	**0**	**2**	**82**	**6.1**	**83**	**1**	**74**	**26**	**34**	**12**	**3**	**2**	**5**	**18**	**0**	**0**	**0**
1993-94	**Vancouver Canucks**	**NHL**	**80**	**6**	**14**	**20**	**6**	**11**	**17**	**109**	**0**	**1**	**0**	**79**	**7.6**	**66**	**0**	**100**	**38**	**4**	**7**	**0**	**0**	**0**	**4**	**0**	**0**	**0**
1994-95	**Vancouver Canucks**	**NHL**	**40**	**0**	**8**	**8**	**0**	**12**	**12**	**129**	**0**	**0**	**0**	**29**	**0.0**	**35**	**0**	**29**	**8**	**14**	**8**	**0**	**1**	**1**	**22**	**0**	**0**	**0**
1995-96	**Vancouver Canucks**	**NHL**	**69**	**2**	**10**	**12**	**2**	**8**	**10**	**130**	**0**	**0**	**0**	**68**	**2.9**	**62**	**0**	**88**	**35**	**9**	**6**	**0**	**0**	**0**	**25**	**0**	**0**	**0**
1996-97	**Vancouver Canucks**	**NHL**	**61**	**1**	**7**	**8**	**1**	**6**	**7**	**118**	**0**	**0**	**0**	**70**	**1.4**	**55**	**0**	**68**	**20**	**7**	....	....	....	....	....	....	....	....
1997-98	**Vancouver Canucks**	**NHL**	**31**	**5**	**2**	**7**	**6**	**2**	**8**	**42**	**0**	**0**	**2**	**29**	**17.2**	**23**	**1**	**41**	**16**	**–3**	....	....	....	....	....	....	....	....
1998-99	**Vancouver Canucks**	**NHL**	**12**	**0**	**2**	**2**	**0**	**2**	**2**	**21**	**0**	**0**	**0**	**7**	**0.0**	**7**	**0**	**7**	**1**	**1**	....	....	....	....	....	....	....	....
	Syracuse Crunch	AHL	20	2	4	6	....	....	....	37	....	....	....	....	....	....	....	....	....	....	....	....	....	....	....	....	....	....
	NHL Totals		**838**	**52**	**152**	**204**	**48**	**118**	**166**	**1571**	**3**	**3**	**7**	**1012**	**5.1**	**799**	**27**	**857**	**223**		**82**	**9**	**10**	**19**	**166**	**1**	**0**	**1**

WHL East First All-Star Team (1985) • NHL All-Rookie Team (1986)

Traded to **Calgary** by **Hartford** with Shane Churla for Neil Sheehy, Carey Wilson and the rights to Lane MacDonald, January 3, 1988. Traded to **Vancouver** by **Calgary** for Ron Stern and Kevan Guy, March 5, 1991. • Missed majority of 1997-98 season recovering from knee injury suffered in game vs. Dallas, December 27, 1997.

• MUSIL, Frantisek

"Frank" D – L. 6'3", 215 lbs. b: Pardubice, Czech., 12/17/1964. Minnesota's 3rd, 38th overall, in 1983.

Season	Club	League	GP	G	A	Pts	AG	AA	APts	PIM	PP	SH	GW	S	%	TGF	PGF	TGA	PGA	+/–	GP	G	A	Pts	PIM	PP	SH	GW
1980-81	HC Tesla Pardubice	Czech.	2	0	0	0	....	....	....	0	....	....	....	....	....	....	....	....	....	....	....	....	....	....	....	....	....	....
	Czechoslovakia	EJC-A	5	0	2	2	....	....	....	6	....	....	....	....	....	....	....	....	....	....	....	....	....	....	....	....	....	....
1981-82	HC Tesla Pardubice	Czech.	35	1	3	4	....	....	....	34	....	....	....	....	....	....	....	....	....	....	....	....	....	....	....	....	....	....
	Czechoslovakia	WJC-A	7	1	1	2	....	....	....	8	....	....	....	....	....	....	....	....	....	....	....	....	....	....	....	....	....	....
	Czechoslovakia	EJC-A	5	1	2	3	....	....	....	12	....	....	....	....	....	....	....	....	....	....	....	....	....	....	....	....	....	....
1982-83	HC Tesla Pardubice	Czech.	33	1	2	3	....	....	....	44	....	....	....	....	....	....	....	....	....	....	....	....	....	....	....	....	....	....
	Czechoslovakia	WJC-A	6	0	2	2	....	....	....	8	....	....	....	....	....	....	....	....	....	....	....	....	....	....	....	....	....	....
	Czechoslovakia	WEC-A	4	0	1	1	....	....	....	6	....	....	....	....	....	....	....	....	....	....	....	....	....	....	....	....	....	....
1983-84	HC Tesla Pardubice	Czech.	37	4	8	12	....	....	....	72	....	....	....	....	....	....	....	....	....	....	....	....	....	....	....	....	....	....
	Czechoslovakia	WJC-A	7	0	2	2	....	....	....	10	....	....	....	....	....	....	....	....	....	....	....	....	....	....	....	....	....	....
1984-85	Czechoslovakia	Can-Cup	5	0	1	1	....	....	....	4	....	....	....	....	....	....	....	....	....	....	....	....	....	....	....	....	....	....
	Dukla Jihlava	Czech.	44	4	6	10	....	....	....	76	....	....	....	....	....	....	....	....	....	....	....	....	....	....	....	....	....	....
	Czechoslovakia	WEC-A	10	1	1	2	....	....	....	12	....	....	....	....	....	....	....	....	....	....	....	....	....	....	....	....	....	....
1985-86	Dukla Jihlava	Czech.	34	4	7	11	....	....	....	42	....	....	....	....	....	....	....	....	....	....	....	....	....	....	....	....	....	....
	Czechoslovakia	WEC-A	10	0	2	2	....	....	....	20	....	....	....	....	....	....	....	....	....	....	....	....	....	....	....	....	....	....
1986-87	**Minnesota North Stars**	**NHL**	**72**	**2**	**9**	**11**	**2**	**7**	**9**	**148**	**0**	**0**	**0**	**83**	**2.4**	**62**	**8**	**87**	**33**	**0**	....	....	....	....	....	....	....	....
1987-88	**Minnesota North Stars**	**NHL**	**80**	**9**	**8**	**17**	**8**	**6**	**14**	**213**	**1**	**1**	**0**	**78**	**11.5**	**72**	**5**	**111**	**42**	**–2**	....	....	....	....	....	....	....	....
1988-89	**Minnesota North Stars**	**NHL**	**55**	**1**	**19**	**20**	**1**	**13**	**14**	**54**	**0**	**0**	**1**	**78**	**1.3**	**52**	**10**	**57**	**19**	**4**	**5**	**1**	**1**	**2**	**4**	**0**	**0**	**0**
1989-90	**Minnesota North Stars**	**NHL**	**56**	**2**	**8**	**10**	**2**	**6**	**8**	**109**	**0**	**0**	**1**	**78**	**2.6**	**56**	**5**	**72**	**21**	**0**	**4**	**0**	**0**	**0**	**14**	**0**	**0**	**0**
1990-91	**Minnesota North Stars**	**NHL**	**8**	**0**	**2**	**2**	**0**	**2**	**2**	**23**	**0**	**0**	**0**	**5**	**0.0**	**4**	**1**	**6**	**3**	**0**	....	....	....	....	....	....	....	....
	Calgary Flames	**NHL**	**67**	**7**	**14**	**21**	**6**	**11**	**17**	**160**	**2**	**0**	**1**	**68**	**10.3**	**60**	**7**	**63**	**22**	**12**	**7**	**0**	**0**	**0**	**10**	**0**	**0**	**0**
	Czechoslovakia	WEC-A	10	2	0	2	....	....	....	40	....	....	....	....	....	....	....	....	....	....	....	....	....	....	....	....	....	....
1991-92	Czechoslovakia	Can-Cup	5	0	0	0	....	....	....	6	....	....	....	....	....	....	....	....	....	....	....	....	....	....	....	....	....	....
	Calgary Flames	**NHL**	**78**	**4**	**8**	**12**	**4**	**6**	**10**	**103**	**1**	**1**	**0**	**71**	**5.6**	**61**	**2**	**89**	**42**	**12**	....	....	....	....	....	....	....	....
	Czechoslovakia	WC-A	7	3	1	4	....	....	....	26	....	....	....	....	....	....	....	....	....	....	....	....	....	....	....	....	....	....
1992-93	**Calgary Flames**	**NHL**	**80**	**6**	**10**	**16**	**5**	**7**	**12**	**131**	**0**	**0**	**1**	**87**	**6.9**	**73**	**5**	**62**	**22**	**28**	**6**	**1**	**1**	**2**	**7**	**0**	**0**	**0**
1993-94	**Calgary Flames**	**NHL**	**75**	**1**	**8**	**9**	**1**	**6**	**7**	**50**	**0**	**0**	**0**	**65**	**1.5**	**70**	**0**	**70**	**38**	**38**	**7**	**0**	**1**	**1**	**4**	**0**	**0**	**0**
	Czech-Republic	WC-A	2	0	0	0	....	....	....	2	....	....	....	....	....	....	....	....	....	....	....	....	....	....	....	....	....	....
1994-95	HC Sparta Praha	Czech-Rep	19	1	4	5	....	....	....	50	....	....	....	....	....	....	....	....	....	....	....	....	....	....	....	....	....	....
	HC Saxonia	Germany	1	0	0	0	....	....	....	2	....	....	....	....	....	....	....	....	....	....	....	....	....	....	....	....	....	....
	Calgary Flames	**NHL**	**35**	**0**	**5**	**5**	**0**	**7**	**7**	**61**	**0**	**0**	**0**	**18**	**0.0**	**20**	**0**	**28**	**14**	**6**	**5**	**0**	**1**	**1**	**0**	**0**	**0**	**0**
1995-96	Karlovy Vary-2	Czech-Rep	16	7	4	11	....	....	....	16	....	....	....	....	....	....	....	....	....	....	....	....	....	....	....	....	....	....
	Ottawa Senators	**NHL**	**65**	**1**	**3**	**4**	**1**	**2**	**3**	**85**	**0**	**0**	**0**	**37**	**2.7**	**37**	**0**	**78**	**31**	**–10**	....	....	....	....	....	....	....	....
1996-97	**Ottawa Senators**	**NHL**	**57**	**0**	**5**	**5**	**0**	**4**	**4**	**58**	**0**	**0**	**0**	**24**	**0.0**	**37**	**0**	**42**	**11**	**6**	....	....	....	....	....	....	....	....
1997-98	Indianapolis Ice	IHL	52	5	8	13	....	....	....	122	....	....	....	....	....	....	....	....	....	....	....	....	....	....	....	....	....	....
	Detroit Vipers	IHL	9	0	0	0	....	....	....	6	....	....	....	....	....	....	....	....	....	....	....	....	....	....	....	....	....	....
	Edmonton Oilers	**NHL**	**17**	**1**	**2**	**3**	**1**	**2**	**3**	**8**	**0**	**1**	**1**	**8**	**12.5**	**11**	**1**	**17**	**8**	**1**	**7**	**0**	**0**	**0**	**6**	**0**	**0**	**0**
1998-99	**Edmonton Oilers**	**NHL**	**39**	**0**	**3**	**3**	**0**	**3**	**3**	**34**	**0**	**0**	**0**	**9**	**0.0**	**15**	**0**	**28**	**13**	**0**	**1**	**0**	**0**	**0**	**2**	**0**	**0**	**0**
99-2000	**Edmonton Oilers**	**NHL**	DID NOT PLAY – INJURED																									
	NHL Totals		**784**	**34**	**104**	**138**	**31**	**82**	**113**	**1237**	**4**	**3**	**5**	**709**	**4.8**	**630**	**44**	**810**	**319**		**42**	**2**	**4**	**6**	**47**	**0**	**0**	**0**

WC-A All-Star Team (1992)

Traded to **Calgary** by **Minnesota** for Brian Glynn, October 26, 1990. Traded to **Ottawa** by **Calgary** for Ottawa's 4th round choice (Chris St. Croix) in 1997 Entry Draft, October 7, 1995. Traded to **Edmonton** by **Ottawa** for Scott Ferguson, March 9, 1998. • Missed entire 1999-2000 season recovering from spinal cord injury suffered in training camp, October 2, 1999.

• MYERS, Hap

Harold Robert D – L. 5'11", 195 lbs. b: Edmonton, Alta., 7/28/1947.

Season	Club	League	GP	G	A	Pts	AG	AA	APts	PIM	PP	SH	GW	S	%	TGF	PGF	TGA	PGA	+/–	GP	G	A	Pts	PIM	PP	SH	GW
1964-65	Edmonton Red Wings	AJHL-B	STATISTICS NOT AVAILABLE																									
	Edmonton Oil Kings	CAHL	STATISTICS NOT AVAILABLE																									
	Edmonton Oil Kings	Mem-Cup	21	0	3	3	....	....	....	17	....	....	....	....	....	....	....	....	....	....	....	....	....	....	....	....	....	....
1965-66	Edmonton Oil Kings	ASHL	40	0	3	3	....	....	....	18	....	....	....	....	....	....	....	....	....	....	11	3	3	6	14	....	....	....
	Edmonton Oil Kings	Mem-Cup	11	0	0	0	....	....	....	10	....	....	....	....	....	....	....	....	....	....	....	....	....	....	....	....	....	....
1966-67	Edmonton Oil Kings	CMJHL	56	6	33	39	....	....	....	86	....	....	....	....	....	....	....	....	....	....	9	0	7	7	30	....	....	....
1967-68	Edmonton Oil Kings	WCJHL	55	13	37	50	....	....	....	98	....	....	....	....	....	....	....	....	....	....	13	3	5	8	26	....	....	....
1968-69	Fort Worth Wings	CHL	70	8	13	21	....	....	....	52	....	....	....	....	....	....	....	....	....	....	....	....	....	....	....	....	....	....
1969-70	Cleveland Barons	AHL	72	9	28	37	....	....	....	61	....	....	....	....	....	....	....	....	....	....	....	....	....	....	....	....	....	....
1970-71	**Buffalo Sabres**	**NHL**	**13**	**0**	**0**	**0**	**0**	**0**	**0**	**6**	**0**	**0**	**0**	**14**	**0.0**	**0**	**0**	**14**	**3**	**–11**	....	....	....	....	....	....	....	....
	Salt Lake Golden Eagles	WHL	43	1	4	5	....	....	....	14	....	....	....	....	....	....	....	....	....	....	....	....	....	....	....	....	....	....

Season	Club	League	REGULAR SEASON GP	G	A	Pts	AG	AA	APts	PIM	PP	SH	GW	S	%	TGF	PGF	TGA	PGA	+/-	PLAYOFFS GP	G	A	Pts	PIM	PP	SH	GW
1971-72	Cincinnati Swords	AHL	67	4	16	20	....	....	....	55	....	....	....	....	....	....	....	....	....	....	10	0	3	3	14	....	....	....
1972-73	Cincinnati Swords	AHL	37	0	9	9	....	....	....	2	....	....	....	....	....	....	....	....	....	....	15	0	4	4	12	....	....	....
1973-74	Cincinnati Swords	AHL	76	6	25	31	....	....	....	51	....	....	....	....	....	....	....	....	....	....	5	0	2	2	8	....	....	....
	NHL Totals		**13**	**0**	**0**	**0**	**0**	**0**	**0**	**6**	**0**	**0**	**0**	**14**	**0.0**	**0**	**0**	**14**	**3**		....	....	....	....	....	....	....	....

Claimed by **Buffalo** (Salt Lake-CHL) from **Detroit** in Reverse Draft, June 10, 1970.

• MYHRES, Brantt

Brantt Robert RW – R. 6'4", 220 lbs. b: Edmonton, Alta., 3/18/1974. Tampa Bay's 5th, 97th overall, in 1992.

Season	Club	League	GP	G	A	Pts	AG	AA	APts	PIM	PP	SH	GW	S	%	TGF	PGF	TGA	PGA	+/-	GP	G	A	Pts	PIM	PP	SH	GW
1989-90	Bobbeyville Barons	AAHA	60	40	62	102	....	....	....	195	....	....	....	....	....	....	....	....	....	....	....	....	....	....	....	....	....	....
1990-91	Portland Winter Hawks	WHL	59	2	7	9	....	....	....	125	....	....	....	....	....	....	....	....	....	....	....	....	....	....	....	....	....	....
1991-92	Portland Winter Hawks	WHL	4	0	2	2	....	....	....	22	....	....	....	....	....	....	....	....	....	....	....	....	....	....	....	....	....	....
	Lethbridge Huricanes	WHL	53	4	11	15	....	....	....	359	....	....	....	....	....	....	....	....	....	....	5	0	0	0	36	....	....	....
1992-93	Lethbridge Hurricanes	WHL	64	13	35	48	....	....	....	277	....	....	....	....	....	....	....	....	....	....	3	0	0	0	11	....	....	....
1993-94	Lethbridge Hurricanes	WHL	34	10	21	31	....	....	....	103	....	....	....	....	....	....	....	....	....	....	....	....	....	....	....	....	....	....
	Spokane Chiefs	WHL	27	10	22	32	....	....	....	139	....	....	....	....	....	....	....	....	....	....	3	1	4	5	7	....	....	....
	Atlanta Knights	IHL	2	0	0	0	....	....	....	17	....	....	....	....	....	....	....	....	....	....	....	....	....	....	....	....	....	....
1994-95	Atlanta Knights	IHL	40	5	5	10	....	....	....	213	....	....	....	....	....	....	....	....	....	....	....	....	....	....	....	....	....	....
	Tampa Bay Lightning	**NHL**	**15**	**2**	**0**	**2**	**4**	**0**	**4**	**81**	**0**	**0**	**1**	**4**	**50.0**	**2**	**0**	**4**	**0**	**−2**	....	....	....	....	....	....	....	....
1995-96	Atlanta Knights	IHL	12	0	2	2	....	....	....	58	....	....	....	....	....	....	....	....	....	....	....	....	....	....	....	....	....	....
1996-97	**Tampa Bay Lightning**	**NHL**	**47**	**3**	**1**	**4**	**3**	**1**	**4**	**136**	**0**	**0**	**1**	**13**	**23.1**	**7**	**0**	**6**	**0**	**1**	....	....	....	....	....	....	....	....
	San Antonio Dragons	IHL	12	0	0	0	....	....	....	98	....	....	....	....	....	....	....	....	....	....	....	....	....	....	....	....	....	....
1997-98	**Philadelphia Flyers**	**NHL**	**23**	**0**	**0**	**0**	**0**	**0**	**0**	**169**	**0**	**0**	**0**	**0**	**0.0**	**1**	**0**	**2**	**0**	**−1**	....	....	....	....	....	....	....	....
	Philadelphia Phantoms	AHL	18	4	4	8	....	....	....	67	....	....	....	....	....	....	....	....	....	....	....	....	....	....	....	....	....	....
1998-99	**San Jose Sharks**	**NHL**	**30**	**1**	**0**	**1**	**1**	**0**	**1**	**116**	**0**	**0**	**0**	**7**	**14.3**	**2**	**0**	**4**	**0**	**−2**	....	....	....	....	....	....	....	....
	Kentucky Thoroughblades	AHL	4	0	0	0	....	....	....	16	....	....	....	....	....	....	....	....	....	....	....	....	....	....	....	....	....	....
99-2000	**San Jose Sharks**	**NHL**	**13**	**0**	**1**	**1**	**0**	**1**	**1**	**97**	**0**	**0**	**0**	**2**	**0.0**	**1**	**0**	**1**	**0**	**0**	....	....	....	....	....	....	....	....
	Kentucky Thoroughblades	AHL	10	1	5	6	....	....	....	18	....	....	....	....	....	....	....	....	....	....	7	0	1	1	21	....	....	....
	NHL Totals		**128**	**6**	**2**	**8**	**8**	**2**	**10**	**599**	**0**	**0**	**2**	**26**	**23.1**	**13**	**0**	**17**	**0**		....	....	....	....	....	....	....	....

Traded to **Edmonton** by **Tampa Bay** with Toronto's 3rd round choice (previously acquired, Edmonton selected Alex Henry) in 1998 Entry Draft for Vladimir Vujtek and Edmonton's 3rd round choice (Dimitri Afanasenkov) in 1998 Entry Draft, July 16, 1997. Traded to **Philadelphia** by **Edmonton** for Jason Bowen, October 15, 1997. Signed as a free agent by **San Jose**, September 11, 1998.

• MYRVOLD, Anders

D – L. 6'2", 200 lbs. b: Lorenskog, Norway, 8/12/1975. Quebec's 6th, 127th overall, in 1993.

Season	Club	League	GP	G	A	Pts	AG	AA	APts	PIM	PP	SH	GW	S	%	TGF	PGF	TGA	PGA	+/-	GP	G	A	Pts	PIM	PP	SH	GW
1991-92	Storhamr IL	Norway	1	0	0	0	....	....	....	4	....	....	....	....	....	....	....	....	....	....	....	....	....	....	....	....	....	....
1992-93	Farjestads BK Stockholm	Sweden	2	0	0	0	....	....	....	0	....	....	....	....	....	....	....	....	....	....	....	....	....	....	....	....	....	....
	Norway	WJC-B	7	5	1	6	....	....	....	10	....	....	....	....	....	....	....	....	....	....	....	....	....	....	....	....	....	....
1993-94	Grums HC	Sweden-2	24	1	0	1	....	....	....	59	....	....	....	....	....	....	....	....	....	....	....	....	....	....	....	....	....	....
	Norway	WJC-B	7	0	2	2	....	....	....	14	....	....	....	....	....	....	....	....	....	....	....	....	....	....	....	....	....	....
	Norway	WC-A	6	1	0	1	....	....	....	6	....	....	....	....	....	....	....	....	....	....	....	....	....	....	....	....	....	....
1994-95	Laval Titan	QMJHL	64	14	50	64	....	....	....	173	....	....	....	....	....	....	....	....	....	....	20	4	10	14	68	....	....	....
	Norway	WJC-B	7	0	3	3	....	....	....	36	....	....	....	....	....	....	....	....	....	....	....	....	....	....	....	....	....	....
	Cornwall Aces	AHL	....	....	....	....	....	....	....	....	....	....	....	....	....	....	....	....	....	....	3	0	1	1	2	....	....	....
1995-96	**Colorado Avalanche**	**NHL**	**4**	**0**	**1**	**1**	**0**	**1**	**1**	**6**	**0**	**0**	**0**	**4**	**0.0**	**1**	**1**	**2**	**0**	**−2**	....	....	....	....	....	....	....	....
	Cornwall Aces	AHL	70	5	24	29	....	....	....	125	....	....	....	....	....	....	....	....	....	....	5	1	0	1	19	....	....	....
1996-97	Hershey Bears	AHL	20	0	3	3	....	....	....	16	....	....	....	....	....	....	....	....	....	....	....	....	....	....	....	....	....	....
	Boston Bruins	**NHL**	**9**	**0**	**2**	**2**	**0**	**2**	**2**	**4**	**0**	**0**	**0**	**8**	**0.0**	**9**	**1**	**9**	**0**	**−1**	....	....	....	....	....	....	....	....
	Providence Bruins	AHL	53	6	15	21	....	....	....	107	....	....	....	....	....	....	....	....	....	....	10	0	1	1	6	....	....	....
1997-98	Providence Bruins	AHL	75	4	21	25	....	....	....	91	....	....	....	....	....	....	....	....	....	....	....	....	....	....	....	....	....	....
1998-99	Djurgardens IF Stockholm	Sweden	29	3	4	7	....	....	....	52	....	....	....	....	....	....	....	....	....	....	....	....	....	....	....	....	....	....
	Djurgardens IF Stockholm	EuroHL	3	0	1	1	....	....	....	4	....	....	....	....	....	....	....	....	....	....	....	....	....	....	....	....	....	....
	AIK Solna Stockholm	Sweden	19	1	3	4	....	....	....	24	....	....	....	....	....	....	....	....	....	....	....	....	....	....	....	....	....	....
	Norway	WC-A	6	0	1	1	....	....	....	10	....	....	....	....	....	....	....	....	....	....	....	....	....	....	....	....	....	....
99-2000	AIK Solna Stockholm	Sweden	49	1	3	4	....	....	....	87	....	....	....	....	....	....	....	....	....	....	....	....	....	....	....	....	....	....
	NHL Totals		**13**	**0**	**3**	**3**	**0**	**3**	**3**	**10**	**0**	**0**	**0**	**12**	**0.0**	**10**	**2**	**11**	**0**		....	....	....	....	....	....	....	....

WJC-B All-Star Team (1993) • Named Best Defenseman at WJC-B (1993, 1994, 1995)

Rights transferred to **Colorado** after **Quebec** franchise relocated, June 21, 1995. Traded to **Boston** by **Colorado** with Landon Wilson for Boston's 1st round choice (Robyn Regehr) in 1998 Entry Draft, November 22, 1996.

• NABOKOV, Dmitri

C – R. 6'2", 209 lbs. b: Novosibirsk, USSR, 1/4/1977. Chicago's 1st, 19th overall, in 1995.

Season	Club	League	GP	G	A	Pts	AG	AA	APts	PIM	PP	SH	GW	S	%	TGF	PGF	TGA	PGA	+/-	GP	G	A	Pts	PIM	PP	SH	GW
1993-94	Krylja Sovetov Moscow	CIS	17	0	2	2	....	....	....	6	....	....	....	....	....	....	....	....	....	....	3	0	0	0	0	....	....	....
1994-95	Krylja Sovetov Moscow	CIS	49	15	12	27	....	....	....	32	....	....	....	....	....	....	....	....	....	....	4	5	0	5	6	....	....	....
1995-96	Krylja Sovetov Moscow	CIS	50	12	14	26	....	....	....	51	....	....	....	....	....	....	....	....	....	....	....	....	....	....	....	....	....	....
	Russia	WJC-A	7	3	5	8	....	....	....	4	....	....	....	....	....	....	....	....	....	....	....	....	....	....	....	....	....	....
1996-97	Krylja Sovetov Moscow	Russia	1	0	0	0	....	....	....	0	....	....	....	....	....	....	....	....	....	....	....	....	....	....	....	....	....	....
	Regina Pats	WHL	50	39	56	95	....	....	....	61	....	....	....	....	....	....	....	....	....	....	5	2	3	5	2	....	....	....
	Indianapolis Ice	IHL	2	0	0	0	....	....	....	0	....	....	....	....	....	....	....	....	....	....	....	....	....	....	....	....	....	....
1997-98	**Chicago Blackhawks**	**NHL**	**25**	**7**	**4**	**11**	**8**	**4**	**12**	**10**	**3**	**0**	**2**	**34**	**20.6**	**19**	**9**	**11**	**0**	**−1**	....	....	....	....	....	....	....	....
	Indianapolis Ice	IHL	46	6	15	21	....	....	....	16	....	....	....	....	....	....	....	....	....	....	5	2	1	3	0	....	....	....
1998-99	**New York Islanders**	**NHL**	**4**	**0**	**2**	**2**	**0**	**2**	**2**	**2**	**0**	**0**	**0**	**4**	**0.0**	**5**	**0**	**1**	**0**	**4**	....	....	....	....	....	....	....	....
	Lowell Lock Monsters	AHL	73	17	25	42	....	....	....	46	....	....	....	....	....	....	....	....	....	....	3	0	1	1	0	....	....	....
99-2000	**New York Islanders**	**NHL**	**26**	**4**	**7**	**11**	**4**	**6**	**10**	**16**	**0**	**0**	**0**	**40**	**10.0**	**20**	**10**	**18**	**0**	**−8**	....	....	....	....	....	....	....	....
	Lowell Lock Monsters	AHL	51	8	26	34	....	....	....	42	....	....	....	....	....	....	....	....	....	....	6	1	2	3	2	....	....	....
	NHL Totals		**55**	**11**	**13**	**24**	**12**	**12**	**24**	**28**	**3**	**0**	**2**	**78**	**14.1**	**44**	**19**	**30**	**0**		....	....	....	....	....	....	....	....

WHL East Second All-Star Team (1997)

Traded to **NY Islanders** by **Chicago** for Jean-Pierre Dumont and Chicago's 5th round choice (later traded to Philadelphia - Philadelphia selected Francis Belanger) in 1998 Entry Draft, June 1, 1998.

• NACHBAUR, Don

Donald Kenneth C – L. 6'2", 200 lbs. b: Kitimat, B.C., 1/30/1959. Hartford's 3rd, 60th overall, in 1979.

Season	Club	League	GP	G	A	Pts	AG	AA	APts	PIM	PP	SH	GW	S	%	TGF	PGF	TGA	PGA	+/-	GP	G	A	Pts	PIM	PP	SH	GW
1976-77	Merritt Centennials	BCJHL	54	22	27	49	....	....	....	31	....	....	....	....	....	....	....	....	....	....	....	....	....	....	....	....	....	....
1977-78	Billings Bighorns	WCJHL	68	23	27	50	....	....	....	128	....	....	....	....	....	....	....	....	....	....	20	*18	7	25	37	....	....	....
1978-79	Billings Bighorns	WHL	69	44	52	96	....	....	....	175	....	....	....	....	....	....	....	....	....	....	8	2	3	5	10	....	....	....
1979-80	Springfield Indians	AHL	70	12	17	29	....	....	....	119	....	....	....	....	....	....	....	....	....	....	....	....	....	....	....	....	....	....
1980-81	**Hartford Whalers**	**NHL**	**77**	**16**	**17**	**33**	**12**	**11**	**23**	**139**	**2**	**0**	**1**	**70**	**22.9**	**44**	**2**	**43**	**0**	**−1**	....	....	....	....	....	....	....	....
1981-82	**Hartford Whalers**	**NHL**	**77**	**5**	**21**	**26**	**4**	**14**	**18**	**117**	**0**	**0**	**0**	**113**	**4.4**	**35**	**5**	**63**	**12**	**−21**	....	....	....	....	....	....	....	....
1982-83	**Edmonton Oilers**	**NHL**	**4**	**0**	**0**	**0**	**0**	**0**	**0**	**17**	**0**	**0**	**0**	**0**	**0.0**	**2**	**0**	**3**	**0**	**−1**	**2**	**0**	**0**	**0**	**7**	**0**	**0**	**0**
	Moncton Alpines	AHL	70	33	32	65	....	....	....	125	....	....	....	....	....	....	....	....	....	....	....	....	....	....	....	....	....	....
1983-84	New Haven Nighthawks	AHL	70	33	32	65	....	....	....	194	....	....	....	....	....	....	....	....	....	....	....	....	....	....	....	....	....	....
1984-85	Hershey Bears	AHL	7	2	3	5	....	....	....	21	....	....	....	....	....	....	....	....	....	....	....	....	....	....	....	....	....	....
1985-86	**Philadelphia Flyers**	**NHL**	**5**	**1**	**1**	**2**	**1**	**1**	**2**	**7**	**0**	**0**	**0**	**4**	**25.0**	**3**	**0**	**0**	**0**	**3**	....	....	....	....	....	....	....	....
	Hershey Bears	AHL	74	23	24	47	....	....	....	301	....	....	....	....	....	....	....	....	....	....	18	5	4	9	70	....	....	....
1986-87	**Philadelphia Flyers**	**NHL**	**23**	**0**	**2**	**2**	**0**	**1**	**1**	**87**	**0**	**0**	**0**	**12**	**0.0**	**4**	**0**	**3**	**0**	**1**	**7**	**1**	**1**	**2**	**15**	**0**	**0**	**1**
	Hershey Bears	AHL	57	18	17	35	....	....	....	274	....	....	....	....	....	....	....	....	....	....	5	0	3	3	47	....	....	....
1987-88	**Philadelphia Flyers**	**NHL**	**20**	**0**	**4**	**4**	**0**	**3**	**3**	**61**	**0**	**0**	**0**	**11**	**0.0**	**5**	**0**	**3**	**0**	**2**	**2**	**0**	**0**	**0**	**2**	**0**	**0**	**0**
	Hershey Bears	AHL	42	19	21	40	....	....	....	174	....	....	....	....	....	....	....	....	....	....	8	4	3	7	47	....	....	....
1988-89	**Philadelphia Flyers**	**NHL**	**15**	**1**	**0**	**1**	**1**	**0**	**1**	**37**	**0**	**0**	**0**	**10**	**10.0**	**2**	**0**	**3**	**0**	**−1**	....	....	....	....	....	....	....	....
	Hershey Bears	AHL	49	24	31	55	....	....	....	172	....	....	....	....	....	....	....	....	....	....	12	0	5	5	58	....	....	....
1989-90	**Philadelphia Flyers**	**NHL**	**2**	**0**	**1**	**1**	**0**	**1**	**1**	**0**	**0**	**0**	**0**	**0**	**0.0**	**1**	**0**	**0**	**0**	**1**	....	....	....	....	....	....	....	....
	Hershey Bears	AHL	30	10	9	19	....	....	....	72	....	....	....	....	....	....	....	....	....	....	....	....	....	....	....	....	....	....
1990-91	EC Graz	Austria	33	18	25	43	....	....	....	9	....	....	....	....	....	....	....	....	....	....	....	....	....	....	....	....	....	....

			REGULAR SEASON																		PLAYOFFS							
Season	Club	League	GP	G	A	Pts	AG	AA	APts	PIM	PP	SH	GW	S	%	TGF	PGF	TGA	PGA	+/-	GP	G	A	Pts	PIM	PP	SH	GW
1991-92	EC Graz	Austria	44	32	29	61	....	....	....	*197	....	....	....	....	....	....	....	....	....	....	....	....	....	....	....	....	....	....
1992-93	EC Graz	Austria	53	35	29	64	....	....	....	....	....	....	....	....	....	....	....	....	....	....	....	....	....	....	....	....	....	....
1993-94	EC Graz	Austria	52	21	20	41	....	....	....	....	....	....	....	....	....	....	....	....	....	....	....	....	....	....	....	....	....	....
	NHL Totals		**223**	**23**	**46**	**69**	**18**	**31**	**49**	**465**	**2**	**0**	**1**	**220**	**10.5**	**96**	**7**	**118**	**12**		**11**	**1**	**1**	**2**	**24**	**0**	**0**	**1**

Traded to **Edmonton** by **Hartford** with Ken Linseman for Risto Siltanen and the rights to Brent Loney, August 19, 1982. Claimed by **LA Kings** from **Edmonton** in Waiver Draft, October 3, 1983. Signed as a free agent by **Philadelphia**, October 4, 1984.

• NAGY, Ladislav

C – L. 5'11", 183 lbs. b: Saca, Czech., 6/1/1979. St. Louis' 6th, 177th overall, in 1997.

Season	Club	League	GP	G	A	Pts	AG	AA	APts	PIM	PP	SH	GW	S	%	TGF	PGF	TGA	PGA	+/-	GP	G	A	Pts	PIM	PP	SH	GW
1996-97	HC Kosice	Slovakia-Jr.	45	29	30	59	....	....	....	105	....	....	....	....	....	....	....	....	....	....	....	....	....	....	....	....	....	....
	Dragon Presov	Slovakia-2	11	6	5	11	....	....	....	....	....	....	....	....	....	....	....	....	....	....	....	....	....	....	....	....	....	....
1997-98	HC Kosice	Slovakia	29	19	15	34	....	....	....	41	....	....	....	....	....	....	....	....	....	....	11	2	4	6	6	....	....	....
1998-99	Halifax Mooseheads	QMJHL	63	71	55	126	....	....	....	148	....	....	....	....	....	....	....	....	....	....	5	3	3	6	18	....	....	....
	Worcester IceCats	AHL	....	....	....	....	....	....	....	....	....	....	....	....	....	....	....	....	....	....	3	2	2	4	0	....	....	....
	Slovakia	WJC-A	6	4	3	7	....	....	....	6	....	....	....	....	....	....	....	....	....	....	....	....	....	....	....	....	....	....
99-2000	**St. Louis Blues**	**NHL**	**11**	**2**	**4**	**6**	**2**	**4**	**6**	**2**	**1**	**0**	**0**	**15**	**13.3**	**8**	**3**	**3**	**0**	**2**	**6**	**1**	**1**	**2**	**0**	**0**	**0**	**0**
	Worcester IceCats	AHL	69	23	28	51	....	....	....	67	....	....	....	....	....	....	....	....	....	....	2	1	0	1	0	....	....	....
	NHL Totals		**11**	**2**	**4**	**6**	**2**	**4**	**6**	**2**	**1**	**0**	**0**	**15**	**13.3**	**8**	**3**	**3**	**0**		**6**	**1**	**1**	**2**	**0**	**0**	**0**	**0**

• NAHRGANG, Jim

James Herbert D – R. 6', 185 lbs. b: Millbank, Ont., 4/17/1951. Detroit's 7th, 86th overall, in 1971.

Season	Club	League	GP	G	A	Pts	AG	AA	APts	PIM	PP	SH	GW	S	%	TGF	PGF	TGA	PGA	+/-	GP	G	A	Pts	PIM	PP	SH	GW
1966-67	New Hamburg Hahns	OHA-C	STATISTICS NOT AVAILABLE																									
1967-68	Ottawa 67's	OHA-Jr.	52	1	9	10	....	....	....	74	....	....	....	....	....	....	....	....	....	....	....	....	....	....	....	....	....	....
1968-69	Ottawa 67's	OHA-Jr.	52	1	7	8	....	....	....	47	....	....	....	....	....	....	....	....	....	....	7	0	0	0	2	....	....	....
1969-70	Kitchener Rangers	OHA-Jr.	51	10	23	33	....	....	....	119	....	....	....	....	....	....	....	....	....	....	6	0	2	2	10	....	....	....
1970-71	Michigan Tech Huskies	WCHA	31	6	13	19	....	....	....	70	....	....	....	....	....	....	....	....	....	....	....	....	....	....	....	....	....	....
1971-72	Michigan Tech Huskies	WCHA	31	8	18	26	....	....	....	66	....	....	....	....	....	....	....	....	....	....	....	....	....	....	....	....	....	....
1972-73	Michigan Tech Huskies	WCHA	36	11	16	27	....	....	....	85	....	....	....	....	....	....	....	....	....	....	....	....	....	....	....	....	....	....
1973-74	Michigan Tech Huskies	WCHA	39	8	24	32	....	....	....	95	....	....	....	....	....	....	....	....	....	....	....	....	....	....	....	....	....	....
1974-75	**Detroit Red Wings**	**NHL**	**1**	**0**	**0**	**0**	**0**	**0**	**0**	**0**	**0**	**0**	**0**	**2**	**0.0**	**0**	**0**	**0**	**0**	**0**	....	....	....	....	....	....	....	....
	Virginia Wings	AHL	71	4	19	23	....	....	....	73	....	....	....	....	....	....	....	....	....	....	5	0	3	3	2	....	....	....
1975-76	**Detroit Red Wings**	**NHL**	**3**	**0**	**1**	**1**	**0**	**1**	**1**	**0**	**0**	**0**	**0**	**2**	**0.0**	**1**	**0**	**7**	**1**	**–5**	....	....	....	....	....	....	....	....
	New Haven Nighthawks	AHL	49	4	11	15	....	....	....	74	....	....	....	....	....	....	....	....	....	....	....	....	....	....	....	....	....	....
1976-77	**Detroit Red Wings**	**NHL**	**53**	**5**	**11**	**16**	**4**	**8**	**12**	**34**	**3**	**1**	**1**	**96**	**5.2**	**40**	**8**	**52**	**8**	**–12**	....	....	....	....	....	....	....	....
	Kansas City Blues	CHL	16	2	6	8	....	....	....	38	....	....	....	....	....	....	....	....	....	....	10	0	4	4	26	....	....	....
1977-78	Kansas City Red Wings	CHL	9	0	3	3	....	....	....	13	....	....	....	....	....	....	....	....	....	....	....	....	....	....	....	....	....	....
	Philadelphia Firebirds	AHL	69	8	22	30	....	....	....	147	....	....	....	....	....	....	....	....	....	....	4	0	1	1	4	....	....	....
	NHL Totals		**57**	**5**	**12**	**17**	**4**	**9**	**13**	**34**	**3**	**1**	**1**	**100**	**5.0**	**41**	**8**	**59**	**9**		....	....	....	....	....	....	....	....

WCHA Second All-Star Team (1973) • WCHA First All-Star Team (1974) • NCAA West First All-American Team (1974) • NCAA Championship All-Tournament Team (1974)

• NAMESTNIKOV, John

John Yevgeny D – R. 5'11", 190 lbs. b: Arzamis-Ig, USSR, 10/9/1971. Vancouver's 5th, 117th overall, in 1991.

Season	Club	League	GP	G	A	Pts	AG	AA	APts	PIM	PP	SH	GW	S	%	TGF	PGF	TGA	PGA	+/-	GP	G	A	Pts	PIM	PP	SH	GW
1988-89	Torpedo Gorky	USSR	2	0	0	0	....	....	....	2	....	....	....	....	....	....	....	....	....	....	....	....	....	....	....	....	....	....
	Soviet Union	EJC-A	6	0	1	1	....	....	....	6	....	....	....	....	....	....	....	....	....	....	....	....	....	....	....	....	....	....
1989-90	Torpedo Gorky	USSR	23	0	0	0	....	....	....	25	....	....	....	....	....	....	....	....	....	....	....	....	....	....	....	....	....	....
	Soviet Union	WJC-A	7	0	1	1	....	....	....	6	....	....	....	....	....	....	....	....	....	....	....	....	....	....	....	....	....	....
1990-91	Torpedo Nizhny	USSR	42	1	2	3	....	....	....	49	....	....	....	....	....	....	....	....	....	....	....	....	....	....	....	....	....	....
1991-92	CSKA Moscow	CIS	42	1	1	2	....	....	....	47	....	....	....	....	....	....	....	....	....	....	....	....	....	....	....	....	....	....
1992-93	CSKA Moscow	CIS	42	5	5	10	....	....	....	68	....	....	....	....	....	....	....	....	....	....	....	....	....	....	....	....	....	....
1993-94	**Vancouver Canucks**	**NHL**	**17**	**0**	**5**	**5**	**0**	**4**	**4**	**10**	**0**	**0**	**0**	**11**	**0.0**	**13**	**2**	**15**	**2**	**–2**	....	....	....	....	....	....	....	....
	Hamilton Canucks	AHL	59	7	27	34	....	....	....	97	....	....	....	....	....	....	....	....	....	....	4	0	2	2	19	....	....	....
1994-95	Syracuse Crunch	AHL	59	11	22	33	....	....	....	59	....	....	....	....	....	....	....	....	....	....	....	....	....	....	....	....	....	....
	Vancouver Canucks	**NHL**	**16**	**0**	**3**	**3**	**0**	**4**	**4**	**4**	**0**	**0**	**0**	**18**	**0.0**	**12**	**3**	**9**	**2**	**2**	**1**	**0**	**0**	**0**	**2**	**0**	**0**	**0**
1995-96	Syracuse Crunch	AHL	59	13	34	47	....	....	....	85	....	....	....	....	....	....	....	....	....	....	15	1	8	9	16	....	....	....
	Vancouver Canucks	**NHL**	....	....	....	....	....	....	....	....	....	....	....	....	....	....	....	....	....	....	**1**	**0**	**0**	**0**	**0**	**0**	**0**	**0**
1996-97	**Vancouver Canucks**	**NHL**	**2**	**0**	**0**	**0**	**0**	**0**	**0**	**4**	**0**	**0**	**0**	**1**	**0.0**	**0**	**0**	**1**	**0**	**–1**	....	....	....	....	....	....	....	....
	Syracuse Crunch	AHL	55	9	37	46	....	....	....	73	....	....	....	....	....	....	....	....	....	....	3	2	0	2	0	....	....	....
1997-98	**New York Islanders**	**NHL**	**6**	**0**	**1**	**1**	**0**	**1**	**1**	**4**	**0**	**0**	**0**	**2**	**0.0**	**4**	**2**	**3**	**0**	**–1**	....	....	....	....	....	....	....	....
	Utah Grizzlies	IHL	62	6	19	25	....	....	....	48	....	....	....	....	....	....	....	....	....	....	4	1	0	1	2	....	....	....
1998-99	Lowell Lock Monsters	AHL	42	12	14	26	....	....	....	42	....	....	....	....	....	....	....	....	....	....	....	....	....	....	....	....	....	....
99-2000	Hartford Wolf Pack	AHL	33	1	9	10	....	....	....	14	....	....	....	....	....	....	....	....	....	....	....	....	....	....	....	....	....	....
	Nashville Predators	**NHL**	**2**	**0**	**0**	**0**	**0**	**0**	**0**	**2**	**0**	**0**	**0**	**3**	**0.0**	....	....	....	....	....	....	....	....	....	....	....	....	....
	Milwaukee Admirals	IHL	12	2	3	5	....	....	....	17	....	....	....	....	....	....	....	....	....	....	3	0	0	0	0	....	....	....
	NHL Totals		**43**	**0**	**9**	**9**	**0**	**9**	**9**	**24**	**0**	**0**	**0**	**35**	**0.0**	**29**	**7**	**28**	**4**		**2**	**0**	**0**	**0**	**2**	**0**	**0**	**0**

Signed as a free agent by **NY Islanders**, July 21, 1997. Signed as a free agent by **NY Rangers**, August 9, 1999. Traded to **Nashville** by **NY Rangers** for Jason Dawe, February 3, 2000.

• NANNE, Lou

Louis Vincent "Sweet Lou from the Soo" D/RW – R. 6'1", 185 lbs. b: Sault Ste. Marie, Ont., 6/2/1941.

Season	Club	League	GP	G	A	Pts	AG	AA	APts	PIM	PP	SH	GW	S	%	TGF	PGF	TGA	PGA	+/-	GP	G	A	Pts	PIM	PP	SH	GW
1960-61	University of Minnesota	WCHA	30	4	12	16	....	....	....	52	....	....	....	....	....	....	....	....	....	....	....	....	....	....	....	....	....	....
1961-62	University of Minnesota	WCHA	22	4	11	15	....	....	....	37	....	....	....	....	....	....	....	....	....	....	....	....	....	....	....	....	....	....
1962-63	University of Minnesota	WCHA	29	14	29	*43	....	....	....	30	....	....	....	....	....	....	....	....	....	....	....	....	....	....	....	....	....	....
1963-64	Rochester Mustangs	USHL	STATISTICS NOT AVAILABLE																									
1964-65	Rochester Mustangs	USHL	STATISTICS NOT AVAILABLE																									
1965-66	Rochester Mustangs	USHL	25	23	22	45	....	....	....	4	....	....	....	....	....	....	....	....	....	....	....	....	....	....	....	....	....	....
1966-67	Rochester Mustangs	USHL	24	11	12	23	....	....	....	8	....	....	....	....	....	....	....	....	....	....	....	....	....	....	....	....	....	....
1967-68	United States	Nat-Team	....	....	....	....	....	....	....	....	....	....	....	....	....	....	....	....	....	....	....	....	....	....	....	....	....	....
	United States	Olympics	7	2	2	4	....	....	....	12	....	....	....	....	....	....	....	....	....	....	....	....	....	....	....	....	....	....
	Minnesota North Stars	**NHL**	**2**	**0**	**1**	**1**	**0**	**1**	**1**	**0**	**0**	**0**	**0**	**0**	**0.0**	**1**	**0**	**1**	**0**	**0**	....	....	....	....	....	....	....	....
1968-69	**Minnesota North Stars**	**NHL**	**41**	**2**	**12**	**14**	**2**	**11**	**13**	**47**	**1**	**1**	**0**	**71**	**2.8**	**51**	**10**	**59**	**9**	**–9**	....	....	....	....	....	....	....	....
	Memphis South Stars	CHL	3	0	1	1	....	....	....	0	....	....	....	....	....	....	....	....	....	....	....	....	....	....	....	....	....	....
	Cleveland Barons	AHL	10	1	2	3	....	....	....	8	....	....	....	....	....	....	....	....	....	....	....	....	....	....	....	....	....	....
1969-70	**Minnesota North Stars**	**NHL**	**74**	**3**	**20**	**23**	**3**	**19**	**22**	**75**	**1**	**0**	**0**	**96**	**3.1**	**66**	**13**	**75**	**14**	**–8**	**5**	**0**	**2**	**2**	**2**	**0**	**0**	**0**
1970-71	**Minnesota North Stars**	**NHL**	**68**	**5**	**11**	**16**	**5**	**9**	**14**	**22**	**0**	**0**	**0**	**61**	**8.2**	**34**	**2**	**49**	**11**	**–6**	**12**	**3**	**6**	**9**	**4**	**0**	**0**	**2**
1971-72	**Minnesota North Stars**	**NHL**	**78**	**21**	**28**	**49**	**21**	**24**	**45**	**27**	**7**	**0**	**6**	**154**	**13.6**	**68**	**21**	**52**	**0**	**–5**	**7**	**0**	**0**	**0**	**0**	**0**	**0**	**0**
1972-73	**Minnesota North Stars**	**NHL**	**74**	**15**	**20**	**35**	**14**	**16**	**30**	**39**	**2**	**0**	**2**	**142**	**10.6**	**68**	**12**	**38**	**1**	**19**	**6**	**1**	**2**	**3**	**0**	**0**	**0**	**0**
1973-74	**Minnesota North Stars**	**NHL**	**76**	**11**	**21**	**32**	**11**	**17**	**28**	**46**	**2**	**0**	**2**	**139**	**7.9**	**90**	**14**	**90**	**13**	**–1**	....	....	....	....	....	....	....	....
1974-75	**Minnesota North Stars**	**NHL**	**49**	**6**	**9**	**15**	**5**	**7**	**12**	**35**	**1**	**0**	**0**	**49**	**12.2**	**43**	**9**	**65**	**7**	**–24**	....	....	....	....	....	....	....	....
1975-76	**Minnesota North Stars**	**NHL**	**79**	**3**	**14**	**17**	**3**	**10**	**13**	**45**	**2**	**0**	**0**	**83**	**3.6**	**53**	**18**	**101**	**32**	**–34**	....	....	....	....	....	....	....	....
	United States	WEC-A	10	1	3	4	....	....	....	26	....	....	....	....	....	....	....	....	....	....	....	....	....	....	....	....	....	....
1976-77	United States	Can-Cup	5	0	2	2	....	....	....	6	....	....	....	....	....	....	....	....	....	....	....	....	....	....	....	....	....	....
	Minnesota North Stars	**NHL**	**68**	**2**	**20**	**22**	**2**	**15**	**17**	**12**	**2**	**0**	**0**	**69**	**2.9**	**74**	**27**	**82**	**11**	**–24**	**2**	**0**	**0**	**0**	**2**	**0**	**0**	**0**
	United States	WEC-A	10	2	2	4	....	....	....	19	....	....	....	....	....	....	....	....	....	....	....	....	....	....	....	....	....	....
1977-78	**Minnesota North Stars**	**NHL**	**26**	**0**	**1**	**1**	**0**	**1**	**1**	**8**	**0**	**0**	**0**	**22**	**0.0**	**14**	**3**	**32**	**7**	**–14**	....	....	....	....	....	....	....	....
	NHL Totals		**635**	**68**	**157**	**225**	**66**	**130**	**196**	**356**	**18**	**1**	**10**	**886**	**7.7**	**562**	**129**	**644**	**105**		**32**	**4**	**10**	**14**	**8**	**0**	**0**	**2**

WCHA First All-Star Team (1963) • NCAA West First All-American Team (1963) • Won Lester Patrick Trophy (1989)

• Played weekend games for Rochester (USHL) during 1963-1965 seasons. Signed as a free agent by **Minnesota**, March, 1968.

• NANTAIS, Rich

Rich Francois LW – L. 5'11", 188 lbs. b: Repentigny, Que., 10/27/1954. Minnesota's 2nd, 24th overall, in 1974.

Season	Club	League	GP	G	A	Pts	AG	AA	APts	PIM	PP	SH	GW	S	%	TGF	PGF	TGA	PGA	+/–	GP	G	A	Pts	PIM	PP	SH	GW
			REGULAR SEASON																		PLAYOFFS							
1970-71	Quebec Remaprts	QJHL	5	0	0	0	....	....	....	2	....	....	....	....	....	....	....	....	....	....	7	0	0	0	2	....	....	....
1971-72	Quebec Remparts	QMJHL	62	25	46	71	....	....	....	*283	....	....	....	....	....	....	....	....	....	....	15	8	12	20	34	....	....	....
1972-73	Quebec Remparts	QMJHL	59	21	27	48	....	....	....	165	....	....	....	....	....	....	....	....	....	....	....	....	....	....	....	....	....	....
	Quebec Remaprts	Mem-Cup	3	2	0	2	....	....	....	2	....	....	....	....	....	....	....	....	....	....	....	....	....	....	....	....	....	....
1973-74	Quebec Remparts	QMJHL	67	64	130	194	....	....	....	213	....	....	....	....	....	....	....	....	....	....	....	....	....	....	....	....	....	....
	Quebec Remaprts	Mem-Cup	4	1	3	4	....	....	....	12	....	....	....	....	....	....	....	....	....	....	....	....	....	....	....	....	....	....
1974-75	**Minnesota North Stars**	**NHL**	**18**	**4**	**1**	**5**	**3**	**1**	**4**	**9**	**0**	**0**	**1**	**13**	**30.8**	**7**	**0**	**6**	**0**	**1**	....	....	....	....	....	....	....	....
	New Haven Nighthawks	AHL	47	21	12	33	....	....	....	145	....	....	....	....	....	....	....	....	....	....	16	3	3	6	44	....	....	....
1975-76	**Minnesota North Stars**	**NHL**	**5**	**0**	**0**	**0**	**0**	**0**	**0**	**17**	**0**	**0**	**0**	**2**	**0.0**	**1**	**1**	**1**	**0**	**–1**	....	....	....	....	....	....	....	....
	New Haven Nighthawks	AHL	38	8	6	14	....	....	....	79	....	....	....	....	....	....	....	....	....	....	....	....	....	....	....	....	....	....
	Springfield Indians	AHL	3	0	1	1	....	....	....	4	....	....	....	....	....	....	....	....	....	....	....	....	....	....	....	....	....	....
	Richmond Robins	AHL	21	3	4	7	....	....	....	39	....	....	....	....	....	....	....	....	....	....	8	2	4	6	*33	....	....	....
1976-77	**Minnesota North Stars**	**NHL**	**40**	**1**	**3**	**4**	**1**	**2**	**3**	**53**	**0**	**0**	**0**	**23**	**4.3**	**9**	**1**	**16**	**0**	**–8**	....	....	....	....	....	....	....	....
1977-78	Fort Worth Texans	CHL	60	11	18	29	....	....	....	197	....	....	....	....	....	....	....	....	....	....	13	3	1	4	*49	....	....	....
	NHL Totals		**63**	**5**	**4**	**9**	**4**	**3**	**7**	**79**	**0**	**0**	**1**	**38**	**13.2**	**17**	**2**	**23**	**0**		....	....	....	....	....	....	....	....

Traded to **Washington** by **New Haven** (AHL) with Alain Langlais for Ron H. Anderson and Bob Gryp, February 23, 1976. Signed as a free agent by **Minnesota**, September, 1976.

• NAPIER, Mark

Mark Robert RW – L. 5'10", 182 lbs. b: Toronto, Ont., 1/28/1957. Montreal's 1st, 10th overall, in 1977.

Season	Club	League	GP	G	A	Pts	AG	AA	APts	PIM	PP	SH	GW	S	%	TGF	PGF	TGA	PGA	+/–	GP	G	A	Pts	PIM	PP	SH	GW
1972-73	Wexford Raiders	OHA-B	44	41	27	68	....	....	....	201	....	....	....	....	....	....	....	....	....	....	....	....	....	....	....	....	....	....
1973-74	Toronto Marlboros	OMJHL	70	47	46	93	....	....	....	63	....	....	....	....	....	....	....	....	....	....	....	....	....	....	....	....	....	....
1974-75	Toronto Marlboros	OMJHL	61	66	64	130	....	....	....	106	....	....	....	....	....	....	....	....	....	....	23	*24	24	*48	13	....	....	....
	Toronto Marlboros	Mem-Cup	4	4	4	8	....	....	....	4	....	....	....	....	....	....	....	....	....	....	....	....	....	....	....	....	....	....
1975-76	Toronto Toros	WHA	78	43	50	93	....	....	....	20	....	....	....	....	....	....	....	....	....	....	....	....	....	....	....	....	....	....
1976-77	Birmingham Bulls	WHA	80	60	36	96	....	....	....	24	....	....	....	....	....	....	....	....	....	....	....	....	....	....	....	....	....	....
1977-78	Birmingham Bulls	WHA	79	33	32	65	....	....	....	9	....	....	....	....	....	....	....	....	....	....	5	0	2	2	14	....	....	....
1978-79♦	**Montreal Canadiens**	**NHL**	**54**	**11**	**20**	**31**	**9**	**14**	**23**	**11**	**2**	**0**	**0**	**73**	**15.1**	**53**	**17**	**20**	**1**	**17**	**12**	**3**	**2**	**5**	**2**	**0**	**0**	**0**
1979-80	**Montreal Canadiens**	**NHL**	**76**	**16**	**33**	**49**	**14**	**24**	**38**	**7**	**4**	**0**	**1**	**123**	**13.0**	**75**	**25**	**40**	**1**	**11**	**10**	**2**	**6**	**8**	**0**	**1**	**0**	**0**
1980-81	**Montreal Canadiens**	**NHL**	**79**	**35**	**36**	**71**	**27**	**24**	**51**	**24**	**5**	**0**	**6**	**185**	**18.9**	**105**	**24**	**48**	**1**	**34**	**3**	**0**	**0**	**0**	**2**	**0**	**0**	**0**
1981-82	**Montreal Canadiens**	**NHL**	**80**	**40**	**41**	**81**	**32**	**27**	**59**	**14**	**9**	**0**	**5**	**186**	**21.5**	**105**	**20**	**39**	**3**	**49**	**5**	**3**	**2**	**5**	**0**	**1**	**1**	**1**
	Canada	WEC-A	9	3	1	4	....	....	....	0	....	....	....	....	....	....	....	....	....	....	....	....	....	....	....	....	....	....
1982-83	**Montreal Canadiens**	**NHL**	**73**	**40**	**27**	**67**	**33**	**19**	**52**	**6**	**3**	**0**	**6**	**171**	**23.4**	**82**	**11**	**51**	**0**	**20**	**3**	**0**	**0**	**0**	**0**	**0**	**0**	**0**
1983-84	**Montreal Canadiens**	**NHL**	**5**	**3**	**2**	**5**	**2**	**1**	**3**	**0**	**0**	**0**	**1**	**11**	**27.3**	**7**	**1**	**6**	**0**	**0**	....	....	....	....	....	....	....	....
	Minnesota North Stars	**NHL**	**58**	**13**	**28**	**41**	**10**	**19**	**29**	**17**	**0**	**0**	**1**	**83**	**15.7**	**55**	**14**	**41**	**2**	**2**	**12**	**3**	**2**	**5**	**0**	**3**	**0**	**0**
1984-85	**Minnesota North Stars**	**NHL**	**39**	**10**	**18**	**28**	**8**	**12**	**20**	**2**	**3**	**1**	**1**	**97**	**10.3**	**43**	**16**	**39**	**6**	**–6**	....	....	....	....	....	....	....	....
♦	**Edmonton Oilers**	**NHL**	**33**	**9**	**26**	**35**	**7**	**18**	**25**	**19**	**3**	**0**	**0**	**50**	**18.0**	**53**	**12**	**29**	**0**	**12**	**18**	**5**	**5**	**10**	**7**	**1**	**0**	**0**
1985-86	**Edmonton Oilers**	**NHL**	**80**	**24**	**32**	**56**	**19**	**22**	**41**	**14**	**3**	**1**	**4**	**117**	**20.5**	**73**	**7**	**54**	**1**	**13**	**10**	**1**	**4**	**5**	**0**	**0**	**0**	**0**
1986-87	**Edmonton Oilers**	**NHL**	**62**	**8**	**13**	**21**	**7**	**9**	**16**	**2**	**0**	**1**	**0**	**88**	**9.1**	**29**	**1**	**35**	**10**	**3**	....	....	....	....	....	....	....	....
	Buffalo Sabres	**NHL**	**15**	**5**	**5**	**10**	**4**	**4**	**8**	**0**	**1**	**0**	**0**	**40**	**12.5**	**16**	**7**	**23**	**9**	**–5**	....	....	....	....	....	....	....	....
1987-88	**Buffalo Sabres**	**NHL**	**47**	**10**	**8**	**18**	**9**	**6**	**15**	**8**	**0**	**1**	**2**	**81**	**12.3**	**27**	**0**	**48**	**18**	**–3**	**6**	**0**	**3**	**3**	**0**	**0**	**0**	**0**
1988-89	**Buffalo Sabres**	**NHL**	**66**	**11**	**17**	**28**	**9**	**12**	**21**	**33**	**0**	**2**	**1**	**92**	**12.0**	**40**	**0**	**68**	**25**	**–3**	**3**	**1**	**0**	**1**	**0**	**0**	**0**	**0**
1989-90	HC Bolzano	Italy	36	68	72	140	....	....	....	6	....	....	....	....	....	....	....	....	....	....	6	8	6	14	2	....	....	....
1990-91	HC Varese	Italy	36	*45	*73	*118	....	....	....	4	....	....	....	....	....	....	....	....	....	....	10	8	18	26	0	....	....	....
1991-92	HC Milano Devils	Alpenliga	20	29	13	42	....	....	....	4	....	....	....	....	....	....	....	....	....	....	....	....	....	....	....	....	....	....
	HC Milano Devils	Italy	11	11	14	25	....	....	....	0	....	....	....	....	....	....	....	....	....	....	12	15	13	28	0	....	....	....
	Canada	Nat-Team	2	1	0	1	....	....	....	0	....	....	....	....	....	....	....	....	....	....	....	....	....	....	....	....	....	....
1992-93	HC Milano Devils	Alpenliga	27	19	19	38	....	....	....	4	....	....	....	....	....	....	....	....	....	....	....	....	....	....	....	....	....	....
	HC Milano Devils	Italy	16	13	23	36	....	....	....	2	....	....	....	....	....	....	....	....	....	....	11	6	9	15	0	....	....	....
	NHL Totals		**767**	**235**	**306**	**541**	**190**	**211**	**401**	**157**	**33**	**6**	**28**	**1397**	**16.8**	**763**	**155**	**541**	**77**		**82**	**18**	**24**	**42**	**11**	**6**	**1**	**1**
	Other Major League Totals		237	136	118	254	....	....	....	53	....	....	....	....	....	....	....	....	....	....	5	0	2	2	14	....	....	....

OMJHL First All-Star Team (1975) • Won Lou Kaplan Trophy (WHA Rookie of the Year) (1976)

Signed as an underage free agent by **Toronto** (WHA), May, 1975. Transferred to **Birmingham** (WHA) after **Toronto** (WHA) franchise relocated, June 30, 1976. Traded to **Minnesota** by **Montreal** with Keith Acton and Toronto's 3rd round choice (previously acquired, Minnesota selected Ken Hodge Jr.) in 1984 Entry Draft for Bobby Smith, October 28, 1983. Traded to **Edmonton** by **Minnesota** for Gord Sherven and Terry Martin, January 24, 1985. Traded to **Buffalo** by **Edmonton** with Lee Fogolin and Edmonton's 4th round choice (John Bradley) in 1987 Entry Draft for Normand Lacombe, Wayne Van Dorp and Buffalo's 4th round choice (Peter Ericksson) in 1987 Entry Draft, March 6, 1987.

• NASH, Tyson

Tyson Scott LW – L. 6', 185 lbs. b: Edmonton, Alta., 3/11/1975. Vancouver's 10th, 247th overall, in 1994.

Season	Club	League	GP	G	A	Pts	AG	AA	APts	PIM	PP	SH	GW	S	%	TGF	PGF	TGA	PGA	+/–	GP	G	A	Pts	PIM	PP	SH	GW
1990-91	Sherwood Park Crusaders	AAHA	40	17	28	43	....	....	....	63	....	....	....	....	....	....	....	....	....	....	....	....	....	....	....	....	....	....
1991-92	Kamloops Blazers	WHL	33	1	6	7	....	....	....	62	....	....	....	....	....	....	....	....	....	....	4	0	0	0	0	....	....	....
	Kamloops Blazers	Mem-Cup	1	0	0	0	....	....	....	0	....	....	....	....	....	....	....	....	....	....	....	....	....	....	....	....	....	....
1992-93	Kamloops Blazers	WHL	61	10	16	26	....	....	....	78	....	....	....	....	....	....	....	....	....	....	13	3	2	5	32	....	....	....
1993-94	Kamloops Blazers	WHL	65	20	36	56	....	....	....	135	....	....	....	....	....	....	....	....	....	....	16	3	4	7	12	....	....	....
	Kamloops Blazers	Mem-Cup	4	1	3	4	....	....	....	6	....	....	....	....	....	....	....	....	....	....	....	....	....	....	....	....	....	....
1994-95	Kamloops Blazers	WHL	63	34	41	75	....	....	....	70	....	....	....	....	....	....	....	....	....	....	21	10	7	17	30	....	....	....
	Kamloops Blazers	Mem-Cup	4	2	4	6	....	....	....	8	....	....	....	....	....	....	....	....	....	....	....	....	....	....	....	....	....	....
1995-96	Syracuse Crunch	AHL	50	4	7	11	....	....	....	58	....	....	....	....	....	....	....	....	....	....	4	0	0	0	11	....	....	....
	Raleigh IceCaps	ECHL	6	1	1	2	....	....	....	8	....	....	....	....	....	....	....	....	....	....	....	....	....	....	....	....	....	....
1996-97	Syracuse Crunch	AHL	77	17	17	34	....	....	....	105	....	....	....	....	....	....	....	....	....	....	3	0	2	2	0	....	....	....
1997-98	Syracuse Crunch	AHL	74	20	20	40	....	....	....	184	....	....	....	....	....	....	....	....	....	....	5	0	2	2	28	....	....	....
1998-99	**St. Louis Blues**	**NHL**	**2**	**0**	**0**	**0**	**0**	**0**	**0**	**5**	**0**	**0**	**0**	**1**	**0.0**	**0**	**0**	**1**	**0**	**–1**	**1**	**0**	**0**	**0**	**2**	**0**	**0**	**0**
	Worcester IceCats	AHL	55	14	22	36	....	....	....	143	....	....	....	....	....	....	....	....	....	....	4	4	1	5	27	....	....	....
99-2000	**St. Louis Blues**	**NHL**	**66**	**4**	**9**	**13**	**4**	**8**	**12**	**150**	**0**	**1**	**1**	**68**	**5.9**	**20**	**1**	**13**	**0**	**6**	**6**	**1**	**0**	**1**	**24**	**0**	**0**	**0**
	NHL Totals		**68**	**4**	**9**	**13**	**4**	**8**	**12**	**155**	**0**	**1**	**1**	**69**	**5.8**	**20**	**1**	**14**	**0**		**7**	**1**	**0**	**1**	**26**	**0**	**0**	**0**

Signed as a free agent by **St. Louis**, July 14, 1998.

• NASLUND, Markus

RW – L. 5'11", 195 lbs. b: Ornskoldsvik, Sweden, 7/30/1973. Pittsburgh's 1st, 16th overall, in 1991.

Season	Club	League	GP	G	A	Pts	AG	AA	APts	PIM	PP	SH	GW	S	%	TGF	PGF	TGA	PGA	+/–	GP	G	A	Pts	PIM	PP	SH	GW
1988-89	Ornskoldsviks IF	Sweden-3	14	7	6	13	....	....	....	....	....	....	....	....	....	....	....	....	....	....	....	....	....	....	....	....	....	....
1989-90	MoDo AIK	Sweden-Jr.	33	43	35	78	....	....	....	20	....	....	....	....	....	....	....	....	....	....	....	....	....	....	....	....	....	....
	Sweden	EJC-A	6	0	0	0	....	....	....	2	....	....	....	....	....	....	....	....	....	....	....	....	....	....	....	....	....	....
1990-91	MoDo AIK	Sweden	32	10	9	19	....	....	....	14	....	....	....	....	....	....	....	....	....	....	....	....	....	....	....	....	....	....
	Sweden	EJC-A	6	14	2	16	....	....	....	14	....	....	....	....	....	....	....	....	....	....	....	....	....	....	....	....	....	....
1991-92	MoDo AIK	Sweden	39	22	18	40	....	....	....	54	....	....	....	....	....	....	....	....	....	....	....	....	....	....	....	....	....	....
	Sweden	WJC-A	7	8	2	10	....	....	....	12	....	....	....	....	....	....	....	....	....	....	....	....	....	....	....	....	....	....
1992-93	MoDo AIK	Sweden-Jr.	2	4	1	5	....	....	....	2	....	....	....	....	....	....	....	....	....	....	....	....	....	....	....	....	....	....
	MoDo AIK	Sweden	39	22	17	39	....	....	....	67	....	....	....	....	....	....	....	....	....	....	3	3	2	5	0	....	....	....
	Sweden	WJC-A	7	13	11	24	....	....	....	33	....	....	....	....	....	....	....	....	....	....	....	....	....	....	....	....	....	....
	Sweden	WC-A	8	1	1	2	....	....	....	14	....	....	....	....	....	....	....	....	....	....	....	....	....	....	....	....	....	....
1993-94	**Pittsburgh Penguins**	**NHL**	**71**	**4**	**7**	**11**	**4**	**5**	**9**	**27**	**1**	**0**	**0**	**80**	**5.0**	**23**	**1**	**25**	**0**	**–3**	....	....	....	....	....	....	....	....
	Cleveland Lumberjacks	IHL	5	1	6	7	....	....	....	4	....	....	....	....	....	....	....	....	....	....	....	....	....	....	....	....	....	....
1994-95	**Pittsburgh Penguins**	**NHL**	**14**	**2**	**2**	**4**	**4**	**3**	**7**	**2**	**0**	**0**	**0**	**13**	**15.4**	**4**	**1**	**3**	**0**	**0**	....	....	....	....	....	....	....	....
	Cleveland Lumberjacks	IHL	7	3	4	7	....	....	....	6	....	....	....	....	....	....	....	....	....	....	4	1	3	4	8	....	....	....
1995-96	**Pittsburgh Penguins**	**NHL**	**66**	**19**	**33**	**52**	**19**	**27**	**46**	**36**	**3**	**0**	**4**	**125**	**15.2**	**71**	**10**	**44**	**0**	**17**	....	....	....	....	....	....	....	....
	Vancouver Canucks	**NHL**	**10**	**3**	**0**	**3**	**3**	**0**	**3**	**6**	**1**	**0**	**1**	**19**	**15.8**	**7**	**3**	**1**	**0**	**3**	**6**	**1**	**2**	**3**	**8**	**1**	**0**	**0**
	Sweden	WC-A	1	0	0	0	....	....	....	0	....	....	....	....	....	....	....	....	....	....	....	....	....	....	....	....	....	....
1996-97	Sweden	W-Cup	1	0	0	0	....	....	....	2	....	....	....	....	....	....	....	....	....	....	....	....	....	....	....	....	....	....
	Vancouver Canucks	**NHL**	**78**	**21**	**20**	**41**	**22**	**18**	**40**	**30**	**4**	**0**	**4**	**120**	**17.5**	**54**	**15**	**54**	**0**	**–15**	....	....	....	....	....	....	....	....
1997-98	**Vancouver Canucks**	**NHL**	**76**	**14**	**20**	**34**	**16**	**20**	**36**	**56**	**2**	**1**	**0**	**106**	**13.2**	**50**	**9**	**40**	**4**	**5**	....	....	....	....	....	....	....	....

			REGULAR SEASON																		PLAYOFFS							
Season	Club	League	GP	G	A	Pts	AG	AA	APts	PIM	PP	SH	GW	S	%	TGF	PGF	TGA	PGA	+/–	GP	G	A	Pts	PIM	PP	SH	GW
1998-99	**Vancouver Canucks**	**NHL**	**80**	**36**	**30**	**66**	**42**	**29**	**71**	**74**	**15**	**2**	**3**	**205**	**17.6**	**88**	**37**	**76**	**12**	**–13**	....	....	....	....	....	....	....	....
	Sweden	WC-A	10	6	4	10	....	....	....	16	....	....	....	....	....	....	....	....	....	....	....	....	....	....	....	....	....	....
99-2000	**Vancouver Canucks**	**NHL**	**82**	**27**	**38**	**65**	**30**	**35**	**65**	**64**	**6**	**2**	**3**	**271**	**10.0**	**88**	**33**	**73**	**13**	**–5**	....	....	....	....	....	....	....	....
	NHL Totals		**477**	**126**	**150**	**276**	**140**	**137**	**277**	**295**	**32**	**5**	**15**	**939**	**13.4**	**385**	**109**	**316**	**29**		**6**	**1**	**2**	**3**	**8**	**1**	**0**	**0**

WJC-A All-Star Team (1993) • Played in NHL All-Star Game (1999)

Traded to **Vancouver** by **Pittsburgh** for Alek Stojanov, March 20, 1996.

• NASLUND, Mats

LW – L. 5'7", 160 lbs. b: Timra, Sweden, 10/31/1959. Montreal's 2nd, 37th overall, in 1979.

Season	Club	League	GP	G	A	Pts	AG	AA	APts	PIM	PP	SH	GW	S	%	TGF	PGF	TGA	PGA	+/–	GP	G	A	Pts	PIM	PP	SH	GW
1975-76	Timra IK	Sweden	3	0	0	0	....	....	....	0	....	....	....	....	....	....	....	....	....	....	....	....	....	....	....	....	....	....
1976-77	Timra IK	Sweden-2	17	15	13	28	....	....	....	....	....	....	....	....	....	....	....	....	....	....	....	....	....	....	....	....	....	....
	Sweden	EJC-A	6	9	3	12	....	....	....	2	....	....	....	....	....	....	....	....	....	....	....	....	....	....	....	....	....	....
1977-78	Timra IF	Sweden	35	13	6	19	....	....	....	14	....	....	....	....	....	....	....	....	....	....	....	....	....	....	....	....	....	....
	Sweden	WJC-A	7	2	8	10	....	....	....	6	....	....	....	....	....	....	....	....	....	....	....	....	....	....	....	....	....	....
1978-79	Brynas IF Gavle	Sweden	36	12	12	24	....	....	....	19	....	....	....	....	....	....	....	....	....	....	....	....	....	....	....	....	....	....
	Sweden	WJC-A	6	3	2	5	....	....	....	6	....	....	....	....	....	....	....	....	....	....	....	....	....	....	....	....	....	....
	Sweden	WEC-A	8	5	2	7	....	....	....	8	....	....	....	....	....	....	....	....	....	....	....	....	....	....	....	....	....	....
1979-80	Brynas IF Gavle	Sweden	36	18	19	37	....	....	....	34	....	....	....	....	....	....	....	....	....	....	7	2	2	4	4	....	....	....
	Sweden	Olympics	7	3	7	10	....	....	....	6	....	....	....	....	....	....	....	....	....	....	....	....	....	....	....	....	....	....
1980-81	Brynas IF Gavle	Sweden	36	17	*25	*42	....	....	....	34	....	....	....	....	....	....	....	....	....	....	....	....	....	....	....	....	....	....
	Sweden	WEC-A	8	0	3	3	....	....	....	6	....	....	....	....	....	....	....	....	....	....	....	....	....	....	....	....	....	....
1981-82	Brynas IF Gavle	Sweden	36	24	18	42	....	....	....	16	....	....	....	....	....	....	....	....	....	....	....	....	....	....	....	....	....	....
	Sweden	WEC-A	10	2	4	6	....	....	....	6	....	....	....	....	....	....	....	....	....	....	....	....	....	....	....	....	....	....
1982-83	**Montreal Canadiens**	**NHL**	**74**	**26**	**45**	**71**	**21**	**31**	**52**	**10**	**1**	**0**	**6**	**122**	**21.3**	**102**	**22**	**46**	**0**	**34**	**3**	**1**	**0**	**1**	**0**	**1**	**0**	**0**
	Sweden	WEC-A	10	3	4	7	....	....	....	2	....	....	....	....	....	....	....	....	....	....	....	....	....	....	....	....	....	....
1983-84	**Montreal Canadiens**	**NHL**	**77**	**29**	**35**	**64**	**23**	**24**	**47**	**4**	**3**	**0**	**1**	**146**	**19.9**	**91**	**24**	**71**	**9**	**5**	**15**	**6**	**8**	**14**	**4**	**3**	**1**	**3**
1984-85	Sweden	Can-Cup	8	2	3	5	....	....	....	6	....	....	....	....	....	....	....	....	....	....	....	....	....	....	....	....	....	....
	Montreal Canadiens	**NHL**	**80**	**42**	**37**	**79**	**34**	**25**	**59**	**14**	**9**	**2**	**8**	**179**	**23.5**	**110**	**38**	**69**	**16**	**19**	**12**	**7**	**4**	**11**	**6**	**3**	**0**	**2**
1985-86♦	**Montreal Canadiens**	**NHL**	**80**	**43**	**67**	**110**	**34**	**45**	**79**	**16**	**19**	**0**	**7**	**223**	**19.3**	**155**	**71**	**76**	**3**	**11**	**20**	**8**	**11**	**19**	**4**	**4**	**0**	**0**
1986-87	**Montreal Canadiens**	**NHL**	**79**	**25**	**55**	**80**	**22**	**40**	**62**	**16**	**10**	**0**	**3**	**173**	**14.5**	**114**	**57**	**60**	**0**	**–3**	**17**	**7**	**15**	**22**	**11**	**4**	**0**	**3**
1987-88	Sweden	Can-Cup	6	1	2	3	....	....	....	2	....	....	....	....	....	....	....	....	....	....	....	....	....	....	....	....	....	....
	Montreal Canadiens	**NHL**	**78**	**24**	**59**	**83**	**20**	**42**	**62**	**14**	**4**	**0**	**2**	**167**	**14.4**	**125**	**49**	**61**	**2**	**17**	**6**	**0**	**7**	**7**	**2**	**0**	**0**	**0**
1988-89	**Montreal Canadiens**	**NHL**	**77**	**33**	**51**	**84**	**28**	**36**	**64**	**14**	**14**	**0**	**4**	**165**	**20.0**	**117**	**43**	**40**	**0**	**34**	**21**	**4**	**11**	**15**	**6**	**1**	**0**	**0**
1989-90	**Montreal Canadiens**	**NHL**	**72**	**21**	**20**	**41**	**18**	**14**	**32**	**19**	**6**	**0**	**3**	**136**	**15.4**	**58**	**14**	**43**	**2**	**3**	**3**	**1**	**1**	**2**	**0**	**0**	**0**	**1**
1990-91	HC Lugano	Switz.	31	27	29	56	....	....	....	....	....	....	....	....	....	....	....	....	....	....	11	4	9	13	....	....	....	....
	Sweden	WEC-A	10	3	5	8	....	....	....	0	....	....	....	....	....	....	....	....	....	....	....	....	....	....	....	....	....	....
1991-92	Sweden	Can-Cup	6	1	3	4	....	....	....	0	....	....	....	....	....	....	....	....	....	....	....	....	....	....	....	....	....	....
	Malmo IF	Sweden	39	15	24	39	....	....	....	10	....	....	....	....	....	....	....	....	....	....	10	3	2	5	0	....	....	....
	Sweden	Olympics	8	1	5	6	....	....	....	27	....	....	....	....	....	....	....	....	....	....	....	....	....	....	....	....	....	....
1992-93	Malmo IF	Sweden	33	11	21	32	....	....	....	10	....	....	....	....	....	....	....	....	....	....	1	0	0	0	0	....	....	....
1993-94	Malmo IF	Sweden	40	14	30	44	....	....	....	8	....	....	....	....	....	....	....	....	....	....	11	2	4	6	4	....	....	....
	Sweden	Olympics	8	0	7	7	....	....	....	0	....	....	....	....	....	....	....	....	....	....	....	....	....	....	....	....	....	....
1994-95	**Boston Bruins**	**NHL**	**34**	**8**	**14**	**22**	**14**	**21**	**35**	**4**	**2**	**0**	**1**	**48**	**16.7**	**34**	**16**	**23**	**1**	**–4**	**5**	**1**	**0**	**1**	**0**	**0**	**0**	**0**
	NHL Totals		**651**	**251**	**383**	**634**	**214**	**278**	**492**	**111**	**68**	**2**	**35**	**1359**	**18.5**	**906**	**334**	**489**	**33**		**102**	**35**	**57**	**92**	**33**	**16**	**1**	**9**

WJC-A All-Star Team (1978) • Swedish World All-Star Team (1979, 1980, 1981, 1982, 1983) • Swedish Player of the Year (1980) • NHL All-Rookie Team (1983) • NHL Second All-Star Team (1986) • Won Lady Byng Trophy (1988) • Played in NHL All-Star Game (1984, 1986, 1988)

Signed as a free agent by **Boston**, February 21, 1994.

• NASREDDINE, Alain

D – L. 6'1", 201 lbs. b: Montreal, Que., 7/10/1975. Florida's 8th, 135th overall, in 1993.

Season	Club	League	GP	G	A	Pts	AG	AA	APts	PIM	PP	SH	GW	S	%	TGF	PGF	TGA	PGA	+/–	GP	G	A	Pts	PIM	PP	SH	GW
1990-91	Montreal-Bourassa	QAAA	35	10	25	35	....	....	....	50	....	....	....	....	....	....	....	....	....	....	....	....	....	....	....	....	....	....
1991-92	Drummondville Voltigeurs	QMJHL	61	1	9	10	....	....	....	78	....	....	....	....	....	....	....	....	....	....	4	0	0	0	17	....	....	....
1992-93	Drummondville Voltigeurs	QMJHL	64	0	14	14	....	....	....	137	....	....	....	....	....	....	....	....	....	....	10	0	1	1	36	....	....	....
1993-94	Chicoutimi Sagueneens	QMJHL	60	3	24	27	....	....	....	218	....	....	....	....	....	....	....	....	....	....	26	2	10	12	118	....	....	....
	Chicoutimi Sagueneens	Mem-Cup	4	0	0	0	....	....	....	8	....	....	....	....	....	....	....	....	....	....	....	....	....	....	....	....	....	....
1994-95	Chicoutimi Sagueneens	QMJHL	67	8	31	39	....	....	....	342	....	....	....	....	....	....	....	....	....	....	13	3	5	8	40	....	....	....
1995-96	Carolina Monarchs	AHL	63	0	5	5	....	....	....	245	....	....	....	....	....	....	....	....	....	....	....	....	....	....	....	....	....	....
1996-97	Carolina Monarchs	AHL	26	0	4	4	....	....	....	109	....	....	....	....	....	....	....	....	....	....	....	....	....	....	....	....	....	....
	Indianapolis Ice	IHL	49	0	2	2	....	....	....	248	....	....	....	....	....	....	....	....	....	....	4	1	1	2	27	....	....	....
1997-98	Indianapolis Ice	IHL	75	1	12	13	....	....	....	258	....	....	....	....	....	....	....	....	....	....	5	0	2	2	12	....	....	....
1998-99	**Chicago Blackhawks**	**NHL**	**7**	**0**	**0**	**0**	**0**	**0**	**0**	**19**	**0**	**0**	**0**	**2**	**0.0**	**2**	**0**	**4**	**0**	**–2**	....	....	....	....	....	....	....	....
	Portland Pirates	AHL	7	0	1	1	....	....	....	36	....	....	....	....	....	....	....	....	....	....	....	....	....	....	....	....	....	....
	Montreal Canadiens	**NHL**	**8**	**0**	**0**	**0**	**0**	**0**	**0**	**33**	**0**	**0**	**0**	**1**	**0.0**	**1**	**0**	**0**	**0**	**1**	....	....	....	....	....	....	....	....
	Fredericton Canadiens	AHL	38	0	10	10	....	....	....	108	....	....	....	....	....	....	....	....	....	....	15	0	3	3	39	....	....	....
99-2000	Quebec Citadelles	AHL	59	1	6	7	....	....	....	178	....	....	....	....	....	....	....	....	....	....	....	....	....	....	....	....	....	....
	Hamilton Bulldogs	AHL	11	0	0	0	....	....	....	12	....	....	....	....	....	....	....	....	....	....	10	1	1	2	14	....	....	....
	NHL Totals		**15**	**0**	**0**	**0**	**0**	**0**	**0**	**52**	**0**	**0**	**0**	**3**	**0.0**	**3**	**0**	**4**	**0**		....	....	....	....	....	....	....	....

QMJHL Second All-Star Team (1995)

Traded to **Chicago** by **Florida** with a conditional choice in 1999 Entry Draft for Ivan Droppa, December 18, 1996. Traded to **Montreal** by **Chicago** with Jeff Hackett, Eric Weinrich and Tampa Bay's 4th round choice (previously acquired, Montreal selected Chris Dyment) in 1999 Entry Draft for Jocelyn Thibault, Dave Manson and Brad Brown, November 16, 1998. Traded to **Edmonton** by **Montreal** with Igor Ulanov for Christian Laflamme and Matthieu Descoteaux, March 9, 2000.

• NATTRESS, Ric

Eric James "Stash" D – R. 6'2", 210 lbs. b: Hamilton, Ont., 5/25/1962. Montreal's 2nd, 27th overall, in 1980.

Season	Club	League	GP	G	A	Pts	AG	AA	APts	PIM	PP	SH	GW	S	%	TGF	PGF	TGA	PGA	+/–	GP	G	A	Pts	PIM	PP	SH	GW
1978-79	Hamilton Huskies	OMHA	40	21	28	49	....	....	....	76	....	....	....	....	....	....	....	....	....	....	....	....	....	....	....	....	....	....
1979-80	Brantford Alexanders	OMJHL	65	3	21	24	....	....	....	94	....	....	....	....	....	....	....	....	....	....	11	1	6	7	38	....	....	....
1980-81	Brantford Alexanders	OMJHL	51	8	34	42	....	....	....	106	....	....	....	....	....	....	....	....	....	....	6	1	4	5	19	....	....	....
1981-82	Brantford Alexanders	OHL	59	11	50	61	....	....	....	126	....	....	....	....	....	....	....	....	....	....	11	3	7	10	17	....	....	....
	Nova Scotia Voyageurs	AHL	....	....	....	....	....	....	....	....	....	....	....	....	....	....	....	....	....	....	5	0	1	1	7	....	....	....
1982-83	**Montreal Canadiens**	**NHL**	**40**	**1**	**3**	**4**	**1**	**2**	**3**	**19**	**0**	**0**	**0**	**44**	**2.3**	**31**	**1**	**25**	**3**	**8**	**3**	**0**	**0**	**0**	**10**	**0**	**0**	**0**
	Nova Scotia Voyageurs	AHL	9	0	4	4	....	....	....	16	....	....	....	....	....	....	....	....	....	....	....	....	....	....	....	....	....	....
1983-84	**Montreal Canadiens**	**NHL**	**34**	**0**	**12**	**12**	**0**	**8**	**8**	**15**	**0**	**0**	**0**	**33**	**0.0**	**32**	**10**	**34**	**1**	**–11**	....	....	....	....	....	....	....	....
1984-85	**Montreal Canadiens**	**NHL**	**5**	**0**	**1**	**1**	**0**	**1**	**1**	**2**	**0**	**0**	**0**	**3**	**0.0**	**3**	**0**	**5**	**0**	**–2**	**2**	**0**	**0**	**0**	**2**	**0**	**0**	**0**
	Sherbrooke Canadiens	AHL	72	8	40	48	....	....	....	37	....	....	....	....	....	....	....	....	....	....	16	4	13	17	20	....	....	....
1985-86	**St. Louis Blues**	**NHL**	**78**	**4**	**20**	**24**	**3**	**13**	**16**	**52**	**1**	**0**	**2**	**124**	**3.2**	**89**	**20**	**98**	**21**	**–8**	**18**	**1**	**4**	**5**	**24**	**0**	**0**	**0**
1986-87	**St. Louis Blues**	**NHL**	**73**	**6**	**22**	**28**	**5**	**16**	**21**	**24**	**2**	**0**	**0**	**133**	**4.5**	**99**	**31**	**132**	**30**	**–34**	**6**	**0**	**0**	**0**	**2**	**0**	**0**	**0**
1987-88	**Calgary Flames**	**NHL**	**63**	**2**	**13**	**15**	**2**	**9**	**11**	**37**	**0**	**0**	**0**	**48**	**4.2**	**67**	**0**	**77**	**24**	**14**	**6**	**1**	**3**	**4**	**0**	**0**	**0**	**0**
1988-89♦	**Calgary Flames**	**NHL**	**38**	**1**	**8**	**9**	**1**	**6**	**7**	**47**	**0**	**0**	**0**	**28**	**3.6**	**34**	**0**	**28**	**6**	**12**	**19**	**0**	**3**	**3**	**20**	**0**	**0**	**0**
1989-90	Calgary Flames	Fr-Tour	4	0	0	0	....	....	....	0	....	....	....	....	....	....	....	....	....	....	....	....	....	....	....	....	....	....
	Calgary Flames	**NHL**	**49**	**1**	**14**	**15**	**1**	**10**	**11**	**26**	**0**	**0**	**0**	**65**	**1.5**	**52**	**2**	**67**	**31**	**14**	**6**	**2**	**0**	**2**	**0**	**0**	**0**	**0**
1990-91	**Calgary Flames**	**NHL**	**58**	**5**	**13**	**18**	**5**	**10**	**15**	**63**	**0**	**0**	**1**	**81**	**6.2**	**57**	**0**	**75**	**17**	**–1**	**7**	**1**	**0**	**1**	**2**	**0**	**0**	**1**
	Canada	WEC-A	7	0	1	1	....	....	....	4	....	....	....	....	....	....	....	....	....	....	....	....	....	....	....	....	....	....
1991-92	**Calgary Flames**	**NHL**	**18**	**0**	**5**	**5**	**0**	**4**	**4**	**31**	**0**	**0**	**0**	**23**	**0.0**	**15**	**0**	**21**	**6**	**0**	....	....	....	....	....	....	....	....
	Toronto Maple Leafs	**NHL**	**36**	**2**	**14**	**16**	**2**	**11**	**13**	**32**	**0**	**0**	**1**	**43**	**4.7**	**41**	**1**	**57**	**16**	**–1**	....	....	....	....	....	....	....	....
1992-93	**Philadelphia Flyers**	**NHL**	**44**	**7**	**10**	**17**	**6**	**7**	**13**	**29**	**0**	**0**	**4**	**57**	**12.3**	**41**	**0**	**60**	**20**	**1**	....	....	....	....	....	....	....	....
	NHL Totals		**536**	**29**	**135**	**164**	**26**	**97**	**123**	**377**	**3**	**0**	**8**	**682**	**4.3**	**561**	**65**	**679**	**175**		**67**	**5**	**10**	**15**	**60**	**0**	**0**	**1**

Rights traded to **St. Louis** by **Montreal** for cash, October 7, 1985. Traded to **Calgary** by **St. Louis** for Calgary's 4th round choice (Andy Rymsha) in 1987 Entry Draft and 5th round choice (Dave Lacoutre) in 1988 Entry Draft, June 13, 1987. Traded to **Toronto** by **Calgary** with Doug Gilmour, Jamie Macoun, Kent Manderville and Rick Wamsley for Gary Leeman, Alexander Godynyuk, Jeff Resse, Michel Petit and Craig Berube, January 2, 1992. Signed as a free agent by **Philadelphia**, August 21, 1992. •Officially announced retirement, October 8, 1993.

• NATYSHAK, Mike

RW – R. 6'2", 201 lbs. b: Belle River, Ont., 11/29/1963. Quebec's 1st, 23rd overall, in 1986 Supplemental Draft.

			REGULAR SEASON																		PLAYOFFS							
Season	Club	League	GP	G	A	Pts	AG	AA	APts	PIM	PP	SH	GW	S	%	TGF	PGF	TGA	PGA	+/-	GP	G	A	Pts	PIM	PP	SH	GW
1979-80	Belle River Canadians	OHA-C	3	0	1	1	....	....	....	0	....	....	....	....	....	....	....	....	....	....	....	....	....	....	....	....	....	....
1980-81	Belle River Canadians	OHA-C	23	5	12	17	....	....	....	95	....	....	....	....	....	....	....	....	....	....	....	....	....	....	....	....	....	....
1981-82	Belle River Canadians	OJHL-C	STATISTICS NOT AVAILABLE																									
1982-83	Windsor Blues	OJHL-B	22	16	18	34	....	....	....	....	....	....	....	....	....	....	....	....	....	....	....	....	....	....	....	....	....	....
1983-84	Bowling Green University	CCHA	19	0	0	0	....	....	....	0	....	....	....	....	....	....	....	....	....	....	....	....	....	....	....	....	....	....
1984-85	Bowling Green University	CCHA	38	4	9	13	....	....	....	79	....	....	....	....	....	....	....	....	....	....	....	....	....	....	....	....	....	....
1985-86	Bowling Green University	CCHA	40	3	5	8	....	....	....	62	....	....	....	....	....	....	....	....	....	....	....	....	....	....	....	....	....	....
1986-87	Bowling Green University	CCHA	45	5	10	15	....	....	....	101	....	....	....	....	....	....	....	....	....	....	....	....	....	....	....	....	....	....
1987-88	**Quebec Nordiques**	**NHL**	**4**	**0**	**0**	**0**	**0**	**0**	**0**	**0**	**0**	**0**	**0**	**0**	**0.0**	**0**	**0**	**1**	**0**	**-1**	....	....	....	....	....	....	....	....
	Fredericton Express	AHL	46	5	9	14	....	....	....	34	....	....	....	....	....	....	....	....	....	....	6	0	3	3	13	....	....	....
1988-89	Fort Wayne Komets	IHL	48	5	9	14	....	....	....	95	....	....	....	....	....	....	....	....	....	....	3	0	0	0	0	....	....	....
	NHL Totals		**4**	**0**	**0**	**0**	**0**	**0**	**0**	**0**	**0**	**0**	**0**	**0**	**0.0**	**0**	**0**	**1**	**0**		....	....	....	....	....	....	....	....

• NAZAROV, Andrei

LW – R. 6'5", 234 lbs. b: Chelyabinsk, USSR, 5/22/1974. San Jose's 2nd, 10th overall, in 1992.

			REGULAR SEASON																		PLAYOFFS							
Season	Club	League	GP	G	A	Pts	AG	AA	APts	PIM	PP	SH	GW	S	%	TGF	PGF	TGA	PGA	+/-	GP	G	A	Pts	PIM	PP	SH	GW
1991-92	Dynamo Moscow	CIS	2	1	0	1	....	....	....	2	....	....	....	....	....	....	....	....	....	....	....	....	....	....	....	....	....	....
	Russia	EJC-A	6	3	1	4	....	....	....	12	....	....	....	....	....	....	....	....	....	....	....	....	....	....	....	....	....	....
1992-93	Dynamo Moscow	CIS	42	8	2	10	....	....	....	79	....	....	....	....	....	....	....	....	....	....	10	1	1	2	8	....	....	....
1993-94	Dynamo Moscow	CIS	6	2	2	4	....	....	....	0	....	....	....	....	....	....	....	....	....	....	....	....	....	....	....	....	....	....
	San Jose Sharks	**NHL**	**1**	**0**	**0**	**0**	**0**	**0**	**0**	**0**	**0**	**0**	**0**	**0**	**0.0**	**0**	**0**	**0**	**0**	**0**	....	....	....	....	....	....	....	....
	Kansas City Blades	IHL	71	15	18	33	....	....	....	64	....	....	....	....	....	....	....	....	....	....	....	....	....	....	....	....	....	....
1994-95	Kansas City Blades	IHL	43	15	10	25	....	....	....	55	....	....	....	....	....	....	....	....	....	....	....	....	....	....	....	....	....	....
	San Jose Sharks	**NHL**	**26**	**3**	**5**	**8**	**5**	**7**	**12**	**94**	**0**	**0**	**0**	**19**	**15.8**	**13**	**2**	**12**	**0**	**-1**	**6**	**0**	**0**	**0**	**9**	**0**	**0**	**0**
1995-96	**San Jose Sharks**	**NHL**	**42**	**7**	**7**	**14**	**7**	**6**	**13**	**62**	**2**	**0**	**1**	**55**	**12.7**	**21**	**7**	**29**	**0**	**-15**	....	....	....	....	....	....	....	....
	Kansas City Blades	IHL	27	4	6	10	....	....	....	118	....	....	....	....	....	....	....	....	....	....	2	0	0	0	2	....	....	....
1996-97	**San Jose Sharks**	**NHL**	**60**	**12**	**15**	**27**	**13**	**13**	**26**	**222**	**1**	**0**	**1**	**116**	**10.3**	**39**	**5**	**38**	**0**	**-4**	....	....	....	....	....	....	....	....
	Kentucky Thoroughblades	AHL	3	1	2	3	....	....	....	4	....	....	....	....	....	....	....	....	....	....	....	....	....	....	....	....	....	....
1997-98	**San Jose Sharks**	**NHL**	**40**	**1**	**1**	**2**	**1**	**1**	**2**	**112**	**0**	**0**	**0**	**31**	**3.2**	**9**	**2**	**11**	**0**	**-4**	....	....	....	....	....	....	....	....
	Tampa Bay Lightning	**NHL**	**14**	**1**	**1**	**2**	**1**	**1**	**2**	**58**	**0**	**0**	**0**	**19**	**5.3**	**3**	**0**	**12**	**0**	**-9**	....	....	....	....	....	....	....	....
	Russia	WC-A	6	1	2	3	....	....	....	10	....	....	....	....	....	....	....	....	....	....	....	....	....	....	....	....	....	....
1998-99	**Tampa Bay Lightning**	**NHL**	**26**	**2**	**0**	**2**	**2**	**0**	**2**	**43**	**0**	**0**	**0**	**18**	**11.1**	**5**	**1**	**9**	**0**	**-5**	....	....	....	....	....	....	....	....
	Calgary Flames	**NHL**	**36**	**5**	**9**	**14**	**6**	**9**	**15**	**30**	**0**	**0**	**2**	**53**	**9.4**	**29**	**8**	**20**	**0**	**1**	....	....	....	....	....	....	....	....
99-2000	**Calgary Flames**	**NHL**	**76**	**10**	**22**	**32**	**11**	**20**	**31**	**78**	**1**	**0**	**1**	**110**	**9.1**	**44**	**4**	**37**	**0**	**3**	....	....	....	....	....	....	....	....
	NHL Totals		**321**	**41**	**60**	**101**	**46**	**57**	**103**	**699**	**4**	**0**	**5**	**421**	**9.7**	**163**	**29**	**168**	**0**		**6**	**0**	**0**	**0**	**9**	**0**	**0**	**0**

Traded to **Tampa Bay** by **San Jose** with Florida's 1st round choice (previously acquired, Tampa Bay selected Vincent Lecavalier) for Bryan Marchment, David Shaw and Tampa Bay's 1st round choice (later traded to Nashville — Nashville selected David Legwand) in 1998 Entry Draft, March 24, 1998. Traded to **Calgary** by **Tampa Bay** for Michael Nylander, January 19, 1999.

• NDUR, Rumun

D – L. 6'2", 222 lbs. b: Zaria, Nigeria, 7/7/1975. Buffalo's 3rd, 69th overall, in 1994.

			REGULAR SEASON																		PLAYOFFS							
Season	Club	League	GP	G	A	Pts	AG	AA	APts	PIM	PP	SH	GW	S	%	TGF	PGF	TGA	PGA	+/-	GP	G	A	Pts	PIM	PP	SH	GW
1990-91	Belmont Bombers	OJHL-D	36	3	11	14	....	....	....	70	....	....	....	....	....	....	....	....	....	....	....	....	....	....	....	....	....	....
1991-92	Sarnia Ranson Bees	OJHL-B	30	2	5	7	....	....	....	46	....	....	....	....	....	....	....	....	....	....	....	....	....	....	....	....	....	....
	Clearwater Steeplejacks	OJHL-C	4	0	4	4	....	....	....	4	....	....	....	....	....	....	....	....	....	....	....	....	....	....	....	....	....	....
1992-93	Guelph Platers	OJHL-B	24	7	8	15	....	....	....	202	....	....	....	....	....	....	....	....	....	....	....	....	....	....	....	....	....	....
	Guelph Storm	OHL	22	1	3	4	....	....	....	30	....	....	....	....	....	....	....	....	....	....	4	0	1	1	4	....	....	....
1993-94	Guelph Storm	OHL	61	6	33	39	....	....	....	176	....	....	....	....	....	....	....	....	....	....	9	4	1	5	24	....	....	....
1994-95	Guelph Storm	OHL	63	10	21	31	....	....	....	187	....	....	....	....	....	....	....	....	....	....	14	0	4	4	28	....	....	....
1995-96	Rochester Americans	AHL	73	2	12	14	....	....	....	306	....	....	....	....	....	....	....	....	....	....	17	1	2	3	33	....	....	....
1996-97	**Buffalo Sabres**	**NHL**	**2**	**0**	**0**	**0**	**0**	**0**	**0**	**2**	**0**	**0**	**0**	**0**	**0.0**	**1**	**0**	**0**	**0**	**1**	....	....	....	....	....	....	....	....
	Rochester Americans	AHL	68	5	11	16	....	....	....	282	....	....	....	....	....	....	....	....	....	....	10	3	1	4	21	....	....	....
1997-98	**Buffalo Sabres**	**NHL**	**1**	**0**	**0**	**0**	**0**	**0**	**0**	**2**	**0**	**0**	**0**	**0**	**0.0**	**0**	**0**	**1**	**0**	**-1**	....	....	....	....	....	....	....	....
	Rochester Americans	AHL	50	1	12	13	....	....	....	207	....	....	....	....	....	....	....	....	....	....	4	0	2	2	16	....	....	....
1998-99	**Buffalo Sabres**	**NHL**	**8**	**0**	**0**	**0**	**0**	**0**	**0**	**16**	**0**	**0**	**0**	**1**	**0.0**	**3**	**0**	**2**	**0**	**1**	....	....	....	....	....	....	....	....
	NY Rangers	**NHL**	**31**	**1**	**3**	**4**	**1**	**3**	**4**	**46**	**0**	**0**	**0**	**21**	**4.8**	**10**	**0**	**15**	**3**	**-2**	....	....	....	....	....	....	....	....
	Hartford Wolf Pack	AHL	6	0	1	1	....	....	....	4	....	....	....	....	....	....	....	....	....	....	....	....	....	....	....	....	....	....
99-2000	**Atlanta Thrashers**	**NHL**	**27**	**1**	**0**	**1**	**1**	**0**	**1**	**71**	**0**	**0**	**0**	**6**	**16.7**	**4**	**0**	**24**	**3**	**-17**	....	....	....	....	....	....	....	....
	Hartford Wolf Pack	AHL	2	0	0	0	....	....	....	0	....	....	....	....	....	....	....	....	....	....	....	....	....	....	....	....	....	....
	NHL Totals		**69**	**2**	**3**	**5**	**2**	**3**	**5**	**137**	**0**	**0**	**0**	**28**	**7.1**	**18**	**0**	**42**	**6**		....	....	....	....	....	....	....	....

Claimed on waivers by **NY Rangers** from **Buffalo**, December 18, 1998. Claimed on waivers by **Atlanta** from **NY Rangers**, December 11, 1999.

• NEATON, Pat

D – L. 6', 180 lbs. b: Redford, MI, 5/21/1971. Pittsburgh's 9th, 145th overall, in 1990.

			REGULAR SEASON																		PLAYOFFS							
Season	Club	League	GP	G	A	Pts	AG	AA	APts	PIM	PP	SH	GW	S	%	TGF	PGF	TGA	PGA	+/-	GP	G	A	Pts	PIM	PP	SH	GW
1987-88	Detroit Little Caesar's	MNHL	71	12	26	38	....	....	....	....	....	....	....	....	....	....	....	....	....	....	....	....	....	....	....	....	....	....
1988-89	Thornhill Thunderbirds	OJHL-B	38	16	42	58	....	....	....	76	....	....	....	....	....	....	....	....	....	....	....	....	....	....	....	....	....	....
1989-90	University of Michigan	CCHA	42	3	23	26	....	....	....	36	....	....	....	....	....	....	....	....	....	....	....	....	....	....	....	....	....	....
1990-91	University of Michigan	CCHA	44	15	28	43	....	....	....	78	....	....	....	....	....	....	....	....	....	....	....	....	....	....	....	....	....	....
	United States	WJC-A	8	4	2	6	....	....	....	6	....	....	....	....	....	....	....	....	....	....	....	....	....	....	....	....	....	....
1991-92	University of Michigan	CCHA	43	10	20	30	....	....	....	62	....	....	....	....	....	....	....	....	....	....	....	....	....	....	....	....	....	....
1992-93	University of Michigan	CCHA	38	10	18	28	....	....	....	37	....	....	....	....	....	....	....	....	....	....	....	....	....	....	....	....	....	....
1993-94	**Pittsburgh Penguins**	**NHL**	**9**	**1**	**1**	**2**	**1**	**1**	**2**	**12**	**1**	**0**	**0**	**11**	**9.1**	**9**	**5**	**2**	**1**	**3**	....	....	....	....	....	....	....	....
	Cleveland Lumberjacks	IHL	71	8	24	32	....	....	....	78	....	....	....	....	....	....	....	....	....	....	....	....	....	....	....	....	....	....
	United States	WC-A	8	2	0	2	....	....	....	12	....	....	....	....	....	....	....	....	....	....	....	....	....	....	....	....	....	....
1994-95	Cleveland Lumberjacks	IHL	2	0	0	0	....	....	....	4	....	....	....	....	....	....	....	....	....	....	....	....	....	....	....	....	....	....
	San Diego Gulls	IHL	71	8	27	35	....	....	....	86	....	....	....	....	....	....	....	....	....	....	5	0	1	1	0	....	....	....
	United States	WC-A	4	1	0	1	....	....	....	8	....	....	....	....	....	....	....	....	....	....	....	....	....	....	....	....	....	....
1995-96	Orlando Solar Bears	IHL	77	8	27	35	....	....	....	148	....	....	....	....	....	....	....	....	....	....	21	3	5	8	34	....	....	....
1996-97	Orlando Solar Bears	IHL	81	17	35	52	....	....	....	68	....	....	....	....	....	....	....	....	....	....	10	0	1	1	13	....	....	....
1997-98	Orlando Solar Bears	IHL	78	11	24	35	....	....	....	114	....	....	....	....	....	....	....	....	....	....	17	3	11	14	12	....	....	....
1998-99	Orlando Solar Bears	IHL	75	5	22	27	....	....	....	98	....	....	....	....	....	....	....	....	....	....	17	2	2	4	14	....	....	....
99-2000	Utah Grizzlies	IHL	80	5	21	26	....	....	....	80	....	....	....	....	....	....	....	....	....	....	5	0	1	1	6	....	....	....
	NHL Totals		**9**	**1**	**1**	**2**	**1**	**1**	**2**	**12**	**1**	**0**	**0**	**11**	**9.1**	**9**	**5**	**2**	**1**		....	....	....	....	....	....	....	....

CCHA Second All-Star Team (1991) • CCHA First All-Star Team (1993)

Signed as a free agent by **Utah** (IHL), August 10, 1999.

• NECHAEV, Viktor

C – L. 6'1", 183 lbs. b: Vostochnaya, USSR, 1/28/1955. Los Angeles' 7th, 132nd overall, in 1982.

			REGULAR SEASON																		PLAYOFFS							
Season	Club	League	GP	G	A	Pts	AG	AA	APts	PIM	PP	SH	GW	S	%	TGF	PGF	TGA	PGA	+/-	GP	G	A	Pts	PIM	PP	SH	GW
1973-74	Sibir Novosibirsk	USSR-2	20	8	8	16	....	....	....	....	....	....	....	....	....	....	....	....	....	....	....	....	....	....	....	....	....	....
1974-75	Sibir Novosibirsk	USSR-2	50	20	12	32	....	....	....	....	....	....	....	....	....	....	....	....	....	....	....	....	....	....	....	....	....	....
1975-76	SKA Leningrad	USSR	12	2	0	2	....	....	....	....	....	....	....	....	....	....	....	....	....	....	....	....	....	....	....	....	....	....
1976-77	SKA Leningrad	USSR	44	18	13	31	....	....	....	....	....	....	....	....	....	....	....	....	....	....	....	....	....	....	....	....	....	....
1977-78	SKA Leningrad	USSR	22	5	1	6	....	....	....	6	....	....	....	....	....	....	....	....	....	....	22	12	13	25	6	....	....	....
1978-79	SKA Leningrad	USSR	28	4	4	8	....	....	....	12	....	....	....	....	....	....	....	....	....	....	....	....	....	....	....	....	....	....
1979-80	SKA Leningrad	USSR	40	17	12	29	....	....	....	....	....	....	....	....	....	....	....	....	....	....	....	....	....	....	....	....	....	....
1980-81	HC Binokar	USSR-2	20	10	7	17	....	....	....	....	....	....	....	....	....	....	....	....	....	....	....	....	....	....	....	....	....	....
1981-82	HC Izhorets	USSR-2	20	16	7	23	....	....	....	....	....	....	....	....	....	....	....	....	....	....	....	....	....	....	....	....	....	....
1982-83	**Los Angeles Kings**	**NHL**	**3**	**1**	**0**	**1**	**1**	**0**	**1**	**0**	**0**	**0**	**0**	**7**	**14.3**	**2**	**0**	**1**	**0**	**1**	....	....	....	....	....	....	....	....
	New Haven Nighthawks	AHL	28	4	7	11	....	....	....	6	....	....	....	....	....	....	....	....	....	....	....	....	....	....	....	....	....	....
	Saginaw Gears	IHL	10	1	4	5	....	....	....	0	....	....	....	....	....	....	....	....	....	....	....	....	....	....	....	....	....	....
1983-84	Dusseldorfer EG	Germany	38	7	9	16	....	....	....	30	....	....	....	....	....	....	....	....	....	....	....	....	....	....	....	....	....	....
	NHL Totals		**3**	**1**	**0**	**1**	**1**	**0**	**1**	**0**	**0**	**0**	**0**	**7**	**14.3**	**2**	**0**	**1**	**0**		....	....	....	....	....	....	....	....

• NECKAR, Stanislav

D – L. 6'1", 212 lbs. b: Ceske Budejovice, Czech., 12/22/1975. Ottawa's 2nd, 29th overall, in 1994.

			REGULAR SEASON																		PLAYOFFS							
Season	Club	League	GP	G	A	Pts	AG	AA	APts	PIM	PP	SH	GW	S	%	TGF	PGF	TGA	PGA	+/–	GP	G	A	Pts	PIM	PP	SH	GW
1991-92	Motor Ceske Budejovice	Czech-Jr.	18	1	3	4	....	....	....	....	....	....	....	....	....	....	....	....	....	....	....	....	....	....	....	....	....	....
1992-93	Motor Ceske Budejovice	Czech.	42	2	9	11	....	....	....	12	....	....	....	....	....	....	....	....	....	....	....	....	....	....	....	....	....	....
	Czech-Republic	WJC-A	7	2	0	2	....	....	....	6	....	....	....	....	....	....	....	....	....	....	....	....	....	....	....	....	....	....
1993-94	HC Ceske Budejovice	Czech-Rep	12	3	2	5	....	....	....	2	....	....	....	....	....	....	....	....	....	....	3	0	0	0	....	....	....	....
1994-95	Detroit Vipers	IHL	15	2	2	4	....	....	....	15	....	....	....	....	....	....	....	....	....	....	....	....	....	....	....	....	....	....
	Ottawa Senators	**NHL**	**48**	**1**	**3**	**4**	**2**	**4**	**6**	**37**	**0**	**0**	**0**	**34**	**2.9**	**38**	**7**	**64**	**13**	**–20**	....	....	....	....	....	....	....	....
1995-96	**Ottawa Senators**	**NHL**	**82**	**3**	**9**	**12**	**3**	**7**	**10**	**54**	**1**	**0**	**0**	**57**	**5.3**	**53**	**1**	**106**	**38**	**–16**	....	....	....	....	....	....	....	....
	Czech-Republic	WC-A	8	1	3	4	....	....	....	2	....	....	....	....	....	....	....	....	....	....	....	....	....	....	....	....	....	....
1996-97	Czech-Republic	W-Cup	3	0	0	0	....	....	....	0	....	....	....	....	....	....	....	....	....	....	....	....	....	....	....	....	....	....
	Ottawa Senators	**NHL**	**5**	**0**	**0**	**0**	**0**	**0**	**0**	**2**	**0**	**0**	**0**	**3**	**0.0**	**5**	**0**	**6**	**3**	**2**	....	....	....	....	....	....	....	....
1997-98	**Ottawa Senators**	**NHL**	**60**	**2**	**2**	**4**	**2**	**2**	**4**	**31**	**0**	**0**	**0**	**43**	**4.7**	**22**	**0**	**51**	**15**	**–14**	**9**	**0**	**0**	**0**	**2**	**0**	**0**	**0**
1998-99	**Ottawa Senators**	**NHL**	**3**	**0**	**2**	**2**	**0**	**2**	**2**	**0**	**0**	**0**	**0**	**2**	**0.0**	**3**	**1**	**3**	**0**	**–1**	....	....	....	....	....	....	....	....
	New York Rangers	**NHL**	**18**	**0**	**0**	**0**	**0**	**0**	**0**	**8**	**0**	**0**	**0**	**8**	**0.0**	**10**	**1**	**11**	**1**	**–1**	....	....	....	....	....	....	....	....
	Phoenix Coyotes	**NHL**	**11**	**0**	**1**	**1**	**0**	**1**	**1**	**10**	**0**	**0**	**0**	**6**	**0.0**	**5**	**0**	**3**	**1**	**3**	**6**	**0**	**1**	**1**	**4**	**0**	**0**	**0**
99-2000	**Phoenix Coyotes**	**NHL**	**66**	**2**	**8**	**10**	**2**	**7**	**9**	**36**	**0**	**0**	**0**	**34**	**5.9**	**43**	**0**	**49**	**7**	**1**	**5**	**0**	**0**	**0**	**0**	**0**	**0**	**0**
	NHL Totals		**293**	**8**	**25**	**33**	**9**	**23**	**32**	**178**	**1**	**0**	**0**	**187**	**4.3**	**179**	**10**	**293**	**78**		**20**	**0**	**1**	**1**	**6**	**0**	**0**	**0**

Traded to **NY Rangers** by **Ottawa** for Bill Berg and NY Rangers' 2nd round choice (later traded to Anaheim, Anaheim selected Jordan Leopold) in 1999 Entry Draft, November 27, 1998. Traded to **Phoenix** by **NY Rangers** for Jason Doig and Phoenix's 6th round choice (Jay Dardis) in 1999 Entry Draft, March 23, 1999.

• NEDOMANSKY, Vaclav

"Big Ned" RW – L. 6'2", 205 lbs. b: Hodonin, Czech., 3/14/1944.

Season	Club	League	GP	G	A	Pts	AG	AA	APts	PIM	PP	SH	GW	S	%	TGF	PGF	TGA	PGA	+/–	GP	G	A	Pts	PIM	PP	SH	GW
1962-1964	Slovan Bratislava	Czech.	STATISTICS NOT AVAILABLE																									
1964-65	Slovan Bratislava	Czech.	STATISTICS NOT AVAILABLE																									
	Czechoslovakia	WEC-A	7	4	2	6	....	....	....	2	....	....	....	....	....	....	....	....	....	....	....	....	....	....	....	....	....	....
1965-66	Slovan Bratislava	Czech.	STATISTICS NOT AVAILABLE																									
	Czechoslovakia	WEC-A	7	5	2	7	....	....	....	8	....	....	....	....	....	....	....	....	....	....	....	....	....	....	....	....	....	....
1966-67	Slovan Bratislava	Czech.	36	*41	29	*70	....	....	....	22	....	....	....	....	....	....	....	....	....	....	....	....	....	....	....	....	....	....
	Czechoslovakia	WEC-A	7	1	2	3	....	....	....	14	....	....	....	....	....	....	....	....	....	....	....	....	....	....	....	....	....	....
1967-68	Slovan Bratislava	Czech.	36	31	15	46	....	....	....	10	....	....	....	....	....	....	....	....	....	....	8	5	6	11	....	....	....	....
	Czechoslovakia	Olympics	7	5	2	7	....	....	....	4	....	....	....	....	....	....	....	....	....	....	....	....	....	....	....	....	....	....
1968-69	Slovan Bratislava	Czech.	36	28	20	48	....	....	....	....	....	....	....	....	....	....	....	....	....	....	....	....	....	....	....	....	....	....
	Czechoslovakia	WEC-A	10	9	2	11	....	....	....	10	....	....	....	....	....	....	....	....	....	....	....	....	....	....	....	....	....	....
1969-70	Slovan Bratislava	Czech.	36	*29	13	42	....	....	....	23	....	....	....	....	....	....	....	....	....	....	....	....	....	....	....	....	....	....
	Czechoslovakia	WEC-A	10	10	7	17	....	....	....	11	....	....	....	....	....	....	....	....	....	....	....	....	....	....	....	....	....	....
1970-71	Slovan Bratislava	Czech.	36	*30	16	*46	....	....	....	....	....	....	....	....	....	....	....	....	....	....	8	8	2	10	....	....	....	....
	Czechoslovakia	WEC-A	10	10	7	17	....	....	....	....	....	....	....	....	....	....	....	....	....	....	....	....	....	....	....	....	....	....
1971-72	Slovan Bratislava	Czech.	36	*35	21	*56	....	....	....	....	....	....	....	....	....	....	....	....	....	....	....	....	....	....	....	....	....	....
	Czechoslovakia	Olympics	6	8	3	11	....	....	....	0	....	....	....	....	....	....	....	....	....	....	....	....	....	....	....	....	....	....
	Czechoslovakia	WEC-A	9	9	6	15	....	....	....	0	....	....	....	....	....	....	....	....	....	....	....	....	....	....	....	....	....	....
1972-73	Slovan Bratislava	Czech.	36	22	17	39	....	....	....	....	....	....	....	....	....	....	....	....	....	....	....	....	....	....	....	....	....	....
	Czechoslovakia	WEC-A	10	9	3	12	....	....	....	2	....	....	....	....	....	....	....	....	....	....	....	....	....	....	....	....	....	....
1973-74	Slovan Bratislava	Czech.	44	*46	28	*74	....	....	....	....	....	....	....	....	....	....	....	....	....	....	....	....	....	....	....	....	....	....
	Czechoslovakia	WEC-A	10	10	3	13	....	....	....	4	....	....	....	....	....	....	....	....	....	....	....	....	....	....	....	....	....	....
1974-75	Toronto Toros	WHA	78	41	40	81	....	....	....	19	....	....	....	....	....	....	....	....	....	....	6	3	1	4	9	....	....	....
1975-76	Toronto Toros	WHA	81	56	42	98	....	....	....	8	....	....	....	....	....	....	....	....	....	....	....	....	....	....	....	....	....	....
1976-77	Birmingham Bulls	WHA	81	36	33	69	....	....	....	10	....	....	....	....	....	....	....	....	....	....	....	....	....	....	....	....	....	....
1977-78	Birmingham Bulls	WHA	12	2	3	5	....	....	....	6	....	....	....	....	....	....	....	....	....	....	....	....	....	....	....	....	....	....
	Detroit Red Wings	**NHL**	**63**	**11**	**17**	**28**	**10**	**13**	**23**	**2**	**5**	**0**	**1**	**107**	**10.3**	**39**	**19**	**37**	**0**	**–17**	**7**	**3**	**5**	**8**	**0**	**1**	**0**	**0**
1978-79	**Detroit Red Wings**	**NHL**	**80**	**38**	**35**	**73**	**33**	**25**	**58**	**19**	**13**	**0**	**2**	**212**	**17.9**	**106**	**50**	**69**	**0**	**–13**	....	....	....	....	....	....	....	....
1979-80	**Detroit Red Wings**	**NHL**	**79**	**35**	**39**	**74**	**30**	**28**	**58**	**13**	**11**	**0**	**5**	**235**	**14.9**	**106**	**41**	**70**	**0**	**–5**	....	....	....	....	....	....	....	....
1980-81	**Detroit Red Wings**	**NHL**	**74**	**12**	**20**	**32**	**9**	**13**	**22**	**30**	**6**	**0**	**0**	**128**	**9.4**	**44**	**17**	**62**	**0**	**–35**	....	....	....	....	....	....	....	....
1981-82	**Detroit Red Wings**	**NHL**	**68**	**12**	**28**	**40**	**9**	**19**	**28**	**22**	**1**	**0**	**0**	**103**	**11.7**	**51**	**16**	**51**	**1**	**–15**	....	....	....	....	....	....	....	....
1982-83	**New York Rangers**	**NHL**	**1**	**1**	**0**	**1**	**1**	**0**	**1**	**0**	....	....	....	....	....	....	....	....	....	....	....	....	....	....	....	....	....	....
	St. Louis Blues	**NHL**	**22**	**2**	**9**	**11**	**2**	**6**	**8**	**2**	**1**	**0**	**0**	**35**	**5.7**	**21**	**15**	**14**	**0**	**–8**	....	....	....	....	....	....	....	....
	New York Rangers	**NHL**	**34**	**11**	**8**	**19**	**9**	**6**	**15**	**0**	**8**	**0**	**3**	**52**	**21.2**	**29**	**20**	**8**	**0**	**1**	....	....	....	....	....	....	....	....
	NHL Totals		**421**	**122**	**156**	**278**	**103**	**110**	**213**	**88**	**45**	**0**	**11**	**872**	**14.0**	**396**	**178**	**311**	**1**		**7**	**3**	**5**	**8**	**0**	**1**	**0**	**0**
	Other Major League Totals		252	135	118	253	....	....	....	43	....	....	....	....	....	....	....	....	....	....	6	3	1	4	9	....	....	....

WEC-A First All-Star Team (1969, 1970, 1974) • Named Best Forward at WEC-A (1974) • Won Paul Daneau Trophy (WHA Most Gentlemanly Player) (1976)

• Scored total of 369 goals in 419 Czech Elite League games. Signed as a free agent by **Toronto** (WHA), July, 1974. Transferred to **Birmingham** (WHA) after **Toronto** (WHA) franchise relocated, June 30, 1976. Traded to **Detroit** by **Birmingham** (WHA) with Tim Sheehy for the loan of Steve Durbano and Dave Hanson and future considerations, November 18, 1977. Signed as a free agent by **NY Rangers** on September 30, 1982. Claimed on waivers by **St. Louis** from **NY Rangers**, October 6, 1982. Traded to **NY Rangers** by **St. Louis** with Glen Hanlon for Andre Dore, January 4, 1983.

• NEDVED, Petr

C – L. 6'3", 195 lbs. b: Liberec, Czech., 12/9/1971. Vancouver's 1st, 2nd overall, in 1990.

Season	Club	League	GP	G	A	Pts	AG	AA	APts	PIM	PP	SH	GW	S	%	TGF	PGF	TGA	PGA	+/–	GP	G	A	Pts	PIM	PP	SH	GW
1988-89	CHZ Litvinov	Czech-Jr.	20	32	19	51	....	....	....	12	....	....	....	....	....	....	....	....	....	....	....	....	....	....	....	....	....	....
1989-90	Seattle Thunderbirds	WHL	71	65	80	145	....	....	....	80	....	....	....	....	....	....	....	....	....	....	11	4	9	13	2	....	....	....
1990-91	**Vancouver Canucks**	**NHL**	**61**	**10**	**6**	**16**	**9**	**5**	**14**	**20**	**1**	**0**	**0**	**97**	**10.3**	**25**	**3**	**45**	**2**	**–21**	**6**	**0**	**1**	**1**	**0**	**0**	**0**	**0**
1991-92	**Vancouver Canucks**	**NHL**	**77**	**15**	**22**	**37**	**14**	**17**	**31**	**36**	**5**	**0**	**1**	**99**	**15.2**	**49**	**11**	**44**	**3**	**–3**	**10**	**1**	**4**	**5**	**16**	**0**	**0**	**0**
1992-93	**Vancouver Canucks**	**NHL**	**84**	**38**	**33**	**71**	**32**	**23**	**55**	**96**	**2**	**1**	**3**	**149**	**25.5**	**106**	**28**	**75**	**17**	**20**	**12**	**2**	**3**	**5**	**2**	**0**	**0**	**0**
1993-94	Canada	Nat-Team	17	19	12	31	....	....	....	16	....	....	....	....	....	....	....	....	....	....	....	....	....	....	....	....	....	....
	Canada	Olympics	8	5	1	6	....	....	....	6	....	....	....	....	....	....	....	....	....	....	....	....	....	....	....	....	....	....
	St. Louis Blues	**NHL**	**19**	**6**	**14**	**20**	**6**	**11**	**17**	**8**	**2**	**0**	**0**	**63**	**9.5**	**27**	**12**	**16**	**3**	**2**	**4**	**0**	**1**	**1**	**4**	**0**	**0**	**0**
1994-95	**New York Rangers**	**NHL**	**46**	**11**	**12**	**23**	**19**	**18**	**37**	**26**	**1**	**0**	**3**	**123**	**8.9**	**35**	**6**	**30**	**0**	**–1**	**10**	**3**	**2**	**5**	**6**	**2**	**0**	**0**
1995-96	**Pittsburgh Penguins**	**NHL**	**80**	**45**	**54**	**99**	**44**	**44**	**88**	**68**	**8**	**1**	**5**	**204**	**22.1**	**129**	**31**	**86**	**25**	**37**	**18**	**10**	**10**	**20**	**16**	**4**	**0**	**2**
1996-97	Czech-Republic	W-Cup	3	0	1	1	....	....	....	8	....	....	....	....	....	....	....	....	....	....	....	....	....	....	....	....	....	....
	Pittsburgh Penguins	**NHL**	**74**	**33**	**38**	**71**	**35**	**34**	**69**	**66**	**12**	**3**	**4**	**189**	**17.5**	**103**	**38**	**88**	**21**	**–2**	**5**	**1**	**2**	**3**	**12**	**0**	**1**	**0**
1997-98	HC Stadion Liberec-2	Czech-Rep	2	0	3	3	....	....	....	....	....	....	....	....	....	....	....	....	....	....	....	....	....	....	....	....	....	....
	HC Novy Jicin-3	Czech-Rep	7	9	16	25	....	....	....	....	....	....	....	....	....	....	....	....	....	....	....	....	....	....	....	....	....	....
	HC Sparta Praha	Czech-Rep	5	2	3	5	....	....	....	8	....	....	....	....	....	....	....	....	....	....	6	0	2	2	52	....	....	....
	Las Vegas Thunder	IHL	3	3	3	6	....	....	....	4	....	....	....	....	....	....	....	....	....	....	....	....	....	....	....	....	....	....
1998-99	Las Vegas Thunder	IHL	13	8	10	18	....	....	....	32	....	....	....	....	....	....	....	....	....	....	....	....	....	....	....	....	....	....
	New York Rangers	**NHL**	**56**	**20**	**27**	**47**	**23**	**26**	**49**	**50**	**9**	**1**	**3**	**153**	**13.1**	**67**	**29**	**51**	**7**	**–6**	....	....	....	....	....	....	....	....
99-2000	**New York Rangers**	**NHL**	**76**	**24**	**44**	**68**	**27**	**41**	**68**	**40**	**6**	**2**	**4**	**201**	**11.9**	**85**	**27**	**72**	**16**	**2**	....	....	....	....	....	....	....	....
	NHL Totals		**573**	**202**	**250**	**452**	**209**	**219**	**428**	**410**	**46**	**8**	**23**	**1278**	**15.8**	**626**	**185**	**507**	**94**		**65**	**17**	**23**	**40**	**56**	**6**	**1**	**2**

Canadian Major Junior Rookie of the Year (1990)

Signed as a free agent by **St. Louis**, March 5, 1994. Traded to **NY Rangers** by **St. Louis** for Esa Tikkanen and Doug Lidster, July 24, 1994. Traded to **Pittsburgh** by **NY Rangers** with Sergei Zubov for Luc Robitaille and Ulf Samuelsson, August 31, 1995. Traded to **NY Rangers** by **Pittsburgh** with Chris Tamer and Sean Pronger for Alexei Kovalev and Harry York, November 25, 1998.

• NEDVED, Zdenek

RW – L. 6', 180 lbs. b: Lany, Czech., 3/3/1975. Toronto's 3rd, 123rd overall, in 1993.

Season	Club	League	GP	G	A	Pts	AG	AA	APts	PIM	PP	SH	GW	S	%	TGF	PGF	TGA	PGA	+/–	GP	G	A	Pts	PIM	PP	SH	GW
1991-92	Poldi Kladno	Czech-Jr.	19	15	12	27	....	....	....	22	....	....	....	....	....	....	....	....	....	....	....	....	....	....	....	....	....	....
1992-93	Sudbury Wolves	OHL	18	3	9	12	....	....	....	6	....	....	....	....	....	....	....	....	....	....	....	....	....	....	....	....	....	....
1993-94	Sudbury Wolves	OHL	60	50	50	100	....	....	....	42	....	....	....	....	....	....	....	....	....	....	10	7	8	15	10	....	....	....
	Czech-Republic	WJC-A	7	4	3	7	....	....	....	10	....	....	....	....	....	....	....	....	....	....	....	....	....	....	....	....	....	....
1994-95	Sudbury Wolves	OHL	59	47	51	98	....	....	....	36	....	....	....	....	....	....	....	....	....	....	18	12	16	28	16	....	....	....
	Czech-Republic	WJC-A	7	4	4	8	....	....	....	10	....	....	....	....	....	....	....	....	....	....	....	....	....	....	....	....	....	....
	Toronto Maple Leafs	**NHL**	**1**	**0**	**0**	**0**	**0**	**0**	**0**	**2**	**0**	**0**	**0**	**0**	**0.0**	**0**	**0**	**0**	**0**	**0**	....	....	....	....	....	....	....	....
1995-96	**Toronto Maple Leafs**	**NHL**	**7**	**1**	**1**	**2**	**1**	**1**	**2**	**6**	**0**	**0**	**0**	**7**	**14.3**	**2**	**1**	**2**	**0**	**–1**	....	....	....	....	....	....	....	....
	St. John's Maple Leafs	AHL	41	13	14	27	....	....	....	22	....	....	....	....	....	....	....	....	....	....	4	2	0	2	0	....	....	....

Season	Club	League	GP	G	A	Pts	AG	AA	APts	PIM	PP	SH	GW	S	%	TGF	PGF	TGA	PGA	+/–	GP	G	A	Pts	PIM	PP	SH	GW
			REGULAR SEASON																		PLAYOFFS							
1996-97	Toronto Maple Leafs	NHL	23	3	5	8	3	4	7	6	1	0	0	22	13.6	16	3	9	0	4	....	....	....	....	....	....	....	....
	St. John's Maple Leafs	AHL	51	9	25	34	....	....	....	34	....	....	....	....	....	....	....	....	....	....	7	2	2	4	6	....	....	....
1997-98	Long Beach Ice Dogs	IHL	19	3	8	11	....	....	....	18	....	....	....	....	....	....	....	....	....	....	....	....	....	....	....	....	....	....
	St. John's Maple Leafs	AHL	45	7	8	15	....	....	....	24	....	....	....	....	....	....	....	....	....	....	3	1	0	1	2	....	....	....
1998-99	HC Sparta Praha	Czech-Rep	10	0	2	2	....	....	....	8	....	....	....	....	....	....	....	....	....	....	....	....	....	....	....	....	....	....
	HC Sparta Praha	EuroHL	3	0	0	0	....	....	....	0	....	....	....	....	....	....	....	....	....	....	....	....	....	....	....	....	....	....
	Lukko Rauma	Finland	30	4	7	11	....	....	....	22	....	....	....	....	....	....	....	....	....	....	....	....	....	....	....	....	....	....
99-2000	Lukko Rauma	Finland	54	28	18	46	....	....	....	50	....	....	....	....	....	....	....	....	....	....	4	0	0	0	2	....	....	....
	NHL Totals		**31**	**4**	**6**	**10**	**4**	**5**	**9**	**14**	**1**	**0**	**0**	**29**	**13.8**	**18**	**4**	**11**	**0**		....	....	....	....	....	....	....	....

• NEEDHAM, Mike

Michael Lawrence RW – R. 5'10", 185 lbs. b: Calgary, Alta., 4/4/1970. Pittsburgh's 7th, 126th overall, in 1989.

Season	Club	League	GP	G	A	Pts	AG	AA	APts	PIM	PP	SH	GW	S	%	TGF	PGF	TGA	PGA	+/–	GP	G	A	Pts	PIM	PP	SH	GW
1985-86	Fort Saskatchewan Rangers	AMHA	49	19	26	45	....	....	....	97	....	....	....	....	....	....	....	....	....	....	....	....	....	....	....	....	....	....
1986-87	Fort Saskatchewan Traders	AJHL	STATISTICS NOT AVAILABLE																									
	Kamloops Blazers	WHL	3	1	2	3	....	....	....	0	....	....	....	....	....	....	....	....	....	....	11	2	1	3	5	....	....	....
1987-88	Kamloops Blazers	WHL	64	31	33	64	....	....	....	93	....	....	....	....	....	....	....	....	....	....	5	0	1	1	5	....	....	....
1988-89	Kamloops Blazers	WHL	49	24	27	51	....	....	....	55	....	....	....	....	....	....	....	....	....	....	16	2	9	11	13	....	....	....
1989-90	Kamloops Blazers	WHL	60	59	66	125	....	....	....	75	....	....	....	....	....	....	....	....	....	....	17	11	13	24	10	....	....	....
	Canada	WJC-A	7	3	4	7	....	....	....	2	....	....	....	....	....	....	....	....	....	....	....	....	....	....	....	....	....	....
	Kamloops Blazers	Mem-Cup	3	1	2	3	....	....	....	2	....	....	....	....	....	....	....	....	....	....	....	....	....	....	....	....	....	....
1990-91	Muskegon Lumberjacks	IHL	65	14	31	45	....	....	....	17	....	....	....	....	....	....	....	....	....	....	5	2	2	4	5	....	....	....
1991-92	Muskegon Lumberjacks	IHL	80	41	37	78	....	....	....	83	....	....	....	....	....	....	....	....	....	....	8	4	4	8	6	....	....	....
♦	**Pittsburgh Penguins**	**NHL**	....	....	....	....	....	....	....	....	....	....	....	....	....	....	....	....	....	....	**5**	**1**	**0**	**1**	**2**	**0**	**0**	**0**
1992-93	**Pittsburgh Penguins**	**NHL**	**56**	**8**	**5**	**13**	**7**	**3**	**10**	**14**	**0**	**0**	**2**	**49**	**16.3**	**21**	**3**	**20**	**1**	**–1**	**9**	**1**	**0**	**1**	**2**	**0**	**0**	**0**
	Cleveland Lumberjacks	IHL	1	2	0	2	....	....	....	0	....	....	....	....	....	....	....	....	....	....	....	....	....	....	....	....	....	....
1993-94	**Pittsburgh Penguins**	**NHL**	**25**	**1**	**0**	**1**	**1**	**0**	**1**	**2**	**0**	**0**	**1**	**6**	**16.7**	**2**	**0**	**2**	**0**	**0**	....	....	....	....	....	....	....	....
	Cleveland Lumberjacks	IHL	6	4	3	7	....	....	....	7	....	....	....	....	....	....	....	....	....	....	....	....	....	....	....	....	....	....
	Dallas Stars	**NHL**	**5**	**0**	**0**	**0**	**0**	**0**	**0**	**0**	**0**	**0**	**0**	**3**	**0.0**	**2**	**1**	**3**	**0**	**–2**	....	....	....	....	....	....	....	....
1994-95	Kalamazoo Wings	IHL	37	9	9	18	....	....	....	31	....	....	....	....	....	....	....	....	....	....	14	5	5	10	11	....	....	....
1995-96	Adirondack Red Wings	AHL	16	5	10	15	....	....	....	12	....	....	....	....	....	....	....	....	....	....	....	....	....	....	....	....	....	....
	NHL Totals		**86**	**9**	**5**	**14**	**8**	**3**	**11**	**16**	**0**	**0**	**3**	**58**	**15.5**	**25**	**4**	**25**	**1**		**14**	**2**	**0**	**2**	**4**	**0**	**0**	**0**

WHL West First All-Star Team (1990)

Traded to **Dallas** by **Pittsburgh** for Jim McKenzie, March 21, 1994.

• NEELY, Bob

Robert Barry "Waldo" LW – L. 6'1", 210 lbs. b: Sarnia, Ont., 11/9/1953. Toronto's 2nd, 10th overall, in 1973.

Season	Club	League	GP	G	A	Pts	AG	AA	APts	PIM	PP	SH	GW	S	%	TGF	PGF	TGA	PGA	+/–	GP	G	A	Pts	PIM	PP	SH	GW
1970-71	Sarnia Black Hawks	OHA-B	STATISTICS NOT AVAILABLE																									
	Hamilton Red Wings	OHA-Jr.	34	4	11	15	....	....	....	129	....	....	....	....	....	....	....	....	....	....	7	0	4	4	4	....	....	....
1971-72	Hamilton Red Wings	OMJHL	17	3	8	11	....	....	....	109	....	....	....	....	....	....	....	....	....	....	....	....	....	....	....	....	....	....
	Peterborough Petes	OMJHL	32	8	22	30	....	....	....	96	....	....	....	....	....	....	....	....	....	....	15	4	8	12	76	....	....	....
	Peterborough Petes	Mem-Cup	3	0	2	2	....	....	....	6	....	....	....	....	....	....	....	....	....	....	....	....	....	....	....	....	....	....
1972-73	Peterborough Petes	OMJHL	55	24	52	76	....	....	....	304	....	....	....	....	....	....	....	....	....	....	17	3	17	20	44	....	....	....
1973-74	**Toronto Maple Leafs**	**NHL**	**54**	**5**	**7**	**12**	**5**	**6**	**11**	**98**	**2**	**0**	**0**	**77**	**6.5**	**45**	**9**	**52**	**2**	**–14**	**4**	**1**	**3**	**4**	**0**	**0**	**0**	**0**
1974-75	**Toronto Maple Leafs**	**NHL**	**57**	**5**	**16**	**21**	**4**	**12**	**16**	**61**	**2**	**0**	**1**	**103**	**4.9**	**64**	**12**	**86**	**16**	**–18**	**3**	**0**	**0**	**0**	**2**	**0**	**0**	**0**
	Oklahoma City Blazers	CHL	9	2	4	6	....	....	....	14	....	....	....	....	....	....	....	....	....	....	....	....	....	....	....	....	....	....
1975-76	**Toronto Maple Leafs**	**NHL**	**69**	**9**	**13**	**22**	**8**	**10**	**18**	**89**	**0**	**0**	**0**	**107**	**8.4**	**64**	**9**	**87**	**17**	**–15**	**10**	**3**	**1**	**4**	**7**	**2**	**0**	**0**
1976-77	**Toronto Maple Leafs**	**NHL**	**70**	**17**	**16**	**33**	**15**	**12**	**27**	**16**	**3**	**0**	**5**	**123**	**13.8**	**72**	**18**	**82**	**11**	**–17**	**9**	**1**	**3**	**4**	**6**	**1**	**0**	**0**
1977-78	**Toronto Maple Leafs**	**NHL**	**11**	**0**	**1**	**1**	**0**	**1**	**1**	**0**	**0**	**0**	**0**	**7**	**0.0**	**3**	**0**	**6**	**0**	**–3**	....	....	....	....	....	....	....	....
	Colorado Rockies	**NHL**	**22**	**3**	**6**	**9**	**3**	**5**	**8**	**2**	**1**	**0**	**0**	**33**	**9.1**	**21**	**8**	**23**	**0**	**–10**	....	....	....	....	....	....	....	....
	Philadelphia Firebirds	AHL	29	6	14	20	....	....	....	47	....	....	....	....	....	....	....	....	....	....	4	1	3	4	2	....	....	....
1978-79	New Brunswick Hawks	AHL	60	17	29	46	....	....	....	55	....	....	....	....	....	....	....	....	....	....	5	0	1	1	0	....	....	....
1979-80	New Brunswick Hawks	AHL	64	14	51	65	....	....	....	46	....	....	....	....	....	....	....	....	....	....	8	1	4	5	2	....	....	....
	NHL Totals		**283**	**39**	**59**	**98**	**35**	**46**	**81**	**266**	**8**	**0**	**6**	**450**	**8.7**	**269**	**56**	**336**	**46**		**26**	**5**	**7**	**12**	**15**	**3**	**0**	**0**

OMJHL First All-Star Team (1973) • AHL First All-Star Team (1980)

Traded to **Colorado** by **Toronto** for cash, January 9, 1978. Traded to **Toronto** by **Colorado** for cash, May 30, 1978.

• NEELY, Cam

Cam Michael RW – R. 6'1", 218 lbs. b: Comox, B.C., 6/6/1965. Vancouver's 1st, 9th overall, in 1983.

Season	Club	League	GP	G	A	Pts	AG	AA	APts	PIM	PP	SH	GW	S	%	TGF	PGF	TGA	PGA	+/–	GP	G	A	Pts	PIM	PP	SH	GW
1981-82	Ridge Meadows Lightning	BCAHA	64	73	68	141	....	....	....	134	....	....	....	....	....	....	....	....	....	....	....	....	....	....	....	....	....	....
1982-83	Portland Winter Hawks	WHL	72	56	64	120	....	....	....	130	....	....	....	....	....	....	....	....	....	....	14	9	11	20	17	....	....	....
	Portland Winter Hawks	Mem-Cup	4	*5	4	9	....	....	....	6	....	....	....	....	....	....	....	....	....	....	....	....	....	....	....	....	....	....
1983-84	Portland Winter Hawks	WHL	19	8	18	26	....	....	....	29	....	....	....	....	....	....	....	....	....	....	....	....	....	....	....	....	....	....
	Vancouver Canucks	**NHL**	**56**	**16**	**15**	**31**	**13**	**10**	**23**	**57**	**3**	**0**	**1**	**87**	**18.4**	**55**	**17**	**39**	**1**	**0**	**4**	**2**	**0**	**2**	**2**	**1**	**0**	**0**
1984-85	**Vancouver Canucks**	**NHL**	**72**	**21**	**18**	**39**	**17**	**12**	**29**	**137**	**4**	**0**	**1**	**138**	**15.2**	**65**	**12**	**79**	**0**	**–26**	....	....	....	....	....	....	....	....
1985-86	**Vancouver Canucks**	**NHL**	**73**	**14**	**20**	**34**	**11**	**13**	**24**	**126**	**6**	**0**	**3**	**113**	**12.4**	**50**	**17**	**63**	**0**	**–30**	**3**	**0**	**0**	**0**	**6**	**0**	**0**	**0**
1986-87	**Boston Bruins**	**NHL**	**75**	**36**	**36**	**72**	**31**	**26**	**57**	**143**	**7**	**0**	**3**	**206**	**17.5**	**105**	**26**	**56**	**0**	**23**	**4**	**5**	**1**	**6**	**8**	**3**	**0**	**0**
1987-88	**Boston Bruins**	**NHL**	**69**	**42**	**27**	**69**	**36**	**19**	**55**	**175**	**11**	**0**	**3**	**207**	**20.3**	**102**	**31**	**41**	**0**	**30**	**23**	**9**	**8**	**17**	**51**	**2**	**0**	**2**
1988-89	**Boston Bruins**	**NHL**	**74**	**37**	**38**	**75**	**31**	**27**	**58**	**190**	**18**	**0**	**6**	**235**	**15.7**	**108**	**40**	**54**	**0**	**14**	**10**	**7**	**2**	**9**	**8**	**4**	**0**	**2**
1989-90	**Boston Bruins**	**NHL**	**76**	**55**	**37**	**92**	**48**	**27**	**75**	**117**	**25**	**0**	**12**	**271**	**20.3**	**128**	**58**	**65**	**5**	**10**	**21**	**12**	**16**	**28**	**51**	**4**	**1**	**2**
1990-91	**Boston Bruins**	**NHL**	**69**	**51**	**40**	**91**	**47**	**30**	**77**	**98**	**18**	**1**	**8**	**262**	**19.5**	**139**	**60**	**57**	**4**	**26**	**19**	**16**	**4**	**20**	**36**	**9**	**0**	**4**
1991-92	**Boston Bruins**	**NHL**	**9**	**9**	**3**	**12**	**8**	**2**	**10**	**16**	**1**	**0**	**2**	**30**	**30.0**	**15**	**1**	**5**	**0**	**9**	....	....	....	....	....	....	....	....
1992-93	**Boston Bruins**	**NHL**	**13**	**11**	**7**	**18**	**9**	**5**	**14**	**25**	**6**	**0**	**1**	**45**	**24.4**	**25**	**10**	**11**	**0**	**4**	**4**	**4**	**1**	**5**	**4**	**1**	**0**	**0**
1993-94	**Boston Bruins**	**NHL**	**49**	**50**	**24**	**74**	**47**	**19**	**66**	**54**	**20**	**0**	**13**	**185**	**27.0**	**109**	**48**	**53**	**4**	**12**	....	....	....	....	....	....	....	....
1994-95	**Boston Bruins**	**NHL**	**42**	**27**	**14**	**41**	**48**	**21**	**69**	**72**	**16**	**0**	**5**	**178**	**15.2**	**64**	**28**	**32**	**3**	**7**	**5**	**2**	**0**	**2**	**2**	**1**	**0**	**1**
1995-96	**Boston Bruins**	**NHL**	**49**	**26**	**20**	**46**	**26**	**16**	**42**	**31**	**7**	**0**	**3**	**191**	**13.6**	**78**	**28**	**47**	**0**	**3**	....	....	....	....	....	....	....	....
	NHL Totals		**726**	**395**	**299**	**694**	**372**	**227**	**599**	**1241**	**142**	**1**	**61**	**2148**	**18.4**	**1043**	**376**	**602**	**17**		**93**	**57**	**32**	**89**	**168**	**25**	**1**	**11**

NHL Second All-Star Team (1988, 1990, 1991, 1994) • Won Bill Masterton Trophy (1994) • Played in NHL All-Star Game (1988, 1989, 1990, 1991, 1996)

Traded to **Boston** by **Vancouver** with Vancouver's 1st round choice (Glen Wesley) in 1987 Entry Draft for Barry Pederson, June 6, 1986. • Missed majority of 1991-92 season recovering from thigh (October 15, 1991) and knee (January, 1992) injuries. • Missed majority of 1992-93 season recovering from knee surgery, September 17, 1992.

• NEILSON, Jim

James Anthony "Chief" D – L. 6'2", 205 lbs. b: Big River, Sask., 11/28/1940.

Season	Club	League	GP	G	A	Pts	AG	AA	APts	PIM	PP	SH	GW	S	%	TGF	PGF	TGA	PGA	+/–	GP	G	A	Pts	PIM	PP	SH	GW
1958-59	Prince Albert Mintos	SJHL	10	1	2	3	....	....	....	6	....	....	....	....	....	....	....	....	....	....	....	....	....	....	....	....	....	....
1959-60	Prince Albert Mintos	SJHL	57	21	28	49	....	....	....	61	....	....	....	....	....	....	....	....	....	....	7	2	2	4	6	....	....	....
1960-61	Prince Albert Mintos	SJHL	59	20	26	46	....	....	....	59	....	....	....	....	....	....	....	....	....	....	....	....	....	....	....	....	....	....
1961-62	Kitchener-Waterloo Beavers	EPHL	70	9	33	42	....	....	....	78	....	....	....	....	....	....	....	....	....	....	7	2	3	5	2	....	....	....
1962-63	**New York Rangers**	**NHL**	**69**	**5**	**11**	**16**	**6**	**11**	**17**	**38**																		
1963-64	**New York Rangers**	**NHL**	**69**	**5**	**24**	**29**	**6**	**25**	**31**	**93**																		
1964-65	**New York Rangers**	**NHL**	**62**	**0**	**13**	**13**	**0**	**13**	**13**	**58**																		
1965-66	**New York Rangers**	**NHL**	**65**	**4**	**19**	**23**	**4**	**18**	**22**	**84**																		
1966-67	**New York Rangers**	**NHL**	**61**	**4**	**11**	**15**	**5**	**11**	**16**	**65**											**4**	**1**	**0**	**1**	**0**	**1**	**0**	**0**
1967-68	**New York Rangers**	**NHL**	**67**	**6**	**29**	**35**	**7**	**29**	**36**	**60**	**2**	**0**	**1**	**172**	**3.5**	**108**	**26**	**71**	**18**	**29**	**6**	**0**	**2**	**2**	**4**	**0**	**0**	**0**
1968-69	**New York Rangers**	**NHL**	**76**	**10**	**34**	**44**	**11**	**30**	**41**	**95**	**3**	**0**	**2**	**274**	**3.6**	**130**	**38**	**97**	**11**	**6**	**4**	**0**	**3**	**3**	**5**	**0**	**0**	**0**
1969-70	**New York Rangers**	**NHL**	**62**	**3**	**20**	**23**	**3**	**19**	**22**	**75**	**0**	**0**	**0**	**204**	**1.5**	**94**	**16**	**66**	**12**	**24**	**6**	**0**	**1**	**1**	**8**	**0**	**0**	**0**
1970-71	**New York Rangers**	**NHL**	**77**	**8**	**24**	**32**	**8**	**20**	**28**	**69**	**2**	**0**	**3**	**200**	**4.0**	**112**	**27**	**73**	**19**	**31**	**13**	**0**	**3**	**3**	**30**	**0**	**0**	**0**
1971-72	**New York Rangers**	**NHL**	**78**	**7**	**30**	**37**	**7**	**26**	**33**	**56**	**2**	**0**	**0**	**183**	**3.8**	**131**	**18**	**97**	**22**	**38**	**10**	**0**	**3**	**3**	**8**	**0**	**0**	**0**
1972-73	**New York Rangers**	**NHL**	**52**	**4**	**16**	**20**	**4**	**13**	**17**	**35**	**0**	**0**	**0**	**99**	**4.0**	**76**	**7**	**60**	**13**	**22**	**10**	**0**	**4**	**4**	**2**	**0**	**0**	**0**
1973-74	**New York Rangers**	**NHL**	**72**	**4**	**7**	**11**	**4**	**6**	**10**	**38**	**2**	**0**	**1**	**103**	**3.9**	**62**	**4**	**77**	**15**	**–4**	**12**	**0**	**1**	**1**	**4**	**0**	**0**	**0**
1974-75	**California Golden Seals**	**NHL**	**72**	**3**	**17**	**20**	**3**	**13**	**16**	**56**	**0**	**0**	**0**	**112**	**2.7**	**77**	**18**	**130**	**25**	**–46**	....	....	....	....	....	....	....	....
1975-76	**California Golden Seals**	**NHL**	**26**	**1**	**6**	**7**	**1**	**4**	**5**	**20**	**1**	**0**	**0**	**41**	**2.4**	**28**	**7**	**34**	**7**	**–6**	....	....	....	....	....	....	....	....

			REGULAR SEASON																		PLAYOFFS							
Season	**Club**	**League**	**GP**	**G**	**A**	**Pts**	**AG**	**AA**	**APts**	**PIM**	**PP**	**SH**	**GW**	**S**	**%**	**TGF**	**PGF**	**TGA**	**PGA**	**+/–**	**GP**	**G**	**A**	**Pts**	**PIM**	**PP**	**SH**	**GW**
1976-77	**Cleveland Barons**	**NHL**	**47**	**3**	**17**	**20**	**3**	**13**	**16**	**42**	**0**	**0**	**0**	**42**	**7.1**	**64**	**3**	**82**	**16**	**–5**	....	....	....	....	....	....	....	....
1977-78	**Cleveland Barons**	**NHL**	**68**	**2**	**21**	**23**	**2**	**16**	**18**	**20**	**0**	**0**	**0**	**51**	**3.9**	**65**	**4**	**109**	**23**	**–25**	....	....	....	....	....	....	....	....
1978-79	Edmonton Oilers	WHA	35	0	5	5	....	....	....	18	....	....	....	....	....	....	....	....	....	....	....	....	....	....	....	....	....	....
	NHL Totals		**1023**	**69**	**299**	**368**	**74**	**267**	**341**	**904**	....	....	....	....	....	....	....	....	....		**65**	**1**	**17**	**18**	**61**	....	....	....
	Other Major League Totals		35	0	5	5	....	....	....	18	....	....	....	....	....	....	....	....	....	....	....	....	....	....	....	....	....	....

NHL Second All-Star Team (1968) • Played in NHL All-Star Game (1967, 1971)

Selected by **LA Sharks** (WHA) in 1972 WHA General Player Draft, February 12, 1972. Claimed by **California** from **NY Rangers** in Intra-League Draft, June 10, 1974. Transferred to **Cleveland** after **California** franchise relocated, August 26, 1976. Placed on **Minnesota** Reserve List after **Cleveland-Minnesota** Dispersal Draft, June 15, 1978. Signed as a free agent by **Edmonton** (WHA), June, 1978.

• NELSON, Gordie

Gordon William D – L. 5′8″, 180 lbs. b: Kinistino, Sask., 5/10/1947.

Season	Club	League	GP	G	A	Pts	AG	AA	APts	PIM	PP	SH	GW	S	%	TGF	PGF	TGA	PGA	+/–	GP	G	A	Pts	PIM	PP	SH	GW
1964-65	Melville Millionaires	SJHL	55	3	16	19	....	....	....	99	....	....	....	....	....	....	....	....	....	....	....	....	....	....	....	....	....	....
1965-66	Melville Millionaires	SJHL	60	11	24	35	....	....	....	91	....	....	....	....	....	....	....	....	....	....	....	....	....	....	....	....	....	....
1966-67	Trois-Rivieres Reds	QJHL	14	3	8	11	....	....	....	35	....	....	....	....	....	....	....	....	....	....	7	2	5	7	19	....	....	....
1967-68	Tulsa Oilers	CPHL	62	4	18	22	....	....	....	114	....	....	....	....	....	....	....	....	....	....	10	0	5	5	4	....	....	....
1968-69	Tulsa Oilers	CHL	71	8	22	30	....	....	....	136	....	....	....	....	....	....	....	....	....	....	7	2	3	5	25	....	....	....
1969-70	**Toronto Maple Leafs**	**NHL**	**3**	**0**	**0**	**0**	**0**	**0**	**0**	**11**	**0**	**0**	**0**	**5**	**0.0**	**3**	**0**	**2**	**1**	**2**	....	....	....	....	....	....	....	....
	Tulsa Oilers	CHL	69	10	38	48	....	....	....	158	....	....	....	....	....	....	....	....	....	....	6	2	4	6	10	....	....	....
1970-71	Tulsa Oilers	CHL	57	4	26	30	....	....	....	23	....	....	....	....	....	....	....	....	....	....	....	....	....	....	....	....	....	....
1971-72	Phoenix Roadrunners	WHL	67	7	35	42	....	....	....	102	....	....	....	....	....	....	....	....	....	....	6	0	2	2	16	....	....	....
1972-73	Phoenix Roadrunners	WHL	9	1	3	4	....	....	....	28	....	....	....	....	....	....	....	....	....	....	....	....	....	....	....	....	....	....
	Portland Buckaroos	WHL	65	5	25	30	....	....	....	143	....	....	....	....	....	....	....	....	....	....	....	....	....	....	....	....	....	....
	NHL Totals		**3**	**0**	**0**	**0**	**0**	**0**	**0**	**11**	**0**	**0**	**0**	**5**	**0.0**	**3**	**0**	**2**	**1**	....	....	....	....	....	....	....	....	....

CHL First All-Star Team (1970)

Signed as a free agent by **Toronto**, December 10, 1969.

• NELSON, Jeff

Jeffrey A.C. C – L. 5′11″, 190 lbs. b: Prince Albert, Sask., 12/18/1972. Washington's 4th, 36th overall, in 1991.

Season	Club	League	GP	G	A	Pts	AG	AA	APts	PIM	PP	SH	GW	S	%	TGF	PGF	TGA	PGA	+/–	GP	G	A	Pts	PIM	PP	SH	GW
1987-88	Prince Albert Midget Raiders	AAHA	31	24	32	56	....	....	....	32	....	....	....	....	....	....	....	....	....	....	....	....	....	....	....	....	....	....
1988-89	Prince Albert Raiders	WHL	71	30	57	87	....	....	....	74	....	....	....	....	....	....	....	....	....	....	4	0	3	3	4	....	....	....
1989-90	Prince Albert Raiders	WHL	72	28	69	97	....	....	....	79	....	....	....	....	....	....	....	....	....	....	14	2	11	13	10	....	....	....
1990-91	Prince Albert Raiders	WHL	72	46	74	120	....	....	....	58	....	....	....	....	....	....	....	....	....	....	3	1	1	2	4	....	....	....
1991-92	Prince Albert Raiders	WHL	64	48	65	113	....	....	....	84	....	....	....	....	....	....	....	....	....	....	9	7	14	21	18	....	....	....
	Canada	WJC-A	7	1	1	2	....	....	....	2	....	....	....	....	....	....	....	....	....	....	....	....	....	....	....	....	....	....
1992-93	Baltimore Skipjacks	AHL	72	14	38	52	....	....	....	12	....	....	....	....	....	....	....	....	....	....	7	1	3	4	2	....	....	....
1993-94	Portland Pirates	AHL	80	34	73	107	....	....	....	92	....	....	....	....	....	....	....	....	....	....	17	10	5	15	20	....	....	....
1994-95	Portland Pirates	AHL	64	33	50	83	....	....	....	57	....	....	....	....	....	....	....	....	....	....	7	1	4	5	8	....	....	....
	Washington Capitals	**NHL**	**10**	**1**	**0**	**1**	**2**	**0**	**2**	**2**	**0**	**0**	**0**	**4**	**25.0**	**2**	**0**	**4**	**0**	**–2**	....	....	....	....	....	....	....	....
1995-96	**Washington Capitals**	**NHL**	**33**	**0**	**7**	**7**	**0**	**6**	**6**	**16**	**0**	**0**	**0**	**21**	**0.0**	**12**	**0**	**9**	**0**	**3**	**3**	**0**	**0**	**0**	**4**	**0**	**0**	**0**
	Portland Pirates	AHL	39	15	32	47	....	....	....	62	....	....	....	....	....	....	....	....	....	....	....	....	....	....	....	....	....	....
1996-97	Grand Rapids Griffins	IHL	82	34	55	89	....	....	....	85	....	....	....	....	....	....	....	....	....	....	5	0	4	4	4	....	....	....
1997-98	Milwaukee Admirals	IHL	52	20	34	54	....	....	....	30	....	....	....	....	....	....	....	....	....	....	10	2	7	9	15	....	....	....
1998-99	**Nashville Predators**	**NHL**	**9**	**2**	**1**	**3**	**2**	**1**	**3**	**2**	**0**	**0**	**0**	**8**	**25.0**	**4**	**0**	**10**	**5**	**–1**	....	....	....	....	....	....	....	....
	Milwaukee Admirals	IHL	70	20	31	51	....	....	....	66	....	....	....	....	....	....	....	....	....	....	2	0	0	0	0	....	....	....
99-2000	Portland Pirates	AHL	73	24	30	54	....	....	....	38	....	....	....	....	....	....	....	....	....	....	1	0	0	0	0	....	....	....
	NHL Totals		**52**	**3**	**8**	**11**	**4**	**7**	**11**	**20**	**0**	**0**	**0**	**33**	**9.1**	**18**	**0**	**23**	**5**		**3**	**0**	**0**	**0**	**4**	**0**	**0**	**0**

• Brother of Todd • Canadian Major Junior Scholastic Player of the Year (1989, 1990) • WHL East Second All-Star Team (1991, 1992)

Traded to **Nashville** by **Washington** for future considerations, August 19, 1998. Traded to **Washington** by **Nashville** for cash, June 21, 1999.

• NELSON, Todd

D – L. 6′, 201 lbs. b: Prince Albert, Sask., 5/11/1969. Pittsburgh's 4th, 79th overall, in 1989.

Season	Club	League	GP	G	A	Pts	AG	AA	APts	PIM	PP	SH	GW	S	%	TGF	PGF	TGA	PGA	+/–	GP	G	A	Pts	PIM	PP	SH	GW
1984-85	Prince Albert Bantam Raiders	SAHA	36	3	18	21	....	....	....	50	....	....	....	....	....	....	....	....	....	....	....	....	....	....	....	....	....	....
1985-86	Prince Albert Midget Raiders	AAHA	36	3	23	26	....	....	....	74	....	....	....	....	....	....	....	....	....	....	....	....	....	....	....	....	....	....
	Prince Albert Raiders	WHL	4	0	0	0	....	....	....	0	....	....	....	....	....	....	....	....	....	....	....	....	....	....	....	....	....	....
1986-87	Prince Albert Raiders	WHL	35	1	6	7	....	....	....	10	....	....	....	....	....	....	....	....	....	....	4	0	0	0	0	....	....	....
1987-88	Prince Albert Raiders	WHL	72	3	21	24	....	....	....	59	....	....	....	....	....	....	....	....	....	....	10	3	2	5	4	....	....	....
1988-89	Prince Albert Raiders	WHL	72	14	45	59	....	....	....	72	....	....	....	....	....	....	....	....	....	....	4	1	3	4	4	....	....	....
1989-90	Prince Albert Raiders	WHL	69	13	42	55	....	....	....	88	....	....	....	....	....	....	....	....	....	....	14	3	12	15	12	....	....	....
1990-91	Muskegon Lumberjacks	IHL	79	4	20	24	....	....	....	32	....	....	....	....	....	....	....	....	....	....	3	0	0	0	4	....	....	....
1991-92	**Pittsburgh Penguins**	**NHL**	**1**	**0**	**0**	**0**	**0**	**0**	**0**	**0**	**0**	**0**	**0**	**0**	**0.0**	**0**	**0**	**0**	**0**	**0**	....	....	....	....	....	....	....	....
	Muskegon Lumberjacks	IHL	80	6	35	41	....	....	....	46	....	....	....	....	....	....	....	....	....	....	14	1	11	12	4	....	....	....
1992-93	Cleveland Lumberjacks	IHL	76	7	35	42	....	....	....	115	....	....	....	....	....	....	....	....	....	....	4	0	2	2	4	....	....	....
1993-94	**Washington Capitals**	**NHL**	**2**	**1**	**0**	**1**	**1**	**0**	**1**	**2**	**1**	**0**	**1**	**1**	**100.0**	**3**	**1**	**1**	**0**	**1**	**4**	**0**	**0**	**0**	**0**	**0**	**0**	**0**
	Portland Pirates	AHL	80	11	34	45	....	....	....	69	....	....	....	....	....	....	....	....	....	....	11	0	6	6	6	....	....	....
1994-95	Portland Pirates	AHL	75	10	35	45	....	....	....	76	....	....	....	....	....	....	....	....	....	....	7	0	4	4	6	....	....	....
1995-96	Hershey Bears	AHL	70	10	40	50	....	....	....	38	....	....	....	....	....	....	....	....	....	....	5	1	2	3	8	....	....	....
1996-97	Grand Rapids Griffins	IHL	81	3	18	21	....	....	....	32	....	....	....	....	....	....	....	....	....	....	5	1	0	1	0	....	....	....
1997-98	Grand Rapids Griffins	IHL	75	6	21	27	....	....	....	36	....	....	....	....	....	....	....	....	....	....	3	0	0	0	2	....	....	....
1998-99	Berlin Capitals	Germany	44	5	10	15	....	....	....	26	....	....	....	....	....	....	....	....	....	....	....	....	....	....	....	....	....	....
99-2000	HIFK Helsinki	EuroHL	1	0	0	0	....	....	....	0	....	....	....	....	....	....	....	....	....	....	....	....	....	....	....	....	....	....
	HIFK Helsinki	Finland	4	1	1	2	....	....	....	2	....	....	....	....	....	....	....	....	....	....	....	....	....	....	....	....	....	....
	Grand Rapids Griffins	IHL	73	2	15	17	....	....	....	47	....	....	....	....	....	....	....	....	....	....	17	0	2	2	10	....	....	....
	NHL Totals		**3**	**1**	**0**	**1**	**1**	**0**	**1**	**2**	**1**	**0**	**1**	**1**	**100.0**	**3**	**1**	**1**	**0**		**4**	**0**	**0**	**0**	**0**	**0**	**0**	**0**

• Brother of Jeff • WHL East Second All-Star Team (1989, 1990)

Signed as a free agent by **Washington**, August 15, 1993. Signed as a free agent by **Grand Rapids** (IHL), July 24, 1996. Signed as a free agent by **Grand Rapids** (IHL), September 30, 1999.

• NEMCHINOV, Sergei

C – L. 6′, 205 lbs. b: Moscow, USSR, 1/14/1964. NY Rangers' 14th, 244th overall, in 1990.

Season	Club	League	GP	G	A	Pts	AG	AA	APts	PIM	PP	SH	GW	S	%	TGF	PGF	TGA	PGA	+/–	GP	G	A	Pts	PIM	PP	SH	GW
1981-82	Krylja Sovetov Moscow	USSR	15	1	0	1	....	....	....	0	....	....	....	....	....	....	....	....	....	....	....	....	....	....	....	....	....	....
	Soviet Union	EJC-A	5	4	2	6	....	....	....	4	....	....	....	....	....	....	....	....	....	....	....	....	....	....	....	....	....	....
1982-83	CSKA Moscow	USSR	11	0	0	0	....	....	....	2	....	....	....	....	....	....	....	....	....	....	....	....	....	....	....	....	....	....
	Soviet Union	WJC-A	7	4	3	7	....	....	....	2	....	....	....	....	....	....	....	....	....	....	....	....	....	....	....	....	....	....
1983-84	CSKA Moscow	USSR	20	6	5	11	....	....	....	4	....	....	....	....	....	....	....	....	....	....	....	....	....	....	....	....	....	....
	Soviet Union	WJC-A	7	5	6	11	....	....	....	2	....	....	....	....	....	....	....	....	....	....	....	....	....	....	....	....	....	....
1984-85	CSKA Moscow	USSR	31	2	4	6	....	....	....	4	....	....	....	....	....	....	....	....	....	....	....	....	....	....	....	....	....	....
1985-86	Krylja Sovetov Moscow	USSR	39	7	12	19	....	....	....	28	....	....	....	....	....	....	....	....	....	....	....	....	....	....	....	....	....	....
1986-87	Krylja Sovetov Moscow	USSR	40	13	9	22	....	....	....	24	....	....	....	....	....	....	....	....	....	....	....	....	....	....	....	....	....	....
	USSR	RV-87	1	0	0	0	....	....	....	4	....	....	....	....	....	....	....	....	....	....	....	....	....	....	....	....	....	....
1987-88	Soviet Union	Can-Cup	5	0	0	0	....	....	....	6	....	....	....	....	....	....	....	....	....	....	....	....	....	....	....	....	....	....
	Krylja Sovetov Moscow	USSR	48	17	11	28	....	....	....	26	....	....	....	....	....	....	....	....	....	....	....	....	....	....	....	....	....	....
1988-89	Krylja Sovetov Moscow	USSR	43	15	14	29	....	....	....	28	....	....	....	....	....	....	....	....	....	....	....	....	....	....	....	....	....	....
	CSKA Moscow	Super-S	7	2	2	4	....	....	....	2	....	....	....	....	....	....	....	....	....	....	....	....	....	....	....	....	....	....
	Soviet Union	WEC-A	7	2	0	2	....	....	....	2	....	....	....	....	....	....	....	....	....	....	....	....	....	....	....	....	....	....
1989-90	Krylja Sovetov Moscow	Fr-Tour	1	0	0	0	....	....	....	0	....	....	....	....	....	....	....	....	....	....	....	....	....	....	....	....	....	....
	Krylja Sovetov Moscow	USSR	48	17	16	33	....	....	....	34	....	....	....	....	....	....	....	....	....	....	....	....	....	....	....	....	....	....
	Krylja Sovetov Moscow	Super-S	5	0	2	2	....	....	....	2	....	....	....	....	....	....	....	....	....	....	....	....	....	....	....	....	....	....
	Soviet Union	WEC-A	10	5	2	7	....	....	....	4	....	....	....	....	....	....	....	....	....	....	....	....	....	....	....	....	....	....

			REGULAR SEASON																		PLAYOFFS							
Season	Club	League	GP	G	A	Pts	AG	AA	APts	PIM	PP	SH	GW	S	%	TGF	PGF	TGA	PGA	+/–	GP	G	A	Pts	PIM	PP	SH	GW
1990-91	Krylja Sovetov Moscow	Fr-Tour	1	1	0	1				0																		
	Krylja Sovetov Moscow	USSR	46	21	24	45				30																		
	CSKA Moscow	Super-S	7	1	6	7				0																		
	Soviet Union	WEC-A	10	2	3	5				2																		
1991-92	**New York Rangers**	**NHL**	**73**	**30**	**28**	**58**	**27**	**21**	**48**	**15**	**2**	**0**	**5**	**124**	**24.2**	**79**	**17**	**61**	**18**	**19**	**13**	**1**	**4**	**5**	**8**	**0**	**0**	**0**
1992-93	**New York Rangers**	**NHL**	**81**	**23**	**31**	**54**	**19**	**21**	**40**	**34**	**0**	**1**	**3**	**144**	**16.0**	**74**	**5**	**74**	**20**	**15**								
1993-94♦	**New York Rangers**	**NHL**	**76**	**22**	**27**	**49**	**20**	**21**	**41**	**36**	**4**	**0**	**6**	**144**	**15.3**	**59**	**11**	**51**	**16**	**13**	**23**	**2**	**5**	**7**	**6**	**0**	**0**	**0**
1994-95	**New York Rangers**	**NHL**	**47**	**7**	**6**	**13**	**12**	**9**	**21**	**16**	**0**	**0**	**3**	**67**	**10.4**	**21**	**1**	**32**	**6**	**–6**	**10**	**4**	**5**	**9**	**2**	**0**	**0**	**1**
1995-96	**New York Rangers**	**NHL**	**78**	**17**	**15**	**32**	**17**	**12**	**29**	**38**	**0**	**0**	**2**	**118**	**14.4**	**43**	**3**	**42**	**11**	**9**	**6**	**0**	**1**	**1**	**2**	**0**	**0**	**0**
1996-97	Russia	W-Cup	5	1	2	3				2																		
	New York Rangers	**NHL**	**63**	**6**	**13**	**19**	**6**	**12**	**18**	**12**	**1**	**0**	**1**	**90**	**6.7**	**29**	**3**	**23**	**2**	**5**								
	Vancouver Canucks	**NHL**	**6**	**2**	**3**	**5**	**2**	**3**	**5**	**4**	**0**	**0**	**1**	**7**	**28.6**	**6**	**1**	**1**	**0**	**4**								
1997-98	**New York Islanders**	**NHL**	**74**	**10**	**19**	**29**	**12**	**19**	**31**	**24**	**2**	**1**	**1**	**94**	**10.6**	**51**	**8**	**61**	**21**	**3**								
	Russia	Olympics	6	1	0	1				0																		
	Russia	WC-A	6	0	1	1				8																		
1998-99	**New York Islanders**	**NHL**	**67**	**8**	**8**	**16**	**9**	**8**	**17**	**22**	**1**	**0**	**0**	**61**	**13.1**	**27**	**2**	**55**	**13**	**–17**								
	New Jersey Devils	**NHL**	**10**	**4**	**0**	**4**	**5**	**0**	**5**	**6**	**1**	**0**	**1**	**13**	**30.8**	**8**	**2**	**4**	**2**	**4**	**4**	**0**	**0**	**0**	**0**	**0**	**0**	**0**
99-2000♦	**New Jersey Devils**	**NHL**	**53**	**10**	**16**	**26**	**11**	**15**	**26**	**18**	**0**	**1**	**1**	**55**	**18.2**	**37**	**5**	**35**	**4**	**1**	**21**	**3**	**2**	**5**	**2**	**1**	**0**	**0**
	NHL Totals		**628**	**139**	**166**	**305**	**140**	**141**	**281**	**225**	**11**	**3**	**24**	**917**	**15.2**	**434**	**58**	**439**	**113**		**77**	**10**	**17**	**27**	**20**	**1**	**0**	**1**

Traded to **Vancouver** by **NY Rangers** with Brian Noonan for Esa Tikkanen and Russ Courtnall, March 8, 1997. Signed as a free agent by **NY Islanders**, July 10, 1997. Traded to **New Jersey** by **NY Islanders** for New Jersey's 4th round choice (later traded to Los Angeles - Los Angeles selected Daniel Johansson) in 1999 Entry Draft, March 22, 1999.

• NEMECEK, Jan

D – R. 6'1", 220 lbs. b: Pisek, Czech., 2/14/1976. Los Angeles' 7th, 215th overall, in 1994.

Season	Club	League	GP	G	A	Pts	AG	AA	APts	PIM	PP	SH	GW	S	%	TGF	PGF	TGA	PGA	+/–	GP	G	A	Pts	PIM	PP	SH	GW
1992-93	Motor Ceske Budejovice	Czech.	15	0	0	0																						
	Czech-Republic	EJC-A	6	0	1	1				2																		
1993-94	HC Ceske Budejovice	Czech-Rep	16	0	1	1				16																		
	Czech-Republic	EJC-A	5	1	0	1				6																		
1994-95	Hull Olympiques	QMJHL	49	10	16	26				48											21	5	9	14	10			
	Hull Olympiques	Mem-Cup	3	0	1	1				0																		
1995-96	Hull Olympiques	QMJHL	57	17	49	66				58											17	2	13	15	10			
	Czech-Republic	WJC-A	6	1	2	3				2																		
1996-97	Mississippi Sea Wolves	ECHL	20	3	9	12				16											3	0	0	0	4			
	Phoenix Roadrunners	IHL	24	1	1	2				2																		
1997-98	Fredericton Canadiens	AHL	65	7	24	31				43											2	0	0	0	0			
1998-99	**Los Angeles Kings**	**NHL**	**6**	**1**	**0**	**1**	**1**	**0**	**1**	**4**	**0**	**0**	**1**	**8**	**12.5**	**3**	**0**	**4**	**0**	**–1**								
	Long Beach Ice Dogs	IHL	66	5	16	21				42																		
99-2000	**Los Angeles Kings**	**NHL**	**1**	**0**	**0**	**0**	**0**	**0**	**0**	**0**	**0**	**0**	**0**	**0**	**0.0**	**0**	**0**	**0**	**0**	**0**								
	Long Beach Ice Dogs	IHL	71	9	15	24				22											6	1	0	1	4			
	NHL Totals		**7**	**1**	**0**	**1**	**1**	**0**	**1**	**4**	**0**	**0**	**1**	**8**	**12.5**	**3**	**0**	**4**	**0**									

QMJHL Second All-Star Team (1996)

• NEMETH, Steve

C – L. 5'8", 170 lbs. b: Calgary, Alta., 2/11/1967. NY Rangers' 10th, 196th overall, in 1985.

Season	Club	League	GP	G	A	Pts	AG	AA	APts	PIM	PP	SH	GW	S	%	TGF	PGF	TGA	PGA	+/–	GP	G	A	Pts	PIM	PP	SH	GW
1982-83	Calgary Royals	AAHA	STATISTICS NOT AVAILABLE																									
	Lethbridge Broncos	WHL	2	0	1	1				0																		
1983-84	Lethbridge Broncos	WHL	68	22	20	42				33											5	1	1	2	2			
1984-85	Lethbridge Broncos	WHL	67	39	55	94				39											4	2	3	5	13			
1985-86	Lethbridge Broncos	WHL	70	42	69	111				47											10	5	5	10	6			
1986-87	Canada	Nat-Team	43	14	7	21				12																		
	Canada	WJC-A	6	4	4	8				4																		
	Kamloops Blazers	WHL	10	10	4	14				0											13	11	9	20	12			
1987-88	**New York Rangers**	**NHL**	**12**	**2**	**0**	**2**	**2**	**0**	**2**	**2**	**0**	**1**	**0**	**12**	**16.7**	**4**	**0**	**10**	**2**	**–4**								
	Colorado Rangers	IHL	57	13	24	37				28											10	2	1	3	8			
1988-89	Canada	Nat-Team	26	6	10	16				10																		
	Denver Rangers	IHL	11	5	2	7				8																		
1989-90	Canada	Nat-Team	73	24	42	66				40																		
1990-91	Krefelder EV	Austria	17	20	15	35				20																		
1991-92	Sheffield Steelers	Britain-2	25	92	94	186				28											6	21	18	39	14			
	Canada	Nat-Team	1	1	0	1				0																		
1992-93	Sheffield Steelers	BH-Cup	10	11	9	20				18																		
	Sheffield Steelers	Britain	32	67	64	131				67																		
1993-94	Sheffield Steelers	BH-Cup	6	11	11	22				4																		
	Sheffield Steelers	Britain	35	40	59	99				67											5	4	6	10	6			
1994-95	Sheffield Steelers	BH-Cup	2	1	2	3				4																		
	Sheffield Steelers	Britain	41	54	51	105				39											7	1	3	4	0			
1995-96	Sheffield Steelers	BH-Cup	9	6	4	10				6																		
	Sheffield Steelers	Britain	31	28	27	55				24											8	5	5	10	10			
1996-97	Sheffield Steelers	BH-Cup	4	0	0	0				0																		
	Sheffield Steelers	Britain	9	0	5	5				4																		
1997-98	Tacoma Sabrecats	WCHL	33	5	8	13				12																		
1998-99	Kingston Hawks	BH-Cup	8	7	6	13				10																		
	Kingston Hawks	Britain	6	2	3	5				4																		
	NHL Totals		**12**	**2**	**0**	**2**	**2**	**0**	**2**	**2**	**0**	**1**	**0**	**12**	**16.7**	**4**	**0**	**10**	**2**									

• NEMIROVSKY, David

RW – R. 6'1", 192 lbs. b: Toronto, Ont., 8/1/1976. Florida's 5th, 84th overall, in 1994.

Season	Club	League	GP	G	A	Pts	AG	AA	APts	PIM	PP	SH	GW	S	%	TGF	PGF	TGA	PGA	+/–	GP	G	A	Pts	PIM	PP	SH	GW
1991-92	Pickering Panthers	OJHL	14	3	10	13				5																		
	Weston Dukes	OJHL	23	6	13	19				2																		
1992-93	Weston Dukes	OJHL	2	0	3	3				0																		
	North York Rangers	OJHL	40	19	23	42				27																		
1993-94	Ottawa 67's	OHL	64	21	31	52				18											17	10	10	20	2			
1994-95	Ottawa 67's	OHL	59	27	29	56				25																		
1995-96	Sarnia Sting	OHL	26	18	27	45				14											10	8	8	16	6			
	Florida Panthers	**NHL**	**9**	**0**	**2**	**2**	**0**	**2**	**2**	**2**	**0**	**0**	**0**	**6**	**0.0**	**2**	**0**	**3**	**0**	**–1**								
	Carolina Monarchs	AHL	5	1	2	3				0																		
1996-97	**Florida Panthers**	**NHL**	**39**	**7**	**7**	**14**	**7**	**6**	**13**	**32**	**1**	**0**	**0**	**53**	**13.2**	**23**	**5**	**17**	**0**	**1**	**3**	**1**	**0**	**1**	**0**	**0**	**0**	**0**
	Carolina Monarchs	AHL	34	21	21	42				18																		
1997-98	**Florida Panthers**	**NHL**	**41**	**9**	**12**	**21**	**11**	**12**	**23**	**8**	**2**	**0**	**1**	**62**	**14.5**	**30**	**12**	**21**	**0**	**–3**								
	Beast of New Haven	AHL	29	10	15	25				10											1	1	0	1	0			
1998-99	**Florida Panthers**	**NHL**	**2**	**0**	**1**	**1**	**0**	**1**	**1**	**0**	**0**	**0**	**0**	**2**	**0.0**	**1**	**0**	**0**	**0**	**1**								
	Fort Wayne Komets	IHL	44	22	13	35				24																		
	St. John's Maple Leafs	AHL	22	3	9	12				18											5	4	1	5	0			
99-2000	St. John's Maple Leafs	AHL	57	18	25	43				69																		
	NHL Totals		**91**	**16**	**22**	**38**	**18**	**21**	**39**	**42**	**3**	**0**	**1**	**123**	**13.0**	**56**	**17**	**41**	**0**		**3**	**1**	**0**	**1**	**0**	**0**	**0**	**0**

Traded to **Toronto** by **Florida** for Jeff Ware, February 17, 1999.

• NESTERENKO, Eric

Eric Paul "Sonja" RW – R. 6'2", 197 lbs. b: Flin Flon, Man., 10/31/1933.

Season	Club	League	GP	G	A	Pts	AG	AA	APts	PIM	PP	SH	GW	S	%	TGF	PGF	TGA	PGA	+/–	GP	G	A	Pts	PIM	PP	SH	GW
1949-50	Toronto Marlboros	OHA-Jr.	1	0	0	0				0																		
1950-51	Toronto Marlboros	OHA-Jr.	46	28	22	50				90											13	7	9	16	27			
1951-52	Toronto Marlboros	OHA-Jr.	52	53	42	95				133											6	2	6	8	12			
	Toronto Maple Leafs	**NHL**	**1**	**0**	**0**	**0**	**0**	**0**	**0**	**0**																		

			REGULAR SEASON																		PLAYOFFS							
Season	Club	League	GP	G	A	Pts	AG	AA	APts	PIM	PP	SH	GW	S	%	TGF	PGF	TGA	PGA	+/–	GP	G	A	Pts	PIM	PP	SH	GW
1952-53	Toronto Marlboros	OHA-Jr.	34	27	21	48				46																		
	Toronto Maple Leafs	**NHL**	**35**	**10**	**6**	**16**	**13**	**7**	**20**	**27**																		
1953-54	**Toronto Maple Leafs**	**NHL**	**68**	**14**	**9**	**23**	**19**	**11**	**30**	**70**											**5**	**0**	**1**	**1**	**9**			
1954-55	**Toronto Maple Leafs**	**NHL**	**62**	**15**	**15**	**30**	**19**	**17**	**36**	**99**											**4**	**0**	**1**	**1**	**6**			
1955-56	**Toronto Maple Leafs**	**NHL**	**40**	**4**	**6**	**10**	**5**	**7**	**12**	**65**																		
	Winnipeg Warriors	WHL	20	8	6	14				27											14	3	7	10	22			
	Winnipeg Warriors	Ed-Cup	3	1	2	3				2																		
1956-57	**Chicago Black Hawks**	**NHL**	**24**	**8**	**15**	**23**	**10**	**16**	**26**	**32**																		
1957-58	**Chicago Black Hawks**	**NHL**	**70**	**20**	**18**	**38**	**25**	**19**	**44**	**104**																		
1958-59	**Chicago Black Hawks**	**NHL**	**70**	**16**	**18**	**34**	**19**	**18**	**37**	**81**											**6**	**2**	**2**	**4**	**8**			
1959-60	**Chicago Black Hawks**	**NHL**	**61**	**13**	**23**	**36**	**15**	**22**	**37**	**71**											**4**	**0**	**0**	**0**	**2**			
1960-61 ♦	**Chicago Black Hawks**	**NHL**	**68**	**19**	**19**	**38**	**22**	**18**	**40**	**125**											**11**	**2**	**3**	**5**	**6**			
1961-62	**Chicago Black Hawks**	**NHL**	**68**	**15**	**14**	**29**	**17**	**13**	**30**	**97**											**12**	**0**	**5**	**5**	**22**			
1962-63	**Chicago Black Hawks**	**NHL**	**67**	**12**	**15**	**27**	**14**	**15**	**29**	**103**											**6**	**2**	**3**	**5**	**8**			
1963-64	**Chicago Black Hawks**	**NHL**	**70**	**7**	**19**	**26**	**9**	**20**	**29**	**93**											**7**	**2**	**1**	**3**	**8**			
1964-65	**Chicago Black Hawks**	**NHL**	**56**	**14**	**16**	**30**	**17**	**16**	**33**	**63**											**14**	**2**	**2**	**4**	**16**			
1965-66	**Chicago Black Hawks**	**NHL**	**67**	**15**	**25**	**40**	**17**	**24**	**41**	**58**											**6**	**1**	**0**	**1**	**4**			
1966-67	**Chicago Black Hawks**	**NHL**	**68**	**14**	**23**	**37**	**16**	**22**	**38**	**38**											**6**	**1**	**2**	**3**	**2**			
1967-68	**Chicago Black Hawks**	**NHL**	**71**	**11**	**25**	**36**	**13**	**25**	**38**	**37**	**1**	**2**	**1**	**93**	**11.8**	**61**	**7**	**66**	**15**	**3**	**10**	**0**	**1**	**1**	**2**	**0**	**0**	**0**
1968-69	**Chicago Black Hawks**	**NHL**	**72**	**15**	**17**	**32**	**16**	**15**	**31**	**29**	**1**	**3**	**1**	**90**	**16.7**	**60**	**6**	**79**	**30**	**5**								
1969-70	**Chicago Black Hawks**	**NHL**	**67**	**16**	**18**	**34**	**17**	**17**	**34**	**26**	**3**	**2**	**3**	**124**	**12.9**	**55**	**8**	**43**	**13**	**17**	**7**	**1**	**2**	**3**	**4**	**0**	**0**	**0**
1970-71	**Chicago Black Hawks**	**NHL**	**76**	**8**	**15**	**23**	**8**	**13**	**21**	**28**	**1**	**0**	**2**	**72**	**11.1**	**40**	**5**	**50**	**28**	**13**	**18**	**0**	**1**	**1**	**19**	**0**	**0**	**0**
1971-72	**Chicago Black Hawks**	**NHL**	**38**	**4**	**8**	**12**	**4**	**7**	**11**	**27**	**1**	**0**	**0**	**25**	**16.0**	**19**	**3**	**15**	**6**	**7**	**8**	**0**	**0**	**0**	**11**	**0**	**0**	**0**
1972-73	HC Lausanne	Switz.	DID NOT PLAY – COACHING																									
1973-74	Chicago Cougars	WHA	29	2	5	7				8																		
1974-75			DID NOT PLAY																									
1975-76	Trail Smoke Eaters	WIHL	40	10	25	35				38																		
1976-77	Trail Smoke Eaters	WIHL	DID NOT PLAY – GENERAL MANAGER																									
	NHL Totals		**1219**	**250**	**324**	**574**	**295**	**322**	**617**	**1273**											**124**	**13**	**24**	**37**	**127**			
	Other Major League Totals		29	2	5	7				8																		

Played in NHL All-Star Game (1961, 1965)

Signed as a free agent by **Toronto**, January 8, 1953. Traded to **Chicago** by **Toronto** with Harry Lumley for $40,000, May 21, 1956. • Played weekend games only during 1956-57 season while attending University of Toronto. Selected by **Dayton-Houston** (WHA) in 1972 WHA General Player Draft, February 12, 1972. WHA rights traded to **Chicago** (WHA) by **Houston** (WHA) for future considerations, June, 1973.

• NETHERY, Lance

C – L. 6'1", 185 lbs. b: Toronto, Ont., 6/28/1957. NY Rangers' 9th, 131st overall, in 1977.

Season	Club	League	GP	G	A	Pts	AG	AA	APts	PIM	PP	SH	GW	S	%	TGF	PGF	TGA	PGA	+/–	GP	G	A	Pts	PIM	PP	SH	GW
1974-75	Burlington Cougars	OHA-B	40	51	69	120																						
1975-76	Cornell University	ECAC	29	18	27	45				16																		
1976-77	Cornell University	ECAC	29	32	46	78				18																		
1977-78	Cornell University	ECAC	26	23	*60	*83				12																		
1978-79	Cornell University	ECAC	27	18	47	65				30																		
	New Haven Nighthawks	AHL	1	0	0	0				0																		
1979-80	New Haven Nighthawks	AHL	74	23	39	62				20											10	3	12	15	2			
1980-81	**New York Rangers**	**NHL**	**33**	**11**	**12**	**23**	**9**	**8**	**17**	**12**	**2**	**0**	**0**	**47**	**23.4**	**31**	**3**	**34**	**6**	**0**	**14**	**5**	**3**	**8**	**9**	**0**	**0**	**1**
	New Haven Nighthawks	AHL	36	18	30	48				8																		
1981-82	New York Rangers	DN-Cup	4	1	0	1																						
	New York Rangers	**NHL**	**5**	**0**	**0**	**0**	**0**	**0**	**0**	**0**	**0**	**0**	**0**	**4**	**0.0**	**0**	**0**	**1**	**0**	**–1**								
	Springfield Indians	AHL	9	5	5	10				0																		
	Edmonton Oilers	**NHL**	**3**	**0**	**2**	**2**	**0**	**1**	**1**	**2**	**0**	**0**	**0**	**1**	**0.0**	**2**	**0**	**1**	**0**	**1**								
	Wichita Wind	CHL	46	35	32	67				26											7	1	4	5	8			
1982-83	HC Duisburg	Germany-2	42	72	84	*156																						
	Wichita Wind	CHL	10	7	5	12				0																		
1983-84	HC Davos	Switz.	40	39	*43	82																						
1984-85	HC Davos	Switz.	34	42	36	78															4	2	1	3				
1985-86	HC Davos	Switz.	36	*46	33	79															5	2	5	7				
	Hershey Bears	AHL	13	5	6	11				2											18	4	9	13	2			
1986-87	HC Davos	Switz.	36	23	31	54															10	*5	7	*12				
1987-88	HC Davos	Switz.	36	37	27	64															4	5	7	12				
1988-89	SC Hericau	Switz-2	STATISTICS NOT AVAILABLE																									
1989-90	SC Herisau	Switz-2	25	25	49	74															10	6	7	13				
1990-91	HC Davos	Switz.	DID NOT PLAY – COACHING																									
	NHL Totals		**41**	**11**	**14**	**25**	**9**	**9**	**18**	**14**	**2**	**0**	**0**	**52**	**21.2**	**33**	**3**	**36**	**6**		**14**	**5**	**3**	**8**	**9**	**0**	**0**	**1**

ECAC Second All-Star Team (1977) • ECAC First All-Star Team (1978, 1979) • NCAA East First All-American Team (1978, 1979)

Traded to **Edmonton** by **NY Rangers** for Eddie Mio, December 11, 1981.

• NEUFELD, Ray

Raymond Matthew RW – R. 6'3", 210 lbs. b: St. Boniface, Man., 4/15/1959. Hartford's 4th, 81st overall, in 1979.

Season	Club	League	GP	G	A	Pts	AG	AA	APts	PIM	PP	SH	GW	S	%	TGF	PGF	TGA	PGA	+/–	GP	G	A	Pts	PIM	PP	SH	GW
1976-77	Flin Flon Bombers	WCJHL	68	13	19	32				63																		
1977-78	Flin Flon Bombers	WCJHL	72	23	46	69				224											15	4	4	8	39			
1978-79	Edmonton Oil Kings	WHL	57	54	48	102				138											8	5	1	6	2			
1979-80	**Hartford Whalers**	**NHL**	**8**	**1**	**0**	**1**	**1**	**0**	**1**	**0**	**0**	**0**	**0**	**4**	**25.0**	**2**	**0**	**5**	**0**	**–3**	**2**	**1**	**0**	**1**	**0**	**0**	**0**	**0**
	Springfield Indians	AHL	73	23	29	52				51																		
1980-81	**Hartford Whalers**	**NHL**	**52**	**5**	**10**	**15**	**4**	**7**	**11**	**44**	**0**	**0**	**0**	**55**	**9.1**	**32**	**3**	**28**	**0**	**1**								
	Binghamton Whalers	AHL	25	7	7	14				43											6	2	0	2	0			
1981-82	**Hartford Whalers**	**NHL**	**19**	**4**	**3**	**7**	**3**	**2**	**5**	**4**	**1**	**0**	**0**	**33**	**12.1**	**11**	**1**	**17**	**0**	**–7**								
	Binghamton Whalers	AHL	61	28	31	59				81											15	*9	8	17	10			
1982-83	**Hartford Whalers**	**NHL**	**80**	**26**	**31**	**57**	**21**	**21**	**42**	**86**	**4**	**0**	**1**	**165**	**15.8**	**77**	**16**	**125**	**30**	**–34**								
1983-84	**Hartford Whalers**	**NHL**	**80**	**27**	**42**	**69**	**22**	**29**	**51**	**97**	**5**	**0**	**5**	**163**	**16.6**	**109**	**36**	**94**	**3**	**–18**								
1984-85	**Hartford Whalers**	**NHL**	**76**	**27**	**35**	**62**	**22**	**24**	**46**	**129**	**12**	**0**	**2**	**176**	**15.3**	**95**	**45**	**81**	**2**	**–29**								
1985-86	**Hartford Whalers**	**NHL**	**16**	**5**	**10**	**15**	**4**	**7**	**11**	**40**	**3**	**0**	**0**	**35**	**14.3**	**26**	**13**	**17**	**1**	**–3**								
	Winnipeg Jets	**NHL**	**60**	**20**	**28**	**48**	**16**	**19**	**35**	**62**	**7**	**0**	**4**	**132**	**15.2**	**80**	**27**	**71**	**1**	**–17**	**3**	**2**	**0**	**2**	**10**	**1**	**0**	**0**
1986-87	**Winnipeg Jets**	**NHL**	**80**	**18**	**18**	**36**	**16**	**13**	**29**	**105**	**5**	**0**	**2**	**134**	**13.4**	**56**	**8**	**61**	**0**	**–13**	**8**	**1**	**1**	**2**	**30**	**0**	**0**	**0**
1987-88	**Winnipeg Jets**	**NHL**	**78**	**18**	**18**	**36**	**15**	**13**	**28**	**169**	**9**	**0**	**2**	**115**	**15.7**	**61**	**30**	**61**	**1**	**–29**	**5**	**2**	**2**	**4**	**6**	**1**	**0**	**0**
1988-89	**Winnipeg Jets**	**NHL**	**31**	**5**	**2**	**7**	**4**	**1**	**5**	**52**	**0**	**0**	**0**	**47**	**10.6**	**20**	**1**	**28**	**0**	**–9**								
	Boston Bruins	**NHL**	**14**	**1**	**3**	**4**	**1**	**2**	**3**	**28**	**0**	**0**	**0**	**16**	**6.3**	**6**	**0**	**8**	**0**	**–2**	**10**	**2**	**3**	**5**	**9**	**0**	**0**	**1**
1989-90	**Boston Bruins**	**NHL**	**1**	**0**	**0**	**0**	**0**	**0**	**0**	**0**	**0**	**0**	**0**	**1**	**0.0**	**0**	**0**	**0**	**0**	**0**								
	Maine Mariners	AHL	76	27	29	56				117																		
	NHL Totals		**595**	**157**	**200**	**357**	**129**	**138**	**267**	**816**	**46**	**0**	**16**	**1076**	**14.6**	**575**	**180**	**596**	**38**		**28**	**8**	**6**	**14**	**55**	**2**	**0**	**1**

Traded to **Winnipeg** by **Hartford** for Dave Babych, November 21, 1985. Traded to **Boston** by **Winnipeg** for Moe Lemay, December 30, 1988.

• NEVIN, Bob

Robert Frank "Nevvy" RW – R. 6', 185 lbs. b: South Porcupine, Ont., 3/18/1938.

Season	Club	League	GP	G	A	Pts	AG	AA	APts	PIM	PP	SH	GW	S	%	TGF	PGF	TGA	PGA	+/–	GP	G	A	Pts	PIM	PP	SH	GW
1953-54	Weston Dukes	OHA-B	STATISTICS NOT AVAILABLE																									
1954-55	Toronto Marlboros	OHA-Jr.	3	0	0	0				0																		
1955-56	Toronto Marlboros	OHA-Jr.	48	34	31	65				34											11	7	4	11	7			
	Toronto Marlboros	Mem-Cup	6	5	0	5				6																		
1956-57	Toronto Marlboros	OHA-Jr.	51	45	29	74				52											9	5	6	11	13			
	Rochester Americans	AHL	1	0	0	0				0																		

			REGULAR SEASON																		PLAYOFFS							
Season	Club	League	GP	G	A	Pts	AG	AA	APts	PIM	PP	SH	GW	S	%	TGF	PGF	TGA	PGA	+/-	GP	G	A	Pts	PIM	PP	SH	GW
1957-58	Toronto Marlboros	OHA-Jr.	50	32	39	71	....	....	....	29	....	....	....	....	....	....	....	....	....	....	13	*13	10	*23	15	....	....	....
	Toronto Maple Leafs	**NHL**	**4**	**0**	**0**	**0**	**0**	**0**	**0**	**0**	....	....	....	....	....	....	....	....	....	....	....	....	....	....	....	....	....	....
	Rochester Americans	AHL	1	0	2	2	....	....	....	2	....	....	....	....	....	....	....	....	....	....	....	....	....	....	....	....	....	....
	Toronto Marlboros	Mem-Cup	4	2	1	3	....	....	....	16	....	....	....	....	....	....	....	....	....	....	....	....	....	....	....	....	....	....
1958-59	**Toronto Maple Leafs**	**NHL**	**2**	**0**	**0**	**0**	**0**	**0**	**0**	**2**	....	....	....	....	....	....	....	....	....	....	....	....	....	....	....	....	....	....
	Chicoutimi Sagueneens	QHL	35	16	8	24	....	....	....	12	....	....	....	....	....	....	....	....	....	....	....	....	....	....	....	....	....	....
	Rochester Americans	AHL	21	3	3	6	....	....	....	6	....	....	....	....	....	....	....	....	....	....	....	....	....	....	....	....	....	....
1959-60	Rochester Americans	AHL	71	32	42	74	....	....	....	10	....	....	....	....	....	....	....	....	....	....	12	6	4	10	4	....	....	....
1960-61	**Toronto Maple Leafs**	**NHL**	**68**	**21**	**37**	**58**	**24**	**36**	**60**	**13**	....	....	....	....	....	....	....	....	....	....	**5**	**1**	**0**	**1**	**2**	**1**	**0**	**0**
1961-62♦	**Toronto Maple Leafs**	**NHL**	**69**	**15**	**30**	**45**	**17**	**29**	**46**	**10**	....	....	....	....	....	....	....	....	....	....	**12**	**2**	**4**	**6**	**6**	**0**	**0**	**0**
1962-63♦	**Toronto Maple Leafs**	**NHL**	**58**	**12**	**21**	**33**	**14**	**21**	**35**	**4**	....	....	....	....	....	....	....	....	....	....	**10**	**3**	**0**	**3**	**2**	**0**	**1**	**2**
1963-64	**Toronto Maple Leafs**	**NHL**	**49**	**7**	**12**	**19**	**9**	**13**	**22**	**26**	....	....	....	....	....	....	....	....	....	....	....	....	....	....	....	....	....	....
	New York Rangers	**NHL**	**14**	**5**	**4**	**9**	**6**	**4**	**10**	**9**	....	....	....	....	....	....	....	....	....	....	....	....	....	....	....	....	....	....
1964-65	**New York Rangers**	**NHL**	**64**	**16**	**14**	**30**	**19**	**14**	**33**	**28**	....	....	....	....	....	....	....	....	....	....	....	....	....	....	....	....	....	....
1965-66	**New York Rangers**	**NHL**	**69**	**29**	**33**	**62**	**33**	**32**	**65**	**10**	....	....	....	....	....	....	....	....	....	....	....	....	....	....	....	....	....	....
1966-67	**New York Rangers**	**NHL**	**67**	**20**	**24**	**44**	**23**	**23**	**46**	**6**	....	....	....	....	....	....	....	....	....	....	**4**	**0**	**3**	**3**	**2**	**0**	**0**	**0**
1967-68	**New York Rangers**	**NHL**	**74**	**28**	**30**	**58**	**33**	**30**	**63**	**20**	**3**	**0**	**4**	**217**	**12.9**	**82**	**17**	**69**	**19**	**15**	**6**	**0**	**3**	**3**	**4**	**0**	**0**	**0**
1968-69	**New York Rangers**	**NHL**	**71**	**31**	**25**	**56**	**33**	**22**	**55**	**14**	**11**	**0**	**6**	**236**	**13.1**	**89**	**33**	**66**	**13**	**3**	**4**	**0**	**2**	**2**	**0**	**0**	**0**	**0**
1969-70	**New York Rangers**	**NHL**	**68**	**18**	**19**	**37**	**20**	**18**	**38**	**8**	**3**	**1**	**4**	**126**	**14.3**	**61**	**18**	**58**	**16**	**1**	**6**	**1**	**1**	**2**	**2**	**1**	**0**	**0**
1970-71	**New York Rangers**	**NHL**	**78**	**21**	**25**	**46**	**21**	**21**	**42**	**10**	**3**	**0**	**3**	**154**	**13.6**	**68**	**14**	**51**	**14**	**17**	**13**	**5**	**3**	**8**	**0**	**1**	**0**	**1**
1971-72	**Minnesota North Stars**	**NHL**	**72**	**15**	**19**	**34**	**15**	**16**	**31**	**6**	**2**	**0**	**2**	**96**	**15.6**	**52**	**10**	**40**	**5**	**7**	**7**	**1**	**1**	**2**	**0**	**0**	**0**	**0**
1972-73	**Minnesota North Stars**	**NHL**	**66**	**5**	**13**	**18**	**5**	**10**	**15**	**0**	**0**	**0**	**1**	**55**	**9.1**	**30**	**7**	**71**	**36**	**–12**	....	....	....	....	....	....	....	....
1973-74	**Los Angeles Kings**	**NHL**	**78**	**20**	**30**	**50**	**19**	**25**	**44**	**12**	**5**	**0**	**6**	**127**	**15.7**	**72**	**16**	**69**	**21**	**8**	**5**	**1**	**0**	**1**	**2**	**0**	**0**	**0**
1974-75	**Los Angeles Kings**	**NHL**	**80**	**31**	**41**	**72**	**27**	**31**	**58**	**19**	**7**	**2**	**3**	**157**	**19.7**	**98**	**18**	**70**	**26**	**36**	**3**	**0**	**0**	**0**	**0**	**0**	**0**	**0**
1975-76	**Los Angeles Kings**	**NHL**	**77**	**13**	**42**	**55**	**11**	**31**	**42**	**14**	**2**	**1**	**0**	**121**	**10.7**	**87**	**25**	**85**	**33**	**10**	**9**	**2**	**1**	**3**	**4**	**0**	**0**	**1**
1976-77	Edmonton Oilers	WHA	13	3	2	5	....	....	....	0	....	....	....	....	....	....	....	....	....	....	....	....	....	....	....	....	....	....
	NHL Totals		**1128**	**307**	**419**	**726**	**329**	**376**	**705**	**211**	....	....	....	....	....	....	....	....	....	....	**84**	**16**	**18**	**34**	**24**	....	....	....
	Other Major League Totals		13	3	2	5	....	....	....	0	....	....	....	....	....	....	....	....	....	....	....	....	....	....	....	....	....	....

Played in NHL All-Star Game (1962, 1963, 1967, 1969)

Traded to **NY Rangers** by **Toronto** with Rod Seiling, Dick Duff, Arnie Brown and Bill Collins for Andy Bathgate and Don McKenney, February 22, 1964. Traded to **Minnesota** by **NY Rangers** for future considerations (Bobby Rousseau, June 8, 1971), May 25, 1971. Selected by **Ontario-Ottawa** (WHA) in 1972 WHA General Player Draft, February 12, 1972. Claimed by **LA Kings** (Springfield-AHL) from **Minnesota** in Reverse Draft, June 13, 1973. Signed as a free agent by **Edmonton** (WHA), October 25, 1976.

• NEWBERRY, John

C – L. 6′, 190 lbs. b: Port Alberni, B.C., 4/8/1962. Montreal's 4th, 45th overall, in 1980.

Season	Club	League	GP	G	A	Pts	AG	AA	APts	PIM	PP	SH	GW	S	%	TGF	PGF	TGA	PGA	+/-	GP	G	A	Pts	PIM	PP	SH	GW
1979-80	Nanaimo Clippers	BCJHL	65	*84	*101	*185	....	....	....	96	....	....	....	....	....	....	....	....	....	....	....	....	....	....	....	....	....	....
	Victoria Cougars	WHL	1	0	2	2	....	....	....	0	....	....	....	....	....	....	....	....	....	....	....	....	....	....	....	....	....	....
1980-81	University of Wisconsin	WCHA	39	30	32	62	....	....	....	77	....	....	....	....	....	....	....	....	....	....	....	....	....	....	....	....	....	....
1981-82	University of Wisconsin	WCHA	39	38	27	65	....	....	....	42	....	....	....	....	....	....	....	....	....	....	....	....	....	....	....	....	....	....
1982-83	Nova Scotia Voyageurs	AHL	71	29	29	58	....	....	....	43	....	....	....	....	....	....	....	....	....	....	6	3	1	4	2	....	....	....
	Montreal Canadiens	**NHL**	....	....	....	....	....	....	....	....	....	....	....	....	....	....	....	....	....	....	**2**	**0**	**0**	**0**	**0**	**0**	**0**	**0**
1983-84	**Montreal Canadiens**	**NHL**	**3**	**0**	**0**	**0**	**0**	**0**	**0**	**0**	**0**	**0**	**0**	**2**	**0.0**	**0**	**0**	**0**	**0**	**0**	....	....	....	....	....	....	....	....
	Nova Scotia Voyageurs	AHL	78	25	37	62	....	....	....	116	....	....	....	....	....	....	....	....	....	....	12	7	12	19	22	....	....	....
1984-85	**Montreal Canadiens**	**NHL**	**16**	**0**	**4**	**4**	**0**	**3**	**3**	**6**	**0**	**0**	**0**	**12**	**0.0**	**9**	**0**	**6**	**0**	**3**	....	....	....	....	....	....	....	....
	Sherbrooke Canadiens	AHL	58	23	40	63	....	....	....	30	....	....	....	....	....	....	....	....	....	....	17	6	*14	*20	18	....	....	....
1985-86	**Hartford Whalers**	**NHL**	**3**	**0**	**0**	**0**	**0**	**0**	**0**	**0**	**0**	**0**	**0**	**4**	**0.0**	**1**	**0**	**5**	**0**	**–4**	....	....	....	....	....	....	....	....
	Binghamton Whalers	AHL	21	6	11	17	....	....	....	38	....	....	....	....	....	....	....	....	....	....	....	....	....	....	....	....	....	....
	Moncton Golden Flames	AHL	44	10	24	34	....	....	....	31	....	....	....	....	....	....	....	....	....	....	9	1	4	5	2	....	....	....
1986-87	Karpat Oulu	Finland	39	16	14	30	....	....	....	63	....	....	....	....	....	....	....	....	....	....	9	3	4	7	17	....	....	....
1987-88	Vastra Frolunda	Sweden-2	34	22	39	61	....	....	....	32	....	....	....	....	....	....	....	....	....	....	10	3	6	9	10	....	....	....
1988-89	Vastra Frolunda	Sweden-2	33	24	22	46	....	....	....	32	....	....	....	....	....	....	....	....	....	....	11	5	5	10	8	....	....	....
1989-90	Orebro IK	Switz-2	17	4	*23	27	....	....	....	29	....	....	....	....	....	....	....	....	....	....	....	....	....	....	....	....	....	....
	EV Zug	Switz.	19	8	5	13	....	....	....	....	....	....	....	....	....	....	....	....	....	....	3	1	0	1	0	....	....	....
1990-91	Uppsala/Almtuna IS	Sweden-2	27	18	18	36	....	....	....	46	....	....	....	....	....	....	....	....	....	....	2	0	1	1	27	....	....	....
1991-92	Uppsala/Almtuna IS	Sweden-2	29	10	25	35	....	....	....	46	....	....	....	....	....	....	....	....	....	....	....	....	....	....	....	....	....	....
1992-93	Murrayfield Racers	BH-Cup	6	7	13	20	....	....	....	28	....	....	....	....	....	....	....	....	....	....	....	....	....	....	....	....	....	....
	Murrayfield Racers	Britain	32	59	85	144	....	....	....	120	....	....	....	....	....	....	....	....	....	....	7	11	13	24	10	....	....	....
	NHL Totals		**22**	**0**	**4**	**4**	**0**	**3**	**3**	**6**	**0**	**0**	**0**	**18**	**0.0**	**10**	**0**	**11**	**0**		**2**	**0**	**0**	**0**	**0**	**0**	**0**	**0**

NCAA Championship All-Tournament Team (1981, 1982) • WCHA First All-Star Team (1982) • NCAA West First All-American Team (1982)

Signed as a free agent by **Hartford**, September 19, 1985.

• NEWELL, Rick

Gordon Richard D – L. 5′11″, 180 lbs. b: Winnipeg, Man., 2/18/1948.

Season	Club	League	GP	G	A	Pts	AG	AA	APts	PIM	PP	SH	GW	S	%	TGF	PGF	TGA	PGA	+/-	GP	G	A	Pts	PIM	PP	SH	GW
1964-65	Winnipeg Rangers	MJHL	35	5	13	18	....	....	....	74	....	....	....	....	....	....	....	....	....	....	5	1	*8	9	15	....	....	....
1965-66	Winnipeg Rangers	MJHL	3	0	2	2	....	....	....	6	....	....	....	....	....	....	....	....	....	....	....	....	....	....	....	....	....	....
1966-67	University of Minnesota-Duluth	WCHA	22	6	13	19	....	....	....	68	....	....	....	....	....	....	....	....	....	....	....	....	....	....	....	....	....	....
1967-68	University of Minnesota-Duluth	WCHA	18	1	7	8	....	....	....	52	....	....	....	....	....	....	....	....	....	....	....	....	....	....	....	....	....	....
1968-69	University of Minnesota-Duluth	WCHA	18	1	6	7	....	....	....	16	....	....	....	....	....	....	....	....	....	....	....	....	....	....	....	....	....	....
1969-70	University of Minnesota-Duluth	WCHA	STATISTICS NOT AVAILABLE																									
	Omaha Knights	CHL	6	0	0	0	....	....	....	4	....	....	....	....	....	....	....	....	....	....	....	....	....	....	....	....	....	....
1970-71	Omaha Knights	CHL	69	6	17	23	....	....	....	110	....	....	....	....	....	....	....	....	....	....	11	1	4	5	4	....	....	....
1971-72	Phoenix Roadrunners	WHL	1	0	0	0	....	....	....	0	....	....	....	....	....	....	....	....	....	....	....	....	....	....	....	....	....	....
	Providence Reds	AHL	19	1	6	7	....	....	....	15	....	....	....	....	....	....	....	....	....	....	....	....	....	....	....	....	....	....
	Omaha Knights	CHL	53	8	21	29	....	....	....	76	....	....	....	....	....	....	....	....	....	....	....	....	....	....	....	....	....	....
1972-73	**Detroit Red Wings**	**NHL**	**3**	**0**	**0**	**0**	**0**	**0**	**0**	**0**	**0**	**0**	**0**	**0**	**0.0**	**1**	**0**	**3**	**1**	**–1**	....	....	....	....	....	....	....	....
	Virginia Wings	AHL	68	24	23	47	....	....	....	125	....	....	....	....	....	....	....	....	....	....	9	2	3	5	6	....	....	....
1973-74	**Detroit Red Wings**	**NHL**	**3**	**0**	**0**	**0**	**0**	**0**	**0**	**0**	**0**	**0**	**0**	**1**	**0.0**	**2**	**0**	**3**	**0**	**–1**	....	....	....	....	....	....	....	....
	Virginia Wings	AHL	50	9	22	31	....	....	....	44	....	....	....	....	....	....	....	....	....	....	....	....	....	....	....	....	....	....
	London Lions	Britain	17	12	11	23	....	....	....	63	....	....	....	....	....	....	....	....	....	....	....	....	....	....	....	....	....	....
1974-75	Phoenix Roadrunners	WHA	25	0	4	4	....	....	....	39	....	....	....	....	....	....	....	....	....	....	5	0	1	1	2	....	....	....
	Tulsa Oilers	CHL	22	5	9	14	....	....	....	24	....	....	....	....	....	....	....	....	....	....	....	....	....	....	....	....	....	....
1975-76	Tucson Mavericks	CHL	57	9	23	32	....	....	....	104	....	....	....	....	....	....	....	....	....	....	....	....	....	....	....	....	....	....
	Syracuse Blazers	NAHL	6	1	3	4	....	....	....	0	....	....	....	....	....	....	....	....	....	....	....	....	....	....	....	....	....	....
1976-77			DID NOT PLAY																									
1977-78	Phoenix Roadrunners	PHL	35	10	32	42	....	....	....	28	....	....	....	....	....	....	....	....	....	....	....	....	....	....	....	....	....	....
	NHL Totals		**6**	**0**	**0**	**0**	**0**	**0**	**0**	**0**	**0**	**0**	**0**	**1**	**0.0**	**3**	**0**	**6**	**1**		....	....	....	....	....	....	....	....
	Other Major League Totals		25	0	4	4	....	....	....	39	....	....	....	....	....	....	....	....	....	....	5	0	1	1	2	....	....	....

PHL Second All-Star Team (1978)

Traded to **Detroit** by **NY Rangers** with Gary Doak for Joe Zanussi and Detroit's 1st round choice (Albert Blanchard) in 1972 Amateur Draft, May 24, 1972. Selected by **Chicago** (WHA) in 1973 WHA Professional Player Draft, June, 1973. WHA rights traded to **Phoenix** (WHA) by **Chicago** (WHA) for future considerations, June, 1974. Traded to **Cleveland** (WHA) by **Phoenix** (WHA) with Rob Watt for Grant Erickson, November, 1975.

• NEWMAN, Dan

Daniel Kenneth LW – L. 6′1″, 195 lbs. b: Windsor, Ont., 1/26/1952.

Season	Club	League	GP	G	A	Pts	AG	AA	APts	PIM	PP	SH	GW	S	%	TGF	PGF	TGA	PGA	+/-	GP	G	A	Pts	PIM	PP	SH	GW
1970-71	St. Clair College	NCAA-3	22	13	17	30	....	....	....	42	....	....	....	....	....	....	....	....	....	....	....	....	....	....	....	....	....	....
1971-72	St. Clair College	NCAA-3	20	28	13	41	....	....	....	....	....	....	....	....	....	....	....	....	....	....	....	....	....	....	....	....	....	....
1972-73	Virginia Wings	AHL	5	1	0	1	....	....	....	0	....	....	....	....	....	....	....	....	....	....	....	....	....	....	....	....	....	....
	Des Moines–Port Huron	IHL	61	8	14	22	....	....	....	27	....	....	....	....	....	....	....	....	....	....	3	0	0	0	0	....	....	....
1973-74	Port Huron Wings	IHL	66	14	16	30	....	....	....	129	....	....	....	....	....	....	....	....	....	....	....	....	....	....	....	....	....	....
1974-75	Port Huron Flags	IHL	72	8	22	30	....	....	....	72	....	....	....	....	....	....	....	....	....	....	5	1	2	3	0	....	....	....
1975-76	Port Huron Flags	IHL	75	39	45	84	....	....	....	114	....	....	....	....	....	....	....	....	....	....	15	6	9	15	35	....	....	....

Season	Club	League	GP	G	A	Pts	AG	AA	APts	PIM	PP	SH	GW	S	%	TGF	PGF	TGA	PGA	+/-	GP	G	A	Pts	PIM	PP	SH	GW
			REGULAR SEASON																		PLAYOFFS							
1976-77	**New York Rangers**	**NHL**	**41**	**9**	**8**	**17**	**8**	**6**	**14**	**37**	**0**	**0**	**1**	**67**	**13.4**	**30**	**3**	**31**	**0**	**–4**	....	....	....	....	....	....	....	....
	New Haven Nighthawks	AHL	33	12	17	29	....	....	....	57	....	....	....	....	....	....	....	....	....	....	....	....	....	....	....	....	....	....
1977-78	**New York Rangers**	**NHL**	**59**	**5**	**13**	**18**	**5**	**10**	**15**	**22**	**0**	**0**	**1**	**81**	**6.2**	**27**	**2**	**36**	**0**	**–11**	**3**	**0**	**0**	**0**	**4**	**0**	**0**	**0**
	New Haven Nighthawks	AHL	8	2	4	6	....	....	....	7	....	....	....	....	....	....	....	....	....	....	....	....	....	....	....	....	....	....
1978-79	**Montreal Canadiens**	**NHL**	**16**	**0**	**2**	**2**	**0**	**1**	**1**	**4**	**0**	**0**	**0**	**9**	**0.0**	**4**	**0**	**5**	**0**	**–1**	....	....	....	....	....	....	....	....
	Nova Scotia Voyageurs	AHL	54	24	22	46	....	....	....	54	....	....	....	....	....	....	....	....	....	....	9	3	1	4	2	....	....	....
1979-80	**Edmonton Oilers**	**NHL**	**10**	**3**	**1**	**4**	**3**	**1**	**4**	**0**	**0**	**0**	**0**	**16**	**18.8**	**5**	**0**	**6**	**0**	**–1**	....	....	....	....	....	....	....	....
	Houston Apollos	CHL	14	5	9	14	....	....	....	4	....	....	....	....	....	....	....	....	....	....	....	....	....	....	....	....	....	....
	Binghamton Dusters	AHL	55	11	17	28	....	....	....	50	....	....	....	....	....	....	....	....	....	....	....	....	....	....	....	....	....	....
	NHL Totals		**126**	**17**	**24**	**41**	**16**	**18**	**34**	**63**	**0**	**0**	**2**	**173**	**9.8**	**66**	**5**	**78**	**0**		**3**	**0**	**0**	**0**	**4**	**0**	**0**	**0**

Signed as a free agent by **Port Huron** (IHL), September, 1972. NHL rights transferred to **NY Rangers** after NHL club signed affiliation agreement with **Port Huron** (IHL), June, 1974. Claimed by **Montreal** from **NY Rangers** in Waiver Draft, October 9, 1978. Traded to **Edmonton** by **Montreal** with Dave Lumley for Edmonton's 2nd round choice (Ric Nattress) in 1980 Entry Draft, June 13, 1979. Traded to **Boston** by **Edmonton** for Bobby Schmautz, December 10, 1979.

• NICHOL, Scott

Scott B. C – R. 5'8", 160 lbs. b: Edmonton, Alta., 12/31/1974. Buffalo's 9th, 272nd overall, in 1993.

Season	Club	League	GP	G	A	Pts	AG	AA	APts	PIM	PP	SH	GW	S	%	TGF	PGF	TGA	PGA	+/-	GP	G	A	Pts	PIM	PP	SH	GW
1991-92	Calgary Midget Flames	AAHA	23	26	16	42	....	....	....	132	....	....	....	....	....	....	....	....	....	....	....	....	....	....	....	....	....	....
1992-93	Portland Winter Hawks	WHL	67	31	33	64	....	....	....	146	....	....	....	....	....	....	....	....	....	....	16	8	8	16	41	....	....	....
1993-94	Portland Winter Hawks	WHL	65	40	53	93	....	....	....	144	....	....	....	....	....	....	....	....	....	....	10	3	8	11	16	....	....	....
1994-95	Rochester Americans	AHL	71	11	16	27	....	....	....	136	....	....	....	....	....	....	....	....	....	....	5	0	3	3	14	....	....	....
1995-96	**Buffalo Sabres**	**NHL**	**2**	**0**	**0**	**0**	**0**	**0**	**0**	**10**	**0**	**0**	**0**	**4**	**0.0**	**0**	**0**	**0**	**0**	**0**	....	....	....	....	....	....	....	....
	Rochester Americans	AHL	62	14	18	32	....	....	....	170	....	....	....	....	....	....	....	....	....	....	19	7	6	13	36	....	....	....
1996-97	Rochester Americans	AHL	68	22	21	43	....	....	....	133	....	....	....	....	....	....	....	....	....	....	10	2	1	3	26	....	....	....
1997-98	**Buffalo Sabres**	**NHL**	**3**	**0**	**0**	**0**	**0**	**0**	**0**	**4**	**0**	**0**	**0**	**5**	**0.0**	**0**	**0**	**0**	**0**	**0**	....	....	....	....	....	....	....	....
	Rochester Americans	AHL	35	13	7	20	....	....	....	113	....	....	....	....	....	....	....	....	....	....	....	....	....	....	....	....	....	....
1998-99	Rochester Americans	AHL	52	13	20	33	....	....	....	120	....	....	....	....	....	....	....	....	....	....	....	....	....	....	....	....	....	....
99-2000	Rochester Americans	AHL	37	7	11	18	....	....	....	141	....	....	....	....	....	....	....	....	....	....	....	....	....	....	....	....	....	....
	NHL Totals		**5**	**0**	**0**	**0**	**0**	**0**	**0**	**14**	**0**	**0**	**0**	**9**	**0.0**	**0**	**0**	**0**	**0**		....	....	....	....	....	....	....	....

• Missed remainder of 1999-2000 season recovering from knee injury suffered in game vs. Saint John (AHL), February 16, 2000.

• NICHOLLS, Bernie

Bernard Irvine "The Pumper Nicholl Kid" C – R. 6', 185 lbs. b: Haliburton, Ont., 6/24/1961. Los Angeles' 6th, 73rd overall, in 1980.

Season	Club	League	GP	G	A	Pts	AG	AA	APts	PIM	PP	SH	GW	S	%	TGF	PGF	TGA	PGA	+/-	GP	G	A	Pts	PIM	PP	SH	GW
1978-79	North York Rangers	OJHL	50	40	62	102	....	....	....	60	....	....	....	....	....	....	....	....	....	....	....	....	....	....	....	....	....	....
	Kingston Canadians	OMJHL	2	0	1	1	....	....	....	0	....	....	....	....	....	....	....	....	....	....	....	....	....	....	....	....	....	....
1979-80	Kingston Canadians	OMJHL	68	36	43	79	....	....	....	85	....	....	....	....	....	....	....	....	....	....	3	1	0	1	10	....	....	....
1980-81	Kingston Canadians	OMJHL	65	63	89	152	....	....	....	109	....	....	....	....	....	....	....	....	....	....	14	8	10	18	17	....	....	....
1981-82	**Los Angeles Kings**	**NHL**	**22**	**14**	**18**	**32**	**11**	**12**	**23**	**27**	**8**	**1**	**1**	**63**	**22.2**	**38**	**14**	**29**	**7**	**2**	**10**	**4**	**0**	**4**	**23**	**0**	**0**	**1**
	New Haven Nighthawks	AHL	55	41	30	71	....	....	....	31	....	....	....	....	....	....	....	....	....	....	....	....	....	....	....	....	....	....
1982-83	**Los Angeles Kings**	**NHL**	**71**	**28**	**22**	**50**	**23**	**15**	**38**	**124**	**12**	**0**	**3**	**171**	**16.4**	**68**	**24**	**83**	**16**	**–23**	....	....	....	....	....	....	....	....
1983-84	**Los Angeles Kings**	**NHL**	**78**	**41**	**54**	**95**	**33**	**37**	**70**	**83**	**8**	**4**	**2**	**255**	**16.1**	**123**	**37**	**136**	**29**	**–21**	....	....	....	....	....	....	....	....
1984-85	**Los Angeles Kings**	**NHL**	**80**	**46**	**54**	**100**	**38**	**37**	**75**	**76**	**15**	**0**	**6**	**329**	**14.0**	**153**	**68**	**89**	**0**	**–4**	**3**	**1**	**1**	**2**	**9**	**0**	**0**	**0**
	Canada	WEC-A	10	0	2	2	....	....	....	12	....	....	....	....	....	....	....	....	....	....	....	....	....	....	....	....	....	....
1985-86	**Los Angeles Kings**	**NHL**	**80**	**36**	**61**	**97**	**29**	**41**	**70**	**78**	**10**	**4**	**0**	**281**	**12.8**	**140**	**49**	**114**	**18**	**–5**	....	....	....	....	....	....	....	....
1986-87	**Los Angeles Kings**	**NHL**	**80**	**33**	**48**	**81**	**29**	**35**	**64**	**101**	**10**	**1**	**2**	**227**	**14.5**	**115**	**47**	**86**	**2**	**–16**	**5**	**2**	**5**	**7**	**6**	**1**	**0**	**0**
1987-88	**Los Angeles Kings**	**NHL**	**65**	**32**	**46**	**78**	**27**	**33**	**60**	**114**	**8**	**7**	**1**	**236**	**13.6**	**125**	**53**	**102**	**32**	**2**	**5**	**2**	**6**	**8**	**11**	**1**	**0**	**0**
1988-89	**Los Angeles Kings**	**NHL**	**79**	**70**	**80**	**150**	**60**	**57**	**117**	**96**	**21**	**8**	**6**	**385**	**18.2**	**194**	**63**	**139**	**38**	**30**	**11**	**7**	**9**	**16**	**12**	**3**	**0**	**1**
1989-90	**Los Angeles Kings**	**NHL**	**47**	**27**	**48**	**75**	**23**	**34**	**57**	**66**	**8**	**0**	**1**	**172**	**15.7**	**96**	**35**	**75**	**8**	**–6**	....	....	....	....	....	....	....	....
	New York Rangers	**NHL**	**32**	**12**	**25**	**37**	**10**	**18**	**28**	**20**	**7**	**0**	**0**	**115**	**10.4**	**56**	**35**	**29**	**5**	**–3**	**10**	**7**	**5**	**12**	**16**	**3**	**0**	**0**
1990-91	**New York Rangers**	**NHL**	**71**	**25**	**48**	**73**	**23**	**37**	**60**	**96**	**8**	**0**	**2**	**163**	**15.3**	**121**	**50**	**67**	**1**	**5**	**5**	**4**	**3**	**7**	**8**	**0**	**0**	**1**
1991-92	**New York Rangers**	**NHL**	**1**	**0**	**0**	**0**	**0**	**0**	**0**	**0**	**0**	**0**	**0**	**2**	**0.0**	**1**	**0**	**2**	**0**	**–1**	....	....	....	....	....	....	....	....
	Edmonton Oilers	**NHL**	**49**	**20**	**29**	**49**	**18**	**22**	**40**	**60**	**7**	**0**	**2**	**115**	**17.4**	**69**	**25**	**40**	**1**	**5**	**16**	**8**	**11**	**19**	**25**	**4**	**0**	**1**
1992-93	**Edmonton Oilers**	**NHL**	**46**	**8**	**32**	**40**	**7**	**22**	**29**	**40**	**4**	**0**	**1**	**86**	**9.3**	**56**	**28**	**46**	**2**	**–16**	....	....	....	....	....	....	....	....
	New Jersey Devils	**NHL**	**23**	**5**	**15**	**20**	**4**	**10**	**14**	**40**	**1**	**0**	**0**	**46**	**10.9**	**33**	**12**	**19**	**1**	**3**	**5**	**0**	**0**	**0**	**6**	**0**	**0**	**0**
1993-94	**New Jersey Devils**	**NHL**	**61**	**19**	**27**	**46**	**18**	**21**	**39**	**86**	**3**	**0**	**1**	**142**	**13.4**	**66**	**17**	**45**	**20**	**24**	**16**	**4**	**9**	**13**	**28**	**2**	**1**	**0**
1994-95	**Chicago Blackhawks**	**NHL**	**48**	**22**	**29**	**51**	**39**	**43**	**82**	**32**	**11**	**2**	**5**	**114**	**19.3**	**74**	**39**	**41**	**10**	**4**	**16**	**1**	**11**	**12**	**8**	**1**	**0**	**0**
1995-96	**Chicago Blackhawks**	**NHL**	**59**	**19**	**41**	**60**	**19**	**34**	**53**	**60**	**6**	**0**	**2**	**100**	**19.0**	**88**	**36**	**50**	**9**	**11**	**10**	**2**	**7**	**9**	**4**	**1**	**0**	**0**
1996-97	**San Jose Sharks**	**NHL**	**65**	**12**	**33**	**45**	**13**	**29**	**42**	**63**	**2**	**1**	**0**	**137**	**8.8**	**60**	**19**	**90**	**28**	**–21**	....	....	....	....	....	....	....	....
1997-98	**San Jose Sharks**	**NHL**	**60**	**6**	**22**	**28**	**7**	**22**	**29**	**26**	**3**	**0**	**0**	**81**	**7.4**	**42**	**12**	**43**	**9**	**–4**	**6**	**0**	**5**	**5**	**8**	**0**	**0**	**0**
1998-99	**San Jose Sharks**	**NHL**	**10**	**0**	**2**	**2**	**0**	**2**	**2**	**4**	**0**	**0**	**0**	**11**	**0.0**	**3**	**2**	**5**	**0**	**–4**	....	....	....	....	....	....	....	....
	NHL Totals		**1127**	**475**	**734**	**1209**	**431**	**561**	**992**	**1292**	**152**	**28**	**35**	**3231**	**14.7**	**1721**	**665**	**1330**	**236**		**118**	**42**	**72**	**114**	**164**	**16**	**1**	**4**

Played in NHL All-Star Game (1984, 1989, 1990)

Traded to **NY Rangers** by **LA Kings** for Tomas Sandstrom and Tony Granato, January 20, 1990. Traded to **Edmonton** by **NY Rangers** with Steven Rice and Louie DeBrusk for Mark Messier and future considerations (Jeff Beukeboom for David Shaw, November 12, 1991), October 4, 1991. Traded to **New Jersey** by **Edmonton** for Zdeno Ciger and Kevin Todd, January 13, 1993. Signed as a free agent by **Chicago**, July 14, 1994. Signed as a free agent by **San Jose**, August 5, 1996.

• NICHOLSON, Neil

Neil Andrew D – R. 5'11", 180 lbs. b: Saint John, N.B., 9/12/1949. Oakland's 6th, 65th overall, in 1969.

Season	Club	League	GP	G	A	Pts	AG	AA	APts	PIM	PP	SH	GW	S	%	TGF	PGF	TGA	PGA	+/-	GP	G	A	Pts	PIM	PP	SH	GW
1966-67	Fredericton Jr. Red Wings	NBJHL	....	9	11	20	....	....	....	39	....	....	....	....	....	....	....	....	....	....	....	....	....	....	....	....	....	....
	Halifax Jr. Canadiens	MJrHL	....	....	....	....	....	....	....	....	....	....	....	....	....	....	....	....	....	....	4	0	1	1	4	....	....	....
1967-68	Fredericton Jr. Red Wings	NBJHL	4	0	2	2	....	....	....	2	....	....	....	....	....	....	....	....	....	....	6	3	5	8	18	....	....	....
	Fredericton Red Wings	SNBHL	31	11	20	31	....	....	....	30	....	....	....	....	....	....	....	....	....	....	5	2	2	4	6	....	....	....
	Fredericton Red Wings	Mem-Cup	6	4	3	7	....	....	....	6	....	....	....	....	....	....	....	....	....	....	....	....	....	....	....	....	....	....
1968-69	London Knights	OHA-Jr.	54	16	26	42	....	....	....	62	....	....	....	....	....	....	....	....	....	....	6	0	2	2	8	....	....	....
1969-70	Providence Reds	AHL	63	3	21	24	....	....	....	120	....	....	....	....	....	....	....	....	....	....	....	....	....	....	....	....	....	....
	Oakland Seals	**NHL**	....	....	....	....	....	....	....	....	....	....	....	....	....	....	....	....	....	....	**2**	**0**	**0**	**0**	**0**	**0**	**0**	**0**
1970-71	Providence Reds	AHL	56	8	16	24	....	....	....	41	....	....	....	....	....	....	....	....	....	....	10	4	1	5	6	....	....	....
1971-72	Providence Reds	AHL	73	18	18	36	....	....	....	21	....	....	....	....	....	....	....	....	....	....	5	2	2	4	4	....	....	....
1972-73	**New York Islanders**	**NHL**	**30**	**3**	**1**	**4**	**3**	**1**	**4**	**23**	**0**	**0**	**0**	**51**	**5.9**	**18**	**0**	**47**	**7**	**–22**	....	....	....	....	....	....	....	....
	New Haven Nighthawks	AHL	43	7	12	19	....	....	....	44	....	....	....	....	....	....	....	....	....	....	....	....	....	....	....	....	....	....
1973-74	**New York Islanders**	**NHL**	**8**	**0**	**0**	**0**	**0**	**0**	**0**	**0**	**0**	**0**	**0**	**2**	**0.0**	**2**	**0**	**0**	**0**	**2**	....	....	....	....	....	....	....	....
	Fort Worth Wings	CHL	47	10	16	26	....	....	....	30	....	....	....	....	....	....	....	....	....	....	4	0	2	2	11	....	....	....
1974-75	Fort Worth Texans	CHL	74	14	47	61	....	....	....	99	....	....	....	....	....	....	....	....	....	....	....	....	....	....	....	....	....	....
1975-76	Fort Worth Texans	CHL	74	16	39	55	....	....	....	119	....	....	....	....	....	....	....	....	....	....	....	....	....	....	....	....	....	....
1976-77	Fort Worth Texans	CHL	65	6	43	49	....	....	....	78	....	....	....	....	....	....	....	....	....	....	6	1	5	6	9	....	....	....
1977-78	**New York Islanders**	**NHL**	**1**	**0**	**0**	**0**	**0**	**0**	**0**	**0**	**0**	**0**	**0**	**2**	**0.0**	**3**	**0**	**1**	**0**	**2**	....	....	....	....	....	....	....	....
	Fort Worth Texans	CHL	69	16	36	52	....	....	....	73	....	....	....	....	....	....	....	....	....	....	14	2	6	8	8	....	....	....
1978-79	Fort Worth Texans	CHL	19	0	13	13	....	....	....	6	....	....	....	....	....	....	....	....	....	....	5	2	0	2	8	....	....	....
1979-80	SC Langnau	Switz.	28	11	8	19	....	....	....	....	....	....	....	....	....	....	....	....	....	....	....	....	....	....	....	....	....	....
1980-81	SC Langnau	Switz.	28	14	17	31	....	....	....	....	....	....	....	....	....	....	....	....	....	....	....	....	....	....	....	....	....	....
1981-82	SC Langnau	Switz-2	STATISTICS NOT AVAILABLE																									
	Dallas Black Hawks	CHL	10	0	0	0	....	....	....	2	....	....	....	....	....	....	....	....	....	....	8	0	2	2	0	....	....	....
1982-83	SC Langnau	Switz.	38	17	12	29	....	....	....	....	....	....	....	....	....	....	....	....	....	....	....	....	....	....	....	....	....	....
	Moncton Alpines	AHL	12	0	2	2	....	....	....	9	....	....	....	....	....	....	....	....	....	....	....	....	....	....	....	....	....	....
1983-84	SC Langnau	Switz.	26	6	13	19	....	....	....	0	....	....	....	....	....	....	....	....	....	....	....	....	....	....	....	....	....	....
1984-85	SC Langnau	Switz.	27	6	8	14	....	....	....	....	....	....	....	....	....	....	....	....	....	....	....	....	....	....	....	....	....	....
	NHL Totals		**39**	**3**	**1**	**4**	**3**	**1**	**4**	**23**	**0**	**0**	**0**	**55**	**5.5**	**23**	**0**	**48**	**7**		**2**	**0**	**0**	**0**	**0**	**0**	**0**	**0**

CHL First All-Star Team (1977)

Claimed by **NY Islanders** from **California** (Salt Lake-CHL) in Inter-League Draft, June 6, 1972.

• NICHOLSON, Paul

LW – L. 6', 190 lbs. b: London, Ont., 2/16/1954. Washington's 4th, 55th overall, in 1974.

Season	Club	League	GP	G	A	Pts	AG	AA	APts	PIM	PP	SH	GW	S	%	TGF	PGF	TGA	PGA	+/–	GP	G	A	Pts	PIM	PP	SH	GW
			REGULAR SEASON																		PLAYOFFS							
1971-72	London Knights	OMJHL	62	18	16	34	....	....	....	50	....	....	....	....	....	....	....	....	....	....	7	1	0	1	7	....	....	....
1972-73	London Knights	OMJHL	60	16	18	34	....	....	....	42	....	....	....	....	....	....	....	....	....	....	....	....	....	....	....	....	....	....
1973-74	London Knights	OMJHL	67	36	33	69	....	....	....	60	....	....	....	....	....	....	....	....	....	....	....	....	....	....	....	....	....	....
1974-75	**Washington Capitals**	**NHL**	**39**	**4**	**5**	**9**	**3**	**4**	**7**	**7**	**0**	**0**	**1**	**46**	**8.7**	**14**	**1**	**42**	**0**	**–29**	....	....	....	....	....	....	....	....
	Richmond Robins	AHL	34	9	13	22	....	....	....	26	....	....	....	....	....	....	....	....	....	....	2	0	0	0	2	....	....	....
1975-76	**Washington Capitals**	**NHL**	**14**	**0**	**2**	**2**	**0**	**1**	**1**	**9**	**0**	**0**	**0**	**10**	**0.0**	**4**	**0**	**9**	**1**	**–4**	....	....	....	....	....	....	....	....
	Richmond Robins	AHL	4	0	0	0	....	....	....	0	....	....	....	....	....	....	....	....	....	....	....	....	....	....	....	....	....	....
	Dayton Gems	IHL	55	35	37	72	....	....	....	76	....	....	....	....	....	....	....	....	....	....	15	11	9	20	15	....	....	....
1976-77	**Washington Capitals**	**NHL**	**9**	**0**	**1**	**1**	**0**	**1**	**1**	**2**	**0**	**0**	**0**	**16**	**0.0**	**1**	**0**	**7**	**0**	**–6**	....	....	....	....	....	....	....	....
	Dayton Gems	IHL	67	28	39	67	....	....	....	50	....	....	....	....	....	....	....	....	....	....	4	1	4	5	2	....	....	....
	Springfield Indians	AHL	1	0	0	0	....	....	....	0	....	....	....	....	....	....	....	....	....	....	....	....	....	....	....	....	....	....
1977-78	Port Huron Flags	IHL	77	34	46	80	....	....	....	54	....	....	....	....	....	....	....	....	....	....	17	9	8	17	6	....	....	....
	NHL Totals		**62**	**4**	**8**	**12**	**3**	**6**	**9**	**18**	**0**	**0**	**1**	**72**	**5.6**	**19**	**1**	**58**	**1**		....	....	....	....	....	....	....	....

• NICKULAS, Eric

C – R. 5'11", 190 lbs. b: Hyannis, MA, 3/25/1975. Boston's 3rd, 99th overall, in 1994.

Season	Club	League	GP	G	A	Pts	AG	AA	APts	PIM	PP	SH	GW	S	%	TGF	PGF	TGA	PGA	+/–	GP	G	A	Pts	PIM	PP	SH	GW
1991-92	Barnstable High School	Hi-School	24	30	25	55	....	....	....	....	....	....	....	....	....	....	....	....	....	....	....	....	....	....	....	....	....	....
1992-93	Tabor Academy Seawolves	Hi-School	28	25	25	50	....	....	....	....	....	....	....	....	....	....	....	....	....	....	....	....	....	....	....	....	....	....
1993-94	Cushing Academy Penguins	Hi-School	25	46	36	82	....	....	....	....	....	....	....	....	....	....	....	....	....	....	....	....	....	....	....	....	....	....
1994-95	University of New Hampshire	H-East	33	15	9	24	....	....	....	32	....	....	....	....	....	....	....	....	....	....	....	....	....	....	....	....	....	....
1995-96	University of New Hampshire	H-East	34	26	12	38	....	....	....	66	....	....	....	....	....	....	....	....	....	....	....	....	....	....	....	....	....	....
1996-97	University of New Hampshire	H-East	39	29	22	51	....	....	....	80	....	....	....	....	....	....	....	....	....	....	....	....	....	....	....	....	....	....
1997-98	Orlando Solar Bears	IHL	76	22	9	31	....	....	....	77	....	....	....	....	....	....	....	....	....	....	6	0	0	0	10	....	....	....
1998-99	**Boston Bruins**	**NHL**	**2**	**0**	**0**	**0**	**0**	**0**	**0**	**0**	**0**	**0**	**0**	**0**	**0.0**	**0**	**0**	**0**	**0**	**0**	**1**	**0**	**0**	**0**	**2**	**0**	**0**	**0**
	Providence Bruins	AHL	75	31	27	58	....	....	....	83	....	....	....	....	....	....	....	....	....	....	18	8	12	20	33	....	....	....
99-2000	**Boston Bruins**	**NHL**	**20**	**5**	**6**	**11**	**6**	**6**	**12**	**12**	**1**	**0**	**0**	**28**	**17.9**	**12**	**2**	**11**	**0**	**–1**	....	....	....	....	....	....	....	....
	Providence Bruins	AHL	40	6	6	12	....	....	....	37	....	....	....	....	....	....	....	....	....	....	12	2	3	5	20	....	....	....
	NHL Totals		**22**	**5**	**6**	**11**	**6**	**6**	**12**	**12**	**1**	**0**	**0**	**28**	**17.9**	**12**	**2**	**11**	**0**		**1**	**0**	**0**	**0**	**2**	**0**	**0**	**0**

• NICOLSON, Graeme

Graeme Butte D – R. 6', 185 lbs. b: North Bay, Ont., 1/13/1958. Boston's 2nd, 35th overall, in 1978.

Season	Club	League	GP	G	A	Pts	AG	AA	APts	PIM	PP	SH	GW	S	%	TGF	PGF	TGA	PGA	+/–	GP	G	A	Pts	PIM	PP	SH	GW
1975-76	Cornwall Royals	QMJHL	72	11	36	47	....	....	....	101	....	....	....	....	....	....	....	....	....	....	....	....	....	....	....	....	....	....
1976-77	Cornwall Royals	QMJHL	64	21	46	67	....	....	....	197	....	....	....	....	....	....	....	....	....	....	12	3	9	12	34	....	....	....
1977-78	Cornwall Royals	QMJHL	62	13	52	65	....	....	....	122	....	....	....	....	....	....	....	....	....	....	9	1	4	5	45	....	....	....
1978-79	**Boston Bruins**	**NHL**	**1**	**0**	**0**	**0**	**0**	**0**	**0**	**0**	**0**	**0**	**0**	**0**	**0.0**	**0**	**0**	**0**	**0**	**0**	....	....	....	....	....	....	....	....
	Rochester Americans	AHL	80	16	35	51	....	....	....	112	....	....	....	....	....	....	....	....	....	....	....	....	....	....	....	....	....	....
1979-80	Binghamton Dusters	AHL	79	7	36	43	....	....	....	151	....	....	....	....	....	....	....	....	....	....	....	....	....	....	....	....	....	....
1980-81			DID NOT PLAY																									
1981-82	**Colorado Rockies**	**NHL**	**41**	**2**	**7**	**9**	**2**	**5**	**7**	**51**	**0**	**0**	**0**	**39**	**5.1**	**30**	**0**	**49**	**3**	**–16**	....	....	....	....	....	....	....	....
	Fort Worth Texans	CHL	30	9	12	21	....	....	....	38	....	....	....	....	....	....	....	....	....	....	....	....	....	....	....	....	....	....
1982-83	**New York Rangers**	**NHL**	**10**	**0**	**0**	**0**	**0**	**0**	**0**	**9**	**0**	**0**	**0**	**3**	**0.0**	**3**	**0**	**9**	**1**	**–5**	....	....	....	....	....	....	....	....
	Tulsa Oilers	CHL	64	19	28	47	....	....	....	166	....	....	....	....	....	....	....	....	....	....	....	....	....	....	....	....	....	....
1983-84	Tulsa Oilers	CHL	62	7	24	31	....	....	....	61	....	....	....	....	....	....	....	....	....	....	9	1	6	7	12	....	....	....
1984-85	Flamboro Mott's Clamatos	OHA-Sr.	6	1	7	8	....	....	....	4	....	....	....	....	....	....	....	....	....	....	....	....	....	....	....	....	....	....
	Binghamton Whalers	AHL	37	3	9	12	....	....	....	53	....	....	....	....	....	....	....	....	....	....	4	0	0	0	2	....	....	....
	NHL Totals		**52**	**2**	**7**	**9**	**2**	**5**	**7**	**60**	**0**	**0**	**0**	**42**	**4.8**	**33**	**0**	**58**	**4**		....	....	....	....	....	....	....	....

QMJHL First All-Star Team (1977) • QMJHL Second All-Star Team (1978) • CHL Second All-Star Team (1984)

• Sat out entire 1980-81 season to become unrestricted free agent. Signed as a free agent by **Colorado**, September 2, 1981. Transferred to **New Jersey** after **Colorado** franchise relocated, June 30, 1982. Claimed by **NY Rangers** from **New Jersey** in Waiver Draft, October 4, 1982. Signed as a free agent by **Washington**, August 17, 1984.

• NIECKAR, Barry

Barry Glenn LW – L. 6'3", 205 lbs. b: Rama, Sask., 12/16/1967.

Season	Club	League	GP	G	A	Pts	AG	AA	APts	PIM	PP	SH	GW	S	%	TGF	PGF	TGA	PGA	+/–	GP	G	A	Pts	PIM	PP	SH	GW
1986-87	Weyburn Red Wings	SJHL	41	12	10	22	....	....	....	115	....	....	....	....	....	....	....	....	....	....	....	....	....	....	....	....	....	....
1987-88	Yorkton Terriers	SJHL	57	27	32	59	....	....	....	188	....	....	....	....	....	....	....	....	....	....	16	11	6	17	65	....	....	....
1988-89			STATISTICS NOT AVAILABLE																									
1989-90	Virginia Lancers	ECHL	5	2	2	4	....	....	....	27	....	....	....	....	....	....	....	....	....	....	....	....	....	....	....	....	....	....
1990-91			STATISTICS NOT AVAILABLE																									
1991-92	Phoenix Roadrunners	IHL	5	0	0	0	....	....	....	9	....	....	....	....	....	....	....	....	....	....	....	....	....	....	....	....	....	....
	Raleigh IceCaps	ECHL	46	10	18	28	....	....	....	229	....	....	....	....	....	....	....	....	....	....	4	4	0	4	22	....	....	....
1992-93	**Hartford Whalers**	**NHL**	**2**	**0**	**0**	**0**	**0**	**0**	**0**	**2**	**0**	**0**	**0**	**1**	**0.0**	**0**	**0**	**2**	**0**	**–2**	....	....	....	....	....	....	....	....
	Springfield Indians	AHL	21	2	4	6	....	....	....	65	....	....	....	....	....	....	....	....	....	....	6	1	0	1	14	....	....	....
1993-94	Springfield Indians	AHL	30	0	2	2	....	....	....	67	....	....	....	....	....	....	....	....	....	....	....	....	....	....	....	....	....	....
	Raleigh IceCaps	ECHL	18	4	6	10	....	....	....	126	....	....	....	....	....	....	....	....	....	....	15	5	7	12	51	....	....	....
1994-95	Saint John Flames	AHL	65	8	7	15	....	....	....	*491	....	....	....	....	....	....	....	....	....	....	4	0	0	0	22	....	....	....
	Calgary Flames	**NHL**	**3**	**0**	**0**	**0**	**0**	**0**	**0**	**12**	**0**	**0**	**0**	**0**	**0.0**	**0**	**0**	**0**	**0**	**0**	....	....	....	....	....	....	....	....
1995-96	Utah Grizzlies	IHL	53	9	15	24	....	....	....	194	....	....	....	....	....	....	....	....	....	....	....	....	....	....	....	....	....	....
	Peoria Rivermen	IHL	10	3	3	6	....	....	....	72	....	....	....	....	....	....	....	....	....	....	12	4	6	10	48	....	....	....
1996-97	**Mighty Ducks of Anaheim**	**NHL**	**2**	**0**	**0**	**0**	**0**	**0**	**0**	**5**	**0**	**0**	**0**	**0**	**0.0**	**0**	**0**	**0**	**0**	**0**	....	....	....	....	....	....	....	....
	Long Beach Ice Dogs	IHL	63	3	10	13	....	....	....	386	....	....	....	....	....	....	....	....	....	....	5	0	0	0	22	....	....	....
1997-98	**Mighty Ducks of Anaheim**	**NHL**	**1**	**0**	**0**	**0**	**0**	**0**	**0**	**2**	**0**	**0**	**0**	**0**	**0.0**	**0**	**0**	**0**	**0**	**0**	....	....	....	....	....	....	....	....
	Cincinnati Mighty Ducks	AHL	75	10	14	24	....	....	....	295	....	....	....	....	....	....	....	....	....	....	....	....	....	....	....	....	....	....
1998-99	Springfield Falcons	AHL	67	11	6	17	....	....	....	270	....	....	....	....	....	....	....	....	....	....	1	0	0	0	2	....	....	....
99-2000	London Knights	Britain	15	2	0	2	....	....	....	100	....	....	....	....	....	....	....	....	....	....	8	2	2	4	29	....	....	....
	NHL Totals		**8**	**0**	**0**	**0**	**0**	**0**	**0**	**21**	**0**	**0**	**0**	**1**	**0.0**	**0**	**0**	**2**	**0**		....	....	....	....	....	....	....	....

Signed as a free agent by **Hartford**, September 25, 1992. Signed as a free agent by **Calgary**, February 11, 1995. Signed as a free agent by **NY Islanders**, August 8, 1995. Signed as a free agent by **Anaheim**, October 2, 1996. Signed as a free agent by **Phoenix**, August 27, 1998.

• NIEDERMAYER, Rob

Rob W. C – L. 6'2", 204 lbs. b: Cassiar, B.C., 12/28/1974. Florida's 1st, 5th overall, in 1993.

Season	Club	League	GP	G	A	Pts	AG	AA	APts	PIM	PP	SH	GW	S	%	TGF	PGF	TGA	PGA	+/–	GP	G	A	Pts	PIM	PP	SH	GW
1989-90	Cranbrook Midget Royals	BCAHA	35	42	40	82	....	....	....	30	....	....	....	....	....	....	....	....	....	....	....	....	....	....	....	....	....	....
1990-91	Medicine Hat Tigers	WHL	71	24	26	50	....	....	....	8	....	....	....	....	....	....	....	....	....	....	12	3	7	10	2	....	....	....
1991-92	Medicine Hat Tigers	WHL	71	32	46	78	....	....	....	77	....	....	....	....	....	....	....	....	....	....	4	2	3	5	2	....	....	....
1992-93	Medicine Hat Tigers	WHL	52	43	34	77	....	....	....	67	....	....	....	....	....	....	....	....	....	....	....	....	....	....	....	....	....	....
	Canada	WJC-A	7	0	2	2	....	....	....	2	....	....	....	....	....	....	....	....	....	....	....	....	....	....	....	....	....	....
1993-94	**Florida Panthers**	**NHL**	**65**	**9**	**17**	**26**	**8**	**13**	**21**	**51**	**3**	**0**	**2**	**67**	**13.4**	**38**	**18**	**31**	**0**	**–11**	....	....	....	....	....	....	....	....
1994-95	Medicine Hat Tigers	WHL	13	9	15	24	....	....	....	14	....	....	....	....	....	....	....	....	....	....	....	....	....	....	....	....	....	....
	Florida Panthers	**NHL**	**48**	**4**	**6**	**10**	**7**	**9**	**16**	**36**	**1**	**0**	**0**	**58**	**6.9**	**26**	**11**	**28**	**0**	**–13**	....	....	....	....	....	....	....	....
1995-96	**Florida Panthers**	**NHL**	**82**	**26**	**35**	**61**	**26**	**29**	**55**	**107**	**11**	**0**	**6**	**155**	**16.8**	**97**	**44**	**54**	**2**	**1**	**22**	**5**	**3**	**8**	**12**	**2**	**0**	**2**
1996-97	**Florida Panthers**	**NHL**	**60**	**14**	**24**	**38**	**15**	**21**	**36**	**54**	**3**	**0**	**2**	**136**	**10.3**	**55**	**16**	**43**	**8**	**4**	**5**	**2**	**1**	**3**	**6**	**1**	**0**	**0**
1997-98	**Florida Panthers**	**NHL**	**33**	**8**	**7**	**15**	**9**	**7**	**16**	**41**	**5**	**0**	**2**	**64**	**12.5**	**27**	**14**	**27**	**5**	**–9**	....	....	....	....	....	....	....	....
1998-99	**Florida Panthers**	**NHL**	**82**	**18**	**33**	**51**	**21**	**32**	**53**	**50**	**6**	**1**	**3**	**142**	**12.7**	**86**	**29**	**89**	**19**	**–13**	....	....	....	....	....	....	....	....
	Canada	WC-A	10	2	1	3	....	....	....	8	....	....	....	....	....	....	....	....	....	....	....	....	....	....	....	....	....	....
99-2000	**Florida Panthers**	**NHL**	**81**	**10**	**23**	**33**	**11**	**21**	**32**	**46**	**1**	**0**	**4**	**135**	**7.4**	**67**	**20**	**75**	**23**	**–5**	**4**	**1**	**0**	**1**	**6**	**0**	**0**	**0**
	NHL Totals		**451**	**89**	**145**	**234**	**97**	**132**	**229**	**385**	**30**	**1**	**19**	**757**	**11.8**	**396**	**152**	**347**	**57**		**31**	**8**	**4**	**12**	**24**	**3**	**0**	**2**

• Brother of Scott • WHL East First All-Star Team (1993)

• Missed majority of 1997-98 season recovering from thumb injury suffered in game vs. Boston (November 26, 1997) and head injury suffered in game vs. Buffalo, March 19, 1998.

• NIEDERMAYER, Scott

Robert Scott D – L. 6'1", 200 lbs. b: Edmonton, Alta., 8/31/1973. New Jersey's 1st, 3rd overall, in 1991.

			REGULAR SEASON																			PLAYOFFS							
Season	Club	League	GP	G	A	Pts	AG	AA	APts	PIM	PP	SH	GW	S	%	TGF	PGF	TGA	PGA	+/–	GP	G	A	Pts	PIM	PP	SH	GW
1988-89	Cranbrook Blazers	BCAHA	62	55	37	92	....	....	....	100	....	....	....	....	....	....	....	....	....	....	....	....	....	....	....	....	....	....
1989-90	Kamloops Blazers	WHL	64	14	55	69	....	....	....	64	....	....	....	....	....	....	....	....	....	....	17	2	14	16	35	....	....	....
	Kamloops Blazers	Mem-Cup	3	1	1	2	....	....	....	2	....	....	....	....	....	....	....	....	....	....	....	....	....	....	....	....	....	....
1990-91	Kamloops Blazers	WHL	57	26	56	82	....	....	....	52	....	....	....	....	....	....	....	....	....	....	....	....	....	....	....	....	....	....
	Canada	WJC-A	7	0	0	0	....	....	....	0	....	....	....	....	....	....	....	....	....	....	....	....	....	....	....	....	....	....
1991-92	Kamloops Blazers	WHL	35	7	32	39	....	....	....	61	....	....	....	....	....	....	....	....	....	....	17	9	14	23	28	....	....	....
	Canada	WJC-A	7	0	0	0	....	....	....	10	....	....	....	....	....	....	....	....	....	....	....	....	....	....	....	....	....	....
	New Jersey Devils	**NHL**	**4**	**0**	**1**	**1**	**0**	**1**	**1**	**2**	**0**	**0**	**0**	**4**	**0.0**	**5**	**0**	**4**	**0**	**1**	....	....	....	....	....	....	....	....
	Kamloops Blazers	Mem-Cup	5	2	5	7	....	....	....	6	....	....	....	....	....	....	....	....	....	....	....	....	....	....	....	....	....	....
1992-93	**New Jersey Devils**	**NHL**	**80**	**11**	**29**	**40**	**9**	**20**	**29**	**47**	**5**	**0**	**0**	**131**	**8.4**	**116**	**36**	**77**	**5**	**8**	**5**	**0**	**3**	**3**	**2**	**0**	**0**	**0**
1993-94	**New Jersey Devils**	**NHL**	**81**	**10**	**36**	**46**	**9**	**28**	**37**	**42**	**5**	**0**	**2**	**135**	**7.4**	**121**	**29**	**77**	**19**	**34**	**20**	**2**	**2**	**4**	**8**	**1**	**0**	**0**
1994-95 ♦	**New Jersey Devils**	**NHL**	**48**	**4**	**15**	**19**	**7**	**22**	**29**	**18**	**4**	**0**	**0**	**52**	**7.7**	**68**	**13**	**50**	**14**	**19**	**20**	**4**	**7**	**11**	**10**	**2**	**0**	**1**
1995-96	**New Jersey Devils**	**NHL**	**79**	**8**	**25**	**33**	**8**	**20**	**28**	**46**	**6**	**0**	**0**	**179**	**4.5**	**102**	**34**	**83**	**20**	**5**	....	....	....	....	....	....	....	....
1996-97	Canada	W-Cup	8	1	3	4	....	....	....	6	....	....	....	....	....	....	....	....	....	....	....	....	....	....	....	....	....	....
	New Jersey Devils	**NHL**	**81**	**5**	**30**	**35**	***5**	**27**	**32**	**64**	**3**	**0**	**3**	**159**	**3.1**	**82**	**24**	**72**	**10**	**–4**	**10**	**2**	**4**	**6**	**6**	**2**	**0**	**1**
1997-98	**New Jersey Devils**	**NHL**	**81**	**14**	**43**	**57**	**16**	**42**	**58**	**27**	**11**	**0**	**1**	**175**	**8.0**	**115**	**53**	**71**	**14**	**5**	**6**	**0**	**2**	**2**	**4**	**0**	**0**	**0**
1998-99	Utah Grizzlies	IHL	5	0	2	2	....	....	....	0	....	....	....	....	....	....	....	....	....	....	....	....	....	....	....	....	....	....
	New Jersey Devils	**NHL**	**72**	**11**	**35**	**46**	**13**	**34**	**47**	**26**	**1**	**1**	**3**	**161**	**6.8**	**103**	**34**	**65**	**12**	**16**	**7**	**1**	**3**	**4**	**18**	**1**	**0**	**0**
99-2000 ♦	**New Jersey Devils**	**NHL**	**71**	**7**	**31**	**38**	**8**	**29**	**37**	**48**	**1**	**0**	**0**	**109**	**6.4**	**93**	**20**	**69**	**15**	**19**	**22**	**5**	**2**	**7**	**10**	**0**	**2**	**1**
	NHL Totals		**597**	**70**	**245**	**315**	**75**	**223**	**298**	**320**	**36**	**1**	**9**	**1105**	**6.3**	**805**	**243**	**568**	**109**		**90**	**14**	**23**	**37**	**58**	**6**	**2**	**3**

• Brother of Rob • WHL West First All-Star Team (1991, 1992) • Canadian Major Junior Scholastic Player of the Year (1991) • WJC-A All-Star Team (1992) • Memorial Cup All-Star Team (1992) • Won Stafford Smythe Memorial Trophy (Memorial Cup Tournament MVP) (1992) • NHL All-Rookie Team (1993) • NHL Second All-Star Team (1998) • Played in NHL All-Star Game (1998)

Signed to 25-game try-out contract by **Utah** (IHL) with **New Jersey** retaining NHL rights, October 19, 1998.

• NIEKAMP, Jim

James Lawrence D – R. 6'1", 185 lbs. b: Detroit, MI, 3/11/1946.

Season	Club	League	GP	G	A	Pts	AG	AA	APts	PIM	PP	SH	GW	S	%	TGF	PGF	TGA	PGA	+/–	GP	G	A	Pts	PIM	PP	SH	GW
1964-65	St-Jerome Alouettes	QJHL	33	10	31	41	....	....	....	....	....	....	....	....	....	....	....	....	....	....	8	1	5	6	38	....	....	....
1965-66	St-Jerome Alouettes	QJHL	32	10	15	25	....	....	....	135	....	....	....	....	....	....	....	....	....	....	5	1	1	2	22	....	....	....
	Hamilton Red Wings	OHA-Jr.	11	1	6	7	....	....	....	55	....	....	....	....	....	....	....	....	....	....	....	....	....	....	....	....	....	....
1966-67	Toledo Blades	IHL	66	6	24	30	....	....	....	163	....	....	....	....	....	....	....	....	....	....	8	0	1	1	12	....	....	....
1967-68	Fort Worth Wings	CPHL	49	6	9	15	....	....	....	76	....	....	....	....	....	....	....	....	....	....	7	0	2	2	24	....	....	....
1968-69	Fort Worth Wings	CHL	63	13	21	34	....	....	....	113	....	....	....	....	....	....	....	....	....	....	....	....	....	....	....	....	....	....
1969-70	Cleveland Barons	AHL	47	6	16	22	....	....	....	114	....	....	....	....	....	....	....	....	....	....	....	....	....	....	....	....	....	....
1970-71	**Detroit Red Wings**	**NHL**	**24**	**0**	**2**	**2**	**0**	**2**	**2**	**27**	**0**	**0**	**0**	**21**	**0.0**	**14**	**1**	**36**	**9**	**–14**	....	....	....	....	....	....	....	....
	Baltimore Clippers	AHL	46	9	29	38	....	....	....	93	....	....	....	....	....	....	....	....	....	....	....	....	....	....	....	....	....	....
1971-72	**Detroit Red Wings**	**NHL**	**5**	**0**	**0**	**0**	**0**	**0**	**0**	**10**	**0**	**0**	**0**	**2**	**0.0**	**3**	**0**	**11**	**5**	**–3**	....	....	....	....	....	....	....	....
	Tidewater Red Wings	AHL	65	6	11	17	....	....	....	216	....	....	....	....	....	....	....	....	....	....	....	....	....	....	....	....	....	....
1972-73	Los Angeles Sharks	WHA	78	7	22	29	....	....	....	155	....	....	....	....	....	....	....	....	....	....	6	2	1	3	10	....	....	....
1973-74	Los Angeles Sharks	WHA	76	2	19	21	....	....	....	95	....	....	....	....	....	....	....	....	....	....	....	....	....	....	....	....	....	....
1974-75	Phoenix Roadrunners	WHA	71	2	26	28	....	....	....	66	....	....	....	....	....	....	....	....	....	....	5	0	0	0	8	....	....	....
1975-76	Phoenix Roadrunners	WHA	79	4	14	18	....	....	....	77	....	....	....	....	....	....	....	....	....	....	5	1	0	1	0	....	....	....
1976-77	Phoenix Roadrunners	WHA	79	1	15	16	....	....	....	91	....	....	....	....	....	....	....	....	....	....	....	....	....	....	....	....	....	....
1977-78	Phoenix Roadrunners	PHL	23	1	11	12	....	....	....	12	....	....	....	....	....	....	....	....	....	....	....	....	....	....	....	....	....	....
	NHL Totals		**29**	**0**	**2**	**2**	**0**	**2**	**2**	**37**	**0**	**0**	**0**	**23**	**0.0**	**17**	**1**	**47**	**14**		....	....	....	....	....	....	....	....
	Other Major League Totals		383	16	96	112	....	....	....	484	....	....	....	....	....	....	....	....	....	....	16	3	1	4	18	....	....	....

QJHL First All-Star Team (1965)

Selected by **LA Sharks** (WHA) in 1972 WHA General Player Draft, February 12, 1972. Traded to **Vancouver** by **Detroit** for Ralph Stewart, March 6, 1972. Transferred to **Michigan** (WHA) after **LA Sharks** (WHA) franchise relocated, April 11, 1974. Traded to **Phoenix** (WHA) by **Michigan** (WHA) for the rights to Danny Gruen, May, 1974.

• NIELSEN, Jeff

RW – L. 6', 200 lbs. b: Grand Rapids, MN, 9/20/1971. NY Rangers' 4th, 69th overall, in 1990.

Season	Club	League	GP	G	A	Pts	AG	AA	APts	PIM	PP	SH	GW	S	%	TGF	PGF	TGA	PGA	+/–	GP	G	A	Pts	PIM	PP	SH	GW
1987-88	Grand Rapids Thunderhawks	Hi-School	21	9	11	20	....	....	....	14	....	....	....	....	....	....	....	....	....	....	....	....	....	....	....	....	....	....
1988-89	Grand Rapids Thunderhawks	Hi-School	25	13	17	30	....	....	....	26	....	....	....	....	....	....	....	....	....	....	....	....	....	....	....	....	....	....
1989-90	Grand Rapids Thunderhawks	Hi-School	28	32	25	*57	....	....	....	....	....	....	....	....	....	....	....	....	....	....	....	....	....	....	....	....	....	....
1990-91	University of Minnesota	WCHA	45	11	14	25	....	....	....	50	....	....	....	....	....	....	....	....	....	....	....	....	....	....	....	....	....	....
1991-92	University of Minnesota	WCHA	41	14	14	28	....	....	....	70	....	....	....	....	....	....	....	....	....	....	....	....	....	....	....	....	....	....
1992-93	University of Minnesota	WCHA	42	21	20	41	....	....	....	80	....	....	....	....	....	....	....	....	....	....	....	....	....	....	....	....	....	....
1993-94	University of Minnesota	WCHA	41	29	16	45	....	....	....	94	....	....	....	....	....	....	....	....	....	....	....	....	....	....	....	....	....	....
1994-95	Binghamton Rangers	AHL	76	24	13	37	....	....	....	139	....	....	....	....	....	....	....	....	....	....	7	0	0	0	22	....	....	....
1995-96	Binghamton Rangers	AHL	64	22	20	42	....	....	....	56	....	....	....	....	....	....	....	....	....	....	4	1	1	2	4	....	....	....
1996-97	**New York Rangers**	**NHL**	**2**	**0**	**0**	**0**	**0**	**0**	**0**	**2**	**0**	**0**	**0**	**1**	**0.0**	**0**	**0**	**1**	**0**	**–1**	....	....	....	....	....	....	....	....
	Binghamton Rangers	AHL	76	27	26	53	....	....	....	71	....	....	....	....	....	....	....	....	....	....	4	0	0	0	7	....	....	....
1997-98	**Mighty Ducks of Anaheim**	**NHL**	**32**	**4**	**5**	**9**	**5**	**5**	**10**	**16**	**0**	**0**	**0**	**36**	**11.1**	**12**	**0**	**17**	**4**	**–1**	....	....	....	....	....	....	....	....
	Cincinnati Mighty Ducks	AHL	18	4	8	12	....	....	....	37	....	....	....	....	....	....	....	....	....	....	....	....	....	....	....	....	....	....
1998-99	**Mighty Ducks of Anaheim**	**NHL**	**80**	**5**	**4**	**9**	**6**	**4**	**10**	**34**	**0**	**0**	**2**	**94**	**5.3**	**16**	**0**	**37**	**9**	**–12**	**4**	**0**	**0**	**0**	**2**	**0**	**0**	**0**
99-2000	**Mighty Ducks of Anaheim**	**NHL**	**79**	**8**	**10**	**18**	**9**	**9**	**18**	**14**	**1**	**0**	**0**	**113**	**7.1**	**28**	**1**	**38**	**15**	**4**	....	....	....	....	....	....	....	....
	United States	WC-A	7	1	1	2	....	....	....	2	....	....	....	....	....	....	....	....	....	....	....	....	....	....	....	....	....	....
	NHL Totals		**193**	**17**	**19**	**36**	**20**	**18**	**38**	**66**	**1**	**0**	**2**	**244**	**7.0**	**56**	**1**	**93**	**28**		**4**	**0**	**0**	**0**	**2**	**0**	**0**	**0**

• Brother of Kirk • WCHA Second All-Star Team (1994)

Signed as a free agent by **Anaheim**, August 18, 1997. Selected by **Minnesota** from **Anaheim** in Expansion Draft, June 23, 2000.

• NIELSEN, Kirk

RW – R. 6'1", 205 lbs. b: Grand Rapids, MN, 10/19/1973. Philadelphia's 1st, 10th overall, in 1994 Supplemental Draft.

Season	Club	League	GP	G	A	Pts	AG	AA	APts	PIM	PP	SH	GW	S	%	TGF	PGF	TGA	PGA	+/–	GP	G	A	Pts	PIM	PP	SH	GW
1989-1992	Grand Rapids Thunderhawks	Hi-School	STATISTICS NOT AVAILABLE																									
1992-93	Harvard University	ECAC	30	2	2	4	....	....	....	38	....	....	....	....	....	....	....	....	....	....	....	....	....	....	....	....	....	....
1993-94	Harvard University	ECAC	32	6	9	15	....	....	....	41	....	....	....	....	....	....	....	....	....	....	....	....	....	....	....	....	....	....
1994-95	Harvard University	ECAC	30	13	8	21	....	....	....	24	....	....	....	....	....	....	....	....	....	....	....	....	....	....	....	....	....	....
1995-96	Harvard University	ECAC	31	12	16	28	....	....	....	66	....	....	....	....	....	....	....	....	....	....	....	....	....	....	....	....	....	....
1996-97	Providence Bruins	AHL	68	12	23	35	....	....	....	30	....	....	....	....	....	....	....	....	....	....	9	2	1	3	2	....	....	....
1997-98	**Boston Bruins**	**NHL**	**6**	**0**	**0**	**0**	**0**	**0**	**0**	**0**	**0**	**0**	**0**	**1**	**0.0**	**0**	**0**	**1**	**0**	**–1**	....	....	....	....	....	....	....	....
	Providence Bruins	AHL	72	19	29	48	....	....	....	40	....	....	....	....	....	....	....	....	....	....	....	....	....	....	....	....	....	....
1998-99	Cincinnati Cyclones	IHL	82	12	22	34	....	....	....	58	....	....	....	....	....	....	....	....	....	....	3	0	0	0	4	....	....	....
	NHL Totals		**6**	**0**	**0**	**0**	**0**	**0**	**0**	**0**	**0**	**0**	**0**	**1**	**0.0**	**0**	**0**	**1**	**0**		....	....	....	....	....	....	....	....

• Brother of Jeff

Signed as a free agent by **Boston**, June 7, 1996.

• NIEMINEN, Ville

LW – L. 5'11", 205 lbs. b: Tampere, Finland, 4/6/1977. Colorado's 4th, 78th overall, in 1997.

Season	Club	League	GP	G	A	Pts	AG	AA	APts	PIM	PP	SH	GW	S	%	TGF	PGF	TGA	PGA	+/–	GP	G	A	Pts	PIM	PP	SH	GW
1994-95	Tappara Tampere	Finland-Jr.	16	11	21	32	....	....	....	47	....	....	....	....	....	....	....	....	....	....	....	....	....	....	....	....	....	....
	Tappara Tampere	Finland	16	0	0	0	....	....	....	0	....	....	....	....	....	....	....	....	....	....	....	....	....	....	....	....	....	....
1995-96	Tappara Tampere	Finland-Jr.	20	20	23	43	....	....	....	63	....	....	....	....	....	....	....	....	....	....	....	....	....	....	....	....	....	....
	Tappara Tampere	Finland	4	0	1	1	....	....	....	8	....	....	....	....	....	....	....	....	....	....	....	....	....	....	....	....	....	....
	KooVee Kouvola	Finland-2	7	2	1	3	....	....	....	4	....	....	....	....	....	....	....	....	....	....	....	....	....	....	....	....	....	....
1996-97	Tappara Tampere	Finland	49	10	13	23	....	....	....	120	....	....	....	....	....	....	....	....	....	....	3	1	0	1	8	....	....	....
	Finland	WJC-A	6	2	5	7	....	....	....	2	....	....	....	....	....	....	....	....	....	....	....	....	....	....	....	....	....	....
1997-98	Hershey Bears	AHL	74	14	22	36	....	....	....	85	....	....	....	....	....	....	....	....	....	....	....	....	....	....	....	....	....	....

Season	Club	League	GP	G	A	Pts	AG	AA	APts	PIM	PP	SH	GW	S	%	TGF	PGF	TGA	PGA	+/–	GP	G	A	Pts	PIM	PP	SH	GW
			REGULAR SEASON																		PLAYOFFS							
1998-99	Hershey Bears	AHL	67	24	19	43	....	....	....	127	....	....	....	....	....	....	....	....	....	....	3	0	1	1	0	....	....	....
99-2000	**Colorado Avalanche**	**NHL**	**1**	**0**	**0**	**0**	**0**	**0**	**0**	**0**	**0**	**0**	**0**	**2**	**0.0**	**0**	**0**	**0**	**0**	**0**	....	....	....	....	....	....	....	....
	Hershey Bears	AHL	74	21	30	51	....	....	....	54	....	....	....	....	....	....	....	....	....	....	9	2	4	6	6	....	....	....
	NHL Totals		**1**	**0**	**0**	**0**	**0**	**0**	**0**	**0**	**0**	**0**	**0**	**2**	**0.0**	**0**	**0**	**0**	**0**		....	....	....	....	....	....	....	....

• NIENHUIS, Kraig

LW – L. 6'2", 205 lbs. b: Sarnia, Ont., 5/9/1961.

Season	Club	League	GP	G	A	Pts	AG	AA	APts	PIM	PP	SH	GW	S	%	TGF	PGF	TGA	PGA	+/–	GP	G	A	Pts	PIM	PP	SH	GW
1980-81	Sarnia Bees	OHA-B	34	7	10	17	....	....	....	24	....	....	....	....	....	....	....	....	....	....	....	....	....	....	....	....	....	....
1981-82	Sarnia Bees	OJHL-B	41	25	27	52	....	....	....	....	....	....	....	....	....	....	....	....	....	....	....	....	....	....	....	....	....	....
1982-83	RPI Engineers	ECAC	24	9	11	20	....	....	....	34	....	....	....	....	....	....	....	....	....	....	....	....	....	....	....	....	....	....
1983-84	RPI Engineers	ECAC	35	10	12	22	....	....	....	26	....	....	....	....	....	....	....	....	....	....	....	....	....	....	....	....	....	....
1984-85	RPI Engineers	ECAC	36	11	10	21	....	....	....	55	....	....	....	....	....	....	....	....	....	....	....	....	....	....	....	....	....	....
1985-86	**Boston Bruins**	**NHL**	**70**	**16**	**14**	**30**	**13**	**9**	**22**	**37**	**3**	**0**	**2**	**120**	**13.3**	**40**	**8**	**52**	**10**	**–10**	**2**	**0**	**0**	**0**	**14**	**0**	**0**	**0**
1986-87	**Boston Bruins**	**NHL**	**16**	**4**	**2**	**6**	**3**	**1**	**4**	**2**	**2**	**0**	**0**	**25**	**16.0**	**9**	**4**	**11**	**1**	**–5**	....	....	....	....	....	....	....	....
	Moncton Golden Flames	AHL	54	10	17	27	....	....	....	44	....	....	....	....	....	....	....	....	....	....	....	....	....	....	....	....	....	....
1987-88	**Boston Bruins**	**NHL**	**1**	**0**	**0**	**0**	**0**	**0**	**0**	**0**	**0**	**0**	**0**	**4**	**0.0**	**0**	**0**	**1**	**0**	**–1**	....	....	....	....	....	....	....	....
	Maine Mariners	AHL	36	16	17	33	....	....	....	57	....	....	....	....	....	....	....	....	....	....	....	....	....	....	....	....	....	....
1988-89	Canada	Nat-Team	4	0	0	0	....	....	....	12	....	....	....	....	....	....	....	....	....	....	....	....	....	....	....	....	....	....
	ESV Kaufbeuren	Germany	35	23	28	51	....	....	....	*80	....	....	....	....	....	....	....	....	....	....	12	15	18	33	30	....	....	....
1989-90	Mannheimer ERC	Germany	13	7	4	11	....	....	....	18	....	....	....	....	....	....	....	....	....	....	....	....	....	....	....	....	....	....
1990-91	KAC Klagenfurt	Austria	30	31	22	53	....	....	....	66	....	....	....	....	....	....	....	....	....	....	....	....	....	....	....	....	....	....
	Albany Choppers	IHL	3	3	1	4	....	....	....	0	....	....	....	....	....	....	....	....	....	....	....	....	....	....	....	....	....	....
1991-92	KAC Klagenfurt	Austria	26	21	15	36	....	....	....	....	....	....	....	....	....	....	....	....	....	....	....	....	....	....	....	....	....	....
1992-93	KAC Klagenfurt	Austria	18	14	13	27	....	....	....	....	....	....	....	....	....	....	....	....	....	....	....	....	....	....	....	....	....	....
1993-94	KAC Klagenfurt	Austria	22	8	12	20	....	....	....	....	....	....	....	....	....	....	....	....	....	....	....	....	....	....	....	....	....	....
1994-95	HK Olimpija Ljubljana	Slovenia	36	53	38	91	....	....	....	93	....	....	....	....	....	....	....	....	....	....	....	....	....	....	....	....	....	....
1995-96	HK Olimpija Ljubljana	Alpenliga	10	9	10	19	....	....	....	8	....	....	....	....	....	....	....	....	....	....	....	....	....	....	....	....	....	....
	HK Olimpija Ljubljana	Slovenia	33	31	25	56	....	....	....	32	....	....	....	....	....	....	....	....	....	....	....	....	....	....	....	....	....	....
	Austria	WC-A	6	0	0	0	....	....	....	12	....	....	....	....	....	....	....	....	....	....	....	....	....	....	....	....	....	....
1996-97	Eisbaren Berlin	Germany	48	12	22	34	....	....	....	79	....	....	....	....	....	....	....	....	....	....	8	0	0	0	10	....	....	....
1997-98	Nottingham Panthers	BH-Cup	12	4	4	8	....	....	....	2	....	....	....	....	....	....	....	....	....	....	....	....	....	....	....	....	....	....
	Nottingham Panthers	Britain	42	21	24	45	....	....	....	43	....	....	....	....	....	....	....	....	....	....	6	0	5	5	8	....	....	....
1998-99	SG Milano-Cortina	Alpenliga	7	4	6	10	....	....	....	12	....	....	....	....	....	....	....	....	....	....	....	....	....	....	....	....	....	....
	Port Huron Border Cats	UHL	29	15	22	37	....	....	....	12	....	....	....	....	....	....	....	....	....	....	7	3	4	7	4	....	....	....
99-2000	Port Huron Border Cats	UHL	37	13	22	35	....	....	....	33	....	....	....	....	....	....	....	....	....	....	....	....	....	....	....	....	....	....
	NHL Totals		**87**	**20**	**16**	**36**	**16**	**10**	**26**	**39**	**5**	**0**	**2**	**149**	**13.4**	**49**	**12**	**64**	**11**		**2**	**0**	**0**	**0**	**14**	**0**	**0**	**0**

Signed as a free agent by **Boston**, May 28, 1985. • Played w/ RHI's LA Blades in 1995 (2-0-2-2-3) and St. Louis Vipers in 1999 (1-0-0-0-0).

• NIEUWENDYK, Joe

C – L. 6'1", 205 lbs. b: Oshawa, Ont., 9/10/1966. Calgary's 2nd, 27th overall, in 1985.

Season	Club	League	GP	G	A	Pts	AG	AA	APts	PIM	PP	SH	GW	S	%	TGF	PGF	TGA	PGA	+/–	GP	G	A	Pts	PIM	PP	SH	GW
1983-84	Pickering Panthers	OJHL-B	38	30	28	58	....	....	....	35	....	....	....	....	....	....	....	....	....	....	....	....	....	....	....	....	....	....
1984-85	Cornell University	ECAC	29	21	24	45	....	....	....	30	....	....	....	....	....	....	....	....	....	....	....	....	....	....	....	....	....	....
1985-86	Cornell University	ECAC	29	26	28	54	....	....	....	67	....	....	....	....	....	....	....	....	....	....	....	....	....	....	....	....	....	....
	Canada	WJC-A	7	5	7	12	....	....	....	6	....	....	....	....	....	....	....	....	....	....	....	....	....	....	....	....	....	....
1986-87	Cornell University	ECAC	23	26	26	52	....	....	....	26	....	....	....	....	....	....	....	....	....	....	....	....	....	....	....	....	....	....
	Canada	Nat-Team	5	2	0	2	....	....	....	0	....	....	....	....	....	....	....	....	....	....	....	....	....	....	....	....	....	....
	Calgary Flames	**NHL**	**9**	**5**	**1**	**6**	**4**	**1**	**5**	**0**	**2**	**0**	**1**	**16**	**31.3**	**8**	**2**	**6**	**0**	**0**	**6**	**2**	**2**	**4**	**0**	**0**	**0**	**0**
1987-88	**Calgary Flames**	**NHL**	**75**	**51**	**41**	**92**	**44**	**29**	**73**	**23**	**31**	**3**	**8**	**212**	**24.1**	**139**	**65**	**82**	**28**	**20**	**8**	**3**	**4**	**7**	**2**	**1**	**0**	**0**
1988-89♦	**Calgary Flames**	**NHL**	**77**	**51**	**31**	**82**	**43**	**22**	**65**	**40**	**19**	**3**	**11**	**215**	**23.7**	**115**	**42**	**67**	**20**	**26**	**22**	**10**	**4**	**14**	**10**	**6**	**0**	**1**
1989-90	Calgary Flames	Fr-Tour	4	0	2	2	....	....	....	2	....	....	....	....	....	....	....	....	....	....	....	....	....	....	....	....	....	....
	Calgary Flames	**NHL**	**79**	**45**	**50**	**95**	**39**	**36**	**75**	**40**	**18**	**0**	**3**	**226**	**19.9**	**137**	**51**	**66**	**12**	**32**	**6**	**4**	**6**	**10**	**4**	**1**	**0**	**0**
	Canada	WEC-A	1	0	0	0	....	....	....	0	....	....	....	....	....	....	....	....	....	....	....	....	....	....	....	....	....	....
1990-91	**Calgary Flames**	**NHL**	**79**	**45**	**40**	**85**	**41**	**30**	**71**	**36**	**22**	**4**	**1**	**222**	**20.3**	**127**	**57**	**71**	**20**	**19**	**7**	**4**	**1**	**5**	**10**	**2**	**0**	**0**
1991-92	**Calgary Flames**	**NHL**	**69**	**22**	**34**	**56**	**20**	**26**	**46**	**55**	**7**	**0**	**2**	**137**	**16.1**	**88**	**33**	**76**	**20**	**–1**	....	....	....	....	....	....	....	....
1992-93	**Calgary Flames**	**NHL**	**79**	**38**	**37**	**75**	**32**	**25**	**57**	**52**	**14**	**0**	**6**	**208**	**18.3**	**113**	**43**	**62**	**1**	**9**	**6**	**3**	**6**	**9**	**10**	**1**	**0**	**0**
1993-94	**Calgary Flames**	**NHL**	**64**	**36**	**39**	**75**	**34**	**30**	**64**	**51**	**14**	**1**	**7**	**191**	**18.8**	**102**	**42**	**43**	**2**	**19**	**6**	**2**	**2**	**4**	**0**	**1**	**0**	**0**
1994-95	**Calgary Flames**	**NHL**	**46**	**21**	**29**	**50**	**37**	**43**	**80**	**33**	**3**	**0**	**4**	**122**	**17.2**	**71**	**27**	**33**	**0**	**11**	**5**	**4**	**3**	**7**	**0**	**2**	**0**	**1**
1995-96	**Dallas Stars**	**NHL**	**52**	**14**	**18**	**32**	**14**	**15**	**29**	**41**	**8**	**0**	**3**	**138**	**10.1**	**50**	**25**	**49**	**7**	**–17**	....	....	....	....	....	....	....	....
1996-97	**Dallas Stars**	**NHL**	**66**	**30**	**21**	**51**	**32**	**19**	**51**	**32**	**8**	**0**	**2**	**173**	**17.3**	**63**	**22**	**47**	**1**	**–5**	**7**	**2**	**2**	**4**	**6**	**0**	**0**	**0**
1997-98	**Dallas Stars**	**NHL**	**73**	**39**	**30**	**69**	**46**	**29**	**75**	**30**	**14**	**0**	**11**	**203**	**19.2**	**88**	**38**	**34**	**0**	**16**	**1**	**1**	**0**	**1**	**0**	**0**	**0**	**0**
	Canada	Olympics	6	2	3	5	....	....	....	2	....	....	....	....	....	....	....	....	....	....	....	....	....	....	....	....	....	....
1998-99♦	**Dallas Stars**	**NHL**	**67**	**28**	**27**	**55**	**33**	**26**	**59**	**34**	**8**	**0**	**8**	**157**	**17.8**	**70**	**27**	**32**	**0**	**11**	**23**	***11**	**10**	**21**	**19**	**3**	**0**	**6**
99-2000	**Dallas Stars**	**NHL**	**48**	**15**	**19**	**34**	**17**	**18**	**35**	**26**	**7**	**0**	**2**	**110**	**13.6**	**46**	**18**	**29**	**0**	**–1**	**23**	**7**	**3**	**10**	**18**	**3**	**0**	**2**
	NHL Totals		**883**	**440**	**417**	**857**	**436**	**349**	**785**	**493**	**175**	**11**	**69**	**2330**	**18.9**	**1217**	**492**	**697**	**111**		**120**	**53**	**43**	**96**	**79**	**20**	**0**	**10**

ECAC First All-Star Team (1986, 1987) • NCAA East First All-American Team (1986, 1987) • NHL All-Rookie Team (1988) • Won Calder Memorial Trophy (1988) • Won Dodge Ram Tough Award (1988) • Won King Clancy Memorial Trophy (1995) • Won Conn Smythe Trophy (1999) • Played in NHL All-Star Game (1988, 1989, 1990, 1994)

Traded to **Dallas** by **Calgary** for Corey Millen and Jarome Iginla, December 19, 1995.

• NIGRO, Frank

C – R. 5'9", 182 lbs. b: Richmond Hill, Ont., 2/11/1960. Toronto's 4th, 93rd overall, in 1979.

Season	Club	League	GP	G	A	Pts	AG	AA	APts	PIM	PP	SH	GW	S	%	TGF	PGF	TGA	PGA	+/–	GP	G	A	Pts	PIM	PP	SH	GW
1976-77	Richmond Hill Rams	OHA-B	40	31	35	66	....	....	....	22	....	....	....	....	....	....	....	....	....	....	....	....	....	....	....	....	....	....
	Peterborough Petes	OMJHL	4	0	1	1	....	....	....	2	....	....	....	....	....	....	....	....	....	....	....	....	....	....	....	....	....	....
1977-78	London Knights	OMJHL	68	35	52	87	....	....	....	37	....	....	....	....	....	....	....	....	....	....	11	7	0	7	6	....	....	....
1978-79	London Knights	OMJHL	63	33	56	89	....	....	....	64	....	....	....	....	....	....	....	....	....	....	6	0	1	1	0	....	....	....
1979-80	London Knights	OMJHL	46	12	26	38	....	....	....	30	....	....	....	....	....	....	....	....	....	....	5	0	0	0	0	....	....	....
1980-81	New Brunswick Hawks	AHL	1	0	0	0	....	....	....	0	....	....	....	....	....	....	....	....	....	....	....	....	....	....	....	....	....	....
1981-82	Cincinnati Tigers	CHL	49	24	26	50	....	....	....	24	....	....	....	....	....	....	....	....	....	....	4	1	3	4	2	....	....	....
1982-83	**Toronto Maple Leafs**	**NHL**	**51**	**6**	**15**	**21**	**5**	**10**	**15**	**23**	**1**	**0**	**0**	**77**	**7.8**	**28**	**5**	**24**	**0**	**–1**	**3**	**0**	**0**	**0**	**2**	**0**	**0**	**0**
	St. Catharines Saints	AHL	30	20	13	33	....	....	....	8	....	....	....	....	....	....	....	....	....	....	....	....	....	....	....	....	....	....
1983-84	**Toronto Maple Leafs**	**NHL**	**17**	**2**	**3**	**5**	**2**	**2**	**4**	**16**	**0**	**0**	**0**	**18**	**11.1**	**8**	**1**	**11**	**0**	**–4**	....	....	....	....	....	....	....	....
	St. Catharines Saints	AHL	41	17	24	41	....	....	....	16	....	....	....	....	....	....	....	....	....	....	7	0	6	6	9	....	....	....
1984-85	HC Gardena-Groden	Italy	26	37	43	80	....	....	....	16	....	....	....	....	....	....	....	....	....	....	4	7	7	14	6	....	....	....
1985-86	HC Merano	Italy	34	68	64	132	....	....	....	6	....	....	....	....	....	....	....	....	....	....	6	7	9	16	0	....	....	....
1986-87	HC Merano	Italy	33	36	51	87	....	....	....	14	....	....	....	....	....	....	....	....	....	....	....	....	....	....	....	....	....	....
1987-88	HC Merano	Italy	35	36	36	72	....	....	....	31	....	....	....	....	....	....	....	....	....	....	8	12	5	17	2	....	....	....
1988-89	HC Varese	Italy	43	39	52	91	....	....	....	12	....	....	....	....	....	....	....	....	....	....	....	....	....	....	....	....	....	....
	Italy	WEC-B	7	2	8	10	....	....	....	10	....	....	....	....	....	....	....	....	....	....	....	....	....	....	....	....	....	....
1989-90	HC Varese	Italy	33	21	50	71	....	....	....	10	....	....	....	....	....	....	....	....	....	....	6	5	5	10	0	....	....	....
	Italy	WEC-B	7	4	*8	12	....	....	....	2	....	....	....	....	....	....	....	....	....	....	....	....	....	....	....	....	....	....
1990-91	HC Varese	Italy	35	39	45	84	....	....	....	7	....	....	....	....	....	....	....	....	....	....	10	12	12	24	0	....	....	....
	Italy	WEC-B	7	5	3	8	....	....	....	0	....	....	....	....	....	....	....	....	....	....	....	....	....	....	....	....	....	....
1991-92	HC Bolzano	Alpenliga	20	12	22	34	....	....	....	2	....	....	....	....	....	....	....	....	....	....	....	....	....	....	....	....	....	....
	HC Bolzano	Italy	18	5	25	30	....	....	....	0	....	....	....	....	....	....	....	....	....	....	7	8	7	15	8	....	....	....
	Italy	Olympics	7	0	3	3	....	....	....	6	....	....	....	....	....	....	....	....	....	....	....	....	....	....	....	....	....	....
	NHL Totals		**68**	**8**	**18**	**26**	**7**	**12**	**19**	**39**	**1**	**0**	**0**	**95**	**8.4**	**36**	**6**	**35**	**0**		**3**	**0**	**0**	**0**	**2**	**0**	**0**	**0**

• Missed remainder of 1980-81 season recovering from knee injury suffered in game vs. Nova Scotia (AHL), October 7, 1980.

• NIINIMAA, Janne

Janne Henrik D – L. 6'1", 220 lbs. b: Raahe, Finland, 5/22/1975. Philadelphia's 1st, 36th overall, in 1993.

Season	Club	League	GP	G	A	Pts	AG	AA	APts	PIM	PP	SH	GW	S	%	TGF	PGF	TGA	PGA	+/–	GP	G	A	Pts	PIM	PP	SH	GW
1990-91	Karpat Oulu	Finland-Jr.	3	1	0	1	....	....	....	2	....	....	....	....	....	....	....	....	....	....	....	....	....	....	....	....	....	....
1991-92	Karput Oulu	Finland-Jr.	3	0	0	0	....	....	....	4	....	....	....	....	....	....	....	....	....	....	....	....	....	....	....	....	....	....
	Finland	WJC-A	5	0	0	0	....	....	....	2	....	....	....	....	....	....	....	....	....	....	....	....	....	....	....	....	....	....
	Karpat Oulu	Finland-2	41	2	11	13	....	....	....	49	....	....	....	....	....	....	....	....	....	....	....	....	....	....	....	....	....	....

Season	Club	League	REGULAR SEASON																		PLAYOFFS							
			GP	G	A	Pts	AG	AA	APts	PIM	PP	SH	GW	S	%	TGF	PGF	TGA	PGA	+/–	GP	G	A	Pts	PIM	PP	SH	GW
1992-93	Karpat Oulu	Finland-Jr.	10	3	9	12	....	....	....	16	....	....	....	....	....	....	....	....	....	....	....	....	....	....	....	....	....	....
	KKP Kiimimki	Finland-3	1	0	2	2	....	....	....	4	....	....	....	....	....	....	....	....	....	....	....	....	....	....	....	....	....	....
	Karpat Oulu	Finland-2	29	2	3	5	....	....	....	14	....	....	....	....	....	....	....	....	....	....	....	....	....	....	....	....	....	....
1993-94	Jokerit Helsinki	Finland-Jr.	10	2	6	8	....	....	....	41	....	....	....	....	....	....	....	....	....	....	....	....	....	....	....	....	....	....
	Finland	WJC-A	7	0	0	0	....	....	....	10	....	....	....	....	....	....	....	....	....	....	....	....	....	....	....	....	....	....
	Jokerit Helsinki	Finland	45	3	8	11	....	....	....	24	....	....	....	....	....	....	....	....	....	....	12	1	1	2	4	....	....	....
1994-95	Jokerit Helsinki	Finland-Jr.	3	1	2	3	....	....	....	4	....	....	....	....	....	....	....	....	....	....	....	....	....	....	....	....	....	....
	Finland	WJC-A	7	2	3	5	....	....	....	6	....	....	....	....	....	....	....	....	....	....	....	....	....	....	....	....	....	....
	Jokerit Helsinki	Finland	42	7	10	17	....	....	....	36	....	....	....	....	....	....	....	....	....	....	10	1	4	5	35	....	....	....
	Finland	WC-A	8	1	2	3	....	....	....	10	....	....	....	....	....	....	....	....	....	....	....	....	....	....	....	....	....	....
1995-96	Jokerit Helsinki	Finland	49	5	15	20	....	....	....	79	....	....	....	....	....	....	....	....	....	....	11	0	2	2	12	....	....	....
	Jokerit Helsinki	Finland-Jr.	....	....	....	....	....	....	....	....	....	....	....	....	....	....	....	....	....	....	2	3	4	7	6	....	....	....
	Finland	WC-A	5	1	0	1	....	....	....	10	....	....	....	....	....	....	....	....	....	....	....	....	....	....	....	....	....	....
1996-97	Finland	W-Cup	2	0	0	0	....	....	....	2	....	....	....	....	....	....	....	....	....	....	....	....	....	....	....	....	....	....
	Philadelphia Flyers	**NHL**	**77**	**4**	**40**	**44**	**4**	**36**	**40**	**58**	**1**	**0**	**2**	**141**	**2.8**	**109**	**35**	**67**	**5**	**12**	**19**	**1**	**12**	**13**	**16**	**1**	**0**	**1**
1997-98	**Philadelphia Flyers**	**NHL**	**66**	**3**	**31**	**34**	**4**	**30**	**34**	**56**	**2**	**0**	**1**	**115**	**2.6**	**84**	**34**	**48**	**4**	**6**	....	....	....	....	....	....	....	....
	Finland	Olympics	6	0	3	3	....	....	....	8	....	....	....	....	....	....	....	....	....	....	....	....	....	....	....	....	....	....
	Edmonton Oilers	**NHL**	**11**	**1**	**8**	**9**	**1**	**8**	**9**	**6**	**1**	**0**	**0**	**19**	**5.3**	**19**	**9**	**7**	**4**	**7**	**11**	**1**	**1**	**2**	**12**	**0**	**0**	**1**
1998-99	**Edmonton Oilers**	**NHL**	**81**	**4**	**24**	**28**	**5**	**23**	**28**	**88**	**2**	**0**	**1**	**142**	**2.8**	**84**	**18**	**88**	**29**	**7**	**4**	**0**	**0**	**0**	**2**	**0**	**0**	**0**
99-2000	**Edmonton Oilers**	**NHL**	**81**	**8**	**25**	**33**	**9**	**23**	**32**	**89**	**2**	**2**	**0**	**133**	**6.0**	**86**	**24**	**79**	**31**	**14**	**5**	**0**	**2**	**2**	**2**	**0**	**0**	**0**
	Finland	WC-A	9	2	1	3	....	....	....	8	....	....	....	....	....	....	....	....	....	....	....	....	....	....	....	....	....	....
	NHL Totals		**316**	**20**	**128**	**148**	**23**	**120**	**143**	**297**	**8**	**2**	**4**	**550**	**3.6**	**382**	**120**	**289**	**73**		**39**	**2**	**15**	**17**	**32**	**1**	**0**	**2**

NHL All-Rookie Team (1997)

Traded to **Edmonton** by **Philadelphia** for Dan McGillis and Edmonton's 2nd round choice (Jason Beckett) in 1998 Entry Draft, March 24, 1998.

• NIKOLISHIN, Andrei

Andrei V. LW – L. 5'11", 214 lbs. b: Vorkuta, USSR, 3/25/1973. Hartford's 2nd, 47th overall, in 1992.

Season	Club	League	GP	G	A	Pts	AG	AA	APts	PIM	PP	SH	GW	S	%	TGF	PGF	TGA	PGA	+/–	GP	G	A	Pts	PIM	PP	SH	GW
1990-91	Dynamo Moscow	USSR	2	0	0	0	....	....	....	0	....	....	....	....	....	....	....	....	....	....	....	....	....	....	....	....	....	....
	Soviet Union	EJC-A	5	3	3	6	....	....	....	4	....	....	....	....	....	....	....	....	....	....	....	....	....	....	....	....	....	....
1991-92	Dynamo Moscow	CIS	18	1	0	1	....	....	....	4	....	....	....	....	....	....	....	....	....	....	....	....	....	....	....	....	....	....
	Russia	WJC-A	7	1	2	3	....	....	....	2	....	....	....	....	....	....	....	....	....	....	....	....	....	....	....	....	....	....
1992-93	Dynamo Moscow	CIS	42	5	7	12	....	....	....	30	....	....	....	....	....	....	....	....	....	....	10	2	1	3	8	....	....	....
	Russia	WC-A	8	1	3	4	....	....	....	8	....	....	....	....	....	....	....	....	....	....	....	....	....	....	....	....	....	....
1993-94	Dynamo Moscow	CIS	41	8	12	20	....	....	....	30	....	....	....	....	....	....	....	....	....	....	9	1	3	4	4	....	....	....
	Russia	Olympics	8	2	5	7	....	....	....	6	....	....	....	....	....	....	....	....	....	....	....	....	....	....	....	....	....	....
	Russia	WC-A	6	0	0	0	....	....	....	4	....	....	....	....	....	....	....	....	....	....	....	....	....	....	....	....	....	....
1994-95	Dynamo Moscow	CIS	12	7	2	9	....	....	....	6	....	....	....	....	....	....	....	....	....	....	....	....	....	....	....	....	....	....
	Hartford Whalers	**NHL**	**39**	**8**	**10**	**18**	**14**	**15**	**29**	**10**	**1**	**1**	**0**	**57**	**14.0**	**28**	**7**	**17**	**3**	**7**	....	....	....	....	....	....	....	....
1995-96	**Hartford Whalers**	**NHL**	**61**	**14**	**37**	**51**	**14**	**30**	**44**	**34**	**4**	**1**	**3**	**83**	**16.9**	**63**	**22**	**55**	**12**	**–2**	....	....	....	....	....	....	....	....
	Russia	WC-A	8	2	3	5	....	....	....	10	....	....	....	....	....	....	....	....	....	....	....	....	....	....	....	....	....	....
1996-97	Russia	W-Cup	4	1	3	4	....	....	....	4	....	....	....	....	....	....	....	....	....	....	....	....	....	....	....	....	....	....
	Hartford Whalers	**NHL**	**12**	**2**	**5**	**7**	**2**	**4**	**6**	**2**	**0**	**0**	**0**	**25**	**8.0**	**10**	**2**	**10**	**0**	**–2**	....	....	....	....	....	....	....	....
	Washington Capitals	**NHL**	**59**	**7**	**14**	**21**	**7**	**12**	**19**	**30**	**1**	**0**	**0**	**73**	**9.6**	**40**	**6**	**39**	**10**	**5**	....	....	....	....	....	....	....	....
	Russia	WC-A	5	0	1	1	....	....	....	6	....	....	....	....	....	....	....	....	....	....	....	....	....	....	....	....	....	....
1997-98	**Washington Capitals**	**NHL**	**38**	**6**	**10**	**16**	**7**	**10**	**17**	**14**	**1**	**0**	**1**	**40**	**15.0**	**21**	**4**	**20**	**4**	**1**	**21**	**1**	**13**	**14**	**12**	**1**	**0**	**0**
	Portland Pirates	AHL	2	0	0	0	....	....	....	2	....	....	....	....	....	....	....	....	....	....	....	....	....	....	....	....	....	....
1998-99	Dynamo Moscow	Russia	4	0	0	0	....	....	....	0	....	....	....	....	....	....	....	....	....	....	....	....	....	....	....	....	....	....
	Washington Capitals	**NHL**	**73**	**8**	**27**	**35**	**9**	**26**	**35**	**28**	**0**	**1**	**1**	**121**	**6.6**	**50**	**10**	**53**	**13**	**0**	....	....	....	....	....	....	....	....
99-2000	**Washington Capitals**	**NHL**	**76**	**11**	**14**	**25**	**12**	**13**	**25**	**28**	**0**	**2**	**2**	**98**	**11.2**	**47**	**5**	**46**	**10**	**6**	**5**	**0**	**2**	**2**	**4**	**0**	**0**	**0**
	Russia	WC-A	4	0	0	0	....	....	....	0	....	....	....	....	....	....	....	....	....	....	....	....	....	....	....	....	....	....
	NHL Totals		**358**	**56**	**117**	**173**	**65**	**110**	**175**	**146**	**7**	**5**	**7**	**497**	**11.3**	**259**	**56**	**240**	**52**		**26**	**1**	**15**	**16**	**16**	**1**	**0**	**0**

CIS First All-Star Team (1994) • CIS Player of the Year (1994)

Traded to **Washington** by **Hartford** for Curtis Leschyshyn, November 9, 1996.

• NIKULIN, Igor

RW – L. 6'1", 200 lbs. b: Cherepovets, USSR, 8/26/1972. Anaheim's 4th, 107th overall, in 1995.

Season	Club	League	GP	G	A	Pts	AG	AA	APts	PIM	PP	SH	GW	S	%	TGF	PGF	TGA	PGA	+/–	GP	G	A	Pts	PIM	PP	SH	GW
1992-93	Severstal Cherepovets	CIS	42	11	11	22	....	....	....	22	....	....	....	....	....	....	....	....	....	....	....	....	....	....	....	....	....	....
1993-94	Severstal Cherepovets	CIS	44	14	15	29	....	....	....	52	....	....	....	....	....	....	....	....	....	....	2	1	0	1	0	....	....	....
1994-95	Severstal Cherepovets	CIS	52	14	12	26	....	....	....	28	....	....	....	....	....	....	....	....	....	....	....	....	....	....	....	....	....	....
1995-96	Severstal Cherepovets	CIS	47	20	13	33	....	....	....	28	....	....	....	....	....	....	....	....	....	....	4	1	0	1	0	....	....	....
	Baltimore Bandits	AHL	4	2	2	4	....	....	....	2	....	....	....	....	....	....	....	....	....	....	....	....	....	....	....	....	....	....
1996-97	Baltimore Bandits	AHL	61	27	25	52	....	....	....	14	....	....	....	....	....	....	....	....	....	....	3	2	1	3	2	....	....	....
	Fort Wayne Komets	IHL	10	1	2	3	....	....	....	4	....	....	....	....	....	....	....	....	....	....	....	....	....	....	....	....	....	....
	Mighty Ducks of Anaheim	**NHL**	....	....	....	....	....	....	....	....	....	....	....	....	....	....	....	....	....	....	**1**	**0**	**0**	**0**	**0**	**0**	**0**	**0**
1997-98	Cincinnati Mighty Ducks	AHL	54	14	11	25	....	....	....	40	....	....	....	....	....	....	....	....	....	....	....	....	....	....	....	....	....	....
1998-99	Cincinnati Mighty Ducks	AHL	74	18	26	44	....	....	....	26	....	....	....	....	....	....	....	....	....	....	3	0	1	1	4	....	....	....
99-2000	Ak Bars Kazan	Russia	5	0	0	0	....	....	....	4	....	....	....	....	....	....	....	....	....	....	....	....	....	....	....	....	....	....
	Severstal Cherepovets	Russia	24	8	6	14	....	....	....	8	....	....	....	....	....	....	....	....	....	....	8	3	3	6	2	....	....	....
	NHL Totals		....	....	....	....	....	....	....	....	....	....	....	....	....	....	....	....	....	....	**1**	**0**	**0**	**0**	**0**	**0**	**0**	**0**

• NILAN, Chris

Christopher John "Knuckles" RW – R. 6', 205 lbs. b: Boston, MA, 2/9/1958. Montreal's 22nd, 231st overall, in 1978.

Season	Club	League	GP	G	A	Pts	AG	AA	APts	PIM	PP	SH	GW	S	%	TGF	PGF	TGA	PGA	+/–	GP	G	A	Pts	PIM	PP	SH	GW
1977-78	Tri-Valley Squires	NEJHL	STATISTICS NOT AVAILABLE																									
1978-79	Northeastern University	ECAC	32	9	17	26	....	....	....	....	....	....	....	....	....	....	....	....	....	....	....	....	....	....	....	....	....	....
1979-80	Nova Scotia Voyageurs	AHL	49	15	10	25	....	....	....	*304	....	....	....	....	....	....	....	....	....	....	....	....	....	....	....	....	....	....
	Montreal Canadiens	**NHL**	**15**	**0**	**2**	**2**	**0**	**1**	**1**	**50**	**0**	**0**	**0**	**8**	**0.0**	**2**	**0**	**3**	**0**	**–1**	**5**	**0**	**0**	**0**	**2**	**0**	**0**	**0**
1980-81	**Montreal Canadiens**	**NHL**	**57**	**7**	**8**	**15**	**5**	**5**	**10**	**262**	**0**	**0**	**1**	**69**	**10.1**	**21**	**1**	**13**	**0**	**7**	**2**	**0**	**0**	**0**	**0**	**0**	**0**	**0**
1981-82	**Montreal Canadiens**	**NHL**	**49**	**7**	**4**	**11**	**6**	**3**	**9**	**204**	**0**	**0**	**1**	**45**	**15.6**	**19**	**1**	**12**	**0**	**6**	**5**	**1**	**1**	**2**	**22**	**0**	**0**	**0**
1982-83	**Montreal Canadiens**	**NHL**	**66**	**6**	**8**	**14**	**5**	**6**	**11**	**213**	**0**	**0**	**0**	**67**	**9.0**	**25**	**0**	**35**	**0**	**–10**	**3**	**0**	**0**	**0**	**5**	**0**	**0**	**0**
1983-84	**Montreal Canadiens**	**NHL**	**76**	**16**	**10**	**26**	**13**	**7**	**20**	***338**	**4**	**0**	**1**	**98**	**16.3**	**46**	**12**	**38**	**0**	**–4**	**15**	**1**	**0**	**1**	***81**	**0**	**0**	**0**
1984-85	**Montreal Canadiens**	**NHL**	**77**	**21**	**16**	**37**	**17**	**11**	**28**	***358**	**1**	**0**	**2**	**98**	**21.4**	**52**	**3**	**46**	**0**	**3**	**12**	**2**	**1**	**3**	**81**	**1**	**0**	**1**
1985-86♦	**Montreal Canadiens**	**NHL**	**72**	**19**	**15**	**34**	**15**	**10**	**25**	**274**	**2**	**0**	**1**	**120**	**15.8**	**63**	**12**	**41**	**0**	**10**	**18**	**1**	**2**	**3**	***141**	**1**	**0**	**0**
1986-87	**Montreal Canadiens**	**NHL**	**44**	**4**	**16**	**20**	**3**	**12**	**15**	**266**	**0**	**0**	**1**	**68**	**5.9**	**31**	**2**	**27**	**0**	**2**	**17**	**3**	**0**	**3**	**75**	**0**	**0**	**0**
1987-88	United States	Can-Cup	5	2	0	2	....	....	....	14	....	....	....	....	....	....	....	....	....	....	....	....	....	....	....	....	....	....
	Montreal Canadiens	**NHL**	**50**	**7**	**5**	**12**	**6**	**4**	**10**	**209**	**0**	**0**	**1**	**68**	**10.3**	**21**	**2**	**21**	**0**	**–2**	....	....	....	....	....	....	....	....
	New York Rangers	**NHL**	**22**	**3**	**5**	**8**	**3**	**4**	**7**	**96**	**0**	**0**	**0**	**20**	**15.0**	**14**	**1**	**13**	**0**	**0**	....	....	....	....	....	....	....	....
1988-89	**New York Rangers**	**NHL**	**38**	**7**	**7**	**14**	**6**	**5**	**11**	**177**	**0**	**0**	**1**	**39**	**17.9**	**23**	**0**	**32**	**1**	**–8**	**4**	**0**	**1**	**1**	**38**	**0**	**0**	**0**
1989-90	**New York Rangers**	**NHL**	**25**	**1**	**2**	**3**	**1**	**1**	**2**	**59**	**0**	**0**	**0**	**24**	**4.2**	**7**	**0**	**15**	**0**	**–8**	**4**	**0**	**1**	**1**	**19**	**0**	**0**	**0**
1990-91	**Boston Bruins**	**NHL**	**41**	**6**	**9**	**15**	**5**	**7**	**12**	**277**	**0**	**0**	**2**	**41**	**14.6**	**28**	**2**	**23**	**1**	**4**	**19**	**0**	**2**	**2**	**62**	**0**	**0**	**0**
1991-92	**Boston Bruins**	**NHL**	**39**	**5**	**5**	**10**	**5**	**4**	**9**	**186**	**0**	**0**	**0**	**33**	**15.2**	**14**	**0**	**19**	**0**	**–5**	....	....	....	....	....	....	....	....
	Montreal Canadiens	**NHL**	**17**	**1**	**3**	**4**	**1**	**2**	**3**	**74**	**0**	**0**	**0**	**22**	**4.5**	**6**	**0**	**7**	**0**	**–1**	**7**	**0**	**1**	**1**	**15**	**0**	**0**	**0**
	NHL Totals		**688**	**110**	**115**	**225**	**91**	**82**	**173**	**3043**	**7**	**0**	**11**	**820**	**13.4**	**372**	**36**	**345**	**2**		**111**	**8**	**9**	**17**	**541**	**2**	**0**	**1**

Traded to **NY Rangers** by **Montreal** with Montreal's 1st round choice (Steven Rice) in 1989 Entry Draft for NY Rangers' 1st round choice (Lindsay Vallis) in 1989 Entry Draft, January 27, 1988. • Missed majority of 1989-90 season recovering from arm injury suffered in game vs. Montreal, November 4, 1989. Traded to **Boston** by **NY Rangers** for Greg Johnston and cash, June 28, 1990. Claimed on waivers by **Montreal** from **Boston**, February 12, 1992.

• NILL, Jim

James Edward RW – R. 6', 185 lbs. b: Hanna, Alta., 4/11/1958. St. Louis' 4th, 89th overall, in 1978.

Season	Club	League	GP	G	A	Pts	AG	AA	APts	PIM	PP	SH	GW	S	%	TGF	PGF	TGA	PGA	+/–	GP	G	A	Pts	PIM	PP	SH	GW
1974-75	Drumheller Falcons	AJHL	58	30	30	60	....	....	....	126	....	....	....	....	....	....	....	....	....	....	12	5	6	11	35	....	....	....
1975-76	Medicine Hat Tigers	WCJHL	62	5	11	16	....	....	....	69	....	....	....	....	....	....	....	....	....	....	9	1	1	2	20	....	....	....
1976-77	Medicine Hat Tigers	WCJHL	71	23	24	47	....	....	....	140	....	....	....	....	....	....	....	....	....	....	4	2	2	4	4	....	....	....
1977-78	Medicine Hat Tigers	WCJHL	72	47	46	93	....	....	....	252	....	....	....	....	....	....	....	....	....	....	12	8	7	15	37	....	....	....

Season	Club	League	GP	G	A	Pts	AG	AA	APts	PIM	PP	SH	GW	S	%	TGF	PGF	TGA	PGA	+/–	GP	G	A	Pts	PIM	PP	SH	GW
			REGULAR SEASON																		PLAYOFFS							
1978-79	University of Calgary	CWUAA	17	8	7	15	....	....	....	36	....	....	....	....	....	....	....	....	....	....	3	1	2	3	4	....	....	....
1979-80	Canada	Nat-Team	45	13	19	32	....	....	....	54	....	....	....	....	....	....	....	....	....	....	....	....	....	....	....	....	....	....
	Canada	Olympics	6	1	2	3	....	....	....	4	....	....	....	....	....	....	....	....	....	....	....	....	....	....	....	....	....	....
1980-81	Salt Lake Golden Eagles	CHL	79	28	34	62	....	....	....	222	....	....	....	....	....	....	....	....	....	....	16	9	8	17	38	....	....	....
1981-82	**St. Louis Blues**	**NHL**	**61**	**9**	**12**	**21**	**7**	**8**	**15**	**127**	**1**	**2**	**0**	**65**	**13.8**	**40**	**2**	**68**	**17**	**–13**	....	....	....	....	....	....	....	....
	Vancouver Canucks	**NHL**	**8**	**1**	**2**	**3**	**1**	**1**	**2**	**5**	**0**	**0**	**1**	**6**	**16.7**	**5**	**0**	**6**	**1**	**0**	**16**	**4**	**3**	**7**	**67**	**1**	**0**	**1**
1982-83	**Vancouver Canucks**	**NHL**	**65**	**7**	**15**	**22**	**6**	**10**	**16**	**136**	**1**	**1**	**0**	**53**	**13.2**	**39**	**7**	**62**	**12**	**–18**	**4**	**0**	**0**	**0**	**6**	**0**	**0**	**0**
1983-84	**Vancouver Canucks**	**NHL**	**51**	**9**	**6**	**15**	**7**	**4**	**11**	**78**	**0**	**0**	**0**	**53**	**17.0**	**25**	**0**	**56**	**24**	**–7**	....	....	....	....	....	....	....	....
	Boston Bruins	**NHL**	**27**	**3**	**2**	**5**	**2**	**1**	**3**	**81**	**0**	**0**	**0**	**19**	**15.8**	**14**	**0**	**24**	**5**	**–5**	**3**	**0**	**0**	**0**	**4**	**0**	**0**	**0**
1984-85	**Boston Bruins**	**NHL**	**49**	**1**	**9**	**10**	**1**	**6**	**7**	**62**	**0**	**0**	**0**	**23**	**4.3**	**12**	**0**	**35**	**12**	**–11**	....	....	....	....	....	....	....	....
	Winnipeg Jets	**NHL**	**20**	**8**	**8**	**16**	**6**	**5**	**11**	**38**	**1**	**0**	**1**	**22**	**36.4**	**22**	**3**	**22**	**5**	**2**	**8**	**0**	**1**	**1**	**28**	**0**	**0**	**0**
1985-86	**Winnipeg Jets**	**NHL**	**61**	**6**	**8**	**14**	**5**	**5**	**10**	**75**	**0**	**0**	**1**	**35**	**17.1**	**26**	**1**	**45**	**14**	**–6**	**3**	**0**	**0**	**0**	**4**	**0**	**0**	**0**
1986-87	**Winnipeg Jets**	**NHL**	**36**	**3**	**4**	**7**	**3**	**3**	**6**	**52**	**1**	**0**	**2**	**12**	**25.0**	**13**	**1**	**15**	**4**	**1**	**3**	**0**	**0**	**0**	**7**	**0**	**0**	**0**
1987-88	**Winnipeg Jets**	**NHL**	**24**	**0**	**1**	**1**	**0**	**1**	**1**	**44**	**0**	**0**	**0**	**13**	**0.0**	**4**	**1**	**12**	**2**	**–7**	....	....	....	....	....	....	....	....
	Moncton Hawks	AHL	3	0	0	0	....	....	....	6	....	....	....	....	....	....	....	....	....	....	....	....	....	....	....	....	....	....
	Detroit Red Wings	**NHL**	**36**	**3**	**11**	**14**	**3**	**8**	**11**	**55**	**0**	**0**	**0**	**25**	**12.0**	**24**	**1**	**29**	**8**	**2**	**16**	**6**	**1**	**7**	**62**	**0**	**1**	**0**
1988-89	**Detroit Red Wings**	**NHL**	**71**	**8**	**7**	**15**	**7**	**5**	**12**	**83**	**0**	**1**	**2**	**39**	**20.5**	**23**	**0**	**33**	**9**	**–1**	**6**	**0**	**0**	**0**	**25**	**0**	**0**	**0**
1989-90	**Detroit Red Wings**	**NHL**	**15**	**0**	**2**	**2**	**0**	**1**	**1**	**18**	**0**	**0**	**0**	**10**	**0.0**	**4**	**0**	**10**	**3**	**–3**	....	....	....	....	....	....	....	....
	Adirondack Red Wings	AHL	20	10	8	18	....	....	....	24	....	....	....	....	....	....	....	....	....	....	....	....	....	....	....	....	....	....
1990-91	Adirondack Red Wings	AHL	32	3	10	13	....	....	....	74	....	....	....	....	....	....	....	....	....	....	2	0	0	0	2	....	....	....
1991-1994	**Ottawa Senators**	**NHL**	DID NOT PLAY – SCOUTING																									
1994-2000	**Detroit Red Wings**	**NHL**	DID NOT PLAY – ASSISTANT GENERAL MANAGER																									
	NHL Totals		**524**	**58**	**87**	**145**	**48**	**58**	**106**	**854**	**4**	**4**	**7**	**375**	**15.5**	**251**	**16**	**417**	**116**		**59**	**10**	**5**	**15**	**203**	**1**	**1**	**1**

CHL Second All-Star Team (1981)

Traded to **Vancouver** by **St. Louis** with Tony Currie, Rick Heinz and St. Louis' 4th round choice (Shawn Kilroy) in 1982 Entry Draft for Glen Hanlon, March 9, 1982. Traded to **Boston** by **Vancouver** for Peter McNab, February 3, 1984. Traded to **Winnipeg** by **Boston** for Morris Lukowich, February 4, 1985. Traded to **Detroit** by **Winnipeg** for Mark Kumpel, January 11, 1988.

• NILSON, Marcus

RW – R. 6'2", 193 lbs. b: Balsta, Sweden, 3/1/1978. Florida's 1st, 20th overall, in 1996.

Season	Club	League	GP	G	A	Pts	AG	AA	APts	PIM	PP	SH	GW	S	%	TGF	PGF	TGA	PGA	+/–	GP	G	A	Pts	PIM	PP	SH	GW
1994-95	Djurgardens IF Stockholm	Sweden-Jr.	24	7	8	15	....	....	....	22	....	....	....	....	....	....	....	....	....	....	....	....	....	....	....	....	....	....
	Sweden	EJC-A	5	4	4	8	....	....	....	0	....	....	....	....	....	....	....	....	....	....	....	....	....	....	....	....	....	....
1995-96	Djurgardens IF Stockholm	Sweden-Jr.	25	19	17	36	....	....	....	46	....	....	....	....	....	....	....	....	....	....	2	1	1	2	12	....	....	....
	Sweden	WJC-A	7	3	5	8	....	....	....	12	....	....	....	....	....	....	....	....	....	....	....	....	....	....	....	....	....	....
	Djurgardens IF Stockholm	Sweden	12	0	0	0	....	....	....	0	....	....	....	....	....	....	....	....	....	....	1	0	0	0	0	....	....	....
	Sweden	EJC-A	5	3	5	8	....	....	....	10	....	....	....	....	....	....	....	....	....	....	....	....	....	....	....	....	....	....
1996-97	Djurgardens IF Stockholm	Sweden	37	0	3	3	....	....	....	33	....	....	....	....	....	....	....	....	....	....	4	0	0	0	0	....	....	....
	Sweden	WJC-A	6	0	4	4	....	....	....	29	....	....	....	....	....	....	....	....	....	....	....	....	....	....	....	....	....	....
1997-98	Djurgardens IF Stockholm	Sweden	41	4	7	11	....	....	....	18	....	....	....	....	....	....	....	....	....	....	15	2	1	3	16	....	....	....
1998-99	**Florida Panthers**	**NHL**	**8**	**1**	**1**	**2**	**1**	**1**	**2**	**5**	**0**	**0**	**1**	**7**	**14.3**	**3**	**0**	**1**	**0**	**2**	....	....	....	....	....	....	....	....
	Beast of New Haven	AHL	69	8	25	33	....	....	....	10	....	....	....	....	....	....	....	....	....	....	....	....	....	....	....	....	....	....
99-2000	**Florida Panthers**	**NHL**	**9**	**0**	**2**	**2**	**0**	**2**	**2**	**2**	**0**	**0**	**0**	**6**	**0.0**	**4**	**0**	**2**	**0**	**2**	....	....	....	....	....	....	....	....
	Louisville Panthers	AHL	64	9	23	32	....	....	....	52	....	....	....	....	....	....	....	....	....	....	4	0	0	0	2	....	....	....
	NHL Totals		**17**	**1**	**3**	**4**	**1**	**3**	**4**	**7**	**0**	**0**	**1**	**13**	**7.7**	**7**	**0**	**3**	**0**		....	....	....	....	....	....	....	....

• NILSSON, Kent

C – L. 6'1", 195 lbs. b: Nynashamn, Sweden, 8/31/1956. Atlanta's 5th, 64th overall, in 1976.

Season	Club	League	GP	G	A	Pts	AG	AA	APts	PIM	PP	SH	GW	S	%	TGF	PGF	TGA	PGA	+/–	GP	G	A	Pts	PIM	PP	SH	GW
1973-74	Djurgardens IF Stockholm	Sweden	8	1	2	3	....	....	....	4	....	....	....	....	....	....	....	....	....	....	14	8	6	14	2	....	....	....
	Sweden	EJC-A	5	8	7	15	....	....	....	2	....	....	....	....	....	....	....	....	....	....	....	....	....	....	....	....	....	....
1974-75	Djurgardens IF Stockholm	Sweden	28	13	12	25	....	....	....	14	....	....	....	....	....	....	....	....	....	....	....	....	....	....	....	....	....	....
	Djurgardens IF Stockholm	Sweden-Q	6	*7	3	10	....	....	....	4	....	....	....	....	....	....	....	....	....	....	....	....	....	....	....	....	....	....
	Sweden	WJC-A	6	3	3	6	....	....	....	....	....	....	....	....	....	....	....	....	....	....	....	....	....	....	....	....	....	....
	Sweden	EJC-A	5	5	5	10	....	....	....	0	....	....	....	....	....	....	....	....	....	....	....	....	....	....	....	....	....	....
1975-76	Djurgardens IF Stockholm	Sweden	36	28	26	*54	....	....	....	10	....	....	....	....	....	....	....	....	....	....	....	....	....	....	....	....	....	....
	Sweden	Nat-Team	5	0	0	0	....	....	....	0	....	....	....	....	....	....	....	....	....	....	....	....	....	....	....	....	....	....
	Sweden	WJC-A	4	1	3	4	....	....	....	2	....	....	....	....	....	....	....	....	....	....	....	....	....	....	....	....	....	....
1976-77	AIK Solna Stockholm	Sweden	36	30	19	49	....	....	....	18	....	....	....	....	....	....	....	....	....	....	....	....	....	....	....	....	....	....
1977-78	Winnipeg Jets	WHA	80	42	65	107	....	....	....	8	....	....	....	....	....	....	....	....	....	....	9	2	8	10	10	....	....	....
1978-79	Winnipeg Jets	WHA	78	39	68	107	....	....	....	8	....	....	....	....	....	....	....	....	....	....	10	3	11	14	4	....	....	....
1979-80	**Atlanta Flames**	**NHL**	**80**	**40**	**53**	**93**	**34**	**39**	**73**	**10**	**14**	**0**	**3**	**217**	**18.4**	**118**	**44**	**77**	**0**	**–3**	**4**	**0**	**0**	**0**	**2**	**0**	**0**	**0**
1980-81	**Calgary Flames**	**NHL**	**80**	**49**	**82**	**131**	**38**	**55**	**93**	**26**	**20**	**0**	**8**	**217**	**22.6**	**164**	**68**	**81**	**0**	**15**	**14**	**3**	**9**	**12**	**2**	**0**	**0**	**0**
1981-82	Sweden	Can-Cup	5	0	2	2	....	....	....	4	....	....	....	....	....	....	....	....	....	....	....	....	....	....	....	....	....	....
	Calgary Flames	**NHL**	**41**	**26**	**29**	**55**	**21**	**19**	**40**	**8**	**13**	**0**	**0**	**103**	**25.2**	**68**	**38**	**50**	**0**	**–20**	**3**	**0**	**3**	**3**	**2**	**0**	**0**	**0**
1982-83	**Calgary Flames**	**NHL**	**80**	**46**	**58**	**104**	**38**	**40**	**78**	**10**	**16**	**4**	**6**	**217**	**21.2**	**149**	**57**	**109**	**22**	**5**	**9**	**1**	**11**	**12**	**2**	**1**	**0**	**0**
1983-84	**Calgary Flames**	**NHL**	**67**	**31**	**49**	**80**	**25**	**33**	**58**	**22**	**7**	**9**	**5**	**181**	**17.1**	**104**	**51**	**100**	**23**	**–24**	....	....	....	....	....	....	....	....
1984-85	Sweden	Can-Cup	8	3	*8	11	....	....	....	4	....	....	....	....	....	....	....	....	....	....	....	....	....	....	....	....	....	....
	Calgary Flames	**NHL**	**77**	**37**	**62**	**99**	**30**	**42**	**72**	**14**	**9**	**3**	**3**	**201**	**18.4**	**129**	**58**	**103**	**28**	**–4**	**3**	**0**	**1**	**1**	**0**	**0**	**0**	**0**
	Sweden	WEC-A	8	6	5	11	....	....	....	6	....	....	....	....	....	....	....	....	....	....	....	....	....	....	....	....	....	....
1985-86	**Minnesota North Stars**	**NHL**	**61**	**16**	**44**	**60**	**13**	**30**	**43**	**10**	**8**	**0**	**2**	**122**	**13.1**	**94**	**52**	**41**	**3**	**4**	**5**	**1**	**4**	**5**	**0**	**0**	**0**	**0**
1986-87	**Minnesota North Stars**	**NHL**	**44**	**13**	**33**	**46**	**11**	**24**	**35**	**12**	**8**	**0**	**1**	**89**	**14.6**	**67**	**29**	**41**	**5**	**2**	....	....	....	....	....	....	....	....
♦	**Edmonton Oilers**	**NHL**	**17**	**5**	**12**	**17**	**4**	**9**	**13**	**4**	**1**	**0**	**0**	**25**	**20.0**	**26**	**4**	**13**	**1**	**10**	**21**	**6**	**13**	**19**	**6**	**2**	**0**	**0**
1987-88	Sweden	Can-Cup	6	0	4	4	....	....	....	4	....	....	....	....	....	....	....	....	....	....	....	....	....	....	....	....	....	....
	HC Bolzano	Italy	35	60	72	132	....	....	....	48	....	....	....	....	....	....	....	....	....	....	8	14	14	28	....	....	....	....
	SC Langnau	Switz.	2	2	0	2	....	....	....	....	....	....	....	....	....	....	....	....	....	....	....	....	....	....	....	....	....	....
1988-89	Djurgardens IF Stockholm	Sweden	35	21	21	42	....	....	....	36	....	....	....	....	....	....	....	....	....	....	1	0	1	1	0	....	....	....
	Sweden	WEC-A	10	3	*11	*14	....	....	....	0	....	....	....	....	....	....	....	....	....	....	....	....	....	....	....	....	....	....
1989-90	EHC Kloten	Switz.	36	21	19	40	....	....	....	....	....	....	....	....	....	....	....	....	....	....	5	4	5	9	....	....	....	....
	Sweden	WEC-A	10	10	2	12	....	....	....	6	....	....	....	....	....	....	....	....	....	....	....	....	....	....	....	....	....	....
1990-91	EHC Kloten	Switz.	33	37	39	76	....	....	....	....	....	....	....	....	....	....	....	....	....	....	8	3	8	11	....	....	....	....
1991-92	EHC Kloten	Switz.	17	11	14	25	....	....	....	8	....	....	....	....	....	....	....	....	....	....	2	0	0	0	2	....	....	....
1992-93	Djurgardens IF Stockholm	Sweden	40	11	20	31	....	....	....	20	....	....	....	....	....	....	....	....	....	....	6	2	3	5	0	....	....	....
1993-94	EC Graz	Alpenliga	30	15	33	48	....	....	....	....	....	....	....	....	....	....	....	....	....	....	....	....	....	....	....	....	....	....
	EC Graz	Austria	27	8	9	17	....	....	....	....	....	....	....	....	....	....	....	....	....	....	....	....	....	....	....	....	....	....
1994-95	VIF Valerengen	Norway	6	1	1	2	....	....	....	8	....	....	....	....	....	....	....	....	....	....	....	....	....	....	....	....	....	....
	Edmonton Oilers	**NHL**	**6**	**1**	**0**	**1**	**2**	**0**	**2**	**0**	**1**	**0**	**0**	**2**	**50.0**	**1**	**1**	**5**	**0**	**–5**	....	....	....	....	....	....	....	....
1995-96	Nynashamns IF	Sweden-3	2	2	3	5	....	....	....	6	....	....	....	....	....	....	....	....	....	....	....	....	....	....	....	....	....	....
1996-97			OUT OF HOCKEY – RETIRED																									
1997-98	CH Majadahonda	Spain	6	8	12	20	....	....	....	....	....	....	....	....	....	....	....	....	....	....	2	3	8	11	....	....	....	....
	NHL Totals		**553**	**264**	**422**	**686**	**216**	**291**	**507**	**116**	**97**	**16**	**28**	**1374**	**19.2**	**920**	**402**	**620**	**82**		**59**	**11**	**41**	**52**	**14**	**3**	**0**	**0**
	Other Major League Totals		158	81	133	214				16											19	5	19	24	14			

Won Lou Kaplan Trophy (WHA Rookie of the Year) (1978) • Won Paul Daneau Trophy (WHA Most Gentlemanly Player) (1979) • Swedish World All-Star Team (1985, 1989, 1990) • Swedish Player of the Year (1989) • Played in NHL All-Star Game (1980, 1981)

Signed as a free agent by **Winnipeg** (WHA), July 29, 1977. Reclaimed by **Atlanta** from **Winnipeg** prior to Expansion Draft, June 9, 1979. Transferred to **Calgary** after **Atlanta** franchise relocated, June 24, 1980. Traded to **Minnesota** by **Calgary** with Calgary's 3rd round choice (Brad Turner) in 1986 Entry Draft for Minnesota's 2nd round choice (Joe Nieuwendyck) in 1985 Entry Draft and 2nd round choice (Stephane Matteau) in 1987 Entry Draft, June 15, 1985. Traded to **Edmonton** by **Minnesota** for cash, March 2, 1987. Signed as a free agent by **Edmonton**, January 26, 1995.

• NILSSON, Ulf

Ulf Gosta C – R. 5'11", 175 lbs. b: Nynashamn, Sweden, 5/11/1950. NY Rangers' 12th, 243rd overall, in 1983.

Season	Club	League	GP	G	A	Pts	AG	AA	APts	PIM	PP	SH	GW	S	%	TGF	PGF	TGA	PGA	+/–	GP	G	A	Pts	PIM	PP	SH	GW
1967-68	AIK Solna Stockholm	Sweden	19	2	1	3	....	....	....	....	....	....	....	....	....	....	....	....	....	....	....	....	....	....	....	....	....	....
1968-69	AIK Solna Stockholm	Sweden	8	2	4	6	....	....	....	0	....	....	....	....	....	....	....	....	....	....	7	1	3	4	4	....	....	....
1969-70	AIK Solna Stockholm	Sweden	14	6	6	12	....	....	....	10	....	....	....	....	....	....	....	....	....	....	14	5	3	8	2	....	....	....
1970-71	AIK Solna Stockholm	Sweden	14	10	3	13	....	....	....	6	....	....	....	....	....	....	....	....	....	....	14	2	4	6	8	....	....	....
1971-72	AIK Solna Stockholm	Sweden	14	5	6	11	....	....	....	2	....	....	....	....	....	....	....	....	....	....	8	5	1	6	2	....	....	....

Season	Club	League	REGULAR SEASON GP	G	A	Pts	AG	AA	APts	PIM	PP	SH	GW	S	%	TGF	PGF	TGA	PGA	+/–	PLAYOFFS GP	G	A	Pts	PIM	PP	SH	GW
1972-73	AIK Solna Stockholm	Sweden	14	11	7	18				4											14	10	8	18	23			
	Sweden	WEC-A	10	5	3	8				4																		
1973-74	AIK Solna Stockholm	Sweden	14	9	9	18				32											15	14	6	20	26			
	Sweden	WEC-A	2	0	0	0				0																		
1974-75	Winnipeg Jets	WHA	78	26	94	120				79																		
1975-76	Winnipeg Jets	WHA	78	38	76	114				84											13	7	*19	26	6			
1976-77	Sweden	Can-Cup	5	1	1	2				6																		
	Winnipeg Jets	WHA	71	39	*85	124				89											20	6	21	27	33			
1977-78	Winnipeg Jets	WHA	73	37	*89	126				89											9	1	*13	14	12			
1978-79	**New York Rangers**	**NHL**	59	27	39	66	23	28	51	21	8	2	5	96	28.1	89	27	53	8	17	2	0	0	0	2	0	0	0
	NHL All-Stars	Chal-Cup	2	0	0	0				0																		
1979-80	**New York Rangers**	**NHL**	50	14	44	58	12	32	44	20	5	0	1	72	19.4	69	22	36	4	15	9	0	6	6	2	0	0	0
1980-81	**New York Rangers**	**NHL**	51	14	25	39	11	17	28	42	1	0	3	80	17.5	59	20	55	13	–3	14	8	8	16	23	3	0	1
1981-82	Sweden	Can-Cup	4	1	2	3				2																		
	Springfield Indians	AHL	2	0	0	0				0																		
1982-83	**New York Rangers**	**NHL**	10	2	4	6	2	3	5	2	0	0	1	9	22.2	7	0	8	0	–1								
	Tulsa Oilers	CHL	3	2	1	3				4																		
	NHL Totals		170	57	112	169	48	80	128	85	14	2	10	257	22.2	224	69	152	25		25	8	14	22	27	3	0	1
	Other Major League Totals		300	140	344	484				341											42	14	53	67	51			

WHA First All-Star Team (1976, 1978) • Won WHA Playoff MVP Trophy (1976) • WHA Second All-Star Team (1977)

Signed as a free agent by **Winnipeg** (WHA), May 3, 1974. Signed as a free agent by **NY Rangers**, June 5, 1978.

• NISTICO, Lou

C – L. 5′7″, 170 lbs. b: Thunder Bay, Ont., 1/25/1953. Minnesota's 7th, 105th overall, in 1973.

Season	Club	League	GP	G	A	Pts	AG	AA	APts	PIM	PP	SH	GW	S	%	TGF	PGF	TGA	PGA	+/–	GP	G	A	Pts	PIM	PP	SH	GW
1967-68	Westfort Hurricanes	TBJHL	22	1	5	6				93																		
	Westfort Hurricanes	Mem-Cup	11	0	1	1				4																		
1968-69	Westfort Hurricanes	TBJHL	36	23	23	46				86																		
	Westfort Hurricanes	Mem-Cup	6	2	4	6				13																		
1969-70	Westfort Hurricanes	TBJHL	23	11	19	30				164																		
	Westfort Hurricanes	Mem-Cup	12	8	7	15				36																		
1970-71	London Knights	OHA-Jr.	45	11	11	22				119											4	0	0	0	29			
1971-72	London Knights	OMJHL	62	22	30	52				193											7	3	7	10	36			
1972-73	London Knights	OMJHL	65	31	64	95				108																		
1973-74	Toronto Toros	WHA	13	1	3	4				14																		
	Jacksonville Barons	AHL	51	12	24	36				109																		
1974-75	Toronto Toros	WHA	29	11	11	22				75											6	6	1	7	19			
	Mohawk Valley Comets	NAHL	42	21	27	48				103																		
1975-76	Toronto Toros	WHA	65	12	22	34				120																		
	Buffalo Norsemen	NAHL	10	9	5	14				49																		
1976-77	Birmingham Bulls	WHA	79	20	36	56				166																		
1977-78	Phoenix Roadrunners	CHL	4	0	0	0				0																		
	Colorado Rockies	**NHL**	3	0	0	0	0	0	0	0	0	0	0	3	0.0	0	0	0	0	0								
	Brantford Alexanders	OHA-Sr.	27	19	16	35				85																		
1978-79	Welland Cougars	OHA-Sr.	40	29	30	59																						
	NHL Totals		3	0	0	0	0	0	0	0	0	0	0	3	0.0	0	0	0	0									
	Other Major League Totals		186	44	72	116				375											6	6	1	7	19			

NAHL Second All-Star Team (1975)

Selected by **Toronto** (WHA) in 1973 WHA Amateur Draft, June, 1973. Transferred to **Birmingham** after **Toronto** (WHA) franchise relocated, June 30, 1976. Traded to **Edmonton** (WHA) by **Birmingham** (WHA) with Jeff Jacques for Pete Laframboise, Dan Ardnt and Chris Evans, September, 1977. Signed as a free agent by **Colorado** to a five-game tryout contract, November 6, 1977.

• NOEL, Claude

C – L. 5′11″, 165 lbs. b: Kirkland Lake, Ont., 10/31/1955.

Season	Club	League	GP	G	A	Pts	AG	AA	APts	PIM	PP	SH	GW	S	%	TGF	PGF	TGA	PGA	+/–	GP	G	A	Pts	PIM	PP	SH	GW
1973-74	North Bay Trappers	NOJHA	44	19	43	62				35																		
1974-75	Kitchener Rangers	OMJHL	70	14	37	51				28																		
1975-76	Buffalo Norsmen	NAHL	74	19	42	61				27											4	1	1	2	2			
1976-77	Hershey Bears	AHL	80	14	32	46				19											6	2	1	3	0			
1977-78	Hershey Bears	AHL	65	13	25	38				18																		
1978-79	Hershey Bears	AHL	76	30	50	80				27											4	1	4	5	0			
1979-80	**Washington Capitals**	**NHL**	7	0	0	0	0	0	0	0	0	0	0	5	0.0	0	0	5	2	–3								
	Hershey Bears	AHL	68	24	38	62				18											16	9	10	19	6			
1980-81	Hershey Bears	AHL	64	14	44	58				50											10	2	2	4	14			
1981-82	SC Bern	Switz.	26	12	12	24				40																		
1982-83	Toledo Goaldiggers	IHL	82	42	82	124				41											11	3	*15	18	4			
1983-84	HC Salzburg	Austria-2	26	31	47	78				28																		
1984-85	Toledo Goaldiggers	IHL	74	16	56	72				30											6	1	2	3	2			
1985-86	Toledo Goaldiggers	IHL	12	1	7	8				4																		
	Kalamazoo Wings	IHL	71	15	38	53				18											6	2	4	6	2			
1986-87	Kalamazoo Wings	IHL	80	33	37	70				28											5	1	2	3	0			
1987-88	Milwaukee Admirals	IHL	56	8	34	42				18																		
1988-1990			OUT OF HOCKEY – RETIRED																									
1990-1991	Roanoke Valley Rebels	ECHL	DID NOT PLAY – COACHING																									
1991-1992	Dayton Bombers	ECHL	DID NOT PLAY – COACHING																									
1992-1998	Michigan K-Wings	IHL	DID NOT PLAY – ASSISTANT COACH																									
1998-2000	Milwaukee Admirals	IHL	DID NOT PLAY – ASSISTANT COACH																									
	NHL Totals		7	0	0	0	0	0	0	0	0	0	0	5	0.0	0	0	5	2									

IHL Second All-Star Team (1983) • Won James Gatschene Memorial Trophy (MVP - IHL) (1983)

Signed as a free agent by **Washington**, October 9, 1979.

• NOLAN, Owen

Owen Liam RW – R. 6′1″, 215 lbs. b: Belfast, Ireland, 2/12/1972. Quebec's 1st, 1st overall, in 1990.

Season	Club	League	GP	G	A	Pts	AG	AA	APts	PIM	PP	SH	GW	S	%	TGF	PGF	TGA	PGA	+/–	GP	G	A	Pts	PIM	PP	SH	GW
1987-88	Thorold Bantam Black Hawks	OMHA	28	53	32	85				24																		
	Thorold Black Hawks	OJHL-B	3	1	0	1				2																		
1988-89	Cornwall Royals	OHL	62	34	25	59				213											18	5	11	16	41			
1989-90	Cornwall Royals	OHL	58	51	59	110				240											6	7	5	12	26			
1990-91	**Quebec Nordiques**	**NHL**	59	3	10	13	3	8	11	109	0	0	0	54	5.6	25	2	43	1	–19								
	Halifax Citadels	AHL	6	4	4	8				11																		
1991-92	**Quebec Nordiques**	**NHL**	75	42	31	73	38	23	61	183	17	0	0	190	22.1	98	31	78	2	–9								
1992-93	**Quebec Nordiques**	**NHL**	73	36	41	77	30	28	58	185	15	0	4	241	14.9	111	42	78	8	–1	5	1	0	1	2	0	0	0
1993-94	**Quebec Nordiques**	**NHL**	6	2	2	4	2	2	4	8	0	0	0	15	13.3	9	3	7	3	2								
1994-95	**Quebec Nordiques**	**NHL**	46	30	19	49	53	28	81	46	13	2	8	137	21.9	61	21	29	10	21	6	2	3	5	6	0	0	0
1995-96	**Colorado Avalanche**	**NHL**	9	4	4	8	4	3	7	9	4	0	0	23	17.4	12	8	8	1	–3								
	San Jose Sharks	**NHL**	72	29	32	61	29	26	55	137	12	1	2	184	15.8	81	32	97	18	–30								
1996-97	**San Jose Sharks**	**NHL**	72	31	32	63	33	28	61	155	10	0	3	225	13.8	85	28	79	3	–19								
	Canada	WC-A	10	4	3	7				31																		

Season	Club	League	GP	G	A	Pts	AG	AA	APts	PIM	PP	SH	GW	S	%	TGF	PGF	TGA	PGA	+/–	GP	G	A	Pts	PIM	PP	SH	GW
			REGULAR SEASON																		PLAYOFFS							
1997-98	**San Jose Sharks**	**NHL**	**75**	**14**	**27**	**41**	**16**	**26**	**42**	**144**	**3**	**1**	**1**	**192**	**7.3**	**52**	**15**	**58**	**19**	**–2**	**6**	**2**	**2**	**4**	**26**	**2**	**0**	**1**
1998-99	**San Jose Sharks**	**NHL**	**78**	**19**	**26**	**45**	**22**	**25**	**47**	**129**	**6**	**2**	**3**	**207**	**9.2**	**72**	**24**	**50**	**18**	**16**	**6**	**1**	**1**	**2**	**6**	**0**	**0**	**0**
99-2000	**San Jose Sharks**	**NHL**	**78**	**44**	**40**	**84**	**50**	**37**	**87**	**110**	**18**	**4**	**6**	**261**	**16.9**	**101**	**44**	**83**	**25**	**–1**	**10**	**8**	**2**	**10**	**6**	**2**	**2**	**3**
	NHL Totals		**643**	**254**	**264**	**518**	**280**	**234**	**514**	**1215**	**98**	**10**	**27**	**1729**	**14.7**	**707**	**250**	**610**	**108**		**33**	**14**	**8**	**22**	**46**	**4**	**2**	**4**

OHL First All-Star Team (1990) • Played in NHL All-Star Game (1992, 1996, 1997, 2000)

• Missed remainder of 1993-94 season recovering from shoulder injury suffered in game vs. Tampa Bay, November 13, 1983. Transferred to **Colorado** after **Quebec** franchise relocated, June 21, 1995. Traded to **San Jose** by **Colorado** for Sandis Ozolinsh, October 26, 1995.

• NOLAN, Ted

Theodore John C – L. 6', 185 lbs. b: Sault Ste. Marie, Ont., 4/7/1958. Detroit's 7th, 78th overall, in 1978.

Season	Club	League	GP	G	A	Pts	AG	AA	APts	PIM	PP	SH	GW	S	%	TGF	PGF	TGA	PGA	+/–	GP	G	A	Pts	PIM	PP	SH	GW
1975-76	Kenora Thistles	NOJHA	60	10	36	46	....	....	....	....	....	....	....	....	....	....	....	....	....	....	....	....	....	....	....	....	....	....
1976-77	Sault Ste. Marie Greyhounds	OMJHL	60	8	16	24	....	....	....	109	....	....	....	....	....	....	....	....	....	....	9	1	2	3	19	....	....	....
1977-78	Sault Ste. Marie Greyhounds	OMJHL	66	14	30	44	....	....	....	106	....	....	....	....	....	....	....	....	....	....	13	1	3	4	20	....	....	....
1978-79	Kansas City Red Wings	CHL	73	12	38	50	....	....	....	66	....	....	....	....	....	....	....	....	....	....	4	1	2	3	0	....	....	....
1979-80	Adirondack Red Wings	AHL	75	16	24	40	....	....	....	106	....	....	....	....	....	....	....	....	....	....	5	0	1	1	0	....	....	....
1980-81	Adirondack Red Wings	AHL	76	22	28	50	....	....	....	86	....	....	....	....	....	....	....	....	....	....	18	6	10	16	11	....	....	....
1981-82	**Detroit Red Wings**	**NHL**	**41**	**4**	**13**	**17**	**3**	**9**	**12**	**45**	**0**	**2**	**0**	**67**	**6.0**	**25**	**2**	**37**	**8**	**–6**	....	....	....	....	....	....	....	....
	Adirondack Red Wings	AHL	39	12	18	30	....	....	....	81	....	....	....	....	....	....	....	....	....	....	....	....	....	....	....	....	....	....
1982-83	Adirondack Red Wings	AHL	78	24	40	64	....	....	....	103	....	....	....	....	....	....	....	....	....	....	6	2	5	7	14	....	....	....
1983-84	**Detroit Red Wings**	**NHL**	**19**	**1**	**2**	**3**	**1**	**1**	**2**	**26**	**0**	**0**	**1**	**15**	**6.7**	**5**	**1**	**16**	**1**	**–11**	....	....	....	....	....	....	....	....
	Adirondack Red Wings	AHL	31	10	16	26	....	....	....	76	....	....	....	....	....	....	....	....	....	....	7	2	3	5	18	....	....	....
1984-85	Rochester Americans	AHL	65	28	34	62	....	....	....	152	....	....	....	....	....	....	....	....	....	....	5	4	0	4	18	....	....	....
1985-86	**Pittsburgh Penguins**	**NHL**	**18**	**1**	**1**	**2**	**1**	**1**	**2**	**34**	**0**	**0**	**0**	**17**	**5.9**	**5**	**1**	**5**	**0**	**–1**	....	....	....	....	....	....	....	....
	Baltimore Skipjacks	AHL	10	4	4	8	....	....	....	19	....	....	....	....	....	....	....	....	....	....	....	....	....	....	....	....	....	....
	NHL Totals		**78**	**6**	**16**	**22**	**5**	**11**	**16**	**105**	**0**	**2**	**1**	**99**	**6.1**	**35**	**4**	**58**	**9**		....	....	....	....	....	....	....	....

Won Jack Adams Award (1997)

Signed as a free agent by **Buffalo**, March 7, 1985. Rights traded to **Pittsburgh** by **Buffalo** for cash, September 16, 1985.

• NOLET, Simon

Simon Laurent RW – R. 5'9", 185 lbs. b: St. Odilon, Que., 11/23/1941.

Season	Club	League	GP	G	A	Pts	AG	AA	APts	PIM	PP	SH	GW	S	%	TGF	PGF	TGA	PGA	+/–	GP	G	A	Pts	PIM	PP	SH	GW
1960-61	Quebec Citadelle	QJHL	11	2	1	3	....	....	....	0	....	....	....	....	....	....	....	....	....	....	....	....	....	....	....	....	....	....
1961-62	Quebec Citadelle	QJHL	39	25	27	52	....	....	....	22	....	....	....	....	....	....	....	....	....	....	10	4	4	8	12	....	....	....
	Quebec Aces	AHL	1	0	0	0	....	....	....	2	....	....	....	....	....	....	....	....	....	....	....	....	....	....	....	....	....	....
	Quebec Citadelle	Mem-Cup	9	2	4	6	....	....	....	2	....	....	....	....	....	....	....	....	....	....	....	....	....	....	....	....	....	....
1962-63	Windsor Maple Leafs	NSSHL	55	53	55	108	....	....	....	30	....	....	....	....	....	....	....	....	....	....	7	5	6	11	14	....	....	....
	Moncton Hawks	NSSHL	....	....	....	....	....	....	....	....	....	....	....	....	....	....	....	....	....	....	12	4	5	9	2	....	....	....
1963-64	Windsor Maple Leafs	NSSHL	68	68	65	133	....	....	....	19	....	....	....	....	....	....	....	....	....	....	8	2	6	8	4	....	....	....
	Windsor Maple Leafs	Al-Cup	11	10	8	18	....	....	....	8	....	....	....	....	....	....	....	....	....	....	....	....	....	....	....	....	....	....
1964-65	Sherbrooke Castors	QSHL	STATISTICS NOT AVAILABLE																									
	Quebec Aces	AHL	2	2	1	3	....	....	....	2	....	....	....	....	....	....	....	....	....	....	....	....	....	....	....	....	....	....
	Sherbrooke Castors	Al-Cup	15	*21	14	*35	....	....	....	4	....	....	....	....	....	....	....	....	....	....	....	....	....	....	....	....	....	....
1965-66	Quebec Aces	AHL	61	16	17	33	....	....	....	12	....	....	....	....	....	....	....	....	....	....	6	0	0	0	2	....	....	....
1966-67	Quebec Aces	AHL	66	32	24	56	....	....	....	28	....	....	....	....	....	....	....	....	....	....	5	1	4	5	4	....	....	....
1967-68	**Philadelphia Flyers**	**NHL**	**4**	**0**	**0**	**0**	**0**	**0**	**0**	**2**	**0**	**0**	**0**	**9**	**0.0**	**0**	**0**	**1**	**0**	**–1**	**1**	**0**	**0**	**0**	**0**	**0**	**0**	**0**
	Quebec Aces	AHL	70	44	52	96	....	....	....	45	....	....	....	....	....	....	....	....	....	....	10	5	10	15	10	....	....	....
1968-69	**Philadelphia Flyers**	**NHL**	**35**	**4**	**10**	**14**	**4**	**9**	**13**	**8**	**2**	**0**	**0**	**77**	**5.2**	**20**	**12**	**18**	**0**	**–10**	....	....	....	....	....	....	....	....
	Quebec Aces	AHL	33	11	21	32	....	....	....	28	....	....	....	....	....	....	....	....	....	....	15	5	3	8	28	....	....	....
1969-70	**Philadelphia Flyers**	**NHL**	**56**	**22**	**22**	**44**	**24**	**21**	**45**	**36**	**6**	**0**	**4**	**163**	**13.5**	**62**	**18**	**32**	**0**	**12**	....	....	....	....	....	....	....	....
	Quebec Aces	AHL	22	13	18	31	....	....	....	14	....	....	....	....	....	....	....	....	....	....	....	....	....	....	....	....	....	....
1970-71	**Philadelphia Flyers**	**NHL**	**74**	**9**	**19**	**28**	**9**	**16**	**25**	**42**	**4**	**0**	**0**	**168**	**5.4**	**44**	**15**	**30**	**0**	**–1**	**4**	**2**	**1**	**3**	**0**	**1**	**0**	**0**
1971-72	**Philadelphia Flyers**	**NHL**	**67**	**23**	**20**	**43**	**23**	**17**	**40**	**22**	**6**	**0**	**5**	**201**	**11.4**	**70**	**27**	**40**	**3**	**6**	....	....	....	....	....	....	....	....
1972-73	**Philadelphia Flyers**	**NHL**	**70**	**16**	**20**	**36**	**15**	**16**	**31**	**6**	**6**	**0**	**0**	**146**	**11.0**	**61**	**28**	**39**	**3**	**–3**	**11**	**3**	**1**	**4**	**4**	**0**	**0**	**0**
1973-74♦	**Philadelphia Flyers**	**NHL**	**52**	**19**	**17**	**36**	**18**	**14**	**32**	**13**	**1**	**0**	**1**	**97**	**19.6**	**51**	**8**	**15**	**0**	**28**	**15**	**1**	**1**	**2**	**4**	**0**	**0**	**0**
1974-75	**Kansas City Scouts**	**NHL**	**72**	**26**	**32**	**58**	**23**	**24**	**47**	**30**	**11**	**2**	**2**	**197**	**13.2**	**76**	**39**	**95**	**6**	**–52**	....	....	....	....	....	....	....	....
1975-76	**Kansas City Scouts**	**NHL**	**41**	**10**	**15**	**25**	**9**	**11**	**20**	**16**	**2**	**0**	**1**	**123**	**8.1**	**35**	**12**	**33**	**1**	**–9**	....	....	....	....	....	....	....	....
	Pittsburgh Penguins	**NHL**	**39**	**9**	**8**	**17**	**8**	**6**	**14**	**2**	**1**	**0**	**1**	**74**	**12.2**	**34**	**6**	**21**	**0**	**7**	**3**	**0**	**0**	**0**	**0**	**0**	**0**	**0**
1976-77	**Colorado Rockies**	**NHL**	**52**	**12**	**19**	**31**	**11**	**15**	**26**	**10**	**1**	**1**	**2**	**105**	**11.4**	**44**	**5**	**52**	**13**	**0**	....	....	....	....	....	....	....	....
	NHL Totals		**562**	**150**	**182**	**332**	**144**	**149**	**293**	**187**	**40**	**3**	**16**	**1360**	**11.0**	**497**	**170**	**376**	**26**		**34**	**6**	**3**	**9**	**8**	**1**	**0**	**0**

AHL Second All-Star Team (1968) • Won John B. Sollenberger Trophy (Top Scorer - AHL) (1968) • Played in NHL All-Star Game (1972, 1975)

NHL rights transferred to **Philadelphia** after NHL club purchased **Quebec** (AHL) franchise, May 8, 1967. Claimed by **Kansas City** from **Philadelphia** in Expansion Draft, June 12, 1974. Traded to **Pittsburgh** by **Kansas City** with Ed Gilbert and Kansas City's 1st round choice (Blair Chapman) in 1976 Amateur Draft for Steve Durbano, Chuck Arnason and Pittsburgh's 1st round choice (Paul Gardner) in 1976 Amateur Draft, January 9, 1976. Transferred to **Colorado** by **Pittsburgh** with Michel Plasse and the loan of Colin Campbell for the 1976-77 season (September 1, 1976) as compensation for Pittsburgh's signing of free agent Denis Herron, August 7, 1976.

• NOONAN, Brian

RW – R. 6'1", 200 lbs. b: Boston, MA, 5/29/1965. Chicago's 10th, 186th overall, in 1983.

Season	Club	League	GP	G	A	Pts	AG	AA	APts	PIM	PP	SH	GW	S	%	TGF	PGF	TGA	PGA	+/–	GP	G	A	Pts	PIM	PP	SH	GW
1982-83	Archbishop Williams High	Hi-School	21	26	17	43	....	....	....	....	....	....	....	....	....	....	....	....	....	....	....	....	....	....	....	....	....	....
1983-84	Archbishop Williams High	Hi-School	17	14	23	37	....	....	....	....	....	....	....	....	....	....	....	....	....	....	....	....	....	....	....	....	....	....
1984-85	New Westminster Bruins	WHL	72	50	66	116	....	....	....	76	....	....	....	....	....	....	....	....	....	....	11	8	7	15	4	....	....	....
1985-86	Nova Scotia Oilers	AHL	2	0	0	0	....	....	....	0	....	....	....	....	....	....	....	....	....	....	....	....	....	....	....	....	....	....
	Saginaw Generals	IHL	76	39	39	78	....	....	....	69	....	....	....	....	....	....	....	....	....	....	11	6	3	9	6	....	....	....
1986-87	Nova Scotia Oilers	AHL	70	25	26	51	....	....	....	30	....	....	....	....	....	....	....	....	....	....	5	3	1	4	4	....	....	....
1987-88	**Chicago Blackhawks**	**NHL**	**77**	**10**	**20**	**30**	**9**	**14**	**23**	**44**	**3**	**0**	**2**	**87**	**11.5**	**64**	**31**	**66**	**6**	**–27**	**3**	**0**	**0**	**0**	**4**	**0**	**0**	**0**
1988-89	**Chicago Blackhawks**	**NHL**	**45**	**4**	**12**	**16**	**3**	**8**	**11**	**28**	**2**	**0**	**0**	**84**	**4.8**	**29**	**7**	**32**	**8**	**–2**	**1**	**0**	**0**	**0**	**0**	**0**	**0**	**0**
	Saginaw Hawks	IHL	19	18	13	31	....	....	....	36	....	....	....	....	....	....	....	....	....	....	1	0	0	0	0	....	....	....
1989-90	**Chicago Blackhawks**	**NHL**	**8**	**0**	**2**	**2**	**0**	**1**	**1**	**6**	**0**	**0**	**0**	**13**	**0.0**	**3**	**0**	**6**	**3**	**0**	....	....	....	....	....	....	....	....
	Indianapolis Ice	IHL	56	40	36	76	....	....	....	85	....	....	....	....	....	....	....	....	....	....	14	6	9	15	20	....	....	....
1990-91	**Chicago Blackhawks**	**NHL**	**7**	**0**	**4**	**4**	**0**	**3**	**3**	**2**	**0**	**0**	**0**	**12**	**0.0**	**4**	**1**	**4**	**0**	**–1**	....	....	....	....	....	....	....	....
	Indianapolis Ice	IHL	59	38	53	91	....	....	....	67	....	....	....	....	....	....	....	....	....	....	7	6	4	10	18	....	....	....
1991-92	**Chicago Blackhawks**	**NHL**	**65**	**19**	**12**	**31**	**17**	**9**	**26**	**81**	**4**	**0**	**0**	**154**	**12.3**	**57**	**15**	**38**	**5**	**9**	**18**	**6**	**9**	**15**	**30**	**3**	**0**	**1**
1992-93	**Chicago Blackhawks**	**NHL**	**63**	**16**	**14**	**30**	**13**	**10**	**23**	**82**	**5**	**0**	**3**	**129**	**12.4**	**47**	**17**	**29**	**2**	**3**	**4**	**3**	**0**	**3**	**4**	**1**	**0**	**0**
1993-94	**Chicago Blackhawks**	**NHL**	**64**	**14**	**21**	**35**	**13**	**16**	**29**	**57**	**8**	**0**	**3**	**134**	**10.4**	**63**	**33**	**28**	**0**	**2**	....	....	....	....	....	....	....	....
♦	**New York Rangers**	**NHL**	**12**	**4**	**2**	**6**	**4**	**2**	**6**	**12**	**2**	**0**	**3**	**26**	**15.4**	**13**	**4**	**4**	**0**	**5**	**22**	**4**	**7**	**11**	**17**	**2**	**0**	**1**
1994-95	**New York Rangers**	**NHL**	**45**	**14**	**13**	**27**	**25**	**19**	**44**	**26**	**7**	**0**	**1**	**95**	**14.7**	**48**	**16**	**46**	**11**	**–3**	**5**	**0**	**0**	**0**	**8**	**0**	**0**	**0**
1995-96	**St. Louis Blues**	**NHL**	**81**	**13**	**22**	**35**	**13**	**18**	**31**	**84**	**3**	**1**	**6**	**131**	**9.9**	**54**	**13**	**62**	**23**	**2**	**13**	**4**	**1**	**5**	**10**	**0**	**0**	**0**
1996-97	**St. Louis Blues**	**NHL**	**13**	**2**	**5**	**7**	**2**	**4**	**6**	**0**	**0**	**0**	**0**	**13**	**15.4**	**8**	**0**	**7**	**1**	**2**	....	....	....	....	....	....	....	....
	New York Rangers	**NHL**	**44**	**6**	**9**	**15**	**6**	**8**	**14**	**28**	**3**	**0**	**1**	**62**	**9.7**	**22**	**10**	**22**	**3**	**–7**	....	....	....	....	....	....	....	....
	Vancouver Canucks	**NHL**	**16**	**4**	**8**	**12**	**4**	**7**	**11**	**6**	**0**	**1**	**0**	**25**	**16.0**	**17**	**3**	**17**	**5**	**2**	....	....	....	....	....	....	....	....
1997-98	**Vancouver Canucks**	**NHL**	**82**	**10**	**15**	**25**	**12**	**15**	**27**	**62**	**1**	**0**	**2**	**87**	**11.5**	**41**	**6**	**67**	**13**	**–19**	....	....	....	....	....	....	....	....
1998-99	**Phoenix Coyotes**	**NHL**	**7**	**0**	**0**	**0**	**0**	**0**	**0**	**0**	**0**	**0**	**0**	**1**	**0.0**	**0**	**0**	**3**	**0**	**–3**	**5**	**0**	**2**	**2**	**4**	**0**	**0**	**0**
	Indianapolis Ice	IHL	65	19	44	63	....	....	....	128	....	....	....	....	....	....	....	....	....	....	....	....	....	....	....	....	....	....
99-2000	Chicago Wolves	IHL	80	30	32	62	....	....	....	80	....	....	....	....	....	....	....	....	....	....	16	4	7	11	10	....	....	....
	NHL Totals		**629**	**116**	**159**	**275**	**121**	**134**	**255**	**518**	**38**	**2**	**21**	**1053**	**11.0**	**470**	**156**	**431**	**80**		**71**	**17**	**19**	**36**	**77**	**6**	**0**	**2**

IHL Second All-Star Team (1990) • IHL First All-Star Team (1991)

Traded to **NY Rangers** by **Chicago** with Stephane Matteau for Tony Amonte and the rights to Matt Oates, March 21, 1994. Signed as a free agent by **St. Louis**, July 24, 1995. Traded to **NY Rangers** by **St. Louis** for Sergio Momesso, November 13, 1996. Traded to **Vancouver** by **NY Rangers** with Sergei Nemchinov for Esa Tikkanen and Russ Courtnall, March 8, 1997. Signed as a free agent by **Phoenix**, March 17, 1999. Signed as a free agent by **Chicago Wolves** (IHL), September 14, 1999.

Season	Club	League	GP	G	A	Pts	AG	AA	APts	PIM	PP	SH	GW	S	%	TGF	PGF	TGA	PGA	+/–	GP	G	A	Pts	PIM	PP	SH	GW
			REGULAR SEASON																		PLAYOFFS							

• NORDMARK, Robert

D – R. 6', 209 lbs. b: Lulea, Sweden, 8/20/1962. St. Louis' 3rd, 59th overall, in 1987.

Season	Club	League	GP	G	A	Pts	AG	AA	APts	PIM	PP	SH	GW	S	%	TGF	PGF	TGA	PGA	+/–	GP	G	A	Pts	PIM	PP	SH	GW
1979-80	Lulea HF	Sweden-2	24	4	2	6	....	....	....	16	....	....	....	....	....	....	....	....	....	....	8	0	0	0	4	....	....	....
	Sweden	EJC-A	5	1	1	2	....	....	....	6	....	....	....	....	....	....	....	....	....	....	....	....	....	....	....	....	....	....
1980-81	Vastra Frolunda	Sweden	34	4	3	7	....	....	....	30	....	....	....	....	....	....	....	....	....	....	2	0	0	0	0	....	....	....
	Sweden	WJC-A	5	0	0	0	....	....	....	2	....	....	....	....	....	....	....	....	....	....	....	....	....	....	....	....	....	....
1981-82	Brynas IF Gavle	Sweden	34	5	5	10	....	....	....	16	....	....	....	....	....	....	....	....	....	....	....	....	....	....	....	....	....	....
	Sweden	WJC-A	7	2	1	3	....	....	....	0	....	....	....	....	....	....	....	....	....	....	....	....	....	....	....	....	....	....
1982-83	Brynas IF Gavle	Sweden	36	8	5	13	....	....	....	32	....	....	....	....	....	....	....	....	....	....	....	....	....	....	....	....	....	....
1983-84	Brynas IF Gavle	Sweden	32	10	15	25	....	....	....	44	....	....	....	....	....	....	....	....	....	....	....	....	....	....	....	....	....	....
1984-85	Lulea HF	Sweden	33	3	9	12	....	....	....	30	....	....	....	....	....	....	....	....	....	....	....	....	....	....	....	....	....	....
1985-86	Lulea HF	Sweden	35	9	15	24	....	....	....	48	....	....	....	....	....	....	....	....	....	....	....	....	....	....	....	....	....	....
	Sweden	WEC-A	8	3	2	5	....	....	....	10	....	....	....	....	....	....	....	....	....	....	....	....	....	....	....	....	....	....
1986-87	Lulea HF	Sweden	32	7	8	15	....	....	....	46	....	....	....	....	....	....	....	....	....	....	3	0	3	3	4	....	....	....
	Sweden	WEC-A	9	1	2	3	....	....	....	16	....	....	....	....	....	....	....	....	....	....	....	....	....	....	....	....	....	....
1987-88	**St. Louis Blues**	**NHL**	**67**	**3**	**18**	**21**	**3**	**13**	**16**	**60**	**2**	**0**	**0**	**78**	**3.8**	**58**	**23**	**50**	**9**	**–6**	....	....	....	....	....	....	....	....
1988-89	**Vancouver Canucks**	**NHL**	**80**	**6**	**35**	**41**	**5**	**25**	**30**	**97**	**5**	**0**	**1**	**156**	**3.8**	**113**	**62**	**62**	**7**	**–4**	**7**	**3**	**2**	**5**	**8**	**2**	**0**	**0**
1989-90	**Vancouver Canucks**	**NHL**	**44**	**2**	**11**	**13**	**2**	**8**	**10**	**34**	**1**	**0**	**0**	**86**	**2.3**	**42**	**20**	**38**	**0**	**–16**	....	....	....	....	....	....	....	....
1990-91	**Vancouver Canucks**	**NHL**	**45**	**2**	**6**	**8**	**2**	**5**	**7**	**63**	**1**	**0**	**0**	**65**	**3.1**	**40**	**13**	**46**	**9**	**–10**	....	....	....	....	....	....	....	....
1991-92	Vasteras IK	Sweden	36	11	6	17	....	....	....	72	....	....	....	....	....	....	....	....	....	....	....	....	....	....	....	....	....	....
1992-93	Vasteras IK	Sweden	24	11	4	15	....	....	....	52	....	....	....	....	....	....	....	....	....	....	3	1	0	1	10	....	....	....
1993-94	Djurgardens IF Stockholm	Sweden	35	5	9	14	....	....	....	62	....	....	....	....	....	....	....	....	....	....	....	....	....	....	....	....	....	....
1994-95	Djurgardens IF Stockholm	Sweden	34	7	11	18	....	....	....	50	....	....	....	....	....	....	....	....	....	....	3	1	0	1	2	....	....	....
	Sweden	WC-A	6	1	1	2	....	....	....	4	....	....	....	....	....	....	....	....	....	....	....	....	....	....	....	....	....	....
1995-96	Lukko Rauma	Finland	43	16	13	29	....	....	....	58	....	....	....	....	....	....	....	....	....	....	8	2	4	6	6	....	....	....
1996-97	ZSC Lions Zurich	Switz.	41	9	17	26	....	....	....	59	....	....	....	....	....	....	....	....	....	....	5	0	2	2	4	....	....	....
1997-98	Djurgardens IF Stockholm	Sweden	11	3	5	8	....	....	....	10	....	....	....	....	....	....	....	....	....	....	6	0	0	0	4	....	....	....
	Djurgardens IF Stockholm	EuroHL	5	1	0	1	....	....	....	6	....	....	....	....	....	....	....	....	....	....	....	....	....	....	....	....	....	....
1998-99	KAC Klagenfurt	Alpenliga	19	8	5	13	....	....	....	4	....	....	....	....	....	....	....	....	....	....	....	....	....	....	....	....	....	....
	KAC Klagenfurt	Austria	22	2	9	11	....	....	....	20	....	....	....	....	....	....	....	....	....	....	....	....	....	....	....	....	....	....
99-2000	Hammarby IF	Sweden-2	37	7	10	17	....	....	....	14	....	....	....	....	....	....	....	....	....	....	2	1	0	1	0	....	....	....
	NHL Totals		**236**	**13**	**70**	**83**	**12**	**51**	**63**	**254**	**9**	**0**	**1**	**385**	**3.4**	**253**	**118**	**196**	**25**		**7**	**3**	**2**	**5**	**8**	**2**	**0**	**0**

Traded to **Vancouver** by **St. Louis** with St. Louis's 2nd round choice (later traded to Montreal - Montreal selected Craig Darby) in 1991 Entry Draft for Dave Richter, September 6, 1988.

• NORDSTROM, Peter

C – L. 6'1", 200 lbs. b: Munkfors, Sweden, 7/26/1974. Boston's 3rd, 78th overall, in 1998.

Season	Club	League	GP	G	A	Pts	AG	AA	APts	PIM	PP	SH	GW	S	%	TGF	PGF	TGA	PGA	+/–	GP	G	A	Pts	PIM	PP	SH	GW
1989-90	IFK Munkfors	Sweden-3	21	2	1	3	....	....	....	8	....	....	....	....	....	....	....	....	....	....	....	....	....	....	....	....	....	....
1990-91	IFK Munkfors	Sweden-3	32	10	18	28	....	....	....	20	....	....	....	....	....	....	....	....	....	....	....	....	....	....	....	....	....	....
1991-92	IFK Munkfors	Sweden-3	31	12	20	32	....	....	....	42	....	....	....	....	....	....	....	....	....	....	....	....	....	....	....	....	....	....
1992-93	IFK Munkfors	Sweden-3	35	19	11	30	....	....	....	44	....	....	....	....	....	....	....	....	....	....	....	....	....	....	....	....	....	....
1993-94	IFK Munkfors	Sweden-3	31	17	26	43	....	....	....	87	....	....	....	....	....	....	....	....	....	....	....	....	....	....	....	....	....	....
1994-95	IFK Munkfors	Sweden-2	21	8	17	25	....	....	....	30	....	....	....	....	....	....	....	....	....	....	....	....	....	....	....	....	....	....
	Leksands IF	Sweden	13	1	0	1	....	....	....	0	....	....	....	....	....	....	....	....	....	....	....	....	....	....	....	....	....	....
1995-96	Farjestads BK Karlstad	Sweden	40	6	5	11	....	....	....	36	....	....	....	....	....	....	....	....	....	....	8	0	3	3	12	....	....	....
1996-97	Farjestads BK Karlstad	Sweden	44	9	5	14	....	....	....	32	....	....	....	....	....	....	....	....	....	....	14	1	2	3	6	....	....	....
1997-98	Farjestads BK Karlstad	Sweden	45	6	19	25	....	....	....	46	....	....	....	....	....	....	....	....	....	....	12	5	7	*12	8	....	....	....
1998-99	Farjestads BK Karlstad	Sweden	21	4	4	8	....	....	....	14	....	....	....	....	....	....	....	....	....	....	4	1	1	2	2	....	....	....
	Farjestads BK Karlstad	EuroHL	2	1	0	1	....	....	....	2	....	....	....	....	....	....	....	....	....	....	....	....	....	....	....	....	....	....
	Boston Bruins	**NHL**	**2**	**0**	**0**	**0**	**0**	**0**	**0**	**0**	**0**	**0**	**0**	**0**	**0.0**	**1**	**0**	**2**	**0**	**–1**	....	....	....	....	....	....	....	....
	Providence Bruins	AHL	13	2	1	3	....	....	....	2	....	....	....	....	....	....	....	....	....	....	....	....	....	....	....	....	....	....
99-2000	Farjestads BK Karlstad	Sweden	45	8	14	22	....	....	....	48	....	....	....	....	....	....	....	....	....	....	7	0	3	3	2	....	....	....
	Sweden	WC-A	7	2	1	3	....	....	....	4	....	....	....	....	....	....	....	....	....	....	....	....	....	....	....	....	....	....
	NHL Totals		**2**	**0**	**0**	**0**	**0**	**0**	**0**	**0**	**0**	**0**	**0**	**0**	**0.0**	**1**	**0**	**2**	**0**		....	....	....	....	....	....	....	....

• NORIS, Joe

Joseph S. C/D – R. 6', 185 lbs. b: Denver, CO, 10/26/1951. Pittsburgh's 2nd, 32nd overall, in 1971.

Season	Club	League	GP	G	A	Pts	AG	AA	APts	PIM	PP	SH	GW	S	%	TGF	PGF	TGA	PGA	+/–	GP	G	A	Pts	PIM	PP	SH	GW
1968-69	Kitchener Rangers	OHA-Jr.	18	5	9	14	....	....	....	21	....	....	....	....	....	....	....	....	....	....	....	....	....	....	....	....	....	....
1969-70	Kitchener Rangers	OHA-Jr.	48	27	19	46	....	....	....	45	....	....	....	....	....	....	....	....	....	....	6	8	6	14	4	....	....	....
1970-71	Toronto Marlboros	OHA-Jr.	42	12	24	36	....	....	....	22	....	....	....	....	....	....	....	....	....	....	13	0	7	7	10	....	....	....
1971-72	**Pittsburgh Penguins**	**NHL**	**35**	**2**	**5**	**7**	**2**	**4**	**6**	**20**	**0**	**0**	**0**	**48**	**4.2**	**22**	**1**	**31**	**2**	**–8**	....	....	....	....	....	....	....	....
	Hershey Bears	AHL	42	8	15	23	....	....	....	37	....	....	....	....	....	....	....	....	....	....	4	1	1	2	8	....	....	....
1972-73	Hershey Bears	AHL	8	2	5	7	....	....	....	9	....	....	....	....	....	....	....	....	....	....	....	....	....	....	....	....	....	....
	San Diego Gulls	WHL	25	3	13	16	....	....	....	14	....	....	....	....	....	....	....	....	....	....	....	....	....	....	....	....	....	....
	St. Louis Blues	**NHL**	**2**	**0**	**0**	**0**	**0**	**0**	**0**	**0**	**0**	**0**	**0**	**0**	**0.0**	**0**	**0**	**2**	**0**	**–2**	....	....	....	....	....	....	....	....
	Denver Spurs	WHL	35	10	18	28	....	....	....	14	....	....	....	....	....	....	....	....	....	....	5	1	2	3	7	....	....	....
1973-74	**Buffalo Sabres**	**NHL**	**18**	**0**	**0**	**0**	**0**	**0**	**0**	**2**	**0**	**0**	**0**	**9**	**0.0**	**7**	**2**	**9**	**0**	**–4**	....	....	....	....	....	....	....	....
	Cincinnati Swords	AHL	28	5	13	18	....	....	....	20	....	....	....	....	....	....	....	....	....	....	5	3	3	6	0	....	....	....
1974-75	Syracuse Eagles	AHL	73	26	36	62	....	....	....	41	....	....	....	....	....	....	....	....	....	....	1	1	1	2	0	....	....	....
1975-76	San Diego Mariners	WHA	80	28	40	68	....	....	....	24	....	....	....	....	....	....	....	....	....	....	11	2	4	6	6	....	....	....
1976-77	United States	Can-Cup	4	0	1	1	....	....	....	6	....	....	....	....	....	....	....	....	....	....	....	....	....	....	....	....	....	....
	San Diego Mariners	WHA	73	35	57	92	....	....	....	30	....	....	....	....	....	....	....	....	....	....	7	2	1	3	6	....	....	....
1977-78	Birmingham Bulls	WHA	45	9	19	28	....	....	....	6	....	....	....	....	....	....	....	....	....	....	....	....	....	....	....	....	....	....
1978-79	San Diego Hawks	PHL	58	27	*77	*104	....	....	....	8	....	....	....	....	....	....	....	....	....	....	....	....	....	....	....	....	....	....
1979-80	EC Graz	Austria	6	2	2	4	....	....	....	2	....	....	....	....	....	....	....	....	....	....	....	....	....	....	....	....	....	....
1980-1992			OUT OF HOCKEY – RETIRED																									
1992-93	San Diego Surf	SCSHL	STATISTICS NOT AVAILABLE																									
	NHL Totals		**55**	**2**	**5**	**7**	**2**	**4**	**6**	**22**	**0**	**0**	**0**	**57**	**3.5**	**29**	**3**	**42**	**2**		....	....	....	....	....	....	....	....
	Other Major League Totals		198	72	116	188	....	....	....	60	....	....	....	....	....	....	....	....	....	....	18	4	5	9	12	....	....	....

PHL First All-Star Team (1979) • PHL MVP (1979)

Selected by **Ontario-Ottawa** (WHA) in 1972 WHA General Player Draft, February 12, 1972. Traded to **St. Louis** by **Pittsburgh** for Jim Shires, January 8, 1973. Claimed by **Buffalo** from **St. Louis** in Intra-League Draft, June 12, 1973. WHA rights claimed on waivers by **Calgary** (WHA) from **Toronto** (WHA), June, 1975. WHA rights traded to **San Diego** (WHA) by **Calgary** (WHA) for Richard Sentes, August, 1975. Signed as a free agent by **Birmingham** (WHA) after **San Diego** (WHA) franchise folded, June, 1977.

• NORRIS, Dwayne

Carl Dwayne RW – R. 5'10", 175 lbs. b: St. John's, Nfld., 1/8/1970. Quebec's 5th, 127th overall, in 1990.

Season	Club	League	GP	G	A	Pts	AG	AA	APts	PIM	PP	SH	GW	S	%	TGF	PGF	TGA	PGA	+/–	GP	G	A	Pts	PIM	PP	SH	GW
1987-88	Notre Dame Hounds	SJHL	55	20	34	54	....	....	....		....	....	....	....	....	....	....	....	....	....	....	....	....	....	....	....	....	....
	Notre Dame Hounds	Cen-Cup	5	4	3	7	....	....	....		....	....	....	....	....	....	....	....	....	....	....	....	....	....	....	....	....	....
1988-89	Michigan State Spartans	CCHA	40	16	21	37	....	....	....	32	....	....	....	....	....	....	....	....	....	....	....	....	....	....	....	....	....	....
1989-90	Michigan State Spartans	CCHA	33	18	25	43	....	....	....	30	....	....	....	....	....	....	....	....	....	....	....	....	....	....	....	....	....	....
	Canada	WJC-A	7	2	4	6	....	....	....	2	....	....	....	....	....	....	....	....	....	....	....	....	....	....	....	....	....	....
1990-91	Michigan State Spartans	CCHA	40	26	25	51	....	....	....	60	....	....	....	....	....	....	....	....	....	....	....	....	....	....	....	....	....	....
1991-92	Michigan State Spartans	CCHA	41	40	38	78	....	....	....	58	....	....	....	....	....	....	....	....	....	....	....	....	....	....	....	....	....	....
1992-93	Halifax Citadels	AHL	50	25	28	53	....	....	....	62	....	....	....	....	....	....	....	....	....	....	....	....	....	....	....	....	....	....
1993-94	Canada	Nat-Team	48	18	14	32	....	....	....	22	....	....	....	....	....	....	....	....	....	....	....	....	....	....	....	....	....	....
	Canada	Olympics	8	2	2	4	....	....	....	4	....	....	....	....	....	....	....	....	....	....	....	....	....	....	....	....	....	....
	Quebec Nordiques	**NHL**	**4**	**1**	**1**	**2**	**1**	**1**	**2**	**4**	**0**	**0**	**0**	**7**	**14.3**	**4**	**2**	**1**	**0**	**1**	....	....	....	....	....	....	....	....
	Cornwall Aces	AHL	9	2	9	11	....	....	....	0	....	....	....	....	....	....	....	....	....	....	13	7	4	11	17	....	....	....
1994-95	Cornwall Aces	AHL	60	30	43	73	....	....	....	61	....	....	....	....	....	....	....	....	....	....	12	7	8	15	4	....	....	....
	Quebec Nordiques	**NHL**	**13**	**1**	**2**	**3**	**2**	**3**	**5**	**2**	**0**	**0**	**1**	**7**	**14.3**	**4**	**0**	**3**	**0**	**1**	....	....	....	....	....	....	....	....
1995-96	Los Angeles Ice Dogs	IHL	14	7	16	23	....	....	....	22	....	....	....	....	....	....	....	....	....	....	....	....	....	....	....	....	....	....
	Mighty Ducks of Anaheim	**NHL**	**3**	**0**	**1**	**1**	**0**	**1**	**1**	**2**	**0**	**0**	**0**	**3**	**0.0**	**1**	**0**	**1**	**0**	**0**	....	....	....	....	....	....	....	....
	Baltimore Bandits	AHL	62	31	55	86	....	....	....	16	....	....	....	....	....	....	....	....	....	....	12	6	9	15	12	....	....	....

			REGULAR SEASON																		PLAYOFFS							
Season	Club	League	GP	G	A	Pts	AG	AA	APts	PIM	PP	SH	GW	S	%	TGF	PGF	TGA	PGA	+/-	GP	G	A	Pts	PIM	PP	SH	GW
1996-97	Kolner Haie	Germany	49	16	28	44	....	....	....	24	....	....	....	....	....	....	....	....	....	....	4	3	0	3	0	....	....	....
	Kolner Haie	EuroHL	6	2	3	5	....	....	....	0	....	....	....	....	....	....	....	....	....	....	....	....	....	....	....	....	....	....
1997-98	Kolner Haie	Germany	42	13	14	27	....	....	....	34	....	....	....	....	....	....	....	....	....	....	3	0	0	0	0	....	....	....
	Kolner Haie	EuroHL	6	1	3	4	....	....	....	2	....	....	....	....	....	....	....	....	....	....	....	....	....	....	....	....	....	....
1998-99	Kolner Haie	Germany	48	16	30	46	....	....	....	62	....	....	....	....	....	....	....	....	....	....	5	2	3	5	8	....	....	....
99-2000	Kolner Haie	Germany	49	17	23	40	....	....	....	70	....	....	....	....	....	....	....	....	....	....	10	4	1	5	12	....	....	....
	NHL Totals		**20**	**2**	**4**	**6**	**3**	**5**	**8**	**8**	**0**	**0**	**1**	**17**	**11.8**	**9**	**2**	**5**	**0**		....	....	....	....	....	....	....	....

CCHA First All-Star Team (1992) • NCAA West First All-American Team (1992) • AHL First All-Star Team (1995) • AHL Second All-Star Team (1996)

Signed as a free agent by **Anaheim**, November 3, 1995.

• NORRISH, Rod

LW – L. 5′10″, 185 lbs. b: Saskatoon, Sask., 11/27/1951. Minnesota's 1st, 21st overall, in 1971.

Season	Club	League	GP	G	A	Pts	AG	AA	APts	PIM	PP	SH	GW	S	%	TGF	PGF	TGA	PGA	+/-	GP	G	A	Pts	PIM	PP	SH	GW
1969-70	Regina Pats	SJHL	50	*37	19	56	....	....	....	11	....	....	....	....	....	....	....	....	....	....	....	....	....	....	....	....	....	....
	Weyburn Red Wings	Mem-Cup	19	8	13	21	....	....	....	7	....	....	....	....	....	....	....	....	....	....	....	....	....	....	....	....	....	....
1970-71	Regina Pats	WCJHL	65	49	32	81	....	....	....	49	....	....	....	....	....	....	....	....	....	....	....	....	....	....	....	....	....	....
1971-72	Cleveland Barons	AHL	39	0	1	1	....	....	....	0	....	....	....	....	....	....	....	....	....	....	6	0	0	0	0	....	....	....
1972-73	Cleveland-Jacksonville Barons	AHL	76	22	33	55	....	....	....	22	....	....	....	....	....	....	....	....	....	....	....	....	....	....	....	....	....	....
1973-74	**Minnesota North Stars**	**NHL**	**9**	**2**	**1**	**3**	**2**	**1**	**3**	**0**	**0**	**0**	**0**	**6**	**33.3**	**3**	**0**	**6**	**0**	**–3**	....	....	....	....	....	....	....	....
	New Haven Nighthawks	AHL	53	19	16	35	....	....	....	11	....	....	....	....	....	....	....	....	....	....	10	1	5	6	2	....	....	....
1974-75	**Minnesota North Stars**	**NHL**	**12**	**1**	**2**	**3**	**1**	**1**	**2**	**2**	**0**	**0**	**0**	**13**	**7.7**	**5**	**3**	**5**	**1**	**–2**	....	....	....	....	....	....	....	....
	New Haven Nighthawks	AHL	52	9	21	30	....	....	....	13	....	....	....	....	....	....	....	....	....	....	16	6	8	14	0	....	....	....
	NHL Totals		**21**	**3**	**3**	**6**	**3**	**2**	**5**	**2**	**0**	**0**	**0**	**19**	**15.8**	**8**	**3**	**11**	**1**		....	....	....	....	....	....	....	....

WCJHL All-Star Team (1971)

• Loaned to **Weyburn** (SJHL) by **Regina** (SJHL) for Memorial Cup playoffs, March, 1970.

• NORSTROM, Mattias

Mattias E.J. D – L. 6′2″, 201 lbs. b: Stockholm, Sweden, 1/2/1972. NY Rangers' 2nd, 48th overall, in 1992.

Season	Club	League	GP	G	A	Pts	AG	AA	APts	PIM	PP	SH	GW	S	%	TGF	PGF	TGA	PGA	+/-	GP	G	A	Pts	PIM	PP	SH	GW
1990-91	Mora IK	Sweden-2	9	1	1	2	....	....	....	6	....	....	....	....	....	....	....	....	....	....	1	0	0	0	2	....	....	....
1991-92	AIK Solna Stockholm	Sweden	39	4	3	7	....	....	....	28	....	....	....	....	....	....	....	....	....	....	3	0	2	2	2	....	....	....
	Sweden	WJC-A	7	0	1	1	....	....	....	10	....	....	....	....	....	....	....	....	....	....	....	....	....	....	....	....	....	....
1992-93	AIK Solna Stockholm	Sweden	22	0	1	1	....	....	....	16	....	....	....	....	....	....	....	....	....	....	....	....	....	....	....	....	....	....
1993-94	**New York Rangers**	**NHL**	**9**	**0**	**2**	**2**	**0**	**2**	**2**	**6**	**0**	**0**	**0**	**3**	**0.0**	**5**	**1**	**4**	**0**	**0**	....	....	....	....	....	....	....	....
	Binghamton Rangers	AHL	55	1	9	10	....	....	....	70	....	....	....	....	....	....	....	....	....	....	....	....	....	....	....	....	....	....
1994-95	Binghamton Rangers	AHL	63	9	10	19	....	....	....	91	....	....	....	....	....	....	....	....	....	....	....	....	....	....	....	....	....	....
	New York Rangers	**NHL**	**9**	**0**	**3**	**3**	**0**	**4**	**4**	**2**	**0**	**0**	**0**	**4**	**0.0**	**10**	**0**	**8**	**0**	**2**	**3**	**0**	**0**	**0**	**0**	**0**	**0**	**0**
1995-96	**New York Rangers**	**NHL**	**25**	**2**	**1**	**3**	**2**	**1**	**3**	**22**	**0**	**0**	**0**	**17**	**11.8**	**14**	**1**	**10**	**2**	**5**	....	....	....	....	....	....	....	....
	Los Angeles Kings	**NHL**	**11**	**0**	**1**	**1**	**0**	**1**	**1**	**18**	**0**	**0**	**0**	**17**	**0.0**	**8**	**3**	**14**	**1**	**–8**	....	....	....	....	....	....	....	....
	Sweden	WC-A	6	0	0	0	....	....	....	6	....	....	....	....	....	....	....	....	....	....	....	....	....	....	....	....	....	....
1996-97	Sweden	W-Cup	4	0	1	1	....	....	....	0	....	....	....	....	....	....	....	....	....	....	....	....	....	....	....	....	....	....
	Los Angeles Kings	**NHL**	**80**	**1**	**21**	**22**	**1**	**19**	**20**	**84**	**0**	**0**	**0**	**106**	**0.9**	**76**	**12**	**76**	**8**	**–4**	....	....	....	....	....	....	....	....
	Sweden	WC-A	11	0	2	2	....	....	....	14	....	....	....	....	....	....	....	....	....	....	....	....	....	....	....	....	....	....
1997-98	**Los Angeles Kings**	**NHL**	**73**	**1**	**12**	**13**	**1**	**12**	**13**	**90**	**0**	**0**	**0**	**61**	**1.6**	**76**	**13**	**73**	**24**	**14**	**4**	**0**	**0**	**0**	**2**	**0**	**0**	**0**
	Sweden	Olympics	4	0	1	1	....	....	....	2	....	....	....	....	....	....	....	....	....	....	....	....	....	....	....	....	....	....
	Sweden	WC-A	1	0	0	0	....	....	....	0	....	....	....	....	....	....	....	....	....	....	....	....	....	....	....	....	....	....
1998-99	**Los Angeles Kings**	**NHL**	**78**	**2**	**5**	**7**	**2**	**5**	**7**	**36**	**0**	**1**	**0**	**61**	**3.3**	**49**	**1**	**78**	**20**	**–10**	....	....	....	....	....	....	....	....
99-2000	**Los Angeles Kings**	**NHL**	**82**	**1**	**13**	**14**	**1**	**12**	**13**	**66**	**0**	**0**	**0**	**62**	**1.6**	**75**	**0**	**84**	**31**	**22**	**4**	**0**	**0**	**0**	**6**	**0**	**0**	**0**
	Sweden	WC-A	6	0	1	1	....	....	....	8	....	....	....	....	....	....	....	....	....	....	....	....	....	....	....	....	....	....
	NHL Totals		**367**	**7**	**58**	**65**	**7**	**56**	**63**	**324**	**0**	**1**	**0**	**331**	**2.1**	**313**	**31**	**347**	**86**		**11**	**0**	**0**	**0**	**8**	**0**	**0**	**0**

Played in NHL All-Star Game (1999)

Traded to **LA Kings** by **NY Rangers** with Ray Ferraro, Ian Laperriere, Nathan Lafayette and NY Rangers' 4th round choice (Sean Blanchard) in 1997 Entry Draft for Marty McSorley, Jari Kurri and Shane Churla, March 14, 1996.

• NORTON, Jeff

Jeffrey Thomas D – L. 6′2″, 200 lbs. b: Acton, MA, 11/25/1965. NY Islanders' 3rd, 62nd overall, in 1984.

Season	Club	League	GP	G	A	Pts	AG	AA	APts	PIM	PP	SH	GW	S	%	TGF	PGF	TGA	PGA	+/-	GP	G	A	Pts	PIM	PP	SH	GW
1983-84	Cushing Academy Penguins	Hi-School	21	22	33	55	....	....	....	....	....	....	....	....	....	....	....	....	....	....	....	....	....	....	....	....	....	....
1984-85	University of Michigan	CCHA	37	8	16	24	....	....	....	103	....	....	....	....	....	....	....	....	....	....	....	....	....	....	....	....	....	....
1985-86	University of Michigan	CCHA	37	15	30	45	....	....	....	99	....	....	....	....	....	....	....	....	....	....	....	....	....	....	....	....	....	....
1986-87	University of Michigan	CCHA	39	12	36	48	....	....	....	92	....	....	....	....	....	....	....	....	....	....	....	....	....	....	....	....	....	....
1987-88	United States	Nat-Team	54	7	22	29	....	....	....	52	....	....	....	....	....	....	....	....	....	....	....	....	....	....	....	....	....	....
	United States	Olympics	6	0	4	4	....	....	....	4	....	....	....	....	....	....	....	....	....	....	....	....	....	....	....	....	....	....
	New York Islanders	**NHL**	**15**	**1**	**6**	**7**	**1**	**4**	**5**	**14**	**1**	**0**	**1**	**18**	**5.6**	**24**	**8**	**22**	**9**	**3**	**3**	**0**	**2**	**2**	**13**	**0**	**0**	**0**
1988-89	**New York Islanders**	**NHL**	**69**	**1**	**30**	**31**	**1**	**21**	**22**	**74**	**1**	**0**	**0**	**126**	**0.8**	**87**	**36**	**104**	**29**	**–24**	....	....	....	....	....	....	....	....
	United States	WEC-A	6	1	0	1	....	....	....	4	....	....	....	....	....	....	....	....	....	....	....	....	....	....	....	....	....	....
1989-90	**New York Islanders**	**NHL**	**60**	**4**	**49**	**53**	**3**	**35**	**38**	**65**	**4**	**0**	**0**	**104**	**3.8**	**108**	**56**	**73**	**12**	**–9**	**4**	**1**	**3**	**4**	**17**	**0**	**0**	**0**
	United States	WEC-A	10	4	1	5	....	....	....	14	....	....	....	....	....	....	....	....	....	....	....	....	....	....	....	....	....	....
1990-91	**New York Islanders**	**NHL**	**44**	**3**	**25**	**28**	**3**	**19**	**22**	**16**	**2**	**1**	**0**	**87**	**3.4**	**64**	**31**	**53**	**7**	**–13**	....	....	....	....	....	....	....	....
1991-92	**New York Islanders**	**NHL**	**28**	**1**	**18**	**19**	**1**	**14**	**15**	**18**	**0**	**1**	**0**	**34**	**2.9**	**51**	**20**	**45**	**16**	**2**	....	....	....	....	....	....	....	....
1992-93	**New York Islanders**	**NHL**	**66**	**12**	**38**	**50**	**10**	**26**	**36**	**45**	**5**	**0**	**0**	**127**	**9.4**	**124**	**55**	**95**	**23**	**–3**	**10**	**1**	**1**	**2**	**4**	**0**	**0**	**0**
1993-94	**San Jose Sharks**	**NHL**	**64**	**7**	**33**	**40**	**6**	**26**	**32**	**36**	**1**	**0**	**0**	**92**	**7.6**	**85**	**20**	**59**	**10**	**16**	**14**	**1**	**5**	**6**	**20**	**0**	**0**	**0**
1994-95	**San Jose Sharks**	**NHL**	**20**	**1**	**9**	**10**	**2**	**13**	**15**	**39**	**0**	**0**	**0**	**21**	**4.8**	**17**	**2**	**16**	**2**	**1**	....	....	....	....	....	....	....	....
	St. Louis Blues	**NHL**	**28**	**2**	**18**	**20**	**4**	**27**	**31**	**33**	**0**	**0**	**1**	**27**	**7.4**	**50**	**10**	**28**	**9**	**21**	**7**	**1**	**1**	**2**	**11**	**0**	**0**	**0**
1995-96	**St. Louis Blues**	**NHL**	**36**	**4**	**7**	**11**	**4**	**6**	**10**	**26**	**0**	**0**	**1**	**33**	**12.1**	**44**	**16**	**33**	**9**	**4**	....	....	....	....	....	....	....	....
	Edmonton Oilers	**NHL**	**30**	**4**	**16**	**20**	**4**	**13**	**17**	**16**	**1**	**0**	**1**	**52**	**7.7**	**57**	**21**	**47**	**16**	**5**	....	....	....	....	....	....	....	....
1996-97	**Edmonton Oilers**	**NHL**	**62**	**2**	**11**	**13**	**2**	**10**	**12**	**42**	**0**	**0**	**0**	**68**	**2.9**	**57**	**14**	**62**	**12**	**–7**	....	....	....	....	....	....	....	....
	Tampa Bay Lightning	**NHL**	**13**	**0**	**5**	**5**	**0**	**4**	**4**	**16**	**0**	**0**	**0**	**13**	**0.0**	**15**	**6**	**12**	**3**	**0**	....	....	....	....	....	....	....	....
1997-98	**Tampa Bay Lightning**	**NHL**	**37**	**4**	**6**	**10**	**5**	**6**	**11**	**26**	**4**	**0**	**0**	**41**	**9.8**	**22**	**9**	**48**	**10**	**–25**	....	....	....	....	....	....	....	....
	Florida Panthers	**NHL**	**19**	**0**	**7**	**7**	**0**	**7**	**7**	**18**	**0**	**0**	**0**	**20**	**0.0**	**12**	**6**	**18**	**5**	**–7**	....	....	....	....	....	....	....	....
1998-99	**Florida Panthers**	**NHL**	**3**	**0**	**0**	**0**	**0**	**0**	**0**	**2**	**0**	**0**	**0**	**2**	**0.0**	**1**	**0**	**1**	**0**	**0**	....	....	....	....	....	....	....	....
	San Jose Sharks	**NHL**	**69**	**4**	**18**	**22**	**5**	**17**	**22**	**42**	**2**	**0**	**1**	**68**	**5.9**	**64**	**28**	**43**	**9**	**2**	**6**	**0**	**7**	**7**	**10**	**0**	**0**	**0**
99-2000	**San Jose Sharks**	**NHL**	**62**	**0**	**20**	**20**	**0**	**19**	**19**	**49**	**0**	**0**	**0**	**45**	**0.0**	**47**	**9**	**52**	**12**	**–2**	**12**	**0**	**1**	**1**	**7**	**0**	**0**	**0**
	NHL Totals		**725**	**50**	**316**	**366**	**51**	**267**	**318**	**577**	**21**	**2**	**5**	**978**	**5.1**	**929**	**347**	**811**	**193**		**56**	**4**	**20**	**24**	**82**	**0**	**0**	**0**

CCHA Second All-Star Team (1987)

• Missed remainder of 1991-92 season recovering from wrist injury suffered in game vs. Buffalo, January 3, 1992. Traded to **San Jose** by **NY Islanders** for San Jose's 3rd round choice (Jason Strudwick) in 1994 Entry Draft, June 20, 1993. Traded to **St. Louis** by **San Jose** with San Jose's 3rd round choice (later traded to Colorado — Colorado selected Rick Berry) in 1997 Entry Draft for Craig Janney and cash, March 6, 1995. Traded to **Edmonton** by **St. Louis** with Donald Dufresne for Igor Kravchuk and Ken Sutton, January 4, 1996. Traded to **Tampa Bay** by **Edmonton** for Drew Bannister and Tampa Bay's 6th round choice (Peter Sarno) in 1997 Entry Draft, March 18, 1997. Traded to **Florida** by **Tampa Bay** with Dino Ciccarelli for Mark Fitzpatrick and Jody Hull, January 15, 1998. Traded to **San Jose** by **Florida** for Alex Hicks and San Jose's 5th round choice (later traded to NY Islanders, NY Islanders selected Adam Johnson) in 1999 Entry Draft, November 11, 1998.

• NORWICH, Craig

Craig Richard D – L. 5′11″, 175 lbs. b: Edina, MN, 12/15/1955. Montreal's 11th, 142nd overall, in 1975.

Season	Club	League	GP	G	A	Pts	AG	AA	APts	PIM	PP	SH	GW	S	%	TGF	PGF	TGA	PGA	+/-	GP	G	A	Pts	PIM	PP	SH	GW
1973-74	Edina Hornets	Hi-School	STATISTICS NOT AVAILABLE																									
1974-75	University of Wisconsin	WCHA	38	11	34	45	....	....	....	24	....	....	....	....	....	....	....	....	....	....	....	....	....	....	....	....	....	....
1975-76	University of Wisconsin	WCHA	32	13	27	40	....	....	....	66	....	....	....	....	....	....	....	....	....	....	....	....	....	....	....	....	....	....
1976-77	University of Wisconsin	WCHA	44	18	65	83	....	....	....	70	....	....	....	....	....	....	....	....	....	....	....	....	....	....	....	....	....	....
1977-78	Cincinnati Stingers	WHA	65	7	23	30	....	....	....	48	....	....	....	....	....	....	....	....	....	....	....	....	....	....	....	....	....	....
	United States	WEC-A	10	1	2	3	....	....	....	2	....	....	....	....	....	....	....	....	....	....	....	....	....	....	....	....	....	....
1978-79	Cincinnati Stingers	WHA	80	6	51	57	....	....	....	73	....	....	....	....	....	....	....	....	....	....	3	0	1	1	4	....	....	....
1979-80	**Winnipeg Jets**	**NHL**	**70**	**10**	**35**	**45**	**8**	**26**	**34**	**36**	**7**	**0**	**0**	**217**	**4.6**	**106**	**44**	**80**	**7**	**–11**	....	....	....	....	....	....	....	....

Season	Club	League	REGULAR SEASON																		PLAYOFFS							
			GP	G	A	Pts	AG	AA	APts	PIM	PP	SH	GW	S	%	TGF	PGF	TGA	PGA	+/–	GP	G	A	Pts	PIM	PP	SH	GW
1980-81	**St. Louis Blues**	**NHL**	**23**	**4**	**12**	**16**	**3**	**8**	**11**	**14**	**3**	**0**	**1**	**64**	**6.3**	**38**	**14**	**24**	**1**	**1**								
	Colorado Rockies	**NHL**	**11**	**3**	**11**	**14**	**2**	**7**	**9**	**10**	**1**	**0**	**0**	**23**	**13.0**	**26**	**9**	**16**	**3**	**4**								
	Fort Worth Texans	CHL	8	0	4	4				6																		
	United States	WEC-A	8	1	0	1				0																		
1981-82	Springfield Indians	AHL	28	5	9	14				26																		
1982-83	HC Gardena-Groden	Italy	31	35	62	97				64																		
1983-84	HC Lausanne	Switz-2	STATISTICS NOT AVAILABLE																									
1984-85	HC Gardena-Groden	Italy	1	2	2	4				2																		
	Adirondack Red Wings	AHL	16	4	7	11				16																		
1985-86	HC Fassa	Italy	31	14	63	77				28											3	0	11	11	4			
1986-87	HC Fassa	Italy	37	14	55	69				82																		
	NHL Totals		**104**	**17**	**58**	**75**	**13**	**41**	**54**	**60**	**11**	**0**	**1**	**304**	**5.6**	**170**	**67**	**120**	**11**									
	Other Major League Totals		145	13	74	87				121											3	0	1	1	4			

WCHA Second All-Star Team (1976) • NCAA West First All-American Team (1976, 1977) • WCHA First All-Star Team (1977) • NCAA Championship All-Tournament Team (1977) • WEC-B All-Star Team (1983)

Selected by **Houston** (WHA) in 1974 WHA Amateur Draft, May, 1974. WHA rights traded to **Cincinnati** (WHA) by **Houston** (WHA) with the rights to Dave Taylor for John Hughes, May, 1977. Claimed by **Winnipeg** from **Cincinnati** (WHA) in WHA Dispersal Draft, June 9, 1979. Traded to **St. Louis** by **Winnipeg** for Rick Bowness, June 19, 1980. Claimed on waivers by **Colorado** from **St. Louis**, February 2, 1981. Signed as a free agent by **NY Rangers**, December, 1981.

• NORWOOD, Lee

Lee Charles D – L. 6'1", 198 lbs. b: Oakland, CA, 2/2/1960. Quebec's 3rd, 62nd overall, in 1979.

Season	Club	League	GP	G	A	Pts	AG	AA	APts	PIM	PP	SH	GW	S	%	TGF	PGF	TGA	PGA	+/–	GP	G	A	Pts	PIM	PP	SH	GW
1977-78	Hull Olympiques	QMJHL	51	3	17	20				83																		
1978-79	Oshawa Generals	OMJHL	61	23	38	61				171											5	2	2	4	17			
1979-80	Oshawa Generals	OMJHL	60	13	39	52				143											6	2	7	9	15			
1980-81	**Quebec Nordiques**	**NHL**	**11**	**1**	**1**	**2**	**1**	**1**	**2**	**9**	**0**	**0**	**0**	**8**	**12.5**	**6**	**2**	**7**	**0**	**–3**	**3**	**0**	**0**	**0**	**2**	**0**	**0**	**0**
	Hershey Bears	AHL	52	11	32	43				78											8	0	4	4	14			
1981-82	**Quebec Nordiques**	**NHL**	**2**	**0**	**0**	**0**	**0**	**0**	**0**	**2**	**0**	**0**	**0**	**1**	**0.0**	**1**	**0**	**0**	**0**	**1**								
	Fredericton Express	AHL	29	6	13	19				74																		
	Washington Capitals	**NHL**	**26**	**7**	**10**	**17**	**6**	**7**	**13**	**125**	**3**	**0**	**1**	**33**	**21.2**	**41**	**16**	**22**	**4**	**7**								
1982-83	**Washington Capitals**	**NHL**	**8**	**0**	**1**	**1**	**0**	**1**	**1**	**14**	**0**	**0**	**0**	**6**	**0.0**	**3**	**1**	**8**	**3**	**–3**								
	Hershey Bears	AHL	67	12	36	48				90											5	0	1	1	2			
1983-84	St. Catharines Saints	AHL	75	13	46	59				91											7	0	5	5	31			
1984-85	Peoria Rivermen	IHL	80	17	60	77				229											18	1	11	12	62			
1985-86	**St. Louis Blues**	**NHL**	**71**	**5**	**24**	**29**	**4**	**16**	**20**	**134**	**2**	**0**	**1**	**111**	**4.5**	**91**	**28**	**81**	**25**	**7**	**19**	**2**	**7**	**9**	**64**	**0**	**0**	**0**
1986-87	**Detroit Red Wings**	**NHL**	**57**	**6**	**21**	**27**	**5**	**15**	**20**	**163**	**4**	**0**	**2**	**101**	**5.9**	**74**	**28**	**95**	**26**	**–23**	**16**	**1**	**6**	**7**	**31**	**0**	**0**	**1**
	Adirondack Red Wings	AHL	3	0	3	3				0																		
1987-88	**Detroit Red Wings**	**NHL**	**51**	**9**	**22**	**31**	**8**	**16**	**24**	**131**	**3**	**0**	**2**	**106**	**8.5**	**80**	**21**	**74**	**19**	**4**	**16**	**2**	**6**	**8**	**40**	**2**	**0**	**0**
1988-89	**Detroit Red Wings**	**NHL**	**66**	**10**	**32**	**42**	**8**	**23**	**31**	**100**	**4**	**1**	**0**	**97**	**10.3**	**109**	**31**	**103**	**31**	**6**	**6**	**1**	**2**	**3**	**16**	**1**	**0**	**0**
1989-90	**Detroit Red Wings**	**NHL**	**64**	**8**	**14**	**22**	**7**	**10**	**17**	**95**	**1**	**0**	**1**	**60**	**13.3**	**76**	**5**	**97**	**40**	**14**								
1990-91	**Detroit Red Wings**	**NHL**	**21**	**3**	**7**	**10**	**3**	**5**	**8**	**50**	**1**	**0**	**0**	**36**	**8.3**	**23**	**4**	**20**	**7**	**6**								
	New Jersey Devils	**NHL**	**28**	**3**	**2**	**5**	**3**	**2**	**5**	**87**	**1**	**0**	**0**	**27**	**11.1**	**25**	**3**	**32**	**9**	**–1**	**4**	**0**	**0**	**0**	**18**	**0**	**0**	**0**
1991-92	**Hartford Whalers**	**NHL**	**6**	**0**	**0**	**0**	**0**	**0**	**0**	**16**	**0**	**0**	**0**	**1**	**0.0**	**2**	**0**	**3**	**1**	**0**								
	St. Louis Blues	**NHL**	**44**	**3**	**11**	**14**	**3**	**8**	**11**	**94**	**1**	**0**	**1**	**51**	**5.9**	**47**	**8**	**35**	**10**	**14**	**1**	**0**	**1**	**1**	**0**	**0**	**0**	**0**
1992-93	**St. Louis Blues**	**NHL**	**32**	**3**	**7**	**10**	**2**	**5**	**7**	**63**	**2**	**0**	**0**	**36**	**8.3**	**36**	**16**	**36**	**11**	**–5**								
1993-94	**Calgary Flames**	**NHL**	**16**	**0**	**1**	**1**	**0**	**1**	**1**	**16**	**0**	**0**	**0**	**10**	**0.0**	**10**	**1**	**10**	**4**	**3**								
	San Diego Gulls	IHL	4	0	0	0				0											8	0	1	1	11			
1994-95			OUT OF HOCKEY – RETIRED																									
1995-96	Chicago Wolves	IHL	21	2	6	8				26																		
	Detroit Vipers	IHL	27	3	11	14				26											5	0	3	3	6			
1996-97	Saginaw Lumber Kings	ColHL	12	3	3	6				8																		
	San Antonio Dragons	IHL	12	0	6	6				10											3	0	0	0	2			
	NHL Totals		**503**	**58**	**153**	**211**	**50**	**110**	**160**	**1099**	**22**	**1**	**8**	**684**	**8.5**	**624**	**164**	**623**	**190**		**65**	**6**	**22**	**28**	**171**	**3**	**0**	**1**

IHL First All-Star Team (1985) • Won Governors' Trophy (Top Defenseman - IHL) (1985)

Traded to **Washington** by **Quebec** with Quebec's 6th round choice (Mats Kilstrom) in 1982 Entry Draft for Tim Tookey and Washington's 7th round choice (Daniel Poudrier) in 1982 Entry Draft, February 1, 1982. Traded to **Toronto** by **Washington** for Dave Shand, October 6, 1983. Signed as a free agent by **St. Louis**, August 13, 1985. Traded to **Detroit** by **St. Louis** for Larry Trader, August 7, 1986. Traded to **New Jersey** by **Detroit** with Detroit's 4th round choice (Scott McCabe) in 1992 Entry Draft for Paul Ysebaert, November 27, 1990. Traded to **Hartford** by **New Jersey** for Hartford's 5th round choice (John Guirestante) in 1993 Entry Draft, October 3, 1991. Traded to **St. Louis** by **Hartford** for St. Louis' 5th round choice (Nolan Pratt) in 1993 Entry Draft, November 13, 1991. • Missed remainder of 1992-93 and majority of 1993-94 seasons recovering from ankle injury suffered in game vs. Detroit, January 21, 1993. Signed as a free agent by **Calgary**, October 22, 1993.

• NOVOSELTSEV, Ivan

LW – L. 6'1", 183 lbs. b: Golitsino, USSR, 1/23/1979. Florida's 5th, 95th overall, in 1997.

Season	Club	League	GP	G	A	Pts	AG	AA	APts	PIM	PP	SH	GW	S	%	TGF	PGF	TGA	PGA	+/–	GP	G	A	Pts	PIM	PP	SH	GW
1995-96	Krylja Sovetov Moscow	CIS-Jr.	STATISTICS NOT AVAILABLE																									
	Krylja Sovetov Moscow	CIS	1	0	0	0				2																		
1996-97	Krylja Sovetov Moscow	Russia	30	0	3	3				18											2	0	0	0	4			
	Krylja Sovetov Moscow-2	Russia-3	19	5	3	8				39																		
1997-98	Sarnia Sting	OHL	53	26	22	48				41											5	1	1	2	8			
1998-99	Sarnia Sting	OHL	68	57	39	96				45											5	2	4	6	6			
99-2000	**Florida Panthers**	**NHL**	**14**	**2**	**1**	**3**	**2**	**1**	**3**	**8**	**2**	**0**	**0**	**8**	**25.0**	**4**	**3**	**4**	**0**	**–3**								
	Louisville Panthers	AHL	47	14	21	35				22											4	1	0	1	6			
	NHL Totals		**14**	**2**	**1**	**3**	**2**	**1**	**3**	**8**	**2**	**0**	**0**	**8**	**25.0**	**4**	**3**	**4**	**0**									

OHL First All-Star Team (1999)

• NOVY, Milan

C – L. 5'10", 196 lbs. b: Kladno, Czech., 9/23/1951. Washington's 2nd, 58th overall, in 1982.

Season	Club	League	GP	G	A	Pts	AG	AA	APts	PIM	PP	SH	GW	S	%	TGF	PGF	TGA	PGA	+/–	GP	G	A	Pts	PIM	PP	SH	GW
1963-1968	SONP Kladno	Czech-Jr.	STATISTICS NOT AVAILABLE																									
1968-71	SONP Kladno	Czech.	STATISTICS NOT AVAILABLE																									
1971-72	SONP Kladno	Czech.	36	19	14	33																						
1972-73	Dukla Jihlava	Czech.	40	*39	17	56				18																		
1973-74	Dukla Jihlava	Czech.	44	34	23	57				18																		
1974-75	Poldi Kladno	Czech.	40	*46	22	68				38																		
	Czechoslovakia	WEC-A	10	4	4	8				4																		
1975-76	Poldi Kladno	Czech.	32	*32	25	*57				14																		
	Czechoslovakia	Olympics	5	5	0	5				0																		
	Czechoslovakia	WEC-A	10	9	6	15				4																		
1976-77	Czechoslovakia	Can-Cup	7	5	3	8				2																		
	Poldi Kladno	Czech.	44	*59	31	*90																						
	Czechoslovakia	WEC-A	10	7	9	16				2																		
1977-78	Poldi Kladno	Czech.	44	40	35	*75				64																		
	Czechoslovakia	WEC-A	9	4	1	5				2																		
1978-79	Poldi Kladno	Czech.	22	24	15	39				4											22	9	8	17				
	Czechoslovakia	WEC-A	5	0	2	2				4																		
1979-80	Poldi Kladno	Czech.	44	36	30	66				20																		
	Czechoslovakia	Olympics	6	7	8	*15				0																		
1980-81	Poldi Kladno	Czech.	16	19	*42	*61				12											28	13	6	19				
	Czechoslovakia	WEC-A	8	6	2	8				2																		
1981-82	Czechoslovakia	Can-Cup	6	1	2	3				7																		
	Poldi Kladno	Czech.	44	29	*38	*67				40																		
	Czechoslovakia	WEC-A	10	3	1	4				6																		
1982-83	**Washington Capitals**	**NHL**	**73**	**18**	**30**	**48**	**15**	**21**	**36**	**16**	**3**	**0**	**3**	**131**	**13.7**	**62**	**16**	**45**	**0**	**1**	**2**	**0**	**0**	**0**	**0**	**0**	**0**	**0**
1983-84	Czechoslovakia	Nat-Team	35	19	8	27				25																		
	ZSC Zurich	Switz.	38	31	23	54																						

			REGULAR SEASON																		PLAYOFFS							
Season	Club	League	GP	G	A	Pts	AG	AA	APts	PIM	PP	SH	GW	S	%	TGF	PGF	TGA	PGA	+/–	GP	G	A	Pts	PIM	PP	SH	GW
1984-85	ZSC Zurich	Switz-2	40	40	44	84	....	....	....	....	....	....	....	....	....	....	....	....	....	....	....	....	....	....	....	....	....	....
1985-86	WEV Wien	Austria	40	31	50	81	....	....	....	16	....	....	....	....	....	....	....	....	....	....	....	....	....	....	....	....	....	....
1986-87	Poldi Kladno	Czech-2	STATISTICS NOT AVAILABLE																									
1987-88	Poldi Kladno	Czech.	47	24	29	53	....	....	....	10	....	....	....	....	....	....	....	....	....	....	....	....	....	....	....	....	....	....
1988-89	Poldi Kladno	Czech.	40	15	19	34	....	....	....	2	....	....	....	....	....	....	....	....	....	....	....	....	....	....	....	....	....	....
	NHL Totals		**73**	**18**	**30**	**48**	**15**	**21**	**36**	**16**	**3**	**0**	**3**	**131**	**13.7**	**62**	**16**	**45**	**0**		**2**	**0**	**0**	**0**	**0**	**0**	**0**	**0**

WEC-A All-Star Team (1976) • Canada Cup All-Star Team (1976) • Czechoslovakian Player of the Year (1977, 1981, 1982)

• NOWAK, Hank

Henry Stanley LW – L. 6'1", 195 lbs. b: Oshawa, Ont., 11/24/1950. Philadelphia's 6th, 87th overall, in 1970.

Season	Club	League	GP	G	A	Pts	AG	AA	APts	PIM	PP	SH	GW	S	%	TGF	PGF	TGA	PGA	+/–	GP	G	A	Pts	PIM	PP	SH	GW
1968-69	Oshawa Generals	OHA-Jr.	26	2	3	5	....	....	....	37	....	....	....	....	....	....	....	....	....	....	....	....	....	....	....	....	....	....
1969-70	Oshawa Generals	OHA-Jr.	53	17	22	39	....	....	....	37	....	....	....	....	....	....	....	....	....	....	6	1	2	3	6	....	....	....
1970-71	Quebec Aces	AHL	49	2	7	9	....	....	....	26	....	....	....	....	....	....	....	....	....	....	1	0	0	0	0	....	....	....
1971-72	Richmond Robins	AHL	62	2	3	5	....	....	....	8	....	....	....	....	....	....	....	....	....	....	....	....	....	....	....	....	....	....
1972-73	Hershey Bears	AHL	66	25	22	47	....	....	....	77	....	....	....	....	....	....	....	....	....	....	7	1	2	3	8	....	....	....
1973-74	**Pittsburgh Penguins**	**NHL**	**13**	**0**	**0**	**0**	**0**	**0**	**0**	**11**	**0**	**0**	**0**	**26**	**0.0**	**1**	**0**	**15**	**0**	**–14**	....	....	....	....	....	....	....	....
	Hershey Bears	AHL	56	32	37	69	....	....	....	90	....	....	....	....	....	....	....	....	....	....	14	3	12	15	14	....	....	....
1974-75	**Detroit Red Wings**	**NHL**	**56**	**8**	**14**	**22**	**7**	**10**	**17**	**69**	**1**	**0**	**0**	**110**	**7.3**	**27**	**2**	**69**	**10**	**–34**	....	....	....	....	....	....	....	....
	Boston Bruins	**NHL**	**21**	**4**	**7**	**11**	**3**	**5**	**8**	**26**	**0**	**0**	**1**	**38**	**10.5**	**13**	**0**	**10**	**5**	**8**	**3**	**1**	**0**	**1**	**0**	**0**	**0**	**0**
1975-76	**Boston Bruins**	**NHL**	**66**	**7**	**3**	**10**	**6**	**2**	**8**	**41**	**0**	**0**	**1**	**60**	**11.7**	**24**	**1**	**26**	**2**	**–1**	**10**	**0**	**0**	**0**	**8**	**0**	**0**	**0**
1976-77	**Boston Bruins**	**NHL**	**24**	**7**	**5**	**12**	**6**	**4**	**10**	**14**	**0**	**0**	**1**	**36**	**19.4**	**19**	**1**	**14**	**0**	**4**	....	....	....	....	....	....	....	....
	Rochester Americans	AHL	35	12	17	29	....	....	....	26	....	....	....	....	....	....	....	....	....	....	....	....	....	....	....	....	....	....
1977-78	Binghamton Dusters	AHL	77	20	24	44	....	....	....	50	....	....	....	....	....	....	....	....	....	....	....	....	....	....	....	....	....	....
1978-79	Philadelphia Firebirds	AHL	32	7	12	19	....	....	....	16	....	....	....	....	....	....	....	....	....	....	....	....	....	....	....	....	....	....
	Cape Cod Freedoms	NEHL	1	0	0	0	....	....	....	0	....	....	....	....	....	....	....	....	....	....	....	....	....	....	....	....	....	....
	Utica Mohawks	NEHL	43	27	43	70	....	....	....	49	....	....	....	....	....	....	....	....	....	....	....	....	....	....	....	....	....	....
1979-80	Saginaw Gears	IHL	12	6	3	9	....	....	....	44	....	....	....	....	....	....	....	....	....	....	....	....	....	....	....	....	....	....
	Toledo Goaldiggers	IHL	65	14	22	36	....	....	....	59	....	....	....	....	....	....	....	....	....	....	4	0	0	0	2	....	....	....
	NHL Totals		**180**	**26**	**29**	**55**	**22**	**21**	**43**	**161**	**1**	**0**	**3**	**270**	**9.6**	**84**	**4**	**134**	**17**		**13**	**1**	**0**	**1**	**8**	**0**	**0**	**0**

Claimed by **Hershey** (AHL) from **Philadelphia** in Reverse Draft, June 8, 1972. Traded to **Pittsburgh** by **Hershey** (AHL) for cash, May 22, 1973. Traded to **Detroit** by **Pittsburgh** with Pittsburgh's 3rd round choice (Dan Mandryk) in 1974 Amateur Draft for Nelson Debenedet, May 27, 1974. Traded to **Boston** by **Detroit** with Earl Anderson for Walt McKechnie and Boston's 3rd round choice (Clarke Hamilton) in 1975 Amateur Draft, February 18, 1975.

• NUMMINEN, Teppo

Teppo Kalevi D – R. 6'1", 195 lbs. b: Tampere, Finland, 7/3/1968. Winnipeg's 2nd, 29th overall, in 1986.

Season	Club	League	GP	G	A	Pts	AG	AA	APts	PIM	PP	SH	GW	S	%	TGF	PGF	TGA	PGA	+/–	GP	G	A	Pts	PIM	PP	SH	GW
1984-85	Tappara Tampere	Finland-Jr.	30	14	17	31	....	....	....	10	....	....	....	....	....	....	....	....	....	....	....	....	....	....	....	....	....	....
	Whitby Lawmen	OJHL	16	3	9	12	....	....	....	0	....	....	....	....	....	....	....	....	....	....	....	....	....	....	....	....	....	....
1985-86	Tappara Tampere	Finland-Jr.	2	0	0	0	....	....	....	0	....	....	....	....	....	....	....	....	....	....	3	0	1	1	2	....	....	....
	Tappara Tampere	Finland	31	2	4	6	....	....	....	6	....	....	....	....	....	....	....	....	....	....	8	0	0	0	0	....	....	....
	Finland	EJC-A	5	3	2	5	....	....	....	4	....	....	....	....	....	....	....	....	....	....	....	....	....	....	....	....	....	....
1986-87	Tappara Tampere	Finland	44	9	9	18	....	....	....	16	....	....	....	....	....	....	....	....	....	....	9	4	1	5	4	....	....	....
	Finland	WEC-A	10	5	0	5	....	....	....	4	....	....	....	....	....	....	....	....	....	....	....	....	....	....	....	....	....	....
1987-88	Finland	Can-Cup	4	1	0	1	....	....	....	2	....	....	....	....	....	....	....	....	....	....	....	....	....	....	....	....	....	....
	Tappara Tampere	Finland	40	10	10	20	....	....	....	29	....	....	....	....	....	....	....	....	....	....	10	6	6	12	6	....	....	....
	Finland	WJC-A	7	5	2	7	....	....	....	4	....	....	....	....	....	....	....	....	....	....	....	....	....	....	....	....	....	....
	Finland	Olympics	6	1	4	5	....	....	....	0	....	....	....	....	....	....	....	....	....	....	....	....	....	....	....	....	....	....
1988-89	**Winnipeg Jets**	**NHL**	**69**	**1**	**14**	**15**	**1**	**10**	**11**	**36**	**0**	**1**	**0**	**85**	**1.2**	**65**	**13**	**73**	**10**	**–11**	....	....	....	....	....	....	....	....
1989-90	**Winnipeg Jets**	**NHL**	**79**	**11**	**32**	**43**	**9**	**23**	**32**	**20**	**1**	**0**	**1**	**105**	**10.5**	**88**	**22**	**92**	**22**	**–4**	**7**	**1**	**2**	**3**	**10**	**0**	**0**	**0**
1990-91	**Winnipeg Jets**	**NHL**	**80**	**8**	**25**	**33**	**7**	**19**	**26**	**28**	**3**	**0**	**0**	**151**	**5.3**	**88**	**31**	**99**	**27**	**–15**	....	....	....	....	....	....	....	....
	Finland	WEC-A	10	1	3	4	....	....	....	10	....	....	....	....	....	....	....	....	....	....	....	....	....	....	....	....	....	....
1991-92	Finland	Can-Cup	6	1	1	2	....	....	....	2	....	....	....	....	....	....	....	....	....	....	....	....	....	....	....	....	....	....
	Winnipeg Jets	**NHL**	**80**	**5**	**34**	**39**	**5**	**26**	**31**	**32**	**4**	**0**	**1**	**143**	**3.5**	**106**	**38**	**85**	**32**	**15**	**7**	**0**	**0**	**0**	**0**	**0**	**0**	**0**
1992-93	**Winnipeg Jets**	**NHL**	**66**	**7**	**30**	**37**	**6**	**21**	**27**	**33**	**3**	**1**	**0**	**103**	**6.8**	**92**	**26**	**96**	**34**	**4**	**6**	**1**	**1**	**2**	**2**	**1**	**0**	**0**
1993-94	**Winnipeg Jets**	**NHL**	**57**	**5**	**18**	**23**	**5**	**14**	**19**	**28**	**4**	**0**	**1**	**89**	**5.6**	**68**	**24**	**108**	**41**	**–23**	....	....	....	....	....	....	....	....
1994-95	TuTo Turku	Finland	12	3	8	11	....	....	....	4	....	....	....	....	....	....	....	....	....	....	....	....	....	....	....	....	....	....
	Winnipeg Jets	**NHL**	**42**	**5**	**16**	**21**	**9**	**24**	**33**	**16**	**2**	**0**	**0**	**86**	**5.8**	**68**	**17**	**60**	**21**	**12**	....	....	....	....	....	....	....	....
1995-96	**Winnipeg Jets**	**NHL**	**74**	**11**	**43**	**54**	**11**	**35**	**46**	**22**	**6**	**0**	**3**	**165**	**6.7**	**115**	**53**	**109**	**43**	**–4**	**6**	**0**	**0**	**0**	**2**	**0**	**0**	**0**
	Finland	WC-A	1	0	1	1	....	....	....	0	....	....	....	....	....	....	....	....	....	....	....	....	....	....	....	....	....	....
1996-97	Finland	W-Cup	2	0	0	0	....	....	....	0	....	....	....	....	....	....	....	....	....	....	....	....	....	....	....	....	....	....
	Phoenix Coyotes	**NHL**	**82**	**2**	**25**	**27**	**2**	**22**	**24**	**28**	**0**	**0**	**0**	**135**	**1.5**	**93**	**20**	**102**	**26**	**–3**	**7**	**3**	**3**	**6**	**0**	**1**	**0**	**1**
	Finland	WC-A	5	2	2	4	....	....	....	6	....	....	....	....	....	....	....	....	....	....	....	....	....	....	....	....	....	....
1997-98	**Phoenix Coyotes**	**NHL**	**82**	**11**	**40**	**51**	**13**	**39**	**52**	**30**	**6**	**0**	**2**	**126**	**8.7**	**101**	**30**	**84**	**38**	**25**	**1**	**0**	**0**	**0**	**0**	**0**	**0**	**0**
	Finland	Olympics	6	1	1	2	....	....	....	2	....	....	....	....	....	....	....	....	....	....	....	....	....	....	....	....	....	....
1998-99	**Phoenix Coyotes**	**NHL**	**82**	**10**	**30**	**40**	**12**	**29**	**41**	**30**	**1**	**0**	**0**	**156**	**6.4**	**89**	**27**	**81**	**22**	**3**	**7**	**2**	**1**	**3**	**4**	**2**	**0**	**0**
99-2000	**Phoenix Coyotes**	**NHL**	**79**	**8**	**34**	**42**	**9**	**32**	**41**	**16**	**2**	**0**	**2**	**126**	**6.3**	**102**	**27**	**75**	**21**	**21**	**5**	**1**	**1**	**2**	**0**	**0**	**0**	**0**
	NHL Totals		**872**	**84**	**341**	**425**	**89**	**294**	**383**	**319**	**32**	**2**	**10**	**1470**	**5.7**	**1075**	**328**	**1064**	**337**		**46**	**8**	**8**	**16**	**18**	**4**	**0**	**1**

WJC-A All-Star Team (1988) • Named Best Defenseman at WJC-A (1988) • WC-A All-Star Team (1997) • Played in NHL All-Star Game (1999, 2000)

Transferred to **Phoenix** after **Winnipeg** franchise relocated, July 1, 1996.

• NURMINEN, Kai

Kai I. LW – L. 6'1", 198 lbs. b: Turku, Finland, 3/29/1969. Los Angeles' 9th, 193rd overall, in 1996.

Season	Club	League	GP	G	A	Pts	AG	AA	APts	PIM	PP	SH	GW	S	%	TGF	PGF	TGA	PGA	+/–	GP	G	A	Pts	PIM	PP	SH	GW
1986-87	TPS Turku	Finland-Jr.	2	0	1	1	....	....	....	0	....	....	....	....	....	....	....	....	....	....	....	....	....	....	....	....	....	....
1987-88	TPS Turku	Finland-Jr.	32	9	7	16	....	....	....	16	....	....	....	....	....	....	....	....	....	....	....	....	....	....	....	....	....	....
1988-89	TPS Turku	Finland-Jr.	22	13	10	23	....	....	....	14	....	....	....	....	....	....	....	....	....	....	....	....	....	....	....	....	....	....
1989-90	TPS Turku	Finalnd-Jr.	22	13	10	23	....	....	....	14	....	....	....	....	....	....	....	....	....	....	....	....	....	....	....	....	....	....
1990-91	TuTo Turku	Finland-2	33	26	20	46	....	....	....	14	....	....	....	....	....	....	....	....	....	....	....	....	....	....	....	....	....	....
1991-92	Kiekko-67	Finland-2	44	44	19	63	....	....	....	34	....	....	....	....	....	....	....	....	....	....	....	....	....	....	....	....	....	....
1992-93	Kiekko-67	Finland-2	8	6	4	10	....	....	....	2	....	....	....	....	....	....	....	....	....	....	....	....	....	....	....	....	....	....
	TPS Turku	Finland	31	4	6	10	....	....	....	13	....	....	....	....	....	....	....	....	....	....	7	1	2	3	0	....	....	....
1993-94	TPS Turku	Finland	45	23	12	35	....	....	....	20	....	....	....	....	....	....	....	....	....	....	11	0	3	3	4	....	....	....
1994-95	HPK Hameenlinna	Finland	49	*30	25	55	....	....	....	40	....	....	....	....	....	....	....	....	....	....	....	....	....	....	....	....	....	....
1995-96	HV-71 Jonkoping	Sweden	40	31	24	55	....	....	....	30	....	....	....	....	....	....	....	....	....	....	4	3	1	4	8	....	....	....
	Finland	WC-A	6	4	2	6	....	....	....	6	....	....	....	....	....	....	....	....	....	....	....	....	....	....	....	....	....	....
1996-97	Finland	W-Cup	2	0	1	1	....	....	....	0	....	....	....	....	....	....	....	....	....	....	....	....	....	....	....	....	....	....
	Los Angeles Kings	**NHL**	**67**	**16**	**11**	**27**	**17**	**10**	**27**	**22**	**4**	**0**	**1**	**112**	**14.3**	**50**	**13**	**41**	**1**	**–3**	....	....	....	....	....	....	....	....
	Finland	WC-A	6	3	0	3	....	....	....	0	....	....	....	....	....	....	....	....	....	....	....	....	....	....	....	....	....	....
1997-98	Vasteras IK	Sweden	23	9	7	16	....	....	....	24	....	....	....	....	....	....	....	....	....	....	....	....	....	....	....	....	....	....
	Jokerit Helsinki	Finland	20	7	9	16	....	....	....	30	....	....	....	....	....	....	....	....	....	....	8	5	3	8	4	....	....	....
1998-99	HC Davos	Switz.	42	26	14	40	....	....	....	26	....	....	....	....	....	....	....	....	....	....	....	....	....	....	....	....	....	....
99-2000	TPS Turku	Finland	54	*41	37	*78	....	....	....	40	....	....	....	....	....	....	....	....	....	....	10	5	*9	*14	0	....	....	....
	TPS Turku	EuroHL	5	4	2	6	....	....	....	4	....	....	....	....	....	....	....	....	....	....	5	2	5	7	4	....	....	....
	NHL Totals		**67**	**16**	**11**	**27**	**17**	**10**	**27**	**22**	**4**	**0**	**1**	**112**	**14.3**	**50**	**13**	**41**	**1**		....	....	....	....	....	....	....	....

Finnish First All-Star Team (1995)

Signed as a free agent by **Minnesota**, May 24, 2000.

• NYLANDER, Michael

C – L. 5'11", 195 lbs. b: Stockholm, Sweden, 10/3/1972. Hartford's 4th, 59th overall, in 1991.

Season	Club	League	GP	G	A	Pts	AG	AA	APts	PIM	PP	SH	GW	S	%	TGF	PGF	TGA	PGA	+/–	GP	G	A	Pts	PIM	PP	SH	GW
1987-88	RA-73	Sweden-3	3	0	0	0	....	....	....	0	....	....	....	....	....	....	....	....	....	....	....	....	....	....	....	....	....	....
1988-89	Huddinge IK	Sweden-Jr.	STATISTICS NOT AVAILABLE																									
1989-90	Huddinge IK	Sweden-2	31	7	15	22	....	....	....	4	....	....	....	....	....	....	....	....	....	....	5	3	0	3	0	....	....	....
	Sweden	EJC-A	6	2	4	6	....	....	....	0	....	....	....	....	....	....	....	....	....	....	....	....	....	....	....	....	....	....

			REGULAR SEASON																		PLAYOFFS							
Season	Club	League	GP	G	A	Pts	AG	AA	APts	PIM	PP	SH	GW	S	%	TGF	PGF	TGA	PGA	+/–	GP	G	A	Pts	PIM	PP	SH	GW
1990-91	Huddinge IK	Sweden-2	33	14	20	34				10											2	0	0	0	0			
	Sweden	WJC-A	7	6	5	11				8																		
1991-92	AIK Solna Stockholm	Sweden	40	11	17	28				30											3	1	4	5	4			
	Sweden	WJC-A	7	*8	*9	*17				6																		
	Sweden	WC-A	6	0	1	1				0																		
1992-93	Hartford Whalers	NHL	59	11	22	33	9	15	24	36	3	0	1	85	12.9	48	13	47	5	–7								
	Springfield Indians	AHL																			3	3	3	6	2			
	Sweden	WC-A	7	1	7	8				4																		
1993-94	Hartford Whalers	NHL	58	11	33	44	10	26	36	24	4	0	1	74	14.9	52	15	40	1	–2								
	Springfield Indians	AHL	4	0	9	9				0																		
	Calgary Flames	NHL	15	2	9	11	2	7	9	6	0	0	0	21	9.5	18	2	6	0	10	3	0	0	0	0	0	0	0
1994-95	JyP-HT Jyvaskyla	Finland	16	11	19	30				63																		
	Calgary Flames	NHL	6	0	1	1	0	1	1	2	0	0	0	2	0.0	5	1	3	0	1	6	0	6	6	2	0	0	0
1995-96	Calgary Flames	NHL	73	17	38	55	17	31	48	20	4	0	6	163	10.4	84	34	52	2	0	4	0	0	0	0	0	0	0
	Sweden	WC-A	3	2	3	5				0																		
1996-97	Sweden	W-Cup	4	2	1	3				0																		
	HC Lugano	Switz.	36	12	43	55				28											8	3	8	11	8			
	Sweden	WC-A	11	6	5	11				6																		
1997-98	Calgary Flames	NHL	65	13	23	36	15	23	38	24	0	0	2	117	11.1	55	13	32	0	10								
	Sweden	Olympics	4	0	0	0				6																		
1998-99	Calgary Flames	NHL	9	2	3	5	2	3	5	2	1	0	0	7	28.6	5	2	2	0	1								
	Tampa Bay Lightning	NHL	24	2	7	9	2	7	9	6	0	0	0	26	7.7	13	5	18	0	–10								
	Sweden	WC-A	10	2	4	6				8																		
99-2000	Tampa Bay Lightning	NHL	11	1	2	3	1	2	3	4	1	0	0	10	10.0	3	2	4	0	–3								
	Chicago Blackhawks	NHL	66	23	28	51	26	26	52	26	4	0	2	112	20.5	73	21	43	0	9								
	Sweden	WC-A	7	1	5	6				6																		
	NHL Totals		386	82	166	248	84	141	225	150	17	0	12	617	13.3	356	108	247	8		13	0	6	6	2	0	0	0

WJC-A All-Star Team (1992) • Named Best Forward at WJC-A (1992) • Swedish Rookie of the Year (1992) • Swedish World All-Star Team (1996, 1997) • WC-A All-Star Team (1997) • Named Best Forward at WC-A (1997)

Traded to **Calgary** by **Hartford** with James Patrick and Zarley Zalapski for Gary Suter, Paul Ranheim and Ted Drury, March 10, 1994. • Missed majority of 1994-95 season recovering from wrist injury suffered in game vs. Detroit, January 26, 1995. Traded to **Tampa Bay** by **Calgary** for Andrei Nazarov, January 19, 1999. Traded to **Chicago** by **Tampa Bay** for Bryan Muir and Reid Simpson, November 12, 1999.

• NYLUND, Gary

D – L. 6'4", 210 lbs. b: Surrey, B.C., 10/28/1963. Toronto's 1st, 3rd overall, in 1982.

Season	Club	League	GP	G	A	Pts	AG	AA	APts	PIM	PP	SH	GW	S	%	TGF	PGF	TGA	PGA	+/–	GP	G	A	Pts	PIM	PP	SH	GW
1978-79	Delta Sun	BCJHL	57	6	29	35				107																		
	Portland Winter Hawks	WHL	2	0	0	0				0																		
1979-80	Portland Winter Hawks	WHL	72	5	21	26				59											8	0	1	1	2			
1980-81	Portland Winter Hawks	WHL	70	6	40	46				186											9	1	7	8	17			
1981-82	Portland Winter Hawks	WHL	65	7	59	66				267											15	3	16	19	74			
	Canada	WJC-A	7	1	3	4				0																		
	Portland Winter Hawks	Mem-Cup	4	0	2	2				10																		
1982-83	Toronto Maple Leafs	NHL	16	0	3	3	0	2	2	16	0	0	0	12	0.0	12	0	14	2	0								
1983-84	Toronto Maple Leafs	NHL	47	2	14	16	2	10	12	103	0	0	0	71	2.8	57	3	109	28	–27								
1984-85	Toronto Maple Leafs	NHL	76	3	17	20	2	12	14	99	0	0	0	61	4.9	64	1	138	38	–37								
1985-86	Toronto Maple Leafs	NHL	79	2	16	18	2	11	13	180	0	0	0	84	2.4	108	3	182	45	–32	10	0	2	2	25	0	0	0
1986-87	Chicago Blackhawks	NHL	80	7	20	27	6	15	21	190	2	0	0	123	5.7	97	11	128	33	–9	4	0	2	2	11	0	0	0
1987-88	Chicago Blackhawks	NHL	76	4	15	19	3	11	14	208	0	0	0	92	4.3	65	1	117	44	–9	5	0	0	0	10	0	0	0
1988-89	Chicago Blackhawks	NHL	23	3	2	5	3	1	4	63	0	0	0	26	11.5	12	2	28	14	–4								
	New York Islanders	NHL	46	4	8	12	3	6	9	74	0	0	0	48	8.3	31	0	70	24	–15								
1989-90	New York Islanders	NHL	64	4	21	25	3	15	18	144	2	0	0	65	6.2	69	7	80	26	8	5	0	2	2	17	0	0	0
1990-91	New York Islanders	NHL	72	2	21	23	2	16	18	105	0	0	0	102	2.0	85	17	103	27	–8								
1991-92	New York Islanders	NHL	7	0	1	1	0	1	1	10	0	0	0	5	0.0	7	2	10	2	–3								
	Capital District Islanders	AHL	4	0	0	0				0																		
1992-93	New York Islanders	NHL	22	1	1	2	1	1	2	43	0	0	0	19	5.3	15	0	21	4	–2								
	Capital District Islanders	AHL	2	0	0	0				0																		
	NHL Totals		608	32	139	171	27	101	128	1235	4	0	0	708	4.5	622	47	1000	287		24	0	6	6	63	0	0	0

WHL First All-Star Team (1982) • Memorial Cup All-Star Team (1982)

Signed as a free agent by **Chicago**, August 27, 1986. Traded to **NY Islanders** by **Chicago** with Marc Bergevin for Steve Konroyd and Bob Bassen, November 25, 1988.

• NYROP, Bill

William D. D – L. 6'2", 205 lbs. b: Washington, DC, 7/23/1952 d: 1/1/1996. Montreal's 7th, 66th overall, in 1972. **USHOF**

Season	Club	League	GP	G	A	Pts	AG	AA	APts	PIM	PP	SH	GW	S	%	TGF	PGF	TGA	PGA	+/–	GP	G	A	Pts	PIM	PP	SH	GW
1967-1970	Edina Hornets	Hi-School	STATISTICS NOT AVAILABLE																									
1970-71	University of Notre Dame	WCHA	30	2	4	6				40																		
1971-72	University of Notre Dame	WCHA	31	3	18	21				44																		
1972-73	University of Notre Dame	WCHA	38	3	21	24				46																		
1973-74	University of Notre Dame	WCHA	33	9	29	38				44																		
1974-75	Nova Scotia Voyageurs	AHL	75	2	22	24				76											6	0	5	5	0			
1975-76♦	Montreal Canadiens	NHL	19	0	3	3	0	2	2	8	0	0	0	23	0.0	28	1	9	3	21	13	0	3	3	12	0	0	0
	Nova Scotia Voyageurs	AHL	52	3	25	28				30																		
1976-77	United States	Can-Cup	5	1	1	2				0																		
♦	Montreal Canadiens	NHL	74	3	19	22	3	15	18	21	0	0	1	47	6.4	85	0	46	3	42	8	1	0	1	4	0	0	0
1977-78♦	Montreal Canadiens	NHL	72	5	21	26	5	16	21	37	1	2	1	69	7.2	108	1	62	11	56	12	0	4	4	6	0	0	0
1978-79			OUT OF HOCKEY – RETIRED																									
1979-80			OUT OF HOCKEY – RETIRED																									
1980-81	Minnesota North Stars	DN-Cup	3	2	1	3				0																		
1981-82	Minnesota North Stars	NHL	42	4	8	12	3	5	8	35	0	1	1	25	16.0	59	1	52	8	14	2	0	0	0	0	0	0	0
1982-83	Kolner EC	Germany	19	3	2	5				8																		
1983-1992			OUT OF HOCKEY – RETIRED																									
1992-93	West Palm Beach Blazers	SunHL	DID NOT PLAY – COACHING																									
	NHL Totals		207	12	51	63	11	38	49	101	1	3	3	164	7.3	280	3	169	25		35	1	7	8	22	0	0	0

WCHA Second All-Star Team (1973) • NCAA West First All-American Team (1973) • WEC-B All-Star Team (1974)

Traded to **Minnesota** by **Montreal** for future considerations, September, 1980. Traded to **Calgary** by **Minnesota** with Steve Christoff and St. Louis' 2nd round choice (previously acquired, Calgary selected Dave Reierson) in 1982 Entry Draft for Willi Plett and Calgary's 4th round choice (Dusan Pasek) in 1982 Entry Draft, June 7, 1982

• NYSTROM, Bob

Robert Thore RW – R. 6'1", 200 lbs. b: Stockholm, Sweden, 10/10/1952. NY Islanders' 3rd, 33rd overall, in 1972.

Season	Club	League	GP	G	A	Pts	AG	AA	APts	PIM	PP	SH	GW	S	%	TGF	PGF	TGA	PGA	+/–	GP	G	A	Pts	PIM	PP	SH	GW
1969-70	Kamloops Rockets	BCJHL	48	16	17	33																						
1970-71	Calgary Centennials	WCJHL	66	15	16	31				153											10	2	3	5	32			
1971-72	Calgary Centennials	WCJHL	64	27	25	52				178											11	3	6	9	27			
1972-73	New York Islanders	NHL	11	1	1	2	1	1	2	10	0	0	0	12	8.3	3	0	14	0	–11								
	New Haven Nighthawks	AHL	60	12	10	22				114																		
1973-74	New York Islanders	NHL	77	21	20	41	20	16	36	118	3	0	5	176	11.9	57	7	67	0	–17								
1974-75	New York Islanders	NHL	76	27	28	55	24	21	45	122	3	0	3	194	13.9	76	10	49	0	17	17	1	3	4	27	0	0	0
1975-76	New York Islanders	NHL	80	23	25	48	20	19	39	106	2	0	4	185	12.4	72	6	42	0	24	13	3	6	9	30	1	0	0
1976-77	New York Islanders	NHL	80	29	27	56	26	21	47	91	5	0	3	207	14.0	80	18	40	0	22	12	0	2	2	7	0	0	0
1977-78	New York Islanders	NHL	80	30	29	59	27	22	49	94	3	0	6	178	16.9	85	6	60	0	19	7	3	1	4	14	1	0	2
1978-79	New York Islanders	NHL	78	19	20	39	16	14	30	113	1	0	5	161	11.8	68	4	46	1	19	10	3	2	5	4	0	0	1
1979-80♦	New York Islanders	NHL	67	21	18	39	18	13	31	94	2	0	4	146	14.4	52	6	42	0	4	20	9	9	18	50	0	0	3
1980-81♦	New York Islanders	NHL	79	14	30	44	11	20	31	145	3	0	0	161	8.7	73	9	58	0	6	18	6	6	12	20	0	0	1
1981-82♦	New York Islanders	NHL	74	22	25	47	17	17	34	103	0	0	4	136	16.2	69	3	53	0	13	15	5	5	10	32	0	0	0
1982-83♦	New York Islanders	NHL	74	10	20	30	8	14	22	98	3	0	3	100	10.0	45	4	35	0	6	20	7	6	13	15	0	0	0

Season	Club	League	GP	G	A	Pts	AG	AA	APts	PIM	PP	SH	GW	S	%	TGF	PGF	TGA	PGA	+/-	GP	G	A	Pts	PIM	PP	SH	GW
			REGULAR SEASON																		PLAYOFFS							
1983-84	New York Islanders	NHL	74	15	29	44	12	20	32	80	1	0	1	134	11.2	75	10	56	0	9	15	0	2	2	8	0	0	0
1984-85	New York Islanders	NHL	36	2	5	7	2	3	5	58	0	0	0	18	11.1	18	1	11	0	6	10	2	2	4	29	0	0	0
1985-86	New York Islanders	NHL	14	1	1	2	1	1	2	16	1	0	0	17	5.9	5	1	8	0	–4	....	....	....	....	....	....	....	....
	NHL Totals		900	235	278	513	203	202	405	1248	27	0	38	1825	12.9	778	85	581	1		157	39	44	83	236	2	0	7

Played in NHL All-Star Game (1977)

• OATES, Adam

C – R. 5'11", 180 lbs. b: Weston, Ont., 8/27/1962.

Season	Club	League	GP	G	A	Pts	AG	AA	APts	PIM	PP	SH	GW	S	%	TGF	PGF	TGA	PGA	+/-	GP	G	A	Pts	PIM	PP	SH	GW
1979-80	Port Credit Titans	OJHL-B	34	30	36	66	....	....	....	41	....	....	....	....	....	....	....	....	....	....	....	....	....	....	....	....	....	....
	Markham Waxers	OJHL-B	9	1	6	7	....	....	....	2	....	....	....	....	....	....	....	....	....	....	....	....	....	....	....	....	....	....
1980-81	Markham Waxers	OJHL-B	43	36	53	89	....	....	....	89	....	....	....	....	....	....	....	....	....	....	....	....	....	....	....	....	....	....
1981-82	Markham Waxers	OJHL-B	40	59	110	169	....	....	....	....	....	....	....	....	....	....	....	....	....	....	....	....	....	....	....	....	....	....
1982-83	RPI Engineers	ECAC	22	9	33	42	....	....	....	8	....	....	....	....	....	....	....	....	....	....	....	....	....	....	....	....	....	....
1983-84	RPI Engineers	ECAC	38	26	57	83	....	....	....	15	....	....	....	....	....	....	....	....	....	....	....	....	....	....	....	....	....	....
1984-85	RPI Engineers	ECAC	38	31	60	91	....	....	....	29	....	....	....	....	....	....	....	....	....	....	....	....	....	....	....	....	....	....
1985-86	Detroit Red Wings	NHL	38	9	11	20	7	7	14	10	1	0	1	49	18.4	30	10	50	6	–24	....	....	....	....	....	....	....	....
	Adirondack Red Wings	AHL	34	18	28	46	....	....	....	4	....	....	....	....	....	....	....	....	....	....	17	7	14	21	4	....	....	....
1986-87	Detroit Red Wings	NHL	76	15	32	47	13	23	36	21	4	0	1	138	10.9	64	16	49	1	0	16	4	7	11	6	0	0	1
1987-88	Detroit Red Wings	NHL	63	14	40	54	12	29	41	20	3	0	3	111	12.6	75	19	41	1	16	16	8	12	20	6	4	0	1
1988-89	Detroit Red Wings	NHL	69	16	62	78	14	44	58	14	2	0	1	127	12.6	106	43	64	0	–1	6	0	8	8	2	0	0	0
1989-90	St. Louis Blues	NHL	80	23	79	102	20	57	77	30	6	2	3	168	13.7	163	73	100	19	9	12	2	12	14	4	1	0	0
1990-91	St. Louis Blues	NHL	61	25	90	115	23	69	92	29	3	1	3	139	18.0	144	55	78	4	15	13	7	13	20	10	2	0	1
1991-92	St. Louis Blues	NHL	54	10	59	69	9	45	54	12	3	0	3	118	8.5	109	41	80	8	–4	....	....	....	....	....	....	....	....
	Boston Bruins	NHL	26	10	20	30	9	15	24	10	3	0	1	73	13.7	46	23	34	6	–5	15	5	14	19	4	3	0	2
1992-93	Boston Bruins	NHL	84	45	*97	142	37	67	104	32	24	1	11	254	17.7	197	85	110	13	15	4	0	9	9	4	0	0	0
1993-94	Boston Bruins	NHL	77	32	80	112	30	62	92	45	16	2	3	197	16.2	159	69	101	21	10	13	3	9	12	8	2	0	0
1994-95	Boston Bruins	NHL	48	12	41	53	21	61	82	8	4	1	2	109	11.0	72	33	57	7	–11	5	1	0	1	2	1	0	0
1995-96	Boston Bruins	NHL	70	25	67	92	25	55	80	18	7	1	2	183	13.7	126	43	100	33	16	5	2	5	7	2	0	1	0
1996-97	Boston Bruins	NHL	63	18	52	70	19	46	65	10	2	2	4	138	13.0	88	21	96	26	–3	....	....	....	....	....	....	....	....
	Washington Capitals	NHL	17	4	8	12	4	7	11	4	1	0	1	22	18.2	23	7	25	7	–2	....	....	....	....	....	....	....	....
1997-98	Washington Capitals	NHL	82	18	58	76	21	57	78	36	3	2	3	121	14.9	114	44	80	16	6	21	6	11	17	8	1	1	1
1998-99	Washington Capitals	NHL	59	12	42	54	14	41	55	22	3	0	0	79	15.2	75	27	59	10	–1	....	....	....	....	....	....	....	....
99-2000	Washington Capitals	NHL	82	15	56	71	17	52	69	14	5	0	6	93	16.1	101	34	77	23	13	5	0	3	3	4	0	0	0
	NHL Totals		1049	303	894	1197	295	737	1032	335	90	12	48	2119	14.3	1692	643	1201	201		131	38	103	141	60	14	2	6

ECAC Second All-Star Team (1984) • NCAA East First All-American Team (1984, 1985) • ECAC First All-Star Team (1985) • NCAA Championship All-Tournament Team (1985) • NHL Second All-Star Team (1991) • Played in NHL All-Star Game (1991, 1992, 1993, 1994, 1997)

Signed as a free agent by **Detroit,** June 28, 1985. Traded to **St. Louis** by **Detroit** with Paul MacLean for Bernie Federko and Tony McKegney, June 15, 1989. Traded to **Boston** by **St. Louis** for Craig Janney and Stephane Quintal, February 7, 1992. Traded to **Washington** by **Boston** with Bill Ranford and Rick Tocchet for Jim Carey, Anson Carter, Jason Allison and Washington's 3rd round choice (Lee Goren) in 1997 Entry Draft, March 1, 1997.

• O'BRIEN, Dennis

Dennis Francis D – L. 6', 195 lbs. b: Port Hope, Ont., 6/10/1949. Minnesota's 2nd, 14th overall, in 1969.

Season	Club	League	GP	G	A	Pts	AG	AA	APts	PIM	PP	SH	GW	S	%	TGF	PGF	TGA	PGA	+/-	GP	G	A	Pts	PIM	PP	SH	GW
1967-68	Coborg Cougars	OHA-B	STATISTICS NOT AVAILABLE																									
1968-69	St. Catharines Black Hawks	OHA-Jr.	52	1	19	20	....	....	....	*235	....	....	....	....	....	....	....	....	....	....	18	1	7	8	72	....	....	....
1969-70	Iowa Stars	CHL	72	2	18	20	....	....	....	*331	....	....	....	....	....	....	....	....	....	....	11	0	2	2	30	....	....	....
1970-71	Minnesota North Stars	NHL	27	3	2	5	3	2	5	29	0	0	0	15	20.0	11	0	17	4	–2	9	0	0	0	20	0	0	0
	Cleveland Barons	AHL	27	1	6	7	....	....	....	100	....	....	....	....	....	....	....	....	....	....	....	....	....	....	....	....	....	....
1971-72	Minnesota North Stars	NHL	70	3	6	9	3	5	8	108	0	0	1	68	4.4	36	3	27	5	11	3	0	1	1	11	0	0	0
1972-73	Minnesota North Stars	NHL	74	3	11	14	3	9	12	75	0	0	0	58	5.2	65	3	63	12	11	6	1	0	1	38	0	0	0
1973-74	Minnesota North Stars	NHL	77	5	12	17	5	10	15	166	0	0	2	66	7.6	67	0	61	4	10	....	....	....	....	....	....	....	....
1974-75	Minnesota North Stars	NHL	56	6	10	16	5	7	12	125	0	1	1	79	7.6	58	6	87	24	–11	....	....	....	....	....	....	....	....
1975-76	Minnesota North Stars	NHL	78	1	14	15	1	10	11	187	0	0	0	72	1.4	58	7	117	40	–26	....	....	....	....	....	....	....	....
1976-77	Minnesota North Stars	NHL	75	6	18	24	5	14	19	114	2	0	1	74	8.1	74	5	116	12	–35	2	0	0	0	4	0	0	0
1977-78	Minnesota North Stars	NHL	13	0	2	2	0	2	2	32	0	0	0	8	0.0	13	2	20	4	–5	....	....	....	....	....	....	....	....
	Colorado Rockies	NHL	16	0	2	2	0	2	2	12	0	0	0	9	0.0	8	0	19	1	–10	....	....	....	....	....	....	....	....
	Cleveland Barons	NHL	23	0	3	3	0	2	2	31	0	0	0	17	0.0	19	0	34	2	–13	....	....	....	....	....	....	....	....
	Boston Bruins	NHL	16	2	3	5	2	2	4	29	0	0	0	15	13.3	23	0	20	3	6	14	0	1	1	28	0	0	0
1978-79	Boston Bruins	NHL	64	2	8	10	2	6	8	107	0	0	0	73	2.7	75	1	83	25	16	....	....	....	....	....	....	....	....
	Rochester Americans	AHL	2	0	0	0	....	....	....	2	....	....	....	....	....	....	....	....	....	....	....	....	....	....	....	....	....	....
1979-80	Boston Bruins	NHL	3	0	0	0	0	0	0	2	0	0	0	2	0.0	0	0	4	0	–4	....	....	....	....	....	....	....	....
	Binghamton Dusters	AHL	6	2	5	7	....	....	....	65	....	....	....	....	....	....	....	....	....	....	....	....	....	....	....	....	....	....
	NHL Totals		592	31	91	122	29	71	100	1017	2	1	5	556	5.6	507	27	668	136		34	1	2	3	101	0	0	0

Claimed on waivers by **Colorado** from **Minnesota**, December 2, 1977. Traded to **Cleveland** by **Colorado** for Mike Christie, January 12, 1978. Claimed on waivers by **Boston** from **Cleveland**, March 10, 1978.

• O'CALLAHAN, Jack

D – R. 6'1", 190 lbs. b: Charleston, MA, 7/24/1957. Chicago's 5th, 96th overall, in 1977.

Season	Club	League	GP	G	A	Pts	AG	AA	APts	PIM	PP	SH	GW	S	%	TGF	PGF	TGA	PGA	+/-	GP	G	A	Pts	PIM	PP	SH	GW
1974-75	Boston College High School	Hi-School	STATISTICS NOT AVAILABLE																									
1975-76	Boston University Jr. Varsity	ECAC	1	0	2	2	....	....	....	0	....	....	....	....	....	....	....	....	....	....	....	....	....	....	....	....	....	....
1976-77	Boston University	ECAC	31	1	23	24	....	....	....	90	....	....	....	....	....	....	....	....	....	....	....	....	....	....	....	....	....	....
1977-78	Boston University	ECAC	31	8	47	55	....	....	....	61	....	....	....	....	....	....	....	....	....	....	....	....	....	....	....	....	....	....
1978-79	Boston University	ECAC	29	6	16	22	....	....	....	72	....	....	....	....	....	....	....	....	....	....	....	....	....	....	....	....	....	....
	United States	WEC-A	8	0	1	1	....	....	....	12	....	....	....	....	....	....	....	....	....	....	....	....	....	....	....	....	....	....
1979-80	United States	Nat-Team	55	7	30	37	....	....	....	85	....	....	....	....	....	....	....	....	....	....	....	....	....	....	....	....	....	....
	United States	Olympics	4	0	1	1	....	....	....	2	....	....	....	....	....	....	....	....	....	....	....	....	....	....	....	....	....	....
1980-81	New Brunswick Hawks	AHL	78	9	25	34	....	....	....	167	....	....	....	....	....	....	....	....	....	....	13	1	6	7	36	....	....	....
1981-82	New Brunswick Hawks	AHL	79	15	33	48	....	....	....	130	....	....	....	....	....	....	....	....	....	....	15	2	6	8	24	....	....	....
1982-83	Chicago Black Hawks	NHL	39	0	11	11	0	8	8	46	0	0	0	45	0.0	31	1	23	2	9	5	0	2	2	2	0	0	0
	Springfield Indians	AHL	35	2	24	26	....	....	....	25	....	....	....	....	....	....	....	....	....	....	....	....	....	....	....	....	....	....
1983-84	Chicago Black Hawks	NHL	70	4	13	17	3	9	12	67	0	0	1	88	4.5	44	1	54	5	–6	2	0	0	0	2	0	0	0
1984-85	Chicago Black Hawks	NHL	66	6	8	14	5	5	10	105	0	0	1	70	8.6	58	2	64	14	6	15	3	5	8	25	0	0	0
1985-86	Chicago Black Hawks	NHL	80	4	19	23	3	13	16	116	0	0	0	86	4.7	84	2	91	14	5	3	0	1	1	4	0	0	0
1986-87	Chicago Blackhawks	NHL	48	1	13	14	1	9	10	59	1	0	0	65	1.5	59	2	53	6	10	2	0	0	0	2	0	0	0
1987-88	New Jersey Devils	NHL	50	7	19	26	6	14	20	97	4	0	1	90	7.8	58	29	37	5	–3	5	1	3	4	6	0	0	0
1988-89	New Jersey Devils	NHL	36	5	21	26	4	15	19	51	5	0	0	96	5.2	49	33	16	0	0	....	....	....	....	....	....	....	....
	United States	WEC-A	10	0	2	2	....	....	....	14	....	....	....	....	....	....	....	....	....	....	....	....	....	....	....	....	....	....
	NHL Totals		389	27	104	131	22	73	95	541	10	0	3	540	5.0	383	70	338	46		32	4	11	15	41	0	0	0

ECAC First All-Star Team (1978, 1979) • NCAA Championship All-Tournament Team (1978) • NCAA Championship Tournament MVP (1978) • NCAA East First All-American Team (1979)

Claimed by **New Jersey** from **Chicago** in Waiver Draft, October 5, 1987.

• O'CONNELL, Mike

Michael Thomas D – R. 5'9", 180 lbs. b: Chicago, IL, 11/25/1955. Chicago's 3rd, 43rd overall, in 1975.

Season	Club	League	GP	G	A	Pts	AG	AA	APts	PIM	PP	SH	GW	S	%	TGF	PGF	TGA	PGA	+/-	GP	G	A	Pts	PIM	PP	SH	GW
1973-74	Kingston Canadians	OMJHL	70	16	43	59	....	....	....	81	....	....	....	....	....	....	....	....	....	....	....	....	....	....	....	....	....	....
1974-75	Kingston Canadians	OMJHL	50	18	55	73	....	....	....	47	....	....	....	....	....	....	....	....	....	....	8	1	3	4	8	....	....	....
1975-76	Dallas Black Hawks	CHL	70	6	37	43	....	....	....	50	....	....	....	....	....	....	....	....	....	....	10	2	*8	10	8	....	....	....
1976-77	Dallas Black Hawks	CHL	63	15	53	68	....	....	....	30	....	....	....	....	....	....	....	....	....	....	5	1	4	5	0	....	....	....
1977-78	Chicago Black Hawks	NHL	6	1	1	2	1	1	2	2	0	0	0	7	14.3	4	0	4	0	0	....	....	....	....	....	....	....	....
	Dallas Black Hawks	CHL	62	6	45	51	....	....	....	75	....	....	....	....	....	....	....	....	....	....	13	1	*11	12	8	....	....	....
1978-79	Chicago Black Hawks	NHL	48	4	22	26	3	16	19	20	1	0	0	83	4.8	66	13	68	14	–1	4	0	0	0	4	0	0	0
	New Brunswick Hawks	AHL	35	5	19	24	....	....	....	19	....	....	....	....	....	....	....	....	....	....	....	....	....	....	....	....	....	....
1979-80	Chicago Black Hawks	NHL	78	8	22	30	7	16	23	52	2	0	2	158	5.1	85	17	93	23	–2	7	0	1	1	0	0	0	0

			REGULAR SEASON																		PLAYOFFS							
Season	Club	League	GP	G	A	Pts	AG	AA	APts	PIM	PP	SH	GW	S	%	TGF	PGF	TGA	PGA	+/–	GP	G	A	Pts	PIM	PP	SH	GW
1980-81	**Chicago Black Hawks**	**NHL**	**34**	**5**	**16**	**21**	**4**	**11**	**15**	**32**	**1**	**1**	**0**	**79**	**6.3**	**54**	**15**	**50**	**16**	**5**	....	....	....	....	....	....	....	....
	Boston Bruins	**NHL**	**48**	**10**	**22**	**32**	**8**	**15**	**23**	**42**	**2**	**1**	**0**	**96**	**10.4**	**75**	**32**	**55**	**11**	**–1**	**3**	**1**	**3**	**4**	**2**	**0**	**1**	**0**
1981-82	United States	Can-Cup	4	1	3	4	....	....	....	2	....	....	....	....	....	....	....	....	....	....	....	....	....	....	....	....	....	....
	Boston Bruins	**NHL**	**80**	**5**	**34**	**39**	**4**	**23**	**27**	**75**	**1**	**0**	**0**	**170**	**2.9**	**142**	**33**	**130**	**29**	**8**	**11**	**2**	**2**	**4**	**20**	**0**	**0**	**0**
1982-83	**Boston Bruins**	**NHL**	**80**	**14**	**39**	**53**	**11**	**27**	**38**	**42**	**7**	**1**	**5**	**168**	**8.3**	**153**	**46**	**90**	**27**	**44**	**17**	**3**	**5**	**8**	**12**	**2**	**0**	**1**
1983-84	**Boston Bruins**	**NHL**	**75**	**18**	**42**	**60**	**14**	**29**	**43**	**42**	**9**	**0**	**1**	**194**	**9.3**	**151**	**52**	**116**	**35**	**18**	**3**	**0**	**0**	**0**	**0**	**0**	**0**	**0**
1984-85	**Boston Bruins**	**NHL**	**78**	**15**	**40**	**55**	**12**	**27**	**39**	**64**	**8**	**0**	**2**	**257**	**5.8**	**149**	**55**	**119**	**28**	**3**	**5**	**1**	**5**	**6**	**0**	**1**	**0**	**0**
	United States	WEC-A	8	1	0	1	....	....	....	2	....	....	....	....	....	....	....	....	....	....	....	....	....	....	....	....	....	....
1985-86	**Boston Bruins**	**NHL**	**63**	**8**	**21**	**29**	**6**	**14**	**20**	**47**	**4**	**1**	**0**	**174**	**4.6**	**99**	**39**	**94**	**26**	**–8**	....	....	....	....	....	....	....	....
	Detroit Red Wings	**NHL**	**13**	**1**	**7**	**8**	**1**	**5**	**6**	**16**	**0**	**1**	**0**	**38**	**2.6**	**23**	**10**	**23**	**4**	**–6**	....	....	....	....	....	....	....	....
1986-87	**Detroit Red Wings**	**NHL**	**77**	**5**	**26**	**31**	**4**	**19**	**23**	**70**	**3**	**1**	**0**	**141**	**3.5**	**104**	**37**	**117**	**25**	**–25**	**16**	**1**	**4**	**5**	**14**	**0**	**0**	**0**
1987-88	**Detroit Red Wings**	**NHL**	**48**	**6**	**13**	**19**	**5**	**9**	**14**	**38**	**0**	**0**	**0**	**68**	**8.8**	**71**	**15**	**53**	**21**	**24**	**10**	**0**	**4**	**4**	**8**	**0**	**0**	**0**
1988-89	**Detroit Red Wings**	**NHL**	**66**	**1**	**15**	**16**	**1**	**11**	**12**	**41**	**0**	**0**	**0**	**49**	**2.0**	**79**	**15**	**104**	**32**	**–8**	**6**	**0**	**0**	**0**	**4**	**0**	**0**	**0**
1989-90	**Detroit Red Wings**	**NHL**	**66**	**4**	**14**	**18**	**3**	**10**	**13**	**22**	**0**	**0**	**0**	**57**	**7.0**	**68**	**6**	**109**	**35**	**–12**	....	....	....	....	....	....	....	....
	NHL Totals		**860**	**105**	**334**	**439**	**84**	**233**	**317**	**605**	**38**	**6**	**10**	**1739**	**6.0**	**1323**	**385**	**1225**	**326**		**82**	**8**	**24**	**32**	**64**	**3**	**1**	**1**

OMJHL First All-Star Team (1975) • CHL First All-Star Team (1977) • Named CHL's Top Defenseman (1977) • Played in NHL All-Star Game (1984)

Traded to **Boston** by **Chicago** for Al Secord, December 18, 1980. Traded to **Detroit** by **Boston** for Reed Larson, March 10, 1986.

• O'CONNOR, Myles

D – L. 5'11", 190 lbs. b: Calgary, Alta., 4/2/1967. New Jersey's 4th, 45th overall, in 1985.

Season	Club	League	GP	G	A	Pts	AG	AA	APts	PIM	PP	SH	GW	S	%	TGF	PGF	TGA	PGA	+/–	GP	G	A	Pts	PIM	PP	SH	GW
1984-85	Notre Dame Hounds	Hi-School	40	20	35	55	....	....	....	40	....	....	....	....	....	....	....	....	....	....	....	....	....	....	....	....	....	....
1985-86	University of Michigan	CCHA	37	6	19	25	....	....	....	73	....	....	....	....	....	....	....	....	....	....	....	....	....	....	....	....	....	....
	Canada	Nat-Team	8	0	0	0	....	....	....	0	....	....	....	....	....	....	....	....	....	....	....	....	....	....	....	....	....	....
1986-87	University of Michigan	CCHA	39	15	39	54	....	....	....	111	....	....	....	....	....	....	....	....	....	....	....	....	....	....	....	....	....	....
1987-88	University of Michigan	CCHA	40	9	25	34	....	....	....	78	....	....	....	....	....	....	....	....	....	....	....	....	....	....	....	....	....	....
1988-89	University of Michigan	CCHA	40	3	31	34	....	....	....	91	....	....	....	....	....	....	....	....	....	....	....	....	....	....	....	....	....	....
	Utica Devils	AHL	1	0	0	0	....	....	....	0	....	....	....	....	....	....	....	....	....	....	....	....	....	....	....	....	....	....
1989-90	Utica Devils	AHL	76	14	33	47	....	....	....	124	....	....	....	....	....	....	....	....	....	....	5	1	2	3	26	....	....	....
1990-91	**New Jersey Devils**	**NHL**	**22**	**3**	**1**	**4**	**3**	**1**	**4**	**41**	**0**	**0**	**0**	**14**	**21.4**	**16**	**1**	**15**	**3**	**3**	....	....	....	....	....	....	....	....
	Utica Devils	AHL	33	6	17	23	....	....	....	62	....	....	....	....	....	....	....	....	....	....	....	....	....	....	....	....	....	....
1991-92	**New Jersey Devils**	**NHL**	**9**	**0**	**2**	**2**	**0**	**2**	**2**	**13**	**0**	**0**	**0**	**13**	**0.0**	**6**	**1**	**9**	**2**	**–2**	....	....	....	....	....	....	....	....
	Utica Devils	AHL	66	9	39	48	....	....	....	184	....	....	....	....	....	....	....	....	....	....	....	....	....	....	....	....	....	....
1992-93	**New Jersey Devils**	**NHL**	**7**	**0**	**0**	**0**	**0**	**0**	**0**	**9**	**0**	**0**	**0**	**4**	**0.0**	**3**	**0**	**10**	**3**	**–4**	....	....	....	....	....	....	....	....
	Utica Devils	AHL	9	1	5	6	....	....	....	10	....	....	....	....	....	....	....	....	....	....	....	....	....	....	....	....	....	....
1993-94	**Mighty Ducks of Anaheim**	**NHL**	**5**	**0**	**1**	**1**	**0**	**1**	**1**	**6**	**0**	**0**	**0**	**7**	**0.0**	**3**	**0**	**3**	**0**	**0**	....	....	....	....	....	....	....	....
	San Diego Gulls	IHL	39	1	13	14	....	....	....	117	....	....	....	....	....	....	....	....	....	....	9	1	4	5	83	....	....	....
1994-95	San Diego Gulls	IHL	16	1	4	5	....	....	....	50	....	....	....	....	....	....	....	....	....	....	5	0	1	1	0	....	....	....
1995-96	Houston Aeros	IHL	80	2	24	26	....	....	....	256	....	....	....	....	....	....	....	....	....	....	....	....	....	....	....	....	....	....
1996-97	Houston Aeros	IHL	3	0	0	0	....	....	....	6	....	....	....	....	....	....	....	....	....	....	....	....	....	....	....	....	....	....
	Cincinnati Cyclones	IHL	62	0	4	4	....	....	....	241	....	....	....	....	....	....	....	....	....	....	3	0	0	0	34	....	....	....
1997-98	Nippon Paper Kushiro	Japan	31	4	11	15	....	....	....	107	....	....	....	....	....	....	....	....	....	....	....	....	....	....	....	....	....	....
	NHL Totals		**43**	**3**	**4**	**7**	**3**	**4**	**7**	**69**	**0**	**0**	**0**	**38**	**7.9**	**28**	**2**	**37**	**8**		....	....	....	....	....	....	....	....

CCHA First All-Star Team (1989) • NCAA West First All-American Team (1989)

Signed as a free agent by **Anaheim**, July 22, 1993. Signed as a free agent by **Houston** (IHL), August 30, 1995. Traded to **Cincinnati** (IHL) by **Houston** (IHL) for future considerations, November 8, 1996.

• ODDLEIFSON, Chris

Christopher Roy C – R. 6'2", 185 lbs. b: Brandon, Man., 9/7/1950. California's 1st, 10th overall, in 1970.

Season	Club	League	GP	G	A	Pts	AG	AA	APts	PIM	PP	SH	GW	S	%	TGF	PGF	TGA	PGA	+/–	GP	G	A	Pts	PIM	PP	SH	GW
1966-67	Winnipeg Monarchs	MJHL	8	3	3	6	....	....	....	10	....	....	....	....	....	....	....	....	....	....	....	....	....	....	....	....	....	....
1967-68			STATISTICS NOT AVAILABLE																									
1968-69	Winnipeg Jets	WCJHL	46	14	30	44	....	....	....	118	....	....	....	....	....	....	....	....	....	....	7	0	2	2	0	....	....	....
1969-70	Winnipeg Jets	WCJHL	59	31	•64	95	....	....	....	243	....	....	....	....	....	....	....	....	....	....	14	8	19	27	90	....	....	....
1970-71	Providence Reds	AHL	66	15	42	57	....	....	....	95	....	....	....	....	....	....	....	....	....	....	10	1	4	5	25	....	....	....
1971-72	Oklahoma City Blazers	CHL	68	18	44	62	....	....	....	134	....	....	....	....	....	....	....	....	....	....	6	0	2	2	12	....	....	....
1972-73	**Boston Bruins**	**NHL**	**6**	**0**	**0**	**0**	**0**	**0**	**0**	**0**	**0**	**0**	**0**	**1**	**0.0**	**0**	**0**	**1**	**0**	**–1**	....	....	....	....	....	....	....	....
	Boston Braves	AHL	63	12	42	54	....	....	....	127	....	....	....	....	....	....	....	....	....	....	10	3	6	9	41	....	....	....
1973-74	**Boston Bruins**	**NHL**	**49**	**10**	**11**	**21**	**10**	**9**	**19**	**25**	**0**	**0**	**1**	**63**	**15.9**	**32**	**0**	**18**	**2**	**16**	....	....	....	....	....	....	....	....
	Vancouver Canucks	**NHL**	**21**	**3**	**5**	**8**	**3**	**4**	**7**	**19**	**1**	**0**	**1**	**22**	**13.6**	**14**	**2**	**20**	**8**	**0**	....	....	....	....	....	....	....	....
1974-75	**Vancouver Canucks**	**NHL**	**60**	**16**	**35**	**51**	**14**	**26**	**40**	**54**	**3**	**0**	**2**	**74**	**21.6**	**68**	**13**	**53**	**15**	**17**	**5**	**0**	**3**	**3**	**2**	**0**	**0**	**0**
1975-76	**Vancouver Canucks**	**NHL**	**80**	**16**	**46**	**62**	**14**	**34**	**48**	**88**	**2**	**2**	**1**	**133**	**12.0**	**94**	**27**	**72**	**22**	**17**	**2**	**1**	**2**	**3**	**0**	**0**	**0**	**0**
1976-77	**Vancouver Canucks**	**NHL**	**80**	**14**	**26**	**40**	**13**	**20**	**33**	**81**	**3**	**1**	**0**	**99**	**14.1**	**64**	**16**	**84**	**18**	**–18**	....	....	....	....	....	....	....	....
1977-78	**Vancouver Canucks**	**NHL**	**78**	**17**	**22**	**39**	**15**	**17**	**32**	**64**	**2**	**1**	**2**	**91**	**18.7**	**60**	**9**	**91**	**22**	**–18**	....	....	....	....	....	....	....	....
1978-79	**Vancouver Canucks**	**NHL**	**67**	**11**	**26**	**37**	**9**	**19**	**28**	**51**	**4**	**0**	**1**	**83**	**13.3**	**54**	**10**	**80**	**21**	**–15**	**3**	**0**	**1**	**1**	**2**	**0**	**0**	**0**
1979-80	**Vancouver Canucks**	**NHL**	**75**	**8**	**20**	**28**	**7**	**15**	**22**	**76**	**1**	**1**	**0**	**62**	**12.9**	**45**	**4**	**90**	**40**	**–9**	**4**	**0**	**0**	**0**	**4**	**0**	**0**	**0**
1980-81	**Vancouver Canucks**	**NHL**	**8**	**0**	**0**	**0**	**0**	**0**	**0**	**6**	**0**	**0**	**0**	**3**	**0.0**	**0**	**0**	**3**	**2**	**–1**	....	....	....	....	....	....	....	....
	Dallas Black Hawks	CHL	46	12	36	48	....	....	....	30	....	....	....	....	....	....	....	....	....	....	5	0	3	3	0	....	....	....
1981-1983	SC Langenthal	Sweden-2	STATISTICS NOT AVAILABLE																									
	NHL Totals		**524**	**95**	**191**	**286**	**85**	**144**	**229**	**464**	**16**	**5**	**8**	**631**	**15.1**	**431**	**81**	**512**	**150**		**14**	**1**	**6**	**7**	**8**	**0**	**0**	**0**

WCJHL First All-Star Team (1970)

Traded to **Boston** by **California** with Rich Leduc for Ivan Boldirev, November 17, 1971. Traded to **Vancouver** by **Boston** with Fred O'Donnell for Bobby Schmautz, February 7, 1974.

• ODELEIN, Lyle

Lyle Theodore D – R. 5'11", 210 lbs. b: Quill Lake, Sask., 7/21/1968. Montreal's 8th, 141st overall, in 1986.

Season	Club	League	GP	G	A	Pts	AG	AA	APts	PIM	PP	SH	GW	S	%	TGF	PGF	TGA	PGA	+/–	GP	G	A	Pts	PIM	PP	SH	GW
1984-85	Regina Pat Canadians	AAHA	26	12	13	25	....	....	....	30	....	....	....	....	....	....	....	....	....	....	....	....	....	....	....	....	....	....
1985-86	Moose Jaw Warriors	WHL	67	9	37	46	....	....	....	117	....	....	....	....	....	....	....	....	....	....	13	1	6	7	34	....	....	....
1986-87	Moose Jaw Warriors	WHL	59	9	50	59	....	....	....	70	....	....	....	....	....	....	....	....	....	....	9	2	5	7	26	....	....	....
1987-88	Moose Jaw Warriors	WHL	63	15	43	58	....	....	....	166	....	....	....	....	....	....	....	....	....	....	....	....	....	....	....	....	....	....
1988-89	Sherbrooke Canadiens	AHL	33	3	4	7	....	....	....	120	....	....	....	....	....	....	....	....	....	....	3	0	2	2	5	....	....	....
	Peoria Rivermen	IHL	36	2	8	10	....	....	....	116	....	....	....	....	....	....	....	....	....	....	....	....	....	....	....	....	....	....
1989-90	**Montreal Canadiens**	**NHL**	**8**	**0**	**2**	**2**	**0**	**1**	**1**	**33**	**0**	**0**	**0**	**1**	**0.0**	**5**	**0**	**6**	**0**	**–1**	....	....	....	....	....	....	....	....
	Sherbrooke Canadiens	AHL	68	7	24	31	....	....	....	265	....	....	....	....	....	....	....	....	....	....	12	6	5	11	79	....	....	....
1990-91	Montreal Canadiens	Fr-Tour	2	0	0	0	....	....	....	2	....	....	....	....	....	....	....	....	....	....	....	....	....	....	....	....	....	....
	Montreal Canadiens	**NHL**	**52**	**0**	**2**	**2**	**0**	**2**	**2**	**259**	**0**	**0**	**0**	**25**	**0.0**	**36**	**1**	**34**	**6**	**7**	**12**	**0**	**0**	**0**	**54**	**0**	**0**	**0**
1991-92	**Montreal Canadiens**	**NHL**	**71**	**1**	**7**	**8**	**1**	**5**	**6**	**212**	**0**	**0**	**0**	**43**	**2.3**	**42**	**0**	**32**	**5**	**15**	**7**	**0**	**0**	**0**	**11**	**0**	**0**	**0**
1992-93♦	**Montreal Canadiens**	**NHL**	**83**	**2**	**14**	**16**	**2**	**10**	**12**	**205**	**0**	**0**	**0**	**79**	**2.5**	**86**	**0**	**69**	**18**	**35**	**20**	**1**	**5**	**6**	**30**	**0**	**0**	**0**
1993-94	**Montreal Canadiens**	**NHL**	**79**	**11**	**29**	**40**	**10**	**22**	**32**	**276**	**6**	**0**	**2**	**116**	**9.5**	**100**	**31**	**87**	**26**	**8**	**7**	**0**	**0**	**0**	**17**	**0**	**0**	**0**
1994-95	**Montreal Canadiens**	**NHL**	**48**	**3**	**7**	**10**	**5**	**10**	**15**	**152**	**0**	**0**	**0**	**74**	**4.1**	**37**	**4**	**54**	**8**	**–13**	....	....	....	....	....	....	....	....
1995-96	**Montreal Canadiens**	**NHL**	**79**	**3**	**14**	**17**	**3**	**11**	**14**	**230**	**0**	**1**	**0**	**74**	**4.1**	**67**	**3**	**72**	**16**	**8**	**6**	**1**	**1**	**2**	**6**	**0**	**1**	**0**
1996-97	Canada	W-Cup	2	0	0	0	....	....	....	0	....	....	....	....	....	....	....	....	....	....	....	....	....	....	....	....	....	....
	New Jersey Devils	**NHL**	**79**	**3**	**13**	**16**	**3**	**12**	**15**	**110**	**1**	**0**	**2**	**93**	**3.2**	**75**	**10**	**54**	**5**	**16**	**10**	**2**	**2**	**4**	**19**	**1**	**0**	**0**
1997-98	**New Jersey Devils**	**NHL**	**79**	**4**	**19**	**23**	**5**	**19**	**24**	**171**	**1**	**0**	**0**	**76**	**5.3**	**71**	**13**	**64**	**17**	**11**	**6**	**1**	**1**	**2**	**21**	**1**	**0**	**1**
1998-99	**New Jersey Devils**	**NHL**	**70**	**5**	**26**	**31**	**6**	**25**	**31**	**114**	**1**	**0**	**0**	**101**	**5.0**	**71**	**20**	**56**	**11**	**6**	**7**	**0**	**3**	**3**	**10**	**0**	**0**	**0**
99-2000	**New Jersey Devils**	**NHL**	**57**	**1**	**15**	**16**	**1**	**14**	**15**	**104**	**0**	**0**	**1**	**59**	**1.7**	**39**	**4**	**46**	**1**	**–10**	....	....	....	....	....	....	....	....
	Phoenix Coyotes	**NHL**	**16**	**1**	**7**	**8**	**1**	**6**	**7**	**19**	**1**	**0**	**0**	**30**	**3.3**	**18**	**4**	**17**	**4**	**1**	**5**	**0**	**0**	**0**	**16**	**0**	**0**	**0**
	NHL Totals		**721**	**34**	**155**	**189**	**37**	**137**	**174**	**1885**	**10**	**1**	**5**	**771**	**4.4**	**647**	**90**	**591**	**117**		**80**	**5**	**12**	**17**	**184**	**2**	**1**	**1**

• Brother of Selmar

Traded to **New Jersey** by **Montreal** for Stephane Richer, August 22, 1996. Traded to **Phoenix** by **New Jersey** for Deron Quint and a conditional choice in 2001 Entry Draft, March 7, 2000. Selected by **Columbus** from **Phoenix** in Expansion Draft, June 23, 2000.

• ODELEIN, Selmar

D – R. 6', 195 lbs. b: Quill Lake, Sask., 4/11/1966. Edmonton's 1st, 21st overall, in 1984.

			REGULAR SEASON																		PLAYOFFS							
Season	Club	League	GP	G	A	Pts	AG	AA	APts	PIM	PP	SH	GW	S	%	TGF	PGF	TGA	PGA	+/–	GP	G	A	Pts	PIM	PP	SH	GW
1982-83	Regina Pat Canadians	SAHA	70	30	84	114	....	....	....	38	....	....	....	....	....	....	....	....	....	....	....	....	....	....	....	....	....	....
	Regina Pats	WHL	1	0	0	0	....	....	....	0	....	....	....	....	....	....	....	....	....	....	....	....	....	....	....	....	....	....
1983-84	Regina Pats	WHL	71	9	42	51	....	....	....	45	....	....	....	....	....	....	....	....	....	....	23	4	11	15	45	....	....	....
1984-85	Regina Pats	WHL	64	24	35	59	....	....	....	121	....	....	....	....	....	....	....	....	....	....	8	2	2	4	13	....	....	....
	Canada	WJC-A	7	1	5	6	....	....	....	8	....	....	....	....	....	....	....	....	....	....	....	....	....	....	....	....	....	....
1985-86	Regina Pats	WHL	36	13	28	41	....	....	....	57	....	....	....	....	....	....	....	....	....	....	8	5	2	7	24	....	....	....
	Canada	WJC-A	7	0	1	1	....	....	....	6	....	....	....	....	....	....	....	....	....	....	....	....	....	....	....	....	....	....
	Edmonton Oilers	**NHL**	**4**	**0**	**0**	**0**	**0**	**0**	**0**	**0**	**0**	**0**	**0**	**2**	**0.0**	**3**	**0**	**2**	**0**	**1**	....	....	....	....	....	....	....	....
1986-87	Nova Scotia Oilers	AHL	2	0	1	1	....	....	....	2	....	....	....	....	....	....	....	....	....	....	....	....	....	....	....	....	....	....
1987-88	**Edmonton Oilers**	**NHL**	**12**	**0**	**2**	**2**	**0**	**1**	**1**	**33**	**0**	**0**	**0**	**17**	**0.0**	**11**	**2**	**12**	**1**	**–2**	....	....	....	....	....	....	....	....
	Nova Scotia Oilers	AHL	43	9	14	23	....	....	....	75	....	....	....	....	....	....	....	....	....	....	5	0	1	1	31	....	....	....
1988-89	**Edmonton Oilers**	**NHL**	**2**	**0**	**0**	**0**	**0**	**0**	**0**	**2**	**0**	**0**	**0**	**0**	**0.0**	**1**	**0**	**2**	**0**	**–1**	....	....	....	....	....	....	....	....
	Cape Breton Oilers	AHL	63	8	21	29	....	....	....	150	....	....	....	....	....	....	....	....	....	....	....	....	....	....	....	....	....	....
1989-90	Canada	Nat-Team	73	7	30	37	....	....	....	69	....	....	....	....	....	....	....	....	....	....	....	....	....	....	....	....	....	....
1990-91	IEV Innsbruck	Austria	38	9	21	30	....	....	....	71	....	....	....	....	....	....	....	....	....	....	....	....	....	....	....	....	....	....
1991-92	VEU Feldkirch	Austria	29	9	18	27	....	....	....	....	....	....	....	....	....	....	....	....	....	....	....	....	....	....	....	....	....	....
1992-93	Nottingham Panthers	Britain	23	17	18	35	....	....	....	48	....	....	....	....	....	....	....	....	....	....	7	5	10	15	12	....	....	....
1993-94	Sheffield Steelers	Britain	25	5	21	26	....	....	....	28	....	....	....	....	....	....	....	....	....	....	4	0	4	4	6	....	....	....
	NHL Totals		**18**	**0**	**2**	**2**	**0**	**1**	**1**	**35**	**0**	**0**	**0**	**19**	**0.0**	**15**	**2**	**16**	**1**		....	....	....	....	....	....	....	....

• Brother of Lyle • WHL Second All-Star Team (1985)

• Missed remainder of 1986-87 season recovering from knee injury suffered in game vs. Adirondack (AHL), October 17, 1986.

• ODGERS, Jeff

Jeffrey J. RW – R. 6', 200 lbs. b: Spy Hill, Sask., 5/31/1969.

Season	Club	League	GP	G	A	Pts	AG	AA	APts	PIM	PP	SH	GW	S	%	TGF	PGF	TGA	PGA	+/–	GP	G	A	Pts	PIM	PP	SH	GW
1985-86	Saskatoon Blazers	AAHA	36	27	29	56	....	....	....	74	....	....	....	....	....	....	....	....	....	....	....	....	....	....	....	....	....	....
1986-87	Brandon Wheat Kings	WHL	70	7	14	21	....	....	....	150	....	....	....	....	....	....	....	....	....	....	....	....	....	....	....	....	....	....
1987-88	Brandon Wheat Kings	WHL	70	17	18	35	....	....	....	202	....	....	....	....	....	....	....	....	....	....	4	1	1	2	14	....	....	....
1988-89	Brandon Wheat Kings	WHL	71	31	29	60	....	....	....	277	....	....	....	....	....	....	....	....	....	....	....	....	....	....	....	....	....	....
1989-90	Brandon Wheat Kings	WHL	64	37	28	65	....	....	....	209	....	....	....	....	....	....	....	....	....	....	....	....	....	....	....	....	....	....
1990-91	Kansas City Blades	IHL	77	12	19	31	....	....	....	318	....	....	....	....	....	....	....	....	....	....	....	....	....	....	....	....	....	....
1991-92	**San Jose Sharks**	**NHL**	**61**	**7**	**4**	**11**	**6**	**3**	**9**	**217**	**0**	**0**	**0**	**64**	**10.9**	**19**	**2**	**39**	**1**	**–21**	....	....	....	....	....	....	....	....
	Kansas City Blades	IHL	12	2	2	4	....	....	....	56	....	....	....	....	....	....	....	....	....	....	4	2	1	3	0	....	....	....
1992-93	**San Jose Sharks**	**NHL**	**66**	**12**	**15**	**27**	**10**	**10**	**20**	**253**	**6**	**0**	**0**	**100**	**12.0**	**47**	**16**	**57**	**0**	**–26**	....	....	....	....	....	....	....	....
1993-94	**San Jose Sharks**	**NHL**	**81**	**13**	**8**	**21**	**12**	**6**	**18**	**222**	**7**	**0**	**0**	**73**	**17.8**	**36**	**19**	**31**	**1**	**–13**	**11**	**0**	**0**	**0**	**11**	**0**	**0**	**0**
1994-95	**San Jose Sharks**	**NHL**	**48**	**4**	**3**	**7**	**7**	**4**	**11**	**117**	**0**	**0**	**1**	**47**	**8.5**	**11**	**0**	**19**	**0**	**–8**	**11**	**1**	**1**	**2**	**23**	**0**	**0**	**0**
1995-96	**San Jose Sharks**	**NHL**	**78**	**12**	**4**	**16**	**12**	**3**	**15**	**192**	**0**	**0**	**1**	**84**	**14.3**	**26**	**0**	**31**	**1**	**–4**	....	....	....	....	....	....	....	....
1996-97	**Boston Bruins**	**NHL**	**80**	**7**	**8**	**15**	**7**	**7**	**14**	**197**	**1**	**0**	**1**	**84**	**8.3**	**22**	**5**	**32**	**0**	**–15**	....	....	....	....	....	....	....	....
1997-98	Providence Bruins	AHL	4	0	0	0	....	....	....	31	....	....	....	....	....	....	....	....	....	....	....	....	....	....	....	....	....	....
	Colorado Avalanche	**NHL**	**68**	**5**	**8**	**13**	**6**	**8**	**14**	**213**	**0**	**0**	**0**	**47**	**10.6**	**17**	**0**	**12**	**0**	**5**	**6**	**0**	**0**	**0**	**25**	**0**	**0**	**0**
1998-99	**Colorado Avalanche**	**NHL**	**75**	**2**	**3**	**5**	**2**	**3**	**5**	**259**	**1**	**0**	**0**	**39**	**5.1**	**11**	**2**	**12**	**0**	**–3**	**15**	**1**	**0**	**1**	**14**	**0**	**0**	**1**
99-2000	**Colorado Avalanche**	**NHL**	**62**	**1**	**2**	**3**	**1**	**2**	**3**	**162**	**0**	**0**	**1**	**29**	**3.4**	**6**	**0**	**13**	**0**	**–7**	**4**	**0**	**0**	**0**	**0**	**0**	**0**	**0**
	NHL Totals		**619**	**63**	**55**	**118**	**63**	**46**	**109**	**1832**	**15**	**0**	**4**	**567**	**11.1**	**195**	**44**	**246**	**3**		**47**	**2**	**1**	**3**	**73**	**0**	**0**	**1**

Signed as a free agent by **San Jose**, September 3, 1991. Traded to **Boston** by **San Jose** with Pittsburgh's 5th round choice (previously acquired, Boston selected Elias Abrahamsson) in 1996 Entry Draft for Al Iafrate, June 21, 1996. Signed as a free agent by **Colorado**, October 24, 1997. Selected by **Minnesota** from **Colorado** in Expansion Draft, June 23, 2000.

• ODJICK, Gino

LW – L. 6'3", 210 lbs. b: Maniwaki, Que., 9/7/1970. Vancouver's 5th, 86th overall, in 1990.

Season	Club	League	GP	G	A	Pts	AG	AA	APts	PIM	PP	SH	GW	S	%	TGF	PGF	TGA	PGA	+/–	GP	G	A	Pts	PIM	PP	SH	GW
1987-88	Hawkesbury Hawks	OJHL	40	2	4	6	....	....	....	167	....	....	....	....	....	....	....	....	....	....	....	....	....	....	....	....	....	....
1988-89	Laval Titan	QMJHL	50	9	15	24	....	....	....	278	....	....	....	....	....	....	....	....	....	....	16	0	9	9	129	....	....	....
	Laval Titan	Mem-Cup	3	0	1	1	....	....	....	5	....	....	....	....	....	....	....	....	....	....	....	....	....	....	....	....	....	....
1989-90	Laval Titan	QMJHL	51	12	26	38	....	....	....	280	....	....	....	....	....	....	....	....	....	....	13	6	5	11	110	....	....	....
	Laval Titan	Mem-Cup	4	0	1	1	....	....	....	10	....	....	....	....	....	....	....	....	....	....	....	....	....	....	....	....	....	....
1990-91	**Vancouver Canucks**	**NHL**	**45**	**7**	**1**	**8**	**6**	**1**	**7**	**296**	**0**	**0**	**0**	**39**	**17.9**	**12**	**0**	**18**	**0**	**–6**	**6**	**0**	**0**	**0**	**18**	**0**	**0**	**0**
	Milwaukee Admirals	IHL	17	7	3	10	....	....	....	102	....	....	....	....	....	....	....	....	....	....	....	....	....	....	....	....	....	....
1991-92	**Vancouver Canucks**	**NHL**	**65**	**4**	**6**	**10**	**4**	**5**	**9**	**348**	**0**	**0**	**0**	**68**	**5.9**	**16**	**1**	**16**	**0**	**–1**	**4**	**0**	**0**	**0**	**6**	**0**	**0**	**0**
1992-93	**Vancouver Canucks**	**NHL**	**75**	**4**	**13**	**17**	**3**	**9**	**12**	**370**	**0**	**0**	**1**	**79**	**5.1**	**28**	**2**	**23**	**0**	**3**	**1**	**0**	**0**	**0**	**0**	**0**	**0**	**0**
1993-94	**Vancouver Canucks**	**NHL**	**76**	**16**	**13**	**29**	**15**	**10**	**25**	**271**	**4**	**0**	**5**	**121**	**13.2**	**48**	**8**	**28**	**1**	**13**	**10**	**0**	**0**	**0**	**18**	**0**	**0**	**0**
1994-95	**Vancouver Canucks**	**NHL**	**23**	**4**	**5**	**9**	**7**	**7**	**14**	**109**	**0**	**0**	**0**	**35**	**11.4**	**12**	**2**	**13**	**0**	**–3**	**5**	**0**	**0**	**0**	**47**	**0**	**0**	**0**
1995-96	**Vancouver Canucks**	**NHL**	**55**	**3**	**4**	**7**	**3**	**3**	**6**	**181**	**0**	**0**	**0**	**59**	**5.1**	**11**	**0**	**27**	**0**	**–16**	**6**	**3**	**1**	**4**	**6**	**0**	**0**	**2**
1996-97	**Vancouver Canucks**	**NHL**	**70**	**5**	**8**	**13**	**5**	**7**	**12**	***371**	**1**	**0**	**0**	**85**	**5.9**	**22**	**3**	**24**	**0**	**–5**	....	....	....	....	....	....	....	....
1997-98	**Vancouver Canucks**	**NHL**	**35**	**3**	**2**	**5**	**4**	**2**	**6**	**181**	**0**	**0**	**1**	**36**	**8.3**	**9**	**0**	**12**	**0**	**–3**	....	....	....	....	....	....	....	....
	New York Islanders	**NHL**	**13**	**0**	**0**	**0**	**0**	**0**	**0**	**31**	**0**	**0**	**0**	**16**	**0.0**	**4**	**2**	**1**	**0**	**1**	....	....	....	....	....	....	....	....
1998-99	**New York Islanders**	**NHL**	**23**	**4**	**3**	**7**	**5**	**3**	**8**	**133**	**1**	**0**	**2**	**28**	**14.3**	**9**	**3**	**8**	**0**	**–2**	....	....	....	....	....	....	....	....
99-2000	**New York Islanders**	**NHL**	**46**	**5**	**10**	**15**	**6**	**9**	**15**	**90**	**0**	**0**	**3**	**91**	**5.5**	**23**	**4**	**26**	**0**	**–7**	....	....	....	....	....	....	....	....
	Philadelphia Flyers	**NHL**	**13**	**3**	**1**	**4**	**3**	**1**	**4**	**10**	**0**	**0**	**1**	**24**	**12.5**	**4**	**0**	**2**	**0**	**2**	....	....	....	....	....	....	....	....
	NHL Totals		**539**	**58**	**66**	**124**	**61**	**57**	**118**	**2391**	**6**	**0**	**13**	**681**	**8.5**	**198**	**25**	**198**	**1**		**32**	**3**	**1**	**4**	**95**	**0**	**0**	**2**

Traded to **NY Islanders** by **Vancouver** for Jason Strudwick, March 23, 1998. Traded to **Philadelphia** by **NY Islanders** for Mikael Andersson and Carolina's 5th round choice (previously acquired, NY Islanders selected Kristofer Ottoson) in 2000 Entry Draft, February 15, 2000.

• O'DONNELL, Fred

Frederick James RW – R. 5'10", 175 lbs. b: Kingston, Ont., 12/6/1949. Minnesota's 4th, 37th overall, in 1969.

Season	Club	League	GP	G	A	Pts	AG	AA	APts	PIM	PP	SH	GW	S	%	TGF	PGF	TGA	PGA	+/–	GP	G	A	Pts	PIM	PP	SH	GW
1966-67	Oshawa Generals	OHA-Jr.	36	6	9	15	....	....	....	44	....	....	....	....	....	....	....	....	....	....	....	....	....	....	....	....	....	....
1967-68	Oshawa Generals	OHA-Jr.	44	24	14	38	....	....	....	72	....	....	....	....	....	....	....	....	....	....	....	....	....	....	....	....	....	....
1968-69	Oshawa Generals	OHA-Jr.	54	31	27	58	....	....	....	124	....	....	....	....	....	....	....	....	....	....	....	....	....	....	....	....	....	....
1969-70	Kingston Aces	OHA-Sr.	36	16	22	38	....	....	....	76	....	....	....	....	....	....	....	....	....	....	....	....	....	....	....	....	....	....
	Oklahoma City Blazers	CHL	2	2	2	4	....	....	....	0	....	....	....	....	....	....	....	....	....	....	....	....	....	....	....	....	....	....
1970-71	Oklahoma City Blazers	CHL	67	23	23	46	....	....	....	158	....	....	....	....	....	....	....	....	....	....	5	4	1	5	30	....	....	....
1971-72	Boston Braves	AHL	62	16	22	38	....	....	....	161	....	....	....	....	....	....	....	....	....	....	....	....	....	....	....	....	....	....
1972-73	**Boston Bruins**	**NHL**	**72**	**10**	**4**	**14**	**9**	**3**	**12**	**55**	**0**	**0**	**2**	**56**	**17.9**	**19**	**0**	**17**	**1**	**3**	**5**	**0**	**1**	**1**	**5**	**0**	**0**	**0**
1973-74	**Boston Bruins**	**NHL**	**43**	**5**	**7**	**12**	**5**	**6**	**11**	**43**	**0**	**0**	**1**	**39**	**12.8**	**20**	**0**	**17**	**0**	**3**	....	....	....	....	....	....	....	....
1974-75	New England Whalers	WHA	76	21	15	36	....	....	....	84	....	....	....	....	....	....	....	....	....	....	3	0	0	0	15	....	....	....
1975-76	New England Whalers	WHA	79	11	11	22	....	....	....	81	....	....	....	....	....	....	....	....	....	....	17	2	5	7	20	....	....	....
	NHL Totals		**115**	**15**	**11**	**26**	**14**	**9**	**23**	**98**	**0**	**0**	**3**	**95**	**15.8**	**39**	**0**	**34**	**1**		**5**	**0**	**1**	**1**	**5**	**0**	**0**	**0**
	Other Major League Totals		155	32	26	58	....	....	....	165	....	....	....	....	....	....	....	....	....	....	20	2	5	7	35	....	....	....

Traded to **Boston** by **Minnesota** to complete transaction that sent Barry Gibbs and Tommy Williams to Boston (May 7, 1969), May 7, 1971. Selected by **Winnipeg** (WHA) in 1972 WHA General Player Draft, February 1972. WHA rights traded to **New England** (WHA) by **Winnipeg** (WHA) for future considerations, June, 1972. Traded to **Vancouver** by **Boston** with Chris Oddleifson for Bobby Schmautz, February 7, 1974. • Suspended by **Vancouver** for refusing to report to NHL club, February 9, 1974. Traded to **Cleveland** (WHA) by **New England** (WHA) with Bob McManama for Wayne Connelly, June, 1976.

• O'DONNELL, Sean

"O.D." D – L. 6'3", 235 lbs. b: Ottawa, Ont., 10/13/1971. Buffalo's 6th, 123rd overall, in 1991.

Season	Club	League	GP	G	A	Pts	AG	AA	APts	PIM	PP	SH	GW	S	%	TGF	PGF	TGA	PGA	+/–	GP	G	A	Pts	PIM	PP	SH	GW
1987-88	Kanata Valley Lasers	OJHL	54	4	25	29	....	....	....	96	....	....	....	....	....	....	....	....	....	....	....	....	....	....	....	....	....	....
1988-89	Sudbury Wolves	OHL	56	1	9	10	....	....	....	49	....	....	....	....	....	....	....	....	....	....	....	....	....	....	....	....	....	....
1989-90	Sudbury Wolves	OHL	64	7	19	26	....	....	....	84	....	....	....	....	....	....	....	....	....	....	7	1	2	3	8	....	....	....
1990-91	Sudbury Wolves	OHL	66	8	23	31	....	....	....	114	....	....	....	....	....	....	....	....	....	....	5	1	4	5	10	....	....	....
1991-92	Rochester Americans	AHL	73	4	9	13	....	....	....	193	....	....	....	....	....	....	....	....	....	....	16	1	2	3	21	....	....	....
1992-93	Rochester Americans	AHL	74	3	18	21	....	....	....	203	....	....	....	....	....	....	....	....	....	....	17	1	6	7	38	....	....	....
1993-94	Rochester Americans	AHL	64	2	10	12	....	....	....	242	....	....	....	....	....	....	....	....	....	....	4	0	1	1	21	....	....	....
1994-95	Phoenix Roadrunners	IHL	61	2	18	20	....	....	....	132	....	....	....	....	....	....	....	....	....	....	9	0	1	1	21	....	....	....
	Los Angeles Kings	**NHL**	**15**	**0**	**2**	**2**	**0**	**3**	**3**	**49**	**0**	**0**	**0**	**12**	**0.0**	**7**	**0**	**14**	**5**	**–2**	....	....	....	....	....	....	....	....
1995-96	**Los Angeles Kings**	**NHL**	**71**	**2**	**5**	**7**	**2**	**4**	**6**	**127**	**0**	**0**	**0**	**65**	**3.1**	**58**	**3**	**79**	**27**	**3**	....	....	....	....	....	....	....	....

			REGULAR SEASON																		PLAYOFFS							
Season	Club	League	GP	G	A	Pts	AG	AA	APts	PIM	PP	SH	GW	S	%	TGF	PGF	TGA	PGA	+/–	GP	G	A	Pts	PIM	PP	SH	GW
1996-97	Los Angeles Kings	NHL	55	5	12	17	5	11	16	144	2	0	0	68	7.4	44	7	61	11	–13	....	....	....	....	....	....	....	....
1997-98	Los Angeles Kings	NHL	80	2	15	17	2	15	17	179	0	0	1	71	2.8	63	7	70	21	7	4	1	0	1	36	0	0	0
1998-99	Los Angeles Kings	NHL	80	1	13	14	1	13	14	186	0	0	0	64	1.6	53	5	69	22	1	....	....	....	....	....	....	....	....
	Canada	WC-A	9	1	2	3	....	....	....	6	....	....	....	....	....	....	....	....	....	....	....	....	....	....	....	....	....	....
99-2000	Los Angeles Kings	NHL	80	2	12	14	2	11	13	114	0	0	1	51	3.9	60	1	79	24	4	4	1	0	1	4	0	0	0
	NHL Totals		381	12	59	71	12	57	69	799	2	0	2	331	3.6	285	23	372	110		8	2	0	2	40	0	0	0

Traded to **LA Kings** by **Buffalo** for Doug Houda, July 26, 1994. Selected by **Minnesota** from **LA Kings** in Expansion Draft, June 23, 2000.

• O'DONOGHUE, Don

Donald Francis RW – R. 5'10", 180 lbs. b: Kingston, Ont., 8/27/1949. Oakland's 3rd, 29th overall, in 1969.

Season	Club	League	GP	G	A	Pts	AG	AA	APts	PIM	PP	SH	GW	S	%	TGF	PGF	TGA	PGA	+/–	GP	G	A	Pts	PIM	PP	SH	GW
1967-68	St. Catharines Black Hawks	OHA-Jr.	54	5	15	20	....	....	....	12	....	....	....	....	....	....	....	....	....	....	5	0	1	1	2	....	....	....
1968-69	St. Catharines Black Hawks	OHA-Jr.	45	9	21	30	....	....	....	61	....	....	....	....	....	....	....	....	....	....	18	4	3	7	32	....	....	....
1969-70	Oakland Seals	NHL	68	5	6	11	5	6	11	21	0	0	1	55	9.1	16	2	47	7	–26	3	0	0	0	0	0	0	0
1970-71	California Golden Seals	NHL	43	11	9	20	11	7	18	10	3	1	0	63	17.5	28	7	64	23	–20	....	....	....	....	....	....	....	....
	Providence Reds	AHL	25	9	8	17	....	....	....	20	....	....	....	....	....	....	....	....	....	....	....	....	....	....	....	....	....	....
1971-72	California Golden Seals	NHL	14	2	2	4	2	2	4	4	0	0	0	11	18.2	6	0	11	1	–4	....	....	....	....	....	....	....	....
	Baltimore Clippers	AHL	23	3	6	9	....	....	....	10	....	....	....	....	....	....	....	....	....	....	....	....	....	....	....	....	....	....
	Boston Braves	AHL	16	0	3	3	....	....	....	0	....	....	....	....	....	....	....	....	....	....	9	0	1	1	7	....	....	....
1972-73	Philadelphia Blazers	WHA	74	16	23	39	....	....	....	43	....	....	....	....	....	....	....	....	....	....	4	0	1	1	0	....	....	....
1973-74	Vancouver Blazers	WHA	49	8	6	14	....	....	....	20	....	....	....	....	....	....	....	....	....	....	....	....	....	....	....	....	....	....
1974-75	Vancouver Blazers	WHA	4	0	0	0	....	....	....	0	....	....	....	....	....	....	....	....	....	....	....	....	....	....	....	....	....	....
	Tulsa Oilers	CHL	46	8	22	30	....	....	....	60	....	....	....	....	....	....	....	....	....	....	2	1	0	1	2	....	....	....
1975-76	Cincinnati Stingers	WHA	20	1	8	9	....	....	....	0	....	....	....	....	....	....	....	....	....	....	....	....	....	....	....	....	....	....
	Hampton Gulls	SHL	45	15	26	41	....	....	....	59	....	....	....	....	....	....	....	....	....	....	9	2	6	8	4	....	....	....
1976-77	Hampton Gulls	SHL	50	16	26	42	....	....	....	46	....	....	....	....	....	....	....	....	....	....	....	....	....	....	....	....	....	....
1977-78	Hampton Gulls	AHL	43	4	8	12	....	....	....	84	....	....	....	....	....	....	....	....	....	....	....	....	....	....	....	....	....	....
	NHL Totals		125	18	17	35	18	15	33	35	3	1	1	129	14.0	50	9	122	31		3	0	0	0	0	0	0	0
	Other Major League Totals		147	25	37	62	....	....	....	63	....	....	....	....	....	....	....	....	....	....	4	0	1	1	0	....	....	....

Selected by **New England** (WHA) in 1972 WHA General Player Draft, February 12, 1972. Traded to **Boston** by **California** with Carol Vadnais for Reggie Leach, Rick Smith and Bob Stewart, February 23, 1972. WHA rights traded to **Philadelphia** (WHA) by **New England** (WHA) for cash, June, 1972. Claimed by **Rochester** (AHL) from **Boston** in Reverse Draft, June 12, 1972. Transferred to **Vancouver** (WHA) after **Philadelphia** (WHA) franchise relocated, May, 1973. Selected by **Cincinnati** (WHA) from **Toronto** (WHA) in 1975 WHA Expansion Draft, June, 1975.

• ODROWSKI, Gerry

Gerald Bernard "Snowy / The Hook" D – L. 5'10", 185 lbs. b: Trout Creek, Ont., 10/4/1938.

Season	Club	League	GP	G	A	Pts	AG	AA	APts	PIM	PP	SH	GW	S	%	TGF	PGF	TGA	PGA	+/–	GP	G	A	Pts	PIM	PP	SH	GW
1955-56	Sundridge Beavers	OHA-I	STATISTICS NOT AVAILABLE																									
1956-57	St. Michael's Majors	OHA-Jr.	52	0	1	1	....	....	....	4	....	....	....	....	....	....	....	....	....	....	....	....	....	....	....	....	....	....
1957-58	Sault Ste. Marie Greyhounds	NOHA	48	4	7	11	....	....	....	20	....	....	....	....	....	....	....	....	....	....	1	0	0	0	0	....	....	....
1958-59	Sault Ste. Marie Greyhounds	NOHA	53	3	12	15	....	....	....	40	....	....	....	....	....	....	....	....	....	....	4	0	0	0	2	....	....	....
1959-60	Sudbury Wolves	EPHL	67	8	21	29	....	....	....	69	....	....	....	....	....	....	....	....	....	....	4	1	8	9	28	....	....	....
1960-61	Detroit Red Wings	NHL	68	1	4	5	1	4	5	45	....	....	....	....	....	....	....	....	....	....	10	0	0	0	4	0	0	0
1961-62	Detroit Red Wings	NHL	69	1	6	7	1	6	7	24	....	....	....	....	....	....	....	....	....	....	....	....	....	....	....	....	....	....
1962-63	Detroit Red Wings	NHL	1	0	0	0	0	0	0	0	....	....	....	....	....	....	....	....	....	....	2	0	0	0	2	0	0	0
	Pittsburgh Hornets	AHL	69	7	23	30	....	....	....	125	....	....	....	....	....	....	....	....	....	....	....	....	....	....	....	....	....	....
1963-64	Quebec Aces	AHL	8	0	0	0	....	....	....	25	....	....	....	....	....	....	....	....	....	....	....	....	....	....	....	....	....	....
	San Francisco Seals	WHL	37	3	12	15	....	....	....	70	....	....	....	....	....	....	....	....	....	....	11	0	3	3	30	....	....	....
1964-65	San Francisco Seals	WHL	70	9	20	29	....	....	....	114	....	....	....	....	....	....	....	....	....	....	....	....	....	....	....	....	....	....
1965-66	San Francisco Seals	WHL	71	7	24	31	....	....	....	102	....	....	....	....	....	....	....	....	....	....	7	0	0	0	4	....	....	....
1966-67	California Seals	WHL	72	8	27	35	....	....	....	64	....	....	....	....	....	....	....	....	....	....	6	0	1	1	10	....	....	....
1967-68	Oakland Seals	NHL	42	4	6	10	5	6	11	10	0	2	2	40	10.0	17	3	28	14	0	....	....	....	....	....	....	....	....
	Vancouver Canucks	WHL	8	2	3	5	....	....	....	6	....	....	....	....	....	....	....	....	....	....	....	....	....	....	....	....	....	....
1968-69	Oakland Seals	NHL	74	5	1	6	5	1	6	24	0	3	0	54	9.3	14	0	44	34	4	7	0	1	1	2	0	0	0
1969-70	San Diego Gulls	WHL	68	6	30	36	....	....	....	78	....	....	....	....	....	....	....	....	....	....	6	0	2	2	12	....	....	....
1970-71	Phoenix Roadrunners	WHL	70	7	28	35	....	....	....	56	....	....	....	....	....	....	....	....	....	....	10	0	5	5	13	....	....	....
1971-72	Phoenix Roadrunners	WHL	20	3	4	7	....	....	....	30	....	....	....	....	....	....	....	....	....	....	....	....	....	....	....	....	....	....
	St. Louis Blues	NHL	55	1	2	3	1	2	3	8	0	1	0	30	3.3	7	0	33	25	–1	11	0	0	0	8	0	0	0
1972-73	Los Angeles Sharks	WHA	78	6	31	37	....	....	....	89	....	....	....	....	....	....	....	....	....	....	6	1	2	3	6	....	....	....
1973-74	Los Angeles Sharks	WHA	77	4	32	36	....	....	....	48	....	....	....	....	....	....	....	....	....	....	....	....	....	....	....	....	....	....
1974-75	Phoenix Roadrunners	WHA	77	5	38	43	....	....	....	77	....	....	....	....	....	....	....	....	....	....	5	0	2	2	0	....	....	....
1975-76	Minnesota Fighting Saints	WHA	37	1	12	13	....	....	....	10	....	....	....	....	....	....	....	....	....	....	....	....	....	....	....	....	....	....
	Winnipeg Jets	WHA	13	0	1	1	....	....	....	6	....	....	....	....	....	....	....	....	....	....	....	....	....	....	....	....	....	....
	NHL Totals		309	12	19	31	13	19	32	111	....	....	....	....	....	....	....	....	....	....	30	0	1	1	16	....	....	....
	Other Major League Totals		282	16	114	130	....	....	....	230	....	....	....	....	....	....	....	....	....	....	11	1	4	5	6	....	....	....

WHL Second All-Star Team (1967)

Traded to **Boston** by **Detroit** for Warren Godfrey, October 10, 1963. Traded to **San Francisco** (WHL) by **Boston** with future considerations (loan of Dallas Smith for 1964-65 season, July 8, 1964) for Cliff Pennington, December 17, 1963. NHL rights transferred to **California** after owners of **San Francisco** (WHL) franchise awarded NHL expansion franchise, April 5, 1966. Traded to **San Diego** (WHL) by **Oakland** for cash, October 1, 1969. Traded to **Phoenix** by **San Diego** (WHL) for cash, October, 1970. Traded to **St. Louis** by **Phoenix** (WHL) for cash, November 28, 1971. Selected by **LA Sharks** (WHA) in 1972 WHA General Player Draft, February 12, 1972. Transferred to **Michigan** (WHA) after **LA Sharks** (WHA) franchise relocated, April 11, 1974. Claimed by **Phoenix** (WHA) from **Michigan** in 1974 WHA Expansion Draft, June, 1974. Claimed by **Minnesota** (WHA) from **Phoenix** (WHA) in WHA Intra-League Draft, May 19, 1975. Traded to **Winnipeg** (WHA) by **Minnesota** (WHA) for Perry Miller, January, 1976.

• O'DWYER, Bill

William M. C – L. 6', 190 lbs. b: Boston, MA, 1/25/1960. Los Angeles' 10th, 157th overall, in 1980.

Season	Club	League	GP	G	A	Pts	AG	AA	APts	PIM	PP	SH	GW	S	%	TGF	PGF	TGA	PGA	+/–	GP	G	A	Pts	PIM	PP	SH	GW
1977-78	Don Bosco Boston	MBAHL	STATISTICS NOT AVAILABLE																									
1978-79	Boston College	ECAC	30	9	30	39	....	....	....	14	....	....	....	....	....	....	....	....	....	....	....	....	....	....	....	....	....	....
1979-80	Boston College	ECAC	33	20	22	42	....	....	....	22	....	....	....	....	....	....	....	....	....	....	....	....	....	....	....	....	....	....
1980-81	Boston College	ECAC	31	20	20	40	....	....	....	6	....	....	....	....	....	....	....	....	....	....	....	....	....	....	....	....	....	....
1981-82	Boston College	ECAC	30	15	26	41	....	....	....	10	....	....	....	....	....	....	....	....	....	....	....	....	....	....	....	....	....	....
1982-83	New Haven Nighthawks	AHL	77	24	23	47	....	....	....	29	....	....	....	....	....	....	....	....	....	....	11	3	4	7	9	....	....	....
1983-84	Los Angeles Kings	NHL	5	0	0	0	0	0	0	0	0	0	0	2	0.0	1	0	0	0	1	....	....	....	....	....	....	....	....
	New Haven Nighthawks	AHL	58	15	42	57	....	....	....	39	....	....	....	....	....	....	....	....	....	....	....	....	....	....	....	....	....	....
1984-85	Los Angeles Kings	NHL	13	1	0	1	1	0	1	15	0	0	0	8	12.5	2	0	4	2	0	....	....	....	....	....	....	....	....
	New Haven Nighthawks	AHL	46	19	24	43	....	....	....	27	....	....	....	....	....	....	....	....	....	....	....	....	....	....	....	....	....	....
1985-86	New Haven Nighthawks	AHL	41	10	15	25	....	....	....	41	....	....	....	....	....	....	....	....	....	....	5	0	1	1	2	....	....	....
1986-87	New Haven Nighthawks	AHL	65	22	42	64	....	....	....	74	....	....	....	....	....	....	....	....	....	....	3	0	0	0	14	....	....	....
1987-88	Boston Bruins	NHL	77	7	10	17	6	7	13	83	1	0	1	98	7.1	33	1	53	18	–3	9	0	0	0	0	0	0	0
1988-89	Boston Bruins	NHL	19	1	2	3	1	1	2	8	0	0	0	18	5.6	4	0	11	3	–4	....	....	....	....	....	....	....	....
1989-90	Boston Bruins	NHL	6	0	1	1	0	1	1	2	0	0	0	7	0.0	1	0	3	0	–2	1	0	0	0	2	0	0	0
	Maine Mariners	AHL	71	26	45	71	....	....	....	56	....	....	....	....	....	....	....	....	....	....	....	....	....	....	....	....	....	....
1990-91	New Haven Nighthawks	AHL	6	2	1	3	....	....	....	2	....	....	....	....	....	....	....	....	....	....	....	....	....	....	....	....	....	....
	Phoenix Roadrunners	IHL	25	3	9	12	....	....	....	12	....	....	....	....	....	....	....	....	....	....	11	7	6	13	0	....	....	....
1991-92	Phoenix Roadrunners	IHL	39	9	17	26	....	....	....	12	....	....	....	....	....	....	....	....	....	....	....	....	....	....	....	....	....	....
	NHL Totals		120	9	13	22	8	9	17	108	1	0	1	133	6.8	41	1	71	23		10	0	0	0	2	0	0	0

ECAC Second All-Star Team (1980, 1981, 1982)

Signed as a free agent by **NY Rangers**, July 13, 1985. Signed as a free agent by **Boston**, August 13, 1987. • Missed majority of the 1988-89 season due to a knee injury. Signed as a free agent by **LA Kings**, July 11, 1990.

• O'FLAHERTY, Gerry

Gerard Joseph LW – L. 5'10", 182 lbs. b: Pittsburgh, PA, 8/31/1950. Toronto's 3rd, 36th overall, in 1970.

Season	Club	League	GP	G	A	Pts	AG	AA	APts	PIM	PP	SH	GW	S	%	TGF	PGF	TGA	PGA	+/–	GP	G	A	Pts	PIM	PP	SH	GW
1967-68	North York Rangers	OHA-B	36	19	24	43	....	....	....	13	....	....	....	....	....	....	....	....	....	....	....	....	....	....	....	....	....	....
1968-69	Kitchener Rangers	OHA-Jr.	22	4	3	7	....	....	....	4	....	....	....	....	....	....	....	....	....	....	....	....	....	....	....	....	....	....
1969-70	Kitchener Rangers	OHA-Jr.	54	40	38	78	....	....	....	30	....	....	....	....	....	....	....	....	....	....	6	6	6	12	8	....	....	....
1970-71	Tulsa Oilers	CHL	70	23	29	52	....	....	....	33	....	....	....	....	....	....	....	....	....	....	....	....	....	....	....	....	....	....

Season	Club	League	REGULAR SEASON																		PLAYOFFS							
			GP	G	A	Pts	AG	AA	APts	PIM	PP	SH	GW	S	%	TGF	PGF	TGA	PGA	+/-	GP	G	A	Pts	PIM	PP	SH	GW
1971-72	**Toronto Maple Leafs**	**NHL**	**2**	**0**	**0**	**0**	**0**	**0**	**0**	**0**	**0**	**0**	**0**	**3**	**0.0**	**0**	**0**	**0**	**0**	**0**	....	....	....	....	....	....	....	....
	Tulsa Oilers	CHL	57	22	30	52	....	....	....	48	....	....	....	....	....	....	....	....	....	....	13	6	*9	15	28	....	....	....
1972-73	**Vancouver Canucks**	**NHL**	**78**	**13**	**17**	**30**	**12**	**13**	**25**	**29**	**0**	**0**	**0**	**135**	**9.6**	**46**	**1**	**84**	**22**	**–17**	....	....	....	....	....	....	....	....
1973-74	**Vancouver Canucks**	**NHL**	**78**	**22**	**20**	**42**	**21**	**16**	**37**	**18**	**2**	**0**	**2**	**142**	**15.5**	**61**	**10**	**76**	**20**	**–5**	....	....	....	....	....	....	....	....
1974-75	**Vancouver Canucks**	**NHL**	**80**	**25**	**17**	**42**	**22**	**13**	**35**	**37**	**3**	**2**	**2**	**164**	**15.2**	**62**	**12**	**70**	**26**	**6**	**5**	**2**	**2**	**4**	**6**	**0**	**0**	**0**
1975-76	**Vancouver Canucks**	**NHL**	**68**	**20**	**18**	**38**	**18**	**13**	**31**	**47**	**0**	**1**	**3**	**129**	**15.5**	**56**	**2**	**71**	**28**	**11**	**2**	**0**	**0**	**0**	**0**	**0**	**0**	**0**
1976-77	United States	Can-Cup	4	0	1	1	....	....	....	0	....	....	....	....	....	....	....	....	....	....	....	....	....	....	....	....	....	....
	Vancouver Canucks	**NHL**	**72**	**12**	**12**	**24**	**11**	**9**	**20**	**20**	**1**	**0**	**2**	**114**	**10.5**	**35**	**8**	**66**	**15**	**–24**	....	....	....	....	....	....	....	....
	Tulsa Oilers	CHL	5	2	3	5	....	....	....	2	....	....	....	....	....	....	....	....	....	....	....	....	....	....	....	....	....	....
1977-78	**Vancouver Canucks**	**NHL**	**59**	**6**	**11**	**17**	**5**	**8**	**13**	**15**	**0**	**1**	**0**	**90**	**6.7**	**27**	**2**	**44**	**14**	**–5**	....	....	....	....	....	....	....	....
	Tulsa Oilers	CHL	10	9	7	16	....	....	....	0	....	....	....	....	....	....	....	....	....	....	....	....	....	....	....	....	....	....
1978-79	**Atlanta Flames**	**NHL**	**1**	**1**	**0**	**1**	**1**	**0**	**1**	**2**	**0**	**0**	**0**	**2**	**50.0**	**1**	**0**	**1**	**0**	**0**	....	....	....	....	....	....	....	....
	Tulsa Oilers	CHL	38	18	24	42	....	....	....	18	....	....	....	....	....	....	....	....	....	....	....	....	....	....	....	....	....	....
	Nova Scotia Voyageurs	AHL	35	8	14	22	....	....	....	18	....	....	....	....	....	....	....	....	....	....	10	2	1	3	6	....	....	....
	NHL Totals		**438**	**99**	**95**	**194**	**90**	**72**	**162**	**168**	**6**	**4**	**9**	**779**	**12.7**	**288**	**35**	**412**	**125**		**7**	**2**	**2**	**4**	**6**	**0**	**0**	**0**

• Son of John (Peanuts)

Claimed by **Vancouver** from **Toronto** in Intra-League Draft, June 5, 1972. Signed as a free agent by **Minnesota**, July 15, 1978. Traded to **Atlanta** by **Minnesota** for cash, October 10, 1978.

• OGILVIE, Brian

Brian Hugh C – R. 5'11", 186 lbs. b: Stettler, Alta., 1/30/1952. Chicago's 2nd, 29th overall, in 1972.

Season	Club	League	GP	G	A	Pts	AG	AA	APts	PIM	PP	SH	GW	S	%	TGF	PGF	TGA	PGA	+/-	GP	G	A	Pts	PIM	PP	SH	GW
1968-69	Red Deer Rustlers	AJHL	2	1	0	1	....	....	....	0	....	....	....	....	....	....	....	....	....	....	....	....	....	....	....	....	....	....
1969-70	Red Deer Rustlers	AJHL	40	24	17	41	....	....	....	52	....	....	....	....	....	....	....	....	....	....	....	....	....	....	....	....	....	....
1970-71	Red Deer Rustlers	AJHL	44	29	47	76	....	....	....	106	....	....	....	....	....	....	....	....	....	....	....	....	....	....	....	....	....	....
	Red Deer Rustlers	Cen-Cup	10	10	11	21	....	....	....	17	....	....	....	....	....	....	....	....	....	....	....	....	....	....	....	....	....	....
1971-72	Vancouver Nats	WCJHL	21	11	18	29	....	....	....	21	....	....	....	....	....	....	....	....	....	....	....	....	....	....	....	....	....	....
	Edmonton Oil Kings	WCJHL	33	23	31	54	....	....	....	40	....	....	....	....	....	....	....	....	....	....	16	7	7	14	24	....	....	....
	Edmonton Oil Kings	Mem-Cup	2	1	1	2	....	....	....	4	....	....	....	....	....	....	....	....	....	....	....	....	....	....	....	....	....	....
1972-73	**Chicago Black Hawks**	**NHL**	**12**	**1**	**2**	**3**	**1**	**2**	**3**	**4**	**1**	**0**	**0**	**12**	**8.3**	**3**	**1**	**4**	**0**	**–2**	....	....	....	....	....	....	....	....
	Dallas Black Hawks	CHL	58	17	25	42	....	....	....	64	....	....	....	....	....	....	....	....	....	....	7	1	2	3	16	....	....	....
1973-74	Dallas Black Hawks	CHL	70	21	33	54	....	....	....	66	....	....	....	....	....	....	....	....	....	....	10	2	2	4	4	....	....	....
1974-75	**St. Louis Blues**	**NHL**	**20**	**5**	**5**	**10**	**4**	**4**	**8**	**4**	**0**	**0**	**2**	**36**	**13.9**	**18**	**7**	**25**	**10**	**–4**	....	....	....	....	....	....	....	....
	Denver Spurs	CHL	34	20	12	32	....	....	....	45	....	....	....	....	....	....	....	....	....	....	2	1	0	1	0	....	....	....
1975-76	**St. Louis Blues**	**NHL**	**9**	**2**	**1**	**3**	**2**	**1**	**3**	**2**	**0**	**0**	**0**	**14**	**14.3**	**3**	**0**	**4**	**0**	**–1**	....	....	....	....	....	....	....	....
	Providence Reds	AHL	47	16	18	34	....	....	....	61	....	....	....	....	....	....	....	....	....	....	3	0	2	2	9	....	....	....
1976-77	**St. Louis Blues**	**NHL**	**3**	**0**	**0**	**0**	**0**	**0**	**0**	**0**	**0**	**0**	**0**	**0**	**0.0**	**0**	**0**	**1**	**0**	**–1**	....	....	....	....	....	....	....	....
	Kansas City Blues	CHL	66	26	28	54	....	....	....	91	....	....	....	....	....	....	....	....	....	....	10	2	4	6	17	....	....	....
1977-78	**St. Louis Blues**	**NHL**	**32**	**6**	**8**	**14**	**5**	**6**	**11**	**12**	**3**	**0**	**0**	**63**	**9.5**	**19**	**4**	**30**	**3**	**–12**	....	....	....	....	....	....	....	....
	Salt Lake Golden Eagles	CHL	15	7	7	14	....	....	....	22	....	....	....	....	....	....	....	....	....	....	....	....	....	....	....	....	....	....
1978-79	**St. Louis Blues**	**NHL**	**14**	**1**	**5**	**6**	**1**	**4**	**5**	**7**	**0**	**0**	**0**	**21**	**4.8**	**6**	**1**	**8**	**0**	**–3**	....	....	....	....	....	....	....	....
	Salt Lake Golden Eagles	CHL	59	26	28	54	....	....	....	72	....	....	....	....	....	....	....	....	....	....	5	0	5	5	8	....	....	....
1979-80	Salt Lake Golden Eagles	CHL	75	30	31	61	....	....	....	88	....	....	....	....	....	....	....	....	....	....	13	5	9	14	16	....	....	....
	NHL Totals		**90**	**15**	**21**	**36**	**13**	**17**	**30**	**29**	**4**	**0**	**2**	**146**	**10.3**	**49**	**13**	**72**	**13**		....	....	....	....	....	....	....	....

AJHL First All-Star Team (1971)

Claimed by **St. Louis** from **Chicago** in Intra-League Draft, June 10, 1974.

• OGRODNICK, John

John Alexander LW – L. 6', 204 lbs. b: Ottawa, Ont., 6/20/1959. Detroit's 4th, 66th overall, in 1979.

Season	Club	League	GP	G	A	Pts	AG	AA	APts	PIM	PP	SH	GW	S	%	TGF	PGF	TGA	PGA	+/-	GP	G	A	Pts	PIM	PP	SH	GW
1976-77	Maple Ridge Bruins	BCJHL	67	54	56	110	....	....	....	63	....	....	....	....	....	....	....	....	....	....	....	....	....	....	....	....	....	....
	New Westminster Bruins	WCJHL	14	2	4	6	....	....	....	0	....	....	....	....	....	....	....	....	....	....	14	3	3	6	2	....	....	....
	New Westminster Bruins	Mem-Cup	5	2	0	2	....	....	....	0	....	....	....	....	....	....	....	....	....	....	....	....	....	....	....	....	....	....
1977-78	New Westminster Bruins	WCJHL	72	59	29	88	....	....	....	47	....	....	....	....	....	....	....	....	....	....	21	14	7	21	14	....	....	....
	New Westminster Bruins	Mem-Cup	5	3	1	4	....	....	....	2	....	....	....	....	....	....	....	....	....	....	....	....	....	....	....	....	....	....
1978-79	New Westminster Bruins	WHL	72	48	36	84	....	....	....	38	....	....	....	....	....	....	....	....	....	....	6	2	0	2	4	....	....	....
	Canada	WJC-A	5	3	0	3	....	....	....	4	....	....	....	....	....	....	....	....	....	....	....	....	....	....	....	....	....	....
1979-80	**Detroit Red Wings**	**NHL**	**41**	**8**	**24**	**32**	**7**	**17**	**24**	**8**	**3**	**0**	**1**	**121**	**6.6**	**55**	**13**	**46**	**0**	**–4**	....	....	....	....	....	....	....	....
	Adirondack Red Wings	AHL	39	13	20	33	....	....	....	21	....	....	....	....	....	....	....	....	....	....	....	....	....	....	....	....	....	....
1980-81	**Detroit Red Wings**	**NHL**	**80**	**35**	**35**	**70**	**27**	**23**	**50**	**14**	**9**	**2**	**2**	**276**	**12.7**	**114**	**37**	**102**	**8**	**–17**	....	....	....	....	....	....	....	....
	Canada	WEC-A	8	3	2	5	....	....	....	0	....	....	....	....	....	....	....	....	....	....	....	....	....	....	....	....	....	....
1981-82	**Detroit Red Wings**	**NHL**	**80**	**28**	**26**	**54**	**22**	**17**	**39**	**28**	**3**	**2**	**3**	**254**	**11.0**	**81**	**18**	**93**	**15**	**–15**	....	....	....	....	....	....	....	....
1982-83	**Detroit Red Wings**	**NHL**	**80**	**41**	**44**	**85**	**34**	**31**	**65**	**30**	**5**	**0**	**2**	**254**	**16.1**	**110**	**20**	**90**	**11**	**11**	....	....	....	....	....	....	....	....
1983-84	**Detroit Red Wings**	**NHL**	**64**	**42**	**36**	**78**	**34**	**25**	**59**	**14**	**19**	**3**	**5**	**252**	**16.7**	**112**	**54**	**89**	**15**	**–16**	**4**	**0**	**0**	**0**	**0**	**0**	**0**	**0**
1984-85	**Detroit Red Wings**	**NHL**	**79**	**55**	**50**	**105**	**45**	**34**	**79**	**30**	**15**	**1**	**6**	**303**	**18.2**	**159**	**54**	**125**	**21**	**1**	**3**	**1**	**1**	**2**	**0**	**0**	**0**	**0**
1985-86	**Detroit Red Wings**	**NHL**	**76**	**38**	**32**	**70**	**30**	**22**	**52**	**18**	**15**	**1**	**2**	**208**	**18.3**	**101**	**44**	**90**	**3**	**–30**	....	....	....	....	....	....	....	....
1986-87	**Detroit Red Wings**	**NHL**	**39**	**12**	**28**	**40**	**10**	**20**	**30**	**6**	**4**	**1**	**1**	**117**	**10.3**	**60**	**23**	**40**	**1**	**–2**	....	....	....	....	....	....	....	....
	Quebec Nordiques	**NHL**	**32**	**11**	**16**	**27**	**9**	**12**	**21**	**4**	**2**	**0**	**1**	**127**	**8.7**	**44**	**20**	**30**	**0**	**–6**	**13**	**9**	**4**	**13**	**6**	**3**	**0**	**2**
1987-88	**New York Rangers**	**NHL**	**64**	**22**	**32**	**54**	**19**	**23**	**42**	**16**	**7**	**0**	**5**	**152**	**14.5**	**85**	**40**	**48**	**0**	**–3**	....	....	....	....	....	....	....	....
1988-89	**New York Rangers**	**NHL**	**60**	**13**	**29**	**42**	**11**	**21**	**32**	**14**	**1**	**0**	**1**	**149**	**8.7**	**58**	**7**	**51**	**0**	**0**	**3**	**2**	**0**	**2**	**0**	**1**	**0**	**0**
	Denver Rangers	IHL	3	2	0	2	....	....	....	0	....	....	....	....	....	....	....	....	....	....	....	....	....	....	....	....	....	....
1989-90	**New York Rangers**	**NHL**	**80**	**43**	**31**	**74**	**37**	**22**	**59**	**44**	**19**	**0**	**8**	**215**	**20.0**	**120**	**55**	**54**	**0**	**11**	**10**	**6**	**3**	**9**	**0**	**3**	**0**	**1**
1990-91	**New York Rangers**	**NHL**	**79**	**31**	**23**	**54**	**28**	**17**	**45**	**10**	**12**	**0**	**4**	**250**	**12.4**	**98**	**32**	**51**	**0**	**15**	**4**	**0**	**0**	**0**	**0**	**0**	**0**	**0**
1991-92	**New York Rangers**	**NHL**	**55**	**17**	**13**	**30**	**15**	**10**	**25**	**22**	**3**	**0**	**4**	**110**	**15.5**	**55**	**18**	**32**	**1**	**6**	**3**	**0**	**0**	**0**	**0**	**0**	**0**	**0**
1992-93	**Detroit Red Wings**	**NHL**	**19**	**6**	**6**	**12**	**5**	**4**	**9**	**2**	**4**	**0**	**0**	**25**	**24.0**	**17**	**11**	**8**	**0**	**–2**	**1**	**0**	**0**	**0**	**0**	**0**	**0**	**0**
	Adirondack Red Wings	AHL	4	2	2	4	....	....	....	0	....	....	....	....	....	....	....	....	....	....	....	....	....	....	....	....	....	....
	NHL Totals		**928**	**402**	**425**	**827**	**333**	**298**	**631**	**260**	**121**	**10**	**45**	**2813**	**14.3**	**1269**	**446**	**949**	**75**		**41**	**18**	**8**	**26**	**6**	**7**	**0**	**3**

NHL First All-Star Team (1985) • Played in NHL All-Star Game (1981, 1982, 1984, 1985, 1986)

Traded to **Quebec** by **Detroit** with Basil McRae and Doug Shedden for Brent Ashton, Gilbert Delorme and Mark Kumpel, January 17, 1987. Traded to **NY Rangers** by **Quebec** with David Shaw for Jeff Jackson and Terry Carkner, September 30, 1987. Signed as a free agent by **Detroit**, September 29, 1992.

• OHLUND, Mattias

D – L. 6'2", 220 lbs. b: Pitea, Sweden, 9/9/1976. Vancouver's 1st, 13th overall, in 1994.

Season	Club	League	GP	G	A	Pts	AG	AA	APts	PIM	PP	SH	GW	S	%	TGF	PGF	TGA	PGA	+/-	GP	G	A	Pts	PIM	PP	SH	GW
1992-93	Pitea IK	Sweden 2	22	0	6	6	....	....	....	16	....	....	....	....	....	....	....	....	....	....	....	....	....	....	....	....	....	....
1993-94	Pitea IK	Sweden 2	28	7	10	17	....	....	....	62	....	....	....	....	....	....	....	....	....	....	....	....	....	....	....	....	....	....
	Sweden	WJC-A	7	0	2	2	....	....	....	2	....	....	....	....	....	....	....	....	....	....	....	....	....	....	....	....	....	....
	Sweden	EJC-A	5	0	6	6	....	....	....	8	....	....	....	....	....	....	....	....	....	....	....	....	....	....	....	....	....	....
1994-95	Lulea HF	Sweden	34	6	10	16	....	....	....	34	....	....	....	....	....	....	....	....	....	....	9	4	0	4	16	....	....	....
	Sweden	WJC-A	7	1	0	1	....	....	....	4	....	....	....	....	....	....	....	....	....	....	....	....	....	....	....	....	....	....
1995-96	Lulea HF	Sweden	38	4	10	14	....	....	....	26	....	....	....	....	....	....	....	....	....	....	13	1	0	1	47	....	....	....
	Sweden	WJC-A	7	0	5	5	....	....	....	32	....	....	....	....	....	....	....	....	....	....	....	....	....	....	....	....	....	....
1996-97	Lulea HF	Sweden	47	7	9	16	....	....	....	38	....	....	....	....	....	....	....	....	....	....	10	1	2	3	8	....	....	....
	Lulea HF	EuroHL	6	0	3	3	....	....	....	0	....	....	....	....	....	....	....	....	....	....	....	....	....	....	....	....	....	....
	Sweden	WC-A	11	2	1	3	....	....	....	12	....	....	....	....	....	....	....	....	....	....	....	....	....	....	....	....	....	....
1997-98	**Vancouver Canucks**	**NHL**	**77**	**7**	**23**	**30**	**8**	**23**	**31**	**76**	**1**	**0**	**0**	**172**	**4.1**	**84**	**19**	**81**	**19**	**3**	....	....	....	....	....	....	....	....
	Sweden	Olympics	4	0	1	1	....	....	....	4	....	....	....	....	....	....	....	....	....	....	....	....	....	....	....	....	....	....
1998-99	**Vancouver Canucks**	**NHL**	**74**	**9**	**26**	**35**	**11**	**25**	**36**	**83**	**2**	**1**	**1**	**129**	**7.0**	**93**	**43**	**97**	**28**	**–19**	....	....	....	....	....	....	....	....
99-2000	**Vancouver Canucks**	**NHL**	**42**	**4**	**16**	**20**	**4**	**15**	**19**	**24**	**2**	**1**	**1**	**63**	**6.3**	**67**	**21**	**55**	**15**	**6**	....	....	....	....	....	....	....	....
	NHL Totals		**193**	**20**	**65**	**85**	**23**	**63**	**86**	**183**	**5**	**2**	**2**	**364**	**5.5**	**244**	**83**	**233**	**62**		....	....	....	....	....	....	....	....

WJC-A All-Star Team (1996) • Named Best Defenseman at WJC-A (1996) • NHL All-Rookie Team (1998) • Played in NHL All-Star Game (1999)

• OJANEN, Janne

Janne Juhani C – L. 6'2", 200 lbs. b: Tampere, Finland, 4/9/1968. New Jersey's 3rd, 45th overall, in 1986.

Season	Club	League	REGULAR SEASON																		PLAYOFFS							
			GP	G	A	Pts	AG	AA	APts	PIM	PP	SH	GW	S	%	TGF	PGF	TGA	PGA	+/–	GP	G	A	Pts	PIM	PP	SH	GW
1984-85	Tappara Tampere	Finland-Jr.	STATISTICS NOT AVAILABLE																									
	Whitby Lawmen	OJHL	15	8	6	14	....	....	....	6	....	....	....	....	....	....	....	....	....	....	....	....	....	....	....	....	....	....
1985-86	Tappara Tampere	Finland-Jr.	14	5	17	22	....	....	....	14	....	....	....	....	....	....	....	....	....	....	5	2	3	5	8	....	....	....
	Tappara Tampere	Finland	3	0	0	0	....	....	....	2	....	....	....	....	....	....	....	....	....	....	....	....	....	....	....	....	....	....
	Finland	EJC-A	5	5	7	12	....	....	....	10	....	....	....	....	....	....	....	....	....	....	....	....	....	....	....	....	....	....
1986-87	Tappara Tampere	Finland	40	18	13	31	....	....	....	16	....	....	....	....	....	....	....	....	....	....	9	4	6	10	2	....	....	....
	Finland	WJC-A	7	2	10	12	....	....	....	6	....	....	....	....	....	....	....	....	....	....	....	....	....	....	....	....	....	....
	Finland	Nat-Team	6	2	1	3	....	....	....	8	....	....	....	....	....	....	....	....	....	....	....	....	....	....	....	....	....	....
	Finland	WEC-A	8	3	3	6	....	....	....	9	....	....	....	....	....	....	....	....	....	....	....	....	....	....	....	....	....	....
1987-88	Finland	Can-Cup	5	0	1	1	....	....	....	0	....	....	....	....	....	....	....	....	....	....	....	....	....	....	....	....	....	....
	Tappara Tampere	Finland	44	21	31	52	....	....	....	30	....	....	....	....	....	....	....	....	....	....	10	4	4	8	12	....	....	....
	Finland	WJC-A	7	6	5	11	....	....	....	16	....	....	....	....	....	....	....	....	....	....	....	....	....	....	....	....	....	....
	Finland	Nat-Team	13	1	4	5	....	....	....	8	....	....	....	....	....	....	....	....	....	....	....	....	....	....	....	....	....	....
	Finland	Olympics	8	2	1	3	....	....	....	4	....	....	....	....	....	....	....	....	....	....	....	....	....	....	....	....	....	....
1988-89	**New Jersey Devils**	**NHL**	**3**	**0**	**1**	**1**	**0**	**1**	**1**	**2**	**0**	**0**	**0**	**1**	**0.0**	**1**	**0**	**2**	**0**	**–1**	....	....	....	....	....	....	....	....
	Utica Devils	AHL	72	23	37	60	....	....	....	10	....	....	....	....	....	....	....	....	....	....	5	0	3	3	0	....	....	....
1989-90	**New Jersey Devils**	**NHL**	**64**	**17**	**13**	**30**	**15**	**9**	**24**	**12**	**1**	**0**	**1**	**76**	**22.4**	**38**	**7**	**37**	**1**	**–5**	....	....	....	....	....	....	....	....
1990-91	Tappara Tampere	Finland	44	15	33	48	....	....	....	36	....	....	....	....	....	....	....	....	....	....	3	1	2	3	6	....	....	....
	Finland	Nat-Team	3	0	2	2	....	....	....	4	....	....	....	....	....	....	....	....	....	....	....	....	....	....	....	....	....	....
1991-92	Finland	Can-Cup	6	2	2	4	....	....	....	2	....	....	....	....	....	....	....	....	....	....	....	....	....	....	....	....	....	....
	Tappara Tampere	Finland	44	21	27	48	....	....	....	24	....	....	....	....	....	....	....	....	....	....	....	....	....	....	....	....	....	....
	New Jersey Devils	**NHL**	....	....	....	....	....	....	....	....	....	....	....	....	....	....	....	....	....	....	**3**	**0**	**2**	**2**	**0**	**0**	**0**	**0**
	Finland	Nat-Team	13	3	2	5	....	....	....	4	....	....	....	....	....	....	....	....	....	....	....	....	....	....	....	....	....	....
1992-93	**New Jersey Devils**	**NHL**	**31**	**4**	**9**	**13**	**3**	**6**	**9**	**14**	**1**	**0**	**1**	**44**	**9.1**	**29**	**14**	**18**	**1**	**–2**	....	....	....	....	....	....	....	....
	Cincinnati Cyclones	IHL	7	1	8	9	....	....	....	0	....	....	....	....	....	....	....	....	....	....	....	....	....	....	....	....	....	....
1993-94	Tappara Tampere	Finland	39	22	24	46	....	....	....	24	....	....	....	....	....	....	....	....	....	....	10	2	*9	11	2	....	....	....
	Finland	Nat-Team	32	9	7	16	....	....	....	36	....	....	....	....	....	....	....	....	....	....	....	....	....	....	....	....	....	....
	Finland	Olympics	8	4	2	6	....	....	....	8	....	....	....	....	....	....	....	....	....	....	....	....	....	....	....	....	....	....
	Finland	WC-A	8	2	2	4	....	....	....	6	....	....	....	....	....	....	....	....	....	....	....	....	....	....	....	....	....	....
1994-95	Tappara Tampere	Finland	50	22	33	55	....	....	....	74	....	....	....	....	....	....	....	....	....	....	....	....	....	....	....	....	....	....
	HC Lugano	Switz.	....	....	....	....	....	....	....	....	....	....	....	....	....	....	....	....	....	....	1	0	1	1	0	....	....	....
	Finland	Nat-Team	12	4	2	6	....	....	....	4	....	....	....	....	....	....	....	....	....	....	....	....	....	....	....	....	....	....
	Finland	WC-A	8	0	4	4	....	....	....	4	....	....	....	....	....	....	....	....	....	....	....	....	....	....	....	....	....	....
1995-96	Tappara Tampere	Finland	45	20	*44	64	....	....	....	34	....	....	....	....	....	....	....	....	....	....	4	2	2	4	2	....	....	....
	Finland	Nat-Team	13	6	8	14	....	....	....	41	....	....	....	....	....	....	....	....	....	....	....	....	....	....	....	....	....	....
	Finland	WC-A	6	2	0	2	....	....	....	6	....	....	....	....	....	....	....	....	....	....	....	....	....	....	....	....	....	....
1996-97	Finland	W-Cup	4	1	1	2	....	....	....	0	....	....	....	....	....	....	....	....	....	....	....	....	....	....	....	....	....	....
	Malmo IF	Sweden	41	10	29	39	....	....	....	28	....	....	....	....	....	....	....	....	....	....	4	0	1	1	4	....	....	....
	Finland	Nat-Team	20	6	12	18	....	....	....	20	....	....	....	....	....	....	....	....	....	....	....	....	....	....	....	....	....	....
	Finland	WC-A	7	2	4	6	....	....	....	6	....	....	....	....	....	....	....	....	....	....	....	....	....	....	....	....	....	....
1997-98	Malmo IF	Sweden	45	11	22	33	....	....	....	25	....	....	....	....	....	....	....	....	....	....	....	....	....	....	....	....	....	....
	Finland	Nat-Team	6	2	2	4	....	....	....	4	....	....	....	....	....	....	....	....	....	....	....	....	....	....	....	....	....	....
1998-99	Tappara Tampere	Finland	54	14	32	46	....	....	....	30	....	....	....	....	....	....	....	....	....	....	....	....	....	....	....	....	....	....
99-2000	Tappara Tampere	Finland	53	18	*47	65	....	....	....	54	....	....	....	....	....	....	....	....	....	....	4	3	7	10	2	....	....	....
	NHL Totals		**98**	**21**	**23**	**44**	**18**	**16**	**34**	**28**	**2**	**0**	**2**	**121**	**17.4**	**68**	**21**	**57**	**2**		**3**	**0**	**2**	**2**	**0**	**0**	**0**	**0**

Finnish Rookie of the Year (1987)

• OKERLUND, Todd

RW – R. 5'11", 200 lbs. b: Burnsville, MN, 9/6/1964. NY Islanders' 8th, 168th overall, in 1982.

Season	Club	League	REGULAR SEASON																		PLAYOFFS							
			GP	G	A	Pts	AG	AA	APts	PIM	PP	SH	GW	S	%	TGF	PGF	TGA	PGA	+/–	GP	G	A	Pts	PIM	PP	SH	GW
1981-82	Burnsville High School	Hi-School	25	12	20	32	....	....	....	8	....	....	....	....	....	....	....	....	....	....	....	....	....	....	....	....	....	....
1982-83	Burnsville High School	Hi-School	STATISTICS NOT AVAILABLE																									
1983-84	University of Minnesota	WCHA	34	11	20	31	....	....	....	18	....	....	....	....	....	....	....	....	....	....	....	....	....	....	....	....	....	....
	United States	WJC-A	7	2	3	5	....	....	....	4	....	....	....	....	....	....	....	....	....	....	....	....	....	....	....	....	....	....
1984-85	University of Minnesota	WCHA	47	16	27	43	....	....	....	80	....	....	....	....	....	....	....	....	....	....	....	....	....	....	....	....	....	....
1985-86	University of Minnesota	WCHA	48	17	32	49	....	....	....	58	....	....	....	....	....	....	....	....	....	....	....	....	....	....	....	....	....	....
1986-87	University of Minnesota	WCHA	4	0	7	7	....	....	....	0	....	....	....	....	....	....	....	....	....	....	....	....	....	....	....	....	....	....
1987-88	United States	Nat-Team	40	9	16	25	....	....	....	34	....	....	....	....	....	....	....	....	....	....	....	....	....	....	....	....	....	....
	United States	Olympics	3	1	0	1	....	....	....	4	....	....	....	....	....	....	....	....	....	....	....	....	....	....	....	....	....	....
	New York Islanders	**NHL**	**4**	**0**	**0**	**0**	**0**	**0**	**0**	**2**	**0**	**0**	**0**	**3**	**0.0**	**0**	**0**	**0**	**0**	**0**	....	....	....	....	....	....	....	....
	Springfield Indians	AHL	13	2	1	3	....	....	....	9	....	....	....	....	....	....	....	....	....	....	....	....	....	....	....	....	....	....
	NHL Totals		**4**	**0**	**0**	**0**	**0**	**0**	**0**	**2**	**0**	**0**	**0**	**3**	**0.0**	**0**	**0**	**0**	**0**		....	....	....	....	....	....	....	....

• Suffered eventual career-ending knee injury in a game vs. Michigan Tech (WCHA), October 18, 1986.

• OKSIUTA, Roman

RW – L. 6'3", 230 lbs. b: Murmansk, USSR, 8/21/1970. NY Rangers' 11th, 202nd overall, in 1989.

Season	Club	League	REGULAR SEASON																		PLAYOFFS							
			GP	G	A	Pts	AG	AA	APts	PIM	PP	SH	GW	S	%	TGF	PGF	TGA	PGA	+/–	GP	G	A	Pts	PIM	PP	SH	GW
1987-88	Khimik Voskresensk	USSR	11	1	0	1	....	....	....	4	....	....	....	....	....	....	....	....	....	....	....	....	....	....	....	....	....	....
	Soviet Union	EJC-A	6	5	6	11	....	....	....	4	....	....	....	....	....	....	....	....	....	....	....	....	....	....	....	....	....	....
1988-89	Khimik Voskresensk	USSR	34	13	3	16	....	....	....	14	....	....	....	....	....	....	....	....	....	....	....	....	....	....	....	....	....	....
	Soviet Union	WJC-A	7	6	3	9	....	....	....	4	....	....	....	....	....	....	....	....	....	....	....	....	....	....	....	....	....	....
1989-90	Khimik Voskresensk	Fr-Tour	1	0	0	0	....	....	....	0	....	....	....	....	....	....	....	....	....	....	....	....	....	....	....	....	....	....
	Khimik Voskresensk	USSR	37	13	6	19	....	....	....	16	....	....	....	....	....	....	....	....	....	....	....	....	....	....	....	....	....	....
	Soviet Union	WJC-A	7	7	2	9	....	....	....	4	....	....	....	....	....	....	....	....	....	....	....	....	....	....	....	....	....	....
1990-91	Khimik Voskresensk	Fr-Tour	1	0	0	0	....	....	....	0	....	....	....	....	....	....	....	....	....	....	....	....	....	....	....	....	....	....
	Khimik Voskresensk	USSR	41	12	8	20	....	....	....	24	....	....	....	....	....	....	....	....	....	....	....	....	....	....	....	....	....	....
	Khimik Voskresensk	Super-S	4	1	2	3	....	....	....	0	....	....	....	....	....	....	....	....	....	....	....	....	....	....	....	....	....	....
1991-92	Khimik Voskresensk	CIS	42	*24	20	*44	....	....	....	28	....	....	....	....	....	....	....	....	....	....	....	....	....	....	....	....	....	....
1992-93	Khimik Voskresensk	CIS	20	11	2	13	....	....	....	42	....	....	....	....	....	....	....	....	....	....	....	....	....	....	....	....	....	....
	Cape Breton Oilers	AHL	43	26	25	51	....	....	....	22	....	....	....	....	....	....	....	....	....	....	16	9	19	28	12	....	....	....
1993-94	**Edmonton Oilers**	**NHL**	**10**	**1**	**2**	**3**	**1**	**2**	**3**	**4**	**0**	**0**	**0**	**18**	**5.6**	**9**	**2**	**8**	**0**	**–1**	....	....	....	....	....	....	....	....
	Cape Breton Oilers	AHL	47	31	22	53	....	....	....	90	....	....	....	....	....	....	....	....	....	....	4	2	2	4	22	....	....	....
1994-95	Cape Breton Oilers	AHL	25	9	7	16	....	....	....	20	....	....	....	....	....	....	....	....	....	....	....	....	....	....	....	....	....	....
	Edmonton Oilers	**NHL**	**26**	**11**	**2**	**13**	**19**	**3**	**22**	**8**	**5**	**0**	**0**	**52**	**21.2**	**20**	**9**	**25**	**0**	**–14**	....	....	....	....	....	....	....	....
	Vancouver Canucks	**NHL**	**12**	**5**	**2**	**7**	**9**	**3**	**12**	**2**	**1**	**0**	**1**	**15**	**33.3**	**11**	**3**	**6**	**0**	**2**	**10**	**2**	**3**	**5**	**0**	**1**	**0**	**0**
1995-96	**Vancouver Canucks**	**NHL**	**56**	**16**	**23**	**39**	**16**	**19**	**35**	**42**	**5**	**0**	**1**	**92**	**17.4**	**70**	**20**	**50**	**2**	**2**	....	....	....	....	....	....	....	....
	Mighty Ducks of Anaheim	**NHL**	**14**	**7**	**5**	**12**	**7**	**4**	**11**	**18**	**6**	**0**	**0**	**27**	**25.9**	**19**	**12**	**5**	**0**	**2**	....	....	....	....	....	....	....	....
	Russia	WC-A	7	3	0	3	....	....	....	2	....	....	....	....	....	....	....	....	....	....	....	....	....	....	....	....	....	....
1996-97	**Mighty Ducks of Anaheim**	**NHL**	**28**	**6**	**7**	**13**	**6**	**6**	**12**	**22**	**2**	**0**	**0**	**48**	**12.5**	**18**	**6**	**24**	**0**	**–12**	....	....	....	....	....	....	....	....
	Pittsburgh Penguins	**NHL**	**7**	**0**	**0**	**0**	**0**	**0**	**0**	**4**	**0**	**0**	**0**	**10**	**0.0**	**2**	**0**	**6**	**0**	**–4**	....	....	....	....	....	....	....	....
1997-98	Furuset Oslo	Norway	10	10	7	17	....	....	....	44	....	....	....	....	....	....	....	....	....	....	....	....	....	....	....	....	....	....
	Fort Wayne Komets	IHL	19	5	8	13	....	....	....	50	....	....	....	....	....	....	....	....	....	....	3	0	0	0	12	....	....	....
1998-99	KalPa Kuopio	Finland	10	4	2	6	....	....	....	55	....	....	....	....	....	....	....	....	....	....	....	....	....	....	....	....	....	....
	Lukko Rauma	Finland	16	0	7	7	....	....	....	79	....	....	....	....	....	....	....	....	....	....	....	....	....	....	....	....	....	....
	NHL Totals		**153**	**46**	**41**	**87**	**58**	**37**	**95**	**100**	**19**	**0**	**2**	**262**	**17.6**	**149**	**52**	**124**	**2**		**10**	**2**	**3**	**5**	**0**	**1**	**0**	**0**

Won Izvestia Trophy (CIS Top Scorer) (1992)

Traded to **Edmonton** by **NY Rangers** with NY Rangers' 3rd round choice (Alexander Kerch) in 1993 Entry Draft for Kevin Lowe, December 11, 1992. Traded to **Vancouver** by **Edmonton** for Jiri Slegr, April 7, 1995. Traded to **Anaheim** by **Vancouver** for Mike Sillinger, March 15, 1996. Traded to **Pittsburgh** by **Anaheim** for Richard Park, March 18, 1997.

			REGULAR SEASON																		PLAYOFFS							
Season	Club	League	GP	G	A	Pts	AG	AA	APts	PIM	PP	SH	GW	S	%	TGF	PGF	TGA	PGA	+/–	GP	G	A	Pts	PIM	PP	SH	GW

• OLAUSSON, Fredrik Fredrik K.G. D – R. 6'2", 198 lbs. b: Dadesjo, Sweden, 10/5/1966. Winnipeg's 4th, 81st overall, in 1985.

Season	Club	League	GP	G	A	Pts	AG	AA	APts	PIM	PP	SH	GW	S	%	TGF	PGF	TGA	PGA	+/–	GP	G	A	Pts	PIM	PP	SH	GW
1982-83	Nybro SK	Sweden-2	31	4	4	8	....	....	....	12	....	....	....	....	....	....	....	....	....	....	....	....	....	....	....	....	....	....
1983-84	Nybro SK	Sweden-2	28	8	14	22	....	....	....	32	....	....	....	....	....	....	....	....	....	....	....	....	....	....	....	....	....	....
	Sweden	EJC-A	5	2	3	5	....	....	....	14	....	....	....	....	....	....	....	....	....	....	....	....	....	....	....	....	....	....
1984-85	Farjestads BK Stockholm	Sweden	29	5	12	17	....	....	....	22	....	....	....	....	....	....	....	....	....	....	3	1	0	1	0	....	....	....
	Sweden	WJC-A	7	1	1	2	....	....	....	4	....	....	....	....	....	....	....	....	....	....	....	....	....	....	....	....	....	....
1985-86	Farjestads BK Stockholm	Sweden	33	4	12	16	....	....	....	22	....	....	....	....	....	....	....	....	....	....	8	3	2	5	6	....	....	....
	Sweden	WJC-A	7	4	2	6	....	....	....	11	....	....	....	....	....	....	....	....	....	....	....	....	....	....	....	....	....	....
	Sweden	WEC-A	10	1	0	1	....	....	....	4	....	....	....	....	....	....	....	....	....	....	....	....	....	....	....	....	....	....
1986-87	**Winnipeg Jets**	**NHL**	72	7	29	36	6	21	27	24	1	0	2	119	5.9	82	21	70	6	–3	10	2	3	5	4	1	0	0
1987-88	**Winnipeg Jets**	**NHL**	38	5	10	15	4	7	11	18	2	0	2	65	7.7	47	15	32	3	3	5	1	1	2	0	0	0	0
1988-89	**Winnipeg Jets**	**NHL**	75	15	47	62	13	33	46	32	4	0	1	178	8.4	148	41	129	28	6	....	....	....	....	....	....	....	....
	Sweden	WEC-A	9	3	1	4	....	....	....	6	....	....	....	....	....	....	....	....	....	....	....	....	....	....	....	....	....	....
1989-90	**Winnipeg Jets**	**NHL**	77	9	46	55	8	33	41	32	3	0	0	147	6.1	116	36	106	25	–1	7	0	2	2	2	0	0	0
1990-91	**Winnipeg Jets**	**NHL**	71	12	29	41	11	22	33	24	5	0	0	168	7.1	95	40	91	14	–22	....	....	....	....	....	....	....	....
1991-92	**Winnipeg Jets**	**NHL**	77	20	42	62	18	32	50	34	13	1	2	227	8.8	108	65	94	20	–31	7	1	5	6	4	1	0	0
1992-93	**Winnipeg Jets**	**NHL**	68	16	41	57	13	28	41	22	11	0	3	165	9.7	110	65	57	8	–4	6	0	2	2	2	0	0	0
1993-94	**Winnipeg Jets**	**NHL**	18	2	5	7	2	4	6	10	1	0	0	41	4.9	20	10	13	0	–3	....	....	....	....	....	....	....	....
	Edmonton Oilers	**NHL**	55	9	19	28	8	15	23	20	6	0	1	85	10.6	72	31	67	22	–4	....	....	....	....	....	....	....	....
1994-95	EV Ehrwald	Austria-2	10	4	3	7	....	....	....	8	....	....	....	....	....	....	....	....	....	....	....	....	....	....	....	....	....	....
	Edmonton Oilers	**NHL**	33	0	10	10	0	15	15	20	0	0	0	52	0.0	35	10	42	13	–4	....	....	....	....	....	....	....	....
1995-96	**Edmonton Oilers**	**NHL**	20	0	6	6	0	5	5	14	0	0	0	20	0.0	19	11	28	6	–14	....	....	....	....	....	....	....	....
	Mighty Ducks of Anaheim	**NHL**	36	2	16	18	2	13	15	24	1	0	0	63	3.2	50	27	20	4	7	....	....	....	....	....	....	....	....
1996-97	**Mighty Ducks of Anaheim**	**NHL**	20	2	9	11	2	8	10	8	1	0	0	35	5.7	28	9	29	5	–5	....	....	....	....	....	....	....	....
	Pittsburgh Penguins	**NHL**	51	7	20	27	7	18	25	24	2	0	3	75	9.3	83	25	44	7	21	4	0	1	1	0	0	0	0
1997-98	**Pittsburgh Penguins**	**NHL**	76	6	27	33	7	26	33	42	2	0	1	89	6.7	96	39	54	10	13	6	0	3	3	2	0	0	0
1998-99	**Mighty Ducks of Anaheim**	**NHL**	74	16	40	56	19	39	58	30	10	0	2	121	13.2	115	65	35	2	17	4	0	2	2	4	0	0	0
99-2000	**Mighty Ducks of Anaheim**	**NHL**	70	15	19	34	17	18	35	28	8	0	1	120	12.5	69	38	44	0	–13	....	....	....	....	....	....	....	....
	NHL Totals		**931**	**143**	**415**	**558**	**137**	**337**	**474**	**406**	**70**	**1**	**18**	**1770**	**8.1**	**1293**	**548**	**955**	**173**		**49**	**4**	**19**	**23**	**18**	**2**	**0**	**0**

Swedish World All-Star Team (1986)

Traded to **Edmonton** by **Winnipeg** with Winnipeg's 7th round choice (Curtis Sheptak) in 1994 Entry Draft for Edmonton's 3rd round choice (Tavis Hansen) in 1994 Entry Draft, December 6, 1993. Claimed on waivers by **Anaheim** from **Edmonton**, January 16, 1996. Traded to **Pittsburgh** by **Anaheim** with Alex Hicks for Shawn Antoski and Dmitri Mironov, November 19, 1996. Signed as a free agent by **Anaheim**, August 28, 1998.

• OLCZYK, Ed Edward Walter C – L. 6'1", 207 lbs. b: Chicago, IL, 8/16/1966. Chicago's 1st, 3rd overall, in 1984.

Season	Club	League	GP	G	A	Pts	AG	AA	APts	PIM	PP	SH	GW	S	%	TGF	PGF	TGA	PGA	+/–	GP	G	A	Pts	PIM	PP	SH	GW
1981-82	Team Illinois All-Stars	MNHL	56	74	95	169	....	....	....	63	....	....	....	....	....	....	....	....	....	....	....	....	....	....	....	....	....	....
1982-83	Stratford Cullitons	OJHL-B	42	*50	*92	*142	....	....	....	54	....	....	....	....	....	....	....	....	....	....	....	....	....	....	....	....	....	....
1983-84	United States	Nat-Team	62	21	47	68	....	....	....	36	....	....	....	....	....	....	....	....	....	....	....	....	....	....	....	....	....	....
	United States	Olympics	6	2	5	7	....	....	....	0	....	....	....	....	....	....	....	....	....	....	....	....	....	....	....	....	....	....
1984-85	**Chicago Black Hawks**	**NHL**	70	20	30	50	16	20	36	67	1	1	2	136	14.7	72	7	59	5	11	15	6	5	11	11	1	1	0
	United States	WEC-A	6	1	6	7	....	....	....	6	....	....	....	....	....	....	....	....	....	....	....	....	....	....	....	....	....	....
1985-86	**Chicago Black Hawks**	**NHL**	79	29	50	79	23	34	57	47	8	1	2	218	13.3	124	37	108	23	2	3	0	0	0	0	0	0	0
	United States	WEC-A	7	4	6	10	....	....	....	12	....	....	....	....	....	....	....	....	....	....	....	....	....	....	....	....	....	....
1986-87	**Chicago Blackhawks**	**NHL**	79	16	35	51	14	25	39	119	2	1	2	181	8.8	67	11	73	13	–4	4	1	1	2	4	0	0	0
	United States	WEC-A	10	4	3	7	....	....	....	10	....	....	....	....	....	....	....	....	....	....	....	....	....	....	....	....	....	....
1987-88	United States	Can-Cup	5	1	1	2	....	....	....	2	....	....	....	....	....	....	....	....	....	....	....	....	....	....	....	....	....	....
	Toronto Maple Leafs	**NHL**	80	42	33	75	36	24	60	55	14	4	3	243	17.3	100	34	132	44	–22	6	5	4	9	2	1	1	1
1988-89	**Toronto Maple Leafs**	**NHL**	80	38	52	90	32	37	69	75	11	2	4	249	15.3	119	39	111	31	0	....	....	....	....	....	....	....	....
	United States	WEC-A	10	4	3	7	....	....	....	10	....	....	....	....	....	....	....	....	....	....	....	....	....	....	....	....	....	....
1989-90	**Toronto Maple Leafs**	**NHL**	79	32	56	88	28	40	68	78	6	0	4	208	15.4	128	36	101	9	0	5	1	2	3	14	0	0	0
1990-91	**Toronto Maple Leafs**	**NHL**	18	4	10	14	4	8	12	13	0	0	0	45	8.9	17	7	21	4	–7	....	....	....	....	....	....	....	....
	Winnipeg Jets	**NHL**	61	26	31	57	24	24	48	69	14	0	2	181	14.4	77	36	61	0	–20	....	....	....	....	....	....	....	....
1991-92	United States	Can-Cup	8	0	3	3	....	....	....	4	....	....	....	....	....	....	....	....	....	....	....	....	....	....	....	....	....	....
	Winnipeg Jets	**NHL**	64	32	33	65	29	25	54	67	12	0	7	245	13.1	101	49	41	0	11	6	2	1	3	4	0	0	1
1992-93	**Winnipeg Jets**	**NHL**	25	8	12	20	7	8	15	26	2	0	0	81	9.9	34	17	28	0	–11	....	....	....	....	....	....	....	....
	New York Rangers	**NHL**	46	13	16	29	11	11	22	26	0	0	1	109	11.9	49	15	25	0	9	....	....	....	....	....	....	....	....
	United States	WC-A	6	1	1	2	....	....	....	18	....	....	....	....	....	....	....	....	....	....	....	....	....	....	....	....	....	....
1993-94♦	**New York Rangers**	**NHL**	37	3	5	8	3	4	7	28	0	0	1	40	7.5	12	2	11	0	–1	1	0	0	0	0	0	0	0
1994-95	**New York Rangers**	**NHL**	20	2	1	3	4	1	5	4	1	0	0	29	6.9	7	1	8	0	–2	....	....	....	....	....	....	....	....
	Winnipeg Jets	**NHL**	13	2	8	10	4	12	16	8	1	0	0	27	7.4	14	5	8	0	1	....	....	....	....	....	....	....	....
1995-96	**Winnipeg Jets**	**NHL**	51	27	22	49	27	18	45	65	16	0	1	147	18.4	69	28	42	1	0	6	1	2	3	6	0	0	0
1996-97	**Los Angeles Kings**	**NHL**	67	21	23	44	22	20	42	45	0	0	5	166	12.7	66	22	75	9	–22	....	....	....	....	....	....	....	....
	Pittsburgh Penguins	**NHL**	12	4	7	11	4	6	10	6	5	1	1	29	13.8	16	4	4	0	8	5	1	0	1	12	0	1	1
1997-98	**Pittsburgh Penguins**	**NHL**	56	11	11	22	13	11	24	35	5	1	1	123	8.9	39	17	38	7	–9	6	2	0	2	4	1	1	1
1998-99	**Chicago Blackhawks**	**NHL**	61	10	15	25	12	14	26	29	2	1	2	88	11.4	41	7	48	11	–3	....	....	....	....	....	....	....	....
	Chicago Wolves	IHL	7	2	2	4	....	....	....	6	....	....	....	....	....	....	....	....	....	....	....	....	....	....	....	....	....	....
99-2000	**Chicago Blackhawks**	**NHL**	33	2	2	4	2	2	4	12	0	0	0	33	6.1	11	1	18	0	–8	....	....	....	....	....	....	....	....
	NHL Totals		**1031**	**342**	**452**	**794**	**315**	**344**	**659**	**874**	**100**	**12**	**38**	**2578**	**13.3**	**1163**	**375**	**1012**	**157**		**57**	**19**	**15**	**34**	**57**	**3**	**4**	**4**

Traded to **Toronto** by **Chicago** with Al Secord for Rick Vaive, Steve Thomas and Bob McGill, September 3, 1987. Traded to **Winnipeg** by **Toronto** with Mark Osborne for Dave Ellett and Paul Fenton, November 10, 1990. Traded to **NY Rangers** by **Winnipeg** for Kris King and Tie Domi, December 28, 1992. • Missed majority of 1993-94 season recovering from thumb injury suffered in game vs. Florida, January 3, 1994. Traded to **Winnipeg** by **NY Rangers** for Winnipeg's 5th round choice (Alexei Vasiliev) in 1995 Entry Draft, April 7, 1995. Signed as a free agent by **LA Kings**, July 8, 1996. Traded to **Pittsburgh** by **LA Kings** for Glen Murray, March 18, 1997. Signed as a free agent by **Chicago**, August 26, 1998. • Missed majority of 1999-2000 season recovering from hernia injury suffered in game vs. Pittsburgh, Oct. 16, 1999.

• OLIVER, David David Lee RW – R. 6', 190 lbs. b: Sechelt, B.C., 4/17/1971. Edmonton's 7th, 144th overall, in 1991.

Season	Club	League	GP	G	A	Pts	AG	AA	APts	PIM	PP	SH	GW	S	%	TGF	PGF	TGA	PGA	+/–	GP	G	A	Pts	PIM	PP	SH	GW
1988-89	Vernon Lakers	BCJHL	58	41	38	79	....	....	....	38	....	....	....	....	....	....	....	....	....	....	....	....	....	....	....	....	....	....
1989-90	Vernon Lakers	BCJHL	58	51	48	99	....	....	....	22	....	....	....	....	....	....	....	....	....	....	....	....	....	....	....	....	....	....
	Vernon Lakers	Cen-Cup	6	3	6	9	....	....	....	0	....	....	....	....	....	....	....	....	....	....	....	....	....	....	....	....	....	....
1990-91	University of Michigan	CCHA	27	13	11	24	....	....	....	34	....	....	....	....	....	....	....	....	....	....	....	....	....	....	....	....	....	....
1991-92	University of Michigan	CCHA	44	31	27	58	....	....	....	32	....	....	....	....	....	....	....	....	....	....	....	....	....	....	....	....	....	....
1992-93	University of Michigan	CCHA	40	35	20	55	....	....	....	18	....	....	....	....	....	....	....	....	....	....	....	....	....	....	....	....	....	....
1993-94	University of Michigan	CCHA	41	28	40	68	....	....	....	16	....	....	....	....	....	....	....	....	....	....	....	....	....	....	....	....	....	....
1994-95	Cape Breton Oilers	AHL	32	11	18	29	....	....	....	8	....	....	....	....	....	....	....	....	....	....	....	....	....	....	....	....	....	....
	Edmonton Oilers	**NHL**	44	16	14	30	28	21	49	20	10	0	0	79	20.3	43	23	31	0	–11	....	....	....	....	....	....	....	....
1995-96	**Edmonton Oilers**	**NHL**	80	20	19	39	20	16	36	34	14	0	0	131	15.3	64	34	53	1	–22	....	....	....	....	....	....	....	....
1996-97	**Edmonton Oilers**	**NHL**	17	1	2	3	1	2	3	4	0	0	0	22	4.5	5	1	12	0	–8	....	....	....	....	....	....	....	....
	New York Rangers	**NHL**	14	2	1	3	2	1	3	4	0	0	0	13	15.4	5	0	3	1	3	3	0	0	0	0	0	0	0
1997-98	Houston Aeros	IHL	78	38	27	65	....	....	....	60	....	....	....	....	....	....	....	....	....	....	4	3	0	3	4	....	....	....
1998-99	**Ottawa Senators**	**NHL**	17	2	5	7	2	5	7	4	0	0	0	18	11.1	9	1	7	0	1	....	....	....	....	....	....	....	....
	Houston Aeros	IHL	37	18	17	35	....	....	....	30	....	....	....	....	....	....	....	....	....	....	19	10	6	16	22	....	....	....
99-2000	**Phoenix Coyotes**	**NHL**	9	1	0	1	1	0	1	2	1	0	0	6	16.7	2	1	1	0	0	....	....	....	....	....	....	....	....
	Houston Aeros	IHL	45	16	11	27	....	....	....	40	....	....	....	....	....	....	....	....	....	....	11	3	4	7	8	....	....	....
	NHL Totals		**181**	**42**	**41**	**83**	**54**	**45**	**99**	**68**	**25**	**0**	**0**	**269**	**15.6**	**128**	**60**	**107**	**2**		**3**	**0**	**0**	**0**	**0**	**0**	**0**	**0**

Centennial Cyup All-Star Team (1990) • CCHA Second All-Star Team (1993) • CCHA First All-Star Team (1994) • NCAA West First All-American Team (1994)

Claimed on waivers by **NY Rangers** from **Edmonton**, February 21, 1997. Signed as a free agent by **Ottawa**, July 2, 1998. Signed as a free agent by **Phoenix**, July 20, 1999.

• OLIVER, Murray Murray Clifford C – L. 5'10", 170 lbs. b: Hamilton, Ont., 11/14/1937.

Season	Club	League	GP	G	A	Pts	AG	AA	APts	PIM	PP	SH	GW	S	%	TGF	PGF	TGA	PGA	+/–	GP	G	A	Pts	PIM	PP	SH	GW
			REGULAR SEASON																		PLAYOFFS							
1953-54	Burlington Jr. Bees	OHA-B	STATISTICS NOT AVAILABLE																									
	Hamilton Tiger Cubs	OHA-Jr.	2	0	2	2	....	....	....	0	....	....	....	....	....	....	....	....	....	....	5	1	0	1	0	....	....	....
1954-55	Hamilton Tiger Cubs	OHA-Jr.	39	5	13	18	....	....	....	19	....	....	....	....	....	....	....	....	....	....	3	2	0	2	0	....	....	....
1955-56	Hamilton Tiger Cubs	OHA-Jr.	5	1	1	2	....	....	....	2	....	....	....	....	....	....	....	....	....	....	....	....	....	....	....	....	....	....
1956-57	Hamilton Tiger Cubs	OHA-Jr.	52	17	42	59	....	....	....	20	....	....	....	....	....	....	....	....	....	....	4	3	1	4	0	....	....	....
1957-58	Hamilton Tiger Cubs	OHA-Jr.	52	34	56	90	....	....	....	37	....	....	....	....	....	....	....	....	....	....	4	2	5	7	8	....	....	....
	Detroit Red Wings	**NHL**	**1**	**0**	**1**	**1**	**0**	**1**	**1**	**0**	....	....	....	....	....	....	....	....	....	....	....	....	....	....	....	....	....	....
1958-59	Edmonton Flyers	WHL	64	33	34	67	....	....	....	35	....	....	....	....	....	....	....	....	....	....	3	1	1	2	0	....	....	....
1959-60	**Detroit Red Wings**	**NHL**	**54**	**20**	**19**	**39**	**23**	**18**	**41**	**16**	....	....	....	....	....	....	....	....	....	....	**6**	**1**	**0**	**1**	**4**	**0**	**0**	**0**
	Edmonton Flyers	WHL	16	8	12	20	....	....	....	6	....	....	....	....	....	....	....	....	....	....	....	....	....	....	....	....	....	....
1960-61	**Detroit Red Wings**	**NHL**	**49**	**11**	**12**	**23**	**13**	**12**	**25**	**8**	....	....	....	....	....	....	....	....	....	....	....	....	....	....	....	....	....	....
	Boston Bruins	**NHL**	**21**	**6**	**10**	**16**	**7**	**10**	**17**	**8**	....	....	....	....	....	....	....	....	....	....	....	....	....	....	....	....	....	....
1961-62	**Boston Bruins**	**NHL**	**70**	**17**	**29**	**46**	**19**	**28**	**47**	**21**	....	....	....	....	....	....	....	....	....	....	....	....	....	....	....	....	....	....
1962-63	**Boston Bruins**	**NHL**	**65**	**22**	**40**	**62**	**26**	**40**	**66**	**38**	....	....	....	....	....	....	....	....	....	....	....	....	....	....	....	....	....	....
1963-64	**Boston Bruins**	**NHL**	**70**	**24**	**44**	**68**	**30**	**47**	**77**	**41**	....	....	....	....	....	....	....	....	....	....	....	....	....	....	....	....	....	....
1964-65	**Boston Bruins**	**NHL**	**65**	**20**	**23**	**43**	**24**	**24**	**48**	**30**	....	....	....	....	....	....	....	....	....	....	....	....	....	....	....	....	....	....
1965-66	**Boston Bruins**	**NHL**	**70**	**18**	**42**	**60**	**20**	**40**	**60**	**30**	....	....	....	....	....	....	....	....	....	....	....	....	....	....	....	....	....	....
1966-67	**Boston Bruins**	**NHL**	**65**	**9**	**26**	**35**	**10**	**25**	**35**	**16**	....	....	....	....	....	....	....	....	....	....	....	....	....	....	....	....	....	....
1967-68	**Toronto Maple Leafs**	**NHL**	**74**	**16**	**21**	**37**	**19**	**21**	**40**	**18**	**2**	**0**	**2**	**155**	**10.3**	**54**	**10**	**42**	**6**	**8**	....	....	....	....	....	....	....	....
1968-69	**Toronto Maple Leafs**	**NHL**	**76**	**14**	**36**	**50**	**15**	**32**	**47**	**16**	**3**	**2**	**3**	**192**	**7.3**	**78**	**11**	**66**	**11**	**12**	**4**	**1**	**2**	**3**	**0**	**0**	**0**	**0**
1969-70	**Toronto Maple Leafs**	**NHL**	**76**	**14**	**33**	**47**	**15**	**31**	**46**	**16**	**5**	**0**	**3**	**200**	**7.0**	**66**	**23**	**75**	**13**	**–19**	....	....	....	....	....	....	....	....
1970-71	**Minnesota North Stars**	**NHL**	**61**	**9**	**23**	**32**	**9**	**19**	**28**	**8**	**3**	**1**	**0**	**115**	**7.8**	**49**	**21**	**58**	**30**	**0**	**12**	**7**	**4**	**11**	**0**	**2**	**0**	**0**
1971-72	**Minnesota North Stars**	**NHL**	**77**	**27**	**29**	**56**	**27**	**25**	**52**	**16**	**7**	**0**	**4**	**191**	**14.1**	**88**	**37**	**50**	**8**	**9**	**7**	**0**	**6**	**6**	**4**	**0**	**0**	**0**
1972-73	**Minnesota North Stars**	**NHL**	**75**	**11**	**31**	**42**	**10**	**25**	**35**	**10**	**2**	**0**	**2**	**174**	**6.3**	**55**	**7**	**68**	**24**	**4**	**6**	**0**	**4**	**4**	**2**	**0**	**0**	**0**
1973-74	**Minnesota North Stars**	**NHL**	**78**	**17**	**20**	**37**	**16**	**16**	**32**	**4**	**3**	**1**	**0**	**146**	**11.6**	**53**	**7**	**95**	**36**	**–13**	....	....	....	....	....	....	....	....
1974-75	**Minnesota North Stars**	**NHL**	**80**	**19**	**15**	**34**	**17**	**11**	**28**	**24**	**3**	**1**	**1**	**137**	**13.9**	**48**	**11**	**109**	**53**	**–19**	....	....	....	....	....	....	....	....
	NHL Totals		**1127**	**274**	**454**	**728**	**300**	**425**	**725**	**320**	....	....	....	....	....	....	....	....	....	....	**35**	**9**	**16**	**25**	**10**	....	....	....

Played in NHL All-Star Game (1963, 1964, 1965, 1967, 1968)

Traded to **Boston** by **Detroit** with Gary Aldcorn and Tom McCarthy for Vic Stasiuk and Leo Labine, January 23, 1961. Traded to **Toronto** by **Boston** with cash for Eddie Shack, May 15, 1967. Traded to **Minnesota** by **Toronto** for Terry O'Malley, the rights to Brian Conacher and cash, May 22, 1970.

• OLIWA, Krzysztof Krzysztof Artur LW – L. 6'5", 235 lbs. b: Tychy, Poland, 4/12/1973. New Jersey's 4th, 65th overall, in 1993.

Season	Club	League	GP	G	A	Pts	AG	AA	APts	PIM	PP	SH	GW	S	%	TGF	PGF	TGA	PGA	+/–	GP	G	A	Pts	PIM	PP	SH	GW
1990-91	GKS Katowski	Poland-Jr.	5	4	4	8	....	....	....	10	....	....	....	....	....	....	....	....	....	....	....	....	....	....	....	....	....	....
1991-92	GKS Tychy	Poland	10	3	7	10	....	....	....	6	....	....	....	....	....	....	....	....	....	....	....	....	....	....	....	....	....	....
	Poland	WJC-B	6	1	1	2	....	....	....	14	....	....	....	....	....	....	....	....	....	....	....	....	....	....	....	....	....	....
1992-93	Welland Cougars	OJHL-B	30	13	21	34	....	....	....	127	....	....	....	....	....	....	....	....	....	....	....	....	....	....	....	....	....	....
1993-94	Albany River Rats	AHL	33	2	4	6	....	....	....	151	....	....	....	....	....	....	....	....	....	....	....	....	....	....	....	....	....	....
	Raleigh IceCaps	ECHL	15	0	2	2	....	....	....	65	....	....	....	....	....	....	....	....	....	....	9	0	0	0	35	....	....	....
1994-95	Albany River Rats	AHL	20	1	1	2	....	....	....	77	....	....	....	....	....	....	....	....	....	....	....	....	....	....	....	....	....	....
	Saint John Flames	AHL	14	1	4	5	....	....	....	79	....	....	....	....	....	....	....	....	....	....	....	....	....	....	....	....	....	....
	Raleigh IceCaps	ECHL	5	0	2	2	....	....	....	32	....	....	....	....	....	....	....	....	....	....	....	....	....	....	....	....	....	....
	Detroit Vipers	IHL	4	0	1	1	....	....	....	24	....	....	....	....	....	....	....	....	....	....	....	....	....	....	....	....	....	....
1995-96	Albany River Rats	AHL	51	5	11	16	....	....	....	217	....	....	....	....	....	....	....	....	....	....	....	....	....	....	....	....	....	....
	Raleigh IceCaps	ECHL	9	1	0	1	....	....	....	53	....	....	....	....	....	....	....	....	....	....	....	....	....	....	....	....	....	....
1996-97	**New Jersey Devils**	**NHL**	**1**	**0**	**0**	**0**	**0**	**0**	**0**	**5**	**0**	**0**	**0**	**0**	**0.0**	**0**	**0**	**1**	**0**	**–1**	....	....	....	....	....	....	....	....
	Albany River Rats	AHL	60	13	14	27	....	....	....	322	....	....	....	....	....	....	....	....	....	....	15	7	1	8	49	....	....	....
1997-98	**New Jersey Devils**	**NHL**	**73**	**2**	**3**	**5**	**2**	**3**	**5**	**295**	**0**	**0**	**2**	**53**	**3.8**	**10**	**0**	**7**	**0**	**3**	**6**	**0**	**0**	**0**	**23**	**0**	**0**	**0**
1998-99	**New Jersey Devils**	**NHL**	**64**	**5**	**7**	**12**	**6**	**7**	**13**	**240**	**0**	**0**	**1**	**59**	**8.5**	**18**	**1**	**13**	**0**	**4**	**1**	**0**	**0**	**0**	**2**	**0**	**0**	**0**
99-2000	**New Jersey Devils**	**NHL**	**69**	**6**	**10**	**16**	**7**	**9**	**16**	**184**	**1**	**0**	**2**	**61**	**9.8**	**23**	**3**	**22**	**0**	**–2**	....	....	....	....	....	....	....	....
	NHL Totals		**207**	**13**	**20**	**33**	**15**	**19**	**34**	**724**	**1**	**0**	**5**	**173**	**7.5**	**51**	**4**	**43**	**0**		**7**	**0**	**0**	**0**	**25**	**0**	**0**	**0**

Traded to **Columbus** by **New Jersey** for Columbus' 3rd round choice in 2001 Entry Draft and future considerations (Turner Stevenson, June 23, 2000), June 12, 2000.

• OLSEN, Darryl Darryl M D – L. 6', 180 lbs. b: Calgary, Alta., 10/7/1966. Calgary's 10th, 185th overall, in 1985.

Season	Club	League	GP	G	A	Pts	AG	AA	APts	PIM	PP	SH	GW	S	%	TGF	PGF	TGA	PGA	+/–	GP	G	A	Pts	PIM	PP	SH	GW
1983-84	Calgary North Stars	AAHA	STATISTICS NOT AVAILABLE																									
	St. Albert Saints	AJHL	STATISTICS NOT AVAILABLE																									
1984-85	St. Albert Saints	AJHL	57	19	48	67	....	....	....	77	....	....	....	....	....	....	....	....	....	....	....	....	....	....	....	....	....	....
1985-86	Northern Michigan University	WCHA	37	5	20	25	....	....	....	46	....	....	....	....	....	....	....	....	....	....	....	....	....	....	....	....	....	....
1986-87	Northern Michigan University	WCHA	37	5	20	25	....	....	....	96	....	....	....	....	....	....	....	....	....	....	....	....	....	....	....	....	....	....
1987-88	Northern Michigan University	WCHA	35	11	20	31	....	....	....	59	....	....	....	....	....	....	....	....	....	....	....	....	....	....	....	....	....	....
1988-89	Northern Michigan University	WCHA	45	16	26	42	....	....	....	88	....	....	....	....	....	....	....	....	....	....	....	....	....	....	....	....	....	....
	Canada	Nat-Team	3	1	0	1	....	....	....	4	....	....	....	....	....	....	....	....	....	....	....	....	....	....	....	....	....	....
1989-90	Salt Lake Golden Eagles	IHL	72	16	50	66	....	....	....	90	....	....	....	....	....	....	....	....	....	....	11	3	6	9	2	....	....	....
1990-91	Salt Lake Golden Eagles	IHL	76	15	40	55	....	....	....	89	....	....	....	....	....	....	....	....	....	....	4	1	5	6	2	....	....	....
1991-92	**Calgary Flames**	**NHL**	**1**	**0**	**0**	**0**	**0**	**0**	**0**	**0**	**0**	**0**	**0**	**3**	**0.0**	**0**	**0**	**2**	**0**	**–2**	....	....	....	....	....	....	....	....
	Salt Lake Golden Eagles	IHL	59	7	33	40	....	....	....	80	....	....	....	....	....	....	....	....	....	....	5	2	1	3	4	....	....	....
1992-93	Providence Bruins	AHL	50	7	27	34	....	....	....	38	....	....	....	....	....	....	....	....	....	....	....	....	....	....	....	....	....	....
	San Diego Gulls	IHL	21	2	8	10	....	....	....	26	....	....	....	....	....	....	....	....	....	....	10	1	3	4	30	....	....	....
1993-94	Salt Lake Golden Eagles	IHL	73	17	32	49	....	....	....	97	....	....	....	....	....	....	....	....	....	....	....	....	....	....	....	....	....	....
1994-95	HC Gardena-Groden	Italy	34	7	18	25	....	....	....	47	....	....	....	....	....	....	....	....	....	....	3	1	0	1	2	....	....	....
	HC Gardena-Groden	EuroHL	5	3	1	4	....	....	....	2	....	....	....	....	....	....	....	....	....	....	....	....	....	....	....	....	....	....
	Houston Aeros	IHL	4	0	1	1	....	....	....	12	....	....	....	....	....	....	....	....	....	....	....	....	....	....	....	....	....	....
1995-96	VSV Villach	Alpenliga	10	1	12	13	....	....	....	10	....	....	....	....	....	....	....	....	....	....	....	....	....	....	....	....	....	....
	VSV Villach	Austria	23	9	19	28	....	....	....	22	....	....	....	....	....	....	....	....	....	....	....	....	....	....	....	....	....	....
1996-97	Nottingham Panthers	BH-Cup	11	6	14	20	....	....	....	8	....	....	....	....	....	....	....	....	....	....	....	....	....	....	....	....	....	....
	Nottingham Panthers	Britain	39	7	21	28	....	....	....	24	....	....	....	....	....	....	....	....	....	....	8	1	2	3	0	....	....	....
1997-98			OUT OF HOCKEY – RETIRED																									
1998-99	Phoenix Mustangs	WCHL	11	0	3	3	....	....	....	12	....	....	....	....	....	....	....	....	....	....	3	0	0	0	6	....	....	....
99-2000	EC Bad Nauheim	Germany-2	19	3	5	8	....	....	....	12	....	....	....	....	....	....	....	....	....	....	....	....	....	....	....	....	....	....
	Amarillo Rattlers	WPHL	10	1	1	2	....	....	....	6	....	....	....	....	....	....	....	....	....	....	....	....	....	....	....	....	....	....
	Corpus Christi IceRays	WPHL	34	9	23	32	....	....	....	24	....	....	....	....	....	....	....	....	....	....	7	0	4	4	10	....	....	....
	NHL Totals		**1**	**0**	**0**	**0**	**0**	**0**	**0**	**0**	**0**	**0**	**0**	**3**	**0.0**	**0**	**0**	**2**	**0**		....	....	....	....	....	....	....	....

WCHA First All-Star Team (1989) • NCAA West First All-American Team (1991)

Signed as a free agent by **Boston**, July 23, 1992. Signed as a free agent by **San Diego** (IHL), February 26, 1993. Signed as a free agent by **Phoenix Mustangs** (WCHL), March 3, 1999. Signed as a free agent by **Amarillo** (WPHL), December 17, 1999. Traded to **Corpus Christi** (WPHL) by **Amarillo** (WPHL) for Todd Norman and future considerations (Greg McEachern, January 14, 2000), January 4, 2000. • Played w/ RHI's Denver Dare Devils in 1996 (24-13-14-27-15).

• OLSSON, Christer D – L. 5'11", 190 lbs. b: Arboga, Sweden, 7/24/1970. St. Louis' 10th, 275th overall, in 1993.

Season	Club	League	GP	G	A	Pts	AG	AA	APts	PIM	PP	SH	GW	S	%	TGF	PGF	TGA	PGA	+/–	GP	G	A	Pts	PIM	PP	SH	GW
1988-89	IFK Arboga	Sweden-3	33	9	10	19	....	....	....	....	....	....	....	....	....	....	....	....	....	....	....	....	....	....	....	....	....	....
1989-90	Mora IK	Sweden-2	21	2	1	3	....	....	....	8	....	....	....	....	....	....	....	....	....	....	....	....	....	....	....	....	....	....
1990-91	Mora IK	Sweden-2	28	4	8	12	....	....	....	20	....	....	....	....	....	....	....	....	....	....	....	....	....	....	....	....	....	....
1991-92	Mora IK	Sweden 2	36	6	10	16	....	....	....	38	....	....	....	....	....	....	....	....	....	....	2	1	0	1	6	....	....	....
1992-93	Brynas IF Gavle	Sweden	22	4	4	8	....	....	....	18	....	....	....	....	....	....	....	....	....	....	....	....	....	....	....	....	....	....
1993-94	Brynas IF Gavle	Sweden	38	7	3	10	....	....	....	50	....	....	....	....	....	....	....	....	....	....	7	0	3	3	6	....	....	....
1994-95	Brynas IF Gavle	Sweden	39	6	5	11	....	....	....	18	....	....	....	....	....	....	....	....	....	....	14	1	3	4	8	....	....	....
	Sweden	WC-A	8	2	1	3	....	....	....	4	....	....	....	....	....	....	....	....	....	....	....	....	....	....	....	....	....	....
1995-96	**St. Louis Blues**	**NHL**	**26**	**2**	**8**	**10**	**2**	**7**	**9**	**14**	**2**	**0**	**0**	**32**	**6.3**	**17**	**13**	**10**	**0**	**–6**	**3**	**0**	**0**	**0**	**0**	**0**	**0**	**0**
	Worcester IceCats	AHL	39	7	7	14	....	....	....	22	....	....	....	....	....	....	....	....	....	....	....	....	....	....	....	....	....	....

			REGULAR SEASON																		PLAYOFFS							
Season	**Club**	**League**	**GP**	**G**	**A**	**Pts**	**AG**	**AA**	**APts**	**PIM**	**PP**	**SH**	**GW**	**S**	**%**	**TGF**	**PGF**	**TGA**	**PGA**	**+/–**	**GP**	**G**	**A**	**Pts**	**PIM**	**PP**	**SH**	**GW**
1996-97	**St. Louis Blues**	**NHL**	**5**	**0**	**1**	**1**	**0**	**1**	**1**	**0**	**0**	**0**	**0**	**2**	**0.0**	**3**	**0**	**3**	**1**	**1**								
	Worcester IceCats	AHL	2	0	0	0				0																		
	Ottawa Senators	**NHL**	**25**	**2**	**3**	**5**	**2**	**3**	**5**	**10**	**1**	**0**	**0**	**24**	**8.3**	**19**	**6**	**20**	**2**	**–5**								
1997-98	Vasteras IK	Sweden	45	13	8	21				54											7	0	1	1	18			
	Sweden	WC-A	10	2	1	3				2																		
1998-99	Vasteras IK	Sweden	47	5	11	16				48											4	0	1	1	4			
	Sweden	WC-A	10	1	2	3				20																		
99-2000	KAC Klagenfurt	IEL	34	7	11	18				63																		
	KAC Klagenfurt	Austria	16	4	10	14				12																		
	NHL Totals		**56**	**4**	**12**	**16**	**4**	**11**	**15**	**24**	**3**	**0**	**0**	**58**	**6.9**	**39**	**19**	**33**	**3**		**3**	**0**	**0**	**0**	**0**	**0**	**0**	**0**

Named Best Defenseman at WC-A (1995)

Traded to **Ottawa** by **St. Louis** for Pavol Demitra, November 27, 1996.

• O'NEIL, Paul

Paul Joseph C/RW – R. 6'1", 185 lbs. b: Charlestown, Mass., 8/24/1953. Vancouver's 6th, 67th overall, in 1973.

Season	Club	League	GP	G	A	Pts	AG	AA	APts	PIM	PP	SH	GW	S	%	TGF	PGF	TGA	PGA	+/–	GP	G	A	Pts	PIM	PP	SH	GW
1971-72	Boston University	ECAC	17	13	14	27				6																		
1972-73	Boston University	ECAC	28	35	19	54				8																		
	United States	WEC-B	7	0	3	3																						
1973-74	**Vancouver Canucks**	**NHL**	**5**	**0**	**0**	**0**	**0**	**0**	**0**	**0**	**0**	**0**	**0**	**2**	**0.0**	**0**	**0**	**2**	**0**	**–2**								
	Seattle Totems	WHL	66	29	17	46				14																		
1974-75	Seattle Totems	CHL	49	16	19	35				17																		
1975-76	**Boston Bruins**	**NHL**	**1**	**0**	**0**	**0**	**0**	**0**	**0**	**0**																		
	Rochester Americans	AHL	49	35	16	51				17											6	4	3	7	4			
1976-77	Hampton Gulls	SHL	48	21	34	55				0																		
1977-78	Hampton Gulls	AHL	36	17	27	44				9																		
	San Diego Mariners	PHL	17	11	9	20				0																		
1978-79	Birmingham Bulls	WHA	1	0	0	0				0																		
	Binghamton Dusters	AHL	5	0	3	3				0																		
	San Diego Hawks	PHL	39	30	14	44				14																		
1979-80	HC Salzburg	Austria	34	55	43	98				28																		
1980-81	Hampton Aces	EHL	33	21	16	37				9																		
	HC Salzburg	Austria	9	7	3	10				0																		
1981-82			STATISTICS NOT AVAILABLE																									
1982-83	Virginia Raiders	ACHL	55	38	41	79				20											1	0	1	1	0			
1983-84	Birmingham–Virginia	ACHL	70	51	72	123				8											4	1	0	1	0			
1984-85	Virginia Lancers	ACHL	47	28	41	69				20																		
1985-86	Virginia Lancers	ACHL	57	34	38	72				18											5	2	2	4	2			
	NHL Totals		**6**	**0**	**0**	**0**	**0**	**0**	**0**	**0**	**0**	**0**	**0**	**2**	**0.0**	**0**	**0**	**2**	**0**									
	Other Major League Totals		1	0	0	0				0																		

ACHL Second All-Star Team (1984) • ACHL MVP (1984)

Selected by **Houston** (WHA) in 1972 WHA General Player Draft, February 12, 1972. Signed as a free agent by **Boston**, October 10, 1975. Signed as a free agent by **Birmingham** (WHA) after **Houston** (WHA) franchise folded, July 6, 1978.

• O'NEILL, Jeff

C – R. 6'1", 190 lbs. b: Richmond Hill, Ont., 2/23/1976. Hartford's 1st, 5th overall, in 1994.

Season	Club	League	GP	G	A	Pts	AG	AA	APts	PIM	PP	SH	GW	S	%	TGF	PGF	TGA	PGA	+/–	GP	G	A	Pts	PIM	PP	SH	GW
1990-91	Richmond Hill-Vaughan Kings	OMHA	78	56	134	190																						
1991-92	Thornhill Thunderbirds	OJHL	43	27	53	80				48																		
1992-93	Guelph Storm	OHL	65	32	47	79				88											5	2	2	4	6			
1993-94	Guelph Storm	OHL	66	45	81	126				95											9	2	11	13	31			
1994-95	Guelph Storm	OHL	57	43	81	124				56											14	8	18	26	34			
	Canada	WJC-A	7	2	4	6				2																		
1995-96	**Hartford Whalers**	**NHL**	**65**	**8**	**19**	**27**	**8**	**16**	**24**	**40**	**1**	**0**	**1**	**65**	**12.3**	**42**	**10**	**48**	**13**	**–3**								
1996-97	**Hartford Whalers**	**NHL**	**72**	**14**	**16**	**30**	**15**	**14**	**29**	**40**	**2**	**1**	**2**	**101**	**13.9**	**38**	**9**	**58**	**5**	**–24**								
	Springfield Falcons	AHL	1	0	0	0				0																		
1997-98	**Carolina Hurricanes**	**NHL**	**74**	**19**	**20**	**39**	**22**	**20**	**42**	**67**	**7**	**1**	**4**	**114**	**16.7**	**53**	**16**	**57**	**12**	**–8**								
1998-99	**Carolina Hurricanes**	**NHL**	**75**	**16**	**15**	**31**	**19**	**14**	**33**	**66**	**4**	**0**	**2**	**121**	**13.2**	**44**	**11**	**31**	**1**	**3**	**6**	**0**	**1**	**1**	**0**	**0**	**0**	**0**
99-2000	**Carolina Hurricanes**	**NHL**	**80**	**25**	**38**	**63**	**28**	**35**	**63**	**72**	**4**	**0**	**7**	**189**	**13.2**	**88**	**34**	**66**	**3**	**–9**								
	NHL Totals		**366**	**82**	**108**	**190**	**92**	**99**	**191**	**285**	**18**	**2**	**16**	**590**	**13.9**	**265**	**80**	**260**	**34**		**6**	**0**	**1**	**1**	**0**	**0**	**0**	**0**

OHL First All-Star Team (1995)

Transferred to **Carolina** after **Hartford** franchise relocated, June 25, 1997.

• ORBAN, Bill

William Terrence C/LW – L. 6', 185 lbs. b: Regina, Sask., 2/20/1944.

Season	Club	League	GP	G	A	Pts	AG	AA	APts	PIM	PP	SH	GW	S	%	TGF	PGF	TGA	PGA	+/–	GP	G	A	Pts	PIM	PP	SH	GW
1962-63	Saskatoon Jr. Quakers	SJHL	49	22	20	42				126																		
	Saskatoon Quakers	SSHL																			3	2	2	4	0			
1963-64	Saskatoon Jr. Quakers	SJHL	53	44	55	99				101											12	16	12	28	15			
1964-65	Fort Wayne Komets	IHL	54	25	36	61				70											10	7	7	14	33			
1965-66	Los Angeles Blades	WHL	72	11	20	31				55																		
1966-67	Los Angeles Blades	WHL	72	14	12	26				33																		
1967-68	**Chicago Black Hawks**	**NHL**	**39**	**3**	**2**	**5**	**3**	**2**	**5**	**17**	**0**	**0**	**0**	**21**	**14.3**	**7**	**1**	**20**	**3**	**–11**	**3**	**0**	**0**	**0**	**0**	**0**	**0**	**0**
1968-69	**Chicago Black Hawks**	**NHL**	**45**	**4**	**6**	**10**	**4**	**5**	**9**	**33**	**0**	**0**	**0**	**38**	**10.5**	**16**	**0**	**27**	**8**	**–3**								
	Minnesota North Stars	**NHL**	**21**	**1**	**5**	**6**	**1**	**4**	**5**	**10**	**0**	**0**	**0**	**24**	**4.2**	**10**	**2**	**9**	**0**	**–1**								
1969-70	**Minnesota North Stars**	**NHL**	**9**	**0**	**2**	**2**	**0**	**2**	**2**	**7**	**0**	**0**	**0**	**3**	**0.0**	**2**	**0**	**7**	**3**	**–2**								
	Iowa Stars	CHL	65	31	44	75				78											10	4	2	6	27			
1970-71	Cleveland Barons	AHL	27	6	9	15				34																		
	Springfield Kings	AHL	8	0	5	5				11											12	10	6	16	16			
1971-72	Springfield Kings	AHL	42	13	18	31				55											5	0	0	0	9			
1972-73	Portland Buckaroos	WHL	18	8	3	11				18																		
1973-74	Tulsa Oilers	CHL	62	16	20	36				38																		
1974-75	Dallas Black Hawks	CHL	72	15	24	39				46											10	5	3	8	2			
	NHL Totals		**114**	**8**	**15**	**23**	**8**	**13**	**21**	**67**	**0**	**0**	**0**	**86**	**9.3**	**35**	**3**	**63**	**14**		**3**	**0**	**0**	**0**	**0**	**0**	**0**	**0**

SJHL Second All-Star Team (1964) • Won WHL Rookie of the Year Award (1966) • CHL Second All-Star Team (1970)

Traded to **Chicago** by **LA Blades** (WHL) for cash, July, 1967. Traded to **Minnesota** by **Chicago** with Tom Reid for Andre Boudrias and Mike McMahon Jr., February 14, 1969. Traded to **LA Kings** (Springfield-AHL) by **Cleveland** (AHL) for Roger Cote, March, 1971. Claimed by **Chicago** from **LA Kings** in Intra-League Draft, June 5, 1972.

• O'REGAN, Tom

Thomas Patrick C/D – L. 5'10", 180 lbs. b: Cambridge, MA, 12/29/1961.

Season	Club	League	GP	G	A	Pts	AG	AA	APts	PIM	PP	SH	GW	S	%	TGF	PGF	TGA	PGA	+/–	GP	G	A	Pts	PIM	PP	SH	GW
1978-79	Mantignon Warriors	Hi-School	24	21	33	54																						
1979-80	Boston University	ECAC	28	9	15	24				31																		
1980-81	Boston University	ECAC	20	10	10	20				41																		
1981-82	Boston University	ECAC	28	18	34	52				67																		
1982-83	Boston University	ECAC	27	15	17	32				43																		
1983-84	**Pittsburgh Penguins**	**NHL**	**51**	**4**	**10**	**14**	**3**	**7**	**10**	**8**	**0**	**0**	**0**	**44**	**9.1**	**16**	**1**	**63**	**26**	**–22**								
	Baltimore Skipjacks	AHL	25	13	14	27				15																		
1984-85	**Pittsburgh Penguins**	**NHL**	**1**	**0**	**0**	**0**	**0**	**0**	**0**	**0**	**0**	**0**	**0**	**1**	**0.0**	**0**	**0**	**2**	**1**	**–1**								
	Baltimore Skipjacks	AHL	62	28	28	56				62											15	4	5	9	0			
1985-86	**Pittsburgh Penguins**	**NHL**	**9**	**1**	**2**	**3**	**1**	**1**	**2**	**2**	**0**	**0**	**0**	**7**	**14.3**	**3**	**0**	**8**	**6**	**1**								
	Baltimore Skipjacks	AHL	61	23	31	54				65																		
1986-87	Adirondack Red Wings	AHL	58	20	42	62				78											11	3	9	12	10			
1987-88	EV Landshut	Germany	36	21	29	50				*110											4	4	1	5				

Season	Club	League	REGULAR SEASON																		PLAYOFFS							
			GP	G	A	Pts	AG	AA	APts	PIM	PP	SH	GW	S	%	TGF	PGF	TGA	PGA	+/–	GP	G	A	Pts	PIM	PP	SH	GW
1988-89	EV Landshut	Germany	36	19	34	53	....	....	....	74	....	....	....	....	....	....	....	....	....	....	3	2	1	3	8	....	....	....
	United States	WEC-A	8	2	1	3	....	....	....	8	....	....	....	....	....	....	....	....	....	....	....	....	....	....	....	....	....	....
1989-90	BSC Preussen Berlin	Germany	34	27	32	59	....	....	....	71	....	....	....	....	....	....	....	....	....	....	6	1	5	6	14	....	....	....
	United States	WEC-A	10	1	1	2	....	....	....	6	....	....	....	....	....	....	....	....	....	....	....	....	....	....	....	....	....	....
1990-91	BSC Preussen Berlin	Germany	43	21	26	47	....	....	....	72	....	....	....	....	....	....	....	....	....	....	8	6	3	9	6	....	....	....
1991-92	BSC Preussen Berlin	Germany	42	20	30	50	....	....	....	93	....	....	....	....	....	....	....	....	....	....	7	3	2	5	6	....	....	....
1992-93	BSC Preussen Berlin	Germany	30	11	18	29	....	....	....	*98	....	....	....	....	....	....	....	....	....	....	....	....	....	....	....	....	....	....
1993-94	BSC Preussen Berlin	Germany	42	18	28	46	....	....	....	66	....	....	....	....	....	....	....	....	....	....	....	....	....	....	....	....	....	....
1994-95	BSC Preussen Berlin	Germany	43	7	43	50	....	....	....	66	....	....	....	....	....	....	....	....	....	....	12	4	9	13	12	....	....	....
	United States	WC-A	6	0	2	2	....	....	....	6	....	....	....	....	....	....	....	....	....	....	....	....	....	....	....	....	....	....
1995-96	Berlin Devils	Germany	45	14	34	48	....	....	....	20	....	....	....	....	....	....	....	....	....	....	13	4	10	14	22	....	....	....
	United States	WC-A	8	0	0	0	....	....	....	4	....	....	....	....	....	....	....	....	....	....	....	....	....	....	....	....	....	....
1996-97	Berlin Capitals	Germany	43	5	18	23	....	....	....	30	....	....	....	....	....	....	....	....	....	....	4	1	1	2	6	....	....	....
	Berlin Capitals	EuroHL	5	0	1	1	....	....	....	33	....	....	....	....	....	....	....	....	....	....	....	....	....	....	....	....	....	....
1997-98	Berlin Capitals	Germany	47	9	22	31	....	....	....	78	....	....	....	....	....	....	....	....	....	....	....	....	....	....	....	....	....	....
	NHL Totals		**61**	**5**	**12**	**17**	**4**	**8**	**12**	**10**	**0**	**0**	**0**	**52**	**9.6**	**19**	**1**	**73**	**33**		....	....	....	....	....	....	....	....

Signed as a free agent by **Pittsburgh**, September 4, 1983. Signed as a free agent by **Detroit**, September 29, 1986.

• O'REILLY, Terry

Terence Joseph James "Taz" RW – R. 6'1", 200 lbs. b: Niagara Falls, Ont., 6/7/1951. Boston's 2nd, 14th overall, in 1971.

Season	Club	League	REGULAR SEASON																		PLAYOFFS							
			GP	G	A	Pts	AG	AA	APts	PIM	PP	SH	GW	S	%	TGF	PGF	TGA	PGA	+/–	GP	G	A	Pts	PIM	PP	SH	GW
1968-69	Oshawa Generals	OHA-Jr.	46	5	15	20	....	....	....	87	....	....	....	....	....	....	....	....	....	....	....	....	....	....	....	....	....	....
1969-70	Oshawa Generals	OHA-Jr.	54	13	36	49	....	....	....	60	....	....	....	....	....	....	....	....	....	....	6	1	5	6	22	....	....	....
1970-71	Oshawa Generals	OHA-Jr.	54	23	42	65	....	....	....	151	....	....	....	....	....	....	....	....	....	....	....	....	....	....	....	....	....	....
1971-72	**Boston Bruins**	**NHL**	**1**	**1**	**0**	**1**	**1**	**0**	**1**	**0**	**0**	**0**	**0**	**2**	**50.0**	**3**	**0**	**0**	**0**	**3**	....	....	....	....	....	....	....	....
	Boston Braves	AHL	60	9	8	17	....	....	....	134	....	....	....	....	....	....	....	....	....	....	9	2	2	4	31	....	....	....
1972-73	**Boston Bruins**	**NHL**	**72**	**5**	**22**	**27**	**5**	**17**	**22**	**109**	**0**	**0**	**1**	**80**	**6.3**	**54**	**0**	**27**	**0**	**27**	**5**	**0**	**0**	**0**	**2**	**0**	**0**	**0**
1973-74	**Boston Bruins**	**NHL**	**76**	**11**	**24**	**35**	**11**	**20**	**31**	**94**	**0**	**0**	**1**	**86**	**12.8**	**55**	**0**	**25**	**0**	**30**	**16**	**2**	**5**	**7**	**38**	**0**	**0**	**0**
1974-75	**Boston Bruins**	**NHL**	**68**	**15**	**20**	**35**	**13**	**15**	**28**	**146**	**2**	**0**	**2**	**93**	**16.1**	**60**	**3**	**42**	**0**	**15**	**3**	**0**	**0**	**0**	**17**	**0**	**0**	**0**
1975-76	**Boston Bruins**	**NHL**	**80**	**23**	**27**	**50**	**20**	**20**	**40**	**150**	**2**	**0**	**2**	**135**	**17.0**	**60**	**4**	**53**	**0**	**3**	**12**	**3**	**1**	**4**	**25**	**0**	**0**	**0**
1976-77	**Boston Bruins**	**NHL**	**79**	**14**	**41**	**55**	**13**	**32**	**45**	**147**	**1**	**1**	**4**	**137**	**10.2**	**85**	**4**	**43**	**0**	**38**	**14**	**5**	**6**	**11**	**28**	**0**	**0**	**1**
1977-78	**Boston Bruins**	**NHL**	**77**	**29**	**61**	**90**	**26**	**47**	**73**	**211**	**5**	**0**	**4**	**166**	**17.5**	**120**	**28**	**52**	**0**	**40**	**15**	**5**	**10**	**15**	**40**	**1**	**0**	**1**
1978-79	**Boston Bruins**	**NHL**	**80**	**26**	**51**	**77**	**22**	**37**	**59**	**205**	**3**	**0**	**5**	**120**	**21.7**	**106**	**23**	**76**	**0**	**7**	**11**	**0**	**6**	**6**	**25**	**0**	**0**	**0**
1979-80	**Boston Bruins**	**NHL**	**71**	**19**	**42**	**61**	**16**	**31**	**47**	**265**	**3**	**0**	**5**	**105**	**18.1**	**87**	**14**	**58**	**2**	**17**	**10**	**3**	**6**	**9**	**69**	**2**	**0**	**1**
1980-81	**Boston Bruins**	**NHL**	**77**	**8**	**35**	**43**	**6**	**23**	**29**	**223**	**0**	**0**	**0**	**84**	**9.5**	**69**	**11**	**63**	**7**	**2**	**3**	**1**	**2**	**3**	**12**	**0**	**0**	**0**
1981-82	**Boston Bruins**	**NHL**	**70**	**22**	**30**	**52**	**17**	**20**	**37**	**213**	**0**	**1**	**3**	**114**	**19.3**	**72**	**4**	**55**	**10**	**23**	**11**	**5**	**4**	**9**	**56**	**0**	**0**	**1**
1982-83	**Boston Bruins**	**NHL**	**19**	**6**	**14**	**20**	**5**	**10**	**15**	**40**	**0**	**1**	**1**	**23**	**26.1**	**28**	**1**	**13**	**2**	**16**	....	....	....	....	....	....	....	....
1983-84	**Boston Bruins**	**NHL**	**58**	**12**	**18**	**30**	**10**	**12**	**22**	**124**	**2**	**0**	**2**	**48**	**25.0**	**44**	**3**	**43**	**11**	**9**	**3**	**0**	**0**	**0**	**14**	**0**	**0**	**0**
1984-85	**Boston Bruins**	**NHL**	**63**	**13**	**17**	**30**	**11**	**12**	**23**	**168**	**0**	**1**	**2**	**61**	**21.3**	**43**	**3**	**66**	**8**	**–18**	**5**	**1**	**2**	**3**	**9**	**0**	**0**	**0**
	NHL Totals		**891**	**204**	**402**	**606**	**176**	**296**	**472**	**2095**	**18**	**4**	**32**	**1254**	**16.3**	**886**	**98**	**616**	**40**		**108**	**25**	**42**	**67**	**335**	**3**	**0**	**4**

Played in NHL All-Star Game (1975, 1978)

• Suspended by NHL for first 10 games of 1982-83 season for assault on referee Andy Van Hellemond, April 25, 1982. • Missed majority of 1982-83 season recovering from finger injury suffered in game vs. NY Islanders (November 18, 1982) and knee injury suffered in game vs. Vancouver, December 31, 1982.

• ORLANDO, Gates

Gates Gaetano "Gates" C – R. 5'8", 180 lbs. b: Montreal, Que., 11/13/1962. Buffalo's 10th, 164th overall, in 1981.

Season	Club	League	REGULAR SEASON																		PLAYOFFS							
			GP	G	A	Pts	AG	AA	APts	PIM	PP	SH	GW	S	%	TGF	PGF	TGA	PGA	+/–	GP	G	A	Pts	PIM	PP	SH	GW
1979-80	Montreal Juniors	QMJHL	70	28	44	72	....	....	....	50	....	....	....	....	....	....	....	....	....	....	9	6	5	11	8	....	....	....
1980-81	Providence College	ECAC	31	24	32	56	....	....	....	45	....	....	....	....	....	....	....	....	....	....	....	....	....	....	....	....	....	....
1981-82	Providence College	ECAC	28	18	18	36	....	....	....	31	....	....	....	....	....	....	....	....	....	....	....	....	....	....	....	....	....	....
1982-83	Providence College	ECAC	40	30	39	69	....	....	....	32	....	....	....	....	....	....	....	....	....	....	....	....	....	....	....	....	....	....
1983-84	Providence College	ECAC	30	21	28	49	....	....	....	....	....	....	....	....	....	....	....	....	....	....	....	....	....	....	....	....	....	....
	Rochester Americans	AHL	11	8	7	15	....	....	....	2	....	....	....	....	....	....	....	....	....	....	18	4	10	14	6	....	....	....
1984-85	**Buffalo Sabres**	**NHL**	**11**	**3**	**6**	**9**	**2**	**4**	**6**	**6**	**1**	**0**	**0**	**22**	**13.6**	**12**	**3**	**6**	**0**	**3**	**5**	**0**	**4**	**4**	**14**	**0**	**0**	**0**
	Rochester Americans	AHL	49	26	30	56	....	....	....	62	....	....	....	....	....	....	....	....	....	....	2	0	1	1	6	....	....	....
1985-86	**Buffalo Sabres**	**NHL**	**60**	**13**	**12**	**25**	**10**	**8**	**18**	**29**	**1**	**2**	**1**	**70**	**18.6**	**32**	**3**	**48**	**12**	**–7**	....	....	....	....	....	....	....	....
	Rochester Americans	AHL	3	4	0	4	....	....	....	10	....	....	....	....	....	....	....	....	....	....	....	....	....	....	....	....	....	....
1986-87	**Buffalo Sabres**	**NHL**	**27**	**2**	**8**	**10**	**2**	**6**	**8**	**16**	**0**	**0**	**0**	**24**	**8.3**	**14**	**0**	**31**	**11**	**–6**	....	....	....	....	....	....	....	....
	Rochester Americans	AHL	44	22	42	64	....	....	....	42	....	....	....	....	....	....	....	....	....	....	18	9	13	*22	14	....	....	....
1987-88	HC Meran	Italy	36	49	44	93	....	....	....	66	....	....	....	....	....	....	....	....	....	....	....	....	....	....	....	....	....	....
	Rochester Americans	AHL	13	4	13	17	....	....	....	18	....	....	....	....	....	....	....	....	....	....	7	2	6	8	6	....	....	....
1988-89	HC Bolzano	Italy	44	57	45	102	....	....	....	66	....	....	....	....	....	....	....	....	....	....	....	....	....	....	....	....	....	....
1989-90	HC Bolzano	Italy	36	64	62	126	....	....	....	18	....	....	....	....	....	....	....	....	....	....	6	8	10	18	6	....	....	....
	Italy	WEC-B	7	9	4	13	....	....	....	6	....	....	....	....	....	....	....	....	....	....	....	....	....	....	....	....	....	....
1990-91	HC Bolzano	Italy	27	39	33	72	....	....	....	29	....	....	....	....	....	....	....	....	....	....	10	8	15	23	12	....	....	....
	Italy	WEC-B	7	8	4	12	....	....	....	2	....	....	....	....	....	....	....	....	....	....	....	....	....	....	....	....	....	....
1991-92	HC Milano Devils	Alpenliga	11	8	7	15	....	....	....	2	....	....	....	....	....	....	....	....	....	....	....	....	....	....	....	....	....	....
	HC Milano Devils	Italy	18	21	22	43	....	....	....	12	....	....	....	....	....	....	....	....	....	....	11	11	17	28	42	....	....	....
	Italy	WC-A	5	0	3	3	....	....	....	4	....	....	....	....	....	....	....	....	....	....	....	....	....	....	....	....	....	....
1992-93	HC Milano Devils	Alpenliga	25	19	27	46	....	....	....	46	....	....	....	....	....	....	....	....	....	....	....	....	....	....	....	....	....	....
	HC Milano Devils	Italy	16	9	18	27	....	....	....	14	....	....	....	....	....	....	....	....	....	....	11	5	9	14	23	....	....	....
	Italy	WC-A	6	1	0	1	....	....	....	2	....	....	....	....	....	....	....	....	....	....	....	....	....	....	....	....	....	....
1993-94	HC Milano Devils	Alpenliga	30	16	31	47	....	....	....	29	....	....	....	....	....	....	....	....	....	....	....	....	....	....	....	....	....	....
	HC Milano Devils	Italy	20	16	*44	*60	....	....	....	10	....	....	....	....	....	....	....	....	....	....	8	8	10	18	27	....	....	....
	Italy	Olympics	7	3	6	9	....	....	....	4	....	....	....	....	....	....	....	....	....	....	....	....	....	....	....	....	....	....
	Italy	WC-A	6	3	4	7	....	....	....	6	....	....	....	....	....	....	....	....	....	....	....	....	....	....	....	....	....	....
1994-95	SC Bern	Switz.	36	24	31	55	....	....	....	58	....	....	....	....	....	....	....	....	....	....	6	3	7	10	8	....	....	....
	Italy	WC-A	6	1	2	3	....	....	....	12	....	....	....	....	....	....	....	....	....	....	....	....	....	....	....	....	....	....
1995-96	SC Bern	Switz.	34	15	26	41	....	....	....	62	....	....	....	....	....	....	....	....	....	....	11	*10	8	18	*45	....	....	....
	Italy	WC-A	6	2	5	7	....	....	....	6	....	....	....	....	....	....	....	....	....	....	....	....	....	....	....	....	....	....
1996-97	SC Bern	Switz.	46	26	*56	*82	....	....	....	34	....	....	....	....	....	....	....	....	....	....	13	7	*10	*17	12	....	....	....
	SC Bern	EuroHL	6	4	6	10	....	....	....	10	....	....	....	....	....	....	....	....	....	....	....	....	....	....	....	....	....	....
	Italy	WC-A	8	5	4	9	....	....	....	14	....	....	....	....	....	....	....	....	....	....	....	....	....	....	....	....	....	....
1997-98	SC Bern	Switz.	38	16	32	48	....	....	....	73	....	....	....	....	....	....	....	....	....	....	7	6	3	9	18	....	....	....
	Italy	Olympics	4	1	2	3	....	....	....	4	....	....	....	....	....	....	....	....	....	....	....	....	....	....	....	....	....	....
	SG Cortina	Italy	....	....	....	....	....	....	....	....	....	....	....	....	....	....	....	....	....	....	2	3	0	3	4	....	....	....
	Italy	WC-A	6	3	2	5	....	....	....	2	....	....	....	....	....	....	....	....	....	....	....	....	....	....	....	....	....	....
1998-99	HC Lugano	Switz.	28	12	20	32	....	....	....	34	....	....	....	....	....	....	....	....	....	....	11	6	5	11	10	....	....	....
	Italy	WC-A	3	0	1	1	....	....	....	4	....	....	....	....	....	....	....	....	....	....	....	....	....	....	....	....	....	....
99-2000	Rochester Jr. Americans	NAJHL	DID NOT PLAY – COACHING																									
	NHL Totals		**98**	**18**	**26**	**44**	**14**	**18**	**32**	**51**	**2**	**2**	**1**	**116**	**15.5**	**58**	**6**	**85**	**23**		**5**	**0**	**4**	**4**	**14**	**0**	**0**	**0**

ECAC First All-Star Team (1984) • Named Best Forward at WEC-B (1990) • WEC-B All-Star Team (1991)

• Named Head Coach of **Adirondack IceHawks** (UHL), June 23, 2000.

• ORLESKI, Dave

David Eugene LW – L. 6'4", 210 lbs. b: Edmonton, Alta., 12/26/1959. Montreal's 6th, 79th overall, in 1979.

Season	Club	League	REGULAR SEASON																		PLAYOFFS							
			GP	G	A	Pts	AG	AA	APts	PIM	PP	SH	GW	S	%	TGF	PGF	TGA	PGA	+/–	GP	G	A	Pts	PIM	PP	SH	GW
1975-76	Edmonton Mets	AAHA	STATISTICS NOT AVAILABLE																									
1976-77	New Westminster Bruins	WCJHL	62	8	14	22	....	....	....	29	....	....	....	....	....	....	....	....	....	....	14	3	4	7	8	....	....	....
	New Westminster Bruins	Mem-Cup	5	2	2	4	....	....	....	14	....	....	....	....	....	....	....	....	....	....	....	....	....	....	....	....	....	....
1977-78	New Westminster Bruins	WCJHL	64	15	35	50	....	....	....	132	....	....	....	....	....	....	....	....	....	....	14	12	9	21	28	....	....	....
1978-79	New Westminster Bruins	WHL	71	27	39	66	....	....	....	128	....	....	....	....	....	....	....	....	....	....	8	3	4	7	2	....	....	....
	Canada	WJC-A	5	2	0	2	....	....	....	0	....	....	....	....	....	....	....	....	....	....	....	....	....	....	....	....	....	....
1979-80	Nova Scotia Voyageurs	AHL	70	24	24	48	....	....	....	32	....	....	....	....	....	....	....	....	....	....	6	0	2	2	0	....	....	....

Season	Club	League	GP	G	A	Pts	AG	AA	APts	PIM	PP	SH	GW	S	%	TGF	PGF	TGA	PGA	+/–	GP	G	A	Pts	PIM	PP	SH	GW
			REGULAR SEASON																		PLAYOFFS							
1980-81	Montreal Canadiens	NHL	1	0	0	0	0	0	0	0	0	0	0	0	0.0	0	0	0	0	0	....	....	....	....	....	....	....	....
	Nova Scotia Voyageurs	AHL	37	8	13	21	....	....	....	44	....	....	....	....	....	....	....	....	....	....	6	2	1	3	7	....	....	....
1981-82	Montreal Canadiens	NHL	1	0	0	0	0	0	0	0	0	0	0	0	0.0	0	0	0	0	0	....	....	....	....	....	....	....	....
	Nova Scotia Voyageurs	AHL	64	14	23	37	....	....	....	15	....	....	....	....	....	....	....	....	....	....	9	1	2	3	6	....	....	....
1982-83	Nova Scotia Voyageurs	AHL	68	30	37	67	....	....	....	28	....	....	....	....	....	....	....	....	....	....	3	1	0	1	0	....	....	....
1983-84	Salt Lake Golden Eagles	CHL	3	0	1	1	....	....	....	4	....	....	....	....	....	....	....	....	....	....	....	....	....	....	....	....	....	....
	Nova Scotia Voyageurs	AHL	20	6	9	15	....	....	....	14	....	....	....	....	....	....	....	....	....	....	12	2	2	4	0	....	....	....
1984-85	Nova Scotia Voyageurs	AHL	2	0	1	1	....	....	....	0	....	....	....	....	....	....	....	....	....	....	....	....	....	....	....	....	....	....
	NHL Totals		**2**	**0**	**0**	**0**	**0**	**0**	**0**	**0**	**0**	**0**	**0**	**0**	**0.0**	**0**	**0**	**0**	**0**		....	....	....	....	....	....	....	....

• ORR, Bobby

Robert Gordon D – L. 6', 197 lbs. b: Parry Sound, Ont., 3/20/1948. **HHOF**

Season	Club	League	GP	G	A	Pts	AG	AA	APts	PIM	PP	SH	GW	S	%	TGF	PGF	TGA	PGA	+/–	GP	G	A	Pts	PIM	PP	SH	GW
1962-63	Oshawa Generals	MTJHL	34	6	15	21	....	....	....	45	....	....	....	....	....	....	....	....	....	....	....	....	....	....	....	....	....	....
1963-64	Oshawa Generals	OHA-Jr.	56	29	43	72	....	....	....	142	....	....	....	....	....	....	....	....	....	....	6	0	7	7	21	....	....	....
1964-65	Oshawa Generals	OHA-Jr.	56	34	59	93	....	....	....	112	....	....	....	....	....	....	....	....	....	....	6	0	6	6	10	....	....	....
1965-66	Oshawa Generals	OHA-Jr.	47	38	56	94	....	....	....	92	....	....	....	....	....	....	....	....	....	....	17	9	19	28	14	....	....	....
	Oshawa Generals	Mem-Cup	12	12	24	36	....	....	....	11	....	....	....	....	....	....	....	....	....	....	....	....	....	....	....	....	....	....
1966-67	Boston Bruins	NHL	61	13	28	41	15	27	42	102	....	....	....	....	....	....	....	....	....	....	....	....	....	....	....	....	....	....
1967-68	Boston Bruins	NHL	46	11	20	31	13	20	33	63	3	0	1	172	6.4	99	28	56	15	30	4	0	2	2	2	0	0	0
1968-69	Boston Bruins	NHL	67	21	43	64	22	38	60	133	4	0	2	285	7.4	163	46	87	35	65	10	1	7	8	10	0	0	0
1969-70♦	Boston Bruins	NHL	76	33	*87	*120	36	83	119	125	11	4	3	413	8.0	192	79	100	41	54	14	9	11	20	14	3	2	1
1970-71	Boston Bruins	NHL	78	37	*102	139	37	86	123	91	5	3	5	392	9.4	258	79	85	30	124	7	5	7	12	25	1	1	1
1971-72♦	Boston Bruins	NHL	76	37	*80	117	37	70	107	106	11	4	4	353	10.5	209	69	83	29	86	15	5	*19	*24	19	4	0	1
1972-73	Team Canada	Summit-72	DID NOT PLAY – INJURED																									
	Boston Bruins	NHL	63	29	72	101	27	58	85	99	7	1	3	282	10.3	173	57	90	30	56	5	1	1	2	7	0	0	0
1973-74	Boston Bruins	NHL	74	32	*90	122	31	75	106	82	11	0	4	384	8.3	229	62	115	32	84	16	4	*14	18	28	1	0	2
1974-75	Boston Bruins	NHL	80	46	*89	*135	40	67	107	101	16	2	4	384	12.0	246	81	129	44	80	3	1	5	6	2	0	1	0
1975-76	Boston Bruins	NHL	10	5	13	18	4	10	14	22	3	1	0	57	8.8	32	13	11	2	10	....	....	....	....	....	....	....	....
1976-77	Canada	Can-Cup	7	2	7	*9	....	....	....	8	....	....	....	....	....	....	....	....	....	....	....	....	....	....	....	....	....	....
	Chicago Black Hawks	NHL	20	4	19	23	4	15	19	25	2	0	0	55	7.3	42	20	20	4	6	....	....	....	....	....	....	....	....
1977-78			DID NOT PLAY – INJURED																									
1978-79	Chicago Black Hawks	NHL	6	2	2	4	2	1	3	4	0	0	0	18	11.1	8	1	5	0	2	....	....	....	....	....	....	....	....
	NHL Totals		**657**	**270**	**645**	**915**	**268**	**550**	**818**	**953**	....	....	....	....	....	....	....	....	....	....	**74**	**26**	**66**	**92**	**107**	....	....	....

NHL Second All-Star Team (1967) • Won Calder Memorial Trophy (1967) • NHL First All-Star Team (1968, 1969, 1970, 1971, 1972, 1973, 1974, 1975) • Won James Norris Trophy (1968, 1969, 1970, 1971, 1972, 1973, 1974,1975) • NHL Plus/Minus Leader (1969, 1970, 1971, 1972, 1974, 1975) • Won Art Ross Trophy (1970, 1975) • Won Hart Trophy (1970, 1971, 1972) • Won Conn Smythe Trophy (1970, 1972) • Won Lester B. Pearson Award (1975) • Canada Cup All-Star Team (1976) • Named Canada Cup MVP (1976) • Won Lester Patrick Trophy (1979) • Played in NHL All-Star Game (1968, 1969, 1970, 1971, 1972, 1973, 1975)

• Missed majority of 1975-76 season recovering from knee injury suffered in training camp, September 22, 1975. Signed as a free agent by **Chicago**, June 24, 1976. • Missed entire 1977-78 season recovering from knee surgery, April 19, 1977.

• ORSZAGH, Vladimir

RW – L. 5'11", 173 lbs. b: Banska Bystrica, Czech., 5/24/1977. NY Islanders' 4th, 106th overall, in 1995.

Season	Club	League	GP	G	A	Pts	AG	AA	APts	PIM	PP	SH	GW	S	%	TGF	PGF	TGA	PGA	+/–	GP	G	A	Pts	PIM	PP	SH	GW
1993-94	Banska Bystrica	Slovakia-Jr.	38	38	27	65	....	....	....	....	....	....	....	....	....	....	....	....	....	....	....	....	....	....	....	....	....	....
1994-95	Banska Bystrica	Slovakia-2	38	18	12	30	....	....	....	....	....	....	....	....	....	....	....	....	....	....	....	....	....	....	....	....	....	....
	Slovakia	WJC-B	7	1	2	3	....	....	....	8	....	....	....	....	....	....	....	....	....	....	....	....	....	....	....	....	....	....
1995-96	Banska Bystrica	Slovakia	31	9	5	14	....	....	....	22	....	....	....	....	....	....	....	....	....	....	....	....	....	....	....	....	....	....
	Slovakia	WJC-A	6	5	1	6	....	....	....	18	....	....	....	....	....	....	....	....	....	....	....	....	....	....	....	....	....	....
1996-97	Utah Grizzlies	IHL	68	12	15	27	....	....	....	30	....	....	....	....	....	....	....	....	....	....	3	0	1	1	4	....	....	....
1997-98	New York Islanders	NHL	11	0	1	1	0	1	1	2	0	0	0	9	0.0	1	0	4	0	–3	....	....	....	....	....	....	....	....
	Utah Grizzlies	IHL	62	13	10	23	....	....	....	60	....	....	....	....	....	....	....	....	....	....	4	2	0	2	0	....	....	....
1998-99	New York Islanders	NHL	12	1	0	1	1	0	1	6	0	0	0	4	....	....	....	....	....	....	....	....	....	....	....	....	....	....
	Lowell Lock Monsters	AHL	68	18	23	41	....	....	....	57	....	....	....	....	....	....	....	....	....	....	3	2	2	4	2	....	....	....
99-2000	New York Islanders	NHL	11	2	1	3	2	1	3	4	0	0	0	16	12.5	3	0	6	4	1	....	....	....	....	....	....	....	....
	Lowell Lock Monsters	AHL	55	8	12	20	....	....	....	22	....	....	....	....	....	....	....	....	....	....	7	3	3	6	2	....	....	....
	NHL Totals		**34**	**3**	**2**	**5**	**3**	**2**	**5**	**12**	**0**	**0**	**0**	**29**	**10.3**	**4**	**0**	**10**	**4**		....	....	....	....	....	....	....	....

• OSBORNE, Keith

Keith J. RW – R. 6'1", 180 lbs. b: Toronto, Ont., 4/2/1969. St. Louis' 1st, 12th overall, in 1987.

Season	Club	League	GP	G	A	Pts	AG	AA	APts	PIM	PP	SH	GW	S	%	TGF	PGF	TGA	PGA	+/–	GP	G	A	Pts	PIM	PP	SH	GW
1985-86	Toronto Red Wings	MTHL	42	48	63	111	....	....	....	36	....	....	....	....	....	....	....	....	....	....	....	....	....	....	....	....	....	....
1986-87	North Bay Centennials	OHL	61	34	55	89	....	....	....	31	....	....	....	....	....	....	....	....	....	....	24	11	11	22	25	....	....	....
1987-88	North Bay Centennials	OHL	30	14	22	36	....	....	....	20	....	....	....	....	....	....	....	....	....	....	4	1	5	6	8	....	....	....
1988-89	North Bay Centennials	OHL	15	11	15	26	....	....	....	12	....	....	....	....	....	....	....	....	....	....	....	....	....	....	....	....	....	....
	Niagara Falls Thunder	OHL	50	34	49	83	....	....	....	45	....	....	....	....	....	....	....	....	....	....	17	12	12	24	36	....	....	....
1989-90	St. Louis Blues	NHL	5	0	2	2	0	1	1	8	0	0	0	4	0.0	3	0	5	0	–2	....	....	....	....	....	....	....	....
	Peoria Rivermen	IHL	56	23	24	47	....	....	....	58	....	....	....	....	....	....	....	....	....	....	5	1	1	2	4	....	....	....
1990-91	Peoria Rivermen	IHL	54	10	20	30	....	....	....	79	....	....	....	....	....	....	....	....	....	....	....	....	....	....	....	....	....	....
	Newmarket Saints	AHL	12	0	3	3	....	....	....	6	....	....	....	....	....	....	....	....	....	....	....	....	....	....	....	....	....	....
1991-92	St. John's Maple Leafs	AHL	53	11	16	27	....	....	....	21	....	....	....	....	....	....	....	....	....	....	4	0	1	1	2	....	....	....
1992-93	Tampa Bay Lightning	NHL	11	1	1	2	1	1	2	8	0	0	1	11	9.1	5	1	5	0	–1	....	....	....	....	....	....	....	....
	Atlanta Knights	IHL	72	40	49	89	....	....	....	91	....	....	....	....	....	....	....	....	....	....	8	1	5	6	2	....	....	....
1993-94	ZSC Lions Zurich	Switz-2	36	26	31	57																						
1994-95	EHC Chur	Switz-2	STATISTICS NOT AVAILABLE																									
1995-96	Peoria Rivermen	IHL	63	23	28	51	....	....	....	64	....	....	....	....	....	....	....	....	....	....	9	5	3	8	12	....	....	....
1996-97	San Antonio Dragons	IHL	52	12	13	25	....	....	....	41	....	....	....	....	....	....	....	....	....	....	....	....	....	....	....	....	....	....
	Utah Grizzlies	IHL	9	3	0	3	....	....	....	4	....	....	....	....	....	....	....	....	....	....	1	0	0	0	0	....	....	....
1997-98	Augsburger Panther	Germany	17	1	5	6	....	....	....	20	....	....	....	....	....	....	....	....	....	....	....	....	....	....	....	....	....	....
	Winston-Salem Ice Hawks	UHL	50	26	35	61	....	....	....	60	....	....	....	....	....	....	....	....	....	....	....	....	....	....	....	....	....	....
1998-99	Saginaw Gears	UHL	73	20	49	69	....	....	....	72	....	....	....	....	....	....	....	....	....	....	....	....	....	....	....	....	....	....
99-2000	Ohio Gears	UHL	70	15	55	70	....	....	....	71	....	....	....	....	....	....	....	....	....	....	....	....	....	....	....	....	....	....
	NHL Totals		**16**	**1**	**3**	**4**	**1**	**2**	**3**	**16**	**0**	**0**	**1**	**15**	**6.7**	**8**	**1**	**10**	**0**		....	....	....	....	....	....	....	....

• Missed majority of 1987-88 season recovering from wrist and ankle injuries suffered in training camp, September, 1987. Traded to **Toronto** by **St. Louis** for Darren Veitch, March 5, 1991. Claimed by **Tampa Bay** from **Toronto** in Expansion Draft, June 18, 1992.

• OSBORNE, Mark

Mark Anatole "Ozzie" LW – L. 6'2", 205 lbs. b: Toronto, Ont., 8/13/1961. Detroit's 2nd, 46th overall, in 1980.

Season	Club	League	GP	G	A	Pts	AG	AA	APts	PIM	PP	SH	GW	S	%	TGF	PGF	TGA	PGA	+/–	GP	G	A	Pts	PIM	PP	SH	GW
1977-78	Toronto Young Nationals	MTHL	58	20	28	48	....	....	....	60	....	....	....	....	....	....	....	....	....	....	....	....	....	....	....	....	....	....
1978-79	Niagara Falls Flyers	OMJHL	62	17	25	42	....	....	....	53	....	....	....	....	....	....	....	....	....	....	20	6	2	8	31	....	....	....
1979-80	Niagara Falls Flyers	OMJHL	52	10	33	43	....	....	....	104	....	....	....	....	....	....	....	....	....	....	10	2	1	3	23	....	....	....
1980-81	Niagara Falls Flyers	OMJHL	54	39	41	80	....	....	....	140	....	....	....	....	....	....	....	....	....	....	12	11	10	21	20	....	....	....
	Adirondack Red Wings	AHL	....	....	....	....	....	....	....	....	....	....	....	....	....	....	....	....	....	....	13	2	3	5	2	....	....	....
1981-82	Detroit Red Wings	NHL	80	26	41	67	21	27	48	61	5	0	3	181	14.4	97	19	88	3	–7	....	....	....	....	....	....	....	....
1982-83	Detroit Red Wings	NHL	80	19	24	43	16	17	33	83	3	0	3	159	11.9	76	17	104	4	–41	....	....	....	....	....	....	....	....
1983-84	New York Rangers	NHL	73	23	28	51	18	19	37	88	6	0	5	139	16.5	85	22	66	4	1	5	0	1	1	7	0	0	0
1984-85	New York Rangers	NHL	23	4	4	8	3	3	6	33	0	0	0	29	13.8	20	2	22	2	–2	3	0	0	0	4	0	0	0
1985-86	New York Rangers	NHL	62	16	24	40	13	16	29	80	5	1	1	134	11.9	58	14	49	10	5	15	2	3	5	26	0	1	1
1986-87	New York Rangers	NHL	58	17	15	32	15	11	26	101	5	0	2	129	13.2	51	15	69	18	–15	....	....	....	....	....	....	....	....
	Toronto Maple Leafs	NHL	16	5	10	15	4	7	11	12	1	0	0	31	16.1	17	5	13	0	–1	9	1	3	4	6	0	0	0
1987-88	Toronto Maple Leafs	NHL	79	23	37	60	20	26	46	102	4	2	0	155	14.8	102	24	102	21	–3	6	1	3	4	16	0	0	1
1988-89	Toronto Maple Leafs	NHL	75	16	30	46	14	21	35	112	5	0	1	118	13.6	88	24	86	17	–5	....	....	....	....	....	....	....	....
1989-90	Toronto Maple Leafs	NHL	78	23	50	73	20	36	56	91	3	1	6	137	16.8	116	32	104	22	2	5	2	3	5	12	0	1	0
1990-91	Toronto Maple Leafs	NHL	18	3	3	6	3	2	5	4	1	1	0	32	9.4	8	1	24	7	–10	....	....	....	....	....	....	....	....
	Winnipeg Jets	NHL	37	8	8	16	7	6	13	59	0	0	2	55	14.5	26	0	31	4	–1	....	....	....	....	....	....	....	....

			REGULAR SEASON																		PLAYOFFS							
Season	Club	League	GP	G	A	Pts	AG	AA	APts	PIM	PP	SH	GW	S	%	TGF	PGF	TGA	PGA	+/-	GP	G	A	Pts	PIM	PP	SH	GW
1991-92	**Winnipeg Jets**	**NHL**	43	4	12	16	4	9	13	65	0	0	0	50	8.0	22	1	30	1	–8	....	....	....	....	....	....	....	....
	Toronto Maple Leafs	**NHL**	11	3	1	4	3	1	4	8	0	2	0	16	18.8	6	0	10	2	–2	....	....	....	....	....	....	....	....
1992-93	**Toronto Maple Leafs**	**NHL**	76	12	14	26	10	10	20	89	0	2	2	110	10.9	36	2	71	30	–7	19	1	1	2	16	0	0	0
1993-94	**Toronto Maple Leafs**	**NHL**	73	9	15	24	8	12	20	145	1	1	2	103	8.7	31	1	41	13	2	18	4	2	6	52	0	2	1
1994-95	**New York Rangers**	**NHL**	37	1	3	4	2	4	6	19	0	0	0	32	3.1	8	0	12	2	–2	7	1	0	1	2	0	0	0
1995-96	Cleveland Lumberjacks	IHL	70	31	38	69	....	....	....	131	....	....	....	....	....	....	....	....	....	....	3	1	2	3	2	....	....	....
1996-97	Cleveland Lumberjacks	IHL	59	7	25	32	....	....	....	96	....	....	....	....	....	....	....	....	....	....	6	1	2	3	14	....	....	....
1997-1998	Cleveland Lumberjacks	IHL	DID NOT PLAY – ASSISTANT COACH																									
	Cleveland Lumberjacks	IHL	3	0	0	0	....	....	....	22	....	....	....	....	....	....	....	....	....	....	....	....	....	....	....	....	....	....
1998-1999	St. Michael's Majors	OHL	DID NOT PLAY – ASSISTANT COACH																									
1999-2000	St. Michael's Majors	OHL	DID NOT PLAY – COACHING																									
	NHL Totals		919	212	319	531	181	227	408	1152	39	10	27	1610	13.2	847	179	922	160		87	12	16	28	141	0	4	3

Traded to **NY Rangers** by **Detroit** with Mike Blaisdell and Willy Huber for Ron Duguay, Eddie Mio and Eddie Johnstone, June 13, 1983. Traded to **Toronto** by **NY Rangers** for Jeff Jackson and Toronto's 3rd round choice (Rob Zamuner) in 1989 Entry Draft, March 5, 1987. Traded to **Winnipeg** by **Toronto** with Ed Olczyk for Dave Ellett and Paul Fenton, November 10, 1989. Traded to **Toronto** by **Winnipeg** for Lucien DeBlois, March 10, 1992. Signed as a free agent by **NY Rangers**, January 25, 1995. • Officially announced retirement and named Assistant Coach of **Cleveland** (IHL), June 19, 1997.

• OSBURN, Randy

Randoulf Allan LW – L. 6', 190 lbs. b: Collingwood, Ont., 11/26/1952. Toronto's 2nd, 27th overall, in 1972.

Season	Club	League	GP	G	A	Pts	AG	AA	APts	PIM	PP	SH	GW	S	%	TGF	PGF	TGA	PGA	+/-	GP	G	A	Pts	PIM	PP	SH	GW
1970-71	Hamilton Red Wings	OHA-Jr.	12	1	4	5	....	....	....	7	....	....	....	....	....	....	....	....	....	....	....	....	....	....	....	....	....	....
	London Knights	OHA-Jr.	42	18	29	47	....	....	....	8	....	....	....	....	....	....	....	....	....	....	4	1	1	2	0	....	....	....
1971-72	London Knights	OMJHL	63	43	57	100	....	....	....	29	....	....	....	....	....	....	....	....	....	....	7	3	8	11	2	....	....	....
1972-73	**Toronto Maple Leafs**	**NHL**	26	0	2	2	0	2	2	0	0	0	0	15	0.0	5	1	9	0	–5	....	....	....	....	....	....	....	....
	Tulsa Oilers	CHL	27	9	11	20	....	....	....	25	....	....	....	....	....	....	....	....	....	....	....	....	....	....	....	....	....	....
1973-74	Oklahoma City Blazers	CHL	72	*37	25	62	....	....	....	13	....	....	....	....	....	....	....	....	....	....	10	3	3	6	4	....	....	....
1974-75	**Philadelphia Flyers**	**NHL**	1	0	0	0	0	0	0	0	0	0	0	0	0.0	0	0	0	0	0	....	....	....	....	....	....	....	....
	Richmond Robins	AHL	13	1	3	4	....	....	....	0	....	....	....	....	....	....	....	....	....	....	....	....	....	....	....	....	....	....
	Philadelphia Firebirds	NAHL	26	12	11	23	....	....	....	10	....	....	....	....	....	....	....	....	....	....	4	1	1	2	5	....	....	....
1975-76	Philadelphia Firebirds	NAHL	69	29	39	68	....	....	....	46	....	....	....	....	....	....	....	....	....	....	16	11	8	19	10	....	....	....
1976-77	Philadelphia Firebirds	NAHL	40	32	26	58	....	....	....	10	....	....	....	....	....	....	....	....	....	....	....	....	....	....	....	....	....	....
1977-78	Philadelphia Firebirds	AHL	78	35	26	61	....	....	....	30	....	....	....	....	....	....	....	....	....	....	4	1	0	1	2	....	....	....
	NHL Totals		27	0	2	2	0	2	2	0	0	0	0	15	0.0	5	1	9	0		....	....	....	....	....	....	....	....

OMJHL Second All-Star Team (1972) • CHL First All-Star Team (1974)

Traded to **Philadelphia** by **Toronto** with Dave Fortier for Bill Flett, May 27, 1974.

• O'SHEA, Danny

Daniel Patrick C – L. 6'1", 190 lbs. b: Toronto, Ont., 6/15/1945.

Season	Club	League	GP	G	A	Pts	AG	AA	APts	PIM	PP	SH	GW	S	%	TGF	PGF	TGA	PGA	+/-	GP	G	A	Pts	PIM	PP	SH	GW
1961-62	Peterborough Petes	OHA-Jr.	47	5	4	9	....	....	....	21	....	....	....	....	....	....	....	....	....	....	....	....	....	....	....	....	....	....
1962-63	Peterborough Petes	OHA-Jr.	30	7	7	14	....	....	....	16	....	....	....	....	....	....	....	....	....	....	....	....	....	....	....	....	....	....
1963-64	Oshawa Generals	OHA-Jr.	55	30	49	79	....	....	....	92	....	....	....	....	....	....	....	....	....	....	6	6	3	9	16	....	....	....
1964-65	Oshawa Generals	OHA-Jr.	24	16	19	35	....	....	....	60	....	....	....	....	....	....	....	....	....	....	6	0	5	5	17	....	....	....
1965-66	Oshawa Generals	OHA-Jr.	48	36	45	81	....	....	....	132	....	....	....	....	....	....	....	....	....	....	17	*15	18	33	47	....	....	....
	Oshawa Generals	Mem-Cup	12	11	14	25	....	....	....	20	....	....	....	....	....	....	....	....	....	....	....	....	....	....	....	....	....	....
1966-67	Canada	Nat-Team	STATISTICS NOT AVAILABLE																									
1967-68	Winnipeg Nats	WCSHL	....	7	5	12	....	....	....	27	....	....	....	....	....	....	....	....	....	....	....	....	....	....	....	....	....	....
1968-69	**Minnesota North Stars**	**NHL**	74	15	34	49	16	30	46	88	4	0	3	157	9.6	72	20	82	4	–26	....	....	....	....	....	....	....	....
1969-70	**Minnesota North Stars**	**NHL**	75	10	24	34	11	22	33	82	4	0	0	136	7.4	61	24	54	13	–4	6	1	0	1	8	0	0	0
1970-71	**Minnesota North Stars**	**NHL**	59	14	12	26	14	10	24	16	0	0	3	155	9.0	35	0	42	4	–3	....	....	....	....	....	....	....	....
	Chicago Black Hawks	**NHL**	18	4	7	11	4	6	10	10	0	0	1	31	12.9	15	2	11	3	5	18	2	5	7	15	0	0	0
1971-72	**Chicago Black Hawks**	**NHL**	48	6	9	15	6	8	14	28	0	0	2	63	9.5	30	2	35	7	0	....	....	....	....	....	....	....	....
	St. Louis Blues	**NHL**	20	3	3	6	3	3	6	11	0	0	0	25	12.0	8	0	18	6	–4	10	0	2	2	36	0	0	0
1972-73	**St. Louis Blues**	**NHL**	75	12	26	38	11	21	32	30	0	2	2	110	10.9	52	2	86	31	–5	5	0	0	0	2	0	0	0
1973-74			DID NOT PLAY																									
1974-75	Minnesota Fighting Saints	WHA	76	16	25	41	....	....	....	47	....	....	....	....	....	....	....	....	....	....	11	0	0	0	6	....	....	....
	NHL Totals		369	64	115	179	65	100	165	265	8	2	11	677	9.5	273	50	328	68		39	3	7	10	61	0	0	0
	Other Major League Totals		76	16	25	41	....	....	....	47	....	....	....	....	....	....	....	....	....	....	11	0	0	0	6	....	....	....

• Brother of Kevin • Played in NHL All-Star Game (1969, 1970)

Traded to **Minnesota** by **Montreal** for Minnesota's 1st round choices in 1970 (Chuck Lefley) and 1971 (Chuck Arnason) Amateur Drafts, June 14, 1967. Traded to **Chicago** by **Minnesota** for Doug Mohns and Terry Caffery, February 22, 1971. Traded to **St. Louis** by **Chicago** for Chris Bordeleau and future considerations (John Garrett, September 19, 1972), February 8, 1972. Selected by **Winnipeg** (WHA) in 1972 WHA General Player Draft, February 13, 1972. • Missed entire 1973-74 season recovering from heart attack suffered in July of 1973 and could not receive medical clearance to play in the NHL. WHA rights traded to **Minnesota** (WHA) by **Winnipeg** (WHA) for future considerations, June, 1974.

• O'SHEA, Kevin

Kevin William RW – R. 6'2", 205 lbs. b: Toronto, Ont., 5/28/1947.

Season	Club	League	GP	G	A	Pts	AG	AA	APts	PIM	PP	SH	GW	S	%	TGF	PGF	TGA	PGA	+/-	GP	G	A	Pts	PIM	PP	SH	GW
1966-67	Cornwall Colts	OHA-B	STATISTICS NOT AVAILABLE																									
	Cornwall Royals	Mem-Cup	12	6	5	11	....	....	....	43	....	....	....	....	....	....	....	....	....	....	....	....	....	....	....	....	....	....
1967-68	St. Lawrence University	ECAC	DID NOT PLAY – FRESHMAN																									
1968-69	Ottawa Nationals	OHA-Sr.	6	3	1	4	....	....	....	32	....	....	....	....	....	....	....	....	....	....	....	....	....	....	....	....	....	....
	Canada	WEC-A	7	0	0	0	....	....	....	23	....	....	....	....	....	....	....	....	....	....	....	....	....	....	....	....	....	....
1969-70	San Diego Gulls	WHL	71	12	22	34	....	....	....	49	....	....	....	....	....	....	....	....	....	....	6	1	2	3	9	....	....	....
1970-71	**Buffalo Sabres**	**NHL**	41	4	4	8	4	3	7	8	0	1	1	33	12.1	13	1	23	0	–11	....	....	....	....	....	....	....	....
1971-72	**Buffalo Sabres**	**NHL**	52	6	9	15	6	8	14	44	0	0	0	56	10.7	21	1	43	4	–19	....	....	....	....	....	....	....	....
	St. Louis Blues	**NHL**	4	0	0	0	0	0	0	2	0	0	0	3	0.0	1	0	2	0	–1	11	2	1	3	10	0	0	1
1972-73	**St. Louis Blues**	**NHL**	37	3	5	8	3	4	7	31	0	0	0	39	7.7	11	1	26	3	–13	1	0	0	0	0	0	0	0
	Denver Spurs	WHL	16	11	7	18	....	....	....	29	....	....	....	....	....	....	....	....	....	....	....	....	....	....	....	....	....	....
1973-74	Phoenix Roadrunners	WHL	54	24	21	45	....	....	....	40	....	....	....	....	....	....	....	....	....	....	9	6	5	*11	0	....	....	....
1974-75	Minnesota Fighting Saints	WHA	68	10	10	20	....	....	....	42	....	....	....	....	....	....	....	....	....	....	....	....	....	....	....	....	....	....
1975-76	Timra IF	Sweden	33	16	5	21	....	....	....	*72	....	....	....	....	....	....	....	....	....	....	....	....	....	....	....	....	....	....
	NHL Totals		134	13	18	31	13	15	28	85	0	1	1	131	9.9	46	3	94	7		12	2	1	3	10	0	0	1
	Other Major League Totals		68	10	10	20	....	....	....	42	....	....	....	....	....	....	....	....	....	....	....	....	....	....	....	....	....	....

• Brother of Danny

Claimed by **San Diego** (WHL) from **NY Rangers** in Reverse Draft, June 12, 1969. Claimed by **Buffalo** from **San Diego** (WHL) in Inter-League Draft, June 9, 1970. Selected by **Minnesota** (WHA) in 1972 WHA General Player Draft, February 12, 1972. Claimed on waivers by **St. Louis** from **Buffalo**, March 3, 1972.

• OSIECKI, Mark

Mark Anthony D – R. 6'2", 200 lbs. b: St. Paul, MN, 7/23/1968. Calgary's 10th, 187th overall, in 1987.

Season	Club	League	GP	G	A	Pts	AG	AA	APts	PIM	PP	SH	GW	S	%	TGF	PGF	TGA	PGA	+/-	GP	G	A	Pts	PIM	PP	SH	GW
1984-85	White Bear Lake Bears	Hi-School	23	13	26	39	....	....	....	....	....	....	....	....	....	....	....	....	....	....	....	....	....	....	....	....	....	....
1985-86	White Bear Lake Bears	Hi-School	24	12	13	25	....	....	....	....	....	....	....	....	....	....	....	....	....	....	....	....	....	....	....	....	....	....
1986-87	University of Wisconsin	WCHA	8	0	1	1	....	....	....	4	....	....	....	....	....	....	....	....	....	....	....	....	....	....	....	....	....	....
1987-88	University of Wisconsin	WCHA	18	0	1	1	....	....	....	22	....	....	....	....	....	....	....	....	....	....	....	....	....	....	....	....	....	....
1988-89	University of Wisconsin	WCHA	44	1	3	4	....	....	....	56	....	....	....	....	....	....	....	....	....	....	....	....	....	....	....	....	....	....
1989-90	University of Wisconsin	WCHA	46	5	38	43	....	....	....	78	....	....	....	....	....	....	....	....	....	....	....	....	....	....	....	....	....	....
1990-91	Salt Lake Golden Eagles	IHL	75	1	24	25	....	....	....	36	....	....	....	....	....	....	....	....	....	....	4	2	0	2	2	....	....	....
1991-92	**Calgary Flames**	**NHL**	50	2	7	9	2	5	7	24	1	0	2	44	4.5	42	4	57	15	–4	....	....	....	....	....	....	....	....
	Salt Lake Golden Eagles	IHL	1	0	0	0	....	....	....	0	....	....	....	....	....	....	....	....	....	....	....	....	....	....	....	....	....	....
	United States	WC-A	6	0	1	1	....	....	....	4	....	....	....	....	....	....	....	....	....	....	....	....	....	....	....	....	....	....
1992-93	**Ottawa Senators**	**NHL**	34	0	4	4	0	3	3	12	0	0	0	20	0.0	18	0	54	15	–21	....	....	....	....	....	....	....	....
	New Haven Senators	AHL	4	0	1	1	....	....	....	0	....	....	....	....	....	....	....	....	....	....	....	....	....	....	....	....	....	....
	Winnipeg Jets	**NHL**	4	1	0	1	1	0	1	2	1	0	0	5	20.0	5	2	2	0	1	....	....	....	....	....	....	....	....
	Minnesota North Stars	**NHL**	5	0	0	0	0	0	0	5	0	0	0	1	0.0	1	0	2	1	0	....	....	....	....	....	....	....	....
1993-94	Kalamazoo Wings	IHL	65	4	14	18	....	....	....	45	....	....	....	....	....	....	....	....	....	....	5	0	0	0	5	....	....	....

			REGULAR SEASON																		PLAYOFFS							
Season	Club	League	GP	G	A	Pts	AG	AA	APts	PIM	PP	SH	GW	S	%	TGF	PGF	TGA	PGA	+/–	GP	G	A	Pts	PIM	PP	SH	GW
1994-95	Detroit Vipers	IHL	4	0	0	0	....	....	....	4	....	....	....	....	....	....	....	....	....	....	....	....	....	....	....	....	....	....
	Minnesota Moose	IHL	39	1	2	3	....	....	....	22	....	....	....	....	....	....	....	....	....	....	2	0	0	0	2	....	....	....
1995-1996	White Bear Lake Bears	Hi-School	DID NOT PLAY – ASSISTANT COACH																									
1996-1997	University of North Dakota	WCHA	DID NOT PLAY – ASSISTANT COACH																									
1997-2000	Green Bay Gamblers	USHL	DID NOT PLAY – COACHING																									
	NHL Totals		**93**	**3**	**11**	**14**	**3**	**8**	**11**	**43**	**2**	**0**	**2**	**70**	**4.3**	**66**	**6**	**115**	**31**		....	....	....	....	....	....	....	....

NCAA Championship All-Tournament Team (1990)

Traded to **Ottawa** by **Calgary** for Chris Lindberg, June 22, 1992. Claimed on waivers by **Winnipeg** from **Ottawa**, February 20, 1993. Traded to **Minnesota** by **Winnipeg** with Winnipeg's 10th round choice (Bill Lang) in 1993 Entry Draft for Minnesota's 9th round choice (Vladimir Potatov) in 1993 Entry Draft, March 20, 1993. Transferred to **Dallas** after **Minnesota** franchise relocated, June 9, 1993.

• O'SULLIVAN, Chris

D – L. 6'2", 205 lbs. b: Dorchester, MA, 5/15/1974. Calgary's 2nd, 30th overall, in 1992.

Season	Club	League	GP	G	A	Pts	AG	AA	APts	PIM	PP	SH	GW	S	%	TGF	PGF	TGA	PGA	+/–	GP	G	A	Pts	PIM	PP	SH	GW
1991-92	Catholic Memorial Knights	Hi-School	26	26	23	49	....	....	....	65	....	....	....	....	....	....	....	....	....	....	....	....	....	....	....	....	....	....
1992-93	Boston University	H-East	5	0	2	2	....	....	....	4	....	....	....	....	....	....	....	....	....	....	....	....	....	....	....	....	....	....
1993-94	Boston University	H-East	32	5	18	23	....	....	....	25	....	....	....	....	....	....	....	....	....	....	....	....	....	....	....	....	....	....
	United States	WJC-A	7	0	3	3	....	....	....	4	....	....	....	....	....	....	....	....	....	....	....	....	....	....	....	....	....	....
1994-95	Boston University	H-East	40	23	33	56	....	....	....	48	....	....	....	....	....	....	....	....	....	....	....	....	....	....	....	....	....	....
	United States	WC-A	6	0	0	0	....	....	....	10	....	....	....	....	....	....	....	....	....	....	....	....	....	....	....	....	....	....
1995-96	Boston University	H-East	37	12	35	47	....	....	....	50	....	....	....	....	....	....	....	....	....	....	....	....	....	....	....	....	....	....
1996-97	**Calgary Flames**	**NHL**	**27**	**2**	**8**	**10**	**2**	**7**	**9**	**2**	**1**	**0**	**1**	**41**	**4.9**	**25**	**15**	**13**	**3**	**0**	....	....	....	....	....	....	....	....
	Saint John Flames	AHL	29	3	8	11	....	....	....	17	....	....	....	....	....	....	....	....	....	....	5	0	4	4	0	....	....	....
1997-98	**Calgary Flames**	**NHL**	**12**	**0**	**2**	**2**	**0**	**2**	**2**	**10**	**0**	**0**	**0**	**12**	**0.0**	**10**	**1**	**5**	**0**	**4**	....	....	....	....	....	....	....	....
	Saint John Flames	AHL	32	4	10	14	....	....	....	2	....	....	....	....	....	....	....	....	....	....	21	2	17	19	18	....	....	....
1998-99	**Calgary Flames**	**NHL**	**10**	**0**	**1**	**1**	**0**	**1**	**1**	**2**	**0**	**0**	**0**	**10**	**0.0**	**3**	**0**	**4**	**0**	**–1**	....	....	....	....	....	....	....	....
	Saint John Flames	AHL	41	7	29	36	....	....	....	24	....	....	....	....	....	....	....	....	....	....	....	....	....	....	....	....	....	....
	Hartford Wolf Pack	AHL	10	1	4	5	....	....	....	0	....	....	....	....	....	....	....	....	....	....	7	1	3	4	11	....	....	....
99-2000	**Vancouver Canucks**	**NHL**	**11**	**0**	**5**	**5**	**0**	**5**	**5**	**2**	**0**	**0**	**0**	**16**	**0.0**	**8**	**3**	**3**	**0**	**2**	....	....	....	....	....	....	....	....
	Syracuse Crunch	AHL	59	18	47	65	....	....	....	24	....	....	....	....	....	....	....	....	....	....	4	0	1	1	0	....	....	....
	United States	WC-A	7	0	1	1	....	....	....	0	....	....	....	....	....	....	....	....	....	....	....	....	....	....	....	....	....	....
	NHL Totals		**60**	**2**	**16**	**18**	**2**	**15**	**17**	**16**	**1**	**0**	**1**	**79**	**2.5**	**46**	**19**	**25**	**3**		....	....	....	....	....	....	....	....

Hockey East First All-Star Team (1995) • NCAA East Second All-American Team (1995) • NCAA Championship All-Tournament Team (1995) • NCAA Championship Tournament MVP (1995)

• Missed majority of 1992-93 season recovering from neck injury suffered in game vs. Boston College, November 11, 1992. Traded to **NY Rangers** by **Calgary** for Lee Sorochan, March 23, 1999..Signed as a free agent by **Vancouver**, August 20, 1999.

• OTEVREL, Jaroslav

LW – L. 6'3", 215 lbs. b: Gottwaldov, Czech., 9/16/1968. San Jose's 8th, 133rd overall, in 1991.

Season	Club	League	GP	G	A	Pts	AG	AA	APts	PIM	PP	SH	GW	S	%	TGF	PGF	TGA	PGA	+/–	GP	G	A	Pts	PIM	PP	SH	GW
1987-88	TJ Gottwaldov	Czech.	32	4	7	11	....	....	....	18	....	....	....	....	....	....	....	....	....	....	....	....	....	....	....	....	....	....
1988-89	TJ Gottwaldov	Czech.	40	14	6	20	....	....	....	37	....	....	....	....	....	....	....	....	....	....	....	....	....	....	....	....	....	....
1989-90	Dukla Trencin	Czech.	43	7	10	17	....	....	....	20	....	....	....	....	....	....	....	....	....	....	....	....	....	....	....	....	....	....
1990-91	ZPS Zlin	Czech.	49	24	26	50	....	....	....	105	....	....	....	....	....	....	....	....	....	....	....	....	....	....	....	....	....	....
1991-92	ZPS Zlin	Czech.	36	14	12	26	....	....	....	44	....	....	....	....	....	....	....	....	....	....	4	0	3	3	0	....	....	....
1992-93	**San Jose Sharks**	**NHL**	**7**	**0**	**2**	**2**	**0**	**1**	**1**	**0**	**0**	**0**	**0**	**4**	**0.0**	**2**	**1**	**7**	**0**	**–6**	....	....	....	....	....	....	....	....
	Kansas City Blades	IHL	62	17	27	44	....	....	....	58	....	....	....	....	....	....	....	....	....	....	6	1	4	5	4	....	....	....
1993-94	**San Jose Sharks**	**NHL**	**9**	**3**	**2**	**5**	**3**	**2**	**5**	**2**	**1**	**0**	**0**	**11**	**27.3**	**6**	**2**	**9**	**0**	**–5**	....	....	....	....	....	....	....	....
	Kansas City Blades	IHL	62	20	33	53	....	....	....	46	....	....	....	....	....	....	....	....	....	....	....	....	....	....	....	....	....	....
1994-95	HC Assat-Pori	Finland	50	13	18	31	....	....	....	26	....	....	....	....	....	....	....	....	....	....	7	1	4	5	2	....	....	....
1995-96	HC Assat-Pori	Finland	43	10	26	36	....	....	....	44	....	....	....	....	....	....	....	....	....	....	....	....	....	....	....	....	....	....
	NHL Totals		**16**	**3**	**4**	**7**	**3**	**3**	**6**	**2**	**1**	**0**	**0**	**15**	**20.0**	**8**	**3**	**16**	**0**		....	....	....	....	....	....	....	....

• Suffered career-ending neck injury in game vs. JyP Jyvaskyla (Finland), February 11, 1996.

• OTTO, Joel

Joel Stuart . C – R. 6'4", 220 lbs. b: Elk River, MN, 10/29/1961.

Season	Club	League	GP	G	A	Pts	AG	AA	APts	PIM	PP	SH	GW	S	%	TGF	PGF	TGA	PGA	+/–	GP	G	A	Pts	PIM	PP	SH	GW
1980-81	Bemidji State Beavers	NCAA	23	5	11	16	....	....	....	10	....	....	....	....	....	....	....	....	....	....	....	....	....	....	....	....	....	....
1981-82	Bemidji State Beavers	NCAA	31	19	33	52	....	....	....	24	....	....	....	....	....	....	....	....	....	....	....	....	....	....	....	....	....	....
1982-83	Bemidji State Beavers	NCAA	37	33	28	61	....	....	....	68	....	....	....	....	....	....	....	....	....	....	....	....	....	....	....	....	....	....
1983-84	Bemidji State Beavers	NCAA	31	32	43	75	....	....	....	32	....	....	....	....	....	....	....	....	....	....	....	....	....	....	....	....	....	....
1984-85	**Calgary Flames**	**NHL**	**17**	**4**	**8**	**12**	**3**	**5**	**8**	**30**	**1**	**0**	**0**	**27**	**14.8**	**20**	**7**	**10**	**0**	**3**	**3**	**2**	**1**	**3**	**10**	**1**	**0**	**1**
	Moncton Golden Flames	AHL	56	27	36	63	....	....	....	89	....	....	....	....	....	....	....	....	....	....	....	....	....	....	....	....	....	....
	United States	WEC-A	10	2	1	3	....	....	....	8	....	....	....	....	....	....	....	....	....	....	....	....	....	....	....	....	....	....
1985-86	**Calgary Flames**	**NHL**	**79**	**25**	**34**	**59**	**20**	**23**	**43**	**188**	**9**	**0**	**2**	**147**	**17.0**	**103**	**32**	**49**	**1**	**23**	**22**	**5**	**10**	**15**	**80**	**3**	**0**	**1**
1986-87	**Calgary Flames**	**NHL**	**68**	**19**	**31**	**50**	**16**	**23**	**39**	**185**	**5**	**0**	**1**	**127**	**15.0**	**91**	**33**	**63**	**13**	**8**	**2**	**0**	**2**	**2**	**6**	**0**	**0**	**0**
1987-88	United States	Can-Cup	5	0	2	2	....	....	....	4	....	....	....	....	....	....	....	....	....	....	....	....	....	....	....	....	....	....
	Calgary Flames	**NHL**	**62**	**13**	**39**	**52**	**11**	**28**	**39**	**194**	**4**	**1**	**4**	**105**	**12.4**	**87**	**26**	**70**	**25**	**16**	**9**	**3**	**2**	**5**	**26**	**1**	**0**	**1**
1988-89♦	**Calgary Flames**	**NHL**	**72**	**23**	**30**	**53**	**19**	**21**	**40**	**213**	**10**	**2**	**2**	**123**	**18.7**	**82**	**35**	**73**	**38**	**12**	**22**	**6**	**13**	**19**	**46**	**2**	**1**	**1**
1989-90	Calgary Flames	Fr-Tour	4	0	0	0	....	....	....	2	....	....	....	....	....	....	....	....	....	....	....	....	....	....	....	....	....	....
	Calgary Flames	**NHL**	**75**	**13**	**20**	**33**	**11**	**14**	**25**	**116**	**7**	**0**	**0**	**96**	**13.5**	**55**	**16**	**70**	**35**	**4**	**6**	**2**	**2**	**4**	**2**	**0**	**0**	**0**
	United States	WEC-A	9	2	4	6	....	....	....	2	....	....	....	....	....	....	....	....	....	....	....	....	....	....	....	....	....	....
1990-91	**Calgary Flames**	**NHL**	**76**	**19**	**20**	**39**	**17**	**15**	**32**	**183**	**7**	**1**	**4**	**109**	**17.4**	**62**	**20**	**79**	**33**	**–4**	**7**	**1**	**2**	**3**	**8**	**0**	**0**	**0**
1991-92	United States	Can-Cup	8	4	0	4	....	....	....	2	....	....	....	....	....	....	....	....	....	....	....	....	....	....	....	....	....	....
	Calgary Flames	**NHL**	**78**	**13**	**21**	**34**	**12**	**16**	**28**	**161**	**5**	**1**	**3**	**105**	**12.4**	**65**	**20**	**99**	**44**	**–10**	....	....	....	....	....	....	....	....
1992-93	**Calgary Flames**	**NHL**	**75**	**19**	**33**	**52**	**16**	**23**	**39**	**150**	**6**	**1**	**4**	**115**	**16.5**	**74**	**23**	**89**	**40**	**2**	**6**	**4**	**2**	**6**	**4**	**0**	**1**	**1**
1993-94	**Calgary Flames**	**NHL**	**81**	**11**	**12**	**23**	**10**	**9**	**19**	**92**	**3**	**1**	**1**	**108**	**10.2**	**38**	**7**	**84**	**36**	**–17**	**3**	**0**	**1**	**1**	**4**	**0**	**0**	**0**
1994-95	**Calgary Flames**	**NHL**	**47**	**8**	**13**	**21**	**14**	**19**	**33**	**130**	**0**	**2**	**2**	**46**	**17.4**	**34**	**2**	**45**	**21**	**8**	**7**	**0**	**3**	**3**	**2**	**0**	**0**	**0**
1995-96	**Philadelphia Flyers**	**NHL**	**67**	**12**	**29**	**41**	**12**	**24**	**36**	**115**	**6**	**1**	**1**	**91**	**13.2**	**64**	**24**	**47**	**18**	**11**	**12**	**3**	**4**	**7**	**11**	**1**	**0**	**1**
1996-97	United States	W-Cup	7	1	2	3	....	....	....	6	....	....	....	....	....	....	....	....	....	....	....	....	....	....	....	....	....	....
	Philadelphia Flyers	**NHL**	**78**	**13**	**19**	**32**	**14**	**17**	**31**	**99**	**0**	**1**	**2**	**105**	**12.4**	**44**	**1**	**49**	**18**	**12**	**18**	**1**	**5**	**6**	**8**	**0**	**0**	**0**
1997-98	**Philadelphia Flyers**	**NHL**	**68**	**3**	**4**	**7**	**4**	**4**	**8**	**78**	**0**	**0**	**0**	**53**	**5.7**	**12**	**0**	**32**	**18**	**–2**	**5**	**0**	**0**	**0**	**0**	**0**	**0**	**0**
	United States	Olympics	4	0	0	0	....	....	....	0	....	....	....	....	....	....	....	....	....	....	....	....	....	....	....	....	....	....
	NHL Totals		**943**	**195**	**313**	**508**	**179**	**241**	**420**	**1934**	**63**	**11**	**26**	**1357**	**14.4**	**831**	**246**	**859**	**340**		**122**	**27**	**47**	**74**	**207**	**8**	**2**	**6**

NCAA (College Div.) West All-American Team (1983, 1984)

Signed as a free agent by **Calgary,** September 11, 1984. Signed as a free agent by **Philadelphia**, July 31, 1995.

• OWCHAR, Dennis

D – R. 5'11", 190 lbs. b: Dryden, Ont., 3/28/1953. Pittsburgh's 4th, 55th overall, in 1973.

Season	Club	League	GP	G	A	Pts	AG	AA	APts	PIM	PP	SH	GW	S	%	TGF	PGF	TGA	PGA	+/–	GP	G	A	Pts	PIM	PP	SH	GW
1969-70	Fort William Hurricanes	TBJHL	STATISTICS NOT AVAILABLE																									
	Fort William Hurricanes	Mem-Cup	12	0	3	3	....	....	....	6	....	....	....	....	....	....	....	....	....	....	....	....	....	....	....	....	....	....
1970-71	Fort William Hurricanes	TBJHL	STATISTICS NOT AVAILABLE																									
1971-72	Fort William Hurricanes	TBJHL	STATISTICS NOT AVAILABLE																									
1972-73	St. Catharines Black Hawks	OMJHL	19	3	13	16	....	....	....	13	....	....	....	....	....	....	....	....	....	....	....	....	....	....	....	....	....	....
	Toronto Marlboros	OMJHL	20	7	8	15	....	....	....	27	....	....	....	....	....	....	....	....	....	....	....	....	....	....	....	....	....	....
	Toronto Marlboros	Mem-Cup	3	0	0	0	....	....	....	5	....	....	....	....	....	....	....	....	....	....	....	....	....	....	....	....	....	....
1973-74	Hershey Bears	AHL	74	16	17	33	....	....	....	51	....	....	....	....	....	....	....	....	....	....	14	1	5	6	14	....	....	....
1974-75	**Pittsburgh Penguins**	**NHL**	**46**	**6**	**11**	**17**	**5**	**8**	**13**	**67**	**0**	**0**	**0**	**62**	**9.7**	**54**	**0**	**56**	**14**	**12**	**6**	**0**	**1**	**1**	**4**	**0**	**0**	**0**
	Hershey Bears	AHL	24	3	14	17	....	....	....	31	....	....	....	....	....	....	....	....	....	....	4	0	1	1	0	....	....	....
1975-76	**Pittsburgh Penguins**	**NHL**	**54**	**5**	**12**	**17**	**4**	**9**	**13**	**19**	**1**	**0**	**0**	**62**	**8.1**	**66**	**3**	**65**	**15**	**13**	**2**	**0**	**0**	**0**	**2**	**0**	**0**	**0**
	Hershey Bears	AHL	7	5	1	6	....	....	....	13	....	....	....	....	....	....	....	....	....	....	....	....	....	....	....	....	....	....
1976-77	**Pittsburgh Penguins**	**NHL**	**46**	**5**	**18**	**23**	**4**	**14**	**18**	**37**	**1**	**0**	**0**	**86**	**5.8**	**57**	**6**	**68**	**10**	**–7**	....	....	....	....	....	....	....	....
1977-78	**Pittsburgh Penguins**	**NHL**	**22**	**2**	**8**	**10**	**2**	**6**	**8**	**23**	**0**	**0**	**0**	**51**	**3.9**	**25**	**0**	**44**	**7**	**–12**	....	....	....	....	....	....	....	....
	Colorado Rockies	**NHL**	**60**	**8**	**23**	**31**	**7**	**18**	**25**	**25**	**2**	**0**	**0**	**120**	**6.7**	**69**	**14**	**122**	**18**	**–49**	**2**	**1**	**0**	**1**	**2**	**0**	**0**	**0**
1978-79	**Colorado Rockies**	**NHL**	**50**	**3**	**13**	**16**	**3**	**9**	**12**	**27**	**1**	**0**	**0**	**77**	**3.9**	**48**	**18**	**78**	**15**	**–33**	....	....	....	....	....	....	....	....

			REGULAR SEASON																		PLAYOFFS							
Season	Club	League	GP	G	A	Pts	AG	AA	APts	PIM	PP	SH	GW	S	%	TGF	PGF	TGA	PGA	+/–	GP	G	A	Pts	PIM	PP	SH	GW
1979-80	**Colorado Rockies**	**NHL**	10	1	0	1	1	0	1	2	0	0	0	7	14.3	4	0	8	1	–3	....	....	....	....	....	....	....	....
	New Haven Nighthawks	AHL	40	6	27	33	....	....	....	26	....	....	....	....	....	....	....	....	....	....	....	....	....	....	....	....	....	....
1980-81	New Haven Nighthawks	AHL	57	2	16	18	....	....	....	67	....	....	....	....	....	....	....	....	....	....	4	0	0	0	5	....	....	....
1981-1986	Thunder Bay Twins	CASH	STATISTICS NOT AVAILABLE																									
1986-87	Thunder Bay Twins	CASH	6	1	5	6	....	....	....	6	....	....	....	....	....	....	....	....	....	....	....	....	....	....	....	....	....	....
	NHL Totals		288	30	85	115	26	64	90	200	5	0	0	465	6.5	323	41	441	80		10	1	1	2	8	0	0	0

Traded to **Colorado** by **Pittsburgh** for Tom Edur, December 2, 1977. Traded to **New Haven** (AHL) by **Colorado** with Larry Skinner for Bobby Sheehan, May 12, 1979.

• OZOLINSH, Sandis

D – L. 6'3", 205 lbs. b: Riga, Latvia, 8/3/1972. San Jose's 3rd, 30th overall, in 1991.

Season	Club	League	GP	G	A	Pts	AG	AA	APts	PIM	PP	SH	GW	S	%	TGF	PGF	TGA	PGA	+/–	GP	G	A	Pts	PIM	PP	SH	GW
1990-91	Dynamo Riga	Fr-Tour	1	0	0	0	....	....	....	0	....	....	....	....	....	....	....	....	....	....	....	....	....	....	....	....	....	....
	Dynamo Riga	USSR	44	0	3	3	....	....	....	51	....	....	....	....	....	....	....	....	....	....	....	....	....	....	....	....	....	....
1991-92	Dynamo Riga	CIS	30	6	0	6	....	....	....	42	....	....	....	....	....	....	....	....	....	....	....	....	....	....	....	....	....	....
	Russia	WJC-A	7	1	5	6	....	....	....	4	....	....	....	....	....	....	....	....	....	....	....	....	....	....	....	....	....	....
	Kansas City Blades	IHL	34	6	9	15	....	....	....	20	....	....	....	....	....	....	....	....	....	....	15	2	5	7	22	....	....	....
1992-93	**San Jose Sharks**	**NHL**	37	7	16	23	6	11	17	40	2	0	0	83	8.4	52	17	67	23	–9	....	....	....	....	....	....	....	....
1993-94	**San Jose Sharks**	**NHL**	81	26	38	64	24	30	54	24	4	0	3	157	16.6	118	36	87	21	16	14	0	10	10	8	0	0	0
1994-95	**San Jose Sharks**	**NHL**	48	9	16	25	16	24	40	30	3	1	2	83	10.8	58	10	62	8	–6	11	3	2	5	6	1	0	0
1995-96	San Francisco Spiders	IHL	2	1	0	1	....	....	....	0	....	....	....	....	....	....	....	....	....	....	....	....	....	....	....	....	....	....
	San Jose Sharks	**NHL**	7	1	3	4	1	2	3	4	1	0	0	21	4.8	12	3	15	8	2	....	....	....	....	....	....	....	....
♦	**Colorado Avalanche**	**NHL**	66	13	37	50	13	30	43	50	7	1	1	145	9.0	124	57	67	0	0	22	5	14	19	16	2	0	1
1996-97	**Colorado Avalanche**	**NHL**	80	23	45	68	24	40	64	88	13	0	4	232	9.9	132	69	60	1	4	17	4	13	17	24	2	0	1
1997-98	**Colorado Avalanche**	**NHL**	66	13	38	51	15	37	52	65	9	0	2	135	9.6	92	54	51	1	–12	7	0	7	7	14	0	0	0
1998-99	**Colorado Avalanche**	**NHL**	39	7	25	32	8	24	32	22	4	0	3	81	8.6	68	32	26	0	10	19	4	8	12	22	3	0	1
99-2000	**Colorado Avalanche**	**NHL**	82	16	36	52	18	33	51	46	6	0	1	210	7.6	128	49	63	1	17	17	5	5	10	20	3	0	1
	NHL Totals		506	115	254	369	125	231	356	369	49	2	16	1147	10.0	784	327	498	63		107	21	59	80	110	11	0	4

NHL First All-Star Team (1997) • Played in NHL All-Star Game (1994, 1997, 1998, 2000)

• Missed remainder of 1992-93 season recovering from knee injury suffered in game vs. Philadelphia, December 30, 1992. Traded to **Colorado** by **San Jose** for Owen Nolan, October 26, 1995. Traded to **Carolina** by **Colorado** with Columbus' 2nd round choice (previously acquired, Carolina selected Tomas Kurka) in 2000 Entry Draft for Nolan Pratt, Carolina's 1st (Vaclav Nedorost) and 2nd (Jared Aulin) round choices in 2000 Entry Draft and Philadelphia's 2nd round choice (previously acquired, Colorado selected Argis Saviels) in 2000 Entry Draft, June 24, 2000.

• PACHAL, Clayton

C/LW – L. 5'10", 185 lbs. b: Yorkton, Sask., 4/21/1956. Boston's 1st, 16th overall, in 1976.

Season	Club	League	GP	G	A	Pts	AG	AA	APts	PIM	PP	SH	GW	S	%	TGF	PGF	TGA	PGA	+/–	GP	G	A	Pts	PIM	PP	SH	GW
1972-73	Estevan Bruins	SJHL	STATISTICS NOT AVAILABLE																									
	New Westminster Bruins	WCJHL	37	2	2	4	....	....	....	67	....	....	....	....	....	....	....	....	....	....	5	0	0	0	16	....	....	....
1973-74	New Westminster Bruins	WCJHL	67	8	11	19	....	....	....	278	....	....	....	....	....	....	....	....	....	....	11	1	1	2	39	....	....	....
1974-75	New Westminster Bruins	WCJHL	65	17	30	47	....	....	....	306	....	....	....	....	....	....	....	....	....	....	17	3	6	9	72	....	....	....
	Canada	WJC-A	3	0	0	0	....	....	....	2	....	....	....	....	....	....	....	....	....	....	....	....	....	....	....	....	....	....
	New Westminster Bruins	Mem-Cup	4	2	1	3	....	....	....	4	....	....	....	....	....	....	....	....	....	....	....	....	....	....	....	....	....	....
1975-76	New Westminster Bruins	WCJHL	65	41	47	88	....	....	....	259	....	....	....	....	....	....	....	....	....	....	15	9	8	17	29	....	....	....
	New Westminster Bruins	Mem-Cup	4	2	0	2	....	....	....	14	....	....	....	....	....	....	....	....	....	....	....	....	....	....	....	....	....	....
1976-77	**Boston Bruins**	**NHL**	1	0	0	0	0	0	0	12	0	0	0	0	0.0	0	0	0	0	0	....	....	....	....	....	....	....	....
	Rochester Americans	AHL	70	8	20	28	....	....	....	150	....	....	....	....	....	....	....	....	....	....	9	4	2	6	2	....	....	....
	Binghamton Dusters	NAHL	1	0	0	0	....	....	....	0	....	....	....	....	....	....	....	....	....	....	....	....	....	....	....	....	....	....
1977-78	**Boston Bruins**	**NHL**	10	0	0	0	0	0	0	14	0	0	0	4	0.0	0	0	1	0	–1	....	....	....	....	....	....	....	....
	Rochester Americans	AHL	61	10	10	20	....	....	....	105	....	....	....	....	....	....	....	....	....	....	6	1	2	3	7	....	....	....
1978-79	**Colorado Rockies**	**NHL**	24	2	3	5	2	2	4	69	1	0	0	19	10.5	13	5	21	2	–11	....	....	....	....	....	....	....	....
	Philadelphia Firebirds	AHL	26	1	4	5	....	....	....	75	....	....	....	....	....	....	....	....	....	....	....	....	....	....	....	....	....	....
1979-80	Cincinnati Stingers	CHL	18	0	2	2	....	....	....	31	....	....	....	....	....	....	....	....	....	....	....	....	....	....	....	....	....	....
	Grand Rapids Owls	IHL	34	8	17	25	....	....	....	64	....	....	....	....	....	....	....	....	....	....	....	....	....	....	....	....	....	....
1980-81	Unity Miners	SAHA-I	STATISTICS NOT AVAILABLE																									
1981-82	Unity Miners	SAHA-I	STATISTICS NOT AVAILABLE																									
1982-83	Wilkie Outlaws	SAHA-I	STATISTICS NOT AVAILABLE																									
1983-84	Rosetown Red Wings	SAHA-I	STATISTICS NOT AVAILABLE																									
	NHL Totals		35	2	3	5	2	2	4	95	1	0	0	23	8.7	13	5	22	2		....	....	....	....	....	....	....	....

Traded to **Colorado** by **Boston** for Mark Suzor, October 11, 1978. Signed as a free agent by **Edmonton**, July, 1979.

• PADDOCK, John

Alvin John RW – R. 6'3", 190 lbs. b: Brandon, Man., 6/9/1954. Washington's 3rd, 37th overall, in 1974.

Season	Club	League	GP	G	A	Pts	AG	AA	APts	PIM	PP	SH	GW	S	%	TGF	PGF	TGA	PGA	+/–	GP	G	A	Pts	PIM	PP	SH	GW
1972-73	Brandon Jr. Bees	MJHL	STATISTICS NOT AVAILABLE																									
	Brandon Wheat Kings	WCJHL	11	3	2	5	....	....	....	6	....	....	....	....	....	....	....	....	....	....	6	2	2	4	4	....	....	....
1973-74	Brandon Wheat Kings	WCJHL	68	34	49	83	....	....	....	228	....	....	....	....	....	....	....	....	....	....	....	....	....	....	....	....	....	....
1974-75	Richmond Robins	AHL	72	26	22	48	....	....	....	296	....	....	....	....	....	....	....	....	....	....	7	5	3	8	38	....	....	....
1975-76	**Washington Capitals**	**NHL**	8	1	1	2	1	1	2	12	0	0	0	5	20.0	3	0	8	0	–5	....	....	....	....	....	....	....	....
	Richmond Robins	AHL	42	11	14	25	....	....	....	98	....	....	....	....	....	....	....	....	....	....	8	0	3	3	5	....	....	....
1976-77	**Philadelphia Flyers**	**NHL**	5	0	0	0	0	0	0	9	0	0	0	3	0.0	1	0	1	0	0	....	....	....	....	....	....	....	....
	Springfield Indians	AHL	61	13	16	29	....	....	....	106	....	....	....	....	....	....	....	....	....	....	....	....	....	....	....	....	....	....
1977-78	Maine Mariners	AHL	61	8	12	20	....	....	....	152	....	....	....	....	....	....	....	....	....	....	6	1	2	3	7	....	....	....
1978-79	Maine Mariners	AHL	79	30	37	67	....	....	....	275	....	....	....	....	....	....	....	....	....	....	10	*9	1	10	13	....	....	....
1979-80	**Philadelphia Flyers**	**NHL**	32	3	7	10	3	5	8	36	0	0	0	29	10.3	16	1	19	0	–4	3	2	0	2	0	0	0	0
1980-81	**Quebec Nordiques**	**NHL**	32	2	5	7	2	3	5	25	0	0	0	32	6.3	13	0	25	5	–7	2	0	0	0	0	0	0	0
	Maine Mariners	AHL	22	8	7	15	....	....	....	53	....	....	....	....	....	....	....	....	....	....	8	10	6	16	48	....	....	....
1981-82	Maine Mariners	AHL	39	6	10	16	....	....	....	123	....	....	....	....	....	....	....	....	....	....	3	0	1	1	18	....	....	....
1982-83	**Philadelphia Flyers**	**NHL**	10	2	1	3	2	1	3	4	0	0	0	14	14.3	6	2	10	0	–6	....	....	....	....	....	....	....	....
	Maine Mariners	AHL	69	30	23	53	....	....	....	188	....	....	....	....	....	....	....	....	....	....	13	2	2	4	18	....	....	....
1983-1984	Maine Mariners	AHL	17	3	6	9	....	....	....	20	....	....	....	....	....	....	....	....	....	....	....	....	....	....	....	....	....	....
1983-1985	Maine Mariners	AHL	DID NOT PLAY – COACHING																									
1985-1989	Hershey Bears	AHL	DID NOT PLAY – COACHING																									
1989-1990	**Philadelphia Flyers**	**NHL**	DID NOT PLAY – ASSISTANT COACH																									
1990-1991	Binghamton Rangers	AHL	DID NOT PLAY – COACHING																									
1991-1995	**Winnipeg Jets**	**NHL**	DID NOT PLAY – COACHING																									
1995-1997	**Winnipeg Jets**	**NHL**	DID NOT PLAY – ASSISTANT GENERAL MANAGER																									
1997-1999	**New York Rangers**	**NHL**	DID NOT PLAY – SCOUTING																									
1999-2000	Hartford Wolf Pack	AHL	DID NOT PLAY – COACHING																									
	NHL Totals		87	8	14	22	8	10	18	86	0	0	0	83	9.6	39	3	63	5		5	2	0	2	0	0	0	0

Traded to **Philadelphia** by **Washington** to complete transaction that sent Bob Sirois to Washington (December 15, 1975), September 1, 1976. Traded to **Quebec** by **Philadelphia** for cash, August 11, 1980. Signed as a free agent by **Philadelphia**, January 4, 1983. Signed as a free agent by **New Jersey**, August 1, 1983.

• PAEK, Jim

D – L. 6'1", 195 lbs. b: Seoul, South Korea, 4/7/1967. Pittsburgh's 9th, 170th overall, in 1985.

Season	Club	League	GP	G	A	Pts	AG	AA	APts	PIM	PP	SH	GW	S	%	TGF	PGF	TGA	PGA	+/–	GP	G	A	Pts	PIM	PP	SH	GW
1983-84	St. Michael's Major Midgets	OMHA	39	8	12	20	....	....	....	86	....	....	....	....	....	....	....	....	....	....	....	....	....	....	....	....	....	....
	St. Michael's Buzzers	OJHL-B	5	0	2	2	....	....	....	8	....	....	....	....	....	....	....	....	....	....	....	....	....	....	....	....	....	....
1984-85	Oshawa Generals	OHL	54	2	13	15	....	....	....	57	....	....	....	....	....	....	....	....	....	....	5	1	0	1	9	....	....	....
1985-86	Oshawa Generals	OHL	64	5	21	26	....	....	....	122	....	....	....	....	....	....	....	....	....	....	6	0	1	1	9	....	....	....
1986-87	Oshawa Generals	OHL	57	5	17	22	....	....	....	75	....	....	....	....	....	....	....	....	....	....	26	1	14	15	43	....	....	....
	Oshawa Generals	Mem-Cup	4	1	0	1	....	....	....	4	....	....	....	....	....	....	....	....	....	....	....	....	....	....	....	....	....	....
1987-88	Muskegon Lumberjacks	IHL	82	7	52	59	....	....	....	141	....	....	....	....	....	....	....	....	....	....	6	0	0	0	29	....	....	....
1988-89	Muskegon Lumberjacks	IHL	80	3	54	57	....	....	....	96	....	....	....	....	....	....	....	....	....	....	14	1	10	11	24	....	....	....
1989-90	Muskegon Lumberjacks	IHL	81	9	41	50	....	....	....	115	....	....	....	....	....	....	....	....	....	....	15	1	10	11	41	....	....	....
1990-91	Canada	Nat-Team	48	2	12	14	....	....	....	24	....	....	....	....	....	....	....	....	....	....	....	....	....	....	....	....	....	....
♦	**Pittsburgh Penguins**	**NHL**	3	0	0	0	0	0	0	9	0	0	0	0	0.0	2	0	0	0	2	8	1	0	1	2	0	0	0
1991-92♦	**Pittsburgh Penguins**	**NHL**	49	1	7	8	1	5	6	36	0	0	0	33	3.0	43	0	50	7	0	19	0	4	4	6	0	0	0

Season	Club	League	GP	G	A	Pts	AG	AA	APts	PIM	PP	SH	GW	S	%	TGF	PGF	TGA	PGA	+/–	GP	G	A	Pts	PIM	PP	SH	GW
			REGULAR SEASON																		PLAYOFFS							
1992-93	**Pittsburgh Penguins**	**NHL**	**77**	**3**	**15**	**18**	**2**	**10**	**12**	**64**	**0**	**0**	**0**	**57**	**5.3**	**72**	**3**	**71**	**15**	**13**	....	....	....	....	....	....	....	....
1993-94	**Pittsburgh Penguins**	**NHL**	**41**	**0**	**4**	**4**	**0**	**3**	**3**	**8**	**0**	**0**	**0**	**24**	**0.0**	**22**	**0**	**30**	**1**	**–7**	....	....	....	....	....	....	....	....
	Los Angeles Kings	**NHL**	**18**	**1**	**1**	**2**	**1**	**1**	**2**	**10**	**0**	**0**	**0**	**11**	**9.1**	**9**	**0**	**11**	**1**	**–1**	....	....	....	....	....	....	....	....
1994-95	**Ottawa Senators**	**NHL**	**29**	**0**	**2**	**2**	**0**	**3**	**3**	**28**	**0**	**0**	**0**	**16**	**0.0**	**14**	**1**	**27**	**9**	**–5**	....	....	....	....	....	....	....	....
1995-96	Houston Aeros	IHL	25	2	5	7	....	....	....	20	....	....	....	....	....	....	....	....	....	....	....	....	....	....	....	....	....	....
	Minnesota Moose	IHL	42	1	11	12	....	....	....	54	....	....	....	....	....	....	....	....	....	....	....	....	....	....	....	....	....	....
1996-97	Manitoba Moose	IHL	9	0	2	2	....	....	....	12	....	....	....	....	....	....	....	....	....	....	....	....	....	....	....	....	....	....
	Cleveland Lumberjacks	IHL	74	3	25	28	....	....	....	36	....	....	....	....	....	....	....	....	....	....	14	0	1	1	2	....	....	....
1997-98	Cleveland Lumberjacks	IHL	75	7	9	16	....	....	....	48	....	....	....	....	....	....	....	....	....	....	10	2	1	3	4	....	....	....
1998-99	Cleveland Lumberjacks	IHL	65	4	11	15	....	....	....	34	....	....	....	....	....	....	....	....	....	....	....	....	....	....	....	....	....	....
	Houston Aeros	IHL	11	0	3	3	....	....	....	2	....	....	....	....	....	....	....	....	....	....	19	2	4	6	10	....	....	....
99-2000	Cleveland Lumberjacks	IHL	69	2	20	22	....	....	....	27	....	....	....	....	....	....	....	....	....	....	9	0	2	2	2	....	....	....
	NHL Totals		**217**	**5**	**29**	**34**	**4**	**22**	**26**	**155**	**0**	**0**	**0**	**141**	**3.5**	**162**	**4**	**189**	**33**		**27**	**1**	**4**	**5**	**8**	**0**	**0**	**0**

Traded to **LA Kings** by **Pittsburgh** with Marty McSorley for Tomas Sandstrom and Shawn McEachern, February 16, 1994. Traded to **Ottawa** by **LA Kings** for Ottawa's 7th round choice (Benoit Larose) in 1995 Entry Draft, June 25, 1994. Traded to **Houston** (IHL) by **Manitoba** (IHL) for Mike Stevens, November 25, 1996. Loaned to **Houston** (IHL) by **Cleveland** (IHL) for Jason Ruff and future considerations, March, 1999.

• PAIEMENT, Rosaire

Joseph Wilfrid Rosaire C – R. 5'11", 170 lbs. b: Earlton, Ont., 8/12/1945.

Season	Club	League	GP	G	A	Pts	AG	AA	APts	PIM	PP	SH	GW	S	%	TGF	PGF	TGA	PGA	+/–	GP	G	A	Pts	PIM	PP	SH	GW
1962-63	New Liskeard Lions	OMHA	STATISTICS NOT AVAILABLE																									
1963-64	Waterloo Siskins	OHA-B	STATISTICS NOT AVAILABLE																									
1964-65	Niagara Falls Flyers	OHA-Jr.	56	13	24	37	....	....	....	40	....	....	....	....	....	....	....	....	....	....	9	0	2	2	5	....	....	....
	Niagara Falls Flyers	Mem-Cup	12	3	4	7	....	....	....	13	....	....	....	....	....	....	....	....	....	....	....	....	....	....	....	....	....	....
1965-66	Niagara Falls Flyers	OHA-Jr.	47	14	25	39	....	....	....	38	....	....	....	....	....	....	....	....	....	....	6	0	1	1	10	....	....	....
1966-67	New Jersey Devils	EHL	72	*61	64	*125	....	....	....	175	....	....	....	....	....	....	....	....	....	....	16	3	11	14	53	....	....	....
1967-68	**Philadelphia Flyers**	**NHL**	**7**	**1**	**0**	**1**	**1**	**0**	**1**	**11**	**0**	**0**	**0**	**11**	**9.1**	**3**	**1**	**1**	**0**	**1**	**3**	**3**	**0**	**3**	**0**	**2**	**0**	**1**
	Quebec Aces	AHL	64	18	30	48	....	....	....	189	....	....	....	....	....	....	....	....	....	....	12	4	6	10	*41	....	....	....
1968-69	**Philadelphia Flyers**	**NHL**	**27**	**2**	**4**	**6**	**2**	**4**	**6**	**52**	**0**	**0**	**0**	**58**	**3.4**	**9**	**0**	**23**	**0**	**–14**	....	....	....	....	....	....	....	....
	Quebec Aces	AHL	42	16	22	38	....	....	....	122	....	....	....	....	....	....	....	....	....	....	15	*9	5	14	35	....	....	....
1969-70	**Philadelphia Flyers**	**NHL**	**9**	**1**	**1**	**2**	**1**	**1**	**2**	**11**	**0**	**0**	**0**	**29**	**3.4**	**1**	**0**	**5**	**0**	**–4**	....	....	....	....	....	....	....	....
	Quebec Aces	AHL	67	28	40	68	....	....	....	*242	....	....	....	....	....	....	....	....	....	....	6	1	1	2	15	....	....	....
1970-71	**Vancouver Canucks**	**NHL**	**78**	**34**	**28**	**62**	**34**	**23**	**57**	**152**	**4**	**1**	**4**	**249**	**13.7**	**84**	**17**	**79**	**24**	**12**	....	....	....	....	....	....	....	....
1971-72	**Vancouver Canucks**	**NHL**	**69**	**10**	**19**	**29**	**10**	**16**	**26**	**117**	**1**	**0**	**1**	**177**	**5.6**	**46**	**3**	**84**	**4**	**–37**	....	....	....	....	....	....	....	....
1972-73	Chicago Cougars	WHA	78	33	36	69	....	....	....	137	....	....	....	....	....	....	....	....	....	....	....	....	....	....	....	....	....	....
1973-74	Chicago Cougars	WHA	78	30	43	73	....	....	....	87	....	....	....	....	....	....	....	....	....	....	18	9	6	15	16	....	....	....
1974-75	Chicago Cougars	WHA	78	26	48	74	....	....	....	97	....	....	....	....	....	....	....	....	....	....	....	....	....	....	....	....	....	....
1975-76	New England Whalers	WHA	80	28	43	71	....	....	....	89	....	....	....	....	....	....	....	....	....	....	17	4	11	15	41	....	....	....
1976-77	New England Whalers	WHA	13	5	2	7	....	....	....	12	....	....	....	....	....	....	....	....	....	....	....	....	....	....	....	....	....	....
	Indianapolis Racers	WHA	67	18	25	43	....	....	....	91	....	....	....	....	....	....	....	....	....	....	9	0	5	5	15	....	....	....
1977-78	Indianapolis Racers	WHA	61	6	24	30	....	....	....	81	....	....	....	....	....	....	....	....	....	....	....	....	....	....	....	....	....	....
	NHL Totals		**190**	**48**	**52**	**100**	**48**	**44**	**92**	**343**	**5**	**1**	**5**	**524**	**9.2**	**143**	**21**	**192**	**28**		**3**	**3**	**0**	**3**	**0**	**2**	**0**	**1**
	Other Major League Totals		455	146	221	367	....	....	....	594	....	....	....	....	....	....	....	....	....	....	44	13	22	35	72	....	....	....

• Brother of Wilf • EHL North First All-Star Team (1967) • EHL North Rookie of the Year (1967) • Won John Carlin Trophy (Top Scorer - EHL) (1967)

Traded to **Philadelphia** by **Boston** for Philadelphia's 1st round choice (Rick MacLeish) in 1970 Amateur Draft, October 18, 1967. Claimed by **Vancouver** from **Philadelphia** in Expansion Draft, June 10, 1970. Selected by **Chicago** (WHA) in 1972 WHA General Player Draft, February 12, 1972. Selected by **Denver** (WHA) from **Chicago** (WHA) in WHA Expansion Draft, May, 1975. Traded to **New England** (WHA) by **Denver** (WHA) for New England's 1st round choice (later traded to Indianapolis — Indianapolis selected Bob Simpson) in WHA Amateur Draft, June 26, 1975. Traded to **Indianapolis** (WHA) by **New England** (WHA) for Gary MacGregor, November, 1976.

• PAIEMENT, Wilf

Wilfrid Jr. RW – R. 6'1", 210 lbs. b: Earlton, Ont., 10/16/1955. Kansas City's 1st, 2nd overall, in 1974.

Season	Club	League	GP	G	A	Pts	AG	AA	APts	PIM	PP	SH	GW	S	%	TGF	PGF	TGA	PGA	+/–	GP	G	A	Pts	PIM	PP	SH	GW
1971-72	Niagara Falls Flyers	OMJHL	34	6	13	19	....	....	....	74	....	....	....	....	....	....	....	....	....	....	6	0	1	1	17	....	....	....
1972-73	St. Catharines Black Hawks	OMJHL	61	18	27	45	....	....	....	173	....	....	....	....	....	....	....	....	....	....	....	....	....	....	....	....	....	....
1973-74	St. Catharines Black Hawks	OMJHL	70	50	73	123	....	....	....	134	....	....	....	....	....	....	....	....	....	....	....	....	....	....	....	....	....	....
	St. Catharines Black Hawks	Mem-Cup	3	1	0	1	....	....	....	17	....	....	....	....	....	....	....	....	....	....	....	....	....	....	....	....	....	....
1974-75	**Kansas City Scouts**	**NHL**	**78**	**26**	**13**	**39**	**23**	**10**	**33**	**101**	**6**	**0**	**3**	**195**	**13.3**	**59**	**21**	**80**	**0**	**–42**	....	....	....	....	....	....	....	....
1975-76	**Kansas City Scouts**	**NHL**	**57**	**21**	**22**	**43**	**18**	**16**	**34**	**121**	**4**	**0**	**3**	**178**	**11.8**	**53**	**18**	**75**	**3**	**–37**	....	....	....	....	....	....	....	....
1976-77	**Colorado Rockies**	**NHL**	**78**	**41**	**40**	**81**	**37**	**31**	**68**	**101**	**9**	**5**	**2**	**287**	**14.3**	**109**	**35**	**102**	**15**	**–13**	....	....	....	....	....	....	....	....
	Canada	WEC-A	10	5	5	10	....	....	....	32	....	....	....	....	....	....	....	....	....	....	....	....	....	....	....	....	....	....
1977-78	**Colorado Rockies**	**NHL**	**80**	**31**	**56**	**87**	**28**	**44**	**72**	**114**	**7**	**2**	**1**	**287**	**10.8**	**126**	**43**	**115**	**18**	**–14**	**2**	**0**	**0**	**0**	**7**	**0**	**0**	**0**
	Canada	WEC-A	10	6	1	7	....	....	....	8	....	....	....	....	....	....	....	....	....	....	....	....	....	....	....	....	....	....
1978-79	**Colorado Rockies**	**NHL**	**65**	**24**	**36**	**60**	**21**	**26**	**47**	**80**	**5**	**0**	**1**	**206**	**11.7**	**79**	**27**	**93**	**11**	**–30**	....	....	....	....	....	....	....	....
	Canada	WEC-A	8	3	3	6	....	....	....	6	....	....	....	....	....	....	....	....	....	....	....	....	....	....	....	....	....	....
1979-80	**Colorado Rockies**	**NHL**	**34**	**10**	**16**	**26**	**8**	**12**	**20**	**41**	**2**	**2**	**1**	**111**	**9.0**	**37**	**11**	**35**	**3**	**–6**	....	....	....	....	....	....	....	....
	Toronto Maple Leafs	**NHL**	**41**	**20**	**28**	**48**	**17**	**20**	**37**	**72**	**8**	**0**	**2**	**159**	**12.6**	**72**	**29**	**48**	**6**	**1**	**3**	**0**	**2**	**2**	**17**	**0**	**0**	**0**
1980-81	**Toronto Maple Leafs**	**NHL**	**77**	**40**	**57**	**97**	**31**	**38**	**69**	**145**	**13**	**3**	**2**	**302**	**13.2**	**133**	**48**	**134**	**42**	**–7**	**3**	**0**	**0**	**0**	**2**	**0**	**0**	**0**
1981-82	**Toronto Maple Leafs**	**NHL**	**69**	**18**	**40**	**58**	**14**	**27**	**41**	**203**	**6**	**1**	**1**	**186**	**9.7**	**80**	**22**	**96**	**17**	**–21**	....	....	....	....	....	....	....	....
	Quebec Nordiques	**NHL**	**8**	**7**	**6**	**13**	**6**	**4**	**10**	**18**	**3**	**2**	**1**	**24**	**29.2**	**16**	**5**	**14**	**2**	**–1**	**14**	**6**	**6**	**12**	**28**	**1**	**0**	**1**
1982-83	**Quebec Nordiques**	**NHL**	**80**	**26**	**38**	**64**	**21**	**26**	**47**	**170**	**6**	**0**	**2**	**191**	**13.6**	**97**	**25**	**93**	**11**	**–10**	**4**	**0**	**1**	**1**	**4**	**0**	**0**	**0**
1983-84	**Quebec Nordiques**	**NHL**	**80**	**39**	**37**	**76**	**31**	**25**	**56**	**121**	**8**	**3**	**3**	**207**	**18.8**	**103**	**19**	**71**	**15**	**28**	**9**	**3**	**1**	**4**	**24**	**0**	**0**	**0**
1984-85	**Quebec Nordiques**	**NHL**	**68**	**23**	**28**	**51**	**19**	**19**	**38**	**165**	**2**	**1**	**4**	**156**	**14.7**	**71**	**9**	**57**	**7**	**12**	**18**	**4**	**2**	**6**	**58**	**0**	**0**	**0**
1985-86	**Quebec Nordiques**	**NHL**	**44**	**7**	**12**	**19**	**6**	**8**	**14**	**145**	**2**	**0**	**0**	**75**	**9.3**	**34**	**5**	**29**	**0**	**0**	....	....	....	....	....	....	....	....
	New York Rangers	**NHL**	**8**	**1**	**6**	**7**	**1**	**4**	**5**	**13**	**0**	**0**	**0**	**14**	**7.1**	**8**	**1**	**5**	**0**	**2**	**16**	**5**	**5**	**10**	**45**	**4**	**0**	**0**
1986-87	**Buffalo Sabres**	**NHL**	**56**	**20**	**17**	**37**	**17**	**12**	**29**	**108**	**2**	**0**	**3**	**117**	**17.1**	**57**	**10**	**46**	**1**	**2**	....	....	....	....	....	....	....	....
1987-88	**Pittsburgh Penguins**	**NHL**	**23**	**2**	**6**	**8**	**2**	**4**	**6**	**39**	**0**	**0**	**0**	**25**	**8.0**	**11**	**0**	**15**	**0**	**–4**	....	....	....	....	....	....	....	....
	Muskegon Lumberjacks	IHL	28	17	18	35	....	....	....	52	....	....	....	....	....	....	....	....	....	....	5	0	2	2	15	....	....	....
	NHL Totals		**946**	**356**	**458**	**814**	**300**	**326**	**626**	**1757**	**83**	**19**	**29**	**2720**	**13.1**	**1145**	**328**	**1108**	**151**		**69**	**18**	**17**	**35**	**185**	**5**	**0**	**1**

• Brother of Rosaire • OMJHL First All-Star Team (1974) • Named Best Forward (Tied with Sergei Makarov) at WEC-A (1979) • Played in NHL All-Star Game (1976, 1977, 1978)

Transferred to **Colorado** after **Kansas City** franchise relocated, July 15, 1976. Traded to **Toronto** by **Colorado** with Pat Hickey for Lanny McDonald and Joel Quenneville, December 29, 1979. Traded to **Quebec** by **Toronto** for Miroslav Frycer and Quebec's 7th round choice (Jeff Triano) in 1982 Entry Draft, March 9, 1982. Traded to **NY Rangers** by **Quebec** for Steve Patrick, February 6, 1986. Claimed by **Buffalo** from **NY Rangers** in Waiver Draft, October 6, 1986. Signed as a free agent by **Pittsburgh**, September 10, 1987.

• PALAZZARI, Doug

Douglas John C – L. 5'5", 170 lbs. b: Eveleth, MN, 11/3/1952.

Season	Club	League	GP	G	A	Pts	AG	AA	APts	PIM	PP	SH	GW	S	%	TGF	PGF	TGA	PGA	+/–	GP	G	A	Pts	PIM	PP	SH	GW
1970-71	Colorado College	WCHA	26	8	17	25	....	....	....	37	....	....	....	....	....	....	....	....	....	....	....	....	....	....	....	....	....	....
1971-72	Colorado College	WCHA	32	32	40	72	....	....	....	42	....	....	....	....	....	....	....	....	....	....	....	....	....	....	....	....	....	....
1972-73	Colorado College	WCHA	27	24	28	52	....	....	....	32	....	....	....	....	....	....	....	....	....	....	....	....	....	....	....	....	....	....
	United States	WEC-B	7	6	*13	*19	....	....	....	....	....	....	....	....	....	....	....	....	....	....	....	....	....	....	....	....	....	....
1973-74	Colorado College	WCHA	28	25	42	67	....	....	....	18	....	....	....	....	....	....	....	....	....	....	....	....	....	....	....	....	....	....
	United States	WEC-B	6	5	4	9	....	....	....	....	....	....	....	....	....	....	....	....	....	....	....	....	....	....	....	....	....	....
1974-75	**St. Louis Blues**	**NHL**	**73**	**14**	**17**	**31**	**12**	**13**	**25**	**19**	**0**	**1**	**1**	**110**	**12.7**	**45**	**8**	**45**	**16**	**8**	**2**	**0**	**0**	**0**	**0**	**0**	**0**	**0**
1975-76	Providence Reds	AHL	55	19	32	51	....	....	....	72	....	....	....	....	....	....	....	....	....	....	3	1	1	2	2	....	....	....
1976-77	United States	Can-Cup	2	0	0	0	....	....	....	2	....	....	....	....	....	....	....	....	....	....	....	....	....	....	....	....	....	....
	St. Louis Blues	**NHL**	**12**	**1**	**0**	**1**	**1**	**0**	**1**	**0**	**0**	**0**	**0**	**11**	**9.1**	**1**	**0**	**5**	**1**	**–3**	....	....	....	....	....	....	....	....
	Kansas City Blues	CHL	41	18	34	52	....	....	....	31	....	....	....	....	....	....	....	....	....	....	....	....	....	....	....	....	....	....
1977-78	**St. Louis Blues**	**NHL**	**3**	**1**	**0**	**1**	**1**	**0**	**1**	**0**	**0**	**0**	**0**	**3**	**33.3**	**1**	**0**	**3**	**0**	**–2**	....	....	....	....	....	....	....	....
	Salt Lake Golden Eagles	CHL	70	*45	*56	*101	....	....	....	82	....	....	....	....	....	....	....	....	....	....	6	2	3	5	18	....	....	....
1978-79	**St. Louis Blues**	**NHL**	**20**	**2**	**3**	**5**	**2**	**2**	**4**	**4**	**0**	**0**	**0**	**16**	**12.5**	**8**	**0**	**17**	**4**	**–5**	....	....	....	....	....	....	....	....
	Salt Lake Golden Eagles	CHL	35	24	32	56	....	....	....	19	....	....	....	....	....	....	....	....	....	....	10	2	*14	*16	11	....	....	....

			REGULAR SEASON																		PLAYOFFS							
Season	Club	League	GP	G	A	Pts	AG	AA	APts	PIM	PP	SH	GW	S	%	TGF	PGF	TGA	PGA	+/–	GP	G	A	Pts	PIM	PP	SH	GW
1979-80	Salt Lake Golden Eagles	CHL	74	*48	*61	*109	....	....	....	62	....	....	....	....	....	....	....	....	....	....	13	7	7	14	6	....	....	....
1980-81	Salt Lake Golden Eagles	CHL	27	16	21	37	....	....	....	57	....	....	....	....	....	....	....	....	....	....	17	7	11	18	15	....	....	....
1981-82	Salt Lake Golden Eagles	CHL	68	34	41	75	....	....	....	44	....	....	....	....	....	....	....	....	....	....	10	11	6	17	13	....	....	....
	NHL Totals		**108**	**18**	**20**	**38**	**16**	**15**	**31**	**23**	**0**	**1**	**1**	**140**	**12.9**	**55**	**8**	**70**	**21**		**2**	**0**	**0**	**0**	**0**	**0**	**0**	**0**

• Son of Aldo. • WCHA First All-Star Team (1972, 1974) • NCAA West First All-American Team (1972, 1974) • CHL First All-Star Team (1978, 1980) • Won Tommy Ivan Trophy (MVP - CHL) (1978, 1980)

Signed as a free agent by **St. Louis**, August, 1974.

• PALFFY, Ziggy

Zigmund RW – L. 5'10", 183 lbs. b: Skalica, Czech., 5/5/1972. NY Islanders' 2nd, 26th overall, in 1991.

Season	Club	League	GP	G	A	Pts	AG	AA	APts	PIM	PP	SH	GW	S	%	TGF	PGF	TGA	PGA	+/–	GP	G	A	Pts	PIM	PP	SH	GW
1990-91	AC Nitra	Czech.	50	34	16	50	....	....	....	18	....	....	....	....	....	....	....	....	....	....	....	....	....	....	....	....	....	....
	Czechoslovakia	WJC-A	7	7	6	13	....	....	....	2	....	....	....	....	....	....	....	....	....	....	....	....	....	....	....	....	....	....
1991-92	Czechoslovakia	Can-Cup	5	1	0	1	....	....	....	2	....	....	....	....	....	....	....	....	....	....	....	....	....	....	....	....	....	....
	Dukla Trencin	Czech.	45	41	33	74	....	....	....	36	....	....	....	....	....	....	....	....	....	....	....	....	....	....	....	....	....	....
	Czechoslovakia	WJC-A	6	3	1	4	....	....	....	6	....	....	....	....	....	....	....	....	....	....	....	....	....	....	....	....	....	....
1992-93	Dukla Trencin	Czech.	43	38	41	79	....	....	....	....	....	....	....	....	....	....	....	....	....	....	....	....	....	....	....	....	....	....
1993-94	**New York Islanders**	**NHL**	**5**	**0**	**0**	**0**	**0**	**0**	**0**	**0**	**0**	**0**	**0**	**5**	**0.0**	**1**	**1**	**6**	**0**	**–6**	....	....	....	....	....	....	....	....
	Salt Lake Golden Eagles	IHL	57	25	32	57	....	....	....	83	....	....	....	....	....	....	....	....	....	....	....	....	....	....	....	....	....	....
	Slovakia	Olympics	8	3	*7	*10	....	....	....	8	....	....	....	....	....	....	....	....	....	....	....	....	....	....	....	....	....	....
1994-95	Denver Grizzlies	IHL	33	20	23	43	....	....	....	40	....	....	....	....	....	....	....	....	....	....	....	....	....	....	....	....	....	....
	New York Islanders	**NHL**	**33**	**10**	**7**	**17**	**18**	**10**	**28**	**6**	**1**	**0**	**1**	**75**	**13.3**	**25**	**5**	**17**	**0**	**3**	....	....	....	....	....	....	....	....
1995-96	**New York Islanders**	**NHL**	**81**	**43**	**44**	**87**	**42**	**36**	**78**	**56**	**17**	**1**	**6**	**257**	**16.7**	**109**	**52**	**84**	**10**	**–17**	....	....	....	....	....	....	....	....
	Slovakia	WC-A	5	2	0	2	....	....	....	10	....	....	....	....	....	....	....	....	....	....	....	....	....	....	....	....	....	....
1996-97	Slovakia	W-Cup	3	1	2	3	....	....	....	2	....	....	....	....	....	....	....	....	....	....	....	....	....	....	....	....	....	....
	Dukla Trencin	Slovakia	1	0	0	0	....	....	....	....	....	....	....	....	....	....	....	....	....	....	....	....	....	....	....	....	....	....
	New York Islanders	**NHL**	**80**	**48**	**42**	**90**	**51**	**37**	**88**	**43**	**6**	**4**	**6**	**292**	**16.4**	**119**	**32**	**77**	**11**	**21**	....	....	....	....	....	....	....	....
1997-98	**New York Islanders**	**NHL**	**82**	**45**	**42**	**87**	**53**	**41**	**94**	**34**	**17**	**2**	**5**	**277**	**16.2**	**118**	**52**	**81**	**13**	**–2**	....	....	....	....	....	....	....	....
1998-99	HK 36 Skalica	Slovakia	9	11	8	19	....	....	....	6	....	....	....	....	....	....	....	....	....	....	....	....	....	....	....	....	....	....
	New York Islanders	**NHL**	**50**	**22**	**28**	**50**	**26**	**27**	**53**	**34**	**5**	**2**	**1**	**168**	**13.1**	**60**	**20**	**51**	**5**	**–6**	....	....	....	....	....	....	....	....
	Slovakia	WC-A	6	5	5	10	....	....	....	6	....	....	....	....	....	....	....	....	....	....	....	....	....	....	....	....	....	....
99-2000	**Los Angeles Kings**	**NHL**	**64**	**27**	**39**	**66**	**30**	**36**	**66**	**32**	**4**	**0**	**3**	**186**	**14.5**	**96**	**31**	**50**	**3**	**18**	**4**	**2**	**0**	**2**	**0**	**0**	**0**	**0**
	NHL Totals		**395**	**195**	**202**	**397**	**220**	**187**	**407**	**205**	**50**	**9**	**22**	**1260**	**15.5**	**528**	**193**	**366**	**42**		**4**	**2**	**0**	**2**	**0**	**0**	**0**	**0**

Czechoslovakian Rookie of the Year (1991) • Czechoslovakian First All-Star Team (1992) • Played in NHL All-Star Game (1998)

Traded to **LA Kings** by **NY Islanders** with Brian Smolinski, Marcel Cousineau and New Jersey's 4th round choice (previously acquired, LA Kings selected Daniel Johanssen) in 1999 Entry Draft for Olli Jokinen, Josh Green, Mathieu Biron and LA Kings' 1st round choice (Taylor Pyatt) in 1999 Entry Draft, June 20, 1999.

• PALMER, Brad

Brad Donald LW – L. 6', 185 lbs. b: Duncan, B.C., 9/14/1961. Minnesota's 1st, 16th overall, in 1980.

Season	Club	League	GP	G	A	Pts	AG	AA	APts	PIM	PP	SH	GW	S	%	TGF	PGF	TGA	PGA	+/–	GP	G	A	Pts	PIM	PP	SH	GW
1977-78	Kelowna Packers	BCJHL	46	20	21	41	....	....	....	32	....	....	....	....	....	....	....	....	....	....	....	....	....	....	....	....	....	....
1978-79	Victoria Cougars	WHL	69	18	15	33	....	....	....	53	....	....	....	....	....	....	....	....	....	....	15	2	7	9	2	....	....	....
1979-80	Victoria Cougars	WHL	72	45	49	94	....	....	....	61	....	....	....	....	....	....	....	....	....	....	17	11	8	19	6	....	....	....
1980-81	Minnesota North Stars	DN-Cup	3	0	0	0	....	....	....	2	....	....	....	....	....	....	....	....	....	....	....	....	....	....	....	....	....	....
	Victoria Cougars	WHL	44	34	53	87	....	....	....	72	....	....	....	....	....	....	....	....	....	....	....	....	....	....	....	....	....	....
	Minnesota North Stars	**NHL**	**23**	**4**	**4**	**8**	**3**	**3**	**6**	**22**	**0**	**0**	**0**	**59**	**6.8**	**17**	**2**	**22**	**1**	**–6**	**19**	**8**	**5**	**13**	**4**	**1**	**2**	**1**
1981-82	**Minnesota North Stars**	**NHL**	**72**	**22**	**23**	**45**	**17**	**15**	**32**	**18**	**7**	**0**	**3**	**180**	**12.2**	**73**	**23**	**64**	**1**	**–13**	**3**	**0**	**0**	**0**	**12**	**0**	**0**	**0**
1982-83	**Boston Bruins**	**NHL**	**73**	**6**	**11**	**17**	**5**	**8**	**13**	**18**	**0**	**0**	**0**	**123**	**4.9**	**25**	**0**	**44**	**12**	**–7**	**7**	**1**	**0**	**1**	**0**	**0**	**1**	**1**
1983-84	Hershey Bears	AHL	62	25	32	57	....	....	....	16	....	....	....	....	....	....	....	....	....	....	....	....	....	....	....	....	....	....
1984-85	EHC Chur	Switz.	10	4	3	7	....	....	....	....	....	....	....	....	....	....	....	....	....	....	....	....	....	....	....	....	....	....
1985-86	Lukko Rauma	Finland	31	16	8	24	....	....	....	10	....	....	....	....	....	....	....	....	....	....	....	....	....	....	....	....	....	....
1986-87	Lukko Rauma	Finland	22	5	6	11	....	....	....	16	....	....	....	....	....	....	....	....	....	....	....	....	....	....	....	....	....	....
1987-88			STATISTICS NOT AVAILABLE																									
1988-89	EHC Lustenau	Austria	32	26	24	50	....	....	....	....	....	....	....	....	....	....	....	....	....	....	....	....	....	....	....	....	....	....
1989-90	EHC Lustenau	Austria	16	8	5	13	....	....	....	4	....	....	....	....	....	....	....	....	....	....	....	....	....	....	....	....	....	....
1990-91			STATISTICS NOT AVAILABLE																									
1991-92	EC Bad Nauheim	Germany-2	14	5	12	17	....	....	....	28	....	....	....	....	....	....	....	....	....	....	....	....	....	....	....	....	....	....
	BSC Preussen Berlin	Germany	6	2	0	2	....	....	....	4	....	....	....	....	....	....	....	....	....	....	....	....	....	....	....	....	....	....
	NHL Totals		**168**	**32**	**38**	**70**	**25**	**26**	**51**	**58**	**7**	**0**	**3**	**362**	**8.8**	**115**	**25**	**130**	**14**		**29**	**9**	**5**	**14**	**16**	**1**	**3**	**2**

Traded to **Boston** by **Minnesota** with Dave Donnelly for Boston agreeing not to select Brian Bellows in 1982 Entry Draft, June 9, 1982.

• PALMER, Rob

Robert Hazen C – L. 6', 190 lbs. b: Detroit, MI, 10/2/1952. Chicago's 6th, 93rd overall, in 1972.

Season	Club	League	GP	G	A	Pts	AG	AA	APts	PIM	PP	SH	GW	S	%	TGF	PGF	TGA	PGA	+/–	GP	G	A	Pts	PIM	PP	SH	GW
1969-70	Detroit Olympics	OJHL	40	*62	*58	*120	....	....	....	26	....	....	....	....	....	....	....	....	....	....	....	....	....	....	....	....	....	....
1970-71	University of Denver	WCHA	36	14	23	37	....	....	....	14	....	....	....	....	....	....	....	....	....	....	....	....	....	....	....	....	....	....
1971-72	University of Denver	WCHA	36	14	25	39	....	....	....	20	....	....	....	....	....	....	....	....	....	....	....	....	....	....	....	....	....	....
1972-73	University of Denver	WCHA	26	18	27	45	....	....	....	8	....	....	....	....	....	....	....	....	....	....	....	....	....	....	....	....	....	....
1973-74	**Chicago Black Hawks**	**NHL**	**1**	**0**	**0**	**0**	**0**	**0**	**0**	**0**	**0**	**0**	**0**	**0**	**0.0**	**0**	**0**	**0**	**0**	**0**	....	....	....	....	....	....	....	....
	Dallas Black Hawks	CHL	49	11	16	27	....	....	....	44	....	....	....	....	....	....	....	....	....	....	10	3	0	3	4	....	....	....
1974-75	**Chicago Black Hawks**	**NHL**	**13**	**0**	**2**	**2**	**0**	**1**	**1**	**2**	**0**	**0**	**0**	**8**	**0.0**	**3**	**0**	**2**	**0**	**1**	....	....	....	....	....	....	....	....
	Dallas Black Hawks	CHL	55	12	34	46	....	....	....	32	....	....	....	....	....	....	....	....	....	....	10	2	9	11	14	....	....	....
1975-76	**Chicago Black Hawks**	**NHL**	**2**	**0**	**1**	**1**	**0**	**1**	**1**	**0**	**0**	**0**	**0**	**0**	**0.0**	**1**	**0**	**0**	**0**	**1**	....	....	....	....	....	....	....	....
	Dallas Black Hawks	CHL	62	14	17	31	....	....	....	56	....	....	....	....	....	....	....	....	....	....	10	4	3	7	2	....	....	....
	NHL Totals		**16**	**0**	**3**	**3**	**0**	**2**	**2**	**2**	**0**	**0**	**0**	**8**	**0.0**	**4**	**0**	**2**	**0**		....	....	....	....	....	....	....	....

WCHA First All-Star Team (1973) • NCAA West First All-American Team (1973)

• PALMER, Robert

Robert Ross D – R. 5'11", 190 lbs. b: Sarnia, Ont., 9/10/1956. Los Angeles' 4th, 85th overall, in 1976.

Season	Club	League	GP	G	A	Pts	AG	AA	APts	PIM	PP	SH	GW	S	%	TGF	PGF	TGA	PGA	+/–	GP	G	A	Pts	PIM	PP	SH	GW
1972-73	Toronto Young Nationals	OHA-B	STATISTICS NOT AVAILABLE																									
1973-74	University of Michigan	WCHA	36	3	12	15	....	....	....	14	....	....	....	....	....	....	....	....	....	....	....	....	....	....	....	....	....	....
1974-75	University of Michigan	WCHA	40	5	15	20	....	....	....	26	....	....	....	....	....	....	....	....	....	....	....	....	....	....	....	....	....	....
1975-76	University of Michigan	WCHA	42	5	16	21	....	....	....	58	....	....	....	....	....	....	....	....	....	....	....	....	....	....	....	....	....	....
1976-77	University of Michigan	WCHA	45	5	37	42	....	....	....	32	....	....	....	....	....	....	....	....	....	....	....	....	....	....	....	....	....	....
	Fort Worth Texans	CHL	3	0	2	2	....	....	....	0	....	....	....	....	....	....	....	....	....	....	5	0	0	0	0	....	....	....
1977-78	**Los Angeles Kings**	**NHL**	**48**	**0**	**3**	**3**	**0**	**2**	**2**	**27**	**0**	**0**	**0**	**38**	**0.0**	**22**	**1**	**31**	**2**	**–8**	**2**	**0**	**0**	**0**	**0**	**0**	**0**	**0**
	Springfield Indians	AHL	19	1	7	8	....	....	....	18	....	....	....	....	....	....	....	....	....	....	....	....	....	....	....	....	....	....
1978-79	**Los Angeles Kings**	**NHL**	**78**	**4**	**41**	**45**	**3**	**30**	**33**	**26**	**2**	**1**	**0**	**130**	**3.1**	**123**	**16**	**154**	**34**	**–13**	**2**	**0**	**0**	**0**	**2**	**0**	**0**	**0**
1979-80	**Los Angeles Kings**	**NHL**	**78**	**4**	**36**	**40**	**3**	**26**	**29**	**18**	**1**	**0**	**0**	**110**	**3.6**	**122**	**9**	**134**	**50**	**29**	**4**	**1**	**2**	**3**	**4**	**0**	**0**	**0**
1980-81	**Los Angeles Kings**	**NHL**	**13**	**0**	**4**	**4**	**0**	**3**	**3**	**13**	**0**	**0**	**0**	**11**	**0.0**	**12**	**0**	**10**	**3**	**5**	....	....	....	....	....	....	....	....
	Houston Apollos	CHL	28	3	10	13	....	....	....	23	....	....	....	....	....	....	....	....	....	....	....	....	....	....	....	....	....	....
	Indianapolis Checkers	CHL	27	1	9	10	....	....	....	16	....	....	....	....	....	....	....	....	....	....	5	1	1	2	0	....	....	....
1981-82	**Los Angeles Kings**	**NHL**	**5**	**0**	**2**	**2**	**0**	**1**	**1**	**0**	**0**	**0**	**0**	**2**	**0.0**	**10**	**0**	**10**	**1**	**1**	....	....	....	....	....	....	....	....
	New Haven Nighthawks	AHL	41	2	23	25	....	....	....	22	....	....	....	....	....	....	....	....	....	....	4	1	4	5	2	....	....	....
1982-83	**New Jersey Devils**	**NHL**	**60**	**1**	**10**	**11**	**1**	**7**	**8**	**21**	**0**	**0**	**0**	**81**	**1.2**	**48**	**6**	**69**	**21**	**–6**	....	....	....	....	....	....	....	....
1983-84	**New Jersey Devils**	**NHL**	**38**	**0**	**5**	**5**	**0**	**3**	**3**	**10**	**0**	**0**	**0**	**18**	**0.0**	**22**	**1**	**48**	**17**	**–10**	....	....	....	....	....	....	....	....
	Maine Mariners	AHL	33	5	10	15	....	....	....	10	....	....	....	....	....	....	....	....	....	....	17	3	10	13	8	....	....	....
1984-85	Maine Mariners	AHL	79	1	23	24	....	....	....	22	....	....	....	....	....	....	....	....	....	....	11	0	3	3	2	....	....	....
1985-86	Maine Mariners	AHL	73	2	10	12	....	....	....	18	....	....	....	....	....	....	....	....	....	....	5	0	0	0	0	....	....	....
	NHL Totals		**320**	**9**	**101**	**110**	**7**	**72**	**79**	**115**	**3**	**1**	**0**	**390**	**2.3**	**359**	**33**	**456**	**128**		**8**	**1**	**2**	**3**	**6**	**0**	**0**	**0**

Signed as a free agent by **New Jersey**, September 9, 1982.

• PANDOLFO, Jay

Jay Paul LW – L. 6'1", 190 lbs. b: Winchester, MA, 12/27/1974. New Jersey's 2nd, 32nd overall, in 1993.

Season	Club	League	GP	G	A	Pts	AG	AA	APts	PIM	PP	SH	GW	S	%	TGF	PGF	TGA	PGA	+/-	GP	G	A	Pts	PIM	PP	SH	GW
			REGULAR SEASON																		PLAYOFFS							
1989-90	Burlington Prep School	Hi-School	23	33	30	63	....	....	....	18	....	....	....	....	....	....	....	....	....	....	....	....	....	....	....	....	....	....
1990-91	Burlington Prep School	Hi-School	20	19	27	46	....	....	....	10	....	....	....	....	....	....	....	....	....	....	....	....	....	....	....	....	....	....
1991-92	Burlington Prep School	Hi-School	20	35	34	69	....	....	....	14	....	....	....	....	....	....	....	....	....	....	....	....	....	....	....	....	....	....
1992-93	Boston University	H-East	37	16	22	38	....	....	....	16	....	....	....	....	....	....	....	....	....	....	....	....	....	....	....	....	....	....
1993-94	Boston University	H-East	37	17	25	42	....	....	....	27	....	....	....	....	....	....	....	....	....	....	....	....	....	....	....	....	....	....
	United States	WJC-A	7	0	0	0	....	....	....	2	....	....	....	....	....	....	....	....	....	....	....	....	....	....	....	....	....	....
1994-95	Boston University	H-East	20	7	13	20	....	....	....	6	....	....	....	....	....	....	....	....	....	....	....	....	....	....	....	....	....	....
1995-96	Boston University	H-East	39	*38	29	67	....	....	....	6	....	....	....	....	....	....	....	....	....	....	....	....	....	....	....	....	....	....
	Albany River Rats	AHL	5	3	1	4	....	....	....	0	....	....	....	....	....	....	....	....	....	....	3	0	0	0	0	....	....	....
1996-97	**New Jersey Devils**	**NHL**	**46**	**6**	**8**	**14**	**6**	**7**	**13**	**6**	**0**	**0**	**1**	**61**	**9.8**	**22**	**2**	**22**	**1**	**–1**	**6**	**0**	**1**	**1**	**0**	**0**	**0**	**0**
	Albany River Rats	AHL	12	3	9	12	....	....	....	0	....	....	....	....	....	....	....	....	....	....	....	....	....	....	....	....	....	....
1997-98	**New Jersey Devils**	**NHL**	**23**	**1**	**3**	**4**	**1**	**3**	**4**	**4**	**0**	**0**	**0**	**23**	**4.3**	**6**	**0**	**10**	**0**	**–4**	**3**	**0**	**2**	**2**	**0**	**0**	**0**	**0**
	Albany River Rats	AHL	51	18	19	37	....	....	....	24	....	....	....	....	....	....	....	....	....	....	....	....	....	....	....	....	....	....
1998-99	**New Jersey Devils**	**NHL**	**70**	**14**	**13**	**27**	**16**	**13**	**29**	**10**	**1**	**1**	**4**	**100**	**14.0**	**45**	**6**	**50**	**14**	**3**	**7**	**1**	**0**	**1**	**0**	**0**	**0**	**0**
	United States	WC-A	2	0	0	0	....	....	....	0	....	....	....	....	....	....	....	....	....	....	....	....	....	....	....	....	....	....
99-2000♦	**New Jersey Devils**	**NHL**	**71**	**7**	**8**	**15**	**8**	**7**	**15**	**4**	**0**	**0**	**0**	**86**	**8.1**	**28**	**0**	**43**	**15**	**0**	**23**	**0**	**5**	**5**	**0**	**0**	**0**	**0**
	NHL Totals		**210**	**28**	**32**	**60**	**31**	**30**	**61**	**24**	**1**	**1**	**5**	**270**	**10.4**	**101**	**8**	**125**	**30**		**39**	**1**	**8**	**9**	**0**	**0**	**0**	**0**

Hockey East First All-Star Team (1996) • NCAA East First All-American Team (1996)

• PANKEWICZ, Greg

RW – R. 6', 185 lbs. b: Drayton Valley, Alta., 11/6/1970.

Season	Club	League	GP	G	A	Pts	AG	AA	APts	PIM	PP	SH	GW	S	%	TGF	PGF	TGA	PGA	+/-	GP	G	A	Pts	PIM	PP	SH	GW
1988-89	Sherwood Park Crusaders	AJHL	53	26	18	44	....	....	....	307	....	....	....	....	....	....	....	....	....	....	....	....	....	....	....	....	....	....
1989-90	Regina Pats	WHL	63	14	24	38	....	....	....	136	....	....	....	....	....	....	....	....	....	....	10	1	3	4	19	....	....	....
1990-91	Regina Pats	WHL	72	39	41	80	....	....	....	134	....	....	....	....	....	....	....	....	....	....	8	4	7	11	12	....	....	....
1991-92	Knoxville Cherokees	ECHL	59	41	39	80	....	....	....	214	....	....	....	....	....	....	....	....	....	....	....	....	....	....	....	....	....	....
1992-93	New Haven Senators	AHL	62	23	20	43	....	....	....	163	....	....	....	....	....	....	....	....	....	....	....	....	....	....	....	....	....	....
1993-94	**Ottawa Senators**	**NHL**	**3**	**0**	**0**	**0**	**0**	**0**	**0**	**2**	**0**	**0**	**0**	**3**	**0.0**	**2**	**0**	**3**	**0**	**–1**	....	....	....	....	....	....	....	....
	P.E.I. Senators	AHL	69	33	29	62	....	....	....	241	....	....	....	....	....	....	....	....	....	....	....	....	....	....	....	....	....	....
1994-95	P.E.I. Senators	AHL	75	37	30	67	....	....	....	161	....	....	....	....	....	....	....	....	....	....	6	1	1	2	24	....	....	....
1995-96	Portland Pirates	AHL	28	9	12	21	....	....	....	99	....	....	....	....	....	....	....	....	....	....	....	....	....	....	....	....	....	....
	Chicago Wolves	IHL	45	9	16	25	....	....	....	164	....	....	....	....	....	....	....	....	....	....	5	4	0	4	8	....	....	....
1996-97	Manitoba Moose	IHL	79	32	34	66	....	....	....	222	....	....	....	....	....	....	....	....	....	....	....	....	....	....	....	....	....	....
1997-98	Manitoba Moose	IHL	76	42	34	76	....	....	....	246	....	....	....	....	....	....	....	....	....	....	3	0	0	0	6	....	....	....
1998-99	**Calgary Flames**	**NHL**	**18**	**0**	**3**	**3**	**0**	**3**	**3**	**20**	**0**	**0**	**0**	**10**	**0.0**	**5**	**0**	**10**	**5**	**0**	....	....	....	....	....	....	....	....
	Saint John Flames	AHL	30	10	14	24	....	....	....	84	....	....	....	....	....	....	....	....	....	....	....	....	....	....	....	....	....	....
	Kentucky Thoroughblades	AHL	10	2	3	5	....	....	....	7	....	....	....	....	....	....	....	....	....	....	11	4	1	5	10	....	....	....
99-2000	Houston Aeros	IHL	62	22	19	41	....	....	....	134	....	....	....	....	....	....	....	....	....	....	5	2	1	3	18	....	....	....
	NHL Totals		**21**	**0**	**3**	**3**	**0**	**3**	**3**	**22**	**0**	**0**	**0**	**13**	**0.0**	**7**	**0**	**13**	**5**		....	....	....	....	....	....	....	....

Signed as a free agent by **Ottawa**, May 27, 1993. Signed as a free agent by **Calgary**, September 1, 1998. Traded to **San Jose** by **Calgary** for cash, March 23, 1999.

• PANTELEEV, Grigori

LW – L. 5'9", 190 lbs. b: Gastello, USSR, 11/13/1972. Boston's 5th, 136th overall, in 1992.

Season	Club	League	GP	G	A	Pts	AG	AA	APts	PIM	PP	SH	GW	S	%	TGF	PGF	TGA	PGA	+/-	GP	G	A	Pts	PIM	PP	SH	GW
1990-91	Dynamo Riga	USSR	23	4	1	5	....	....	....	4	....	....	....	....	....	....	....	....	....	....	....	....	....	....	....	....	....	....
1991-92	Dynamo Riga	CIS	26	4	8	12	....	....	....	4	....	....	....	....	....	....	....	....	....	....	....	....	....	....	....	....	....	....
1992-93	**Boston Bruins**	**NHL**	**39**	**8**	**6**	**14**	**7**	**4**	**11**	**12**	**2**	**0**	**1**	**45**	**17.8**	**24**	**6**	**24**	**0**	**–6**	....	....	....	....	....	....	....	....
	Providence Bruins	AHL	39	17	30	47	....	....	....	22	....	....	....	....	....	....	....	....	....	....	3	0	0	0	10	....	....	....
1993-94	**Boston Bruins**	**NHL**	**10**	**0**	**0**	**0**	**0**	**0**	**0**	**0**	**0**	**0**	**0**	**8**	**0.0**	**1**	**0**	**3**	**0**	**–2**	....	....	....	....	....	....	....	....
	Providence Bruins	AHL	55	24	26	50	....	....	....	20	....	....	....	....	....	....	....	....	....	....	....	....	....	....	....	....	....	....
1994-95	**Boston Bruins**	**NHL**	**1**	**0**	**0**	**0**	**0**	**0**	**0**	**0**	**0**	**0**	**0**	**0**	**0.0**	**0**	**0**	**0**	**0**	**0**	....	....	....	....	....	....	....	....
	Providence Bruins	AHL	70	20	23	43	....	....	....	36	....	....	....	....	....	....	....	....	....	....	13	8	11	19	6	....	....	....
1995-96	**New York Islanders**	**NHL**	**4**	**0**	**0**	**0**	**0**	**0**	**0**	**0**	**0**	**0**	**0**	**1**	**0.0**	**0**	**0**	**3**	**0**	**–3**	....	....	....	....	....	....	....	....
	Utah Grizzlies	IHL	33	11	25	36	....	....	....	18	....	....	....	....	....	....	....	....	....	....	....	....	....	....	....	....	....	....
	Las Vegas Thunder	IHL	29	15	21	36	....	....	....	14	....	....	....	....	....	....	....	....	....	....	15	4	7	11	2	....	....	....
1996-97	San Antonio Dragons	IHL	81	25	37	62	....	....	....	41	....	....	....	....	....	....	....	....	....	....	9	4	2	6	4	....	....	....
1997-98	San Antonio Dragons	IHL	19	2	13	15	....	....	....	8	....	....	....	....	....	....	....	....	....	....	....	....	....	....	....	....	....	....
	Orlando Solar Bears	IHL	63	27	29	56	....	....	....	44	....	....	....	....	....	....	....	....	....	....	17	6	9	15	2	....	....	....
1998-99	Orlando Solar Bears	IHL	77	25	37	62	....	....	....	51	....	....	....	....	....	....	....	....	....	....	17	8	8	16	4	....	....	....
99-2000	Hannover Scorpions	Germany	67	21	30	51	....	....	....	63	....	....	....	....	....	....	....	....	....	....	....	....	....	....	....	....	....	....
	Latvia	WC-A	7	1	1	2	....	....	....	2	....	....	....	....	....	....	....	....	....	....	....	....	....	....	....	....	....	....
	NHL Totals		**54**	**8**	**6**	**14**	**7**	**4**	**11**	**12**	**2**	**0**	**1**	**54**	**14.8**	**25**	**6**	**30**	**0**		....	....	....	....	....	....	....	....

Signed as a free agent by **NY Islanders**, September 20, 1995.

• PAPPIN, Jim

James Joseph RW – R. 6', 190 lbs. b: Sudbury, Ont., 9/10/1939.

Season	Club	League	GP	G	A	Pts	AG	AA	APts	PIM	PP	SH	GW	S	%	TGF	PGF	TGA	PGA	+/-	GP	G	A	Pts	PIM	PP	SH	GW
1958-59	Toronto Marlboros	OHA-Jr.	54	17	18	35	....	....	....	86	....	....	....	....	....	....	....	....	....	....	5	2	3	5	4	....	....	....
1959-60	Toronto Marlboros	OHA-Jr.	48	40	34	74	....	....	....	126	....	....	....	....	....	....	....	....	....	....	4	3	0	3	20	....	....	....
	Sudbury Wolves	EPHL	4	1	0	1	....	....	....	4	....	....	....	....	....	....	....	....	....	....	3	0	1	1	0	....	....	....
1960-61	Sudbury Wolves	EPHL	46	17	20	37	....	....	....	74	....	....	....	....	....	....	....	....	....	....	....	....	....	....	....	....	....	....
	Rochester Americans	AHL	22	7	4	11	....	....	....	4	....	....	....	....	....	....	....	....	....	....	....	....	....	....	....	....	....	....
1961-62	Rochester Americans	AHL	69	28	21	49	....	....	....	105	....	....	....	....	....	....	....	....	....	....	2	1	0	1	2	....	....	....
1962-63	Rochester Americans	AHL	72	34	23	57	....	....	....	100	....	....	....	....	....	....	....	....	....	....	2	1	2	3	2	....	....	....
1963-64♦	**Toronto Maple Leafs**	**NHL**	**50**	**11**	**8**	**19**	**14**	**8**	**22**	**33**	....	....	....	....	....	....	....	....	....	....	**11**	**0**	**0**	**0**	**0**	**0**	**0**	**0**
	Rochester Americans	AHL	16	10	6	16	....	....	....	16	....	....	....	....	....	....	....	....	....	....	....	....	....	....	....	....	....	....
1964-65	**Toronto Maple Leafs**	**NHL**	**44**	**9**	**9**	**18**	**11**	**9**	**20**	**33**	....	....	....	....	....	....	....	....	....	....	....	....	....	....	....	....	....	....
	Rochester Americans	AHL	22	14	11	25	....	....	....	36	....	....	....	....	....	....	....	....	....	....	10	*11	5	16	32	....	....	....
1965-66	**Toronto Maple Leafs**	**NHL**	**7**	**0**	**3**	**3**	**0**	**3**	**3**	**8**	....	....	....	....	....	....	....	....	....	....	....	....	....	....	....	....	....	....
	Rochester Americans	AHL	63	36	51	87	....	....	....	116	....	....	....	....	....	....	....	....	....	....	12	*8	3	11	13	....	....	....
1966-67♦	**Toronto Maple Leafs**	**NHL**	**64**	**21**	**11**	**32**	**24**	**11**	**35**	**89**	....	....	....	....	....	....	....	....	....	....	**12**	***7**	**8**	***15**	**12**	**3**	**0**	**1**
	Rochester Americans	AHL	6	4	3	7	....	....	....	4	....	....	....	....	....	....	....	....	....	....	....	....	....	....	....	....	....	....
1967-68	**Toronto Maple Leafs**	**NHL**	**58**	**13**	**15**	**28**	**15**	**15**	**30**	**37**	**2**	**0**	**1**	**117**	**11.1**	**45**	**18**	**27**	**0**	**0**	....	....	....	....	....	....	....	....
	Rochester Americans	AHL	5	1	5	6	....	....	....	16	....	....	....	....	....	....	....	....	....	....	11	2	6	8	32	....	....	....
1968-69	**Chicago Black Hawks**	**NHL**	**75**	**30**	**40**	**70**	**32**	**36**	**68**	**49**	**3**	**0**	**4**	**208**	**14.4**	**98**	**27**	**72**	**8**	**7**	....	....	....	....	....	....	....	....
1969-70	**Chicago Black Hawks**	**NHL**	**66**	**28**	**25**	**53**	**31**	**23**	**54**	**68**	**9**	**0**	**7**	**158**	**17.7**	**81**	**27**	**37**	**0**	**17**	**8**	**3**	**2**	**5**	**6**	**1**	**0**	**0**
1970-71	**Chicago Black Hawks**	**NHL**	**58**	**22**	**23**	**45**	**22**	**19**	**41**	**40**	**7**	**0**	**2**	**113**	**19.5**	**62**	**22**	**33**	**2**	**9**	**18**	**10**	**4**	**14**	**24**	**2**	**0**	**1**
1971-72	**Chicago Black Hawks**	**NHL**	**64**	**27**	**21**	**48**	**27**	**18**	**45**	**38**	**1**	**1**	**5**	**145**	**18.6**	**65**	**7**	**65**	**10**	**3**	**8**	**2**	**5**	**7**	**4**	**0**	**1**	**1**
1972-73	**Chicago Black Hawks**	**NHL**	**76**	**41**	**51**	**92**	**39**	**41**	**80**	**82**	**7**	**2**	**4**	**182**	**22.5**	**126**	**27**	**82**	**8**	**25**	**16**	**8**	**7**	**15**	**24**	**1**	**0**	**1**
1973-74	**Chicago Black Hawks**	**NHL**	**78**	**32**	**41**	**73**	**31**	**34**	**65**	**76**	**8**	**1**	**8**	**160**	**20.0**	**107**	**30**	**65**	**13**	**25**	**11**	**3**	**6**	**9**	**29**	**0**	**0**	**2**
1974-75	**Chicago Black Hawks**	**NHL**	**71**	**36**	**27**	**63**	**32**	**20**	**52**	**94**	**7**	**2**	**5**	**158**	**22.8**	**94**	**25**	**84**	**14**	**–1**	**8**	**0**	**2**	**2**	**2**	**0**	**0**	**0**
1975-76	**California Golden Seals**	**NHL**	**32**	**6**	**13**	**19**	**5**	**10**	**15**	**12**	**2**	**0**	**0**	**72**	**8.3**	**30**	**15**	**31**	**0**	**–16**	....	....	....	....	....	....	....	....
1976-77	**Cleveland Barons**	**NHL**	**24**	**2**	**8**	**10**	**2**	**6**	**8**	**8**	**0**	**0**	**1**	**28**	**7.1**	**19**	**5**	**9**	**0**	**5**	....	....	....	....	....	....	....	....
	NHL Totals		**767**	**278**	**295**	**573**	**285**	**253**	**538**	**667**	....	....	....	....	....	....	....	....	....	....	**92**	**33**	**34**	**67**	**101**	....	....	....

AHL Second All-Star Team (1966) • Played in NHL All-Star Game (1964, 1968, 1973, 1974, 1975)

Traded to **Chicago** by **Toronto** for Pierre Pilote, May 23, 1968. Traded to **California** by **Chicago** with Chicago's 3rd round choice (Guy Lash) in 1977 Amateur Draft for Joey Johnston, June 1, 1975. Transferred to **Cleveland** after **California** franchise relocated, August 26, 1976.

• PARADISE, Bob

Robert Harvey D – L. 6'1", 205 lbs. b: St. Paul, MN, 4/22/1944. **USHOF**

Season	Club	League	GP	G	A	Pts	AG	AA	APts	PIM	PP	SH	GW	S	%	TGF	PGF	TGA	PGA	+/-	GP	G	A	Pts	PIM	PP	SH	GW
1961-62	St. Paul Saints	Hi-School	STATISTICS NOT AVAILABLE																									
1962-1966	St. Mary's College	NAIA	STATISTICS NOT AVAILABLE																									
1966-67	Muskegon Mohawks	IHL	42	5	6	11	....	....	....	47											....	....	....	....	....	....	....	....

			REGULAR SEASON																		PLAYOFFS							
Season	Club	League	GP	G	A	Pts	AG	AA	APts	PIM	PP	SH	GW	S	%	TGF	PGF	TGA	PGA	+/-	GP	G	A	Pts	PIM	PP	SH	GW
1967-68	Minnesota Nationals	USHL	24	2	6	8	....	....	....	43	....	....	....	....	....	....	....	....	....	....	....	....	....	....	....	....	....	....
	United States	Olympics	6	0	0	0	....	....	....	0	....	....	....	....	....	....	....	....	....	....	....	....	....	....	....	....	....	....
1968-69	United States	Nat-Team	STATISTICS NOT AVAILABLE																									
	United States	WEC-A	8	0	0	0	....	....	....	30	....	....	....	....	....	....	....	....	....	....	....	....	....	....	....	....	....	....
1969-70	Omaha Knights	CHL	61	3	14	17	....	....	....	98	....	....	....	....	....	....	....	....	....	....	12	0	2	2	27	....	....	....
1970-71	Montreal Voyageurs	AHL	72	0	9	9	....	....	....	107	....	....	....	....	....	....	....	....	....	....	3	0	0	0	0	....	....	....
1971-72	**Minnesota North Stars**	**NHL**	**6**	**0**	**0**	**0**	**0**	**0**	**0**	**6**	**0**	**0**	**0**	**1**	**0.0**	**1**	**0**	**0**	**0**	**1**	**4**	**0**	**0**	**0**	**2**	**0**	**0**	**0**
	Seattle Totems	WHL	54	5	8	13	....	....	....	80	....	....	....	....	....	....	....	....	....	....	....	....	....	....	....	....	....	....
	Cleveland Barons	AHL	4	0	0	0	....	....	....	0	....	....	....	....	....	....	....	....	....	....	....	....	....	....	....	....	....	....
1972-73	**Atlanta Flames**	**NHL**	**71**	**1**	**7**	**8**	**1**	**6**	**7**	**103**	**0**	**0**	**1**	**53**	**1.9**	**42**	**0**	**76**	**14**	**-20**	....	....	....	....	....	....	....	....
1973-74	**Atlanta Flames**	**NHL**	**18**	**0**	**1**	**1**	**0**	**1**	**1**	**13**	**0**	**0**	**0**	**8**	**0.0**	**8**	**0**	**19**	**4**	**-7**	....	....	....	....	....	....	....	....
	Pittsburgh Penguins	**NHL**	**38**	**2**	**7**	**9**	**2**	**6**	**8**	**39**	**1**	**0**	**0**	**35**	**5.7**	**39**	**4**	**44**	**6**	**-3**	....	....	....	....	....	....	....	....
1974-75	**Pittsburgh Penguins**	**NHL**	**78**	**3**	**15**	**18**	**3**	**11**	**14**	**109**	**0**	**0**	**0**	**55**	**5.5**	**88**	**4**	**104**	**18**	**-2**	**6**	**0**	**1**	**1**	**17**	**0**	**0**	**0**
1975-76	**Pittsburgh Penguins**	**NHL**	**9**	**0**	**0**	**0**	**0**	**0**	**0**	**4**	**0**	**0**	**0**	**4**	**0.0**	**4**	**0**	**15**	**4**	**-7**	....	....	....	....	....	....	....	....
	Washington Capitals	**NHL**	**48**	**0**	**8**	**8**	**0**	**6**	**6**	**42**	**0**	**0**	**0**	**26**	**0.0**	**38**	**3**	**83**	**7**	**-41**	....	....	....	....	....	....	....	....
1976-77	**Washington Capitals**	**NHL**	**22**	**0**	**5**	**5**	**0**	**4**	**4**	**20**	**0**	**0**	**0**	**15**	**0.0**	**20**	**0**	**30**	**7**	**-3**	....	....	....	....	....	....	....	....
	Springfield Indians	AHL	14	0	4	4	....	....	....	18	....	....	....	....	....	....	....	....	....	....	....	....	....	....	....	....	....	....
	United States	WEC-A	9	0	0	0	....	....	....	8	....	....	....	....	....	....	....	....	....	....	....	....	....	....	....	....	....	....
1977-78	**Pittsburgh Penguins**	**NHL**	**64**	**2**	**10**	**12**	**2**	**8**	**10**	**53**	**0**	**0**	**0**	**34**	**5.9**	**54**	**0**	**107**	**23**	**-30**	....	....	....	....	....	....	....	....
1978-79	**Pittsburgh Penguins**	**NHL**	**14**	**0**	**1**	**1**	**0**	**1**	**1**	**4**	**0**	**0**	**0**	**4**	**0.0**	**9**	**0**	**13**	**0**	**-4**	**2**	**0**	**0**	**0**	**0**	**0**	**0**	**0**
	Binghamton Dusters	AHL	16	0	1	1	....	....	....	12	....	....	....	....	....	....	....	....	....	....	....	....	....	....	....	....	....	....
	NHL Totals		**368**	**8**	**54**	**62**	**8**	**43**	**51**	**393**	**1**	**0**	**1**	**235**	**3.4**	**303**	**11**	**491**	**83**		**12**	**0**	**1**	**1**	**19**	**0**	**0**	**0**

Signed as a free agent by **Montreal**, June, 1970. Traded to **Minnesota** by **Montreal** with the rights to Gary Gambucci for cash, May, 1971. Traded to **Atlanta** by **Minnesota** for cash, June 6, 1972. Traded to **Pittsburgh** by **Atlanta** with Chuck Arnason for Al McDonough, January 4, 1974. Traded to **Washington** by **Pittsburgh** for Washington's 2nd round choice (Greg Malone) in 1976 Amateur Draft, November 26, 1975. Traded to **Pittsburgh** by **Washington** for the rights to Don Awrey, October 1, 1977.

• PARISE, Jean-Paul

"J.P." LW – L. 5'9", 175 lbs. b: Smooth Rock Falls, Ont., 12/11/1941.

Season	Club	League	GP	G	A	Pts	AG	AA	APts	PIM	PP	SH	GW	S	%	TGF	PGF	TGA	PGA	+/-	GP	G	A	Pts	PIM	PP	SH	GW
1961-62	Niagara Falls Flyers	OHA	38	8	20	28	....	....	....	28	....	....	....	....	....	....	....	....	....	....	....	....	....	....	....	....	....	....
	Kingston Frontenacs	EPHL	1	0	0	0	....	....	....	0	....	....	....	....	....	....	....	....	....	....	....	....	....	....	....	....	....	....
1962-63	Kingston Frontenacs	EPHL	64	11	17	28	....	....	....	64	....	....	....	....	....	....	....	....	....	....	5	0	0	0	6	....	....	....
1963-64	Minneapolis Bruins	CPHL	72	27	36	63	....	....	....	77	....	....	....	....	....	....	....	....	....	....	5	1	2	3	10	....	....	....
1964-65	Minneapolis Bruins	CPHL	70	17	56	73	....	....	....	106	....	....	....	....	....	....	....	....	....	....	5	5	1	6	0	....	....	....
1965-66	**Boston Bruins**	**NHL**	**3**	**0**	**0**	**0**	**0**	**0**	**0**	**0**	....	....	....	....	....	....	....	....	....	....	....	....	....	....	....	....	....	....
	Oklahoma City Blazers	CPHL	69	19	30	49	....	....	....	137	....	....	....	....	....	....	....	....	....	....	7	*6	3	9	2	....	....	....
1966-67	**Boston Bruins**	**NHL**	**18**	**2**	**2**	**4**	**2**	**2**	**4**	**10**	....	....	....	....	....	....	....	....	....	....	....	....	....	....	....	....	....	....
	Oklahoma City Blazers	CPHL	42	11	22	33	....	....	....	98	....	....	....	....	....	....	....	....	....	....	11	1	9	10	32	....	....	....
1967-68	**Toronto Maple Leafs**	**NHL**	**1**	**0**	**1**	**1**	**0**	**1**	**1**	**0**	**0**	**0**	**0**	**1**	**0.0**	**1**	**0**	**1**	**0**	**0**	....	....	....	....	....	....	....	....
	Rochester Americans	AHL	30	10	18	28	....	....	....	37	....	....	....	....	....	....	....	....	....	....	....	....	....	....	....	....	....	....
	Minnesota North Stars	**NHL**	**43**	**11**	**16**	**27**	**13**	**16**	**29**	**27**	**1**	**0**	**3**	**110**	**10.0**	**46**	**8**	**53**	**5**	**-10**	**14**	**2**	**5**	**7**	**10**	**0**	**1**	**0**
1968-69	**Minnesota North Stars**	**NHL**	**76**	**22**	**27**	**49**	**23**	**24**	**47**	**57**	**7**	**1**	**3**	**196**	**11.2**	**71**	**18**	**108**	**11**	**-44**	....	....	....	....	....	....	....	....
1969-70	**Minnesota North Stars**	**NHL**	**74**	**24**	**48**	**72**	**26**	**45**	**71**	**72**	**6**	**1**	**1**	**168**	**14.3**	**104**	**31**	**82**	**6**	**-3**	**6**	**3**	**2**	**5**	**2**	**2**	**0**	**0**
1970-71	**Minnesota North Stars**	**NHL**	**73**	**11**	**23**	**34**	**11**	**19**	**30**	**60**	**1**	**1**	**3**	**191**	**5.8**	**52**	**11**	**57**	**1**	**-15**	**12**	**3**	**3**	**6**	**22**	**2**	**0**	**1**
1971-72	**Minnesota North Stars**	**NHL**	**71**	**19**	**18**	**37**	**19**	**16**	**35**	**70**	**6**	**0**	**3**	**183**	**10.4**	**60**	**15**	**35**	**0**	**10**	**7**	**3**	**3**	**6**	**6**	**2**	**0**	**0**
1972-73	Team Canada	Summit-72	6	2	2	4	....	....	....	*28	....	....	....	....	....	....	....	....	....	....	....	....	....	....	....	....	....	....
	Minnesota North Stars	**NHL**	**78**	**27**	**48**	**75**	**25**	**38**	**63**	**96**	**6**	**0**	**4**	**188**	**14.4**	**100**	**20**	**64**	**2**	**18**	**6**	**0**	**0**	**0**	**9**	**0**	**0**	**0**
1973-74	**Minnesota North Stars**	**NHL**	**78**	**18**	**37**	**55**	**17**	**31**	**48**	**42**	**2**	**0**	**1**	**188**	**9.6**	**83**	**16**	**77**	**2**	**-8**	....	....	....	....	....	....	....	....
1974-75	**Minnesota North Stars**	**NHL**	**38**	**9**	**16**	**25**	**8**	**12**	**20**	**40**	**1**	**0**	**0**	**65**	**13.8**	**43**	**9**	**56**	**4**	**-18**	....	....	....	....	....	....	....	....
	New York Islanders	**NHL**	**41**	**14**	**16**	**30**	**12**	**12**	**24**	**22**	**4**	**0**	**1**	**88**	**15.9**	**46**	**11**	**25**	**0**	**10**	**17**	**8**	**8**	**16**	**22**	**4**	**0**	**1**
1975-76	**New York Islanders**	**NHL**	**80**	**22**	**35**	**57**	**19**	**26**	**45**	**80**	**5**	**2**	**4**	**152**	**14.5**	**91**	**31**	**50**	**2**	**12**	**13**	**4**	**6**	**10**	**10**	**1**	**0**	**0**
1976-77	**New York Islanders**	**NHL**	**80**	**25**	**31**	**56**	**23**	**24**	**47**	**46**	**5**	**0**	**7**	**147**	**17.0**	**91**	**25**	**41**	**1**	**26**	**11**	**4**	**4**	**8**	**6**	**1**	**0**	**0**
1977-78	**New York Islanders**	**NHL**	**39**	**12**	**16**	**28**	**11**	**12**	**23**	**12**	**1**	**0**	**0**	**68**	**17.6**	**44**	**3**	**22**	**0**	**19**	....	....	....	....	....	....	....	....
	Cleveland Barons	**NHL**	**40**	**9**	**13**	**22**	**8**	**10**	**18**	**27**	**1**	**0**	**0**	**61**	**14.8**	**33**	**3**	**46**	**1**	**-15**	....	....	....	....	....	....	....	....
1978-79	**Minnesota North Stars**	**NHL**	**57**	**13**	**9**	**22**	**11**	**7**	**18**	**45**	**1**	**0**	**0**	**73**	**17.8**	**47**	**21**	**39**	**1**	**-12**	....	....	....	....	....	....	....	....
	NHL Totals		**890**	**238**	**356**	**594**	**228**	**295**	**523**	**706**	....	....	....	....	....	....	....	....	....		**86**	**27**	**31**	**58**	**87**	....	....	....

CHL Second All-Star Team (1966)

Played in NHL All-Star Game (1970, 1973)

Claimed by **Oakland** from **Boston** in Expansion Draft, June 6, 1967. Traded to **Toronto** (Rochester-AHL) by **Oakland** with Bryan Hextall Jr. for Gerry Ehman, October 12, 1967. Traded to **Minnesota** by **Toronto** (Rochester-AHL) with Milan Marcetta for Murray Hall, Ted Taylor, Len Lunde, Don Johns, Duke Harris and the loan of Carl Wetzel, December 23, 1967. Traded to **NY Islanders** by **Minnesota** for Doug Rombough and Ernie Hicke, January 5, 1975. Traded to **Cleveland** by **NY Islanders** with Jean Potvin for Wayne Merrick, Darcy Reiger and Cleveland's 4th round choice (draft choice cancelled by the Cleveland-Minnesota merger) in 1978 Amateur Draft, January 10, 1978. Placed on **Minnesota** Reserve List after **Cleveland-Minnesota** Dispersal Draft, June 5, 1978.

• PARIZEAU, Michel

Michel Gerard C – L. 5'10", 165 lbs. b: Montreal, Que., 4/9/1948. NY Rangers' 3rd, 10th overall, in 1965.

Season	Club	League	GP	G	A	Pts	AG	AA	APts	PIM	PP	SH	GW	S	%	TGF	PGF	TGA	PGA	+/-	GP	G	A	Pts	PIM	PP	SH	GW
1964-65	Montreal Metros	MMJHL	STATISTICS NOT AVAILABLE																									
1965-66	Drummondville Rangers	QJHL	STATISTICS NOT AVAILABLE																									
1966-67	Drummondville Rangers	QJHL	45	23	45	68	....	....	....	51	....	....	....	....	....	....	....	....	....	....	3	2	1	3	0	....	....	....
1967-68	Drummondville Rangers	QJHL	50	29	62	91	....	....	....	62	....	....	....	....	....	....	....	....	....	....	10	7	12	19	2	....	....	....
	Drummondville Rangers	Mem-Cup	4	2	4	6	....	....	....	0	....	....	....	....	....	....	....	....	....	....	....	....	....	....	....	....	....	....
1968-69	Omaha Knights	CHL	71	22	39	61	....	....	....	20	....	....	....	....	....	....	....	....	....	....	7	1	3	4	0	....	....	....
1969-70	Omaha Knights	CHL	71	13	16	29	....	....	....	30	....	....	....	....	....	....	....	....	....	....	12	7	3	10	9	....	....	....
1970-71	Omaha Knights	CHL	72	35	49	84	....	....	....	43	....	....	....	....	....	....	....	....	....	....	11	4	7	11	11	....	....	....
1971-72	**St. Louis Blues**	**NHL**	**21**	**1**	**2**	**3**	**1**	**2**	**3**	**8**	**1**	**0**	**0**	**14**	**7.1**	**4**	**1**	**5**	**1**	**-1**	....	....	....	....	....	....	....	....
	Philadelphia Flyers	**NHL**	**37**	**2**	**12**	**14**	**2**	**10**	**12**	**10**	**1**	**0**	**1**	**39**	**5.1**	**21**	**9**	**21**	**3**	**-6**	....	....	....	....	....	....	....	....
1972-73	Quebec Nordiques	WHA	75	25	48	73	....	....	....	50	....	....	....	....	....	....	....	....	....	....	....	....	....	....	....	....	....	....
1973-74	Quebec Nordiques	WHA	78	26	34	60	....	....	....	39	....	....	....	....	....	....	....	....	....	....	....	....	....	....	....	....	....	....
1974-75	Quebec Nordiques	WHA	78	28	46	74	....	....	....	69	....	....	....	....	....	....	....	....	....	....	15	2	4	6	10	....	....	....
1975-76	Quebec Nordiques	WHA	58	12	27	39	....	....	....	22	....	....	....	....	....	....	....	....	....	....	....	....	....	....	....	....	....	....
	Indianapolis Racers	WHA	23	13	15	28	....	....	....	20	....	....	....	....	....	....	....	....	....	....	7	4	4	8	6	....	....	....
1976-77	Indianapolis Racers	WHA	75	18	37	55	....	....	....	39	....	....	....	....	....	....	....	....	....	....	8	3	6	9	8	....	....	....
1977-78	Indianapolis Racers	WHA	70	13	27	40	....	....	....	47	....	....	....	....	....	....	....	....	....	....	....	....	....	....	....	....	....	....
1978-79	Indianapolis Racers	WHA	22	4	9	13	....	....	....	4	....	....	....	....	....	....	....	....	....	....	....	....	....	....	....	....	....	....
	Cincinnati Stingers	WHA	30	3	9	12	....	....	....	28	....	....	....	....	....	....	....	....	....	....	3	1	0	1	0	....	....	....
1979-80	Syracuse Firebirds	AHL	DID NOT PLAY – COACHING																									
	NHL Totals		**58**	**3**	**14**	**17**	**3**	**12**	**15**	**18**	**2**	**0**	**1**	**53**	**5.7**	**25**	**10**	**26**	**4**		....	....	....	....	....	....	....	....
	Other Major League Totals		509	142	252	394	....	....	....	318	....	....	....	....	....	....	....	....	....	....	33	10	14	24	24	....	....	....

CHL First All-Star Team (1971)

Claimed by **St. Louis** from **NY Rangers** in Intra-League Draft, June 8, 1971. Claimed on waivers by **Philadelphia** from **St. Louis**, December 8, 1971. Selected by **Quebec** (WHA) in 1972 WHA General Player Draft, February 12, 1972. Traded to **Indianapolis** (WHA) by **Quebec** (WHA) for Michel Dubois, Bill Prentice and Bob Fitchner, February, 1976. Signed as a free agent by **Cincinnati** (WHA) after **Indianapolis** (WHA) franchise folded, December 15, 1978.

• PARK, Brad

Douglas Bradford D – L. 6', 200 lbs. b: Toronto, Ont., 7/6/1948. NY Rangers' 1st, 2nd overall, in 1966. **HHOF**

Season	Club	League	GP	G	A	Pts	AG	AA	APts	PIM	PP	SH	GW	S	%	TGF	PGF	TGA	PGA	+/-	GP	G	A	Pts	PIM	PP	SH	GW
1965-66	Toronto Westclairs	OHA-B	STATISTICS NOT AVAILABLE																									
	Toronto Marlboros	OHA-Jr.	33	0	14	14	....	....	....	48	....	....	....	....	....	....	....	....	....	....	14	1	0	1	38	....	....	....
1966-67	Toronto Marlboros	OHA-Jr.	28	4	15	19	....	....	....	73	....	....	....	....	....	....	....	....	....	....	8	4	3	7	17	....	....	....
1967-68	Toronto Marlboros	OHA-Jr.	50	10	33	43	....	....	....	120	....	....	....	....	....	....	....	....	....	....	5	0	6	6	37	....	....	....
	Toronto Marlboros	OHA-Jr.	1	0	0	0	....	....	....	0	....	....	....	....	....	....	....	....	....	....	....	....	....	....	....	....	....	....
1968-69	**New York Rangers**	**NHL**	**54**	**3**	**23**	**26**	**3**	**20**	**23**	**70**	**2**	**0**	**0**	**103**	**2.9**	**71**	**14**	**48**	**3**	**12**	**4**	**0**	**2**	**2**	**7**	**0**	**0**	**0**
	Buffalo Bisons	AHL	17	2	12	14	....	....	....	49	....	....	....	....	....	....	....	....	....	....	....	....	....	....	....	....	....	....
1969-70	**New York Rangers**	**NHL**	**60**	**11**	**26**	**37**	**12**	**24**	**36**	**98**	**6**	**1**	**2**	**161**	**6.8**	**105**	**32**	**62**	**12**	**23**	**5**	**1**	**2**	**3**	**11**	**1**	**0**	**0**

Season	Club	League	REGULAR SEASON GP	G	A	Pts	AG	AA	APts	PIM	PP	SH	GW	S	%	TGF	PGF	TGA	PGA	+/–	PLAYOFFS GP	G	A	Pts	PIM	PP	SH	GW
1970-71	New York Rangers	NHL	68	7	37	44	7	31	38	114	3	0	0	199	3.5	114	39	63	13	25	13	0	4	4	42	0	0	0
1971-72	New York Rangers	NHL	75	24	49	73	24	43	67	130	8	2	4	263	9.1	159	42	70	15	62	16	4	7	11	21	2	0	1
1972-73	Team Canada	Summit-72	8	1	4	5	....	....	....	2	....	....	....	....	....	....	....	....	....	....	....	....	....	....	....	....	....	....
	New York Rangers	NHL	52	10	43	53	9	34	43	51	4	0	1	142	7.0	99	24	56	12	31	10	2	5	7	8	1	0	1
1973-74	New York Rangers	NHL	78	25	57	82	24	47	71	148	4	0	4	227	11.0	168	57	115	22	18	13	4	8	12	38	1	0	1
1974-75	New York Rangers	NHL	65	13	44	57	11	33	44	104	8	0	2	189	6.9	155	63	111	25	6	3	1	4	5	2	0	0	0
1975-76	New York Rangers	NHL	13	2	4	6	2	3	5	23	0	0	1	28	7.1	20	10	21	7	–4	....	....	....	....	....	....	....	....
	Boston Bruins	NHL	43	16	37	53	14	28	42	95	7	1	2	163	9.8	119	43	66	13	23	11	3	8	11	14	1	1	0
1976-77	Boston Bruins	NHL	77	12	55	67	11	42	53	67	4	1	4	238	5.0	178	42	116	27	47	14	2	10	12	4	0	0	0
1977-78	Boston Bruins	NHL	80	22	57	79	20	44	64	79	9	0	3	225	9.8	199	46	118	33	68	15	9	11	20	14	4	0	0
1978-79	Boston Bruins	NHL	40	7	32	39	6	23	29	10	3	0	0	96	7.3	87	34	35	10	28	11	1	4	5	8	0	0	1
1979-80	Boston Bruins	NHL	32	5	16	21	4	12	16	27	2	0	2	67	7.5	53	19	31	8	11	10	3	6	9	4	0	0	0
1980-81	Boston Bruins	NHL	78	14	52	66	11	35	46	111	10	0	2	201	7.0	166	78	106	39	21	3	1	3	4	11	1	0	0
1981-82	Boston Bruins	NHL	75	14	42	56	11	28	39	82	8	0	1	159	8.8	150	59	113	33	11	11	1	4	5	4	0	0	1
1982-83	Boston Bruins	NHL	76	10	26	36	8	18	26	82	5	0	0	127	7.9	110	30	85	25	20	16	3	9	12	18	1	0	1
1983-84	Detroit Red Wings	NHL	80	5	53	58	4	36	40	85	4	0	0	140	3.6	144	68	122	17	–29	3	0	3	3	0	0	0	0
1984-85	Detroit Red Wings	NHL	67	13	30	43	11	20	31	53	6	0	0	92	14.1	97	38	76	2	–15	3	0	0	0	11	0	0	0
	NHL Totals		1113	213	683	896	192	521	713	1429	93	5	28	2820	7.6	2194	738	1414	316		161	35	90	125	217	12	1	6

OHA-Jr. Second All-Star Team (1968) • NHL First All-Star Team (1970, 1972, 1974, 1976, 1978) • NHL Second All-Star Team (1971, 1973) • Won Bill Masterton Trophy (1984) • Played in NHL All-Star Game (1970, 1971, 1972, 1973, 1974, 1975, 1976, 1977, 1978)

Traded to **Boston** by **NY Rangers** with Jean Ratelle and Joe Zanussi for Phil Esposito and Carol Vadnais, November 7, 1975. Signed as a free agent by **Detroit**, August 9, 1983.

• PARK, Richard

C – R. 5′11″, 190 lbs. b: Seoul, S. Korea, 5/27/1976. Pittsburgh's 2nd, 50th overall, in 1994.

Season	Club	League	GP	G	A	Pts	AG	AA	APts	PIM	PP	SH	GW	S	%	TGF	PGF	TGA	PGA	+/–	GP	G	A	Pts	PIM	PP	SH	GW
1991-92	Toronto Young Nationals	MTHL	76	49	58	107	....	....	....	91	....	....	....	....	....	....	....	....	....	....	....	....	....	....	....	....	....	....
1992-93	Belleville Bulls	OHL	66	23	38	61	....	....	....	38	....	....	....	....	....	....	....	....	....	....	5	0	0	0	14	....	....	....
1993-94	Belleville Bulls	OHL	59	27	49	76	....	....	....	70	....	....	....	....	....	....	....	....	....	....	12	3	5	8	18	....	....	....
	United States	WJC-A	7	3	2	5	....	....	....	4	....	....	....	....	....	....	....	....	....	....	....	....	....	....	....	....	....	....
1994-95	Belleville Bulls	OHL	45	28	51	79	....	....	....	35	....	....	....	....	....	....	....	....	....	....	16	9	18	27	12	....	....	....
	United States	WJC-A	7	1	7	8	....	....	....	29	....	....	....	....	....	....	....	....	....	....	....	....	....	....	....	....	....	....
	Pittsburgh Penguins	NHL	1	0	1	1	0	1	1	2	0	0	0	4	0.0	1	0	1	1	1	3	0	0	0	2	0	0	0
1995-96	Belleville Bulls	OHL	6	7	6	13	....	....	....	2	....	....	....	....	....	....	....	....	....	....	14	18	12	30	10	....	....	....
	Pittsburgh Penguins	NHL	56	4	6	10	4	5	9	36	0	1	1	62	6.5	18	1	23	9	3	1	0	0	0	0	0	0	0
1996-97	Pittsburgh Penguins	NHL	1	0	0	0	0	0	0	0	0	0	0	1	0.0	0	0	1	0	–1	....	....	....	....	....	....	....	....
	Cleveland Lumberjacks	IHL	50	12	15	27	....	....	....	30	....	....	....	....	....	....	....	....	....	....	....	....	....	....	....	....	....	....
	Mighty Ducks of Anaheim	NHL	11	1	1	2	1	1	2	10	0	0	0	9	11.1	4	0	4	0	0	11	0	1	1	2	0	0	0
1997-98	Mighty Ducks of Anaheim	NHL	15	0	2	2	0	2	2	8	0	0	0	14	0.0	5	0	8	0	–3	....	....	....	....	....	....	....	....
	Cincinnati Mighty Ducks	AHL	56	17	26	43	....	....	....	36	....	....	....	....	....	....	....	....	....	....	....	....	....	....	....	....	....	....
1998-99	Philadelphia Flyers	NHL	7	0	0	0	0	0	0	0	0	0	0	5	0.0	0	0	1	0	–1	....	....	....	....	....	....	....	....
	Philadelphia Phantoms	AHL	75	41	42	83	....	....	....	33	....	....	....	....	....	....	....	....	....	....	16	9	6	15	4	....	....	....
99-2000	Utah Grizzlies	IHL	82	28	32	60	....	....	....	36	....	....	....	....	....	....	....	....	....	....	5	1	0	1	0	....	....	....
	NHL Totals		91	5	10	15	5	9	14	56	0	1	1	95	5.3	28	1	38	10		15	0	1	1	4	0	0	0

AHL Second All-Star Team (1999)

Traded to **Anaheim** by **Pittsburgh** for Roman Oksiuta, March 18, 1997. Signed as a free agent by **Philadelphia**, August 24, 1998. Signed as a free agent by **Utah** (IHL), September 22, 1999.

• PARKER, Jeff

Jeffrey Lee RW – R. 6′3″, 194 lbs. b: St. Paul, MN, 9/7/1964. Buffalo's 9th, 111th overall, in 1982.

Season	Club	League	GP	G	A	Pts	AG	AA	APts	PIM	PP	SH	GW	S	%	TGF	PGF	TGA	PGA	+/–	GP	G	A	Pts	PIM	PP	SH	GW
1982-83	White Bear Lake Bears	Hi-School	28	14	14	28	....	....	....	....	....	....	....	....	....	....	....	....	....	....	....	....	....	....	....	....	....	....
1983-84	Michigan State Spartans	CCHA	44	8	13	21	....	....	....	82	....	....	....	....	....	....	....	....	....	....	....	....	....	....	....	....	....	....
1984-85	Michigan State Spartans	CCHA	42	10	12	22	....	....	....	89	....	....	....	....	....	....	....	....	....	....	....	....	....	....	....	....	....	....
1985-86	Michigan State Spartans	CCHA	41	15	20	35	....	....	....	88	....	....	....	....	....	....	....	....	....	....	....	....	....	....	....	....	....	....
1986-87	Buffalo Sabres	NHL	15	3	3	6	3	2	5	7	0	0	0	10	30.0	11	1	10	1	1	....	....	....	....	....	....	....	....
	Rochester Americans	AHL	54	14	8	22	....	....	....	75	....	....	....	....	....	....	....	....	....	....	14	1	3	4	19	....	....	....
1987-88	Buffalo Sabres	NHL	4	0	2	2	0	1	1	2	0	0	0	0	0.0	2	0	4	1	–1	....	....	....	....	....	....	....	....
	Rochester Americans	AHL	34	13	31	44	....	....	....	69	....	....	....	....	....	....	....	....	....	....	2	1	1	2	0	....	....	....
1988-89	Buffalo Sabres	NHL	57	9	9	18	8	6	14	82	0	0	2	78	11.5	30	1	44	18	3	5	0	0	0	26	0	0	0
	Rochester Americans	AHL	6	2	4	6	....	....	....	9	....	....	....	....	....	....	....	....	....	....	....	....	....	....	....	....	....	....
1989-90	Buffalo Sabres	NHL	61	4	5	9	3	4	7	70	0	0	0	61	6.6	23	2	35	5	–9	....	....	....	....	....	....	....	....
1990-91	Muskegon Lumberjacks	IHL	11	1	7	8	....	....	....	13	....	....	....	....	....	....	....	....	....	....	....	....	....	....	....	....	....	....
	Hartford Whalers	NHL	4	0	0	0	0	0	0	2	0	0	0	4	0.0	0	0	6	4	–2	....	....	....	....	....	....	....	....
	NHL Totals		141	16	19	35	14	13	27	163	0	0	2	153	10.5	66	4	99	29		5	0	0	0	26	0	0	0

NCAA Championship All-Tournament Team (1986)

Traded to **Winnipeg** by **Buffalo** with Phil Housley, Scott Arneil and Buffalo's 1st round choice (Keith Tkachuk) in 1990 Entry Draft for Dale Hawerchuk, Winnipeg's 1st round choice (Brad May) in 1990 Entry Draft and future considerations, June 16, 1990. Signed as a free agent by **Pittsburgh**, February 5, 1991. Traded to **Harford** by **Pittsburgh** with John Cullen and Zarley Zalapski for Ron Francis, Grant Jennings and Ulf Samuelsson, March 4, 1991.

• PARKER, Scott

RW – R. 6′4″, 220 lbs. b: Hanford, CA, 1/29/1978. Colorado's 4th, 20th overall, in 1998.

Season	Club	League	GP	G	A	Pts	AG	AA	APts	PIM	PP	SH	GW	S	%	TGF	PGF	TGA	PGA	+/–	GP	G	A	Pts	PIM	PP	SH	GW
1993-94	Alaska Artic Ice	AAHL	34	8	12	20	....	....	....	86	....	....	....	....	....	....	....	....	....	....	....	....	....	....	....	....	....	....
1994-95	Spokane Braves	KIJHL	43	7	21	28	....	....	....	128	....	....	....	....	....	....	....	....	....	....	....	....	....	....	....	....	....	....
1995-96	Kelowna Rockets	WHL	64	3	4	7	....	....	....	159	....	....	....	....	....	....	....	....	....	....	6	0	0	0	12	....	....	....
1996-97	Kelowna Rockets	WHL	68	18	8	26	....	....	....	*330	....	....	....	....	....	....	....	....	....	....	6	0	2	2	4	....	....	....
1997-98	Kelowna Rockets	WHL	71	30	22	52	....	....	....	243	....	....	....	....	....	....	....	....	....	....	7	6	0	6	23	....	....	....
1998-99	Colorado Rockies	NHL	27	0	0	0	0	0	0	71	0	0	0	3	0.0	0	0	3	0	–3	....	....	....	....	....	....	....	....
	Hershey Bears	AHL	32	4	3	7	....	....	....	143	....	....	....	....	....	....	....	....	....	....	4	0	0	0	6	....	....	....
99-2000	Hershey Bears	AHL	68	12	7	19	....	....	....	206	....	....	....	....	....	....	....	....	....	....	11	1	1	2	56	....	....	....
	NHL Totals		27	0	0	0	0	0	0	71	0	0	0	3	0.0	0	0	3	0		....	....	....	....	....	....	....	....

• Re-entered NHL draft. Originally New Jersey's 6th choice, 63rd overall, in 1996 Entry Draft.

• PARKS, Greg

Greg Roy C – R. 5′9″, 180 lbs. b: Edmonton, Alta., 3/25/1967.

Season	Club	League	GP	G	A	Pts	AG	AA	APts	PIM	PP	SH	GW	S	%	TGF	PGF	TGA	PGA	+/–	GP	G	A	Pts	PIM	PP	SH	GW
1982-83	Edmonton Jaycees	AAHA	STATISTICS NOT AVAILABLE																									
1983-84	St. Albert Saints	AJHL	58	35	40	75	....	....	....	113	....	....	....	....	....	....	....	....	....	....	....	....	....	....	....	....	....	....
1984-85	St. Albert Saints	AJHL	48	36	74	110	....	....	....	200	....	....	....	....	....	....	....	....	....	....	....	....	....	....	....	....	....	....
1985-86	Bowling Green University	CCHA	41	16	26	42	....	....	....	43	....	....	....	....	....	....	....	....	....	....	....	....	....	....	....	....	....	....
1986-87	Bowling Green University	CCHA	45	23	27	50	....	....	....	52	....	....	....	....	....	....	....	....	....	....	....	....	....	....	....	....	....	....
1987-88	Bowling Green University	CCHA	45	30	44	74	....	....	....	84	....	....	....	....	....	....	....	....	....	....	....	....	....	....	....	....	....	....
1988-89	Bowling Green University	CCHA	47	32	42	74	....	....	....	98	....	....	....	....	....	....	....	....	....	....	....	....	....	....	....	....	....	....
1989-90	Karpat Oulu	Finland-2	16	4	6	10	....	....	....	22	....	....	....	....	....	....	....	....	....	....	....	....	....	....	....	....	....	....
	Johnstown Chiefs	ECHL	8	5	9	14	....	....	....	7	....	....	....	....	....	....	....	....	....	....	....	....	....	....	....	....	....	....
	Springfield Indians	AHL	49	22	32	54	....	....	....	30	....	....	....	....	....	....	....	....	....	....	18	9	*13	*22	22	....	....	....
1990-91	New York Islanders	NHL	20	1	2	3	1	2	3	4	0	0	0	10	10.0	6	0	6	0	0	....	....	....	....	....	....	....	....
	Capital District Islanders	AHL	48	32	43	75	....	....	....	67	....	....	....	....	....	....	....	....	....	....	....	....	....	....	....	....	....	....
1991-92	New York Islanders	NHL	1	0	0	0	0	0	0	2	0	0	0	0	0.0	0	0	0	0	0	....	....	....	....	....	....	....	....
	Capital District Islanders	AHL	70	36	57	93	....	....	....	84	....	....	....	....	....	....	....	....	....	....	7	5	8	13	4	....	....	....
1992-93	Leksands IF	Sweden	39	21	19	40	....	....	....	66	....	....	....	....	....	....	....	....	....	....	1	0	0	0	4	....	....	....
	Canada	Nat-Team	9	2	2	4	....	....	....	4	....	....	....	....	....	....	....	....	....	....	....	....	....	....	....	....	....	....
	New York Islanders	NHL	2	0	0	0	0	0	0	0	0	0	0	3	0.0	0	0	0	0	0	2	0	0	0	0	0	0	0
1993-94	Leksands IF	Sweden	39	21	18	39	....	....	....	44	....	....	....	....	....	....	....	....	....	....	4	3	1	4	....	....	....	....
	Canada	Nat-Team	13	1	1	2	....	....	....	112	....	....	....	....	....	....	....	....	....	....	....	....	....	....	....	....	....	....
	Canada	Olympics	8	1	2	3	....	....	....	10	....	....	....	....	....	....	....	....	....	....	....	....	....	....	....	....	....	....
1994-95	Krefelder EV	Germany	10	2	7	9	....	....	....	8	....	....	....	....	....	....	....	....	....	....	1	0	0	0	0	....	....	....

Season	Club	League	REGULAR SEASON																		PLAYOFFS							
			GP	G	A	Pts	AG	AA	APts	PIM	PP	SH	GW	S	%	TGF	PGF	TGA	PGA	+/–	GP	G	A	Pts	PIM	PP	SH	GW
1995-96	Brynas IF Gavle	Sweden	22	10	12	22	....	....	....	22	....	....	....	....	....	....	....	....	....	....	....	....	....	....	....	....	....	....
	Canada	Nat-Team	7	0	0	0	....	....	....	6	....	....	....	....	....	....	....	....	....	....	....	....	....	....	....	....	....	....
1996-97	SC Langnau	Switz-2	42	36	40	76	....	....	....	53	....	....	....	....	....	....	....	....	....	....	8	5	5	10	39	....	....	....
1997-98	SC Langnau	Switz-2	40	30	40	70	....	....	....	56	....	....	....	....	....	....	....	....	....	....	....	....	....	....	....	....	....	....
1998-99	SC Langnau	Switz.	29	13	24	37	....	....	....	26	....	....	....	....	....	....	....	....	....	....	....	....	....	....	....	....	....	....
99-2000	Leksands IF	Sweden	36	16	13	29	....	....	....	52	....	....	....	....	....	....	....	....	....	....	....	....	....	....	....	....	....	....
	Canada	Nat-Team	4	1	3	4	....	....	....	0	....	....	....	....	....	....	....	....	....	....	....	....	....	....	....	....	....	....
	NHL Totals		**23**	**1**	**2**	**3**	**1**	**2**	**3**	**6**	**0**	**0**	**0**	**13**	**7.7**	**6**	**0**	**6**	**0**		**2**	**0**	**0**	**0**	**0**	**0**	**0**	**0**

CCHA First All-Star Team (1989) • NCAA West First All-American Team (1989)

Signed as a free agent by **NY Islanders**, August 13, 1990.

• PARRISH, Mark

LW – R. 5'11", 191 lbs. b: Edina, MN, 2/2/1977. Colorado's 3rd, 79th overall, in 1996.

Season	Club	League	GP	G	A	Pts	AG	AA	APts	PIM	PP	SH	GW	S	%	TGF	PGF	TGA	PGA	+/–	GP	G	A	Pts	PIM	PP	SH	GW
1994-95	Jefferson Jaguars	Hi-School	27	40	20	60	....	....	....	42	....	....	....	....	....	....	....	....	....	....	....	....	....	....	....	....	....	....
1995-96	St. Cloud State Huskies	WCHA	39	15	13	28	....	....	....	30	....	....	....	....	....	....	....	....	....	....	....	....	....	....	....	....	....	....
	United States	WJC-A	6	1	3	4	....	....	....	2	....	....	....	....	....	....	....	....	....	....	....	....	....	....	....	....	....	....
1996-97	St. Cloud State Huskies	WCHA	35	*27	15	42	....	....	....	60	....	....	....	....	....	....	....	....	....	....	....	....	....	....	....	....	....	....
	United States	WJC-A	6	5	2	7	....	....	....	8	....	....	....	....	....	....	....	....	....	....	....	....	....	....	....	....	....	....
1997-98	Seattle Thunderbirds	WHL	54	54	38	92	....	....	....	29	....	....	....	....	....	....	....	....	....	....	5	2	3	5	2	....	....	....
	United States	WC-A	6	0	0	0	....	....	....	4	....	....	....	....	....	....	....	....	....	....	....	....	....	....	....	....	....	....
	Beast of New Haven	AHL	1	1	0	1	....	....	....	2	....	....	....	....	....	....	....	....	....	....	....	....	....	....	....	....	....	....
1998-99	**Florida Panthers**	**NHL**	**73**	**24**	**13**	**37**	**28**	**13**	**41**	**25**	**5**	**0**	**5**	**129**	**18.6**	**60**	**18**	**48**	**0**	**–6**	....	....	....	....	....	....	....	....
	Beast of New Haven	AHL	2	1	0	1	....	....	....	0	....	....	....	....	....	....	....	....	....	....	....	....	....	....	....	....	....	....
99-2000	**Florida Panthers**	**NHL**	**81**	**26**	**18**	**44**	**29**	**17**	**46**	**39**	**6**	**0**	**3**	**152**	**17.1**	**65**	**20**	**44**	**0**	**1**	**4**	**0**	**1**	**1**	**0**	**0**	**0**	**0**
	NHL Totals		**154**	**50**	**31**	**81**	**57**	**30**	**87**	**64**	**11**	**0**	**8**	**281**	**17.8**	**125**	**38**	**92**	**0**		**4**	**0**	**1**	**1**	**0**	**0**	**0**	**0**

NCAA West Second All-American Team (1997) • WHL West First All-Star Team (1998)

Rights traded to **Florida** by **Colorado** with Anaheim's 3rd round choice (previously acquired, Florida selected Lance Ward) in 1998 Entry Draft for Tom Fitzgerald, March 24, 1998. Traded to **NY Islanders** by **Florida** with Oleg Kvasha for Roberto Luongo and Olli Jokinen, June 24, 2000.

• PASEK, Dusan

C – L. 6'1", 200 lbs. b: Bratislava, Czech., 9/7/1960 d: 3/15/1998. Minnesota's 4th, 81st overall, in 1982.

Season	Club	League	GP	G	A	Pts	AG	AA	APts	PIM	PP	SH	GW	S	%	TGF	PGF	TGA	PGA	+/–	GP	G	A	Pts	PIM	PP	SH	GW
1969-1972	BEZ Bratislava	Czech-Jr.	STATISTICS NOT AVAILABLE																									
1972-1977	Slovan Bratislava	Czech-Jr.	STATISTICS NOT AVAILABLE																									
1977-78	Slovan Bratislava	Czech.	5	0	1	1	....	....	....	0	....	....	....	....	....	....	....	....	....	....	....	....	....	....	....	....	....	....
	Czechoslovakia	EJC-A	5	6	4	10	....	....	....	4	....	....	....	....	....	....	....	....	....	....	....	....	....	....	....	....	....	....
1978-79	Slovan Bratislava	Czech.	36	9	12	21	....	....	....	18	....	....	....	....	....	....	....	....	....	....	....	....	....	....	....	....	....	....
	Czechoslovakia	WJC-A	6	2	0	2	....	....	....	2	....	....	....	....	....	....	....	....	....	....	....	....	....	....	....	....	....	....
1979-80	Slovan Bratislava	Czech.	40	18	1	19	....	....	....	22	....	....	....	....	....	....	....	....	....	....	....	....	....	....	....	....	....	....
	Czechoslovakia	WJC-A	5	6	1	7	....	....	....	4	....	....	....	....	....	....	....	....	....	....	....	....	....	....	....	....	....	....
1980-81	Slovan Bratislava	Czech.	34	22	10	32	....	....	....	12	....	....	....	....	....	....	....	....	....	....	....	....	....	....	....	....	....	....
1981-82	Czechoslovakia	Can-Cup	6	0	2	2	....	....	....	2	....	....	....	....	....	....	....	....	....	....	....	....	....	....	....	....	....	....
	Slovan Bratislava	Czech-2	STATISTICS NOT AVAILABLE																									
	Czechoslovakia	WEC-A	10	1	2	3	....	....	....	4	....	....	....	....	....	....	....	....	....	....	....	....	....	....	....	....	....	....
1982-83	Slovan Bratislava	Czech-2	43	23	23	46	....	....	....	62	....	....	....	....	....	....	....	....	....	....	....	....	....	....	....	....	....	....
	Czechoslovakia	WEC-A	10	3	2	5	....	....	....	6	....	....	....	....	....	....	....	....	....	....	....	....	....	....	....	....	....	....
1983-84	Slovan Bratislava	Czech.	40	28	19	47	....	....	....	62	....	....	....	....	....	....	....	....	....	....	....	....	....	....	....	....	....	....
	Czechoslovakia	Olympics	7	0	4	4	....	....	....	2	....	....	....	....	....	....	....	....	....	....	....	....	....	....	....	....	....	....
1984-85	Czechoslovakia	Can-Cup	5	0	0	0	....	....	....	4	....	....	....	....	....	....	....	....	....	....	....	....	....	....	....	....	....	....
	Slovan Bratislava	Czech.	40	23	14	37	....	....	....	60	....	....	....	....	....	....	....	....	....	....	....	....	....	....	....	....	....	....
	Czechoslovakia	WEC-A	10	3	3	6	....	....	....	6	....	....	....	....	....	....	....	....	....	....	....	....	....	....	....	....	....	....
1985-86	Dukla Islau	Czech.	45	13	11	24	....	....	....	44	....	....	....	....	....	....	....	....	....	....	....	....	....	....	....	....	....	....
	Czechoslovakia	WEC-A	10	4	3	7	....	....	....	16	....	....	....	....	....	....	....	....	....	....	....	....	....	....	....	....	....	....
1986-87	Slovan Bratislava	Czech.	32	18	*27	45	....	....	....	*81	....	....	....	....	....	....	....	....	....	....	6	3	2	5	....	....	....	....
	Czechoslovakia	WEC-A	10	6	2	8	....	....	....	2	....	....	....	....	....	....	....	....	....	....	....	....	....	....	....	....	....	....
1987-88	Czechoslovakia	Can-Cup	6	4	1	5	....	....	....	12	....	....	....	....	....	....	....	....	....	....	....	....	....	....	....	....	....	....
	Slovan Bratislava	Czech.	40	19	18	37	....	....	....	81	....	....	....	....	....	....	....	....	....	....	....	....	....	....	....	....	....	....
	Czechoslovakia	Olympics	8	6	5	11	....	....	....	8	....	....	....	....	....	....	....	....	....	....	....	....	....	....	....	....	....	....
1988-89	**Minnesota North Stars**	**NHL**	**48**	**4**	**10**	**14**	**3**	**7**	**10**	**30**	**1**	**0**	**0**	**86**	**4.7**	**29**	**8**	**29**	**0**	**–8**	**2**	**1**	**0**	**1**	**0**	**0**	**0**	**0**
1989-90	Kalamazoo Wings	IHL	20	10	14	24	....	....	....	6	....	....	....	....	....	....	....	....	....	....	....	....	....	....	....	....	....	....
1990-91	Slovan Bratislava	Czech.	11	11	5	16	....	....	....	20	....	....	....	....	....	....	....	....	....	....	....	....	....	....	....	....	....	....
	HC Asiago	Italy	34	35	41	76	....	....	....	22	....	....	....	....	....	....	....	....	....	....	3	5	1	6	0	....	....	....
	HC Ambri-Piotta	Switz.	1	2	1	3	....	....	....	0	....	....	....	....	....	....	....	....	....	....	5	1	1	2	9	....	....	....
1991-92	HC Fassa	Alpenliga	18	19	22	41	....	....	....	45	....	....	....	....	....	....	....	....	....	....	....	....	....	....	....	....	....	....
	HC Fassa	Italy	17	15	25	40	....	....	....	12	....	....	....	....	....	....	....	....	....	....	8	7	8	15	10	....	....	....
	HC Fassa	Italy	25	22	33	55	....	....	....	22	....	....	....	....	....	....	....	....	....	....	8	7	8	15	10	....	....	....
1992-93	KalPa Kuopio	Finland	10	2	4	6	....	....	....	16	....	....	....	....	....	....	....	....	....	....	....	....	....	....	....	....	....	....
	KalPa Kuopio	Finland	10	2	4	6	....	....	....	16	....	....	....	....	....	....	....	....	....	....	....	....	....	....	....	....	....	....
	NHL Totals		**48**	**4**	**10**	**14**	**3**	**7**	**10**	**30**	**1**	**0**	**0**	**86**	**4.7**	**29**	**8**	**29**	**0**		**2**	**1**	**0**	**1**	**0**	**0**	**0**	**0**

Czechoslovakian First All-Star Team (1988)

• PASIN, Dave

RW – R. 6'1", 205 lbs. b: Edmonton, Alta., 7/8/1966. Boston's 1st, 19th overall, in 1984.

Season	Club	League	GP	G	A	Pts	AG	AA	APts	PIM	PP	SH	GW	S	%	TGF	PGF	TGA	PGA	+/–	GP	G	A	Pts	PIM	PP	SH	GW
1981-82	Edmonton Legionaires	AAHA	STATISTICS NOT AVAILABLE																									
1982-83	Prince Albert Raiders	WHL	62	40	42	82	....	....	....	48	....	....	....	....	....	....	....	....	....	....	....	....	....	....	....	....	....	....
1983-84	Prince Albert Raiders	WHL	71	68	54	122	....	....	....	68	....	....	....	....	....	....	....	....	....	....	5	1	4	5	0	....	....	....
1984-85	Prince Albert Raiders	WHL	65	64	52	116	....	....	....	88	....	....	....	....	....	....	....	....	....	....	10	10	11	21	10	....	....	....
	Prince Albert Raiders	Mem-Cup	5	4	7	11	....	....	....	4	....	....	....	....	....	....	....	....	....	....	....	....	....	....	....	....	....	....
1985-86	**Boston Bruins**	**NHL**	**71**	**18**	**19**	**37**	**14**	**13**	**27**	**50**	**4**	**0**	**3**	**116**	**15.5**	**57**	**12**	**47**	**1**	**–1**	**3**	**0**	**1**	**1**	**0**	**0**	**0**	**0**
1986-87	Moncton Golden Flames	AHL	66	27	25	52	....	....	....	47	....	....	....	....	....	....	....	....	....	....	6	1	1	2	14	....	....	....
1987-88	Maine Mariners	AHL	30	8	14	22	....	....	....	39	....	....	....	....	....	....	....	....	....	....	8	4	3	7	13	....	....	....
1988-89	Maine Mariners	AHL	11	2	5	7	....	....	....	6	....	....	....	....	....	....	....	....	....	....	....	....	....	....	....	....	....	....
	Los Angeles Kings	**NHL**	**5**	**0**	**0**	**0**	**0**	**0**	**0**	**0**	**0**	**0**	**0**	**2**	**0.0**	**1**	**0**	**2**	**0**	**–1**	....	....	....	....	....	....	....	....
	New Haven Nighthawks	AHL	48	25	23	48	....	....	....	42	....	....	....	....	....	....	....	....	....	....	17	8	8	16	47	....	....	....
1989-90	New Haven Nighthawks	AHL	7	7	4	11	....	....	....	14	....	....	....	....	....	....	....	....	....	....	....	....	....	....	....	....	....	....
	HC Fribourg	Switz.	12	4	7	11	....	....	....	....	....	....	....	....	....	....	....	....	....	....	....	....	....	....	....	....	....	....
	Springfield Indians	AHL	11	2	3	5	....	....	....	2	....	....	....	....	....	....	....	....	....	....	3	1	2	3	2	....	....	....
1990-91	New Haven Nighthawks	AHL	39	13	25	38	....	....	....	57	....	....	....	....	....	....	....	....	....	....	....	....	....	....	....	....	....	....
	Phoenix Roadrunners	IHL	13	4	3	7	....	....	....	24	....	....	....	....	....	....	....	....	....	....	9	3	4	7	8	....	....	....
1991-92	HC Gardena-Groden	Italy-2	30	51	30	81	....	....	....	33	....	....	....	....	....	....	....	....	....	....	....	....	....	....	....	....	....	....
1992-93	HC Bolzano	Alpenliga	18	12	12	24	....	....	....	100	....	....	....	....	....	....	....	....	....	....	....	....	....	....	....	....	....	....
	HC Bolzano	Italy	32	31	46	77	....	....	....	52	....	....	....	....	....	....	....	....	....	....	8	4	5	9	7	....	....	....
1993-94	HC Bolzano	Alpenliga	29	29	34	63	....	....	....	74	....	....	....	....	....	....	....	....	....	....	....	....	....	....	....	....	....	....
	HC Bolzano	Italy	15	12	27	39	....	....	....	37	....	....	....	....	....	....	....	....	....	....	6	5	7	12	14	....	....	....
1994-95	HC Bolzano	Alpenliga	18	20	25	45	....	....	....	38	....	....	....	....	....	....	....	....	....	....	....	....	....	....	....	....	....	....
	HC Bolzono	Italy	32	31	*46	*77	....	....	....	52	....	....	....	....	....	....	....	....	....	....	10	12	19	31	28	....	....	....
1995-96	San Francisco Spiders	IHL	26	5	9	14	....	....	....	16	....	....	....	....	....	....	....	....	....	....	....	....	....	....	....	....	....	....

Season	Club	League	GP	G	A	Pts	AG	AA	APts	PIM	PP	SH	GW	S	%	TGF	PGF	TGA	PGA	+/–	GP	G	A	Pts	PIM	PP	SH	GW
			REGULAR SEASON																		PLAYOFFS							
1996-97	HC Bolzano	Alpenliga	38	23	28	51				127																		
	HC Davos	Switz.	2	3	1	4				6											6	4	3	7	16			
1997-98	HC Thurgau	Switz-2	9	3	8	11																						
	NHL Totals		**76**	**18**	**19**	**37**	**14**	**13**	**27**	**50**	**4**	**0**	**3**	**118**	**15.3**	**58**	**12**	**49**	**1**		**3**	**0**	**1**	**1**	**0**	**0**	**0**	**0**

WHL East Second All-Star Team (1985)

• Missed majority of 1987-88 season recovering from eye injury suffered in practice, November 12, 1987. Rights traded to **LA Kings** by **Boston** for Paul Guay, November 3, 1988. Claimed on waivers by **NY Islanders** from **LA Kings**, March 6, 1990. • Played w/ RHI's Oakland Skates in 1996 (6-3-2-5-6).

• PASLAWSKI, Greg

Gregory Stephen RW – R. 5'11", 190 lbs. b: Kindersley, Sask., 8/25/1961.

Season	Club	League	GP	G	A	Pts	AG	AA	APts	PIM	PP	SH	GW	S	%	TGF	PGF	TGA	PGA	+/–	GP	G	A	Pts	PIM	PP	SH	GW
1979-80	Prince Albert Raiders	SJHL	58	17	32	49				142																		
1980-81	Prince Albert Raiders	SJHL	59	55	60	115				106																		
	Prince Albert Raiders	Cen-Cup																										
1981-82	Nova Scotia Voyageurs	AHL	43	15	11	26				31																		
1982-83	Nova Scotia Voyageurs	AHL	75	46	42	88				32											6	1	3	4	8			
1983-84	**Montreal Canadiens**	**NHL**	**26**	**1**	**4**	**5**	**1**	**3**	**4**	**4**	**0**	**0**	**0**	**27**	**3.7**	**10**	**0**	**15**	**0**	**–5**								
	St. Louis Blues	**NHL**	**34**	**8**	**6**	**14**	**6**	**4**	**10**	**17**	**1**	**0**	**0**	**36**	**22.2**	**20**	**3**	**15**	**2**	**4**	**9**	**1**	**0**	**1**	**2**	**0**	**0**	**0**
1984-85	**St. Louis Blues**	**NHL**	**72**	**22**	**20**	**42**	**18**	**14**	**32**	**21**	**7**	**0**	**2**	**159**	**13.8**	**60**	**15**	**39**	**0**	**6**	**3**	**0**	**0**	**0**	**2**	**0**	**0**	**0**
1985-86	**St. Louis Blues**	**NHL**	**56**	**22**	**11**	**33**	**18**	**7**	**25**	**18**	**1**	**1**	**2**	**150**	**14.7**	**47**	**10**	**56**	**7**	**–12**	**17**	**10**	**7**	**17**	**13**	**2**	**0**	**0**
1986-87	**St. Louis Blues**	**NHL**	**76**	**29**	**35**	**64**	**25**	**25**	**50**	**27**	**5**	**1**	**7**	**204**	**14.2**	**95**	**27**	**78**	**11**	**1**	**6**	**1**	**1**	**2**	**4**	**0**	**0**	**0**
1987-88	**St. Louis Blues**	**NHL**	**17**	**2**	**1**	**3**	**2**	**1**	**3**	**4**	**0**	**0**	**1**	**30**	**6.7**	**6**	**2**	**20**	**2**	**–14**	**3**	**1**	**1**	**2**	**2**	**1**	**0**	**0**
1988-89	**St. Louis Blues**	**NHL**	**75**	**26**	**26**	**52**	**22**	**18**	**40**	**18**	**8**	**0**	**3**	**179**	**14.5**	**79**	**26**	**61**	**16**	**8**	**9**	**2**	**1**	**3**	**2**	**1**	**0**	**0**
1989-90	**Winnipeg Jets**	**NHL**	**71**	**18**	**30**	**48**	**15**	**21**	**36**	**14**	**7**	**0**	**6**	**122**	**14.8**	**80**	**25**	**63**	**4**	**–4**	**7**	**1**	**3**	**4**	**0**	**0**	**0**	**0**
1990-91	**Winnipeg Jets**	**NHL**	**43**	**9**	**10**	**19**	**8**	**8**	**16**	**10**	**1**	**0**	**1**	**66**	**13.6**	**32**	**9**	**29**	**0**	**–6**								
	Buffalo Sabres	**NHL**	**12**	**2**	**1**	**3**	**2**	**1**	**3**	**4**	**0**	**0**	**1**	**9**	**22.2**	**6**	**0**	**6**	**0**	**0**								
1991-92	**Quebec Nordiques**	**NHL**	**80**	**28**	**17**	**45**	**25**	**13**	**38**	**18**	**5**	**1**	**4**	**134**	**20.9**	**68**	**20**	**82**	**22**	**–12**								
1992-93	**Philadelphia Flyers**	**NHL**	**60**	**14**	**19**	**33**	**12**	**13**	**25**	**12**	**4**	**0**	**0**	**90**	**15.6**	**56**	**10**	**46**	**0**	**0**								
	Calgary Flames	**NHL**	**13**	**4**	**5**	**9**	**3**	**3**	**6**	**0**	**0**	**0**	**1**	**19**	**21.1**	**13**	**4**	**6**	**0**	**3**	**6**	**3**	**0**	**3**	**0**	**0**	**0**	**1**
1993-94	**Calgary Flames**	**NHL**	**15**	**2**	**0**	**2**	**2**	**0**	**2**	**2**	**0**	**0**	**1**	**13**	**15.4**	**7**	**2**	**9**	**0**	**–4**								
	Peoria Rivermen	IHL	29	16	16	32				12											6	3	3	6	0			
1994-95	Peoria Rivermen	IHL	69	26	43	69				15											9	9	1	10	4			
1995-96	Peoria Rivermen	IHL	60	16	27	43				22											1	0	0	0	0			
	NHL Totals		**650**	**187**	**185**	**372**	**159**	**131**	**290**	**169**	**39**	**3**	**29**	**1238**	**15.1**	**579**	**153**	**525**	**64**		**60**	**19**	**13**	**32**	**25**	**4**	**0**	**1**

Signed as a free agent by **Montreal**, October 5, 1981. Traded to **St. Louis** by **Montreal** with Gilbert Delorme and Doug Wickenheiser for Perry Turnbull, December 21, 1983. • Missed remainder of 1987-88 season recovering from back surgery, November, 1987. Traded to **Winnipeg** by **St. Louis** with Montreal's 3rd round choice (previously acquired, Winnipeg selected Kris Draper) in 1989 Entry Draft for NY Rangers' 3rd round choice (previously acquired, St. Louis selected Denny Felsner) in 1989 Entry Draft and Winnipeg's 2nd round choice (Steve Staios) in 1991 Entry Draft, June 17, 1989. Traded to **Buffalo** by **Winnipeg** for cash, February 4, 1991. Claimed by **San Jose** from **Buffalo** in Expansion Draft, May 30, 1991. Traded to **Quebec** by **San Jose** for Tony Hrkac, May 31, 1991. Signed as a free agent by **Philadelphia**, August 25, 1992. Traded to **Calgary** by **Philadelphia** for Calgary's 9th round choice (E.J. Bradley) in 1993 Entry Draft, March 18, 1993. • Played w/ RHI's St. Louis Vipers in 1999 (1-1-3-4-0).

• PATERA, Pavel

C – L. 6'1", 181 lbs. b: Kladno, Czech., 9/6/1971. Dallas' 4th, 153rd overall, in 1998.

Season	Club	League	GP	G	A	Pts	AG	AA	APts	PIM	PP	SH	GW	S	%	TGF	PGF	TGA	PGA	+/–	GP	G	A	Pts	PIM	PP	SH	GW
1990-91	Poldi Kladno	Czech.	3	0	0	0																						
1991-92	Poldi Kladno	Czech.	38	12	13	25				26											8	8	4	12	0			
1992-93	Poldi Kladno	Czech.	42	9	23	32																						
1993-94	Poldi Kladno	Czech-Rep	43	21	39	60															11	5	10	15				
1994-95	Poldi Kladno	Czech-Rep	43	26	49	75				24											11	5	7	12	6			
1995-96	Poldi Kladno	Czech-Rep	40	24	31	55				38											8	3	1	4	34			
1996-97	AIK Solna Stockholm	Sweden	50	19	24	43				44											7	2	3	5	6			
1997-98	AIK Solna Stockholm	Sweden	46	8	17	25				50																		
1998-99	HC Slovnaft Vsetin	Czech-Rep	52	16	37	53				58											12	5	*10	15				
	Czech-Republic	WC-A	12	3	4	7				6																		
99-2000	**Dallas Stars**	**NHL**	**12**	**1**	**4**	**5**	**1**	**4**	**5**	**4**	**0**	**0**	**0**	**18**	**5.6**	**6**	**1**	**6**	**0**	**–1**								
	HC Slovnaft Vsetin	Czech-Rep	29	8	14	22				36											9	3	4	7	8			
	Czech Republic	WC-A	9	1	1	2				4																		
	NHL Totals		**12**	**1**	**4**	**5**	**1**	**4**	**5**	**4**	**0**	**0**	**0**	**18**	**5.6**	**6**	**1**	**6**	**0**									

Traded to **Minnesota** by **Dallas** with Aaron Gavey, Dallas' 8th round choice (Eric Johansson) in 2000 Entry Draft and Minnesota's 4th round choice (previously acquired) in 2002 Entry Draft for Brad Lukowich and Minnesota's 3rd and 9th round choices in 2001 Entry Draft, June 25, 2000.

• PATERSON, Joe

Joseph Andrew LW – L. 6'2", 207 lbs. b: Toronto, Ont., 6/25/1960. Detroit's 5th, 87th overall, in 1979.

Season	Club	League	GP	G	A	Pts	AG	AA	APts	PIM	PP	SH	GW	S	%	TGF	PGF	TGA	PGA	+/–	GP	G	A	Pts	PIM	PP	SH	GW
1976-77	Weston Dodgers	OJHL	43	12	18	30				84																		
1977-78	London Knights	OMJHL	68	17	16	33				100											11	3	2	5	36			
1978-79	London Knights	OMJHL	59	22	19	41				158											7	2	3	5	13			
1979-80	London Knights	OMJHL	62	21	50	71				156											5	4	2	6	4			
	Kalamazoo Wings	IHL	4	1	2	3				2											3	2	1	3	11			
1980-81	**Detroit Red Wings**	**NHL**	**38**	**2**	**5**	**7**	**2**	**3**	**5**	**53**	**0**	**0**	**0**	**36**	**5.6**	**14**	**0**	**10**	**0**	**4**								
	Adirondack Red Wings	AHL	39	9	16	25				68																		
1981-82	**Detroit Red Wings**	**NHL**	**3**	**0**	**0**	**0**	**0**	**0**	**0**	**0**	**0**	**0**	**0**	**1**	**0.0**	**1**	**0**	**0**	**0**	**1**								
	Adirondack Red Wings	AHL	74	22	28	50				132											5	1	4	5	6			
1982-83	**Detroit Red Wings**	**NHL**	**33**	**2**	**1**	**3**	**2**	**1**	**3**	**14**	**0**	**0**	**1**	**18**	**11.1**	**5**	**0**	**14**	**1**	**–8**								
	Adirondack Red Wings	AHL	36	11	10	21				85											6	1	2	3	21			
1983-84	**Detroit Red Wings**	**NHL**	**41**	**2**	**5**	**7**	**2**	**3**	**5**	**148**	**0**	**0**	**0**	**26**	**7.7**	**13**	**0**	**13**	**0**	**0**	**3**	**0**	**0**	**0**	**7**	**0**	**0**	**0**
	Adirondack Red Wings	AHL	20	10	15	25				43																		
1984-85	**Philadelphia Flyers**	**NHL**	**6**	**0**	**0**	**0**	**0**	**0**	**0**	**31**	**0**	**0**	**0**	**4**	**0.0**	**0**	**0**	**1**	**0**	**–1**	**17**	**3**	**4**	**7**	**70**	**1**	**0**	**0**
	Hershey Bears	AHL	67	26	27	53				173																		
1985-86	**Philadelphia Flyers**	**NHL**	**5**	**0**	**0**	**0**	**0**	**0**	**0**	**12**	**0**	**0**	**0**	**4**	**0.0**	**2**	**0**	**1**	**0**	**1**								
	Hershey Bears	AHL	20	5	10	15				68																		
	Los Angeles Kings	**NHL**	**47**	**9**	**18**	**27**	**7**	**12**	**19**	**153**	**2**	**0**	**1**	**75**	**12.0**	**45**	**12**	**41**	**1**	**–7**								
1986-87	**Los Angeles Kings**	**NHL**	**45**	**2**	**1**	**3**	**2**	**1**	**3**	**158**	**0**	**0**	**1**	**30**	**6.7**	**5**	**0**	**20**	**0**	**–15**	**2**	**0**	**0**	**0**	**0**	**0**	**0**	**0**
1987-88	**Los Angeles Kings**	**NHL**	**32**	**1**	**3**	**4**	**1**	**2**	**3**	**113**	**0**	**0**	**0**	**20**	**5.0**	**6**	**0**	**16**	**0**	**–10**								
	New York Rangers	**NHL**	**21**	**1**	**3**	**4**	**1**	**2**	**3**	**63**	**0**	**0**	**0**	**9**	**11.1**	**7**	**0**	**12**	**1**	**–4**								
1988-89	**New York Rangers**	**NHL**	**20**	**0**	**1**	**1**	**0**	**1**	**1**	**84**	**0**	**0**	**0**	**8**	**0.0**	**2**	**0**	**5**	**0**	**–3**								
	Denver Rangers	IHL	9	5	4	9				31																		
1989-90	Flint Spirits	IHL	69	21	26	47				198											4	0	1	1	2			
1990-91	Binghamton Rangers	AHL	80	16	35	51				221											10	5	3	8	25			
1991-92	Binghamton Rangers	AHL	49	7	10	17				115											5	0	0	0	4			
	Phoenix Roadrunners	IHL	2	0	0	0				2																		
1992-1995	Adirondack Red Wings	AHL	DID NOT PLAY – ASSISTANT COACH																									
1995-1997	Sault Ste. Marie Greyhounds	OHL	DID NOT PLAY – COACHING																									
1997-1999	Beast of New Haven	AHL	DID NOT PLAY – ASSISTANT COACH																									
1999-2000	Louisville Panthers	AHL	DID NOT PLAY – COACHING																									
	NHL Totals		**291**	**19**	**37**	**56**	**17**	**25**	**42**	**829**	**2**	**0**	**3**	**231**	**8.2**	**100**	**12**	**133**	**3**		**22**	**3**	**4**	**7**	**77**	**1**	**0**	**0**

Traded to **Philadelphia** by **Detroit** with Murray Craven for Darryl Sittler, October 10, 1984. Trade to **LA Kings** by **Philadelphia** for Philadelphia's 4th round choice (previously acquired, Philadelphia selected Mark Bar) in 1986 Entry Draft, December 18, 1985. Traded to **NY Rangers** by **LA Kings** for Gord Walker and Mike Siltala, January 21, 1988.

• PATERSON, Mark

D – L. 5'11", 180 lbs. b: Ottawa, Ont., 2/22/1964. Hartford's 2nd, 35th overall, in 1982.

Season	Club	League	GP	G	A	Pts	AG	AA	APts	PIM	PP	SH	GW	S	%	TGF	PGF	TGA	PGA	+/–	GP	G	A	Pts	PIM	PP	SH	GW
1979-80	Nepean Royals	OMHA	STATISTICS NOT AVAILABLE																									
	Nepean Raiders	OJHL	1	0	0	0				0																		
1980-81	Nepean Raiders	OJHL	50	6	13	19				98																		
1981-82	Ottawa 67's	OHL	64	4	13	17				59											17	1	5	6	40			

			REGULAR SEASON																		PLAYOFFS							
Season	**Club**	**League**	**GP**	**G**	**A**	**Pts**	**AG**	**AA**	**APts**	**PIM**	**PP**	**SH**	**GW**	**S**	**%**	**TGF**	**PGF**	**TGA**	**PGA**	**+/–**	**GP**	**G**	**A**	**Pts**	**PIM**	**PP**	**SH**	**GW**
1982-83	Ottawa 67's	OHL	57	7	14	21	....	....	....	140	....	....	....	....	....	....	....	....	....	....	9	1	4	5	31	....	....	....
	Hartford Whalers	**NHL**	**2**	**0**	**0**	**0**	**0**	**0**	**0**	**0**	**0**	**0**	**0**	**1**	**0.0**	**0**	**0**	**1**	**0**	**–1**	....	....	....	....	....	....	....	....
1983-84	Ottawa 67's	OHL	45	8	16	24	....	....	....	114	....	....	....	....	....	....	....	....	....	....	13	2	7	9	16	....	....	....
	Canada	WJC-A	7	0	2	2	....	....	....	10	....	....	....	....	....	....	....	....	....	....	....	....	....	....	....	....	....	....
	Hartford Whalers	**NHL**	**9**	**2**	**0**	**2**	**2**	**0**	**2**	**4**	**0**	**0**	**0**	**10**	**20.0**	**13**	**0**	**9**	**0**	**4**	....	....	....	....	....	....	....	....
	Ottawa 67's	Mem-Cup	5	0	2	2	....	....	....	8	....	....	....	....	....	....	....	....	....	....	....	....	....	....	....	....	....	....
1984-85	**Hartford Whalers**	**NHL**	**13**	**1**	**3**	**4**	**1**	**2**	**3**	**24**	**0**	**0**	**0**	**9**	**11.1**	**9**	**0**	**16**	**1**	**–6**	....	....	....	....	....	....	....	....
	Binghamton Whalers	AHL	44	2	18	20	....	....	....	74	....	....	....	....	....	....	....	....	....	....	8	0	0	0	18	....	....	....
1985-86	**Hartford Whalers**	**NHL**	**5**	**0**	**0**	**0**	**0**	**0**	**0**	**5**	**0**	**0**	**0**	**0**	**0.0**	**0**	**0**	**5**	**0**	**–5**	....	....	....	....	....	....	....	....
	Binghamton Whalers	AHL	67	2	16	18	....	....	....	121	....	....	....	....	....	....	....	....	....	....	6	0	0	0	6	....	....	....
1986-87	Moncton Golden Flames	AHL	70	6	21	27	....	....	....	112	....	....	....	....	....	....	....	....	....	....	3	0	0	0	0	....	....	....
1987-88	Saginaw Hawks	IHL	23	1	5	6	....	....	....	55	....	....	....	....	....	....	....	....	....	....	8	0	4	4	15	....	....	....
1988-89	Saginaw Hawks	IHL	17	1	3	4	....	....	....	42	....	....	....	....	....	....	....	....	....	....	....	....	....	....	....	....	....	....
	NHL Totals		**29**	**3**	**3**	**6**	**3**	**2**	**5**	**33**	**0**	**0**	**0**	**20**	**15.0**	**22**	**0**	**31**	**1**		....	....	....	....	....	....	....	....

Traded to **Calgary** by **Hartford** for Yves Courteau, October 7, 1986.

• PATERSON, Rick

David Rick C – R. 5'9", 187 lbs. b: Kingston, Ont., 2/10/1958. Chicago's 3rd, 46th overall, in 1978.

Season	Club	League	GP	G	A	Pts	AG	AA	APts	PIM	PP	SH	GW	S	%	TGF	PGF	TGA	PGA	+/–	GP	G	A	Pts	PIM	PP	SH	GW
1973-74	Cornwall Royals	QMJHL	60	1	14	15	....	....	....	5	....	....	....	....	....	....	....	....	....	....	....	....	....	....	....	....	....	....
1974-75	Cornwall Royals	QMJHL	68	18	20	38	....	....	....	50	....	....	....	....	....	....	....	....	....	....	....	....	....	....	....	....	....	....
1975-76	Cornwall Royals	QMJHL	71	20	60	80	....	....	....	59	....	....	....	....	....	....	....	....	....	....	....	....	....	....	....	....	....	....
1976-77	Cornwall Royals	QMJHL	72	31	63	94	....	....	....	90	....	....	....	....	....	....	....	....	....	....	12	6	9	15	22	....	....	....
1977-78	Cornwall Royals	QMJHL	71	58	80	138	....	....	....	105	....	....	....	....	....	....	....	....	....	....	9	3	7	10	27	....	....	....
	Canada	WJC-A	6	1	2	3	....	....	....	0	....	....	....	....	....	....	....	....	....	....	....	....	....	....	....	....	....	....
1978-79	New Brunswick Hawks	AHL	73	21	19	40	....	....	....	30	....	....	....	....	....	....	....	....	....	....	5	0	1	1	9	....	....	....
	Chicago Black Hawks	**NHL**	....	....	....	....	....	....	....	....	....	....	....	....	....	....	....	....	....	....	**1**	**0**	**1**	**1**	**0**	**0**	**0**	**0**
1979-80	**Chicago Black Hawks**	**NHL**	**11**	**0**	**2**	**2**	**0**	**1**	**1**	**0**	**0**	**0**	**0**	**11**	**0.0**	**4**	**0**	**4**	**0**	**0**	**7**	**0**	**0**	**0**	**5**	**0**	**0**	**0**
	New Brunswick Hawks	AHL	55	22	30	52	....	....	....	18	....	....	....	....	....	....	....	....	....	....	12	5	6	11	9	....	....	....
1980-81	**Chicago Black Hawks**	**NHL**	**49**	**8**	**2**	**10**	**6**	**1**	**7**	**18**	**1**	**2**	**1**	**38**	**21.1**	**18**	**2**	**41**	**23**	**–2**	**2**	**1**	**0**	**1**	**0**	**0**	**1**	**0**
	New Brunswick Hawks	AHL	21	7	8	15	....	....	....	6	....	....	....	....	....	....	....	....	....	....	....	....	....	....	....	....	....	....
1981-82	**Chicago Black Hawks**	**NHL**	**48**	**4**	**7**	**11**	**3**	**5**	**8**	**8**	**0**	**0**	**1**	**45**	**8.9**	**17**	**0**	**60**	**41**	**–2**	**15**	**3**	**2**	**5**	**21**	**0**	**0**	**0**
	New Brunswick Hawks	AHL	30	8	16	24	....	....	....	45	....	....	....	....	....	....	....	....	....	....	....	....	....	....	....	....	....	....
1982-83	**Chicago Black Hawks**	**NHL**	**79**	**14**	**9**	**23**	**11**	**6**	**17**	**14**	**1**	**3**	**2**	**78**	**17.9**	**33**	**2**	**76**	**44**	**–1**	**13**	**1**	**1**	**2**	**4**	**0**	**1**	**1**
1983-84	**Chicago Black Hawks**	**NHL**	**72**	**7**	**6**	**13**	**6**	**4**	**10**	**41**	**0**	**0**	**0**	**64**	**10.9**	**33**	**0**	**83**	**37**	**–13**	**5**	**1**	**1**	**2**	**6**	**0**	**1**	**0**
1984-85	**Chicago Black Hawks**	**NHL**	**79**	**7**	**12**	**19**	**6**	**8**	**14**	**25**	**0**	**3**	**1**	**53**	**13.2**	**31**	**0**	**63**	**38**	**6**	**15**	**1**	**5**	**6**	**15**	**0**	**0**	**0**
1985-86	**Chicago Black Hawks**	**NHL**	**70**	**9**	**3**	**12**	**7**	**2**	**9**	**24**	**0**	**5**	**0**	**36**	**25.0**	**17**	**0**	**50**	**32**	**–1**	**3**	**0**	**0**	**0**	**0**	**0**	**0**	**0**
1986-87	**Chicago Blackhawks**	**NHL**	**22**	**1**	**2**	**3**	**1**	**1**	**2**	**6**	**0**	**1**	**0**	**4**	**25.0**	**5**	**0**	**12**	**8**	**1**	....	....	....	....	....	....	....	....
	Nova Scotia Oilers	AHL	31	5	7	12	....	....	....	2	....	....	....	....	....	....	....	....	....	....	5	0	1	1	10	....	....	....
1987-88	Saginaw Hawks	IHL	82	19	26	45	....	....	....	83	....	....	....	....	....	....	....	....	....	....	10	2	4	6	16	....	....	....
	NHL Totals		**430**	**50**	**43**	**93**	**40**	**28**	**68**	**136**	**2**	**14**	**5**	**329**	**15.2**	**158**	**4**	**389**	**223**		**61**	**7**	**10**	**17**	**51**	**0**	**3**	**1**

• PATEY, Doug

Douglas Edward RW – R. 5'11", 180 lbs. b: Toronto, Ont., 12/28/1956. Washington's 5th, 73rd overall, in 1976.

Season	Club	League	GP	G	A	Pts	AG	AA	APts	PIM	PP	SH	GW	S	%	TGF	PGF	TGA	PGA	+/–	GP	G	A	Pts	PIM	PP	SH	GW
1973-74	Dixie Beehives	OJHL	42	31	30	61	....	....	....	28	....	....	....	....	....	....	....	....	....	....	....	....	....	....	....	....	....	....
1974-75	Sault Ste. Marie Greyhounds	OMJHL	64	31	28	59	....	....	....	20	....	....	....	....	....	....	....	....	....	....	....	....	....	....	....	....	....	....
1975-76	Sault Ste. Marie Greyhounds	OMJHL	59	45	65	110	....	....	....	52	....	....	....	....	....	....	....	....	....	....	12	5	10	15	8	....	....	....
1976-77	**Washington Capitals**	**NHL**	**37**	**3**	**1**	**4**	**3**	**1**	**4**	**6**	**0**	**0**	**0**	**43**	**7.0**	**9**	**0**	**24**	**0**	**–15**	....	....	....	....	....	....	....	....
	Dayton Gems	IHL	38	11	16	27	....	....	....	23	....	....	....	....	....	....	....	....	....	....	4	1	1	2	2	....	....	....
1977-78	**Washington Capitals**	**NHL**	**2**	**0**	**1**	**1**	**0**	**1**	**1**	**0**	**0**	**0**	**0**	**0**	**0.0**	**1**	**0**	**0**	**0**	**1**	....	....	....	....	....	....	....	....
	Hershey Bears	AHL	79	27	33	60	....	....	....	23	....	....	....	....	....	....	....	....	....	....	....	....	....	....	....	....	....	....
1978-79	**Washington Capitals**	**NHL**	**6**	**1**	**0**	**1**	**1**	**0**	**1**	**2**	**0**	**0**	**0**	**6**	**16.7**	**1**	**0**	**3**	**0**	**–2**	....	....	....	....	....	....	....	....
	Hershey Bears	AHL	74	22	24	46	....	....	....	16	....	....	....	....	....	....	....	....	....	....	4	1	0	1	0	....	....	....
1979-80	Cincinnati Stingers	CHL	14	5	9	14	....	....	....	2	....	....	....	....	....	....	....	....	....	....	....	....	....	....	....	....	....	....
	Houston Apollos	CHL	33	15	15	30	....	....	....	16	....	....	....	....	....	....	....	....	....	....	....	....	....	....	....	....	....	....
1980-81	SaPKo Savonlinna	Finland-2	12	12	6	18	....	....	....	14	....	....	....	....	....	....	....	....	....	....	....	....	....	....	....	....	....	....
	NHL Totals		**45**	**4**	**2**	**6**	**4**	**2**	**6**	**8**	**0**	**0**	**0**	**49**	**8.2**	**11**	**0**	**27**	**0**		....	....	....	....	....	....	....	....

• Brother of Larry

Claimed by **Edmonton** from **Washington** in Expansion Draft, June 13, 1979.

• PATEY, Larry

Larry James C – L. 6'1", 185 lbs. b: Toronto, Ont., 3/19/1953. California's 7th, 130th overall, in 1973.

Season	Club	League	GP	G	A	Pts	AG	AA	APts	PIM	PP	SH	GW	S	%	TGF	PGF	TGA	PGA	+/–	GP	G	A	Pts	PIM	PP	SH	GW
1972-73	Braintree Bruins	NEJHL	47	36	27	63	....	....	....	....	....	....	....	....	....	....	....	....	....	....	....	....	....	....	....	....	....	....
1973-74	**California Golden Seals**	**NHL**	**1**	**0**	**0**	**0**	**0**	**0**	**0**	**0**	**0**	**0**	**0**	**0**	**0.0**	**0**	**0**	**0**	**0**	**0**	....	....	....	....	....	....	....	....
	Salt Lake Golden Eagles	WHL	76	40	43	83	....	....	....	91	....	....	....	....	....	....	....	....	....	....	5	2	2	4	15	....	....	....
1974-75	**California Golden Seals**	**NHL**	**79**	**25**	**20**	**45**	**22**	**15**	**37**	**68**	**8**	**1**	**4**	**156**	**16.0**	**62**	**20**	**73**	**11**	**–20**	....	....	....	....	....	....	....	....
1975-76	**California Golden Seals**	**NHL**	**18**	**4**	**4**	**8**	**3**	**3**	**6**	**23**	**1**	**0**	**0**	**25**	**16.0**	**11**	**4**	**15**	**0**	**–8**	....	....	....	....	....	....	....	....
	St. Louis Blues	**NHL**	**53**	**8**	**6**	**14**	**7**	**4**	**11**	**26**	**2**	**1**	**0**	**80**	**10.0**	**22**	**4**	**35**	**5**	**–12**	**3**	**1**	**1**	**2**	**2**	**1**	**0**	**1**
1976-77	**St. Louis Blues**	**NHL**	**80**	**21**	**29**	**50**	**19**	**22**	**41**	**41**	**1**	**2**	**2**	**134**	**15.7**	**62**	**3**	**70**	**22**	**11**	**4**	**1**	**0**	**1**	**0**	**0**	**0**	**0**
1977-78	**St. Louis Blues**	**NHL**	**80**	**17**	**17**	**34**	**15**	**13**	**28**	**29**	**3**	**0**	**3**	**129**	**13.2**	**46**	**5**	**76**	**15**	**–20**	....	....	....	....	....	....	....	....
1978-79	**St. Louis Blues**	**NHL**	**78**	**15**	**19**	**34**	**13**	**14**	**27**	**60**	**0**	**2**	**2**	**124**	**12.1**	**42**	**1**	**100**	**32**	**–27**	....	....	....	....	....	....	....	....
1979-80	**St. Louis Blues**	**NHL**	**78**	**17**	**17**	**34**	**14**	**12**	**26**	**76**	**0**	**3**	**3**	**144**	**11.8**	**42**	**0**	**77**	**17**	**–18**	**3**	**1**	**0**	**1**	**2**	**0**	**0**	**0**
1980-81	**St. Louis Blues**	**NHL**	**80**	**22**	**23**	**45**	**17**	**15**	**32**	**107**	**0**	**8**	**3**	**125**	**17.6**	**54**	**0**	**82**	**30**	**2**	**11**	**2**	**4**	**6**	**30**	**0**	**0**	**0**
1981-82	**St. Louis Blues**	**NHL**	**70**	**14**	**12**	**26**	**11**	**8**	**19**	**97**	**1**	**4**	**2**	**109**	**12.8**	**40**	**1**	**86**	**37**	**–10**	**10**	**2**	**4**	**6**	**13**	**0**	**1**	**0**
1982-83	**St. Louis Blues**	**NHL**	**67**	**9**	**12**	**21**	**7**	**8**	**15**	**80**	**0**	**3**	**0**	**72**	**12.5**	**28**	**0**	**71**	**37**	**–6**	**4**	**1**	**0**	**1**	**4**	**0**	**0**	**0**
1983-84	**St. Louis Blues**	**NHL**	**17**	**0**	**1**	**1**	**0**	**1**	**1**	**8**	**0**	**0**	**0**	**9**	**0.0**	**1**	**0**	**31**	**18**	**–12**	....	....	....	....	....	....	....	....
	New York Rangers	**NHL**	**9**	**1**	**2**	**3**	**1**	**1**	**2**	**4**	**0**	**1**	**0**	**6**	**16.7**	**6**	**0**	**9**	**3**	**0**	**4**	**0**	**1**	**1**	**6**	**0**	**0**	**0**
1984-85	**New York Rangers**	**NHL**	**7**	**0**	**1**	**1**	**0**	**1**	**1**	**12**	**0**	**0**	**0**	**2**	**0.0**	**1**	**0**	**7**	**0**	**–6**	**1**	**0**	**0**	**0**	**0**	**0**	**0**	**0**
	New Haven Nighthawks	AHL	62	14	14	28	....	....	....	43	....	....	....	....	....	....	....	....	....	....	....	....	....	....	....	....	....	....
	NHL Totals		**717**	**153**	**163**	**316**	**129**	**117**	**246**	**631**	**16**	**25**	**19**	**1115**	**13.7**	**417**	**38**	**732**	**227**		**40**	**8**	**10**	**18**	**57**	**1**	**1**	**1**

• Brother of Doug • Won WHL Rookie of the Year Award (1974)

Traded to **St. Louis** by **California** with California's 3rd round choice (later traded back to California - California/Cleveland selected Reg Kerr) in 1977 Amateur Draft for Wayne Merrick, November 24, 1975. Traded to **NY Rangers** by **St. Louis** with Bob Brooke for Dave Barr and NY Rangers' 3rd round choice (Alan Perry) in 1984 Entry Draft and cash, March 5, 1984.

• PATRICK, Craig

RW – L. 6', 190 lbs. b: Detroit, MI, 5/20/1946. **USHOF**

Season	Club	League	GP	G	A	Pts	AG	AA	APts	PIM	PP	SH	GW	S	%	TGF	PGF	TGA	PGA	+/–	GP	G	A	Pts	PIM	PP	SH	GW
1963-64	Lachine Maroons	MMJHL	43	12	31	43	....	....	....	12	....	....	....	....	....	....	....	....	....	....	....	....	....	....	....	....	....	....
	Montreal NDG Monarchs	Mem-Cup	4	4	1	5	....	....	....	0	....	....	....	....	....	....	....	....	....	....	....	....	....	....	....	....	....	....
1964-65	Montreal Jr. Canadiens	OHA-Jr.	56	13	18	31	....	....	....	18	....	....	....	....	....	....	....	....	....	....	7	1	0	1	2	....	....	....
1965-66	Los Angeles Hechter Hawks	CalHL	9	15	8	23	....	....	....	4	....	....	....	....	....	....	....	....	....	....	....	....	....	....	....	....	....	....
1966-67	University of Denver	WCHA	30	18	16	34	....	....	....	6	....	....	....	....	....	....	....	....	....	....	....	....	....	....	....	....	....	....
1967-68	University of Denver	WCHA	34	23	26	49	....	....	....	12	....	....	....	....	....	....	....	....	....	....	....	....	....	....	....	....	....	....
1968-69	University of Denver	WCHA	17	7	8	15	....	....	....	6	....	....	....	....	....	....	....	....	....	....	....	....	....	....	....	....	....	....
1969-70	University of Denver	WCHA	5	9	7	16	....	....	....	....	....	....	....	....	....	....	....	....	....	....	....	....	....	....	....	....	....	....
	United States	Nat-Team	6	0	3	3	....	....	....	0	....	....	....	....	....	....	....	....	....	....	....	....	....	....	....	....	....	....
	United States	WEC-B	7	8	5	13	....	....	....	2	....	....	....	....	....	....	....	....	....	....	....	....	....	....	....	....	....	....
1970-71	United States	Nat-Team	STATISTICS NOT AVAILABLE																									
	Montreal Voyageurs	AHL	3	0	1	1	....	....	....	0	....	....	....	....	....	....	....	....	....	....	....	....	....	....	....	....	....	....
	United States	WEC-A	10	3	2	5	....	....	....	2	....	....	....	....	....	....	....	....	....	....	....	....	....	....	....	....	....	....
1971-72	**California Golden Seals**	**NHL**	**59**	**8**	**3**	**11**	**8**	**3**	**11**	**12**	**0**	**0**	**0**	**73**	**11.0**	**20**	**1**	**51**	**8**	**–24**	....	....	....	....	....	....	....	....
	Baltimore Clippers	AHL	12	3	0	3	....	....	....	0	....	....	....	....	....	....	....	....	....	....	....	....	....	....	....	....	....	....
1972-73	**California Golden Seals**	**NHL**	**71**	**20**	**22**	**42**	**19**	**17**	**36**	**6**	**2**	**1**	**0**	**152**	**13.2**	**69**	**15**	**108**	**22**	**–32**	....	....	....	....	....	....	....	....
1973-74	**California Golden Seals**	**NHL**	**59**	**10**	**20**	**30**	**10**	**16**	**26**	**17**	**2**	**0**	**1**	**95**	**10.5**	**48**	**11**	**72**	**5**	**–30**	....	....	....	....	....	....	....	....

			REGULAR SEASON																		PLAYOFFS							
Season	Club	League	GP	G	A	Pts	AG	AA	APts	PIM	PP	SH	GW	S	%	TGF	PGF	TGA	PGA	+/–	GP	G	A	Pts	PIM	PP	SH	GW
1974-75	**California Golden Seals**	**NHL**	**14**	**2**	**1**	**3**	**2**	**1**	**3**	**0**	**0**	**0**	**0**	**15**	**13.3**	**4**	**0**	**13**	**1**	**–8**	....	....	....	....	....	....	....	....
	St. Louis Blues	**NHL**	**43**	**6**	**9**	**15**	**5**	**7**	**12**	**6**	**0**	**0**	**2**	**58**	**10.3**	**32**	**3**	**30**	**7**	**6**	**2**	**0**	**1**	**1**	**0**	**0**	**0**	**0**
1975-76	**Kansas City Scouts**	**NHL**	**80**	**17**	**18**	**35**	**15**	**13**	**28**	**14**	**3**	**1**	**0**	**143**	**11.9**	**63**	**10**	**109**	**32**	**–24**	....	....	....	....	....	....	....	....
1976-77	United States	Can-Cup	5	2	2	4	....	....	....	0	....	....	....	....	....	....	....	....	....	....	....	....	....	....	....	....	....	....
	Washington Capitals	**NHL**	**28**	**7**	**10**	**17**	**6**	**8**	**14**	**2**	**1**	**0**	**0**	**47**	**14.9**	**25**	**10**	**29**	**4**	**–10**	....	....	....	....	....	....	....	....
	Minnesota Fighting Saints	WHA	30	6	11	17	....	....	....	6	....	....	....	....	....	....	....	....	....	....	....	....	....	....	....	....	....	....
1977-78	**Washington Capitals**	**NHL**	**44**	**1**	**7**	**8**	**1**	**5**	**6**	**4**	**1**	**0**	**0**	**43**	**2.3**	**19**	**2**	**26**	**1**	**–8**	....	....	....	....	....	....	....	....
	Hershey Bears	AHL	27	5	4	9	....	....	....	4	....	....	....	....	....	....	....	....	....	....	....	....	....	....	....	....	....	....
1978-79	**Washington Capitals**	**NHL**	**3**	**1**	**1**	**2**	**1**	**1**	**2**	**0**	**0**	**0**	**0**	**3**	**33.3**	**2**	**0**	**3**	**0**	**–1**	....	....	....	....	....	....	....	....
	Tulsa Oilers	CHL	69	22	23	45	....	....	....	12	....	....	....	....	....	....	....	....	....	....	....	....	....	....	....	....	....	....
	United States	WEC-A	8	0	3	3	....	....	....	2	....	....	....	....	....	....	....	....	....	....	....	....	....	....	....	....	....	....
1979-80	Los Angeles Blades	PHL	7	0	1	1	....	....	....	27	....	....	....	....	....	....	....	....	....	....	....	....	....	....	....	....	....	....
1980-81	**New York Rangers**	**NHL**	DID NOT PLAY – ASSISTANT GENERAL MANAGER																									
1981-1986	**New York Rangers**	**NHL**	DID NOT PLAY – GENERAL MANAGER																									
1986-1989	University of Denver	WCHA	DID NOT PLAY – GENERAL MANAGER																									
1989-2000	**Pittsburgh Penguins**	**NHL**	DID NOT PLAY – GENERAL MANAGER																									
	NHL Totals		**401**	**72**	**91**	**163**	**67**	**71**	**138**	**61**	**9**	**2**	**3**	**629**	**11.4**	**282**	**52**	**441**	**80**		**2**	**0**	**1**	**1**	**0**	**0**	**0**	**0**
	Other Major League Totals		30	6	11	17	....	....	....	6	....	....	....	....	....	....	....	....	....	....	....	....	....	....	....	....	....	....

• Son of Lynn • Brother of Glenn • Won Lester Patrick Trophy (2000)

Signed as a free agent to five-game amateur tryout contract by **Montreal Voyageurs** (AHL), February 24, 1971. Signed as a free agent by **California**, October 6, 1971. Selected by **Miami-Philadelphia** (WHA) in 1972 WHA General Player Draft, February 12, 1972. Traded to **St. Louis** by **California** with Stan Gilbertson for Warren Williams and Dave Gardner, November 11, 1974. Traded to **Kansas City** by **St. Louis** with Denis Dupere and cash for Lynn Powis and Kansas City's 2nd round choice (Brian Sutter) in 1976 Amateur Draft, June 18, 1975. WHA rights traded to **Minnesota** (WHA) by **Calgary** (WHA) for future considerations, June, 1976. Signed as a free agent by **Washington** after **Minnesota** (WHA) franchise folded, February 1, 1977.
• Served as University of Denver's Director of Athletics, 1986-1989.

• PATRICK, Glenn

Glenn Curtiss D – L. 6'2", 190 lbs. b: New York, NY, 4/26/1950.

1968-1970	University of Denver	WCHA	STATISTICS NOT AVAILABLE																									
1970-71	University of Denver	WCHA	STATISTICS NOT AVAILABLE																									
	Kansas City Blues	CHL	3	0	0	0	....	....	....	0	....	....	....	....	....	....	....	....	....	....	....	....	....	....	....	....	....	....
1971-72	Columbus Seals	IHL	52	1	8	9	....	....	....	89	....	....	....	....	....	....	....	....	....	....	....	....	....	....	....	....	....	....
	Denver Spurs	WHL	5	0	1	1	....	....	....	6	....	....	....	....	....	....	....	....	....	....	9	0	2	2	21	....	....	....
1972-73	Denver Spurs	WHL	72	5	21	26	....	....	....	125	....	....	....	....	....	....	....	....	....	....	5	0	1	1	0	....	....	....
1973-74	**St. Louis Blues**	**NHL**	**1**	**0**	**0**	**0**	**0**	**0**	**0**	**2**	**0**	**0**	**0**	**0**	**0.0**	**0**	**0**	**1**	**0**	**–1**	....	....	....	....	....	....	....	....
	Denver Spurs	WHL	68	7	24	31	....	....	....	163	....	....	....	....	....	....	....	....	....	....	....	....	....	....	....	....	....	....
1974-75	**California Golden Seals**	**NHL**	**2**	**0**	**0**	**0**	**0**	**0**	**0**	**0**	**0**	**0**	**0**	**2**	**0.0**	**0**	**0**	**3**	**1**	**–2**	....	....	....	....	....	....	....	....
	Salt Lake Golden Eagles	CHL	75	2	26	28	....	....	....	151	....	....	....	....	....	....	....	....	....	....	11	1	2	3	31	....	....	....
1975-76	Salt Lake Golden Eagles	CHL	63	7	18	25	....	....	....	140	....	....	....	....	....	....	....	....	....	....	5	0	0	0	0	....	....	....
1976-77	**Cleveland Barons**	**NHL**	**35**	**2**	**3**	**5**	**2**	**2**	**4**	**70**	**0**	**0**	**0**	**26**	**7.7**	**22**	**0**	**40**	**7**	**–11**	....	....	....	....	....	....	....	....
	Salt Lake Golden Eagles	CHL	14	0	7	7	....	....	....	46	....	....	....	....	....	....	....	....	....	....	....	....	....	....	....	....	....	....
	Edmonton Oilers	WHA	23	0	4	4	....	....	....	62	....	....	....	....	....	....	....	....	....	....	2	0	0	0	0	....	....	....
1977-78	Hampton Gulls	AHL	13	0	1	1	....	....	....	21	....	....	....	....	....	....	....	....	....	....	....	....	....	....	....	....	....	....
	Hershey Bears	AHL	13	1	8	9	....	....	....	15	....	....	....	....	....	....	....	....	....	....	....	....	....	....	....	....	....	....
	United States	Nat-Team	9	1	3	4	....	....	....	4	....	....	....	....	....	....	....	....	....	....	....	....	....	....	....	....	....	....
	United States	WEC-A	9	1	3	4	....	....	....	4	....	....	....	....	....	....	....	....	....	....	....	....	....	....	....	....	....	....
1978-79	Hampton Aces	NEHL	11	0	1	1	....	....	....	11	....	....	....	....	....	....	....	....	....	....	....	....	....	....	....	....	....	....
1979-1982			OUT OF HOCKEY – RETIRED																									
1982-1984	Peoria Prancers	IHL	DID NOT PLAY – COACHING																									
1984-1992			OUT OF HOCKEY – RETIRED																									
1992-1994	Hampton Roads Admirals	ECHL	DID NOT PLAY – ASSISTANT COACH																									
1994-1997	**Pittsburgh Penguins**	**NHL**	DID NOT PLAY																									
1997-1999	Syracuse Crunch	AHL	DID NOT PLAY – ASSISTANT COACH																									
1999-2000	Wilkes-Barre Penguins	AHL	DID NOT PLAY – COACHING																									
	NHL Totals		**38**	**2**	**3**	**5**	**2**	**2**	**4**	**72**	**0**	**0**	**0**	**28**	**7.1**	**22**	**0**	**44**	**8**		....	....	....	....	....	....	....	....
	Other Major League Totals		23	0	4	4	....	....	....	62	....	....	....	....	....	....	....	....	....	....	2	0	0	0	0	....	....	....

• Son of Lynn • Brother of Craig

Signed as a free agent by **St. Louis**, March 10, 1970. Selected by **Miami-Philadelphia** (WHA) in 1972 WHA General Player Draft, February 12, 1972. Traded to **California** by **St. Louis** for Ron Serafini, July 18, 1974. Transferred to **Cleveland** after **California** franchise relocated, August 26, 1976. Signed as a free agent by **Edmonton** (WHA) after being released by Cleveland, February 10, 1977.

• PATRICK, James

James Alan "Jeep" D – R. 6'2", 198 lbs. b: Winnipeg, Man., 6/14/1963. NY Rangers' 1st, 9th overall, in 1981.

1980-81	Prince Albert Raiders	SJHL	59	21	61	82	....	....	....	162	....	....	....	....	....	....	....	....	....	....	....	....	....	....	....	....	....	....
	Prince Albert Raiders	Cen-Cup	....	....	....	....	....	....	....	....	....	....	....	....	....	....	....	....	....	....	....	....	....	....	....	....	....	....
1981-82	University of North Dakota	WCHA	42	5	24	29	....	....	....	26	....	....	....	....	....	....	....	....	....	....	....	....	....	....	....	....	....	....
	Canada	WJC-A	7	0	2	2	....	....	....	6	....	....	....	....	....	....	....	....	....	....	....	....	....	....	....	....	....	....
1982-83	University of North Dakota	WCHA	36	12	36	48	....	....	....	29	....	....	....	....	....	....	....	....	....	....	....	....	....	....	....	....	....	....
	Canada	WJC-A	7	0	2	2	....	....	....	4	....	....	....	....	....	....	....	....	....	....	....	....	....	....	....	....	....	....
	Canada	WEC-A	9	1	1	2	....	....	....	10	....	....	....	....	....	....	....	....	....	....	....	....	....	....	....	....	....	....
1983-84	Canada	Nat-Team	63	7	24	31	....	....	....	52	....	....	....	....	....	....	....	....	....	....	....	....	....	....	....	....	....	....
	Canada	Olympics	7	0	3	3	....	....	....	4	....	....	....	....	....	....	....	....	....	....	....	....	....	....	....	....	....	....
	New York Rangers	**NHL**	**12**	**1**	**7**	**8**	**1**	**5**	**6**	**2**	**0**	**0**	**0**	**15**	**6.7**	**18**	**5**	**10**	**3**	**6**	**5**	**0**	**3**	**3**	**2**	**0**	**0**	**0**
1984-85	**New York Rangers**	**NHL**	**75**	**8**	**28**	**36**	**6**	**19**	**25**	**71**	**4**	**1**	**1**	**101**	**7.9**	**94**	**25**	**105**	**19**	**–17**	**3**	**0**	**0**	**0**	**4**	**0**	**0**	**0**
1985-86	**New York Rangers**	**NHL**	**75**	**14**	**29**	**43**	**11**	**19**	**30**	**88**	**2**	**1**	**1**	**131**	**10.7**	**100**	**34**	**85**	**33**	**14**	**16**	**1**	**5**	**6**	**34**	**0**	**0**	**0**
1986-87	**New York Rangers**	**NHL**	**78**	**10**	**45**	**55**	**9**	**33**	**42**	**62**	**5**	**0**	**0**	**143**	**7.0**	**125**	**37**	**95**	**20**	**13**	**6**	**1**	**2**	**3**	**2**	**2**	**0**	**1**
	Canada	WEC-A	8	0	1	1	....	....	....	2	....	....	....	....	....	....	....	....	....	....	....	....	....	....	....	....	....	....
1987-88	Canada	Can-Cup	6	0	1	1	....	....	....	2	....	....	....	....	....	....	....	....	....	....	....	....	....	....	....	....	....	....
	New York Rangers	**NHL**	**70**	**17**	**45**	**62**	**14**	**32**	**46**	**52**	**9**	**0**	**1**	**187**	**9.1**	**120**	**52**	**78**	**26**	**16**	....	....	....	....	....	....	....	....
1988-89	**New York Rangers**	**NHL**	**68**	**11**	**36**	**47**	**9**	**25**	**34**	**41**	**6**	**0**	**2**	**147**	**7.5**	**107**	**49**	**80**	**25**	**3**	**4**	**0**	**1**	**1**	**2**	**0**	**0**	**0**
	Canada	WEC-A	10	2	2	4	....	....	....	8	....	....	....	....	....	....	....	....	....	....	....	....	....	....	....	....	....	....
1989-90	**New York Rangers**	**NHL**	**73**	**14**	**43**	**57**	**12**	**31**	**43**	**50**	**9**	**0**	**0**	**136**	**10.3**	**125**	**54**	**99**	**32**	**4**	**10**	**3**	**8**	**11**	**0**	**2**	**0**	**1**
1990-91	**New York Rangers**	**NHL**	**74**	**10**	**49**	**59**	**9**	**37**	**46**	**58**	**6**	**0**	**2**	**138**	**7.2**	**115**	**60**	**83**	**23**	**–5**	**6**	**0**	**0**	**0**	**6**	**0**	**0**	**0**
1991-92	**New York Rangers**	**NHL**	**80**	**14**	**57**	**71**	**13**	**43**	**56**	**54**	**6**	**0**	**1**	**148**	**9.5**	**143**	**52**	**82**	**25**	**34**	**13**	**0**	**7**	**7**	**12**	**0**	**0**	**0**
1992-93	**New York Rangers**	**NHL**	**60**	**5**	**21**	**26**	**4**	**14**	**18**	**61**	**3**	**0**	**0**	**99**	**5.1**	**82**	**28**	**80**	**27**	**1**	....	....	....	....	....	....	....	....
1993-94	**New York Rangers**	**NHL**	**6**	**0**	**3**	**3**	**0**	**2**	**2**	**2**	**0**	**0**	**0**	**6**	**0.0**	**4**	**1**	**4**	**2**	**1**	....	....	....	....	....	....	....	....
	Hartford Whalers	**NHL**	**47**	**8**	**20**	**28**	**7**	**16**	**23**	**32**	**4**	**1**	**2**	**65**	**12.3**	**54**	**24**	**57**	**15**	**–12**	....	....	....	....	....	....	....	....
	Calgary Flames	**NHL**	**15**	**2**	**2**	**4**	**2**	**2**	**4**	**6**	**1**	**0**	**0**	**20**	**10.0**	**14**	**2**	**9**	**3**	**6**	**7**	**0**	**1**	**1**	**6**	**0**	**0**	**0**
1994-95	**Calgary Flames**	**NHL**	**43**	**0**	**10**	**10**	**0**	**15**	**15**	**14**	**0**	**0**	**0**	**43**	**0.0**	**34**	**3**	**44**	**10**	**–3**	**5**	**0**	**1**	**1**	**0**	**0**	**0**	**0**
1995-96	**Calgary Flames**	**NHL**	**80**	**3**	**32**	**35**	**3**	**26**	**29**	**30**	**1**	**0**	**0**	**116**	**2.6**	**81**	**31**	**79**	**32**	**3**	**4**	**0**	**0**	**0**	**2**	**0**	**0**	**0**
1996-97	**Calgary Flames**	**NHL**	**19**	**3**	**1**	**4**	**3**	**1**	**4**	**6**	**1**	**0**	**0**	**22**	**13.6**	**15**	**2**	**16**	**5**	**2**	....	....	....	....	....	....	....	....
1997-98	**Calgary Flames**	**NHL**	**60**	**6**	**11**	**17**	**7**	**11**	**18**	**26**	**1**	**0**	**1**	**57**	**10.5**	**54**	**8**	**64**	**16**	**–2**	....	....	....	....	....	....	....	....
	Canada	WC-A	6	0	1	1	....	....	....	0	....	....	....	....	....	....	....	....	....	....	....	....	....	....	....	....	....	....
1998-99	**Buffalo Sabres**	**NHL**	**45**	**1**	**7**	**8**	**1**	**7**	**8**	**16**	**0**	**0**	**0**	**31**	**3.2**	**25**	**0**	**22**	**9**	**12**	**20**	**0**	**1**	**1**	**12**	**0**	**0**	**0**
99-2000	**Buffalo Sabres**	**NHL**	**66**	**5**	**8**	**13**	**6**	**7**	**13**	**22**	**0**	**0**	**3**	**40**	**12.5**	**38**	**0**	**43**	**13**	**8**	**5**	**0**	**1**	**1**	**2**	**0**	**0**	**0**
	NHL Totals		**1046**	**132**	**454**	**586**	**117**	**345**	**462**	**693**	**58**	**3**	**14**	**1645**	**8.0**	**1348**	**467**	**1135**	**338**		**104**	**5**	**30**	**35**	**84**	**4**	**0**	**2**

• Brother of Steve • WCHA Second All-Star Team (1982) • NCAA Chamionship All-Tournament Team (1982) • WCHA First All-Star Team (1983) • NCAA West All American Team (1983)

Traded to **Hartford** by **NY Rangers** with Darren Turcotte for Steve Larmer, Nick Kypreos, Barry Richter and Hartford's 6th round choice (Yuri Litvinov) in 1994 Entry Draft, November 2, 1993. Traded to **Calgary** by **Hartford** with Zarley Zalapski and Michael Nylander for Gary Suter, Paul Ranheim and Ted Drury, March 10, 1994. • Missed remainder of 1996-97 season recovering from knee injury originally suffered in game vs. Pittsburgh, October 24, 1996. Signed as a free agent by **Buffalo**, October 7, 1998.

• PATRICK, Steve
Stephen Gary "Steepashakis" RW – R. 6'4", 206 lbs. b: Winnipeg, Man., 2/4/1961. Buffalo's 1st, 20th overall, in 1980.

Season	Club	League	GP	G	A	Pts	AG	AA	APts	PIM	PP	SH	GW	S	%	TGF	PGF	TGA	PGA	+/-	Playoffs GP	G	A	Pts	PIM	PP	SH	GW
1978-79	Brandon Wheat Kings	WHL	52	23	31	54	....	....	....	105	....	....	....	....	....	....	....	....	....	....	22	6	12	18	44	....	....	....
	Brandon Wheat Kings	Mem-Cup	5	1	1	2	....	....	....	6	....	....	....	....	....	....	....	....	....	....	....	....	....	....	....	....	....	....
1979-80	Brandon Wheat Kings	WHL	71	28	38	66	....	....	....	185	....	....	....	....	....	....	....	....	....	....	11	6	6	12	19	....	....	....
1980-81	Brandon Wheat Kings	WHL	34	29	30	59	....	....	....	56	....	....	....	....	....	....	....	....	....	....	....	....	....	....	....	....	....	....
	Buffalo Sabres	**NHL**	**30**	**1**	**7**	**8**	**1**	**5**	**6**	**25**	**0**	**0**	**0**	**35**	**2.9**	**16**	**1**	**14**	**0**	**1**	**5**	**0**	**1**	**1**	**6**	**0**	**0**	**0**
1981-82	**Buffalo Sabres**	**NHL**	**41**	**8**	**8**	**16**	**6**	**5**	**11**	**64**	**0**	**0**	**0**	**52**	**15.4**	**23**	**1**	**23**	**4**	**3**	....	....	....	....	....	....	....	....
	Rochester Americans	AHL	38	11	9	20	....	....	....	15	....	....	....	....	....	....	....	....	....	....	5	3	2	5	12	....	....	....
1982-83	**Buffalo Sabres**	**NHL**	**56**	**9**	**13**	**22**	**7**	**9**	**16**	**26**	**0**	**0**	**1**	**63**	**14.3**	**37**	**2**	**37**	**6**	**4**	**2**	**0**	**0**	**0**	**0**	**0**	**0**	**0**
1983-84	**Buffalo Sabres**	**NHL**	**11**	**1**	**4**	**5**	**1**	**3**	**4**	**6**	**0**	**0**	**0**	**11**	**9.1**	**7**	**0**	**9**	**0**	**–2**	**1**	**0**	**0**	**0**	**0**	**0**	**0**	**0**
	Rochester Americans	AHL	30	8	14	22	....	....	....	33	....	....	....	....	....	....	....	....	....	....	13	2	1	3	18	....	....	....
1984-85	**Buffalo Sabres**	**NHL**	**14**	**2**	**2**	**4**	**2**	**1**	**3**	**4**	**0**	**0**	**0**	**12**	**16.7**	**5**	**0**	**8**	**0**	**–3**	....	....	....	....	....	....	....	....
	New York Rangers	**NHL**	**43**	**11**	**18**	**29**	**9**	**12**	**21**	**63**	**4**	**0**	**0**	**63**	**17.5**	**48**	**14**	**40**	**1**	**–5**	**1**	**0**	**0**	**0**	**0**	**0**	**0**	**0**
1985-86	**New York Rangers**	**NHL**	**28**	**4**	**3**	**7**	**3**	**2**	**5**	**37**	**0**	**0**	**0**	**20**	**20.0**	**10**	**0**	**17**	**0**	**–7**	....	....	....	....	....	....	....	....
	Quebec Nordiques	**NHL**	**27**	**4**	**13**	**17**	**3**	**9**	**12**	**17**	**1**	**0**	**0**	**29**	**13.8**	**35**	**11**	**23**	**0**	**1**	**3**	**0**	**0**	**0**	**6**	**0**	**0**	**0**
	NHL Totals		**250**	**40**	**68**	**108**	**32**	**46**	**78**	**242**	**5**	**0**	**1**	**285**	**14.0**	**181**	**29**	**171**	**11**		**12**	**0**	**1**	**1**	**12**	**0**	**0**	**0**

• Brother of James

Traded to **NY Rangers** by **Buffalo** with Jim Wiemer for Dave Maloney and Chris Renaud, December 6, 1984. Traded to **Quebec** by **NY Rangers** for Wilf Paiement, February 6, 1986.

• PATTERSON, Colin
Colin Alexander W – R. 6'2", 195 lbs. b: Rexdale, Ont., 5/11/1960.

Season	Club	League	GP	G	A	Pts	AG	AA	APts	PIM	PP	SH	GW	S	%	TGF	PGF	TGA	PGA	+/-	Playoffs GP	G	A	Pts	PIM	PP	SH	GW
1979-80	Royal York Royals	OJHL	41	30	60	*90	....	....	....	44	....	....	....	....	....	....	....	....	....	....	....	....	....	....	....	....	....	....
1980-81	Clarkson College	ECAC	34	20	31	51	....	....	....	8	....	....	....	....	....	....	....	....	....	....	....	....	....	....	....	....	....	....
1981-82	Clarkson College	ECAC	34	21	31	52	....	....	....	32	....	....	....	....	....	....	....	....	....	....	....	....	....	....	....	....	....	....
1982-83	Clarkson College	ECAC	31	23	29	52	....	....	....	30	....	....	....	....	....	....	....	....	....	....	....	....	....	....	....	....	....	....
	Colorado Flames	CHL	7	1	1	2	....	....	....	0	....	....	....	....	....	....	....	....	....	....	3	0	0	0	15	....	....	....
1983-84	**Calgary Flames**	**NHL**	**56**	**13**	**14**	**27**	**10**	**10**	**20**	**15**	**0**	**1**	**1**	**87**	**14.9**	**38**	**0**	**34**	**13**	**17**	**11**	**1**	**1**	**2**	**6**	**0**	**0**	**0**
	Colorado Flames	CHL	6	2	3	5	....	....	....	9	....	....	....	....	....	....	....	....	....	....	....	....	....	....	....	....	....	....
1984-85	**Calgary Flames**	**NHL**	**57**	**22**	**21**	**43**	**18**	**14**	**32**	**5**	**3**	**0**	**2**	**104**	**21.2**	**67**	**10**	**54**	**17**	**20**	**4**	**0**	**0**	**0**	**5**	**0**	**0**	**0**
1985-86	**Calgary Flames**	**NHL**	**61**	**14**	**13**	**27**	**11**	**9**	**20**	**22**	**0**	**0**	**1**	**84**	**16.7**	**47**	**1**	**67**	**29**	**8**	**19**	**6**	**3**	**9**	**10**	**1**	**1**	**1**
1986-87	**Calgary Flames**	**NHL**	**68**	**13**	**13**	**26**	**11**	**9**	**20**	**41**	**0**	**1**	**3**	**78**	**16.7**	**51**	**2**	**62**	**20**	**7**	**6**	**0**	**2**	**2**	**2**	**0**	**0**	**0**
1987-88	**Calgary Flames**	**NHL**	**39**	**7**	**11**	**18**	**6**	**8**	**14**	**28**	**0**	**0**	**0**	**37**	**18.9**	**35**	**1**	**47**	**20**	**7**	**9**	**1**	**0**	**1**	**8**	**0**	**1**	**0**
1988-89♦	**Calgary Flames**	**NHL**	**74**	**14**	**24**	**38**	**12**	**17**	**29**	**56**	**0**	**0**	**1**	**103**	**13.6**	**68**	**1**	**63**	**40**	**44**	**22**	**3**	**10**	**13**	**24**	**0**	**0**	**0**
1989-90	Calgary Flames	Fr-Tour	3	0	0	0	....	....	....	4	....	....	....	....	....	....	....	....	....	....	....	....	....	....	....	....	....	....
	Calgary Flames	**NHL**	**61**	**5**	**3**	**8**	**4**	**2**	**6**	**20**	**0**	**0**	**0**	**56**	**8.9**	**20**	**0**	**44**	**20**	**–4**	....	....	....	....	....	....	....	....
1990-91	**Calgary Flames**	**NHL**	....	....	....	....	....	....	....	....	....	....	....	....	....	....	....	....	....	....	**1**	**0**	**0**	**0**	**0**	**0**	**0**	**0**
1991-92	**Buffalo Sabres**	**NHL**	**52**	**4**	**8**	**12**	**4**	**6**	**10**	**30**	**0**	**2**	**0**	**33**	**12.1**	**20**	**0**	**41**	**17**	**–4**	**5**	**1**	**0**	**1**	**0**	**0**	**0**	**0**
1992-93	**Buffalo Sabres**	**NHL**	**36**	**4**	**2**	**6**	**3**	**1**	**4**	**22**	**0**	**1**	**0**	**30**	**13.3**	**11**	**0**	**25**	**12**	**–2**	**8**	**0**	**1**	**1**	**2**	**0**	**0**	**0**
1993-94	HK Olimpija Ljubljana	Slovenia	14	32	51	83	....	....	....	....	....	....	....	....	....	....	....	....	....	....	6	4	8	12	....	....	....	....
	NHL Totals		**504**	**96**	**109**	**205**	**79**	**76**	**155**	**239**	**3**	**5**	**8**	**612**	**15.7**	**357**	**15**	**437**	**188**		**85**	**12**	**17**	**29**	**57**	**1**	**2**	**1**

ECAC Second All-Star Team (1983) • NCAA East First All-American Team (1983)

Signed as a free agent by **Calgary**, March 24, 1983. • Missed entire 1990-91 regular season recovering from knee surgery, October 12, 1990. Traded to **Buffalo** by **Calgary** for future considerations, October 24, 1991.

• PATTERSON, Dennis
Dennis Gordon D – L. 5'8", 175 lbs. b: Peterborough, Ont., 1/9/1950. Minnesota's 3rd, 34th overall, in 1970.

Season	Club	League	GP	G	A	Pts	AG	AA	APts	PIM	PP	SH	GW	S	%	TGF	PGF	TGA	PGA	+/-	Playoffs GP	G	A	Pts	PIM	PP	SH	GW
1967-68	Chatham Maroons	OHA-B	STATISTICS NOT AVAILABLE																									
1968-69	Peterborough Petes	OHA-Jr.	54	5	17	22	....	....	....	56	....	....	....	....	....	....	....	....	....	....	10	0	2	2	12	....	....	....
1969-70	Peterborough Petes	OHA-Jr.	54	8	29	37	....	....	....	84	....	....	....	....	....	....	....	....	....	....	6	0	3	3	6	....	....	....
1970-71	Clinton Comets	EHL	72	6	30	36	....	....	....	93	....	....	....	....	....	....	....	....	....	....	....	....	....	....	....	....	....	....
	Cleveland Barons	AHL	9	0	2	2	....	....	....	4	....	....	....	....	....	....	....	....	....	....	8	0	1	1	22	....	....	....
1971-72	Cleveland Barons	AHL	76	3	17	20	....	....	....	62	....	....	....	....	....	....	....	....	....	....	6	0	1	1	12	....	....	....
1972-73	Cleveland Barons	AHL	42	1	11	12	....	....	....	40	....	....	....	....	....	....	....	....	....	....	....	....	....	....	....	....	....	....
1973-74	New Haven Eagles	AHL	70	8	25	33	....	....	....	69	....	....	....	....	....	....	....	....	....	....	10	1	3	4	4	....	....	....
1974-75	**Kansas City Scouts**	**NHL**	**66**	**1**	**5**	**6**	**1**	**4**	**5**	**39**	**0**	**0**	**0**	**53**	**1.9**	**41**	**2**	**113**	**17**	**–57**	....	....	....	....	....	....	....	....
	Baltimore Clippers	AHL	12	1	3	4	....	....	....	6	....	....	....	....	....	....	....	....	....	....	....	....	....	....	....	....	....	....
1975-76	**Kansas City Scouts**	**NHL**	**69**	**5**	**16**	**21**	**4**	**12**	**16**	**28**	**0**	**0**	**0**	**76**	**6.6**	**60**	**7**	**98**	**17**	**–28**	....	....	....	....	....	....	....	....
	Springfield Indians	AHL	10	0	5	5	....	....	....	12	....	....	....	....	....	....	....	....	....	....	....	....	....	....	....	....	....	....
1976-77	Rhode Island Reds	AHL	51	3	18	21	....	....	....	22	....	....	....	....	....	....	....	....	....	....	....	....	....	....	....	....	....	....
	Edmonton Oilers	WHA	23	0	2	2	....	....	....	2	....	....	....	....	....	....	....	....	....	....	....	....	....	....	....	....	....	....
1977-78	Maine Mariners	AHL	78	3	24	27	....	....	....	26	....	....	....	....	....	....	....	....	....	....	12	0	3	3	22	....	....	....
1978-79	Maine Mariners	AHL	74	3	29	32	....	....	....	112	....	....	....	....	....	....	....	....	....	....	10	1	4	5	32	....	....	....
1979-80	**Philadelphia Flyers**	**NHL**	**3**	**0**	**1**	**1**	**0**	**1**	**1**	**0**	**0**	**0**	**0**	**3**	**0.0**	**1**	**0**	**2**	**0**	**–1**	....	....	....	....	....	....	....	....
	Maine Mariners	AHL	67	2	25	27	....	....	....	72	....	....	....	....	....	....	....	....	....	....	10	2	6	8	20	....	....	....
1980-81	Maine Mariners	AHL	70	3	26	29	....	....	....	74	....	....	....	....	....	....	....	....	....	....	....	....	....	....	....	....	....	....
1981-82	Maine Mariners	AHL	51	1	14	15	....	....	....	111	....	....	....	....	....	....	....	....	....	....	4	0	0	0	12	....	....	....
1982-83	Maine Mariners	AHL	76	1	19	20	....	....	....	71	....	....	....	....	....	....	....	....	....	....	17	0	4	4	9	....	....	....
	NHL Totals		**138**	**6**	**22**	**28**	**5**	**17**	**22**	**67**	**0**	**0**	**0**	**132**	**4.5**	**102**	**9**	**213**	**34**		....	....	....	....	....	....	....	....
	Other Major League Totals		23	0	2	2	....	....	....	2	....	....	....	....	....	....	....	....	....	....	....	....	....	....	....	....	....	....

AHL Second All-Star Team (1979, 1980, 1981)

Claimed by **Kansas City** from **Minnesota** in Expansion Draft, June 12, 1974. Signed as a free agent by **Edmonton** (WHA), September, 1976. Signed as a free agent by **Philadelphia**, August 8, 1979.

• PATTERSON, Ed
RW – R. 6'2", 213 lbs. b: Delta, B.C., 11/14/1972. Pittsburgh's 7th, 148th overall, in 1991.

Season	Club	League	GP	G	A	Pts	AG	AA	APts	PIM	PP	SH	GW	S	%	TGF	PGF	TGA	PGA	+/-	Playoffs GP	G	A	Pts	PIM	PP	SH	GW
1987-88	South Delta Selects	BCAHA	50	40	70	110	....	....	....	60	....	....	....	....	....	....	....	....	....	....	....	....	....	....	....	....	....	....
1988-89	Seattle Thunderbirds	WHL	46	4	6	10	....	....	....	55	....	....	....	....	....	....	....	....	....	....	....	....	....	....	....	....	....	....
1989-90	Seattle Thunderbirds	WHL	18	9	2	11	....	....	....	19	....	....	....	....	....	....	....	....	....	....	....	....	....	....	....	....	....	....
	Swift Current Broncos	WHL	15	1	3	4	....	....	....	0	....	....	....	....	....	....	....	....	....	....	4	0	0	0	2	....	....	....
1990-91	Swift Current Broncos	WHL	7	2	7	9	....	....	....	0	....	....	....	....	....	....	....	....	....	....	....	....	....	....	....	....	....	....
	Kamloops Blazers	WHL	55	14	33	47	....	....	....	134	....	....	....	....	....	....	....	....	....	....	5	0	0	0	7	....	....	....
1991-92	Kamloops Blazers	WHL	38	19	25	44	....	....	....	100	....	....	....	....	....	....	....	....	....	....	1	0	0	0	0	....	....	....
	Kamloops Blazers	Mem-Cup	5	0	2	2	....	....	....	2	....	....	....	....	....	....	....	....	....	....	....	....	....	....	....	....	....	....
1992-93	Cleveland Lumberjacks	IHL	63	4	16	20	....	....	....	131	....	....	....	....	....	....	....	....	....	....	3	1	1	2	2	....	....	....
1993-94	**Pittsburgh Penguins**	**NHL**	**27**	**3**	**1**	**4**	**3**	**1**	**4**	**10**	**0**	**0**	**0**	**15**	**20.0**	**4**	**0**	**11**	**2**	**–5**	....	....	....	....	....	....	....	....
	Cleveland Lumberjacks	IHL	55	21	32	53	....	....	....	73	....	....	....	....	....	....	....	....	....	....	....	....	....	....	....	....	....	....
1994-95	Cleveland Lumberjacks	IHL	58	13	17	30	....	....	....	93	....	....	....	....	....	....	....	....	....	....	4	1	2	3	6	....	....	....
1995-96	**Pittsburgh Penguins**	**NHL**	**35**	**0**	**2**	**2**	**0**	**2**	**2**	**38**	**0**	**0**	**0**	**17**	**0.0**	**2**	**0**	**11**	**4**	**–5**	....	....	....	....	....	....	....	....
1996-97	**Pittsburgh Penguins**	**NHL**	**6**	**0**	**0**	**0**	**0**	**0**	**0**	**8**	**0**	**0**	**0**	**2**	**0.0**	**1**	**0**	**2**	**1**	**0**	....	....	....	....	....	....	....	....
	Cleveland Lumberjacks	IHL	40	6	12	18	....	....	....	75	....	....	....	....	....	....	....	....	....	....	13	2	4	6	61	....	....	....
1997-98	Grand Rapids Griffins	IHL	81	12	31	43	....	....	....	226	....	....	....	....	....	....	....	....	....	....	3	2	1	3	8	....	....	....
1998-99	Cincinnati Cyclones	IHL	73	8	25	33	....	....	....	227	....	....	....	....	....	....	....	....	....	....	3	1	0	1	4	....	....	....
99-2000	Grand Rapids Griffins	IHL	74	20	21	41	....	....	....	141	....	....	....	....	....	....	....	....	....	....	5	4	0	4	2	....	....	....
	NHL Totals		**68**	**3**	**3**	**6**	**3**	**3**	**6**	**56**	**0**	**0**	**0**	**34**	**8.8**	**7**	**0**	**24**	**7**		....	....	....	....	....	....	....	....

Signed as a free agent by **Grand Rapids** (IHL), September 14, 1999.

• PAVELICH, Mark
Mark Thomas "Weber" C – R. 5'8", 170 lbs. b: Eveleth, MN, 2/28/1958.

Season	Club	League	GP	G	A	Pts	AG	AA	APts	PIM	PP	SH	GW	S	%	TGF	PGF	TGA	PGA	+/-	Playoffs GP	G	A	Pts	PIM	PP	SH	GW
1976-77	University of Minnesota-Duluth	WCHA	37	12	7	19	....	....	....	8	....	....	....	....	....	....	....	....	....	....	....	....	....	....	....	....	....	....
1977-78	University of Minnesota-Duluth	WCHA	36	14	30	44	....	....	....	44	....	....	....	....	....	....	....	....	....	....	....	....	....	....	....	....	....	....
1978-79	University of Minnesota-Duluth	WCHA	37	31	48	79	....	....	....	52	....	....	....	....	....	....	....	....	....	....	....	....	....	....	....	....	....	....

			REGULAR SEASON																		PLAYOFFS							
Season	Club	League	GP	G	A	Pts	AG	AA	APts	PIM	PP	SH	GW	S	%	TGF	PGF	TGA	PGA	+/–	GP	G	A	Pts	PIM	PP	SH	GW
1979-80	United States	Nat-Team	53	15	30	45	....	....	....	12	....	....	....	....	....	....	....	....	....	....	....	....	....	....	....	....	....	....
	United States	Olympics	7	1	6	7	....	....	....	2	....	....	....	....	....	....	....	....	....	....	....	....	....	....	....	....	....	....
1980-81	HC Lugano	Switz.	60	24	49	73	....	....	....	....	....	....	....	....	....	....	....	....	....	....	....	....	....	....	....	....	....	....
	United States	WEC-A	8	2	3	5	....	....	....	4	....	....	....	....	....	....	....	....	....	....	....	....	....	....	....	....	....	....
1981-82	**New York Rangers**	**NHL**	79	33	43	76	26	29	55	67	12	3	3	180	18.3	113	34	83	25	21	6	1	5	6	0	0	0	0
1982-83	**New York Rangers**	**NHL**	78	37	38	75	30	26	56	52	10	2	6	154	24.0	107	33	71	17	20	9	4	5	9	12	2	0	2
1983-84	**New York Rangers**	**NHL**	77	29	53	82	23	36	59	96	12	1	2	164	17.7	118	41	92	26	11	5	2	4	6	0	0	1	0
1984-85	**New York Rangers**	**NHL**	48	14	31	45	11	21	32	29	6	0	3	91	15.4	66	27	45	7	1	3	0	3	3	2	0	0	0
1985-86	**New York Rangers**	**NHL**	59	20	20	40	16	13	29	82	8	0	3	104	19.2	59	23	40	1	–3	....	....	....	....	....	....	....	....
1986-87	**Minnesota North Stars**	**NHL**	12	4	6	10	3	4	7	10	0	0	0	25	16.0	19	4	9	1	7	....	....	....	....	....	....	....	....
	Dundee Rockets	Britain	1	0	2	2	....	....	....	0	....	....	....	....	....	....	....	....	....	....	....	....	....	....	....	....	....	....
1987-88	HC Bolzano	Italy	36	31	44	75	....	....	....	19	....	....	....	....	....	....	....	....	....	....	8	9	13	22	8	....	....	....
1988-89	HC Bolzano	Italy	44	23	34	57	....	....	....	42	....	....	....	....	....	....	....	....	....	....	....	....	....	....	....	....	....	....
1989-90			DID NOT PLAY																									
1990-91			DID NOT PLAY																									
1991-92	**San Jose Sharks**	**NHL**	2	0	1	1	0	1	1	4	0	0	0	0	0.0	1	0	3	0	–2	....	....	....	....	....	....	....	....
	NHL Totals		355	137	192	329	109	130	239	340	48	6	17	718	19.1	483	162	343	77		23	7	17	24	14	2	1	2

WCHA First All-Star Team (1979) • NCAA West First All-American Team (1979)

Signed as a free agent by **NY Rangers**, June 5, 1981. Traded to **Minnesota** by **NY Rangers** for Minnesota's 2nd round choice (Troy Mallette) in 1988 Entry Draft, October 24, 1986. Signed as a free agent by **San Jose**, August 9, 1991.

• PAVESE, Jim

James Peter D – L. 6'2", 205 lbs. b: New York, NY, 5/8/1962. St. Louis' 2nd, 54th overall, in 1980.

Season	Club	League	GP	G	A	Pts	AG	AA	APts	PIM	PP	SH	GW	S	%	TGF	PGF	TGA	PGA	+/–	GP	G	A	Pts	PIM	PP	SH	GW
1975-76	Suffolk Royals	NYJHL	42	1	9	10	....	....	....	72	....	....	....	....	....	....	....	....	....	....	....	....	....	....	....	....	....	....
1976-77	Suffolk Royals	NYJHL	32	6	31	37	....	....	....	32	....	....	....	....	....	....	....	....	....	....	....	....	....	....	....	....	....	....
1977-78	Suffolk Royals	NYJHL	34	18	40	58	....	....	....	102	....	....	....	....	....	....	....	....	....	....	....	....	....	....	....	....	....	....
1978-79	Peterborough Jr. Bees	OJHL	34	8	32	40	....	....	....	106	....	....	....	....	....	....	....	....	....	....	....	....	....	....	....	....	....	....
	Peterborough Petes	OMJHL	16	1	1	2	....	....	....	22	....	....	....	....	....	....	....	....	....	....	2	0	0	0	0	....	....	....
1979-80	Kitchener Rangers	OMJHL	68	10	26	36	....	....	....	206	....	....	....	....	....	....	....	....	....	....	....	....	....	....	....	....	....	....
1980-81	Kitchener Rangers	OMJHL	19	3	12	15	....	....	....	93	....	....	....	....	....	....	....	....	....	....	....	....	....	....	....	....	....	....
	Sault Ste. Marie Greyhounds	OMJHL	43	3	25	28	....	....	....	127	....	....	....	....	....	....	....	....	....	....	19	1	3	4	69	....	....	....
1981-82	Sault Ste. Marie Greyhounds	OHL	26	4	21	25	....	....	....	110	....	....	....	....	....	....	....	....	....	....	13	2	12	14	38	....	....	....
	St. Louis Blues	**NHL**	42	2	9	11	2	6	8	101	0	0	1	29	6.9	40	1	66	13	–14	3	0	3	3	2	0	0	0
	Salt Lake Golden Eagles	CHL	....	....	....	....	....	....	....	....	....	....	....	....	....	....	....	....	....	....	1	0	0	0	17	....	....	....
1982-83	**St. Louis Blues**	**NHL**	24	0	2	2	0	1	1	45	0	0	0	9	0.0	19	0	30	0	–11	4	0	0	0	6	0	0	0
	Salt Lake Golden Eagles	CHL	36	5	6	11	....	....	....	165	....	....	....	....	....	....	....	....	....	....	4	1	3	4	2	....	....	....
1983-84	**St. Louis Blues**	**NHL**	4	0	1	1	0	1	1	19	0	0	0	1	0.0	3	0	4	0	–1	....	....	....	....	....	....	....	....
	Montana Magic	CHL	47	1	19	20	....	....	....	147	....	....	....	....	....	....	....	....	....	....	....	....	....	....	....	....	....	....
1984-85	**St. Louis Blues**	**NHL**	51	2	5	7	2	3	5	69	0	0	1	27	7.4	31	1	35	1	–4	1	0	0	0	5	0	0	0
1985-86	**St. Louis Blues**	**NHL**	69	4	7	11	3	5	8	116	1	0	0	51	7.8	61	3	80	19	–3	19	0	2	2	51	0	0	0
1986-87	**St. Louis Blues**	**NHL**	69	2	9	11	2	7	9	127	0	0	0	45	4.4	39	1	74	15	–21	2	0	0	0	2	0	0	0
1987-88	**St. Louis Blues**	**NHL**	4	0	1	1	0	1	1	8	0	0	0	3	0.0	1	0	4	2	–1	....	....	....	....	....	....	....	....
	New York Rangers	**NHL**	14	0	1	1	0	1	1	48	0	0	0	13	0.0	5	0	14	2	–7	....	....	....	....	....	....	....	....
	Colorado Rangers	IHL	1	0	0	0	....	....	....	2	....	....	....	....	....	....	....	....	....	....	....	....	....	....	....	....	....	....
	Detroit Red Wings	**NHL**	7	0	3	3	0	2	2	21	0	0	0	4	0.0	8	1	7	3	3	4	0	1	1	15	0	0	0
	New Haven Nighthawks	AHL	1	0	1	1	....	....	....	0	....	....	....	....	....	....	....	....	....	....	....	....	....	....	....	....	....	....
1988-89	**Detroit Red Wings**	**NHL**	39	3	6	9	3	4	7	130	0	0	0	27	11.1	35	0	44	8	–1	....	....	....	....	....	....	....	....
	Hartford Whalers	**NHL**	5	0	0	0	0	0	0	5	0	0	0	6	0.0	1	0	2	0	–1	1	0	0	0	0	0	0	0
1989-90			DID NOT PLAY																									
1990-91	New Haven Nighthawks	AHL	55	4	14	18	....	....	....	73	....	....	....	....	....	....	....	....	....	....	....	....	....	....	....	....	....	....
	NHL Totals		328	13	44	57	12	31	43	689	1	0	2	215	6.0	243	7	360	63		34	0	6	6	81	0	0	0

Traded to **NY Rangers** by **St. Louis** for future considerations, October 23, 1987. Traded to **Detroit** by **NY Rangers** for future considerations, March 8, 1988. Traded to **Hartford** by **Detroit** for Torrie Robertson, March 7, 1989.

• PAYNE, Davis

LW – L. 6'2", 205 lbs. b: Port Alberni, B.C., 9/24/1970. Edmonton's 6th, 140th overall, in 1989.

Season	Club	League	GP	G	A	Pts	AG	AA	APts	PIM	PP	SH	GW	S	%	TGF	PGF	TGA	PGA	+/–	GP	G	A	Pts	PIM	PP	SH	GW
1986-87	Kamloops Lions	BCAHA	48	25	35	60	....	....	....	....	....	....	....	....	....	....	....	....	....	....	....	....	....	....	....	....	....	....
1987-88	Kamloops Chiefs	RMJHL	53	58	64	122	....	....	....	....	....	....	....	....	....	....	....	....	....	....	....	....	....	....	....	....	....	....
1988-89	Michigan Tech Huskies	WCHA	35	5	3	8	....	....	....	39	....	....	....	....	....	....	....	....	....	....	....	....	....	....	....	....	....	....
1989-90	Michigan Tech Huskies	WCHA	30	11	10	21	....	....	....	81	....	....	....	....	....	....	....	....	....	....	....	....	....	....	....	....	....	....
1990-91	Michigan Tech Huskies	WCHA	41	15	20	35	....	....	....	82	....	....	....	....	....	....	....	....	....	....	....	....	....	....	....	....	....	....
1991-92	Michigan Tech Huskies	WCHA	24	6	1	7	....	....	....	71	....	....	....	....	....	....	....	....	....	....	....	....	....	....	....	....	....	....
1992-93	Greensboro Monarchs	ECHL	57	15	20	35	....	....	....	178	....	....	....	....	....	....	....	....	....	....	1	0	0	0	4	....	....	....
1993-94	Greensboro Monarchs	ECHL	36	17	17	34	....	....	....	139	....	....	....	....	....	....	....	....	....	....	8	2	1	3	27	....	....	....
	Phoenix Roadrunners	IHL	22	6	3	9	....	....	....	51	....	....	....	....	....	....	....	....	....	....	....	....	....	....	....	....	....	....
	Rochester Americans	AHL	2	0	0	0	....	....	....	5	....	....	....	....	....	....	....	....	....	....	3	0	2	2	0	....	....	....
1994-95	Greensboro Monarchs	ECHL	62	25	36	61	....	....	....	195	....	....	....	....	....	....	....	....	....	....	17	7	10	17	38	....	....	....
	Providence Bruins	AHL	2	1	0	1	....	....	....	0	....	....	....	....	....	....	....	....	....	....	....	....	....	....	....	....	....	....
1995-96	**Boston Bruins**	**NHL**	7	0	0	0	0	0	0	7	0	0	0	2	0.0	0	0	0	0	0	....	....	....	....	....	....	....	....
	Providence Bruins	AHL	51	17	22	39	....	....	....	72	....	....	....	....	....	....	....	....	....	....	4	1	4	5	2	....	....	....
1996-97	**Boston Bruins**	**NHL**	15	0	1	1	0	1	1	7	0	0	0	8	0.0	2	1	7	2	–4	....	....	....	....	....	....	....	....
	Providence Bruins	AHL	57	18	15	33	....	....	....	104	....	....	....	....	....	....	....	....	....	....	....	....	....	....	....	....	....	....
1997-98	Providence Bruins	AHL	3	0	0	0	....	....	....	0	....	....	....	....	....	....	....	....	....	....	....	....	....	....	....	....	....	....
	San Antonio Dragons	IHL	59	15	10	25	....	....	....	117	....	....	....	....	....	....	....	....	....	....	....	....	....	....	....	....	....	....
1998-99	Greenville Growl	ECHL	43	19	20	39	....	....	....	96	....	....	....	....	....	....	....	....	....	....	....	....	....	....	....	....	....	....
99-2000	Greenville Growl	ECHL	48	22	25	47	....	....	....	104	....	....	....	....	....	....	....	....	....	....	5	0	0	0	6	....	....	....
	NHL Totals		22	0	1	1	0	1	1	14	0	0	0	10	0.0	2	1	7	2		....	....	....	....	....	....	....	....

Signed as a free agent by **Boston**, September 6, 1995.

• PAYNE, Steve

Steven John LW – L. 6'2", 210 lbs. b: Toronto, Ont., 8/16/1958. Minnesota's 2nd, 19th overall, in 1978.

Season	Club	League	GP	G	A	Pts	AG	AA	APts	PIM	PP	SH	GW	S	%	TGF	PGF	TGA	PGA	+/–	GP	G	A	Pts	PIM	PP	SH	GW
1976-77	Ottawa 67's	OMJHL	61	25	26	51	....	....	....	22	....	....	....	....	....	....	....	....	....	....	19	4	14	18	5	....	....	....
	Ottawa 67's	Mem-Cup	5	1	0	1	....	....	....	0	....	....	....	....	....	....	....	....	....	....	....	....	....	....	....	....	....	....
1977-78	Ottawa 67's	OMJHL	52	57	37	94	....	....	....	22	....	....	....	....	....	....	....	....	....	....	16	12	8	20	4	....	....	....
1978-79	**Minnesota North Stars**	**NHL**	70	23	17	40	20	12	32	29	3	0	2	165	13.9	63	11	57	0	–5	....	....	....	....	....	....	....	....
	Oklahoma City Stars	CHL	5	3	4	7	....	....	....	2	....	....	....	....	....	....	....	....	....	....	....	....	....	....	....	....	....	....
	Canada	WEC-A	7	2	0	2	....	....	....	2	....	....	....	....	....	....	....	....	....	....	....	....	....	....	....	....	....	....
1979-80	**Minnesota North Stars**	**NHL**	80	42	43	85	36	31	67	40	16	0	2	233	18.0	138	47	55	1	37	15	7	7	14	9	3	0	3
1980-81	Minnesota North Stars	DN-Cup	2	0	0	0	....	....	....	0	....	....	....	....	....	....	....	....	....	....	....	....	....	....	....	....	....	....
	Minnesota North Stars	**NHL**	76	30	28	58	23	19	42	88	11	0	2	243	12.3	105	49	42	0	14	19	17	12	29	6	6	0	4
1981-82	**Minnesota North Stars**	**NHL**	74	33	45	78	26	30	56	76	11	0	3	239	13.8	115	40	56	1	20	4	4	2	6	2	2	0	0
1982-83	**Minnesota North Stars**	**NHL**	80	30	39	69	25	27	52	53	14	1	2	199	15.1	112	48	75	2	–9	9	3	6	9	19	1	0	0
1983-84	**Minnesota North Stars**	**NHL**	78	28	31	59	22	21	43	49	7	0	2	174	16.1	94	27	71	2	–2	15	3	6	9	18	1	0	2
1984-85	**Minnesota North Stars**	**NHL**	76	29	22	51	24	15	39	61	14	0	4	224	12.9	75	31	59	1	–14	9	1	2	3	6	0	0	0
1985-86	**Minnesota North Stars**	**NHL**	22	8	4	12	6	3	9	8	3	0	2	60	13.3	19	7	12	0	0	....	....	....	....	....	....	....	....
1986-87	**Minnesota North Stars**	**NHL**	48	4	6	10	3	4	7	19	0	0	0	67	6.0	22	4	30	0	–12	....	....	....	....	....	....	....	....
1987-88	**Minnesota North Stars**	**NHL**	9	1	3	4	1	2	3	12	0	0	0	15	6.7	7	3	5	0	–1	....	....	....	....	....	....	....	....
	Kalamazoo Wings	IHL	5	3	5	8	....	....	....	6	....	....	....	....	....	....	....	....	....	....	....	....	....	....	....	....	....	....
	NHL Totals		613	228	238	466	186	164	350	435	79	1	19	1619	14.1	750	267	462	7		71	35	35	70	60	13	0	9

Played in NHL All-Star Game (1980, 1985)

			REGULAR SEASON																		PLAYOFFS							
Season	Club	League	GP	G	A	Pts	AG	AA	APts	PIM	PP	SH	GW	S	%	TGF	PGF	TGA	PGA	+/–	GP	G	A	Pts	PIM	PP	SH	GW

• PAYNTER, Kent Kent Douglas D – L. 6', 183 lbs. b: Summerside, P.E.I., 4/17/1965. Chicago's 9th, 165th overall, in 1983.

Season	Club	League	GP	G	A	Pts	AG	AA	APts	PIM	PP	SH	GW	S	%	TGF	PGF	TGA	PGA	+/–	GP	G	A	Pts	PIM	PP	SH	GW
1981-82	Summerside Capitals	MJrHL	35	7	23	30	....	....	....	65	....	....	....	....	....	....	....	....	....	....	....	....	....	....	....	....	....	....
1982-83	Kitchener Rangers	OHL	65	4	11	15	....	....	....	97	....	....	....	....	....	....	....	....	....	....	12	1	0	1	20	....	....	....
1983-84	Kitchener Rangers	OHL	65	9	27	36	....	....	....	94	....	....	....	....	....	....	....	....	....	....	16	4	9	13	18	....	....	....
	Kitchener Rangers	Mem-Cup	4	0	3	3	....	....	....	6	....	....	....	....	....	....	....	....	....	....	....	....	....	....	....	....	....	....
1984-85	Kitchener Rangers	OHL	58	7	28	35	....	....	....	93	....	....	....	....	....	....	....	....	....	....	4	2	1	3	4	....	....	....
1985-86	Nova Scotia Oilers	AHL	23	1	2	3	....	....	....	36	....	....	....	....	....	....	....	....	....	....	....	....	....	....	....	....	....	....
	Saginaw Generals	IHL	4	0	1	1	....	....	....	2	....	....	....	....	....	....	....	....	....	....	....	....	....	....	....	....	....	....
1986-87	Nova Scotia Oilers	AHL	66	2	6	8	....	....	....	57	....	....	....	....	....	....	....	....	....	....	2	0	0	0	0	....	....	....
1987-88	**Chicago Blackhawks**	**NHL**	**2**	**0**	**0**	**0**	**0**	**0**	**0**	**2**	**0**	**0**	**0**	**0**	**0.0**	**0**	**0**	**0**	**0**	**0**	....	....	....	....	....	....	....	....
	Saginaw Hawks	IHL	74	8	20	28	....	....	....	141	....	....	....	....	....	....	....	....	....	....	10	0	1	1	30	....	....	....
1988-89	**Chicago Blackhawks**	**NHL**	**1**	**0**	**0**	**0**	**0**	**0**	**0**	**2**	**0**	**0**	**0**	**0**	**0.0**	**0**	**0**	**1**	**0**	**–1**	....	....	....	....	....	....	....	....
	Saginaw Hawks	IHL	69	12	14	26	....	....	....	148	....	....	....	....	....	....	....	....	....	....	6	2	2	4	17	....	....	....
1989-90	**Washington Capitals**	**NHL**	**13**	**1**	**2**	**3**	**1**	**1**	**2**	**18**	**0**	**0**	**0**	**15**	**6.7**	**11**	**1**	**19**	**2**	**–7**	**3**	**0**	**0**	**0**	**10**	**0**	**0**	**0**
	Baltimore Skipjacks	AHL	60	7	20	27	....	....	....	110	....	....	....	....	....	....	....	....	....	....	11	5	6	1	34	....	....	....
1990-91	**Washington Capitals**	**NHL**	**1**	**0**	**0**	**0**	**0**	**0**	**0**	**15**	**0**	**0**	**0**	**0**	**0.0**	**0**	**0**	**0**	**0**	**0**	**1**	**0**	**0**	**0**	**0**	**0**	**0**	**0**
	Baltimore Skipjacks	AHL	43	10	17	27	....	....	....	64	....	....	....	....	....	....	....	....	....	....	6	2	1	3	8	....	....	....
1991-92	**Winnipeg Jets**	**NHL**	**5**	**0**	**0**	**0**	**0**	**0**	**0**	**4**	**0**	**0**	**0**	**6**	**0.0**	**2**	**0**	**3**	**0**	**–1**	....	....	....	....	....	....	....	....
	Moncton Hawks	AHL	62	3	30	33	....	....	....	71	....	....	....	....	....	....	....	....	....	....	11	2	6	8	25	....	....	....
1992-93	**Ottawa Senators**	**NHL**	**6**	**0**	**0**	**0**	**0**	**0**	**0**	**20**	**0**	**0**	**0**	**3**	**0.0**	**2**	**0**	**13**	**4**	**–7**	....	....	....	....	....	....	....	....
	New Haven Senators	AHL	48	7	17	24	....	....	....	81	....	....	....	....	....	....	....	....	....	....	....	....	....	....	....	....	....	....
1993-94	**Ottawa Senators**	**NHL**	**9**	**0**	**1**	**1**	**0**	**1**	**1**	**8**	**0**	**0**	**0**	**8**	**0.0**	**4**	**1**	**16**	**7**	**–6**	....	....	....	....	....	....	....	....
	P.E.I. Senators	AHL	63	6	20	26	....	....	....	125	....	....	....	....	....	....	....	....	....	....	....	....	....	....	....	....	....	....
1994-95	Milwaukee Admirals	IHL	73	3	22	25	....	....	....	104	....	....	....	....	....	....	....	....	....	....	5	2	3	5	8	....	....	....
1995-96	Milwaukee Admirals	IHL	79	9	19	28	....	....	....	147	....	....	....	....	....	....	....	....	....	....	5	0	2	2	10	....	....	....
1996-97	Milwaukee Admirals	IHL	77	10	28	38	....	....	....	97	....	....	....	....	....	....	....	....	....	....	3	1	1	2	4	....	....	....
1997-98	Milwaukee Admirals	IHL	15	0	6	6	....	....	....	14	....	....	....	....	....	....	....	....	....	....	....	....	....	....	....	....	....	....
	Indianapolis Ice	IHL	37	3	7	10	....	....	....	36	....	....	....	....	....	....	....	....	....	....	5	0	1	1	4	....	....	....
	NHL Totals		**37**	**1**	**3**	**4**	**1**	**2**	**3**	**69**	**0**	**0**	**0**	**32**	**3.1**	**19**	**2**	**52**	**13**		**4**	**0**	**0**	**0**	**10**	**0**	**0**	**0**

Signed as a free agent by **Washington**, August 21, 1989. Traded to **Winnipeg** by **Washington** with Tyler Larter and Bob Joyce for Craig Duncanson, Brent Hughes, and Simon Wheeldon, May 21, 1991. Claimed by **Ottawa** from **Winnipeg** in Expansion Draft, June 18, 1992.

• PEAKE, Pat Patrick M. C – R. 6'1", 195 lbs. b: Rochester, MI, 5/28/1973. Washington's 1st, 14th overall, in 1991.

Season	Club	League	GP	G	A	Pts	AG	AA	APts	PIM	PP	SH	GW	S	%	TGF	PGF	TGA	PGA	+/–	GP	G	A	Pts	PIM	PP	SH	GW
1989-90	Detroit Compuware	NAJHL	34	33	44	77	....	....	....	48	....	....	....	....	....	....	....	....	....	....	....	....	....	....	....	....	....	....
1990-91	Detroit Ambassadors	OHL	63	39	51	90	....	....	....	54	....	....	....	....	....	....	....	....	....	....	....	....	....	....	....	....	....	....
1991-92	Detroit Ambassadors	OHL	53	41	52	93	....	....	....	44	....	....	....	....	....	....	....	....	....	....	7	8	9	17	10	....	....	....
	United States	WJC-A	7	5	1	6	....	....	....	4	....	....	....	....	....	....	....	....	....	....	....	....	....	....	....	....	....	....
	Baltimore Skipjacks	AHL	3	1	0	1	....	....	....	4	....	....	....	....	....	....	....	....	....	....	....	....	....	....	....	....	....	....
1992-93	Detroit Jr. Red Wings	OHL	46	58	78	136	....	....	....	64	....	....	....	....	....	....	....	....	....	....	2	1	3	4	2	....	....	....
	United States	WJC-A	7	4	9	13	....	....	....	18	....	....	....	....	....	....	....	....	....	....	....	....	....	....	....	....	....	....
1993-94	**Washington Capitals**	**NHL**	**49**	**11**	**18**	**29**	**10**	**14**	**24**	**39**	**3**	**0**	**1**	**91**	**12.1**	**40**	**15**	**24**	**0**	**1**	**8**	**0**	**1**	**1**	**8**	**0**	**0**	**0**
	Portland Pirates	AHL	4	0	5	5	....	....	....	2	....	....	....	....	....	....	....	....	....	....	....	....	....	....	....	....	....	....
1994-95	**Washington Capitals**	**NHL**	**18**	**0**	**4**	**4**	**0**	**6**	**6**	**12**	**0**	**0**	**0**	**30**	**0.0**	**5**	**3**	**8**	**0**	**–6**	....	....	....	....	....	....	....	....
	Portland Pirates	AHL	5	1	3	4	....	....	....	2	....	....	....	....	....	....	....	....	....	....	4	0	3	3	6	....	....	....
1995-96	**Washington Capitals**	**NHL**	**62**	**17**	**19**	**36**	**17**	**16**	**33**	**46**	**8**	**0**	**3**	**129**	**13.2**	**56**	**27**	**23**	**1**	**7**	**5**	**2**	**1**	**3**	**12**	**2**	**0**	**0**
1996-97	**Washington Capitals**	**NHL**	**4**	**0**	**0**	**0**	**0**	**0**	**0**	**4**	**0**	**0**	**0**	**9**	**0.0**	**2**	**1**	**0**	**0**	**1**	....	....	....	....	....	....	....	....
	Portland Pirates	AHL	3	0	2	2	....	....	....	0	....	....	....	....	....	....	....	....	....	....	....	....	....	....	....	....	....	....
1997-98	**Washington Capitals**	**NHL**	**1**	**0**	**0**	**0**	**0**	**0**	**0**	**4**	**0**	**0**	**0**	**0**	**0.0**	**0**	**0**	**0**	**0**	**0**	....	....	....	....	....	....	....	....
	NHL Totals		**134**	**28**	**41**	**69**	**27**	**36**	**63**	**105**	**11**	**0**	**4**	**259**	**10.8**	**103**	**46**	**55**	**1**		**13**	**2**	**2**	**4**	**20**	**2**	**0**	**0**

OHL First All-Star Team (1993) • Canadian Major Junior First All-Star Team (1993) • Canadian Major Junior Player of the Year (1993)

• Suffered eventual career-ending heel injury in game vs Pittsburgh, April 26, 1996.

• PEARSON, Mel George Alexander Melvin LW – L. 5'10", 175 lbs. b: Flin Flon, Man., 4/29/1938 d: 1/9/1999.

Season	Club	League	GP	G	A	Pts	AG	AA	APts	PIM	PP	SH	GW	S	%	TGF	PGF	TGA	PGA	+/–	GP	G	A	Pts	PIM	PP	SH	GW
1955-56	Flin Flon Bombers	SJHL	48	26	23	49	....	....	....	32	....	....	....	....	....	....	....	....	....	....	12	1	0	1	6	....	....	....
	Flin Flon Bombers	Mem-Cup	7	2	2	4	....	....	....	2	....	....	....	....	....	....	....	....	....	....	....	....	....	....	....	....	....	....
1956-57	Flin Flon Bombers	SJHL	56	*59	49	108	....	....	....	86	....	....	....	....	....	....	....	....	....	....	10	*13	9	*22	6	....	....	....
1957-58	Trois-Rivieres Lions	QHL	54	17	28	45	....	....	....	60	....	....	....	....	....	....	....	....	....	....	....	....	....	....	....	....	....	....
	Providence Reds	AHL	10	1	2	3	....	....	....	0	....	....	....	....	....	....	....	....	....	....	....	....	....	....	....	....	....	....
	Fort Williams Canadiens	Mem-Cup	17	10	10	20	....	....	....	17	....	....	....	....	....	....	....	....	....	....	....	....	....	....	....	....	....	....
1958-59	Vancouver Canucks	WHL	70	16	33	49	....	....	....	35	....	....	....	....	....	....	....	....	....	....	8	1	2	3	11	....	....	....
1959-60	**New York Rangers**	**NHL**	**23**	**1**	**5**	**6**	**1**	**5**	**6**	**13**	....	....	....	....	....	....	....	....	....	....	....	....	....	....	....	....	....	....
	Trois-Rivieres Lions	EPHL	43	21	23	44	....	....	....	26	....	....	....	....	....	....	....	....	....	....	....	....	....	....	....	....	....	....
1960-61	Kitchener-Waterloo Beavers	EPHL	69	20	27	47	....	....	....	62	....	....	....	....	....	....	....	....	....	....	7	1	1	2	10	....	....	....
1961-62	**New York Rangers**	**NHL**	**3**	**0**	**0**	**0**	**0**	**0**	**0**	**2**	....	....	....	....	....	....	....	....	....	....	....	....	....	....	....	....	....	....
	Kitchener-Waterloo Beavers	EPHL	66	23	38	61	....	....	....	44	....	....	....	....	....	....	....	....	....	....	7	1	0	1	10	....	....	....
1962-63	**New York Rangers**	**NHL**	**5**	**1**	**0**	**1**	**1**	**0**	**1**	**6**	....	....	....	....	....	....	....	....	....	....	....	....	....	....	....	....	....	....
	Baltimore Clippers	AHL	67	13	29	42	....	....	....	40	....	....	....	....	....	....	....	....	....	....	3	1	1	2	4	....	....	....
1963-64	Baltimore Clippers	AHL	68	8	22	30	....	....	....	35	....	....	....	....	....	....	....	....	....	....	....	....	....	....	....	....	....	....
1964-65	**New York Rangers**	**NHL**	**5**	**0**	**0**	**0**	**0**	**0**	**0**	**4**	....	....	....	....	....	....	....	....	....	....	....	....	....	....	....	....	....	....
	St. Paul Rangers	CPHL	61	24	46	70	....	....	....	30	....	....	....	....	....	....	....	....	....	....	11	5	7	12	20	....	....	....
1965-66	Buffalo Bisons	AHL	72	18	40	58	....	....	....	30	....	....	....	....	....	....	....	....	....	....	....	....	....	....	....	....	....	....
1966-67	Los Angeles Blades	WHL	68	17	45	62	....	....	....	24	....	....	....	....	....	....	....	....	....	....	....	....	....	....	....	....	....	....
1967-68	**Pittsburgh Penguins**	**NHL**	**2**	**0**	**1**	**1**	**0**	**1**	**1**	**0**	**0**	**0**	**0**	**2**	**0.0**	**1**	**0**	**2**	**0**	**–1**	....	....	....	....	....	....	....	....
	Portland Buckaroos	WHL	68	19	20	39	....	....	....	16	....	....	....	....	....	....	....	....	....	....	12	1	4	5	7	....	....	....
1968-69	Portland Buckaroos	WHL	74	19	26	45	....	....	....	44	....	....	....	....	....	....	....	....	....	....	11	0	1	1	10	....	....	....
1969-70	Portland Buckaroos	WHL	72	26	22	48	....	....	....	24	....	....	....	....	....	....	....	....	....	....	11	2	4	6	30	....	....	....
1970-71	Portland Buckaroos	WHL	72	23	19	42	....	....	....	52	....	....	....	....	....	....	....	....	....	....	11	1	6	7	10	....	....	....
1971-72	Portland Buckaroos	WHL	72	21	38	59	....	....	....	45	....	....	....	....	....	....	....	....	....	....	11	1	1	2	17	....	....	....
1972-73	Minnesota Fighting Saints	WHA	70	8	12	20	....	....	....	12	....	....	....	....	....	....	....	....	....	....	5	2	0	2	0	....	....	....
	NHL Totals		**38**	**2**	**6**	**8**	**2**	**6**	**8**	**25**	....	....	....	....	....	....	....	....	....	....	....	....	....	....	....	....	....	....
	Other Major League Totals		70	8	12	20	....	....	....	12	....	....	....	....	....	....	....	....	....	....	5	2	0	2	0	....	....	....

Traded to **Chicago** by **NY Rangers** with Dave Richardson, Tracy Pratt and Dick Meissner for John McKenzie and Ray Cullen, June 4, 1965. Claimed by **Pittsburgh** from **Chicago** in Expansion Draft, June 6, 1967. Loaned to **Portland** (WHL) by **Pittsburgh** for cash, October, 1967. Traded to **Portland** (WHL) by **Pittsburgh** for cash, August, 1969. Selected by **Dayton-Houston** (WHA) in 1972 WHA General Player Draft, February 12, 1972. Traded to **Minnesota** (WHA) by **Houston** (WHA) for future considerations and cash, September, 1972.

• PEARSON, Rob Robert Gordon RW – R. 6'3", 198 lbs. b: Oshawa, Ont., 3/8/1971. Toronto's 2nd, 12th overall, in 1989.

Season	Club	League	GP	G	A	Pts	AG	AA	APts	PIM	PP	SH	GW	S	%	TGF	PGF	TGA	PGA	+/–	GP	G	A	Pts	PIM	PP	SH	GW
1987-88	Oshawa Legionaires	OMHA	72	68	65	133	....	....	....	188	....	....	....	....	....	....	....	....	....	....	....	....	....	....	....	....	....	....
1988-89	Belleville Bulls	OHL	26	8	12	20	....	....	....	51	....	....	....	....	....	....	....	....	....	....	....	....	....	....	....	....	....	....
1989-90	Belleville Bulls	OHL	58	48	40	88	....	....	....	174	....	....	....	....	....	....	....	....	....	....	11	5	5	10	26	....	....	....
1990-91	Belleville Bulls	OHL	10	6	3	9	....	....	....	27	....	....	....	....	....	....	....	....	....	....	....	....	....	....	....	....	....	....
	Oshawa Generals	OHL	41	57	52	109	....	....	....	76	....	....	....	....	....	....	....	....	....	....	16	16	17	33	39	....	....	....
	Newmarket Saints	AHL	3	0	0	0	....	....	....	29	....	....	....	....	....	....	....	....	....	....	....	....	....	....	....	....	....	....
1991-92	**Toronto Maple Leafs**	**NHL**	**47**	**14**	**10**	**24**	**13**	**8**	**21**	**58**	**6**	**0**	**0**	**79**	**17.7**	**30**	**14**	**32**	**0**	**–16**	....	....	....	....	....	....	....	....
	St. John's Maple Leafs	AHL	27	15	14	29	....	....	....	107	....	....	....	....	....	....	....	....	....	....	13	5	4	9	40	....	....	....
1992-93	**Toronto Maple Leafs**	**NHL**	**78**	**23**	**14**	**37**	**19**	**10**	**29**	**211**	**8**	**0**	**3**	**164**	**14.0**	**66**	**21**	**48**	**1**	**–2**	**14**	**2**	**2**	**4**	**31**	**0**	**0**	**0**
1993-94	**Toronto Maple Leafs**	**NHL**	**67**	**12**	**18**	**30**	**11**	**14**	**25**	**189**	**1**	**0**	**4**	**119**	**10.1**	**49**	**13**	**42**	**0**	**–6**	**14**	**1**	**0**	**1**	**32**	**0**	**0**	**0**
1994-95	**Washington Capitals**	**NHL**	**32**	**0**	**6**	**6**	**0**	**9**	**9**	**96**	**0**	**0**	**0**	**34**	**0.0**	**9**	**2**	**13**	**0**	**–6**	**3**	**1**	**0**	**1**	**17**	**0**	**0**	**1**
1995-96	Portland Pirates	AHL	44	18	24	42	....	....	....	143	....	....	....	....	....	....	....	....	....	....	....	....	....	....	....	....	....	....
	St. Louis Blues	**NHL**	**27**	**6**	**4**	**10**	**6**	**3**	**9**	**54**	**1**	**0**	**1**	**51**	**11.8**	**17**	**4**	**10**	**1**	**4**	**2**	**0**	**0**	**0**	**14**	**0**	**0**	**0**

Season	Club	League	REGULAR SEASON																		PLAYOFFS							
			GP	G	A	Pts	AG	AA	APts	PIM	PP	SH	GW	S	%	TGF	PGF	TGA	PGA	+/–	GP	G	A	Pts	PIM	PP	SH	GW
1996-97	St. Louis Blues	NHL	18	1	2	3	1	2	3	37	0	0	0	14	7.1	5	2	8	0	–5								
	Worcester IceCats	AHL	46	11	16	27				199											5	3	0	3	16			
1997-98	Cleveland Lumberjacks	IHL	46	17	14	31				118											10	6	4	10	43			
1998-99	Cleveland Lumberjacks	IHL	20	3	10	13				27																		
	Orlando Solar Bears	IHL	11	6	2	8				41											17	8	6	14	24			
99-2000	Long Beach Ice Dogs	IHL	60	17	23	40				145											4	0	0	0	8			
	NHL Totals		**269**	**56**	**54**	**110**	**50**	**46**	**96**	**645**	**16**	**0**	**8**	**461**	**12.1**	**176**	**56**	**153**	**2**		**33**	**4**	**2**	**6**	**94**	**0**	**0**	**1**

OHL First All-Star Team (1991)

Traded to **Washington** by **Toronto** with Philadelphia's 1st round choice (previously acquired, Washington selected Nolan Baumgartner) in 1994 Entry Draft for Mike Ridley and St. Louis' 1st round choice (previously acquired, Toronto selected Eric Fichaud) in 1994 Entry Draft, June 28, 1994. Traded to **St. Louis** by **Washington** for Denis Chasse, January 29, 1996. Signed as a free agent by **Lonf Beach** (IHL), August 5, 1999.

• PEARSON, Scott

LW – L. 6'1", 205 lbs. b: Cornwall, Ont., 12/19/1969. Toronto's 1st, 6th overall, in 1988.

Season	Club	League	GP	G	A	Pts	AG	AA	APts	PIM	PP	SH	GW	S	%	TGF	PGF	TGA	PGA	+/–	GP	G	A	Pts	PIM	PP	SH	GW
1984-85	Cornwall Midget Royals	OMHA	60	40	40	80				60																		
1985-86	Kingston Canadians	OHL	63	16	23	39				56																		
1986-87	Kingston Canadians	OHL	62	30	24	54				101											9	3	3	6	42			
1987-88	Kingston Canadians	OHL	46	26	32	58				117																		
1988-89	Kingston Raiders	OHL	13	9	8	17				34																		
	Niagara Falls Thunder	OHL	32	26	34	60				90											17	14	10	24	53			
	Toronto Maple Leafs	**NHL**	**9**	**0**	**1**	**1**	**0**	**1**	**1**	**2**	**0**	**0**	**0**	**6**	**0.0**	**2**	**0**	**2**	**0**	**0**								
1989-90	**Toronto Maple Leafs**	**NHL**	**41**	**5**	**10**	**15**	**4**	**7**	**11**	**90**	**0**	**0**	**1**	**66**	**7.6**	**24**	**4**	**27**	**0**	**–7**	**2**	**2**	**0**	**2**	**10**	**0**	**0**	**0**
	Newmarket Saints	AHL	18	12	11	23				64																		
1990-91	**Toronto Maple Leafs**	**NHL**	**12**	**0**	**0**	**0**	**0**	**0**	**0**	**20**	**0**	**0**	**0**	**13**	**0.0**	**1**	**0**	**6**	**0**	**–5**								
	Quebec Nordiques	**NHL**	**35**	**11**	**4**	**15**	**10**	**3**	**13**	**86**	**0**	**0**	**0**	**61**	**18.0**	**25**	**2**	**27**	**0**	**–4**								
	Halifax Citadels	AHL	24	12	15	27				44																		
1991-92	**Quebec Nordiques**	**NHL**	**10**	**1**	**2**	**3**	**1**	**2**	**3**	**14**	**0**	**0**	**0**	**14**	**7.1**	**4**	**1**	**8**	**0**	**–5**								
	Halifax Citadels	AHL	5	2	1	3				4																		
1992-93	**Quebec Nordiques**	**NHL**	**41**	**13**	**1**	**14**	**11**	**1**	**12**	**95**	**0**	**0**	**1**	**45**	**28.9**	**20**	**0**	**17**	**0**	**3**	**3**	**0**	**0**	**0**	**0**	**0**	**0**	**0**
	Halifax Citadels	AHL	5	3	1	4				25																		
1993-94	**Edmonton Oilers**	**NHL**	**72**	**19**	**18**	**37**	**18**	**14**	**32**	**165**	**3**	**0**	**7**	**160**	**11.9**	**54**	**10**	**48**	**0**	**–4**								
1994-95	**Edmonton Oilers**	**NHL**	**28**	**1**	**4**	**5**	**2**	**6**	**8**	**54**	**0**	**0**	**0**	**21**	**4.8**	**6**	**0**	**17**	**0**	**–11**								
	Buffalo Sabres	**NHL**	**14**	**2**	**1**	**3**	**4**	**1**	**5**	**20**	**0**	**0**	**0**	**19**	**10.5**	**6**	**0**	**9**	**0**	**–3**	**5**	**0**	**0**	**0**	**4**	**0**	**0**	**0**
1995-96	**Buffalo Sabres**	**NHL**	**27**	**4**	**0**	**4**	**4**	**0**	**4**	**67**	**0**	**0**	**1**	**26**	**15.4**	**4**	**0**	**8**	**0**	**–4**								
	Rochester Americans	AHL	26	8	8	16				113																		
1996-97	**Toronto Maple Leafs**	**NHL**	**1**	**0**	**0**	**0**	**0**	**0**	**0**	**2**	**0**	**0**	**0**	**0**	**0.0**	**0**	**0**	**0**	**0**	**0**								
	St. John's Maple Leafs	AHL	14	5	2	7				26											9	5	2	7	14			
1997-98	Chicago Wolves	IHL	78	34	17	51				225											22	12	6	18	50			
1998-99	Chicago Wolves	IHL	62	23	13	36				154											8	4	1	5	*50			
99-2000	**New York Islanders**	**NHL**	**2**	**0**	**1**	**1**	**0**	**1**	**1**	**0**	**0**	**0**	**0**	**5**	**0.0**	**2**	**0**	**1**	**0**	**1**								
	Chicago Wolves	IHL	77	19	14	33				124											16	5	5	10	28			
	NHL Totals		**292**	**56**	**42**	**98**	**54**	**36**	**90**	**615**	**3**	**0**	**10**	**436**	**12.8**	**148**	**17**	**170**	**0**		**10**	**2**	**0**	**2**	**14**	**0**	**0**	**0**

Traded to **Quebec** by **Toronto** with Toronto's 2nd round choices in 1991 (later traded to Washington — Washington selected Eric Lavigne) and 1992 (Tuomas Gronman) Entry Drafts for Aaron Broten, Lucien Deblois and Michel Petit, November 17, 1990. Traded to **Edmonton** by **Quebec** for Martin Gelinas and Edmonton's 6th round choice (Nicholas Checco) in 1993 Entry Draft, June 20, 1993. Traded to **Buffalo** by **Edmonton** for Ken Sutton, April 7, 1995. Signed as a free agent by **Toronto**, July 24, 1996. • Missed majority of 1996-97 season recovering from abdominal surgery, November, 1996. Signed as a free agent by **NY Islanders**, August 9, 1999.

• PECA, Michael

Michael Anthony C – R. 5'11", 181 lbs. b: Toronto, Ont., 3/26/1974. Vancouver's 2nd, 40th overall, in 1992.

Season	Club	League	GP	G	A	Pts	AG	AA	APts	PIM	PP	SH	GW	S	%	TGF	PGF	TGA	PGA	+/–	GP	G	A	Pts	PIM	PP	SH	GW
1989-90	Toronto Young Nationals	MTHL	39	42	53	95				40																		
1990-91	Sudbury Wolves	OHL	62	14	27	41				24											5	1	0	1	7			
1991-92	Sudbury Wolves	OHL	39	16	34	50				61																		
	Ottawa 67's	OHL	27	8	17	25				32											11	6	10	16	6			
1992-93	Ottawa 67's	OHL	55	38	64	102				80																		
	Hamilton Canucks	AHL	9	6	3	9				11																		
1993-94	Ottawa 67's	OHL	55	50	63	113				101											17	7	22	29	30			
	Vancouver Canucks	**NHL**	**4**	**0**	**0**	**0**	**0**	**0**	**0**	**2**	**0**	**0**	**0**	**5**	**0.0**	**0**	**0**	**1**	**0**	**–1**								
1994-95	Syracuse Crunch	AHL	35	10	24	34				75																		
	Vancouver Canucks	**NHL**	**33**	**6**	**6**	**12**	**11**	**9**	**20**	**30**	**2**	**0**	**1**	**46**	**13.0**	**21**	**7**	**25**	**5**	**–6**	**5**	**0**	**1**	**1**	**8**	**0**	**0**	**0**
1995-96	**Buffalo Sabres**	**NHL**	**68**	**11**	**20**	**31**	**11**	**16**	**27**	**67**	**4**	**3**	**1**	**109**	**10.1**	**50**	**14**	**55**	**18**	**–1**								
1996-97	**Buffalo Sabres**	**NHL**	**79**	**20**	**29**	**49**	**21**	**26**	**47**	**80**	**5**	**6**	**4**	**137**	**14.6**	**73**	**14**	**65**	**32**	**26**	**10**	**0**	**2**	**2**	**8**	**0**	**0**	**0**
1997-98	**Buffalo Sabres**	**NHL**	**61**	**18**	**22**	**40**	**21**	**22**	**43**	**57**	**6**	**5**	**1**	**132**	**13.6**	**63**	**22**	**49**	**20**	**12**	**13**	**3**	**2**	**5**	**8**	**0**	**0**	**1**
1998-99	**Buffalo Sabres**	**NHL**	**82**	**27**	**29**	**56**	**32**	**28**	**60**	**81**	**10**	**0**	**8**	**199**	**13.6**	**79**	**28**	**73**	**29**	**7**	**21**	**5**	**8**	**13**	**18**	**2**	**1**	**0**
99-2000	**Buffalo Sabres**	**NHL**	**73**	**20**	**21**	**41**	**22**	**19**	**41**	**67**	**2**	**0**	**3**	**144**	**13.9**	**55**	**12**	**57**	**20**	**6**	**5**	**0**	**1**	**1**	**4**	**0**	**0**	**0**
	NHL Totals		**400**	**102**	**127**	**229**	**118**	**120**	**238**	**384**	**29**	**14**	**18**	**772**	**13.2**	**341**	**97**	**325**	**124**		**54**	**8**	**14**	**22**	**46**	**2**	**1**	**1**

Won Frank J. Selke Trophy (1997)

Traded to **Buffalo** by **Vancouver** with Mike Wilson and Vancouver's 1st round choice (Jay McKee) in 1995 Entry Draft for Alexander Mogilny and Buffalo's 5th round choice (Todd Norman) in 1995 Entry Draft, July 8, 1995.

• PEDERSEN, Allen

Allen Bentley D – L. 6'3", 210 lbs. b: Fort Saskatchewan, Alta., 1/13/1965. Boston's 5th, 105th overall, in 1983.

Season	Club	League	GP	G	A	Pts	AG	AA	APts	PIM	PP	SH	GW	S	%	TGF	PGF	TGA	PGA	+/–	GP	G	A	Pts	PIM	PP	SH	GW
1981-82	Fort Saskatchewan Rangers	AAHA	STATISTICS NOT AVAILABLE																									
1982-83	Medicine Hat Tigers	WHL	63	3	10	13				49											5	0	0	0	7			
1983-84	Medicine Hat Tigers	WHL	44	0	11	11				47											14	0	2	2	24			
1984-85	Medicine Hat Tigers	WHL	72	6	16	22				66											10	0	0	0	9			
1985-86	Moncton Golden Flames	AHL	59	1	8	9				39											3	0	0	0	0			
1986-87	**Boston Bruins**	**NHL**	**79**	**1**	**11**	**12**	**1**	**8**	**9**	**71**	**0**	**0**	**0**	**56**	**1.8**	**63**	**0**	**99**	**21**	**–15**	**4**	**0**	**0**	**0**	**4**	**0**	**0**	**0**
1987-88	**Boston Bruins**	**NHL**	**78**	**0**	**6**	**6**	**0**	**4**	**4**	**90**	**0**	**0**	**0**	**43**	**0.0**	**45**	**0**	**57**	**18**	**6**	**21**	**0**	**0**	**0**	**34**	**0**	**0**	**0**
1988-89	**Boston Bruins**	**NHL**	**51**	**0**	**6**	**6**	**0**	**4**	**4**	**69**	**0**	**0**	**0**	**24**	**0.0**	**37**	**0**	**63**	**23**	**–3**	**10**	**0**	**0**	**0**	**2**	**0**	**0**	**0**
1989-90	**Boston Bruins**	**NHL**	**68**	**1**	**2**	**3**	**1**	**1**	**2**	**71**	**0**	**0**	**0**	**32**	**3.1**	**50**	**1**	**69**	**15**	**–5**	**21**	**0**	**0**	**0**	**41**	**0**	**0**	**0**
1990-91	**Boston Bruins**	**NHL**	**57**	**2**	**6**	**8**	**2**	**5**	**7**	**107**	**0**	**0**	**0**	**34**	**5.9**	**42**	**0**	**42**	**15**	**15**	**8**	**0**	**0**	**0**	**10**	**0**	**0**	**0**
	Maine Mariners	AHL	15	0	6	6				18											2	0	1	1	2			
1991-92	**Minnesota North Stars**	**NHL**	**29**	**0**	**1**	**1**	**0**	**1**	**1**	**10**	**0**	**0**	**0**	**17**	**0.0**	**16**	**0**	**22**	**5**	**–1**								
1992-93	**Hartford Whalers**	**NHL**	**59**	**1**	**4**	**5**	**1**	**3**	**4**	**60**	**0**	**0**	**0**	**16**	**6.3**	**43**	**0**	**81**	**38**	**0**								
1993-94	**Hartford Whalers**	**NHL**	**7**	**0**	**0**	**0**	**0**	**0**	**0**	**9**	**0**	**0**	**0**	**1**	**0.0**	**3**	**0**	**4**	**0**	**–1**								
	Springfield Indians	AHL	45	2	4	6				28											3	0	1	1	6			
1994-95	Atlanta Knights	IHL	71	0	5	5				61											5	0	0	0	2			
1995-1996	Atlanta Knights	IHL	DID NOT PLAY – ASSISTANT COACH																									
1996-2000	Pensacola Ice Pilots	ECHL	DID NOT PLAY – COACHING																									
	NHL Totals		**428**	**5**	**36**	**41**	**5**	**26**	**31**	**487**	**0**	**0**	**0**	**223**	**2.2**	**299**	**1**	**437**	**135**		**64**	**0**	**0**	**0**	**91**	**0**	**0**	**0**

Claimed by **Minnesota** from **Boston** in Expansion Draft, May 30, 1991. Traded to **Hartford** by **Minnesota** for Hartford's 6th round choice (Rick Mrozik) in 1993 Entry Draft, June 15, 1992.

• PEDERSON, Barry

Barry Alan C – R. 5'11", 185 lbs. b: Big River, Sask., 3/13/1961. Boston's 1st, 18th overall, in 1980.

Season	Club	League	GP	G	A	Pts	AG	AA	APts	PIM	PP	SH	GW	S	%	TGF	PGF	TGA	PGA	+/–	GP	G	A	Pts	PIM	PP	SH	GW
1976-77	Nanaimo Clippers	BCJHL	64	44	74	118				31																		
1977-78	Nanaimo Clippers	BCJHL	63	51	102	153				68																		
	Victoria Cougars	WCJHL	3	1	4	5				2																		
1978-79	Victoria Cougars	WHL	72	31	53	84				41																		
1979-80	Victoria Cougars	WHL	72	52	88	140				50											16	13	14	27	31			
1980-81	Victoria Cougars	WHL	55	65	82	147				65											15	15	21	36	10			
	Boston Bruins	**NHL**	**9**	**1**	**4**	**5**	**1**	**3**	**4**	**6**	**1**	**0**	**0**	**20**	**5.0**	**8**	**5**	**9**	**1**	**–5**								
	Victoria Cougars	Mem-Cup	4	4	1	5				6																		

			REGULAR SEASON																		PLAYOFFS							
Season	Club	League	GP	G	A	Pts	AG	AA	APts	PIM	PP	SH	GW	S	%	TGF	PGF	TGA	PGA	+/–	GP	G	A	Pts	PIM	PP	SH	GW
1981-82	Boston Bruins	NHL	80	44	48	92	35	32	67	53	13	4	7	197	22.3	121	40	72	18	27	11	7	11	18	2	1	0	2
1982-83	Boston Bruins	NHL	77	46	61	107	38	42	80	47	15	1	10	212	21.7	144	47	79	20	38	17	14	18	32	21	1	1	2
1983-84	Boston Bruins	NHL	80	39	77	116	31	53	84	64	10	3	7	236	16.5	152	61	93	29	27	3	0	1	1	2	0	0	0
1984-85	Boston Bruins	NHL	22	4	8	12	3	5	8	10	0	2	0	35	11.4	18	8	24	3	–11	....	....	....	....	....	....	....	....
1985-86	Boston Bruins	NHL	79	29	47	76	23	32	55	60	12	0	6	192	15.1	122	51	80	28	19	3	1	0	1	0	0	0	0
1986-87	Vancouver Canucks	NHL	79	24	52	76	21	38	59	50	6	0	3	184	13.0	109	46	108	32	–13	....	....	....	....	....	....	....	....
	Canada	WEC-A	10	2	3	5	....	....	....	2	....	....	....	....	....	....	....	....	....	....	....	....	....	....	....	....	....	....
1987-88	Vancouver Canucks	NHL	76	19	52	71	16	37	53	92	4	1	1	163	11.7	100	40	89	31	2	....	....	....	....	....	....	....	....
1988-89	Vancouver Canucks	NHL	62	15	26	41	13	18	31	22	7	1	0	98	15.3	60	20	56	21	5	....	....	....	....	....	....	....	....
1989-90	Vancouver Canucks	NHL	16	2	7	9	2	5	7	10	0	0	0	22	9.1	12	3	18	6	–3	....	....	....	....	....	....	....	....
	Pittsburgh Penguins	NHL	38	4	18	22	3	13	16	29	1	0	1	58	6.9	45	18	46	9	–10	....	....	....	....	....	....	....	....
1990-91♦	Pittsburgh Penguins	NHL	46	6	8	14	5	6	11	21	1	0	1	26	23.1	22	2	27	9	2	....	....	....	....	....	....	....	....
1991-92	Hartford Whalers	NHL	5	2	2	4	2	2	4	0	1	0	0	6	33.3	7	4	6	1	–2	....	....	....	....	....	....	....	....
	Boston Bruins	NHL	32	3	6	9	3	5	8	8	1	0	0	41	7.3	14	3	26	10	–5	....	....	....	....	....	....	....	....
	Maine Mariners	AHL	14	5	13	18	....	....	....	6	....	....	....	....	....	....	....	....	....	....	....	....	....	....	....	....	....	....
	NHL Totals		701	238	416	654	196	291	487	472	72	12	36	1490	16.0	934	348	733	218		34	22	30	52	25	2	1	4

WHL Second All-Star Team (1980) • WHL All-Star Team (1981) • Played in NHL All-Star Game (1983, 1984)

• Missed majority of 1984-85 season recovering from surgery to remove begnin tumour from shoulder, December, 1985. Traded to **Vancouver** by **Boston** for Cam Neely and Vancouver's 1st round choice (Glen Wesley) in 1987 Entry Draft, June 6, 1986. Traded to **Pittsburgh** by **Vancouver** with Rod Buskas and Tony Tanti for Dave Capuano, Andrew McBain and Dan Quinn, January 8, 1990. Signed as a free agent by **Hartford**, September 5, 1991. Traded to **Boston** by **Hartford** for future considerations, November 14, 1991.

• PEDERSON, Denis

Denis Erlo C – R. 6'2", 205 lbs. b: Prince Albert, Sask., 9/10/1975. New Jersey's 1st, 13th overall, in 1993.

Season	Club	League	GP	G	A	Pts	AG	AA	APts	PIM	PP	SH	GW	S	%	TGF	PGF	TGA	PGA	+/–	GP	G	A	Pts	PIM	PP	SH	GW
1990-91	Prince Albert Mintos	AAHA	30	25	17	42	....	....	....	84	....	....	....	....	....	....	....	....	....	....	....	....	....	....	....	....	....	....
1991-92	Prince Albert Mintos	AAHA	21	33	25	58	....	....	....	40	....	....	....	....	....	....	....	....	....	....	....	....	....	....	....	....	....	....
	Prince Albert Raiders	WHL	10	0	0	0	....	....	....	6	....	....	....	....	....	....	....	....	....	....	7	0	1	1	13	....	....	....
1992-93	Prince Albert Raiders	WHL	72	33	40	73	....	....	....	134	....	....	....	....	....	....	....	....	....	....	....	....	....	....	....	....	....	....
1993-94	Prince Albert Raiders	WHL	71	53	45	98	....	....	....	157	....	....	....	....	....	....	....	....	....	....	....	....	....	....	....	....	....	....
1994-95	Prince Albert Raiders	WHL	63	30	38	68	....	....	....	122	....	....	....	....	....	....	....	....	....	....	15	11	14	25	14	....	....	....
	Canada	WJC-A	7	2	2	4	....	....	....	0	....	....	....	....	....	....	....	....	....	....	....	....	....	....	....	....	....	....
	Albany River Rats	AHL	....	....	....	....	....	....	....	....	....	....	....	....	....	....	....	....	....	....	3	0	0	0	2	....	....	....
1995-96	New Jersey Devils	NHL	10	3	1	4	3	1	4	0	1	0	2	6	50.0	5	1	5	0	–1	....	....	....	....	....	....	....	....
	Albany River Rats	AHL	68	28	43	71	....	....	....	104	....	....	....	....	....	....	....	....	....	....	4	1	2	3	0	....	....	....
1996-97	New Jersey Devils	NHL	70	12	20	32	13	18	31	62	3	0	3	106	11.3	43	6	30	0	7	9	0	0	0	2	0	0	0
	Albany River Rats	AHL	3	1	3	4	....	....	....	7	....	....	....	....	....	....	....	....	....	....	....	....	....	....	....	....	....	....
1997-98	New Jersey Devils	NHL	80	15	13	28	18	13	31	97	7	0	1	135	11.1	44	17	40	7	–6	6	1	1	2	2	0	1	0
1998-99	New Jersey Devils	NHL	76	11	12	23	13	12	25	66	3	0	1	145	7.6	45	14	54	13	–10	3	0	1	1	0	0	0	0
99-2000	New Jersey Devils	NHL	35	3	3	6	3	3	6	16	0	0	0	41	7.3	7	0	20	6	–7	....	....	....	....	....	....	....	....
	Vancouver Canucks	NHL	12	3	2	5	3	2	5	2	0	0	1	15	20.0	7	1	9	4	1	....	....	....	....	....	....	....	....
	NHL Totals		283	47	51	98	53	49	102	243	14	0	8	448	10.5	151	39	158	30		18	1	2	3	4	0	1	0

WHL East Second All-Star Team (1994)

Traded to **Vancouver** by **New Jersey** with Brendan Morrison for Alexander Mogilny, March 14, 2000.

• PEDERSON, Mark

LW – L. 6'2", 196 lbs. b: Prelate, Sask., 1/14/1968. Montreal's 1st, 15th overall, in 1986.

Season	Club	League	GP	G	A	Pts	AG	AA	APts	PIM	PP	SH	GW	S	%	TGF	PGF	TGA	PGA	+/–	GP	G	A	Pts	PIM	PP	SH	GW
1983-84	Medicine Hat Cable Vision	AAHA	42	43	47	90	....	....	....	64	....	....	....	....	....	....	....	....	....	....	....	....	....	....	....	....	....	....
	Medicine Hat Tigers	WHL	3	0	0	0	....	....	....	0	....	....	....	....	....	....	....	....	....	....	....	....	....	....	....	....	....	....
1984-85	Medicine Hat Tigers	WHL	71	42	40	82	....	....	....	63	....	....	....	....	....	....	....	....	....	....	10	3	2	5	0	....	....	....
1985-86	Medicine Hat Tigers	WHL	72	46	60	106	....	....	....	46	....	....	....	....	....	....	....	....	....	....	25	12	6	18	25	....	....	....
1986-87	Medicine Hat Tigers	WHL	69	56	46	102	....	....	....	58	....	....	....	....	....	....	....	....	....	....	20	*19	7	26	14	....	....	....
	Medicine Hat Tigers	Mem-Cup	5	0	3	3	....	....	....	6	....	....	....	....	....	....	....	....	....	....	....	....	....	....	....	....	....	....
1987-88	Medicine Hat Tigers	WHL	62	53	58	111	....	....	....	55	....	....	....	....	....	....	....	....	....	....	16	*13	6	19	16	....	....	....
	Canada	WJC-A	7	1	2	3	....	....	....	4	....	....	....	....	....	....	....	....	....	....	....	....	....	....	....	....	....	....
	Medicine Hat Tigers	Mem-Cup	5	*5	4	9	....	....	....	4	....	....	....	....	....	....	....	....	....	....	....	....	....	....	....	....	....	....
1988-89	Sherbrooke Canadiens	AHL	75	43	38	81	....	....	....	53	....	....	....	....	....	....	....	....	....	....	6	7	5	12	4	....	....	....
1989-90	Montreal Canadiens	NHL	9	0	2	2	0	1	1	2	0	0	0	10	0.0	3	0	3	0	0	2	0	0	0	0	0	0	0
	Sherbrooke Canadiens	AHL	72	53	42	95	....	....	....	60	....	....	....	....	....	....	....	....	....	....	11	10	8	18	19	....	....	....
1990-91	Montreal Canadiens	Fr-Tour	4	2	0	2	....	....	....	2	....	....	....	....	....	....	....	....	....	....	....	....	....	....	....	....	....	....
	Philadelphia Flyers	NHL	12	2	1	3	2	1	3	5	1	0	0	14	14.3	6	2	12	0	–8	....	....	....	....	....	....	....	....
	Montreal Canadiens	NHL	47	8	15	23	7	11	18	18	4	0	2	62	12.9	32	14	15	0	3	....	....	....	....	....	....	....	....
1991-92	Philadelphia Flyers	NHL	58	15	25	40	14	19	33	22	4	0	3	94	16.0	57	19	25	1	14	....	....	....	....	....	....	....	....
1992-93	Philadelphia Flyers	NHL	14	3	4	7	2	3	5	6	1	0	0	21	14.3	8	4	6	0	–2	....	....	....	....	....	....	....	....
	San Jose Sharks	NHL	27	7	3	10	6	2	8	22	1	0	0	42	16.7	15	5	30	0	–20	....	....	....	....	....	....	....	....
1993-94	Detroit Red Wings	NHL	2	0	0	0	0	0	0	2	0	0	0	0	0.0	0	0	1	0	–1	....	....	....	....	....	....	....	....
	Adirondack Red Wings	AHL	62	52	45	97	....	....	....	37	....	....	....	....	....	....	....	....	....	....	12	4	7	11	10	....	....	....
1994-95	Kalamazoo Wings	IHL	75	31	32	63	....	....	....	47	....	....	....	....	....	....	....	....	....	....	16	8	4	12	2	....	....	....
1995-96	VSV Villach	Austria	34	28	32	60	....	....	....	52	....	....	....	....	....	....	....	....	....	....	....	....	....	....	....	....	....	....
1996-97	Farjestads BK Karlstad	Sweden	30	7	4	11	....	....	....	26	....	....	....	....	....	....	....	....	....	....	....	....	....	....	....	....	....	....
	Farjestads BK Karlstad	EuroHL	5	1	1	2	....	....	....	4	....	....	....	....	....	....	....	....	....	....	....	....	....	....	....	....	....	....
	ZSC Lions Zurich	Switz.	9	7	3	10	....	....	....	4	....	....	....	....	....	....	....	....	....	....	5	1	3	4	30	....	....	....
1997-98	Hannover Scorpions	Germany	47	20	38	58	....	....	....	61	....	....	....	....	....	....	....	....	....	....	4	0	1	1	2	....	....	....
1998-99	Krefeld Pinguine	Germany	50	21	27	48	....	....	....	40	....	....	....	....	....	....	....	....	....	....	4	3	1	4	4	....	....	....
99-2000	Krefeld Pinguine	Germany	44	20	17	37	....	....	....	80	....	....	....	....	....	....	....	....	....	....	3	2	0	2	4	....	....	....
	NHL Totals		169	35	50	85	31	37	68	77	11	0	5	243	14.4	121	44	92	1		2	0	0	0	0	0	0	0

WHL East First All-Star Team (1987) • WHL East Second All-Star Team (1988) • AHL First All-Star Team (1990, 1994)

Traded to **Philadelphia** by **Montreal** for Philadelphia's 2nd round choice (Jim Campbell) in 1991 Entry Draft, March 15, 1991. Traded to **San Jose** by **Philadelphia** with future considerations for Dave Snuggerud, December 19, 1992. Signed as a free agent by **Detroit**, August 23, 1993.

• PEDERSON, Tom

Thomas S. D – R. 5'9", 175 lbs. b: Bloomington, MN, 1/14/1970. Minnesota's 12th, 217th overall, in 1989.

Season	Club	League	GP	G	A	Pts	AG	AA	APts	PIM	PP	SH	GW	S	%	TGF	PGF	TGA	PGA	+/–	GP	G	A	Pts	PIM	PP	SH	GW
1987-88	Jefferson Jaguars	Hi-School	22	16	27	43	....	....	....	....	....	....	....	....	....	....	....	....	....	....	....	....	....	....	....	....	....	....
1988-89	University of Minnesota	WCHA	36	4	20	24	....	....	....	40	....	....	....	....	....	....	....	....	....	....	....	....	....	....	....	....	....	....
	United States	WJC-A	7	2	8	10	....	....	....	4	....	....	....	....	....	....	....	....	....	....	....	....	....	....	....	....	....	....
1989-90	University of Minnesota	WCHA	43	8	30	38	....	....	....	58	....	....	....	....	....	....	....	....	....	....	....	....	....	....	....	....	....	....
1990-91	University of Minnesota	WCHA	36	12	20	32	....	....	....	46	....	....	....	....	....	....	....	....	....	....	....	....	....	....	....	....	....	....
	United States	WEC-A	9	0	4	4	....	....	....	10	....	....	....	....	....	....	....	....	....	....	....	....	....	....	....	....	....	....
1991-92	United States	Nat-Team	44	3	11	14	....	....	....	41	....	....	....	....	....	....	....	....	....	....	....	....	....	....	....	....	....	....
	Kansas City Blades	IHL	20	6	9	15	....	....	....	16	....	....	....	....	....	....	....	....	....	....	13	1	6	7	14	....	....	....
1992-93	San Jose Sharks	NHL	44	7	13	20	6	9	15	31	2	0	2	102	6.9	45	21	56	16	–16	....	....	....	....	....	....	....	....
	Kansas City Blades	IHL	26	6	15	21	....	....	....	10	....	....	....	....	....	....	....	....	....	....	12	1	6	7	2	....	....	....
1993-94	San Jose Sharks	NHL	74	6	19	25	6	15	21	31	3	0	1	185	3.2	88	31	82	28	3	14	1	6	7	2	0	1	0
	Kansas City Blades	IHL	7	3	1	4	....	....	....	0	....	....	....	....	....	....	....	....	....	....	....	....	....	....	....	....	....	....
1994-95	San Jose Sharks	NHL	47	5	11	16	9	16	25	31	0	0	0	59	8.5	45	13	62	16	–14	10	0	5	5	8	0	0	0
1995-96	San Jose Sharks	NHL	60	1	4	5	1	3	4	40	1	0	1	59	1.7	51	9	67	16	–9	....	....	....	....	....	....	....	....
	United States	WC-A	8	1	0	1	....	....	....	2	....	....	....	....	....	....	....	....	....	....	....	....	....	....	....	....	....	....
1996-97	Seibu-Tetsudo Tokyo	Japan	29	10	28	38	....	....	....	24	....	....	....	....	....	....	....	....	....	....	....	....	....	....	....	....	....	....
	Toronto Maple Leafs	NHL	15	1	2	3	1	2	3	9	1	0	0	23	4.3	14	7	8	1	0	....	....	....	....	....	....	....	....
	St. John's Maple Leafs	AHL	1	0	4	4	....	....	....	2	....	....	....	....	....	....	....	....	....	....	....	....	....	....	....	....	....	....
	Utah Grizzlies	IHL	10	1	2	3	....	....	....	8	....	....	....	....	....	....	....	....	....	....	7	1	3	4	4	....	....	....

Season	Club	League	REGULAR SEASON																		PLAYOFFS							
			GP	G	A	Pts	AG	AA	APts	PIM	PP	SH	GW	S	%	TGF	PGF	TGA	PGA	+/-	GP	G	A	Pts	PIM	PP	SH	GW
1997-98	Fort Wayne Komets	IHL	78	12	24	36	....	....	....	87	....	....	....	....	....	....	....	....	....	....	4	2	0	2	4	....	....	....
1998-99	Hannover Scorpions	Germany	50	10	22	32	....	....	....	53	....	....	....	....	....	....	....	....	....	....	....	....	....	....	....	....	....	....
99-2000	Hannover Scorpions	Germany	21	3	5	8	....	....	....	12	....	....	....	....	....	....	....	....	....	....	....	....	....	....	....	....	....	....
	NHL Totals		**240**	**20**	**49**	**69**	**23**	**45**	**68**	**142**	**7**	**0**	**4**	**428**	**4.7**	**243**	**81**	**275**	**77**		**24**	**1**	**11**	**12**	**10**	**0**	**1**	**0**

Claimed by **San Jose** from **Minnesota** in Dispersal Draft, May 30, 1991. Signed as a free agent by **Toronto**, December 11, 1996.

• PELENSKY, Perry

RW – R. 5'11", 180 lbs. b: Edmonton, Alta., 5/22/1962. Chicago's 4th, 75th overall, in 1981.

Season	Club	League	GP	G	A	Pts	AG	AA	APts	PIM	PP	SH	GW	S	%	TGF	PGF	TGA	PGA	+/-	GP	G	A	Pts	PIM	PP	SH	GW
1979-80	Fort Saskatchewan Traders	SJHL	59	55	59	114	....	....	....	105	....	....	....	....	....	....	....	....	....	....	....	....	....	....	....	....	....	....
	Portland Winter Hawks	WHL	....	....	....	....	....	....	....	....	....	....	....	....	....	....	....	....	....	....	5	0	0	0	0	....	....	....
1980-81	Portland Winter Hawks	WHL	65	35	32	67	....	....	....	124	....	....	....	....	....	....	....	....	....	....	9	7	2	9	30	....	....	....
1981-82	Portland Winter Hawks	WHL	71	40	46	86	....	....	....	192	....	....	....	....	....	....	....	....	....	....	15	10	5	15	41	....	....	....
	Portland Winter Hawks	Mem-Cup	4	1	0	1	....	....	....	11	....	....	....	....	....	....	....	....	....	....	....	....	....	....	....	....	....	....
1982-83	Springfield Indians	AHL	80	15	25	40	....	....	....	89	....	....	....	....	....	....	....	....	....	....	....	....	....	....	....	....	....	....
1983-84	**Chicago Black Hawks**	**NHL**	**4**	**0**	**0**	**0**	**0**	**0**	**0**	**5**	**0**	**0**	**0**	**4**	**0.0**	**1**	**0**	**1**	**0**	**0**	....	....	....	....	....	....	....	....
	Springfield Indians	AHL	73	22	16	38	....	....	....	185	....	....	....	....	....	....	....	....	....	....	4	0	1	1	9	....	....	....
1984-85	Milwaukee Admirals	IHL	82	21	39	60	....	....	....	222	....	....	....	....	....	....	....	....	....	....	....	....	....	....	....	....	....	....
	NHL Totals		**4**	**0**	**0**	**0**	**0**	**0**	**0**	**5**	**0**	**0**	**0**	**4**	**0.0**	**1**	**0**	**1**	**0**		....	....	....	....	....	....	....	....

• PELLERIN, Scott

Scott Jacque-Frederick LW – L. 5'11", 189 lbs. b: Shediac, N.B., 1/9/1970. New Jersey's 4th, 47th overall, in 1989.

Season	Club	League	GP	G	A	Pts	AG	AA	APts	PIM	PP	SH	GW	S	%	TGF	PGF	TGA	PGA	+/-	GP	G	A	Pts	PIM	PP	SH	GW
1985-86	Moncton Flyers	NBAHA	STATISTICS NOT AVAILABLE																									
1986-87	Notre Dame Midget Hounds	SAHA	72	62	68	130	....	....	....	98	....	....	....	....	....	....	....	....	....	....	....	....	....	....	....	....	....	....
1987-88	Notre Dame Hounds	SJHL	57	37	49	86	....	....	....	139	....	....	....	....	....	....	....	....	....	....	....	....	....	....	....	....	....	....
	Notre Dame Hounds	Cen-Cup	5	*5	1	6	....	....	....	....	....	....	....	....	....	....	....	....	....	....	....	....	....	....	....	....	....	....
1988-89	University of Maine	H-East	45	29	33	62	....	....	....	92	....	....	....	....	....	....	....	....	....	....	....	....	....	....	....	....	....	....
1989-90	University of Maine	H-East	42	22	34	56	....	....	....	68	....	....	....	....	....	....	....	....	....	....	....	....	....	....	....	....	....	....
	Canada	WJC-A	7	2	0	2	....	....	....	2	....	....	....	....	....	....	....	....	....	....	....	....	....	....	....	....	....	....
1990-91	University of Maine	H-East	43	23	25	48	....	....	....	60	....	....	....	....	....	....	....	....	....	....	....	....	....	....	....	....	....	....
1991-92	University of Maine	H-East	37	*32	25	57	....	....	....	54	....	....	....	....	....	....	....	....	....	....	....	....	....	....	....	....	....	....
	Utica Devils	AHL	....	....	....	....	....	....	....	....	....	....	....	....	....	....	....	....	....	....	3	1	0	1	0	....	....	....
1992-93	**New Jersey Devils**	**NHL**	**45**	**10**	**11**	**21**	**8**	**8**	**16**	**41**	**1**	**2**	**0**	**60**	**16.7**	**29**	**1**	**45**	**16**	**–1**	....	....	....	....	....	....	....	....
	Utica Devils	AHL	27	15	18	33	....	....	....	33	....	....	....	....	....	....	....	....	....	....	2	0	1	1	0	....	....	....
1993-94	**New Jersey Devils**	**NHL**	**1**	**0**	**0**	**0**	**0**	**0**	**0**	**2**	**0**	**0**	**0**	**0**	**0.0**	**0**	**0**	**0**	**0**	**0**	....	....	....	....	....	....	....	....
	Albany River Rats	AHL	73	28	46	74	....	....	....	84	....	....	....	....	....	....	....	....	....	....	5	2	1	3	11	....	....	....
1994-95	Albany River Rats	AHL	74	23	33	56	....	....	....	95	....	....	....	....	....	....	....	....	....	....	14	6	4	10	8	....	....	....
1995-96	**New Jersey Devils**	**NHL**	**6**	**2**	**1**	**3**	**2**	**1**	**3**	**0**	**0**	**0**	**0**	**9**	**22.2**	**4**	**0**	**3**	**0**	**1**	....	....	....	....	....	....	....	....
	Albany River Rats	AHL	75	35	47	82	....	....	....	142	....	....	....	....	....	....	....	....	....	....	4	0	3	3	10	....	....	....
1996-97	**St. Louis Blues**	**NHL**	**54**	**8**	**10**	**18**	**8**	**9**	**17**	**35**	**0**	**2**	**2**	**76**	**10.5**	**32**	**0**	**34**	**14**	**12**	**6**	**0**	**0**	**0**	**6**	**0**	**0**	**0**
	Worcester IceCats	AHL	24	10	16	26	....	....	....	37	....	....	....	....	....	....	....	....	....	....	....	....	....	....	....	....	....	....
1997-98	**St. Louis Blues**	**NHL**	**80**	**8**	**21**	**29**	**9**	**21**	**30**	**62**	**1**	**1**	**0**	**96**	**8.3**	**47**	**1**	**58**	**26**	**14**	**10**	**0**	**2**	**2**	**10**	**0**	**0**	**0**
1998-99	**St. Louis Blues**	**NHL**	**80**	**20**	**21**	**41**	**23**	**20**	**43**	**42**	**0**	**5**	**4**	**138**	**14.5**	**59**	**4**	**78**	**24**	**1**	**8**	**1**	**0**	**1**	**4**	**0**	**0**	**0**
99-2000	**St. Louis Blues**	**NHL**	**80**	**8**	**15**	**23**	**9**	**14**	**23**	**48**	**0**	**2**	**2**	**120**	**6.7**	**42**	**2**	**55**	**24**	**9**	**7**	**0**	**0**	**0**	**2**	**0**	**0**	**0**
	NHL Totals		**346**	**56**	**79**	**135**	**59**	**73**	**132**	**230**	**2**	**12**	**8**	**499**	**11.2**	**213**	**8**	**273**	**104**		**31**	**1**	**2**	**3**	**22**	**0**	**0**	**0**

Hockey East First All-Star Team (1992) • NCAA East First All-American Team (1992) • Won Hobey Baker Memorial Award (Top U.S. Collegiate Player) (1992)

Signed as a free agent by **St. Louis**, July 10, 1996. Selected by **Minnesota** from **St. Louis** in Expansion Draft, June 23, 2000.

• PELLETIER, Roger

Joseph Georges Roger D – R. 5'11", 195 lbs. b: Montreal, Que., 6/22/1945.

Season	Club	League	GP	G	A	Pts	AG	AA	APts	PIM	PP	SH	GW	S	%	TGF	PGF	TGA	PGA	+/-	GP	G	A	Pts	PIM	PP	SH	GW
1962-63	Quebec Citadelle	QJHL	....	....	....	....	....	....	....	....	....	....	....	....	....	....	....	....	....	....	10	0	3	3	12	....	....	....
1963-64	Quebec Citadelle	QJHL	....	....	....	....	....	....	....	....	....	....	....	....	....	....	....	....	....	....	7	0	1	1	15	....	....	....
1964-65	Quebec Citadelle	QJHL	5	0	0	0	....	....	....	14	....	....	....	....	....	....	....	....	....	....	5	0	0	0	14	....	....	....
1965-66	Thetford Mines Aces	QSHL	38	7	17	24	....	....	....	*266	....	....	....	....	....	....	....	....	....	....	12	2	2	4	54	....	....	....
	Quebec Aces	AHL	1	0	1	1	....	....	....	0	....	....	....	....	....	....	....	....	....	....	....	....	....	....	....	....	....	....
1966-67	Quebec Aces	AHL	31	0	1	1	....	....	....	24	....	....	....	....	....	....	....	....	....	....	3	0	0	0	4	....	....	....
1967-68	**Philadelphia Flyers**	**NHL**	**1**	**0**	**0**	**0**	**0**	**0**	**0**	**0**	**0**	**0**	**0**	**0**	**0.0**	**0**	**0**	**0**	**0**	**0**	....	....	....	....	....	....	....	....
	Quebec Aces	AHL	56	5	8	13	....	....	....	42	....	....	....	....	....	....	....	....	....	....	15	0	0	0	8	....	....	....
1968-69	Quebec Aces	AHL	64	2	14	16	....	....	....	66	....	....	....	....	....	....	....	....	....	....	4	0	0	0	6	....	....	....
1969-70	Quebec Aces	AHL	44	3	4	7	....	....	....	26	....	....	....	....	....	....	....	....	....	....	6	0	0	0	2	....	....	....
1970-71	Quebec Aces	AHL	71	3	14	17	....	....	....	123	....	....	....	....	....	....	....	....	....	....	1	0	0	0	0	....	....	....
1971-72	Richmond Robins	AHL	58	5	11	16	....	....	....	62	....	....	....	....	....	....	....	....	....	....	....	....	....	....	....	....	....	....
1972-73	Richmond Robins	AHL	76	6	18	24	....	....	....	93	....	....	....	....	....	....	....	....	....	....	4	1	0	1	6	....	....	....
1973-74	Richmond Robins	AHL	41	1	7	8	....	....	....	49	....	....	....	....	....	....	....	....	....	....	....	....	....	....	....	....	....	....
	Springfield Kings	AHL	26	1	12	13	....	....	....	37	....	....	....	....	....	....	....	....	....	....	....	....	....	....	....	....	....	....
	NHL Totals		**1**	**0**	**0**	**0**	**0**	**0**	**0**	**0**	**0**	**0**	**0**	**0**	**0.0**	**0**	**0**	**0**	**0**		....	....	....	....	....	....	....	....

• Regular season totals for Quebec (QJHL) in 1962-63, 1963-64 and 1964-65 seasons unavailable. NHL rights transferred to **Philadelphia** after NHL club purchased **Quebec** (AHL) franchise, May 8, 1967. Claimed by **Quebec** (AHL) from **Philadelphia** in Reverse Draft, June 12, 1969. Traded to **Springfield** (AHL) by **Richmond** (AHL) for Doug Volmar, February, 1974.

• PELOFFY, Andre

Andre Charles C – L. 5'8", 160 lbs. b: Sote, France, 2/25/1951. NY Rangers' 12th, 111th overall, in 1971.

Season	Club	League	GP	G	A	Pts	AG	AA	APts	PIM	PP	SH	GW	S	%	TGF	PGF	TGA	PGA	+/-	GP	G	A	Pts	PIM	PP	SH	GW
1968-69	Laval Saints	MMJHL	STATISTICS NOT AVAILABLE																									
1969-70	Laval Saints	MMJHL	56	37	43	80	....	....	....	67	....	....	....	....	....	....	....	....	....	....	....	....	....	....	....	....	....	....
1970-71	Rosemount Nationale	QJHL	60	49	69	118	....	....	....	67	....	....	....	....	....	....	....	....	....	....	....	....	....	....	....	....	....	....
1971-72	New Haven Blades	EHL	42	32	44	76	....	....	....	31	....	....	....	....	....	....	....	....	....	....	7	2	5	7	0	....	....	....
	Providence Reds	AHL	2	1	2	3	....	....	....	0	....	....	....	....	....	....	....	....	....	....	....	....	....	....	....	....	....	....
1972-73	Providence Reds	AHL	62	16	23	39	....	....	....	24	....	....	....	....	....	....	....	....	....	....	3	2	1	3	2	....	....	....
1973-74	Providence Reds	AHL	72	26	45	71	....	....	....	52	....	....	....	....	....	....	....	....	....	....	14	7	5	12	12	....	....	....
1974-75	**Washington Capitals**	**NHL**	**9**	**0**	**0**	**0**	**0**	**0**	**0**	**0**	**0**	**0**	**0**	**7**	**0.0**	**2**	**1**	**9**	**0**	**–8**	....	....	....	....	....	....	....	....
	Richmond Robins	AHL	62	29	44	73	....	....	....	84	....	....	....	....	....	....	....	....	....	....	7	0	4	4	2	....	....	....
1975-76	Richmond Robins	AHL	67	29	30	59	....	....	....	78	....	....	....	....	....	....	....	....	....	....	8	2	1	3	8	....	....	....
1976-77	Springfield Indians	AHL	79	42	57	*99	....	....	....	106	....	....	....	....	....	....	....	....	....	....	....	....	....	....	....	....	....	....
1977-78	New England Whalers	WHA	10	2	0	2	....	....	....	2	....	....	....	....	....	....	....	....	....	....	2	0	0	0	0	....	....	....
	Springfield Indians	AHL	67	33	55	88	....	....	....	73	....	....	....	....	....	....	....	....	....	....	4	2	3	5	8	....	....	....
1978-79	Springfield Indians	AHL	77	28	48	76	....	....	....	138	....	....	....	....	....	....	....	....	....	....	....	....	....	....	....	....	....	....
1979-80	ASG Tours	France	28	42	24	66	....	....	....	....	....	....	....	....	....	....	....	....	....	....	....	....	....	....	....	....	....	....
1980-81	VSV Villach	Austria	34	45	42	87	....	....	....	79	....	....	....	....	....	....	....	....	....	....	....	....	....	....	....	....	....	....
	Springfield Indians	AHL	7	2	0	2	....	....	....	6	....	....	....	....	....	....	....	....	....	....	6	2	5	7	2	....	....	....
	France	WEC-C	7	7	8	15	....	....	....	6	....	....	....	....	....	....	....	....	....	....	....	....	....	....	....	....	....	....
1981-82	VSV Villach	Austria	34	29	45	74	....	....	....	....	....	....	....	....	....	....	....	....	....	....	10	15	13	28	....	....	....	....
	France	WEC-C	7	7	4	11	....	....	....	6	....	....	....	....	....	....	....	....	....	....	....	....	....	....	....	....	....	....
1982-83	HC St-Gervais	France	28	42	45	87	....	....	....	....	....	....	....	....	....	....	....	....	....	....	....	....	....	....	....	....	....	....
	France	WEC-C	7	7	11	18	....	....	....	4	....	....	....	....	....	....	....	....	....	....	....	....	....	....	....	....	....	....
1983-84	HC St-Gervais	France	28	36	39	75	....	....	....	....	....	....	....	....	....	....	....	....	....	....	....	....	....	....	....	....	....	....
1984-85	HC St-Gervais	France	30	25	*44	69	....	....	....	....	....	....	....	....	....	....	....	....	....	....	....	....	....	....	....	....	....	....
	France	WEC-C	1	2	0	2	....	....	....	0	....	....	....	....	....	....	....	....	....	....	....	....	....	....	....	....	....	....
1985-86	HC St-Gervais	France	28	27	50	77	....	....	....	....	....	....	....	....	....	....	....	....	....	....	....	....	....	....	....	....	....	....
	France	WEC-B	7	3	0	3	....	....	....	0	....	....	....	....	....	....	....	....	....	....	....	....	....	....	....	....	....	....
1986-87	HC St-Gervais	France-2	STATISTICS NOT AVAILABLE																									
	France	WEC-B	7	2	2	4	....	....	....	4	....	....	....	....	....	....	....	....	....	....	....	....	....	....	....	....	....	....
1987-88	Paris Francais Volants	France	29	30	34	64	....	....	....	20	....	....	....	....	....	....	....	....	....	....	....	....	....	....	....	....	....	....
	France	Olympics	6	0	2	2	....	....	....	0	....	....	....	....	....	....	....	....	....	....	....	....	....	....	....	....	....	....
1988-89	Paris Francais Volants	France	38	14	19	33	....	....	....	20	....	....	....	....	....	....	....	....	....	....	....	....	....	....	....	....	....	....

Season	Club	League	REGULAR SEASON																		PLAYOFFS							
			GP	G	A	Pts	AG	AA	APts	PIM	PP	SH	GW	S	%	TGF	PGF	TGA	PGA	+/-	GP	G	A	Pts	PIM	PP	SH	GW
1989-90	Paris Francais Volants	France	19	2	3	5	....	....	....	18	....	....	....	....	....	....	....	....	....	....	4	0	1	1	0	....	....	....
1990-1992	Paris Francais Volants	France	DID NOT PLAY – ASSISTANT COACH																									
1993-1996	Paris Francais Volants	France	DID NOT PLAY – COACHING																									
	NHL Totals		**9**	**0**	**0**	**0**	**0**	**0**	**0**	**0**	**0**	**0**	**0**	**7**	**0.0**	**2**	**1**	**9**	**0**		....	....	....	....	....	....	....	....
	Other Major League Totals		10	2	0	2	....	....	....	2	....	....	....	....	....	....	....	....	....	....	2	0	0	0	0	....	....	....

EHL North Rookie of the Year (1972) • Won John B. Sollenberger Trophy (Top Scorer - AHL) (1977) • WEC-C All-Star Team (1981, 1983)

Selected by **Quebec** (WHA) in 1972 WHA General Player Draft, February 12, 1972. Traded to **Washington** by **NY Rangers** for cash, July 29, 1974. Signed as a free agent by **New England** (WHA), August, 1977.

• PELTONEN, Ville

LW – L. 5'11", 180 lbs. b: Vantaa, Finland, 3/24/1973. San Jose's 4th, 58th overall, in 1993.

Season	Club	League	GP	G	A	Pts	AG	AA	APts	PIM	PP	SH	GW	S	%	TGF	PGF	TGA	PGA	+/-	GP	G	A	Pts	PIM	PP	SH	GW
1990-91	HIFK Helsinki	Finland-Jr.	36	21	16	37	....	....	....	16	....	....	....	....	....	....	....	....	....	....	7	2	3	5	10	....	....	....
	Finland	EJC-A	5	4	4	8	....	....	....	2	....	....	....	....	....	....	....	....	....	....	....	....	....	....	....	....	....	....
1991-92	HIFK Helsinki	Finland-Jr.	37	28	23	51	....	....	....	28	....	....	....	....	....	....	....	....	....	....	4	0	2	2	0	....	....	....
	HIFK Helsinki	Finland	6	0	0	0	....	....	....	0	....	....	....	....	....	....	....	....	....	....	....	....	....	....	....	....	....	....
1992-93	HIFK Helsinki	Finland-Jr.	2	4	2	6	....	....	....	4	....	....	....	....	....	....	....	....	....	....	....	....	....	....	....	....	....	....
	HIFK Helsinki	Finland	46	13	24	37	....	....	....	16	....	....	....	....	....	....	....	....	....	....	4	0	2	2	2	....	....	....
	Finland	WJC-A	7	5	6	11	....	....	....	20	....	....	....	....	....	....	....	....	....	....	....	....	....	....	....	....	....	....
1993-94	HIFK Helsinki	Finland	43	16	22	38	....	....	....	14	....	....	....	....	....	....	....	....	....	....	3	0	0	0	2	....	....	....
	Finland	Nat-Team	19	6	4	10	....	....	....	6	....	....	....	....	....	....	....	....	....	....	....	....	....	....	....	....	....	....
	Finland	Olympics	8	4	3	7	....	....	....	0	....	....	....	....	....	....	....	....	....	....	....	....	....	....	....	....	....	....
	Finland	WC-A	8	4	1	5	....	....	....	4	....	....	....	....	....	....	....	....	....	....	....	....	....	....	....	....	....	....
1994-95	HIFK Helsinki	Finland	45	20	16	36	....	....	....	16	....	....	....	....	....	....	....	....	....	....	3	0	0	0	0	....	....	....
	Finland	Nat-Team	16	3	3	6	....	....	....	4	....	....	....	....	....	....	....	....	....	....	....	....	....	....	....	....	....	....
	Finland	WC-A	8	6	5	11	....	....	....	4	....	....	....	....	....	....	....	....	....	....	....	....	....	....	....	....	....	....
1995-96	**San Jose Sharks**	**NHL**	**31**	**2**	**11**	**13**	**2**	**9**	**11**	**14**	**0**	**0**	**0**	**58**	**3.4**	**26**	**4**	**34**	**5**	**–7**	....	....	....	....	....	....	....	....
	Kansas City Blades	IHL	29	5	13	18	....	....	....	8	....	....	....	....	....	....	....	....	....	....	....	....	....	....	....	....	....	....
	Finland	Nat-Team	1	0	0	0	....	....	....	0	....	....	....	....	....	....	....	....	....	....	....	....	....	....	....	....	....	....
	Finland	WC-A	6	3	2	5	....	....	....	6	....	....	....	....	....	....	....	....	....	....	....	....	....	....	....	....	....	....
1996-97	Finland	W-Cup	4	1	3	4	....	....	....	0	....	....	....	....	....	....	....	....	....	....	....	....	....	....	....	....	....	....
	San Jose Sharks	**NHL**	**28**	**2**	**3**	**5**	**2**	**3**	**5**	**0**	**1**	**0**	**0**	**35**	**5.7**	**13**	**1**	**22**	**2**	**–8**	....	....	....	....	....	....	....	....
	Kentucky Thoroughblades	AHL	40	22	30	52	....	....	....	21	....	....	....	....	....	....	....	....	....	....	....	....	....	....	....	....	....	....
	Finland	Nat-Team	3	0	1	1	....	....	....	2	....	....	....	....	....	....	....	....	....	....	....	....	....	....	....	....	....	....
	Finland	WC-A	7	2	2	4	....	....	....	0	....	....	....	....	....	....	....	....	....	....	....	....	....	....	....	....	....	....
1997-98	Vastra Frolunda	Sweden	45	22	29	*51	....	....	....	44	....	....	....	....	....	....	....	....	....	....	7	4	2	6	0	....	....	....
	Finland	Nat-Team	16	4	8	12	....	....	....	10	....	....	....	....	....	....	....	....	....	....	....	....	....	....	....	....	....	....
	Finland	Olympics	6	2	1	3	....	....	....	6	....	....	....	....	....	....	....	....	....	....	....	....	....	....	....	....	....	....
	Finland	WC-A	10	4	6	10	....	....	....	8	....	....	....	....	....	....	....	....	....	....	....	....	....	....	....	....	....	....
1998-99	**Nashville Predators**	**NHL**	**14**	**5**	**5**	**10**	**6**	**5**	**11**	**2**	**1**	**0**	**0**	**31**	**16.1**	**13**	**5**	**7**	**0**	**1**	....	....	....	....	....	....	....	....
	Finland	WC-A	12	2	3	5	....	....	....	2	....	....	....	....	....	....	....	....	....	....	....	....	....	....	....	....	....	....
99-2000	**Nashville Predators**	**NHL**	**79**	**6**	**22**	**28**	**7**	**20**	**27**	**22**	**2**	**0**	**2**	**125**	**4.8**	**48**	**12**	**37**	**0**	**–1**	....	....	....	....	....	....	....	....
	Finland	WC-A	9	0	4	4	....	....	....	2	....	....	....	....	....	....	....	....	....	....	....	....	....	....	....	....	....	....
	NHL Totals		**152**	**15**	**41**	**56**	**17**	**37**	**54**	**38**	**4**	**0**	**2**	**249**	**6.0**	**100**	**22**	**100**	**7**		....	....	....	....	....	....	....	....

Finnish Rookie of the Year (1993) • WC-A All-Star Team (1995)

Traded to **Nashville** by **San Jose** for Nashville's 5th round choice (later traded to Phoenix - Phoenix selected Josh Blackburn) in 1998 Entry Draft, June 26, 1998. • Missed majority of 1998-99 season recovering from shoulder surgery, December 10, 1998.

• PELUSO, Mike

Mike David LW – L. 6'4", 225 lbs. b: Pengilly, MN, 11/8/1965. New Jersey's 10th, 190th overall, in 1984.

Season	Club	League	GP	G	A	Pts	AG	AA	APts	PIM	PP	SH	GW	S	%	TGF	PGF	TGA	PGA	+/-	GP	G	A	Pts	PIM	PP	SH	GW
1983-84	Greenway Raiders	Hi-School	12	5	15	20	....	....	....	30	....	....	....	....	....	....	....	....	....	....	....	....	....	....	....	....	....	....
1984-85	Stratford Cullitons	OJHL-B	40	10	35	45	....	....	....	114	....	....	....	....	....	....	....	....	....	....	....	....	....	....	....	....	....	....
1985-86	University of Alaska-Anchorage	G-North	32	2	11	13	....	....	....	59	....	....	....	....	....	....	....	....	....	....	....	....	....	....	....	....	....	....
1986-87	University of Alaska-Anchorage	G-North	30	5	21	26	....	....	....	68	....	....	....	....	....	....	....	....	....	....	....	....	....	....	....	....	....	....
1987-88	University of Alaska-Anchorage	G-North	35	4	33	37	....	....	....	76	....	....	....	....	....	....	....	....	....	....	....	....	....	....	....	....	....	....
1988-89	University of Alaska-Anchorage	G-North	33	10	27	37	....	....	....	75	....	....	....	....	....	....	....	....	....	....	....	....	....	....	....	....	....	....
1989-90	**Chicago Blackhawks**	**NHL**	**2**	**0**	**0**	**0**	**0**	**0**	**0**	**15**	**0**	**0**	**0**	**0**	**0.0**	**0**	**0**	**0**	**0**	**0**	....	....	....	....	....	....	....	....
	Indianapolis Ice	IHL	75	7	10	17	....	....	....	279	....	....	....	....	....	....	....	....	....	....	14	0	1	1	58	....	....	....
1990-91	**Chicago Blackhawks**	**NHL**	**53**	**6**	**1**	**7**	**5**	**1**	**6**	**320**	**2**	**0**	**0**	**29**	**20.7**	**12**	**2**	**13**	**0**	**–3**	**3**	**0**	**0**	**0**	**2**	**0**	**0**	**0**
	Indianapolis Ice	IHL	6	2	1	3	....	....	....	21	....	....	....	....	....	....	....	....	....	....	5	0	2	2	40	....	....	....
1991-92	**Chicago Blackhawks**	**NHL**	**63**	**6**	**3**	**9**	**5**	**2**	**7**	***408**	**2**	**0**	**0**	**32**	**18.8**	**15**	**3**	**13**	**2**	**1**	**17**	**1**	**2**	**3**	**8**	**0**	**0**	**1**
	Indianapolis Ice	IHL	4	0	1	1	....	....	....	15	....	....	....	....	....	....	....	....	....	....	....	....	....	....	....	....	....	....
1992-93	**Ottawa Senators**	**NHL**	**81**	**15**	**10**	**25**	**12**	**7**	**19**	**318**	**2**	**0**	**1**	**93**	**16.1**	**34**	**5**	**64**	**0**	**–35**	....	....	....	....	....	....	....	....
1993-94	**New Jersey Devils**	**NHL**	**69**	**4**	**16**	**20**	**4**	**12**	**16**	**238**	**0**	**0**	**0**	**44**	**9.1**	**33**	**0**	**15**	**1**	**19**	**17**	**1**	**0**	**1**	***64**	**0**	**0**	**1**
1994-95♦	**New Jersey Devils**	**NHL**	**46**	**2**	**9**	**11**	**4**	**13**	**17**	**167**	**0**	**0**	**1**	**27**	**7.4**	**19**	**0**	**14**	**0**	**5**	**20**	**1**	**2**	**3**	**8**	**0**	**0**	**0**
1995-96	**New Jersey Devils**	**NHL**	**57**	**3**	**8**	**11**	**3**	**7**	**10**	**146**	**0**	**0**	**0**	**41**	**7.3**	**17**	**1**	**12**	**0**	**4**	....	....	....	....	....	....	....	....
1996-97	**New Jersey Devils**	**NHL**	**20**	**0**	**2**	**2**	**0**	**2**	**2**	**68**	**0**	**0**	**0**	**14**	**0.0**	**3**	**0**	**3**	**0**	**0**	....	....	....	....	....	....	....	....
	St. Louis Blues	**NHL**	**44**	**2**	**3**	**5**	**2**	**3**	**5**	**158**	**0**	**0**	**0**	**23**	**8.7**	**7**	**0**	**7**	**0**	**0**	**5**	**0**	**0**	**0**	**25**	**0**	**0**	**0**
1997-98	**Calgary Flames**	**NHL**	**23**	**0**	**0**	**0**	**0**	**0**	**0**	**113**	**0**	**0**	**0**	**8**	**0.0**	**0**	**0**	**6**	**0**	**–6**	....	....	....	....	....	....	....	....
	NHL Totals		**458**	**38**	**52**	**90**	**35**	**47**	**82**	**1951**	**6**	**0**	**2**	**311**	**12.2**	**140**	**11**	**147**	**3**		**62**	**3**	**4**	**7**	**107**	**0**	**0**	**2**

Signed as a free agent by **Chicago**, September 7, 1989. Claimed by **Ottawa** from **Chicago** in Expansion Draft, June 18, 1992. Traded to **New Jersey** by **Ottawa** to complete transaction that sent Craig Billington, Troy Mallette and New Jersey's 4th round choice (Cosmo Dupaul) in 1993 Entry Draft to Ottawa (June 20, 1993), June 26, 1993. Traded to **St. Louis** by **New Jersey** with Ricard Persson for Ken Sutton and St. Louis' 2nd round choice (Brett Clouthier) in 1999 Entry Draft, November 26, 1996. Transferred to **NY Rangers** from **St. Louis** as compensation for St. Louis' signing of Larry Pleau as head coach, June 21, 1997. Claimed by **Calgary** from **NY Rangers** in NHL Waiver Draft, September 28, 1997. • Suffered eventual career-ending neck injury suffered in game vs. Phoenix, December 22, 1997. • Officially announced retirement, December 30, 1997.

• PELYK, Mike

Michael Joseph "Mike Mikita" D – L. 6'1", 190 lbs. b: Toronto, Ont., 9/29/1947. Toronto's 3rd, 17th overall, in 1964.

Season	Club	League	GP	G	A	Pts	AG	AA	APts	PIM	PP	SH	GW	S	%	TGF	PGF	TGA	PGA	+/-	GP	G	A	Pts	PIM	PP	SH	GW
1963-64	Toronto Midget Marlboros	MTHL	STATISTICS NOT AVAILABLE																									
1964-65	York Steel	OHA-B	25	2	21	23	....	....	....	....	....	....	....	....	....	....	....	....	....	....	....	....	....	....	....	....	....	....
1965-66	Toronto Westclairs	OHA-B	STATISTICS NOT AVAILABLE																									
	Toronto Marlboros	OHA-Jr.	17	0	3	3	....	....	....	20	....	....	....	....	....	....	....	....	....	....	....	....	....	....	....	....	....	....
1966-67	Toronto Marlboros	OHA-Jr.	48	2	18	20	....	....	....	146	....	....	....	....	....	....	....	....	....	....	17	3	10	13	35	....	....	....
	Toronto Marlboros	Mem-Cup	9	0	4	4	....	....	....	*37	....	....	....	....	....	....	....	....	....	....	....	....	....	....	....	....	....	....
1967-68	**Toronto Maple Leafs**	**NHL**	**24**	**0**	**3**	**3**	**0**	**3**	**3**	**55**	**0**	**0**	**0**	**18**	**0.0**	**16**	**1**	**13**	**1**	**3**	....	....	....	....	....	....	....	....
	Tulsa Oilers	CPHL	47	0	16	16	....	....	....	131	....	....	....	....	....	....	....	....	....	....	....	....	....	....	....	....	....	....
1968-69	**Toronto Maple Leafs**	**NHL**	**65**	**3**	**9**	**12**	**3**	**8**	**11**	**146**	**0**	**0**	**0**	**67**	**4.5**	**59**	**2**	**71**	**12**	**–2**	**4**	**0**	**0**	**0**	**8**	**0**	**0**	**0**
1969-70	**Toronto Maple Leafs**	**NHL**	**36**	**1**	**3**	**4**	**1**	**3**	**4**	**37**	**0**	**0**	**0**	**47**	**2.1**	**16**	**0**	**36**	**10**	**–10**	....	....	....	....	....	....	....	....
1970-71	**Toronto Maple Leafs**	**NHL**	**73**	**5**	**21**	**26**	**5**	**18**	**23**	**54**	**0**	**0**	**1**	**78**	**6.4**	**71**	**7**	**64**	**17**	**17**	**6**	**0**	**0**	**0**	**10**	**0**	**0**	**0**
1971-72	**Toronto Maple Leafs**	**NHL**	**46**	**1**	**4**	**5**	**1**	**3**	**4**	**44**	**0**	**0**	**0**	**58**	**1.7**	**28**	**3**	**49**	**22**	**–2**	**5**	**0**	**0**	**0**	**8**	**0**	**0**	**0**
1972-73	**Toronto Maple Leafs**	**NHL**	**72**	**3**	**16**	**19**	**3**	**13**	**16**	**118**	**0**	**0**	**1**	**113**	**2.7**	**89**	**9**	**118**	**18**	**–20**	....	....	....	....	....	....	....	....
1973-74	**Toronto Maple Leafs**	**NHL**	**71**	**12**	**19**	**31**	**12**	**16**	**28**	**94**	**0**	**0**	**1**	**115**	**10.4**	**77**	**8**	**83**	**19**	**5**	**4**	**0**	**0**	**0**	**4**	**0**	**0**	**0**
1974-75	Vancouver Blazers	WHA	75	14	26	40	....	....	....	121	....	....	....	....	....	....	....	....	....	....	....	....	....	....	....	....	....	....
1975-76	Cincinnati Stingers	WHA	75	10	23	33	....	....	....	117	....	....	....	....	....	....	....	....	....	....	....	....	....	....	....	....	....	....
1976-77	**Toronto Maple Leafs**	**NHL**	**13**	**0**	**2**	**2**	**0**	**2**	**2**	**4**	**0**	**0**	**0**	**9**	**0.0**	**9**	**0**	**22**	**9**	**–4**	**9**	**0**	**2**	**2**	**4**	**0**	**0**	**0**
	Dallas Black Hawks	CHL	62	9	26	35	....	....	....	73	....	....	....	....	....	....	....	....	....	....	....	....	....	....	....	....	....	....
1977-78	**Toronto Maple Leafs**	**NHL**	**41**	**1**	**11**	**12**	**1**	**8**	**9**	**14**	**1**	**0**	**0**	**40**	**2.5**	**34**	**3**	**40**	**10**	**1**	**12**	**0**	**1**	**1**	**7**	**0**	**0**	**0**
	Tulsa Oilers	CHL	32	2	12	14	....	....	....	35	....	....	....	....	....	....	....	....	....	....	....	....	....	....	....	....	....	....
	NHL Totals		**441**	**26**	**88**	**114**	**26**	**74**	**100**	**566**	**1**	**0**	**3**	**545**	**4.8**	**399**	**33**	**496**	**118**		**40**	**0**	**3**	**3**	**41**	**0**	**0**	**0**
	Other Major League Totals		150	24	49	73	....	....	....	238	....	....	....	....	....	....	....	....	....	....	....	....	....	....	....	....	....	....

Selected by **Minnesota** (WHA) in 1972 WHA General Player Draft, February 12, 1972. WHA rights traded to **Cincinnati** (WHA) by **Minnesota** (WHA) for future considerations, June, 1974. Loaned to **Vancouver** (WHA) by **Cincinnati** (WHA) for 1974-75 season, June, 1974. Rights traded to **Toronto** by **Cincinnati** (WHA) with the rights to Randy Carlyle for cash, June, 1976.

• PENNEY, Chad

LW – L. 6', 195 lbs. b: Labrador City, Nfld., 9/18/1973. Ottawa's 2nd, 25th overall, in 1992.

			REGULAR SEASON																		PLAYOFFS							
Season	Club	League	GP	G	A	Pts	AG	AA	APts	PIM	PP	SH	GW	S	%	TGF	PGF	TGA	PGA	+/-	GP	G	A	Pts	PIM	PP	SH	GW
1989-90	Dartmouth Oland Exports	NSAHA	45	41	54	95	....	....	....	....	....	....	....	....	....	....	....	....	....	....	....	....	....	....	....	....	....	....
1990-91	North Bay Centennials	OHL	66	33	34	67	....	....	....	56	....	....	....	....	....	....	....	....	....	....	10	2	6	8	12	....	....	....
1991-92	North Bay Centennials	OHL	57	25	27	52	....	....	....	90	....	....	....	....	....	....	....	....	....	....	21	13	17	30	9	....	....	....
	Canada	WJC-A	7	0	0	0	....	....	....	2	....	....	....	....	....	....	....	....	....	....	....	....	....	....	....	....	....	....
1992-93	North Bay Centennials	OHL	18	8	7	15	....	....	....	19	....	....	....	....	....	....	....	....	....	....	....	....	....	....	....	....	....	....
	Sault Ste. Marie Greyhounds	OHL	48	29	44	73	....	....	....	67	....	....	....	....	....	....	....	....	....	....	18	7	10	17	18	....	....	....
	Sault Ste. Marie Greyhounds	Mem-Cup	4	*5	2	7	....	....	....	6	....	....	....	....	....	....	....	....	....	....	....	....	....	....	....	....	....	....
1993-94	**Ottawa Senators**	**NHL**	3	0	0	0	0	0	0	2	0	0	0	2	0.0	1	0	3	0	–2	....	....	....	....	....	....	....	....
	P.E.I. Senators	AHL	73	20	30	50	....	....	....	66	....	....	....	....	....	....	....	....	....	....	....	....	....	....	....	....	....	....
1994-95	P.E.I. Senators	AHL	66	16	16	32	....	....	....	19	....	....	....	....	....	....	....	....	....	....	11	2	2	4	2	....	....	....
1995-96	P.E.I. Senators	AHL	79	23	37	60	....	....	....	48	....	....	....	....	....	....	....	....	....	....	3	1	1	2	0	....	....	....
1996-97	Manchester Storm	BH-Cup	1	1	0	1	....	....	....	0	....	....	....	....	....	....	....	....	....	....	....	....	....	....	....	....	....	....
	Manchester Storm	Britain	39	9	16	25	....	....	....	48	....	....	....	....	....	....	....	....	....	....	6	1	1	2	6	....	....	....
	Manchester Storm	EuroHL	4	0	2	2	....	....	....	25	....	....	....	....	....	....	....	....	....	....	....	....	....	....	....	....	....	....
1997-98	Kentucky Thoroughblades	AHL	78	16	21	37	....	....	....	43	....	....	....	....	....	....	....	....	....	....	2	0	0	0	0	....	....	....
1998-99	Colorado Gold Kings	WCHL	67	31	46	77	....	....	....	58	....	....	....	....	....	....	....	....	....	....	3	0	2	2	4	....	....	....
	NHL Totals		3	0	0	0	0	0	0	2	0	0	0	2	0.0	1	0	3	0		....	....	....	....	....	....	....	....

Memorial Cup All-Star Team (1993)

• PEPLINSKI, Jim

James Desmond RW – R. 6'3", 210 lbs. b: Renfrew, Ont., 10/24/1960. Atlanta's 5th, 75th overall, in 1979.

Season	Club	League	GP	G	A	Pts	AG	AA	APts	PIM	PP	SH	GW	S	%	TGF	PGF	TGA	PGA	+/-	GP	G	A	Pts	PIM	PP	SH	GW
1976-77	South Ottawa Canadians	OMHA	22	22	33	55	....	....	....	42	....	....	....	....	....	....	....	....	....	....	....	....	....	....	....	....	....	....
1977-78	Toronto Marlboros	OMJHL	66	13	28	41	....	....	....	44	....	....	....	....	....	....	....	....	....	....	5	2	2	4	26	....	....	....
1978-79	Toronto Marlboros	OMJHL	66	23	32	55	....	....	....	88	....	....	....	....	....	....	....	....	....	....	3	0	1	1	0	....	....	....
1979-80	Toronto Marlboros	OMJHL	67	35	66	101	....	....	....	89	....	....	....	....	....	....	....	....	....	....	4	1	2	3	15	....	....	....
1980-81	**Calgary Flames**	**NHL**	80	13	25	38	10	17	27	108	1	0	2	107	12.1	54	6	50	0	–2	16	2	3	5	41	0	0	0
1981-82	**Calgary Flames**	**NHL**	74	30	37	67	24	25	49	115	3	3	5	141	21.3	90	13	100	23	0	3	1	0	1	13	1	0	0
1982-83	**Calgary Flames**	**NHL**	80	15	26	41	12	18	30	134	1	0	1	147	10.2	73	5	77	4	–5	8	1	1	2	45	0	0	0
1983-84	**Calgary Flames**	**NHL**	74	11	22	33	9	15	24	114	0	0	1	149	7.4	54	6	70	1	–21	11	3	4	7	21	0	0	0
1984-85	**Calgary Flames**	**NHL**	80	16	29	45	13	20	33	111	0	0	1	174	9.2	67	0	77	22	12	4	1	3	4	11	0	0	0
1985-86	**Calgary Flames**	**NHL**	77	24	35	59	19	24	43	214	0	1	3	161	14.9	84	0	71	18	31	22	5	9	14	107	0	0	0
1986-87	**Calgary Flames**	**NHL**	80	18	32	50	16	23	39	181	0	2	3	145	12.4	72	0	77	18	13	6	1	0	1	24	0	0	0
1987-88	**Calgary Flames**	**NHL**	75	20	31	51	17	22	39	234	0	2	4	128	15.6	70	0	68	18	20	9	0	5	5	45	0	0	0
	Canada	Olympics	7	0	1	1	....	....	....	6	....	....	....	....	....	....	....	....	....	....	....	....	....	....	....	....	....	....
1988-89♦	**Calgary Flames**	**NHL**	79	13	25	38	11	18	29	241	0	0	2	103	12.6	48	0	42	0	6	20	1	6	7	75	0	0	0
1989-90	Calgary Flames	Fr-Tour	4	0	1	1	....	....	....	0	....	....	....	....	....	....	....	....	....	....	....	....	....	....	....	....	....	....
	Calgary Flames	**NHL**	6	1	0	1	1	0	1	4	0	0	0	12	8.3	3	0	4	0	–1	....	....	....	....	....	....	....	....
1990-1994			OUT OF HOCKEY – RETIRED																									
1994-95	**Calgary Flames**	**NHL**	6	0	1	1	0	1	1	11	0	0	0	5	0.0	3	0	5	0	–2	....	....	....	....	....	....	....	....
	NHL Totals		711	161	263	424	132	183	315	1467	5	8	22	1272	12.7	618	30	641	104		99	15	31	46	382	1	0	0

Transferred to **Calgary** after **Atlanta** franchise relocated, June 24, 1980. Signed as a free agent by **Calgary**, April 6, 1995.

• PERLINI, Fred

C – L. 6'2", 175 lbs. b: Sault Ste. Marie, Ont., 4/12/1962. Toronto's 8th, 158th overall, in 1980.

Season	Club	League	GP	G	A	Pts	AG	AA	APts	PIM	PP	SH	GW	S	%	TGF	PGF	TGA	PGA	+/-	GP	G	A	Pts	PIM	PP	SH	GW
1978-79	Sault Ste. Marie Legionaires	OMHA	27	57	50	107	....	....	....	....	....	....	....	....	....	....	....	....	....	....	....	....	....	....	....	....	....	....
1979-80	Toronto Marlboros	OMJHL	67	13	18	31	....	....	....	12	....	....	....	....	....	....	....	....	....	....	4	0	1	1	5	....	....	....
1980-81	Toronto Marlboros	OMJHL	35	37	29	66	....	....	....	48	....	....	....	....	....	....	....	....	....	....	5	0	0	0	4	....	....	....
1981-82	Toronto Marlboros	OHL	68	47	64	111	....	....	....	75	....	....	....	....	....	....	....	....	....	....	10	4	9	13	9	....	....	....
	Toronto Maple Leafs	**NHL**	7	2	3	5	2	2	4	0	1	0	0	12	16.7	8	3	7	0	–2	....	....	....	....	....	....	....	....
1982-83	St. Catharines Saints	AHL	76	8	22	30	....	....	....	24	....	....	....	....	....	....	....	....	....	....	....	....	....	....	....	....	....	....
1983-84	**Toronto Maple Leafs**	**NHL**	1	0	0	0	0	0	0	0	0	0	0	3	0.0	0	0	0	0	0	....	....	....	....	....	....	....	....
	St. Catharines Saints	AHL	79	21	31	52	....	....	....	67	....	....	....	....	....	....	....	....	....	....	7	1	1	2	17	....	....	....
1984-85	St. Catharines Saints	AHL	77	21	28	49	....	....	....	26	....	....	....	....	....	....	....	....	....	....	....	....	....	....	....	....	....	....
1985-86	Baltimore Skipjacks	AHL	25	6	4	10	....	....	....	6	....	....	....	....	....	....	....	....	....	....	....	....	....	....	....	....	....	....
1986-87	Nottingham Panthers	Aut-Cup	3	4	5	9	....	....	....	6	....	....	....	....	....	....	....	....	....	....	....	....	....	....	....	....	....	....
	Nottingham Panthers	Britain	35	89	82	171	....	....	....	135	....	....	....	....	....	....	....	....	....	....	4	6	8	14	8	....	....	....
1987-88	Fife Flyers	Aut-Cup	5	17	7	24	....	....	....	15	....	....	....	....	....	....	....	....	....	....	....	....	....	....	....	....	....	....
	Fife Flyers	Britain	35	103	73	176	....	....	....	34	....	....	....	....	....	....	....	....	....	....	8	*20	14	34	0	....	....	....
1988-89	Deeside Dragons	Britain-2	24	103	69	172	....	....	....	42	....	....	....	....	....	....	....	....	....	....	....	....	....	....	....	....	....	....
1989-90	Trafford Metros	Britain-2	25	81	59	140	....	....	....	14	....	....	....	....	....	....	....	....	....	....	....	....	....	....	....	....	....	....
1990-91	Blackburn Black Hawks	Britain-2	21	83	49	132	....	....	....	48	....	....	....	....	....	....	....	....	....	....	....	....	....	....	....	....	....	....
	Telford Tigers	Britain-2	5	9	8	17	....	....	....	2	....	....	....	....	....	....	....	....	....	....	....	....	....	....	....	....	....	....
1991-92	Streatham Redskins	Aut-Cup	4	16	7	23	....	....	....	4	....	....	....	....	....	....	....	....	....	....	....	....	....	....	....	....	....	....
	Streatham Redskins	Britain-2	23	93	53	146	....	....	....	42	....	....	....	....	....	....	....	....	....	....	6	12	4	16	8	....	....	....
1992-93	Streatham Redskins	Aut-Cup	3	10	3	13	....	....	....	4	....	....	....	....	....	....	....	....	....	....	....	....	....	....	....	....	....	....
	Streatham Redskins	Britain-2	31	135	91	226	....	....	....	20	....	....	....	....	....	....	....	....	....	....	6	17	9	26	4	....	....	....
1993-94	Lee Valley Lions	Britain-2	20	71	47	118	....	....	....	26	....	....	....	....	....	....	....	....	....	....	....	....	....	....	....	....	....	....
	Basingstroke Beavers	Britain	1	0	0	0	....	....	....	0	....	....	....	....	....	....	....	....	....	....	....	....	....	....	....	....	....	....
1994-95	Guildford Flames	Aut-Cup	6	12	16	28	....	....	....	12	....	....	....	....	....	....	....	....	....	....	....	....	....	....	....	....	....	....
	Guildford Flames	Britain-2	44	78	57	135	....	....	....	40	....	....	....	....	....	....	....	....	....	....	....	....	....	....	....	....	....	....
1995-96	Guildford Flames	BH-Cup	8	11	6	17	....	....	....	33	....	....	....	....	....	....	....	....	....	....	....	....	....	....	....	....	....	....
	Guildford Flames	Britain-2	50	90	56	146	....	....	....	51	....	....	....	....	....	....	....	....	....	....	....	....	....	....	....	....	....	....
1996-97	Guildford Flames	BH-Cup	2	2	1	3	....	....	....	2	....	....	....	....	....	....	....	....	....	....	....	....	....	....	....	....	....	....
	Guildford Flames	Britain	27	32	18	50	....	....	....	14	....	....	....	....	....	....	....	....	....	....	10	8	6	14	0	....	....	....
	NHL Totals		8	2	3	5	2	2	4	0	1	0	0	15	13.3	8	3	7	0		....	....	....	....	....	....	....	....

• PERREAULT, Gilbert

C – L. 6'1", 180 lbs. b: Victoriaville, Que., 11/13/1950. Buffalo's 1st, 1st overall, in 1970. **HHOF**

Season	Club	League	GP	G	A	Pts	AG	AA	APts	PIM	PP	SH	GW	S	%	TGF	PGF	TGA	PGA	+/-	GP	G	A	Pts	PIM	PP	SH	GW
1966-67	Thetford Mines Canadiens	QJHL	45	25	40	65	....	....	....	8	....	....	....	....	....	....	....	....	....	....	11	7	15	22	0	....	....	....
	Thetford Mines Canadiens	Mem-Cup	19	15	11	26	....	....	....	2	....	....	....	....	....	....	....	....	....	....	....	....	....	....	....	....	....	....
1967-68	Montreal Jr. Canadiens	OHA-Jr.	47	15	34	49	....	....	....	10	....	....	....	....	....	....	....	....	....	....	11	8	9	17	5	....	....	....
1968-69	Montreal Jr. Canadiens	OHA-Jr.	54	37	60	97	....	....	....	29	....	....	....	....	....	....	....	....	....	....	14	5	10	15	10	....	....	....
	Montreal Jr. Canadiens	Mem-Cup	8	3	12	15	....	....	....	4	....	....	....	....	....	....	....	....	....	....	....	....	....	....	....	....	....	....
1969-70	Montreal Jr. Canadiens	OHA-Jr.	54	51	70	121	....	....	....	26	....	....	....	....	....	....	....	....	....	....	16	*17	*21	*38	4	....	....	....
	Montreal Jr. Canadiens	Mem-Cup	12	17	19	36	....	....	....	16	....	....	....	....	....	....	....	....	....	....	....	....	....	....	....	....	....	....
1970-71	**Buffalo Sabres**	**NHL**	78	38	34	72	38	28	66	19	14	0	5	210	18.1	105	48	97	1	–39	....	....	....	....	....	....	....	....
1971-72	**Buffalo Sabres**	**NHL**	76	26	48	74	26	42	68	24	11	0	1	218	11.9	105	50	100	5	–40	....	....	....	....	....	....	....	....
1972-73	Team Canada	Summit-72	2	1	1	2	....	....	....	0	....	....	....	....	....	....	....	....	....	....	....	....	....	....	....	....	....	....
	Buffalo Sabres	**NHL**	78	28	60	88	26	48	74	10	8	0	7	234	12.0	126	43	74	2	11	6	3	7	10	2	1	0	1
1973-74	**Buffalo Sabres**	**NHL**	55	18	33	51	17	27	44	10	6	0	7	163	11.0	84	29	66	3	–8	....	....	....	....	....	....	....	....
1974-75	**Buffalo Sabres**	**NHL**	68	39	57	96	34	43	77	36	12	0	8	245	15.9	139	60	78	0	1	17	6	9	15	10	4	0	1
1975-76	**Buffalo Sabres**	**NHL**	80	44	69	113	39	52	91	36	14	0	4	237	18.6	142	57	68	0	17	9	4	4	8	4	0	0	0
1976-77	Canada	Can-Cup	7	4	4	8	....	....	....	2	....	....	....	....	....	....	....	....	....	....	....	....	....	....	....	....	....	....
	Buffalo Sabres	**NHL**	80	39	56	95	35	43	78	30	7	2	9	195	20.0	120	42	75	7	10	6	1	8	9	4	0	0	0
1977-78	**Buffalo Sabres**	**NHL**	79	41	48	89	37	37	74	20	7	0	7	192	21.4	122	36	68	0	18	8	3	2	5	0	0	0	1
1978-79	**Buffalo Sabres**	**NHL**	79	27	58	85	23	42	65	20	6	0	4	172	15.7	116	39	65	0	12	3	1	0	1	2	1	0	0
	NHL All-Stars	Chal-Cup	3	1	1	2	....	....	....	2	....	....	....	....	....	....	....	....	....	....	....	....	....	....	....	....	....	....
1979-80	**Buffalo Sabres**	**NHL**	80	40	66	106	34	48	82	57	10	0	5	180	22.2	153	57	65	1	32	14	10	11	21	8	3	0	2
1980-81	**Buffalo Sabres**	**NHL**	56	20	39	59	16	26	42	56	5	0	3	150	13.3	92	34	59	4	3	8	2	10	12	2	0	0	0
1981-82	Canada	Can-Cup	4	3	6	9	....	....	....	2	....	....	....	....	....	....	....	....	....	....	....	....	....	....	....	....	....	....
	Buffalo Sabres	**NHL**	62	31	42	73	24	28	52	40	2	0	4	155	20.0	103	22	71	9	19	4	0	7	7	0	0	0	0

Season	Club	League	GP	G	A	Pts	AG	AA	APts	PIM	PP	SH	GW	S	%	TGF	PGF	TGA	PGA	+/–	GP	G	A	Pts	PIM	PP	SH	GW
			REGULAR SEASON																		PLAYOFFS							
1982-83	Buffalo Sabres	NHL	77	30	46	76	25	32	57	34	8	2	5	192	15.6	112	34	95	7	–10	10	0	7	7	8	0	0	0
1983-84	Buffalo Sabres	NHL	73	31	59	90	25	40	65	32	8	2	7	165	18.8	115	37	80	21	19								
1984-85	Buffalo Sabres	NHL	78	30	53	83	24	36	60	42	10	1	1	172	17.4	117	44	82	18	9	5	3	5	8	4	1	0	0
1985-86	Buffalo Sabres	NHL	72	21	39	60	17	26	43	28	5	1	3	164	12.8	83	23	80	10	–10								
1986-87	Buffalo Sabres	NHL	20	9	7	16	8	5	13	6	1	0	1	35	25.7	23	6	26	7	–2								
	NHL Totals		1191	512	814	1326	448	603	1051	500	134	8	81	3079	16.6	1857	661	1249	95		90	33	70	103	44	10	0	5

OHA-Jr. First All-Star Team (1969, 1970) • Won Calder Memorial Trophy (1971) • Won Lady Byng Trophy (1973) • NHL Second All-Star Team (1976, 1977) • Canada Cup All-Star Team (1981) • Played in NHL All-Star Game (1971, 1977, 1978, 1980, 1984) • Officially announced retirement, November 24, 1986.

• PERREAULT, Yanic

C – L. 5'11", 188 lbs. b: Sherbrooke, Que., 4/4/1971. Toronto's 1st, 47th overall, in 1991.

Season	Club	League	GP	G	A	Pts	AG	AA	APts	PIM	PP	SH	GW	S	%	TGF	PGF	TGA	PGA	+/–	GP	G	A	Pts	PIM	PP	SH	GW
1987-88	Montreal L'est Cantonniers	QAAA	42	70	57	127																						
1988-89	Trois-Rivieres Draveurs	QMJHL	70	53	55	108				48																		
1989-90	Trois-Rivieres Draveurs	QMJHL	63	51	63	114				75											7	6	5	11	19			
1990-91	Trois-Rivieres Draveurs	QMJHL	67	*87	98	*185				103											6	4	7	11	6			
1991-92	St. John's Maple Leafs	AHL	62	38	38	76				19											16	7	8	15	4			
1992-93	St. John's Maple Leafs	AHL	79	49	46	95				56											9	4	5	9	2			
1993-94	**Toronto Maple Leafs**	**NHL**	13	3	3	6	3	2	5	0	2	0	0	24	12.5	7	2	4	0	1								
	St. John's Maple Leafs	AHL	62	45	60	105				38											11	*12	6	18	14			
1994-95	Phoenix Roadrunners	IHL	68	51	48	99				52																		
	Los Angeles Kings	**NHL**	26	2	5	7	4	7	11	20	0	0	1	43	4.7	14	2	9	0	3								
1995-96	**Los Angeles Kings**	**NHL**	78	25	24	49	25	20	45	16	8	3	7	175	14.3	63	23	56	5	–11								
	Canada	WC-A	8	6	3	9				0																		
1996-97	**Los Angeles Kings**	**NHL**	41	11	14	25	12	12	24	20	1	1	0	98	11.2	33	6	38	11	0								
1997-98	**Los Angeles Kings**	**NHL**	79	28	20	48	33	20	53	32	3	2	3	206	13.6	73	12	77	22	6	4	1	2	3	6	1	0	0
1998-99	**Los Angeles Kings**	**NHL**	64	10	17	27	12	16	28	30	2	2	1	113	8.8	45	11	49	12	–3								
	Toronto Maple Leafs	**NHL**	12	7	8	15	8	8	16	12	2	1	2	28	25.0	22	6	7	1	10	17	3	6	9	6	0	0	2
99-2000	**Toronto Maple Leafs**	**NHL**	58	18	27	45	20	25	45	22	5	0	4	114	15.8	51	16	35	3	3	1	0	1	1	0	0	0	0
	NHL Totals		371	104	118	222	117	110	227	152	23	9	18	801	13.0	308	78	275	54		22	4	9	13	12	1	0	2

Canadian Major Junior Rookie of the Year (1989) • QMJHL First All-Star Team (1991)

Traded to **LA Kings** by **Toronto** for LA Kings' 4th round choice (later traded to Philadelphia — later traded to LA Kings — LA Kings selected Mikael Simons) in 1996 Entry Draft, July 11, 1994. Traded to **Toronto** by **Los Angeles** for Jason Podollan and Toronto's 3rd round choice (Cory Campbell) in 1999 Entry Draft, March 23, 1999. • Missed majority of 1999-2000 season recovering from arm injury suffered in game vs. Pittsburgh, December 4, 1999.

• PERRY, Brian

Brian Thomas C – L. 5'11", 180 lbs. b: Aldershot, England, 4/6/1944.

Season	Club	League	GP	G	A	Pts	AG	AA	APts	PIM	PP	SH	GW	S	%	TGF	PGF	TGA	PGA	+/–	GP	G	A	Pts	PIM	PP	SH	GW
1963-64	Owen Sound Greys	OHA-B	40	44	41	*85																						
1964-65	New York Rovers	EHL	8	1	0	1				4																		
	New Glasgow Rangers	NSSHL	....	12	12	24				12																		
1965-66	New Haven Blades	EHL	71	39	49	88				28											3	0	2	2	0			
	Providence Reds	AHL	8	3	1	4				2																		
1966-67	Providence Reds	AHL	62	23	30	53				10																		
1967-68	Providence Reds	AHL	71	31	38	69				36											8	0	9	9	8			
1968-69	**Oakland Seals**	**NHL**	61	10	21	31	11	19	30	10	0	0	1	75	13.3	42	6	42	0	–6	6	1	1	2	4	0	0	0
1969-70	**Oakland Seals**	**NHL**	34	6	8	14	6	7	13	14	0	0	0	41	14.6	21	5	19	0	–3	2	0	0	0	0	0	0	0
	Providence Reds	AHL	24	10	17	27				4																		
1970-71	**Buffalo Sabres**	**NHL**	1	0	0	0	0	0	0	0	0	0	0	0	0.0	0	0	0	0	0								
	Seattle Totems	WHL	47	12	11	23				24																		
1971-72	Providence Reds	AHL	76	24	25	49				52											5	1	4	5	2			
1972-73	New York Raiders	WHA	74	13	20	33				30																		
1973-74	New York-Jersey Knights	WHA	71	20	11	31				19																		
1974-75	Syracuse Blazers	NAHL	73	32	56	88				102																		
	San Diego Mariners	WHA																			6	1	2	3	6			
	NHL Totals		96	16	29	45	17	26	43	24	0	0	1	116	13.8	63	11	61	0		8	1	1	2	4	0	0	0
	Other Major League Totals		145	33	31	64				49											6	1	2	3	6			

Claimed by **Oakland** from **Providence** (AHL) in Inter-League Draft, June 6, 1968. Claimed by **Buffalo** from **Oakland** in Expansion Draft, June 10, 1970. Claimed by **Providence** (AHL) from **Buffalo** in Reverse Draft, June, 1971. Selected by **NY Raiders** (WHA) in 1972 WHA General Player Draft, February 12, 1972. Transferred to **San Diego** (WHA) after **New York-Jersey** (WHA) franchise relocated, April 30, 1974.

• PERSSON, Ricard

Ricard Lars "Rico" D – L. 6'2", 205 lbs. b: Ostersund, Sweden, 8/24/1969. New Jersey's 2nd, 23rd overall, in 1987.

Season	Club	League	GP	G	A	Pts	AG	AA	APts	PIM	PP	SH	GW	S	%	TGF	PGF	TGA	PGA	+/–	GP	G	A	Pts	PIM	PP	SH	GW
1984-85	Ostersunds IK	Sweden-2	13	0	3	3				6																		
1985-86	Ostersunds IK	Sweden-2	24	2	2	4				16																		
1986-87	Ostersunds IK	Sweden-2	31	10	11	21				28																		
	Sweden	EJC-A	7	2	1	3				0																		
1987-88	Leksands IF	Sweden	31	2	0	2				8											2	0	1	1	2			
1988-89	Leksands IF	Swéden	33	2	4	6				28											9	0	1	1	6			
1989-90	Leksands IF	Sweden	43	9	10	19				62											3	0	0	0	6			
1990-91	Leksands IF	Sweden	37	6	9	15				42																		
1991-92	Leksands IF	Sweden	21	0	7	7				28																		
1992-93	Leksands IF	Sweden	36	7	15	22				63											2	0	2	2	0			
1993-94	Malmo IF	Sweden	40	11	9	20				38											11	2	0	2	12			
1994-95	Malmo IF	Sweden	31	3	13	16				38											9	0	2	2	8			
	Albany River Rats	AHL	3	0	0	0				0											9	3	5	8	7			
1995-96	**New Jersey Devils**	**NHL**	12	2	1	3	2	1	3	8	1	0	0	41	4.9	10	3	3	1	5								
	Albany River Rats	AHL	67	15	31	46				59											4	0	0	0	7			
1996-97	**New Jersey Devils**	**NHL**	1	0	0	0	0	0	0	0	0	0	0	2	0.0	0	0	0	0	0								
	Albany River Rats	AHL	13	1	4	5				8																		
	St. Louis Blues	**NHL**	53	4	8	12	4	7	11	45	1	0	0	68	5.9	42	5	43	4	–2	6	0	0	0	27	0	0	0
1997-98	**St. Louis Blues**	**NHL**	1	0	0	0	0	0	0	0	0	0	0	0	0.0	0	0	0	0	0								
	Worcester IceCats	AHL	32	2	16	18				58											10	3	7	10	24			
1998-99	**St. Louis Blues**	**NHL**	54	1	12	13	1	12	13	94	0	0	0	52	1.9	46	3	49	10	4	13	0	3	3	17	0	0	0
	Worcester IceCats	AHL	19	6	4	10				42																		
99-2000	**St. Louis Blues**	**NHL**	41	0	8	8	0	7	7	38	0	0	0	30	0.0	20	1	22	1	–2	3	1	0	1	0	0	0	0
	Worcester IceCats	AHL	2	0	1	1				0																		
	Sweden	WC-A	7	0	0	0				6																		
	NHL Totals		162	7	29	36	7	27	34	185	2	0	0	193	3.6	118	12	117	16		22	1	3	4	44	0	0	0

Traded to **St. Louis** by **New Jersey** with Mike Peluso for Ken Sutton and St. Louis' 2nd round choice (Brett Clouthier) in 1999 Entry Draft, November 26, 1996. Signed as a free agent by **Ottawa**, July 12, 2000.

• PERSSON, Stefan

Stefan E. D – L. 6'1", 189 lbs. b: Umea, Sweden, 12/22/1954. NY Islanders' 13th, 214th overall, in 1974.

Season	Club	League	GP	G	A	Pts	AG	AA	APts	PIM	PP	SH	GW	S	%	TGF	PGF	TGA	PGA	+/–	GP	G	A	Pts	PIM	PP	SH	GW
1970-71	Pitea IF	Sweden-2	8	0	1	1																						
1971-72	Pitea IF	Sweden-2	18	5	1	6																						
1972-73	Pitea IF	Sweden-2	16	6	7	13																						
	Sweden	EJC-A	5	2	1	3				14																		
1973-74	Brynas IF Gavle	Sweden	14	1	3	4				8											21	4	3	7	38			
1974-75	Brynas IF Gavle	Sweden	30	5	7	12				34											6	1	0	1	2			
	Sweden	Nat-Team	11	0	1	1				0																		
1975-76	Brynas IF Gavle	Sweden	34	8	9	17				51											4	0	2	2	10			

			REGULAR SEASON																		PLAYOFFS							
Season	Club	League	GP	G	A	Pts	AG	AA	APts	PIM	PP	SH	GW	S	%	TGF	PGF	TGA	PGA	+/-	GP	G	A	Pts	PIM	PP	SH	GW
1976-77	Brynas IF Gavle	Sweden	31	5	13	18	....	....	....	70	....	....	....	....	....	....	....	....	....	....	4	1	0	1	2	....	....	....
	Sweden	Nat-Team	18	4	1	5	....	....	....	34	....	....	....	....	....	....	....	....	....	....	....	....	....	....	....	....	....	....
	Sweden	WEC-A	10	2	0	2	....	....	....	20	....	....	....	....	....	....	....	....	....	....	....	....	....	....	....	....	....	....
1977-78	**New York Islanders**	**NHL**	**66**	**6**	**50**	**56**	**5**	**39**	**44**	**54**	**3**	**0**	**0**	**77**	**7.8**	**128**	**66**	**52**	**9**	**19**	**7**	**0**	**2**	**2**	**6**	**0**	**0**	**0**
1978-79	**New York Islanders**	**NHL**	**78**	**10**	**56**	**66**	**9**	**41**	**50**	**57**	**6**	**0**	**1**	**113**	**8.8**	**162**	**78**	**62**	**16**	**38**	**10**	**0**	**4**	**4**	**8**	**0**	**0**	**0**
1979-80♦	**New York Islanders**	**NHL**	**73**	**4**	**35**	**39**	**3**	**26**	**29**	**76**	**2**	**0**	**0**	**91**	**4.4**	**100**	**47**	**49**	**9**	**13**	**21**	**5**	**10**	**15**	**16**	**4**	**0**	**0**
1980-81♦	**New York Islanders**	**NHL**	**80**	**9**	**52**	**61**	**7**	**35**	**42**	**82**	**6**	**0**	**2**	**120**	**7.5**	**166**	**86**	**75**	**19**	**24**	**7**	**0**	**5**	**5**	**6**	**0**	**0**	**0**
1981-82	Sweden	Can-Cup	5	0	0	0	....	....	....	2	....	....	....	....	....	....	....	....	....	....	....	....	....	....	....	....	....	....
♦	**New York Islanders**	**NHL**	**70**	**6**	**37**	**43**	**5**	**25**	**30**	**99**	**3**	**0**	**2**	**107**	**5.6**	**135**	**55**	**73**	**28**	**35**	**13**	**1**	**14**	**15**	**9**	**1**	**0**	**0**
1982-83♦	**New York Islanders**	**NHL**	**70**	**4**	**25**	**29**	**3**	**17**	**20**	**71**	**2**	**0**	**0**	**80**	**5.0**	**95**	**34**	**59**	**10**	**12**	**18**	**1**	**5**	**6**	**18**	**1**	**0**	**0**
1983-84	**New York Islanders**	**NHL**	**75**	**9**	**24**	**33**	**7**	**16**	**23**	**65**	**4**	**0**	**2**	**95**	**9.5**	**127**	**36**	**89**	**28**	**30**	**16**	**0**	**6**	**6**	**2**	**0**	**0**	**0**
1984-85	**New York Islanders**	**NHL**	**54**	**3**	**19**	**22**	**2**	**13**	**15**	**30**	**3**	**0**	**0**	**56**	**5.4**	**83**	**22**	**68**	**15**	**8**	**10**	**0**	**4**	**4**	**4**	**0**	**0**	**0**
1985-86	**New York Islanders**	**NHL**	**56**	**1**	**19**	**20**	**1**	**13**	**14**	**40**	**1**	**0**	**0**	**46**	**2.2**	**75**	**28**	**69**	**19**	**–3**	....	....	....	....	....	....	....	....
1986-87	Boras HC	Sweden-3	32	5	18	23	....	....	....	....	....	....	....	....	....	....	....	....	....	....	....	....	....	....	....	....	....	....
1987-88	Boras HC	Sweden-3	12	3	7	10	....	....	....	....	....	....	....	....	....	....	....	....	....	....	....	....	....	....	....	....	....	....
1988-89			OUT OF HOCKEY – RETIRED																									
1989-90	Boras HC	Sweden-3	32	7	23	30	....	....	....	125	....	....	....	....	....	....	....	....	....	....	....	....	....	....	....	....	....	....
	NHL Totals		**622**	**52**	**317**	**369**	**42**	**225**	**267**	**574**	**30**	**0**	**7**	**785**	**6.6**	**1071**	**452**	**596**	**153**		**102**	**7**	**50**	**57**	**69**	**6**	**0**	**0**

• PESUT, George

George Matthew D – L. 6'1", 205 lbs. b: Saskatoon, Sask., 6/17/1953. St. Louis' 2nd, 24th overall, in 1973.

Season	Club	League	GP	G	A	Pts	AG	AA	APts	PIM	PP	SH	GW	S	%	TGF	PGF	TGA	PGA	+/-	GP	G	A	Pts	PIM	PP	SH	GW
1970-71	Saskatoon Macs	SAHA	STATISTICS NOT AVAILABLE																									
1971-72	Victoria Cougars	WCJHL	38	3	13	16	....	....	....	83	....	....	....	....	....	....	....	....	....	....	....	....	....	....	....	....	....	....
	Flin Flon Bombers	WCJHL	25	3	8	11	....	....	....	73	....	....	....	....	....	....	....	....	....	....	....	....	....	....	....	....	....	....
	Saskatoon Blades	WCJHL	2	0	0	0	....	....	....	4	....	....	....	....	....	....	....	....	....	....	....	....	....	....	....	....	....	....
1972-73	Saskatoon Blades	WCJHL	68	12	25	37	....	....	....	98	....	....	....	....	....	....	....	....	....	....	....	....	....	....	....	....	....	....
1973-74	Denver Spurs	WHL	7	0	2	2	....	....	....	19	....	....	....	....	....	....	....	....	....	....	....	....	....	....	....	....	....	....
	Richmond Robins	AHL	38	3	5	8	....	....	....	4	....	....	....	....	....	....	....	....	....	....	....	....	....	....	....	....	....	....
1974-75	Richmond Robins	AHL	8	0	1	1	....	....	....	7	....	....	....	....	....	....	....	....	....	....	....	....	....	....	....	....	....	....
	California Golden Seals	**NHL**	**47**	**0**	**13**	**13**	**0**	**10**	**10**	**73**	**0**	**0**	**0**	**33**	**0.0**	**48**	**7**	**65**	**8**	**–16**	....	....	....	....	....	....	....	....
1975-76	**California Golden Seals**	**NHL**	**45**	**3**	**9**	**12**	**3**	**7**	**10**	**57**	**2**	**0**	**0**	**35**	**8.6**	**31**	**14**	**29**	**4**	**–8**	....	....	....	....	....	....	....	....
1976-77	Calgary Cowboys	WHA	17	2	0	2	....	....	....	2	....	....	....	....	....	....	....	....	....	....	....	....	....	....	....	....	....	....
	Tidewater Sharks	SHL	14	4	6	10	....	....	....	19	....	....	....	....	....	....	....	....	....	....	....	....	....	....	....	....	....	....
	Erie Blades	NAHL	25	5	7	12	....	....	....	62	....	....	....	....	....	....	....	....	....	....	9	2	1	3	6	....	....	....
1977-78			STATISTICS NOT AVAILABLE																									
1978-79	HC Davos	Switz-2	STATISTICS NOT AVAILABLE																									
1979-80	HC Davos	Switz-2	28	28	20	48	....	....	....	100	....	....	....	....	....	....	....	....	....	....	....	....	....	....	....	....	....	....
1980-81	Wichita Wind	CHL	53	6	21	27	....	....	....	33	....	....	....	....	....	....	....	....	....	....	16	3	4	7	39	....	....	....
1981-82	Hamburger EV	Germany-2	STATISTICS NOT AVAILABLE																									
1982-83	BSC Preussen Berlin	Germany-2	STATISTICS NOT AVAILABLE																									
1983-84	BSC Preussen Berlin	Germany-2	32	14	19	33	....	....	....	30	....	....	....	....	....	....	....	....	....	....	10	2	5	7	12	....	....	....
1984-85	BSC Preussen Berlin	Germany-2	42	25	37	62	....	....	....	72	....	....	....	....	....	....	....	....	....	....	17	5	12	17	14	....	....	....
1985-86	HC Chamonix	France	STATISTICS NOT AVAILABLE																									
1986-87	BSC Preussen Berlin	Germany-2	53	3	32	35	....	....	....	41	....	....	....	....	....	....	....	....	....	....	....	....	....	....	....	....	....	....
1987-88	SV Bayreuth	Germany-2	12	3	8	11	....	....	....	24	....	....	....	....	....	....	....	....	....	....	....	....	....	....	....	....	....	....
1988-89	ERC Nurnberg	Germany-2	33	5	30	35	....	....	....	46	....	....	....	....	....	....	....	....	....	....	....	....	....	....	....	....	....	....
1989-90	ERC Nurnberg	Germany-2	28	6	29	35	....	....	....	24	....	....	....	....	....	....	....	....	....	....	....	....	....	....	....	....	....	....
1990-91	ECD Sauerland	Germany-2	33	16	39	55	....	....	....	36	....	....	....	....	....	....	....	....	....	....	....	....	....	....	....	....	....	....
1991-92	EC Kassel	Germany-2	38	9	24	33	....	....	....	34	....	....	....	....	....	....	....	....	....	....	....	....	....	....	....	....	....	....
1992-93	EC Kassel	Germany-2	12	1	9	10	....	....	....	14	....	....	....	....	....	....	....	....	....	....	....	....	....	....	....	....	....	....
1993-94	BSC Preussen Berlin	Germany-2	DID NOT PLAY – COACHING																									
	NHL Totals		**92**	**3**	**22**	**25**	**3**	**17**	**20**	**130**	**2**	**0**	**0**	**68**	**4.4**	**79**	**21**	**94**	**12**		....	....	....	....	....	....	....	....
	Other Major League Totals		17	2	0	2	....	....	....	2	....	....	....	....	....	....	....	....	....	....	....	....	....	....	....	....	....	....

WCJHL First All-Star Team (1973)

Selected by **Cleveland** (WHA) in 1973 WHA Amateur Draft, June, 1973. Traded to **Philadelphia** by **St. Louis** for Bob Stumpf, November, 1973. Traded to **California** by **Philadelphia** for the rights to Ron Chipperfield, December 11, 1974. WHA rights traded to **Calgary** (WHA) by **Cleveland** (WHA) for future considerations, June, 1976.

• PETERS, Garry

Garry Lorne C – L. 5'10", 185 lbs. b: Regina, Sask., 10/9/1942.

Season	Club	League	GP	G	A	Pts	AG	AA	APts	PIM	PP	SH	GW	S	%	TGF	PGF	TGA	PGA	+/-	GP	G	A	Pts	PIM	PP	SH	GW
1959-60	Regina Pats	SJHL	37	9	6	15	....	....	....	39	....	....	....	....	....	....	....	....	....	....	....	....	....	....	....	....	....	....
1960-61	Regina Pats	SJHL	57	36	46	82	....	....	....	94	....	....	....	....	....	....	....	....	....	....	10	*10	*12	*22	8	....	....	....
	Regina Pats	Mem-Cup	6	2	2	4	....	....	....	2	....	....	....	....	....	....	....	....	....	....	....	....	....	....	....	....	....	....
1961-62	Regina Pats	SJHL	56	45	*69	*114	....	....	....	68	....	....	....	....	....	....	....	....	....	....	16	10	14	24	4	....	....	....
1962-63	Regina Pats	SJHL	50	37	39	76	....	....	....	100	....	....	....	....	....	....	....	....	....	....	4	1	0	1	15	....	....	....
	Hull-Ottawa Canadiens	EPHL	4	0	1	1	....	....	....	2	....	....	....	....	....	....	....	....	....	....	1	0	0	0	0	....	....	....
	Estevan Bruins	Mem-Cup	6	4	0	4	....	....	....	*25	....	....	....	....	....	....	....	....	....	....	....	....	....	....	....	....	....	....
1963-64	Omaha Knights	CPHL	72	32	49	81	....	....	....	82	....	....	....	....	....	....	....	....	....	....	10	5	9	14	17	....	....	....
1964-65	**Montreal Canadiens**	**NHL**	**13**	**0**	**2**	**2**	**0**	**2**	**2**	**6**	....	....	....	....	....	....	....	....	....	....	....	....	....	....	....	....	....	....
	Quebec Aces	AHL	4	1	2	3	....	....	....	4	....	....	....	....	....	....	....	....	....	....	....	....	....	....	....	....	....	....
	Omaha Knights	CPHL	43	21	23	44	....	....	....	56	....	....	....	....	....	....	....	....	....	....	....	....	....	....	....	....	....	....
1965-66	**New York Rangers**	**NHL**	**63**	**7**	**3**	**10**	**8**	**3**	**11**	**42**	....	....	....	....	....	....	....	....	....	....	....	....	....	....	....	....	....	....
1966-67	**Montreal Canadiens**	**NHL**	**4**	**0**	**1**	**1**	**0**	**1**	**1**	**2**	....	....	....	....	....	....	....	....	....	....	....	....	....	....	....	....	....	....
	Houston Apollos	CPHL	50	21	31	52	....	....	....	90	....	....	....	....	....	....	....	....	....	....	....	....	....	....	....	....	....	....
1967-68	**Philadelphia Flyers**	**NHL**	**31**	**7**	**5**	**12**	**8**	**5**	**13**	**22**	**1**	**0**	**1**	**79**	**8.9**	**16**	**4**	**20**	**6**	**–2**	....	....	....	....	....	....	....	....
1968-69	**Philadelphia Flyers**	**NHL**	**66**	**8**	**6**	**14**	**8**	**5**	**13**	**49**	**1**	**1**	**2**	**166**	**4.8**	**21**	**3**	**55**	**17**	**–20**	**4**	**1**	**1**	**2**	**16**	**0**	**0**	**1**
1969-70	**Philadelphia Flyers**	**NHL**	**59**	**6**	**10**	**16**	**6**	**9**	**15**	**69**	**1**	**0**	**0**	**102**	**5.9**	**20**	**3**	**43**	**17**	**–9**	....	....	....	....	....	....	....	....
1970-71	**Philadelphia Flyers**	**NHL**	**73**	**6**	**7**	**13**	**6**	**6**	**12**	**69**	**0**	**2**	**2**	**135**	**4.4**	**17**	**0**	**47**	**16**	**–14**	**4**	**1**	**1**	**2**	**15**	**0**	**0**	**0**
1971-72♦	**Boston Bruins**	**NHL**	**2**	**0**	**0**	**0**	**0**	**0**	**0**	**2**	**0**	**0**	**0**	**1**	**0.0**	**0**	**0**	**0**	**0**	**0**	**1**	**0**	**0**	**0**	**0**	**0**	**0**	**0**
	Boston Braves	AHL	58	39	34	73	....	....	....	118	....	....	....	....	....	....	....	....	....	....	8	1	2	3	4	....	....	....
1972-73	New York Raiders	WHA	23	2	7	9	....	....	....	24	....	....	....	....	....	....	....	....	....	....	....	....	....	....	....	....	....	....
1973-74	New York-Jersey Knights	WHA	34	2	5	7	....	....	....	18	....	....	....	....	....	....	....	....	....	....	....	....	....	....	....	....	....	....
	NHL Totals		**311**	**34**	**34**	**68**	**36**	**31**	**67**	**261**	....	....	....	....	....	....	....	....	....		**9**	**2**	**2**	**4**	**31**	....	....	....
	Other Major League Totals		57	4	12	16	....	....	....	42	....	....	....	....	....	....	....	....	....	....	....	....	....	....	....	....	....	....

SJHL First All-Star Team (1962) • Shared Ken McKenzie Trophy (Rookie of the Year - CPHL) with Poul Popiel (1964) • AHL First All-Star Team (1972) • Won Les Cunningham Award (MVP - AHL) (1972)

Traded to **NY Rangers** by **Montreal** with Cesare Maniago for Earl Ingarfield, Noel Price, Gord Labossiere, Dave McComb and cash, June 8, 1965. Traded to **Montreal** by **NY Rangers** with Ted Taylor for Red Berenson, June 13, 1966. Claimed by **Philadelphia** from **Montreal** in Expansion Draft, June 6, 1967. • Missed majority of 1967-68 season recovering from eye injury suffered in game vs. NY Rangers, December 25, 1967. Claimed by **Boston** from **Philadelphia** in Intra-League Draft, June 8, 1971. Selected by **NY Raiders** (WHA) in 1972 WHA General Player Draft, February 12, 1972. Claimed by **NY Islanders** from **Boston** in Expansion Draft, June 6, 1972.

• PETERS, Jimmy Jr.

James Stephen C – L. 6'2", 185 lbs. b: Montreal, Que., 6/20/1944.

Season	Club	League	GP	G	A	Pts	AG	AA	APts	PIM	PP	SH	GW	S	%	TGF	PGF	TGA	PGA	+/-	GP	G	A	Pts	PIM	PP	SH	GW
1961-62	Hamilton Red Wings	OHA-Jr.	42	4	9	13	....	....	....	4	....	....	....	....	....	....	....	....	....	....	10	2	2	4	7	....	....	....
	Hamilton Red Wings	Mem-Cup	13	2	6	8	....	....	....	0	....	....	....	....	....	....	....	....	....	....	....	....	....	....	....	....	....	....
1962-63	Hamilton Red Wings	OHA-Jr.	50	9	24	33	....	....	....	12	....	....	....	....	....	....	....	....	....	....	5	3	3	6	4	....	....	....
1963-64	Hamilton Red Wings	OHA-Jr.	54	31	45	76	....	....	....	6	....	....	....	....	....	....	....	....	....	....	....	....	....	....	....	....	....	....
	Cincinnati Wings	CPHL	5	3	0	3	....	....	....	0	....	....	....	....	....	....	....	....	....	....	....	....	....	....	....	....	....	....
1964-65	Hamilton Red Wings	OHA-Jr.	51	36	65	101	....	....	....	12	....	....	....	....	....	....	....	....	....	....	....	....	....	....	....	....	....	....
	Detroit Red Wings	**NHL**	**1**	**0**	**0**	**0**	**0**	**0**	**0**	**0**	....	....	....	....	....	....	....	....	....	....	....	....	....	....	....	....	....	....
	Memphis Wings	CPHL	8	0	1	1	....	....	....	2	....	....	....	....	....	....	....	....	....	....	....	....	....	....	....	....	....	....
1965-66	**Detroit Red Wings**	**NHL**	**6**	**1**	**1**	**2**	**1**	**1**	**2**	**2**	....	....	....	....	....	....	....	....	....	....	....	....	....	....	....	....	....	....
	Memphis Wings	CPHL	64	15	28	43	....	....	....	2	....	....	....	....	....	....	....	....	....	....	....	....	....	....	....	....	....	....

Season	Club	League	GP	G	A	Pts	AG	AA	APts	PIM	PP	SH	GW	S	%	TGF	PGF	TGA	PGA	+/-	GP	G	A	Pts	PIM	PP	SH	GW
			REGULAR SEASON																		PLAYOFFS							
1966-67	**Detroit Red Wings**	**NHL**	2	0	0	0	0	0	0	0	....	....	....	....	....	....	....	....	....	....	....	....	....	....	....	....	....	....
	Pittsburgh Hornets	AHL	16	2	5	7	....	....	....	0	....	....	....	....	....	....	....	....	....	....	....	....	....	....	....	....	....	....
	Memphis Wings	CPHL	51	6	19	25	....	....	....	10	....	....	....	....	....	....	....	....	....	....	7	1	2	3	2	....	....	....
1967-68	**Detroit Red Wings**	**NHL**	45	5	6	11	6	6	12	8	1	0	1	36	13.9	12	3	21	2	–10	....	....	....	....	....	....	....	....
	Fort Worth Wings	CPHL	20	10	18	28	....	....	....	13	....	....	....	....	....	....	....	....	....	....	....	....	....	....	....	....	....	....
1968-69	**Los Angeles Kings**	**NHL**	76	10	15	25	11	13	24	28	1	0	1	109	9.2	38	5	74	31	–10	11	0	2	2	2	0	0	0
1969-70	**Los Angeles Kings**	**NHL**	74	15	9	24	16	8	24	10	2	3	2	118	12.7	33	5	69	28	–13	....	....	....	....	....	....	....	....
1970-71	Springfield Kings	AHL	26	5	14	19	....	....	....	9	....	....	....	....	....	....	....	....	....	....	....	....	....	....	....	....	....	....
	Denver Spurs	WHL	42	8	22	30	....	....	....	6	....	....	....	....	....	....	....	....	....	....	5	2	2	4	2	....	....	....
1971-72	Seattle Totems	WHL	63	16	36	52	....	....	....	8	....	....	....	....	....	....	....	....	....	....	....	....	....	....	....	....	....	....
1972-73	**Los Angeles Kings**	**NHL**	77	4	5	9	4	4	8	0	1	1	0	40	10.0	10	2	35	24	–3	....	....	....	....	....	....	....	....
1973-74	**Los Angeles Kings**	**NHL**	25	2	0	2	2	0	2	0	0	0	0	19	10.5	2	0	16	12	–2	....	....	....	....	....	....	....	....
	Portland Buckaroos	WHL	42	7	15	22	....	....	....	15	....	....	....	....	....	....	....	....	....	....	10	4	3	7	0	....	....	....
1974-75	**Los Angeles Kings**	**NHL**	3	0	0	0	0	0	0	0	0	0	0	1	0.0	0	0	1	1	0	....	....	....	....	....	....	....	....
	Springfield Indians	AHL	69	24	37	61	....	....	....	10	....	....	....	....	....	....	....	....	....	....	15	6	0	6	4	....	....	....
1975-76	Fort Worth Texans	CHL	76	16	30	46	....	....	....	17	....	....	....	....	....	....	....	....	....	....	....	....	....	....	....	....	....	....
	NHL Totals		309	37	36	73	40	32	72	48	....	....	....	....	....	....	....	....	....	....	11	0	2	2	2	....	....	....

• Son of Jimmy Sr.

Traded to **LA Kings** by **Detroit** for Terry Sawchuk, October 10, 1968. Traded to **Denver** (WHL) by **LA Kings** with LA Kings holding right of recall for Ed Hoekstra, December, 1970.

• PETERS, Steve

Steve Alan C – L. 5'11", 186 lbs. b: Peterborough, Ont., 1/23/1960. Colorado's 2nd, 64th overall, in 1979.

Season	Club	League	GP	G	A	Pts	AG	AA	APts	PIM	PP	SH	GW	S	%	TGF	PGF	TGA	PGA	+/-	GP	G	A	Pts	PIM	PP	SH	GW
1976-77	Peterborough Petes	OMJHL	62	6	10	16	....	....	....	48	....	....	....	....	....	....	....	....	....	....	4	1	2	3	8	....	....	....
1977-78	Niagara Falls Flyers	OMJHL	67	18	38	56	....	....	....	49	....	....	....	....	....	....	....	....	....	....	....	....	....	....	....	....	....	....
1978-79	Oshawa Generals	OMJHL	64	36	56	92	....	....	....	70	....	....	....	....	....	....	....	....	....	....	5	1	7	8	0	....	....	....
1979-80	Oshawa Generals	OMJHL	21	13	14	27	....	....	....	22	....	....	....	....	....	....	....	....	....	....	....	....	....	....	....	....	....	....
	Windsor Spitfires	OMJHL	39	24	30	54	....	....	....	22	....	....	....	....	....	....	....	....	....	....	16	4	15	19	14	....	....	....
	Colorado Rockies	**NHL**	2	0	1	1	0	1	1	0	0	0	0	0	0.0	1	0	0	0	1	....	....	....	....	....	....	....	....
	Fort Worth Texans	CHL	....	....	....	....	....	....	....	....	....	....	....	....	....	....	....	....	....	....	2	0	0	0	0	....	....	....
1980-81	Fort Worth Texans	CHL	34	4	5	9	....	....	....	30	....	....	....	....	....	....	....	....	....	....	....	....	....	....	....	....	....	....
	Muskegon Mohawks	IHL	38	6	20	26	....	....	....	8	....	....	....	....	....	....	....	....	....	....	3	1	0	1	5	....	....	....
1981-82	Fort Worth Texans	CHL	79	13	28	41	....	....	....	15	....	....	....	....	....	....	....	....	....	....	....	....	....	....	....	....	....	....
1982-83	Muskegon Mohawks	IHL	80	38	58	96	....	....	....	35	....	....	....	....	....	....	....	....	....	....	4	0	4	4	2	....	....	....
1983-84	SC Riessersee	Germany	46	22	29	51	....	....	....	60	....	....	....	....	....	....	....	....	....	....	....	....	....	....	....	....	....	....
1984-85	EHC Chur	Switz.	33	13	10	23	....	....	....	....	....	....	....	....	....	....	....	....	....	....	....	....	....	....	....	....	....	....
1985-86	SaiPa Lappeenranta	Finland	32	6	8	14	....	....	....	58	....	....	....	....	....	....	....	....	....	....	....	....	....	....	....	....	....	....
1986-87	HIFK Helsinki	Finland	40	9	4	13	....	....	....	22	....	....	....	....	....	....	....	....	....	....	5	1	2	3	4	....	....	....
1987-88	KooKoo Kouvola	Finland	44	9	18	27	....	....	....	52	....	....	....	....	....	....	....	....	....	....	....	....	....	....	....	....	....	....
	Miami Valley Sabres	AAHL	12	4	4	8	....	....	....	12	....	....	....	....	....	....	....	....	....	....	....	....	....	....	....	....	....	....
1988-89	Tappara Tampere	Finland	38	5	14	19	....	....	....	28	....	....	....	....	....	....	....	....	....	....	8	0	0	0	18	....	....	....
1989-90	SaiPa Lappeenranta	Finland	43	4	11	15	....	....	....	28	....	....	....	....	....	....	....	....	....	....	....	....	....	....	....	....	....	....
	NHL Totals		2	0	1	1	0	1	1	0	0	0	0	0	0.0	1	0	0	0		....	....	....	....	....	....	....	....

• PETERSON, Brent

LW – L. 6'3", 200 lbs. b: Calgary, Alta., 7/20/1972. Tampa Bay's 1st, 3rd overall, in 1993 Supplemental Draft.

Season	Club	League	GP	G	A	Pts	AG	AA	APts	PIM	PP	SH	GW	S	%	TGF	PGF	TGA	PGA	+/-	GP	G	A	Pts	PIM	PP	SH	GW
1990-91	Thunder Bay Flyers	USHL	48	27	40	67	....	....	....	10	....	....	....	....	....	....	....	....	....	....	10	8	9	17	4	....	....	....
1991-92	Michigan Tech Huskies	WCHA	39	11	9	20	....	....	....	18	....	....	....	....	....	....	....	....	....	....	....	....	....	....	....	....	....	....
1992-93	Michigan Tech Huskies	WCHA	37	24	18	42	....	....	....	32	....	....	....	....	....	....	....	....	....	....	....	....	....	....	....	....	....	....
1993-94	Michigan Tech Huskies	WCHA	43	25	21	46	....	....	....	30	....	....	....	....	....	....	....	....	....	....	....	....	....	....	....	....	....	....
1994-95	Michigan Tech Huskies	WCHA	39	20	16	36	....	....	....	27	....	....	....	....	....	....	....	....	....	....	....	....	....	....	....	....	....	....
1995-96	Atlanta Knights	IHL	69	9	19	28	....	....	....	33	....	....	....	....	....	....	....	....	....	....	3	0	0	0	0	....	....	....
1996-97	**Tampa Bay Lightning**	**NHL**	17	2	0	2	2	0	2	4	0	0	0	11	18.2	2	0	7	1	–4	....	....	....	....	....	....	....	....
	Adirondack Red Wings	AHL	52	22	23	45	....	....	....	56	....	....	....	....	....	....	....	....	....	....	4	3	1	4	2	....	....	....
1997-98	**Tampa Bay Lightning**	**NHL**	19	5	0	5	6	0	6	2	0	0	0	15	33.3	7	0	10	1	–2	....	....	....	....	....	....	....	....
	Milwaukee Admirals	IHL	63	20	39	59	....	....	....	48	....	....	....	....	....	....	....	....	....	....	8	5	3	8	22	....	....	....
1998-99	**Tampa Bay Lighning**	**NHL**	20	2	1	3	2	1	3	0	0	0	0	16	12.5	4	0	6	0	–2	....	....	....	....	....	....	....	....
	Cleveland Lumberjacks	IHL	18	6	7	13	....	....	....	31	....	....	....	....	....	....	....	....	....	....	....	....	....	....	....	....	....	....
	Grand Rapids Griffins	IHL	17	7	5	12	....	....	....	14	....	....	....	....	....	....	....	....	....	....	....	....	....	....	....	....	....	....
99-2000	Milwaukee Admirals	IHL	66	8	24	32	....	....	....	62	....	....	....	....	....	....	....	....	....	....	3	3	2	5	4	....	....	....
	NHL Totals		56	9	1	10	10	1	11	6	0	0	0	42	21.4	13	0	23	2		....	....	....	....	....	....	....	....

Claimed by **Hartford** from **Vancouver** in Waiver Draft, October 5, 1987. Traded to **Pittsburgh** by **Tampa Bay** for cash, March 18, 1999. Signed as a free agent by **Nashville**, July 24, 1999.

• PETERSON, Brent

Brent Ronald C – R. 6', 190 lbs. b: Calgary, Alta., 2/15/1958. Detroit's 2nd, 12th overall, in 1978.

Season	Club	League	GP	G	A	Pts	AG	AA	APts	PIM	PP	SH	GW	S	%	TGF	PGF	TGA	PGA	+/-	GP	G	A	Pts	PIM	PP	SH	GW
1973-74	Calgary Royals	AAHA	STATISTICS NOT AVAILABLE																									
1974-75	Edmonton Oil Kings	WCJHL	66	17	26	43	....	....	....	44	....	....	....	....	....	....	....	....	....	....	....	....	....	....	....	....	....	....
1975-76	Edmonton Oil Kings	WCJHL	70	22	39	61	....	....	....	57	....	....	....	....	....	....	....	....	....	....	5	4	2	6	7	....	....	....
1976-77	Portland Winter Hawks	WCJHL	69	34	78	112	....	....	....	98	....	....	....	....	....	....	....	....	....	....	10	3	8	11	8	....	....	....
1977-78	Portland Winter Hawks	WCJHL	51	33	50	83	....	....	....	95	....	....	....	....	....	....	....	....	....	....	3	1	1	2	2	....	....	....
1978-79	**Detroit Red Wings**	**NHL**	5	0	0	0	0	0	0	0	0	0	0	7	0.0	1	0	1	0	0	....	....	....	....	....	....	....	....
1979-80	**Detroit Red Wings**	**NHL**	18	1	2	3	1	1	2	2	0	0	0	6	16.7	5	0	7	1	–1	....	....	....	....	....	....	....	....
	Adirondack Red Wings	AHL	52	9	22	31	....	....	....	61	....	....	....	....	....	....	....	....	....	....	5	0	0	0	6	....	....	....
1980-81	**Detroit Red Wings**	**NHL**	53	6	18	24	5	12	17	24	1	0	1	40	15.0	33	5	40	14	2	....	....	....	....	....	....	....	....
	Adirondack Red Wings	AHL	3	1	0	1	....	....	....	10	....	....	....	....	....	....	....	....	....	....	....	....	....	....	....	....	....	....
1981-82	**Detroit Red Wings**	**NHL**	15	1	0	1	1	0	1	6	0	0	0	10	10.0	2	0	16	8	–6	....	....	....	....	....	....	....	....
	Buffalo Sabres	**NHL**	46	9	5	14	7	3	10	43	0	0	0	41	22.0	25	7	29	8	–3	4	1	0	1	12	1	0	0
1982-83	**Buffalo Sabres**	**NHL**	75	13	24	37	11	17	28	38	1	1	0	98	13.3	57	5	57	15	10	10	1	2	3	28	0	0	1
1983-84	**Buffalo Sabres**	**NHL**	70	9	12	21	7	8	15	52	0	0	0	81	11.1	35	2	47	17	3	3	0	1	1	4	0	0	0
1984-85	**Buffalo Sabres**	**NHL**	74	12	22	34	10	15	25	47	2	1	2	104	11.5	45	4	37	14	18	5	0	0	0	6	0	0	0
1985-86	**Vancouver Canucks**	**NHL**	77	8	23	31	6	15	21	94	0	3	2	86	9.3	65	15	95	35	–10	3	2	0	2	9	1	0	0
1986-87	**Vancouver Canucks**	**NHL**	69	7	15	22	6	11	17	77	2	1	2	71	9.9	34	3	82	37	–14	....	....	....	....	....	....	....	....
1987-88	**Hartford Whalers**	**NHL**	52	2	7	9	2	5	7	40	0	0	0	33	6.1	12	1	41	21	–9	4	0	0	0	2	0	0	0
1988-89	**Hartford Whalers**	**NHL**	66	4	13	17	3	9	12	61	0	0	2	56	7.1	22	0	60	40	2	2	0	1	1	4	0	0	0
1989-1991	**Hartford Whalers**	**NHL**	DID NOT PLAY – ASSISTANT COACH																									
1991-1998	Portland Winter Hawks	WHL	DID NOT PLAY – COACHING																									
1998-2000	**Nashville Predators**	**NHL**	DID NOT PLAY – ASSISTANT COACH																									
	NHL Totals		620	72	141	213	59	96	155	484	6	6	9	633	11.4	336	42	512	210		31	4	4	8	65	2	0	1

Traded to **Buffalo** by **Detroit** with Mike Foligno and Dale McCourt for Danny Gare, Jim Schoenfeld and Derek Smith, December 2, 1981. Claimed by **Vanouver** from **Buffalo** in Waiver Draft, October 7, 1985.

• PETIT, Michel

D – R. 6'1", 205 lbs. b: St. Malo, Que., 2/12/1964. Vancouver's 1st, 11th overall, in 1982.

Season	Club	League	GP	G	A	Pts	AG	AA	APts	PIM	PP	SH	GW	S	%	TGF	PGF	TGA	PGA	+/-	GP	G	A	Pts	PIM	PP	SH	GW
1979-80	Ste-Foy Gouverneurs	QAAA	35	4	9	13	....	....	....	....	....	....	....	....	....	....	....	....	....	....	....	....	....	....	....	....	....	....
1980-81	Ste-Foy Gouverneurs	QAAA	48	10	45	55	....	....	....	84	....	....	....	....	....	....	....	....	....	....	....	....	....	....	....	....	....	....
1981-82	Sherbrooke Castors	QMJHL	63	10	39	49	....	....	....	106	....	....	....	....	....	....	....	....	....	....	22	5	20	25	24	....	....	....
	Sherbrooke Castors	Mem-Cup	5	1	5	6	....	....	....	16	....	....	....	....	....	....	....	....	....	....	....	....	....	....	....	....	....	....
1982-83	St-Jean Castors	QMJHL	62	19	67	86	....	....	....	196	....	....	....	....	....	....	....	....	....	....	3	0	0	0	35	....	....	....
	Vancouver Canucks	**NHL**	2	0	0	0	0	0	0	0	0	0	0	1	0.0	0	0	4	0	–4	....	....	....	....	....	....	....	....
1983-84	**Vancouver Canucks**	**NHL**	44	6	9	15	5	6	11	53	5	0	0	78	7.7	52	17	42	1	–6	1	0	0	0	0	0	0	0
	Canada	Nat-Team	19	3	10	13	....	....	....	58	....	....	....	....	....	....	....	....	....	....	....	....	....	....	....	....	....	....
1984-85	**Vancouver Canucks**	**NHL**	69	5	26	31	4	18	22	127	1	1	1	96	5.2	90	26	101	11	–26	....	....	....	....	....	....	....	....
1985-86	**Vancouver Canucks**	**NHL**	32	1	6	7	1	4	5	27	1	0	0	43	2.3	24	7	28	5	–6	....	....	....	....	....	....	....	....
	Fredericton Express	AHL	25	0	13	13	....	....	....	79	....	....	....	....	....	....	....	....	....	....	....	....	....	....	....	....	....	....

Season	Club	League	REGULAR SEASON GP	G	A	Pts	AG	AA	APts	PIM	PP	SH	GW	S	%	TGF	PGF	TGA	PGA	+/–	PLAYOFFS GP	G	A	Pts	PIM	PP	SH	GW
1986-87	Vancouver Canucks	NHL	69	12	13	25	10	9	19	131	4	0	1	116	10.3	85	18	100	28	–5								
1987-88	Vancouver Canucks	NHL	10	0	3	3	0	2	2	35	0	0	0	13	0.0	11	6	12	3	–4								
	New York Rangers	NHL	64	9	24	33	8	17	25	223	2	0	3	96	9.4	89	26	81	21	3								
1988-89	New York Rangers	NHL	69	8	25	33	7	18	25	154	5	0	1	132	6.1	101	25	129	38	–15	4	0	2	2	27	0	0	0
1989-90	Quebec Nordiques	NHL	63	12	24	36	10	17	27	215	5	0	0	137	8.8	86	41	124	41	–38								
	Canada	WEC-A	8	0	1	1				8																		
1990-91	Quebec Nordiques	NHL	19	4	7	11	4	5	9	47	3	0	0	39	10.3	24	12	35	8	–15								
	Toronto Maple Leafs	NHL	54	9	19	28	8	14	22	132	3	1	2	95	9.5	70	26	93	30	–19								
1991-92	Toronto Maple Leafs	NHL	34	1	13	14	1	10	11	85	1	0	1	61	1.6	32	9	51	11	–17								
	Calgary Flames	NHL	36	3	10	13	3	8	11	79	3	0	0	68	4.4	33	6	37	12	2								
1992-93	Calgary Flames	NHL	35	3	9	12	2	6	8	54	2	0	0	58	5.2	27	4	30	2	–5								
1993-94	Calgary Flames	NHL	63	2	21	23	2	16	18	110	0	0	0	103	1.9	62	12	64	19	5								
1994-95	Los Angeles Kings	NHL	40	5	12	17	9	18	27	84	2	0	0	70	7.1	61	9	61	13	4								
1995-96	Los Angeles Kings	NHL	9	0	1	1	0	1	1	27	0	0	0	12	0.0	7	1	7	0	–1								
	Tampa Bay Lightning	NHL	45	4	7	11	4	6	10	108	0	0	1	56	7.1	43	15	51	13	–10	6	0	0	0	20	0	0	0
1996-97	Edmonton Oilers	NHL	18	2	4	6	2	4	6	20	0	0	0	30	6.7	12	2	26	3	–13								
	Philadelphia Flyers	NHL	20	0	3	3	0	3	3	51	0	0	0	13	0.0	17	0	21	6	2	3	0	0	0	6	0	0	0
1997-98	Detroit Vipers	IHL	9	2	3	5				24																		
	Phoenix Coyotes	NHL	32	4	2	6	5	2	7	77	1	0	0	34	11.8	21	2	28	5	–4	5	0	0	0	8	0	0	0
1998-99	Las Vegas Thunder	IHL	6	0	1	1				10																		
99-2000	Frankfurt Lions	Germany	29	9	9	18				83											5	1	1	2	22			
	NHL Totals		**827**	**90**	**238**	**328**	**85**	**184**	**269**	**1839**	**38**	**2**	**10**	**1351**	**6.7**	**947**	**264**	**1125**	**270**		**19**	**0**	**2**	**2**	**61**	**0**	**0**	**0**

QMJHL First All-Star Team (1982, 1983)

Traded to **NY Rangers** by **Vancouver** for Willie Huber and Larry Melnyk, November 4, 1987. Traded to **Quebec** by **NY Rangers** for Randy Moller, October 5, 1989. Traded to **Toronto** by **Quebec** with Aaron Broten and Lucien Deblois for Scott Pearson and Toronto's 2nd round choices in 1991 (later traded to Washington — Washington selected Eric Lavigne) and 1992 (Tuomas Gronman) Entry Drafts, November 17, 1990. Traded to **Calgary** by **Toronto** with Craig Berube, Alexander Godynyuk, Gary Leeman and Jeff Reese for Doug Gilmour, Jamie Macoun, Ric Nattress, Rick Wamsley and Kent Manderville, January 2, 1992. Signed as a free agent by **LA Kings**, June 16, 1994. Traded to **Tampa Bay** by **LA Kings** for Steven Finn, November 13, 1995. Signed as a free agent by **Edmonton**, October 24, 1996. Claimed on waivers by **Philadelphia** from **Edmonton**, January 17, 1997. Signed as a free agent by **Phoenix**, November 25, 1997.
• Missed majority of 1998-99 season recovering from head injury suffered in game vs. Utah (IHL), October 17, 1998.

• PETRENKO, Sergei

LW – L. 6', 176 lbs. b: Kharkov, USSR, 9/10/1968. Buffalo's 5th, 168th overall, in 1993.

Season	Club	League	GP	G	A	Pts	AG	AA	APts	PIM	PP	SH	GW	S	%	TGF	PGF	TGA	PGA	+/–	GP	G	A	Pts	PIM	PP	SH	GW
1987-88	Dynamo Moscow	USSR	31	2	5	7				4																		
1988-89	Dynamo Moscow	USSR	23	4	6	10				6																		
1989-90	Dynamo Moscow	Fr-Tour	1	0	0	0				0																		
	Dynamo Moscow	USSR	33	5	4	9				8																		
	Dynamo Moscow	Super-S	5	1	1	2				2																		
1990-91	Dynamo Moscow	Fr-Tour	1	0	0	0				0																		
	Dynamo Moscow	USSR	43	14	13	27				10																		
	Dynamo Moscow	Super-S	DID NOT PLAY																									
1991-92	Dynamo Moscow	CIS	31	9	10	19				10																		
	Russia	Olympics	8	3	2	5				0																		
	Russia	WC-A	6	1	0	1				2																		
1992-93	Dynamo Moscow	CIS	36	12	12	24				10											10	4	5	9	6			
	Russia	WC-A	4	0	1	1				2																		
1993-94	Buffalo Sabres	NHL	14	0	4	4	0	3	3	0	0	0	0	7	0.0	6	2	7	0	–3								
	Rochester Americans	AHL	38	16	15	31				8																		
1994-95	Rochester Americans	AHL	43	12	16	28				16																		
1995-96	Dynamo Moscow	CIS	22	8	7	15				14																		
1996-97	HC Davos	Switz.	41	19	23	42				20											1	0	0	0	0			
	Russia	WC-A	4	2	2	4				4																		
1997-98	Dynamo Moscow	EuroHL	10	7	2	9				4																		
	Dynamo Moscow	Russia	44	14	19	33				8																		
	Russia	WC-A	6	2	4	6				2																		
1998-99	Dynamo Moscow	Russia	40	11	24	35				36											6	0	1	1	0			
	Russia	WC-A	6	2	4	6				2																		
99-2000	HC Vitkovice	Czech-Rep	29	7	9	16				4																		
	Metallurg Novokuznetsk	Russia	11	3	2	5				6											10	1	2	3	4			
	NHL Totals		**14**	**0**	**4**	**4**	**0**	**3**	**3**	**0**	**0**	**0**	**0**	**7**	**0.0**	**6**	**2**	**7**	**0**									

• PETROV, Oleg

RW – L. 5'8", 175 lbs. b: Moscow, USSR, 4/18/1971. Montreal's 9th, 127th overall, in 1991.

Season	Club	League	GP	G	A	Pts	AG	AA	APts	PIM	PP	SH	GW	S	%	TGF	PGF	TGA	PGA	+/–	GP	G	A	Pts	PIM	PP	SH	GW
1988-89	CSKA Moscow	USSR-Jr.	STATISTICS NOT AVAILABLE																									
	Soviet Union	EJC-A	6	1	4	5				4																		
1989-90	CSKA Moscow	USSR	30	4	7	11				4																		
	CSKA Moscow	Super-S	1	1	0	1				0																		
1990-91	CSKA Moscow	Fr-Tour	1	0	0	0				0																		
	CSKA Moscow	USSR	43	7	4	11				8																		
1991-92	CSKA Moscow	CIS	42	10	16	26				8																		
1992-93♦	Montreal Canadiens	NHL	9	2	1	3	2	1	3	10	0	0	1	20	10.0	6	1	4	1	2	1	0	0	0	0	0	0	0
	Fredericton Canadiens	AHL	55	26	29	55				36											5	4	1	5	0			
1993-94	Montreal Canadiens	NHL	55	12	15	27	11	12	23	2	1	0	1	107	11.2	38	5	26	0	7	2	0	0	0	0	0	0	0
	Fredericton Canadiens	AHL	23	8	20	28				18																		
1994-95	Montreal Canadiens	NHL	12	2	3	5	4	4	8	4	0	0	0	26	7.7	5	1	11	0	–7								
	Fredericton Canadiens	AHL	17	7	11	18				12											17	5	6	11	10			
1995-96	Montreal Canadiens	NHL	36	4	7	11	4	6	10	23	0	0	2	44	9.1	16	3	23	1	–9	5	0	1	1	0	0	0	0
	Fredericton Canadiens	AHL	22	12	18	30				71											6	2	6	8	0			
1996-97	HC Ambri-Piotta	Switz.	45	24	28	52				44																		
	HC Meran	Italy	12	5	12	17				4																		
1997-98	HC Ambri-Piotta	Switz.	40	30	*63	*93				60											14	11	11	22	40			
	Russia	WC-A	6	3	3	6				4																		
1998-99	HC Ambri-Piotta	Switz.	45	35	*52	*87				52											15	9	11	*20	32			
	Russia	WC-A	6	0	2	2				4																		
99-2000	Montreal Canadiens	NHL	44	2	24	26	2	22	24	8	1	0	0	96	2.1	35	7	18	0	10								
	Quebec Citadelles	AHL	16	7	7	14				4																		
	Russia	WC-A	6	1	1	2				4																		
	NHL Totals		**156**	**22**	**50**	**72**	**23**	**45**	**68**	**47**	**2**	**0**	**4**	**293**	**7.5**	**100**	**17**	**82**	**2**		**8**	**0**	**1**	**1**	**0**	**0**	**0**	**0**

NHL All-Rookie Team (1994)

Signed as a free agent by **Montreal**, July 15, 1999.

• PETROVICKY, Robert

C – L. 5'11", 172 lbs. b: Kosice, Czech., 10/26/1973. Hartford's 1st, 9th overall, in 1992.

Season	Club	League	GP	G	A	Pts	AG	AA	APts	PIM	PP	SH	GW	S	%	TGF	PGF	TGA	PGA	+/–	GP	G	A	Pts	PIM	PP	SH	GW
1990-91	Dukla Trencin	Czech.	33	9	14	23				12																		
	Czechoslovakia	EJC-A	5	1	7	8				4																		
1991-92	Dukla Trencin	Czech.	46	25	36	61				28																		
	Czechoslovakia	WJC-A	7	3	6	9				10																		
1992-93	Hartford Whalers	NHL	42	3	6	9	2	4	6	45	0	0	0	41	7.3	18	4	24	0	–10								
	Springfield Indians	AHL	16	5	3	8				39											15	5	6	11	14			
1993-94	Dukla Trencin	Slovakia	1	0	0	0				0																		
	Hartford Whalers	NHL	33	6	5	11	6	4	10	39	1	0	0	33	18.2	12	2	12	1	–1								
	Springfield Indians	AHL	30	16	8	24				39											4	0	2	2	4			
	Slovakia	Olympics	8	1	6	7				18																		

Season	Club	League	GP	G	A	Pts	AG	AA	APts	PIM	PP	SH	GW	S	%	TGF	PGF	TGA	PGA	+/–	Playoffs GP	G	A	Pts	PIM	PP	SH	GW
1994-95	Springfield Falcons	AHL	74	30	52	82	....	....	....	121	....	....	....	....	....	....	....	....	....	....	....	....	....	....	....	....	....	....
	Hartford Whalers	**NHL**	**2**	**0**	**0**	**0**	**0**	**0**	**0**	**0**	**0**	**0**	**0**	**1**	**0.0**	**0**	**0**	**0**	**0**	**0**	....	....	....	....	....	....	....	....
	Slovakia	WC-B	6	4	7	11	....	....	....	8	....	....	....	....	....	....	....	....	....	....	....	....	....	....	....	....	....	....
1995-96	Springfield Falcons	AHL	9	4	8	12	....	....	....	18	....	....	....	....	....	....	....	....	....	....	....	....	....	....	....	....	....	....
	Detroit Vipers	IHL	12	5	3	8	....	....	....	16	....	....	....	....	....	....	....	....	....	....	....	....	....	....	....	....	....	....
	Dallas Stars	**NHL**	**5**	**1**	**1**	**2**	**1**	**1**	**2**	**0**	**1**	**0**	**1**	**3**	**33.3**	**4**	**3**	**0**	**0**	**1**	....	....	....	....	....	....	....	....
	Michigan K-Wings	IHL	50	23	23	46	....	....	....	63	....	....	....	....	....	....	....	....	....	....	7	3	1	4	16	....	....	....
	Slovakia	WC-A	5	0	1	1	....	....	....	0	....	....	....	....	....	....	....	....	....	....	....	....	....	....	....	....	....	....
1996-97	**St. Louis Blues**	**NHL**	**44**	**7**	**12**	**19**	**7**	**11**	**18**	**10**	**0**	**0**	**1**	**54**	**13.0**	**29**	**6**	**22**	**1**	**2**	**2**	**0**	**0**	**0**	**0**	**0**	**0**	**0**
	Worcester IceCats	AHL	12	5	4	9	....	....	....	19	....	....	....	....	....	....	....	....	....	....	....	....	....	....	....	....	....	....
1997-98	Worcester IceCats	AHL	65	27	34	61	....	....	....	97	....	....	....	....	....	....	....	....	....	....	10	3	4	7	12	....	....	....
	Slovakia	Olympics	4	2	1	3	....	....	....	0	....	....	....	....	....	....	....	....	....	....	....	....	....	....	....	....	....	....
1998-99	Grand Rapids Griffins	IHL	49	26	32	58	....	....	....	87	....	....	....	....	....	....	....	....	....	....	....	....	....	....	....	....	....	....
	Tampa Bay Lightning	**NHL**	**28**	**3**	**4**	**7**	**4**	**4**	**8**	**6**	**0**	**0**	**0**	**32**	**9.4**	**9**	**0**	**17**	**0**	**–8**	....	....	....	....	....	....	....	....
99-2000	**Tampa Bay Lightning**	**NHL**	**43**	**7**	**10**	**17**	**8**	**9**	**17**	**14**	**1**	**0**	**0**	**50**	**14.0**	**24**	**5**	**17**	**0**	**2**	....	....	....	....	....	....	....	....
	Grand Rapids Griffins	IHL	7	5	3	8	....	....	....	4	....	....	....	....	....	....	....	....	....	....	....	....	....	....	....	....	....	....
	NHL Totals		**197**	**27**	**38**	**65**	**28**	**33**	**61**	**114**	**3**	**0**	**2**	**214**	**12.6**	**96**	**20**	**92**	**2**		**2**	**0**	**0**	**0**	**0**	**0**	**0**	**0**

Czechoslovakian First All-Star Team (1992) • WC-B All-Star Team (1995)

Traded to **Dallas** by **Hartford** for Dan Kesa, November 29, 1995. Signed as a free agent by **St. Louis**, September 6, 1996. Signed as a free agent by **Tampa Bay**, February 15, 1999.

• PETTERSSON, Jorgen

LW – L. 6'2", 185 lbs. b: Gothenburg, Sweden, 7/11/1956.

Season	Club	League	GP	G	A	Pts	AG	AA	APts	PIM	PP	SH	GW	S	%	TGF	PGF	TGA	PGA	+/–	Playoffs GP	G	A	Pts	PIM	PP	SH	GW
1973-74	Vastra Frolunda	Sweden-2	13	0	2	2	....	....	....	2	....	....	....	....	....	....	....	....	....	....	15	3	3	6	2	....	....	....
1974-75	Vastra Frolunda	Sweden	29	19	3	22	....	....	....	4	....	....	....	....	....	....	....	....	....	....	....	....	....	....	....	....	....	....
	Sweden	WJC-A	DID NOT PLAY																									
	Sweden	EJC-A	5	3	2	5	....	....	....	0	....	....	....	....	....	....	....	....	....	....	....	....	....	....	....	....	....	....
1975-76	Vastra Frolunda	Sweden	29	18	8	26	....	....	....	6	....	....	....	....	....	....	....	....	....	....	....	....	....	....	....	....	....	....
	Sweden	WJC-A	4	2	1	3	....	....	....	0	....	....	....	....	....	....	....	....	....	....	....	....	....	....	....	....	....	....
1976-77	Vastra Frolunda	Sweden	19	15	4	19	....	....	....	4	....	....	....	....	....	....	....	....	....	....	....	....	....	....	....	....	....	....
1977-78	Vastra Frolunda	Sweden	16	5	8	13	....	....	....	8	....	....	....	....	....	....	....	....	....	....	....	....	....	....	....	....	....	....
1978-79	Vastra Frolunda	Sweden	35	23	11	34	....	....	....	12	....	....	....	....	....	....	....	....	....	....	....	....	....	....	....	....	....	....
1979-80	Vastra Frolunda	Sweden	33	17	15	32	....	....	....	18	....	....	....	....	....	....	....	....	....	....	8	4	*4	*8	8	....	....	....
1980-81	**St. Louis Blues**	**NHL**	**62**	**37**	**36**	**73**	**29**	**24**	**53**	**24**	**8**	**0**	**5**	**172**	**21.5**	**100**	**26**	**60**	**0**	**14**	**11**	**4**	**3**	**7**	**0**	**1**	**0**	**2**
1981-82	Sweden	Can-Cup	5	0	0	0	....	....	....	0	....	....	....	....	....	....	....	....	....	....	....	....	....	....	....	....	....	....
	St. Louis Blues	**NHL**	**77**	**38**	**31**	**69**	**30**	**21**	**51**	**28**	**8**	**0**	**2**	**227**	**16.7**	**92**	**29**	**72**	**1**	**–8**	**7**	**1**	**2**	**3**	**0**	**1**	**0**	**0**
1982-83	**St. Louis Blues**	**NHL**	**74**	**35**	**38**	**73**	**29**	**26**	**55**	**4**	**7**	**3**	**4**	**201**	**17.4**	**93**	**29**	**87**	**13**	**–10**	**4**	**1**	**1**	**2**	**0**	**1**	**0**	**0**
	Sweden	WEC-A	10	2	0	2	....	....	....	4	....	....	....	....	....	....	....	....	....	....	....	....	....	....	....	....	....	....
1983-84	**St. Louis Blues**	**NHL**	**77**	**28**	**34**	**62**	**22**	**23**	**45**	**29**	**7**	**0**	**7**	**212**	**13.2**	**83**	**25**	**69**	**9**	**–2**	**11**	**7**	**3**	**10**	**2**	**2**	**0**	**1**
1984-85	**St. Louis Blues**	**NHL**	**75**	**23**	**32**	**55**	**19**	**22**	**41**	**20**	**8**	**0**	**3**	**180**	**12.8**	**90**	**34**	**50**	**2**	**8**	**3**	**1**	**1**	**2**	**0**	**0**	**0**	**0**
1985-86	**Hartford Whalers**	**NHL**	**23**	**5**	**5**	**10**	**4**	**3**	**7**	**2**	**2**	**0**	**0**	**27**	**18.5**	**13**	**7**	**22**	**4**	**–12**	....	....	....	....	....	....	....	....
	Washington Capitals	**NHL**	**47**	**8**	**16**	**24**	**6**	**11**	**17**	**10**	**2**	**0**	**3**	**74**	**10.8**	**35**	**10**	**32**	**3**	**–4**	**8**	**1**	**2**	**3**	**2**	**1**	**0**	**0**
1986-87	Vastra Frolunda	Sweden-2	27	14	13	27	....	....	....	10	....	....	....	....	....	....	....	....	....	....	2	0	0	0	0	....	....	....
1987-88	Vastra Frolunda	Sweden-2	35	22	21	43	....	....	....	18	....	....	....	....	....	....	....	....	....	....	11	6	5	11	2	....	....	....
1988-89	Vastra Frolunda	Sweden-2	36	23	30	53	....	....	....	10	....	....	....	....	....	....	....	....	....	....	8	7	6	13	8	....	....	....
1989-90	Vastra Frolunda	Sweden	36	13	11	24	....	....	....	16	....	....	....	....	....	....	....	....	....	....	....	....	....	....	....	....	....	....
1990-91	Vastra Frolunda	Sweden	1	0	0	0	....	....	....	0	....	....	....	....	....	....	....	....	....	....	....	....	....	....	....	....	....	....
	Hanhals HF	Sweden-2	29	16	19	35	....	....	....	18	....	....	....	....	....	....	....	....	....	....	....	....	....	....	....	....	....	....
1991-1993			OUT OF HOCKEY – RETIRED																									
1993-94	Harryda HC	Sweden-3	32	31	34	65	....	....	....	16	....	....	....	....	....	....	....	....	....	....	....	....	....	....	....	....	....	....
1994-95	Kungsbacka HC	Sweden-3	8	4	7	11	....	....	....	8	....	....	....	....	....	....	....	....	....	....	....	....	....	....	....	....	....	....
	NHL Totals		**435**	**174**	**192**	**366**	**139**	**130**	**269**	**117**	**42**	**3**	**24**	**1093**	**15.9**	**506**	**160**	**392**	**32**		**44**	**15**	**12**	**27**	**4**	**6**	**0**	**3**

Signed as a free agent by **St. Louis**, May 8, 1980. Traded to **Hartford** by **St. Louis** with Mike Luit for Mark Johnson and Greg Millen, February 21, 1985. Traded to **Washington** by **Hartford** for Doug Jarvis, December 6, 1985.

• PHAIR, Lyle

LW – L. 6'1", 190 lbs. b: Pilot Mound, Man., 8/31/1961.

Season	Club	League	GP	G	A	Pts	AG	AA	APts	PIM	PP	SH	GW	S	%	TGF	PGF	TGA	PGA	+/–	Playoffs GP	G	A	Pts	PIM	PP	SH	GW
1979-80	Selkirk Steelers	MJHL	48	41	50	91	....	....	....	....	....	....	....	....	....	....	....	....	....	....	....	....	....	....	....	....	....	....
1980-81	Selkirk Steelers	MJHL	48	21	48	69	....	....	....	....	....	....	....	....	....	....	....	....	....	....	....	....	....	....	....	....	....	....
1981-82	Michigan State Spartans	CCHA	42	19	24	43	....	....	....	49	....	....	....	....	....	....	....	....	....	....	....	....	....	....	....	....	....	....
1982-83	Michigan State Spartans	CCHA	42	20	15	35	....	....	....	64	....	....	....	....	....	....	....	....	....	....	....	....	....	....	....	....	....	....
1983-84	Michigan State Spartans	CCHA	45	15	16	31	....	....	....	58	....	....	....	....	....	....	....	....	....	....	....	....	....	....	....	....	....	....
1984-85	Michigan State Spartans	CCHA	43	23	27	50	....	....	....	86	....	....	....	....	....	....	....	....	....	....	....	....	....	....	....	....	....	....
1985-86	**Los Angeles Kings**	**NHL**	**15**	**0**	**1**	**1**	**0**	**1**	**1**	**2**	**0**	**0**	**0**	**11**	**0.0**	**4**	**0**	**17**	**1**	**–12**	....	....	....	....	....	....	....	....
	New Haven Nighthawks	AHL	35	9	9	18	....	....	....	15	....	....	....	....	....	....	....	....	....	....	2	0	1	1	0	....	....	....
1986-87	**Los Angeles Kings**	**NHL**	**5**	**2**	**0**	**2**	**2**	**0**	**2**	**2**	**0**	**0**	**0**	**4**	**50.0**	**3**	**0**	**4**	**0**	**–1**	....	....	....	....	....	....	....	....
	New Haven Nighthawks	AHL	65	19	27	46	....	....	....	77	....	....	....	....	....	....	....	....	....	....	7	0	3	3	13	....	....	....
1987-88	**Los Angeles Kings**	**NHL**	**28**	**4**	**6**	**10**	**3**	**4**	**7**	**8**	**0**	**0**	**0**	**35**	**11.4**	**17**	**3**	**20**	**1**	**–5**	**1**	**0**	**0**	**0**	**0**	**0**	**0**	**0**
	New Haven Nighthawks	AHL	45	15	12	27	....	....	....	26	....	....	....	....	....	....	....	....	....	....	....	....	....	....	....	....	....	....
1988-89	New Haven Nighthawks	AHL	11	2	3	5	....	....	....	4	....	....	....	....	....	....	....	....	....	....	....	....	....	....	....	....	....	....
	Utica Devils	AHL	58	5	19	24	....	....	....	24	....	....	....	....	....	....	....	....	....	....	3	0	0	0	2	....	....	....
	NHL Totals		**48**	**6**	**7**	**13**	**5**	**5**	**10**	**12**	**0**	**0**	**0**	**50**	**12.0**	**24**	**3**	**41**	**2**		**1**	**0**	**0**	**0**	**0**	**0**	**0**	**0**

NCAA Championship All-Tournament Team (1984)

Signed as a free agent by **LA Kings**, June 7, 1985. Traded to **New Jersey** by **LA Kings** for cash, December 13, 1988.

• PHILLIPOFF, Harold

Harold M LW – L. 6'3", 220 lbs. b: Kamsack, Sask., 7/14/1956. Atlanta's 2nd, 10th overall, in 1976.

Season	Club	League	GP	G	A	Pts	AG	AA	APts	PIM	PP	SH	GW	S	%	TGF	PGF	TGA	PGA	+/–	Playoffs GP	G	A	Pts	PIM	PP	SH	GW
1973-74	Bellingham Blazers	BCJHL	61	27	35	62	....	....	....	182	....	....	....	....	....	....	....	....	....	....	....	....	....	....	....	....	....	....
	New Westminster Bruins	WCJHL	2	1	0	1	....	....	....	0	....	....	....	....	....	....	....	....	....	....	11	0	1	1	45	....	....	....
1974-75	New Westminster Bruins	WCJHL	70	26	32	58	....	....	....	280	....	....	....	....	....	....	....	....	....	....	18	6	12	18	94	....	....	....
	New Westminster Bruins	Mem-Cup	4	1	1	2	....	....	....	12	....	....	....	....	....	....	....	....	....	....	....	....	....	....	....	....	....	....
1975-76	New Westminster Bruins	WCJHL	67	38	51	89	....	....	....	146	....	....	....	....	....	....	....	....	....	....	15	7	9	16	28	....	....	....
	New Westminster Bruins	Mem-Cup	4	3	1	4	....	....	....	7	....	....	....	....	....	....	....	....	....	....	....	....	....	....	....	....	....	....
1976-77	Nova Scotia Voyageurs	AHL	67	6	16	22	....	....	....	155	....	....	....	....	....	....	....	....	....	....	12	1	2	3	8	....	....	....
1977-78	**Atlanta Flames**	**NHL**	**67**	**17**	**36**	**53**	**15**	**28**	**43**	**128**	**2**	**0**	**2**	**132**	**12.9**	**85**	**12**	**46**	**0**	**27**	**2**	**0**	**1**	**1**	**2**	**0**	**0**	**0**
1978-79	**Atlanta Flames**	**NHL**	**51**	**9**	**17**	**26**	**8**	**12**	**20**	**113**	**0**	**0**	**2**	**66**	**13.6**	**38**	**0**	**33**	**0**	**5**	....	....	....	....	....	....	....	....
	Chicago Black Hawks	**NHL**	**14**	**0**	**4**	**4**	**0**	**3**	**3**	**6**	**0**	**0**	**0**	**13**	**0.0**	**8**	**2**	**10**	**0**	**–4**	**4**	**0**	**1**	**1**	**7**	**0**	**0**	**0**
1979-80	**Chicago Black Hawks**	**NHL**	**9**	**0**	**0**	**0**	**0**	**0**	**0**	**20**	**0**	**0**	**0**	**2**	**0.0**	**1**	**0**	**4**	**0**	**–3**	....	....	....	....	....	....	....	....
1980-81	Dallas Black Hawks	CHL	75	26	37	63	....	....	....	121	....	....	....	....	....	....	....	....	....	....	2	4	0	4	7	....	....	....
1981-82	Oklahoma City Stars	CHL	13	1	5	6	....	....	....	44	....	....	....	....	....	....	....	....	....	....	....	....	....	....	....	....	....	....
	Fredericton Express	AHL	58	19	28	47	....	....	....	122	....	....	....	....	....	....	....	....	....	....	....	....	....	....	....	....	....	....
	NHL Totals		**141**	**26**	**57**	**83**	**23**	**43**	**66**	**267**	**2**	**0**	**4**	**213**	**12.2**	**132**	**14**	**93**	**0**		**6**	**0**	**2**	**2**	**9**	**0**	**0**	**0**

Memorial Cup All-Star Team (1976)

Traded to **Chicago** by **Atlanta** with Pat Ribble, Greg Fox, Tom Lysiak and Miles Zaharko for Ivan Boldirev, Phil Russell and Darcy Rota, March 13, 1979. Traded to **Vancouver** by **Chicago** with Dave Logan for Ron Sedlbauer, December 21, 1979.

• PHILLIPS, Chris

D – L. 6'3", 215 lbs. b: Fort McMurray, Alta., 3/9/1978. Ottawa's 1st, 1st overall, in 1996.

Season	Club	League	GP	G	A	Pts	AG	AA	APts	PIM	PP	SH	GW	S	%	TGF	PGF	TGA	PGA	+/–	Playoffs GP	G	A	Pts	PIM	PP	SH	GW
1992-93	Fort McMurray Bantam Barons	AAHA	STATISTICS NOT AVAILABLE																									
1993-94	Fort McMurray Oil Barons	AJHL	56	6	16	22	....	....	....	72	....	....	....	....	....	....	....	....	....	....	10	0	3	3	16	....	....	....
1994-95	Fort McMurray Oil Barons	AJHL	48	16	32	48	....	....	....	127	....	....	....	....	....	....	....	....	....	....	11	4	2	6	10	....	....	....
1995-96	Prince Albert Raiders	WHL	61	10	30	40	....	....	....	97	....	....	....	....	....	....	....	....	....	....	18	2	12	14	30	....	....	....
	Canada	WJC-A	6	0	0	0	....	....	....	0	....	....	....	....	....	....	....	....	....	....	....	....	....	....	....	....	....	....

Season	Club	League	GP	G	A	Pts	AG	AA	APts	PIM	PP	SH	GW	S	%	TGF	PGF	TGA	PGA	+/–	GP	G	A	Pts	PIM	PP	SH	GW
			REGULAR SEASON																		PLAYOFFS							
1996-97	Prince Albert Raiders	WHL	32	3	23	26	....	....	....	58	....	....	....	....	....	....	....	....	....	....	....	....	....	....	....	....	....	....
	Canada	WJC-A	7	0	1	1	....	....	....	4	....	....	....	....	....	....	....	....	....	....	....	....	....	....	....	....	....	....
	Lethbridge Hurricanes	WHL	26	4	18	22	....	....	....	28	....	....	....	....	....	....	....	....	....	....	19	4	*21	25	20	....	....	....
	Lethbridge Hurricanes	Mem-Cup	5	2	3	5	....	....	....	14	....	....	....	....	....	....	....	....	....	....	....	....	....	....	....	....	....	....
1997-98	**Ottawa Senators**	**NHL**	**72**	**5**	**11**	**16**	**6**	**11**	**17**	**38**	**2**	**0**	**2**	**107**	**4.7**	**56**	**19**	**40**	**5**	**2**	**11**	**0**	**2**	**2**	**2**	**0**	**0**	**0**
1998-99	**Ottawa Senators**	**NHL**	**34**	**3**	**3**	**6**	**4**	**3**	**7**	**32**	**2**	**0**	**0**	**51**	**5.9**	**26**	**7**	**27**	**3**	**–5**	**3**	**0**	**0**	**0**	**0**	**0**	**0**	**0**
99-2000	**Ottawa Senators**	**NHL**	**65**	**5**	**14**	**19**	**6**	**13**	**19**	**39**	**0**	**0**	**1**	**96**	**5.2**	**59**	**10**	**41**	**4**	**12**	**6**	**0**	**1**	**1**	**4**	**0**	**0**	**0**
	Canada	WC-A	9	0	0	0	....	....	....	2	....	....	....	....	....	....	....	....	....	....	....	....	....	....	....	....	....	....
	NHL Totals		**171**	**13**	**28**	**41**	**16**	**27**	**43**	**109**	**4**	**0**	**3**	**254**	**5.1**	**141**	**36**	**108**	**12**		**20**	**0**	**3**	**3**	**6**	**0**	**0**	**0**

WJC-A All-Star Team (1997) • WHL East First All-Star Team (1997) • Canadian Major Junior First All-Star Team (1997)

• Missed majority of 1998-99 season recovering from ankle injury suffered in game vs. Buffalo, December 30, 1998.

• PICARD, Michel

LW – L. 5'11", 190 lbs. b: Beauport, Que., 11/7/1969. Hartford's 8th, 178th overall, in 1989.

Season	Club	League	GP	G	A	Pts	AG	AA	APts	PIM	PP	SH	GW	S	%	TGF	PGF	TGA	PGA	+/–	GP	G	A	Pts	PIM	PP	SH	GW
1985-86	Ste-Foy Gouverneurs	QAAA	42	53	34	87	....	....	....	....	....	....	....	....	....	....	....	....	....	....	....	....	....	....	....	....	....	....
1986-87	Trois-Rivieres Draveurs	QMJHL	66	33	35	68	....	....	....	53	....	....	....	....	....	....	....	....	....	....	....	....	....	....	....	....	....	....
1987-88	Trois-Rivieres Draveurs	QMJHL	69	40	55	95	....	....	....	71	....	....	....	....	....	....	....	....	....	....	....	....	....	....	....	....	....	....
1988-89	Trois-Rivieres Draveurs	QMJHL	66	59	81	140	....	....	....	170	....	....	....	....	....	....	....	....	....	....	4	1	3	4	2	....	....	....
1989-90	Binghamton Whalers	AHL	67	16	24	40	....	....	....	98	....	....	....	....	....	....	....	....	....	....	....	....	....	....	....	....	....	....
1990-91	**Hartford Whalers**	**NHL**	**5**	**1**	**0**	**1**	**1**	**0**	**1**	**2**	**0**	**0**	**0**	**7**	**14.3**	**2**	**0**	**4**	**0**	**–2**	....	....	....	....	....	....	....	....
	Springfield Indians	AHL	77	*56	40	96	....	....	....	61	....	....	....	....	....	....	....	....	....	....	18	8	13	21	18	....	....	....
1991-92	**Hartford Whalers**	**NHL**	**25**	**3**	**5**	**8**	**3**	**4**	**7**	**6**	**1**	**0**	**0**	**41**	**7.3**	**13**	**3**	**12**	**0**	**–2**	....	....	....	....	....	....	....	....
	Springfield Indians	AHL	40	21	17	38	....	....	....	44	....	....	....	....	....	....	....	....	....	....	11	2	0	2	34	....	....	....
1992-93	**San Jose Sharks**	**NHL**	**25**	**4**	**0**	**4**	**3**	**0**	**3**	**24**	**2**	**0**	**0**	**32**	**12.5**	**9**	**2**	**24**	**0**	**–17**	....	....	....	....	....	....	....	....
	Kansas City Blades	IHL	33	7	10	17	....	....	....	51	....	....	....	....	....	....	....	....	....	....	12	3	2	5	20	....	....	....
1993-94	Portland Pirates	AHL	61	41	44	85	....	....	....	99	....	....	....	....	....	....	....	....	....	....	17	11	10	21	22	....	....	....
1994-95	P.E.I. Senators	AHL	57	32	57	89	....	....	....	58	....	....	....	....	....	....	....	....	....	....	8	4	4	8	6	....	....	....
	Ottawa Senators	**NHL**	**24**	**5**	**8**	**13**	**9**	**12**	**21**	**14**	**1**	**0**	**0**	**33**	**15.2**	**17**	**6**	**12**	**0**	**–1**	....	....	....	....	....	....	....	....
1995-96	**Ottawa Senators**	**NHL**	**17**	**2**	**6**	**8**	**2**	**5**	**7**	**10**	**0**	**0**	**1**	**21**	**9.5**	**13**	**5**	**9**	**0**	**–1**	....	....	....	....	....	....	....	....
	P.E.I. Senators	AHL	55	37	45	82	....	....	....	79	....	....	....	....	....	....	....	....	....	....	5	5	1	6	2	....	....	....
1996-97	Vastra Frolunda	Sweden	3	0	1	1	....	....	....	0	....	....	....	....	....	....	....	....	....	....	....	....	....	....	....	....	....	....
	Grand Rapids Griffins	IHL	82	46	55	101	....	....	....	58	....	....	....	....	....	....	....	....	....	....	5	2	0	2	10	....	....	....
1997-98	Grand Rapids Griffins	IHL	58	28	41	69	....	....	....	42	....	....	....	....	....	....	....	....	....	....	....	....	....	....	....	....	....	....
	St. Louis Blues	**NHL**	**16**	**1**	**8**	**9**	**1**	**8**	**9**	**29**	**0**	**0**	**0**	**19**	**5.3**	**11**	**1**	**7**	**0**	**3**	....	....	....	....	....	....	....	....
1998-99	**St. Louis Blues**	**NHL**	**45**	**11**	**11**	**22**	**13**	**11**	**24**	**16**	**0**	**0**	**2**	**69**	**15.9**	**41**	**10**	**26**	**0**	**5**	**5**	**0**	**0**	**0**	**2**	**0**	**0**	**0**
	Grand Rapids Griffins	IHL	6	2	2	4	....	....	....	2	....	....	....	....	....	....	....	....	....	....	....	....	....	....	....	....	....	....
99-2000	Grand Rapids Griffins	IHL	65	33	35	68	....	....	....	50	....	....	....	....	....	....	....	....	....	....	17	8	10	*18	4	....	....	....
	Edmonton Oilers	**NHL**	**2**	**0**	**0**	**0**	**0**	**0**	**0**	**2**	**0**	**0**	**0**	**2**	**0.0**	**0**	**0**	**0**	**0**	**0**	....	....	....	....	....	....	....	....
	NHL Totals		**159**	**27**	**38**	**65**	**32**	**40**	**72**	**103**	**4**	**0**	**3**	**224**	**12.1**	**106**	**27**	**94**	**0**		**5**	**0**	**0**	**0**	**2**	**0**	**0**	**0**

QMJHL Second All-Star Team (1989) • AHL First All-Star Team (1991, 1995) • AHL Second All-Star Team (1994) • IHL First All-Star Team (1997)

Traded to **San Jose** by **Hartford** for future considerations (Yvon Corriveau, January 21, 1993), October 9, 1992. Signed as a free agent by **Ottawa**, June 16, 1994. Traded to **Washington** by **Ottawa** for cash, May 21, 1996. Signed as a free agent by **St. Louis**, January 5, 1998. Signed as a free agent by **Edmonton**, December 2, 1999.

• PICARD, Noel

Jean Noel D – R. 6'1", 185 lbs. b: Montreal, Que., 12/25/1938.

Season	Club	League	GP	G	A	Pts	AG	AA	APts	PIM	PP	SH	GW	S	%	TGF	PGF	TGA	PGA	+/–	GP	G	A	Pts	PIM	PP	SH	GW
1960-61	Jersey Devils	EHL	55	2	6	8	....	....	....	55	....	....	....	....	....	....	....	....	....	....	....	....	....	....	....	....	....	....
1961-62	Montreal Olympics	QSHL	18	3	7	10	....	....	....	8	....	....	....	....	....	....	....	....	....	....	6	1	3	4	17	....	....	....
	Montreal Olympics	Al-Cup	15	2	6	8	....	....	....	38	....	....	....	....	....	....	....	....	....	....	....	....	....	....	....	....	....	....
1962-63	Montreal Olympics	QSHL	STATISTICS NOT AVAILABLE																									
	Sherbrooke Castors	QSHL	....	....	....	....	....	....	....	....	....	....	....	....	....	....	....	....	....	....	1	0	0	0	0	....	....	....
1963-64	Omaha Knights	CPHL	59	4	25	29	....	....	....	147	....	....	....	....	....	....	....	....	....	....	9	1	2	3	12	....	....	....
1964-65♦	**Montreal Canadiens**	**NHL**	**16**	**0**	**7**	**7**	**0**	**7**	**7**	**33**	....	....	....	....	....	....	....	....	....	....	**3**	**0**	**1**	**1**	**0**	**0**	**0**	**0**
	Omaha Knights	CPHL	50	13	23	36	....	....	....	142	....	....	....	....	....	....	....	....	....	....	....	....	....	....	....	....	....	....
1965-66	Houston Apollos	CPHL	58	3	15	18	....	....	....	186	....	....	....	....	....	....	....	....	....	....	....	....	....	....	....	....	....	....
1966-67	Seattle Totems	WHL	63	3	24	27	....	....	....	135	....	....	....	....	....	....	....	....	....	....	10	2	5	7	16	....	....	....
	Providence Reds	AHL	9	0	3	3	....	....	....	17	....	....	....	....	....	....	....	....	....	....	....	....	....	....	....	....	....	....
1967-68	**St. Louis Blues**	**NHL**	**66**	**1**	**10**	**11**	**1**	**10**	**11**	**142**	**0**	**0**	**1**	**120**	**0.8**	**54**	**7**	**65**	**14**	**–4**	**13**	**0**	**3**	**3**	**46**	**0**	**0**	**0**
1968-69	**St. Louis Blues**	**NHL**	**67**	**5**	**19**	**24**	**5**	**17**	**22**	**131**	**0**	**0**	**1**	**136**	**3.7**	**70**	**10**	**54**	**13**	**19**	**12**	**1**	**4**	**5**	**30**	**0**	**0**	**0**
1969-70	**St. Louis Blues**	**NHL**	**39**	**1**	**4**	**5**	**1**	**4**	**5**	**88**	**1**	**0**	**0**	**31**	**3.2**	**27**	**3**	**28**	**4**	**0**	**16**	**0**	**2**	**2**	**65**	**0**	**0**	**0**
1970-71	**St. Louis Blues**	**NHL**	**75**	**3**	**8**	**11**	**3**	**7**	**10**	**119**	**0**	**0**	**1**	**128**	**2.3**	**73**	**0**	**91**	**20**	**2**	**6**	**1**	**1**	**2**	**26**	**1**	**0**	**0**
1971-72	**St. Louis Blues**	**NHL**	**15**	**1**	**5**	**6**	**1**	**4**	**5**	**50**	**0**	**0**	**0**	**34**	**2.9**	**15**	**0**	**15**	**1**	**1**	....	....	....	....	....	....	....	....
1972-73	**St. Louis Blues**	**NHL**	**16**	**1**	**0**	**1**	**1**	**0**	**1**	**10**	**0**	**0**	**0**	**19**	**5.3**	**7**	**0**	**9**	**0**	**–2**	....	....	....	....	....	....	....	....
	Atlanta Flames	**NHL**	**41**	**0**	**10**	**10**	**0**	**8**	**8**	**43**	**0**	**0**	**0**	**37**	**0.0**	**29**	**1**	**35**	**1**	**–6**	....	....	....	....	....	....	....	....
	NHL Totals		**335**	**12**	**63**	**75**	**12**	**57**	**69**	**616**	....	....	....	....	....	....	....	....	....	....	**50**	**2**	**11**	**13**	**167**	....	....	....

• Brother of Roger • Played in NHL All-Star Game (1969)

Claimed by **St. Louis** from **Montreal** in Expansion Draft, June 6, 1967. Claimed on waivers by **Atlanta** from **St. Louis**, November 25, 1972.

• PICARD, Robert

Robert Rene Joseph D – L. 6'2", 207 lbs. b: Montreal, Que., 5/25/1957. Washington's 1st, 3rd overall, in 1977.

Season	Club	League	GP	G	A	Pts	AG	AA	APts	PIM	PP	SH	GW	S	%	TGF	PGF	TGA	PGA	+/–	GP	G	A	Pts	PIM	PP	SH	GW
1973-74	Montreal Red-White-Blue	QMJHL	70	7	46	53	....	....	....	*296	....	....	....	....	....	....	....	....	....	....	....	....	....	....	....	....	....	....
1974-75	Montreal Red-White-Blue	QMJHL	70	13	74	87	....	....	....	339	....	....	....	....	....	....	....	....	....	....	....	....	....	....	....	....	....	....
1975-76	Montreal Juniors	QMJHL	72	14	67	81	....	....	....	282	....	....	....	....	....	....	....	....	....	....	6	2	9	11	25	....	....	....
1976-77	Montreal Juniors	QMJHL	70	32	60	92	....	....	....	267	....	....	....	....	....	....	....	....	....	....	13	2	10	12	20	....	....	....
1977-78	**Washington Capitals**	**NHL**	**75**	**10**	**27**	**37**	**9**	**21**	**30**	**101**	**2**	**0**	**4**	**170**	**5.9**	**69**	**12**	**106**	**23**	**–26**	....	....	....	....	....	....	....	....
	Canada	WEC-A	10	1	2	3	....	....	....	4	....	....	....	....	....	....	....	....	....	....	....	....	....	....	....	....	....	....
1978-79	**Washington Capitals**	**NHL**	**77**	**21**	**44**	**65**	**18**	**32**	**50**	**85**	**8**	**0**	**2**	**243**	**8.6**	**153**	**48**	**138**	**36**	**3**	....	....	....	....	....	....	....	....
	NHL All-Stars	Chal-Cup	DID NOT PLAY																									
	Canada	WEC-A	7	0	0	0	....	....	....	2	....	....	....	....	....	....	....	....	....	....	....	....	....	....	....	....	....	....
1979-80	**Washington Capitals**	**NHL**	**78**	**11**	**43**	**54**	**9**	**31**	**40**	**122**	**5**	**0**	**1**	**212**	**5.2**	**141**	**48**	**135**	**21**	**–21**	....	....	....	....	....	....	....	....
1980-81	**Toronto Maple Leafs**	**NHL**	**59**	**6**	**19**	**25**	**5**	**13**	**18**	**68**	**2**	**0**	**0**	**160**	**3.8**	**81**	**28**	**112**	**27**	**–32**	....	....	....	....	....	....	....	....
	Montreal Canadiens	**NHL**	**8**	**2**	**2**	**4**	**2**	**1**	**3**	**6**	**1**	**0**	**0**	**12**	**16.7**	**7**	**3**	**5**	**0**	**–1**	**1**	**0**	**0**	**0**	**0**	**0**	**0**	**0**
1981-82	**Montreal Canadiens**	**NHL**	**62**	**2**	**26**	**28**	**2**	**17**	**19**	**106**	**2**	**0**	**0**	**132**	**1.5**	**82**	**24**	**47**	**6**	**17**	**5**	**1**	**1**	**2**	**7**	**0**	**0**	**0**
1982-83	**Montreal Canadiens**	**NHL**	**64**	**7**	**31**	**38**	**6**	**21**	**27**	**60**	**1**	**0**	**1**	**117**	**6.0**	**105**	**18**	**83**	**27**	**31**	**3**	**0**	**0**	**0**	**0**	**0**	**0**	**0**
1983-84	**Montreal Canadiens**	**NHL**	**7**	**0**	**2**	**2**	**0**	**1**	**1**	**0**	**0**	**0**	**0**	**7**	**0.0**	**7**	**2**	**6**	**0**	**–1**	....	....	....	....	....	....	....	....
	Winnipeg Jets	**NHL**	**62**	**6**	**16**	**22**	**5**	**11**	**16**	**34**	**1**	**1**	**1**	**126**	**4.8**	**87**	**7**	**106**	**35**	**9**	**3**	**0**	**0**	**0**	**12**	**0**	**0**	**0**
1984-85	**Winnipeg Jets**	**NHL**	**78**	**12**	**22**	**34**	**10**	**15**	**25**	**107**	**0**	**0**	**3**	**151**	**7.9**	**123**	**10**	**123**	**41**	**31**	**8**	**2**	**2**	**4**	**8**	**1**	**0**	**0**
1985-86	**Winnipeg Jets**	**NHL**	**20**	**2**	**5**	**7**	**2**	**3**	**5**	**17**	**0**	**0**	**1**	**40**	**5.0**	**26**	**2**	**34**	**8**	**–2**	....	....	....	....	....	....	....	....
	Quebec Nordiques	**NHL**	**48**	**7**	**27**	**34**	**6**	**18**	**24**	**36**	**1**	**1**	**0**	**131**	**5.3**	**101**	**43**	**79**	**19**	**–2**	**3**	**0**	**2**	**2**	**2**	**0**	**0**	**0**
1986-87	**Quebec Nordiques**	**NHL**	**78**	**8**	**20**	**28**	**7**	**15**	**22**	**71**	**1**	**1**	**3**	**163**	**4.9**	**73**	**16**	**101**	**27**	**–17**	**13**	**2**	**10**	**12**	**10**	**1**	**0**	**0**
1987-88	**Quebec Nordiques**	**NHL**	**65**	**3**	**13**	**16**	**3**	**9**	**12**	**103**	**0**	**1**	**1**	**110**	**2.7**	**64**	**7**	**103**	**45**	**–1**	....	....	....	....	....	....	....	....
1988-89	**Quebec Nordiques**	**NHL**	**74**	**7**	**14**	**21**	**6**	**10**	**16**	**61**	**2**	**1**	**1**	**102**	**6.9**	**71**	**12**	**119**	**32**	**–28**	....	....	....	....	....	....	....	....
1989-90	**Quebec Nordiques**	**NHL**	**24**	**0**	**5**	**5**	**0**	**4**	**4**	**28**	**0**	**0**	**0**	**25**	**0.0**	**24**	**2**	**36**	**9**	**–5**	....	....	....	....	....	....	....	....
	Detroit Red Wings	**NHL**	**20**	**0**	**3**	**3**	**0**	**2**	**2**	**20**	**0**	**0**	**0**	**14**	**0.0**	**17**	**2**	**20**	**7**	**2**	....	....	....	....	....	....	....	....
	NHL Totals		**899**	**104**	**319**	**423**	**90**	**224**	**314**	**1025**	**26**	**5**	**18**	**1915**	**5.4**	**1231**	**284**	**1353**	**363**		**36**	**5**	**15**	**20**	**39**	**2**	**0**	**0**

QMJHL Second All-Star Team (1975) • QMJHL West First All-Star Team (1976) • QMJHL First All-Star Team (1977) • Played in NHL All-Star Game (1980, 1981)

Traded to **Toronto** by **Washington** with Tim Coulis and Washington's 2nd round choice (Bob McGill) in 1980 Entry Draft for Mike Palmateer and Toronto's 3rd round choice (Torrie Robertson) in 1980 Entry Draft, June 11, 1980. Traded to **Montreal** by **Toronto** for Michel Larocque, March 10, 1981. Traded to **Winnipeg** by **Montreal** for Winnipeg's 3rd round choice (Patrick Roy) in 1984 Entry Draft, November 4, 1983. Traded to **Quebec** by **Winnipeg** for Mario Marois, November 27, 1985. Traded to **Detroit** by **Quebec** with Greg C. Adams for Tony McKegney, December 4, 1989.

			REGULAR SEASON																		PLAYOFFS							
Season	Club	League	GP	G	A	Pts	AG	AA	APts	PIM	PP	SH	GW	S	%	TGF	PGF	TGA	PGA	+/–	GP	G	A	Pts	PIM	PP	SH	GW

• PICARD, Roger

Adrien Roger RW – R. 6', 200 lbs. b: Montreal, Que., 1/13/1935.

Season	Club	League	GP	G	A	Pts	AG	AA	APts	PIM	PP	SH	GW	S	%	TGF	PGF	TGA	PGA	+/–	GP	G	A	Pts	PIM	PP	SH	GW
1955-56	Montreal Lakeshore Royals	MMJHL	33	22	20	42	....	....	....	28	....	....	....	....	....	....	....	....	....	....	....	....	....	....	....	....	....	....
1956-57	Montreal Lakeshore Royals	MMJHL	33	12	21	33	....	....	....	28	....	....	....	....	....	....	....	....	....	....	....	....	....	....	....	....	....	....
1957-1960	Granby Victorias	QSHL	STATISTICS NOT AVAILABLE																									
1960-61	Granby Victorias	QSHL	28	13	10	23	....	....	....	21	....	....	....	....	....	....	....	....	....	....	9	10	4	14	4	....	....	....
1961-62	Sherbrooke Castors	ETSHL	20	6	9	15	....	....	....	20	....	....	....	....	....	....	....	....	....	....	7	6	5	11	8	....	....	....
	Montreal Olympics	Al-Cup	16	7	8	15	....	....	....	14	....	....	....	....	....	....	....	....	....	....	....	....	....	....	....	....	....	....
1962-63	Montreal Olympics	QSHL	STATISTICS NOT AVAILABLE																									
1963-64	Montreal Olympics	QSHL	STATISTICS NOT AVAILABLE																									
1964-65	Drummondville Eagles	QSHL	STATISTICS NOT AVAILABLE																									
1965-66	Drummondville Eagles	QSHL	38	20	33	53	....	....	....	20	....	....	....	....	....	....	....	....	....	....	5	1	3	4	20	....	....	....
1966-67	Drummondville Eagles	QSHL	41	21	33	54	....	....	....	47	....	....	....	....	....	....	....	....	....	....	9	0	6	6	21	....	....	....
	Drummondville Eagles	Al-Cup	11	3	6	9	....	....	....	22	....	....	....	....	....	....	....	....	....	....	....	....	....	....	....	....	....	....
1967-68	**St. Louis Blues**	**NHL**	**15**	**2**	**2**	**4**	**2**	**2**	**4**	**21**	**0**	**0**	**0**	**45**	**4.4**	**5**	**0**	**9**	**0**	**–4**	....	....	....	....	....	....	....	....
	Kansas City Blues	CPHL	43	15	28	43	....	....	....	82	....	....	....	....	....	....	....	....	....	....	7	0	10	10	21	....	....	....
1968-69	Denver Spurs	WHL	26	6	3	9	....	....	....	8	....	....	....	....	....	....	....	....	....	....	....	....	....	....	....	....	....	....
	Buffalo Bisons	AHL	11	5	4	9	....	....	....	4	....	....	....	....	....	....	....	....	....	....	....	....	....	....	....	....	....	....
	Omaha Knights	CHL	31	9	11	20	....	....	....	41	....	....	....	....	....	....	....	....	....	....	1	0	0	0	0	....	....	....
	NHL Totals		**15**	**2**	**2**	**4**	**2**	**2**	**4**	**21**	**0**	**0**	**0**	**45**	**4.4**	**5**	**0**	**9**	**0**		....	....	....	....	....	....	....	....

• Brother of Noel

Signed as a free agent by **St. Louis**, June 6, 1967.

• PICHETTE, Dave

D – L. 6'3", 190 lbs. b: Grand Falls, Nfld., 2/4/1960.

Season	Club	League	GP	G	A	Pts	AG	AA	APts	PIM	PP	SH	GW	S	%	TGF	PGF	TGA	PGA	+/–	GP	G	A	Pts	PIM	PP	SH	GW
1978-79	Quebec Remparts	QMJHL	57	10	16	26	....	....	....	134	....	....	....	....	....	....	....	....	....	....	6	1	1	2	35	....	....	....
1979-80	Quebec Remparts	QMJHL	56	8	19	27	....	....	....	129	....	....	....	....	....	....	....	....	....	....	5	1	3	4	8	....	....	....
1980-81	**Quebec Nordiques**	**NHL**	**46**	**4**	**16**	**20**	**3**	**11**	**14**	**62**	**2**	**0**	**0**	**47**	**8.5**	**60**	**14**	**50**	**7**	**3**	**1**	**0**	**0**	**0**	**14**	**0**	**0**	**0**
	Hershey Bears	AHL	20	2	3	5	....	....	....	37	....	....	....	....	....	....	....	....	....	....	....	....	....	....	....	....	....	....
1981-82	**Quebec Nordiques**	**NHL**	**67**	**7**	**30**	**37**	**6**	**20**	**26**	**152**	**3**	**0**	**0**	**84**	**8.3**	**131**	**51**	**94**	**13**	**–1**	**16**	**2**	**4**	**6**	**22**	**1**	**0**	**1**
1982-83	**Quebec Nordiques**	**NHL**	**53**	**3**	**21**	**24**	**2**	**15**	**17**	**49**	**0**	**0**	**0**	**62**	**4.8**	**92**	**27**	**62**	**6**	**9**	**2**	**0**	**1**	**1**	**0**	**0**	**0**	**0**
	Fredericton Express	AHL	16	3	11	14	....	....	....	14	....	....	....	....	....	....	....	....	....	....	....	....	....	....	....	....	....	....
1983-84	**Quebec Nordiques**	**NHL**	**23**	**2**	**7**	**9**	**2**	**5**	**7**	**12**	**0**	**0**	**0**	**34**	**5.9**	**28**	**8**	**20**	**2**	**2**	....	....	....	....	....	....	....	....
	Fredericton Express	AHL	10	2	1	3	....	....	....	13	....	....	....	....	....	....	....	....	....	....	....	....	....	....	....	....	....	....
	St. Louis Blues	**NHL**	**23**	**0**	**11**	**11**	**0**	**7**	**7**	**6**	**0**	**0**	**0**	**37**	**0.0**	**37**	**16**	**30**	**4**	**–5**	**9**	**1**	**2**	**3**	**18**	**0**	**0**	**0**
1984-85	**New Jersey Devils**	**NHL**	**71**	**17**	**40**	**57**	**14**	**27**	**41**	**41**	**8**	**0**	**2**	**140**	**12.1**	**101**	**43**	**86**	**8**	**–20**	....	....	....	....	....	....	....	....
1985-86	**New Jersey Devils**	**NHL**	**33**	**7**	**12**	**19**	**6**	**8**	**14**	**22**	**4**	**0**	**1**	**59**	**11.9**	**56**	**22**	**45**	**0**	**–11**	....	....	....	....	....	....	....	....
	Maine Mariners	AHL	25	4	15	19	....	....	....	28	....	....	....	....	....	....	....	....	....	....	....	....	....	....	....	....	....	....
1986-87	Maine Mariners	AHL	61	6	16	22	....	....	....	69	....	....	....	....	....	....	....	....	....	....	....	....	....	....	....	....	....	....
1987-88	**New York Rangers**	**NHL**	**6**	**1**	**3**	**4**	**1**	**2**	**3**	**4**	**0**	**0**	**0**	**7**	**14.3**	**6**	**4**	**5**	**0**	**–3**	....	....	....	....	....	....	....	....
	New Haven Nighthawks	AHL	46	10	21	31	....	....	....	37	....	....	....	....	....	....	....	....	....	....	....	....	....	....	....	....	....	....
1988-89	Cape Breton Oilers	AHL	39	5	21	26	....	....	....	20	....	....	....	....	....	....	....	....	....	....	....	....	....	....	....	....	....	....
1989-90	Krefelder EV	Germany-2	15	3	15	18	....	....	....	48	....	....	....	....	....	....	....	....	....	....	....	....	....	....	....	....	....	....
	Halifax Citadels	AHL	58	3	18	21	....	....	....	65	....	....	....	....	....	....	....	....	....	....	....	....	....	....	....	....	....	....
	NHL Totals		**322**	**41**	**140**	**181**	**34**	**95**	**129**	**348**	**17**	**0**	**3**	**470**	**8.7**	**511**	**185**	**392**	**40**		**28**	**3**	**7**	**10**	**54**	**1**	**0**	**1**

Signed as a free agent by **Quebec**, October 31, 1979. Traded to **St. Louis** by **Quebec** for Andre Dore, February 10, 1984. Claimed by **New Jersey** from **St. Louis** in Waiver Draft, October 9, 1984.

• PIERCE, Randy

Randy Stephen RW – R. 5'11", 187 lbs. b: Arnprior, Ont., 11/23/1957. Colorado's 3rd, 47th overall, in 1977.

Season	Club	League	GP	G	A	Pts	AG	AA	APts	PIM	PP	SH	GW	S	%	TGF	PGF	TGA	PGA	+/–	GP	G	A	Pts	PIM	PP	SH	GW
1974-75	Smiths Falls Bears	OJHL	STATISTICS NOT AVAILABLE																									
1975-76	Sudbury Wolves	OMJHL	56	21	44	65	....	....	....	72	....	....	....	....	....	....	....	....	....	....	15	9	16	25	13	....	....	....
1976-77	Sudbury Wolves	OMJHL	60	38	60	98	....	....	....	67	....	....	....	....	....	....	....	....	....	....	6	2	3	5	7	....	....	....
1977-78	**Colorado Rockies**	**NHL**	**35**	**9**	**10**	**19**	**8**	**8**	**16**	**15**	**1**	**0**	**3**	**60**	**15.0**	**33**	**9**	**24**	**0**	**0**	**2**	**0**	**0**	**0**	**0**	**0**	**0**	**0**
	Hampton Gulls	AHL	3	0	1	1	....	....	....	2	....	....	....	....	....	....	....	....	....	....	....	....	....	....	....	....	....	....
	Phoenix Roadrunners	CHL	12	3	1	4	....	....	....	11	....	....	....	....	....	....	....	....	....	....	....	....	....	....	....	....	....	....
1978-79	**Colorado Rockies**	**NHL**	**70**	**19**	**17**	**36**	**16**	**12**	**28**	**35**	**4**	**1**	**3**	**145**	**13.1**	**58**	**18**	**68**	**7**	**–21**	....	....	....	....	....	....	....	....
	Philadelphia Firebirds	AHL	1	0	0	0	....	....	....	0	....	....	....	....	....	....	....	....	....	....	....	....	....	....	....	....	....	....
1979-80	**Colorado Rockies**	**NHL**	**75**	**16**	**23**	**39**	**14**	**17**	**31**	**100**	**0**	**0**	**1**	**171**	**9.4**	**59**	**9**	**62**	**1**	**–11**	....	....	....	....	....	....	....	....
1980-81	**Colorado Rockies**	**NHL**	**55**	**9**	**21**	**30**	**7**	**14**	**21**	**52**	**3**	**0**	**3**	**124**	**7.3**	**48**	**18**	**65**	**7**	**–28**	....	....	....	....	....	....	....	....
1981-82	**Colorado Rockies**	**NHL**	**5**	**0**	**0**	**0**	**0**	**0**	**0**	**4**	**0**	**0**	**0**	**7**	**0.0**	**0**	**0**	**1**	**0**	**–1**	....	....	....	....	....	....	....	....
	Fort Worth Texans	CHL	15	6	6	12	....	....	....	19	....	....	....	....	....	....	....	....	....	....	....	....	....	....	....	....	....	....
1982-83	**New Jersey Devils**	**NHL**	**3**	**0**	**0**	**0**	**0**	**0**	**0**	**0**	**0**	**0**	**0**	**2**	**0.0**	**2**	**0**	**2**	**0**	**0**	....	....	....	....	....	....	....	....
	Wichita Wind	CHL	14	4	8	12	....	....	....	4	....	....	....	....	....	....	....	....	....	....	....	....	....	....	....	....	....	....
	Binghamton Whalers	AHL	46	14	41	55	....	....	....	33	....	....	....	....	....	....	....	....	....	....	2	0	1	1	0	....	....	....
1983-84	**Hartford Whalers**	**NHL**	**17**	**6**	**3**	**9**	**5**	**2**	**7**	**9**	**0**	**1**	**0**	**25**	**24.0**	**14**	**0**	**16**	**7**	**5**	....	....	....	....	....	....	....	....
	Binghamton Whalers	AHL	46	22	24	46	....	....	....	41	....	....	....	....	....	....	....	....	....	....	....	....	....	....	....	....	....	....
1984-85	**Hartford Whalers**	**NHL**	**17**	**3**	**2**	**5**	**2**	**1**	**3**	**8**	**0**	**0**	**0**	**24**	**12.5**	**9**	**0**	**21**	**8**	**–4**	....	....	....	....	....	....	....	....
	Binghamton Whalers	AHL	31	6	10	16	....	....	....	45	....	....	....	....	....	....	....	....	....	....	6	2	1	3	6	....	....	....
1985-86	Salt Lake Golden Eagles	IHL	20	5	5	10	....	....	....	25	....	....	....	....	....	....	....	....	....	....	....	....	....	....	....	....	....	....
	NHL Totals		**277**	**62**	**76**	**138**	**52**	**54**	**106**	**223**	**8**	**2**	**10**	**558**	**11.1**	**223**	**54**	**259**	**30**		**2**	**0**	**0**	**0**	**0**	**0**	**0**	**0**

Transferred to **New Jersey** after **Colorado** franchise relocated, June 30, 1982. Signed as a free agent by **Hartford**, October 6, 1983.

• PILON, Richard

Richard B. D – L. 6', 205 lbs. b: Saskatoon, Sask., 4/30/1968. NY Islanders' 9th, 143rd overall, in 1986.

Season	Club	League	GP	G	A	Pts	AG	AA	APts	PIM	PP	SH	GW	S	%	TGF	PGF	TGA	PGA	+/–	GP	G	A	Pts	PIM	PP	SH	GW
1984-85	Prince Albert Midget Raiders	SAHA	26	3	11	14	....	....	....	41	....	....	....	....	....	....	....	....	....	....	....	....	....	....	....	....	....	....
1985-86	Prince Albert Midget Raiders	SAHA	35	3	28	31	....	....	....	142	....	....	....	....	....	....	....	....	....	....	....	....	....	....	....	....	....	....
	Prince Albert Raiders	WHL	6	0	0	0	....	....	....	0	....	....	....	....	....	....	....	....	....	....	....	....	....	....	....	....	....	....
1986-87	Prince Albert Raiders	WHL	68	4	21	25	....	....	....	192	....	....	....	....	....	....	....	....	....	....	7	1	6	7	17	....	....	....
1987-88	Prince Albert Raiders	WHL	65	13	34	47	....	....	....	177	....	....	....	....	....	....	....	....	....	....	9	0	6	6	38	....	....	....
1988-89	**New York Islanders**	**NHL**	**62**	**0**	**14**	**14**	**0**	**10**	**10**	**242**	**0**	**0**	**0**	**47**	**0.0**	**53**	**9**	**74**	**21**	**–9**	....	....	....	....	....	....	....	....
1989-90	**New York Islanders**	**NHL**	**14**	**0**	**2**	**2**	**0**	**1**	**1**	**31**	**0**	**0**	**0**	**5**	**0.0**	**8**	**0**	**17**	**11**	**2**	....	....	....	....	....	....	....	....
1990-91	**New York Islanders**	**NHL**	**60**	**1**	**4**	**5**	**1**	**3**	**4**	**126**	**0**	**0**	**0**	**33**	**3.0**	**41**	**1**	**76**	**24**	**–12**	....	....	....	....	....	....	....	....
1991-92	**New York Islanders**	**NHL**	**65**	**1**	**6**	**7**	**1**	**5**	**6**	**183**	**0**	**0**	**0**	**27**	**3.7**	**57**	**2**	**85**	**29**	**–1**	....	....	....	....	....	....	....	....
1992-93	**New York Islanders**	**NHL**	**44**	**1**	**3**	**4**	**1**	**2**	**3**	**164**	**0**	**0**	**0**	**20**	**5.0**	**28**	**0**	**52**	**20**	**–4**	**15**	**0**	**0**	**0**	**50**	**0**	**0**	**0**
	Capital District Islanders	AHL	6	0	1	1	....	....	....	8	....	....	....	....	....	....	....	....	....	....	....	....	....	....	....	....	....	....
1993-94	**New York Islanders**	**NHL**	**28**	**1**	**4**	**5**	**1**	**3**	**4**	**75**	**0**	**0**	**0**	**20**	**5.0**	**17**	**0**	**31**	**10**	**–4**	....	....	....	....	....	....	....	....
	Salt Lake Golden Eagles	IHL	2	0	0	0	....	....	....	8	....	....	....	....	....	....	....	....	....	....	....	....	....	....	....	....	....	....
1994-95	**New York Islanders**	**NHL**	**20**	**1**	**1**	**2**	**2**	**1**	**3**	**40**	**0**	**0**	**0**	**11**	**9.1**	**8**	**1**	**14**	**4**	**–3**	....	....	....	....	....	....	....	....
1995-96	**New York Islanders**	**NHL**	**27**	**0**	**3**	**3**	**0**	**2**	**2**	**72**	**0**	**0**	**0**	**7**	**0.0**	**14**	**0**	**30**	**7**	**–9**	....	....	....	....	....	....	....	....
1996-97	**New York Islanders**	**NHL**	**52**	**1**	**4**	**5**	**1**	**4**	**5**	**179**	**0**	**0**	**0**	**17**	**5.9**	**37**	**0**	**42**	**9**	**4**	....	....	....	....	....	....	....	....
1997-98	**New York Islanders**	**NHL**	**76**	**0**	**7**	**7**	**0**	**7**	**7**	**291**	**0**	**0**	**0**	**37**	**0.0**	**38**	**0**	**57**	**20**	**1**	....	....	....	....	....	....	....	....
1998-99	**New York Islanders**	**NHL**	**52**	**0**	**4**	**4**	**0**	**4**	**4**	**88**	**0**	**0**	**0**	**27**	**0.0**	**22**	**0**	**43**	**13**	**–8**	....	....	....	....	....	....	....	....
99-2000	**New York Islanders**	**NHL**	**9**	**0**	**2**	**2**	**0**	**2**	**2**	**34**	**0**	**0**	**0**	**0**	**0.0**	**5**	**0**	**11**	**4**	**–2**	....	....	....	....	....	....	....	....
	New York Rangers	**NHL**	**45**	**0**	**4**	**4**	**0**	**4**	**4**	**36**	**0**	**0**	**0**	**16**	**0.0**	**27**	**0**	**39**	**12**	**0**	....	....	....	....	....	....	....	....
	NHL Totals		**554**	**6**	**58**	**64**	**7**	**48**	**55**	**1561**	**0**	**0**	**0**	**267**	**2.2**	**355**	**13**	**571**	**184**		**15**	**0**	**0**	**0**	**50**	**0**	**0**	**0**

WHL East Second All-Star Team (1988)

• Missed remainder of 1989-90 season recovering from eye injury suffered in game vs. Detroit, November 4, 1989. • Missed majority of 1993-94 season recovering from shoulder injury originally suffered in game vs. Boston, November 13, 1993. • Missed remainder of 1994-95 and majority of 1995-96 seasons recovering from wrist injury suffered in game vs. Quebec, April 18, 1995. Claimed by **NY Rangers** from **NY Islanders** on waivers, December 1, 1999.

• PILOTE, Pierre

Joseph Albert Pierre Paul "Pete" D – L. 5'10", 178 lbs. b: Kenogami, Que., 12/11/1931. **HHOF**

			REGULAR SEASON																		PLAYOFFS							
Season	**Club**	**League**	**GP**	**G**	**A**	**Pts**	**AG**	**AA**	**APts**	**PIM**	**PP**	**SH**	**GW**	**S**	**%**	**TGF**	**PGF**	**TGA**	**PGA**	**+/–**	**GP**	**G**	**A**	**Pts**	**PIM**	**PP**	**SH**	**GW**
1950-51	St. Catharines Teepees	OHA-Jr.	54	13	13	26	....	....	....	*230	....	....	....	....	....	....	....	....	....	....	9	2	2	4	23	....	....	....
1951-52	St. Catharines Teepees	OHA-Jr.	52	21	32	53	....	....	....	139	....	....	....	....	....	....	....	....	....	....	14	3	12	15	*50	....	....	....
	Buffalo Bisons	AHL	2	0	1	1	....	....	....	4	....	....	....	....	....	....	....	....	....	....	....	....	....	....	....	....	....	....
1952-53	Buffalo Bisons	AHL	61	2	14	16	....	....	....	85	....	....	....	....	....	....	....	....	....	....	....	....	....	....	....	....	....	....
1953-54	Buffalo Bisons	AHL	67	2	28	30	....	....	....	108	....	....	....	....	....	....	....	....	....	....	3	0	0	0	6	....	....	....
1954-55	Buffalo Bisons	AHL	63	10	28	38	....	....	....	120	....	....	....	....	....	....	....	....	....	....	10	0	4	4	18	....	....	....
1955-56	**Chicago Black Hawks**	**NHL**	**20**	**3**	**5**	**8**	**4**	**6**	**10**	**34**	....	....	....	....	....	....	....	....	....	....	....	....	....	....	....	....	....	....
	Buffalo Bisons	AHL	43	0	11	11	....	....	....	118	....	....	....	....	....	....	....	....	....	....	5	0	2	2	4	....	....	....
1956-57	**Chicago Black Hawks**	**NHL**	**70**	**3**	**14**	**17**	**4**	**15**	**19**	**117**	....	....	....	....	....	....	....	....	....	....	....	....	....	....	....	....	....	....
1957-58	**Chicago Black Hawks**	**NHL**	**70**	**6**	**24**	**30**	**7**	**25**	**32**	**91**	....	....	....	....	....	....	....	....	....	....	....	....	....	....	....	....	....	....
1958-59	**Chicago Black Hawks**	**NHL**	**70**	**7**	**30**	**37**	**8**	**30**	**38**	**79**	....	....	....	....	....	....	....	....	....	....	**6**	**0**	**2**	**2**	**10**	**0**	**0**	**0**
1959-60	**Chicago Black Hawks**	**NHL**	**70**	**7**	**38**	**45**	**8**	**37**	**45**	**100**	....	....	....	....	....	....	....	....	....	....	**4**	**0**	**1**	**1**	**8**	**0**	**0**	**0**
1960-61 ♦	**Chicago Black Hawks**	**NHL**	**70**	**6**	**29**	**35**	**7**	**28**	**35**	***165**	....	....	....	....	....	....	....	....	....	....	**12**	**3**	***12**	***15**	**8**	**1**	**0**	**0**
1961-62	**Chicago Black Hawks**	**NHL**	**59**	**7**	**35**	**42**	**8**	**34**	**42**	**97**	....	....	....	....	....	....	....	....	....	....	**12**	**0**	**7**	**7**	**8**	**0**	**0**	**0**
1962-63	**Chicago Black Hawks**	**NHL**	**59**	**8**	**18**	**26**	**9**	**18**	**27**	**57**	....	....	....	....	....	....	....	....	....	....	**6**	**0**	**8**	**8**	**8**	**0**	**0**	**0**
1963-64	**Chicago Black Hawks**	**NHL**	**70**	**7**	**46**	**53**	**9**	**49**	**58**	**84**	....	....	....	....	....	....	....	....	....	....	**7**	**2**	**6**	**8**	**6**	**0**	**0**	**1**
1964-65	**Chicago Black Hawks**	**NHL**	**68**	**14**	**45**	**59**	**17**	**47**	**64**	**162**	....	....	....	....	....	....	....	....	....	....	**12**	**0**	**7**	**7**	**22**	**0**	**0**	**0**
1965-66	**Chicago Black Hawks**	**NHL**	**51**	**2**	**34**	**36**	**2**	**33**	**35**	**60**	....	....	....	....	....	....	....	....	....	....	**6**	**0**	**2**	**2**	**10**	**0**	**0**	**0**
1966-67	**Chicago Black Hawks**	**NHL**	**70**	**6**	**46**	**52**	**7**	**45**	**52**	**90**	....	....	....	....	....	....	....	....	....	....	**6**	**2**	**4**	**6**	**6**	**0**	**0**	**0**
1967-68	**Chicago Black Hawks**	**NHL**	**74**	**1**	**36**	**37**	**1**	**36**	**37**	**69**	**0**	**0**	**0**	**69**	**1.4**	**98**	**22**	**97**	**13**	**–8**	**11**	**1**	**3**	**4**	**12**	**1**	**0**	**0**
1968-69	**Toronto Maple Leafs**	**NHL**	**69**	**3**	**18**	**21**	**3**	**16**	**19**	**46**	**1**	**0**	**0**	**48**	**6.3**	**67**	**13**	**64**	**15**	**5**	**4**	**0**	**1**	**1**	**4**	**0**	**0**	**0**
	NHL Totals		**890**	**80**	**418**	**498**	**94**	**419**	**513**	**1251**	....	....	....	....	....	....	....	....	....	....	**86**	**8**	**53**	**61**	**102**	....	....	....

NHL Second All-Star Team (1960, 1961, 1962) • NHL First All-Star Team (1963, 1964, 1965, 1966, 1967) • Won James Norris Trophy (1963, 1964, 1965) • Played in NHL All-Star Game (1960, 1961, 1962, 1963, 1964, 1965, 1967, 1968)

Traded to **Toronto** by **Chicago** for Jim Pappin, May 23, 1968.

• PINDER, Gerry

Allan Gerald LW – R. 5'8", 165 lbs. b: Saskatoon, Sask., 9/15/1948.

Season	**Club**	**League**	**GP**	**G**	**A**	**Pts**	**AG**	**AA**	**APts**	**PIM**	**PP**	**SH**	**GW**	**S**	**%**	**TGF**	**PGF**	**TGA**	**PGA**	**+/–**	**GP**	**G**	**A**	**Pts**	**PIM**	**PP**	**SH**	**GW**
1964-65	Nutana Nats	SAHA	STATISTICS NOT AVAILABLE																									
	Saskatoon Blade Bees	SJHL-B	1	0	0	0	....	....	....	0	....	....	....	....	....	....	....	....	....	....	....	....	....	....	....	....	....	....
1965-66	Saskatoon Blades	SJHL	58	34	47	81	....	....	....	66	....	....	....	....	....	....	....	....	....	....	5	1	2	3	9	....	....	....
1966-67	Saskatoon Blades	CMJHL	55	*78	62	*140	....	....	....	95	....	....	....	....	....	....	....	....	....	....	4	4	1	5	4	....	....	....
1967-68	Winnipeg Nationals	WCSHL	25	11	14	25	....	....	....	12	....	....	....	....	....	....	....	....	....	....	....	....	....	....	....	....	....	....
	Canada	Olympics	7	1	0	1	....	....	....	2	....	....	....	....	....	....	....	....	....	....	....	....	....	....	....	....	....	....
1968-69	Canada	Nat-Team	STATISTICS NOT AVAILABLE																									
	Canada	WEC-A	10	3	1	4	....	....	....	14	....	....	....	....	....	....	....	....	....	....	....	....	....	....	....	....	....	....
1969-70	**Chicago Black Hawks**	**NHL**	**75**	**19**	**20**	**39**	**21**	**19**	**40**	**41**	**4**	**1**	**3**	**169**	**11.2**	**71**	**16**	**36**	**4**	**23**	**8**	**0**	**4**	**4**	**4**	**0**	**0**	**0**
1970-71	**Chicago Black Hawks**	**NHL**	**74**	**13**	**18**	**31**	**13**	**15**	**28**	**35**	**1**	**0**	**2**	**102**	**12.7**	**59**	**19**	**42**	**0**	**–2**	**9**	**0**	**0**	**0**	**2**	**0**	**0**	**0**
1971-72	**California Golden Seals**	**NHL**	**74**	**23**	**31**	**54**	**23**	**27**	**50**	**59**	**7**	**1**	**1**	**140**	**16.4**	**77**	**25**	**78**	**8**	**–18**	....	....	....	....	....	....	....	....
1972-73	Cleveland Crusaders	WHA	78	30	36	66	....	....	....	21	....	....	....	....	....	....	....	....	....	....	9	2	9	11	30	....	....	....
1973-74	Cleveland Crusaders	WHA	73	23	33	56	....	....	....	90	....	....	....	....	....	....	....	....	....	....	1	0	0	0	0	....	....	....
1974-75	Cleveland Crusaders	WHA	74	13	28	41	....	....	....	71	....	....	....	....	....	....	....	....	....	....	5	3	1	4	6	....	....	....
1975-76	Cleveland Crusaders	WHA	79	21	30	51	....	....	....	118	....	....	....	....	....	....	....	....	....	....	3	0	0	0	4	....	....	....
1976-77	San Diego Mariners	WHA	44	6	13	19	....	....	....	36	....	....	....	....	....	....	....	....	....	....	....	....	....	....	....	....	....	....
	Maine Nordiques	NAHL	11	6	3	9	....	....	....	4	....	....	....	....	....	....	....	....	....	....	10	8	2	10	12	....	....	....
1977-78	Edmonton Oilers	WHA	5	0	1	1	....	....	....	0	....	....	....	....	....	....	....	....	....	....	....	....	....	....	....	....	....	....
	NHL Totals		**223**	**55**	**69**	**124**	**57**	**61**	**118**	**135**	**12**	**2**	**6**	**411**	**13.4**	**207**	**60**	**156**	**12**		**17**	**0**	**4**	**4**	**6**	**0**	**0**	**0**
	Other Major League Totals		353	93	141	234	....	....	....	336	....	....	....	....	....	....	....	....	....	....	18	5	10	15	40	....	....	....

CMJHL First All-Star Team (1967)

Traded to **California** by **Chicago** with Gerry Desjardins and Kerry Bond for Gary Smith, September 9, 1971. Selected by **Calgary-Cleveland** (WHA) in 1972 WHA General Player Draft, February 12, 1972. Traded to **San Diego** (WHA) by **Cleveland-Minnesota** (WHA) with Paul Shymr for Ray Adduono and Bob Wall, September, 1976. Signed as a free agent by **Edmonton** (WHA) after **San Diego** (WHA) franchise folded, June, 1977.

• PIRUS, Alex

Joseph Alexander RW – R. 6'1", 205 lbs. b: Toronto, Ont., 1/12/1955. Minnesota's 3rd, 41st overall, in 1975.

Season	**Club**	**League**	**GP**	**G**	**A**	**Pts**	**AG**	**AA**	**APts**	**PIM**	**PP**	**SH**	**GW**	**S**	**%**	**TGF**	**PGF**	**TGA**	**PGA**	**+/–**	**GP**	**G**	**A**	**Pts**	**PIM**	**PP**	**SH**	**GW**
1972-73	Richmond Hill Rams	OHA-B	44	40	44	84	....	....	....	97	....	....	....	....	....	....	....	....	....	....	....	....	....	....	....	....	....	....
1973-74	University of Notre Dame	WCHA	28	8	16	24	....	....	....	22	....	....	....	....	....	....	....	....	....	....	....	....	....	....	....	....	....	....
1974-75	University of Notre Dame	WCHA	37	23	32	55	....	....	....	94	....	....	....	....	....	....	....	....	....	....	....	....	....	....	....	....	....	....
1975-76	University of Notre Dame	WCHA	38	26	18	44	....	....	....	65	....	....	....	....	....	....	....	....	....	....	....	....	....	....	....	....	....	....
1976-77	**Minnesota North Stars**	**NHL**	**79**	**20**	**17**	**37**	**18**	**13**	**31**	**47**	**1**	**0**	**1**	**128**	**15.6**	**45**	**4**	**61**	**0**	**–20**	**2**	**0**	**1**	**1**	**2**	**0**	**0**	**0**
1977-78	**Minnesota North Stars**	**NHL**	**61**	**9**	**6**	**15**	**8**	**5**	**13**	**38**	**1**	**0**	**1**	**89**	**10.1**	**28**	**3**	**50**	**0**	**–25**	....	....	....	....	....	....	....	....
	Fort Worth Texans	CHL	18	9	6	15	....	....	....	4	....	....	....	....	....	....	....	....	....	....	14	6	2	8	11	....	....	....
1978-79	**Minnesota North Stars**	**NHL**	**15**	**1**	**3**	**4**	**1**	**2**	**3**	**9**	**0**	**0**	**0**	**14**	**7.1**	**8**	**1**	**15**	**0**	**–8**	....	....	....	....	....	....	....	....
	Oklahoma City Stars	CHL	51	16	16	32	....	....	....	33	....	....	....	....	....	....	....	....	....	....	....	....	....	....	....	....	....	....
1979-80	**Detroit Red Wings**	**NHL**	**4**	**0**	**2**	**2**	**0**	**1**	**1**	**0**	**0**	**0**	**0**	**0**	**0.0**	**2**	**0**	**2**	**0**	**0**	....	....	....	....	....	....	....	....
	Oklahoma City Stars	CHL	62	23	23	46	....	....	....	49	....	....	....	....	....	....	....	....	....	....	....	....	....	....	....	....	....	....
1980-81	Indianapolis Checkers	CHL	79	25	46	71	....	....	....	78	....	....	....	....	....	....	....	....	....	....	5	3	2	5	4	....	....	....
	NHL Totals		**159**	**30**	**28**	**58**	**27**	**21**	**48**	**94**	**2**	**0**	**2**	**231**	**13.0**	**83**	**8**	**128**	**0**		**2**	**0**	**1**	**1**	**2**	**0**	**0**	**0**

Traded to **Detroit** by **Minnesota** for cash, January 3, 1980. Traded to **Minnesota** by **Detroit** for cash, June 6, 1980. Traded to **NY Islanders** by **Minnesota** for future considerations, July 4, 1980.

• PITLICK, Lance

D – R. 6', 205 lbs. b: Minneapolis, MN, 11/5/1967. Minnesota's 10th, 180th overall, in 1986.

Season	**Club**	**League**	**GP**	**G**	**A**	**Pts**	**AG**	**AA**	**APts**	**PIM**	**PP**	**SH**	**GW**	**S**	**%**	**TGF**	**PGF**	**TGA**	**PGA**	**+/–**	**GP**	**G**	**A**	**Pts**	**PIM**	**PP**	**SH**	**GW**
1984-85	Robbinsdale-Cooper Hawks	Hi-School	23	8	4	12	....	....	....	....	....	....	....	....	....	....	....	....	....	....	....	....	....	....	....	....	....	....
1985-86	Robbinsdale-Cooper Hawks	Hi-School	21	17	8	25	....	....	....	247	....	....	....	....	....	....	....	....	....	....	....	....	....	....	....	....	....	....
1986-87	University of Minnesota	WCHA	45	0	9	9	....	....	....	88	....	....	....	....	....	....	....	....	....	....	....	....	....	....	....	....	....	....
1987-88	University of Minnesota	WCHA	38	3	9	12	....	....	....	76	....	....	....	....	....	....	....	....	....	....	....	....	....	....	....	....	....	....
1988-89	University of Minnesota	WCHA	47	4	9	13	....	....	....	95	....	....	....	....	....	....	....	....	....	....	....	....	....	....	....	....	....	....
1989-90	University of Minnesota	WCHA	14	3	2	5	....	....	....	26	....	....	....	....	....	....	....	....	....	....	....	....	....	....	....	....	....	....
1990-91	Hershey Bears	AHL	64	6	15	21	....	....	....	75	....	....	....	....	....	....	....	....	....	....	3	0	0	0	9	....	....	....
1991-92	United States	Nat-Team	19	0	1	1	....	....	....	38	....	....	....	....	....	....	....	....	....	....	....	....	....	....	....	....	....	....
	Hershey Bears	AHL	4	0	0	0	....	....	....	6	....	....	....	....	....	....	....	....	....	....	3	0	0	0	4	....	....	....
1992-93	Hershey Bears	AHL	53	5	10	15	....	....	....	77	....	....	....	....	....	....	....	....	....	....	....	....	....	....	....	....	....	....
1993-94	Hershey Bears	AHL	58	4	13	17	....	....	....	93	....	....	....	....	....	....	....	....	....	....	11	1	0	1	11	....	....	....
1994-95	P.E.I. Senators	AHL	61	8	19	27	....	....	....	55	....	....	....	....	....	....	....	....	....	....	11	1	4	5	10	....	....	....
	Ottawa Senators	**NHL**	**15**	**0**	**1**	**1**	**0**	**1**	**1**	**6**	**0**	**0**	**0**	**11**	**0.0**	**5**	**1**	**12**	**3**	**–5**	....	....	....	....	....	....	....	....
1995-96	**Ottawa Senators**	**NHL**	**28**	**1**	**6**	**7**	**1**	**5**	**6**	**20**	**0**	**0**	**0**	**13**	**7.7**	**14**	**0**	**26**	**4**	**–8**	....	....	....	....	....	....	....	....
	P.E.I. Senators	AHL	29	4	10	14	....	....	....	39	....	....	....	....	....	....	....	....	....	....	5	0	0	0	0	....	....	....
1996-97	**Ottawa Senators**	**NHL**	**66**	**5**	**5**	**10**	**5**	**4**	**9**	**91**	**0**	**0**	**1**	**54**	**9.3**	**38**	**0**	**54**	**18**	**2**	**7**	**0**	**0**	**0**	**4**	**0**	**0**	**0**
1997-98	**Ottawa Senators**	**NHL**	**69**	**2**	**7**	**9**	**2**	**7**	**9**	**50**	**0**	**0**	**0**	**66**	**3.0**	**43**	**0**	**45**	**10**	**8**	**11**	**0**	**1**	**1**	**17**	**0**	**0**	**0**
1998-99	**Ottawa Senators**	**NHL**	**50**	**3**	**6**	**9**	**4**	**6**	**10**	**33**	**0**	**0**	**0**	**34**	**8.8**	**32**	**0**	**33**	**8**	**7**	**2**	**0**	**0**	**0**	**0**	**0**	**0**	**0**
99-2000	**Florida Panthers**	**NHL**	**62**	**3**	**5**	**8**	**3**	**5**	**8**	**44**	**0**	**0**	**1**	**26**	**11.5**	**49**	**0**	**52**	**10**	**7**	**4**	**0**	**1**	**1**	**0**	**0**	**0**	**0**
	NHL Totals		**290**	**14**	**30**	**44**	**15**	**28**	**43**	**244**	**0**	**0**	**2**	**204**	**6.9**	**181**	**1**	**222**	**53**		**24**	**0**	**2**	**2**	**21**	**0**	**0**	**0**

Signed as a free agent by **Philadelphia**, September 5, 1990. Signed as a free agent by **Ottawa**, June 22, 1994. Signed as a free agent by **Florida**, July 21, 1999.

• PITTIS, Domenic

C – L. 5'11", 190 lbs. b: Calgary, Alta., 10/1/1974. Pittsburgh's 2nd, 52nd overall, in 1993.

Season	**Club**	**League**	**GP**	**G**	**A**	**Pts**	**AG**	**AA**	**APts**	**PIM**	**PP**	**SH**	**GW**	**S**	**%**	**TGF**	**PGF**	**TGA**	**PGA**	**+/–**	**GP**	**G**	**A**	**Pts**	**PIM**	**PP**	**SH**	**GW**
1990-91	Calgary Buffaloes	AAHA	35	23	54	77	....	....	....	43	....	....	....	....	....	....	....	....	....	....	....	....	....	....	....	....	....	....
1991-92	Lethbridge Hurricanes	WHL	65	6	17	23	....	....	....	18	....	....	....	....	....	....	....	....	....	....	5	0	2	2	4	....	....	....
1992-93	Lethbridge Hurricanes	WHL	66	46	73	119	....	....	....	69	....	....	....	....	....	....	....	....	....	....	4	3	3	6	8	....	....	....

			REGULAR SEASON																		PLAYOFFS							
Season	Club	League	GP	G	A	Pts	AG	AA	APts	PIM	PP	SH	GW	S	%	TGF	PGF	TGA	PGA	+/–	GP	G	A	Pts	PIM	PP	SH	GW
1993-94	Lethbridge Hurricanes	WHL	72	58	69	127	....	....	....	93	....	....	....	....	....	....	....	....	....	....	8	4	11	15	16	....	....	....
1994-95	Cleveland Lumberjacks	IHL	62	18	32	50	....	....	....	66	....	....	....	....	....	....	....	....	....	....	3	0	2	2	2	....	....	....
1995-96	Cleveland Lumberjacks	IHL	74	10	28	38	....	....	....	100	....	....	....	....	....	....	....	....	....	....	3	0	0	0	2	....	....	....
1996-97	**Pittsburgh Penguins**	**NHL**	**1**	**0**	**0**	**0**	**0**	**0**	**0**	**0**	**0**	**0**	**0**	**0**	**0.0**	**0**	**0**	**1**	**0**	**–1**	....	....	....	....	....	....	....	....
	Long Beach Ice Dogs	IHL	65	23	43	66	....	....	....	91	....	....	....	....	....	....	....	....	....	....	18	5	9	14	26	....	....	....
1997-98	Syracuse Crunch	AHL	75	23	41	64	....	....	....	90	....	....	....	....	....	....	....	....	....	....	5	1	3	4	4	....	....	....
1998-99	**Buffalo Sabres**	**NHL**	**3**	**0**	**0**	**0**	**0**	**0**	**0**	**2**	**0**	**0**	**0**	**1**	**0.0**	**2**	**2**	**0**	**0**	**0**	....	....	....	....	....	....	....	....
	Rochester Americans	AHL	76	38	66	*104	....	....	....	108	....	....	....	....	....	....	....	....	....	....	20	7	*14	*21	40	....	....	....
99-2000	**Buffalo Sabres**	**NHL**	**7**	**1**	**0**	**1**	**1**	**0**	**1**	**6**	**0**	**0**	**0**	**6**	**16.7**	**3**	**0**	**2**	**0**	**1**	....	....	....	....	....	....	....	....
	Rochester Americans	AHL	53	17	48	65	....	....	....	85	....	....	....	....	....	....	....	....	....	....	21	4	*26	*30	28	....	....	....
	NHL Totals		**11**	**1**	**0**	**1**	**1**	**0**	**1**	**8**	**0**	**0**	**0**	**7**	**14.3**	**5**	**2**	**3**	**0**		....	....	....	....	....	....	....	....

WHL East Second All-Star Team (1994) • Won John P. Sollenberger Trophy (Top Scorer - AHL) (1999)

Signed as a free agent by **Buffalo**, August 10, 1998.

• PIVONKA, Michal

C – L. 6'2", 200 lbs. b: Kladno, Czech., 1/28/1966. Washington's 3rd, 59th overall, in 1984.

Season	Club	League	GP	G	A	Pts	AG	AA	APts	PIM	PP	SH	GW	S	%	TGF	PGF	TGA	PGA	+/–	GP	G	A	Pts	PIM	PP	SH	GW
1982-83	Dukla Jihlava	Czech-Jr.	STATISTICS NOT AVAILABLE																									
	Czechoslovakia	EJC-A	5	4	5	9	....	....	....	14	....	....	....	....	....	....	....	....	....	....	....	....	....	....	....	....	....	....
1983-84	Dukla Jihlava	Czech-Jr.	STATISTICS NOT AVAILABLE																									
	Czechoslovakia	WJC-A	7	1	2	3	....	....	....	0	....	....	....	....	....	....	....	....	....	....	....	....	....	....	....	....	....	....
	Czechoslovakia	EJC-A	5	3	4	7	....	....	....	2	....	....	....	....	....	....	....	....	....	....	....	....	....	....	....	....	....	....
1984-85	Dukla Jihlava	Czech.	33	8	11	19	....	....	....	18	....	....	....	....	....	....	....	....	....	....	....	....	....	....	....	....	....	....
	Czechoslovakia	WJC-A	7	9	4	13	....	....	....	14	....	....	....	....	....	....	....	....	....	....	....	....	....	....	....	....	....	....
	Czechoslovakia	WEC-A	10	0	1	1	....	....	....	0	....	....	....	....	....	....	....	....	....	....	....	....	....	....	....	....	....	....
1985-86	Dukla Jihlava	Czech.	42	5	13	18	....	....	....	18	....	....	....	....	....	....	....	....	....	....	....	....	....	....	....	....	....	....
	Czechoslovakia	WJC-A	7	5	5	10	....	....	....	10	....	....	....	....	....	....	....	....	....	....	....	....	....	....	....	....	....	....
	Czechoslovakia	WEC-A	10	2	1	3	....	....	....	8	....	....	....	....	....	....	....	....	....	....	....	....	....	....	....	....	....	....
1986-87	**Washington Capitals**	**NHL**	**73**	**18**	**25**	**43**	**16**	**18**	**34**	**41**	**4**	**0**	**2**	**117**	**15.4**	**65**	**23**	**62**	**1**	**–19**	**7**	**1**	**1**	**2**	**2**	**0**	**0**	**0**
1987-88	**Washington Capitals**	**NHL**	**71**	**11**	**23**	**34**	**9**	**16**	**25**	**28**	**3**	**0**	**0**	**96**	**11.5**	**57**	**24**	**32**	**0**	**1**	**14**	**4**	**9**	**13**	**4**	**2**	**0**	**0**
1988-89	**Washington Capitals**	**NHL**	**52**	**8**	**19**	**27**	**7**	**13**	**20**	**30**	**1**	**0**	**1**	**73**	**11.0**	**42**	**9**	**24**	**0**	**9**	**6**	**3**	**1**	**4**	**10**	**0**	**1**	**0**
	Baltimore Skipjacks	AHL	31	12	24	36	....	....	....	19	....	....	....	....	....	....	....	....	....	....	....	....	....	....	....	....	....	....
1989-90	Washington Capitals	Fr-Tour	4	0	0	0	....	....	....	2	....	....	....	....	....	....	....	....	....	....	....	....	....	....	....	....	....	....
	Washington Capitals	**NHL**	**77**	**25**	**39**	**64**	**21**	**28**	**49**	**54**	**10**	**3**	**0**	**149**	**16.8**	**80**	**27**	**79**	**19**	**–7**	**11**	**0**	**2**	**2**	**6**	**0**	**0**	**0**
1990-91	**Washington Capitals**	**NHL**	**79**	**20**	**50**	**70**	**18**	**38**	**56**	**34**	**6**	**0**	**4**	**172**	**11.6**	**94**	**31**	**65**	**5**	**3**	**11**	**2**	**3**	**5**	**8**	**0**	**0**	**0**
1991-92	Czechoslovakia	Can-Cup	5	0	3	3	....	....	....	2	....	....	....	....	....	....	....	....	....	....	....	....	....	....	....	....	....	....
	Washington Capitals	**NHL**	**80**	**23**	**57**	**80**	**21**	**43**	**64**	**47**	**7**	**4**	**2**	**177**	**13.0**	**111**	**38**	**78**	**15**	**10**	**7**	**1**	**5**	**6**	**13**	**1**	**0**	**1**
1992-93	**Washington Capitals**	**NHL**	**69**	**21**	**53**	**74**	**17**	**37**	**54**	**66**	**6**	**1**	**5**	**147**	**14.3**	**105**	**37**	**71**	**17**	**14**	**6**	**0**	**2**	**2**	**0**	**0**	**0**	**0**
1993-94	**Washington Capitals**	**NHL**	**82**	**14**	**36**	**50**	**13**	**28**	**41**	**38**	**5**	**0**	**4**	**138**	**10.1**	**72**	**26**	**59**	**15**	**2**	**7**	**4**	**4**	**8**	**4**	**1**	**0**	**0**
1994-95	KAC Klagenfurt	Austria	7	2	4	6	....	....	....	4	....	....	....	....	....	....	....	....	....	....	....	....	....	....	....	....	....	....
	Washington Capitals	**NHL**	**46**	**10**	**23**	**33**	**18**	**34**	**52**	**50**	**4**	**2**	**2**	**80**	**12.5**	**53**	**26**	**36**	**12**	**3**	**7**	**1**	**4**	**5**	**21**	**0**	**0**	**0**
1995-96	Detroit Vipers	IHL	7	1	9	10	....	....	....	19	....	....	....	....	....	....	....	....	....	....	....	....	....	....	....	....	....	....
	Washington Capitals	**NHL**	**73**	**16**	**65**	**81**	**16**	**53**	**69**	**36**	**6**	**2**	**5**	**168**	**9.5**	**100**	**33**	**66**	**17**	**18**	**6**	**3**	**2**	**5**	**18**	**1**	**0**	**0**
1996-97	**Washington Capitals**	**NHL**	**54**	**7**	**16**	**23**	**7**	**14**	**21**	**22**	**2**	**0**	**1**	**83**	**8.4**	**47**	**11**	**58**	**7**	**–15**	....	....	....	....	....	....	....	....
1997-98	**Washington Capitals**	**NHL**	**33**	**3**	**6**	**9**	**4**	**6**	**10**	**20**	**0**	**0**	**1**	**38**	**7.9**	**16**	**5**	**10**	**4**	**5**	**13**	**0**	**3**	**3**	**0**	**0**	**0**	**0**
1998-99	**Washington Capitals**	**NHL**	**36**	**5**	**6**	**11**	**6**	**6**	**12**	**12**	**2**	**0**	**0**	**30**	**16.7**	**16**	**4**	**21**	**3**	**–6**	....	....	....	....	....	....	....	....
99-2000	Kansas City Blades	IHL	52	16	34	50	....	....	....	38	....	....	....	....	....	....	....	....	....	....	....	....	....	....	....	....	....	....
	NHL Totals		**825**	**181**	**418**	**599**	**173**	**334**	**507**	**478**	**56**	**12**	**27**	**1468**	**12.3**	**858**	**294**	**661**	**115**		**95**	**19**	**36**	**55**	**86**	**5**	**1**	**1**

EJC-A All-Star Team (1983) • WJC-A All-Star Team (1985, 1986) • Named Best Forward at WJC-A (1985)

• Missed majority of 1997-98 season recovering from wrist injury suffered in game vs. Pittsburgh, November 12, 1997. • Missed majority of 1998-99 season recovering from groin injury suffered in game vs. Buffalo, February 7, 1998. Signed as a free agent by **Kansas City** (IHL), September 27, 1999.

• PLAGER, Barclay

Barclay Graham D – L. 5'11", 175 lbs. b: Kirkland Lake, Ont., 3/26/1941 d: 2/6/1988.

Season	Club	League	GP	G	A	Pts	AG	AA	APts	PIM	PP	SH	GW	S	%	TGF	PGF	TGA	PGA	+/–	GP	G	A	Pts	PIM	PP	SH	GW
1957-58	Quebec Baronets	QJHL	STATISTICS NOT AVAILABLE																									
	Peterborough Petes	OHA-Jr.	4	0	0	0	....	....	....	2	....	....	....	....	....	....	....	....	....	....	....	....	....	....	....	....	....	....
1958-59	Peterborough Petes	OHA-Jr.	54	4	16	20	....	....	....	252	....	....	....	....	....	....	....	....	....	....	19	6	6	12	*74	....	....	....
	Peterborough Petes	Mem-Cup	12	0	2	2	....	....	....	58	....	....	....	....	....	....	....	....	....	....	....	....	....	....	....	....	....	....
1959-60	Peterborough Petes	OHA-Jr.	48	8	27	35	....	....	....	165	....	....	....	....	....	....	....	....	....	....	12	1	7	8	37	....	....	....
1960-61	Peterborough Petes	OHA-Jr.	48	11	33	44	....	....	....	*155	....	....	....	....	....	....	....	....	....	....	3	0	0	0	23	....	....	....
	Hull-Ottawa Canadiens	EPHL	3	0	0	0	....	....	....	2	....	....	....	....	....	....	....	....	....	....	....	....	....	....	....	....	....	....
1961-62	Quebec Aces	AHL	1	0	1	1	....	....	....	2	....	....	....	....	....	....	....	....	....	....	....	....	....	....	....	....	....	....
	Hull-Ottawa Canadiens	EPHL	60	8	16	24	....	....	....	102	....	....	....	....	....	....	....	....	....	....	10	1	1	2	22	....	....	....
1962-63	Pittsburgh Hornets	AHL	13	0	1	1	....	....	....	15	....	....	....	....	....	....	....	....	....	....	....	....	....	....	....	....	....	....
	Edmonton Flyers	WHL	52	2	18	20	....	....	....	67	....	....	....	....	....	....	....	....	....	....	....	....	....	....	....	....	....	....
1963-64	Omaha Knights	CPHL	70	14	*61	75	....	....	....	*208	....	....	....	....	....	....	....	....	....	....	10	2	*11	13	29	....	....	....
1964-65	Springfield Indians	AHL	39	2	16	18	....	....	....	65	....	....	....	....	....	....	....	....	....	....	....	....	....	....	....	....	....	....
1965-66	Springfield Indians	AHL	58	11	20	31	....	....	....	54	....	....	....	....	....	....	....	....	....	....	6	1	0	1	0	....	....	....
1966-67	Springfield Indians	AHL	36	6	12	18	....	....	....	60	....	....	....	....	....	....	....	....	....	....	....	....	....	....	....	....	....	....
	Omaha Knights	CPHL	11	1	10	11	....	....	....	39	....	....	....	....	....	....	....	....	....	....	12	3	8	11	*42	....	....	....
1967-68	Buffalo Bisons	AHL	20	2	13	15	....	....	....	37	....	....	....	....	....	....	....	....	....	....	....	....	....	....	....	....	....	....
	St. Louis Blues	**NHL**	**49**	**5**	**15**	**20**	**6**	**15**	**21**	***153**	**2**	**0**	**1**	**61**	**8.2**	**50**	**10**	**38**	**2**	**4**	**18**	**2**	**5**	**7**	***73**	**0**	**1**	**0**
1968-69	**St. Louis Blues**	**NHL**	**61**	**4**	**26**	**30**	**4**	**23**	**27**	**120**	**0**	**0**	**1**	**88**	**4.5**	**73**	**14**	**36**	**8**	**31**	**12**	**0**	**4**	**4**	**31**	**0**	**0**	**0**
1969-70	**St. Louis Blues**	**NHL**	**75**	**6**	**26**	**32**	**6**	**24**	**30**	**128**	**1**	**1**	**1**	**97**	**6.2**	**71**	**13**	**79**	**23**	**2**	**13**	**0**	**2**	**2**	**20**	**0**	**0**	**0**
1970-71	**St. Louis Blues**	**NHL**	**69**	**4**	**20**	**24**	**4**	**17**	**21**	**172**	**1**	**0**	**0**	**87**	**4.6**	**82**	**15**	**75**	**19**	**11**	**6**	**0**	**3**	**3**	**10**	**0**	**0**	**0**
1971-72	**St. Louis Blues**	**NHL**	**78**	**7**	**22**	**29**	**7**	**19**	**26**	**176**	**1**	**2**	**0**	**128**	**5.5**	**105**	**21**	**118**	**40**	**6**	**11**	**1**	**4**	**5**	**21**	**1**	**0**	**1**
1972-73	**St. Louis Blues**	**NHL**	**68**	**8**	**25**	**33**	**7**	**20**	**27**	**102**	**3**	**0**	**2**	**131**	**6.1**	**83**	**14**	**98**	**29**	**0**	**5**	**0**	**1**	**1**	**0**	**0**	**0**	**0**
1973-74	**St. Louis Blues**	**NHL**	**72**	**6**	**20**	**26**	**6**	**16**	**22**	**99**	**1**	**0**	**0**	**104**	**5.8**	**71**	**12**	**107**	**37**	**–11**	....	....	....	....	....	....	....	....
1974-75	**St. Louis Blues**	**NHL**	**76**	**4**	**24**	**28**	**3**	**18**	**21**	**96**	**0**	**0**	**1**	**88**	**4.5**	**87**	**11**	**106**	**50**	**20**	**2**	**0**	**1**	**1**	**14**	**0**	**0**	**0**
1975-76	**St. Louis Blues**	**NHL**	**64**	**0**	**8**	**8**	**0**	**6**	**6**	**67**	**0**	**0**	**0**	**32**	**0.0**	**42**	**3**	**78**	**33**	**–6**	**1**	**0**	**0**	**0**	**13**	**0**	**0**	**0**
1976-77	**St. Louis Blues**	**NHL**	**2**	**0**	**1**	**1**	**0**	**1**	**1**	**2**	**0**	**0**	**0**	**2**	**0.0**	**3**	**0**	**2**	**0**	**1**	....	....	....	....	....	....	....	....
	Kansas City Blues	CHL	75	6	42	48	....	....	....	157	....	....	....	....	....	....	....	....	....	....	9	2	4	6	12	....	....	....
1977-78	Salt Lake Golden Eagles	CHL	46	2	19	21	....	....	....	80	....	....	....	....	....	....	....	....	....	....	....	....	....	....	....	....	....	....
	NHL Totals		**614**	**44**	**187**	**231**	**43**	**159**	**202**	**1115**	**9**	**3**	**6**	**818**	**5.4**	**667**	**113**	**737**	**241**		**68**	**3**	**20**	**23**	**182**	**1**	**1**	**1**

• Brother of Bill and Bob • OHA-Jr. First All-Team (1961) • CPHL First All-Star Team (1964) • Named Top Defenseman - CPHL(1964) • CHL Second All-Star Team (1977) • Won Tommy Ivan Trophy (MVP - CHL) (1977)

Played in NHL All-Star Game (1970, 1971, 1973, 1974)

Claimed by **Detroit** from **Montreal** in Intra-League Draft, June 4, 1962. Traded to **Springfield** (AHL) by **Detroit** for cash, August, 1964. NHL rights transferred to **LA Kings** after NHL club purchased **Springfield** (AHL) franchise, May, 1967. Traded to **NY Rangers** by **LA Kings** for Trevor Fahey, Ken Turlick and Jim Murray, June 16, 1967. Traded to **St. Louis** by **NY Rangers** with Red Berenson for Ron Stewart and Ron Attwell, November 29, 1967.

• PLAGER, Bill

William Ronald D – R. 5'9", 175 lbs. b: Kirkland Lake, Ont., 7/6/1945.

Season	Club	League	GP	G	A	Pts	AG	AA	APts	PIM	PP	SH	GW	S	%	TGF	PGF	TGA	PGA	+/–	GP	G	A	Pts	PIM	PP	SH	GW
1962-63	Peterborough Petes	OHA-Jr.	49	1	5	6	....	....	....	94	....	....	....	....	....	....	....	....	....	....	6	0	0	0	0	....	....	....
1963-64	Lachine Maroons	MMJHL	40	6	34	40	....	....	....	*187	....	....	....	....	....	....	....	....	....	....	....	....	....	....	....	....	....	....
	Notre Dame Monarchs	Mem-Cup	4	0	1	1	....	....	....	20	....	....	....	....	....	....	....	....	....	....	....	....	....	....	....	....	....	....
1964-65	Peterborough Petes	OHA-Jr.	27	4	3	7	....	....	....	77	....	....	....	....	....	....	....	....	....	....	12	0	3	3	31	....	....	....
1965-66	Peterborough Petes	OHA-Jr.	47	1	21	22	....	....	....	190	....	....	....	....	....	....	....	....	....	....	6	0	1	1	14	....	....	....
1966-67	Houston Apollos	CPHL	51	4	13	17	....	....	....	130	....	....	....	....	....	....	....	....	....	....	6	0	1	1	14	....	....	....
1967-68	**Minnesota North Stars**	**NHL**	**32**	**0**	**2**	**2**	**0**	**2**	**2**	**30**	**0**	**0**	**0**	**12**	**0.0**	**9**	**1**	**25**	**1**	**–16**	**12**	**0**	**2**	**2**	**8**	**0**	**0**	**0**
	Memphis South Stars	CPHL	30	0	7	7	....	....	....	51	....	....	....	....	....	....	....	....	....	....	....	....	....	....	....	....	....	....
1968-69	**St. Louis Blues**	**NHL**	**2**	**0**	**0**	**0**	**0**	**0**	**0**	**2**	**0**	**0**	**0**	**3**	**0.0**	**0**	**0**	**0**	**0**	**0**	**4**	**0**	**0**	**0**	**4**	**0**	**0**	**0**
	Kansas City Blues	CHL	35	1	4	5	....	....	....	66	....	....	....	....	....	....	....	....	....	....	4	0	1	1	6	....	....	....

			REGULAR SEASON																		PLAYOFFS							
Season	Club	League	GP	G	A	Pts	AG	AA	APts	PIM	PP	SH	GW	S	%	TGF	PGF	TGA	PGA	+/–	GP	G	A	Pts	PIM	PP	SH	GW
1969-70	**St. Louis Blues**	**NHL**	**24**	**1**	**4**	**5**	**1**	**4**	**5**	**30**	**0**	**0**	**0**	**23**	**4.3**	**12**	**2**	**16**	**1**	**–5**	**3**	**0**	**0**	**0**	**0**	**0**	**0**	**0**
	Buffalo Bisons	AHL	48	2	28	30	....	....	....	91	....	....	....	....	....	....	....	....	....	....	....	....	....	....	....	....	....	....
1970-71	**St. Louis Blues**	**NHL**	**36**	**0**	**3**	**3**	**0**	**2**	**2**	**45**	**0**	**0**	**0**	**24**	**0.0**	**14**	**0**	**14**	**0**	**0**	**1**	**0**	**0**	**0**	**2**	**0**	**0**	**0**
	Kansas City Blues	CHL	7	0	0	0	....	....	....	31	....	....	....	....	....	....	....	....	....	....	....	....	....	....	....	....	....	....
1971-72	**St. Louis Blues**	**NHL**	**65**	**1**	**11**	**12**	**1**	**9**	**10**	**64**	**0**	**0**	**1**	**63**	**1.6**	**40**	**3**	**66**	**14**	**–15**	**11**	**0**	**0**	**0**	**12**	**0**	**0**	**0**
	Denver Spurs	WHL	8	0	5	5	....	....	....	18	....	....	....	....	....	....	....	....	....	....	....	....	....	....	....	....	....	....
1972-73	**Atlanta Flames**	**NHL**	**76**	**2**	**11**	**13**	**2**	**9**	**11**	**92**	**0**	**0**	**0**	**60**	**3.3**	**40**	**1**	**72**	**15**	**–18**	....	....	....	....	....	....	....	....
1973-74	**Minnesota North Stars**	**NHL**	**1**	**0**	**0**	**0**	**0**	**0**	**0**	**2**	**0**	**0**	**0**	**0**	**0.0**	**0**	**0**	**1**	**0**	**–1**	....	....	....	....	....	....	....	....
	New Haven Nighthawks	AHL	67	4	33	37	....	....	....	122	....	....	....	....	....	....	....	....	....	....	10	1	5	6	8	....	....	....
1974-75	**Minnesota North Stars**	**NHL**	**7**	**0**	**0**	**0**	**0**	**0**	**0**	**8**	**0**	**0**	**0**	**10**	**0.0**	**6**	**0**	**13**	**4**	**–3**	....	....	....	....	....	....	....	....
	New Haven Nighthawks	AHL	64	6	27	33	....	....	....	101	....	....	....	....	....	....	....	....	....	....	16	0	4	4	23	....	....	....
1975-76	**Minnesota North Stars**	**NHL**	**20**	**0**	**3**	**3**	**0**	**2**	**2**	**21**	**0**	**0**	**0**	**9**	**0.0**	**6**	**0**	**16**	**5**	**–5**	....	....	....	....	....	....	....	....
	New Haven Nighthawks	AHL	48	3	14	17	....	....	....	58	....	....	....	....	....	....	....	....	....	....	3	0	1	1	4	....	....	....
1976-77	Erie Blades	NAHL	64	5	25	30	....	....	....	65	....	....	....	....	....	....	....	....	....	....	....	....	....	....	....	....	....	....
	NHL Totals		**263**	**4**	**34**	**38**	**4**	**28**	**32**	**294**	**0**	**0**	**1**	**204**	**2.0**	**127**	**7**	**223**	**40**		**31**	**0**	**2**	**2**	**26**	**0**	**0**	**0**

• Brother of Barclay and Bob • AHL Second All-Star Team (1975)

Traded to **Minnesota** by **Montreal** with the rights to Barrie Meissner and Leo Thiffault for Bryan Watson, June 6, 1967. Claimed by **NY Rangers** from **Minnesota** in Intra-League Draft, June 12, 1968. Traded to **St. Louis** by **NY Rangers** with Camille Henry and Robbie Irons for Don Caley and Wayne Rivers, June 13, 1968. Claimed by **Atlanta** from **St. Louis** in Expansion Draft, June 6, 1972. Claimed by **Minnesota** from **Atlanta** in Intra-League Draft, June 12, 1973.

• PLAGER, Bob　Robert Bryant　D – L. 5'11", 195 lbs.　b: Kirkland Lake, Ont., 3/11/1943.

Season	Club	League	GP	G	A	Pts	AG	AA	APts	PIM	PP	SH	GW	S	%	TGF	PGF	TGA	PGA	+/–	GP	G	A	Pts	PIM	PP	SH	GW
1958-59	Kirkland Lake Legion	NOHA	STATISTICS NOT AVAILABLE																									
1959-60	Guelph Biltmores	OHA-Jr.	44	0	1	1	....	....	....	37	....	....	....	....	....	....	....	....	....	....	5	0	1	1	4	....	....	....
1960-61	Guelph Royals	OHA-Jr.	43	3	12	15	....	....	....	99	....	....	....	....	....	....	....	....	....	....	14	3	8	11	73	....	....	....
1961-62	Guelph Royals	OHA-Jr.	50	5	22	27	....	....	....	*161	....	....	....	....	....	....	....	....	....	....	....	....	....	....	....	....	....	....
	Kitchener Frontenacs	EPHL	3	0	0	0	....	....	....	2	....	....	....	....	....	....	....	....	....	....	....	....	....	....	....	....	....	....
1962-63	Guelph Royals	OHA-Jr.	45	11	28	39	....	....	....	97	....	....	....	....	....	....	....	....	....	....	....	....	....	....	....	....	....	....
	Baltimore Clippers	AHL	4	0	0	0	....	....	....	6	....	....	....	....	....	....	....	....	....	....	2	0	0	0	10	....	....	....
1963-64	St. Paul Rangers	CPHL	61	13	35	48	....	....	....	158	....	....	....	....	....	....	....	....	....	....	8	3	6	9	21	....	....	....
1964-65	**New York Rangers**	**NHL**	**10**	**0**	**0**	**0**	**0**	**0**	**0**	**18**	....	....	....	....	....	....	....	....	....	....	....	....	....	....	....	....	....	....
	Vancouver Canucks	WHL	31	5	12	17	....	....	....	103	....	....	....	....	....	....	....	....	....	....	....	....	....	....	....	....	....	....
	Baltimore Clippers	AHL	19	2	12	14	....	....	....	27	....	....	....	....	....	....	....	....	....	....	5	0	0	0	6	....	....	....
1965-66	**New York Rangers**	**NHL**	**18**	**0**	**5**	**5**	**0**	**5**	**5**	**22**	....	....	....	....	....	....	....	....	....	....	....	....	....	....	....	....	....	....
	Minnesota Rangers	CPHL	44	7	12	19	....	....	....	145	....	....	....	....	....	....	....	....	....	....	....	....	....	....	....	....	....	....
1966-67	**New York Rangers**	**NHL**	**1**	**0**	**0**	**0**	**0**	**0**	**0**	**0**	....	....	....	....	....	....	....	....	....	....	....	....	....	....	....	....	....	....
	Baltimore Clippers	AHL	63	3	16	19	....	....	....	*169	....	....	....	....	....	....	....	....	....	....	9	0	5	5	15	....	....	....
1967-68	**St. Louis Blues**	**NHL**	**53**	**2**	**5**	**7**	**2**	**5**	**7**	**86**	**0**	**0**	**0**	**52**	**3.8**	**41**	**3**	**62**	**13**	**–11**	**18**	**1**	**2**	**3**	**69**	**0**	**0**	**0**
1968-69	**St. Louis Blues**	**NHL**	**32**	**0**	**7**	**7**	**0**	**6**	**6**	**43**	**0**	**0**	**0**	**46**	**0.0**	**28**	**0**	**25**	**7**	**10**	**9**	**0**	**4**	**4**	**47**	**0**	**0**	**0**
	Kansas City Blues	CHL	5	1	3	4	....	....	....	16	....	....	....	....	....	....	....	....	....	....	....	....	....	....	....	....	....	....
1969-70	**St. Louis Blues**	**NHL**	**64**	**3**	**11**	**14**	**3**	**10**	**13**	**113**	**0**	**0**	**0**	**83**	**3.6**	**43**	**1**	**60**	**20**	**2**	**16**	**0**	**3**	**3**	**46**	**0**	**0**	**0**
1970-71	**St. Louis Blues**	**NHL**	**70**	**1**	**19**	**20**	**1**	**16**	**17**	**114**	**0**	**0**	**1**	**70**	**1.4**	**66**	**2**	**87**	**32**	**9**	**6**	**0**	**2**	**2**	**4**	**0**	**0**	**0**
1971-72	**St. Louis Blues**	**NHL**	**50**	**4**	**7**	**11**	**4**	**6**	**10**	**81**	**0**	**0**	**0**	**59**	**6.8**	**49**	**2**	**72**	**24**	**–1**	**11**	**1**	**4**	**5**	**5**	**0**	**0**	**0**
1972-73	**St. Louis Blues**	**NHL**	**77**	**2**	**31**	**33**	**2**	**25**	**27**	**107**	**0**	**0**	**1**	**117**	**1.7**	**94**	**7**	**128**	**40**	**–1**	**5**	**0**	**2**	**2**	**2**	**0**	**0**	**0**
1973-74	**St. Louis Blues**	**NHL**	**61**	**3**	**10**	**13**	**3**	**8**	**11**	**48**	**0**	**1**	**1**	**78**	**3.8**	**58**	**0**	**70**	**21**	**9**	....	....	....	....	....	....	....	....
1974-75	**St. Louis Blues**	**NHL**	**73**	**1**	**14**	**15**	**1**	**10**	**11**	**53**	**0**	**0**	**0**	**85**	**1.2**	**74**	**1**	**106**	**43**	**10**	**2**	**0**	**0**	**0**	**20**	**0**	**0**	**0**
1975-76	**St. Louis Blues**	**NHL**	**63**	**3**	**8**	**11**	**3**	**6**	**9**	**90**	**0**	**1**	**1**	**43**	**7.0**	**66**	**3**	**86**	**40**	**17**	**3**	**0**	**0**	**0**	**2**	**0**	**0**	**0**
1976-77	**St. Louis Blues**	**NHL**	**54**	**1**	**9**	**10**	**1**	**7**	**8**	**23**	**0**	**0**	**0**	**64**	**1.6**	**36**	**3**	**50**	**8**	**–9**	**4**	**0**	**0**	**0**	**0**	**0**	**0**	**0**
	Kansas City Blues	CHL	4	0	2	2	....	....	....	15	....	....	....	....	....	....	....	....	....	....	....	....	....	....	....	....	....	....
1977-78	**St. Louis Blues**	**NHL**	**18**	**0**	**0**	**0**	**0**	**0**	**0**	**4**	**0**	**0**	**0**	**15**	**0.0**	**6**	**0**	**17**	**3**	**–8**	....	....	....	....	....	....	....	....
	Salt Lake Golden Eagles	CHL	11	0	3	3	....	....	....	52	....	....	....	....	....	....	....	....	....	....	6	0	3	3	6	....	....	....
	NHL Totals		**644**	**20**	**126**	**146**	**20**	**104**	**124**	**802**	....	....	....	....	....	....	....	....	....	....	**74**	**2**	**17**	**19**	**195**	....	....	....

• Brother of Barclay and Bill

Traded to **St. Louis** by **NY Rangers** with Gary Sabourin, Tim Ecclestone and Gord Kannegiesser for Rod Seiling, June 6, 1967.

• PLANTE, Cam　D – L. 6'1", 195 lbs.　b: Brandon, Man., 3/12/1964. Toronto's 5th, 133rd overall, in 1983.

Season	Club	League	GP	G	A	Pts	AG	AA	APts	PIM	PP	SH	GW	S	%	TGF	PGF	TGA	PGA	+/–	GP	G	A	Pts	PIM	PP	SH	GW
1979-80	Brandon Midget Kings	MAHA	STATISTICS NOT AVAILABLE																									
1980-81	Brandon Wheat Kings	WHL	70	3	14	17	....	....	....	17	....	....	....	....	....	....	....	....	....	....	5	0	2	2	0	....	....	....
1981-82	Brandon Wheat Kings	WHL	36	4	12	16	....	....	....	22	....	....	....	....	....	....	....	....	....	....	4	0	6	6	4	....	....	....
1982-83	Brandon Wheat Kings	WHL	56	19	56	75	....	....	....	71	....	....	....	....	....	....	....	....	....	....	....	....	....	....	....	....	....	....
1983-84	Brandon Wheat Kings	WHL	72	22	118	140	....	....	....	96	....	....	....	....	....	....	....	....	....	....	11	4	16	20	14	....	....	....
1984-85	**Toronto Maple Leafs**	**NHL**	**2**	**0**	**0**	**0**	**0**	**0**	**0**	**0**	**0**	**0**	**0**	**0**	**0.0**	**0**	**0**	**0**	**0**	**0**	....	....	....	....	....	....	....	....
	St. Catharines Saints	AHL	54	5	31	36	....	....	....	42	....	....	....	....	....	....	....	....	....	....	....	....	....	....	....	....	....	....
1985-86	St. Catharines Saints	AHL	49	6	15	21	....	....	....	28	....	....	....	....	....	....	....	....	....	....	5	0	3	3	2	....	....	....
1986-87	Newmarket Saints	AHL	19	3	4	7	....	....	....	14	....	....	....	....	....	....	....	....	....	....	....	....	....	....	....	....	....	....
	Milwaukee Admirals	IHL	56	7	47	54	....	....	....	44	....	....	....	....	....	....	....	....	....	....	5	2	2	4	4	....	....	....
1987-88	Newmarket Saints	AHL	18	2	8	10	....	....	....	14	....	....	....	....	....	....	....	....	....	....	....	....	....	....	....	....	....	....
	VSV Villach	Austria	11	2	10	12	....	....	....	14	....	....	....	....	....	....	....	....	....	....	....	....	....	....	....	....	....	....
	HC Basel	Switz-2	20	9	26	35	....	....	....	....	....	....	....	....	....	....	....	....	....	....	....	....	....	....	....	....	....	....
1988-89	HC Davos	Switz.	3	3	2	5	....	....	....	....	....	....	....	....	....	....	....	....	....	....	....	....	....	....	....	....	....	....
1989-90	Krefelder EV	Germany-2	12	1	19	20	....	....	....	10	....	....	....	....	....	....	....	....	....	....	....	....	....	....	....	....	....	....
	Fort Wayne Komets	IHL	61	7	42	49	....	....	....	45	....	....	....	....	....	....	....	....	....	....	7	1	6	7	2	....	....	....
1990-91	Kansas City Blades	IHL	43	6	14	20	....	....	....	34	....	....	....	....	....	....	....	....	....	....	....	....	....	....	....	....	....	....
1991-92	Thunder Bay Thunder Hawks	ColHL	54	16	57	73	....	....	....	32	....	....	....	....	....	....	....	....	....	....	13	0	8	8	6	....	....	....
1992-93	Norwich-Peterborough Pirates	BH-Cup	8	9	26	35	....	....	....	16	....	....	....	....	....	....	....	....	....	....	....	....	....	....	....	....	....	....
	Norwich-Peterborough Pirates	Britain	25	14	52	66	....	....	....	93	....	....	....	....	....	....	....	....	....	....	6	5	7	12	20	....	....	....
1993-94	Peterborough Pirates	BH-Cup	8	9	26	35	....	....	....	16	....	....	....	....	....	....	....	....	....	....	....	....	....	....	....	....	....	....
	Peterborough Pirates	Britain	37	13	55	68	....	....	....	56	....	....	....	....	....	....	....	....	....	....	6	10	15	25	6	....	....	....
1994-95	Peterborough Pirates	BH-Cup	6	4	8	12	....	....	....	8	....	....	....	....	....	....	....	....	....	....	....	....	....	....	....	....	....	....
	Peterborough Pirates	Britain	34	22	52	74	....	....	....	60	....	....	....	....	....	....	....	....	....	....	3	3	6	9	18	....	....	....
1995-96	Peterborough Pirates	BH-Cup	6	4	7	11	....	....	....	24	....	....	....	....	....	....	....	....	....	....	....	....	....	....	....	....	....	....
	Peterborough Pirates	Britain	16	4	32	36	....	....	....	93	....	....	....	....	....	....	....	....	....	....	....	....	....	....	....	....	....	....
	Chelmsford Chieftans	Britain	10	8	15	23	....	....	....	22	....	....	....	....	....	....	....	....	....	....	....	....	....	....	....	....	....	....
	Humberside Hawks	Britain	9	3	5	8	....	....	....	18	....	....	....	....	....	....	....	....	....	....	7	2	14	16	8	....	....	....
1996-97	Wichita Thunder	CHL	55	12	63	75	....	....	....	74	....	....	....	....	....	....	....	....	....	....	9	2	7	9	18	....	....	....
1997-98	Wichita Thunder	CHL	67	8	62	70	....	....	....	112	....	....	....	....	....	....	....	....	....	....	14	0	8	8	16	....	....	....
	NHL Totals		**2**	**0**	**0**	**0**	**0**	**0**	**0**	**0**	**0**	**0**	**0**	**0**	**0.0**	**0**	**0**	**0**	**0**		....	....	....	....	....	....	....	....

WHL East All-Star Team (1984) • Played w/ RHI's St. Louis Vipers in 1995 (19-3-24-27-24) and Denver Dare Devils in 1996 (27-11-34-45-26).

• PLANTE, Dan　Daniel L.　RW – R. 5'11", 202 lbs.　b: Hayward, WI, 10/5/1971. NY Islanders' 3rd, 48th overall, in 1990.

Season	Club	League	GP	G	A	Pts	AG	AA	APts	PIM	PP	SH	GW	S	%	TGF	PGF	TGA	PGA	+/–	GP	G	A	Pts	PIM	PP	SH	GW
1988-89	Edina Hornets	Hi-School	27	10	26	36	....	....	....	23	....	....	....	....	....	....	....	....	....	....	....	....	....	....	....	....	....	....
1989-90	Edina Hornets	Hi-School	24	8	18	26	....	....	....	12	....	....	....	....	....	....	....	....	....	....	....	....	....	....	....	....	....	....
1990-91	University of Wisconsin	WCHA	33	1	2	3	....	....	....	54	....	....	....	....	....	....	....	....	....	....	....	....	....	....	....	....	....	....
1991-92	University of Wisconsin	WCHA	36	13	13	26	....	....	....	107	....	....	....	....	....	....	....	....	....	....	....	....	....	....	....	....	....	....
1992-93	University of Wisconsin	WCHA	42	26	31	57	....	....	....	142	....	....	....	....	....	....	....	....	....	....	....	....	....	....	....	....	....	....
1993-94	**New York Islanders**	**NHL**	**12**	**0**	**1**	**1**	**0**	**1**	**1**	**4**	**0**	**0**	**0**	**9**	**0.0**	**2**	**0**	**4**	**0**	**–2**	**1**	**1**	**0**	**1**	**2**	**0**	**0**	**0**
	Salt Lake Golden Eagles	IHL	66	7	17	24	....	....	....	148	....	....	....	....	....	....	....	....	....	....	....	....	....	....	....	....	....	....
1994-95	Denver Grizzlies	IHL	2	0	0	0	....	....	....	4	....	....	....	....	....	....	....	....	....	....	....	....	....	....	....	....	....	....
1995-96	**New York Islanders**	**NHL**	**73**	**5**	**3**	**8**	**5**	**2**	**7**	**50**	**0**	**2**	**0**	**103**	**4.9**	**16**	**1**	**64**	**27**	**–22**	....	....	....	....	....	....	....	....
	United States	WC-A	7	1	1	2	....	....	....	0	....	....	....	....	....	....	....	....	....	....	....	....	....	....	....	....	....	....

			REGULAR SEASON																		PLAYOFFS							
Season	Club	League	GP	G	A	Pts	AG	AA	APts	PIM	PP	SH	GW	S	%	TGF	PGF	TGA	PGA	+/–	GP	G	A	Pts	PIM	PP	SH	GW
1996-97	**New York Islanders**	**NHL**	**67**	**4**	**9**	**13**	**4**	**8**	**12**	**75**	**0**	**2**	**0**	**61**	**6.6**	**21**	**0**	**36**	**9**	**–6**	....	....	....	....	....	....	....	....
	United States	WC-A	8	1	1	2	....	....	....	6	....	....	....	....	....	....	....	....	....	....	....	....	....	....	....	....	....	....
1997-98	**New York Islanders**	**NHL**	**7**	**0**	**1**	**1**	**0**	**1**	**1**	**6**	**0**	**0**	**0**	**7**	**0.0**	**1**	**0**	**2**	**0**	**–1**	....	....	....	....	....	....	....	....
	Utah Grizzlies	IHL	73	22	27	49	....	....	....	125	....	....	....	....	....	....	....	....	....	....	4	0	2	2	14	....	....	....
1998-99	Chicago Wolves	IHL	81	21	12	33	....	....	....	119	....	....	....	....	....	....	....	....	....	....	10	1	5	6	10	....	....	....
99-2000	Chicago Wolves	IHL	79	11	11	22	....	....	....	71	....	....	....	....	....	....	....	....	....	....	16	3	5	8	14	....	....	....
	NHL Totals		**159**	**9**	**14**	**23**	**9**	**12**	**21**	**135**	**0**	**4**	**0**	**180**	**5.0**	**40**	**1**	**106**	**36**		**1**	**1**	**0**	**1**	**2**	**0**	**0**	**0**

• Missed remainder of 1994-95 season recovering from knee injury suffered in game vs. Houston (IHL), October 2, 1994. Signed as a free agent by **Chicago** (IHL), July 21, 1999.

• PLANTE, Derek

C – L. 5'11", 181 lbs. b: Cloquet, MN, 1/17/1971. Buffalo's 7th, 161st overall, in 1989.

Season	Club	League	GP	G	A	Pts	AG	AA	APts	PIM	PP	SH	GW	S	%	TGF	PGF	TGA	PGA	+/–	GP	G	A	Pts	PIM	PP	SH	GW
1987-88	Cloquet Lumberjacks	Hi-School	23	16	25	41	....	....	....	....	....	....	....	....	....	....	....	....	....	....	....	....	....	....	....	....	....	....
1988-89	Cloquet Lumberjacks	Hi-School	24	30	33	63	....	....	....	....	....	....	....	....	....	....	....	....	....	....	....	....	....	....	....	....	....	....
	Madison Capitols	USHL	STATISTICS NOT AVAILABLE																									
1989-90	University of Minnesota-Duluth	WCHA	28	10	11	21	....	....	....	12	....	....	....	....	....	....	....	....	....	....	....	....	....	....	....	....	....	....
1990-91	University of Minnesota-Duluth	WCHA	36	23	20	43	....	....	....	6	....	....	....	....	....	....	....	....	....	....	....	....	....	....	....	....	....	....
	United States	WJC-A	7	1	2	3	....	....	....	4	....	....	....	....	....	....	....	....	....	....	....	....	....	....	....	....	....	....
1991-92	University of Minnesota-Duluth	WCHA	37	27	36	63	....	....	....	28	....	....	....	....	....	....	....	....	....	....	....	....	....	....	....	....	....	....
	United States	WC-A	6	0	1	1	....	....	....	0	....	....	....	....	....	....	....	....	....	....	....	....	....	....	....	....	....	....
1992-93	University of Minnesota-Duluth	WCHA	37	*36	*56	*92	....	....	....	30	....	....	....	....	....	....	....	....	....	....	....	....	....	....	....	....	....	....
	United States	WC-A	6	1	0	1	....	....	....	2	....	....	....	....	....	....	....	....	....	....	....	....	....	....	....	....	....	....
1993-94	**Buffalo Sabres**	**NHL**	**77**	**21**	**35**	**56**	**20**	**27**	**47**	**24**	**8**	**1**	**2**	**147**	**14.3**	**81**	**42**	**40**	**5**	**4**	**7**	**1**	**0**	**1**	**0**	**0**	**0**	**0**
	United States	Nat-Team	2	0	1	1	....	....	....	0	....	....	....	....	....	....	....	....	....	....	....	....	....	....	....	....	....	....
1994-95	**Buffalo Sabres**	**NHL**	**47**	**3**	**19**	**22**	**5**	**28**	**33**	**12**	**2**	**0**	**0**	**94**	**3.2**	**29**	**13**	**29**	**9**	**–4**	....	....	....	....	....	....	....	....
1995-96	**Buffalo Sabres**	**NHL**	**76**	**23**	**33**	**56**	**23**	**27**	**50**	**28**	**4**	**0**	**5**	**203**	**11.3**	**78**	**22**	**78**	**18**	**–4**	....	....	....	....	....	....	....	....
	United States	WC-A	8	1	1	2	....	....	....	4	....	....	....	....	....	....	....	....	....	....	....	....	....	....	....	....	....	....
1996-97	**Buffalo Sabres**	**NHL**	**82**	**27**	**26**	**53**	**29**	**23**	**52**	**24**	**5**	**0**	**6**	**191**	**14.1**	**82**	**19**	**62**	**13**	**14**	**12**	**4**	**6**	**10**	**4**	**1**	**0**	**2**
1997-98	**Buffalo Sabres**	**NHL**	**72**	**13**	**21**	**34**	**15**	**21**	**36**	**26**	**5**	**0**	**1**	**150**	**8.7**	**51**	**16**	**52**	**25**	**8**	**11**	**0**	**3**	**3**	**10**	**0**	**0**	**0**
1998-99	**Buffalo Sabres**	**NHL**	**41**	**4**	**11**	**15**	**5**	**11**	**16**	**12**	**0**	**0**	**0**	**66**	**6.1**	**24**	**6**	**20**	**5**	**3**	....	....	....	....	....	....	....	....
♦	**Dallas Stars**	**NHL**	**10**	**2**	**3**	**5**	**2**	**3**	**5**	**4**	**1**	**0**	**0**	**24**	**8.3**	**9**	**3**	**5**	**0**	**1**	**6**	**1**	**0**	**1**	**4**	**0**	**0**	**0**
99-2000	**Dallas Stars**	**NHL**	**16**	**1**	**1**	**2**	**1**	**1**	**2**	**2**	**1**	**0**	**0**	**17**	**5.9**	**4**	**1**	**7**	**0**	**–4**	....	....	....	....	....	....	....	....
	Michigan K-Wings	IHL	13	0	4	4	....	....	....	2	....	....	....	....	....	....	....	....	....	....	....	....	....	....	....	....	....	....
	Chicago Blackhawks	**NHL**	**17**	**1**	**1**	**2**	**1**	**1**	**2**	**2**	**0**	**0**	**0**	**14**	**7.1**	**5**	**1**	**5**	**0**	**–1**	....	....	....	....	....	....	....	....
	Chicago Wolves	IHL	4	2	1	3	....	....	....	2	....	....	....	....	....	....	....	....	....	....	8	3	1	4	6	....	....	....
	United States	WC-A	7	1	1	2	....	....	....	4	....	....	....	....	....	....	....	....	....	....	....	....	....	....	....	....	....	....
	NHL Totals		**438**	**95**	**150**	**245**	**101**	**142**	**243**	**134**	**26**	**1**	**14**	**906**	**10.5**	**363**	**123**	**298**	**75**		**36**	**6**	**9**	**15**	**18**	**1**	**0**	**2**

WCHA Second All-Star Team (1992) • WCHA First All-Star Team (1993) • NCAA West First All-American Team (1993)

Traded to **Dallas** by **Buffalo** for Dallas' 2nd round choice (Michael Zigomanis) in 1999 Entry Draft, March 23, 1999. Traded to **Chicago** by **Dallas** with Kevin Dean and Dallas' 2nd round choice in 2001 Entry Draft for Sylvain Cote and Dave Manson, February 8, 2000.

• PLANTE, Pierre

Pierre Renald RW – R. 6'1", 190 lbs. b: Valleyfield, Que., 5/14/1951. Philadelphia's 2nd, 9th overall, in 1971.

Season	Club	League	GP	G	A	Pts	AG	AA	APts	PIM	PP	SH	GW	S	%	TGF	PGF	TGA	PGA	+/–	GP	G	A	Pts	PIM	PP	SH	GW
1968-69	Drummondville Rangers	QJHL	44	11	13	24	....	....	....	35	....	....	....	....	....	....	....	....	....	....	10	2	10	12	12	....	....	....
1969-70	Drummondville Rangers	QJHL	51	51	51	102	....	....	....	186	....	....	....	....	....	....	....	....	....	....	1	1	0	1	7	....	....	....
1970-71	Drummondville Rangers	QJHL	58	38	50	88	....	....	....	251	....	....	....	....	....	....	....	....	....	....	6	1	9	10	14	....	....	....
1971-72	**Philadelphia Flyers**	**NHL**	**24**	**1**	**0**	**1**	**1**	**0**	**1**	**15**	**0**	**0**	**0**	**24**	**4.2**	**4**	**1**	**14**	**0**	**–11**	....	....	....	....	....	....	....	....
	Richmond Robins	AHL	47	10	17	27	....	....	....	51	....	....	....	....	....	....	....	....	....	....	....	....	....	....	....	....	....	....
1972-73	**Philadelphia Flyers**	**NHL**	**2**	**0**	**3**	**3**	**0**	**2**	**2**	**0**	**0**	**0**	**0**	**5**	**0.0**	**4**	**0**	**1**	**0**	**3**	....	....	....	....	....	....	....	....
	Richmond Robins	AHL	30	9	11	20	....	....	....	56	....	....	....	....	....	....	....	....	....	....	....	....	....	....	....	....	....	....
	St. Louis Blues	**NHL**	**49**	**12**	**13**	**25**	**11**	**10**	**21**	**56**	**0**	**0**	**1**	**90**	**13.3**	**46**	**6**	**33**	**1**	**8**	**5**	**2**	**0**	**2**	**15**	**0**	**0**	**0**
1973-74	**St. Louis Blues**	**NHL**	**78**	**26**	**28**	**54**	**25**	**23**	**48**	**85**	**8**	**0**	**3**	**151**	**17.2**	**77**	**24**	**68**	**1**	**–14**	....	....	....	....	....	....	....	....
1974-75	**St. Louis Blues**	**NHL**	**80**	**34**	**32**	**66**	**30**	**24**	**54**	**125**	**4**	**0**	**4**	**162**	**21.0**	**100**	**16**	**70**	**2**	**16**	**2**	**0**	**0**	**0**	**8**	**0**	**0**	**0**
1975-76	**St. Louis Blues**	**NHL**	**74**	**14**	**19**	**33**	**12**	**14**	**26**	**77**	**5**	**0**	**2**	**125**	**11.2**	**53**	**14**	**61**	**0**	**–22**	**3**	**0**	**0**	**0**	**6**	**0**	**0**	**0**
1976-77	**St. Louis Blues**	**NHL**	**76**	**18**	**20**	**38**	**16**	**15**	**31**	**77**	**4**	**0**	**3**	**124**	**14.5**	**68**	**17**	**55**	**0**	**–4**	**4**	**0**	**0**	**0**	**2**	**0**	**0**	**0**
1977-78	**Chicago Black Hawks**	**NHL**	**77**	**10**	**18**	**28**	**9**	**14**	**23**	**59**	**0**	**0**	**2**	**104**	**9.6**	**44**	**2**	**63**	**19**	**–2**	**1**	**0**	**0**	**0**	**0**	**0**	**0**	**0**
1978-79	**New York Rangers**	**NHL**	**70**	**6**	**25**	**31**	**5**	**18**	**23**	**37**	**0**	**0**	**1**	**84**	**7.1**	**53**	**4**	**63**	**25**	**11**	**18**	**0**	**6**	**6**	**20**	**0**	**0**	**0**
1979-80	**Quebec Nordiques**	**NHL**	**69**	**4**	**14**	**18**	**3**	**10**	**13**	**68**	**0**	**0**	**1**	**82**	**4.9**	**29**	**1**	**70**	**28**	**–14**	....	....	....	....	....	....	....	....
	Syracuse Firebirds	AHL	3	0	0	0	....	....	....	2	....	....	....	....	....	....	....	....	....	....	....	....	....	....	....	....	....	....
	NHL Totals		**599**	**125**	**172**	**297**	**112**	**130**	**242**	**599**	**21**	**0**	**17**	**951**	**13.1**	**478**	**85**	**498**	**76**		**33**	**2**	**6**	**8**	**51**	**0**	**0**	**0**

QJHL First All-Star Team (1970)

Traded to **St. Louis** by **Philadelphia** with Brent Hughes for Andre Dupont and St. Louis' 3rd round choice (Bob Stumpf) in 1973 Amateur Draft, December 14, 1972. Traded to **Chicago** by **St. Louis** for Dick Redmond, August 9, 1977. Traded to **Minnesota** by **Chicago** to complete transaction that sent Doug Hicks to Chicago (March 14, 1978), May 4, 1978. Claimed on waivers by **Detroit** from **Minnesota**, September 13, 1978. Claimed by **NY Rangers** from **Detroit** in Waiver Draft, October 2, 1978. Claimed by **Quebec** from **NY Rangers** in Expansion Draft, June 13, 1979.

• PLANTERY, Mark

Mark P. D – L. 6'1", 185 lbs. b: St. Catharines, Ont., 8/14/1959.

Season	Club	League	GP	G	A	Pts	AG	AA	APts	PIM	PP	SH	GW	S	%	TGF	PGF	TGA	PGA	+/–	GP	G	A	Pts	PIM	PP	SH	GW
1975-76	Thorold Black Hawks	OHA-B	40	6	28	34	....	....	....	85	....	....	....	....	....	....	....	....	....	....	....	....	....	....	....	....	....	....
1976-77	St. Catharines Fincups	OMJHL	54	1	23	24	....	....	....	112	....	....	....	....	....	....	....	....	....	....	9	0	0	0	13	....	....	....
	Canada	WJC-A	7	0	1	1	....	....	....	6	....	....	....	....	....	....	....	....	....	....	....	....	....	....	....	....	....	....
1977-78	Hamilton Fincups	OMJHL	51	0	6	6	....	....	....	91	....	....	....	....	....	....	....	....	....	....	20	1	2	3	29	....	....	....
1978-79	Brantford Alexanders	OMJHL	37	4	19	23	....	....	....	98	....	....	....	....	....	....	....	....	....	....	....	....	....	....	....	....	....	....
	Windsor Spitfires	OMJHL	27	3	15	18	....	....	....	43	....	....	....	....	....	....	....	....	....	....	7	0	2	2	17	....	....	....
1979-80	Tulsa Oilers	CHL	67	6	26	32	....	....	....	102	....	....	....	....	....	....	....	....	....	....	3	0	0	0	2	....	....	....
1980-81	**Winnipeg Jets**	**NHL**	**25**	**1**	**5**	**6**	**1**	**3**	**4**	**14**	**0**	**0**	**0**	**18**	**5.6**	**23**	**1**	**34**	**2**	**–10**	....	....	....	....	....	....	....	....
	Tulsa Oilers	CHL	50	3	15	18	....	....	....	77	....	....	....	....	....	....	....	....	....	....	....	....	....	....	....	....	....	....
1981-82	Tulsa Oilers	CHL	76	9	40	49	....	....	....	65	....	....	....	....	....	....	....	....	....	....	3	1	0	1	0	....	....	....
1982-83	Sherbrooke Jets	AHL	75	6	25	31	....	....	....	51	....	....	....	....	....	....	....	....	....	....	....	....	....	....	....	....	....	....
1983-84	HC Gardena-Groden	Italy	28	4	20	24	....	....	....	53	....	....	....	....	....	....	....	....	....	....	6	7	8	15	6	....	....	....
1984-85	Toledo Goaldiggers	IHL	33	1	15	16	....	....	....	37	....	....	....	....	....	....	....	....	....	....	....	....	....	....	....	....	....	....
	Flint Generals	IHL	44	3	17	20	....	....	....	44	....	....	....	....	....	....	....	....	....	....	4	0	0	0	5	....	....	....
1985-86	Milwaukee Admirals	IHL	1	0	0	0	....	....	....	0	....	....	....	....	....	....	....	....	....	....	....	....	....	....	....	....	....	....
	NHL Totals		**25**	**1**	**5**	**6**	**1**	**3**	**4**	**14**	**0**	**0**	**0**	**18**	**5.6**	**23**	**1**	**34**	**2**		....	....	....	....	....	....	....	....

Signed as a free agent by **Winnipeg**, October 5, 1979.

• PLAVSIC, Adrien

D – L. 6'1", 200 lbs. b: Montreal, Que., 1/13/1970. St. Louis' 2nd, 30th overall, in 1988.

Season	Club	League	GP	G	A	Pts	AG	AA	APts	PIM	PP	SH	GW	S	%	TGF	PGF	TGA	PGA	+/–	GP	G	A	Pts	PIM	PP	SH	GW
1986-87	Lac St-Louis Lions	QAAA	42	8	27	35	....	....	....	22	....	....	....	....	....	....	....	....	....	....	....	....	....	....	....	....	....	....
1987-88	University of New Hampshire	H-East	30	5	6	11	....	....	....	45	....	....	....	....	....	....	....	....	....	....	....	....	....	....	....	....	....	....
1988-89	Canada	Nat-Team	62	5	10	15	....	....	....	25	....	....	....	....	....	....	....	....	....	....	....	....	....	....	....	....	....	....
1989-90	**St. Louis Blues**	**NHL**	**4**	**0**	**1**	**1**	**0**	**1**	**1**	**2**	**0**	**0**	**0**	**1**	**0.0**	**4**	**0**	**1**	**0**	**3**	....	....	....	....	....	....	....	....
	Canada	WJC-A	7	0	1	1	....	....	....	8	....	....	....	....	....	....	....	....	....	....	....	....	....	....	....	....	....	....
	Peoria Rivermen	IHL	51	7	14	21	....	....	....	87	....	....	....	....	....	....	....	....	....	....	....	....	....	....	....	....	....	....
	Vancouver Canucks	**NHL**	**11**	**3**	**2**	**5**	**3**	**1**	**4**	**8**	**2**	**0**	**0**	**13**	**23.1**	**10**	**2**	**10**	**0**	**–2**	....	....	....	....	....	....	....	....
	Milwaukee Admirals	IHL	3	1	2	3	....	....	....	14	....	....	....	....	....	....	....	....	....	....	6	1	3	4	6	....	....	....
1990-91	**Vancouver Canucks**	**NHL**	**48**	**2**	**10**	**12**	**2**	**8**	**10**	**62**	**0**	**0**	**0**	**69**	**2.9**	**33**	**10**	**48**	**2**	**–23**	....	....	....	....	....	....	....	....
1991-92	Canada	Nat-Team	38	7	8	15	....	....	....	44	....	....	....	....	....	....	....	....	....	....	....	....	....	....	....	....	....	....
	Canada	Olympics	8	0	2	2	....	....	....	0	....	....	....	....	....	....	....	....	....	....	....	....	....	....	....	....	....	....
	Vancouver Canucks	**NHL**	**16**	**1**	**9**	**10**	**1**	**7**	**8**	**14**	**0**	**0**	**0**	**21**	**4.8**	**23**	**6**	**21**	**8**	**4**	**13**	**1**	**7**	**8**	**4**	**0**	**0**	**0**
1992-93	**Vancouver Canucks**	**NHL**	**57**	**6**	**21**	**27**	**5**	**14**	**19**	**53**	**5**	**0**	**2**	**62**	**9.7**	**86**	**22**	**51**	**15**	**28**	....	....	....	....	....	....	....	....
1993-94	**Vancouver Canucks**	**NHL**	**47**	**1**	**9**	**10**	**1**	**7**	**8**	**6**	**0**	**0**	**1**	**41**	**2.4**	**24**	**4**	**38**	**13**	**–5**	....	....	....	....	....	....	....	....
	Hamilton Canucks	AHL	2	0	0	0	....	....	....	0	....	....	....	....	....	....	....	....	....	....	....	....	....	....	....	....	....	....

			REGULAR SEASON																		PLAYOFFS							
Season	Club	League	GP	G	A	Pts	AG	AA	APts	PIM	PP	SH	GW	S	%	TGF	PGF	TGA	PGA	+/–	GP	G	A	Pts	PIM	PP	SH	GW
1994-95	**Vancouver Canucks**	**NHL**	**3**	**0**	**1**	**1**	**0**	**1**	**1**	**4**	**0**	**0**	**0**	**11**	**0.0**	**4**	**0**	**1**	**0**	**3**	....	....	....	....	....	....	....	....
	Tampa Bay Lightning	**NHL**	**15**	**2**	**1**	**3**	**4**	**1**	**5**	**4**	**0**	**0**	**0**	**24**	**8.3**	**14**	**2**	**7**	**0**	**5**	....	....	....	....	....	....	....	....
1995-96	**Tampa Bay Lightning**	**NHL**	**7**	**1**	**2**	**3**	**1**	**2**	**3**	**6**	**0**	**0**	**0**	**4**	**25.0**	**7**	**0**	**2**	**0**	**5**	....	....	....	....	....	....	....	....
	Atlanta Knights	IHL	68	5	34	39	....	....	....	32	....	....	....	....	....	....	....	....	....	....	3	0	1	1	4	....	....	....
1996-97	**Mighty Ducks of Anaheim**	**NHL**	**6**	**0**	**0**	**0**	**0**	**0**	**0**	**2**	**0**	**0**	**0**	**3**	**0.0**	**4**	**4**	**6**	**1**	**–5**	....	....	....	....	....	....	....	....
	Long Beach Ice Dogs	IHL	69	7	28	35	....	....	....	86	....	....	....	....	....	....	....	....	....	....	18	0	9	9	10	....	....	....
1997-98	Revier Lowen	Germany	36	4	15	19	....	....	....	28	....	....	....	....	....	....	....	....	....	....	....	....	....	....	....	....	....	....
1998-99	ZSC Lions Zurich	Switz.	28	3	21	24	....	....	....	18	....	....	....	....	....	....	....	....	....	....	....	....	....	....	....	....	....	....
99-2000	ZSC Lions Zurich	Switz.	42	12	16	28	....	....	....	83	....	....	....	....	....	....	....	....	....	....	15	4	6	10	18	....	....	....
	NHL Totals		**214**	**16**	**56**	**72**	**17**	**42**	**59**	**161**	**7**	**0**	**3**	**249**	**6.4**	**209**	**50**	**185**	**39**		**13**	**1**	**7**	**8**	**4**	**0**	**0**	**0**

Traded to **Vancouver** by **St. Louis** with Montreal's 1st round choice (previously acquired, Vancouver selected Shawn Antoski) in 1990 Entry Draft and St. Louis' 2nd round choice (later traded to Montreal — Montreal selected Craig Darby) in 1991 Entry Draft for Rich Sutter, Harold Snepsts and St. Louis' 2nd round choice (previously acquired, St. Louis selected Craig Johnson) in 1990 Entry Draft, March 6, 1990. Traded to **Tampa Bay** by **Vancouver** for Tampa Bay's 5th round choice (David Darguzas) in 1997 Entry Draft, March 23, 1995. Signed as a free agent by **Anaheim**, September 6, 1996.

• PLAYFAIR, Jim

James D – L. 6'4", 200 lbs. b: Fort St. James, B.C., 5/22/1964. Edmonton's 1st, 20th overall, in 1982.

Season	Club	League	GP	G	A	Pts	AG	AA	APts	PIM	PP	SH	GW	S	%	TGF	PGF	TGA	PGA	+/–	GP	G	A	Pts	PIM	PP	SH	GW
1980-81	Fort Saskatchewan Traders	AJHL	31	2	17	19	....	....	....	105	....	....	....	....	....	....	....	....	....	....	....	....	....	....	....	....	....	....
1981-82	Portland Winter Hawks	WHL	70	4	13	17	....	....	....	121	....	....	....	....	....	....	....	....	....	....	15	1	2	3	21	....	....	....
	Portland Winter Hawks	Mem-Cup	4	0	0	0	....	....	....	12	....	....	....	....	....	....	....	....	....	....	....	....	....	....	....	....	....	....
1982-83	Portland Winter Hawks	WHL	63	8	27	35	....	....	....	218	....	....	....	....	....	....	....	....	....	....	14	0	5	5	16	....	....	....
	Portland Winter Hawks	Mem-Cup	4	0	3	3	....	....	....	18	....	....	....	....	....	....	....	....	....	....	....	....	....	....	....	....	....	....
1983-84	Portland Winter Hawks	WHL	16	5	6	11	....	....	....	38	....	....	....	....	....	....	....	....	....	....	....	....	....	....	....	....	....	....
	Calgary Wranglers	WHL	46	6	9	15	....	....	....	96	....	....	....	....	....	....	....	....	....	....	4	0	1	1	2	....	....	....
	Edmonton Oilers	**NHL**	**2**	**1**	**1**	**2**	**1**	**1**	**2**	**2**	**0**	**0**	**0**	**2**	**50.0**	**4**	**0**	**0**	**0**	**4**	....	....	....	....	....	....	....	....
1984-85	Nova Scotia Voyageurs	AHL	41	0	4	4	....	....	....	107	....	....	....	....	....	....	....	....	....	....	....	....	....	....	....	....	....	....
1985-86	Nova Scotia Oilers	AHL	73	2	12	14	....	....	....	160	....	....	....	....	....	....	....	....	....	....	....	....	....	....	....	....	....	....
1986-87	Nova Scotia Oilers	AHL	60	1	21	22	....	....	....	82	....	....	....	....	....	....	....	....	....	....	....	....	....	....	....	....	....	....
1987-88	**Chicago Blackhawks**	**NHL**	**12**	**1**	**3**	**4**	**1**	**2**	**3**	**21**	**1**	**0**	**0**	**11**	**9.1**	**14**	**2**	**8**	**0**	**4**	....	....	....	....	....	....	....	....
	Saginaw Hawks	IHL	50	5	21	26	....	....	....	133	....	....	....	....	....	....	....	....	....	....	....	....	....	....	....	....	....	....
1988-89	**Chicago Blackhawks**	**NHL**	**7**	**0**	**0**	**0**	**0**	**0**	**0**	**28**	**0**	**0**	**0**	**1**	**0.0**	**2**	**0**	**1**	**0**	**1**	....	....	....	....	....	....	....	....
	Saginaw Hawks	IHL	23	3	6	9	....	....	....	73	....	....	....	....	....	....	....	....	....	....	6	0	2	2	20	....	....	....
1989-90	Indianapolis Ice	IHL	67	7	24	31	....	....	....	137	....	....	....	....	....	....	....	....	....	....	14	1	5	6	24	....	....	....
1990-91	Indianapolis Ice	IHL	23	3	4	7	....	....	....	31	....	....	....	....	....	....	....	....	....	....	....	....	....	....	....	....	....	....
1991-92	Indianapolis Ice	IHL	23	1	1	2	....	....	....	53	....	....	....	....	....	....	....	....	....	....	....	....	....	....	....	....	....	....
1992-1993	Indianapolis Ice	IHL	DID NOT PLAY – ASSISTANT COACH																									
1993-1996	Dayton Bombers	ECHL	DID NOT PLAY – COACHING																									
1996-1999	Michigan K-Wings	IHL	DID NOT PLAY – ASSISTANT COACH																									
1999-2000	Michigan K-Wings	IHL	DID NOT PLAY – ASSISTANT COACH																									
	Michigan K-Wings	IHL	DID NOT PLAY – COACHING																									
	NHL Totals		**21**	**2**	**4**	**6**	**2**	**3**	**5**	**51**	**1**	**0**	**0**	**14**	**14.3**	**20**	**2**	**9**	**0**		....	....	....	....	....	....	....	....

• Brother of Larry

Signed as a free agent by **Chicago**, July 31, 1987. • Named Head Coach of **Michigan** (IHL), January 24, 2000.

• PLAYFAIR, Larry

Larry William D – L. 6'4", 205 lbs. b: Fort St. James, B.C., 6/23/1958. Buffalo's 1st, 13th overall, in 1978.

Season	Club	League	GP	G	A	Pts	AG	AA	APts	PIM	PP	SH	GW	S	%	TGF	PGF	TGA	PGA	+/–	GP	G	A	Pts	PIM	PP	SH	GW
1974-75	Langely Lords	BCJHL	STATISTICS NOT AVAILABLE																									
	Kamloops Blazers	WCJHL	1	0	0	0	....	....	....	0	....	....	....	....	....	....	....	....	....	....	....	....	....	....	....	....	....	....
1975-76	Langley Lords	BCJHL	72	10	20	30	....	....	....	162	....	....	....	....	....	....	....	....	....	....	....	....	....	....	....	....	....	....
	Kamloops Blazers	WCJHL	3	0	0	0	....	....	....	0	....	....	....	....	....	....	....	....	....	....	....	....	....	....	....	....	....	....
1976-77	Portland Winter Hawks	WCJHL	65	2	17	19	....	....	....	199	....	....	....	....	....	....	....	....	....	....	8	0	0	0	4	....	....	....
1977-78	Portland Winter Hawks	WCJHL	71	13	19	32	....	....	....	402	....	....	....	....	....	....	....	....	....	....	8	0	2	2	58	....	....	....
1978-79	**Buffalo Sabres**	**NHL**	**26**	**0**	**3**	**3**	**0**	**2**	**2**	**60**	**0**	**0**	**0**	**12**	**0.0**	**18**	**1**	**17**	**1**	**1**	....	....	....	....	....	....	....	....
	Hershey Bears	AHL	45	0	12	12	....	....	....	148	....	....	....	....	....	....	....	....	....	....	....	....	....	....	....	....	....	....
1979-80	**Buffalo Sabres**	**NHL**	**79**	**2**	**10**	**12**	**2**	**7**	**9**	**145**	**0**	**0**	**0**	**32**	**6.3**	**50**	**0**	**38**	**1**	**13**	**14**	**0**	**2**	**2**	**29**	**0**	**0**	**0**
1980-81	**Buffalo Sabres**	**NHL**	**75**	**3**	**9**	**12**	**2**	**6**	**8**	**169**	**0**	**0**	**1**	**54**	**5.6**	**59**	**0**	**56**	**1**	**4**	**8**	**0**	**0**	**0**	**26**	**0**	**0**	**0**
1981-82	**Buffalo Sabres**	**NHL**	**77**	**6**	**10**	**16**	**5**	**7**	**12**	**258**	**0**	**0**	**0**	**68**	**8.8**	**62**	**0**	**79**	**12**	**–5**	**4**	**0**	**0**	**0**	**22**	**0**	**0**	**0**
1982-83	**Buffalo Sabres**	**NHL**	**79**	**4**	**13**	**17**	**3**	**9**	**12**	**180**	**0**	**0**	**0**	**75**	**5.3**	**79**	**2**	**91**	**19**	**5**	**5**	**0**	**1**	**1**	**11**	**0**	**0**	**0**
1983-84	**Buffalo Sabres**	**NHL**	**76**	**5**	**11**	**16**	**4**	**7**	**11**	**211**	**0**	**0**	**0**	**67**	**7.5**	**67**	**5**	**72**	**14**	**4**	**3**	**0**	**0**	**0**	**0**	**0**	**0**	**0**
1984-85	**Buffalo Sabres**	**NHL**	**72**	**3**	**14**	**17**	**2**	**10**	**12**	**157**	**0**	**0**	**1**	**64**	**4.7**	**48**	**0**	**59**	**8**	**–3**	**5**	**0**	**3**	**3**	**9**	**0**	**0**	**0**
1985-86	**Buffalo Sabres**	**NHL**	**47**	**1**	**2**	**3**	**1**	**1**	**2**	**100**	**0**	**0**	**0**	**35**	**2.9**	**29**	**0**	**49**	**12**	**–8**	....	....	....	....	....	....	....	....
	Los Angeles Kings	**NHL**	**14**	**0**	**1**	**1**	**0**	**1**	**1**	**26**	**0**	**0**	**0**	**6**	**0.0**	**10**	**1**	**30**	**7**	**–14**	....	....	....	....	....	....	....	....
1986-87	**Los Angeles Kings**	**NHL**	**37**	**2**	**7**	**9**	**2**	**5**	**7**	**181**	**0**	**0**	**0**	**20**	**10.0**	**33**	**0**	**39**	**5**	**–1**	....	....	....	....	....	....	....	....
1987-88	**Los Angeles Kings**	**NHL**	**54**	**0**	**7**	**7**	**0**	**5**	**5**	**197**	**0**	**0**	**0**	**20**	**0.0**	**34**	**0**	**52**	**5**	**–13**	**3**	**0**	**0**	**0**	**14**	**0**	**0**	**0**
1988-89	**Los Angeles Kings**	**NHL**	**6**	**0**	**3**	**3**	**0**	**2**	**2**	**16**	**0**	**0**	**0**	**4**	**0.0**	**5**	**0**	**2**	**0**	**3**	....	....	....	....	....	....	....	....
	Buffalo Sabres	**NHL**	**42**	**0**	**3**	**3**	**0**	**2**	**2**	**110**	**0**	**0**	**0**	**6**	**0.0**	**17**	**0**	**32**	**5**	**–10**	**1**	**0**	**0**	**0**	**0**	**0**	**0**	**0**
1989-90	**Buffalo Sabres**	**NHL**	**4**	**0**	**1**	**1**	**0**	**1**	**1**	**2**	**0**	**0**	**0**	**0**	**0.0**	**1**	**0**	**3**	**0**	**–2**	....	....	....	....	....	....	....	....
	NHL Totals		**688**	**26**	**94**	**120**	**21**	**65**	**86**	**1812**	**0**	**0**	**2**	**463**	**5.6**	**512**	**9**	**619**	**90**		**43**	**0**	**6**	**6**	**111**	**0**	**0**	**0**

• Brother of Jim • WCJHL All-Star Team (1978)

Traded to **LA Kings** by **Buffalo** with Sean McKenna and Ken Baumgartner for Brian Engblom and Doug Smith, Januray 30, 1986. Traded to **Buffalo** by **LA Kings** for Bob Logan and Buffalo's 9th round choice (Jim Glacin) in 1989 Entry Draft, Ocotber 21, 1988.

• PLEAU, Larry

Lawrence Winslow C – L. 6'1", 190 lbs. b: Lynn, MA, 1/29/1947.

Season	Club	League	GP	G	A	Pts	AG	AA	APts	PIM	PP	SH	GW	S	%	TGF	PGF	TGA	PGA	+/–	GP	G	A	Pts	PIM	PP	SH	GW
1963-64	Notre Dame Monarchs	MMJHL	44	8	22	30	....	....	....	33	....	....	....	....	....	....	....	....	....	....	18	5	10	15	12	....	....	....
	Notre Dame Monarchs	Mem-Cup	13	4	10	14	....	....	....	14	....	....	....	....	....	....	....	....	....	....	....	....	....	....	....	....	....	....
1964-65	Montreal Jr. Canadiens	OHA-Jr.	55	9	17	26	....	....	....	24	....	....	....	....	....	....	....	....	....	....	7	0	0	0	10	....	....	....
1965-66	Montreal Jr. Canadiens	OHA-Jr.	40	13	11	24	....	....	....	47	....	....	....	....	....	....	....	....	....	....	10	0	6	6	6	....	....	....
1966-67	Montreal Jr. Canadiens	OHA-Jr.	45	20	32	52	....	....	....	34	....	....	....	....	....	....	....	....	....	....	4	0	2	2	2	....	....	....
1967-68	United States	Nat-Team	STATISTICS NOT AVAILABLE																									
	United States	Olympics	7	2	4	6	....	....	....	2	....	....	....	....	....	....	....	....	....	....	....	....	....	....	....	....	....	....
1968-69	Jersey Devils	EHL	66	37	44	81	....	....	....	53	....	....	....	....	....	....	....	....	....	....	....	....	....	....	....	....	....	....
	United States	WEC-A	10	5	0	5	....	....	....	8	....	....	....	....	....	....	....	....	....	....	....	....	....	....	....	....	....	....
1969-70	**Montreal Canadiens**	**NHL**	**20**	**1**	**0**	**1**	**1**	**0**	**1**	**0**	**0**	**1**	**0**	**19**	**5.3**	**3**	**0**	**12**	**8**	**–1**	....	....	....	....	....	....	....	....
	Montreal Voyageurs	AHL	50	15	16	31	....	....	....	19	....	....	....	....	....	....	....	....	....	....	....	....	....	....	....	....	....	....
1970-71	**Montreal Canadiens**	**NHL**	**19**	**1**	**5**	**6**	**1**	**4**	**5**	**8**	**0**	**0**	**1**	**24**	**4.2**	**7**	**0**	**24**	**9**	**–8**	....	....	....	....	....	....	....	....
1971-72	**Montreal Canadiens**	**NHL**	**55**	**7**	**10**	**17**	**7**	**9**	**16**	**19**	**0**	**0**	**2**	**67**	**10.4**	**25**	**0**	**25**	**4**	**4**	**4**	**0**	**0**	**0**	**0**	**0**	**0**	**0**
	Nova Scotia Voyageurs	AHL	11	7	6	13	....	....	....	19	....	....	....	....	....	....	....	....	....	....	....	....	....	....	....	....	....	....
1972-73	New England Whalers	WHA	78	39	48	87	....	....	....	42	....	....	....	....	....	....	....	....	....	....	15	12	7	19	15	....	....	....
1973-74	New England Whalers	WHA	77	26	43	69	....	....	....	35	....	....	....	....	....	....	....	....	....	....	2	2	0	2	0	....	....	....
1974-75	New England Whalers	WHA	78	30	34	64	....	....	....	50	....	....	....	....	....	....	....	....	....	....	6	2	3	5	14	....	....	....
1975-76	New England Whalers	WHA	75	29	45	74	....	....	....	21	....	....	....	....	....	....	....	....	....	....	14	5	7	12	0	....	....	....
1976-77	New England Whalers	WHA	78	11	21	32	....	....	....	22	....	....	....	....	....	....	....	....	....	....	5	1	0	1	0	....	....	....
1977-78	New England Whalers	WHA	54	16	18	34	....	....	....	4	....	....	....	....	....	....	....	....	....	....	14	5	4	9	8	....	....	....
1978-79	New England Whalers	WHA	28	6	6	12	....	....	....	6	....	....	....	....	....	....	....	....	....	....	10	2	1	3	0	....	....	....
	Springfield Indians	AHL	5	1	3	4	....	....	....	0	....	....	....	....	....	....	....	....	....	....	....	....	....	....	....	....	....	....
	NHL Totals		**94**	**9**	**15**	**24**	**9**	**13**	**22**	**27**	**0**	**1**	**3**	**110**	**8.2**	**35**	**0**	**61**	**21**		**4**	**0**	**0**	**0**	**0**	**0**	**0**	**0**
	Other Major League Totals		468	157	215	372	....	....	....	180	....	....	....	....	....	....	....	....	....	....	66	29	22	51	37	....	....	....

EHL North Rookie of the Year (1969)

Selected by **New England** (WHA) in 1972 WHA General Player Draft, February 12, 1972. Claimed by **Toronto** from **Montreal** in Intra-League Draft, June 5, 1972.

• PLETT, Willi

RW – R. 6'3", 205 lbs. b: Asuncion, Paraguay, 6/7/1955. Atlanta's 4th, 80th overall, in 1975.

Season	Club	League	GP	G	A	Pts	AG	AA	APts	PIM	PP	SH	GW	S	%	TGF	PGF	TGA	PGA	+/–	GP	G	A	Pts	PIM	PP	SH	GW
			REGULAR SEASON																		PLAYOFFS							
1974-75	Niagara Falls Flyers	OJHL	STATISTICS NOT AVAILABLE																									
	St. Catharines Black Hawks	OMJHL	22	6	8	14	....	....	....	63	....	....	....	....	....	....	....	....	....	....	4	1	1	2	42	....	....	....
1975-76	**Atlanta Flames**	**NHL**	**4**	**0**	**0**	**0**	**0**	**0**	**0**	**0**	**0**	**0**	**0**	**5**	**0.0**	**1**	**0**	**1**	**0**	**0**	....	....	....	....	....	....	....	....
	Tulsa Oilers	CHL	73	30	20	50	....	....	....	163	....	....	....	....	....	....	....	....	....	....	9	*5	4	9	21	....	....	....
1976-77	**Atlanta Flames**	**NHL**	**64**	**33**	**23**	**56**	**30**	**18**	**48**	**123**	**5**	**0**	**6**	**156**	**21.2**	**91**	**22**	**54**	**0**	**15**	**3**	**1**	**0**	**1**	**19**	**0**	**0**	**0**
	Tulsa Oilers	CHL	14	8	4	12	....	....	....	68	....	....	....	....	....	....	....	....	....	....	....	....	....	....	....	....	....	....
1977-78	**Atlanta Flames**	**NHL**	**78**	**22**	**21**	**43**	**20**	**16**	**36**	**171**	**2**	**0**	**3**	**191**	**11.5**	**82**	**14**	**74**	**0**	**–6**	....	....	....	....	....	....	....	....
1978-79	**Atlanta Flames**	**NHL**	**74**	**23**	**20**	**43**	**20**	**14**	**34**	**213**	**0**	**0**	**4**	**164**	**14.0**	**78**	**6**	**59**	**0**	**13**	**2**	**1**	**0**	**1**	**29**	**0**	**0**	**0**
1979-80	**Atlanta Flames**	**NHL**	**76**	**13**	**19**	**32**	**11**	**14**	**25**	**231**	**0**	**0**	**2**	**119**	**10.9**	**56**	**1**	**59**	**0**	**–4**	**4**	**1**	**0**	**1**	**15**	**1**	**0**	**0**
1980-81	**Calgary Flames**	**NHL**	**78**	**38**	**30**	**68**	**30**	**20**	**50**	**239**	**8**	**0**	**4**	**159**	**23.9**	**121**	**44**	**72**	**0**	**5**	**15**	**8**	**4**	**12**	**89**	**5**	**0**	**3**
1981-82	**Calgary Flames**	**NHL**	**78**	**21**	**36**	**57**	**17**	**24**	**41**	**288**	**5**	**0**	**2**	**152**	**13.8**	**112**	**37**	**97**	**0**	**–22**	**3**	**1**	**2**	**3**	**39**	**1**	**0**	**0**
1982-83	**Minnesota North Stars**	**NHL**	**71**	**25**	**14**	**39**	**20**	**10**	**30**	**170**	**8**	**0**	**3**	**125**	**20.0**	**72**	**27**	**57**	**0**	**–12**	**9**	**1**	**3**	**4**	**38**	**0**	**0**	**0**
1983-84	**Minnesota North Stars**	**NHL**	**73**	**15**	**23**	**38**	**12**	**16**	**28**	**316**	**1**	**0**	**1**	**103**	**14.6**	**65**	**4**	**68**	**1**	**–6**	**16**	**6**	**2**	**8**	**51**	**1**	**0**	**0**
1984-85	**Minnesota North Stars**	**NHL**	**47**	**14**	**14**	**28**	**11**	**10**	**21**	**157**	**1**	**0**	**1**	**83**	**16.9**	**43**	**11**	**28**	**0**	**4**	**9**	**3**	**6**	**9**	**67**	**1**	**0**	**0**
1985-86	**Minnesota North Stars**	**NHL**	**59**	**10**	**7**	**17**	**8**	**5**	**13**	**231**	**4**	**0**	**0**	**72**	**13.9**	**28**	**8**	**41**	**1**	**–20**	**5**	**0**	**1**	**1**	**45**	**0**	**0**	**0**
1986-87	**Minnesota North Stars**	**NHL**	**67**	**6**	**5**	**11**	**5**	**4**	**9**	**263**	**0**	**0**	**1**	**50**	**12.0**	**22**	**2**	**20**	**1**	**1**	....	....	....	....	....	....	....	....
1987-88	**Boston Bruins**	**NHL**	**65**	**2**	**3**	**5**	**2**	**2**	**4**	**170**	**1**	**0**	**0**	**29**	**6.9**	**14**	**2**	**22**	**0**	**–10**	**17**	**2**	**4**	**6**	**74**	**0**	**0**	**1**
	NHL Totals		**834**	**222**	**215**	**437**	**186**	**153**	**339**	**2572**	**35**	**0**	**27**	**1408**	**15.8**	**785**	**178**	**652**	**3**		**83**	**24**	**22**	**46**	**466**	**9**	**0**	**4**

Won Calder Memorial Trophy (1977)

Transferred to **Calgary** after **Atlanta** franchise relocated, June 24, 1980. Traded to **Minnesota** by **Calgary** with Calgary's 4th round choice (Dusan Pasek) in 1982 Entry Draft for Steve Christoff, Bill Nyrop and St. Louis' 2nd round choice (previously acquired, Calgary selected Dave Reierson) in 1982 Entry Draft, June 7, 1982. Traded to **NY Rangers** by **Minnesota** for Pat Price, September 8, 1987. Claimed by **Boston** from **NY Rangers** in Waiver Draft, October 5, 1987.

• PLUMB, Rob

Robert Edwin LW – L. 5'8", 166 lbs. b: Kingston, Ont., 8/29/1957. Detroit's 10th, 163rd overall, in 1977.

Season	Club	League	GP	G	A	Pts	AG	AA	APts	PIM	PP	SH	GW	S	%	TGF	PGF	TGA	PGA	+/–	GP	G	A	Pts	PIM	PP	SH	GW
1974-75	Kingston Canadians	OMJHL	58	9	16	25	....	....	....	41	....	....	....	....	....	....	....	....	....	....	8	2	4	6	9	....	....	....
1975-76	Kingston Canadians	OMJHL	26	6	5	11	....	....	....	20	....	....	....	....	....	....	....	....	....	....	4	0	0	0	12	....	....	....
1976-77	Kingston Canadians	OMJHL	64	20	31	51	....	....	....	73	....	....	....	....	....	....	....	....	....	....	13	8	4	12	18	....	....	....
1977-78	**Detroit Red Wings**	**NHL**	**7**	**2**	**1**	**3**	**2**	**1**	**3**	**0**	**1**	**0**	**0**	**7**	**28.6**	**4**	**2**	**7**	**1**	**–4**	....	....	....	....	....	....	....	....
	Kansas City Red Wings	CHL	55	18	11	29	....	....	....	34	....	....	....	....	....	....	....	....	....	....	....	....	....	....	....	....	....	....
1978-79	**Detroit Red Wings**	**NHL**	**7**	**1**	**1**	**2**	**1**	**1**	**2**	**2**	**0**	**0**	**0**	**4**	**25.0**	**4**	**1**	**4**	**0**	**–1**	....	....	....	....	....	....	....	....
	Kansas City Red Wings	CHL	44	17	20	37	....	....	....	16	....	....	....	....	....	....	....	....	....	....	4	0	0	0	0	....	....	....
1979-80	Adirondack Red Wings	AHL	18	1	2	3	....	....	....	8	....	....	....	....	....	....	....	....	....	....	....	....	....	....	....	....	....	....
	Kalamazoo Wings	IHL	56	24	44	68	....	....	....	39	....	....	....	....	....	....	....	....	....	....	13	4	4	8	24	....	....	....
1980-81	Kalamazoo Wings	IHL	82	54	55	109	....	....	....	70	....	....	....	....	....	....	....	....	....	....	8	3	1	4	4	....	....	....
1981-82	EHC Dubendorfer	Switz-2	38	52	33	*85	....	....	....	....	....	....	....	....	....	....	....	....	....	....	....	....	....	....	....	....	....	....
1982-83	EHC Dubendorfer	Switz-2	38	37	39	76	....	....	....	....	....	....	....	....	....	....	....	....	....	....	....	....	....	....	....	....	....	....
1983-84	EHC Dubendorfer	Switz-2	38	43	38	81	....	....	....	....	....	....	....	....	....	....	....	....	....	....	....	....	....	....	....	....	....	....
1984-85	EHC Dubendorfer	Switz-2	38	45	*60	105	....	....	....	....	....	....	....	....	....	....	....	....	....	....	....	....	....	....	....	....	....	....
1985-86	ZSC Zurich	Switz.	35	19	20	39	....	....	....	....	....	....	....	....	....	....	....	....	....	....	....	....	....	....	....	....	....	....
1986-87	EHC Uzwil	Switz-3	STATISTICS NOT AVAILABLE																									
1987-88	EHC Uzwil	Switz-2	38	22	13	35	....	....	....	....	....	....	....	....	....	....	....	....	....	....	....	....	....	....	....	....	....	....
	NHL Totals		**14**	**3**	**2**	**5**	**3**	**2**	**5**	**2**	**1**	**0**	**0**	**11**	**27.3**	**8**	**3**	**11**	**1**		....	....	....	....	....	....	....	....

• Brother of Ron • IHL Second All-Star Team (1981)

• PLUMB, Ron

Ronald William D – L. 5'10", 175 lbs. b: Kingston, Ont., 7/17/1950. Boston's 3rd, 9th overall, in 1970.

Season	Club	League	GP	G	A	Pts	AG	AA	APts	PIM	PP	SH	GW	S	%	TGF	PGF	TGA	PGA	+/–	GP	G	A	Pts	PIM	PP	SH	GW
1967-68	Peterborough Petes	OHA-Jr.	47	3	19	22	....	....	....	38	....	....	....	....	....	....	....	....	....	....	5	0	2	2	7	....	....	....
1968-69	Peterborough Petes	OHA-Jr.	53	4	10	14	....	....	....	57	....	....	....	....	....	....	....	....	....	....	10	2	1	3	19	....	....	....
1969-70	Peterborough Petes	OHA-Jr.	54	16	29	45	....	....	....	77	....	....	....	....	....	....	....	....	....	....	6	2	3	5	19	....	....	....
1970-71	Oklahoma City Blazers	CHL	72	3	19	22	....	....	....	73	....	....	....	....	....	....	....	....	....	....	5	0	0	0	12	....	....	....
1971-72	Oklahoma City Blazers	CHL	72	10	42	52	....	....	....	90	....	....	....	....	....	....	....	....	....	....	6	1	2	3	8	....	....	....
1972-73	Philadelphia Blazers	WHA	78	10	41	51	....	....	....	66	....	....	....	....	....	....	....	....	....	....	4	0	2	2	13	....	....	....
1973-74	Vancouver Blazers	WHA	75	6	32	38	....	....	....	40	....	....	....	....	....	....	....	....	....	....	....	....	....	....	....	....	....	....
1974-75	San Diego Mariners	WHA	78	10	38	48	....	....	....	56	....	....	....	....	....	....	....	....	....	....	10	2	3	5	19	....	....	....
1975-76	Cincinnati Stingers	WHA	80	10	36	46	....	....	....	31	....	....	....	....	....	....	....	....	....	....	....	....	....	....	....	....	....	....
1976-77	Cincinnati Stingers	WHA	79	11	58	69	....	....	....	52	....	....	....	....	....	....	....	....	....	....	4	1	2	3	0	....	....	....
1977-78	Cincinnati Stingers	WHA	54	13	34	47	....	....	....	45	....	....	....	....	....	....	....	....	....	....	....	....	....	....	....	....	....	....
	New England Whalers	WHA	27	1	9	10	....	....	....	18	....	....	....	....	....	....	....	....	....	....	14	1	5	6	16	....	....	....
1978-79	New England Whalers	WHA	78	4	16	20	....	....	....	33	....	....	....	....	....	....	....	....	....	....	9	1	3	4	0	....	....	....
1979-80	**Hartford Whalers**	**NHL**	**26**	**3**	**4**	**7**	**3**	**3**	**6**	**14**	**0**	**0**	**0**	**38**	**7.9**	**35**	**1**	**26**	**2**	**10**	....	....	....	....	....	....	....	....
	Springfield Indians	AHL	52	2	20	22	....	....	....	42	....	....	....	....	....	....	....	....	....	....	....	....	....	....	....	....	....	....
1980-81	Springfield Indians	AHL	79	11	51	62	....	....	....	150	....	....	....	....	....	....	....	....	....	....	7	3	6	9	8	....	....	....
1981-82	Springfield Indians	AHL	80	4	31	35	....	....	....	56	....	....	....	....	....	....	....	....	....	....	....	....	....	....	....	....	....	....
1982-83	Fife Flyers	Scotland	PLAYER/COACH – STATISTICS UNAVAILABLE																									
1983-84	Fife Flyers	Scotland	PLAYER/COACH – STATISTICS UNAVAILABLE																									
1984-85	Fife Flyers	Britain	36	26	54	80	....	....	....	88	....	....	....	....	....	....	....	....	....	....	6	3	15	18	10	....	....	....
1985-86	Fife Flyers	Britain	36	20	51	71	....	....	....	76	....	....	....	....	....	....	....	....	....	....	5	0	4	4	8	....	....	....
	NHL Totals		**26**	**3**	**4**	**7**	**3**	**3**	**6**	**14**	**0**	**0**	**0**	**38**	**7.9**	**35**	**1**	**26**	**2**		....	....	....	....	....	....	....	....
	Other Major League Totals		549	65	264	329				341											41	5	15	20	48			

• Brother of Rob • OHA-Jr. First All-Star Team (1970) • CHL First All-Star Team (1972) • WHA First All-Star Team (1977) • Won Dennis A. Murphy Trophy (WHA Top Defenseman) (1977)

Selected by **Miami-Philadelphia** (WHA) in 1972 WHA General Player Draft, February 12, 1972. Transferred to **Vancouver** (WHA) after **Philadelphia** (WHA) franchise relocated, May, 1973. Traded to **Cincinnati** (WHA) by **Vancouver** (WHA) for future considerations, August, 1974. Loaned to **San Diego** (WHA) by **Cincinnati** (WHA) for 1974-75 season, August, 1974. Traded to **New England** (WHA) by **Cincinnati** (WHA) for Greg Carroll, February, 1978. Rights retained by **Hartford** prior to Expansion Draft, June 9, 1979.

• POAPST, Steve

Steve Ray D – L. 6', 200 lbs. b: Cornwall, Ont., 1/3/1969.

Season	Club	League	GP	G	A	Pts	AG	AA	APts	PIM	PP	SH	GW	S	%	TGF	PGF	TGA	PGA	+/–	GP	G	A	Pts	PIM	PP	SH	GW
1986-87	Smith Falls Bears	OJHL	54	10	27	37	....	....	....	94	....	....	....	....	....	....	....	....	....	....	....	....	....	....	....	....	....	....
1987-88	Colgate University	ECAC	32	3	13	16	....	....	....	22	....	....	....	....	....	....	....	....	....	....	....	....	....	....	....	....	....	....
1988-89	Colgate University	ECAC	30	0	5	5	....	....	....	38	....	....	....	....	....	....	....	....	....	....	....	....	....	....	....	....	....	....
1989-90	Colgate University	ECAC	38	4	15	19	....	....	....	54	....	....	....	....	....	....	....	....	....	....	....	....	....	....	....	....	....	....
1990-91	Colgate University	ECAC	32	6	15	21	....	....	....	43	....	....	....	....	....	....	....	....	....	....	....	....	....	....	....	....	....	....
1991-92	Hampton Roads Admirals	ECHL	55	8	20	28	....	....	....	29	....	....	....	....	....	....	....	....	....	....	14	1	4	5	12	....	....	....
1992-93	Hampton Roads Admirals	ECHL	63	10	35	45	....	....	....	57	....	....	....	....	....	....	....	....	....	....	4	0	1	1	4	....	....	....
	Baltimore Skipjacks	AHL	7	0	1	1	....	....	....	4	....	....	....	....	....	....	....	....	....	....	7	0	3	3	6	....	....	....
1993-94	Portland Pirates	AHL	78	14	21	35	....	....	....	47	....	....	....	....	....	....	....	....	....	....	12	0	3	3	8	....	....	....
1994-95	Portland Pirates	AHL	71	8	22	30	....	....	....	60	....	....	....	....	....	....	....	....	....	....	7	0	1	1	16	....	....	....
1995-96	**Washington Capitals**	**NHL**	**3**	**1**	**0**	**1**	**1**	**0**	**1**	**0**	**0**	**0**	**1**	**2**	**50.0**	**1**	**0**	**2**	**0**	**–1**	**6**	**0**	**0**	**0**	**0**	**0**	**0**	**0**
	Portland Pirates	AHL	70	10	24	34	....	....	....	79	....	....	....	....	....	....	....	....	....	....	20	2	6	8	16	....	....	....
1996-97	Portland Pirates	AHL	47	1	20	21	....	....	....	34	....	....	....	....	....	....	....	....	....	....	5	0	1	1	6	....	....	....
1997-98	Portland Pirates	AHL	76	8	29	37	....	....	....	46	....	....	....	....	....	....	....	....	....	....	10	2	3	5	8	....	....	....
1998-99	**Washington Capitals**	**NHL**	**22**	**0**	**0**	**0**	**0**	**0**	**0**	**8**	**0**	**0**	**0**	**11**	**0.0**	**3**	**0**	**14**	**3**	**–8**	....	....	....	....	....	....	....	....
	Portland Pirates	AHL	54	3	21	24	....	....	....	36	....	....	....	....	....	....	....	....	....	....	....	....	....	....	....	....	....	....
99-2000	Portland Pirates	AHL	58	0	14	14	....	....	....	20	....	....	....	....	....	....	....	....	....	....	3	1	0	1	2	....	....	....
	NHL Totals		**25**	**1**	**0**	**1**	**1**	**0**	**1**	**8**	**0**	**0**	**1**	**13**	**7.7**	**4**	**0**	**16**	**3**		**6**	**0**	**0**	**0**	**0**	**0**	**0**	**0**

ECHL First All-Star Team (1993)

Signed as a free agent by **Washington**, February 4, 1995. • Played w/ RHI's New England Stingers in 1994 (20-6-23-29-47).

• POCZA, Harvie

Harvie Dwight LW – L. 6'2", 200 lbs. b: Lethbridge, Alta., 9/22/1959. Washington's 3rd, 67th overall, in 1979.

Season	Club	League	GP	G	A	Pts	AG	AA	APts	PIM	PP	SH	GW	S	%	TGF	PGF	TGA	PGA	+/–	GP	G	A	Pts	PIM	PP	SH	GW
			REGULAR SEASON																		PLAYOFFS							
1975-76	Lethbridge Y's Men	AAHA	STATISTICS NOT AVAILABLE																									
	The Pas Blue Devils	AJHL	5	1	1	2	....	....	....	0	....	....	....	....	....	....	....	....	....	....	....	....	....	....	....	....	....	....
1976-77	Pincher Creek Panthers	AJHL	57	23	36	59	....	....	....	187	....	....	....	....	....	....	....	....	....	....	....	....	....	....	....	....	....	....
	Calgary Centennials	WCJHL	10	4	5	9	....	....	....	9	....	....	....	....	....	....	....	....	....	....	....	....	....	....	....	....	....	....
1977-78	Billings Bighorns	WCJHL	71	34	32	66	....	....	....	168	....	....	....	....	....	....	....	....	....	....	19	9	11	20	60	....	....	....
1978-79	Billings Bighorns	WHL	72	42	55	97	....	....	....	151	....	....	....	....	....	....	....	....	....	....	8	1	4	5	8	....	....	....
1979-80	**Washington Capitals**	**NHL**	**1**	**0**	**0**	**0**	**0**	**0**	**0**	**0**	**0**	**0**	**0**	**2**	**0.0**	**0**	**0**	**0**	**0**	**0**	....	....	....	....	....	....	....	....
	Port Huron Flags	IHL	13	9	7	16	....	....	....	11	....	....	....	....	....	....	....	....	....	....	....	....	....	....	....	....	....	....
	Hershey Bears	AHL	59	13	12	25	....	....	....	28	....	....	....	....	....	....	....	....	....	....	8	4	3	7	22	....	....	....
1980-81	Hershey Bears	AHL	78	27	18	45	....	....	....	108	....	....	....	....	....	....	....	....	....	....	10	10	2	12	21	....	....	....
1981-82	**Washington Capitals**	**NHL**	**2**	**0**	**0**	**0**	**0**	**0**	**0**	**2**	**0**	**0**	**0**	**1**	**0.0**	**1**	**0**	**3**	**0**	**–2**	....	....	....	....	....	....	....	....
	Hershey Bears	AHL	61	29	23	52	....	....	....	116	....	....	....	....	....	....	....	....	....	....	5	1	1	2	0	....	....	....
1982-83	Hershey Bears	AHL	77	13	29	42	....	....	....	85	....	....	....	....	....	....	....	....	....	....	5	1	2	3	9	....	....	....
	NHL Totals		**3**	**0**	**0**	**0**	**0**	**0**	**0**	**2**	**0**	**0**	**0**	**3**	**0.0**	**1**	**0**	**3**	**0**		....	....	....	....	....	....	....	....

• PODDUBNY, Walt

Walter Michael LW – L. 6'1", 210 lbs. b: Thunder Bay, Ont., 2/14/1960. Edmonton's 4th, 90th overall, in 1980.

Season	Club	League	GP	G	A	Pts	AG	AA	APts	PIM	PP	SH	GW	S	%	TGF	PGF	TGA	PGA	+/–	GP	G	A	Pts	PIM	PP	SH	GW
1978-79	Thunder Bay Kings	TBAHA	STATISTICS NOT AVAILABLE																									
	Brandon Wheat Kings	WHL	20	11	11	22	....	....	....	12	....	....	....	....	....	....	....	....	....	....	....	....	....	....	....	....	....	....
1979-80	Kitchener Rangers	OMJHL	19	3	9	12	....	....	....	35	....	....	....	....	....	....	....	....	....	....	....	....	....	....	....	....	....	....
	Kingston Canadians	OMJHL	43	30	17	47	....	....	....	36	....	....	....	....	....	....	....	....	....	....	3	0	2	2	0	....	....	....
1980-81	Milwaukee Admirals	IHL	5	4	2	6	....	....	....	4	....	....	....	....	....	....	....	....	....	....	....	....	....	....	....	....	....	....
	Wichita Wind	CHL	70	21	29	50	....	....	....	207	....	....	....	....	....	....	....	....	....	....	11	1	6	7	26	....	....	....
1981-82	**Edmonton Oilers**	**NHL**	**4**	**0**	**0**	**0**	**0**	**0**	**0**	**0**	**0**	**0**	**0**	**2**	**0.0**	**0**	**0**	**1**	**0**	**–1**	....	....	....	....	....	....	....	....
	Wichita Wind	CHL	60	35	46	81	....	....	....	79	....	....	....	....	....	....	....	....	....	....	....	....	....	....	....	....	....	....
	Toronto Maple Leafs	**NHL**	**11**	**3**	**4**	**7**	**2**	**3**	**5**	**8**	**1**	**0**	**0**	**22**	**13.6**	**13**	**4**	**10**	**1**	**0**	....	....	....	....	....	....	....	....
1982-83	**Toronto Maple Leafs**	**NHL**	**72**	**28**	**31**	**59**	**23**	**21**	**44**	**71**	**9**	**0**	**3**	**163**	**17.2**	**76**	**16**	**52**	**0**	**8**	**4**	**3**	**1**	**4**	**0**	**2**	**0**	**1**
1983-84	**Toronto Maple Leafs**	**NHL**	**38**	**11**	**14**	**25**	**9**	**10**	**19**	**48**	**4**	**0**	**0**	**77**	**14.3**	**32**	**10**	**35**	**0**	**–13**	....	....	....	....	....	....	....	....
1984-85	**Toronto Maple Leafs**	**NHL**	**32**	**5**	**15**	**20**	**4**	**10**	**14**	**26**	**1**	**0**	**0**	**51**	**9.8**	**26**	**5**	**20**	**0**	**1**	....	....	....	....	....	....	....	....
	St. Catharines Saints	AHL	8	5	7	12	....	....	....	10	....	....	....	....	....	....	....	....	....	....	....	....	....	....	....	....	....	....
1985-86	**Toronto Maple Leafs**	**NHL**	**33**	**12**	**22**	**34**	**10**	**15**	**25**	**25**	**5**	**0**	**1**	**76**	**15.8**	**43**	**16**	**21**	**0**	**6**	**9**	**4**	**1**	**5**	**4**	**0**	**0**	**3**
	St. Catharines Saints	AHL	37	28	27	55	....	....	....	52	....	....	....	....	....	....	....	....	....	....	....	....	....	....	....	....	....	....
1986-87	**New York Rangers**	**NHL**	**75**	**40**	**47**	**87**	**35**	**34**	**69**	**49**	**11**	**0**	**5**	**253**	**15.8**	**115**	**38**	**62**	**1**	**16**	**6**	**0**	**0**	**0**	**8**	**0**	**0**	**0**
1987-88	**New York Rangers**	**NHL**	**77**	**38**	**50**	**88**	**32**	**36**	**68**	**76**	**13**	**0**	**4**	**202**	**18.8**	**121**	**65**	**54**	**0**	**2**	....	....	....	....	....	....	....	....
1988-89	**Quebec Nordiques**	**NHL**	**72**	**38**	**37**	**75**	**32**	**26**	**58**	**107**	**14**	**0**	**2**	**197**	**19.3**	**102**	**52**	**69**	**1**	**–18**	....	....	....	....	....	....	....	....
1989-90	**New Jersey Devils**	**NHL**	**33**	**4**	**10**	**14**	**3**	**7**	**10**	**28**	**1**	**0**	**0**	**50**	**8.0**	**21**	**6**	**19**	**0**	**–4**	....	....	....	....	....	....	....	....
	Utica Devils	AHL	2	1	2	3	....	....	....	0	....	....	....	....	....	....	....	....	....	....	....	....	....	....	....	....	....	....
1990-91	**New Jersey Devils**	**NHL**	**14**	**4**	**6**	**10**	**4**	**5**	**9**	**10**	**0**	**0**	**0**	**22**	**18.2**	**14**	**2**	**4**	**0**	**8**	....	....	....	....	....	....	....	....
1991-92	**New Jersey Devils**	**NHL**	**7**	**1**	**2**	**3**	**1**	**2**	**3**	**6**	**0**	**0**	**0**	**9**	**11.1**	**3**	**1**	**3**	**0**	**–1**	....	....	....	....	....	....	....	....
1992-93	EC Bad Nauheim	Germany-2	44	35	41	76	....	....	....	149	....	....	....	....	....	....	....	....	....	....	9	5	*15	*20	15	....	....	....
1993-94	HC Fassa	Alpenliga	9	2	3	5	....	....	....	19	....	....	....	....	....	....	....	....	....	....	....	....	....	....	....	....	....	....
	EC Bad Nauheim	Germany-2	37	40	46	86	....	....	....	115	....	....	....	....	....	....	....	....	....	....	....	....	....	....	....	....	....	....
1994-95	Worcester IceCats	AHL	34	7	6	13	....	....	....	32	....	....	....	....	....	....	....	....	....	....	....	....	....	....	....	....	....	....
1995-1996	Daytona Breakers	SunHL	DID NOT PLAY – COACHING																									
1996-1997	Worcester IceCats	AHL	DID NOT PLAY – ASSISTANT COACH																									
1997-2000	Anchorage Aces	WCHL	DID NOT PLAY – COACHING																									
	NHL Totals		**468**	**184**	**238**	**422**	**155**	**169**	**324**	**454**	**59**	**0**	**15**	**1124**	**16.4**	**566**	**215**	**350**	**3**		**19**	**7**	**2**	**9**	**12**	**2**	**0**	**4**

Played in NHL All-Star Game (1989)

Traded to **Toronto** by **Edmonton** with Phil Drouillard for Laurie Boschman, March 9, 1982. Traded to **NY Rangers** by **Toronto** for Mike Allison, August 18, 1986. Traded to **Quebec** by **NY Rangers** with Jari Gronstad, Bruce Bell and the NY Rangers' 4th round choice (Eric Dubois) in 1989 Entry Draft for Jason Lafreniere and Normand Rochefort, August 1, 1988. Traded to **New Jersey** by **Quebec** with Quebec's 4th round choice (Mike Bodnarchuk) in 1990 Entry Draft for Joe Cirella, Claude Loiselle and New Jersey's 8th round choice (Alexander Karpovtsev) in 1990 Entry Draft, June 17, 1989. • Resigned as Head Coach of **Anchorage** (WCHL), June 14, 1999. • Re-hired as Head Coach of **Anchorage** (WCHL), November 10, 1999. • Played w/ RHI's Las Vegas Flash in 1994 (19-21-26-47-32) and Orlando Rollergators in 1995 (10-7-10-17-12).

• PODEIN, Shjon

LW – L. 6'2", 200 lbs. b: Rochester, MN, 3/5/1968. Edmonton's 9th, 166th overall, in 1988.

Season	Club	League	GP	G	A	Pts	AG	AA	APts	PIM	PP	SH	GW	S	%	TGF	PGF	TGA	PGA	+/–	GP	G	A	Pts	PIM	PP	SH	GW
1985-86	John Marshall Rockets	Hi-School	25	34	30	64	....	....	....		....	....	....	....	....	....	....	....	....	....	....	....	....	....	....	....	....	....
1986-87	U.S. International University	NCAA-2	6	0	1	1	....	....	....	0	....	....	....	....	....	....	....	....	....	....	....	....	....	....	....	....	....	....
	Rochester Mustangs	USHL	STATISTICS NOT AVAILABLE																									
1987-88	University of Minnesota-Duluth	WCHA	30	4	4	8	....	....	....	48	....	....	....	....	....	....	....	....	....	....	....	....	....	....	....	....	....	....
1988-89	University of Minnesota-Duluth	WCHA	36	7	5	12	....	....	....	46	....	....	....	....	....	....	....	....	....	....	....	....	....	....	....	....	....	....
1989-90	University of Minnesota-Duluth	WCHA	35	21	18	39	....	....	....	36	....	....	....	....	....	....	....	....	....	....	....	....	....	....	....	....	....	....
1990-91	Cape Breton Oilers	AHL	63	14	15	29	....	....	....	65	....	....	....	....	....	....	....	....	....	....	4	0	0	0	5	....	....	....
1991-92	Cape Breton Oilers	AHL	80	30	24	54	....	....	....	46	....	....	....	....	....	....	....	....	....	....	5	3	1	4	2	....	....	....
1992-93	**Edmonton Oilers**	**NHL**	**40**	**13**	**6**	**19**	**11**	**4**	**15**	**25**	**2**	**1**	**1**	**64**	**20.3**	**26**	**4**	**25**	**1**	**–2**	....	....	....	....	....	....	....	....
	Cape Breton Oilers	AHL	38	18	21	39	....	....	....	32	....	....	....	....	....	....	....	....	....	....	9	2	2	4	29	....	....	....
	United States	WC-A	6	1	3	4	....	....	....	8	....	....	....	....	....	....	....	....	....	....	....	....	....	....	....	....	....	....
1993-94	**Edmonton Oilers**	**NHL**	**28**	**3**	**5**	**8**	**3**	**4**	**7**	**8**	**0**	**0**	**0**	**26**	**11.5**	**11**	**0**	**8**	**0**	**3**	....	....	....	....	....	....	....	....
	Cape Breton Oilers	AHL	5	4	4	8	....	....	....	4	....	....	....	....	....	....	....	....	....	....	....	....	....	....	....	....	....	....
	United States	WC-A	8	3	1	4	....	....	....	14	....	....	....	....	....	....	....	....	....	....	....	....	....	....	....	....	....	....
1994-95	**Philadelphia Flyers**	**NHL**	**44**	**3**	**7**	**10**	**5**	**10**	**15**	**33**	**0**	**0**	**1**	**48**	**6.3**	**18**	**0**	**22**	**2**	**–2**	**15**	**1**	**3**	**4**	**10**	**0**	**0**	**0**
1995-96	**Philadelphia Flyers**	**NHL**	**79**	**15**	**10**	**25**	**15**	**8**	**23**	**89**	**0**	**4**	**4**	**115**	**13.0**	**41**	**2**	**27**	**13**	**25**	**12**	**1**	**2**	**3**	**50**	**0**	**0**	**1**
1996-97	**Philadelphia Flyers**	**NHL**	**82**	**14**	**18**	**32**	**15**	**16**	**31**	**41**	**0**	**0**	**4**	**153**	**9.2**	**41**	**1**	**52**	**19**	**7**	**19**	**4**	**3**	**7**	**16**	**0**	**0**	**1**
1997-98	**Philadelphia Flyers**	**NHL**	**82**	**11**	**13**	**24**	**13**	**13**	**26**	**53**	**1**	**1**	**2**	**126**	**8.7**	**34**	**3**	**41**	**18**	**8**	**5**	**0**	**0**	**0**	**10**	**0**	**0**	**0**
	United States	WC-A	4	0	0	0	....	....	....	4	....	....	....	....	....	....	....	....	....	....	....	....	....	....	....	....	....	....
1998-99	**Philadelphia Flyers**	**NHL**	**14**	**1**	**0**	**1**	**1**	**0**	**1**	**0**	**0**	**0**	**0**	**26**	**3.8**	**2**	**0**	**8**	**4**	**–2**	....	....	....	....	....	....	....	....
	Colorado Avalanche	**NHL**	**41**	**2**	**6**	**8**	**2**	**6**	**8**	**24**	**0**	**0**	**0**	**49**	**4.1**	**12**	**0**	**24**	**9**	**–3**	**19**	**1**	**1**	**2**	**12**	**0**	**0**	**0**
99-2000	**Colorado Avalanche**	**NHL**	**75**	**11**	**8**	**19**	**12**	**7**	**19**	**29**	**0**	**1**	**3**	**104**	**10.6**	**28**	**0**	**40**	**24**	**12**	**17**	**5**	**0**	**5**	**8**	**0**	**0**	**1**
	NHL Totals		**485**	**73**	**73**	**146**	**77**	**68**	**145**	**302**	**3**	**7**	**15**	**711**	**10.3**	**213**	**10**	**247**	**90**		**87**	**12**	**9**	**21**	**106**	**0**	**0**	**3**

Signed as a free agent by **Philadelphia**, July 27, 1994. Traded to **Colorado** by **Philadelphia** for Keith Jones, November 12, 1998.

• PODLOSKI, Ray

C – L. 6'2", 210 lbs. b: Edmonton, Alta., 1/5/1966. Boston's 2nd, 40th overall, in 1984.

Season	Club	League	GP	G	A	Pts	AG	AA	APts	PIM	PP	SH	GW	S	%	TGF	PGF	TGA	PGA	+/–	GP	G	A	Pts	PIM	PP	SH	GW
1982-83	Red Deer Rustlers	AJHL	59	49	49	98	....	....	....	47	....	....	....	....	....	....	....	....	....	....	1	0	0	0	2	....	....	....
	Portland Winter Hawks	WHL	2	0	1	1	....	....	....	0	....	....	....	....	....	....	....	....	....	....	1	0	0	0	2	....	....	....
	Portland Winter Hawks	Mem-Cup	1	0	0	0	....	....	....	0	....	....	....	....	....	....	....	....	....	....	....	....	....	....	....	....	....	....
1983-84	Portland Winter Hawks	WHL	66	46	50	96	....	....	....	44	....	....	....	....	....	....	....	....	....	....	14	8	14	22	14	....	....	....
1984-85	Portland Winter Hawks	WHL	67	63	75	138	....	....	....	41	....	....	....	....	....	....	....	....	....	....	6	3	1	4	7	....	....	....
1985-86	Portland Winter Hawks	WHL	66	59	75	134	....	....	....	68	....	....	....	....	....	....	....	....	....	....	7	1	9	10	8	....	....	....
	Portland Winter Hawks	Mem-Cup	4	2	5	7	....	....	....	2	....	....	....	....	....	....	....	....	....	....	....	....	....	....	....	....	....	....
1986-87	Moncton Golden Flames	AHL	70	23	27	50	....	....	....	12	....	....	....	....	....	....	....	....	....	....	3	0	0	0	15	....	....	....
1987-88	Maine Mariners	AHL	36	12	20	32	....	....	....	12	....	....	....	....	....	....	....	....	....	....	5	1	2	3	19	....	....	....
1988-89	**Boston Bruins**	**NHL**	**8**	**0**	**1**	**1**	**0**	**1**	**1**	**17**	**0**	**0**	**0**	**3**	**0.0**	**1**	**0**	**2**	**0**	**–1**	....	....	....	....	....	....	....	....
	Maine Mariners	AHL	71	20	34	54	....	....	....	70	....	....	....	....	....	....	....	....	....	....	....	....	....	....	....	....	....	....
1989-90	Canada	Nat-Team	58	18	16	34	....	....	....	38	....	....	....	....	....	....	....	....	....	....	....	....	....	....	....	....	....	....
1990-91	EHC Nurnberg	Germany-2	52	59	65	124	....	....	....	58	....	....	....	....	....	....	....	....	....	....	....	....	....	....	....	....	....	....
1991-92	EHC Nurnberg	Germany-2	41	31	48	79	....	....	....	64	....	....	....	....	....	....	....	....	....	....	....	....	....	....	....	....	....	....
1992-93	KAC Klagenfurt	Alpenliga	30	26	35	61	....	....	....	45	....	....	....	....	....	....	....	....	....	....	....	....	....	....	....	....	....	....
	KAC Klagenfurt	Austria	19	9	15	24	....	....	....		....	....	....	....	....	....	....	....	....	....	....	....	....	....	....	....	....	....
1993-94	HC Bolzano	Alpenliga	26	14	16	30	....	....	....	6	....	....	....	....	....	....	....	....	....	....	....	....	....	....	....	....	....	....
	HC Bolzano	Italy	17	13	21	34	....	....	....	43	....	....	....	....	....	....	....	....	....	....	8	1	4	5	5	....	....	....

			REGULAR SEASON																		PLAYOFFS							
Season	Club	League	GP	G	A	Pts	AG	AA	APts	PIM	PP	SH	GW	S	%	TGF	PGF	TGA	PGA	+/–	GP	G	A	Pts	PIM	PP	SH	GW
1994-95	EHC Lustenau	Austria	20	21	10	31	....	....	....	28	....	....	....	....	....	....	....	....	....	....	3	0	0	0	2	....	....	....
	HC Asiago	Italy	6	7	8	15	....	....	....	2	....	....	....	....	....	....	....	....	....	....	2	3	3	6	0	....	....	....
1995-96	EHC Lustenau	Alpenliga	8	10	11	21	....	....	....	0	....	....	....	....	....	....	....	....	....	....	....	....	....	....	....	....	....	....
	EHC Lustenau	Austria	25	15	26	41	....	....	....	20	....	....	....	....	....	....	....	....	....	....	....	....	....	....	....	....	....	....
1996-97	EC Kapfenberg	Austria-2	STATISTICS NOT AVAILABLE																									
	EHC Lustenau	Austria-2	....	....	....	....	....	....	....	....	....	....	....	....	....	....	....	....	....	....	5	5	4	9	2	....	....	....
1997-98	Kassel Huskies	Germany	22	10	8	18	....	....	....	18	....	....	....	....	....	....	....	....	....	....	....	....	....	....	....	....	....	....
	KAC Klagenfurt	Austria	8	6	3	9	....	....	....	2	....	....	....	....	....	....	....	....	....	....	....	....	....	....	....	....	....	....
1998-99	VSV Villach	Alpenliga	33	25	27	52	....	....	....	4	....	....	....	....	....	....	....	....	....	....	....	....	....	....	....	....	....	....
	VSV Villach	Austria	23	7	12	19	....	....	....	6	....	....	....	....	....	....	....	....	....	....	....	....	....	....	....	....	....	....
	Austria	WC-A	6	1	0	1	....	....	....	2	....	....	....	....	....	....	....	....	....	....	....	....	....	....	....	....	....	....
99-2000	Vojens IF Lions	Denmark	25	18	11	29	....	....	....	18	....	....	....	....	....	....	....	....	....	....	6	1	0	1	2	....	....	....
	NHL Totals		**8**	**0**	**1**	**1**	**0**	**1**	**1**	**17**	**0**	**0**	**0**	**3**	**0.0**	**1**	**0**	**2**	**0**		....	....	....	....	....	....	....	....

• PODOLLAN, Jason

RW – R. 6'1", 198 lbs. b: Vernon, B.C., 2/18/1976. Florida's 3rd, 31st overall, in 1994.

Season	Club	League	GP	G	A	Pts	AG	AA	APts	PIM	PP	SH	GW	S	%	TGF	PGF	TGA	PGA	+/–	GP	G	A	Pts	PIM	PP	SH	GW
1990-91	Sherwood Park Flyers	AAHA	61	105	111	216	....	....	....	133	....	....	....	....	....	....	....	....	....	....	....	....	....	....	....	....	....	....
1991-92	Penticton Panthers	BCJHL	59	20	26	46	....	....	....	66	....	....	....	....	....	....	....	....	....	....	....	....	....	....	....	....	....	....
	Spokane Chiefs	WHL	2	0	0	0	....	....	....	2	....	....	....	....	....	....	....	....	....	....	10	3	1	4	16	....	....	....
1992-93	Spokane Chiefs	WHL	72	36	33	69	....	....	....	108	....	....	....	....	....	....	....	....	....	....	10	4	4	8	14	....	....	....
1993-94	Spokane Chiefs	WHL	69	29	37	66	....	....	....	108	....	....	....	....	....	....	....	....	....	....	3	3	0	3	2	....	....	....
1994-95	Spokane Chiefs	WHL	72	43	41	84	....	....	....	102	....	....	....	....	....	....	....	....	....	....	11	5	7	12	18	....	....	....
	Cincinnati Cyclones	IHL	....	....	....	....	....	....	....	....	....	....	....	....	....	....	....	....	....	....	3	0	0	0	2	....	....	....
1995-96	Spokane Chiefs	WHL	56	37	25	62	....	....	....	103	....	....	....	....	....	....	....	....	....	....	18	*21	12	33	28	....	....	....
	Canada	WJC-A	6	2	3	5	....	....	....	2	....	....	....	....	....	....	....	....	....	....	....	....	....	....	....	....	....	....
1996-97	**Florida Panthers**	**NHL**	**19**	**1**	**1**	**2**	**1**	**1**	**2**	**4**	**1**	**0**	**0**	**20**	**5.0**	**6**	**3**	**6**	**0**	**–3**	....	....	....	....	....	....	....	....
	Carolina Monarchs	AHL	39	21	25	46	....	....	....	36	....	....	....	....	....	....	....	....	....	....	....	....	....	....	....	....	....	....
	Toronto Maple Leafs	**NHL**	**10**	**0**	**3**	**3**	**0**	**3**	**3**	**6**	**0**	**0**	**0**	**10**	**0.0**	**6**	**0**	**8**	**0**	**–2**	....	....	....	....	....	....	....	....
	St. John's Maple Leafs	AHL	....	....	....	....	....	....	....	....	....	....	....	....	....	....	....	....	....	....	11	2	3	5	6	....	....	....
1997-98	St. John's Maple Leafs	AHL	70	30	31	61	....	....	....	116	....	....	....	....	....	....	....	....	....	....	4	1	0	1	10	....	....	....
1998-99	**Toronto Maple Leafs**	**NHL**	**4**	**0**	**0**	**0**	**0**	**0**	**0**	**0**	**0**	**0**	**0**	**2**	**0.0**	**1**	**0**	**1**	**0**	**0**	....	....	....	....	....	....	....	....
	St. John's Maple Leafs	AHL	68	42	26	68	....	....	....	65	....	....	....	....	....	....	....	....	....	....	....	....	....	....	....	....	....	....
	Los Angeles Kings	**NHL**	**6**	**0**	**0**	**0**	**0**	**0**	**0**	**5**	**0**	**0**	**0**	**7**	**0.0**	**1**	**0**	**4**	**0**	**–3**	....	....	....	....	....	....	....	....
	Long Beach Ice Dogs	IHL	8	5	3	8	....	....	....	2	....	....	....	....	....	....	....	....	....	....	6	1	2	3	4	....	....	....
99-2000	**Los Angeles Kings**	**NHL**	**1**	**0**	**1**	**1**	**0**	**1**	**1**	**2**	**0**	**0**	**0**	**2**	**0.0**	**1**	**1**	**0**	**0**	**0**	....	....	....	....	....	....	....	....
	Lowell Lock Monsters	AHL	71	29	26	55	....	....	....	91	....	....	....	....	....	....	....	....	....	....	4	0	0	0	4	....	....	....
	NHL Totals		**40**	**1**	**5**	**6**	**1**	**5**	**6**	**17**	**1**	**0**	**0**	**41**	**2.4**	**15**	**4**	**19**	**0**		....	....	....	....	....	....	....	....

WHL West Second All-Star Team (1996)

Traded to **Toronto** by **Florida** for Kirk Muller, March 18, 1997. Traded to **Los Angeles** by **Toronto** with Toronto's 3rd round choice (Cory Campbell) in 1999 Entry Draft for Yanic Perreault, March 23, 1999.

• POESCHEK, Rudy

Rudolph Leopold "Pot Pie" RW/D – R. 6'2", 218 lbs. b: Kamloops, B.C., 9/29/1966. NY Rangers' 12th, 238th overall, in 1985.

Season	Club	League	GP	G	A	Pts	AG	AA	APts	PIM	PP	SH	GW	S	%	TGF	PGF	TGA	PGA	+/–	GP	G	A	Pts	PIM	PP	SH	GW
1982-83	Vernon Lakers	BCJHL	54	4	10	14	....	....	....	100	....	....	....	....	....	....	....	....	....	....	....	....	....	....	....	....	....	....
1983-84	Revelstoke Rangers	BCJHL	22	5	21	26	....	....	....	107	....	....	....	....	....	....	....	....	....	....	....	....	....	....	....	....	....	....
	Kamloops Blazers	WHL	47	3	9	12	....	....	....	93	....	....	....	....	....	....	....	....	....	....	8	0	2	2	7	....	....	....
	Kamloops Blazers	Mem-Cup	2	0	0	0	....	....	....	7	....	....	....	....	....	....	....	....	....	....	....	....	....	....	....	....	....	....
1984-85	Kamloops Blazers	WHL	34	6	7	13	....	....	....	100	....	....	....	....	....	....	....	....	....	....	15	0	3	3	56	....	....	....
1985-86	Kamloops Blazers	WHL	32	3	13	16	....	....	....	92	....	....	....	....	....	....	....	....	....	....	16	3	7	10	40	....	....	....
	Kamloops Blazers	Mem-Cup	5	1	1	2	....	....	....	13	....	....	....	....	....	....	....	....	....	....	....	....	....	....	....	....	....	....
1986-87	Kamloops Blazers	WHL	54	13	18	31	....	....	....	153	....	....	....	....	....	....	....	....	....	....	15	2	4	6	37	....	....	....
1987-88	**New York Rangers**	**NHL**	**1**	**0**	**0**	**0**	**0**	**0**	**0**	**2**	**0**	**0**	**0**	**1**	**0.0**	**0**	**0**	**0**	**0**	**0**	....	....	....	....	....	....	....	....
	Colorado Rangers	IHL	82	7	31	38	....	....	....	210	....	....	....	....	....	....	....	....	....	....	12	2	2	4	31	....	....	....
1988-89	**New York Rangers**	**NHL**	**52**	**0**	**2**	**2**	**0**	**1**	**1**	**199**	**0**	**0**	**0**	**17**	**0.0**	**7**	**0**	**15**	**0**	**–8**	....	....	....	....	....	....	....	....
	Colorado Rangers	IHL	2	0	0	0	....	....	....	6	....	....	....	....	....	....	....	....	....	....	....	....	....	....	....	....	....	....
1989-90	**New York Rangers**	**NHL**	**15**	**0**	**0**	**0**	**0**	**0**	**0**	**55**	**0**	**0**	**0**	**1**	**0.0**	**1**	**0**	**2**	**0**	**–1**	....	....	....	....	....	....	....	....
	Flint Spirits	IHL	38	8	13	21	....	....	....	109	....	....	....	....	....	....	....	....	....	....	4	0	0	0	16	....	....	....
1990-91	Binghamton Rangers	AHL	38	1	3	4	....	....	....	162	....	....	....	....	....	....	....	....	....	....	....	....	....	....	....	....	....	....
	Winnipeg Jets	**NHL**	**1**	**0**	**0**	**0**	**0**	**0**	**0**	**5**	**0**	**0**	**0**	**0**	**0.0**	**0**	**0**	**0**	**0**	**0**	....	....	....	....	....	....	....	....
	Moncton Hawks	AHL	23	2	4	6	....	....	....	67	....	....	....	....	....	....	....	....	....	....	9	1	1	2	41	....	....	....
1991-92	**Winnipeg Jets**	**NHL**	**4**	**0**	**0**	**0**	**0**	**0**	**0**	**17**	**0**	**0**	**0**	**1**	**0.0**	**0**	**0**	**5**	**0**	**–5**	....	....	....	....	....	....	....	....
	Moncton Hawks	AHL	63	4	18	22	....	....	....	170	....	....	....	....	....	....	....	....	....	....	11	0	2	2	48	....	....	....
1992-93	St. John's Maple Leafs	AHL	78	7	24	31	....	....	....	189	....	....	....	....	....	....	....	....	....	....	9	0	4	4	13	....	....	....
1993-94	**Tampa Bay Lightning**	**NHL**	**71**	**3**	**6**	**9**	**3**	**5**	**8**	**118**	**0**	**0**	**1**	**46**	**6.5**	**27**	**0**	**27**	**3**	**3**	....	....	....	....	....	....	....	....
1994-95	**Tampa Bay Lightning**	**NHL**	**25**	**1**	**1**	**2**	**2**	**1**	**3**	**92**	**0**	**0**	**0**	**14**	**7.1**	**7**	**0**	**8**	**1**	**0**	....	....	....	....	....	....	....	....
1995-96	**Tampa Bay Lightning**	**NHL**	**57**	**1**	**3**	**4**	**1**	**2**	**3**	**88**	**0**	**0**	**0**	**36**	**2.8**	**16**	**1**	**24**	**7**	**–2**	**3**	**0**	**0**	**0**	**12**	**0**	**0**	**0**
1996-97	**Tampa Bay Lightning**	**NHL**	**60**	**0**	**6**	**6**	**0**	**5**	**5**	**120**	**0**	**0**	**0**	**30**	**0.0**	**25**	**0**	**47**	**19**	**–3**	....	....	....	....	....	....	....	....
1997-98	**St. Louis Blues**	**NHL**	**50**	**1**	**7**	**8**	**1**	**7**	**8**	**64**	**0**	**0**	**0**	**29**	**3.4**	**27**	**2**	**36**	**6**	**–5**	**2**	**0**	**0**	**0**	**6**	**0**	**0**	**0**
1998-99	**St. Louis Blues**	**NHL**	**16**	**0**	**0**	**0**	**0**	**0**	**0**	**33**	**0**	**0**	**0**	**8**	**0.0**	**7**	**0**	**8**	**1**	**0**	....	....	....	....	....	....	....	....
99-2000	**St. Louis Blues**	**NHL**	**12**	**0**	**0**	**0**	**0**	**0**	**0**	**24**	**0**	**0**	**0**	**8**	**0.0**	**3**	**0**	**7**	**1**	**–3**	....	....	....	....	....	....	....	....
	Worcester IceCats	AHL	5	0	0	0	....	....	....	4	....	....	....	....	....	....	....	....	....	....	....	....	....	....	....	....	....	....
	Houston Aeros	IHL	32	2	6	8	....	....	....	51	....	....	....	....	....	....	....	....	....	....	....	....	....	....	....	....	....	....
	NHL Totals		**364**	**6**	**25**	**31**	**7**	**21**	**28**	**817**	**0**	**0**	**1**	**191**	**3.1**	**120**	**3**	**179**	**38**		**5**	**0**	**0**	**0**	**18**	**0**	**0**	**0**

Traded to **Winnipeg** by **NY Rangers** for Guy Larose, January 22, 1991. Signed as a free agent by **Toronto**, July 8, 1992. Signed as a free agent by **Tampa Bay**, August 10, 1993. Signed as a free agent by **St. Louis**, July 31, 1997. Loaned to **Houston** (IHL) by **St. Louis**, November 11, 1999.

• POLANIC, Tom

Thomas Joseph D – L. 6'3", 205 lbs. b: Toronto, Ont., 4/2/1943.

Season	Club	League	GP	G	A	Pts	AG	AA	APts	PIM	PP	SH	GW	S	%	TGF	PGF	TGA	PGA	+/–	GP	G	A	Pts	PIM	PP	SH	GW
1960-61	St. Michael's Buzzers	OHA-B	STATISTICS NOT AVAILABLE																									
	St. Michael's Majors	OHA-Jr.	11	0	0	0	....	....	....	8	....	....	....	....	....	....	....	....	....	....	1	0	0	0	0	....	....	....
1961-62	St. Michael's Majors	MTJHL	23	9	10	19	....	....	....	24	....	....	....	....	....	....	....	....	....	....	12	0	11	11	23	....	....	....
	St. Michael's Majors	Mem-Cup	5	0	1	1	....	....	....	25	....	....	....	....	....	....	....	....	....	....	....	....	....	....	....	....	....	....
1962-63	University of Michigan	WCHA	DID NOT PLAY – FRESHMAN																									
1963-64	University of Michigan	WCHA	....	8	38	46	....	....	....	92	....	....	....	....	....	....	....	....	....	....	....	....	....	....	....	....	....	....
1964-65	University of Michigan	WCHA	....	5	12	17	....	....	....	56	....	....	....	....	....	....	....	....	....	....	....	....	....	....	....	....	....	....
1965-66	Charlotte Checkers	EHL	64	7	24	31	....	....	....	101	....	....	....	....	....	....	....	....	....	....	9	1	4	5	23	....	....	....
	Tulsa Oilers	CPHL	2	0	1	1	....	....	....	0	....	....	....	....	....	....	....	....	....	....	....	....	....	....	....	....	....	....
1966-67	Tulsa Oilers	CPHL	19	0	1	1	....	....	....	25	....	....	....	....	....	....	....	....	....	....	....	....	....	....	....	....	....	....
	Victoria Maple Leafs	WHL	46	1	13	14	....	....	....	69	....	....	....	....	....	....	....	....	....	....	....	....	....	....	....	....	....	....
1967-68	Phoenix Roadrunners	WHL	70	3	10	13	....	....	....	136	....	....	....	....	....	....	....	....	....	....	4	1	0	1	6	....	....	....
1968-69	Phoenix Roadrunners	WHL	74	5	17	22	....	....	....	*187	....	....	....	....	....	....	....	....	....	....	....	....	....	....	....	....	....	....
1969-70	**Minnesota North Stars**	**NHL**	**16**	**0**	**2**	**2**	**0**	**2**	**2**	**53**	**0**	**0**	**0**	**4**	**0.0**	**5**	**0**	**10**	**0**	**–5**	**5**	**1**	**1**	**2**	**4**	**0**	**0**	**0**
	Iowa Stars	CHL	44	1	8	9	....	....	....	88	....	....	....	....	....	....	....	....	....	....	8	0	1	1	8	....	....	....
1970-71	**Minnesota North Stars**	**NHL**	**3**	**0**	**0**	**0**	**0**	**0**	**0**	**0**	**0**	**0**	**0**	**2**	**0.0**	**1**	**0**	**1**	**0**	**0**	....	....	....	....	....	....	....	....
	Cleveland Barons	AHL	68	2	20	22	....	....	....	154	....	....	....	....	....	....	....	....	....	....	8	0	3	3	35	....	....	....
1971-72	Orillia Terriers	OHA-Sr.	31	6	24	30	....	....	....	67	....	....	....	....	....	....	....	....	....	....	....	....	....	....	....	....	....	....
1972-73	Orillia Terriers	OHA-Sr.	35	4	13	17	....	....	....	87	....	....	....	....	....	....	....	....	....	....	....	....	....	....	....	....	....	....
1973-74	Orillia Terriers	OHA-Sr.	33	2	27	29	....	....	....	63	....	....	....	....	....	....	....	....	....	....	....	....	....	....	....	....	....	....

Season	Club	League	REGULAR SEASON																		PLAYOFFS							
			GP	G	A	Pts	AG	AA	APts	PIM	PP	SH	GW	S	%	TGF	PGF	TGA	PGA	+/–	GP	G	A	Pts	PIM	PP	SH	GW
1974-75	Brantford Forresters	OHA-Sr.	39	3	18	21	....	....	....	65	....	....	....	....	....	....	....	....	....	....	....	....	....	....	....	....	....	....
1975-76			OUT OF HOCKEY – RETIRED																									
1976-77	Barrie Flyers	OHA-Sr.	30	1	14	15	....	....	....	31	....	....	....	....	....	....	....	....	....	....	....	....	....	....	....	....	....	....
	NHL Totals		**19**	**0**	**2**	**2**	**0**	**2**	**2**	**53**	**0**	**0**	**0**	**6**	**0.0**	**6**	**0**	**11**	**0**		**5**	**1**	**1**	**2**	**4**	**0**	**0**	**0**

WCHA First All-Star Team (1964) • NCAA West First All-American Team (1964) • NCAA Championship All-Tournament Team (1964) • WCHA Second All-Star Team (1965) • OHA-Sr. First All-Star Team (1973, 1974)

Traded to **Phoenix** (WHL) by **Toronto** for cash, September 12, 1967. Traded to **Minnesota** by **Phoenix** (WHL) for Brian D. Smith and Milan Marcetta, February 11, 1969.

• POLICH, Mike

Michael J. C/LW – L. 5'8", 170 lbs. b: Hibbing, MN, 12/19/1952.

Season	Club	League	GP	G	A	Pts	AG	AA	APts	PIM	PP	SH	GW	S	%	TGF	PGF	TGA	PGA	+/–	GP	G	A	Pts	PIM	PP	SH	GW
1971-72	University of Minnesota	WCHA	32	8	5	13	....	....	....	14	....	....	....	....	....	....	....	....	....	....	....	....	....	....	....	....	....	....
1972-73	University of Minnesota	WCHA	34	18	14	32	....	....	....	34	....	....	....	....	....	....	....	....	....	....	....	....	....	....	....	....	....	....
1973-74	University of Minnesota	WCHA	40	19	33	52	....	....	....	36	....	....	....	....	....	....	....	....	....	....	....	....	....	....	....	....	....	....
	United States	WEC-B	....	7	5	12	....	....	....	....	....	....	....	....	....	....	....	....	....	....	....	....	....	....	....	....	....	....
1974-75	University of Minnesota	WCHA	42	25	37	62	....	....	....	84	....	....	....	....	....	....	....	....	....	....	....	....	....	....	....	....	....	....
	United States	WEC-A	10	2	5	7	....	....	....	34	....	....	....	....	....	....	....	....	....	....	....	....	....	....	....	....	....	....
1975-76	Nova Scotia Voyageurs	AHL	75	24	19	43	....	....	....	66	....	....	....	....	....	....	....	....	....	....	9	4	5	9	6	....	....	....
1976-77	United States	Can-Cup	5	1	1	2	....	....	....	4	....	....	....	....	....	....	....	....	....	....	....	....	....	....	....	....	....	....
	Nova Scotia Voyageurs	AHL	69	19	41	60	....	....	....	48	....	....	....	....	....	....	....	....	....	....	11	4	4	8	6	....	....	....
♦	**Montreal Canadiens**	**NHL**	....	....	....	....	....	....	....	....	....	....	....	....	....	....	....	....	....	....	**5**	**0**	**0**	**0**	**0**	**0**	**0**	**0**
1977-78	**Montreal Canadiens**	**NHL**	**1**	**0**	**0**	**0**	**0**	**0**	**0**	**0**	**0**	**0**	**0**	**0**	**0.0**	**0**	**0**	**0**	**0**	**0**	....	....	....	....	....	....	....	....
	Nova Scotia Voyageurs	AHL	79	22	38	60	....	....	....	70	....	....	....	....	....	....	....	....	....	....	11	2	6	8	4	....	....	....
1978-79	**Minnesota North Stars**	**NHL**	**73**	**6**	**10**	**16**	**5**	**7**	**12**	**18**	**0**	**0**	**0**	**66**	**9.1**	**28**	**1**	**59**	**19**	**–13**	....	....	....	....	....	....	....	....
	Oklahoma City Stars	CHL	9	0	7	7	....	....	....	0	....	....	....	....	....	....	....	....	....	....	....	....	....	....	....	....	....	....
1979-80	**Minnesota North Stars**	**NHL**	**78**	**10**	**14**	**24**	**8**	**10**	**18**	**20**	**0**	**0**	**1**	**94**	**10.6**	**34**	**0**	**61**	**27**	**0**	**15**	**2**	**1**	**3**	**2**	**0**	**0**	**0**
1980-81	Minnesota North Stars	DN-Cup	2	2	0	2	....	....	....	0	....	....	....	....	....	....	....	....	....	....	....	....	....	....	....	....	....	....
	Minnesota North Stars	**NHL**	**74**	**8**	**5**	**13**	**6**	**3**	**9**	**19**	**0**	**1**	**0**	**58**	**13.8**	**19**	**1**	**59**	**39**	**–2**	**3**	**0**	**0**	**0**	**0**	**0**	**0**	**0**
	NHL Totals		**226**	**24**	**29**	**53**	**19**	**20**	**39**	**57**	**0**	**1**	**1**	**218**	**11.0**	**81**	**2**	**179**	**85**		**23**	**2**	**1**	**3**	**2**	**0**	**0**	**0**

NCAA Championship All-Tournament Team (1974) • WCHA First All-Star Team (1975) • NCAA West First All-American Team (1975)

Signed as a free agent by **Montreal**, September 27, 1975. Signed as a free agent by **Minnesota**, September 6, 1978.

• POLIS, Greg

Gregory Linn "Pole Cat" LW – L. 6', 195 lbs. b: Westlock, Alta., 8/8/1950. Pittsburgh's 1st, 7th overall, in 1970.

Season	Club	League	GP	G	A	Pts	AG	AA	APts	PIM	PP	SH	GW	S	%	TGF	PGF	TGA	PGA	+/–	GP	G	A	Pts	PIM	PP	SH	GW
1966-67	Estevan Bruins	CMJHL	54	12	20	32	....	....	....	83	....	....	....	....	....	....	....	....	....	....	13	1	5	6	12	....	....	....
1967-68	Estevan Bruins	WCJHL	59	35	32	67	....	....	....	124	....	....	....	....	....	....	....	....	....	....	13	3	6	9	20	....	....	....
	Estevan Bruins	Mem-Cup	12	1	4	5	....	....	....	8	....	....	....	....	....	....	....	....	....	....	....	....	....	....	....	....	....	....
1968-69	Estevan Bruins	WCJHL	60	40	85	125	....	....	....	94	....	....	....	....	....	....	....	....	....	....	12	4	6	10	8	....	....	....
1969-70	Estevan Bruins	WCJHL	60	48	56	104	....	....	....	69	....	....	....	....	....	....	....	....	....	....	5	2	1	3	2	....	....	....
1970-71	**Pittsburgh Penguins**	**NHL**	**61**	**18**	**15**	**33**	**18**	**13**	**31**	**40**	**5**	**0**	**2**	**157**	**11.5**	**56**	**17**	**45**	**0**	**–6**	....	....	....	....	....	....	....	....
1971-72	**Pittsburgh Penguins**	**NHL**	**76**	**30**	**19**	**49**	**30**	**16**	**46**	**38**	**8**	**0**	**0**	**208**	**14.4**	**74**	**20**	**58**	**0**	**–4**	**4**	**0**	**2**	**2**	**0**	**0**	**0**	**0**
1972-73	**Pittsburgh Penguins**	**NHL**	**78**	**26**	**23**	**49**	**24**	**18**	**42**	**36**	**8**	**0**	**2**	**221**	**11.8**	**73**	**23**	**82**	**0**	**–32**	....	....	....	....	....	....	....	....
1973-74	**Pittsburgh Penguins**	**NHL**	**41**	**14**	**13**	**27**	**13**	**11**	**24**	**32**	**5**	**0**	**1**	**163**	**8.6**	**35**	**13**	**40**	**0**	**–18**	....	....	....	....	....	....	....	....
	St. Louis Blues	**NHL**	**37**	**8**	**12**	**20**	**8**	**10**	**18**	**24**	**3**	**0**	**0**	**122**	**6.6**	**31**	**9**	**29**	**0**	**–7**	....	....	....	....	....	....	....	....
1974-75	**New York Rangers**	**NHL**	**76**	**26**	**15**	**41**	**23**	**11**	**34**	**55**	**4**	**0**	**4**	**213**	**12.2**	**63**	**13**	**48**	**1**	**3**	**3**	**0**	**0**	**0**	**6**	**0**	**0**	**0**
1975-76	**New York Rangers**	**NHL**	**79**	**15**	**21**	**36**	**13**	**16**	**29**	**77**	**0**	**0**	**1**	**158**	**9.5**	**50**	**3**	**58**	**3**	**–8**	....	....	....	....	....	....	....	....
1976-77	**New York Rangers**	**NHL**	**77**	**16**	**23**	**39**	**14**	**18**	**32**	**44**	**3**	**0**	**2**	**187**	**8.6**	**58**	**4**	**66**	**12**	**0**	....	....	....	....	....	....	....	....
1977-78	**New York Rangers**	**NHL**	**37**	**7**	**16**	**23**	**6**	**12**	**18**	**12**	**0**	**4**	**1**	**72**	**9.7**	**32**	**1**	**44**	**10**	**–3**	....	....	....	....	....	....	....	....
1978-79	**New York Rangers**	**NHL**	**6**	**1**	**1**	**2**	**1**	**1**	**2**	**8**	**0**	**0**	**0**	**10**	**10.0**	**4**	**0**	**3**	**0**	**1**	....	....	....	....	....	....	....	....
	Washington Capitals	**NHL**	**19**	**12**	**6**	**18**	**10**	**4**	**14**	**6**	**6**	**0**	**1**	**46**	**26.1**	**28**	**9**	**18**	**2**	**3**	....	....	....	....	....	....	....	....
	New Haven Nighthawks	AHL	10	3	3	6	....	....	....	0	....	....	....	....	....	....	....	....	....	....	....	....	....	....	....	....	....	....
1979-80	**Washington Capitals**	**NHL**	**28**	**1**	**5**	**6**	**1**	**4**	**5**	**19**	**0**	**0**	**0**	**30**	**3.3**	**15**	**1**	**22**	**2**	**–6**	....	....	....	....	....	....	....	....
	Hershey Bears	AHL	9	0	2	2	....	....	....	2	....	....	....	....	....	....	....	....	....	....	....	....	....	....	....	....	....	....
1980-81	Hershey Bears	AHL	2	1	0	1	....	....	....	5	....	....	....	....	....	....	....	....	....	....	....	....	....	....	....	....	....	....
	NHL Totals		**615**	**174**	**169**	**343**	**161**	**134**	**295**	**391**	**42**	**4**	**14**	**1587**	**11.0**	**519**	**113**	**513**	**30**		**7**	**0**	**2**	**2**	**6**	**0**	**0**	**0**

WCJHL All-Star Team (1969, 1970) • Played in NHL All-Star Game (1971, 1972, 1973)

Traded to **St. Louis** by **Pittsburgh** with Bryan Watson and Pittsburgh's 2nd round choice (Bob Hess) in 1974 Amateur Draft for Steve Durbano, Ab DeMarco Jr. and Bob Kelly, January 17, 1974. Traded to **NY Rangers** by **St. Louis** for Larry Sacharuk and NY Rangers' 1st round choice (Lucien Deblois) in 1977 Entry Draft, August 29, 1974. Claimed on waivers by **Washington** from **NY Rangers**, January 15, 1979.

• POLONICH, Dennis

Dennis Daniel C/RW – R. 5'6", 166 lbs. b: Foam Lake, Sask., 12/4/1953. Detroit's 8th, 118th overall, in 1973.

Season	Club	League	GP	G	A	Pts	AG	AA	APts	PIM	PP	SH	GW	S	%	TGF	PGF	TGA	PGA	+/–	GP	G	A	Pts	PIM	PP	SH	GW
1970-71	Foam Lake Lakers	SAHA-I	STATISTICS NOT AVAILABLE																									
1971-72	Flin Flon Bombers	WCJHL	65	9	21	30	....	....	....	200	....	....	....	....	....	....	....	....	....	....	7	0	1	1	41	....	....	....
1972-73	Flin Flon Bombers	WCJHL	68	26	48	74	....	....	....	222	....	....	....	....	....	....	....	....	....	....	9	1	5	6	38	....	....	....
1973-74	London Lions	Britain	67	17	43	60	....	....	....	57	....	....	....	....	....	....	....	....	....	....	....	....	....	....	....	....	....	....
1974-75	**Detroit Red Wings**	**NHL**	**4**	**0**	**0**	**0**	**0**	**0**	**0**	**0**	**0**	**0**	**0**	**4**	**0.0**	**0**	**0**	**1**	**0**	**–1**	....	....	....	....	....	....	....	....
	Virginia Wings	AHL	60	14	20	34	....	....	....	194	....	....	....	....	....	....	....	....	....	....	5	0	2	2	30	....	....	....
1975-76	**Detroit Red Wings**	**NHL**	**57**	**11**	**12**	**23**	**10**	**9**	**19**	**302**	**1**	**0**	**0**	**97**	**11.3**	**30**	**4**	**36**	**1**	**–9**	....	....	....	....	....	....	....	....
	Kalamazoo Wings	IHL	5	1	8	9	....	....	....	32	....	....	....	....	....	....	....	....	....	....	....	....	....	....	....	....	....	....
1976-77	**Detroit Red Wings**	**NHL**	**79**	**18**	**28**	**46**	**16**	**22**	**38**	**274**	**6**	**1**	**1**	**183**	**9.8**	**67**	**19**	**73**	**5**	**–20**	....	....	....	....	....	....	....	....
1977-78	**Detroit Red Wings**	**NHL**	**79**	**16**	**19**	**35**	**15**	**15**	**30**	**254**	**5**	**0**	**0**	**128**	**12.5**	**63**	**18**	**50**	**0**	**–5**	**7**	**1**	**0**	**1**	**19**	**0**	**0**	**0**
1978-79	**Detroit Red Wings**	**NHL**	**62**	**10**	**12**	**22**	**9**	**9**	**18**	**208**	**1**	**0**	**0**	**80**	**12.5**	**44**	**9**	**45**	**0**	**–10**	....	....	....	....	....	....	....	....
1979-80	**Detroit Red Wings**	**NHL**	**66**	**2**	**8**	**10**	**2**	**6**	**8**	**127**	**0**	**0**	**0**	**61**	**3.3**	**22**	**1**	**43**	**7**	**–15**	....	....	....	....	....	....	....	....
1980-81	**Detroit Red Wings**	**NHL**	**32**	**2**	**2**	**4**	**2**	**1**	**3**	**77**	**0**	**0**	**0**	**27**	**7.4**	**8**	**2**	**26**	**6**	**–14**	....	....	....	....	....	....	....	....
	Adirondack Red Wings	AHL	40	16	13	29	....	....	....	99	....	....	....	....	....	....	....	....	....	....	14	9	5	14	95	....	....	....
1981-82	Adirondack Red Wings	AHL	80	30	26	56	....	....	....	202	....	....	....	....	....	....	....	....	....	....	5	2	2	4	0	....	....	....
1982-83	**Detroit Red Wings**	**NHL**	**11**	**0**	**1**	**1**	**0**	**1**	**1**	**0**	**0**	**0**	**0**	**7**	**0.0**	**1**	**0**	**7**	**2**	**–4**	....	....	....	....	....	....	....	....
	Adirondack Red Wings	AHL	61	18	22	40	....	....	....	128	....	....	....	....	....	....	....	....	....	....	6	2	2	4	10	....	....	....
1983-84	Adirondack Red Wings	AHL	66	14	26	40	....	....	....	122	....	....	....	....	....	....	....	....	....	....	....	....	....	....	....	....	....	....
1984-85	Adirondack Red Wings	AHL	53	18	17	35	....	....	....	133	....	....	....	....	....	....	....	....	....	....	....	....	....	....	....	....	....	....
1985-86	Muskegon Lumberjacks	IHL	78	32	36	68	....	....	....	222	....	....	....	....	....	....	....	....	....	....	14	8	10	18	36	....	....	....
1986-87	Muskegon Lumberjacks	IHL	22	2	9	11	....	....	....	24	....	....	....	....	....	....	....	....	....	....	....	....	....	....	....	....	....	....
	NHL Totals		**390**	**59**	**82**	**141**	**54**	**63**	**117**	**1242**	**13**	**1**	**1**	**587**	**10.1**	**235**	**53**	**281**	**21**		**7**	**1**	**0**	**1**	**19**	**0**	**0**	**0**

• POOLEY, Paul

Paul Robert C – R. 6', 175 lbs. b: Exeter, Ont., 8/2/1960.

Season	Club	League	GP	G	A	Pts	AG	AA	APts	PIM	PP	SH	GW	S	%	TGF	PGF	TGA	PGA	+/–	GP	G	A	Pts	PIM	PP	SH	GW
1977-78	North York Rangers	OJHL	STATISTICS NOT AVAILABLE																									
	Kingston Canadians	OMJHL	4	0	0	0	....	....	....	2	....	....	....	....	....	....	....	....	....	....	4	2	0	2	0	....	....	....
1978-79	North York Rangers	OJHL	STATISTICS NOT AVAILABLE																									
	Kingston Canadians	OMJHL	....	....	....	....	....	....	....	....	....	....	....	....	....	....	....	....	....	....	11	3	7	10	4	....	....	....
1979-80	North York Rangers	OJHL	32	15	22	37	....	....	....	25	....	....	....	....	....	....	....	....	....	....	....	....	....	....	....	....	....	....
1980-81	Ohio State University	CCHA	38	28	30	58	....	....	....	41	....	....	....	....	....	....	....	....	....	....	....	....	....	....	....	....	....	....
1981-82	Ohio State University	CCHA	34	21	24	45	....	....	....	34	....	....	....	....	....	....	....	....	....	....	....	....	....	....	....	....	....	....
1982-83	Ohio State University	CCHA	30	24	29	53	....	....	....	48	....	....	....	....	....	....	....	....	....	....	....	....	....	....	....	....	....	....
1983-84	Ohio State University	CCHA	41	32	64	*96	....	....	....	40	....	....	....	....	....	....	....	....	....	....	....	....	....	....	....	....	....	....
1984-85	**Winnipeg Jets**	**NHL**	**12**	**0**	**2**	**2**	**0**	**1**	**1**	**0**	**0**	**0**	**0**	**1**	**0.0**	**2**	**0**	**2**	**1**	**1**	....	....	....	....	....	....	....	....
	Sherbrooke Canadiens	AHL	57	18	17	35	....	....	....	16	....	....	....	....	....	....	....	....	....	....	17	2	2	4	7	....	....	....
1985-86	**Winnipeg Jets**	**NHL**	**3**	**0**	**1**	**1**	**0**	**1**	**1**	**0**	**0**	**0**	**0**	**2**	**0.0**	**2**	**0**	**2**	**1**	**1**	....	....	....	....	....	....	....	....
	Sherbrooke Canadiens	AHL	70	20	21	41	....	....	....	31	....	....	....	....	....	....	....	....	....	....	....	....	....	....	....	....	....	....
1986-87	Fort Wayne Komets	IHL	77	28	44	72	....	....	....	47	....	....	....	....	....	....	....	....	....	....	2	1	3	2	2	....	....	....
1987-88			OUT OF HOCKEY – RETIRED																									

			REGULAR SEASON																		PLAYOFFS							
Season	Club	League	GP	G	A	Pts	AG	AA	APts	PIM	PP	SH	GW	S	%	TGF	PGF	TGA	PGA	+/–	GP	G	A	Pts	PIM	PP	SH	GW
1988-1991	Ohio State University	H-East	DID NOT PLAY – ASSISTANT COACH																									
1991-1994	Lake Superior State	CCHA	DID NOT PLAY – ASSISTANT COACH																									
1994-2000	Providence College	H-East	DID NOT PLAY – COACHING																									
	NHL Totals		**15**	**0**	**3**	**3**	**0**	**2**	**2**	**0**	**0**	**0**	**0**	**3**	**0.0**	**4**	**0**	**4**	**2**		....	....	....	....	....	....	....	....

CCHA Second All-Star Team (1981) • CCHA First All-Star Team (1984) • NCAA West First All-American Team (1984)

Signed as a free agent by **Winnipeg**, May 24, 1984.

• POPEIN, Larry

Lawrence Thomas "Pope" C – L. 5'10", 165 lbs. b: Yorkton, Sask., 8/11/1930.

Season	Club	League	GP	G	A	Pts	AG	AA	APts	PIM	PP	SH	GW	S	%	TGF	PGF	TGA	PGA	+/–	GP	G	A	Pts	PIM	PP	SH	GW
1947-48	Moose Jaw Canucks	SJHL	27	21	12	33	....	....	....	6	....	....	....	....	....	....	....	....	....	....	4	4	0	4	7	....	....	....
	Moose Jaw Canucks	Mem-Cup	5	0	0	0	....	....	....	0	....	....	....	....	....	....	....	....	....	....	....	....	....	....	....	....	....	....
1948-49	Moose Jaw Canucks	WCJHL	26	21	12	33	....	....	....	34	....	....	....	....	....	....	....	....	....	....	8	5	2	7	0	....	....	....
1949-50	Moose Jaw Canucks	WCJHL	37	36	22	58	....	....	....	4	....	....	....	....	....	....	....	....	....	....	4	5	2	7	0	....	....	....
1950-51	Regina Capitals	WCMHL	54	21	19	40	....	....	....	14	....	....	....	....	....	....	....	....	....	....	....	....	....	....	....	....	....	....
1951-52	Vancouver Canucks	PCHL	69	32	36	68	....	....	....	14	....	....	....	....	....	....	....	....	....	....	....	....	....	....	....	....	....	....
1952-53	Vancouver Canucks	WHL	70	25	44	69	....	....	....	23	....	....	....	....	....	....	....	....	....	....	9	5	10	15	0	....	....	....
1953-54	Vancouver Canucks	WHL	70	34	32	66	....	....	....	22	....	....	....	....	....	....	....	....	....	....	10	4	7	11	4	....	....	....
1954-55	**New York Rangers**	**NHL**	**70**	**11**	**17**	**28**	**14**	**19**	**33**	**27**	....	....	....	....	....	....	....	....	....	....	....	....	....	....	....	....	....	....
1955-56	**New York Rangers**	**NHL**	**64**	**14**	**25**	**39**	**19**	**30**	**49**	**37**	....	....	....	....	....	....	....	....	....	....	**5**	**0**	**1**	**1**	**2**	**0**	**0**	**0**
1956-57	**New York Rangers**	**NHL**	**67**	**11**	**19**	**30**	**14**	**21**	**35**	**20**	....	....	....	....	....	....	....	....	....	....	**5**	**0**	**3**	**3**	**0**	**0**	**0**	**0**
1957-58	**New York Rangers**	**NHL**	**70**	**12**	**22**	**34**	**15**	**23**	**38**	**22**	....	....	....	....	....	....	....	....	....	....	**6**	**1**	**0**	**1**	**4**	**0**	**0**	**0**
1958-59	**New York Rangers**	**NHL**	**61**	**13**	**21**	**34**	**15**	**21**	**36**	**28**	....	....	....	....	....	....	....	....	....	....	....	....	....	....	....	....	....	....
1959-60	**New York Rangers**	**NHL**	**66**	**14**	**22**	**36**	**16**	**21**	**37**	**16**	....	....	....	....	....	....	....	....	....	....	....	....	....	....	....	....	....	....
1960-61	**New York Rangers**	**NHL**	**4**	**0**	**1**	**1**	**0**	**1**	**1**	**0**	....	....	....	....	....	....	....	....	....	....	....	....	....	....	....	....	....	....
	Vancouver Canucks	WHL	69	19	48	67	....	....	....	12	....	....	....	....	....	....	....	....	....	....	9	1	3	4	0	....	....	....
1961-62	Vancouver Canucks	WHL	59	9	22	31	....	....	....	12	....	....	....	....	....	....	....	....	....	....	10	0	3	3	2	....	....	....
1962-63	Vancouver Canucks	WHL	65	15	21	36	....	....	....	24	....	....	....	....	....	....	....	....	....	....	7	0	1	1	4	....	....	....
1963-64	Vancouver Canucks	WHL	39	8	11	19	....	....	....	18	....	....	....	....	....	....	....	....	....	....	....	....	....	....	....	....	....	....
1964-65	Vancouver Canucks	WHL	59	7	9	16	....	....	....	12	....	....	....	....	....	....	....	....	....	....	5	0	1	1	2	....	....	....
1965-66	Vancouver Canucks	WHL	68	16	15	31	....	....	....	20	....	....	....	....	....	....	....	....	....	....	7	2	3	5	2	....	....	....
1966-67	Vancouver Canucks	WHL	71	22	26	48	....	....	....	18	....	....	....	....	....	....	....	....	....	....	3	1	1	2	2	....	....	....
1967-68	Vancouver Canucks	WHL	27	6	6	12	....	....	....	4	....	....	....	....	....	....	....	....	....	....	....	....	....	....	....	....	....	....
	Oakland Seals	**NHL**	**47**	**5**	**14**	**19**	**6**	**14**	**20**	**12**	**0**	**1**	**0**	**51**	**9.8**	**23**	**3**	**53**	**16**	**–17**	....	....	....	....	....	....	....	....
1968-69	Omaha Knights	CHL	57	1	4	5	....	....	....	16	....	....	....	....	....	....	....	....	....	....	7	1	0	1	0	....	....	....
1969-70	Omaha Knights	CHL	2	0	0	0	....	....	....	0	....	....	....	....	....	....	....	....	....	....	....	....	....	....	....	....	....	....
	NHL Totals		**449**	**80**	**141**	**221**	**99**	**150**	**249**	**162**	....	....	....	....	....	....	....	....	....	....	**16**	**1**	**4**	**5**	**6**	....	....	....

• WCJHL First All-Star Team (1950) • WCMHL Rookie-of-the-Year (1951)

Claimed by **NY Rangers** (Baltimore-AHL) from **NY Rangers** in Reverse Draft, June 13, 1966. Traded to **Oakland** by **NY Rangers** for cash, December, 1967. Traded to **NY Rangers** by **Oakland** for cash, May 14, 1968. • Named playing-coach of **Omaha** (CHL), August 29, 1968.

• POPIEL, Poul

Poul Peter D – L. 5'10", 175 lbs. b: Sollested, Denmark, 2/28/1943.

Season	Club	League	GP	G	A	Pts	AG	AA	APts	PIM	PP	SH	GW	S	%	TGF	PGF	TGA	PGA	+/–	GP	G	A	Pts	PIM	PP	SH	GW
1960-61	St. Catharines Teepees	OHA-Jr.	38	2	9	11	....	....	....	74	....	....	....	....	....	....	....	....	....	....	3	0	1	1	2	....	....	....
1961-62	St. Catharines Teepees	OHA-Jr.	49	3	16	19	....	....	....	128	....	....	....	....	....	....	....	....	....	....	6	0	0	0	11	....	....	....
1962-63	St. Catharines Black Hawks	OHA-Jr.	50	11	34	45	....	....	....	131	....	....	....	....	....	....	....	....	....	....	....	....	....	....	....	....	....	....
	Buffalo Bisons	AHL	2	0	1	1	....	....	....	2	....	....	....	....	....	....	....	....	....	....	....	....	....	....	....	....	....	....
1963-64	Buffalo Bisons	AHL	4	0	0	0	....	....	....	4	....	....	....	....	....	....	....	....	....	....	....	....	....	....	....	....	....	....
	St. Louis Braves	CPHL	54	9	14	23	....	....	....	78	....	....	....	....	....	....	....	....	....	....	6	0	1	1	17	....	....	....
1964-65	Buffalo Bisons	AHL	48	7	12	19	....	....	....	76	....	....	....	....	....	....	....	....	....	....	9	0	1	1	29	....	....	....
1965-66	**Boston Bruins**	**NHL**	**3**	**0**	**1**	**1**	**0**	**1**	**1**	**2**	....	....	....	....	....	....	....	....	....	....	....	....	....	....	....	....	....	....
	Hershey Bears	AHL	63	6	26	32	....	....	....	101	....	....	....	....	....	....	....	....	....	....	3	0	0	0	2	....	....	....
1966-67	Hershey Bears	AHL	63	5	27	32	....	....	....	134	....	....	....	....	....	....	....	....	....	....	5	1	0	1	10	....	....	....
1967-68	**Los Angeles Kings**	**NHL**	**1**	**0**	**0**	**0**	**0**	**0**	**0**	**0**	**0**	**0**	**0**	**3**	**0.0**	**0**	**0**	**2**	**1**	**–1**	**3**	**1**	**0**	**1**	**4**	**0**	**0**	**0**
	Springfield Kings	AHL	72	8	27	35	....	....	....	180	....	....	....	....	....	....	....	....	....	....	4	0	0	0	4	....	....	....
1968-69	Springfield Kings	AHL	13	0	10	10	....	....	....	19	....	....	....	....	....	....	....	....	....	....	....	....	....	....	....	....	....	....
	Detroit Red Wings	**NHL**	**62**	**2**	**13**	**15**	**2**	**12**	**14**	**82**	**0**	**0**	**2**	**99**	**2.0**	**58**	**1**	**53**	**6**	**10**	....	....	....	....	....	....	....	....
1969-70	Cleveland Barons	AHL	22	3	15	18	....	....	....	14	....	....	....	....	....	....	....	....	....	....	....	....	....	....	....	....	....	....
	Detroit Red Wings	**NHL**	**32**	**0**	**4**	**4**	**0**	**4**	**4**	**29**	**0**	**0**	**0**	**22**	**0.0**	**16**	**2**	**9**	**0**	**5**	**1**	**0**	**0**	**0**	**0**	**0**	**0**	**0**
1970-71	**Vancouver Canucks**	**NHL**	**78**	**10**	**22**	**32**	**10**	**18**	**28**	**61**	**2**	**0**	**2**	**136**	**7.4**	**70**	**12**	**60**	**11**	**9**	....	....	....	....	....	....	....	....
1971-72	**Vancouver Canucks**	**NHL**	**38**	**1**	**1**	**2**	**1**	**1**	**2**	**36**	**0**	**0**	**0**	**32**	**3.1**	**5**	**0**	**37**	**21**	**–11**	....	....	....	....	....	....	....	....
	Rochester Americans	AHL	12	7	4	11	....	....	....	10	....	....	....	....	....	....	....	....	....	....	....	....	....	....	....	....	....	....
1972-73	Houston Aeros	WHA	74	16	48	64	....	....	....	158	....	....	....	....	....	....	....	....	....	....	10	2	9	11	23	....	....	....
1973-74	Houston Aeros	WHA	78	7	41	48	....	....	....	126	....	....	....	....	....	....	....	....	....	....	14	1	*14	15	22	....	....	....
1974-75	Houston Aeros	WHA	78	11	53	64	....	....	....	22	....	....	....	....	....	....	....	....	....	....	13	1	10	11	34	....	....	....
1975-76	Houston Aeros	WHA	78	10	36	46	....	....	....	71	....	....	....	....	....	....	....	....	....	....	17	3	5	8	16	....	....	....
1976-77	Houston Aeros	WHA	80	12	56	68	....	....	....	87	....	....	....	....	....	....	....	....	....	....	11	0	7	7	10	....	....	....
1977-78	Houston Aeros	WHA	80	6	31	37	....	....	....	53	....	....	....	....	....	....	....	....	....	....	6	0	2	2	13	....	....	....
1978-79	IEV Innsbruck	Austria	34	6	28	34	....	....	....	99	....	....	....	....	....	....	....	....	....	....	....	....	....	....	....	....	....	....
1979-80	**Edmonton Oilers**	**NHL**	**10**	**0**	**0**	**0**	**0**	**0**	**0**	**0**	**0**	**0**	**0**	**12**	**0.0**	**5**	**1**	**11**	**2**	**–5**	....	....	....	....	....	....	....	....
	Houston Apollos	CHL	57	2	27	29	....	....	....	28	....	....	....	....	....	....	....	....	....	....	6	0	1	1	10	....	....	....
1980-81			DID NOT PLAY																									
1981-82	Muskegon Mohawks	IHL	12	0	4	4	....	....	....	10	....	....	....	....	....	....	....	....	....	....	....	....	....	....	....	....	....	....
	NHL Totals		**224**	**13**	**41**	**54**	**13**	**36**	**49**	**210**	....	....	....	....	....	....	....	....	....	....	**4**	**1**	**0**	**1**	**4**	....	....	....
	Other Major League Totals		468	62	265	327	....	....	....	517	....	....	....	....	....	....	....	....	....	....	71	7	47	54	118	....	....	....

Shared Ken McKenzie Trophy (Rookie of the Year - CPHL) with Garry Peters (1964) • WHA Second All-Star Team (1975, 1977)

Claimed by **Boston** from **Chicago** in Intra-League Draft, June 9, 1965. Claimed by **LA Kings** from **Boston** in Expansion Draft, June 6, 1967. Traded to **Detroit** by **LA Kings** for Ron C. Anderson, November 12, 1968. Claimed by **Vancouver** from **Detroit** in Expansion Draft, June 10, 1970. Selected by **Dayton-Houston** (WHA) in 1972 WHA General Player Draft, February 12, 1972. Signed as a free agent by **Edmonton**, November 2, 1979.

• POPOVIC, Peter

D – L. 6'6", 235 lbs. b: Koping, Sweden, 2/10/1968. Montreal's 5th, 93rd overall, in 1988.

Season	Club	League	GP	G	A	Pts	AG	AA	APts	PIM	PP	SH	GW	S	%	TGF	PGF	TGA	PGA	+/–	GP	G	A	Pts	PIM	PP	SH	GW
1986-87	Vasteras IK	Sweden 2	24	1	2	3	....	....	....	10	....	....	....	....	....	....	....	....	....	....	12	2	8	10	6	....	....	....
1987-88	Vasteras IK	Sweden-2	28	3	17	20	....	....	....	16	....	....	....	....	....	....	....	....	....	....	15	1	4	5	20	....	....	....
1988-89	Vasteras IK	Sweden	22	1	4	5	....	....	....	32	....	....	....	....	....	....	....	....	....	....	....	....	....	....	....	....	....	....
1989-90	Vasteras IK	Sweden	30	2	10	12	....	....	....	24	....	....	....	....	....	....	....	....	....	....	2	0	1	1	2	....	....	....
1990-91	Vasteras IK	Sweden	40	3	2	5	....	....	....	62	....	....	....	....	....	....	....	....	....	....	4	0	0	0	4	....	....	....
1991-92	Vasteras IK	Sweden	34	7	10	17	....	....	....	30	....	....	....	....	....	....	....	....	....	....	....	....	....	....	....	....	....	....
1992-93	Vasteras IK	Sweden	39	6	12	18	....	....	....	46	....	....	....	....	....	....	....	....	....	....	3	0	1	1	2	....	....	....
	Sweden	WC-A	8	0	1	1	....	....	....	2	....	....	....	....	....	....	....	....	....	....	....	....	....	....	....	....	....	....
1993-94	**Montreal Canadiens**	**NHL**	**47**	**2**	**12**	**14**	**2**	**9**	**11**	**26**	**1**	**0**	**0**	**58**	**3.4**	**43**	**11**	**32**	**10**	**10**	**6**	**0**	**1**	**1**	**0**	**0**	**0**	**0**
1994-95	Vasteras IK	Sweden	11	0	3	3	....	....	....	10	....	....	....	....	....	....	....	....	....	....	....	....	....	....	....	....	....	....
	Montreal Canadiens	**NHL**	**33**	**0**	**5**	**5**	**0**	**7**	**7**	**8**	**0**	**0**	**0**	**23**	**0.0**	**11**	**0**	**27**	**6**	**–10**	....	....	....	....	....	....	....	....
1995-96	**Montreal Canadiens**	**NHL**	**76**	**2**	**12**	**14**	**2**	**10**	**12**	**69**	**0**	**0**	**0**	**59**	**3.4**	**82**	**8**	**87**	**34**	**21**	**6**	**0**	**2**	**2**	**4**	**0**	**0**	**0**
1996-97	Sweden	W-Cup	3	0	0	0	....	....	....	2	....	....	....	....	....	....	....	....	....	....	....	....	....	....	....	....	....	....
	Montreal Canadiens	**NHL**	**78**	**1**	**13**	**14**	**1**	**12**	**13**	**32**	**0**	**0**	**0**	**82**	**1.2**	**71**	**2**	**87**	**27**	**9**	**3**	**0**	**0**	**0**	**2**	**0**	**0**	**0**
1997-98	**Montreal Canadiens**	**NHL**	**69**	**2**	**6**	**8**	**2**	**6**	**8**	**38**	**0**	**0**	**0**	**40**	**5.0**	**37**	**0**	**63**	**20**	**–6**	**10**	**1**	**1**	**2**	**2**	**0**	**0**	**0**
1998-99	**New York Rangers**	**NHL**	**68**	**1**	**4**	**5**	**1**	**4**	**5**	**40**	**0**	**0**	**0**	**64**	**1.6**	**45**	**3**	**70**	**16**	**–12**	....	....	....	....	....	....	....	....
99-2000	**Pittsburgh Penguins**	**NHL**	**54**	**1**	**5**	**6**	**1**	**5**	**6**	**30**	**0**	**0**	**0**	**23**	**4.3**	**26**	**1**	**49**	**16**	**–8**	**10**	**0**	**0**	**0**	**10**	**0**	**0**	**0**
	NHL Totals		**425**	**9**	**57**	**66**	**9**	**53**	**62**	**243**	**1**	**0**	**0**	**349**	**2.6**	**315**	**25**	**415**	**129**		**35**	**1**	**4**	**5**	**18**	**0**	**0**	**0**

Traded to **NY Rangers** by **Montreal** for Sylvain Blouin and NY Rangers' 6th round choice (later traded to Phoenix - Phoenix selected Erik Leverstrom) in 1999 Entry Draft, June 30, 1998. Traded to **Pittsburgh** by **NY Rangers** for Kevin Hatcher, September 30, 1999. Signed as a free agent by **Boston**, July 2, 2000.

			REGULAR SEASON																		PLAYOFFS							
Season	**Club**	**League**	**GP**	**G**	**A**	**Pts**	**AG**	**AA**	**APts**	**PIM**	**PP**	**SH**	**GW**	**S**	**%**	**TGF**	**PGF**	**TGA**	**PGA**	**+/–**	**GP**	**G**	**A**	**Pts**	**PIM**	**PP**	**SH**	**GW**

• PORVARI, Jukka

RW – L. 5'11", 175 lbs. b: Tampere, Finland, 1/19/1954.

Season	Club	League	GP	G	A	Pts	AG	AA	APts	PIM	PP	SH	GW	S	%	TGF	PGF	TGA	PGA	+/–	GP	G	A	Pts	PIM	PP	SH	GW
1973-74	Tappara Tampere	Finland-Jr.	STATISTICS NOT AVAILABLE																									
	Finland	WJC-A	5	1	1	2	....	....	....	0	....	....	....	....	....	....	....	....	....	....	....	....	....	....	....	....	....	....
1974-75	Tappara Tampere	Finland	36	7	9	16	....	....	....	2	....	....	....	....	....	....	....	....	....	....	....	....	....	....	....	....	....	....
1975-76	Tappara Tampere	Finland	36	10	10	20	....	....	....	4	....	....	....	....	....	....	....	....	....	....	4	0	2	2	4	....	....	....
1976-77	Tappara Tampere	Finland	36	17	16	33	....	....	....	20	....	....	....	....	....	....	....	....	....	....	6	3	5	8	5	....	....	....
	Finland	WEC-A	10	3	3	6	....	....	....	2	....	....	....	....	....	....	....	....	....	....	....	....	....	....	....	....	....	....
1977-78	Tappara Tampere	Finland	26	11	7	18	....	....	....	18	....	....	....	....	....	....	....	....	....	....	8	1	1	2	16	....	....	....
	Finland	WEC-A	10	3	1	4	....	....	....	8	....	....	....	....	....	....	....	....	....	....	....	....	....	....	....	....	....	....
1978-79	Tappara Tampere	Finland	35	20	22	42	....	....	....	38	....	....	....	....	....	....	....	....	....	....	10	*9	4	13	0	....	....	....
	Finland	WEC-A	8	4	2	6	....	....	....	8	....	....	....	....	....	....	....	....	....	....	....	....	....	....	....	....	....	....
1979-80	Tappara Tampere	Finland	31	19	15	34	....	....	....	36	....	....	....	....	....	....	....	....	....	....	7	4	0	4	0	....	....	....
	Finland	Nat-Team	19	9	6	15	....	....	....	10	....	....	....	....	....	....	....	....	....	....	....	....	....	....	....	....	....	....
	Finland	Olympics	7	7	4	11	....	....	....	4	....	....	....	....	....	....	....	....	....	....	....	....	....	....	....	....	....	....
1980-81	Tappara Tampere	Finland	36	14	18	32	....	....	....	22	....	....	....	....	....	....	....	....	....	....	8	4	6	10	6	....	....	....
	Finland	WEC-A	8	3	0	3	....	....	....	8	....	....	....	....	....	....	....	....	....	....	....	....	....	....	....	....	....	....
1981-82	Finland	Can-Cup	5	1	0	1	....	....	....	0	....	....	....	....	....	....	....	....	....	....	....	....	....	....	....	....	....	....
	Colorado Rockies	**NHL**	**31**	**2**	**6**	**8**	**2**	**4**	**6**	**0**	**0**	**0**	**0**	**45**	**4.4**	**16**	**1**	**42**	**5**	**–22**	....	....	....	....	....	....	....	....
	Fort Worth Texans	CHL	2	0	0	0	....	....	....	0	....	....	....	....	....	....	....	....	....	....	....	....	....	....	....	....	....	....
1982-83	**New Jersey Devils**	**NHL**	**8**	**1**	**3**	**4**	**1**	**2**	**3**	**4**	**0**	**0**	**0**	**10**	**10.0**	**4**	**1**	**4**	**0**	**–1**	....	....	....	....	....	....	....	....
	Wichita Wind	CHL	11	2	3	5	....	....	....	0	....	....	....	....	....	....	....	....	....	....	....	....	....	....	....	....	....	....
	KAC Klagenfurt	Austria	14	13	10	23	....	....	....	18	....	....	....	....	....	....	....	....	....	....	....	....	....	....	....	....	....	....
1983-84	TPS Turku	Finland	37	18	8	26	....	....	....	16	....	....	....	....	....	....	....	....	....	....	10	5	1	6	4	....	....	....
1984-85	TPS Turku	Finland	36	27	16	43	....	....	....	26	....	....	....	....	....	....	....	....	....	....	10	*7	2	9	12	....	....	....
1985-86	TPS Turku	Finland	36	9	9	18	....	....	....	12	....	....	....	....	....	....	....	....	....	....	7	0	3	3	0	....	....	....
	NHL Totals		**39**	**3**	**9**	**12**	**3**	**6**	**9**	**4**	**0**	**0**	**0**	**55**	**5.5**	**20**	**2**	**46**	**5**		....	....	....	....	....	....	....	....

Finnish First All-Star Team (1978, 1980, 1981)

Signed as a free agent by **Colorado**, July 8, 1981. Transferred to **New Jersey** after **Colorado** franchise relocated, June 30, 1982.

• POSA, Victor

LW/D – L. 6', 195 lbs. b: Bari, Italy, 11/5/1966. Chicago's 7th, 137th overall, in 1985.

Season	Club	League	GP	G	A	Pts	AG	AA	APts	PIM	PP	SH	GW	S	%	TGF	PGF	TGA	PGA	+/–	GP	G	A	Pts	PIM	PP	SH	GW
1982-83	Henry Carr Crusaders	OJHL-B	35	2	16	18	....	....	....	178	....	....	....	....	....	....	....	....	....	....	....	....	....	....	....	....	....	....
	Markham Waxers	OJHL	1	0	1	1	....	....	....	0	....	....	....	....	....	....	....	....	....	....	....	....	....	....	....	....	....	....
1983-84	Henry Carr Crusaders	OJHL-B	25	16	21	37	....	....	....	139	....	....	....	....	....	....	....	....	....	....	....	....	....	....	....	....	....	....
1984-85	University of Wisconsin	WCHA	33	1	5	6	....	....	....	47	....	....	....	....	....	....	....	....	....	....	....	....	....	....	....	....	....	....
1985-86	Toronto Marlboros	OHL	48	28	34	62	....	....	....	116	....	....	....	....	....	....	....	....	....	....	....	....	....	....	....	....	....	....
	Chicago Black Hawks	**NHL**	**2**	**0**	**0**	**0**	**0**	**0**	**0**	**2**	**0**	**0**	**0**	**1**	**0.0**	**0**	**0**	**0**	**0**	**0**	....	....	....	....	....	....	....	....
1986-87	Nova Scotia Oilers	AHL	2	1	0	1	....	....	....	2	....	....	....	....	....	....	....	....	....	....	....	....	....	....	....	....	....	....
	Saginaw Generals	IHL	61	13	27	40	....	....	....	203	....	....	....	....	....	....	....	....	....	....	7	1	0	1	34	....	....	....
1987-88	Saginaw Hawks	IHL	2	0	0	0	....	....	....	0	....	....	....	....	....	....	....	....	....	....	....	....	....	....	....	....	....	....
	Flint Spirits	IHL	9	1	0	1	....	....	....	36	....	....	....	....	....	....	....	....	....	....	....	....	....	....	....	....	....	....
	Peoria Rivermen	IHL	10	0	2	2	....	....	....	106	....	....	....	....	....	....	....	....	....	....	....	....	....	....	....	....	....	....
1988-89	Flint Spirits	IHL	3	0	0	0	....	....	....	21	....	....	....	....	....	....	....	....	....	....	....	....	....	....	....	....	....	....
	Carolina Thunderbirds	EHL	10	4	4	8	....	....	....	41	....	....	....	....	....	....	....	....	....	....	....	....	....	....	....	....	....	....
1989-90			OUT OF HOCKEY – RETIRED																									
1990-91	SIJ Rotterdam	Holland	1	0	0	0	....	....	....	32	....	....	....	....	....	....	....	....	....	....	....	....	....	....	....	....	....	....
	Winston-Salem Thunderbirds	ECHL	9	1	4	5	....	....	....	41	....	....	....	....	....	....	....	....	....	....	....	....	....	....	....	....	....	....
	Richmond Renegades	ECHL	20	4	9	13	....	....	....	102	....	....	....	....	....	....	....	....	....	....	....	....	....	....	....	....	....	....
1991-92	Michigan Falcons	ColHL	37	14	40	54	....	....	....	131	....	....	....	....	....	....	....	....	....	....	....	....	....	....	....	....	....	....
1992-93	Detroit Falcons	ColHL	39	15	16	31	....	....	....	102	....	....	....	....	....	....	....	....	....	....	6	0	1	1	30	....	....	....
1993-94	Huntsville Blast	ECHL	9	1	3	4	....	....	....	33	....	....	....	....	....	....	....	....	....	....	....	....	....	....	....	....	....	....
1994-95			DID NOT PLAY																									
1995-96	Winston-Salem Mammoths	SHL	21	4	5	9	....	....	....	36	....	....	....	....	....	....	....	....	....	....	....	....	....	....	....	....	....	....
	NHL Totals		**2**	**0**	**0**	**0**	**0**	**0**	**0**	**2**	**0**	**0**	**0**	**1**	**0.0**	**0**	**0**	**0**	**0**		....	....	....	....	....	....	....	....

• POSAVAD, Mike

D – R. 5'11", 195 lbs. b: Brantford, Ont., 1/3/1964. St. Louis' 1st, 50th overall, in 1982.

Season	Club	League	GP	G	A	Pts	AG	AA	APts	PIM	PP	SH	GW	S	%	TGF	PGF	TGA	PGA	+/–	GP	G	A	Pts	PIM	PP	SH	GW
1979-80	Brantford Penguins	OJHL-B	43	11	22	33	....	....	....	16	....	....	....	....	....	....	....	....	....	....	....	....	....	....	....	....	....	....
1980-81	Peterborough Petes	OMJHL	58	3	12	15	....	....	....	55	....	....	....	....	....	....	....	....	....	....	....	....	....	....	....	....	....	....
1981-82	Peterborough Petes	OHL	64	7	23	30	....	....	....	110	....	....	....	....	....	....	....	....	....	....	9	3	4	7	15	....	....	....
1982-83	Peterborough Petes	OHL	70	1	36	37	....	....	....	68	....	....	....	....	....	....	....	....	....	....	4	0	2	2	2	....	....	....
	Salt Lake Golden Eagles	CHL	1	0	0	0	....	....	....	0	....	....	....	....	....	....	....	....	....	....	....	....	....	....	....	....	....	....
1983-84	Peterborough Petes	OHL	63	3	25	28	....	....	....	78	....	....	....	....	....	....	....	....	....	....	8	3	2	5	8	....	....	....
1984-85	Peoria Rivermen	IHL	67	2	19	21	....	....	....	58	....	....	....	....	....	....	....	....	....	....	19	1	5	6	42	....	....	....
1985-86	**St. Louis Blues**	**NHL**	**6**	**0**	**0**	**0**	**0**	**0**	**0**	**0**	**0**	**0**	**0**	**2**	**0.0**	**0**	**0**	**1**	**0**	**–1**	....	....	....	....	....	....	....	....
	Peoria Rivermen	IHL	72	1	17	18	....	....	....	75	....	....	....	....	....	....	....	....	....	....	11	0	1	1	13	....	....	....
1986-87	**St. Louis Blues**	**NHL**	**2**	**0**	**0**	**0**	**0**	**0**	**0**	**0**	**0**	**0**	**0**	**0**	**0.0**	**2**	**0**	**1**	**0**	**1**	....	....	....	....	....	....	....	....
	Peoria Rivermen	IHL	77	2	15	17	....	....	....	77	....	....	....	....	....	....	....	....	....	....	....	....	....	....	....	....	....	....
1987-88	Peoria Rivermen	IHL	27	0	4	4	....	....	....	23	....	....	....	....	....	....	....	....	....	....	....	....	....	....	....	....	....	....
	NHL Totals		**8**	**0**	**0**	**0**	**0**	**0**	**0**	**0**	**0**	**0**	**0**	**2**	**0.0**	**2**	**0**	**2**	**0**		....	....	....	....	....	....	....	....

OHL Second All-Star Team (1982)

• POSMYK, Marek

D – R. 6'5", 228 lbs. b: Jihlava, Czech., 9/15/1978. Toronto's 1st, 36th overall, in 1996.

Season	Club	League	GP	G	A	Pts	AG	AA	APts	PIM	PP	SH	GW	S	%	TGF	PGF	TGA	PGA	+/–	GP	G	A	Pts	PIM	PP	SH	GW
1994-95	Dukla Jihlava	Czech-Jr.	16	1	3	4	....	....	....	....	....	....	....	....	....	....	....	....	....	....	....	....	....	....	....	....	....	....
1995-96	Dukla Jihlava	Czech-Jr.	16	6	5	11	....	....	....	....	....	....	....	....	....	....	....	....	....	....	....	....	....	....	....	....	....	....
	Czech-Republic	WJC-A	5	1	0	1	....	....	....	2	....	....	....	....	....	....	....	....	....	....	....	....	....	....	....	....	....	....
	Dukla Jihlava	Czech.	18	1	2	3	....	....	....	....	....	....	....	....	....	....	....	....	....	....	1	0	0	0	....	....	....	....
1996-97	Dukla Jihlava	Czech-Rep	24	1	7	8	....	....	....	44	....	....	....	....	....	....	....	....	....	....	....	....	....	....	....	....	....	....
	Czech-Republic	WJC-A	1	0	0	0	....	....	....	0	....	....	....	....	....	....	....	....	....	....	....	....	....	....	....	....	....	....
	St. John's Maple Leafs	AHL	2	0	0	0	....	....	....	2	....	....	....	....	....	....	....	....	....	....	....	....	....	....	....	....	....	....
1997-98	Czech-Republic	WJC-A	7	1	2	3	....	....	....	8	....	....	....	....	....	....	....	....	....	....	....	....	....	....	....	....	....	....
	Sarnia Sting	OHL	48	8	16	24	....	....	....	94	....	....	....	....	....	....	....	....	....	....	5	0	2	2	6	....	....	....
	St. John's Maple Leafs	AHL	3	0	0	0	....	....	....	4	....	....	....	....	....	....	....	....	....	....	....	....	....	....	....	....	....	....
1998-99	St. John's Maple Leafs	AHL	41	1	0	1	....	....	....	36	....	....	....	....	....	....	....	....	....	....	....	....	....	....	....	....	....	....
99-2000	**Tampa Bay Lightning**	**NHL**	**18**	**1**	**2**	**3**	**1**	**2**	**3**	**20**	**0**	**0**	**0**	**22**	**4.5**	**15**	**0**	**14**	**0**	**1**	....	....	....	....	....	....	....	....
	Detroit Vipers	IHL	1	0	1	1	....	....	....	0	....	....	....	....	....	....	....	....	....	....	....	....	....	....	....	....	....	....
	NHL Totals		**18**	**1**	**2**	**3**	**1**	**2**	**3**	**20**	**0**	**0**	**0**	**22**	**4.5**	**15**	**0**	**14**	**0**		....	....	....	....	....	....	....	....

Traded to **Tampa Bay** by **Toronto** with Mike Johnson, Toronto's 5th (Pavel Sedov) and 6th (Aaron Gionet) round choices in 2000 Entry Draft and future considerations for Darcy Tucker, Tampa Bay's 4th round choice (Miguel Delisle) in 2000 Entry Draft and future considerations, February 9, 2000.

• POTI, Tom

Thomas Emilio D – L. 6'3", 215 lbs. b: Worcester, MA, 3/22/1977. Edmonton's 4th, 59th overall, in 1996.

Season	Club	League	GP	G	A	Pts	AG	AA	APts	PIM	PP	SH	GW	S	%	TGF	PGF	TGA	PGA	+/–	GP	G	A	Pts	PIM	PP	SH	GW
1991-92	Mass Central Chiefs	MBAHL	STATISTICS NOT AVAILABLE																									
1992-93	St. Peter's-Marian High	Hi-School	55	25	46	71	....	....	....	....	....	....	....	....	....	....	....	....	....	....	....	....	....	....	....	....	....	....
1993-94	Cushing Academy Penguins	Hi-School	30	10	35	45	....	....	....	....	....	....	....	....	....	....	....	....	....	....	....	....	....	....	....	....	....	....
1994-95	Cushing Academy Penguins	Hi-School	36	17	54	71	....	....	....	35	....	....	....	....	....	....	....	....	....	....	....	....	....	....	....	....	....	....
	Central Mass Outlaws	MBAHL	8	8	10	18	....	....	....	....	....	....	....	....	....	....	....	....	....	....	....	....	....	....	....	....	....	....
1995-96	Cushing Academy Penguins	Hi-School	29	14	59	73	....	....	....	18	....	....	....	....	....	....	....	....	....	....	....	....	....	....	....	....	....	....
	United States	WJC-A	6	0	3	3	....	....	....	0	....	....	....	....	....	....	....	....	....	....	....	....	....	....	....	....	....	....
1996-97	Boston University	H-East	38	4	17	21	....	....	....	54	....	....	....	....	....	....	....	....	....	....	....	....	....	....	....	....	....	....
	United States	WJC-A	6	1	2	3	....	....	....	4	....	....	....	....	....	....	....	....	....	....	....	....	....	....	....	....	....	....

			REGULAR SEASON																		PLAYOFFS							
Season	Club	League	GP	G	A	Pts	AG	AA	APts	PIM	PP	SH	GW	S	%	TGF	PGF	TGA	PGA	+/–	GP	G	A	Pts	PIM	PP	SH	GW
1997-98	Boston University	H-East	38	13	29	42	....	....	....	60	....	....	....	....	....	....	....	....	....	....	....	....	....	....	....	....	....	....
1998-99	**Edmonton Oilers**	**NHL**	**73**	**5**	**16**	**21**	**6**	**15**	**21**	**42**	**2**	**0**	**3**	**94**	**5.3**	**71**	**16**	**60**	**15**	**10**	**4**	**0**	**1**	**1**	**2**	**0**	**0**	**0**
99-2000	**Edmonton Oilers**	**NHL**	**76**	**9**	**26**	**35**	**10**	**24**	**34**	**65**	**2**	**1**	**1**	**125**	**7.2**	**94**	**26**	**73**	**13**	**8**	**5**	**0**	**1**	**1**	**0**	**0**	**0**	**0**
	NHL Totals		**149**	**14**	**42**	**56**	**16**	**39**	**55**	**107**	**4**	**1**	**4**	**219**	**6.4**	**165**	**42**	**133**	**28**		**9**	**0**	**2**	**2**	**2**	**0**	**0**	**0**

NCAA Championship All-Tournament Team (1997) • Hockey East First All-Star Team (1998) • NCAA East First All-American Team (1998) • NHL All-Rookie Team (1999)

• POTOMSKI, Barry

LW – L. 6'2", 215 lbs. b: Windsor, Ont., 11/24/1972.

Season	Club	League	GP	G	A	Pts	AG	AA	APts	PIM	PP	SH	GW	S	%	TGF	PGF	TGA	PGA	+/–	GP	G	A	Pts	PIM	PP	SH	GW
1988-89	Windsor Riversides	OMHA	56	24	22	46	....	....	....	....	....	....	....	....	....	....	....	....	....	....	....	....	....	....	....	....	....	....
1989-90	Tillsonburg Titans	OJHL-B	32	11	17	28	....	....	....	158	....	....	....	....	....	....	....	....	....	....	....	....	....	....	....	....	....	....
	London Knights	OHL	9	0	2	2	....	....	....	18	....	....	....	....	....	....	....	....	....	....	....	....	....	....	....	....	....	....
1990-91	London Knights	OHL	65	14	17	31	....	....	....	202	....	....	....	....	....	....	....	....	....	....	7	0	2	2	10	....	....	....
1991-92	London Knights	OHL	61	19	32	51	....	....	....	224	....	....	....	....	....	....	....	....	....	....	10	5	1	6	22	....	....	....
1992-93	Erie Panthers	ECHL	5	1	1	2	....	....	....	31	....	....	....	....	....	....	....	....	....	....	....	....	....	....	....	....	....	....
	Toledo Storm	ECHL	43	5	18	23	....	....	....	184	....	....	....	....	....	....	....	....	....	....	14	5	2	7	73	....	....	....
1993-94	Toledo Storm	ECHL	13	9	4	13	....	....	....	81	....	....	....	....	....	....	....	....	....	....	....	....	....	....	....	....	....	....
	Adirondack Red Wings	AHL	50	9	5	14	....	....	....	224	....	....	....	....	....	....	....	....	....	....	11	1	1	2	44	....	....	....
1994-95	Phoenix Roadrunners	IHL	42	5	6	11	....	....	....	171	....	....	....	....	....	....	....	....	....	....	....	....	....	....	....	....	....	....
1995-96	**Los Angeles Kings**	**NHL**	**33**	**3**	**2**	**5**	**3**	**2**	**5**	**104**	**1**	**0**	**0**	**23**	**13.0**	**10**	**2**	**15**	**0**	**–7**	....	....	....	....	....	....	....	....
	Phoenix Roadrunners	IHL	24	5	2	7	....	....	....	74	....	....	....	....	....	....	....	....	....	....	3	1	0	1	8	....	....	....
1996-97	**Los Angeles Kings**	**NHL**	**26**	**3**	**2**	**5**	**3**	**2**	**5**	**93**	**0**	**0**	**1**	**18**	**16.7**	**7**	**0**	**15**	**0**	**–8**	....	....	....	....	....	....	....	....
	Phoenix Roadrunners	IHL	28	2	11	13	....	....	....	58	....	....	....	....	....	....	....	....	....	....	....	....	....	....	....	....	....	....
1997-98	**San Jose Sharks**	**NHL**	**9**	**0**	**1**	**1**	**0**	**1**	**1**	**30**	**0**	**0**	**0**	**4**	**0.0**	**2**	**0**	**1**	**0**	**1**	....	....	....	....	....	....	....	....
	Las Vegas Thunder	IHL	31	3	2	5	....	....	....	143	....	....	....	....	....	....	....	....	....	....	4	1	0	1	13	....	....	....
1998-99	Adirondack Red Wings	AHL	75	9	7	16	....	....	....	220	....	....	....	....	....	....	....	....	....	....	1	0	0	0	2	....	....	....
99-2000	Long Beach Ice Dogs	IHL	1	0	0	0	....	....	....	0	....	....	....	....	....	....	....	....	....	....	....	....	....	....	....	....	....	....
	San Diego Gulls	WCHL	51	13	30	43	....	....	....	211	....	....	....	....	....	....	....	....	....	....	9	4	4	8	12	....	....	....
	NHL Totals		**68**	**6**	**5**	**11**	**6**	**5**	**11**	**227**	**1**	**0**	**1**	**45**	**13.3**	**19**	**2**	**31**	**0**		....	....	....	....	....	....	....	....

Signed as a free agent by **LA Kings**, July 7, 1994. Signed as a free agent by **San Jose**, August 15, 1997. Signed as a free agent by **Detroit**, August 13, 1998. • Played w/ RHI's Anaheim Bullfrogs in 1993 (13-5-14-19-56).

• POTVIN, Denis

Denis Charles D – L. 6', 205 lbs. b: Ottawa, Ont., 10/29/1953. NY Islanders' 1st, 1st overall, in 1973. **HHOF**

Season	Club	League	GP	G	A	Pts	AG	AA	APts	PIM	PP	SH	GW	S	%	TGF	PGF	TGA	PGA	+/–	GP	G	A	Pts	PIM	PP	SH	GW
1968-69	Ottawa 67's	OHA-Jr.	46	12	25	37	....	....	....	83	....	....	....	....	....	....	....	....	....	....	....	....	....	....	....	....	....	....
1969-70	Ottawa 67's	OHA-Jr.	42	13	18	31	....	....	....	97	....	....	....	....	....	....	....	....	....	....	5	2	1	3	9	....	....	....
1970-71	Ottawa 67's	OHA-Jr.	57	20	58	78	....	....	....	200	....	....	....	....	....	....	....	....	....	....	11	4	6	10	26	....	....	....
1971-72	Ottawa 67's	OMJHL	48	15	45	60	....	....	....	188	....	....	....	....	....	....	....	....	....	....	....	....	....	....	....	....	....	....
1972-73	Ottawa 67's	OMJHL	61	35	88	123	....	....	....	232	....	....	....	....	....	....	....	....	....	....	9	6	10	16	22	....	....	....
1973-74	**New York Islanders**	**NHL**	**77**	**17**	**37**	**54**	**16**	**31**	**47**	**175**	**6**	**0**	**3**	**209**	**8.1**	**114**	**29**	**141**	**40**	**–16**	....	....	....	....	....	....	....	....
1974-75	**New York Islanders**	**NHL**	**79**	**21**	**55**	**76**	**18**	**41**	**59**	**105**	**5**	**2**	**4**	**211**	**10.0**	**153**	**48**	**111**	**34**	**28**	**17**	**5**	**9**	**14**	**30**	**3**	**1**	**0**
1975-76	**New York Islanders**	**NHL**	**78**	**31**	**67**	**98**	**27**	**50**	**77**	**100**	**18**	**0**	**4**	**256**	**12.1**	**168**	**85**	**104**	**33**	**12**	**13**	**5**	***14**	**19**	**32**	**2**	**0**	**1**
1976-77	Canada	Can-Cup	7	1	8	*9	....	....	....	16	....	....	....	....	....	....	....	....	....	....	....	....	....	....	....	....	....	....
	New York Islanders	**NHL**	**80**	**25**	**55**	**80**	**23**	**42**	**65**	**103**	**7**	**1**	**4**	**241**	**10.4**	**173**	**56**	**92**	**17**	**42**	**12**	**6**	**4**	**10**	**20**	**2**	**0**	**0**
1977-78	**New York Islanders**	**NHL**	**80**	**30**	**64**	**94**	**27**	**50**	**77**	**81**	**9**	**0**	**6**	**288**	**10.4**	**204**	**70**	**107**	**30**	**57**	**7**	**2**	**2**	**4**	**6**	**0**	**0**	**0**
1978-79	**New York Islanders**	**NHL**	**73**	**31**	**70**	**101**	**27**	**51**	**78**	**58**	**12**	**3**	**2**	**237**	**13.1**	**203**	**75**	**91**	**34**	**71**	**10**	**4**	**7**	**11**	**8**	**0**	**0**	**1**
	NHL All-Stars	Chal-Cup	2	0	0	0	....	....	....	0	....	....	....	....	....	....	....	....	....	....	....	....	....	....	....	....	....	....
1979-80 ◆	**New York Islanders**	**NHL**	**31**	**8**	**33**	**41**	**7**	**24**	**31**	**44**	**4**	**0**	**0**	**98**	**8.2**	**72**	**26**	**48**	**15**	**13**	**21**	**6**	**13**	**19**	**24**	**4**	**0**	**1**
1980-81 ◆	**New York Islanders**	**NHL**	**74**	**20**	**56**	**76**	**16**	**37**	**53**	**104**	**9**	**0**	**4**	**206**	**9.7**	**190**	**85**	**108**	**41**	**38**	**18**	**8**	**17**	**25**	**16**	**6**	**1**	**2**
1981-82	Canada	Can-Cup	7	2	5	7	....	....	....	12	....	....	....	....	....	....	....	....	....	....	....	....	....	....	....	....	....	....
◆	**New York Islanders**	**NHL**	**60**	**24**	**37**	**61**	**19**	**25**	**44**	**83**	**11**	**1**	**4**	**169**	**14.2**	**148**	**56**	**77**	**23**	**38**	**19**	**5**	**16**	**21**	**30**	**3**	**0**	**0**
1982-83 ◆	**New York Islanders**	**NHL**	**69**	**12**	**54**	**66**	**10**	**38**	**48**	**60**	**4**	**1**	**1**	**191**	**6.3**	**140**	**55**	**81**	**28**	**32**	**20**	**8**	**12**	**20**	**22**	**4**	**0**	**1**
1983-84	**New York Islanders**	**NHL**	**78**	**22**	**63**	**85**	**18**	**43**	**61**	**87**	**11**	**1**	**3**	**246**	**8.9**	**178**	**50**	**105**	**32**	**55**	**20**	**1**	**5**	**6**	**28**	**1**	**0**	**0**
1984-85	**New York Islanders**	**NHL**	**77**	**17**	**51**	**68**	**14**	**35**	**49**	**96**	**6**	**0**	**1**	**198**	**8.6**	**161**	**45**	**117**	**37**	**36**	**10**	**3**	**2**	**5**	**10**	**1**	**0**	**1**
1985-86	**New York Islanders**	**NHL**	**74**	**21**	**38**	**59**	**17**	**26**	**43**	**78**	**8**	**1**	**4**	**168**	**12.5**	**133**	**39**	**93**	**33**	**34**	**3**	**0**	**1**	**1**	**0**	**0**	**0**	**0**
	Canada	WEC-A	7	1	4	5	....	....	....	6	....	....	....	....	....	....	....	....	....	....	....	....	....	....	....	....	....	....
1986-87	**New York Islanders**	**NHL**	**58**	**12**	**30**	**42**	**10**	**22**	**32**	**70**	**8**	**0**	**1**	**147**	**8.2**	**93**	**44**	**78**	**23**	**–6**	**10**	**2**	**2**	**4**	**21**	**1**	**0**	**0**
1987-88	**New York Islanders**	**NHL**	**72**	**19**	**32**	**51**	**16**	**23**	**39**	**112**	**9**	**0**	**3**	**188**	**10.1**	**121**	**46**	**74**	**25**	**26**	**5**	**1**	**4**	**5**	**6**	**1**	**0**	**0**
	NHL Totals		**1060**	**310**	**742**	**1052**	**265**	**538**	**803**	**1356**	**127**	**10**	**44**	**3053**	**10.2**	**2251**	**809**	**1427**	**445**		**185**	**56**	**108**	**164**	**253**	**28**	**2**	**7**

• Brother of Jean • OMJHL First All-Star Team (1971, 1972, 1973) • Won Calder Memorial Trophy (1974) • NHL First All-Star Team (1975, 1976, 1978, 1979, 1981) • Won James Norris Trophy (1976, 1978, 1979) • NHL Second All-Star Team (1977, 1984) • Played in NHL All-Star Game (1974, 1975, 1976, 1977, 1978, 1981, 1983, 1984, 1988)

• Missed majority of 1979-80 season recovering from thumb injury suffered in game vs. Edmonton, November 30, 1979.

• POTVIN, Jean

Jean Rene D – R. 5'11", 188 lbs. b: Ottawa, Ont., 3/25/1949.

Season	Club	League	GP	G	A	Pts	AG	AA	APts	PIM	PP	SH	GW	S	%	TGF	PGF	TGA	PGA	+/–	GP	G	A	Pts	PIM	PP	SH	GW
1966-67	Hull Volants	QJHL	45	22	27	49	....	....	....	115	....	....	....	....	....	....	....	....	....	....	....	....	....	....	....	....	....	....
1967-68	Ottawa 67's	OHA-Jr.	54	18	17	35	....	....	....	138	....	....	....	....	....	....	....	....	....	....	....	....	....	....	....	....	....	....
1968-69	Ottawa 67's	OHA-Jr.	54	17	23	40	....	....	....	116	....	....	....	....	....	....	....	....	....	....	7	1	7	8	20	....	....	....
1969-70	Springfield Kings	AHL	61	3	5	8	....	....	....	42	....	....	....	....	....	....	....	....	....	....	14	0	2	2	24	....	....	....
1970-71	**Los Angeles Kings**	**NHL**	**4**	**1**	**3**	**4**	**1**	**2**	**3**	**2**	**0**	**0**	**0**	**5**	**20.0**	**8**	**1**	**3**	**1**	**5**	....	....	....	....	....	....	....	....
	Springfield Kings	AHL	60	9	23	32	....	....	....	94	....	....	....	....	....	....	....	....	....	....	12	2	10	12	17	....	....	....
1971-72	**Los Angeles Kings**	**NHL**	**39**	**2**	**3**	**5**	**2**	**3**	**5**	**35**	**0**	**0**	**1**	**55**	**3.6**	**25**	**3**	**67**	**6**	**–39**	....	....	....	....	....	....	....	....
	Philadelphia Flyers	**NHL**	**29**	**3**	**12**	**15**	**3**	**10**	**13**	**6**	**2**	**0**	**1**	**23**	**13.0**	**22**	**16**	**13**	**1**	**–6**	....	....	....	....	....	....	....	....
1972-73	**Philadelphia Flyers**	**NHL**	**35**	**3**	**9**	**12**	**3**	**7**	**10**	**10**	**1**	**0**	**1**	**27**	**11.1**	**25**	**12**	**17**	**3**	**–1**	....	....	....	....	....	....	....	....
	New York Islanders	**NHL**	**10**	**0**	**3**	**3**	**0**	**2**	**2**	**12**	**0**	**0**	**0**	**18**	**0.0**	**15**	**2**	**22**	**6**	**–3**	....	....	....	....	....	....	....	....
1973-74	**New York Islanders**	**NHL**	**78**	**5**	**23**	**28**	**5**	**19**	**24**	**100**	**2**	**0**	**0**	**114**	**4.4**	**85**	**28**	**99**	**16**	**–26**	....	....	....	....	....	....	....	....
1974-75	**New York Islanders**	**NHL**	**73**	**9**	**24**	**33**	**8**	**18**	**26**	**59**	**6**	**1**	**4**	**115**	**7.8**	**85**	**39**	**56**	**7**	**–3**	**15**	**2**	**4**	**6**	**9**	**0**	**0**	**0**
1975-76	**New York Islanders**	**NHL**	**78**	**17**	**55**	**72**	**15**	**41**	**56**	**74**	**9**	**1**	**2**	**167**	**10.2**	**139**	**82**	**48**	**7**	**16**	**13**	**0**	**1**	**1**	**2**	**0**	**0**	**0**
1976-77	**New York Islanders**	**NHL**	**79**	**10**	**36**	**46**	**9**	**28**	**37**	**26**	**1**	**1**	**0**	**124**	**8.1**	**86**	**37**	**38**	**3**	**14**	**11**	**0**	**4**	**4**	**6**	**0**	**0**	**0**
1977-78	**New York Islanders**	**NHL**	**34**	**1**	**10**	**11**	**1**	**8**	**9**	**8**	**0**	**0**	**0**	**36**	**2.8**	**33**	**1**	**27**	**6**	**11**	....	....	....	....	....	....	....	....
	Cleveland Barons	**NHL**	**40**	**3**	**14**	**17**	**3**	**11**	**14**	**30**	**0**	**0**	**1**	**85**	**3.5**	**58**	**6**	**76**	**20**	**–4**	....	....	....	....	....	....	....	....
1978-79	**Minnesota North Stars**	**NHL**	**64**	**5**	**16**	**21**	**4**	**12**	**16**	**65**	**2**	**2**	**1**	**89**	**5.6**	**67**	**11**	**73**	**7**	**–10**	....	....	....	....	....	....	....	....
	Oklahoma City Stars	CHL	9	3	7	10	....	....	....	10	....	....	....	....	....	....	....	....	....	....	....	....	....	....	....	....	....	....
1979-80	**New York Islanders**	**NHL**	**32**	**2**	**13**	**15**	**2**	**9**	**11**	**26**	**2**	**0**	**0**	**49**	**4.1**	**36**	**10**	**49**	**11**	**–12**	....	....	....	....	....	....	....	....
1980-81	**New York Islanders**	**NHL**	**18**	**2**	**3**	**5**	**2**	**2**	**4**	**25**	**2**	**0**	**1**	**16**	**12.5**	**14**	**3**	**17**	**2**	**–4**	....	....	....	....	....	....	....	....
	NHL Totals		**613**	**63**	**224**	**287**	**58**	**172**	**230**	**478**	**27**	**5**	**12**	**923**	**6.8**	**698**	**251**	**605**	**96**		**39**	**2**	**9**	**11**	**17**	**0**	**0**	**0**

• Brother of Denis

Signed as a free agent by **LA Kings** (Springfield-AHL), November 15, 1969. Traded to **Philadelphia** by **LA Kings** with Eddie Joyal, Bill Flett and Ross Lonsberry for Bill Lesuk, Jim Johnson and Serge Bernier, January 28, 1972. Traded to **NY Islanders** by **Philadelphia** with future considerations (Glen Irwin, May 18, 1973) for Terry Crisp, March 5, 1973. Traded to **Cleveland** by **NY Islanders** with Jean-Paul Parise for Wayne Merrick, Darcy Reiger and Cleveland's 4th round choice (draft choice cancelled by the Cleveland-Minnesota merger) in the 1978 Amateur Draft, January 10, 1978. Placed on **Minnesota** Reserve List after **Cleveland-Minnesota** Dispersal Draft, June 15, 1978. Signed as a free agent by **NY Islanders**, June 10, 1979.

• POTVIN, Marc

Marc R. RW – R. 6'1", 200 lbs. b: Ottawa, Ont., 1/29/1967. Detroit's 9th, 169th overall, in 1986.

Season	Club	League	GP	G	A	Pts	AG	AA	APts	PIM	PP	SH	GW	S	%	TGF	PGF	TGA	PGA	+/–	GP	G	A	Pts	PIM	PP	SH	GW
1985-86	Stratford Cullitons	OJHL-B	39	22	43	65	....	....	....	180	....	....	....	....	....	....	....	....	....	....	....	....	....	....	....	....	....	....
1986-87	Bowling Green University	CCHA	43	5	15	20	....	....	....	74	....	....	....	....	....	....	....	....	....	....	....	....	....	....	....	....	....	....
1987-88	Bowling Green University	CCHA	45	15	21	36	....	....	....	80	....	....	....	....	....	....	....	....	....	....	....	....	....	....	....	....	....	....
1988-89	Bowling Green University	CCHA	46	23	12	35	....	....	....	63	....	....	....	....	....	....	....	....	....	....	....	....	....	....	....	....	....	....
1989-90	Bowling Green University	CCHA	40	19	17	36	....	....	....	72	....	....	....	....	....	....	....	....	....	....	....	....	....	....	....	....	....	....
	Adirondack Red Wings	AHL	5	2	1	3	....	....	....	9	....	....	....	....	....	....	....	....	....	....	4	0	1	1	23	....	....	....
1990-91	**Detroit Red Wings**	**NHL**	**9**	**0**	**0**	**0**	**0**	**0**	**0**	**55**	**0**	**0**	**0**	**13**	**0.0**	**3**	**0**	**7**	**0**	**–4**	**6**	**0**	**0**	**0**	**32**	**0**	**0**	**0**
	Adirondack Red Wings	AHL	63	9	13	22	....	....	....	*365	....	....	....	....	....	....	....	....	....	....	....	....	....	....	....	....	....	....

Season	Club	League	GP	G	A	Pts	AG	AA	APts	PIM	PP	SH	GW	S	%	TGF	PGF	TGA	PGA	+/–	GP	G	A	Pts	PIM	PP	SH	GW
			REGULAR SEASON																		PLAYOFFS							
1991-92	**Detroit Red Wings**	**NHL**	**5**	**1**	**0**	**1**	**1**	**0**	**1**	**52**	**0**	**0**	**0**	**4**	**25.0**	**1**	**0**	**3**	**0**	**–2**	**1**	**0**	**0**	**0**	**0**	**0**	**0**	**0**
	Adirondack Red Wings	AHL	51	13	16	29	....	....	....	314	....	....	....	....	....	....	....	....	....	....	19	5	4	9	57	....	....	....
1992-93	Adirondack Red Wings	AHL	37	8	12	20	....	....	....	109	....	....	....	....	....	....	....	....	....	....	....	....	....	....	....	....	....	....
	Los Angeles Kings	**NHL**	**20**	**0**	**1**	**1**	**0**	**1**	**1**	**61**	**0**	**0**	**0**	**7**	**0.0**	**1**	**0**	**11**	**0**	**–10**	**1**	**0**	**0**	**0**	**0**	**0**	**0**	**0**
1993-94	**Los Angeles Kings**	**NHL**	**3**	**0**	**0**	**0**	**0**	**0**	**0**	**26**	**0**	**0**	**0**	**1**	**0.0**	**0**	**0**	**3**	**0**	**–3**	....	....	....	....	....	....	....	....
	Hartford Whalers	**NHL**	**51**	**2**	**3**	**5**	**2**	**2**	**4**	**246**	**0**	**0**	**0**	**25**	**8.0**	**7**	**1**	**11**	**0**	**–5**	....	....	....	....	....	....	....	....
1994-95	**Boston Bruins**	**NHL**	**6**	**0**	**1**	**1**	**0**	**1**	**1**	**4**	**0**	**0**	**0**	**4**	**0.0**	**1**	**0**	**0**	**0**	**1**	....	....	....	....	....	....	....	....
	Providence Bruins	AHL	21	4	14	18	....	....	....	84	....	....	....	....	....	....	....	....	....	....	12	2	4	6	25	....	....	....
1995-96	**Boston Bruins**	**NHL**	**27**	**0**	**0**	**0**	**0**	**0**	**0**	**12**	**0**	**0**	**0**	**14**	**0.0**	**1**	**0**	**3**	**0**	**–2**	**5**	**0**	**1**	**1**	**18**	**0**	**0**	**0**
	Providence Bruins	AHL	48	9	9	18	....	....	....	118	....	....	....	....	....	....	....	....	....	....	....	....	....	....	....	....	....	....
1996-97	Portland Pirates	AHL	71	17	15	32	....	....	....	222	....	....	....	....	....	....	....	....	....	....	5	0	0	0	12	....	....	....
1997-98	Chicago Wolves	IHL	81	4	8	12	....	....	....	170	....	....	....	....	....	....	....	....	....	....	10	0	0	0	22	....	....	....
1998-1999	Adirondack Red Wings	AHL	DID NOT PLAY – ASSISTANT COACH																									
1999-2000	Mississippi Sea Wolves	ECHL	DID NOT PLAY – COACHING																									
	NHL Totals		**121**	**3**	**5**	**8**	**3**	**4**	**7**	**456**	**0**	**0**	**0**	**68**	**4.4**	**14**	**1**	**38**	**0**		**13**	**0**	**1**	**1**	**50**	**0**	**0**	**0**

Traded to **LA Kings** by **Detroit** with Jimmy Carson and Gary Shuchuk for Paul Coffey, Sylvain Couturier and Jim Hiller, January 29, 1993. Traded to **Hartford** by **LA Kings** for Doug Houda, November 3, 1993. Signed as a free agent by **Boston**, June 29, 1994. • Named Head Coach of **Springfield** (AHL), July 12, 2000.

• POUDRIER, Daniel

D – L. 6'2", 175 lbs. b: Thetford Mines, Que., 2/15/1964. Quebec's 6th, 131st overall, in 1982.

Season	Club	League	GP	G	A	Pts	AG	AA	APts	PIM	PP	SH	GW	S	%	TGF	PGF	TGA	PGA	+/–	GP	G	A	Pts	PIM	PP	SH	GW
1979-80	Montreal L'est Cantonniers	QAAA	32	4	13	17	....	....	....	....	....	....	....	....	....	....	....	....	....	....	....	....	....	....	....	....	....	....
1980-81	Montreal West Cantonniers	QAAA	26	8	8	16	....	....	....	18	....	....	....	....	....	....	....	....	....	....	....	....	....	....	....	....	....	....
1981-82	Shawinigan Cataractes	QMJHL	64	6	18	24	....	....	....	20	....	....	....	....	....	....	....	....	....	....	14	1	1	2	2	....	....	....
1982-83	Shawinigan Cataractes	QMJHL	67	6	28	34	....	....	....	31	....	....	....	....	....	....	....	....	....	....	10	1	2	3	2	....	....	....
1983-84	Drummondville Voltigeurs	QMJHL	64	7	28	35	....	....	....	15	....	....	....	....	....	....	....	....	....	....	10	2	3	5	4	....	....	....
1984-85	Fredericton Express	AHL	1	0	0	0	....	....	....	0	....	....	....	....	....	....	....	....	....	....	....	....	....	....	....	....	....	....
	Muskegon Mohawks	IHL	82	9	30	39	....	....	....	12	....	....	....	....	....	....	....	....	....	....	17	2	6	8	2	....	....	....
1985-86	**Quebec Nordiques**	**NHL**	**13**	**1**	**5**	**6**	**1**	**3**	**4**	**10**	**0**	**0**	**1**	**6**	**16.7**	**11**	**1**	**11**	**3**	**2**	....	....	....	....	....	....	....	....
	Fredericton Express	AHL	65	5	26	31	....	....	....	9	....	....	....	....	....	....	....	....	....	....	6	0	3	3	0	....	....	....
1986-87	**Quebec Nordiques**	**NHL**	**6**	**0**	**0**	**0**	**0**	**0**	**0**	**0**	**0**	**0**	**0**	**2**	**0.0**	**3**	**0**	**5**	**0**	**–2**	....	....	....	....	....	....	....	....
	Fredericton Express	AHL	69	8	18	26	....	....	....	11	....	....	....	....	....	....	....	....	....	....	....	....	....	....	....	....	....	....
1987-88	**Quebec Nordiques**	**NHL**	**6**	**0**	**0**	**0**	**0**	**0**	**0**	**0**	**0**	**0**	**0**	**0**	**0.0**	**4**	**3**	**3**	**1**	**–1**	....	....	....	....	....	....	....	....
	Fredericton Express	AHL	66	13	30	43	....	....	....	18	....	....	....	....	....	....	....	....	....	....	11	2	5	7	2	....	....	....
1988-89	Halifax Citadels	AHL	7	2	4	6	....	....	....	2	....	....	....	....	....	....	....	....	....	....	3	0	0	0	2	....	....	....
	HC Mont Blanc	France	18	7	5	12	....	....	....	8	....	....	....	....	....	....	....	....	....	....	....	....	....	....	....	....	....	....
1989-90	Canada	Nat-Team	40	4	7	11	....	....	....	2	....	....	....	....	....	....	....	....	....	....	....	....	....	....	....	....	....	....
	WEV Wien	Austria	11	5	6	11	....	....	....	6	....	....	....	....	....	....	....	....	....	....	....	....	....	....	....	....	....	....
1990-91	EV Fussen	Germany-2	47	30	42	72	....	....	....	22	....	....	....	....	....	....	....	....	....	....	....	....	....	....	....	....	....	....
1991-92	EHC Klostersee	Germany-3	17	20	16	36	....	....	....	6	....	....	....	....	....	....	....	....	....	....	13	13	17	30	4	....	....	....
	St. Thomas Wildcats	ColHL	9	1	1	2	....	....	....	0	....	....	....	....	....	....	....	....	....	....	....	....	....	....	....	....	....	....
1992-93	EHC Klostersee	Germany-3	17	20	16	36	....	....	....	6	....	....	....	....	....	....	....	....	....	....	....	....	....	....	....	....	....	....
1993-94	Thetford Mines Coyotes	QSPHL	PLAYER/COACH – STATISTICS UNAVAILABLE																									
1994-95	EC Wolfsberg	Germany-2	STATISTICS NOT AVAILABLE																									
1995-96	EHC Eisbaren Berlin	Germany	27	4	6	10	....	....	....	2	....	....	....	....	....	....	....	....	....	....	....	....	....	....	....	....	....	....
1996-97	TSV Erding	Germany-2	47	17	25	42	....	....	....	38	....	....	....	....	....	....	....	....	....	....	12	8	5	13	....	....	....	....
1997-98	TSV Erding	Germany-2	58	10	29	39	....	....	....	8	....	....	....	....	....	....	....	....	....	....	....	....	....	....	....	....	....	....
1998-99	TSV Erding	Germany-2	44	6	22	28	....	....	....	10	....	....	....	....	....	....	....	....	....	....	14	4	7	11	8	....	....	....
99-2000	EV Landshut	Germany-2	26	7	8	15	....	....	....	2	....	....	....	....	....	....	....	....	....	....	....	....	....	....	....	....	....	....
	NHL Totals		**25**	**1**	**5**	**6**	**1**	**3**	**4**	**10**	**0**	**0**	**1**	**8**	**12.5**	**18**	**4**	**19**	**4**		....	....	....	....	....	....	....	....

• POULIN, Daniel

D – R. 5'11", 185 lbs. b: Robertsville, Que., 9/19/1957. Montreal's 18th, 167th overall, in 1977.

Season	Club	League	GP	G	A	Pts	AG	AA	APts	PIM	PP	SH	GW	S	%	TGF	PGF	TGA	PGA	+/–	GP	G	A	Pts	PIM	PP	SH	GW
1974-75	Chicoutimi Sagueneens	QMJHL	68	15	46	61	....	....	....	43	....	....	....	....	....	....	....	....	....	....	....	....	....	....	....	....	....	....
1975-76	Chicoutimi Sagueneens	QMJHL	72	18	55	73	....	....	....	24	....	....	....	....	....	....	....	....	....	....	....	....	....	....	....	....	....	....
1976-77	Chicoutimi Sagueneens	QMJHL	72	21	74	95	....	....	....	50	....	....	....	....	....	....	....	....	....	....	....	....	....	....	....	....	....	....
1977-78	Kalamazoo Wings	IHL	43	7	20	27	....	....	....	44	....	....	....	....	....	....	....	....	....	....	....	....	....	....	....	....	....	....
	Muskegon Mohawks	IHL	2	0	1	1	....	....	....	0	....	....	....	....	....	....	....	....	....	....	....	....	....	....	....	....	....	....
1978-79	Erie Blades	EHL	68	35	53	88	....	....	....	79	....	....	....	....	....	....	....	....	....	....	....	....	....	....	....	....	....	....
1979-80	Erie Blades	EHL	65	33	*66	99	....	....	....	36	....	....	....	....	....	....	....	....	....	....	9	3	*12	15	12	....	....	....
1980-81	Oklahoma City Stars	CHL	58	16	32	48	....	....	....	32	....	....	....	....	....	....	....	....	....	....	3	0	0	0	0	....	....	....
1981-82	**Minnesota North Stars**	**NHL**	**3**	**1**	**1**	**2**	**1**	**1**	**2**	**2**	**0**	**0**	**0**	**8**	**12.5**	**4**	**1**	**3**	**1**	**1**	....	....	....	....	....	....	....	....
	Nashville South Stars	CHL	76	29	56	85	....	....	....	104	....	....	....	....	....	....	....	....	....	....	3	2	2	4	2	....	....	....
1982-83	EHC Biel-Bienne	Switz.	38	32	27	59	....	....	....	....	....	....	....	....	....	....	....	....	....	....	....	....	....	....	....	....	....	....
1983-84	EHC Biel-Bienne	Swirz.	40	30	34	64	....	....	....	....	....	....	....	....	....	....	....	....	....	....	....	....	....	....	....	....	....	....
1984-85	EHC Biel-Bienne	Switz.	35	26	30	56	....	....	....	....	....	....	....	....	....	....	....	....	....	....	3	1	4	5	....	....	....	....
1985-86	EHC Biel-Bienne	Switz.	36	27	35	62	....	....	....	....	....	....	....	....	....	....	....	....	....	....	....	....	....	....	....	....	....	....
1986-87	EHC Biel-Bienne	Switz.	36	14	20	34	....	....	....	....	....	....	....	....	....	....	....	....	....	....	....	....	....	....	....	....	....	....
1987-88	EHC Biel-Bienne	Switz.	36	18	25	43	....	....	....	....	....	....	....	....	....	....	....	....	....	....	....	....	....	....	....	....	....	....
1988-89	EHC Biel-Bienne	Switz.	36	19	20	39	....	....	....	....	....	....	....	....	....	....	....	....	....	....	2	1	0	1	....	....	....	....
1989-90	HC Davos	Switz-2	36	17	16	33	....	....	....	....	....	....	....	....	....	....	....	....	....	....	6	2	7	9	....	....	....	....
	NHL Totals		**3**	**1**	**1**	**2**	**1**	**1**	**2**	**2**	**0**	**0**	**0**	**8**	**12.5**	**4**	**1**	**3**	**1**		....	....	....	....	....	....	....	....

QMJHL East First All-Star Team (1976) • EHL First All-Star Team (1979, 1980) • CHL First All-Star Team (1982) • Won Bobby Orr Trophy (CHL's Top Defenseman) (1982)

Signed as a free agent by **Minnesota**, June 16, 1980.

• POULIN, Dave

David James C – L. 5'11", 190 lbs. b: Timmins, Ont., 12/17/1958.

Season	Club	League	GP	G	A	Pts	AG	AA	APts	PIM	PP	SH	GW	S	%	TGF	PGF	TGA	PGA	+/–	GP	G	A	Pts	PIM	PP	SH	GW
1975-76	Mississagua Reps	MTHL	STATISTICS NOT AVAILABLE																									
1976-77	Dixie Beehives	OHA-B	STATISTICS NOT AVAILABLE																									
1977-78	Dixie Beehives	OHA-B	34	28	31	59	....	....	....	59	....	....	....	....	....	....	....	....	....	....	....	....	....	....	....	....	....	....
1978-79	University of Notre Dame	WCHA	37	28	31	59	....	....	....	32	....	....	....	....	....	....	....	....	....	....	....	....	....	....	....	....	....	....
1979-80	University of Notre Dame	WCHA	24	19	24	43	....	....	....	46	....	....	....	....	....	....	....	....	....	....	....	....	....	....	....	....	....	....
1980-81	University of Notre Dame	WCHA	35	13	22	35	....	....	....	53	....	....	....	....	....	....	....	....	....	....	....	....	....	....	....	....	....	....
1981-82	University of Notre Dame	WCHA	39	29	30	59	....	....	....	44	....	....	....	....	....	....	....	....	....	....	....	....	....	....	....	....	....	....
1982-83	Rogle BK Angelholm	Sweden-2	32	35	27	62	....	....	....	64	....	....	....	....	....	....	....	....	....	....	....	....	....	....	....	....	....	....
	Philadelphia Flyers	**NHL**	**2**	**2**	**0**	**2**	**2**	**0**	**2**	**2**	**0**	**1**	**1**	**4**	**50.0**	**2**	**0**	**2**	**1**	**1**	**3**	**1**	**3**	**4**	**9**	**0**	**0**	**0**
	Maine Mariners	AHL	16	7	9	16	....	....	....	2	....	....	....	....	....	....	....	....	....	....	....	....	....	....	....	....	....	....
1983-84	**Philadelphia Flyers**	**NHL**	**73**	**31**	**45**	**76**	**25**	**31**	**56**	**47**	**6**	**3**	**6**	**185**	**16.8**	**113**	**22**	**86**	**26**	**31**	**3**	**0**	**0**	**0**	**2**	**0**	**0**	**0**
1984-85	**Philadelphia Flyers**	**NHL**	**73**	**30**	**44**	**74**	**24**	**30**	**54**	**59**	**1**	**4**	**5**	**174**	**17.2**	**104**	**16**	**78**	**33**	**43**	**11**	**3**	**5**	**8**	**6**	**0**	**2**	**0**
1985-86	**Philadelphia Flyers**	**NHL**	**79**	**27**	**42**	**69**	**22**	**28**	**50**	**49**	**2**	**6**	**2**	**181**	**14.9**	**100**	**19**	**99**	**38**	**20**	**5**	**2**	**0**	**2**	**2**	**1**	**0**	**0**
1986-87	**Philadelphia Flyers**	**NHL**	**75**	**25**	**45**	**70**	**22**	**33**	**55**	**53**	**1**	**3**	**5**	**155**	**16.1**	**96**	**10**	**75**	**36**	**47**	**15**	**3**	**3**	**6**	**14**	**1**	**1**	**0**
	NHL All-Stars	RV-87	2	1	1	2	....	....	....	0	....	....	....	....	....	....	....	....	....	....	....	....	....	....	....	....	....	....
1987-88	**Philadelphia Flyers**	**NHL**	**68**	**19**	**32**	**51**	**16**	**23**	**39**	**32**	**1**	**5**	**3**	**125**	**15.2**	**62**	**5**	**79**	**39**	**17**	**7**	**2**	**6**	**8**	**4**	**1**	**0**	**1**
1988-89	**Philadelphia Flyers**	**NHL**	**69**	**18**	**17**	**35**	**15**	**12**	**27**	**49**	**1**	**5**	**4**	**81**	**22.2**	**52**	**3**	**76**	**31**	**4**	**19**	**6**	**5**	**11**	**16**	**0**	**2**	**2**
1989-90	**Philadelphia Flyers**	**NHL**	**28**	**9**	**8**	**17**	**8**	**6**	**14**	**12**	**0**	**0**	**1**	**46**	**19.6**	**20**	**0**	**30**	**15**	**5**	....	....	....	....	....	....	....	....
	Boston Bruins	**NHL**	**32**	**6**	**19**	**25**	**5**	**14**	**19**	**12**	**0**	**1**	**0**	**42**	**14.3**	**37**	**4**	**33**	**11**	**11**	**18**	**8**	**5**	**13**	**8**	**2**	**0**	**2**
1990-91	**Boston Bruins**	**NHL**	**31**	**8**	**12**	**20**	**7**	**9**	**16**	**25**	**0**	**2**	**0**	**60**	**13.3**	**29**	**2**	**32**	**10**	**5**	**16**	**0**	**9**	**9**	**20**	**0**	**0**	**0**
1991-92	**Boston Bruins**	**NHL**	**18**	**4**	**4**	**8**	**4**	**3**	**7**	**18**	**0**	**1**	**1**	**31**	**12.9**	**11**	**1**	**19**	**7**	**–2**	**15**	**3**	**3**	**6**	**22**	**1**	**0**	**1**
1992-93	**Boston Bruins**	**NHL**	**84**	**16**	**33**	**49**	**13**	**23**	**36**	**62**	**0**	**5**	**0**	**112**	**14.3**	**69**	**2**	**75**	**37**	**29**	**4**	**1**	**1**	**2**	**10**	**0**	**1**	**0**

			REGULAR SEASON																		PLAYOFFS							
Season	Club	League	GP	G	A	Pts	AG	AA	APts	PIM	PP	SH	GW	S	%	TGF	PGF	TGA	PGA	+/–	GP	G	A	Pts	PIM	PP	SH	GW
1993-94	**Washington Capitals**	**NHL**	**63**	**6**	**19**	**25**	**6**	**15**	**21**	**52**	**0**	**1**	**0**	**64**	**9.4**	**35**	**0**	**67**	**31**	**–1**	**11**	**2**	**2**	**4**	**19**	**0**	**0**	**0**
1994-95	**Washington Capitals**	**NHL**	**29**	**4**	**5**	**9**	**7**	**7**	**14**	**10**	**0**	**2**	**0**	**30**	**13.3**	**15**	**1**	**24**	**12**	**2**	**2**	**0**	**0**	**0**	**0**	**0**	**0**	**0**
1995-2000	University of Notre Dame	CCHA	DID NOT PLAY – COACHING																									
	NHL Totals		**724**	**205**	**325**	**530**	**176**	**234**	**410**	**482**	**12**	**39**	**28**	**1290**	**15.9**	**745**	**85**	**775**	**327**		**129**	**31**	**42**	**73**	**132**	**6**	**6**	**6**

CCHA Second All-Star Team (1982) • Won Frank J. Selke Trophy (1987) • Won King Clancy Memorial Trophy (1993) • Played in NHL All-Star Game (1986, 1988)

Signed as a free agent by **Philadelphia**, March 8, 1983. Traded to **Boston** by **Philadelphia** for Ken Linseman, January 16, 1990. • Missed majority of 1991-92 season recovering from groin injury suffered in training camp that required surgery, December 6, 1991. Signed as a free agent by **Washington**, August 3, 1993.

• POULIN, Patrick

C – L. 6'1", 218 lbs. b: Vanier, Que., 4/23/1973. Hartford's 1st, 9th overall, in 1991.

Season	Club	League	GP	G	A	Pts	AG	AA	APts	PIM	PP	SH	GW	S	%	TGF	PGF	TGA	PGA	+/–	GP	G	A	Pts	PIM	PP	SH	GW
1988-89	Ste-Foy Gouverneurs	QAAA	42	28	42	70	....	....	....	44	....	....	....	....	....	....	....	....	....	....	13	13	23	36	24	....	....	....
1989-90	St-Hyacinthe Laser	QMJHL	60	25	26	51	....	....	....	55	....	....	....	....	....	....	....	....	....	....	12	1	9	10	5	....	....	....
1990-91	St-Hyacinthe Laser	QMJHL	56	32	38	70	....	....	....	82	....	....	....	....	....	....	....	....	....	....	4	0	2	2	23	....	....	....
1991-92	St-Hyacinthe Laser	QMJHL	56	52	86	*138	....	....	....	58	....	....	....	....	....	....	....	....	....	....	5	2	2	4	4	....	....	....
	Canada	WJC-A	7	2	2	4	....	....	....	2	....	....	....	....	....	....	....	....	....	....	....	....	....	....	....	....	....	....
	Hartford Whalers	**NHL**	**1**	**0**	**0**	**0**	**0**	**0**	**0**	**2**	**0**	**0**	**0**	**0**	**0.0**	**1**	**0**	**2**	**0**	**–1**	**7**	**2**	**1**	**3**	**0**	**1**	**0**	**0**
	Springfield Indians	AHL	....	....	....	....	....	....	....	....	....	....	....	....	....	....	....	....	....	....	1	0	0	0	0	....	....	....
1992-93	**Hartford Whalers**	**NHL**	**81**	**20**	**31**	**51**	**17**	**21**	**38**	**37**	**4**	**0**	**2**	**160**	**12.5**	**73**	**19**	**74**	**1**	**–19**	....	....	....	....	....	....	....	....
1993-94	**Hartford Whalers**	**NHL**	**9**	**2**	**1**	**3**	**2**	**1**	**3**	**11**	**1**	**0**	**0**	**13**	**15.4**	**2**	**1**	**9**	**0**	**–8**	....	....	....	....	....	....	....	....
	Chicago Blackhawks	**NHL**	**58**	**12**	**13**	**25**	**11**	**10**	**21**	**40**	**1**	**0**	**3**	**83**	**14.5**	**30**	**4**	**26**	**0**	**0**	**4**	**0**	**0**	**0**	**0**	**0**	**0**	**0**
1994-95	**Chicago Blackhawks**	**NHL**	**45**	**15**	**15**	**30**	**27**	**22**	**49**	**53**	**4**	**0**	**2**	**77**	**19.5**	**49**	**14**	**23**	**1**	**13**	**16**	**4**	**1**	**5**	**8**	**1**	**0**	**0**
1995-96	**Chicago Blackhawks**	**NHL**	**38**	**7**	**8**	**15**	**7**	**7**	**14**	**16**	**1**	**0**	**0**	**40**	**17.5**	**23**	**1**	**15**	**0**	**7**	....	....	....	....	....	....	....	....
	Indianapolis Ice	IHL	1	0	1	1	....	....	....	0	....	....	....	....	....	....	....	....	....	....	....	....	....	....	....	....	....	....
	Tampa Bay Lightning	**NHL**	**8**	**0**	**1**	**1**	**0**	**1**	**1**	**0**	**0**	**0**	**0**	**11**	**0.0**	**2**	**0**	**2**	**0**	**0**	**2**	**0**	**0**	**0**	**0**	**0**	**0**	**0**
1996-97	**Tampa Bay Lightning**	**NHL**	**73**	**12**	**14**	**26**	**13**	**12**	**25**	**56**	**2**	**3**	**1**	**124**	**9.7**	**36**	**7**	**67**	**22**	**–16**	....	....	....	....	....	....	....	....
1997-98	**Tampa Bay Lightning**	**NHL**	**44**	**2**	**7**	**9**	**2**	**7**	**9**	**19**	**0**	**0**	**0**	**49**	**4.1**	**14**	**0**	**37**	**20**	**–3**	....	....	....	....	....	....	....	....
	Montreal Canadiens	**NHL**	**34**	**4**	**6**	**10**	**5**	**6**	**11**	**8**	**0**	**1**	**1**	**39**	**10.3**	**19**	**2**	**26**	**8**	**–1**	**3**	**0**	**0**	**0**	**0**	**0**	**0**	**0**
1998-99	**Montreal Canadiens**	**NHL**	**81**	**8**	**17**	**25**	**9**	**16**	**25**	**21**	**0**	**1**	**1**	**87**	**9.2**	**40**	**0**	**44**	**10**	**6**	....	....	....	....	....	....	....	....
99-2000	**Montreal Canadiens**	**NHL**	**82**	**10**	**5**	**15**	**11**	**5**	**16**	**17**	**0**	**1**	**2**	**82**	**12.2**	**21**	**1**	**51**	**16**	**–15**	....	....	....	....	....	....	....	....
	NHL Totals		**554**	**92**	**118**	**210**	**104**	**108**	**212**	**280**	**13**	**6**	**12**	**765**	**12.0**	**310**	**49**	**376**	**78**		**32**	**6**	**2**	**8**	**8**	**2**	**0**	**0**

QMJHL First All-Star Team (1992) • Canadian Major Junior Player of the Year (1992)

Traded to **Chicago** by **Hartford** with Eric Weinrich for Steve Larmer and Bryan Marchment, November 2, 1993. Traded to **Tampa Bay** by **Chicago** with Igor Ulanov and Chicago's 2nd round choice (later traded to New Jersey — New Jersey selected Pierre Dagenais) in 1996 Entry Draft for Enrico Ciccone and Tampa Bay's 2nd round choice (Jeff Paul) in 1996 Entry Draft, March 20, 1996. Traded to **Montreal** by **Tampa Bay** with Mick Vukota and Igor Ulanov for Stephane Richer, Darcy Tucker and David Wilkie, January 15, 1998.

• POUZAR, Jaroslav

LW – L. 5'11", 200 lbs. b: Cakovec, Czech., 1/23/1952. Edmonton's 4th, 83rd overall, in 1982.

Season	Club	League	GP	G	A	Pts	AG	AA	APts	PIM	PP	SH	GW	S	%	TGF	PGF	TGA	PGA	+/–	GP	G	A	Pts	PIM	PP	SH	GW
1970-1972	Motor Ceske Budejovice	Czech.	STATISTICS NOT AVAILABLE																									
1972-73	Motor Ceske Budejovice	Czech.	40	23	6	29	....	....	....	....	....	....	....	....	....	....	....	....	....	....	....	....	....	....	....	....	....	....
1973-74	Motor Ceske Budejovice	Czech.	40	25	8	33	....	....	....	....	....	....	....	....	....	....	....	....	....	....	....	....	....	....	....	....	....	....
1975-76	Motor Ceske Budejovice	Czech.	30	14	7	21	....	....	....	38	....	....	....	....	....	....	....	....	....	....	....	....	....	....	....	....	....	....
	Czechoslovakia	Olympics	5	1	1	2	....	....	....	2	....	....	....	....	....	....	....	....	....	....	....	....	....	....	....	....	....	....
	Czechoslovakia	WEC-A	8	2	3	5	....	....	....	0	....	....	....	....	....	....	....	....	....	....	....	....	....	....	....	....	....	....
1976-77	Czechoslovakia	Can-Cup	5	2	0	2	....	....	....	4	....	....	....	....	....	....	....	....	....	....	....	....	....	....	....	....	....	....
	Motor Ceske Budejovice	Czech.	44	29	15	44	....	....	....	....	....	....	....	....	....	....	....	....	....	....	....	....	....	....	....	....	....	....
	Czechoslovakia	WEC-A	10	4	4	8	....	....	....	14	....	....	....	....	....	....	....	....	....	....	....	....	....	....	....	....	....	....
1977-78	Motor Ceske Budejovice	Czech.	43	*42	20	62	....	....	....	....	....	....	....	....	....	....	....	....	....	....	....	....	....	....	....	....	....	....
	Czechoslovakia	WEC-A	10	7	1	8	....	....	....	4	....	....	....	....	....	....	....	....	....	....	....	....	....	....	....	....	....	....
1978-79	Motor Ceske Budejovice	Czech.	23	10	7	17	....	....	....	38	....	....	....	....	....	....	....	....	....	....	15	10	4	14	....	....	....	....
	Czechoslovakia	WEC-A	8	4	3	7	....	....	....	6	....	....	....	....	....	....	....	....	....	....	....	....	....	....	....	....	....	....
1979-80	Motor Ceske Budejovice	Czech.	44	39	23	62	....	....	....	48	....	....	....	....	....	....	....	....	....	....	23	10	10	20	31	....	....	....
	Czechoslovakia	Olympics	6	8	5	13	....	....	....	8	....	....	....	....	....	....	....	....	....	....	....	....	....	....	....	....	....	....
1980-81	Motor Ceske Budejovice	Czech.	42	29	23	52	....	....	....	45	....	....	....	....	....	....	....	....	....	....	28	8	5	13	....	....	....	....
	Czechoslovakia	WEC-A	7	1	1	2	....	....	....	2	....	....	....	....	....	....	....	....	....	....	....	....	....	....	....	....	....	....
1981-82	Czechoslovakia	Can-Cup	6	1	1	2	....	....	....	4	....	....	....	....	....	....	....	....	....	....	....	....	....	....	....	....	....	....
	Motor Ceske Budejovice	Czech	34	19	17	36	....	....	....	32	....	....	....	....	....	....	....	....	....	....	....	....	....	....	....	....	....	....
	Czechoslovakia	WEC-A	10	3	1	4	....	....	....	6	....	....	....	....	....	....	....	....	....	....	....	....	....	....	....	....	....	....
1982-83	**Edmonton Oilers**	**NHL**	**74**	**15**	**18**	**33**	**12**	**12**	**24**	**57**	**2**	**0**	**2**	**86**	**17.4**	**53**	**7**	**29**	**0**	**17**	**1**	**2**	**0**	**2**	**0**	**1**	**0**	**1**
1983-84♦	**Edmonton Oilers**	**NHL**	**67**	**13**	**19**	**32**	**10**	**13**	**23**	**44**	**2**	**0**	**0**	**87**	**14.9**	**83**	**15**	**51**	**0**	**17**	**14**	**1**	**2**	**3**	**12**	**0**	**0**	**1**
1984-85♦	**Edmonton Oilers**	**NHL**	**33**	**4**	**8**	**12**	**3**	**5**	**8**	**28**	**0**	**0**	**1**	**36**	**11.1**	**20**	**3**	**14**	**0**	**3**	**9**	**2**	**1**	**3**	**2**	**0**	**0**	**0**
1985-86	ECD Iserlohn	Germany	36	17	26	43	....	....	....	39	....	....	....	....	....	....	....	....	....	....	8	3	5	8	....	....	....	....
1986-87	ECD Iserlohn	Germany	35	29	32	61	....	....	....	30	....	....	....	....	....	....	....	....	....	....	3	3	6	9	....	....	....	....
♦	**Edmonton Oilers**	**NHL**	**12**	**2**	**3**	**5**	**2**	**2**	**4**	**6**	**0**	**0**	**1**	**11**	**18.2**	**10**	**0**	**7**	**0**	**3**	**5**	**1**	**1**	**2**	**2**	**0**	**0**	**0**
1987-88	ECD Iserlohn	Germany	26	16	18	34	....	....	....	15	....	....	....	....	....	....	....	....	....	....	....	....	....	....	....	....	....	....
	SB Rosenheim	Germany	7	3	7	10	....	....	....	14	....	....	....	....	....	....	....	....	....	....	5	1	4	5	0	....	....	....
1988-89	SB Rosenheim	Germany	36	20	34	54	....	....	....	26	....	....	....	....	....	....	....	....	....	....	11	10	10	*20	22	....	....	....
1989-90	SB Rosenheim	Germany	35	9	31	40	....	....	....	32	....	....	....	....	....	....	....	....	....	....	11	2	7	9	28	....	....	....
1990-91	Augsburger EV	Germany-2	33	17	46	63	....	....	....	26	....	....	....	....	....	....	....	....	....	....	18	18	16	34	16	....	....	....
1991-92	SB Rosenheim	Germany	5	1	2	3	....	....	....	4	....	....	....	....	....	....	....	....	....	....	....	....	....	....	....	....	....	....
	NHL Totals		**186**	**34**	**48**	**82**	**27**	**32**	**59**	**135**	**4**	**0**	**4**	**220**	**15.5**	**166**	**25**	**101**	**0**		**29**	**6**	**4**	**10**	**16**	**1**	**0**	**2**

• POWIS, Geoff

Geoff Charles C – L. 6'1", 170 lbs. b: Winnipeg, Man., 6/14/1945.

Season	Club	League	GP	G	A	Pts	AG	AA	APts	PIM	PP	SH	GW	S	%	TGF	PGF	TGA	PGA	+/–	GP	G	A	Pts	PIM	PP	SH	GW
1963-64	Moose Jaw Canucks	SJHL	48	23	21	44	....	....	....	45	....	....	....	....	....	....	....	....	....	....	5	0	1	1	2	....	....	....
1964-65	Moose Jaw Canucks	SJHL	49	39	38	77	....	....	....	100	....	....	....	....	....	....	....	....	....	....	....	....	....	....	....	....	....	....
1965-66	Moose Jaw Canucks	SJHL	54	46	44	90	....	....	....	53	....	....	....	....	....	....	....	....	....	....	3	1	1	2	0	....	....	....
1966-67	St. Louis Braves	CPHL	57	8	15	23	....	....	....	23	....	....	....	....	....	....	....	....	....	....	....	....	....	....	....	....	....	....
1967-68	**Chicago Black Hawks**	**NHL**	**2**	**0**	**0**	**0**	**0**	**0**	**0**	**0**	**0**	**0**	**0**	**0**	**0.0**	**0**	**0**	**0**	**0**	**0**	....	....	....	....	....	....	....	....
	Dallas Black Hawks	CPHL	60	15	30	45	....	....	....	20	....	....	....	....	....	....	....	....	....	....	5	0	1	1	0	....	....	....
1968-69	Port Huron Flags	IHL	71	48	36	84	....	....	....	28	....	....	....	....	....	....	....	....	....	....	3	4	2	6	2	....	....	....
1969-70	Port Huron Flags	IHL	67	31	40	71	....	....	....	54	....	....	....	....	....	....	....	....	....	....	15	7	7	14	13	....	....	....
1970-71	Port Huron–Toledo Hornets	IHL	52	21	22	43	....	....	....	30	....	....	....	....	....	....	....	....	....	....	....	....	....	....	....	....	....	....
1971-72	Toledo Hornets	IHL	27	5	15	20	....	....	....	6	....	....	....	....	....	....	....	....	....	....	....	....	....	....	....	....	....	....
1972-73	Seattle Totems	WHL	4	0	1	1	....	....	....	2	....	....	....	....	....	....	....	....	....	....	....	....	....	....	....	....	....	....
	Cranbrook Royals	WIHL	50	36	32	68	....	....	....	....	....	....	....	....	....	....	....	....	....	....	....	....	....	....	....	....	....	....
1973-74	Cranbrook Royals	WIHL	46	28	39	67	....	....	....	....	....	....	....	....	....	....	....	....	....	....	....	....	....	....	....	....	....	....
1974-75	Cranbrook Royals	WIHL	12	4	4	8	....	....	....	0	....	....	....	....	....	....	....	....	....	....	....	....	....	....	....	....	....	....
1975-76	Cranbrook Royals	WIHL	24	10	13	23	....	....	....	22	....	....	....	....	....	....	....	....	....	....	....	....	....	....	....	....	....	....
	NHL Totals		**2**	**0**	**0**	**0**	**0**	**0**	**0**	**0**	**0**	**0**	**0**	**0**	**0.0**	**0**	**0**	**0**	**0**		....	....	....	....	....	....	....	....

IHL First All-Star Team (1969) • WIHL Second All-Star Team (1973)

• POWIS, Lynn

Trevor Lynn C – L. 6', 175 lbs. b: Maryfield, Sask., 7/7/1949. Montreal's 7th, 68th overall, in 1969.

Season	Club	League	GP	G	A	Pts	AG	AA	APts	PIM	PP	SH	GW	S	%	TGF	PGF	TGA	PGA	+/–	GP	G	A	Pts	PIM	PP	SH	GW
1965-66	Melville Millionaires	SJHL	16	0	2	2	....	....	....	4	....	....	....	....	....	....	....	....	....	....	....	....	....	....	....	....	....	....
1966-67	Moose Jaw Canucks	CMJHL	52	13	18	31	....	....	....	17	....	....	....	....	....	....	....	....	....	....	14	5	4	9	4	....	....	....
1967-68	University of Denver	WCHA	DID NOT PLAY – FRESHMAN																									
1968-69	University of Denver	WCHA	30	17	12	29	....	....	....	21	....	....	....	....	....	....	....	....	....	....	....	....	....	....	....	....	....	....
1969-70	University of Denver	WCHA	5	2	3	5	....	....	....	12	....	....	....	....	....	....	....	....	....	....	....	....	....	....	....	....	....	....
1970-71	Denver Spurs	WHL	59	14	13	27	....	....	....	13	....	....	....	....	....	....	....	....	....	....	....	....	....	....	....	....	....	....
1971-72	Nova Scotia Voyageurs	AHL	38	5	6	11	....	....	....	19	....	....	....	....	....	....	....	....	....	....	15	0	2	2	0	....	....	....
1972-73	Omaha Knights	CHL	72	34	40	74	....	....	....	49	....	....	....	....	....	....	....	....	....	....	11	2	5	7	8	....	....	....

			REGULAR SEASON																		PLAYOFFS							
Season	Club	League	GP	G	A	Pts	AG	AA	APts	PIM	PP	SH	GW	S	%	TGF	PGF	TGA	PGA	+/–	GP	G	A	Pts	PIM	PP	SH	GW
1973-74	**Chicago Black Hawks**	**NHL**	**57**	**8**	**13**	**21**	**8**	**11**	**19**	**6**	**1**	**0**	**2**	**71**	**11.3**	**30**	**4**	**17**	**1**	**10**	**1**	**0**	**0**	**0**	**0**	**0**	**0**	**0**
1974-75	**Kansas City Scouts**	**NHL**	**73**	**11**	**20**	**31**	**10**	**15**	**25**	**19**	**3**	**0**	**0**	**149**	**7.4**	**39**	**18**	**79**	**4**	**–54**								
1975-76	Providence Reds	AHL	52	30	31	61				54																		
	Calgary Cowboys	WHA	21	4	10	14				2											10	5	4	9	12			
1976-77	Calgary Cowboys	WHA	63	30	30	60				40																		
1977-78	Indianapolis Racers	WHA	14	4	6	10				2																		
	Winnipeg Jets	WHA	55	12	19	31				16											3	2	1	3	7			
1978-79	EV Duisburg	Germany-2	STATISTICS NOT AVAILABLE																									
1979-80	EV Duisburg	Germany	39	28	37	65				*162																		
1980-81	EV Duisburg	Germany	17	12	12	24				62																		
1981-82	EV Fussen	Germany	32	17	22	39				82																		
1982-83	HC Alleghe	Italy	19	17	26	43				18																		
	NHL Totals		**130**	**19**	**33**	**52**	**18**	**26**	**44**	**25**	**4**	**0**	**2**	**220**	**8.6**	**69**	**22**	**96**	**5**		**1**	**0**	**0**	**0**	**0**	**0**	**0**	**0**
	Other Major League Totals		153	50	65	115				60											13	7	5	12	19			

Selected by **Dayton-Houston** (WHA) in 1972 WHA General Player Draft, February 12, 1972. Traded to **Atlanta** by **Montreal** for cash, June 9, 1972. Traded to **Chicago** by **Atlanta** for Mike Baumgartner, August 30, 1973. Claimed by **Kansas City** from **Chicago** in Expansion Draft, June 12, 1974. Traded to **St. Louis** by **Kansas City** with Kansas City's 2nd round choice (Brian Sutter) in 1976 Amateur Draft for Craig Patrick and Denis Dupere, June 18, 1975. Traded to **Calgary** (WHA) by **Providence** (AHL) for future considerations, February, 1976. Signed as a free agent by **Indianapolis** (WHA) after **Calgary** (WHA) franchise folded, May 31, 1977. Signed as a free agent by **Winnipeg** (WHA) following release by **Indianapolis** (WHA), December, 1977.

• PRAJSLER, Petr

D – L. 6'2", 200 lbs. b: Hradec Kralove, Czech., 9/21/1965. Los Angeles' 5th, 93rd overall, in 1985.

Season	Club	League	GP	G	A	Pts	AG	AA	APts	PIM	PP	SH	GW	S	%	TGF	PGF	TGA	PGA	+/–	GP	G	A	Pts	PIM	PP	SH	GW
1982-83	Czechoslovakia	EJC-A	5	1	0	1				4																		
1983-84	Tesla Pardubice	Czech-Jr.	STATISTICS NOT AVAILABLE																									
1984-85	Tesla Pardubice	Czech.	29	4	1	5				24																		
	Czechoslovakia	WJC-A	6	1	2	3				4																		
1985-86	Tesla Pardubice	Czech.	27	5	5	10				24																		
1986-87	Tesla Pardubice	Czech.	41	3	4	7				49																		
1987-88	**Los Angeles Kings**	**NHL**	**7**	**0**	**0**	**0**	**0**	**0**	**0**	**2**	**0**	**0**	**0**	**2**	**0.0**	**4**	**0**	**2**	**0**	**2**								
	New Haven Nighthawks	AHL	41	3	8	11				58																		
1988-89	**Los Angeles Kings**	**NHL**	**2**	**0**	**3**	**3**	**0**	**2**	**2**	**0**	**0**	**0**	**0**	**1**	**0.0**	**6**	**2**	**0**	**0**	**4**	**1**	**0**	**0**	**0**	**0**	**0**	**0**	**0**
	New Haven Nighthawks	AHL	43	4	6	10				96											16	3	3	6	34			
1989-90	**Los Angeles Kings**	**NHL**	**34**	**3**	**7**	**10**	**3**	**5**	**8**	**47**	**1**	**0**	**0**	**49**	**6.1**	**38**	**19**	**33**	**5**	**–9**	**3**	**0**	**0**	**0**	**0**	**0**	**0**	**0**
	New Haven Nighthawks	AHL	6	1	7	8				2																		
1990-91	Phoenix Roadrunners	IHL	77	13	34	47				140											9	1	9	10	18			
1991-92	**Boston Bruins**	**NHL**	**3**	**0**	**0**	**0**	**0**	**0**	**0**	**2**	**0**	**0**	**0**	**3**	**0.0**	**0**	**0**	**1**	**0**	**–1**								
	Maine Mariners	AHL	61	12	33	45				88																		
1992-93	Hradec Kralove	Czech-2	35	5	9	14																						
1993-94	Hradec Kralove-2	Czech-Rep	17	0	4	4																						
	NHL Totals		**46**	**3**	**10**	**13**	**3**	**7**	**10**	**51**	**1**	**0**	**0**	**55**	**5.5**	**48**	**21**	**36**	**5**		**4**	**0**	**0**	**0**	**0**	**0**	**0**	**0**

Signed as a free agent by **Boston**, August 1, 1991.

• PRATT, Kelly

Kelly Edward RW – R. 5'9", 170 lbs. b: High Prairie, Alta., 2/8/1953.

Season	Club	League	GP	G	A	Pts	AG	AA	APts	PIM	PP	SH	GW	S	%	TGF	PGF	TGA	PGA	+/–	GP	G	A	Pts	PIM	PP	SH	GW
1969-70	Red Deer Rustlers	AJHL	29	3	4	7				56																		
1970-71	Kamloops Rockets	BCJHL	STATISTICS NOT AVAILABLE																									
1971-72	Swift Current Broncos	WCJHL	63	36	29	65				114																		
1972-73	Swift Current Broncos	WCJHL	65	45	37	82				91																		
1973-74	Winnipeg Jets	WHA	46	4	6	10				50																		
	Jacksonville Barons	AHL	16	2	6	8				24																		
1974-75	**Pittsburgh Penguins**	**NHL**	**22**	**0**	**6**	**6**	**0**	**4**	**4**	**15**	**0**	**0**	**0**	**28**	**0.0**	**10**	**2**	**10**	**3**	**1**								
	Hershey Bears	AHL	31	7	10	17				97											8	0	2	2	14			
1975-76	Hershey Bears	AHL	62	13	25	38				96											1	0	0	0	0			
1976-77	Hershey Bears	AHL	31	2	5	7				21																		
1977-78	Hampton Gulls	AHL	11	1	0	1				26																		
	San Diego Mariners	PCL	23	10	15	25				20																		
1978-79	Spokane Flyers	PHL	18	5	5	10				32																		
	Los Angeles Blades	PHL	9	6	2	8				9																		
	San Diego Hawks	PHL	16	3	4	7				4																		
	NHL Totals		**22**	**0**	**6**	**6**	**0**	**4**	**4**	**15**	**0**	**0**	**0**	**28**	**0.0**	**10**	**2**	**10**	**3**									
	Other Major League Totals		46	4	6	10				50																		

Selected by **Winnipeg** (WHA) in 1973 WHA Amateur Draft, June, 1973. Signed as a free agent by **Pittsburgh**, July 15, 1974. Traded to **Hershey** (AHL) by **Pittsburgh** for cash, August 28, 1975.

• PRATT, Nolan

D – L. 6'2", 200 lbs. b: Fort McMurray, Alta., 8/14/1975. Hartford's 4th, 115th overall, in 1993.

Season	Club	League	GP	G	A	Pts	AG	AA	APts	PIM	PP	SH	GW	S	%	TGF	PGF	TGA	PGA	+/–	GP	G	A	Pts	PIM	PP	SH	GW
1991-92	Bonnyville Pontiacs	AJHL	STATISTICS NOT AVAILABLE																									
	Portland Winter Hawks	WHL	22	2	9	11				13											6	1	3	4	12			
1992-93	Portland Winter Hawks	WHL	70	4	19	23				97											16	2	7	9	31			
1993-94	Portland Winter Hawks	WHL	72	4	32	36				105											10	1	2	3	14			
1994-95	Portland Winter Hawks	WHL	72	6	37	43				196											9	1	6	7	10			
1995-96	Springfield Falcons	AHL	62	2	6	8				72											2	0	0	0	0			
	Richmond Renegades	ECHL	4	1	0	1				2																		
1996-97	**Hartford Whalers**	**NHL**	**9**	**0**	**2**	**2**	**0**	**2**	**2**	**6**	**0**	**0**	**0**	**4**	**0.0**	**4**	**0**	**6**	**2**	**0**								
	Springfield Falcons	AHL	66	1	18	19				127											17	0	3	3	18			
1997-98	**Carolina Hurricanes**	**NHL**	**23**	**0**	**2**	**2**	**0**	**2**	**2**	**44**	**0**	**0**	**0**	**11**	**0.0**	**10**	**0**	**14**	**2**	**–2**								
	Beast of New Haven	AHL	54	3	15	18				135																		
1998-99	**Carolina Hurricanes**	**NHL**	**61**	**1**	**14**	**15**	**1**	**13**	**14**	**95**	**0**	**0**	**1**	**46**	**2.2**	**44**	**3**	**30**	**4**	**15**	**3**	**0**	**0**	**0**	**2**	**0**	**0**	**0**
99-2000	**Carolina Hurricanes**	**NHL**	**64**	**3**	**1**	**4**	**3**	**1**	**4**	**90**	**0**	**0**	**1**	**47**	**6.4**	**29**	**1**	**61**	**11**	**–22**								
	NHL Totals		**157**	**4**	**19**	**23**	**4**	**18**	**22**	**235**	**0**	**0**	**2**	**108**	**3.7**	**87**	**4**	**111**	**19**		**3**	**0**	**0**	**0**	**2**	**0**	**0**	**0**

Transferred to **Carolina** after **Hartford** franchise relocated, June 25, 1997. Traded to **Colorado** by **Carolina** with Carolina's 1st (Vaclav Nedorost) and 2nd (Jared Aulin) round choices in 2000 Entry Draft and Philadelphia's 2nd round choice (previously acquired, Colorado selected Argis Saviels) in 2000 Entry Draft for Sandis Ozolinsh and Columbus' 2nd round choice (previously acquired, Carolina selected Tomas Kurka) in 2000 Entry Draft, June 24, 2000.

• PRATT, Tracy

Tracy Arnold D – L. 6'2", 195 lbs. b: New York City, NY, 3/8/1943.

Season	Club	League	GP	G	A	Pts	AG	AA	APts	PIM	PP	SH	GW	S	%	TGF	PGF	TGA	PGA	+/–	GP	G	A	Pts	PIM	PP	SH	GW
1959-60	Vancouver Prep College	Hi-School	STATISTICS NOT AVAILABLE																									
1960-61	Flin Flon Bombers	SJHL	59	3	13	16				83																		
1961-62	Flin Flon Bombers	SJHL	51	7	16	23				143											10	2	4	6	36			
1962-63	Brandon Wheat Kings	MJHL	33	10	17	27				132											10	3	8	11	38			
	Brandon Wheat Kings	Mem-Cup	9	2	4	6				*35																		
1963-64	St. Paul Rangers	CPHL	52	4	15	19				128											11	0	0	0	*49			
1964-65	St. Paul Rangers	CPHL	66	15	25	40				200											9	1	2	3	27			
1965-66	St. Louis Braves	CPHL	70	2	23	25				*206											5	1	2	3	6			
1966-67	Portland Buckaroos	WHL	63	0	10	10				92											4	0	1	1	4			
1967-68	**Oakland Seals**	**NHL**	**34**	**0**	**5**	**5**	**0**	**5**	**5**	**90**	**0**	**0**	**0**	**35**	**0.0**	**23**	**2**	**48**	**9**	**–18**								
	Vancouver Canucks	WHL	29	1	8	9				73																		
1968-69	Vancouver Canucks	WHL	45	2	10	12				74																		
	Pittsburgh Penguins	**NHL**	**18**	**0**	**5**	**5**	**0**	**4**	**4**	**34**	**0**	**0**	**0**	**10**	**0.0**	**23**	**3**	**16**	**2**	**6**								
1969-70	**Pittsburgh Penguins**	**NHL**	**65**	**5**	**7**	**12**	**5**	**7**	**12**	**124**	**0**	**0**	**1**	**73**	**6.8**	**35**	**4**	**73**	**13**	**–29**	**10**	**0**	**1**	**1**	**51**	**0**	**0**	**0**
1970-71	**Buffalo Sabres**	**NHL**	**76**	**1**	**7**	**8**	**1**	**6**	**7**	**179**	**0**	**0**	**0**	**34**	**2.9**	**64**	**2**	**102**	**23**	**–17**								
1971-72	**Buffalo Sabres**	**NHL**	**27**	**0**	**10**	**10**	**0**	**9**	**9**	**52**	**0**	**0**	**0**	**31**	**0.0**	**32**	**1**	**40**	**9**	**0**								
	Cincinnati Swords	AHL	16	0	11	11				40																		
1972-73	**Buffalo Sabres**	**NHL**	**74**	**1**	**15**	**16**	**1**	**12**	**13**	**116**	**0**	**0**	**0**	**63**	**1.6**	**79**	**2**	**92**	**24**	**9**	**6**	**0**	**0**	**0**	**6**	**0**	**0**	**0**

			REGULAR SEASON																		PLAYOFFS							
Season	Club	League	GP	G	A	Pts	AG	AA	APts	PIM	PP	SH	GW	S	%	TGF	PGF	TGA	PGA	+/–	GP	G	A	Pts	PIM	PP	SH	GW
1973-74	**Buffalo Sabres**	**NHL**	**33**	**0**	**7**	**7**	**0**	**6**	**6**	**52**	**0**	**0**	**0**	**20**	**0.0**	**46**	**0**	**45**	**8**	**9**	....	....	....	....	....	....	....	....
	Vancouver Canucks	**NHL**	**45**	**3**	**8**	**11**	**3**	**7**	**10**	**44**	**0**	**0**	**0**	**30**	**10.0**	**47**	**0**	**82**	**24**	**–11**	....	....	....	....	....	....	....	....
1974-75	**Vancouver Canucks**	**NHL**	**79**	**5**	**17**	**22**	**4**	**13**	**17**	**145**	**0**	**0**	**0**	**100**	**5.0**	**100**	**7**	**123**	**36**	**6**	**3**	**0**	**0**	**0**	**5**	**0**	**0**	**0**
1975-76	**Vancouver Canucks**	**NHL**	**52**	**1**	**5**	**6**	**1**	**4**	**5**	**72**	**1**	**0**	**0**	**44**	**2.3**	**40**	**2**	**70**	**25**	**–7**	**2**	**0**	**0**	**0**	**0**	**0**	**0**	**0**
1976-77	**Colorado Rockies**	**NHL**	**66**	**1**	**10**	**11**	**1**	**8**	**9**	**110**	**0**	**0**	**0**	**53**	**1.9**	**57**	**4**	**113**	**33**	**–27**	....	....	....	....	....	....	....	....
	Toronto Maple Leafs	**NHL**	**11**	**0**	**1**	**1**	**0**	**1**	**1**	**8**	**0**	**0**	**0**	**4**	**0.0**	**2**	**0**	**10**	**1**	**–7**	**4**	**0**	**0**	**0**	**0**	**0**	**0**	**0**
	NHL Totals		**580**	**17**	**97**	**114**	**16**	**82**	**98**	**1026**	**1**	**0**	**1**	**497**	**3.4**	**548**	**27**	**814**	**207**		**25**	**0**	**1**	**1**	**62**	**0**	**0**	**0**

• Son of Walter (Babe) • Played in NHL All-Star Game (1975)

Traded to **Chicago** by **NY Rangers** with Dave Richardson, Dick Meissner and Mel Pearson for John McKenzie and Ray Cullen, June 4, 1965. Claimed by **Oakland** from **Chicago** in Expansion Draft, June 6, 1967. Traded to **Pittsburgh** by **Oakland** with George Swarbrick and Bryan Watson for Earl Ingarfield, Gene Ubriaco and Dick Mattiussi, January 30, 1969. Claimed by **Buffalo** from **Pittsburgh** in Expansion Draft, June 10, 1970. Traded to **Vancouver** by **Buffalo** with John Gould for Jerry Korab, December 27, 1973. Signed as a free agent by **Colorado**, September 12, 1976. Traded to **Toronto** by **Colorado** for Toronto's 3rd round choice (Randy Pierce) in 1977 Amateur Draft, March 8, 1977.

• PRENTICE, Dean

Dean Sutherland LW – L. 5'11", 180 lbs. b: Schumacher, Ont., 10/5/1932.

Season	Club	League	GP	G	A	Pts	AG	AA	APts	PIM	PP	SH	GW	S	%	TGF	PGF	TGA	PGA	+/–	GP	G	A	Pts	PIM	PP	SH	GW
1950-51	Guelph Biltmores	OHA-Jr.	51	20	16	36	....	....	....	26	....	....	....	....	....	....	....	....	....	....	4	1	1	2	15	....	....	....
1951-52	Guelph Biltmores	OHA-Jr.	51	48	27	75	....	....	....	68	....	....	....	....	....	....	....	....	....	....	23	*21	10	31	28	....	....	....
	Guelph Biltmores	Mem-Cup	12	13	5	18	....	....	....	14	....	....	....	....	....	....	....	....	....	....	....	....	....	....	....	....	....	....
1952-53	Guelph Biltmores	OHA-Jr.	5	1	1	2	....	....	....	16	....	....	....	....	....	....	....	....	....	....	....	....	....	....	....	....	....	....
	New York Rangers	**NHL**	**55**	**6**	**3**	**9**	**8**	**4**	**12**	**20**	....	....	....	....	....	....	....	....	....	....	....	....	....	....	....	....	....	....
1953-54	**New York Rangers**	**NHL**	**52**	**4**	**13**	**17**	**5**	**16**	**21**	**18**	....	....	....	....	....	....	....	....	....	....	....	....	....	....	....	....	....	....
1954-55	**New York Rangers**	**NHL**	**70**	**16**	**15**	**31**	**21**	**17**	**38**	**20**	....	....	....	....	....	....	....	....	....	....	....	....	....	....	....	....	....	....
1955-56	**New York Rangers**	**NHL**	**70**	**24**	**18**	**42**	**33**	**21**	**54**	**44**	....	....	....	....	....	....	....	....	....	....	**5**	**1**	**0**	**1**	**2**	**0**	**0**	**0**
1956-57	**New York Rangers**	**NHL**	**68**	**19**	**23**	**42**	**24**	**25**	**49**	**38**	....	....	....	....	....	....	....	....	....	....	**5**	**0**	**2**	**2**	**4**	**0**	**0**	**0**
1957-58	**New York Rangers**	**NHL**	**38**	**13**	**9**	**22**	**16**	**9**	**25**	**14**	....	....	....	....	....	....	....	....	....	....	**6**	**1**	**3**	**4**	**4**	**0**	**0**	**0**
1958-59	**New York Rangers**	**NHL**	**70**	**17**	**33**	**50**	**20**	**33**	**53**	**11**	....	....	....	....	....	....	....	....	....	....	....	....	....	....	....	....	....	....
1959-60	**New York Rangers**	**NHL**	**70**	**32**	**34**	**66**	**38**	**33**	**71**	**43**	....	....	....	....	....	....	....	....	....	....	....	....	....	....	....	....	....	....
1960-61	**New York Rangers**	**NHL**	**56**	**20**	**25**	**45**	**23**	**24**	**47**	**17**	....	....	....	....	....	....	....	....	....	....	....	....	....	....	....	....	....	....
1961-62	**New York Rangers**	**NHL**	**68**	**22**	**38**	**60**	**25**	**37**	**62**	**20**	....	....	....	....	....	....	....	....	....	....	**3**	**0**	**2**	**2**	**0**	**0**	**0**	**0**
1962-63	**New York Rangers**	**NHL**	**49**	**13**	**25**	**38**	**15**	**25**	**40**	**18**	....	....	....	....	....	....	....	....	....	....	....	....	....	....	....	....	....	....
	Boston Bruins	**NHL**	**19**	**6**	**9**	**15**	**7**	**9**	**16**	**4**	....	....	....	....	....	....	....	....	....	....	....	....	....	....	....	....	....	....
1963-64	**Boston Bruins**	**NHL**	**70**	**23**	**16**	**39**	**29**	**17**	**46**	**37**	....	....	....	....	....	....	....	....	....	....	....	....	....	....	....	....	....	....
1964-65	**Boston Bruins**	**NHL**	**31**	**14**	**9**	**23**	**17**	**9**	**26**	**12**	....	....	....	....	....	....	....	....	....	....	....	....	....	....	....	....	....	....
1965-66	**Boston Bruins**	**NHL**	**50**	**7**	**22**	**29**	**8**	**21**	**29**	**10**	....	....	....	....	....	....	....	....	....	....	....	....	....	....	....	....	....	....
	Detroit Red Wings	**NHL**	**19**	**6**	**9**	**15**	**7**	**9**	**16**	**8**	....	....	....	....	....	....	....	....	....	....	**12**	**5**	**5**	**10**	**4**	**2**	**0**	**0**
1966-67	**Detroit Red Wings**	**NHL**	**68**	**23**	**22**	**45**	**27**	**21**	**48**	**18**	....	....	....	....	....	....	....	....	....	....	....	....	....	....	....	....	....	....
1967-68	**Detroit Red Wings**	**NHL**	**69**	**17**	**38**	**55**	**20**	**38**	**58**	**42**	**4**	**1**	**2**	**174**	**9.8**	**77**	**14**	**71**	**15**	**7**	....	....	....	....	....	....	....	....
1968-69	**Detroit Red Wings**	**NHL**	**74**	**14**	**20**	**34**	**15**	**18**	**33**	**18**	**2**	**1**	**1**	**191**	**7.3**	**51**	**6**	**77**	**24**	**–8**	....	....	....	....	....	....	....	....
1969-70	**Pittsburgh Penguins**	**NHL**	**75**	**26**	**25**	**51**	**28**	**23**	**51**	**14**	**12**	**0**	**2**	**205**	**12.7**	**74**	**28**	**66**	**0**	**–20**	**10**	**2**	**5**	**7**	**8**	**1**	**0**	**0**
1970-71	**Pittsburgh Penguins**	**NHL**	**69**	**21**	**17**	**38**	**21**	**14**	**35**	**18**	**7**	**0**	**2**	**135**	**15.6**	**60**	**22**	**46**	**0**	**–8**	....	....	....	....	....	....	....	....
1971-72	**Minnesota North Stars**	**NHL**	**71**	**20**	**27**	**47**	**20**	**23**	**43**	**14**	**7**	**0**	**1**	**207**	**9.7**	**62**	**16**	**42**	**0**	**4**	**7**	**3**	**0**	**3**	**0**	**0**	**0**	**1**
1972-73	**Minnesota North Stars**	**NHL**	**73**	**26**	**16**	**42**	**24**	**13**	**37**	**22**	**5**	**0**	**5**	**168**	**15.5**	**56**	**9**	**44**	**0**	**3**	**6**	**1**	**0**	**1**	**16**	**1**	**0**	**0**
1973-74	**Minnesota North Stars**	**NHL**	**24**	**2**	**3**	**5**	**2**	**2**	**4**	**4**	**0**	**0**	**0**	**36**	**5.6**	**9**	**0**	**20**	**0**	**–11**	....	....	....	....	....	....	....	....
1974-75	New Haven Nighthawks	AHL	DID NOT PLAY – COACHING																									
1975-76			OUT OF HOCKEY – RETIRED																									
1976-77	Traverse City Bays	USHL	28	5	22	27	....	....	....	4	....	....	....	....	....	....	....	....	....	....	....	....	....	....	....	....	....	....
	NHL Totals		**1378**	**391**	**469**	**860**	**453**	**461**	**914**	**484**	....	....	....	....	....	....	....	....	....		**54**	**13**	**17**	**30**	**38**	....	....	....

• Brother of Eric • NHL Second All-Star Team (1960) • Played in NHL All-Star Game (1957, 1961, 1963, 1970)

Traded to **Boston** by **NY Rangers** for Don McKenney and Dick Meissner, February 4, 1963. • Terms of transaction stipulated that Meissner would report to the NY Rangers following the 1962-63 season. • Missed remainder of 1964-65 season recovering from back injury suffered in game vs. Chicago, December 27, 1964. Traded to **Detroit** by **Boston** with Leo Boivin for Gary Doak, Ron Murphy, Bill Lesuk and future considerations (Steve Atkinson June 6, 1966), February 16, 1966. Claimed by **Pittsburgh** from **Detroit** in Intra-League Draft, June 11, 1969. Traded to **Minnesota** by **Pittsburgh** for cash, October 6, 1971.

• PRESLEY, Wayne

RW – R. 5'11", 195 lbs. b: Dearborn, MI, 3/23/1965. Chicago's 2nd, 39th overall, in 1983.

Season	Club	League	GP	G	A	Pts	AG	AA	APts	PIM	PP	SH	GW	S	%	TGF	PGF	TGA	PGA	+/–	GP	G	A	Pts	PIM	PP	SH	GW
1981-82	Detroit Little Caesar's	MNHL	61	35	56	91	....	....	....	146	....	....	....	....	....	....	....	....	....	....	....	....	....	....	....	....	....	....
1982-83	Kitchener Rangers	OHL	70	39	48	87	....	....	....	99	....	....	....	....	....	....	....	....	....	....	12	1	4	5	9	....	....	....
1983-84	Kitchener Rangers	OHL	70	63	76	139	....	....	....	156	....	....	....	....	....	....	....	....	....	....	16	12	16	28	38	....	....	....
	Kitchener Rangers	Mem-Cup	4	3	2	5	....	....	....	7	....	....	....	....	....	....	....	....	....	....	....	....	....	....	....	....	....	....
1984-85	Kitchener Rangers	OHL	31	25	21	46	....	....	....	77	....	....	....	....	....	....	....	....	....	....	....	....	....	....	....	....	....	....
	Sault Ste. Marie Greyhounds	OHL	11	5	9	14	....	....	....	14	....	....	....	....	....	....	....	....	....	....	16	13	9	22	13	....	....	....
	Chicago Black Hawks	**NHL**	**3**	**0**	**1**	**1**	**0**	**1**	**1**	**0**	**0**	**0**	**0**	**0**	**0.0**	**1**	**0**	**0**	**0**	**1**	....	....	....	....	....	....	....	....
	Sault Ste. Marie Greyhounds	Mem-Cup	4	2	2	4	....	....	....	4	....	....	....	....	....	....	....	....	....	....	....	....	....	....	....	....	....	....
1985-86	**Chicago Black Hawks**	**NHL**	**38**	**7**	**8**	**15**	**6**	**5**	**11**	**38**	**0**	**0**	**1**	**56**	**12.5**	**30**	**0**	**36**	**0**	**–6**	**3**	**0**	**0**	**0**	**0**	**0**	**0**	**0**
	Nova Scotia Oilers	AHL	29	6	9	15	....	....	....	22	....	....	....	....	....	....	....	....	....	....	....	....	....	....	....	....	....	....
1986-87	**Chicago Blackhawks**	**NHL**	**80**	**32**	**29**	**61**	**28**	**21**	**49**	**114**	**7**	**0**	**4**	**167**	**19.2**	**85**	**22**	**81**	**0**	**–18**	**4**	**1**	**0**	**1**	**9**	**0**	**0**	**0**
1987-88	United States	Can-Cup	5	1	0	1	....	....	....	12	....	....	....	....	....	....	....	....	....	....	....	....	....	....	....	....	....	....
	Chicago Blackhawks	**NHL**	**42**	**12**	**10**	**22**	**10**	**7**	**17**	**52**	**4**	**0**	**1**	**89**	**13.5**	**33**	**12**	**35**	**1**	**–13**	**5**	**0**	**0**	**0**	**4**	**0**	**0**	**0**
1988-89	**Chicago Blackhawks**	**NHL**	**72**	**21**	**19**	**40**	**18**	**13**	**31**	**100**	**4**	**3**	**4**	**132**	**15.9**	**52**	**14**	**56**	**15**	**–3**	**14**	**7**	**5**	**12**	**18**	**1**	**3**	**1**
1989-90	**Chicago Blackhawks**	**NHL**	**49**	**6**	**7**	**13**	**5**	**5**	**10**	**69**	**1**	**0**	**0**	**75**	**8.0**	**27**	**5**	**46**	**5**	**–19**	**19**	**9**	**6**	**15**	**29**	**1**	**1**	**1**
1990-91	**Chicago Blackhawks**	**NHL**	**71**	**15**	**19**	**34**	**14**	**14**	**28**	**122**	**1**	**0**	**3**	**141**	**10.6**	**55**	**13**	**35**	**4**	**11**	**6**	**0**	**1**	**1**	**38**	**0**	**0**	**0**
1991-92	**San Jose Sharks**	**NHL**	**47**	**8**	**14**	**22**	**7**	**11**	**18**	**76**	**3**	**0**	**0**	**114**	**7.0**	**28**	**14**	**47**	**4**	**–29**	....	....	....	....	....	....	....	....
	Buffalo Sabres	**NHL**	**12**	**2**	**2**	**4**	**2**	**2**	**4**	**57**	**0**	**0**	**1**	**21**	**9.5**	**9**	**1**	**8**	**2**	**2**	**7**	**3**	**3**	**6**	**14**	**0**	**0**	**0**
1992-93	**Buffalo Sabres**	**NHL**	**79**	**15**	**17**	**32**	**12**	**12**	**24**	**96**	**0**	**1**	**2**	**97**	**15.5**	**49**	**4**	**58**	**18**	**5**	**8**	**1**	**0**	**1**	**6**	**0**	**1**	**1**
1993-94	**Buffalo Sabres**	**NHL**	**65**	**17**	**8**	**25**	**16**	**6**	**22**	**103**	**1**	**5**	**1**	**93**	**18.3**	**41**	**3**	**35**	**15**	**18**	**7**	**2**	**1**	**3**	**14**	**1**	**0**	**1**
1994-95	**Buffalo Sabres**	**NHL**	**46**	**14**	**5**	**19**	**25**	**7**	**32**	**41**	**0**	**5**	**2**	**90**	**15.6**	**27**	**2**	**39**	**19**	**5**	**5**	**3**	**1**	**4**	**8**	**0**	**1**	**1**
1995-96	**New York Rangers**	**NHL**	**61**	**4**	**6**	**10**	**4**	**5**	**9**	**71**	**0**	**1**	**2**	**85**	**4.7**	**19**	**0**	**34**	**22**	**7**	....	....	....	....	....	....	....	....
	Toronto Maple Leafs	**NHL**	**19**	**2**	**2**	**4**	**2**	**2**	**4**	**14**	**1**	**0**	**0**	**28**	**7.1**	**7**	**2**	**19**	**10**	**–4**	**5**	**0**	**0**	**0**	**2**	**0**	**0**	**0**
1996-97	St. John's Maple Leafs	AHL	2	0	0	0	....	....	....	0	....	....	....	....	....	....	....	....	....	....	....	....	....	....	....	....	....	....
	Detroit Vipers	IHL	42	7	16	23	....	....	....	80	....	....	....	....	....	....	....	....	....	....	18	0	4	4	50	....	....	....
1997-98	Detroit Vipers	IHL	16	1	5	6	....	....	....	47	....	....	....	....	....	....	....	....	....	....	23	4	6	10	60	....	....	....
	NHL Totals		**684**	**155**	**147**	**302**	**149**	**111**	**260**	**953**	**22**	**15**	**21**	**1188**	**13.0**	**463**	**92**	**529**	**115**		**83**	**26**	**17**	**43**	**142**	**3**	**6**	**5**

OHL First All-Star Team (1984)

Traded to **San Jose** by **Chicago** for San Jose's 3rd round choice (Bogdan Savenko) in 1993 Entry Draft, September 20, 1991. Traded to **Buffalo** by **San Jose** for Dave Snuggerud, March 9, 1992. Signed as a free agent by **NY Rangers**, August 31, 1995. Traded to **Toronto** by **NY Rangers** for Sergio Momesso, February 29, 1996.

• PRESTON, Rich

Richard John "Cool Hand Luke" RW – R. 6', 185 lbs. b: Regina, Sask., 5/22/1952.

Season	Club	League	GP	G	A	Pts	AG	AA	APts	PIM	PP	SH	GW	S	%	TGF	PGF	TGA	PGA	+/–	GP	G	A	Pts	PIM	PP	SH	GW
1969-70	Regina Pats	SJHL	36	15	15	30	....	....	....	4	....	....	....	....	....	....	....	....	....	....	....	....	....	....	....	....	....	....
1970-71	University of Denver	WCHA	17	0	1	1	....	....	....	0	....	....	....	....	....	....	....	....	....	....	....	....	....	....	....	....	....	....
1971-72	University of Denver	WCHA	33	3	11	14	....	....	....	18	....	....	....	....	....	....	....	....	....	....	....	....	....	....	....	....	....	....
1972-73	University of Denver	WCHA	39	23	25	48	....	....	....	24	....	....	....	....	....	....	....	....	....	....	....	....	....	....	....	....	....	....
1973-74	University of Denver	WCHA	38	20	25	45	....	....	....	36	....	....	....	....	....	....	....	....	....	....	....	....	....	....	....	....	....	....
1974-75	Houston Aeros	WHA	78	20	21	41	....	....	....	10	....	....	....	....	....	....	....	....	....	....	13	1	6	7	6	....	....	....
1975-76	Houston Aeros	WHA	77	22	33	55	....	....	....	33	....	....	....	....	....	....	....	....	....	....	17	4	6	10	8	....	....	....
1976-77	Houston Aeros	WHA	80	38	41	79	....	....	....	54	....	....	....	....	....	....	....	....	....	....	11	3	5	8	10	....	....	....
1977-78	Houston Aeros	WHA	73	25	25	50	....	....	....	52	....	....	....	....	....	....	....	....	....	....	....	....	....	....	....	....	....	....
1978-79	Winnipeg Jets	WHA	80	28	32	60	....	....	....	88	....	....	....	....	....	....	....	....	....	....	10	8	5	13	15	....	....	....
1979-80	**Chicago Black Hawks**	**NHL**	**80**	**31**	**30**	**61**	**26**	**22**	**48**	**70**	**12**	**2**	**5**	**205**	**15.1**	**106**	**38**	**75**	**23**	**16**	**7**	**0**	**3**	**3**	**2**	**0**	**0**	**0**
1980-81	**Chicago Black Hawks**	**NHL**	**47**	**7**	**14**	**21**	**5**	**9**	**14**	**24**	**3**	**0**	**1**	**100**	**7.0**	**46**	**14**	**72**	**25**	**–15**	**3**	**0**	**1**	**1**	**0**	**0**	**0**	**0**
1981-82	**Chicago Black Hawks**	**NHL**	**75**	**15**	**28**	**43**	**12**	**19**	**31**	**30**	**1**	**1**	**1**	**122**	**12.3**	**84**	**15**	**94**	**25**	**0**	**15**	**2**	**4**	**6**	**21**	**0**	**0**	**0**
1982-83	**Chicago Black Hawks**	**NHL**	**79**	**25**	**28**	**53**	**20**	**19**	**39**	**64**	**4**	**0**	**2**	**161**	**15.5**	**97**	**23**	**80**	**20**	**14**	**13**	**2**	**7**	**9**	**25**	**0**	**0**	**1**

			REGULAR SEASON																		PLAYOFFS							
Season	**Club**	**League**	**GP**	**G**	**A**	**Pts**	**AG**	**AA**	**APts**	**PIM**	**PP**	**SH**	**GW**	**S**	**%**	**TGF**	**PGF**	**TGA**	**PGA**	**+/-**	**GP**	**G**	**A**	**Pts**	**PIM**	**PP**	**SH**	**GW**
1983-84	**Chicago Black Hawks**	**NHL**	**75**	**10**	**18**	**28**	**8**	**12**	**20**	**50**	**3**	**1**	**1**	**109**	**9.2**	**59**	**11**	**91**	**22**	**–21**	**5**	**0**	**1**	**1**	**4**	**0**	**0**	**0**
1984-85	**New Jersey Devils**	**NHL**	**75**	**12**	**15**	**27**	**10**	**10**	**20**	**26**	**1**	**0**	**1**	**106**	**11.3**	**48**	**6**	**85**	**19**	**–24**	....	....	....	....	....	....	....	....
1985-86	**New Jersey Devils**	**NHL**	**76**	**19**	**22**	**41**	**15**	**15**	**30**	**65**	**3**	**0**	**2**	**117**	**16.2**	**70**	**19**	**82**	**34**	**3**	....	....	....	....	....	....	....	....
1986-87	**Chicago Blackhawks**	**NHL**	**73**	**8**	**9**	**17**	**7**	**7**	**14**	**19**	**0**	**0**	**1**	**55**	**14.5**	**30**	**2**	**59**	**23**	**–8**	**4**	**0**	**2**	**2**	**4**	**0**	**0**	**0**
1987-1991			OUT OF HOCKEY – RETIRED																									
1991-1995	**Chicago Blackhawks**	**NHL**	DID NOT PLAY – ASSISTANT COACH																									
1995-1997	Regina Pats	WHL	DID NOT PLAY – COACHING																									
1997-2000	**Calgary Flames**	**NHL**	DID NOT PLAY – ASSISTANT COACH																									
	NHL Totals		**580**	**127**	**164**	**291**	**103**	**113**	**216**	**348**	**27**	**4**	**14**	**975**	**13.0**	**540**	**128**	**638**	**191**		**47**	**4**	**18**	**22**	**56**	**0**	**0**	**1**
	Other Major League Totals		388	133	152	285	....	....	....	237	....	....	....	....	....	....	....	....	....	....	51	16	22	38	39	....	....	....

Won WHA Playoff MVP Trophy (1979)

Selected by **Houston** (WHA) in 1973 WHA Professional Player Draft, June, 1973. Traded to **Winnipeg** (WHA) by **Houston** (WHA) for cash, July 6, 1978. Claimed by **Chicago** from **Winnipeg** in Expansion Draft, June 13, 1979. Traded to **New Jersey** by **Chicago** with Don Dietrich and Chicago's 2nd round choice (Eric Weinrich) in 1985 Entry Draft for Bob MacMillan and New Jersey's 5th round choice (Rick Herbert) in 1985 Entry Draft, June 19, 1984. Signed as a free agent by **Chicago**, July 14, 1986. • Named Assistant Coach of **San Jose**, June 25, 2000.

• PRESTON, Yves

LW – L. 5'11", 180 lbs. b: Montreal, Que., 6/14/1956.

Season	Club	League	GP	G	A	Pts	AG	AA	APts	PIM	PP	SH	GW	S	%	TGF	PGF	TGA	PGA	+/-	GP	G	A	Pts	PIM	PP	SH	GW
1973-74	Chicoutimi Sagueneens	QMJHL	70	26	33	59	....	....	....	60	....	....	....	....	....	....	....	....	....	....	....	....	....	....	....	....	....	....
1974-75	Laval Nationales	QMJHL	64	18	33	51	....	....	....	44	....	....	....	....	....	....	....	....	....	....	....	....	....	....	....	....	....	....
1975-76	Laval Nationales	QMJHL	63	29	42	71	....	....	....	45	....	....	....	....	....	....	....	....	....	....	....	....	....	....	....	....	....	....
1976-77	Milwaukee Admirals	USHL	15	17	13	30	....	....	....	2	....	....	....	....	....	....	....	....	....	....	....	....	....	....	....	....	....	....
	Dayton Gems	IHL	10	0	0	0	....	....	....	2	....	....	....	....	....	....	....	....	....	....	....	....	....	....	....	....	....	....
1977-78	Milwaukee Admirals	IHL	80	37	37	74	....	....	....	51	....	....	....	....	....	....	....	....	....	....	1	0	0	0	0	....	....	....
1978-79	**Philadelphia Flyers**	**NHL**	**9**	**3**	**1**	**4**	**3**	**1**	**4**	**0**	**0**	**0**	**1**	**7**	**42.9**	**6**	**2**	**6**	**0**	**–2**	....	....	....	....	....	....	....	....
	Maine Mariners	AHL	73	35	32	67	....	....	....	38	....	....	....	....	....	....	....	....	....	....	10	6	4	10	19	....	....	....
1979-80	Maine Mariners	AHL	71	23	24	47	....	....	....	51	....	....	....	....	....	....	....	....	....	....	12	1	4	5	17	....	....	....
1980-81	**Philadelphia Flyers**	**NHL**	**19**	**4**	**2**	**6**	**3**	**1**	**4**	**4**	**1**	**0**	**1**	**13**	**30.8**	**9**	**1**	**7**	**0**	**1**	....	....	....	....	....	....	....	....
	Wichita Wind	CHL	31	4	11	15	....	....	....	25	....	....	....	....	....	....	....	....	....	....	4	0	3	3	21	....	....	....
1981-82	Milwaukee Admirals	IHL	70	25	29	54	....	....	....	23	....	....	....	....	....	....	....	....	....	....	5	1	1	2	0	....	....	....
1982-83	Milwaukee Admirals	IHL	67	35	53	88	....	....	....	17	....	....	....	....	....	....	....	....	....	....	11	4	3	7	6	....	....	....
1983-84	Milwaukee Admirals	IHL	82	36	49	85	....	....	....	37	....	....	....	....	....	....	....	....	....	....	4	0	2	2	0	....	....	....
	NHL Totals		**28**	**7**	**3**	**10**	**6**	**2**	**8**	**4**	**1**	**0**	**2**	**20**	**35.0**	**15**	**3**	**13**	**0**		....	....	....	....	....	....	....	....

IHL Second All-Star Team (1978) • AHL First All-Star Team (1979)

Signed as a free agent by **Philadelphia**, October 9, 1978.

• PRIAKIN, Sergei

RW – L. 6'3", 210 lbs. b: Moscow, Soviet Union, 12/7/1963. Calgary's 12th, 252nd overall, in 1988.

Season	Club	League	GP	G	A	Pts	AG	AA	APts	PIM	PP	SH	GW	S	%	TGF	PGF	TGA	PGA	+/-	GP	G	A	Pts	PIM	PP	SH	GW
1980-81	Soviet Union	EJC-A	5	4	2	6	....	....	....	4	....	....	....	....	....	....	....	....	....	....	....	....	....	....	....	....	....	....
1981-82	Kralja Sovetov Moscow	USSR	43	4	5	9	....	....	....	23	....	....	....	....	....	....	....	....	....	....	....	....	....	....	....	....	....	....
	Kralja Sovetov Moscow	USSR-Jr.	STATISTICS NOT AVAILABLE																									
	Soviet Union	WJC-A	7	2	1	3	....	....	....	4	....	....	....	....	....	....	....	....	....	....	....	....	....	....	....	....	....	....
1982-83	Kralja Sovetov Moscow	USSR	35	11	9	20	....	....	....	18	....	....	....	....	....	....	....	....	....	....	....	....	....	....	....	....	....	....
	Soviet Union	WJC-A	7	2	4	6	....	....	....	13	....	....	....	....	....	....	....	....	....	....	....	....	....	....	....	....	....	....
1983-84	Kralja Sovetov Moscow	USSR	44	18	13	31	....	....	....	24	....	....	....	....	....	....	....	....	....	....	....	....	....	....	....	....	....	....
1984-85	Kralja Sovetov Moscow	USSR	32	14	9	23	....	....	....	10	....	....	....	....	....	....	....	....	....	....	....	....	....	....	....	....	....	....
1985-86	Kralja Sovetov Moscow	USSR	39	12	13	25	....	....	....	16	....	....	....	....	....	....	....	....	....	....	....	....	....	....	....	....	....	....
1986-87	Kralja Sovetov Moscow	USSR	40	12	20	32	....	....	....	18	....	....	....	....	....	....	....	....	....	....	....	....	....	....	....	....	....	....
	USSR	RV-87	2	0	0	0	....	....	....	12	....	....	....	....	....	....	....	....	....	....	....	....	....	....	....	....	....	....
	Soviet Union	WEC-A	8	0	2	2	....	....	....	8	....	....	....	....	....	....	....	....	....	....	....	....	....	....	....	....	....	....
1987-88	Soviet Union	Can-Cup	9	0	2	2	....	....	....	6	....	....	....	....	....	....	....	....	....	....	....	....	....	....	....	....	....	....
	Kralja Sovetov Moscow	USSR	44	10	15	25	....	....	....	16	....	....	....	....	....	....	....	....	....	....	....	....	....	....	....	....	....	....
1988-89	Kralja Sovetov Moscow	USSR	44	11	15	26	....	....	....	23	....	....	....	....	....	....	....	....	....	....	....	....	....	....	....	....	....	....
◆	**Calgary Flames**	**NHL**	**2**	**0**	**0**	**0**	**0**	**0**	**0**	**2**	**0**	**0**	**0**	**2**	**0.0**	**1**	**0**	**0**	**0**	**1**	**1**	**0**	**0**	**0**	**0**	**0**	**0**	**0**
1989-90	Calgary Flames	Fr-Tour	4	1	1	2	....	....	....	0	....	....	....	....	....	....	....	....	....	....	....	....	....	....	....	....	....	....
	Calgary Flames	**NHL**	**20**	**2**	**2**	**4**	**2**	**1**	**3**	**0**	**0**	**0**	**1**	**17**	**11.8**	**8**	**0**	**15**	**0**	**–7**	....	....	....	....	....	....	....	....
	Salt Lake Golden Eagles	IHL	3	1	0	1	....	....	....	0	....	....	....	....	....	....	....	....	....	....	....	....	....	....	....	....	....	....
	Soviet Union	WEC-A	3	0	1	1	....	....	....	2	....	....	....	....	....	....	....	....	....	....	....	....	....	....	....	....	....	....
1990-91	**Calgary Flames**	**NHL**	**24**	**1**	**6**	**7**	**1**	**5**	**6**	**0**	**0**	**0**	**0**	**26**	**3.8**	**11**	**0**	**14**	**0**	**–3**	....	....	....	....	....	....	....	....
	Salt Lake Golden Eagles	IHL	18	5	12	17	....	....	....	2	....	....	....	....	....	....	....	....	....	....	....	....	....	....	....	....	....	....
1991-92	ZSC Lions Zurich	Switz-2	42	21	25	46	....	....	....	24	....	....	....	....	....	....	....	....	....	....	....	....	....	....	....	....	....	....
1992-93	Kralja Sovetov Moscow	CIS	20	4	4	8	....	....	....	10	....	....	....	....	....	....	....	....	....	....	....	....	....	....	....	....	....	....
	ZSC Lions Zurich	Switz	23	12	5	17	....	....	....	12	....	....	....	....	....	....	....	....	....	....	4	2	1	3	4	....	....	....
1993-94	ZSC Lions Zurich	Switz	29	19	15	34	....	....	....	20	....	....	....	....	....	....	....	....	....	....	....	....	....	....	....	....	....	....
1994-95	Kiekko-Espoo	Finland	50	13	20	33	....	....	....	49	....	....	....	....	....	....	....	....	....	....	4	1	4	5	0	....	....	....
1995-96	Kiekko-Espoo	Finland	49	9	24	33	....	....	....	53	....	....	....	....	....	....	....	....	....	....	....	....	....	....	....	....	....	....
1996-97	Blues Espoo	Finland	50	15	25	40	....	....	....	53	....	....	....	....	....	....	....	....	....	....	4	0	0	0	2	....	....	....
1997-98	Blues Espoo	Finland	46	11	24	35	....	....	....	24	....	....	....	....	....	....	....	....	....	....	8	3	3	6	0	....	....	....
	NHL Totals		**46**	**3**	**8**	**11**	**3**	**6**	**9**	**2**	**0**	**0**	**1**	**45**	**6.7**	**20**	**0**	**29**	**0**		**1**	**0**	**0**	**0**	**0**	**0**	**0**	**0**

• PRICE, Noel

Garry Noel D – L. 6', 190 lbs. b: Brockville, Ont., 12/9/1935.

Season	Club	League	GP	G	A	Pts	AG	AA	APts	PIM	PP	SH	GW	S	%	TGF	PGF	TGA	PGA	+/-	GP	G	A	Pts	PIM	PP	SH	GW
1952-53	St. Michael's Majors	OHA-Jr.	44	0	4	4	....	....	....	120	....	....	....	....	....	....	....	....	....	....	17	1	4	5	28	....	....	....
1953-54	St. Michael's Majors	OHA-Jr.	58	6	5	11	....	....	....	157	....	....	....	....	....	....	....	....	....	....	8	1	2	3	31	....	....	....
1954-55	St. Michael's Majors	OHA-Jr.	47	4	11	15	....	....	....	129	....	....	....	....	....	....	....	....	....	....	5	1	2	3	12	....	....	....
1955-56	St. Michael's Majors	OHA-Jr.	46	10	22	32	....	....	....	84	....	....	....	....	....	....	....	....	....	....	8	1	0	1	8	....	....	....
1956-57	Rochester Americans	AHL	1	1	1	2	....	....	....	0	....	....	....	....	....	....	....	....	....	....	10	0	1	1	16	....	....	....
	Winnipeg Warriors	WHL	70	5	22	27	....	....	....	142	....	....	....	....	....	....	....	....	....	....	....	....	....	....	....	....	....	....
1957-58	**Toronto Maple Leafs**	**NHL**	**1**	**0**	**0**	**0**	**0**	**0**	**0**	**5**											....	....	....	....	....	....	....	....
	Rochester Americans	AHL	69	4	20	24	....	....	....	153	....	....	....	....	....	....	....	....	....	....	....	....	....	....	....	....	....	....
1958-59	**Toronto Maple Leafs**	**NHL**	**28**	**0**	**0**	**0**	**0**	**0**	**0**	**4**											**5**	**0**	**0**	**0**	**2**	**0**	**0**	**0**
1959-60	**New York Rangers**	**NHL**	**6**	**0**	**0**	**0**	**0**	**0**	**0**	**2**											....	....	....	....	....	....	....	....
	Springfield Indians	AHL	31	0	6	6	....	....	....	52	....	....	....	....	....	....	....	....	....	....	10	1	3	4	20	....	....	....
1960-61	**New York Rangers**	**NHL**	**1**	**0**	**0**	**0**	**0**	**0**	**0**	**2**											....	....	....	....	....	....	....	....
	Springfield Indians	AHL	71	6	21	27	....	....	....	97	....	....	....	....	....	....	....	....	....	....	8	1	4	5	30	....	....	....
1961-62	Springfield Indians	AHL	47	4	19	23	....	....	....	75	....	....	....	....	....	....	....	....	....	....	....	....	....	....	....	....	....	....
	Detroit Red Wings	**NHL**	**20**	**0**	**1**	**1**	**0**	**1**	**1**	**6**											....	....	....	....	....	....	....	....
1962-63	Baltimore Clippers	AHL	68	7	29	36	....	....	....	103	....	....	....	....	....	....	....	....	....	....	3	0	0	0	4	....	....	....
1963-64	Baltimore Clippers	AHL	72	6	35	41	....	....	....	109	....	....	....	....	....	....	....	....	....	....	....	....	....	....	....	....	....	....
1964-65	Baltimore Clippers	AHL	72	4	35	39	....	....	....	78	....	....	....	....	....	....	....	....	....	....	5	0	2	2	4	....	....	....
1965-66◆	**Montreal Canadiens**	**NHL**	**15**	**0**	**6**	**6**	**0**	**6**	**6**	**8**											**3**	**0**	**1**	**1**	**0**	**0**	**0**	**0**
	Quebec Aces	AHL	55	8	20	28	....	....	....	48	....	....	....	....	....	....	....	....	....	....	....	....	....	....	....	....	....	....
1966-67	**Montreal Canadiens**	**NHL**	**24**	**0**	**3**	**3**	**0**	**3**	**3**	**8**											....	....	....	....	....	....	....	....
	Quebec Aces	AHL	47	3	23	26	....	....	....	60	....	....	....	....	....	....	....	....	....	....	5	1	4	5	2	....	....	....
1967-68	**Pittsburgh Penguins**	**NHL**	**70**	**6**	**27**	**33**	**7**	**27**	**34**	**48**	**1**	**0**	**2**	**187**	**3.2**	**97**	**17**	**105**	**18**	**–7**	....	....	....	....	....	....	....	....
1968-69	**Pittsburgh Penguins**	**NHL**	**73**	**2**	**18**	**20**	**2**	**16**	**18**	**61**	**1**	**0**	**0**	**152**	**1.3**	**65**	**13**	**99**	**17**	**–30**	....	....	....	....	....	....	....	....
1969-70	Springfield Kings	AHL	72	10	44	54	....	....	....	58	....	....	....	....	....	....	....	....	....	....	14	1	3	4	14	....	....	....
1970-71	**Los Angeles Kings**	**NHL**	**62**	**1**	**19**	**20**	**1**	**16**	**17**	**29**	**0**	**0**	**0**	**88**	**1.1**	**63**	**11**	**77**	**10**	**–15**	....	....	....	....	....	....	....	....
1971-72	Springfield Kings	AHL	9	1	3	4	....	....	....	6	....	....	....	....	....	....	....	....	....	....	....	....	....	....	....	....	....	....
	Nova Scotia Voyageurs	AHL	64	3	26	29	....	....	....	81	....	....	....	....	....	....	....	....	....	....	15	4	7	11	16	....	....	....
1972-73	**Atlanta Flames**	**NHL**	**54**	**1**	**13**	**14**	**1**	**10**	**11**	**38**	**0**	**0**	**0**	**70**	**1.4**	**51**	**11**	**61**	**14**	**–7**	....	....	....	....	....	....	....	....
1973-74	**Atlanta Flames**	**NHL**	**62**	**0**	**13**	**13**	**0**	**11**	**11**	**38**	**0**	**0**	**0**	**93**	**0.0**	**56**	**2**	**82**	**17**	**–11**	**4**	**0**	**0**	**0**	**6**	**0**	**0**	**0**

			REGULAR SEASON																		PLAYOFFS							
Season	Club	League	GP	G	A	Pts	AG	AA	APts	PIM	PP	SH	GW	S	%	TGF	PGF	TGA	PGA	+/–	GP	G	A	Pts	PIM	PP	SH	GW
1974-75	**Atlanta Flames**	**NHL**	**80**	**4**	**14**	**18**	**3**	**10**	**13**	**82**	**1**	**1**	**0**	**101**	**4.0**	**66**	**6**	**81**	**21**	**0**	....	....	....	....	....	....	....	....
1975-76	**Atlanta Flames**	**NHL**	**3**	**0**	**0**	**0**	**0**	**0**	**0**	**2**	**0**	**0**	**0**	**1**	**0.0**	**0**	**0**	**0**	**0**	**0**	....	....	....	....	....	....	....	....
	Nova Scotia Voyageurs	AHL	73	2	37	39	....	....	....	55	....	....	....	....	....	....	....	....	....	....	8	0	7	7	12	....	....	....
	NHL Totals		**499**	**14**	**114**	**128**	**14**	**100**	**114**	**333**	....	....	....	....	....	....	....	....	....	....	**12**	**0**	**1**	**1**	**8**	....	....	....

WHL Prairie Division Second All-Star Team (1957) • AHL Second All-Star Team (1966) • AHL First All-Star Team (1970, 1972, 1976) • Won Eddie Shore Award (Outstanding Defenseman - AHL) (1970, 1972, 1976) • Played in NHL All-Star Game (1967)

Traded to **NY Rangers** by **Toronto** for Hank Ciesla, Bill Kennedy and future considerations, October 3, 1959. Traded to **Detroit** by **NY Rangers** for Pete Goegan, February 16, 1962. Traded to **NY Rangers** by **Detroit** for Pete Goegan, October 8, 1962. Traded to **Montreal** by **NY Rangers** with Earl Ingarfield, Gord Labossiere, Dave McComb and cash for Cesare Maniago and Garry Peters, June 8, 1965. Claimed by **Pittsburgh** from **Montreal** in Expansion Draft, June 6, 1967. Claimed by **LA Kings** (Springfield-AHL) from **Pittsburgh** in Reverse Draft, June 12, 1969. Traded to **Montreal** by **LA Kings** with Denis DeJordy, Dale Hoganson and Doug Robinson for Rogie Vachon, November 4, 1971. Traded to **Atlanta** by **Montreal** for cash and future considerations, August 14, 1972.

• PRICE, Pat

Shaun Patrick D – L. 6'2", 200 lbs. b: Nelson, B.C., 3/24/1955. NY Islanders' 1st, 11th overall, in 1975.

Season	Club	League	GP	G	A	Pts	AG	AA	APts	PIM	PP	SH	GW	S	%	TGF	PGF	TGA	PGA	+/–	GP	G	A	Pts	PIM	PP	SH	GW
1970-71	Saskatoon Blades	WCJHL	66	2	16	18	....	....	....	56	....	....	....	....	....	....	....	....	....	....	5	0	3	3	2	....	....	....
1971-72	Saskatoon Blades	WCJHL	66	10	48	58	....	....	....	85	....	....	....	....	....	....	....	....	....	....	8	0	3	3	25	....	....	....
1972-73	Saskatoon Blades	WCJHL	67	12	56	68	....	....	....	134	....	....	....	....	....	....	....	....	....	....	16	4	17	21	24	....	....	....
1973-74	Saskatoon Blades	WCJHL	68	27	68	95	....	....	....	147	....	....	....	....	....	....	....	....	....	....	6	3	4	7	13	....	....	....
1974-75	Team Canada	Summit-74	DID NOT PLAY																									
	Vancouver Blazers	WHA	68	5	29	34	....	....	....	15	....	....	....	....	....	....	....	....	....	....	....	....	....	....	....	....	....	....
1975-76	**New York Islanders**	**NHL**	**4**	**0**	**2**	**2**	**0**	**1**	**1**	**2**	**0**	**0**	**0**	**4**	**0.0**	**6**	**0**	**2**	**0**	**4**	....	....	....	....	....	....	....	....
	Fort Worth Texans	CHL	72	6	44	50	....	....	....	119	....	....	....	....	....	....	....	....	....	....	....	....	....	....	....	....	....	....
1976-77	**New York Islanders**	**NHL**	**71**	**3**	**22**	**25**	**3**	**17**	**20**	**25**	**2**	**0**	**0**	**82**	**3.7**	**81**	**19**	**37**	**1**	**26**	**10**	**0**	**1**	**1**	**2**	**0**	**0**	**0**
1977-78	**New York Islanders**	**NHL**	**52**	**2**	**10**	**12**	**2**	**8**	**10**	**27**	**0**	**0**	**1**	**50**	**4.0**	**60**	**5**	**30**	**0**	**25**	**5**	**0**	**1**	**1**	**2**	**0**	**0**	**0**
	Rochester Americans	AHL	5	2	1	3	....	....	....	9	....	....	....	....	....	....	....	....	....	....	....	....	....	....	....	....	....	....
1978-79	**New York Islanders**	**NHL**	**55**	**3**	**11**	**14**	**3**	**8**	**11**	**50**	**0**	**0**	**0**	**48**	**6.3**	**60**	**4**	**38**	**0**	**18**	**7**	**0**	**1**	**1**	**25**	**0**	**0**	**0**
1979-80	**Edmonton Oilers**	**NHL**	**75**	**11**	**21**	**32**	**9**	**15**	**24**	**134**	**2**	**0**	**0**	**95**	**11.6**	**98**	**16**	**113**	**35**	**4**	**3**	**0**	**0**	**0**	**11**	**0**	**0**	**0**
1980-81	**Edmonton Oilers**	**NHL**	**59**	**8**	**24**	**32**	**6**	**16**	**22**	**193**	**0**	**0**	**0**	**90**	**8.9**	**82**	**22**	**91**	**24**	**–7**	....	....	....	....	....	....	....	....
	Pittsburgh Penguins	**NHL**	**13**	**0**	**10**	**10**	**0**	**7**	**7**	**33**	**0**	**0**	**0**	**25**	**0.0**	**18**	**2**	**17**	**3**	**2**	**5**	**1**	**1**	**2**	**21**	**0**	**0**	**0**
1981-82	**Pittsburgh Penguins**	**NHL**	**77**	**7**	**31**	**38**	**6**	**21**	**27**	**322**	**2**	**0**	**0**	**107**	**6.5**	**98**	**13**	**107**	**24**	**2**	**5**	**0**	**0**	**0**	**28**	**0**	**0**	**0**
1982-83	**Pittsburgh Penguins**	**NHL**	**38**	**1**	**11**	**12**	**1**	**8**	**9**	**104**	**0**	**0**	**0**	**57**	**1.8**	**36**	**8**	**63**	**16**	**–19**	....	....	....	....	....	....	....	....
	Quebec Nordiques	**NHL**	**14**	**1**	**2**	**3**	**1**	**1**	**2**	**28**	**0**	**0**	**0**	**8**	**12.5**	**18**	**0**	**28**	**7**	**–3**	**4**	**0**	**0**	**0**	**14**	**0**	**0**	**0**
1983-84	**Quebec Nordiques**	**NHL**	**72**	**3**	**25**	**28**	**2**	**17**	**19**	**188**	**0**	**0**	**2**	**59**	**5.1**	**107**	**16**	**93**	**22**	**20**	**9**	**1**	**0**	**1**	**10**	**0**	**0**	**0**
1984-85	**Quebec Nordiques**	**NHL**	**68**	**1**	**26**	**27**	**1**	**18**	**19**	**118**	**0**	**0**	**0**	**55**	**1.8**	**80**	**3**	**84**	**24**	**17**	**17**	**0**	**4**	**4**	**51**	**0**	**0**	**0**
1985-86	**Quebec Nordiques**	**NHL**	**54**	**3**	**13**	**16**	**2**	**9**	**11**	**82**	**0**	**0**	**0**	**49**	**6.1**	**54**	**3**	**73**	**22**	**0**	**3**	**0**	**1**	**1**	**4**	**0**	**0**	**0**
1986-87	**Quebec Nordiques**	**NHL**	**47**	**0**	**6**	**6**	**0**	**4**	**4**	**81**	**0**	**0**	**0**	**22**	**0.0**	**27**	**0**	**42**	**8**	**–7**	....	....	....	....	....	....	....	....
	Fredericton Express	AHL	7	0	0	0	....	....	....	14	....	....	....	....	....	....	....	....	....	....	....	....	....	....	....	....	....	....
	New York Rangers	**NHL**	**13**	**0**	**2**	**2**	**0**	**1**	**1**	**49**	**0**	**0**	**0**	**4**	**0.0**	**5**	**0**	**19**	**6**	**–8**	**6**	**0**	**1**	**1**	**27**	**0**	**0**	**0**
1987-88	**Minnesota North Stars**	**NHL**	**14**	**0**	**2**	**2**	**0**	**1**	**1**	**20**	**0**	**0**	**0**	**10**	**0.0**	**7**	**0**	**19**	**9**	**–3**	....	....	....	....	....	....	....	....
	Kalamazoo Wings	IHL	2	1	1	2	....	....	....	15	....	....	....	....	....	....	....	....	....	....	....	....	....	....	....	....	....	....
	NHL Totals		**726**	**43**	**218**	**261**	**36**	**152**	**188**	**1456**	**6**	**0**	**3**	**765**	**5.6**	**837**	**111**	**856**	**201**		**74**	**2**	**10**	**12**	**195**	**0**	**0**	**0**
	Other Major League Totals		68	5	29	34	....	....	....	15	....	....	....	....	....	....	....	....	....	....	....	....	....	....	....	....	....	....

WCJHL First All-Star Team (1974)

Selected by **Vancouver** (WHA) in 1974 WHA Amateur Draft, May, 1974. Claimed by **Edmonton** from **NY Islanders** in Expansion Draft, June 13, 1979. Traded to **Pittsburgh** by **Edmonton** for Pat Hughes, March 10, 1981. Claimed on waivers by **Quebec** from **Pittsburgh**, December 31, 1982. Traded to **NY Rangers** by **Quebec** for Lane Lambert, March 5, 1987. Traded to **Minnesota** by **NY Rangers** for Willi Plett, September 8, 1987.

• PRICE, Tom

Thomas Edward D – L. 6'1", 190 lbs. b: Toronto, Ont., 7/12/1954. California's 5th, 57th overall, in 1974.

Season	Club	League	GP	G	A	Pts	AG	AA	APts	PIM	PP	SH	GW	S	%	TGF	PGF	TGA	PGA	+/–	GP	G	A	Pts	PIM	PP	SH	GW
1972-73	London Knights	OMJHL	62	4	10	14	....	....	....	104	....	....	....	....	....	....	....	....	....	....	....	....	....	....	....	....	....	....
1973-74	Ottawa 67's	OMJHL	61	7	33	40	....	....	....	80	....	....	....	....	....	....	....	....	....	....	7	2	1	3	10	....	....	....
1974-75	**California Golden Seals**	**NHL**	**3**	**0**	**0**	**0**	**0**	**0**	**0**	**4**	**0**	**0**	**0**	**2**	**0.0**	**1**	**0**	**3**	**1**	**–1**	....	....	....	....	....	....	....	....
	Salt Lake Golden Eagles	CHL	52	2	16	18	....	....	....	91	....	....	....	....	....	....	....	....	....	....	1	0	0	0	2	....	....	....
1975-76	**California Golden Seals**	**NHL**	**5**	**0**	**0**	**0**	**0**	**0**	**0**	**0**	**0**	**0**	**0**	**5**	**0.0**	**1**	**0**	**10**	**0**	**–9**	....	....	....	....	....	....	....	....
	Salt Lake Golden Eagles	CHL	59	11	15	26	....	....	....	77	....	....	....	....	....	....	....	....	....	....	5	1	1	2	2	....	....	....
1976-77	**Cleveland Barons**	**NHL**	**2**	**0**	**0**	**0**	**0**	**0**	**0**	**0**	**0**	**0**	**0**	**2**	**0.0**	**0**	**0**	**4**	**0**	**–4**	....	....	....	....	....	....	....	....
	Salt Lake Golden Eagles	CHL	55	3	21	24	....	....	....	71	....	....	....	....	....	....	....	....	....	....	....	....	....	....	....	....	....	....
	Pittsburgh Penguins	**NHL**	**7**	**0**	**2**	**2**	**0**	**2**	**2**	**4**	**0**	**0**	**0**	**7**	**0.0**	**4**	**1**	**3**	**0**	**0**	....	....	....	....	....	....	....	....
1977-78	**Pittsburgh Penguins**	**NHL**	**10**	**0**	**0**	**0**	**0**	**0**	**0**	**0**	**0**	**0**	**0**	**3**	**0.0**	**2**	**0**	**6**	**0**	**–4**	....	....	....	....	....	....	....	....
	Grand Rapids Owls	IHL	9	1	8	9	....	....	....	30	....	....	....	....	....	....	....	....	....	....	....	....	....	....	....	....	....	....
	Binghamton Dusters	AHL	31	1	6	7	....	....	....	39	....	....	....	....	....	....	....	....	....	....	....	....	....	....	....	....	....	....
	Springfield Indians	AHL	21	0	9	9	....	....	....	23	....	....	....	....	....	....	....	....	....	....	4	1	2	2	6	....	....	....
1978-79	**Pittsburgh Penguins**	**NHL**	**2**	**0**	**0**	**0**	**0**	**0**	**0**	**4**	**0**	**0**	**0**	**0**	**0.0**	**0**	**0**	**2**	**0**	**–2**	....	....	....	....	....	....	....	....
	Binghamton Dusters	AHL	70	14	31	45	....	....	....	62	....	....	....	....	....	....	....	....	....	....	10	1	7	8	16	....	....	....
1979-80	Syracuse Firebirds	AHL	68	4	34	38	....	....	....	58	....	....	....	....	....	....	....	....	....	....	4	1	4	5	0	....	....	....
1980-81	Springfield Indians	AHL	51	2	24	26	....	....	....	56	....	....	....	....	....	....	....	....	....	....	....	....	....	....	....	....	....	....
1981-82	New Haven Nighthawks	AHL	57	3	20	23	....	....	....	52	....	....	....	....	....	....	....	....	....	....	4	0	0	0	2	....	....	....
1982-83	Saginaw Gears	IHL	26	1	8	9	....	....	....	18	....	....	....	....	....	....	....	....	....	....	....	....	....	....	....	....	....	....
1983-84	New Haven Nighthawks	AHL	77	2	23	25	....	....	....	54	....	....	....	....	....	....	....	....	....	....	....	....	....	....	....	....	....	....
1984-85			DID NOT PLAY																									
1985-86	New Haven Nighthawks	AHL	8	0	2	2	....	....	....	8	....	....	....	....	....	....	....	....	....	....	....	....	....	....	....	....	....	....
	NHL Totals		**29**	**0**	**2**	**2**	**0**	**2**	**2**	**12**	**0**	**0**	**0**	**19**	**0.0**	**8**	**1**	**28**	**1**		....	....	....	....	....	....	....	....

Transferred to **Cleveland** after **California** franchise relocated, August 26, 1976. Signed as a free agent by **Pittsburgh** following release by **Cleveland**, Februray 28, 1977.

• PRIESTLAY, Ken

C – L. 5'10", 190 lbs. b: Richmond, B.C., 8/24/1967. Buffalo's 5th, 98th overall, in 1985.

Season	Club	League	GP	G	A	Pts	AG	AA	APts	PIM	PP	SH	GW	S	%	TGF	PGF	TGA	PGA	+/–	GP	G	A	Pts	PIM	PP	SH	GW
1982-83	Nanaimo Clippers	BCJHL	STATISTICS NOT AVAILABLE																									
1983-84	Victoria Cougars	WHL	55	10	18	28	....	....	....	31	....	....	....	....	....	....	....	....	....	....	....	....	....	....	....	....	....	....
1984-85	Victoria Cougars	WHL	50	25	37	62	....	....	....	48	....	....	....	....	....	....	....	....	....	....	....	....	....	....	....	....	....	....
1985-86	Victoria Cougars	WHL	72	73	72	145	....	....	....	45	....	....	....	....	....	....	....	....	....	....	....	....	....	....	....	....	....	....
	Rochester Americans	AHL	4	0	2	2	....	....	....	0	....	....	....	....	....	....	....	....	....	....	....	....	....	....	....	....	....	....
1986-87	Victoria Cougars	WHL	33	43	39	82	....	....	....	37	....	....	....	....	....	....	....	....	....	....	....	....	....	....	....	....	....	....
	Buffalo Sabres	**NHL**	**34**	**11**	**6**	**17**	**9**	**4**	**13**	**8**	**3**	**0**	**0**	**49**	**22.4**	**30**	**14**	**14**	**1**	**3**	....	....	....	....	....	....	....	....
	Rochester Americans	AHL	....	....	....	....	....	....	....	....	....	....	....	....	....	....	....	....	....	....	8	3	2	5	4	....	....	....
1987-88	**Buffalo Sabres**	**NHL**	**33**	**5**	**12**	**17**	**4**	**9**	**13**	**35**	**1**	**1**	**0**	**63**	**7.9**	**38**	**15**	**37**	**10**	**–4**	**6**	**0**	**0**	**0**	**11**	**0**	**0**	**0**
	Rochester Americans	AHL	43	27	24	51	....	....	....	47	....	....	....	....	....	....	....	....	....	....	....	....	....	....	....	....	....	....
1988-89	**Buffalo Sabres**	**NHL**	**15**	**2**	**0**	**2**	**2**	**0**	**2**	**2**	**0**	**0**	**0**	**20**	**10.0**	**6**	**2**	**19**	**7**	**–8**	**3**	**0**	**0**	**0**	**2**	**0**	**0**	**0**
	Rochester Americans	AHL	64	56	37	93	....	....	....	60	....	....	....	....	....	....	....	....	....	....	....	....	....	....	....	....	....	....
1989-90	**Buffalo Sabres**	**NHL**	**35**	**7**	**7**	**14**	**6**	**5**	**11**	**14**	**1**	**0**	**1**	**66**	**10.6**	**23**	**5**	**23**	**4**	**–1**	**5**	**0**	**0**	**0**	**8**	**0**	**0**	**0**
	Rochester Americans	AHL	40	19	39	58	....	....	....	46	....	....	....	....	....	....	....	....	....	....	....	....	....	....	....	....	....	....
1990-91	Canada	Nat-Team	40	20	26	46	....	....	....	34	....	....	....	....	....	....	....	....	....	....	....	....	....	....	....	....	....	....
	Pittsburgh Penguins	**NHL**	**2**	**0**	**1**	**1**	**0**	**1**	**1**	**0**	**0**	**0**	**0**	**2**	**0.0**	**1**	**0**	**1**	**0**	**0**	....	....	....	....	....	....	....	....
1991-92♦	**Pittsburgh Penguins**	**NHL**	**49**	**2**	**8**	**10**	**2**	**6**	**8**	**4**	**0**	**0**	**0**	**20**	**10.0**	**14**	**4**	**10**	**5**	**5**	....	....	....	....	....	....	....	....
	Muskegon Lumberjacks	IHL	13	4	11	15	....	....	....	6	....	....	....	....	....	....	....	....	....	....	13	5	11	16	10	....	....	....
1992-93	Cleveland Lumberjacks	IHL	66	33	36	69	....	....	....	72	....	....	....	....	....	....	....	....	....	....	4	2	1	3	4	....	....	....
1993-94	Kalamazoo Wings	IHL	25	9	5	14	....	....	....	34	....	....	....	....	....	....	....	....	....	....	5	2	1	3	2	....	....	....
1994-95	Sheffield Steelers	Britain	28	55	32	87	....	....	....	18	....	....	....	....	....	....	....	....	....	....	8	9	8	17	32	....	....	....
1995-96	Sheffield Steelers	BH-Cup	13	22	20	42	....	....	....	12	....	....	....	....	....	....	....	....	....	....	....	....	....	....	....	....	....	....
	Sheffield Steelers	Britain	36	58	40	98	....	....	....	28	....	....	....	....	....	....	....	....	....	....	8	8	5	13	4	....	....	....
1996-97	Sheffield Steelers	BH-Cup	10	7	12	19	....	....	....	2	....	....	....	....	....	....	....	....	....	....	....	....	....	....	....	....	....	....
	Sheffield Steelers	Britain	34	25	12	37	....	....	....	24	....	....	....	....	....	....	....	....	....	....	8	4	5	9	2	....	....	....

Season	Club	League	REGULAR SEASON																		PLAYOFFS							
			GP	G	A	Pts	AG	AA	APts	PIM	PP	SH	GW	S	%	TGF	PGF	TGA	PGA	+/–	GP	G	A	Pts	PIM	PP	SH	GW
1997-98	Sheffield Steelers	BH-Cup	11	8	9	17	....	....	....	6	....	....	....	....	....	....	....	....	....	....	....	....	....	....	....	....	....	....
	Sheffield Steelers	Britain	27	11	24	35	....	....	....	24	....	....	....	....	....	....	....	....	....	....	9	3	3	6	2	....	....	....
1998-99	Sheffield Steelers	BH-Cup	10	4	10	14	....	....	....	4	....	....	....	....	....	....	....	....	....	....	....	....	....	....	....	....	....	....
	Sheffield Steelers	Britain	41	19	24	43	....	....	....	12	....	....	....	....	....	....	....	....	....	....	6	4	2	6	0	....	....	....
99-2000	Powell River Regals	X-Games	STATISTICS NOT AVAILABLE																									
	Powell River Regals	Al-Cup	4	2	3	5	....	....	....	4	....	....	....	....	....	....	....	....	....	....	....	....	....	....	....	....	....	....
	NHL Totals		**168**	**27**	**34**	**61**	**23**	**25**	**48**	**63**	**5**	**1**	**1**	**220**	**12.3**	**112**	**40**	**104**	**27**		**14**	**0**	**0**	**0**	**21**	**0**	**0**	**0**

WHL West Second All-Star Team (1986, 1987)

Traded to **Pittsburgh** by **Buffalo** for Tony Tanti, March 5, 1991.

• PRIMEAU, Keith

C – L. 6'4", 210 lbs. b: Toronto, Ont., 11/24/1971. Detroit's 1st, 3rd overall, in 1990.

Season	Club	League	GP	G	A	Pts	AG	AA	APts	PIM	PP	SH	GW	S	%	TGF	PGF	TGA	PGA	+/–	GP	G	A	Pts	PIM	PP	SH	GW
1986-87	Whitby Flyers	OMHA	65	69	80	149	....	....	....	116	....	....	....	....	....	....	....	....	....	....	....	....	....	....	....	....	....	....
1987-88	Hamilton Kilty B's	OJHL-B	19	19	17	36	....	....	....	16	....	....	....	....	....	....	....	....	....	....	....	....	....	....	....	....	....	....
	Hamilton Steelhawks	OHL	47	6	6	12	....	....	....	69	....	....	....	....	....	....	....	....	....	....	11	0	2	2	2	....	....	....
1988-89	Niagara Falls Thunder	OHL	48	20	35	55	....	....	....	56	....	....	....	....	....	....	....	....	....	....	17	9	16	25	12	....	....	....
1989-90	Niagara Falls Thunder	OHL	65	*57	70	*127	....	....	....	97	....	....	....	....	....	....	....	....	....	....	16	*16	17	*33	49	....	....	....
1990-91	**Detroit Red Wings**	**NHL**	**58**	**3**	**12**	**15**	**3**	**9**	**12**	**106**	**0**	**0**	**1**	**33**	**9.1**	**24**	**3**	**33**	**0**	**–12**	**5**	**1**	**1**	**2**	**25**	**0**	**0**	**0**
	Adirondack Red Wings	AHL	6	3	5	8	....	....	....	8	....	....	....	....	....	....	....	....	....	....	....	....	....	....	....	....	....	....
1991-92	**Detroit Red Wings**	**NHL**	**35**	**6**	**10**	**16**	**5**	**8**	**13**	**83**	**0**	**0**	**0**	**27**	**22.2**	**24**	**1**	**16**	**2**	**9**	**11**	**0**	**0**	**0**	**14**	**0**	**0**	**0**
	Adirondack Red Wings	AHL	42	21	24	45	....	....	....	89	....	....	....	....	....	....	....	....	....	....	9	1	7	8	27	....	....	....
1992-93	**Detroit Red Wings**	**NHL**	**73**	**15**	**17**	**32**	**12**	**12**	**24**	**152**	**4**	**1**	**2**	**75**	**20.0**	**49**	**16**	**44**	**5**	**–6**	**7**	**0**	**2**	**2**	**26**	**0**	**0**	**0**
1993-94	**Detroit Red Wings**	**NHL**	**78**	**31**	**42**	**73**	**29**	**33**	**62**	**173**	**7**	**3**	**4**	**155**	**20.0**	**112**	**29**	**62**	**13**	**34**	**7**	**0**	**2**	**2**	**6**	**0**	**0**	**0**
1994-95	**Detroit Red Wings**	**NHL**	**45**	**15**	**27**	**42**	**27**	**40**	**67**	**99**	**1**	**0**	**3**	**96**	**15.6**	**57**	**13**	**31**	**4**	**17**	**17**	**4**	**5**	**9**	**45**	**2**	**0**	**0**
1995-96	**Detroit Red Wings**	**NHL**	**74**	**27**	**25**	**52**	**27**	**20**	**47**	**168**	**6**	**2**	**7**	**150**	**18.0**	**97**	**38**	**46**	**6**	**19**	**17**	**1**	**4**	**5**	**28**	**0**	**0**	**0**
1996-97	Canada	W-Cup	5	0	0	0	....	....	....	21	....	....	....	....	....	....	....	....	....	....	....	....	....	....	....	....	....	....
	Hartford Whalers	**NHL**	**75**	**26**	**25**	**51**	**28**	**22**	**50**	**161**	**6**	**3**	**2**	**169**	**15.4**	**78**	**21**	**71**	**11**	**–3**	....	....	....	....	....	....	....	....
	Canada	WC-A	11	3	3	6	....	....	....	14	....	....	....	....	....	....	....	....	....	....	....	....	....	....	....	....	....	....
1997-98	**Carolina Hurricanes**	**NHL**	**81**	**26**	**37**	**63**	**30**	**36**	**66**	**110**	**7**	**3**	**2**	**180**	**14.4**	**103**	**30**	**73**	**19**	**19**	....	....	....	....	....	....	....	....
	Canada	Olympics	6	2	1	3	....	....	....	4	....	....	....	....	....	....	....	....	....	....	....	....	....	....	....	....	....	....
	Canada	WC-A	6	3	1	4	....	....	....	4	....	....	....	....	....	....	....	....	....	....	....	....	....	....	....	....	....	....
1998-99	**Carolina Hurricanes**	**NHL**	**78**	**30**	**32**	**62**	**35**	**31**	**66**	**75**	**9**	**1**	**5**	**178**	**16.9**	**89**	**24**	**75**	**18**	**8**	**6**	**0**	**3**	**3**	**6**	**0**	**0**	**0**
99-2000	**Philadelphia Flyers**	**NHL**	**23**	**7**	**10**	**17**	**8**	**9**	**17**	**31**	**1**	**0**	**1**	**51**	**13.7**	**23**	**3**	**14**	**4**	**10**	**18**	**2**	**11**	**13**	**13**	**0**	**0**	**1**
	NHL Totals		**620**	**186**	**237**	**423**	**204**	**220**	**424**	**1158**	**41**	**13**	**27**	**1114**	**16.7**	**656**	**178**	**465**	**82**		**88**	**8**	**28**	**36**	**163**	**2**	**0**	**1**

• Brother of Wayne • OHL Second All-Star Team (1990) • Played in NHL All-Star Game (1999)

Traded to **Hartford** by **Detroit** with Paul Coffey and Detroit's 1st round choice (Nikos Tselios) in 1997 Entry Draft for Brendan Shanahan and Brian Glynn, October 9, 1996. Transferred to **Carolina** after **Hartford** franchise relocated, June 25, 1997. • Sat out majority of 1999-2000 season in contract dispute with Carolina management. Traded to **Philadelphia** by **Carolina** with Carolina's 5th round choice (later traded to NY Islanders - NY Islanders selected Kristofer Ottoston) in 2000 Entry Draft for Rod Brind'Amour, Jean-Marc Pelletier and Philadelphia's 2nd round choice (later traded to Colorado - Colorado selected Argis Saviels) in 2000 Entry Draft, January 23, 2000.

• PRIMEAU, Kevin

RW – R. 6', 180 lbs. b: Edmonton, Alta., 1/3/1956.

Season	Club	League	GP	G	A	Pts	AG	AA	APts	PIM	PP	SH	GW	S	%	TGF	PGF	TGA	PGA	+/–	GP	G	A	Pts	PIM	PP	SH	GW
1974-75	University of Alberta	CWUAA	33	12	15	27	....	....	....	23	....	....	....	....	....	....	....	....	....	....	....	....	....	....	....	....	....	....
1975-76	University of Alberta	CWUAA	34	10	10	20	....	....	....	29	....	....	....	....	....	....	....	....	....	....	....	....	....	....	....	....	....	....
1976-77	University of Alberta	CWUAA	34	20	14	34	....	....	....	49	....	....	....	....	....	....	....	....	....	....	....	....	....	....	....	....	....	....
1977-78	University of Alberta	CWUAA	25	13	16	29	....	....	....	36	....	....	....	....	....	....	....	....	....	....	....	....	....	....	....	....	....	....
	Edmonton Oilers	WHA	7	0	1	1	....	....	....	2	....	....	....	....	....	....	....	....	....	....	2	0	0	0	2	....	....	....
1978-79	HC Davos	Switz-2	STATISTICS NOT AVAILABLE																									
1979-80	EHC Visp	Switz-2	STATISTICS NOT AVAILABLE																									
	Canada	Nat-Team	41	16	11	27	....	....	....	18	....	....	....	....	....	....	....	....	....	....	....	....	....	....	....	....	....	....
	Canada	Olympics	6	4	1	5	....	....	....	6	....	....	....	....	....	....	....	....	....	....	....	....	....	....	....	....	....	....
1980-81	EHC Visp	Switz-2	STATISTICS NOT AVAILABLE																									
	Vancouver Canucks	**NHL**	**2**	**0**	**0**	**0**	**0**	**0**	**0**	**4**	**0**	**0**	**0**	**0**	**0.0**	**0**	**0**	**0**	**0**	**0**	....	....	....	....	....	....	....	....
	Dallas Black Hawks	CHL	45	14	9	23	....	....	....	22	....	....	....	....	....	....	....	....	....	....	....	....	....	....	....	....	....	....
	NHL Totals		**2**	**0**	**0**	**0**	**0**	**0**	**0**	**4**	**0**	**0**	**0**	**0**	**0.0**	**0**	**0**	**0**	**0**		....	....	....	....	....	....	....	....
	Other Major League Totals		7	0	1	1	....	....	....	2	....	....	....	....	....	....	....	....	....	....	2	0	0	0	2	....	....	....

Signed as a free agent by **Edmonton** (WHA), March 5, 1977. Signed as a free agent by **Vancouver**, 1980.

• PRIMEAU, Wayne

C – L. 6'3", 220 lbs. b: Scarborough, Ont., 6/4/1976. Buffalo's 1st, 17th overall, in 1994.

Season	Club	League	GP	G	A	Pts	AG	AA	APts	PIM	PP	SH	GW	S	%	TGF	PGF	TGA	PGA	+/–	GP	G	A	Pts	PIM	PP	SH	GW
1991-92	Whitby Flyers	OMHA	63	36	50	86	....	....	....	96	....	....	....	....	....	....	....	....	....	....	....	....	....	....	....	....	....	....
1992-93	Owen Sound Platers	OHL	66	10	27	37	....	....	....	108	....	....	....	....	....	....	....	....	....	....	8	1	4	5	0	....	....	....
1993-94	Owen Sound Platers	OHL	65	25	50	75	....	....	....	75	....	....	....	....	....	....	....	....	....	....	9	1	6	7	8	....	....	....
1994-95	Owen Sound Platers	OHL	66	34	62	96	....	....	....	84	....	....	....	....	....	....	....	....	....	....	10	4	9	13	15	....	....	....
	Buffalo Sabres	**NHL**	**1**	**1**	**0**	**1**	**2**	**0**	**2**	**0**	**0**	**0**	**1**	**2**	**50.0**	**1**	**0**	**3**	**0**	**–2**	....	....	....	....	....	....	....	....
1995-96	Owen Sound Platers	OHL	28	15	29	44	....	....	....	52	....	....	....	....	....	....	....	....	....	....	....	....	....	....	....	....	....	....
	Oshawa Generals	OHL	24	12	13	25	....	....	....	33	....	....	....	....	....	....	....	....	....	....	3	2	3	5	2	....	....	....
	Buffalo Sabres	**NHL**	**2**	**0**	**0**	**0**	**0**	**0**	**0**	**0**	**0**	**0**	**0**	**0**	**0.0**	**0**	**0**	**0**	**0**	**0**	....	....	....	....	....	....	....	....
	Rochester Americans	AHL	8	2	3	5	....	....	....	6	....	....	....	....	....	....	....	....	....	....	17	3	1	4	11	....	....	....
1996-97	**Buffalo Sabres**	**NHL**	**45**	**2**	**4**	**6**	**2**	**4**	**6**	**64**	**1**	**0**	**0**	**25**	**8.0**	**7**	**1**	**8**	**0**	**–2**	**9**	**0**	**0**	**0**	**6**	**0**	**0**	**0**
	Rochester Americans	AHL	24	9	5	14	....	....	....	27	....	....	....	....	....	....	....	....	....	....	1	0	0	0	0	....	....	....
1997-98	**Buffalo Sabres**	**NHL**	**69**	**6**	**6**	**12**	**7**	**6**	**13**	**87**	**2**	**0**	**1**	**51**	**11.8**	**24**	**4**	**18**	**7**	**9**	**14**	**1**	**3**	**4**	**6**	**0**	**0**	**0**
1998-99	**Buffalo Sabres**	**NHL**	**67**	**5**	**8**	**13**	**6**	**8**	**14**	**38**	**0**	**0**	**0**	**55**	**9.1**	**23**	**4**	**26**	**1**	**–6**	**19**	**3**	**4**	**7**	**6**	**1**	**0**	**0**
99-2000	**Buffalo Sabres**	**NHL**	**41**	**5**	**7**	**12**	**6**	**6**	**12**	**38**	**2**	**0**	**1**	**40**	**12.5**	**17**	**5**	**20**	**0**	**–8**	....	....	....	....	....	....	....	....
	Tampa Bay Lightning	**NHL**	**17**	**2**	**3**	**5**	**2**	**3**	**5**	**25**	**0**	**0**	**0**	**35**	**5.7**	**9**	**0**	**14**	**1**	**–4**	....	....	....	....	....	....	....	....
	NHL Totals		**242**	**21**	**28**	**49**	**25**	**27**	**52**	**252**	**5**	**0**	**3**	**208**	**10.1**	**81**	**14**	**89**	**9**		**42**	**4**	**7**	**11**	**18**	**1**	**0**	**0**

• Brother of Keith • Traded to **Tampa Bay** by **Buffalo** with Cory Sarich, Brian Holzinger and Buffalo's 3rd round choice (Alexandre Kharitonov) in 2000 Entry Draft for Chris Gratton and Tampa Bay's 2nd round choice in 2001 Entry Draft, March 9, 2000.

• PROBERT, Bob

Robert A. LW – L. 6'3", 225 lbs. b: Windsor, Ont., 6/5/1965. Detroit's 3rd, 46th overall, in 1983.

Season	Club	League	GP	G	A	Pts	AG	AA	APts	PIM	PP	SH	GW	S	%	TGF	PGF	TGA	PGA	+/–	GP	G	A	Pts	PIM	PP	SH	GW
1981-82	Windsor Club 240	OMHA	55	60	40	100	....	....	....	40	....	....	....	....	....	....	....	....	....	....	....	....	....	....	....	....	....	....
1982-83	Brantford Alexanders	OHL	51	12	16	28	....	....	....	133	....	....	....	....	....	....	....	....	....	....	8	2	2	4	23	....	....	....
1983-84	Brantford Alexanders	OHL	65	35	28	63	....	....	....	189	....	....	....	....	....	....	....	....	....	....	6	0	3	3	16	....	....	....
1984-85	Hamilton Steelhawks	OHL	4	0	1	1	....	....	....	21	....	....	....	....	....	....	....	....	....	....	....	....	....	....	....	....	....	....
	Sault Ste. Marie Greyhounds	OHL	44	20	52	72	....	....	....	172	....	....	....	....	....	....	....	....	....	....	15	6	11	17	60	....	....	....
	Sault Ste. Marie Greyhounds	Mem-Cup	4	1	2	3	....	....	....	34	....	....	....	....	....	....	....	....	....	....	....	....	....	....	....	....	....	....
1985-86	**Detroit Red Wings**	**NHL**	**44**	**8**	**13**	**21**	**6**	**9**	**15**	**186**	**3**	**0**	**0**	**46**	**17.4**	**30**	**9**	**35**	**0**	**–14**	....	....	....	....	....	....	....	....
	Adirondack Red Wings	AHL	32	12	15	27	....	....	....	152	....	....	....	....	....	....	....	....	....	....	10	2	3	5	68	....	....	....
1986-87	**Detroit Red Wings**	**NHL**	**63**	**13**	**11**	**24**	**11**	**8**	**19**	**221**	**2**	**0**	**0**	**56**	**23.2**	**27**	**5**	**28**	**0**	**–6**	**16**	**3**	**4**	**7**	**63**	**1**	**0**	**1**
	Adirondack Red Wings	AHL	7	1	4	5	....	....	....	15	....	....	....	....	....	....	....	....	....	....	....	....	....	....	....	....	....	....
1987-88	**Detroit Red Wings**	**NHL**	**74**	**29**	**33**	**62**	**25**	**24**	**49**	***398**	**15**	**0**	**5**	**126**	**23.0**	**111**	**42**	**53**	**0**	**16**	**16**	**8**	**13**	**21**	**51**	**5**	**0**	**1**
1988-89	**Detroit Red Wings**	**NHL**	**25**	**4**	**2**	**6**	**3**	**1**	**4**	**106**	**1**	**0**	**0**	**23**	**17.4**	**13**	**6**	**18**	**0**	**–11**	....	....	....	....	....	....	....	....
1989-90	**Detroit Red Wings**	**NHL**	**4**	**3**	**0**	**3**	**3**	**0**	**3**	**21**	**0**	**0**	**1**	**12**	**25.0**	**5**	**0**	**5**	**0**	**0**	....	....	....	....	....	....	....	....
1990-91	**Detroit Red Wings**	**NHL**	**55**	**16**	**23**	**39**	**15**	**17**	**32**	**315**	**4**	**0**	**3**	**88**	**18.2**	**63**	**22**	**44**	**0**	**–3**	**6**	**1**	**2**	**3**	**50**	**0**	**0**	**0**
1991-92	**Detroit Red Wings**	**NHL**	**63**	**20**	**24**	**44**	**18**	**18**	**36**	**276**	**8**	**0**	**1**	**96**	**20.8**	**76**	**24**	**36**	**0**	**16**	**11**	**1**	**6**	**7**	**28**	**0**	**0**	**0**
1992-93	**Detroit Red Wings**	**NHL**	**80**	**14**	**29**	**43**	**12**	**20**	**32**	**292**	**6**	**0**	**3**	**128**	**10.9**	**64**	**20**	**53**	**0**	**–9**	**7**	**0**	**3**	**3**	**10**	**0**	**0**	**0**
1993-94	**Detroit Red Wings**	**NHL**	**66**	**7**	**10**	**17**	**6**	**8**	**14**	**275**	**1**	**0**	**0**	**105**	**6.7**	**29**	**2**	**28**	**0**	**–1**	**7**	**1**	**1**	**2**	**8**	**0**	**0**	**0**
1994-95	**Chicago Blackhawks**	**NHL**	DID NOT PLAY – SUSPENDED																									
1995-96	**Chicago Blackhawks**	**NHL**	**78**	**19**	**21**	**40**	**19**	**17**	**36**	**237**	**1**	**0**	**3**	**97**	**19.6**	**61**	**9**	**37**	**0**	**15**	**10**	**0**	**2**	**2**	**23**	**0**	**0**	**0**
1996-97	**Chicago Blackhawks**	**NHL**	**82**	**9**	**14**	**23**	**10**	**12**	**22**	**326**	**1**	**0**	**3**	**111**	**8.1**	**47**	**12**	**38**	**0**	**–3**	**6**	**2**	**1**	**3**	**41**	**0**	**0**	**0**

			REGULAR SEASON																		PLAYOFFS							
Season	Club	League	GP	G	A	Pts	AG	AA	APts	PIM	PP	SH	GW	S	%	TGF	PGF	TGA	PGA	+/–	GP	G	A	Pts	PIM	PP	SH	GW
1997-98	**Chicago Blackhawks**	**NHL**	**14**	**2**	**1**	**3**	**2**	**1**	**3**	**48**	**2**	**0**	**0**	**18**	**11.1**	**3**	**2**	**8**	**0**	**–7**	....	....	....	....	....	....	....	....
1998-99	**Chicago Blackhawks**	**NHL**	**78**	**7**	**14**	**21**	**8**	**13**	**21**	**206**	**0**	**0**	**3**	**87**	**8.0**	**34**	**6**	**40**	**1**	**–11**	....	....	....	....	....	....	....	....
99-2000	**Chicago Blackhawks**	**NHL**	**69**	**4**	**11**	**15**	**4**	**10**	**14**	**114**	**0**	**0**	**0**	**38**	**10.5**	**34**	**2**	**23**	**1**	**10**	....	....	....	....	....	....	....	....
	NHL Totals		**795**	**155**	**206**	**361**	**142**	**158**	**300**	**3021**	**44**	**0**	**22**	**1031**	**15.0**	**597**	**161**	**446**	**2**		**79**	**16**	**32**	**48**	**274**	**6**	**0**	**2**

Played in NHL All-Star Game (1988)

Signed as a free agent by **Chicago**, July 23, 1994. • Suspended for entire 1994-95 season for violating NHL substance abuse policy, September 2, 1994. • majority of 1997-98 season recovering from rotator cuff injury suffered in game vs. Detroit, November 16, 1997.

• PROCHAZKA, Martin

RW – R. 5'11", 180 lbs. b: Slany, Czech., 3/3/1972. Toronto's 6th, 135th overall, in 1991.

Season	Club	League	GP	G	A	Pts	AG	AA	APts	PIM	PP	SH	GW	S	%	TGF	PGF	TGA	PGA	+/–	GP	G	A	Pts	PIM	PP	SH	GW
1989-90	Poldi Kladno	Czech.	49	18	12	30	....	....	....	....	....	....	....	....	....	....	....	....	....	....	....	....	....	....	....	....	....	....
	Czechoslovakia	WJC-A	7	5	2	7	....	....	....	2	....	....	....	....	....	....	....	....	....	....	....	....	....	....	....	....	....	....
	Czechoslovakia	EJC-A	6	2	4	6	....	....	....	6	....	....	....	....	....	....	....	....	....	....	....	....	....	....	....	....	....	....
1990-91	Poldi Kladno	Czech.	50	19	10	29	....	....	....	21	....	....	....	....	....	....	....	....	....	....	....	....	....	....	....	....	....	....
	Czechoslovakia	WJC-A	7	4	1	5	....	....	....	0	....	....	....	....	....	....	....	....	....	....	....	....	....	....	....	....	....	....
1991-92	Dukla Jihlava	Czech.	44	18	11	29	....	....	....	2	....	....	....	....	....	....	....	....	....	....	....	....	....	....	....	....	....	....
	Czechoslovakia	WJC-A	7	0	2	2	....	....	....	0	....	....	....	....	....	....	....	....	....	....	....	....	....	....	....	....	....	....
1992-93	Poldi Kladno	Czech.	46	26	12	38	....	....	....	....	....	....	....	....	....	....	....	....	....	....	....	....	....	....	....	....	....	....
1993-94	Poldi Kladno	Czech-Rep	43	24	16	40	....	....	....	0	....	....	....	....	....	....	....	....	....	....	2	2	0	2	....	....	....	....
1994-95	Poldi Kladno	Czech-Rep	41	25	33	58	....	....	....	18	....	....	....	....	....	....	....	....	....	....	11	8	4	12	4	....	....	....
	Czech-Republic	WC-A	8	2	1	3	....	....	....	2	....	....	....	....	....	....	....	....	....	....	....	....	....	....	....	....	....	....
1995-96	Poldi Kladno	Czech-Rep	37	15	27	42	....	....	....	....	....	....	....	....	....	....	....	....	....	....	8	2	4	6	....	....	....	....
	Czech-Republic	WC-A	6	3	3	6	....	....	....	2	....	....	....	....	....	....	....	....	....	....	....	....	....	....	....	....	....	....
1996-97	Czech-Republic	W-Cup	2	0	0	0	....	....	....	0	....	....	....	....	....	....	....	....	....	....	....	....	....	....	....	....	....	....
	AIK Solna Stockholm	Sweden	49	16	23	39	....	....	....	38	....	....	....	....	....	....	....	....	....	....	7	2	3	5	8	....	....	....
	Czech-Republic	WC-A	9	7	7	14	....	....	....	4	....	....	....	....	....	....	....	....	....	....	....	....	....	....	....	....	....	....
1997-98	**Toronto Maple Leafs**	**NHL**	**29**	**2**	**4**	**6**	**2**	**4**	**6**	**8**	**0**	**0**	**0**	**40**	**5.0**	**13**	**4**	**11**	**1**	**–1**	....	....	....	....	....	....	....	....
	Czech-Republic	Olympics	6	1	1	2	....	....	....	0	....	....	....	....	....	....	....	....	....	....	....	....	....	....	....	....	....	....
	Czech-Republic	WC-A	9	3	5	8	....	....	....	14	....	....	....	....	....	....	....	....	....	....	....	....	....	....	....	....	....	....
1998-99	HC Slovnaft Vsetin	Czech-Rep	47	20	29	49	....	....	....	12	....	....	....	....	....	....	....	....	....	....	12	*10	9	*19	....	....	....	....
	Czech-Republic	WC-A	12	2	4	6	....	....	....	0	....	....	....	....	....	....	....	....	....	....	....	....	....	....	....	....	....	....
99-2000	**Atlanta Thrashers**	**NHL**	**3**	**0**	**1**	**1**	**0**	**1**	**1**	**0**	**0**	**0**	**0**	**5**	**0.0**	**1**	**0**	**2**	**0**	**–1**	....	....	....	....	....	....	....	....
	HC Slovnaft Vsetin	Czech-Rep	31	10	10	20	....	....	....	16	....	....	....	....	....	....	....	....	....	....	9	2	0	2	0	....	....	....
	Czech-Republic	WC-A	9	2	3	5	....	....	....	6	....	....	....	....	....	....	....	....	....	....	....	....	....	....	....	....	....	....
	NHL Totals		**32**	**2**	**5**	**7**	**2**	**5**	**7**	**8**	**0**	**0**	**0**	**45**	**4.4**	**14**	**4**	**13**	**1**		....	....	....	....	....	....	....	....

WC-A All-Star Team (1997) • Named WC-A MVP (2000)

Traded to **Atlanta** by **Toronto** for Atlanta's 6th round choice in 2001 Entry Draft, July 15, 1999.

• PROKHOROV, Vitali

LW – L. 5'9", 185 lbs. b: Moscow, USSR, 12/25/1966. St. Louis' 3rd, 64th overall, in 1992.

Season	Club	League	GP	G	A	Pts	AG	AA	APts	PIM	PP	SH	GW	S	%	TGF	PGF	TGA	PGA	+/–	GP	G	A	Pts	PIM	PP	SH	GW
1983-84	Spartak Moscow	USSR	5	0	0	0	....	....	....	0	....	....	....	....	....	....	....	....	....	....	....	....	....	....	....	....	....	....
1984-85	Spartak Moscow	USSR	31	1	1	2	....	....	....	10	....	....	....	....	....	....	....	....	....	....	....	....	....	....	....	....	....	....
1985-86	Spartak Moscow	USSR	29	3	9	12	....	....	....	4	....	....	....	....	....	....	....	....	....	....	....	....	....	....	....	....	....	....
1986-87	Spartak Moscow	USSR	27	1	6	7	....	....	....	2	....	....	....	....	....	....	....	....	....	....	....	....	....	....	....	....	....	....
1987-88	Spartak Moscow	USSR	19	5	0	5	....	....	....	4	....	....	....	....	....	....	....	....	....	....	....	....	....	....	....	....	....	....
1988-89	Spartak Moscow	USSR	37	11	5	16	....	....	....	10	....	....	....	....	....	....	....	....	....	....	....	....	....	....	....	....	....	....
1989-90	Spartak Moscow	Fr-Tour	1	0	0	0	....	....	....	0	....	....	....	....	....	....	....	....	....	....	....	....	....	....	....	....	....	....
	Spartak Moscow	USSR	43	13	8	21	....	....	....	35	....	....	....	....	....	....	....	....	....	....	....	....	....	....	....	....	....	....
1990-91	Spartak Moscow	Fr-Tour	1	0	1	1	....	....	....	0	....	....	....	....	....	....	....	....	....	....	....	....	....	....	....	....	....	....
	Spartak Moscow	USSR	43	21	10	31	....	....	....	29	....	....	....	....	....	....	....	....	....	....	....	....	....	....	....	....	....	....
1991-92	Soviet Union	Can-Cup	5	1	2	3	....	....	....	4	....	....	....	....	....	....	....	....	....	....	....	....	....	....	....	....	....	....
	Spartak Moscow	CIS	38	13	19	32	....	....	....	68	....	....	....	....	....	....	....	....	....	....	....	....	....	....	....	....	....	....
	Russia	Olympics	8	2	4	6	....	....	....	6	....	....	....	....	....	....	....	....	....	....	....	....	....	....	....	....	....	....
	Russia	WC-A	6	0	3	3	....	....	....	4	....	....	....	....	....	....	....	....	....	....	....	....	....	....	....	....	....	....
1992-93	**St. Louis Blues**	**NHL**	**26**	**4**	**1**	**5**	**3**	**1**	**4**	**15**	**0**	**0**	**1**	**21**	**19.0**	**8**	**2**	**10**	**0**	**–4**	....	....	....	....	....	....	....	....
1993-94	**St. Louis Blues**	**NHL**	**55**	**15**	**10**	**25**	**14**	**8**	**22**	**20**	**3**	**0**	**1**	**85**	**17.6**	**30**	**4**	**32**	**0**	**–6**	**4**	**0**	**0**	**0**	**0**	**0**	**0**	**0**
	Peoria Rivermen	IHL	19	13	10	23	....	....	....	16	....	....	....	....	....	....	....	....	....	....	....	....	....	....	....	....	....	....
1994-95	Spartak Moscow	CIS	8	1	4	5	....	....	....	8	....	....	....	....	....	....	....	....	....	....	....	....	....	....	....	....	....	....
	St. Louis Blues	**NHL**	**2**	**0**	**0**	**0**	**0**	**0**	**0**	**0**	**0**	**0**	**0**	**0**	**0.0**	**1**	**0**	**0**	**0**	**1**	....	....	....	....	....	....	....	....
	Peoria Rivermen	IHL	20	6	3	9	....	....	....	6	....	....	....	....	....	....	....	....	....	....	9	4	7	11	6	....	....	....
1995-96	Farjestads BK Stockholm	Sweden	37	7	11	18	....	....	....	61	....	....	....	....	....	....	....	....	....	....	8	2	0	2	31	....	....	....
1996-97			STATISTICS NOT AVAILABLE																									
1997-98	Spartak Moscow	Russia	46	*21	14	35	....	....	....	90	....	....	....	....	....	....	....	....	....	....	....	....	....	....	....	....	....	....
1998-99	HC Davos	Switz.	3	0	1	1	....	....	....	2	....	....	....	....	....	....	....	....	....	....	....	....	....	....	....	....	....	....
	CSKA Moscow	Russia	12	5	5	10	....	....	....	22	....	....	....	....	....	....	....	....	....	....	....	....	....	....	....	....	....	....
	AK Bars Kazan	Russia	16	2	4	6	....	....	....	8	....	....	....	....	....	....	....	....	....	....	9	2	1	3	27	....	....	....
99-2000	Metallurg Magnitogorsk	Russia	20	8	11	19	....	....	....	8	....	....	....	....	....	....	....	....	....	....	12	5	4	9	2	....	....	....
	Metallurg Magnitogorsk	EuroHL	5	2	3	5	....	....	....	0	....	....	....	....	....	....	....	....	....	....	2	0	0	0	0	....	....	....
	NHL Totals		**83**	**19**	**11**	**30**	**17**	**9**	**26**	**35**	**3**	**0**	**2**	**106**	**17.9**	**39**	**6**	**42**	**0**		**4**	**0**	**0**	**0**	**0**	**0**	**0**	**0**

• PROKOPEC, Mike

RW – R. 6'2", 190 lbs. b: Toronto, Ont., 5/17/1974. Chicago's 7th, 161st overall, in 1992.

Season	Club	League	GP	G	A	Pts	AG	AA	APts	PIM	PP	SH	GW	S	%	TGF	PGF	TGA	PGA	+/–	GP	G	A	Pts	PIM	PP	SH	GW
1990-91	Barrie Colts	OJHL-B	39	17	20	37	....	....	....	63	....	....	....	....	....	....	....	....	....	....	....	....	....	....	....	....	....	....
1991-92	Cornwall Royals	OHL	59	12	15	27	....	....	....	75	....	....	....	....	....	....	....	....	....	....	6	0	0	0	0	....	....	....
1992-93	Newmarket Royals	OHL	40	6	14	20	....	....	....	70	....	....	....	....	....	....	....	....	....	....	....	....	....	....	....	....	....	....
	Guelph Storm	OHL	28	10	14	24	....	....	....	27	....	....	....	....	....	....	....	....	....	....	5	1	0	1	14	....	....	....
1993-94	Guelph Storm	OHL	66	52	58	110	....	....	....	93	....	....	....	....	....	....	....	....	....	....	9	12	4	16	17	....	....	....
1994-95	Indianapolis Ice	IHL	70	21	12	33	....	....	....	80	....	....	....	....	....	....	....	....	....	....	....	....	....	....	....	....	....	....
1995-96	**Chicago Blackhawks**	**NHL**	**9**	**0**	**0**	**0**	**0**	**0**	**0**	**5**	**0**	**0**	**0**	**5**	**0.0**	**1**	**0**	**5**	**0**	**–4**	....	....	....	....	....	....	....	....
	Indianapolis Ice	IHL	67	18	22	40	....	....	....	131	....	....	....	....	....	....	....	....	....	....	5	2	0	2	4	....	....	....
1996-97	**Chicago Blackhawks**	**NHL**	**6**	**0**	**0**	**0**	**0**	**0**	**0**	**6**	**0**	**0**	**0**	**2**	**0.0**	**1**	**0**	**2**	**0**	**–1**	....	....	....	....	....	....	....	....
	Indianapolis Ice	IHL	57	13	18	31	....	....	....	143	....	....	....	....	....	....	....	....	....	....	....	....	....	....	....	....	....	....
	Detroit Vipers	IHL	3	2	0	2	....	....	....	4	....	....	....	....	....	....	....	....	....	....	8	2	1	3	14	....	....	....
1997-98	Worcester IceCats	AHL	62	21	25	46	....	....	....	112	....	....	....	....	....	....	....	....	....	....	11	1	2	3	10	....	....	....
1998-99	Detroit Vipers	IHL	75	25	28	53	....	....	....	125	....	....	....	....	....	....	....	....	....	....	10	3	6	9	26	....	....	....
99-2000	Manitoba Moose	IHL	68	23	21	44	....	....	....	100	....	....	....	....	....	....	....	....	....	....	....	....	....	....	....	....	....	....
	NHL Totals		**15**	**0**	**0**	**0**	**0**	**0**	**0**	**11**	**0**	**0**	**0**	**7**	**0.0**	**2**	**0**	**7**	**0**		....	....	....	....	....	....	....	....

Traded to **Ottawa** by **Chicago** for Denis Chasse, the rights to Kevin Bolibruck and future considerations, March 18, 1997. Signed as a free agent by **Manitoba** (IHL), August 24, 1999.

• PRONGER, Chris

Chris Robert D – L. 6'6", 220 lbs. b: Dryden, Ont., 10/10/1974. Hartford's 1st, 2nd overall, in 1993.

Season	Club	League	GP	G	A	Pts	AG	AA	APts	PIM	PP	SH	GW	S	%	TGF	PGF	TGA	PGA	+/–	GP	G	A	Pts	PIM	PP	SH	GW
1990-91	Stratford Cullitons	OJHL-B	48	15	37	52	....	....	....	132	....	....	....	....	....	....	....	....	....	....	....	....	....	....	....	....	....	....
1991-92	Peterborough Petes	OHL	63	17	45	62	....	....	....	90	....	....	....	....	....	....	....	....	....	....	10	1	8	9	28	....	....	....
1992-93	Peterborough Petes	OHL	61	15	62	77	....	....	....	108	....	....	....	....	....	....	....	....	....	....	21	15	25	40	51	....	....	....
	Canada	WJC-A	7	1	3	4	....	....	....	6	....	....	....	....	....	....	....	....	....	....	....	....	....	....	....	....	....	....
	Peterborough Petes	Mem-Cup	5	1	5	6	....	....	....	8	....	....	....	....	....	....	....	....	....	....	....	....	....	....	....	....	....	....
1993-94	**Hartford Whalers**	**NHL**	**81**	**5**	**25**	**30**	**5**	**19**	**24**	**113**	**2**	**0**	**0**	**174**	**2.9**	**81**	**22**	**99**	**37**	**–3**	....	....	....	....	....	....	....	....
1994-95	**Hartford Whalers**	**NHL**	**43**	**5**	**9**	**14**	**9**	**13**	**22**	**54**	**3**	**0**	**1**	**94**	**5.3**	**40**	**11**	**55**	**14**	**–12**	....	....	....	....	....	....	....	....
1995-96	**St. Louis Blues**	**NHL**	**78**	**7**	**18**	**25**	**7**	**15**	**22**	**110**	**3**	**1**	**1**	**138**	**5.1**	**86**	**29**	**106**	**31**	**–18**	**13**	**1**	**5**	**6**	**16**	**0**	**0**	**0**
1996-97	**St. Louis Blues**	**NHL**	**79**	**11**	**24**	**35**	**12**	**21**	**33**	**143**	**4**	**0**	**0**	**147**	**7.5**	**103**	**26**	**90**	**28**	**15**	**6**	**1**	**1**	**2**	**22**	**0**	**0**	**0**
	Canada	WC-A	9	0	2	2	....	....	....	12	....	....	....	....	....	....	....	....	....	....	....	....	....	....	....	....	....	....

			REGULAR SEASON																		PLAYOFFS							
Season	Club	League	GP	G	A	Pts	AG	AA	APts	PIM	PP	SH	GW	S	%	TGF	PGF	TGA	PGA	+/-	GP	G	A	Pts	PIM	PP	SH	GW
1997-98	**St. Louis Blues**	**NHL**	**81**	**9**	**27**	**36**	**11**	**26**	**37**	**180**	**1**	**0**	**2**	**145**	**6.2**	**118**	**15**	**84**	**28**	**47**	**10**	**1**	**9**	**10**	**26**	**0**	**0**	**0**
	Canada	Olympics	6	0	0	0				4																		
1998-99	**St. Louis Blues**	**NHL**	**67**	**13**	**33**	**46**	**15**	**32**	**47**	**113**	**8**	**0**	**0**	**172**	**7.6**	**109**	**44**	**88**	**26**	**3**	**13**	**1**	**4**	**5**	**28**	**1**	**0**	**0**
99-2000	**St. Louis Blues**	**NHL**	**79**	**14**	**48**	**62**	**16**	**45**	**61**	**92**	**8**	**0**	**3**	**192**	**7.3**	**147**	**50**	**72**	**27**	**52**	**7**	**3**	**4**	**7**	**32**	**2**	**0**	**2**
	NHL Totals		**508**	**64**	**184**	**248**	**75**	**171**	**246**	**805**	**29**	**1**	**7**	**1062**	**6.0**	**684**	**197**	**594**	**191**		**49**	**7**	**23**	**30**	**124**	**3**	**0**	**2**

• Brother of Sean • OHL First All-Star Team (1993) • Canadian Major Junior First All-Star Team (1993) • Canadian Major Junior Defenseman of the Year (1993) • NHL All-Rookie Team (1994) • NHL Second All-Star Team (1998) • Won Bud Ice Plus/Minus Award (1998) • NHL First All-Star Team (2000) • Won James Norris Trophy (2000) • Won Hart Trophy (2000) • Played in NHL All-Star Game (1999, 2000)

Traded to **St. Louis** by **Hartford** for Brendan Shanahan, July 27, 1995.

• PRONGER, Sean

Sean James C – L. 6'2", 205 lbs. b: Dryden, Ont., 11/30/1972. Vancouver's 3rd, 51st overall, in 1991.

Season	Club	League	GP	G	A	Pts	AG	AA	APts	PIM	PP	SH	GW	S	%	TGF	PGF	TGA	PGA	+/-	GP	G	A	Pts	PIM	PP	SH	GW
1988-89	Kenora Boise	NOJHA	33	38	30	68																						
1989-90	Thunder Bay Flyers	USHL	48	18	34	52				61																		
1990-91	Bowling Green University	CCHA	40	3	7	10				30																		
1991-92	Bowling Green University	CCHA	34	9	7	16				28																		
1992-93	Bowling Green University	CCHA	39	23	23	46				35																		
1993-94	Bowling Green University	CCHA	38	17	17	34				38																		
1994-95	Knoxville Cherokees	ECHL	34	18	23	41				55																		
	Greensboro Monarchs	ECHL	2	0	2	2				0																		
	San Diego Gulls	IHL	8	0	0	0				2																		
1995-96	**Mighty Ducks of Anaheim**	**NHL**	**7**	**0**	**1**	**1**	**0**	**1**	**1**	**6**	**0**	**0**	**0**	**3**	**0.0**	**2**	**0**	**2**	**0**	**0**								
	Baltimore Bandits	AHL	72	16	17	33				61											12	3	7	10	16			
1996-97	**Mighty Ducks of Anaheim**	**NHL**	**39**	**7**	**7**	**14**	**7**	**6**	**13**	**20**	**1**	**0**	**1**	**43**	**16.3**	**23**	**2**	**18**	**3**	**6**	**9**	**0**	**2**	**2**	**4**	**0**	**0**	**0**
	Baltimore Bandits	AHL	41	26	17	43				17																		
1997-98	**Mighty Ducks of Anaheim**	**NHL**	**62**	**5**	**15**	**20**	**6**	**15**	**21**	**30**	**1**	**0**	**2**	**68**	**7.4**	**35**	**11**	**37**	**4**	**-9**								
	Pittsburgh Penguins	**NHL**	**5**	**1**	**0**	**1**	**1**	**0**	**1**	**2**	**0**	**0**	**1**	**5**	**20.0**	**2**	**0**	**3**	**0**	**-1**	**5**	**0**	**0**	**0**	**4**	**0**	**0**	**0**
1998-99	**Pittsburgh Penguins**	**NHL**	**2**	**0**	**0**	**0**	**0**	**0**	**0**	**0**	**0**	**0**	**0**	**3**	**0.0**	**0**	**0**	**0**	**0**	**0**								
	Houston Aeros	IHL	16	11	7	18				32																		
	New York Rangers	**NHL**	**14**	**0**	**3**	**3**	**0**	**3**	**3**	**4**	**0**	**0**	**0**	**3**	**0.0**	**3**	**0**	**6**	**0**	**-3**								
	Los Angeles Kings	**NHL**	**13**	**0**	**1**	**1**	**0**	**1**	**1**	**4**	**0**	**0**	**0**	**8**	**0.0**	**3**	**0**	**1**	**0**	**2**								
99-2000	**Boston Bruins**	**NHL**	**11**	**0**	**1**	**1**	**0**	**1**	**1**	**13**	**0**	**0**	**0**	**7**	**0.0**	**2**	**0**	**6**	**0**	**-4**								
	Providence Bruins	AHL	51	11	18	29				26																		
	Manitoba Moose	IHL	14	3	5	8				21											2	0	1	1	2			
	NHL Totals		**153**	**13**	**28**	**41**	**14**	**27**	**41**	**79**	**2**	**0**	**4**	**140**	**9.3**	**70**	**13**	**73**	**7**		**14**	**0**	**2**	**2**	**8**	**0**	**0**	**0**

• Brother of Chris

Signed as a free agent by **Anaheim**, February 14, 1995. Traded to **Pittsburgh** by **Anaheim** for the rights to Patrick Lalime, March 24, 1998. Traded to **NY Rangers** by **Pittsburgh** with Chris Tamer and Petr Nedved for Alexei Kovalev and Harry York, November 25, 1998. Traded to **Los Angeles** by **NY Rangers** for Eric Lacroix, February 12, 1999. Signed as a free agent by **Boston**, August 25, 1999. Traded to **Manitoba** (IHL) by **Providence** (AHL) with Keith McCambridge for Terry Hollinger, March 16, 2000 with Boston retaining Pronger's NHL rights.

• PRONOVOST, Andre

Andre Joseph Armand Andre LW – L. 5'10", 188 lbs. b: Shawinigan Falls, Que., 7/9/1936.

Season	Club	League	GP	G	A	Pts	AG	AA	APts	PIM	PP	SH	GW	S	%	TGF	PGF	TGA	PGA	+/-	GP	G	A	Pts	PIM	PP	SH	GW
1953-54	Verdun Jr. Canadiens	QJHL	54	31	46	77				28											8	3	2	5	2			
1954-55	Montreal Jr. Canadiens	QJHL	42	22	13	35				60											5	1	3	4	4			
1955-56	Montreal Jr. Canadiens	QJHL	STATISTICS NOT AVAILABLE																									
	Shawinigan Cataracts	QHL	3	0	1	1				4																		
	Montreal Jr. Canadiens	Mem-Cup	10	1	4	5				12																		
1956-57♦	**Montreal Canadiens**	**NHL**	**64**	**10**	**11**	**21**	**13**	**12**	**25**	**58**											**8**	**1**	**0**	**1**	**4**			
	Shawinigan Cataracts	QHL	7	2	2	4				11																		
1957-58♦	**Montreal Canadiens**	**NHL**	**66**	**16**	**12**	**28**	**20**	**12**	**32**	**55**											**10**	**2**	**0**	**2**	**16**			
1958-59♦	**Montreal Canadiens**	**NHL**	**70**	**9**	**14**	**23**	**11**	**14**	**25**	**48**											**11**	**2**	**1**	**3**	**6**			
1959-60♦	**Montreal Canadiens**	**NHL**	**69**	**12**	**19**	**31**	**14**	**18**	**32**	**61**											**8**	**1**	**2**	**3**	**0**			
1960-61	**Montreal Canadiens**	**NHL**	**21**	**1**	**5**	**6**	**1**	**5**	**6**	**4**																		
	Boston Bruins	**NHL**	**47**	**11**	**11**	**22**	**13**	**11**	**24**	**30**																		
1961-62	**Boston Bruins**	**NHL**	**70**	**15**	**8**	**23**	**17**	**8**	**25**	**74**																		
1962-63	**Boston Bruins**	**NHL**	**21**	**0**	**2**	**2**	**0**	**2**	**2**	**6**																		
	Detroit Red Wings	**NHL**	**47**	**13**	**5**	**18**	**15**	**5**	**20**	**18**											**11**	**1**	**4**	**5**	**6**			
1963-64	**Detroit Red Wings**	**NHL**	**70**	**7**	**16**	**23**	**9**	**17**	**26**	**54**											**14**	**4**	**3**	**7**	**26**			
1964-65	**Detroit Red Wings**	**NHL**	**3**	**0**	**1**	**1**	**0**	**1**	**1**	**0**																		
	Pittsburgh Hornets	AHL	22	2	5	7				4																		
	Memphis Wings	CPHL	55	23	38	61				75																		
1965-66	Pittsburgh Hornets	AHL	72	25	21	46				64											3	0	1	1	0			
1966-67	Memphis Wings	CPHL	70	25	42	67				85											7	1	1	2	19			
1967-68	**Minnesota North Stars**	**NHL**	**8**	**0**	**0**	**0**	**0**	**0**	**0**	**0**	**0**	**0**	**0**	**6**	**0.0**	**1**	**0**	**2**	**1**	**0**	**8**	**0**	**1**	**1**	**0**	**0**	**0**	**0**
	Memphis South Stars	CPHL	60	20	18	38				43											3	2	1	3	0			
1968-69	Phoenix Roadrunners	WHL	51	18	14	32				31																		
	Baltimore Clippers	AHL	25	1	4	5				2											4	0	0	0	0			
1969-70	Muskegon Mohawks	IHL	71	50	57	107				55											6	0	3	3	8			
1970-71	Muskegon Mohawks	IHL	60	18	24	42				24											6	2	0	2	2			
1971-72	Jersey Devils	EHL	5	2	1	3				2																		
	NHL Totals		**556**	**94**	**104**	**198**	**113**	**105**	**218**	**408**											**70**	**11**	**11**	**22**	**58**			

IHL First All-Star Team (1970) • Played in NHL All-Star Game (1957, 1958, 1959, 1960)

Traded to **Boston** by **Montreal** for Jean-Guy Gendron, November 27, 1960. Traded to **Detroit** by **Boston** for Forbes Kennedy, December 3, 1962. Claimed by **Minnesota** from **Detroit** in Expansion Draft, June 6, 1967. Traded to **Baltimore** (AHL) by **Phoenix** (AHL) for Bob Cunningham, February, 1969.

• PRONOVOST, Jean

Jean Joseph Jean Denis RW – R. 6', 185 lbs. b: Shawinigan Falls, Que., 12/18/1945.

Season	Club	League	GP	G	A	Pts	AG	AA	APts	PIM	PP	SH	GW	S	%	TGF	PGF	TGA	PGA	+/-	GP	G	A	Pts	PIM	PP	SH	GW
1963-64	Victoriaville Bruins	QJHL	9	8	4	12				4																		
	Victoriaville Bruins	Mem-Cup	3	0	0	0																						
1964-65	Niagara Falls Flyers	OHA-Jr.	54	30	40	70				40											11	4	8	12	8			
	Niagara Falls Flyers	Mem-Cup	13	7	12	19				2																		
1965-66	Niagara Falls Flyers	OHA-Jr.	48	18	34	52				47																		
1966-67	Oklahoma City Blazers	CPHL	68	21	24	45				81											11	5	2	7	12			
1967-68	Oklahoma City Blazers	CPHL	49	25	25	50				41											7	3	4	7	6			
1968-69	**Pittsburgh Penguins**	**NHL**	**76**	**16**	**25**	**41**	**17**	**22**	**39**	**41**	**4**	**2**	**1**	**199**	**8.0**	**57**	**14**	**50**	**3**	**-4**								
1969-70	**Pittsburgh Penguins**	**NHL**	**72**	**20**	**21**	**41**	**22**	**20**	**42**	**45**	**5**	**0**	**6**	**222**	**9.0**	**57**	**16**	**44**	**1**	**-2**	**10**	**3**	**4**	**7**	**2**	**1**	**1**	**0**
1970-71	**Pittsburgh Penguins**	**NHL**	**78**	**21**	**24**	**45**	**21**	**20**	**41**	**35**	**4**	**0**	**2**	**225**	**9.3**	**70**	**15**	**54**	**7**	**8**								
1971-72	**Pittsburgh Penguins**	**NHL**	**68**	**30**	**23**	**53**	**30**	**20**	**50**	**12**	**3**	**1**	**3**	**214**	**14.0**	**75**	**18**	**51**	**9**	**15**	**4**	**1**	**1**	**2**	**0**	**0**	**1**	**0**
1972-73	**Pittsburgh Penguins**	**NHL**	**66**	**21**	**22**	**43**	**20**	**17**	**37**	**16**	**2**	**1**	**5**	**192**	**10.9**	**68**	**16**	**78**	**11**	**-15**								
1973-74	**Pittsburgh Penguins**	**NHL**	**77**	**40**	**32**	**72**	**39**	**26**	**65**	**22**	**8**	**4**	**2**	**248**	**16.1**	**107**	**27**	**82**	**11**	**9**								
1974-75	**Pittsburgh Penguins**	**NHL**	**78**	**43**	**32**	**75**	**38**	**24**	**62**	**37**	**11**	**1**	**9**	**275**	**15.6**	**108**	**28**	**81**	**14**	**13**	**9**	**3**	**3**	**6**	**6**	**0**	**0**	**0**
1975-76	**Pittsburgh Penguins**	**NHL**	**80**	**52**	**52**	**104**	**46**	**39**	**85**	**24**	**13**	**2**	**3**	**299**	**17.4**	**148**	**51**	**92**	**11**	**16**	**3**	**0**	**0**	**0**	**2**	**0**	**0**	**0**
1976-77	**Pittsburgh Penguins**	**NHL**	**79**	**33**	**31**	**64**	**30**	**24**	**54**	**24**	**7**	**1**	**6**	**217**	**15.2**	**89**	**25**	**79**	**23**	**8**	**3**	**2**	**1**	**3**	**2**	**1**	**0**	**0**
	Canada	WEC-A	7	2	2	4				0																		
1977-78	**Pittsburgh Penguins**	**NHL**	**79**	**40**	**25**	**65**	**36**	**19**	**55**	**50**	**12**	**2**	**5**	**219**	**18.3**	**102**	**36**	**106**	**24**	**-16**								
	Canada	WEC-A	10	2	3	5				0																		
1978-79	**Atlanta Flames**	**NHL**	**75**	**28**	**39**	**67**	**24**	**28**	**52**	**30**	**4**	**2**	**8**	**151**	**18.5**	**86**	**22**	**48**	**5**	**21**	**2**	**2**	**0**	**2**	**0**	**1**	**0**	**0**
1979-80	**Atlanta Flames**	**NHL**	**80**	**24**	**19**	**43**	**20**	**14**	**34**	**12**	**6**	**0**	**3**	**119**	**20.2**	**66**	**14**	**72**	**32**	**12**	**4**	**0**	**0**	**0**	**2**	**0**	**0**	**0**
1980-81	**Washington Capitals**	**NHL**	**80**	**22**	**36**	**58**	**17**	**24**	**41**	**61**	**6**	**1**	**4**	**188**	**11.7**	**91**	**34**	**88**	**22**	**-9**								
1981-82	**Washington Capitals**	**NHL**	**10**	**1**	**2**	**3**	**1**	**1**	**2**	**4**	**0**	**0**	**0**	**15**	**6.7**	**6**	**1**	**13**	**1**	**-7**								
	Hershey Bears	AHL	64	35	31	66				18											5	1	1	2	0			
1982-1988			OUT OF HOCKEY – RETIRED																									

Season	Club	League	GP	G	A	Pts	AG	AA	APts	PIM	PP	SH	GW	S	%	TGF	PGF	TGA	PGA	+/-	GP	G	A	Pts	PIM	PP	SH	GW
			REGULAR SEASON																		PLAYOFFS							
1988-1994	McGill University	OUAA	DID NOT PLAY – COACHING																									
1994-1996	Shawinigan Cataractes	QMJHL	DID NOT PLAY – COACHING																									
1996-1998	Quebec Rafales	IHL	DID NOT PLAY – COACHING																									
	NHL Totals		**998**	**391**	**383**	**774**	**361**	**298**	**659**	**413**	**85**	**17**	**57**	**2783**	**14.0**	**1130**	**317**	**938**	**174**		**35**	**11**	**9**	**20**	**14**	**3**	**2**	**0**

• Brother of Marcel and Claude • 1963-64 Victoriaville (QJHL) statistics are playoff totals only. Regular season totals unavailable. Played in NHL All-Star Game (1975, 1976, 1977, 1978)

Traded to **Pittsburgh** by **Boston** with John Arbour for cash, May 21, 1968. Traded to **Atlanta** by **Pittsburgh** for Gregg Sheppard, September 6, 1978. Transferred to **Calgary** after **Atlanta** franchise relocated, June 23, 1980. Traded to **Washington** by **Calgary** for cash, July 1, 1980.

• PRONOVOST, Marcel

Joseph Rene Marcel D – L. 6', 190 lbs. b: Lac-de-Tortue, Que., 6/15/1930. HHOF

Season	Club	League	GP	G	A	Pts	AG	AA	APts	PIM	PP	SH	GW	S	%	TGF	PGF	TGA	PGA	+/-	GP	G	A	Pts	PIM	PP	SH	GW
1947-48	Windsor Spitfires	OHA-Jr.	33	6	18	24	....	....	....	61	....	....	....	....	....	....	....	....	....	....	12	1	3	4	28	....	....	....
	Detroit Auto Club	IHL	19	5	3	8	....	....	....	53	....	....	....	....	....	....	....	....	....	....	....	....	....	....	....	....	....	....
1948-49	Windsor Spitfires	OHA-Jr.	42	14	23	37	....	....	....	126	....	....	....	....	....	....	....	....	....	....	4	1	5	6	2	....	....	....
	Detroit Auto Club	IHL	9	4	4	8	....	....	....	24	....	....	....	....	....	....	....	....	....	....	6	3	1	4	15	....	....	....
1949-50	Omaha Knights	USHL	69	13	39	52	....	....	....	100	....	....	....	....	....	....	....	....	....	....	7	4	*9	*13	9	....	....	....
♦	**Detroit Red Wings**	**NHL**	....	....	....	....	....	....	....	....	....	....	....	....	....	....	....	....	....	....	**9**	**0**	**1**	**1**	**10**	....	....	....
1950-51	**Detroit Red Wings**	**NHL**	**37**	**1**	**6**	**7**	**1**	**7**	**8**	**20**	....	....	....	....	....	....	....	....	....	....	**6**	**0**	**0**	**0**	**0**	....	....	....
	Indianapolis Capitols	AHL	34	9	23	32	....	....	....	44	....	....	....	....	....	....	....	....	....	....	....	....	....	....	....	....	....	....
1951-52♦	**Detroit Red Wings**	**NHL**	**69**	**7**	**11**	**18**	**9**	**13**	**22**	**50**	....	....	....	....	....	....	....	....	....	....	**8**	**0**	**1**	**1**	**10**	....	....	....
1952-53	**Detroit Red Wings**	**NHL**	**68**	**8**	**19**	**27**	**10**	**23**	**33**	**72**	....	....	....	....	....	....	....	....	....	....	**6**	**0**	**0**	**0**	**6**	....	....	....
1953-54♦	**Detroit Red Wings**	**NHL**	**57**	**6**	**12**	**18**	**8**	**15**	**23**	**50**	....	....	....	....	....	....	....	....	....	....	**12**	**2**	**3**	**5**	**12**	....	....	....
1954-55♦	**Detroit Red Wings**	**NHL**	**70**	**9**	**25**	**34**	**12**	**29**	**41**	**90**	....	....	....	....	....	....	....	....	....	....	**11**	**1**	**2**	**3**	**6**	....	....	....
1955-56	**Detroit Red Wings**	**NHL**	**68**	**4**	**13**	**17**	**5**	**15**	**20**	**46**	....	....	....	....	....	....	....	....	....	....	**10**	**0**	**2**	**2**	**8**	....	....	....
1956-57	**Detroit Red Wings**	**NHL**	**70**	**7**	**9**	**16**	**9**	**10**	**19**	**38**	....	....	....	....	....	....	....	....	....	....	**5**	**0**	**0**	**0**	**6**	....	....	....
1957-58	**Detroit Red Wings**	**NHL**	**62**	**2**	**18**	**20**	**2**	**19**	**21**	**52**	....	....	....	....	....	....	....	....	....	....	**4**	**0**	**1**	**1**	**4**	....	....	....
1958-59	**Detroit Red Wings**	**NHL**	**69**	**11**	**21**	**32**	**13**	**21**	**34**	**44**	....	....	....	....	....	....	....	....	....	....	....	....	....	....	....	....	....	....
1959-60	**Detroit Red Wings**	**NHL**	**69**	**7**	**17**	**24**	**8**	**16**	**24**	**38**	....	....	....	....	....	....	....	....	....	....	**6**	**1**	**1**	**2**	**2**	....	....	....
1960-61	**Detroit Red Wings**	**NHL**	**70**	**6**	**11**	**17**	**7**	**11**	**18**	**44**	....	....	....	....	....	....	....	....	....	....	**9**	**2**	**3**	**5**	**0**	....	....	....
1961-62	**Detroit Red Wings**	**NHL**	**70**	**4**	**14**	**18**	**5**	**13**	**18**	**38**	....	....	....	....	....	....	....	....	....	....	....	....	....	....	....	....	....	....
1962-63	**Detroit Red Wings**	**NHL**	**69**	**4**	**9**	**13**	**5**	**9**	**14**	**48**	....	....	....	....	....	....	....	....	....	....	**11**	**1**	**4**	**5**	**8**	....	....	....
1963-64	**Detroit Red Wings**	**NHL**	**67**	**3**	**17**	**20**	**4**	**18**	**22**	**42**	....	....	....	....	....	....	....	....	....	....	**14**	**0**	**2**	**2**	**14**	....	....	....
1964-65	**Detroit Red Wings**	**NHL**	**68**	**1**	**15**	**16**	**1**	**15**	**16**	**45**	....	....	....	....	....	....	....	....	....	....	**7**	**0**	**3**	**3**	**4**	....	....	....
1965-66	**Toronto Maple Leafs**	**NHL**	**54**	**2**	**8**	**10**	**2**	**8**	**10**	**34**	....	....	....	....	....	....	....	....	....	....	**4**	**0**	**0**	**0**	**6**	....	....	....
1966-67♦	**Toronto Maple Leafs**	**NHL**	**58**	**2**	**12**	**14**	**2**	**12**	**14**	**28**	....	....	....	....	....	....	....	....	....	....	**12**	**1**	**0**	**1**	**8**	....	....	....
1967-68	**Toronto Maple Leafs**	**NHL**	**70**	**3**	**17**	**20**	**3**	**17**	**20**	**48**	**0**	**0**	**1**	**70**	**4.3**	**70**	**0**	**82**	**12**	**0**	....	....	....	....	....	....	....	....
1968-69	**Toronto Maple Leafs**	**NHL**	**34**	**1**	**2**	**3**	**1**	**2**	**3**	**20**	**0**	**0**	**0**	**18**	**5.6**	**18**	**1**	**26**	**7**	**–2**	....	....	....	....	....	....	....	....
1969-70	**Toronto Maple Leafs**	**NHL**	**7**	**0**	**1**	**1**	**0**	**1**	**1**	**4**	**0**	**0**	**0**	**2**	**0.0**	**10**	**0**	**6**	**1**	**5**	....	....	....	....	....	....	....	....
	Tulsa Oilers	CHL	53	1	16	17	....	....	....	24	....	....	....	....	....	....	....	....	....	....	2	0	0	0	0	....	....	....
1970-71	Tulsa Oilers	CHL	17	0	0	0	....	....	....	4	....	....	....	....	....	....	....	....	....	....	....	....	....	....	....	....	....	....
	NHL Totals		**1206**	**88**	**257**	**345**	**107**	**274**	**381**	**851**	....	....	....	....	....	....	....	....	....	....	**134**	**8**	**23**	**31**	**104**	....	....	....

• Brother of Claude and Jean • USHL First All-Star Team (1950) • Won Outstanding Rookie Cup (Top Rookie - USHL) (1950) • AHL Second All-Star Team (1951) • NHL Second All-Star Team (1958, 1959) • NHL First All-Star Team (1960, 1961) • Played in NHL All-Star Game (1950, 1954, 1955, 1957, 1958, 1959, 1960, 1961, 1963, 1965, 1968)

Traded to **Toronto** by **Detroit** with Aut Erickson, Larry Jeffrey, Ed Joyal and Lowell MacDonald for Billy Harris, Gary Jarrett and Andy Bathgate, May 20, 1965. • Named playing-coach of **Tulsa** (CHL) by **Toronto**, September 12, 1969.

• PROPP, Brian

Brian Phillip LW – L. 5'10", 195 lbs. b: Lanigan, Sask., 2/15/1959. Philadelphia's 1st, 14th overall, in 1979.

Season	Club	League	GP	G	A	Pts	AG	AA	APts	PIM	PP	SH	GW	S	%	TGF	PGF	TGA	PGA	+/-	GP	G	A	Pts	PIM	PP	SH	GW
1975-76	Melville Millionaires	SJHL	57	76	*92	*168	....	....	....	36	....	....	....	....	....	....	....	....	....	....	....	....	....	....	....	....	....	....
1976-77	Brandon Wheat Kings	WCJHL	72	55	80	135	....	....	....	47	....	....	....	....	....	....	....	....	....	....	16	*14	12	26	5	....	....	....
1977-78	Brandon Wheat Kings	WCJHL	70	70	*112	*182	....	....	....	200	....	....	....	....	....	....	....	....	....	....	8	7	6	13	12	....	....	....
1978-79	Brandon Wheat Kings	WCJHL	71	*94	*100	*194	....	....	....	127	....	....	....	....	....	....	....	....	....	....	22	15	23	*38	40	....	....	....
	Canada	WJC-A	5	2	1	3	....	....	....	2	....	....	....	....	....	....	....	....	....	....	....	....	....	....	....	....	....	....
	Brandon Wheat Kings	Mem-Cup	5	4	*7	11	....	....	....	6	....	....	....	....	....	....	....	....	....	....	....	....	....	....	....	....	....	....
1979-80	**Philadelphia Flyers**	**NHL**	**80**	**34**	**41**	**75**	**29**	**30**	**59**	**54**	**4**	**0**	**3**	**209**	**16.3**	**118**	**23**	**51**	**1**	**45**	**19**	**5**	**10**	**15**	**29**	**3**	**0**	**0**
1980-81	**Philadelphia Flyers**	**NHL**	**79**	**26**	**40**	**66**	**20**	**27**	**47**	**110**	**6**	**0**	**5**	**194**	**13.4**	**104**	**34**	**43**	**0**	**27**	**12**	**6**	**6**	**12**	**32**	**0**	**0**	**0**
1981-82	**Philadelphia Flyers**	**NHL**	**80**	**44**	**47**	**91**	**35**	**31**	**66**	**117**	**13**	**0**	**6**	**290**	**15.2**	**130**	**49**	**65**	**3**	**19**	**4**	**2**	**2**	**4**	**4**	**0**	**0**	**1**
	Canada	WEC-A	10	3	1	4	....	....	....	4	....	....	....	....	....	....	....	....	....	....	....	....	....	....	....	....	....	....
1982-83	**Philadelphia Flyers**	**NHL**	**80**	**40**	**42**	**82**	**33**	**29**	**62**	**72**	**13**	**1**	**12**	**250**	**16.0**	**108**	**28**	**59**	**14**	**35**	**3**	**1**	**2**	**3**	**8**	**1**	**0**	**0**
	Canada	WEC-A	10	4	4	8	....	....	....	6	....	....	....	....	....	....	....	....	....	....	....	....	....	....	....	....	....	....
1983-84	**Philadelphia Flyers**	**NHL**	**79**	**39**	**53**	**92**	**31**	**36**	**67**	**37**	**11**	**1**	**4**	**301**	**13.0**	**141**	**29**	**89**	**26**	**49**	**3**	**0**	**1**	**1**	**6**	**0**	**0**	**0**
1984-85	**Philadelphia Flyers**	**NHL**	**76**	**43**	**54**	**97**	**35**	**37**	**72**	**43**	**12**	**7**	**4**	**258**	**16.7**	**141**	**39**	**85**	**29**	**46**	**19**	**8**	**10**	**18**	**6**	**4**	**1**	**2**
1985-86	**Philadelphia Flyers**	**NHL**	**72**	**40**	**57**	**97**	**32**	**38**	**70**	**47**	**11**	**2**	**5**	**317**	**12.6**	**153**	**64**	**88**	**23**	**24**	**5**	**0**	**2**	**2**	**4**	**0**	**0**	**0**
1986-87	**Philadelphia Flyers**	**NHL**	**53**	**31**	**36**	**67**	**27**	**26**	**53**	**45**	**8**	**5**	**5**	**208**	**14.9**	**93**	**29**	**45**	**20**	**39**	**26**	**12**	**16**	**28**	**10**	**5**	**1**	**3**
1987-88	Canada	Can-Cup	9	2	2	4	....	....	....	2	....	....	....	....	....	....	....	....	....	....	....	....	....	....	....	....	....	....
	Philadelphia Flyers	**NHL**	**74**	**27**	**49**	**76**	**23**	**35**	**58**	**76**	**7**	**2**	**6**	**257**	**10.5**	**119**	**49**	**86**	**24**	**8**	**7**	**4**	**2**	**6**	**8**	**0**	**0**	**0**
1988-89	**Philadelphia Flyers**	**NHL**	**77**	**32**	**46**	**78**	**27**	**33**	**60**	**37**	**13**	**2**	**5**	**245**	**13.1**	**123**	**52**	**78**	**23**	**16**	**18**	**14**	**9**	**23**	**14**	**5**	**1**	**1**
1989-90	**Philadelphia Flyers**	**NHL**	**40**	**13**	**15**	**28**	**11**	**11**	**22**	**31**	**5**	**0**	**0**	**108**	**12.0**	**40**	**14**	**30**	**7**	**3**	....	....	....	....	....	....	....	....
	Boston Bruins	**NHL**	**14**	**3**	**9**	**12**	**3**	**6**	**9**	**10**	**0**	**1**	**0**	**45**	**6.7**	**19**	**6**	**16**	**5**	**2**	**20**	**4**	**9**	**13**	**2**	**1**	**0**	**2**
1990-91	Minnesota North Stars	Fr-Tour	3	0	1	1	....	....	....	8	....	....	....	....	....	....	....	....	....	....	....	....	....	....	....	....	....	....
	Minnesota North Stars	**NHL**	**79**	**26**	**47**	**73**	**24**	**36**	**60**	**58**	**9**	**0**	**1**	**171**	**15.2**	**110**	**49**	**66**	**12**	**7**	**23**	**8**	**15**	**23**	**28**	**8**	**0**	**3**
1991-92	**Minnesota North Stars**	**NHL**	**51**	**12**	**23**	**35**	**11**	**17**	**28**	**49**	**4**	**0**	**0**	**115**	**10.4**	**56**	**23**	**37**	**1**	**–3**	**1**	**0**	**0**	**0**	**0**	**0**	**0**	**0**
1992-93	**Minnesota North Stars**	**NHL**	**17**	**3**	**3**	**6**	**2**	**2**	**4**	**0**	**1**	**0**	**1**	**35**	**8.6**	**10**	**7**	**15**	**2**	**–10**	....	....	....	....	....	....	....	....
	Canada	Nat-Team	3	3	1	4	....	....	....	2	....	....	....	....	....	....	....	....	....	....	....	....	....	....	....	....	....	....
	HC Lugano	Switz.	24	21	6	27	....	....	....	32	....	....	....	....	....	....	....	....	....	....	9	5	1	6	28	....	....	....
1993-94	**Hartford Whalers**	**NHL**	**65**	**12**	**17**	**29**	**11**	**13**	**24**	**44**	**3**	**1**	**2**	**108**	**11.1**	**39**	**11**	**43**	**18**	**3**	....	....	....	....	....	....	....	....
1994-95	HC Anglet	France-2	27	32	19	51	....	....	....	74	....	....	....	....	....	....	....	....	....	....	....	....	....	....	....	....	....	....
	NHL Totals		**1016**	**425**	**579**	**1004**	**354**	**407**	**761**	**830**	**120**	**22**	**59**	**3111**	**13.7**	**1504**	**506**	**896**	**208**		**160**	**64**	**84**	**148**	**151**	**27**	**3**	**12**

WCJHL All-Star Team (1977, 1978) • WHL All-Star Team (1979) • Played in NHL All-Star Game (1980, 1982, 1984, 1986, 1990)

Traded to **Boston** by **Philadelphia** for Boston's 2nd round choice (Terran Sandwith) in 1990 Entry Draft, March 2, 1990. Signed as a free agent by **Minnesota**, July 25, 1990. Signed as a free agent by **Hartford**, October 4, 1993.

• PROSPAL, Vaclav

C – L. 6'2", 195 lbs. b: Ceske-Budejovice, Czech., 2/17/1975. Philadelphia's 2nd, 71st overall, in 1993.

Season	Club	League	GP	G	A	Pts	AG	AA	APts	PIM	PP	SH	GW	S	%	TGF	PGF	TGA	PGA	+/-	GP	G	A	Pts	PIM	PP	SH	GW
1991-92	Motor Ceske Budjevoice	Czech-Jr.	36	16	16	32	....	....	....	12	....	....	....	....	....	....	....	....	....	....	....	....	....	....	....	....	....	....
1992-93	Motor Ceske Budejovice	Czech-Jr.	32	26	31	57	....	....	....	24	....	....	....	....	....	....	....	....	....	....	....	....	....	....	....	....	....	....
	Czech-Republic	EJC-A	6	4	7	11	....	....	....	2	....	....	....	....	....	....	....	....	....	....	....	....	....	....	....	....	....	....
1993-94	Hershey Bears	AHL	55	14	21	35	....	....	....	38	....	....	....	....	....	....	....	....	....	....	2	0	0	0	2	....	....	....
	Czech-Republic	WJC-A	7	1	1	2	....	....	....	16	....	....	....	....	....	....	....	....	....	....	....	....	....	....	....	....	....	....
1994-95	Hershey Bears	AHL	69	13	32	45	....	....	....	36	....	....	....	....	....	....	....	....	....	....	2	1	0	1	4	....	....	....
	Czech-Republic	WJC-A	7	3	7	10	....	....	....	2	....	....	....	....	....	....	....	....	....	....	....	....	....	....	....	....	....	....
1995-96	Hershey Bears	AHL	68	15	36	51	....	....	....	59	....	....	....	....	....	....	....	....	....	....	5	2	4	6	2	....	....	....
1996-97	**Philadelphia Flyers**	**NHL**	**18**	**5**	**10**	**15**	**5**	**9**	**14**	**4**	**0**	**0**	**0**	**35**	**14.3**	**22**	**10**	**9**	**0**	**3**	**5**	**1**	**3**	**4**	**4**	**0**	**0**	**0**
	Philadelphia Phantoms	AHL	63	32	63	95	....	....	....	70	....	....	....	....	....	....	....	....	....	....	....	....	....	....	....	....	....	....
1997-98	**Philadelphia Flyers**	**NHL**	**41**	**5**	**13**	**18**	**6**	**13**	**19**	**17**	**4**	**0**	**0**	**60**	**8.3**	**25**	**13**	**23**	**1**	**–10**	....	....	....	....	....	....	....	....
	Ottawa Senators	**NHL**	**15**	**1**	**6**	**7**	**1**	**6**	**7**	**4**	**0**	**0**	**0**	**28**	**3.6**	**9**	**4**	**6**	**0**	**–1**	**6**	**0**	**0**	**0**	**0**	**0**	**0**	**0**

			REGULAR SEASON																		PLAYOFFS							
Season	**Club**	**League**	**GP**	**G**	**A**	**Pts**	**AG**	**AA**	**APts**	**PIM**	**PP**	**SH**	**GW**	**S**	**%**	**TGF**	**PGF**	**TGA**	**PGA**	**+/–**	**GP**	**G**	**A**	**Pts**	**PIM**	**PP**	**SH**	**GW**
1998-99	**Ottawa Senators**	**NHL**	**79**	**10**	**26**	**36**	**12**	**25**	**37**	**58**	**2**	**0**	**3**	**114**	**8.8**	**50**	**12**	**30**	**0**	**8**	**4**	**0**	**0**	**0**	**0**	**0**	**0**	**0**
99-2000	**Ottawa Senators**	**NHL**	**79**	**22**	**33**	**55**	**25**	**31**	**56**	**40**	**5**	**0**	**4**	**204**	**10.8**	**80**	**25**	**58**	**1**	**–2**	**6**	**0**	**4**	**4**	**4**	**0**	**0**	**0**
	Czech-Republic	WC-A	9	3	4	7	....	....	....	8	....	....	....	....	....	....	....	....	....	....	....	....	....	....	....	....	....	....
	NHL Totals		**232**	**43**	**88**	**131**	**49**	**84**	**133**	**123**	**11**	**0**	**7**	**441**	**9.8**	**186**	**64**	**126**	**2**		**21**	**1**	**7**	**8**	**8**	**0**	**0**	**0**

AHL First All-Star Team (1997)

Traded to **Ottawa** by **Philadelphia** with Pat Falloon and Dallas' 2nd round choice (previously acquired, Ottawa selected Chris Bala) in 1998 Entry Draft for Alexandre Daigle, January 17, 1998.

• PROULX, Christian

D – L. 6', 185 lbs. b: Sherbrooke, Que., 12/10/1973. Montreal's 9th, 164th overall, in 1992.

Season	Club	League	GP	G	A	Pts	AG	AA	APts	PIM	PP	SH	GW	S	%	TGF	PGF	TGA	PGA	+/–	GP	G	A	Pts	PIM	PP	SH	GW
1988-89	Montreal L'est Cantonniers	QAAA	36	2	4	6	....	....	....	....	....	....	....	....	....	....	....	....	....	....	....	....	....	....	....	....	....	....
1989-90	Montreal L'est Cantonniers	QAAA	41	4	19	23	....	....	....	....	....	....	....	....	....	....	....	....	....	....	....	....	....	....	....	....	....	....
1990-91	St-Jean Castors	QMJHL	67	1	8	9	....	....	....	73	....	....	....	....	....	....	....	....	....	....	....	....	....	....	....	....	....	....
1991-92	St-Jean Castors	QMJHL	68	1	17	18	....	....	....	180	....	....	....	....	....	....	....	....	....	....	....	....	....	....	....	....	....	....
1992-93	St-Jean Castors	QMJHL	70	3	34	37	....	....	....	147	....	....	....	....	....	....	....	....	....	....	4	0	0	0	12	....	....	....
	Fredericton Canadiens	AHL	2	1	0	1	....	....	....	2	....	....	....	....	....	....	....	....	....	....	4	0	0	0	0	....	....	....
1993-94	**Montreal Canadiens**	**NHL**	**7**	**1**	**2**	**3**	**1**	**2**	**3**	**20**	**0**	**0**	**0**	**11**	**9.1**	**6**	**1**	**5**	**0**	**0**	....	....	....	....	....	....	....	....
	Fredericton Canadiens	AHL	70	2	12	14	....	....	....	183	....	....	....	....	....	....	....	....	....	....	....	....	....	....	....	....	....	....
1994-95	Fredericton Canadiens	AHL	75	1	9	10	....	....	....	184	....	....	....	....	....	....	....	....	....	....	9	0	1	1	8	....	....	....
1995-96	San Francisco Spiders	IHL	80	1	15	16	....	....	....	154	....	....	....	....	....	....	....	....	....	....	4	0	0	0	6	....	....	....
1996-97	Milwaukee Admirals	IHL	74	3	4	7	....	....	....	145	....	....	....	....	....	....	....	....	....	....	1	0	0	0	2	....	....	....
1997-98	Hershey Bears	AHL	32	2	2	4	....	....	....	76	....	....	....	....	....	....	....	....	....	....	....	....	....	....	....	....	....	....
	Milwaukee Admirals	IHL	31	4	6	10	....	....	....	84	....	....	....	....	....	....	....	....	....	....	10	0	1	1	20	....	....	....
1998-99	HC Asiago	Alpenliga	29	3	12	15	....	....	....	106	....	....	....	....	....	....	....	....	....	....	18	3	9	12	97	....	....	....
99-2000	EC Bad Tolz	Germany-2	44	9	18	27	....	....	....	192	....	....	....	....	....	....	....	....	....	....	....	....	....	....	....	....	....	....
	NHL Totals		**7**	**1**	**2**	**3**	**1**	**2**	**3**	**20**	**0**	**0**	**0**	**11**	**9.1**	**6**	**1**	**5**	**0**		....	....	....	....	....	....	....	....

• PROVOST, Claude

Claude Joseph Antoine RW – R. 5'9", 168 lbs. b: Montreal, Que., 9/17/1933 d: 4/17/1984.

Season	Club	League	GP	G	A	Pts	AG	AA	APts	PIM	PP	SH	GW	S	%	TGF	PGF	TGA	PGA	+/–	GP	G	A	Pts	PIM	PP	SH	GW
1951-52	Montreal Nationale	QJHL	49	24	29	53	....	....	....	46	....	....	....	....	....	....	....	....	....	....	9	5	2	7	4	....	....	....
1952-53	Montreal Jr. Canadiens	QJHL	46	24	36	60	....	....	....	29	....	....	....	....	....	....	....	....	....	....	7	6	5	11	10	....	....	....
1953-54	Montreal Jr. Canadiens	QJHL	48	45	39	84	....	....	....	83	....	....	....	....	....	....	....	....	....	....	8	3	8	11	16	....	....	....
1954-55	Shawinigan Cataracts	QHL	61	25	23	48	....	....	....	44	....	....	....	....	....	....	....	....	....	....	13	6	3	9	6	....	....	....
	Shawinigan Cataracts	Ed-Cup	7	2	2	4	....	....	....	4	....	....	....	....	....	....	....	....	....	....	....	....	....	....	....	....	....	....
1955-56♦	**Montreal Canadiens**	**NHL**	**60**	**13**	**16**	**29**	**18**	**19**	**37**	**30**	....	....	....	....	....	....	....	....	....	....	**10**	**3**	**3**	**6**	**12**	....	....	....
	Shawinigan Cataracts	QHL	9	7	8	15	....	....	....	12	....	....	....	....	....	....	....	....	....	....	....	....	....	....	....	....	....	....
1956-57♦	**Montreal Canadiens**	**NHL**	**67**	**16**	**14**	**30**	**21**	**15**	**36**	**24**	....	....	....	....	....	....	....	....	....	....	**10**	**0**	**1**	**1**	**8**	....	....	....
1957-58♦	**Montreal Canadiens**	**NHL**	**70**	**19**	**32**	**51**	**23**	**33**	**56**	**71**	....	....	....	....	....	....	....	....	....	....	**10**	**1**	**3**	**4**	**8**	....	....	....
1958-59♦	**Montreal Canadiens**	**NHL**	**69**	**16**	**22**	**38**	**19**	**22**	**41**	**37**	....	....	....	....	....	....	....	....	....	....	**11**	**6**	**2**	**8**	**2**	....	....	....
1959-60♦	**Montreal Canadiens**	**NHL**	**70**	**17**	**29**	**46**	**20**	**28**	**48**	**42**	....	....	....	....	....	....	....	....	....	....	**8**	**1**	**1**	**2**	**0**	....	....	....
1960-61	**Montreal Canadiens**	**NHL**	**49**	**11**	**4**	**15**	**13**	**4**	**17**	**32**	....	....	....	....	....	....	....	....	....	....	**6**	**1**	**3**	**4**	**4**	....	....	....
1961-62	**Montreal Canadiens**	**NHL**	**70**	**33**	**29**	**62**	**38**	**28**	**66**	**22**	....	....	....	....	....	....	....	....	....	....	**6**	**2**	**2**	**4**	**2**	....	....	....
1962-63	**Montreal Canadiens**	**NHL**	**67**	**20**	**30**	**50**	**23**	**30**	**53**	**26**	....	....	....	....	....	....	....	....	....	....	**5**	**0**	**1**	**1**	**2**	....	....	....
1963-64	**Montreal Canadiens**	**NHL**	**68**	**15**	**17**	**32**	**19**	**18**	**37**	**37**	....	....	....	....	....	....	....	....	....	....	**7**	**2**	**2**	**4**	**22**	....	....	....
1964-65♦	**Montreal Canadiens**	**NHL**	**70**	**27**	**37**	**64**	**33**	**38**	**71**	**28**	....	....	....	....	....	....	....	....	....	....	**13**	**2**	**6**	**8**	**12**	....	....	....
1965-66♦	**Montreal Canadiens**	**NHL**	**70**	**19**	**36**	**55**	**22**	**34**	**56**	**38**	....	....	....	....	....	....	....	....	....	....	**10**	**2**	**3**	**5**	**2**	....	....	....
1966-67	**Montreal Canadiens**	**NHL**	**64**	**11**	**13**	**24**	**13**	**13**	**26**	**16**	....	....	....	....	....	....	....	....	....	....	**7**	**1**	**1**	**2**	**0**	....	....	....
1967-68♦	**Montreal Canadiens**	**NHL**	**73**	**14**	**30**	**44**	**16**	**30**	**46**	**26**	**2**	**3**	**3**	**170**	**8.2**	**60**	**4**	**66**	**27**	**17**	**13**	**2**	**8**	**10**	**10**	**1**	**0**	**1**
1968-69♦	**Montreal Canadiens**	**NHL**	**73**	**13**	**15**	**28**	**14**	**13**	**27**	**18**	**0**	**1**	**5**	**184**	**7.1**	**48**	**0**	**66**	**30**	**12**	**10**	**2**	**2**	**4**	**2**	**0**	**0**	**0**
1969-70	**Montreal Canadiens**	**NHL**	**65**	**10**	**11**	**21**	**11**	**10**	**21**	**22**	**0**	**0**	**1**	**120**	**8.3**	**34**	**0**	**57**	**29**	**6**	....	....	....	....	....	....	....	....
1970-71	Rosemount Nationale	QJHL	DID NOT PLAY – COACHING																									
	NHL Totals		**1005**	**254**	**335**	**589**	**303**	**335**	**638**	**469**	....	....	....	....	....	....	....	....	....	....	**126**	**25**	**38**	**63**	**86**	....	....	....

NHL First All-Star Team (1965) • Won Bill Masterton Trophy (1968) • Played in NHL All-Star Game (1956, 1957, 1958, 1959, 1960, 1961, 1962, 1963, 1964, 1965, 1967)

Traded to **LA Kings** by **Montreal** for cash, June 8, 1971.

• PRPIC, Joel

Joel Melvin C – L. 6'7", 225 lbs. b: Sudbury, Ont., 9/25/1974. Boston's 9th, 233rd overall, in 1993.

Season	Club	League	GP	G	A	Pts	AG	AA	APts	PIM	PP	SH	GW	S	%	TGF	PGF	TGA	PGA	+/–	GP	G	A	Pts	PIM	PP	SH	GW
1991-92	Sudbury Cubs	NOJHA	1	0	0	0	....	....	....	0	....	....	....	....	....	....	....	....	....	....	....	....	....	....	....	....	....	....
1992-93	Waterloo Siskins	OJHL-B	45	17	43	60	....	....	....	160	....	....	....	....	....	....	....	....	....	....	....	....	....	....	....	....	....	....
1993-94	St. Lawrence University	ECAC	31	2	4	6	....	....	....	90	....	....	....	....	....	....	....	....	....	....	....	....	....	....	....	....	....	....
1994-95	St. Lawrence University	ECAC	32	7	10	17	....	....	....	62	....	....	....	....	....	....	....	....	....	....	....	....	....	....	....	....	....	....
1995-96	St. Lawrence University	ECAC	32	3	10	13	....	....	....	77	....	....	....	....	....	....	....	....	....	....	....	....	....	....	....	....	....	....
1996-97	St. Lawrence University	ECAC	34	10	8	18	....	....	....	57	....	....	....	....	....	....	....	....	....	....	....	....	....	....	....	....	....	....
1997-98	**Boston Bruins**	**NHL**	**1**	**0**	**0**	**0**	**0**	**0**	**0**	**2**	**0**	**0**	**0**	**0**	**0.0**	**0**	**0**	**0**	**0**	**0**	....	....	....	....	....	....	....	....
	Providence Bruins	AHL	73	17	18	35	....	....	....	53	....	....	....	....	....	....	....	....	....	....	....	....	....	....	....	....	....	....
1998-99	Providence Bruins	AHL	75	14	16	30	....	....	....	163	....	....	....	....	....	....	....	....	....	....	18	4	6	10	48	....	....	....
99-2000	**Boston Bruins**	**NHL**	**14**	**0**	**3**	**3**	**0**	**3**	**3**	**0**	**0**	**0**	**0**	**13**	**0.0**	**4**	**0**	**10**	**0**	**–6**	....	....	....	....	....	....	....	....
	Providence Bruins	AHL	70	9	20	29	....	....	....	143	....	....	....	....	....	....	....	....	....	....	14	3	4	7	58	....	....	....
	NHL Totals		**15**	**0**	**3**	**3**	**0**	**3**	**3**	**2**	**0**	**0**	**0**	**13**	**0.0**	**4**	**0**	**10**	**0**		....	....	....	....	....	....	....	....

• PRYOR, Chris

Christopher M. D – R. 5'11", 210 lbs. b: St. Paul, MN, 1/23/1961.

Season	Club	League	GP	G	A	Pts	AG	AA	APts	PIM	PP	SH	GW	S	%	TGF	PGF	TGA	PGA	+/–	GP	G	A	Pts	PIM	PP	SH	GW
1978-79	Hill-Murray Pioneers	Hi-School	STATISTICS NOT AVAILABLE																									
1979-80	University of New Hampshire	ECAC	27	9	13	22	....	....	....	27	....	....	....	....	....	....	....	....	....	....	....	....	....	....	....	....	....	....
1980-81	University of New Hampshire	ECAC	33	10	27	37	....	....	....	36	....	....	....	....	....	....	....	....	....	....	....	....	....	....	....	....	....	....
1981-82	University of New Hampshire	ECAC	35	3	16	19	....	....	....	36	....	....	....	....	....	....	....	....	....	....	....	....	....	....	....	....	....	....
1982-83	University of New Hampshire	ECAC	34	4	9	13	....	....	....	23	....	....	....	....	....	....	....	....	....	....	....	....	....	....	....	....	....	....
1983-84	Salt Lake Golden Eagles	CHL	72	7	21	28	....	....	....	215	....	....	....	....	....	....	....	....	....	....	5	1	2	3	11	....	....	....
1984-85	**Minnesota North Stars**	**NHL**	**4**	**0**	**0**	**0**	**0**	**0**	**0**	**16**	**0**	**0**	**0**	**2**	**0.0**	**0**	**0**	**4**	**2**	**–2**	....	....	....	....	....	....	....	....
	Springfield Indians	AHL	77	3	21	24	....	....	....	158	....	....	....	....	....	....	....	....	....	....	....	....	....	....	....	....	....	....
1985-86	**Minnesota North Stars**	**NHL**	**7**	**0**	**1**	**1**	**0**	**1**	**1**	**0**	**0**	**0**	**0**	**8**	**0.0**	**4**	**0**	**6**	**2**	**0**	....	....	....	....	....	....	....	....
	Springfield Indians	AHL	55	4	16	20	....	....	....	104	....	....	....	....	....	....	....	....	....	....	....	....	....	....	....	....	....	....
1986-87	**Minnesota North Stars**	**NHL**	**50**	**1**	**3**	**4**	**1**	**2**	**3**	**49**	**0**	**0**	**0**	**20**	**5.0**	**27**	**1**	**50**	**18**	**–6**	....	....	....	....	....	....	....	....
	Springfield Indians	AHL	5	0	2	2	....	....	....	17	....	....	....	....	....	....	....	....	....	....	....	....	....	....	....	....	....	....
1987-88	**Minnesota North Stars**	**NHL**	**3**	**0**	**0**	**0**	**0**	**0**	**0**	**6**	**0**	**0**	**0**	**3**	**0.0**	**0**	**0**	**1**	**0**	**–1**	....	....	....	....	....	....	....	....
	Kalamazoo Wings	IHL	56	4	16	20	....	....	....	171	....	....	....	....	....	....	....	....	....	....	....	....	....	....	....	....	....	....
	New York Islanders	**NHL**	**1**	**0**	**0**	**0**	**0**	**0**	**0**	**2**	**0**	**0**	**0**	**1**	**0.0**	**1**	**0**	**0**	**0**	**1**	....	....	....	....	....	....	....	....
1988-89	**New York Islanders**	**NHL**	**7**	**0**	**0**	**0**	**0**	**0**	**0**	**25**	**0**	**0**	**0**	**2**	**0.0**	**2**	**0**	**11**	**3**	**–6**	....	....	....	....	....	....	....	....
	Springfield Indians	AHL	54	3	6	9	....	....	....	205	....	....	....	....	....	....	....	....	....	....	....	....	....	....	....	....	....	....
1989-90	**New York Islanders**	**NHL**	**10**	**0**	**0**	**0**	**0**	**0**	**0**	**24**	**0**	**0**	**0**	**2**	**0.0**	**0**	**0**	**8**	**1**	**–7**	....	....	....	....	....	....	....	....
	Springfield Indians	AHL	60	3	7	10	....	....	....	105	....	....	....	....	....	....	....	....	....	....	18	1	3	4	12	....	....	....
1990-91	Capital District Islanders	AHL	41	1	8	9	....	....	....	94	....	....	....	....	....	....	....	....	....	....	....	....	....	....	....	....	....	....
1991-92	Capital District Islanders	AHL	22	0	3	3	....	....	....	12	....	....	....	....	....	....	....	....	....	....	7	2	2	4	18	....	....	....
1992-93	Capital District Islanders	AHL	3	0	0	0	....	....	....	6	....	....	....	....	....	....	....	....	....	....	....	....	....	....	....	....	....	....
	NHL Totals		**82**	**1**	**4**	**5**	**1**	**3**	**4**	**122**	**0**	**0**	**0**	**38**	**2.6**	**34**	**1**	**80**	**26**		....	....	....	....	....	....	....	....

Signed as a free agent by **Minnesota**, January 10, 1985. Traded to **NY Islanders** by **Minnesota** with Minnesota's 7th round choice (Brett Harkins) in 1989 Entry Draft for Gord Dineen, March 8, 1988.

• PULFORD, Bob

Robert Jesse "Pully" LW – L. 5'11", 188 lbs. b: Newton Robinson, Ont., 3/31/1936. **HHOF**

			REGULAR SEASON																		PLAYOFFS							
Season	Club	League	GP	G	A	Pts	AG	AA	APts	PIM	PP	SH	GW	S	%	TGF	PGF	TGA	PGA	+/–	GP	G	A	Pts	PIM	PP	SH	GW
1953-54	Weston Dukes	OHA-B	STATISTICS NOT AVAILABLE																									
	Toronto Marlboros	OHA-Jr.	17	5	9	14	....	....	....	12	....	....	....	....	....	....	....	....	....	....	15	4	7	11	12	....	....	....
1954-55	Toronto Marlboros	OHA-Jr.	47	24	22	46	....	....	....	43	....	....	....	....	....	....	....	....	....	....	13	7	10	17	29	....	....	....
	Toronto Marlboros	Mem-Cup	11	5	4	9	....	....	....	15	....	....	....	....	....	....	....	....	....	....	....	....	....	....	....	....	....	....
1955-56	Toronto Marlboros	OHA-Jr.	48	30	25	55	....	....	....	87	....	....	....	....	....	....	....	....	....	....	11	*16	8	*24	2	....	....	....
	Toronto Marlboros	Mem-Cup	13	13	8	21	....	....	....	16	....	....	....	....	....	....	....	....	....	....	....	....	....	....	....	....	....	....
1956-57	**Toronto Maple Leafs**	**NHL**	**65**	**11**	**11**	**22**	**14**	**12**	**26**	**32**	....	....	....	....	....	....	....	....	....	....	....	....	....	....	....	....	....	....
1957-58	**Toronto Maple Leafs**	**NHL**	**70**	**14**	**17**	**31**	**17**	**17**	**34**	**48**	....	....	....	....	....	....	....	....	....	....	....	....	....	....	....	....	....	....
1958-59	**Toronto Maple Leafs**	**NHL**	**70**	**23**	**14**	**37**	**28**	**14**	**42**	**53**	....	....	....	....	....	....	....	....	....	....	**12**	**4**	**4**	**8**	**8**	....	....	....
1959-60	**Toronto Maple Leafs**	**NHL**	**70**	**24**	**28**	**52**	**28**	**27**	**55**	**81**	....	....	....	....	....	....	....	....	....	....	**10**	**4**	**1**	**5**	**10**	....	....	....
1960-61	**Toronto Maple Leafs**	**NHL**	**40**	**11**	**18**	**29**	**13**	**17**	**30**	**41**	....	....	....	....	....	....	....	....	....	....	**5**	**0**	**0**	**0**	**8**	....	....	....
1961-62♦	**Toronto Maple Leafs**	**NHL**	**70**	**18**	**21**	**39**	**21**	**20**	**41**	**98**	....	....	....	....	....	....	....	....	....	....	**12**	**7**	**1**	**8**	**24**	....	....	....
1962-63♦	**Toronto Maple Leafs**	**NHL**	**70**	**19**	**25**	**44**	**22**	**25**	**47**	**49**	....	....	....	....	....	....	....	....	....	....	**10**	**2**	**5**	**7**	**14**	....	....	....
1963-64♦	**Toronto Maple Leafs**	**NHL**	**70**	**18**	**30**	**48**	**22**	**32**	**54**	**73**	....	....	....	....	....	....	....	....	....	....	**14**	**5**	**3**	**8**	**20**	....	....	....
1964-65	**Toronto Maple Leafs**	**NHL**	**65**	**19**	**20**	**39**	**23**	**20**	**43**	**46**	....	....	....	....	....	....	....	....	....	....	**6**	**1**	**1**	**2**	**16**	....	....	....
1965-66	**Toronto Maple Leafs**	**NHL**	**70**	**28**	**28**	**56**	**32**	**27**	**59**	**51**	....	....	....	....	....	....	....	....	....	....	**4**	**1**	**1**	**2**	**12**	....	....	....
1966-67♦	**Toronto Maple Leafs**	**NHL**	**67**	**17**	**28**	**45**	**20**	**27**	**47**	**28**	....	....	....	....	....	....	....	....	....	....	**12**	**1**	***10**	**11**	**12**	....	....	....
1967-68	**Toronto Maple Leafs**	**NHL**	**74**	**20**	**30**	**50**	**23**	**30**	**53**	**40**	**4**	**3**	**3**	**229**	**8.7**	**69**	**14**	**71**	**9**	**–7**	....	....	....	....	....	....	....	....
1968-69	**Toronto Maple Leafs**	**NHL**	**72**	**11**	**23**	**34**	**12**	**20**	**32**	**20**	**3**	**1**	**1**	**179**	**6.1**	**53**	**9**	**77**	**24**	**–9**	**4**	**0**	**0**	**0**	**2**	**0**	**0**	**0**
1969-70	**Toronto Maple Leafs**	**NHL**	**74**	**18**	**19**	**37**	**20**	**18**	**38**	**31**	**3**	**0**	**1**	**227**	**7.9**	**62**	**21**	**84**	**19**	**–24**	....	....	....	....	....	....	....	....
1970-71	**Los Angeles Kings**	**NHL**	**59**	**17**	**26**	**43**	**17**	**22**	**39**	**53**	**6**	**1**	**2**	**170**	**10.0**	**63**	**19**	**83**	**24**	**–15**	....	....	....	....	....	....	....	....
1971-72	**Los Angeles Kings**	**NHL**	**73**	**13**	**24**	**37**	**13**	**21**	**34**	**48**	**2**	**1**	**0**	**170**	**7.6**	**57**	**14**	**99**	**31**	**–25**	....	....	....	....	....	....	....	....
1972-73	**Los Angeles Kings**	**NHL**	DID NOT PLAY – COACHING																									
	NHL Totals		**1079**	**281**	**362**	**643**	**325**	**349**	**674**	**792**	....	....	....	....	....	....	....	....	....		**89**	**25**	**26**	**51**	**126**	....	....	....

Won Jack Adams Award (1975) • Played in NHL All-Star Game (1960, 1962, 1963, 1964, 1968)

Traded to **LA Kings** by **Toronto** for Garry Monahan and Brian Murphy, September 3, 1970.

• PULKKINEN, Dave

David Joel John LW/D – R. 6', 195 lbs. b: Kapuskasing, Ont., 5/18/1949. St. Louis' 8th, 77th overall, in 1969.

Season	Club	League	GP	G	A	Pts	AG	AA	APts	PIM	PP	SH	GW	S	%	TGF	PGF	TGA	PGA	+/–	GP	G	A	Pts	PIM	PP	SH	GW
1968-69	Oshawa Generals	OHA-Jr.	54	17	19	36	....	....	....	50	....	....	....	....	....	....	....	....	....	....	....	....	....	....	....	....	....	....
1969-70	Kansas City Blues	CHL	11	1	2	3	....	....	....	0	....	....	....	....	....	....	....	....	....	....	....	....	....	....	....	....	....	....
	Port Huron Flags	IHL	43	11	16	27	....	....	....	51	....	....	....	....	....	....	....	....	....	....	....	....	....	....	....	....	....	....
1970-71	Port Huron–Toledo	IHL	25	3	12	15	....	....	....	8	....	....	....	....	....	....	....	....	....	....	....	....	....	....	....	....	....	....
	Dayton Gems	IHL	1	0	0	0	....	....	....	0	....	....	....	....	....	....	....	....	....	....	....	....	....	....	....	....	....	....
1971-72	Kansas City Blues	CHL	70	12	46	58	....	....	....	49	....	....	....	....	....	....	....	....	....	....	....	....	....	....	....	....	....	....
1972-73	**New York Islanders**	**NHL**	**2**	**0**	**0**	**0**	**0**	**0**	**0**	**0**	**0**	**0**	**0**	**0**	**0.0**	**0**	**0**	**1**	**0**	**–1**	....	....	....	....	....	....	....	....
	New Haven Nighthawks	AHL	75	25	41	66	....	....	....	55	....	....	....	....	....	....	....	....	....	....	....	....	....	....	....	....	....	....
1973-74	Baltimore Clippers	AHL	60	11	24	35	....	....	....	39	....	....	....	....	....	....	....	....	....	....	2	0	1	1	0	....	....	....
1974-75	Syracuse Eagles	AHL	11	0	3	3	....	....	....	4	....	....	....	....	....	....	....	....	....	....	....	....	....	....	....	....	....	....
	NHL Totals		**2**	**0**	**0**	**0**	**0**	**0**	**0**	**0**	**0**	**0**	**0**	**0**	**0.0**	**0**	**0**	**1**	**0**		....	....	....	....	....	....	....	....

Claimed on waivers by **Toledo** (IHL) from **Port Huron** (IHL), November, 1970. Traded to **Dayton** (IHL) by **Toledo** (IHL) for cash, December, 1970. Traded to **NY Islanders** by **St. Louis** for cash, August, 1972.

• PURINTON, Dale

D – L. 6'2", 190 lbs. b: Fort Wayne, IN, 10/11/1976. NY Rangers' 5th, 117th overall, in 1995.

Season	Club	League	GP	G	A	Pts	AG	AA	APts	PIM	PP	SH	GW	S	%	TGF	PGF	TGA	PGA	+/–	GP	G	A	Pts	PIM	PP	SH	GW
1992-93	Moose Jaw Midget Warriors	SAHA	34	1	16	17	....	....	....	107	....	....	....	....	....	....	....	....	....	....	....	....	....	....	....	....	....	....
	Moose Jaw Warriors	WHL	2	0	0	0	....	....	....	2	....	....	....	....	....	....	....	....	....	....	....	....	....	....	....	....	....	....
1993-94	Vernon Lakers	BCJHL	42	1	6	7	....	....	....	194	....	....	....	....	....	....	....	....	....	....	....	....	....	....	....	....	....	....
1994-95	Tacoma Rockets	WHL	65	0	8	8	....	....	....	291	....	....	....	....	....	....	....	....	....	....	3	0	0	0	13	....	....	....
1995-96	Kelowna Rockets	WHL	22	1	4	5	....	....	....	88	....	....	....	....	....	....	....	....	....	....	....	....	....	....	....	....	....	....
	Lethbridge Hurricanes	WHL	37	3	6	9	....	....	....	144	....	....	....	....	....	....	....	....	....	....	4	1	1	2	25	....	....	....
1996-97	Lethbridge Hurricanes	WHL	51	6	26	32	....	....	....	254	....	....	....	....	....	....	....	....	....	....	18	3	5	8	*88	....	....	....
1997-98	Hartford Wolf Pack	AHL	17	0	0	0	....	....	....	95	....	....	....	....	....	....	....	....	....	....	....	....	....	....	....	....	....	....
	Charlotte Checkers	ECHL	34	3	5	8	....	....	....	186	....	....	....	....	....	....	....	....	....	....	....	....	....	....	....	....	....	....
1998-99	Hartford Wolf Pack	AHL	45	1	3	4	....	....	....	306	....	....	....	....	....	....	....	....	....	....	7	0	2	2	24	....	....	....
99-2000	**New York Rangers**	**NHL**	**1**	**0**	**0**	**0**	**0**	**0**	**0**	**7**	**0**	**0**	**0**	**1**	**0.0**	**0**	**0**	**1**	**0**	**–1**	....	....	....	....	....	....	....	....
	Hartford Wolf Pack	AHL	62	4	4	8	....	....	....	415	....	....	....	....	....	....	....	....	....	....	23	0	3	3	*87	....	....	....
	NHL Totals		**1**	**0**	**0**	**0**	**0**	**0**	**0**	**7**	**0**	**0**	**0**	**1**	**0.0**	**0**	**0**	**1**	**0**		....	....	....	....	....	....	....	....

• PURVES, John

RW – R. 6'1", 201 lbs. b: Toronto, Ont., 2/12/1968. Washington's 6th, 103rd overall, in 1986.

Season	Club	League	GP	G	A	Pts	AG	AA	APts	PIM	PP	SH	GW	S	%	TGF	PGF	TGA	PGA	+/–	GP	G	A	Pts	PIM	PP	SH	GW
1983-84	North York Rangers	MTHL	40	24	35	59	....	....	....	58	....	....	....	....	....	....	....	....	....	....	....	....	....	....	....	....	....	....
1984-85	Belleville Bulls	OHL	55	15	14	29	....	....	....	39	....	....	....	....	....	....	....	....	....	....	....	....	....	....	....	....	....	....
1985-86	Belleville Bulls	OHL	16	3	9	12	....	....	....	6	....	....	....	....	....	....	....	....	....	....	....	....	....	....	....	....	....	....
	Hamilton Steelhawks	OHL	36	13	28	41	....	....	....	36	....	....	....	....	....	....	....	....	....	....	9	2	0	2	12	....	....	....
1986-87	Hamilton Steelhawks	OHL	28	12	11	23	....	....	....	37	....	....	....	....	....	....	....	....	....	....	....	....	....	....	....	....	....	....
1987-88	Hamilton Steelhawks	OHL	64	39	44	83	....	....	....	65	....	....	....	....	....	....	....	....	....	....	14	7	18	25	4	....	....	....
1988-89	Niagara Falls Thunder	OHL	5	5	11	16	....	....	....	2	....	....	....	....	....	....	....	....	....	....	....	....	....	....	....	....	....	....
	North Bay Centennials	OHL	42	34	52	86	....	....	....	38	....	....	....	....	....	....	....	....	....	....	12	14	12	26	16	....	....	....
1989-90	Baltimore Skipjacks	AHL	75	29	35	64	....	....	....	12	....	....	....	....	....	....	....	....	....	....	9	5	7	12	4	....	....	....
1990-91	**Washington Capitals**	**NHL**	**7**	**1**	**0**	**1**	**1**	**0**	**1**	**0**	**0**	**0**	**1**	**8**	**12.5**	**3**	**0**	**6**	**0**	**–3**	....	....	....	....	....	....	....	....
	Baltimore Skipjacks	AHL	53	22	29	51	....	....	....	27	....	....	....	....	....	....	....	....	....	....	6	2	3	5	0	....	....	....
1991-92	Baltimore Skipjacks	AHL	78	43	46	89	....	....	....	47	....	....	....	....	....	....	....	....	....	....	....	....	....	....	....	....	....	....
1992-93	ESV Kaufbeuren	Germany	43	15	17	32	....	....	....	34	....	....	....	....	....	....	....	....	....	....	....	....	....	....	....	....	....	....
1993-94	Fort Wayne Komets	IHL	69	38	48	86	....	....	....	29	....	....	....	....	....	....	....	....	....	....	18	10	14	24	12	....	....	....
1994-95	Fort Wayne Komets	IHL	60	30	33	63	....	....	....	16	....	....	....	....	....	....	....	....	....	....	4	4	1	5	6	....	....	....
1995-96	San Francisco Spiders	IHL	75	56	49	105	....	....	....	32	....	....	....	....	....	....	....	....	....	....	4	0	3	3	0	....	....	....
1996-97	Kansas City Blades	IHL	66	25	47	72	....	....	....	17	....	....	....	....	....	....	....	....	....	....	3	0	0	0	0	....	....	....
1997-98	Kansas City Blades	IHL	21	6	10	16	....	....	....	9	....	....	....	....	....	....	....	....	....	....	....	....	....	....	....	....	....	....
	San Antonio Dragons	IHL	59	22	21	43	....	....	....	12	....	....	....	....	....	....	....	....	....	....	....	....	....	....	....	....	....	....
1998-99	Utah Grizzlies	IHL	80	24	39	63	....	....	....	24	....	....	....	....	....	....	....	....	....	....	....	....	....	....	....	....	....	....
99-2000	Utah Grizzlies	IHL	78	36	27	63	....	....	....	40	....	....	....	....	....	....	....	....	....	....	5	1	0	1	2	....	....	....
	NHL Totals		**7**	**1**	**0**	**1**	**1**	**0**	**1**	**0**	**0**	**0**	**1**	**8**	**12.5**	**3**	**0**	**6**	**0**		....	....	....	....	....	....	....	....

OHL Second All-Star Team (1989) • IHL Second All-Star Team (1996)

• PUSHOR, Jamie

James M. D – R. 6'3", 224 lbs. b: Lethbridge, Alta., 2/11/1973. Detroit's 2nd, 32nd overall, in 1991.

Season	Club	League	GP	G	A	Pts	AG	AA	APts	PIM	PP	SH	GW	S	%	TGF	PGF	TGA	PGA	+/–	GP	G	A	Pts	PIM	PP	SH	GW
1988-89	Lethbridge Y's Men	AAHA	37	1	8	9	....	....	....	20	....	....	....	....	....	....	....	....	....	....	....	....	....	....	....	....	....	....
	Lethbridge Hurricanes	WHL	2	0	0	0	....	....	....	0	....	....	....	....	....	....	....	....	....	....	....	....	....	....	....	....	....	....
1989-90	Lethbridge Y's Men	AAHA	35	6	27	33	....	....	....	92	....	....	....	....	....	....	....	....	....	....	....	....	....	....	....	....	....	....
	Lethbridge Hurricanes	WHL	10	0	2	2	....	....	....	2	....	....	....	....	....	....	....	....	....	....	16	0	0	0	63	....	....	....
1990-91	Lethbridge Hurricanes	WHL	71	1	13	14	....	....	....	202	....	....	....	....	....	....	....	....	....	....	....	....	....	....	....	....	....	....
1991-92	Lethbridge Hurricanes	WHL	49	2	15	17	....	....	....	232	....	....	....	....	....	....	....	....	....	....	5	0	0	0	33	....	....	....
1992-93	Lethbridge Hurricanes	WHL	72	6	22	28	....	....	....	200	....	....	....	....	....	....	....	....	....	....	4	0	1	1	9	....	....	....
1993-94	Adirondack Red Wings	AHL	73	1	17	18	....	....	....	124	....	....	....	....	....	....	....	....	....	....	12	0	0	0	22	....	....	....
1994-95	Adirondack Red Wings	AHL	58	2	11	13	....	....	....	129	....	....	....	....	....	....	....	....	....	....	4	0	1	1	0	....	....	....
1995-96	**Detroit Red Wings**	**NHL**	**5**	**0**	**1**	**1**	**0**	**1**	**1**	**17**	**0**	**0**	**0**	**6**	**0.0**	**4**	**0**	**4**	**2**	**2**	....	....	....	....	....	....	....	....
	Adirondack Red Wings	AHL	65	2	16	18	....	....	....	126	....	....	....	....	....	....	....	....	....	....	3	0	0	0	5	....	....	....
1996-97♦	**Detroit Red Wings**	**NHL**	**75**	**4**	**7**	**11**	**4**	**6**	**10**	**129**	**0**	**0**	**0**	**63**	**6.3**	**46**	**1**	**56**	**12**	**1**	**5**	**0**	**1**	**1**	**5**	**0**	**0**	**0**

Season	Club	League	GP	G	A	Pts	AG	AA	APts	PIM	PP	SH	GW	S	%	TGF	PGF	TGA	PGA	+/–	GP	G	A	Pts	PIM	PP	SH	GW
			REGULAR SEASON																		**PLAYOFFS**							
1997-98	**Detroit Red Wings**	**NHL**	**54**	**2**	**5**	**7**	**2**	**5**	**7**	**71**	**0**	**0**	**0**	**43**	**4.7**	**33**	**1**	**44**	**14**	**2**								
	Mighty Ducks of Anaheim	**NHL**	**10**	**0**	**2**	**2**	**0**	**2**	**2**	**10**	**0**	**0**	**0**	**8**	**0.0**	**8**	**0**	**12**	**5**	**1**	....	....	....	....	....	....	....	....
1998-99	**Mighty Ducks of Anaheim**	**NHL**	**70**	**1**	**2**	**3**	**1**	**2**	**3**	**112**	**0**	**0**	**0**	**75**	**1.3**	**26**	**1**	**69**	**24**	**–20**	**4**	**0**	**0**	**0**	**6**	**0**	**0**	**0**
99-2000	**Dallas Stars**	**NHL**	**62**	**0**	**8**	**8**	**0**	**7**	**7**	**53**	**0**	**0**	**0**	**27**	**0.0**	**21**	**0**	**21**	**0**	**0**	**5**	**0**	**0**	**0**	**5**	**0**	**0**	**0**
	NHL Totals		**276**	**7**	**25**	**32**	**7**	**23**	**30**	**392**	**0**	**0**	**0**	**222**	**3.2**	**138**	**3**	**206**	**57**		**14**	**0**	**1**	**1**	**16**	**0**	**0**	**0**

Traded to **Anaheim** by **Detroit** with Detroit's 4th round choice (Viktor Wallin) in 1998 Entry Draft for Dmitri Mironov, March 24, 1998. Claimed by **Atlanta** from **Anaheim** in Expansion Draft, June 25, 1999. Traded to **Dallas** by **Atlanta** for Jason Botterill, July 15, 1999. Selected by **Columbus** from **Dallas** in Expansion Draft, June 23, 2000.

• PYATT, Nelson

Frederick Nelson C – L. 6', 175 lbs. b: Port Arthur, Ont., 9/9/1953. Detroit's 2nd, 39th overall, in 1973.

Season	Club	League	GP	G	A	Pts	AG	AA	APts	PIM	PP	SH	GW	S	%	TGF	PGF	TGA	PGA	+/–	GP	G	A	Pts	PIM	PP	SH	GW
1970-71	Thunder Bay Marrs	TBJHL	STATISTICS NOT AVAILABLE																									
	Thunder Bay Marrs	Cen-Cup	5	3	4	7	....	....	....	7	....	....	....	....	....	....	....	....	....	....	....	....	....	....	....	....	....	....
1971-72	Oshawa Generals	OMJHL	54	17	29	46	....	....	....	27	....	....	....	....	....	....	....	....	....	....	12	3	3	6	10	....	....	....
1972-73	Oshawa Generals	OMJHL	26	13	19	32	....	....	....	7	....	....	....	....	....	....	....	....	....	....	....	....	....	....	....	....	....	....
1973-74	**Detroit Red Wings**	**NHL**	**5**	**0**	**0**	**0**	**0**	**0**	**0**	**0**	**0**	**0**	**0**	**1**	**0.0**	**0**	**0**	**2**	**0**	**–2**	....	....	....	....	....	....	....	....
	London Lions	Britain	61	35	28	63	....	....	....	4	....	....	....	....	....	....	....	....	....	....	....	....	....	....	....	....	....	....
1974-75	**Detroit Red Wings**	**NHL**	**9**	**0**	**0**	**0**	**0**	**0**	**0**	**2**	**0**	**0**	**0**	**6**	**0.0**	**1**	**0**	**3**	**0**	**–2**	....	....	....	....	....	....	....	....
	Virginia Wings	AHL	14	3	4	7	....	....	....	12	....	....	....	....	....	....	....	....	....	....	....	....	....	....	....	....	....	....
	Washington Capitals	**NHL**	**16**	**6**	**4**	**10**	**5**	**3**	**8**	**21**	**0**	**0**	**1**	**33**	**18.2**	**11**	**4**	**28**	**7**	**–14**	....	....	....	....	....	....	....	....
1975-76	**Washington Capitals**	**NHL**	**77**	**26**	**23**	**49**	**23**	**17**	**40**	**14**	**5**	**0**	**0**	**151**	**17.2**	**70**	**16**	**120**	**10**	**–56**	....	....	....	....	....	....	....	....
1976-77	**Colorado Rockies**	**NHL**	**77**	**23**	**22**	**45**	**21**	**17**	**38**	**20**	**2**	**0**	**4**	**158**	**14.6**	**60**	**7**	**72**	**2**	**–17**	....	....	....	....	....	....	....	....
1977-78	**Colorado Rockies**	**NHL**	**71**	**9**	**12**	**21**	**8**	**9**	**17**	**8**	**1**	**0**	**0**	**87**	**10.3**	**31**	**4**	**50**	**0**	**–23**	....	....	....	....	....	....	....	....
1978-79	**Colorado Rockies**	**NHL**	**28**	**2**	**2**	**4**	**2**	**1**	**3**	**2**	**0**	**0**	**0**	**34**	**5.9**	**7**	**0**	**24**	**0**	**–17**	....	....	....	....	....	....	....	....
	Philadelphia Firebirds	AHL	7	3	1	4	....	....	....	0	....	....	....	....	....	....	....	....	....	....	....	....	....	....	....	....	....	....
1979-80	**Colorado Rockies**	**NHL**	**13**	**5**	**0**	**5**	**4**	**0**	**4**	**2**	**0**	**0**	**0**	**20**	**25.0**	**7**	**0**	**13**	**1**	**–5**	....	....	....	....	....	....	....	....
	Fort Worth Texans	CHL	45	20	17	37	....	....	....	11	....	....	....	....	....	....	....	....	....	....	15	5	1	6	2	....	....	....
1980-81	VER Selb	Germany-2	STATISTICS NOT AVAILABLE																									
1981-82	VER Selb	Germany-2	46	80	30	110	....	....	....	32	....	....	....	....	....	....	....	....	....	....	....	....	....	....	....	....	....	....
1982-83	WEV Wein	Austria	24	28	24	52	....	....	....	25	....	....	....	....	....	....	....	....	....	....	....	....	....	....	....	....	....	....
	NHL Totals		**296**	**71**	**63**	**134**	**63**	**47**	**110**	**69**	**8**	**0**	**5**	**490**	**14.5**	**187**	**31**	**312**	**20**		....	....	....	....	....	....	....	....

Traded to **Washington** by **Detroit** for Washington's 3rd round choice (Allen Cameron) in 1975 Amateur Draft, February 28, 1975. Signed as a free agent by **Colorado**, September 1, 1976.

• QUENNEVILLE, Joel

Joel Norman "Herbie" D – L. 6'1", 200 lbs. b: Windsor, Ont., 9/15/1958. Toronto's 1st, 21st overall, in 1978.

Season	Club	League	GP	G	A	Pts	AG	AA	APts	PIM	PP	SH	GW	S	%	TGF	PGF	TGA	PGA	+/–	GP	G	A	Pts	PIM	PP	SH	GW
1974-75	Windsor Blues	OHA-B	42	11	10	21	....	....	....	15	....	....	....	....	....	....	....	....	....	....	....	....	....	....	....	....	....	....
1975-76	Windsor Spitfires	OMJHL	66	15	33	48	....	....	....	61	....	....	....	....	....	....	....	....	....	....	....	....	....	....	....	....	....	....
1976-77	Windsor Spitfires	OMJHL	65	19	59	78	....	....	....	169	....	....	....	....	....	....	....	....	....	....	9	6	5	11	112	....	....	....
1977-78	Windsor Spitfires	OMJHL	66	27	76	103	....	....	....	114	....	....	....	....	....	....	....	....	....	....	6	2	3	5	17	....	....	....
1978-79	**Toronto Maple Leafs**	**NHL**	**61**	**2**	**9**	**11**	**2**	**7**	**9**	**60**	**0**	**0**	**1**	**56**	**3.6**	**41**	**2**	**42**	**10**	**7**	**6**	**0**	**1**	**1**	**4**	**0**	**0**	**0**
	New Brunswick Hawks	AHL	16	1	10	11	....	....	....	10	....	....	....	....	....	....	....	....	....	....	....	....	....	....	....	....	....	....
1979-80	**Toronto Maple Leafs**	**NHL**	**32**	**1**	**4**	**5**	**1**	**3**	**4**	**24**	**1**	**0**	**0**	**56**	**1.8**	**25**	**2**	**33**	**8**	**–2**	....	....	....	....	....	....	....	....
	Colorado Rockies	**NHL**	**35**	**5**	**7**	**12**	**4**	**5**	**9**	**26**	**1**	**0**	**0**	**62**	**8.1**	**32**	**8**	**46**	**1**	**–21**	....	....	....	....	....	....	....	....
1980-81	**Colorado Rockies**	**NHL**	**71**	**10**	**24**	**34**	**8**	**16**	**24**	**86**	**3**	**0**	**1**	**107**	**9.3**	**91**	**28**	**106**	**19**	**–24**	....	....	....	....	....	....	....	....
1981-82	**Colorado Rockies**	**NHL**	**64**	**5**	**10**	**15**	**4**	**7**	**11**	**55**	**0**	**0**	**0**	**67**	**7.5**	**49**	**4**	**93**	**19**	**–29**	....	....	....	....	....	....	....	....
1982-83	**New Jersey Devils**	**NHL**	**74**	**5**	**12**	**17**	**4**	**8**	**12**	**46**	**0**	**1**	**0**	**85**	**5.9**	**66**	**3**	**106**	**30**	**–13**	....	....	....	....	....	....	....	....
1983-84	**Hartford Whalers**	**NHL**	**80**	**5**	**8**	**13**	**4**	**5**	**9**	**95**	**0**	**2**	**0**	**67**	**7.5**	**77**	**1**	**139**	**52**	**–11**	....	....	....	....	....	....	....	....
1984-85	**Hartford Whalers**	**NHL**	**79**	**6**	**16**	**22**	**5**	**11**	**16**	**96**	**0**	**0**	**2**	**75**	**8.0**	**80**	**2**	**135**	**42**	**–15**	....	....	....	....	....	....	....	....
1985-86	**Hartford Whalers**	**NHL**	**71**	**5**	**20**	**25**	**4**	**13**	**17**	**83**	**1**	**0**	**1**	**49**	**10.2**	**84**	**1**	**100**	**38**	**21**	**10**	**0**	**2**	**2**	**12**	**0**	**0**	**0**
1986-87	**Hartford Whalers**	**NHL**	**37**	**3**	**7**	**10**	**3**	**5**	**8**	**24**	**0**	**1**	**1**	**19**	**15.8**	**31**	**0**	**44**	**20**	**7**	**6**	**0**	**0**	**0**	**0**	**0**	**0**	**0**
1987-88	**Hartford Whalers**	**NHL**	**77**	**1**	**8**	**9**	**1**	**6**	**7**	**44**	**0**	**0**	**0**	**42**	**2.4**	**44**	**0**	**95**	**38**	**–13**	**6**	**0**	**2**	**2**	**2**	**0**	**0**	**0**
1988-89	**Hartford Whalers**	**NHL**	**69**	**4**	**7**	**11**	**3**	**5**	**8**	**32**	**0**	**0**	**0**	**45**	**8.9**	**53**	**1**	**77**	**28**	**3**	**4**	**0**	**3**	**3**	**4**	**0**	**0**	**0**
1989-90	**Hartford Whalers**	**NHL**	**44**	**1**	**4**	**5**	**1**	**3**	**4**	**34**	**0**	**0**	**0**	**17**	**5.9**	**35**	**0**	**37**	**11**	**9**	....	....	....	....	....	....	....	....
1990-91	**Washington Capitals**	**NHL**	**9**	**1**	**0**	**1**	**1**	**0**	**1**	**0**	**0**	**0**	**0**	**3**	**33.3**	**1**	**0**	**9**	**0**	**–8**	....	....	....	....	....	....	....	....
	Baltimore Skipjacks	AHL	59	6	13	19	....	....	....	58	....	....	....	....	....	....	....	....	....	....	6	1	1	2	6	....	....	....
1991-92	St. John's Maple Leafs	AHL	73	7	23	30	....	....	....	58	....	....	....	....	....	....	....	....	....	....	16	0	1	1	10	....	....	....
1992-1993	St. John's Maple Leafs	AHL	DID NOT PLAY – ASSISTANT COACH																									
1993-1994	Springfield Indians	AHL	DID NOT PLAY – COACHING																									
1994-1997	**Colorado Avalanche**	**NHL**	DID NOT PLAY – ASSISTANT COACH																									
1997-2000	**St. Louis Blues**	**NHL**	DID NOT PLAY – COACHING																									
	NHL Totals		**803**	**54**	**136**	**190**	**45**	**94**	**139**	**705**	**6**	**4**	**6**	**750**	**7.2**	**709**	**52**	**1062**	**316**		**32**	**0**	**8**	**8**	**22**	**0**	**0**	**0**

OMJHL Second All-Star Team (1978) • AHL Second All-Star Team (1992) • Won Jack Adams Award (2000)

Traded to **Colorado** by **Toronto** with Lanny McDonald for Pat Hickey and Wilf Paiement, December 29, 1979. Transferred to **New Jersey** after **Colorado** franchise relocated, June 30, 1982. Traded to **Calgary** by **New Jersey** with Steve Tambellini for Phil Russell and Mel Bridgman, June 20, 1983. Traded to **Hartford** by **Calgary** with Richie Dunn for Mickey Volcan, July 5, 1983. • Missed majority of the 1986-87 season recovering from shoulder injury suffered in game vs. Boston, December 18, 1986. Traded to **Washington** by **Hartford** for cash, October 3, 1990. Signed as a free agent by **Toronto**, July 30, 1991.

• QUINN, Dan

Daniel Peter C – L. 5'11", 182 lbs. b: Ottawa, Ont., 6/1/1965. Calgary's 1st, 13th overall, in 1983.

Season	Club	League	GP	G	A	Pts	AG	AA	APts	PIM	PP	SH	GW	S	%	TGF	PGF	TGA	PGA	+/–	GP	G	A	Pts	PIM	PP	SH	GW
1980-81	London Diamonds	OHA-B	42	28	38	66	....	....	....	78	....	....	....	....	....	....	....	....	....	....	....	....	....	....	....	....	....	....
	Rockland Remparts	QJHL	2	0	0	0	....	....	....	0	....	....	....	....	....	....	....	....	....	....	....	....	....	....	....	....	....	....
1981-82	Belleville Bulls	OHL	67	19	32	51	....	....	....	41	....	....	....	....	....	....	....	....	....	....	....	....	....	....	....	....	....	....
1982-83	Belleville Bulls	OHL	70	59	88	147	....	....	....	27	....	....	....	....	....	....	....	....	....	....	4	2	6	8	2	....	....	....
1983-84	Belleville Bulls	OHL	24	23	36	59	....	....	....	12	....	....	....	....	....	....	....	....	....	....	....	....	....	....	....	....	....	....
	Calgary Flames	**NHL**	**54**	**19**	**33**	**52**	**15**	**22**	**37**	**20**	**11**	**0**	**1**	**103**	**18.4**	**68**	**32**	**48**	**9**	**–3**	**8**	**3**	**5**	**8**	**4**	**1**	**0**	**0**
1984-85	**Calgary Flames**	**NHL**	**74**	**20**	**38**	**58**	**16**	**26**	**42**	**22**	**7**	**0**	**3**	**143**	**14.0**	**85**	**33**	**54**	**11**	**9**	**3**	**0**	**0**	**0**	**0**	**0**	**0**	**0**
1985-86	**Calgary Flames**	**NHL**	**78**	**30**	**42**	**72**	**24**	**28**	**52**	**44**	**17**	**3**	**3**	**191**	**15.7**	**96**	**44**	**102**	**38**	**–12**	**18**	**8**	**7**	**15**	**10**	**5**	**1**	**2**
1986-87	**Calgary Flames**	**NHL**	**16**	**3**	**6**	**9**	**3**	**4**	**7**	**14**	**1**	**0**	**0**	**27**	**11.1**	**12**	**7**	**11**	**0**	**–6**	....	....	....	....	....	....	....	....
	Pittsburgh Penguins	**NHL**	**64**	**28**	**43**	**71**	**24**	**31**	**55**	**40**	**10**	**3**	**4**	**157**	**17.8**	**92**	**30**	**76**	**28**	**14**	....	....	....	....	....	....	....	....
	Canada	WEC-A	10	2	2	4	....	....	....	12	....	....	....	....	....	....	....	....	....	....	....	....	....	....	....	....	....	....
1987-88	**Pittsburgh Penguins**	**NHL**	**70**	**40**	**39**	**79**	**34**	**28**	**62**	**50**	**21**	**1**	**4**	**235**	**17.0**	**119**	**62**	**111**	**46**	**–8**	....	....	....	....	....	....	....	....
1988-89	**Pittsburgh Penguins**	**NHL**	**79**	**34**	**60**	**94**	**29**	**43**	**72**	**102**	**16**	**0**	**4**	**200**	**17.0**	**132**	**74**	**107**	**12**	**–37**	**11**	**6**	**3**	**9**	**10**	**4**	**0**	**1**
1989-90	**Pittsburgh Penguins**	**NHL**	**41**	**9**	**20**	**29**	**8**	**14**	**22**	**22**	**5**	**0**	**2**	**86**	**10.5**	**44**	**22**	**50**	**13**	**–15**	....	....	....	....	....	....	....	....
	Vancouver Canucks	**NHL**	**37**	**16**	**18**	**34**	**14**	**13**	**27**	**27**	**6**	**0**	**3**	**95**	**16.8**	**43**	**18**	**36**	**9**	**–2**	....	....	....	....	....	....	....	....
1990-91	**Vancouver Canucks**	**NHL**	**64**	**18**	**31**	**49**	**16**	**24**	**40**	**46**	**8**	**0**	**3**	**157**	**11.5**	**71**	**35**	**77**	**13**	**–28**	....	....	....	....	....	....	....	....
	St. Louis Blues	**NHL**	**14**	**4**	**7**	**11**	**4**	**5**	**9**	**20**	**4**	**0**	**2**	**26**	**15.4**	**13**	**8**	**10**	**0**	**–5**	**13**	**4**	**7**	**11**	**32**	**2**	**0**	**1**
1991-92	**Philadelphia Flyers**	**NHL**	**67**	**11**	**26**	**37**	**10**	**20**	**30**	**26**	**6**	**0**	**1**	**101**	**10.9**	**55**	**26**	**42**	**0**	**–13**	....	....	....	....	....	....	....	....
1992-93	**Minnesota North Stars**	**NHL**	**11**	**0**	**4**	**4**	**0**	**3**	**3**	**6**	**0**	**0**	**0**	**20**	**0.0**	**6**	**4**	**7**	**1**	**–4**	....	....	....	....	....	....	....	....
1993-94	SC Bern	Switz.	25	13	18	31	....	....	....	56	....	....	....	....	....	....	....	....	....	....	....	....	....	....	....	....	....	....
	Ottawa Senators	**NHL**	**13**	**7**	**0**	**7**	**6**	**0**	**6**	**6**	**2**	**0**	**3**	**31**	**22.6**	**14**	**4**	**17**	**7**	**0**	....	....	....	....	....	....	....	....
1994-95	EV Zug	Switz.	7	7	6	13	....	....	....	26	....	....	....	....	....	....	....	....	....	....	....	....	....	....	....	....	....	....
	Los Angeles Kings	**NHL**	**44**	**14**	**17**	**31**	**25**	**25**	**50**	**32**	**2**	**0**	**4**	**78**	**17.9**	**41**	**9**	**38**	**3**	**–3**	....	....	....	....	....	....	....	....
1995-96	**Ottawa Senators**	**NHL**	**28**	**6**	**18**	**24**	**6**	**15**	**21**	**24**	**4**	**0**	**0**	**62**	**9.7**	**33**	**12**	**32**	**3**	**–8**	....	....	....	....	....	....	....	....
	Detroit Vipers	IHL	4	0	5	5	....	....	....	2	....	....	....	....	....	....	....	....	....	....	....	....	....	....	....	....	....	....
	Philadelphia Flyers	**NHL**	**35**	**7**	**14**	**21**	**7**	**11**	**18**	**22**	**3**	**0**	**0**	**47**	**14.9**	**34**	**16**	**16**	**0**	**2**	**12**	**1**	**4**	**5**	**6**	**1**	**0**	**0**
1996-97	**Pittsburgh Penguins**	**NHL**	**16**	**0**	**3**	**3**	**0**	**3**	**3**	**10**	**0**	**0**	**0**	**16**	**0.0**	**8**	**2**	**15**	**3**	**–6**	....	....	....	....	....	....	....	....
	NHL Totals		**805**	**266**	**419**	**685**	**241**	**315**	**556**	**533**	**123**	**7**	**37**	**1775**	**15.0**	**966**	**438**	**849**	**196**		**65**	**22**	**26**	**48**	**62**	**13**	**1**	**4**

Traded to **Pittsburgh** by **Calgary** for Mike Bullard, November 12, 1986. Traded to **Vancouver** by **Pittsburgh** with Dave Capuano and Andrew McBain for Rod Buskas, Barry Pederson and Tony Tanti, January 8, 1990. Traded to **St. Louis** by **Vancouver** with Garth Butcher for Geoff Courtnall, Robert Dirk, Sergio Momesso, Cliff Ronning and St. Louis' 5th round choice (Brian Loney) in 1992 Entry Draft, March 5, 1991. Traded to **Philadelphia** by **St. Louis** with Rod Brind'Amour for Ron Sutter and Murray Baron, September 22, 1991. Signed as a free agent by **Minnesota**, October 4, 1992. Signed as a free agent by **Ottawa**, March 15, 1994. Signed as a free agent by **LA Kings**, September 3, 1994. Signed as a free agent by **Ottawa**, August 1, 1995. Traded to **Philadelphia** by **Ottawa** for cash, January 23, 1996. Signed as a free agent by **Pittsburgh**, July 17, 1996.

			REGULAR SEASON																		PLAYOFFS							
Season	Club	League	GP	G	A	Pts	AG	AA	APts	PIM	PP	SH	GW	S	%	TGF	PGF	TGA	PGA	+/–	GP	G	A	Pts	PIM	PP	SH	GW

• QUINN, Pat John Brian Patrick D – L. 6'3", 205 lbs. b: Hamilton, Ont., 1/29/1943.

Season	Club	League	GP	G	A	Pts	AG	AA	APts	PIM	PP	SH	GW	S	%	TGF	PGF	TGA	PGA	+/–	GP	G	A	Pts	PIM	PP	SH	GW
1958-59	Hamilton Tiger Cubs	OHA-Jr.	20	0	1	1	....	....	....	34	....	....	....	....	....	....	....	....	....	....	....	....	....	....	....	....	....	....
1959-60	Hamilton Tiger Cubs	OHA-Jr.	27	0	1	1	....	....	....	58	....	....	....	....	....	....	....	....	....	....	....	....	....	....	....	....	....	....
1960-61	Hamilton Kilty B's	OHA-B	STATISTICS NOT AVAILABLE																									
1961-62	Hamilton Kilty B's	OHA-B	STATISTICS NOT AVAILABLE																									
1962-63	Edmonton Oil Kings	CAHL	STATISTICS NOT AVAILABLE																									
	Edmonton Oil Kings	Mem-Cup	19	2	10	12	....	....	....	49	....	....	....	....	....	....	....	....	....	....								
1963-64	Knoxville Knights	EHL	72	6	31	37	....	....	....	217	....	....	....	....	....	....	....	....	....	....	8	1	3	4	34	....	....	....
1964-65	Tulsa Oilers	CPHL	70	3	32	35	....	....	....	202	....	....	....	....	....	....	....	....	....	....	3	0	0	0	9	....	....	....
1965-66	Memphis Wings	CPHL	67	2	16	18	....	....	....	135	....	....	....	....	....	....	....	....	....	....	....	....	....	....	....	....	....	....
1966-67	Houston Apollos	CPHL	15	0	3	3	....	....	....	66	....	....	....	....	....	....	....	....	....	....	....	....	....	....	....	....	....	....
	Seattle Totems	WHL	35	1	3	4	....	....	....	49	....	....	....	....	....	....	....	....	....	....	5	0	0	0	2	....	....	....
1967-68	Tulsa Oilers	CPHL	51	3	15	18	....	....	....	178	....	....	....	....	....	....	....	....	....	....	11	1	4	5	19	....	....	....
1968-69	**Toronto Maple Leafs**	**NHL**	**40**	**2**	**7**	**9**	**2**	**6**	**8**	**95**	**0**	**0**	**1**	**42**	**4.8**	**39**	**1**	**33**	**5**	**10**	**4**	**0**	**0**	**0**	**13**	**0**	**0**	**0**
	Tulsa Oilers	CHL	17	0	6	6	....	....	....	25	....	....	....	....	....	....	....	....	....	....	....	....	....	....	....	....	....	....
1969-70	**Toronto Maple Leafs**	**NHL**	**59**	**0**	**5**	**5**	**0**	**5**	**5**	**88**	**0**	**0**	**0**	**47**	**0.0**	**35**	**0**	**67**	**18**	**–14**	....	....	....	....	....	....	....	....
	Tulsa Oilers	CHL	2	0	1	1	....	....	....	6	....	....	....	....	....	....	....	....	....	....	....	....	....	....	....	....	....	....
1970-71	**Vancouver Canucks**	**NHL**	**76**	**2**	**11**	**13**	**2**	**9**	**11**	**149**	**0**	**0**	**0**	**76**	**2.6**	**69**	**0**	**103**	**36**	**2**	....	....	....	....	....	....	....	....
1971-72	**Vancouver Canucks**	**NHL**	**57**	**2**	**3**	**5**	**2**	**3**	**5**	**63**	**0**	**0**	**0**	**37**	**5.4**	**32**	**1**	**71**	**12**	**–28**	....	....	....	....	....	....	....	....
1972-73	**Atlanta Flames**	**NHL**	**78**	**2**	**18**	**20**	**2**	**14**	**16**	**113**	**0**	**1**	**1**	**88**	**2.3**	**67**	**4**	**82**	**21**	**2**	....	....	....	....	....	....	....	....
1973-74	**Atlanta Flames**	**NHL**	**77**	**5**	**27**	**32**	**5**	**22**	**27**	**94**	**0**	**0**	**1**	**93**	**5.4**	**86**	**1**	**92**	**22**	**15**	**4**	**0**	**0**	**0**	**6**	**0**	**0**	**0**
1974-75	**Atlanta Flames**	**NHL**	**80**	**2**	**19**	**21**	**2**	**14**	**16**	**156**	**0**	**0**	**0**	**68**	**2.9**	**76**	**1**	**94**	**31**	**12**	....	....	....	....	....	....	....	....
1975-76	**Atlanta Flames**	**NHL**	**80**	**2**	**11**	**13**	**2**	**8**	**10**	**134**	**0**	**1**	**0**	**58**	**3.4**	**70**	**1**	**77**	**13**	**5**	**2**	**0**	**1**	**1**	**2**	**0**	**0**	**0**
1976-77	**Atlanta Flames**	**NHL**	**59**	**1**	**12**	**13**	**1**	**9**	**10**	**58**	**0**	**0**	**0**	**29**	**3.4**	**47**	**0**	**66**	**12**	**–7**	**1**	**0**	**0**	**0**	**0**	**0**	**0**	**0**
	NHL Totals		**606**	**18**	**113**	**131**	**18**	**90**	**108**	**950**	**0**	**2**	**3**	**538**	**3.3**	**521**	**9**	**685**	**170**		**11**	**0**	**1**	**1**	**21**	**0**	**0**	**0**

Won Jack Adams Award (1980)

Claimed by **Montreal** from **Detroit** in Intra-League Draft, June 15, 1966. Traded to **St. Louis** by **Montreal** with Ron Attwell for cash, June 14, 1967. Traded to **Toronto** by **St. Louis** for cash, March 25, 1968. Claimed by **Vancouver** from **Toronto** in Expansion Draft, June 10, 1970. Claimed by **Atlanta** from **Vancouver** in Expansion Draft, June 6, 1972.

• QUINNEY, Ken RW – R. 5'10", 186 lbs. b: New Westminster, B.C., 5/23/1965. Quebec's 9th, 203rd overall, in 1984.

Season	Club	League	GP	G	A	Pts	AG	AA	APts	PIM	PP	SH	GW	S	%	TGF	PGF	TGA	PGA	+/–	GP	G	A	Pts	PIM	PP	SH	GW
1981-82	Calgary Wranglers	WHL	63	11	17	28	....	....	....	55	....	....	....	....	....	....	....	....	....	....	2	0	0	0	15	....	....	....
1982-83	Calgary Wranglers	WHL	71	26	25	51	....	....	....	71	....	....	....	....	....	....	....	....	....	....	16	6	1	7	46	....	....	....
1983-84	Calgary Wranglers	WHL	71	64	54	118	....	....	....	38	....	....	....	....	....	....	....	....	....	....	4	5	2	7	0	....	....	....
1984-85	Calgary Wranglers	WHL	56	47	67	114	....	....	....	65	....	....	....	....	....	....	....	....	....	....	7	6	4	10	15	....	....	....
1985-86	Fredericton Express	AHL	61	11	26	37	....	....	....	34	....	....	....	....	....	....	....	....	....	....	6	2	2	4	9	....	....	....
1986-87	**Quebec Nordiques**	**NHL**	**25**	**2**	**7**	**9**	**2**	**5**	**7**	**16**	**1**	**0**	**0**	**22**	**9.1**	**13**	**2**	**11**	**2**	**2**	....	....	....	....	....	....	....	....
	Fredericton Express	AHL	48	14	27	41	....	....	....	20	....	....	....	....	....	....	....	....	....	....	....	....	....	....	....	....	....	....
1987-88	**Quebec Nordiques**	**NHL**	**15**	**2**	**2**	**4**	**2**	**1**	**3**	**5**	**1**	**0**	**0**	**20**	**10.0**	**6**	**2**	**8**	**1**	**–3**	....	....	....	....	....	....	....	....
	Fredericton Express	AHL	58	37	39	76	....	....	....	39	....	....	....	....	....	....	....	....	....	....	13	3	5	8	35	....	....	....
1988-89	Halifax Citadels	AHL	72	41	49	90	....	....	....	65	....	....	....	....	....	....	....	....	....	....	4	3	0	3	0	....	....	....
1989-90	Halifax Citadels	AHL	44	9	16	25	....	....	....	63	....	....	....	....	....	....	....	....	....	....	2	0	0	0	2	....	....	....
1990-91	**Quebec Nordiques**	**NHL**	**19**	**3**	**4**	**7**	**3**	**3**	**6**	**2**	**1**	**0**	**0**	**19**	**15.8**	**17**	**4**	**16**	**1**	**–2**	....	....	....	....	....	....	....	....
	Halifax Citadels	AHL	44	20	20	40	....	....	....	76	....	....	....	....	....	....	....	....	....	....	....	....	....	....	....	....	....	....
1991-92	Adirondack Red Wings	AHL	63	31	29	60	....	....	....	33	....	....	....	....	....	....	....	....	....	....	19	7	12	19	9	....	....	....
1992-93	Adirondack Red Wings	AHL	63	32	34	66	....	....	....	15	....	....	....	....	....	....	....	....	....	....	10	2	9	11	9	....	....	....
1993-94	Las Vegas Thunder	IHL	79	*55	53	108	....	....	....	52	....	....	....	....	....	....	....	....	....	....	5	3	3	6	2	....	....	....
1994-95	Las Vegas Thunder	IHL	78	40	42	82	....	....	....	40	....	....	....	....	....	....	....	....	....	....	10	3	2	5	9	....	....	....
1995-96	Las Vegas Thunder	IHL	66	33	36	69	....	....	....	59	....	....	....	....	....	....	....	....	....	....	9	2	5	7	15	....	....	....
1996-97	Las Vegas Thunder	IHL	71	27	36	63	....	....	....	39	....	....	....	....	....	....	....	....	....	....	2	0	0	0	0	....	....	....
1997-98	Las Vegas Thunder	IHL	82	34	57	91	....	....	....	19	....	....	....	....	....	....	....	....	....	....	4	1	2	3	2	....	....	....
1998-99	Frankfurt Lions	Germany	36	12	17	29	....	....	....	26	....	....	....	....	....	....	....	....	....	....	8	2	3	5	27	....	....	....
	Frankfurt Lions	EuroHL	2	0	0	0	....	....	....	0	....	....	....	....	....	....	....	....	....	....	....	....	....	....	....	....	....	....
99-2000	Frankfurt Lions	Germany	56	17	16	33	....	....	....	30	....	....	....	....	....	....	....	....	....	....	....	....	....	....	....	....	....	....
	Frankfurt Lions	Germany	56	17	16	33	....	....	....	51	....	....	....	....	....	....	....	....	....	....	5	0	2	2	4	....	....	....
	NHL Totals		**59**	**7**	**13**	**20**	**7**	**9**	**16**	**23**	**3**	**0**	**0**	**61**	**11.5**	**36**	**8**	**35**	**4**		....	....	....	....	....	....	....	....

WHL East First All-Star Team (1985) • IHL First All-Star Team (1994) • IHL Second All-Star Team (1998)

Signed as a free agent by **Detroit**, August 12, 1991.

• QUINT, Deron Deron Timothy D – L. 6'2", 219 lbs. b: Durham, NH, 3/12/1976. Winnipeg's 1st, 30th overall, in 1994.

Season	Club	League	GP	G	A	Pts	AG	AA	APts	PIM	PP	SH	GW	S	%	TGF	PGF	TGA	PGA	+/–	GP	G	A	Pts	PIM	PP	SH	GW
1990-91	Cardigan High School	Hi-School	31	67	54	121	....	....	....	....	....	....	....	....	....	....	....	....	....	....	....	....	....	....	....	....	....	....
1991-92	Cardigan High School	Hi-School	21	111	58	169	....	....	....	....	....	....	....	....	....	....	....	....	....	....	....	....	....	....	....	....	....	....
1992-93	Tabor Academy Seawolves	Hi-School	28	15	26	41	....	....	....	30	....	....	....	....	....	....	....	....	....	....	1	0	2	2	0	....	....	....
1993-94	Seattle Thunderbirds	WHL	63	15	29	44	....	....	....	47	....	....	....	....	....	....	....	....	....	....	9	4	12	16	8	....	....	....
	United States	WJC-A	7	0	1	1	....	....	....	2	....	....	....	....	....	....	....	....	....	....	....	....	....	....	....	....	....	....
1994-95	Seattle Thunderbirds	WHL	65	29	60	89	....	....	....	82	....	....	....	....	....	....	....	....	....	....	3	1	2	3	6	....	....	....
	United States	WJC-A	7	3	3	6	....	....	....	6	....	....	....	....	....	....	....	....	....	....	....	....	....	....	....	....	....	....
1995-96	**Winnipeg Jets**	**NHL**	**51**	**5**	**13**	**18**	**5**	**11**	**16**	**22**	**2**	**0**	**0**	**97**	**5.2**	**64**	**15**	**52**	**1**	**–2**	....	....	....	....	....	....	....	....
	Springfield Falcons	AHL	11	2	3	5	....	....	....	4	....	....	....	....	....	....	....	....	....	....	10	2	3	5	6	....	....	....
	Seattle Thunderbirds	WHL	....	....	....	....	....	....	....	....	....	....	....	....	....	....	....	....	....	....	5	4	1	5	6	....	....	....
1996-97	**Phoenix Coyotes**	**NHL**	**27**	**3**	**11**	**14**	**3**	**10**	**13**	**4**	**1**	**0**	**0**	**63**	**4.8**	**34**	**18**	**20**	**0**	**–4**	**7**	**0**	**2**	**2**	**0**	**0**	**0**	**0**
	Springfield Falcons	AHL	43	6	18	24	....	....	....	20	....	....	....	....	....	....	....	....	....	....	12	2	7	9	4	....	....	....
1997-98	**Phoenix Coyotes**	**NHL**	**32**	**4**	**7**	**11**	**5**	**7**	**12**	**16**	**1**	**0**	**1**	**61**	**6.6**	**27**	**10**	**24**	**1**	**–6**	....	....	....	....	....	....	....	....
	Springfield Falcons	AHL	8	1	7	8	....	....	....	10	....	....	....	....	....	....	....	....	....	....	1	0	0	0	0	....	....	....
1998-99	**Phoenix Coyotes**	**NHL**	**60**	**5**	**8**	**13**	**6**	**8**	**14**	**20**	**2**	**0**	**0**	**94**	**5.3**	**35**	**13**	**35**	**3**	**–10**	....	....	....	....	....	....	....	....
99-2000	**Phoenix Coyotes**	**NHL**	**50**	**3**	**7**	**10**	**3**	**6**	**9**	**22**	**0**	**0**	**1**	**88**	**3.4**	**35**	**5**	**32**	**2**	**0**	....	....	....	....	....	....	....	....
	New Jersey Devils	**NHL**	**4**	**1**	**0**	**1**	**1**	**0**	**1**	**2**	**0**	**0**	**0**	**6**	**16.7**	**2**	**0**	**4**	**0**	**–2**	....	....	....	....	....	....	....	....
	NHL Totals		**224**	**21**	**46**	**67**	**23**	**42**	**65**	**86**	**6**	**0**	**2**	**409**	**5.1**	**197**	**61**	**167**	**7**		**7**	**0**	**2**	**2**	**0**	**0**	**0**	**0**

WHL West First All-Star Team (1995)

Transferred to **Phoenix** after **Winnipeg** franchise relocated, July 1, 1996. Traded to **New Jersey** by **Phoenix** with a conditional choice in 2001 Entry Draft for Lyle Odelein, March 7, 2000.

• QUINTAL, Stephane D – R. 6'3", 230 lbs. b: Boucherville, Que., 10/22/1968. Boston's 2nd, 14th overall, in 1987.

Season	Club	League	GP	G	A	Pts	AG	AA	APts	PIM	PP	SH	GW	S	%	TGF	PGF	TGA	PGA	+/–	GP	G	A	Pts	PIM	PP	SH	GW
1984-85	Richelieu Regents	QAAA	41	1	10	11	....	....	....	....	....	....	....	....	....	....	....	....	....	....	....	....	....	....	....	....	....	....
1985-86	Granby Bisons	QMJHL	67	2	17	19	....	....	....	144	....	....	....	....	....	....	....	....	....	....	....	....	....	....	....	....	....	....
1986-87	Granby Bisons	QMJHL	67	13	41	54	....	....	....	178	....	....	....	....	....	....	....	....	....	....	8	0	9	9	10	....	....	....
1987-88	Hull Olympiques	QMJHL	38	13	23	36	....	....	....	138	....	....	....	....	....	....	....	....	....	....	19	7	12	19	30	....	....	....
	Hull Olympiques	Mem-Cup	4	2	1	3	....	....	....	0	....	....	....	....	....	....	....	....	....	....	....	....	....	....	....	....	....	....
1988-89	**Boston Bruins**	**NHL**	**26**	**0**	**1**	**1**	**0**	**1**	**1**	**29**	**0**	**0**	**0**	**23**	**0.0**	**13**	**1**	**19**	**2**	**–5**	....	....	....	....	....	....	....	....
	Maine Mariners	AHL	16	4	10	14	....	....	....	28	....	....	....	....	....	....	....	....	....	....	....	....	....	....	....	....	....	....
1989-90	**Boston Bruins**	**NHL**	**38**	**2**	**2**	**4**	**2**	**1**	**3**	**22**	**0**	**0**	**0**	**43**	**4.7**	**14**	**1**	**26**	**2**	**–11**	....	....	....	....	....	....	....	....
	Maine Mariners	AHL	37	4	16	20	....	....	....	27	....	....	....	....	....	....	....	....	....	....	....	....	....	....	....	....	....	....
1990-91	**Boston Bruins**	**NHL**	**45**	**2**	**6**	**8**	**2**	**5**	**7**	**89**	**1**	**0**	**0**	**54**	**3.7**	**34**	**2**	**34**	**4**	**2**	**3**	**0**	**1**	**1**	**7**	**0**	**0**	**0**
	Maine Mariners	AHL	23	1	5	6	....	....	....	30	....	....	....	....	....	....	....	....	....	....	....	....	....	....	....	....	....	....
1991-92	**Boston Bruins**	**NHL**	**49**	**4**	**10**	**14**	**4**	**8**	**12**	**77**	**0**	**0**	**0**	**52**	**7.7**	**36**	**4**	**44**	**4**	**–8**	....	....	....	....	....	....	....	....
	St. Louis Blues	**NHL**	**26**	**0**	**6**	**6**	**0**	**5**	**5**	**32**	**0**	**0**	**0**	**19**	**0.0**	**23**	**2**	**32**	**8**	**–3**	**4**	**1**	**2**	**3**	**6**	**1**	**0**	**0**
1992-93	**St. Louis Blues**	**NHL**	**75**	**1**	**10**	**11**	**1**	**7**	**8**	**100**	**0**	**0**	**1**	**81**	**1.2**	**56**	**4**	**76**	**18**	**–6**	**9**	**0**	**0**	**0**	**8**	**0**	**0**	**0**
1993-94	**Winnipeg Jets**	**NHL**	**81**	**8**	**18**	**26**	**7**	**14**	**21**	**119**	**1**	**1**	**1**	**154**	**5.2**	**80**	**15**	**145**	**55**	**–25**	....	....	....	....	....	....	....	....
1994-95	**Winnipeg Jets**	**NHL**	**43**	**6**	**17**	**23**	**11**	**25**	**36**	**78**	**3**	**0**	**2**	**107**	**5.6**	**67**	**18**	**63**	**14**	**0**	....	....	....	....	....	....	....	....
1995-96	**Montreal Canadiens**	**NHL**	**68**	**2**	**14**	**16**	**2**	**11**	**13**	**117**	**0**	**1**	**1**	**104**	**1.9**	**72**	**15**	**83**	**22**	**–4**	**6**	**0**	**1**	**1**	**6**	**0**	**0**	**0**

			REGULAR SEASON																			PLAYOFFS							
Season	Club	League	GP	G	A	Pts	AG	AA	APts	PIM	PP	SH	GW	S	%	TGF	PGF	TGA	PGA	+/–	GP	G	A	Pts	PIM	PP	SH	GW
1996-97	**Montreal Canadiens**	**NHL**	**71**	**7**	**15**	**22**	**7**	**13**	**20**	**100**	**1**	**0**	**0**	**139**	**5.0**	**80**	**7**	**109**	**37**	**1**	**5**	**0**	**1**	**1**	**6**	**0**	**0**	**0**
1997-98	**Montreal Canadiens**	**NHL**	**71**	**6**	**10**	**16**	**7**	**10**	**17**	**97**	**0**	**0**	**0**	**88**	**6.8**	**61**	**2**	**68**	**22**	**13**	**9**	**0**	**2**	**2**	**4**	**0**	**0**	**0**
1998-99	**Montreal Canadiens**	**NHL**	**82**	**8**	**19**	**27**	**9**	**18**	**27**	**84**	**1**	**1**	**4**	**159**	**5.0**	**70**	**9**	**101**	**17**	**–23**								
	Canada	WC-A	10	3	2	5				4																		
99-2000	**New York Rangers**	**NHL**	**75**	**2**	**14**	**16**	**2**	**13**	**15**	**77**	**0**	**0**	**1**	**102**	**2.0**	**57**	**7**	**74**	**14**	**–10**								
	NHL Totals		**750**	**48**	**142**	**190**	**54**	**131**	**185**	**1021**	**7**	**4**	**9**	**1125**	**4.3**	**663**	**87**	**874**	**219**		**36**	**1**	**7**	**8**	**37**	**1**	**0**	**0**

QMJHL First All-Star Team (1987)

Traded to **St. Louis** by **Boston** with Craig Janney for Adam Oates, February 7, 1992. Traded to **Winnipeg** by **St. Louis** with Nelson Emerson for Phil Housley, September 24, 1993. Traded to **Montreal** by **Winnipeg** for Montreal's 2nd round choice (Jason Doig) in 1995 Entry Draft, July 8, 1995. Signed as a free agent by **NY Rangers**, July 13, 1999.

• QUINTIN, Jean-Francois

LW – L. 6', 187 lbs. b: St. Jean, Que., 5/28/1969. Minnesota's 4th, 75th overall, in 1989.

Season	Club	League	GP	G	A	Pts	AG	AA	APts	PIM	PP	SH	GW	S	%	TGF	PGF	TGA	PGA	+/–	GP	G	A	Pts	PIM	PP	SH	GW
1985-86	Richelieu Riverains	QAAA	38	34	46	80																						
1986-87	Shawinigan Cataractes	QMJHL	43	1	9	10				17																		
1987-88	Shawinigan Cataractes	QMJHL	70	28	70	98				143											11	5	8	13	26			
1988-89	Shawinigan Cataractes	QMJHL	69	52	100	152				105											10	9	15	24	16			
1989-90	Kalamazoo Wings	IHL	68	20	18	38				38											10	8	4	12	14			
1990-91	Kalamazoo Wings	IHL	78	31	43	74				64											9	1	5	6	11			
1991-92	**San Jose Sharks**	**NHL**	**8**	**3**	**0**	**3**	**3**	**0**	**3**	**0**	**0**	**0**	**0**	**12**	**25.0**	**5**	**0**	**3**	**0**	**2**								
	Kansas City Blades	IHL	21	4	6	10				29											13	2	10	12	29			
1992-93	**San Jose Sharks**	**NHL**	**14**	**2**	**5**	**7**	**2**	**3**	**5**	**4**	**0**	**0**	**0**	**12**	**16.7**	**9**	**4**	**9**	**0**	**–4**								
	Kansas City Blades	IHL	64	20	29	49				169											11	2	1	3	16			
1993-94	Kansas City Blades	IHL	41	14	19	33				117																		
1994-95	Kansas City Blades	IHL	63	23	35	58				130											19	2	9	11	57			
1995-96	Kansas City Blades	IHL	77	26	35	61				158											5	0	3	3	20			
1996-97	Kansas City Blades	IHL	21	3	5	8				49											2	0	0	0	2			
1997-98	Kansas City Blades	IHL	79	22	37	59				126											11	3	6	9	34			
1998-99	HK Olimpija Ljubljana	Slovenia	19	14	16	30																						
99-2000	Star Bulls Rosenheim	Germany	66	21	43	64				*225																		
	NHL Totals		**22**	**5**	**5**	**10**	**5**	**3**	**8**	**4**	**0**	**0**	**0**	**24**	**20.8**	**14**	**4**	**12**	**0**									

QMJHL Second All-Star Team (1989)

Claimed by **San Jose** from **Minnesota** in Dispersal Draft, May 30, 1991.

• RACHUNEK, Karel

D – R. 6'2", 202 lbs. b: Gottwaldov, Czech., 8/27/1979. Ottawa's 8th, 229th overall, in 1997.

Season	Club	League	GP	G	A	Pts	AG	AA	APts	PIM	PP	SH	GW	S	%	TGF	PGF	TGA	PGA	+/–	GP	G	A	Pts	PIM	PP	SH	GW
1995-96	ZPS Zlin	Czech-Jr.	38	8	11	19																						
1996-97	ZPS Zlin	Czech-Jr.	27	2	11	13																						
1997-98	ZPS Zlin	Czech-Rep	27	1	2	3				16																		
1998-99	ZPS Zlin	Czech-Rep	39	3	9	12				88											6	0	0	0				
	Czech-Republic	WJC-A	6	1	3	4				4																		
99-2000	**Ottawa Senators**	**NHL**	**6**	**0**	**0**	**0**	**0**	**0**	**0**	**2**	**0**	**0**	**0**	**3**	**0.0**	**2**	**0**	**2**	**0**	**0**								
	Grand Rapids Griffins	IHL	62	6	20	26				64											9	0	5	5	6			
	NHL Totals		**6**	**0**	**0**	**0**	**0**	**0**	**0**	**2**	**0**	**0**	**0**	**3**	**0.0**	**2**	**0**	**2**	**0**									

• RACINE, Yves

D – L. 6', 205 lbs. b: Matane, Que., 2/7/1969. Detroit's 1st, 11th overall, in 1987.

Season	Club	League	GP	G	A	Pts	AG	AA	APts	PIM	PP	SH	GW	S	%	TGF	PGF	TGA	PGA	+/–	GP	G	A	Pts	PIM	PP	SH	GW
1984-85	Ste-Foy Gouverneurs	QAAA	26	3	6	9																						
1985-86	Ste-Foy Gouverneurs	QAAA	42	4	38	42				66																		
	North Bay Hoppers	NOJHA	1	0	0	0				0																		
1986-87	Longueuil Chevaliers	QMJHL	70	7	43	50				50											20	3	11	14	14			
	Longueuil Chevaliers	Mem-Cup	5	0	0	0				0																		
1987-88	Victoriaville Tigres	QMJHL	69	10	84	94				150											5	0	0	0	13			
	Adirondack Red Wings	AHL																			9	4	2	6	2			
1988-89	Victoriaville Tigres	QMJHL	63	23	85	108				95											16	3	*30	*33	41			
	Canada	WJC-A	7	0	0	0				6																		
	Adirondack Red Wings	AHL																			2	1	1	2	0			
1989-90	**Detroit Red Wings**	**NHL**	**28**	**4**	**9**	**13**	**3**	**6**	**9**	**23**	**1**	**0**	**0**	**49**	**8.2**	**30**	**9**	**24**	**0**	**–3**								
	Adirondack Red Wings	AHL	46	8	27	35				31																		
1990-91	**Detroit Red Wings**	**NHL**	**62**	**7**	**40**	**47**	**6**	**30**	**36**	**33**	**2**	**0**	**1**	**131**	**5.3**	**82**	**27**	**57**	**3**	**1**	**7**	**2**	**0**	**2**	**0**	**2**	**0**	**0**
	Adirondack Red Wings	AHL	16	3	9	12				10																		
	Canada	WEC-A	4	0	0	0				0																		
1991-92	**Detroit Red Wings**	**NHL**	**61**	**2**	**22**	**24**	**2**	**17**	**19**	**94**	**1**	**0**	**0**	**103**	**1.9**	**69**	**18**	**69**	**12**	**–6**	**11**	**2**	**1**	**3**	**10**	**1**	**0**	**1**
1992-93	**Detroit Red Wings**	**NHL**	**80**	**9**	**31**	**40**	**7**	**21**	**28**	**80**	**5**	**0**	**0**	**163**	**5.5**	**114**	**38**	**79**	**13**	**10**	**7**	**1**	**3**	**4**	**27**	**0**	**0**	**0**
1993-94	**Philadelphia Flyers**	**NHL**	**67**	**9**	**43**	**52**	**8**	**33**	**41**	**48**	**5**	**1**	**1**	**142**	**6.3**	**102**	**45**	**87**	**19**	**–11**								
	Canada	WC-A	8	1	2	3				8																		
1994-95	**Montreal Canadiens**	**NHL**	**47**	**4**	**7**	**11**	**7**	**10**	**17**	**42**	**2**	**0**	**1**	**63**	**6.3**	**48**	**15**	**55**	**21**	**–1**								
1995-96	**Montreal Canadiens**	**NHL**	**25**	**0**	**3**	**3**	**0**	**2**	**2**	**26**	**0**	**0**	**0**	**16**	**0.0**	**12**	**3**	**23**	**7**	**–7**								
	San Jose Sharks	**NHL**	**32**	**1**	**16**	**17**	**1**	**13**	**14**	**28**	**0**	**0**	**0**	**35**	**2.9**	**45**	**10**	**50**	**12**	**–3**								
1996-97	Kentucky Thoroughblades	AHL	4	0	1	1				2																		
	Quebec Rafales	IHL	6	0	4	4				4																		
	Calgary Flames	**NHL**	**46**	**1**	**15**	**16**	**1**	**13**	**14**	**24**	**1**	**0**	**0**	**82**	**1.2**	**55**	**20**	**32**	**1**	**4**								
1997-98	**Tampa Bay Lightning**	**NHL**	**60**	**0**	**8**	**8**	**0**	**8**	**8**	**41**	**0**	**0**	**0**	**76**	**0.0**	**31**	**8**	**59**	**13**	**–23**								
1998-99	Jokerit Helsinki	Finland	52	8	18	26				108											3	1	0	1	6			
	Jokerit Helsinki	EuroHL	6	1	0	1				18											2	1	1	2	6			
99-2000	Adler Mannheim	Germany	54	5	21	26				90											5	0	1	1	43			
	Adler Mannheim	EuroHL	6	0	1	1				8																		
	NHL Totals		**508**	**37**	**194**	**231**	**35**	**153**	**188**	**439**	**17**	**1**	**3**	**860**	**4.3**	**588**	**193**	**535**	**101**		**25**	**5**	**4**	**9**	**37**	**3**	**0**	**1**

QMJHL First-All Star Team (1988, 1989)

Traded to **Philadelphia** by **Detroit** with Detroit's 4th round choice (Sebastien Vallee) in 1994 Entry Draft for Terry Carkner, October 5, 1993. Traded to **Montreal** by **Philadelphia** for Kevin Haller, June 29, 1994. Claimed on waivers by **San Jose** from **Montreal**, January 23, 1996. Traded to **Calgary** by **San Jose** for cash, December 17, 1996. Signed as a free agent by **Tampa Bay**, July 16, 1997.

• RAFALSKI, Brian

Brian Christopher D – R. 5'9", 200 lbs. b: Dearborn, MI, 9/28/1973.

Season	Club	League	GP	G	A	Pts	AG	AA	APts	PIM	PP	SH	GW	S	%	TGF	PGF	TGA	PGA	+/–	GP	G	A	Pts	PIM	PP	SH	GW
1990-91	Madison Capitols	USHL	47	12	11	23				28																		
1991-92	University of Wisconsin	WCHA	34	3	14	17				34																		
1992-93	University of Wisconsin	WCHA	32	0	13	13				10																		
1993-94	University of Wisconsin	WCHA	37	6	17	23				26																		
1994-95	University of Wisconsin	WCHA	43	11	34	45				48																		
1995-96	Brynas IF Gavle	Sweden	22	1	8	9				14																		
	Brynas IF Gavle	Sweden-2	18	3	6	9				12											9	0	1	1	2			
1996-97	HPK Hameenlinna	Finland	49	11	24	35				26											10	6	5	11	4			
1997-98	HIFK Helsinki	Finland	40	13	10	23				20											9	5	6	11	0			

			REGULAR SEASON																		PLAYOFFS							
Season	**Club**	**League**	**GP**	**G**	**A**	**Pts**	**AG**	**AA**	**APts**	**PIM**	**PP**	**SH**	**GW**	**S**	**%**	**TGF**	**PGF**	**TGA**	**PGA**	**+/–**	**GP**	**G**	**A**	**Pts**	**PIM**	**PP**	**SH**	**GW**
1998-99	HIFK Helsinki	Finland	53	19	34	53	....	....	....	18	....	....	....	....	....	....	....	....	....	....	11	5	*9	*14	4	....	....	....
	HIFK Helsinki	EuroHL	6	4	6	10	....	....	....	10	....	....	....	....	....	....	....	....	....	....	4	1	0	1	2	....	....	....
	United States	WC-Q	3	0	1	1	....	....	....	0	....	....	....	....	....	....	....	....	....	....	....	....	....	....	....	....	....	....
99-2000♦	**New Jersey Devils**	**NHL**	**75**	**5**	**27**	**32**	**6**	**25**	**31**	**28**	**1**	**0**	**1**	**128**	**3.9**	**91**	**23**	**48**	**1**	**21**	**23**	**2**	**6**	**8**	**8**	**0**	**0**	**1**
	NHL Totals		**75**	**5**	**27**	**32**	**6**	**25**	**31**	**28**	**1**	**0**	**1**	**128**	**3.9**	**91**	**23**	**48**	**1**		**23**	**2**	**6**	**8**	**8**	**0**	**0**	**1**

WCHA First All-Star Team (1995) • NCAA West First All-American Team (1995) • Finnish Elite League First All-Star Team (1998, 1999) • Named Best Defender in Finnish Elite League (1998, 1999) • NHL All-Rookie Team (2000)

Signed as a free agent by **New Jersey**, May 7, 1999.

• RAGLAN, Herb

RW – R. 6', 205 lbs. b: Peterborough, Ont., 8/5/1967. St. Louis' 1st, 37th overall, in 1985.

Season	Club	League	GP	G	A	Pts	AG	AA	APts	PIM	PP	SH	GW	S	%	TGF	PGF	TGA	PGA	+/–	GP	G	A	Pts	PIM	PP	SH	GW
1983-84	Peterborough Legionaires	OJHL-B	26	39	21	60	....	....	....	60	....	....	....	....	....	....	....	....	....	....	....	....	....	....	....	....	....	....
1984-85	Kingston Canadians	OHL	58	20	22	42	....	....	....	166	....	....	....	....	....	....	....	....	....	....	....	....	....	....	....	....	....	....
1985-86	Kingston Canadians	OHL	28	10	9	19	....	....	....	88	....	....	....	....	....	....	....	....	....	....	10	5	2	7	30	....	....	....
	St. Louis Blues	**NHL**	**7**	**0**	**0**	**0**	**0**	**0**	**0**	**5**	**0**	**0**	**0**	**4**	**0.0**	**0**	**0**	**3**	**0**	**–3**	**10**	**1**	**1**	**2**	**24**	**0**	**0**	**0**
1986-87	**St. Louis Blues**	**NHL**	**62**	**6**	**10**	**16**	**5**	**7**	**12**	**159**	**0**	**0**	**0**	**58**	**10.3**	**28**	**0**	**22**	**0**	**6**	**4**	**0**	**0**	**0**	**2**	**0**	**0**	**0**
1987-88	**St. Louis Blues**	**NHL**	**73**	**10**	**15**	**25**	**9**	**11**	**20**	**190**	**0**	**0**	**2**	**95**	**10.5**	**37**	**0**	**47**	**0**	**–10**	**10**	**1**	**3**	**4**	**11**	**0**	**0**	**0**
1988-89	**St. Louis Blues**	**NHL**	**50**	**7**	**10**	**17**	**6**	**7**	**13**	**144**	**0**	**0**	**1**	**86**	**8.1**	**22**	**0**	**30**	**0**	**–8**	**8**	**1**	**2**	**3**	**13**	**0**	**0**	**0**
1989-90	**St. Louis Blues**	**NHL**	**11**	**0**	**1**	**1**	**0**	**1**	**1**	**21**	**0**	**0**	**0**	**13**	**0.0**	**2**	**0**	**7**	**0**	**–5**	....	....	....	....	....	....	....	....
1990-91	**St. Louis Blues**	**NHL**	**32**	**3**	**3**	**6**	**3**	**2**	**5**	**52**	**0**	**0**	**1**	**29**	**10.3**	**12**	**0**	**8**	**0**	**4**	....	....	....	....	....	....	....	....
	Quebec Nordiques	**NHL**	**15**	**1**	**3**	**4**	**1**	**2**	**3**	**30**	**0**	**0**	**0**	**19**	**5.3**	**6**	**0**	**5**	**0**	**1**	....	....	....	....	....	....	....	....
1991-92	**Quebec Nordiques**	**NHL**	**62**	**6**	**14**	**20**	**5**	**11**	**16**	**120**	**0**	**0**	**0**	**79**	**7.6**	**25**	**1**	**30**	**1**	**–5**	....	....	....	....	....	....	....	....
1992-93	Halifax Citadels	AHL	28	3	9	12	....	....	....	83	....	....	....	....	....	....	....	....	....	....	....	....	....	....	....	....	....	....
	Tampa Bay Lightning	**NHL**	**2**	**0**	**0**	**0**	**0**	**0**	**0**	**2**	**0**	**0**	**0**	**0**	**0.0**	**0**	**0**	**0**	**0**	**0**	....	....	....	....	....	....	....	....
	Atlanta Knights	IHL	24	4	10	14	....	....	....	139	....	....	....	....	....	....	....	....	....	....	9	3	3	6	32	....	....	....
1993-94	Kalamazoo Wings	IHL	29	6	11	17	....	....	....	112	....	....	....	....	....	....	....	....	....	....	5	0	0	0	32	....	....	....
	Ottawa Senators	**NHL**	**29**	**0**	**0**	**0**	**0**	**0**	**0**	**52**	**0**	**0**	**0**	**13**	**0.0**	**0**	**0**	**13**	**0**	**–13**	....	....	....	....	....	....	....	....
1994-95	Kalamazoo Wings	IHL	31	4	4	8	....	....	....	94	....	....	....	....	....	....	....	....	....	....	6	0	0	0	15	....	....	....
1995-96	Brantford Smoke	ColHL	69	46	38	84	....	....	....	267	....	....	....	....	....	....	....	....	....	....	12	9	6	15	58	....	....	....
1996-97	Central Texas Stampede	WPHL	33	14	18	32	....	....	....	131	....	....	....	....	....	....	....	....	....	....	10	7	3	10	30	....	....	....
	Brantford Smoke	ColHL	11	5	4	9	....	....	....	33	....	....	....	....	....	....	....	....	....	....	2	3	1	4	4	....	....	....
1997-98	Brantford Smoke	UHL	17	8	10	18	....	....	....	38	....	....	....	....	....	....	....	....	....	....	....	....	....	....	....	....	....	....
	NHL Totals		**343**	**33**	**56**	**89**	**29**	**41**	**70**	**775**	**0**	**0**	**4**	**396**	**8.3**	**132**	**1**	**165**	**1**		**32**	**3**	**6**	**9**	**50**	**0**	**0**	**0**

• Son of Rags (Clare)

• Missed remainder of 1989-90 season recovering from wrist injury suffered in game vs. Quebec, November 4, 1989. Traded to **Quebec** by **St. Louis** with Tony Twist and Andy Rymsha for Darin Kimble, February 4, 1991. Traded to **Tampa Bay** by **Quebec** for Martin Simard, Steve Tuttle and Michel Mongeau, February 12, 1993. Signed as a free agent by **Ottawa**, January 1, 1994.

• RAGNARSSON, Marcus

Lars Johan Marcus D – L. 6'1", 215 lbs. b: Ostervala, Sweden, 8/13/1971. San Jose's 5th, 99th overall, in 1992.

Season	Club	League	GP	G	A	Pts	AG	AA	APts	PIM	PP	SH	GW	S	%	TGF	PGF	TGA	PGA	+/–	GP	G	A	Pts	PIM	PP	SH	GW
1986-87	Ostervala IF	Sweden-3	28	1	6	7	....	....	....	....	....	....	....	....	....	....	....	....	....	....	....	....	....	....	....	....	....	....
1987-88	Ostervala IF	Sweden-3	25	3	12	15	....	....	....	....	....	....	....	....	....	....	....	....	....	....	....	....	....	....	....	....	....	....
1988-89	Ostervala IF	Sweden-3	30	15	14	29	....	....	....	....	....	....	....	....	....	....	....	....	....	....	....	....	....	....	....	....	....	....
1989-90	Nacka HK	Sweden-2	9	2	3	5	....	....	....	4	....	....	....	....	....	....	....	....	....	....	....	....	....	....	....	....	....	....
	Djurgardens IF Stockholm	Sweden	13	0	2	2	....	....	....	0	....	....	....	....	....	....	....	....	....	....	1	0	0	0	0	....	....	....
1990-91	Djurgardens IF Stockholm	Sweden	35	4	1	5	....	....	....	12	....	....	....	....	....	....	....	....	....	....	7	0	0	0	6	....	....	....
1991-92	Djurgardens IF Stockholm	Sweden	40	8	5	13	....	....	....	14	....	....	....	....	....	....	....	....	....	....	10	0	1	1	4	....	....	....
1992-93	Djurgardens IF Stockholm	Sweden	35	3	3	6	....	....	....	53	....	....	....	....	....	....	....	....	....	....	6	0	3	3	8	....	....	....
1993-94	Djurgardens IF Stockholm	Sweden	19	0	4	4	....	....	....	24	....	....	....	....	....	....	....	....	....	....	....	....	....	....	....	....	....	....
1994-95	Djurgardens IF Stockholm	Sweden	38	7	9	16	....	....	....	20	....	....	....	....	....	....	....	....	....	....	3	0	0	0	4	....	....	....
	Sweden	WC-A	4	0	0	0	....	....	....	4	....	....	....	....	....	....	....	....	....	....	....	....	....	....	....	....	....	....
1995-96	**San Jose Sharks**	**NHL**	**71**	**8**	**31**	**39**	**8**	**25**	**33**	**42**	**4**	**0**	**0**	**94**	**8.5**	**100**	**37**	**90**	**3**	**–24**	....	....	....	....	....	....	....	....
1996-97	**San Jose Sharks**	**NHL**	**69**	**3**	**14**	**17**	**3**	**12**	**15**	**63**	**2**	**0**	**0**	**57**	**5.3**	**62**	**13**	**90**	**23**	**–18**	....	....	....	....	....	....	....	....
	Sweden	WC-A	11	2	1	3	....	....	....	10	....	....	....	....	....	....	....	....	....	....	....	....	....	....	....	....	....	....
1997-98	**San Jose Sharks**	**NHL**	**79**	**5**	**20**	**25**	**6**	**20**	**26**	**65**	**3**	**0**	**2**	**91**	**5.5**	**67**	**18**	**77**	**17**	**–11**	**6**	**0**	**0**	**0**	**4**	**0**	**0**	**0**
	Sweden	Olympics	3	0	1	1	....	....	....	0	....	....	....	....	....	....	....	....	....	....	....	....	....	....	....	....	....	....
1998-99	**San Jose Sharks**	**NHL**	**74**	**0**	**13**	**13**	**0**	**13**	**13**	**66**	**0**	**0**	**0**	**87**	**0.0**	**61**	**12**	**65**	**23**	**7**	**6**	**0**	**1**	**1**	**6**	**0**	**0**	**0**
99-2000	**San Jose Sharks**	**NHL**	**63**	**3**	**13**	**16**	**3**	**12**	**15**	**38**	**0**	**0**	**0**	**60**	**5.0**	**59**	**10**	**56**	**20**	**13**	**12**	**0**	**3**	**3**	**10**	**0**	**0**	**0**
	NHL Totals		**356**	**19**	**91**	**110**	**20**	**82**	**102**	**274**	**9**	**0**	**2**	**389**	**4.9**	**349**	**90**	**378**	**86**		**24**	**0**	**4**	**4**	**20**	**0**	**0**	**0**

• RAMAGE, Rob

Robert George D – R. 6'2", 200 lbs. b: Byron, Ont., 1/11/1959. Colorado's 1st, 1st overall, in 1979.

Season	Club	League	GP	G	A	Pts	AG	AA	APts	PIM	PP	SH	GW	S	%	TGF	PGF	TGA	PGA	+/–	GP	G	A	Pts	PIM	PP	SH	GW
1975-76	London Knights	OMJHL	65	12	31	43	....	....	....	113	....	....	....	....	....	....	....	....	....	....	5	0	1	1	11	....	....	....
1976-77	London Knights	OMJHL	65	15	58	73	....	....	....	177	....	....	....	....	....	....	....	....	....	....	20	3	11	14	55	....	....	....
	Canada	WJC-A	7	0	1	1	....	....	....	6	....	....	....	....	....	....	....	....	....	....	....	....	....	....	....	....	....	....
1977-78	London Knights	OMJHL	59	17	48	65	....	....	....	162	....	....	....	....	....	....	....	....	....	....	11	4	5	9	29	....	....	....
	Canada	WJC-A	6	1	3	4	....	....	....	6	....	....	....	....	....	....	....	....	....	....	....	....	....	....	....	....	....	....
1978-79	Birmingham Bulls	WHA	80	12	36	48	....	....	....	165	....	....	....	....	....	....	....	....	....	....	....	....	....	....	....	....	....	....
1979-80	**Colorado Rockies**	**NHL**	**75**	**8**	**20**	**28**	**7**	**15**	**22**	**135**	**4**	**0**	**3**	**218**	**3.7**	**87**	**21**	**126**	**20**	**–40**	....	....	....	....	....	....	....	....
1980-81	**Colorado Rockies**	**NHL**	**79**	**20**	**42**	**62**	**16**	**28**	**44**	**193**	**12**	**1**	**3**	**289**	**6.9**	**141**	**63**	**164**	**40**	**–46**	....	....	....	....	....	....	....	....
	Canada	WEC-A	8	0	1	1	....	....	....	0	....	....	....	....	....	....	....	....	....	....	....	....	....	....	....	....	....	....
1981-82	**Colorado Rockies**	**NHL**	**80**	**13**	**29**	**42**	**10**	**19**	**29**	**201**	**6**	**0**	**0**	**270**	**4.8**	**113**	**35**	**153**	**28**	**–47**	....	....	....	....	....	....	....	....
1982-83	**St. Louis Blues**	**NHL**	**78**	**16**	**35**	**51**	**13**	**24**	**37**	**193**	**7**	**0**	**3**	**279**	**5.7**	**143**	**47**	**138**	**33**	**–9**	**4**	**0**	**3**	**3**	**22**	**0**	**0**	**0**
1983-84	**St. Louis Blues**	**NHL**	**80**	**15**	**45**	**60**	**12**	**31**	**43**	**121**	**9**	**0**	**3**	**266**	**5.6**	**155**	**64**	**161**	**59**	**–11**	**11**	**1**	**8**	**9**	**32**	**1**	**0**	**1**
1984-85	**St. Louis Blues**	**NHL**	**80**	**7**	**31**	**38**	**6**	**21**	**27**	**178**	**1**	**0**	**0**	**285**	**2.5**	**136**	**41**	**142**	**40**	**–7**	**3**	**1**	**3**	**4**	**6**	**0**	**1**	**0**
1985-86	**St. Louis Blues**	**NHL**	**77**	**10**	**56**	**66**	**8**	**38**	**46**	**171**	**7**	**0**	**2**	**227**	**4.4**	**158**	**52**	**131**	**43**	**18**	**19**	**1**	**10**	**11**	**66**	**0**	**0**	**0**
1986-87	**St. Louis Blues**	**NHL**	**59**	**11**	**28**	**39**	**9**	**20**	**29**	**108**	**6**	**0**	**3**	**160**	**6.9**	**95**	**41**	**86**	**20**	**–12**	**6**	**2**	**2**	**4**	**21**	**2**	**0**	**0**
1987-88	**St. Louis Blues**	**NHL**	**67**	**8**	**34**	**42**	**7**	**24**	**31**	**127**	**5**	**0**	**0**	**203**	**3.9**	**108**	**46**	**117**	**35**	**–20**	....	....	....	....	....	....	....	....
	Calgary Flames	**NHL**	**12**	**1**	**6**	**7**	**1**	**4**	**5**	**37**	**1**	**0**	**0**	**12**	**8.3**	**26**	**2**	**16**	**8**	**16**	**9**	**1**	**3**	**4**	**21**	**1**	**0**	**0**
1988-89♦	**Calgary Flames**	**NHL**	**68**	**3**	**13**	**16**	**3**	**9**	**12**	**156**	**2**	**0**	**0**	**91**	**3.3**	**67**	**9**	**48**	**16**	**26**	**20**	**1**	**11**	**12**	**26**	**1**	**0**	**0**
1989-90	**Toronto Maple Leafs**	**NHL**	**80**	**8**	**41**	**49**	**7**	**29**	**36**	**202**	**3**	**0**	**1**	**196**	**4.1**	**144**	**48**	**130**	**33**	**–1**	**5**	**1**	**2**	**3**	**20**	**0**	**0**	**0**
1990-91	**Toronto Maple Leafs**	**NHL**	**80**	**10**	**25**	**35**	**9**	**19**	**28**	**173**	**5**	**0**	**2**	**169**	**5.9**	**104**	**28**	**102**	**28**	**2**	....	....	....	....	....	....	....	....
1991-92	**Minnesota North Stars**	**NHL**	**34**	**4**	**5**	**9**	**4**	**4**	**8**	**69**	**2**	**0**	**0**	**63**	**6.3**	**40**	**15**	**31**	**2**	**–4**	....	....	....	....	....	....	....	....
1992-93	**Tampa Bay Lightning**	**NHL**	**66**	**5**	**12**	**17**	**4**	**8**	**12**	**138**	**5**	**0**	**0**	**115**	**4.3**	**47**	**20**	**66**	**18**	**–21**	....	....	....	....	....	....	....	....
♦	**Montreal Canadiens**	**NHL**	**8**	**0**	**1**	**1**	**0**	**1**	**1**	**8**	**0**	**0**	**0**	**16**	**0.0**	**5**	**0**	**12**	**4**	**–3**	**7**	**0**	**0**	**0**	**4**	**0**	**0**	**0**
1993-94	**Montreal Canadiens**	**NHL**	**6**	**0**	**1**	**1**	**0**	**1**	**1**	**2**	**0**	**0**	**0**	**5**	**0.0**	**3**	**0**	**4**	**0**	**–1**	....	....	....	....	....	....	....	....
	Philadelphia Flyers	**NHL**	**15**	**0**	**1**	**1**	**0**	**1**	**1**	**14**	**0**	**0**	**0**	**18**	**0.0**	**3**	**0**	**21**	**7**	**–11**	....	....	....	....	....	....	....	....
	NHL Totals		**1044**	**139**	**425**	**564**	**116**	**296**	**412**	**2226**	**75**	**1**	**20**	**2882**	**4.8**	**1575**	**532**	**1648**	**434**		**84**	**8**	**42**	**50**	**218**	**5**	**1**	**1**
	Other Major League Totals		80	12	36	48	....	....	....	165	....	....	....	....	....	....	....	....	....	....	....	....	....	....	....	....	....	....

OMJHL First All-Star Team (1978) • WHA First All-Star Team (1979) • Played in NHL All-Star Game (1981, 1984, 1986, 1988)

Signed as an underage free agent by **Birmingham** (WHA), June, 1978. Traded to **St. Louis** by **New Jersey** for St. Louis' 1st round choice (John MacLean) in 1983 Entry Draft, June 9, 1982. Traded to **Calgary** by **St. Louis** with Rick Wamsley for Brett Hull and Steve Bozek, March 7, 1988. Traded to **Toronto** by **Calgary** for Toronto's 2nd round choice (Kent Manderville) in 1989 Entry Draft June 16, 1989. Claimed by **Minnesota** from **Toronto** in Expansion Draft, May 30, 1991. Claimed by **Tampa Bay** from **Minnesota** in Expansion Draft, June 18, 1992. Traded to **Montreal** by **Tampa Bay** for Eric Charron, Alain Cote and future considerations (Donald Dufresne, June 18, 1993), March 20, 1993. Traded to **Philadelphia** by **Montreal** for cash, November 28, 1993.

• RAMSAY, Craig

Craig Edward "Rammer" LW – L. 5'10", 175 lbs. b: Weston, Ont., 3/17/1951. Buffalo's 2nd, 19th overall, in 1971.

Season	Club	League	GP	G	A	Pts	AG	AA	APts	PIM	PP	SH	GW	S	%	TGF	PGF	TGA	PGA	+/–	GP	G	A	Pts	PIM	PP	SH	GW
1967-68	Peterborough Petes	OHA-Jr.	40	6	13	19	....	....	....	21	....	....	....	....	....	....	....	....	....	....	5	0	0	0	4	....	....	....
1968-69	Peterborough Petes	OHA-Jr.	54	11	28	39	....	....	....	20	....	....	....	....	....	....	....	....	....	....	10	1	2	3	9	....	....	....
1969-70	Peterborough Petes	OHA-Jr.	54	27	41	68	....	....	....	18	....	....	....	....	....	....	....	....	....	....	6	1	3	4	7	....	....	....
1970-71	Peterborough Petes	OHA-Jr.	58	30	76	106	....	....	....	25	....	....	....	....	....	....	....	....	....	....	5	2	2	4	2	....	....	....

			REGULAR SEASON																		PLAYOFFS							
Season	Club	League	GP	G	A	Pts	AG	AA	APts	PIM	PP	SH	GW	S	%	TGF	PGF	TGA	PGA	+/–	GP	G	A	Pts	PIM	PP	SH	GW
1971-72	Cincinnati Swords	AHL	19	5	7	12	....	....	....	4	....	....	....	....	....	....	....	....	....	....	....	....	....	....	....	....	....	....
	Buffalo Sabres	**NHL**	57	6	10	16	6	9	15	0	0	0	2	43	14.0	32	3	28	4	5	....	....	....	....	....	....	....	....
1972-73	**Buffalo Sabres**	**NHL**	76	11	17	28	10	13	23	15	0	1	1	89	12.4	46	0	46	13	13	6	1	1	2	0	0	0	0
1973-74	**Buffalo Sabres**	**NHL**	78	20	26	46	19	21	40	0	1	2	3	154	13.0	69	4	85	37	17	....	....	....	....	....	....	....	....
1974-75	**Buffalo Sabres**	**NHL**	80	26	38	64	23	28	51	26	1	7	7	200	13.0	90	5	77	43	51	17	5	7	12	2	1	1	1
1975-76	**Buffalo Sabres**	**NHL**	80	22	49	71	19	37	56	34	1	1	0	134	16.4	100	9	76	29	44	9	1	2	3	2	0	1	0
1976-77	**Buffalo Sabres**	**NHL**	80	20	41	61	18	32	50	20	2	3	2	145	13.8	92	15	68	28	37	6	0	4	4	0	0	0	0
1977-78	**Buffalo Sabres**	**NHL**	80	28	43	71	25	33	58	18	2	5	3	159	17.6	105	17	73	23	38	8	3	1	4	9	1	0	1
1978-79	**Buffalo Sabres**	**NHL**	80	26	31	57	22	22	44	10	4	3	3	113	23.0	90	19	88	38	21	3	1	0	1	2	0	0	0
1979-80	**Buffalo Sabres**	**NHL**	80	21	39	60	18	28	46	18	5	0	4	103	20.4	84	20	82	33	15	10	0	6	6	4	0	0	0
1980-81	**Buffalo Sabres**	**NHL**	80	24	35	59	19	23	42	12	1	1	3	110	21.8	87	3	69	24	39	8	2	4	6	4	0	0	1
1981-82	**Buffalo Sabres**	**NHL**	80	16	35	51	13	23	36	8	0	1	2	109	14.7	68	4	83	33	14	4	1	1	2	0	0	0	1
1982-83	**Buffalo Sabres**	**NHL**	64	11	18	29	9	12	21	7	0	3	1	87	12.6	41	2	42	17	14	10	2	3	5	4	0	0	0
1983-84	**Buffalo Sabres**	**NHL**	76	9	17	26	7	12	19	17	0	0	0	97	9.3	47	2	64	22	3	3	0	1	1	0	0	0	0
1984-85	**Buffalo Sabres**	**NHL**	79	12	21	33	10	14	24	16	0	0	1	71	16.9	51	4	53	23	17	5	1	1	2	0	0	0	0
1985-1986	**Buffalo Sabres**	**NHL**	DID NOT PLAY – ASSISTANT COACH																									
1986-1987	**Buffalo Sabres**	**NHL**	DID NOT PLAY – COACHING																									
	Buffalo Sabres	**NHL**	DID NOT PLAY – ASSISTANT GENERAL MANAGER																									
1987-1993	**Buffalo Sabres**	**NHL**	DID NOT PLAY – ASSISTANT GENERAL MANAGER																									
1993-1995	**Florida Panthers**	**NHL**	DID NOT PLAY – ASSISTANT COACH																									
1995-1996	**Dallas Stars**	**NHL**	DID NOT PLAY – SCOUTING																									
1996-1998	**Ottawa Senators**	**NHL**	DID NOT PLAY – ASSISTANT COACH																									
1998-2000	**Philadelphia Flyers**	**NHL**	DID NOT PLAY – ASSISTANT COACH																									
	NHL Totals		1070	252	420	672	218	307	525	201	17	27	32	1614	15.6	1002	107	934	367		89	17	31	48	27	2	2	4

Won Frank J. Selke Trophy (1985) • Played in NHL All-Star Game (1976)

• Named Assistant Coach of **Philadelphia Flyers**, July 7, 1998. • Named interim Head Coach of **Philadelphia**, February 20, 2000. •Named Head Coach of **Philadelphia**, June 13, 2000.

• RAMSEY, Mike

Michael Allan D – L. 6'3", 195 lbs. b: Minneapolis, MN, 12/3/1960. Buffalo's 1st, 11th overall, in 1979.

Season	Club	League	GP	G	A	Pts	AG	AA	APts	PIM	PP	SH	GW	S	%	TGF	PGF	TGA	PGA	+/–	GP	G	A	Pts	PIM	PP	SH	GW
1978-79	University of Minnesota	WCHA	26	6	11	17	....	....	....	30	....	....	....	....	....	....	....	....	....	....	....	....	....	....	....	....	....	....
	United States	WJC-A	5	1	1	2	....	....	....	10	....	....	....	....	....	....	....	....	....	....	....	....	....	....	....	....	....	....
1979-80	United States	Nat-Team	56	11	22	33	....	....	....	55	....	....	....	....	....	....	....	....	....	....	....	....	....	....	....	....	....	....
	United States	Olympics	7	0	2	2	....	....	....	8	....	....	....	....	....	....	....	....	....	....	....	....	....	....	....	....	....	....
	Buffalo Sabres	**NHL**	13	1	6	7	1	4	5	6	0	0	1	17	5.9	17	1	8	1	9	13	1	2	3	12	1	0	1
1980-81	**Buffalo Sabres**	**NHL**	72	3	14	17	2	9	11	56	0	0	0	50	6.0	45	7	27	5	16	8	0	3	3	20	0	0	0
1981-82	**Buffalo Sabres**	**NHL**	80	7	23	30	6	15	21	56	2	0	0	94	7.4	102	8	96	20	18	4	1	1	2	14	0	0	0
	United States	WEC-A	7	1	0	1	....	....	....	8	....	....	....	....	....	....	....	....	....	....	....	....	....	....	....	....	....	....
1982-83	**Buffalo Sabres**	**NHL**	77	8	30	38	7	21	28	55	1	1	1	116	6.9	109	12	101	24	20	10	4	4	8	15	0	0	1
1983-84	**Buffalo Sabres**	**NHL**	72	9	22	31	7	15	22	82	1	0	4	134	6.7	96	12	88	31	27	3	0	1	1	6	0	0	0
1984-85	United States	Can-Cup	6	1	1	2	....	....	....	6	....	....	....	....	....	....	....	....	....	....	....	....	....	....	....	....	....	....
	Buffalo Sabres	**NHL**	79	8	22	30	6	15	21	102	3	0	2	160	5.0	115	27	85	28	31	5	0	1	1	23	0	0	0
1985-86	**Buffalo Sabres**	**NHL**	76	7	21	28	6	14	20	117	1	0	1	154	4.5	104	14	124	35	1	....	....	....	....	....	....	....	....
1986-87	**Buffalo Sabres**	**NHL**	80	8	31	39	7	23	30	109	2	1	0	154	5.2	110	22	151	64	1	....	....	....	....	....	....	....	....
	NHL All-Stars	RV-87	2	0	0	0	....	....	....	0	....	....	....	....	....	....	....	....	....	....	....	....	....	....	....	....	....	....
1987-88	United States	Can-Cup	5	0	1	1	....	....	....	2	....	....	....	....	....	....	....	....	....	....	....	....	....	....	....	....	....	....
	Buffalo Sabres	**NHL**	63	5	16	21	4	11	15	77	1	0	0	94	5.3	76	16	103	49	6	6	0	3	3	29	0	0	0
1988-89	**Buffalo Sabres**	**NHL**	56	2	14	16	2	10	12	84	0	0	1	63	3.2	62	6	75	24	5	5	1	0	1	11	1	0	0
1989-90	**Buffalo Sabres**	**NHL**	73	4	21	25	3	15	18	47	1	0	2	91	4.4	86	9	85	29	21	6	0	1	1	8	0	0	0
1990-91	**Buffalo Sabres**	**NHL**	71	6	14	20	5	11	16	46	0	0	1	87	6.9	80	1	100	35	14	5	1	0	1	12	0	0	1
1991-92	**Buffalo Sabres**	**NHL**	66	3	14	17	3	11	14	67	0	0	1	55	5.5	52	3	84	43	8	7	0	2	2	8	0	0	0
1992-93	**Buffalo Sabres**	**NHL**	33	2	8	10	2	5	7	20	0	0	0	27	7.4	29	0	33	8	4	....	....	....	....	....	....	....	....
	Pittsburgh Penguins	**NHL**	12	1	2	3	1	1	2	8	0	0	0	8	12.5	20	0	9	2	13	12	0	6	6	4	0	0	0
1993-94	**Pittsburgh Penguins**	**NHL**	65	2	2	4	2	2	4	22	0	0	0	31	6.5	31	0	51	16	–4	1	0	0	0	0	0	0	0
1994-95	**Detroit Red Wings**	**NHL**	33	1	2	3	2	3	5	23	0	0	0	29	3.4	24	1	19	7	11	15	0	1	1	4	0	0	0
1995-96	**Detroit Red Wings**	**NHL**	47	2	4	6	2	3	5	35	0	0	0	35	5.7	35	0	28	10	17	15	0	4	4	10	0	0	0
1996-97	**Detroit Red Wings**	**NHL**	2	0	0	0	0	0	0	0	0	0	0	3	0.0	1	0	2	1	0	....	....	....	....	....	....	....	....
1997-2000	**Buffalo Sabres**	**NHL**	DID NOT PLAY – ASSISTANT COACH																									
	NHL Totals		1070	79	266	345	68	188	256	1012	12	2	14	1402	5.6	1194	139	1269	432		115	8	29	37	176	2	0	3

Played in NHL All-Star Game (1982, 1983, 1985, 1986)

Traded to **Pittsburgh** by **Buffalo** for Bob Errey, March 22, 1993. Signed as a free agent by **Detroit**, August 3, 1994.

• RAMSEY, Wayne

D – L. 6', 185 lbs. b: Hamiota, Man., 1/31/1957. Buffalo's 5th, 104th overall, in 1977.

Season	Club	League	GP	G	A	Pts	AG	AA	APts	PIM	PP	SH	GW	S	%	TGF	PGF	TGA	PGA	+/–	GP	G	A	Pts	PIM	PP	SH	GW
1973-74	Brandon Travellers	MJHL	15	0	9	9	....	....	....	35	....	....	....	....	....	....	....	....	....	....	....	....	....	....	....	....	....	....
	Brandon Wheat Kings	WCJHL	53	1	11	12	....	....	....	37	....	....	....	....	....	....	....	....	....	....	....	....	....	....	....	....	....	....
1974-75	Brandon Wheat Kings	WCJHL	21	1	0	1	....	....	....	17	....	....	....	....	....	....	....	....	....	....	5	1	2	3	7	....	....	....
1975-76	Brandon Wheat Kings	WCJHL	63	11	37	48	....	....	....	75	....	....	....	....	....	....	....	....	....	....	5	0	2	2	6	....	....	....
1976-77	Brandon Wheat Kings	WCJHL	72	16	60	76	....	....	....	136	....	....	....	....	....	....	....	....	....	....	16	4	*16	20	33	....	....	....
1977-78	**Buffalo Sabres**	**NHL**	2	0	0	0	0	0	0	0	0	0	0	0	0.0	0	0	0	0	0	....	....	....	....	....	....	....	....
	Hershey Bears	AHL	56	10	18	28	....	....	....	35	....	....	....	....	....	....	....	....	....	....	....	....	....	....	....	....	....	....
1978-79	Springfield Indians	AHL	15	4	5	9	....	....	....	8	....	....	....	....	....	....	....	....	....	....	....	....	....	....	....	....	....	....
	Milwaukee Admirals	IHL	3	1	2	3	....	....	....	2	....	....	....	....	....	....	....	....	....	....	....	....	....	....	....	....	....	....
	Toledo Goaldiggers	IHL	61	9	30	39	....	....	....	63	....	....	....	....	....	....	....	....	....	....	6	0	4	4	6	....	....	....
1979-80	Rochester Americans	AHL	68	6	29	35	....	....	....	58	....	....	....	....	....	....	....	....	....	....	....	....	....	....	....	....	....	....
1980-81	Port Huron Flags	IHL	61	9	29	38	....	....	....	53	....	....	....	....	....	....	....	....	....	....	4	1	1	2	4	....	....	....
	NHL Totals		2	0	0	0	0	0	0	0	0	0	0	0	0.0	0	0	0	0		....	....	....	....	....	....	....	....

Traded to **Toledo** (IHL) by **Milwaukee** (IHL) for Paul Tantardini, December, 1978.

• RANHEIM, Paul

Paul S. LW – R. 6'1", 210 lbs. b: St. Louis, MO, 1/25/1966. Calgary's 3rd, 38th overall, in 1984.

Season	Club	League	GP	G	A	Pts	AG	AA	APts	PIM	PP	SH	GW	S	%	TGF	PGF	TGA	PGA	+/–	GP	G	A	Pts	PIM	PP	SH	GW
1982-83	Edina Hornets	Hi-School	26	12	25	37	....	....	....	4	....	....	....	....	....	....	....	....	....	....	....	....	....	....	....	....	....	....
1983-84	Edina Hornets	Hi-School	26	16	24	40	....	....	....	6	....	....	....	....	....	....	....	....	....	....	....	....	....	....	....	....	....	....
1984-85	University of Wisconsin	WCHA	42	11	11	22	....	....	....	40	....	....	....	....	....	....	....	....	....	....	....	....	....	....	....	....	....	....
1985-86	University of Wisconsin	WCHA	33	17	17	34	....	....	....	34	....	....	....	....	....	....	....	....	....	....	....	....	....	....	....	....	....	....
	United States	WJC-A	7	6	3	9	....	....	....	8	....	....	....	....	....	....	....	....	....	....	....	....	....	....	....	....	....	....
1986-87	University of Wisconsin	WCHA	42	24	35	59	....	....	....	54	....	....	....	....	....	....	....	....	....	....	....	....	....	....	....	....	....	....
1987-88	University of Wisconsin	WCHA	44	36	26	62	....	....	....	63	....	....	....	....	....	....	....	....	....	....	....	....	....	....	....	....	....	....
1988-89	**Calgary Flames**	**NHL**	5	0	0	0	0	0	0	0	0	0	0	4	0.0	2	0	5	0	–3	....	....	....	....	....	....	....	....
	Salt Lake Golden Eagles	IHL	75	*68	29	97	....	....	....	16	....	....	....	....	....	....	....	....	....	....	14	5	5	10	8	....	....	....
1989-90	Calgary Flames	Fr-Tour	4	2	0	2	....	....	....	0	....	....	....	....	....	....	....	....	....	....	....	....	....	....	....	....	....	....
	Calgary Flames	**NHL**	80	26	28	54	22	20	42	23	1	3	4	197	13.2	72	5	51	11	27	6	1	3	4	2	0	0	0
	United States	WEC-A	9	4	0	4	....	....	....	6	....	....	....	....	....	....	....	....	....	....	....	....	....	....	....	....	....	....
1990-91	**Calgary Flames**	**NHL**	39	14	16	30	13	12	25	4	2	0	2	108	13.0	56	14	32	10	20	7	2	2	4	0	0	0	0
1991-92	**Calgary Flames**	**NHL**	80	23	20	43	21	15	36	32	1	3	3	159	14.5	65	6	59	16	16	....	....	....	....	....	....	....	....
	United States	WC-A	6	2	1	3	....	....	....	2	....	....	....	....	....	....	....	....	....	....	....	....	....	....	....	....	....	....
1992-93	**Calgary Flames**	**NHL**	83	21	22	43	17	15	32	26	3	4	1	179	11.7	59	9	96	42	–4	6	0	1	1	0	0	0	0
1993-94	**Calgary Flames**	**NHL**	67	10	14	24	9	11	20	20	0	2	2	110	9.1	37	2	68	26	–7	....	....	....	....	....	....	....	....
	Hartford Whalers	**NHL**	15	0	3	3	0	2	2	2	0	0	0	21	0.0	5	0	20	4	–11	....	....	....	....	....	....	....	....
1994-95	**Hartford Whalers**	**NHL**	47	6	14	20	11	21	32	10	0	0	1	73	8.2	24	1	41	15	–3	....	....	....	....	....	....	....	....
1995-96	**Hartford Whalers**	**NHL**	73	10	20	30	10	16	26	14	0	1	1	126	7.9	39	2	56	17	–2	....	....	....	....	....	....	....	....
1996-97	**Hartford Whalers**	**NHL**	67	10	11	21	11	10	21	18	0	3	1	96	10.4	30	1	61	19	–13	....	....	....	....	....	....	....	....
	United States	WC-A	8	2	0	2	....	....	....	2	....	....	....	....	....	....	....	....	....	....	....	....	....	....	....	....	....	....

			REGULAR SEASON																		PLAYOFFS							
Season	Club	League	GP	G	A	Pts	AG	AA	APts	PIM	PP	SH	GW	S	%	TGF	PGF	TGA	PGA	+/–	GP	G	A	Pts	PIM	PP	SH	GW
1997-98	**Carolina Hurricanes**	**NHL**	**73**	**5**	**9**	**14**	**6**	**9**	**15**	**28**	**0**	**1**	**2**	**77**	**6.5**	**17**	**0**	**42**	**14**	**–11**	....	....	....	....	....	....	....	....
1998-99	**Carolina Hurricanes**	**NHL**	**78**	**9**	**10**	**19**	**11**	**10**	**21**	**39**	**0**	**2**	**1**	**67**	**13.4**	**25**	**0**	**38**	**17**	**4**	**6**	**0**	**0**	**0**	**2**	**0**	**0**	**0**
99-2000	**Carolina Hurricanes**	**NHL**	**79**	**9**	**13**	**22**	**10**	**12**	**22**	**6**	**0**	**0**	**2**	**98**	**9.2**	**29**	**3**	**59**	**19**	**–14**	....	....	....	....	....	....	....	....
	NHL Totals		**786**	**143**	**180**	**323**	**141**	**153**	**294**	**222**	**7**	**19**	**20**	**1315**	**10.9**	**460**	**43**	**628**	**210**		**25**	**3**	**6**	**9**	**4**	**0**	**0**	**0**

WCHA Second All-Star Team (1987) • NCAA West First All-American Team (1988) • WCHA First All-Star Team (1988) • IHL Second All-Star Team (1989) • Won Garry F. Longman Memorial Trophy (Top Rookie - IHL) (1989)

• Missed majority of 1989-90 season recovering from ankle injury suffered in game vs. Minnesota, December 11, 1990. Traded to **Hartford** by **Calgary** with Gary Suter and Ted Drury for James Patrick, Zarley Zalapski and Michael Nylander, March 10, 1994. Transferred to **Carolina** after **Hartford** franchise relocated, June 25, 1997. Traded to **Philadelphia** by **Carolina** for Philadelphia's 8th round choice in 2002 Entry Draft, May 31, 2000.

• RASMUSSEN, Erik

C – L. 6'2", 205 lbs. b: Minneapolis, MN, 3/28/1977. Buffalo's 1st, 7th overall, in 1996.

Season	Club	League	GP	G	A	Pts	AG	AA	APts	PIM	PP	SH	GW	S	%	TGF	PGF	TGA	PGA	+/–	GP	G	A	Pts	PIM	PP	SH	GW
1992-93	St. Louis Park High School	Hi-School	23	16	24	40	....	....	....	50	....	....	....	....	....	....	....	....	....	....	....	....	....	....	....	....	....	....
1993-94	St. Louis Park High School	Hi-School	18	25	18	43	....	....	....	80	....	....	....	....	....	....	....	....	....	....	....	....	....	....	....	....	....	....
1994-95	St. Louis Park High School	Hi-School	23	19	33	52	....	....	....	80	....	....	....	....	....	....	....	....	....	....	....	....	....	....	....	....	....	....
1995-96	University of Minnesota	WCHA	40	16	32	48	....	....	....	55	....	....	....	....	....	....	....	....	....	....	....	....	....	....	....	....	....	....
	United States	WJC-A	6	0	1	1	....	....	....	16	....	....	....	....	....	....	....	....	....	....	....	....	....	....	....	....	....	....
1996-97	University of Minnesota	WCHA	34	15	12	27	....	....	....	*123	....	....	....	....	....	....	....	....	....	....	....	....	....	....	....	....	....	....
	United States	WJC-A	6	4	5	*9	....	....	....	4	....	....	....	....	....	....	....	....	....	....	....	....	....	....	....	....	....	....
1997-98	**Buffalo Sabres**	**NHL**	**21**	**2**	**3**	**5**	**2**	**3**	**5**	**14**	**0**	**0**	**0**	**28**	**7.1**	**12**	**0**	**10**	**0**	**2**	....	....	....	....	....	....	....	....
	Rochester Americans	AHL	53	9	14	23	....	....	....	83	....	....	....	....	....	....	....	....	....	....	1	0	0	0	5	....	....	....
1998-99	**Buffalo Sabres**	**NHL**	**42**	**3**	**7**	**10**	**4**	**7**	**11**	**37**	**0**	**0**	**0**	**40**	**7.5**	**18**	**0**	**16**	**4**	**6**	**21**	**2**	**4**	**6**	**18**	**0**	**0**	**1**
	Rochester Americans	AHL	37	12	14	26	....	....	....	47	....	....	....	....	....	....	....	....	....	....	....	....	....	....	....	....	....	....
99-2000	**Buffalo Sabres**	**NHL**	**67**	**8**	**6**	**14**	**9**	**6**	**15**	**43**	**0**	**0**	**2**	**76**	**10.5**	**26**	**2**	**24**	**1**	**1**	**3**	**0**	**0**	**0**	**4**	**0**	**0**	**0**
	NHL Totals		**130**	**13**	**16**	**29**	**15**	**16**	**31**	**94**	**0**	**0**	**2**	**144**	**9.0**	**56**	**2**	**50**	**5**		**24**	**2**	**4**	**6**	**22**	**0**	**0**	**1**

• RATCHUK, Peter

D – L. 6'1", 185 lbs. b: Buffalo, NY, 9/10/1977. Colorado's 1st, 25th overall, in 1996.

Season	Club	League	GP	G	A	Pts	AG	AA	APts	PIM	PP	SH	GW	S	%	TGF	PGF	TGA	PGA	+/–	GP	G	A	Pts	PIM	PP	SH	GW
1994-95	Lawrence Academy	Hi-School	31	8	15	23	....	....	....	18	....	....	....	....	....	....	....	....	....	....	....	....	....	....	....	....	....	....
1995-96	Shattuck-St. Mary's Sabres	Hi-School	35	22	28	50	....	....	....	24	....	....	....	....	....	....	....	....	....	....	....	....	....	....	....	....	....	....
1996-97	Bowling Green University	CCHA	35	9	12	21	....	....	....	14	....	....	....	....	....	....	....	....	....	....	....	....	....	....	....	....	....	....
1997-98	Hull Olympiques	QMJHL	60	23	31	54	....	....	....	34	....	....	....	....	....	....	....	....	....	....	11	3	6	9	8	....	....	....
1998-99	**Florida Panthers**	**NHL**	**24**	**1**	**1**	**2**	**1**	**1**	**2**	**10**	**0**	**0**	**0**	**34**	**2.9**	**10**	**1**	**12**	**2**	**–1**	....	....	....	....	....	....	....	....
	Beast of New Haven	AHL	53	7	20	27	....	....	....	44	....	....	....	....	....	....	....	....	....	....	....	....	....	....	....	....	....	....
99-2000	Louisville Panthers	AHL	76	9	17	26	....	....	....	64	....	....	....	....	....	....	....	....	....	....	4	1	2	3	0	....	....	....
	NHL Totals		**24**	**1**	**1**	**2**	**1**	**1**	**2**	**10**	**0**	**0**	**0**	**34**	**2.9**	**10**	**1**	**12**	**2**		....	....	....	....	....	....	....	....

Signed as a free agent by **Florida**, June 15, 1998.

• RATELLE, Jean

Joseph Gilbert Yvan Jean C – L. 6'1", 180 lbs. b: Lac Ste. Jean, Que., 10/3/1940. **HHOF**

Season	Club	League	GP	G	A	Pts	AG	AA	APts	PIM	PP	SH	GW	S	%	TGF	PGF	TGA	PGA	+/–	GP	G	A	Pts	PIM	PP	SH	GW
1958-59	Guelph Biltmores	OHA-Jr.	54	20	31	51	....	....	....	11	....	....	....	....	....	....	....	....	....	....	10	5	4	9	2	....	....	....
1959-60	Guelph Biltmores	OHA-Jr.	48	39	47	86	....	....	....	15	....	....	....	....	....	....	....	....	....	....	5	3	5	8	4	....	....	....
	Trois-Rivieres Lions	EPHL	3	3	5	8	....	....	....	0	....	....	....	....	....	....	....	....	....	....	4	0	3	3	0	....	....	....
1960-61	Guelph Royals	OHA-Jr.	47	40	*61	101	....	....	....	10	....	....	....	....	....	....	....	....	....	....	14	6	11	17	6	....	....	....
	New York Rangers	**NHL**	**3**	**2**	**1**	**3**	**2**	**1**	**3**	**0**	....	....	....	....	....	....	....	....	....	....	....	....	....	....	....	....	....	....
1961-62	**New York Rangers**	**NHL**	**31**	**4**	**8**	**12**	**5**	**8**	**13**	**4**	....	....	....	....	....	....	....	....	....	....	....	....	....	....	....	....	....	....
	Kitchener-Waterloo Beavers	EPHL	32	10	29	39	....	....	....	8	....	....	....	....	....	....	....	....	....	....	7	2	6	8	2	....	....	....
1962-63	**New York Rangers**	**NHL**	**48**	**11**	**9**	**20**	**13**	**9**	**22**	**8**	....	....	....	....	....	....	....	....	....	....	....	....	....	....	....	....	....	....
	Baltimore Clippers	AHL	20	11	8	19	....	....	....	0	....	....	....	....	....	....	....	....	....	....	3	0	0	0	0	....	....	....
1963-64	**New York Rangers**	**NHL**	**15**	**0**	**7**	**7**	**0**	**7**	**7**	**6**	....	....	....	....	....	....	....	....	....	....	....	....	....	....	....	....	....	....
	Baltimore Clippers	AHL	57	20	26	46	....	....	....	2	....	....	....	....	....	....	....	....	....	....	....	....	....	....	....	....	....	....
1964-65	**New York Rangers**	**NHL**	**54**	**14**	**21**	**35**	**17**	**22**	**39**	**14**	....	....	....	....	....	....	....	....	....	....	....	....	....	....	....	....	....	....
	Baltimore Clippers	AHL	8	9	4	13	....	....	....	6	....	....	....	....	....	....	....	....	....	....	....	....	....	....	....	....	....	....
1965-66	**New York Rangers**	**NHL**	**67**	**21**	**30**	**51**	**24**	**29**	**53**	**10**	....	....	....	....	....	....	....	....	....	....	....	....	....	....	....	....	....	....
1966-67	**New York Rangers**	**NHL**	**41**	**6**	**5**	**11**	**7**	**5**	**12**	**4**	....	....	....	....	....	....	....	....	....	....	**4**	**0**	**0**	**0**	**2**	**0**	**0**	**0**
1967-68	**New York Rangers**	**NHL**	**74**	**32**	**46**	**78**	**37**	**46**	**83**	**18**	**10**	**0**	**5**	**180**	**17.8**	**98**	**25**	**50**	**0**	**23**	**6**	**0**	**4**	**4**	**2**	**0**	**0**	**0**
1968-69	**New York Rangers**	**NHL**	**75**	**32**	**46**	**78**	**34**	**41**	**75**	**26**	**8**	**0**	**4**	**204**	**15.7**	**110**	**36**	**58**	**0**	**16**	**4**	**1**	**0**	**1**	**0**	**1**	**0**	**0**
1969-70	**New York Rangers**	**NHL**	**75**	**32**	**42**	**74**	**35**	**39**	**74**	**28**	**10**	**0**	**6**	**198**	**16.2**	**93**	**29**	**57**	**1**	**8**	**6**	**1**	**3**	**4**	**0**	**0**	**0**	**0**
1970-71	**New York Rangers**	**NHL**	**78**	**26**	**46**	**72**	**26**	**39**	**65**	**14**	**6**	**1**	**3**	**203**	**12.8**	**93**	**26**	**41**	**2**	**28**	**13**	**2**	**9**	**11**	**8**	**0**	**0**	**0**
1971-72	**New York Rangers**	**NHL**	**63**	**46**	**63**	**109**	**46**	**55**	**101**	**4**	**5**	**1**	**6**	**183**	**25.1**	**140**	**39**	**41**	**1**	**61**	**6**	**0**	**1**	**1**	**0**	**0**	**0**	**0**
1972-73	Team Canada	Summit-72	6	1	3	4	....	....	....	0	....	....	....	....	....	....	....	....	....	....	....	....	....	....	....	....	....	....
	New York Rangers	**NHL**	**78**	**41**	**53**	**94**	**39**	**42**	**81**	**12**	**11**	**0**	**4**	**241**	**17.0**	**123**	**35**	**67**	**3**	**24**	**10**	**2**	**7**	**9**	**0**	**1**	**0**	**0**
1973-74	**New York Rangers**	**NHL**	**68**	**28**	**39**	**67**	**27**	**32**	**59**	**16**	**6**	**0**	**3**	**165**	**17.0**	**95**	**34**	**60**	**4**	**5**	**13**	**2**	**4**	**6**	**0**	**0**	**0**	**1**
1974-75	**New York Rangers**	**NHL**	**79**	**36**	**55**	**91**	**32**	**41**	**73**	**26**	**15**	**0**	**6**	**205**	**17.6**	**129**	**63**	**65**	**0**	**1**	**3**	**1**	**5**	**6**	**2**	**1**	**0**	**0**
1975-76	**New York Rangers**	**NHL**	**13**	**5**	**10**	**15**	**4**	**7**	**11**	**2**	**2**	**0**	**1**	**28**	**17.9**	**20**	**9**	**12**	**3**	**2**	....	....	....	....	....	....	....	....
	Boston Bruins	**NHL**	**67**	**31**	**59**	**90**	**27**	**44**	**71**	**16**	**15**	**1**	**3**	**186**	**16.7**	**115**	**50**	**66**	**18**	**17**	**12**	**8**	**8**	**16**	**4**	**5**	**0**	**1**
1976-77	**Boston Bruins**	**NHL**	**78**	**33**	**61**	**94**	**30**	**47**	**77**	**22**	**8**	**1**	**6**	**186**	**17.7**	**117**	**27**	**75**	**4**	**19**	**14**	**5**	**12**	**17**	**4**	**1**	**0**	**1**
1977-78	**Boston Bruins**	**NHL**	**80**	**25**	**59**	**84**	**23**	**46**	**69**	**10**	**3**	**0**	**5**	**158**	**15.8**	**112**	**16**	**53**	**6**	**49**	**15**	**3**	**7**	**10**	**0**	**0**	**0**	**0**
1978-79	**Boston Bruins**	**NHL**	**80**	**27**	**45**	**72**	**23**	**33**	**56**	**12**	**11**	**0**	**5**	**137**	**19.7**	**100**	**32**	**61**	**10**	**17**	**11**	**7**	**6**	**13**	**2**	**2**	**0**	**2**
1979-80	**Boston Bruins**	**NHL**	**67**	**28**	**45**	**73**	**24**	**33**	**57**	**8**	**14**	**0**	**1**	**145**	**19.3**	**98**	**38**	**53**	**4**	**11**	**3**	**0**	**0**	**0**	**0**	**0**	**0**	**0**
1980-81	**Boston Bruins**	**NHL**	**47**	**11**	**26**	**37**	**9**	**17**	**26**	**16**	**4**	**0**	**2**	**62**	**17.7**	**52**	**19**	**26**	**11**	**18**	**3**	**0**	**0**	**0**	**0**	**0**	**0**	**0**
	NHL Totals		**1281**	**491**	**776**	**1267**	**484**	**643**	**1127**	**276**	....	....	....	....	....	....	....	....	....	....	**123**	**32**	**66**	**98**	**24**	....	....	....

OHA-Jr. Second All-Star Team (1961) • Won Bill Masterton Trophy (1971) • NHL Second All-Star Team (1972) • Won Lady Byng Trophy (1972, 1976) • Won Lester B. Pearson Award (1972) • Played in NHL All-Star Game (1970, 1971, 1972, 1973, 1980)

Traded to **Boston** by **NY Rangers** with Brad Park and Joe Zanussi for Phil Esposito and Carol Vadnais, November 7, 1975.

• RATHJE, Mike

Mike Steven D – L. 6'5", 230 lbs. b: Mannville, Alta., 5/11/1974. San Jose's 1st, 3rd overall, in 1992.

Season	Club	League	GP	G	A	Pts	AG	AA	APts	PIM	PP	SH	GW	S	%	TGF	PGF	TGA	PGA	+/–	GP	G	A	Pts	PIM	PP	SH	GW
1989-90	Sherwood Park Crusaders	AAHA	33	6	11	17	....	....	....	30	....	....	....	....	....	....	....	....	....	....	....	....	....	....	....	....	....	....
1990-91	Medicine Hat Tigers	WHL	64	1	16	17	....	....	....	28	....	....	....	....	....	....	....	....	....	....	12	0	4	4	2	....	....	....
1991-92	Medicine Hat Tigers	WHL	67	11	23	34	....	....	....	99	....	....	....	....	....	....	....	....	....	....	4	0	1	1	2	....	....	....
1992-93	Medicine Hat Tigers	WHL	57	12	37	49	....	....	....	103	....	....	....	....	....	....	....	....	....	....	10	3	3	6	12	....	....	....
	Canada	WJC-A	7	2	2	4	....	....	....	12	....	....	....	....	....	....	....	....	....	....	....	....	....	....	....	....	....	....
	Kansas City Blades	IHL	....	....	....	....	....	....	....	....	....	....	....	....	....	....	....	....	....	....	5	0	0	0	12	....	....	....
1993-94	**San Jose Sharks**	**NHL**	**47**	**1**	**9**	**10**	**1**	**7**	**8**	**59**	**1**	**0**	**0**	**30**	**3.3**	**26**	**3**	**42**	**10**	**–9**	**1**	**0**	**0**	**0**	**0**	**0**	**0**	**0**
	Kansas City Blades	IHL	6	0	2	2	....	....	....	0	....	....	....	....	....	....	....	....	....	....	....	....	....	....	....	....	....	....
1994-95	**San Jose Sharks**	**NHL**	**42**	**2**	**7**	**9**	**4**	**10**	**14**	**29**	**0**	**0**	**0**	**38**	**5.3**	**42**	**5**	**53**	**15**	**–1**	**11**	**5**	**2**	**7**	**4**	**5**	**0**	**0**
	Kansas City Blades	IHL	6	0	1	1	....	....	....	7	....	....	....	....	....	....	....	....	....	....	....	....	....	....	....	....	....	....
1995-96	**San Jose Sharks**	**NHL**	**27**	**0**	**7**	**7**	**0**	**6**	**6**	**14**	**0**	**0**	**0**	**26**	**0.0**	**24**	**9**	**46**	**15**	**–16**	....	....	....	....	....	....	....	....
	Kansas City Blades	IHL	36	6	11	17	....	....	....	34	....	....	....	....	....	....	....	....	....	....	....	....	....	....	....	....	....	....
1996-97	**San Jose Sharks**	**NHL**	**31**	**0**	**8**	**8**	**0**	**7**	**7**	**21**	**0**	**0**	**0**	**22**	**0.0**	**26**	**3**	**31**	**7**	**–1**	....	....	....	....	....	....	....	....
1997-98	**San Jose Sharks**	**NHL**	**81**	**3**	**12**	**15**	**4**	**12**	**16**	**59**	**1**	**0**	**0**	**61**	**4.9**	**55**	**6**	**83**	**30**	**–4**	**6**	**1**	**0**	**1**	**6**	**1**	**0**	**0**
1998-99	**San Jose Sharks**	**NHL**	**82**	**5**	**9**	**14**	**6**	**9**	**15**	**36**	**2**	**0**	**1**	**67**	**7.5**	**68**	**11**	**71**	**29**	**15**	**6**	**0**	**0**	**0**	**4**	**0**	**0**	**0**
99-2000	**San Jose Sharks**	**NHL**	**66**	**2**	**14**	**16**	**2**	**13**	**15**	**31**	**0**	**0**	**0**	**46**	**4.3**	**49**	**9**	**67**	**25**	**–2**	**12**	**1**	**3**	**4**	**8**	**0**	**0**	**0**
	NHL Totals		**376**	**13**	**66**	**79**	**17**	**64**	**81**	**249**	**4**	**0**	**1**	**290**	**4.5**	**290**	**46**	**393**	**131**		**36**	**7**	**5**	**12**	**22**	**6**	**0**	**0**

WHL East Second All-Star Team (1992, 1993)

• Missed majority of 1996-97 season recovering from groin injury suffered in game vs. Dallas, November 8, 1996.

Season	Club	League	GP	G	A	Pts	AG	AA	APts	PIM	PP	SH	GW	S	%	TGF	PGF	TGA	PGA	+/-	GP	G	A	Pts	PIM	PP	SH	GW
			REGULAR SEASON																		PLAYOFFS							

• RATHWELL, Jake

John Donald RW – L. 6', 190 lbs. b: Temiscominque, Que., 8/12/1947.

Season	Club	League	GP	G	A	Pts	AG	AA	APts	PIM	PP	SH	GW	S	%	TGF	PGF	TGA	PGA	+/-	GP	G	A	Pts	PIM	PP	SH	GW
1966-67	Verdun Maple Leafs	QJHL	STATISTICS NOT AVAILABLE																									
	Verdun Maple Leafs	Mem-Cup	4	4	1	5	....	....	....	4	....	....	....	....	....	....	....	....	....	....	....	....	....	....	....	....	....	....
1967-68	Espanola Bruins	OHA-B	STATISTICS NOT AVAILABLE																		....	....	....	....	....	....	....	....
	Kitchener Rangers	OHA-Jr.	9	0	0	0	....	....	....	7	....	....	....	....	....	....	....	....	....	....	....	....	....	....	....	....	....	....
	Peterborough Petes	OHA-Jr.	14	2	2	4	....	....	....	4	....	....	....	....	....	....	....	....	....	....	....	....	....	....	....	....	....	....
1968-69	Clinton Comets	EHL	72	18	26	44	....	....	....	104	....	....	....	....	....	....	....	....	....	....	17	5	6	11	30	....	....	....
1969-70	Clinton Comets	EHL	74	*56	43	99	....	....	....	151	....	....	....	....	....	....	....	....	....	....	17	11	12	23	27	....	....	....
	Iowa Stars	CHL	....	....	....	....	....	....	....	....	....	....	....	....	....	....	....	....	....	....	3	0	0	0	4	....	....	....
1970-71	Salt Lake Golden Eagles	WHL	71	20	19	39	....	....	....	66	....	....	....	....	....	....	....	....	....	....	....	....	....	....	....	....	....	....
1971-72	Salt Lake Golden Eagles	WHL	30	5	6	11	....	....	....	20	....	....	....	....	....	....	....	....	....	....	....	....	....	....	....	....	....	....
	Portland Buckaroos	WHL	16	8	5	13	....	....	....	17	....	....	....	....	....	....	....	....	....	....	....	....	....	....	....	....	....	....
	Cincinnati Swords	AHL	14	6	6	12	....	....	....	4	....	....	....	....	....	....	....	....	....	....	10	2	2	4	17	....	....	....
1972-73	Cincinnati Swords	AHL	76	27	44	71	....	....	....	78	....	....	....	....	....	....	....	....	....	....	15	4	8	12	22	....	....	....
1973-74	San Diego Gulls	WHL	37	6	10	16	....	....	....	25	....	....	....	....	....	....	....	....	....	....	....	....	....	....	....	....	....	....
	Rochester Americans	AHL	26	5	5	10	....	....	....	24	....	....	....	....	....	....	....	....	....	....	5	2	2	4	10	....	....	....
1974-75	**Boston Bruins**	**NHL**	**1**	**0**	**0**	**0**	**0**	**0**	**0**	**0**	**0**	**0**	**0**	**0**	**0.0**	**0**	**0**	**0**	**0**	**0**	....	....	....	....	....	....	....	....
	Rochester Americans	AHL	68	10	12	22	....	....	....	45	....	....	....	....	....	....	....	....	....	....	10	2	0	2	4	....	....	....
	NHL Totals		**1**	**0**	**0**	**0**	**0**	**0**	**0**	**0**	**0**	**0**	**0**	**0**	**0.0**	**0**	**0**	**0**	**0**		....	....	....	....	....	....	....	....

Won WHL Rookie of the Year Award (1971)

Traded to **Minnesota** by **Montreal** for cash, June, 1968. Claimed by **Salt Lake** (CHL) from **Minnesota** in Reverse Draft, June 10, 1970. Traded to **Portland** (WHL) by **California** (Salt Lake-WHL) with Guyle Fielder for Lyle Bradley and Fred Hilts, January, 1972. Traded to **Buffalo** (Cincinnati-AHL) by **Portland** for cash, March, 1972. Traded to **St. Louis** by **Buffalo** for Paul Curtis, June 14, 1973. Traded to **Boston** by **St. Louis** with St. Louis' 2nd round choice (Mark Howe) in 1974 Amateur Draft and cash for Don Awrey, October 5, 1973.

• RATUSHNY, Dan

Dan Paul D – R. 6'1", 205 lbs. b: Nepean, Ont., 10/29/1970. Winnipeg's 2nd, 25th overall, in 1989.

Season	Club	League	GP	G	A	Pts	AG	AA	APts	PIM	PP	SH	GW	S	%	TGF	PGF	TGA	PGA	+/-	GP	G	A	Pts	PIM	PP	SH	GW
1987-88	Nepean Raiders	OJHL	54	8	20	28	....	....	....	116	....	....	....	....	....	....	....	....	....	....	....	....	....	....	....	....	....	....
1988-89	Cornell University	ECAC	28	2	13	15	....	....	....	50	....	....	....	....	....	....	....	....	....	....	....	....	....	....	....	....	....	....
	Canada	Nat-Team	2	0	0	0	....	....	....	2	....	....	....	....	....	....	....	....	....	....	....	....	....	....	....	....	....	....
1989-90	Cornell University	ECAC	26	5	14	19	....	....	....	54	....	....	....	....	....	....	....	....	....	....	....	....	....	....	....	....	....	....
	Canada	WJC-A	7	2	2	4	....	....	....	4	....	....	....	....	....	....	....	....	....	....	....	....	....	....	....	....	....	....
1990-91	Cornell University	ECAC	26	7	24	31	....	....	....	52	....	....	....	....	....	....	....	....	....	....	....	....	....	....	....	....	....	....
	Canada	Nat-Team	12	0	1	1	....	....	....	6	....	....	....	....	....	....	....	....	....	....	....	....	....	....	....	....	....	....
1991-92	Canada	Nat-Team	58	5	13	18	....	....	....	50	....	....	....	....	....	....	....	....	....	....	....	....	....	....	....	....	....	....
	Canada	Olympics	8	0	0	0	....	....	....	4	....	....	....	....	....	....	....	....	....	....	....	....	....	....	....	....	....	....
	EHC Olten	Switz.	2	0	0	0	....	....	....	0	....	....	....	....	....	....	....	....	....	....	....	....	....	....	....	....	....	....
1992-93	Fort Wayne Komets	IHL	63	6	19	25	....	....	....	48	....	....	....	....	....	....	....	....	....	....	....	....	....	....	....	....	....	....
	Vancouver Canucks	**NHL**	**1**	**0**	**1**	**1**	**0**	**1**	**1**	**2**	**0**	**0**	**0**	**2**	**0.0**	**2**	**0**	**2**	**0**	**0**	....	....	....	....	....	....	....	....
1993-94	Hamilton Canucks	AHL	62	8	31	39	....	....	....	22	....	....	....	....	....	....	....	....	....	....	4	0	0	0	4	....	....	....
1994-95	Fort Wayne Komets	IHL	72	3	25	28	....	....	....	46	....	....	....	....	....	....	....	....	....	....	4	0	1	1	8	....	....	....
1995-96	Peoria Rivermen	IHL	45	7	15	22	....	....	....	45	....	....	....	....	....	....	....	....	....	....	12	3	4	7	10	....	....	....
	Carolina Monarchs	AHL	23	5	10	15	....	....	....	28	....	....	....	....	....	....	....	....	....	....	....	....	....	....	....	....	....	....
1996-97	Quebec Rafales	IHL	50	14	23	37	....	....	....	34	....	....	....	....	....	....	....	....	....	....	....	....	....	....	....	....	....	....
1997-98	Quebec Rafales	IHL	20	3	9	12	....	....	....	22	....	....	....	....	....	....	....	....	....	....	....	....	....	....	....	....	....	....
	Albany River Rats	AHL	39	8	5	13	....	....	....	10	....	....	....	....	....	....	....	....	....	....	9	0	3	3	8	....	....	....
1998-99	Kansas City Blades	IHL	70	9	32	41	....	....	....	38	....	....	....	....	....	....	....	....	....	....	3	0	0	0	4	....	....	....
99-2000	Seibu Tetsudo Tokyo	Japan	27	2	11	13	....	....	....	....	....	....	....	....	....	....	....	....	....	....	9	2	3	5	8	....	....	....
	NHL Totals		**1**	**0**	**1**	**1**	**0**	**1**	**1**	**2**	**0**	**0**	**0**	**2**	**0.0**	**2**	**0**	**2**	**0**		....	....	....	....	....	....	....	....

ECAC First All-Star Team (1990, 1991)

Traded to **Vancouver** by **Winnipeg** for Vancouver's 9th round choice (Harijs Vitolinsh) in 1993 Entry Draft, March 22, 1993.

• RAUSSE, Errol

Errol Andrew LW – L. 5'10", 180 lbs. b: Quesnel, B.C., 5/18/1959. Washington's 2nd, 24th overall, in 1979.

Season	Club	League	GP	G	A	Pts	AG	AA	APts	PIM	PP	SH	GW	S	%	TGF	PGF	TGA	PGA	+/-	GP	G	A	Pts	PIM	PP	SH	GW
1975-76	Langley Lords	BCJHL	66	34	49	83	....	....	....	47	....	....	....	....	....	....	....	....	....	....	....	....	....	....	....	....	....	....
1976-77	Kamloops Chiefs	WCJHL	68	22	18	40	....	....	....	21	....	....	....	....	....	....	....	....	....	....	5	0	2	2	0	....	....	....
1977-78	Seattle Breakers	WCJHL	72	62	92	154	....	....	....	60	....	....	....	....	....	....	....	....	....	....	....	....	....	....	....	....	....	....
1978-79	Seattle Thunderbirds	WHL	71	65	47	112	....	....	....	17	....	....	....	....	....	....	....	....	....	....	....	....	....	....	....	....	....	....
	Canada	WJC-A	5	1	1	2	....	....	....	2	....	....	....	....	....	....	....	....	....	....	....	....	....	....	....	....	....	....
1979-80	**Washington Capitals**	**NHL**	**24**	**6**	**2**	**8**	**5**	**1**	**6**	**0**	**0**	**0**	**0**	**24**	**25.0**	**12**	**0**	**8**	**0**	**4**	....	....	....	....	....	....	....	....
	Hershey Bears	AHL	53	14	17	31	....	....	....	2	....	....	....	....	....	....	....	....	....	....	11	7	7	14	2	....	....	....
1980-81	**Washington Capitals**	**NHL**	**5**	**1**	**1**	**2**	**1**	**1**	**2**	**0**	**0**	**0**	**0**	**3**	**33.3**	**3**	**0**	**2**	**0**	**1**	....	....	....	....	....	....	....	....
	Hershey Bears	AHL	57	19	27	46	....	....	....	18	....	....	....	....	....	....	....	....	....	....	10	2	6	8	2	....	....	....
1981-82	**Washington Capitals**	**NHL**	**2**	**0**	**0**	**0**	**0**	**0**	**0**	**0**	**0**	**0**	**0**	**0**	**0.0**	**0**	**0**	**2**	**0**	**–2**	....	....	....	....	....	....	....	....
	Hershey Bears	AHL	59	18	25	43	....	....	....	6	....	....	....	....	....	....	....	....	....	....	5	0	4	4	2	....	....	....
1982-83	Hershey Bears	AHL	79	25	35	60	....	....	....	18	....	....	....	....	....	....	....	....	....	....	5	1	2	3	2	....	....	....
1983-84	SG Cortina	Italy	28	29	31	60	....	....	....	8	....	....	....	....	....	....	....	....	....	....	7	9	7	16	8	....	....	....
1984-85	HC Alleghe	Italy	26	39	45	84	....	....	....	10	....	....	....	....	....	....	....	....	....	....	8	11	14	*25	10	....	....	....
1985-86	HC Alleghe	Italy	35	43	60	103	....	....	....	56	....	....	....	....	....	....	....	....	....	....	4	5	6	11	0	....	....	....
1986-87	HC Alleghe	Italy	37	37	47	84	....	....	....	26	....	....	....	....	....	....	....	....	....	....	....	....	....	....	....	....	....	....
1987-88	HC Alleghe	Italy	36	43	50	93	....	....	....	22	....	....	....	....	....	....	....	....	....	....	10	9	17	26	4	....	....	....
1988-89	HC Alleghe	Italy	30	37	30	67	....	....	....	12	....	....	....	....	....	....	....	....	....	....	....	....	....	....	....	....	....	....
1989-90	HC Alleghe	Italy	35	31	39	70	....	....	....	28	....	....	....	....	....	....	....	....	....	....	10	5	25	30	6	....	....	....
1990-91	HC Alleghe	Italy	30	21	36	57	....	....	....	4	....	....	....	....	....	....	....	....	....	....	6	3	2	5	0	....	....	....
1991-92	HC Alleghe	Alpenliga	18	19	13	32	....	....	....	2	....	....	....	....	....	....	....	....	....	....	....	....	....	....	....	....	....	....
	HC Alleghe	Italy	18	8	20	28	....	....	....	4	....	....	....	....	....	....	....	....	....	....	9	7	9	16	2	....	....	....
1992-93	HC Alleghe	Alpenliga	28	16	28	44	....	....	....	14	....	....	....	....	....	....	....	....	....	....	....	....	....	....	....	....	....	....
	HC Alleghe	Italy	16	5	18	23	....	....	....	0	....	....	....	....	....	....	....	....	....	....	9	6	5	11	4	....	....	....
1993-94	HC Alleghe	Alpenliga	29	11	18	29	....	....	....	10	....	....	....	....	....	....	....	....	....	....	....	....	....	....	....	....	....	....
	HC Alleghe	Italy	7	4	4	8	....	....	....	2	....	....	....	....	....	....	....	....	....	....	3	1	1	2	4	....	....	....
	NHL Totals		**31**	**7**	**3**	**10**	**6**	**2**	**8**	**0**	**0**	**0**	**0**	**27**	**25.9**	**15**	**0**	**12**	**0**		....	....	....	....	....	....	....	....

• RAUTAKALLIO, Pekka

D – L. 5'11", 185 lbs. b: Pori, Finland, 7/25/1953.

Season	Club	League	GP	G	A	Pts	AG	AA	APts	PIM	PP	SH	GW	S	%	TGF	PGF	TGA	PGA	+/-	GP	G	A	Pts	PIM	PP	SH	GW
1968-69	Assat Pori	Finland	10	2	1	3	....	....	....	0	....	....	....	....	....	....	....	....	....	....	....	....	....	....	....	....	....	....
1969-70	Assat Pori	Finland	22	9	2	11	....	....	....	2	....	....	....	....	....	....	....	....	....	....	....	....	....	....	....	....	....	....
1970-71	Assat Pori	Finland	31	6	5	11	....	....	....	18	....	....	....	....	....	....	....	....	....	....	....	....	....	....	....	....	....	....
1971-72	Assat Pori	Finland	32	10	8	18	....	....	....	14	....	....	....	....	....	....	....	....	....	....	....	....	....	....	....	....	....	....
	Finland	WEC-A	4	0	0	0	....	....	....	0	....	....	....	....	....	....	....	....	....	....	....	....	....	....	....	....	....	....
1972-73	Assat Pori	Finland	34	23	12	35	....	....	....	21	....	....	....	....	....	....	....	....	....	....	....	....	....	....	....	....	....	....
	Finland	WEC-A	7	0	0	0	....	....	....	4	....	....	....	....	....	....	....	....	....	....	....	....	....	....	....	....	....	....
1973-74	Assat Pori	Finland	32	9	12	21	....	....	....	8	....	....	....	....	....	....	....	....	....	....	....	....	....	....	....	....	....	....
1974-75	Assat Pori	Finland	36	9	13	22	....	....	....	19	....	....	....	....	....	....	....	....	....	....	....	....	....	....	....	....	....	....
	Finland	WEC-A	10	0	3	3	....	....	....	0	....	....	....	....	....	....	....	....	....	....	....	....	....	....	....	....	....	....
1975-76	Phoenix Roadrunners	WHA	73	11	39	50	....	....	....	8	....	....	....	....	....	....	....	....	....	....	5	0	2	2	0	....	....	....
1976-77	Finland	Can-Cup	5	2	2	4	....	....	....	2	....	....	....	....	....	....	....	....	....	....	....	....	....	....	....	....	....	....
	Phoenix Roadrunners	WHA	78	4	31	35	....	....	....	8	....	....	....	....	....	....	....	....	....	....	....	....	....	....	....	....	....	....
	Finland	WEC-A	10	3	4	7	....	....	....	2	....	....	....	....	....	....	....	....	....	....	....	....	....	....	....	....	....	....
1977-78	Assat Pori	Finland	36	16	21	37	....	....	....	16	....	....	....	....	....	....	....	....	....	....	9	5	4	9	0	....	....	....
	Finland	WEC-A	10	4	3	7	....	....	....	2	....	....	....	....	....	....	....	....	....	....	....	....	....	....	....	....	....	....
1978-79	Assat Pori	Finland	36	25	28	53	....	....	....	26	....	....	....	....	....	....	....	....	....	....	8	5	9	14	2	....	....	....
	Finland	WEC-A	7	2	1	3	....	....	....	2	....	....	....	....	....	....	....	....	....	....	....	....	....	....	....	....	....	....
1979-80	**Atlanta Flames**	**NHL**	**79**	**5**	**25**	**30**	**4**	**18**	**22**	**18**	**1**	**0**	**1**	**104**	**4.8**	**100**	**18**	**60**	**0**	**22**	**4**	**0**	**1**	**1**	**2**	**0**	**0**	**0**

Season	Club	League	REGULAR SEASON GP	G	A	Pts	AG	AA	APts	PIM	PP	SH	GW	S	%	TGF	PGF	TGA	PGA	+/–	PLAYOFFS GP	G	A	Pts	PIM	PP	SH	GW
1980-81	**Calgary Flames**	**NHL**	**76**	**11**	**45**	**56**	**9**	**30**	**39**	**64**	**3**	**0**	**1**	**129**	**8.5**	**118**	**34**	**88**	**3**	**–1**	**16**	**2**	**4**	**6**	**6**	**1**	**0**	**0**
1981-82	Finland	Can-Cup	5	0	1	1	....	....	....	2	....	....	....	....	....	....	....	....	....	....	....	....	....	....	....	....	....	....
	Calgary Flames	**NHL**	**80**	**17**	**51**	**68**	**13**	**34**	**47**	**40**	**5**	**0**	**3**	**176**	**9.7**	**151**	**44**	**129**	**14**	**–8**	**3**	**0**	**0**	**0**	**0**	**0**	**0**	**0**
1982-83	HIFK Helsinki	Finland	36	16	16	32	....	....	....	16	....	....	....	....	....	....	....	....	....	....	9	6	4	10	10	....	....	....
	Finland	WEC-A	10	1	7	8	....	....	....	0	....	....	....	....	....	....	....	....	....	....	....	....	....	....	....	....	....	....
1983-84	HIFK Helsinki	Finland	33	9	21	30	....	....	....	10	....	....	....	....	....	....	....	....	....	....	2	0	2	2	0	....	....	....
1984-85	HIFK Helsinki	Finland	29	12	18	30	....	....	....	18	....	....	....	....	....	....	....	....	....	....	....	....	....	....	....	....	....	....
1985-86	HIFK Helsinki	Finland	34	13	23	36	....	....	....	8	....	....	....	....	....	....	....	....	....	....	10	3	0	3	10	....	....	....
1986-87	HIFK Helsinki	Finland	42	15	25	40	....	....	....	10	....	....	....	....	....	....	....	....	....	....	5	5	1	6	5	....	....	....
1987-88	HC Rapperswil-Jona	Switz-2	36	15	18	33	....	....	....	....	....	....	....	....	....	....	....	....	....	....	....	....	....	....	....	....	....	....
	NHL Totals		**235**	**33**	**121**	**154**	**26**	**82**	**108**	**122**	**9**	**0**	**5**	**409**	**8.1**	**369**	**96**	**277**	**17**		**23**	**2**	**5**	**7**	**8**	**1**	**0**	**0**
	Other Major League Totals		151	15	70	85	....	....	....	16	....	....	....	....	....	....	....	....	....	....	5	0	2	2	0	....	....	....

EJC-A All-Star Team (1971) • Named Best Defenseman at EJC-A (1971) • Finnish First All-Star Team (1975, 1978, 1979, 1983, 1986) • Played in NHL All-Star Game (1982)

Signed as a free agent by **Phoenix** (WHA), June 16, 1975. Signed as a free agent by **Atlanta**, June 5, 1979. Transferred to **Calgary** after **Atlanta** franchise relocated, June 24, 1980.

• RAVLICH, Matt

Matthew Joseph D – L. 5'10", 185 lbs. b: Sault Ste. Marie, Ont., 7/12/1938.

Season	Club	League	GP	G	A	Pts	AG	AA	APts	PIM	PP	SH	GW	S	%	TGF	PGF	TGA	PGA	+/–	GP	G	A	Pts	PIM	PP	SH	GW
1954-55	Woodstock Athletics	OHA-B	STATISTICS NOT AVAILABLE																									
	Galt Black Hawks	OHA-Jr.	3	1	1	2	....	....	....	0	....	....	....	....	....	....	....	....	....	....	....	....	....	....	....	....	....	....
1955-56	St. Catharines Teepees	OHA-Jr.	48	2	15	17	....	....	....	188	....	....	....	....	....	....	....	....	....	....	6	0	0	0	11	....	....	....
1956-57	St. Catharines Teepees	OHA-Jr.	52	7	27	34	....	....	....	137	....	....	....	....	....	....	....	....	....	....	14	9	12	21	4	....	....	....
1957-58	St. Catharines Teepees	OHA-Jr.	49	38	35	73	....	....	....	105	....	....	....	....	....	....	....	....	....	....	8	3	7	10	15	....	....	....
1958-59	Trois-Rivieres Ducs	QJHL	61	14	31	45	....	....	....	58	....	....	....	....	....	....	....	....	....	....	8	2	3	5	7	....	....	....
1959-60	Sault Ste. Marie Greyhounds	EPHL	70	18	37	55	....	....	....	94	....	....	....	....	....	....	....	....	....	....	....	....	....	....	....	....	....	....
1960-61	Sault Ste. Marie Greyhounds	EPHL	55	5	25	30	....	....	....	104	....	....	....	....	....	....	....	....	....	....	12	0	2	2	0	....	....	....
1961-62	Providence Reds	AHL	69	10	29	39	....	....	....	112	....	....	....	....	....	....	....	....	....	....	3	0	2	2	0	....	....	....
1962-63	**Boston Bruins**	**NHL**	**2**	**1**	**0**	**1**	**1**	**0**	**1**	**0**	....	....	....	....	....	....	....	....	....	....	....	....	....	....	....	....	....	....
	Providence Reds	AHL	70	7	38	45	....	....	....	97	....	....	....	....	....	....	....	....	....	....	6	0	2	2	8	....	....	....
1963-64	Providence Reds	AHL	69	8	31	39	....	....	....	79	....	....	....	....	....	....	....	....	....	....	3	2	2	4	2	....	....	....
1964-65	Buffalo Bisons	AHL	8	1	5	6	....	....	....	12	....	....	....	....	....	....	....	....	....	....	....	....	....	....	....	....	....	....
	Chicago Black Hawks	**NHL**	**61**	**3**	**16**	**19**	**4**	**16**	**20**	**80**	....	....	....	....	....	....	....	....	....	....	**14**	**1**	**4**	**5**	**14**	**1**	**0**	**0**
1965-66	**Chicago Black Hawks**	**NHL**	**62**	**0**	**16**	**16**	**0**	**15**	**15**	**78**	....	....	....	....	....	....	....	....	....	....	**6**	**0**	**1**	**1**	**2**	**0**	**0**	**0**
1966-67	**Chicago Black Hawks**	**NHL**	**62**	**0**	**3**	**3**	**0**	**3**	**3**	**39**	....	....	....	....	....	....	....	....	....	....	....	....	....	....	....	....	....	....
1967-68	Dallas Black Hawks	CPHL	15	1	8	9	....	....	....	55	....	....	....	....	....	....	....	....	....	....	5	0	1	1	2	....	....	....
	Chicago Black Hawks	**NHL**	....	....	....	....	....	....	....	....	....	....	....	....	....	....	....	....	....	....	**4**	**0**	**0**	**0**	**0**	**0**	**0**	**0**
1968-69	**Chicago Black Hawks**	**NHL**	**60**	**2**	**12**	**14**	**2**	**11**	**13**	**57**	**0**	**0**	**0**	**74**	**2.7**	**69**	**1**	**66**	**18**	**20**	....	....	....	....	....	....	....	....
	Dallas Black Hawks	CHL	9	0	4	4	....	....	....	16	....	....	....	....	....	....	....	....	....	....	8	0	3	3	6	....	....	....
1969-70	**Detroit Red Wings**	**NHL**	**46**	**0**	**6**	**6**	**0**	**6**	**6**	**33**	**0**	**0**	**0**	**25**	**0.0**	**31**	**0**	**26**	**2**	**7**	....	....	....	....	....	....	....	....
	Los Angeles Kings	**NHL**	**21**	**3**	**7**	**10**	**3**	**7**	**10**	**34**	**0**	**0**	**1**	**19**	**15.8**	**24**	**2**	**36**	**6**	**–8**	....	....	....	....	....	....	....	....
1970-71	**Los Angeles Kings**	**NHL**	**66**	**3**	**16**	**19**	**3**	**13**	**16**	**41**	**0**	**0**	**1**	**57**	**5.3**	**68**	**14**	**88**	**20**	**–14**	....	....	....	....	....	....	....	....
1971-72	Seattle Totems	WHL	8	0	2	2	....	....	....	2	....	....	....	....	....	....	....	....	....	....	....	....	....	....	....	....	....	....
	Boston Bruins	**NHL**	**25**	**0**	**1**	**1**	**0**	**1**	**1**	**2**	**0**	**0**	**0**	**13**	**0.0**	**13**	**0**	**9**	**0**	**4**	....	....	....	....	....	....	....	....
	Boston Braves	AHL	20	1	6	7	....	....	....	14	....	....	....	....	....	....	....	....	....	....	8	1	3	4	14	....	....	....
1972-73	**Boston Bruins**	**NHL**	**5**	**0**	**1**	**1**	**0**	**1**	**1**	**0**	**0**	**0**	**0**	**1**	**0.0**	**1**	**0**	**7**	**1**	**–5**	....	....	....	....	....	....	....	....
	Boston Braves	AHL	67	5	15	20	....	....	....	71	....	....	....	....	....	....	....	....	....	....	9	2	4	6	21	....	....	....
1973-74	Boston Braves	AHL	50	4	20	24	....	....	....	21	....	....	....	....	....	....	....	....	....	....	....	....	....	....	....	....	....	....
	NHL Totals		**410**	**12**	**78**	**90**	**13**	**73**	**86**	**364**	....	....	....	....	....	....	....	....	....	....	**24**	**1**	**5**	**6**	**16**	....	....	....

Claimed by **Boston** from **Chicago** (Sault Ste. Marie-EPHL) in Inter-League Draft, June 12, 1961. Traded to **Chicago** by **Boston** with Jerry Toppazzini for Murray Balfour and Mike Draper, June 9, 1964. • Missed remainder of 1966-67 season and majority of 1967-68 recovering from leg injury suffered in game vs. Detroit, March 28, 1967. Claimed by **Detroit** from **Chicago** in Intra-League Draft, June 11, 1969. Traded to **LA Kings** by **Detroit** with Gary Monahan and Brian Gibbons for Dale Rolfe, Gary Croteau and Larry Johnston, February 20, 1970. Claimed on waivers by **Boston** from **LA Kings**, November 3, 1971.

• RAY, Rob

Robert John RW – L. 6', 203 lbs. b: Stirling, Ont., 6/8/1968. Buffalo's 5th, 97th overall, in 1988.

Season	Club	League	GP	G	A	Pts	AG	AA	APts	PIM	PP	SH	GW	S	%	TGF	PGF	TGA	PGA	+/–	GP	G	A	Pts	PIM	PP	SH	GW
1983-84	Trenton Bobcats	OJHL-B	40	11	10	21	....	....	....	57	....	....	....	....	....	....	....	....	....	....	....	....	....	....	....	....	....	....
1984-85	Whitby Lawmen	OJHL	35	5	10	15	....	....	....	318	....	....	....	....	....	....	....	....	....	....	....	....	....	....	....	....	....	....
1985-86	Cornwall Royals	OHL	53	6	13	19	....	....	....	253	....	....	....	....	....	....	....	....	....	....	6	0	0	0	26	....	....	....
1986-87	Cornwall Royals	OHL	46	17	20	37	....	....	....	158	....	....	....	....	....	....	....	....	....	....	5	1	1	2	16	....	....	....
1987-88	Cornwall Royals	OHL	61	11	41	52	....	....	....	179	....	....	....	....	....	....	....	....	....	....	11	2	3	5	33	....	....	....
1988-89	Rochester Americans	AHL	74	11	18	29	....	....	....	*446	....	....	....	....	....	....	....	....	....	....	....	....	....	....	....	....	....	....
1989-90	**Buffalo Sabres**	**NHL**	**27**	**2**	**1**	**3**	**2**	**1**	**3**	**99**	**0**	**0**	**0**	**20**	**10.0**	**8**	**0**	**10**	**0**	**–2**	....	....	....	....	....	....	....	....
	Rochester Americans	AHL	43	2	13	15	....	....	....	335	....	....	....	....	....	....	....	....	....	....	17	1	3	4	115	....	....	....
1990-91	**Buffalo Sabres**	**NHL**	**66**	**8**	**8**	**16**	**7**	**6**	**13**	***350**	**0**	**0**	**1**	**54**	**14.8**	**24**	**1**	**34**	**0**	**–11**	**6**	**1**	**1**	**2**	**56**	**0**	**0**	**1**
	Rochester Americans	AHL	8	1	1	2	....	....	....	15	....	....	....	....	....	....	....	....	....	....	....	....	....	....	....	....	....	....
1991-92	**Buffalo Sabres**	**NHL**	**63**	**5**	**3**	**8**	**5**	**2**	**7**	**354**	**0**	**0**	**0**	**29**	**17.2**	**10**	**1**	**18**	**0**	**–9**	**7**	**0**	**0**	**0**	**2**	**0**	**0**	**0**
1992-93	**Buffalo Sabres**	**NHL**	**68**	**3**	**2**	**5**	**2**	**1**	**3**	**211**	**1**	**0**	**0**	**28**	**10.7**	**9**	**1**	**11**	**0**	**–3**	....	....	....	....	....	....	....	....
1993-94	**Buffalo Sabres**	**NHL**	**82**	**3**	**4**	**7**	**3**	**3**	**6**	**274**	**0**	**0**	**0**	**34**	**8.8**	**15**	**0**	**13**	**0**	**2**	**7**	**1**	**0**	**1**	**43**	**0**	**0**	**0**
1994-95	**Buffalo Sabres**	**NHL**	**47**	**0**	**3**	**3**	**0**	**4**	**4**	**173**	**0**	**0**	**0**	**7**	**0.0**	**6**	**0**	**10**	**0**	**–4**	**5**	**0**	**0**	**0**	**14**	**0**	**0**	**0**
1995-96	**Buffalo Sabres**	**NHL**	**71**	**3**	**6**	**9**	**3**	**5**	**8**	**287**	**0**	**0**	**0**	**21**	**14.3**	**12**	**0**	**20**	**0**	**–8**	....	....	....	....	....	....	....	....
1996-97	**Buffalo Sabres**	**NHL**	**82**	**7**	**3**	**10**	**7**	**3**	**10**	**286**	**0**	**0**	**1**	**45**	**15.6**	**18**	**0**	**16**	**1**	**3**	**12**	**0**	**1**	**1**	**28**	**0**	**0**	**0**
1997-98	**Buffalo Sabres**	**NHL**	**63**	**2**	**4**	**6**	**2**	**4**	**6**	**234**	**1**	**0**	**1**	**19**	**10.5**	**14**	**2**	**10**	**0**	**2**	**10**	**0**	**0**	**0**	**24**	**0**	**0**	**0**
1998-99	**Buffalo Sabres**	**NHL**	**76**	**0**	**4**	**4**	**0**	**4**	**4**	***261**	**0**	**0**	**0**	**23**	**0.0**	**7**	**0**	**9**	**0**	**–2**	**5**	**1**	**0**	**1**	**0**	**0**	**0**	**1**
99-2000	**Buffalo Sabres**	**NHL**	**69**	**1**	**3**	**4**	**1**	**3**	**4**	**158**	**0**	**0**	**0**	**17**	**5.9**	**8**	**0**	**8**	**0**	**0**	....	....	....	....	....	....	....	....
	NHL Totals		**714**	**34**	**41**	**75**	**32**	**36**	**68**	**2687**	**2**	**0**	**3**	**297**	**11.4**	**131**	**5**	**159**	**1**		**52**	**3**	**2**	**5**	**167**	**0**	**0**	**2**

Won King Clancy Memorial Trophy (1999)

• REASONER, Marty

C – L. 6'1", 203 lbs. b: Rochester, NY, 2/26/1977. St. Louis' 1st, 14th overall, in 1996.

Season	Club	League	GP	G	A	Pts	AG	AA	APts	PIM	PP	SH	GW	S	%	TGF	PGF	TGA	PGA	+/–	GP	G	A	Pts	PIM	PP	SH	GW
1993-94	Deerfield Spartans	Hi-School	22	27	25	52	....	....	....	....	....	....	....	....	....	....	....	....	....	....	....	....	....	....	....	....	....	....
1994-95	Deerfield Spartans	Hi-School	26	25	32	57	....	....	....	14	....	....	....	....	....	....	....	....	....	....	....	....	....	....	....	....	....	....
1995-96	Boston College	H-East	34	16	29	45	....	....	....	32	....	....	....	....	....	....	....	....	....	....	....	....	....	....	....	....	....	....
	United States	WJC-A	6	3	2	5	....	....	....	10	....	....	....	....	....	....	....	....	....	....	....	....	....	....	....	....	....	....
1996-97	Boston College	H-East	35	20	24	44	....	....	....	31	....	....	....	....	....	....	....	....	....	....	....	....	....	....	....	....	....	....
	United States	WJC-A	6	1	3	4	....	....	....	4	....	....	....	....	....	....	....	....	....	....	....	....	....	....	....	....	....	....
1997-98	Boston College	H-East	42	*33	40	*73	....	....	....	56	....	....	....	....	....	....	....	....	....	....	....	....	....	....	....	....	....	....
1998-99	**St. Louis Blues**	**NHL**	**22**	**3**	**7**	**10**	**4**	**7**	**11**	**8**	**1**	**0**	**0**	**33**	**9.1**	**19**	**9**	**8**	**0**	**2**	....	....	....	....	....	....	....	....
	Worcester IceCats	AHL	44	17	22	39	....	....	....	24	....	....	....	....	....	....	....	....	....	....	4	2	1	3	6	....	....	....
99-2000	**St. Louis Blues**	**NHL**	**32**	**10**	**14**	**24**	**11**	**13**	**24**	**20**	**3**	**0**	**0**	**51**	**19.6**	**34**	**12**	**13**	**0**	**9**	**7**	**2**	**1**	**3**	**4**	**1**	**0**	**0**
	Worcester IceCats	AHL	44	23	28	51	....	....	....	39	....	....	....	....	....	....	....	....	....	....	....	....	....	....	....	....	....	....
	NHL Totals		**54**	**13**	**21**	**34**	**15**	**20**	**35**	**28**	**4**	**0**	**0**	**84**	**15.5**	**53**	**21**	**21**	**0**		**7**	**2**	**1**	**3**	**4**	**1**	**0**	**0**

Hockey East First All-Star Team (1997, 1998) • NCAA East First All-American Team (1998) • NCAA Championship All-Tournament Team (1998)

• REAUME, Marc

Marc Avellin D – L. 6'1", 185 lbs. b: La Salle, Ont., 2/7/1934.

Season	Club	League	GP	G	A	Pts	AG	AA	APts	PIM	PP	SH	GW	S	%	TGF	PGF	TGA	PGA	+/–	GP	G	A	Pts	PIM	PP	SH	GW
1950-51	St. Michael's Buzzers	OHA-B	STATISTICS NOT AVAILABLE																									
	St. Michael's Majors	OHA-Jr.	5	0	0	0	....	....	....	2	....	....	....	....	....	....	....	....	....	....	....	....	....	....	....	....	....	....
1951-52	St. Michael's Majors	OHA-Jr.	46	11	16	27	....	....	....	44	....	....	....	....	....	....	....	....	....	....	7	1	2	3	8	....	....	....
1952-53	St. Michael's Majors	OHA-Jr.	46	5	16	21	....	....	....	75	....	....	....	....	....	....	....	....	....	....	17	0	3	3	16	....	....	....
1953-54	St. Michael's Majors	OHA-Jr.	54	14	27	41	....	....	....	24	....	....	....	....	....	....	....	....	....	....	8	3	6	9	6	....	....	....
1954-55	**Toronto Maple Leafs**	**NHL**	**1**	**0**	**0**	**0**	**0**	**0**	**0**	**4**	....	....	....	....	....	....	....	....	....	....	**4**	**0**	**0**	**0**	**2**	**0**	**0**	**0**
	Pittsburgh Hornets	AHL	57	5	7	12	....	....	....	63	....	....	....	....	....	....	....	....	....	....	6	0	0	0	4	....	....	....

Season	Club	League	REGULAR SEASON																		PLAYOFFS							
			GP	G	A	Pts	AG	AA	APts	PIM	PP	SH	GW	S	%	TGF	PGF	TGA	PGA	+/–	GP	G	A	Pts	PIM	PP	SH	GW
1955-56	**Toronto Maple Leafs**	NHL	48	0	12	12	0	14	14	50	....	....	....	....	....	....	....	....	....	....	5	0	2	2	6	0	0	0
	Pittsburgh Hornets	AHL	16	2	5	7	....	....	....	24	....	....	....	....	....	....	....	....	....	....	....	....	....	....	....	....	....	....
1956-57	**Toronto Maple Leafs**	NHL	63	6	14	20	8	15	23	81	....	....	....	....	....	....	....	....	....	....	....	....	....	....	....	....	....	....
1957-58	**Toronto Maple Leafs**	NHL	68	1	7	8	1	7	8	49	....	....	....	....	....	....	....	....	....	....	....	....	....	....	....	....	....	....
1958-59	**Toronto Maple Leafs**	NHL	51	1	5	6	1	5	6	67	....	....	....	....	....	....	....	....	....	....	10	0	0	0	0	0	0	0
1959-60	**Toronto Maple Leafs**	NHL	36	0	1	1	0	1	1	6	....	....	....	....	....	....	....	....	....	....	....	....	....	....	....	....	....	....
	Detroit Red Wings	NHL	9	0	1	1	0	1	1	2	....	....	....	....	....	....	....	....	....	....	2	0	0	0	0	0	0	0
1960-61	**Detroit Red Wings**	NHL	38	0	1	1	0	1	1	8	....	....	....	....	....	....	....	....	....	....	....	....	....	....	....	....	....	....
	Hershey Bears	AHL	33	2	7	9	....	....	....	30	....	....	....	....	....	....	....	....	....	....	8	0	1	1	4	....	....	....
1961-62	Hershey Bears	AHL	70	3	18	21	....	....	....	42	....	....	....	....	....	....	....	....	....	....	7	1	2	3	6	....	....	....
1962-63	Hershey Bears	AHL	69	5	23	28	....	....	....	42	....	....	....	....	....	....	....	....	....	....	13	2	4	6	34	....	....	....
1963-64	**Montreal Canadiens**	NHL	3	0	0	0	0	0	0	2	....	....	....	....	....	....	....	....	....	....	....	....	....	....	....	....	....	....
	Hershey Bears	AHL	69	5	23	28	....	....	....	45	....	....	....	....	....	....	....	....	....	....	6	1	0	1	2	....	....	....
1964-65	Tulsa Oilers	CPHL	68	4	28	32	....	....	....	31	....	....	....	....	....	....	....	....	....	....	12	0	7	7	6	....	....	....
1965-66	Rochester Americans	AHL	2	0	3	3	....	....	....	2	....	....	....	....	....	....	....	....	....	....	....	....	....	....	....	....	....	....
	Tulsa Oilers	CPHL	68	8	25	33	....	....	....	43	....	....	....	....	....	....	....	....	....	....	11	1	0	1	0	....	....	....
1966-67	Tulsa Oilers	CPHL	62	7	18	25	....	....	....	59	....	....	....	....	....	....	....	....	....	....	....	....	....	....	....	....	....	....
	Rochester Americans	AHL	2	0	0	0	....	....	....	0	....	....	....	....	....	....	....	....	....	....	....	....	....	....	....	....	....	....
1967-68	Rochester Americans	AHL	70	8	22	30	....	....	....	40	....	....	....	....	....	....	....	....	....	....	11	2	4	6	10	....	....	....
1968-69	Rochester Americans	AHL	11	0	6	6	....	....	....	2	....	....	....	....	....	....	....	....	....	....	....	....	....	....	....	....	....	....
	Vancouver Canucks	WHL	59	4	19	23	....	....	....	31	....	....	....	....	....	....	....	....	....	....	8	3	7	10	2	....	....	....
1969-70	Vancouver Canucks	WHL	72	10	25	35	....	....	....	36	....	....	....	....	....	....	....	....	....	....	11	2	11	13	6	....	....	....
1970-71	**Vancouver Canucks**	NHL	27	0	2	2	0	2	2	4	0	0	0	19	0.0	12	0	24	6	–6	....	....	....	....	....	....	....	....
	Rochester Americans	AHL	6	0	3	3	....	....	....	6	....	....	....	....	....	....	....	....	....	....	....	....	....	....	....	....	....	....
	NHL Totals		344	8	43	51	10	46	56	273	....	....	....	....	....	....	....	....	....	....	21	0	2	2	8	....	....	....

AHL First All-Star Team (1963) • Won Eddie Shore Award (Outstanding Defenseman - AHL) (1963) • CPHL Second All-Star Team (1966) • AHL Second All-Star Team (1968) • WHL First All-Star Team (1970) • Won Hal Laycoe Cup (WHL Top Defenseman) (1970)

Traded to **Detroit** by **Toronto** for Red Kelly, February 10, 1960. Traded to **Hershey** (AHL) by **Detroit** with Pete Conacher and Jack McIntyre for Howie Young, January, 1961. Traded to **Montreal** by **Hershey** (AHL) for Ralph Keller and the loan of Chuck Hamilton, June 11, 1963. Claimed by **Toronto** (Tulsa-CHL) from **Montreal** in Inter-League Draft, June 9, 1964. Rights transferred to **Vancouver** (WHL) after WHL club purchased **Rochester** (AHL) franchise, August 13, 1968. NHL rights transferred to **Vancouver** after NHL club purchased **Vancouver** (WHL) franchise, December 19, 1969. • Suffered career-ending leg injury in automobile accident, January 24, 1971.

• RECCHI, Mark

Mark L. RW – L. 5'10", 185 lbs. b: Kamloops, B.C., 2/1/1968. Pittsburgh's 4th, 67th overall, in 1988.

Season	Club	League	GP	G	A	Pts	AG	AA	APts	PIM	PP	SH	GW	S	%	TGF	PGF	TGA	PGA	+/–	GP	G	A	Pts	PIM	PP	SH	GW
1983-84	Kamloops Chevys	BCAHA	STATISTICS NOT AVAILABLE																									
1984-85	Langley Eagles	BCJHL	51	26	39	65	....	....	....	39	....	....	....	....	....	....	....	....	....	....	....	....	....	....	....	....	....	....
	New Westminster Bruins	WHL	4	1	0	1	....	....	....	0	....	....	....	....	....	....	....	....	....	....	....	....	....	....	....	....	....	....
1985-86	New Westminster Bruins	WHL	72	21	40	61	....	....	....	55	....	....	....	....	....	....	....	....	....	....	....	....	....	....	....	....	....	....
1986-87	Kamloops Blazers	WHL	40	26	50	76	....	....	....	63	....	....	....	....	....	....	....	....	....	....	13	3	16	19	17	....	....	....
1987-88	Kamloops Blazers	WHL	62	61	*93	154	....	....	....	75	....	....	....	....	....	....	....	....	....	....	17	10	*21	*31	18	....	....	....
	Canada	WJC-A	7	0	5	5	....	....	....	4	....	....	....	....	....	....	....	....	....	....	....	....	....	....	....	....	....	....
1988-89	**Pittsburgh Penguins**	NHL	15	1	1	2	1	1	2	0	0	0	0	11	9.1	4	0	6	0	–2	....	....	....	....	....	....	....	....
	Muskegon Lumberjacks	IHL	63	50	49	99	....	....	....	86	....	....	....	....	....	....	....	....	....	....	14	7	*14	*21	28	....	....	....
1989-90	**Pittsburgh Penguins**	NHL	74	30	37	67	26	27	53	44	6	2	4	143	21.0	88	18	72	8	6	....	....	....	....	....	....	....	....
	Muskegon Lumberjacks	IHL	4	7	4	11	....	....	....	2	....	....	....	....	....	....	....	....	....	....	....	....	....	....	....	....	....	....
	Canada	WEC-A	5	0	2	2	....	....	....	2	....	....	....	....	....	....	....	....	....	....	....	....	....	....	....	....	....	....
1990-91 ♦	**Pittsburgh Penguins**	NHL	78	40	73	113	37	56	93	48	12	0	9	184	21.7	151	58	108	15	0	24	10	24	34	33	5	0	2
1991-92	**Pittsburgh Penguins**	NHL	58	33	37	70	30	28	58	78	16	1	4	156	21.2	100	49	83	16	–16	....	....	....	....	....	....	....	....
	Philadelphia Flyers	NHL	22	10	17	27	9	13	22	18	4	0	1	54	18.5	36	19	31	9	–5	....	....	....	....	....	....	....	....
1992-93	**Philadelphia Flyers**	NHL	84	53	70	123	44	48	92	95	15	4	6	274	19.3	163	57	116	11	1	....	....	....	....	....	....	....	....
	Canada	WC-A	8	2	5	7	....	....	....	2	....	....	....	....	....	....	....	....	....	....	....	....	....	....	....	....	....	....
1993-94	**Philadelphia Flyers**	NHL	84	40	67	107	37	52	89	46	11	0	5	217	18.4	155	56	107	6	–2	....	....	....	....	....	....	....	....
1994-95	**Philadelphia Flyers**	NHL	10	2	3	5	4	4	8	12	1	0	2	17	11.8	6	3	9	0	–6	....	....	....	....	....	....	....	....
	Montreal Canadiens	NHL	39	14	29	43	25	43	68	16	8	0	1	104	13.5	58	18	45	2	–3	....	....	....	....	....	....	....	....
1995-96	**Montreal Canadiens**	NHL	82	28	50	78	28	41	69	69	11	2	6	191	14.7	115	43	59	7	20	6	3	3	6	0	3	0	0
1996-97	**Montreal Canadiens**	NHL	82	34	46	80	36	41	77	58	7	2	3	202	16.8	112	34	103	24	–1	5	4	2	6	2	0	0	0
	Canada	WC-A	9	3	3	6	....	....	....	0	....	....	....	....	....	....	....	....	....	....	....	....	....	....	....	....	....	....
1997-98	**Montreal Canadiens**	NHL	82	32	42	74	38	41	79	51	9	1	6	216	14.8	107	48	59	11	11	10	4	8	12	6	0	0	2
	Canada	Olympics	5	0	2	2	....	....	....	0	....	....	....	....	....	....	....	....	....	....	....	....	....	....	....	....	....	....
1998-99	**Montreal Canadiens**	NHL	61	12	35	47	14	34	48	28	3	0	2	152	7.9	67	32	48	9	–4	....	....	....	....	....	....	....	....
	Philadelphia Flyers	NHL	10	4	2	6	5	2	7	6	0	0	0	19	21.1	11	4	11	1	–3	6	0	1	1	2	0	0	0
99-2000	**Philadelphia Flyers**	NHL	82	28	*63	91	32	59	91	50	7	1	5	223	12.6	123	56	58	11	20	18	6	12	18	6	2	0	1
	NHL Totals		863	361	572	933	366	490	856	619	110	13	54	2163	16.7	1296	495	915	130		69	27	50	77	49	10	0	5

WHL West All-Star Team (1988) • IHL Second All-Star Team (1989) • NHL Second All-Star Team (1992) • Played in NHL All-Star Game (1991, 1993, 1994, 1997, 1998, 1999, 2000)

Traded to **Philadelphia** by **Pittsburgh** with Brian Benning and LA Kings' 1st round choice (previously acquired, Philadelphia selected Jason Bowen) in 1992 Entry Draft for Rick Tocchet, Kjell Samuelsson, Ken Wregget and Philadelphia's 3rd round choice (Dave Roche) in 1993 Entry Draft, February 19, 1992. Traded to **Montreal** by **Philadelphia** with Philadelphia's 3rd round choice (Martin Hohenberger) in 1995 Entry Draft for Eric Desjardins, Gilbert Dionne and John LeClair, February 9, 1995. Traded to **Philadelphia** by **Montreal** for Danius Zubrus, Philadelphia's 2nd round choice (Matt Carkner) in 1999 Entry Draft and NY Islanders' 6th round choice (previously acquired, Montreal selected Scott Selig) in 2000 Entry Draft, March 10, 1999.

• REDDEN, Wade

D – L. 6'2", 205 lbs. b: Lloydminster, Sask., 6/12/1977. NY Islanders' 1st, 2nd overall, in 1995.

Season	Club	League	GP	G	A	Pts	AG	AA	APts	PIM	PP	SH	GW	S	%	TGF	PGF	TGA	PGA	+/–	GP	G	A	Pts	PIM	PP	SH	GW
1992-93	Lloydminster Blazers	SJHL	34	4	11	15	....	....	....	64	....	....	....	....	....	....	....	....	....	....	....	....	....	....	....	....	....	....
1993-94	Brandon Wheat Kings	WHL	63	4	35	39	....	....	....	98	....	....	....	....	....	....	....	....	....	....	14	2	4	6	10	....	....	....
1994-95	Brandon Wheat Kings	WHL	64	14	46	60	....	....	....	83	....	....	....	....	....	....	....	....	....	....	18	5	10	15	8	....	....	....
	Canada	WJC-A	7	3	2	5	....	....	....	0	....	....	....	....	....	....	....	....	....	....	....	....	....	....	....	....	....	....
	Brandon Wheat Kings	Mem-Cup	4	0	4	4	....	....	....	4	....	....	....	....	....	....	....	....	....	....	....	....	....	....	....	....	....	....
1995-96	Brandon Wheat Kings	WHL	51	9	45	54	....	....	....	55	....	....	....	....	....	....	....	....	....	....	19	5	10	15	19	....	....	....
	Canada	WJC-A	6	0	2	2	....	....	....	2	....	....	....	....	....	....	....	....	....	....	....	....	....	....	....	....	....	....
	Brandon Wheat Kings	Mem-Cup	4	1	2	3	....	....	....	0	....	....	....	....	....	....	....	....	....	....	....	....	....	....	....	....	....	....
1996-97	**Ottawa Senators**	NHL	82	6	24	30	6	21	27	41	2	0	1	102	5.9	75	22	66	14	1	7	1	3	4	2	0	0	0
1997-98	**Ottawa Senators**	NHL	80	8	14	22	9	14	23	27	3	0	2	103	7.8	67	13	54	17	17	9	0	2	2	2	0	0	0
1998-99	**Ottawa Senators**	NHL	72	8	21	29	9	20	29	54	3	0	1	127	6.3	81	22	71	19	7	4	1	2	3	2	1	0	0
	Canada	WC-A	10	1	2	3	....	....	....	6	....	....	....	....	....	....	....	....	....	....	....	....	....	....	....	....	....	....
99-2000	**Ottawa Senators**	NHL	81	10	26	36	11	24	35	49	3	0	2	163	6.1	97	29	83	14	–1	....	....	....	....	....	....	....	....
	NHL Totals		315	32	85	117	35	79	114	171	11	0	6	495	6.5	320	86	274	64		20	2	7	9	6	1	0	0

WHL East Second All-Star Team (1995) • WHL East First All-Star Team (1996) • Memorial Cup All-Star Team (1996)

Traded to **Ottawa** by **NY Islanders** with Damian Rhodes for Don Beaupre, Martin Straka and Bryan Berard, January 23, 1996.

• REDMOND, Craig

Craig Sanford D – L. 5'11", 190 lbs. b: Dawson Creek, B.C., 9/22/1965. Los Angeles' 1st, 6th overall, in 1984.

Season	Club	League	GP	G	A	Pts	AG	AA	APts	PIM	PP	SH	GW	S	%	TGF	PGF	TGA	PGA	+/–	GP	G	A	Pts	PIM	PP	SH	GW
1980-81	Abbotsford Flyers	BCJHL	40	15	22	37	....	....	....	....	....	....	....	....	....	....	....	....	....	....	....	....	....	....	....	....	....	....
1981-82	Abbotsford Flyers	BCJHL	45	30	76	106	....	....	....	41	....	....	....	....	....	....	....	....	....	....	....	....	....	....	....	....	....	....
1982-83	University of Denver	WCHA	34	16	38	54	....	....	....	44	....	....	....	....	....	....	....	....	....	....	....	....	....	....	....	....	....	....
1983-84	Canada	Nat-Team	55	10	11	21	....	....	....	38	....	....	....	....	....	....	....	....	....	....	....	....	....	....	....	....	....	....
	Canada	Olympics	7	2	0	2	....	....	....	4	....	....	....	....	....	....	....	....	....	....	....	....	....	....	....	....	....	....
1984-85	**Los Angeles Kings**	NHL	79	6	33	39	5	22	27	57	1	0	0	113	5.3	102	23	101	14	–8	3	1	0	1	2	0	0	0
1985-86	**Los Angeles Kings**	NHL	73	6	18	24	5	12	17	57	3	0	0	116	5.2	71	19	99	13	–34	....	....	....	....	....	....	....	....
	Canada	WEC-A	10	3	2	5	....	....	....	16	....	....	....	....	....	....	....	....	....	....	....	....	....	....	....	....	....	....
1986-87	**Los Angeles Kings**	NHL	16	1	7	8	1	5	6	8	0	0	0	18	5.6	19	5	19	4	–1	....	....	....	....	....	....	....	....
	New Haven Nighthawks	AHL	5	2	2	4	....	....	....	6	....	....	....	....	....	....	....	....	....	....	....	....	....	....	....	....	....	....
1987-88	**Los Angeles Kings**	NHL	2	0	0	0	0	0	0	0	0	0	0	5	0.0	0	0	4	0	–4	....	....	....	....	....	....	....	....
	New Haven Nighthawks	AHL	DID NOT PLAY – SUSPENDED																									

			REGULAR SEASON																		PLAYOFFS							
Season	Club	League	GP	G	A	Pts	AG	AA	APts	PIM	PP	SH	GW	S	%	TGF	PGF	TGA	PGA	+/-	GP	G	A	Pts	PIM	PP	SH	GW
1988-89	Denver Rangers	IHL	10	0	13	13	....	....	....	6	....	....	....	....	....	....	....	....	....	....	....	....	....	....	....	....	....	....
	Edmonton Oilers	**NHL**	**21**	**3**	**10**	**13**	**3**	**7**	**10**	**12**	**3**	**0**	**0**	**29**	**10.3**	**26**	**16**	**24**	**4**	**–10**	....	....	....	....	....	....	....	....
	Cape Breton Oilers	AHL	44	13	22	35	....	....	....	28	....	....	....	....	....	....	....	....	....	....	....	....	....	....	....	....	....	....
1989-1995	OUT OF HOCKEY – RETIRED																											
1995-96	Cape Breton Oilers	AHL	43	2	18	20	....	....	....	80	....	....	....	....	....	....	....	....	....	....	....	....	....	....	....	....	....	....
	Atlanta Knights	IHL	25	0	5	5	....	....	....	18	....	....	....	....	....	....	....	....	....	....	3	0	1	1	0	....	....	....
	NHL Totals		**191**	**16**	**68**	**84**	**14**	**46**	**60**	**134**	**7**	**0**	**0**	**281**	**5.7**	**218**	**63**	**247**	**35**		**3**	**1**	**0**	**1**	**2**	**0**	**0**	**0**

• Suspended by **LA Kings** for refusing to report to **New Haven** (AHL), October 15, 1987. Traded to **Edmonton** by **LA Kings** for John Miner, August 10, 1988. Claimed by **NY Rangers** from **Edmonton** in Waiver Draft, October 3, 1988. Claimed on waivers by **Edmonton** from **NY Rangers**, November 1, 1988.

• REDMOND, Dick

Richard John D – L. 5'11", 178 lbs. b: Kirkland Lake, Ont., 8/14/1949. Minnesota's 1st, 5th overall, in 1969.

Season	Club	League	GP	G	A	Pts	AG	AA	APts	PIM	PP	SH	GW	S	%	TGF	PGF	TGA	PGA	+/-	GP	G	A	Pts	PIM	PP	SH	GW
1966-67	Peterborough Petes	OHA-Jr.	40	2	7	9	....	....	....	77	....	....	....	....	....	....	....	....	....	....	6	0	2	2	2	....	....	....
1967-68	Peterborough Petes	OHA-Jr.	52	7	28	35	....	....	....	84	....	....	....	....	....	....	....	....	....	....	5	3	0	3	2	....	....	....
1968-69	Peterborough Petes	OHA-Jr.	6	2	2	4	....	....	....	44	....	....	....	....	....	....	....	....	....	....	....	....	....	....	....	....	....	....
	St. Catharines Black Hawks	OHA-Jr.	44	31	43	74	....	....	....	136	....	....	....	....	....	....	....	....	....	....	18	11	17	28	35	....	....	....
1969-70	**Minnesota North Stars**	**NHL**	**7**	**0**	**1**	**1**	**0**	**1**	**1**	**4**	**0**	**0**	**0**	**10**	**0.0**	**2**	**1**	**2**	**0**	**–1**	....	....	....	....	....	....	....	....
	Iowa Stars	CHL	56	7	23	30	....	....	....	65	....	....	....	....	....	....	....	....	....	....	11	2	8	10	26	....	....	....
1970-71	**Minnesota North Stars**	**NHL**	**9**	**0**	**2**	**2**	**0**	**2**	**2**	**16**	**0**	**0**	**0**	**11**	**0.0**	**2**	**0**	**6**	**2**	**–2**	....	....	....	....	....	....	....	....
	Cleveland Barons	AHL	49	6	13	19	....	....	....	69	....	....	....	....	....	....	....	....	....	....	....	....	....	....	....	....	....	....
	California Golden Seals	**NHL**	**11**	**2**	**4**	**6**	**2**	**3**	**5**	**12**	**1**	**0**	**0**	**35**	**5.7**	**25**	**5**	**29**	**3**	**–6**	....	....	....	....	....	....	....	....
1971-72	**California Golden Seals**	**NHL**	**74**	**10**	**35**	**45**	**10**	**30**	**40**	**76**	**1**	**0**	**0**	**254**	**3.9**	**111**	**36**	**102**	**17**	**–10**	....	....	....	....	....	....	....	....
1972-73	**California Golden Seals**	**NHL**	**24**	**3**	**13**	**16**	**3**	**10**	**13**	**22**	**1**	**0**	**0**	**63**	**4.8**	**29**	**9**	**44**	**9**	**–15**	....	....	....	....	....	....	....	....
	Chicago Black Hawks	**NHL**	**52**	**9**	**19**	**28**	**8**	**15**	**23**	**4**	**3**	**0**	**1**	**140**	**6.4**	**51**	**18**	**31**	**0**	**2**	**13**	**4**	**2**	**6**	**2**	**0**	**0**	**2**
1973-74	**Chicago Black Hawks**	**NHL**	**76**	**17**	**42**	**59**	**16**	**35**	**51**	**69**	**5**	**0**	**4**	**246**	**6.9**	**117**	**40**	**58**	**7**	**26**	**11**	**1**	**7**	**8**	**8**	**1**	**0**	**0**
1974-75	**Chicago Black Hawks**	**NHL**	**80**	**14**	**43**	**57**	**12**	**32**	**44**	**90**	**6**	**0**	**1**	**310**	**4.5**	**150**	**50**	**128**	**34**	**6**	**8**	**2**	**3**	**5**	**0**	**1**	**0**	**0**
1975-76	**Chicago Black Hawks**	**NHL**	**53**	**9**	**27**	**36**	**8**	**20**	**28**	**25**	**5**	**0**	**1**	**165**	**5.5**	**78**	**26**	**60**	**9**	**1**	**4**	**0**	**2**	**2**	**4**	**0**	**0**	**0**
1976-77	**Chicago Black Hawks**	**NHL**	**80**	**22**	**25**	**47**	**20**	**19**	**39**	**30**	**9**	**0**	**2**	**211**	**10.4**	**95**	**30**	**123**	**18**	**–40**	**2**	**0**	**1**	**1**	**0**	**0**	**0**	**0**
1977-78	**St. Louis Blues**	**NHL**	**28**	**4**	**11**	**15**	**4**	**8**	**12**	**16**	**2**	**0**	**0**	**93**	**4.3**	**25**	**13**	**31**	**5**	**–14**	....	....	....	....	....	....	....	....
	Atlanta Flames	**NHL**	**42**	**7**	**11**	**18**	**6**	**8**	**14**	**16**	**5**	**0**	**1**	**86**	**8.1**	**64**	**20**	**38**	**6**	**12**	**2**	**1**	**0**	**1**	**0**	**0**	**0**	**0**
1978-79	**Boston Bruins**	**NHL**	**64**	**7**	**26**	**33**	**6**	**19**	**25**	**21**	**4**	**0**	**1**	**144**	**4.9**	**88**	**38**	**68**	**18**	**0**	**11**	**1**	**3**	**4**	**2**	**0**	**1**	**0**
1979-80	**Boston Bruins**	**NHL**	**76**	**14**	**33**	**47**	**12**	**24**	**36**	**39**	**6**	**0**	**5**	**166**	**8.4**	**135**	**41**	**75**	**18**	**37**	**10**	**0**	**3**	**3**	**9**	**0**	**0**	**0**
1980-81	**Boston Bruins**	**NHL**	**78**	**15**	**20**	**35**	**12**	**13**	**25**	**60**	**6**	**2**	**0**	**152**	**9.9**	**97**	**24**	**91**	**22**	**4**	**3**	**0**	**1**	**1**	**2**	**0**	**0**	**0**
1981-82	**Boston Bruins**	**NHL**	**17**	**0**	**0**	**0**	**0**	**0**	**0**	**4**	**0**	**0**	**0**	**14**	**0.0**	**5**	**0**	**14**	**2**	**–7**	**2**	**0**	**0**	**0**	**0**	**0**	**0**	**0**
	Erie Blades	AHL	31	8	12	20	....	....	....	14	....	....	....	....	....	....	....	....	....	....	....	....	....	....	....	....	....	....
	NHL Totals		**771**	**133**	**312**	**445**	**119**	**239**	**358**	**504**	**54**	**2**	**16**	**2100**	**6.3**	**1074**	**351**	**900**	**170**		**66**	**9**	**22**	**31**	**27**	**2**	**1**	**2**

• Brother of Mickey • OHA-Jr. First All-Star Team (1969)

Traded to **California** by **Minnesota** with Tommy Williams for Ted Hampson and Wayne Muloin, March 7, 1971. Traded to **Chicago** by **California** with the rights to Bobby Sheehan for Darryl Maggs, December 5, 1972. Traded to **St. Louis** by **Chicago** for Pierre Plante, August 9, 1977. Traded to **Atlanta** by **St. Louis** with Yves Belanger, Bob MacMillan and St. Louis' 2nd round choice (Mike Perovich) in 1979 Entry Draft for Phil Myre, Curt Bennett and Barry Gibbs, December 12, 1977. Traded to **Boston** by **Atlanta** for Gregg Sheppard, September 6, 1978.

• REDMOND, Keith

LW – L. 6'3", 208 lbs. b: Richmond Hill, Ont., 10/25/1972. Los Angeles' 2nd, 79th overall, in 1991.

Season	Club	League	GP	G	A	Pts	AG	AA	APts	PIM	PP	SH	GW	S	%	TGF	PGF	TGA	PGA	+/-	GP	G	A	Pts	PIM	PP	SH	GW
1988-89	Nepean Raiders	OJHL	59	3	12	15	....	....	....	110	....	....	....	....	....	....	....	....	....	....	....	....	....	....	....	....	....	....
1989-90	Nepean Raiders	OJHL	40	14	10	24	....	....	....	169	....	....	....	....	....	....	....	....	....	....	....	....	....	....	....	....	....	....
1990-91	Bowling Green University	CCHA	35	1	3	4	....	....	....	72	....	....	....	....	....	....	....	....	....	....	....	....	....	....	....	....	....	....
1991-92	Bowling Green University	CCHA	8	0	0	0	....	....	....	14	....	....	....	....	....	....	....	....	....	....	....	....	....	....	....	....	....	....
	Belleville Bulls	OHL	16	1	7	8	....	....	....	52	....	....	....	....	....	....	....	....	....	....	....	....	....	....	....	....	....	....
	Detroit Jr. Red Wings	OHL	25	6	12	18	....	....	....	61	....	....	....	....	....	....	....	....	....	....	7	1	3	4	49	....	....	....
1992-93	Phoenix Roadrunners	IHL	53	6	10	16	....	....	....	285	....	....	....	....	....	....	....	....	....	....	....	....	....	....	....	....	....	....
	Muskegon Fury	ColHL	4	1	0	1	....	....	....	46	....	....	....	....	....	....	....	....	....	....	....	....	....	....	....	....	....	....
1993-94	**Los Angeles Kings**	**NHL**	**12**	**1**	**0**	**1**	**1**	**0**	**1**	**20**	**0**	**0**	**0**	**9**	**11.1**	**1**	**0**	**4**	**0**	**–3**	....	....	....	....	....	....	....	....
	Phoenix Roadrunners	IHL	43	8	10	18	....	....	....	196	....	....	....	....	....	....	....	....	....	....	....	....	....	....	....	....	....	....
1994-95	Phoenix Roadrunners	IHL	20	0	3	3	....	....	....	81	....	....	....	....	....	....	....	....	....	....	6	2	1	3	29	....	....	....
1995-96	Phoenix Roadrunners	IHL	34	5	3	8	....	....	....	164	....	....	....	....	....	....	....	....	....	....	1	0	0	0	0	....	....	....
	NHL Totals		**12**	**1**	**0**	**1**	**1**	**0**	**1**	**20**	**0**	**0**	**0**	**9**	**11.1**	**1**	**0**	**4**	**0**		....	....	....	....	....	....	....	....

• REDMOND, Mickey

Michael Edward RW – R. 5'11", 185 lbs. b: Kirkland Lake, Ont., 12/27/1947.

Season	Club	League	GP	G	A	Pts	AG	AA	APts	PIM	PP	SH	GW	S	%	TGF	PGF	TGA	PGA	+/-	GP	G	A	Pts	PIM	PP	SH	GW
1963-64	Peterborough Petes	OHA-Jr.	53	21	17	38	....	....	....	26	....	....	....	....	....	....	....	....	....	....	4	1	2	3	2	....	....	....
1964-65	Peterborough Petes	OHA-Jr.	52	23	20	43	....	....	....	30	....	....	....	....	....	....	....	....	....	....	12	9	1	10	11	....	....	....
1965-66	Peterborough Petes	OHA-Jr.	48	41	51	92	....	....	....	31	....	....	....	....	....	....	....	....	....	....	6	4	1	5	6	....	....	....
1966-67	Peterborough Petes	OHA-Jr.	48	*51	44	95	....	....	....	44	....	....	....	....	....	....	....	....	....	....	6	2	5	7	14	....	....	....
	Houston Apollos	CPHL	....	....	....	....	....	....	....	....	....	....	....	....	....	....	....	....	....	....	5	3	2	5	2	....	....	....
1967-68♦	**Montreal Canadiens**	**NHL**	**41**	**6**	**5**	**11**	**7**	**5**	**12**	**4**	**1**	**0**	**0**	**52**	**11.5**	**16**	**5**	**9**	**0**	**2**	**2**	**0**	**0**	**0**	**0**	**0**	**0**	**0**
	Houston Apollos	CPHL	15	9	8	17	....	....	....	9	....	....	....	....	....	....	....	....	....	....	....	....	....	....	....	....	....	....
1968-69♦	**Montreal Canadiens**	**NHL**	**65**	**9**	**15**	**24**	**9**	**13**	**22**	**12**	**1**	**0**	**0**	**118**	**7.6**	**39**	**4**	**19**	**0**	**16**	**14**	**2**	**3**	**5**	**2**	**0**	**1**	**1**
1969-70	**Montreal Canadiens**	**NHL**	**75**	**27**	**27**	**54**	**29**	**25**	**54**	**61**	**3**	**0**	**2**	**279**	**9.7**	**83**	**18**	**42**	**0**	**23**	....	....	....	....	....	....	....	....
1970-71	**Montreal Canadiens**	**NHL**	**40**	**14**	**15**	**29**	**14**	**13**	**27**	**35**	**2**	**0**	**1**	**116**	**12.1**	**47**	**13**	**22**	**0**	**12**	....	....	....	....	....	....	....	....
	Detroit Red Wings	**NHL**	**21**	**6**	**8**	**14**	**6**	**7**	**13**	**7**	**2**	**0**	**1**	**68**	**8.8**	**22**	**8**	**16**	**0**	**–2**	....	....	....	....	....	....	....	....
1971-72	**Detroit Red Wings**	**NHL**	**78**	**42**	**29**	**71**	**42**	**25**	**67**	**34**	**10**	**0**	**5**	**271**	**15.5**	**104**	**37**	**80**	**0**	**–13**	....	....	....	....	....	....	....	....
1972-73	Team Canada	Summit-72	1	0	0	0	....	....	....	0	....	....	....	....	....	....	....	....	....	....	....	....	....	....	....	....	....	....
	Detroit Red Wings	**NHL**	**76**	**52**	**41**	**93**	**49**	**33**	**82**	**24**	**15**	**0**	**7**	**363**	**14.3**	**124**	**47**	**73**	**2**	**6**	....	....	....	....	....	....	....	....
1973-74	**Detroit Red Wings**	**NHL**	**76**	**51**	**26**	**77**	**49**	**21**	**70**	**14**	**21**	**0**	**9**	**296**	**17.2**	**111**	**45**	**89**	**2**	**–21**	....	....	....	....	....	....	....	....
1974-75	**Detroit Red Wings**	**NHL**	**29**	**15**	**12**	**27**	**13**	**9**	**22**	**18**	**5**	**0**	**1**	**93**	**16.1**	**44**	**23**	**33**	**0**	**–12**	....	....	....	....	....	....	....	....
1975-76	**Detroit Red Wings**	**NHL**	**37**	**11**	**17**	**28**	**10**	**13**	**23**	**10**	**2**	**0**	**3**	**123**	**8.9**	**40**	**15**	**42**	**0**	**–17**	....	....	....	....	....	....	....	....
	NHL Totals		**538**	**233**	**195**	**428**	**228**	**164**	**392**	**219**	**62**	**0**	**29**	**1779**	**13.1**	**630**	**215**	**425**	**4**		**16**	**2**	**3**	**5**	**2**	**0**	**1**	**1**

• Brother of Dick • OHA-Jr. First All-Star Team (1966, 1967) • NHL First All-Star Team (1973) • NHL Second All-Star Team (1974) • Played in NHL All-Star Game (1974)

Traded to **Detroit** by **Montreal** with Guy Charron and Bill Collins for Frank Mahovlich, January 13, 1971.

• REEDS, Mark

RW – R. 5'10", 190 lbs. b: Burlington, Ont., 1/24/1960. St. Louis' 3rd, 86th overall, in 1979.

Season	Club	League	GP	G	A	Pts	AG	AA	APts	PIM	PP	SH	GW	S	%	TGF	PGF	TGA	PGA	+/-	GP	G	A	Pts	PIM	PP	SH	GW
1976-77	Markham Waxers	OHA-B	24	18	22	40	....	....	....	83	....	....	....	....	....	....	....	....	....	....	....	....	....	....	....	....	....	....
	Toronto Marlboros	OMJHL	18	6	7	13	....	....	....	6	....	....	....	....	....	....	....	....	....	....	....	....	....	....	....	....	....	....
1977-78	Peterborough Petes	OMJHL	68	11	27	38	....	....	....	67	....	....	....	....	....	....	....	....	....	....	8	1	1	2	12	....	....	....
	Peterborough Petes	Mem-Cup	3	0	0	0	....	....	....	2	....	....	....	....	....	....	....	....	....	....	....	....	....	....	....	....	....	....
1978-79	Peterborough Petes	OMJHL	66	25	25	50	....	....	....	96	....	....	....	....	....	....	....	....	....	....	11	0	5	5	19	....	....	....
	Peterborough Petes	Mem-Cup	5	0	3	3	....	....	....	9	....	....	....	....	....	....	....	....	....	....	....	....	....	....	....	....	....	....
1979-80	Peterborough Petes	OMJHL	54	34	45	79	....	....	....	51	....	....	....	....	....	....	....	....	....	....	14	9	10	19	19	....	....	....
	Canada	WJC-A	5	1	0	1	....	....	....	2	....	....	....	....	....	....	....	....	....	....	....	....	....	....	....	....	....	....
	Peterborough Petes	Mem-Cup	5	3	3	6	....	....	....	2	....	....	....	....	....	....	....	....	....	....	....	....	....	....	....	....	....	....
1980-81	Salt Lake Golden Eagles	CHL	74	15	45	60	....	....	....	81	....	....	....	....	....	....	....	....	....	....	17	5	8	13	28	....	....	....
1981-82	**St. Louis Blues**	**NHL**	**9**	**1**	**3**	**4**	**1**	**2**	**3**	**0**	**0**	**0**	**0**	**8**	**12.5**	**6**	**0**	**3**	**0**	**3**	**10**	**0**	**1**	**1**	**2**	**0**	**0**	**0**
	Salt Lake Golden Eagles	CHL	59	22	24	46	....	....	....	55	....	....	....	....	....	....	....	....	....	....	....	....	....	....	....	....	....	....
1982-83	**St. Louis Blues**	**NHL**	**20**	**5**	**14**	**19**	**4**	**10**	**14**	**6**	**0**	**0**	**1**	**34**	**14.7**	**26**	**3**	**17**	**2**	**8**	**4**	**1**	**0**	**1**	**2**	**0**	**0**	**0**
	Salt Lake Golden Eagles	CHL	55	16	26	42	....	....	....	32	....	....	....	....	....	....	....	....	....	....	....	....	....	....	....	....	....	....
1983-84	**St. Louis Blues**	**NHL**	**65**	**11**	**14**	**25**	**9**	**10**	**19**	**23**	**3**	**1**	**0**	**72**	**15.3**	**33**	**5**	**48**	**17**	**–3**	**11**	**3**	**3**	**6**	**15**	**0**	**1**	**1**
1984-85	**St. Louis Blues**	**NHL**	**80**	**9**	**30**	**39**	**7**	**20**	**27**	**25**	**0**	**1**	**4**	**98**	**9.2**	**56**	**0**	**73**	**25**	**8**	**3**	**0**	**0**	**0**	**0**	**0**	**0**	**0**
1985-86	**St. Louis Blues**	**NHL**	**78**	**10**	**28**	**38**	**8**	**19**	**27**	**28**	**0**	**0**	**2**	**108**	**9.3**	**56**	**2**	**77**	**34**	**11**	**19**	**4**	**4**	**8**	**2**	**0**	**0**	**1**
1986-87	**St. Louis Blues**	**NHL**	**68**	**9**	**16**	**25**	**8**	**12**	**20**	**16**	**1**	**0**	**0**	**106**	**8.5**	**39**	**5**	**80**	**26**	**–20**	**6**	**0**	**1**	**1**	**2**	**0**	**0**	**0**
1987-88	**Hartford Whalers**	**NHL**	**38**	**0**	**7**	**7**	**0**	**5**	**5**	**31**	**0**	**0**	**0**	**36**	**0.0**	**13**	**0**	**35**	**9**	**–13**	....	....	....	....	....	....	....	....

			REGULAR SEASON																		PLAYOFFS							
Season	Club	League	GP	G	A	Pts	AG	AA	APts	PIM	PP	SH	GW	S	%	TGF	PGF	TGA	PGA	+/–	GP	G	A	Pts	PIM	PP	SH	GW
1988-89	**Hartford Whalers**	**NHL**	**7**	**0**	**2**	**2**	**0**	**1**	**1**	**6**	**0**	**0**	**0**	**6**	**0.0**	**2**	**0**	**4**	**1**	**–1**	....	....	....	....	....	....	....	....
	Binghamton Whalers	AHL	69	26	34	60	....	....	....	18	....	....	....	....	....	....	....	....	....	....	....	....	....	....	....	....	....	....
1989-90	HC Fiemme	Italy	34	34	59	93	....	....	....	6	....	....	....	....	....	....	....	....	....	....	10	13	25	38	6	....	....	....
1990-91	HC Fiemme	Italy	36	8	47	55	....	....	....	18	....	....	....	....	....	....	....	....	....	....	6	2	13	15	4	....	....	....
1991-1992	Peoria Rivermen	IHL	DID NOT PLAY – ASSISTANT COACH																									
1992-1993	Peoria Rivermen	IHL	DID NOT PLAY – ASSISTANT COACH																									
	Peoria Rivermen	IHL	16	4	2	6	....	....	....	8	....	....	....	....	....	....	....	....	....	....	1	0	0	0	0	....	....	....
1993-1996	Peoria Rivermen	IHL	DID NOT PLAY – ASSISTANT COACH																									
1996-1999	Peoria Rivermen	ECHL	DID NOT PLAY – COACHING																									
1999-2000	Missouri River Otters	UHL	DID NOT PLAY – COACHING																									
	NHL Totals		**365**	**45**	**114**	**159**	**37**	**79**	**116**	**135**	**4**	**2**	**7**	**468**	**9.6**	**231**	**15**	**337**	**114**		**53**	**8**	**9**	**17**	**23**	**0**	**1**	**2**

Memorial Cup All-Star Team (1980)

Traded to **Hartford** by **St. Louis** for Hartford's 3rd round choice (Blair Atcheynum) in 1989 Entry Draft, October 5, 1987.

• REEKIE, Joe

D – L. 6'3", 220 lbs. b: Victoria, B.C., 2/22/1965. Buffalo's 6th, 119th overall, in 1985.

Season	Club	League	GP	G	A	Pts	AG	AA	APts	PIM	PP	SH	GW	S	%	TGF	PGF	TGA	PGA	+/–	GP	G	A	Pts	PIM	PP	SH	GW
1981-82	Nepean Raiders	OJHL	16	2	5	7	....	....	....	4	....	....	....	....	....	....	....	....	....	....	....	....	....	....	....	....	....	....
1982-83	Pembroke Lumber Kings	OJHL	7	2	1	3	....	....	....	16	....	....	....	....	....	....	....	....	....	....	....	....	....	....	....	....	....	....
	North Bay Centennials	OHL	59	2	9	11	....	....	....	49	....	....	....	....	....	....	....	....	....	....	8	0	1	1	11	....	....	....
1983-84	North Bay Centennials	OHL	9	1	0	1	....	....	....	18	....	....	....	....	....	....	....	....	....	....	....	....	....	....	....	....	....	....
	Cornwall Royals	OHL	53	6	27	33	....	....	....	166	....	....	....	....	....	....	....	....	....	....	3	0	0	0	4	....	....	....
1984-85	Cornwall Royals	OHL	65	19	63	82	....	....	....	134	....	....	....	....	....	....	....	....	....	....	9	4	13	17	18	....	....	....
1985-86	**Buffalo Sabres**	**NHL**	**3**	**0**	**0**	**0**	**0**	**0**	**0**	**14**	**0**	**0**	**0**	**1**	**0.0**	**2**	**0**	**4**	**0**	**–2**	....	....	....	....	....	....	....	....
	Rochester Americans	AHL	77	3	25	28	....	....	....	178	....	....	....	....	....	....	....	....	....	....	....	....	....	....	....	....	....	....
1986-87	**Buffalo Sabres**	**NHL**	**56**	**1**	**8**	**9**	**1**	**6**	**7**	**82**	**0**	**0**	**0**	**56**	**1.8**	**59**	**4**	**74**	**25**	**6**	....	....	....	....	....	....	....	....
	Rochester Americans	AHL	22	0	6	6	....	....	....	52	....	....	....	....	....	....	....	....	....	....	....	....	....	....	....	....	....	....
1987-88	**Buffalo Sabres**	**NHL**	**30**	**1**	**4**	**5**	**1**	**3**	**4**	**68**	**0**	**0**	**0**	**23**	**4.3**	**28**	**0**	**39**	**8**	**–3**	**2**	**0**	**0**	**0**	**4**	**0**	**0**	**0**
1988-89	**Buffalo Sabres**	**NHL**	**15**	**1**	**3**	**4**	**1**	**2**	**3**	**26**	**1**	**0**	**0**	**14**	**7.1**	**19**	**1**	**18**	**6**	**6**	....	....	....	....	....	....	....	....
	Rochester Americans	AHL	21	1	2	3	....	....	....	56	....	....	....	....	....	....	....	....	....	....	....	....	....	....	....	....	....	....
1989-90	**New York Islanders**	**NHL**	**31**	**1**	**8**	**9**	**1**	**6**	**7**	**43**	**0**	**0**	**1**	**22**	**4.5**	**35**	**1**	**38**	**17**	**13**	....	....	....	....	....	....	....	....
	Springfield Indians	AHL	15	1	4	5	....	....	....	24	....	....	....	....	....	....	....	....	....	....	....	....	....	....	....	....	....	....
1990-91	**New York Islanders**	**NHL**	**66**	**3**	**16**	**19**	**3**	**12**	**15**	**96**	**0**	**0**	**2**	**70**	**4.3**	**65**	**3**	**76**	**31**	**17**	....	....	....	....	....	....	....	....
	Capital District Islanders	AHL	2	1	0	1	....	....	....	0	....	....	....	....	....	....	....	....	....	....	....	....	....	....	....	....	....	....
1991-92	**New York Islanders**	**NHL**	**54**	**4**	**12**	**16**	**4**	**9**	**13**	**85**	**0**	**0**	**0**	**59**	**6.8**	**64**	**3**	**75**	**29**	**15**	....	....	....	....	....	....	....	....
	Capital District Islanders	AHL	3	2	2	4	....	....	....	2	....	....	....	....	....	....	....	....	....	....	....	....	....	....	....	....	....	....
1992-93	**Tampa Bay Lightning**	**NHL**	**42**	**2**	**11**	**13**	**2**	**8**	**10**	**69**	**0**	**0**	**0**	**53**	**3.8**	**40**	**2**	**56**	**20**	**2**	....	....	....	....	....	....	....	....
1993-94	**Tampa Bay Lightning**	**NHL**	**73**	**1**	**11**	**12**	**1**	**9**	**10**	**127**	**0**	**0**	**0**	**88**	**1.1**	**55**	**0**	**73**	**26**	**8**	....	....	....	....	....	....	....	....
	Washington Capitals	**NHL**	**12**	**0**	**5**	**5**	**0**	**4**	**4**	**29**	**0**	**0**	**0**	**10**	**0.0**	**15**	**0**	**12**	**4**	**7**	**11**	**2**	**1**	**3**	**29**	**0**	**1**	**1**
1994-95	**Washington Capitals**	**NHL**	**48**	**1**	**6**	**7**	**2**	**9**	**11**	**97**	**0**	**0**	**0**	**52**	**1.9**	**35**	**1**	**37**	**13**	**10**	**7**	**0**	**0**	**0**	**2**	**0**	**0**	**0**
1995-96	**Washington Capitals**	**NHL**	**78**	**3**	**7**	**10**	**3**	**6**	**9**	**149**	**0**	**0**	**0**	**52**	**5.8**	**54**	**0**	**63**	**16**	**7**	....	....	....	....	....	....	....	....
1996-97	**Washington Capitals**	**NHL**	**65**	**1**	**8**	**9**	**1**	**7**	**8**	**107**	**0**	**0**	**0**	**65**	**1.5**	**48**	**1**	**58**	**19**	**8**	....	....	....	....	....	....	....	....
1997-98	**Washington Capitals**	**NHL**	**68**	**2**	**8**	**10**	**2**	**8**	**10**	**70**	**0**	**0**	**1**	**59**	**3.4**	**52**	**1**	**52**	**16**	**15**	**21**	**1**	**2**	**3**	**20**	**0**	**0**	**0**
1998-99	**Washington Capitals**	**NHL**	**73**	**0**	**10**	**10**	**0**	**10**	**10**	**68**	**0**	**0**	**0**	**81**	**0.0**	**63**	**2**	**76**	**26**	**11**	....	....	....	....	....	....	....	....
99-2000	**Washington Capitals**	**NHL**	**59**	**0**	**7**	**7**	**0**	**6**	**6**	**50**	**0**	**0**	**0**	**32**	**0.0**	**48**	**1**	**40**	**14**	**21**	**5**	**0**	**1**	**1**	**2**	**0**	**0**	**0**
	NHL Totals		**773**	**21**	**124**	**145**	**22**	**105**	**127**	**1180**	**1**	**0**	**4**	**737**	**2.8**	**682**	**20**	**791**	**270**		**46**	**3**	**4**	**7**	**57**	**0**	**1**	**1**

• Re-entered NHL draft. Originally Hartford's 8th choice, 128th overall, in 1983 Entry Draft.

• Missed majority of 1987-88 and 1988-89 seasons recovering from knee injury originally suffered in game vs. Toronto, November 11, 1987. Traded to **NY Islanders** by **Buffalo** for NY Islanders' 6th round choice (Bill Pye) in 1989 Entry Draft, June 17, 1989. Claimed by **Tampa Bay** from **NY Islanders** in Expansion Draft, June 18, 1992. Traded to **Washington** by **Tampa Bay** for Enrico Ciccone, Washington's 3rd round choice (later traded to Anaheim - Anaheim selected Craig Reichert) in 1994 Entry Draft and the return of conditional draft choice transferred in the Pat Elynuik trade, March 21, 1994.

• REGEHR, Robyn

D – L. 6'2", 225 lbs. b: Recife, Brazil, 4/19/1980. Colorado's 3rd, 19th overall, in 1998.

Season	Club	League	GP	G	A	Pts	AG	AA	APts	PIM	PP	SH	GW	S	%	TGF	PGF	TGA	PGA	+/–	GP	G	A	Pts	PIM	PP	SH	GW
1995-96	Prince Albert Mintos	SAHA	59	8	24	32	....	....	....	157	....	....	....	....	....	....	....	....	....	....	....	....	....	....	....	....	....	....
1996-97	Kamloops Blazers	WHL	64	4	19	23	....	....	....	96	....	....	....	....	....	....	....	....	....	....	5	0	1	1	18	....	....	....
1997-98	Kamloops Blazers	WHL	65	4	10	14	....	....	....	120	....	....	....	....	....	....	....	....	....	....	5	0	3	3	8	....	....	....
1998-99	Kamloops Blazers	WHL	54	12	20	32	....	....	....	130	....	....	....	....	....	....	....	....	....	....	12	1	4	5	21	....	....	....
	Canada	WJC-A	7	0	0	0	....	....	....	2	....	....	....	....	....	....	....	....	....	....	....	....	....	....	....	....	....	....
99-2000	**Calgary Flames**	**NHL**	**57**	**5**	**7**	**12**	**6**	**6**	**12**	**46**	**2**	**0**	**0**	**64**	**7.8**	**39**	**5**	**50**	**14**	**–2**	....	....	....	....	....	....	....	....
	Saint John Flames	AHL	5	0	0	0	....	....	....	0	....	....	....	....	....	....	....	....	....	....	....	....	....	....	....	....	....	....
	Canada	WC-A	6	0	0	0	....	....	....	2	....	....	....	....	....	....	....	....	....	....	....	....	....	....	....	....	....	....
	NHL Totals		**57**	**5**	**7**	**12**	**6**	**6**	**12**	**46**	**2**	**0**	**0**	**64**	**7.8**	**39**	**5**	**50**	**14**		....	....	....	....	....	....	....	....

WHL West First All-Star Team (1999)

Traded to **Calgary** by **Colorado** with Rene Corbet, Wade Belak and Colorado's 2nd round compensatory choice (Jarret Stoll) in 2000 Entry Draft for Theoren Fleury and Chris Dingman, February 28, 1999.

• REGIER, Darcy

Darcy John D – L. 5'11", 190 lbs. b: Swift Current, Sask., 11/27/1956. California's 5th, 77th overall, in 1976.

Season	Club	League	GP	G	A	Pts	AG	AA	APts	PIM	PP	SH	GW	S	%	TGF	PGF	TGA	PGA	+/–	GP	G	A	Pts	PIM	PP	SH	GW
1973-74	Prince Albert Raiders	SJHL	40	1	8	9	....	....	....	59	....	....	....	....	....	....	....	....	....	....	6	0	2	2	4	....	....	....
1974-75	Lethbridge Broncos	WCJHL	67	11	25	36	....	....	....	78	....	....	....	....	....	....	....	....	....	....	6	0	3	3	9	....	....	....
1975-76	Lethbridge Broncos	WCJHL	53	5	22	27	....	....	....	125	....	....	....	....	....	....	....	....	....	....	7	1	1	2	9	....	....	....
1976-77	Salt Lake Golden Eagles	CHL	68	5	22	27	....	....	....	123	....	....	....	....	....	....	....	....	....	....	....	....	....	....	....	....	....	....
1977-78	**Cleveland Barons**	**NHL**	**15**	**0**	**1**	**1**	**0**	**1**	**1**	**28**	**0**	**0**	**0**	**8**	**0.0**	**6**	**0**	**14**	**3**	**–5**	....	....	....	....	....	....	....	....
	Binghamton Dusters	AHL	5	0	1	1	....	....	....	2	....	....	....	....	....	....	....	....	....	....	....	....	....	....	....	....	....	....
	Phoenix Roadrunners	CHL	16	0	5	5	....	....	....	43	....	....	....	....	....	....	....	....	....	....	....	....	....	....	....	....	....	....
	Fort Worth Texans	CHL	38	2	6	8	....	....	....	37	....	....	....	....	....	....	....	....	....	....	14	2	6	8	24	....	....	....
1978-79	Fort Worth Texans	CHL	59	1	15	16	....	....	....	98	....	....	....	....	....	....	....	....	....	....	5	0	1	1	2	....	....	....
1979-80	Indianapolis Checkers	CHL	79	0	18	18	....	....	....	52	....	....	....	....	....	....	....	....	....	....	7	0	1	1	20	....	....	....
1980-81	Indianapolis Checkers	CHL	76	2	18	20	....	....	....	77	....	....	....	....	....	....	....	....	....	....	5	0	1	1	27	....	....	....
1981-82	Indianapolis Checkers	CHL	80	4	17	21	....	....	....	98	....	....	....	....	....	....	....	....	....	....	13	1	4	5	20	....	....	....
1982-83	**New York Islanders**	**NHL**	**6**	**0**	**0**	**0**	**0**	**0**	**0**	**7**	**0**	**0**	**0**	**3**	**0.0**	**1**	**0**	**2**	**1**	**0**	....	....	....	....	....	....	....	....
	Indianapolis Checkers	CHL	74	3	28	31	....	....	....	102	....	....	....	....	....	....	....	....	....	....	11	0	4	4	21	....	....	....
1983-84	**New York Islanders**	**NHL**	**5**	**0**	**1**	**1**	**0**	**1**	**1**	**0**	**0**	**0**	**0**	**6**	**0.0**	**4**	**0**	**2**	**0**	**2**	....	....	....	....	....	....	....	....
	Indianapolis Checkers	CHL	68	4	12	16	....	....	....	112	....	....	....	....	....	....	....	....	....	....	10	1	1	2	13	....	....	....
	NHL Totals		**26**	**0**	**2**	**2**	**0**	**2**	**2**	**35**	**0**	**0**	**0**	**17**	**0.0**	**11**	**0**	**18**	**4**		....	....	....	....	....	....	....	....

SJHL First All-Star Team • CHL First All-Star Team (1983)

Rights transferred to **Cleveland** after **California** franchise relocated, August 26, 1976. Traded to **NY Islanders** by **Cleveland** with Wayne Merrick and Cleveland's 4th round choice (draft choice cancelled by the Cleveland-Minnesota merger) in 1978 Entry Draft for Jean-Paul Parise and Jean Potvin, January 10, 1978.

• REICHEL, Robert

C – L. 5'10", 185 lbs. b: Litvinov, Czech., 6/25/1971. Calgary's 5th, 70th overall, in 1989.

Season	Club	League	GP	G	A	Pts	AG	AA	APts	PIM	PP	SH	GW	S	%	TGF	PGF	TGA	PGA	+/–	GP	G	A	Pts	PIM	PP	SH	GW
1987-88	CHZ Litvinov	Czech.	36	17	10	27	....	....	....	8	....	....	....	....	....	....	....	....	....	....	....	....	....	....	....	....	....	....
	Czechoslovakia	WJC-A	7	3	8	11	....	....	....	2	....	....	....	....	....	....	....	....	....	....	....	....	....	....	....	....	....	....
	Czechoslovakia	EJC-A	6	8	4	12	....	....	....	6	....	....	....	....	....	....	....	....	....	....	....	....	....	....	....	....	....	....
1988-89	CHZ Litvinov	Czech.	44	23	25	48	....	....	....	32	....	....	....	....	....	....	....	....	....	....	....	....	....	....	....	....	....	....
	Czechoslovakia	WJC-A	7	4	4	8	....	....	....	4	....	....	....	....	....	....	....	....	....	....	....	....	....	....	....	....	....	....
	Czechoslovakia	EJC-A	6	14	7	21	....	....	....	22	....	....	....	....	....	....	....	....	....	....	....	....	....	....	....	....	....	....
1989-90	CHZ Litvinov	Czech.	44	*43	28	*71	....	....	....	....	....	....	....	....	....	....	....	....	....	....	8	6	6	12	....	....	....	....
	Czechoslovakia	WJC-A	7	*11	10	*21	....	....	....	4	....	....	....	....	....	....	....	....	....	....	....	....	....	....	....	....	....	....
	Czechoslovakia	WEC-A	10	5	6	11	....	....	....	4	....	....	....	....	....	....	....	....	....	....	....	....	....	....	....	....	....	....

			REGULAR SEASON																		PLAYOFFS							
Season	**Club**	**League**	**GP**	**G**	**A**	**Pts**	**AG**	**AA**	**APts**	**PIM**	**PP**	**SH**	**GW**	**S**	**%**	**TGF**	**PGF**	**TGA**	**PGA**	**+/–**	**GP**	**G**	**A**	**Pts**	**PIM**	**PP**	**SH**	**GW**
1990-91	**Calgary Flames**	**NHL**	**66**	**19**	**22**	**41**	**17**	**17**	**34**	**22**	**3**	**0**	**3**	**131**	**14.5**	**58**	**17**	**24**	**0**	**17**	**6**	**1**	**1**	**2**	**0**	**1**	**0**	**0**
	Czechoslovakia	WEC-A	8	2	4	6				10																		
1991-92	Czechoslovakia	Can-Cup	5	1	2	3				6																		
	Calgary Flames	**NHL**	**77**	**20**	**34**	**54**	**18**	**26**	**44**	**32**	**8**	**0**	**3**	**181**	**11.0**	**77**	**36**	**41**	**1**	**1**								
	Czechoslovakia	WC-A	8	1	3	4				2																		
1992-93	**Calgary Flames**	**NHL**	**80**	**40**	**48**	**88**	**33**	**33**	**66**	**54**	**12**	**0**	**5**	**238**	**16.8**	**127**	**49**	**54**	**1**	**25**	**6**	**2**	**4**	**6**	**2**	**2**	**0**	**0**
1993-94	**Calgary Flames**	**NHL**	**84**	**40**	**53**	**93**	**37**	**41**	**78**	**58**	**14**	**0**	**6**	**249**	**16.1**	**118**	**49**	**51**	**2**	**20**	**7**	**0**	**5**	**5**	**0**	**0**	**0**	**0**
1994-95	Frankfurt Lions	Germany	21	19	24	43				41																		
	Calgary Flames	**NHL**	**48**	**18**	**17**	**35**	**32**	**25**	**57**	**28**	**5**	**0**	**2**	**160**	**11.3**	**50**	**20**	**32**	**0**	**–2**	**7**	**2**	**4**	**6**	**4**	**0**	**0**	**1**
1995-96	Frankfurt Lions	Germany	46	47	54	101				84											3	1	3	4	0			
	Czech-Republic	WC-A	8	4	4	8				0																		
1996-97	Czech-Republic	W-Cup	3	1	0	1				0																		
	Calgary Flames	**NHL**	**70**	**16**	**27**	**43**	**17**	**24**	**41**	**22**	**6**	**0**	**3**	**181**	**8.8**	**57**	**22**	**38**	**1**	**–2**								
	New York Islanders	**NHL**	**12**	**5**	**14**	**19**	**5**	**12**	**17**	**4**	**0**	**1**	**0**	**33**	**15.2**	**22**	**5**	**10**	**0**	**7**								
	Czech-Republic	WC-A	9	1	4	5				4																		
1997-98	**New York Islanders**	**NHL**	**82**	**25**	**40**	**65**	**29**	**39**	**68**	**32**	**8**	**0**	**2**	**201**	**12.4**	**97**	**48**	**61**	**1**	**–11**								
	Czech-Republic	Olympics	6	3	0	3				0																		
	Czech-Republic	WC-A	8	0	4	4				0																		
1998-99	**New York Islanders**	**NHL**	**70**	**19**	**37**	**56**	**22**	**36**	**58**	**50**	**5**	**1**	**1**	**186**	**10.2**	**77**	**36**	**58**	**2**	**–15**								
	Phoenix Coyotes	**NHL**	**13**	**7**	**6**	**13**	**8**	**6**	**14**	**4**	**3**	**0**	**3**	**50**	**14.0**	**17**	**5**	**11**	**1**	**2**	**7**	**1**	**3**	**4**	**2**	**0**	**0**	**0**
99-2000	HC Chemopetrol Litvinov	Czech-Rep	45	25	32	57				24											7	3	4	7	2			
	Czech-Republic	WC-A	9	2	3	5				4																		
	NHL Totals		**602**	**209**	**298**	**507**	**218**	**259**	**477**	**306**	**64**	**2**	**28**	**1610**	**13.0**	**700**	**287**	**380**	**9**		**33**	**6**	**17**	**23**	**8**	**3**	**0**	**1**

EJC-A All-Star Team (1988, 1989) • WJC-A All-Star Team (1990) • Named Best Forward at WJC-A (1990) • Czechoslovakian First All-Star Team (1990) • WEC-A All-Star Team (1990) • WC-A All-Star Team (1996)

Traded to **NY Islanders** by **Calgary** for Marty McInnis, Tyrone Garner and Calgary's 6th round choice (previously acquired, Calgary selected Ilja Demidov) in 1997 Entry Draft, March 18, 1997. Traded to **Phoenix** by **NY Islanders** with NY Islanders' 3rd round choice (Jason Jaspers) in 1999 Entry Draft and Ottawa's 4th round choice (previously acquired, Phoenix selected Preston Mizzi) in 1999 Entry Draft for Brad Isbister and Phoenix's 3rd round choice (Brian Collins) in 1999 Entry Draft, March 20, 1999.

• REICHERT, Craig

Craig Steven RW – R. 6'1", 200 lbs. b: Winnipeg, Man., 5/11/1974. Anaheim's 3rd, 67th overall, in 1994.

Season	Club	League	GP	G	A	Pts	AG	AA	APts	PIM	PP	SH	GW	S	%	TGF	PGF	TGA	PGA	+/–	GP	G	A	Pts	PIM	PP	SH	GW
1990-91	Calgary Buffaloes	AAHA	47	32	36	68				54											13	13	28	41	27			
1991-92	Spokane Chiefs	WHL	68	13	20	33				56											4	1	0	1	4			
1992-93	Red Deer Rebels	WHL	66	32	33	65				62											4	3	1	4	2			
1993-94	Red Deer Rebels	WHL	72	52	67	119				153											4	2	2	4	8			
1994-95	San Diego Gulls	IHL	49	4	12	16				28																		
1995-96	Baltimore Bandits	AHL	68	10	17	27				50											1	0	0	0	0			
1996-97	**Mighty Ducks of Anaheim**	**NHL**	**3**	**0**	**0**	**0**	**0**	**0**	**0**	**0**	**0**	**0**	**0**	**3**	**0.0**	**0**	**0**	**2**	**0**	**–2**								
	Baltimore Bandits	AHL	77	22	53	75				54											3	0	2	2	0			
1997-98	Cincinnati Mighty Ducks	AHL	78	28	59	87				28																		
1998-99	Cincinnati Mighty Ducks	AHL	72	28	41	69				56											3	2	0	2	0			
99-2000	Louisville Panthers	AHL	72	16	42	58				41											4	1	1	2	2			
	NHL Totals		**3**	**0**	**0**	**0**	**0**	**0**	**0**	**0**	**0**	**0**	**0**	**3**	**0.0**	**0**	**0**	**2**	**0**									

Signed as a free agent by **Florida**, July 21, 1999.

• REID, Dave

David William LW – L. 6'1", 217 lbs. b: Toronto, Ont., 5/15/1964. Boston's 4th, 60th overall, in 1982.

Season	Club	League	GP	G	A	Pts	AG	AA	APts	PIM	PP	SH	GW	S	%	TGF	PGF	TGA	PGA	+/–	GP	G	A	Pts	PIM	PP	SH	GW
1979-80	Royal York Royals	OJHL	41	4	7	11				93																		
1980-81	Mississauga Reps	MTHL	39	21	28	49																						
	Dixie Beehives	OHA-B	4	2	3	5				0																		
1981-82	Peterborough Petes	OHL	68	10	32	42				41											9	2	3	5	11			
1982-83	Peterborough Petes	OHL	70	23	34	57				33											4	3	1	4	0			
1983-84	Peterborough Petes	OHL	60	33	64	97				12																		
	Boston Bruins	**NHL**	**8**	**1**	**0**	**1**	**1**	**0**	**1**	**2**	**0**	**0**	**0**	**4**	**25.0**	**3**	**0**	**2**	**0**	**1**								
1984-85	**Boston Bruins**	**NHL**	**35**	**14**	**13**	**27**	**11**	**9**	**20**	**27**	**2**	**0**	**5**	**52**	**26.9**	**39**	**10**	**30**	**0**	**–1**	**5**	**1**	**0**	**1**	**0**	**0**	**0**	**0**
	Hershey Bears	AHL	43	10	14	24				6																		
1985-86	**Boston Bruins**	**NHL**	**37**	**10**	**10**	**20**	**8**	**7**	**15**	**10**	**4**	**0**	**1**	**53**	**18.9**	**34**	**15**	**17**	**0**	**2**								
	Moncton Golden Flames	AHL	26	14	18	32				4																		
1986-87	**Boston Bruins**	**NHL**	**12**	**3**	**3**	**6**	**3**	**2**	**5**	**0**	**0**	**0**	**0**	**19**	**15.8**	**6**	**0**	**7**	**0**	**–1**	**2**	**0**	**0**	**0**	**0**	**0**	**0**	**0**
	Moncton Golden Flames	AHL	40	12	22	34				23											5	0	1	1	0			
1987-88	**Boston Bruins**	**NHL**	**3**	**0**	**0**	**0**	**0**	**0**	**0**	**0**	**0**	**0**	**0**	**2**	**0.0**	**0**	**0**	**0**	**0**	**0**								
	Maine Mariners	AHL	63	21	37	58				40											10	6	7	13	0			
1988-89	**Toronto Maple Leafs**	**NHL**	**77**	**9**	**21**	**30**	**8**	**15**	**23**	**22**	**1**	**1**	**0**	**87**	**10.3**	**49**	**5**	**61**	**29**	**12**								
1989-90	**Toronto Maple Leafs**	**NHL**	**70**	**9**	**19**	**28**	**8**	**14**	**22**	**9**	**0**	**4**	**1**	**97**	**9.3**	**41**	**0**	**80**	**31**	**–8**	**3**	**0**	**0**	**0**	**0**	**0**	**0**	**0**
1990-91	**Toronto Maple Leafs**	**NHL**	**69**	**15**	**13**	**28**	**14**	**10**	**24**	**18**	**1**	**8**	**0**	**110**	**13.6**	**41**	**4**	**77**	**30**	**–10**								
1991-92	**Boston Bruins**	**NHL**	**43**	**7**	**7**	**14**	**6**	**5**	**11**	**27**	**2**	**1**	**0**	**70**	**10.0**	**32**	**5**	**33**	**11**	**5**	**15**	**2**	**5**	**7**	**4**	**0**	**0**	**1**
	Maine Mariners	AHL	12	1	5	6				4																		
1992-93	**Boston Bruins**	**NHL**	**65**	**20**	**16**	**36**	**17**	**11**	**28**	**10**	**1**	**5**	**2**	**116**	**17.2**	**52**	**3**	**67**	**30**	**12**								
1993-94	**Boston Bruins**	**NHL**	**83**	**6**	**17**	**23**	**6**	**13**	**19**	**25**	**0**	**2**	**1**	**145**	**4.1**	**46**	**0**	**66**	**30**	**10**	**13**	**2**	**1**	**3**	**2**	**0**	**1**	**0**
1994-95	**Boston Bruins**	**NHL**	**38**	**5**	**5**	**10**	**9**	**7**	**16**	**10**	**0**	**0**	**0**	**47**	**10.6**	**16**	**0**	**16**	**8**	**8**	**5**	**0**	**0**	**0**	**0**	**0**	**0**	**0**
	Providence Bruins	AHL	7	3	0	3				0																		
1995-96	**Boston Bruins**	**NHL**	**63**	**23**	**21**	**44**	**23**	**17**	**40**	**4**	**1**	**6**	**3**	**160**	**14.4**	**58**	**3**	**67**	**26**	**14**	**5**	**0**	**2**	**2**	**2**	**0**	**0**	**0**
1996-97	**Dallas Stars**	**NHL**	**82**	**19**	**20**	**39**	**20**	**18**	**38**	**10**	**1**	**1**	**4**	**135**	**14.1**	**50**	**2**	**55**	**19**	**12**	**7**	**1**	**0**	**1**	**4**	**0**	**0**	**0**
1997-98	**Dallas Stars**	**NHL**	**65**	**6**	**12**	**18**	**7**	**12**	**19**	**14**	**3**	**0**	**1**	**90**	**6.7**	**29**	**12**	**45**	**13**	**–15**	**5**	**0**	**3**	**3**	**2**	**0**	**0**	**0**
1998-99♦	**Dallas Stars**	**NHL**	**73**	**6**	**11**	**17**	**7**	**11**	**18**	**16**	**1**	**0**	**1**	**81**	**7.4**	**26**	**3**	**28**	**5**	**0**	**23**	**2**	**8**	**10**	**14**	**0**	**0**	**0**
99-2000	**Colorado Avalanche**	**NHL**	**65**	**11**	**7**	**18**	**12**	**6**	**18**	**28**	**0**	**0**	**3**	**86**	**12.8**	**37**	**3**	**34**	**12**	**12**	**17**	**1**	**3**	**4**	**0**	**0**	**0**	**0**
	NHL Totals		**888**	**164**	**195**	**359**	**160**	**157**	**317**	**232**	**17**	**28**	**22**	**1354**	**12.1**	**559**	**65**	**685**	**244**		**100**	**9**	**22**	**31**	**28**	**0**	**1**	**1**

Signed as a free agent by **Toronto**, June 23, 1988. Signed as a free agent by **Boston**, December 1, 1991. Signed as a free agent by **Dallas**, July 11, 1996. Signed as a free agent by **Colorado**, October 6, 1999.

• REID, Tom

Allan Thomas D – L. 6'1", 200 lbs. b: Fort Erie, Ont., 6/24/1946.

Season	Club	League	GP	G	A	Pts	AG	AA	APts	PIM	PP	SH	GW	S	%	TGF	PGF	TGA	PGA	+/–	GP	G	A	Pts	PIM	PP	SH	GW
1963-64	Fort Frances Royals	MJHL	27	2	5	7				45											10	1	1	2	24			
1964-65	St. Catharines Black Hawks	OHA-Jr.	56	4	13	17				106											5	1	0	1	11			
1965-66	St. Catharines Black Hawks	OHA-Jr.	45	3	15	18				74											7	0	0	0	44			
1966-67	St. Catharines Black Hawks	OHA-Jr.	45	5	19	24				120											4	0	2	2	2			
	St. Louis Braves	CPHL	1	0	0	0				0																		
1967-68	**Chicago Black Hawks**	**NHL**	**56**	**0**	**4**	**4**	**0**	**4**	**4**	**25**	**0**	**0**	**0**	**24**	**0.0**	**18**	**0**	**30**	**13**	**1**	**9**	**0**	**0**	**0**	**2**	**0**	**0**	**0**
	Dallas Black Hawks	CPHL	3	0	1	1				0																		
1968-69	**Chicago Black Hawks**	**NHL**	**30**	**0**	**3**	**3**	**0**	**3**	**3**	**12**	**0**	**0**	**0**	**6**	**0.0**	**12**	**0**	**18**	**2**	**–4**								
	Dallas Black Hawks	CHL	3	0	1	1				4																		
	Minnesota North Stars	**NHL**	**18**	**0**	**4**	**4**	**0**	**4**	**4**	**38**	**0**	**0**	**0**	**16**	**0.0**	**16**	**2**	**32**	**5**	**–13**								
1969-70	**Minnesota North Stars**	**NHL**	**66**	**1**	**7**	**8**	**1**	**7**	**8**	**51**	**0**	**0**	**1**	**89**	**1.1**	**63**	**2**	**86**	**15**	**–10**	**6**	**0**	**1**	**1**	**4**	**0**	**0**	**0**
	Iowa Stars	CHL	9	0	5	5				8																		
1970-71	**Minnesota North Stars**	**NHL**	**73**	**3**	**14**	**17**	**3**	**12**	**15**	**62**	**0**	**0**	**1**	**111**	**2.7**	**72**	**4**	**99**	**25**	**–6**	**12**	**0**	**6**	**6**	**20**	**0**	**0**	**0**
1971-72	**Minnesota North Stars**	**NHL**	**78**	**6**	**15**	**21**	**6**	**13**	**19**	**107**	**1**	**0**	**1**	**111**	**5.4**	**86**	**8**	**88**	**23**	**13**	**7**	**1**	**4**	**5**	**17**	**0**	**0**	**0**
1972-73	**Minnesota North Stars**	**NHL**	**60**	**1**	**13**	**14**	**1**	**10**	**11**	**50**	**0**	**0**	**0**	**79**	**1.3**	**78**	**3**	**77**	**17**	**15**	**6**	**0**	**2**	**2**	**4**	**0**	**0**	**0**
1973-74	**Minnesota North Stars**	**NHL**	**76**	**4**	**19**	**23**	**4**	**16**	**20**	**81**	**0**	**0**	**0**	**118**	**3.4**	**82**	**3**	**134**	**33**	**–22**								
1974-75	**Minnesota North Stars**	**NHL**	**74**	**1**	**5**	**6**	**1**	**4**	**5**	**103**	**0**	**0**	**1**	**98**	**1.0**	**65**	**1**	**147**	**44**	**–39**								

			REGULAR SEASON																		PLAYOFFS							
Season	**Club**	**League**	**GP**	**G**	**A**	**Pts**	**AG**	**AA**	**APts**	**PIM**	**PP**	**SH**	**GW**	**S**	**%**	**TGF**	**PGF**	**TGA**	**PGA**	**+/–**	**GP**	**G**	**A**	**Pts**	**PIM**	**PP**	**SH**	**GW**
1975-76	**Minnesota North Stars**	**NHL**	**69**	**0**	**15**	**15**	**0**	**11**	**11**	**52**	**0**	**0**	**0**	**90**	**0.0**	**59**	**20**	**102**	**39**	**–24**	....	....	....	....	....	....	....	....
1976-77	**Minnesota North Stars**	**NHL**	**65**	**0**	**8**	**8**	**0**	**6**	**6**	**52**	**0**	**0**	**0**	**45**	**0.0**	**56**	**4**	**101**	**33**	**–16**	**2**	**0**	**0**	**0**	**2**	**0**	**0**	**0**
1977-78	**Minnesota North Stars**	**NHL**	**36**	**1**	**6**	**7**	**1**	**5**	**6**	**21**	**0**	**0**	**1**	**26**	**3.8**	**24**	**1**	**66**	**17**	**–26**	....	....	....	....	....	....	....	....
	NHL Totals		**701**	**17**	**113**	**130**	**17**	**95**	**112**	**654**	**1**	**0**	**5**	**813**	**2.1**	**631**	**48**	**980**	**266**		**42**	**1**	**13**	**14**	**49**	**0**	**0**	**0**

OHA-Jr. First All-Star Team (1967)

Traded to **Minnesota** by **Chicago** with Bill Orban for Andre Boudrias and Mike McMahon Jr., February 14, 1969.

• REIERSON, Dave

David D – R. 6', 185 lbs. b: Bashaw, Alta., 8/30/1964. Calgary's 1st, 29th overall, in 1982.

Season	Club	League	GP	G	A	Pts	AG	AA	APts	PIM	PP	SH	GW	S	%	TGF	PGF	TGA	PGA	+/–	GP	G	A	Pts	PIM	PP	SH	GW
1980-81	Prince Albert Raiders	SJHL	73	14	39	53	....	....	....	....	....	....	....	....	....	....	....	....	....	....	....	....	....	....	....	....	....	....
	Prince Albert Raiders	Cen-Cup	STATISTICS NOT AVAILABLE																									
1981-82	Prince Albert Raiders	SJHL	60	20	51	71	....	....	....	163	....	....	....	....	....	....	....	....	....	....	27	3	25	28	42	....	....	....
1982-83	Michigan Tech Huskies	CCHA	38	2	14	16	....	....	....	52	....	....	....	....	....	....	....	....	....	....	....	....	....	....	....	....	....	....
1983-84	Michigan Tech Huskies	CCHA	38	4	15	19	....	....	....	63	....	....	....	....	....	....	....	....	....	....	....	....	....	....	....	....	....	....
1984-85	Michigan Tech Huskies	CCHA	36	5	27	32	....	....	....	76	....	....	....	....	....	....	....	....	....	....	....	....	....	....	....	....	....	....
1985-86	Michigan Tech Huskies	WCHA	39	7	16	23	....	....	....	51	....	....	....	....	....	....	....	....	....	....	....	....	....	....	....	....	....	....
1986-87	Canada	Nat-Team	61	1	17	18	....	....	....	36	....	....	....	....	....	....	....	....	....	....	....	....	....	....	....	....	....	....
	Moncton Golden Flames	AHL	....	....	....	....	....	....	....	....	....	....	....	....	....	....	....	....	....	....	6	0	1	1	12	....	....	....
1987-88	Canada	Nat-Team	32	2	8	10	....	....	....	18	....	....	....	....	....	....	....	....	....	....	....	....	....	....	....	....	....	....
	Salt Lake Golden Eagles	IHL	48	10	19	29	....	....	....	42	....	....	....	....	....	....	....	....	....	....	16	2	14	16	30	....	....	....
1988-89	**Calgary Flames**	**NHL**	**2**	**0**	**0**	**0**	**0**	**0**	**0**	**2**	**0**	**0**	**0**	**1**	**0.0**	**2**	**0**	**1**	**0**	**1**	....	....	....	....	....	....	....	....
	Salt Lake Golden Eagles	IHL	76	7	46	53	....	....	....	70	....	....	....	....	....	....	....	....	....	....	13	1	8	9	12	....	....	....
1989-90	Tappara Tampere	Finland	32	7	5	12	....	....	....	28	....	....	....	....	....	....	....	....	....	....	7	0	2	2	12	....	....	....
	Canada	Nat-Team	6	0	1	1	....	....	....	0	....	....	....	....	....	....	....	....	....	....	....	....	....	....	....	....	....	....
1990-91	Canada	Nat-Team	8	0	1	1	....	....	....	6	....	....	....	....	....	....	....	....	....	....	....	....	....	....	....	....	....	....
	Tappara Tampere	Finland	41	1	8	9	....	....	....	18	....	....	....	....	....	....	....	....	....	....	3	0	0	0	2	....	....	....
1991-92	HC Amiens	France	14	2	6	8	....	....	....	28	....	....	....	....	....	....	....	....	....	....	20	6	8	14	12	....	....	....
1992-93	HC Amiens	France	14	14	12	26	....	....	....	18	....	....	....	....	....	....	....	....	....	....	....	....	....	....	....	....	....	....
1993-94	HC Amiens	France	26	12	18	30	....	....	....	36	....	....	....	....	....	....	....	....	....	....	6	1	5	6	8	....	....	....
1994-95	Hannover Scorpions	Germany	43	8	14	22	....	....	....	38	....	....	....	....	....	....	....	....	....	....	5	1	0	1	2	....	....	....
1995-96	Hannover Scorpions	Germany	37	5	11	16	....	....	....	28	....	....	....	....	....	....	....	....	....	....	....	....	....	....	....	....	....	....
	Augsburger Panther	Germany	7	2	2	4	....	....	....	6	....	....	....	....	....	....	....	....	....	....	7	1	1	2	4	....	....	....
1996-97	HC Amiens	France	31	5	10	15	....	....	....	30	....	....	....	....	....	....	....	....	....	....	10	2	0	2	8	....	....	....
1997-98	HC Amiens	France	40	10	20	30	....	....	....	48	....	....	....	....	....	....	....	....	....	....	....	....	....	....	....	....	....	....
	HC Amiens	EuroHL	6	1	2	3	....	....	....	8	....	....	....	....	....	....	....	....	....	....	....	....	....	....	....	....	....	....
1998-99	HC Amiens	France	48	10	15	25	....	....	....	61	....	....	....	....	....	....	....	....	....	....	....	....	....	....	....	....	....	....
	NHL Totals		**2**	**0**	**0**	**0**	**0**	**0**	**0**	**2**	**0**	**0**	**0**	**1**	**0.0**	**2**	**0**	**1**	**0**		....	....	....	....	....	....	....	....

• REINHART, Paul

Paul Gerard "Rhino" D – L. 5'11", 205 lbs. b: Kitchener, Ont., 1/6/1960. Atlanta's 1st, 12th overall, in 1979.

Season	Club	League	GP	G	A	Pts	AG	AA	APts	PIM	PP	SH	GW	S	%	TGF	PGF	TGA	PGA	+/–	GP	G	A	Pts	PIM	PP	SH	GW
1974-75	Kitchener Greenshirts	OMHA	30	4	16	20	....	....	....	16	....	....	....	....	....	....	....	....	....	....	....	....	....	....	....	....	....	....
1975-76	Kitchener Rangers	OMJHL	53	6	33	39	....	....	....	42	....	....	....	....	....	....	....	....	....	....	8	1	2	3	4	....	....	....
1976-77	Kitchener Rangers	OMJHL	51	4	14	18	....	....	....	16	....	....	....	....	....	....	....	....	....	....	3	0	2	2	4	....	....	....
1977-78	Kitchener Rangers	OMJHL	47	17	28	45	....	....	....	15	....	....	....	....	....	....	....	....	....	....	9	4	6	10	29	....	....	....
1978-79	Kitchener Rangers	OMJHL	66	51	78	129	....	....	....	57	....	....	....	....	....	....	....	....	....	....	10	3	10	13	16	....	....	....
1979-80	**Atlanta Flames**	**NHL**	**79**	**9**	**38**	**47**	**8**	**28**	**36**	**31**	**4**	**0**	**1**	**130**	**6.9**	**118**	**31**	**78**	**2**	**11**	....	....	....	....	....	....	....	....
1980-81	**Calgary Flames**	**NHL**	**74**	**18**	**49**	**67**	**14**	**33**	**47**	**52**	**10**	**0**	**0**	**122**	**14.8**	**156**	**54**	**105**	**13**	**10**	**16**	**1**	**14**	**15**	**16**	**1**	**0**	**0**
1981-82	Canada	Can-Cup	2	0	0	0	....	....	....	2	....	....	....	....	....	....	....	....	....	....	....	....	....	....	....	....	....	....
	Calgary Flames	**NHL**	**62**	**13**	**48**	**61**	**10**	**32**	**42**	**17**	**8**	**0**	**0**	**116**	**11.2**	**131**	**50**	**115**	**35**	**1**	**3**	**0**	**1**	**1**	**2**	**0**	**0**	**0**
	Canada	WEC-A	7	1	5	6	....	....	....	4	....	....	....	....	....	....	....	....	....	....	....	....	....	....	....	....	....	....
1982-83	**Calgary Flames**	**NHL**	**78**	**17**	**58**	**75**	**14**	**40**	**54**	**28**	**5**	**0**	**1**	**152**	**11.2**	**154**	**59**	**125**	**31**	**1**	**9**	**6**	**3**	**9**	**2**	**4**	**1**	**0**
	Canada	WEC-A	6	2	4	6	....	....	....	2	....	....	....	....	....	....	....	....	....	....	....	....	....	....	....	....	....	....
1983-84	**Calgary Flames**	**NHL**	**27**	**6**	**15**	**21**	**5**	**10**	**15**	**10**	**3**	**0**	**1**	**92**	**6.5**	**44**	**13**	**51**	**10**	**–10**	**11**	**6**	**11**	**17**	**2**	**0**	**1**	**0**
1984-85	**Calgary Flames**	**NHL**	**75**	**23**	**46**	**69**	**19**	**31**	**50**	**18**	**12**	**2**	**5**	**173**	**13.3**	**153**	**55**	**149**	**54**	**3**	**4**	**1**	**1**	**2**	**0**	**0**	**0**	**0**
1985-86	**Calgary Flames**	**NHL**	**32**	**8**	**25**	**33**	**6**	**17**	**23**	**15**	**4**	**0**	**2**	**58**	**13.8**	**65**	**26**	**52**	**17**	**4**	**21**	**5**	**13**	**18**	**4**	**4**	**0**	**0**
1986-87	**Calgary Flames**	**NHL**	**76**	**15**	**53**	**68**	**13**	**39**	**52**	**22**	**7**	**0**	**2**	**120**	**12.5**	**133**	**50**	**96**	**20**	**7**	**4**	**0**	**1**	**1**	**6**	**0**	**0**	**0**
1987-88	**Calgary Flames**	**NHL**	**14**	**0**	**4**	**4**	**0**	**3**	**3**	**10**	**0**	**0**	**0**	**22**	**0.0**	**20**	**7**	**18**	**5**	**0**	**8**	**2**	**7**	**9**	**6**	**1**	**0**	**0**
1988-89	**Vancouver Canucks**	**NHL**	**64**	**7**	**50**	**57**	**6**	**35**	**41**	**44**	**3**	**0**	**1**	**133**	**5.3**	**121**	**60**	**80**	**15**	**–4**	**7**	**2**	**3**	**5**	**4**	**1**	**0**	**2**
1989-90	**Vancouver Canucks**	**NHL**	**67**	**17**	**40**	**57**	**15**	**29**	**44**	**30**	**9**	**1**	**1**	**139**	**12.2**	**118**	**48**	**89**	**21**	**2**	....	....	....	....	....	....	....	....
	NHL Totals		**648**	**133**	**426**	**559**	**110**	**297**	**407**	**277**	**65**	**3**	**14**	**1257**	**10.6**	**1213**	**453**	**958**	**223**		**83**	**23**	**54**	**77**	**42**	**11**	**2**	**2**

Played in NHL All-Star Game (1985, 1989)

Transferred to **Calgary** after **Atlanta** franchise relocated, June 24, 1980. Traded to **Vancouver** by **Calgary** with Steve Bozek for Vancouver's 3rd round choice (Veli-Pekka Kautonen) in 1989 Entry Draft, September 6, 1988.

• REINPRECHT, Steve

C – L. 6', 190 lbs. b: Edmonton, AB, 5/7/1976.

Season	Club	League	GP	G	A	Pts	AG	AA	APts	PIM	PP	SH	GW	S	%	TGF	PGF	TGA	PGA	+/–	GP	G	A	Pts	PIM	PP	SH	GW
1992-93	Edmonton S.S. Athletics	AAHA	71	48	77	125	....	....	....	....	....	....	....	....	....	....	....	....	....	....	....	....	....	....	....	....	....	....
1993-1995	St. Albert Saints	AJHL	STATISTICS NOT AVAILABLE																									
1995-96	St. Albert Saints	AJHL	32	24	36	60	....	....	....	....	....	....	....	....	....	....	....	....	....	....	....	....	....	....	....	....	....	....
1996-97	University of Wisconsin	WCHA	38	11	9	20	....	....	....	12	....	....	....	....	....	....	....	....	....	....	....	....	....	....	....	....	....	....
1997-98	University of Wisconsin	WCHA	41	19	24	43	....	....	....	18	....	....	....	....	....	....	....	....	....	....	....	....	....	....	....	....	....	....
1998-99	University of Wisconsin	WCHA	38	16	17	33	....	....	....	14	....	....	....	....	....	....	....	....	....	....	....	....	....	....	....	....	....	....
99-2000	University of Wisconsin	WCHA	37	26	40	*66	....	....	....	14	....	....	....	....	....	....	....	....	....	....	....	....	....	....	....	....	....	....
	Los Angeles Kings	**NHL**	**1**	**0**	**0**	**0**	**0**	**0**	**0**	**2**	**0**	**0**	**0**	**0**	**0.0**	**0**	**0**	**0**	**0**	**0**	....	....	....	....	....	....	....	....
	NHL Totals		**1**	**0**	**0**	**0**	**0**	**0**	**0**	**2**	**0**	**0**	**0**	**0**	**0.0**	**0**	**0**	**0**	**0**		....	....	....	....	....	....	....	....

WCHA First All-Star Team (2000) • NCAA West First All-American Team (2000)

Signed as a free agent by **LA Kings**, March 31, 2000.

• REIRDEN, Todd

D – L. 6'4", 205 lbs. b: Arlington Heights, IL, 6/25/1971. New Jersey's 14th, 242nd overall, in 1990.

Season	Club	League	GP	G	A	Pts	AG	AA	APts	PIM	PP	SH	GW	S	%	TGF	PGF	TGA	PGA	+/–	GP	G	A	Pts	PIM	PP	SH	GW
1987-88	Deerfield Spartans	Hi-School	22	19	32	51	....	....	....	....	....	....	....	....	....	....	....	....	....	....	....	....	....	....	....	....	....	....
	Chicago Young Americans	MNHL	STATISTICS NOT AVAILABLE																									
1988-89	Tabor Academy Seawolves	Hi-School	22	6	16	22	....	....	....	....	....	....	....	....	....	....	....	....	....	....	....	....	....	....	....	....	....	....
1989-90	Tabor Academy Seawolves	Hi-School	22	10	28	38	....	....	....	....	....	....	....	....	....	....	....	....	....	....	....	....	....	....	....	....	....	....
1990-91	Bowling Green University	CCHA	28	1	5	6	....	....	....	22	....	....	....	....	....	....	....	....	....	....	....	....	....	....	....	....	....	....
1991-92	Bowling Green University	CCHA	33	8	7	15	....	....	....	34	....	....	....	....	....	....	....	....	....	....	....	....	....	....	....	....	....	....
1992-93	Bowling Green University	CCHA	41	8	17	25	....	....	....	48	....	....	....	....	....	....	....	....	....	....	....	....	....	....	....	....	....	....
1993-94	Bowling Green University	CCHA	38	7	23	30	....	....	....	56	....	....	....	....	....	....	....	....	....	....	....	....	....	....	....	....	....	....
1994-95	Albany River Rats	AHL	2	0	1	1	....	....	....	2	....	....	....	....	....	....	....	....	....	....	....	....	....	....	....	....	....	....
	Raleigh Icecaps	ECHL	26	2	13	15	....	....	....	33	....	....	....	....	....	....	....	....	....	....	....	....	....	....	....	....	....	....
	Tallahassee Tiger Sharks	ECHL	43	5	25	30	....	....	....	61	....	....	....	....	....	....	....	....	....	....	13	2	5	7	40	....	....	....
1995-96	Tallahassee Tiger Sharks	ECHL	7	1	3	4	....	....	....	10	....	....	....	....	....	....	....	....	....	....	....	....	....	....	....	....	....	....
	Jacksonville Lizard Kings	ECHL	15	1	10	11	....	....	....	41	....	....	....	....	....	....	....	....	....	....	1	0	2	2	4	....	....	....
	Chicago Wolves	IHL	31	0	2	2	....	....	....	39	....	....	....	....	....	....	....	....	....	....	9	0	2	2	16	....	....	....
1996-97	Chicago Wolves	IHL	57	3	10	13	....	....	....	108	....	....	....	....	....	....	....	....	....	....	....	....	....	....	....	....	....	....
	San Antonio Dragons	IHL	23	2	5	7	....	....	....	51	....	....	....	....	....	....	....	....	....	....	9	0	1	1	17	....	....	....
1997-98	San Antonio Dragons	IHL	70	5	14	19	....	....	....	132	....	....	....	....	....	....	....	....	....	....	....	....	....	....	....	....	....	....
	Fort Wayne Komets	IHL	11	2	2	4	....	....	....	16	....	....	....	....	....	....	....	....	....	....	4	0	2	2	4	....	....	....

			REGULAR SEASON																		PLAYOFFS							
Season	**Club**	**League**	**GP**	**G**	**A**	**Pts**	**AG**	**AA**	**APts**	**PIM**	**PP**	**SH**	**GW**	**S**	**%**	**TGF**	**PGF**	**TGA**	**PGA**	**+/–**	**GP**	**G**	**A**	**Pts**	**PIM**	**PP**	**SH**	**GW**
1998-99	**Edmonton Oilers**	**NHL**	**17**	**2**	**3**	**5**	**2**	**3**	**5**	**20**	**0**	**0**	**0**	**26**	**7.7**	**13**	**5**	**11**	**2**	**–1**	....	....	....	....	....	....	....	....
	Hamilton Bulldogs	AHL	58	9	25	34	....	....	....	84	....	....	....	....	....	....	....	....	....	....	11	0	5	5	6	....	....	....
99-2000	**St. Louis Blues**	**NHL**	**56**	**4**	**21**	**25**	**4**	**19**	**23**	**32**	**0**	**0**	**1**	**77**	**5.2**	**62**	**11**	**34**	**1**	**18**	**4**	**0**	**1**	**1**	**0**	**0**	**0**	**0**
	NHL Totals		**73**	**6**	**24**	**30**	**6**	**22**	**28**	**52**	**0**	**0**	**1**	**103**	**5.8**	**75**	**16**	**45**	**3**		**4**	**0**	**1**	**1**	**0**	**0**	**0**	**0**

Signed as a free agent by **Edmonton**, September 17, 1998. Claimed on waivers by **St. Louis** from **Edmonton**, September 30, 1999.

• RENAUD, Mark

Mark Joseph D – L. 6', 185 lbs. b: Windsor, Ont., 2/21/1959. Hartford's 5th, 102nd overall, in 1979.

Season	Club	League	GP	G	A	Pts	AG	AA	APts	PIM	PP	SH	GW	S	%	TGF	PGF	TGA	PGA	+/–	GP	G	A	Pts	PIM	PP	SH	GW
1975-76	Windsor Spitfires	OMJHL	66	3	15	18	....	....	....	42	....	....	....	....	....	....	....	....	....	....	....	....	....	....	....	....	....	....
1976-77	Niagara Falls Flyers	OMJHL	66	7	25	32	....	....	....	30	....	....	....	....	....	....	....	....	....	....	....	....	....	....	....	....	....	....
1977-78	Niagara Falls Flyers	OMJHL	68	6	24	30	....	....	....	57	....	....	....	....	....	....	....	....	....	....	....	....	....	....	....	....	....	....
1978-79	Niagara Falls Flyers	OMJHL	68	10	56	66	....	....	....	89	....	....	....	....	....	....	....	....	....	....	20	4	17	21	30	....	....	....
1979-80	**Hartford Whalers**	**NHL**	**13**	**0**	**2**	**2**	**0**	**1**	**1**	**4**	**0**	**0**	**0**	**9**	**0.0**	**9**	**0**	**10**	**0**	**–1**	....	....	....	....	....	....	....	....
	Springfield Indians	AHL	61	3	16	19	....	....	....	39	....	....	....	....	....	....	....	....	....	....	....	....	....	....	....	....	....	....
1980-81	**Hartford Whalers**	**NHL**	**4**	**1**	**0**	**1**	**1**	**0**	**1**	**0**	**0**	**0**	**0**	**1**	**100.0**	**2**	**0**	**3**	**1**	**0**	....	....	....	....	....	....	....	....
	Binghamton Whalers	AHL	73	6	44	50	....	....	....	56	....	....	....	....	....	....	....	....	....	....	6	0	2	2	2	....	....	....
1981-82	**Hartford Whalers**	**NHL**	**48**	**1**	**17**	**18**	**1**	**11**	**12**	**39**	**0**	**0**	**0**	**72**	**1.4**	**54**	**9**	**77**	**15**	**–17**	....	....	....	....	....	....	....	....
	Binghamton Whalers	AHL	33	3	19	22	....	....	....	70	....	....	....	....	....	....	....	....	....	....	....	....	....	....	....	....	....	....
1982-83	**Hartford Whalers**	**NHL**	**77**	**3**	**28**	**31**	**2**	**19**	**21**	**37**	**1**	**0**	**0**	**87**	**3.4**	**77**	**14**	**128**	**23**	**–42**	....	....	....	....	....	....	....	....
1983-84	**Buffalo Sabres**	**NHL**	**10**	**1**	**3**	**4**	**1**	**2**	**3**	**6**	**0**	**0**	**0**	**11**	**9.1**	**6**	**0**	**5**	**0**	**1**	....	....	....	....	....	....	....	....
	Rochester Americans	AHL	64	9	33	42	....	....	....	52	....	....	....	....	....	....	....	....	....	....	15	2	8	10	39	....	....	....
1984-85	Rochester Americans	AHL	80	8	34	42	....	....	....	56	....	....	....	....	....	....	....	....	....	....	5	0	0	0	2	....	....	....
	NHL Totals		**152**	**6**	**50**	**56**	**5**	**33**	**38**	**86**	**1**	**0**	**0**	**180**	**3.3**	**148**	**23**	**223**	**39**		....	....	....	....	....	....	....	....

Claimed by **Buffalo** from **Hartford** in Waiver Draft, October 3, 1983.

• RENBERG, Mikael

Bo Mikael RW – L. 6'2", 218 lbs. b: Pitea, Sweden, 5/5/1972. Philadelphia's 3rd, 40th overall, in 1990.

Season	Club	League	GP	G	A	Pts	AG	AA	APts	PIM	PP	SH	GW	S	%	TGF	PGF	TGA	PGA	+/–	GP	G	A	Pts	PIM	PP	SH	GW
1988-89	Pitea HC	Sweden-2	12	6	3	9	....	....	....	....	....	....	....	....	....	....	....	....	....	....	....	....	....	....	....	....	....	....
1989-90	Pitea HC	Sweden-2	29	15	19	34	....	....	....	....	....	....	....	....	....	....	....	....	....	....	....	....	....	....	....	....	....	....
	Sweden	EJC-A	6	7	1	8	....	....	....	6	....	....	....	....	....	....	....	....	....	....	....	....	....	....	....	....	....	....
1990-91	Lulea HF	Sweden	29	11	6	17	....	....	....	12	....	....	....	....	....	....	....	....	....	....	5	1	1	2	4	....	....	....
1991-92	Lulea HF	Sweden	38	8	15	23	....	....	....	20	....	....	....	....	....	....	....	....	....	....	2	0	0	0	0	....	....	....
	Sweden	WJC-A	7	6	4	10	....	....	....	8	....	....	....	....	....	....	....	....	....	....	....	....	....	....	....	....	....	....
1992-93	Lulea HF	Sweden	39	19	13	32	....	....	....	61	....	....	....	....	....	....	....	....	....	....	11	4	4	8	4	....	....	....
	Sweden	WC-A	8	5	3	8	....	....	....	6	....	....	....	....	....	....	....	....	....	....	....	....	....	....	....	....	....	....
1993-94	**Philadelphia Flyers**	**NHL**	**83**	**38**	**44**	**82**	**35**	**34**	**69**	**36**	**9**	**0**	**1**	**195**	**19.5**	**119**	**42**	**69**	**0**	**8**	....	....	....	....	....	....	....	....
1994-95	Lulea HF	Sweden	10	9	4	13	....	....	....	16	....	....	....	....	....	....	....	....	....	....	....	....	....	....	....	....	....	....
	Philadelphia Flyers	**NHL**	**47**	**26**	**31**	**57**	**46**	**46**	**92**	**20**	**8**	**0**	**4**	**143**	**18.2**	**75**	**21**	**35**	**1**	**20**	**15**	**6**	**7**	**13**	**6**	**2**	**0**	**0**
1995-96	**Philadelphia Flyers**	**NHL**	**51**	**23**	**20**	**43**	**23**	**16**	**39**	**45**	**9**	**0**	**4**	**198**	**11.6**	**68**	**28**	**33**	**1**	**8**	**11**	**3**	**6**	**9**	**14**	**1**	**0**	**0**
1996-97	**Philadelphia Flyers**	**NHL**	**77**	**22**	**37**	**59**	**23**	**33**	**56**	**65**	**1**	**0**	**4**	**249**	**8.8**	**99**	**13**	**50**	**0**	**36**	**18**	**5**	**6**	**11**	**4**	**2**	**0**	**0**
1997-98	**Tampa Bay Lightning**	**NHL**	**68**	**16**	**22**	**38**	**19**	**22**	**41**	**34**	**6**	**3**	**0**	**175**	**9.1**	**51**	**21**	**72**	**5**	**–37**	....	....	....	....	....	....	....	....
	Sweden	Olympics	4	1	2	3	....	....	....	4	....	....	....	....	....	....	....	....	....	....	....	....	....	....	....	....	....	....
	Sweden	WC-A	10	5	3	8	....	....	....	5	....	....	....	....	....	....	....	....	....	....	....	....	....	....	....	....	....	....
1998-99	**Tampa Bay Lightning**	**NHL**	**20**	**4**	**8**	**12**	**5**	**8**	**13**	**4**	**2**	**0**	**0**	**42**	**9.5**	**21**	**7**	**18**	**2**	**–2**	....	....	....	....	....	....	....	....
	Philadelphia Flyers	**NHL**	**46**	**11**	**15**	**26**	**13**	**14**	**27**	**14**	**4**	**0**	**2**	**112**	**9.8**	**38**	**10**	**21**	**0**	**7**	**6**	**0**	**1**	**1**	**0**	**0**	**0**	**0**
99-2000	**Philadelphia Flyers**	**NHL**	**62**	**8**	**21**	**29**	**9**	**19**	**28**	**30**	**3**	**0**	**1**	**106**	**7.5**	**48**	**17**	**32**	**0**	**–1**	....	....	....	....	....	....	....	....
	Phoenix Coyotes	**NHL**	**10**	**2**	**4**	**6**	**2**	**4**	**6**	**2**	**0**	**0**	**0**	**16**	**12.5**	**6**	**1**	**5**	**0**	**0**	**5**	**1**	**2**	**3**	**4**	**0**	**0**	**1**
	NHL Totals		**464**	**150**	**202**	**352**	**175**	**196**	**371**	**250**	**42**	**3**	**16**	**1236**	**12.1**	**525**	**160**	**335**	**9**		**55**	**15**	**22**	**37**	**28**	**5**	**0**	**1**

WC-A All-Star Team (1993) • NHL All-Rookie Team (1994)

Traded to **Tampa Bay** by **Philadelphia** with Karl Dykhuis for Philadelphia's 1st round choices (previously acquired by Tampa Bay) in 1998 (Simon Gagne), 1999 (Maxime Ouellet), 2000 and 2001 Entry Drafts, August 20, 1997. Traded to **Philadelphia** by **Tampa Bay** with Daymond Langkow for Chris Gratton and Mike Sillinger, December 12, 1998. Traded to **Phoenix** by **Philadelphia** for Rick Tocchet, March 8, 2000.

• REYNOLDS, Bobby

Robert Dehart LW – L. 5'11", 175 lbs. b: Flint, MI, 7/14/1967. Toronto's 10th, 190th overall, in 1985.

Season	Club	League	GP	G	A	Pts	AG	AA	APts	PIM	PP	SH	GW	S	%	TGF	PGF	TGA	PGA	+/–	GP	G	A	Pts	PIM	PP	SH	GW
1983-84	St. Clair Shores Falcons	NAJHL	60	25	34	59	....	....	....	....	....	....	....	....	....	....	....	....	....	....	....	....	....	....	....	....	....	....
1984-85	St. Clair Shores Falcons	NAJHL	43	20	30	50	....	....	....	....	....	....	....	....	....	....	....	....	....	....	....	....	....	....	....	....	....	....
1985-86	Michigan State Spartans	CCHA	45	9	10	19	....	....	....	26	....	....	....	....	....	....	....	....	....	....	....	....	....	....	....	....	....	....
1986-87	Michigan State Spartans	CCHA	40	20	13	33	....	....	....	40	....	....	....	....	....	....	....	....	....	....	....	....	....	....	....	....	....	....
	United States	WJC-A	7	3	3	6	....	....	....	8	....	....	....	....	....	....	....	....	....	....	....	....	....	....	....	....	....	....
1987-88	Michigan State Spartans	CCHA	46	42	25	67	....	....	....	52	....	....	....	....	....	....	....	....	....	....	....	....	....	....	....	....	....	....
1988-89	Michigan State Spartans	CCHA	47	36	41	77	....	....	....	78	....	....	....	....	....	....	....	....	....	....	....	....	....	....	....	....	....	....
1989-90	**Toronto Maple Leafs**	**NHL**	**7**	**1**	**1**	**2**	**1**	**1**	**2**	**0**	**0**	**0**	**0**	**13**	**7.7**	**2**	**0**	**5**	**0**	**–3**	....	....	....	....	....	....	....	....
	Newmarket Saints	AHL	66	22	28	50	....	....	....	55	....	....	....	....	....	....	....	....	....	....	....	....	....	....	....	....	....	....
1990-91	Newmarket Saints	AHL	65	24	22	46	....	....	....	59	....	....	....	....	....	....	....	....	....	....	....	....	....	....	....	....	....	....
	Baltimore Skipjacks	AHL	14	4	9	13	....	....	....	8	....	....	....	....	....	....	....	....	....	....	6	2	2	4	10	....	....	....
1991-92	Baltimore Skipjacks	AHL	53	12	18	30	....	....	....	39	....	....	....	....	....	....	....	....	....	....	....	....	....	....	....	....	....	....
	Kalamazoo Wings	IHL	13	8	10	18	....	....	....	19	....	....	....	....	....	....	....	....	....	....	12	5	4	9	4	....	....	....
1992-93	ECD Sauerland	Germany-2	45	54	69	123	....	....	....	97	....	....	....	....	....	....	....	....	....	....	....	....	....	....	....	....	....	....
1993-94	ECD Sauerland	Germany-2	52	45	47	92	....	....	....	84	....	....	....	....	....	....	....	....	....	....	....	....	....	....	....	....	....	....
1994-95	HC Courmaosta	EuroHL	16	15	24	39	....	....	....	4	....	....	....	....	....	....	....	....	....	....	....	....	....	....	....	....	....	....
	HC Courmaosta	Italy	16	9	14	23	....	....	....	6	....	....	....	....	....	....	....	....	....	....	....	....	....	....	....	....	....	....
	KAC Klagenfurt	Germany	7	2	5	7	....	....	....	6	....	....	....	....	....	....	....	....	....	....	7	4	5	9	29	....	....	....
1995-96	Ratinger Lowen	Germany	46	41	32	73	....	....	....	36	....	....	....	....	....	....	....	....	....	....	3	1	1	2	0	....	....	....
1996-97	Ratinger Lowen	Germany	48	21	16	37	....	....	....	28	....	....	....	....	....	....	....	....	....	....	6	1	1	2	52	....	....	....
1997-98	Ratinger Lowen	Germany	27	9	13	22	....	....	....	12	....	....	....	....	....	....	....	....	....	....	....	....	....	....	....	....	....	....
	ZSC Lions Zurich	Switz.	11	4	5	9	....	....	....	2	....	....	....	....	....	....	....	....	....	....	....	....	....	....	....	....	....	....
1998-99	Flint Generals	UHL	4	4	2	6	....	....	....	0	....	....	....	....	....	....	....	....	....	....	....	....	....	....	....	....	....	....
	Detroit Vipers	IHL	67	21	20	41	....	....	....	60	....	....	....	....	....	....	....	....	....	....	10	2	4	6	6	....	....	....
99-2000	Flint Generals	UHL	32	22	37	59	....	....	....	18	....	....	....	....	....	....	....	....	....	....	....	....	....	....	....	....	....	....
	Houston Aeros	IHL	51	13	21	34	....	....	....	21	....	....	....	....	....	....	....	....	....	....	11	3	0	3	10	....	....	....
	NHL Totals		**7**	**1**	**1**	**2**	**1**	**1**	**2**	**0**	**0**	**0**	**0**	**13**	**7.7**	**2**	**0**	**5**	**0**		....	....	....	....	....	....	....	....

CCHA Second All-Star Team (1988, 1989) • NCAA West First All-American Team (1989)

Traded to **Washington** by **Toronto** for Rob Mendel, March 5, 1991. Signed as a free agent by **Houston** (IHL), December 29, 1999. • Played w/ RHI's Detroit Mustangs in 1995 (24-27-35-62-15).

• RHEAUME, Pascal

LW – L. 6'1", 209 lbs. b: Quebec, Que., 6/21/1973.

Season	Club	League	GP	G	A	Pts	AG	AA	APts	PIM	PP	SH	GW	S	%	TGF	PGF	TGA	PGA	+/–	GP	G	A	Pts	PIM	PP	SH	GW
1990-91	Ste-Foy Gouverneurs	QAAA	37	20	38	58	....	....	....	25	....	....	....	....	....	....	....	....	....	....	....	....	....	....	....	....	....	....
1991-92	Trois-Rivieres Draveurs	QMJHL	65	17	20	37	....	....	....	84	....	....	....	....	....	....	....	....	....	....	14	5	4	9	23	....	....	....
1992-93	Sherbrooke Faucons	QMJHL	65	28	34	62	....	....	....	88	....	....	....	....	....	....	....	....	....	....	14	6	5	11	31	....	....	....
1993-94	Albany River Rats	AHL	55	17	18	35	....	....	....	43	....	....	....	....	....	....	....	....	....	....	5	0	1	1	0	....	....	....
1994-95	Albany River Rats	AHL	78	19	25	44	....	....	....	46	....	....	....	....	....	....	....	....	....	....	14	3	6	9	19	....	....	....
1995-96	Albany River Rats	AHL	68	26	42	68	....	....	....	50	....	....	....	....	....	....	....	....	....	....	4	1	2	3	2	....	....	....
1996-97	**New Jersey Devils**	**NHL**	**2**	**1**	**0**	**1**	**1**	**0**	**1**	**0**	**0**	**0**	**0**	**5**	**20.0**	**1**	**0**	**0**	**0**	**1**	....	....	....	....	....	....	....	....
	Albany River Rats	AHL	51	22	23	45	....	....	....	40	....	....	....	....	....	....	....	....	....	....	16	2	8	10	16	....	....	....
1997-98	**St. Louis Blues**	**NHL**	**48**	**6**	**9**	**15**	**7**	**9**	**16**	**35**	**1**	**0**	**0**	**45**	**13.3**	**33**	**8**	**21**	**0**	**4**	**10**	**1**	**3**	**4**	**8**	**1**	**0**	**0**

Season	Club	League	REGULAR SEASON																		PLAYOFFS							
			GP	G	A	Pts	AG	AA	APts	PIM	PP	SH	GW	S	%	TGF	PGF	TGA	PGA	+/-	GP	G	A	Pts	PIM	PP	SH	GW
1998-99	St. Louis Blues	NHL	60	9	18	27	11	17	28	24	2	0	0	85	10.6	41	5	26	0	10	5	1	0	1	4	0	0	0
99-2000	St. Louis Blues	NHL	7	1	1	2	1	1	2	6	0	0	0	5	20.0	2	0	4	0	−2								
	Worcester IceCats	AHL	7	1	1	2				4																		
	NHL Totals		117	17	28	45	20	27	47	65	3	0	0	140	12.1	77	13	51	0		15	2	3	5	12	1	0	0

Brother of Manon

Signed as a free agent by **New Jersey**, October 1, 1993. Claimed by **St. Louis** from **New Jersey** in NHL Waiver Draft, September 28, 1997. • Missed majority of 1999-2000 season recovering from shoulder surgery, August, 1999.

• RIBBLE, Pat

Patrick Wayne D – L. 6'4", 210 lbs. b: Leamington, Ont., 4/26/1954. Atlanta's 3rd, 58th overall, in 1974.

Season	Club	League	GP	G	A	Pts	AG	AA	APts	PIM	PP	SH	GW	S	%	TGF	PGF	TGA	PGA	+/-	GP	G	A	Pts	PIM	PP	SH	GW
1972-73	Oshawa Generals	OMJHL	61	11	27	38				110																		
1973-74	Oshawa Generals	OMJHL	70	8	16	24				134																		
1974-75	Oshawa Generals	OMJHL	77	5	17	22				164											6	0	1	1	23			
1975-76	**Atlanta Flames**	**NHL**	3	0	0	0	0	0	0	0	0	0	0	0	0.0	2	0	2	0	0								
	Tulsa Oilers	CHL	73	3	22	25				98											9	0	3	3	10			
1976-77	**Atlanta Flames**	**NHL**	23	2	2	4	2	2	4	31	0	0	0	31	6.5	19	0	23	3	−1	2	0	0	0	6	0	0	0
	Tulsa Oilers	CHL	51	9	20	29				140																		
1977-78	**Atlanta Flames**	**NHL**	80	5	12	17	5	9	14	68	1	0	0	106	4.7	83	2	105	28	4	2	0	1	1	2	0	0	0
	Canada	WEC-A	10	0	0	0				15																		
1978-79	**Atlanta Flames**	**NHL**	66	5	16	21	4	12	16	69	0	0	0	70	7.1	77	0	78	19	18								
	Chicago Black Hawks	**NHL**	12	1	3	4	1	2	3	8	0	0	1	12	8.3	11	0	4	0	7	4	0	0	0	4	0	0	0
1979-80	**Chicago Black Hawks**	**NHL**	23	1	2	3	1	1	2	14	0	0	0	15	6.7	11	1	19	1	−8								
	Toronto Maple Leafs	**NHL**	13	0	2	2	0	1	1	8	0	0	0	11	0.0	10	0	22	3	−9								
	Washington Capitals	**NHL**	19	1	5	6	1	4	5	30	0	0	0	15	6.7	17	0	20	5	2								
1980-81	Washington Capitals	DN-Cup	3	1	1	2				6																		
	Washington Capitals	**NHL**	67	3	15	18	2	10	12	103	3	0	1	115	2.6	98	32	121	42	−13								
1981-82	**Washington Capitals**	**NHL**	12	1	2	3	1	1	2	14	0	0	0	15	6.7	11	0	17	2	−4								
	Calgary Flames	**NHL**	3	0	0	0	0	0	0	2	0	0	0	6	0.0	3	0	1	0	2								
	Oklahoma City Stars	CHL	43	1	9	10				44											2	0	0	0	6			
1982-83	**Calgary Flames**	**NHL**	28	0	1	1	0	1	1	18	0	0	0	14	0.0	18	0	39	9	−12								
	Colorado Flames	CHL	10	1	4	5				8																		
1983-84	Colorado Flames	CHL	53	4	27	31				60											6	0	2	2	4			
1984-85	Indianapolis Checkers	IHL	24	10	14	24				18											7	0	2	2	4			
	Salt Lake Golden Eagles	IHL	54	4	23	27				50																		
1985-86	Indianapolis Checkers	IHL	52	6	21	27				45											2	0	1	1	2			
1986-87	Salt Lake Golden Eagles	IHL	80	9	19	28				55											17	1	5	6	2			
	NHL Totals		349	19	60	79	17	43	60	365	4	0	2	410	4.6	360	35	451	112		8	0	1	1	12	0	0	0

CHL Second All-Star Team (1977, 1984)

Traded to **Chicago** by **Atlanta** with Tom Lysiak, Harold Phillipoff, Greg Fox and Miles Zaharko for Ivan Boldirev, Phil Russell and Darcy Rota, March 13, 1979. Traded to **Toronto** by **Chicago** for Dave Hutchison, January 10, 1980. Traded to **Washington** by **Toronto** for Mike Kaszycki, February 16, 1980. Traded to **Calgary** by **Washington** with Washington's 2nd round choice (later traded to Montreal — Montreal selected Todd Francis) in 1983 Entry Draft for Randy Holt and Bobby Gould, November 25, 1981.

• RIBEIRO, Mike

C – L. 5'11", 165 lbs. b: Montreal, Que., 2/10/1980. Montreal's 2nd, 45th overall, in 1998.

Season	Club	League	GP	G	A	Pts	AG	AA	APts	PIM	PP	SH	GW	S	%	TGF	PGF	TGA	PGA	+/-	GP	G	A	Pts	PIM	PP	SH	GW
1996-97	Montreal L'est Cantonniers	QAAA	43	32	57	89				48																		
1997-98	Rouyn-Noranda Huskies	QMJHL	67	40	*85	125				55											6	3	1	4	0			
1998-99	Rouyn-Noranda Huskies	QMJHL	69	*67	*100	*167				137											11	5	11	16	12			
	Fredericton Canadiens	AHL																			5	0	1	1	2			
99-2000	**Montreal Canadiens**	**NHL**	19	1	1	2	1	1	2	2	1	0	0	18	5.6	4	4	6	0	−6								
	Quebec Citadelles	AHL	3	0	0	0				2																		
	Canada	WJC-A	7	0	2	2				0																		
	Rouyn-Noranda Huskies	QMJHL	2	1	3	4				0																		
	Quebec Remparts	QMJHL	21	17	28	45				30											11	3	20	23	38			
	NHL Totals		19	1	1	2	1	1	2	2	1	0	0	18	5.6	4	4	6	0									

QMJHL Second All-Star Team (1998) • QMJHL First All-Star Team (1999) • Canadian Major Junior First All-Star Team (1999)

• RICCI, Mike

C – L. 6', 190 lbs. b: Scarborough, Ont., 10/27/1971. Philadelphia's 1st, 4th overall, in 1990.

Season	Club	League	GP	G	A	Pts	AG	AA	APts	PIM	PP	SH	GW	S	%	TGF	PGF	TGA	PGA	+/-	GP	G	A	Pts	PIM	PP	SH	GW
1986-87	Toronto Midget Marlboros	MTHL	38	39	42	81				27																		
1987-88	Mississauga Reps	MTHL	STATISTICS NOT AVAILABLE																									
	Peterborough Petes	OHL	41	24	37	61				20											8	5	5	10	4			
1988-89	Peterborough Petes	OHL	60	54	52	106				43											17	19	16	35	18			
	Canada	WJC-A	7	5	2	7				6																		
	Peterborough Petes	Mem-Cup	5	3	1	4				8																		
1989-90	Peterborough Petes	OHL	60	52	64	116				39											12	5	7	12	26			
	Canada	WJC-A	5	0	4	4				0																		
1990-91	**Philadelphia Flyers**	**NHL**	68	21	20	41	19	15	34	64	9	0	4	121	17.4	69	28	58	9	−8								
1991-92	**Philadelphia Flyers**	**NHL**	78	20	36	56	18	27	45	93	11	2	0	149	13.4	83	29	90	26	−10								
1992-93	**Quebec Nordiques**	**NHL**	77	27	51	78	22	35	57	123	12	1	10	142	19.0	123	58	75	18	8	6	0	6	6	8	0	0	0
1993-94	**Quebec Nordiques**	**NHL**	83	30	21	51	28	16	44	113	13	3	6	138	21.7	82	32	80	21	−9								
	Canada	WC-A	8	2	1	3				8																		
1994-95	**Quebec Nordiques**	**NHL**	48	15	21	36	27	31	58	40	9	0	1	73	20.5	56	25	35	9	5	6	1	3	4	8	0	0	0
1995-96♦	**Colorado Avalanche**	**NHL**	62	6	21	27	6	17	23	52	3	0	1	73	8.2	60	29	41	11	1	22	6	11	17	18	3	0	1
1996-97	**Colorado Avalanche**	**NHL**	63	13	19	32	14	17	31	59	5	0	3	74	17.6	55	22	36	0	−3	17	2	4	6	17	0	0	1
1997-98	**Colorado Avalanche**	**NHL**	6	0	4	4	0	4	4	2	0	0	0	5	0.0	4	0	4	0	0								
	San Jose Sharks	**NHL**	59	9	14	23	11	14	25	30	5	0	2	86	10.5	40	16	41	13	−4	6	1	3	4	6	0	0	0
1998-99	**San Jose Sharks**	**NHL**	82	13	26	39	15	25	40	68	2	1	2	98	13.3	48	10	52	15	1	6	2	3	5	10	1	0	0
99-2000	**San Jose Sharks**	**NHL**	82	20	24	44	22	22	44	60	10	0	5	134	14.9	62	20	39	11	14	12	5	1	6	2	3	0	1
	NHL Totals		708	174	257	431	182	223	405	704	79	7	34	1093	15.9	682	269	551	133		75	17	31	48	69	7	0	3

OHL Second All-Star Team (1989) • Canadian Major Junior Player of the Year (1990) • OHL First All-Star Team (1990)

Traded to **Quebec** by **Philadelphia** with Steve Duchesne, Peter Forsberg, Kerry Huffman, Ron Hextall, Philadelphia's 1st round choice (Jocelyn Thibault) in 1993 Entry Draft, $15,000,000 and future considerations (Chris Simon and Philadelphia's 1st round choice (later traded to Toronto - later traded to Washington - Washington selected Nolan Baumgartner) in 1994 Entry Draft, July 21, 1992) for Eric Lindros, June 30, 1992. Transferred to **Colorado** after **Quebec** franchise relocated, June 21, 1995. Traded to **San Jose** by **Colorado** with Colorado's 2nd round choice (later traded to Buffalo - Buffalo selected Jaroslav Kristek) in 1998 Entry Draft for Shean Donovan and San Jose's 1st round choice (Alex Tanguay) in 1998 Entry Draft, November 21, 1997.

• RICE, Steven

RW – R. 6', 217 lbs. b: Kitchener, Ont., 5/26/1971. NY Rangers' 1st, 20th overall, in 1989.

Season	Club	League	GP	G	A	Pts	AG	AA	APts	PIM	PP	SH	GW	S	%	TGF	PGF	TGA	PGA	+/-	GP	G	A	Pts	PIM	PP	SH	GW
1986-87	Waterloo Majors	OMHA	32	17	16	33				87																		
	Waterloo Siskins	OJHL	7	4	1	5				10																		
1987-88	Kitchener Rangers	OHL	59	11	14	25				43											4	0	1	1	0			
1988-89	Kitchener Rangers	OHL	64	36	30	66				42											5	2	1	3	8			
1989-90	Kitchener Rangers	OHL	58	39	37	76				102											16	4	8	12	24			
	Canada	WJC-A	7	2	0	2				16																		
	Kitchener Rangers	Mem-Cup	5	4	4	8				10																		
1990-91	Kitchener Rangers	OHL	29	30	30	60				43											6	5	6	11	2			
	Canada	WJC-A	7	4	1	5				8																		
	New York Rangers	**NHL**	11	1	1	2	1	1	2	4	0	0	0	12	8.3	4	0	2	0	2	2	2	1	3	6	1	0	0
	Binghamton Rangers	AHL	8	4	1	5				12											5	2	0	2	2			
1991-92	**Edmonton Oilers**	**NHL**	3	0	0	0	0	0	0	2	0	0	0	2	0.0	0	0	2	0	−2								
	Cape Breton Oilers	AHL	45	32	20	52				38											5	4	4	8	10			
1992-93	**Edmonton Oilers**	**NHL**	28	2	5	7	2	3	5	28	0	0	0	29	6.9	11	0	16	1	−4								
	Cape Breton Oilers	AHL	51	34	28	62				63											14	4	6	10	22			

			REGULAR SEASON																		PLAYOFFS							
Season	**Club**	**League**	**GP**	**G**	**A**	**Pts**	**AG**	**AA**	**APts**	**PIM**	**PP**	**SH**	**GW**	**S**	**%**	**TGF**	**PGF**	**TGA**	**PGA**	**+/–**	**GP**	**G**	**A**	**Pts**	**PIM**	**PP**	**SH**	**GW**
1993-94	**Edmonton Oilers**	**NHL**	**63**	**17**	**15**	**32**	**16**	**12**	**28**	**36**	**6**	**0**	**1**	**129**	**13.2**	**58**	**20**	**48**	**0**	**–10**	....	....	....	....	....	....	....	....
1994-95	**Hartford Whalers**	**NHL**	**40**	**11**	**10**	**21**	**19**	**15**	**34**	**61**	**4**	**0**	**1**	**57**	**19.3**	**30**	**9**	**19**	**0**	**2**	....	....	....	....	....	....	....	....
1995-96	**Hartford Whalers**	**NHL**	**59**	**10**	**12**	**22**	**10**	**10**	**20**	**47**	**1**	**0**	**2**	**108**	**9.3**	**39**	**10**	**33**	**0**	**–4**	....	....	....	....	....	....	....	....
1996-97	**Hartford Whalers**	**NHL**	**78**	**21**	**14**	**35**	**22**	**12**	**34**	**59**	**5**	**0**	**2**	**159**	**13.2**	**60**	**17**	**54**	**0**	**–11**	....	....	....	....	....	....	....	....
1997-98	**Carolina Hurricanes**	**NHL**	**47**	**2**	**4**	**6**	**2**	**4**	**6**	**38**	**0**	**0**	**0**	**39**	**5.1**	**8**	**1**	**23**	**0**	**–16**	....	....	....	....	....	....	....	....
	NHL Totals		**329**	**64**	**61**	**125**	**72**	**57**	**129**	**275**	**16**	**0**	**6**	**535**	**12.0**	**210**	**57**	**197**	**1**		**2**	**2**	**1**	**3**	**6**	**1**	**0**	**0**

Memorial Cup All-Star Team (1990) • OHL Second All-Star Team (1991) • AHL Second All-Star Team (1993)

Traded to **Edmonton** by **NY Rangers** with Bernie Nicholls and Louie DeBrusk for Mark Messier and future considerations (Jeff Beukeboom for David Shaw, November 12, 1991), October 4, 1991. Signed as a free agent by **Hartford**, August 18, 1994. Transferred to **Carolina** after **Hartford** franchise relocated, June 25, 1997.

• RICHARD, Henri

Joseph Henri "The Pocket Rocket" C – R. 5'7", 160 lbs. b: Montreal, Que., 2/29/1936. **HHOF**

Season	Club	League	GP	G	A	Pts	AG	AA	APts	PIM	PP	SH	GW	S	%	TGF	PGF	TGA	PGA	+/–	GP	G	A	Pts	PIM	PP	SH	GW
1951-52	Montreal Nationale	QJHL	49	23	32	55	....	....	....	35	....	....	....	....	....	....	....	....	....	....	4	1	0	1	0	....	....	....
1952-53	Montreal Nationale	QJHL	46	27	36	63	....	....	....	55	....	....	....	....	....	....	....	....	....	....	7	4	5	9	4	....	....	....
	Montreal Royals	QMHL	1	0	0	0	....	....	....	0	....	....	....	....	....	....	....	....	....	....	....	....	....	....	....	....	....	....
1953-54	Montreal Jr. Canadiens	QJHL	54	*56	*53	*109	....	....	....	85	....	....	....	....	....	....	....	....	....	....	7	6	7	13	6	....	....	....
1954-55	Montreal Jr. Canadiens	QJHL	44	*33	33	*66	....	....	....	65	....	....	....	....	....	....	....	....	....	....	4	3	1	4	2	....	....	....
1955-56♦	**Montreal Canadiens**	**NHL**	**64**	**19**	**21**	**40**	**26**	**25**	**51**	**46**	....	....	....	....	....	....	....	....	....	....	**10**	**4**	**4**	**8**	**21**	....	....	....
1956-57♦	**Montreal Canadiens**	**NHL**	**63**	**18**	**36**	**54**	**23**	**40**	**63**	**71**	....	....	....	....	....	....	....	....	....	....	**10**	**2**	**6**	**8**	**10**	....	....	....
1957-58♦	**Montreal Canadiens**	**NHL**	**67**	**28**	***52**	**80**	**35**	**54**	**89**	**56**	....	....	....	....	....	....	....	....	....	....	**10**	**1**	**7**	**8**	**11**	....	....	....
1958-59♦	**Montreal Canadiens**	**NHL**	**63**	**21**	**30**	**51**	**25**	**30**	**55**	**33**	....	....	....	....	....	....	....	....	....	....	**11**	**3**	**8**	**11**	**13**	....	....	....
1959-60♦	**Montreal Canadiens**	**NHL**	**70**	**30**	**43**	**73**	**36**	**42**	**78**	**66**	....	....	....	....	....	....	....	....	....	....	**8**	**3**	**9**	***12**	**9**	....	....	....
1960-61	**Montreal Canadiens**	**NHL**	**70**	**24**	**44**	**68**	**28**	**43**	**71**	**91**	....	....	....	....	....	....	....	....	....	....	**6**	**2**	**4**	**6**	**22**	....	....	....
1961-62	**Montreal Canadiens**	**NHL**	**54**	**21**	**29**	**50**	**24**	**28**	**52**	**48**	....	....	....	....	....	....	....	....	....	....	....	....	....	....	....	....	....	....
1962-63	**Montreal Canadiens**	**NHL**	**67**	**23**	***50**	**73**	**27**	**50**	**77**	**57**	....	....	....	....	....	....	....	....	....	....	**5**	**1**	**1**	**2**	**2**	....	....	....
1963-64	**Montreal Canadiens**	**NHL**	**66**	**14**	**39**	**53**	**17**	**41**	**58**	**73**	....	....	....	....	....	....	....	....	....	....	**7**	**1**	**1**	**2**	**9**	....	....	....
1964-65♦	**Montreal Canadiens**	**NHL**	**53**	**23**	**29**	**52**	**28**	**30**	**58**	**43**	....	....	....	....	....	....	....	....	....	....	**13**	**7**	**4**	**11**	**24**	....	....	....
1965-66♦	**Montreal Canadiens**	**NHL**	**62**	**22**	**39**	**61**	**25**	**37**	**62**	**47**	....	....	....	....	....	....	....	....	....	....	**8**	**1**	**4**	**5**	**2**	....	....	....
1966-67	**Montreal Canadiens**	**NHL**	**65**	**21**	**34**	**55**	**24**	**33**	**57**	**28**	....	....	....	....	....	....	....	....	....	....	**10**	**4**	**6**	**10**	**2**	....	....	....
1967-68♦	**Montreal Canadiens**	**NHL**	**54**	**9**	**19**	**28**	**10**	**19**	**29**	**16**	**2**	**0**	**3**	**123**	**7.3**	**36**	**9**	**23**	**0**	**4**	**13**	**4**	**4**	**8**	**4**	**1**	**0**	**0**
1968-69♦	**Montreal Canadiens**	**NHL**	**64**	**15**	**37**	**52**	**16**	**33**	**49**	**45**	**2**	**0**	**0**	**210**	**7.1**	**78**	**7**	**48**	**2**	**25**	**14**	**2**	**4**	**6**	**8**	**0**	**0**	**0**
1969-70	**Montreal Canadiens**	**NHL**	**62**	**16**	**36**	**52**	**17**	**34**	**51**	**61**	**2**	**0**	**4**	**204**	**7.8**	**72**	**8**	**40**	**0**	**24**	....	....	....	....	....	....	....	....
1970-71♦	**Montreal Canadiens**	**NHL**	**75**	**12**	**37**	**49**	**12**	**31**	**43**	**46**	**1**	**0**	**1**	**226**	**5.3**	**59**	**5**	**43**	**2**	**13**	**20**	**5**	**7**	**12**	**20**	**0**	**0**	**1**
1971-72	**Montreal Canadiens**	**NHL**	**75**	**12**	**32**	**44**	**12**	**28**	**40**	**48**	**0**	**0**	**1**	**175**	**6.9**	**66**	**6**	**51**	**1**	**10**	**6**	**0**	**3**	**3**	**4**	**0**	**0**	**0**
1972-73♦	**Montreal Canadiens**	**NHL**	**71**	**8**	**35**	**43**	**7**	**28**	**35**	**21**	**0**	**0**	**2**	**133**	**6.0**	**58**	**1**	**24**	**1**	**34**	**17**	**6**	**4**	**10**	**14**	**0**	**0**	**2**
1973-74	**Montreal Canadiens**	**NHL**	**75**	**19**	**36**	**55**	**18**	**30**	**48**	**28**	**1**	**0**	**3**	**175**	**10.9**	**73**	**4**	**63**	**1**	**7**	**6**	**2**	**2**	**4**	**2**	**0**	**0**	**0**
1974-75	**Montreal Canadiens**	**NHL**	**16**	**3**	**10**	**13**	**3**	**7**	**10**	**4**	**0**	**0**	**0**	**33**	**9.1**	**20**	**1**	**10**	**0**	**9**	**6**	**1**	**2**	**3**	**4**	**0**	**0**	**0**
	NHL Totals		**1256**	**358**	**688**	**1046**	**413**	**663**	**1076**	**928**	....	....	....	....	....	....	....	....	....	....	**180**	**49**	**80**	**129**	**181**	....	....	....

• Brother of Maurice • NHL First All-Star Team (1958) • NHL Second All-Star Team (1959, 1961, 1963) • Won Bill Masterton Trophy (1974)

Played in NHL All-Star Game (1956, 1957, 1958, 1959, 1960, 1961, 1963, 1965, 1967, 1974)

Signed as a free agent by **Montreal**, October 13, 1955.

• RICHARD, Jacques

Jacques A.G. LW – L. 5'11", 180 lbs. b: Quebec City, Que., 10/7/1952. Atlanta's 1st, 2nd overall, in 1972.

Season	Club	League	GP	G	A	Pts	AG	AA	APts	PIM	PP	SH	GW	S	%	TGF	PGF	TGA	PGA	+/–	GP	G	A	Pts	PIM	PP	SH	GW
1967-68	Quebec Remparts	QJHL	50	18	18	36	....	....	....	....	....	....	....	....	....	....	....	....	....	....	....	....	....	....	....	....	....	....
1968-69	Quebec Remparts	QJHL	50	23	40	63	....	....	....	78	....	....	....	....	....	....	....	....	....	....	....	....	....	....	....	....	....	....
1969-70	Quebec Remparts	QJHL	53	62	64	126	....	....	....	170	....	....	....	....	....	....	....	....	....	....	27	28	25	53	86	....	....	....
	Quebec Remparts	Mem-Cup	12	17	10	27	....	....	....	*48	....	....	....	....	....	....	....	....	....	....	....	....	....	....	....	....	....	....
1970-71	Quebec Remparts	QJHL	55	53	60	113	....	....	....	125	....	....	....	....	....	....	....	....	....	....	14	18	17	35	42	....	....	....
	Quebec Remparts	Mem-Cup	7	6	7	13	....	....	....	8	....	....	....	....	....	....	....	....	....	....	....	....	....	....	....	....	....	....
1971-72	Quebec Remparts	QMJHL	61	*71	89	*160	....	....	....	100	....	....	....	....	....	....	....	....	....	....	15	11	*26	*37	23	....	....	....
1972-73	**Atlanta Flames**	**NHL**	**74**	**13**	**18**	**31**	**12**	**14**	**26**	**32**	**4**	**0**	**2**	**165**	**7.9**	**48**	**15**	**57**	**0**	**–24**	....	....	....	....	....	....	....	....
1973-74	**Atlanta Flames**	**NHL**	**78**	**27**	**16**	**43**	**26**	**13**	**39**	**45**	**7**	**0**	**1**	**270**	**10.0**	**79**	**31**	**66**	**0**	**–18**	**4**	**0**	**0**	**0**	**2**	**0**	**0**	**0**
1974-75	**Atlanta Flames**	**NHL**	**63**	**17**	**12**	**29**	**15**	**9**	**24**	**31**	**3**	**0**	**1**	**172**	**9.9**	**44**	**12**	**49**	**1**	**–16**	....	....	....	....	....	....	....	....
1975-76	**Buffalo Sabres**	**NHL**	**73**	**12**	**23**	**35**	**11**	**17**	**28**	**31**	**3**	**0**	**5**	**104**	**11.5**	**62**	**11**	**47**	**0**	**4**	**9**	**1**	**1**	**2**	**7**	**0**	**0**	**0**
1976-77	**Buffalo Sabres**	**NHL**	**21**	**2**	**0**	**2**	**2**	**0**	**2**	**16**	**0**	**0**	**0**	**20**	**10.0**	**6**	**0**	**9**	**0**	**–3**	....	....	....	....	....	....	....	....
	Hershey Bears	AHL	44	20	25	45	....	....	....	42	....	....	....	....	....	....	....	....	....	....	6	3	0	3	2	....	....	....
1977-78	Hershey Bears	AHL	54	25	23	48	....	....	....	29	....	....	....	....	....	....	....	....	....	....	....	....	....	....	....	....	....	....
1978-79	**Buffalo Sabres**	**NHL**	**61**	**10**	**15**	**25**	**9**	**11**	**20**	**26**	**0**	**0**	**1**	**85**	**11.8**	**37**	**3**	**26**	**0**	**8**	**3**	**1**	**0**	**1**	**0**	**0**	**0**	**1**
1979-80	**Quebec Nordiques**	**NHL**	**14**	**3**	**12**	**15**	**3**	**9**	**12**	**4**	**0**	**0**	**0**	**45**	**6.7**	**18**	**8**	**19**	**2**	**–7**	....	....	....	....	....	....	....	....
	Rochester Americans	AHL	37	13	23	36	....	....	....	37	....	....	....	....	....	....	....	....	....	....	....	....	....	....	....	....	....	....
1980-81	**Quebec Nordiques**	**NHL**	**78**	**52**	**51**	**103**	**41**	**34**	**75**	**39**	**16**	**0**	**5**	**261**	**19.9**	**136**	**58**	**91**	**4**	**–9**	**5**	**2**	**4**	**6**	**14**	**1**	**0**	**0**
1981-82	**Quebec Nordiques**	**NHL**	**59**	**15**	**26**	**41**	**12**	**17**	**29**	**77**	**1**	**3**	**1**	**124**	**12.1**	**63**	**20**	**59**	**7**	**–9**	**10**	**1**	**0**	**1**	**9**	**0**	**0**	**0**
1982-83	**Quebec Nordiques**	**NHL**	**35**	**9**	**14**	**23**	**7**	**10**	**17**	**6**	**1**	**0**	**1**	**60**	**15.0**	**31**	**6**	**33**	**8**	**0**	**4**	**0**	**0**	**0**	**2**	**0**	**0**	**0**
	Fredericton Express	AHL	19	16	15	31	....	....	....	16	....	....	....	....	....	....	....	....	....	....	....	....	....	....	....	....	....	....
	NHL Totals		**556**	**160**	**187**	**347**	**138**	**134**	**272**	**307**	**35**	**3**	**17**	**1306**	**12.3**	**524**	**164**	**456**	**22**		**35**	**5**	**5**	**10**	**34**	**1**	**0**	**1**

QJHL First All-Star Team (1971) • QMJHL First All-Star Team (1972)

Traded to **Buffalo** by **Atlanta** for Larry Carriere and Buffalo's 1st round choice (later traded to Washington - Washington selected Greg Carroll) in 1976 Amateur Draft and cash, October 1, 1975. Signed as a free agent by **Quebec**, February 12, 1980.

• RICHARD, Jean-Marc

D – L. 5'11", 178 lbs. b: St.-Raymond, Que., 10/8/1966.

Season	Club	League	GP	G	A	Pts	AG	AA	APts	PIM	PP	SH	GW	S	%	TGF	PGF	TGA	PGA	+/–	GP	G	A	Pts	PIM	PP	SH	GW
1982-83	Ste-Foy Gouverneurs	QAAA	47	2	7	9	....	....	....	21	....	....	....	....	....	....	....	....	....	....	....	....	....	....	....	....	....	....
1983-84	Chicoutimi Sagueneens	QMJHL	61	1	20	21	....	....	....	41	....	....	....	....	....	....	....	....	....	....	....	....	....	....	....	....	....	....
1984-85	Chicoutimi Sagueneens	QMJHL	68	10	61	71	....	....	....	57	....	....	....	....	....	....	....	....	....	....	....	....	....	....	....	....	....	....
1985-86	Chicoutimi Sagueneens	QMJHL	72	20	87	107	....	....	....	111	....	....	....	....	....	....	....	....	....	....	9	3	5	8	14	....	....	....
1986-87	Chicoutimi Sagueneens	QMJHL	67	21	81	102	....	....	....	105	....	....	....	....	....	....	....	....	....	....	16	6	25	31	28	....	....	....
1987-88	**Quebec Nordiques**	**NHL**	**4**	**2**	**1**	**3**	**2**	**1**	**3**	**2**	**1**	**0**	**0**	**5**	**40.0**	**3**	**2**	**4**	**0**	**–3**	....	....	....	....	....	....	....	....
	Fredericton Express	AHL	68	14	42	56	....	....	....	52	....	....	....	....	....	....	....	....	....	....	7	2	1	3	4	....	....	....
1988-89	Halifax Citadels	AHL	57	8	25	33	....	....	....	38	....	....	....	....	....	....	....	....	....	....	4	1	0	1	4	....	....	....
1989-90	**Quebec Nordiques**	**NHL**	**1**	**0**	**0**	**0**	**0**	**0**	**0**	**0**	**0**	**0**	**0**	**0**	**0.0**	**0**	**0**	**1**	**0**	**–1**	....	....	....	....	....	....	....	....
	Halifax Citadels	AHL	40	1	24	25	....	....	....	38	....	....	....	....	....	....	....	....	....	....	....	....	....	....	....	....	....	....
1990-91	Halifax Citadels	AHL	80	7	41	48	....	....	....	76	....	....	....	....	....	....	....	....	....	....	....	....	....	....	....	....	....	....
	Fort Wayne Komets	IHL	1	0	0	0	....	....	....	0	....	....	....	....	....	....	....	....	....	....	19	3	9	12	8	....	....	....
1991-92	Fort Wayne Komets	IHL	82	18	68	86	....	....	....	109	....	....	....	....	....	....	....	....	....	....	7	0	5	5	20	....	....	....
1992-93	San Diego Gulls	IHL	6	1	0	1	....	....	....	4	....	....	....	....	....	....	....	....	....	....	....	....	....	....	....	....	....	....
	Fort Wayne Komets	IHL	52	10	33	43	....	....	....	48	....	....	....	....	....	....	....	....	....	....	12	6	11	17	6	....	....	....
1993-94	Las Vegas Thunder	IHL	59	15	33	48	....	....	....	44	....	....	....	....	....	....	....	....	....	....	5	0	3	3	0	....	....	....
1994-95	Las Vegas Thunder	IHL	81	16	41	57	....	....	....	76	....	....	....	....	....	....	....	....	....	....	10	0	3	3	4	....	....	....
1995-96	Las Vegas Thunder	IHL	82	12	40	52	....	....	....	92	....	....	....	....	....	....	....	....	....	....	15	1	7	8	23	....	....	....
1996-97	Quebec Rafales	IHL	56	8	26	34	....	....	....	31	....	....	....	....	....	....	....	....	....	....	9	1	1	2	10	....	....	....
1997-98	Frankfurt Lions	Germany	48	4	17	21	....	....	....	40	....	....	....	....	....	....	....	....	....	....	7	1	2	3	2	....	....	....
1998-99	Frankfurt Lions	Germany	49	8	18	26	....	....	....	74	....	....	....	....	....	....	....	....	....	....	8	1	0	1	12	....	....	....
	Frankfurt Lions	EuroHL	6	0	1	1	....	....	....	6	....	....	....	....	....	....	....	....	....	....	....	....	....	....	....	....	....	....
99-2000	Frankfurt Lions	Germany	56	4	23	27	....	....	....	36	....	....	....	....	....	....	....	....	....	....	5	0	0	0	0	....	....	....
	NHL Totals		**5**	**2**	**1**	**3**	**2**	**1**	**3**	**2**	**1**	**0**	**0**	**5**	**40.0**	**3**	**2**	**5**	**0**		....	....	....	....	....	....	....	....

QMJHL First All-Star Team (1986, 1987) • IHL First All-Star Team (1992, 1994) • Won Governors' Trophy (Top Defenseman - IHL) (1992)

Signed as a free agent by **Quebec**, April 13, 1987. Signed as a free agent by **Fort Wayne** (IHL), September, 1991.

REGULAR SEASON / PLAYOFFS

• RICHARD, Mike

Michael C – L. 5'10", 190 lbs. b: Scarborough, Ont., 7/9/1966.

Season	Club	League	GP	G	A	Pts	AG	AA	APts	PIM	PP	SH	GW	S	%	TGF	PGF	TGA	PGA	+/-	GP	G	A	Pts	PIM	PP	SH	GW
1982-83	Don Mills Flyers	MTHL	40	25	30	55	....	....	....	10	....	....	....	....	....	....	....	....	....	....	....	....	....	....	....	....	....	....
1983-84	Toronto Marlboros	OHL	66	19	17	36	....	....	....	12	....	....	....	....	....	....	....	....	....	....	9	2	1	3	0	....	....	....
1984-85	Toronto Marlboros	OHL	66	31	41	72	....	....	....	15	....	....	....	....	....	....	....	....	....	....	5	0	0	0	11	....	....	....
1985-86	Toronto Marlboros	OHL	63	32	48	80	....	....	....	28	....	....	....	....	....	....	....	....	....	....	4	1	1	2	2	....	....	....
1986-87	Toronto Marlboros	OHL	66	*57	50	107	....	....	....	38	....	....	....	....	....	....	....	....	....	....	....	....	....	....	....	....	....	....
	Baltimore Skipjacks	AHL	9	5	2	7	....	....	....	2	....	....	....	....	....	....	....	....	....	....	....	....	....	....	....	....	....	....
	Baltimore Skipjacks	AHL	9	5	2	7	....	....	....	2	....	....	....	....	....	....	....	....	....	....	....	....	....	....	....	....	....	....
1987-88	**Washington Capitals**	**NHL**	**4**	**0**	**0**	**0**	**0**	**0**	**0**	**0**	**0**	**0**	**0**	**5**	**0.0**	**1**	**1**	**1**	**0**	**–1**	....	....	....	....	....	....	....	....
	Binghamton Whalers	AHL	72	46	48	94	....	....	....	23	....	....	....	....	....	....	....	....	....	....	4	0	3	3	4	....	....	....
1988-89	Baltimore Skipjacks	AHL	80	44	63	107	....	....	....	51	....	....	....	....	....	....	....	....	....	....	....	....	....	....	....	....	....	....
1989-90	Washington Capitals	Fr-Tour	1	0	0	0	....	....	....	0	....	....	....	....	....	....	....	....	....	....	....	....	....	....	....	....	....	....
	Washington Capitals	**NHL**	**3**	**0**	**2**	**2**	**0**	**1**	**1**	**0**	**0**	**0**	**0**	**5**	**0.0**	**6**	**2**	**5**	**1**	**0**	....	....	....	....	....	....	....	....
	Baltimore Skipjacks	AHL	53	41	42	83	....	....	....	14	....	....	....	....	....	....	....	....	....	....	11	4	*13	17	6	....	....	....
1990-91	ZSC Lions Zurich	Switz.	36	28	23	51	....	....	....	....	....	....	....	....	....	....	....	....	....	....	4	1	5	6	4	....	....	....
1991-92	HC Milano Devils	Alpenliga	18	18	26	44	....	....	....	4	....	....	....	....	....	....	....	....	....	....	....	....	....	....	....	....	....	....
	HC Milano Devils	Italy	18	20	26	46	....	....	....	4	....	....	....	....	....	....	....	....	....	....	12	7	11	18	4	....	....	....
1992-93	EHC Olten	Switz-2	36	46	46	*92	....	....	....	....	....	....	....	....	....	....	....	....	....	....	....	....	....	....	....	....	....	....
1993-94	EHC Olten	Switz	35	29	19	48	....	....	....	50	....	....	....	....	....	....	....	....	....	....	....	....	....	....	....	....	....	....
1994-95	EHC Olten	Switz-2	32	31	38	69	....	....	....	62	....	....	....	....	....	....	....	....	....	....	....	....	....	....	....	....	....	....
1995-96	SC Rapperswil-Jona	Switz.	36	27	*38	65	....	....	....	14	....	....	....	....	....	....	....	....	....	....	4	0	3	3	7	....	....	....
1996-97	SC Rapperswil-Jona	Switz.	41	17	31	48	....	....	....	30	....	....	....	....	....	....	....	....	....	....	3	1	0	1	0	....	....	....
1997-98	SC Rapperswil-Jona	Switz.	22	12	19	31	....	....	....	25	....	....	....	....	....	....	....	....	....	....	7	5	4	9	4	....	....	....
1998-99	SC Rapperswil-Jona	Switz.	41	26	32	58	....	....	....	49	....	....	....	....	....	....	....	....	....	....	5	1	2	3	2	....	....	....
99-2000	SC Rapperswil-Jona	Switz.	45	23	29	52	....	....	....	42	....	....	....	....	....	....	....	....	....	....	6	3	4	7	10	....	....	....
	NHL Totals		**7**	**0**	**2**	**2**	**0**	**1**	**1**	**0**	**0**	**0**	**0**	**10**	**0.0**	**7**	**3**	**6**	**1**		....	....	....	....	....	....	....	....

Won Dudley "Red" Garrett Memorial Award (Top Rookie - AHL) (1987) • AHL Second All-Star Team (1990)

Signed as a free agent by **Washington**, October 9, 1987.

• RICHARDS, Todd

Todd M. D – R. 6', 194 lbs. b: Robindale, MN, 10/20/1966. Montreal's 3rd, 33rd overall, in 1985.

Season	Club	League	GP	G	A	Pts	AG	AA	APts	PIM	PP	SH	GW	S	%	TGF	PGF	TGA	PGA	+/-	GP	G	A	Pts	PIM	PP	SH	GW
1984-85	Armstrong High School	Hi-School	24	10	23	33	....	....	....	24	....	....	....	....	....	....	....	....	....	....	....	....	....	....	....	....	....	....
1985-86	University of Minnesota	WCHA	38	6	23	29	....	....	....	38	....	....	....	....	....	....	....	....	....	....	....	....	....	....	....	....	....	....
1986-87	University of Minnesota	WCHA	49	8	43	51	....	....	....	70	....	....	....	....	....	....	....	....	....	....	....	....	....	....	....	....	....	....
1987-88	University of Minnesota	WCHA	34	10	30	40	....	....	....	26	....	....	....	....	....	....	....	....	....	....	....	....	....	....	....	....	....	....
1988-89	University of Minnesota	WCHA	46	6	32	38	....	....	....	60	....	....	....	....	....	....	....	....	....	....	....	....	....	....	....	....	....	....
1989-90	Sherbrooke Canadiens	AHL	71	6	18	24	....	....	....	73	....	....	....	....	....	....	....	....	....	....	5	1	2	3	6	....	....	....
1990-91	Montreal Canadiens	Fr-Tour	2	0	0	0	....	....	....	2	....	....	....	....	....	....	....	....	....	....	....	....	....	....	....	....	....	....
	Fredericton Canadiens	AHL	3	0	1	1	....	....	....	2	....	....	....	....	....	....	....	....	....	....	....	....	....	....	....	....	....	....
	Hartford Whalers	**NHL**	**2**	**0**	**4**	**4**	**0**	**3**	**3**	**2**	**0**	**0**	**0**	**4**	**0.0**	**5**	**5**	**6**	**2**	**–4**	**6**	**0**	**0**	**0**	**2**	**0**	**0**	**0**
	Springfield Indians	AHL	71	10	41	51	....	....	....	62	....	....	....	....	....	....	....	....	....	....	14	2	8	10	2	....	....	....
1991-92	**Hartford Whalers**	**NHL**	**6**	**0**	**0**	**0**	**0**	**0**	**0**	**2**	**0**	**0**	**0**	**3**	**0.0**	**6**	**2**	**6**	**0**	**–2**	**5**	**0**	**3**	**3**	**4**	**0**	**0**	**0**
	Springfield Indians	AHL	43	6	23	29	....	....	....	33	....	....	....	....	....	....	....	....	....	....	8	0	3	3	2	....	....	....
1992-93	Springfield Indians	AHL	78	13	42	55	....	....	....	53	....	....	....	....	....	....	....	....	....	....	9	1	5	6	2	....	....	....
1993-94	Las Vegas Thunder	IHL	80	11	35	46	....	....	....	122	....	....	....	....	....	....	....	....	....	....	5	1	4	5	18	....	....	....
1994-95	Las Vegas Thunder	IHL	80	12	49	61	....	....	....	130	....	....	....	....	....	....	....	....	....	....	9	1	2	3	6	....	....	....
1995-96	Orlando Solar Bears	IHL	81	19	54	73	....	....	....	59	....	....	....	....	....	....	....	....	....	....	23	4	9	13	8	....	....	....
1996-97	Orlando Solar Bears	IHL	82	9	36	45	....	....	....	134	....	....	....	....	....	....	....	....	....	....	10	0	1	1	4	....	....	....
1997-98	Orlando Solar Bears	IHL	75	6	37	43	....	....	....	68	....	....	....	....	....	....	....	....	....	....	17	3	8	11	13	....	....	....
1998-99	Orlando Solar Bears	IHL	67	11	26	37	....	....	....	61	....	....	....	....	....	....	....	....	....	....	16	3	7	10	14	....	....	....
99-2000	Orlando Solar Bears	IHL	43	7	18	25	....	....	....	26	....	....	....	....	....	....	....	....	....	....	6	0	5	5	4	....	....	....
	NHL Totals		**8**	**0**	**4**	**4**	**0**	**3**	**3**	**4**	**0**	**0**	**0**	**7**	**0.0**	**11**	**7**	**12**	**2**		**11**	**0**	**3**	**3**	**6**	**0**	**0**	**0**

WCHA Second All-Star Team (1987, 1988, 1989) • NCAA Championship All-Tournament Team (1989) • IHL Second All-Star Team (1994) • IHL First All-Star Team (1995, 1996) • Won Governors' Trophy (Top Defenseman - IHL) (1995)

Traded to **Hartford** by **Montreal** for future considerations, October 11, 1990.

• RICHARDS, Travis

Travis J. D – L. 6'1", 185 lbs. b: Crystal, MN, 3/22/1970. Minnesota's 6th, 169th overall, in 1988.

Season	Club	League	GP	G	A	Pts	AG	AA	APts	PIM	PP	SH	GW	S	%	TGF	PGF	TGA	PGA	+/-	GP	G	A	Pts	PIM	PP	SH	GW
1986-87	Armstrong High School	Hi-School	22	6	16	22	....	....	....	20	....	....	....	....	....	....	....	....	....	....	....	....	....	....	....	....	....	....
1987-88	Armstrong High School	Hi-School	24	14	14	28	....	....	....	....	....	....	....	....	....	....	....	....	....	....	....	....	....	....	....	....	....	....
1988-89	Armstrong High School	Hi-School	STATISTICS NOT AVAILABLE																									
1989-90	University of Minnesota	WCHA	45	4	24	28	....	....	....	38	....	....	....	....	....	....	....	....	....	....	....	....	....	....	....	....	....	....
1990-91	University of Minnesota	WCHA	45	9	25	34	....	....	....	28	....	....	....	....	....	....	....	....	....	....	....	....	....	....	....	....	....	....
1991-92	University of Minnesota	WCHA	41	10	22	32	....	....	....	65	....	....	....	....	....	....	....	....	....	....	....	....	....	....	....	....	....	....
1992-93	University of Minnesota	WCHA	42	12	26	38	....	....	....	52	....	....	....	....	....	....	....	....	....	....	....	....	....	....	....	....	....	....
	United States	WC-A	5	0	1	1	....	....	....	0	....	....	....	....	....	....	....	....	....	....	....	....	....	....	....	....	....	....
1993-94	United States	Nat-Team	51	1	11	12	....	....	....	38	....	....	....	....	....	....	....	....	....	....	....	....	....	....	....	....	....	....
	United States	Olympics	8	0	0	0	....	....	....	2	....	....	....	....	....	....	....	....	....	....	....	....	....	....	....	....	....	....
	Kalamazoo Wings	IHL	19	2	10	12	....	....	....	20	....	....	....	....	....	....	....	....	....	....	4	1	1	2	0	....	....	....
1994-95	**Dallas Stars**	**NHL**	**2**	**0**	**0**	**0**	**0**	**0**	**0**	**0**	**0**	**0**	**0**	**1**	**0.0**	**0**	**0**	**0**	**0**	**0**	....	....	....	....	....	....	....	....
	Kalamazoo Wings	IHL	63	4	16	20	....	....	....	53	....	....	....	....	....	....	....	....	....	....	15	1	5	6	12	....	....	....
1995-96	**Dallas Stars**	**NHL**	**1**	**0**	**0**	**0**	**0**	**0**	**0**	**2**	**0**	**0**	**0**	**0**	**0.0**	**0**	**0**	**1**	**0**	**–1**	....	....	....	....	....	....	....	....
	Michigan K-Wings	IHL	65	8	15	23	....	....	....	55	....	....	....	....	....	....	....	....	....	....	9	2	2	4	4	....	....	....
1996-97	Grand Rapids Griffins	IHL	77	10	13	23	....	....	....	83	....	....	....	....	....	....	....	....	....	....	5	1	3	4	2	....	....	....
1997-98	Grand Rapids Griffins	IHL	81	12	20	32	....	....	....	70	....	....	....	....	....	....	....	....	....	....	3	1	1	2	4	....	....	....
1998-99	Grand Rapids Griffins	IHL	82	9	23	32	....	....	....	84	....	....	....	....	....	....	....	....	....	....	....	....	....	....	....	....	....	....
99-2000	Grand Rapids Griffins	IHL	71	5	23	28	....	....	....	47	....	....	....	....	....	....	....	....	....	....	17	1	7	8	18	....	....	....
	NHL Totals		**3**	**0**	**0**	**0**	**0**	**0**	**0**	**2**	**0**	**0**	**0**	**1**	**0.0**	**0**	**0**	**1**	**0**		....	....	....	....	....	....	....	....

WCHA Second All-Star Team (1992, 1993) • IHL First All-Star Team (1995, 1996) • Won Governors' Trophy (Outstanding Defenseman - IHL) (1995)

Rights transferred to **Dallas** after **Minnesota** franchise relocated, June 9, 1993.

• RICHARDSON, Dave

David George LW – L. 5'9", 175 lbs. b: St. Boniface, Man., 12/11/1940.

Season	Club	League	GP	G	A	Pts	AG	AA	APts	PIM	PP	SH	GW	S	%	TGF	PGF	TGA	PGA	+/-	GP	G	A	Pts	PIM	PP	SH	GW
1957-58	Brandon Wheat Kings	MJHL	28	3	7	10	....	....	....	39	....	....	....	....	....	....	....	....	....	....	....	....	....	....	....	....	....	....
1958-59	Winnipeg Rangers	MJHL	31	10	13	23	....	....	....	60	....	....	....	....	....	....	....	....	....	....	4	0	1	1	9	....	....	....
1959-60	Winnipeg Rangers	MJHL	26	19	17	36	....	....	....	*121	....	....	....	....	....	....	....	....	....	....	12	6	*30	*36	10	....	....	....
1960-61	Winnipeg Rangers	MJHL	29	17	31	48	....	....	....	65	....	....	....	....	....	....	....	....	....	....	....	....	....	....	....	....	....	....
	Seattle Totems	WHL	2	0	0	0	....	....	....	4	....	....	....	....	....	....	....	....	....	....	....	....	....	....	....	....	....	....
	Winnipeg Maroons	Al-Cup	4	0	2	2	....	....	....	12	....	....	....	....	....	....	....	....	....	....	....	....	....	....	....	....	....	....
	Edmonton Oil Kings	Mem-Cup	4	2	1	3	....	....	....	0	....	....	....	....	....	....	....	....	....	....	....	....	....	....	....	....	....	....
1961-62	Los Angeles Blades	WHL	3	0	1	1	....	....	....	0	....	....	....	....	....	....	....	....	....	....	....	....	....	....	....	....	....	....
	Fort Wayne Komets	IHL	65	24	47	71	....	....	....	166	....	....	....	....	....	....	....	....	....	....	....	....	....	....	....	....	....	....
1962-63	Sudbury Wolves	EPHL	72	29	38	67	....	....	....	117	....	....	....	....	....	....	....	....	....	....	8	3	1	4	8	....	....	....
1963-64	**New York Rangers**	**NHL**	**34**	**3**	**1**	**4**	**4**	**1**	**5**	**21**	....	....	....	....	....	....	....	....	....	....	....	....	....	....	....	....	....	....
	Baltimore Clippers	AHL	37	9	15	24	....	....	....	88	....	....	....	....	....	....	....	....	....	....	....	....	....	....	....	....	....	....
1964-65	**New York Rangers**	**NHL**	**7**	**0**	**1**	**1**	**0**	**1**	**1**	**4**	....	....	....	....	....	....	....	....	....	....	....	....	....	....	....	....	....	....
	St. Paul Rangers	CPHL	8	3	2	5	....	....	....	10	....	....	....	....	....	....	....	....	....	....	....	....	....	....	....	....	....	....
	Baltimore Clippers	AHL	47	17	23	.40	....	....	....	89	....	....	....	....	....	....	....	....	....	....	3	0	0	0	2	....	....	....
1965-66	**Chicago Black Hawks**	**NHL**	**3**	**0**	**0**	**0**	**0**	**0**	**0**	**2**	....	....	....	....	....	....	....	....	....	....	....	....	....	....	....	....	....	....
	Buffalo Bisons	AHL	35	11	14	25	....	....	....	58	....	....	....	....	....	....	....	....	....	....	....	....	....	....	....	....	....	....
	St. Louis Braves	CPHL	6	1	3	4	....	....	....	2	....	....	....	....	....	....	....	....	....	....	....	....	....	....	....	....	....	....

			REGULAR SEASON																		PLAYOFFS							
Season	Club	League	GP	G	A	Pts	AG	AA	APts	PIM	PP	SH	GW	S	%	TGF	PGF	TGA	PGA	+/-	GP	G	A	Pts	PIM	PP	SH	GW
1966-67	Buffalo Bisons	AHL	71	13	35	48	....	....	....	54	....	....	....	....	....	....	....	....	....	....	....	....	....	....	....	....	....	....
1967-68	Memphis–Fort Worth	CPHL	46	21	28	49	....	....	....	71	....	....	....	....	....	....	....	....	....	....	13	3	6	9	17	....	....	....
	Detroit Red Wings	**NHL**	**1**	**0**	**0**	**0**	**0**	**0**	**0**	**0**	**0**	**0**	**0**	**0**	**0.0**	**0**	**0**	**0**	**0**	**0**	....	....	....	....	....	....	....	....
1968-69	San Diego Gulls	WHL	51	9	12	21	....	....	....	55	....	....	....	....	....	....	....	....	....	....	....	....	....	....	....	....	....	....
1969-70	San Diego Gulls	WHL	24	4	6	10	....	....	....	35	....	....	....	....	....	....	....	....	....	....	....	....	....	....	....	....	....	....
1970-71			DID NOT PLAY																									
1971-72	St. Boniface Mohawks	CCHL	STATISTICS NOT AVAILABLE																									
1972-73	St. Boniface Mohawks	CCHL	24	33	55	*88	....	....	....	27	....	....	....	....	....	....	....	....	....	....	....	....	....	....	....	....	....	....
1973-74	Warroad Lakers	CCHL	24	14	14	28	....	....	....	....	....	....	....	....	....	....	....	....	....	....	....	....	....	....	....	....	....	....
	NHL Totals		**45**	**3**	**2**	**5**	**4**	**2**	**6**	**27**	....	....	....	....	**0.0**	....	....	....	....		....	....	....	....	....	....	....	....

Won Garry F. Longman Memorial Trophy (Top Rookie - IHL) (1962)

Traded to **Chicago** by **NY Rangers** with Tracy Pratt, Mel Pearson and Dick Meissner for Ray Cullen and John McKenzie, June 4, 1965. Claimed by **Minnesota** from **Chicago** in Expansion Draft, June 6, 1967. Traded to **Detroit** by **Minnesota** with Jean-Guy Talbot for Duke Harris and Bob McCord, October 19, 1967.

• RICHARDSON, Glen

Glen Gordon LW – L. 6'2", 200 lbs. b: Barrie, Ont., 9/20/1955. Vancouver's 4th, 64th overall, in 1975.

Season	Club	League	GP	G	A	Pts	AG	AA	APts	PIM	PP	SH	GW	S	%	TGF	PGF	TGA	PGA	+/-	GP	G	A	Pts	PIM	PP	SH	GW
1972-73	Kitchener Rangers	OMJHL	40	4	6	10	....	....	....	25	....	....	....	....	....	....	....	....	....	....	....	....	....	....	....	....	....	....
1973-74	Hamilton Fincups	OMJHL	65	11	17	28	....	....	....	54	....	....	....	....	....	....	....	....	....	....	....	....	....	....	....	....	....	....
1974-75	Hamilton Fincups	OMJHL	66	29	43	72	....	....	....	119	....	....	....	....	....	....	....	....	....	....	17	9	12	21	8	....	....	....
1975-76	**Vancouver Canucks**	**NHL**	**24**	**3**	**6**	**9**	**3**	**4**	**7**	**19**	**0**	**0**	**0**	**27**	**11.1**	**15**	**1**	**15**	**0**	**–1**	....	....	....	....	....	....	....	....
	Tulsa Oilers	CHL	45	10	16	26	....	....	....	27	....	....	....	....	....	....	....	....	....	....	9	4	1	5	4	....	....	....
1976-77	Tulsa Oilers	CHL	72	24	38	62	....	....	....	27	....	....	....	....	....	....	....	....	....	....	9	1	2	3	4	....	....	....
1977-78	Tulsa Oilers	CHL	69	11	18	29	....	....	....	24	....	....	....	....	....	....	....	....	....	....	7	2	1	3	12	....	....	....
	NHL Totals		**24**	**3**	**6**	**9**	**3**	**4**	**7**	**19**	**0**	**0**	**0**	**27**	**11.1**	**15**	**1**	**15**	**0**		....	....	....	....	....	....	....	....

• RICHARDSON, Ken

Kenneth William C – L. 6', 190 lbs. b: North Bay, Ont., 4/12/1951.

Season	Club	League	GP	G	A	Pts	AG	AA	APts	PIM	PP	SH	GW	S	%	TGF	PGF	TGA	PGA	+/-	GP	G	A	Pts	PIM	PP	SH	GW
1968-69	Peterborough Petes	OHA-Jr.	54	7	12	19	....	....	....	27	....	....	....	....	....	....	....	....	....	....	10	1	1	2	5	....	....	....
1969-70	Smiths Falls Bears	OJHL	40	24	16	40	....	....	....	77	....	....	....	....	....	....	....	....	....	....	....	....	....	....	....	....	....	....
	Peterborough Petes	OHA-Jr.	....	....	....	....	....	....	....	....	....	....	....	....	....	....	....	....	....	....	6	0	0	0	5	....	....	....
1970-71	Smiths Falls Bears	OJHL	44	30	32	62	....	....	....	97	....	....	....	....	....	....	....	....	....	....	....	....	....	....	....	....	....	....
	Peterborough Petes	OHA-Jr.	....	....	....	....	....	....	....	....	....	....	....	....	....	....	....	....	....	....	5	0	1	1	10	....	....	....
1971-72	Laurentian University	OUAA	26	16	10	26	....	....	....	21	....	....	....	....	....	....	....	....	....	....	....	....	....	....	....	....	....	....
1972-73	Laurentian University	OUAA	25	14	7	21	....	....	....	37	....	....	....	....	....	....	....	....	....	....	....	....	....	....	....	....	....	....
1973-74	Columbus Owls	IHL	58	11	22	33	....	....	....	29	....	....	....	....	....	....	....	....	....	....	4	5	2	7	10	....	....	....
1974-75	**St. Louis Blues**	**NHL**	**21**	**5**	**7**	**12**	**4**	**5**	**9**	**12**	**1**	**0**	**1**	**26**	**19.2**	**16**	**2**	**10**	**0**	**4**	....	....	....	....	....	....	....	....
	Denver Spurs	CHL	30	10	11	21	....	....	....	20	....	....	....	....	....	....	....	....	....	....	2	2	1	3	0	....	....	....
1975-76	Providence Reds	AHL	3	0	1	1	....	....	....	4	....	....	....	....	....	....	....	....	....	....	....	....	....	....	....	....	....	....
	Oklahoma City Blazers	CHL	70	19	33	52	....	....	....	17	....	....	....	....	....	....	....	....	....	....	4	1	0	1	0	....	....	....
1976-77	Kansas City Blues	CHL	74	20	27	47	....	....	....	17	....	....	....	....	....	....	....	....	....	....	10	2	3	5	2	....	....	....
1977-78	**St. Louis Blues**	**NHL**	**12**	**2**	**5**	**7**	**2**	**4**	**6**	**2**	**0**	**0**	**0**	**14**	**14.3**	**9**	**0**	**6**	**1**	**4**	....	....	....	....	....	....	....	....
	Salt Lake Golden Eagles	CHL	59	16	23	39	....	....	....	26	....	....	....	....	....	....	....	....	....	....	6	3	0	3	2	....	....	....
1978-79	**St. Louis Blues**	**NHL**	**16**	**1**	**1**	**2**	**1**	**1**	**2**	**2**	**0**	**0**	**0**	**6**	**16.7**	**5**	**0**	**26**	**16**	**–5**	....	....	....	....	....	....	....	....
	Salt Lake Golden Eagles	CHL	58	7	10	17	....	....	....	15	....	....	....	....	....	....	....	....	....	....	10	3	1	4	0	....	....	....
1979-80	Salt Lake Golden Eagles	CHL	61	4	16	20	....	....	....	24	....	....	....	....	....	....	....	....	....	....	11	0	1	1	2	....	....	....
	NHL Totals		**49**	**8**	**13**	**21**	**7**	**10**	**17**	**16**	**1**	**0**	**1**	**46**	**17.4**	**30**	**2**	**42**	**17**		....	....	....	....	....	....	....	....

Signed as a free agent by **St. Louis** (Columbus-IHL), September, 1973.

• RICHARDSON, Luke

Luke Glen D – L. 6'3", 210 lbs. b: Ottawa, Ont., 3/26/1969. Toronto's 1st, 7th overall, in 1987.

Season	Club	League	GP	G	A	Pts	AG	AA	APts	PIM	PP	SH	GW	S	%	TGF	PGF	TGA	PGA	+/-	GP	G	A	Pts	PIM	PP	SH	GW
1984-85	Ottawa Golden Knights	OJHL	35	5	26	31	....	....	....	72	....	....	....	....	....	....	....	....	....	....	....	....	....	....	....	....	....	....
1985-86	Peterborough Petes	OHL	63	6	18	24	....	....	....	57	....	....	....	....	....	....	....	....	....	....	16	2	1	3	50	....	....	....
1986-87	Peterborough Petes	OHL	59	13	32	45	....	....	....	70	....	....	....	....	....	....	....	....	....	....	12	0	5	5	24	....	....	....
	Canada	WJC-A	6	0	0	0	....	....	....	0	....	....	....	....	....	....	....	....	....	....	....	....	....	....	....	....	....	....
1987-88	**Toronto Maple Leafs**	**NHL**	**78**	**4**	**6**	**10**	**3**	**4**	**7**	**90**	**0**	**0**	**0**	**49**	**8.2**	**48**	**1**	**93**	**21**	**–25**	**2**	**0**	**0**	**0**	**0**	**0**	**0**	**0**
1988-89	**Toronto Maple Leafs**	**NHL**	**55**	**2**	**7**	**9**	**2**	**5**	**7**	**106**	**0**	**0**	**0**	**59**	**3.4**	**42**	**1**	**76**	**20**	**–15**	....	....	....	....	....	....	....	....
1989-90	**Toronto Maple Leafs**	**NHL**	**67**	**4**	**14**	**18**	**3**	**10**	**13**	**122**	**0**	**0**	**0**	**80**	**5.0**	**76**	**6**	**83**	**12**	**–1**	**5**	**0**	**0**	**0**	**22**	**0**	**0**	**0**
1990-91	**Toronto Maple Leafs**	**NHL**	**78**	**1**	**9**	**10**	**1**	**7**	**8**	**238**	**0**	**0**	**0**	**68**	**1.5**	**46**	**1**	**102**	**29**	**–28**	....	....	....	....	....	....	....	....
1991-92	**Edmonton Oilers**	**NHL**	**75**	**2**	**19**	**21**	**2**	**14**	**16**	**118**	**0**	**0**	**0**	**85**	**2.4**	**64**	**7**	**101**	**35**	**–9**	**16**	**0**	**5**	**5**	**45**	**0**	**0**	**0**
1992-93	**Edmonton Oilers**	**NHL**	**82**	**3**	**10**	**13**	**2**	**7**	**9**	**142**	**0**	**2**	**0**	**78**	**3.8**	**55**	**2**	**107**	**36**	**–18**	....	....	....	....	....	....	....	....
1993-94	**Edmonton Oilers**	**NHL**	**69**	**2**	**6**	**8**	**2**	**5**	**7**	**131**	**0**	**0**	**0**	**92**	**2.2**	**47**	**0**	**83**	**23**	**–13**	....	....	....	....	....	....	....	....
	Canada	WC-A	8	0	1	1	....	....	....	6	....	....	....	....	....	....	....	....	....	....	....	....	....	....	....	....	....	....
1994-95	**Edmonton Oilers**	**NHL**	**46**	**3**	**10**	**13**	**5**	**15**	**20**	**40**	**1**	**1**	**1**	**51**	**5.9**	**40**	**4**	**72**	**30**	**–6**	....	....	....	....	....	....	....	....
1995-96	**Edmonton Oilers**	**NHL**	**82**	**2**	**9**	**11**	**2**	**7**	**9**	**108**	**0**	**0**	**0**	**61**	**3.3**	**55**	**4**	**113**	**35**	**–27**	....	....	....	....	....	....	....	....
	Canada	WC-A	8	0	0	0	....	....	....	12	....	....	....	....	....	....	....	....	....	....	....	....	....	....	....	....	....	....
1996-97	**Edmonton Oilers**	**NHL**	**82**	**1**	**11**	**12**	**1**	**10**	**11**	**91**	**0**	**0**	**0**	**67**	**1.5**	**68**	**3**	**80**	**24**	**9**	**12**	**0**	**2**	**2**	**14**	**0**	**0**	**0**
1997-98	**Philadelphia Flyers**	**NHL**	**81**	**2**	**3**	**5**	**2**	**3**	**5**	**139**	**2**	**0**	**0**	**57**	**3.5**	**51**	**4**	**62**	**22**	**7**	**5**	**0**	**0**	**0**	**0**	**0**	**0**	**0**
1998-99	**Philadelphia Flyers**	**NHL**	**78**	**0**	**6**	**6**	**0**	**6**	**6**	**106**	**0**	**0**	**0**	**49**	**0.0**	**37**	**0**	**65**	**25**	**–3**	....	....	....	....	....	....	....	....
99-2000	**Philadelphia Flyers**	**NHL**	**74**	**2**	**5**	**7**	**2**	**5**	**7**	**140**	**0**	**0**	**1**	**50**	**4.0**	**41**	**0**	**37**	**10**	**14**	**18**	**0**	**1**	**1**	**41**	**0**	**0**	**0**
	NHL Totals		**947**	**28**	**115**	**143**	**27**	**98**	**125**	**1571**	**3**	**3**	**2**	**846**	**3.3**	**670**	**33**	**1074**	**322**		**58**	**0**	**8**	**8**	**122**	**0**	**0**	**0**

Traded to **Edmonton** by **Toronto** with Vincent Damphousse, Peter Ing, Scott Thornton, future considerations and cash for Grant Fuhr, Glenn Anderson and Craig Berube, September 19, 1991. Signed as a free agent by **Philadelphia**, July 23, 1997.

• RICHER, Bob

Robert Roger C – L. 5'10", 175 lbs. b: Cowansville, Que., 3/5/1951. Buffalo's 4th, 47th overall, in 1971.

Season	Club	League	GP	G	A	Pts	AG	AA	APts	PIM	PP	SH	GW	S	%	TGF	PGF	TGA	PGA	+/-	GP	G	A	Pts	PIM	PP	SH	GW
1969-70	Trois-Rivieres Ducs	QJHL	50	22	29	51	....	....	....	87	....	....	....	....	....	....	....	....	....	....	....	....	....	....	....	....	....	....
1970-71	Trois-Rivieres Ducs	QJHL	62	47	44	91	....	....	....	130	....	....	....	....	....	....	....	....	....	....	11	6	1	7	15	....	....	....
1971-72	Cincinnati Swords	AHL	1	0	0	0	....	....	....	2	....	....	....	....	....	....	....	....	....	....	....	....	....	....	....	....	....	....
	Charlotte Checkers	EHL	71	44	31	75	....	....	....	62	....	....	....	....	....	....	....	....	....	....	15	7	9	16	37	....	....	....
1972-73	**Buffalo Sabres**	**NHL**	**3**	**0**	**0**	**0**	**0**	**0**	**0**	**0**	**0**	**0**	**0**	**0**	**0.0**	**0**	**0**	**0**	**0**	**0**	....	....	....	....	....	....	....	....
	Cincinnati Swords	AHL	63	11	10	21	....	....	....	12	....	....	....	....	....	....	....	....	....	....	1	0	0	0	5	....	....	....
1973-74	Cincinnati Swords	AHL	71	9	11	20	....	....	....	25	....	....	....	....	....	....	....	....	....	....	5	0	0	0	0	....	....	....
	NHL Totals		**3**	**0**	**0**	**0**	**0**	**0**	**0**	**0**	**0**	**0**	**0**	**0**	**0.0**	**0**	**0**	**0**	**0**		....	....	....	....	....	....	....	....

• RICHER, Stephane

Stephane Jean-Gilles D – R. 5'11", 190 lbs. b: Hull, Que., 4/28/1966.

Season	Club	League	GP	G	A	Pts	AG	AA	APts	PIM	PP	SH	GW	S	%	TGF	PGF	TGA	PGA	+/-	GP	G	A	Pts	PIM	PP	SH	GW
1982-83	Montreal Concordia	QAAA	48	9	37	46	....	....	....	....	....	....	....	....	....	....	....	....	....	....	....	....	....	....	....	....	....	....
1983-84	Hull Olympiques	QMJHL	70	8	38	46	....	....	....	42	....	....	....	....	....	....	....	....	....	....	....	....	....	....	....	....	....	....
1984-85	Hull Olympiques	QMJHL	62	21	56	77	....	....	....	98	....	....	....	....	....	....	....	....	....	....	....	....	....	....	....	....	....	....
1985-86	Hull Olympiques	QMJHL	71	14	52	66	....	....	....	166	....	....	....	....	....	....	....	....	....	....	....	....	....	....	....	....	....	....
	Hull Olympiques	Mem-Cup	5	0	0	0	....	....	....	4	....	....	....	....	....	....	....	....	....	....	....	....	....	....	....	....	....	....
1986-87	Hull Olympiques	QMJHL	33	6	22	28	....	....	....	74	....	....	....	....	....	....	....	....	....	....	8	3	4	7	17	....	....	....
1987-88	Baltimore Skipjacks	AHL	22	0	3	3	....	....	....	6	....	....	....	....	....	....	....	....	....	....	....	....	....	....	....	....	....	....
	Sherbrooke Canadiens	AHL	41	4	7	11	....	....	....	46	....	....	....	....	....	....	....	....	....	....	5	1	0	1	10	....	....	....
1988-89	Sherbrooke Canadiens	AHL	70	7	26	33	....	....	....	158	....	....	....	....	....	....	....	....	....	....	6	1	2	3	18	....	....	....
1989-90	Sherbrooke Canadiens	AHL	60	10	12	22	....	....	....	85	....	....	....	....	....	....	....	....	....	....	12	4	9	13	16	....	....	....
1990-91	New Haven Nighthawks	AHL	3	0	1	1	....	....	....	0	....	....	....	....	....	....	....	....	....	....	....	....	....	....	....	....	....	....
	Phoenix Roadrunners	IHL	67	11	38	49	....	....	....	48	....	....	....	....	....	....	....	....	....	....	11	4	6	10	6	....	....	....
1991-92	Fredericton Canadiens	AHL	80	17	47	64	....	....	....	74	....	....	....	....	....	....	....	....	....	....	7	0	5	5	18	....	....	....
1992-93	**Tampa Bay Lightning**	**NHL**	**3**	**0**	**0**	**0**	**0**	**0**	**0**	**0**	**0**	**0**	**0**	**2**	**0.0**	**1**	**0**	**4**	**0**	**–3**	....	....	....	....	....	....	....	....
	Atlanta Knights	IHL	3	0	4	4	....	....	....	4	....	....	....	....	....	....	....	....	....	....	....	....	....	....	....	....	....	....
	Boston Bruins	**NHL**	**21**	**1**	**4**	**5**	**1**	**3**	**4**	**18**	**0**	**0**	**1**	**22**	**4.5**	**9**	**0**	**16**	**1**	**–6**	**3**	**0**	**0**	**0**	**0**	**0**	**0**	**0**
	Providence Bruins	AHL	53	8	20	28	....	....	....	60	....	....	....	....	....	....	....	....	....	....	....	....	....	....	....	....	....	....

Season	Club	League	REGULAR SEASON GP	G	A	Pts	AG	AA	APts	PIM	PP	SH	GW	S	%	TGF	PGF	TGA	PGA	+/–	PLAYOFFS GP	G	A	Pts	PIM	PP	SH	GW
1993-94	**Florida Panthers**	**NHL**	**2**	**0**	**1**	**1**	**0**	**1**	**1**	**0**	**0**	**0**	**0**	**3**	**0.0**	**2**	**2**	**2**	**1**	**–1**	....	....	....	....	....	....	....	....
	Cincinnati Cyclones	IHL	66	9	55	64	....	....	....	80	....	....	....	....	....	....	....	....	....	....	11	2	9	11	26	....	....	....
1994-95	Cincinnati Cyclones	IHL	80	16	53	69	....	....	....	67	....	....	....	....	....	....	....	....	....	....	10	2	7	9	18	....	....	....
	Florida Panthers	**NHL**	**1**	**0**	**0**	**0**	**0**	**0**	**0**	**2**	**0**	**0**	**0**	**0**	**0.0**	**0**	**0**	**0**	**0**	**0**	....	....	....	....	....	....	....	....
1995-96	Adler Mannheim	Germany	50	11	30	41	....	....	....	62	....	....	....	....	....	....	....	....	....	....	8	1	4	5	0	....	....	....
1996-97	Adler Mannheim	Germany	49	10	19	29	....	....	....	65	....	....	....	....	....	....	....	....	....	....	9	0	4	4	10	....	....	....
1997-98	Adler Mannheim	Germany	48	6	25	31	....	....	....	64	....	....	....	....	....	....	....	....	....	....	8	3	6	9	4	....	....	....
	Adler Mannheim	EuroHL	5	0	2	2	....	....	....	29	....	....	....	....	....	....	....	....	....	....	....	....	....	....	....	....	....	....
1998-99	Adler Mannheim	Germany	51	13	29	42	....	....	....	90	....	....	....	....	....	....	....	....	....	....	12	2	8	10	38	....	....	....
	Adler Mannheim	EuroHL	4	1	2	3	....	....	....	2	....	....	....	....	....	....	....	....	....	....	4	1	2	3	2	....	....	....
99-2000	Adler Mannheim	Germany	43	10	18	28	....	....	....	46	....	....	....	....	....	....	....	....	....	....	5	0	2	2	16	....	....	....
	Adler Mannheim	EuroHL	5	1	2	3	....	....	....	18	....	....	....	....	....	....	....	....	....	....	....	....	....	....	....	....	....	....
	NHL Totals		**27**	**1**	**5**	**6**	**1**	**4**	**5**	**20**	**0**	**0**	**1**	**27**	**3.7**	**12**	**2**	**22**	**2**		**3**	**0**	**0**	**0**	**0**	**0**	**0**	**0**

AHL Second All-Star Team (1992) • IHL Second All-Star Team (1994, 1995)

Signed as a free agent by **Montreal**, January 9, 1988. Signed as a free agent by **LA Kings**, July 11, 1990. Signed as a free agent by **Montreal**, September 17, 1991. Signed as a free agent by **Tampa Bay**, July 29, 1992. Traded to **Boston** by **Tampa Bay** for Bob Beers, October 28, 1992. Claimed by **Florida** from **Boston** in Expansion Draft, June 24, 1993.

• RICHER, Stephane

RW – R. 6'2", 215 lbs. b: Ripon, Que., 6/7/1966. Montreal's 3rd, 29th overall, in 1984.

Season	Club	League	GP	G	A	Pts	AG	AA	APts	PIM	PP	SH	GW	S	%	TGF	PGF	TGA	PGA	+/–	GP	G	A	Pts	PIM	PP	SH	GW
1982-83	Laval Insulaires	QAAA	48	47	54	101	....	....	....	86	....	....	....	....	....	....	....	....	....	....	....	....	....	....	....	....	....	....
1983-84	Granby Bisons	QMJHL	67	39	37	76	....	....	....	58	....	....	....	....	....	....	....	....	....	....	3	1	1	2	4	....	....	....
1984-85	Granby Bisons	QMJHL	30	30	27	57	....	....	....	31	....	....	....	....	....	....	....	....	....	....	....	....	....	....	....	....	....	....
	Canada	WJC-A	7	4	3	7	....	....	....	2	....	....	....	....	....	....	....	....	....	....	....	....	....	....	....	....	....	....
	Chicoutimi Sagueneens	QMJHL	27	31	32	63	....	....	....	40	....	....	....	....	....	....	....	....	....	....	12	13	13	26	25	....	....	....
	Montreal Canadiens	**NHL**	**1**	**0**	**0**	**0**	**0**	**0**	**0**	**0**	**0**	**0**	**0**	**0**	**0.0**	**0**	**0**	**0**	**0**	**0**	....	....	....	....	....	....	....	....
	Sherbrooke Canadiens	AHL	....	....	....	....	....	....	....	....	....	....	....	....	....	....	....	....	....	....	9	6	3	9	10	....	....	....
1985-86♦	**Montreal Canadiens**	**NHL**	**65**	**21**	**16**	**37**	**17**	**11**	**28**	**50**	**5**	**0**	**2**	**112**	**18.8**	**57**	**24**	**32**	**0**	**1**	**16**	**4**	**1**	**5**	**23**	**3**	**0**	**1**
1986-87	**Montreal Canadiens**	**NHL**	**57**	**20**	**19**	**39**	**17**	**14**	**31**	**80**	**4**	**0**	**3**	**109**	**18.3**	**54**	**14**	**30**	**1**	**11**	**5**	**3**	**2**	**5**	**0**	**0**	**0**	**1**
	Sherbrooke Canadiens	AHL	12	10	4	14	....	....	....	11	....	....	....	....	....	....	....	....	....	....	....	....	....	....	....	....	....	....
1987-88	**Montreal Canadiens**	**NHL**	**72**	**50**	**28**	**78**	**43**	**20**	**63**	**72**	**16**	**0**	**11**	**263**	**19.0**	**103**	**42**	**50**	**1**	**12**	**8**	**7**	**5**	**12**	**6**	**1**	**0**	**2**
1988-89	**Montreal Canadiens**	**NHL**	**68**	**25**	**35**	**60**	**21**	**25**	**46**	**61**	**11**	**0**	**6**	**214**	**11.7**	**77**	**33**	**40**	**0**	**4**	**21**	**6**	**5**	**11**	**14**	**2**	**0**	**3**
1989-90	**Montreal Canadiens**	**NHL**	**75**	**51**	**40**	**91**	**44**	**29**	**73**	**46**	**9**	**0**	**8**	**269**	**19.0**	**111**	**31**	**45**	**0**	**35**	**9**	**7**	**3**	**10**	**2**	**1**	**0**	**1**
1990-91	Montreal Canadiens	Fr-Tour	4	2	1	3	....	....	....	8	....	....	....	....	....	....	....	....	....	....	....	....	....	....	....	....	....	....
	Montreal Canadiens	**NHL**	**75**	**31**	**30**	**61**	**28**	**23**	**51**	**53**	**9**	**0**	**4**	**221**	**14.0**	**76**	**22**	**54**	**0**	**0**	**13**	**9**	**5**	**14**	**6**	**1**	**0**	**1**
1991-92	**New Jersey Devils**	**NHL**	**74**	**29**	**35**	**64**	**26**	**26**	**52**	**25**	**5**	**1**	**6**	**240**	**12.1**	**91**	**28**	**67**	**3**	**–1**	**7**	**1**	**2**	**3**	**0**	**0**	**0**	**0**
1992-93	**New Jersey Devils**	**NHL**	**78**	**38**	**35**	**73**	**32**	**24**	**56**	**44**	**7**	**1**	**7**	**286**	**13.3**	**101**	**34**	**72**	**4**	**–1**	**5**	**2**	**2**	**4**	**2**	**1**	**0**	**0**
1993-94	**New Jersey Devils**	**NHL**	**80**	**36**	**36**	**72**	**34**	**28**	**62**	**16**	**7**	**3**	**9**	**217**	**16.6**	**97**	**21**	**52**	**7**	**31**	**20**	**7**	**5**	**12**	**6**	**3**	**0**	**2**
1994-95♦	**New Jersey Devils**	**NHL**	**45**	**23**	**16**	**39**	**41**	**24**	**65**	**10**	**1**	**2**	**5**	**133**	**17.3**	**48**	**8**	**35**	**3**	**8**	**19**	**6**	**15**	**21**	**2**	**3**	**1**	**2**
1995-96	**New Jersey Devils**	**NHL**	**73**	**20**	**12**	**32**	**20**	**10**	**30**	**30**	**3**	**4**	**3**	**192**	**10.4**	**42**	**7**	**57**	**14**	**–8**	....	....	....	....	....	....	....	....
1996-97	**Montreal Canadiens**	**NHL**	**63**	**22**	**24**	**46**	**23**	**21**	**44**	**32**	**2**	**0**	**2**	**126**	**17.5**	**63**	**15**	**52**	**4**	**0**	**5**	**0**	**0**	**0**	**0**	**0**	**0**	**0**
1997-98	**Montreal Canadiens**	**NHL**	**14**	**5**	**4**	**9**	**6**	**4**	**10**	**5**	**2**	**0**	**0**	**24**	**20.8**	**13**	**6**	**6**	**0**	**1**	....	....	....	....	....	....	....	....
	Tampa Bay Lightning	**NHL**	**26**	**9**	**11**	**20**	**11**	**11**	**22**	**36**	**3**	**0**	**2**	**71**	**12.7**	**29**	**10**	**29**	**3**	**–7**	....	....	....	....	....	....	....	....
1998-99	**Tampa Bay Lightning**	**NHL**	**64**	**12**	**21**	**33**	**14**	**20**	**34**	**22**	**3**	**2**	**1**	**139**	**8.6**	**51**	**12**	**63**	**14**	**–10**	....	....	....	....	....	....	....	....
99-2000	**Tampa Bay Lightning**	**NHL**	**20**	**7**	**5**	**12**	**8**	**5**	**13**	**4**	**1**	**0**	**0**	**47**	**14.9**	**20**	**5**	**13**	**0**	**2**	....	....	....	....	....	....	....	....
	Detroit Vipers	IHL	2	0	0	0	....	....	....	0	....	....	....	....	....	....	....	....	....	....	....	....	....	....	....	....	....	....
	St. Louis Blues	**NHL**	**36**	**8**	**17**	**25**	**9**	**16**	**25**	**14**	**4**	**0**	**1**	**63**	**12.7**	**32**	**14**	**11**	**0**	**7**	**3**	**1**	**0**	**1**	**0**	**0**	**0**	**0**
	NHL Totals		**986**	**407**	**384**	**791**	**394**	**311**	**705**	**600**	**92**	**13**	**70**	**2726**	**14.9**	**1065**	**326**	**708**	**54**		**131**	**53**	**45**	**98**	**61**	**15**	**1**	**13**

QMJHL Rookie of the Year (1984) • QMJHL Second All-Star Team (1985) • Played in NHL All-Star Game (1990)

Traded to **New Jersey** by **Montreal** with Tom Chorske for Kirk Muller and Rollie Melanson, September 20, 1991. Traded to **Montreal** by **New Jersey** for Lyle Odelein, August 22, 1996. Traded to **Tampa Bay** by **Montreal** with Darcy Tucker and David Wilkie for Patrick Poulin, Mick Vukota and Igor Ulanov, January 15, 1998. Traded to **St. Louis** by **Tampa Bay** for Rich Parent and Chris McAlpine, January 13, 2000.

• RICHMOND, Steve

Steven L. D – L. 6'1", 205 lbs. b: Chicago, IL, 12/11/1959.

Season	Club	League	GP	G	A	Pts	AG	AA	APts	PIM	PP	SH	GW	S	%	TGF	PGF	TGA	PGA	+/–	GP	G	A	Pts	PIM	PP	SH	GW
1977-78	Evanston Eagles	Hi-School	STATISTICS NOT AVAILABLE																									
1978-79	University of Michigan	CCHA	34	2	5	7	....	....	....	38	....	....	....	....	....	....	....	....	....	....	....	....	....	....	....	....	....	....
1979-80	University of Michigan	CCHA	38	10	19	29	....	....	....	26	....	....	....	....	....	....	....	....	....	....	....	....	....	....	....	....	....	....
1980-81	University of Michigan	CCHA	39	22	32	54	....	....	....	56	....	....	....	....	....	....	....	....	....	....	....	....	....	....	....	....	....	....
1981-82	University of Michigan	CCHA	38	6	30	36	....	....	....	68	....	....	....	....	....	....	....	....	....	....	....	....	....	....	....	....	....	....
1982-83	Tulsa Oilers	CHL	68	5	13	18	....	....	....	187	....	....	....	....	....	....	....	....	....	....	....	....	....	....	....	....	....	....
1983-84	**New York Rangers**	**NHL**	**26**	**2**	**5**	**7**	**2**	**3**	**5**	**110**	**0**	**0**	**0**	**16**	**12.5**	**24**	**0**	**21**	**3**	**6**	**4**	**0**	**0**	**0**	**12**	**0**	**0**	**0**
	Tulsa Oilers	CHL	38	1	17	18	....	....	....	114	....	....	....	....	....	....	....	....	....	....	....	....	....	....	....	....	....	....
1984-85	**New York Rangers**	**NHL**	**34**	**0**	**5**	**5**	**0**	**3**	**3**	**90**	**0**	**0**	**0**	**14**	**0.0**	**21**	**1**	**42**	**6**	**–16**	....	....	....	....	....	....	....	....
	New Haven Nighthawks	AHL	37	3	10	13	....	....	....	122	....	....	....	....	....	....	....	....	....	....	....	....	....	....	....	....	....	....
1985-86	**New York Rangers**	**NHL**	**17**	**0**	**2**	**2**	**0**	**1**	**1**	**63**	**0**	**0**	**0**	**8**	**0.0**	**10**	**0**	**8**	**0**	**2**	....	....	....	....	....	....	....	....
	New Haven Nighthawks	AHL	11	2	6	8	....	....	....	32	....	....	....	....	....	....	....	....	....	....	....	....	....	....	....	....	....	....
	Detroit Red Wings	**NHL**	**29**	**1**	**2**	**3**	**1**	**1**	**2**	**82**	**0**	**0**	**0**	**18**	**5.6**	**13**	**1**	**35**	**5**	**–18**	....	....	....	....	....	....	....	....
	Adirondack Red Wings	AHL	20	1	7	8	....	....	....	23	....	....	....	....	....	....	....	....	....	....	17	2	9	11	34	....	....	....
1986-87	**New Jersey Devils**	**NHL**	**44**	**1**	**7**	**8**	**1**	**5**	**6**	**143**	**0**	**0**	**0**	**31**	**3.2**	**34**	**0**	**55**	**9**	**–12**	....	....	....	....	....	....	....	....
1987-88	Utica Devils	AHL	79	6	27	33	....	....	....	141	....	....	....	....	....	....	....	....	....	....	....	....	....	....	....	....	....	....
	Flint Spirits	IHL	2	0	2	2	....	....	....	2	....	....	....	....	....	....	....	....	....	....	16	2	9	11	57	....	....	....
1988-89	**Los Angeles Kings**	**NHL**	**9**	**0**	**2**	**2**	**0**	**1**	**1**	**26**	**0**	**0**	**0**	**1**	**0.0**	**6**	**0**	**7**	**3**	**2**	....	....	....	....	....	....	....	....
	New Haven Nighthawks	AHL	49	6	35	41	....	....	....	114	....	....	....	....	....	....	....	....	....	....	17	3	10	13	84	....	....	....
1989-90	Flint Spirits	IHL	10	1	3	4	....	....	....	19	....	....	....	....	....	....	....	....	....	....	4	0	1	1	16	....	....	....
1990-91	San Diego Gulls	IHL	12	3	7	10	....	....	....	19	....	....	....	....	....	....	....	....	....	....	....	....	....	....	....	....	....	....
	NHL Totals		**159**	**4**	**23**	**27**	**4**	**14**	**18**	**514**	**0**	**0**	**0**	**88**	**4.5**	**108**	**2**	**168**	**26**		**4**	**0**	**0**	**0**	**12**	**0**	**0**	**0**

Signed as a free agent by **NY Rangers**, June 22, 1982. Traded to **Detroit** by **NY Rangers** for Mike McEwen, December 26, 1985. Traded to **New Jersey** by **Detroit** for Sam St.Laurent, August 18, 1986. Signed as a free agent by **LA Kings**, July, 1988.

• RICHTER, Barry

D – L. 6'2", 200 lbs. b: Madison, WI, 9/11/1970. Hartford's 2nd, 32nd overall, in 1988.

Season	Club	League	GP	G	A	Pts	AG	AA	APts	PIM	PP	SH	GW	S	%	TGF	PGF	TGA	PGA	+/–	GP	G	A	Pts	PIM	PP	SH	GW
1986-87	Culver Academy Eagles	Hi-School	39	15	30	45	....	....	....	....	....	....	....	....	....	....	....	....	....	....	....	....	....	....	....	....	....	....
1987-88	Culver Academy Eagles	Hi-School	35	24	29	53	....	....	....	18	....	....	....	....	....	....	....	....	....	....	....	....	....	....	....	....	....	....
1988-89	Culver Academy Eagles	Hi-School	19	21	29	50	....	....	....	16	....	....	....	....	....	....	....	....	....	....	....	....	....	....	....	....	....	....
	United States	WJC-A	7	0	0	0	....	....	....	2	....	....	....	....	....	....	....	....	....	....	....	....	....	....	....	....	....	....
1989-90	University of Wisconsin	WCHA	42	13	23	36	....	....	....	36	....	....	....	....	....	....	....	....	....	....	....	....	....	....	....	....	....	....
	United States	WJC-A	7	3	1	4	....	....	....	0	....	....	....	....	....	....	....	....	....	....	....	....	....	....	....	....	....	....
1990-91	University of Wisconsin	WCHA	43	15	20	35	....	....	....	42	....	....	....	....	....	....	....	....	....	....	....	....	....	....	....	....	....	....
1991-92	University of Wisconsin	WCHA	39	10	25	35	....	....	....	62	....	....	....	....	....	....	....	....	....	....	....	....	....	....	....	....	....	....
	United States	WC-A	4	1	0	1	....	....	....	4	....	....	....	....	....	....	....	....	....	....	....	....	....	....	....	....	....	....
1992-93	University of Wisconsin	WCHA	42	14	32	46	....	....	....	74	....	....	....	....	....	....	....	....	....	....	....	....	....	....	....	....	....	....
	United States	WC-A	6	0	0	0	....	....	....	8	....	....	....	....	....	....	....	....	....	....	....	....	....	....	....	....	....	....
1993-94	United States	Nat-Team	56	7	16	23	....	....	....	50	....	....	....	....	....	....	....	....	....	....	....	....	....	....	....	....	....	....
	United States	Olympics	8	0	3	3	....	....	....	4	....	....	....	....	....	....	....	....	....	....	....	....	....	....	....	....	....	....
	United States	WC-A	7	0	0	0	....	....	....	6	....	....	....	....	....	....	....	....	....	....	....	....	....	....	....	....	....	....
	Binghamton Rangers	AHL	21	0	9	9	....	....	....	12	....	....	....	....	....	....	....	....	....	....	....	....	....	....	....	....	....	....
1994-95	Binghamton Rangers	AHL	73	15	41	56	....	....	....	54	....	....	....	....	....	....	....	....	....	....	11	4	5	9	12	....	....	....
1995-96	**New York Rangers**	**NHL**	**4**	**0**	**1**	**1**	**0**	**1**	**1**	**0**	**0**	**0**	**0**	**3**	**0.0**	**2**	**0**	**1**	**1**	**2**	....	....	....	....	....	....	....	....
	Binghamton Rangers	AHL	69	20	61	81	....	....	....	64	....	....	....	....	....	....	....	....	....	....	3	0	3	3	0	....	....	....
1996-97	**Boston Bruins**	**NHL**	**50**	**5**	**13**	**18**	**5**	**12**	**17**	**32**	**1**	**0**	**0**	**79**	**6.3**	**54**	**16**	**50**	**5**	**–7**	....	....	....	....	....	....	....	....
	Providence Bruins	AHL	19	2	6	8	....	....	....	4	....	....	....	....	....	....	....	....	....	....	10	4	4	8	4	....	....	....
1997-98	Providence Bruins	AHL	75	16	29	45	....	....	....	47	....	....	....	....	....	....	....	....	....	....	....	....	....	....	....	....	....	....

			REGULAR SEASON																		PLAYOFFS							
Season	Club	League	GP	G	A	Pts	AG	AA	APts	PIM	PP	SH	GW	S	%	TGF	PGF	TGA	PGA	+/-	GP	G	A	Pts	PIM	PP	SH	GW
1998-99	**New York Islanders**	**NHL**	**72**	**6**	**18**	**24**	**7**	**17**	**24**	**34**	**0**	**0**	**2**	**111**	**5.4**	**71**	**27**	**56**	**8**	**-4**	....	....	....	....	....	....	....	....
	United States	WC-A	6	2	0	2	....	....	....	0	....	....	....	....	....	....	....	....	....	....	....	....	....	....	....	....	....	....
99-2000	**Montreal Canadiens**	**NHL**	**23**	**0**	**2**	**2**	**0**	**2**	**2**	**8**	**0**	**0**	**0**	**13**	**0.0**	**8**	**2**	**11**	**0**	**-5**	....	....	....	....	....	....	....	....
	Quebec Citadelles	AHL	2	0	0	0	....	....	....	0	....	....	....	....	....	....	....	....	....	....	....	....	....	....	....	....	....	....
	Manitoba Moose	IHL	19	5	4	9	....	....	....	6	....	....	....	....	....	....	....	....	....	....	2	1	1	2	0	....	....	....
	NHL Totals		**149**	**11**	**34**	**45**	**12**	**32**	**44**	**74**	**1**	**0**	**2**	**206**	**5.3**	**135**	**45**	**118**	**14**		....	....	....	....	....	....	....	....

NCAA Championship All-Tournament Team (1992) • WCHA First All-Star Team (1993) • NCAA West First All-American Team (1993) • AHL First All-Star Team (1996) • Won Eddie Shore Award (Outstanding Defenseman — AHL) (1996)

Traded to **NY Rangers** by **Hartford** with Steve Larmer, Nick Kypreos and Hartford's 6th round choice (Yuri Litvinov) in 1994 Entry Draft for Darren Turcotte and James Patrick, November 2, 1993. Signed as a free agent by **Boston**, July 19, 1996. Signed as a free agent by **NY Islanders**, August 17, 1998. Signed as a free agent by **Montreal**, August 20, 1999. Loaned to **Manitoba** (IHL) by **Montreal** for loan of Patrice Tardif to **Quebec** (AHL), March 3, 2000.

• RICHTER, Dave

D – R. 6'5", 225 lbs. b: St. Boniface, Man., 4/8/1960. Minnesota's 10th, 205th overall, in 1980.

Season	Club	League	GP	G	A	Pts	AG	AA	APts	PIM	PP	SH	GW	S	%	TGF	PGF	TGA	PGA	+/-	GP	G	A	Pts	PIM	PP	SH	GW
1978-79	St. Boniface Saints	MJHL	STATISTICS NOT AVAILABLE																									
1979-80	University of Michigan	WCHA	34	0	4	4	....	....	....	54	....	....	....	....	....	....	....	....	....	....	....	....	....	....	....	....	....	....
1980-81	University of Michigan	WCHA	36	2	13	15	....	....	....	56	....	....	....	....	....	....	....	....	....	....	....	....	....	....	....	....	....	....
1981-82	University of Michigan	WCHA	36	9	12	21	....	....	....	78	....	....	....	....	....	....	....	....	....	....	....	....	....	....	....	....	....	....
	Minnesota North Stars	**NHL**	**3**	**0**	**0**	**0**	**0**	**0**	**0**	**11**	**0**	**0**	**0**	**1**	**0.0**	**1**	**0**	**1**	**0**	**0**	....	....	....	....	....	....	....	....
	Nashville South Stars	CHL	2	0	1	1	....	....	....	0	....	....	....	....	....	....	....	....	....	....	....	....	....	....	....	....	....	....
1982-83	**Minnesota North Stars**	**NHL**	**6**	**0**	**0**	**0**	**0**	**0**	**0**	**4**	**0**	**0**	**0**	**3**	**0.0**	**5**	**0**	**5**	**0**	**0**	....	....	....	....	....	....	....	....
	Birmingham South Stars	CHL	69	6	17	23	....	....	....	211	....	....	....	....	....	....	....	....	....	....	13	3	1	4	36	....	....	....
1983-84	**Minnesota North Stars**	**NHL**	**42**	**2**	**3**	**5**	**2**	**2**	**4**	**132**	**0**	**0**	**0**	**22**	**9.1**	**19**	**0**	**33**	**6**	**-8**	**8**	**0**	**0**	**0**	**20**	**0**	**0**	**0**
	Salt Lake Golden Eagles	CHL	10	1	4	5	....	....	....	39	....	....	....	....	....	....	....	....	....	....	....	....	....	....	....	....	....	....
1984-85	**Minnesota North Stars**	**NHL**	**55**	**2**	**8**	**10**	**2**	**5**	**7**	**221**	**0**	**0**	**0**	**29**	**6.9**	**30**	**0**	**55**	**28**	**3**	**9**	**1**	**0**	**1**	**39**	**0**	**0**	**0**
	Springfield Indians	AHL	3	0	0	0	....	....	....	2	....	....	....	....	....	....	....	....	....	....	....	....	....	....	....	....	....	....
1985-86	**Minnesota North Stars**	**NHL**	**14**	**0**	**3**	**3**	**0**	**2**	**2**	**29**	**0**	**0**	**0**	**5**	**0.0**	**5**	**0**	**13**	**2**	**-6**	....	....	....	....	....	....	....	....
	Philadelphia Flyers	**NHL**	**50**	**0**	**2**	**2**	**0**	**1**	**1**	**138**	**0**	**0**	**0**	**17**	**0.0**	**22**	**0**	**32**	**8**	**-2**	**5**	**0**	**0**	**0**	**21**	**0**	**0**	**0**
1986-87	**Vancouver Canucks**	**NHL**	**78**	**2**	**15**	**17**	**2**	**11**	**13**	**172**	**0**	**0**	**0**	**31**	**6.5**	**72**	**0**	**102**	**28**	**-2**	....	....	....	....	....	....	....	....
1987-88	**Vancouver Canucks**	**NHL**	**49**	**2**	**4**	**6**	**2**	**3**	**5**	**224**	**0**	**0**	**0**	**18**	**11.1**	**31**	**1**	**49**	**14**	**-5**	....	....	....	....	....	....	....	....
1988-89	**St. Louis Blues**	**NHL**	**66**	**1**	**5**	**6**	**1**	**4**	**5**	**99**	**0**	**0**	**0**	**23**	**4.3**	**33**	**0**	**77**	**23**	**-21**	....	....	....	....	....	....	....	....
1989-90	**St. Louis Blues**	**NHL**	**2**	**0**	**0**	**0**	**0**	**0**	**0**	**0**	**0**	**0**	**0**	**3**	**0.0**	**0**	**0**	**2**	**0**	**-2**	....	....	....	....	....	....	....	....
	Peoria Rivermen	IHL	9	1	4	5	....	....	....	30	....	....	....	....	....	....	....	....	....	....	....	....	....	....	....	....	....	....
	WEV Wien	Austria	10	0	0	0	....	....	....	2	....	....	....	....	....	....	....	....	....	....	....	....	....	....	....	....	....	....
	Phoenix Roadrunners	IHL	20	0	5	5	....	....	....	49	....	....	....	....	....	....	....	....	....	....	....	....	....	....	....	....	....	....
	Baltimore Skipjacks	AHL	13	0	1	1	....	....	....	13	....	....	....	....	....	....	....	....	....	....	....	....	....	....	....	....	....	....
1990-91	Albany Choppers	IHL	41	0	1	1	....	....	....	128	....	....	....	....	....	....	....	....	....	....	....	....	....	....	....	....	....	....
	Capital District Islanders	AHL	3	0	1	1	....	....	....	0	....	....	....	....	....	....	....	....	....	....	....	....	....	....	....	....	....	....
	NHL Totals		**365**	**9**	**40**	**49**	**9**	**28**	**37**	**1030**	**0**	**0**	**0**	**152**	**5.9**	**218**	**1**	**369**	**109**		**22**	**1**	**0**	**1**	**80**	**0**	**0**	**0**

CHL Second All-Star Team (1983)

Traded to **Philadelphia** by **Minnesota** with Bo Berglund for Ed Hospodar and Todd Bergen, November 29, 1985. Traded to **Vancouver** by **Philadelphia** with Rich Sutter and Vancouver's 3rd round choice (previously acquired, Vancouver selected Don Gibson) in 1986 Entry Draft for J.J. Daigneault, Vancouver's 2nd round choice (Kent Hawley) in 1986 Entry Draft and Vancouver's 5th round choice (later traded back to Vancouver - Vancouver selected Sean Fabian) in 1987 Entry Draft, June 6, 1986. Traded to **St. Louis** by **Vancouver** for Robert Nordmark and St. Louis's 2nd round choice (later traded to Montreal - Montreal selected Craig Darby), September 6, 1988.

• RIDLEY, Mike

Michael Owen Guy C – L. 6', 195 lbs. b: Winnipeg, Man., 7/8/1963.

Season	Club	League	GP	G	A	Pts	AG	AA	APts	PIM	PP	SH	GW	S	%	TGF	PGF	TGA	PGA	+/-	GP	G	A	Pts	PIM	PP	SH	GW
1982-83	St. Boniface Saints	MJHL	48	91	100	191	....	....	....	36	....	....	....	....	....	....	....	....	....	....	....	....	....	....	....	....	....	....
1983-84	University of Manitoba	GPAC	46	39	41	80	....	....	....	....	....	....	....	....	....	....	....	....	....	....	....	....	....	....	....	....	....	....
1984-85	University of Manitoba	GPAC	23	23	36	59	....	....	....	40	....	....	....	....	....	....	....	....	....	....	7	6	2	8	38	....	....	....
1985-86	**New York Rangers**	**NHL**	**80**	**22**	**43**	**65**	**18**	**29**	**47**	**69**	**7**	**0**	**6**	**150**	**14.7**	**97**	**31**	**96**	**30**	**0**	**16**	**6**	**8**	**14**	**26**	**2**	**0**	**1**
1986-87	**New York Rangers**	**NHL**	**38**	**16**	**20**	**36**	**14**	**15**	**29**	**20**	**4**	**0**	**1**	**81**	**19.8**	**50**	**17**	**48**	**5**	**-10**	....	....	....	....	....	....	....	....
	Washington Capitals	**NHL**	**40**	**15**	**19**	**34**	**13**	**14**	**27**	**20**	**6**	**0**	**3**	**68**	**22.1**	**51**	**13**	**42**	**3**	**-1**	**7**	**2**	**1**	**3**	**6**	**0**	**0**	**1**
1987-88	**Washington Capitals**	**NHL**	**70**	**28**	**31**	**59**	**24**	**22**	**46**	**22**	**12**	**0**	**3**	**134**	**20.9**	**94**	**38**	**58**	**3**	**1**	**14**	**6**	**5**	**11**	**10**	**1**	**0**	**0**
1988-89	**Washington Capitals**	**NHL**	**80**	**41**	**48**	**89**	**35**	**34**	**69**	**49**	**16**	**0**	**9**	**187**	**21.9**	**117**	**45**	**57**	**2**	**17**	**6**	**0**	**5**	**5**	**2**	**0**	**0**	**0**
1989-90	Washington Capitals	Fr-Tour	4	2	0	2	....	....	....	10	....	....	....	....	....	....	....	....	....	....	....	....	....	....	....	....	....	....
	Washington Capitals	**NHL**	**74**	**30**	**43**	**73**	**26**	**31**	**57**	**27**	**8**	**3**	**3**	**124**	**24.2**	**94**	**26**	**94**	**26**	**0**	**14**	**3**	**4**	**7**	**8**	**0**	**1**	**0**
1990-91	**Washington Capitals**	**NHL**	**79**	**23**	**48**	**71**	**21**	**37**	**58**	**26**	**6**	**5**	**4**	**155**	**14.8**	**105**	**32**	**87**	**23**	**9**	**11**	**3**	**4**	**7**	**8**	**1**	**0**	**1**
1991-92	**Washington Capitals**	**NHL**	**80**	**29**	**40**	**69**	**26**	**30**	**56**	**38**	**5**	**5**	**3**	**123**	**23.6**	**99**	**27**	**103**	**34**	**3**	**7**	**0**	**11**	**11**	**0**	**0**	**0**	**0**
1992-93	**Washington Capitals**	**NHL**	**84**	**26**	**56**	**82**	**22**	**39**	**61**	**44**	**6**	**2**	**3**	**148**	**17.6**	**124**	**48**	**118**	**47**	**5**	**6**	**1**	**5**	**6**	**0**	**1**	**0**	**0**
1993-94	**Washington Capitals**	**NHL**	**81**	**26**	**44**	**70**	**24**	**34**	**58**	**24**	**10**	**2**	**4**	**144**	**18.1**	**105**	**35**	**84**	**29**	**15**	**11**	**4**	**6**	**10**	**6**	**0**	**0**	**0**
1994-95	**Toronto Maple Leafs**	**NHL**	**48**	**10**	**27**	**37**	**18**	**40**	**58**	**14**	**2**	**2**	**1**	**88**	**11.4**	**50**	**11**	**47**	**9**	**1**	**7**	**3**	**1**	**4**	**2**	**1**	**0**	**1**
1995-96	**Vancouver Canucks**	**NHL**	**37**	**6**	**15**	**21**	**6**	**12**	**18**	**29**	**2**	**0**	**1**	**32**	**18.8**	**30**	**8**	**35**	**10**	**-3**	**5**	**0**	**0**	**0**	**2**	**0**	**0**	**0**
1996-97	**Vancouver Canucks**	**NHL**	**75**	**20**	**32**	**52**	**21**	**28**	**49**	**42**	**3**	**0**	**5**	**79**	**25.3**	**78**	**15**	**67**	**4**	**0**	....	....	....	....	....	....	....	....
1997-98	Manitoba Moose	IHL	4	2	2	4	....	....	....	0	....	....	....	....	....	....	....	....	....	....	....	....	....	....	....	....	....	....
	NHL Totals		**866**	**292**	**466**	**758**	**268**	**365**	**633**	**424**	**87**	**19**	**46**	**1513**	**19.3**	**1094**	**346**	**936**	**225**		**104**	**28**	**50**	**78**	**70**	**6**	**1**	**4**

Canadian University Player of the Year; CIAU All-Canadian, GPAC MVP and First All-Star Team (1984) • CIAU All-Canadian, GPAC First All-Star Team (1985) • NHL All-Rookie Team (1986)

Played in NHL All-Star Game (1989)

Signed as a free agent by **NY Rangers**, September 26, 1985. Traded to **Washington** by **NY Rangers** with Bob Crawford and Kelly Miller for Bob Carpenter and Washington's 2nd round choice (Jason Prosofsky) in 1989 Entry Draft, January 1, 1987. Traded to **Toronto** by **Washington** with St. Louis' 1st round choice (previously acquired, Toronto selected Eric Fichaud) in 1994 Entry Draft for Rob Pearson and Philadelphia's 1st round choice (previously acquired, Washington selected Nolan Baumgartner) in 1994 Entry Draft, June 28, 1994. Traded to **Vancouver** by **Toronto** for Sergio Momesso, July 8, 1995.

• RILEY, Bill

James William RW – R. 5'11", 195 lbs. b: Amherst, N.S., 9/20/1950.

Season	Club	League	GP	G	A	Pts	AG	AA	APts	PIM	PP	SH	GW	S	%	TGF	PGF	TGA	PGA	+/-	GP	G	A	Pts	PIM	PP	SH	GW
1968-69	Amherst Ramblers	MJrHL	48	32	32	64	....	....	....	....	....	....	....	....	....	....	....	....	....	....	....	....	....	....	....	....	....	....
1969-70	Amherst Ramblers	MJrHL	30	34	28	62	....	....	....	....	....	....	....	....	....	....	....	....	....	....	1	0	0	0	0	....	....	....
1970-71	Amherst Square M's	MJrHL-B	STATISTICS NOT AVAILABLE																									
1971-72	Kitmat Eagles	BCSHL	STATISTICS NOT AVAILABLE																									
1972-73	Kitmat Eagles	BCSHL	40	56	32	*88	....	....	....	....	....	....	....	....	....	....	....	....	....	....	....	....	....	....	....	....	....	....
1973-74	Kitmat Eagles	BCSHL	40	76	42	*118	....	....	....	....	....	....	....	....	....	....	....	....	....	....	....	....	....	....	....	....	....	....
1974-75	**Washington Capitals**	**NHL**	**1**	**0**	**0**	**0**	**0**	**0**	**0**	**0**	**0**	**0**	**0**	**0**	**0.0**	**0**	**0**	**1**	**0**	**-1**	....	....	....	....	....	....	....	....
	Dayton Gems	IHL	63	12	16	28	....	....	....	279	....	....	....	....	....	....	....	....	....	....	14	5	0	5	29	....	....	....
1975-76	Dayton Gems	IHL	69	35	31	66	....	....	....	301	....	....	....	....	....	....	....	....	....	....	15	6	10	16	54	....	....	....
1976-77	**Washington Capitals**	**NHL**	**43**	**13**	**14**	**27**	**12**	**11**	**23**	**124**	**5**	**0**	**2**	**45**	**28.9**	**43**	**13**	**26**	**0**	**4**	....	....	....	....	....	....	....	....
	Dayton Gems	IHL	30	19	15	34	....	....	....	69	....	....	....	....	....	....	....	....	....	....	....	....	....	....	....	....	....	....
1977-78	**Washington Capitals**	**NHL**	**57**	**13**	**12**	**25**	**12**	**9**	**21**	**125**	**5**	**0**	**0**	**67**	**19.4**	**42**	**14**	**43**	**0**	**-15**	....	....	....	....	....	....	....	....
1978-79	**Washington Capitals**	**NHL**	**24**	**2**	**2**	**4**	**2**	**1**	**3**	**64**	**0**	**0**	**0**	**24**	**8.3**	**5**	**0**	**11**	**0**	**-6**	....	....	....	....	....	....	....	....
	Hershey Bears	AHL	51	15	15	30	....	....	....	118	....	....	....	....	....	....	....	....	....	....	4	1	0	1	8	....	....	....
1979-80	**Winnipeg Jets**	**NHL**	**14**	**3**	**2**	**5**	**3**	**1**	**4**	**7**	**2**	**0**	**1**	**11**	**27.3**	**8**	**4**	**4**	**0**	**0**	....	....	....	....	....	....	....	....
	Nova Scotia Voyageurs	AHL	63	31	33	64	....	....	....	157	....	....	....	....	....	....	....	....	....	....	4	0	0	0	2	....	....	....
1980-81	New Brunswick Hawks	AHL	46	12	25	37	....	....	....	107	....	....	....	....	....	....	....	....	....	....	12	3	3	6	49	....	....	....
1981-82	New Brunswick Hawks	AHL	80	32	30	62	....	....	....	104	....	....	....	....	....	....	....	....	....	....	15	8	8	16	6	....	....	....
1982-83	Moncton Alpines	AHL	73	33	30	63	....	....	....	134	....	....	....	....	....	....	....	....	....	....	....	....	....	....	....	....	....	....
1983-84	Nova Scotia Voyageurs	AHL	78	24	24	48	....	....	....	79	....	....	....	....	....	....	....	....	....	....	12	2	5	7	8	....	....	....
1984-85	Moncton Jr. Midland Hawks	MJrHL	DID NOT PLAY – COACHING																									
1985-86	Moncton Junction Club	MCIHL	STATISTICS NOT AVAILABLE																									
1986-87	St. John's Capitals	Nfld-Sr.	44	29	33	62	....	....	....	....	....	....	....	....	....	....	....	....	....	....	....	....	....	....	....	....	....	....

Season	Club	League	REGULAR SEASON																		PLAYOFFS							
			GP	G	A	Pts	AG	AA	APts	PIM	PP	SH	GW	S	%	TGF	PGF	TGA	PGA	+/–	GP	G	A	Pts	PIM	PP	SH	GW
1987-88	St. John's Capitals	Nfld-Sr.	37	39	63	102	....	....	....	43	....	....	....	....	....	....	....	....	....	....	....	....	....	....	....	....	....	....
1988-89	St. John's Capitals	Nfld-Sr.	29	25	36	61	....	....	....	....	....	....	....	....	....	....	....	....	....	....	....	....	....	....	....	....	....	....
1989-90	Amherst Ramblers	MJrHL	DID NOT PLAY – COACHING																									
	NHL Totals		**139**	**31**	**30**	**61**	**29**	**22**	**51**	**320**	**12**	**0**	**3**	**147**	**21.1**	**98**	**31**	**85**	**0**		....	....	....	....	....	....	....	....

Signed as a free agent by **Washington** to a five-game tryout contract, December 20, 1974. Signed as a free agent by **Washington**, January 19, 1977. Claimed by **Winnipeg** from **Washington** in Expansion Draft, June 3, 1979. Signed as a free agent by **Toronto**, February 25, 1981.

• RIOUX, Gerry

RW – R. 5'11", 195 lbs. b: Iroquois Falls, Ont., 2/17/1959.

Season	Club	League	GP	G	A	Pts	AG	AA	APts	PIM	PP	SH	GW	S	%	TGF	PGF	TGA	PGA	+/–	GP	G	A	Pts	PIM	PP	SH	GW
1976-77	Sault Ste. Marie Greyhounds	OMJHL	61	5	15	20	....	....	....	126	....	....	....	....	....	....	....	....	....	....	9	1	0	1	23	....	....	....
1977-78	Sault Ste. Marie Greyhounds	OMJHL	25	0	4	4	....	....	....	28	....	....	....	....	....	....	....	....	....	....	....	....	....	....	....	....	....	....
	Niagara Falls Flyers	OMJHL	29	2	5	7	....	....	....	34	....	....	....	....	....	....	....	....	....	....	....	....	....	....	....	....	....	....
1978-79	Windsor Spitfires	OMJHL	65	11	14	25	....	....	....	195	....	....	....	....	....	....	....	....	....	....	7	0	3	0	11	....	....	....
1979-80	**Winnipeg Jets**	**NHL**	**8**	**0**	**0**	**0**	**0**	**0**	**0**	**6**	**0**	**0**	**0**	**4**	**0.0**	**0**	**0**	**2**	**0**	**–2**	....	....	....	....	....	....	....	....
	Tulsa Oilers	CHL	57	9	11	20	....	....	....	172	....	....	....	....	....	....	....	....	....	....	....	....	....	....	....	....	....	....
1980-81	Tulsa Oilers	CHL	22	2	2	4	....	....	....	48	....	....	....	....	....	....	....	....	....	....	....	....	....	....	....	....	....	....
	Fort Wayne Komets	IHL	3	0	1	1	....	....	....	0	....	....	....	....	....	....	....	....	....	....	....	....	....	....	....	....	....	....
	NHL Totals		**8**	**0**	**0**	**0**	**0**	**0**	**0**	**6**	**0**	**0**	**0**	**4**	**0.0**	**0**	**0**	**2**	**0**		....	....	....	....	....	....	....	....

Signed as a free agent by **Winnipeg**, October, 1979.

• RIOUX, Pierre

RW – R. 5'9", 165 lbs. b: Quebec City, Que., 2/1/1962.

Season	Club	League	GP	G	A	Pts	AG	AA	APts	PIM	PP	SH	GW	S	%	TGF	PGF	TGA	PGA	+/–	GP	G	A	Pts	PIM	PP	SH	GW
1977-78	Ste-Foy Gouverneurs	QAAA	39	22	27	49	....	....	....	....	....	....	....	....	....	....	....	....	....	....	....	....	....	....	....	....	....	....
1978-79	Ste-Foy Gouverneurs	QAAA	39	38	59	97	....	....	....	....	....	....	....	....	....	....	....	....	....	....	....	....	....	....	....	....	....	....
1979-80	Shawinigan Cataractes	QMJHL	70	27	47	74	....	....	....	24	....	....	....	....	....	....	....	....	....	....	7	2	2	4	4	....	....	....
1980-81	Shawinigan Cataractes	QMJHL	69	53	77	130	....	....	....	16	....	....	....	....	....	....	....	....	....	....	5	2	3	5	6	....	....	....
1981-82	Shawinigan Cataractes	QMJHL	57	*66	86	152	....	....	....	50	....	....	....	....	....	....	....	....	....	....	14	15	26	41	8	....	....	....
	Canada	WJC-A	7	3	3	6	....	....	....	4	....	....	....	....	....	....	....	....	....	....	....	....	....	....	....	....	....	....
1982-83	**Calgary Flames**	**NHL**	**14**	**1**	**2**	**3**	**1**	**1**	**2**	**4**	**0**	**0**	**0**	**9**	**11.1**	**4**	**0**	**8**	**1**	**–3**	....	....	....	....	....	....	....	....
	Colorado Flames	CHL	59	26	36	62	....	....	....	18	....	....	....	....	....	....	....	....	....	....	....	....	....	....	....	....	....	....
1983-84	Colorado Flames	CHL	65	37	46	83	....	....	....	22	....	....	....	....	....	....	....	....	....	....	6	2	7	9	4	....	....	....
1984-85	Moncton Golden Flames	AHL	69	25	66	91	....	....	....	14	....	....	....	....	....	....	....	....	....	....	....	....	....	....	....	....	....	....
1985-86	EV Zug	Switz-2	....	....	....	....	....	....	....	....	....	....	....	....	....	....	....	....	....	....	....	....	....	....	....	....	....	....
	Moncton Golden Flames	AHL	5	0	0	0	....	....	....	0	....	....	....	....	....	....	....	....	....	....	....	....	....	....	....	....	....	....
	Binghamton Whalers	AHL	6	0	2	2	....	....	....	0	....	....	....	....	....	....	....	....	....	....	....	....	....	....	....	....	....	....
1986-87	Krefelder EV	Germany-2	46	*72	73	*145	....	....	....	50	....	....	....	....	....	....	....	....	....	....	13	23	31	54	9	....	....	....
1987-88	KalPa Kuopio	Finland	41	21	20	41	....	....	....	44	....	....	....	....	....	....	....	....	....	....	....	....	....	....	....	....	....	....
1988-89	Ratingen Lowen	Germany-2	33	29	46	75	....	....	....	21	....	....	....	....	....	....	....	....	....	....	12	7	18	25	15	....	....	....
1989-90	SV Bayrueth	Germany-2	36	*57	51	108	....	....	....	8	....	....	....	....	....	....	....	....	....	....	18	24	27	51	8	....	....	....
1990-91	SV Bayrueth	Germany-2	50	57	71	128	....	....	....	78	....	....	....	....	....	....	....	....	....	....	....	....	....	....	....	....	....	....
1991-92	SV Bayrueth	Germany-2	29	22	42	64	....	....	....	22	....	....	....	....	....	....	....	....	....	....	14	7	16	23	2	....	....	....
1992-93	SV Bayrueth	Germany-2	45	41	52	93	....	....	....	14	....	....	....	....	....	....	....	....	....	....	....	....	....	....	....	....	....	....
1993-94	Dusseldorfer EG	Germany	42	12	24	36	....	....	....	8	....	....	....	....	....	....	....	....	....	....	....	....	....	....	....	....	....	....
1994-95	Dusseldorfer EG	Germany	43	17	37	54	....	....	....	8	....	....	....	....	....	....	....	....	....	....	10	1	10	11	6	....	....	....
1995-96	Heilbronner EC	Germany-2	46	43	69	112	....	....	....	34	....	....	....	....	....	....	....	....	....	....	9	5	9	14	4	....	....	....
	Augsburg Panther	Germany	1	1	1	2	....	....	....	0	....	....	....	....	....	....	....	....	....	....	....	....	....	....	....	....	....	....
1996-97	Heilbronner EC	Germany-2	21	13	25	38	....	....	....	4	....	....	....	....	....	....	....	....	....	....	....	....	....	....	....	....	....	....
	Augsburger Panther	Germany	27	14	16	30	....	....	....	2	....	....	....	....	....	....	....	....	....	....	4	3	1	4	0	....	....	....
1997-98	Augsburger Panther	Germany	50	22	28	50	....	....	....	4	....	....	....	....	....	....	....	....	....	....	....	....	....	....	....	....	....	....
1998-99	Augsburger Panther	Germany	49	18	23	41	....	....	....	6	....	....	....	....	....	....	....	....	....	....	5	4	2	6	0	....	....	....
99-2000	Kassel Huskies	Germany	24	3	10	13	....	....	....	4	....	....	....	....	....	....	....	....	....	....	8	0	3	3	4	....	....	....
	NHL Totals		**14**	**1**	**2**	**3**	**1**	**1**	**2**	**4**	**0**	**0**	**0**	**9**	**11.1**	**4**	**0**	**8**	**1**		....	....	....	....	....	....	....	....

QMJHL First All-Star Team (1982) • AHL First All-Star Team (1985)

Signed as a free agent by **Calgary**, August 24, 1982.

• RISEBROUGH, Doug

Douglas John C – L. 5'11", 180 lbs. b: Guelph, Ont., 1/29/1954. Montreal's 2nd, 7th overall, in 1974.

Season	Club	League	GP	G	A	Pts	AG	AA	APts	PIM	PP	SH	GW	S	%	TGF	PGF	TGA	PGA	+/–	GP	G	A	Pts	PIM	PP	SH	GW
1971-72	Guelph GMCs	OJHL	56	19	33	52	....	....	....	127	....	....	....	....	....	....	....	....	....	....	....	....	....	....	....	....	....	....
1972-73	Guelph Biltmores	OJHL	60	*47	*60	*107	....	....	....	229	....	....	....	....	....	....	....	....	....	....	....	....	....	....	....	....	....	....
1973-74	Kitchener Rangers	OMJHL	46	25	27	52	....	....	....	114	....	....	....	....	....	....	....	....	....	....	....	....	....	....	....	....	....	....
1974-75	**Montreal Canadiens**	**NHL**	**64**	**15**	**32**	**47**	**13**	**24**	**37**	**198**	**2**	**0**	**2**	**111**	**13.5**	**69**	**7**	**35**	**0**	**27**	**11**	**3**	**5**	**8**	**37**	**0**	**0**	**0**
	Nova Scotia Voyageurs	AHL	7	5	4	9	....	....	....	55	....	....	....	....	....	....	....	....	....	....	....	....	....	....	....	....	....	....
1975-76♦	**Montreal Canadiens**	**NHL**	**80**	**16**	**28**	**44**	**14**	**21**	**35**	**180**	**1**	**0**	**3**	**143**	**11.2**	**64**	**11**	**36**	**1**	**18**	**13**	**0**	**3**	**3**	**30**	**0**	**0**	**0**
1976-77♦	**Montreal Canadiens**	**NHL**	**78**	**22**	**38**	**60**	**20**	**29**	**49**	**132**	**1**	**0**	**6**	**142**	**15.5**	**80**	**11**	**36**	**0**	**33**	**12**	**2**	**3**	**5**	**16**	**0**	**0**	**0**
1977-78♦	**Montreal Canadiens**	**NHL**	**72**	**18**	**23**	**41**	**16**	**18**	**34**	**97**	**1**	**0**	**3**	**115**	**15.7**	**66**	**6**	**34**	**4**	**30**	**15**	**2**	**2**	**4**	**17**	**0**	**1**	**1**
1978-79♦	**Montreal Canadiens**	**NHL**	**48**	**10**	**15**	**25**	**9**	**11**	**20**	**62**	**0**	**0**	**2**	**83**	**12.0**	**42**	**0**	**22**	**2**	**22**	**15**	**1**	**6**	**7**	**32**	**0**	**0**	**1**
1979-80	**Montreal Canadiens**	**NHL**	**44**	**8**	**10**	**18**	**7**	**7**	**14**	**81**	**0**	**0**	**0**	**82**	**9.8**	**26**	**1**	**30**	**3**	**–2**	....	....	....	....	....	....	....	....
1980-81	**Montreal Canadiens**	**NHL**	**48**	**13**	**21**	**34**	**10**	**14**	**24**	**93**	**1**	**0**	**1**	**94**	**13.8**	**41**	**5**	**34**	**5**	**7**	**3**	**1**	**0**	**1**	**0**	**1**	**0**	**0**
1981-82	**Montreal Canadiens**	**NHL**	**59**	**15**	**18**	**33**	**12**	**12**	**24**	**116**	**2**	**2**	**2**	**80**	**18.8**	**50**	**5**	**33**	**11**	**23**	**5**	**2**	**1**	**3**	**11**	**0**	**0**	**0**
1982-83	**Calgary Flames**	**NHL**	**71**	**21**	**37**	**58**	**17**	**26**	**43**	**138**	**3**	**0**	**1**	**145**	**14.5**	**79**	**5**	**89**	**28**	**13**	**9**	**1**	**3**	**4**	**18**	**0**	**0**	**0**
1983-84	**Calgary Flames**	**NHL**	**77**	**23**	**28**	**51**	**18**	**19**	**37**	**161**	**0**	**1**	**3**	**161**	**14.3**	**78**	**3**	**94**	**30**	**11**	**11**	**2**	**1**	**3**	**25**	**0**	**0**	**0**
1984-85	**Calgary Flames**	**NHL**	**15**	**7**	**5**	**12**	**6**	**3**	**9**	**49**	**0**	**1**	**4**	**33**	**21.2**	**14**	**0**	**13**	**9**	**10**	**4**	**0**	**3**	**3**	**12**	**0**	**0**	**0**
1985-86	**Calgary Flames**	**NHL**	**62**	**15**	**28**	**43**	**12**	**19**	**31**	**169**	**0**	**3**	**1**	**92**	**16.3**	**58**	**0**	**65**	**29**	**22**	**22**	**7**	**9**	**16**	**38**	**0**	**1**	**1**
1986-87	**Calgary Flames**	**NHL**	**22**	**2**	**3**	**5**	**2**	**2**	**4**	**66**	**0**	**0**	**0**	**19**	**10.5**	**9**	**0**	**20**	**9**	**–2**	**4**	**0**	**1**	**1**	**2**	**0**	**0**	**0**
	NHL Totals		**740**	**185**	**286**	**471**	**156**	**205**	**361**	**1542**	**11**	**7**	**28**	**1300**	**14.2**	**676**	**54**	**541**	**131**		**124**	**21**	**37**	**58**	**238**	**1**	**2**	**3**

Traded to **Calgary** by **Montreal** with Montreal's 2nd round choice (later traded to Minnesota — Minnesota selected Frantisek Musil) in 1983 Entry Draft for Washington's 2nd round choice (previously acquired, Montreal selected Todd Francis) in 1983 Entry Draft and Calgary's 3rd round choice (Graeme Bonar) in 1984 Entry Draft, September 11, 1982.

• RISSLING, Gary

Gary Daniel LW – L. 5'9", 175 lbs. b: Saskatoon, Sask., 8/8/1956.

Season	Club	League	GP	G	A	Pts	AG	AA	APts	PIM	PP	SH	GW	S	%	TGF	PGF	TGA	PGA	+/–	GP	G	A	Pts	PIM	PP	SH	GW
1973-74	Spruce Grove Mets	AJHL	46	29	31	60	....	....	....	132	....	....	....	....	....	....	....	....	....	....	....	....	....	....	....	....	....	....
1974-75	Spruce Grove Mets	AJHL	5	2	2	4	....	....	....	2	....	....	....	....	....	....	....	....	....	....	....	....	....	....	....	....	....	....
	Edmonton Oil Kings	WCJHL	69	19	35	54	....	....	....	228	....	....	....	....	....	....	....	....	....	....	....	....	....	....	....	....	....	....
1975-76	Edmonton Oil Kings	WCJHL	18	5	9	14	....	....	....	25	....	....	....	....	....	....	....	....	....	....	....	....	....	....	....	....	....	....
	Calgary Centennials	WCJHL	47	29	38	67	....	....	....	196	....	....	....	....	....	....	....	....	....	....	....	....	....	....	....	....	....	....
1976-77	Calgary Wranglers	WCJHL	68	40	40	80	....	....	....	317	....	....	....	....	....	....	....	....	....	....	9	9	7	16	12	....	....	....
1977-78	Port Huron Flags	IHL	79	29	34	63	....	....	....	341	....	....	....	....	....	....	....	....	....	....	17	7	10	17	131	....	....	....
1978-79	**Washington Capitals**	**NHL**	**26**	**3**	**3**	**6**	**3**	**2**	**5**	**127**	**1**	**0**	**1**	**16**	**18.8**	**11**	**1**	**15**	**0**	**–5**	....	....	....	....	....	....	....	....
	Hershey Bears	AHL	52	14	20	34	....	....	....	337	....	....	....	....	....	....	....	....	....	....	4	0	0	0	18	....	....	....
1979-80	**Washington Capitals**	**NHL**	**11**	**0**	**1**	**1**	**0**	**1**	**1**	**49**	**0**	**0**	**0**	**5**	**0.0**	**1**	**0**	**7**	**0**	**–6**	....	....	....	....	....	....	....	....
	Hershey Bears	AHL	46	16	24	40	....	....	....	279	....	....	....	....	....	....	....	....	....	....	14	3	5	8	*87	....	....	....
1980-81	Hershey Bears	AHL	4	1	1	2	....	....	....	74	....	....	....	....	....	....	....	....	....	....	....	....	....	....	....	....	....	....
	Birmingham Bulls	CHL	19	5	7	12	....	....	....	161	....	....	....	....	....	....	....	....	....	....	....	....	....	....	....	....	....	....
	Pittsburgh Penguins	**NHL**	**25**	**1**	**0**	**1**	**1**	**0**	**1**	**143**	**0**	**0**	**0**	**16**	**6.3**	**1**	**0**	**5**	**0**	**–4**	**5**	**0**	**1**	**1**	**4**	**0**	**0**	**0**
1981-82	**Pittsburgh Penguins**	**NHL**	**16**	**0**	**0**	**0**	**0**	**0**	**0**	**55**	**0**	**0**	**0**	**1**	**0.0**	**1**	**0**	**3**	**0**	**–2**	....	....	....	....	....	....	....	....
	Erie Blades	AHL	29	7	15	22	....	....	....	185	....	....	....	....	....	....	....	....	....	....	....	....	....	....	....	....	....	....
1982-83	**Pittsburgh Penguins**	**NHL**	**40**	**5**	**4**	**9**	**4**	**3**	**7**	**128**	**0**	**0**	**0**	**35**	**14.3**	**10**	**1**	**28**	**2**	**–17**	....	....	....	....	....	....	....	....
	Baltimore Skipjacks	AHL	38	14	17	31	....	....	....	136	....	....	....	....	....	....	....	....	....	....	....	....	....	....	....	....	....	....
1983-84	**Pittsburgh Penguins**	**NHL**	**47**	**4**	**13**	**17**	**3**	**9**	**12**	**297**	**1**	**0**	**1**	**40**	**10.0**	**24**	**5**	**32**	**4**	**–9**	....	....	....	....	....	....	....	....
	Baltimore Skipjacks	AHL	30	12	13	25	....	....	....	47	....	....	....	....	....	....	....	....	....	....	....	....	....	....	....	....	....	....

			REGULAR SEASON																		PLAYOFFS							
Season	Club	League	GP	G	A	Pts	AG	AA	APts	PIM	PP	SH	GW	S	%	TGF	PGF	TGA	PGA	+/–	GP	G	A	Pts	PIM	PP	SH	GW
1984-85	**Pittsburgh Penguins**	**NHL**	**56**	**10**	**9**	**19**	**8**	**6**	**14**	**209**	**0**	**0**	**0**	**52**	**19.2**	**30**	**1**	**38**	**3**	**–6**								
	Baltimore Skipjacks	AHL	22	9	17	26				60																		
1985-86	Baltimore Skipjacks	AHL	76	19	34	53				340																		
1986-87	Baltimore Skipjacks	AHL	66	15	23	38				285																		
	NHL Totals		**221**	**23**	**30**	**53**	**19**	**21**	**40**	**1008**	**2**	**0**	**2**	**165**	**13.9**	**78**	**8**	**128**	**9**		**5**	**0**	**1**	**1**	**4**	**0**	**0**	**0**

Signed as a free agent by **Washington**, December 4, 1978. Traded to **Pittsburgh** by **Washington** for Pittsburgh's 5th round choice (Peter Sidorkiewicz) in 1981 Entry Draft, January 2, 1981.

• RITCHIE, Bob

Robert LW – L. 5'10", 170 lbs. b: Laverlochere, Que., 2/20/1955. Philadelphia's 2nd, 54th overall, in 1975.

			REGULAR SEASON																		PLAYOFFS							
Season	Club	League	GP	G	A	Pts	AG	AA	APts	PIM	PP	SH	GW	S	%	TGF	PGF	TGA	PGA	+/–	GP	G	A	Pts	PIM	PP	SH	GW
1971-72	Sorel Black Hawks	QMJHL	62	18	24	42				31											4	1	1	2	15			
1972-73	Sorel Black Hawks	QMJHL	50	13	30	43				20																		
1973-74	Sorel Black Hawks	QMJHL	70	37	58	95				23																		
1974-75	Sorel Black Hawks	QMJHL	72	55	56	111				48																		
1975-76	Richmond Robins	AHL	42	12	10	22				19																		
1976-77	**Philadelphia Flyers**	**NHL**	**1**	**0**	**0**	**0**	**0**	**0**	**0**	**0**	**0**	**0**	**0**	**1**	**0.0**	**0**	**0**	**0**	**0**	**0**								
	Springfield Indians	AHL	54	19	25	44				20																		
	Detroit Red Wings	**NHL**	**17**	**6**	**2**	**8**	**5**	**2**	**7**	**10**	**1**	**0**	**0**	**33**	**18.2**	**12**	**3**	**25**	**3**	**–13**								
1977-78	**Detroit Red Wings**	**NHL**	**11**	**2**	**2**	**4**	**2**	**2**	**4**	**0**	**1**	**0**	**0**	**18**	**11.1**	**5**	**2**	**4**	**0**	**–1**								
	Kansas City Red Wings	CHL	52	15	21	36				16																		
	NHL Totals		**29**	**8**	**4**	**12**	**7**	**4**	**11**	**10**	**2**	**0**	**0**	**52**	**15.4**	**17**	**5**	**29**	**3**									

Traded to **Detroit** by **Philadelphia** with Terry Murray, Steve Coates and Dave Kelly for Rick Lapointe and Mike Korney, February 17, 1977.

• RITCHIE, Byron

C – L. 5'10", 185 lbs. b: Burnaby, B.C., 4/24/1977. Hartford's 6th, 165th overall, in 1995.

			REGULAR SEASON																		PLAYOFFS							
Season	Club	League	GP	G	A	Pts	AG	AA	APts	PIM	PP	SH	GW	S	%	TGF	PGF	TGA	PGA	+/–	GP	G	A	Pts	PIM	PP	SH	GW
1992-93	North Delta Bantam Selects	BCAHA	60	102	151	253				147																		
1993-94	Lethbridge Hurricanes	WHL	44	4	11	15				44											6	0	0	0	14			
1994-95	Lethbridge Hurricanes	WHL	58	22	28	50				132																		
1995-96	Lethbridge Hurricanes	WHL	66	55	51	106				163											4	0	2	2	4			
	Springfield Falcons	AHL	6	2	1	3				4											8	0	3	3	0			
1996-97	Lethbridge Hurricanes	WHL	63	50	76	126				115											18	*16	12	*28	28			
1997-98	Beast of New Haven	AHL	65	13	18	31				97																		
1998-99	**Carolina Hurricanes**	**NHL**	**3**	**0**	**0**	**0**	**0**	**0**	**0**	**0**	**0**	**0**	**0**	**0**	**0.0**	**0**	**0**	**0**	**0**	**0**								
	Beast of New Haven	AHL	66	24	33	57				139																		
99-2000	**Carolina Hurricanes**	**NHL**	**26**	**0**	**2**	**2**	**0**	**2**	**2**	**17**	**0**	**0**	**0**	**13**	**0.0**	**3**	**1**	**12**	**0**	**–10**								
	Cincinnati Cyclones	IHL	34	8	13	21				81											10	1	6	7	32			
	NHL Totals		**29**	**0**	**2**	**2**	**0**	**2**	**2**	**17**	**0**	**0**	**0**	**13**	**0.0**	**3**	**1**	**12**	**0**									

WHL East Second All-Star Team (1996, 1997)

Rights transferred to **Carolina** after **Hartford** franchise relocated, June 25, 1997.

• RIVARD, Bob

Joseph Robert C/LW – L. 5'8", 155 lbs. b: Sherbrooke, Que., 8/1/1939.

			REGULAR SEASON																		PLAYOFFS							
Season	Club	League	GP	G	A	Pts	AG	AA	APts	PIM	PP	SH	GW	S	%	TGF	PGF	TGA	PGA	+/–	GP	G	A	Pts	PIM	PP	SH	GW
1958-59	Peterborough Petes	OHA-Jr.	10	3	2	5				4											19	0	2	2	0			
	Peterborough Petes	Mem-Cup	12	4	0	4				0																		
1959-60	Peterborough Petes	OHA-Jr.	48	22	31	53				18											12	8	11	19	10			
	Montreal Royals	EPHL																			4	0	0	0	2			
1960-61	Toledo–Indianapolis	IHL	40	20	25	45				23																		
1961-62	Indianapolis Chiefs	IHL	68	40	51	91				33																		
1962-63	Fort Wayne Komets	IHL	70	20	36	56				25											11	8	2	10	6			
1963-64	Fort Wayne Komets	IHL	70	34	62	96				38											12	3	11	14	4			
1964-65	Fort Wayne Komets	IHL	70	46	70	116				44											9	7	8	15	2			
1965-66	Fort Wayne Komets	IHL	70	42	*91	*133				32											6	4	5	9	2			
1966-67	Quebec Aces	AHL	71	22	40	62				22											5	3	2	5	0			
1967-68	**Pittsburgh Penguins**	**NHL**	**27**	**5**	**12**	**17**	**6**	**12**	**18**	**4**	**1**	**0**	**1**	**62**	**8.1**	**21**	**4**	**19**	**2**	**0**								
	Baltimore Clippers	AHL	41	14	24	38				12																		
1968-69	Quebec Aces	AHL	34	3	16	19				18																		
	Baltimore Clippers	AHL	39	17	21	38				22											4	0	3	3	2			
1969-70	Baltimore Clippers	AHL	68	21	35	56				16											5	2	3	5	0			
1970-71	Baltimore Clippers	AHL	68	26	16	42				16											6	1	2	3	6			
1971-72	Baltimore Clippers	AHL	75	23	35	58				18											18	*10	*15	*25	8			
1972-73	Baltimore Clippers	AHL	76	25	50	75				28																		
1973-74	Baltimore Clippers	AHL	76	36	56	92				48											9	4	5	9	0			
1974-75	Baltimore Clippers	AHL	46	14	23	37				26																		
	Fort Wayne Komets	IHL	24	7	14	21				16																		
1975-76	Lindsay Lancers	OHA-Sr.	30	12	17	29				14																		
	NHL Totals		**27**	**5**	**12**	**17**	**6**	**12**	**18**	**4**	**1**	**0**	**1**	**62**	**8.1**	**21**	**4**	**19**	**2**									

IHL First All-Star Team (1965) • IHL Second All-Star Team (1966) • Won Leo P. Lamoureux Memorial Trophy (Top Scorer - IHL) (1966) • Won Dudley "Red" Garrett Memorial Award (Top Rookie - AHL) (1967)

Claimed by **Pittsburgh** from **Montreal** in Expansion Draft, June 6, 1967. Loaned to **Philadelphia** by **Pittsburgh** for cash, September, 1968. Traded to **Baltimore** (AHL) by **Pittsburgh** to complete transaction that sent Jim Morrison to Pittsburgh (October, 1969), November, 1969.

• RIVERS, Jamie

D – L. 6', 197 lbs. b: Ottawa, Ont., 3/16/1975. St. Louis' 2nd, 63rd overall, in 1993.

			REGULAR SEASON																		PLAYOFFS							
Season	Club	League	GP	G	A	Pts	AG	AA	APts	PIM	PP	SH	GW	S	%	TGF	PGF	TGA	PGA	+/–	GP	G	A	Pts	PIM	PP	SH	GW
1989-90	Ottawa South Canadians	OMHA	50	26	46	72				46																		
1990-91	Ottawa Jr. Senators	OJHL	55	4	30	34				74																		
1991-92	Sudbury Wolves	OHL	55	3	13	16				20											8	0	0	0	0			
1992-93	Sudbury Wolves	OHL	62	12	43	55				20											14	7	19	26	4			
1993-94	Sudbury Wolves	OHL	65	32	*89	121				58											10	1	9	10	14			
1994-95	Sudbury Wolves	OHL	46	9	56	65				30											18	7	26	33	22			
	Canada	WJC-A	7	3	3	6				2																		
1995-96	**St. Louis Blues**	**NHL**	**3**	**0**	**0**	**0**	**0**	**0**	**0**	**2**	**0**	**0**	**0**	**5**	**0.0**	**0**	**0**	**1**	**0**	**–1**								
	Worcester IceCats	AHL	75	7	45	52				130											4	0	1	1	4			
1996-97	**St. Louis Blues**	**NHL**	**15**	**2**	**5**	**7**	**2**	**4**	**6**	**6**	**1**	**0**	**0**	**9**	**22.2**	**11**	**5**	**11**	**1**	**–4**								
	Worcester IceCats	AHL	63	8	35	43				83											5	1	2	3	14			
1997-98	**St. Louis Blues**	**NHL**	**59**	**2**	**4**	**6**	**2**	**4**	**6**	**36**	**1**	**0**	**1**	**53**	**3.8**	**31**	**8**	**18**	**0**	**5**								
1998-99	**St. Louis Blues**	**NHL**	**76**	**2**	**5**	**7**	**2**	**5**	**7**	**47**	**1**	**0**	**0**	**78**	**2.6**	**40**	**8**	**37**	**2**	**–3**	**9**	**1**	**1**	**2**	**2**	**1**	**0**	**1**
99-2000	**New York Islanders**	**NHL**	**75**	**1**	**16**	**17**	**1**	**15**	**16**	**84**	**1**	**0**	**0**	**95**	**1.1**	**54**	**8**	**75**	**25**	**–4**								
	NHL Totals		**228**	**7**	**30**	**37**	**7**	**28**	**35**	**175**	**4**	**0**	**1**	**240**	**2.9**	**136**	**29**	**142**	**28**		**9**	**1**	**1**	**2**	**2**	**1**	**0**	**1**

• Brother of Shawn • OHL First All-Star Team (1994) • Canadian Major Junior Second All-Star Team (1994) • OHL Second All-Star Team (1995) • AHL Second All-Star Team (1997)

Claimed by **NY Islanders** from **St. Louis** in NHL Waiver Draft, September 27, 1999.

• RIVERS, Shawn

Shawn Hamilton D – L. 5'10", 185 lbs. b: Ottawa, Ont., 1/30/1971.

			REGULAR SEASON																		PLAYOFFS							
Season	Club	League	GP	G	A	Pts	AG	AA	APts	PIM	PP	SH	GW	S	%	TGF	PGF	TGA	PGA	+/–	GP	G	A	Pts	PIM	PP	SH	GW
1987-88	Ottawa Jr. Senators	OJHL	53	13	47	60				38											20	8	15	23	10			
1988-89	St. Lawrence University	ECAC	36	3	23	26				20																		
1989-90	St. Lawrence University	ECAC	26	3	14	17				29																		
1990-91	Sudbury Wolves	OHL	66	18	33	51				43											5	2	7	9	0			
1991-92	Sudbury Wolves	OHL	64	26	54	80				34											11	0	4	4	10			
1992-93	**Tampa Bay Lightning**	**NHL**	**4**	**0**	**2**	**2**	**0**	**1**	**1**	**2**	**0**	**0**	**0**	**3**	**0.0**	**2**	**0**	**4**	**0**	**–2**								
	Atlanta Knights	IHL	78	9	34	43				101											9	1	3	4	8			
1993-94	Atlanta Knights	IHL	76	6	30	36				88											12	1	4	5	21			
1994-95	Chicago Wolves	IHL	68	8	29	37				69											3	0	1	1	0			

			REGULAR SEASON																		PLAYOFFS							
Season	**Club**	**League**	**GP**	**G**	**A**	**Pts**	**AG**	**AA**	**APts**	**PIM**	**PP**	**SH**	**GW**	**S**	**%**	**TGF**	**PGF**	**TGA**	**PGA**	**+/–**	**GP**	**G**	**A**	**Pts**	**PIM**	**PP**	**SH**	**GW**
1995-96	Chicago Wolves	IHL	21	3	4	7	....	....	....	22	....	....	....	....	....	....	....	....	....	....	....	....	....	....	....	....	....	....
	Atlanta Knights	IHL	45	2	16	18	....	....	....	22	....	....	....	....	....	....	....	....	....	....	....	....	....	....	....	....	....	....
	Syracuse Crunch	AHL	5	0	2	2	....	....	....	2	....	....	....	....	....	....	....	....	....	....	16	1	6	7	14	....	....	....
1996-97	Augsburger Panther	Germany	48	8	20	28	....	....	....	22	....	....	....	....	....	....	....	....	....	....	4	1	2	3	0	....	....	....
1997-98	EHC Kloten	Switz.	13	0	6	6	....	....	....	16	....	....	....	....	....	....	....	....	....	....	7	0	0	0	10	....	....	....
	San Antonio Dragons	IHL	14	2	4	6	....	....	....	6	....	....	....	....	....	....	....	....	....	....	....	....	....	....	....	....	....	....
	Lake Charles Ice Pirates	WPHL	5	3	3	6	....	....	....	2	....	....	....	....	....	....	....	....	....	....	....	....	....	....	....	....	....	....
	Springfield Falcons	AHL	3	0	0	0	....	....	....	0	....	....	....	....	....	....	....	....	....	....	....	....	....	....	....	....	....	....
1998-99	SG Cortina	Alpenliga	STATISTICS NOT AVAILABLE																									
	NHL Totals		**4**	**0**	**2**	**2**	**0**	**1**	**1**	**2**	**0**	**0**	**0**	**3**	**0.0**	**2**	**0**	**4**	**0**		....	....	....	....	....	....	....	....

• Brother of Jamie

Signed as a free agent by **Tampa Bay**, June 29, 1992.

• RIVERS, Wayne

John Wayne RW – R. 5'9", 177 lbs. b: Hamilton, Ont., 2/1/1942.

1959-60	Hamilton Kilty B's	OHA-B	STATISTICS NOT AVAILABLE																									
	Hamilton Tiger Cubs	OHA-Jr.	2	0	0	0	....	....	....	2	....	....	....	....	....	....	....	....	....	....	....	....	....	....	....	....	....	....
1960-61	Hamilton Red Wings	OHA-Jr.	41	13	18	31	....	....	....	38	....	....	....	....	....	....	....	....	....	....	4	0	0	0	21	....	....	....
1961-62	Hamilton Red Wings	OHA-Jr.	48	14	15	29	....	....	....	55	....	....	....	....	....	....	....	....	....	....	10	2	1	3	20	....	....	....
	Detroit Red Wings	**NHL**	**2**	**0**	**0**	**0**	**0**	**0**	**0**	**0**	....	....	....	....	....	....	....	....	....	....	....	....	....	....	....	....	....	....
	Hershey Bears	AHL	1	0	0	0	....	....	....	0	....	....	....	....	....	....	....	....	....	....	....	....	....	....	....	....	....	....
	Hamilton Red Wings	Mem-Cup	14	10	5	15	....	....	....	*43	....	....	....	....	....	....	....	....	....	....	....	....	....	....	....	....	....	....
1962-63	Hershey Bears	AHL	52	15	31	46	....	....	....	42	....	....	....	....	....	....	....	....	....	....	12	0	0	0	13	....	....	....
1963-64	**Boston Bruins**	**NHL**	**12**	**2**	**7**	**9**	**2**	**7**	**9**	**6**	....	....	....	....	....	....	....	....	....	....	....	....	....	....	....	....	....	....
	Hershey Bears	AHL	36	20	6	26	....	....	....	24	....	....	....	....	....	....	....	....	....	....	....	....	....	....	....	....	....	....
1964-65	**Boston Bruins**	**NHL**	**58**	**6**	**17**	**23**	**7**	**17**	**24**	**72**	....	....	....	....	....	....	....	....	....	....	....	....	....	....	....	....	....	....
	Hershey Bears	AHL	14	6	8	14	....	....	....	0	....	....	....	....	....	....	....	....	....	....	....	....	....	....	....	....	....	....
1965-66	**Boston Bruins**	**NHL**	**2**	**1**	**1**	**2**	**1**	**1**	**2**	**2**	....	....	....	....	....	....	....	....	....	....	....	....	....	....	....	....	....	....
	Hershey Bears	AHL	65	37	30	67	....	....	....	81	....	....	....	....	....	....	....	....	....	....	3	1	0	1	2	....	....	....
1966-67	**Boston Bruins**	**NHL**	**8**	**2**	**1**	**3**	**2**	**1**	**3**	**6**	....	....	....	....	....	....	....	....	....	....	....	....	....	....	....	....	....	....
	Hershey Bears	AHL	54	30	37	67	....	....	....	59	....	....	....	....	....	....	....	....	....	....	5	0	2	2	4	....	....	....
1967-68	**St. Louis Blues**	**NHL**	**22**	**4**	**4**	**8**	**5**	**4**	**9**	**8**	**1**	**0**	**0**	**53**	**7.5**	**16**	**4**	**15**	**1**	**–2**	....	....	....	....	....	....	....	....
	Kansas City Blues	CPHL	50	25	37	62	....	....	....	41	....	....	....	....	....	....	....	....	....	....	7	*6	1	7	9	....	....	....
1968-69	**New York Rangers**	**NHL**	**4**	**0**	**0**	**0**	**0**	**0**	**0**	**0**	**0**	**0**	**0**	**1**	**0.0**	**0**	**0**	**1**	**0**	**–1**	....	....	....	....	....	....	....	....
	Buffalo Bisons	AHL	67	30	37	67	....	....	....	35	....	....	....	....	....	....	....	....	....	....	6	3	5	8	0	....	....	....
1969-70	Buffalo Bisons	AHL	68	27	34	61	....	....	....	58	....	....	....	....	....	....	....	....	....	....	14	3	9	12	6	....	....	....
	Omaha Knights	CHL	....	....	....	....	....	....	....	....	....	....	....	....	....	....	....	....	....	....	6	3	4	7	7	....	....	....
1970-71	Baltimore Clippers	AHL	65	38	37	75	....	....	....	66	....	....	....	....	....	....	....	....	....	....	6	3	2	5	6	....	....	....
1971-72	Springfield Kings	AHL	68	*48	33	81	....	....	....	67	....	....	....	....	....	....	....	....	....	....	5	0	3	3	4	....	....	....
1972-73	New York Raiders	WHA	75	37	40	77	....	....	....	47	....	....	....	....	....	....	....	....	....	....	....	....	....	....	....	....	....	....
1973-74	New York-Jersey Knights	WHA	73	30	27	57	....	....	....	20	....	....	....	....	....	....	....	....	....	....	....	....	....	....	....	....	....	....
1974-75	San Diego Mariners	WHA	78	54	53	107	....	....	....	52	....	....	....	....	....	....	....	....	....	....	5	3	1	4	8	....	....	....
1975-76	San Diego Mariners	WHA	71	19	25	44	....	....	....	24	....	....	....	....	....	....	....	....	....	....	11	4	4	8	4	....	....	....
1976-77	San Diego Mariners	WHA	60	18	31	49	....	....	....	40	....	....	....	....	....	....	....	....	....	....	7	1	1	2	2	....	....	....
1977-78	San Francisco Shamrocks	PHL	32	11	22	33	....	....	....	7	....	....	....	....	....	....	....	....	....	....	....	....	....	....	....	....	....	....
1978-79	San Francisco Shamrocks	PHL	15	4	5	9	....	....	....	25	....	....	....	....	....	....	....	....	....	....	....	....	....	....	....	....	....	....
	NHL Totals		**108**	**15**	**30**	**45**	**17**	**30**	**47**	**94**	....	....	....	....	....	....	....	....	....		....	....	....	....	....	....	....	....
	Other Major League Totals		357	158	176	334	....	....	....	183	....	....	....	....	....	....	....	....	....	....	23	8	6	14	14	....	....	....

AHL Second All-Star Team (1967, 1971) • CPHL Second All-Star Team (1968) • AHL First All-Star Team (1972)

Claimed by **Boston** from **Detroit**(Hershey-AHL) in Inter-League Draft, June 4, 1963. Claimed by **St. Louis** from **Boston** in Expansion Draft, June 6, 1967. Traded to **NY Rangers** by **St. Louis** with Don Caley for Camille Henry, Bill Plager and Robbie Irons, June 13, 1968. Traded to **LA Kings** (Springfield-AHL) by **NY Rangers** (Baltimore-AHL) for Mike McMahon, October, 1971. Selected by **Ontario-Ottawa** (WHA) in 1972 WHA General Player Draft, February 12, 1972. Traded to **NY Raiders** (WHA) by **Ottawa** (WHA) for future considerations, July, 1972. Transferred to **San Diego** (WHA) after **New York-Jersey** (WHA) franchise relocated, April 30, 1974.

• RIVET, Craig

Craig A. D – R. 6'2", 197 lbs. b: North Bay, Ont., 9/13/1974. Montreal's 4th, 68th overall, in 1992.

1990-91	Barrie Colts	OJHL-B	42	9	17	26	....	....	....	55	....	....	....	....	....	....	....	....	....	....	....	....	....	....	....	....	....	....
1991-92	Kingston Frontenacs	OHL	66	5	21	26	....	....	....	97	....	....	....	....	....	....	....	....	....	....	....	....	....	....	....	....	....	....
1992-93	Kingston Frontenacs	OHL	64	19	55	74	....	....	....	117	....	....	....	....	....	....	....	....	....	....	16	5	7	12	39	....	....	....
1993-94	Kingston Frontenacs	OHL	61	12	52	64	....	....	....	100	....	....	....	....	....	....	....	....	....	....	6	0	3	3	6	....	....	....
	Fredericton Canadiens	AHL	4	0	2	2	....	....	....	2	....	....	....	....	....	....	....	....	....	....	....	....	....	....	....	....	....	....
1994-95	Fredericton Canadiens	AHL	78	5	27	32	....	....	....	126	....	....	....	....	....	....	....	....	....	....	12	0	4	4	17	....	....	....
	Montreal Canadiens	**NHL**	**5**	**0**	**1**	**1**	**0**	**1**	**1**	**5**	**0**	**0**	**0**	**2**	**0.0**	**2**	**0**	**0**	**0**	**2**	....	....	....	....	....	....	....	....
1995-96	**Montreal Canadiens**	**NHL**	**19**	**1**	**4**	**5**	**1**	**3**	**4**	**54**	**0**	**0**	**0**	**9**	**11.1**	**11**	**0**	**7**	**0**	**4**	....	....	....	....	....	....	....	....
	Fredericton Canadiens	AHL	49	5	18	23	....	....	....	189	....	....	....	....	....	....	....	....	....	....	6	0	0	0	12	....	....	....
1996-97	**Montreal Canadiens**	**NHL**	**35**	**0**	**4**	**4**	**0**	**4**	**4**	**54**	**0**	**0**	**0**	**24**	**0.0**	**27**	**0**	**23**	**3**	**7**	**5**	**0**	**1**	**1**	**14**	**0**	**0**	**0**
	Fredericton Canadiens	AHL	23	3	12	15	....	....	....	99	....	....	....	....	....	....	....	....	....	....	....	....	....	....	....	....	....	....
1997-98	**Montreal Canadiens**	**NHL**	**61**	**0**	**2**	**2**	**0**	**2**	**2**	**93**	**0**	**0**	**0**	**26**	**0.0**	**21**	**0**	**32**	**8**	**–3**	**5**	**0**	**0**	**0**	**2**	**0**	**0**	**0**
1998-99	**Montreal Canadiens**	**NHL**	**66**	**2**	**8**	**10**	**2**	**8**	**10**	**66**	**0**	**0**	**0**	**39**	**5.1**	**29**	**0**	**39**	**7**	**–3**	....	....	....	....	....	....	....	....
99-2000	**Montreal Canadiens**	**NHL**	**61**	**3**	**14**	**17**	**3**	**13**	**16**	**76**	**0**	**0**	**1**	**71**	**4.2**	**46**	**2**	**43**	**10**	**11**	....	....	....	....	....	....	....	....
	NHL Totals		**247**	**6**	**33**	**39**	**6**	**31**	**37**	**348**	**0**	**0**	**1**	**171**	**3.5**	**136**	**2**	**144**	**28**		**10**	**0**	**1**	**1**	**16**	**0**	**0**	**0**

• RIZZUTO, Garth

Garth Alexander C – L. 5'10", 175 lbs. b: Trail, B.C., 9/11/1947.

1965-66	Moose Jaw Canucks	SJHL	22	5	11	16	....	....	....	16	....	....	....	....	....	....	....	....	....	....	5	0	2	2	14	....	....	....
1966-67	Moose Jaw Canucks	CMJHL	55	24	31	55	....	....	....	133	....	....	....	....	....	....	....	....	....	....	14	7	16	23	59	....	....	....
1967-68	Dallas Black Hawks	CPHL	47	5	14	19	....	....	....	17	....	....	....	....	....	....	....	....	....	....	5	2	1	3	4	....	....	....
1968-69	Dallas Black Hawks	CHL	72	30	29	59	....	....	....	71	....	....	....	....	....	....	....	....	....	....	11	2	4	6	10	....	....	....
1969-70	Dallas Black Hawks	CHL	72	20	42	62	....	....	....	55	....	....	....	....	....	....	....	....	....	....	....	....	....	....	....	....	....	....
1970-71	**Vancouver Canucks**	**NHL**	**37**	**3**	**4**	**7**	**3**	**3**	**6**	**16**	**1**	**0**	**0**	**33**	**9.1**	**9**	**2**	**26**	**3**	**–16**	....	....	....	....	....	....	....	....
	Rochester Americans	AHL	22	8	12	20	....	....	....	56	....	....	....	....	....	....	....	....	....	....	....	....	....	....	....	....	....	....
1971-72	Seattle Totems	WHL	23	4	15	19	....	....	....	36	....	....	....	....	....	....	....	....	....	....	....	....	....	....	....	....	....	....
	Rochester Americans	AHL	36	6	8	14	....	....	....	11	....	....	....	....	....	....	....	....	....	....	....	....	....	....	....	....	....	....
1972-73	Winnipeg Jets	WHA	61	10	10	20	....	....	....	32	....	....	....	....	....	....	....	....	....	....	14	0	1	1	14	....	....	....
1973-74	Winnipeg Jets	WHA	41	3	4	7	....	....	....	8	....	....	....	....	....	....	....	....	....	....	....	....	....	....	....	....	....	....
1974-75	Nelson Maple Leafs	WIHL	6	4	7	11	....	....	....	34	....	....	....	....	....	....	....	....	....	....	....	....	....	....	....	....	....	....
	NHL Totals		**37**	**3**	**4**	**7**	**3**	**3**	**6**	**16**	**1**	**0**	**0**	**33**	**9.1**	**9**	**2**	**26**	**3**		....	....	....	....	....	....	....	....
	Other Major League Totals		102	13	14	27	....	....	....	40	....	....	....	....	....	....	....	....	....	....	14	0	1	1	14	....	....	....

Claimed by **Vancouver** from **Chicago** in Expansion Draft, June 10, 1970. Signed as a free agent by **Winnipeg** (WHA), July 19, 1972.

• ROBERGE, Mario

LW – L. 5'11", 193 lbs. b: Quebec City, Que., 1/25/1964.

1981-82	Quebec Remparts	QMJHL	8	0	3	3	....	....	....	2	....	....	....	....	....	....	....	....	....	....	....	....	....	....	....	....	....	....
1982-83	Quebec Remparts	QMJHL	69	3	27	30	....	....	....	153	....	....	....	....	....	....	....	....	....	....	....	....	....	....	....	....	....	....
1983-84	Quebec Remparts	QMJHL	60	12	28	40	....	....	....	253	....	....	....	....	....	....	....	....	....	....	5	0	1	1	22	....	....	....
1984-85	Riviere-du-Loup 3 L's	RHL	STATISTICS NOT AVAILABLE																									
1985-86	Riviere-du-Loup 3 L's	RHL	31	16	41	57	....	....	....	94	....	....	....	....	....	....	....	....	....	....	....	....	....	....	....	....	....	....
	St. John's Capitals	Nfld-Sr.	2	1	0	1	....	....	....	2	....	....	....	....	....	....	....	....	....	....	....	....	....	....	....	....	....	....
1986-87	Virginia Lancers	ACHL	52	25	43	68	....	....	....	178	....	....	....	....	....	....	....	....	....	....	12	5	9	14	62	....	....	....
1987-88	Port-aux-Basques Mariners	Nfld.	37	24	64	88	....	....	....	152	....	....	....	....	....	....	....	....	....	....	....	....	....	....	....	....	....	....
1988-89	Sherbrooke Canadiens	AHL	58	4	9	13	....	....	....	249	....	....	....	....	....	....	....	....	....	....	6	0	2	2	8	....	....	....
1989-90	Sherbrooke Canadiens	AHL	73	13	27	40	....	....	....	247	....	....	....	....	....	....	....	....	....	....	12	5	2	7	53	....	....	....

			REGULAR SEASON																		PLAYOFFS							
Season	Club	League	GP	G	A	Pts	AG	AA	APts	PIM	PP	SH	GW	S	%	TGF	PGF	TGA	PGA	+/–	GP	G	A	Pts	PIM	PP	SH	GW
1990-91	**Montreal Canadiens**	**NHL**	**5**	**0**	**0**	**0**	**0**	**0**	**0**	**21**	**0**	**0**	**0**	**2**	**0.0**	**0**	**0**	**2**	**0**	**–2**	**12**	**0**	**0**	**0**	**24**	**0**	**0**	**0**
	Fredericton Canadiens	AHL	68	12	27	39	....	....	....	*365	....	....	....	....	....	....	....	....	....	....	2	0	2	2	5	....	....	....
1991-92	**Montreal Canadiens**	**NHL**	**20**	**2**	**1**	**3**	**2**	**1**	**3**	**62**	**0**	**0**	**0**	**7**	**28.6**	**4**	**0**	**1**	**0**	**3**	....	....	....	....	....	....	....	....
	Fredericton Canadiens	AHL	6	1	2	3	....	....	....	20	....	....	....	....	....	....	....	....	....	....	7	0	2	2	20	....	....	....
1992-93♦	**Montreal Canadiens**	**NHL**	**50**	**4**	**4**	**8**	**3**	**3**	**6**	**142**	**0**	**0**	**3**	**23**	**17.4**	**14**	**1**	**11**	**0**	**2**	**3**	**0**	**0**	**0**	**0**	**0**	**0**	**0**
1993-94	**Montreal Canadiens**	**NHL**	**28**	**1**	**2**	**3**	**1**	**2**	**3**	**55**	**0**	**0**	**0**	**5**	**20.0**	**4**	**0**	**6**	**0**	**–2**	....	....	....	....	....	....	....	....
1994-95	**Montreal Canadiens**	**NHL**	**9**	**0**	**0**	**0**	**0**	**0**	**0**	**34**	**0**	**0**	**0**	**0**	**0.0**	**0**	**0**	**2**	**0**	**–2**	....	....	....	....	....	....	....	....
	Fredericton Canadiens	AHL	28	8	12	20	....	....	....	91	....	....	....	....	....	....	....	....	....	....	6	1	1	2	6	....	....	....
1995-96	Fredericton Canadiens	AHL	74	9	24	33	....	....	....	205	....	....	....	....	....	....	....	....	....	....	4	0	2	2	14	....	....	....
1996-97	Quebec Rafales	IHL	68	8	17	25	....	....	....	256	....	....	....	....	....	....	....	....	....	....	5	0	1	1	5	....	....	....
1997-98			DID NOT PLAY																									
1998-99	St-Georges Garaga	QSPHL	34	5	24	29	....	....	....	214	....	....	....	....	....	....	....	....	....	....	....	....	....	....	....	....	....	....
99-2000	St-Georges Garaga	QSPHL	26	5	22	27	....	....	....	106	....	....	....	....	....	....	....	....	....	....	....	....	....	....	....	....	....	....
	Mohawk Valley Prowlers	UHL	36	7	14	21	....	....	....	100	....	....	....	....	....	....	....	....	....	....	7	0	3	3	27	....	....	....
	NHL Totals		**112**	**7**	**7**	**14**	**6**	**6**	**12**	**314**	**0**	**0**	**3**	**37**	**18.9**	**22**	**1**	**22**	**0**		**15**	**0**	**0**	**0**	**24**	**0**	**0**	**0**

• Brother of Serge

Signed as a free agent by **Montreal**, October 5, 1988. Signed as a free agent by **Mohawk Valley** (UHL), January 10, 2000.

• ROBERGE, Serge

RW – R. 6'1", 195 lbs. b: Quebec City, Que., 3/31/1965.

Season	Club	League	GP	G	A	Pts	AG	AA	APts	PIM	PP	SH	GW	S	%	TGF	PGF	TGA	PGA	+/–	GP	G	A	Pts	PIM	PP	SH	GW
1982-83	Quebec Remparts	QMJHL	9	0	0	0	....	....	....	30	....	....	....	....	....	....	....	....	....	....	....	....	....	....	....	....	....	....
	Hull Olympiques	QMJHL	22	0	4	4	....	....	....	115	....	....	....	....	....	....	....	....	....	....	....	....	....	....	....	....	....	....
1983-84	Drummondville Voltigeurs	QMJHL	58	1	7	8	....	....	....	287	....	....	....	....	....	....	....	....	....	....	10	0	2	2	*105	....	....	....
1984-85	Drummondville Voltigeurs	QMJHL	45	8	19	27	....	....	....	299	....	....	....	....	....	....	....	....	....	....	....	....	....	....	....	....	....	....
1985-86	Riviere-du-Loup 3 L's	RHL	31	6	8	14	....	....	....	180	....	....	....	....	....	....	....	....	....	....	....	....	....	....	....	....	....	....
	St. John's Capitals	Nfld-Sr.	2	0	0	0	....	....	....	12	....	....	....	....	....	....	....	....	....	....	....	....	....	....	....	....	....	....
1986-87	Virginia Lancers	ACHL	49	9	16	25	....	....	....	*353	....	....	....	....	....	....	....	....	....	....	12	4	2	6	*104	....	....	....
1987-88	Port aux Basques Mariners	Nfld-Sr.	12	5	3	8	....	....	....	....	....	....	....	....	....	....	....	....	....	....	....	....	....	....	....	....	....	....
	Sherbrooke Canadiens	AHL	30	0	1	1	....	....	....	130	....	....	....	....	....	....	....	....	....	....	5	0	0	0	21	....	....	....
1988-89	Sherbrooke Canadiens	AHL	65	5	7	12	....	....	....	352	....	....	....	....	....	....	....	....	....	....	6	0	1	1	10	....	....	....
1989-90	Sherbrooke Canadiens	AHL	66	8	5	13	....	....	....	*343	....	....	....	....	....	....	....	....	....	....	12	2	0	2	44	....	....	....
1990-91	**Quebec Nordiques**	**NHL**	**9**	**0**	**0**	**0**	**0**	**0**	**0**	**24**	**0**	**0**	**0**	**0**	**0.0**	**1**	**0**	**1**	**0**	**0**	....	....	....	....	....	....	....	....
	Halifax Citadels	AHL	52	0	5	5	....	....	....	152	....	....	....	....	....	....	....	....	....	....	....	....	....	....	....	....	....	....
1991-92	Halifax Citadels	AHL	66	2	8	10	....	....	....	319	....	....	....	....	....	....	....	....	....	....	....	....	....	....	....	....	....	....
1992-93	Halifax Citadels	AHL	16	2	2	4	....	....	....	34	....	....	....	....	....	....	....	....	....	....	....	....	....	....	....	....	....	....
	Utica Devils	AHL	28	0	3	3	....	....	....	85	....	....	....	....	....	....	....	....	....	....	1	0	0	0	0	....	....	....
1993-94	Cape Breton Oilers	AHL	51	3	5	8	....	....	....	130	....	....	....	....	....	....	....	....	....	....	1	0	0	0	0	....	....	....
1994-95	Cornwall Aces	AHL	73	0	3	3	....	....	....	342	....	....	....	....	....	....	....	....	....	....	11	0	0	0	29	....	....	....
1995-96	Rochester Americans	AHL	32	0	1	1	....	....	....	42	....	....	....	....	....	....	....	....	....	....	....	....	....	....	....	....	....	....
	Fredericton Canadiens	AHL	14	1	1	2	....	....	....	45	....	....	....	....	....	....	....	....	....	....	7	0	0	0	10	....	....	....
1996-97	Quebec Rafales	IHL	61	2	4	6	....	....	....	273	....	....	....	....	....	....	....	....	....	....	....	....	....	....	....	....	....	....
1997-98	Quebec Rafales	IHL	35	2	0	2	....	....	....	115	....	....	....	....	....	....	....	....	....	....	....	....	....	....	....	....	....	....
1998-99	Pont-Rouge Grand Portneuf	QSPHL	5	1	2	3	....	....	....	23	....	....	....	....	....	....	....	....	....	....	....	....	....	....	....	....	....	....
	Mohawk Valley Prowlers	UHL	61	7	4	11	....	....	....	268	....	....	....	....	....	....	....	....	....	....	....	....	....	....	....	....	....	....
99-2000	Mohawk Valley Prowlers	UHL	54	3	7	10	....	....	....	207	....	....	....	....	....	....	....	....	....	....	7	2	2	4	34	....	....	....
	NHL Totals		**9**	**0**	**0**	**0**	**0**	**0**	**0**	**24**	**0**	**0**	**0**	**0**	**0.0**	**1**	**0**	**1**	**0**		....	....	....	....	....	....	....	....

• Brother of Mario

Signed as a free agent by **Montreal**, January 25, 1988. Signed as a free agent by **Quebec**, December 28, 1990. • Played w/ RHI's Las Vegas Flash in 1994 (3-0-0-0-2); Montreal Roadrunners in 1994 (11-1-2-3-35) and 1997 (24-2-9-11-73).

• ROBERT, Rene

Rene Paul RW – R. 5'10", 184 lbs. b: Trois Rivieres, Que., 12/31/1948.

Season	Club	League	GP	G	A	Pts	AG	AA	APts	PIM	PP	SH	GW	S	%	TGF	PGF	TGA	PGA	+/–	GP	G	A	Pts	PIM	PP	SH	GW
1965-66	Trois-Rivieres Leafs	QJHL	42	13	38	51	....	....	....	31	....	....	....	....	....	....	....	....	....	....	5	0	2	2	7	....	....	....
1966-67	Trois-Rivieres Leafs	QJHL	41	34	32	66	....	....	....	73	....	....	....	....	....	....	....	....	....	....	11	5	12	17	15	....	....	....
1967-68	Trois-Rivieres Leafs	QJHL	49	*69	74	143	....	....	....		....	....	....	....	....	....	....	....	....	....	4	3	5	8	4	....	....	....
	Tulsa Oilers	CPHL	3	0	2	2	....	....	....	0	....	....	....	....	....	....	....	....	....	....	2	0	4	4	14	....	....	....
1968-69	Tulsa Oilers	CHL	59	21	30	51	....	....	....	57	....	....	....	....	....	....	....	....	....	....	7	4	3	7	2	....	....	....
1969-70	Vancouver Canucks	WHL	5	0	0	0	....	....	....	2	....	....	....	....	....	....	....	....	....	....	....	....	....	....	....	....	....	....
	Rochester Americans	AHL	49	23	40	63	....	....	....	57	....	....	....	....	....	....	....	....	....	....	....	....	....	....	....	....	....	....
1970-71	**Toronto Maple Leafs**	**NHL**	**5**	**0**	**0**	**0**	**0**	**0**	**0**	**0**	**0**	**0**	**0**	**8**	**0.0**	**1**	**0**	**3**	**0**	**–2**	....	....	....	....	....	....	....	....
	Tulsa Oilers	CHL	58	26	36	62	....	....	....	85	....	....	....	....	....	....	....	....	....	....	....	....	....	....	....	....	....	....
	Phoenix Roadrunners	WHL	7	4	3	7	....	....	....	6	....	....	....	....	....	....	....	....	....	....	10	5	3	8	7	....	....	....
1971-72	**Pittsburgh Penguins**	**NHL**	**49**	**7**	**11**	**18**	**7**	**9**	**16**	**42**	**3**	**0**	**2**	**71**	**9.9**	**28**	**12**	**29**	**2**	**–11**	....	....	....	....	....	....	....	....
	Buffalo Sabres	**NHL**	**12**	**6**	**3**	**9**	**6**	**3**	**9**	**2**	**3**	**0**	**0**	**42**	**14.3**	**15**	**8**	**12**	**0**	**–5**	....	....	....	....	....	....	....	....
1972-73	**Buffalo Sabres**	**NHL**	**75**	**40**	**43**	**83**	**38**	**34**	**72**	**83**	**9**	**0**	**6**	**265**	**15.1**	**119**	**43**	**60**	**0**	**16**	**6**	**5**	**3**	**8**	**2**	**1**	**0**	**1**
1973-74	**Buffalo Sabres**	**NHL**	**76**	**21**	**44**	**65**	**20**	**36**	**56**	**71**	**3**	**0**	**5**	**245**	**8.6**	**109**	**39**	**86**	**0**	**–16**	....	....	....	....	....	....	....	....
1974-75	**Buffalo Sabres**	**NHL**	**74**	**40**	**60**	**100**	**35**	**45**	**80**	**75**	**14**	**0**	**3**	**264**	**15.2**	**145**	**65**	**77**	**3**	**6**	**16**	**5**	**8**	**13**	**16**	**0**	**0**	**3**
1975-76	**Buffalo Sabres**	**NHL**	**72**	**35**	**52**	**87**	**31**	**39**	**70**	**53**	**11**	**0**	**4**	**273**	**12.8**	**135**	**59**	**59**	**0**	**17**	**9**	**3**	**2**	**5**	**6**	**0**	**0**	**0**
1976-77	**Buffalo Sabres**	**NHL**	**80**	**33**	**40**	**73**	**30**	**31**	**61**	**46**	**5**	**0**	**4**	**250**	**13.2**	**120**	**41**	**52**	**0**	**27**	**6**	**5**	**2**	**7**	**20**	**1**	**0**	**0**
1977-78	**Buffalo Sabres**	**NHL**	**67**	**25**	**48**	**73**	**23**	**37**	**60**	**25**	**7**	**0**	**4**	**209**	**12.0**	**110**	**34**	**57**	**0**	**19**	**7**	**2**	**0**	**2**	**23**	**0**	**0**	**0**
1978-79	**Buffalo Sabres**	**NHL**	**68**	**22**	**40**	**62**	**19**	**29**	**48**	**46**	**1**	**0**	**6**	**206**	**10.7**	**86**	**35**	**63**	**0**	**–12**	**3**	**2**	**2**	**4**	**4**	**0**	**0**	**0**
1979-80	**Colorado Rockies**	**NHL**	**69**	**28**	**35**	**63**	**24**	**26**	**50**	**79**	**10**	**0**	**0**	**248**	**11.3**	**95**	**42**	**88**	**15**	**–20**	....	....	....	....	....	....	....	....
1980-81	**Colorado Rockies**	**NHL**	**28**	**8**	**11**	**19**	**6**	**7**	**13**	**30**	**4**	**0**	**0**	**66**	**12.1**	**29**	**12**	**32**	**2**	**–13**	....	....	....	....	....	....	....	....
	Toronto Maple Leafs	**NHL**	**14**	**6**	**7**	**13**	**5**	**5**	**10**	**8**	**1**	**0**	**1**	**43**	**14.0**	**22**	**10**	**9**	**2**	**5**	**3**	**0**	**2**	**2**	**2**	**0**	**0**	**0**
1981-82	**Toronto Maple Leafs**	**NHL**	**55**	**13**	**24**	**37**	**10**	**16**	**26**	**37**	**2**	**0**	**1**	**120**	**10.8**	**59**	**26**	**58**	**14**	**–11**	....	....	....	....	....	....	....	....
	NHL Totals		**744**	**284**	**418**	**702**	**254**	**317**	**571**	**597**	**73**	**0**	**36**	**2310**	**12.3**	**1073**	**426**	**685**	**38**		**50**	**22**	**19**	**41**	**73**	**2**	**0**	**4**

QJHL First All-Star Team (1968) • NHL Second All-Star Team (1975) • Played in NHL All-Star Game (1973, 1975)

Signed as a free agent by **Toronto** (Tulsa-CHL) to a five-game tryout contract, March 20, 1968. Traded to **Vancouver** (WHL) by **Toronto** with Brad Selwood for Ron Ward, May, 1969. Traded to **Toronto** by **Vancouver** (WHL) for cash, May 15, 1970. Claimed by **Buffalo** from **Toronto** in Intra-League Draft, June 8, 1971. Claimed by **Pittsburgh** from **Buffalo** in Intra-League Draft, June 8, 1971. Traded to **Buffalo** by **Pittsburgh** for Eddie Shack, March 4, 1972. Traded to **Colorado** by **Buffalo** for John Van Boxmeer, October 5, 1979. Traded to **Toronto** by **Colorado** for Toronto's 3rd round choice (Uli Hiemer) in the 1981 Entry Draft, January 30, 1981.

• ROBERTO, Phil

Phillip Joseph RW – R. 6'1", 190 lbs. b: Niagara Falls, Ont., 1/1/1949.

Season	Club	League	GP	G	A	Pts	AG	AA	APts	PIM	PP	SH	GW	S	%	TGF	PGF	TGA	PGA	+/–	GP	G	A	Pts	PIM	PP	SH	GW
1965-66	Niagara Falls Canucks	OHA-B	STATISTICS NOT AVAILABLE																									
	Niagara Falls Flyers	OHA-Jr.	2	2	0	2	....	....	....	0	....	....	....	....	....	....	....	....	....	....	6	1	1	2	6	....	....	....
1966-67	Niagara Falls Canucks	OHA-B	STATISTICS NOT AVAILABLE																									
	Niagara Falls Flyers	OHA-Jr.	14	1	0	1	....	....	....	6	....	....	....	....	....	....	....	....	....	....	....	....	....	....	....	....	....	....
1967-68	Niagara Falls Flyers	OHA-Jr.	53	19	20	39	....	....	....	92	....	....	....	....	....	....	....	....	....	....	19	13	14	27	*71	....	....	....
	Niagara Falls Flyers	Mem-Cup	10	4	8	12	....	....	....	15	....	....	....	....	....	....	....	....	....	....	....	....	....	....	....	....	....	....
1968-69	Niagara Falls Flyers	OHA-Jr.	52	29	65	94	....	....	....	152	....	....	....	....	....	....	....	....	....	....	14	7	15	22	38	....	....	....
1969-70	**Montreal Canadiens**	**NHL**	**8**	**0**	**1**	**1**	**0**	**1**	**1**	**8**	**0**	**0**	**0**	**5**	**0.0**	**3**	**1**	**1**	**0**	**1**	....	....	....	....	....	....	....	....
	Montreal Voyageurs	AHL	54	20	19	39	....	....	....	160	....	....	....	....	....	....	....	....	....	....	8	3	1	4	19	....	....	....
1970-71♦	**Montreal Canadiens**	**NHL**	**39**	**14**	**7**	**21**	**14**	**6**	**20**	**76**	**2**	**0**	**3**	**88**	**15.9**	**29**	**2**	**23**	**6**	**10**	**15**	**0**	**1**	**1**	**36**	**0**	**0**	**0**
	Montreal Voyageurs	AHL	32	19	22	41	....	....	....	127	....	....	....	....	....	....	....	....	....	....	....	....	....	....	....	....	....	....
1971-72	**Montreal Canadiens**	**NHL**	**27**	**3**	**2**	**5**	**3**	**2**	**5**	**22**	**0**	**0**	**0**	**35**	**8.6**	**10**	**0**	**9**	**2**	**3**	....	....	....	....	....	....	....	....
	St. Louis Blues	**NHL**	**49**	**12**	**13**	**25**	**12**	**11**	**23**	**76**	**0**	**0**	**0**	**170**	**7.1**	**40**	**3**	**44**	**6**	**–1**	**11**	**7**	**6**	**13**	**29**	**3**	**0**	**1**
1972-73	**St. Louis Blues**	**NHL**	**77**	**20**	**22**	**42**	**19**	**17**	**36**	**99**	**2**	**0**	**5**	**275**	**7.3**	**69**	**8**	**90**	**17**	**–12**	**5**	**2**	**1**	**3**	**4**	**0**	**0**	**0**
1973-74	**St. Louis Blues**	**NHL**	**15**	**1**	**1**	**2**	**1**	**1**	**2**	**10**	**0**	**0**	**0**	**14**	**7.1**	**3**	**1**	**11**	**5**	**–4**	....	....	....	....	....	....	....	....
	Denver Spurs	WHL	8	5	4	9	....	....	....	40	....	....	....	....	....	....	....	....	....	....	....	....	....	....	....	....	....	....

			REGULAR SEASON																		PLAYOFFS							
Season	**Club**	**League**	**GP**	**G**	**A**	**Pts**	**AG**	**AA**	**APts**	**PIM**	**PP**	**SH**	**GW**	**S**	**%**	**TGF**	**PGF**	**TGA**	**PGA**	**+/-**	**GP**	**G**	**A**	**Pts**	**PIM**	**PP**	**SH**	**GW**
1974-75	**St. Louis Blues**	**NHL**	7	0	2	2	0	1	1	2	0	0	0	5	0.0	3	1	7	2	-3	....	....	....	....	....	....	....	....
	Denver Spurs	CHL	8	3	2	5	....	....	....	12	....	....	....	....	....	....	....	....	....	....	....	....	....	....	....	....	....	....
	Detroit Red Wings	**NHL**	46	13	27	40	11	20	31	30	5	0	2	113	11.5	55	19	50	4	-10	....	....	....	....	....	....	....	....
1975-76	**Detroit Red Wings**	**NHL**	37	1	7	8	1	5	6	68	0	0	0	55	1.8	19	2	25	6	-2	....	....	....	....	....	....	....	....
	Kansas City Scouts	**NHL**	37	7	15	22	6	11	17	42	3	0	0	89	7.9	35	12	52	18	-11	....	....	....	....	....	....	....	....
1976-77	**Colorado Rockies**	**NHL**	22	1	5	6	1	4	5	23	0	0	0	38	2.6	8	0	25	6	-11	....	....	....	....	....	....	....	....
	Cleveland Barons	**NHL**	21	3	4	7	3	3	6	8	0	0	0	32	9.4	13	0	20	0	-7	....	....	....	....	....	....	....	....
1977-78	Birmingham Bulls	WHA	53	8	20	28	....	....	....	91	....	....	....	....	....	....	....	....	....	....	4	1	0	1	20	....	....	....
	NHL Totals		385	75	106	181	71	82	153	464	12	0	10	919	8.2	287	49	357	72		31	9	8	17	69	3	0	1
	Other Major League Totals		53	8	20	28	....	....	....	91	....	....	....	....	....	....	....	....	....	....	4	1	0	1	20	....	....	....

OHA-Jr. Second All-Star Team (1969)

Traded to **St. Louis** by **Montreal** for Jimmy Roberts, December 13, 1971. Selected by **New England** (WHA) in 1972 WHA General Player Draft, February 12, 1972. Traded to **Detroit** by **St. Louis** with St. Louis's 3rd round choice (Blair Davidson) in 1975 Amateur Draft for Red Berenson, December 30, 1974. Traded to **Kansas City** by **Detroit** for Buster Harvey, January 14, 1976. Transferred to **Colorado** after **Kansas City** franchise relocated, July 15, 1976. Signed as a free agent by **Cleveland** after securing release from **Colorado**, December 24, 1976. Signed as a free agent by **Birmingham** (WHA), July, 1977.

• ROBERTS, David

David L. LW – L. 6', 185 lbs. b: Alameda, CA, 5/28/1970. St. Louis' 5th, 114th overall, in 1989.

Season	Club	League	GP	G	A	Pts	AG	AA	APts	PIM	PP	SH	GW	S	%	TGF	PGF	TGA	PGA	+/-	GP	G	A	Pts	PIM	PP	SH	GW
1986-87	Avon Farms Winged Beavers	Hi-School	17	6	9	15	....	....	....	....	....	....	....	....	....	....	....	....	....	....	....	....	....	....	....	....	....	....
1987-88	Avon Farms Winged Beavers	Hi-School	25	18	39	57	....	....	....	....	....	....	....	....	....	....	....	....	....	....	....	....	....	....	....	....	....	....
1988-89	Avon Farms Winged Beavers	Hi-School	25	28	48	76	....	....	....	....	....	....	....	....	....	....	....	....	....	....	....	....	....	....	....	....	....	....
1989-90	University of Michigan	CCHA	42	21	32	53	....	....	....	46	....	....	....	....	....	....	....	....	....	....	....	....	....	....	....	....	....	....
1990-91	University of Michigan	CCHA	43	26	45	71	....	....	....	58	....	....	....	....	....	....	....	....	....	....	....	....	....	....	....	....	....	....
1991-92	University of Michigan	CCHA	44	16	42	58	....	....	....	68	....	....	....	....	....	....	....	....	....	....	....	....	....	....	....	....	....	....
1992-93	University of Michigan	CCHA	40	27	38	65	....	....	....	40	....	....	....	....	....	....	....	....	....	....	....	....	....	....	....	....	....	....
1993-94	United States	Nat-Team	49	17	28	45	....	....	....	68	....	....	....	....	....	....	....	....	....	....	....	....	....	....	....	....	....	....
	United States	Olympics	8	1	5	6	....	....	....	4	....	....	....	....	....	....	....	....	....	....	....	....	....	....	....	....	....	....
	St. Louis Blues	**NHL**	1	0	0	0	0	0	0	2	0	0	0	1	0.0	0	0	0	0	0	3	0	0	0	12	0	0	0
	Peoria Rivermen	IHL	10	4	6	10	....	....	....	4	....	....	....	....	....	....	....	....	....	....	....	....	....	....	....	....	....	....
1994-95	Peoria Rivermen	IHL	65	30	38	68	....	....	....	65	....	....	....	....	....	....	....	....	....	....	....	....	....	....	....	....	....	....
	St. Louis Blues	**NHL**	19	6	5	11	11	7	18	10	3	0	2	41	14.6	15	5	8	0	2	6	0	0	0	4	0	0	0
1995-96	**St. Louis Blues**	**NHL**	28	1	6	7	1	5	6	12	1	0	1	35	2.9	12	3	17	1	-7	....	....	....	....	....	....	....	....
	Worcester IceCats	AHL	22	8	17	25	....	....	....	46	....	....	....	....	....	....	....	....	....	....	....	....	....	....	....	....	....	....
	Edmonton Oilers	**NHL**	6	2	4	6	2	3	5	6	0	0	0	12	16.7	5	0	5	0	0	....	....	....	....	....	....	....	....
1996-97	**Vancouver Canucks**	**NHL**	58	10	17	27	11	15	26	51	1	1	1	74	13.5	38	5	29	7	11	....	....	....	....	....	....	....	....
1997-98	**Vancouver Canucks**	**NHL**	13	1	1	2	1	1	2	4	0	0	0	14	7.1	3	0	6	2	-1	....	....	....	....	....	....	....	....
	Syracuse Crunch	AHL	37	17	22	39	....	....	....	44	....	....	....	....	....	....	....	....	....	....	5	2	1	3	2	....	....	....
1998-99	Michigan K-Wings	IHL	75	32	38	70	....	....	....	77	....	....	....	....	....	....	....	....	....	....	4	1	2	3	2	....	....	....
99-2000	EV Zug	Switz.	40	15	21	36	....	....	....	100	....	....	....	....	....	....	....	....	....	....	11	3	4	7	16	....	....	....
	NHL Totals		125	20	33	53	26	31	57	85	5	1	4	177	11.3	73	13	65	10		9	0	0	0	16	0	0	0

• Son of Doug • CCHA Second All-Star Team (1991, 1993) • NCAA West Second All-American Team (1991)

Traded to **Edmonton** by **St. Louis** for future considerations, March 12, 1996. Signed as a free agent by **Vancouver**, July 31, 1996. Signed as a free agent by **Dallas**, July 31, 1998.

• ROBERTS, Doug

Douglas William RW – R. 6'2", 212 lbs. b: Detroit, MI, 10/28/1942.

Season	Club	League	GP	G	A	Pts	AG	AA	APts	PIM	PP	SH	GW	S	%	TGF	PGF	TGA	PGA	+/-	GP	G	A	Pts	PIM	PP	SH	GW
1962-63	Michigan State Spartans	WCHA	23	7	6	13	....	....	....	....	....	....	....	....	....	....	....	....	....	....	....	....	....	....	....	....	....	....
1963-64	Michigan State Spartans	WCHA	22	21	14	35	....	....	....	16	....	....	....	....	....	....	....	....	....	....	....	....	....	....	....	....	....	....
1964-65	Michigan State Spartans	WCHA	29	28	33	61	....	....	....	42	....	....	....	....	....	....	....	....	....	....	....	....	....	....	....	....	....	....
1965-66	Memphis Wings	CPHL	70	20	40	60	....	....	....	71	....	....	....	....	....	....	....	....	....	....	....	....	....	....	....	....	....	....
	Detroit Red Wings	**NHL**	1	0	0	0	0	0	0	0	....	....	....	....	....	....	....	....	....	....	....	....	....	....	....	....	....	....
1966-67	**Detroit Red Wings**	**NHL**	13	3	1	4	3	1	4	0	....	....	....	....	....	....	....	....	....	....	....	....	....	....	....	....	....	....
	Memphis Wings	CPHL	57	11	18	29	....	....	....	116	....	....	....	....	....	....	....	....	....	....	....	....	....	....	....	....	....	....
1967-68	**Detroit Red Wings**	**NHL**	37	8	9	17	9	9	18	12	1	0	1	60	13.3	28	7	21	0	0	....	....	....	....	....	....	....	....
	Fort Worth Wings	CPHL	28	8	17	25	....	....	....	73	....	....	....	....	....	....	....	....	....	....	13	5	8	13	16	....	....	....
1968-69	**Oakland Seals**	**NHL**	76	1	19	20	1	17	18	79	0	0	0	114	0.9	103	17	122	23	-13	7	0	1	1	34	0	0	0
1969-70	**Oakland Seals**	**NHL**	76	6	25	31	6	23	29	107	0	0	1	137	4.4	94	21	126	16	-37	4	0	2	2	6	0	0	0
1970-71	**California Golden Seals**	**NHL**	78	4	13	17	4	11	15	94	1	0	0	128	3.1	65	7	134	20	-56	....	....	....	....	....	....	....	....
1971-72	**Boston Bruins**	**NHL**	3	1	0	1	1	0	1	0	0	0	0	3	33.3	1	0	0	0	1	....	....	....	....	....	....	....	....
	Boston Braves	AHL	74	35	40	75	....	....	....	107	....	....	....	....	....	....	....	....	....	....	9	1	4	5	21	....	....	....
1972-73	**Boston Bruins**	**NHL**	45	4	7	11	4	6	10	7	0	0	2	67	6.0	26	2	11	0	13	5	2	0	2	6	0	0	0
	Boston Braves	AHL	7	2	3	5	....	....	....	0	....	....	....	....	....	....	....	....	....	....	....	....	....	....	....	....	....	....
1973-74	**Boston Bruins**	**NHL**	7	0	1	1	0	1	1	2	0	0	0	11	0.0	3	0	1	0	2	....	....	....	....	....	....	....	....
	Detroit Red Wings	**NHL**	57	12	25	37	12	21	33	33	2	0	1	84	14.3	52	4	57	0	-9	....	....	....	....	....	....	....	....
1974-75	**Detroit Red Wings**	**NHL**	26	4	4	8	3	3	6	8	4	0	0	26	15.4	20	10	18	1	-7	....	....	....	....	....	....	....	....
	Virginia Wings	AHL	31	7	11	18	....	....	....	32	....	....	....	....	....	....	....	....	....	....	5	0	2	2	4	....	....	....
1975-76	New England Whalers	WHA	76	4	13	17	....	....	....	51	....	....	....	....	....	....	....	....	....	....	17	1	1	2	8	....	....	....
1976-77	New England Whalers	WHA	64	3	18	21	....	....	....	33	....	....	....	....	....	....	....	....	....	....	2	0	0	0	0	....	....	....
	Rhode Island Reds	AHL	8	2	4	6	....	....	....	4	....	....	....	....	....	....	....	....	....	....	....	....	....	....	....	....	....	....
1977-78	Jokerit Helsinki	Finland	31	4	2	6	....	....	....	38	....	....	....	....	....	....	....	....	....	....	....	....	....	....	....	....	....	....
1978-79			OUT OF HOCKEY – RETIRED																									
1979-1980	Connecticut College	ECAC-2	DID NOT PLAY – FRONT OFFICE STAFF																									
1980-2000	Connecticut College	ECAC-2	DID NOT PLAY – COACHING																									
	NHL Totals		419	43	104	147	43	92	135	342	....	....	....	....	....	....	....	....	....	....	16	2	3	5	46	....	....	....
	Other Major League Totals		140	7	31	38	....	....	....	84	....	....	....	....	....	....	....	....	....	....	19	1	1	2	8	....	....	....

• Brother of Gordie • Father of David • WCHA Second All-Star Team (1965) • NCAA West First All-American Team (1965) • Won Ken McKenzie Trophy (Rookie of the Year - CPHL) (1966) • Played in NHL All-Star Game (1971)

Signed as a free agent by **Detroit**, June 12, 1965. Traded to **Oakland** by **Detroit** with Gary Jarrett, Howie Young and Chris Worthy for Bob Baun and Ron Harris, May 27, 1968. Traded to **Boston** by **California** for cash, September 4, 1971. Traded to **Detroit** by **Boston** for cash, November 23, 1973. Selected by **LA Sharks** (WHA) in 1972 WHA General Player Draft, February 12, 1972. Signed as a free agent by **New England** (WHA), September, 1975.

• ROBERTS, Gary

Gary R. LW – L. 6'1", 200 lbs. b: North York, Ont., 5/23/1966. Calgary's 1st, 12th overall, in 1984.

Season	Club	League	GP	G	A	Pts	AG	AA	APts	PIM	PP	SH	GW	S	%	TGF	PGF	TGA	PGA	+/-	GP	G	A	Pts	PIM	PP	SH	GW
1980-81	Whitby Legionaires	OMHA	STATISTICS NOT AVAILABLE																									
	Hamilton Kilty B's	OHA-B	3	0	1	1	....	....	....	0	....	....	....	....	....	....	....	....	....	....	....	....	....	....	....	....	....	....
1981-82	Whitby Selects	OMHA	44	55	31	86	....	....	....	133	....	....	....	....	....	....	....	....	....	....	....	....	....	....	....	....	....	....
1982-83	Ottawa 67's	OHL	53	12	8	20	....	....	....	83	....	....	....	....	....	....	....	....	....	....	5	1	0	1	19	....	....	....
1983-84	Ottawa 67's	OHL	48	27	30	57	....	....	....	144	....	....	....	....	....	....	....	....	....	....	13	10	7	17	62	....	....	....
	Ottawa 67's	Mem-Cup	5	1	4	5	....	....	....	18	....	....	....	....	....	....	....	....	....	....	....	....	....	....	....	....	....	....
1984-85	Ottawa 67's	OHL	59	44	62	106	....	....	....	186	....	....	....	....	....	....	....	....	....	....	5	2	8	10	10	....	....	....
	Moncton Golden Flames	AHL	7	4	2	6	....	....	....	7	....	....	....	....	....	....	....	....	....	....	....	....	....	....	....	....	....	....
1985-86	Ottawa 67's	OHL	24	26	25	51	....	....	....	83	....	....	....	....	....	....	....	....	....	....	....	....	....	....	....	....	....	....
	Canada	WJC-A	7	6	3	9	....	....	....	6	....	....	....	....	....	....	....	....	....	....	....	....	....	....	....	....	....	....
	Guelph Platers	OHL	23	18	15	33	....	....	....	65	....	....	....	....	....	....	....	....	....	....	20	18	13	31	43	....	....	....
	Guelph Platers	Mem-Cup	4	4	1	5	....	....	....	14	....	....	....	....	....	....	....	....	....	....	....	....	....	....	....	....	....	....
1986-87	**Calgary Flames**	**NHL**	32	5	10	15	4	7	11	85	0	0	0	38	13.2	23	1	16	0	6	2	0	0	0	4	0	0	0
	Moncton Golden Flames	AHL	38	20	18	38	....	....	....	72	....	....	....	....	....	....	....	....	....	....	....	....	....	....	....	....	....	....
1987-88	**Calgary Flames**	**NHL**	74	13	15	28	11	11	22	282	0	0	1	118	11.0	60	1	47	12	24	9	2	3	5	29	0	0	0
1988-89♦	**Calgary Flames**	**NHL**	71	22	16	38	19	11	30	250	0	1	2	123	17.9	60	1	34	7	32	22	5	7	12	57	0	0	0
1989-90	Calgary Flames	Fr-Tour	4	1	0	1	....	....	....	6	....	....	....	....	....	....	....	....	....	....	....	....	....	....	....	....	....	....
	Calgary Flames	**NHL**	78	39	33	72	34	24	58	222	5	0	5	175	22.3	107	19	64	7	31	6	2	5	7	41	0	0	0
1990-91	**Calgary Flames**	**NHL**	80	22	31	53	20	24	44	252	0	0	3	132	16.7	75	3	68	11	15	7	1	3	4	18	0	0	0
1991-92	**Calgary Flames**	**NHL**	76	53	37	90	48	28	76	207	15	0	2	196	27.0	121	33	79	23	32	....	....	....	....	....	....	....	....

Season	Club	League	GP	G	A	Pts	AG	AA	APts	PIM	PP	SH	GW	S	%	TGF	PGF	TGA	PGA	+/–	GP	G	A	Pts	PIM	PP	SH	GW
			REGULAR SEASON																		PLAYOFFS							
1992-93	**Calgary Flames**	**NHL**	**58**	**38**	**41**	**79**	**32**	**28**	**60**	**172**	**8**	**3**	**4**	**166**	**22.9**	**104**	**26**	**55**	**9**	**32**	**5**	**1**	**6**	**7**	**43**	**1**	**0**	**0**
1993-94	**Calgary Flames**	**NHL**	**73**	**41**	**43**	**84**	**38**	**33**	**71**	**145**	**12**	**3**	**5**	**202**	**20.3**	**128**	**49**	**63**	**21**	**37**	**7**	**2**	**6**	**8**	**24**	**1**	**0**	**1**
1994-95	**Calgary Flames**	**NHL**	**8**	**2**	**2**	**4**	**4**	**3**	**7**	**43**	**2**	**0**	**0**	**20**	**10.0**	**8**	**5**	**3**	**1**	**1**	....	....	....	....	....	....	....	....
1995-96	**Calgary Flames**	**NHL**	**35**	**22**	**20**	**42**	**22**	**16**	**38**	**78**	**9**	**0**	**5**	**84**	**26.2**	**51**	**21**	**16**	**1**	**15**	....	....	....	....	....	....	....	....
1996-97	**Calgary Flames**	**NHL**	DID NOT PLAY – INJURED																									
1997-98	**Carolina Hurricanes**	**NHL**	**61**	**20**	**29**	**49**	**23**	**28**	**51**	**103**	**4**	**0**	**2**	**106**	**18.9**	**65**	**20**	**46**	**4**	**3**	....	....	....	....	....	....	....	....
1998-99	**Carolina Hurricanes**	**NHL**	**77**	**14**	**28**	**42**	**16**	**27**	**43**	**178**	**1**	**1**	**4**	**138**	**10.1**	**62**	**15**	**54**	**9**	**2**	**6**	**1**	**1**	**2**	**8**	**0**	**0**	**0**
99-2000	**Carolina Hurricanes**	**NHL**	**69**	**23**	**30**	**53**	**26**	**28**	**54**	**62**	**12**	**0**	**1**	**150**	**15.3**	**78**	**26**	**64**	**2**	**–10**	....	....	....	....	....	....	....	....
	NHL Totals		**792**	**314**	**335**	**649**	**297**	**268**	**565**	**2079**	**68**	**8**	**34**	**1648**	**19.1**	**942**	**220**	**609**	**107**		**64**	**14**	**31**	**45**	**224**	**2**	**0**	**1**

OHL Second All-Star Team (1985, 1986) • Won Bill Masterton Memorial Trophy (1996) • Played in NHL All-Star Game (1992, 1993)

• Missed remainder of 1994-95 and majority of 1995-96 seasons recovering from neck injury suffered in game vs. Toronto, February 4, 1995. • Missed remainder of 1995-96 and entire 1996-97 seasons recovering from neck injury suffered in game vs. Vancouver, April 3, 1996. Traded to **Carolina** by **Calgary** with Trevor Kidd for Andrew Cassels and Jean-Sebastien Giguere, August 25, 1997. Signed as a free agent by **Toronto**, July 4, 2000.

• ROBERTS, Gordie

Gordon Douglas D – L. 6'1", 195 lbs. b: Detroit, MI, 10/2/1957. Montreal's 7th, 54th overall, in 1977. **USHOF**

Season	Club	League	GP	G	A	Pts	AG	AA	APts	PIM	PP	SH	GW	S	%	TGF	PGF	TGA	PGA	+/–	GP	G	A	Pts	PIM	PP	SH	GW
1973-74	Detroit Jr. Red Wings	OJHL	70	25	55	80	....	....	....	340	....	....	....	....	....	....	....	....	....	....	....	....	....	....	....	....	....	....
1974-75	Victoria Cougars	WHL	53	19	45	64	....	....	....	145	....	....	....	....	....	....	....	....	....	....	12	1	9	10	42	....	....	....
1975-76	New England Whalers	WHA	77	3	19	22	....	....	....	102	....	....	....	....	....	....	....	....	....	....	17	2	9	11	36	....	....	....
1976-77	New England Whalers	WHA	77	13	33	46	....	....	....	169	....	....	....	....	....	....	....	....	....	....	5	2	2	4	6	....	....	....
1977-78	New England Whalers	WHA	78	15	46	61	....	....	....	118	....	....	....	....	....	....	....	....	....	....	14	0	5	5	29	....	....	....
1978-79	New England Whalers	WHA	79	11	46	57	....	....	....	113	....	....	....	....	....	....	....	....	....	....	10	0	4	4	10	....	....	....
1979-80	**Hartford Whalers**	**NHL**	**80**	**8**	**28**	**36**	**7**	**20**	**27**	**89**	**1**	**0**	**1**	**107**	**7.5**	**135**	**16**	**133**	**20**	**6**	**3**	**1**	**1**	**2**	**2**	**0**	**0**	**0**
1980-81	**Hartford Whalers**	**NHL**	**27**	**2**	**11**	**13**	**2**	**7**	**9**	**81**	**1**	**0**	**0**	**36**	**5.6**	**36**	**6**	**58**	**13**	**–15**	....	....	....	....	....	....	....	....
	Minnesota North Stars	**NHL**	**50**	**6**	**31**	**37**	**5**	**21**	**26**	**94**	**3**	**0**	**0**	**83**	**7.2**	**73**	**21**	**66**	**16**	**2**	**19**	**1**	**5**	**6**	**17**	**0**	**1**	**0**
1981-82	**Minnesota North Stars**	**NHL**	**79**	**4**	**30**	**34**	**3**	**20**	**23**	**119**	**0**	**0**	**0**	**104**	**3.8**	**127**	**33**	**119**	**24**	**–1**	**4**	**0**	**3**	**3**	**27**	**0**	**0**	**0**
	United States	WEC-A	7	3	4	7	....	....	....	12	....	....	....	....	....	....	....	....	....	....	....	....	....	....	....	....	....	....
1982-83	**Minnesota North Stars**	**NHL**	**80**	**3**	**41**	**44**	**2**	**28**	**30**	**103**	**2**	**0**	**1**	**127**	**2.4**	**135**	**35**	**108**	**26**	**18**	**9**	**1**	**5**	**6**	**14**	**0**	**0**	**0**
1983-84	**Minnesota North Stars**	**NHL**	**77**	**8**	**45**	**53**	**6**	**31**	**37**	**132**	**1**	**1**	**0**	**131**	**6.1**	**147**	**35**	**136**	**38**	**14**	**15**	**3**	**7**	**10**	**23**	**1**	**1**	**0**
1984-85	United States	Can-Cup	6	1	0	1	....	....	....	6	....	....	....	....	....	....	....	....	....	....	....	....	....	....	....	....	....	....
	Minnesota North Stars	**NHL**	**78**	**6**	**36**	**42**	**5**	**24**	**29**	**112**	**1**	**0**	**0**	**142**	**4.2**	**104**	**32**	**122**	**38**	**–12**	**9**	**1**	**6**	**7**	**6**	**0**	**0**	**0**
1985-86	**Minnesota North Stars**	**NHL**	**76**	**2**	**21**	**23**	**2**	**14**	**16**	**101**	**0**	**0**	**0**	**66**	**3.0**	**101**	**4**	**106**	**23**	**14**	**5**	**0**	**4**	**4**	**8**	**0**	**0**	**0**
1986-87	**Minnesota North Stars**	**NHL**	**67**	**3**	**10**	**13**	**3**	**7**	**10**	**68**	**0**	**0**	**1**	**43**	**7.0**	**61**	**1**	**111**	**44**	**–7**	....	....	....	....	....	....	....	....
	United States	WEC-A	10	0	1	1	....	....	....	33	....	....	....	....	....	....	....	....	....	....	....	....	....	....	....	....	....	....
1987-88	**Minnesota North Stars**	**NHL**	**48**	**1**	**10**	**11**	**1**	**7**	**8**	**103**	**0**	**0**	**0**	**33**	**3.0**	**37**	**3**	**80**	**29**	**–17**	....	....	....	....	....	....	....	....
	Philadelphia Flyers	**NHL**	**11**	**1**	**2**	**3**	**1**	**1**	**2**	**15**	**0**	**0**	**0**	**9**	**11.1**	**19**	**2**	**13**	**3**	**7**	....	....	....	....	....	....	....	....
	St. Louis Blues	**NHL**	**11**	**1**	**3**	**4**	**1**	**2**	**3**	**25**	**0**	**0**	**0**	**10**	**10.0**	**14**	**1**	**19**	**6**	**0**	**10**	**1**	**2**	**3**	**33**	**0**	**0**	**0**
1988-89	**St. Louis Blues**	**NHL**	**77**	**2**	**24**	**26**	**2**	**17**	**19**	**90**	**0**	**0**	**0**	**52**	**3.8**	**91**	**12**	**111**	**39**	**7**	**10**	**1**	**7**	**8**	**8**	**0**	**0**	**0**
1989-90	**St. Louis Blues**	**NHL**	**75**	**3**	**14**	**17**	**3**	**10**	**13**	**140**	**0**	**0**	**0**	**56**	**5.4**	**71**	**6**	**101**	**24**	**–12**	**10**	**0**	**2**	**2**	**26**	**0**	**0**	**0**
1990-91	**St. Louis Blues**	**NHL**	**3**	**0**	**1**	**1**	**0**	**1**	**1**	**8**	**0**	**0**	**0**	**2**	**0.0**	**2**	**0**	**3**	**0**	**–1**	....	....	....	....	....	....	....	....
	Peoria Rivermen	IHL	6	0	8	8	....	....	....	4	....	....	....	....	....	....	....	....	....	....	....	....	....	....	....	....	....	....
♦	**Pittsburgh Penguins**	**NHL**	**61**	**3**	**12**	**15**	**3**	**9**	**12**	**70**	**0**	**0**	**0**	**22**	**13.6**	**67**	**0**	**69**	**20**	**18**	**24**	**1**	**2**	**3**	**63**	**0**	**0**	**0**
1991-92♦	**Pittsburgh Penguins**	**NHL**	**73**	**2**	**22**	**24**	**2**	**17**	**19**	**87**	**1**	**0**	**1**	**29**	**6.9**	**78**	**4**	**72**	**17**	**19**	**19**	**0**	**2**	**2**	**32**	**0**	**0**	**0**
1992-93	**Boston Bruins**	**NHL**	**65**	**5**	**12**	**17**	**4**	**8**	**12**	**105**	**0**	**0**	**1**	**40**	**12.5**	**74**	**6**	**67**	**22**	**23**	**4**	**0**	**0**	**0**	**6**	**0**	**0**	**0**
1993-94	**Boston Bruins**	**NHL**	**59**	**1**	**6**	**7**	**1**	**5**	**6**	**40**	**0**	**0**	**0**	**19**	**5.3**	**30**	**0**	**47**	**4**	**–13**	**12**	**0**	**1**	**1**	**8**	**0**	**0**	**0**
1994-95	Chicago Wolves	IHL	68	6	22	28	....	....	....	80	....	....	....	....	....	....	....	....	....	....	3	0	0	0	4	....	....	....
1995-96	Minnesota Moose	IHL	37	1	12	13	....	....	....	44	....	....	....	....	....	....	....	....	....	....	....	....	....	....	....	....	....	....
	NHL Totals		**1097**	**61**	**359**	**420**	**53**	**249**	**302**	**1582**	**10**	**1**	**5**	**1111**	**5.5**	**1402**	**217**	**1541**	**406**		**153**	**10**	**47**	**57**	**273**	**1**	**2**	**0**
	Other Major League Totals		311	42	144	186	....	....	....	502	....	....	....	....	....	....	....	....	....	....	46	4	20	24	81	....	....	....

• Brother of Doug

Signed as an underage free agent by **New England** (WHA), August, 1975. Claimed by **Hartford** from **Montreal** in Expansion Draft, June 22, 1979. Traded to **Minnesota** by **Hartford** for Mike Fidler, December 16, 1980. Traded to **Philadelphia** by **Minnesota** for future considerations, February 8, 1988. Traded to **St. Louis** by **Philadelphia** for future considerations, March 8, 1988. Traded to **Pittsburgh** by **St. Louis** for Pittsburgh's 11th round choice (Wade Saltzman) in 1992 Entry Draft, October 2, 1990. Signed as a free agent by **Boston**, July 23, 1992.

• ROBERTS, Jim

James Drew LW – L. 6'1", 198 lbs. b: Toronto, Ont., 6/8/1956. Minnesota's 2nd, 31st overall, in 1976.

Season	Club	League	GP	G	A	Pts	AG	AA	APts	PIM	PP	SH	GW	S	%	TGF	PGF	TGA	PGA	+/–	GP	G	A	Pts	PIM	PP	SH	GW
1972-73	Owen Sound Greyhounds	OHA-B	STATISTICS NOT AVAILABLE																									
1973-74	Ottawa 67's	OMJHL	64	13	18	31	....	....	....	44	....	....	....	....	....	....	....	....	....	....	7	2	0	2	2	....	....	....
1974-75	Ottawa 67's	OMJHL	60	22	40	62	....	....	....	58	....	....	....	....	....	....	....	....	....	....	7	0	0	0	0	....	....	....
1975-76	Ottawa 67's	OMJHL	64	27	56	83	....	....	....	62	....	....	....	....	....	....	....	....	....	....	12	3	9	12	6	....	....	....
1976-77	**Minnesota North Stars**	**NHL**	**53**	**11**	**8**	**19**	**10**	**6**	**16**	**14**	**1**	**0**	**0**	**73**	**15.1**	**33**	**3**	**39**	**0**	**–9**	**2**	**0**	**0**	**0**	**0**	**0**	**0**	**0**
	New Haven Nighthawks	AHL	10	7	3	10	....	....	....	6	....	....	....	....	....	....	....	....	....	....	....	....	....	....	....	....	....	....
1977-78	**Minnesota North Stars**	**NHL**	**42**	**4**	**14**	**18**	**4**	**11**	**15**	**19**	**0**	**0**	**0**	**75**	**5.3**	**36**	**11**	**43**	**4**	**–14**								
	Fort Worth Texans	CHL	33	15	7	22	....	....	....	12	....	....	....	....	....	....	....	....	....	....	....	....	....	....	....	....	....	....
1978-79	**Minnesota North Stars**	**NHL**	**11**	**2**	**1**	**3**	**2**	**1**	**3**	**0**	**0**	**0**	**0**	**8**	**25.0**	**5**	**1**	**9**	**0**	**–5**								
	Oklahoma City Stars	CHL	66	21	22	43	....	....	....	34	....	....	....	....	....	....	....	....	....	....	....	....	....	....	....	....	....	....
1979-80	Cincinnati Stingers	CHL	26	8	10	18	....	....	....	11	....	....	....	....	....	....	....	....	....	....	....	....	....	....	....	....	....	....
	Maine Mariners	AHL	48	17	16	33	....	....	....	22	....	....	....	....	....	....	....	....	....	....	9	1	2	3	0	....	....	....
	NHL Totals		**106**	**17**	**23**	**40**	**16**	**18**	**34**	**33**	**1**	**0**	**0**	**156**	**10.9**	**74**	**15**	**91**	**4**		**2**	**0**	**0**	**0**	**0**	**0**	**0**	**0**

Claimed by **Winnipeg** from **Minnesota** in Expansion Draft, June 13, 1979.

• ROBERTS, Jimmy

James Wilfred D/RW – R. 5'10", 185 lbs. b: Toronto, Ont., 4/9/1940.

Season	Club	League	GP	G	A	Pts	AG	AA	APts	PIM	PP	SH	GW	S	%	TGF	PGF	TGA	PGA	+/–	GP	G	A	Pts	PIM	PP	SH	GW
1958-59	Peterborough Petes	OHA-Jr.	54	2	8	10	....	....	....	34	....	....	....	....	....	....	....	....	....	....	19	0	0	0	2	....	....	....
	Peterborough Petes	Mem-Cup	12	2	1	3	....	....	....	2	....	....	....	....	....	....	....	....	....	....	....	....	....	....	....	....	....	....
1959-60	Peterborough Petes	OHA-Jr.	48	6	21	27	....	....	....	55	....	....	....	....	....	....	....	....	....	....	12	2	7	9	18	....	....	....
	Montreal Royals	EPHL	....	....	....	....	....	....	....	....	....	....	....	....	....	....	....	....	....	....	4	0	0	0	4	....	....	....
1960-61	Montreal Royals	EPHL	51	7	18	25	....	....	....	55	....	....	....	....	....	....	....	....	....	....	....	....	....	....	....	....	....	....
1961-62	Hull-Ottawa Canadiens	EPHL	67	11	28	39	....	....	....	42	....	....	....	....	....	....	....	....	....	....	13	3	0	3	18	....	....	....
1962-63	Hull-Ottawa Canadiens	EPHL	72	2	27	29	....	....	....	78	....	....	....	....	....	....	....	....	....	....	3	0	0	0	10	....	....	....
	Cleveland Barons	AHL	....	....	....	....	....	....	....	....	....	....	....	....	....	....	....	....	....	....	1	0	0	0	2	....	....	....
1963-64	**Montreal Canadiens**	**NHL**	**15**	**0**	**1**	**1**	**0**	**1**	**1**	**2**	....	....	....	....	....	....	....	....	....	....	**7**	**0**	**1**	**1**	**14**	**0**	**0**	**0**
	Cleveland Barons	AHL	9	1	3	4	....	....	....	4	....	....	....	....	....	....	....	....	....	....	....	....	....	....	....	....	....	....
	Quebec Aces	AHL	2	0	0	0	....	....	....	2	....	....	....	....	....	....	....	....	....	....	....	....	....	....	....	....	....	....
	Omaha Knights	CPHL	46	18	19	37	....	....	....	47	....	....	....	....	....	....	....	....	....	....	....	....	....	....	....	....	....	....
1964-65♦	**Montreal Canadiens**	**NHL**	**70**	**3**	**10**	**13**	**4**	**10**	**14**	**40**	....	....	....	....	....	....	....	....	....	....	**13**	**0**	**0**	**0**	**30**	**0**	**0**	**0**
1965-66♦	**Montreal Canadiens**	**NHL**	**70**	**5**	**5**	**10**	**6**	**5**	**11**	**20**	....	....	....	....	....	....	....	....	....	....	**10**	**1**	**1**	**2**	**10**	**0**	**1**	**0**
1966-67	**Montreal Canadiens**	**NHL**	**63**	**3**	**0**	**3**	**3**	**0**	**3**	**16**	....	....	....	....	....	....	....	....	....	....	**4**	**1**	**0**	**1**	**0**	**0**	**0**	**0**
1967-68	**St. Louis Blues**	**NHL**	**74**	**14**	**23**	**37**	**16**	**23**	**39**	**66**	**3**	**1**	**1**	**164**	**8.5**	**77**	**27**	**81**	**23**	**–8**	**18**	**4**	**1**	**5**	**20**	**0**	**0**	**1**
1968-69	**St. Louis Blues**	**NHL**	**72**	**14**	**19**	**33**	**15**	**17**	**32**	**81**	**2**	**1**	**1**	**129**	**10.9**	**63**	**13**	**64**	**27**	**13**	**12**	**1**	**4**	**5**	**10**	**0**	**0**	**0**
1969-70	**St. Louis Blues**	**NHL**	**76**	**13**	**17**	**30**	**14**	**16**	**30**	**51**	**1**	**2**	**4**	**165**	**7.9**	**65**	**11**	**59**	**23**	**18**	**16**	**2**	**3**	**5**	**29**	**0**	**0**	**0**
1970-71	**St. Louis Blues**	**NHL**	**72**	**13**	**18**	**31**	**13**	**15**	**28**	**77**	**2**	**1**	**0**	**123**	**10.6**	**78**	**16**	**85**	**30**	**7**	**6**	**2**	**1**	**3**	**11**	**0**	**0**	**0**
1971-72	**St. Louis Blues**	**NHL**	**26**	**5**	**7**	**12**	**5**	**6**	**11**	**4**	**1**	**2**	**0**	**46**	**10.9**	**28**	**5**	**28**	**9**	**4**								
	Montreal Canadiens	**NHL**	**51**	**7**	**15**	**22**	**7**	**13**	**20**	**53**	**0**	**3**	**1**	**69**	**10.1**	**40**	**2**	**46**	**11**	**3**	**6**	**1**	**0**	**1**	**0**	**0**	**0**	**1**
1972-73♦	**Montreal Canadiens**	**NHL**	**77**	**14**	**18**	**32**	**13**	**14**	**27**	**28**	**0**	**1**	**3**	**104**	**13.5**	**76**	**1**	**56**	**14**	**33**	**17**	**0**	**2**	**2**	**22**	**0**	**0**	**0**
1973-74	**Montreal Canadiens**	**NHL**	**67**	**8**	**16**	**24**	**8**	**13**	**21**	**39**	**0**	**1**	**2**	**97**	**8.2**	**76**	**0**	**71**	**22**	**27**	**6**	**0**	**0**	**0**	**4**	**0**	**0**	**0**
1974-75	**Montreal Canadiens**	**NHL**	**79**	**5**	**13**	**18**	**4**	**10**	**14**	**52**	**0**	**2**	**0**	**85**	**5.9**	**61**	**3**	**67**	**27**	**18**	**11**	**2**	**2**	**4**	**2**	**0**	**0**	**0**
1975-76♦	**Montreal Canadiens**	**NHL**	**74**	**13**	**8**	**21**	**11**	**6**	**17**	**35**	**0**	**0**	**1**	**80**	**16.3**	**33**	**0**	**39**	**13**	**7**	**13**	**3**	**1**	**4**	**2**	**0**	**1**	**0**
1976-77♦	**Montreal Canadiens**	**NHL**	**45**	**5**	**14**	**19**	**4**	**11**	**15**	**18**	**0**	**1**	**1**	**56**	**8.9**	**35**	**0**	**19**	**6**	**22**	**14**	**3**	**0**	**3**	**6**	**0**	**1**	**1**
1977-78	**St. Louis Blues**	**NHL**	**75**	**4**	**10**	**14**	**4**	**8**	**12**	**39**	**0**	**0**	**1**	**70**	**5.7**	**49**	**5**	**87**	**23**	**–20**	....	....	....	....	....	....	....	....
1978-1984	**Buffalo Sabres**	**NHL**	DID NOT PLAY – ASSISTANT COACH																									
1984-1988	**Pittsburgh Penguins**	**NHL**	DID NOT PLAY – ASSISTANT COACH																									

			REGULAR SEASON																		PLAYOFFS							
Season	Club	League	GP	G	A	Pts	AG	AA	APts	PIM	PP	SH	GW	S	%	TGF	PGF	TGA	PGA	+/-	GP	G	A	Pts	PIM	PP	SH	GW
1988-1991	Springfield Indians	AHL	DID NOT PLAY – COACHING																									
1991-1992	**Hartford Whalers**	**NHL**	DID NOT PLAY – COACHING																									
1992-1994			OUT OF HOCKEY – RETIRED																									
1994-1996	Worcester IceCats	AHL	DID NOT PLAY – COACHING																									
1996-2000	**St. Louis Blues**	**NHL**	DID NOT PLAY – ASSISTANT COACH																									
	NHL Totals		**1006**	**126**	**194**	**320**	**127**	**168**	**295**	**621**	....	....	....	....	....	....	....	....	....	....	**153**	**20**	**16**	**36**	**160**	....	....	....

Played in NHL All-Star Game (1965, 1969, 1970)

Claimed by **St. Louis** from **Montreal** in Expansion Draft, June 6, 1967. Traded to **Montreal** by **St. Louis** for Phil Roberto, December 13, 1971. Traded to **St. Louis** by **Montreal** for St. Louis' 3rd round choice (Murray Meyers) in 1979 Amateur Draft, August 18, 1977. • Served as Head Coach with **Buffalo** (21-16-8) in 1981-82. • Served as interim Head Coach with **St. Louis** (3-3-3) in 1996-97.

• ROBERTSON, Geordie

Geordie Jay "Robbie" RW – R. 6', 165 lbs. b: Victoria, B.C., 8/1/1959.

Season	Club	League	GP	G	A	Pts	AG	AA	APts	PIM	PP	SH	GW	S	%	TGF	PGF	TGA	PGA	+/-	GP	G	A	Pts	PIM	PP	SH	GW
1975-76	Nanaimo Clippers	BCJHL	STATISTICS NOT AVAILABLE																									
	Victoria Cougars	WCJHL	3	3	2	5	....	....	....	0	....	....	....	....	....	....	....	....	....	....	....	....	....	....	....	....	....	....
1976-77	Victoria Cougars	WCJHL	72	39	44	83	....	....	....	107	....	....	....	....	....	....	....	....	....	....	....	....	....	....	....	....	....	....
1977-78	Victoria Cougars	WCJHL	61	64	72	136	....	....	....	85	....	....	....	....	....	....	....	....	....	....	13	15	11	26	42	....	....	....
1978-79	Victoria Cougars	WHL	54	31	42	73	....	....	....	94	....	....	....	....	....	....	....	....	....	....	14	15	10	25	22	....	....	....
1979-80	Rochester Americans	AHL	55	26	26	52	....	....	....	66	....	....	....	....	....	....	....	....	....	....	4	1	4	5	2	....	....	....
1980-81	Rochester Americans	AHL	20	3	3	6	....	....	....	19	....	....	....	....	....	....	....	....	....	....	....	....	....	....	....	....	....	....
1981-82	Rochester Americans	AHL	46	14	15	29	....	....	....	45	....	....	....	....	....	....	....	....	....	....	9	1	3	4	13	....	....	....
1982-83	**Buffalo Sabres**	**NHL**	**5**	**1**	**2**	**3**	**1**	**1**	**2**	**7**	**0**	**0**	**0**	**10**	**10.0**	**5**	**4**	**2**	**0**	**–1**	....	....	....	....	....	....	....	....
	Rochester Americans	AHL	72	46	73	119	....	....	....	83	....	....	....	....	....	....	....	....	....	....	16	8	6	14	23	....	....	....
1983-84	Rochester Americans	AHL	64	37	54	91	....	....	....	103	....	....	....	....	....	....	....	....	....	....	18	9	9	18	42	....	....	....
1984-85	Rochester Americans	AHL	70	27	48	75	....	....	....	91	....	....	....	....	....	....	....	....	....	....	5	0	1	1	4	....	....	....
1985-86	Adirondack Red Wings	AHL	79	36	56	92	....	....	....	99	....	....	....	....	....	....	....	....	....	....	15	4	6	10	25	....	....	....
1986-87	Adirondack Red Wings	AHL	63	28	41	69	....	....	....	94	....	....	....	....	....	....	....	....	....	....	....	....	....	....	....	....	....	....
1987-88	JyP-HT Jyvaskyla	Finland	34	14	6	20	....	....	....	28	....	....	....	....	....	....	....	....	....	....	....	....	....	....	....	....	....	....
	Adirondack Red Wings	AHL	30	11	15	26	....	....	....	24	....	....	....	....	....	....	....	....	....	....	6	1	2	3	14	....	....	....
1988-89	Rochester Americans	AHL	32	11	12	23	....	....	....	12	....	....	....	....	....	....	....	....	....	....	....	....	....	....	....	....	....	....
	NHL Totals		**5**	**1**	**2**	**3**	**1**	**1**	**2**	**7**	**0**	**0**	**0**	**10**	**10.0**	**5**	**4**	**2**	**0**		....	....	....	....	....	....	....	....

• Brother of Torrie

Signed as a free agent by **Buffalo**, September 5, 1979. Signed as a free agent by **Detroit**, July 9, 1985.

• ROBERTSON, Torrie

Torrie Andrew LW – L. 5'11", 200 lbs. b: Victoria, B.C., 8/2/1961. Washington's 3rd, 55th overall, in 1980.

Season	Club	League	GP	G	A	Pts	AG	AA	APts	PIM	PP	SH	GW	S	%	TGF	PGF	TGA	PGA	+/-	GP	G	A	Pts	PIM	PP	SH	GW
1976-77	Nanaimo Clippers	BCJHL	STATISTICS NOT AVAILABLE																									
	Victoria Cougars	WCJHL	1	0	0	0	....	....	....	0	....	....	....	....	....	....	....	....	....	....	....	....	....	....	....	....	....	....
1977-78	Nanaimo Clippers	BCJHL	34	15	15	30	....	....	....	198	....	....	....	....	....	....	....	....	....	....	....	....	....	....	....	....	....	....
1978-79	Victoria Cougars	WHL	69	18	23	41	....	....	....	141	....	....	....	....	....	....	....	....	....	....	15	1	2	3	29	....	....	....
1979-80	Victoria Cougars	WHL	72	23	24	47	....	....	....	298	....	....	....	....	....	....	....	....	....	....	17	5	7	12	117	....	....	....
1980-81	Victoria Cougars	WHL	59	45	66	111	....	....	....	274	....	....	....	....	....	....	....	....	....	....	15	10	13	23	55	....	....	....
	Washington Capitals	**NHL**	**3**	**0**	**0**	**0**	**0**	**0**	**0**	**0**	**0**	**0**	**0**	**3**	**0.0**	**0**	**0**	**2**	**0**	**–2**	....	....	....	....	....	....	....	....
	Victoria Cougars	Mem-Cup	4	2	2	4	....	....	....	6	....	....	....	....	....	....	....	....	....	....	....	....	....	....	....	....	....	....
1981-82	**Washington Capitals**	**NHL**	**54**	**8**	**13**	**21**	**6**	**9**	**15**	**204**	**3**	**0**	**0**	**46**	**17.4**	**28**	**6**	**23**	**0**	**–1**	....	....	....	....	....	....	....	....
	Hershey Bears	AHL	21	5	3	8	....	....	....	60	....	....	....	....	....	....	....	....	....	....	....	....	....	....	....	....	....	....
1982-83	**Washington Capitals**	**NHL**	**5**	**2**	**0**	**2**	**2**	**0**	**2**	**4**	**0**	**0**	**0**	**5**	**40.0**	**3**	**0**	**5**	**0**	**–2**	....	....	....	....	....	....	....	....
	Hershey Bears	AHL	69	21	33	54	....	....	....	187	....	....	....	....	....	....	....	....	....	....	5	1	2	3	8	....	....	....
1983-84	**Hartford Whalers**	**NHL**	**66**	**7**	**13**	**20**	**6**	**9**	**15**	**198**	**0**	**0**	**2**	**61**	**11.5**	**35**	**2**	**42**	**0**	**–9**	....	....	....	....	....	....	....	....
1984-85	**Hartford Whalers**	**NHL**	**74**	**11**	**30**	**41**	**9**	**20**	**29**	**337**	**1**	**0**	**3**	**72**	**15.3**	**58**	**14**	**57**	**0**	**–13**	....	....	....	....	....	....	....	....
1985-86	**Hartford Whalers**	**NHL**	**76**	**13**	**24**	**37**	**10**	**16**	**26**	**358**	**3**	**0**	**0**	**89**	**14.6**	**50**	**11**	**50**	**0**	**–11**	**10**	**1**	**0**	**1**	**67**	**0**	**0**	**0**
1986-87	**Hartford Whalers**	**NHL**	**20**	**1**	**0**	**1**	**1**	**0**	**1**	**98**	**0**	**0**	**1**	**19**	**5.3**	**6**	**0**	**12**	**0**	**–6**	....	....	....	....	....	....	....	....
1987-88	**Hartford Whalers**	**NHL**	**63**	**2**	**8**	**10**	**2**	**6**	**8**	**293**	**0**	**0**	**1**	**46**	**4.3**	**17**	**0**	**17**	**0**	**0**	**6**	**0**	**1**	**1**	**6**	**0**	**0**	**0**
1988-89	**Hartford Whalers**	**NHL**	**27**	**2**	**4**	**6**	**2**	**3**	**5**	**84**	**0**	**0**	**1**	**21**	**9.5**	**9**	**1**	**11**	**0**	**–3**	....	....	....	....	....	....	....	....
	Detroit Red Wings	**NHL**	**12**	**2**	**2**	**4**	**2**	**1**	**3**	**63**	**0**	**0**	**0**	**5**	**40.0**	**6**	**0**	**6**	**0**	**0**	**6**	**1**	**0**	**1**	**17**	**0**	**0**	**0**
1989-90	**Detroit Red Wings**	**NHL**	**42**	**1**	**5**	**6**	**1**	**4**	**5**	**112**	**0**	**0**	**0**	**20**	**5.0**	**11**	**0**	**14**	**0**	**–3**	....	....	....	....	....	....	....	....
	Adirondack Red Wings	AHL	27	3	13	16	....	....	....	47	....	....	....	....	....	....	....	....	....	....	6	1	1	2	33	....	....	....
1990-91	Rochester Americans	AHL	1	0	1	1	....	....	....	0	....	....	....	....	....	....	....	....	....	....	....	....	....	....	....	....	....	....
	Albany Choppers	IHL	1	0	0	0	....	....	....	0	....	....	....	....	....	....	....	....	....	....	....	....	....	....	....	....	....	....
	NHL Totals		**442**	**49**	**99**	**148**	**41**	**68**	**109**	**1751**	**7**	**0**	**8**	**387**	**12.7**	**223**	**34**	**239**	**0**		**22**	**2**	**1**	**3**	**90**	**0**	**0**	**0**

• Brother of Geordie • WHL Second All-Star Team (1980)

Traded to **Hartford** by **Washington** for Greg C. Adams, October 3, 1983. Traded to **Detroit** by **Hartford** for Jim Pavese, March 7, 1989.

• ROBERTSSON, Bert

Bert Erik Johan D – L. 6'3", 210 lbs. b: Sodertalje, Sweden, 6/30/1974. Vancouver's 8th, 254th overall, in 1993.

Season	Club	League	GP	G	A	Pts	AG	AA	APts	PIM	PP	SH	GW	S	%	TGF	PGF	TGA	PGA	+/-	GP	G	A	Pts	PIM	PP	SH	GW
1992-93	Sodertalje SK	Sweden-Jr.	12	1	5	6	....	....	....	20	....	....	....	....	....	....	....	....	....	....	....	....	....	....	....	....	....	....
	Sodertalje SK	Sweden-2	23	2	1	3	....	....	....	24	....	....	....	....	....	....	....	....	....	....	2	0	0	0	0	....	....	....
1993-94	Sodertalje SK	Sweden-2	28	0	1	1	....	....	....	12	....	....	....	....	....	....	....	....	....	....	1	0	0	0	0	....	....	....
1994-95	Sodertalje SK	Sweden-Jr.	11	2	3	5	....	....	....	4	....	....	....	....	....	....	....	....	....	....	....	....	....	....	....	....	....	....
	Sodertalje SK	Sweden-2	23	1	2	3	....	....	....	24	....	....	....	....	....	....	....	....	....	....	3	0	1	1	2	....	....	....
1995-96	Syracuse Crunch	AHL	65	1	7	8	....	....	....	109	....	....	....	....	....	....	....	....	....	....	16	0	1	1	26	....	....	....
1996-97	Syracuse Crunch	AHL	80	4	9	13	....	....	....	132	....	....	....	....	....	....	....	....	....	....	3	1	0	1	4	....	....	....
1997-98	**Vancouver Canucks**	**NHL**	**30**	**2**	**4**	**6**	**2**	**4**	**6**	**24**	**0**	**0**	**0**	**19**	**10.5**	**12**	**0**	**11**	**1**	**2**	....	....	....	....	....	....	....	....
	Syracuse Crunch	AHL	42	5	9	14	....	....	....	87	....	....	....	....	....	....	....	....	....	....	3	0	0	0	6	....	....	....
1998-99	**Vancouver Canucks**	**NHL**	**39**	**2**	**2**	**4**	**2**	**2**	**4**	**13**	**0**	**0**	**0**	**13**	**15.4**	**5**	**0**	**14**	**2**	**–7**	....	....	....	....	....	....	....	....
	Syracuse Crunch	AHL	8	1	0	1	....	....	....	21	....	....	....	....	....	....	....	....	....	....	....	....	....	....	....	....	....	....
99-2000	**Edmonton Oilers**	**NHL**	**52**	**0**	**4**	**4**	**0**	**4**	**4**	**34**	**0**	**0**	**0**	**31**	**0.0**	**16**	**1**	**21**	**3**	**–3**	**5**	**0**	**0**	**0**	**0**	**0**	**0**	**0**
	Hamilton Bulldogs	AHL	6	0	3	3	....	....	....	12	....	....	....	....	....	....	....	....	....	....	....	....	....	....	....	....	....	....
	NHL Totals		**121**	**4**	**10**	**14**	**4**	**10**	**14**	**71**	**0**	**0**	**0**	**63**	**6.3**	**33**	**1**	**46**	**6**		**5**	**0**	**0**	**0**	**0**	**0**	**0**	**0**

Signed as a free agent by **Edmonton**, August 19, 1999. Selected by **Columbus** from **Edmonton** in Expansion Draft, June 23, 2000.

• ROBIDAS, Stephane

D – R. 5'10", 180 lbs. b: Sherbrooke, Que., 3/3/1977. Montreal's 7th, 164th overall, in 1995.

Season	Club	League	GP	G	A	Pts	AG	AA	APts	PIM	PP	SH	GW	S	%	TGF	PGF	TGA	PGA	+/-	GP	G	A	Pts	PIM	PP	SH	GW
1992-93	Magog Cantonniers	QAAA	41	3	12	15	....	....	....	....	....	....	....	....	....	....	....	....	....	....	....	....	....	....	....	....	....	....
1993-94	Shawinigan Cataractes	QMJHL	67	3	18	21	....	....	....	33	....	....	....	....	....	....	....	....	....	....	1	0	0	0	0	....	....	....
1994-95	Shawinigan Cataractes	QMJHL	71	13	56	69	....	....	....	44	....	....	....	....	....	....	....	....	....	....	15	7	12	19	4	....	....	....
1995-96	Shawinigan Cataractes	QMJHL	67	23	56	79	....	....	....	53	....	....	....	....	....	....	....	....	....	....	6	1	5	6	10	....	....	....
1996-97	Shawinigan Cataractes	QMJHL	67	24	51	75	....	....	....	59	....	....	....	....	....	....	....	....	....	....	7	4	6	10	14	....	....	....
1997-98	Fredericton Canadiens	AHL	79	10	21	31	....	....	....	50	....	....	....	....	....	....	....	....	....	....	4	0	2	2	0	....	....	....
1998-99	Fredericton Canadiens	AHL	79	8	33	41	....	....	....	59	....	....	....	....	....	....	....	....	....	....	15	1	5	6	10	....	....	....
99-2000	**Montreal Canadiens**	**NHL**	**1**	**0**	**0**	**0**	**0**	**0**	**0**	**0**	**0**	**0**	**0**	**0**	**0.0**	**0**	**0**	**0**	**0**	**0**	....	....	....	....	....	....	....	....
	Quebec Citadelles	AHL	76	14	31	45	....	....	....	36	....	....	....	....	....	....	....	....	....	....	3	0	1	1	0	....	....	....
	NHL Totals		**1**	**0**	**0**	**0**	**0**	**0**	**0**	**0**	**0**	**0**	**0**	**0**	**0.0**	**0**	**0**	**0**	**0**		....	....	....	....	....	....	....	....

QMJHL First All-Star Team (1996, 1997)

• ROBIDOUX, Florent

LW – L. 6'2", 190 lbs. b: Treheme, Man., 5/5/1960.

Season	Club	League	GP	G	A	Pts	AG	AA	APts	PIM	PP	SH	GW	S	%	TGF	PGF	TGA	PGA	+/-	GP	G	A	Pts	PIM	PP	SH	GW
1977-78	Estevan Bruins	SJHL	59	29	34	63	....	....	....	99	....	....	....	....	....	....	....	....	....	....	....	....	....	....	....	....	....	....
	New Westminster Bruins	WCJHL	8	1	1	2	....	....	....	12	....	....	....	....	....	....	....	....	....	....	16	1	4	5	35	....	....	....
1978-79	Portland Winter Hawks	WHL	70	36	41	77	....	....	....	73	....	....	....	....	....	....	....	....	....	....	25	11	16	27	20	....	....	....
1979-80	Portland Winter Hawks	WHL	70	43	57	100	....	....	....	157	....	....	....	....	....	....	....	....	....	....	8	5	2	7	10	....	....	....

			REGULAR SEASON																			PLAYOFFS							
Season	Club	League	GP	G	A	Pts	AG	AA	APts	PIM	PP	SH	GW	S	%	TGF	PGF	TGA	PGA	+/–	GP	G	A	Pts	PIM	PP	SH	GW
1980-81	Chicago Black Hawks	NHL	39	6	2	8	5	1	6	75	1	0	0	31	19.4	11	2	15	0	–6	....	....	....	....	....	....	....	....
	New Brunswick Hawks	AHL	35	12	11	23	....	....	....	110	....	....	....	....	....	....	....	....	....	....	13	2	7	9	38	....	....	....
1981-82	Chicago Black Hawks	NHL	4	1	2	3	1	1	2	0	0	0	0	4	25.0	3	0	1	0	2	....	....	....	....	....	....	....	....
	New Brunswick Hawks	AHL	69	31	35	66	....	....	....	200	....	....	....	....	....	....	....	....	....	....	15	*9	10	19	21	....	....	....
1982-83	Chicago Black Hawks	NHL	DID NOT PLAY – INJURED																									
1983-84	Chicago Black Hawks	NHL	9	0	0	0	0	0	0	0	0	0	0	2	0.0	0	0	3	0	–3	....	....	....	....	....	....	....	....
	Springfield Indians	AHL	68	26	22	48	....	....	....	123	....	....	....	....	....	....	....	....	....	....	4	0	1	1	6	....	....	....
1984-85	Milwaukee Admirals	IHL	76	29	35	64	....	....	....	184	....	....	....	....	....	....	....	....	....	....	....	....	....	....	....	....	....	....
1985-86	Hershey Bears	AHL	47	6	3	9	....	....	....	81	....	....	....	....	....	....	....	....	....	....	3	0	0	0	15	....	....	....
1986-87	Milwaukee Admirals	IHL	15	2	7	9	....	....	....	16	....	....	....	....	....	....	....	....	....	....	6	3	3	6	13	....	....	....
	NHL Totals		52	7	4	11	6	2	8	75	1	0	0	37	18.9	14	2	19	0		....	....	....	....	....	....	....	....

WHL All-Star Team (1980)

Signed as a free agent by **Chicago**, October 20, 1979. • Missed entire 1982-83 season recovering from injuries suffered in automobile accident, July, 1982. Signed as a free agent by **Philadelphia**, October 8, 1985.

• ROBINSON, Doug

Douglas Garnet LW – L. 6'2", 197 lbs. b: St. Catharines, Ont., 8/27/1940.

Season	Club	League	GP	G	A	Pts	AG	AA	APts	PIM	PP	SH	GW	S	%	TGF	PGF	TGA	PGA	+/–	GP	G	A	Pts	PIM	PP	SH	GW
1955-56	Collingwood Cobras	OHA-B	STATISTICS NOT AVAILABLE																									
1956-57	Guelph Biltmores	OHA-Jr.	52	9	7	16	....	....	....	8	....	....	....	....	....	....	....	....	....	....	10	1	2	3	14	....	....	....
	Guelph Biltmores	Mem-Cup	6	1	2	3	....	....	....	2	....	....	....	....	....	....	....	....	....	....	....	....	....	....	....	....	....	....
1957-58	Guelph Biltmores	OHA-Jr.	6	2	1	3	....	....	....	2	....	....	....	....	....	....	....	....	....	....	....	....	....	....	....	....	....	....
	St. Catharines Teepees	OHA-Jr.	....	....	....	....	....	....	....	....	....	....	....	....	....	....	....	....	....	....	6	0	1	1	0	....	....	....
1958-59	St. Catharines Teepees	OHA-Jr.	52	12	11	23	....	....	....	10	....	....	....	....	....	....	....	....	....	....	7	0	3	3	0	....	....	....
1959-60	St. Catharines Teepees	OHA-Jr.	48	15	20	35	....	....	....	4	....	....	....	....	....	....	....	....	....	....	17	3	4	7	6	....	....	....
	St. Catharines Teepees	Mem-Cup	14	7	3	10	....	....	....	4	....	....	....	....	....	....	....	....	....	....	....	....	....	....	....	....	....	....
1960-61	St. Catharines Teepees	OHA-Jr.	48	36	30	66	....	....	....	22	....	....	....	....	....	....	....	....	....	....	6	3	1	4	20	....	....	....
	Sault Ste. Marie Thunderbirds	EPHL	....	....	....	....	....	....	....	....	....	....	....	....	....	....	....	....	....	....	1	0	0	0	2	....	....	....
1961-62	Sault Ste. Marie Thunderbirds	EPHL	70	33	26	59	....	....	....	32	....	....	....	....	....	....	....	....	....	....	....	....	....	....	....	....	....	....
	Buffalo Bisons	AHL	....	....	....	....	....	....	....	....	....	....	....	....	....	....	....	....	....	....	2	0	0	0	0	....	....	....
1962-63	Buffalo Bisons	AHL	72	36	37	73	....	....	....	8	....	....	....	....	....	....	....	....	....	....	13	*10	4	14	2	....	....	....
1963-64	Buffalo Bisons	AHL	46	22	27	49	....	....	....	22	....	....	....	....	....	....	....	....	....	....	....	....	....	....	....	....	....	....
	Chicago Black Hawks	NHL	....	....	....	....	....	....	....	....	....	....	....	....	....	....	....	....	....	....	4	0	0	0	0	0	0	0
1964-65	Chicago Black Hawks	NHL	40	2	9	11	2	9	11	8	....	....	....	....	....	....	....	....	....	....	....	....	....	....	....	....	....	....
	New York Rangers	NHL	21	8	14	22	10	14	24	2	....	....	....	....	....	....	....	....	....	....	....	....	....	....	....	....	....	....
1965-66	New York Rangers	NHL	51	8	12	20	9	11	20	8	....	....	....	....	....	....	....	....	....	....	....	....	....	....	....	....	....	....
	Baltimore Clippers	AHL	5	2	2	4	....	....	....	0	....	....	....	....	....	....	....	....	....	....	....	....	....	....	....	....	....	....
1966-67	New York Rangers	NHL	1	0	0	0	0	0	0	0	....	....	....	....	....	....	....	....	....	....	....	....	....	....	....	....	....	....
	Baltimore Clippers	AHL	63	39	33	72	....	....	....	89	....	....	....	....	....	....	....	....	....	....	9	4	6	10	2	....	....	....
1967-68	Los Angeles Kings	NHL	34	9	9	18	10	9	19	6	1	0	0	63	14.3	29	3	22	0	4	7	4	3	7	0	0	0	0
	Springfield Kings	AHL	36	21	25	46	....	....	....	0	....	....	....	....	....	....	....	....	....	....	....	....	....	....	....	....	....	....
1968-69	Los Angeles Kings	NHL	31	2	10	12	2	9	11	2	0	0	0	43	4.7	21	2	23	0	–4	....	....	....	....	....	....	....	....
	Springfield Kings	AHL	42	14	20	34	....	....	....	6	....	....	....	....	....	....	....	....	....	....	....	....	....	....	....	....	....	....
1969-70	Springfield Kings	AHL	70	45	41	86	....	....	....	26	....	....	....	....	....	....	....	....	....	....	14	5	3	8	0	....	....	....
1970-71	Los Angeles Kings	NHL	61	15	13	28	15	11	26	8	3	0	3	85	17.6	42	5	45	0	–8	....	....	....	....	....	....	....	....
1971-72	Seattle Totems	WHL	9	7	1	8	....	....	....	0	....	....	....	....	....	....	....	....	....	....	....	....	....	....	....	....	....	....
	Nova Scotia Voyageurs	AHL	27	10	17	27	....	....	....	4	....	....	....	....	....	....	....	....	....	....	....	....	....	....	....	....	....	....
	NHL Totals		239	44	67	111	48	63	111	34	....	....	....	....	....	....	....	....	....	....	11	4	3	7	0	....	....	....

• Father of Rob • AHL Second All-Star Team (1963) • Won Dudley "Red" Garrett Memorial Award (Top Rookie - AHL) (1963) • AHL First All-Star Team (1970)

Traded to **NY Rangers** by **Chicago** with Wayne Hillman and John Brenneman for Camille Henry, Don Johns, Billy Taylor and Wally Chevrier, February 4, 1965. Claimed by **LA Kings** from **NY Rangers** in Expansion Draft, June 6, 1967. Traded to **Montreal** by **LA Kings** with Denis Dejordy, Dale Hoganson and Noel Price for Rogie Vachon, November 4, 1971.

• ROBINSON, Larry

Larry Clark "Big Bird" D – L. 6'4", 225 lbs. b: Winchester, Ont., 6/2/1951. Montreal's 4th, 20th overall, in 1971. **HHOF**

Season	Club	League	GP	G	A	Pts	AG	AA	APts	PIM	PP	SH	GW	S	%	TGF	PGF	TGA	PGA	+/–	GP	G	A	Pts	PIM	PP	SH	GW
1968-69	Haliburton Hawks	OMHA	STATISTICS NOT AVAILABLE																									
1969-70	Brockville Braves	OJHL	40	22	29	51	....	....	....	74	....	....	....	....	....	....	....	....	....	....	....	....	....	....	....	....	....	....
	Ottawa M&W Rangers	Cen-Cup	5	2	1	3	....	....	....	2	....	....	....	....	....	....	....	....	....	....	....	....	....	....	....	....	....	....
1970-71	Kitchener Rangers	OMJHL	61	12	39	51	....	....	....	65	....	....	....	....	....	....	....	....	....	....	4	1	2	3	5	....	....	....
1971-72	Nova Scotia Voyageurs	AHL	74	10	14	24	....	....	....	54	....	....	....	....	....	....	....	....	....	....	15	2	10	12	31	....	....	....
1972-73	Nova Scotia Voyageurs	AHL	38	6	33	39	....	....	....	33	....	....	....	....	....	....	....	....	....	....	....	....	....	....	....	....	....	....
♦	Montreal Canadiens	NHL	36	2	4	6	2	3	5	20	0	0	1	36	5.6	23	1	19	0	3	11	1	4	5	9	0	0	1
1973-74	Montreal Canadiens	NHL	78	6	20	26	6	16	22	66	0	0	1	98	6.1	111	6	92	19	32	6	0	1	1	26	0	0	0
1974-75	Montreal Canadiens	NHL	80	14	47	61	12	35	47	76	1	0	2	102	13.7	142	17	83	19	61	11	0	4	4	27	0	0	0
1975-76♦	Montreal Canadiens	NHL	80	10	30	40	9	22	31	59	2	0	0	130	7.7	113	16	63	16	50	13	3	3	6	10	0	0	1
1976-77	Canada	Can-Cup	7	0	0	0	....	....	....	0	....	....	....	....	....	....	....	....	....	....	....	....	....	....	....	....	....	....
♦	Montreal Canadiens	NHL	77	19	66	85	17	51	68	45	3	0	3	199	9.5	218	34	74	10	120	14	2	10	12	12	1	0	0
1977-78♦	Montreal Canadiens	NHL	80	13	52	65	12	40	52	39	3	2	5	154	8.4	196	45	107	27	71	15	4	*17	*21	6	2	0	0
1978-79♦	Montreal Canadiens	NHL	67	16	45	61	14	33	47	33	4	0	1	147	10.9	156	41	82	17	50	16	6	9	15	8	1	0	1
	NHL All-Stars	Chal-Cup	3	1	0	1	....	....	....	0	....	....	....	....	....	....	....	....	....	....	....	....	....	....	....	....	....	....
1979-80	Montreal Canadiens	NHL	72	14	61	75	12	45	57	39	6	0	3	133	10.5	173	59	106	30	38	10	0	4	4	2	0	0	0
1980-81	Montreal Canadiens	NHL	65	12	38	50	9	25	34	37	7	0	2	130	9.2	151	35	97	27	46	3	0	1	1	2	0	0	0
	Canada	WEC-A	6	1	1	2	....	....	....	2	....	....	....	....	....	....	....	....	....	....	....	....	....	....	....	....	....	....
1981-82	Canada	Can-Cup	7	0	1	1	....	....	....	2	....	....	....	....	....	....	....	....	....	....	....	....	....	....	....	....	....	....
	Montreal Canadiens	NHL	71	12	47	59	9	31	40	41	5	1	0	141	8.5	165	33	104	29	57	5	0	1	1	8	0	0	0
1982-83	Montreal Canadiens	NHL	71	14	49	63	11	34	45	33	6	0	1	147	9.5	151	41	116	39	33	3	0	0	0	2	0	0	0
1983-84	Montreal Canadiens	NHL	74	9	34	43	7	23	30	39	4	0	1	141	6.4	127	40	117	34	4	15	0	5	5	22	0	0	0
1984-85	Canada	Can-Cup	8	1	2	3	....	....	....	2	....	....	....	....	....	....	....	....	....	....	....	....	....	....	....	....	....	....
	Montreal Canadiens	NHL	76	14	33	47	11	22	33	44	6	0	3	120	11.7	136	32	97	26	33	12	3	8	11	8	1	0	0
1985-86♦	Montreal Canadiens	NHL	78	19	63	82	15	42	57	39	10	0	1	167	11.4	191	65	127	30	29	20	0	13	13	22	0	0	0
1986-87	Montreal Canadiens	NHL	70	13	37	50	11	27	38	44	6	0	3	122	10.7	129	41	74	10	24	17	3	17	20	6	2	0	0
1987-88	Montreal Canadiens	NHL	53	6	34	40	5	24	29	30	2	0	1	96	6.3	105	31	59	11	26	11	1	4	5	4	0	0	0
1988-89	Montreal Canadiens	NHL	74	4	26	30	3	18	21	22	0	0	0	79	5.1	99	23	60	7	23	21	2	8	10	12	0	0	0
1989-90	Los Angeles Kings	NHL	64	7	32	39	6	23	29	34	1	0	1	80	8.8	112	28	101	24	7	10	2	3	5	10	0	0	0
1990-91	Los Angeles Kings	NHL	62	1	22	23	1	17	18	16	0	0	0	70	1.4	84	13	72	23	22	12	1	4	5	15	0	0	0
1991-92	Los Angeles Kings	NHL	56	3	10	13	3	8	11	37	0	0	0	46	6.5	53	7	66	21	1	2	0	0	0	0	0	0	0
1992-1995	New Jersey Devils	NHL	DID NOT PLAY – ASSISTANT COACH																									
1995-1998	Los Angeles Kings	NHL	DID NOT PLAY – COACHING																									
1999-2000	New Jersey Devils	NHL	DID NOT PLAY – ASSISTANT COACH																									
	New Jersey Devils	NHL	DID NOT PLAY – COACHING																									
	NHL Totals		1384	208	750	958	175	539	714	793	66	3	29	2338	8.9	2635	608	1716	419		227	28	116	144	211	7	0	3

• Brother of Moe • NHL First All-Star Team (1977, 1979, 1980) • Won James Norris Trophy (1977, 1980) • NHL Plus/Minus Leader (1977) • NHL Second All-Star Team (1978, 1981, 1986) • Won Conn Smythe Trophy (1978) • WEC-A All-Star Team (1981) • Named Best Defenseman at WEC-A (1981) • Played in NHL All-Star Game (1974, 1976, 1977, 1978, 1980, 1982, 1986, 1988, 1989, 1992)

• Played left wing and center for **Brockville** (OJHL). Signed as a free agent by **LA Kings**, July 26, 1989. • Named Assistant Coach of **New Jersey**, May 26, 1999. • Named interim Head Coach of **New Jersey**, March 23, 2000. • Named Head Coach of **New Jersey**, June 30, 1999.

• ROBINSON, Moe

Morris D – L. 6'4", 175 lbs. b: Winchester, Ont., 5/29/1957. Montreal's 6th, 49th overall, in 1977.

			REGULAR SEASON																		PLAYOFFS							
Season	Club	League	GP	G	A	Pts	AG	AA	APts	PIM	PP	SH	GW	S	%	TGF	PGF	TGA	PGA	+/-	GP	G	A	Pts	PIM	PP	SH	GW
1975-76	Gloucester Rangers	OHA-B	STATISTICS NOT AVAILABLE																									
1976-77	Kingston Canadians	OMJHL	48	5	15	20	....	....	....	35	....	....	....	....	....	....	....	....	....	....	....	....	....	....	....	....	....	....
1977-78	Nova Scotia Voyageurs	AHL	75	6	23	29	....	....	....	68	....	....	....	....	....	....	....	....	....	....	11	0	1	1	7	....	....	....
1978-79	Nova Scotia Voyageurs	AHL	78	4	23	27	....	....	....	92	....	....	....	....	....	....	....	....	....	....	9	1	1	2	6	....	....	....
1979-80	**Montreal Canadiens**	**NHL**	1	0	0	0	0	0	0	0	0	0	0	0	0.0	0	0	0	0	0	....	....	....	....	....	....	....	....
	Nova Scotia Voyageurs	AHL	64	5	35	40	....	....	....	82	....	....	....	....	....	....	....	....	....	....	6	0	2	2	4	....	....	....
1980-81	Oklahoma City Stars	CHL	56	4	22	26	....	....	....	55	....	....	....	....	....	....	....	....	....	....	3	0	2	2	0	....	....	....
	NHL Totals		1	0	0	0	0	0	0	0	0	0	0	0	0.0	0	0	0	0		....	....	....	....	....	....	....	....

• Brother of Larry

• ROBINSON, Rob

Robert Douglas D – L. 6'1", 214 lbs. b: St. Catharines, Ont., 4/19/1967. St. Louis' 6th, 117th overall, in 1987.

Season	Club	League	GP	G	A	Pts	AG	AA	APts	PIM	PP	SH	GW	S	%	TGF	PGF	TGA	PGA	+/-	GP	G	A	Pts	PIM	PP	SH	GW
1983-84	St. Catharines Legionaires	OMHA	STATISTICS NOT AVAILABLE																									
	St. Catharines Falcons	OJHL-B	12	1	3	4	....	....	....	12	....	....	....	....	....	....	....	....	....	....	....	....	....	....	....	....	....	....
1984-85	St. Catharines Falcons	OJHL-B	40	5	29	34	....	....	....	28	....	....	....	....	....	....	....	....	....	....	....	....	....	....	....	....	....	....
1985-86	University of Miami-Ohio	CCHA	38	1	9	10	....	....	....	24	....	....	....	....	....	....	....	....	....	....	....	....	....	....	....	....	....	....
1986-87	University of Miami-Ohio	CCHA	33	3	5	8	....	....	....	32	....	....	....	....	....	....	....	....	....	....	....	....	....	....	....	....	....	....
1987-88	University of Miami-Ohio	CCHA	35	1	3	4	....	....	....	56	....	....	....	....	....	....	....	....	....	....	....	....	....	....	....	....	....	....
1988-89	University of Miami-Ohio	CCHA	30	3	4	7	....	....	....	42	....	....	....	....	....	....	....	....	....	....	....	....	....	....	....	....	....	....
	Peoria Rivermen	IHL	11	2	0	2	....	....	....	6	....	....	....	....	....	....	....	....	....	....	....	....	....	....	....	....	....	....
1989-90	Peoria Rivermen	IHL	60	2	11	13	....	....	....	72	....	....	....	....	....	....	....	....	....	....	5	0	1	1	10	....	....	....
1990-91	Peoria Rivermen	IHL	79	2	21	23	....	....	....	42	....	....	....	....	....	....	....	....	....	....	19	0	6	6	8	....	....	....
1991-92	**St. Louis Blues**	**NHL**	22	0	1	1	0	1	1	8	0	0	0	9	0.0	8	0	14	2	–4	....	....	....	....	....	....	....	....
	Peoria Rivermen	IHL	35	1	10	11	....	....	....	29	....	....	....	....	....	....	....	....	....	....	10	0	2	2	12	....	....	....
1992-93	Peoria Rivermen	IHL	34	0	4	4	....	....	....	38	....	....	....	....	....	....	....	....	....	....	....	....	....	....	....	....	....	....
1993-94	Kalamazoo Wings	IHL	67	3	12	15	....	....	....	32	....	....	....	....	....	....	....	....	....	....	5	0	0	0	2	....	....	....
1994-95	Houston Aeros	IHL	70	3	12	15	....	....	....	54	....	....	....	....	....	....	....	....	....	....	4	0	1	1	4	....	....	....
1995-96	Syracuse Crunch	AHL	40	2	6	8	....	....	....	12	....	....	....	....	....	....	....	....	....	....	16	0	2	2	2	....	....	....
1996-97	VEU Feldkirch	Austria	55	4	6	10	....	....	....	30	....	....	....	....	....	....	....	....	....	....	....	....	....	....	....	....	....	....
1997-98	Frankfurt Lions	Germany	43	0	9	9	....	....	....	51	....	....	....	....	....	....	....	....	....	....	7	0	2	2	29	....	....	....
1998-99	Manchester Storm	Britain	42	1	11	12	....	....	....	22	....	....	....	....	....	....	....	....	....	....	7	0	1	1	6	....	....	....
99-2000	Manchester Storm	BH-Cup	11	0	1	1	....	....	....	2	....	....	....	....	....	....	....	....	....	....	....	....	....	....	....	....	....	....
	Manchester Storm	Britain	36	1	5	6	....	....	....	32	....	....	....	....	....	....	....	....	....	....	5	0	1	1	0	....	....	....
	NHL Totals		22	0	1	1	0	1	1	8	0	0	0	9	0.0	8	0	14	2		....	....	....	....	....	....	....	....

• Son of Doug • IHL Second All-Star Team (1991)

Traded to **Tampa Bay** by **St. Louis** with Pat Jablonski, Darin Kimble and Steve Tuttle for future considerations, June 19, 1992.

• ROBINSON, Scott

RW – R. 6'2", 180 lbs. b: 100 Mile House, B.C., 3/29/1964.

Season	Club	League	GP	G	A	Pts	AG	AA	APts	PIM	PP	SH	GW	S	%	TGF	PGF	TGA	PGA	+/-	GP	G	A	Pts	PIM	PP	SH	GW
1981-82	100 Mile House Pioneers	RMAHA	STATISTICS NOT AVAILABLE																									
1982-83	Seattle Breakers	WHL	63	14	13	27	....	....	....	151	....	....	....	....	....	....	....	....	....	....	4	3	0	3	9	....	....	....
1983-84	Seattle Breakers	WHL	44	17	18	35	....	....	....	105	....	....	....	....	....	....	....	....	....	....	5	0	1	1	25	....	....	....
1984-85	Seattle Breakers	WHL	64	44	53	97	....	....	....	106	....	....	....	....	....	....	....	....	....	....	....	....	....	....	....	....	....	....
1985-86	University of Calgary	CWUAA	18	3	9	12	....	....	....	61	....	....	....	....	....	....	....	....	....	....	2	1	1	2	10	....	....	....
1986-87	University of Calgary	CWUAA	19	12	14	26	....	....	....	95	....	....	....	....	....	....	....	....	....	....	5	3	3	6	10	....	....	....
1987-88	University of Calgary	CWUAA	21	14	14	28	....	....	....	64	....	....	....	....	....	....	....	....	....	....	6	3	4	7	12	....	....	....
1988-89	Kalamazoo Wings	IHL	49	14	17	31	....	....	....	129	....	....	....	....	....	....	....	....	....	....	6	1	2	3	21	....	....	....
1989-90	**Minnesota North Stars**	**NHL**	1	0	0	0	0	0	0	2	0	0	0	0	0.0	0	0	0	0	0	....	....	....	....	....	....	....	....
	Kalamazoo Wings	IHL	48	13	12	25	....	....	....	97	....	....	....	....	....	....	....	....	....	....	10	4	7	11	21	....	....	....
1990-91	Kalamazoo Wings	IHL	27	7	9	16	....	....	....	36	....	....	....	....	....	....	....	....	....	....	11	2	1	3	32	....	....	....
1991-92	Kalamazoo Wings	IHL	78	29	27	56	....	....	....	58	....	....	....	....	....	....	....	....	....	....	11	2	6	8	*86	....	....	....
1992-93	Milwaukee Admirals	IHL	27	13	10	23	....	....	....	33	....	....	....	....	....	....	....	....	....	....	....	....	....	....	....	....	....	....
	NHL Totals		1	0	0	0	0	0	0	2	0	0	0	0	0.0	0	0	0	0		....	....	....	....	....	....	....	....

WHL West Second All-Star Team (1985)

Signed as a free agent by **Minnesota**, September 27, 1988.

• ROBITAILLE, Luc

"Lucky" LW – L. 6'1", 215 lbs. b: Montreal, Que., 2/17/1966. Los Angeles' 9th, 171st overall, in 1984.

Season	Club	League	GP	G	A	Pts	AG	AA	APts	PIM	PP	SH	GW	S	%	TGF	PGF	TGA	PGA	+/-	GP	G	A	Pts	PIM	PP	SH	GW
1982-83	Bourassa-Angevins	QAAA	48	36	57	93	....	....	....	....	....	....	....	....	....	....	....	....	....	....	....	....	....	....	....	....	....	....
1983-84	Hull Olympiques	QMJHL	70	32	53	85	....	....	....	48	....	....	....	....	....	....	....	....	....	....	....	....	....	....	....	....	....	....
1984-85	Hull Olympiques	QMJHL	64	55	94	149	....	....	....	115	....	....	....	....	....	....	....	....	....	....	5	4	2	6	27	....	....	....
1985-86	Hull Olympiques	QMJHL	63	68	123	191	....	....	....	91	....	....	....	....	....	....	....	....	....	....	15	17	27	44	28	....	....	....
	Canada	WJC-A	7	3	5	8	....	....	....	2	....	....	....	....	....	....	....	....	....	....	....	....	....	....	....	....	....	....
	Hull Olympiques	Mem-Cup	5	*8	5	13	....	....	....	8	....	....	....	....	....	....	....	....	....	....	....	....	....	....	....	....	....	....
1986-87	**Los Angeles Kings**	**NHL**	79	45	39	84	39	28	67	28	18	0	3	199	22.6	125	53	91	1	–18	5	1	4	5	2	0	0	0
1987-88	**Los Angeles Kings**	**NHL**	80	53	58	111	45	42	87	82	17	0	6	220	24.1	156	72	94	1	–9	5	2	5	7	18	2	0	1
1988-89	**Los Angeles Kings**	**NHL**	78	46	52	98	39	37	76	65	10	0	4	237	19.4	143	38	111	11	5	11	2	6	8	10	0	0	1
1989-90	**Los Angeles Kings**	**NHL**	80	52	49	101	45	35	80	38	20	0	7	210	24.8	141	46	88	1	8	10	5	5	10	10	1	0	1
1990-91	**Los Angeles Kings**	**NHL**	76	45	46	91	41	35	76	68	11	0	5	229	19.7	136	41	68	1	28	12	12	4	16	22	5	0	2
1991-92	Canada	Can-Cup	8	1	2	3	....	....	....	10	....	....	....	....	....	....	....	....	....	....	....	....	....	....	....	....	....	....
	Los Angeles Kings	**NHL**	80	44	63	107	40	48	88	95	26	0	6	240	18.3	137	67	81	7	–4	6	3	4	7	12	1	0	1
1992-93	**Los Angeles Kings**	**NHL**	84	63	62	125	53	43	96	100	24	2	8	265	23.8	167	59	110	20	18	24	9	13	22	28	4	0	2
1993-94	**Los Angeles Kings**	**NHL**	83	44	42	86	41	33	74	86	24	0	3	267	16.5	134	73	84	3	–20	....	....	....	....	....	....	....	....
	Canada	WC-A	8	4	4	8	....	....	....	2	....	....	....	....	....	....	....	....	....	....	....	....	....	....	....	....	....	....
1994-95	**Pittsburgh Penguins**	**NHL**	46	23	19	42	41	28	69	37	5	0	3	109	21.1	70	20	45	5	10	12	7	4	11	26	0	0	2
1995-96	**New York Rangers**	**NHL**	77	23	46	69	23	38	61	80	11	0	4	223	10.3	103	42	48	0	13	11	1	5	6	8	0	0	0
1996-97	**New York Rangers**	**NHL**	69	24	24	48	25	21	46	48	5	0	4	200	12.0	81	24	41	0	16	15	4	7	11	4	0	0	0
1997-98	**Los Angeles Kings**	**NHL**	57	16	24	40	19	24	43	66	5	0	7	130	12.3	60	24	31	0	5	4	1	2	3	6	0	0	0
1998-99	**Los Angeles Kings**	**NHL**	82	39	35	74	46	34	80	54	11	0	7	292	13.4	93	28	68	2	–1	....	....	....	....	....	....	....	....
99-2000	**Los Angeles Kings**	**NHL**	71	36	38	74	41	35	76	68	13	0	7	221	16.3	99	38	50	0	11	4	2	2	4	6	0	0	0
	NHL Totals		1042	553	597	1150	538	481	1019	915	200	2	74	3042	18.2	1645	625	1010	52		119	49	61	110	152	13	0	10

QMJHL Second All-Star Team (1985) • QMJHL First All-Star Team (1986) • Canadian Major Junior Player of the Year (1986) • NHL All-Rookie Team (1987) • Won Calder Memorial Trophy (1987) • NHL Second All-Star Team (1987, 1992) • NHL First All-Star Team (1988, 1989, 1990, 1991, 1993) • Played in NHL All-Star Game (1988, 1989, 1990, 1991, 1992, 1993, 1999)

Traded to **Pittsburgh** by **LA Kings** for Rick Tocchet and Pittsburgh's 2nd round choice (Pavel Rosa) in 1995 Entry Draft, July 29, 1994. Traded to **NY Rangers** by **Pittsburgh** with Ulf Samuelsson for Petr Nedved and Sergei Zubov, August 31, 1995. Traded to **LA Kings** by **NY Rangers** for Kevin Stevens, August 28, 1997.

• ROBITAILLE, Mike

Michael James David D – R. 5'11", 195 lbs. b: Midland, Ont., 2/12/1948.

Season	Club	League	GP	G	A	Pts	AG	AA	APts	PIM	PP	SH	GW	S	%	TGF	PGF	TGA	PGA	+/-	GP	G	A	Pts	PIM	PP	SH	GW
1963-64	Kitchener Greenshirts	OHA-B	STATISTICS NOT AVAILABLE																									
	Kitchener Rangers	OHA-Jr.	1	0	0	0	....	....	....	0	....	....	....	....	....	....	....	....	....	....	....	....	....	....	....	....	....	....
1964-65	Kitchener Greenshirts	OHA-B	STATISTICS NOT AVAILABLE																									
	Kitchener Rangers	OHA-Jr.	37	2	8	10	....	....	....	83	....	....	....	....	....	....	....	....	....	....	....	....	....	....	....	....	....	....
1965-66	Kitchener Greenshirts	OHA-B	STATISTICS NOT AVAILABLE																									
	Kitchener Rangers	OHA-Jr.	1	0	0	0	....	....	....	0	....	....	....	....	....	....	....	....	....	....	....	....	....	....	....	....	....	....
1966-67	Kitchener Rangers	OHA-Jr.	48	7	30	37	....	....	....	70	....	....	....	....	....	....	....	....	....	....	13	2	6	8	15	....	....	....
1967-68	Kitchener Rangers	OHA-Jr.	51	20	51	71	....	....	....	77	....	....	....	....	....	....	....	....	....	....	14	4	10	14	34	....	....	....
1968-69	Omaha Knights	CHL	43	5	35	40	....	....	....	52	....	....	....	....	....	....	....	....	....	....	7	1	3	4	9	....	....	....
1969-70	**New York Rangers**	**NHL**	4	0	0	0	0	0	0	8	0	0	0	2	0.0	1	1	0	0	0	....	....	....	....	....	....	....	....
	Omaha Knights	CHL	64	12	46	58	....	....	....	115	....	....	....	....	....	....	....	....	....	....	12	2	*14	16	15	....	....	....
	Buffalo Bisons	AHL	....	....	....	....	....	....	....	....	....	....	....	....	....	....	....	....	....	....	5	0	4	4	14	....	....	....

			REGULAR SEASON																		PLAYOFFS							
Season	Club	League	GP	G	A	Pts	AG	AA	APts	PIM	PP	SH	GW	S	%	TGF	PGF	TGA	PGA	+/–	GP	G	A	Pts	PIM	PP	SH	GW
1970-71	**New York Rangers**	**NHL**	**11**	**1**	**1**	**2**	**1**	**1**	**2**	**7**	**1**	**0**	**0**	**12**	**8.3**	**3**	**1**	**3**	**0**	**–1**	....	....	....	....	....	....	....	....
	Omaha Knights	CHL	13	0	9	9	....	....	....	32	....	....	....	....	....	....	....	....	....	....	....	....	....	....	....	....	....	....
	Detroit Red Wings	**NHL**	**23**	**4**	**8**	**12**	**4**	**7**	**11**	**22**	**2**	**0**	**0**	**37**	**10.8**	**28**	**12**	**37**	**7**	**–14**	....	....	....	....	....	....	....	....
1971-72	**Buffalo Sabres**	**NHL**	**31**	**2**	**10**	**12**	**2**	**9**	**11**	**22**	**1**	**0**	**0**	**62**	**3.2**	**23**	**13**	**29**	**5**	**–14**	....	....	....	....	....	....	....	....
	Cincinnati Swords	AHL	8	0	1	1	....	....	....	12	....	....	....	....	....	....	....	....	....	....	....	....	....	....	....	....	....	....
1972-73	**Buffalo Sabres**	**NHL**	**65**	**4**	**17**	**21**	**4**	**13**	**17**	**40**	**0**	**0**	**0**	**182**	**2.2**	**74**	**8**	**60**	**3**	**9**	**6**	**0**	**0**	**0**	**0**	**0**	**0**	**0**
1973-74	**Buffalo Sabres**	**NHL**	**71**	**2**	**18**	**20**	**2**	**15**	**17**	**60**	**2**	**0**	**0**	**185**	**1.1**	**83**	**9**	**91**	**19**	**2**	....	....	....	....	....	....	....	....
1974-75	**Buffalo Sabres**	**NHL**	**3**	**0**	**1**	**1**	**0**	**1**	**1**	**0**	**0**	**0**	**0**	**4**	**0.0**	**5**	**0**	**7**	**4**	**2**	....	....	....	....	....	....	....	....
	Vancouver Canucks	**NHL**	**63**	**2**	**22**	**24**	**2**	**16**	**18**	**31**	**0**	**0**	**0**	**157**	**1.3**	**85**	**14**	**83**	**29**	**17**	**5**	**0**	**1**	**1**	**2**	**0**	**0**	**0**
1975-76	**Vancouver Canucks**	**NHL**	**71**	**8**	**19**	**27**	**7**	**14**	**21**	**69**	**2**	**0**	**0**	**164**	**4.9**	**90**	**16**	**95**	**29**	**8**	**2**	**0**	**0**	**0**	**2**	**0**	**0**	**0**
1976-77	**Vancouver Canucks**	**NHL**	**40**	**0**	**9**	**9**	**0**	**7**	**7**	**21**	**0**	**0**	**0**	**54**	**0.0**	**39**	**7**	**57**	**12**	**–13**	....	....	....	....	....	....	....	....
	NHL Totals		**382**	**23**	**105**	**128**	**22**	**83**	**105**	**280**	**8**	**0**	**0**	**859**	**2.7**	**431**	**81**	**462**	**108**		**13**	**0**	**1**	**1**	**4**	**0**	**0**	**0**

OHA-Jr. Second All-Star Team (1967) • OHA-Jr. First All-Star Team (1968) • CHL First All-Star Team (1970) • Named CHL's Top Defenseman (1970)

Traded to **Detroit** by **NY Rangers** with Arnie Brown and Tom Miller for Bruce MacGregor and Larry Brown, February 2, 1971. Traded to **Buffalo** by **Detroit** with Don Luce for Joe Daley, May 25, 1971. Traded to **Vancouver** by **Buffalo** with Gerry Meehan for Jocelyn Guevremont and Bryan McSheffrey, October 14, 1974. • Suffered career-ending neck injury in game vs. Pittsburgh, February 11, 1977.

• ROBITAILLE, Randy

C – L. 5'11", 190 lbs. b: Ottawa, Ont., 10/12/1975.

Season	Club	League	GP	G	A	Pts	AG	AA	APts	PIM	PP	SH	GW	S	%	TGF	PGF	TGA	PGA	+/–	GP	G	A	Pts	PIM	PP	SH	GW
1993-94	Ottawa Jr. Senators	OJHL	57	33	55	88	....	....	....	31	....	....	....	....	....	....	....	....	....	....	....	....	....	....	....	....	....	....
1994-95	Ottawa Jr. Senators	OJHL	54	48	77	125	....	....	....	111	....	....	....	....	....	....	....	....	....	....	....	....	....	....	....	....	....	....
1995-96	University of Miami-Ohio	CCHA	36	14	31	45	....	....	....	26	....	....	....	....	....	....	....	....	....	....	....	....	....	....	....	....	....	....
1996-97	University of Miami-Ohio	CCHA	39	27	34	61	....	....	....	44	....	....	....	....	....	....	....	....	....	....	....	....	....	....	....	....	....	....
	Boston Bruins	**NHL**	**1**	**0**	**0**	**0**	**0**	**0**	**0**	**0**	**0**	**0**	**0**	**0**	**0.0**	**0**	**0**	**0**	**0**	**0**	....	....	....	....	....	....	....	....
1997-98	**Boston Bruins**	**NHL**	**4**	**0**	**0**	**0**	**0**	**0**	**0**	**0**	**0**	**0**	**0**	**5**	**0.0**	**2**	**0**	**4**	**0**	**–2**	....	....	....	....	....	....	....	....
	Providence Bruins	AHL	48	15	29	44	....	....	....	16	....	....	....	....	....	....	....	....	....	....	....	....	....	....	....	....	....	....
1998-99	**Boston Bruins**	**NHL**	**4**	**0**	**2**	**2**	**0**	**2**	**2**	**0**	**0**	**0**	**0**	**5**	**0.0**	**2**	**2**	**1**	**0**	**–1**	**1**	**0**	**0**	**0**	**0**	**0**	**0**	**0**
	Providence Bruins	AHL	74	28	*74	102	....	....	....	34	....	....	....	....	....	....	....	....	....	....	19	6	*14	20	20	....	....	....
99-2000	**Nashville Predators**	**NHL**	**69**	**11**	**14**	**25**	**12**	**13**	**25**	**10**	**2**	**0**	**1**	**113**	**9.7**	**44**	**25**	**32**	**0**	**–13**	....	....	....	....	....	....	....	....
	NHL Totals		**78**	**11**	**16**	**27**	**12**	**15**	**27**	**10**	**2**	**0**	**1**	**123**	**8.9**	**48**	**27**	**37**	**0**		**1**	**0**	**0**	**0**	**0**	**0**	**0**	**0**

CCHA First All-Star Team (1997) • NCAA West First All-American Team (1997) • AHL First All-Star Team (1999) • Won Les Cunningham Award (MVP - AHL) (1999)

Signed as a free agent by **Boston**, March 27, 1997. Traded to **Atlanta** by **Boston** for Peter Ferraro, June 25, 1999. Traded to **Nashville** by **Atlanta** for Denny Lambert, August 16, 1999.

• ROCHE, Dave

C – L. 6'4", 230 lbs. b: Lindsay, Ont., 6/13/1975. Pittsburgh's 3rd, 62nd overall, in 1993.

Season	Club	League	GP	G	A	Pts	AG	AA	APts	PIM	PP	SH	GW	S	%	TGF	PGF	TGA	PGA	+/–	GP	G	A	Pts	PIM	PP	SH	GW
1990-91	Peterborough Jr. Petes	OJHL-B	40	22	17	39	....	....	....	86	....	....	....	....	....	....	....	....	....	....	....	....	....	....	....	....	....	....
1991-92	Peterborough Petes	OHL	62	10	17	27	....	....	....	134	....	....	....	....	....	....	....	....	....	....	10	0	0	0	34	....	....	....
1992-93	Peterborough Petes	OHL	56	40	60	100	....	....	....	105	....	....	....	....	....	....	....	....	....	....	21	14	15	29	42	....	....	....
	Peterborough Petes	Mem-Cup	5	4	1	5	....	....	....	*29	....	....	....	....	....	....	....	....	....	....	....	....	....	....	....	....	....	....
1993-94	Peterborough Petes	OHL	34	15	22	37	....	....	....	127	....	....	....	....	....	....	....	....	....	....	....	....	....	....	....	....	....	....
	Windsor Spitfires	OHL	29	14	20	34	....	....	....	73	....	....	....	....	....	....	....	....	....	....	4	1	1	2	15	....	....	....
1994-95	Windsor Spitfires	OHL	66	55	59	114	....	....	....	180	....	....	....	....	....	....	....	....	....	....	10	9	6	15	16	....	....	....
1995-96	**Pittsburgh Penguins**	**NHL**	**71**	**7**	**7**	**14**	**7**	**6**	**13**	**130**	**0**	**0**	**1**	**65**	**10.8**	**24**	**1**	**28**	**0**	**–5**	**16**	**2**	**7**	**9**	**26**	**0**	**0**	**0**
1996-97	**Pittsburgh Penguins**	**NHL**	**61**	**5**	**5**	**10**	**5**	**4**	**9**	**155**	**2**	**0**	**0**	**53**	**9.4**	**15**	**4**	**24**	**0**	**–13**	....	....	....	....	....	....	....	....
	Cleveland Lumberjacks	IHL	18	5	5	10	....	....	....	25	....	....	....	....	....	....	....	....	....	....	13	6	3	9	*87	....	....	....
1997-98	Syracuse Crunch	AHL	73	12	20	32	....	....	....	307	....	....	....	....	....	....	....	....	....	....	5	2	0	2	10	....	....	....
1998-99	**Calgary Flames**	**NHL**	**36**	**3**	**3**	**6**	**4**	**3**	**7**	**44**	**1**	**0**	**2**	**30**	**10.0**	**8**	**1**	**8**	**0**	**–1**	....	....	....	....	....	....	....	....
	Saint John Flames	AHL	7	0	3	3	....	....	....	6	....	....	....	....	....	....	....	....	....	....	....	....	....	....	....	....	....	....
99-2000	**Calgary Flames**	**NHL**	**2**	**0**	**0**	**0**	**0**	**0**	**0**	**5**	**0**	**0**	**0**	**3**	**0.0**	**0**	**0**	**1**	**0**	**–1**	....	....	....	....	....	....	....	....
	Saint John Flames	AHL	67	22	21	43	....	....	....	130	....	....	....	....	....	....	....	....	....	....	3	0	1	1	8	....	....	....
	NHL Totals		**170**	**15**	**15**	**30**	**16**	**13**	**29**	**334**	**3**	**0**	**3**	**151**	**9.9**	**47**	**6**	**61**	**0**		**16**	**2**	**7**	**9**	**26**	**0**	**0**	**0**

OHL First All-Star Team (1995)

Traded to **Calgary** by **Pittsburgh** with Ken Wregget for German Titov and Todd Hlushko, June 17, 1998.

• ROCHEFORT, Leon

Leon Joseph Fernand RW – R. 6', 185 lbs. b: Cap de la Madeleine, Que., 5/4/1939.

Season	Club	League	GP	G	A	Pts	AG	AA	APts	PIM	PP	SH	GW	S	%	TGF	PGF	TGA	PGA	+/–	GP	G	A	Pts	PIM	PP	SH	GW
1954-55	Trois-Rivieres Kitner	QAAA	20	15	21	36	....	....	....	....	....	....	....	....	....	....	....	....	....	....	....	....	....	....	....	....	....	....
1955-56	Trois-Rivieres Lions	QJHL	STATISTICS NOT AVAILABLE																									
1956-57	Trois-Rivieres Lions	QJHL	STATISTICS NOT AVAILABLE																									
1957-58	Guelph Biltmores	OHA-Jr.	52	17	18	35	....	....	....	19	....	....	....	....	....	....	....	....	....	....	....	....	....	....	....	....	....	....
1958-59	Guelph Biltmores	OHA-Jr.	54	16	19	35	....	....	....	16	....	....	....	....	....	....	....	....	....	....	10	8	4	12	4	....	....	....
1959-60	Trois-Rivieres Lions	EPHL	70	27	22	49	....	....	....	35	....	....	....	....	....	....	....	....	....	....	4	0	0	0	9	....	....	....
1960-61	**New York Rangers**	**NHL**	**1**	**0**	**0**	**0**	**0**	**0**	**0**	**0**	....	....	....	....	....	....	....	....	....	....	....	....	....	....	....	....	....	....
	Kitchener-Waterloo Beavers	EPHL	65	20	18	38	....	....	....	33	....	....	....	....	....	....	....	....	....	....	7	3	1	4	14	....	....	....
1961-62	Kitchener-Waterloo Beavers	EPHL	69	33	27	60	....	....	....	29	....	....	....	....	....	....	....	....	....	....	....	....	....	....	....	....	....	....
1962-63	**New York Rangers**	**NHL**	**23**	**5**	**4**	**9**	**6**	**4**	**10**	**6**	....	....	....	....	....	....	....	....	....	....	....	....	....	....	....	....	....	....
	Baltimore Clippers	AHL	50	14	20	34	....	....	....	12	....	....	....	....	....	....	....	....	....	....	....	....	....	....	....	....	....	....
1963-64	**Montreal Canadiens**	**NHL**	**3**	**0**	**0**	**0**	**0**	**0**	**0**	**0**	....	....	....	....	....	....	....	....	....	....	....	....	....	....	....	....	....	....
	Quebec Aces	AHL	71	27	25	52	....	....	....	14	....	....	....	....	....	....	....	....	....	....	9	4	3	7	2	....	....	....
1964-65	**Montreal Canadiens**	**NHL**	**9**	**2**	**0**	**2**	**2**	**0**	**2**	**0**	....	....	....	....	....	....	....	....	....	....	....	....	....	....	....	....	....	....
	Quebec Aces	AHL	41	18	21	39	....	....	....	12	....	....	....	....	....	....	....	....	....	....	5	0	3	3	6	....	....	....
1965-66♦	**Montreal Canadiens**	**NHL**	**1**	**0**	**1**	**1**	**0**	**1**	**1**	**0**	....	....	....	....	....	....	....	....	....	....	**4**	**1**	**1**	**2**	**4**	**0**	**0**	**0**
	Quebec Aces	AHL	71	35	37	72	....	....	....	12	....	....	....	....	....	....	....	....	....	....	6	5	3	8	0	....	....	....
1966-67	**Montreal Canadiens**	**NHL**	**27**	**9**	**7**	**16**	**10**	**7**	**17**	**6**	....	....	....	....	....	....	....	....	....	....	**10**	**1**	**1**	**2**	**4**	**0**	**0**	**0**
	Quebec Aces	AHL	8	3	2	5	....	....	....	2	....	....	....	....	....	....	....	....	....	....	....	....	....	....	....	....	....	....
1967-68	**Philadelphia Flyers**	**NHL**	**74**	**21**	**21**	**42**	**24**	**21**	**45**	**16**	**4**	**2**	**1**	**237**	**8.9**	**57**	**12**	**54**	**8**	**–1**	**7**	**2**	**0**	**2**	**2**	**0**	**0**	**1**
1968-69	**Philadelphia Flyers**	**NHL**	**65**	**14**	**21**	**35**	**15**	**19**	**34**	**10**	**3**	**0**	**0**	**148**	**9.5**	**43**	**18**	**32**	**0**	**–7**	**3**	**0**	**0**	**0**	**0**	**0**	**0**	**0**
1969-70	**Los Angeles Kings**	**NHL**	**76**	**9**	**23**	**32**	**10**	**22**	**32**	**14**	**1**	**0**	**1**	**190**	**4.7**	**55**	**25**	**67**	**7**	**–30**	....	....	....	....	....	....	....	....
1970-71♦	**Montreal Canadiens**	**NHL**	**57**	**5**	**10**	**15**	**5**	**8**	**13**	**4**	**0**	**3**	**1**	**33**	**15.2**	**22**	**0**	**30**	**19**	**11**	**10**	**0**	**0**	**0**	**6**	**0**	**0**	**0**
	Montreal Voyageurs	AHL	10	1	6	7	....	....	....	0	....	....	....	....	....	....	....	....	....	....	....	....	....	....	....	....	....	....
1971-72	**Detroit Red Wings**	**NHL**	**64**	**17**	**12**	**29**	**17**	**10**	**27**	**10**	**0**	**0**	**3**	**97**	**17.5**	**40**	**3**	**45**	**9**	**1**	....	....	....	....	....	....	....	....
1972-73	**Detroit Red Wings**	**NHL**	**20**	**2**	**4**	**6**	**2**	**3**	**5**	**2**	**0**	**0**	**0**	**23**	**8.7**	**9**	**1**	**9**	**1**	**0**	....	....	....	....	....	....	....	....
	Atlanta Flames	**NHL**	**54**	**9**	**18**	**27**	**8**	**14**	**22**	**10**	**1**	**0**	**0**	**130**	**6.9**	**38**	**8**	**34**	**0**	**–4**	....	....	....	....	....	....	....	....
1973-74	**Atlanta Flames**	**NHL**	**56**	**10**	**12**	**22**	**10**	**10**	**20**	**13**	**1**	**0**	**1**	**107**	**9.3**	**41**	**5**	**52**	**4**	**–12**	....	....	....	....	....	....	....	....
1974-75	**Vancouver Canucks**	**NHL**	**76**	**18**	**11**	**29**	**16**	**8**	**24**	**2**	**2**	**0**	**3**	**124**	**14.5**	**45**	**7**	**47**	**4**	**–5**	**5**	**0**	**2**	**2**	**0**	**0**	**0**	**0**
1975-76	**Vancouver Canucks**	**NHL**	**11**	**0**	**3**	**3**	**0**	**2**	**2**	**0**	**0**	**0**	**0**	**13**	**0.0**	**4**	**0**	**10**	**2**	**–4**	....	....	....	....	....	....	....	....
	Tulsa Oilers	CHL	60	25	40	65	....	....	....	2	....	....	....	....	....	....	....	....	....	....	9	2	5	7	6	....	....	....
	NHL Totals		**617**	**121**	**147**	**268**	**125**	**129**	**254**	**93**	....	....	....	....	....	....	....	....	....	....	**39**	**4**	**4**	**8**	**16**	....	....	....

Played in NHL All-Star Game (1968)

Traded to **Montreal** by **NY Rangers** with Dave Balon, Len Ronson and Gump Worsley for Phil Goyette, Don Marshall and Jacques Plante, June 4, 1963. Claimed by **Philadelphia** from **Montreal** in Expansion Draft, June 6, 1967. Traded to **NY Rangers** by **Philadelphia** with Don Blackburn for Reggie Fleming, June 6, 1969. Traded to **LA Kings** by **NY Rangers** with Dennis Hextall for Real Lemieux, June 9, 1969. Traded to **Montreal** by **LA Kings** with Wayne Thomas and Gregg Boddy for Larry Mickey, Lucien Grenier and Jack Norris, May 22, 1970. Traded to **Detroit** by **Montreal** for Kerry Ketter and cash, May 25, 1971. Traded to **Atlanta** by **Detroit** for Bill Hogaboam, November 28, 1972. Traded to **Vancouver** by **Atlanta** for cash, October 4, 1974.

• ROCHEFORT, Normand

D – L. 6'1", 214 lbs. b: Trois-Rivières, Que., 1/28/1961. Quebec's 1st, 24th overall, in 1980.

Season	Club	League	GP	G	A	Pts	AG	AA	APts	PIM	PP	SH	GW	S	%	TGF	PGF	TGA	PGA	+/–	GP	G	A	Pts	PIM	PP	SH	GW
1977-78	Trois-Rivieres Draveurs	QMJHL	72	9	37	46	....	....	....	36	....	....	....	....	....	....	....	....	....	....	....	....	....	....	....	....	....	....
	Trois-Rivieres Draveurs	Mem-Cup	3	0	1	1	....	....	....	2	....	....	....	....	....	....	....	....	....	....	....	....	....	....	....	....	....	....
1978-79	Trois-Rivieres Draveurs	QMJHL	72	17	57	74	....	....	....	30	....	....	....	....	....	....	....	....	....	....	13	3	11	14	17	....	....	....
	Trois-Rivieres Draveurs	Mem-Cup	4	0	2	2	....	....	....	6	....	....	....	....	....	....	....	....	....	....	....	....	....	....	....	....	....	....

Season	Club	League	GP	G	A	Pts	AG	AA	APts	PIM	PP	SH	GW	S	%	TGF	PGF	TGA	PGA	+/–	GP	G	A	Pts	PIM	PP	SH	GW
			REGULAR SEASON																		PLAYOFFS							
1979-80	Trois-Rivieres Draveurs	QMJHL	20	5	25	30	....	....	....	22	....	....	....	....	....	....	....	....	....	....	....	....	....	....	....	....	....	....
	Quebec Remparts	QMJHL	52	8	39	47	....	....	....	68	....	....	....	....	....	....	....	....	....	....	5	1	3	4	8	....	....	....
1980-81	Quebec Remparts	QMJHL	9	2	6	8	....	....	....	14	....	....	....	....	....	....	....	....	....	....	....	....	....	....	....	....	....	....
	Quebec Nordiques	**NHL**	**56**	**3**	**7**	**10**	**2**	**5**	**7**	**51**	**0**	**0**	**0**	**77**	**3.9**	**63**	**6**	**85**	**17**	**–11**	**5**	**0**	**0**	**0**	**4**	**0**	**0**	**0**
1981-82	**Quebec Nordiques**	**NHL**	**72**	**4**	**14**	**18**	**3**	**9**	**12**	**115**	**0**	**0**	**1**	**105**	**3.8**	**102**	**6**	**102**	**25**	**19**	**16**	**0**	**2**	**2**	**10**	**0**	**0**	**0**
1982-83	**Quebec Nordiques**	**NHL**	**62**	**6**	**17**	**23**	**5**	**12**	**17**	**40**	**1**	**0**	**1**	**104**	**5.8**	**99**	**16**	**94**	**22**	**11**	**1**	**0**	**0**	**0**	**2**	**0**	**0**	**0**
1983-84	**Quebec Nordiques**	**NHL**	**75**	**2**	**22**	**24**	**2**	**15**	**17**	**47**	**0**	**0**	**1**	**84**	**2.4**	**104**	**5**	**93**	**35**	**41**	**6**	**1**	**0**	**1**	**6**	**0**	**0**	**0**
1984-85	**Quebec Nordiques**	**NHL**	**73**	**3**	**21**	**24**	**2**	**14**	**16**	**74**	**1**	**0**	**1**	**113**	**2.7**	**95**	**6**	**107**	**30**	**12**	**18**	**2**	**1**	**3**	**8**	**0**	**0**	**1**
1985-86	**Quebec Nordiques**	**NHL**	**26**	**5**	**4**	**9**	**4**	**3**	**7**	**30**	**2**	**0**	**0**	**51**	**9.8**	**35**	**5**	**28**	**7**	**9**	....	....	....	....	....	....	....	....
1986-87	**Quebec Nordiques**	**NHL**	**70**	**6**	**9**	**15**	**5**	**7**	**12**	**46**	**0**	**0**	**0**	**92**	**6.5**	**74**	**4**	**85**	**17**	**2**	**13**	**2**	**1**	**3**	**26**	**0**	**0**	**1**
	NHL All-Stars	RV-87	1	0	0	0	....	....	....	0	....	....	....	....	....	....	....	....	....	....	....	....	....	....	....	....	....	....
1987-88	Canada	Can-Cup	9	1	2	3	....	....	....	8	....	....	....	....	....	....	....	....	....	....	....	....	....	....	....	....	....	....
	Quebec Nordiques	**NHL**	**46**	**3**	**10**	**13**	**3**	**7**	**10**	**49**	**0**	**1**	**0**	**70**	**4.3**	**66**	**20**	**77**	**29**	**–2**	....	....	....	....	....	....	....	....
1988-89	**New York Rangers**	**NHL**	**11**	**1**	**5**	**6**	**1**	**4**	**5**	**18**	**0**	**0**	**1**	**14**	**7.1**	**12**	**1**	**13**	**2**	**0**	....	....	....	....	....	....	....	....
1989-90	**New York Rangers**	**NHL**	**31**	**3**	**1**	**4**	**3**	**1**	**4**	**24**	**0**	**0**	**1**	**30**	**10.0**	**26**	**0**	**37**	**13**	**2**	**10**	**2**	**1**	**3**	**26**	**0**	**1**	**0**
	Flint Spirits	IHL	7	3	2	5	....	....	....	4	....	....	....	....	....	....	....	....	....	....	....	....	....	....	....	....	....	....
1990-91	**New York Rangers**	**NHL**	**44**	**3**	**7**	**10**	**3**	**5**	**8**	**35**	**0**	**0**	**0**	**34**	**8.8**	**33**	**0**	**38**	**15**	**10**	....	....	....	....	....	....	....	....
1991-92	**New York Rangers**	**NHL**	**26**	**0**	**2**	**2**	**0**	**2**	**2**	**31**	**0**	**0**	**0**	**18**	**0.0**	**11**	**0**	**23**	**2**	**–10**	....	....	....	....	....	....	....	....
1992-93	Eisbaren Berlin	Germany	17	4	2	6	....	....	....	21	....	....	....	....	....	....	....	....	....	....	....	....	....	....	....	....	....	....
1993-94	**Tampa Bay Lightning**	**NHL**	**6**	**0**	**0**	**0**	**0**	**0**	**0**	**10**	**0**	**0**	**0**	**4**	**0.0**	**2**	**0**	**5**	**2**	**–1**	....	....	....	....	....	....	....	....
	Atlanta Knights	IHL	65	5	7	12	....	....	....	43	....	....	....	....	....	....	....	....	....	....	13	0	2	2	6	....	....	....
1994-95	Denver Grizzlies	IHL	77	4	13	17	....	....	....	46	....	....	....	....	....	....	....	....	....	....	17	1	4	5	12	....	....	....
1995-96	San Francisco Spiders	IHL	77	3	12	15	....	....	....	45	....	....	....	....	....	....	....	....	....	....	4	0	0	0	2	....	....	....
1996-97	Kansas City Blades	IHL	77	7	14	21	....	....	....	28	....	....	....	....	....	....	....	....	....	....	3	1	0	1	2	....	....	....
1997-98	Kansas City Blades	IHL	52	1	3	4	....	....	....	48	....	....	....	....	....	....	....	....	....	....	11	1	2	3	8	....	....	....
	NHL Totals		**598**	**39**	**119**	**158**	**33**	**84**	**117**	**570**	**4**	**1**	**6**	**796**	**4.9**	**722**	**69**	**787**	**216**		**69**	**7**	**5**	**12**	**82**	**0**	**1**	**2**

Memorial Cup All-Star Team (1979) • QMJHL Second All-Star Team (1980)

Traded to **NY Rangers** by **Quebec** with Jason Lafreniere for Bruce Bell, Jari Gronstrand, Walt Poddubny and NY Rangers' 4th round choice (Eric Dubois) in 1989 Entry Draft, August 1, 1988. Signed as a free agent by **Tampa Bay**, September 27, 1993.

• RODGERS, Marc

RW – R. 5'9", 185 lbs. b: Shawville, Que., 3/16/1972.

Season	Club	League	GP	G	A	Pts	AG	AA	APts	PIM	PP	SH	GW	S	%	TGF	PGF	TGA	PGA	+/–	GP	G	A	Pts	PIM	PP	SH	GW
1986-87	L'Outaouaus Frontaliers	QAAA	42	16	18	34	....	....	....	....	....	....	....	....	....	....	....	....	....	....	....	....	....	....	....	....	....	....
1987-88	L'Outaouaus Frontaliers	QAAA	38	30	37	67	....	....	....	....	....	....	....	....	....	....	....	....	....	....	....	....	....	....	....	....	....	....
1988-89	Granby Bisons	QMJHL	65	11	21	32	....	....	....	70	....	....	....	....	....	....	....	....	....	....	4	0	2	2	44	....	....	....
1989-90	Granby Bisons	QMJHL	61	24	31	55	....	....	....	155	....	....	....	....	....	....	....	....	....	....	....	....	....	....	....	....	....	....
1990-91	Granby Bisons	QMJHL	64	28	49	77	....	....	....	41	....	....	....	....	....	....	....	....	....	....	....	....	....	....	....	....	....	....
1991-92	Granby Bisons	QMJHL	36	30	57	87	....	....	....	49	....	....	....	....	....	....	....	....	....	....	....	....	....	....	....	....	....	....
	Verdun College Francais	QMJHL	29	14	19	33	....	....	....	0	....	....	....	....	....	....	....	....	....	....	18	3	13	16	26	....	....	....
1992-93	Wheeling Thunderbirds	ECHL	64	23	40	63	....	....	....	91	....	....	....	....	....	....	....	....	....	....	6	1	1	2	8	....	....	....
1993-94	Knoxville Cherokees	ECHL	27	12	18	30	....	....	....	83	....	....	....	....	....	....	....	....	....	....	....	....	....	....	....	....	....	....
	Las Vegas Thunder	IHL	40	7	7	14	....	....	....	110	....	....	....	....	....	....	....	....	....	....	4	0	2	2	17	....	....	....
1994-95	Las Vegas Thunder	IHL	58	17	19	36	....	....	....	131	....	....	....	....	....	....	....	....	....	....	10	2	6	8	25	....	....	....
1995-96	Las Vegas Thunder	IHL	51	13	16	29	....	....	....	65	....	....	....	....	....	....	....	....	....	....	....	....	....	....	....	....	....	....
	Utah Grizzlies	IHL	31	6	14	20	....	....	....	51	....	....	....	....	....	....	....	....	....	....	21	4	4	8	16	....	....	....
1996-97	Utah Grizzlies	IHL	5	2	2	4	....	....	....	10	....	....	....	....	....	....	....	....	....	....	....	....	....	....	....	....	....	....
	Quebec Rafales	IHL	70	25	42	67	....	....	....	115	....	....	....	....	....	....	....	....	....	....	9	1	9	10	14	....	....	....
1997-98	Quebec Rafales	IHL	61	20	22	42	....	....	....	61	....	....	....	....	....	....	....	....	....	....	....	....	....	....	....	....	....	....
	Chicago Wolves	IHL	11	5	5	10	....	....	....	22	....	....	....	....	....	....	....	....	....	....	22	9	9	18	10	....	....	....
1998-99	Adirondack Red Wings	AHL	80	19	38	57	....	....	....	66	....	....	....	....	....	....	....	....	....	....	3	0	0	0	10	....	....	....
99-2000	**Detroit Red Wings**	**NHL**	**21**	**1**	**1**	**2**	**1**	**1**	**2**	**10**	**0**	**0**	**0**	**17**	**5.9**	**7**	**0**	**10**	**0**	**–3**	....	....	....	....	....	....	....	....
	Manitoba Moose	IHL	34	8	10	18	....	....	....	77	....	....	....	....	....	....	....	....	....	....	2	1	0	1	6	....	....	....
	NHL Totals		**21**	**1**	**1**	**2**	**1**	**1**	**2**	**10**	**0**	**0**	**0**	**17**	**5.9**	**7**	**0**	**10**	**0**		....	....	....	....	....	....	....	....

Signed as a free agent by **Detroit**, August 3, 1998.

• ROENICK, Jeremy

Jeremy Shaffer C – R. 6', 192 lbs. b: Boston, MA, 1/17/1970. Chicago's 1st, 8th overall, in 1988.

Season	Club	League	GP	G	A	Pts	AG	AA	APts	PIM	PP	SH	GW	S	%	TGF	PGF	TGA	PGA	+/–	GP	G	A	Pts	PIM	PP	SH	GW
1986-87	Thayer Academy	Hi-School	24	31	34	65	....	....	....	....	....	....	....	....	....	....	....	....	....	....	....	....	....	....	....	....	....	....
1987-88	Thayer Academy	Hi-School	24	34	50	84	....	....	....	....	....	....	....	....	....	....	....	....	....	....	....	....	....	....	....	....	....	....
	United States	WJC-A	7	5	4	9	....	....	....	4	....	....	....	....	....	....	....	....	....	....	....	....	....	....	....	....	....	....
1988-89	Hull Olympiques	QMJHL	28	34	36	70	....	....	....	14	....	....	....	....	....	....	....	....	....	....	....	....	....	....	....	....	....	....
	United States	WJC-A	7	8	8	*16	....	....	....	0	....	....	....	....	....	....	....	....	....	....	....	....	....	....	....	....	....	....
	Chicago Blackhawks	**NHL**	**20**	**9**	**9**	**18**	**8**	**6**	**14**	**4**	**2**	**0**	**0**	**52**	**17.3**	**26**	**7**	**16**	**1**	**4**	**10**	**1**	**3**	**4**	**7**	**1**	**0**	**1**
1989-90	**Chicago Blackhawks**	**NHL**	**78**	**26**	**40**	**66**	**22**	**29**	**51**	**54**	**6**	**0**	**4**	**173**	**15.0**	**86**	**28**	**64**	**8**	**2**	**20**	**11**	**7**	**18**	**8**	**4**	**0**	**1**
1990-91	**Chicago Blackhawks**	**NHL**	**79**	**41**	**53**	**94**	**38**	**40**	**78**	**80**	**15**	**4**	**10**	**194**	**21.1**	**140**	**61**	**52**	**11**	**38**	**6**	**3**	**5**	**8**	**4**	**1**	**0**	**1**
	United States	WEC-A	9	5	6	11	....	....	....	8	....	....	....	....	....	....	....	....	....	....	....	....	....	....	....	....	....	....
1991-92	United States	Can-Cup	8	4	2	6	....	....	....	4	....	....	....	....	....	....	....	....	....	....	....	....	....	....	....	....	....	....
	Chicago Blackhawks	**NHL**	**80**	**53**	**50**	**103**	**48**	**38**	**86**	**98**	**22**	**3**	**13**	**234**	**22.6**	**128**	**57**	**63**	**15**	**23**	**18**	**12**	**10**	**22**	**12**	**4**	**0**	**3**
1992-93	**Chicago Blackhawks**	**NHL**	**84**	**50**	**57**	**107**	**42**	**39**	**81**	**86**	**22**	**3**	**3**	**255**	**19.6**	**132**	**67**	**64**	**14**	**15**	**4**	**1**	**2**	**3**	**2**	**0**	**0**	**0**
1993-94	**Chicago Blackhawks**	**NHL**	**84**	**46**	**61**	**107**	**43**	**47**	**90**	**125**	**24**	**5**	**5**	**281**	**16.4**	**135**	**52**	**91**	**29**	**21**	**6**	**1**	**6**	**7**	**2**	**0**	**0**	**1**
1994-95	Kolner Haie	Germany	3	3	1	4	....	....	....	2	....	....	....	....	....	....	....	....	....	....	....	....	....	....	....	....	....	....
	Chicago Blackhawks	**NHL**	**33**	**10**	**24**	**34**	**18**	**35**	**53**	**14**	**5**	**0**	**1**	**93**	**10.8**	**58**	**33**	**29**	**9**	**5**	**8**	**1**	**2**	**3**	**16**	**0**	**0**	**0**
1995-96	**Chicago Blackhawks**	**NHL**	**66**	**32**	**35**	**67**	**31**	**29**	**60**	**109**	**12**	**4**	**2**	**171**	**18.7**	**92**	**36**	**64**	**17**	**9**	**10**	**5**	**7**	**12**	**2**	**1**	**0**	**1**
1996-97	**Phoenix Coyotes**	**NHL**	**72**	**29**	**40**	**69**	**31**	**36**	**67**	**115**	**10**	**3**	**7**	**228**	**12.7**	**91**	**33**	**76**	**11**	**–7**	**6**	**2**	**4**	**6**	**4**	**0**	**0**	**0**
1997-98	**Phoenix Coyotes**	**NHL**	**79**	**24**	**32**	**56**	**28**	**31**	**59**	**103**	**6**	**1**	**3**	**182**	**13.2**	**88**	**38**	**66**	**21**	**5**	**6**	**5**	**3**	**8**	**4**	**2**	**2**	**2**
	United States	Olympics	4	0	1	1	....	....	....	6	....	....	....	....	....	....	....	....	....	....	....	....	....	....	....	....	....	....
1998-99	**Phoenix Coyotes**	**NHL**	**78**	**24**	**48**	**72**	**28**	**46**	**74**	**130**	**4**	**0**	**3**	**203**	**11.8**	**91**	**29**	**60**	**5**	**7**	**1**	**0**	**0**	**0**	**0**	**0**	**0**	**0**
99-2000	**Phoenix Coyotes**	**NHL**	**75**	**34**	**44**	**78**	**38**	**41**	**79**	**102**	**6**	**3**	**12**	**192**	**17.7**	**100**	**23**	**71**	**5**	**11**	**5**	**2**	**2**	**4**	**10**	**1**	**0**	**0**
	NHL Totals		**828**	**378**	**493**	**871**	**375**	**417**	**792**	**1020**	**134**	**26**	**63**	**2258**	**16.7**	**1167**	**464**	**716**	**146**		**100**	**44**	**51**	**95**	**71**	**14**	**2**	**10**

WJC-A All-Star Team (1989) • QMJHL Second All-Star Team (1989) • Canada Cup All-Star Team (1991) • Played in NHL All-Star Game (1991, 1992, 1993, 1994, 1999, 2000)

Traded to **Phoenix** by **Chicago** for Alexei Zhamnov, Craig Mills and Phoenix's 1st round choice (Ty Jones) in 1997 Entry Draft, August 16, 1996.

• ROEST, Stacy

C – R. 5'9", 192 lbs. b: Lethbridge, Alta., 3/15/1974.

Season	Club	League	GP	G	A	Pts	AG	AA	APts	PIM	PP	SH	GW	S	%	TGF	PGF	TGA	PGA	+/–	GP	G	A	Pts	PIM	PP	SH	GW
1990-91	Lethbridge Y's Men	AMHL	34	22	50	72	....	....	....	38	....	....	....	....	....	....	....	....	....	....	....	....	....	....	....	....	....	....
	Medicine Hat Tigers	WHL	5	1	2	3	....	....	....	0	....	....	....	....	....	....	....	....	....	....	12	5	5	10	4	....	....	....
1991-92	Medicine Hat Tigers	WHL	72	22	43	65	....	....	....	20	....	....	....	....	....	....	....	....	....	....	4	2	1	3	0	....	....	....
1992-93	Medicine Hat Tigers	WHL	72	33	73	106	....	....	....	30	....	....	....	....	....	....	....	....	....	....	10	3	10	13	6	....	....	....
1993-94	Medicine Hat Tigers	WHL	72	48	72	120	....	....	....	48	....	....	....	....	....	....	....	....	....	....	3	1	0	1	4	....	....	....
1994-95	Medicine Hat Tigers	WHL	69	37	78	115	....	....	....	32	....	....	....	....	....	....	....	....	....	....	5	2	7	9	2	....	....	....
	Adirondack Red Wings	AHL	3	0	0	0	....	....	....	0	....	....	....	....	....	....	....	....	....	....	....	....	....	....	....	....	....	....
1995-96	Adirondack Red Wings	AHL	76	16	39	55	....	....	....	40	....	....	....	....	....	....	....	....	....	....	3	0	0	0	0	....	....	....
1996-97	Adirondack Red Wings	AHL	78	25	41	66	....	....	....	30	....	....	....	....	....	....	....	....	....	....	4	1	1	2	0	....	....	....
1997-98	Adirondack Red Wings	AHL	80	34	58	92	....	....	....	30	....	....	....	....	....	....	....	....	....	....	3	2	1	3	6	....	....	....
1998-99	**Detroit Red Wings**	**NHL**	**59**	**4**	**8**	**12**	**5**	**8**	**13**	**14**	**0**	**0**	**1**	**50**	**8.0**	**14**	**1**	**20**	**0**	**–7**	....	....	....	....	....	....	....	....
	Adirondack Red Wings	AHL	2	0	1	1	....	....	....	0	....	....	....	....	....	....	....	....	....	....	....	....	....	....	....	....	....	....
99-2000	**Detroit Red Wings**	**NHL**	**49**	**7**	**9**	**16**	**8**	**8**	**16**	**12**	**1**	**0**	**1**	**56**	**12.5**	**23**	**1**	**23**	**0**	**–1**	**3**	**0**	**0**	**0**	**0**	**0**	**0**	**0**
	NHL Totals		**108**	**11**	**17**	**28**	**13**	**16**	**29**	**26**	**1**	**0**	**2**	**106**	**10.4**	**37**	**2**	**43**	**0**		**3**	**0**	**0**	**0**	**0**	**0**	**0**	**0**

WHL East First All-Star Team (1994) • WHL East Second All-Star Team (1995)

Signed as a free agent by **Detroit**, June 9, 1997. Selected by **Minnesota** from **Detroit** in Expansion Draft, June 23, 2000.

• ROGERS, John

Alfred John RW – R. 5'11", 175 lbs. b: Paradise Hills, Sask., 4/10/1953. Minnesota's 2nd, 25th overall, in 1973.

			REGULAR SEASON																		PLAYOFFS							
Season	Club	League	GP	G	A	Pts	AG	AA	APts	PIM	PP	SH	GW	S	%	TGF	PGF	TGA	PGA	+/–	GP	G	A	Pts	PIM	PP	SH	GW
1969-70	Edmonton Maple Leafs	AJHL	44	30	21	51	....	....	....	150	....	....	....	....	....	....	....	....	....	....	....	....	....	....	....	....	....	....
	Weyburn Red Wings	Mem-Cup	5	1	1	2	....	....	....	9	....	....	....	....	....	....	....	....	....	....	....	....	....	....	....	....	....	....
1970-71	Edmonton Oil Kings	WCJHL	47	27	16	43	....	....	....	218	....	....	....	....	....	....	....	....	....	....	17	7	5	12	56	....	....	....
1971-72	Edmonton Oil Kings	WCJHL	46	26	27	53	....	....	....	236	....	....	....	....	....	....	....	....	....	....	14	7	3	10	14	....	....	....
	Edmonton Oil Kings	Mem-Cup	2	0	0	0	....	....	....	4	....	....	....	....	....	....	....	....	....	....	....	....	....	....	....	....	....	....
1972-73	Edmonton Oil Kings	WCJHL	68	63	41	104	....	....	....	219	....	....	....	....	....	....	....	....	....	....	11	13	11	24	56	....	....	....
1973-74	**Minnesota North Stars**	**NHL**	**10**	**2**	**4**	**6**	**2**	**3**	**5**	**0**	**0**	**0**	**0**	**13**	**15.4**	**7**	**0**	**7**	**1**	**1**	....	....	....	....	....	....	....	....
	New Haven Nighthawks	AHL	54	16	18	34	....	....	....	73	....	....	....	....	....	....	....	....	....	....	10	1	1	2	0	....	....	....
1974-75	**Minnesota North Stars**	**NHL**	**4**	**0**	**0**	**0**	**0**	**0**	**0**	**0**	**0**	**0**	**0**	**2**	**0.0**	**0**	**0**	**1**	**0**	**–1**	....	....	....	....	....	....	....	....
	New Haven Nighthawks	AHL	54	16	18	34	....	....	....	41	....	....	....	....	....	....	....	....	....	....	2	0	0	0	0	....	....	....
1975-76	Edmonton Oilers	WHA	44	9	8	17	....	....	....	34	....	....	....	....	....	....	....	....	....	....	....	....	....	....	....	....	....	....
	Spokane Flyers	WIHL	6	6	2	8	....	....	....	0	....	....	....	....	....	....	....	....	....	....	....	....	....	....	....	....	....	....
	NHL Totals		**14**	**2**	**4**	**6**	**2**	**3**	**5**	**0**	**0**	**0**	**0**	**15**	**13.3**	**7**	**0**	**8**	**1**		....	....	....	....	....	....	....	....
	Other Major League Totals		44	9	8	17	....	....	....	34	....	....	....	....	....	....	....	....	....	....	....	....	....	....	....	....	....	....

Selected by **Edmonton** (WHA) in 1973 WHA Amateur Draft, June, 1973.

• ROGERS, Mike

Michael R. C – L. 5'9", 170 lbs. b: Calgary, Alta., 10/24/1954. Vancouver's 4th, 77th overall, in 1974.

Season	Club	League	GP	G	A	Pts	AG	AA	APts	PIM	PP	SH	GW	S	%	TGF	PGF	TGA	PGA	+/–	GP	G	A	Pts	PIM	PP	SH	GW
1971-72	Calgary Centennials	WCJHL	66	27	30	57	....	....	....	19	....	....	....	....	....	....	....	....	....	....	13	2	4	6	2	....	....	....
1972-73	Calgary Centennials	WCJHL	67	54	58	112	....	....	....	44	....	....	....	....	....	....	....	....	....	....	6	8	5	13	2	....	....	....
1973-74	Calgary Centennials	WCJHL	66	67	73	140	....	....	....	32	....	....	....	....	....	....	....	....	....	....	14	13	16	29	6	....	....	....
1974-75	Edmonton Oilers	WHA	78	35	48	83	....	....	....	2	....	....	....	....	....	....	....	....	....	....	....	....	....	....	....	....	....	....
1975-76	Edmonton Oilers	WHA	44	12	15	27	....	....	....	10	....	....	....	....	....	....	....	....	....	....	....	....	....	....	....	....	....	....
	New England Whalers	WHA	36	18	14	32	....	....	....	10	....	....	....	....	....	....	....	....	....	....	17	5	8	13	2	....	....	....
1976-77	New England Whalers	WHA	78	25	57	82	....	....	....	10	....	....	....	....	....	....	....	....	....	....	5	1	1	2	2	....	....	....
1977-78	New England Whalers	WHA	80	28	43	71	....	....	....	46	....	....	....	....	....	....	....	....	....	....	14	5	6	11	8	....	....	....
1978-79	New England Whalers	WHA	80	27	45	72	....	....	....	31	....	....	....	....	....	....	....	....	....	....	10	2	6	8	2	....	....	....
1979-80	**Hartford Whalers**	**NHL**	**80**	**44**	**61**	**105**	**38**	**45**	**83**	**10**	**3**	**2**	**0**	**229**	**19.2**	**133**	**30**	**79**	**5**	**29**	**3**	**0**	**3**	**3**	**0**	**0**	**0**	**0**
1980-81	**Hartford Whalers**	**NHL**	**80**	**40**	**65**	**105**	**31**	**43**	**74**	**32**	**10**	**4**	**1**	**242**	**16.5**	**133**	**45**	**150**	**40**	**–22**	....	....	....	....	....	....	....	....
	Canada	WEC-A	6	0	1	1	....	....	....	4	....	....	....	....	....	....	....	....	....	....	....	....	....	....	....	....	....	....
1981-82	**New York Rangers**	**NHL**	**80**	**38**	**65**	**103**	**30**	**43**	**73**	**43**	**6**	**1**	**2**	**213**	**17.8**	**138**	**48**	**113**	**25**	**2**	**9**	**1**	**6**	**7**	**2**	**0**	**0**	**0**
1982-83	**New York Rangers**	**NHL**	**71**	**29**	**47**	**76**	**24**	**33**	**57**	**28**	**7**	**5**	**5**	**199**	**14.6**	**99**	**41**	**86**	**18**	**–10**	**1**	**0**	**0**	**0**	**0**	**0**	**0**	**0**
1983-84	**New York Rangers**	**NHL**	**78**	**23**	**38**	**61**	**18**	**26**	**44**	**45**	**6**	**3**	**2**	**186**	**12.4**	**89**	**39**	**93**	**19**	**–24**	**1**	**0**	**0**	**0**	**0**	**0**	**0**	**0**
1984-85	**New York Rangers**	**NHL**	**78**	**26**	**38**	**64**	**21**	**26**	**47**	**24**	**5**	**1**	**1**	**143**	**18.2**	**90**	**32**	**92**	**9**	**–25**	**3**	**0**	**4**	**4**	**4**	**0**	**0**	**0**
1985-86	**New York Rangers**	**NHL**	**9**	**1**	**3**	**4**	**1**	**2**	**3**	**2**	**1**	**0**	**1**	**20**	**5.0**	**7**	**2**	**3**	**0**	**2**	....	....	....	....	....	....	....	....
	New Haven Nighthawks	AHL	20	9	15	24	....	....	....	28	....	....	....	....	....	....	....	....	....	....	....	....	....	....	....	....	....	....
	Edmonton Oilers	**NHL**	**8**	**1**	**0**	**1**	**1**	**0**	**1**	**0**	**0**	**0**	**0**	**6**	**16.7**	**2**	**0**	**4**	**0**	**–2**	....	....	....	....	....	....	....	....
	Nova Scotia Oilers	AHL	33	15	28	43	....	....	....	14	....	....	....	....	....	....	....	....	....	....	....	....	....	....	....	....	....	....
1986-87	HC Ambri-Piotta	Switz.	36	19	18	37	....	....	....	....	....	....	....	....	....	....	....	....	....	....	....	....	....	....	....	....	....	....
	NHL Totals		**484**	**202**	**317**	**519**	**164**	**218**	**382**	**184**	**38**	**16**	**12**	**1238**	**16.3**	**691**	**237**	**620**	**116**		**17**	**1**	**13**	**14**	**6**	**0**	**0**	**0**
	Other Major League Totals		396	145	222	367	....	....	....	109	....	....	....	....	....	....	....	....	....	....	46	13	21	34	14	....	....	....

Won Paul Daneau Trophy (WHA Most Gentlemanly Player) (1975) • Played in NHL All-Star Game (1981)

Selected by **Edmonton** (WHA) in 1974 WHA Amateur Draft, May, 1974. Traded to **New England** (WHA) by **Edmonton** (WHA) with future considerations for Wayne Carleton, January, 1976. Rights retained by **Hartford** prior to Expansion Draft, June 9, 1979. Traded to **NY Rangers** by **Hartford** with Hartford's 10th round choice (Simo Saarinen) in 1982 Entry Draft for Chris Kotsopoulos, Gerry McDonald and Doug Sulliman, October 2, 1981. Traded to **Edmonton** by **NY Rangers** for Larry Melnyk and Todd Strueby, December 20, 1985.

• ROHLICEK, Jeff

C – L. 6', 180 lbs. b: Park Ridge, IL, 1/27/1966. Vancouver's 2nd, 31st overall, in 1984.

Season	Club	League	GP	G	A	Pts	AG	AA	APts	PIM	PP	SH	GW	S	%	TGF	PGF	TGA	PGA	+/–	GP	G	A	Pts	PIM	PP	SH	GW
1981-82	Chicago Jets	MNHL	35	57	73	130	....	....	....	....	....	....	....	....	....	....	....	....	....	....	....	....	....	....	....	....	....	....
1982-83	Main West High School	Hi-School	25	60	60	120	....	....	....	....	....	....	....	....	....	....	....	....	....	....	....	....	....	....	....	....	....	....
1983-84	Portland Winter Hawks	WHL	71	44	53	97	....	....	....	22	....	....	....	....	....	....	....	....	....	....	14	13	8	21	10	....	....	....
1984-85	Portland Winter Hawks	WHL	16	5	13	18	....	....	....	2	....	....	....	....	....	....	....	....	....	....	....	....	....	....	....	....	....	....
	United States	WJC-A	7	0	2	2	....	....	....	2	....	....	....	....	....	....	....	....	....	....	....	....	....	....	....	....	....	....
	Kelowna Wings	WHL	49	34	39	73	....	....	....	24	....	....	....	....	....	....	....	....	....	....	6	3	6	9	2	....	....	....
1985-86	Spokane Chiefs	WHL	57	50	52	102	....	....	....	39	....	....	....	....	....	....	....	....	....	....	9	6	2	8	16	....	....	....
1986-87	Fredericton Express	AHL	70	19	37	56	....	....	....	22	....	....	....	....	....	....	....	....	....	....	....	....	....	....	....	....	....	....
1987-88	**Vancouver Canucks**	**NHL**	**7**	**0**	**0**	**0**	**0**	**0**	**0**	**4**	**0**	**0**	**0**	**2**	**0.0**	**0**	**0**	**4**	**0**	**–4**	....	....	....	....	....	....	....	....
	Fredericton Express	AHL	65	26	31	57	....	....	....	50	....	....	....	....	....	....	....	....	....	....	....	....	....	....	....	....	....	....
1988-89	**Vancouver Canucks**	**NHL**	**2**	**0**	**0**	**0**	**0**	**0**	**0**	**4**	**0**	**0**	**0**	**2**	**0.0**	**0**	**0**	**0**	**0**	**0**	....	....	....	....	....	....	....	....
	Milwaukee Admirals	IHL	78	47	63	110	....	....	....	106	....	....	....	....	....	....	....	....	....	....	11	6	6	12	8	....	....	....
1989-90	Milwaukee Admirals	IHL	53	22	26	48	....	....	....	37	....	....	....	....	....	....	....	....	....	....	....	....	....	....	....	....	....	....
	Springfield Indians	AHL	12	1	2	3	....	....	....	4	....	....	....	....	....	....	....	....	....	....	7	3	2	5	6	....	....	....
1990-91	New Haven Nighthawks	AHL	4	1	1	2	....	....	....	6	....	....	....	....	....	....	....	....	....	....	....	....	....	....	....	....	....	....
	Phoenix Roadrunners	IHL	74	29	31	60	....	....	....	67	....	....	....	....	....	....	....	....	....	....	10	7	6	13	12	....	....	....
1991-92	Phoenix Roadrunners	IHL	23	5	11	16	....	....	....	32	....	....	....	....	....	....	....	....	....	....	....	....	....	....	....	....	....	....
	Indianapolis Ice	IHL	59	25	32	57	....	....	....	28	....	....	....	....	....	....	....	....	....	....	....	....	....	....	....	....	....	....
1992-93	Milwaukee Admirals	IHL	11	1	1	2	....	....	....	8	....	....	....	....	....	....	....	....	....	....	....	....	....	....	....	....	....	....
	Toledo Storm	ECHL	8	5	8	13	....	....	....	14	....	....	....	....	....	....	....	....	....	....	....	....	....	....	....	....	....	....
	Adirondack Red Wings	AHL	29	6	16	22	....	....	....	20	....	....	....	....	....	....	....	....	....	....	11	4	5	9	10	....	....	....
1993-94	Toledo Storm	ECHL	57	28	54	82	....	....	....	36	....	....	....	....	....	....	....	....	....	....	....	....	....	....	....	....	....	....
	Nashville Knights	ECHL	4	1	1	2	....	....	....	24	....	....	....	....	....	....	....	....	....	....	2	1	0	1	2	....	....	....
1994-95	Chicago Wolves	IHL	18	4	4	8	....	....	....	13	....	....	....	....	....	....	....	....	....	....	....	....	....	....	....	....	....	....
	Fort Wayne Komets	IHL	22	9	14	23	....	....	....	8	....	....	....	....	....	....	....	....	....	....	4	1	2	3	4	....	....	....
1995-96	Fort Wayne Komets	IHL	38	8	12	20	....	....	....	34	....	....	....	....	....	....	....	....	....	....	....	....	....	....	....	....	....	....
1996-97	Mississippi Sea Wolves	ECHL	69	34	56	90	....	....	....	34	....	....	....	....	....	....	....	....	....	....	3	1	3	4	4	....	....	....
1997-98	Mississippi Sea Wolves	ECHL	29	7	15	22	....	....	....	30	....	....	....	....	....	....	....	....	....	....	....	....	....	....	....	....	....	....
	NHL Totals		**9**	**0**	**0**	**0**	**0**	**0**	**0**	**8**	**0**	**0**	**0**	**4**	**0.0**	**0**	**0**	**4**	**0**		....	....	....	....	....	....	....	....

WHL West Second All-Star Team (1985) • IHL First All-Star Team (1989)

Traded to **NY Islanders** by **Vancouver** for Jack Capuano, March 6, 1990. • Played w/ RHI's Chicago Cheetahs in 1994 (20-20-31-51-14) and 1995 (22-20-41-61-3).

• ROHLIN, Leif

Leif J. D – L. 6'1", 198 lbs. b: Vasteras, Sweden, 2/26/1968. Vancouver's 2nd, 33rd overall, in 1988.

Season	Club	League	GP	G	A	Pts	AG	AA	APts	PIM	PP	SH	GW	S	%	TGF	PGF	TGA	PGA	+/–	GP	G	A	Pts	PIM	PP	SH	GW
1986-87	Vasteras IK	Sweden 2	27	2	5	7	....	....	....	12	....	....	....	....	....	....	....	....	....	....	12	0	2	2	8	....	....	....
1987-88	Vasteras IK	Sweden-2	30	2	15	17	....	....	....	46	....	....	....	....	....	....	....	....	....	....	7	0	4	4	8	....	....	....
	Sweden	WJC-A	7	1	1	2	....	....	....	10	....	....	....	....	....	....	....	....	....	....	....	....	....	....	....	....	....	....
1988-89	Vasteras IK	Sweden	22	3	7	10	....	....	....	18	....	....	....	....	....	....	....	....	....	....	....	....	....	....	....	....	....	....
1989-90	Vasteras IK	Sweden	32	3	6	9	....	....	....	40	....	....	....	....	....	....	....	....	....	....	2	0	0	0	2	....	....	....
1990-91	Vasteras IK	Sweden	40	4	10	14	....	....	....	46	....	....	....	....	....	....	....	....	....	....	4	0	1	1	8	....	....	....
1991-92	Vasteras IK	Sweden	39	4	6	10	....	....	....	52	....	....	....	....	....	....	....	....	....	....	....	....	....	....	....	....	....	....
1992-93	Vasteras IK	Sweden	37	5	7	12	....	....	....	24	....	....	....	....	....	....	....	....	....	....	2	0	0	0	0	....	....	....
1993-94	Vasteras IK	Sweden	40	6	14	20	....	....	....	26	....	....	....	....	....	....	....	....	....	....	4	0	1	1	6	....	....	....
	Sweden	Olympics	8	0	1	1	....	....	....	10	....	....	....	....	....	....	....	....	....	....	....	....	....	....	....	....	....	....
1994-95	Vasteras IK	Sweden	39	15	15	30	....	....	....	46	....	....	....	....	....	....	....	....	....	....	4	2	0	2	2	....	....	....
	Sweden	WC-A	8	0	3	3	....	....	....	0	....	....	....	....	....	....	....	....	....	....	....	....	....	....	....	....	....	....
1995-96	**Vancouver Canucks**	**NHL**	**56**	**6**	**16**	**22**	**6**	**13**	**19**	**32**	**1**	**0**	**0**	**72**	**8.3**	**68**	**24**	**56**	**12**	**0**	**5**	**0**	**0**	**0**	**0**	**0**	**0**	**0**
1996-97	Sweden	W-Cup	1	0	0	0	....	....	....	2	....	....	....	....	....	....	....	....	....	....	....	....	....	....	....	....	....	....
	Vancouver Canucks	**NHL**	**40**	**2**	**8**	**10**	**2**	**7**	**9**	**8**	**0**	**0**	**0**	**37**	**5.4**	**32**	**2**	**31**	**5**	**4**	....	....	....	....	....	....	....	....

Season	Club	League	GP	G	A	Pts	AG	AA	APts	PIM	PP	SH	GW	S	%	TGF	PGF	TGA	PGA	+/-	GP	G	A	Pts	PIM	PP	SH	GW
			REGULAR SEASON																		PLAYOFFS							
1997-98	HC Ambri-Piotta	Switz.	40	7	29	36	....	....	....	28	....	....	....	....	....	....	....	....	....	....	14	3	4	7	32	....	....	....
1998-99	HC Ambri-Piotta	Switz.	45	8	31	39	....	....	....	58	....	....	....	....	....	....	....	....	....	....	15	4	9	13	18	....	....	....
99-2000	HC Ambri-Piotta	Switz.	45	5	21	26	....	....	....	56	....	....	....	....	....	....	....	....	....	....	7	1	3	4	8	....	....	....
	NHL Totals		**96**	**8**	**24**	**32**	**8**	**20**	**28**	**40**	**1**	**0**	**0**	**109**	**7.3**	**100**	**26**	**87**	**17**		**5**	**0**	**0**	**0**	**0**	**0**	**0**	**0**

• ROHLOFF, Jon

Jon Richard D – R. 5'11", 221 lbs. b: Mankato, MN, 10/3/1969. Boston's 7th, 186th overall, in 1988.

Season	Club	League	GP	G	A	Pts	AG	AA	APts	PIM	PP	SH	GW	S	%	TGF	PGF	TGA	PGA	+/-	GP	G	A	Pts	PIM	PP	SH	GW
1985-86	St. Paul Vulcans	USHL	STATISTICS NOT AVAILABLE																									
1986-87	Grand Rapids Thunderhawks	Hi-School	21	12	23	35	....	....	....	16	....	....	....	....	....	....	....	....	....	....	....	....	....	....	....	....	....	....
1987-88	Grand Rapids Thunderhawks	Hi-School	28	10	13	23	....	....	....	....	....	....	....	....	....	....	....	....	....	....	....	....	....	....	....	....	....	....
1988-89	University of Minnesota-Duluth	WCHA	39	1	2	3	....	....	....	44	....	....	....	....	....	....	....	....	....	....	....	....	....	....	....	....	....	....
1989-90	University of Minnesota-Duluth	WCHA	5	0	1	1	....	....	....	6	....	....	....	....	....	....	....	....	....	....	....	....	....	....	....	....	....	....
1990-91	University of Minnesota-Duluth	WCHA	32	6	11	17	....	....	....	38	....	....	....	....	....	....	....	....	....	....	....	....	....	....	....	....	....	....
1991-92	University of Minnesota-Duluth	WCHA	27	9	9	18	....	....	....	48	....	....	....	....	....	....	....	....	....	....	....	....	....	....	....	....	....	....
1992-93	University of Minnesota-Duluth	WCHA	36	15	20	35	....	....	....	87	....	....	....	....	....	....	....	....	....	....	....	....	....	....	....	....	....	....
1993-94	Providence Bruins	AHL	55	12	23	35	....	....	....	59	....	....	....	....	....	....	....	....	....	....	....	....	....	....	....	....	....	....
1994-95	Providence Bruins	AHL	4	2	1	3	....	....	....	6	....	....	....	....	....	....	....	....	....	....	....	....	....	....	....	....	....	....
	Boston Bruins	**NHL**	**34**	**3**	**8**	**11**	**5**	**12**	**17**	**39**	**0**	**0**	**1**	**51**	**5.9**	**22**	**2**	**22**	**3**	**1**	**5**	**0**	**0**	**0**	**6**	**0**	**0**	**0**
1995-96	**Boston Bruins**	**NHL**	**79**	**1**	**12**	**13**	**1**	**10**	**11**	**59**	**1**	**0**	**0**	**106**	**0.9**	**58**	**14**	**58**	**6**	**–8**	**5**	**1**	**2**	**3**	**2**	**1**	**0**	**0**
1996-97	**Boston Bruins**	**NHL**	**37**	**3**	**5**	**8**	**3**	**4**	**7**	**31**	**1**	**0**	**0**	**69**	**4.3**	**29**	**8**	**42**	**7**	**–14**	....	....	....	....	....	....	....	....
	Providence Bruins	AHL	3	1	1	2	....	....	....	0	....	....	....	....	....	....	....	....	....	....	....	....	....	....	....	....	....	....
	United States	WC-A	8	0	2	2	....	....	....	10	....	....	....	....	....	....	....	....	....	....	....	....	....	....	....	....	....	....
1997-98	Providence Bruins	AHL	58	6	17	23	....	....	....	46	....	....	....	....	....	....	....	....	....	....	....	....	....	....	....	....	....	....
1998-99	Kentucky Thoroughblades	AHL	12	0	1	1	....	....	....	8	....	....	....	....	....	....	....	....	....	....	....	....	....	....	....	....	....	....
	Kansas City Blades	IHL	41	5	13	18	....	....	....	42	....	....	....	....	....	....	....	....	....	....	3	0	0	0	18	....	....	....
99-2000	Kansas City Blades	IHL	44	5	18	23	....	....	....	38	....	....	....	....	....	....	....	....	....	....	....	....	....	....	....	....	....	....
	NHL Totals		**150**	**7**	**25**	**32**	**9**	**26**	**35**	**129**	**2**	**0**	**1**	**226**	**3.1**	**109**	**24**	**122**	**16**		**10**	**1**	**2**	**3**	**8**	**1**	**0**	**0**

WCHA Second All-Star Team (1993)

Signed as a free agent by **San Jose**, July 23, 1998.

• ROLFE, Dale

Dale Roland Carl "Goat" D – L. 6'4", 210 lbs. b: Timmins, Ont., 4/30/1940.

Season	Club	League	GP	G	A	Pts	AG	AA	APts	PIM	PP	SH	GW	S	%	TGF	PGF	TGA	PGA	+/-	GP	G	A	Pts	PIM	PP	SH	GW
1956-57	Barrie Flyers	OHA-Jr.	52	18	16	34	....	....	....	37	....	....	....	....	....	....	....	....	....	....	3	0	0	0	2	....	....	....
1957-58	Barrie Flyers	OHA-Jr.	50	5	22	27	....	....	....	83	....	....	....	....	....	....	....	....	....	....	4	0	0	0	8	....	....	....
1958-59	Barrie Flyers	OHA-Jr.	44	9	25	34	....	....	....	132	....	....	....	....	....	....	....	....	....	....	6	1	4	5	24	....	....	....
1959-60	Barrie Flyers	OHA-Jr.	48	8	39	47	....	....	....	127	....	....	....	....	....	....	....	....	....	....	6	1	6	7	25	....	....	....
	Boston Bruins	**NHL**	**3**	**0**	**0**	**0**	**0**	**0**	**0**	**0**	....	....	....	....	....	....	....	....	....	....	....	....	....	....	....	....	....	....
	Kingston Frontenacs	EPHL	2	0	1	1	....	....	....	2	....	....	....	....	....	....	....	....	....	....	....	....	....	....	....	....	....	....
1960-61	Portland Buckaroos	WHL	70	4	12	16	....	....	....	52	....	....	....	....	....	....	....	....	....	....	14	2	5	7	8	....	....	....
1961-62	Portland Buckaroos	WHL	70	7	15	22	....	....	....	65	....	....	....	....	....	....	....	....	....	....	7	1	2	3	8	....	....	....
1962-63	Hershey Bears	AHL	53	3	9	12	....	....	....	78	....	....	....	....	....	....	....	....	....	....	11	1	3	4	26	....	....	....
1963-64	Springfield Indians	AHL	71	2	16	18	....	....	....	103	....	....	....	....	....	....	....	....	....	....	....	....	....	....	....	....	....	....
1964-65	Springfield Indians	AHL	69	10	25	35	....	....	....	68	....	....	....	....	....	....	....	....	....	....	....	....	....	....	....	....	....	....
1965-66	Springfield Indians	AHL	71	5	27	32	....	....	....	94	....	....	....	....	....	....	....	....	....	....	6	0	1	1	16	....	....	....
1966-67	Springfield Indians	AHL	67	14	35	49	....	....	....	94	....	....	....	....	....	....	....	....	....	....	....	....	....	....	....	....	....	....
1967-68	**Los Angeles Kings**	**NHL**	**68**	**3**	**13**	**16**	**3**	**13**	**16**	**84**	**1**	**0**	**0**	**93**	**3.2**	**72**	**6**	**95**	**19**	**–10**	**7**	**0**	**1**	**1**	**14**	**0**	**0**	**0**
	Springfield Kings	AHL	6	1	5	6	....	....	....	2	....	....	....	....	....	....	....	....	....	....	....	....	....	....	....	....	....	....
1968-69	**Los Angeles Kings**	**NHL**	**75**	**3**	**19**	**22**	**3**	**17**	**20**	**85**	**0**	**0**	**0**	**151**	**2.0**	**76**	**7**	**116**	**23**	**–24**	**10**	**0**	**4**	**4**	**8**	**0**	**0**	**0**
1969-70	**Los Angeles Kings**	**NHL**	**55**	**1**	**9**	**10**	**1**	**8**	**9**	**77**	**0**	**0**	**0**	**115**	**0.9**	**43**	**5**	**94**	**31**	**–25**	....	....	....	....	....	....	....	....
	Detroit Red Wings	**NHL**	**20**	**2**	**9**	**11**	**2**	**8**	**10**	**12**	**0**	**0**	**1**	**62**	**3.2**	**27**	**4**	**21**	**7**	**9**	**4**	**0**	**2**	**2**	**8**	**0**	**0**	**0**
1970-71	**Detroit Red Wings**	**NHL**	**44**	**3**	**9**	**12**	**3**	**7**	**10**	**48**	**0**	**0**	**0**	**90**	**3.3**	**44**	**5**	**65**	**13**	**–13**	....	....	....	....	....	....	....	....
	New York Rangers	**NHL**	**14**	**0**	**7**	**7**	**0**	**6**	**6**	**23**	**0**	**0**	**0**	**28**	**0.0**	**22**	**2**	**15**	**6**	**11**	**13**	**0**	**1**	**1**	**14**	**0**	**0**	**0**
1971-72	**New York Rangers**	**NHL**	**68**	**2**	**14**	**16**	**2**	**12**	**14**	**67**	**0**	**0**	**0**	**166**	**1.2**	**93**	**3**	**64**	**15**	**41**	**16**	**4**	**3**	**7**	**16**	**0**	**0**	**1**
1972-73	**New York Rangers**	**NHL**	**72**	**7**	**25**	**32**	**7**	**20**	**27**	**74**	**1**	**0**	**0**	**159**	**4.4**	**124**	**13**	**89**	**19**	**41**	**8**	**0**	**5**	**5**	**6**	**0**	**0**	**0**
1973-74	**New York Rangers**	**NHL**	**48**	**3**	**12**	**15**	**3**	**10**	**13**	**56**	**0**	**1**	**0**	**98**	**3.1**	**74**	**3**	**68**	**13**	**16**	**13**	**1**	**8**	**9**	**23**	**0**	**0**	**0**
1974-75	**New York Rangers**	**NHL**	**42**	**1**	**8**	**9**	**1**	**6**	**7**	**30**	**1**	**0**	**0**	**56**	**1.8**	**47**	**3**	**43**	**11**	**12**	....	....	....	....	....	....	....	....
	NHL Totals		**509**	**25**	**125**	**150**	**25**	**107**	**132**	**556**	....	....	....	....	....	....	....	....	....		**71**	**5**	**24**	**29**	**89**	....	....	....

OHA-Jr. First Team All-Star (1960) • AHL First All-Star Team (1967)

Traded to **Springfield** (AHL) by **Boston** with Bruce Gamble, Terry Gray and Randy Miller for Bob McCord, June, 1963. NHL rights transferred to **LA Kings** after NHL club purchased **Springfield** (AHL) franchise, May, 1967. Traded to **Detroit** by **LA Kings** with Gary Croteau and Larry Johnston for Garry Monahan, Matt Ravlich and Brian Gibbons, February 20, 1970. Traded to **NY Rangers** by **Detroit** for Jim Krulicki, March 2, 1971.

• ROLSTON, Brian

Brian Lee C – L. 6'2", 200 lbs. b: Flint, MI, 2/21/1973. New Jersey's 2nd, 11th overall, in 1991.

Season	Club	League	GP	G	A	Pts	AG	AA	APts	PIM	PP	SH	GW	S	%	TGF	PGF	TGA	PGA	+/-	GP	G	A	Pts	PIM	PP	SH	GW
1989-90	Detroit Compuware	NAJHL	40	36	37	73	....	....	....	57	....	....	....	....	....	....	....	....	....	....	....	....	....	....	....	....	....	....
1990-91	Detroit Compuware	NAJHL	36	49	46	95	....	....	....	14	....	....	....	....	....	....	....	....	....	....	....	....	....	....	....	....	....	....
	United States	WJC-A	8	1	5	6	....	....	....	0	....	....	....	....	....	....	....	....	....	....	....	....	....	....	....	....	....	....
1991-92	Lake Superior State	CCHA	37	14	23	37	....	....	....	14	....	....	....	....	....	....	....	....	....	....	....	....	....	....	....	....	....	....
	United States	WJC-A	7	3	3	6	....	....	....	2	....	....	....	....	....	....	....	....	....	....	....	....	....	....	....	....	....	....
1992-93	Lake Superior State	CCHA	39	33	31	64	....	....	....	20	....	....	....	....	....	....	....	....	....	....	....	....	....	....	....	....	....	....
	United States	WJC-A	7	6	2	8	....	....	....	2	....	....	....	....	....	....	....	....	....	....	....	....	....	....	....	....	....	....
1993-94	United States	Nat-Team	41	20	28	48	....	....	....	36	....	....	....	....	....	....	....	....	....	....	....	....	....	....	....	....	....	....
	United States	Olympics	8	7	0	7	....	....	....	8	....	....	....	....	....	....	....	....	....	....	....	....	....	....	....	....	....	....
	Albany River Rats	AHL	17	5	5	10	....	....	....	8	....	....	....	....	....	....	....	....	....	....	5	1	2	3	0	....	....	....
1994-95	Albany River Rats	AHL	18	9	11	20	....	....	....	10	....	....	....	....	....	....	....	....	....	....	....	....	....	....	....	....	....	....
♦	**New Jersey Devils**	**NHL**	**40**	**7**	**11**	**18**	**12**	**16**	**28**	**17**	**2**	**0**	**3**	**92**	**7.6**	**28**	**5**	**18**	**0**	**5**	**6**	**2**	**1**	**3**	**4**	**1**	**0**	**0**
1995-96	**New Jersey Devils**	**NHL**	**58**	**13**	**11**	**24**	**13**	**9**	**22**	**8**	**3**	**1**	**4**	**139**	**9.4**	**40**	**10**	**29**	**8**	**9**	....	....	....	....	....	....	....	....
	United States	WC-A	8	3	4	7	....	....	....	4	....	....	....	....	....	....	....	....	....	....	....	....	....	....	....	....	....	....
1996-97	United States	W-Cup	1	0	0	0	....	....	....	0	....	....	....	....	....	....	....	....	....	....	....	....	....	....	....	....	....	....
	New Jersey Devils	**NHL**	**81**	**18**	**27**	**45**	**19**	**24**	**43**	**20**	**2**	**2**	**3**	**237**	**7.6**	**64**	**14**	**50**	**6**	**6**	**10**	**4**	**1**	**5**	**6**	**1**	**2**	**0**
1997-98	**New Jersey Devils**	**NHL**	**76**	**16**	**14**	**30**	**19**	**14**	**33**	**16**	**0**	**2**	**1**	**185**	**8.6**	**48**	**7**	**49**	**15**	**7**	**6**	**1**	**0**	**1**	**2**	**0**	**1**	**0**
1998-99	**New Jersey Devils**	**NHL**	**82**	**24**	**33**	**57**	**28**	**32**	**60**	**14**	**5**	**5**	**3**	**210**	**11.4**	**76**	**21**	**70**	**26**	**11**	**7**	**1**	**0**	**1**	**2**	**0**	**1**	**0**
99-2000	**New Jersey Devils**	**NHL**	**11**	**3**	**1**	**4**	**3**	**1**	**4**	**0**	**1**	**0**	**2**	**33**	**9.1**	**8**	**3**	**8**	**1**	**–2**	....	....	....	....	....	....	....	....
	Colorado Avalanche	**NHL**	**50**	**8**	**10**	**18**	**9**	**9**	**18**	**12**	**1**	**0**	**3**	**107**	**7.5**	**25**	**7**	**28**	**4**	**–6**	....	....	....	....	....	....	....	....
	Boston Bruins	**NHL**	**16**	**5**	**4**	**9**	**6**	**4**	**10**	**6**	**3**	**0**	**1**	**66**	**7.6**	**15**	**7**	**16**	**4**	**–4**	....	....	....	....	....	....	....	....
	NHL Totals		**414**	**94**	**111**	**205**	**109**	**109**	**218**	**93**	**17**	**10**	**20**	**1069**	**8.8**	**304**	**74**	**268**	**64**		**29**	**8**	**2**	**10**	**14**	**2**	**4**	**0**

NCAA Championship All-Tournament Team (1992, 1993) • CCHA First All-Star Team (1993) • NCAA West Second All-American Team (1993)

Traded to **Colorado** by **New Jersey** with New Jersey's 1st round choice (later traded to Boston - Boston selected Martin Samuelsson) and future considerations for Claude Lemieux and Colorado's 1st (David Hale) and 2nd (Matt DeMarchi) round choices in 2000 Entry Draft, November 3, 1999. Traded to **Boston** by **Colorado** with Martin Grenier, Sami Pahlsson and New Jersey's 1st round choice (previously acquired, Boston selected Martin Samuelsson) in 2000 Entry Draft for Ray Bourque and Dave Andreychuk, March 6, 2000.

• ROMANCHYCH, Larry

Lawrence Brian "Swoop" RW – R. 6'1", 180 lbs. b: Vancouver, B.C., 9/7/1949. Chicago's 2nd, 24th overall, in 1969.

Season	Club	League	GP	G	A	Pts	AG	AA	APts	PIM	PP	SH	GW	S	%	TGF	PGF	TGA	PGA	+/-	GP	G	A	Pts	PIM	PP	SH	GW
1967-68	Brandon Wheat Kings	WCJHL	53	20	23	43	....	....	....	24	....	....	....	....	....	....	....	....	....	....	8	1	4	5	2	....	....	....
1968-69	Flin Flon Bombers	WCJHL	55	31	25	56	....	....	....	40	....	....	....	....	....	....	....	....	....	....	18	11	8	19	6	....	....	....
1969-70	Dallas Black Hawks	CHL	57	21	12	33	....	....	....	38	....	....	....	....	....	....	....	....	....	....	....	....	....	....	....	....	....	....
1970-71	**Chicago Black Hawks**	**NHL**	**10**	**0**	**2**	**2**	**0**	**2**	**2**	**2**	**0**	**0**	**0**	**10**	**0.0**	**2**	**1**	**1**	**0**	**0**	....	....	....	....	....	....	....	....
	Dallas Black Hawks	CHL	65	18	34	52	....	....	....	26	....	....	....	....	....	....	....	....	....	....	10	2	4	6	4	....	....	....
1971-72	Dallas Black Hawks	CHL	60	21	23	44	....	....	....	31	....	....	....	....	....	....	....	....	....	....	12	3	4	7	28	....	....	....
1972-73	**Atlanta Flames**	**NHL**	**70**	**18**	**30**	**48**	**17**	**24**	**41**	**39**	**4**	**0**	**2**	**157**	**11.5**	**72**	**15**	**68**	**0**	**–11**	....	....	....	....	....	....	....	....
1973-74	**Atlanta Flames**	**NHL**	**73**	**22**	**29**	**51**	**21**	**24**	**45**	**33**	**7**	**0**	**4**	**159**	**13.8**	**72**	**25**	**54**	**0**	**–7**	**4**	**2**	**2**	**4**	**4**	**0**	**0**	**0**
1974-75	**Atlanta Flames**	**NHL**	**53**	**8**	**12**	**20**	**7**	**9**	**16**	**16**	**2**	**0**	**0**	**64**	**12.5**	**43**	**20**	**33**	**1**	**–9**	....	....	....	....	....	....	....	....

			REGULAR SEASON																		PLAYOFFS							
Season	Club	League	GP	G	A	Pts	AG	AA	APts	PIM	PP	SH	GW	S	%	TGF	PGF	TGA	PGA	+/-	GP	G	A	Pts	PIM	PP	SH	GW
1975-76	Atlanta Flames	NHL	67	16	19	35	14	14	28	8	6	0	2	110	14.5	57	20	44	0	–7	2	0	0	0	0	0	0	0
1976-77	Atlanta Flames	NHL	25	4	5	9	4	4	8	4	0	0	0	42	9.5	12	2	13	0	–3	1	0	0	0	0	0	0	0
	Tulsa Oilers	CHL	37	20	28	48	....	....	....	18	....	....	....	....	....	....	....	....	....	....	....	....	....	....	....	....	....	....
1977-78	Maine Mariners	AHL	79	17	34	51	....	....	....	23	....	....	....	....	....	....	....	....	....	....	12	*8	4	12	6	....	....	....
	NHL Totals		298	68	97	165	63	77	140	102	19	0	8	542	12.5	258	83	213	1		7	2	2	4	4	0	0	0

Claimed by **Atlanta** from **Chicago** in Expansion Draft, June 6, 1972.

• ROMANIUK, Russell

Russell J. LW – L. 6', 195 lbs. b: Winnipeg, Man., 6/9/1970. Winnipeg's 2nd, 31st overall, in 1988.

Season	Club	League	GP	G	A	Pts	AG	AA	APts	PIM	PP	SH	GW	S	%	TGF	PGF	TGA	PGA	+/-	GP	G	A	Pts	PIM	PP	SH	GW
1987-88	St. Boniface Saints	MJHL	38	46	34	80	....	....	....	46	....	....	....	....	....	....	....	....	....	....	....	....	....	....	....	....	....	....
1988-89	University of North Dakota	WCHA	39	17	14	31	....	....	....	32	....	....	....	....	....	....	....	....	....	....	....	....	....	....	....	....	....	....
	Canada	Nat-Team	3	1	0	1	....	....	....	0	....	....	....	....	....	....	....	....	....	....	....	....	....	....	....	....	....	....
1989-90	University of North Dakota	WCHA	45	36	15	51	....	....	....	54	....	....	....	....	....	....	....	....	....	....	....	....	....	....	....	....	....	....
1990-91	University of North Dakota	WCHA	39	40	28	68	....	....	....	30	....	....	....	....	....	....	....	....	....	....	....	....	....	....	....	....	....	....
1991-92	Winnipeg Jets	NHL	27	3	5	8	3	4	7	18	2	0	1	32	9.4	12	6	4	0	2	....	....	....	....	....	....	....	....
	Moncton Hawks	AHL	45	16	15	31	....	....	....	25	....	....	....	....	....	....	....	....	....	....	10	5	4	9	19	....	....	....
1992-93	Winnipeg Jets	NHL	28	3	1	4	2	1	3	22	0	0	1	20	15.0	14	3	11	0	0	1	0	0	0	0	0	0	0
	Moncton Hawks	AHL	28	18	8	26	....	....	....	40	....	....	....	....	....	....	....	....	....	....	5	0	4	4	2	....	....	....
	Fort Wayne Komets	IHL	4	2	0	2	....	....	....	7	....	....	....	....	....	....	....	....	....	....	....	....	....	....	....	....	....	....
1993-94	Canada	Nat-Team	34	8	9	17	....	....	....	17	....	....	....	....	....	....	....	....	....	....	....	....	....	....	....	....	....	....
	Winnipeg Jets	NHL	24	4	8	12	4	6	10	6	3	0	0	36	11.1	16	5	24	2	–11	....	....	....	....	....	....	....	....
	Moncton Hawks	AHL	18	16	8	24	....	....	....	24	....	....	....	....	....	....	....	....	....	....	17	2	6	8	30	....	....	....
1994-95	Winnipeg Jets	NHL	6	0	0	0	0	0	0	0	0	0	0	3	0.0	0	0	4	1	–3	....	....	....	....	....	....	....	....
	Springfield Falcons	AHL	17	5	7	12	....	....	....	29	....	....	....	....	....	....	....	....	....	....	....	....	....	....	....	....	....	....
1995-96	Philadelphia Flyers	NHL	17	3	0	3	3	0	3	17	1	0	0	13	23.1	8	3	7	0	–2	1	0	0	0	0	0	0	0
	Hershey Bears	AHL	27	19	10	29	....	....	....	43	....	....	....	....	....	....	....	....	....	....	....	....	....	....	....	....	....	....
1996-97	Manitoba Moose	IHL	46	14	13	27	....	....	....	43	....	....	....	....	....	....	....	....	....	....	....	....	....	....	....	....	....	....
1997-98	Manitoba Moose	IHL	5	0	1	1	....	....	....	8	....	....	....	....	....	....	....	....	....	....	....	....	....	....	....	....	....	....
	Long Beach Ice Dogs	IHL	49	16	11	27	....	....	....	37	....	....	....	....	....	....	....	....	....	....	....	....	....	....	....	....	....	....
	Las Vegas Thunder	IHL	22	6	4	10	....	....	....	10	....	....	....	....	....	....	....	....	....	....	4	2	2	4	4	....	....	....
1998-99	Las Vegas Thunder	IHL	82	43	20	63	....	....	....	91	....	....	....	....	....	....	....	....	....	....	....	....	....	....	....	....	....	....
99-2000	Nurnberg Ice Tigers	Germany	68	17	17	34	....	....	....	40	....	....	....	....	....	....	....	....	....	....	....	....	....	....	....	....	....	....
	Nurnberg Ice Tigers	EuroHL	6	5	3	8	....	....	....	2	....	....	....	....	....	....	....	....	....	....	2	0	0	0	0	....	....	....
	NHL Totals		102	13	14	27	12	11	23	63	6	0	2	104	12.5	50	17	50	3		2	0	0	0	0	0	0	0

WCHA First All-Star Team (1991)

Traded to **Philadelphia** by **Winnipeg** for Jeff Finley, June 27, 1995. Traded to **Long Beach** (IHL) by **Manitoba** (IHL) for Brian Chapman, October 16, 1997. IHL rights acquired by **Utah** (IHL) from **Las Vegas** (IHL) with Brad Miller, Scott Hollis and Kevin Kaminski after Las Vegas franchise folded, July 6, 1999.

• ROMBOUGH, Doug

Douglas George C – L. 6'3", 215 lbs. b: Fergus, Ont., 7/8/1950. Buffalo's 8th, 97th overall, in 1970.

Season	Club	League	GP	G	A	Pts	AG	AA	APts	PIM	PP	SH	GW	S	%	TGF	PGF	TGA	PGA	+/-	GP	G	A	Pts	PIM	PP	SH	GW
1967-68	Fort Erie Otters	OHA-B	STATISTICS NOT AVAILABLE																									
1968-69	St. Catharines Black Hawks	OHA-Jr.	53	12	13	25	....	....	....	15	....	....	....	....	....	....	....	....	....	....	17	1	1	2	2	....	....	....
1969-70	St. Catharines Black Hawks	OHA-Jr.	53	14	13	27	....	....	....	36	....	....	....	....	....	....	....	....	....	....	10	2	4	6	2	....	....	....
1970-71	Flint Generals	IHL	65	22	36	58	....	....	....	26	....	....	....	....	....	....	....	....	....	....	7	1	5	6	2	....	....	....
1971-72	Cincinnati Swords	AHL	76	22	26	48	....	....	....	42	....	....	....	....	....	....	....	....	....	....	10	4	4	8	22	....	....	....
1972-73	Buffalo Sabres	NHL	5	2	0	2	2	0	2	0	0	0	0	3	66.7	2	0	0	0	2	....	....	....	....	....	....	....	....
	Cincinnati Swords	AHL	66	28	43	71	....	....	....	48	....	....	....	....	....	....	....	....	....	....	14	*10	8	18	26	....	....	....
1973-74	Buffalo Sabres	NHL	46	6	9	15	6	7	13	27	0	0	1	38	15.8	22	2	18	0	2	....	....	....	....	....	....	....	....
	New York Islanders	NHL	12	3	1	4	3	1	4	8	2	0	0	19	15.8	7	2	4	0	1	....	....	....	....	....	....	....	....
1974-75	New York Islanders	NHL	28	5	6	11	4	4	8	6	0	0	0	35	14.3	18	4	8	0	6	....	....	....	....	....	....	....	....
	Minnesota North Stars	NHL	40	6	9	15	5	7	12	33	0	0	1	63	9.5	22	5	17	1	1	....	....	....	....	....	....	....	....
1975-76	Minnesota North Stars	NHL	19	2	2	4	2	1	3	6	0	0	1	9	22.2	3	0	11	4	–4	....	....	....	....	....	....	....	....
	New Haven Nighthawks	AHL	42	5	20	25	....	....	....	28	....	....	....	....	....	....	....	....	....	....	3	0	0	0	0	....	....	....
1976-77	New Haven Nighthawks	AHL	4	0	0	0	....	....	....	0	....	....	....	....	....	....	....	....	....	....	....	....	....	....	....	....	....	....
	Dallas Black Hawks	CHL	70	21	25	46	....	....	....	24	....	....	....	....	....	....	....	....	....	....	5	1	0	1	0	....	....	....
1977-78	Fort Worth Texans	CHL	73	23	34	57	....	....	....	38	....	....	....	....	....	....	....	....	....	....	14	3	3	6	9	....	....	....
	NHL Totals		150	24	27	51	22	20	42	80	2	0	3	167	14.4	74	13	58	5		....	....	....	....	....	....	....	....

Traded to **NY Islanders** by **Buffalo** for Brian Spencer, March 10, 1974. Traded to **Minnesota** by **NY Islanders** with Ernie Hicke for Jean-Paul Parise, January 5, 1975.

• ROMINSKI, Dale

RW – R. 6'2", 200 lbs. b: Farmington Hills, MI, 10/1/1975.

Season	Club	League	GP	G	A	Pts	AG	AA	APts	PIM	PP	SH	GW	S	%	TGF	PGF	TGA	PGA	+/-	GP	G	A	Pts	PIM	PP	SH	GW
1993-94	Brother Rice High School	Hi-School	25	25	20	45	....	....	....	....	....	....	....	....	....	....	....	....	....	....	....	....	....	....	....	....	....	....
1994-95	Detroit Compuware	NAJHL	40	21	21	42	....	....	....	30	....	....	....	....	....	....	....	....	....	....	....	....	....	....	....	....	....	....
1995-96	University of Michigan	CCHA	35	8	7	15	....	....	....	37	....	....	....	....	....	....	....	....	....	....	....	....	....	....	....	....	....	....
1996-97	University of Michigan	CCHA	38	6	7	13	....	....	....	58	....	....	....	....	....	....	....	....	....	....	....	....	....	....	....	....	....	....
1997-98	University of Michigan	CCHA	46	10	14	24	....	....	....	102	....	....	....	....	....	....	....	....	....	....	....	....	....	....	....	....	....	....
1998-99	University of Michigan	CCHA	41	15	8	23	....	....	....	80	....	....	....	....	....	....	....	....	....	....	....	....	....	....	....	....	....	....
99-2000	Tampa Bay Lightning	NHL	3	0	1	1	0	1	1	2	0	0	0	0	0.0	1	0	0	0	1	....	....	....	....	....	....	....	....
	Detroit Vipers	IHL	78	14	15	29	....	....	....	68	....	....	....	....	....	....	....	....	....	....	....	....	....	....	....	....	....	....
	NHL Totals		3	0	1	1	0	1	1	2	0	0	0	0	0.0	1	0	0	0		....	....	....	....	....	....	....	....

Signed as a free agent by **Tampa Bay**, August 31, 1999.

• RONAN, Ed

Edward RW – R. 6', 197 lbs. b: Quincy, MA, 3/21/1968. Montreal's 13th, 227th overall, in 1987.

Season	Club	League	GP	G	A	Pts	AG	AA	APts	PIM	PP	SH	GW	S	%	TGF	PGF	TGA	PGA	+/-	GP	G	A	Pts	PIM	PP	SH	GW
1986-87	Andover Academy	Hi-School	22	10	22	32	....	....	....	10	....	....	....	....	....	....	....	....	....	....	....	....	....	....	....	....	....	....
1987-88	Boston University	H-East	31	2	5	7	....	....	....	20	....	....	....	....	....	....	....	....	....	....	....	....	....	....	....	....	....	....
1988-89	Boston University	H-East	36	4	11	15	....	....	....	34	....	....	....	....	....	....	....	....	....	....	....	....	....	....	....	....	....	....
1989-90	Boston University	H-East	44	17	23	40	....	....	....	50	....	....	....	....	....	....	....	....	....	....	....	....	....	....	....	....	....	....
1990-91	Boston University	H-East	41	16	19	35	....	....	....	38	....	....	....	....	....	....	....	....	....	....	....	....	....	....	....	....	....	....
1991-92	Montreal Canadiens	NHL	3	0	0	0	0	0	0	0	0	0	0	1	0.0	0	0	0	0	0	....	....	....	....	....	....	....	....
	Fredericton Canadiens	AHL	78	25	34	59	....	....	....	82	....	....	....	....	....	....	....	....	....	....	7	5	1	6	6	....	....	....
1992-93♦	Montreal Canadiens	NHL	53	5	7	12	4	5	9	20	0	0	1	54	9.3	23	0	20	3	6	14	2	3	5	10	0	0	0
	Fredericton Canadiens	AHL	16	10	5	15	....	....	....	15	....	....	....	....	....	....	....	....	....	....	5	2	4	6	6	....	....	....
1993-94	Montreal Canadiens	NHL	61	6	8	14	6	6	12	42	0	0	1	49	12.2	24	1	21	1	3	7	1	0	1	0	0	0	0
1994-95	Montreal Canadiens	NHL	30	1	4	5	2	6	8	12	0	0	0	14	7.1	7	0	19	5	–7	....	....	....	....	....	....	....	....
1995-96	Winnipeg Jets	NHL	17	0	0	0	0	0	0	16	0	0	0	13	0.0	2	0	13	8	–3	....	....	....	....	....	....	....	....
	Springfield Falcons	AHL	31	8	16	24	....	....	....	50	....	....	....	....	....	....	....	....	....	....	10	7	6	13	4	....	....	....
1996-97	Buffalo Sabres	NHL	18	1	4	5	1	4	5	11	0	0	0	10	10.0	8	0	4	0	4	6	1	0	1	6	0	0	1
	Rochester Americans	AHL	47	13	21	34	....	....	....	62	....	....	....	....	....	....	....	....	....	....	....	....	....	....	....	....	....	....
1997-98	Providence Bruins	AHL	49	13	15	28	....	....	....	48	....	....	....	....	....	....	....	....	....	....	....	....	....	....	....	....	....	....
	NHL Totals		182	13	23	36	13	21	34	101	0	0	2	141	9.2	64	1	77	17		27	4	3	7	16	0	0	1

Signed as a free agent by **Winnipeg**, October 13, 1995. Signed as a free agent by **Buffalo**, September 5, 1996.

• RONNING, Cliff

Clifford John "Ace" C – L. 5'8", 170 lbs. b: Burnaby, B.C., 10/1/1965. St. Louis' 9th, 134th overall, in 1984.

Season	Club	League	GP	G	A	Pts	AG	AA	APts	PIM	PP	SH	GW	S	%	TGF	PGF	TGA	PGA	+/-	GP	G	A	Pts	PIM	PP	SH	GW
1982-83	New Westminster Royals	BCJHL	52	83	68	151	....	....	....	22	....	....	....	....	....	....	....	....	....	....	....	....	....	....	....	....	....	....
1983-84	New Westminster Bruins	WHL	71	69	67	136	....	....	....	10	....	....	....	....	....	....	....	....	....	....	9	8	13	21	10	....	....	....
1984-85	New Westminster Bruins	WHL	70	*89	108	*197	....	....	....	20	....	....	....	....	....	....	....	....	....	....	11	10	14	24	4	....	....	....
1985-86	Canada	Nat-Team	71	55	63	118	....	....	....	....	....	....	....	....	....	....	....	....	....	....	....	....	....	....	....	....	....	....
	St. Louis Blues	NHL	....	....	....	....	....	....	....	....	....	....	....	....	....	....	....	....	....	....	5	1	1	2	2	1	0	0
1986-87	Canada	Nat-Team	26	17	16	33	....	....	....	12	....	....	....	....	....	....	....	....	....	....	....	....	....	....	....	....	....	....
	St. Louis Blues	NHL	42	11	14	25	9	10	19	6	2	0	2	68	16.2	31	9	23	0	–1	4	0	1	1	0	0	0	0

			REGULAR SEASON																		PLAYOFFS							
Season	Club	League	GP	G	A	Pts	AG	AA	APts	PIM	PP	SH	GW	S	%	TGF	PGF	TGA	PGA	+/–	GP	G	A	Pts	PIM	PP	SH	GW
1987-88	**St. Louis Blues**	**NHL**	**26**	**5**	**8**	**13**	**4**	**6**	**10**	**12**	**1**	**0**	**1**	**38**	**13.2**	**16**	**6**	**4**	**0**	**6**	....	....	....	....	....	....	....	....
1988-89	**St. Louis Blues**	**NHL**	**64**	**24**	**31**	**55**	**20**	**22**	**42**	**18**	**16**	**0**	**1**	**150**	**16.0**	**68**	**41**	**25**	**1**	**3**	**7**	**1**	**3**	**4**	**0**	**1**	**0**	**0**
	Peoria Rivermen	IHL	12	11	20	31	....	....	....	8	....	....	....	....	....	....	....	....	....	....	....	....	....	....	....	....	....	....
1989-90	HC Asiago	Italy	36	67	49	116	....	....	....	25	....	....	....	....	....	....	....	....	....	....	6	7	12	19	4	....	....	....
1990-91	**St. Louis Blues**	**NHL**	**48**	**14**	**18**	**32**	**13**	**14**	**27**	**10**	**5**	**0**	**2**	**81**	**17.3**	**50**	**29**	**19**	**0**	**2**	....	....	....	....	....	....	....	....
	Vancouver Canucks	**NHL**	**11**	**6**	**6**	**12**	**5**	**5**	**10**	**0**	**2**	**0**	**0**	**32**	**18.8**	**22**	**12**	**12**	**0**	**–2**	**6**	**6**	**3**	**9**	**12**	**2**	**0**	**2**
	Canada	WEC-A	10	1	4	5	....	....	....	8	....	....	....	....	....	....	....	....	....	....	....	....	....	....	....	....	....	....
1991-92	**Vancouver Canucks**	**NHL**	**80**	**24**	**47**	**71**	**22**	**36**	**58**	**42**	**6**	**0**	**2**	**216**	**11.1**	**97**	**33**	**48**	**2**	**18**	**13**	**8**	**5**	**13**	**6**	**1**	**0**	**1**
1992-93	**Vancouver Canucks**	**NHL**	**79**	**29**	**56**	**85**	**24**	**39**	**63**	**30**	**10**	**0**	**2**	**209**	**13.9**	**102**	**33**	**50**	**0**	**19**	**12**	**2**	**9**	**11**	**6**	**0**	**0**	**0**
1993-94	**Vancouver Canucks**	**NHL**	**76**	**25**	**43**	**68**	**23**	**33**	**56**	**42**	**10**	**0**	**4**	**197**	**12.7**	**106**	**49**	**51**	**1**	**7**	**24**	**5**	**10**	**15**	**16**	**2**	**0**	**2**
1994-95	**Vancouver Canucks**	**NHL**	**41**	**6**	**19**	**25**	**11**	**28**	**39**	**27**	**3**	**0**	**2**	**93**	**6.5**	**40**	**20**	**24**	**0**	**–4**	**11**	**3**	**5**	**8**	**2**	**1**	**0**	**2**
1995-96	**Vancouver Canucks**	**NHL**	**79**	**22**	**45**	**67**	**22**	**37**	**59**	**42**	**5**	**0**	**1**	**187**	**11.8**	**92**	**18**	**59**	**1**	**16**	**6**	**0**	**2**	**2**	**6**	**0**	**0**	**0**
1996-97	**Phoenix Coyotes**	**NHL**	**69**	**19**	**32**	**51**	**20**	**28**	**48**	**26**	**8**	**0**	**2**	**171**	**11.1**	**71**	**30**	**50**	**0**	**–9**	**7**	**0**	**7**	**7**	**12**	**0**	**0**	**0**
1997-98	**Phoenix Coyotes**	**NHL**	**80**	**11**	**44**	**55**	**13**	**43**	**56**	**36**	**3**	**0**	**0**	**197**	**5.6**	**72**	**30**	**40**	**3**	**5**	**6**	**1**	**3**	**4**	**4**	**0**	**0**	**0**
1998-99	**Phoenix Coyotes**	**NHL**	**7**	**2**	**5**	**7**	**2**	**5**	**7**	**2**	**2**	**0**	**1**	**18**	**11.1**	**8**	**4**	**1**	**0**	**3**	....	....	....	....	....	....	....	....
	Nashville Predators	**NHL**	**72**	**18**	**35**	**53**	**21**	**34**	**55**	**40**	**8**	**0**	**3**	**239**	**7.5**	**65**	**24**	**48**	**1**	**–6**	....	....	....	....	....	....	....	....
99-2000	**Nashville Predators**	**NHL**	**82**	**26**	**36**	**62**	**29**	**33**	**62**	**34**	**7**	**0**	**2**	**248**	**10.5**	**78**	**31**	**60**	**0**	**–13**	....	....	....	....	....	....	....	....
	NHL Totals		**856**	**242**	**439**	**681**	**238**	**373**	**611**	**367**	**88**	**0**	**25**	**2144**	**11.3**	**918**	**369**	**514**	**9**		**101**	**27**	**49**	**76**	**66**	**8**	**0**	**7**

WHL First All-Star Team (1985)

Traded to **Vancouver** by **St. Louis** with Geoff Courtnall, Robert Dirk, Sergio Momesso and St. Louis' 5th round choice (Brian Loney) in 1992 Entry Draft for Dan Quinn and Garth Butcher, March 5, 1991. Signed as a free agent by **Phoenix**, July 1, 1996. Traded to **Nashville** by **Phoenix** with Richard Lintner for cash, October 31, 1998.

• RONSON, Len

Leonard Keith LW – L. 5'9", 175 lbs. b: Brantford, Ont., 7/8/1936.

Season	Club	League	GP	G	A	Pts	AG	AA	APts	PIM	PP	SH	GW	S	%	TGF	PGF	TGA	PGA	+/–	GP	G	A	Pts	PIM	PP	SH	GW
1954-55	Galt Black Hawks	OHA-Jr.	49	15	21	36	....	....	....	84	....	....	....	....	....	....	....	....	....	....	4	0	1	1	6	....	....	....
1955-56	St. Catharines Teepees	OHA-Jr.	48	9	8	17	....	....	....	69	....	....	....	....	....	....	....	....	....	....	6	0	0	0	7	....	....	....
1956-57	Hamilton Tiger Cubs	OHA-Jr.	1	0	0	0	....	....	....	0	....	....	....	....	....	....	....	....	....	....	....	....	....	....	....	....	....	....
	Chatham Maroons	OHA-Sr.	18	2	2	4	....	....	....	26	....	....	....	....	....	....	....	....	....	....	....	....	....	....	....	....	....	....
	Indianapolis–Huntington	IHL	39	7	6	13	....	....	....	31	....	....	....	....	....	....	....	....	....	....	4	1	0	1	0	....	....	....
1957-58	Fort Wayne Komets	IHL	61	26	31	57	....	....	....	13	....	....	....	....	....	....	....	....	....	....	4	1	2	3	2	....	....	....
1958-59	Fort Wayne Komets	IHL	60	39	58	97	....	....	....	38	....	....	....	....	....	....	....	....	....	....	11	8	6	14	4	....	....	....
1959-60	Fort Wayne Komets	IHL	68	*62	47	109	....	....	....	53	....	....	....	....	....	....	....	....	....	....	13	7	10	*17	2	....	....	....
1960-61	**New York Rangers**	**NHL**	**13**	**2**	**1**	**3**	**2**	**1**	**3**	**10**	....	....	....	....	....	....	....	....	....	....	....	....	....	....	....	....	....	....
	Buffalo Bisons	AHL	2	0	0	0	....	....	....	2	....	....	....	....	....	....	....	....	....	....	....	....	....	....	....	....	....	....
	Kitchener-Waterloo Beavers	EPHL	32	17	10	27	....	....	....	4	....	....	....	....	....	....	....	....	....	....	7	2	0	2	14	....	....	....
1961-62	Kitchener-Waterloo Beavers	EPHL	61	34	44	78	....	....	....	25	....	....	....	....	....	....	....	....	....	....	7	3	4	7	22	....	....	....
1962-63	Baltimore Clippers	AHL	45	7	15	22	....	....	....	20	....	....	....	....	....	....	....	....	....	....	....	....	....	....	....	....	....	....
	Sudbury Wolves	EPHL	16	8	17	25	....	....	....	6	....	....	....	....	....	....	....	....	....	....	8	3	4	7	6	....	....	....
1963-64	Cleveland Barons	AHL	2	0	1	1	....	....	....	4	....	....	....	....	....	....	....	....	....	....	3	1	0	1	0	....	....	....
	Omaha Knights	CPHL	63	29	47	76	....	....	....	45	....	....	....	....	....	....	....	....	....	....	10	*8	8	*16	0	....	....	....
1964-65	Providence Reds	AHL	71	25	21	46	....	....	....	24	....	....	....	....	....	....	....	....	....	....	....	....	....	....	....	....	....	....
1965-66	Portland Buckaroos	WHL	68	18	13	31	....	....	....	6	....	....	....	....	....	....	....	....	....	....	14	5	2	7	6	....	....	....
1966-67	San Diego Gulls	WHL	71	32	35	67	....	....	....	22	....	....	....	....	....	....	....	....	....	....	....	....	....	....	....	....	....	....
1967-68	San Diego Gulls	WHL	72	*45	35	80	....	....	....	53	....	....	....	....	....	....	....	....	....	....	7	2	5	7	4	....	....	....
1968-69	**Oakland Seals**	**NHL**	**5**	**0**	**0**	**0**	**0**	**0**	**0**	**0**	**0**	**0**	**0**	**6**	**0.0**	**2**	**1**	**4**	**0**	**–3**	....	....	....	....	....	....	....	....
	San Diego Gulls	WHL	47	24	17	41	....	....	....	34	....	....	....	....	....	....	....	....	....	....	7	1	5	6	0	....	....	....
1969-70	San Diego Gulls	WHL	72	*51	37	88	....	....	....	48	....	....	....	....	....	....	....	....	....	....	6	6	4	10	13	....	....	....
1970-71	San Diego Gulls	WHL	72	21	35	56	....	....	....	39	....	....	....	....	....	....	....	....	....	....	6	2	3	5	2	....	....	....
1971-72	San Diego Gulls	WHL	68	21	33	54	....	....	....	37	....	....	....	....	....	....	....	....	....	....	4	0	0	0	0	....	....	....
	Fort Worth Wings	CHL	4	2	3	5	....	....	....	0	....	....	....	....	....	....	....	....	....	....	....	....	....	....	....	....	....	....
1972-73	San Diego Gulls	WHL	44	12	18	30	....	....	....	14	....	....	....	....	....	....	....	....	....	....	6	3	2	5	0	....	....	....
	NHL Totals		**18**	**2**	**1**	**3**	**2**	**1**	**3**	**10**	....	....	....	....	....	....	....	....	....	....	....	....	....	....	....	....	....	....

IHL Second All-Star Team (1959) • IHL First All-Star Team (1960) • EPHL Second All-Star Team (1962) • WHL First All-Star Team (1968, 1970)

Traded to **Montreal** by **NY Rangers** with Dave Balon, Leon Rochefort and Gump Worsley for Phil Goyette, Don Marshall and Jacques Plante, June 4, 1963. Traded to **Portland** (WHL) by **Montreal** for cash, July, 1965. Traded to **San Diego** (WHL) by **Portland** (WHL), August, 1966. Claimed by **Montreal** from **San Diego** (WHL) in Reverse Draft, June, 1968. Traded to **Oakland** by **Montreal** for cash, August, 1968. Traded to **San Diego** (WHL) by **Oakland** for cash, November, 1968. Loaned to **Fort Worth** (CHL) by **San Diego** (WHL) for cash, December, 1971 and recalled, January, 1972.

• ROONEY, Steve

Steven Paul LW – L. 6'2", 205 lbs. b: Canton, MA, 6/28/1962. Montreal's 8th, 88th overall, in 1981.

Season	Club	League	GP	G	A	Pts	AG	AA	APts	PIM	PP	SH	GW	S	%	TGF	PGF	TGA	PGA	+/–	GP	G	A	Pts	PIM	PP	SH	GW
1979-80	Canton High School	Hi-School	STATISTICS NOT AVAILABLE																									
1980-81	Wexford Raiders	OHA-B	36	13	20	33	....	....	....	58	....	....	....	....	....	....	....	....	....	....	....	....	....	....	....	....	....	....
1981-82	Providence College	ECAC	31	7	10	17	....	....	....	41	....	....	....	....	....	....	....	....	....	....	....	....	....	....	....	....	....	....
1982-83	Providence College	ECAC	42	10	20	30	....	....	....	31	....	....	....	....	....	....	....	....	....	....	....	....	....	....	....	....	....	....
1983-84	Providence College	ECAC	33	11	16	27	....	....	....	46	....	....	....	....	....	....	....	....	....	....	....	....	....	....	....	....	....	....
1984-85	Providence College	H-East	31	7	10	17	....	....	....	41	....	....	....	....	....	....	....	....	....	....	....	....	....	....	....	....	....	....
	Montreal Canadiens	**NHL**	**3**	**1**	**0**	**1**	**1**	**0**	**1**	**7**	**1**	**0**	**0**	**3**	**33.3**	**2**	**1**	**2**	**0**	**–1**	**11**	**2**	**2**	**4**	**19**	**0**	**0**	**0**
1985-86 ♦	**Montreal Canadiens**	**NHL**	**38**	**2**	**3**	**5**	**2**	**2**	**4**	**114**	**1**	**0**	**0**	**24**	**8.3**	**14**	**3**	**15**	**0**	**–4**	**1**	**0**	**0**	**0**	**0**	**0**	**0**	**0**
1986-87	**Montreal Canadiens**	**NHL**	**2**	**0**	**0**	**0**	**0**	**0**	**0**	**22**	**0**	**0**	**0**	**2**	**0.0**	**0**	**0**	**0**	**0**	**0**	....	....	....	....	....	....	....	....
	Sherbrooke Canadiens	AHL	22	4	11	15	....	....	....	66	....	....	....	....	....	....	....	....	....	....	....	....	....	....	....	....	....	....
	Winnipeg Jets	**NHL**	**30**	**2**	**3**	**5**	**2**	**2**	**4**	**57**	**0**	**0**	**1**	**23**	**8.7**	**8**	**0**	**12**	**0**	**–4**	**8**	**0**	**0**	**0**	**34**	**0**	**0**	**0**
1987-88	**Winnipeg Jets**	**NHL**	**56**	**7**	**6**	**13**	**6**	**4**	**10**	**217**	**0**	**0**	**0**	**62**	**11.3**	**19**	**2**	**15**	**0**	**2**	**5**	**1**	**0**	**1**	**33**	**0**	**0**	**0**
1988-89	**New Jersey Devils**	**NHL**	**25**	**3**	**1**	**4**	**3**	**1**	**4**	**79**	**0**	**0**	**1**	**23**	**13.0**	**5**	**1**	**13**	**0**	**–9**	....	....	....	....	....	....	....	....
1989-90	Utica Devils	AHL	59	9	16	25	....	....	....	134	....	....	....	....	....	....	....	....	....	....	5	0	1	1	19	....	....	....
1990-91	Phoenix Roadrunners	IHL	11	2	5	7	....	....	....	76	....	....	....	....	....	....	....	....	....	....	....	....	....	....	....	....	....	....
	New Haven Nighthawks	AHL	44	14	17	31	....	....	....	141	....	....	....	....	....	....	....	....	....	....	....	....	....	....	....	....	....	....
1991-92	Maine Mariners	AHL	13	2	3	5	....	....	....	17	....	....	....	....	....	....	....	....	....	....	....	....	....	....	....	....	....	....
	NHL Totals		**154**	**15**	**13**	**28**	**14**	**9**	**23**	**496**	**2**	**0**	**2**	**137**	**10.9**	**48**	**7**	**57**	**0**		**25**	**3**	**2**	**5**	**86**	**0**	**0**	**0**

• Missed majority of 1985-86 season recovering from shoulder injury suffered in game vs. Calgary, Novemmber 23, 1985. Traded to **Winnipeg** by **Montreal** for Winnipeg's 3rd round choice (Francois Gravel) in 1987 Entry Draft, January 8, 1987. Traded to **New Jersey** by **Winnipeg** with Winnipeg's 3rd round choice (Brad Bombardir) in 1990 Entry Draft for Alain Chevrier and New Jersey's 7th round choice (Doug Evans) in 1989 Entry Draft, July 19, 1988.

• ROOT, Bill

William John D – R. 6', 210 lbs. b: Toronto, Ont., 9/6/1959.

Season	Club	League	GP	G	A	Pts	AG	AA	APts	PIM	PP	SH	GW	S	%	TGF	PGF	TGA	PGA	+/–	GP	G	A	Pts	PIM	PP	SH	GW
1975-76	Don Mills Flyers	MTHL	46	6	39	45	....	....	....	102	....	....	....	....	....	....	....	....	....	....	....	....	....	....	....	....	....	....
1976-77	Niagara Falls Flyers	OMJHL	66	3	19	22	....	....	....	114	....	....	....	....	....	....	....	....	....	....	....	....	....	....	....	....	....	....
1977-78	Niagara Falls Flyers	OMJHL	67	6	11	17	....	....	....	61	....	....	....	....	....	....	....	....	....	....	....	....	....	....	....	....	....	....
1978-79	Niagara Falls Flyers	OMJHL	67	4	31	35	....	....	....	119	....	....	....	....	....	....	....	....	....	....	20	4	7	11	42	....	....	....
1979-80	Nova Scotia Voyageurs	AHL	55	4	15	19	....	....	....	57	....	....	....	....	....	....	....	....	....	....	6	1	1	2	2	....	....	....
1980-81	Nova Scotia Voyageurs	AHL	63	3	12	15	....	....	....	76	....	....	....	....	....	....	....	....	....	....	6	0	1	1	2	....	....	....
1981-82	Nova Scotia Voyageurs	AHL	77	6	25	31	....	....	....	105	....	....	....	....	....	....	....	....	....	....	9	1	0	1	4	....	....	....
1982-83	**Montreal Canadiens**	**NHL**	**46**	**2**	**3**	**5**	**2**	**2**	**4**	**24**	**0**	**0**	**0**	**44**	**4.5**	**42**	**2**	**44**	**9**	**5**	....	....	....	....	....	....	....	....
	Nova Scotia Voyageurs	AHL	24	0	7	7	....	....	....	29	....	....	....	....	....	....	....	....	....	....	....	....	....	....	....	....	....	....
1983-84	**Montreal Canadiens**	**NHL**	**72**	**4**	**13**	**17**	**3**	**9**	**12**	**45**	**1**	**1**	**0**	**71**	**5.6**	**90**	**2**	**75**	**13**	**26**	....	....	....	....	....	....	....	....
1984-85	**Toronto Maple Leafs**	**NHL**	**35**	**1**	**1**	**2**	**1**	**1**	**2**	**23**	**0**	**0**	**0**	**34**	**2.9**	**25**	**0**	**65**	**15**	**–25**	....	....	....	....	....	....	....	....
	St. Catharines Saints	AHL	28	5	9	14	....	....	....	10	....	....	....	....	....	....	....	....	....	....	....	....	....	....	....	....	....	....
1985-86	**Toronto Maple Leafs**	**NHL**	**27**	**0**	**1**	**1**	**0**	**1**	**1**	**29**	**0**	**0**	**0**	**34**	**0.0**	**28**	**5**	**48**	**17**	**–8**	**7**	**0**	**2**	**2**	**13**	**0**	**0**	**0**
	St. Catharines Saints	AHL	14	7	4	11	....	....	....	11	....	....	....	....	....	....	....	....	....	....	....	....	....	....	....	....	....	....
1986-87	**Toronto Maple Leafs**	**NHL**	**34**	**3**	**3**	**6**	**3**	**2**	**5**	**37**	**1**	**0**	**0**	**31**	**9.7**	**24**	**1**	**47**	**15**	**–9**	**13**	**1**	**0**	**1**	**12**	**0**	**0**	**0**
	Newmarket Saints	AHL	32	4	11	15	....	....	....	23	....	....	....	....	....	....	....	....	....	....	....	....	....	....	....	....	....	....
1987-88	**St. Louis Blues**	**NHL**	**9**	**0**	**0**	**0**	**0**	**0**	**0**	**6**	**0**	**0**	**0**	**6**	**0.0**	**4**	**0**	**13**	**2**	**–7**	....	....	....	....	....	....	....	....
	Philadelphia Flyers	**NHL**	**24**	**1**	**2**	**3**	**1**	**1**	**2**	**16**	**1**	**0**	**0**	**13**	**7.7**	**13**	**2**	**9**	**1**	**3**	**2**	**0**	**0**	**0**	**0**	**0**	**0**	**0**

			REGULAR SEASON																		PLAYOFFS							
Season	Club	League	GP	G	A	Pts	AG	AA	APts	PIM	PP	SH	GW	S	%	TGF	PGF	TGA	PGA	+/–	GP	G	A	Pts	PIM	PP	SH	GW
1988-89	Newmarket Saints	AHL	66	10	22	32	....	....	....	39	....	....	....	....	....	....	....	....	....	....	5	0	0	0	18	....	....	....
1989-90	Newmarket Saints	AHL	47	8	7	15	....	....	....	20	....	....	....	....	....	....	....	....	....	....	....	....	....	....	....	....	....	....
1990-91	Newmarket Saints	AHL	36	2	4	6	....	....	....	39	....	....	....	....	....	....	....	....	....	....	....	....	....	....	....	....	....	....
	NHL Totals		**247**	**11**	**23**	**34**	**10**	**16**	**26**	**180**	**3**	**1**	**0**	**233**	**4.7**	**226**	**12**	**301**	**72**		**22**	**1**	**2**	**3**	**25**	**0**	**0**	**0**

Signed as a free agent by **Montreal**, October 4, 1979. Traded to **Toronto** by **Montreal** with Montreal's 2nd round choice (Darryl Shannon) in 1986 Entry Draft for Dom Campedelli, August 21, 1984. Traded to **Hartford** by **Toronto** for Dave Semenko, September 8, 1987. Claimed by **St. Louis** from **Hartford** in Waiver Draft, October 5, 1987. Claimed on waivers by **Philadelphia** from **St. Louis**, November 26, 1987. Traded to **Toronto** by **Philadelphia** for Mike Stothers, June 21, 1988.

• ROSA, Pavel

RW – R. 6', 195 lbs. b: Most, Czech., 6/7/1977. Los Angeles' 3rd, 50th overall, in 1995.

Season	Club	League	GP	G	A	Pts	AG	AA	APts	PIM	PP	SH	GW	S	%	TGF	PGF	TGA	PGA	+/–	GP	G	A	Pts	PIM	PP	SH	GW
1994-95	HC Litvinov-Jr.	Czech-Rep	40	56	42	98	....	....	....	....	....	....	....	....	....	....	....	....	....	....	....	....	....	....	....	....	....	....
	HC Litvinov	Czech-Rep	2	0	0	0	....	....	....	0	....	....	....	....	....	....	....	....	....	....	1	0	0	0	0	....	....	....
	Czech-Republic	EJC-A	5	8	3	11	....	....	....	0	....	....	....	....	....	....	....	....	....	....	....	....	....	....	....	....	....	....
1995-96	Hull Olympiques	QMJHL	61	46	70	116	....	....	....	39	....	....	....	....	....	....	....	....	....	....	18	14	22	36	25	....	....	....
	Czech-Republic	WJC-A	6	0	0	0	....	....	....	2	....	....	....	....	....	....	....	....	....	....	....	....	....	....	....	....	....	....
1996-97	Hull Olympiques	QMJHL	68	*63	*90	*153	....	....	....	66	....	....	....	....	....	....	....	....	....	....	14	18	13	31	16	....	....	....
	Hull Olympiques	Mem-Cup	4	3	5	8	....	....	....	2	....	....	....	....	....	....	....	....	....	....	....	....	....	....	....	....	....	....
1997-98	Fredericton Canadiens	AHL	1	0	0	0	....	....	....	0	....	....	....	....	....	....	....	....	....	....	....	....	....	....	....	....	....	....
	Long Beach Ice Dogs	IHL	2	0	1	1	....	....	....	0	....	....	....	....	....	....	....	....	....	....	1	1	1	2	0	....	....	....
1998-99	**Los Angeles Kings**	**NHL**	**29**	**4**	**12**	**16**	**5**	**12**	**17**	**6**	**0**	**0**	**0**	**61**	**6.6**	**24**	**6**	**18**	**0**	**0**	....	....	....	....	....	....	....	....
	Long Beach Ice Dogs	IHL	31	17	13	30	....	....	....	28	....	....	....	....	....	....	....	....	....	....	6	1	2	3	0	....	....	....
99-2000	**Los Angeles Kings**	**NHL**	**3**	**0**	**0**	**0**	**0**	**0**	**0**	**0**	**0**	**0**	**0**	**1**	**0.0**	**0**	**0**	**1**	**0**	**–1**	....	....	....	....	....	....	....	....
	Long Beach Ice Dogs	IHL	74	22	31	53	....	....	....	76	....	....	....	....	....	....	....	....	....	....	6	2	2	4	4	....	....	....
	NHL Totals		**32**	**4**	**12**	**16**	**5**	**12**	**17**	**6**	**0**	**0**	**0**	**62**	**6.5**	**24**	**6**	**19**	**0**		....	....	....	....	....	....	....	....

QMJHL First All-Star Team (1997) • Canadian Major Junior First All-Star Team (1997)

• Missed majority of 1997-98 season recovering from head injury originally suffered in training camp, September, 1997.

• ROTA, Darcy

Darcy Irwin LW – L. 5'11", 180 lbs. b: Vancouver, B.C., 2/16/1953. Chicago's 1st, 13th overall, in 1973.

Season	Club	League	GP	G	A	Pts	AG	AA	APts	PIM	PP	SH	GW	S	%	TGF	PGF	TGA	PGA	+/–	GP	G	A	Pts	PIM	PP	SH	GW
1970-71	Edmonton Oil Kings	WCJHL	64	43	39	82	....	....	....	60	....	....	....	....	....	....	....	....	....	....	17	13	10	23	15	....	....	....
	Edmonton Oil Kings	Mem-Cup	2	0	0	0	....	....	....	4	....	....	....	....	....	....	....	....	....	....	....	....	....	....	....	....	....	....
1971-72	Edmonton Oil Kings	WCJHL	67	51	54	105	....	....	....	68	....	....	....	....	....	....	....	....	....	....	16	8	9	17	11	....	....	....
	Edmonton Oil Kings	Mem-Cup	2	1	1	2	....	....	....	2	....	....	....	....	....	....	....	....	....	....	....	....	....	....	....	....	....	....
1972-73	Edmonton Oil Kings	WCJHL	68	*73	56	129	....	....	....	104	....	....	....	....	....	....	....	....	....	....	4	5	4	9	14	....	....	....
1973-74	**Chicago Black Hawks**	**NHL**	**74**	**21**	**12**	**33**	**20**	**10**	**30**	**58**	**6**	**0**	**3**	**120**	**17.5**	**54**	**13**	**25**	**0**	**16**	**11**	**3**	**0**	**3**	**11**	**0**	**0**	**0**
1974-75	**Chicago Black Hawks**	**NHL**	**78**	**22**	**22**	**44**	**19**	**16**	**35**	**93**	**5**	**0**	**2**	**158**	**13.9**	**66**	**9**	**56**	**0**	**1**	**7**	**0**	**1**	**1**	**24**	**0**	**0**	**0**
1975-76	**Chicago Black Hawks**	**NHL**	**79**	**20**	**17**	**37**	**18**	**13**	**31**	**73**	**4**	**0**	**2**	**201**	**10.0**	**71**	**16**	**63**	**0**	**–8**	**4**	**1**	**0**	**1**	**2**	**1**	**0**	**0**
1976-77	**Chicago Black Hawks**	**NHL**	**76**	**24**	**22**	**46**	**22**	**17**	**39**	**82**	**4**	**0**	**3**	**148**	**16.2**	**72**	**13**	**66**	**0**	**–7**	**2**	**0**	**0**	**0**	**0**	**0**	**0**	**0**
1977-78	**Chicago Black Hawks**	**NHL**	**78**	**17**	**20**	**37**	**15**	**15**	**30**	**67**	**3**	**0**	**1**	**107**	**15.9**	**46**	**10**	**31**	**0**	**5**	**4**	**0**	**0**	**0**	**2**	**0**	**0**	**0**
1978-79	**Chicago Black Hawks**	**NHL**	**63**	**13**	**17**	**30**	**11**	**12**	**23**	**77**	**1**	**0**	**1**	**116**	**11.2**	**40**	**3**	**47**	**0**	**–10**	....	....	....	....	....	....	....	....
	Atlanta Flames	**NHL**	**13**	**9**	**5**	**14**	**8**	**4**	**12**	**21**	**0**	**0**	**0**	**27**	**33.3**	**16**	**1**	**13**	**1**	**3**	**2**	**0**	**1**	**1**	**26**	**0**	**0**	**0**
1979-80	**Atlanta Flames**	**NHL**	**44**	**10**	**8**	**18**	**8**	**6**	**14**	**49**	**0**	**0**	**1**	**70**	**14.3**	**30**	**3**	**24**	**0**	**3**	....	....	....	....	....	....	....	....
	Vancouver Canucks	**NHL**	**26**	**5**	**6**	**11**	**4**	**4**	**8**	**29**	**0**	**0**	**2**	**53**	**9.4**	**15**	**3**	**24**	**3**	**–9**	**4**	**2**	**0**	**2**	**8**	**0**	**0**	**0**
1980-81	**Vancouver Canucks**	**NHL**	**80**	**25**	**31**	**56**	**19**	**21**	**40**	**124**	**7**	**0**	**5**	**178**	**14.0**	**87**	**18**	**61**	**2**	**10**	**3**	**2**	**1**	**3**	**14**	**1**	**0**	**0**
1981-82	**Vancouver Canucks**	**NHL**	**51**	**20**	**20**	**40**	**16**	**13**	**29**	**139**	**2**	**0**	**0**	**80**	**25.0**	**50**	**11**	**33**	**0**	**6**	**17**	**6**	**3**	**9**	**54**	**2**	**0**	**1**
1982-83	**Vancouver Canucks**	**NHL**	**73**	**42**	**39**	**81**	**34**	**27**	**61**	**88**	**9**	**0**	**5**	**173**	**24.3**	**104**	**30**	**61**	**0**	**13**	**3**	**0**	**0**	**0**	**6**	**0**	**0**	**0**
1983-84	**Vancouver Canucks**	**NHL**	**59**	**28**	**20**	**48**	**22**	**14**	**36**	**73**	**6**	**0**	**0**	**127**	**22.0**	**71**	**22**	**62**	**1**	**–12**	**3**	**0**	**1**	**1**	**0**	**0**	**0**	**0**
	NHL Totals		**794**	**256**	**239**	**495**	**216**	**172**	**388**	**973**	**47**	**0**	**25**	**1558**	**16.4**	**722**	**152**	**566**	**7**		**60**	**14**	**7**	**21**	**147**	**4**	**0**	**1**

WCJHL Second All-Star Team (1972) • WCJHL First All-Star Team (1973) • Played in NHL All-Star Game (1984)

Traded to **Atlanta** by **Chicago** with Ivan Boldirev and Phil Russell for Tom Lysiak, Pat Ribble, Harold Phillipoff, Greg Fox and Miles Zaharko, March 13, 1979. Traded to **Vancouver** by **Atlanta** with Ivan Boldirev for Don Lever and Brad Smith, February 8, 1980.

• ROTA, Randy

Randy Frank C/LW – L. 5'8", 170 lbs. b: Creston, B.C., 8/16/1950. California's 3rd, 33rd overall, in 1970.

Season	Club	League	GP	G	A	Pts	AG	AA	APts	PIM	PP	SH	GW	S	%	TGF	PGF	TGA	PGA	+/–	GP	G	A	Pts	PIM	PP	SH	GW
1967-68	Kamloops Rockets	BCJHL	40	*45	28	73	....	....	....	22	....	....	....	....	....	....	....	....	....	....	....	....	....	....	....	....	....	....
1968-69	Calgary Centennials	WCJHL	33	20	18	38	....	....	....	2	....	....	....	....	....	....	....	....	....	....	11	0	3	3	....	....	....	....
1969-70	Calgary Centennials	WCJHL	60	43	47	90	....	....	....	43	....	....	....	....	....	....	....	....	....	....	15	3	8	11	12	....	....	....
1970-71	Providence Reds	AHL	68	31	34	65	....	....	....	31	....	....	....	....	....	....	....	....	....	....	10	4	3	7	4	....	....	....
1971-72	Nova Scotia Voyageurs	AHL	72	32	23	55	....	....	....	24	....	....	....	....	....	....	....	....	....	....	15	6	4	10	2	....	....	....
1972-73	**Montreal Canadiens**	**NHL**	**2**	**1**	**1**	**2**	**1**	**1**	**2**	**0**	**0**	**0**	**1**	**4**	**25.0**	**3**	**0**	**1**	**0**	**2**	....	....	....	....	....	....	....	....
	Nova Scotia Voyageurs	AHL	73	34	38	72	....	....	....	23	....	....	....	....	....	....	....	....	....	....	13	*10	7	17	10	....	....	....
1973-74	**Los Angeles Kings**	**NHL**	**58**	**10**	**6**	**16**	**10**	**5**	**15**	**16**	**0**	**0**	**0**	**93**	**10.8**	**29**	**5**	**34**	**2**	**–8**	**5**	**0**	**1**	**1**	**0**	**0**	**0**	**0**
1974-75	**Kansas City Scouts**	**NHL**	**80**	**15**	**18**	**33**	**13**	**13**	**26**	**30**	**3**	**0**	**0**	**182**	**8.2**	**52**	**14**	**81**	**4**	**–39**	....	....	....	....	....	....	....	....
1975-76	**Kansas City Scouts**	**NHL**	**71**	**12**	**14**	**26**	**11**	**10**	**21**	**14**	**2**	**0**	**1**	**146**	**8.2**	**39**	**8**	**70**	**1**	**–38**	....	....	....	....	....	....	....	....
1976-77	**Colorado Rockies**	**NHL**	**1**	**0**	**0**	**0**	**0**	**0**	**0**	**0**	**0**	**0**	**0**	**0**	**0.0**	**0**	**0**	**0**	**0**	**0**	....	....	....	....	....	....	....	....
	Oklahoma City Blazers	CHL	12	4	4	8	....	....	....	5	....	....	....	....	....	....	....	....	....	....	....	....	....	....	....	....	....	....
	Edmonton Oilers	WHA	40	9	6	15	....	....	....	8	....	....	....	....	....	....	....	....	....	....	5	3	2	5	0	....	....	....
1977-78	Edmonton Oilers	WHA	53	8	22	30	....	....	....	12	....	....	....	....	....	....	....	....	....	....	5	1	1	2	4	....	....	....
	NHL Totals		**212**	**38**	**39**	**77**	**35**	**29**	**64**	**60**	**5**	**0**	**2**	**425**	**8.9**	**123**	**27**	**186**	**7**		**5**	**0**	**1**	**1**	**0**	**0**	**0**	**0**
	Other Major League Totals		93	17	28	45	....	....	....	20	....	....	....	....	....	....	....	....	....	....	10	4	3	7	4	....	....	....

Traded to **Montreal** by **California** for Lyle Carter and John French, October, 1971. Traded to **LA Kings** by **Montreal** with Bob Murdoch for LA Kings's 1st round choice (Mario Tremblay) in 1974 Amateur Draft and cash, May 29, 1973. Claimed by **Kansas City** from **LA Kings** in Expansion Draft, June 12, 1974. Transferred to **Colorado** after **Kansas City** franchise relocated, July 15, 1976. Traded to **Edmonton** (WHA) by **Colorado** for cash, November, 1976.

• ROULSTON, Tom

Thomas Irwin C/RW – R. 6'1", 184 lbs. b: Winnipeg, Man., 11/20/1957. St. Louis' 3rd, 45th overall, in 1977.

Season	Club	League	GP	G	A	Pts	AG	AA	APts	PIM	PP	SH	GW	S	%	TGF	PGF	TGA	PGA	+/–	GP	G	A	Pts	PIM	PP	SH	GW
1975-76	Spruce Grove Mets	AJHL	5	3	1	4	....	....	....	4	....	....	....	....	....	....	....	....	....	....	....	....	....	....	....	....	....	....
	Edmonton Oil Kings	WCJHL	1	0	0	0	....	....	....	0	....	....	....	....	....	....	....	....	....	....	....	....	....	....	....	....	....	....
	Winnipeg Clubs	WCJHL	60	18	17	35	....	....	....	56	....	....	....	....	....	....	....	....	....	....	6	2	2	4	4	....	....	....
1976-77	Winnipeg Monarchs	WCJHL	72	56	53	109	....	....	....	35	....	....	....	....	....	....	....	....	....	....	7	5	3	8	23	....	....	....
1977-78	Salt Lake Golden Eagles	CHL	21	2	1	3	....	....	....	2	....	....	....	....	....	....	....	....	....	....	....	....	....	....	....	....	....	....
	Port Huron Flags	IHL	49	27	36	63	....	....	....	24	....	....	....	....	....	....	....	....	....	....	16	*17	7	24	10	....	....	....
1978-79	Dallas Black Hawks	CHL	73	26	29	55	....	....	....	57	....	....	....	....	....	....	....	....	....	....	9	*6	6	12	11	....	....	....
1979-80	Houston Apollos	CHL	72	29	41	70	....	....	....	46	....	....	....	....	....	....	....	....	....	....	6	2	4	6	4	....	....	....
1980-81	**Edmonton Oilers**	**NHL**	**11**	**1**	**1**	**2**	**1**	**1**	**2**	**2**	**0**	**0**	**0**	**9**	**11.1**	**7**	**0**	**13**	**3**	**–3**	....	....	....	....	....	....	....	....
	Wichita Wind	CHL	69	*63	44	107	....	....	....	93	....	....	....	....	....	....	....	....	....	....	18	15	11	*26	44	....	....	....
1981-82	**Edmonton Oilers**	**NHL**	**35**	**11**	**3**	**14**	**9**	**2**	**11**	**22**	**0**	**1**	**0**	**54**	**20.4**	**20**	**3**	**25**	**2**	**–6**	**5**	**1**	**0**	**1**	**2**	**0**	**0**	**0**
	Wichita Wind	CHL	30	22	28	50	....	....	....	40	....	....	....	....	....	....	....	....	....	....	....	....	....	....	....	....	....	....
1982-83	**Edmonton Oilers**	**NHL**	**67**	**19**	**21**	**40**	**16**	**15**	**31**	**24**	**2**	**0**	**2**	**107**	**17.8**	**63**	**8**	**30**	**4**	**29**	**16**	**1**	**2**	**3**	**0**	**0**	**0**	**0**
1983-84	**Edmonton Oilers**	**NHL**	**24**	**5**	**7**	**12**	**4**	**5**	**9**	**16**	**1**	**0**	**0**	**38**	**13.2**	**19**	**3**	**17**	**1**	**0**	....	....	....	....	....	....	....	....
	Pittsburgh Penguins	**NHL**	**53**	**11**	**17**	**28**	**9**	**12**	**21**	**8**	**3**	**0**	**0**	**110**	**10.0**	**45**	**17**	**61**	**2**	**–31**	....	....	....	....	....	....	....	....
1984-85	Baltimore Skipjacks	AHL	78	31	39	70	....	....	....	48	....	....	....	....	....	....	....	....	....	....	15	4	8	12	6	....	....	....
1985-86	**Pittsburgh Penguins**	**NHL**	**5**	**0**	**0**	**0**	**0**	**0**	**0**	**2**	**0**	**0**	**0**	**6**	**0.0**	**1**	**0**	**3**	**0**	**–2**	....	....	....	....	....	....	....	....
	Baltimore Skipjacks	AHL	73	38	49	87	....	....	....	38	....	....	....	....	....	....	....	....	....	....	....	....	....	....	....	....	....	....
1986-87	HC Salzburg	Austria	19	18	19	37	....	....	....	28	....	....	....	....	....	....	....	....	....	....	....	....	....	....	....	....	....	....
	EV Landshut	Germany	16	21	11	32	....	....	....	8	....	....	....	....	....	....	....	....	....	....	4	2	1	3	....	....	....	....
1987-88	SB Rosenheim	Germany	10	6	9	15	....	....	....	8	....	....	....	....	....	....	....	....	....	....	11	4	4	8	0	....	....	....

Season	Club	League	REGULAR SEASON GP	G	A	Pts	AG	AA	APts	PIM	PP	SH	GW	S	%	TGF	PGF	TGA	PGA	+/–	PLAYOFFS GP	G	A	Pts	PIM	PP	SH	GW
1988-89	HC Fiemme	Italy	36	40	47	87	....	....	....	26	....	....	....	....	....	....	....	....	....	....	....	....	....	....	....	....	....	....
	HC Davos	Switz.	1	0	1	1	....	....	....	0	....	....	....	....	....	....	....	....	....	....	10	10	8	18	....	....	....	....
1989-1994			OUT OF HOCKEY – RETIRED																									
1994-95	Wichita Thunder	CHL	23	11	19	30	....	....	....	8	....	....	....	....	....	....	....	....	....	....	11	13	11	24	10	....	....	....
	NHL Totals		**195**	**47**	**49**	**96**	**39**	**35**	**74**	**74**	**6**	**1**	**2**	**324**	**14.5**	**155**	**31**	**149**	**12**		**21**	**2**	**2**	**4**	**2**	**0**	**0**	**0**

CHL First All-Star Team (1981)

Traded to **Edmonton** by **St. Louis** with Risto Siltanen for Joe Micheletti, August 7, 1979. Traded to **Pittsburgh** by **Edmonton** for Kevin McClelland and Pittsburgh's 6th round choice (Emanuel Viveiros) in 1984 Entry Draft, December 5, 1983.

• ROUPE, Magnus

LW – L. 6', 189 lbs. b: Stockholm, Sweden, 3/23/1963. Philadelphia's 9th, 182nd overall, in 1982.

Season	Club	League	GP	G	A	Pts	AG	AA	APts	PIM	PP	SH	GW	S	%	TGF	PGF	TGA	PGA	+/–	GP	G	A	Pts	PIM	PP	SH	GW
1977-78	Gislaveds SK	Sweden-3	6	3	1	4	....	....	....	....	....	....	....	....	....	....	....	....	....	....	....	....	....	....	....	....	....	....
1978-79	Gislaveds SK	Sweden-3	15	6	6	12	....	....	....	....	....	....	....	....	....	....	....	....	....	....	....	....	....	....	....	....	....	....
1979-80	Farjestads BK	Sweden-Jr.	STATISTICS NOT AVAILABLE																									
1980-81	Gislaveds IK	Sweden-2	STATISTICS NOT AVAILABLE																									
	Sweden	EJC-A	5	2	2	4	....	....	....	6	....	....	....	....	....	....	....	....	....	....	....	....	....	....	....	....	....	....
1981-82	Farjestads BK Karlstad	Sweden	24	5	3	8	....	....	....	8	....	....	....	....	....	....	....	....	....	....	2	0	0	0	0	....	....	....
	Sweden	WJC-A	7	7	3	10	....	....	....	4	....	....	....	....	....	....	....	....	....	....	....	....	....	....	....	....	....	....
1982-83	Farjestads BK Karlstad	Sweden	29	7	4	11	....	....	....	16	....	....	....	....	....	....	....	....	....	....	6	1	1	2	8	....	....	....
	Sweden	WJC-A	6	1	2	3	....	....	....	....	....	....	....	....	....	....	....	....	....	....	....	....	....	....	....	....	....	....
1983-84	Farjestads BK Karlstad	Sweden	36	2	3	5	....	....	....	38	....	....	....	....	....	....	....	....	....	....	....	....	....	....	....	....	....	....
1984-85	Farjestads BK Karlstad	Sweden	31	9	6	15	....	....	....	16	....	....	....	....	....	....	....	....	....	....	3	1	0	1	0	....	....	....
1985-86	Farjestads BK Karlstad	Sweden	35	11	10	21	....	....	....	38	....	....	....	....	....	....	....	....	....	....	8	3	2	5	18	....	....	....
1986-87	Farjestads BK Karlstad	Sweden	31	11	6	17	....	....	....	58	....	....	....	....	....	....	....	....	....	....	7	0	2	2	10	....	....	....
1987-88	Sweden	Can-Cup	5	1	1	2	....	....	....	4	....	....	....	....	....	....	....	....	....	....	....	....	....	....	....	....	....	....
	Philadelphia Flyers	**NHL**	**33**	**2**	**4**	**6**	**2**	**3**	**5**	**32**	**1**	**0**	**0**	**37**	**5.4**	**11**	**2**	**15**	**0**	**–6**	....	....	....	....	....	....	....	....
	Hershey Bears	AHL	23	6	16	22	....	....	....	10	....	....	....	....	....	....	....	....	....	....	11	3	4	7	31	....	....	....
1988-89	**Philadelphia Flyers**	**NHL**	**7**	**1**	**1**	**2**	**1**	**1**	**2**	**10**	**0**	**0**	**0**	**15**	**6.7**	**2**	**0**	**1**	**0**	**1**	....	....	....	....	....	....	....	....
	Hershey Bears	AHL	12	2	6	8	....	....	....	17	....	....	....	....	....	....	....	....	....	....	....	....	....	....	....	....	....	....
	Farjestads BK Karlstad	Sweden	18	9	4	13	....	....	....	58	....	....	....	....	....	....	....	....	....	....	2	0	1	1	6	....	....	....
1989-90	Farjestads BK Karlstad	Sweden	39	19	17	36	....	....	....	66	....	....	....	....	....	....	....	....	....	....	9	1	2	3	14	....	....	....
	Sweden	WEC-A	10	0	3	3	....	....	....	8	....	....	....	....	....	....	....	....	....	....	....	....	....	....	....	....	....	....
1990-91	Farjestads BK Karlstad	Sweden	39	9	10	19	....	....	....	54	....	....	....	....	....	....	....	....	....	....	8	2	5	7	12	....	....	....
1991-92	Farjestads BK Karlstad	Sweden	39	3	9	12	....	....	....	22	....	....	....	....	....	....	....	....	....	....	6	0	0	0	4	....	....	....
1992-93	Arvika HC	Sweden-2	31	23	18	41	....	....	....	30	....	....	....	....	....	....	....	....	....	....	....	....	....	....	....	....	....	....
1993-94	Arvika HC	Sweden-2	32	22	19	41	....	....	....	72	....	....	....	....	....	....	....	....	....	....	....	....	....	....	....	....	....	....
1994-95	Grums IK	Sweden-2	32	13	22	35	....	....	....	*75	....	....	....	....	....	....	....	....	....	....	....	....	....	....	....	....	....	....
1995-96	Grums IK	Sweden-2	32	19	29	48	....	....	....	36	....	....	....	....	....	....	....	....	....	....	5	6	4	10	4	....	....	....
1996-97	Grums IK	Sweden-2	31	17	23	40	....	....	....	63	....	....	....	....	....	....	....	....	....	....	2	0	1	1	2	....	....	....
1997-98	Eisbaren Berlin	Germany	34	3	4	7	....	....	....	22	....	....	....	....	....	....	....	....	....	....	6	0	0	0	0	....	....	....
1998-99	Grums IK	Sweden-2	27	9	13	22	....	....	....	82	....	....	....	....	....	....	....	....	....	....	....	....	....	....	....	....	....	....
	NHL Totals		**40**	**3**	**5**	**8**	**3**	**4**	**7**	**42**	**1**	**0**	**0**	**52**	**5.8**	**13**	**2**	**16**	**0**		....	....	....	....	....	....	....	....

• ROUSE, Bob

Robert J. D – R. 6'2", 215 lbs. b: Surrey, B.C., 6/18/1964. Minnesota's 3rd, 80th overall, in 1982.

Season	Club	League	GP	G	A	Pts	AG	AA	APts	PIM	PP	SH	GW	S	%	TGF	PGF	TGA	PGA	+/–	GP	G	A	Pts	PIM	PP	SH	GW
1980-81	Billings Bighorns	WHL	70	0	13	13	....	....	....	116	....	....	....	....	....	....	....	....	....	....	5	0	0	0	2	....	....	....
1981-82	Billings Bighorns	WHL	71	7	22	29	....	....	....	209	....	....	....	....	....	....	....	....	....	....	5	0	2	2	10	....	....	....
1982-83	Nanaimo Islanders	WHL	29	7	20	27	....	....	....	86	....	....	....	....	....	....	....	....	....	....	....	....	....	....	....	....	....	....
	Lethbridge Broncos	WHL	42	8	30	38	....	....	....	82	....	....	....	....	....	....	....	....	....	....	20	2	13	15	55	....	....	....
	Lethbridge Broncos	Mem-Cup	3	1	2	3	....	....	....	10	....	....	....	....	....	....	....	....	....	....	....	....	....	....	....	....	....	....
1983-84	Lethbridge Broncos	WHL	71	18	42	60	....	....	....	101	....	....	....	....	....	....	....	....	....	....	5	0	1	1	28	....	....	....
	Minnesota North Stars	**NHL**	**1**	**0**	**0**	**0**	**0**	**0**	**0**	**0**	**0**	**0**	**0**	**0**	**0.0**	**0**	**0**	**0**	**0**	**0**	....	....	....	....	....	....	....	....
1984-85	**Minnesota North Stars**	**NHL**	**63**	**2**	**9**	**11**	**2**	**6**	**8**	**113**	**0**	**0**	**0**	**80**	**2.5**	**48**	**1**	**83**	**22**	**–14**	....	....	....	....	....	....	....	....
	Springfield Indians	AHL	8	0	3	3	....	....	....	6	....	....	....	....	....	....	....	....	....	....	....	....	....	....	....	....	....	....
1985-86	**Minnesota North Stars**	**NHL**	**75**	**1**	**14**	**15**	**1**	**9**	**10**	**151**	**0**	**0**	**1**	**91**	**1.1**	**97**	**2**	**112**	**32**	**15**	**3**	**0**	**0**	**0**	**0**	**0**	**0**	**0**
1986-87	**Minnesota North Stars**	**NHL**	**72**	**2**	**10**	**12**	**2**	**7**	**9**	**179**	**0**	**0**	**0**	**71**	**2.8**	**63**	**1**	**103**	**47**	**6**	....	....	....	....	....	....	....	....
	Canada	WEC-A	4	0	0	0	....	....	....	4	....	....	....	....	....	....	....	....	....	....	....	....	....	....	....	....	....	....
1987-88	**Minnesota North Stars**	**NHL**	**74**	**0**	**12**	**12**	**0**	**9**	**9**	**168**	**0**	**0**	**0**	**62**	**0.0**	**48**	**1**	**125**	**48**	**–30**	....	....	....	....	....	....	....	....
1988-89	**Minnesota North Stars**	**NHL**	**66**	**4**	**13**	**17**	**3**	**9**	**12**	**124**	**0**	**0**	**1**	**66**	**6.1**	**59**	**0**	**92**	**28**	**–5**	....	....	....	....	....	....	....	....
	Washington Capitals	**NHL**	**13**	**0**	**2**	**2**	**0**	**1**	**1**	**36**	**0**	**0**	**0**	**19**	**0.0**	**16**	**3**	**16**	**5**	**2**	**6**	**2**	**0**	**2**	**4**	**0**	**0**	**0**
1989-90	Washington Capitals	Fr-Tour	4	0	0	0	....	....	....	4	....	....	....	....	....	....	....	....	....	....	....	....	....	....	....	....	....	....
	Washington Capitals	**NHL**	**70**	**4**	**16**	**20**	**3**	**11**	**14**	**123**	**0**	**0**	**2**	**72**	**5.6**	**73**	**7**	**93**	**25**	**–2**	**15**	**2**	**3**	**5**	**47**	**1**	**0**	**0**
1990-91	**Washington Capitals**	**NHL**	**47**	**5**	**15**	**20**	**5**	**11**	**16**	**65**	**1**	**0**	**0**	**50**	**10.0**	**44**	**4**	**57**	**10**	**–7**	....	....	....	....	....	....	....	....
	Toronto Maple Leafs	**NHL**	**13**	**2**	**4**	**6**	**2**	**3**	**5**	**10**	**1**	**0**	**0**	**15**	**13.3**	**14**	**3**	**28**	**6**	**–11**	....	....	....	....	....	....	....	....
1991-92	**Toronto Maple Leafs**	**NHL**	**79**	**3**	**19**	**22**	**3**	**14**	**17**	**97**	**1**	**0**	**0**	**115**	**2.6**	**68**	**9**	**112**	**33**	**–20**	....	....	....	....	....	....	....	....
1992-93	**Toronto Maple Leafs**	**NHL**	**82**	**3**	**11**	**14**	**2**	**8**	**10**	**130**	**0**	**1**	**1**	**78**	**3.8**	**64**	**2**	**84**	**29**	**7**	**21**	**3**	**8**	**11**	**29**	**1**	**0**	**1**
1993-94	**Toronto Maple Leafs**	**NHL**	**63**	**5**	**11**	**16**	**5**	**9**	**14**	**101**	**1**	**1**	**0**	**77**	**6.5**	**57**	**8**	**66**	**25**	**8**	**18**	**0**	**3**	**3**	**29**	**0**	**0**	**0**
1994-95	**Detroit Red Wings**	**NHL**	**48**	**1**	**7**	**8**	**2**	**10**	**12**	**36**	**0**	**0**	**1**	**51**	**2.0**	**45**	**4**	**41**	**14**	**14**	**18**	**0**	**3**	**3**	**8**	**0**	**0**	**0**
1995-96	**Detroit Red Wings**	**NHL**	**58**	**0**	**6**	**6**	**0**	**5**	**5**	**48**	**0**	**0**	**0**	**49**	**0.0**	**39**	**0**	**43**	**9**	**5**	**7**	**0**	**1**	**1**	**4**	**0**	**0**	**0**
1996-97♦	**Detroit Red Wings**	**NHL**	**70**	**4**	**9**	**13**	**4**	**8**	**12**	**58**	**0**	**2**	**0**	**70**	**5.7**	**44**	**0**	**49**	**13**	**8**	**20**	**0**	**0**	**0**	**55**	**0**	**0**	**0**
1997-98♦	**Detroit Red Wings**	**NHL**	**71**	**1**	**11**	**12**	**1**	**11**	**12**	**57**	**0**	**0**	**0**	**54**	**1.9**	**38**	**1**	**61**	**15**	**–9**	**22**	**0**	**3**	**3**	**16**	**0**	**0**	**0**
1998-99	**San Jose Sharks**	**NHL**	**70**	**0**	**11**	**11**	**0**	**11**	**11**	**44**	**0**	**0**	**0**	**75**	**0.0**	**45**	**5**	**57**	**17**	**0**	**6**	**0**	**0**	**0**	**6**	**0**	**0**	**0**
99-2000	**San Jose Sharks**	**NHL**	**26**	**0**	**1**	**1**	**0**	**1**	**1**	**19**	**0**	**0**	**0**	**20**	**0.0**	**12**	**1**	**20**	**6**	**–3**	....	....	....	....	....	....	....	....
	NHL Totals		**1061**	**37**	**181**	**218**	**35**	**143**	**178**	**1559**	**4**	**4**	**6**	**1115**	**3.3**	**874**	**52**	**1242**	**384**		**136**	**7**	**21**	**28**	**198**	**2**	**0**	**1**

WHL East First All-Star Team (1984)

Traded to **Washington** by **Minnesota** with Dino Ciccarelli for Mike Gartner and Larry Murphy, March 7, 1989. Traded to **Toronto** by **Washington** with Peter Zezel for Al Iafrate, January 16, 1991. Signed as a free agent by **Detroit**, August 5, 1994. Signed as a free agent by **San Jose**, July 13, 1998. • Officially released by **San Jose**, December 26, 1999.

• ROUSSEAU, Bobby

Joseph Jean Paul Robert RW – R. 5'10", 178 lbs. b: Montreal, Que., 7/26/1940.

Season	Club	League	GP	G	A	Pts	AG	AA	APts	PIM	PP	SH	GW	S	%	TGF	PGF	TGA	PGA	+/–	GP	G	A	Pts	PIM	PP	SH	GW
1954-55	Quebec Citadelle	QJHL	STATISTICS NOT AVAILABLE																									
1955-56	St-Jean Beavers	MMJHL	STATISTICS NOT AVAILABLE																									
	St-Jean Braves	QJHL	44	*53	32	85	....	....	....	25	....	....	....	....	....	....	....	....	....	....	....	....	....	....	....	....	....	....
1956-57	Hull-Ottawa Canadiens	OHA-Jr.	28	7	15	22	....	....	....	18	....	....	....	....	....	....	....	....	....	....	....	....	....	....	....	....	....	....
	Hull-Ottawa Canadiens	EOHL	15	4	2	6	....	....	....	2	....	....	....	....	....	....	....	....	....	....	....	....	....	....	....	....	....	....
	Hull-Ottawa Canadiens	Mem-Cup	8	7	4	11	....	....	....	8	....	....	....	....	....	....	....	....	....	....	....	....	....	....	....	....	....	....
1957-58	Hull-Ottawa Canadiens	OHA-Jr.	27	24	27	51	....	....	....	64	....	....	....	....	....	....	....	....	....	....	....	....	....	....	....	....	....	....
	Hull-Ottawa Canadiens	EOHL	36	26	26	52	....	....	....	14	....	....	....	....	....	....	....	....	....	....	....	....	....	....	....	....	....	....
	Hull-Ottawa Canadiens	Mem-Cup	13	7	17	24	....	....	....	6	....	....	....	....	....	....	....	....	....	....	....	....	....	....	....	....	....	....
1958-59	Hull-Ottawa Canadiens	X-Games	STATISTICS NOT AVAILABLE																									
	Hull-Ottawa Canadiens	EOHL	18	7	18	25	....	....	....	26	....	....	....	....	....	....	....	....	....	....	3	1	1	2	2	....	....	....
	Rochester Americans	AHL	2	0	0	0	....	....	....	0	....	....	....	....	....	....	....	....	....	....	....	....	....	....	....	....	....	....
	Hull-Ottawa Canadiens	Mem-Cup	9	2	6	8	....	....	....	19	....	....	....	....	....	....	....	....	....	....	....	....	....	....	....	....	....	....
1959-60	Brockville Jr. Canadiens	MMJHL	STATISTICS NOT AVAILABLE																									
	Canada	Olympics	7	5	4	9	....	....	....	2	....	....	....	....	....	....	....	....	....	....	....	....	....	....	....	....	....	....
	Hull-Ottawa Canadiens	EPHL	4	4	2	6	....	....	....	4	....	....	....	....	....	....	....	....	....	....	....	....	....	....	....	....	....	....
	Brockville Jr. Canadiens	Mem-Cup	13	14	9	23	....	....	....	14	....	....	....	....	....	....	....	....	....	....	....	....	....	....	....	....	....	....
1960-61	**Montreal Canadiens**	**NHL**	**15**	**1**	**2**	**3**	**1**	**2**	**3**	**4**	....	....	....	....	....	....	....	....	....	....	....	....	....	....	....	....	....	....
	Hull-Ottawa Canadiens	EPHL	38	34	26	60	....	....	....	18	....	....	....	....	....	....	....	....	....	....	14	*12	7	*19	10	....	....	....
1961-62	**Montreal Canadiens**	**NHL**	**70**	**21**	**24**	**45**	**24**	**23**	**47**	**26**	....	....	....	....	....	....	....	....	....	....	**6**	**0**	**2**	**2**	**0**	**0**	**0**	**0**
1962-63	**Montreal Canadiens**	**NHL**	**62**	**19**	**18**	**37**	**22**	**18**	**40**	**15**	....	....	....	....	....	....	....	....	....	....	**5**	**0**	**1**	**1**	**2**	**0**	**0**	**0**
1963-64	**Montreal Canadiens**	**NHL**	**70**	**25**	**31**	**56**	**31**	**33**	**64**	**32**	....	....	....	....	....	....	....	....	....	....	**7**	**1**	**1**	**2**	**2**	**0**	**1**	**1**
1964-65♦	**Montreal Canadiens**	**NHL**	**66**	**12**	**35**	**47**	**14**	**36**	**50**	**26**	....	....	....	....	....	....	....	....	....	....	**13**	**5**	**8**	**13**	**24**	**5**	**0**	**2**

Season	Club	League	REGULAR SEASON																			PLAYOFFS							
			GP	G	A	Pts	AG	AA	APts	PIM	PP	SH	GW	S	%	TGF	PGF	TGA	PGA	+/–	GP	G	A	Pts	PIM	PP	SH	GW
1965-66♦	**Montreal Canadiens**	**NHL**	**70**	**30**	***48**	**78**	**34**	**46**	**80**	**20**	....	....	....	....	....	....	....	....	....	....	**10**	**4**	**4**	**8**	**6**	**2**	**0**	**0**
1966-67	**Montreal Canadiens**	**NHL**	**68**	**19**	**44**	**63**	**22**	**43**	**65**	**58**	....	....	....	....	....	....	....	....	....	....	**10**	**1**	**7**	**8**	**4**	**1**	**0**	**1**
1967-68♦	**Montreal Canadiens**	**NHL**	**74**	**19**	**46**	**65**	**22**	**46**	**68**	**47**	**7**	**1**	**5**	**183**	**10.4**	**97**	**40**	**47**	**2**	**12**	**13**	**2**	**4**	**6**	**8**	**0**	**0**	**1**
1968-69♦	**Montreal Canadiens**	**NHL**	**76**	**30**	**40**	**70**	**32**	**36**	**68**	**59**	**3**	**0**	**8**	**278**	**10.8**	**112**	**28**	**69**	**12**	**27**	**14**	**3**	**2**	**5**	**8**	**0**	**2**	**1**
1969-70	**Montreal Canadiens**	**NHL**	**72**	**24**	**34**	**58**	**26**	**32**	**58**	**30**	**5**	**2**	**4**	**228**	**10.5**	**91**	**30**	**80**	**22**	**3**	....	....	....	....	....	....	....	....
1970-71	**Minnesota North Stars**	**NHL**	**63**	**4**	**20**	**24**	**4**	**17**	**21**	**12**	**0**	**0**	**0**	**122**	**3.3**	**30**	**3**	**25**	**1**	**3**	**12**	**2**	**6**	**8**	**0**	**1**	**0**	**1**
1971-72	**New York Rangers**	**NHL**	**78**	**21**	**36**	**57**	**21**	**31**	**52**	**12**	**4**	**1**	**6**	**180**	**11.7**	**96**	**46**	**49**	**7**	**8**	**16**	**6**	**11**	**17**	**7**	**0**	**0**	**1**
1972-73	**New York Rangers**	**NHL**	**78**	**8**	**37**	**45**	**7**	**29**	**36**	**14**	**2**	**0**	**3**	**150**	**5.3**	**72**	**37**	**37**	**3**	**1**	**10**	**2**	**3**	**5**	**4**	**0**	**0**	**0**
1973-74	**New York Rangers**	**NHL**	**72**	**10**	**41**	**51**	**10**	**34**	**44**	**4**	**6**	**0**	**0**	**87**	**11.5**	**75**	**49**	**24**	**0**	**2**	**12**	**1**	**8**	**9**	**4**	**1**	**0**	**0**
1974-75	**New York Rangers**	**NHL**	**8**	**2**	**2**	**4**	**2**	**1**	**3**	**0**	**2**	**0**	**1**	**9**	**22.2**	**6**	**5**	**3**	**0**	**–2**	....	....	....	....	....	....	....	....
	NHL Totals		**942**	**245**	**458**	**703**	**272**	**427**	**699**	**359**	....	....	....	....	....	....	....	....	....	....	**128**	**27**	**57**	**84**	**69**	....	....	....

• Brother of Roland and Guy • EPHL Second All-Star Team (1961) • Won Calder Memorial Trophy (1962) • NHL Second All-Star Team (1966) • Played in NHL All-Star Game (1965, 1967, 1969)

• Hull-Ottawa played partial schedule against OHA-Jr. teams in 1956-57 and 1957-58 that counted for the opposition only. Traded to **Minnesota** by **Montreal** for Claude Larose, June 10, 1970. Traded to **NY Rangers** by **Minnesota** to complete transaction that sent Bob Nevin to Minnesota (May 25, 1971), June 8, 1971.

• ROUTHIER, Jean-Marc

RW – R. 6'2", 190 lbs. b: Quebec City, Que., 2/2/1968. Quebec's 2nd, 39th overall, in 1986.

Season	Club	League	GP	G	A	Pts	AG	AA	APts	PIM	PP	SH	GW	S	%	TGF	PGF	TGA	PGA	+/–	GP	G	A	Pts	PIM	PP	SH	GW
1984-85	Ste-Foy Gouverneurs	QAAA	41	13	22	35	....	....	....	68	....	....	....	....	....	....	....	....	....	....	....	....	....	....	....	....	....	....
1985-86	Hull Olympiques	QMJHL	71	18	16	34	....	....	....	111	....	....	....	....	....	....	....	....	....	....	15	3	6	9	27	....	....	....
	Hull Olympiques	Mem-Cup	5	3	0	3	....	....	....	4	....	....	....	....	....	....	....	....	....	....	....	....	....	....	....	....	....	....
1986-87	Hull Olympiques	QMJHL	59	17	18	35	....	....	....	98	....	....	....	....	....	....	....	....	....	....	....	....	....	....	....	....	....	....
1987-88	Victoriaville Tigres	QMJHL	57	16	28	44	....	....	....	267	....	....	....	....	....	....	....	....	....	....	2	0	0	0	5	....	....	....
1988-89	Halifax Citadels	AHL	52	13	13	26	....	....	....	189	....	....	....	....	....	....	....	....	....	....	4	1	1	2	16	....	....	....
1989-90	**Quebec Nordiques**	**NHL**	**8**	**0**	**0**	**0**	**0**	**0**	**0**	**9**	**0**	**0**	**0**	**8**	**0.0**	**0**	**0**	**3**	**0**	**–3**	....	....	....	....	....	....	....	....
	Halifax Citadels	AHL	17	4	8	12	....	....	....	29	....	....	....	....	....	....	....	....	....	....	....	....	....	....	....	....	....	....
1990-1997			OUT OF HOCKEY – RETIRED																									
1997-98	Quebec Aces	QSPHL	19	7	17	24	....	....	....	43	....	....	....	....	....	....	....	....	....	....								
1998-99	St-Pierre Becquets	QCSHL	STATISTICS NOT AVAILABLE																									
99-2000	St-Pierre Becquets	QCSHL	10	6	2	8	....	....	....	2	....	....	....	....	....	....	....	....	....	....	....	....	....	....	....	....	....	....
	NHL Totals		**8**	**0**	**0**	**0**	**0**	**0**	**0**	**9**	**0**	**0**	**0**	**8**	**0.0**	**0**	**0**	**3**	**0**		....	....	....	....	....	....	....	....

• ROWE, Mike

Michael A. D – L. 6'1", 208 lbs. b: Kingston, Ont., 3/8/1965. Pittsburgh's 3rd, 59th overall, in 1983.

Season	Club	League	GP	G	A	Pts	AG	AA	APts	PIM	PP	SH	GW	S	%	TGF	PGF	TGA	PGA	+/–	GP	G	A	Pts	PIM	PP	SH	GW
1980-81	Hawkesbury Hawks	OJHL	47	5	13	18	....	....	....	183	....	....	....	....	....	....	....	....	....	....	....	....	....	....	....	....	....	....
1981-82	Toronto Marlboros	OHL	58	4	4	8	....	....	....	214	....	....	....	....	....	....	....	....	....	....	10	0	0	0	63	....	....	....
1982-83	Toronto Marlboros	OHL	64	4	29	33	....	....	....	262	....	....	....	....	....	....	....	....	....	....	4	0	1	1	19	....	....	....
1983-84	Toronto Marlboros	OHL	59	9	36	45	....	....	....	208	....	....	....	....	....	....	....	....	....	....	9	0	5	5	45	....	....	....
1984-85	Toronto Marlboros	OHL	66	17	34	51	....	....	....	202	....	....	....	....	....	....	....	....	....	....	....	....	....	....	....	....	....	....
	Pittsburgh Penguins	**NHL**	**6**	**0**	**0**	**0**	**0**	**0**	**0**	**7**	**0**	**0**	**0**	**6**	**0.0**	**2**	**0**	**12**	**3**	**–7**	....	....	....	....	....	....	....	....
	Baltimore Clippers	AHL	....	....	....	....	....	....	....	....	....	....	....	....	....	....	....	....	....	....	3	0	0	0	0	....	....	....
1985-86	**Pittsburgh Penguins**	**NHL**	**3**	**0**	**0**	**0**	**0**	**0**	**0**	**4**	**0**	**0**	**0**	**5**	**0.0**	**0**	**0**	**1**	**0**	**–1**	....	....	....	....	....	....	....	....
	Baltimore Skipjacks	AHL	67	0	5	5	....	....	....	107	....	....	....	....	....	....	....	....	....	....	....	....	....	....	....	....	....	....
1986-87	**Pittsburgh Penguins**	**NHL**	**2**	**0**	**0**	**0**	**0**	**0**	**0**	**0**	**0**	**0**	**0**	**1**	**0.0**	**0**	**0**	**2**	**0**	**–2**	....	....	....	....	....	....	....	....
	Baltimore Skipjacks	AHL	79	1	18	19	....	....	....	64	....	....	....	....	....	....	....	....	....	....	....	....	....	....	....	....	....	....
1987-88	Muskegon Lumberjacks	IHL	80	8	21	29	....	....	....	137	....	....	....	....	....	....	....	....	....	....	6	0	0	0	13	....	....	....
1988-89	Whitley Warriors	Britain	35	34	86	120	....	....	....	122	....	....	....	....	....	....	....	....	....	....	5	6	5	11	24	....	....	....
1989-90	Fife Flyers	Aut-Cup	6	4	8	12	....	....	....	24	....	....	....	....	....	....	....	....	....	....	....	....	....	....	....	....	....	....
	Fife Flyers	Britain	29	22	30	52	....	....	....	107	....	....	....	....	....	....	....	....	....	....	5	1	4	5	24	....	....	....
1990-91	Basingstoke Beavers	Aut-Cup	6	3	4	7	....	....	....	47	....	....	....	....	....	....	....	....	....	....	....	....	....	....	....	....	....	....
	Basingstoke Beavers	Britain	36	39	63	102	....	....	....	*239	....	....	....	....	....	....	....	....	....	....	....	....	....	....	....	....	....	....
	Murrayfield Racers	Britain	....	....	....	....	....	....	....	....	....	....	....	....	....	....	....	....	....	....	7	6	7	13	18	....	....	....
1991-92	Whitley Warriors	Aut-Cup	8	4	15	19	....	....	....	22	....	....	....	....	....	....	....	....	....	....	....	....	....	....	....	....	....	....
	Whitley Warriors	Britain	36	32	48	80	....	....	....	146	....	....	....	....	....	....	....	....	....	....	7	2	7	9	12	....	....	....
1992-93	Whitley Warriors	BH-Cup	11	5	19	24	....	....	....	28	....	....	....	....	....	....	....	....	....	....	....	....	....	....	....	....	....	....
	Whitley Warriors	Britain	34	17	61	78	....	....	....	100	....	....	....	....	....	....	....	....	....	....	6	1	7	8	10	....	....	....
1993-94	Whitley Warriors	BH-Cup	11	5	19	24	....	....	....	28	....	....	....	....	....	....	....	....	....	....	....	....	....	....	....	....	....	....
	Whitley Warriors	Britain	43	16	53	69	....	....	....	110	....	....	....	....	....	....	....	....	....	....	5	0	1	1	23	....	....	....
1994-95	Whitley Warriors	BH-Cup	2	0	0	0	....	....	....	2	....	....	....	....	....	....	....	....	....	....	....	....	....	....	....	....	....	....
	Whitley Warriors	Britain	37	9	30	39	....	....	....	100	....	....	....	....	....	....	....	....	....	....	6	2	6	8	43	....	....	....
	NHL Totals		**11**	**0**	**0**	**0**	**0**	**0**	**0**	**11**	**0**	**0**	**0**	**12**	**0.0**	**2**	**0**	**15**	**3**		....	....	....	....	....	....	....	....

• ROWE, Tom

Thomas John RW – R. 6', 190 lbs. b: Lynn, MA, 5/23/1956. Washington's 3rd, 37th overall, in 1976.

Season	Club	League	GP	G	A	Pts	AG	AA	APts	PIM	PP	SH	GW	S	%	TGF	PGF	TGA	PGA	+/–	GP	G	A	Pts	PIM	PP	SH	GW
1973-74	London Knights	OMJHL	70	30	39	69	....	....	....	99	....	....	....	....	....	....	....	....	....	....	....	....	....	....	....	....	....	....
1974-75	London Knights	OMJHL	63	19	15	34	....	....	....	137	....	....	....	....	....	....	....	....	....	....	....	....	....	....	....	....	....	....
1975-76	London Knights	OMJHL	60	39	55	94	....	....	....	98	....	....	....	....	....	....	....	....	....	....	5	1	3	4	14	....	....	....
1976-77	**Washington Capitals**	**NHL**	**12**	**1**	**2**	**3**	**1**	**2**	**3**	**2**	**0**	**0**	**0**	**22**	**4.5**	**9**	**2**	**13**	**0**	**–6**	....	....	....	....	....	....	....	....
	Springfield Indians	AHL	67	19	23	42	....	....	....	117	....	....	....	....	....	....	....	....	....	....	....	....	....	....	....	....	....	....
	United States	WEC-A	2	0	0	0	....	....	....	2	....	....	....	....	....	....	....	....	....	....	....	....	....	....	....	....	....	....
1977-78	**Washington Capitals**	**NHL**	**63**	**13**	**8**	**21**	**12**	**6**	**18**	**82**	**1**	**0**	**0**	**116**	**11.2**	**31**	**1**	**48**	**0**	**–18**	....	....	....	....	....	....	....	....
1978-79	**Washington Capitals**	**NHL**	**69**	**31**	**30**	**61**	**27**	**22**	**49**	**137**	**4**	**0**	**4**	**205**	**15.1**	**93**	**20**	**79**	**0**	**–6**	....	....	....	....	....	....	....	....
1979-80	**Washington Capitals**	**NHL**	**41**	**10**	**17**	**27**	**8**	**12**	**20**	**76**	**4**	**0**	**2**	**107**	**9.3**	**47**	**17**	**40**	**1**	**–9**	....	....	....	....	....	....	....	....
	Hartford Whalers	**NHL**	**20**	**6**	**4**	**10**	**5**	**3**	**8**	**30**	**1**	**0**	**1**	**41**	**14.6**	**17**	**1**	**19**	**0**	**–3**	**3**	**2**	**0**	**2**	**0**	**0**	**0**	**0**
1980-81	**Hartford Whalers**	**NHL**	**74**	**13**	**28**	**41**	**10**	**19**	**29**	**190**	**1**	**0**	**1**	**143**	**9.1**	**65**	**9**	**66**	**0**	**–10**	....	....	....	....	....	....	....	....
1981-82	**Hartford Whalers**	**NHL**	**21**	**4**	**0**	**4**	**3**	**0**	**3**	**36**	**1**	**1**	**0**	**47**	**8.5**	**5**	**1**	**18**	**3**	**–11**	....	....	....	....	....	....	....	....
	Binghamton Whalers	AHL	8	5	3	8	....	....	....	36	....	....	....	....	....	....	....	....	....	....	....	....	....	....	....	....	....	....
	Washington Capitals	**NHL**	**6**	**1**	**1**	**2**	**1**	**1**	**2**	**18**	**0**	**0**	**0**	**9**	**11.1**	**4**	**0**	**4**	**0**	**0**	....	....	....	....	....	....	....	....
	Hershey Bears	AHL	34	17	17	34	....	....	....	89	....	....	....	....	....	....	....	....	....	....	5	3	4	7	33	....	....	....
1982-83	**Detroit Red Wings**	**NHL**	**51**	**6**	**10**	**16**	**5**	**7**	**12**	**44**	**0**	**0**	**1**	**65**	**9.2**	**28**	**2**	**43**	**0**	**–17**	....	....	....	....	....	....	....	....
	Adirondack Red Wings	AHL	20	16	7	23	....	....	....	26	....	....	....	....	....	....	....	....	....	....	....	....	....	....	....	....	....	....
1983-84	Moncton Alpines	AHL	50	28	16	44	....	....	....	86	....	....	....	....	....	....	....	....	....	....	....	....	....	....	....	....	....	....
	NHL Totals		**357**	**85**	**100**	**185**	**72**	**72**	**144**	**615**	**12**	**1**	**9**	**755**	**11.3**	**299**	**53**	**330**	**4**		**3**	**2**	**0**	**2**	**0**	**0**	**0**	**0**

Traded to **Hartford** by **Washington** for Al Hangsleben, January 17, 1980. Signed as a free agent by **Washington**, January 31, 1982. Signed as a free agent by **Detroit**, August 9, 1982. Signed as a free agent by **Edmonton**, September 29, 1983.

• ROY, Andre

Andre C. LW – L. 6'4", 213 lbs. b: Port Chester, NY, 2/8/1975. Boston's 5th, 151st overall, in 1994.

Season	Club	League	GP	G	A	Pts	AG	AA	APts	PIM	PP	SH	GW	S	%	TGF	PGF	TGA	PGA	+/–	GP	G	A	Pts	PIM	PP	SH	GW
1992-93	Carleton Place Kings	OJHL-B	40	16	15	31	....	....	....	80	....	....	....	....	....	....	....	....	....	....	....	....	....	....	....	....	....	....
1993-94	Beauport Harfangs	QMJHL	33	6	7	13	....	....	....	125	....	....	....	....	....	....	....	....	....	....	....	....	....	....	....	....	....	....
	Chicoutimi Sagueneens	QMJHL	32	4	14	18	....	....	....	152	....	....	....	....	....	....	....	....	....	....	25	3	6	9	94	....	....	....
	Chicoutimi Sagueneens	Mem-Cup	4	2	0	2	....	....	....	2	....	....	....	....	....	....	....	....	....	....	....	....	....	....	....	....	....	....
1994-95	Chicoutimi Sagueneens	QMJHL	20	15	8	23	....	....	....	90	....	....	....	....	....	....	....	....	....	....	....	....	....	....	....	....	....	....
	Drummondville Voltigeurs	QMJHL	34	18	13	31	....	....	....	233	....	....	....	....	....	....	....	....	....	....	4	2	0	2	34	....	....	....
1995-96	**Boston Bruins**	**NHL**	**3**	**0**	**0**	**0**	**0**	**0**	**0**	**0**	**0**	**0**	**0**	**0**	**0.0**	**0**	**0**	**0**	**0**	**0**	....	....	....	....	....	....	....	....
	Providence Bruins	AHL	58	7	8	15	....	....	....	167	....	....	....	....	....	....	....	....	....	....	1	0	0	0	10	....	....	....
1996-97	**Boston Bruins**	**NHL**	**10**	**0**	**2**	**2**	**0**	**2**	**2**	**12**	**0**	**0**	**0**	**12**	**0.0**	**2**	**0**	**7**	**0**	**–5**	....	....	....	....	....	....	....	....
	Providence Bruins	AHL	50	17	11	28	....	....	....	234	....	....	....	....	....	....	....	....	....	....	....	....	....	....	....	....	....	....

			REGULAR SEASON																		PLAYOFFS							
Season	Club	League	GP	G	A	Pts	AG	AA	APts	PIM	PP	SH	GW	S	%	TGF	PGF	TGA	PGA	+/–	GP	G	A	Pts	PIM	PP	SH	GW
1997-98	Providence Bruins	AHL	36	3	11	14	....	....	....	154	....	....	....	....	....	....	....	....	....	....	....	....	....	....	....	....	....	....
	Charlotte Checkers	ECHL	27	10	8	18	....	....	....	132	....	....	....	....	....	....	....	....	....	....	7	2	3	5	34	....	....	....
1998-99	Fort Wayne Komets	IHL	65	15	6	21	....	....	....	*395	....	....	....	....	....	....	....	....	....	....	2	0	0	0	11	....	....	....
99-2000	**Ottawa Senators**	**NHL**	**73**	**4**	**3**	**7**	**4**	**3**	**7**	**145**	**0**	**0**	**1**	**39**	**10.3**	**17**	**0**	**14**	**0**	**3**	**5**	**0**	**0**	**0**	**2**	**0**	**0**	**0**
	NHL Totals		**86**	**4**	**5**	**9**	**4**	**5**	**9**	**157**	**0**	**0**	**1**	**51**	**7.8**	**19**	**0**	**21**	**0**		**5**	**0**	**0**	**0**	**2**	**0**	**0**	**0**

Signed as a free agent by **Ottawa**, April 28, 1999.

• ROY, Jean-Yves

RW – L. 5'10", 180 lbs. b: Rosemere, Que., 2/17/1969.

Season	Club	League	GP	G	A	Pts	AG	AA	APts	PIM	PP	SH	GW	S	%	TGF	PGF	TGA	PGA	+/–	GP	G	A	Pts	PIM	PP	SH	GW
1985-86	Laval Laurentides	QAAA	42	20	27	47	....	....	....	....	....	....	....	....	....	....	....	....	....	....	....	....	....	....	....	....	....	....
1986-1989			STATISTICS NOT AVAILABLE																									
1989-90	University of Maine	H-East	46	*39	26	65	....	....	....	52	....	....	....	....	....	....	....	....	....	....	....	....	....	....	....	....	....	....
1990-91	University of Maine	H-East	43	37	45	82	....	....	....	62	....	....	....	....	....	....	....	....	....	....	....	....	....	....	....	....	....	....
1991-92	University of Maine	H-East	35	32	24	56	....	....	....	62	....	....	....	....	....	....	....	....	....	....	....	....	....	....	....	....	....	....
	Canada	Nat-Team	13	10	4	14	....	....	....	6	....	....	....	....	....	....	....	....	....	....	....	....	....	....	....	....	....	....
1992-93	Canada	Nat-Team	23	9	6	15	....	....	....	35	....	....	....	....	....	....	....	....	....	....	....	....	....	....	....	....	....	....
	Binghamton Rangers	AHL	49	13	15	28	....	....	....	21	....	....	....	....	....	....	....	....	....	....	14	5	2	7	4	....	....	....
1993-94	Binghamton Rangers	AHL	65	41	24	65	....	....	....	33	....	....	....	....	....	....	....	....	....	....	....	....	....	....	....	....	....	....
	Canada	Nat-Team	6	3	2	5	....	....	....	2	....	....	....	....	....	....	....	....	....	....	....	....	....	....	....	....	....	....
	Canada	Olympics	8	1	0	1	....	....	....	0	....	....	....	....	....	....	....	....	....	....	....	....	....	....	....	....	....	....
1994-95	Binghamton Rangers	AHL	67	41	36	77	....	....	....	28	....	....	....	....	....	....	....	....	....	....	11	4	6	10	12	....	....	....
	New York Rangers	**NHL**	**3**	**1**	**0**	**1**	**2**	**0**	**2**	**2**	**0**	**0**	**0**	**8**	**12.5**	**1**	**0**	**2**	**0**	**–1**	....	....	....	....	....	....	....	....
1995-96	**Ottawa Senators**	**NHL**	**4**	**1**	**1**	**2**	**1**	**1**	**2**	**2**	**0**	**0**	**0**	**6**	**16.7**	**4**	**0**	**1**	**0**	**3**	....	....	....	....	....	....	....	....
	P.E.I. Senators	AHL	67	40	55	95	....	....	....	64	....	....	....	....	....	....	....	....	....	....	5	4	8	12	6	....	....	....
1996-97	**Boston Bruins**	**NHL**	**52**	**10**	**15**	**25**	**11**	**13**	**24**	**22**	**2**	**0**	**1**	**100**	**10.0**	**43**	**7**	**48**	**4**	**–8**	....	....	....	....	....	....	....	....
	Providence Bruins	AHL	27	9	16	25	....	....	....	30	....	....	....	....	....	....	....	....	....	....	10	2	7	9	2	....	....	....
1997-98	**Boston Bruins**	**NHL**	**2**	**0**	**0**	**0**	**0**	**0**	**0**	**0**	**0**	**0**	**0**	**1**	**0.0**	**0**	**0**	**0**	**0**	**0**	....	....	....	....	....	....	....	....
	Providence Bruins	AHL	65	28	34	62	....	....	....	60	....	....	....	....	....	....	....	....	....	....	....	....	....	....	....	....	....	....
1998-99	VSV Villach	Alpenliga	29	25	27	52	....	....	....	26	....	....	....	....	....	....	....	....	....	....	....	....	....	....	....	....	....	....
	VSV Villach	Austria	23	13	20	33	....	....	....	20	....	....	....	....	....	....	....	....	....	....	....	....	....	....	....	....	....	....
	Canada	Nat-Team	5	4	3	7	....	....	....	6	....	....	....	....	....	....	....	....	....	....	....	....	....	....	....	....	....	....
99-2000	Kolner Haie	Germany	56	22	21	43	....	....	....	53	....	....	....	....	....	....	....	....	....	....	10	2	4	6	8	....	....	....
	NHL Totals		**61**	**12**	**16**	**28**	**14**	**14**	**28**	**26**	**2**	**0**	**1**	**115**	**10.4**	**48**	**7**	**51**	**4**		....	....	....	....	....	....	....	....

NCAA East Second All-American Team (1990) • Hockey East First All-Star Team (1991) • NCAA East First All-American Team (1991, 1992) • NCAA Championship All-Tournament Team (1991) • Hockey East Second All-Star Team (1992)

Signed as a free agent by **NY Rangers**, July 20, 1992. Traded to **Ottawa** by **NY Rangers** for Steve Larouche, October 5, 1995. Signed as a free agent by **Boston**, July 15, 1996.

• ROY, Stephane

C – L. 6', 190 lbs. b: Ste. Foy, Que., 6/29/1967. Minnesota's 1st, 51st overall, in 1985.

Season	Club	League	GP	G	A	Pts	AG	AA	APts	PIM	PP	SH	GW	S	%	TGF	PGF	TGA	PGA	+/–	GP	G	A	Pts	PIM	PP	SH	GW
1982-83	Ste-Foy Gouverneurs	QAAA	43	21	39	60	....	....	....	....	....	....	....	....	....	....	....	....	....	....	....	....	....	....	....	....	....	....
1983-84	Chicoutimi Sagueneens	QMJHL	67	12	26	38	....	....	....	25	....	....	....	....	....	....	....	....	....	....	....	....	....	....	....	....	....	....
1984-85	Chicoutimi Sagueneens	QMJHL	41	21	27	48	....	....	....	18	....	....	....	....	....	....	....	....	....	....	....	....	....	....	....	....	....	....
	Granby Bisons	QMJHL	27	7	26	33	....	....	....	16	....	....	....	....	....	....	....	....	....	....	....	....	....	....	....	....	....	....
1985-86	Granby Bisons	QMJHL	61	33	52	85	....	....	....	68	....	....	....	....	....	....	....	....	....	....	....	....	....	....	....	....	....	....
	Canada	Nat-Team	10	0	1	1	....	....	....	4	....	....	....	....	....	....	....	....	....	....	....	....	....	....	....	....	....	....
1986-87	Granby Bisons	QMJHL	45	23	44	67	....	....	....	54	....	....	....	....	....	....	....	....	....	....	7	2	3	5	50	....	....	....
	Canada	Nat-Team	9	1	2	3	....	....	....	4	....	....	....	....	....	....	....	....	....	....	....	....	....	....	....	....	....	....
	Canada	WJC-A	6	0	1	1	....	....	....	6	....	....	....	....	....	....	....	....	....	....	....	....	....	....	....	....	....	....
1987-88	**Minnesota North Stars**	**NHL**	**12**	**1**	**0**	**1**	**1**	**0**	**1**	**0**	**0**	**0**	**0**	**14**	**7.1**	**2**	**0**	**9**	**1**	**–6**	....	....	....	....	....	....	....	....
	Kalamazoo Wings	IHL	58	21	12	33	....	....	....	52	....	....	....	....	....	....	....	....	....	....	5	1	2	3	11	....	....	....
1988-89	Halifax Citadels	AHL	42	8	16	24	....	....	....	28	....	....	....	....	....	....	....	....	....	....	1	0	0	0	0	....	....	....
	Kalamazoo Wings	IHL	20	5	4	9	....	....	....	27	....	....	....	....	....	....	....	....	....	....	....	....	....	....	....	....	....	....
1989-90	HC Nice	France-3	12	15	8	23	....	....	....	38	....	....	....	....	....	....	....	....	....	....	....	....	....	....	....	....	....	....
1990-91	Canada	Nat-Team	52	22	22	44	....	....	....	6	....	....	....	....	....	....	....	....	....	....	....	....	....	....	....	....	....	....
1991-92	Canada	Nat-Team	49	10	24	34	....	....	....	15	....	....	....	....	....	....	....	....	....	....	....	....	....	....	....	....	....	....
1992-93	Canada	Nat-Team	55	12	31	43	....	....	....	38	....	....	....	....	....	....	....	....	....	....	....	....	....	....	....	....	....	....
1993-94	EHC Olten	Switz	3	1	2	3	....	....	....	2	....	....	....	....	....	....	....	....	....	....	....	....	....	....	....	....	....	....
1994-95	EHC Olten	Switz-2	STATISTICS NOT AVAILABLE																									
1995-96	Memphis River Kings	CHL	60	18	44	62	....	....	....	33	....	....	....	....	....	....	....	....	....	....	6	1	2	3	8	....	....	....
1996-97	Memphis River Kings	CHL	38	16	28	44	....	....	....	25	....	....	....	....	....	....	....	....	....	....	....	....	....	....	....	....	....	....
	Anchorage Aces	WPHL	22	3	12	15	....	....	....	27	....	....	....	....	....	....	....	....	....	....	....	....	....	....	....	....	....	....
1997-98	Macon Whoopee	CHL	4	1	6	7	....	....	....	8	....	....	....	....	....	....	....	....	....	....	....	....	....	....	....	....	....	....
	Quebec Aces	QSPHL	8	2	5	7	....	....	....	6	....	....	....	....	....	....	....	....	....	....	....	....	....	....	....	....	....	....
1998-99	Abilene Aviators	WPHL	29	9	18	27	....	....	....	13	....	....	....	....	....	....	....	....	....	....	....	....	....	....	....	....	....	....
99-2000	Pocatiere Seigneurs	QCSHL	36	13	23	36	....	....	....	22	....	....	....	....	....	....	....	....	....	....	3	0	0	0	2	....	....	....
	NHL Totals		**12**	**1**	**0**	**1**	**1**	**0**	**1**	**0**	**0**	**0**	**0**	**14**	**7.1**	**2**	**0**	**9**	**1**		....	....	....	....	....	....	....	....

• Brother of Patrick

Traded to **Quebec** by **Minnesota** for future considerations, December 15, 1988. • Played w/ RHI's Denver Dare Devils in 1996 (18-12-14-26-18).

• ROYER, Remi

D – R. 6'2", 200 lbs. b: Donnacona, Que., 2/12/1978. Chicago's 1st, 31st overall, in 1996.

Season	Club	League	GP	G	A	Pts	AG	AA	APts	PIM	PP	SH	GW	S	%	TGF	PGF	TGA	PGA	+/–	GP	G	A	Pts	PIM	PP	SH	GW
1993-94	Ste-Foy Gouverneurs	QAAA	44	8	24	32	....	....	....	....	....	....	....	....	....	....	....	....	....	....	....	....	....	....	....	....	....	....
1994-95	Victoriaville Tigres	QMJHL	57	3	17	20	....	....	....	144	....	....	....	....	....	....	....	....	....	....	4	0	1	1	7	....	....	....
1995-96	Victoriaville Tigres	QMJHL	43	12	14	26	....	....	....	209	....	....	....	....	....	....	....	....	....	....	....	....	....	....	....	....	....	....
	St-Hyacinthe Laser	QMJHL	19	10	9	19	....	....	....	80	....	....	....	....	....	....	....	....	....	....	12	1	4	5	29	....	....	....
1996-97	Rouyn-Noranda Huskies	QMJHL	29	3	12	15	....	....	....	85	....	....	....	....	....	....	....	....	....	....	....	....	....	....	....	....	....	....
	Indianapolis Ice	IHL	10	0	1	1	....	....	....	17	....	....	....	....	....	....	....	....	....	....	....	....	....	....	....	....	....	....
1997-98	Rouyn-Noranda Huskies	QMJHL	66	20	48	68	....	....	....	205	....	....	....	....	....	....	....	....	....	....	6	1	3	4	8	....	....	....
	Indianapolis Ice	IHL	5	0	2	2	....	....	....	4	....	....	....	....	....	....	....	....	....	....	5	1	2	3	12	....	....	....
1998-99	**Chicago Blackhawks**	**NHL**	**18**	**0**	**0**	**0**	**0**	**0**	**0**	**67**	**0**	**0**	**0**	**24**	**0.0**	**4**	**1**	**15**	**2**	**–10**	....	....	....	....	....	....	....	....
	Indianapolis Ice	IHL	54	4	15	19	....	....	....	164	....	....	....	....	....	....	....	....	....	....	7	0	0	0	44	....	....	....
	Portland Pirates	AHL	2	0	1	1	....	....	....	2	....	....	....	....	....	....	....	....	....	....	....	....	....	....	....	....	....	....
99-2000	Cleveland Lumberjacks	IHL	57	3	13	16	....	....	....	204	....	....	....	....	....	....	....	....	....	....	8	1	1	2	12	....	....	....
	NHL Totals		**18**	**0**	**0**	**0**	**0**	**0**	**0**	**67**	**0**	**0**	**0**	**24**	**0.0**	**4**	**1**	**15**	**2**		....	....	....	....	....	....	....	....

QMJHL First All-Star Team (1998)

• ROZSIVAL, Michal

D – R. 6'1", 200 lbs. b: Vlasim, Czech., 9/3/1978. Pittsburgh's 5th, 105th overall, in 1996.

Season	Club	League	GP	G	A	Pts	AG	AA	APts	PIM	PP	SH	GW	S	%	TGF	PGF	TGA	PGA	+/–	GP	G	A	Pts	PIM	PP	SH	GW
1994-95	Dukla Jihlava-Jr.	Czech-Rep	31	8	13	21	....	....	....	....	....	....	....	....	....	....	....	....	....	....	....	....	....	....	....	....	....	....
1995-96	Dukla Jihlava	Czech-Rep	36	3	4	7	....	....	....	....	....	....	....	....	....	....	....	....	....	....	....	....	....	....	....	....	....	....
1996-97	Swift Current Broncos	WHL	63	8	31	39	....	....	....	80	....	....	....	....	....	....	....	....	....	....	10	0	6	6	15	....	....	....
1997-98	Swift Current Broncos	WHL	71	14	55	69	....	....	....	122	....	....	....	....	....	....	....	....	....	....	12	0	5	5	33	....	....	....
1998-99	Syracuse Crunch	AHL	49	3	22	25	....	....	....	72	....	....	....	....	....	....	....	....	....	....	....	....	....	....	....	....	....	....
99-2000	**Pittsburgh Penguins**	**NHL**	**75**	**4**	**17**	**21**	**4**	**16**	**20**	**48**	**1**	**0**	**1**	**73**	**5.5**	**66**	**5**	**65**	**15**	**11**	**2**	**0**	**0**	**0**	**4**	**0**	**0**	**0**
	NHL Totals		**75**	**4**	**17**	**21**	**4**	**16**	**20**	**48**	**1**	**0**	**1**	**73**	**5.5**	**66**	**5**	**65**	**15**		**2**	**0**	**0**	**0**	**4**	**0**	**0**	**0**

WHL East First All-Star Team (1998)

• RUCCHIN, Steve

Steven Andrew C – L. 6'3", 215 lbs. b: Thunder Bay, Ont., 7/4/1971. Anaheim's 1st, 2nd overall, in 1994 Supplemental Draft.

Season	Club	League	GP	G	A	Pts	AG	AA	APts	PIM	PP	SH	GW	S	%	TGF	PGF	TGA	PGA	+/–	GP	G	A	Pts	PIM	PP	SH	GW
1989-90	Frederick Banting High School	Hi-School	STATISTICS NOT AVAILABLE																									
	Thamesford Trojans	OJHL-D	2	1	2	3	....	....	....	0	....	....	....	....	....	....	....	....	....	....	....	....	....	....	....	....	....	....
1990-91	University of Western Ontario	OUAA	34	13	16	29	....	....	....	14	....	....	....	....	....	....	....	....	....	....	....	....	....	....	....	....	....	....

			REGULAR SEASON																		PLAYOFFS							
Season	Club	League	GP	G	A	Pts	AG	AA	APts	PIM	PP	SH	GW	S	%	TGF	PGF	TGA	PGA	+/–	GP	G	A	Pts	PIM	PP	SH	GW
1991-92	University of Western Ontario...	OUAA	37	28	34	62				36																		
1992-93	University of Western Ontario...	OUAA	34	22	26	48				16																		
1993-94	University of Western Ontario...	OUAA	35	30	23	53				30																		
1994-95	San Diego Gulls	IHL	41	11	15	26				14																		
	Mighty Ducks of Anaheim...	**NHL**	**43**	**6**	**11**	**17**	**11**	**16**	**27**	**23**	**0**	**0**	**1**	**59**	**10.2**	**24**	**0**	**27**	**10**	**7**								
1995-96	**Mighty Ducks of Anaheim...**	**NHL**	**64**	**19**	**25**	**44**	**19**	**20**	**39**	**12**	**8**	**1**	**4**	**113**	**16.8**	**65**	**30**	**53**	**21**	**3**								
1996-97	**Mighty Ducks of Anaheim...**	**NHL**	**79**	**19**	**48**	**67**	**20**	**43**	**63**	**24**	**6**	**1**	**2**	**153**	**12.4**	**105**	**32**	**63**	**16**	**26**	**8**	**1**	**2**	**3**	**10**	**0**	**0**	**0**
1997-98	**Mighty Ducks of Anaheim...**	**NHL**	**72**	**17**	**36**	**53**	**20**	**35**	**55**	**13**	**8**	**1**	**3**	**131**	**13.0**	**82**	**24**	**72**	**22**	**8**								
	Canada	WC-A	6	1	2	3				2																		
1998-99	**Mighty Ducks of Anaheim...**	**NHL**	**69**	**23**	**39**	**62**	**27**	**38**	**65**	**22**	**5**	**1**	**5**	**145**	**15.9**	**105**	**48**	**66**	**20**	**11**	**4**	**0**	**3**	**3**	**0**	**0**	**0**	**0**
99-2000	**Mighty Ducks of Anaheim...**	**NHL**	**71**	**19**	**38**	**57**	**21**	**35**	**56**	**16**	**10**	**0**	**2**	**131**	**14.5**	**98**	**37**	**71**	**19**	**9**								
	NHL Totals		**398**	**103**	**197**	**300**	**118**	**187**	**305**	**110**	**37**	**4**	**17**	**732**	**14.1**	**479**	**171**	**352**	**108**		**12**	**1**	**5**	**6**	**10**	**0**	**0**	**0**

• RUCINSKI, Mike

Michael J. D – L. 5'11", 179 lbs. b: Trenton, MI, 3/30/1975. Hartford's 8th, 217th overall, in 1995.

Season	Club	League	GP	G	A	Pts	AG	AA	APts	PIM	PP	SH	GW	S	%	TGF	PGF	TGA	PGA	+/–	GP	G	A	Pts	PIM	PP	SH	GW
1991-92	Detroit Little Caesars	MNHL	29	4	15	19				38																		
1992-93	Detroit Jr. Red Wings	OHL	66	6	13	19				59											15	0	4	4	12			
1993-94	Detroit Jr. Red Wings	OHL	66	2	26	28				58											17	0	7	7	15			
1994-95	Detroit Jr. Red Wings	OHL	64	9	18	27				61											21	3	3	6	8			
	Detroit Jr. Red Wings	Mem-Cup	5	1	0	1				2																		
1995-96	Detroit Whalers	OHL	51	10	26	36				65											11	2	4	6	14			
1996-97	Richmond Renegades	ECHL	61	20	23	43				85											8	2	6	8	18			
	Springfield Falcons	AHL	6	0	1	1				0																		
1997-98	**Carolina Hurricanes**	**NHL**	**9**	**0**	**1**	**1**	**0**	**1**	**1**	**2**	**0**	**0**	**0**	**3**	**0.0**	**3**	**0**	**3**	**0**	**0**								
	Beast of New Haven	AHL	65	5	17	22				50											1	0	0	0	0			
	Cleveland Lumberjacks	IHL	2	0	0	0				4																		
1998-99	**Carolina Hurricanes**	**NHL**	**15**	**0**	**1**	**1**	**0**	**1**	**1**	**8**	**0**	**0**	**0**	**8**	**0.0**	**4**	**0**	**4**	**1**	**1**								
	Beast of New Haven	AHL	23	2	6	8				27																		
	Florida Everblades	ECHL	16	2	5	7				13																		
	Charlotte Checkers	ECHL	16	6	10	16				4																		
	United States	WC-Q	3	1	1	2				14																		
99-2000	Cincinnati Cyclones	IHL	66	3	10	13				34											11	0	0	0	28			
	NHL Totals		**24**	**0**	**2**	**2**	**0**	**2**	**2**	**10**	**0**	**0**	**0**	**11**	**0.0**	**7**	**0**	**7**	**1**									

Rights transferred to **Carolina** after **Hartford** franchise relocated, June 25, 1997.

• RUCINSKI, Mike

C – L. 5'11", 190 lbs. b: Wheeling, IL, 12/12/1963.

Season	Club	League	GP	G	A	Pts	AG	AA	APts	PIM	PP	SH	GW	S	%	TGF	PGF	TGA	PGA	+/–	GP	G	A	Pts	PIM	PP	SH	GW
1982-83	Chicago Jets	NAJHL	50	*103	88	*191																						
1983-84	University of Illinois-Chicago	CCHA	33	17	26	43				12																		
1984-85	University of Illinois-Chicago	CCHA	40	29	32	61				28																		
1985-86	University of Illinois-Chicago	CCHA	37	16	31	47				18																		
1986-87	Moncton Golden Flames	AHL	42	5	9	14				14																		
	Salt Lake Golden Eagles	IHL	29	16	25	41				19											17	9	*18	*27	28			
1987-88	Saginaw Hawks	IHL	44	19	31	50				32											10	1	9	10	10			
	Chicago Blackhawks	**NHL**																			**2**	**0**	**0**	**0**	**0**	**0**	**0**	**0**
1988-89	**Chicago Blackhawks**	**NHL**	**1**	**0**	**0**	**0**	**0**	**0**	**0**	**0**	**0**	**0**	**0**	**0**	**0.0**	**0**	**0**	**0**	**0**	**0**								
	Saginaw Hawks	IHL	81	35	72	107				40											6	2	4	6	14			
1989-90	Indianapolis Ice	IHL	80	28	41	69				27											13	3	8	11	8			
	NHL Totals		**1**	**0**	**0**	**0**	**0**	**0**	**0**	**0**	**0**	**0**	**0**	**0**	**0.0**	**0**	**0**	**0**	**0**	**0**	**2**	**0**	**0**	**0**	**0**	**0**	**0**	**0**

Signed as a free agent by **Calgary**, August 10, 1986. Signed as a free agent by **Chicago**, July 8, 1987.

• RUCINSKY, Martin

LW – L. 6'1", 205 lbs. b: Most, Czech., 3/11/1971. Edmonton's 2nd, 20th overall, in 1991.

Season	Club	League	GP	G	A	Pts	AG	AA	APts	PIM	PP	SH	GW	S	%	TGF	PGF	TGA	PGA	+/–	GP	G	A	Pts	PIM	PP	SH	GW
1988-89	CHZ Litvinov	Czech.	3	1	0	1				2																		
1989-90	CHZ Litvinov	Czech.	39	12	6	18															8	5	3	8				
1990-91	CHZ Litvinov	Czech.	56	24	20	44				69																		
	Czechoslovakia	WJC-A	7	9	5	14				2																		
1991-92	Czechoslovakia	Can-Cup	4	0	2	2				4																		
	Edmonton Oilers	**NHL**	**2**	**0**	**0**	**0**	**0**	**0**	**0**	**0**	**0**	**0**	**0**	**1**	**0.0**	**0**	**0**	**3**	**0**	**–3**								
	Cape Breton Oilers	AHL	35	11	12	23				34																		
	Quebec Nordiques	**NHL**	**4**	**1**	**1**	**2**	**1**	**1**	**2**	**2**	**0**	**0**	**0**	**4**	**25.0**	**3**	**0**	**2**	**0**	**1**								
	Halifax Citadels	AHL	7	1	1	2				6																		
1992-93	**Quebec Nordiques**	**NHL**	**77**	**18**	**30**	**48**	**15**	**21**	**36**	**51**	**4**	**0**	**1**	**133**	**13.5**	**74**	**21**	**41**	**4**	**16**	**6**	**1**	**1**	**2**	**4**	**1**	**0**	**0**
1993-94	**Quebec Nordiques**	**NHL**	**60**	**9**	**23**	**32**	**8**	**18**	**26**	**58**	**4**	**0**	**1**	**96**	**9.4**	**49**	**17**	**30**	**2**	**4**								
	Czech-Republic	WC-A	6	2	2	4				8																		
1994-95	HC Chemopetrol Litvinov	Czech-Rep	13	12	10	22				54																		
	Quebec Nordiques	**NHL**	**20**	**3**	**6**	**9**	**5**	**9**	**14**	**14**	**0**	**0**	**0**	**32**	**9.4**	**12**	**0**	**9**	**2**	**5**								
1995-96	HC Petra Vsetin	Czech-Rep	1	1	1	2				0																		
	Colorado Avalanche	**NHL**	**22**	**4**	**11**	**15**	**4**	**9**	**13**	**14**	**0**	**0**	**1**	**39**	**10.3**	**21**	**3**	**10**	**2**	**10**								
	Montreal Canadiens	**NHL**	**56**	**25**	**35**	**60**	**25**	**29**	**54**	**54**	**9**	**2**	**3**	**142**	**17.6**	**81**	**28**	**64**	**19**	**8**								
1996-97	Czech-Republic	W-Cup	3	0	0	0				2																		
	Montreal Canadiens	**NHL**	**70**	**28**	**27**	**55**	**30**	**24**	**54**	**62**	**6**	**3**	**3**	**172**	**16.3**	**74**	**22**	**69**	**18**	**1**	**5**	**0**	**0**	**0**	**4**	**0**	**0**	**0**
1997-98	**Montreal Canadiens**	**NHL**	**78**	**21**	**32**	**53**	**25**	**31**	**56**	**84**	**5**	**3**	**3**	**192**	**10.9**	**76**	**22**	**50**	**9**	**13**	**10**	**3**	**0**	**3**	**4**	**1**	**0**	**0**
	Czech-Republic	Olympics	6	3	1	4				4																		
1998-99	HC Chemopetrol Litvinov	Czech-Rep	3	2	2	4				0																		
	Montreal Canadiens	**NHL**	**73**	**17**	**17**	**34**	**20**	**16**	**36**	**50**	**5**	**0**	**1**	**180**	**9.4**	**48**	**19**	**64**	**10**	**–25**								
	Czech-Republic	WC-A	12	4	6	10				16																		
99-2000	**Montreal Canadiens**	**NHL**	**80**	**25**	**24**	**49**	**28**	**22**	**50**	**70**	**7**	**1**	**4**	**242**	**10.3**	**78**	**33**	**55**	**11**	**1**								
	NHL Totals		**542**	**151**	**206**	**357**	**161**	**180**	**341**	**459**	**40**	**9**	**17**	**1233**	**12.2**	**516**	**165**	**397**	**77**		**21**	**4**	**1**	**5**	**12**	**2**	**0**	**0**

WJC-A All-Star Team (1991) • WC-A All-Star Team (1999) • Played in NHL All-Star Game (2000)

Traded to **Quebec** by **Edmonton** for Ron Tugnutt and Brad Zavisha, March 10, 1992. Transferred to **Colorado** after **Quebec** franchise relocated, June 21, 1995. Traded to **Montreal** by **Colorado** with Andrei Kovalenko and Jocelyn Thibault for Patrick Roy and Mike Keane, December 6, 1995.

• RUFF, Jason

Jason C. LW – L. 6'2", 192 lbs. b: Kelowna, B.C., 1/27/1970. St. Louis' 3rd, 96th overall, in 1990.

Season	Club	League	GP	G	A	Pts	AG	AA	APts	PIM	PP	SH	GW	S	%	TGF	PGF	TGA	PGA	+/–	GP	G	A	Pts	PIM	PP	SH	GW
1986-87	Kelowna Packers	BCJHL	45	16	14	30				48																		
1987-88	Lethbridge Hurricanes	WHL	69	25	22	47				109																		
1988-89	Lethbridge Hurricanes	WHL	69	42	38	80				127											7	2	3	5	28			
1989-90	Lethbridge Hurricanes	WHL	72	55	64	119				114											19	9	10	19	18			
1990-91	Lethbridge Hurricanes	WHL	66	61	75	136				154											16	12	17	29	18			
	Peoria Rivermen	IHL																			5	0	0	0	2			
1991-92	Peoria Rivermen	IHL	67	27	45	72				148											10	7	7	14	19			
1992-93	**St. Louis Blues**	**NHL**	**7**	**2**	**1**	**3**	**2**	**1**	**3**	**8**	**1**	**0**	**1**	**7**	**28.6**	**6**	**3**	**4**	**0**	**–1**								
	Peoria Rivermen	IHL	40	22	21	43				81																		
	Tampa Bay Lightning	**NHL**	**1**	**0**	**0**	**0**	**0**	**0**	**0**	**0**	**0**	**0**	**0**	**1**	**0.0**	**0**	**0**	**0**	**0**	**0**								
	Atlanta Knights	IHL	26	11	14	25				90											7	2	1	3	26			
1993-94	**Tampa Bay Lightning**	**NHL**	**6**	**1**	**2**	**3**	**1**	**2**	**3**	**2**	**0**	**0**	**0**	**14**	**7.1**	**4**	**0**	**2**	**0**	**2**								
	Atlanta Knights	IHL	71	24	25	49				122											14	6	*17	23	41			
1994-95	Atlanta Knights	IHL	64	42	34	76				161											3	3	1	4	10			
1995-96	Atlanta Knights	IHL	59	39	33	72				135											2	0	0	0	16			
1996-97	Quebec Rafales	IHL	80	35	50	85				93											9	8	5	13	10			
1997-98	Quebec Rafales	IHL	54	21	24	45				77																		
	Cleveland Lumberjacks	IHL	6	2	3	5				9											10	6	6	12	4			

Season	Club	League	GP	G	A	Pts	AG	AA	APts	PIM	PP	SH	GW	S	%	TGF	PGF	TGA	PGA	+/-	GP	G	A	Pts	PIM	PP	SH	GW
			REGULAR SEASON																		PLAYOFFS							
1998-99	Cleveland Lumberjacks	IHL	44	13	27	40	....	....	....	57	....	....	....	....	....	....	....	....	....	....	....	....	....	....	....	....	....	....
	Houston Aeros	IHL	1	0	0	0	....	....	....	0	....	....	....	....	....	....	....	....	....	....	19	5	5	10	12	....	....	....
99-2000	Frankfurt Lions	Germany	47	19	24	43	....	....	....	71	....	....	....	....	....	....	....	....	....	....	4	1	0	1	2	....	....	....
	NHL Totals		**14**	**3**	**3**	**6**	**3**	**3**	**6**	**10**	**1**	**0**	**1**	**22**	**13.6**	**10**	**3**	**6**	**0**		....	....	....	....	....	....	....	....

WHL East First All-Star Team (1991)

Traded to **Tampa Bay** by **St. Louis** for Doug Crossman, Basil McRae and Tampa Bay's 4th round choice (Andrei Petrakov) in 1996 Entry Draft, January 28, 1993. • Played w/ RHI's Anaheim Bullfrogs in 1993 (2-0-2-2-8).

• RUFF, Lindy

Lindy Cameron D/LW – L. 6'2", 201 lbs. b: Warburg, Alta., 2/17/1960. Buffalo's 2nd, 32nd overall, in 1979.

Season	Club	League	GP	G	A	Pts	AG	AA	APts	PIM	PP	SH	GW	S	%	TGF	PGF	TGA	PGA	+/-	GP	G	A	Pts	PIM	PP	SH	GW
1976-77	Taber Golden Suns	AJHL	60	13	33	46	....	....	....	112	....	....	....	....	....	....	....	....	....	....	....	....	....	....	....	....	....	....
	Lethbridge Broncos	WCJHL	2	0	2	2	....	....	....	0	....	....	....	....	....	....	....	....	....	....	....	....	....	....	....	....	....	....
1977-78	Lethbridge Broncos	WCJHL	66	9	24	33	....	....	....	219	....	....	....	....	....	....	....	....	....	....	8	2	8	10	4	....	....	....
1978-79	Lethbridge Broncos	WHL	24	9	18	27	....	....	....	108	....	....	....	....	....	....	....	....	....	....	6	0	1	1	0	....	....	....
1979-80	**Buffalo Sabres**	**NHL**	**63**	**5**	**14**	**19**	**4**	**10**	**14**	**38**	**1**	**0**	**0**	**77**	**6.5**	**56**	**18**	**40**	**0**	**-2**	**8**	**1**	**1**	**2**	**19**	**0**	**0**	**0**
1980-81	**Buffalo Sabres**	**NHL**	**65**	**8**	**18**	**26**	**6**	**12**	**18**	**121**	**1**	**0**	**2**	**97**	**8.2**	**70**	**14**	**54**	**1**	**3**	**6**	**3**	**1**	**4**	**23**	**1**	**0**	**1**
1981-82	**Buffalo Sabres**	**NHL**	**79**	**16**	**32**	**48**	**13**	**21**	**34**	**194**	**3**	**0**	**6**	**183**	**8.7**	**101**	**25**	**87**	**12**	**1**	**4**	**0**	**0**	**0**	**28**	**0**	**0**	**0**
1982-83	**Buffalo Sabres**	**NHL**	**60**	**12**	**17**	**29**	**10**	**12**	**22**	**130**	**2**	**0**	**1**	**110**	**10.9**	**60**	**9**	**43**	**7**	**15**	**10**	**4**	**2**	**6**	**47**	**0**	**0**	**0**
1983-84	**Buffalo Sabres**	**NHL**	**58**	**14**	**31**	**45**	**11**	**21**	**32**	**101**	**3**	**0**	**4**	**126**	**11.1**	**72**	**14**	**50**	**7**	**15**	**3**	**1**	**0**	**1**	**9**	**0**	**0**	**0**
1984-85	**Buffalo Sabres**	**NHL**	**39**	**13**	**11**	**24**	**11**	**7**	**18**	**45**	**2**	**0**	**2**	**71**	**18.3**	**36**	**6**	**33**	**2**	**-1**	**5**	**2**	**4**	**6**	**15**	**1**	**0**	**0**
1985-86	**Buffalo Sabres**	**NHL**	**54**	**20**	**12**	**32**	**16**	**8**	**24**	**158**	**5**	**1**	**4**	**131**	**15.3**	**58**	**13**	**44**	**7**	**8**	....	....	....	....	....	....	....	....
1986-87	**Buffalo Sabres**	**NHL**	**50**	**6**	**14**	**20**	**5**	**10**	**15**	**74**	**0**	**1**	**1**	**95**	**6.3**	**43**	**7**	**67**	**19**	**-12**	....	....	....	....	....	....	....	....
1987-88	**Buffalo Sabres**	**NHL**	**77**	**2**	**23**	**25**	**2**	**16**	**18**	**179**	**0**	**0**	**0**	**106**	**1.9**	**47**	**5**	**86**	**35**	**-9**	**6**	**0**	**2**	**2**	**23**	**0**	**0**	**0**
1988-89	**Buffalo Sabres**	**NHL**	**63**	**6**	**11**	**17**	**5**	**8**	**13**	**86**	**0**	**0**	**0**	**69**	**8.7**	**41**	**3**	**78**	**23**	**-17**	....	....	....	....	....	....	....	....
	New York Rangers	**NHL**	**13**	**0**	**5**	**5**	**0**	**4**	**4**	**31**	**0**	**0**	**0**	**19**	**0.0**	**13**	**4**	**19**	**4**	**-6**	**2**	**0**	**0**	**0**	**17**	**0**	**0**	**0**
1989-90	**New York Rangers**	**NHL**	**56**	**3**	**6**	**9**	**3**	**4**	**7**	**80**	**0**	**0**	**2**	**59**	**5.1**	**24**	**3**	**38**	**7**	**-10**	**8**	**0**	**3**	**3**	**12**	**0**	**0**	**0**
1990-91	**New York Rangers**	**NHL**	**14**	**0**	**1**	**1**	**0**	**1**	**1**	**27**	**0**	**0**	**0**	**10**	**0.0**	**2**	**0**	**4**	**0**	**-2**	....	....	....	....	....	....	....	....
1991-92	Rochester Americans	AHL	62	10	24	34	....	....	....	110	....	....	....	....	....	....	....	....	....	....	13	0	4	4	18	....	....	....
1992-93	San Diego Gulls	IHL	81	10	32	42	....	....	....	100	....	....	....	....	....	....	....	....	....	....	14	1	6	7	26	....	....	....
1993-1997	**Florida Panthers**	**NHL**	DID NOT PLAY – ASSISTANT COACH																									
1997-2000	**Buffalo Sabres**	**NHL**	DID NOT PLAY – COACHING																									
	NHL Totals		**691**	**105**	**195**	**300**	**86**	**134**	**220**	**1264**	**17**	**2**	**22**	**1153**	**9.1**	**623**	**121**	**643**	**124**		**52**	**11**	**13**	**24**	**193**	**2**	**0**	**1**

Traded to **NY Rangers** by **Buffalo** for NY Rangers' 5th round choice (Richard Smehlik) in 1990 Entry Draft, March 7, 1989. Signed as a free agent by **San Diego** (IHL), August 24, 1992.

• RUHNKE, Kent

RW – R. 6'1", 190 lbs. b: Toronto, Ont., 9/18/1952.

Season	Club	League	GP	G	A	Pts	AG	AA	APts	PIM	PP	SH	GW	S	%	TGF	PGF	TGA	PGA	+/-	GP	G	A	Pts	PIM	PP	SH	GW
1971-72	University of Toronto	OUAA	20	9	6	15	....	....	....	10	....	....	....	....	....	....	....	....	....	....	....	....	....	....	....	....	....	....
1972-73	University of Toronto	OUAA	20	22	13	35	....	....	....	6	....	....	....	....	....	....	....	....	....	....	....	....	....	....	....	....	....	....
1973-74	University of Toronto	OUAA	20	27	13	40	....	....	....	8	....	....	....	....	....	....	....	....	....	....	....	....	....	....	....	....	....	....
	Barrie Flyers	OHA-Sr.	1	1	0	1	....	....	....	0	....	....	....	....	....	....	....	....	....	....	....	....	....	....	....	....	....	....
1974-75	University of Toronto	OUAA	20	10	5	15	....	....	....	10	....	....	....	....	....	....	....	....	....	....	....	....	....	....	....	....	....	....
1975-76	University of Toronto	OUAA	20	29	15	44	....	....	....	6	....	....	....	....	....	....	....	....	....	....	....	....	....	....	....	....	....	....
	Boston Bruins	**NHL**	**2**	**0**	**1**	**1**	**0**	**1**	**1**	**0**	**0**	**0**	**0**	**2**	**0.0**	**1**	**0**	**0**	**0**	**1**	....	....	....	....	....	....	....	....
1976-77	Winnipeg Jets	WHA	51	11	11	22	....	....	....	2	....	....	....	....	....	....	....	....	....	....	....	....	....	....	....	....	....	....
1977-78	Winnipeg Jets	WHA	21	8	9	17	....	....	....	2	....	....	....	....	....	....	....	....	....	....	5	2	0	2	0	....	....	....
	Binghamto Dusters	AHL	47	14	20	34	....	....	....	2	....	....	....	....	....	....	....	....	....	....	....	....	....	....	....	....	....	....
1978-79	SC Riessersee	Germany	49	42	37	79	....	....	....	4	....	....	....	....	....	....	....	....	....	....	....	....	....	....	....	....	....	....
1979-80			STATISTICS NOT AVAILABLE																									
1980-1981	ZSC Zurich	Switz.	PLAYER/COACH – STATISTICS UNAVAILABLE																									
1981-1982	ZSC Zurich	Switz.	DID NOT PLAY – COACHING																									
	EHC Biel-Bienne	Switz.	DID NOT PLAY – COACHING																									
1982-1984	EHC Biel-Bienne	Switz.	DID NOT PLAY – COACHING																									
1983-1985	Dalhousie University	AUAA	DID NOT PLAY – COACHING																									
1985-1987	HC Fribourg-Gotteron	Switz.	DID NOT PLAY – COACHING																									
1987-1988	EHC Olten	Switz.	DID NOT PLAY – COACHING																									
1988-1989	EHC Olten	Switz.	DID NOT PLAY – COACHING																									
	EHC Olten	Switz.	2	1	1	2	....	....	....	....	....	....	....	....	....	....	....	....	....	....								
1989-1990	EHC Olten	Switz.	DID NOT PLAY – COACHING																									
	EHC Olten	Switz.	2	0	1	1	....	....	....	0																		
1990-1991	EV Zug	Switz.	DID NOT PLAY – COACHING																									
1991-1992			STATISTICS NOT AVAILABLE																									
1992-1994	EHC Olten	Switz.	DID NOT PLAY – COACHING																									
	NHL Totals		**2**	**0**	**1**	**1**	**0**	**1**	**1**	**0**	**0**	**0**	**0**	**2**	**0.0**	**1**	**0**	**0**	**0**		....	....	....	....	....	....	....	....
	Other Major League Totals		72	19	20	39	....	....	....	4	....	....	....	....	....	....	....	....	....	....	5	2	0	2	0	....	....	....

Signed to five-game try-out contract by **Boston**, March, 1976. Signed as a free agent by **Winnipeg** (WHA), July, 1976. • Played as an emergency injury replacement while coaching **EHC Olten** (Switz.) in 1988-89 and 1990-91.

• RUMBLE, Darren

Darren W. D – L. 6'1", 200 lbs. b: Barrie, Ont., 1/23/1969. Philadelphia's 1st, 20th overall, in 1987.

Season	Club	League	GP	G	A	Pts	AG	AA	APts	PIM	PP	SH	GW	S	%	TGF	PGF	TGA	PGA	+/-	GP	G	A	Pts	PIM	PP	SH	GW
1985-86	Barrie Colts	OJHL-B	46	14	32	46	....	....	....	91	....	....	....	....	....	....	....	....	....	....	....	....	....	....	....	....	....	....
1986-87	Kitchener Rangers	OHL	64	11	32	43	....	....	....	44	....	....	....	....	....	....	....	....	....	....	4	0	1	1	9	....	....	....
1987-88	Kitchener Rangers	OHL	55	15	50	65	....	....	....	64	....	....	....	....	....	....	....	....	....	....	....	....	....	....	....	....	....	....
1988-89	Kitchener Rangers	OHL	46	11	28	39	....	....	....	25	....	....	....	....	....	....	....	....	....	....	5	1	0	1	2	....	....	....
1989-90	Hershey Bears	AHL	57	2	13	15	....	....	....	31	....	....	....	....	....	....	....	....	....	....	....	....	....	....	....	....	....	....
1990-91	**Philadelphia Flyers**	**NHL**	**3**	**1**	**0**	**1**	**1**	**0**	**1**	**0**	**0**	**0**	**0**	**2**	**50.0**	**2**	**0**	**1**	**0**	**1**	....	....	....	....	....	....	....	....
	Hershey Bears	AHL	73	6	35	41	....	....	....	48	....	....	....	....	....	....	....	....	....	....	3	0	5	5	2	....	....	....
1991-92	Hershey Bears	AHL	79	12	54	66	....	....	....	118	....	....	....	....	....	....	....	....	....	....	6	0	3	3	2	....	....	....
1992-93	**Ottawa Senators**	**NHL**	**69**	**3**	**13**	**16**	**2**	**9**	**11**	**61**	**0**	**0**	**0**	**92**	**3.3**	**38**	**4**	**75**	**17**	**-24**	....	....	....	....	....	....	....	....
	New Haven Senators	AHL	2	1	0	1	....	....	....	0	....	....	....	....	....	....	....	....	....	....	....	....	....	....	....	....	....	....
1993-94	**Ottawa Senators**	**NHL**	**70**	**6**	**9**	**15**	**6**	**7**	**13**	**116**	**0**	**0**	**0**	**95**	**6.3**	**40**	**3**	**125**	**38**	**-50**	....	....	....	....	....	....	....	....
	P.E.I. Senators	AHL	3	2	0	2	....	....	....	0	....	....	....	....	....	....	....	....	....	....	....	....	....	....	....	....	....	....
1994-95	P.E.I. Senators	AHL	70	7	46	53	....	....	....	77	....	....	....	....	....	....	....	....	....	....	11	0	6	6	4	....	....	....
1995-96	**Philadelphia Flyers**	**NHL**	**5**	**0**	**0**	**0**	**0**	**0**	**0**	**4**	**0**	**0**	**0**	**7**	**0.0**	**3**	**0**	**3**	**0**	**0**	....	....	....	....	....	....	....	....
	Hershey Bears	AHL	58	13	37	50	....	....	....	83	....	....	....	....	....	....	....	....	....	....	5	0	0	0	6	....	....	....
1996-97	**Philadelphia Flyers**	**NHL**	**10**	**0**	**0**	**0**	**0**	**0**	**0**	**0**	**0**	**0**	**0**	**9**	**0.0**	**6**	**1**	**7**	**0**	**-2**	....	....	....	....	....	....	....	....
	Philadelphia Phantoms	AHL	72	18	44	62	....	....	....	83	....	....	....	....	....	....	....	....	....	....	7	0	3	3	19	....	....	....
1997-98	Adler Mannheim	Germany	21	2	7	9	....	....	....	18	....	....	....	....	....	....	....	....	....	....	....	....	....	....	....	....	....	....
	Adler Mannheim	EuroHL	4	0	1	1	....	....	....	4	....	....	....	....	....	....	....	....	....	....	....	....	....	....	....	....	....	....
	San Antonio Dragons	IHL	46	7	22	29	....	....	....	47	....	....	....	....	....	....	....	....	....	....	....	....	....	....	....	....	....	....
1998-99	Utah Grizzlies	IHL	10	1	4	5	....	....	....	10	....	....	....	....	....	....	....	....	....	....	....	....	....	....	....	....	....	....
	Grand Rapids Griffins	IHL	53	6	22	28	....	....	....	44	....	....	....	....	....	....	....	....	....	....	....	....	....	....	....	....	....	....
99-2000	Grand Rapids Griffins	IHL	29	3	10	13	....	....	....	20	....	....	....	....	....	....	....	....	....	....	....	....	....	....	....	....	....	....
	Worcester IceCats	AHL	39	0	17	17	....	....	....	31	....	....	....	....	....	....	....	....	....	....	9	0	2	2	6	....	....	....
	NHL Totals		**157**	**10**	**22**	**32**	**9**	**16**	**25**	**181**	**0**	**0**	**0**	**205**	**4.9**	**89**	**8**	**211**	**55**		....	....	....	....	....	....	....	....

AHL Second All-Star Team (1995) • AHL First All-Star Team (1997) • Won Eddie Shore Award (Outstanding Defenseman — AHL) (1997)

Claimed by **Ottawa** from **Philadelphia** in Expansion Draft, June 18, 1992. Signed as a free agent by **Philadelphia**, July 31, 1995.

• RUNDQVIST, Thomas

Per Thomas C – L. 6'3", 195 lbs. b: Vimmerby, Sweden, 5/4/1960. Montreal's 12th, 206th overall, in 1983.

			REGULAR SEASON																			PLAYOFFS							
Season	Club	League	GP	G	A	Pts	AG	AA	APts	PIM	PP	SH	GW	S	%	TGF	PGF	TGA	PGA	+/–	GP	G	A	Pts	PIM	PP	SH	GW
1975-76	Vimmerby IF	Sweden-3	14	6	0	6	....	....	....	....	....	....	....	....	....	....	....	....	....	....	....	....	....	....	....	....	....	....
1976-77	Vimmerby IF	Sweden-3	22	29	13	42	....	....	....	....	....	....	....	....	....	....	....	....	....	....	....	....	....	....	....	....	....	....
1977-78	Vimmerby IF	Sweden-3	DID NOT PLAY – INJURED																									
	Sweden	EJC-A	5	3	2	5	....	....	....	2	....	....	....	....	....	....	....	....	....	....	....	....	....	....	....	....	....	....
1978-79	Farjestads BK Karlstad	Sweden	15	2	5	7	....	....	....	8	....	....	....	....	....	....	....	....	....	....	....	0	1	1	2	....	....	....
1979-80	Farjestads BK Karlstad	Sweden	36	9	6	15	....	....	....	28	....	....	....	....	....	....	....	....	....	....	....	....	....	....	....	....	....	....
	Sweden	WJC-A	5	1	2	3	....	....	....	6	....	....	....	....	....	....	....	....	....	....	....	....	....	....	....	....	....	....
1980-81	Farjestads BK Karlstad	Sweden	36	15	19	34	....	....	....	22	....	....	....	....	....	....	....	....	....	....	7	1	2	3	0	....	....	....
1981-82	Farjestads BK Karlstad	Sweden	36	14	13	27	....	....	....	30	....	....	....	....	....	....	....	....	....	....	2	0	1	1	2	....	....	....
	Sweden	WEC-A	9	1	2	3	....	....	....	2	....	....	....	....	....	....	....	....	....	....	....	....	....	....	....	....	....	....
1982-83	Farjestads BK Karlstad	Sweden	36	22	21	43	....	....	....	28	....	....	....	....	....	....	....	....	....	....	8	3	*8	11	6	....	....	....
	Sweden	WEC-A	10	1	3	4	....	....	....	2	....	....	....	....	....	....	....	....	....	....	....	....	....	....	....	....	....	....
1983-84	Farjestads BK Karlstad	Sweden	36	13	22	35	....	....	....	38	....	....	....	....	....	....	....	....	....	....	....	....	....	....	....	....	....	....
1984-85	**Montreal Canadiens**	**NHL**	**2**	**0**	**1**	**1**	**0**	**1**	**1**	**0**	**0**	**0**	**0**	**1**	**0.0**	**1**	**0**	**0**	**0**	**1**	....	....	....	....	....	....	....	....
	Sherbrooke Canadiens	AHL	73	19	39	58	....	....	....	16	....	....	....	....	....	....	....	....	....	....	17	*5	14	19	4	....	....	....
1985-86	Farjestads BK Karlstad	Sweden	32	9	17	26	....	....	....	27	....	....	....	....	....	....	....	....	....	....	8	2	4	6	2	....	....	....
	Sweden	WEC-A	10	2	3	5	....	....	....	8	....	....	....	....	....	....	....	....	....	....	....	....	....	....	....	....	....	....
1986-87	Farjestads BK Karlstad	Sweden	35	13	22	35	....	....	....	38	....	....	....	....	....	....	....	....	....	....	7	2	5	7	2	....	....	....
	Sweden	WEC-A	10	1	2	3	....	....	....	4	....	....	....	....	....	....	....	....	....	....	....	....	....	....	....	....	....	....
1987-88	Sweden	Can-Cup	6	0	2	2	....	....	....	10	....	....	....	....	....	....	....	....	....	....	....	....	....	....	....	....	....	....
	Farjestads BK Karlstad	Sweden	40	15	22	37	....	....	....	40	....	....	....	....	....	....	....	....	....	....	9	3	7	10	6	....	....	....
	Sweden	Olympics	8	0	3	3	....	....	....	0	....	....	....	....	....	....	....	....	....	....	....	....	....	....	....	....	....	....
1988-89	Farjestads BK Karlstad	Sweden	37	15	26	41	....	....	....	44	....	....	....	....	....	....	....	....	....	....	2	2	1	3	2	....	....	....
	Sweden	WEC-A	9	1	2	3	....	....	....	6	....	....	....	....	....	....	....	....	....	....	....	....	....	....	....	....	....	....
1989-90	Farjestads BK Karlstad	Sweden	40	16	29	45	....	....	....	30	....	....	....	....	....	....	....	....	....	....	10	8	4	12	0	....	....	....
	Sweden	WEC-A	10	3	8	11	....	....	....	6	....	....	....	....	....	....	....	....	....	....	....	....	....	....	....	....	....	....
1990-91	Farjestads BK Karlstad	Sweden	39	12	21	33	....	....	....	22	....	....	....	....	....	....	....	....	....	....	8	5	*7	*12	6	....	....	....
	Sweden	WEC-A	10	6	4	10	....	....	....	4	....	....	....	....	....	....	....	....	....	....	....	....	....	....	....	....	....	....
1991-92	Sweden	Can-Cup	6	2	2	4	....	....	....	2	....	....	....	....	....	....	....	....	....	....	....	....	....	....	....	....	....	....
	Farjestads BK Karlstad	Sweden	39	10	28	38	....	....	....	54	....	....	....	....	....	....	....	....	....	....	6	3	2	5	8	....	....	....
	Sweden	Olympics	8	3	4	7	....	....	....	8	....	....	....	....	....	....	....	....	....	....	....	....	....	....	....	....	....	....
1992-93	Farjestads BK Karlstad	Sweden	37	8	17	25	....	....	....	40	....	....	....	....	....	....	....	....	....	....	3	0	0	0	2	....	....	....
	Sweden	WC-A	8	1	4	5	....	....	....	0	....	....	....	....	....	....	....	....	....	....	....	....	....	....	....	....	....	....
1993-94	VEU Feldkirch	Alpenliga	27	9	20	29	....	....	....	10	....	....	....	....	....	....	....	....	....	....	....	....	....	....	....	....	....	....
	VEU Feldkirch	Austria	26	11	18	29	....	....	....	8	....	....	....	....	....	....	....	....	....	....	....	....	....	....	....	....	....	....
1994-95	VEU Feldkirch	Austria	28	9	15	24	....	....	....	32	....	....	....	....	....	....	....	....	....	....	8	2	3	5	6	....	....	....
1995-96	VEU Feldkirch	Alpenliga	5	2	9	11	....	....	....	2	....	....	....	....	....	....	....	....	....	....	....	....	....	....	....	....	....	....
	VEU Feldkirch	Austria	34	13	30	43	....	....	....	33	....	....	....	....	....	....	....	....	....	....	....	....	....	....	....	....	....	....
1996-97	VEU Feldkirch	Alpenliga	41	9	25	34	....	....	....	53	....	....	....	....	....	....	....	....	....	....	....	....	....	....	....	....	....	....
	VEU Feldkirch	Austria	11	2	9	11	....	....	....	8	....	....	....	....	....	....	....	....	....	....	....	....	....	....	....	....	....	....
1997-98	VEU Feldkirch	Alpenliga	21	6	9	15	....	....	....	6	....	....	....	....	....	....	....	....	....	....	....	....	....	....	....	....	....	....
	VEU Feldkirch	EuroHL	10	6	7	13	....	....	....	4	....	....	....	....	....	....	....	....	....	....	....	....	....	....	....	....	....	....
	VEU Feldkirch	Austria	27	2	16	18	....	....	....	8	....	....	....	....	....	....	....	....	....	....	....	....	....	....	....	....	....	....
	NHL Totals		**2**	**0**	**1**	**1**	**0**	**1**	**1**	**0**	**0**	**0**	**0**	**1**	**0.0**	**1**	**0**	**0**	**0**		....	....	....	....	....	....	....	....

Swedish World All-Star Team (1988, 1989, 1990, 1991) • Swedish Player of the Year (1991) • WEC-A All-Star Team (1991)

• RUOTSALAINEN, Reijo

Reijo Juhani "Rex" D – R. 5'8", 170 lbs. b: Oulu, Finland, 4/1/1960. NY Rangers' 5th, 119th overall, in 1980.

Season	Club	League	GP	G	A	Pts	AG	AA	APts	PIM	PP	SH	GW	S	%	TGF	PGF	TGA	PGA	+/–	GP	G	A	Pts	PIM	PP	SH	GW
1975-76	Karpat Oulu	Finland-2	STATISTICS NOT AVAILABLE																									
	Finland	EJC-A	3	1	0	1	....	....	....	0	....	....	....	....	....	....	....	....	....	....	....	....	....	....	....	....	....	....
1976-77	Karpat Oulu	Finland-2	36	23	35	58	....	....	....	14	....	....	....	....	....	....	....	....	....	....	6	2	6	8	0	....	....	....
	Finland	WJC-A	7	2	4	6	....	....	....	6	....	....	....	....	....	....	....	....	....	....	....	....	....	....	....	....	....	....
1977-78	Karpat Oulu	Finland	30	9	14	23	....	....	....	4	....	....	....	....	....	....	....	....	....	....	....	....	....	....	....	....	....	....
	Finland	WJC-A	6	3	3	6	....	....	....	2	....	....	....	....	....	....	....	....	....	....	....	....	....	....	....	....	....	....
	Finland	WEC-A	9	2	0	2	....	....	....	2	....	....	....	....	....	....	....	....	....	....	....	....	....	....	....	....	....	....
1978-79	Karpat Oulu	Finland	36	14	8	22	....	....	....	47	....	....	....	....	....	....	....	....	....	....	....	....	....	....	....	....	....	....
	Finland	WJC-A	6	0	3	3	....	....	....	0	....	....	....	....	....	....	....	....	....	....	....	....	....	....	....	....	....	....
	Finland	WEC-A	6	2	0	2	....	....	....	2	....	....	....	....	....	....	....	....	....	....	....	....	....	....	....	....	....	....
1979-80	Karpat Oulu	Finland	30	15	13	28	....	....	....	31	....	....	....	....	....	....	....	....	....	....	6	5	2	7	0	....	....	....
	Finland	WJC-A	5	4	3	7	....	....	....	2	....	....	....	....	....	....	....	....	....	....	....	....	....	....	....	....	....	....
1980-81	Karpat Oulu	Finland	36	28	23	51	....	....	....	28	....	....	....	....	....	....	....	....	....	....	12	*7	4	11	6	....	....	....
	Finland	WEC-A	8	3	4	7	....	....	....	4	....	....	....	....	....	....	....	....	....	....	....	....	....	....	....	....	....	....
1981-82	Finland	Can-Cup	5	0	1	1	....	....	....	2	....	....	....	....	....	....	....	....	....	....	....	....	....	....	....	....	....	....
	New York Rangers	DN-Cup	4	1	*6	*7	....	....	....	....	....	....	....	....	....	....	....	....	....	....	....	....	....	....	....	....	....	....
	New York Rangers	**NHL**	**78**	**18**	**38**	**56**	**14**	**25**	**39**	**27**	**7**	**0**	**3**	**247**	**7.3**	**128**	**43**	**72**	**5**	**18**	**10**	**4**	**5**	**9**	**2**	**2**	**0**	**1**
1982-83	**New York Rangers**	**NHL**	**77**	**16**	**53**	**69**	**13**	**37**	**50**	**22**	**5**	**0**	**4**	**230**	**7.0**	**141**	**44**	**77**	**7**	**27**	**9**	**4**	**2**	**6**	**6**	**1**	**0**	**1**
1983-84	**New York Rangers**	**NHL**	**74**	**20**	**39**	**59**	**16**	**27**	**43**	**26**	**5**	**0**	**4**	**287**	**7.0**	**130**	**40**	**79**	**6**	**17**	**5**	**1**	**1**	**2**	**2**	**1**	**0**	**1**
1984-85	**New York Rangers**	**NHL**	**80**	**28**	**45**	**73**	**23**	**31**	**54**	**32**	**10**	**0**	**2**	**255**	**11.0**	**123**	**53**	**99**	**2**	**–27**	**3**	**2**	**0**	**2**	**6**	**1**	**0**	**0**
	Finland	WEC-A	10	0	4	4	....	....	....	6	....	....	....	....	....	....	....	....	....	....	....	....	....	....	....	....	....	....
1985-86	**New York Rangers**	**NHL**	**80**	**17**	**42**	**59**	**14**	**28**	**42**	**47**	**6**	**0**	**2**	**228**	**7.5**	**130**	**49**	**62**	**3**	**22**	**16**	**0**	**8**	**8**	**6**	**0**	**0**	**0**
1986-87	SC Bern	Switz.	36	26	28	54	....	....	....	....	....	....	....	....	....	....	....	....	....	....	....	....	....	....	....	....	....	....
	♦ **Edmonton Oilers**	**NHL**	**16**	**5**	**8**	**13**	**4**	**6**	**10**	**6**	**3**	**0**	**1**	**52**	**9.6**	**33**	**10**	**17**	**2**	**8**	**21**	**2**	**5**	**7**	**10**	**1**	**0**	**1**
1987-88	Finland	Can-Cup	4	0	0	0	....	....	....	2	....	....	....	....	....	....	....	....	....	....	....	....	....	....	....	....	....	....
	HV-71 Jonkoping	Sweden	40	10	22	32	....	....	....	26	....	....	....	....	....	....	....	....	....	....	2	0	1	1	2	....	....	....
	Finland	Olympics	8	4	2	6	....	....	....	0	....	....	....	....	....	....	....	....	....	....	....	....	....	....	....	....	....	....
1988-89	SC Bern	Switz.	36	17	30	47	....	....	....	....	....	....	....	....	....	....	....	....	....	....	9	4	8	12	....	....	....	....
	Finland	WEC-A	10	2	4	6	....	....	....	6	....	....	....	....	....	....	....	....	....	....	....	....	....	....	....	....	....	....
1989-90	**New Jersey Devils**	**NHL**	**31**	**2**	**5**	**7**	**2**	**4**	**6**	**14**	**1**	**0**	**0**	**52**	**3.8**	**27**	**10**	**24**	**3**	**–4**	....	....	....	....	....	....	....	....
	♦ **Edmonton Oilers**	**NHL**	**10**	**1**	**7**	**8**	**1**	**5**	**6**	**6**	**0**	**0**	**0**	**28**	**3.6**	**16**	**8**	**11**	**2**	**–1**	**22**	**2**	**11**	**13**	**12**	**1**	**0**	**0**
1990-91	SC Bern	Switz.	36	13	25	38	....	....	....	....	....	....	....	....	....	....	....	....	....	....	10	5	9	14	....	....	....	....
1991-92	SC Bern	Switz.	35	7	16	23	....	....	....	28	....	....	....	....	....	....	....	....	....	....	11	4	4	8	....	....	....	....
1992-93	SC Bern	Switz.	31	7	16	23	....	....	....	38	....	....	....	....	....	....	....	....	....	....	5	1	2	3	8	....	....	....
1993-94	Karpat Oulu	Finland-2	4	1	5	6	....	....	....	6	....	....	....	....	....	....	....	....	....	....	....	....	....	....	....	....	....	....
	Tappara Tampere	Finland	6	2	4	6	....	....	....	2	....	....	....	....	....	....	....	....	....	....	9	1	2	3	6	....	....	....
1994-95	SC Bern	Switz.	19	3	7	10	....	....	....	28	....	....	....	....	....	....	....	....	....	....	6	1	5	6	4	....	....	....
1995-96	ZSC Lions Zurich	Switz.	18	4	11	15	....	....	....	4	....	....	....	....	....	....	....	....	....	....	....	....	....	....	....	....	....	....
	KalPa Kuopio	Finland	16	3	5	8	....	....	....	4	....	....	....	....	....	....	....	....	....	....	....	....	....	....	....	....	....	....
1996-97	Karpat Oulu	Finland-2	17	1	5	6	....	....	....	14	....	....	....	....	....	....	....	....	....	....	3	0	1	1	0	....	....	....
	Karpat Oulu	Finland-Q	6	0	3	3	....	....	....	0	....	....	....	....	....	....	....	....	....	....	....	....	....	....	....	....	....	....
1997-98	Karpat Oulu	Finland-2	44	8	23	31	....	....	....	42	....	....	....	....	....	....	....	....	....	....	5	1	1	2	4	....	....	....
	Karpat Oulu	Finland-Q	9	1	5	6	....	....	....	6	....	....	....	....	....	....	....	....	....	....	....	....	....	....	....	....	....	....
	NHL Totals		**446**	**107**	**237**	**344**	**87**	**163**	**250**	**180**	**37**	**0**	**16**	**1379**	**7.8**	**728**	**257**	**441**	**30**		**86**	**15**	**32**	**47**	**44**	**7**	**0**	**4**

WJC-A All-Star Team (1980) • Named Best Defenseman at WJC-A (1980) • Finnish First All-Star Team (1980, 1981) • Played in NHL All-Star Game (1986)

Traded to **Edmonton** by **NY Rangers** with Clark Donatelli, Ville Kentala and Jim Wiemer for Mike Golden, Don Jackson, Miloslav Horava and future considerations (Stu Kulak, March 10, 1987, October 23, 1986. Claimed by **New Jersey** from **Edmonton** in Waiver Draft, October 5, 1987. Traded to **Edmonton** by **New Jersey** for Jeff Sharples, March 6, 1990.

• RUPP, Duane

Duane Edward Franklin D – L. 6'1", 195 lbs. b: MacNutt, Sask., 3/29/1938.

Season	Club	League	GP	G	A	Pts	AG	AA	APts	PIM	PP	SH	GW	S	%	TGF	PGF	TGA	PGA	+/–	GP	G	A	Pts	PIM	PP	SH	GW
1955-56	Melville Millionaires	SJHL	1	0	1	1	....	....	....	0	....	....	....	....	....	....	....	....	....	....	....	....	....	....	....	....	....	....
1956-57	Flin Flon Bombers	SJHL	55	4	20	24	....	....	....	20	....	....	....	....	....	....	....	....	....	....	10	2	1	3	2	....	....	....
	Flin Flon Bombers	Mem-Cup	17	0	1	1	....	....	....	8	....	....	....	....	....	....	....	....	....	....	....	....	....	....	....	....	....	....

Season	Club	League	GP	G	A	Pts	AG	AA	APts	PIM	PP	SH	GW	S	%	TGF	PGF	TGA	PGA	+/–	GP	G	A	Pts	PIM	PP	SH	GW
			REGULAR SEASON																		PLAYOFFS							
1957-58	Flin Flon Bombers	SJHL	55	9	25	34	....	....	....	27	....	....	....	....	....	....	....	....	....	....	12	0	0	0	4	....	....	....
1958-59	Indianapolis–Fort Wayne	IHL	58	5	11	16	....	....	....	22	....	....	....	....	....	....	....	....	....	....	11	0	1	1	11	....	....	....
1959-60	Fort Wayne Komets	IHL	67	10	44	54	....	....	....	22	....	....	....	....	....	....	....	....	....	....	13	1	6	7	8	....	....	....
1960-61	Kitchener-Waterloo Beavers	EPHL	69	10	14	24	....	....	....	26	....	....	....	....	....	....	....	....	....	....	7	1	1	2	6	....	....	....
1961-62	Springfield Indians	AHL	27	7	9	16	....	....	....	10	....	....	....	....	....	....	....	....	....	....	....	....	....	....	....	....	....	....
	Vancouver Canucks	WHL	35	3	13	16	....	....	....	14	....	....	....	....	....	....	....	....	....	....	....	....	....	....	....	....	....	....
1962-63	**New York Rangers**	**NHL**	**2**	**0**	**0**	**0**	**0**	**0**	**0**	**0**	....	....	....	....	....	....	....	....	....	....	....	....	....	....	....	....	....	....
	Baltimore Clippers	AHL	71	4	17	21	....	....	....	42	....	....	....	....	....	....	....	....	....	....	3	0	2	2	11	....	....	....
1963-64	Baltimore Clippers	AHL	61	2	9	11	....	....	....	65	....	....	....	....	....	....	....	....	....	....	....	....	....	....	....	....	....	....
	Rochester Americans	AHL	15	1	4	5	....	....	....	16	....	....	....	....	....	....	....	....	....	....	2	0	1	1	0	....	....	....
1964-65	**Toronto Maple Leafs**	**NHL**	**2**	**0**	**0**	**0**	**0**	**0**	**0**	**0**	....	....	....	....	....	....	....	....	....	....	....	....	....	....	....	....	....	....
	Rochester Americans	AHL	71	4	30	34	....	....	....	50	....	....	....	....	....	....	....	....	....	....	10	1	7	8	18	....	....	....
1965-66	**Toronto Maple Leafs**	**NHL**	**2**	**0**	**1**	**1**	**0**	**1**	**1**	**0**	....	....	....	....	....	....	....	....	....	....	....	....	....	....	....	....	....	....
	Rochester Americans	AHL	70	7	34	41	....	....	....	86	....	....	....	....	....	....	....	....	....	....	12	0	8	8	30	....	....	....
1966-67	**Toronto Maple Leafs**	**NHL**	**3**	**0**	**0**	**0**	**0**	**0**	**0**	**0**	....	....	....	....	....	....	....	....	....	....	....	....	....	....	....	....	....	....
	Rochester Americans	AHL	59	7	35	42	....	....	....	84	....	....	....	....	....	....	....	....	....	....	13	0	5	5	13	....	....	....
1967-68	**Toronto Maple Leafs**	**NHL**	**71**	**1**	**8**	**9**	**1**	**8**	**9**	**42**	**0**	**0**	**0**	**79**	**1.3**	**69**	**1**	**63**	**11**	**16**	....	....	....	....	....	....	....	....
1968-69	**Minnesota North Stars**	**NHL**	**29**	**2**	**1**	**3**	**2**	**1**	**3**	**8**	**1**	**0**	**0**	**36**	**5.6**	**25**	**4**	**36**	**6**	**–9**	....	....	....	....	....	....	....	....
	Cleveland Barons	AHL	13	3	6	9	....	....	....	38	....	....	....	....	....	....	....	....	....	....	....	....	....	....	....	....	....	....
	Pittsburgh Penguins	**NHL**	**30**	**3**	**10**	**13**	**3**	**9**	**12**	**24**	**0**	**0**	**0**	**69**	**4.3**	**35**	**14**	**41**	**7**	**–13**	....	....	....	....	....	....	....	....
1969-70	**Pittsburgh Penguins**	**NHL**	**64**	**2**	**14**	**16**	**2**	**13**	**15**	**18**	**1**	**0**	**0**	**105**	**1.9**	**63**	**22**	**78**	**26**	**–11**	**6**	**2**	**2**	**4**	**2**	**0**	**0**	**0**
1970-71	**Pittsburgh Penguins**	**NHL**	**59**	**5**	**28**	**33**	**5**	**23**	**28**	**34**	**1**	**0**	**1**	**152**	**3.3**	**83**	**36**	**68**	**11**	**–10**	....	....	....	....	....	....	....	....
1971-72	**Pittsburgh Penguins**	**NHL**	**34**	**4**	**18**	**22**	**4**	**16**	**20**	**32**	**0**	**0**	**0**	**91**	**4.4**	**54**	**6**	**62**	**14**	**0**	**4**	**0**	**0**	**0**	**6**	**0**	**0**	**0**
	Hershey Bears	AHL	38	2	21	23	....	....	....	36	....	....	....	....	....	....	....	....	....	....	....	....	....	....	....	....	....	....
1972-73	**Pittsburgh Penguins**	**NHL**	**78**	**7**	**13**	**20**	**7**	**10**	**17**	**62**	**2**	**1**	**2**	**132**	**5.3**	**102**	**22**	**106**	**23**	**–3**	....	....	....	....	....	....	....	....
1973-74	Hershey Bears	AHL	67	7	27	34	....	....	....	32	....	....	....	....	....	....	....	....	....	....	14	1	5	6	8	....	....	....
1974-75	Vancouver Blazers	WHA	72	3	26	29	....	....	....	45	....	....	....	....	....	....	....	....	....	....	....	....	....	....	....	....	....	....
1975-76	Calgary Cowboys	WHA	42	0	16	16	....	....	....	33	....	....	....	....	....	....	....	....	....	....	7	0	2	2	8	....	....	....
	Rochester Americans	AHL	4	1	6	7	....	....	....	2	....	....	....	....	....	....	....	....	....	....	....	....	....	....	....	....	....	....
1976-77	Rochester Americans	AHL	41	3	8	11	....	....	....	12	....	....	....	....	....	....	....	....	....	....	2	0	0	0	0	....	....	....
	NHL Totals		**374**	**24**	**93**	**117**	**24**	**81**	**105**	**220**	....	....	....	....	....	....	....	....	....		**10**	**2**	**2**	**4**	**8**	....	....	....
	Other Major League Totals		114	3	42	45	....	....	....	78	....	....	....	....	....	....	....	....	....	....	7	0	2	2	8	....	....	....

AHL Second All-Star Team (1966, 1967, 1974) • Played in NHL All-Star Game (1968)

Loaned to **Toronto** (Rochester-AHL) by **NY Rangers** (Baltimore-AHL) for cash, February 23, 1964. Traded to **Toronto** (Rochester-AHL) by **NY Rangers** with Ed Ehrenverth for Lou Angotti and Ed Lawson, June 25, 1964. Claimed by **Minnesota** from **Toronto** in Intra-League Draft, June 12, 1968. Traded to **Pittsburgh** by **Minnesota** for Leo Boivin, January 24, 1969. Signed as a free agent by **Vancouver** (WHA), June, 1974. Transferred to **Calgary** (WHA) after **Vancouver** (WHA) franchise relocated, May, 1975.

• RUSKOWSKI, Terry

Terry Wallace "Roscoe" C – L. 5'10", 178 lbs. b: Prince Albert, Sask., 12/31/1954. Chicago's 4th, 70th overall, in 1974.

Season	Club	League	GP	G	A	Pts	AG	AA	APts	PIM	PP	SH	GW	S	%	TGF	PGF	TGA	PGA	+/–	GP	G	A	Pts	PIM	PP	SH	GW
1971-72	Swift Current Broncos	WCJHL	67	13	38	51	....	....	....	177	....	....	....	....	....	....	....	....	....	....	....	....	....	....	....	....	....	....
1972-73	Swift Current Broncos	WCJHL	53	25	64	89	....	....	....	136	....	....	....	....	....	....	....	....	....	....	....	....	....	....	....	....	....	....
1973-74	Swift Current Broncos	WCJHL	68	40	93	133	....	....	....	243	....	....	....	....	....	....	....	....	....	....	13	5	*23	28	23	....	....	....
1974-75	Houston Aeros	WHA	71	10	36	46	....	....	....	134	....	....	....	....	....	....	....	....	....	....	13	4	2	6	15	....	....	....
1975-76	Houston Aeros	WHA	65	14	35	49	....	....	....	100	....	....	....	....	....	....	....	....	....	....	16	6	10	16	*64	....	....	....
1976-77	Houston Aeros	WHA	80	24	60	84	....	....	....	146	....	....	....	....	....	....	....	....	....	....	11	6	11	17	*67	....	....	....
1977-78	Houston Aeros	WHA	78	15	57	72	....	....	....	170	....	....	....	....	....	....	....	....	....	....	4	1	1	2	5	....	....	....
1978-79	Winnipeg Jets	WHA	75	20	66	86	....	....	....	211	....	....	....	....	....	....	....	....	....	....	8	1	*12	13	23	....	....	....
1979-80	**Chicago Black Hawks**	**NHL**	**74**	**15**	**55**	**70**	**13**	**40**	**53**	**252**	**6**	**1**	**3**	**90**	**16.7**	**94**	**33**	**82**	**28**	**7**	**4**	**0**	**0**	**0**	**22**	**0**	**0**	**0**
1980-81	**Chicago Black Hawks**	**NHL**	**72**	**8**	**51**	**59**	**6**	**34**	**40**	**225**	**2**	**0**	**2**	**88**	**9.1**	**80**	**22**	**103**	**26**	**–19**	**3**	**0**	**2**	**2**	**11**	**0**	**0**	**0**
1981-82	**Chicago Black Hawks**	**NHL**	**60**	**7**	**30**	**37**	**6**	**20**	**26**	**120**	**2**	**0**	**0**	**69**	**10.1**	**62**	**19**	**67**	**11**	**–13**	**11**	**1**	**2**	**3**	**53**	**0**	**0**	**0**
1982-83	**Chicago Black Hawks**	**NHL**	**5**	**0**	**2**	**2**	**0**	**1**	**1**	**12**	**0**	**0**	**0**	**4**	**0.0**	**2**	**0**	**2**	**0**	**0**	....	....	....	....	....	....	....	....
	Los Angeles Kings	**NHL**	**71**	**14**	**30**	**44**	**11**	**21**	**32**	**127**	**4**	**1**	**2**	**71**	**19.7**	**64**	**11**	**94**	**25**	**–16**	....	....	....	....	....	....	....	....
1983-84	**Los Angeles Kings**	**NHL**	**77**	**7**	**25**	**32**	**6**	**17**	**23**	**89**	**0**	**2**	**1**	**51**	**13.7**	**43**	**4**	**83**	**20**	**–24**	....	....	....	....	....	....	....	....
1984-85	**Los Angeles Kings**	**NHL**	**78**	**16**	**33**	**49**	**13**	**22**	**35**	**144**	**2**	**0**	**2**	**74**	**21.6**	**79**	**11**	**82**	**16**	**2**	**3**	**0**	**2**	**2**	**0**	**0**	**0**	**0**
1985-86	**Pittsburgh Penguins**	**NHL**	**73**	**26**	**37**	**63**	**21**	**25**	**46**	**162**	**11**	**0**	**7**	**91**	**28.6**	**115**	**56**	**50**	**1**	**10**	....	....	....	....	....	....	....	....
1986-87	**Pittsburgh Penguins**	**NHL**	**70**	**14**	**37**	**51**	**12**	**27**	**39**	**145**	**5**	**0**	**2**	**71**	**19.7**	**89**	**38**	**43**	**0**	**8**	....	....	....	....	....	....	....	....
1987-88	**Minnesota North Stars**	**NHL**	**47**	**5**	**12**	**17**	**4**	**9**	**13**	**76**	**2**	**0**	**0**	**33**	**15.2**	**25**	**6**	**43**	**9**	**–15**	....	....	....	....	....	....	....	....
1988-89	**Minnesota North Stars**	**NHL**	**3**	**1**	**1**	**2**	**1**	**1**	**2**	**2**	**0**	**0**	**0**	**2**	**50.0**	**2**	**0**	**1**	**0**	**1**	....	....	....	....	....	....	....	....
1989-1991	Saskatoon Blades	WHL	DID NOT PLAY – COACHING																									
1991-1994	Columbus Chill	ECHL	DID NOT PLAY – COACHING																									
1994-1996	Houston Aeros	IHL	DID NOT PLAY – COACHING																									
1996-1999			OUT OF HOCKEY – RETIRED																									
1999-2000	Knoxville Speed	UHL	DID NOT PLAY – COACHING																									
	NHL Totals		**630**	**113**	**313**	**426**	**93**	**217**	**310**	**1354**	**34**	**4**	**19**	**644**	**17.5**	**655**	**200**	**650**	**136**		**21**	**1**	**6**	**7**	**86**	**0**	**0**	**0**
	Other Major League Totals		369	83	254	337	....	....	....	761	....	....	....	....	....	....	....	....	....	....	52	18	36	54	174	....	....	....

Selected by **Houston** (WHA) in 1974 WHA Amateur Draft, May, 1974. Traded to **Winnipeg** (WHA) by **Houston** (WHA) for cash, July, 1978. Reclaimed by **Chicago** from **Winnipeg** prior to Expansion Draft, June 9, 1979. Traded to **LA Kings** by **Chicago** for Larry Goodenough and LA Kings's 3rd round choice (Trent Yawney) in 1984 Entry Draft, October 24, 1982. Signed as a free agent by **Pittsburgh**, October 3, 1985. Signed as a free agent by **Minnesota**, July, 1987.

• RUSSELL, Cam

Cameron D – L. 6'4", 200 lbs. b: Halifax, N.S., 1/12/1969. Chicago's 3rd, 50th overall, in 1987.

Season	Club	League	GP	G	A	Pts	AG	AA	APts	PIM	PP	SH	GW	S	%	TGF	PGF	TGA	PGA	+/–	GP	G	A	Pts	PIM	PP	SH	GW
1984-85	Dartmouth Mounties	NSAHA	STATISTICS NOT AVAILABLE																									
1985-86	Hull Olympiques	QMJHL	56	3	4	7	....	....	....	24	....	....	....	....	....	....	....	....	....	....	15	0	2	2	4	....	....	....
	Hull Olympiques	Mem-Cup	5	0	0	0	....	....	....	7	....	....	....	....	....	....	....	....	....	....	....	....	....	....	....	....	....	....
1986-87	Hull Olympiques	QMJHL	66	3	16	19	....	....	....	119	....	....	....	....	....	....	....	....	....	....	8	0	1	1	16	....	....	....
1987-88	Hull Olympiques	QMJHL	53	9	18	27	....	....	....	141	....	....	....	....	....	....	....	....	....	....	19	2	5	7	39	....	....	....
	Hull Olympiques	Mem-Cup	4	0	2	2	....	....	....	6	....	....	....	....	....	....	....	....	....	....	....	....	....	....	....	....	....	....
1988-89	Hull Olympiques	QMJHL	66	8	32	40	....	....	....	109	....	....	....	....	....	....	....	....	....	....	9	2	6	8	6	....	....	....
1989-90	**Chicago Blackhawks**	**NHL**	**19**	**0**	**1**	**1**	**0**	**1**	**1**	**27**	**0**	**0**	**0**	**10**	**0.0**	**9**	**1**	**13**	**2**	**–3**	**1**	**0**	**0**	**0**	**0**	**0**	**0**	**0**
	Indianapolis Ice	IHL	46	3	15	18	....	....	....	114	....	....	....	....	....	....	....	....	....	....	9	0	1	1	24	....	....	....
1990-91	**Chicago Blackhawks**	**NHL**	**3**	**0**	**0**	**0**	**0**	**0**	**0**	**5**	**0**	**0**	**0**	**0**	**0.0**	**2**	**0**	**1**	**0**	**1**	**1**	**0**	**0**	**0**	**0**	**0**	**0**	**0**
	Indianapolis Ice	IHL	53	5	9	14	....	....	....	125	....	....	....	....	....	....	....	....	....	....	6	0	2	2	30	....	....	....
1991-92	**Chicago Blackhawks**	**NHL**	**19**	**0**	**0**	**0**	**0**	**0**	**0**	**34**	**0**	**0**	**0**	**9**	**0.0**	**2**	**0**	**12**	**2**	**–8**	**12**	**0**	**2**	**2**	**2**	**0**	**0**	**0**
	Indianapolis Ice	IHL	41	4	9	13	....	....	....	78	....	....	....	....	....	....	....	....	....	....	....	....	....	....	....	....	....	....
1992-93	**Chicago Blackhawks**	**NHL**	**67**	**2**	**4**	**6**	**2**	**3**	**5**	**151**	**0**	**0**	**0**	**49**	**4.1**	**32**	**2**	**32**	**7**	**5**	**4**	**0**	**0**	**0**	**0**	**0**	**0**	**0**
1993-94	**Chicago Blackhawks**	**NHL**	**67**	**1**	**7**	**8**	**1**	**5**	**6**	**200**	**0**	**0**	**0**	**41**	**2.4**	**37**	**0**	**31**	**4**	**10**	....	....	....	....	....	....	....	....
1994-95	**Chicago Blackhawks**	**NHL**	**33**	**1**	**3**	**4**	**2**	**4**	**6**	**88**	**0**	**0**	**0**	**18**	**5.6**	**17**	**1**	**12**	**0**	**4**	**16**	**0**	**3**	**3**	**8**	**0**	**0**	**0**
1995-96	**Chicago Blackhawks**	**NHL**	**61**	**2**	**2**	**4**	**2**	**2**	**4**	**129**	**0**	**0**	**0**	**22**	**9.1**	**26**	**0**	**19**	**1**	**8**	**6**	**0**	**0**	**0**	**2**	**0**	**0**	**0**
1996-97	**Chicago Blackhawks**	**NHL**	**44**	**1**	**1**	**2**	**1**	**1**	**2**	**65**	**0**	**0**	**0**	**19**	**5.3**	**10**	**0**	**19**	**1**	**–8**	**4**	**0**	**0**	**0**	**4**	**0**	**0**	**0**
1997-98	**Chicago Blackhawks**	**NHL**	**41**	**1**	**1**	**2**	**1**	**1**	**2**	**79**	**0**	**0**	**1**	**18**	**5.6**	**16**	**0**	**14**	**1**	**3**	....	....	....	....	....	....	....	....
1998-99	**Chicago Blackhawks**	**NHL**	**7**	**0**	**0**	**0**	**0**	**0**	**0**	**10**	**0**	**0**	**0**	**1**	**0.0**	**2**	**0**	**1**	**0**	**1**	....	....	....	....	....	....	....	....
	Colorado Avalanche	**NHL**	**35**	**1**	**2**	**3**	**1**	**2**	**3**	**84**	**0**	**0**	**0**	**14**	**7.1**	**13**	**0**	**22**	**4**	**–5**	....	....	....	....	....	....	....	....
99-2000	**Colorado Avalanche**	**NHL**	DID NOT PLAY – INJURED																									
	Halifax Moosehaeds	QMJHL	DID NOT PLAY – ASSISTANT COACH																									
	NHL Totals		**396**	**9**	**21**	**30**	**10**	**19**	**29**	**872**	**0**	**0**	**1**	**201**	**4.5**	**166**	**4**	**176**	**22**		**44**	**0**	**5**	**5**	**16**	**0**	**0**	**0**

Traded to **Colorado** by **Chicago** for Roman Vopat and Los Angeles' 6th round choice (previously acquired, later traded to Ottawa, Ottawa selected Martin Brusek) in 1999 Entry Draft, November 10, 1998. • Missed remainder of 1998-99 and entire 1999-2000 seasons recovering from torn rotator cuff suffered in game vs. Philadelphia, February 14, 1999.

• RUSSELL, Phil

Philip Douglas D – R. 6'2", 205 lbs. b: Edmonton, Alta., 7/21/1952. Chicago's 1st, 13th overall, in 1972.

Season	Club	League	GP	G	A	Pts	AG	AA	APts	PIM	PP	SH	GW	S	%	TGF	PGF	TGA	PGA	+/–	GP	G	A	Pts	PIM	PP	SH	GW
1970-71	Edmonton Oil Kings	WCJHL	34	4	16	20	....	....	....	113	....	....	....	....	....	....	....	....	....	....	17	1	7	8	47	....	....	....
1971-72	Edmonton Oil Kings	WCJHL	64	14	45	59	....	....	....	*331	....	....	....	....	....	....	....	....	....	....	16	1	9	10	15	....	....	....
	Edmonton Oil Kings	Mem-Cup	2	0	0	0	....	....	....	0	....	....	....	....	....	....	....	....	....	....	....	....	....	....	....	....	....	....

			REGULAR SEASON																		PLAYOFFS							
Season	Club	League	GP	G	A	Pts	AG	AA	APts	PIM	PP	SH	GW	S	%	TGF	PGF	TGA	PGA	+/–	GP	G	A	Pts	PIM	PP	SH	GW
1972-73	**Chicago Black Hawks**	**NHL**	**76**	**6**	**19**	**25**	**6**	**15**	**21**	**156**	**1**	**0**	**0**	**119**	**5.0**	**99**	**7**	**72**	**11**	**31**	**16**	**0**	**3**	**3**	**49**	**0**	**0**	**0**
1973-74	**Chicago Black Hawks**	**NHL**	**75**	**10**	**25**	**35**	**10**	**21**	**31**	**184**	**0**	**1**	**0**	**123**	**8.1**	**112**	**8**	**61**	**4**	**47**	**9**	**0**	**1**	**1**	**41**	**0**	**0**	**0**
1974-75	**Chicago Black Hawks**	**NHL**	**80**	**5**	**24**	**29**	**4**	**18**	**22**	**260**	**1**	**0**	**1**	**187**	**2.7**	**108**	**24**	**100**	**23**	**7**	**8**	**1**	**3**	**4**	**23**	**0**	**0**	**0**
1975-76	**Chicago Black Hawks**	**NHL**	**74**	**9**	**29**	**38**	**8**	**22**	**30**	**194**	**7**	**0**	**0**	**180**	**5.0**	**102**	**26**	**119**	**23**	**–20**	**4**	**0**	**1**	**1**	**17**	**0**	**0**	**0**
1976-77	**Chicago Black Hawks**	**NHL**	**76**	**9**	**36**	**45**	**8**	**28**	**36**	**233**	**1**	**0**	**2**	**178**	**5.1**	**124**	**31**	**120**	**28**	**1**	**2**	**0**	**1**	**1**	**2**	**0**	**0**	**0**
	Canada	WEC-A	10	0	3	3	....	....	....	16	....	....	....	....	....	....	....	....	....	....	....	....	....	....	....	....	....	....
1977-78	**Chicago Black Hawks**	**NHL**	**57**	**6**	**20**	**26**	**5**	**15**	**20**	**139**	**0**	**1**	**1**	**132**	**4.5**	**79**	**12**	**62**	**14**	**19**	....	....	....	....	....	....	....	....
1978-79	**Chicago Black Hawks**	**NHL**	**66**	**8**	**23**	**31**	**7**	**17**	**24**	**122**	**1**	**1**	**1**	**147**	**5.4**	**78**	**16**	**97**	**28**	**–7**	....	....	....	....	....	....	....	....
	Atlanta Flames	**NHL**	**13**	**1**	**6**	**7**	**1**	**4**	**5**	**28**	**1**	**0**	**0**	**19**	**5.3**	**24**	**5**	**24**	**6**	**1**	**2**	**0**	**0**	**0**	**9**	**0**	**0**	**0**
1979-80	**Atlanta Flames**	**NHL**	**80**	**5**	**31**	**36**	**4**	**23**	**27**	**115**	**1**	**0**	**1**	**104**	**4.8**	**104**	**6**	**103**	**19**	**14**	**4**	**0**	**1**	**1**	**6**	**0**	**0**	**0**
1980-81	**Calgary Flames**	**NHL**	**80**	**6**	**23**	**29**	**5**	**15**	**20**	**104**	**1**	**1**	**1**	**109**	**5.5**	**127**	**9**	**155**	**54**	**17**	**16**	**2**	**7**	**9**	**29**	**0**	**0**	**0**
1981-82	**Calgary Flames**	**NHL**	**71**	**4**	**25**	**29**	**3**	**17**	**20**	**110**	**0**	**0**	**0**	**114**	**3.5**	**101**	**2**	**142**	**49**	**6**	**3**	**0**	**1**	**1**	**2**	**0**	**0**	**0**
1982-83	**Calgary Flames**	**NHL**	**78**	**13**	**18**	**31**	**11**	**12**	**23**	**112**	**0**	**1**	**2**	**116**	**11.2**	**96**	**0**	**120**	**26**	**2**	**9**	**1**	**4**	**5**	**24**	**0**	**0**	**0**
1983-84	**New Jersey Devils**	**NHL**	**76**	**9**	**22**	**31**	**7**	**15**	**22**	**96**	**0**	**0**	**0**	**123**	**7.3**	**81**	**9**	**128**	**29**	**–27**	....	....	....	....	....	....	....	....
1984-85	**New Jersey Devils**	**NHL**	**66**	**4**	**16**	**20**	**3**	**11**	**14**	**110**	**0**	**1**	**0**	**73**	**5.5**	**66**	**2**	**112**	**34**	**–14**	....	....	....	....	....	....	....	....
1985-86	**New Jersey Devils**	**NHL**	**30**	**2**	**3**	**5**	**2**	**2**	**4**	**51**	**0**	**0**	**0**	**22**	**9.1**	**20**	**1**	**46**	**10**	**–17**	....	....	....	....	....	....	....	....
	Buffalo Sabres	**NHL**	**12**	**2**	**3**	**5**	**2**	**2**	**4**	**12**	**0**	**0**	**0**	**15**	**13.3**	**7**	**0**	**18**	**3**	**–8**	....	....	....	....	....	....	....	....
	Canada	WEC-A	8	0	1	1	....	....	....	10	....	....	....	....	....	....	....	....	....	....	....	....	....	....	....	....	....	....
1986-87	**Buffalo Sabres**	**NHL**	**6**	**0**	**2**	**2**	**0**	**1**	**1**	**12**	**0**	**0**	**0**	**2**	**0.0**	**6**	**0**	**8**	**2**	**0**	....	....	....	....	....	....	....	....
	EHC Olten	Switz.	5	0	1	1	....	....	....	....	....	....	....	....	....	....	....	....	....	....	....	....	....	....	....	....	....	....
1987-88	Kalamazoo Wings	IHL	27	2	9	11	....	....	....	35	....	....	....	....	....	....	....	....	....	....	....	....	....	....	....	....	....	....
	NHL Totals		**1016**	**99**	**325**	**424**	**86**	**238**	**324**	**2038**	**14**	**6**	**9**	**1763**	**5.6**	**1334**	**158**	**1487**	**363**		**73**	**4**	**22**	**26**	**202**	**0**	**0**	**0**

WCJHL All-Star Team (1972) • Played in NHL All-Star Game (1976, 1977, 1985)

Traded to **Atlanta** by **Chicago** with Ivan Boldirev and Darcy Rota for Tom Lysiak, Pat Ribble, Harold Phillipoff, Greg Fox and Miles Zaharko, March 13, 1979. Transferred to **Calgary** after **Atlanta** franchise relocated, June 24, 1980. Traded to **New Jersey** by **Calgary** with Mel Bridgman for Steve Tambellini and Joel Quenneville, June 20, 1983. Traded to **Buffalo** by **New Jersey** for Buffalo's 12th round choice (Doug Kirton) in 1986 Entry Draft, March 11, 1986.

• RUUTTU, Christian

C – L. 5'11", 194 lbs. b: Lappeenranta, Finland, 2/20/1964. Buffalo's 9th, 139th overall, in 1983.

Season	Club	League	GP	G	A	Pts	AG	AA	APts	PIM	PP	SH	GW	S	%	TGF	PGF	TGA	PGA	+/–	GP	G	A	Pts	PIM	PP	SH	GW
1980-81	HC Assat-Pori	Finland-Jr.	4	1	1	2	....	....	....	2	....	....	....	....	....	....	....	....	....	....	....	....	....	....	....	....	....	....
1981-82	Belmont Hill Hillies	Hi-School	STATISTICS NOT AVAILABLE																									
1982-83	HC Assat-Pori	Finland-Jr.	5	2	6	8	....	....	....	12	....	....	....	....	....	....	....	....	....	....	....	....	....	....	....	....	....	....
	Finland	WJC-A	7	2	2	4	....	....	....	14	....	....	....	....	....	....	....	....	....	....	....	....	....	....	....	....	....	....
	HC Assat-Pori	Finland	36	15	18	33	....	....	....	34	....	....	....	....	....	....	....	....	....	....	....	....	....	....	....	....	....	....
1983-84	HC Assat-Pori	Finland-Jr.	2	0	2	2	....	....	....	12	....	....	....	....	....	....	....	....	....	....	....	....	....	....	....	....	....	....
	HC Assat-Pori	Finland	37	18	42	60	....	....	....	72	....	....	....	....	....	....	....	....	....	....	9	2	5	7	12	....	....	....
	Finland	WJC-A	7	0	1	1	....	....	....	8	....	....	....	....	....	....	....	....	....	....	....	....	....	....	....	....	....	....
1984-85	HC Assat-Pori	Finland-Jr.	1	3	0	3	....	....	....	0	....	....	....	....	....	....	....	....	....	....	....	....	....	....	....	....	....	....
	HC Assat-Pori	Finland	32	14	32	46	....	....	....	34	....	....	....	....	....	....	....	....	....	....	8	1	6	7	8	....	....	....
	Finland	WEC-A	6	1	1	2	....	....	....	16	....	....	....	....	....	....	....	....	....	....	....	....	....	....	....	....	....	....
1985-86	HIFK Helsinki	Finland	36	16	38	54	....	....	....	47	....	....	....	....	....	....	....	....	....	....	10	3	6	9	8	....	....	....
	Finland	WEC-A	10	2	5	7	....	....	....	12	....	....	....	....	....	....	....	....	....	....	....	....	....	....	....	....	....	....
1986-87	**Buffalo Sabres**	**NHL**	**76**	**22**	**43**	**65**	**19**	**31**	**50**	**62**	**3**	**1**	**1**	**167**	**13.2**	**96**	**31**	**67**	**11**	**9**	....	....	....	....	....	....	....	....
	Finland	WEC-A	10	0	0	0	....	....	....	18	....	....	....	....	....	....	....	....	....	....	....	....	....	....	....	....	....	....
1987-88	Finland	Can-Cup	5	2	1	3	....	....	....	10	....	....	....	....	....	....	....	....	....	....	....	....	....	....	....	....	....	....
	Buffalo Sabres	**NHL**	**73**	**26**	**45**	**71**	**22**	**32**	**54**	**85**	**8**	**1**	**4**	**185**	**14.1**	**95**	**39**	**86**	**27**	**–3**	**6**	**2**	**5**	**7**	**4**	**1**	**0**	**0**
1988-89	**Buffalo Sabres**	**NHL**	**67**	**14**	**46**	**60**	**12**	**33**	**45**	**98**	**5**	**0**	**1**	**149**	**9.4**	**84**	**30**	**64**	**23**	**13**	**2**	**0**	**0**	**0**	**2**	**0**	**0**	**0**
1989-90	**Buffalo Sabres**	**NHL**	**75**	**19**	**41**	**60**	**16**	**29**	**45**	**66**	**4**	**1**	**2**	**160**	**11.9**	**81**	**17**	**83**	**28**	**9**	**6**	**0**	**0**	**0**	**4**	**0**	**0**	**0**
	Finland	WEC-A	9	5	3	8	....	....	....	4	....	....	....	....	....	....	....	....	....	....	....	....	....	....	....	....	....	....
1990-91	**Buffalo Sabres**	**NHL**	**77**	**16**	**34**	**50**	**15**	**26**	**41**	**96**	**2**	**3**	**1**	**155**	**10.3**	**78**	**26**	**90**	**32**	**–6**	**6**	**1**	**3**	**4**	**29**	**0**	**1**	**0**
	Finland	WEC-A	10	7	3	10	....	....	....	10	....	....	....	....	....	....	....	....	....	....	....	....	....	....	....	....	....	....
1991-92	Finland	Can-Cup	6	1	5	6	....	....	....	4	....	....	....	....	....	....	....	....	....	....	....	....	....	....	....	....	....	....
	Buffalo Sabres	**NHL**	**70**	**4**	**21**	**25**	**4**	**16**	**20**	**76**	**0**	**2**	**1**	**108**	**3.7**	**42**	**12**	**74**	**37**	**–7**	**3**	**0**	**0**	**0**	**6**	**0**	**0**	**0**
	Finland	WC-A	5	0	1	1	....	....	....	6	....	....	....	....	....	....	....	....	....	....	....	....	....	....	....	....	....	....
1992-93	**Chicago Blackhawks**	**NHL**	**84**	**17**	**37**	**54**	**14**	**25**	**39**	**134**	**3**	**1**	**6**	**187**	**9.1**	**76**	**20**	**62**	**20**	**14**	**4**	**0**	**0**	**0**	**2**	**0**	**0**	**0**
1993-94	**Chicago Blackhawks**	**NHL**	**54**	**9**	**20**	**29**	**8**	**16**	**24**	**68**	**1**	**1**	**1**	**96**	**9.4**	**36**	**8**	**46**	**14**	**–4**	**6**	**0**	**0**	**0**	**2**	**0**	**0**	**0**
	Finland	WC-A	4	2	2	4	....	....	....	4	....	....	....	....	....	....	....	....	....	....	....	....	....	....	....	....	....	....
1994-95	HIFK Helsinki	Finland	20	4	8	12	....	....	....	24	....	....	....	....	....	....	....	....	....	....	....	....	....	....	....	....	....	....
	Chicago Blackhawks	**NHL**	**20**	**2**	**5**	**7**	**4**	**7**	**11**	**6**	**0**	**0**	**1**	**25**	**8.0**	**10**	**0**	**10**	**3**	**3**	....	....	....	....	....	....	....	....
	Vancouver Canucks	**NHL**	**25**	**5**	**6**	**11**	**9**	**9**	**18**	**23**	**0**	**0**	**1**	**44**	**11.4**	**17**	**1**	**9**	**4**	**11**	**9**	**1**	**1**	**2**	**0**	**0**	**1**	**0**
1995-96	Vastra Frolunda	Sweden	32	13	25	38	....	....	....	98	....	....	....	....	....	....	....	....	....	....	12	4	7	11	24	....	....	....
	Finland	WC-A	6	0	2	2	....	....	....	2	....	....	....	....	....	....	....	....	....	....	....	....	....	....	....	....	....	....
1996-97	Finland	W-Cup	4	1	0	1	....	....	....	2	....	....	....	....	....	....	....	....	....	....	....	....	....	....	....	....	....	....
	ZSC Lions Zurich	Switz-2	42	31	40	71	....	....	....	72	....	....	....	....	....	....	....	....	....	....	11	5	9	14	6	....	....	....
1997-98	HIFK Helsinki	Finland	44	11	28	39	....	....	....	32	....	....	....	....	....	....	....	....	....	....	9	3	3	6	8	....	....	....
1998-99	Blues Espoo	Finland	45	14	22	36	....	....	....	40	....	....	....	....	....	....	....	....	....	....	....	....	....	....	....	....	....	....
	NHL Totals		**621**	**134**	**298**	**432**	**123**	**224**	**347**	**714**	**26**	**10**	**19**	**1276**	**10.5**	**615**	**184**	**591**	**199**		**42**	**4**	**9**	**13**	**49**	**1**	**2**	**0**

Finnish First All-Star Team (1986) • Played in NHL All-Star Game (1988)

Traded to **Winnipeg** by **Buffalo** with future considerations for Stephane Beauregard, June 15, 1992. Traded to **Chicago** by **Winnipeg** for Stephane Beauregard, August 10, 1992. Traded to **Vancouver** by **Chicago** for Murray Craven, March 10, 1995.

• RUUTU, Jarkko

LW – L. 6'2", 194 lbs. b: Vantaa, Finland, 8/23/1975. Vancouver's 3rd, 68th overall, in 1998.

Season	Club	League	GP	G	A	Pts	AG	AA	APts	PIM	PP	SH	GW	S	%	TGF	PGF	TGA	PGA	+/–	GP	G	A	Pts	PIM	PP	SH	GW
1991-92	HIFK Helsinki	Finland-Jr.	1	0	0	0	....	....	....	0	....	....	....	....	....	....	....	....	....	....	....	....	....	....	....	....	....	....
1992-93	HIFK Helsinki-B	Finland-Jr.	33	26	21	47	....	....	....	53	....	....	....	....	....	....	....	....	....	....	....	....	....	....	....	....	....	....
	HIFK Helsinki	Finland-Jr.	1	0	0	0	....	....	....	0	....	....	....	....	....	....	....	....	....	....	....	....	....	....	....	....	....	....
1993-94	HIFK Helsinki	Finland-Jr.	19	9	12	21	....	....	....	44	....	....	....	....	....	....	....	....	....	....	....	....	....	....	....	....	....	....
1994-95	HIFK Helsinki	Finland-Jr.	35	26	22	48	....	....	....	117	....	....	....	....	....	....	....	....	....	....	....	....	....	....	....	....	....	....
1995-96	Michigan Tech Huskies	WCHA	39	12	10	22	....	....	....	96	....	....	....	....	....	....	....	....	....	....	....	....	....	....	....	....	....	....
1996-97	HIFK Helsinki	Finland	48	11	10	21	....	....	....	*155	....	....	....	....	....	....	....	....	....	....	....	....	....	....	....	....	....	....
1997-98	HIFK Helsinki	Finland	37	10	10	20	....	....	....	87	....	....	....	....	....	....	....	....	....	....	8	*7	4	11	10	....	....	....
1998-99	HIFK Helsinki	Finland	25	10	4	14	....	....	....	136	....	....	....	....	....	....	....	....	....	....	9	0	2	2	43	....	....	....
	HIFK Helsinki	EuroHL	5	1	2	3	....	....	....	8	....	....	....	....	....	....	....	....	....	....	....	....	....	....	....	....	....	....
99-2000	**Vancouver Canucks**	**NHL**	**8**	**0**	**1**	**1**	**0**	**1**	**1**	**6**	**0**	**0**	**0**	**4**	**0.0**	**2**	**0**	**3**	**0**	**–1**	....	....	....	....	....	....	....	....
	Syracuse Crunch	AHL	65	26	32	58	....	....	....	164	....	....	....	....	....	....	....	....	....	....	4	3	1	4	8	....	....	....
	NHL Totals		**8**	**0**	**1**	**1**	**0**	**1**	**1**	**6**	**0**	**0**	**0**	**4**	**0.0**	**2**	**0**	**3**	**0**		....	....	....	....	....	....	....	....

• RUZICKA, Vladimir

"Rosie" C – L. 6'3", 215 lbs. b: Most, Czech., 6/6/1963. Toronto's 5th, 73rd overall, in 1982.

Season	Club	League	GP	G	A	Pts	AG	AA	APts	PIM	PP	SH	GW	S	%	TGF	PGF	TGA	PGA	+/–	GP	G	A	Pts	PIM	PP	SH	GW
1969-1978	CHZ Litvinov	Czech-Jr.	STATISTICS NOT AVAILABLE																									
1978-79	CHZ Litvinov	Czech-Jr.	STATISTICS NOT AVAILABLE																									
	Czechoslovakia	EJC-A	3	1	2	3	....	....	....	2	....	....	....	....	....	....	....	....	....	....	....	....	....	....	....	....	....	....
1979-80	CHZ Litvinov	Czech.	9	1	1	2	....	....	....	0	....	....	....	....	....	....	....	....	....	....	....	....	....	....	....	....	....	....
1980-81	CHZ Litvinov	Czech.	41	12	13	25	....	....	....	10	....	....	....	....	....	....	....	....	....	....	....	....	....	....	....	....	....	....
	Czechoslovakia	WJC-A	5	5	0	5	....	....	....	2	....	....	....	....	....	....	....	....	....	....	....	....	....	....	....	....	....	....
	Czechoslovakia	EJC-A	5	8	8	16	....	....	....	18	....	....	....	....	....	....	....	....	....	....	....	....	....	....	....	....	....	....
1981-82	CHZ Litvinov	Czech.	44	27	22	49	....	....	....	50	....	....	....	....	....	....	....	....	....	....	....	....	....	....	....	....	....	....
	Czechoslovakia	WJC-A	7	8	1	9	....	....	....	6	....	....	....	....	....	....	....	....	....	....	....	....	....	....	....	....	....	....
1982-83	CHZ Litvinov	Czech.	43	22	24	46	....	....	....	40	....	....	....	....	....	....	....	....	....	....	....	....	....	....	....	....	....	....
	Czechoslovakia	WJC-A	7	12	8	*20	....	....	....	6	....	....	....	....	....	....	....	....	....	....	....	....	....	....	....	....	....	....
	Czechoslovakia	WEC-A	10	3	1	4	....	....	....	4	....	....	....	....	....	....	....	....	....	....	....	....	....	....	....	....	....	....
1983-84	CHZ Litvinov	Czech.	44	*31	23	*54	....	....	....	50	....	....	....	....	....	....	....	....	....	....	....	....	....	....	....	....	....	....
	Czechoslovakia	Olympics	7	4	6	10	....	....	....	0	....	....	....	....	....	....	....	....	....	....	....	....	....	....	....	....	....	....

Season	Club	League	REGULAR SEASON																		PLAYOFFS							
			GP	G	A	Pts	AG	AA	APts	PIM	PP	SH	GW	S	%	TGF	PGF	TGA	PGA	+/–	GP	G	A	Pts	PIM	PP	SH	GW
1984-85	Czechoslovakia	Can-Cup	5	0	0	0	....	....	....	2	....	....	....	....	....	....	....	....	....	....	....	....	....	....	....	....	....	....
	CHZ Litvinov	Czech.	41	38	22	60	....	....	....	29	....	....	....	....	....	....	....	....	....	....	....	....	....	....	....	....	....	....
	Czechoslovakia	WEC-A	10	8	3	11	....	....	....	0	....	....	....	....	....	....	....	....	....	....	....	....	....	....	....	....	....	....
1985-86	CHZ Litvinov	Czech.	43	41	32	73	....	....	....	....	....	....	....	....	....	....	....	....	....	....	....	....	....	....	....	....	....	....
	Czechoslovakia	WEC-A	10	4	11	15	....	....	....	6	....	....	....	....	....	....	....	....	....	....	....	....	....	....	....	....	....	....
1986-87	CHZ Litvinov	Czech.	39	29	21	50	....	....	....	46	....	....	....	....	....	....	....	....	....	....	....	....	....	....	....	....	....	....
	Czechoslovakia	WEC-A	10	3	3	6	....	....	....	10	....	....	....	....	....	....	....	....	....	....	....	....	....	....	....	....	....	....
1987-88	Czechoslovakia	Can-Cup	6	2	0	2	....	....	....	0	....	....	....	....	....	....	....	....	....	....	....	....	....	....	....	....	....	....
	Dukla Trencin	Czech.	44	*38	27	65	....	....	....	70	....	....	....	....	....	....	....	....	....	....	....	....	....	....	....	....	....	....
	Czechoslovakia	Olympics	8	4	3	7	....	....	....	12	....	....	....	....	....	....	....	....	....	....	....	....	....	....	....	....	....	....
1988-89	Dukla Trencin	Czech.	45	*46	38	*84	....	....	....	42	....	....	....	....	....	....	....	....	....	....	....	....	....	....	....	....	....	....
	Czechoslovakia	WEC-A	10	7	7	14	....	....	....	2	....	....	....	....	....	....	....	....	....	....	....	....	....	....	....	....	....	....
1989-90	CHZ Litvinov	Czech.	32	21	23	44	....	....	....	....	....	....	....	....	....	....	....	....	....	....	....	....	....	....	....	....	....	....
	Edmonton Oilers	**NHL**	**25**	**11**	**6**	**17**	**9**	**4**	**13**	**10**	**4**	**0**	**1**	**52**	**21.2**	**24**	**13**	**32**	**0**	**–21**	....	....	....	....	....	....	....	....
1990-91	**Boston Bruins**	**NHL**	**29**	**8**	**8**	**16**	**7**	**6**	**13**	**19**	**4**	**0**	**0**	**51**	**15.7**	**22**	**7**	**14**	**0**	**1**	**17**	**2**	**11**	**13**	**0**	**1**	**0**	**2**
1991-92	**Boston Bruins**	**NHL**	**77**	**39**	**36**	**75**	**36**	**27**	**63**	**48**	**18**	**0**	**6**	**228**	**17.1**	**106**	**54**	**63**	**1**	**–10**	**13**	**2**	**3**	**5**	**2**	**2**	**0**	**0**
1992-93	**Boston Bruins**	**NHL**	**60**	**19**	**22**	**41**	**16**	**15**	**31**	**38**	**7**	**0**	**2**	**146**	**13.0**	**60**	**23**	**43**	**0**	**–6**	....	....	....	....	....	....	....	....
1993-94	**Ottawa Senators**	**NHL**	**42**	**5**	**13**	**18**	**5**	**10**	**15**	**14**	**4**	**0**	**0**	**64**	**7.8**	**32**	**16**	**37**	**0**	**–21**	....	....	....	....	....	....	....	....
1994-95	Slavia Praha	Czech-Rep	41	27	24	51	....	....	....	....	....	....	....	....	....	....	....	....	....	....	3	2	0	2	....	....	....	....
1995-96	Slavia Praha	Czech-Rep	37	21	*44	*65	....	....	....	....	....	....	....	....	....	....	....	....	....	....	5	2	1	3	....	....	....	....
1996-97	Slavia Praha	Czech-Rep	44	22	32	54	....	....	....	40	....	....	....	....	....	....	....	....	....	....	....	....	....	....	....	....	....	....
1997-98	Slavia Praha	Czech-Rep	49	20	40	60	....	....	....	60	....	....	....	....	....	....	....	....	....	....	5	0	6	6	6	....	....	....
	Czech-Republic	Olympics	6	3	0	3	....	....	....	0	....	....	....	....	....	....	....	....	....	....	....	....	....	....	....	....	....	....
1998-99	Slavia Praha	Czech-Rep	50	25	31	56	....	....	....	67	....	....	....	....	....	....	....	....	....	....	....	....	....	....	....	....	....	....
99-2000	Slavia Praha	Czech-Rep	21	5	8	13	....	....	....	16	....	....	....	....	....	....	....	....	....	....	....	....	....	....	....	....	....	....
	NHL Totals		**233**	**82**	**85**	**167**	**73**	**62**	**135**	**129**	**37**	**0**	**9**	**541**	**15.2**	**244**	**113**	**189**	**1**		**30**	**4**	**14**	**18**	**2**	**3**	**0**	**2**

EJC-A All-Star Team (1981) • WJC-A All-Star Team (1982, 1983) • WEC-A All-Star Team (1985) • Czechoslovakian Player of the Year (1986, 1988) • Czechoslovakian First All-Star Team (1988, 1989)

Traded to **Edmonton** by **Toronto** for Edmonton's 4th round choice (Greg Walters) in 1990 Entry Draft, December 21, 1989. Traded to **Boston** by **Edmonton** for Greg Hawgood, October 22, 1990. Signed as a free agent by **Ottawa**, August 12, 1993.

• RYAN, Terry

LW – L. 6'1", 202 lbs. b: St. John's, Nfld., 1/14/1977. Montreal's 1st, 8th overall, in 1995.

Season	Club	League	GP	G	A	Pts	AG	AA	APts	PIM	PP	SH	GW	S	%	TGF	PGF	TGA	PGA	+/–	GP	G	A	Pts	PIM	PP	SH	GW
1991-92	Quesnel Millionaires	RMJHL	49	26	41	67	....	....	....	217	....	....	....	....	....	....	....	....	....	....	....	....	....	....	....	....	....	....
1992-93	Quesnel Millionaires	RMJHL	29	31	25	56	....	....	....	222	....	....	....	....	....	....	....	....	....	....	....	....	....	....	....	....	....	....
	Vernon Lakers	BCJHL	9	5	6	11	....	....	....	15	....	....	....	....	....	....	....	....	....	....	....	....	....	....	....	....	....	....
	Tri-City Americans	WHL	1	0	0	0	....	....	....	0	....	....	....	....	....	....	....	....	....	....	1	0	1	1	5	....	....	....
1993-94	Tri-City Americans	WHL	61	16	17	33	....	....	....	176	....	....	....	....	....	....	....	....	....	....	4	0	1	1	25	....	....	....
1994-95	Tri-City Americans	WHL	70	50	60	110	....	....	....	207	....	....	....	....	....	....	....	....	....	....	17	12	15	27	36	....	....	....
1995-96	Tri-City Americans	WHL	59	32	37	69	....	....	....	133	....	....	....	....	....	....	....	....	....	....	5	0	0	0	4	....	....	....
	Fredericton Canadiens	AHL	....	....	....	....	....	....	....	....	....	....	....	....	....	....	....	....	....	....	3	0	0	0	2	....	....	....
1996-97	Red Deer Rebels	WHL	16	13	22	35	....	....	....	10	....	....	....	....	....	....	....	....	....	....	16	18	6	24	32	....	....	....
	Montreal Canadiens	**NHL**	**3**	**0**	**0**	**0**	**0**	**0**	**0**	**0**	**0**	**0**	**0**	**0**	**0.0**	**0**	**0**	**0**	**0**	**0**	....	....	....	....	....	....	....	....
1997-98	**Montreal Canadiens**	**NHL**	**4**	**0**	**0**	**0**	**0**	**0**	**0**	**31**	**0**	**0**	**0**	**0**	**0.0**	**0**	**0**	**0**	**0**	**0**	....	....	....	....	....	....	....	....
	Fredericton Canadiens	AHL	71	21	18	39	....	....	....	256	....	....	....	....	....	....	....	....	....	....	3	1	1	2	0	....	....	....
1998-99	**Montreal Canadiens**	**NHL**	**1**	**0**	**0**	**0**	**0**	**0**	**0**	**5**	**0**	**0**	**0**	**0**	**0.0**	**0**	**0**	**0**	**0**	**0**	....	....	....	....	....	....	....	....
	Fredericton Canadiens	AHL	55	16	27	43	....	....	....	189	....	....	....	....	....	....	....	....	....	....	11	1	3	4	10	....	....	....
99-2000	Utah Grizzlies	IHL	6	0	3	3	....	....	....	24	....	....	....	....	....	....	....	....	....	....	....	....	....	....	....	....	....	....
	Long Beach Ice Dogs	IHL	1	0	0	0	....	....	....	4	....	....	....	....	....	....	....	....	....	....	....	....	....	....	....	....	....	....
	St. John's Maple Leafs	AHL	50	7	17	24	....	....	....	176	....	....	....	....	....	....	....	....	....	....	....	....	....	....	....	....	....	....
	NHL Totals		**8**	**0**	**0**	**0**	**0**	**0**	**0**	**36**	**0**	**0**	**0**	**0**	**0.0**	**0**	**0**	**0**	**0**		....	....	....	....	....	....	....	....

WHL West Second All-Star Team (1995)

Signed as a free agent by **Utah** (IHL) with **Montreal** retaining NHL rights, October 15, 1999. Signed as a free agent by **St. John's** (AHL) following release by Utah (IHL) with **Montreal** retaining NHL rights, November 12, 1999.

• RYCHEL, Warren

Warren Stanley LW – L. 6', 205 lbs. b: Tecumseh, Ont., 5/12/1967.

Season	Club	League	GP	G	A	Pts	AG	AA	APts	PIM	PP	SH	GW	S	%	TGF	PGF	TGA	PGA	+/–	GP	G	A	Pts	PIM	PP	SH	GW
1983-84	Essex 73's	OJHL-C	24	11	16	27	....	....	....	86	....	....	....	....	....	....	....	....	....	....	....	....	....	....	....	....	....	....
1984-85	Sudbury Wolves	OHL	35	5	8	13	....	....	....	74	....	....	....	....	....	....	....	....	....	....	....	....	....	....	....	....	....	....
	Guelph Platers	OHL	29	1	3	4	....	....	....	48	....	....	....	....	....	....	....	....	....	....	....	....	....	....	....	....	....	....
1985-86	Guelph Platers	OHL	38	14	5	19	....	....	....	119	....	....	....	....	....	....	....	....	....	....	....	....	....	....	....	....	....	....
	Ottawa 67's	OHL	29	11	18	29	....	....	....	54	....	....	....	....	....	....	....	....	....	....	....	....	....	....	....	....	....	....
1986-87	Ottawa 67's	OHL	28	11	7	18	....	....	....	57	....	....	....	....	....	....	....	....	....	....	....	....	....	....	....	....	....	....
	Kitchener Rangers	OHL	21	5	5	10	....	....	....	39	....	....	....	....	....	....	....	....	....	....	4	0	0	0	9	....	....	....
1987-88	Peoria Rivermen	IHL	7	2	1	3	....	....	....	7	....	....	....	....	....	....	....	....	....	....	....	....	....	....	....	....	....	....
	Saginaw Hawks	IHL	51	2	7	9	....	....	....	113	....	....	....	....	....	....	....	....	....	....	1	0	0	0	0	....	....	....
1988-89	**Chicago Blackhawks**	**NHL**	**2**	**0**	**0**	**0**	**0**	**0**	**0**	**17**	**0**	**0**	**0**	**3**	**0.0**	**0**	**0**	**1**	**0**	**–1**	....	....	....	....	....	....	....	....
	Saginaw Hawks	IHL	50	15	14	29	....	....	....	226	....	....	....	....	....	....	....	....	....	....	6	0	0	0	51	....	....	....
1989-90	Indianapolis Ice	IHL	77	23	16	39	....	....	....	374	....	....	....	....	....	....	....	....	....	....	14	1	3	4	64	....	....	....
1990-91	Indianapolis Ice	IHL	68	33	30	63	....	....	....	338	....	....	....	....	....	....	....	....	....	....	5	2	1	3	30	....	....	....
	Chicago Blackhawks	**NHL**	....	....	....	....	....	....	....	....	....	....	....	....	....	....	....	....	....	....	**3**	**1**	**3**	**4**	**2**	**1**	**0**	**1**
1991-92	Moncton Hawks	AHL	36	14	15	29	....	....	....	211	....	....	....	....	....	....	....	....	....	....	....	....	....	....	....	....	....	....
	Kalamazoo Wings	IHL	45	15	20	35	....	....	....	165	....	....	....	....	....	....	....	....	....	....	8	0	3	3	51	....	....	....
1992-93	**Los Angeles Kings**	**NHL**	**70**	**6**	**7**	**13**	**5**	**5**	**10**	**314**	**0**	**0**	**1**	**67**	**9.0**	**20**	**2**	**42**	**9**	**–15**	**23**	**6**	**7**	**13**	**39**	**0**	**0**	**2**
1993-94	**Los Angeles Kings**	**NHL**	**80**	**10**	**9**	**19**	**9**	**7**	**16**	**322**	**0**	**0**	**3**	**105**	**9.5**	**32**	**1**	**52**	**2**	**–19**	....	....	....	....	....	....	....	....
1994-95	**Los Angeles Kings**	**NHL**	**7**	**0**	**0**	**0**	**0**	**0**	**0**	**19**	**0**	**0**	**0**	**7**	**0.0**	**1**	**0**	**6**	**0**	**–5**	....	....	....	....	....	....	....	....
	Toronto Maple Leafs	**NHL**	**26**	**1**	**6**	**7**	**2**	**9**	**11**	**101**	**0**	**0**	**0**	**34**	**2.9**	**11**	**0**	**10**	**0**	**1**	**3**	**0**	**0**	**0**	**0**	**0**	**0**	**0**
1995-96♦	**Colorado Avalanche**	**NHL**	**52**	**6**	**2**	**8**	**6**	**2**	**8**	**147**	**0**	**0**	**1**	**45**	**13.3**	**13**	**0**	**7**	**0**	**6**	**12**	**1**	**0**	**1**	**23**	**0**	**0**	**0**
1996-97	**Mighty Ducks of Anaheim**	**NHL**	**70**	**10**	**7**	**17**	**11**	**6**	**17**	**218**	**1**	**1**	**1**	**59**	**16.9**	**29**	**1**	**22**	**0**	**6**	**11**	**0**	**2**	**2**	**19**	**0**	**0**	**0**
1997-98	**Mighty Ducks of Anaheim**	**NHL**	**63**	**5**	**6**	**11**	**6**	**6**	**12**	**198**	**1**	**0**	**0**	**62**	**8.1**	**23**	**5**	**29**	**1**	**–10**	....	....	....	....	....	....	....	....
	Colorado Avalanche	**NHL**	**8**	**0**	**0**	**0**	**0**	**0**	**0**	**23**	**0**	**0**	**0**	**4**	**0.0**	**0**	**0**	**1**	**0**	**–1**	**6**	**0**	**0**	**0**	**24**	**0**	**0**	**0**
1998-99	**Colorado Avalanche**	**NHL**	**28**	**0**	**2**	**2**	**0**	**2**	**2**	**63**	**0**	**0**	**0**	**15**	**0.0**	**4**	**0**	**1**	**0**	**3**	**12**	**0**	**1**	**1**	**14**	**0**	**0**	**0**
	NHL Totals		**406**	**38**	**39**	**77**	**39**	**37**	**76**	**1422**	**2**	**1**	**6**	**401**	**9.5**	**133**	**9**	**171**	**12**		**70**	**8**	**13**	**21**	**121**	**1**	**0**	**3**

Signed as a free agent by **Chicago**, September 19, 1986. Traded to **Winnipeg** by **Chicago** with Troy Murray for Bryan Marchment and Chris Norton, July 22, 1991. Traded to **Minnesota** by **Winnipeg** for Tony Joseph, December 30, 1991. Signed as a free agent by **LA Kings**, October 1, 1992. Traded to **Washington** by **LA Kings** for Randy Burridge, February 10, 1995. Traded to **Toronto** by **Washington** for Toronto's 4th round choice (Sebastien Charpentier) in 1995 Entry Draft, February 10, 1995. Traded to **Colorado** by **Toronto** for cash, October 2, 1995. Signed as a free agent by **Anaheim**, August 21, 1996. Traded to **Colorado** by **Anaheim** with future considerations for Josef Marha, March 24, 1998.

• RYMSHA, Andy

Andrew Anthony D – L. 6'3", 210 lbs. b: St. Catharines, Ont., 12/10/1968. St. Louis' 5th, 82nd overall, in 1987.

Season	Club	League	GP	G	A	Pts	AG	AA	APts	PIM	PP	SH	GW	S	%	TGF	PGF	TGA	PGA	+/–	GP	G	A	Pts	PIM	PP	SH	GW
1985-86	St. Catharines Falcons	OJHL-B	39	6	13	19	....	....	....	170	....	....	....	....	....	....	....	....	....	....	....	....	....	....	....	....	....	....
1986-87	Western Michigan University	CCHA	41	7	12	19	....	....	....	60	....	....	....	....	....	....	....	....	....	....	....	....	....	....	....	....	....	....
1987-88	Western Michigan University	CCHA	42	5	6	11	....	....	....	114	....	....	....	....	....	....	....	....	....	....	....	....	....	....	....	....	....	....
1988-89	Western Michigan University	CCHA	35	3	4	7	....	....	....	139	....	....	....	....	....	....	....	....	....	....	....	....	....	....	....	....	....	....
1989-90	Western Michigan University	CCHA	37	1	10	11	....	....	....	108	....	....	....	....	....	....	....	....	....	....	....	....	....	....	....	....	....	....
1990-91	Halifax Citadels	AHL	12	1	2	3	....	....	....	22	....	....	....	....	....	....	....	....	....	....	....	....	....	....	....	....	....	....
	Peoria Rivermen	IHL	45	2	9	11	....	....	....	64	....	....	....	....	....	....	....	....	....	....	....	....	....	....	....	....	....	....
1991-92	**Quebec Nordiques**	**NHL**	**6**	**0**	**0**	**0**	**0**	**0**	**0**	**23**	**0**	**0**	**0**	**4**	**0.0**	**1**	**0**	**4**	**0**	**–3**	....	....	....	....	....	....	....	....
	Halifax Citadels	AHL	44	4	7	11	....	....	....	54	....	....	....	....	....	....	....	....	....	....	....	....	....	....	....	....	....	....
	New Haven Nighthawks	AHL	16	0	5	5	....	....	....	20	....	....	....	....	....	....	....	....	....	....	....	....	....	....	....	....	....	....
1992-93	Canada	Nat-Team	6	8	2	10	....	....	....	16	....	....	....	....	....	....	....	....	....	....	....	....	....	....	....	....	....	....
	Halifax Citadels	AHL	43	4	6	10	....	....	....	62	....	....	....	....	....	....	....	....	....	....	....	....	....	....	....	....	....	....

			REGULAR SEASON																		PLAYOFFS							
Season	Club	League	GP	G	A	Pts	AG	AA	APts	PIM	PP	SH	GW	S	%	TGF	PGF	TGA	PGA	+/–	GP	G	A	Pts	PIM	PP	SH	GW
1993-94	Detroit Falcons	ColHL	48	24	38	62	....	....	....	48	....	....	....	....	....	....	....	....	....	....	....	....	....	....	....	....	....	....
	Bracknell Bees	Britain	14	16	13	29	....	....	....	40	....	....	....	....	....	....	....	....	....	....	....	....	....	....	....	....	....	....
1994-95	WEV Wein	Austria	29	21	21	42	....	....	....	*124	....	....	....	....	....	....	....	....	....	....	3	3	0	3	6	....	....	....
	HC Asiago	Italy	8	4	7	11	....	....	....	18	....	....	....	....	....	....	....	....	....	....	....	....	....	....	....	....	....	....
1995-96	San Francisco Spiders	IHL	76	33	27	60	....	....	....	84	....	....	....	....	....	....	....	....	....	....	4	0	2	2	8	....	....	....
1996-97	Kaufbeuren Adler	Germany	26	8	12	20	....	....	....	68	....	....	....	....	....	....	....	....	....	....	....	....	....	....	....	....	....	....
	HC Ajoie	Switz-2	13	6	6	12	....	....	....	58	....	....	....	....	....	....	....	....	....	....	9	1	4	5	26	....	....	....
1997-98	WSV Sterzing	Italy	12	7	8	15	....	....	....	40	....	....	....	....	....	....	....	....	....	....	....	....	....	....	....	....	....	....
	Star Bulls Rosenheim	Germany	43	16	17	33	....	....	....	116	....	....	....	....	....	....	....	....	....	....	....	....	....	....	....	....	....	....
1998-99	Schwenningen Wild Wings	Germany	50	23	16	39	....	....	....	*246	....	....	....	....	....	....	....	....	....	....	....	....	....	....	....	....	....	....
99-2000	Krefeld Pinguine	Germany	49	11	9	20	....	....	....	192	....	....	....	....	....	....	....	....	....	....	3	1	0	1	50	....	....	....
	NHL Totals		**6**	**0**	**0**	**0**	**0**	**0**	**0**	**23**	**0**	**0**	**0**	**4**	**0.0**	**1**	**0**	**4**	**0**		....	....	....	....	....	....	....	....

Traded to **Quebec** by **St. Louis** with Tony Twist and Herb Raglan for Darin Kimble, February 4, 1991. • Played w/ RHI's Portland Rge 1994 (22-16-46-62-98), New Jersey 1995 (23-23-24-47-102), 1996 (17-19-26-45-42), 1997 (13-11-11-22-22) and Buffalo Wings 1996 (4-3-9-12-31).

• SAARINEN, Simo

D – L. 5'8", 185 lbs. b: Helsinki, Finland, 2/14/1963. NY Rangers' 10th, 193rd overall, in 1982.

Season	Club	League	GP	G	A	Pts	AG	AA	APts	PIM	PP	SH	GW	S	%	TGF	PGF	TGA	PGA	+/–	GP	G	A	Pts	PIM	PP	SH	GW
1980-81	HIFK Helsinki	Finland-Jr.	21	9	9	18	....	....	....	31	....	....	....	....	....	....	....	....	....	....	....	....	....	....	....	....	....	....
	HIFK Helsinki	Finland	20	1	0	1	....	....	....	4	....	....	....	....	....	....	....	....	....	....	2	0	0	0	0	....	....	....
1981-82	HIFK Helsinki	Finland	36	5	10	15	....	....	....	20	....	....	....	....	....	....	....	....	....	....	8	1	3	4	6	....	....	....
	Finland	WJC-A	7	3	3	6	....	....	....	6	....	....	....	....	....	....	....	....	....	....	....	....	....	....	....	....	....	....
1982-83	HIFK Helsinki	Finland	36	9	6	15	....	....	....	24	....	....	....	....	....	....	....	....	....	....	9	0	1	1	14	....	....	....
	Finland	WJC-A	7	3	3	6	....	....	....	4	....	....	....	....	....	....	....	....	....	....	....	....	....	....	....	....	....	....
1983-84	HIFK Helsinki	Finland	36	7	7	14	....	....	....	32	....	....	....	....	....	....	....	....	....	....	2	0	0	0	0	....	....	....
	Finland	Olympics	6	1	0	1	....	....	....	14	....	....	....	....	....	....	....	....	....	....	....	....	....	....	....	....	....	....
1984-85	**New York Rangers**	**NHL**	**8**	**0**	**0**	**0**	**0**	**0**	**0**	**0**	**0**	**0**	**0**	**8**	**0.0**	**5**	**1**	**8**	**0**	**–4**	....	....	....	....	....	....	....	....
1985-86	New Haven Nighthawks	AHL	13	3	4	7	....	....	....	11	....	....	....	....	....	....	....	....	....	....	....	....	....	....	....	....	....	....
1986-87	HIFK Helsinki	Finland	36	1	6	7	....	....	....	12	....	....	....	....	....	....	....	....	....	....	5	1	1	2	2	....	....	....
1987-88	HIFK Helsinki	Finland	39	8	11	19	....	....	....	29	....	....	....	....	....	....	....	....	....	....	6	2	2	4	2	....	....	....
	Finland	Olympics	7	0	2	2	....	....	....	4	....	....	....	....	....	....	....	....	....	....	....	....	....	....	....	....	....	....
1988-89	HIFK Helsinki	Finland	34	1	7	8	....	....	....	14	....	....	....	....	....	....	....	....	....	....	2	0	1	1	0	....	....	....
	Finland	WEC-A	5	0	0	0	....	....	....	2	....	....	....	....	....	....	....	....	....	....	....	....	....	....	....	....	....	....
1989-90	HIFK Helsinki	Finland	41	9	11	20	....	....	....	38	....	....	....	....	....	....	....	....	....	....	2	0	1	1	2	....	....	....
	Finland	WEC-A	7	0	3	3	....	....	....	8	....	....	....	....	....	....	....	....	....	....	....	....	....	....	....	....	....	....
1990-91	HIFK Helsinki	Finland	27	3	7	10	....	....	....	12	....	....	....	....	....	....	....	....	....	....	....	....	....	....	....	....	....	....
1991-92	HIFK Helsinki	Finland	43	5	18	23	....	....	....	14	....	....	....	....	....	....	....	....	....	....	7	0	0	0	0	....	....	....
	Finland	Olympics	5	0	1	1	....	....	....	6	....	....	....	....	....	....	....	....	....	....	....	....	....	....	....	....	....	....
1992-93	HIFK Helsinki	Finland	46	7	5	12	....	....	....	22	....	....	....	....	....	....	....	....	....	....	4	0	3	3	0	....	....	....
1993-94	HIFK Helsinki	Finland	40	4	5	9	....	....	....	38	....	....	....	....	....	....	....	....	....	....	3	0	1	1	0	....	....	....
1994-95	HIFK Helsinki	Finland	42	7	7	14	....	....	....	40	....	....	....	....	....	....	....	....	....	....	3	0	0	0	2	....	....	....
1995-96	HIFK Helsinki	Finland	30	4	3	7	....	....	....	32	....	....	....	....	....	....	....	....	....	....	1	1	0	1	0	....	....	....
	NHL Totals		**8**	**0**	**0**	**0**	**0**	**0**	**0**	**0**	**0**	**0**	**0**	**8**	**0.0**	**5**	**1**	**8**	**0**		....	....	....	....	....	....	....	....

WJC-A All-Star Team (1983) • Finnish First All-Star Team (1988)

• Missed remainder of 1984-85 and majority of 1985-86 seasons recovering from knee injury suffered in game vs. LA Kings, November 11, 1984.

• SABOL, Shaun

D – L. 6'3", 230 lbs. b: Minneapolis, MN, 7/13/1966. Philadelphia's 9th, 209th overall, in 1986.

Season	Club	League	GP	G	A	Pts	AG	AA	APts	PIM	PP	SH	GW	S	%	TGF	PGF	TGA	PGA	+/–	GP	G	A	Pts	PIM	PP	SH	GW
1983-84	St. Paul Vulcans	USHL	47	6	10	16	....	....	....	32	....	....	....	....	....	....	....	....	....	....	....	....	....	....	....	....	....	....
1984-85	St. Paul Vulcans	USHL	47	4	13	17	....	....	....	137	....	....	....	....	....	....	....	....	....	....	....	....	....	....	....	....	....	....
1985-86	St. Paul Vulcans	USHL	46	10	19	29	....	....	....	129	....	....	....	....	....	....	....	....	....	....	....	....	....	....	....	....	....	....
1986-87	University of Wisconsin	WCHA	40	7	16	23	....	....	....	98	....	....	....	....	....	....	....	....	....	....	....	....	....	....	....	....	....	....
1987-88	University of Wisconsin	WCHA	8	4	3	7	....	....	....	10	....	....	....	....	....	....	....	....	....	....	....	....	....	....	....	....	....	....
	Hershey Bears	AHL	51	1	9	10	....	....	....	66	....	....	....	....	....	....	....	....	....	....	2	0	0	0	5	....	....	....
1988-89	Hershey Bears	AHL	58	7	11	18	....	....	....	134	....	....	....	....	....	....	....	....	....	....	12	0	2	2	35	....	....	....
1989-90	**Philadelphia Flyers**	**NHL**	**2**	**0**	**0**	**0**	**0**	**0**	**0**	**0**	**0**	**0**	**0**	**2**	**0.0**	**1**	**0**	**1**	**0**	**0**	....	....	....	....	....	....	....	....
	Hershey Bears	AHL	46	6	16	22	....	....	....	49	....	....	....	....	....	....	....	....	....	....	....	....	....	....	....	....	....	....
1990-91	Hershey Bears	AHL	59	6	13	19	....	....	....	136	....	....	....	....	....	....	....	....	....	....	7	0	1	1	34	....	....	....
1991-92	Binghamton Rangers	AHL	72	5	19	24	....	....	....	123	....	....	....	....	....	....	....	....	....	....	11	1	2	3	10	....	....	....
	NHL Totals		**2**	**0**	**0**	**0**	**0**	**0**	**0**	**0**	**0**	**0**	**0**	**2**	**0.0**	**1**	**0**	**1**	**0**		....	....	....	....	....	....	....	....

Traded to **NY Rangers** by **Philadelphia** for future considerations, August 5, 1991.

• SABOURIN, Gary

Gary Bruce RW – R. 5'11", 180 lbs. b: Parry Sound, Ont., 12/4/1943.

Season	Club	League	GP	G	A	Pts	AG	AA	APts	PIM	PP	SH	GW	S	%	TGF	PGF	TGA	PGA	+/–	GP	G	A	Pts	PIM	PP	SH	GW
1961-62	Orangeville Crushers	OHA-B	STATISTICS NOT AVAILABLE																									
1962-63	Guelph Royals	OHA-Jr.	42	14	26	40	....	....	....	119	....	....	....	....	....	....	....	....	....	....	....	....	....	....	....	....	....	....
1963-64	Kitchener Rangers	OHA-Jr.	53	16	34	50	....	....	....	111	....	....	....	....	....	....	....	....	....	....	....	....	....	....	....	....	....	....
	St. Paul Rangers	CPHL	6	2	1	3	....	....	....	9	....	....	....	....	....	....	....	....	....	....	2	0	0	0	0	....	....	....
1964-65	St. Paul Rangers	CPHL	59	16	22	38	....	....	....	92	....	....	....	....	....	....	....	....	....	....	11	0	7	7	16	....	....	....
1965-66	Minnesota Rangers	CPHL	66	11	30	41	....	....	....	118	....	....	....	....	....	....	....	....	....	....	7	3	1	4	16	....	....	....
1966-67	Omaha Knights	CPHL	70	23	25	48	....	....	....	121	....	....	....	....	....	....	....	....	....	....	12	2	2	4	12	....	....	....
1967-68	**St. Louis Blues**	**NHL**	**50**	**13**	**10**	**23**	**15**	**10**	**25**	**50**	**0**	**2**	**2**	**121**	**10.7**	**36**	**2**	**25**	**2**	**11**	**18**	**4**	**2**	**6**	**30**	**1**	**0**	**1**
	Kansas City Blues	CPHL	18	8	10	18	....	....	....	16	....	....	....	....	....	....	....	....	....	....	....	....	....	....	....	....	....	....
1968-69	**St. Louis Blues**	**NHL**	**75**	**25**	**23**	**48**	**27**	**20**	**47**	**58**	**3**	**0**	**3**	**228**	**11.0**	**61**	**12**	**27**	**1**	**23**	**12**	**6**	**5**	**11**	**12**	**1**	**2**	**0**
1969-70	**St. Louis Blues**	**NHL**	**72**	**28**	**14**	**42**	**31**	**13**	**44**	**61**	**11**	**0**	**5**	**246**	**11.4**	**78**	**37**	**50**	**0**	**–9**	**16**	**5**	**0**	**5**	**10**	**0**	**1**	**1**
1970-71	**St. Louis Blues**	**NHL**	**59**	**14**	**17**	**31**	**14**	**14**	**28**	**56**	**2**	**0**	**2**	**160**	**8.8**	**48**	**8**	**36**	**0**	**4**	....	....	....	....	....	....	....	....
1971-72	**St. Louis Blues**	**NHL**	**77**	**28**	**17**	**45**	**28**	**15**	**43**	**52**	**4**	**0**	**7**	**236**	**11.9**	**63**	**13**	**48**	**1**	**3**	**11**	**3**	**3**	**6**	**6**	**0**	**0**	**0**
1972-73	**St. Louis Blues**	**NHL**	**76**	**21**	**27**	**48**	**20**	**21**	**41**	**30**	**1**	**0**	**2**	**240**	**8.8**	**68**	**9**	**64**	**0**	**–5**	**5**	**1**	**1**	**2**	**0**	**0**	**0**	**1**
1973-74	**St. Louis Blues**	**NHL**	**54**	**7**	**23**	**30**	**7**	**19**	**26**	**27**	**1**	**0**	**0**	**126**	**5.6**	**46**	**8**	**47**	**0**	**–9**	....	....	....	....	....	....	....	....
1974-75	**Toronto Maple Leafs**	**NHL**	**55**	**5**	**18**	**23**	**4**	**13**	**17**	**26**	**1**	**0**	**0**	**114**	**4.4**	**33**	**7**	**43**	**4**	**–13**	....	....	....	....	....	....	....	....
1975-76	**California Golden Seals**	**NHL**	**76**	**21**	**28**	**49**	**18**	**21**	**39**	**33**	**4**	**0**	**3**	**172**	**12.2**	**71**	**19**	**59**	**0**	**–7**	....	....	....	....	....	....	....	....
1976-77	**Cleveland Barons**	**NHL**	**33**	**7**	**11**	**18**	**6**	**8**	**14**	**4**	**2**	**0**	**1**	**76**	**9.2**	**27**	**6**	**27**	**0**	**–6**	....	....	....	....	....	....	....	....
	NHL Totals		**627**	**169**	**188**	**357**	**170**	**154**	**324**	**397**	**29**	**2**	**25**	**1719**	**9.8**	**531**	**121**	**426**	**8**		**62**	**19**	**11**	**30**	**58**	**2**	**3**	**3**

• Brother of Bob • Played in NHL All-Star Game (1970, 1971)

Traded to **St. Louis** by **NY Rangers** with Bob Plager, Gord Kannegiesser and Tim Ecclestone for Rod Seiling, June 6, 1967. Traded to **Toronto** by **St. Louis** for Eddie Johnston, May 27, 1974. Traded to **California** by **Toronto** for Stan Weir, June 20, 1975. Transferred to **Cleveland** after **California** franchise relocated, August 26, 1976.

• SABOURIN, Ken

D – L. 6'3", 205 lbs. b: Scarborough, Ont., 4/28/1966. Calgary's 2nd, 33rd overall, in 1984.

Season	Club	League	GP	G	A	Pts	AG	AA	APts	PIM	PP	SH	GW	S	%	TGF	PGF	TGA	PGA	+/–	GP	G	A	Pts	PIM	PP	SH	GW
1981-82	Don Mills Flyers	MTHL	40	10	20	30	....	....	....	....	....	....	....	....	....	....	....	....	....	....	....	....	....	....	....	....	....	....
1982-83	Sault Ste. Marie Greyhounds	OHL	58	0	8	8	....	....	....	90	....	....	....	....	....	....	....	....	....	....	10	0	0	0	14	....	....	....
1983-84	Sault Ste. Marie Greyhounds	OHL	63	7	14	21	....	....	....	157	....	....	....	....	....	....	....	....	....	....	9	0	1	1	25	....	....	....
1984-85	Sault Ste. Marie Greyhounds	OHL	63	5	19	24	....	....	....	139	....	....	....	....	....	....	....	....	....	....	16	1	4	5	10	....	....	....
	Sault Ste. Marie Greyhounds	Mem-Cup	4	0	2	2	....	....	....	2	....	....	....	....	....	....	....	....	....	....	....	....	....	....	....	....	....	....
1985-86	Sault Ste. Marie Greyhounds	OHL	25	1	5	6	....	....	....	77	....	....	....	....	....	....	....	....	....	....	....	....	....	....	....	....	....	....
	Cornwall Royals	OHL	37	3	12	15	....	....	....	94	....	....	....	....	....	....	....	....	....	....	6	1	2	3	6	....	....	....
	Moncton Golden Flames	AHL	3	0	0	0	....	....	....	0	....	....	....	....	....	....	....	....	....	....	6	0	1	1	2	....	....	....
1986-87	Moncton Golden Flames	AHL	75	1	10	11	....	....	....	166	....	....	....	....	....	....	....	....	....	....	6	0	1	1	27	....	....	....
1987-88	Salt Lake Golden Eagles	IHL	71	2	8	10	....	....	....	186	....	....	....	....	....	....	....	....	....	....	16	1	6	7	57	....	....	....
1988-89♦	**Calgary Flames**	**NHL**	**6**	**0**	**1**	**1**	**0**	**1**	**1**	**26**	**0**	**0**	**0**	**2**	**0.0**	**6**	**0**	**3**	**0**	**3**	**1**	**0**	**0**	**0**	**0**	**0**	**0**	**0**
	Salt Lake Golden Eagles	IHL	74	2	18	20	....	....	....	197	....	....	....	....	....	....	....	....	....	....	11	0	1	1	26	....	....	....

Season	Club	League	GP	G	A	Pts	AG	AA	APts	PIM	PP	SH	GW	S	%	TGF	PGF	TGA	PGA	+/–	GP	G	A	Pts	PIM	PP	SH	GW
			REGULAR SEASON																		PLAYOFFS							
1989-90	Calgary Flames	Fr-Tour	3	0	0	0	....	....	....	6	....	....	....	....	....	....	....	....	....	....	....	....	....	....	....	....	....	....
	Calgary Flames	**NHL**	**5**	**0**	**0**	**0**	**0**	**0**	**0**	**10**	**0**	**0**	**0**	**3**	**0.0**	**5**	**0**	**4**	**0**	**1**	....	....	....	....	....	....	....	....
	Salt Lake Golden Eagles	IHL	76	5	19	24	....	....	....	336	....	....	....	....	....	....	....	....	....	....	11	0	2	2	40	....	....	....
1990-91	**Calgary Flames**	**NHL**	**16**	**1**	**3**	**4**	**1**	**2**	**3**	**36**	**0**	**0**	**0**	**9**	**11.1**	**15**	**0**	**8**	**2**	**9**	....	....	....	....	....	....	....	....
	Salt Lake Golden Eagles	IHL	28	2	15	17	....	....	....	77	....	....	....	....	....	....	....	....	....	....	....	....	....	....	....	....	....	....
	Washington Capitals	**NHL**	**28**	**1**	**4**	**5**	**1**	**3**	**4**	**81**	**0**	**0**	**0**	**14**	**7.1**	**22**	**0**	**17**	**1**	**6**	**11**	**0**	**0**	**0**	**34**	**0**	**0**	**0**
1991-92	**Washington Capitals**	**NHL**	**19**	**0**	**0**	**0**	**0**	**0**	**0**	**48**	**0**	**0**	**0**	**12**	**0.0**	**7**	**0**	**13**	**1**	**–5**	....	....	....	....	....	....	....	....
	Baltimore Skipjacks	AHL	30	3	8	11	....	....	....	106	....	....	....	....	....	....	....	....	....	....	....	....	....	....	....	....	....	....
1992-93	Baltimore Skipjacks	AHL	30	5	14	19	....	....	....	68	....	....	....	....	....	....	....	....	....	....	....	....	....	....	....	....	....	....
	Salt Lake Golden Eagles	IHL	52	2	11	13	....	....	....	140	....	....	....	....	....	....	....	....	....	....	....	....	....	....	....	....	....	....
1993-94	Milwaukee Admirals	IHL	81	6	13	19	....	....	....	279	....	....	....	....	....	....	....	....	....	....	4	0	0	0	10	....	....	....
1994-95	Milwaukee Admirals	IHL	75	3	16	19	....	....	....	297	....	....	....	....	....	....	....	....	....	....	15	1	1	2	69	....	....	....
1995-96	Milwaukee Admirals	IHL	82	2	8	10	....	....	....	252	....	....	....	....	....	....	....	....	....	....	5	0	1	1	24	....	....	....
1996-97	Milwaukee Admirals	IHL	81	2	9	11	....	....	....	233	....	....	....	....	....	....	....	....	....	....	3	0	0	0	2	....	....	....
1997-98	Milwaukee Admirals	IHL	71	1	5	6	....	....	....	172	....	....	....	....	....	....	....	....	....	....	10	0	1	1	55	....	....	....
1998-99	Orlando Solar Bears	IHL	72	3	4	7	....	....	....	248	....	....	....	....	....	....	....	....	....	....	14	0	0	0	49	....	....	....
	NHL Totals		**74**	**2**	**8**	**10**	**2**	**6**	**8**	**201**	**0**	**0**	**0**	**40**	**5.0**	**55**	**0**	**45**	**4**		**12**	**0**	**0**	**0**	**34**	**0**	**0**	**0**

Traded to **Washington** by **Calgary** for Paul Fenton, January 24, 1991. Traded to **Calgary** by **Washington** for future considerations, December 16, 1992. Traded to **Quebec** by **Washington** with Paul MacDermid for Mike Hough, January 20, 1993.

• SACCO, David

RW – R. 6', 180 lbs. b: Malden, MA, 7/31/1970. Toronto's 9th, 195th overall, in 1988.

Season	Club	League	GP	G	A	Pts	AG	AA	APts	PIM	PP	SH	GW	S	%	TGF	PGF	TGA	PGA	+/–	GP	G	A	Pts	PIM	PP	SH	GW
1987-88	Medford Mustangs	Hi-School	STATISTICS NOT AVAILABLE																									
1988-89	Boston University	H-East	35	14	29	43	....	....	....	40	....	....	....	....	....	....	....	....	....	....	....	....	....	....	....	....	....	....
1989-90	Boston University	H-East	3	0	4	4	....	....	....	2	....	....	....	....	....	....	....	....	....	....	....	....	....	....	....	....	....	....
1990-91	Boston University	H-East	40	21	40	61	....	....	....	24	....	....	....	....	....	....	....	....	....	....	....	....	....	....	....	....	....	....
1991-92	Boston University	H-East	34	13	32	45	....	....	....	30	....	....	....	....	....	....	....	....	....	....	....	....	....	....	....	....	....	....
1992-93	Boston University	H-East	40	25	37	62	....	....	....	86	....	....	....	....	....	....	....	....	....	....	....	....	....	....	....	....	....	....
	United States	WC-A	6	0	0	0	....	....	....	0	....	....	....	....	....	....	....	....	....	....	....	....	....	....	....	....	....	....
1993-94	United States	Nat-Team	32	8	20	28	....	....	....	88	....	....	....	....	....	....	....	....	....	....	....	....	....	....	....	....	....	....
	United States	Olympics	8	3	5	8	....	....	....	12	....	....	....	....	....	....	....	....	....	....	....	....	....	....	....	....	....	....
	Toronto Maple Leafs	**NHL**	**4**	**1**	**1**	**2**	**1**	**1**	**2**	**4**	**1**	**0**	**0**	**4**	**25.0**	**2**	**2**	**2**	**0**	**–2**	....	....	....	....	....	....	....	....
	St. John's Maple Leafs	AHL	5	3	1	4	....	....	....	2	....	....	....	....	....	....	....	....	....	....	....	....	....	....	....	....	....	....
1994-95	San Diego Gulls	IHL	45	11	25	36	....	....	....	57	....	....	....	....	....	....	....	....	....	....	4	3	1	4	0	....	....	....
	Mighty Ducks of Anaheim	**NHL**	**8**	**0**	**2**	**2**	**0**	**3**	**3**	**0**	**0**	**0**	**0**	**5**	**0.0**	**4**	**1**	**6**	**0**	**–3**	....	....	....	....	....	....	....	....
1995-96	**Mighty Ducks of Anaheim**	**NHL**	**23**	**4**	**10**	**14**	**4**	**8**	**12**	**18**	**2**	**0**	**0**	**26**	**15.4**	**22**	**7**	**14**	**0**	**1**	....	....	....	....	....	....	....	....
	Baltimore Bandits	AHL	25	14	16	30	....	....	....	18	....	....	....	....	....	....	....	....	....	....	2	0	1	1	4	....	....	....
1996-97	Baltimore Bandits	AHL	51	18	38	56	....	....	....	30	....	....	....	....	....	....	....	....	....	....	1	0	2	2	0	....	....	....
1997-98	SC Bern	Switz.	16	5	12	17	....	....	....	47	....	....	....	....	....	....	....	....	....	....	....	....	....	....	....	....	....	....
	SC Bern	EuroHL	3	0	0	0	....	....	....	0	....	....	....	....	....	....	....	....	....	....	....	....	....	....	....	....	....	....
	NHL Totals		**35**	**5**	**13**	**18**	**5**	**12**	**17**	**22**	**3**	**0**	**0**	**35**	**14.3**	**28**	**10**	**22**	**0**		....	....	....	....	....	....	....	....

• Brother of Joe • NCAA East First All-American Team (1992, 1993) • Hockey East First All-Star Team (1992, 1993)

Traded to **Anaheim** by **Toronto** for Terry Yake, September 28, 1994. Signed as a free agent by **NY Islanders**, September 6, 1996.

• SACCO, Joe

Joseph W. RW – L. 6'1", 190 lbs. b: Medford, MA, 2/4/1969. Toronto's 4th, 71st overall, in 1987.

Season	Club	League	GP	G	A	Pts	AG	AA	APts	PIM	PP	SH	GW	S	%	TGF	PGF	TGA	PGA	+/–	GP	G	A	Pts	PIM	PP	SH	GW
1985-86	Medford Mustangs	Hi-School	20	30	30	60	....	....	....	....	....	....	....	....	....	....	....	....	....	....	....	....	....	....	....	....	....	....
1986-87	Medford Mustangs	Hi-School	21	22	32	54	....	....	....	....	....	....	....	....	....	....	....	....	....	....	....	....	....	....	....	....	....	....
1987-88	Boston University	H-East	34	16	20	36	....	....	....	40	....	....	....	....	....	....	....	....	....	....	....	....	....	....	....	....	....	....
1988-89	Boston University	H-East	33	21	19	40	....	....	....	66	....	....	....	....	....	....	....	....	....	....	....	....	....	....	....	....	....	....
	United States	WJC-A	7	3	1	4	....	....	....	2	....	....	....	....	....	....	....	....	....	....	....	....	....	....	....	....	....	....
1989-90	Boston University	H-East	44	28	24	52	....	....	....	70	....	....	....	....	....	....	....	....	....	....	....	....	....	....	....	....	....	....
	United States	WEC-A	10	1	1	2	....	....	....	2	....	....	....	....	....	....	....	....	....	....	....	....	....	....	....	....	....	....
1990-91	**Toronto Maple Leafs**	**NHL**	**20**	**0**	**5**	**5**	**0**	**4**	**4**	**2**	**0**	**0**	**0**	**20**	**0.0**	**7**	**3**	**11**	**2**	**–5**	....	....	....	....	....	....	....	....
	Newmarket Saints	AHL	49	18	17	35	....	....	....	24	....	....	....	....	....	....	....	....	....	....	....	....	....	....	....	....	....	....
	United States	WEC-A	10	1	0	1	....	....	....	6	....	....	....	....	....	....	....	....	....	....	....	....	....	....	....	....	....	....
1991-92	United States	Nat-Team	50	11	26	37	....	....	....	61	....	....	....	....	....	....	....	....	....	....	....	....	....	....	....	....	....	....
	United States	Olympics	8	0	2	2	....	....	....	0	....	....	....	....	....	....	....	....	....	....	....	....	....	....	....	....	....	....
	United States	WC-A	6	1	0	1	....	....	....	4	....	....	....	....	....	....	....	....	....	....	....	....	....	....	....	....	....	....
	Toronto Maple Leafs	**NHL**	**17**	**7**	**4**	**11**	**6**	**3**	**9**	**4**	**0**	**0**	**1**	**40**	**17.5**	**16**	**0**	**8**	**0**	**8**	....	....	....	....	....	....	....	....
	St. John's Maple Leafs	AHL	....	....	....	....	....	....	....	....	....	....	....	....	....	....	....	....	....	....	1	1	1	2	0	....	....	....
1992-93	**Toronto Maple Leafs**	**NHL**	**23**	**4**	**4**	**8**	**3**	**3**	**6**	**8**	**0**	**0**	**0**	**38**	**10.5**	**13**	**2**	**16**	**1**	**–4**	....	....	....	....	....	....	....	....
	St. John's Maple Leafs	AHL	37	14	16	30	....	....	....	45	....	....	....	....	....	....	....	....	....	....	7	6	4	10	2	....	....	....
1993-94	**Mighty Ducks of Anaheim**	**NHL**	**84**	**19**	**18**	**37**	**18**	**14**	**32**	**61**	**3**	**1**	**2**	**206**	**9.2**	**52**	**10**	**70**	**17**	**–11**	....	....	....	....	....	....	....	....
	United States	WC-A	8	0	1	1	....	....	....	14	....	....	....	....	....	....	....	....	....	....	....	....	....	....	....	....	....	....
1994-95	**Mighty Ducks of Anaheim**	**NHL**	**41**	**10**	**8**	**18**	**18**	**12**	**30**	**23**	**2**	**0**	**0**	**77**	**13.0**	**22**	**4**	**33**	**7**	**–8**	....	....	....	....	....	....	....	....
1995-96	**Mighty Ducks of Anaheim**	**NHL**	**76**	**13**	**14**	**27**	**13**	**11**	**24**	**40**	....	....	....	....	....	....	....	....	....	....	....	....	....	....	....	....	....	....
	United States	WC-A	8	2	4	6	....	....	....	2	....	....	....	....	....	....	....	....	....	....	....	....	....	....	....	....	....	....
1996-97	**Mighty Ducks of Anaheim**	**NHL**	**77**	**12**	**17**	**29**	**13**	**15**	**28**	**35**	**1**	**1**	**2**	**131**	**9.2**	**38**	**2**	**50**	**15**	**1**	**11**	**2**	**0**	**2**	**2**	**0**	**0**	**0**
1997-98	**Mighty Ducks of Anaheim**	**NHL**	**55**	**8**	**11**	**19**	**9**	**11**	**20**	**24**	**0**	**2**	**2**	**90**	**8.9**	**27**	**1**	**40**	**13**	**–1**	....	....	....	....	....	....	....	....
	New York Islanders	**NHL**	**25**	**3**	**3**	**6**	**4**	**3**	**7**	**10**	**0**	**0**	**0**	**32**	**9.4**	**9**	**0**	**11**	**3**	**1**	....	....	....	....	....	....	....	....
1998-99	**New York Islanders**	**NHL**	**73**	**3**	**0**	**3**	**4**	**0**	**4**	**45**	**0**	**1**	**2**	**84**	**3.6**	**10**	**0**	**45**	**11**	**–24**	....	....	....	....	....	....	....	....
99-2000	**Washington Capitals**	**NHL**	**79**	**7**	**16**	**23**	**8**	**15**	**23**	**50**	**0**	**0**	**1**	**117**	**6.0**	**38**	**2**	**44**	**15**	**7**	**5**	**0**	**0**	**0**	**4**	**0**	**0**	**0**
	NHL Totals		**570**	**86**	**100**	**186**	**96**	**91**	**187**	**302**	**6**	**5**	**10**	**835**	**10.3**	**232**	**24**	**328**	**84**		**16**	**2**	**0**	**2**	**6**	**0**	**0**	**0**

• Brother of David

Claimed by **Anaheim** from **Toronto** in Expansion Draft, June 24, 1993. Traded to **NY Islanders** by **Anaheim** with J.J. Daigneault and Mark Janssens for Travis Green, Doug Houda and Tony Tuzzolino, February 6, 1998. Signed as a free agent by **Washington**, August 9, 1999.

• SACHARUK, Larry

Lawrence D – R. 6', 200 lbs. b: Saskatoon, Sask., 9/16/1952. NY Rangers' 3rd, 21st overall, in 1972.

Season	Club	League	GP	G	A	Pts	AG	AA	APts	PIM	PP	SH	GW	S	%	TGF	PGF	TGA	PGA	+/–	GP	G	A	Pts	PIM	PP	SH	GW
1967-68	Saskatoon Blades	WCJHL	34	6	2	8	....	....	....	4	....	....	....	....	....	....	....	....	....	....	7	1	1	2	0	....	....	....
1968-69	Saskatoon Blades	WCJHL	56	5	11	16	....	....	....	39	....	....	....	....	....	....	....	....	....	....	4	1	1	2	0	....	....	....
1969-70	Niagara Falls Flyers	OHA-Jr.	51	19	18	37	....	....	....	47	....	....	....	....	....	....	....	....	....	....	....	....	....	....	....	....	....	....
1970-71	Saskatoon Blades	WCJHL	59	27	58	85	....	....	....	42	....	....	....	....	....	....	....	....	....	....	5	2	3	5	15	....	....	....
1971-72	Saskatoon Blades	WCJHL	65	50	36	86	....	....	....	57	....	....	....	....	....	....	....	....	....	....	8	6	7	13	12	....	....	....
1972-73	**New York Rangers**	**NHL**	**8**	**1**	**0**	**1**	**1**	**0**	**1**	**0**	**0**	**0**	**0**	**9**	**11.1**	**4**	**0**	**5**	**0**	**–1**	....	....	....	....	....	....	....	....
	Providence Reds	AHL	64	14	35	49	....	....	....	42	....	....	....	....	....	....	....	....	....	....	4	0	1	1	0	....	....	....
1973-74	**New York Rangers**	**NHL**	**23**	**2**	**4**	**6**	**2**	**3**	**5**	**4**	**1**	**0**	**2**	**50**	**4.0**	**20**	**5**	**16**	**1**	**0**	....	....	....	....	....	....	....	....
	Providence Reds	AHL	42	27	35	62	....	....	....	26	....	....	....	....	....	....	....	....	....	....	15	1	*14	15	4	....	....	....
1974-75	**St. Louis Blues**	**NHL**	**76**	**20**	**22**	**42**	**17**	**16**	**33**	**24**	**11**	**0**	**1**	**207**	**9.7**	**87**	**32**	**69**	**5**	**–9**	**2**	**1**	**1**	**2**	**2**	**0**	**0**	**0**
1975-76	**New York Rangers**	**NHL**	**42**	**6**	**7**	**13**	**5**	**5**	**10**	**14**	**4**	**0**	**2**	**70**	**8.6**	**32**	**21**	**26**	**1**	**–14**	....	....	....	....	....	....	....	....
1976-77	**New York Rangers**	**NHL**	**2**	**0**	**0**	**0**	**0**	**0**	**0**	**0**	**0**	**0**	**0**	**2**	**0.0**	**1**	**1**	**1**	**0**	**–1**	....	....	....	....	....	....	....	....
	New Haven Nighthawks	AHL	55	23	31	54	....	....	....	18	....	....	....	....	....	....	....	....	....	....	....	....	....	....	....	....	....	....
1977-78	New Haven Nighthawks	AHL	72	19	37	56	....	....	....	12	....	....	....	....	....	....	....	....	....	....	11	0	5	5	0	....	....	....
1978-79	Indianapolis Racers	WHA	15	2	9	11	....	....	....	25	....	....	....	....	....	....	....	....	....	....	....	....	....	....	....	....	....	....
1979-80	Birmingham Bulls	CHL	80	11	29	40	....	....	....	28	....	....	....	....	....	....	....	....	....	....	4	0	0	0	0	....	....	....

			REGULAR SEASON																		PLAYOFFS							
Season	Club	League	GP	G	A	Pts	AG	AA	APts	PIM	PP	SH	GW	S	%	TGF	PGF	TGA	PGA	+/–	GP	G	A	Pts	PIM	PP	SH	GW
1980-81	IEV Innsbruck	Austria	34	35	23	58	....	....	....	34	....	....	....	....	....	....	....	....	....	....	....	....	....	....	....	....	....	....
1981-82	WAT Stadlau	Austria	21	12	10	22	....	....	....	....	....	....	....	....	....	....	....	....	....	....	3	1	1	2	....	....	....	....
1982-83	Birmingham Eagles	Britain	6	14	8	22	....	....	....	16	....	....	....	....	....	....	....	....	....	....	....	....	....	....	....	....	....	....
	NHL Totals		**151**	**29**	**33**	**62**	**25**	**24**	**49**	**42**	**16**	**0**	**5**	**338**	**8.6**	**144**	**59**	**117**	**7**		**2**	**1**	**1**	**2**	**2**	**0**	**0**	**0**
	Other Major League Totals		15	2	9	11	....	....	....	25	....	....	....	....	....	....	....	....	....	....	....	....	....	....	....	....	....	....

WCJHL Second All-Star Team (1972)

Selected by **NY Raiders** (WHA) in 1972 WHA General Player Draft, February 12, 1972. Traded to **NY Rangers** by **St. Louis** for Bob MacMillan, September 20, 1975. Traded to **St. Louis** by **NY Rangers** with NY Rangers' 1st round choice (Lucien DeBlois) in 1977 Amateur Draft for Greg Polis, August 29, 1974. Signed as a free agent by **Indianapolis** (WHA), July, 1978.

• SAGANIUK, Rocky

Rocky Ray RW/C – R. 5'8", 185 lbs. b: Myrnam, Alta., 10/15/1957. Toronto's 4th, 29th overall, in 1977.

Season	Club	League	GP	G	A	Pts	AG	AA	APts	PIM	PP	SH	GW	S	%	TGF	PGF	TGA	PGA	+/–	GP	G	A	Pts	PIM	PP	SH	GW
1974-75	Taber Golden Suns	AJHL	50	21	32	53	....	....	....	124	....	....	....	....	....	....	....	....	....	....	....	....	....	....	....	....	....	....
1975-76	Taber Golden Suns	AJHL	49	42	32	74	....	....	....	169	....	....	....	....	....	....	....	....	....	....	....	....	....	....	....	....	....	....
	Kamloops Chiefs	WCJHL	4	0	0	0	....	....	....	0	....	....	....	....	....	....	....	....	....	....	....	....	....	....	....	....	....	....
	Lethbridge Broncos	WCJHL	6	2	1	3	....	....	....	0	....	....	....	....	....	....	....	....	....	....	5	2	1	3	6	....	....	....
1976-77	Lethbridge Broncos	WCJHL	72	60	48	108	....	....	....	203	....	....	....	....	....	....	....	....	....	....	15	6	5	11	21	....	....	....
1977-78	Dallas Black Hawks	CHL	42	16	13	29	....	....	....	71	....	....	....	....	....	....	....	....	....	....	....	....	....	....	....	....	....	....
1978-79	**Toronto Maple Leafs**	**NHL**	**16**	**3**	**5**	**8**	**3**	**4**	**7**	**9**	**1**	**0**	**1**	**30**	**10.0**	**15**	**4**	**10**	**0**	**1**	**3**	**1**	**0**	**1**	**5**	**0**	**0**	**0**
	New Brunswick Hawks	AHL	62	*47	29	76	....	....	....	91	....	....	....	....	....	....	....	....	....	....	....	....	....	....	....	....	....	....
1979-80	**Toronto Maple Leafs**	**NHL**	**75**	**24**	**23**	**47**	**20**	**17**	**37**	**52**	**3**	**0**	**4**	**164**	**14.6**	**67**	**9**	**63**	**0**	**–5**	**3**	**0**	**0**	**0**	**10**	**0**	**0**	**0**
1980-81	**Toronto Maple Leafs**	**NHL**	**71**	**12**	**18**	**30**	**9**	**12**	**21**	**52**	**2**	**0**	**3**	**113**	**10.6**	**51**	**9**	**58**	**0**	**–16**	....	....	....	....	....	....	....	....
1981-82	**Toronto Maple Leafs**	**NHL**	**65**	**17**	**16**	**33**	**13**	**11**	**24**	**49**	**0**	**0**	**1**	**100**	**17.0**	**47**	**0**	**63**	**0**	**–16**	....	....	....	....	....	....	....	....
1982-83	**Toronto Maple Leafs**	**NHL**	**3**	**0**	**0**	**0**	**0**	**0**	**0**	**2**	**0**	**0**	**0**	**0**	**0.0**	**0**	**0**	**3**	**0**	**–3**	....	....	....	....	....	....	....	....
	St. Catharines Saints	AHL	61	26	23	49	....	....	....	83	....	....	....	....	....	....	....	....	....	....	....	....	....	....	....	....	....	....
1983-84	**Pittsburgh Penguins**	**NHL**	**29**	**1**	**3**	**4**	**1**	**2**	**3**	**37**	**0**	**0**	**0**	**30**	**3.3**	**7**	**0**	**23**	**4**	**–12**	....	....	....	....	....	....	....	....
	Baltimore Skipjacks	AHL	5	1	1	2	....	....	....	0	....	....	....	....	....	....	....	....	....	....	....	....	....	....	....	....	....	....
1984-85	St. Catharines Saints	AHL	4	1	1	2	....	....	....	11	....	....	....	....	....	....	....	....	....	....	....	....	....	....	....	....	....	....
1985-86	Flamboro Flames	OHA-Sr.	STATISTICS NOT AVAILABLE																									
1986-87	Brantford Motts Clamatos	OHA-Sr.	33	21	22	43	....	....	....	55	....	....	....	....	....	....	....	....	....	....	....	....	....	....	....	....	....	....
1987-88	Ayr Bruins	Britain	14	19	20	39	....	....	....	50	....	....	....	....	....	....	....	....	....	....	13	8	8	16	32	....	....	....
1988-89	Ayr Bruins	Aut-Cup	5	3	11	14	....	....	....	25	....	....	....	....	....	....	....	....	....	....	....	....	....	....	....	....	....	....
	Ayr Bruins	Britain	8	8	8	16	....	....	....	32	....	....	....	....	....	....	....	....	....	....	....	....	....	....	....	....	....	....
1989-1990	Ayr Bruins	Britain	DID NOT PLAY – COACHING																									
1990-1991	Peterborough Pirates	Britain	DID NOT PLAY – COACHING																									
1991-1992	Peterborough Pirates	Britain	DID NOT PLAY – COACHING																									
	Peterborough Pirates	Britain	4	6	4	10	....	....	....	2	....	....	....	....	....	....	....	....	....	....	....	....	....	....	....	....	....	....
1992-1993	Peterborough Pirates	Britain	DID NOT PLAY – COACHING																									
1993-1994	Murrayfield Racers	Britain	DID NOT PLAY – COACHING																									
	Murrayfield Racers	Britain	3	4	3	7	....	....	....	4	....	....	....	....	....	....	....	....	....	....	....	....	....	....	....	....	....	....
1994-1995	Durham Wasps	BH-Cup	2	0	1	1	....	....	....	6	....	....	....	....	....	....	....	....	....	....	....	....	....	....	....	....	....	....
	Durham Wasps	Britain	2	1	2	3	....	....	....	6	....	....	....	....	....	....	....	....	....	....	....	....	....	....	....	....	....	....
	Blackburn Black Hawks	Britain	DID NOT PLAY – COACHING																									
	NHL Totals		**259**	**57**	**65**	**122**	**46**	**46**	**92**	**201**	**6**	**0**	**9**	**437**	**13.0**	**187**	**22**	**220**	**4**		**6**	**1**	**0**	**1**	**15**	**0**	**0**	**0**

AHL First All-Star Team (1979) • Won Les Cunningham Award (MVP - AHL) (1979)

Traded to **Pittsburgh** by **Toronto** with Vincent Tremblay for Pat Graham and Nick Ricci, August 15, 1983. Signed as a free agent by **Toronto**, August 21, 1984. • Served as player/coach in 1991-92; 1993-94 and 1994-95.

• ST. AMOUR, Martin

LW – L. 6'3", 194 lbs. b: Montreal, Que., 1/30/1970. Montreal's 2nd, 34th overall, in 1988.

Season	Club	League	GP	G	A	Pts	AG	AA	APts	PIM	PP	SH	GW	S	%	TGF	PGF	TGA	PGA	+/–	GP	G	A	Pts	PIM	PP	SH	GW
1986-87	Laval-Laurentides Regents	QAAA	42	55	95	150	....	....	....	58	....	....	....	....	....	....	....	....	....	....	....	....	....	....	....	....	....	....
1987-88	Verdun Jr. Canadiens	QMJHL	61	20	50	70	....	....	....	111	....	....	....	....	....	....	....	....	....	....	....	....	....	....	....	....	....	....
1988-89	Verdun Jr. Canadiens	QMJHL	28	19	17	36	....	....	....	87	....	....	....	....	....	....	....	....	....	....	....	....	....	....	....	....	....	....
	Trois-Rivieres Draveurs	QMJHL	26	8	21	29	....	....	....	69	....	....	....	....	....	....	....	....	....	....	4	1	2	3	0	....	....	....
1989-90	Trois-Rivieres Draveurs	QMJHL	60	57	79	136	....	....	....	162	....	....	....	....	....	....	....	....	....	....	7	7	9	16	19	....	....	....
	Sherbrooke Canadiens	AHL	....	....	....	....	....	....	....	....	....	....	....	....	....	....	....	....	....	....	1	0	0	0	0	....	....	....
1990-91	Fredericton Canadiens	AHL	45	13	16	29	....	....	....	51	....	....	....	....	....	....	....	....	....	....	1	0	0	0	0	....	....	....
1991-92	Cincinnati Cyclones	ECHL	60	44	44	88	....	....	....	183	....	....	....	....	....	....	....	....	....	....	9	4	9	13	18	....	....	....
1992-93	**Ottawa Senators**	**NHL**	**1**	**0**	**0**	**0**	**0**	**0**	**0**	**2**	**0**	**0**	**0**	**2**	**0.0**	**0**	**0**	**0**	**0**	**0**	....	....	....	....	....	....	....	....
	New Haven Senators	AHL	71	21	39	60	....	....	....	78	....	....	....	....	....	....	....	....	....	....	....	....	....	....	....	....	....	....
1993-94	P.E.I. Senators	AHL	37	13	12	25	....	....	....	65	....	....	....	....	....	....	....	....	....	....	....	....	....	....	....	....	....	....
	Providence Bruins	AHL	12	0	3	3	....	....	....	22	....	....	....	....	....	....	....	....	....	....	....	....	....	....	....	....	....	....
1994-95	Whitley Warriors	BH-Cup	8	14	12	26	....	....	....	61	....	....	....	....	....	....	....	....	....	....	....	....	....	....	....	....	....	....
	Whitley Warriors	Britain	2	1	1	2	....	....	....	16	....	....	....	....	....	....	....	....	....	....	....	....	....	....	....	....	....	....
	Moncton Labatt Ice	NSSHL	STATISTICS NOT AVAILABLE																									
1995-96	San Francisco Spiders	IHL	4	0	2	2	....	....	....	6	....	....	....	....	....	....	....	....	....	....	....	....	....	....	....	....	....	....
	Los Angeles Ice Dogs	IHL	1	0	0	0	....	....	....	0	....	....	....	....	....	....	....	....	....	....	....	....	....	....	....	....	....	....
	San Diego Gulls	WCHL	53	*61	48	*109	....	....	....	....	....	....	....	....	....	....	....	....	....	....	9	6	7	13	10	....	....	....
1996-97	HC Amiens	France	7	3	4	7	....	....	....	12	....	....	....	....	....	....	....	....	....	....	....	....	....	....	....	....	....	....
	San Diego Gulls	WCHL	59	*60	67	*127	....	....	....	170	....	....	....	....	....	....	....	....	....	....	8	*8	4	12	23	....	....	....
1997-98	San Diego Gulls	WCHL	61	35	44	79	....	....	....	203	....	....	....	....	....	....	....	....	....	....	12	*11	7	18	28	....	....	....
1998-99	San Diego Gulls	WCHL	59	15	31	46	....	....	....	176	....	....	....	....	....	....	....	....	....	....	12	2	7	9	18	....	....	....
99-2000	San Diego Gulls	WCHL	23	6	10	16	....	....	....	80	....	....	....	....	....	....	....	....	....	....	....	....	....	....	....	....	....	....
	NHL Totals		**1**	**0**	**0**	**0**	**0**	**0**	**0**	**2**	**0**	**0**	**0**	**2**	**0.0**	**0**	**0**	**0**	**0**		....	....	....	....	....	....	....	....

WCHL First All-Star Team (1996, 1997) • Named WCHL's MVP (1997)

Signed as a free agent by **Ottawa**, July 16, 1992.

• ST. LAURENT, Andre

Andre L. C – R. 5'10", 180 lbs. b: Rouyn-Noranda, Que., 2/16/1953. NY Islanders' 3rd, 49th overall, in 1973.

Season	Club	League	GP	G	A	Pts	AG	AA	APts	PIM	PP	SH	GW	S	%	TGF	PGF	TGA	PGA	+/–	GP	G	A	Pts	PIM	PP	SH	GW
1970-71	Montreal Jr. Canadiens	QJHL	60	13	27	40	....	....	....	127	....	....	....	....	....	....	....	....	....	....	11	2	6	8	55	....	....	....
1971-72	Montreal Jr. Canadiens	OMJHL	63	18	34	52	....	....	....	161	....	....	....	....	....	....	....	....	....	....	....	....	....	....	....	....	....	....
1972-73	Montreal Red-White-Blue	QMJHL	64	52	48	100	....	....	....	245	....	....	....	....	....	....	....	....	....	....	4	1	2	3	0	....	....	....
1973-74	**New York Islanders**	**NHL**	**42**	**5**	**9**	**14**	**5**	**7**	**12**	**18**	**0**	**0**	**0**	**75**	**6.7**	**17**	**1**	**15**	**0**	**1**	....	....	....	....	....	....	....	....
	Fort Worth Wings	CHL	32	14	19	33	....	....	....	53	....	....	....	....	....	....	....	....	....	....	5	2	2	4	12	....	....	....
1974-75	**New York Islanders**	**NHL**	**78**	**14**	**27**	**41**	**12**	**20**	**32**	**60**	**1**	**0**	**0**	**186**	**7.5**	**62**	**7**	**33**	**0**	**22**	**15**	**2**	**2**	**4**	**6**	**1**	**0**	**0**
1975-76	**New York Islanders**	**NHL**	**67**	**9**	**17**	**26**	**8**	**13**	**21**	**56**	**0**	**0**	**2**	**101**	**8.9**	**38**	**2**	**23**	**1**	**14**	**13**	**1**	**5**	**6**	**15**	**0**	**0**	**0**
	Fort Worth Texans	CHL	3	1	2	3	....	....	....	2	....	....	....	....	....	....	....	....	....	....	....	....	....	....	....	....	....	....
1976-77	**New York Islanders**	**NHL**	**72**	**10**	**13**	**23**	**9**	**10**	**19**	**55**	**2**	**0**	**3**	**96**	**10.4**	**41**	**4**	**29**	**0**	**8**	**12**	**1**	**2**	**3**	**6**	**0**	**0**	**1**
1977-78	**New York Islanders**	**NHL**	**2**	**0**	**0**	**0**	**0**	**0**	**0**	**2**	**0**	**0**	**0**	**5**	**0.0**	**0**	**0**	**0**	**0**	**0**	....	....	....	....	....	....	....	....
	Detroit Red Wings	**NHL**	**77**	**31**	**39**	**70**	**28**	**30**	**58**	**108**	**10**	**0**	**4**	**193**	**16.1**	**90**	**30**	**66**	**13**	**7**	**7**	**1**	**1**	**2**	**4**	**0**	**0**	**0**
1978-79	**Detroit Red Wings**	**NHL**	**76**	**18**	**31**	**49**	**15**	**22**	**37**	**124**	**4**	**1**	**1**	**158**	**11.4**	**66**	**22**	**91**	**16**	**–31**	....	....	....	....	....	....	....	....
1979-80	**Los Angeles Kings**	**NHL**	**77**	**6**	**24**	**30**	**5**	**17**	**22**	**88**	**1**	**0**	**0**	**121**	**5.0**	**42**	**9**	**62**	**16**	**–13**	**4**	**1**	**0**	**1**	**0**	**0**	**1**	**1**
1980-81	**Los Angeles Kings**	**NHL**	**22**	**10**	**6**	**16**	**8**	**4**	**12**	**63**	**0**	**0**	**2**	**33**	**30.3**	**20**	**0**	**12**	**0**	**8**	**3**	**0**	**1**	**1**	**9**	**0**	**0**	**0**
	Fort Worth Texans	CHL	12	1	14	15	....	....	....	36	....	....	....	....	....	....	....	....	....	....	....	....	....	....	....	....	....	....
	Houston Apollos	CHL	3	1	0	1	....	....	....	4	....	....	....	....	....	....	....	....	....	....	....	....	....	....	....	....	....	....
1981-82	**Los Angeles Kings**	**NHL**	**16**	**2**	**4**	**6**	**2**	**3**	**5**	**28**	**0**	**1**	**0**	**27**	**7.4**	**10**	**1**	**19**	**12**	**2**	....	....	....	....	....	....	....	....
	New Haven Nighthawks	AHL	28	7	9	16	....	....	....	58	....	....	....	....	....	....	....	....	....	....	....	....	....	....	....	....	....	....
	Pittsburgh Penguins	**NHL**	**18**	**8**	**5**	**13**	**6**	**3**	**9**	**4**	**1**	**0**	**1**	**33**	**24.2**	**20**	**2**	**21**	**8**	**5**	**5**	**2**	**1**	**3**	**8**	**0**	**0**	**0**
1982-83	**Pittsburgh Penguins**	**NHL**	**70**	**13**	**9**	**22**	**11**	**6**	**17**	**105**	....	....	....	....	....	....	....	....	....	....	....	....	....	....	....	....	....	....
1983-84	**Pittsburgh Penguins**	**NHL**	**8**	**2**	**0**	**2**	**2**	**0**	**2**	**21**	....	....	....	....	....	....	....	....	....	....	....	....	....	....	....	....	....	....
	Detroit Red Wings	**NHL**	**19**	**1**	**3**	**4**	**1**	**2**	**3**	**17**	....	....	....	....	....	....	....	....	....	....	....	....	....	....	....	....	....	....
	Adirondack Red Wings	AHL	50	26	43	69	....	....	....	129	....	....	....	....	....	....	....	....	....	....	7	4	4	8	23	....	....	....
1984-85	Adirondack Red Wings	AHL	35	10	23	33	....	....	....	68	....	....	....	....	....	....	....	....	....	....	....	....	....	....	....	....	....	....

			REGULAR SEASON																		PLAYOFFS							
Season	**Club**	**League**	**GP**	**G**	**A**	**Pts**	**AG**	**AA**	**APts**	**PIM**	**PP**	**SH**	**GW**	**S**	**%**	**TGF**	**PGF**	**TGA**	**PGA**	**+/–**	**GP**	**G**	**A**	**Pts**	**PIM**	**PP**	**SH**	**GW**
1985-86	Rogle BK Angelhorn	Sweden-2	32	17	29	46	....	....	....	76	....	....	....	....	....	....	....	....	....	....	5	1	1	2	12	....	....	....
1986-87	HC Rouen	France-2	STATISTICS NOT AVAILABLE																									
1987-88	HC Rouen	France	24	16	35	51	....	....	....	24	....	....	....	....	....	....	....	....	....	....	....	....	....	....	....	....	....	....
1988-89	HC Clermont	France-2	21	43	29	72	....	....	....	43	....	....	....	....	....	....	....	....	....	....	....	....	....	....	....	....	....	....
1989-90	HC Bordeaux	France	1	0	0	0	....	....	....	2	....	....	....	....	....	....	....	....	....	....	....	....	....	....	....	....	....	....
	NHL Totals		**644**	**129**	**187**	**316**	**112**	**137**	**249**	**749**	**19**	**2**	**13**	**1028**	**12.5**	**406**	**78**	**371**	**66**		**59**	**8**	**12**	**20**	**48**	**1**	**1**	**2**

Traded to **Detroit** by **NY Islanders** for Michel Bergeron, October 20, 1977. Traded to **LA Kings** by **Detroit** with Detroit's 1st round choice (Larry Murphy) in 1980 Entry Draft and 1st round choice (Doug Smith) in 1981 Entry Draft for Dale McCourt, August 22, 1979. Claimed on waivers by **Pittsburgh** from **LA Kings**, February 23, 1982. Traded to **Detroit** by **Pittsburgh** for future considerations, October 24, 1983.

• ST. LOUIS, Martin

RW – L. 5'9", 185 lbs. b: Laval, Que., 6/18/1975.

Season	Club	League	GP	G	A	Pts	AG	AA	APts	PIM	PP	SH	GW	S	%	TGF	PGF	TGA	PGA	+/–	GP	G	A	Pts	PIM	PP	SH	GW
1991-92	Laval-Laurentides Regents	QAAA	42	29	74	103	....	....	....	....	....	....	....	....	....	....	....	....	....	....	....	....	....	....	....	....	....	....
1992-93	Hawkesbury Hawks	OJHL	31	37	50	87	....	....	....	70	....	....	....	....	....	....	....	....	....	....	....	....	....	....	....	....	....	....
1993-94	University of Vermont	ECAC	33	15	36	51	....	....	....	24	....	....	....	....	....	....	....	....	....	....	....	....	....	....	....	....	....	....
1994-95	University of Vermont	ECAC	35	23	48	71	....	....	....	36	....	....	....	....	....	....	....	....	....	....	....	....	....	....	....	....	....	....
1995-96	University of Vermont	ECAC	35	29	56	85	....	....	....	38	....	....	....	....	....	....	....	....	....	....	....	....	....	....	....	....	....	....
1996-97	University of Vermont	ECAC	36	24	*36	60	....	....	....	65	....	....	....	....	....	....	....	....	....	....	....	....	....	....	....	....	....	....
1997-98	Cleveland Lumberjacks	IHL	56	16	34	50	....	....	....	24	....	....	....	....	....	....	....	....	....	....	....	....	....	....	....	....	....	....
	Saint John Flames	AHL	25	15	11	26	....	....	....	20	....	....	....	....	....	....	....	....	....	....	20	5	15	20	16	....	....	....
1998-99	**Calgary Flames**	**NHL**	**13**	**1**	**1**	**2**	**1**	**1**	**2**	**10**	**0**	**0**	**0**	**14**	**7.1**	**5**	**1**	**6**	**0**	**–2**	....	....	....	....	....	....	....	....
	Saint John Flames	AHL	53	28	34	62	....	....	....	30	....	....	....	....	....	....	....	....	....	....	7	4	4	8	2	....	....	....
99-2000	**Calgary Flames**	**NHL**	**56**	**3**	**15**	**18**	**3**	**14**	**17**	**22**	**0**	**0**	**1**	**73**	**4.1**	**27**	**3**	**47**	**18**	**–5**	....	....	....	....	....	....	....	....
	Saint John Flames	AHL	17	15	11	26	....	....	....	14	....	....	....	....	....	....	....	....	....	....	....	....	....	....	....	....	....	....
	NHL Totals		**69**	**4**	**16**	**20**	**4**	**15**	**19**	**32**	**0**	**0**	**1**	**87**	**4.6**	**32**	**4**	**53**	**18**		....	....	....	....	....	....	....	....

ECAC First All-Star Team (1995, 1996, 1997) • NCAA East First All-American Team (1995, 1996, 1997) • NCAA Championship All-Tournament Team (1996)

Signed as a free agent by **Calgary**, February 19, 1998.

• ST. MARSEILLE, Frank

Francis Leo RW – R. 5'11", 180 lbs. b: Levack, Ont., 12/14/1939.

Season	Club	League	GP	G	A	Pts	AG	AA	APts	PIM	PP	SH	GW	S	%	TGF	PGF	TGA	PGA	+/–	GP	G	A	Pts	PIM	PP	SH	GW
1954-1961	Levack Huskies	NOHA	STATISTICS NOT AVAILABLE																									
1961-62	Levack Huskies	NOHA	STATISTICS NOT AVAILABLE																									
	New Haven Blades	EHL	3	0	0	0	....	....	....	9	....	....	....	....	....	....	....	....	....	....	....	....	....	....	....	....	....	....
1962-63	Chatham Maroons	OHA-Sr.	45	17	22	39	....	....	....	49	....	....	....	....	....	....	....	....	....	....	10	4	1	5	4	....	....	....
	Sudbury Wolves	EPHL	3	0	2	2	....	....	....	0	....	....	....	....	....	....	....	....	....	....	....	....	....	....	....	....	....	....
1963-64	Chatham Maroons	IHL	70	31	33	64	....	....	....	21	....	....	....	....	....	....	....	....	....	....	....	....	....	....	....	....	....	....
1964-65	Port Huron Flags	IHL	70	38	59	97	....	....	....	57	....	....	....	....	....	....	....	....	....	....	7	2	5	7	24	....	....	....
1965-66	Port Huron Flags	IHL	68	45	45	90	....	....	....	28	....	....	....	....	....	....	....	....	....	....	9	6	6	12	12	....	....	....
1966-67	Port Huron Flags	IHL	72	41	77	118	....	....	....	46	....	....	....	....	....	....	....	....	....	....	....	....	....	....	....	....	....	....
1967-68	Kansas City Blues	CPHL	11	7	8	15	....	....	....	0	....	....	....	....	....	....	....	....	....	....	....	....	....	....	....	....	....	....
	St. Louis Blues	**NHL**	**57**	**16**	**16**	**32**	**19**	**16**	**35**	**12**	**1**	**0**	**1**	**147**	**10.9**	**40**	**6**	**23**	**0**	**11**	**18**	**5**	**8**	**13**	**0**	**4**	**0**	**0**
1968-69	**St. Louis Blues**	**NHL**	**72**	**12**	**26**	**38**	**13**	**23**	**36**	**22**	**3**	**0**	**3**	**169**	**7.1**	**55**	**16**	**19**	**0**	**20**	**12**	**3**	**3**	**6**	**2**	**0**	**0**	**0**
1969-70	**St. Louis Blues**	**NHL**	**74**	**16**	**43**	**59**	**17**	**40**	**57**	**18**	**3**	**0**	**1**	**166**	**9.6**	**90**	**47**	**46**	**0**	**–3**	**15**	**6**	**7**	**13**	**4**	**3**	**1**	**0**
1970-71	**St. Louis Blues**	**NHL**	**77**	**19**	**32**	**51**	**19**	**27**	**46**	**26**	**3**	**0**	**5**	**217**	**8.8**	**72**	**26**	**42**	**0**	**4**	**6**	**2**	**1**	**3**	**4**	**2**	**0**	**1**
1971-72	**St. Louis Blues**	**NHL**	**78**	**16**	**36**	**52**	**16**	**31**	**47**	**32**	**1**	**0**	**1**	**228**	**7.0**	**67**	**15**	**48**	**1**	**5**	**11**	**3**	**5**	**8**	**6**	**1**	**0**	**0**
1972-73	**St. Louis Blues**	**NHL**	**45**	**7**	**18**	**25**	**7**	**14**	**21**	**8**	**3**	**0**	**0**	**119**	**5.9**	**38**	**11**	**33**	**0**	**–6**	....	....	....	....	....	....	....	....
	Los Angeles Kings	**NHL**	**29**	**7**	**4**	**11**	**7**	**3**	**10**	**2**	**2**	**0**	**2**	**65**	**10.8**	**20**	**4**	**17**	**0**	**–1**	....	....	....	....	....	....	....	....
1973-74	**Los Angeles Kings**	**NHL**	**78**	**14**	**36**	**50**	**13**	**30**	**43**	**40**	**2**	**0**	**1**	**190**	**7.4**	**71**	**14**	**62**	**6**	**1**	**5**	**0**	**0**	**0**	**0**	**0**	**0**	**0**
1974-75	**Los Angeles Kings**	**NHL**	**80**	**17**	**36**	**53**	**15**	**27**	**42**	**46**	**0**	**0**	**1**	**168**	**10.1**	**72**	**10**	**54**	**4**	**12**	**3**	**0**	**1**	**1**	**0**	**0**	**0**	**0**
1975-76	**Los Angeles Kings**	**NHL**	**68**	**10**	**16**	**26**	**9**	**12**	**21**	**20**	**2**	**0**	**1**	**66**	**15.2**	**33**	**10**	**37**	**0**	**–14**	**9**	**0**	**0**	**0**	**0**	**0**	**0**	**0**
1976-77	**Los Angeles Kings**	**NHL**	**49**	**6**	**22**	**28**	**5**	**17**	**22**	**16**	**1**	**0**	**0**	**74**	**8.1**	**46**	**7**	**39**	**1**	**1**	**9**	**1**	**0**	**1**	**2**	**0**	**0**	**0**
	Fort Worth Texans	CHL	16	6	12	18	....	....	....	4	....	....	....	....	....	....	....	....	....	....	....	....	....	....	....	....	....	....
1977-78	Nova Scotia Voyageurs	AHL	74	14	14	28	....	....	....	38	....	....	....	....	....	....	....	....	....	....	11	3	2	5	0	....	....	....
	NHL Totals		**707**	**140**	**285**	**425**	**140**	**240**	**380**	**242**	**21**	**0**	**16**	**1609**	**8.7**	**604**	**166**	**420**	**12**		**88**	**20**	**25**	**45**	**18**	**10**	**1**	**1**

IHL Second All-Star Team (1967) • Played in NHL All-Star Game (1970)

Signed as a free agent by **St. Louis**, November 23, 1967. Traded to **LA Kings** by **St. Louis** for Paul Curtis, January 22, 1973.

• ST. SAUVEUR, Claude

C – L. 6'1", 185 lbs. b: Sherbrooke, Que., 1/2/1952. California's 4th, 54th overall, in 1972.

Season	Club	League	GP	G	A	Pts	AG	AA	APts	PIM	PP	SH	GW	S	%	TGF	PGF	TGA	PGA	+/–	GP	G	A	Pts	PIM	PP	SH	GW
1969-70	Sherbrooke Castors	QJHL	26	23	18	41	....	....	....	6	....	....	....	....	....	....	....	....	....	....	....	....	....	....	....	....	....	....
1970-71	Sherbrooke Castors	QJHL	62	52	67	119	....	....	....	80	....	....	....	....	....	....	....	....	....	....	10	11	9	20	10	....	....	....
1971-72	Sherbrooke Castors	QMJHL	60	53	58	111	....	....	....	97	....	....	....	....	....	....	....	....	....	....	4	1	2	3	4	....	....	....
1972-73	Roanoke Valley Rebels	EHL	62	55	52	107	....	....	....	99	....	....	....	....	....	....	....	....	....	....	16	11	13	24	0	....	....	....
	Philadelphia Blazers	WHA	2	1	0	1	....	....	....	0	....	....	....	....	....	....	....	....	....	....	....	....	....	....	....	....	....	....
1973-74	Vancouver Blazers	WHA	70	38	30	68	....	....	....	55	....	....	....	....	....	....	....	....	....	....	....	....	....	....	....	....	....	....
1974-75	Vancouver Blazers	WHA	76	24	23	47	....	....	....	32	....	....	....	....	....	....	....	....	....	....	....	....	....	....	....	....	....	....
1975-76	**Atlanta Flames**	**NHL**	**79**	**24**	**24**	**48**	**21**	**18**	**39**	**23**	**11**	**0**	**2**	**171**	**14.0**	**67**	**32**	**41**	**0**	**–6**	**2**	**0**	**0**	**0**	**0**	**0**	**0**	**0**
1976-77	Calgary Cowboys	WHA	17	0	3	3	....	....	....	2	....	....	....	....	....	....	....	....	....	....	....	....	....	....	....	....	....	....
	Tidewater Sharks	SHL	6	5	7	12	....	....	....	0	....	....	....	....	....	....	....	....	....	....	....	....	....	....	....	....	....	....
	Edmonton Oilers	WHA	15	5	7	12	....	....	....	2	....	....	....	....	....	....	....	....	....	....	5	1	0	1	0	....	....	....
1977-78	Indianapolis Racers	WHA	72	36	42	78	....	....	....	24	....	....	....	....	....	....	....	....	....	....	....	....	....	....	....	....	....	....
1978-79	Indianapolis Racers	WHA	17	4	2	6	....	....	....	12	....	....	....	....	....	....	....	....	....	....	....	....	....	....	....	....	....	....
	Cincinnati Stingers	WHA	16	4	5	9	....	....	....	4	....	....	....	....	....	....	....	....	....	....	....	....	....	....	....	....	....	....
1979-80	Milwaukee Admirals	IHL	43	38	57	95	....	....	....	91	....	....	....	....	....	....	....	....	....	....	1	0	0	0	0	....	....	....
1980-81	Milwaukee Admirals	IHL	54	34	28	62	....	....	....	88	....	....	....	....	....	....	....	....	....	....	5	2	3	5	6	....	....	....
1981-82	Yukijirushi Sapporo	Japan	30	10	28	38	....	....	....	....	....	....	....	....	....	....	....	....	....	....	....	....	....	....	....	....	....	....
	NHL Totals		**79**	**24**	**24**	**48**	**21**	**18**	**39**	**23**	**11**	**0**	**2**	**171**	**14.0**	**67**	**32**	**41**	**0**		**2**	**0**	**0**	**0**	**0**	**0**	**0**	**0**
	Other Major League Totals		285	112	112	224	....	....	....	131	....	....	....	....	....	....	....	....	....	....	5	1	0	1	0	....	....	....

QMJHL First All-Star Team (1972) • EHL Rookie of the Year (1973) • IHL Second All-Star Team (1980)

Selected by **Miami-Philadelphia** (WHA) in 1972 WHA General Player Draft, February 12, 1972. Transferred to **Vancouver** (WHA) after **Philadelphia** (WHA) franchise relocated, May, 1973. Traded to **Atlanta** by **California** for cash, September 23, 1975. WHA rights transferred to **Calgary** (WHA) after **Vancouver** (WHA) franchise relocated, May 7, 1975. Traded to **Edmonton** (WHA) by **Calgary** (WHA) with Wayne Connelly for cash, January, 1977. Traded to **Indianapolis** (WHA) by **Edmonton** (WHA) with Barry Wilkins, Rusty Patenaude and Kevin Devine for Blair MacDonald, Dave Inkpen and Mike Zuke, September, 1977. Signed as a free agent by **Cincinnati** (WHA) after **Indianapolis** (WHA) franchise folded, December 15, 1978.

• SAKIC, Joe

C – L. 5'11", 192 lbs. b: Burnaby, B.C., 7/7/1969. Quebec's 2nd, 15th overall, in 1987.

Season	Club	League	GP	G	A	Pts	AG	AA	APts	PIM	PP	SH	GW	S	%	TGF	PGF	TGA	PGA	+/–	GP	G	A	Pts	PIM	PP	SH	GW
1985-86	Burnaby BC Selects	BCAHA	80	83	73	156	....	....	....	96	....	....	....	....	....	....	....	....	....	....	....	....	....	....	....	....	....	....
	Lethbridge Broncos	WHL	3	0	0	0	....	....	....	0	....	....	....	....	....	....	....	....	....	....	....	....	....	....	....	....	....	....
1986-87	Swift Current Broncos	WHL	72	60	73	133	....	....	....	31	....	....	....	....	....	....	....	....	....	....	4	0	1	1	0	....	....	....
	Canada	Nat-Team	1	0	0	0	....	....	....	0	....	....	....	....	....	....	....	....	....	....	....	....	....	....	....	....	....	....
1987-88	Swift Current Broncos	WHL	64	*78	82	*160	....	....	....	64	....	....	....	....	....	....	....	....	....	....	10	11	13	24	12	....	....	....
	Canada	WJC-A	7	3	1	4	....	....	....	2	....	....	....	....	....	....	....	....	....	....	....	....	....	....	....	....	....	....
1988-89	**Quebec Nordiques**	**NHL**	**70**	**23**	**39**	**62**	**19**	**28**	**47**	**24**	**10**	**0**	**2**	**148**	**15.5**	**96**	**59**	**85**	**12**	**–36**	....	....	....	....	....	....	....	....
1989-90	**Quebec Nordiques**	**NHL**	**80**	**39**	**63**	**102**	**34**	**45**	**79**	**27**	**8**	**1**	**2**	**234**	**16.7**	**139**	**58**	**132**	**11**	**–40**	....	....	....	....	....	....	....	....
1990-91	**Quebec Nordiques**	**NHL**	**80**	**48**	**61**	**109**	**44**	**47**	**91**	**24**	**12**	**3**	**7**	**245**	**19.6**	**132**	**48**	**164**	**54**	**–26**	....	....	....	....	....	....	....	....
	Canada	WEC-A	10	6	5	11	....	....	....	0	....	....	....	....	....	....	....	....	....	....	....	....	....	....	....	....	....	....
1991-92	**Quebec Nordiques**	**NHL**	**69**	**29**	**65**	**94**	**26**	**49**	**75**	**20**	**6**	**3**	**1**	**217**	**13.4**	**124**	**46**	**97**	**24**	**5**	....	....	....	....	....	....	....	....
1992-93	**Quebec Nordiques**	**NHL**	**78**	**48**	**57**	**105**	**40**	**39**	**79**	**40**	**20**	**2**	**4**	**264**	**18.2**	**150**	**76**	**104**	**27**	**–3**	**6**	**3**	**3**	**6**	**2**	**1**	**0**	**0**
1993-94	**Quebec Nordiques**	**NHL**	**84**	**28**	**64**	**92**	**26**	**50**	**76**	**18**	**10**	**1**	**9**	**279**	**10.0**	**121**	**49**	**105**	**25**	**–8**	....	....	....	....	....	....	....	....
	Canada	WC-A	8	4	3	7	....	....	....	0	....	....	....	....	....	....	....	....	....	....	....	....	....	....	....	....	....	....
1994-95	**Quebec Nordiques**	**NHL**	**47**	**19**	**43**	**62**	**34**	**64**	**98**	**30**	**3**	**2**	**5**	**157**	**12.1**	**82**	**36**	**49**	**10**	**7**	**6**	**4**	**1**	**5**	**0**	**1**	**1**	**1**
1995-96♦	**Colorado Avalanche**	**NHL**	**82**	**51**	**69**	**120**	**50**	**57**	**107**	**44**	**17**	**6**	**7**	**339**	**15.0**	**159**	**74**	**85**	**14**	**14**	**22**	***18**	**16**	***34**	**14**	**6**	**0**	**6**

Season	Club	League	GP	G	A	Pts	AG	AA	APts	PIM	PP	SH	GW	S	%	TGF	PGF	TGA	PGA	+/–	GP	G	A	Pts	PIM	PP	SH	GW
			REGULAR SEASON																		PLAYOFFS							
1996-97	Canada	W-Cup	8	2	2	4	....	....	....	6	....	....	....	....	....	....	....	....	....	....	....	....	....	....	....	....	....	....
	Colorado Avalanche	**NHL**	**65**	**22**	**52**	**74**	**23**	**46**	**69**	**34**	**10**	**2**	**5**	**261**	**8.4**	**107**	**58**	**67**	**8**	**–10**	**17**	**8**	***17**	**25**	**14**	**3**	**0**	**0**
1997-98	**Colorado Avalanche**	**NHL**	**64**	**27**	**36**	**63**	**32**	**35**	**67**	**50**	**12**	**1**	**2**	**254**	**10.6**	**90**	**45**	**53**	**8**	**0**	**6**	**2**	**3**	**5**	**6**	**0**	**1**	**2**
	Canada	Olympics	4	1	2	3	....	....	....	4	....	....	....	....	....	....	....	....	....	....	....	....	....	....	....	....	....	....
1998-99	**Colorado Avalanche**	**NHL**	**73**	**41**	**55**	**96**	**48**	**53**	**101**	**29**	**12**	**5**	**6**	**255**	**16.1**	**133**	**54**	**77**	**21**	**23**	**19**	**6**	**13**	**19**	**8**	**1**	**1**	**1**
99-2000	**Colorado Avalanche**	**NHL**	**60**	**28**	**53**	**81**	**32**	**49**	**81**	**28**	**5**	**1**	**5**	**242**	**11.6**	**113**	**37**	**52**	**6**	**30**	**17**	**2**	**7**	**9**	**8**	**2**	**0**	**0**
	NHL Totals		**852**	**403**	**657**	**1060**	**408**	**562**	**970**	**368**	**125**	**27**	**55**	**2895**	**13.9**	**1446**	**640**	**1070**	**220**		**93**	**43**	**60**	**103**	**52**	**14**	**3**	**10**

WHL East Second All-Star Team (1987) • Canadian Major Junior Player of the Year (1988) • WHL East First All-Star Team (1988) • Won Conn Smythe Trophy (1996) • Played in NHL All-Star Game (1990, 1991, 1992, 1993, 1994, 1996, 1998, 2000)

Transferred to **Colorado** after **Quebec** franchise relocated, June 21, 1995.

• SALEI, Ruslan

D – L. 6'2", 205 lbs. b: Minsk, USSR, 11/2/1974. Anaheim's 1st, 9th overall, in 1996.

Season	Club	League	GP	G	A	Pts	AG	AA	APts	PIM	PP	SH	GW	S	%	TGF	PGF	TGA	PGA	+/–	GP	G	A	Pts	PIM	PP	SH	GW
1992-93	Dynamo Minsk	CIS	9	1	0	1	....	....	....	10	....	....	....	....	....	....	....	....	....	....	....	....	....	....	....	....	....	....
1993-94	Tivali Minsk	CIS	39	2	3	5	....	....	....	50	....	....	....	....	....	....	....	....	....	....	....	....	....	....	....	....	....	....
	Belarus	WC-C1	6	1	1	2	....	....	....	10	....	....	....	....	....	....	....	....	....	....	....	....	....	....	....	....	....	....
1994-95	Tivali Minsk	CIS	51	4	2	6	....	....	....	44	....	....	....	....	....	....	....	....	....	....	....	....	....	....	....	....	....	....
	Belarus	WC-C1	4	0	1	1	....	....	....	4	....	....	....	....	....	....	....	....	....	....	....	....	....	....	....	....	....	....
1995-96	Las Vegas Thunder	IHL	76	7	23	30	....	....	....	123	....	....	....	....	....	....	....	....	....	....	15	3	7	10	18	....	....	....
1996-97	**Mighty Ducks of Anaheim**	**NHL**	**30**	**0**	**1**	**1**	**0**	**1**	**1**	**37**	**0**	**0**	**0**	**14**	**0.0**	**12**	**1**	**20**	**1**	**–8**	....	....	....	....	....	....	....	....
	Baltimore Bandits	AHL	12	1	4	5	....	....	....	12	....	....	....	....	....	....	....	....	....	....	....	....	....	....	....	....	....	....
	Las Vegas Thunder	IHL	8	0	2	2	....	....	....	24	....	....	....	....	....	....	....	....	....	....	3	2	1	3	6	....	....	....
1997-98	**Mighty Ducks of Anaheim**	**NHL**	**66**	**5**	**10**	**15**	**6**	**10**	**16**	**70**	**1**	**0**	**0**	**104**	**4.8**	**53**	**12**	**49**	**15**	**7**	....	....	....	....	....	....	....	....
	Cincinnati Mighty Ducks	AHL	6	3	6	9	....	....	....	14	....	....	....	....	....	....	....	....	....	....	....	....	....	....	....	....	....	....
	Belarus	Olympics	7	1	0	1	....	....	....	4	....	....	....	....	....	....	....	....	....	....	....	....	....	....	....	....	....	....
	Belarus	WC-A	2	1	0	1	....	....	....	2	....	....	....	....	....	....	....	....	....	....	....	....	....	....	....	....	....	....
1998-99	**Mighty Ducks of Anaheim**	**NHL**	**74**	**2**	**14**	**16**	**2**	**13**	**15**	**65**	**1**	**0**	**0**	**123**	**1.6**	**63**	**18**	**73**	**29**	**1**	**3**	**0**	**0**	**0**	**4**	**0**	**0**	**0**
99-2000	**Mighty Ducks of Anaheim**	**NHL**	**71**	**5**	**5**	**10**	**6**	**5**	**11**	**94**	**1**	**0**	**0**	**116**	**4.3**	**53**	**5**	**77**	**32**	**3**	....	....	....	....	....	....	....	....
	Belarus	WC-A	6	0	1	1	....	....	....	4	....	....	....	....	....	....	....	....	....	....	....	....	....	....	....	....	....	....
	NHL Totals		**241**	**12**	**30**	**42**	**14**	**29**	**43**	**266**	**3**	**0**	**0**	**357**	**3.4**	**181**	**36**	**219**	**77**		**3**	**0**	**0**	**0**	**4**	**0**	**0**	**0**

• SALESKI, Don

Donald Patrick "Big Bird" RW – R. 6'3", 205 lbs. b: Moose Jaw, Sask., 11/10/1949. Philadelphia's 6th, 64th overall, in 1969.

Season	Club	League	GP	G	A	Pts	AG	AA	APts	PIM	PP	SH	GW	S	%	TGF	PGF	TGA	PGA	+/–	GP	G	A	Pts	PIM	PP	SH	GW
1966-67	Regina Pats	CMJHL	38	3	2	5	....	....	....	6	....	....	....	....	....	....	....	....	....	....	3	0	0	0	0	....	....	....
1967-68	Regina Pats	WCJHL	58	6	9	15	....	....	....	34	....	....	....	....	....	....	....	....	....	....	....	....	....	....	....	....	....	....
1968-69	Regina Pats	SJHL	40	33	25	58	....	....	....	117	....	....	....	....	....	....	....	....	....	....	....	....	....	....	....	....	....	....
	Regina Pats	Mem-Cup	11	6	6	12	....	....	....	19	....	....	....	....	....	....	....	....	....	....	....	....	....	....	....	....	....	....
1969-70	Regina Pats	SJHL	STATISTICS NOT AVAILABLE																									
	Winnipeg Jets	WCJHL	2	1	0	1	....	....	....	12	....	....	....	....	....	....	....	....	....	....	....	....	....	....	....	....	....	....
	Saskatoon Blades	WCJHL	3	0	1	1	....	....	....	4	....	....	....	....	....	....	....	....	....	....	....	....	....	....	....	....	....	....
1970-71	Quebec Aces	AHL	72	9	7	16	....	....	....	51	....	....	....	....	....	....	....	....	....	....	1	0	0	0	0	....	....	....
1971-72	**Philadelphia Flyers**	**NHL**	**1**	**0**	**0**	**0**	**0**	**0**	**0**	**0**	**0**	**0**	**0**	**2**	**0.0**	**0**	**0**	**1**	**0**	**–1**	....	....	....	....	....	....	....	....
	Richmond Robins	AHL	73	22	35	57	....	....	....	111	....	....	....	....	....	....	....	....	....	....	....	....	....	....	....	....	....	....
1972-73	**Philadelphia Flyers**	**NHL**	**78**	**12**	**9**	**21**	**11**	**7**	**18**	**205**	**1**	**1**	**2**	**158**	**7.6**	**36**	**3**	**57**	**4**	**–20**	**11**	**1**	**2**	**3**	**4**	**0**	**0**	**0**
1973-74♦	**Philadelphia Flyers**	**NHL**	**77**	**15**	**25**	**40**	**14**	**21**	**35**	**131**	**2**	**2**	**3**	**157**	**9.6**	**60**	**8**	**32**	**1**	**21**	**17**	**2**	**7**	**9**	**24**	**0**	**0**	**0**
1974-75♦	**Philadelphia Flyers**	**NHL**	**63**	**10**	**18**	**28**	**9**	**13**	**22**	**107**	**0**	**0**	**2**	**113**	**8.8**	**39**	**1**	**34**	**3**	**7**	**17**	**2**	**3**	**5**	**25**	**0**	**0**	**1**
1975-76	**Philadelphia Flyers**	**NHL**	**78**	**21**	**26**	**47**	**18**	**19**	**37**	**68**	**1**	**1**	**4**	**224**	**9.4**	**74**	**7**	**47**	**13**	**33**	**16**	**6**	**5**	**11**	**47**	**0**	**1**	**1**
1976-77	**Philadelphia Flyers**	**NHL**	**74**	**22**	**16**	**38**	**20**	**12**	**32**	**33**	**2**	**2**	**6**	**156**	**14.1**	**68**	**8**	**51**	**15**	**24**	**10**	**0**	**0**	**0**	**12**	**0**	**0**	**0**
1977-78	**Philadelphia Flyers**	**NHL**	**70**	**27**	**18**	**45**	**25**	**14**	**39**	**44**	**5**	**4**	**1**	**163**	**16.6**	**69**	**10**	**40**	**15**	**34**	**11**	**2**	**0**	**2**	**19**	**0**	**0**	**1**
1978-79	**Philadelphia Flyers**	**NHL**	**35**	**11**	**5**	**16**	**9**	**4**	**13**	**14**	**1**	**1**	**2**	**75**	**14.7**	**25**	**4**	**24**	**6**	**3**	....	....	....	....	....	....	....	....
	Colorado Rockies	**NHL**	**16**	**2**	**0**	**2**	**2**	**0**	**2**	**4**	**0**	**0**	**0**	**50**	**4.0**	**5**	**1**	**20**	**6**	**–10**	....	....	....	....	....	....	....	....
1979-80	**Colorado Rockies**	**NHL**	**51**	**8**	**8**	**16**	**7**	**6**	**13**	**23**	**0**	**0**	**0**	**68**	**11.8**	**31**	**4**	**54**	**10**	**–17**	....	....	....	....	....	....	....	....
	Fort Worth Texans	CHL	19	9	6	15	....	....	....	18	....	....	....	....	....	....	....	....	....	....	14	5	6	11	20	....	....	....
	NHL Totals		**543**	**128**	**125**	**253**	**115**	**96**	**211**	**629**	**12**	**11**	**20**	**1166**	**11.0**	**407**	**46**	**360**	**73**		**82**	**13**	**17**	**30**	**131**	**0**	**1**	**3**

Traded to **Colorado** by **Philadelphia** for future considerations, March 3, 1979.

• SALMING, Borje

Borje Anders "King" D – L. 6'1", 193 lbs. b: Kiruna, Sweden, 4/17/1951. **HHOF**

Season	Club	League	GP	G	A	Pts	AG	AA	APts	PIM	PP	SH	GW	S	%	TGF	PGF	TGA	PGA	+/–	GP	G	A	Pts	PIM	PP	SH	GW
1967-68	Kiruna AIF	Sweden-2	STATISTICS NOT AVAILABLE																									
	Sweden	EJC-A	5	1	0	1	....	....	....	4	....	....	....	....	....	....	....	....	....	....	....	....	....	....	....	....	....	....
1968-69	Kiruna AIF	Sweden-2	STATISTICS NOT AVAILABLE																									
	Sweden	EJC-A	5	0	0	0	....	....	....	8	....	....	....	....	....	....	....	....	....	....	....	....	....	....	....	....	....	....
1969-70	Kiruna AIF	Sweden-2	STATISTICS NOT AVAILABLE																									
1970-71	Brynas IF Gavle	Sweden	14	0	5	5	....	....	....	6	....	....	....	....	....	....	....	....	....	....	13	2	1	3	16	....	....	....
1971-72	Brynas IF Gavle	Sweden	14	1	1	2	....	....	....	20	....	....	....	....	....	....	....	....	....	....	14	0	4	4	30	....	....	....
	Sweden	WEC-A	4	0	0	0	....	....	....	6	....	....	....	....	....	....	....	....	....	....	....	....	....	....	....	....	....	....
1972-73	Brynas IF Gavle	Sweden	14	2	3	5	....	....	....	10	....	....	....	....	....	....	....	....	....	....	12	3	1	4	24	....	....	....
	Sweden	WEC-A	10	4	6	10	....	....	....	8	....	....	....	....	....	....	....	....	....	....	....	....	....	....	....	....	....	....
1973-74	**Toronto Maple Leafs**	**NHL**	**76**	**5**	**34**	**39**	**5**	**28**	**33**	**48**	**3**	**0**	**0**	**130**	**3.8**	**115**	**22**	**78**	**23**	**38**	**4**	**0**	**1**	**1**	**4**	**0**	**0**	**0**
1974-75	**Toronto Maple Leafs**	**NHL**	**60**	**12**	**25**	**37**	**10**	**19**	**29**	**34**	**4**	**1**	**1**	**136**	**8.8**	**96**	**22**	**109**	**39**	**4**	**7**	**0**	**4**	**4**	**6**	**0**	**0**	**0**
1975-76	**Toronto Maple Leafs**	**NHL**	**78**	**16**	**41**	**57**	**14**	**31**	**45**	**70**	**8**	**0**	**1**	**194**	**8.2**	**177**	**53**	**134**	**43**	**33**	**10**	**3**	**4**	**7**	**9**	**1**	**0**	**0**
1976-77	Sweden	Can-Cup	5	4	3	7	....	....	....	2	....	....	....	....	....	....	....	....	....	....	....	....	....	....	....	....	....	....
	Toronto Maple Leafs	**NHL**	**76**	**12**	**66**	**78**	**11**	**51**	**62**	**46**	**1**	**0**	**0**	**186**	**6.5**	**182**	**48**	**120**	**31**	**45**	**9**	**3**	**6**	**9**	**6**	**2**	**0**	**0**
1977-78	**Toronto Maple Leafs**	**NHL**	**80**	**16**	**60**	**76**	**15**	**47**	**62**	**70**	**6**	**0**	**5**	**258**	**6.2**	**157**	**50**	**111**	**34**	**30**	**6**	**2**	**2**	**4**	**6**	**0**	**0**	**1**
1978-79	**Toronto Maple Leafs**	**NHL**	**78**	**17**	**56**	**73**	**15**	**41**	**56**	**76**	**4**	**0**	**2**	**230**	**7.4**	**149**	**46**	**103**	**36**	**36**	**6**	**0**	**1**	**1**	**8**	**0**	**0**	**0**
	NHL All-Stars	Chal-Cup	3	0	0	0	....	....	....	2	....	....	....	....	....	....	....	....	....	....	....	....	....	....	....	....	....	....
1979-80	**Toronto Maple Leafs**	**NHL**	**74**	**19**	**52**	**71**	**16**	**38**	**54**	**94**	**4**	**0**	**1**	**222**	**8.6**	**174**	**56**	**155**	**41**	**4**	**3**	**1**	**1**	**2**	**2**	**1**	**0**	**0**
1980-81	**Toronto Maple Leafs**	**NHL**	**72**	**5**	**61**	**66**	**4**	**41**	**45**	**154**	**1**	**1**	**1**	**210**	**2.4**	**146**	**58**	**131**	**43**	**0**	**3**	**0**	**2**	**2**	**4**	**0**	**0**	**0**
1981-82	Sweden	Can-Cup	5	0	2	2	....	....	....	10	....	....	....	....	....	....	....	....	....	....	....	....	....	....	....	....	....	....
	Toronto Maple Leafs	**NHL**	**69**	**12**	**44**	**56**	**9**	**29**	**38**	**170**	**1**	**0**	**0**	**175**	**6.9**	**143**	**37**	**155**	**53**	**4**	....	....	....	....	....	....	....	....
1982-83	**Toronto Maple Leafs**	**NHL**	**69**	**7**	**38**	**45**	**6**	**26**	**32**	**104**	**2**	**1**	**0**	**110**	**6.4**	**129**	**40**	**131**	**39**	**–3**	**4**	**1**	**4**	**5**	**10**	**1**	**0**	**0**
1983-84	**Toronto Maple Leafs**	**NHL**	**68**	**5**	**38**	**43**	**4**	**26**	**30**	**92**	**2**	**1**	**0**	**160**	**3.1**	**121**	**33**	**182**	**60**	**–34**	....	....	....	....	....	....	....	....
1984-85	**Toronto Maple Leafs**	**NHL**	**73**	**6**	**33**	**39**	**5**	**22**	**27**	**76**	**3**	**0**	**0**	**181**	**3.3**	**115**	**39**	**147**	**45**	**–26**	....	....	....	....	....	....	....	....
1985-86	**Toronto Maple Leafs**	**NHL**	**41**	**7**	**15**	**22**	**6**	**10**	**16**	**48**	**3**	**1**	**1**	**71**	**9.9**	**67**	**24**	**66**	**16**	**–7**	**10**	**1**	**6**	**7**	**14**	**0**	**0**	**0**
1986-87	**Toronto Maple Leafs**	**NHL**	**56**	**4**	**16**	**20**	**3**	**12**	**15**	**42**	**0**	**1**	**1**	**71**	**5.6**	**89**	**8**	**92**	**28**	**17**	**13**	**0**	**3**	**3**	**14**	**0**	**0**	**0**
1987-88	**Toronto Maple Leafs**	**NHL**	**66**	**2**	**24**	**26**	**2**	**17**	**19**	**82**	**1**	**0**	**0**	**92**	**2.2**	**105**	**18**	**114**	**34**	**7**	**6**	**1**	**3**	**4**	**8**	**0**	**0**	**0**
1988-89	**Toronto Maple Leafs**	**NHL**	**63**	**3**	**17**	**20**	**3**	**12**	**15**	**86**	**1**	**0**	**0**	**58**	**5.2**	**75**	**13**	**92**	**37**	**7**	....	....	....	....	....	....	....	....
	Sweden	WEC-A	8	1	1	2	....	....	....	8	....	....	....	....	....	....	....	....	....	....	....	....	....	....	....	....	....	....
1989-90	**Detroit Red Wings**	**NHL**	**49**	**2**	**17**	**19**	**2**	**12**	**14**	**52**	**2**	**0**	**0**	**52**	**3.8**	**71**	**13**	**57**	**19**	**20**	....	....	....	....	....	....	....	....
1990-91	AIK Solna Stockholm	Sweden	36	4	9	13	....	....	....	46	....	....	....	....	....	....	....	....	....	....	....	....	....	....	....	....	....	....
1991-92	Sweden	Can-Cup	6	0	0	0	....	....	....	10	....	....	....	....	....	....	....	....	....	....	....	....	....	....	....	....	....	....
	AIK Solna Stockholm	Sweden	38	6	14	20	....	....	....	*98	....	....	....	....	....	....	....	....	....	....	3	0	2	2	6	....	....	....
	Sweden	Olympics	8	4	3	7	....	....	....	4	....	....	....	....	....	....	....	....	....	....	....	....	....	....	....	....	....	....
1992-93	AIK Solna Stockholm	Sweden	6	1	0	1	....	....	....	10	....	....	....	....	....	....	....	....	....	....	....	....	....	....	....	....	....	....
	NHL Totals		**1148**	**150**	**637**	**787**	**130**	**462**	**592**	**1344**	**46**	**6**	**13**	**2536**	**5.9**	**2111**	**580**	**1977**	**621**		**81**	**12**	**37**	**49**	**91**	**5**	**0**	**1**

Named Best Defenseman at EJC-A (1969) • WEC-A All-Star Team (1973) • NHL Second All-Star Team (1975, 1976, 1978, 1979, 1980) • Canada Cup All-Star Team (1976) • NHL First All-Star Team (1977) • Swedish World All-Star Team (1989) • Played in NHL All-Star Game (1976, 1977, 1978)

Signed as a free agent by **Toronto**, May 12, 1973. Signed as a free agent by **Detroit**, June 12, 1989.

Season	Club	League	REGULAR SEASON																		PLAYOFFS							
			GP	G	A	Pts	AG	AA	APts	PIM	PP	SH	GW	S	%	TGF	PGF	TGA	PGA	+/–	GP	G	A	Pts	PIM	PP	SH	GW

• SALO, Sami D – R. 6'3", 192 lbs. b: Turku, Finland, 9/2/1974. Ottawa's 7th, 239th overall, in 1996.

Season	Club	League	GP	G	A	Pts	AG	AA	APts	PIM	PP	SH	GW	S	%	TGF	PGF	TGA	PGA	+/–	GP	G	A	Pts	PIM	PP	SH	GW
1991-92	Kiekko-67 Turku	Finland-Jr.	23	4	5	9	....	....	....	26	....	....	....	....	....	....	....	....	....	....	....	....	....	....	....	....	....	....
1992-93	Kiekko Turku-2	Finland-Jr.	21	9	4	13	....	....	....	4	....	....	....	....	....	....	....	....	....	....	....	....	....	....	....	....	....	....
	Kiekko-67 Turku	Finland-Jr.	13	6	2	8	....	....	....	2	....	....	....	....	....	....	....	....	....	....	....	....	....	....	....	....	....	....
1993-94	TPS Turku	Finland-Jr.	36	7	13	20	....	....	....	16	....	....	....	....	....	....	....	....	....	....	7	0	1	1	10	....	....	....
1994-95	TPS Turku	Finland-Jr.	14	1	3	4	....	....	....	6	....	....	....	....	....	....	....	....	....	....	....	....	....	....	....	....	....	....
	Kiekko-67 Turku	Finland-2	19	4	2	6	....	....	....	4	....	....	....	....	....	....	....	....	....	....	....	....	....	....	....	....	....	....
	TPS Turku	Finland	7	1	2	3	....	....	....	8	....	....	....	....	....	....	....	....	....	....	1	0	0	0	0	....	....	....
1995-96	TPS Turku	Finland	47	7	14	21	....	....	....	32	....	....	....	....	....	....	....	....	....	....	11	1	3	4	8	....	....	....
1996-97	TPS Turku	Finland	48	9	6	15	....	....	....	10	....	....	....	....	....	....	....	....	....	....	10	2	3	5	4	....	....	....
1997-98	Jokerit Helsinki	Finland	35	3	5	8	....	....	....	10	....	....	....	....	....	....	....	....	....	....	8	0	1	1	2	....	....	....
1998-99	**Ottawa Senators**	**NHL**	**61**	**7**	**12**	**19**	**8**	**12**	**20**	**24**	**2**	**0**	**1**	**106**	**6.6**	**68**	**21**	**35**	**8**	**20**	**4**	**0**	**0**	**0**	**0**	**0**	**0**	**0**
	Detroit Vipers	IHL	5	0	2	2	....	....	....	0	....	....	....	....	....	....	....	....	....	....	....	....	....	....	....	....	....	....
99-2000	**Ottawa Senators**	**NHL**	**37**	**6**	**8**	**14**	**7**	**7**	**14**	**2**	**3**	**0**	**1**	**85**	**7.1**	**39**	**10**	**30**	**7**	**6**	**6**	**1**	**1**	**2**	**0**	**1**	**0**	**0**
	NHL Totals		**98**	**13**	**20**	**33**	**15**	**19**	**34**	**26**	**5**	**0**	**2**	**191**	**6.8**	**107**	**31**	**65**	**15**		**10**	**1**	**1**	**2**	**0**	**1**	**0**	**0**

NHL All-Rookie Team (1999) • Missed majority of 1999-2000 season recovering from wrist injury originally suffered in game vs. Philadelphia, November 28, 1999.

• SALOVAARA, Barry Barry John D – R. 5'10", 180 lbs. b: Cooksville, Ont., 1/7/1948.

Season	Club	League	GP	G	A	Pts	AG	AA	APts	PIM	PP	SH	GW	S	%	TGF	PGF	TGA	PGA	+/–	GP	G	A	Pts	PIM	PP	SH	GW
1965-66	St. Catharines Black Hawks	OHA-Jr.	47	3	13	16	....	....	....	67	....	....	....	....	....	....	....	....	....	....	7	0	2	2	8	....	....	....
1966-67	St. Catharines Black Hawks	OHA-Jr.	48	7	18	25	....	....	....	99	....	....	....	....	....	....	....	....	....	....	6	1	1	2	4	....	....	....
1967-68	St. Catharines Black Hawks	OHA-Jr.	38	6	20	26	....	....	....	96	....	....	....	....	....	....	....	....	....	....	....	....	....	....	....	....	....	....
1968-69	Greensboro Generals	EHL	57	6	15	21	....	....	....	106	....	....	....	....	....	....	....	....	....	....	8	0	1	1	19	....	....	....
	Dallas Black Hawks	CHL	4	0	1	1	....	....	....	8	....	....	....	....	....	....	....	....	....	....	....	....	....	....	....	....	....	....
1969-70	Greensboro Generals	EHL	74	11	35	46	....	....	....	141	....	....	....	....	....	....	....	....	....	....	16	1	13	14	45	....	....	....
1970-71	Greensboro Generals	EHL	72	15	53	68	....	....	....	95	....	....	....	....	....	....	....	....	....	....	9	0	7	7	29	....	....	....
1971-72	Fort Worth Wings	CHL	34	3	14	17	....	....	....	42	....	....	....	....	....	....	....	....	....	....	....	....	....	....	....	....	....	....
	Tidewater Red Wings	AHL	36	0	13	13	....	....	....	36	....	....	....	....	....	....	....	....	....	....	....	....	....	....	....	....	....	....
1972-73	Tidewater Red Wings	AHL	76	4	26	30	....	....	....	92	....	....	....	....	....	....	....	....	....	....	13	3	1	4	16	....	....	....
1973-74	Baltimore Clippers	AHL	70	8	25	33	....	....	....	95	....	....	....	....	....	....	....	....	....	....	9	1	5	6	22	....	....	....
1974-75	**Detroit Red Wings**	**NHL**	**27**	**0**	**2**	**2**	**0**	**1**	**1**	**18**	**0**	**0**	**0**	**18**	**0.0**	**15**	**0**	**31**	**5**	**–11**	....	....	....	....	....	....	....	....
	Virginia Wings	AHL	43	2	17	19	....	....	....	50	....	....	....	....	....	....	....	....	....	....	5	1	0	1	7	....	....	....
1975-76	**Detroit Red Wings**	**NHL**	**63**	**2**	**11**	**13**	**2**	**8**	**10**	**52**	**1**	**0**	**1**	**57**	**3.5**	**36**	**1**	**48**	**6**	**–7**	....	....	....	....	....	....	....	....
	New Haven Nighthawks	AHL	6	1	3	4	....	....	....	14	....	....	....	....	....	....	....	....	....	....	....	....	....	....	....	....	....	....
1976-1978	KAC Klagenfurt	Austria	64	22	31	53	....	....	....	115	....	....	....	....	....	....	....	....	....	....	....	....	....	....	....	....	....	....
1977-78			STATISTICS NOT AVAILABLE																									
1978-79	KooVee Tampere	Finland	35	7	7	14	....	....	....	51	....	....	....	....	....	....	....	....	....	....	....	....	....	....	....	....	....	....
	NHL Totals		**90**	**2**	**13**	**15**	**2**	**9**	**11**	**70**	**1**	**0**	**1**	**75**	**2.7**	**51**	**1**	**79**	**11**		....	....	....	....	....	....	....	....

Traded to **Detroit** (Tidewater-AHL) by **Chicago** (Greensboro-EHL) for cash, June 15, 1971. • Statistics for KAC Klagenfurt (Austria) represent combined totals for 1976--77 and 1977-78 seasons.

• SALVIAN, Dave David Clifford RW – L. 5'10", 170 lbs. b: Toronto, Ont., 9/9/1955. NY Islanders' 2nd, 29th overall, in 1975.

Season	Club	League	GP	G	A	Pts	AG	AA	APts	PIM	PP	SH	GW	S	%	TGF	PGF	TGA	PGA	+/–	GP	G	A	Pts	PIM	PP	SH	GW
1972-73	St. Catharines Black Hawks	OMJHL	51	12	12	24	....	....	....	66	....	....	....	....	....	....	....	....	....	....	....	....	....	....	....	....	....	....
1973-74	St. Catharines Black Hawks	OMJHL	66	36	61	97	....	....	....	113	....	....	....	....	....	....	....	....	....	....	....	....	....	....	....	....	....	....
1974-75	St. Catharines Black Hawks	OMJHL	57	44	48	92	....	....	....	81	....	....	....	....	....	....	....	....	....	....	1	0	0	0	2	....	....	....
1975-76	Fort Worth Texans	CHL	74	38	21	59	....	....	....	72	....	....	....	....	....	....	....	....	....	....	....	....	....	....	....	....	....	....
1976-77	Fort Worth Texans	CHL	75	36	24	60	....	....	....	57	....	....	....	....	....	....	....	....	....	....	6	1	2	3	2	....	....	....
	New York Islanders	**NHL**	....	....	....	....	....	....	....	....	....	....	....	....	....	....	....	....	....	....	**1**	**0**	**1**	**1**	**2**	**0**	**0**	**0**
1977-78	Fort Worth Texans	CHL	68	12	22	34	....	....	....	58	....	....	....	....	....	....	....	....	....	....	14	3	3	6	10	....	....	....
1978-79	Fort Worth Texans	CHL	56	11	13	24	....	....	....	45	....	....	....	....	....	....	....	....	....	....	....	....	....	....	....	....	....	....
	Fort Wayne Komets	IHL	14	1	2	3	....	....	....	2	....	....	....	....	....	....	....	....	....	....	13	3	3	6	6	....	....	....
1979-80	Dallas Black Hawks	CHL	76	24	19	43	....	....	....	22	....	....	....	....	....	....	....	....	....	....	....	....	....	....	....	....	....	....
	NHL Totals		....	....	....	....	....	....	....	....	....	....	....	....	....	....	....	....	....		**1**	**0**	**1**	**1**	**2**	**0**	**0**	**0**

OMJHL Second All-Star Team (1975)

• SAMPSON, Gary Gary Edward LW – L. 6', 190 lbs. b: Atikokan, Ont., 8/24/1959.

Season	Club	League	GP	G	A	Pts	AG	AA	APts	PIM	PP	SH	GW	S	%	TGF	PGF	TGA	PGA	+/–	GP	G	A	Pts	PIM	PP	SH	GW
1977-78	International Falls High	Hi-School	STATISTICS NOT AVAILABLE																									
1978-79	Boston College	ECAC	30	10	18	28	....	....	....	4	....	....	....	....	....	....	....	....	....	....	....	....	....	....	....	....	....	....
1979-80	Boston College	ECAC	24	6	18	24	....	....	....	8	....	....	....	....	....	....	....	....	....	....	....	....	....	....	....	....	....	....
1980-81	Boston College	ECAC	31	8	16	24	....	....	....	8	....	....	....	....	....	....	....	....	....	....	....	....	....	....	....	....	....	....
1981-82	Boston College	ECAC	21	7	11	18	....	....	....	22	....	....	....	....	....	....	....	....	....	....	....	....	....	....	....	....	....	....
1982-83	United States	Nat-Team	40	11	20	31	....	....	....	8	....	....	....	....	....	....	....	....	....	....	....	....	....	....	....	....	....	....
1983-84	United States	Nat-Team	57	21	18	39	....	....	....	10	....	....	....	....	....	....	....	....	....	....	....	....	....	....	....	....	....	....
	United States	Olympics	6	1	2	3	....	....	....	2	....	....	....	....	....	....	....	....	....	....	....	....	....	....	....	....	....	....
	Washington Capitals	**NHL**	**15**	**1**	**1**	**2**	**1**	**1**	**2**	**6**	**0**	**0**	**0**	**17**	**5.9**	**5**	**0**	**4**	**0**	**1**	**8**	**1**	**0**	**1**	**0**	**0**	**0**	**0**
1984-85	**Washington Capitals**	**NHL**	**46**	**10**	**15**	**25**	**8**	**10**	**18**	**13**	**0**	**1**	**0**	**53**	**18.9**	**38**	**0**	**23**	**5**	**20**	**4**	**0**	**0**	**0**	**0**	**0**	**0**	**0**
	Binghamton Whalers	AHL	5	2	2	4	....	....	....	2	....	....	....	....	....	....	....	....	....	....	....	....	....	....	....	....	....	....
1985-86	**Washington Capitals**	**NHL**	**19**	**1**	**4**	**5**	**1**	**3**	**4**	**2**	**0**	**0**	**1**	**17**	**5.9**	**5**	**1**	**9**	**2**	**–3**	....	....	....	....	....	....	....	....
	Binghamton Whalers	AHL	49	9	21	30	....	....	....	16	....	....	....	....	....	....	....	....	....	....	6	2	2	4	4	....	....	....
1986-87	**Washington Capitals**	**NHL**	**25**	**1**	**2**	**3**	**1**	**1**	**2**	**4**	**0**	**0**	**0**	**14**	**7.1**	**6**	**0**	**19**	**4**	**–9**	....	....	....	....	....	....	....	....
	Binghamton Whalers	AHL	37	12	16	28	....	....	....	10	....	....	....	....	....	....	....	....	....	....	11	4	2	6	0	....	....	....
1987-88	Baltimore Skipjacks	AHL	16	2	4	6	....	....	....	4	....	....	....	....	....	....	....	....	....	....	....	....	....	....	....	....	....	....
	NHL Totals		**105**	**13**	**22**	**35**	**11**	**15**	**26**	**25**	**0**	**1**	**1**	**101**	**12.9**	**54**	**1**	**55**	**11**		**12**	**1**	**0**	**1**	**0**	**0**	**0**	**0**

Signed as a free agent by **Washington**, February 21, 1984.

• SAMSONOV, Sergei Sergei Victorovian LW – R. 5'8", 184 lbs. b: Moscow, USSR, 10/27/1978. Boston's 2nd, 8th overall, in 1997.

Season	Club	League	GP	G	A	Pts	AG	AA	APts	PIM	PP	SH	GW	S	%	TGF	PGF	TGA	PGA	+/–	GP	G	A	Pts	PIM	PP	SH	GW
1994-95	CSKA Moscow	CIS-Jr.	50	110	72	182	....	....	....	....	....	....	....	....	....	....	....	....	....	....	....	....	....	....	....	....	....	....
	CSKA Moscow	CIS	13	2	2	4	....	....	....	14	....	....	....	....	....	....	....	....	....	....	2	0	0	0	0	....	....	....
	Russia	EJC-A	5	2	4	6	....	....	....	0	....	....	....	....	....	....	....	....	....	....	....	....	....	....	....	....	....	....
1995-96	CSKA Moscow	CIS	51	21	17	38	....	....	....	12	....	....	....	....	....	....	....	....	....	....	3	1	1	2	4	....	....	....
	Russia	WJC-A	7	4	2	6	....	....	....	0	....	....	....	....	....	....	....	....	....	....	....	....	....	....	....	....	....	....
	Russia	EJC-A	5	3	2	5	....	....	....	4	....	....	....	....	....	....	....	....	....	....	....	....	....	....	....	....	....	....
1996-97	Detroit Vipers	IHL	73	29	35	64	....	....	....	18	....	....	....	....	....	....	....	....	....	....	19	8	4	12	12	....	....	....
	Russia	WJC-A	6	6	1	7	....	....	....	0	....	....	....	....	....	....	....	....	....	....	....	....	....	....	....	....	....	....
1997-98	**Boston Bruins**	**NHL**	**81**	**22**	**25**	**47**	**26**	**24**	**50**	**8**	**7**	**0**	**3**	**159**	**13.8**	**64**	**22**	**33**	**0**	**9**	**6**	**2**	**5**	**7**	**0**	**0**	**0**	**1**
1998-99	**Boston Bruins**	**NHL**	**79**	**25**	**26**	**51**	**29**	**25**	**54**	**18**	**6**	**0**	**8**	**160**	**15.6**	**77**	**30**	**53**	**0**	**–6**	**11**	**3**	**1**	**4**	**0**	**0**	**0**	**0**
99-2000	**Boston Bruins**	**NHL**	**77**	**19**	**26**	**45**	**21**	**24**	**45**	**4**	**6**	**0**	**3**	**145**	**13.1**	**70**	**25**	**51**	**0**	**–6**	....	....	....	....	....	....	....	....
	NHL Totals		**237**	**66**	**77**	**143**	**76**	**73**	**149**	**30**	**19**	**0**	**14**	**464**	**14.2**	**211**	**77**	**137**	**0**		**17**	**5**	**6**	**11**	**0**	**0**	**0**	**1**

EJC-A All-Star Team (1995, 1996) • Named Best Forward at EJC-A (1995) • WJC-A All-Star Team (1997) • Won Garry F. Longman Memorial Trophy (Top Rookie - IHL) (1997) • NHL All-Rookie Team (1998) • Won Calder Memorial Trophy (1998)

• SAMUELSSON, Kjell Kjell William Alf D – R. 6'6", 235 lbs. b: Tingsryd, Sweden, 10/18/1958. NY Rangers' 5th, 119th overall, in 1984.

Season	Club	League	GP	G	A	Pts	AG	AA	APts	PIM	PP	SH	GW	S	%	TGF	PGF	TGA	PGA	+/–	GP	G	A	Pts	PIM	PP	SH	GW
1976-77	Tingsryds AIF	Sweden-2	22	1	2	3	....	....	....	....	....	....	....	....	....	....	....	....	....	....	....	....	....	....	....	....	....	....
1977-78	Tingsryds AIF	Sweden-2	20	3	0	3	....	....	....	41	....	....	....	....	....	....	....	....	....	....	....	....	....	....	....	....	....	....
1978-79	Tingsryds AIF	Sweden-2	24	3	4	7	....	....	....	67	....	....	....	....	....	....	....	....	....	....	....	....	....	....	....	....	....	....
1979-80	Tingsryds AIF	Sweden-2	26	5	4	9	....	....	....	45	....	....	....	....	....	....	....	....	....	....	....	....	....	....	....	....	....	....
1980-81	Tingsryds AIF	Sweden-2	35	6	7	13	....	....	....	61	....	....	....	....	....	....	....	....	....	....	2	0	1	1	14	....	....	....

			REGULAR SEASON																		PLAYOFFS							
Season	Club	League	GP	G	A	Pts	AG	AA	APts	PIM	PP	SH	GW	S	%	TGF	PGF	TGA	PGA	+/–	GP	G	A	Pts	PIM	PP	SH	GW
1981-82	Tingsryds AIF	Sweden-2	33	11	14	25				68											3	0	2	2	2			
1982-83	Tingsryds AIF	Sweden-2	32	11	6	17				57																		
1983-84	Leksands IF	Sweden	36	6	6	12				59																		
1984-85	Leksands IF	Sweden	35	9	5	14				34																		
1985-86	**New York Rangers**	**NHL**	**9**	**0**	**0**	**0**	**0**	**0**	**0**	**10**	**0**	**0**	**0**	**7**	**0.0**	**4**	**0**	**8**	**3**	**–1**	**9**	**0**	**1**	**1**	**8**	**0**	**0**	**0**
	New Haven Nighthawks	AHL	56	6	21	27				87											3	0	0	0	10			
1986-87	**New York Rangers**	**NHL**	**30**	**2**	**6**	**8**	**2**	**4**	**6**	**50**	**0**	**0**	**0**	**20**	**10.0**	**39**	**7**	**39**	**5**	**–2**								
	Philadelphia Flyers	**NHL**	**46**	**1**	**6**	**7**	**1**	**4**	**5**	**86**	**0**	**0**	**0**	**28**	**3.6**	**35**	**2**	**52**	**10**	**–9**	**26**	**0**	**4**	**4**	**25**	**0**	**0**	**0**
1987-88	**Philadelphia Flyers**	**NHL**	**74**	**6**	**24**	**30**	**5**	**17**	**22**	**184**	**3**	**0**	**0**	**118**	**5.1**	**117**	**29**	**92**	**32**	**28**	**7**	**2**	**5**	**7**	**23**	**0**	**0**	**1**
1988-89	**Philadelphia Flyers**	**NHL**	**69**	**3**	**14**	**17**	**3**	**10**	**13**	**140**	**0**	**1**	**0**	**60**	**5.0**	**80**	**3**	**108**	**44**	**13**	**19**	**1**	**3**	**4**	**24**	**0**	**0**	**0**
1989-90	**Philadelphia Flyers**	**NHL**	**66**	**5**	**17**	**22**	**4**	**12**	**16**	**91**	**0**	**0**	**1**	**88**	**5.7**	**88**	**4**	**110**	**46**	**20**								
1990-91	**Philadelphia Flyers**	**NHL**	**78**	**9**	**19**	**28**	**8**	**14**	**22**	**82**	**1**	**0**	**3**	**101**	**8.9**	**74**	**7**	**112**	**49**	**4**								
	Sweden	WEC-A	10	2	2	4				12																		
1991-92	Sweden	Can-Cup	6	1	0	1				16																		
	Philadelphia Flyers	**NHL**	**54**	**4**	**9**	**13**	**4**	**7**	**11**	**76**	**0**	**0**	**0**	**63**	**6.3**	**44**	**2**	**69**	**28**	**1**								
	♦ **Pittsburgh Penguins**	**NHL**	**20**	**1**	**2**	**3**	**1**	**2**	**3**	**34**	**0**	**0**	**1**	**28**	**3.6**	**21**	**0**	**31**	**10**	**0**	**15**	**0**	**3**	**3**	**12**	**0**	**0**	**0**
1992-93	**Pittsburgh Penguins**	**NHL**	**63**	**3**	**6**	**9**	**2**	**4**	**6**	**106**	**0**	**0**	**1**	**63**	**4.8**	**61**	**3**	**64**	**31**	**25**	**12**	**0**	**3**	**3**	**2**	**0**	**0**	**0**
1993-94	**Pittsburgh Penguins**	**NHL**	**59**	**5**	**8**	**13**	**5**	**6**	**11**	**118**	**1**	**0**	**0**	**57**	**8.8**	**61**	**5**	**59**	**21**	**18**	**6**	**0**	**0**	**0**	**26**	**0**	**0**	**0**
1994-95	**Pittsburgh Penguins**	**NHL**	**41**	**1**	**6**	**7**	**2**	**9**	**11**	**54**	**0**	**0**	**0**	**37**	**2.7**	**39**	**2**	**52**	**23**	**8**	**11**	**0**	**1**	**1**	**32**	**0**	**0**	**0**
1995-96	**Philadelphia Flyers**	**NHL**	**75**	**3**	**11**	**14**	**3**	**9**	**12**	**81**	**0**	**0**	**1**	**62**	**4.8**	**70**	**1**	**67**	**18**	**20**	**12**	**1**	**0**	**1**	**24**	**0**	**0**	**0**
1996-97	**Philadelphia Flyers**	**NHL**	**34**	**4**	**3**	**7**	**4**	**3**	**7**	**47**	**0**	**0**	**0**	**36**	**11.1**	**31**	**0**	**19**	**5**	**17**	**5**	**0**	**0**	**0**	**2**	**0**	**0**	**0**
1997-98	**Philadelphia Flyers**	**NHL**	**49**	**0**	**3**	**3**	**0**	**3**	**3**	**28**	**0**	**0**	**0**	**23**	**0.0**	**27**	**0**	**33**	**15**	**9**	**1**	**0**	**0**	**0**	**0**	**0**	**0**	**0**
1998-99	VEU Feldkirch	EuroHL	2	0	1	1				0																		
	Tampa Bay Lightning	**NHL**	**46**	**1**	**4**	**5**	**1**	**4**	**5**	**38**	**0**	**0**	**0**	**22**	**4.5**	**29**	**1**	**53**	**19**	**–6**								
99-2000	Trenton Titans	ECHL	DID NOT PLAY – ASSISTANT COACH																									
	NHL Totals		**813**	**48**	**138**	**186**	**45**	**108**	**153**	**1225**	**5**	**1**	**7**	**813**	**5.9**	**820**	**66**	**968**	**359**		**123**	**4**	**20**	**24**	**178**	**0**	**0**	**1**

Played in NHL All-Star Game (1988)

Traded to **Philadelphia** by **NY Rangers** with NY Rangers' 2nd round choice (Patrik Juhlin) in 1989 Entry Draft for Bob Froese, December 18, 1986. Traded to **Pittsburgh** by **Philadelphia** with Rick Tocchet, Ken Wregget and Philadelphia's 3rd round choice (Dave Roche) in 1993 Entry Draft for Mark Recchi, Brian Benning and LA Kings' 1st round choice (previously acquired, Philadelphia selected Jason Bowen) in 1992 Entry Draft, February 19, 1992. Signed as a free agent by **Philadelphia**, August 31, 1995. Signed as a free agent by **Tampa Bay**, October 14, 1998.
• Officially announced retirement, April 18, 1998.

• SAMUELSSON, Ulf

D – L. 6'1", 205 lbs. b: Fagersta, Sweden, 3/26/1964. Hartford's 4th, 67th overall, in 1982.

Season	Club	League	GP	G	A	Pts	AG	AA	APts	PIM	PP	SH	GW	S	%	TGF	PGF	TGA	PGA	+/–	GP	G	A	Pts	PIM	PP	SH	GW
1980-81	Fagersta AIK	Sweden-3	22	11	5	16																						
1981-82	Leksands IF	Sweden	31	3	1	4				40																		
	Sweden	WJC-A	7	1	2	3				18																		
	Sweden	EJC-A	5	2	1	3				10																		
1982-83	Leksands IF	Sweden	33	9	6	15				72																		
	Sweden	WJC-A	1	0	1	1																						
1983-84	Leksands IF	Sweden	36	5	11	16				53																		
	Sweden	WJC-A	7	1	4	5				18																		
1984-85	**Hartford Whalers**	**NHL**	**41**	**2**	**6**	**8**	**2**	**4**	**6**	**83**	**0**	**0**	**0**	**32**	**6.3**	**41**	**3**	**53**	**9**	**–6**								
	Binghamton Whalers	AHL	36	5	11	16				92																		
	Sweden	WEC-A	9	1	2	3				22																		
1985-86	**Hartford Whalers**	**NHL**	**80**	**5**	**19**	**24**	**4**	**13**	**17**	**174**	**0**	**1**	**1**	**72**	**6.9**	**103**	**13**	**109**	**26**	**7**	**10**	**1**	**2**	**3**	**38**	**0**	**0**	**1**
1986-87	**Hartford Whalers**	**NHL**	**78**	**2**	**31**	**33**	**2**	**23**	**25**	**162**	**0**	**0**	**0**	**104**	**1.9**	**120**	**18**	**111**	**37**	**28**	**5**	**0**	**1**	**1**	**41**	**-2**	**0**	**0**
	NHL All-Stars	RV-87	2	0	0	0				0																		
1987-88	**Hartford Whalers**	**NHL**	**76**	**8**	**33**	**41**	**7**	**24**	**31**	**159**	**3**	**0**	**0**	**156**	**5.1**	**96**	**32**	**113**	**39**	**–10**	**5**	**0**	**0**	**0**	**8**	**0**	**0**	**0**
1988-89	**Hartford Whalers**	**NHL**	**71**	**9**	**26**	**35**	**8**	**18**	**26**	**181**	**3**	**0**	**2**	**122**	**7.4**	**111**	**34**	**87**	**33**	**23**	**4**	**0**	**2**	**2**	**4**	**0**	**0**	**0**
1989-90	**Hartford Whalers**	**NHL**	**55**	**2**	**11**	**13**	**2**	**8**	**10**	**177**	**0**	**0**	**0**	**57**	**3.5**	**57**	**4**	**57**	**19**	**15**	**7**	**1**	**0**	**1**	**2**	**0**	**0**	**0**
	Sweden	WEC-A	7	2	0	2				18																		
1990-91	**Hartford Whalers**	**NHL**	**62**	**3**	**18**	**21**	**3**	**14**	**17**	**174**	**0**	**0**	**0**	**110**	**2.7**	**62**	**4**	**57**	**12**	**13**								
	♦ **Pittsburgh Penguins**	**NHL**	**14**	**1**	**4**	**5**	**1**	**3**	**4**	**37**	**0**	**0**	**0**	**15**	**6.7**	**15**	**0**	**15**	**4**	**4**	**20**	**3**	**2**	**5**	**34**	**1**	**0**	**1**
1991-92	Sweden	Can-Cup	3	0	0	0				4																		
	♦ **Pittsburgh Penguins**	**NHL**	**62**	**1**	**14**	**15**	**1**	**11**	**12**	**206**	**1**	**0**	**1**	**75**	**1.3**	**69**	**9**	**83**	**25**	**2**	**21**	**0**	**2**	**2**	**39**	**0**	**0**	**0**
1992-93	**Pittsburgh Penguins**	**NHL**	**77**	**3**	**26**	**29**	**2**	**18**	**20**	**249**	**0**	**0**	**1**	**96**	**3.1**	**116**	**14**	**100**	**34**	**36**	**12**	**1**	**5**	**6**	**24**	**0**	**0**	**0**
1993-94	**Pittsburgh Penguins**	**NHL**	**80**	**5**	**24**	**29**	**5**	**19**	**24**	**199**	**1**	**0**	**0**	**106**	**4.7**	**111**	**17**	**102**	**31**	**23**	**6**	**0**	**1**	**1**	**18**	**0**	**0**	**0**
1994-95	Leksands IF	Sweden	2	0	0	0				8																		
	Pittsburgh Penguins	**NHL**	**44**	**1**	**15**	**16**	**2**	**22**	**24**	**113**	**0**	**0**	**0**	**47**	**2.1**	**57**	**8**	**63**	**25**	**11**	**7**	**0**	**2**	**2**	**8**	**0**	**0**	**0**
1995-96	**New York Rangers**	**NHL**	**74**	**1**	**18**	**19**	**1**	**15**	**16**	**122**	**0**	**0**	**0**	**66**	**1.5**	**63**	**8**	**68**	**22**	**9**	**11**	**1**	**5**	**6**	**16**	**0**	**0**	**0**
1996-97	**New York Rangers**	**NHL**	**73**	**6**	**11**	**17**	**6**	**10**	**16**	**138**	**1**	**0**	**1**	**77**	**7.8**	**53**	**4**	**67**	**21**	**3**	**15**	**0**	**2**	**2**	**30**	**0**	**0**	**0**
1997-98	**New York Rangers**	**NHL**	**73**	**3**	**9**	**12**	**4**	**9**	**13**	**122**	**0**	**0**	**2**	**59**	**5.1**	**38**	**1**	**54**	**18**	**1**								
	Sweden	Olympics	3	0	1	1				4																		
1998-99	**New York Rangers**	**NHL**	**67**	**4**	**8**	**12**	**5**	**8**	**13**	**93**	**0**	**0**	**0**	**37**	**10.8**	**56**	**3**	**66**	**19**	**6**								
	Detroit Red Wings	**NHL**	**4**	**0**	**0**	**0**	**0**	**0**	**0**	**6**	**0**	**0**	**0**	**2**	**0.0**	**0**	**0**	**2**	**1**	**–1**	**9**	**0**	**3**	**3**	**10**	**0**	**0**	**0**
99-2000	**Philadelphia Flyers**	**NHL**	**49**	**1**	**2**	**3**	**1**	**2**	**3**	**58**	**0**	**0**	**1**	**17**	**5.9**	**31**	**1**	**29**	**7**	**8**								
	NHL Totals		**1080**	**57**	**275**	**332**	**56**	**221**	**277**	**2453**	**9**	**1**	**9**	**1250**	**4.6**	**1199**	**173**	**1236**	**382**		**132**	**7**	**27**	**34**	**272**	**-1**	**0**	**2**

EJC-A All-Star Team (1982)

Traded to **Pittsburgh** by **Hartford** with Ron Francis and Grant Jennings for John Cullen, Jeff Parker and Zarley Zalapski, March 4, 1991. Traded to **NY Rangers** by **Pittsburgh** with Luc Robitaille for Petr Nedved and Sergei Zubov, August 31, 1995. Traded to **Detroit** by **NY Rangers** for Detroit's 2nd round choice (David Inman) in 1999 Entry Draft and NY Rangers' 3rd round choice (previously acquired, NY Rangers' selected Johan Asplund) in 2000 Entry Draft, March 23, 1999. Traded to **Atlanta** by **Detroit** for future considerations, June 25, 1999. Signed as a free agent by **Philadelphia**, October 19, 1999.

• SANDELIN, Scott

Scott A. D – R. 6', 200 lbs. b: Hibbing, MN, 8/8/1964. Montreal's 5th, 40th overall, in 1982.

Season	Club	League	GP	G	A	Pts	AG	AA	APts	PIM	PP	SH	GW	S	%	TGF	PGF	TGA	PGA	+/–	GP	G	A	Pts	PIM	PP	SH	GW
1981-82	Hibbing Blue Jackets	Hi-School	20	5	15	20				30																		
1982-83	University of North Dakota	WCHA	21	0	4	4				10																		
1983-84	University of North Dakota	WCHA	41	4	23	27				24																		
	United States	WJC-A	7	0	1	1				10																		
1984-85	University of North Dakota	WCHA	38	4	17	21				30																		
1985-86	University of North Dakota	WCHA	40	7	31	38				38																		
	Sherbrooke Canadiens	AHL	6	0	2	2				2																		
	United States	WEC-A	10	2	0	2				2																		
1986-87	**Montreal Canadiens**	**NHL**	**1**	**0**	**0**	**0**	**0**	**0**	**0**	**0**	**0**	**0**	**0**	**0**	**0.0**	**1**	**0**	**0**	**0**	**1**								
	Sherbrooke Canadiens	AHL	74	7	22	29				35											16	2	4	6	2			
1987-88	**Montreal Canadiens**	**NHL**	**8**	**0**	**1**	**1**	**0**	**1**	**1**	**2**	**0**	**0**	**0**	**5**	**0.0**	**8**	**1**	**7**	**0**	**0**								
	Sherbrooke Canadiens	AHL	58	8	14	22				35											4	0	2	2	0			
1988-89	Sherbrooke Canadiens	AHL	12	0	9	9				8																		
	Hershey Bears	AHL	39	6	9	15				38											8	2	1	3	4			
1989-90	Hershey Bears	AHL	70	4	27	31				38																		
1990-91	**Philadelphia Flyers**	**NHL**	**15**	**0**	**3**	**3**	**0**	**2**	**2**	**0**	**0**	**0**	**0**	**4**	**0.0**	**11**	**2**	**12**	**0**	**–3**								
	Hershey Bears	AHL	39	3	10	13				21											7	1	2	3	0			
1991-92	**Minnesota North Stars**	**NHL**	**1**	**0**	**0**	**0**	**0**	**0**	**0**	**0**	**0**	**0**	**0**	**1**	**0.0**	**0**	**0**	**1**	**0**	**–1**								
	Kalamazoo Wings	IHL	49	3	18	21				32											11	1	1	2	2			
1992-1993	Fargo-Moorhead Express	AmHA	DID NOT PLAY – COACHING																									
1993-1994	Fargo-Moorhead Jr. Kings	MWJHL	DID NOT PLAY – COACHING																									
1994-2000	University of North Dakota	WCHA	DID NOT PLAY – ASSISTANT COACH																									
	NHL Totals		**25**	**0**	**4**	**4**	**0**	**3**	**3**	**2**	**0**	**0**	**0**	**10**	**0.0**	**20**	**3**	**20**	**0**									

WCHA First All-Star Team (1986)

Traded to **Philadelphia** by **Montreal** for J.J. Daigneault, November 7, 1988. Signed as a free agent by **Minnesota**, August 21, 1991.

• SANDERSON, Derek

Derek Michael "Turk" C – L. 6', 185 lbs. b: Niagara Falls, Ont., 6/16/1946.

			REGULAR SEASON																		PLAYOFFS							
Season	Club	League	GP	G	A	Pts	AG	AA	APts	PIM	PP	SH	GW	S	%	TGF	PGF	TGA	PGA	+/-	GP	G	A	Pts	PIM	PP	SH	GW
1961-62	Niagara Falls Canucks	OHA-B	STATISTICS NOT AVAILABLE																									
1962-63	Niagara Falls Canucks	OHA-B	STATISTICS NOT AVAILABLE																									
	Niagara Falls Flyers	OHA-Jr.	2	0	0	0				10											1	0	0	0	0			
	Niagara Falls Flyers	Mem-Cup	1	0	0	0				0																		
1963-64	Niagara Falls Flyers	OHA-Jr.	42	12	15	27				42											4	0	1	1	0			
1964-65	Niagara Falls Flyers	OHA-Jr.	55	19	46	65				128											11	9	8	17	26			
1965-66	Niagara Falls Flyers	OHA-Jr.	48	33	43	76				*238											6	6	0	6	*72			
	Boston Bruins	**NHL**	**2**	**0**	**0**	**0**	**0**	**0**	**0**	**0**																		
	Oklahoma City Blazers	CPHL	2	1	0	1				0											4	0	4	4	5			
	Niagara Falls Flyers	Mem-Cup	11	7	6	13				*78																		
1966-67	Niagara Falls Flyers	OHA-Jr.	47	41	*60	*101				193											13	8	*17	25	*70			
	Boston Bruins	**NHL**	**2**	**0**	**0**	**0**	**0**	**0**	**0**	**0**																		
	Oklahoma City Blazers	CPHL																			2	0	0	0	0			
1967-68	**Boston Bruins**	**NHL**	**71**	**24**	**25**	**49**	**28**	**25**	**53**	**98**	**4**	**1**	**6**	**187**	**12.8**	**60**	**6**	**50**	**7**	**11**	**4**	**0**	**2**	**2**	**9**	**0**	**0**	**0**
1968-69	**Boston Bruins**	**NHL**	**61**	**26**	**22**	**48**	**28**	**20**	**48**	**146**	**1**	**3**	**3**	**194**	**13.4**	**62**	**6**	**41**	**20**	**35**	**9**	***8**	**2**	**10**	**36**	**0**	**2**	**3**
1969-70♦	**Boston Bruins**	**NHL**	**50**	**18**	**23**	**41**	**20**	**22**	**42**	**118**	**5**	**5**	**2**	**179**	**10.1**	**56**	**15**	**54**	**21**	**8**	**14**	**5**	**4**	**9**	***72**	**1**	**0**	**2**
1970-71	**Boston Bruins**	**NHL**	**71**	**29**	**34**	**63**	**29**	**28**	**57**	**130**	**1**	**6**	**0**	**217**	**13.4**	**82**	**3**	**69**	**29**	**39**	**7**	**2**	**1**	**3**	**13**	**0**	**0**	**0**
1971-72♦	**Boston Bruins**	**NHL**	**78**	**25**	**33**	**58**	**25**	**29**	**54**	**108**	**0**	**7**	**2**	**198**	**12.6**	**73**	**1**	**86**	**39**	**25**	**11**	**1**	**1**	**2**	**44**	**0**	**1**	**0**
1972-73	Philadelphia Blazers	WHA	8	3	3	6				69																		
	Boston Bruins	**NHL**	**25**	**5**	**10**	**15**	**5**	**8**	**13**	**38**	**0**	**2**	**0**	**41**	**12.2**	**18**	**0**	**20**	**13**	**11**	**5**	**1**	**2**	**3**	**13**	**0**	**0**	**0**
1973-74	**Boston Bruins**	**NHL**	**29**	**8**	**12**	**20**	**8**	**10**	**18**	**48**	**0**	**0**	**1**	**64**	**12.5**	**31**	**2**	**23**	**11**	**17**								
	Boston Braves	AHL	3	4	3	7				2																		
1974-75	**New York Rangers**	**NHL**	**75**	**25**	**25**	**50**	**22**	**19**	**41**	**106**	**3**	**2**	**3**	**188**	**13.3**	**80**	**10**	**83**	**23**	**10**	**3**	**0**	**0**	**0**	**0**	**0**	**0**	**0**
1975-76	**New York Rangers**	**NHL**	**8**	**0**	**0**	**0**	**0**	**0**	**0**	**4**	**0**	**0**	**0**	**29**	**0.0**	**0**	**0**	**13**	**5**	**–8**								
	St. Louis Blues	**NHL**	**65**	**24**	**43**	**67**	**21**	**32**	**53**	**59**	**6**	**6**	**1**	**171**	**14.0**	**86**	**23**	**90**	**40**	**13**	**3**	**1**	**0**	**1**	**0**	**1**	**0**	**0**
1976-77	**St. Louis Blues**	**NHL**	**32**	**8**	**13**	**21**	**7**	**10**	**17**	**26**	**3**	**0**	**2**	**53**	**15.1**	**27**	**9**	**27**	**1**	**–8**								
	Kansas City Blues	CHL	8	4	3	7				6																		
	Vancouver Canucks	**NHL**	**16**	**7**	**9**	**16**	**6**	**7**	**13**	**30**	**2**	**2**	**1**	**21**	**33.3**	**25**	**8**	**17**	**5**	**5**								
1977-78	**Pittsburgh Penguins**	**NHL**	**13**	**3**	**1**	**4**	**3**	**1**	**4**	**0**	**1**	**0**	**0**	**11**	**27.3**	**5**	**1**	**15**	**5**	**–6**								
	Tulsa Oilers	CHL	4	0	0	0				0																		
	Kansas City Red Wings	CHL	4	1	3	4				0																		
	NHL Totals		**598**	**202**	**250**	**452**	**202**	**211**	**413**	**911**											**56**	**18**	**12**	**30**	**187**			
	Other Major League Totals		8	3	3	6				69																		

OHA-Jr. Second All-Star Team (1966) • OHA-Jr. First All-Star Team (1967) • Won Calder Memorial Trophy (1968)

Selected by **Miami-Philadelphia** (WHA) in 1972 WHA General Player Draft, February 12, 1972. Signed as a free agent by **Boston** after securing release from **Philadelphia** (WHA), February, 1973. Traded to **NY Rangers** by **Boston** for Walt McKechnie, June 12, 1974. Traded to **St. Louis** by **NY Rangers** for NY Rangers' 1st round choice (previously acquired, NY Rangers selected Lucien DeBlois) in 1977 Amateur Draft, October 30, 1975. Traded to **Vancouver** by **St. Louis** for cash, February 18, 1977. Signed as a free agent by **Pittsburgh**, March 14, 1978.

• SANDERSON, Geoff

Geoff M. LW – L. 6', 190 lbs. b: Hay River, N.W.T., 2/1/1972. Hartford's 2nd, 36th overall, in 1990.

Season	Club	League	GP	G	A	Pts	AG	AA	APts	PIM	PP	SH	GW	S	%	TGF	PGF	TGA	PGA	+/-	GP	G	A	Pts	PIM	PP	SH	GW
1987-88	St. Albert Royals	AAHA	45	65	55	120				175																		
1988-89	Swift Current Broncos	WHL	58	17	11	28				16											12	3	5	8	6			
	Swift Current Broncos	Mem-Cup	2	0	0	0				0																		
1989-90	Swift Current Broncos	WHL	70	32	62	94				56											4	1	4	5	8			
1990-91	Swift Current Broncos	WHL	70	62	50	112				57											3	1	2	3	4			
	Hartford Whalers	**NHL**	**2**	**1**	**0**	**1**	**1**	**0**	**1**	**0**	**0**	**0**	**0**	**2**	**50.0**	**1**	**0**	**3**	**0**	**–2**	**3**	**0**	**0**	**0**	**0**	**0**	**0**	**0**
	Springfield Indians	AHL																			1	0	0	0	2			
1991-92	**Hartford Whalers**	**NHL**	**64**	**13**	**18**	**31**	**12**	**14**	**26**	**18**	**2**	**0**	**1**	**98**	**13.3**	**49**	**5**	**59**	**20**	**5**	**7**	**1**	**0**	**1**	**2**	**0**	**0**	**0**
1992-93	**Hartford Whalers**	**NHL**	**82**	**46**	**43**	**89**	**38**	**30**	**68**	**28**	**21**	**2**	**4**	**271**	**17.0**	**113**	**53**	**92**	**11**	**–21**								
	Canada	WC-A	8	3	3	6				2																		
1993-94	**Hartford Whalers**	**NHL**	**82**	**41**	**26**	**67**	**38**	**20**	**58**	**42**	**15**	**1**	**6**	**266**	**15.4**	**98**	**40**	**74**	**3**	**–13**								
	Canada	WC-A	8	4	2	6				8																		
1994-95	HPK Hameenlinna	Finland	12	6	4	10				24																		
	Hartford Whalers	**NHL**	**46**	**18**	**14**	**32**	**32**	**21**	**53**	**24**	**4**	**0**	**4**	**170**	**10.6**	**42**	**16**	**37**	**1**	**–10**								
1995-96	**Hartford Whalers**	**NHL**	**81**	**34**	**31**	**65**	**33**	**25**	**58**	**40**	**6**	**0**	**7**	**314**	**10.8**	**88**	**30**	**66**	**8**	**0**								
1996-97	**Hartford Whalers**	**NHL**	**82**	**36**	**31**	**67**	**38**	**28**	**66**	**29**	**12**	**1**	**4**	**297**	**12.1**	**90**	**35**	**65**	**1**	**–9**								
	Canada	WC-A	11	3	2	5				2																		
1997-98	**Carolina Hurricanes**	**NHL**	**40**	**7**	**10**	**17**	**8**	**10**	**18**	**14**	**2**	**0**	**0**	**96**	**7.3**	**29**	**11**	**23**	**1**	**–4**								
	Vancouver Canucks	**NHL**	**9**	**0**	**3**	**3**	**0**	**3**	**3**	**4**	**0**	**0**	**0**	**29**	**0.0**	**5**	**1**	**5**	**0**	**–1**								
	Buffalo Sabres	**NHL**	**26**	**4**	**5**	**9**	**5**	**5**	**10**	**20**	**0**	**0**	**2**	**72**	**5.6**	**17**	**7**	**5**	**1**	**6**	**14**	**3**	**1**	**4**	**4**	**1**	**0**	**1**
1998-99	**Buffalo Sabres**	**NHL**	**75**	**12**	**18**	**30**	**14**	**17**	**31**	**22**	**1**	**0**	**1**	**155**	**7.7**	**46**	**11**	**28**	**1**	**8**	**19**	**4**	**6**	**10**	**14**	**0**	**0**	**1**
99-2000	**Buffalo Sabres**	**NHL**	**67**	**13**	**13**	**26**	**15**	**12**	**27**	**22**	**4**	**0**	**3**	**136**	**9.6**	**38**	**7**	**29**	**2**	**4**	**5**	**0**	**2**	**2**	**8**	**0**	**0**	**0**
	NHL Totals		**656**	**225**	**212**	**437**	**234**	**185**	**419**	**263**	**67**	**4**	**32**	**1906**	**11.8**	**616**	**216**	**486**	**49**		**48**	**8**	**9**	**17**	**28**	**1**	**0**	**2**

Played in NHL All-Star Game (1994, 1997)

Transferred to **Carolina** after **Hartford** franchise relocated, June 25, 1997. Traded to **Vancouver** by **Carolina** with Sean Burke and Enrico Ciccone for Kirk McLean and Martin Gelinas, January 3, 1998. Traded to **Buffalo** by **Vancouver** for Brad May and Buffalo's 3rd round choice (later traded to Tampa Bay - Tampa Bay selected Jimmie Olvestad) in 1999 Entry Draft, February 4, 1998. Selected by **Columbus** from **Buffalo** in Expansion Draft, June 23, 2000.

• SANDLAK, Jim

James J. RW – R. 6'4", 219 lbs. b: Kitchener, Ont., 12/12/1966. Vancouver's 1st, 4th overall, in 1985.

Season	Club	League	GP	G	A	Pts	AG	AA	APts	PIM	PP	SH	GW	S	%	TGF	PGF	TGA	PGA	+/-	GP	G	A	Pts	PIM	PP	SH	GW
1982-83	Kitchener Dutchmen	OJHL	38	26	25	51				100																		
	Kitchener Rangers	OHL	1	0	0	0				0																		
1983-84	London Knights	OHL	68	23	18	41				143											8	1	11	12	13			
1984-85	London Knights	OHL	58	40	24	64				128											8	3	2	5	14			
	Canada	WJC-A	5	1	0	1				6																		
1985-86	London Knights	OHL	16	8	14	22				38											5	2	3	5	24			
	Vancouver Canucks	**NHL**	**23**	**1**	**3**	**4**	**1**	**2**	**3**	**10**	**0**	**0**	**0**	**34**	**2.9**	**9**	**3**	**10**	**0**	**–4**	**3**	**0**	**1**	**1**	**0**	**0**	**0**	**0**
	Canada	WJC-A	7	5	7	12				16																		
1986-87	**Vancouver Canucks**	**NHL**	**78**	**15**	**21**	**36**	**13**	**15**	**28**	**66**	**2**	**0**	**3**	**114**	**13.2**	**57**	**19**	**42**	**0**	**–4**								
1987-88	**Vancouver Canucks**	**NHL**	**49**	**16**	**15**	**31**	**14**	**11**	**25**	**81**	**6**	**0**	**2**	**96**	**16.7**	**52**	**21**	**41**	**1**	**–9**								
	Fredericton Express	AHL	24	10	15	25				47																		
1988-89	**Vancouver Canucks**	**NHL**	**72**	**20**	**20**	**40**	**17**	**14**	**31**	**99**	**9**	**0**	**4**	**164**	**12.2**	**64**	**20**	**36**	**0**	**8**	**6**	**1**	**1**	**2**	**2**	**0**	**0**	**0**
1989-90	**Vancouver Canucks**	**NHL**	**70**	**15**	**8**	**23**	**13**	**6**	**19**	**104**	**1**	**0**	**2**	**135**	**11.1**	**41**	**7**	**49**	**0**	**–15**								
1990-91	**Vancouver Canucks**	**NHL**	**59**	**7**	**6**	**13**	**6**	**5**	**11**	**125**	**4**	**0**	**0**	**88**	**8.0**	**22**	**7**	**35**	**0**	**–20**								
1991-92	**Vancouver Canucks**	**NHL**	**66**	**16**	**24**	**40**	**15**	**18**	**33**	**176**	**3**	**0**	**2**	**122**	**13.1**	**58**	**10**	**27**	**1**	**22**	**13**	**4**	**6**	**10**	**22**	**2**	**0**	**0**
1992-93	**Vancouver Canucks**	**NHL**	**59**	**10**	**18**	**28**	**8**	**12**	**20**	**122**	**1**	**0**	**1**	**104**	**9.6**	**44**	**14**	**35**	**7**	**2**	**6**	**2**	**2**	**4**	**4**	**0**	**0**	**0**
1993-94	**Hartford Whalers**	**NHL**	**27**	**6**	**2**	**8**	**6**	**2**	**8**	**32**	**2**	**0**	**1**	**32**	**18.8**	**16**	**2**	**9**	**1**	**6**								
1994-95	**Hartford Whalers**	**NHL**	**13**	**0**	**0**	**0**	**0**	**0**	**0**	**0**	**0**	**0**	**0**	**13**	**0.0**	**2**	**0**	**12**	**0**	**–10**								
1995-96	**Vancouver Canucks**	**NHL**	**33**	**4**	**2**	**6**	**4**	**2**	**6**	**6**	**0**	**1**	**1**	**44**	**9.1**	**13**	**1**	**18**	**3**	**–3**	**5**	**0**	**0**	**0**	**2**	**0**	**0**	**0**
	Syracuse Crunch	AHL	12	6	1	7				16																		
1996-97	Detroit Vipers	IHL	DID NOT PLAY – ASSISTANT COACH																									
1997-98	ERC Ingolstadt	Germany-2	18	6	9	15				85											3	0	1	1	2			
	NHL Totals		**549**	**110**	**119**	**229**	**97**	**87**	**184**	**821**	**28**	**1**	**16**	**946**	**11.6**	**378**	**104**	**314**	**13**		**33**	**7**	**10**	**17**	**30**	**2**	**0**	**0**

Named Best Forward at WJC-A (1986) • NHL All-Rookie Team (1987)

Traded to **Hartford** by **Vancouver** to complete transaction that sent Murray Craven to Vancouver (March 22, 1993), May 17, 1993. Signed as a free agent by **Vancouver**, October 1, 1995.

• SANDSTROM, Tomas

RW – L. 6'2", 205 lbs. b: Jakobstad, Finland, 9/4/1964. NY Rangers' 2nd, 36th overall, in 1982.

			REGULAR SEASON																		PLAYOFFS							
Season	Club	League	GP	G	A	Pts	AG	AA	APts	PIM	PP	SH	GW	S	%	TGF	PGF	TGA	PGA	+/–	GP	G	A	Pts	PIM	PP	SH	GW
1979-80	Fagersta HK	Sweden-2	6	1	1	2	....	....	....	0	....	....	....	....	....	....	....	....	....	....	....	....	....	....	....	....	....	....
1980-81	Fagersta HK	Sweden-2	20	23	5	28	....	....	....	....	....	....	....	....	....	....	....	....	....	....	....	....	....	....	....	....	....	....
1981-82	Fagersta HK	Sweden-2	32	28	11	39	....	....	....	74	....	....	....	....	....	....	....	....	....	....	....	....	....	....	....	....	....	....
	Sweden	EJC-A	5	5	2	7	....	....	....	16	....	....	....	....	....	....	....	....	....	....	....	....	....	....	....	....	....	....
1982-83	Brynas IF Gavle	Sweden	36	23	14	37	....	....	....	50	....	....	....	....	....	....	....	....	....	....	....	....	....	....	....	....	....	....
	Sweden	WJC-A	7	9	3	12	....	....	....	....	....	....	....	....	....	....	....	....	....	....	....	....	....	....	....	....	....	....
1983-84	Brynas IF Gavle	Sweden	34	19	10	29	....	....	....	81	....	....	....	....	....	....	....	....	....	....	....	....	....	....	....	....	....	....
	Sweden	WJC-A	7	4	3	7	....	....	....	12	....	....	....	....	....	....	....	....	....	....	....	....	....	....	....	....	....	....
	Sweden	Olympics	7	2	1	3	....	....	....	6	....	....	....	....	....	....	....	....	....	....	....	....	....	....	....	....	....	....
1984-85	Sweden	Can-Cup	8	1	1	2	....	....	....	2	....	....	....	....	....	....	....	....	....	....	....	....	....	....	....	....	....	....
	New York Rangers	NHL	74	29	29	58	24	20	44	51	5	0	3	190	15.3	84	25	58	2	3	3	0	2	2	0	0	0	0
	Sweden	WEC-A	10	3	6	9	....	....	....	18	....	....	....	....	....	....	....	....	....	....	....	....	....	....	....	....	....	....
1985-86	New York Rangers	NHL	73	25	29	54	20	19	39	109	8	2	1	238	10.5	80	39	53	8	–4	16	4	6	10	20	0	0	1
1986-87	New York Rangers	NHL	64	40	34	74	35	25	60	60	13	0	5	240	16.7	100	36	56	0	8	6	1	2	3	20	0	0	0
	NHL All-Stars	RV-87	1	0	0	0	....	....	....	0	....	....	....	....	....	....	....	....	....	....	....	....	....	....	....	....	....	....
	Sweden	WEC-A	8	4	6	10	....	....	....	6	....	....	....	....	....	....	....	....	....	....	....	....	....	....	....	....	....	....
1987-88	New York Rangers	NHL	69	28	40	68	24	29	53	95	11	0	3	204	13.7	109	52	67	4	–6	....	....	....	....	....	....	....	....
1988-89	New York Rangers	NHL	79	32	56	88	27	40	67	148	11	2	4	240	13.3	132	52	90	15	5	4	3	2	5	12	2	0	0
	Sweden	WEC-A	10	4	3	7	....	....	....	14	....	....	....	....	....	....	....	....	....	....	....	....	....	....	....	....	....	....
1989-90	New York Rangers	NHL	48	19	19	38	16	14	30	100	6	0	3	166	11.4	53	24	40	1	–10	....	....	....	....	....	....	....	....
	Los Angeles Kings	NHL	28	13	20	33	11	14	25	28	1	1	0	83	15.7	45	16	35	5	–1	10	5	4	9	19	0	0	0
1990-91	Los Angeles Kings	NHL	68	45	44	89	41	34	75	106	16	0	6	221	20.4	128	41	60	0	27	10	4	4	8	14	3	0	0
1991-92	Sweden	Can-Cup	6	1	2	3	....	....	....	8	....	....	....	....	....	....	....	....	....	....	....	....	....	....	....	....	....	....
	Los Angeles Kings	NHL	49	17	22	39	15	17	32	70	5	0	4	147	11.6	58	18	43	1	–2	6	0	3	3	8	0	0	0
1992-93	Los Angeles Kings	NHL	39	25	27	52	21	19	40	57	8	0	3	134	18.7	71	25	34	0	12	24	8	17	25	12	2	0	2
1993-94	Los Angeles Kings	NHL	51	17	24	41	16	19	35	59	4	0	2	121	14.0	68	32	51	3	–12	....	....	....	....	....	....	....	....
	Pittsburgh Penguins	NHL	27	6	11	17	6	9	15	24	0	0	1	72	8.3	25	2	22	4	5	6	0	0	0	4	0	0	0
1994-95	Malmo IF Gavle	Sweden	12	10	5	15	....	....	....	14	....	....	....	....	....	....	....	....	....	....	....	....	....	....	....	....	....	....
	Pittsburgh Penguins	NHL	47	21	23	44	37	34	71	42	4	1	3	116	18.1	56	17	51	13	1	12	3	3	6	16	2	0	0
1995-96	Pittsburgh Penguins	NHL	58	35	35	70	34	29	63	69	17	1	2	187	18.7	120	59	64	7	4	18	4	2	6	30	0	0	1
1996-97	Pittsburgh Penguins	NHL	40	9	15	24	10	13	23	33	1	1	0	73	12.3	38	10	30	6	4	....	....	....	....	....	....	....	....
♦	Detroit Red Wings	NHL	34	9	9	18	10	8	18	36	0	1	2	66	13.6	32	10	26	6	2	20	0	4	4	24	0	0	0
1997-98	Mighty Ducks of Anaheim	NHL	77	9	8	17	11	8	19	64	2	1	0	136	6.6	40	13	54	2	–25	....	....	....	....	....	....	....	....
	Sweden	Olympics	4	0	1	1	....	....	....	0	....	....	....	....	....	....	....	....	....	....	....	....	....	....	....	....	....	....
1998-99	Mighty Ducks of Anaheim	NHL	58	15	17	32	18	16	34	42	7	0	2	107	14.0	40	16	39	10	–5	4	0	0	0	4	0	0	0
99-2000	Malmo IF	Sweden	42	16	13	29	....	....	....	28	....	....	....	....	....	....	....	....	....	....	....	6	3	2	5	10	....	....	....
	NHL Totals		983	394	462	856	376	367	743	1193	119	10	44	2741	14.4	1279	487	873	87		139	32	49	81	183	9	0	4

EJC-A All-Star Team (1982) • Named Best Forward at EJC-A (1982) • WJC-A All-Star Team (1983) • Named Best Forward at WJC-A (1983) • NHL All-Rookie Team (1985) • Played in NHL All-Star Game (1988, 1991)

Traded to **LA Kings** by **NY Rangers** with Tony Granato for Bernie Nicholls, January 20, 1990. Traded to **Pittsburgh** by **LA Kings** with Shawn McEachern for Marty McSorley and Jim Paek, February 16, 1994. Traded to **Detroit** by **Pittsburgh** for Greg Johnson, January 27, 1997. Signed as a free agent by **Anaheim**, October 20, 1997.

• SANDWITH, Terran

D – L. 6'4", 210 lbs. b: Edmonton, Alta., 4/17/1972. Philadelphia's 4th, 42nd overall, in 1990.

			REGULAR SEASON																		PLAYOFFS							
Season	Club	League	GP	G	A	Pts	AG	AA	APts	PIM	PP	SH	GW	S	%	TGF	PGF	TGA	PGA	+/–	GP	G	A	Pts	PIM	PP	SH	GW
1987-88	Hobbema Hawks	AJHL	58	5	8	13	....	....	....	106	....	....	....	....	....	....	....	....	....	....	....	....	....	....	....	....	....	....
1988-89	Tri-City Americans	WHL	31	0	0	0	....	....	....	29	....	....	....	....	....	....	....	....	....	....	6	0	0	0	4	....	....	....
1989-90	Tri-City Americans	WHL	70	4	14	18	....	....	....	92	....	....	....	....	....	....	....	....	....	....	7	0	2	2	14	....	....	....
1990-91	Tri-City Americans	WHL	46	5	17	22	....	....	....	132	....	....	....	....	....	....	....	....	....	....	7	1	0	1	14	....	....	....
1991-92	Brandon Wheat Kings	WHL	41	6	14	20	....	....	....	115	....	....	....	....	....	....	....	....	....	....	....	....	....	....	....	....	....	....
	Saskatoon Blades	WHL	18	2	5	7	....	....	....	53	....	....	....	....	....	....	....	....	....	....	18	2	1	3	28	....	....	....
1992-93	Hershey Bears	AHL	61	1	12	13	....	....	....	140	....	....	....	....	....	....	....	....	....	....	....	....	....	....	....	....	....	....
1993-94	Hershey Bears	AHL	62	3	5	8	....	....	....	169	....	....	....	....	....	....	....	....	....	....	2	0	1	1	4	....	....	....
1994-95	Hershey Bears	AHL	11	1	1	2	....	....	....	32	....	....	....	....	....	....	....	....	....	....	....	....	....	....	....	....	....	....
	Kansas City Blades	IHL	25	0	3	3	....	....	....	73	....	....	....	....	....	....	....	....	....	....	....	....	....	....	....	....	....	....
1995-96	Canada	Nat-Team	47	3	12	15	....	....	....	63	....	....	....	....	....	....	....	....	....	....	....	....	....	....	....	....	....	....
	Cape Breton Oilers	AHL	5	0	2	2	....	....	....	4	....	....	....	....	....	....	....	....	....	....	....	....	....	....	....	....	....	....
1996-97	Hamilton Bulldogs	AHL	78	3	6	9	....	....	....	213	....	....	....	....	....	....	....	....	....	....	22	0	2	2	27	....	....	....
1997-98	Edmonton Oilers	NHL	8	0	0	0	0	0	0	6	0	0	0	4	0.0	3	0	8	1	–4	....	....	....	....	....	....	....	....
	Hamilton Bulldogs	AHL	54	4	8	12	....	....	....	131	....	....	....	....	....	....	....	....	....	....	9	0	0	0	10	....	....	....
1998-99	Cincinnati Mighty Ducks	AHL	40	0	6	6	....	....	....	77	....	....	....	....	....	....	....	....	....	....	....	....	....	....	....	....	....	....
99-2000	St. John's Maple Leafs	AHL	78	1	10	11	....	....	....	155	....	....	....	....	....	....	....	....	....	....	....	....	....	....	....	....	....	....
	NHL Totals		8	0	0	0	0	0	0	6	0	0	0	4	0.0	3	0	8	1		....	....	....	....	....	....	....	....

Signed as a free agent by **Edmonton**, April 10, 1996. Signed as a free agent by **Anaheim**, July 13, 1998. Signed as a free agent by **Toronto**, July 2, 1999. • Played w/ RHI's LA Blades in 1995 (11-4-7-11-35).

• SANIPASS, Everett

LW – L. 6'2", 204 lbs. b: Big Cove, N.B., 2/13/1968. Chicago's 1st, 14th overall, in 1986.

			REGULAR SEASON																		PLAYOFFS							
Season	Club	League	GP	G	A	Pts	AG	AA	APts	PIM	PP	SH	GW	S	%	TGF	PGF	TGA	PGA	+/–	GP	G	A	Pts	PIM	PP	SH	GW
1983-84	Moncton Flyers	NBAHA	37	43	26	69	....	....	....	....	....	....	....	....	....	....	....	....	....	....	....	....	....	....	....	....	....	....
1984-85	Verdun Jr. Canadiens	QMJHL	38	8	11	19	....	....	....	84	....	....	....	....	....	....	....	....	....	....	12	2	5	7	66	....	....	....
	Verdun Jr. Canadiens	Mem-Cup	2	1	0	1	....	....	....	2	....	....	....	....	....	....	....	....	....	....	....	....	....	....	....	....	....	....
1985-86	Verdun Jr. Canadiens	QMJHL	67	23	66	89	....	....	....	320	....	....	....	....	....	....	....	....	....	....	5	0	2	2	16	....	....	....
1986-87	Verdun Jr. Canadiens	QMJHL	23	17	34	51	....	....	....	165	....	....	....	....	....	....	....	....	....	....	....	....	....	....	....	....	....	....
	Canada	WJC-A	6	3	2	5	....	....	....	8	....	....	....	....	....	....	....	....	....	....	....	....	....	....	....	....	....	....
	Granby Bisons	QMJHL	12	17	14	31	....	....	....	55	....	....	....	....	....	....	....	....	....	....	8	6	4	10	48	....	....	....
	Chicago Blackhawks	NHL	7	1	3	4	1	2	3	2	0	0	0	9	11.1	6	0	3	0	3	....	....	....	....	....	....	....	....
1987-88	Chicago Blackhawks	NHL	57	8	12	20	7	9	16	126	0	0	0	55	14.5	27	4	32	0	–9	2	2	0	2	2	0	0	0
1988-89	Chicago Blackhawks	NHL	50	6	9	15	5	6	11	164	0	0	2	51	11.8	26	6	28	1	–7	3	0	0	0	2	0	0	0
	Saginaw Hawks	IHL	23	9	12	21	....	....	....	76	....	....	....	....	....	....	....	....	....	....	....	....	....	....	....	....	....	....
1989-90	Chicago Blackhawks	NHL	12	2	2	4	2	1	3	17	0	0	0	16	12.5	7	0	8	1	0	....	....	....	....	....	....	....	....
	Indianapolis Ice	IHL	33	15	13	28	....	....	....	121	....	....	....	....	....	....	....	....	....	....	....	....	....	....	....	....	....	....
	Quebec Nordiques	NHL	9	3	3	6	3	2	5	8	2	0	0	16	18.8	9	5	8	0	–4	....	....	....	....	....	....	....	....
1990-91	Quebec Nordiques	NHL	29	5	5	10	5	4	9	41	1	0	0	38	13.2	13	2	26	0	–15	....	....	....	....	....	....	....	....
	Halifax Citadels	AHL	14	11	7	18	....	....	....	41	....	....	....	....	....	....	....	....	....	....	....	....	....	....	....	....	....	....
1991-92	Halifax Citadels	AHL	7	3	5	8	....	....	....	31	....	....	....	....	....	....	....	....	....	....	....	....	....	....	....	....	....	....
1992-93	Halifax Citadels	AHL	9	1	3	4	....	....	....	36	....	....	....	....	....	....	....	....	....	....	....	....	....	....	....	....	....	....
1993-94	Richibucto Schooners	NBSHL	....	....	....	....	....	....	....	....	....	....	....	....	....	....	....	....	....	....	7	10	9	19	25	....	....	....
1994-95	East Hants Penguins	NSSHL	21	9	21	30	....	....	....	....	....	....	....	....	....	....	....	....	....	....	....	....	....	....	....	....	....	....
	NHL Totals		164	25	34	59	23	24	47	358	3	0	2	185	13.5	88	17	105	2		5	2	0	2	4	0	0	0

QMJHL First All-Star Team (1987)

Traded to **Quebec** by **Chicago** with Mario Doyon and Dan Vincelette for Greg Millen, Michel Goulet and Quebec's 6th round choice (Kevin St.Jacques) in 1991 Entry Draft, March 5, 1990.
• Suffered eventual career-ending back injury in game vs. Philadelphia, January 17, 1991.

• SAPRYKIN, Oleg

C – L. 6', 195 lbs. b: Moscow, USSR, 2/12/1981. Calgary's 1st, 11th overall, in 1999.

			REGULAR SEASON																		PLAYOFFS							
Season	Club	League	GP	G	A	Pts	AG	AA	APts	PIM	PP	SH	GW	S	%	TGF	PGF	TGA	PGA	+/–	GP	G	A	Pts	PIM	PP	SH	GW
1997-98	CSKA Moscow	Russia	20	0	2	2	....	....	....	8	....	....	....	....	....	....	....	....	....	....	....	....	....	....	....	....	....	....
	CSKA Moscow	Russia-2	15	0	3	3	....	....	....	6	....	....	....	....	....	....	....	....	....	....	....	....	....	....	....	....	....	....
1998-99	Seattle Thunderbirds	WHL	66	47	46	93	....	....	....	107	....	....	....	....	....	....	....	....	....	....	11	5	11	16	36	....	....	....
99-2000	Seattle Thunderbirds	WHL	48	30	36	66	....	....	....	91	....	....	....	....	....	....	....	....	....	....	6	3	3	6	37	....	....	....
	Calgary Flames	**NHL**	**4**	**0**	**1**	**1**	**0**	**1**	**1**	**2**	**0**	**0**	**0**	**2**	**0.0**	**3**	**3**	**4**	**0**	**–4**	....	....	....	....	....	....	....	....
	NHL Totals		**4**	**0**	**1**	**1**	**0**	**1**	**1**	**2**	**0**	**0**	**0**	**2**	**0.0**	**3**	**3**	**4**	**0**		....	....	....	....	....	....	....	....

WHL West Second All-Star Team (1999, 2000)

• SARAULT, Yves

LW – L. 6', 200 lbs. b: Valleyfield, Que., 12/23/1972. Montreal's 4th, 61st overall, in 1991.

			REGULAR SEASON																		PLAYOFFS							
Season	Club	League	GP	G	A	Pts	AG	AA	APts	PIM	PP	SH	GW	S	%	TGF	PGF	TGA	PGA	+/–	GP	G	A	Pts	PIM	PP	SH	GW
1988-89	Lac St-Louis Lions	QAAA	42	23	30	53	....	....	....	64	....	....	....	....	....	....	....	....	....	....	....	....	....	....	....	....	....	....
1989-90	Victoriaville Tigres	QMJHL	70	12	28	40	....	....	....	140	....	....	....	....	....	....	....	....	....	....	16	0	3	3	26	....	....	....
1990-91	St-Jean Lynx	QMJHL	56	22	24	46	....	....	....	113	....	....	....	....	....	....	....	....	....	....	....	....	....	....	....	....	....	....
1991-92	St-Jean Lynx	QMJHL	50	28	38	66	....	....	....	96	....	....	....	....	....	....	....	....	....	....	....	....	....	....	....	....	....	....
	Trois-Rivieres Draveurs	QMJHL	18	15	14	29	....	....	....	12	....	....	....	....	....	....	....	....	....	....	15	10	10	20	18	....	....	....
1992-93	Fredericton Canadiens	AHL	59	14	17	31	....	....	....	41	....	....	....	....	....	....	....	....	....	....	3	0	1	1	2	....	....	....
	Wheeling Thunderbirds	ECHL	2	1	3	4	....	....	....	0	....	....	....	....	....	....	....	....	....	....	....	....	....	....	....	....	....	....
1993-94	Fredericton Canadiens	AHL	60	13	14	27	....	....	....	72	....	....	....	....	....	....	....	....	....	....	....	....	....	....	....	....	....	....
1994-95	Fredericton Canadiens	AHL	69	24	21	45	....	....	....	96	....	....	....	....	....	....	....	....	....	....	13	2	1	3	33	....	....	....
	Montreal Canadiens	**NHL**	**8**	**0**	**1**	**1**	**0**	**1**	**1**	**0**	**0**	**0**	**0**	**9**	**0.0**	**1**	**0**	**2**	**0**	**–1**	....	....	....	....	....	....	....	....
1995-96	**Montreal Canadiens**	**NHL**	**14**	**0**	**0**	**0**	**0**	**0**	**0**	**4**	**0**	**0**	**0**	**14**	**0.0**	**0**	**0**	**7**	**0**	**–7**	....	....	....	....	....	....	....	....
	Calgary Flames	**NHL**	**11**	**2**	**1**	**3**	**2**	**1**	**3**	**4**	**0**	**0**	**1**	**12**	**16.7**	**6**	**1**	**7**	**0**	**–2**	....	....	....	....	....	....	....	....
	Saint John Flames	AHL	26	10	12	22	....	....	....	34	....	....	....	....	....	....	....	....	....	....	16	6	2	8	33	....	....	....
1996-97	**Colorado Avalanche**	**NHL**	**28**	**2**	**1**	**3**	**2**	**1**	**3**	**6**	**0**	**0**	**0**	**41**	**4.9**	**6**	**1**	**5**	**0**	**0**	**5**	**0**	**0**	**0**	**2**	**0**	**0**	**0**
	Hershey Bears	AHL	6	2	3	5	....	....	....	8	....	....	....	....	....	....	....	....	....	....	....	....	....	....	....	....	....	....
1997-98	**Colorado Avalanche**	**NHL**	**2**	**1**	**0**	**1**	**1**	**0**	**1**	**0**	**0**	**0**	**0**	**1**	**100.0**	**1**	**0**	**0**	**0**	**1**	....	....	....	....	....	....	....	....
	Hershey Bears	AHL	63	23	36	59	....	....	....	43	....	....	....	....	....	....	....	....	....	....	7	1	2	3	14	....	....	....
1998-99	**Ottawa Senators**	**NHL**	**11**	**0**	**1**	**1**	**0**	**1**	**1**	**4**	**0**	**0**	**0**	**7**	**0.0**	**1**	**0**	**0**	**0**	**1**	....	....	....	....	....	....	....	....
	Detroit Vipers	IHL	36	11	12	23	....	....	....	52	....	....	....	....	....	....	....	....	....	....	11	7	2	9	40	....	....	....
99-2000	**Ottawa Senators**	**NHL**	**11**	**0**	**2**	**2**	**0**	**2**	**2**	**7**	**0**	**0**	**0**	**13**	**0.0**	**2**	**0**	**5**	**0**	**–3**	....	....	....	....	....	....	....	....
	Grand Rapids Griffins	IHL	62	17	26	43	....	....	....	77	....	....	....	....	....	....	....	....	....	....	17	7	4	11	32	....	....	....
	NHL Totals		**85**	**5**	**6**	**11**	**5**	**6**	**11**	**25**	**0**	**0**	**1**	**97**	**5.2**	**17**	**2**	**26**	**0**		**5**	**0**	**0**	**0**	**2**	**0**	**0**	**0**

QMJHL Second All-Star Team (1992)

Traded to **Calgary** by **Montreal** with Craig Ferguson for Calgary's 8th round choice (Petr Kubos) in 1997 Entry Draft, November 26, 1995. Signed as a free agent by **Colorado**, September 13, 1996. Signed as a free agent by **Ottawa**, August 7, 1998.

• SARGENT, Gary

Gary Alan D – L. 5'10", 210 lbs. b: Red Lake, MN, 2/8/1954. Los Angeles' 1st, 48th overall, in 1974.

			REGULAR SEASON																		PLAYOFFS							
Season	Club	League	GP	G	A	Pts	AG	AA	APts	PIM	PP	SH	GW	S	%	TGF	PGF	TGA	PGA	+/–	GP	G	A	Pts	PIM	PP	SH	GW
1972-73	Bemidji State Beavers	NAIA	30	23	24	47	....	....	....	....	....	....	....	....	....	....	....	....	....	....	....	....	....	....	....	....	....	....
	United States	WEC-B	7	1	4	5	....	....	....	0	....	....	....	....	....	....	....	....	....	....	....	....	....	....	....	....	....	....
1973-74	Fargo-Moorhead Sugar Kings	MWJHL	47	37	46	83	....	....	....	78	....	....	....	....	....	....	....	....	....	....	....	....	....	....	....	....	....	....
	United States	WJC-A	3	0	2	2	....	....	....	0	....	....	....	....	....	....	....	....	....	....	....	....	....	....	....	....	....	....
1974-75	Springfield Indians	AHL	27	7	17	24	....	....	....	46	....	....	....	....	....	....	....	....	....	....	....	....	....	....	....	....	....	....
1975-76	**Los Angeles Kings**	**NHL**	**63**	**8**	**16**	**24**	**7**	**12**	**19**	**36**	**3**	**0**	**1**	**87**	**9.2**	**59**	**10**	**59**	**7**	**–3**	....	....	....	....	....	....	....	....
1976-77	United States	Can-Cup	5	0	0	0	....	....	....	2	....	....	....	....	....	....	....	....	....	....	....	....	....	....	....	....	....	....
	Los Angeles Kings	**NHL**	**80**	**14**	**40**	**54**	**13**	**31**	**44**	**65**	**8**	**0**	**2**	**200**	**7.0**	**151**	**54**	**118**	**28**	**7**	**9**	**3**	**4**	**7**	**6**	**2**	**0**	**0**
1977-78	**Los Angeles Kings**	**NHL**	**72**	**7**	**34**	**41**	**6**	**26**	**32**	**52**	**3**	**0**	**1**	**182**	**3.8**	**133**	**41**	**95**	**21**	**18**	**2**	**0**	**0**	**0**	**0**	**0**	**0**	**0**
1978-79	**Minnesota North Stars**	**NHL**	**79**	**12**	**32**	**44**	**10**	**23**	**33**	**39**	**8**	**0**	**1**	**182**	**6.6**	**145**	**43**	**135**	**23**	**–10**	....	....	....	....	....	....	....	....
1979-80	**Minnesota North Stars**	**NHL**	**52**	**13**	**21**	**34**	**11**	**15**	**26**	**22**	**3**	**0**	**1**	**129**	**10.1**	**91**	**32**	**54**	**7**	**12**	**4**	**2**	**1**	**3**	**2**	**1**	**0**	**1**
1980-81	Minnesota North Stars	DN-Cup	3	0	0	0	....	....	....	2	....	....	....	....	....	....	....	....	....	....	....	....	....	....	....	....	....	....
	Minnesota North Stars	**NHL**	**23**	**4**	**7**	**11**	**3**	**5**	**8**	**36**	**2**	**0**	**0**	**42**	**9.5**	**31**	**11**	**24**	**3**	**–1**	....	....	....	....	....	....	....	....
1981-82	**Minnesota North Stars**	**NHL**	**15**	**0**	**5**	**5**	**0**	**3**	**3**	**18**	**0**	**0**	**0**	**24**	**0.0**	**25**	**8**	**13**	**1**	**5**	....	....	....	....	....	....	....	....
1982-83	**Minnesota North Stars**	**NHL**	**18**	**3**	**6**	**9**	**2**	**4**	**6**	**5**	**1**	**0**	**0**	**30**	**10.0**	**27**	**8**	**19**	**5**	**5**	**5**	**0**	**2**	**2**	**0**	**0**	**0**	**0**
	NHL Totals		**402**	**61**	**161**	**222**	**52**	**119**	**171**	**273**	**28**	**0**	**6**	**876**	**7.0**	**662**	**207**	**517**	**95**		**20**	**5**	**7**	**12**	**8**	**3**	**0**	**1**

First Team NAIA All-American (1973)

Signed as a free agent by **Minnesota** from **LA Kings**, June 30, 1978. LA Kings received Rick Hampton, Steve Jensen and Dave Gardner as compensation.

• SARICH, Cory

D – R. 6'3", 175 lbs. b: Saskatoon, Sask., 8/16/1978. Buffalo's 2nd, 27th overall, in 1996.

			REGULAR SEASON																		PLAYOFFS							
Season	Club	League	GP	G	A	Pts	AG	AA	APts	PIM	PP	SH	GW	S	%	TGF	PGF	TGA	PGA	+/–	GP	G	A	Pts	PIM	PP	SH	GW
1994-95	Saskatoon Blazers	SAHA	31	5	22	27	....	....	....	99	....	....	....	....	....	....	....	....	....	....	....	....	....	....	....	....	....	....
	Saskatoon Blades	WHL	6	0	0	0	....	....	....	4	....	....	....	....	....	....	....	....	....	....	3	0	1	1	0	....	....	....
1995-96	Saskatoon Blades	WHL	59	5	18	23	....	....	....	54	....	....	....	....	....	....	....	....	....	....	3	0	0	0	4	....	....	....
1996-97	Saskatoon Blades	WHL	58	6	27	33	....	....	....	158	....	....	....	....	....	....	....	....	....	....	....	....	....	....	....	....	....	....
	Canada	WJC-A	7	0	0	0	....	....	....	6	....	....	....	....	....	....	....	....	....	....	....	....	....	....	....	....	....	....
1997-98	Saskatoon Blades	WHL	33	5	24	29	....	....	....	90	....	....	....	....	....	....	....	....	....	....	....	....	....	....	....	....	....	....
	Canada	WJC-A	7	0	1	1	....	....	....	6	....	....	....	....	....	....	....	....	....	....	....	....	....	....	....	....	....	....
	Seattle Thunderbirds	WHL	13	3	16	19	....	....	....	47	....	....	....	....	....	....	....	....	....	....	0	0	0	0	0	....	....	....
1998-99	**Buffalo Sabres**	**NHL**	**4**	**0**	**0**	**0**	**0**	**0**	**0**	**0**	**0**	**0**	**0**	**2**	**0.0**	**5**	**0**	**2**	**0**	**3**	....	....	....	....	....	....	....	....
	Rochester Americans	AHL	77	3	26	29	....	....	....	82	....	....	....	....	....	....	....	....	....	....	20	2	4	6	14	....	....	....
99-2000	**Buffalo Sabres**	**NHL**	**42**	**0**	**4**	**4**	**0**	**4**	**4**	**35**	**0**	**0**	**0**	**49**	**0.0**	**28**	**1**	**30**	**5**	**2**	....	....	....	....	....	....	....	....
	Rochester Americans	AHL	15	0	6	6	....	....	....	44	....	....	....	....	....	....	....	....	....	....	....	....	....	....	....	....	....	....
	Tampa Bay Lightning	**NHL**	**17**	**0**	**2**	**2**	**0**	**2**	**2**	**42**	**0**	**0**	**0**	**20**	**0.0**	**10**	**1**	**24**	**7**	**–8**	....	....	....	....	....	....	....	....
	NHL Totals		**63**	**0**	**6**	**6**	**0**	**6**	**6**	**77**	**0**	**0**	**0**	**71**	**0.0**	**43**	**2**	**56**	**12**		....	....	....	....	....	....	....	....

WHL West Second All-Star Team (1998)

Traded to **Tampa Bay** by **Buffalo** with Wayne Primeau, Brian Holzinger and Buffalo's 3rd round choice (Alexandre Kharitonov) in 2000 Entry Draft for Chris Gratton and Tampa Bay's 2nd round choice in 2001 Entry Draft, March 9, 2000.

• SARNER, Craig

Craig Brian RW – L. 5'11", 185 lbs. b: St. Paul, MN, 6/20/1949.

			REGULAR SEASON																		PLAYOFFS							
Season	Club	League	GP	G	A	Pts	AG	AA	APts	PIM	PP	SH	GW	S	%	TGF	PGF	TGA	PGA	+/–	GP	G	A	Pts	PIM	PP	SH	GW
1968-69	University of Minnesota	WCHA	28	5	0	5	....	....	....	4	....	....	....	....	....	....	....	....	....	....	....	....	....	....	....	....	....	....
1969-70	University of Minnesota	WCHA	33	13	10	23	....	....	....	2	....	....	....	....	....	....	....	....	....	....	....	....	....	....	....	....	....	....
1970-71	University of Minnesota	WCHA	29	12	19	31	....	....	....	17	....	....	....	....	....	....	....	....	....	....	....	....	....	....	....	....	....	....
1971-72	United States	Nat-Team	STATISTICS NOT AVAILABLE																									
	United States	Olympics	6	4	6	10	....	....	....	0	....	....	....	....	....	....	....	....	....	....	....	....	....	....	....	....	....	....
	United States	WEC-B	6	4	4	8	....	....	....	....	....	....	....	....	....	....	....	....	....	....	....	....	....	....	....	....	....	....
	Oklahoma City Blazers	CHL	5	1	0	1	....	....	....	0	....	....	....	....	....	....	....	....	....	....	....	....	....	....	....	....	....	....
1972-73	Boston Braves	AHL	74	27	27	54	....	....	....	16	....	....	....	....	....	....	....	....	....	....	5	2	3	5	2	....	....	....
1973-74	Boston Braves	AHL	66	15	26	41	....	....	....	18	....	....	....	....	....	....	....	....	....	....	....	....	....	....	....	....	....	....
1974-75	**Boston Bruins**	**NHL**	**7**	**0**	**0**	**0**	**0**	**0**	**0**	**0**	**0**	**0**	**0**	**5**	**0.0**	**3**	**0**	**7**	**1**	**–3**	....	....	....	....	....	....	....	....
	Rochester Americans	AHL	47	14	13	27	....	....	....	26	....	....	....	....	....	....	....	....	....	....	12	4	3	7	4	....	....	....
1975-76	Minnesota Fighting Saints	WHA	1	0	0	0	....	....	....	0	....	....	....	....	....	....	....	....	....	....	....	....	....	....	....	....	....	....
	United States	Nat-Team	STATISTICS NOT AVAILABLE																									
	United States	WEC-A	10	2	1	3	....	....	....	13	....	....	....	....	....	....	....	....	....	....	....	....	....	....	....	....	....	....
1976-77	Kolner EC	Germany	41	35	26	61	....	....	....	100	....	....	....	....	....	....	....	....	....	....	....	....	....	....	....	....	....	....
1977-78	Kolner EC	Germany	46	49	42	91	....	....	....	....	....	....	....	....	....	....	....	....	....	....	....	....	....	....	....	....	....	....
1978-79	EHC Eisbaren Berlin	Germany	46	52	64	116	....	....	....	68	....	....	....	....	....	....	....	....	....	....	8	1	1	2	4	....	....	....
	United States	WEC-A	8	1	1	2	....	....	....	4	....	....	....	....	....	....	....	....	....	....	....	....	....	....	....	....	....	....
1979-80	HC Davos	Switz.	36	19	10	29	....	....	....	....	....	....	....	....	....	....	....	....	....	....	....	....	....	....	....	....	....	....

Season	Club	League	GP	G	A	Pts	AG	AA	APts	PIM	PP	SH	GW	S	%	TGF	PGF	TGA	PGA	+/–	PO GP	PO G	PO A	PO Pts	PO PIM	PO PP	PO SH	PO GW
			REGULAR SEASON																		PLAYOFFS							
1980-81	HC Davos	Switz.	36	16	14	30																						
1981-1982	HC Davos	Switz.	DID NOT PLAY – COACHING																									
1982-1984	SC Bern	Switz.	DID NOT PLAY – COACHING																									
1984-1985	Schwenninger ERC	Germany	DID NOT PLAY – COACHING																									
	NHL Totals		**7**	**0**	**0**	**0**	**0**	**0**	**0**	**0**	**0**	**0**	**0**	**5**	**0.0**	**3**	**0**	**7**	**1**									
	Other Major League Totals		1	0	0	0				0																		

Selected by **Minnesota** (WHA) in 1972 WHA General Player Draft, February 12, 1972. Signed as a free agent by **Boston**, March, 1972.

• SARRAZIN, Dick

Richard Andre RW – R. 6', 185 lbs. b: St. Gabriel-de-Brandon, Que., 1/22/1946.

Season	Club	League	GP	G	A	Pts	AG	AA	APts	PIM	PP	SH	GW	S	%	TGF	PGF	TGA	PGA	+/–	PO GP	PO G	PO A	PO Pts	PO PIM	PO PP	PO SH	PO GW
1963-64	St-Jerome Alouettes	QJHL	44	15	28	43				6																		
1964-65	St-Jerome Alouettes	QJHL	36	29	25	54				14											8	5	7	12	2			
1965-66	St-Jerome Alouettes	QJHL	48	27	37	64				55											5	0	3	3	2			
1966-67	Johnstown–Jersey	EHL	69	26	28	54				20											16	3	4	7	2			
1967-68	Quebec Aces	AHL	69	17	19	36				27											15	3	4	7	2			
1968-69	**Philadelphia Flyers**	**NHL**	**54**	**16**	**30**	**46**	**17**	**27**	**44**	**14**	**6**	**1**	**3**	**128**	**12.5**	**59**	**23**	**49**	**6**	**–7**	**4**	**0**	**0**	**0**	**0**	**0**	**0**	**0**
	Quebec Aces	AHL	19	7	6	13				4																		
1969-70	**Philadelphia Flyers**	**NHL**	**18**	**1**	**1**	**2**	**1**	**1**	**2**	**4**	**1**	**0**	**0**	**32**	**3.1**	**10**	**3**	**10**	**1**	**–2**								
	Quebec Aces	AHL	50	10	20	30				18											6	0	1	1	2			
1970-71	Quebec Aces	AHL	70	21	53	74				39											10	5	6	11	23			
1971-72	**Philadelphia Flyers**	**NHL**	**28**	**3**	**4**	**7**	**3**	**3**	**6**	**4**	**1**	**0**	**1**	**38**	**7.9**	**14**	**6**	**10**	**2**	**0**								
	Richmond Robins	AHL	42	11	11	22				4																		
1972-73	New England Whalers	WHA	35	4	7	11				0																		
	Chicago Cougars	WHA	33	3	8	11				2																		
1973-74	Jacksonville Barons	AHL	76	20	34	54				18																		
1974-75	Syracuse Eagles	AHL	75	33	37	70				6											1	0	2	2	0			
1975-76	Baltimore Clippers	AHL	55	14	13	27				14																		
	NHL Totals		**100**	**20**	**35**	**55**	**21**	**31**	**52**	**22**	**8**	**1**	**4**	**198**	**10.1**	**83**	**32**	**69**	**9**		**4**	**0**	**0**	**0**	**0**	**0**	**0**	**0**
	Other Major League Totals		68	7	15	22				2																		

Signed as a free agent by **Jersey** (EHL) after being released by **Johnstown** (EHL), November, 1966. Traded to **Philadelphia** (Quebec-AHL) by **Detroit** for cash, October, 1967. Selected by **New England** (WHA) in 1972 WHA General Player Draft, February 12, 1972. Traded to **Chicago** (WHA) by **New England** (WHA) for cash and future considerations, January, 1973. Selected by **Phoenix** (WHA) from **Chicago** (WHA) in 1974 WHA Expansion Draft, May 30, 1974.

• SASSER, Grant

C – R. 5'10", 175 lbs. b: Portland, OR, 2/13/1964. Pittsburgh's 4th, 94th overall, in 1982.

Season	Club	League	GP	G	A	Pts	AG	AA	APts	PIM	PP	SH	GW	S	%	TGF	PGF	TGA	PGA	+/–	PO GP	PO G	PO A	PO Pts	PO PIM	PO PP	PO SH	PO GW
1980-81	Fort Saskatchewan Traders	AJHL	54	33	49	82				49																		
1981-82	Portland Winter Hawks	WHL	49	19	23	42				32											15	5	6	11	13			
	Portland Winter Hawks	Mem-Cup	4	0	1	1				0																		
1982-83	Portland Winter Hawks	WHL	70	54	65	119				39											14	12	15	27	4			
	Portland Winter Hawks	Mem-Cup	4	3	4	7				0																		
1983-84	Portland Winter Hawks	WHL	66	44	69	113				24											14	5	8	13	2			
	Pittsburgh Penguins	**NHL**	**3**	**0**	**0**	**0**	**0**	**0**	**0**	**0**	**0**	**0**	**0**	**2**	**0.0**	**1**	**0**	**3**	**0**	**–2**								
1984-85	Baltimore Skipjacks	AHL	60	5	7	12				12																		
	Muskegon Mohawks	IHL	10	1	4	5				18																		
	NHL Totals		**3**	**0**	**0**	**0**	**0**	**0**	**0**	**0**	**0**	**0**	**0**	**2**	**0.0**	**1**	**0**	**3**	**0**									

• SATAN, Miroslav

LW – L. 6'1", 195 lbs. b: Topolcany, Czech., 10/22/1974. Edmonton's 6th, 111th overall, in 1993.

Season	Club	League	GP	G	A	Pts	AG	AA	APts	PIM	PP	SH	GW	S	%	TGF	PGF	TGA	PGA	+/–	PO GP	PO G	PO A	PO Pts	PO PIM	PO PP	PO SH	PO GW
1991-92	HC Topocalny	Czech-Jr.	31	30	22	52																						
	HC Topocalny	Czech-2	9	2	1	3				6																		
1992-93	Dukla Trencin	Czech.	38	11	6	17																						
1993-94	Dukla Trencin	Slovakia	30	32	16	48				16																		
	Slovakia	WJC-C	4	6	7	13				4																		
	Slovakia	Olympics	8	*9	0	9				0																		
	Slovakia	WC-C1	6	7	1	8				18																		
1994-95	Cape Breton Oilers	AHL	25	24	16	40				15																		
	Detroit Vipers	IHL	8	1	3	4				4																		
	San Diego Gulls	IHL	6	0	2	2				6																		
	Slovakia	WC-B	7	7	6	13				4																		
1995-96	**Edmonton Oilers**	**NHL**	**62**	**18**	**17**	**35**	**18**	**14**	**32**	**22**	**6**	**0**	**4**	**113**	**15.9**	**57**	**19**	**39**	**1**	**0**								
	Slovakia	WC-A	5	0	3	3				6																		
1996-97	Slovakia	W-Cup	3	0	0	0				2																		
	Edmonton Oilers	**NHL**	**64**	**17**	**11**	**28**	**18**	**10**	**28**	**22**	**5**	**0**	**2**	**90**	**18.9**	**41**	**13**	**32**	**0**	**–4**								
	Buffalo Sabres	**NHL**	**12**	**8**	**2**	**10**	**8**	**2**	**10**	**4**	**2**	**0**	**1**	**29**	**27.6**	**12**	**3**	**8**	**0**	**1**	**7**	**0**	**0**	**0**	**0**	**0**	**0**	**0**
1997-98	**Buffalo Sabres**	**NHL**	**79**	**22**	**24**	**46**	**26**	**24**	**50**	**34**	**9**	**0**	**4**	**139**	**15.8**	**64**	**25**	**38**	**1**	**2**	**14**	**5**	**4**	**9**	**4**	**4**	**0**	**1**
1998-99	**Buffalo Sabres**	**NHL**	**81**	**40**	**26**	**66**	**47**	**25**	**72**	**44**	**13**	**3**	**6**	**208**	**19.2**	**88**	**29**	**44**	**9**	**24**	**12**	**3**	**5**	**8**	**2**	**1**	**0**	**1**
99-2000	Dukla Trencin	Slovakia	3	2	8	10				2																		
	Buffalo Sabres	**NHL**	**81**	**33**	**34**	**67**	**37**	**32**	**69**	**32**	**5**	**3**	**5**	**265**	**12.5**	**98**	**27**	**69**	**14**	**16**	**5**	**3**	**2**	**5**	**0**	**0**	**0**	**0**
	Slovakia	WC-A	9	10	2	12				14																		
	NHL Totals		**379**	**138**	**114**	**252**	**154**	**107**	**261**	**158**	**40**	**6**	**22**	**844**	**16.4**	**360**	**116**	**230**	**25**		**38**	**11**	**11**	**22**	**6**	**5**	**0**	**2**

Named Best Forward at WC-C1 (1994) • WC-B All-Star Team (1995) • WJC-A All-Star Team (2000) • Named Best Forward at WC-A (2000) • Played in NHL All-Star Game (2000)

Traded to **Buffalo** by **Edmonton** for Barrie Moore and Craig Millar, March 18, 1997.

• SATHER, Glen

Glen Cameron "Slats" LW – L. 5'11", 180 lbs. b: High River, Alta., 9/2/1943. **HHOF**

Season	Club	League	GP	G	A	Pts	AG	AA	APts	PIM	PP	SH	GW	S	%	TGF	PGF	TGA	PGA	+/–	PO GP	PO G	PO A	PO Pts	PO PIM	PO PP	PO SH	PO GW
1960-61	Wainwright Elks	AMHA	STATISTICS NOT AVAILABLE																									
	Wainwright Commandos	BRSHL	STATISTICS NOT AVAILABLE																									
1961-62	Edmonton Oil Kings	CAHL	STATISTICS NOT AVAILABLE																									
	Edmonton Oil Kings	Mem-Cup	19	5	5	10				14																		
1962-63	Edmonton Oil Kings	CAHL	STATISTICS NOT AVAILABLE																									
	Edmonton Oil Kings	Mem-Cup	20	9	13	22				26																		
1963-64	Edmonton Oil Kings	CAHL	40	31	34	65				30											1	0	0	0	0			
	Edmonton Oil Kings	Mem-Cup	19	8	17	25				30																		
1964-65	Memphis Wings	CPHL	69	19	29	48				98																		
1965-66	Oklahoma City Blazers	CPHL	64	13	12	25				76											9	4	4	8	14			
1966-67	Oklahoma City Blazers	CPHL	57	14	19	33				147											11	2	6	8	24			
	Boston Bruins	**NHL**	**5**	**0**	**0**	**0**	**0**	**0**	**0**	**0**																		
1967-68	**Boston Bruins**	**NHL**	**65**	**8**	**12**	**20**	**9**	**12**	**21**	**34**	**0**	**2**	**1**	**55**	**14.5**	**33**	**4**	**39**	**19**	**9**	**3**	**0**	**0**	**0**	**0**	**0**	**0**	**0**
1968-69	**Boston Bruins**	**NHL**	**76**	**4**	**11**	**15**	**4**	**10**	**14**	**67**	**0**	**1**	**1**	**51**	**7.8**	**25**	**1**	**46**	**26**	**4**	**10**	**0**	**0**	**0**	**18**	**0**	**0**	**0**
1969-70	**Pittsburgh Penguins**	**NHL**	**76**	**12**	**14**	**26**	**13**	**13**	**26**	**114**	**2**	**0**	**0**	**127**	**9.4**	**36**	**8**	**67**	**26**	**–13**	**10**	**0**	**2**	**2**	**17**	**0**	**0**	**0**
1970-71	**Pittsburgh Penguins**	**NHL**	**46**	**8**	**3**	**11**	**8**	**2**	**10**	**96**	**1**	**1**	**0**	**64**	**12.5**	**13**	**2**	**27**	**16**	**0**								
	New York Rangers	**NHL**	**31**	**2**	**0**	**2**	**2**	**0**	**2**	**52**	**0**	**0**	**1**	**18**	**11.1**	**3**	**0**	**14**	**11**	**0**	**13**	**0**	**1**	**1**	**18**	**0**	**0**	**0**
1971-72	**New York Rangers**	**NHL**	**76**	**5**	**9**	**14**	**5**	**8**	**13**	**77**	**0**	**0**	**0**	**52**	**9.6**	**18**	**1**	**40**	**21**	**–2**	**16**	**0**	**1**	**1**	**22**	**0**	**0**	**0**
1972-73	**New York Rangers**	**NHL**	**77**	**11**	**15**	**26**	**10**	**12**	**22**	**64**	**1**	**1**	**2**	**69**	**15.9**	**47**	**1**	**37**	**7**	**16**	**9**	**0**	**0**	**0**	**7**	**0**	**0**	**0**
1973-74	**New York Rangers**	**NHL**	**2**	**0**	**0**	**0**	**0**	**0**	**0**	**0**	**0**	**0**	**0**	**0**	**0.0**	**0**	**0**	**0**	**0**	**0**								
	St. Louis Blues	**NHL**	**69**	**15**	**29**	**44**	**14**	**24**	**38**	**82**	**4**	**0**	**5**	**106**	**14.2**	**62**	**17**	**69**	**15**	**–9**								
1974-75	**Montreal Canadiens**	**NHL**	**63**	**6**	**10**	**16**	**5**	**7**	**12**	**44**	**0**	**1**	**0**	**23**	**26.1**	**29**	**1**	**23**	**9**	**14**	**11**	**1**	**1**	**2**	**4**	**0**	**0**	**0**
1975-76	**Minnesota North Stars**	**NHL**	**72**	**9**	**10**	**19**	**8**	**7**	**15**	**94**	**1**	**0**	**1**	**73**	**12.3**	**32**	**3**	**63**	**26**	**–8**								
1976-77	Edmonton Oilers	WHA	81	19	34	53				77											5	1	1	2	2			
1977-1979	Edmonton Oilers	WHA	DID NOT PLAY – COACHING																									
1979-1989	**Edmonton Oilers**	**NHL**	DID NOT PLAY – COACHING																									

Season	Club	League	REGULAR SEASON GP	G	A	Pts	AG	AA	APts	PIM	PP	SH	GW	S	%	TGF	PGF	TGA	PGA	+/-	PLAYOFFS GP	G	A	Pts	PIM	PP	SH	GW
1989-1994	**Edmonton Oilers**	**NHL**	DID NOT PLAY – GENERAL MANAGER																									
1993-1994	**Edmonton Oilers**	**NHL**	DID NOT PLAY – COACHING																									
1994-2000	**Edmonton Oilers**	**NHL**	DID NOT PLAY – GENERAL MANAGER																									
	NHL Totals		**658**	**80**	**113**	**193**	**78**	**95**	**173**	**724**	....	....	....	....	....	....	....	....	....		**72**	**1**	**5**	**6**	**86**	....	....	....
	Other Major League Totals		81	19	34	53	....	....	....	77	....	....	....	....	....	....	....	....	....	....	5	1	1	2	2	....	....	....

CAHL First All-Star Team (1964) • Won Jack Adams Award (1986)

Claimed by **Boston** from **Memphis** (CHL) in Inter-League Draft, June 8, 1965. Selected by **Pittsburgh** from **Boston** in Intra-League Draft, June 11, 1969. Traded to **NY Rangers** by **Pittsburgh** for Syl Apps Jr. and Sheldon Kannegiesser, January 26, 1971. Selected by **Edmonton** (WHA) in 1972 WHA General Player Draft, February 12, 1972. Traded to **St. Louis** by **NY Rangers** with Rene Villemure for Jack Egers, October 28, 1973. Traded to **Montreal** by **St. Louis** to complete transaction that sent Rik Wilson to St. Louis (May 27, 1974), June 14, 1974. Traded to **Minnesota** by **Montreal** for Minnesota's 3rd round choice (Alain Cote) in 1977 Amateur Draft and cash, July 9, 1975 • Named General Manager of **NY Rangers**, June 1, 2000..

• SAUNDERS, Bernie

LW – R. 6', 190 lbs. b: Montreal, Que., 6/21/1956.

Season	Club	League	GP	G	A	Pts	AG	AA	APts	PIM	PP	SH	GW	S	%	TGF	PGF	TGA	PGA	+/-	GP	G	A	Pts	PIM	PP	SH	GW
1976-77	Western Michigan University	CCHA	37	24	16	40	....	....	....	24	....	....	....	....	....	....	....	....	....	....	....	....	....	....	....	....	....	....
1977-78	Western Michigan University	CCHA	33	22	29	51	....	....	....	30	....	....	....	....	....	....	....	....	....	....	....	....	....	....	....	....	....	....
1978-79	Western Michigan University	CCHA	36	23	21	44	....	....	....	11	....	....	....	....	....	....	....	....	....	....	....	....	....	....	....	....	....	....
	Kalamazoo Wings	IHL	3	1	3	4	....	....	....	0	....	....	....	....	....	....	....	....	....	....	....	....	....	....	....	....	....	....
1979-80	**Quebec Nordiques**	**NHL**	**4**	**0**	**0**	**0**	**0**	**0**	**0**	**0**	**0**	**0**	**0**	**4**	**0.0**	**1**	**0**	**2**	**0**	**–1**	....	....	....	....	....	....	....	....
	Cincinnati Stingers	CHL	29	13	11	24	....	....	....	16	....	....	....	....	....	....	....	....	....	....	....	....	....	....	....	....	....	....
	Syracuse Firebirds	AHL	38	23	17	40	....	....	....	29	....	....	....	....	....	....	....	....	....	....	4	1	0	1	2	....	....	....
1980-81	**Quebec Nordiques**	**NHL**	**6**	**0**	**1**	**1**	**0**	**1**	**1**	**8**	**0**	**0**	**0**	**5**	**0.0**	**1**	**0**	**2**	**0**	**–1**	....	....	....	....	....	....	....	....
	Nova Scotia Voyageurs	AHL	69	17	21	38	....	....	....	88	....	....	....	....	....	....	....	....	....	....	6	1	1	2	4	....	....	....
1981-82	Kalamazoo Wings	IHL	70	38	37	75	....	....	....	57	....	....	....	....	....	....	....	....	....	....	5	3	2	5	6	....	....	....
1982-83			DID NOT PLAY																									
1983-84	Kalamazoo Wings	IHL	1	0	0	0	....	....	....	0	....	....	....	....	....	....	....	....	....	....	....	....	....	....	....	....	....	....
	NHL Totals		**10**	**0**	**1**	**1**	**0**	**1**	**1**	**8**	**0**	**0**	**0**	**9**	**0.0**	**2**	**0**	**4**	**0**		....	....	....	....	....	....	....	....

CCHA Second All-Star Team (1978)

Signed as a free agent by **Quebec**, May 29, 1979.

• SAUNDERS, David

LW – L. 6'1", 195 lbs. b: Ottawa, Ont., 5/20/1966. Vancouver's 3rd, 52nd overall, in 1984.

Season	Club	League	GP	G	A	Pts	AG	AA	APts	PIM	PP	SH	GW	S	%	TGF	PGF	TGA	PGA	+/-	GP	G	A	Pts	PIM	PP	SH	GW
1982-83	Pembroke Lumber Kings	OJHL	48	26	27	53	....	....	....	42	....	....	....	....	....	....	....	....	....	....	....	....	....	....	....	....	....	....
1983-84	St. Lawrence University	ECAC	32	10	21	31	....	....	....	24	....	....	....	....	....	....	....	....	....	....	....	....	....	....	....	....	....	....
1984-85	St. Lawrence University	ECAC	27	7	9	16	....	....	....	16	....	....	....	....	....	....	....	....	....	....	....	....	....	....	....	....	....	....
1985-86	St. Lawrence University	ECAC	29	15	19	34	....	....	....	26	....	....	....	....	....	....	....	....	....	....	....	....	....	....	....	....	....	....
1986-87	St. Lawrence University	ECAC	34	18	34	52	....	....	....	44	....	....	....	....	....	....	....	....	....	....	....	....	....	....	....	....	....	....
1987-88	**Vancouver Canucks**	**NHL**	**56**	**7**	**13**	**20**	**6**	**9**	**15**	**10**	**1**	**0**	**3**	**100**	**7.0**	**30**	**7**	**50**	**12**	**–15**	....	....	....	....	....	....	....	....
	Fredericton Express	AHL	14	9	7	16	....	....	....	6	....	....	....	....	....	....	....	....	....	....	8	1	0	1	12	....	....	....
	Flint Spirits	IHL	8	5	5	10	....	....	....	2	....	....	....	....	....	....	....	....	....	....	....	....	....	....	....	....	....	....
1988-89	Milwaukee Admirals	IHL	21	6	12	18	....	....	....	21	....	....	....	....	....	....	....	....	....	....	....	....	....	....	....	....	....	....
	Canada	Nat-Team	6	1	3	4	....	....	....	2	....	....	....	....	....	....	....	....	....	....	....	....	....	....	....	....	....	....
1989-90	Sport Vassa	Finland-2	37	28	18	46	....	....	....	115	....	....	....	....	....	....	....	....	....	....	....	....	....	....	....	....	....	....
	NHL Totals		**56**	**7**	**13**	**20**	**6**	**9**	**15**	**10**	**1**	**0**	**3**	**100**	**7.0**	**30**	**7**	**50**	**12**		....	....	....	....	....	....	....	....

• SAUVE, Jean-Francois

"Frankie" C – L. 5'6", 175 lbs. b: Ste. Genevieve, Que., 1/23/1960.

Season	Club	League	GP	G	A	Pts	AG	AA	APts	PIM	PP	SH	GW	S	%	TGF	PGF	TGA	PGA	+/-	GP	G	A	Pts	PIM	PP	SH	GW
1976-77	Lac St-Louis Lions	QAAA	40	44	79	123	....	....	....	....	....	....	....	....	....	....	....	....	....	....	....	....	....	....	....	....	....	....
1977-78	Trois-Rivieres Draveurs	QMJHL	6	2	3	5	....	....	....	0	....	....	....	....	....	....	....	....	....	....	....	....	....	....	....	....	....	....
	Trois-Rivieres Draveurs	Mem-Cup	4	0	1	1	....	....	....	0	....	....	....	....	....	....	....	....	....	....	....	....	....	....	....	....	....	....
1978-79	Trois-Rivieres Draveurs	QMJHL	72	65	111	*176	....	....	....	31	....	....	....	....	....	....	....	....	....	....	13	*19	*19	*38	4	....	....	....
	Trois-Rivieres Draveurs	Mem-Cup	4	2	3	5	....	....	....	0	....	....	....	....	....	....	....	....	....	....	....	....	....	....	....	....	....	....
1979-80	Trois-Rivieres Draveurs	QMJHL	72	63	*124	*187	....	....	....	31	....	....	....	....	....	....	....	....	....	....	7	5	9	14	0	....	....	....
	Rochester Americans	AHL	3	1	1	2	....	....	....	0	....	....	....	....	....	....	....	....	....	....	4	1	2	3	2	....	....	....
1980-81	**Buffalo Sabres**	**NHL**	**20**	**5**	**9**	**14**	**4**	**6**	**10**	**12**	**3**	**0**	**0**	**26**	**19.2**	**20**	**8**	**14**	**0**	**–2**	**5**	**2**	**0**	**2**	**0**	**1**	**0**	**0**
	Rochester Americans	AHL	56	29	54	83	....	....	....	21	....	....	....	....	....	....	....	....	....	....	....	....	....	....	....	....	....	....
1981-82	**Buffalo Sabres**	**NHL**	**69**	**19**	**36**	**55**	**15**	**24**	**39**	**46**	**5**	**0**	**1**	**119**	**16.0**	**85**	**31**	**47**	**0**	**7**	**2**	**0**	**2**	**2**	**0**	**0**	**0**	**0**
	Rochester Americans	AHL	7	5	8	13	....	....	....	4	....	....	....	....	....	....	....	....	....	....	....	....	....	....	....	....	....	....
1982-83	**Buffalo Sabres**	**NHL**	**9**	**0**	**4**	**4**	**0**	**3**	**3**	**9**	**0**	**0**	**0**	**15**	**0.0**	**5**	**1**	**4**	**0**	**0**	....	....	....	....	....	....	....	....
	Rochester Americans	AHL	73	30	69	99	....	....	....	10	....	....	....	....	....	....	....	....	....	....	16	7	*21	*28	2	....	....	....
1983-84	**Quebec Nordiques**	**NHL**	**39**	**10**	**17**	**27**	**8**	**12**	**20**	**2**	**5**	**0**	**0**	**43**	**23.3**	**39**	**26**	**9**	**0**	**4**	**9**	**2**	**5**	**7**	**2**	**2**	**0**	**1**
	Fredericton Express	AHL	26	19	31	50	....	....	....	23	....	....	....	....	....	....	....	....	....	....	....	....	....	....	....	....	....	....
1984-85	**Quebec Nordiques**	**NHL**	**64**	**13**	**29**	**42**	**11**	**20**	**31**	**21**	**8**	**0**	**1**	**85**	**15.3**	**71**	**43**	**18**	**1**	**11**	**18**	**5**	**5**	**10**	**8**	**2**	**0**	**0**
1985-86	**Quebec Nordiques**	**NHL**	**75**	**16**	**40**	**56**	**13**	**27**	**40**	**20**	**13**	**0**	**1**	**100**	**16.0**	**74**	**64**	**23**	**0**	**–13**	**2**	**0**	**0**	**0**	**0**	**0**	**0**	**0**
1986-87	**Quebec Nordiques**	**NHL**	**14**	**2**	**3**	**5**	**2**	**2**	**4**	**4**	**2**	**0**	**0**	**14**	**14.3**	**10**	**10**	**4**	**0**	**–4**	....	....	....	....	....	....	....	....
	HC Fribourg	Switz.	36	33	*53	*86	....	....	....	....	....	....	....	....	....	....	....	....	....	....	....	....	....	....	....	....	....	....
1987-88	HC Fribourg	Switz.	36	35	*47	82	....	....	....	....	....	....	....	....	....	....	....	....	....	....	....	....	....	....	....	....	....	....
1988-89	HC Fribourg	Switz.	36	24	35	59	....	....	....	....	....	....	....	....	....	....	....	....	....	....	2	0	2	2	....	....	....	....
	Adirondack Red Wings	AHL	16	7	19	26	....	....	....	18	....	....	....	....	....	....	....	....	....	....	17	6	12	18	6	....	....	....
1989-90	ASG Tours	France	35	43	*62	*105	....	....	....	32	....	....	....	....	....	....	....	....	....	....	....	....	....	....	....	....	....	....
1990-91	ASG Tours	France	23	21	29	50	....	....	....	22	....	....	....	....	....	....	....	....	....	....	3	3	0	3	0	....	....	....
	NHL Totals		**290**	**65**	**138**	**203**	**53**	**94**	**147**	**114**	**36**	**0**	**3**	**402**	**16.2**	**304**	**183**	**119**	**1**		**36**	**9**	**12**	**21**	**10**	**5**	**0**	**1**

• Brother of Bob • QMJHL Second All-Star Team (1979) • QMJHL First All-Star Team (1980) • AHL Second All-Star Team (1981)

Signed as a free agent by **Buffalo**, November 1, 1979. Traded to **Quebec** by **Buffalo** with Tony McKegney, Andre Savard and Buffalo's 3rd round choice (Iiro Jarvi) in 1983 Entry Draft for Real Cloutier and Quebec's 1st round choice (Adam Creighton) in 1983 Entry Draft, June 8, 1983.

• SAVAGE, Andre

Andre Ronald C – R. 6', 195 lbs. b: Ottawa, Ont., 5/27/1975.

Season	Club	League	GP	G	A	Pts	AG	AA	APts	PIM	PP	SH	GW	S	%	TGF	PGF	TGA	PGA	+/-	GP	G	A	Pts	PIM	PP	SH	GW
1992-93	Gloucester Rangers	OJHL	54	34	34	68	....	....	....	38	....	....	....	....	....	....	....	....	....	....	....	....	....	....	....	....	....	....
1993-94	Gloucester Rangers	OJHL	57	43	74	117	....	....	....	44	....	....	....	....	....	....	....	....	....	....	....	....	....	....	....	....	....	....
1994-95	Michigan Tech Huskies	WCHA	39	7	17	24	....	....	....	56	....	....	....	....	....	....	....	....	....	....	....	....	....	....	....	....	....	....
1995-96	Michigan Tech Huskies	WCHA	38	13	27	40	....	....	....	42	....	....	....	....	....	....	....	....	....	....	....	....	....	....	....	....	....	....
1996-97	Michigan Tech Huskies	WCHA	37	18	20	38	....	....	....	34	....	....	....	....	....	....	....	....	....	....	....	....	....	....	....	....	....	....
1997-98	Michigan Tech Huskies	WCHA	33	14	27	41	....	....	....	34	....	....	....	....	....	....	....	....	....	....	....	....	....	....	....	....	....	....
1998-99	**Boston Bruins**	**NHL**	**6**	**1**	**0**	**1**	**1**	**0**	**1**	**0**	**0**	**0**	**0**	**8**	**12.5**	**2**	**0**	**0**	**0**	**2**	....	....	....	....	....	....	....	....
	Providence Bruins	AHL	63	27	42	69	....	....	....	54	....	....	....	....	....	....	....	....	....	....	5	0	1	1	0	....	....	....
99-2000	**Boston Bruins**	**NHL**	**43**	**7**	**13**	**20**	**8**	**12**	**20**	**10**	**2**	**0**	**1**	**70**	**10.0**	**30**	**8**	**30**	**0**	**–8**	....	....	....	....	....	....	....	....
	Providence Bruins	AHL	30	15	17	32	....	....	....	22	....	....	....	....	....	....	....	....	....	....	14	6	7	13	22	....	....	....
	NHL Totals		**49**	**8**	**13**	**21**	**9**	**12**	**21**	**10**	**2**	**0**	**1**	**78**	**10.3**	**32**	**8**	**30**	**0**		....	....	....	....	....	....	....	....

WCHA First All-Star Team (1998)

Signed as a free agent by **Boston**, June 18, 1998.

• SAVAGE, Brian

RW – L. 6'2", 192 lbs. b: Sudbury, Ont., 2/24/1971. Montreal's 11th, 171st overall, in 1991.

Season	Club	League	GP	G	A	Pts	AG	AA	APts	PIM	PP	SH	GW	S	%	TGF	PGF	TGA	PGA	+/-	GP	G	A	Pts	PIM	PP	SH	GW
1989-90	Sudbury Cubs	NOJHA	32	45	40	85	....	....	....	61	....	....	....	....	....	....	....	....	....	....	....	....	....	....	....	....	....	....
1990-91	University of Miami-Ohio	CCHA	28	5	6	11	....	....	....	26	....	....	....	....	....	....	....	....	....	....	....	....	....	....	....	....	....	....
1991-92	University of Miami-Ohio	CCHA	40	24	16	40	....	....	....	43	....	....	....	....	....	....	....	....	....	....	....	....	....	....	....	....	....	....
1992-93	University of Miami-Ohio	CCHA	38	*37	21	58	....	....	....	44	....	....	....	....	....	....	....	....	....	....	....	....	....	....	....	....	....	....
	Canada	Nat-Team	9	3	0	3	....	....	....	12	....	....	....	....	....	....	....	....	....	....	....	....	....	....	....	....	....	....
	Canada	WC-A	8	1	0	1	....	....	....	2	....	....	....	....	....	....	....	....	....	....	....	....	....	....	....	....	....	....

Season	Club	League	REGULAR SEASON GP	G	A	Pts	AG	AA	APts	PIM	PP	SH	GW	S	%	TGF	PGF	TGA	PGA	+/–	PLAYOFFS GP	G	A	Pts	PIM	PP	SH	GW
1993-94	Canada	Nat-Team	51	20	26	46				38																		
	Canada	Olympics	8	2	2	4				6																		
	Montreal Canadiens	**NHL**	**3**	**1**	**0**	**1**	**1**	**0**	**1**	**0**	**0**	**0**	**0**	**3**	**33.3**	**1**	**0**	**1**	**0**	**0**	**3**	**0**	**2**	**2**	**0**	**0**	**0**	**0**
	Fredericton Canadiens	AHL	17	12	15	27				4																		
1994-95	**Montreal Canadiens**	**NHL**	**37**	**12**	**7**	**19**	**21**	**10**	**31**	**27**	**0**	**0**	**0**	**64**	**18.8**	**30**	**2**	**27**	**4**	**5**								
1995-96	**Montreal Canadiens**	**NHL**	**75**	**25**	**8**	**33**	**25**	**7**	**32**	**28**	**4**	**0**	**4**	**150**	**16.7**	**55**	**16**	**47**	**0**	**–8**	**6**	**0**	**2**	**2**	**2**	**0**	**0**	**0**
1996-97	**Montreal Canadiens**	**NHL**	**81**	**23**	**37**	**60**	**24**	**33**	**57**	**39**	**5**	**0**	**2**	**219**	**10.5**	**80**	**20**	**74**	**0**	**–14**	**5**	**1**	**1**	**2**	**0**	**0**	**0**	**0**
1997-98	**Montreal Canadiens**	**NHL**	**64**	**26**	**17**	**43**	**30**	**17**	**47**	**36**	**8**	**0**	**7**	**152**	**17.1**	**60**	**16**	**33**	**0**	**11**	**9**	**0**	**2**	**2**	**6**	**0**	**0**	**0**
1998-99	**Montreal Canadiens**	**NHL**	**54**	**16**	**10**	**26**	**19**	**10**	**29**	**20**	**5**	**0**	**4**	**124**	**12.9**	**34**	**12**	**37**	**1**	**–14**								
	Canada	WC-A	8	3	3	6				6																		
99-2000	**Montreal Canadiens**	**NHL**	**38**	**17**	**12**	**29**	**19**	**11**	**30**	**19**	**6**	**1**	**5**	**107**	**15.9**	**42**	**14**	**32**	**0**	**–4**								
	NHL Totals		**352**	**120**	**91**	**211**	**139**	**88**	**227**	**169**	**28**	**1**	**22**	**819**	**14.7**	**302**	**80**	**251**	**5**		**23**	**1**	**7**	**8**	**8**	**0**	**0**	**0**

CCHA First All-Star Team (1993) • NCAA West Second All-American Team (1993)

• Missed majority of 1999-2000 season recovering from neck injury suffered in game vs. LA Kings, November 20, 1999.

• SAVAGE, Joel

Joel Robert RW – R. 5'11", 205 lbs. b: Surrey, B.C., 12/25/1969. Buffalo's 1st, 13th overall, in 1988.

Season	Club	League	GP	G	A	Pts	AG	AA	APts	PIM	PP	SH	GW	S	%	TGF	PGF	TGA	PGA	+/–	GP	G	A	Pts	PIM	PP	SH	GW
1985-86	Kelowna Packers	BCJHL	43	10	12	22				76											11	2	1	3	6			
1986-87	Victoria Cougars	WHL	68	14	13	27				48											5	2	0	2	0			
1987-88	Victoria Cougars	WHL	69	37	32	69				73																		
1988-89	Victoria Cougars	WHL	60	17	30	47				95											6	1	1	2	8			
1989-90	Rochester Americans	AHL	43	6	7	13				39											5	0	1	1	4			
1990-91	**Buffalo Sabres**	**NHL**	**3**	**0**	**1**	**1**	**0**	**1**	**1**	**0**	**0**	**0**	**0**	**2**	**0.0**	**2**	**1**	**3**	**0**	**–2**								
	Rochester Americans	AHL	61	25	19	44				45											15	3	3	6	8			
1991-92	Rochester Americans	AHL	59	8	14	22				39											9	2	0	2	8			
1992-93	Rochester Americans	AHL	6	1	1	2				6											3	0	0	0	12			
	Fort Wayne Komets	IHL	46	21	16	37				60											10	3	5	8	22			
1993-94	Fort Wayne Komets	IHL	31	2	11	13				29																		
	San Diego Gulls	IHL	20	0	2	2				4																		
	Kalamazoo Wings	IHL	4	2	1	3				0											2	0	0	0	4			
1994-95	Canada	Nat-Team	37	10	17	27				47																		
1995-96	Star Bulls Rosenheim	Germany	50	16	38	54				62											4	0	3	3	18			
	Canada	Nat-Team	2	0	0	0				0																		
1996-97	Star Bulls Rosenheim	Germany	46	8	19	27				108											3	0	2	2	2			
1997-98	HC Lugano	Switz.	11	1	3	4				8																		
	Frankfurt Lions	Germany	27	7	14	21				40																		
1998-99	Frankfurt Lions	Germany	49	13	11	24				56											8	4	3	7	8			
	Frankfurt Lions	EuroHL	5	2	4	6				10																		
99-2000	Adler Mannheim	Germany	47	10	13	23				61											5	0	0	0	4			
	Adler Mannheim	EuroHL	6	0	0	0				6																		
	NHL Totals		**3**	**0**	**1**	**1**	**0**	**1**	**1**	**0**	**0**	**0**	**0**	**2**	**0.0**	**2**	**1**	**3**	**0**									

WHL West Second All-Star Team (1988)

Signed as a free agent by **Anaheim**, September 19, 1993.

• SAVAGE, Reggie

Reginald D. C – L. 5'10", 192 lbs. b: Montreal, Que., 5/1/1970. Washington's 1st, 15th overall, in 1988.

Season	Club	League	GP	G	A	Pts	AG	AA	APts	PIM	PP	SH	GW	S	%	TGF	PGF	TGA	PGA	+/–	GP	G	A	Pts	PIM	PP	SH	GW
1985-86	Richelieu Regents	QAAA	40	38	26	64																						
1986-87	Richelieu Regents	QAAA	42	82	57	139				44																		
1987-88	Victoriaville Tigres	QMJHL	68	68	54	122				77											5	2	3	5	8			
1988-89	Victoriaville Tigres	QMJHL	54	58	55	113				178											16	15	13	28	52			
	Canada	WJC-A	7	4	5	9				4																		
1989-90	Victoriaville Tigres	QMJHL	63	51	43	94				79											16	13	10	23	40			
1990-91	**Washington Capitals**	**NHL**	**1**	**0**	**0**	**0**	**0**	**0**	**0**	**0**	**0**	**0**	**0**	**2**	**0.0**	**0**	**0**	**1**	**0**	**–1**								
	Baltimore Skipjacks	AHL	62	32	29	61				10											6	1	1	2	6			
1991-92	Baltimore Skipjacks	AHL	77	42	28	70				51																		
1992-93	**Washington Capitals**	**NHL**	**16**	**2**	**3**	**5**	**2**	**2**	**4**	**12**	**2**	**0**	**0**	**20**	**10.0**	**9**	**4**	**9**	**0**	**–4**								
	Baltimore Skipjacks	AHL	40	37	18	55				28																		
1993-94	**Quebec Nordiques**	**NHL**	**17**	**3**	**4**	**7**	**3**	**3**	**6**	**16**	**1**	**0**	**0**	**25**	**12.0**	**9**	**3**	**3**	**0**	**3**								
	Cornwall Aces	AHL	33	21	13	34				56																		
1994-95	Cornwall Aces	AHL	34	13	7	20				56											14	5	6	11	40			
1995-96	Atlanta Knights	IHL	66	22	14	36				118																		
	Syracuse Crunch	AHL	10	9	5	14				28											16	9	6	15	54			
1996-97	Springfield Falcons	AHL	68	32	25	57				103											17	6	7	13	24			
1997-98	Kansas City Blades	IHL	51	6	10	16				60																		
	San Antonio Dragons	IHL	22	6	12	18				24																		
	Orlando Solar Bears	IHL	10	5	5	10				18											17	2	9	11	60			
1998-99	HC Asiago	Alpenliga	27	25	27	52				69																		
	HC Asiago	Italy	16	18	15	33				8											2	1	0	1	22			
99-2000	Syracuse Crunch	AHL	78	36	34	70				135											4	0	0	0	8			
	NHL Totals		**34**	**5**	**7**	**12**	**5**	**5**	**10**	**28**	**3**	**0**	**0**	**47**	**10.6**	**18**	**7**	**13**	**0**									

Traded to **Quebec** by **Washington** with Paul MacDermid for Mike Hough, June 20, 1993. Signed as a free agent by **Phoenix**, August 28, 1996. Signed as a free agent by **Vancouver**, June 17, 1999. Signed as a free agent by **Columbus**, June 2, 2000.

• SAVARD, Andre

C – L. 6'1", 185 lbs. b: Temiscamingue, Que., 2/9/1953. Boston's 1st, 6th overall, in 1973.

Season	Club	League	GP	G	A	Pts	AG	AA	APts	PIM	PP	SH	GW	S	%	TGF	PGF	TGA	PGA	+/–	GP	G	A	Pts	PIM	PP	SH	GW
1968-69	D'amos Cometes	QAAA	STATISTICS NOT AVAILABLE																									
1969-70	Quebec Remparts	QJHL	56	23	60	83				126											15	9	13	22	30			
	Quebec Remparts	Mem-Cup	12	8	9	17				37																		
1970-71	Quebec Remparts	QJHL	61	50	89	139				150											14	9	17	26	56			
	Quebec Remparts	Mem-Cup	6	2	*7	9				9																		
1971-72	Quebec Remparts	QMJHL	33	32	46	78				107																		
1972-73	Quebec Remparts	QMJHL	56	67	84	*151				147											15	8	*24	*42	33			
	Quebec Remparts	Mem-Cup	3	2	3	5				18																		
1973-74	**Boston Bruins**	**NHL**	**72**	**16**	**14**	**30**	**15**	**12**	**27**	**39**	**0**	**0**	**1**	**88**	**18.2**	**41**	**1**	**24**	**0**	**16**	**16**	**3**	**2**	**5**	**24**	**0**	**0**	**0**
1974-75	**Boston Bruins**	**NHL**	**77**	**19**	**25**	**44**	**17**	**19**	**36**	**45**	**0**	**0**	**2**	**150**	**12.7**	**62**	**2**	**47**	**3**	**16**	**3**	**1**	**1**	**2**	**2**	**0**	**0**	**1**
1975-76	**Boston Bruins**	**NHL**	**79**	**17**	**23**	**40**	**15**	**17**	**32**	**60**	**0**	**0**	**3**	**182**	**9.3**	**58**	**2**	**56**	**4**	**4**	**12**	**1**	**4**	**5**	**9**	**0**	**0**	**0**
1976-77	**Buffalo Sabres**	**NHL**	**80**	**25**	**35**	**60**	**23**	**27**	**50**	**30**	**4**	**0**	**4**	**160**	**15.6**	**89**	**17**	**69**	**6**	**9**	**6**	**0**	**1**	**1**	**2**	**0**	**0**	**0**
1977-78	**Buffalo Sabres**	**NHL**	**80**	**19**	**20**	**39**	**17**	**15**	**32**	**40**	**2**	**0**	**0**	**127**	**15.0**	**56**	**5**	**51**	**1**	**1**	**6**	**0**	**0**	**0**	**4**	**0**	**0**	**0**
1978-79	**Buffalo Sabres**	**NHL**	**65**	**18**	**22**	**40**	**15**	**16**	**31**	**20**	**2**	**2**	**1**	**97**	**18.6**	**59**	**6**	**59**	**8**	**–2**	**3**	**0**	**2**	**2**	**2**	**0**	**0**	**0**
1979-80	**Buffalo Sabres**	**NHL**	**33**	**3**	**10**	**13**	**3**	**7**	**10**	**16**	**0**	**0**	**2**	**36**	**8.3**	**16**	**0**	**14**	**2**	**4**	**8**	**1**	**1**	**2**	**2**	**0**	**0**	**0**
	Rochester Americans	AHL	25	11	17	28				4																		
1980-81	**Buffalo Sabres**	**NHL**	**79**	**31**	**43**	**74**	**24**	**29**	**53**	**63**	**2**	**2**	**4**	**149**	**20.8**	**110**	**24**	**65**	**11**	**32**	**8**	**4**	**2**	**6**	**17**	**1**	**0**	**0**
1981-82	**Buffalo Sabres**	**NHL**	**62**	**18**	**20**	**38**	**14**	**13**	**27**	**24**	**2**	**1**	**3**	**118**	**15.3**	**50**	**4**	**60**	**19**	**5**	**4**	**0**	**1**	**1**	**5**	**0**	**0**	**0**
1982-83	**Buffalo Sabres**	**NHL**	**68**	**16**	**25**	**41**	**13**	**17**	**30**	**28**	**3**	**2**	**2**	**122**	**13.1**	**53**	**7**	**45**	**10**	**11**	**10**	**0**	**4**	**4**	**8**	**0**	**0**	**0**
1983-84	**Quebec Nordiques**	**NHL**	**60**	**20**	**24**	**44**	**16**	**16**	**32**	**38**	**0**	**2**	**2**	**100**	**20.0**	**58**	**2**	**65**	**26**	**17**	**9**	**3**	**0**	**3**	**2**	**0**	**2**	**1**
1984-85	**Quebec Nordiques**	**NHL**	**35**	**9**	**10**	**19**	**7**	**7**	**14**	**8**	**1**	**1**	**1**	**55**	**16.4**	**25**	**2**	**44**	**18**	**–3**								
1985-1987	Fredericton Express	AHL	DID NOT PLAY – COACHING																									
1987-1988	**Quebec Nordiques**	**NHL**	DID NOT PLAY – COACHING																									
1988-1991	**Quebec Nordiques**	**NHL**	DID NOT PLAY – SCOUTING																									

Season	Club	League	GP	G	A	Pts	AG	AA	APts	PIM	PP	SH	GW	S	%	TGF	PGF	TGA	PGA	+/–	GP	G	A	Pts	PIM	PP	SH	GW
			REGULAR SEASON																		PLAYOFFS							
1991-1994	Quebec Nordiques	NHL	DID NOT PLAY – ASSISTANT COACH																									
1994-1999	Ottawa Senators	NHL	DID NOT PLAY – SCOUTING																									
1999-2000	Ottawa Senators	NHL	DID NOT PLAY – ASSISTANT COACH																									
	NHL Totals		**790**	**211**	**271**	**482**	**179**	**195**	**374**	**411**	**16**	**10**	**25**	**1384**	**15.2**	**677**	**72**	**599**	**108**		**85**	**13**	**18**	**31**	**77**	**1**	**2**	**2**

QJHL Second All-Star Team (1971) • QMJHL First All-Star Team (1973)

Signed as a free agent by **Buffalo**, June 11, 1976. Traded to **Quebec** by **Buffalo** with Tony McKegney, Jean Sauve and Buffalo's 3rd round choice (Iiro Jarvi) in 1983 Entry Draft for Real Cloutier and Quebec's 1st round choice (Adam Creighton) in 1983 Entry Draft, June 8, 1983.

• SAVARD, Denis

Denis Joseph C – R. 5'10", 175 lbs. b: Pointe Gatineau, Que., 2/4/1961. Chicago's 1st, 3rd overall, in 1980. **HHOF**

Season	Club	League	GP	G	A	Pts	AG	AA	APts	PIM	PP	SH	GW	S	%	TGF	PGF	TGA	PGA	+/–	GP	G	A	Pts	PIM	PP	SH	GW
1977-78	Montreal Juniors	QMJHL	72	37	79	116				22																		
1978-79	Montreal Juniors	QMJHL	70	46	*112	158				88											11	5	6	11	46			
1979-80	Montreal Juniors	QMJHL	72	63	118	181				93											10	7	16	23	8			
1980-81	**Chicago Black Hawks**	**NHL**	**76**	**28**	**47**	**75**	**22**	**31**	**53**	**47**	**4**	**0**	**3**	**159**	**17.6**	**102**	**20**	**64**	**9**	**27**	**3**	**0**	**0**	**0**	**0**	**0**	**0**	**0**
1981-82	**Chicago Black Hawks**	**NHL**	**80**	**32**	**87**	**119**	**25**	**58**	**83**	**82**	**8**	**0**	**4**	**231**	**13.9**	**149**	**57**	**95**	**3**	**0**	**15**	**11**	**7**	**18**	**52**	**5**	**0**	**2**
1982-83	**Chicago Black Hawks**	**NHL**	**78**	**35**	**86**	**121**	**29**	**60**	**89**	**99**	**13**	**0**	**4**	**213**	**16.4**	**153**	**61**	**67**	**1**	**26**	**13**	**8**	**9**	**17**	**22**	**3**	**0**	**1**
1983-84	**Chicago Black Hawks**	**NHL**	**75**	**37**	**57**	**94**	**30**	**39**	**69**	**71**	**12**	**0**	**5**	**210**	**17.6**	**121**	**53**	**83**	**2**	**–13**	**5**	**1**	**3**	**4**	**9**	**0**	**0**	**0**
1984-85	**Chicago Black Hawks**	**NHL**	**79**	**38**	**67**	**105**	**31**	**46**	**77**	**56**	**7**	**0**	**1**	**266**	**14.3**	**133**	**47**	**70**	**0**	**16**	**15**	**9**	**20**	**29**	**20**	**3**	**0**	**0**
1985-86	**Chicago Black Hawks**	**NHL**	**80**	**47**	**69**	**116**	**38**	**47**	**85**	**111**	**14**	**1**	**8**	**279**	**16.8**	**149**	**47**	**103**	**8**	**7**	**3**	**4**	**1**	**5**	**6**	**2**	**0**	**0**
1986-87	**Chicago Blackhawks**	**NHL**	**70**	**40**	**50**	**90**	**35**	**36**	**71**	**108**	**7**	**0**	**7**	**237**	**16.9**	**116**	**38**	**68**	**5**	**15**	**4**	**1**	**0**	**1**	**12**	**0**	**0**	**0**
1987-88	**Chicago Blackhawks**	**NHL**	**80**	**44**	**87**	**131**	**38**	**63**	**101**	**95**	**14**	**7**	**6**	**270**	**16.3**	**158**	**77**	**112**	**35**	**4**	**5**	**4**	**3**	**7**	**17**	**0**	**1**	**1**
1988-89	**Chicago Blackhawks**	**NHL**	**58**	**23**	**59**	**82**	**19**	**42**	**61**	**110**	**7**	**5**	**1**	**182**	**12.6**	**106**	**52**	**87**	**28**	**–5**	**16**	**8**	**11**	**19**	**10**	**2**	**1**	**1**
1989-90	**Chicago Blackhawks**	**NHL**	**60**	**27**	**53**	**80**	**23**	**38**	**61**	**56**	**10**	**2**	**4**	**181**	**14.9**	**97**	**39**	**64**	**14**	**8**	**20**	**7**	**15**	**22**	**41**	**4**	**0**	**1**
1990-91	Montreal Canadiens	Fr-Tour	4	3	3	6				4																		
	Montreal Canadiens	**NHL**	**70**	**28**	**31**	**59**	**26**	**24**	**50**	**52**	**7**	**2**	**0**	**187**	**15.0**	**76**	**29**	**51**	**3**	**–1**	**13**	**2**	**11**	**13**	**35**	**1**	**0**	**0**
1991-92	**Montreal Canadiens**	**NHL**	**77**	**28**	**42**	**70**	**25**	**32**	**57**	**73**	**12**	**1**	**5**	**174**	**16.1**	**92**	**40**	**51**	**5**	**6**	**11**	**3**	**9**	**12**	**8**	**1**	**0**	**0**
1992-93♦	**Montreal Canadiens**	**NHL**	**63**	**16**	**34**	**50**	**13**	**23**	**36**	**90**	**4**	**1**	**2**	**99**	**16.2**	**63**	**19**	**55**	**12**	**1**	**14**	**0**	**5**	**5**	**4**	**0**	**0**	**0**
1993-94	**Tampa Bay Lightning**	**NHL**	**74**	**18**	**28**	**46**	**17**	**22**	**39**	**106**	**2**	**1**	**2**	**181**	**9.9**	**69**	**21**	**71**	**22**	**–1**								
1994-95	**Tampa Bay Lightning**	**NHL**	**31**	**6**	**11**	**17**	**11**	**16**	**27**	**10**	**1**	**0**	**1**	**56**	**10.7**	**18**	**6**	**22**	**4**	**–6**								
	Chicago Blackhawks	**NHL**	**12**	**4**	**4**	**8**	**7**	**6**	**13**	**8**	**1**	**0**	**0**	**26**	**15.4**	**13**	**5**	**7**	**2**	**3**	**16**	**7**	**11**	**18**	**10**	**3**	**0**	**0**
1995-96	**Chicago Blackhawks**	**NHL**	**69**	**13**	**35**	**48**	**13**	**29**	**42**	**102**	**2**	**0**	**1**	**110**	**11.8**	**65**	**15**	**30**	**0**	**20**	**10**	**1**	**2**	**3**	**8**	**0**	**0**	**0**
1996-97	**Chicago Blackhawks**	**NHL**	**64**	**9**	**18**	**27**	**10**	**16**	**26**	**60**	**2**	**0**	**2**	**82**	**11.0**	**40**	**15**	**37**	**2**	**–10**	**6**	**0**	**2**	**2**	**2**	**0**	**0**	**0**
1997-2000	**Chicago Blackhawks**	**NHL**	DID NOT PLAY – ASSISTANT COACH																									
	NHL Totals		**1196**	**473**	**865**	**1338**	**412**	**628**	**1040**	**1336**	**127**	**20**	**56**	**3143**	**15.0**	**1720**	**641**	**1137**	**155**		**169**	**66**	**109**	**175**	**256**	**24**	**2**	**6**

QMJHL First All-Star Team (1980) • NHL Second All-Star Team (1983) • Played in NHL All-Star Game (1982, 1983, 1984, 1986, 1988, 1991, 1996)

Traded to **Montreal** by **Chicago** for Chris Chelios and Montreal's 2nd round choice (Michael Pomichter) in 1991 Entry Draft, June 29, 1990. Signed as a free agent by **Tampa Bay**, July 29, 1993. Traded to **Chicago** by **Tampa Bay** for Chicago's 6th round choice (Xavier Delisle) in 1996 Entry Draft, April 6, 1995. • Started 1998-99 season as Chicago's Special Development Coach and was named Assistant Coach on December 3, 1998.

• SAVARD, Jean

C – R. 5'11", 172 lbs. b: Verdun, Que., 4/26/1957. Chicago's 2nd, 19th overall, in 1977.

Season	Club	League	GP	G	A	Pts	AG	AA	APts	PIM	PP	SH	GW	S	%	TGF	PGF	TGA	PGA	+/–	GP	G	A	Pts	PIM	PP	SH	GW
1974-75	Montreal Red-White-Blue	QMJHL	72	35	24	59				44																		
1975-76	Quebec Remparts	QMJHL	.68	25	42	67				58																		
1976-77	Quebec Remparts	QMJHL	72	*84	96	*180				110																		
1977-78	**Chicago Black Hawks**	**NHL**	**31**	**7**	**11**	**18**	**6**	**8**	**14**	**20**	**2**	**0**	**2**	**37**	**18.9**	**24**	**3**	**15**	**0**	**6**								
	Dallas Black Hawks	CHL	41	17	18	35				28											13	4	4	8	32			
1978-79	**Chicago Black Hawks**	**NHL**	**11**	**0**	**1**	**1**	**0**	**1**	**1**	**9**	**0**	**0**	**0**	**7**	**0.0**	**1**	**0**	**3**	**0**	**–2**								
	New Brunswick Hawks	AHL	60	26	29	55				85											5	2	2	4	0			
1979-80	**Hartford Whalers**	**NHL**	**1**	**0**	**0**	**0**	**0**	**0**	**0**	**0**	**0**	**0**	**0**	**1**	**0.0**	**0**	**0**	**0**	**0**	**0**								
	Springfield Indians	AHL	78	28	43	71				60																		
1980-81	Binghamton Whalers	AHL	52	13	27	40				70																		
1981-82	ZSC Zurich	Switz.	28	28	22	50				20																		
1982-83	ZSC Zurich	Switz-2	STATISTICS NOT AVAILABLE																									
	Salt Lake Golden Eagles	CHL	3	0	2	2				4																		
1983-84	HC Salzburg	Austria	STATISTICS NOT AVAILABLE																									
1984-85	HC Salzburg	Austria	11	9	10	19				48																		
1985-86	EHC Waldkraiburg	Germany-2	STATISTICS NOT AVAILABLE																									
	NHL Totals		**43**	**7**	**12**	**19**	**6**	**9**	**15**	**29**	**2**	**0**	**2**	**45**	**15.6**	**25**	**3**	**18**	**0**									

QMJHL First All-Star Team (1977)

Claimed by **Hartford** from **Chicago** in Expansion Draft, June 13, 1979.

• SAVARD, Marc

C – L. 5'10", 184 lbs. b: Ottawa, Ont., 7/17/1977. NY Rangers' 3rd, 91st overall, in 1995.

Season	Club	League	GP	G	A	Pts	AG	AA	APts	PIM	PP	SH	GW	S	%	TGF	PGF	TGA	PGA	+/–	GP	G	A	Pts	PIM	PP	SH	GW
1992-93	Metcalfe Jets	OJHL-B	36	*44	55	*99				38																		
1993-94	Oshawa Generals	OHL	61	18	39	57				20											5	4	3	7	8			
1994-95	Oshawa Generals	OHL	66	43	96	*139				78											7	5	6	11	8			
1995-96	Oshawa Generals	OHL	48	28	59	87				77											5	4	5	9	6			
1996-97	Oshawa Generals	OHL	64	43	*87	*130				94											18	13	*24	*37	20			
	Oshawa Generals	Mem-Cup	4	0	6	6				4																		
1997-98	**New York Rangers**	**NHL**	**28**	**1**	**5**	**6**	**1**	**5**	**6**	**4**	**0**	**0**	**0**	**32**	**3.1**	**9**	**5**	**9**	**1**	**–4**								
	Hartford Wolf Pack	AHL	58	21	53	74				66											15	8	19	27	24			
1998-99	**New York Rangers**	**NHL**	**70**	**9**	**36**	**45**	**11**	**35**	**46**	**38**	**4**	**0**	**1**	**116**	**7.8**	**55**	**22**	**40**	**0**	**–7**								
	Hartford Wolf Pack	AHL	9	3	10	13				16											7	1	12	13	16			
99-2000	**Calgary Flames**	**NHL**	**78**	**22**	**31**	**53**	**25**	**29**	**54**	**56**	**4**	**0**	**3**	**184**	**12.0**	**72**	**22**	**52**	**0**	**–2**								
	NHL Totals		**176**	**32**	**72**	**104**	**37**	**69**	**106**	**98**	**8**	**0**	**4**	**332**	**9.6**	**136**	**49**	**101**	**1**									

OHL Second All-Star Team (1995)

Traded to **Calgary** by **NY Rangers** with NY Rangers 1st round choice (Oleg Saprykin) in 1999 Entry Draft for the rights to Jan Hlavac and Calgary's 1st (Jamie Lundmark) and 3rd (later traded back to Calgary - Calgary selected Craig Andersson) round choices in 1999 Entry Draft, June 26, 1999.

• SAVARD, Serge

Serge A. "The Senator" D – L. 6'3", 210 lbs. b: Montreal, Que., 1/22/1946. **HHOF**

Season	Club	League	GP	G	A	Pts	AG	AA	APts	PIM	PP	SH	GW	S	%	TGF	PGF	TGA	PGA	+/–	GP	G	A	Pts	PIM	PP	SH	GW
1963-64	Montreal Jr. Canadiens	OHA-Jr.	56	3	31	34				72											17	1	7	8	30			
1964-65	Montreal Jr. Canadiens	OHA-Jr.	56	14	33	47				81											7	2	3	5	8			
	Omaha Knights	CPHL	2	0	0	0				0											4	0	1	1	4			
1965-66	Montreal Jr. Canadiens	OHA-Jr.	20	8	10	18				33											10	1	4	5	20			
1966-67	**Montreal Canadiens**	**NHL**	**2**	**0**	**0**	**0**	**0**	**0**	**0**	**0**																		
	Houston Apollos	CPHL	68	7	25	32				155											5	1	3	4	17			
	Quebec Aces	AHL																			1	0	0	0	2			
1967-68♦	**Montreal Canadiens**	**NHL**	**67**	**2**	**13**	**15**	**2**	**13**	**15**	**34**	**1**	**0**	**0**	**59**	**3.4**	**51**	**5**	**40**	**7**	**13**	**6**	**2**	**0**	**2**	**0**	**0**	**2**	**1**
1968-69♦	**Montreal Canadiens**	**NHL**	**74**	**8**	**23**	**31**	**8**	**20**	**28**	**73**	**0**	**0**	**2**	**98**	**8.2**	**93**	**4**	**62**	**6**	**33**	**14**	**4**	**6**	**10**	**24**	**1**	**1**	**0**
1969-70	**Montreal Canadiens**	**NHL**	**64**	**12**	**19**	**31**	**13**	**18**	**31**	**38**	**5**	**3**	**2**	**151**	**7.9**	**96**	**26**	**92**	**26**	**4**								
1970-71♦	**Montreal Canadiens**	**NHL**	**37**	**5**	**10**	**15**	**5**	**8**	**13**	**30**	**0**	**1**	**0**	**55**	**9.1**	**48**	**6**	**40**	**9**	**11**								
1971-72	**Montreal Canadiens**	**NHL**	**23**	**1**	**8**	**9**	**1**	**7**	**8**	**16**	**0**	**0**	**0**	**45**	**2.2**	**43**	**6**	**21**	**5**	**21**	**6**	**0**	**0**	**0**	**10**	**0**	**0**	**0**
1972-73	Team Canada	Summit-72	5	0	2	2				0																		
♦	**Montreal Canadiens**	**NHL**	**74**	**7**	**32**	**39**	**7**	**25**	**32**	**58**	**2**	**1**	**0**	**106**	**6.6**	**147**	**14**	**85**	**22**	**70**	**17**	**3**	**8**	**11**	**22**	**0**	**0**	**0**
1973-74	**Montreal Canadiens**	**NHL**	**67**	**4**	**14**	**18**	**4**	**12**	**16**	**49**	**1**	**0**	**1**	**98**	**4.1**	**105**	**17**	**98**	**30**	**20**	**6**	**1**	**1**	**2**	**4**	**0**	**0**	**0**
1974-75	**Montreal Canadiens**	**NHL**	**80**	**20**	**40**	**60**	**17**	**30**	**47**	**64**	**7**	**1**	**2**	**165**	**12.1**	**171**	**37**	**97**	**34**	**71**	**11**	**1**	**7**	**8**	**2**	**0**	**0**	**0**
1975-76♦	**Montreal Canadiens**	**NHL**	**71**	**8**	**39**	**47**	**7**	**29**	**36**	**38**	**1**	**1**	**1**	**112**	**7.1**	**125**	**19**	**75**	**21**	**52**	**13**	**3**	**6**	**9**	**6**	**1**	**1**	**2**
1976-77	Canada	Can-Cup	7	0	3	3				0																		
♦	**Montreal Canadiens**	**NHL**	**78**	**9**	**33**	**42**	**8**	**25**	**33**	**35**	**0**	**0**	**1**	**110**	**8.2**	**168**	**18**	**93**	**22**	**79**	**14**	**2**	**7**	**9**	**2**	**1**	**0**	**1**
1977-78♦	**Montreal Canadiens**	**NHL**	**77**	**8**	**34**	**42**	**7**	**26**	**33**	**24**	**4**	**0**	**1**	**103**	**7.8**	**155**	**33**	**88**	**28**	**62**	**15**	**1**	**7**	**8**	**8**	**0**	**0**	**0**

			REGULAR SEASON																		PLAYOFFS							
Season	Club	League	GP	G	A	Pts	AG	AA	APts	PIM	PP	SH	GW	S	%	TGF	PGF	TGA	PGA	+/-	GP	G	A	Pts	PIM	PP	SH	GW
1978-79♦	**Montreal Canadiens**	**NHL**	**80**	**7**	**26**	**33**	**6**	**19**	**25**	**30**	**1**	**2**	**0**	**82**	**8.5**	**135**	**12**	**104**	**27**	**46**	**16**	**2**	**7**	**9**	**6**	**1**	**0**	**1**
	NHL All-Stars	Chal-Cup	3	0	0	0				0																		
1979-80	**Montreal Canadiens**	**NHL**	**46**	**5**	**8**	**13**	**4**	**6**	**10**	**18**	**0**	**0**	**1**	**45**	**11.1**	**58**	**8**	**68**	**16**	**–2**	**2**	**0**	**0**	**0**	**0**	**0**	**0**	**0**
1980-81	**Montreal Canadiens**	**NHL**	**77**	**4**	**13**	**17**	**3**	**9**	**12**	**30**	**0**	**0**	**1**	**63**	**6.3**	**93**	**1**	**108**	**28**	**12**	**3**	**0**	**0**	**0**	**0**	**0**	**0**	**0**
1981-82	**Winnipeg Jets**	**NHL**	**47**	**2**	**5**	**7**	**2**	**3**	**5**	**26**	**0**	**0**	**1**	**41**	**4.9**	**67**	**0**	**94**	**19**	**–8**	**4**	**0**	**0**	**0**	**2**	**0**	**0**	**0**
1982-83	**Winnipeg Jets**	**NHL**	**76**	**4**	**16**	**20**	**3**	**11**	**14**	**29**	**0**	**0**	**0**	**51**	**7.8**	**88**	**1**	**155**	**44**	**–24**	**3**	**0**	**0**	**0**	**2**	**0**	**0**	**0**
	NHL Totals		**1040**	**106**	**333**	**439**	**97**	**261**	**358**	**592**											**130**	**19**	**49**	**68**	**88**			

OHA-Jr. Second All-Star Team (1966) • CPHL Second All-Star Team (1967) • Won Ken McKenzie Trophy (Rookie of the Year - CPHL) (1967) • Won Conn Smythe Trophy (1969) • NHL Second All-Star Team (1979) • Won Bill Masterton Trophy (1979) • Played in NHL All-Star Game (1970, 1973, 1977, 1978)

• Missed majority of 1965-66 season recovering from knee surgery, July, 1965. • Missed remainder of 1969-70 and majority of 1970-71 seasons recovering from leg injury suffered in game vs. NY Rangers, March 11, 1970. • Missed remainder of 1970-71 and majority of 1971-72 seasons recovering from leg injury suffered in game vs. Toronto, January 30, 1971. Claimed by **Winnipeg** from **Montreal** in Waiver Draft, October 5, 1981.

• SAVOIA, Ryan

C – R. 6'1", 204 lbs. b: Thorold, Ont., 5/6/1973.

Season	Club	League	GP	G	A	Pts	AG	AA	APts	PIM	PP	SH	GW	S	%	TGF	PGF	TGA	PGA	+/-	GP	G	A	Pts	PIM	PP	SH	GW
1989-90	Thorold Eagles	OJHL-B	40	13	16	29				14																		
1990-91	Thorold Eagles	OJHL-B	35	13	20	33				28																		
1991-92	Thorold Eagles	OJHL-B	41	26	24	50				46																		
1992-93	Thorold Eagles	OJHL-B	39	27	41	68				74																		
1993-94	Thorold Eagles	OJHL-B	39	51	51	102				48																		
1994-95	Brock University	OUAA	38	35	48	83				24																		
	Cleveland Lumberjacks	IHL	1	0	0	0				0																		
1995-96	Cleveland Lumberjacks	IHL	49	6	7	13				31																		
1996-97	Johnstown Chiefs	ECHL	60	35	44	79				100																		
	Cleveland Lumberjacks	IHL	4	1	0	1				2																		
	Fort Wayne Komets	IHL	8	0	2	2				2																		
1997-98	HIFK Helsinki	Finland	1	0	0	0				0																		
	Syracuse Crunch	AHL	7	0	4	4				2																		
	Johnstown Chiefs	ECHL	6	1	5	6				0																		
1998-99	**Pittsburgh Penguins**	**NHL**	**3**	**0**	**0**	**0**	**0**	**0**	**0**	**0**	**0**	**0**	**0**	**0**	**0.0**	**0**	**0**	**1**	**0**	**–1**								
	Syracuse Crunch	AHL	54	9	22	31				40																		
99-2000	Canada	Nat-Team	56	21	30	51				91																		
	NHL Totals		**3**	**0**	**0**	**0**	**0**	**0**	**0**	**0**	**0**	**0**	**0**	**0**	**0.0**	**0**	**0**	**1**	**0**									

Signed as a free agent by **Pittsburgh**, April 7, 1995.

• SAWYER, Kevin

Kevin John LW – L. 6'2", 205 lbs. b: Christina Lake, B.C., 2/21/1974.

Season	Club	League	GP	G	A	Pts	AG	AA	APts	PIM	PP	SH	GW	S	%	TGF	PGF	TGA	PGA	+/-	GP	G	A	Pts	PIM	PP	SH	GW
1991-92	Grand Forks Border Bruins	KIJHL	24	9	11	20				200																		
	Kelowna Spartans	BCJHL	3	0	0	0				9																		
	Vernon Lakers	BCJHL	12	0	1	1				18																		
	Penticton Panthers	BCJHL	3	0	0	0				13																		
1992-93	Spokane Chiefs	WHL	62	4	3	7				274												8	1	1	2	13			
1993-94	Spokane Chiefs	WHL	60	10	15	25				350												3	0	1	1	6			
1994-95	Spokane Chiefs	WHL	54	7	9	16				365												11	2	0	2	58			
	Peoria Rivermen	IHL																			2	0	0	0	12			
1995-96	**St. Louis Blues**	**NHL**	**6**	**0**	**0**	**0**	**0**	**0**	**0**	**23**	**0**	**0**	**0**	**1**	**0.0**	**0**	**0**	**2**	**0**	**–2**								
	Worcester IceCats	AHL	41	3	4	7				268																		
	Boston Bruins	**NHL**	**2**	**0**	**0**	**0**	**0**	**0**	**0**	**5**	**0**	**0**	**0**	**0**	**0.0**	**1**	**0**	**0**	**0**	**1**								
	Providence Bruins	AHL	4	0	0	0				29												4	0	1	1	9			
1996-97	**Boston Bruins**	**NHL**	**2**	**0**	**0**	**0**	**0**	**0**	**0**	**0**	**0**	**0**	**0**	**0**	**0.0**	**0**	**0**	**0**	**0**	**0**								
	Providence Bruins	AHL	60	8	9	17				367												6	0	0	0	32			
1997-98	Michigan K-Wings	IHL	60	2	5	7				*398												3	0	0	0	23			
1998-99	Worcester IceCats	AHL	70	8	14	22				299												4	0	1	1	4			
99-2000	**Phoenix Coyotes**	**NHL**	**3**	**0**	**0**	**0**	**0**	**0**	**0**	**12**	**0**	**0**	**0**	**0**	**0.0**	**1**	**0**	**0**	**0**	**1**								
	Springfield Falcons	AHL	56	4	8	12				321												4	0	0	0	6			
	NHL Totals		**13**	**0**	**0**	**0**	**0**	**0**	**0**	**40**	**0**	**0**	**0**	**1**	**0.0**	**2**	**0**	**2**	**0**									

Signed as a free agent by **St. Louis**, February 28, 1995. Traded to **Boston** by **St. Louis** with Steve Staios for Steve Leach, March 8, 1996. Signed as a free agent by **Dallas**, August 19, 1997. Signed as a free agent by **St. Louis**, September 4, 1998. Signed as a free agent by **Phoenix**, August 15, 1999. Signed as a free agent by **Anaheim**, July 13, 2000.

• SCAMURRA, Peter

Peter Vincent D – L. 6'3", 185 lbs. b: Buffalo, NY, 2/23/1955. Washington's 2nd, 19th overall, in 1975.

Season	Club	League	GP	G	A	Pts	AG	AA	APts	PIM	PP	SH	GW	S	%	TGF	PGF	TGA	PGA	+/-	GP	G	A	Pts	PIM	PP	SH	GW
1972-73	Niagara Falls Flyers	OJHL	55	12	30	42				48																		
1973-74	University of Wisconsin	WCHA	13	2	1	3				12																		
	Peterborough Petes	OMJHL	35	3	11	14				12																		
	Canada	WJC-A	5	1	0	1				8																		
1974-75	Peterborough Petes	OMJHL	62	12	40	52				45												11	2	5	7	12			
1975-76	**Washington Capitals**	**NHL**	**58**	**2**	**13**	**15**	**2**	**10**	**12**	**33**	**1**	**0**	**0**	**49**	**4.1**	**44**	**3**	**92**	**13**	**–38**								
	Richmond Robins	AHL	18	2	1	3				12																		
1976-77	**Washington Capitals**	**NHL**	**21**	**0**	**2**	**2**	**0**	**2**	**2**	**8**	**0**	**0**	**0**	**19**	**0.0**	**13**	**1**	**20**	**2**	**–6**								
	Springfield Indians	AHL	11	2	5	7				6																		
1977-78	Binghamton Dusters	AHL	13	2	2	4				20																		
1978-79	**Washington Capitals**	**NHL**	**30**	**3**	**5**	**8**	**3**	**4**	**7**	**12**	**0**	**1**	**0**	**26**	**11.5**	**33**	**1**	**61**	**16**	**–13**								
1979-80	**Washington Capitals**	**NHL**	**23**	**3**	**5**	**8**	**3**	**4**	**7**	**6**	**1**	**0**	**0**	**16**	**18.8**	**18**	**2**	**22**	**5**	**–1**								
1980-81	SaiPa Lappeenranta	Finland	14	1	3	4				10																		
	Binghamton Whalers	AHL	6	1	2	3				4																		
	NHL Totals		**132**	**8**	**25**	**33**	**8**	**20**	**28**	**59**	**2**	**1**	**0**	**110**	**7.3**	**108**	**7**	**195**	**36**									

OMJHL Second All-Star Team (1975)

• SCATCHARD, Dave

C – R. 6'2", 220 lbs. b: Hinton, Alta., 2/20/1976. Vancouver's 3rd, 42nd overall, in 1994.

Season	Club	League	GP	G	A	Pts	AG	AA	APts	PIM	PP	SH	GW	S	%	TGF	PGF	TGA	PGA	+/-	GP	G	A	Pts	PIM	PP	SH	GW
1991-92	Salmon Arm Selects	BCAHA	65	98	100	198				167																		
1992-93	Kimberley Dynamiters	BCJHL	51	20	23	43				61																		
1993-94	Portland Winter Hawks	WHL	47	9	11	20				46												10	2	1	3	4			
1994-95	Portland Winter Hawks	WHL	71	20	30	50				148												8	0	3	3	21			
1995-96	Portland Winter Hawks	WHL	59	19	28	47				146												7	1	8	9	14			
	Syracuse Crunch	AHL	1	0	0	0				0												15	2	5	7	29			
1996-97	Syracuse Crunch	AHL	26	8	7	15				65																		
1997-98	**Vancouver Canucks**	**NHL**	**76**	**13**	**11**	**24**	**15**	**11**	**26**	**165**	**0**	**0**	**1**	**85**	**15.3**	**30**	**2**	**35**	**3**	**–4**								
1998-99	**Vancouver Canucks**	**NHL**	**82**	**13**	**13**	**26**	**15**	**13**	**28**	**140**	**0**	**2**	**2**	**130**	**10.0**	**33**	**3**	**59**	**17**	**–12**								
99-2000	**Vancouver Canucks**	**NHL**	**21**	**0**	**4**	**4**	**0**	**4**	**4**	**24**	**0**	**0**	**0**	**25**	**0.0**	**7**	**0**	**13**	**3**	**–3**								
	New York Islanders	**NHL**	**44**	**12**	**14**	**26**	**13**	**13**	**26**	**93**	**0**	**1**	**1**	**103**	**11.7**	**30**	**0**	**35**	**5**	**0**								
	NHL Totals		**223**	**38**	**42**	**80**	**43**	**41**	**84**	**422**	**0**	**3**	**4**	**343**	**11.1**	**100**	**5**	**142**	**28**									

Traded to **NY Islanders** by **Vancouver** with Kevin Weekes and Bill Muckalt for Felix Potvin and NY Islanders' compensatory 2nd (later traded to New Jersey - New Jersey selected Teemu Laine) and 3rd (Thatcher Bell) round choices in 2000 Entry Draft, December 19, 1999.

• SCEVIOUR, Darin

RW – R. 5'10", 185 lbs. b: Lacombe, Alta., 11/30/1965. Chicago's 5th, 101st overall, in 1984.

Season	Club	League	GP	G	A	Pts	AG	AA	APts	PIM	PP	SH	GW	S	%	TGF	PGF	TGA	PGA	+/-	GP	G	A	Pts	PIM	PP	SH	GW
1981-82	Red Deer Rustlers	AAHA	64	55	67	122				87																		
1982-83	Lethbridge Broncos	WHL	64	9	17	26				45												17	8	0	8	9			
	Lethbridge Broncos	Mem-Cup	1	0	0	0				0																		
1983-84	Lethbridge Broncos	WHL	71	37	28	65				28												5	2	2	4	0			
1984-85	Lethbridge Broncos	WHL	67	39	36	75				37												4	2	2	4	0			

			REGULAR SEASON																		PLAYOFFS							
Season	Club	League	GP	G	A	Pts	AG	AA	APts	PIM	PP	SH	GW	S	%	TGF	PGF	TGA	PGA	+/–	GP	G	A	Pts	PIM	PP	SH	GW
1985-86	Nova Scotia Oilers	AHL	31	4	3	7				6																		
	Saginaw Generals	IHL	24	9	11	20				7											11	8	5	13	5			
1986-87	**Chicago Blackhawks**	**NHL**	**1**	**0**	**0**	**0**	**0**	**0**	**0**	**0**	**0**	**0**	**0**	**1**	**0.0**	**0**	**0**	**0**	**0**	**0**								
	Canada	Nat-Team	5	2	0	2				17																		
	Saginaw Generals	IHL	37	13	18	31				4											10	10	2	12	0			
1987-88	EV Duisburg	Germany-2	19	41	38	79															19	35	34	69				
1988-89	Neusser SC	Germany-2	30	30	32	62				14																		
1989-90	EHC Essen-West	Germany-2	36	40	49	89				30											13	14	19	33	10			
1990-91	EHC Essen-West	Germany-2	48	42	45	87				48																		
	NHL Totals		**1**	**0**	**0**	**0**	**0**	**0**	**0**	**0**	**0**	**0**	**0**	**1**	**0.0**	**0**	**0**	**0**	**0**									

• SCHAEFER, Peter

LW – L. 5'11", 195 lbs. b: Yellow Grass, Sask., 7/12/1977. Vancouver's 3rd, 66th overall, in 1995.

Season	Club	League	GP	G	A	Pts	AG	AA	APts	PIM	PP	SH	GW	S	%	TGF	PGF	TGA	PGA	+/–	GP	G	A	Pts	PIM	PP	SH	GW
1993-94	Yorkton Mallers	AAHA	32	27	14	41				133																		
	Brandon Wheat Kings	WHL	2	1	0	1				0																		
1994-95	Brandon Wheat Kings	WHL	68	27	32	59				34											18	5	3	8	18			
	Brandon Wheat Kings	Mem-Cup	4	3	0	3				0																		
1995-96	Brandon Wheat Kings	WHL	69	47	61	108				53											19	10	13	23	5			
	Brandon Wheat Kings	Mem-Cup	4	2	0	2				2																		
1996-97	Brandon Wheat Kings	WHL	61	49	74	123				85											6	1	4	5	4			
	Syracuse Crunch	AHL	5	0	3	3				0											3	1	3	4	14			
1997-98	Syracuse Crunch	AHL	73	19	44	63				41											5	2	1	3	2			
1998-99	**Vancouver Canucks**	**NHL**	**25**	**4**	**4**	**8**	**5**	**4**	**9**	**8**	**1**	**0**	**1**	**24**	**16.7**	**12**	**4**	**13**	**4**	**–1**								
	Syracuse Crunch	AHL	41	10	19	29				66																		
99-2000	**Vancouver Canucks**	**NHL**	**71**	**16**	**15**	**31**	**18**	**14**	**32**	**20**	**2**	**2**	**4**	**101**	**15.8**	**48**	**12**	**57**	**21**	**0**								
	Syracuse Crunch	AHL	2	0	0	0				2																		
	Canada	WC-A	8	1	0	1				4																		
	NHL Totals		**96**	**20**	**19**	**39**	**23**	**18**	**41**	**28**	**3**	**2**	**5**	**125**	**16.0**	**60**	**16**	**70**	**25**									

WHL East First All-Star Team (1996, 1997) • Canadian Major Junior First All-Star Team (1997)

• SCHAMEHORN, Kevin

Kevin Dean RW – R. 5'9", 185 lbs. b: Calgary, Alta., 7/28/1956. Detroit's 4th, 58th overall, in 1976.

Season	Club	League	GP	G	A	Pts	AG	AA	APts	PIM	PP	SH	GW	S	%	TGF	PGF	TGA	PGA	+/–	GP	G	A	Pts	PIM	PP	SH	GW
1973-74	Bellingham Blazers	BCJHL	58	17	8	25				293																		
	New Westminster Bruins	WCJHL	2	1	1	2				7											4	0	0	0	0			
1974-75	New Westminster Bruins	WCJHL	37	14	6	20				175											18	7	11	18	13			
	New Westminster Bruins	Mem-Cup	3	0	3	3				14																		
1975-76	New Westminster Bruins	WCJHL	62	32	42	74				276											17	8	9	17	68			
	New Westminster Bruins	Mem-Cup	4	0	0	0				24																		
1976-77	**Detroit Red Wings**	**NHL**	**3**	**0**	**0**	**0**	**0**	**0**	**0**	**9**	**0**	**0**	**0**	**1**	**0.0**	**0**	**0**	**1**	**0**	**–1**								
	Kalamazoo Wings	IHL	77	27	32	59				314											10	3	9	12	76			
1977-78	Kansas City Red Wings	CHL	36	5	3	8				113																		
	Kalamazoo Wings	IHL	39	18	14	32				144											7	1	3	4	65			
1978-79	Kalamazoo Wings	IHL	80	45	57	102				245											15	*15	9	24	60			
1979-80	**Detroit Red Wings**	**NHL**	**2**	**0**	**0**	**0**	**0**	**0**	**0**	**4**	**0**	**0**	**0**	**0**	**0.0**	**1**	**0**	**3**	**0**	**–2**								
	Adirondack Red Wings	AHL	60	10	13	23				145											5	0	0	0	13			
1980-81	**Los Angeles Kings**	**NHL**	**5**	**0**	**0**	**0**	**0**	**0**	**0**	**4**	**0**	**0**	**0**	**2**	**0.0**	**0**	**0**	**1**	**0**	**–1**								
	Rochester Americans	AHL	27	6	10	16				44																		
	Houston Apollos	CHL	26	7	9	16				43																		
1981-82	Kalamazoo Wings	IHL	75	38	27	65				113											5	1	2	3	25			
1982-83	Kalamazoo Wings	IHL	58	38	29	67				78											9	6	3	9	24			
1983-84	Kalamazoo Wings	IHL	76	37	31	68				154											3	0	2	2	9			
1984-85	Kalamazoo Wings	IHL	80	35	43	78				154											11	4	3	7	31			
1985-86	Milwaukee Admirals	IHL	82	47	34	81				101											5	1	3	4	4			
1986-87	Milwaukee Admirals	IHL	82	35	35	70				102											6	3	3	6	6			
1987-88	Milwaukee Admirals	IHL	57	17	19	36				122																		
	Flint Spirits	IHL	19	3	11	14				32																		
1988-89			STATISTICS NOT AVAILABLE																									
1989-90	Kalamazoo Wings	IHL	9	1	2	3				0																		
	NHL Totals		**10**	**0**	**0**	**0**	**0**	**0**	**0**	**17**	**0**	**0**	**0**	**3**	**0.0**	**1**	**0**	**5**	**0**									

Signed as a free agent by **LA Kings**, October 18, 1980. Traded to **Milwaukee** (IHL) by **Kalamazoo** (IHL) for John Flesch, October, 1985.

• SCHASTLIVY, Petr

LW – L. 6'1", 204 lbs. b: Angarsk, USSR, 4/18/1979. Ottawa's 5th, 101st overall, in 1998.

Season	Club	League	GP	G	A	Pts	AG	AA	APts	PIM	PP	SH	GW	S	%	TGF	PGF	TGA	PGA	+/–	GP	G	A	Pts	PIM	PP	SH	GW
1996-97	Yermak Angarsk-2	Russia-3	STATISTICS NOT AVAILABLE																									
1997-98	Torpedo Yaroslavl-2	Russia-3	47	15	9	24				34																		
	Torpedo Yaroslavl	Russia	4	0	0	0				0																		
1998-99	Torpedo Yaroslavl	Russia	40	6	1	7				28											6	0	0	0	2			
	Russia	WC-A	7	3	4	7				4																		
99-2000	**Ottawa Senators**	**NHL**	**13**	**2**	**5**	**7**	**2**	**5**	**7**	**2**	**1**	**0**	**1**	**22**	**9.1**	**9**	**2**	**3**	**0**	**4**	**1**	**0**	**0**	**0**	**0**	**0**	**0**	**0**
	Grand Rapids Griffins	IHL	46	16	12	28				10											17	8	7	15	6			
	NHL Totals		**13**	**2**	**5**	**7**	**2**	**5**	**7**	**2**	**1**	**0**	**1**	**22**	**9.1**	**9**	**2**	**3**	**0**		**1**	**0**	**0**	**0**	**0**	**0**	**0**	**0**

• SCHELLA, John

John Edward D – R. 6', 180 lbs. b: Port Arthur, Ont., 5/9/1947.

Season	Club	League	GP	G	A	Pts	AG	AA	APts	PIM	PP	SH	GW	S	%	TGF	PGF	TGA	PGA	+/–	GP	G	A	Pts	PIM	PP	SH	GW
1963-64	Fort William Canadiens	TBJHL	24	2	0	2				34											11	1	3	4	57			
	Fort William Canadiens	Mem-Cup	4	0	1	1				7																		
1964-65	Fort William Canadiens	TBJHL	24	6	16	22				131																		
	Fort William Beavers	TBSHL	2	0	0	0				0																		
1965-66	Fort William Canadiens	TBJHL	30	8	29	37				136																		
	Fort William Canadiens	Mem-Cup	7	2	0	2				6																		
1966-67	Peterborough Petes	OHA-Jr.	47	11	11	22				182											6	2	3	5	12			
1967-68	Houston Apollos	CPHL	39	5	2	7				110																		
1968-69	Denver Spurs	WHL	69	4	22	26				152																		
1969-70	Denver Spurs	WHL	67	7	30	37				198																		
1970-71	**Vancouver Canucks**	**NHL**	**38**	**0**	**5**	**5**	**0**	**4**	**4**	**58**	**0**	**0**	**0**	**29**	**0.0**	**17**	**0**	**40**	**18**	**–5**								
	Rochester Americans	AHL	33	3	14	17				118																		
1971-72	**Vancouver Canucks**	**NHL**	**77**	**2**	**13**	**15**	**2**	**11**	**13**	**166**	**0**	**0**	**0**	**107**	**1.9**	**59**	**2**	**127**	**41**	**–29**								
1972-73	Houston Aeros	WHA	77	2	24	26				*239											10	0	2	2	12			
1973-74	Houston Aeros	WHA	73	12	19	31				170											14	2	6	8	42			
1974-75	Houston Aeros	WHA	78	10	42	52				176											13	0	8	8	12			
1975-76	Houston Aeros	WHA	74	6	32	38				106											17	1	6	7	38			
1976-77	Houston Aeros	WHA	20	0	6	6				28											6	1	2	3	6			
1977-78	Houston Aeros	WHA	63	9	20	29				125											6	0	1	1	33			
1978-79	San Diego Mariners	PCL	58	6	21	27				145																		
	Binghamton Dusters	AHL	2	1	1	2				0											10	0	0	0	12			
	NHL Totals		**115**	**2**	**18**	**20**	**2**	**15**	**17**	**224**	**0**	**0**	**0**	**136**	**1.5**	**76**	**2**	**167**	**59**									
	Other Major League Totals		385	39	143	182				844											66	4	25	29	143			

Claimed by **Vancouver** from **Montreal** in Expansion Draft, June 10, 1970. Selected by **Dayton-Houston** (WHA) in 1972 WHA General Player Draft, February 12, 1972. Claimed by **NY Islanders** from **Vancouver** in Expansion Draft, June 6, 1972. • Missed majority of 1976-77 season recovering from thumb injury and spinal disc surgery.

• SCHINKEL, Ken Kenneth Calvin RW – R. 5'10", 172 lbs. b: Jansen, Sask., 11/27/1932.

			REGULAR SEASON																		PLAYOFFS							
Season	Club	League	GP	G	A	Pts	AG	AA	APts	PIM	PP	SH	GW	S	%	TGF	PGF	TGA	PGA	+/–	GP	G	A	Pts	PIM	PP	SH	GW
1951-52	Lindsay Bears	OHA-B	STATISTICS NOT AVAILABLE																									
1952-53	St. Catharines Teepees	OHA-Jr.	56	21	22	43				34											3	0	1	1	0			
1953-54	Springfield Indians	QHL	39	3	14	17				6																		
	Syracuse Warriors	AHL	28	7	14	21				4																		
1954-55	Pembroke Lumber Kings	NOHA	57	9	23	32				18											5	1	1	2	2			
1955-56	Springfield Indians	AHL	57	18	16	34				42																		
1956-57	Springfield Indians	AHL	64	22	36	58				2																		
1957-58	Springfield Indians	AHL	70	11	27	38				40											13	3	3	6	2			
1958-59	Springfield Indians	AHL	70	*43	42	85				19																		
1959-60	**New York Rangers**	**NHL**	**69**	**13**	**16**	**29**	**15**	**16**	**31**	**27**																		
1960-61	**New York Rangers**	**NHL**	**38**	**2**	**6**	**8**	**2**	**6**	**8**	**18**																		
	Springfield Indians	AHL	28	13	8	21				25											7	3	3	6	9			
1961-62	**New York Rangers**	**NHL**	**65**	**7**	**21**	**28**	**8**	**20**	**28**	**17**											**2**	**1**	**0**	**1**	**0**	**0**	**0**	**0**
1962-63	**New York Rangers**	**NHL**	**69**	**6**	**9**	**15**	**7**	**9**	**16**	**15**																		
1963-64	**New York Rangers**	**NHL**	**4**	**0**	**0**	**0**	**0**	**0**	**0**	**0**																		
	Baltimore Clippers	AHL	64	23	33	56				35																		
1964-65	Baltimore Clippers	AHL	72	30	41	71				16											5	1	2	3	0			
1965-66	Baltimore Clippers	AHL	72	30	45	75				31																		
1966-67	**New York Rangers**	**NHL**	**20**	**6**	**3**	**9**	**7**	**3**	**10**	**0**											**4**	**0**	**1**	**1**	**0**	**0**	**0**	**0**
	Baltimore Clippers	AHL	51	25	31	56				29																		
1967-68	**Pittsburgh Penguins**	**NHL**	**57**	**14**	**25**	**39**	**16**	**25**	**41**	**19**	**2**	**0**	**3**	**185**	**7.6**	**54**	**12**	**63**	**11**	**–10**								
1968-69	**Pittsburgh Penguins**	**NHL**	**76**	**18**	**34**	**52**	**19**	**30**	**49**	**18**	**8**	**1**	**2**	**226**	**8.0**	**71**	**25**	**90**	**5**	**–39**								
1969-70	**Pittsburgh Penguins**	**NHL**	**72**	**20**	**25**	**45**	**22**	**23**	**45**	**19**	**4**	**0**	**5**	**225**	**8.9**	**62**	**18**	**73**	**3**	**–26**	**10**	**4**	**1**	**5**	**4**	**1**	**0**	**0**
1970-71	**Pittsburgh Penguins**	**NHL**	**50**	**15**	**19**	**34**	**15**	**16**	**31**	**6**	**3**	**0**	**1**	**120**	**12.5**	**48**	**23**	**44**	**0**	**–19**								
1971-72	**Pittsburgh Penguins**	**NHL**	**74**	**15**	**30**	**45**	**15**	**26**	**41**	**8**	**1**	**0**	**1**	**154**	**9.7**	**65**	**15**	**63**	**3**	**–10**	**3**	**2**	**0**	**2**	**0**	**0**	**0**	**0**
1972-73	**Pittsburgh Penguins**	**NHL**	**42**	**11**	**10**	**21**	**10**	**8**	**18**	**16**	**1**	**0**	**2**	**79**	**13.9**	**29**	**6**	**36**	**3**	**–10**								
	NHL Totals		**636**	**127**	**198**	**325**	**136**	**182**	**318**	**163**											**19**	**7**	**2**	**9**	**4**			

AHL Second All-Star Team (1959) • Played in NHL All-Star Game (1968, 1969)

Traded to **NY Rangers** by **Springfield** (AHL) for future considerations, June, 1959. Claimed by **Pittsburgh** from **NY Rangers** in Expansion Draft, June 6, 1967.

• SCHLEGEL, Brad Brad Wilfred D – R. 5'10", 188 lbs. b: Kitchener, Ont., 7/22/1968. Washington's 8th, 144th overall, in 1988.

Season	Club	League	GP	G	A	Pts	AG	AA	APts	PIM	PP	SH	GW	S	%	TGF	PGF	TGA	PGA	+/–	GP	G	A	Pts	PIM	PP	SH	GW
1984-85	Kitchener Dutchmen	OMHA	40	30	50	80				70																		
	Kitchener Ranger B's	OJHL-B	1	0	0	0				0																		
1985-86	London Knights	OHL	62	2	13	15				35											5	0	0	0	4			
1986-87	London Knights	OHL	65	4	23	27				24																		
1987-88	London Knights	OHL	66	13	63	76				49											12	8	17	25	6			
1988-89	Canada	Nat-Team	60	2	22	24				30																		
1989-90	Canada	Nat-Team	72	7	25	32				44																		
1990-91	Canada	Nat-Team	59	8	20	28				64																		
	Canada	WEC-A	10	0	1	1				6																		
1991-92	Canada	Nat-Team	61	3	18	21				84																		
	Canada	Olympics	8	1	2	3				4																		
	Washington Capitals	**NHL**	**15**	**0**	**1**	**1**	**0**	**1**	**1**	**0**	**0**	**0**	**0**	**7**	**0.0**	**6**	**1**	**10**	**1**	**–4**	**7**	**0**	**1**	**1**	**2**	**0**	**0**	**0**
	Baltimore Skipjacks	AHL	2	0	1	1				0																		
	Canada	WC-A	3	0	0	0				2																		
1992-93	**Washington Capitals**	**NHL**	**7**	**0**	**1**	**1**	**0**	**1**	**1**	**6**	**0**	**0**	**0**	**8**	**0.0**	**3**	**0**	**3**	**1**	**1**								
	Baltimore Skipjacks	AHL	61	3	20	23				40											7	0	5	5	6			
1993-94	**Calgary Flames**	**NHL**	**26**	**1**	**6**	**7**	**1**	**5**	**6**	**4**	**0**	**0**	**0**	**24**	**4.2**	**14**	**3**	**21**	**6**	**–4**								
	Saint John Flames	AHL	21	2	8	10				6											7	0	1	1	6			
	Canada	Nat-Team	4	0	0	0				2																		
	Canada	Olympics	8	0	0	0				6																		
1994-95	VSV Villach	Austria	28	7	26	33				40											12	1	11	12	44			
	Canada	Nat-Team	4	0	1	1				2																		
	Canada	WC-A	8	0	3	3				12																		
1995-96	VSV Villach	Alpenliga	24	5	18	23				18																		
	EHC Hannover	Germany	26	1	16	17				34											2	0	0	0	0			
1996-97	VSV Villach	Alpenliga	49	3	29	32				103																		
1997-98	VSV Villach	Alpenliga	19	5	14	19				32																		
	VSV Villach	Austria	19	1	13	14				10											5	1	3	4	4			
1998-99	VSV Villach	Alpenliga	32	7	20	27				18																		
	VSV Villach	Austria	23	1	8	9				34																		
99-2000	VSV Villach	IEL	31	3	8	11				63																		
	VSV Villach	EuroHL	6	0	0	0				4																		
	VSV Villach	Austria	15	0	4	4				12																		
	NHL Totals		**48**	**1**	**8**	**9**	**1**	**7**	**8**	**10**	**0**	**0**	**0**	**39**	**2.6**	**23**	**4**	**34**	**8**		**7**	**0**	**1**	**1**	**2**	**0**	**0**	**0**

OHL Second All-Star Team (1988)

Traded to **Calgary** by **Washington** for Calgary's 7th round choice (Andrew Brunette) in 1993 Entry Draft, June 26, 1993.

• SCHLIEBENER, Andy Andreas D – L. 6', 200 lbs. b: Ottawa, Ont., 8/16/1962. Vancouver's 2nd, 49th overall, in 1980.

Season	Club	League	GP	G	A	Pts	AG	AA	APts	PIM	PP	SH	GW	S	%	TGF	PGF	TGA	PGA	+/–	GP	G	A	Pts	PIM	PP	SH	GW
1978-79	Stratford Cullitons	OHA-B	42	20	31	51				17																		
1979-80	Peterborough Petes	OMJHL	68	8	20	28				47											14	2	8	10	6			
1980-81	Peterborough Petes	OMJHL	68	9	48	57				144											5	1	3	4	4			
1981-82	Peterborough Petes	OHL	14	1	9	10				25																		
	Niagara Falls Flyers	OHL	27	6	26	32				33											5	3	5	8	14			
	Dallas Black Hawks	CHL	8	2	2	4				4											9	0	4	4	10			
	Vancouver Canucks	**NHL**	**22**	**0**	**1**	**1**	**0**	**1**	**1**	**10**	**0**	**0**	**0**	**19**	**0.0**	**13**	**0**	**27**	**3**	**–11**	**3**	**0**	**0**	**0**	**0**	**0**	**0**	**0**
1982-83	Fredericton Express	AHL	76	4	15	19				20											10	0	3	3	7			
1983-84	**Vancouver Canucks**	**NHL**	**51**	**2**	**10**	**12**	**2**	**7**	**9**	**48**	**0**	**0**	**0**	**62**	**3.2**	**42**	**8**	**49**	**6**	**–9**	**3**	**0**	**0**	**0**	**0**	**0**	**0**	**0**
	Fredericton Express	AHL	27	1	6	7				27																		
1984-85	**Vancouver Canucks**	**NHL**	**11**	**0**	**0**	**0**	**0**	**0**	**0**	**16**	**0**	**0**	**0**	**6**	**0.0**	**3**	**0**	**17**	**3**	**–11**								
	Fredericton Express	AHL	47	1	11	12				58																		
1985-86	Fredericton Express	AHL	73	3	9	12				60											6	0	1	1	10			
	NHL Totals		**84**	**2**	**11**	**13**	**2**	**8**	**10**	**74**	**0**	**0**	**0**	**87**	**2.3**	**58**	**8**	**93**	**12**		**6**	**0**	**0**	**0**	**0**	**0**	**0**	**0**

• SCHMAUTZ, Bobby Robert James "Dr. Hook" RW – R. 5'9", 172 lbs. b: Saskatoon, Sask., 3/28/1945.

Season	Club	League	GP	G	A	Pts	AG	AA	APts	PIM	PP	SH	GW	S	%	TGF	PGF	TGA	PGA	+/–	GP	G	A	Pts	PIM	PP	SH	GW
1962-63	Saskatoon Jr. Quakers	SJHL	54	28	31	59				42																		
	Saskatoon Quakers	SSHL																			7	1	1	2	0			
1963-64	Saskatoon Jr. Quakers	SJHL	60	55	43	98				114											12	12	12	24	20			
1964-65	Saskatoon Blades	SJHL	44	45	34	79				113											5	4	4	8	10			
	Los Angeles Blades	WHL	5	0	1	1				0																		
1965-66	Los Angeles Blades	WHL	70	7	16	23				27																		
1966-67	Los Angeles Blades	WHL	37	3	7	10				19																		
1967-68	**Chicago Black Hawks**	**NHL**	**13**	**3**	**2**	**5**	**3**	**2**	**5**	**6**	**0**	**0**	**1**	**27**	**11.1**	**9**	**0**	**11**	**3**	**1**	**11**	**2**	**3**	**5**	**2**	**0**	**0**	**1**
	Dallas Black Hawks	CPHL	54	23	23	46				83																		
1968-69	**Chicago Black Hawks**	**NHL**	**63**	**9**	**7**	**16**	**9**	**6**	**15**	**37**	**3**	**0**	**1**	**81**	**11.1**	**32**	**9**	**29**	**1**	**–5**								
1969-70	Salt Lake–Seattle	WHL	66	32	27	59				89											3	0	2	2	5			
1970-71	Seattle Totems	WHL	42	16	21	37				59																		
	Vancouver Canucks	**NHL**	**26**	**5**	**5**	**10**	**5**	**4**	**9**	**14**	**0**	**0**	**0**	**64**	**7.8**	**18**	**1**	**17**	**2**	**2**								

Season	Club	League	REGULAR SEASON																		PLAYOFFS							
			GP	G	A	Pts	AG	AA	APts	PIM	PP	SH	GW	S	%	TGF	PGF	TGA	PGA	+/–	GP	G	A	Pts	PIM	PP	SH	GW
1971-72	**Vancouver Canucks**	**NHL**	**60**	**12**	**13**	**25**	**12**	**11**	**23**	**82**	**1**	**0**	**0**	**137**	**8.8**	**40**	**5**	**50**	**5**	**–10**	....	....	....	....	....	....	....	....
	Rochester Americans	AHL	7	7	8	15	....	....	....	8	....	....	....	....	....	....	....	....	....	....	....	....	....	....	....	....	....	....
1972-73	**Vancouver Canucks**	**NHL**	**77**	**38**	**33**	**71**	**36**	**26**	**62**	**137**	**5**	**0**	**5**	**263**	**14.4**	**100**	**25**	**104**	**12**	**–17**	....	....	....	....	....	....	....	....
1973-74	**Vancouver Canucks**	**NHL**	**49**	**26**	**19**	**45**	**25**	**16**	**41**	**58**	**8**	**2**	**3**	**164**	**15.9**	**63**	**21**	**58**	**16**	**0**	....	....	....	....	....	....	....	....
	Boston Bruins	**NHL**	**27**	**7**	**13**	**20**	**7**	**11**	**18**	**31**	**1**	**0**	**1**	**62**	**11.3**	**34**	**5**	**23**	**0**	**6**	**16**	**3**	**6**	**9**	**44**	**0**	**0**	**0**
1974-75	**Boston Bruins**	**NHL**	**56**	**21**	**30**	**51**	**18**	**22**	**40**	**63**	**1**	**0**	**2**	**156**	**13.5**	**80**	**12**	**56**	**11**	**23**	**3**	**1**	**5**	**6**	**6**	**0**	**0**	**0**
1975-76	**Boston Bruins**	**NHL**	**75**	**28**	**34**	**62**	**25**	**25**	**50**	**116**	**7**	**0**	**7**	**243**	**11.5**	**105**	**44**	**62**	**14**	**13**	**11**	**2**	**8**	**10**	**13**	**0**	**0**	**1**
1976-77	**Boston Bruins**	**NHL**	**57**	**23**	**29**	**52**	**21**	**22**	**43**	**62**	**4**	**0**	**2**	**177**	**13.0**	**89**	**19**	**46**	**1**	**25**	**14**	***11**	**1**	**12**	**10**	**4**	**0**	**1**
1977-78	**Boston Bruins**	**NHL**	**54**	**27**	**27**	**54**	**25**	**21**	**46**	**87**	**4**	**3**	**6**	**174**	**15.5**	**73**	**23**	**33**	**7**	**24**	**15**	**7**	**8**	**15**	**11**	**2**	**0**	**1**
1978-79	**Boston Bruins**	**NHL**	**65**	**20**	**22**	**42**	**17**	**16**	**33**	**77**	**6**	**1**	**4**	**199**	**10.1**	**69**	**24**	**73**	**27**	**–1**	**11**	**2**	**2**	**4**	**6**	**1**	**0**	**0**
1979-80	**Boston Bruins**	**NHL**	**20**	**8**	**6**	**14**	**7**	**4**	**11**	**8**	**4**	**0**	**0**	**40**	**20.0**	**24**	**10**	**17**	**2**	**–1**	....	....	....	....	....	....	....	....
	Edmonton Oilers	**NHL**	**29**	**8**	**8**	**16**	**7**	**6**	**13**	**20**	**2**	**0**	**0**	**46**	**17.4**	**21**	**4**	**21**	**0**	**–4**	....	....	....	....	....	....	....	....
	Colorado Rockies	**NHL**	**20**	**9**	**4**	**13**	**8**	**3**	**11**	**53**	**2**	**1**	**1**	**66**	**13.6**	**22**	**6**	**29**	**3**	**–10**	....	....	....	....	....	....	....	....
1980-81	**Vancouver Canucks**	**NHL**	**73**	**27**	**34**	**61**	**21**	**23**	**44**	**137**	**9**	**0**	**3**	**205**	**13.2**	**95**	**36**	**65**	**1**	**–5**	**3**	**0**	**0**	**0**	**0**	**0**	**0**	**0**
	NHL Totals		**764**	**271**	**286**	**557**	**246**	**218**	**464**	**988**	**57**	**7**	**36**	**2104**	**12.9**	**874**	**244**	**694**	**105**		**84**	**28**	**33**	**61**	**92**	**7**	**0**	**4**

• Brother of Cliff • SJHL Second All-Star Team (1964) • SJHL First All-Star Team (1965) • Played in NHL All-Star Game (1973, 1974)

Traded to **Seattle** (WHL) by **Chicago** (LA Blades-WHL) with Marc Boileau for cash with Chicago retaining NHL rights, August 10, 1967. Claimed by **St. Louis** from **Chicago** in Intra-League Draft, June 11, 1969. Traded to **Montreal** by **St. Louis** with Norm Beaudin for Ernie Wakely, June 27, 1969. Traded to **Salt Lake** (WHL) by **Montreal** for cash, August, 1969. Traded to **Seattle** (WHL) by **Salt Lake** (WHL) for Guyle Fielder, November 15, 1969. Traded to **Vancouver** by **Seattle** (WHL) for the loan of Jim Wiste and Ed Hatoum for the remainder of the 1970-71 season, February 9, 1971. Traded to **Boston** by **Vancouver** for Fred O'Donnell and Chris Oddleifson, February 7, 1974. Traded to **Edmonton** by **Boston** for Dan Newman, December 10, 1979. Traded to **Colorado** by **Edmonton** for Don Ashby, February 25, 1980. Signed as a free agent by **Vancouver**, October 2, 1980.

• SCHMAUTZ, Cliff

Clifford Harvey RW – R. 5'10", 165 lbs. b: Saskatoon, Sask., 3/17/1939.

Season	Club	League	GP	G	A	Pts	AG	AA	APts	PIM	PP	SH	GW	S	%	TGF	PGF	TGA	PGA	+/–	GP	G	A	Pts	PIM	PP	SH	GW
1956-57	Saskatoon Jr. Quakers	SJHL	47	9	10	19	....	....	....	65	....	....	....	....	....	....	....	....	....	....	....	....	....	....	....	....	....	....
1957-58	Saskatoon Jr. Quakers	SJHL	33	10	16	26	....	....	....	58	....	....	....	....	....	....	....	....	....	....	....	....	....	....	....	....	....	....
1958-59	Weyburn–Moose Jaw	SJHL	42	33	32	65	....	....	....	90	....	....	....	....	....	....	....	....	....	....	....	....	....	....	....	....	....	....
	Nelson Maple Leafs	WIHL	2	0	1	1	....	....	....	6	....	....	....	....	....	....	....	....	....	....	....	....	....	....	....	....	....	....
1959-60	Omaha Knights	IHL	63	32	20	52	....	....	....	91	....	....	....	....	....	....	....	....	....	....	....	....	....	....	....	....	....	....
	Calgary Stampeders	WHL	5	1	1	2	....	....	....	11	....	....	....	....	....	....	....	....	....	....	....	....	....	....	....	....	....	....
1960-61	Sault Ste. Marie Thunderbirds	EPHL	70	32	20	52	....	....	....	91	....	....	....	....	....	....	....	....	....	....	12	7	6	13	4	....	....	....
1961-62	Sault Ste. Marie Thunderbirds	EPHL	24	6	9	15	....	....	....	24	....	....	....	....	....	....	....	....	....	....	....	....	....	....	....	....	....	....
	Buffalo Bisons	AHL	43	14	13	27	....	....	....	29	....	....	....	....	....	....	....	....	....	....	4	0	0	0	12	....	....	....
1962-63	Buffalo Bisons	AHL	64	24	15	39	....	....	....	24	....	....	....	....	....	....	....	....	....	....	13	8	4	12	4	....	....	....
1963-64	Buffalo Bisons	AHL	26	3	7	10	....	....	....	6	....	....	....	....	....	....	....	....	....	....	....	....	....	....	....	....	....	....
	Portland Buckaroos	WHL	34	7	7	14	....	....	....	22	....	....	....	....	....	....	....	....	....	....	5	2	3	5	2	....	....	....
1964-65	Portland Buckaroos	WHL	66	17	42	59	....	....	....	84	....	....	....	....	....	....	....	....	....	....	10	3	2	5	0	....	....	....
1965-66	Portland Buckaroos	WHL	72	*46	58	*104	....	....	....	47	....	....	....	....	....	....	....	....	....	....	14	9	7	16	17	....	....	....
1966-67	Portland Buckaroos	WHL	66	28	29	57	....	....	....	53	....	....	....	....	....	....	....	....	....	....	4	2	1	3	2	....	....	....
1967-68	Portland Buckaroos	WHL	69	26	33	59	....	....	....	36	....	....	....	....	....	....	....	....	....	....	12	*7	4	11	4	....	....	....
1968-69	Portland Buckaroos	WHL	53	27	29	56	....	....	....	28	....	....	....	....	....	....	....	....	....	....	11	*10	4	*14	4	....	....	....
1969-70	Portland Buckaroos	WHL	70	40	33	73	....	....	....	23	....	....	....	....	....	....	....	....	....	....	11	6	6	12	6	....	....	....
1970-71	**Buffalo Sabres**	**NHL**	**26**	**5**	**7**	**12**	**5**	**6**	**11**	**10**	**2**	**0**	**0**	**44**	**11.4**	**19**	**11**	**19**	**0**	**–11**	....	....	....	....	....	....	....	....
	Philadelphia Flyers	**NHL**	**30**	**8**	**12**	**20**	**8**	**10**	**18**	**23**	**0**	**0**	**2**	**65**	**12.3**	**30**	**11**	**16**	**0**	**3**	....	....	....	....	....	....	....	....
1971-72	Portland Buckaroos	WHL	68	40	37	77	....	....	....	44	....	....	....	....	....	....	....	....	....	....	11	6	2	8	2	....	....	....
1972-73	Portland Buckaroos	WHL	54	30	21	51	....	....	....	47	....	....	....	....	....	....	....	....	....	....	....	....	....	....	....	....	....	....
1973-74			DID NOT PLAY																									
1974-75	Portland Buckaroos	WIHL	34	11	8	19	....	....	....	8	....	....	....	....	....	....	....	....	....	....	....	....	....	....	....	....	....	....
	NHL Totals		**56**	**13**	**19**	**32**	**13**	**16**	**29**	**33**	**2**	**0**	**2**	**109**	**11.9**	**49**	**22**	**35**	**0**		....	....	....	....	....	....	....	....

• Brother of Bobby • WHL First All-Star Team (1966) • WHL Second All-Star Team (1972)

Traded to **Portland** (WHL) by **Buffalo** (AHL) for Pat Hannigan, December, 1963. Claimed by **Buffalo** from **Portland** (WHL) in Inter-League Draft, June 9, 1970. Claimed on waivers by **Philadelphia** from **Buffalo**, December 28, 1970. Traded to **Portland** (WHL) by **Philadelphia** for cash, September, 1971.

• SCHMIDT, Norm

Norman W. D – R. 5'11", 190 lbs. b: Sault Ste. Marie, Ont., 1/24/1963. Pittsburgh's 3rd, 70th overall, in 1981.

Season	Club	League	GP	G	A	Pts	AG	AA	APts	PIM	PP	SH	GW	S	%	TGF	PGF	TGA	PGA	+/–	GP	G	A	Pts	PIM	PP	SH	GW
1979-80	Sault Ste. Marie Thunderbirds	NOJHA	18	8	16	24	....	....	....	....	....	....	....	....	....	....	....	....	....	....	....	....	....	....	....	....	....	....
1980-81	Oshawa Generals	OMJHL	65	12	25	37	....	....	....	73	....	....	....	....	....	....	....	....	....	....	11	2	5	7	25	....	....	....
1981-82	Oshawa Generals	OHL	67	13	48	61	....	....	....	172	....	....	....	....	....	....	....	....	....	....	....	....	....	....	....	....	....	....
1982-83	Oshawa Generals	OHL	61	21	49	70	....	....	....	114	....	....	....	....	....	....	....	....	....	....	17	4	16	20	47	....	....	....
	Oshawa Generals	Mem-Cup	5	4	1	5	....	....	....	10	....	....	....	....	....	....	....	....	....	....	....	....	....	....	....	....	....	....
1983-84	**Pittsburgh Penguins**	**NHL**	**34**	**6**	**12**	**18**	**5**	**8**	**13**	**12**	**0**	**0**	**0**	**56**	**10.7**	**38**	**5**	**39**	**5**	**–1**	....	....	....	....	....	....	....	....
	Baltimore Skipjacks	AHL	43	4	12	16	....	....	....	31	....	....	....	....	....	....	....	....	....	....	....	....	....	....	....	....	....	....
1984-85	Baltimore Skipjacks	AHL	33	0	22	22	....	....	....	31	....	....	....	....	....	....	....	....	....	....	....	....	....	....	....	....	....	....
1985-86	**Pittsburgh Penguins**	**NHL**	**66**	**15**	**14**	**29**	**12**	**9**	**21**	**57**	**3**	**0**	**0**	**141**	**10.6**	**87**	**20**	**78**	**18**	**7**	....	....	....	....	....	....	....	....
1986-87	**Pittsburgh Penguins**	**NHL**	**20**	**1**	**5**	**6**	**1**	**4**	**5**	**4**	**1**	**0**	**0**	**32**	**3.1**	**16**	**5**	**22**	**3**	**–8**	....	....	....	....	....	....	....	....
	Baltimore Skipjacks	AHL	36	4	7	11	....	....	....	25	....	....	....	....	....	....	....	....	....	....	....	....	....	....	....	....	....	....
1987-88	**Pittsburgh Penguins**	**NHL**	**5**	**1**	**2**	**3**	**1**	**1**	**2**	**0**	**0**	**0**	**0**	**13**	**7.7**	**8**	**5**	**2**	**0**	**1**	....	....	....	....	....	....	....	....
	NHL Totals		**125**	**23**	**33**	**56**	**19**	**22**	**41**	**73**	**4**	**0**	**0**	**242**	**9.5**	**149**	**35**	**141**	**26**		....	....	....	....	....	....	....	....

OHL Second All-Star Team (1983)

• Suffered career-ending back injury in game vs. Philadelphia, October 18, 1987.

• SCHNEIDER, Andy

LW – L. 5'9", 170 lbs. b: Edmonton, Alta., 3/29/1972.

Season	Club	League	GP	G	A	Pts	AG	AA	APts	PIM	PP	SH	GW	S	%	TGF	PGF	TGA	PGA	+/–	GP	G	A	Pts	PIM	PP	SH	GW
1987-88	Edmonton Scott Pump	AAHA	35	26	49	75	....	....	....	44	....	....	....	....	....	....	....	....	....	....	....	....	....	....	....	....	....	....
1988-89	Seattle Thunderbirds	WHL	69	7	26	33	....	....	....	43	....	....	....	....	....	....	....	....	....	....	....	....	....	....	....	....	....	....
1989-90	Seattle Thunderbirds	WHL	28	10	12	22	....	....	....	55	....	....	....	....	....	....	....	....	....	....	....	....	....	....	....	....	....	....
	Swift Current Broncos	WHL	42	16	21	37	....	....	....	43	....	....	....	....	....	....	....	....	....	....	....	....	....	....	....	....	....	....
1990-91	Swift Current Broncos	WHL	69	12	74	86	....	....	....	103	....	....	....	....	....	....	....	....	....	....	3	0	0	0	2	....	....	....
1991-92	Swift Current Broncos	WHL	63	44	60	104	....	....	....	120	....	....	....	....	....	....	....	....	....	....	8	4	9	13	8	....	....	....
	Canada	WJC-A	7	0	0	0	....	....	....	6	....	....	....	....	....	....	....	....	....	....	....	....	....	....	....	....	....	....
1992-93	Swift Current Broncos	WHL	38	19	66	85	....	....	....	78	....	....	....	....	....	....	....	....	....	....	17	13	*26	*39	40	....	....	....
	New Haven Senators	AHL	19	2	2	4	....	....	....	13	....	....	....	....	....	....	....	....	....	....	....	....	....	....	....	....	....	....
	Swift Current Broncos	Mem-Cup	4	2	5	7	....	....	....	4	....	....	....	....	....	....	....	....	....	....	....	....	....	....	....	....	....	....
1993-94	**Ottawa Senators**	**NHL**	**10**	**0**	**0**	**0**	**0**	**0**	**0**	**15**	**0**	**0**	**0**	**4**	**0.0**	**0**	**0**	**6**	**0**	**–6**	....	....	....	....	....	....	....	....
	P.E.I. Senators	AHL	61	15	46	61	....	....	....	119	....	....	....	....	....	....	....	....	....	....	....	....	....	....	....	....	....	....
1994-95	Leksands IF	Sweden	39	6	8	14	....	....	....	71	....	....	....	....	....	....	....	....	....	....	4	1	1	2	31	....	....	....
	Canada	Nat-Team	3	1	0	1	....	....	....	0	....	....	....	....	....	....	....	....	....	....	....	....	....	....	....	....	....	....
	P.E.I. Senators	AHL	10	1	5	6	....	....	....	25	....	....	....	....	....	....	....	....	....	....	11	5	5	10	11	....	....	....
1995-96	Minnesota Moose	IHL	81	12	28	40	....	....	....	85	....	....	....	....	....	....	....	....	....	....	....	....	....	....	....	....	....	....
1996-97	Manitoba Moose	IHL	79	14	37	51	....	....	....	142	....	....	....	....	....	....	....	....	....	....	....	....	....	....	....	....	....	....
1997-98	Revier Lowen	Germany	26	3	12	15	....	....	....	46	....	....	....	....	....	....	....	....	....	....	....	....	....	....	....	....	....	....
	Schwenningen Wild Wings	Germany	22	7	13	20	....	....	....	91	....	....	....	....	....	....	....	....	....	....	....	....	....	....	....	....	....	....
1998-99	Schwenningen Wild Wings	Germany	52	17	29	46	....	....	....	90	....	....	....	....	....	....	....	....	....	....	....	....	....	....	....	....	....	....
99-2000	Schwenningen Wild Wings	Germany	68	19	35	54	....	....	....	82	....	....	....	....	....	....	....	....	....	....	....	....	....	....	....	....	....	....
	NHL Totals		**10**	**0**	**0**	**0**	**0**	**0**	**0**	**15**	**0**	**0**	**0**	**4**	**0.0**	**0**	**0**	**6**	**0**		....	....	....	....	....	....	....	....

WHL East Second All-Star Team (1993)

Signed as a free agent by **Ottawa**, October 9, 1992.

• SCHNEIDER, Mathieu

D – L. 5'10", 192 lbs. b: New York, NY, 6/12/1969. Montreal's 4th, 44th overall, in 1987.

			REGULAR SEASON																		PLAYOFFS							
Season	Club	League	GP	G	A	Pts	AG	AA	APts	PIM	PP	SH	GW	S	%	TGF	PGF	TGA	PGA	+/–	GP	G	A	Pts	PIM	PP	SH	GW
1985-86	Mount St. Charles Mounties	Hi-School	19	3	27	30	....	....	....	....	....	....	....	....	....	....	....	....	....	....	....	....	....	....	....	....	....	....
1986-87	Cornwall Royals	OHL	63	7	29	36	....	....	....	75	....	....	....	....	....	....	....	....	....	....	5	0	0	0	22	....	....	....
1987-88	Cornwall Royals	OHL	48	21	40	61	....	....	....	83	....	....	....	....	....	....	....	....	....	....	11	2	6	8	14	....	....	....
	United States	WJC-A	7	0	2	2	....	....	....	16	....	....	....	....	....	....	....	....	....	....	....	....	....	....	....	....	....	....
	Montreal Canadiens	**NHL**	**4**	**0**	**0**	**0**	**0**	**0**	**0**	**2**	**0**	**0**	**0**	**2**	**0.0**	**1**	**0**	**2**	**0**	**–1**	....	....	....	....	....	....	....	....
	Sherbrooke Canadiens	AHL	....	....	....	....	....	....	....	....	....	....	....	....	....	....	....	....	....	....	3	0	3	3	12	....	....	....
1988-89	Cornwall Royals	OHL	59	16	57	73	....	....	....	96	....	....	....	....	....	....	....	....	....	....	18	7	20	27	30	....	....	....
1989-90	**Montreal Canadiens**	**NHL**	**44**	**7**	**14**	**21**	**6**	**10**	**16**	**25**	**5**	**0**	**1**	**84**	**8.3**	**57**	**16**	**53**	**14**	**2**	**9**	**1**	**3**	**4**	**31**	**1**	**0**	**0**
	Sherbrooke Canadiens	AHL	28	6	13	19	....	....	....	20	....	....	....	....	....	....	....	....	....	....	....	....	....	....	....	....	....	....
1990-91	Montreal Canadiens	Fr-Tour	3	0	1	1	....	....	....	12	....	....	....	....	....	....	....	....	....	....	....	....	....	....	....	....	....	....
	Montreal Canadiens	**NHL**	**69**	**10**	**20**	**30**	**9**	**15**	**24**	**63**	**5**	**0**	**3**	**164**	**6.1**	**98**	**33**	**75**	**17**	**7**	**13**	**2**	**7**	**9**	**18**	**1**	**0**	**0**
1991-92	**Montreal Canadiens**	**NHL**	**78**	**8**	**24**	**32**	**7**	**18**	**25**	**72**	**2**	**0**	**1**	**194**	**4.1**	**107**	**41**	**75**	**19**	**10**	**10**	**1**	**4**	**5**	**6**	**1**	**0**	**0**
1992-93♦	**Montreal Canadiens**	**NHL**	**60**	**13**	**31**	**44**	**11**	**21**	**32**	**91**	**3**	**0**	**2**	**169**	**7.7**	**100**	**33**	**82**	**23**	**8**	**11**	**1**	**2**	**3**	**16**	**0**	**0**	**0**
1993-94	**Montreal Canadiens**	**NHL**	**75**	**20**	**32**	**52**	**19**	**25**	**44**	**62**	**11**	**0**	**4**	**193**	**10.4**	**119**	**48**	**86**	**30**	**15**	**1**	**0**	**0**	**0**	**0**	**0**	**0**	**0**
1994-95	**Montreal Canadiens**	**NHL**	**30**	**5**	**15**	**20**	**9**	**22**	**31**	**49**	**2**	**0**	**0**	**82**	**6.1**	**39**	**13**	**38**	**9**	**–3**	....	....	....	....	....	....	....	....
	New York Islanders	**NHL**	**13**	**3**	**6**	**9**	**5**	**9**	**14**	**30**	**1**	**0**	**2**	**36**	**8.3**	**20**	**7**	**26**	**8**	**–5**	....	....	....	....	....	....	....	....
1995-96	**New York Islanders**	**NHL**	**65**	**11**	**36**	**47**	**11**	**30**	**41**	**93**	**7**	**0**	**1**	**155**	**7.1**	**103**	**49**	**103**	**31**	**–18**	....	....	....	....	....	....	....	....
	Toronto Maple Leafs	**NHL**	**13**	**2**	**5**	**7**	**2**	**4**	**6**	**10**	**0**	**0**	**0**	**36**	**5.6**	**18**	**12**	**10**	**2**	**–2**	**6**	**0**	**4**	**4**	**8**	**0**	**0**	**0**
1996-97	United States	W-Cup	7	2	0	2	....	....	....	8	....	....	....	....	....	....	....	....	....	....	....	....	....	....	....	....	....	....
	Toronto Maple Leafs	**NHL**	**26**	**5**	**7**	**12**	**5**	**6**	**11**	**20**	**1**	**0**	**1**	**63**	**7.9**	**37**	**10**	**27**	**3**	**3**	....	....	....	....	....	....	....	....
1997-98	**Toronto Maple Leafs**	**NHL**	**76**	**11**	**26**	**37**	**13**	**25**	**38**	**44**	**4**	**1**	**1**	**181**	**6.1**	**89**	**32**	**89**	**20**	**–12**	....	....	....	....	....	....	....	....
	United States	Olympics	4	0	0	0	....	....	....	6	....	....	....	....	....	....	....	....	....	....	....	....	....	....	....	....	....	....
1998-99	**New York Rangers**	**NHL**	**75**	**10**	**24**	**34**	**12**	**23**	**35**	**71**	**5**	**0**	**2**	**159**	**6.3**	**85**	**38**	**80**	**14**	**–19**	....	....	....	....	....	....	....	....
99-2000	**New York Rangers**	**NHL**	**80**	**10**	**20**	**30**	**11**	**19**	**30**	**78**	**3**	**0**	**1**	**228**	**4.4**	**95**	**35**	**77**	**11**	**–6**	....	....	....	....	....	....	....	....
	NHL Totals		**708**	**115**	**260**	**375**	**120**	**227**	**347**	**710**	**49**	**1**	**19**	**1746**	**6.6**	**968**	**367**	**823**	**201**		**50**	**5**	**20**	**25**	**79**	**3**	**0**	**0**

OHL First All-Star Team (1988, 1989 • Played in NHL All-Star Game (1996)

Traded to **NY Islanders** by **Montreal** with Kirk Muller and Craig Darby for Pierre Turgeon and Vladimir Malakhov, April 5, 1995. Traded to **Toronto** by **NY Islanders** with Wendel Clark and D.J. Smith for Darby Hendrickson, Sean Haggerty, Kenny Jonsson and Toronto's 1st round choice (Roberto Luongo) in 1997 Entry Draft, March 13, 1996. • Missed majority of 1996-97 season recovering from groin injury suffered in game vs. St. Louis, December 27, 1996. Rights traded to **NY Rangers** by **Toronto** for Alexander Karpovtsev and NY Rangers' 4th round choice (Mirko Murovic) in 1999 Entry Draft, October 14, 1998. Selected by **Columbus** from **NY Rangers** in Expansion Draft, June 23, 2000.

• SCHOCK, Danny

Daniel Patrick LW – L. 5'11", 180 lbs. b: Terrace Bay, Ont., 12/30/1948. Boston's 1st, 12th overall, in 1968.

Season	Club	League	GP	G	A	Pts	AG	AA	APts	PIM	PP	SH	GW	S	%	TGF	PGF	TGA	PGA	+/–	GP	G	A	Pts	PIM	PP	SH	GW
1965-66	St. Thomas Stars	OHA-B	STATISTICS NOT AVAILABLE																									
1966-67	Estevan Bruins	CMJHL	55	29	29	58	....	....	....	66	....	....	....	....	....	....	....	....	....	....	12	5	1	6	30	....	....	....
1967-68	Estevan Bruins	WCJHL	52	33	30	63	....	....	....	159	....	....	....	....	....	....	....	....	....	....	14	6	15	21	10	....	....	....
	Estevan Bruins	Mem-Cup	14	7	*11	18	....	....	....	12	....	....	....	....	....	....	....	....	....	....	....	....	....	....	....	....	....	....
1968-69	Oklahoma City Blazers	CHL	66	20	32	52	....	....	....	52	....	....	....	....	....	....	....	....	....	....	12	3	6	9	21	....	....	....
1969-70	Oklahoma City Blazers	CHL	3	1	0	1	....	....	....	8	....	....	....	....	....	....	....	....	....	....	....	....	....	....	....	....	....	....
	Salt Lake Golden Eagles	WHL	55	20	18	38	....	....	....	12	....	....	....	....	....	....	....	....	....	....	....	....	....	....	....	....	....	....
♦	**Boston Bruins**	**NHL**	....	....	....	....	....	....	....	....	....	....	....	....	....	....	....	....	....	....	**1**	**0**	**0**	**0**	**0**	**0**	**0**	**0**
1970-71	**Boston Bruins**	**NHL**	**6**	**0**	**0**	**0**	**0**	**0**	**0**	**0**	**0**	**0**	**0**	**1**	**0.0**	**0**	**0**	**1**	**0**	**–1**	....	....	....	....	....	....	....	....
	Philadelphia Flyers	**NHL**	**14**	**1**	**2**	**3**	**1**	**2**	**3**	**0**	**0**	**0**	**0**	**7**	**14.3**	**6**	**0**	**5**	**0**	**1**	....	....	....	....	....	....	....	....
	Quebec Aces	AHL	7	2	1	3	....	....	....	0	....	....	....	....	....	....	....	....	....	....	....	....	....	....	....	....	....	....
1971-72	Richmond Robins	AHL	74	24	17	41	....	....	....	36	....	....	....	....	....	....	....	....	....	....	....	....	....	....	....	....	....	....
1972-73	Richmond Robins	AHL	74	48	36	84	....	....	....	37	....	....	....	....	....	....	....	....	....	....	4	1	3	4	0	....	....	....
1973-74	Richmond Robins	AHL	54	23	28	51	....	....	....	8	....	....	....	....	....	....	....	....	....	....	5	0	2	2	0	....	....	....
1974-75	Syracuse Eagles	AHL	4	3	0	3	....	....	....	0	....	....	....	....	....	....	....	....	....	....	....	....	....	....	....	....	....	....
	Greensboro Generals	SHL	24	5	18	23	....	....	....	2	....	....	....	....	....	....	....	....	....	....	....	....	....	....	....	....	....	....
	Syracuse Blazers	NAHL	3	0	1	1	....	....	....	2	....	....	....	....	....	....	....	....	....	....	....	....	....	....	....	....	....	....
1975-76			DID NOT PLAY																									
1976-77	Richmond Wildcats	SHL	1	0	0	0	....	....	....	0	....	....	....	....	....	....	....	....	....	....	....	....	....	....	....	....	....	....
	NHL Totals		**20**	**1**	**2**	**3**	**1**	**2**	**3**	**0**	**0**	**0**	**0**	**8**	**12.5**	**6**	**0**	**6**	**0**		**1**	**0**	**0**	**0**	**0**	**0**	**0**	**0**

• Brother of Ron

Traded to **Philadelphia** by **Boston** with Rick MacLeish for Mike Walton, February 1, 1971.

• SCHOCK, Ron

Ronald Lawrence C – L. 5'11", 180 lbs. b: Chapleau, Ont., 12/19/1943.

Season	Club	League	GP	G	A	Pts	AG	AA	APts	PIM	PP	SH	GW	S	%	TGF	PGF	TGA	PGA	+/–	GP	G	A	Pts	PIM	PP	SH	GW
1961-62	Niagara Falls Flyers	OHA-Jr.	50	18	27	45	....	....	....	17	....	....	....	....	....	....	....	....	....	....	26	10	22	32	29	....	....	....
1962-63	Niagara Falls Flyers	OHA-Jr.	46	23	48	71	....	....	....	66	....	....	....	....	....	....	....	....	....	....	9	5	11	16	19	....	....	....
	Kingston Frontenacs	EPHL	1	0	1	1	....	....	....	0	....	....	....	....	....	....	....	....	....	....	....	....	....	....	....	....	....	....
	Niagara Falls Flyers	Mem-Cup	16	9	15	24	....	....	....	23	....	....	....	....	....	....	....	....	....	....	....	....	....	....	....	....	....	....
1963-64	Niagara Falls Flyers	OHA-Jr.	44	38	36	74	....	....	....	30	....	....	....	....	....	....	....	....	....	....	4	2	1	3	2	....	....	....
	Boston Bruins	**NHL**	**5**	**1**	**2**	**3**	**1**	**2**	**3**	**0**	....	....	....	....	....	....	....	....	....	....	....	....	....	....	....	....	....	....
	Minneapolis Bruins	CPHL	....	....	....	....	....	....	....	....	....	....	....	....	....	....	....	....	....	....	2	0	3	3	0	....	....	....
1964-65	**Boston Bruins**	**NHL**	**33**	**4**	**7**	**11**	**5**	**7**	**12**	**14**	....	....	....	....	....	....	....	....	....	....	....	....	....	....	....	....	....	....
1965-66	**Boston Bruins**	**NHL**	**24**	**2**	**2**	**4**	**2**	**2**	**4**	**6**	....	....	....	....	....	....	....	....	....	....	....	....	....	....	....	....	....	....
	San Francisco Seals	WHL	43	11	21	32	....	....	....	28	....	....	....	....	....	....	....	....	....	....	7	1	5	6	6	....	....	....
1966-67	**Boston Bruins**	**NHL**	**66**	**10**	**20**	**30**	**12**	**20**	**32**	**8**	....	....	....	....	....	....	....	....	....	....	....	....	....	....	....	....	....	....
1967-68	**St. Louis Blues**	**NHL**	**55**	**9**	**9**	**18**	**10**	**9**	**19**	**17**	**4**	**0**	**1**	**116**	**7.8**	**28**	**9**	**37**	**1**	**–17**	**12**	**1**	**2**	**3**	**0**	**0**	**0**	**1**
	Kansas City Blues	CPHL	10	2	8	10	....	....	....	2	....	....	....	....	....	....	....	....	....	....	....	....	....	....	....	....	....	....
1968-69	**St. Louis Blues**	**NHL**	**67**	**12**	**27**	**39**	**13**	**24**	**37**	**14**	**4**	**0**	**3**	**157**	**7.6**	**51**	**11**	**39**	**2**	**3**	**12**	**1**	**2**	**3**	**6**	**0**	**0**	**0**
1969-70	**Pittsburgh Penguins**	**NHL**	**76**	**8**	**21**	**29**	**9**	**20**	**29**	**40**	**4**	**1**	**1**	**160**	**5.0**	**49**	**17**	**54**	**15**	**–7**	**10**	**1**	**6**	**7**	**7**	**0**	**0**	**0**
1970-71	**Pittsburgh Penguins**	**NHL**	**71**	**14**	**26**	**40**	**14**	**22**	**36**	**20**	**2**	**2**	**1**	**148**	**9.5**	**50**	**8**	**62**	**22**	**2**	....	....	....	....	....	....	....	....
1971-72	**Pittsburgh Penguins**	**NHL**	**77**	**17**	**29**	**46**	**17**	**25**	**42**	**22**	**3**	**2**	**1**	**151**	**11.3**	**60**	**11**	**96**	**37**	**–10**	**4**	**1**	**0**	**1**	**6**	**0**	**0**	**0**
1972-73	**Pittsburgh Penguins**	**NHL**	**78**	**13**	**36**	**49**	**12**	**29**	**41**	**23**	**2**	**3**	**1**	**143**	**9.1**	**63**	**7**	**94**	**26**	**–12**	....	....	....	....	....	....	....	....
1973-74	**Pittsburgh Penguins**	**NHL**	**77**	**14**	**29**	**43**	**13**	**24**	**37**	**22**	**0**	**2**	**3**	**138**	**10.1**	**55**	**5**	**100**	**23**	**–27**	....	....	....	....	....	....	....	....
1974-75	**Pittsburgh Penguins**	**NHL**	**80**	**23**	**63**	**86**	**20**	**47**	**67**	**36**	**3**	**2**	**3**	**172**	**13.4**	**113**	**18**	**100**	**27**	**22**	**9**	**0**	**4**	**4**	**10**	**0**	**0**	**0**
1975-76	**Pittsburgh Penguins**	**NHL**	**80**	**18**	**44**	**62**	**16**	**33**	**49**	**28**	**2**	**1**	**3**	**161**	**11.2**	**82**	**7**	**94**	**21**	**2**	**3**	**0**	**1**	**1**	**0**	**0**	**0**	**0**
1976-77	**Pittsburgh Penguins**	**NHL**	**80**	**17**	**32**	**49**	**15**	**25**	**40**	**10**	**3**	**1**	**4**	**154**	**11.0**	**69**	**8**	**85**	**18**	**–6**	**3**	**0**	**1**	**1**	**0**	**0**	**0**	**0**
1977-78	**Buffalo Sabres**	**NHL**	**40**	**4**	**4**	**8**	**4**	**3**	**7**	**0**	**0**	**0**	**2**	**19**	**21.1**	**10**	**0**	**16**	**1**	**–5**	**2**	**0**	**0**	**0**	**0**	**0**	**0**	**0**
1978-79	Hershey Bears	AHL	79	21	45	66	....	....	....	21	....	....	....	....	....	....	....	....	....	....	4	0	2	2	0	....	....	....
1979-80	Rochester Americans	AHL	40	10	18	28	....	....	....	12	....	....	....	....	....	....	....	....	....	....	....	....	....	....	....	....	....	....
	NHL Totals		**909**	**166**	**351**	**517**	**163**	**292**	**455**	**260**	....	....	....	....	....	....	....	....	....	....	**55**	**4**	**16**	**20**	**29**	....	....	....

• Brother of Danny

Claimed by **St. Louis** from **Boston** in Expansion Draft, June 6, 1967. Traded to **Pittsburgh** by **St. Louis** with Craig Cameron for Lou Angotti and Pittsburgh's 1st round choice (Gene Carr) in 1971 Amateur Draft, June 6, 1969. Traded to **Buffalo** by **Pittsburgh** for Brian Spencer, September 20, 1977.

• SCHOENFELD, Jim

James Grant D – L. 6'2", 200 lbs. b: Galt, Ont., 9/4/1952. Buffalo's 1st, 5th overall, in 1972.

Season	Club	League	GP	G	A	Pts	AG	AA	APts	PIM	PP	SH	GW	S	%	TGF	PGF	TGA	PGA	+/–	GP	G	A	Pts	PIM	PP	SH	GW
1969-70	Owen Sound Grays	OHA-B	STATISTICS NOT AVAILABLE																									
	London Knights	OHA-Jr.	16	1	4	5	....	....	....	81	....	....	....	....	....	....	....	....	....	....	....	....	....	....	....	....	....	....
	Hamilton Red Wings	OHA-Jr.	32	2	12	14	....	....	....	54	....	....	....	....	....	....	....	....	....	....	....	....	....	....	....	....	....	....
1970-71	Hamilton Red Wings	OHA-Jr.	25	3	19	22	....	....	....	120	....	....	....	....	....	....	....	....	....	....	....	....	....	....	....	....	....	....
	Niagara Falls Flyers	OMJHL	30	3	9	12	....	....	....	85	....	....	....	....	....	....	....	....	....	....	....	....	....	....	....	....	....	....
1971-72	Niagara Falls Flyers	OMJHL	40	6	46	52	....	....	....	215	....	....	....	....	....	....	....	....	....	....	6	0	0	0	32	....	....	....
1972-73	**Buffalo Sabres**	**NHL**	**66**	**4**	**15**	**19**	**4**	**12**	**16**	**178**	**1**	**0**	**0**	**91**	**4.4**	**84**	**6**	**78**	**12**	**12**	**6**	**2**	**1**	**3**	**4**	**0**	**0**	**0**
1973-74	**Buffalo Sabres**	**NHL**	**28**	**1**	**8**	**9**	**1**	**7**	**8**	**56**	**0**	**0**	**0**	**49**	**2.0**	**27**	**1**	**43**	**8**	**–9**	....	....	....	....	....	....	....	....
	Cincinnati Swords	AHL	2	0	2	2	....	....	....	4	....	....	....	....	....	....	....	....	....	....	....	....	....	....	....	....	....	....
1974-75	**Buffalo Sabres**	**NHL**	**68**	**1**	**19**	**20**	**1**	**14**	**15**	**184**	**0**	**0**	**0**	**148**	**0.7**	**109**	**3**	**101**	**30**	**35**	**17**	**1**	**4**	**5**	**38**	**1**	**0**	**0**

Season	Club	League	REGULAR SEASON																		PLAYOFFS							
			GP	G	A	Pts	AG	AA	APts	PIM	PP	SH	GW	S	%	TGF	PGF	TGA	PGA	+/–	GP	G	A	Pts	PIM	PP	SH	GW
1975-76	**Buffalo Sabres**	**NHL**	**56**	**2**	**22**	**24**	**2**	**16**	**18**	**114**	**0**	**0**	**0**	**112**	**1.8**	**103**	**3**	**82**	**22**	**40**	**8**	**0**	**3**	**3**	**33**	**0**	**0**	**0**
1976-77	**Buffalo Sabres**	**NHL**	**65**	**7**	**25**	**32**	**6**	**19**	**25**	**97**	**2**	**0**	**2**	**181**	**3.9**	**115**	**17**	**88**	**18**	**28**	**6**	**0**	**0**	**0**	**12**	**0**	**0**	**0**
1977-78	**Buffalo Sabres**	**NHL**	**60**	**2**	**20**	**22**	**2**	**15**	**17**	**89**	**0**	**0**	**0**	**114**	**1.8**	**101**	**10**	**81**	**14**	**24**	**8**	**0**	**1**	**1**	**28**	**0**	**0**	**0**
1978-79	**Buffalo Sabres**	**NHL**	**46**	**8**	**17**	**25**	**7**	**12**	**19**	**67**	**6**	**0**	**0**	**99**	**8.1**	**81**	**15**	**77**	**19**	**8**	**3**	**0**	**1**	**1**	**0**	**0**	**0**	**0**
1979-80	**Buffalo Sabres**	**NHL**	**77**	**9**	**27**	**36**	**8**	**20**	**28**	**72**	**4**	**0**	**1**	**114**	**7.9**	**130**	**11**	**88**	**29**	**60**	**14**	**0**	**3**	**3**	**18**	**0**	**0**	**0**
1980-81	**Buffalo Sabres**	**NHL**	**71**	**8**	**25**	**33**	**6**	**17**	**23**	**110**	**3**	**0**	**0**	**101**	**7.9**	**115**	**7**	**111**	**31**	**28**	**8**	**0**	**0**	**0**	**14**	**0**	**0**	**0**
1981-82	**Buffalo Sabres**	**NHL**	**13**	**3**	**2**	**5**	**2**	**1**	**3**	**30**	**0**	**0**	**1**	**21**	**14.3**	**14**	**0**	**11**	**2**	**5**	....	....	....	....	....	....	....	....
	Detroit Red Wings	**NHL**	**39**	**5**	**9**	**14**	**4**	**6**	**10**	**69**	**0**	**0**	**0**	**87**	**5.7**	**49**	**1**	**58**	**12**	**2**	....	....	....	....	....	....	....	....
1982-83	**Detroit Red Wings**	**NHL**	**57**	**1**	**10**	**11**	**1**	**7**	**8**	**18**	**0**	**0**	**1**	**68**	**1.5**	**46**	**2**	**80**	**22**	**–14**	....	....	....	....	....	....	....	....
1983-84	**Boston Bruins**	**NHL**	**39**	**0**	**2**	**2**	**0**	**1**	**1**	**20**	**0**	**0**	**0**	**35**	**0.0**	**41**	**0**	**33**	**10**	**18**	....	....	....	....	....	....	....	....
1984-85	Rochester Americans	AHL	DID NOT PLAY – COACHING																									
	Buffalo Sabres	**NHL**	**34**	**0**	**3**	**3**	**0**	**2**	**2**	**28**	**0**	**0**	**0**	**37**	**0.0**	**27**	**0**	**42**	**15**	**0**	**5**	**0**	**0**	**0**	**4**	**0**	**0**	**0**
	NHL Totals		**719**	**51**	**204**	**255**	**44**	**149**	**193**	**1132**	**16**	**0**	**5**	**1257**	**4.1**	**1042**	**76**	**973**	**244**		**75**	**3**	**13**	**16**	**151**	**1**	**0**	**0**

OMJHL Second All-Star Team (1972) • NHL Second All-Star Team (1980) • Played in NHL All-Star Game (1977, 1980)

• Missed majority of 1973-74 season recovering from neck surgery, November 10, 1973. Traded to **Detroit** by **Buffalo** with Danny Gare and Derek Smith for Mike Foligno, Dale McCourt and Brent Peterson, December 2, 1981. Signed as a free agent by **Boston**, August 19, 1983. Signed as a free agent by **Buffalo**, December 6, 1984.

• SCHOFIELD, Dwight

Dwight Hamilton D – L. 6'3", 195 lbs. b: Waltham, MA, 3/25/1956. Detroit's 5th, 76th overall, in 1976.

Season	Club	League	GP	G	A	Pts	AG	AA	APts	PIM	PP	SH	GW	S	%	TGF	PGF	TGA	PGA	+/–	GP	G	A	Pts	PIM	PP	SH	GW
1974-75	London Knights	OMJHL	70	6	16	22	....	....	....	124	....	....	....	....	....	....	....	....	....	....	....	....	....	....	....	....	....	....
1975-76	London Knights	OMJHL	59	14	29	43	....	....	....	121	....	....	....	....	....	....	....	....	....	....	5	0	1	1	15	....	....	....
1976-77	**Detroit Red Wings**	**NHL**	**3**	**1**	**0**	**1**	**1**	**0**	**1**	**2**	**0**	**0**	**0**	**3**	**33.3**	**3**	**0**	**3**	**0**	**0**	....	....	....	....	....	....	....	....
	Kalamazoo Wings	IHL	73	20	41	61	....	....	....	180	....	....	....	....	....	....	....	....	....	....	10	4	7	11	61	....	....	....
1977-78	Kansas City Red Wings	CHL	22	3	7	10	....	....	....	58	....	....	....	....	....	....	....	....	....	....	....	....	....	....	....	....	....	....
	Kalamazoo Wings	IHL	3	3	6	9	....	....	....	21	....	....	....	....	....	....	....	....	....	....	....	....	....	....	....	....	....	....
1978-79	Kansas City Red Wings	CHL	13	1	4	5	....	....	....	20	....	....	....	....	....	....	....	....	....	....	....	....	....	....	....	....	....	....
	Kalamazoo Wings	IHL	47	8	29	37	....	....	....	199	....	....	....	....	....	....	....	....	....	....	....	....	....	....	....	....	....	....
	Fort Wayne Komets	IHL	14	2	3	5	....	....	....	54	....	....	....	....	....	....	....	....	....	....	13	0	9	9	28	....	....	....
1979-80	Dayton Gems	IHL	71	15	47	62	....	....	....	257	....	....	....	....	....	....	....	....	....	....	....	....	....	....	....	....	....	....
	Tulsa Oilers	CHL	1	0	0	0	....	....	....	0	....	....	....	....	....	....	....	....	....	....	....	....	....	....	....	....	....	....
1980-81	Milwaukee Admirals	IHL	82	18	41	59	....	....	....	327	....	....	....	....	....	....	....	....	....	....	7	2	5	7	28	....	....	....
1981-82	Nova Scotia Voyageurs	AHL	75	7	24	31	....	....	....	*335	....	....	....	....	....	....	....	....	....	....	9	1	3	4	41	....	....	....
1982-83	**Montreal Canadiens**	**NHL**	**2**	**0**	**0**	**0**	**0**	**0**	**0**	**7**	**0**	**0**	**0**	**0**	**0.0**	**1**	**0**	**0**	**0**	**1**	....	....	....	....	....	....	....	....
	Nova Scotia Voyageurs	AHL	73	10	21	31	....	....	....	248	....	....	....	....	....	....	....	....	....	....	7	0	3	3	21	....	....	....
1983-84	**St. Louis Blues**	**NHL**	**70**	**4**	**10**	**14**	**3**	**7**	**10**	**219**	**0**	**0**	**1**	**48**	**8.3**	**51**	**6**	**55**	**7**	**–3**	**4**	**0**	**0**	**0**	**26**	**0**	**0**	**0**
	Toledo Goaldiggers	IHL	3	2	2	4	....	....	....	4	....	....	....	....	....	....	....	....	....	....	....	....	....	....	....	....	....	....
1984-85	**St. Louis Blues**	**NHL**	**43**	**1**	**4**	**5**	**1**	**3**	**4**	**184**	**0**	**0**	**0**	**14**	**7.1**	**9**	**0**	**13**	**0**	**–4**	**2**	**0**	**0**	**0**	**15**	**0**	**0**	**0**
1985-86	**Washington Capitals**	**NHL**	**50**	**1**	**2**	**3**	**1**	**1**	**2**	**127**	**0**	**0**	**0**	**13**	**7.7**	**17**	**0**	**12**	**0**	**5**	**3**	**0**	**0**	**0**	**14**	**0**	**0**	**0**
1986-87	**Pittsburgh Penguins**	**NHL**	**25**	**1**	**6**	**7**	**1**	**4**	**5**	**59**	**0**	**0**	**0**	**9**	**11.1**	**24**	**1**	**21**	**2**	**4**	....	....	....	....	....	....	....	....
	Baltimore Skipjacks	AHL	20	1	5	6	....	....	....	58	....	....	....	....	....	....	....	....	....	....	....	....	....	....	....	....	....	....
1987-88	**Winnipeg Jets**	**NHL**	**18**	**0**	**0**	**0**	**0**	**0**	**0**	**33**	**0**	**0**	**0**	**3**	**0.0**	**3**	**0**	**6**	**0**	**–3**	....	....	....	....	....	....	....	....
	Kalamazoo Wings	IHL	34	2	7	9	....	....	....	150	....	....	....	....	....	....	....	....	....	....	....	....	....	....	....	....	....	....
	NHL Totals		**211**	**8**	**22**	**30**	**7**	**15**	**22**	**631**	**0**	**0**	**1**	**90**	**8.9**	**108**	**7**	**110**	**9**		**9**	**0**	**0**	**0**	**55**	**0**	**0**	**0**

Signed as a free agent by **Montreal**, September 20, 1982. Claimed by **St. Louis** from **Montreal** in Waiver Draft, October 3, 1983. Claimed by **Washington** from **St. Louis** in Waiver Draft, October 7, 1985. Traded to **Pittsburgh** by **Washington** for cash, October 8, 1986. Signed as a free agent by **Winnipeg**, July, 1987.

• SCHREIBER, Wally

RW – R. 5'11", 180 lbs. b: Edmonton, Alta., 4/15/1962. Washington's 5th, 152nd overall, in 1982.

Season	Club	League	GP	G	A	Pts	AG	AA	APts	PIM	PP	SH	GW	S	%	TGF	PGF	TGA	PGA	+/–	GP	G	A	Pts	PIM	PP	SH	GW
1980-81	Fort Saskatchewan Traders	SJHL	55	39	41	80	....	....	....	105	....	....	....	....	....	....	....	....	....	....	....	....	....	....	....	....	....	....
1981-82	Regina Pats	WHL	68	56	68	124	....	....	....	68	....	....	....	....	....	....	....	....	....	....	20	12	12	24	34	....	....	....
1982-83	Fort Wayne Komets	IHL	67	24	34	58	....	....	....	23	....	....	....	....	....	....	....	....	....	....	....	....	....	....	....	....	....	....
1983-84	Fort Wayne Komets	IHL	82	47	66	*113	....	....	....	44	....	....	....	....	....	....	....	....	....	....	6	3	3	6	6	....	....	....
1984-85	Fort Wayne Komets	IHL	81	51	58	109	....	....	....	45	....	....	....	....	....	....	....	....	....	....	13	3	7	10	10	....	....	....
1985-86	Fort Wayne Komets	IHL	72	37	52	89	....	....	....	38	....	....	....	....	....	....	....	....	....	....	15	10	8	18	6	....	....	....
1986-87	Canada	Nat-Team	70	40	37	77	....	....	....	27	....	....	....	....	....	....	....	....	....	....	....	....	....	....	....	....	....	....
1987-88	Canada	Nat-Team	61	24	15	39	....	....	....	34	....	....	....	....	....	....	....	....	....	....	....	....	....	....	....	....	....	....
	WEV Wein	Austria	6	0	2	2	....	....	....	0	....	....	....	....	....	....	....	....	....	....	....	....	....	....	....	....	....	....
	Canada	Olympics	8	1	2	3	....	....	....	2	....	....	....	....	....	....	....	....	....	....	....	....	....	....	....	....	....	....
	Minnesota North Stars	**NHL**	**16**	**6**	**5**	**11**	**5**	**4**	**9**	**2**	**1**	**2**	**1**	**29**	**20.7**	**18**	**5**	**21**	**4**	**–4**	....	....	....	....	....	....	....	....
1988-89	**Minnesota North Stars**	**NHL**	**25**	**2**	**5**	**7**	**2**	**4**	**6**	**10**	**1**	**0**	**1**	**41**	**4.9**	**11**	**5**	**22**	**11**	**–5**	....	....	....	....	....	....	....	....
	Fort Wayne Komets	IHL	32	15	16	31	....	....	....	51	....	....	....	....	....	....	....	....	....	....	....	....	....	....	....	....	....	....
	Kalamazoo Wings	IHL	5	5	7	12	....	....	....	2	....	....	....	....	....	....	....	....	....	....	....	....	....	....	....	....	....	....
1989-90	Schwenninger ERC	Germany	36	25	29	54	....	....	....	28	....	....	....	....	....	....	....	....	....	....	10	7	13	20	4	....	....	....
	Canada	Nat-Team	5	1	0	1	....	....	....	2	....	....	....	....	....	....	....	....	....	....	....	....	....	....	....	....	....	....
1990-91	Schwenninger ERC	Germany	37	26	43	69	....	....	....	34	....	....	....	....	....	....	....	....	....	....	4	1	4	5	0	....	....	....
1991-92	Schwenninger ERC	Germany	44	32	43	75	....	....	....	31	....	....	....	....	....	....	....	....	....	....	2	0	1	1	27	....	....	....
	Canada	Nat-Team	3	1	2	3	....	....	....	2	....	....	....	....	....	....	....	....	....	....	....	....	....	....	....	....	....	....
	Canada	Olympics	8	2	2	4	....	....	....	2	....	....	....	....	....	....	....	....	....	....	....	....	....	....	....	....	....	....
1992-93	Schwenninger ERC	Germany	44	23	31	54	....	....	....	28	....	....	....	....	....	....	....	....	....	....	7	2	5	7	2	....	....	....
1993-94	EC Hedos Munich	Germany	44	25	30	55	....	....	....	27	....	....	....	....	....	....	....	....	....	....	10	5	11	16	2	....	....	....
	Canada	Nat-Team	4	1	3	4	....	....	....	0	....	....	....	....	....	....	....	....	....	....	....	....	....	....	....	....	....	....
	Canada	Olympics	8	1	0	1	....	....	....	2	....	....	....	....	....	....	....	....	....	....	....	....	....	....	....	....	....	....
1994-95	EV Landshut	Germany	42	27	27	54	....	....	....	26	....	....	....	....	....	....	....	....	....	....	18	11	*15	*26	26	....	....	....
	Canada	Nat-Team	3	1	0	1	....	....	....	2	....	....	....	....	....	....	....	....	....	....	....	....	....	....	....	....	....	....
1995-96	EV Landshut	Germany	50	25	30	55	....	....	....	46	....	....	....	....	....	....	....	....	....	....	11	5	9	14	22	....	....	....
1996-97	EV Landshut	Germany	47	22	29	51	....	....	....	12	....	....	....	....	....	....	....	....	....	....	7	1	9	10	2	....	....	....
1997-98	EV Landshut	Germany	48	17	19	36	....	....	....	43	....	....	....	....	....	....	....	....	....	....	6	1	6	7	2	....	....	....
1998-99	EV Landshut	Germany	50	19	37	56	....	....	....	20	....	....	....	....	....	....	....	....	....	....	3	0	1	1	0	....	....	....
99-2000	Hannover Scorpions	Germany	67	23	46	69	....	....	....	24	....	....	....	....	....	....	....	....	....	....	....	....	....	....	....	....	....	....
	NHL Totals		**41**	**8**	**10**	**18**	**7**	**8**	**15**	**12**	**2**	**2**	**2**	**70**	**11.4**	**29**	**10**	**43**	**15**		....	....	....	....	....	....	....	....

IHL First All-Star Team (1984, 1985) • Won Leo P. Lamoureux Memorial Trophy (Top Scorer - IHL) (1984) • IHL Second All-Star Team (1986)

Signed as a free agent by **Minnesota**, May 26, 1987.

• SCHULTE, Paxton

Paxton J. LW – L. 6'2", 217 lbs. b: Onaway, Alta., 7/16/1972. Quebec's 7th, 124th overall, in 1992.

Season	Club	League	GP	G	A	Pts	AG	AA	APts	PIM	PP	SH	GW	S	%	TGF	PGF	TGA	PGA	+/–	GP	G	A	Pts	PIM	PP	SH	GW
1988-89	St. Albert Raiders	AAHA	28	22	35	57	....	....	....	38	....	....	....	....	....	....	....	....	....	....	....	....	....	....	....	....	....	....
1989-90	Sherwood Park Crusaders	AJHL	56	28	38	66	....	....	....	151	....	....	....	....	....	....	....	....	....	....	....	....	....	....	....	....	....	....
1990-91	University of North Dakota	WCHA	38	2	4	6	....	....	....	32	....	....	....	....	....	....	....	....	....	....	....	....	....	....	....	....	....	....
1991-92	Spokane Chiefs	WHL	70	42	42	84	....	....	....	172	....	....	....	....	....	....	....	....	....	....	10	2	8	10	48	....	....	....
1992-93	Spokane Chiefs	WHL	45	38	35	73	....	....	....	142	....	....	....	....	....	....	....	....	....	....	10	5	6	11	12	....	....	....
1993-94	**Quebec Nordiques**	**NHL**	**1**	**0**	**0**	**0**	**0**	**0**	**0**	**2**	**0**	**0**	**0**	**0**	**0.0**	**0**	**0**	**0**	**0**	**0**	....	....	....	....	....	....	....	....
	Cornwall Aces	AHL	56	15	15	30	....	....	....	102	....	....	....	....	....	....	....	....	....	....	....	....	....	....	....	....	....	....
1994-95	Cornwall Aces	AHL	74	14	22	36	....	....	....	217	....	....	....	....	....	....	....	....	....	....	14	3	3	6	29	....	....	....
1995-96	Cornwall Aces	AHL	69	25	31	56	....	....	....	171	....	....	....	....	....	....	....	....	....	....	....	....	....	....	....	....	....	....
	Saint John Flames	AHL	14	4	5	9	....	....	....	25	....	....	....	....	....	....	....	....	....	....	14	4	7	11	40	....	....	....
1996-97	**Calgary Flames**	**NHL**	**1**	**0**	**0**	**0**	**0**	**0**	**0**	**2**	**0**	**0**	**0**	**1**	**0.0**	**1**	**0**	**0**	**0**	**1**	....	....	....	....	....	....	....	....
	Saint John Flames	AHL	71	14	23	37	....	....	....	274	....	....	....	....	....	....	....	....	....	....	4	2	0	2	35	....	....	....
1997-98	Saint John Flames	AHL	59	8	17	25	....	....	....	133	....	....	....	....	....	....	....	....	....	....	....	....	....	....	....	....	....	....
	Las Vegas Thunder	IHL	10	0	1	1	....	....	....	32	....	....	....	....	....	....	....	....	....	....	4	0	0	0	4	....	....	....

			REGULAR SEASON																		PLAYOFFS							
Season	Club	League	GP	G	A	Pts	AG	AA	APts	PIM	PP	SH	GW	S	%	TGF	PGF	TGA	PGA	+/–	GP	G	A	Pts	PIM	PP	SH	GW
1998-99	Bracknell Bees	BH-Cup	8	1	5	6	....	....	....	49	....	....	....	....	....	....	....	....	....	....	....	....	....	....	....	....	....	....
	Bracknell Bees	Britain	36	9	10	19	....	....	....	153	....	....	....	....	....	....	....	....	....	....	3	0	0	0	14	....	....	....
99-2000	Bracknell Bees	BH-Cup	10	4	8	12	....	....	....	43	....	....	....	....	....	....	....	....	....	....	....	....	....	....	....	....	....	....
	Bracknell Bees	Britain	34	11	19	30	....	....	....	96	....	....	....	....	....	....	....	....	....	....	6	3	2	5	4	....	....	....
	NHL Totals		**2**	**0**	**0**	**0**	**0**	**0**	**0**	**4**	**0**	**0**	**0**	**1**	**0.0**	**1**	**0**	**0**	**0**		....	....	....	....	....	....	....	....

Transferred to **Colorado** after **Quebec** franchise relocated, July 1, 1995. Traded to **Calgary** by **Colorado** for Vesa Viitakoski, March 19, 1996.

• SCHULTZ, Dave

David William "The Hammer" LW – L. 6'1", 190 lbs. b: Waldheim, Sask., 10/14/1949. Philadelphia's 5th, 52nd overall, in 1969.

Season	Club	League	GP	G	A	Pts	AG	AA	APts	PIM	PP	SH	GW	S	%	TGF	PGF	TGA	PGA	+/–	GP	G	A	Pts	PIM	PP	SH	GW
1966-67	North Battleford Beavers	SAHA	STATISTICS NOT AVAILABLE																									
	Swift Current Broncos	X-Games	26	19	13	32	....	....	....	....	....	....	....	....	....	....	....	....	....	....	....	....	....	....	....	....	....	....
1967-68	Swift Current Broncos	WCJHL	59	35	34	69	....	....	....	138	....	....	....	....	....	....	....	....	....	....	....	....	....	....	....	....	....	....
1968-69	Swift Current Broncos	WCJHL	33	16	16	32	....	....	....	65	....	....	....	....	....	....	....	....	....	....	....	....	....	....	....	....	....	....
	Sorel Black Hawks	MMJHL	18	15	19	34	....	....	....	61	....	....	....	....	....	....	....	....	....	....	....	....	....	....	....	....	....	....
	Sorel Black Hawks	Mem-Cup	STATISTICS NOT AVAILABLE																									
1969-70	Salem Rebels	EHL	67	32	37	69	....	....	....	*356	....	....	....	....	....	....	....	....	....	....	5	2	3	5	23	....	....	....
	Quebec Aces	AHL	8	0	0	0	....	....	....	13	....	....	....	....	....	....	....	....	....	....	....	....	....	....	....	....	....	....
1970-71	Quebec Aces	AHL	71	14	23	37	....	....	....	*382	....	....	....	....	....	....	....	....	....	....	1	0	0	0	15	....	....	....
1971-72	**Philadelphia Flyers**	**NHL**	**1**	**0**	**0**	**0**	**0**	**0**	**0**	**0**	**0**	**0**	**0**	**0**	**0.0**	**1**	**0**	**1**	**0**	**0**	....	....	....	....	....	....	....	....
	Richmond Robins	AHL	76	18	28	46	....	....	....	*392	....	....	....	....	....	....	....	....	....	....	....	....	....	....	....	....	....	....
1972-73	**Philadelphia Flyers**	**NHL**	**76**	**9**	**12**	**21**	**8**	**9**	**17**	***259**	**0**	**0**	**2**	**63**	**14.3**	**29**	**0**	**25**	**0**	**4**	**11**	**1**	**0**	**1**	***51**	**0**	**0**	**0**
1973-74♦	**Philadelphia Flyers**	**NHL**	**73**	**20**	**16**	**36**	**19**	**13**	**32**	***348**	**2**	**0**	**3**	**95**	**21.1**	**48**	**2**	**20**	**0**	**26**	**17**	**2**	**4**	**6**	***139**	**0**	**0**	**1**
1974-75♦	**Philadelphia Flyers**	**NHL**	**76**	**9**	**17**	**26**	**8**	**13**	**21**	***472**	**0**	**0**	**0**	**93**	**9.7**	**46**	**2**	**28**	**0**	**16**	**17**	**2**	**3**	**5**	***83**	**0**	**0**	**0**
1975-76	**Philadelphia Flyers**	**NHL**	**71**	**13**	**19**	**32**	**11**	**14**	**25**	**307**	**0**	**0**	**3**	**91**	**14.3**	**48**	**0**	**24**	**0**	**24**	**16**	**2**	**2**	**4**	***90**	**0**	**0**	**0**
1976-77	**Los Angeles Kings**	**NHL**	**76**	**10**	**20**	**30**	**9**	**15**	**24**	**232**	**2**	**0**	**2**	**122**	**8.2**	**51**	**6**	**53**	**0**	**–8**	**9**	**1**	**1**	**2**	**45**	**1**	**0**	**0**
1977-78	**Los Angeles Kings**	**NHL**	**8**	**2**	**0**	**2**	**2**	**0**	**2**	***27**	**0**	**0**	**0**	**10**	**20.0**	**4**	**0**	**3**	**0**	**1**	....	....	....	....	....	....	....	....
	Pittsburgh Penguins	**NHL**	**66**	**9**	**25**	**34**	**8**	**19**	**27**	***378**	**0**	**0**	**1**	**102**	**8.8**	**56**	**3**	**62**	**0**	**–9**	....	....	....	....	....	....	....	....
1978-79	**Pittsburgh Penguins**	**NHL**	**47**	**4**	**9**	**13**	**3**	**7**	**10**	**157**	**0**	**0**	**0**	**50**	**8.0**	**24**	**0**	**27**	**1**	**–2**	....	....	....	....	....	....	....	....
	Buffalo Sabres	**NHL**	**28**	**2**	**3**	**5**	**2**	**2**	**4**	**86**	**0**	**0**	**0**	**16**	**12.5**	**7**	**1**	**18**	**0**	**–12**	**3**	**0**	**2**	**2**	**4**	**0**	**0**	**0**
1979-80	**Buffalo Sabres**	**NHL**	**13**	**1**	**0**	**1**	**1**	**0**	**1**	**28**	**0**	**0**	**0**	**1**	**100.0**	**2**	**0**	**2**	**0**	**0**	....	....	....	....	....	....	....	....
	Rochester Americans	AHL	56	10	14	24	....	....	....	248	....	....	....	....	....	....	....	....	....	....	4	1	0	1	12	....	....	....
	NHL Totals		**535**	**79**	**121**	**200**	**71**	**92**	**163**	**2294**	**4**	**0**	**11**	**643**	**12.3**	**316**	**14**	**263**	**1**		**73**	**8**	**12**	**20**	**412**	**1**	**0**	**1**

Traded to **LA Kings** by **Philadelphia** for LA Kings' 4th round pick (Yves Guillemette) in 1977 Amateur Draft and 2nd choice (later traded to Colorado — Colorado selected Merlin Malinowski) in 1978 Amateur Draft, September 29, 1976. Traded to **Pittsburgh** by **LA Kings** with Gene Carr and LA Kings' 4th round choice (Shane Pearsall) in 1978 Amateur Draft for Hartland Monahan and Syl Apps Jr., November 2, 1977. Traded to **Buffalo** by **Pittsburgh** for Gary McAdam, February 6, 1979.

• SCHULTZ, Ray

D – L. 6'2", 200 lbs. b: Red Deer, Alta., 11/14/1976. Ottawa's 8th, 184th overall, in 1995.

Season	Club	League	GP	G	A	Pts	AG	AA	APts	PIM	PP	SH	GW	S	%	TGF	PGF	TGA	PGA	+/–	GP	G	A	Pts	PIM	PP	SH	GW
1992-93	Edmonton S.S. Athletics	AAHA	STATISTICS NOT AVAILABLE																									
1993-94	Edmonton S.S. Athletics	AAHA	31	3	24	27	....	....	....	94	....	....	....	....	....	....	....	....	....	....	....	....	....	....	....	....	....	....
	Tri-City Americans	WHL	3	0	0	0	....	....	....	11	....	....	....	....	....	....	....	....	....	....	....	....	....	....	....	....	....	....
1994-95	Tri-City Americans	WHL	63	1	8	9	....	....	....	209	....	....	....	....	....	....	....	....	....	....	11	0	0	0	16	....	....	....
1995-96	Calgary Hitmen	WHL	66	3	17	20	....	....	....	282	....	....	....	....	....	....	....	....	....	....	....	....	....	....	....	....	....	....
1996-97	Calgary Hitmen	WHL	32	3	17	20	....	....	....	141	....	....	....	....	....	....	....	....	....	....	....	....	....	....	....	....	....	....
	Kelowna Rockets	WHL	23	3	11	14	....	....	....	63	....	....	....	....	....	....	....	....	....	....	6	0	2	2	12	....	....	....
1997-98	**New York Islanders**	**NHL**	**13**	**0**	**1**	**1**	**0**	**1**	**1**	**45**	**0**	**0**	**0**	**4**	**0.0**	**5**	**0**	**2**	**0**	**3**	....	....	....	....	....	....	....	....
	Kentucky Thoroughblades	AHL	51	2	4	6	....	....	....	179	....	....	....	....	....	....	....	....	....	....	1	0	0	0	25	....	....	....
1998-99	**New York Islanders**	**NHL**	**4**	**0**	**0**	**0**	**0**	**0**	**0**	**7**	**0**	**0**	**0**	**2**	**0.0**	**1**	**0**	**3**	**0**	**–2**	....	....	....	....	....	....	....	....
	Lowell Lock Monsters	AHL	54	0	3	3	....	....	....	184	....	....	....	....	....	....	....	....	....	....	1	0	0	0	4	....	....	....
99-2000	**New York Islanders**	**NHL**	**9**	**0**	**1**	**1**	**0**	**1**	**1**	**30**	**0**	**0**	**0**	**2**	**0.0**	**5**	**0**	**4**	**0**	**1**	....	....	....	....	....	....	....	....
	Kansas City Blades	IHL	65	5	5	10	....	....	....	208	....	....	....	....	....	....	....	....	....	....	....	....	....	....	....	....	....	....
	NHL Totals		**26**	**0**	**2**	**2**	**0**	**2**	**2**	**82**	**0**	**0**	**0**	**8**	**0.0**	**11**	**0**	**9**	**0**		....	....	....	....	....	....	....	....

Signed as a free agent by **NY Islanders**, June 9, 1997.

• SCHURMAN, Maynard

Maynard F. "M.F." LW – L. 6'3", 205 lbs. b: Summerdale, P.E.I., 7/16/1957.

Season	Club	League	GP	G	A	Pts	AG	AA	APts	PIM	PP	SH	GW	S	%	TGF	PGF	TGA	PGA	+/–	GP	G	A	Pts	PIM	PP	SH	GW
1975-76	Mount Allison University	AUAA	20	3	1	4	....	....	....	4	....	....	....	....	....	....	....	....	....	....	....	....	....	....	....	....	....	....
1976-77	Mount Allison University	AUAA	20	14	13	27	....	....	....	23	....	....	....	....	....	....	....	....	....	....	....	....	....	....	....	....	....	....
1977-78	Spokane Flyers	WIHL	56	20	42	62	....	....	....	113	....	....	....	....	....	....	....	....	....	....	....	....	....	....	....	....	....	....
1978-79	Maine Mariners	AHL	10	0	0	0	....	....	....	15	....	....	....	....	....	....	....	....	....	....	....	....	....	....	....	....	....	....
	Milwaukee Admirals	IHL	61	23	30	53	....	....	....	83	....	....	....	....	....	....	....	....	....	....	8	3	2	5	0	....	....	....
1979-80	**Hartford Whalers**	**NHL**	**7**	**0**	**0**	**0**	**0**	**0**	**0**	**0**	**0**	**0**	**0**	**5**	**0.0**	**0**	**0**	**1**	**0**	**–1**	....	....	....	....	....	....	....	....
	Springfield Indians	AHL	64	5	15	20	....	....	....	24	....	....	....	....	....	....	....	....	....	....	....	....	....	....	....	....	....	....
1980-81	Hampton Aces	EHL	66	13	43	56	....	....	....	49	....	....	....	....	....	....	....	....	....	....	....	....	....	....	....	....	....	....
1981-82	Charlottetown Islanders	PEI-Sr.	STATISTICS NOT AVAILABLE																									
1982-83	Wichita Wind	CHL	38	14	19	33	....	....	....	24	....	....	....	....	....	....	....	....	....	....	....	....	....	....	....	....	....	....
1983-84	Maine Mariners	AHL	43	5	15	20	....	....	....	50	....	....	....	....	....	....	....	....	....	....	....	....	....	....	....	....	....	....
1984-1992			OUT OF HOCKEY – RETIRED																									
1992-93	San Diego Surf	SCSHL	STATISTICS NOT AVAILABLE																									
	NHL Totals		**7**	**0**	**0**	**0**	**0**	**0**	**0**	**0**	**0**	**0**	**0**	**5**	**0.0**	**0**	**0**	**1**	**0**		....	....	....	....	....	....	....	....

Signed as a free agent by **Philadelphia**, September, 1978. Claimed by **Hartford** from **Philadelphia** in Expansion Draft, June 13, 1979.

• SCHUTT, Rod

Rodney G. LW – L. 5'10", 185 lbs. b: Bancroft, Ont., 10/13/1956. Montreal's 2nd, 13th overall, in 1976.

Season	Club	League	GP	G	A	Pts	AG	AA	APts	PIM	PP	SH	GW	S	%	TGF	PGF	TGA	PGA	+/–	GP	G	A	Pts	PIM	PP	SH	GW
1972-73	Pembroke Lumber Kings	OJHL	55	31	55	86	....	....	....	61	....	....	....	....	....	....	....	....	....	....	....	....	....	....	....	....	....	....
1973-74	Sudbury Wolves	OMJHL	67	15	41	56	....	....	....	47	....	....	....	....	....	....	....	....	....	....	4	0	0	0	2	....	....	....
1974-75	Sudbury Wolves	OMJHL	69	43	61	104	....	....	....	66	....	....	....	....	....	....	....	....	....	....	15	13	9	22	2	....	....	....
1975-76	Sudbury Wolves	OMJHL	63	72	63	135	....	....	....	42	....	....	....	....	....	....	....	....	....	....	17	18	16	34	13	....	....	....
1976-77	Nova Scotia Voyageurs	AHL	80	33	51	84	....	....	....	56	....	....	....	....	....	....	....	....	....	....	12	8	8	16	4	....	....	....
1977-78	**Montreal Canadiens**	**NHL**	**2**	**0**	**0**	**0**	**0**	**0**	**0**	**0**	**0**	**0**	**0**	**0**	**0.0**	**0**	**0**	**0**	**0**	**0**	....	....	....	....	....	....	....	....
	Nova Scotia Voyageurs	AHL	77	36	44	80	....	....	....	57	....	....	....	....	....	....	....	....	....	....	11	4	7	11	2	....	....	....
1978-79	**Pittsburgh Penguins**	**NHL**	**74**	**24**	**21**	**45**	**21**	**15**	**36**	**33**	**3**	**0**	**2**	**181**	**13.3**	**74**	**21**	**63**	**1**	**–9**	**7**	**2**	**0**	**2**	**4**	**0**	**0**	**0**
1979-80	**Pittsburgh Penguins**	**NHL**	**73**	**18**	**21**	**39**	**15**	**15**	**30**	**43**	**3**	**0**	**2**	**170**	**10.6**	**60**	**14**	**54**	**0**	**–8**	**5**	**2**	**1**	**3**	**6**	**0**	**0**	**0**
1980-81	**Pittsburgh Penguins**	**NHL**	**80**	**25**	**35**	**60**	**19**	**23**	**42**	**55**	**11**	**0**	**5**	**206**	**12.1**	**88**	**27**	**75**	**1**	**–13**	**5**	**3**	**3**	**6**	**16**	**1**	**0**	**1**
1981-82	**Pittsburgh Penguins**	**NHL**	**35**	**9**	**12**	**21**	**7**	**8**	**15**	**42**	**0**	**0**	**3**	**73**	**12.3**	**29**	**2**	**24**	**0**	**3**	**5**	**1**	**2**	**3**	**0**	**0**	**0**	**0**
	Erie Blades	AHL	35	12	15	27	....	....	....	40	....	....	....	....	....	....	....	....	....	....	....	....	....	....	....	....	....	....
1982-83	**Pittsburgh Penguins**	**NHL**	**5**	**0**	**0**	**0**	**0**	**0**	**0**	**0**	**0**	**0**	**0**	**6**	**0.0**	**1**	**0**	**3**	**0**	**–2**	....	....	....	....	....	....	....	....
	Baltimore Skipjacks	AHL	64	34	53	87	....	....	....	24	....	....	....	....	....	....	....	....	....	....	....	....	....	....	....	....	....	....
1983-84	**Pittsburgh Penguins**	**NHL**	**11**	**1**	**3**	**4**	**1**	**2**	**3**	**4**	**0**	**0**	**0**	**13**	**7.7**	**6**	**1**	**5**	**0**	**0**	....	....	....	....	....	....	....	....
	Baltimore Skipjacks	AHL	36	15	19	34	....	....	....	48	....	....	....	....	....	....	....	....	....	....	10	3	1	4	22	....	....	....
1984-85	Muskegon Mohawks	IHL	79	44	46	90	....	....	....	58	....	....	....	....	....	....	....	....	....	....	17	10	13	23	10	....	....	....
1985-86	**Toronto Maple Leafs**	**NHL**	**6**	**0**	**0**	**0**	**0**	**0**	**0**	**0**	**0**	**0**	**0**	**2**	**0.0**	**0**	**0**	**2**	**0**	**–2**	....	....	....	....	....	....	....	....
	St. Catharines Saints	AHL	70	21	28	49	....	....	....	44	....	....	....	....	....	....	....	....	....	....	13	7	4	11	18	....	....	....
	NHL Totals		**286**	**77**	**92**	**169**	**63**	**63**	**126**	**177**	**17**	**0**	**12**	**651**	**11.8**	**258**	**65**	**226**	**2**		**22**	**8**	**6**	**14**	**26**	**1**	**0**	**1**

OMJHL First All-Star Team (1975, 1976) • Won Dudley "Red" Garrett Memorial Award (Top Rookie - AHL) (1977)

Traded to **Pittsburgh** by **Montreal** for Pittsburgh's 1st round choice (Mark Hunter) in 1981 Entry Draft, October 18, 1978. Signed as a free agent by **Toronto**, October 3, 1985.

• SCISSONS, Scott

Scott E. C – L. 6'1", 201 lbs. b: Saskatoon, Sask., 10/29/1971. NY Islanders' 1st, 6th overall, in 1990.

Season	Club	League	GP	G	A	Pts	AG	AA	APts	PIM	PP	SH	GW	S	%	TGF	PGF	TGA	PGA	+/–	GP	G	A	Pts	PIM	PP	SH	GW
1985-86	Saskatoon Flyers	SAHA	65	45	55	100	....	....	....	45	....	....	....	....	....	....	....	....	....	....	....	....	....	....	....	....	....	....
1986-87	Saskatoon Flyers	SAHA	62	55	65	120	....	....	....	50	....	....	....	....	....	....	....	....	....	....	....	....	....	....	....	....	....	....
1987-88	Saskatoon Contacts	SAHA	29	23	16	39	....	....	....	51	....	....	....	....	....	....	....	....	....	....	....	....	....	....	....	....	....	....

			REGULAR SEASON																		PLAYOFFS							
Season	Club	League	GP	G	A	Pts	AG	AA	APts	PIM	PP	SH	GW	S	%	TGF	PGF	TGA	PGA	+/–	GP	G	A	Pts	PIM	PP	SH	GW
1988-89	Saskatoon Blades	WHL	71	30	56	86	....	....	....	65	....	....	....	....	....	....	....	....	....	....	7	0	4	4	16	....	....	....
	Saskatoon Blades	Mem-Cup	4	2	0	2	....	....	....	4	....	....	....	....	....	....	....	....	....	....	....	....	....	....	....	....	....	....
1989-90	Saskatoon Blades	WHL	61	40	47	87	....	....	....	81	....	....	....	....	....	....	....	....	....	....	10	3	8	11	6	....	....	....
1990-91	Saskatoon Blades	WHL	57	24	53	77	....	....	....	61	....	....	....	....	....	....	....	....	....	....	....	....	....	....	....	....	....	....
	New York Islanders	**NHL**	**1**	**0**	**0**	**0**	**0**	**0**	**0**	**0**	**0**	**0**	**0**	**1**	**0.0**	**0**	**0**	**0**	**0**	**0**	....	....	....	....	....	....	....	....
1991-92	Canada	Nat-Team	26	4	8	12	....	....	....	31	....	....	....	....	....	....	....	....	....	....	....	....	....	....	....	....	....	....
1992-93	Capital District Islanders	AHL	43	14	30	44	....	....	....	33	....	....	....	....	....	....	....	....	....	....	4	0	0	0	0	....	....	....
	New York Islanders	**NHL**	....	....	....	....	....	....	....	....	....	....	....	....	....	....	....	....	....	....	**1**	**0**	**0**	**0**	**0**	**0**	**0**	**0**
1993-94	**New York Islanders**	**NHL**	**1**	**0**	**0**	**0**	**0**	**0**	**0**	**0**	**0**	**0**	**0**	**0**	**0.0**	**0**	**0**	**0**	**0**	**0**	....	....	....	....	....	....	....	....
	Salt Lake Golden Eagles	IHL	72	10	26	36	....	....	....	123	....	....	....	....	....	....	....	....	....	....	....	....	....	....	....	....	....	....
1994-95	Denver Grizzlies	IHL	7	2	3	5	....	....	....	6	....	....	....	....	....	....	....	....	....	....	....	....	....	....	....	....	....	....
	Minnesota Moose	IHL	23	7	9	16	....	....	....	6	....	....	....	....	....	....	....	....	....	....	....	....	....	....	....	....	....	....
	NHL Totals		**2**	**0**	**0**	**0**	**0**	**0**	**0**	**0**	**0**	**0**	**0**	**1**	**0.0**	**0**	**0**	**0**	**0**		**1**	**0**	**0**	**0**	**0**	**0**	**0**	**0**

• SCOVILLE, Darryl

D – L. 6'3", 214 lbs. b: Swift Current, SK, 10/13/1975.

Season	Club	League	GP	G	A	Pts	AG	AA	APts	PIM	PP	SH	GW	S	%	TGF	PGF	TGA	PGA	+/–	GP	G	A	Pts	PIM	PP	SH	GW
1994-95	Lebret Eagles	SJHL	STATISTICS NOT AVAILABLE																									
1995-96	Merrimack College	H-East	34	6	20	26	....	....	....	54	....	....	....	....	....	....	....	....	....	....	....	....	....	....	....	....	....	....
1996-97	Merrimack College	H-East	35	7	16	23	....	....	....	71	....	....	....	....	....	....	....	....	....	....	....	....	....	....	....	....	....	....
1997-98	Merrimack College	H-East	38	4	26	30	....	....	....	84	....	....	....	....	....	....	....	....	....	....	....	....	....	....	....	....	....	....
1998-99	Saint John Flames	AHL	61	1	7	8	....	....	....	66	....	....	....	....	....	....	....	....	....	....	7	1	2	3	13	....	....	....
99-2000	**Calgary Flames**	**NHL**	**6**	**0**	**0**	**0**	**0**	**0**	**0**	**2**	**0**	**0**	**0**	**1**	**0.0**	**3**	**0**	**2**	**0**	**1**	....	....	....	....	....	....	....	....
	Saint John Flames	AHL	64	11	25	36	....	....	....	99	....	....	....	....	....	....	....	....	....	....	3	1	2	3	0	....	....	....
	NHL Totals		**6**	**0**	**0**	**0**	**0**	**0**	**0**	**2**	**0**	**0**	**0**	**1**	**0.0**	**3**	**0**	**2**	**0**		....	....	....	....	....	....	....	....

Signed as a free agent by **Calgary**, June 12, 1998

• SCREMIN, Claudio

Claudio Franceso D – R. 6'2", 205 lbs. b: Burnaby, B.C., 5/28/1968. Washington's 12th, 204th overall, in 1988.

Season	Club	League	GP	G	A	Pts	AG	AA	APts	PIM	PP	SH	GW	S	%	TGF	PGF	TGA	PGA	+/–	GP	G	A	Pts	PIM	PP	SH	GW
1984-85	B.C. Wrigley Midgets	BCAHA	71	24	100	124	....	....	....	....	....	....	....	....	....	....	....	....	....	....	....	....	....	....	....	....	....	....
1985-86	Richmond Sockeyes	BCJHL	48	5	29	34	....	....	....	57	....	....	....	....	....	....	....	....	....	....	....	....	....	....	....	....	....	....
1986-87	University of Maine	H-East	15	0	1	1	....	....	....	2	....	....	....	....	....	....	....	....	....	....	....	....	....	....	....	....	....	....
1987-88	University of Maine	H-East	44	6	18	24	....	....	....	22	....	....	....	....	....	....	....	....	....	....	....	....	....	....	....	....	....	....
1988-89	University of Maine	H-East	45	5	24	29	....	....	....	42	....	....	....	....	....	....	....	....	....	....	....	....	....	....	....	....	....	....
1989-90	University of Maine	H-East	45	4	26	30	....	....	....	14	....	....	....	....	....	....	....	....	....	....	....	....	....	....	....	....	....	....
1990-91	Kansas City Blades	IHL	77	7	14	21	....	....	....	60	....	....	....	....	....	....	....	....	....	....	....	....	....	....	....	....	....	....
1991-92	**San Jose Sharks**	**NHL**	**13**	**0**	**0**	**0**	**0**	**0**	**0**	**25**	**0**	**0**	**0**	**18**	**0.0**	**9**	**0**	**17**	**4**	**–4**	....	....	....	....	....	....	....	....
	Kansas City Blades	IHL	70	5	23	28	....	....	....	44	....	....	....	....	....	....	....	....	....	....	15	1	6	7	14	....	....	....
1992-93	**San Jose Sharks**	**NHL**	**4**	**0**	**1**	**1**	**0**	**1**	**1**	**4**	**0**	**0**	**0**	**4**	**0.0**	**6**	**0**	**9**	**2**	**–1**	....	....	....	....	....	....	....	....
	Kansas City Blades	IHL	75	10	22	32	....	....	....	93	....	....	....	....	....	....	....	....	....	....	12	0	5	5	18	....	....	....
1993-94	HC Varese	Alpenliga	28	10	12	22	....	....	....	20	....	....	....	....	....	....	....	....	....	....	....	....	....	....	....	....	....	....
	HC Varese	Italy	7	2	4	6	....	....	....	11	....	....	....	....	....	....	....	....	....	....	....	....	....	....	....	....	....	....
	Kansas City Blades	IHL	38	7	17	24	....	....	....	39	....	....	....	....	....	....	....	....	....	....	....	....	....	....	....	....	....	....
1994-95	Kansas City Blades	IHL	61	8	30	38	....	....	....	29	....	....	....	....	....	....	....	....	....	....	20	8	12	20	14	....	....	....
1995-96	Kansas City Blades	IHL	79	6	47	53	....	....	....	83	....	....	....	....	....	....	....	....	....	....	5	0	1	1	6	....	....	....
1996-97	Kansas City Blades	IHL	69	7	25	32	....	....	....	71	....	....	....	....	....	....	....	....	....	....	3	1	1	2	2	....	....	....
1997-98	Kansas City Blades	IHL	81	12	46	58	....	....	....	66	....	....	....	....	....	....	....	....	....	....	11	2	12	14	4	....	....	....
1998-99	Hannover Scorpions	Germany	52	7	17	24	....	....	....	40	....	....	....	....	....	....	....	....	....	....	....	....	....	....	....	....	....	....
99-2000	London Knights	BH-Cup	11	4	10	14	....	....	....	12	....	....	....	....	....	....	....	....	....	....	....	....	....	....	....	....	....	....
	London Knights	Britain	36	6	24	30	....	....	....	16	....	....	....	....	....	....	....	....	....	....	8	3	8	11	10	....	....	....
	NHL Totals		**17**	**0**	**1**	**1**	**0**	**1**	**1**	**29**	**0**	**0**	**0**	**22**	**0.0**	**15**	**0**	**26**	**6**		....	....	....	....	....	....	....	....

Rights traded to **Minnesota** by **Washington** for Don Beaupre, November 1, 1988. Signed as a free agent by **San Jose**, September 3, 1991.

• SCRUTON, Howard

D – L. 6'3", 190 lbs. b: Toronto, Ont., 10/6/1962.

Season	Club	League	GP	G	A	Pts	AG	AA	APts	PIM	PP	SH	GW	S	%	TGF	PGF	TGA	PGA	+/–	GP	G	A	Pts	PIM	PP	SH	GW
1978-79	St. Michael's Buzzers	OHA-B	65	4	24	28	....	....	....	174	....	....	....	....	....	....	....	....	....	....	....	....	....	....	....	....	....	....
1979-80	Niagara Falls Flyers	OMJHL	51	1	3	4	....	....	....	76	....	....	....	....	....	....	....	....	....	....	10	1	2	3	14	....	....	....
1980-81	Niagara Falls Flyers	OMJHL	28	5	9	14	....	....	....	56	....	....	....	....	....	....	....	....	....	....	....	....	....	....	....	....	....	....
	Kingston Canadians	OMJHL	25	0	10	10	....	....	....	23	....	....	....	....	....	....	....	....	....	....	14	0	4	4	25	....	....	....
1981-82	Kingston Canadians	OHL	56	6	29	35	....	....	....	80	....	....	....	....	....	....	....	....	....	....	....	....	....	....	....	....	....	....
	New Haven Nighthawks	AHL	1	1	0	1	....	....	....	0	....	....	....	....	....	....	....	....	....	....	2	0	0	0	0	....	....	....
1982-83	**Los Angeles Kings**	**NHL**	**4**	**0**	**4**	**4**	**0**	**3**	**3**	**9**	**0**	**0**	**0**	**4**	**0.0**	**5**	**0**	**10**	**1**	**–4**	....	....	....	....	....	....	....	....
	New Haven Nighthawks	AHL	74	6	7	13	....	....	....	40	....	....	....	....	....	....	....	....	....	....	12	0	1	1	12	....	....	....
1983-84	New Haven Nighthawks	AHL	33	1	4	5	....	....	....	21	....	....	....	....	....	....	....	....	....	....	....	....	....	....	....	....	....	....
1984-85	New Haven Nighthawks	AHL	74	1	6	7	....	....	....	31	....	....	....	....	....	....	....	....	....	....	....	....	....	....	....	....	....	....
	NHL Totals		**4**	**0**	**4**	**4**	**0**	**3**	**3**	**9**	**0**	**0**	**0**	**4**	**0.0**	**5**	**0**	**10**	**1**		....	....	....	....	....	....	....	....

Signed as a free agent by **LA Kings**, August 5, 1981.

• SEABROOKE, Glen

C – L. 6', 190 lbs. b: Peterborough, Ont., 9/11/1967. Philadelphia's 1st, 21st overall, in 1985.

Season	Club	League	GP	G	A	Pts	AG	AA	APts	PIM	PP	SH	GW	S	%	TGF	PGF	TGA	PGA	+/–	GP	G	A	Pts	PIM	PP	SH	GW
1982-83	Peterborough Jr. Petes	OJHL-B	36	9	17	26	....	....	....	30	....	....	....	....	....	....	....	....	....	....	....	....	....	....	....	....	....	....
1983-84	Peterborough Travelways	OMHA	29	36	31	67	....	....	....	31	....	....	....	....	....	....	....	....	....	....	....	....	....	....	....	....	....	....
	Peterborough Lumber	OJHL-B	5	3	2	5	....	....	....	4	....	....	....	....	....	....	....	....	....	....	....	....	....	....	....	....	....	....
1984-85	Peterborough Petes	OHL	45	21	13	34	....	....	....	49	....	....	....	....	....	....	....	....	....	....	16	3	5	8	4	....	....	....
1985-86	Peterborough Petes	OHL	19	8	12	20	....	....	....	33	....	....	....	....	....	....	....	....	....	....	14	9	7	16	14	....	....	....
1986-87	Peterborough Petes	OHL	48	30	39	69	....	....	....	29	....	....	....	....	....	....	....	....	....	....	4	3	3	6	6	....	....	....
	Philadelphia Flyers	**NHL**	**10**	**1**	**4**	**5**	**1**	**3**	**4**	**2**	**0**	**0**	**0**	**10**	**10.0**	**8**	**3**	**3**	**0**	**2**	....	....	....	....	....	....	....	....
1987-88	**Philadelphia Flyers**	**NHL**	**6**	**0**	**1**	**1**	**0**	**1**	**1**	**2**	**0**	**0**	**0**	**3**	**0.0**	**2**	**1**	**2**	**0**	**–1**	....	....	....	....	....	....	....	....
	Hershey Bears	AHL	73	32	46	78	....	....	....	39	....	....	....	....	....	....	....	....	....	....	7	4	5	9	2	....	....	....
1988-89	**Philadelphia Flyers**	**NHL**	**3**	**0**	**1**	**1**	**0**	**1**	**1**	**0**	**0**	**0**	**0**	**0**	**0.0**	**1**	**0**	**2**	**0**	**–1**	....	....	....	....	....	....	....	....
	Hershey Bears	AHL	51	23	15	38	....	....	....	19	....	....	....	....	....	....	....	....	....	....	....	....	....	....	....	....	....	....
	NHL Totals		**19**	**1**	**6**	**7**	**1**	**5**	**6**	**4**	**0**	**0**	**0**	**13**	**7.7**	**11**	**4**	**7**	**0**		....	....	....	....	....	....	....	....

• SECORD, Al

Alan William LW – L. 6'1", 205 lbs. b: Sudbury, Ont., 3/3/1958. Boston's 1st, 16th overall, in 1978.

Season	Club	League	GP	G	A	Pts	AG	AA	APts	PIM	PP	SH	GW	S	%	TGF	PGF	TGA	PGA	+/–	GP	G	A	Pts	PIM	PP	SH	GW
1974-75	Wexford Raiders	OJHL	41	5	13	18	....	....	....	104	....	....	....	....	....	....	....	....	....	....	....	....	....	....	....	....	....	....
1975-76	Hamilton Fincups	OMJHL	63	9	13	22	....	....	....	117	....	....	....	....	....	....	....	....	....	....	12	0	2	2	24	....	....	....
1976-77	St. Catharines Fincups	OMJHL	57	32	34	66	....	....	....	343	....	....	....	....	....	....	....	....	....	....	14	4	3	7	46	....	....	....
	Canada	WJC-A	7	2	2	4	....	....	....	8	....	....	....	....	....	....	....	....	....	....	....	....	....	....	....	....	....	....
1977-78	Hamilton Fincups	OMJHL	59	28	22	50	....	....	....	185	....	....	....	....	....	....	....	....	....	....	20	8	11	19	71	....	....	....
1978-79	**Boston Bruins**	**NHL**	**71**	**16**	**7**	**23**	**14**	**5**	**19**	**125**	**0**	**0**	**0**	**80**	**20.0**	**33**	**0**	**26**	**0**	**7**	**4**	**0**	**0**	**0**	**4**	**0**	**0**	**0**
	Rochester Americans	AHL	4	4	2	6	....	....	....	40	....	....	....	....	....	....	....	....	....	....	....	....	....	....	....	....	....	....
1979-80	**Boston Bruins**	**NHL**	**77**	**23**	**16**	**39**	**20**	**12**	**32**	**170**	**1**	**0**	**2**	**155**	**14.8**	**68**	**2**	**47**	**1**	**20**	**10**	**0**	**3**	**3**	**65**	**0**	**0**	**0**
1980-81	**Boston Bruins**	**NHL**	**18**	**0**	**3**	**3**	**0**	**2**	**2**	**42**	**0**	**0**	**0**	**11**	**0.0**	**5**	**1**	**2**	**0**	**2**	....	....	....	....	....	....	....	....
	Springfield Indians	AHL	8	3	5	8	....	....	....	21	....	....	....	....	....	....	....	....	....	....	....	....	....	....	....	....	....	....
	Chicago Black Hawks	**NHL**	**41**	**13**	**9**	**22**	**10**	**6**	**16**	**145**	**3**	**0**	**2**	**111**	**11.7**	**38**	**11**	**32**	**1**	**–4**	**3**	**4**	**0**	**4**	**14**	**0**	**0**	**0**
1981-82	**Chicago Black Hawks**	**NHL**	**80**	**44**	**31**	**75**	**35**	**21**	**56**	**303**	**14**	**0**	**6**	**215**	**20.5**	**135**	**53**	**99**	**0**	**–17**	**15**	**2**	**5**	**7**	**61**	**2**	**0**	**1**
1982-83	**Chicago Black Hawks**	**NHL**	**80**	**54**	**32**	**86**	**44**	**22**	**66**	**180**	**20**	**0**	**6**	**239**	**22.6**	**155**	**56**	**66**	**1**	**34**	**12**	**4**	**7**	**11**	**66**	**1**	**0**	**0**
1983-84	**Chicago Black Hawks**	**NHL**	**14**	**4**	**4**	**8**	**3**	**3**	**6**	**77**	**1**	**0**	**3**	**35**	**11.4**	**23**	**9**	**7**	**0**	**7**	**5**	**3**	**4**	**7**	**28**	**0**	**0**	**1**
1984-85	**Chicago Black Hawks**	**NHL**	**51**	**15**	**11**	**26**	**12**	**7**	**19**	**193**	**6**	**0**	**2**	**110**	**13.6**	**60**	**20**	**40**	**0**	**0**	**15**	**7**	**9**	**16**	**42**	**1**	**0**	**1**
1985-86	**Chicago Black Hawks**	**NHL**	**80**	**40**	**36**	**76**	**32**	**24**	**56**	**201**	**12**	**0**	**3**	**210**	**19.0**	**139**	**48**	**84**	**1**	**8**	**2**	**0**	**2**	**2**	**26**	**0**	**0**	**0**
1986-87	**Chicago Blackhawks**	**NHL**	**77**	**29**	**29**	**58**	**25**	**21**	**46**	**196**	**5**	**0**	**3**	**179**	**16.2**	**86**	**20**	**86**	**0**	**–20**	**4**	**0**	**0**	**0**	**21**	**0**	**0**	**0**
	Canada	WEC-A	10	0	2	2	....	....	....	16	....	....	....	....	....	....	....	....	....	....	....	....	....	....	....	....	....	....
1987-88	**Toronto Maple Leafs**	**NHL**	**74**	**15**	**27**	**42**	**13**	**19**	**32**	**221**	**2**	**0**	**0**	**149**	**10.1**	**80**	**21**	**80**	**0**	**–21**	**6**	**1**	**0**	**1**	**16**	**0**	**0**	**0**

			REGULAR SEASON																		PLAYOFFS							
Season	Club	League	GP	G	A	Pts	AG	AA	APts	PIM	PP	SH	GW	S	%	TGF	PGF	TGA	PGA	+/–	GP	G	A	Pts	PIM	PP	SH	GW
1988-89	**Toronto Maple Leafs**	**NHL**	**40**	**5**	**10**	**15**	**4**	**7**	**11**	**71**	**1**	**0**	**1**	**52**	**9.6**	**20**	**5**	**28**	**0**	**–13**	....	....	....	....	....	....	....	....
	Philadelphia Flyers	**NHL**	**20**	**1**	**0**	**1**	**1**	**0**	**1**	**38**	**0**	**0**	**0**	**15**	**6.7**	**3**	**0**	**10**	**0**	**–7**	**14**	**0**	**4**	**4**	**31**	**0**	**0**	**0**
1989-90	**Chicago Blackhawks**	**NHL**	**43**	**14**	**7**	**21**	**12**	**5**	**17**	**131**	**1**	**0**	**0**	**68**	**20.6**	**36**	**1**	**30**	**0**	**5**	**12**	**0**	**0**	**0**	**8**	**0**	**0**	**0**
1990-1994			OUT OF HOCKEY – RETIRED																									
1994-95	Chicago Wolves	IHL	59	13	20	33	....	....	....	195	....	....	....	....	....	....	....	....	....	....	3	1	1	2	19	....	....	....
1995-96	Chicago Wolves	IHL	47	8	8	16	....	....	....	108	....	....	....	....	....	....	....	....	....	....	9	1	0	4	4	....	....	....
	NHL Totals		**766**	**273**	**222**	**495**	**225**	**154**	**379**	**2093**	**66**	**0**	**28**	**1629**	**16.8**	**881**	**247**	**637**	**4**		**102**	**21**	**34**	**55**	**382**	**4**	**0**	**3**

Played in NHL All-Star Game (1982, 1983)

Traded to **Chicago** by **Boston** for Mike O'Connell, December 18, 1980. Traded to **Toronto** by **Chicago** with Ed Olczyk for Rick Vaive, Steve Thomas and Bob McGill, September 3, 1987. Traded to **Philadelphia** by **Toronto** for Philadelphia's 5th round choice (Keith Carney) in 1989 Entry Draft, February 7, 1989. Signed as a free agent by **Chicago**, August 7, 1989. Signed as a free agent by **Chicago Wolves** (IHL), September 10, 1994. • Played w/ RHI's Chicago Cheetahs in 1994 (18-11-14-25-45).

• SEDLBAUER, Ron

Ronald Andrew "Twilight" LW – L. 6'3", 195 lbs. b: Burlington, Ont., 10/22/1954. Vancouver's 1st, 23rd overall, in 1974.

Season	Club	League	GP	G	A	Pts	AG	AA	APts	PIM	PP	SH	GW	S	%	TGF	PGF	TGA	PGA	+/–	GP	G	A	Pts	PIM	PP	SH	GW
1971-72	Hamilton Red Wings	OMJHL	61	18	8	26	....	....	....	43	....	....	....	....	....	....	....	....	....	....	....	....	....	....	....	....	....	....
1972-73	Hamilton Red Wings	OMJHL	58	13	20	33	....	....	....	92	....	....	....	....	....	....	....	....	....	....	....	....	....	....	....	....	....	....
1973-74	Kitchener Rangers	OMJHL	54	29	25	54	....	....	....	83	....	....	....	....	....	....	....	....	....	....	....	....	....	....	....	....	....	....
1974-75	**Vancouver Canucks**	**NHL**	**26**	**3**	**4**	**7**	**3**	**3**	**6**	**17**	**0**	**0**	**1**	**43**	**7.0**	**12**	**1**	**15**	**0**	**–4**	**5**	**0**	**0**	**0**	**10**	**0**	**0**	**0**
	Seattle Totems	CHL	53	23	13	36	....	....	....	100	....	....	....	....	....	....	....	....	....	....	....	....	....	....	....	....	....	....
1975-76	**Vancouver Canucks**	**NHL**	**56**	**19**	**13**	**32**	**17**	**10**	**27**	**66**	**5**	**0**	**3**	**135**	**14.1**	**60**	**20**	**48**	**4**	**–4**	**2**	**0**	**0**	**0**	**0**	**0**	**0**	**0**
	Tulsa Oilers	CHL	4	1	1	2	....	....	....	9	....	....	....	....	....	....	....	....	....	....	....	....	....	....	....	....	....	....
1976-77	**Vancouver Canucks**	**NHL**	**70**	**18**	**20**	**38**	**16**	**15**	**31**	**29**	**0**	**1**	**3**	**129**	**14.0**	**54**	**3**	**49**	**10**	**12**	....	....	....	....	....	....	....	....
	Tulsa Oilers	CHL	8	4	6	10	....	....	....	28	....	....	....	....	....	....	....	....	....	....	....	....	....	....	....	....	....	....
1977-78	**Vancouver Canucks**	**NHL**	**62**	**18**	**12**	**30**	**16**	**9**	**25**	**25**	**1**	**0**	**1**	**119**	**15.1**	**43**	**6**	**52**	**9**	**–6**	....	....	....	....	....	....	....	....
	Tulsa Oilers	CHL	5	6	1	7	....	....	....	2	....	....	....	....	....	....	....	....	....	....	....	....	....	....	....	....	....	....
1978-79	**Vancouver Canucks**	**NHL**	**79**	**40**	**16**	**56**	**34**	**12**	**46**	**26**	**15**	**0**	**5**	**225**	**17.8**	**87**	**35**	**86**	**0**	**–34**	**3**	**0**	**1**	**1**	**9**	**0**	**0**	**0**
1979-80	**Vancouver Canucks**	**NHL**	**32**	**10**	**4**	**14**	**8**	**3**	**11**	**7**	**0**	**0**	**0**	**74**	**13.5**	**28**	**5**	**28**	**0**	**–5**	....	....	....	....	....	....	....	....
	Chicago Black Hawks	**NHL**	**45**	**13**	**10**	**23**	**11**	**7**	**18**	**14**	**1**	**0**	**0**	**132**	**9.8**	**48**	**7**	**40**	**0**	**1**	**7**	**1**	**1**	**2**	**6**	**1**	**0**	**1**
1980-81	**Chicago Black Hawks**	**NHL**	**39**	**12**	**3**	**15**	**9**	**2**	**11**	**12**	**3**	**0**	**0**	**69**	**17.4**	**25**	**7**	**25**	**0**	**–7**	....	....	....	....	....	....	....	....
	Toronto Maple Leafs	**NHL**	**21**	**10**	**4**	**14**	**8**	**3**	**11**	**14**	**5**	**0**	**2**	**45**	**22.2**	**24**	**12**	**15**	**0**	**–3**	**2**	**0**	**1**	**1**	**2**	**0**	**0**	**0**
1981-82	Cincinnati Tigers	CHL	73	27	20	47	....	....	....	49	....	....	....	....	....	....	....	....	....	....	4	3	0	3	0	....	....	....
	NHL Totals		**430**	**143**	**86**	**229**	**122**	**64**	**186**	**210**	**30**	**1**	**15**	**971**	**14.7**	**381**	**96**	**358**	**23**		**19**	**1**	**3**	**4**	**27**	**1**	**0**	**1**

Traded to **Chicago** by **Vancouver** for Dave Logan and Harold Phillipoff, December 21, 1979. Traded to **Toronto** by **Chicago** for cash, February 18, 1981.

• SEFTEL, Steve

Steven J. LW – L. 6'3", 200 lbs. b: Kitchener, Ont., 5/14/1968. Washington's 2nd, 40th overall, in 1986.

Season	Club	League	GP	G	A	Pts	AG	AA	APts	PIM	PP	SH	GW	S	%	TGF	PGF	TGA	PGA	+/–	GP	G	A	Pts	PIM	PP	SH	GW
1984-85	Kitchener Midget Greenshirts	OMHA	69	58	52	110	....	....	....	176	....	....	....	....	....	....	....	....	....	....	....	....	....	....	....	....	....	....
1985-86	Kingston Canadians	OHL	42	11	16	27	....	....	....	53	....	....	....	....	....	....	....	....	....	....	....	....	....	....	....	....	....	....
1986-87	Kingston Canadians	OHL	54	21	43	64	....	....	....	55	....	....	....	....	....	....	....	....	....	....	12	1	4	5	9	....	....	....
1987-88	Kingston Canadians	OHL	66	32	43	75	....	....	....	51	....	....	....	....	....	....	....	....	....	....	....	....	....	....	....	....	....	....
	Binghamton Whalers	AHL	3	0	0	0	....	....	....	2	....	....	....	....	....	....	....	....	....	....	....	....	....	....	....	....	....	....
1988-89	Baltimore Skipjacks	AHL	58	12	15	27	....	....	....	70	....	....	....	....	....	....	....	....	....	....	....	....	....	....	....	....	....	....
1989-90	Baltimore Skipjacks	AHL	74	10	19	29	....	....	....	52	....	....	....	....	....	....	....	....	....	....	12	4	3	7	10	....	....	....
1990-91	**Washington Capitals**	**NHL**	**4**	**0**	**0**	**0**	**0**	**0**	**0**	**2**	**0**	**0**	**0**	**2**	**0.0**	**0**	**0**	**2**	**0**	**–2**	....	....	....	....	....	....	....	....
	Baltimore Skipjacks	AHL	66	22	22	44	....	....	....	46	....	....	....	....	....	....	....	....	....	....	6	0	0	0	14	....	....	....
1991-92	Baltimore Skipjacks	AHL	18	2	6	8	....	....	....	27	....	....	....	....	....	....	....	....	....	....	....	....	....	....	....	....	....	....
	NHL Totals		**4**	**0**	**0**	**0**	**0**	**0**	**0**	**2**	**0**	**0**	**0**	**2**	**0.0**	**0**	**0**	**2**	**0**		....	....	....	....	....	....	....	....

• SEGUIN, Dan

Daniel George LW – L. 5'8", 165 lbs. b: Sudbury, Ont., 6/7/1948.

Season	Club	League	GP	G	A	Pts	AG	AA	APts	PIM	PP	SH	GW	S	%	TGF	PGF	TGA	PGA	+/–	GP	G	A	Pts	PIM	PP	SH	GW
1964-65	Kitchener Greenshirts	OHA-B	STATISTICS NOT AVAILABLE																									
	Kitchener Rangers	OHA-Jr.	1	0	0	0	....	....	....	0	....	....	....	....	....	....	....	....	....	....	....	....	....	....	....	....	....	....
1965-66	Kitchener Greenshirts	OHA-B	STATISTICS NOT AVAILABLE																									
1966-67	Kitchener Rangers	OHA-Jr.	48	13	32	45	....	....	....	78	....	....	....	....	....	....	....	....	....	....	13	1	3	4	21	....	....	....
1967-68	Kitchener Rangers	OHA-Jr.	43	20	49	69	....	....	....	65	....	....	....	....	....	....	....	....	....	....	19	10	15	25	62	....	....	....
1968-69	Memphis South Stars	CHL	72	25	32	57	....	....	....	60	....	....	....	....	....	....	....	....	....	....	....	....	....	....	....	....	....	....
1969-70	Iowa Stars	CHL	72	20	49	69	....	....	....	43	....	....	....	....	....	....	....	....	....	....	10	3	7	10	12	....	....	....
1970-71	**Minnesota North Stars**	**NHL**	**11**	**1**	**1**	**2**	**1**	**1**	**2**	**4**	**0**	**0**	**0**	**4**	**25.0**	**3**	**0**	**4**	**2**	**1**	....	....	....	....	....	....	....	....
	Vancouver Canucks	**NHL**	**25**	**0**	**5**	**5**	**0**	**4**	**4**	**46**	**0**	**0**	**0**	**17**	**0.0**	**5**	**1**	**15**	**1**	**–10**	....	....	....	....	....	....	....	....
	Rochester Americans	AHL	14	3	3	6	....	....	....	4	....	....	....	....	....	....	....	....	....	....	....	....	....	....	....	....	....	....
1971-72	Rochester Americans	AHL	66	15	24	39	....	....	....	82	....	....	....	....	....	....	....	....	....	....	....	....	....	....	....	....	....	....
1972-73	Seattle Totems	WHL	72	32	47	79	....	....	....	66	....	....	....	....	....	....	....	....	....	....	....	....	....	....	....	....	....	....
1973-74	**Vancouver Canucks**	**NHL**	**1**	**1**	**0**	**1**	**1**	**0**	**1**	**0**	**0**	**0**	**0**	**3**	**33.3**	**2**	**0**	**1**	**0**	**1**	....	....	....	....	....	....	....	....
	Seattle Totems	WHL	67	26	35	61	....	....	....	54	....	....	....	....	....	....	....	....	....	....	....	....	....	....	....	....	....	....
1974-75	Seattle Totems	CHL	73	*37	47	84	....	....	....	26	....	....	....	....	....	....	....	....	....	....	....	....	....	....	....	....	....	....
1975-76	Tulsa Oilers	CHL	62	22	28	50	....	....	....	56	....	....	....	....	....	....	....	....	....	....	9	1	1	2	2	....	....	....
1976-77	Rhode Island Reds	AHL	80	27	37	64	....	....	....	31	....	....	....	....	....	....	....	....	....	....	....	....	....	....	....	....	....	....
1977-78			REINSTATED AS AN AMATEUR																									
1978-79	Stratford Perths	OHA-Sr.	42	30	48	78	....	....	....	....	....	....	....	....	....	....	....	....	....	....	....	....	....	....	....	....	....	....
1979-80	Stratford Combines	OHA-Sr.	40	30	64	94	....	....	....	....	....	....	....	....	....	....	....	....	....	....	....	....	....	....	....	....	....	....
	NHL Totals		**37**	**2**	**6**	**8**	**2**	**5**	**7**	**50**	**0**	**0**	**0**	**24**	**8.3**	**10**	**1**	**20**	**3**		....	....	....	....	....	....	....	....

CHL Second All-Star Team (1970, 1975) • WHL First All-Star Team (1973)

Traded to **Minnesota** by **NY Rangers** with Wayne Hillman and Joey Johnston for Dave Balon, June 12, 1968. Claimed on waivers by **Vancouver** from **Minnesota**, November 23, 1970. Traded to **Rhode Island** (AHL) by **Vancouver** for cash, October, 1976.

• SEGUIN, Steve

Steven Joseph W – L. 6'2", 200 lbs. b: Cornwall, Ont., 4/10/1964. Los Angeles' 2nd, 48th overall, in 1982.

Season	Club	League	GP	G	A	Pts	AG	AA	APts	PIM	PP	SH	GW	S	%	TGF	PGF	TGA	PGA	+/–	GP	G	A	Pts	PIM	PP	SH	GW
1979-80	Cornwall Midget Royals	OMHA	55	61	48	109	....	....	....	....	....	....	....	....	....	....	....	....	....	....	....	....	....	....	....	....	....	....
1980-81	Kingston Voyageurs	OHA-B	1	0	1	1	....	....	....	4	....	....	....	....	....	....	....	....	....	....	....	....	....	....	....	....	....	....
	Kingston Canadians	OMJHL	49	8	8	16	....	....	....	18	....	....	....	....	....	....	....	....	....	....	....	....	....	....	....	....	....	....
1981-82	Kingston Canadians	OHL	62	23	31	54	....	....	....	75	....	....	....	....	....	....	....	....	....	....	4	0	2	2	4	....	....	....
1982-83	Kingston Canadians	OHL	19	8	17	25	....	....	....	42	....	....	....	....	....	....	....	....	....	....	....	....	....	....	....	....	....	....
	Peterborough Petes	OHL	44	16	30	46	....	....	....	22	....	....	....	....	....	....	....	....	....	....	4	0	1	1	2	....	....	....
1983-84	Peterborough Petes	OHL	67	55	51	106	....	....	....	84	....	....	....	....	....	....	....	....	....	....	8	8	8	16	11	....	....	....
1984-85	**Los Angeles Kings**	**NHL**	**5**	**0**	**0**	**0**	**0**	**0**	**0**	**9**	**0**	**0**	**0**	**5**	**0.0**	**0**	**0**	**5**	**0**	**–5**	....	....	....	....	....	....	....	....
	New Haven Nighthawks	AHL	58	18	7	25	....	....	....	39	....	....	....	....	....	....	....	....	....	....	....	....	....	....	....	....	....	....
1985-86	New Haven Nighthawks	AHL	2	0	0	0	....	....	....	0	....	....	....	....	....	....	....	....	....	....	....	....	....	....	....	....	....	....
	Hershey Bears	AHL	75	25	29	54	....	....	....	91	....	....	....	....	....	....	....	....	....	....	15	2	0	2	22	....	....	....
1986-87	Smiths Falls Rideaus	OHA-Sr.	STATISTICS NOT AVAILABLE																									
1987-88	Hershey Bears	AHL	1	0	0	0	....	....	....	0	....	....	....	....	....	....	....	....	....	....	....	....	....	....	....	....	....	....
	Baltimore Skipjacks	AHL	45	17	18	35	....	....	....	63	....	....	....	....	....	....	....	....	....	....	....	....	....	....	....	....	....	....
1988-89	Smiths Falls Rideaus	SLVHL	STATISTICS NOT AVAILABLE																									
	NHL Totals		**5**	**0**	**0**	**0**	**0**	**0**	**0**	**9**	**0**	**0**	**0**	**5**	**0.0**	**0**	**0**	**5**	**0**		....	....	....	....	....	....	....	....

Traded to **Philadelphia** by **LA Kings** with LA Kings' 2nd round choice (Jukka Seppo) in 1986 Entry Draft for Paul Guay and Philadelphia's 4th round choice (Sylvain Couturier) in 1986 Entry Draft, October 11, 1985.

• SEILING, Ric

Richard James RW/C – R. 6'1", 180 lbs. b: Elmira, Ont., 12/15/1957. Buffalo's 1st, 14th overall, in 1977.

Season	Club	League	GP	G	A	Pts	AG	AA	APts	PIM	PP	SH	GW	S	%	TGF	PGF	TGA	PGA	+/–	GP	G	A	Pts	PIM	PP	SH	GW
1974-75	Hamilton Red Wings	OMJHL	68	33	30	63	....	....	....	74	....	....	....	....	....	....	....	....	....	....	17	13	5	18	25	....	....	....
1975-76	Hamilton Fincups	OMJHL	59	35	51	86	....	....	....	49	....	....	....	....	....	....	....	....	....	....	14	14	13	27	19	....	....	....
	Hamilton Fincups	Mem-Cup	3	3	6	*9	....	....	....	2	....	....	....	....	....	....	....	....	....	....	....	....	....	....	....	....	....	....

Season	Club	League	GP	G	A	Pts	AG	AA	APts	PIM	PP	SH	GW	S	%	TGF	PGF	TGA	PGA	+/-	GP	G	A	Pts	PIM	PP	SH	GW
			REGULAR SEASON																		PLAYOFFS							
1976-77	St. Catharines Fincups	OMJHL	62	49	61	110	....	....	....	103	....	....	....	....	....	....	....	....	....	....	14	6	6	12	36	....	....	....
	Canada	WJC-A	7	3	1	4	....	....	....	10	....	....	....	....	....	....	....	....	....	....	....	....	....	....	....	....	....	....
1977-78	**Buffalo Sabres**	**NHL**	**80**	**19**	**19**	**38**	**17**	**15**	**32**	**33**	**2**	**0**	**4**	**114**	**16.7**	**64**	**5**	**46**	**0**	**13**	**8**	**0**	**2**	**2**	**7**	**0**	**0**	**0**
1978-79	**Buffalo Sabres**	**NHL**	**78**	**20**	**22**	**42**	**17**	**16**	**33**	**56**	**2**	**0**	**4**	**136**	**14.7**	**68**	**9**	**51**	**7**	**15**	**3**	**0**	**1**	**1**	**2**	**0**	**0**	**0**
1979-80	**Buffalo Sabres**	**NHL**	**80**	**25**	**35**	**60**	**21**	**26**	**47**	**54**	**5**	**1**	**2**	**155**	**16.1**	**102**	**14**	**66**	**8**	**30**	**14**	**5**	**4**	**9**	**6**	**0**	**0**	**0**
1980-81	**Buffalo Sabres**	**NHL**	**74**	**30**	**27**	**57**	**23**	**18**	**41**	**80**	**2**	**1**	**4**	**140**	**21.4**	**80**	**11**	**65**	**16**	**20**	**8**	**2**	**2**	**4**	**2**	**0**	**0**	**0**
1981-82	**Buffalo Sabres**	**NHL**	**57**	**22**	**25**	**47**	**17**	**17**	**34**	**58**	**7**	**1**	**3**	**112**	**19.6**	**69**	**21**	**54**	**13**	**7**	**4**	**1**	**1**	**2**	**2**	**1**	**0**	**0**
1982-83	**Buffalo Sabres**	**NHL**	**75**	**19**	**22**	**41**	**16**	**15**	**31**	**41**	**6**	**0**	**2**	**127**	**15.0**	**80**	**18**	**74**	**14**	**2**	**10**	**2**	**3**	**5**	**6**	**0**	**0**	**0**
1983-84	**Buffalo Sabres**	**NHL**	**78**	**13**	**22**	**35**	**10**	**15**	**25**	**42**	**0**	**3**	**0**	**135**	**9.6**	**65**	**3**	**67**	**15**	**10**	**3**	**0**	**0**	**0**	**2**	**0**	**0**	**0**
1984-85	**Buffalo Sabres**	**NHL**	**73**	**16**	**15**	**31**	**13**	**10**	**23**	**86**	**2**	**3**	**3**	**118**	**13.6**	**59**	**5**	**49**	**25**	**30**	**5**	**4**	**1**	**5**	**4**	**0**	**0**	**0**
1985-86	**Buffalo Sabres**	**NHL**	**69**	**12**	**13**	**25**	**10**	**9**	**19**	**74**	**0**	**0**	**1**	**85**	**14.1**	**38**	**2**	**59**	**18**	**–5**	....	....	....	....	....	....	....	....
1986-87	**Detroit Red Wings**	**NHL**	**74**	**3**	**8**	**11**	**3**	**6**	**9**	**49**	**0**	**0**	**0**	**35**	**8.6**	**17**	**0**	**55**	**34**	**–4**	**7**	**0**	**0**	**0**	**5**	**0**	**0**	**0**
1987-88	Adirondack Red Wings	AHL	70	16	13	29	....	....	....	34	....	....	....	....	....	....	....	....	....	....	9	2	2	4	47	....	....	....
	NHL Totals		**738**	**179**	**208**	**387**	**147**	**147**	**294**	**573**	**26**	**9**	**23**	**1157**	**15.5**	**642**	**88**	**586**	**150**		**62**	**14**	**14**	**28**	**36**	**1**	**0**	**0**

• Brother of Rod • Memorial Cup All-Star Team (1976)

Traded to **Detroit** by **Buffalo** for future considerations, October 7, 1986.

• SEILING, Rod

Rodney Albert "Sod" D – L. 6', 195 lbs. b: Kitchener, Ont., 11/14/1944.

Season	Club	League	GP	G	A	Pts	AG	AA	APts	PIM	PP	SH	GW	S	%	TGF	PGF	TGA	PGA	+/-	GP	G	A	Pts	PIM	PP	SH	GW
1960-61	St. Michael's Buzzers	OHA-B	STATISTICS NOT AVAILABLE																									
	St. Michael's Majors	OHA-Jr.	3	0	0	0	....	....	....	2	....	....	....	....	....	....	....	....	....	....	4	0	0	0	0	....	....	....
1961-62	St. Michael's Majors	MTJHL	31	24	26	50	....	....	....	14	....	....	....	....	....	....	....	....	....	....	4	2	1	3	0	....	....	....
	St. Michael's Majors	Mem-Cup	5	2	2	4	....	....	....	11	....	....	....	....	....	....	....	....	....	....	....	....	....	....	....	....	....	....
1962-63	Neil McNeil Maroons	MTJHL	38	29	48	77	....	....	....	32	....	....	....	....	....	....	....	....	....	....	10	4	10	14	14	....	....	....
1962-63	**Toronto Maple Leafs**	**NHL**	**1**	**0**	**1**	**1**	**0**	**1**	**1**	**0**	....	....	....	....	....	....	....	....	....	....	....	....	....	....	....	....	....	....
	Sudbury Wolves	EPHL	3	2	2	4	....	....	....	0	....	....	....	....	....	....	....	....	....	....	....	....	....	....	....	....	....	....
	Rochester Americans	AHL	1	1	0	1	....	....	....	0	....	....	....	....	....	....	....	....	....	....	....	....	....	....	....	....	....	....
	Neil McNeil Maroons	Mem-Cup	6	1	3	4	....	....	....	2	....	....	....	....	....	....	....	....	....	....	....	....	....	....	....	....	....	....
1963-64	Toronto Marlboros	OHA-Jr.	41	13	54	67	....	....	....	74	....	....	....	....	....	....	....	....	....	....	9	5	14	19	14	....	....	....
	Canada	Olympics	7	4	2	6	....	....	....	6	....	....	....	....	....	....	....	....	....	....	....	....	....	....	....	....	....	....
	Rochester Americans	AHL	2	0	0	0	....	....	....	0	....	....	....	....	....	....	....	....	....	....	....	....	....	....	....	....	....	....
	New York Rangers	**NHL**	**2**	**0**	**1**	**1**	**0**	**1**	**1**	**0**	....	....	....	....	....	....	....	....	....	....	....	....	....	....	....	....	....	....
	Toronto Marlboros	Mem-Cup	10	7	7	14	....	....	....	10	....	....	....	....	....	....	....	....	....	....	....	....	....	....	....	....	....	....
1964-65	**New York Rangers**	**NHL**	**68**	**4**	**22**	**26**	**5**	**23**	**28**	**44**	....	....	....	....	....	....	....	....	....	....	....	....	....	....	....	....	....	....
1965-66	**New York Rangers**	**NHL**	**52**	**5**	**10**	**15**	**6**	**9**	**15**	**24**	....	....	....	....	....	....	....	....	....	....	....	....	....	....	....	....	....	....
	Minnesota Rangers	CPHL	13	3	5	8	....	....	....	4	....	....	....	....	....	....	....	....	....	....	....	....	....	....	....	....	....	....
1966-67	**New York Rangers**	**NHL**	**12**	**1**	**1**	**2**	**1**	**1**	**2**	**6**	....	....	....	....	....	....	....	....	....	....	....	....	....	....	....	....	....	....
	Baltimore Clippers	AHL	46	10	20	30	....	....	....	38	....	....	....	....	....	....	....	....	....	....	9	2	2	4	14	....	....	....
1967-68	**New York Rangers**	**NHL**	**71**	**5**	**11**	**16**	**6**	**11**	**17**	**44**	**0**	**0**	**1**	**119**	**4.2**	**69**	**5**	**48**	**7**	**23**	**6**	**1**	**1**	**2**	**4**	**0**	**0**	**0**
1968-69	**New York Rangers**	**NHL**	**73**	**4**	**17**	**21**	**4**	**15**	**19**	**73**	**0**	**0**	**1**	**154**	**2.6**	**85**	**16**	**82**	**19**	**6**	**4**	**1**	**0**	**1**	**2**	**0**	**0**	**0**
1969-70	**New York Rangers**	**NHL**	**76**	**5**	**21**	**26**	**5**	**20**	**25**	**68**	**0**	**0**	**0**	**176**	**2.8**	**113**	**10**	**80**	**18**	**41**	**2**	**0**	**0**	**0**	**0**	**0**	**0**	**0**
1970-71	**New York Rangers**	**NHL**	**68**	**5**	**22**	**27**	**5**	**18**	**23**	**34**	**0**	**0**	**3**	**137**	**3.6**	**85**	**13**	**58**	**16**	**30**	**13**	**1**	**0**	**1**	**12**	**0**	**0**	**0**
1971-72	**New York Rangers**	**NHL**	**78**	**5**	**36**	**41**	**5**	**31**	**36**	**62**	**0**	**1**	**2**	**168**	**3.0**	**127**	**7**	**92**	**25**	**53**	**16**	**1**	**4**	**5**	**10**	**1**	**0**	**0**
1972-73	Team Canada	Summit-72	3	0	0	0	....	....	....	0	....	....	....	....	....	....	....	....	....	....	....	....	....	....	....	....	....	....
	New York Rangers	**NHL**	**72**	**9**	**33**	**42**	**8**	**26**	**34**	**36**	**1**	**1**	**2**	**155**	**5.8**	**125**	**12**	**90**	**20**	**43**	....	....	....	....	....	....	....	....
1973-74	**New York Rangers**	**NHL**	**68**	**7**	**23**	**30**	**7**	**19**	**26**	**32**	**0**	**0**	**0**	**104**	**6.7**	**98**	**6**	**96**	**20**	**16**	**13**	**0**	**2**	**2**	**19**	**0**	**0**	**0**
1974-75	**New York Rangers**	**NHL**	**4**	**0**	**1**	**1**	**0**	**1**	**1**	**0**	**0**	**0**	**0**	**4**	**0.0**	**1**	**0**	**7**	**2**	**–4**	....	....	....	....	....	....	....	....
	Washington Capitals	**NHL**	**1**	**0**	**0**	**0**	**0**	**0**	**0**	**0**	**0**	**0**	**0**	**2**	**0.0**	**0**	**0**	**0**	**0**	**0**	....	....	....	....	....	....	....	....
	Toronto Maple Leafs	**NHL**	**60**	**5**	**12**	**17**	**4**	**9**	**13**	**40**	**1**	**1**	**1**	**94**	**5.3**	**76**	**7**	**89**	**28**	**8**	**7**	**0**	**0**	**0**	**0**	**0**	**0**	**0**
1975-76	**Toronto Maple Leafs**	**NHL**	**77**	**3**	**16**	**19**	**3**	**12**	**15**	**46**	**0**	**0**	**0**	**108**	**2.8**	**78**	**3**	**96**	**32**	**11**	**10**	**0**	**1**	**1**	**6**	**0**	**0**	**0**
1976-77	**St. Louis Blues**	**NHL**	**79**	**3**	**26**	**29**	**3**	**20**	**23**	**36**	**2**	**0**	**1**	**142**	**2.1**	**100**	**14**	**118**	**33**	**1**	**4**	**0**	**0**	**0**	**2**	**0**	**0**	**0**
1977-78	**St. Louis Blues**	**NHL**	**78**	**1**	**11**	**12**	**1**	**8**	**9**	**40**	**0**	**0**	**0**	**98**	**1.0**	**54**	**3**	**129**	**30**	**–48**	....	....	....	....	....	....	....	....
1978-79	**St. Louis Blues**	**NHL**	**3**	**0**	**1**	**1**	**0**	**1**	**1**	**4**	**0**	**0**	**0**	**3**	**0.0**	**2**	**0**	**5**	**2**	**–1**	....	....	....	....	....	....	....	....
	Atlanta Flames	**NHL**	**36**	**0**	**4**	**4**	**0**	**3**	**3**	**12**	**0**	**0**	**0**	**28**	**0.0**	**29**	**0**	**29**	**8**	**8**	**2**	**0**	**0**	**0**	**0**	**0**	**0**	**0**
	NHL Totals		**979**	**62**	**269**	**331**	**63**	**229**	**292**	**601**	....	....	....	....	....	....	....	....	....	....	**77**	**4**	**8**	**12**	**55**	....	....	....

• Brother of Ric • OHA-Jr. Second All-Star Team (1964) • Played in NHL All-Star Game (1972)

Traded to **NY Rangers** by **Toronto** with Dick Duff, Bob Nevin, Arnie Brown and Bill Collins for Andy Bathgate and Don McKenney, February 22, 1964. Claimed by **St. Louis** from **NY Rangers** in Expansion Draft, June 6, 1967. Traded to **NY Rangers** by **St. Louis** for Gary Sabourin, Bob Plager, Gord Kannegiesser and Tim Ecclestone, June 6, 1967. Claimed on waivers by **Washington** from **NY Rangers**, October 29, 1974. Traded to **Toronto** by **Washington** for Tim Ecclestone and Willie Brossart, November 2, 1974. Signed as a free agent by **St. Louis**, September 9, 1976. Traded to **Atlanta** by **St. Louis** for cash, November 4, 1978.

• SEJBA, Jiri

LW – L. 5'10", 185 lbs. b: Pardubice, Czech., 7/22/1962. Buffalo's 9th, 182nd overall, in 1985.

Season	Club	League	GP	G	A	Pts	AG	AA	APts	PIM	PP	SH	GW	S	%	TGF	PGF	TGA	PGA	+/-	GP	G	A	Pts	PIM	PP	SH	GW
1979-80	Tesla Pardubice	Czech.	12	5	4	9	....	....	....	4	....	....	....	....	....	....	....	....	....	....	....	....	....	....	....	....	....	....
1980-81	Tesla Pardubice	Czech.	28	14	4	18	....	....	....	14	....	....	....	....	....	....	....	....	....	....	....	....	....	....	....	....	....	....
1981-82	Tesla Pardubice	Czech.	40	24	18	42	....	....	....	33	....	....	....	....	....	....	....	....	....	....	....	....	....	....	....	....	....	....
1982-83	Tesla Pardubice	Czech.	44	21	18	39	....	....	....	32	....	....	....	....	....	....	....	....	....	....	....	....	....	....	....	....	....	....
1983-84	Tesla Pardubice	Czech.	44	15	10	25	....	....	....	21	....	....	....	....	....	....	....	....	....	....	....	....	....	....	....	....	....	....
1984-85	Dukla Jihlava	Czech.	41	19	9	28	....	....	....	40	....	....	....	....	....	....	....	....	....	....	....	....	....	....	....	....	....	....
	Czechoslovakia	WEC-A	9	4	3	7	....	....	....	2	....	....	....	....	....	....	....	....	....	....	....	....	....	....	....	....	....	....
1985-86	Dukla Jihlava	Czech.	43	17	9	26	....	....	....	18	....	....	....	....	....	....	....	....	....	....	....	....	....	....	....	....	....	....
	Czechoslovakia	WEC-A	9	2	2	4	....	....	....	6	....	....	....	....	....	....	....	....	....	....	....	....	....	....	....	....	....	....
1986-87	Tesla Pardubice	Czech.	34	23	11	34	....	....	....	....	....	....	....	....	....	....	....	....	....	....	....	....	....	....	....	....	....	....
	Czechoslovakia	WEC-A	10	1	3	4	....	....	....	12	....	....	....	....	....	....	....	....	....	....	....	....	....	....	....	....	....	....
1987-88	Czechoslovakia	Can-Cup	5	1	2	3	....	....	....	2	....	....	....	....	....	....	....	....	....	....	....	....	....	....	....	....	....	....
	Tesla Pardubice	Czech.	23	10	15	25	....	....	....	....	....	....	....	....	....	....	....	....	....	....	....	....	....	....	....	....	....	....
	Czechoslovakia	Olympics	8	3	1	4	....	....	....	16	....	....	....	....	....	....	....	....	....	....	....	....	....	....	....	....	....	....
1988-89	Tesla Pardubice	Czech.	44	38	21	59	....	....	....	68	....	....	....	....	....	....	....	....	....	....	....	....	....	....	....	....	....	....
	Czechoslovakia	WEC-A	10	0	1	1	....	....	....	8	....	....	....	....	....	....	....	....	....	....	....	....	....	....	....	....	....	....
1989-90	Tesla Pardubice	Czech.	26	11	14	25	....	....	....	....	....	....	....	....	....	....	....	....	....	....	....	....	....	....	....	....	....	....
1990-91	**Buffalo Sabres**	**NHL**	**11**	**0**	**2**	**2**	**0**	**2**	**2**	**8**	**0**	**0**	**0**	**10**	**0.0**	**4**	**0**	**9**	**0**	**–5**	....	....	....	....	....	....	....	....
	Rochester Americans	AHL	31	15	13	28	....	....	....	54	....	....	....	....	....	....	....	....	....	....	14	6	7	13	29	....	....	....
1991-92	Rochester Americans	AHL	59	27	31	58	....	....	....	36	....	....	....	....	....	....	....	....	....	....	2	0	0	0	0	....	....	....
1992-93	Jokerit Helsinki	Finland	46	16	10	26	....	....	....	40	....	....	....	....	....	....	....	....	....	....	3	1	1	2	0	....	....	....
1993-94	Tesla Pardubice	Czech-Rep	42	12	18	30	....	....	....	0	....	....	....	....	....	....	....	....	....	....	....	....	....	....	....	....	....	....
1994-95	Tesla Pardubice	Czech-Rep	36	16	16	32	....	....	....	....	....	....	....	....	....	....	....	....	....	....	....	....	....	....	....	....	....	....
1995-96	Slovan Bratislava	Slovakia	36	11	17	28	....	....	....	44	....	....	....	....	....	....	....	....	....	....	....	....	....	....	....	....	....	....
1996-97	Slovan Bratislava	Slovakia	43	8	23	31	....	....	....	....	....	....	....	....	....	....	....	....	....	....	2	3	1	4	....	....	....	....
	Slovan Bratislava	EuroHL	6	3	7	*10	....	....	....	6	....	....	....	....	....	....	....	....	....	....	2	0	0	0	2	....	....	....
1997-98	Moskitos Essen	Germany-3	60	16	30	46	....	....	....	40	....	....	....	....	....	....	....	....	....	....	....	....	....	....	....	....	....	....
1998-99	Moskitos Essen	Germany-2	48	17	14	31	....	....	....	56	....	....	....	....	....	....	....	....	....	....	....	....	....	....	....	....	....	....
99-2000	Moskitos Essen	Germany	58	5	13	18	....	....	....	37	....	....	....	....	....	....	....	....	....	....	....	....	....	....	....	....	....	....
	NHL Totals		**11**	**0**	**2**	**2**	**0**	**2**	**2**	**8**	**0**	**0**	**0**	**10**	**0.0**	**4**	**0**	**9**	**0**		....	....	....	....	....	....	....	....

• SELANNE, Teemu

Teemu I. RW – R. 6', 200 lbs. b: Helsinki, Finland, 7/3/1970. Winnipeg's 1st, 10th overall, in 1988.

Season	Club	League	GP	G	A	Pts	AG	AA	APts	PIM	PP	SH	GW	S	%	TGF	PGF	TGA	PGA	+/-	GP	G	A	Pts	PIM	PP	SH	GW
1986-87	Jokerit Helsinki	Finland-Jr.	33	10	12	22	....	....	....	8	....	....	....	....	....	....	....	....	....	....	....	....	....	....	....	....	....	....
1987-88	Jokerit Helsinki	Finland-Jr.	33	*43	23	*66	....	....	....	18	....	....	....	....	....	....	....	....	....	....	5	4	3	7	2	....	....	....
	Jokerit Helsinki	Finland-2	5	1	1	2	....	....	....	0	....	....	....	....	....	....	....	....	....	....	....	....	....	....	....	....	....	....
	Finland	EJC-A	6	7	9	16	....	....	....	8	....	....	....	....	....	....	....	....	....	....	....	....	....	....	....	....	....	....

			REGULAR SEASON																		PLAYOFFS							
Season	Club	League	GP	G	A	Pts	AG	AA	APts	PIM	PP	SH	GW	S	%	TGF	PGF	TGA	PGA	+/–	GP	G	A	Pts	PIM	PP	SH	GW
1988-89	Army Sports Academy	Finland-Jr.	3	3	1	4	....	....	....	2	....	....	....	....	....	....	....	....	....	....	....	....	....	....	....	....	....	....
	Jokerit Helsinki	Finland-Jr.	3	8	8	16	....	....	....	4	....	....	....	....	....	....	....	....	....	....	....	....	....	....	....	....	....	....
	Jokerit Helsinki	Finland-2	34	35	33	68	....	....	....	12	....	....	....	....	....	....	....	....	....	....	5	7	3	10	4	....	....	....
	Finland	WJC-A	7	5	5	10	....	....	....	10	....	....	....	....	....	....	....	....	....	....	....	....	....	....	....	....	....	....
1989-90	Jokerit Helsinki	Finland	11	4	8	12	....	....	....	0	....	....	....	....	....	....	....	....	....	....	....	....	....	....	....	....	....	....
1990-91	Jokerit Helsinki	Finland-Jr.	1	0	0	0	....	....	....	0	....	....	....	....	....	....	....	....	....	....	....	....	....	....	....	....	....	....
	Jokerit Helsinki	Finland	42	33	25	58	....	....	....	12	....	....	....	....	....	....	....	....	....	....	....	....	....	....	....	....	....	....
	Finland	WEC-A	10	6	5	11	....	....	....	2	....	....	....	....	....	....	....	....	....	....	....	....	....	....	....	....	....	....
1991-92	Finland	Can-Cup	6	1	1	2	....	....	....	2	....	....	....	....	....	....	....	....	....	....	....	....	....	....	....	....	....	....
	Jokerit Helsinki	Finland	44	*39	23	62	....	....	....	20	....	....	....	....	....	....	....	....	....	....	10	*10	7	*17	18	....	....	....
	Finland	Olympics	8	7	4	11	....	....	....	6	....	....	....	....	....	....	....	....	....	....	....	....	....	....	....	....	....	....
1992-93	**Winnipeg Jets**	**NHL**	**84**	***76**	**56**	**132**	**64**	**39**	**103**	**45**	**24**	**0**	**7**	**387**	**19.6**	**165**	**67**	**93**	**3**	**8**	**6**	**4**	**2**	**6**	**2**	**2**	**0**	**2**
1993-94	**Winnipeg Jets**	**NHL**	**51**	**25**	**29**	**54**	**23**	**22**	**45**	**22**	**11**	**0**	**2**	**191**	**13.1**	**81**	**38**	**66**	**0**	**–23**	....	....	....	....	....	....	....	....
1994-95	Jokerit Helsinki	Finland	20	7	12	19	....	....	....	6	....	....	....	....	....	....	....	....	....	....	....	....	....	....	....	....	....	....
	Winnipeg Jets	**NHL**	**45**	**22**	**26**	**48**	**39**	**38**	**77**	**2**	**8**	**2**	**1**	**167**	**13.2**	**75**	**32**	**44**	**2**	**1**	....	....	....	....	....	....	....	....
1995-96	**Winnipeg Jets**	**NHL**	**51**	**24**	**48**	**72**	**24**	**39**	**63**	**18**	**6**	**1**	**4**	**163**	**14.7**	**98**	**47**	**52**	**4**	**3**	....	....	....	....	....	....	....	....
	Mighty Ducks of Anaheim	**NHL**	**28**	**16**	**20**	**36**	**16**	**16**	**32**	**4**	**3**	**0**	**1**	**104**	**15.4**	**48**	**23**	**24**	**1**	**2**	....	....	....	....	....	....	....	....
	Finland	WC-A	6	5	3	8	....	....	....	0	....	....	....	....	....	....	....	....	....	....	....	....	....	....	....	....	....	....
1996-97	Finland	W-Cup	4	3	2	5	....	....	....	0	....	....	....	....	....	....	....	....	....	....	....	....	....	....	....	....	....	....
	Mighty Ducks of Anaheim	**NHL**	**78**	**51**	**58**	**109**	**54**	**52**	**106**	**34**	**11**	**1**	**8**	**273**	**18.7**	**137**	**46**	**70**	**7**	**28**	**11**	**7**	**3**	**10**	**4**	**3**	**0**	**1**
1997-98	**Mighty Ducks of Anaheim**	**NHL**	**73**	***52**	**34**	**86**	**61**	**33**	**94**	**30**	**10**	**1**	**10**	**268**	**19.4**	**112**	**34**	**72**	**6**	**12**	....	....	....	....	....	....	....	....
	Finland	Olympics	5	4	6	*10	....	....	....	8	....	....	....	....	....	....	....	....	....	....	....	....	....	....	....	....	....	....
1998-99	**Mighty Ducks of Anaheim**	**NHL**	**75**	***47**	**60**	**107**	**55**	**58**	**113**	**30**	**25**	**0**	**7**	**281**	**16.7**	**139**	**70**	**53**	**2**	**18**	**4**	**2**	**2**	**4**	**2**	**1**	**0**	**0**
	Finland	WC-A	11	3	8	11	....	....	....	2	....	....	....	....	....	....	....	....	....	....	....	....	....	....	....	....	....	....
99-2000	**Mighty Ducks of Anaheim**	**NHL**	**79**	**33**	**52**	**85**	**37**	**48**	**85**	**12**	**8**	**0**	**6**	**236**	**14.0**	**117**	**43**	**70**	**2**	**6**	....	....	....	....	....	....	....	....
	NHL Totals		**564**	**346**	**383**	**729**	**373**	**345**	**718**	**197**	**106**	**5**	**46**	**2070**	**16.7**	**972**	**400**	**544**	**27**		**21**	**13**	**7**	**20**	**8**	**6**	**0**	**3**

EJC-A All-Star Team (1988) • Won Calder Memorial Trophy (1993) • NHL First All-Star Team (1993, 1997) • NHL All-Rookie Team (1993) • NHL Second All-Star Team (1998, 1999) • Won Maurice "Rocket" Richard Trophy (1999) • WC-A All-Star Team (1999) • WC-A MVP (1999) • Played in NHL All-Star Game (1993, 1994, 1996, 1997, 1998, 1999, 2000)

• Missed majority of 1989-90 season recovering from leg injury suffered in game vs. HIFK Helsinki, October 19, 1989. Traded to **Anaheim** by **Winnipeg** with Marc Chouinard and Winnipeg's 4th round choice (later traded to Toronto - later traded to Montreal - Montreal selected Kim Staal) in 1996 Entry Draft for Chad Kilger, Oleg Tverdovsky and Anaheim's 3rd round choice (Per-Anton Lundstrom) in 1996 Entry Draft, February 7, 1996.

• SELBY, Brit

Robert Britt LW – L. 5'10", 175 lbs. b: Kingston, Ont., 3/27/1945.

Season	Club	League	GP	G	A	Pts	AG	AA	APts	PIM	PP	SH	GW	S	%	TGF	PGF	TGA	PGA	+/–	GP	G	A	Pts	PIM	PP	SH	GW
1960-61	Lakeshore Maroons	OHA-B	....	....	....	....	....	....	....	....	....	....	....	....	....	....	....	....	....	....	....	....	....	....	....	....	....	....
	Toronto Marlboros	OHA-Jr.	2	0	0	0	....	....	....	0	....	....	....	....	....	....	....	....	....	....	....	....	....	....	....	....	....	....
1961-62	Lakeshore Maroons	OHA-B	STATISTICS NOT AVAILABLE																									
	Toronto Marlboros	OHA-Jr.	3	1	1	2	....	....	....	0	....	....	....	....	....	....	....	....	....	....	....	....	....	....	....	....	....	....
1962-63	Toronto Marlboros	OHA-Jr.	33	24	15	39	....	....	....	22	....	....	....	....	....	....	....	....	....	....	11	6	11	17	28	....	....	....
1963-64	Toronto Marlboros	OHA-Jr.	48	24	28	52	....	....	....	34	....	....	....	....	....	....	....	....	....	....	9	2	3	5	4	....	....	....
	Toronto Marlboros	Mem-Cup	12	8	11	19	....	....	....	10	....	....	....	....	....	....	....	....	....	....	....	....	....	....	....	....	....	....
1964-65	Toronto Marlboros	OHA-Jr.	52	45	43	88	....	....	....	58	....	....	....	....	....	....	....	....	....	....	19	*11	10	21	18	....	....	....
	Toronto Maple Leafs	**NHL**	**3**	**2**	**0**	**2**	**2**	**0**	**2**	**2**	....	....	....	....	....	....	....	....	....	....	....	....	....	....	....	....	....	....
1965-66	**Toronto Maple Leafs**	**NHL**	**61**	**14**	**13**	**27**	**16**	**12**	**28**	**26**	....	....	....	....	....	....	....	....	....	....	**4**	**0**	**0**	**0**	**0**	**0**	**0**	**0**
1966-67	**Toronto Maple Leafs**	**NHL**	**6**	**1**	**1**	**2**	**1**	**1**	**2**	**0**	....	....	....	....	....	....	....	....	....	....	....	....	....	....	....	....	....	....
	Vancouver Canucks	WHL	15	5	1	6	....	....	....	12	....	....	....	....	....	....	....	....	....	....	....	....	....	....	....	....	....	....
1967-68	**Philadelphia Flyers**	**NHL**	**56**	**15**	**15**	**30**	**17**	**15**	**32**	**24**	**4**	**0**	**1**	**88**	**17.0**	**45**	**9**	**39**	**0**	**–3**	**7**	**1**	**1**	**2**	**4**	**0**	**0**	**0**
1968-69	**Philadelphia Flyers**	**NHL**	**63**	**10**	**13**	**23**	**11**	**12**	**23**	**23**	**1**	**0**	**3**	**116**	**8.6**	**37**	**4**	**57**	**13**	**–11**	....	....	....	....	....	....	....	....
	Toronto Maple Leafs	**NHL**	**14**	**2**	**2**	**4**	**2**	**2**	**4**	**19**	**0**	**0**	**0**	**18**	**11.1**	**8**	**2**	**7**	**1**	**0**	**4**	**0**	**0**	**0**	**4**	**0**	**0**	**0**
1969-70	**Toronto Maple Leafs**	**NHL**	**74**	**10**	**13**	**23**	**11**	**12**	**23**	**40**	**1**	**0**	**3**	**88**	**11.4**	**46**	**7**	**65**	**21**	**–5**	....	....	....	....	....	....	....	....
1970-71	**Toronto Maple Leafs**	**NHL**	**11**	**0**	**1**	**1**	**0**	**1**	**1**	**6**	**0**	**0**	**0**	**7**	**0.0**	**1**	**0**	**7**	**3**	**–3**	....	....	....	....	....	....	....	....
	St. Louis Blues	**NHL**	**56**	**1**	**4**	**5**	**1**	**3**	**4**	**23**	**0**	**0**	**0**	**33**	**3.0**	**14**	**1**	**25**	**2**	**–10**	**1**	**0**	**0**	**0**	**0**	**0**	**0**	**0**
1971-72	**St. Louis Blues**	**NHL**	**6**	**0**	**0**	**0**	**0**	**0**	**0**	**0**	**0**	**0**	**0**	**7**	**0.0**	**3**	**0**	**5**	**0**	**–2**	....	....	....	....	....	....	....	....
	Kansas City Blues	CHL	63	11	24	35	....	....	....	82	....	....	....	....	....	....	....	....	....	....	....	....	....	....	....	....	....	....
1972-73	Quebec Nordiques	WHA	7	0	1	1	....	....	....	4	....	....	....	....	....	....	....	....	....	....	....	....	....	....	....	....	....	....
	New England Whalers	WHA	65	13	29	42	....	....	....	48	....	....	....	....	....	....	....	....	....	....	13	3	4	7	13	....	....	....
1973-74	Toronto Toros	WHA	64	9	17	26	....	....	....	21	....	....	....	....	....	....	....	....	....	....	10	1	3	4	2	....	....	....
1974-75	Toronto Toros	WHA	17	1	4	5	....	....	....	0	....	....	....	....	....	....	....	....	....	....	....	....	....	....	....	....	....	....
	NHL Totals		**350**	**55**	**62**	**117**	**61**	**58**	**119**	**163**	....	....	....	....	....	....	....	....	....		**16**	**1**	**1**	**2**	**8**	....	....	....
	Other Major League Totals		153	23	51	74	....	....	....	73	....	....	....	....	....	....	....	....	....	....	23	4	7	11	15	....	....	....

Won Calder Memorial Trophy (1966)

Claimed by **Philadelphia** from **Toronto** in Expansion Draft, June 6, 1967. Traded to **Toronto** by **Philadelphia** with Forbes Kennedy for Gerry Meehan, Bill Sutherland and Mike Byers, March 2, 1969. Traded to **St. Louis** by **Toronto** for Bob Baun, November 13, 1970. Selected by **Dayton-Houston** (WHA) in 1972 WHA General Player Draft, February 12, 1972. WHA rights traded to **Quebec** (WHA) by **Houston** (WHA) for future considerations, June, 1972. Traded to **Philadelphia** (WHA) by **Quebec** (WHA) with Jean Gravel for Frank Golembrosky and Michel Rouleau, October, 1972. Traded to **New England** (WHA) by **Philadelphia** (WHA) for Bob Brown, October, 1972. Traded to **Toronto** (WHA) by **New England** (WHA) for Bob Charlebois, September, 1973.

• SELF, Steve

C – L. 5'9", 170 lbs. b: Peterborough, Ont., 5/9/1950.

Season	Club	League	GP	G	A	Pts	AG	AA	APts	PIM	PP	SH	GW	S	%	TGF	PGF	TGA	PGA	+/–	GP	G	A	Pts	PIM	PP	SH	GW
1971-72	Colby College White Mules	NCAA-3	20	29	28	57	....	....	....	....	....	....	....	....	....	....	....	....	....	....	....	....	....	....	....	....	....	....
1972-73	New England–Greensboro	EHL	77	50	40	90	....	....	....	92	....	....	....	....	....	....	....	....	....	....	7	2	2	4	0	....	....	....
1973-74	Greensboro Generals	SHL	11	5	4	9	....	....	....	19	....	....	....	....	....	....	....	....	....	....	....	....	....	....	....	....	....	....
	Flint–Dayton	IHL	51	23	22	45	....	....	....	48	....	....	....	....	....	....	....	....	....	....	4	4	4	8	0	....	....	....
1974-75	Dayton Gems	IHL	74	56	47	103	....	....	....	77	....	....	....	....	....	....	....	....	....	....	14	7	7	14	6	....	....	....
1975-76	Dayton Gems	IHL	78	36	37	73	....	....	....	91	....	....	....	....	....	....	....	....	....	....	15	10	8	18	8	....	....	....
1976-77	**Washington Capitals**	**NHL**	**3**	**0**	**0**	**0**	**0**	**0**	**0**	**0**	**0**	**0**	**0**	**3**	**0.0**	**1**	**0**	**4**	**0**	**–3**	....	....	....	....	....	....	....	....
	Dayton Gems	IHL	78	44	41	85	....	....	....	33	....	....	....	....	....	....	....	....	....	....	4	0	1	1	0	....	....	....
	NHL Totals		**3**	**0**	**0**	**0**	**0**	**0**	**0**	**0**	**0**	**0**	**0**	**3**	**0.0**	**1**	**0**	**4**	**0**		....	....	....	....	....	....	....	....

NCAA (College Div.) East All-American Team (1972)

Signed as a free agent by **Washington** to a three-game tryout contract, October 10, 1976.

• SELIVANOV, Alex

Alexandre RW – L. 6', 208 lbs. b: Moscow, USSR, 3/23/1971. Philadelphia's 4th, 140th overall, in 1994.

Season	Club	League	GP	G	A	Pts	AG	AA	APts	PIM	PP	SH	GW	S	%	TGF	PGF	TGA	PGA	+/–	GP	G	A	Pts	PIM	PP	SH	GW
1988-89	Spartak Moscow	USSR	1	0	0	0	....	....	....	0	....	....	....	....	....	....	....	....	....	....	....	....	....	....	....	....	....	....
1989-90	Spartak Moscow	USSR	4	0	0	0	....	....	....	0	....	....	....	....	....	....	....	....	....	....	....	....	....	....	....	....	....	....
1990-91	Spartak Moscow	USSR	21	3	1	4	....	....	....	6	....	....	....	....	....	....	....	....	....	....	....	....	....	....	....	....	....	....
1991-92	Spartak Moscow	CIS	31	6	7	13	....	....	....	16	....	....	....	....	....	....	....	....	....	....	....	....	....	....	....	....	....	....
1992-93	Spartak Moscow	CIS	42	12	19	31	....	....	....	66	....	....	....	....	....	....	....	....	....	....	3	2	0	2	2	....	....	....
1993-94	Spartak Moscow	CIS	45	30	11	41	....	....	....	50	....	....	....	....	....	....	....	....	....	....	6	5	1	6	2	....	....	....
1994-95	Atlanta Knights	IHL	4	0	3	3	....	....	....	2	....	....	....	....	....	....	....	....	....	....	....	....	....	....	....	....	....	....
	Chicago Wolves	IHL	14	4	1	5	....	....	....	8	....	....	....	....	....	....	....	....	....	....	....	....	....	....	....	....	....	....
	Tampa Bay Lightning	**NHL**	**43**	**10**	**6**	**16**	**18**	**9**	**27**	**14**	**4**	**0**	**3**	**94**	**10.6**	**32**	**10**	**24**	**0**	**–2**	....	....	....	....	....	....	....	....
1995-96	**Tampa Bay Lightning**	**NHL**	**79**	**31**	**21**	**52**	**30**	**17**	**47**	**93**	**13**	**0**	**5**	**215**	**14.4**	**79**	**29**	**47**	**0**	**3**	**6**	**2**	**2**	**4**	**6**	**0**	**0**	**1**
1996-97	**Tampa Bay Lightning**	**NHL**	**69**	**15**	**18**	**33**	**16**	**16**	**32**	**61**	**3**	**0**	**4**	**187**	**8.0**	**53**	**17**	**40**	**1**	**–3**	....	....	....	....	....	....	....	....
1997-98	**Tampa Bay Lightning**	**NHL**	**70**	**16**	**19**	**35**	**19**	**19**	**38**	**85**	**4**	**0**	**3**	**206**	**7.8**	**50**	**19**	**70**	**1**	**–38**	....	....	....	....	....	....	....	....
1998-99	**Tampa Bay Lightning**	**NHL**	**43**	**6**	**13**	**19**	**7**	**13**	**20**	**18**	**1**	**0**	**0**	**120**	**5.0**	**32**	**11**	**29**	**0**	**–8**	....	....	....	....	....	....	....	....
	Cleveland Lumberjacks	IHL	2	0	1	1	....	....	....	4	....	....	....	....	....	....	....	....	....	....	....	....	....	....	....	....	....	....
	Edmonton Oilers	**NHL**	**29**	**8**	**6**	**14**	**9**	**6**	**15**	**24**	**1**	**0**	**1**	**57**	**14.0**	**19**	**6**	**13**	**0**	**0**	**2**	**0**	**1**	**1**	**2**	**0**	**0**	**0**
99-2000	**Edmonton Oilers**	**NHL**	**67**	**27**	**20**	**47**	**30**	**19**	**49**	**46**	**10**	**0**	**5**	**122**	**22.1**	**67**	**25**	**40**	**0**	**2**	**5**	**0**	**0**	**0**	**8**	**0**	**0**	**0**
	NHL Totals		**400**	**113**	**103**	**216**	**129**	**99**	**228**	**341**	**36**	**0**	**21**	**1001**	**11.3**	**332**	**117**	**263**	**2**		**13**	**2**	**3**	**5**	**16**	**0**	**0**	**1**

Traded to **Tampa Bay** by **Philadelphia** for Philadelphia's 4th round choice (previously acquired, Philadelphia selected Radovan Somik) in 1995 Entry Draft, September 6, 1994. Traded to **Edmonton** by **Tampa Bay** for Alexandre Daigle, January 29, 1999.

			REGULAR SEASON																		PLAYOFFS							
Season	Club	League	GP	G	A	Pts	AG	AA	APts	PIM	PP	SH	GW	S	%	TGF	PGF	TGA	PGA	+/–	GP	G	A	Pts	PIM	PP	SH	GW

• SELWOOD, Brad

Bradley Wayne D – L. 6'1", 200 lbs. b: Leamington, Ont., 3/18/1948. Toronto's 1st, 10th overall, in 1968.

Season	Club	League	GP	G	A	Pts	AG	AA	APts	PIM	PP	SH	GW	S	%	TGF	PGF	TGA	PGA	+/–	GP	G	A	Pts	PIM	PP	SH	GW
1966-67	Thornhill Rattlers	OHA-B	STATISTICS NOT AVAILABLE																									
1967-68	Niagara Falls Flyers	OHA-Jr.	54	10	23	33				75											19	6	11	17	35			
	Niagara Falls Flyers	Mem-Cup	10	1	3	4				16																		
1968-69	Tulsa Oilers	CHL	70	7	32	39				118																		
1969-70	Vancouver Canucks	WHL	72	9	24	33				93											11	1	9	10	26			
1970-71	**Toronto Maple Leafs**	**NHL**	**28**	**2**	**10**	**12**	**2**	**8**	**10**	**13**	**2**	**0**	**0**	**31**	**6.5**	**25**	**6**	**30**	**4**	**–7**								
	Tulsa Oilers	CHL	13	1	1	2				4																		
1971-72	**Toronto Maple Leafs**	**NHL**	**72**	**4**	**17**	**21**	**4**	**15**	**19**	**58**	**2**	**0**	**1**	**108**	**3.7**	**58**	**9**	**58**	**16**	**7**	**5**	**0**	**0**	**0**	**4**	**0**	**0**	**0**
1972-73	New England Whalers	WHA	75	13	21	34				114											15	3	5	8	22			
1973-74	New England Whalers	WHA	76	9	28	37				91											7	0	2	2	11			
1974-75	Team Canada	Summit-74	4	0	0	0				4																		
	New England Whalers	WHA	77	4	35	39				117											5	1	0	1	11			
1975-76	New England Whalers	WHA	40	2	10	12				28											17	2	2	4	27			
1976-77	New England Whalers	WHA	41	4	12	16				71											5	0	0	0	2			
1977-78	New England Whalers	WHA	80	6	25	31				88											14	0	3	3	8			
1978-79	New England Whalers	WHA	42	4	12	16				47																		
1979-80	**Los Angeles Kings**	**NHL**	**63**	**1**	**13**	**14**	**1**	**9**	**10**	**82**	**1**	**0**	**0**	**78**	**1.3**	**63**	**17**	**88**	**28**	**–14**	**1**	**0**	**0**	**0**	**0**	**0**	**0**	**0**
1980-81	Houston Apollos	CHL	30	0	9	9				37																		
	Fort Worth Texans	CHL	33	2	14	16				53											5	0	0	0	4			
1981-82	New Haven Nighthawks	AHL	23	2	4	6				30																		
	NHL Totals		**163**	**7**	**40**	**47**	**7**	**32**	**39**	**153**	**5**	**0**	**1**	**217**	**3.2**	**146**	**32**	**176**	**48**		**6**	**0**	**0**	**0**	**4**	**0**	**0**	**0**
	Other Major League Totals		431	42	143	185				556											63	6	12	18	81			

Won WHL Rookie of the Year Award (1970)

Traded to **Vancouver** (WHL) by **Toronto** with Rene Robert for Ron Ward, May, 1969. Traded to **Toronto** by **Vancouver** (WHL) for cash, May, 1970. Selected by **New England** (WHA) in 1972 WHA General Player Draft, February 12, 1972. Claimed by **Montreal** from **Toronto** in Intra-League Draft, June 5, 1972. Reclaimed by **Montreal** from **Hartford** prior to Expansion Draft, June 9, 1979. Traded to **LA Kings** by **Montreal** with Montreal's 4th round choice (David Gans) in 1982 Entry Draft for LA Kings' 4th round choice (John Devoe) in 1982 Entry Draft, September 14, 1979.

• SEMAK, Alexander

C – R. 5'10", 185 lbs. b: Ufa, USSR, 2/11/1966. New Jersey's 12th, 207th overall, in 1988.

Season	Club	League	GP	G	A	Pts	AG	AA	APts	PIM	PP	SH	GW	S	%	TGF	PGF	TGA	PGA	+/–	GP	G	A	Pts	PIM	PP	SH	GW
1982-83	Ufa Salavat	USSR	13	2	1	3				4																		
	Soviet Union	EJC-A	5	3	3	6				8																		
1983-84	Ufa Salavat	USSR-2	STATISTICS NOT AVAILABLE																									
	Soviet Union	WJC-A	7	0	4	4				2																		
	Soviet Union	EJC-A	5	9	8	17				10																		
1984-85	Ufa Salavat	USSR-2	47	19	17	36				64																		
	Soviet Union	WJC-A	7	7	4	11				12																		
1985-86	Ufa Salavat	USSR	22	9	7	16				22																		
	Soviet Union	WJC-A	7	3	6	9				4																		
1986-87	Dynamo Moscow	USSR	40	20	8	28				32																		
	USSR	RV-87	2	0	0	0				0																		
	Soviet Union	WEC-A	10	1	0	1				4																		
1987-88	Soviet Union	Can-Cup	7	3	0	3				10																		
	Dynamo Moscow	USSR	47	21	14	35				40																		
1988-89	Dynamo Moscow	USSR	44	18	10	28				22																		
1989-90	Dynamo Moscow	Fr-Tour	1	2	0	2				0																		
	Dynamo Moscow	USSR	43	23	11	34				33																		
	Dynamo Moscow	Super-S	5	1	2	3				2																		
	Soviet Union	WEC-A	10	2	2	4				6																		
1990-91	Dynamo Moscow	Fr-Tour	1	1	0	1				2																		
	Dynamo Moscow	USSR	46	17	21	38				48																		
	Dynamo Moscow	Super-S	7	3	4	7				2																		
	Soviet Union	WEC-A	10	5	5	10				8																		
1991-92	Soviet Union	Can-Cup	5	2	1	3				7																		
	Dynamo Moscow	CIS	26	10	13	23				26																		
	New Jersey Devils	**NHL**	**25**	**5**	**6**	**11**	**5**	**5**	**10**	**0**	**0**	**0**	**1**	**45**	**11.1**	**18**	**2**	**11**	**0**	**5**	**1**	**0**	**0**	**0**	**0**	**0**	**0**	**0**
	Utica Devils	AHL	7	3	2	5				0																		
1992-93	**New Jersey Devils**	**NHL**	**82**	**37**	**42**	**79**	**31**	**29**	**60**	**70**	**4**	**1**	**6**	**217**	**17.1**	**102**	**17**	**75**	**14**	**24**	**5**	**1**	**1**	**2**	**0**	**0**	**0**	**0**
1993-94	**New Jersey Devils**	**NHL**	**54**	**12**	**17**	**29**	**11**	**13**	**24**	**22**	**2**	**2**	**2**	**88**	**13.6**	**38**	**12**	**23**	**3**	**6**	**2**	**0**	**0**	**0**	**0**	**0**	**0**	**0**
1994-95	Ufa Salavat	CIS	9	9	6	15				4																		
	New Jersey Devils	**NHL**	**19**	**2**	**6**	**8**	**4**	**9**	**13**	**13**	**0**	**0**	**0**	**32**	**6.3**	**13**	**3**	**15**	**1**	**–4**								
	Tampa Bay Lightning	**NHL**	**22**	**5**	**5**	**10**	**9**	**7**	**16**	**12**	**0**	**0**	**1**	**39**	**12.8**	**12**	**2**	**13**	**0**	**–3**								
1995-96	**New York Islanders**	**NHL**	**69**	**20**	**14**	**34**	**20**	**11**	**31**	**68**	**6**	**0**	**2**	**128**	**15.6**	**49**	**15**	**38**	**0**	**–4**								
1996-97	Russia	W-Cup	1	0	0	0				0																		
	Vancouver Canucks	**NHL**	**18**	**2**	**1**	**3**	**2**	**1**	**3**	**2**	**1**	**0**	**0**	**12**	**16.7**	**5**	**1**	**6**	**0**	**–2**								
	Syracuse Crunch	AHL	23	10	14	24				12																		
	Las Vegas Thunder	IHL	13	11	13	24				10											3	0	4	4	4			
1997-98	Chicago Wolves	IHL	67	26	35	61				90											22	10	*17	*27	35			
1998-99	Albany River Rats	AHL	70	20	42	62				62											5	0	2	2	4			
99-2000	EHC Freiburg	Germany-2	42	27	47	74				84											10	12	12	24				
	NHL Totals		**289**	**83**	**91**	**174**	**82**	**75**	**157**	**187**	**13**	**3**	**12**	**561**	**14.8**	**237**	**52**	**181**	**18**		**8**	**1**	**1**	**2**	**0**	**0**	**0**	**0**

Named Best Forward at EJC-A (1984) • USSR First All-Star Team (1991) • Won "Bud" Poile Trophy (Playoff MVP - IHL) (1998)

Traded to **Tampa Bay** by **New Jersey** with Ben Hankinson for Shawn Chambers and Danton Cole, March 14, 1995. Traded to **NY Islanders** by **Tampa Bay** for NY Islanders' 5th round choice (Karel Betik) in 1997 Entry Draft, September 14, 1995. Claimed by **Vancouver** from **NY Islanders** in NHL Waiver Draft, September 30, 1996.

• SEMCHUK, Brandy

Thomas Brandy RW – R. 6'1", 185 lbs. b: Calgary, Alta., 9/22/1971. Los Angeles' 2nd, 28th overall, in 1990.

Season	Club	League	GP	G	A	Pts	AG	AA	APts	PIM	PP	SH	GW	S	%	TGF	PGF	TGA	PGA	+/–	GP	G	A	Pts	PIM	PP	SH	GW
1985-86	Calgary Royals	AAHA	65	55	50	105				90																		
1986-87	Calgary Royals	AAHA	70	52	55	107				100																		
1987-88	Calgary Canucks	AJHL	90	44	42	86				120																		
1988-89	Canada	Nat-Team	42	11	11	22				14																		
1989-90	Canada	Nat-Team	60	9	15	24				14																		
1990-91	Lethbridge Hurricanes	WHL	14	9	8	17				10											15	8	5	13	18			
	New Haven Nighthawks	AHL	21	1	4	5				6																		
1991-92	Phoenix Roadrunners	IHL	15	1	5	6				6																		
	Raleigh IceCaps	ECHL	5	1	2	3				16											2	1	0	1	4			
1992-93	**Los Angeles Kings**	**NHL**	**1**	**0**	**0**	**0**	**0**	**0**	**0**	**2**	**0**	**0**	**0**	**0**	**0.0**	**0**	**0**	**0**	**0**	**0**								
	Phoenix Roadrunners	IHL	56	13	12	25				58																		
1993-94	Erie Panthers	ECHL	44	17	15	32				37																		
	Phoenix Roadrunners	IHL	2	0	0	0				6																		
1994-95	Nashville Knights	ECHL	9	3	2	5				2																		
	San Antonio Iguanas	CHL	30	18	16	34				34											13	1	5	6	33			
1995-96	San Antonio Iguanas	CHL	12	5	2	7				43																		
1996-97	San Antonio Iguanas	CHL	10	4	6	10				2																		
	Columbus Cottonmouths	CHL	13	5	5	10				8											3	0	1	1	12			
1997-98	Shreveport Mudbugs	WPHL	34	20	11	31				33																		
	Fresno Fighting Falcons	WCHL	25	20	18	38				21											5	2	3	5	0			
1998-99	Fresno Fighting Falcons	WCHL	39	10	11	21				40																		
	NHL Totals		**1**	**0**	**0**	**0**	**0**	**0**	**0**	**2**	**0**	**0**	**0**	**0**	**0.0**	**0**	**0**	**0**	**0**									

Season	Club	League	GP	G	A	Pts	AG	AA	APts	PIM	PP	SH	GW	S	%	TGF	PGF	TGA	PGA	+/-	GP	G	A	Pts	PIM	PP	SH	GW
			REGULAR SEASON																		PLAYOFFS							

• SEMENKO, Dave

David John "Sammy" LW – L. 6'3", 200 lbs. b: Winnipeg, Man., 7/12/1957. Minnesota's 2nd, 25th overall, in 1977.

Season	Club	League	GP	G	A	Pts	AG	AA	APts	PIM	PP	SH	GW	S	%	TGF	PGF	TGA	PGA	+/-	GP	G	A	Pts	PIM	PP	SH	GW
1974-75	Brandon Travellers	MJHL	42	11	17	28	....	....	....	55	....	....	....	....	....	....	....	....	....	....	....	....	....	....	....	....	....	....
	Brandon Wheat Kings	WCJHL	12	2	1	3	....	....	....	12	....	....	....	....	....	....	....	....	....	....	4	0	0	0	0	....	....	....
1975-76	Brandon Wheat Kings	WCJHL	72	8	5	13	....	....	....	194	....	....	....	....	....	....	....	....	....	....	5	0	0	0	0	....	....	....
1976-77	Brandon Wheat Kings	WCJHL	61	27	33	60	....	....	....	265	....	....	....	....	....	....	....	....	....	....	16	3	4	7	61	....	....	....
1977-78	Brandon Wheat Kings	WCJHL	7	10	5	15	....	....	....	40	....	....	....	....	....	....	....	....	....	....	....	....	....	....	....	....	....	....
	Edmonton Oilers	WHA	65	6	6	12	....	....	....	140	....	....	....	....	....	....	....	....	....	....	5	0	0	0	8	....	....	....
1978-79	Edmonton Oilers	WHA	77	10	14	24	....	....	....	158	....	....	....	....	....	....	....	....	....	....	11	4	2	6	29	....	....	....
1979-80	**Edmonton Oilers**	**NHL**	**67**	**6**	**7**	**13**	**5**	**5**	**10**	**135**	**1**	**0**	**1**	**43**	**14.0**	**26**	**5**	**34**	**0**	**-13**	**3**	**0**	**0**	**0**	**2**	**0**	**0**	**0**
1980-81	**Edmonton Oilers**	**NHL**	**58**	**11**	**8**	**19**	**9**	**5**	**14**	**80**	**4**	**0**	**2**	**42**	**26.2**	**29**	**11**	**22**	**0**	**-4**	**8**	**0**	**0**	**0**	**5**	**0**	**0**	**0**
	Wichita Wind	CHL	14	1	2	3	....	....	....	40	....	....	....	....	....	....	....	....	....	....	....	....	....	....	....	....	....	....
1981-82	**Edmonton Oilers**	**NHL**	**59**	**12**	**12**	**24**	**9**	**8**	**17**	**194**	**4**	**0**	**1**	**54**	**22.2**	**45**	**12**	**26**	**0**	**7**	**4**	**0**	**0**	**0**	**2**	**0**	**0**	**0**
1982-83	**Edmonton Oilers**	**NHL**	**75**	**12**	**15**	**27**	**10**	**10**	**20**	**141**	**0**	**0**	**1**	**69**	**17.4**	**62**	**7**	**36**	**0**	**19**	**15**	**1**	**1**	**2**	**69**	**0**	**0**	**0**
1983-84♦	**Edmonton Oilers**	**NHL**	**52**	**6**	**11**	**17**	**5**	**7**	**12**	**118**	**0**	**0**	**2**	**39**	**15.4**	**34**	**2**	**23**	**0**	**9**	**19**	**5**	**5**	**10**	**44**	**0**	**0**	**1**
1984-85♦	**Edmonton Oilers**	**NHL**	**69**	**6**	**12**	**18**	**5**	**8**	**13**	**172**	**0**	**0**	**1**	**50**	**12.0**	**34**	**2**	**27**	**0**	**5**	**14**	**0**	**0**	**0**	**39**	**0**	**0**	**0**
1985-86	**Edmonton Oilers**	**NHL**	**69**	**6**	**12**	**18**	**5**	**8**	**13**	**141**	**0**	**0**	**0**	**51**	**11.8**	**40**	**3**	**38**	**0**	**-1**	**6**	**0**	**0**	**0**	**32**	**0**	**0**	**0**
1986-87	**Edmonton Oilers**	**NHL**	**5**	**0**	**0**	**0**	**0**	**0**	**0**	**0**	**0**	**0**	**0**	**1**	**0.0**	**2**	**0**	**2**	**0**	**0**	....	....	....	....	....	....	....	....
	Hartford Whalers	**NHL**	**51**	**4**	**8**	**12**	**3**	**6**	**9**	**87**	**0**	**0**	**0**	**31**	**12.9**	**21**	**3**	**25**	**0**	**-7**	**4**	**0**	**0**	**0**	**15**	**0**	**0**	**0**
1987-88	**Toronto Maple Leafs**	**NHL**	**70**	**2**	**3**	**5**	**2**	**2**	**4**	**107**	**0**	**0**	**0**	**12**	**16.7**	**8**	**3**	**13**	**0**	**-8**	....	....	....	....	....	....	....	....
	NHL Totals		**575**	**65**	**88**	**153**	**53**	**59**	**112**	**1175**	**9**	**0**	**8**	**392**	**16.6**	**301**	**48**	**246**	**0**		**73**	**6**	**6**	**12**	**208**	**0**	**0**	**1**
	Other Major League Totals		142	16	20	36	....	....	....	298	....	....	....	....	....	....	....	....	....	....	16	4	2	6	37	....	....	....

Selected by **Houston** (WHA) in 1977 WHA Amateur Draft, May, 1977. WHA rights traded to **Edmonton** (WHA) by **Houston** (WHA) for future considerations, November, 1978. Reclaimed by **Minnesota** from **Edmonton** prior to Expansion Draft, June 9, 1979. Traded to **Edmonton** by **Minnesota** for Edmonton's 2nd (Neal Broten) and 3rd (Kevin Maxwell) round choices in 1979 Entry Draft, August 9, 1979. Traded to **Hartford** by **Edmonton** for Hartford's 3rd round choice (Trevor Sim) in 1988 Entry Draft, December 12, 1986. Traded to **Toronto** by **Hartford** for Bill Root, September 8, 1987.

• SEMENOV, Anatoli

C/LW – L. 6'2", 190 lbs. b: Moscow, USSR, 3/5/1962. Edmonton's 5th, 120th overall, in 1989.

Season	Club	League	GP	G	A	Pts	AG	AA	APts	PIM	PP	SH	GW	S	%	TGF	PGF	TGA	PGA	+/-	GP	G	A	Pts	PIM	PP	SH	GW
1979-80	Dynamo Moscow	USSR	8	3	0	3	....	....	....	2	....	....	....	....	....	....	....	....	....	....	....	....	....	....	....	....	....	....
	Soviet Union	EJC-A	5	1	3	4	....	....	....	6	....	....	....	....	....	....	....	....	....	....	....	....	....	....	....	....	....	....
1980-81	Dynamo Moscow	USSR	47	18	14	32	....	....	....	18	....	....	....	....	....	....	....	....	....	....	....	....	....	....	....	....	....	....
	Soviet Union	WJC-A	5	3	2	5	....	....	....	6	....	....	....	....	....	....	....	....	....	....	....	....	....	....	....	....	....	....
1981-82	Dynamo Moscow	USSR	44	12	14	26	....	....	....	28	....	....	....	....	....	....	....	....	....	....	....	....	....	....	....	....	....	....
	Soviet Union	WJC-A	7	5	8	13	....	....	....	22	....	....	....	....	....	....	....	....	....	....	....	....	....	....	....	....	....	....
1982-83	Dynamo Moscow	USSR	44	22	18	40	....	....	....	26	....	....	....	....	....	....	....	....	....	....	....	....	....	....	....	....	....	....
	USSR	Super-S	3	1	0	1	....	....	....	2	....	....	....	....	....	....	....	....	....	....	....	....	....	....	....	....	....	....
1983-84	Dynamo Moscow	USSR	19	10	5	15	....	....	....	14	....	....	....	....	....	....	....	....	....	....	....	....	....	....	....	....	....	....
1984-85	Soviet Union	Can-Cup	6	3	1	4	....	....	....	2	....	....	....	....	....	....	....	....	....	....	....	....	....	....	....	....	....	....
	Dynamo Moscow	USSR	30	17	12	29	....	....	....	32	....	....	....	....	....	....	....	....	....	....	....	....	....	....	....	....	....	....
1985-86	Dynamo Moscow	USSR	32	18	17	35	....	....	....	19	....	....	....	....	....	....	....	....	....	....	....	....	....	....	....	....	....	....
	Dynamo Moscow	Super-S	DID NOT PLAY																									
1986-87	Dynamo Moscow	USSR	40	15	29	44	....	....	....	32	....	....	....	....	....	....	....	....	....	....	....	....	....	....	....	....	....	....
	USSR	RV-87	1	1	0	1	....	....	....	0	....	....	....	....	....	....	....	....	....	....	....	....	....	....	....	....	....	....
	Soviet Union	WEC-A	10	2	1	3	....	....	....	16	....	....	....	....	....	....	....	....	....	....	....	....	....	....	....	....	....	....
1987-88	Soviet Union	Can-Cup	9	2	5	7	....	....	....	2	....	....	....	....	....	....	....	....	....	....	....	....	....	....	....	....	....	....
	Dynamo Moscow	USSR	32	17	8	25	....	....	....	22	....	....	....	....	....	....	....	....	....	....	....	....	....	....	....	....	....	....
	Soviet Union	Olympics	8	2	4	6	....	....	....	6	....	....	....	....	....	....	....	....	....	....	....	....	....	....	....	....	....	....
1988-89	Dynamo Moscow	USSR	31	9	12	21	....	....	....	24	....	....	....	....	....	....	....	....	....	....	....	....	....	....	....	....	....	....
	Dynamo Riga	Super-S	7	1	3	4	....	....	....	0	....	....	....	....	....	....	....	....	....	....	....	....	....	....	....	....	....	....
1989-90	Dynamo Moscow	Fr-Tour	1	1	1	2	....	....	....	0	....	....	....	....	....	....	....	....	....	....	....	....	....	....	....	....	....	....
	Dynamo Moscow	USSR	48	13	20	33	....	....	....	16	....	....	....	....	....	....	....	....	....	....	....	....	....	....	....	....	....	....
	Dynamo Moscow	Super-S	5	1	1	2	....	....	....	2	....	....	....	....	....	....	....	....	....	....	....	....	....	....	....	....	....	....
♦	**Edmonton Oilers**	**NHL**	....	....	....	....	....	....	....	....	....	....	....	....	....	....	....	....	....	....	**2**	**0**	**0**	**0**	**0**	**0**	**0**	**0**
1990-91	**Edmonton Oilers**	**NHL**	**57**	**15**	**16**	**31**	**14**	**12**	**26**	**26**	**3**	**1**	**1**	**101**	**14.9**	**56**	**9**	**37**	**7**	**17**	**12**	**5**	**5**	**10**	**6**	**0**	**0**	**0**
1991-92	**Edmonton Oilers**	**NHL**	**59**	**20**	**22**	**42**	**18**	**17**	**35**	**16**	**3**	**0**	**3**	**105**	**19.0**	**60**	**12**	**53**	**17**	**12**	**8**	**1**	**1**	**2**	**6**	**0**	**0**	**0**
1992-93	**Tampa Bay Lightning**	**NHL**	**13**	**2**	**3**	**5**	**2**	**2**	**4**	**4**	**0**	**0**	**0**	**14**	**14.3**	**9**	**3**	**11**	**0**	**-5**	....	....	....	....	....	....	....	....
	Vancouver Canucks	**NHL**	**62**	**10**	**34**	**44**	**8**	**23**	**31**	**28**	**3**	**2**	**1**	**88**	**11.4**	**76**	**19**	**56**	**20**	**21**	**12**	**1**	**3**	**4**	**0**	**0**	**0**	**0**
1993-94	**Mighty Ducks of Anaheim**	**NHL**	**49**	**11**	**19**	**30**	**10**	**15**	**25**	**12**	**4**	**0**	**2**	**103**	**10.7**	**46**	**18**	**42**	**10**	**-4**	....	....	....	....	....	....	....	....
1994-95	**Mighty Ducks of Anaheim**	**NHL**	**15**	**3**	**4**	**7**	**5**	**6**	**11**	**4**	**2**	**0**	**0**	**33**	**9.1**	**9**	**2**	**21**	**4**	**-10**	....	....	....	....	....	....	....	....
	Philadelphia Flyers	**NHL**	**26**	**1**	**2**	**3**	**2**	**3**	**5**	**6**	**0**	**0**	**0**	**36**	**2.8**	**9**	**4**	**7**	**0**	**-2**	**15**	**2**	**4**	**6**	**0**	**0**	**0**	**0**
1995-96	**Philadelphia Flyers**	**NHL**	**44**	**3**	**13**	**16**	**3**	**11**	**14**	**14**	**0**	**0**	**2**	**55**	**5.5**	**19**	**1**	**15**	**0**	**3**	....	....	....	....	....	....	....	....
	Mighty Ducks of Anaheim	**NHL**	**12**	**1**	**9**	**10**	**1**	**7**	**8**	**10**	**0**	**0**	**0**	**24**	**4.2**	**17**	**10**	**11**	**0**	**-4**	....	....	....	....	....	....	....	....
1996-97	**Buffalo Sabres**	**NHL**	**25**	**2**	**4**	**6**	**2**	**4**	**6**	**2**	**1**	**0**	**1**	**21**	**9.5**	**9**	**2**	**17**	**7**	**-3**	....	....	....	....	....	....	....	....
1997-98	Avtomobilist Yekaterinburg	Russia	8	0	0	0	....	....	....	0	....	....	....	....	....	....	....	....	....	....	....	....	....	....	....	....	....	....
	NHL Totals		**362**	**68**	**126**	**194**	**65**	**100**	**165**	**122**	**16**	**3**	**10**	**580**	**11.7**	**310**	**80**	**270**	**65**		**49**	**9**	**13**	**22**	**12**	**0**	**0**	**0**

USSR First All-Star Team (1985)

Claimed by **Tampa Bay** from **Edmonton** in Expansion Draft, June 18, 1992. Traded to **Vancouver** by **Tampa Bay** for Dave Capuano and Vancouver's 4th round choice (later traded to New Jersey — later traded to Calgary — Calgary selected Ryan Duthie) in 1994 Entry Draft, November 3, 1992. Claimed by **Anaheim** from **Vancouver** in Expansion Draft, June 24, 1993. Traded to **Philadelphia** by **Anaheim** for Milos Holan, March 8, 1995. Traded to **Anaheim** by **Philadelphia** with Mike Crowley for Brian Wesenberg, March 19, 1996. Signed as a free agent by **Buffalo**, September 17, 1996.

• SEPPA, Jyrki

D – L. 6'1", 190 lbs. b: Tampere, Finland, 11/14/1961. Winnipeg's 3rd, 43rd overall, in 1981.

Season	Club	League	GP	G	A	Pts	AG	AA	APts	PIM	PP	SH	GW	S	%	TGF	PGF	TGA	PGA	+/-	GP	G	A	Pts	PIM	PP	SH	GW
1978-79	Ilves Tampere	Finland-Jr.	23	1	5	6	....	....	....	34	....	....	....	....	....	....	....	....	....	....	....	....	....	....	....	....	....	....
1979-80	Ilves Tampere	Finland-Jr.	30	1	1	2	....	....	....	26	....	....	....	....	....	....	....	....	....	....	....	....	....	....	....	....	....	....
1980-81	Ilves Tampere	Finland	34	3	4	7	....	....	....	14	....	....	....	....	....	....	....	....	....	....	2	0	0	0	5	....	....	....
	Finland	WJC-A	5	2	0	2	....	....	....	4	....	....	....	....	....	....	....	....	....	....	....	....	....	....	....	....	....	....
1981-82	Jokerit Helsinki	Finland	31	6	1	7	....	....	....	12	....	....	....	....	....	....	....	....	....	....	....	....	....	....	....	....	....	....
1982-83	Sherbrooke Jets	AHL	72	2	13	15	....	....	....	66	....	....	....	....	....	....	....	....	....	....	....	....	....	....	....	....	....	....
1983-84	**Winnipeg Jets**	**NHL**	**13**	**0**	**2**	**2**	**0**	**1**	**1**	**6**	**0**	**0**	**0**	**7**	**0.0**	**5**	**2**	**12**	**0**	**-9**	....	....	....	....	....	....	....	....
	Sherbrooke Jets	AHL	60	5	35	40	....	....	....	43	....	....	....	....	....	....	....	....	....	....	....	....	....	....	....	....	....	....
1984-85	HPK Hameenlinna	Finland-2	23	4	3	7	....	....	....	24	....	....	....	....	....	....	....	....	....	....	....	....	....	....	....	....	....	....
1985-86	Jokerit Helsinki	Finland	32	2	7	9	....	....	....	36	....	....	....	....	....	....	....	....	....	....	....	....	....	....	....	....	....	....
	NHL Totals		**13**	**0**	**2**	**2**	**0**	**1**	**1**	**6**	**0**	**0**	**0**	**7**	**0.0**	**5**	**2**	**12**	**0**		....	....	....	....	....	....	....	....

• SERAFINI, Ron

Ronald William D – R. 5'11", 180 lbs. b: Highland Park, MI, 10/31/1953. California's 2nd, 50th overall, in 1973.

Season	Club	League	GP	G	A	Pts	AG	AA	APts	PIM	PP	SH	GW	S	%	TGF	PGF	TGA	PGA	+/-	GP	G	A	Pts	PIM	PP	SH	GW
1970-71	Detroit Jr. Red Wings	OJHL	STATISTICS NOT AVAILABLE																									
	Detroit Jr. Red Wings	Cen-Cup	12	3	3	6	....	....	....	33	....	....	....	....	....	....	....	....	....	....	....	....	....	....	....	....	....	....
1971-72	St. Catharines Black Hawks	OMJHL	61	6	17	23	....	....	....	164	....	....	....	....	....	....	....	....	....	....	5	0	1	1	4	....	....	....
1972-73	St. Catharines Black Hawks	OMJHL	63	17	25	42	....	....	....	221	....	....	....	....	....	....	....	....	....	....	....	....	....	....	....	....	....	....
1973-74	**California Golden Seals**	**NHL**	**2**	**0**	**0**	**0**	**0**	**0**	**0**	**2**	**0**	**0**	**0**	**0**	**0.0**	**2**	**0**	**5**	**1**	**-2**	....	....	....	....	....	....	....	....
	Salt Lake Golden Eagles	WHL	74	8	31	39	....	....	....	202	....	....	....	....	....	....	....	....	....	....	5	0	0	0	2	....	....	....
1974-75	Denver Spurs	CHL	75	7	21	28	....	....	....	83	....	....	....	....	....	....	....	....	....	....	2	0	1	1	9	....	....	....
1975-76	Tucson Mavericks	CHL	20	1	3	4	....	....	....	39	....	....	....	....	....	....	....	....	....	....	....	....	....	....	....	....	....	....
	Cincinnati Stingers	WHA	16	0	2	2	....	....	....	15	....	....	....	....	....	....	....	....	....	....	....	....	....	....	....	....	....	....
	Hampton Gulls	SHL	27	4	20	24	....	....	....	20	....	....	....	....	....	....	....	....	....	....	9	1	7	8	10	....	....	....

			REGULAR SEASON																		PLAYOFFS							
Season	Club	League	GP	G	A	Pts	AG	AA	APts	PIM	PP	SH	GW	S	%	TGF	PGF	TGA	PGA	+/-	GP	G	A	Pts	PIM	PP	SH	GW
1976-77	Salt Lake Golden Eagles	CHL	31	3	5	8				29																		
	Oklahoma City Blazers	CHL	10	1	0	1				17																		
	Winston-Salem Polar Bears	SHL	8	1	2	3				4																		
	Hampton Gulls	SHL	9	0	6	6				10																		
1977-78	VEU Feldkirch	Austria	22	10	12	22				51																		
	NHL Totals		**2**	**0**	**0**	**0**	**0**	**0**	**0**	**2**	**0**	**0**	**0**	**0**	**0.0**	**2**	**0**	**5**	**1**									
	Other Major League Totals		16	0	2	2				15																		

Selected by **Cleveland** (WHA) in 1973 WHA Amateur Draft, June, 1973. Traded to **St. Louis** by **California** for Glenn Patrick, July 18, 1974. WHA rights claimed by **Phoenix** (WHA) from **Cleveland** (WHA) in WHA Expansion Draft, June, 1975. Traded to **Cincinnati** (WHA) by **Phoenix** (WHA) for Gary Veneruzzo, November, 1975.

• SEROWIK, Jeff

Jeff M. D – R. 6′1″, 210 lbs. b: Manchester, NH, 1/10/1967. Toronto's 5th, 85th overall, in 1985.

Season	Club	League	GP	G	A	Pts	AG	AA	APts	PIM	PP	SH	GW	S	%	TGF	PGF	TGA	PGA	+/-	GP	G	A	Pts	PIM	PP	SH	GW
1983-84	Manchester West Wildcats	Hi-School	21	12	12	24																						
1984-85	Lawrence Academy	Hi-School	24	8	25	33																						
1985-86	Lawrence Academy	Hi-School	STATISTICS NOT AVAILABLE																									
1986-87	Providence College	H-East	33	3	8	11				22																		
1987-88	Providence College	H-East	33	3	9	12				44																		
1988-89	Providence College	H-East	35	3	14	17				48																		
1989-90	Providence College	H-East	35	6	19	25				34																		
1990-91	**Toronto Maple Leafs**	**NHL**	**1**	**0**	**0**	**0**	**0**	**0**	**0**	**0**	**0**	**0**	**0**	**1**	**0.0**	**0**	**0**	**0**	**0**	**0**								
	Newmarket Saints	AHL	60	8	15	23				45																		
1991-92	St. John's Maple Leafs	AHL	78	11	34	45				60											16	4	9	13	22			
1992-93	St. John's Maple Leafs	AHL	77	19	35	54				92											9	1	5	6	8			
1993-94	Cincinnati Cyclones	IHL	79	6	21	27				98											7	0	1	1	8			
1994-95	**Boston Bruins**	**NHL**	**1**	**0**	**0**	**0**	**0**	**0**	**0**	**0**	**0**	**0**	**0**	**0**	**0.0**	**1**	**0**	**0**	**0**	**1**								
	Providence Bruins	AHL	78	28	34	62				102											13	4	6	10	10			
1995-96	Indianapolis Ice	IHL	69	20	23	43				86																		
	Las Vegas Thunder	IHL	13	7	6	13				18											15	6	5	11	16			
1996-97	Las Vegas Thunder	IHL	42	5	19	24				34											3	0	0	0	4			
1997-98	Kansas City Blades	IHL	77	14	35	49				50											11	2	5	7	12			
1998-99	**Pittsburgh Penguins**	**NHL**	**26**	**0**	**6**	**6**	**0**	**6**	**6**	**16**	**0**	**0**	**0**	**26**	**0.0**	**15**	**5**	**18**	**4**	**–4**								
99-2000	**Pittsburgh Penguins**	**NHL**	DID NOT PLAY – INJURED																									
	NHL Totals		**28**	**0**	**6**	**6**	**0**	**6**	**6**	**16**	**0**	**0**	**0**	**27**	**0.0**	**16**	**5**	**18**	**4**									

Hockey East Second All-Star Team (1990) • Won Eddie Shore Award (Outstanding Defenseman - AHL) (1995)

Signed as a free agent by **Florida**, July 20, 1993. Signed as a free agent by **Boston**, June 29, 1994. Signed as a free agent by **Chicago**, August 10, 1995. Signed as a free agent by **Pittsburgh**, October 8, 1998. • Missed remainder of 1998-99 and entire 1999-2000 seasons recovering from head injury suffered in game vs. Florida, December 30, 1998.

• SERVINIS, George

LW – L. 5′11″, 180 lbs. b: Toronto, Ont., 4/29/1962.

Season	Club	League	GP	G	A	Pts	AG	AA	APts	PIM	PP	SH	GW	S	%	TGF	PGF	TGA	PGA	+/-	GP	G	A	Pts	PIM	PP	SH	GW
1979-80	Wexford Warriors	OMHA	32	17	22	39				60																		
	Wexford Raiders	OJHL	16	2	12	14				9																		
1980-81	Wexford Raiders	OJHL	42	29	35	64				92																		
1981-82	Aurora Tigers	OJHL	55	62	55	117																						
1982-83	RPI Engineers	ECAC	28	35	29	64				22																		
1983-84	RPI Engineers	ECAC	12	5	13	18				14																		
	Canada	Nat-Team	43	13	11	24				33																		
1984-85	RPI Engineers	ECAC	35	34	25	59				44																		
1985-86	Springfield Indians	AHL	30	2	14	16				19																		
1986-87	Indianapolis Checkers	IHL	70	41	54	95				54																		
1987-88	**Minnesota North Stars**	**NHL**	**5**	**0**	**0**	**0**	**0**	**0**	**0**	**0**	**0**	**0**	**0**	**8**	**0.0**	**0**	**0**	**2**	**0**	**–2**								
	Kalamazoo Wings	IHL	49	34	21	55				54											6	3	1	4	2			
1988-89	VSV Villach	Austria	37	32	35	67																						
	NHL Totals		**5**	**0**	**0**	**0**	**0**	**0**	**0**	**0**	**0**	**0**	**0**	**8**	**0.0**	**0**	**0**	**2**	**0**									

NCAA Championship All-Tournament Team (1985)

Signed as a free agent by **Minnesota**, August 13, 1985.

• SEVCIK, Jaroslav

LW – R. 5′9″, 170 lbs. b: Brno, Czech., 5/15/1965. Quebec's 9th, 177th overall, in 1987.

Season	Club	League	GP	G	A	Pts	AG	AA	APts	PIM	PP	SH	GW	S	%	TGF	PGF	TGA	PGA	+/-	GP	G	A	Pts	PIM	PP	SH	GW
1982-83	Dukla Trencin	Czech-Jr.	STATISTICS NOT AVAILABLE																									
	Czechoslovakia	EJC-A	5	1	2	3				0																		
1983-84	Dukla Trencin	Czech-Jr.	STATISTICS NOT AVAILABLE																									
1984-85	Dukla Trencin	Czech.	31	3	4	7				6																		
	Czechoslovakia	WJC-A	7	1	0	1				2																		
1985-86	Dukla Trencin	Czech.	22	0	1	1				6																		
1986-87	Zetor Brno	Czech.	42	14	9	23				14																		
1987-88	Fredericton Express	AHL	32	9	7	16				6																		
1988-89	Halifax Citadels	AHL	78	17	41	58				17											4	1	1	2	2			
1989-90	**Quebec Nordiques**	**NHL**	**13**	**0**	**2**	**2**	**0**	**1**	**1**	**2**	**0**	**0**	**0**	**9**	**0.0**	**5**	**1**	**9**	**0**	**–5**								
	Halifax Citadels	AHL	50	17	17	34				36											3	0	1	1	0			
1990-91	Halifax Citadels	AHL	66	16	26	42				22																		
1991-92	SC Rapperswil-Jona	Switz-2	10	5	3	8				14																		
1992-93	Nottingham Panthers	Britain	7	9	9	18				0																		
	SIJ Rotterdam	Holland	22	13	18	31				26											5	2	4	6	0			
1993-94	SIJ Nijmegan	Holland	27	14	23	37				26											2	0	2	2	0			
1994-95	VSV Villach	Austria	28	11	*43	54				18											12	5	9	14	12			
1995-96	Ratinger Lowen	Germany	17	3	10	13				8																		
	KAC Klagenfurt	Austria	26	11	24	35				12																		
1996-97	EC Kapfenberg	Austria	41	13	16	29				45																		
1997-98	EC Kapfenberg	Austria	28	5	14	19				12																		
1998-99	SV Bayreuth	Germany-2	56	30	36	66				26																		
99-2000	SIJ Amsterdam	Holland	17	7	6	13															6	2	2	4	6			
	NHL Totals		**13**	**0**	**2**	**2**	**0**	**1**	**1**	**2**	**0**	**0**	**0**	**9**	**0.0**	**5**	**1**	**9**	**0**									

• SEVERYN, Brent

LW – L. 6′2″, 211 lbs. b: Vegreville, Alta., 2/22/1966. Winnipeg's 5th, 99th overall, in 1984.

Season	Club	League	GP	G	A	Pts	AG	AA	APts	PIM	PP	SH	GW	S	%	TGF	PGF	TGA	PGA	+/-	GP	G	A	Pts	PIM	PP	SH	GW
1982-83	Vegreville Rangers	AJHL	21	20	22	42				10																		
1983-84	Seattle Thunderbirds	WHL	72	14	22	36				49											5	2	1	3	2			
1984-85	Seattle Thunderbirds	WHL	26	7	16	23				57																		
	Brandon Wheat Kings	WHL	41	8	32	40				54																		
1985-86	Saskatoon Blades	WHL	9	1	4	5				38																		
	Seattle Thunderbirds	WHL	33	11	20	31				164											5	0	4	4	4			
1986-87	University of Alberta	CWUAA	43	7	19	26				171																		
1987-88	University of Alberta	CWUAA	46	21	29	50				178																		
1988-89	Halifax Citadels	AHL	47	2	12	14				141																		
1989-90	**Quebec Nordiques**	**NHL**	**35**	**0**	**2**	**2**	**0**	**1**	**1**	**42**	**0**	**0**	**0**	**28**	**0.0**	**16**	**0**	**38**	**3**	**–19**								
	Halifax Citadels	AHL	43	6	9	15				105											6	1	2	3	49			
1990-91	Halifax Citadels	AHL	50	7	26	33				202																		
1991-92	Utica Devils	AHL	80	11	33	44				211											4	0	1	1	4			
1992-93	Utica Devils	AHL	77	20	32	52				240											5	0	0	0	35			
1993-94	**Florida Panthers**	**NHL**	**67**	**4**	**7**	**11**	**4**	**5**	**9**	**156**	**1**	**0**	**1**	**93**	**4.3**	**37**	**6**	**45**	**13**	**–1**								
1994-95	**Florida Panthers**	**NHL**	**9**	**1**	**1**	**2**	**2**	**1**	**3**	**37**	**1**	**0**	**0**	**10**	**10.0**	**4**	**2**	**6**	**1**	**–3**								
	New York Islanders	**NHL**	**19**	**1**	**3**	**4**	**2**	**4**	**6**	**34**	**0**	**0**	**0**	**22**	**4.5**	**12**	**0**	**13**	**2**	**1**								

			REGULAR SEASON																		PLAYOFFS							
Season	**Club**	**League**	**GP**	**G**	**A**	**Pts**	**AG**	**AA**	**APts**	**PIM**	**PP**	**SH**	**GW**	**S**	**%**	**TGF**	**PGF**	**TGA**	**PGA**	**+/–**	**GP**	**G**	**A**	**Pts**	**PIM**	**PP**	**SH**	**GW**
1995-96	**New York Islanders**	**NHL**	**65**	**1**	**8**	**9**	**1**	**7**	**8**	**180**	**0**	**0**	**0**	**40**	**2.5**	**36**	**0**	**48**	**15**	**3**								
1996-97	**Colorado Avalanche**	**NHL**	**66**	**1**	**4**	**5**	**1**	**4**	**5**	**193**	**0**	**0**	**0**	**55**	**1.8**	**10**	**0**	**16**	**0**	**–6**	**8**	**0**	**0**	**0**	**12**	**0**	**0**	**0**
1997-98	**Mighty Ducks of Anaheim**	**NHL**	**37**	**1**	**3**	**4**	**1**	**3**	**4**	**133**	**0**	**0**	**0**	**27**	**3.7**	**9**	**0**	**12**	**0**	**–3**								
1998-99	**Dallas Stars**	**NHL**	**30**	**1**	**2**	**3**	**1**	**2**	**3**	**50**	**0**	**0**	**0**	**22**	**4.5**	**4**	**0**	**6**	**0**	**–2**								
	Michigan K-Wings	IHL	3	0	0	0				0																		
99-2000	Munich Barons	Germany	18	2	6	8				42											12	0	3	3	14			
	NHL Totals		**328**	**10**	**30**	**40**	**12**	**27**	**39**	**825**	**2**	**0**	**1**	**297**	**3.4**	**128**	**8**	**184**	**34**		**8**	**0**	**0**	**0**	**12**	**0**	**0**	**0**

AHL First All-Star Team (1993)

Signed as a free agent by **Quebec**, July 15, 1988. Traded to **New Jersey** by **Quebec** for Dave Marcinyshyn, June 3, 1991. Traded to **Winnipeg** by **New Jersey** for Winnipeg's 6th round choice (Ryan Smart) in 1994 Entry Draft, September 30, 1993. Traded to **Florida** by **Winnipeg** for Milan Tichy, October 3, 1993. Traded to **NY Islanders** by **Florida** for NY Islanders' 4th round choice (Dave Duerden) in 1995 Entry Draft, March 3, 1995. Traded to **Colorado** by **NY Islanders** for Colorado's 3rd round choice (later traded to Calgary - later traded to Hartford/Carolina - Carolina selected Francis Lessard) in 1997 Entry Draft, September 4, 1996. Claimed by **Anaheim** from **Colorado** in NHL Waiver Draft, September 28, 1997. • Missed majority of 1997-98 season recovering from back injury suffered in game vs. Detroit, October 22, 1997. Signed as a free agent by **Dallas**, August 26, 1998.

• SEVIGNY, Pierre

LW – L. 6′, 195 lbs. b: Trois-Rivières, Que., 9/8/1971. Montreal's 4th, 51st overall, in 1989.

Season	Club	League	GP	G	A	Pts	AG	AA	APts	PIM	PP	SH	GW	S	%	TGF	PGF	TGA	PGA	+/–	GP	G	A	Pts	PIM	PP	SH	GW
1987-88	Montreal L'est Cantonniers	QAAA	40	43	78	121				72																		
1988-89	Verdun Jr. Canadiens	QMJHL	67	27	43	70				88																		
1989-90	St-Hyacinthe Laser	QMJHL	67	47	72	119				205											12	8	8	16	42			
1990-91	St-Hyacinthe Laser	QMJHL	60	36	46	82				203																		
	Canada	WJC-A	7	4	2	6				8																		
1991-92	Fredericton Canadiens	AHL	74	22	37	59				145											7	1	1	2	26			
1992-93	Fredericton Canadiens	AHL	80	36	40	76				113											5	1	1	2	2			
1993-94	**Montreal Canadiens**	**NHL**	**43**	**4**	**5**	**9**	**4**	**4**	**8**	**42**	**1**	**0**	**1**	**19**	**21.1**	**17**	**1**	**10**	**0**	**6**	**3**	**0**	**1**	**1**	**0**	**0**	**0**	**0**
1994-95	**Montreal Canadiens**	**NHL**	**19**	**0**	**0**	**0**	**0**	**0**	**0**	**15**	**0**	**0**	**0**	**6**	**0.0**	**1**	**0**	**6**	**0**	**–5**								
1995-96	Fredericton Canadiens	AHL	76	39	42	81				188											10	5	9	14	20			
1996-97	**Montreal Canadiens**	**NHL**	**13**	**0**	**0**	**0**	**0**	**0**	**0**	**5**	**0**	**0**	**0**	**1**	**0.0**	**1**	**0**	**1**	**0**	**0**								
	Fredericton Canadiens	AHL	32	9	17	26				58																		
1997-98	**New York Rangers**	**NHL**	**3**	**0**	**0**	**0**	**0**	**0**	**0**	**2**	**0**	**0**	**0**	**1**	**0.0**	**1**	**0**	**1**	**0**	**0**								
	Hartford Wolf Pack	AHL	40	18	13	31				94											12	3	5	8	14			
1998-99	Long Beach Ice Dogs	IHL	6	1	3	4				7																		
	Orlando Solar Bears	IHL	43	11	21	32				44											15	4	5	9	32			
99-2000	Quebec Citadelles	AHL	78	24	43	67				154											3	3	0	3	17			
	NHL Totals		**78**	**4**	**5**	**9**	**4**	**4**	**8**	**64**	**1**	**0**	**1**	**27**	**14.8**	**20**	**1**	**18**	**0**		**3**	**0**	**1**	**1**	**0**	**0**	**0**	**0**

QMJHL First All-Star Team (1981) • QMJHL Second All-Star Team (1990, 1991)

Signed as a free agent by **NY Rangers**, August 26, 1997

• SHACK, Eddie

Edward Steven Phillip "The Entertainer" LW – L. 6′1″, 200 lbs. b: Sudbury, Ont., 2/11/1937.

Season	Club	League	GP	G	A	Pts	AG	AA	APts	PIM	PP	SH	GW	S	%	TGF	PGF	TGA	PGA	+/–	GP	G	A	Pts	PIM	PP	SH	GW
1952-53	Guelph Biltmores	OHA-Jr.	21	2	6	8				45																		
1953-54	Guelph Biltmores	OHA-Jr.	54	13	9	22				46											1	1	0	1	4			
1954-55	Guelph Biltmores	OHA-Jr.	19	6	7	13				35											2	0	0	0	4			
1955-56	Guelph Biltmores	OHA-Jr.	48	23	49	72				93											3	1	0	1	10			
1956-57	Guelph Biltmores	OHA-Jr.	52	47	*57	104				129											10	4	10	14	53			
	Guelph Biltmores	Mem-Cup	6	2	2	4				26																		
1957-58	Providence Reds	AHL	35	16	18	34				98																		
1958-59	**New York Rangers**	**NHL**	**67**	**7**	**14**	**21**	**8**	**14**	**22**	**109**																		
1959-60	**New York Rangers**	**NHL**	**62**	**8**	**10**	**18**	**9**	**10**	**19**	**110**																		
	Springfield Indians	AHL	9	3	4	7				10																		
1960-61	**New York Rangers**	**NHL**	**12**	**1**	**2**	**3**	**1**	**2**	**3**	**17**																		
	Toronto Maple Leafs	**NHL**	**55**	**14**	**14**	**28**	**16**	**13**	**29**	**90**											**4**	**0**	**0**	**0**	**2**	**0**	**0**	**0**
1961-62♦	**Toronto Maple Leafs**	**NHL**	**44**	**7**	**14**	**21**	**8**	**13**	**21**	**62**											**9**	**0**	**0**	**0**	**18**	**0**	**0**	**0**
1962-63♦	**Toronto Maple Leafs**	**NHL**	**63**	**16**	**9**	**25**	**19**	**9**	**28**	**97**											**10**	**2**	**1**	**3**	**11**	**0**	**0**	**2**
1963-64♦	**Toronto Maple Leafs**	**NHL**	**64**	**11**	**10**	**21**	**14**	**10**	**24**	**128**											**13**	**0**	**1**	**1**	**25**	**0**	**0**	**0**
1964-65	**Toronto Maple Leafs**	**NHL**	**67**	**5**	**9**	**14**	**6**	**9**	**15**	**68**											**5**	**1**	**0**	**1**	**8**	**0**	**0**	**0**
1965-66	**Toronto Maple Leafs**	**NHL**	**63**	**26**	**17**	**43**	**30**	**16**	**46**	**88**											**4**	**2**	**1**	**3**	**33**	**1**	**0**	**0**
	Rochester Americans	AHL	8	3	4	7				12																		
1966-67♦	**Toronto Maple Leafs**	**NHL**	**63**	**11**	**14**	**25**	**13**	**14**	**27**	**58**											**8**	**0**	**0**	**0**	**8**	**0**	**0**	**0**
1967-68	**Boston Bruins**	**NHL**	**70**	**23**	**19**	**42**	**27**	**19**	**46**	**107**	**4**	**0**	**6**	**195**	**11.8**	**60**	**8**	**52**	**1**	**1**	**4**	**0**	**1**	**1**	**6**	**0**	**0**	**0**
1968-69	**Boston Bruins**	**NHL**	**50**	**11**	**11**	**22**	**12**	**10**	**22**	**74**	**1**	**0**	**3**	**125**	**8.8**	**34**	**4**	**29**	**1**	**2**	**9**	**0**	**2**	**2**	**23**	**0**	**0**	**0**
1969-70	**Los Angeles Kings**	**NHL**	**73**	**22**	**12**	**34**	**24**	**11**	**35**	**113**	**4**	**0**	**2**	**203**	**10.8**	**54**	**10**	**83**	**1**	**–38**								
1970-71	**Los Angeles Kings**	**NHL**	**11**	**2**	**2**	**4**	**2**	**2**	**4**	**8**	**0**	**0**	**1**	**13**	**15.4**	**6**	**3**	**7**	**1**	**–3**								
	Buffalo Sabres	**NHL**	**56**	**25**	**17**	**42**	**25**	**14**	**39**	**93**	**10**	**0**	**4**	**192**	**13.0**	**69**	**34**	**65**	**1**	**–29**								
1971-72	**Buffalo Sabres**	**NHL**	**50**	**11**	**14**	**25**	**11**	**12**	**23**	**34**	**4**	**0**	**0**	**92**	**12.0**	**42**	**19**	**34**	**0**	**–11**								
	Pittsburgh Penguins	**NHL**	**18**	**5**	**9**	**14**	**5**	**8**	**13**	**12**	**4**	**0**	**2**	**47**	**10.6**	**24**	**11**	**8**	**0**	**5**	**4**	**0**	**1**	**1**	**15**	**0**	**0**	**0**
1972-73	**Pittsburgh Penguins**	**NHL**	**74**	**25**	**20**	**45**	**23**	**16**	**39**	**84**	**8**	**0**	**3**	**192**	**13.0**	**76**	**30**	**57**	**1**	**–10**								
1973-74	**Toronto Maple Leafs**	**NHL**	**59**	**7**	**8**	**15**	**7**	**7**	**14**	**74**	**4**	**0**	**1**	**78**	**9.0**	**36**	**8**	**27**	**0**	**1**	**4**	**1**	**0**	**1**	**2**	**0**	**0**	**0**
1974-75	**Toronto Maple Leafs**	**NHL**	**26**	**2**	**1**	**3**	**2**	**1**	**3**	**11**	**1**	**0**	**0**	**18**	**11.1**	**3**	**2**	**10**	**1**	**–8**								
	Oklahoma City Blazers	CHL	8	3	4	7				10																		
1975-76			REINSTATED AS AN AMATEUR																									
1976-77	Whitby Warriors	OHA-Sr.	9	5	4	9				8																		
	NHL Totals		**1047**	**239**	**226**	**465**	**262**	**210**	**472**	**1437**											**74**	**6**	**7**	**13**	**151**			

Played in NHL All-Star Game (1962, 1963, 1964)

Traded to **Detroit** by **NY Rangers** with Bill Gadsby for Red Kelly and Billy McNeill, February 5, 1960. • Kelly and McNeill refused to report and transaction was cancelled, February 7, 1960. Traded to **Toronto** by **NY Rangers** for Pat Hannigan and Johnny Wilson, November 7, 1960. Traded to **Boston** by **Toronto** for Murray Oliver and cash, May 15, 1967. Traded to **LA Kings** by **Boston** with Ross Lonsberry for Ken Turlik and LA Kings' 1st round choices in 1971 (Ron Jones) and 1973 (Andre Savard) Amateur Drafts, May 14, 1969. Traded to **Buffalo** by **LA Kings** with Dick Duff for Mike McMahon Jr. and future considerations, November 25, 1970. Traded to **Pittsburgh** by **Buffalo** for Rene Robert, March 4, 1972. Traded to **Toronto** by **Pittsburgh** for cash, July 3, 1973.

• SHAFRANOV, Konstantin

RW – L. 5′11″, 176 lbs. b: Kamengorsk, USSR, 9/11/1968. St. Louis' 10th, 229th overall, in 1996.

Season	Club	League	GP	G	A	Pts	AG	AA	APts	PIM	PP	SH	GW	S	%	TGF	PGF	TGA	PGA	+/–	GP	G	A	Pts	PIM	PP	SH	GW
1989-90	Torpedo Ust-Kamenogorsk	USSR	28	6	8	14				16																		
1990-91	Torpedo Ust-Kamenogorsk	USSR	40	16	6	22				32																		
1991-92	Torpedo Ust-Kamenogorsk	CIS	36	10	6	16				40																		
1992-93	Torpedo Ust-Kamenogorsk	CIS	42	19	19	38				26											1	0	1	1	0			
	Kazakhstan	WC-C	7	10	9	19				4																		
1993-94	Detroit Falcons	ColHL	4	3	2	5				0																		
	Torpedo Ust-Kamenogorsk	CIS	27	18	21	39				6																		
	Kazakhstan	WC-C1	6	7	5	12				44																		
1994-95	Metallurg Magnitogorsk	CIS	47	21	30	51				24											7	5	4	9	12			
1995-96	Metallurg Magnitogorsk	CIS	6	3	3	6				0																		
	Fort Wayne Komets	IHL	74	46	28	74				26											5	1	2	3	4			
1996-97	**St. Louis Blues**	**NHL**	**5**	**2**	**1**	**3**	**2**	**1**	**3**	**0**	**0**	**0**	**0**	**8**	**25.0**	**3**	**0**	**2**	**0**	**1**								
	Worcester IceCats	AHL	62	23	25	48				16											5	0	2	2	0			
1997-98	Fort Wayne Komets	IHL	67	28	52	80				50											4	2	4	6	2			
	Kazakhstan	Olympics	7	4	3	7				6																		
	Kazakhstan	WC-A	3	0	0	0				0																		
1998-99	Mettalurg Magnitogorsk	Russia	28	4	9	13				4											8	2	3	5	2			
	Mettalurg Magnitogorsk	EuroHL	9	3	9	12				4											5	0	1	1	2			
	Fort Wayne Komets	IHL																			2	0	1	1	0			

			REGULAR SEASON																		PLAYOFFS							
Season	Club	League	GP	G	A	Pts	AG	AA	APts	PIM	PP	SH	GW	S	%	TGF	PGF	TGA	PGA	+/–	GP	G	A	Pts	PIM	PP	SH	GW
99-2000	Grand Rapids Griffins	IHL	24	3	8	11				15																		
	Providence Bruins	AHL	8	0	4	4				0																		
	Fort Wayne Komets	UHL	20	15	15	30				6											13	6	8	14	8			
	NHL Totals		**5**	**2**	**1**	**3**	**2**	**1**	**3**	**0**	**0**	**0**	**0**	**8**	**25.0**	**3**	**0**	**2**	**0**									

Won Garry F. Longman Memorial Trophy (Top Rookie - IHL) (1996) • IHL Second All-Star Team (1998)

• SHAKES, Paul

Paul Steven D – R. 5'10", 175 lbs. b: Collingwood, Ont., 9/4/1952. California's 3rd, 38th overall, in 1972.

Season	Club	League	GP	G	A	Pts	AG	AA	APts	PIM	PP	SH	GW	S	%	TGF	PGF	TGA	PGA	+/–	GP	G	A	Pts	PIM	PP	SH	GW
1969-70	St. Catharines Black Hawks	OHA-Jr.	42	7	24	31				50											10	3	11	14	8			
1970-71	St. Catharines Black Hawks	OHA-Jr.	60	14	57	71				49											15	4	19	23	4			
1971-72	St. Catharines Black Hawks	OMJHL	61	20	48	68				61											5	0	2	2	4			
1972-73	Salt Lake Golden Eagles	WHL	71	11	31	42				59											9	1	3	4	8			
1973-74	**California Golden Seals**	**NHL**	**21**	**0**	**4**	**4**	**0**	**3**	**3**	**12**	**0**	**0**	**0**	**29**	**0.0**	**14**	**0**	**30**	**3**	**–13**								
	Salt Lake Golden Eagles	WHL	54	3	35	38				40											5	0	1	1	7			
1974-75	Springfield Indians	AHL	74	11	32	43				60											17	4	9	13	17			
1975-76	Salt Lake Golden Eagles	CHL	26	3	16	19				16																		
	NHL Totals		**21**	**0**	**4**	**4**	**0**	**3**	**3**	**12**	**0**	**0**	**0**	**29**	**0.0**	**14**	**0**	**30**	**3**									

OMJHL First All-Star Team (1972)

• SHALDYBIN, Yevgeny

D – L. 6'2", 198 lbs. b: Novosibirsk, USSR, 7/29/1975. Boston's 6th, 151st overall, in 1995.

Season	Club	League	GP	G	A	Pts	AG	AA	APts	PIM	PP	SH	GW	S	%	TGF	PGF	TGA	PGA	+/–	GP	G	A	Pts	PIM	PP	SH	GW
1993-94	Torpedo Yaroslavl	CIS	14	0	0	0				0																		
1994-95	Torpedo Yaroslavl	CIS	42	2	5	7				10											4	0	1	1	0			
1995-96	Torpedo Yaroslavl	CIS	41	0	2	2				10											3	0	1	1	2			
1996-97	**Boston Bruins**	**NHL**	**3**	**1**	**0**	**1**	**1**	**0**	**1**	**0**	**0**	**0**	**0**	**5**	**20.0**	**1**	**0**	**3**	**0**	**–2**								
	Providence Bruins	AHL	65	4	13	17				28											3	0	0	0	0			
1997-98	Providence Bruins	AHL	63	5	7	12				54																		
1998-99	Providence Bruins	AHL	1	0	0	0				0																		
	Las Vegas Thunder	IHL	13	1	3	4				6																		
	Binghamton Icemen	UHL	61	14	38	52				38																		
99-2000	Torpedo Nizhny Novgorod	Russia	4	0	0	0				2																		
	Binghamton Icemen	UHL	71	16	52	68				36											6	1	4	5	8			
	NHL Totals		**3**	**1**	**0**	**1**	**1**	**0**	**1**	**0**	**0**	**0**	**0**	**5**	**20.0**	**1**	**0**	**3**	**0**									

• SHANAHAN, Brendan

LW – R. 6'3", 218 lbs. b: Mimico, Ont., 1/23/1969. New Jersey's 1st, 2nd overall, in 1987.

Season	Club	League	GP	G	A	Pts	AG	AA	APts	PIM	PP	SH	GW	S	%	TGF	PGF	TGA	PGA	+/–	GP	G	A	Pts	PIM	PP	SH	GW
1984-85	Mississagua Reps	MTHL	36	20	21	41				26																		
	Dixie Beehives	OJHL	1	0	0	0				0																		
1985-86	London Knights	OHL	59	28	34	62				70											5	5	5	10	5			
1986-87	London Knights	OHL	56	39	53	92				92																		
	Canada	WJC-A	6	4	3	7				4																		
1987-88	**New Jersey Devils**	**NHL**	**65**	**7**	**19**	**26**	**6**	**14**	**20**	**131**	**2**	**0**	**2**	**72**	**9.7**	**34**	**11**	**43**	**0**	**–20**	**12**	**2**	**1**	**3**	**44**	**1**	**0**	**0**
1988-89	**New Jersey Devils**	**NHL**	**68**	**22**	**28**	**50**	**19**	**20**	**39**	**115**	**9**	**0**	**0**	**152**	**14.5**	**73**	**27**	**44**	**0**	**2**								
1989-90	**New Jersey Devils**	**NHL**	**73**	**30**	**42**	**72**	**26**	**30**	**56**	**137**	**8**	**0**	**5**	**196**	**15.3**	**115**	**35**	**66**	**1**	**15**	**6**	**3**	**3**	**6**	**20**	**1**	**0**	**1**
1990-91	**New Jersey Devils**	**NHL**	**75**	**29**	**37**	**66**	**27**	**28**	**55**	**141**	**7**	**0**	**2**	**195**	**14.9**	**91**	**31**	**58**	**2**	**4**	**7**	**3**	**5**	**8**	**12**	**2**	**0**	**0**
1991-92	Canada	Can-Cup	8	2	0	2				6																		
	St. Louis Blues	**NHL**	**80**	**33**	**36**	**69**	**30**	**27**	**57**	**171**	**13**	**0**	**2**	**215**	**15.3**	**105**	**44**	**65**	**1**	**–3**	**6**	**2**	**3**	**5**	**14**	**1**	**0**	**0**
1992-93	**St. Louis Blues**	**NHL**	**71**	**51**	**43**	**94**	**43**	**30**	**73**	**174**	**18**	**0**	**8**	**232**	**22.0**	**131**	**61**	**61**	**1**	**10**	**11**	**4**	**3**	**7**	**18**	**2**	**0**	**0**
1993-94	**St. Louis Blues**	**NHL**	**81**	**52**	**50**	**102**	**49**	**39**	**88**	**211**	**15**	**7**	**8**	**397**	**13.1**	**145**	**69**	**106**	**21**	**–9**	**4**	**2**	**5**	**7**	**4**	**0**	**0**	**0**
	Canada	WC-A	6	4	3	7				6																		
1994-95	Dusseldorfer EG	Germany	3	5	3	8				4																		
	St. Louis Blues	**NHL**	**45**	**20**	**21**	**41**	**35**	**31**	**66**	**136**	**6**	**2**	**6**	**153**	**13.1**	**56**	**15**	**46**	**12**	**7**	**5**	**4**	**5**	**9**	**14**	**1**	**0**	**1**
1995-96	**Hartford Whalers**	**NHL**	**74**	**44**	**34**	**78**	**43**	**28**	**71**	**125**	**17**	**2**	**6**	**280**	**15.7**	**109**	**51**	**78**	**22**	**2**								
1996-97	Canada	W-Cup	7	3	3	6				8																		
	Hartford Whalers	**NHL**	**2**	**1**	**0**	**1**	**1**	**0**	**1**	**0**	**0**	**1**	**0**	**13**	**7.7**	**2**	**0**	**1**	**0**	**1**								
♦	**Detroit Red Wings**	**NHL**	**79**	**46**	**41**	**87**	**49**	**37**	**86**	**131**	**20**	**2**	**7**	**323**	**14.2**	**126**	**49**	**52**	**6**	**31**	**20**	**9**	**8**	**17**	**43**	**2**	**0**	**2**
1997-98♦	**Detroit Red Wings**	**NHL**	**75**	**28**	**29**	**57**	**33**	**28**	**61**	**154**	**15**	**1**	**9**	**266**	**10.5**	**80**	**36**	**45**	**7**	**6**	**20**	**5**	**4**	**9**	**22**	**3**	**0**	**2**
	Canada	Olympics	6	2	0	2				0																		
1998-99	**Detroit Red Wings**	**NHL**	**81**	**31**	**27**	**58**	**36**	**26**	**62**	**123**	**5**	**0**	**5**	**288**	**10.8**	**89**	**32**	**57**	**2**	**2**	**10**	**3**	**7**	**10**	**6**	**1**	**0**	**1**
99-2000	**Detroit Red Wings**	**NHL**	**78**	**41**	**37**	**78**	**46**	**34**	**80**	**105**	**13**	**1**	**9**	**283**	**14.5**	**115**	**42**	**56**	**7**	**24**	**9**	**3**	**2**	**5**	**10**	**0**	**0**	**0**
	NHL Totals		**947**	**435**	**444**	**879**	**443**	**372**	**815**	**1854**	**148**	**16**	**69**	**3065**	**14.2**	**1271**	**503**	**778**	**82**		**110**	**40**	**46**	**86**	**207**	**14**	**0**	**7**

NHL First All-Star Team (1994, 2000) • Played in NHL All-Star Game (1994, 1996, 1997, 1998, 1999, 2000)

Signed as a free agent by **St. Louis**, July 25, 1991. Traded to **Hartford** by **St. Louis** for Chris Pronger, July 27, 1995. Traded to **Detroit** by **Hartford** with Brian Glynn for Paul Coffey, Keith Primeau and Detroit's 1st round choice (Nikos Tselios) in 1997 Entry Draft, October 9, 1996.

• SHANAHAN, Sean

Sean Bryan C/RW – R. 6'3", 205 lbs. b: Toronto, Ont., 2/8/1951.

Season	Club	League	GP	G	A	Pts	AG	AA	APts	PIM	PP	SH	GW	S	%	TGF	PGF	TGA	PGA	+/–	GP	G	A	Pts	PIM	PP	SH	GW
1968-69	Kitchener Rangers	OHA-Jr.	50	3	8	11				37																		
1969-70	Markham Waxers	OHA-B	STATISTICS NOT AVAILABLE																									
	Toronto Marlboros	OHA-Jr.	19	2	4	6				5																		
1970-71	Toronto Marlboros	OHA-Jr.	6	0	0	0				0																		
	Oshawa Generals	OMJHL	24	1	4	5				14																		
1971-72	Providence College	ECAC	23	13	15	28																						
1972-73	Providence College	ECAC	25	13	23	36				8																		
1973-74	Nova Scotia Voyageurs	AHL	63	13	14	27				65											6	1	0	1	6			
1974-75	Nova Scotia Voyageurs	AHL	67	12	10	22				159											6	0	0	0	58			
1975-76	**Montreal Canadiens**	**NHL**	**4**	**0**	**0**	**0**	**0**	**0**	**0**	**0**	**0**	**0**	**0**	**0**	**0.0**	**0**	**0**	**1**	**0**	**–1**								
	Nova Scotia Voyageurs	AHL	64	18	26	44				91											9	4	6	10	11			
1976-77	**Colorado Rockies**	**NHL**	**30**	**1**	**3**	**4**	**1**	**2**	**3**	**40**	**0**	**0**	**0**	**33**	**3.0**	**10**	**0**	**21**	**0**	**–11**								
	Rhode Island Reds	AHL	10	0	1	1				11																		
	Dallas Black Hawks	CHL	7	0	0	0				25											5	1	0	1	19			
1977-78	**Boston Bruins**	**NHL**	**6**	**0**	**0**	**0**	**0**	**0**	**0**	**7**	**0**	**0**	**0**	**2**	**0.0**	**1**	**0**	**2**	**0**	**–1**								
	Rochester Americans	AHL	66	20	23	43				156											6	2	3	5	10			
1978-79	Cincinnati Stingers	WHA	4	0	0	0				7																		
	NHL Totals		**40**	**1**	**3**	**4**	**1**	**2**	**3**	**47**	**0**	**0**	**0**	**35**	**2.9**	**11**	**0**	**24**	**0**									
	Other Major League Totals		4	0	0	0				7																		

Signed as a free agent by **Montreal**, September, 1973. Traded to **Colorado** by **Montreal** with Ron Andruff for cash, September 13, 1976. Signed as a free agent by **Boston**, October 13, 1977. Signed as a free agent by **Detroit**, June 6, 1978. Signed to 10-game tryout contract by **Cincinnati** (WHA) , October 24, 1978.

• SHAND, Dave

David Alistair D – R. 6'2", 200 lbs. b: Cold Lake, Alta., 8/11/1956. Atlanta's 1st, 8th overall, in 1976.

Season	Club	League	GP	G	A	Pts	AG	AA	APts	PIM	PP	SH	GW	S	%	TGF	PGF	TGA	PGA	+/–	GP	G	A	Pts	PIM	PP	SH	GW
1971-72	Camp Borden Forces	OMHA	STATISTICS NOT AVAILABLE																									
1972-73	Toronto Young Nationals	OHA-B	STATISTICS NOT AVAILABLE																									
1973-74	University of Michigan	WCHA	34	2	8	10				50																		
1974-75	University of Michigan	WCHA	10	0	4	4				20																		
	Peterborough Petes	OMJHL	33	4	11	15				30											11	1	4	5	17			
1975-76	Peterborough Petes	OMJHL	62	9	37	46				169																		
1976-77	**Atlanta Flames**	**NHL**	**55**	**5**	**11**	**16**	**4**	**8**	**12**	**62**	**0**	**0**	**1**	**79**	**6.3**	**51**	**1**	**42**	**13**	**21**	**3**	**0**	**0**	**0**	**33**	**0**	**0**	**0**
	Nova Scotia Voyageurs	AHL	9	0	5	5				21																		
1977-78	**Atlanta Flames**	**NHL**	**80**	**2**	**23**	**25**	**2**	**18**	**20**	**94**	**0**	**0**	**0**	**83**	**2.4**	**85**	**4**	**81**	**23**	**23**	**2**	**0**	**0**	**0**	**4**	**0**	**0**	**0**
	Canada	WEC-A	10	0	3	3				6																		

Season	Club	League	REGULAR SEASON																			PLAYOFFS							
			GP	G	A	Pts	AG	AA	APts	PIM	PP	SH	GW	S	%	TGF	PGF	TGA	PGA	+/–	GP	G	A	Pts	PIM	PP	SH	GW
1978-79	**Atlanta Flames**	**NHL**	**79**	**4**	**22**	**26**	**3**	**16**	**19**	**64**	**0**	**1**	**0**	**81**	**4.9**	**107**	**1**	**104**	**21**	**23**	**2**	**0**	**0**	**0**	**20**	**0**	**0**	**0**
	Canada	WEC-A	7	0	0	0	....	....	....	8	....	....	....	....	....	....	....	....	....	....	....	....	....	....	....	....	....	....
1979-80	**Atlanta Flames**	**NHL**	**74**	**3**	**7**	**10**	**3**	**5**	**8**	**104**	**0**	**0**	**1**	**47**	**6.4**	**54**	**0**	**65**	**12**	**1**	**4**	**0**	**1**	**1**	**0**	**0**	**0**	**0**
1980-81	**Toronto Maple Leafs**	**NHL**	**47**	**0**	**4**	**4**	**0**	**3**	**3**	**60**	**0**	**0**	**0**	**31**	**0.0**	**36**	**4**	**63**	**17**	**–14**	**3**	**0**	**0**	**0**	**0**	**0**	**0**	**0**
	New Brunswick Hawks	AHL	2	0	0	0	....	....	....	2	....	....	....	....	....	....	....	....	....	....	....	....	....	....	....	....	....	....
1981-82	Cincinnati Tigers	CHL	76	8	37	45	....	....	....	206	....	....	....	....	....	....	....	....	....	....	4	0	4	4	9	....	....	....
1982-83	**Toronto Maple Leafs**	**NHL**	**1**	**0**	**1**	**1**	**0**	**1**	**1**	**2**	**0**	**0**	**0**	**0**	**0.0**	**2**	**0**	**0**	**0**	**2**	**4**	**1**	**0**	**1**	**13**	**0**	**0**	**0**
	St. Catharines Saints	AHL	69	9	32	41	....	....	....	154	....	....	....	....	....	....	....	....	....	....	....	....	....	....	....	....	....	....
1983-84	**Washington Capitals**	**NHL**	**72**	**4**	**15**	**19**	**3**	**10**	**13**	**124**	**0**	**0**	**0**	**53**	**7.5**	**66**	**3**	**45**	**5**	**23**	**8**	**0**	**1**	**1**	**13**	**0**	**0**	**0**
	Hershey Bears	AHL	2	0	1	1	....	....	....	2	....	....	....	....	....	....	....	....	....	....	....	....	....	....	....	....	....	....
1984-85	**Washington Capitals**	**NHL**	**13**	**1**	**1**	**2**	**1**	**1**	**2**	**34**	**0**	**0**	**0**	**13**	**7.7**	**6**	**0**	**5**	**0**	**1**	....	....	....	....	....	....	....	....
	Binghamton Whalers	AHL	8	0	1	1	....	....	....	10	....	....	....	....	....	....	....	....	....	....	....	....	....	....	....	....	....	....
1985-86	KAC Klagenfurt	Austria	44	11	21	32	....	....	....	110	....	....	....	....	....	....	....	....	....	....	....	....	....	....	....	....	....	....
1986-87	KAC Klagenfurt	Austria	26	4	21	25	....	....	....	95	....	....	....	....	....	....	....	....	....	....	....	....	....	....	....	....	....	....
1987-88	KAC Klagenfurt	Austria	21	1	18	19	....	....	....	*73	....	....	....	....	....	....	....	....	....	....	....	....	....	....	....	....	....	....
1988-89	KAC Klagenfurt	Austria	39	5	25	30	....	....	....	98	....	....	....	....	....	....	....	....	....	....	....	....	....	....	....	....	....	....
	NHL Totals		**421**	**19**	**84**	**103**	**16**	**62**	**78**	**544**	**0**	**1**	**2**	**387**	**4.9**	**407**	**13**	**405**	**91**		**26**	**1**	**2**	**3**	**83**	**0**	**0**	**0**

OMJHL Second All-Star Team (1976) • CHL Second All-Star Team (1982)

Transferred to **Calgary** after **Atlanta** franchise relocated, June 24, 1980. Traded to **Toronto** by **Calgary** with Calgary's 3rd round choice (later traded to Washington — Washington selected Torrie Robertson) in 1980 Entry Draft for Toronto's 2nd round choice (Kevin LaVallee) in 1980 Entry Draft, June 10, 1980. Traded to **Washington** by **Toronto** for Lee Norwood, October 6, 1983.

• SHANK, Daniel

RW – R. 5'10", 190 lbs. b: Montreal, Que., 5/12/1967.

Season	Club	League	GP	G	A	Pts	AG	AA	APts	PIM	PP	SH	GW	S	%	TGF	PGF	TGA	PGA	+/–	GP	G	A	Pts	PIM	PP	SH	GW
1983-84	Longueuil College Francais	QJHL-B	STATISTICS NOT AVAILABLE																									
1984-85	Longueuil Chevaliers	QMJHL	55	26	29	55	....	....	....	139	....	....	....	....	....	....	....	....	....	....	....	....	....	....	....	....	....	....
1985-86	Longueuil Chevaliers	QMJHL	7	3	4	7	....	....	....	19	....	....	....	....	....	....	....	....	....	....	....	....	....	....	....	....	....	....
	Shawinigan Cataractes	QMJHL	9	2	5	7	....	....	....	34	....	....	....	....	....	....	....	....	....	....	....	....	....	....	....	....	....	....
	Chicoutimi Sagueneens	QMJHL	42	32	33	65	....	....	....	150	....	....	....	....	....	....	....	....	....	....	....	....	....	....	....	....	....	....
1986-87	Laval Titan	QMJHL	37	23	35	58	....	....	....	90	....	....	....	....	....	....	....	....	....	....	....	....	....	....	....	....	....	....
	Hull Olympiques	QMJHL	9	3	8	11	....	....	....	56	....	....	....	....	....	....	....	....	....	....	....	....	....	....	....	....	....	....
1987-88	Hull Olympiques	QMJHL	42	23	34	57	....	....	....	274	....	....	....	....	....	....	....	....	....	....	5	3	2	5	16	....	....	....
	Hull Olympiques	Mem-Cup	4	2	3	5	....	....	....	16	....	....	....	....	....	....	....	....	....	....	....	....	....	....	....	....	....	....
1988-89	Adirondack Red Wings	AHL	42	5	20	25	....	....	....	113	....	....	....	....	....	....	....	....	....	....	17	11	8	19	102	....	....	....
1989-90	**Detroit Red Wings**	**NHL**	**57**	**11**	**13**	**24**	**9**	**9**	**18**	**143**	**0**	**0**	**1**	**61**	**18.0**	**32**	**0**	**31**	**0**	**1**	....	....	....	....	....	....	....	....
	Adirondack Red Wings	AHL	14	8	8	16	....	....	....	36	....	....	....	....	....	....	....	....	....	....	....	....	....	....	....	....	....	....
1990-91	**Detroit Red Wings**	**NHL**	**7**	**0**	**1**	**1**	**0**	**1**	**1**	**14**	**0**	**0**	**0**	**4**	**0.0**	**5**	**0**	**5**	**0**	**0**	....	....	....	....	....	....	....	....
	Adirondack Red Wings	AHL	60	26	49	75	....	....	....	278	....	....	....	....	....	....	....	....	....	....	....	....	....	....	....	....	....	....
1991-92	Adirondack Red Wings	AHL	27	13	21	34	....	....	....	112	....	....	....	....	....	....	....	....	....	....	....	....	....	....	....	....	....	....
	Hartford Whalers	**NHL**	**13**	**2**	**0**	**2**	**2**	**0**	**2**	**18**	**0**	**0**	**0**	**10**	**20.0**	**4**	**2**	**6**	**0**	**–4**	**5**	**0**	**0**	**0**	**22**	**0**	**0**	**0**
	Springfield Indians	AHL	31	9	19	28	....	....	....	83	....	....	....	....	....	....	....	....	....	....	8	8	0	8	48	....	....	....
1992-93	San Diego Gulls	IHL	77	39	53	92	....	....	....	*495	....	....	....	....	....	....	....	....	....	....	14	5	10	15	*131	....	....	....
1993-94	San Diego Gulls	IHL	63	27	36	63	....	....	....	273	....	....	....	....	....	....	....	....	....	....	....	....	....	....	....	....	....	....
	Phoenix Roadrunners	IHL	7	4	6	10	....	....	....	26	....	....	....	....	....	....	....	....	....	....	....	....	....	....	....	....	....	....
1994-95	Minnesota Moose	IHL	19	4	11	15	....	....	....	30	....	....	....	....	....	....	....	....	....	....	....	....	....	....	....	....	....	....
	Detroit Vipers	IHL	54	44	27	71	....	....	....	142	....	....	....	....	....	....	....	....	....	....	5	2	2	4	6	....	....	....
1995-96	Las Vegas Thunder	IHL	49	36	29	65	....	....	....	191	....	....	....	....	....	....	....	....	....	....	....	....	....	....	....	....	....	....
	Detroit Vipers	IHL	29	14	19	33	....	....	....	96	....	....	....	....	....	....	....	....	....	....	12	4	5	9	38	....	....	....
1996-97	San Antonio Dragons	IHL	81	33	58	91	....	....	....	293	....	....	....	....	....	....	....	....	....	....	9	3	3	6	32	....	....	....
1997-98	San Antonio Dragons	IHL	80	39	43	82	....	....	....	141	....	....	....	....	....	....	....	....	....	....	....	....	....	....	....	....	....	....
1998-99	Frankfurt Lions	Germany	9	2	5	7	....	....	....	12	....	....	....	....	....	....	....	....	....	....	8	3	2	5	33	....	....	....
	Phoenix Mustangs	WCHL	17	13	16	29	....	....	....	26	....	....	....	....	....	....	....	....	....	....	....	....	....	....	....	....	....	....
99-2000	Phoenix Mustangs	WCHL	48	23	40	63	....	....	....	198	....	....	....	....	....	....	....	....	....	....	12	6	6	12	38	....	....	....
	NHL Totals		**77**	**13**	**14**	**27**	**11**	**10**	**21**	**175**	**0**	**0**	**1**	**75**	**17.3**	**41**	**2**	**42**	**0**		**5**	**0**	**0**	**0**	**22**	**0**	**0**	**0**

IHL First All-Star Team (1993)

Signed as a free agent by **Detroit**, May 26, 1989. Traded to **Hartford** by **Detroit** for Chris Tancill, December 18, 1991. Signed as a free agent by **Phoenix Mustangs** (WCHL), November 5, 1999. • Played w/ RHI's San Diego Barracudas in 1993 (14-28-31-59-107); Phoenix Cobras in 1994 (15-17-30-47-66); Anaheim Bullfrogs in 1995 (19-24-48-72-74); Orlando Roller Blades in 1996 (28-31-50-81-52) and Orlando Jackals in 1997 (17-19-47-66-23).

• SHANNON, Darrin

Darrin A. LW – L. 6'2", 210 lbs. b: Barrie, Ont., 12/8/1969. Pittsburgh's 1st, 4th overall, in 1988.

Season	Club	League	GP	G	A	Pts	AG	AA	APts	PIM	PP	SH	GW	S	%	TGF	PGF	TGA	PGA	+/–	GP	G	A	Pts	PIM	PP	SH	GW
1984-85	Alliston Hornets	OJHL-C	36	28	33	61	....	....	....	2	....	....	....	....	....	....	....	....	....	....	....	....	....	....	....	....	....	....
1985-86	Barrie Colts	OJHL-B	40	13	22	35	....	....	....	21	....	....	....	....	....	....	....	....	....	....	....	....	....	....	....	....	....	....
1986-87	Windsor Spitfires	OHL	60	16	67	83	....	....	....	116	....	....	....	....	....	....	....	....	....	....	14	4	6	10	8	....	....	....
1987-88	Windsor Spitfires	OHL	43	33	41	74	....	....	....	49	....	....	....	....	....	....	....	....	....	....	12	6	12	18	9	....	....	....
	Windsor Spitfires	Mem-Cup	4	2	3	5	....	....	....	16	....	....	....	....	....	....	....	....	....	....	....	....	....	....	....	....	....	....
1988-89	Windsor Spitfires	OHL	54	33	48	81	....	....	....	47	....	....	....	....	....	....	....	....	....	....	4	1	6	7	2	....	....	....
	Canada	WJC-A	7	1	3	4	....	....	....	10	....	....	....	....	....	....	....	....	....	....	....	....	....	....	....	....	....	....
	Buffalo Sabres	**NHL**	**3**	**0**	**0**	**0**	**0**	**0**	**0**	**0**	**0**	**0**	**0**	**0**	**0.0**	**0**	**0**	**2**	**0**	**–2**	**2**	**0**	**0**	**0**	**0**	**0**	**0**	**0**
1989-90	**Buffalo Sabres**	**NHL**	**17**	**2**	**7**	**9**	**2**	**5**	**7**	**4**	**0**	**0**	**0**	**20**	**10.0**	**12**	**0**	**7**	**1**	**6**	**6**	**0**	**1**	**1**	**4**	**0**	**0**	**0**
	Rochester Americans	AHL	50	20	23	43	....	....	....	25	....	....	....	....	....	....	....	....	....	....	9	4	1	5	2	....	....	....
1990-91	**Buffalo Sabres**	**NHL**	**34**	**8**	**6**	**14**	**7**	**5**	**12**	**12**	**1**	**0**	**0**	**56**	**14.3**	**20**	**1**	**37**	**7**	**–11**	**6**	**1**	**2**	**3**	**4**	**0**	**0**	**0**
	Rochester Americans	AHL	49	26	34	60	....	....	....	56	....	....	....	....	....	....	....	....	....	....	10	3	5	8	22	....	....	....
1991-92	**Buffalo Sabres**	**NHL**	**1**	**0**	**1**	**1**	**0**	**1**	**1**	**0**	**0**	**0**	**0**	**2**	**0.0**	**1**	**0**	**0**	**0**	**1**	....	....	....	....	....	....	....	....
	Winnipeg Jets	**NHL**	**68**	**13**	**26**	**39**	**12**	**20**	**32**	**41**	**3**	**0**	**3**	**91**	**14.3**	**63**	**20**	**55**	**17**	**5**	**7**	**0**	**1**	**1**	**10**	**0**	**0**	**0**
1992-93	**Winnipeg Jets**	**NHL**	**84**	**20**	**40**	**60**	**17**	**28**	**45**	**91**	**12**	**0**	**2**	**116**	**17.2**	**107**	**40**	**97**	**26**	**–4**	**6**	**2**	**4**	**6**	**6**	**1**	**0**	**0**
1993-94	**Winnipeg Jets**	**NHL**	**77**	**21**	**37**	**58**	**20**	**29**	**49**	**87**	**9**	**0**	**2**	**124**	**16.9**	**73**	**26**	**85**	**20**	**–18**	....	....	....	....	....	....	....	....
1994-95	**Winnipeg Jets**	**NHL**	**19**	**5**	**3**	**8**	**9**	**4**	**13**	**14**	**3**	**0**	**1**	**26**	**19.2**	**18**	**13**	**16**	**5**	**–6**	....	....	....	....	....	....	....	....
1995-96	**Winnipeg Jets**	**NHL**	**63**	**5**	**18**	**23**	**5**	**15**	**20**	**28**	**0**	**0**	**1**	**74**	**6.8**	**40**	**7**	**48**	**10**	**–5**	**6**	**1**	**0**	**1**	**6**	**0**	**0**	**0**
1996-97	**Phoenix Coyotes**	**NHL**	**82**	**11**	**13**	**24**	**12**	**12**	**24**	**41**	**1**	**0**	**2**	**104**	**10.6**	**48**	**5**	**59**	**20**	**4**	**7**	**3**	**1**	**4**	**4**	**0**	**0**	**1**
1997-98	**Phoenix Coyotes**	**NHL**	**58**	**2**	**12**	**14**	**2**	**12**	**14**	**26**	**0**	**0**	**0**	**57**	**3.5**	**24**	**0**	**38**	**18**	**4**	**5**	**0**	**1**	**1**	**4**	**0**	**0**	**0**
1998-99	Grand Rapids Griffins	IHL	10	1	5	6	....	....	....	12	....	....	....	....	....	....	....	....	....	....	....	....	....	....	....	....	....	....
99-2000	St. John's Maple Leafs	AHL	8	2	0	2	....	....	....	2	....	....	....	....	....	....	....	....	....	....	....	....	....	....	....	....	....	....
	Chicago Wolves	IHL	9	1	3	4	....	....	....	6	....	....	....	....	....	....	....	....	....	....	....	....	....	....	....	....	....	....
	NHL Totals		**506**	**87**	**163**	**250**	**86**	**131**	**217**	**344**	**29**	**0**	**11**	**670**	**13.0**	**406**	**112**	**444**	**124**		**45**	**7**	**10**	**17**	**38**	**1**	**0**	**1**

• Brother of Darryl • Canadian Major Junior Scholastic Player of the Year (1988)

Traded to **Buffalo** by **Pittsburgh** with Doug Bodger for Tom Barrasso and Buffalo's 3rd round choice (Joe Dziedzic) in 1990 Entry Draft, November 12, 1988. Traded to **Winnipeg** by **Buffalo** with Mike Hartman and Dean Kennedy for Dave McLlwain, Gord Donnelly, Winnipeg's 5th round choice (Yuri Khmylev) in 1992 Entry Draft and future considerations, October 11, 1991. Transferred to **Phoenix** after **Winnipeg** franchise relocated, July 1, 1996. • Missed majority of 1998-99 season recovering from knee surgery, June 1998. Signed as a free agent by **Grand Rapids** (IHL), February 18, 1999. Signed as a free agent by **Toronto**, August 25, 1999.

• SHANNON, Darryl

D – L. 6'2", 208 lbs. b: Barrie, Ont., 6/21/1968. Toronto's 2nd, 36th overall, in 1986.

Season	Club	League	GP	G	A	Pts	AG	AA	APts	PIM	PP	SH	GW	S	%	TGF	PGF	TGA	PGA	+/–	GP	G	A	Pts	PIM	PP	SH	GW
1983-84	Alliston Hornets	OJHL-C	30	18	22	40	....	....	....	70	....	....	....	....	....	....	....	....	....	....	....	....	....	....	....	....	....	....
1984-85	Barrie Colts	OJHL-B	39	5	23	28	....	....	....	50	....	....	....	....	....	....	....	....	....	....	....	....	....	....	....	....	....	....
	Richmond Hill Dynes	OJHL	1	0	0	0	....	....	....	0	....	....	....	....	....	....	....	....	....	....	....	....	....	....	....	....	....	....
1985-86	Windsor Spitfires	OHL	57	6	21	27	....	....	....	52	....	....	....	....	....	....	....	....	....	....	16	5	6	11	22	....	....	....
1986-87	Windsor Spitfires	OHL	64	23	27	50	....	....	....	83	....	....	....	....	....	....	....	....	....	....	14	4	8	12	18	....	....	....
1987-88	Windsor Spitfires	OHL	60	16	67	83	....	....	....	116	....	....	....	....	....	....	....	....	....	....	12	3	8	11	17	....	....	....
	Windsor Spitfires	Mem-Cup	4	0	7	7	....	....	....	8	....	....	....	....	....	....	....	....	....	....	....	....	....	....	....	....	....	....
1988-89	**Toronto Maple Leafs**	**NHL**	**14**	**1**	**3**	**4**	**1**	**2**	**3**	**6**	**0**	**0**	**0**	**16**	**6.3**	**19**	**2**	**13**	**1**	**5**	....	....	....	....	....	....	....	....
	Newmarket Saints	AHL	61	5	24	29	....	....	....	37	....	....	....	....	....	....	....	....	....	....	5	0	3	3	10	....	....	....

			REGULAR SEASON																		PLAYOFFS							
Season	Club	League	GP	G	A	Pts	AG	AA	APts	PIM	PP	SH	GW	S	%	TGF	PGF	TGA	PGA	+/-	GP	G	A	Pts	PIM	PP	SH	GW
1989-90	Toronto Maple Leafs	NHL	10	0	1	1	0	1	1	12	0	0	0	16	0.0	5	0	15	0	–10	....	....	....	....	....	....	....	....
	Newmarket Saints	AHL	47	4	15	19	....	....	....	58	....	....	....	....	....	....	....	....	....	....	....	....	....	....	....	....	....	....
1990-91	Toronto Maple Leafs	NHL	10	0	1	1	0	1	1	0	0	0	0	3	0.0	5	0	4	0	1	....	....	....	....	....	....	....	....
	Newmarket Saints	AHL	47	2	14	16	....	....	....	51	....	....	....	....	....	....	....	....	....	....	....	....	....	....	....	....	....	....
1991-92	Toronto Maple Leafs	NHL	48	2	8	10	2	6	8	23	1	0	0	50	4.0	22	7	34	2	–17	....	....	....	....	....	....	....	....
1992-93	Toronto Maple Leafs	NHL	16	0	0	0	0	0	0	11	0	0	0	10	0.0	3	0	9	1	–5	....	....	....	....	....	....	....	....
	St. John's Maple Leafs	AHL	7	1	1	2	....	....	....	4	....	....	....	....	....	....	....	....	....	....	....	....	....	....	....	....	....	....
1993-94	Winnipeg Jets	NHL	20	0	4	4	0	3	3	18	0	0	0	14	0.0	11	1	20	4	–6	....	....	....	....	....	....	....	....
	Moncton Hawks	AHL	37	1	10	11	....	....	....	62	....	....	....	....	....	....	....	....	....	....	20	1	7	8	32	....	....	....
1994-95	Winnipeg Jets	NHL	40	5	9	14	9	13	22	48	0	1	0	42	11.9	26	0	30	5	1	....	....	....	....	....	....	....	....
1995-96	Winnipeg Jets	NHL	48	2	7	9	2	6	8	72	0	0	0	34	5.9	34	1	50	22	5	....	....	....	....	....	....	....	....
	Buffalo Sabres	NHL	26	2	6	8	2	5	7	20	0	0	0	25	8.0	31	2	35	16	10	....	....	....	....	....	....	....	....
1996-97	Buffalo Sabres	NHL	82	4	19	23	4	17	21	112	1	0	1	94	4.3	78	4	74	23	23	12	2	3	5	8	1	0	0
1997-98	Buffalo Sabres	NHL	76	3	19	22	4	19	23	56	1	0	1	85	3.5	71	14	57	26	26	15	2	4	6	8	0	1	0
1998-99	Buffalo Sabres	NHL	71	3	12	15	4	12	16	52	1	0	0	80	3.8	67	6	50	17	28	2	0	0	0	0	0	0	0
99-2000	Atlanta Thrashers	NHL	49	5	13	18	6	12	18	65	1	0	1	66	7.6	42	13	57	14	–14	....	....	....	....	....	....	....	....
	Calgary Flames	NHL	27	1	8	9	1	7	8	22	0	0	0	46	2.2	33	14	40	8	–13	....	....	....	....	....	....	....	....
	NHL Totals		537	28	110	138	35	104	139	517	5	1	3	581	4.8	447	64	488	139		29	4	7	11	16	1	1	0

• Brother of Darrin • OHL Second All-Star Team (1987) • OHL First All-Star Team (1988)

Signed as a free agent by **Winnipeg**, June 30, 1993. Traded to **Buffalo** by **Winnipeg** with Michal Grosek for Craig Muni, February 15, 1996. Claimed by **Atlanta** from **Buffalo** in Expansion Draft, June 25, 1999. Traded to **Calgary** by **Atlanta** with Jason Botterill for Hnat Domenichelli and Dmitri Vlasenkov, February 11, 2000.

• SHANTZ, Jeff

Jeffrey Davis C – R. 6', 195 lbs. b: Duchess, Alta., 10/10/1973. Chicago's 2nd, 36th overall, in 1992.

Season	Club	League	GP	G	A	Pts	AG	AA	APts	PIM	PP	SH	GW	S	%	TGF	PGF	TGA	PGA	+/-	GP	G	A	Pts	PIM	PP	SH	GW
1989-90	Medicine Hat Midget Tigers	AAHA	36	18	31	49	....	....	....	30	....	....	....	....	....	....	....	....	....	....	....	....	....	....	....	....	....	....
	Regina Pats	WHL	1	0	0	0	....	....	....	0	....	....	....	....	....	....	....	....	....	....	....	....	....	....	....	....	....	....
1990-91	Regina Pats	WHL	69	16	21	37	....	....	....	22	....	....	....	....	....	....	....	....	....	....	8	2	2	4	2	....	....	....
1991-92	Regina Pats	WHL	72	39	50	89	....	....	....	35	....	....	....	....	....	....	....	....	....	....	....	....	....	....	....	....	....	....
1992-93	Regina Pats	WHL	64	29	54	83	....	....	....	75	....	....	....	....	....	....	....	....	....	....	13	2	12	14	14	....	....	....
	Canada	WJC-A	7	2	4	6	....	....	....	2	....	....	....	....	....	....	....	....	....	....	....	....	....	....	....	....	....	....
1993-94	Chicago Blackhawks	NHL	52	3	13	16	3	10	13	30	0	0	0	56	5.4	19	1	34	2	–14	6	0	0	0	6	0	0	0
	Indianapolis Ice	IHL	19	5	9	14	....	....	....	20	....	....	....	....	....	....	....	....	....	....	....	....	....	....	....	....	....	....
1994-95	Indianapolis Ice	IHL	32	9	15	24	....	....	....	20	....	....	....	....	....	....	....	....	....	....	....	....	....	....	....	....	....	....
	Chicago Blackhawks	NHL	45	6	12	18	11	18	29	33	0	2	0	58	10.3	24	4	12	3	11	16	3	1	4	2	0	0	0
1995-96	Chicago Blackhawks	NHL	78	6	14	20	6	11	17	24	1	2	0	72	8.3	29	1	39	23	12	10	2	3	5	6	0	0	0
1996-97	Chicago Blackhawks	NHL	69	9	21	30	10	19	29	28	0	1	1	86	10.5	41	3	42	15	11	6	0	4	4	6	0	0	0
1997-98	Chicago Blackhawks	NHL	61	11	20	31	13	20	33	36	1	2	2	69	15.9	38	8	43	13	0	....	....	....	....	....	....	....	....
1998-99	Chicago Blackhawks	NHL	7	1	0	1	1	0	1	4	0	0	0	5	20.0	1	0	5	3	–1	....	....	....	....	....	....	....	....
	Calgary Flames	NHL	69	12	17	29	14	16	30	40	1	1	3	77	15.6	50	1	68	34	15	....	....	....	....	....	....	....	....
99-2000	Calgary Flames	NHL	74	13	18	31	15	17	32	30	6	0	1	112	11.6	53	23	72	29	–13	....	....	....	....	....	....	....	....
	NHL Totals		455	61	115	176	73	111	184	225	9	8	7	535	11.4	255	41	315	122		38	5	8	13	20	0	0	0

WHL East First All-Star Team (1993)

Traded to **Calgary** by **Chicago** with Steve Dubinsky for Marty McInnis, Jamie Allison and Eric Andersson, October 27, 1998.

• SHARIFIJANOV, Vadim

RW – L. 6', 205 lbs. b: Ufa, USSR, 12/23/1975. New Jersey's 1st, 25th overall, in 1994.

Season	Club	League	GP	G	A	Pts	AG	AA	APts	PIM	PP	SH	GW	S	%	TGF	PGF	TGA	PGA	+/-	GP	G	A	Pts	PIM	PP	SH	GW
1991-92	Ufa Salavat	CIS-Jr.	STATISTICS NOT AVAILABLE																									
	Russia	EJC-A	6	8	1	9	....	....	....	8	....	....	....	....	....	....	....	....	....	....	....	....	....	....	....	....	....	....
1992-93	Ufa Salavat	CIS	37	6	4	10	....	....	....	16	....	....	....	....	....	....	....	....	....	....	2	1	0	1	0	....	....	....
	Russia	EJC-A	6	3	5	8	....	....	....	6	....	....	....	....	....	....	....	....	....	....	....	....	....	....	....	....	....	....
1993-94	Ufa Salavat	CIS	46	10	6	16	....	....	....	36	....	....	....	....	....	....	....	....	....	....	5	3	0	3	4	....	....	....
1994-95	CSKA Moscow	CIS	34	7	3	10	....	....	....	26	....	....	....	....	....	....	....	....	....	....	2	0	0	0	0	....	....	....
	Albany River Rats	AHL	1	1	1	2	....	....	....	0	....	....	....	....	....	....	....	....	....	....	9	3	3	6	10	....	....	....
1995-96	Albany River Rats	AHL	69	14	28	42	....	....	....	28	....	....	....	....	....	....	....	....	....	....	....	....	....	....	....	....	....	....
1996-97	New Jersey Devils	NHL	2	0	0	0	0	0	0	0	0	0	0	4	0.0	0	0	0	0	0	....	....	....	....	....	....	....	....
	Albany River Rats	AHL	70	14	27	41	....	....	....	89	....	....	....	....	....	....	....	....	....	....	10	3	3	6	6	....	....	....
1997-98	Albany River Rats	AHL	72	23	27	50	....	....	....	69	....	....	....	....	....	....	....	....	....	....	12	4	9	13	6	....	....	....
1998-99	New Jersey Devils	NHL	53	11	16	27	13	15	28	28	1	0	2	71	15.5	39	6	26	4	11	4	0	0	0	0	0	0	0
	Albany River Rats	AHL	2	1	1	2	....	....	....	0	....	....	....	....	....	....	....	....	....	....	....	....	....	....	....	....	....	....
99-2000	New Jersey Devils	NHL	20	3	4	7	3	4	7	8	0	0	0	20	15.0	8	0	14	0	–6	....	....	....	....	....	....	....	....
	Vancouver Canucks	NHL	17	2	1	3	2	1	3	14	1	0	0	26	7.7	7	4	10	0	–7	....	....	....	....	....	....	....	....
	NHL Totals		92	16	21	37	18	20	38	50	2	0	2	121	13.2	54	10	50	4		4	0	0	0	0	0	0	0

Traded to **Vancouver** by **New Jersey** with New Jersey's 3rd round choice (Tim Branham) in 2000 Entry Draft for NY Islanders' compensatory 2nd round choice (previously acquired, New Jersey selected Teemu Laine) in 2000 Entry Draft and Atlanta's third round choice (previously acquired, New Jersey selected Max Birbraer) in 2000 Entry Draft, January 14, 2000.

• SHARPLES, Jeff

Jeffrey D. D – L. 6'1", 195 lbs. b: Terrace, B.C., 7/28/1967. Detroit's 2nd, 29th overall, in 1985.

Season	Club	League	GP	G	A	Pts	AG	AA	APts	PIM	PP	SH	GW	S	%	TGF	PGF	TGA	PGA	+/-	GP	G	A	Pts	PIM	PP	SH	GW
1982-83	Terrace Titans	BCAHA	STATISTICS NOT AVAILABLE																									
1983-84	Kelowna Wings	WHL	72	9	24	33	....	....	....	51	....	....	....	....	....	....	....	....	....	....	....	....	....	....	....	....	....	....
1984-85	Kelowna Wings	WHL	72	12	41	53	....	....	....	90	....	....	....	....	....	....	....	....	....	....	6	0	1	1	6	....	....	....
1985-86	Spokane Chiefs	WHL	3	0	0	0	....	....	....	4	....	....	....	....	....	....	....	....	....	....	....	....	....	....	....	....	....	....
	Portland Winter Hawks	WHL	19	2	6	8	....	....	....	44	....	....	....	....	....	....	....	....	....	....	15	2	6	8	6	....	....	....
	Portland Winter Hawks	Mem-Cup	4	0	4	4	....	....	....	6	....	....	....	....	....	....	....	....	....	....	....	....	....	....	....	....	....	....
1986-87	Portland Winter Hawks	WHL	44	25	35	60	....	....	....	92	....	....	....	....	....	....	....	....	....	....	20	7	15	22	23	....	....	....
	Detroit Red Wings	NHL	3	0	1	1	0	1	1	2	0	0	0	1	0.0	2	0	2	0	0	2	0	0	0	2	0	0	0
1987-88	Detroit Red Wings	NHL	56	10	25	35	9	18	27	42	2	0	0	94	10.6	78	27	41	3	13	4	0	3	3	4	0	0	0
	Adirondack Red Wings	AHL	4	2	1	3	....	....	....	4	....	....	....	....	....	....	....	....	....	....	....	....	....	....	....	....	....	....
1988-89	Detroit Red Wings	NHL	46	4	9	13	3	6	9	26	3	0	0	48	8.3	46	14	29	2	5	1	0	0	0	0	0	0	0
	Adirondack Red Wings	AHL	10	0	4	4	....	....	....	8	....	....	....	....	....	....	....	....	....	....	....	....	....	....	....	....	....	....
1989-90	Adirondack Red Wings	AHL	9	2	5	7	....	....	....	6	....	....	....	....	....	....	....	....	....	....	....	....	....	....	....	....	....	....
	Cape Breton Oilers	AHL	38	4	13	17	....	....	....	28	....	....	....	....	....	....	....	....	....	....	....	....	....	....	....	....	....	....
	Utica Devils	AHL	13	2	5	7	....	....	....	19	....	....	....	....	....	....	....	....	....	....	5	1	2	3	15	....	....	....
1990-91	Utica Devils	AHL	64	16	29	45	....	....	....	42	....	....	....	....	....	....	....	....	....	....	....	....	....	....	....	....	....	....
1991-92	Capital District Islanders	AHL	31	3	12	15	....	....	....	18	....	....	....	....	....	....	....	....	....	....	7	6	5	11	4	....	....	....
1992-93	Kansas City Blades	IHL	39	5	21	26	....	....	....	43	....	....	....	....	....	....	....	....	....	....	8	0	0	0	6	....	....	....
1993-94	Las Vegas Thunder	IHL	68	18	32	50	....	....	....	68	....	....	....	....	....	....	....	....	....	....	5	2	1	3	6	....	....	....
1994-95	Las Vegas Thunder	IHL	72	20	33	53	....	....	....	63	....	....	....	....	....	....	....	....	....	....	10	4	4	8	18	....	....	....
1995-96	Las Vegas Thunder	IHL	41	6	14	20	....	....	....	56	....	....	....	....	....	....	....	....	....	....	....	....	....	....	....	....	....	....
	Utah Grizzlies	IHL	31	2	15	17	....	....	....	18	....	....	....	....	....	....	....	....	....	....	21	3	10	13	16	....	....	....
1996-97	Utah Grizzlies	IHL	49	9	26	35	....	....	....	54	....	....	....	....	....	....	....	....	....	....	7	0	2	2	10	....	....	....
1997-98	Utah Grizzlies	IHL	76	10	28	38	....	....	....	82	....	....	....	....	....	....	....	....	....	....	4	1	1	2	6	....	....	....
1998-99	Utah Grizzlies	IHL	78	8	29	37	....	....	....	93	....	....	....	....	....	....	....	....	....	....	....	....	....	....	....	....	....	....
99-2000	Utah Grizzlies	IHL	33	2	9	11	....	....	....	49	....	....	....	....	....	....	....	....	....	....	....	....	....	....	....	....	....	....
	NHL Totals		105	14	35	49	12	25	37	70	5	0	0	143	9.8	126	41	72	5		7	0	3	3	6	0	0	0

WHL West Second All-Star Team (1985)

Traded to **Edmonton** by **Detroit** with Petr Klima, Joe Murphy and Adam Graves for Jimmy Carson, Kevin McClelland and Edmonton's 5th round choice (later traded to Montreal — Montreal selected Brad Layzell) in 1991 Entry Draft, November 2, 1989. Traded to **New Jersey** by **Edmonton** for Reijo Ruotsalainen, March 6, 1990. • Missed majority of 1991-92 season in retirement. • Missed majority of 1999-2000 season recovering from head injury suffered in game vs. Detroit (IHL), January 5, 2000.

			REGULAR SEASON																		PLAYOFFS							
Season	**Club**	**League**	**GP**	**G**	**A**	**Pts**	**AG**	**AA**	**APts**	**PIM**	**PP**	**SH**	**GW**	**S**	**%**	**TGF**	**PGF**	**TGA**	**PGA**	**+/–**	**GP**	**G**	**A**	**Pts**	**PIM**	**PP**	**SH**	**GW**

• SHARPLEY, Glen

Glen Stuart C – R. 6', 190 lbs. b: York, Ont., 9/6/1956. Minnesota's 1st, 3rd overall, in 1976.

Season	Club	League	GP	G	A	Pts	AG	AA	APts	PIM	PP	SH	GW	S	%	TGF	PGF	TGA	PGA	+/–	GP	G	A	Pts	PIM	PP	SH	GW
1973-74	Hull Festivals	QMJHL	52	14	30	44	....	....	....	64	....	....	....	....	....	....	....	....	....	....	....	....	....	....	....	....	....	....
1974-75	Hull Festivals	QMJHL	68	24	45	69	....	....	....	99	....	....	....	....	....	....	....	....	....	....	....	....	....	....	....	....	....	....
1975-76	Hull Festivals	QMJHL	69	60	74	134	....	....	....	99	....	....	....	....	....	....	....	....	....	....	....	....	....	....	....	....	....	....
1976-77	**Minnesota North Stars**	**NHL**	**80**	**25**	**32**	**57**	**23**	**25**	**48**	**48**	**2**	**1**	**6**	**206**	**12.1**	**67**	**13**	**93**	**18**	**–21**	**2**	**0**	**0**	**0**	**4**	**0**	**0**	**0**
1977-78	**Minnesota North Stars**	**NHL**	**79**	**22**	**33**	**55**	**20**	**26**	**46**	**42**	**6**	**0**	**3**	**215**	**10.2**	**76**	**24**	**107**	**22**	**–33**	....	....	....	....	....	....	....	....
	Canada	WEC-A	10	1	3	4	....	....	....	16	....	....	....	....	....	....	....	....	....	....	....	....	....	....	....	....	....	....
1978-79	**Minnesota North Stars**	**NHL**	**80**	**19**	**34**	**53**	**16**	**25**	**41**	**30**	**5**	**0**	**1**	**162**	**11.7**	**81**	**18**	**88**	**7**	**–18**	....	....	....	....	....	....	....	....
1979-80	**Minnesota North Stars**	**NHL**	**51**	**20**	**27**	**47**	**17**	**20**	**37**	**38**	**6**	**0**	**0**	**109**	**18.3**	**62**	**16**	**49**	**2**	**–1**	**9**	**1**	**6**	**7**	**4**	**0**	**0**	**0**
1980-81	Minnesota North Stars	DN-Cup	3	2	0	2	....	....	....	0	....	....	....	....	....	....	....	....	....	....	....	....	....	....	....	....	....	....
	Minnesota North Stars	**NHL**	**28**	**12**	**12**	**24**	**9**	**8**	**17**	**18**	**6**	**0**	**0**	**52**	**23.1**	**32**	**11**	**25**	**0**	**–4**	....	....	....	....	....	....	....	....
	Chicago Black Hawks	**NHL**	**35**	**10**	**16**	**26**	**8**	**11**	**19**	**12**	**4**	**0**	**0**	**64**	**15.6**	**44**	**12**	**39**	**13**	**6**	**1**	**0**	**2**	**2**	**0**	**0**	**0**	**0**
1981-82	**Chicago Black Hawks**	**NHL**	**36**	**9**	**7**	**16**	**7**	**5**	**12**	**11**	**0**	**0**	**2**	**38**	**23.7**	**24**	**1**	**31**	**10**	**2**	**15**	**6**	**3**	**9**	**16**	**0**	**0**	**0**
1982-83	**Chicago Black Hawks**	**NHL**	DID NOT PLAY – INJURED																									
1983-84	EHC Arosa	Switz.	STATISTICS NOT AVAILABLE																									
1984-85	**Chicago Black Hawks**	**NHL**	DID NOT PLAY – INJURED																									
1985-86	Baltimore Skipjacks	AHL	7	0	3	3	....	....	....	4	....	....	....	....	....	....	....	....	....	....	....	....	....	....	....	....	....	....
	Peoria Rivermen	IHL	50	26	37	63	....	....	....	32	....	....	....	....	....	....	....	....	....	....	....	....	....	....	....	....	....	....
1986-87	Salt Lake Golden Eagles	IHL	32	10	15	25	....	....	....	14	....	....	....	....	....	....	....	....	....	....	....	....	....	....	....	....	....	....
	Dundee Rockets	Britain	15	31	40	71	....	....	....	49	....	....	....	....	....	....	....	....	....	....	5	6	13	19	10	....	....	....
	NHL Totals		**389**	**117**	**161**	**278**	**100**	**120**	**220**	**199**	**29**	**1**	**12**	**846**	**13.8**	**386**	**95**	**432**	**72**		**27**	**7**	**11**	**18**	**24**	**0**	**0**	**0**

QMJHL West First All-Star Team (1976)

Traded to **Chicago** by **Minnesota** for Ken Solheim and Chicago's 2nd round choice (Tom Hirsch) in 1981 Entry Draft, December 29, 1980. • Suffered eventual NHL career-ending eye injury in game vs. Washington, December 17, 1981. Doctors refused to grant permission to return to active playing duty in the NHL.

• SHAUNESSY, Scott

D/LW – L. 6'4", 220 lbs. b: Newport, RI, 1/22/1964. Quebec's 9th, 200th overall, in 1983.

Season	Club	League	GP	G	A	Pts	AG	AA	APts	PIM	PP	SH	GW	S	%	TGF	PGF	TGA	PGA	+/–	GP	G	A	Pts	PIM	PP	SH	GW
1982-83	St. John's Prep School	Hi-School	23	7	32	39	....	....	....	....	....	....	....	....	....	....	....	....	....	....	....	....	....	....	....	....	....	....
1983-84	Boston University	ECAC	40	6	22	28	....	....	....	48	....	....	....	....	....	....	....	....	....	....	....	....	....	....	....	....	....	....
1984-85	Boston University	H-East	42	7	15	22	....	....	....	87	....	....	....	....	....	....	....	....	....	....	....	....	....	....	....	....	....	....
1985-86	Boston University	H-East	38	6	13	19	....	....	....	31	....	....	....	....	....	....	....	....	....	....	....	....	....	....	....	....	....	....
1986-87	Boston University	H-East	32	2	13	15	....	....	....	71	....	....	....	....	....	....	....	....	....	....	....	....	....	....	....	....	....	....
	Quebec Nordiques	**NHL**	**3**	**0**	**0**	**0**	**0**	**0**	**0**	**7**	**0**	**0**	**0**	**0**	**0.0**	**0**	**0**	**1**	**0**	**–1**	....	....	....	....	....	....	....	....
1987-88	Fredericton Express	AHL	60	0	9	9	....	....	....	257	....	....	....	....	....	....	....	....	....	....	1	0	0	0	2	....	....	....
1988-89	**Quebec Nordiques**	**NHL**	**4**	**0**	**0**	**0**	**0**	**0**	**0**	**16**	**0**	**0**	**0**	**0**	**0.0**	**1**	**0**	**2**	**1**	**0**	....	....	....	....	....	....	....	....
	Halifax Citadels	AHL	41	3	10	13	....	....	....	106	....	....	....	....	....	....	....	....	....	....	....	....	....	....	....	....	....	....
1989-90	Halifax Citadels	AHL	27	3	5	8	....	....	....	105	....	....	....	....	....	....	....	....	....	....	....	....	....	....	....	....	....	....
	Fort Wayne Komets	IHL	45	3	9	12	....	....	....	267	....	....	....	....	....	....	....	....	....	....	5	0	1	1	31	....	....	....
1990-91	Albany Choppers	IHL	34	3	9	12	....	....	....	126	....	....	....	....	....	....	....	....	....	....	....	....	....	....	....	....	....	....
	Muskegon Lumberjacks	IHL	23	1	4	5	....	....	....	104	....	....	....	....	....	....	....	....	....	....	5	0	0	0	21	....	....	....
1991-92	Fort Wayne Komets	IHL	53	3	8	11	....	....	....	243	....	....	....	....	....	....	....	....	....	....	7	0	1	1	27	....	....	....
1992-93	Cincinnati Cyclones	IHL	71	2	7	9	....	....	....	222	....	....	....	....	....	....	....	....	....	....	....	....	....	....	....	....	....	....
1993-1996			OUT OF HOCKEY – RETIRED																									
1996-97	Austin Ice Bats	WPHL	32	3	4	7	....	....	....	138	....	....	....	....	....	....	....	....	....	....	6	3	0	3	22	....	....	....
1997-98	Tupelo T-Rex	WPHL	DID NOT PLAY																									
1998-99	Fort Worth Brahmas	WPHL	55	9	14	23	....	....	....	190	....	....	....	....	....	....	....	....	....	....	12	0	3	3	26	....	....	....
	NHL Totals		**7**	**0**	**0**	**0**	**0**	**0**	**0**	**23**	**0**	**0**	**0**	**0**	**0.0**	**1**	**0**	**3**	**1**		....	....	....	....	....	....	....	....

Hockey East Second All-Star Team (1985) • Hockey East First All-Star Team (1986)

• Retired following 1992-93 season to recover from back surgery. Signed as a free agent by **Austin** (WPHL), November 1, 1996. • Also served as Executive Director of Austin Ice Bats (WPHL) during 1996-97 season. Signed as a free agent by **Fort Worth** (WPHL), October 28, 1998.

• SHAW, Brad

D – R. 6', 190 lbs. b: Cambridge, Ont., 4/28/1964. Detroit's 5th, 86th overall, in 1982.

Season	Club	League	GP	G	A	Pts	AG	AA	APts	PIM	PP	SH	GW	S	%	TGF	PGF	TGA	PGA	+/–	GP	G	A	Pts	PIM	PP	SH	GW
1980-81	Kitchener Greenshirts	OMHA	62	14	58	72	....	....	....	14	....	....	....	....	....	....	....	....	....	....	....	....	....	....	....	....	....	....
1981-82	Ottawa 67's	OHL	68	13	59	72	....	....	....	24	....	....	....	....	....	....	....	....	....	....	15	1	13	14	4	....	....	....
1982-83	Ottawa 67's	OHL	63	12	66	78	....	....	....	24	....	....	....	....	....	....	....	....	....	....	9	2	9	11	4	....	....	....
	Canada	WJC-A	7	1	1	2	....	....	....	2	....	....	....	....	....	....	....	....	....	....	....	....	....	....	....	....	....	....
1983-84	Ottawa 67's	OHL	68	11	71	82	....	....	....	75	....	....	....	....	....	....	....	....	....	....	13	2	*27	29	9	....	....	....
	Canada	WJC-A	7	0	2	2	....	....	....	0	....	....	....	....	....	....	....	....	....	....	....	....	....	....	....	....	....	....
	Ottawa 67's	Mem-Cup	5	1	4	5	....	....	....	2	....	....	....	....	....	....	....	....	....	....	....	....	....	....	....	....	....	....
1984-85	Binghamton Whalers	AHL	24	1	10	11	....	....	....	4	....	....	....	....	....	....	....	....	....	....	8	1	8	9	6	....	....	....
	Salt Lake Golden Eagles	IHL	44	3	29	32	....	....	....	25	....	....	....	....	....	....	....	....	....	....	....	....	....	....	....	....	....	....
1985-86	**Hartford Whalers**	**NHL**	**8**	**0**	**2**	**2**	**0**	**1**	**1**	**4**	**0**	**0**	**0**	**17**	**0.0**	**8**	**3**	**6**	**0**	**–1**	....	....	....	....	....	....	....	....
	Binghamton Whalers	AHL	64	10	44	54	....	....	....	33	....	....	....	....	....	....	....	....	....	....	5	0	2	2	6	....	....	....
1986-87	**Hartford Whalers**	**NHL**	**2**	**0**	**0**	**0**	**0**	**0**	**0**	**0**	**0**	**0**	**0**	**2**	**0.0**	**1**	**0**	**1**	**0**	**0**	....	....	....	....	....	....	....	....
	Binghamton Whalers	AHL	77	9	30	39	....	....	....	43	....	....	....	....	....	....	....	....	....	....	12	1	8	9	2	....	....	....
1987-88	**Hartford Whalers**	**NHL**	**1**	**0**	**0**	**0**	**0**	**0**	**0**	**0**	**0**	**0**	**0**	**1**	**0.0**	**1**	**1**	**1**	**0**	**–1**	....	....	....	....	....	....	....	....
	Binghamton Whalers	AHL	73	12	50	62	....	....	....	50	....	....	....	....	....	....	....	....	....	....	4	0	5	5	4	....	....	....
1988-89	HC Varese	Italy	35	10	30	40	....	....	....	44	....	....	....	....	....	....	....	....	....	....	11	4	8	12	13	....	....	....
	Canada	Nat-Team	4	1	0	1	....	....	....	2	....	....	....	....	....	....	....	....	....	....	....	....	....	....	....	....	....	....
	Hartford Whalers	**NHL**	**3**	**1**	**0**	**1**	**1**	**0**	**1**	**0**	**1**	**0**	**0**	**2**	**50.0**	**3**	**1**	**1**	**0**	**1**	**3**	**1**	**0**	**1**	**0**	**0**	**0**	**0**
1989-90	**Hartford Whalers**	**NHL**	**64**	**3**	**32**	**35**	**3**	**23**	**26**	**30**	**3**	**0**	**0**	**65**	**4.6**	**82**	**28**	**72**	**20**	**2**	**7**	**2**	**5**	**7**	**0**	**1**	**0**	**0**
1990-91	**Hartford Whalers**	**NHL**	**72**	**4**	**28**	**32**	**4**	**21**	**25**	**29**	**2**	**0**	**1**	**129**	**3.1**	**88**	**40**	**81**	**23**	**–10**	**6**	**1**	**2**	**3**	**2**	**0**	**0**	**0**
1991-92	**Hartford Whalers**	**NHL**	**62**	**3**	**22**	**25**	**3**	**17**	**20**	**44**	**0**	**0**	**0**	**100**	**3.0**	**77**	**31**	**63**	**18**	**1**	**3**	**0**	**1**	**1**	**4**	**0**	**0**	**0**
1992-93	**Ottawa Senators**	**NHL**	**81**	**7**	**34**	**41**	**6**	**23**	**29**	**34**	**4**	**0**	**0**	**166**	**4.2**	**106**	**49**	**160**	**56**	**–47**	....	....	....	....	....	....	....	....
1993-94	**Ottawa Senators**	**NHL**	**66**	**4**	**19**	**23**	**4**	**15**	**19**	**59**	**1**	**0**	**0**	**113**	**3.5**	**63**	**20**	**116**	**32**	**–41**	....	....	....	....	....	....	....	....
1994-95	**Ottawa Senators**	**NHL**	**2**	**0**	**0**	**0**	**0**	**0**	**0**	**0**	**0**	**0**	**0**	**3**	**0.0**	**3**	**0**	**1**	**1**	**3**	....	....	....	....	....	....	....	....
	Atlanta Knights	IHL	26	1	18	19	....	....	....	17	....	....	....	....	....	....	....	....	....	....	5	3	4	7	9	....	....	....
1995-96	Detroit Vipers	IHL	79	7	54	61	....	....	....	46	....	....	....	....	....	....	....	....	....	....	8	2	3	5	8	....	....	....
1996-97	Detroit Vipers	IHL	59	6	32	38	....	....	....	30	....	....	....	....	....	....	....	....	....	....	21	2	9	11	10	....	....	....
1997-98	Detroit Vipers	IHL	64	2	33	35	....	....	....	47	....	....	....	....	....	....	....	....	....	....	23	1	11	12	30	....	....	....
1998-99	Detroit Vipers	IHL	61	10	35	45	....	....	....	44	....	....	....	....	....	....	....	....	....	....	....	....	....	....	....	....	....	....
	Washington Capitals	**NHL**	**4**	**0**	**0**	**0**	**0**	**0**	**0**	**4**	**0**	**0**	**0**	**5**	**0.0**	**3**	**1**	**3**	**1**	**0**	....	....	....	....	....	....	....	....
	St. Louis Blues	**NHL**	**12**	**0**	**0**	**0**	**0**	**0**	**0**	**4**	**0**	**0**	**0**	**10**	**0.0**	**3**	**0**	**4**	**1**	**0**	**4**	**0**	**0**	**0**	**0**	**0**	**0**	**0**
99-2000	**Tampa Bay Lightning**	**NHL**	DID NOT PLAY – ASSISTANT COACH																									
	NHL Totals		**377**	**22**	**137**	**159**	**21**	**100**	**121**	**208**	**11**	**0**	**1**	**613**	**3.6**	**438**	**174**	**509**	**152**		**23**	**4**	**8**	**12**	**6**	**1**	**0**	**0**

OHL First All-Star Team (1984) • Won Eddie Shore Award (Outstanding Defenseman - AHL) (1987) • NHL All-Rookie Team (1990) • IHL First All-Star Team (1997)

Traded to **Hartford** by **Detroit** for Hartford's 8th round choice (Urban Nordin) in 1984 Entry Draft, May 29, 1984. Traded to **New Jersey** by **Hartford** for cash, June 13, 1992. Claimed by **Ottawa** from **New Jersey** in Expansion Draft, June 18, 1992. Signed as a free agent by **Ottawa**, March 8, 1999. Claimed on waivers by **Washington** from **Ottawa**, March 10, 1999. Traded to **St. Louis** by **Washington** with Washington's 8th round choice (Colin Hemingway) in 1999 Entry Draft for St. Louis' 6th round choice (Kyle Clark) in 1999 Entry Draft, March 18, 1999. • Named Head Coach of **Detroit Vipers** (IHL), May 24, 2000.

• SHAW, David

David William Martin D – R. 6'2", 205 lbs. b: St. Thomas, Ont., 5/25/1964. Quebec's 1st, 13th overall, in 1982.

Season	Club	League	GP	G	A	Pts	AG	AA	APts	PIM	PP	SH	GW	S	%	TGF	PGF	TGA	PGA	+/–	GP	G	A	Pts	PIM	PP	SH	GW
1980-81	Stratford Cullitons	OHA-B	41	12	19	31	....	....	....	30	....	....	....	....	....	....	....	....	....	....	....	....	....	....	....	....	....	....
1981-82	Kitchener Rangers	OHL	68	6	25	31	....	....	....	94	....	....	....	....	....	....	....	....	....	....	15	2	2	4	51	....	....	....
	Kitchener Rangers	Mem-Cup	5	0	2	2	....	....	....	8	....	....	....	....	....	....	....	....	....	....	....	....	....	....	....	....	....	....
1982-83	Kitchener Rangers	OHL	57	18	56	74	....	....	....	78	....	....	....	....	....	....	....	....	....	....	12	2	10	12	18	....	....	....
	Quebec Nordiques	**NHL**	**2**	**0**	**0**	**0**	**0**	**0**	**0**	**0**	**0**	**0**	**0**	**0**	**0.0**	**0**	**0**	**1**	**0**	**–1**	....	....	....	....	....	....	....	....

			REGULAR SEASON																		PLAYOFFS							
Season	Club	League	GP	G	A	Pts	AG	AA	APts	PIM	PP	SH	GW	S	%	TGF	PGF	TGA	PGA	+/–	GP	G	A	Pts	PIM	PP	SH	GW
1983-84	Kitchener Rangers	OHL	58	14	34	48	....	....	....	73	....	....	....	....	....	....	....	....	....	....	16	4	9	13	12	....	....	....
	Quebec Nordiques	**NHL**	**3**	**0**	**0**	**0**	**0**	**0**	**0**	**0**	**0**	**0**	**0**	**3**	**0.0**	**2**	**0**	**0**	**0**	**2**	....	....	....	....	....	....	....	....
	Kitchener Rangers	Mem-Cup	4	3	7	10	....	....	....	4	....	....	....	....	....	....	....	....	....	....	....	....	....	....	....	....	....	....
1984-85	**Quebec Nordiques**	**NHL**	**14**	**0**	**0**	**0**	**0**	**0**	**0**	**11**	**0**	**0**	**0**	**10**	**0.0**	**4**	**0**	**9**	**0**	**–5**	....	....	....	....	....	....	....	....
	Fredericton Express	AHL	48	7	6	13	....	....	....	73	....	....	....	....	....	....	....	....	....	....	2	0	0	0	7	....	....	....
1985-86	**Quebec Nordiques**	**NHL**	**73**	**7**	**19**	**26**	**6**	**13**	**19**	**78**	**2**	**0**	**2**	**126**	**5.6**	**105**	**18**	**94**	**21**	**14**	....	....	....	....	....	....	....	....
1986-87	**Quebec Nordiques**	**NHL**	**75**	**0**	**19**	**19**	**0**	**14**	**14**	**69**	**0**	**0**	**0**	**136**	**0.0**	**55**	**15**	**99**	**24**	**–35**	....	....	....	....	....	....	....	....
1987-88	**New York Rangers**	**NHL**	**68**	**7**	**25**	**32**	**6**	**18**	**24**	**100**	**5**	**0**	**1**	**141**	**5.0**	**95**	**47**	**93**	**37**	**–8**	....	....	....	....	....	....	....	....
1988-89	**New York Rangers**	**NHL**	**63**	**6**	**11**	**17**	**5**	**8**	**13**	**88**	**3**	**1**	**1**	**85**	**7.1**	**84**	**10**	**85**	**25**	**14**	**4**	**0**	**2**	**2**	**30**	**0**	**0**	**0**
1989-90	**New York Rangers**	**NHL**	**22**	**2**	**10**	**12**	**2**	**7**	**9**	**22**	**1**	**1**	**0**	**24**	**8.3**	**24**	**6**	**31**	**10**	**–3**	....	....	....	....	....	....	....	....
1990-91	**New York Rangers**	**NHL**	**77**	**2**	**10**	**12**	**2**	**8**	**10**	**89**	**0**	**0**	**1**	**61**	**3.3**	**77**	**0**	**105**	**36**	**8**	**6**	**0**	**0**	**0**	**11**	**0**	**0**	**0**
1991-92	**New York Rangers**	**NHL**	**10**	**0**	**1**	**1**	**0**	**1**	**1**	**15**	**0**	**0**	**0**	**6**	**0.0**	**7**	**0**	**10**	**4**	**1**	....	....	....	....	....	....	....	....
	Edmonton Oilers	**NHL**	**12**	**1**	**1**	**2**	**1**	**1**	**2**	**8**	**0**	**0**	**0**	**15**	**6.7**	**3**	**0**	**16**	**5**	**–8**	....	....	....	....	....	....	....	....
	Minnesota North Stars	**NHL**	**37**	**0**	**7**	**7**	**0**	**5**	**5**	**49**	**0**	**0**	**0**	**49**	**0.0**	**38**	**12**	**33**	**2**	**–5**	**7**	**2**	**2**	**4**	**10**	**1**	**0**	**0**
1992-93	**Boston Bruins**	**NHL**	**77**	**10**	**14**	**24**	**8**	**10**	**18**	**108**	**1**	**1**	**1**	**122**	**8.2**	**79**	**12**	**75**	**18**	**10**	**4**	**0**	**1**	**1**	**6**	**0**	**0**	**0**
1993-94	**Boston Bruins**	**NHL**	**55**	**1**	**9**	**10**	**1**	**7**	**8**	**85**	**0**	**0**	**0**	**107**	**0.9**	**43**	**1**	**67**	**14**	**–11**	**13**	**1**	**2**	**3**	**16**	**0**	**0**	**1**
1994-95	**Boston Bruins**	**NHL**	**44**	**3**	**4**	**7**	**5**	**6**	**11**	**36**	**1**	**0**	**0**	**58**	**5.2**	**29**	**4**	**41**	**7**	**–9**	**5**	**0**	**1**	**1**	**4**	**0**	**0**	**0**
1995-96	**Tampa Bay Lightning**	**NHL**	**66**	**1**	**11**	**12**	**1**	**9**	**10**	**64**	**0**	**0**	**0**	**90**	**1.1**	**62**	**7**	**66**	**16**	**5**	**6**	**0**	**1**	**1**	**4**	**0**	**0**	**0**
1996-97	**Tampa Bay Lightning**	**NHL**	**57**	**1**	**10**	**11**	**1**	**9**	**10**	**72**	**0**	**0**	**0**	**59**	**1.7**	**45**	**11**	**39**	**6**	**1**	....	....	....	....	....	....	....	....
1997-98	**Tampa Bay Lightning**	**NHL**	**14**	**0**	**2**	**2**	**0**	**2**	**2**	**12**	**0**	**0**	**0**	**12**	**0.0**	**5**	**0**	**12**	**5**	**–2**	....	....	....	....	....	....	....	....
	Las Vegas Thunder	IHL	26	6	13	19	....	....	....	28	....	....	....	....	....	....	....	....	....	....	....	....	....	....	....	....	....	....
1998-99	Las Vegas Thunder	IHL	24	3	10	13	....	....	....	22	....	....	....	....	....	....	....	....	....	....	....	....	....	....	....	....	....	....
	NHL Totals		**769**	**41**	**153**	**194**	**38**	**118**	**156**	**906**	**13**	**3**	**6**	**1104**	**3.7**	**757**	**143**	**876**	**230**		**45**	**3**	**9**	**12**	**81**	**1**	**0**	**1**

OHL First All-Star Team (1984) • Memorial Cup All-Star Team (1984)

Traded to **NY Rangers** by **Quebec** with John Ogrodnick for Jeff Jackson and Terry Carkner, September 30, 1987. • Missed majority of 1989-90 season recovering from shoulder injury suffered in game vs. Quebec, November 2, 1989. Traded to **Edmonton** by **NY Rangers** for Jeff Beukeboom to complete transaction that sent Mark Messier to NY Rangers for Bernie Nicholls, Steven Rice and Louie DeBrusk (October 4, 1991), November 12, 1991..Traded to **Minnesota** by **Edmonton** for Brian Glynn, January 21, 1992. Traded to **Boston** by **Minnesota** for future considerations, September 2, 1992. Traded to **Tampa Bay** by **Boston** for Detroit's 3rd round choice (previously acquired, Boston selected Jason Doyle) in 1996 Entry Draft, August 17, 1995. Traded to **San Jose** by **Tampa Bay** with Bryan Marchment and Tampa Bay's 1st round choice (later traded to Nashville - Nashville selected David Legwand) in 1998 Entry Draft for Andrei Nazarov and Florida's 1st round choice (previously acquired, Tampa Bay selected Vincent Lecavalier) in 1998 Entry Draft, March 24, 1998.

• SHEDDEN, Doug

Douglas Arthur C – R. 6', 185 lbs. b: Wallaceburg, Ont., 4/29/1961. Pittsburgh's 4th, 93rd overall, in 1980.

Season	Club	League	GP	G	A	Pts	AG	AA	APts	PIM	PP	SH	GW	S	%	TGF	PGF	TGA	PGA	+/–	GP	G	A	Pts	PIM	PP	SH	GW
1976-77	Barrie Co-Op	OMHA	53	53	72	125	....	....	....	....	....	....	....	....	....	....	....	....	....	....	....	....	....	....	....	....	....	....
1977-78	Guelph Platers	OJHL	STATISTICS NOT AVAILABLE																									
	Hamilton Fincups	OMJHL	32	1	9	10	....	....	....	32	....	....	....	....	....	....	....	....	....	....	9	1	2	3	2	....	....	....
	Guelph Platers	Cen-Cup	....	....	....	....	....	....	....	....	....	....	....	....	....	....	....	....	....	....	....	....	....	....	....	....	....	....
	Kitchener Rangers	OMJHL	18	5	7	12	....	....	....	14	....	....	....	....	....	....	....	....	....	....	....	....	....	....	....	....	....	....
1978-79	Kitchener Rangers	OMJHL	66	16	42	58	....	....	....	29	....	....	....	....	....	....	....	....	....	....	10	3	0	3	6	....	....	....
1979-80	Kitchener Rangers	OMJHL	16	10	16	26	....	....	....	26	....	....	....	....	....	....	....	....	....	....	....	....	....	....	....	....	....	....
	Sault Ste. Marie Greyhounds	OMJHL	45	30	44	74	....	....	....	59	....	....	....	....	....	....	....	....	....	....	....	....	....	....	....	....	....	....
1980-81	Sault Ste. Marie Greyhounds	OMJHL	66	51	72	123	....	....	....	114	....	....	....	....	....	....	....	....	....	....	19	16	22	38	10	....	....	....
1981-82	**Pittsburgh Penguins**	**NHL**	**38**	**10**	**15**	**25**	**8**	**10**	**18**	**12**	**4**	**0**	**2**	**76**	**13.2**	**41**	**17**	**26**	**0**	**–2**	....	....	....	....	....	....	....	....
	Erie Blades	AHL	17	4	6	10	....	....	....	14	....	....	....	....	....	....	....	....	....	....	....	....	....	....	....	....	....	....
1982-83	**Pittsburgh Penguins**	**NHL**	**80**	**24**	**43**	**67**	**20**	**30**	**50**	**54**	**4**	**1**	**2**	**175**	**13.7**	**101**	**33**	**97**	**9**	**–20**	....	....	....	....	....	....	....	....
1983-84	**Pittsburgh Penguins**	**NHL**	**67**	**22**	**35**	**57**	**18**	**24**	**42**	**20**	**6**	**1**	**1**	**159**	**13.8**	**83**	**31**	**100**	**10**	**–38**	....	....	....	....	....	....	....	....
1984-85	**Pittsburgh Penguins**	**NHL**	**80**	**35**	**32**	**67**	**29**	**22**	**51**	**30**	**12**	**0**	**3**	**203**	**17.2**	**95**	**43**	**103**	**0**	**–51**	....	....	....	....	....	....	....	....
1985-86	**Pittsburgh Penguins**	**NHL**	**67**	**32**	**34**	**66**	**26**	**23**	**49**	**32**	**19**	**0**	**5**	**179**	**17.9**	**114**	**55**	**66**	**0**	**–7**	....	....	....	....	....	....	....	....
	Detroit Red Wings	**NHL**	**11**	**2**	**3**	**5**	**2**	**2**	**4**	**2**	**2**	**0**	**0**	**33**	**6.1**	**15**	**6**	**10**	**0**	**–1**	....	....	....	....	....	....	....	....
1986-87	**Detroit Red Wings**	**NHL**	**33**	**6**	**12**	**18**	**5**	**9**	**14**	**6**	**1**	**0**	**1**	**51**	**11.8**	**35**	**7**	**25**	**0**	**3**	....	....	....	....	....	....	....	....
	Adirondack Red Wings	AHL	5	2	2	4	....	....	....	4	....	....	....	....	....	....	....	....	....	....	....	....	....	....	....	....	....	....
	Quebec Nordiques	**NHL**	**16**	**0**	**2**	**2**	**0**	**1**	**1**	**8**	**0**	**0**	**0**	**29**	**0.0**	**4**	**0**	**9**	**0**	**–5**	....	....	....	....	....	....	....	....
	Fredericton Express	AHL	15	12	6	18	....	....	....	0	....	....	....	....	....	....	....	....	....	....	....	....	....	....	....	....	....	....
1987-88	Baltimore Skipjacks	AHL	80	37	51	88	....	....	....	32	....	....	....	....	....	....	....	....	....	....	....	....	....	....	....	....	....	....
1988-89	**Toronto Maple Leafs**	**NHL**	**1**	**0**	**0**	**0**	**0**	**0**	**0**	**2**	**0**	**0**	**0**	**2**	**0.0**	**0**	**0**	**1**	**0**	**–1**	....	....	....	....	....	....	....	....
	Newmarket Saints	AHL	29	14	26	40	....	....	....	6	....	....	....	....	....	....	....	....	....	....	....	....	....	....	....	....	....	....
1989-90	Newmarket Saints	AHL	47	26	33	59	....	....	....	12	....	....	....	....	....	....	....	....	....	....	....	....	....	....	....	....	....	....
1990-91	**Toronto Maple Leafs**	**NHL**	**23**	**8**	**10**	**18**	**7**	**8**	**15**	**10**	**4**	**0**	**0**	**35**	**22.9**	**28**	**10**	**16**	**0**	**2**	....	....	....	....	....	....	....	....
	Newmarket Saints	AHL	47	15	34	49	....	....	....	16	....	....	....	....	....	....	....	....	....	....	....	....	....	....	....	....	....	....
1991-92	HC Bolzano-Bozen	Alpenliga	17	17	10	27	....	....	....	4	....	....	....	....	....	....	....	....	....	....	....	....	....	....	....	....	....	....
	HC Bolzano-Bozen	Italy	29	28	22	50	....	....	....	22	....	....	....	....	....	....	....	....	....	....	....	....	....	....	....	....	....	....
	HC Davos	Switz-2	5	10	9	19	....	....	....	....	....	....	....	....	....	....	....	....	....	....	10	3	12	15	....	....	....	....
1992-1993	Muskegon Fury	ColHL	21	16	21	37	....	....	....	18	....	....	....	....	....	....	....	....	....	....	....	....	....	....	....	....	....	....
1992-1995	Wichita Thunder	CHL	DID NOT PLAY – COACHING																									
1995-1999	Louisiana IceGators	ECHL	DID NOT PLAY – COACHING																									
1999-2000	Flint Generals	UHL	DID NOT PLAY – COACHING																									
	NHL Totals		**416**	**139**	**186**	**325**	**115**	**129**	**244**	**176**	**52**	**2**	**14**	**942**	**14.8**	**516**	**202**	**453**	**19**		....	....	....	....	....	....	....	....

Traded to **Detroit** by **Pittsburgh** for Ron Duguay, March 11, 1986. Traded to **Quebec** by **Detroit** with Basil McRae and John Ogrodnick for Brent Ashton, Gilbert Delorme and Mark Kumpel, January 17, 1987. Signed as a free agent by **Toronto**, August 4, 1988. • Named Head Coach of **Memphis** (CHL), June 19, 2000.

• SHEEHAN, Bobby

Robert Richard C – L. 5'7", 155 lbs. b: Weymouth, MA, 1/11/1949. Montreal's 3rd, 32nd overall, in 1969.

Season	Club	League	GP	G	A	Pts	AG	AA	APts	PIM	PP	SH	GW	S	%	TGF	PGF	TGA	PGA	+/–	GP	G	A	Pts	PIM	PP	SH	GW
1966-67	Halifax Jr. Canadians	MJrHL	50	*64	51	115	....	....	....	21	....	....	....	....	....	....	....	....	....	....	17	*24	*28	*52	19	....	....	....
1967-68	Halifax Jr. Canadians	MJrHL	44	51	47	98	....	....	....	25	....	....	....	....	....	....	....	....	....	....	4	6	5	11	0	....	....	....
1968-69	St. Catharines Black Hawks	OHA-Jr.	44	44	41	85	....	....	....	6	....	....	....	....	....	....	....	....	....	....	18	10	13	23	2	....	....	....
1969-70	**Montreal Canadiens**	**NHL**	**16**	**2**	**1**	**3**	**2**	**1**	**3**	**2**	**0**	**0**	**0**	**20**	**10.0**	**5**	**0**	**5**	**0**	**0**	....	....	....	....	....	....	....	....
	Montreal Voyageurs	AHL	46	16	27	43	....	....	....	8	....	....	....	....	....	....	....	....	....	....	8	2	2	4	4	....	....	....
1970-71 ♦	**Montreal Canadiens**	**NHL**	**29**	**6**	**5**	**11**	**6**	**4**	**10**	**2**	**1**	**0**	**1**	**33**	**18.2**	**13**	**3**	**6**	**0**	**4**	**6**	**0**	**0**	**0**	**0**	**0**	**0**	**0**
	Montreal Voyageurs	AHL	35	24	21	45	....	....	....	14	....	....	....	....	....	....	....	....	....	....	....	....	....	....	....	....	....	....
1971-72	**California Golden Seals**	**NHL**	**78**	**20**	**26**	**46**	**20**	**22**	**42**	**12**	**2**	**1**	**3**	**170**	**11.8**	**59**	**10**	**70**	**4**	**–17**	....	....	....	....	....	....	....	....
1972-73	New York Raiders	WHA	75	35	53	88	....	....	....	17	....	....	....	....	....	....	....	....	....	....	....	....	....	....	....	....	....	....
1973-74	New York-Jersey Knights	WHA	50	12	8	20	....	....	....	8	....	....	....	....	....	....	....	....	....	....	....	....	....	....	....	....	....	....
	Edmonton Oilers	WHA	10	1	3	4	....	....	....	6	....	....	....	....	....	....	....	....	....	....	....	....	....	....	....	....	....	....
1974-75	Edmonton Oilers	WHA	77	19	39	58	....	....	....	16	....	....	....	....	....	....	....	....	....	....	....	....	....	....	....	....	....	....
1975-76	**Chicago Black Hawks**	**NHL**	**78**	**11**	**20**	**31**	**10**	**15**	**25**	**8**	**2**	**0**	**0**	**129**	**8.5**	**39**	**7**	**36**	**0**	**–4**	**4**	**0**	**0**	**0**	**0**	**0**	**0**	**0**
1976-77	**Detroit Red Wings**	**NHL**	**34**	**5**	**4**	**9**	**4**	**3**	**7**	**2**	**0**	**0**	**0**	**45**	**11.1**	**12**	**0**	**24**	**2**	**–10**	....	....	....	....	....	....	....	....
	Rhode Island Reds	AHL	36	28	26	54	....	....	....	18	....	....	....	....	....	....	....	....	....	....	....	....	....	....	....	....	....	....
1977-78	Indianapolis Racers	WHA	29	8	7	15	....	....	....	6	....	....	....	....	....	....	....	....	....	....	....	....	....	....	....	....	....	....
	New Haven Nighthawks	AHL	43	13	26	39	....	....	....	14	....	....	....	....	....	....	....	....	....	....	15	7	5	12	4	....	....	....
1978-79	New Haven Nighthawks	AHL	70	33	48	81	....	....	....	26	....	....	....	....	....	....	....	....	....	....	....	....	....	....	....	....	....	....
	New York Rangers	**NHL**	....	....	....	....	....	....	....	....	**0**	**0**	**0**	**0**	**0.0**	**0**	**0**	**0**	**0**	**0**	**15**	**4**	**3**	**7**	**8**	**1**	**0**	**0**
1979-80	New Haven Nighthawks	AHL	13	8	7	15	....	....	....	2	....	....	....	....	....	....	....	....	....	....	....	....	....	....	....	....	....	....
	Colorado Rockies	**NHL**	**30**	**3**	**4**	**7**	**3**	**3**	**6**	**2**	**1**	**0**	**0**	**39**	**7.7**	**14**	**1**	**24**	**4**	**–7**	....	....	....	....	....	....	....	....
	Fort Worth Texans	CHL	31	18	20	38	....	....	....	14	....	....	....	....	....	....	....	....	....	....	....	....	....	....	....	....	....	....
1980-81	**Colorado Rockies**	**NHL**	**41**	**1**	**3**	**4**	**1**	**2**	**3**	**10**	**0**	**0**	**0**	**28**	**3.6**	**9**	**0**	**18**	**4**	**–5**	....	....	....	....	....	....	....	....
	United States	WEC-A	8	1	1	2	....	....	....	0	....	....	....	....	....	....	....	....	....	....	....	....	....	....	....	....	....	....

			REGULAR SEASON																		PLAYOFFS							
Season	Club	League	GP	G	A	Pts	AG	AA	APts	PIM	PP	SH	GW	S	%	TGF	PGF	TGA	PGA	+/–	GP	G	A	Pts	PIM	PP	SH	GW
1981-82	Los Angeles Kings	NHL	4	0	0	0	0	0	0	2	0	0	0	7	0.0	0	0	3	1	–2								
	New Haven Nighthawks	AHL	74	21	17	38				32											4	0	2	2	0			
1982-83	Binghamton Whalers	AHL	48	7	18	25				6											5	1	1	2	0			
	NHL Totals		310	48	63	111	46	50	96	40	6	1	4	471	10.2	151	21	186	15		25	4	3	7	8	1	0	0
	Other Major League Totals		241	75	110	185				53																		

AHL Second All-Star Team (1979)

Traded to **California** by **Montreal** for cash, May 25, 1971. Selected by **New England** (WHA) in 1972 WHA General Player Draft, February 12, 1972. Rights traded to **Chicago** by **California** with Dick Redmond for Darryl Maggs, December 5, 1972. WHA rights traded to **NY Raiders** (WHA) by **New England** (WHA) for NY Raiders' 1st (Glenn Goldup) and 4th (Tom Colley) round choices in 1973 WHA Amateur Draft, August, 1972. Traded to **Edmonton** (WHA) by **New York-Jersey** (WHA) for future considerations (Bob Falkenberg, May, 1974), March, 1974. Signed as a free agent by **Detroit**, October 8, 1976. Signed as a free agent by **Indianapolis** (WHA), July, 1977. Signed as a free agent by **NY Rangers**, October 1, 1978. Traded to **Colorado** by **New Haven** (AHL) for Dennis Owchar and Larry Skinner, May 12, 1979. Signed as a free agent by **LA Kings**, July 8, 1981.

• SHEEHY, Neil

D – R. 6'2", 214 lbs. b: International Falls, MN, 2/9/1960.

Season	Club	League	GP	G	A	Pts	AG	AA	APts	PIM	PP	SH	GW	S	%	TGF	PGF	TGA	PGA	+/–	GP	G	A	Pts	PIM	PP	SH	GW
1979-80	Harvard University	ECAC	13	0	0	0				10																		
1980-81	Harvard University	ECAC	26	4	8	12				22																		
1981-82	Harvard University	ECAC	30	7	11	18				46																		
1982-83	Harvard University	ECAC	34	5	13	18				48																		
1983-84	Calgary Flames	NHL	1	1	0	1	1	0	1	2	0	0	0	1	100.0	1	0	1	0	0	4	0	0	0	4	0	0	0
	Colorado Flames	CHL	74	5	18	23				151																		
1984-85	Calgary Flames	NHL	31	3	4	7	2	3	5	109	0	0	0	42	7.1	28	0	25	2	5								
	Moncton Golden Flames	AHL	34	6	9	15				101																		
	United States	WEC-A	8	0	0	0				14																		
1985-86	Calgary Flames	NHL	65	2	16	18	2	11	13	271	1	0	0	59	3.4	59	8	74	22	–1	22	0	2	2	79	0	0	0
	Moncton Golden Flames	AHL	4	1	1	2				21																		
1986-87	Calgary Flames	NHL	54	4	6	10	3	4	7	151	0	0	0	45	8.9	49	0	49	11	11	6	0	0	0	21	0	0	0
1987-88	Calgary Flames	NHL	36	2	6	8	2	4	6	73	0	0	0	27	7.4	43	0	44	17	16								
	Hartford Whalers	NHL	26	1	4	5	1	3	4	116	0	0	0	13	7.7	19	2	25	5	–3	1	0	0	0	7	0	0	0
1988-89	Washington Capitals	NHL	72	3	4	7	3	3	6	179	0	0	0	22	13.6	41	0	62	20	–1	6	0	0	0	19	0	0	0
1989-90	Washington Capitals	Fr-Tour	3	0	0	0				0																		
	Washington Capitals	NHL	59	1	5	6	1	4	5	291	0	0	0	32	3.1	35	0	36	9	8	13	0	1	1	92	0	0	0
1990-91	Washington Capitals	NHL																			2	0	0	0	19	0	0	0
1991-92	Calgary Flames	NHL	35	1	2	3	1	2	3	119	0	0	0	19	5.3	20	0	33	6	–7								
	Salt Lake Golden Eagles	IHL	6	0	0	0				34																		
	United States	WC-A	6	0	0	0				2																		
1992-93	HK Olimpija Ljubljana	EuroHL	STATISTICS NOT AVAILABLE																									
	HK Olimpija Ljubljana	Slovenia	STATISTICS NOT AVAILABLE																									
1993-94	HK Olimpija Ljubljana	Alpenliga	23	14	23	37				89																		
	NHL Totals		379	18	47	65	16	34	50	1311	1	0	0	260	6.9	295	10	349	92		54	0	3	3	241	0	0	0

• Brother of Tim

Signed as a free agent by **Calgary**, August 16, 1983. Traded to **Hartford** by **Calgary** with Carey Wilson and rights to Lane MacDonald for Dana Murzyn and Shane Churla, January 3, 1988. Traded to **Washington** by **Hartford** with Mike Millar for Grant Jennings and Ed Kastelic, July 6, 1988. Signed as a free agent by **Calgary**, September 3, 1991.

• SHEEHY, Tim

Timothy Kane RW – R. 6'1", 185 lbs. b: Fort Frances, Ont., 9/3/1948. **USHOF**

Season	Club	League	GP	G	A	Pts	AG	AA	APts	PIM	PP	SH	GW	S	%	TGF	PGF	TGA	PGA	+/–	GP	G	A	Pts	PIM	PP	SH	GW
1967-68	Boston College	ECAC	30	27	30	57																						
1968-69	Boston College	ECAC	26	19	41	60				36																		
	United States	WEC-A	10	1	4	5				8																		
1969-70	Boston College	ECAC	24	28	40	68				20																		
1970-71	United States	Nat-Team	STATISTICS NOT AVAILABLE																									
	United States	WEC-A	10	1	2	3				6																		
1971-72	United States	Nat-Team	STATISTICS NOT AVAILABLE																									
	United States	Olympics	6	4	1	5				0																		
1972-73	New England Whalers	WHA	78	33	38	71				30											15	9	14	23	13			
1973-74	New England Whalers	WHA	77	29	29	58				22											7	4	2	6	4			
1974-75	New England Whalers	WHA	52	20	13	33				18																		
	Edmonton Oilers	WHA	29	8	20	28				4																		
1975-76	Edmonton Oilers	WHA	81	34	31	65				17											4	2	2	4	0			
1976-77	Edmonton Oilers	WHA	28	15	8	23				4																		
	Birmingham Bulls	WHA	50	26	21	47				44																		
1977-78	Birmingham Bulls	WHA	13	4	2	6				5																		
	Detroit Red Wings	NHL	15	0	0	0	0	0	0	0	0	0	0	17	0.0	4	2	15	0	–13								
	Kansas City Red Wings	CHL	16	2	6	8				4																		
	New England Whalers	WHA	25	8	11	19				12											13	1	3	4	9			
1978-79	Springfield Indians	AHL	49	9	19	28				17																		
	Utica Mohawks	NEHL	21	14	12	26				21																		
1979-80	Hartford Whalers	NHL	12	2	1	3	2	1	3	0	0	0	0	15	13.3	7	0	1	0	6								
	Cincinnati Stingers	CHL	10	4	5	9				4																		
	Springfield Indians	AHL	52	25	21	46				10																		
	NHL Totals		27	2	1	3	2	1	3	0	0	0	0	32	6.3	11	2	16	0									
	Other Major League Totals		433	177	173	350				156											39	16	21	37	26			

• Brother of Neil • ECAC Second All-Star Team (1969) • NCAA East First All-American Team (1969, 1970) • ECAC First All-Star Team (1970)

Selected by **New England** (WHA) in 1972 WHA General Player Draft, February 12, 1972. Traded to **Edmonton** (WHA) by **New England** (WHA) for Ron Climie, February, 1975. Traded to **Birmingham** (WHA) by **Edmonton** (WHA) for Gavin Kirk and Tom Simpson, December, 1976. Traded to **Detroit** by **Birmingham** (WHA) with Vaclav Nedomansky for the loan of Steve Durbano and Dave Hanson and future considerations, November 18, 1977. Traded to **New England** (WHA) by **Detroit** for cash, February 12, 1978.

• SHELTON, Doug

Wayne Douglas RW – R. 5'10", 175 lbs. b: Woodstock, Ont., 6/27/1945.

Season	Club	League	GP	G	A	Pts	AG	AA	APts	PIM	PP	SH	GW	S	%	TGF	PGF	TGA	PGA	+/–	GP	G	A	Pts	PIM	PP	SH	GW
1962-63	Ingersoll Rockets	OHA-B	STATISTICS NOT AVAILABLE																									
1963-64	St. Catharines Black Hawks	OHA-Jr.	56	3	9	12				16											13	0	0	0	0			
1964-65	St. Catharines Black Hawks	OHA-Jr.	56	8	8	16				16											5	0	0	0	4			
1965-66	St. Catharines Black Hawks	OHA-Jr.	48	36	24	60				16											7	1	2	3	10			
	St. Louis Braves	CPHL																			2	0	0	0	0			
1966-67	St. Louis Braves	CPHL	68	11	23	34				4																		
1967-68	Chicago Black Hawks	NHL	5	0	1	1	0	1	1	2	0	0	0	1	0.0	1	0	4	0	–3								
	Dallas Black Hawks	CPHL	65	19	39	58				22											5	0	2	2	0			
1968-69	Dallas Black Hawks	CHL	69	17	27	44				30											11	3	4	7	10			
1969-70	Denver Spurs	WHL	20	2	3	5				0																		
	Springfield Kings	AHL	28	1	4	5				4											14	4	8	12	6			
	NHL Totals		5	0	1	1	0	1	1	2	0	0	0	1	0.0	1	0	4	0									

Traded to **Minnesota** by **Chicago** to complete transaction that sent Andre Boudrias to Chicago (February 14, 1969), June, 1969. Claimed by **Denver** (WHL) from **Minnesota** in Reverse Draft, June 12, 1969. Traded to **LA Kings** (Springfield-AHL) by **Denver** (WHL) for cash, February, 1970.

• SHEPPARD, Gregg

Gregory Wayne C – L. 5'8", 170 lbs. b: North Battleford, Sask., 4/23/1949.

Season	Club	League	GP	G	A	Pts	AG	AA	APts	PIM	PP	SH	GW	S	%	TGF	PGF	TGA	PGA	+/–	GP	G	A	Pts	PIM	PP	SH	GW
1965-66	North Battleford North Stars	SAHA	STATISTICS NOT AVAILABLE																									
	Estevan Bruins	SJHL	1	1	1	2				0											1	0	0	0	0			
	Estevan Bruins	Mem-Cup	1	1	0	1				0																		
1966-67	Estevan Bruins	CMJHL	52	44	24	68				14											12	11	9	20	4			
1967-68	Estevan Bruins	WCJHL	58	35	46	81				68											14	13	7	20	6			
	Estevan Bruins	Mem-Cup	14	12	11	23				18																		

			REGULAR SEASON																		PLAYOFFS							
Season	Club	League	GP	G	A	Pts	AG	AA	APts	PIM	PP	SH	GW	S	%	TGF	PGF	TGA	PGA	+/-	GP	G	A	Pts	PIM	PP	SH	GW
1968-69	Estevan Bruins	WCJHL	54	42	42	84	....	....	....	33	....	....	....	....	....	....	....	....	....	....	10	1	7	8	0	....	....	....
	Oklahoma City Blazers	CHL	4	0	0	0	....	....	....	0	....	....	....	....	....	....	....	....	....	....	....	....	....	....	....	....	....	....
1969-70	Oklahoma City Blazers	CHL	65	26	29	55	....	....	....	19	....	....	....	....	....	....	....	....	....	....	....	....	....	....	....	....	....	....
	Salt Lake Golden Eagles	WHL	5	0	0	0	....	....	....	2	....	....	....	....	....	....	....	....	....	....	....	....	....	....	....	....	....	....
1970-71	Oklahoma City Blazers	CHL	68	25	50	75	....	....	....	45	....	....	....	....	....	....	....	....	....	....	5	2	3	5	5	....	....	....
1971-72	Oklahoma City Blazers	CHL	72	*41	52	93	....	....	....	43	....	....	....	....	....	....	....	....	....	....	6	4	7	11	4	....	....	....
1972-73	**Boston Bruins**	**NHL**	64	24	26	50	23	21	44	18	0	2	3	151	15.9	62	0	30	5	37	5	2	1	3	0	0	1	1
	Boston Braves	AHL	8	5	5	10	....	....	....	2	....	....	....	....	....	....	....	....	....	....	....	....	....	....	....	....	....	....
1973-74	**Boston Bruins**	**NHL**	75	16	31	47	15	26	41	21	0	3	3	168	9.5	70	1	71	25	23	16	11	8	19	4	0	2	2
1974-75	**Boston Bruins**	**NHL**	76	30	48	78	26	36	62	19	5	7	4	249	12.0	125	25	80	23	43	3	3	1	4	5	0	0	0
1975-76	**Boston Bruins**	**NHL**	70	31	43	74	27	32	59	28	5	2	4	222	14.0	117	44	75	26	24	12	5	6	11	6	1	0	1
1976-77	**Boston Bruins**	**NHL**	77	31	36	67	28	28	56	20	8	1	5	247	12.6	96	34	82	23	3	14	5	7	12	8	1	1	2
1977-78	**Boston Bruins**	**NHL**	54	23	36	59	21	28	49	24	5	1	7	160	14.4	79	25	56	21	19	15	2	10	12	6	0	0	0
1978-79	**Pittsburgh Penguins**	**NHL**	60	15	22	37	13	16	29	9	3	1	2	134	11.2	64	18	65	27	8	7	1	2	3	0	1	0	0
1979-80	**Pittsburgh Penguins**	**NHL**	76	13	24	37	11	17	28	20	3	0	2	136	9.6	67	17	97	25	–22	5	1	1	2	0	0	0	0
1980-81	**Pittsburgh Penguins**	**NHL**	47	11	17	28	9	11	20	49	3	0	1	85	12.9	42	12	77	34	–13	5	2	4	6	2	1	0	0
1981-82	**Pittsburgh Penguins**	**NHL**	58	11	10	21	9	7	16	35	0	0	1	81	13.6	38	2	75	48	9	....	....	....	....	....	....	....	....
	NHL Totals		**657**	**205**	**293**	**498**	**182**	**222**	**404**	**243**	**32**	**17**	**32**	**1633**	**12.6**	**760**	**178**	**708**	**257**		**82**	**32**	**40**	**72**	**31**	**4**	**4**	**6**

CHL Second All-Star Team (1971) • CHL First All-Star Team (1972) • Won Tommy Ivan Trophy (MVP - CHL) (1972) • Played in NHL All-Star Game (1976)

Traded to **Atlanta** by **Boston** for Dick Redmond, September 6, 1978. Traded to **Pittsburgh** by **Atlanta** for Jean Pronovost, September 6, 1978.

• SHEPPARD, Ray

Raymond G. RW – R. 6'1", 195 lbs. b: Pembroke, Ont., 5/27/1966. Buffalo's 3rd, 60th overall, in 1984.

Season	Club	League	GP	G	A	Pts	AG	AA	APts	PIM	PP	SH	GW	S	%	TGF	PGF	TGA	PGA	+/-	GP	G	A	Pts	PIM	PP	SH	GW
1982-83	Brockville Braves	OJHL	48	27	36	63	....	....	....	81	....	....	....	....	....	....	....	....	....	....	....	....	....	....	....	....	....	....
1983-84	Cornwall Royals	OHL	68	44	36	80	....	....	....	69	....	....	....	....	....	....	....	....	....	....	....	....	....	....	....	....	....	....
1984-85	Cornwall Royals	OHL	49	25	33	58	....	....	....	51	....	....	....	....	....	....	....	....	....	....	9	2	12	14	4	....	....	....
1985-86	Cornwall Royals	OHL	63	*81	61	*142	....	....	....	25	....	....	....	....	....	....	....	....	....	....	6	7	4	11	0	....	....	....
1986-87	Rochester Americans	AHL	55	18	13	31	....	....	....	11	....	....	....	....	....	....	....	....	....	....	15	12	3	15	2	....	....	....
1987-88	**Buffalo Sabres**	**NHL**	74	38	27	65	32	19	51	14	15	0	5	173	22.0	84	32	58	0	–6	6	1	1	2	2	1	0	0
1988-89	**Buffalo Sabres**	**NHL**	67	22	21	43	19	15	34	15	7	0	4	147	15.0	79	30	57	1	–7	1	0	1	1	0	0	0	0
1989-90	**Buffalo Sabres**	**NHL**	18	4	2	6	3	1	4	0	1	0	1	31	12.9	11	3	5	0	3	....	....	....	....	....	....	....	....
	Rochester Americans	AHL	5	3	5	8	....	....	....	2	....	....	....	....	....	....	....	....	....	....	17	8	7	15	9	....	....	....
1990-91	**New York Rangers**	**NHL**	59	24	23	47	22	17	39	21	7	0	5	129	18.6	63	23	32	0	8	....	....	....	....	....	....	....	....
1991-92	**Detroit Red Wings**	**NHL**	74	36	26	62	33	20	53	27	11	1	4	178	20.2	90	27	56	0	7	11	6	2	8	4	3	0	0
1992-93	**Detroit Red Wings**	**NHL**	70	32	34	66	27	23	50	29	10	0	1	183	17.5	92	36	50	1	7	7	2	3	5	0	2	0	0
1993-94	**Detroit Red Wings**	**NHL**	82	52	41	93	49	32	81	26	19	0	5	260	20.0	124	46	68	3	13	7	2	1	3	4	0	0	0
1994-95	**Detroit Red Wings**	**NHL**	43	30	10	40	53	15	68	17	11	0	5	125	24.0	60	24	27	2	11	17	4	3	7	5	2	0	0
1995-96	**Detroit Red Wings**	**NHL**	5	2	2	4	2	2	4	2	0	0	1	9	22.2	5	2	3	0	0	....	....	....	....	....	....	....	....
	San Jose Sharks	**NHL**	51	27	19	46	27	16	43	10	12	0	4	170	15.9	63	24	62	4	–19	....	....	....	....	....	....	....	....
	Florida Panthers	**NHL**	14	8	2	10	8	2	10	4	2	0	2	52	15.4	11	3	8	0	0	21	8	8	16	4	3	0	0
1996-97	**Florida Panthers**	**NHL**	68	29	31	60	31	28	59	4	13	0	7	226	12.8	78	31	43	0	4	5	2	0	2	0	1	0	0
1997-98	**Florida Panthers**	**NHL**	61	14	17	31	16	17	33	21	5	0	1	136	10.3	52	25	40	0	–13	....	....	....	....	....	....	....	....
	Carolina Hurricanes	**NHL**	10	4	2	6	5	2	7	2	2	0	1	33	12.1	12	5	5	0	2	....	....	....	....	....	....	....	....
1998-99	**Carolina Hurricanes**	**NHL**	74	25	33	58	29	32	61	16	5	0	4	188	13.3	78	24	50	0	4	6	5	1	6	2	1	0	1
99-2000	**Florida Panthers**	**NHL**	47	10	10	20	11	9	20	4	5	0	2	74	13.5	32	12	24	0	–4	....	....	....	....	....	....	....	....
	NHL Totals		**817**	**357**	**300**	**657**	**367**	**250**	**617**	**212**	**125**	**1**	**52**	**2114**	**16.9**	**934**	**347**	**588**	**11**		**81**	**30**	**20**	**50**	**21**	**13**	**0**	**1**

OHL First All-Star Team (1986) • NHL All-Rookie Team (1988)

• Missed majority of 1989-90 season recovering from ankle injury suffered in game vs. Quebec, January 31, 1990. Traded to **NY Rangers** by **Buffalo** for cash and future considerations, July 9, 1990. Signed as a free agent by **Detroit**, August 5, 1991. Traded to **San Jose** by **Detroit** for Igor Larionov and future considerations, October 24, 1995. Traded to **Florida** by **San Jose** with San Jose's 4th round choice (Joey Tetarenko) in 1996 Entry Draft for Florida's 2nd (later traded to Chicago - Chicago selected Geoff Peters) and 4th (Matt Bradley) round choices in 1996 Entry Draft, March 16, 1996. Traded to **Carolina** by **Florida** for Kirk McLean, March 24, 1998.

• SHERVEN, Gord

Gord R.G. C – R. 6', 185 lbs. b: Gravelbourg, Sask., 8/21/1963. Edmonton's 9th, 197th overall, in 1981.

Season	Club	League	GP	G	A	Pts	AG	AA	APts	PIM	PP	SH	GW	S	%	TGF	PGF	TGA	PGA	+/-	GP	G	A	Pts	PIM	PP	SH	GW
1980-81	Weyburn Red Wings	SJHL	44	35	34	69	....	....	....	....	....	....	....	....	....	....	....	....	....	....	....	....	....	....	....	....	....	....
1981-82	University of North Dakota	WCHA	46	18	25	43	....	....	....	16	....	....	....	....	....	....	....	....	....	....	....	....	....	....	....	....	....	....
1982-83	University of North Dakota	WCHA	36	12	21	33	....	....	....	16	....	....	....	....	....	....	....	....	....	....	....	....	....	....	....	....	....	....
	Canada	WJC-A	7	1	3	4	....	....	....	0	....	....	....	....	....	....	....	....	....	....	....	....	....	....	....	....	....	....
	Canada	WEC-A	9	2	1	3	....	....	....	2	....	....	....	....	....	....	....	....	....	....	....	....	....	....	....	....	....	....
1983-84	Canada	Nat-Team	46	9	13	22	....	....	....	13	....	....	....	....	....	....	....	....	....	....	....	....	....	....	....	....	....	....
	Edmonton Oilers	**NHL**	2	1	0	1	1	0	1	0	0	0	0	5	20.0	1	0	0	0	1	....	....	....	....	....	....	....	....
1984-85	**Edmonton Oilers**	**NHL**	37	9	7	16	7	5	12	10	1	0	1	49	18.4	22	2	22	0	–2	....	....	....	....	....	....	....	....
	Nova Scotia Voyageurs	AHL	5	4	5	9	....	....	....	5	....	....	....	....	....	....	....	....	....	....	....	....	....	....	....	....	....	....
	Minnesota North Stars	**NHL**	32	2	12	14	2	8	10	8	0	0	1	49	4.1	21	0	33	15	3	3	0	0	0	0	0	0	0
1985-86	**Minnesota North Stars**	**NHL**	13	0	2	2	0	1	1	11	0	0	0	8	0.0	4	0	8	5	1	....	....	....	....	....	....	....	....
	Springfield Indians	AHL	11	3	7	10	....	....	....	8	....	....	....	....	....	....	....	....	....	....	....	....	....	....	....	....	....	....
	Edmonton Oilers	**NHL**	5	1	1	2	1	1	2	4	0	0	0	6	16.7	2	0	2	0	0	....	....	....	....	....	....	....	....
	Nova Scotia Oilers	AHL	38	14	17	31	....	....	....	4	....	....	....	....	....	....	....	....	....	....	....	....	....	....	....	....	....	....
1986-87	Canada	Nat-Team	56	14	22	36	....	....	....	30	....	....	....	....	....	....	....	....	....	....	....	....	....	....	....	....	....	....
	Hartford Whalers	**NHL**	7	0	0	0	0	0	0	0	0	0	0	7	0.0	0	0	6	0	–6	....	....	....	....	....	....	....	....
1987-88	Canada	Nat-Team	53	12	16	28	....	....	....	26	....	....	....	....	....	....	....	....	....	....	....	....	....	....	....	....	....	....
	Canada	Olympics	8	4	4	8	....	....	....	4	....	....	....	....	....	....	....	....	....	....	....	....	....	....	....	....	....	....
	Hartford Whalers	**NHL**	1	0	0	0	0	0	0	0	0	0	0	2	0.0	0	0	0	0	0	....	....	....	....	....	....	....	....
1988-89	SB Rosenheim	Germany-2	25	13	19	32	....	....	....	12	....	....	....	....	....	....	....	....	....	....	7	3	4	7	6	....	....	....
1989-90	SB Rosenheim	Germany-2	36	*38	21	59	....	....	....	20	....	....	....	....	....	....	....	....	....	....	10	8	4	12	14	....	....	....
1990-91	SB Rosenheim	Germany-2	43	33	44	77	....	....	....	42	....	....	....	....	....	....	....	....	....	....	11	*16	8	*24	6	....	....	....
	EHC Kloten	Switz-2	1	2	1	3	....	....	....	0	....	....	....	....	....	....	....	....	....	....	....	....	....	....	....	....	....	....
1991-92	SB Rosenheim	Germany-2	37	19	40	59	....	....	....	26	....	....	....	....	....	....	....	....	....	....	10	3	8	11	8	....	....	....
	Canada	Nat-Team	3	0	1	1	....	....	....	0	....	....	....	....	....	....	....	....	....	....	....	....	....	....	....	....	....	....
1992-93	ZSC Lions Zurich	Switz.	36	20	13	33	....	....	....	24	....	....	....	....	....	....	....	....	....	....	4	2	3	5	6	....	....	....
1993-94	EC Hedos Munich	Germany	43	21	27	48	....	....	....	29	....	....	....	....	....	....	....	....	....	....	....	....	....	....	....	....	....	....
1994-95	Munich Mad Dogs	Germany	27	16	21	37	....	....	....	12	....	....	....	....	....	....	....	....	....	....	....	....	....	....	....	....	....	....
	Star Bulls Rosenheim	Germany	15	4	16	20	....	....	....	10	....	....	....	....	....	....	....	....	....	....	7	3	5	8	2	....	....	....
	Canada	Nat-Team	1	0	0	0	....	....	....	0	....	....	....	....	....	....	....	....	....	....	....	....	....	....	....	....	....	....
1995-96	Dusseldorfer EG	Germany	50	20	42	62	....	....	....	36	....	....	....	....	....	....	....	....	....	....	13	6	9	15	4	....	....	....
1996-97	Dusseldorfer EG	Germany	40	13	17	30	....	....	....	12	....	....	....	....	....	....	....	....	....	....	4	1	2	3	6	....	....	....
1997-98	Dusseldorfer EG	Germany	44	9	15	24	....	....	....	14	....	....	....	....	....	....	....	....	....	....	3	0	1	1	2	....	....	....
1998-99	Star Bulls Rosenheim	Germany	46	13	24	37	....	....	....	28	....	....	....	....	....	....	....	....	....	....	....	....	....	....	....	....	....	....
99-2000	Star Bulls Rosenheim	Germany	57	23	31	54	....	....	....	24	....	....	....	....	....	....	....	....	....	....	....	....	....	....	....	....	....	....
	NHL Totals		**97**	**13**	**22**	**35**	**11**	**15**	**26**	**33**	**1**	**0**	**2**	**126**	**10.3**	**50**	**2**	**71**	**20**		**3**	**0**	**0**	**0**	**0**	**0**	**0**	**0**

Traded to **Minnesota** by **Edmonton** with Terry Martin for Mark Napier, January 24, 1985. Traded to **Edmonton** by **Minnesota** with Don Biggs for Marc Habscheid, Don Barber and Emanuel Viveiros, December 20, 1985. Claimed by **Hartford** from **Edmonton** in Waiver Draft, October 6, 1986. • Munich Mad Dogs (Germany) folded after 27 games during 1994-95 season.

• SHEVALIER, Jeff

Jeffrey D. LW – L. 5'11", 180 lbs. b: Mississauga, Ont., 3/14/1974. Los Angeles' 4th, 111th overall, in 1992.

Season	Club	League	GP	G	A	Pts	AG	AA	APts	PIM	PP	SH	GW	S	%	TGF	PGF	TGA	PGA	+/-	GP	G	A	Pts	PIM	PP	SH	GW
1989-90	Acton Sabres	OJHL-C	33	30	34	64	....	....	....	59	....	....	....	....	....	....	....	....	....	....	....	....	....	....	....	....	....	....
1990-91	Acton Sabres	OJHL-C	28	29	31	60	....	....	....	62	....	....	....	....	....	....	....	....	....	....	....	....	....	....	....	....	....	....
	Georgetown Raiders	OJHL-B	12	11	11	22	....	....	....	8	....	....	....	....	....	....	....	....	....	....	....	....	....	....	....	....	....	....
	Oakville Blades	OJHL-B	5	1	4	5	....	....	....	0	....	....	....	....	....	....	....	....	....	....	....	....	....	....	....	....	....	....
1991-92	North Bay Centennials	OHL	64	28	29	57	....	....	....	26	....	....	....	....	....	....	....	....	....	....	21	5	11	16	25	....	....	....
1992-93	North Bay Centennials	OHL	62	59	54	113	....	....	....	46	....	....	....	....	....	....	....	....	....	....	2	1	2	3	4	....	....	....

Season	Club	League	REGULAR SEASON GP	G	A	Pts	AG	AA	APts	PIM	PP	SH	GW	S	%	TGF	PGF	TGA	PGA	+/–	PLAYOFFS GP	G	A	Pts	PIM	PP	SH	GW
1993-94	North Bay Centennials	OHL	64	52	49	101	....	....	....	52	....	....	....	....	....	....	....	....	....	....	17	8	14	22	18	....	....	....
	North Bay Centennials	Mem-Cup	1	0	0	0	....	....	....	2	....	....	....	....	....	....	....	....	....	....	....	....	....	....	....	....	....	....
1994-95	Phoenix Roadrunners	IHL	68	31	39	70	....	....	....	44	....	....	....	....	....	....	....	....	....	....	9	5	4	9	0	....	....	....
1994-95	**Los Angeles Kings**	**NHL**	**1**	**1**	**0**	**1**	**2**	**0**	**2**	**0**	**0**	**0**	**0**	**1**	**100.0**	**1**	**0**	**0**	**0**	**1**	....	....	....	....	....	....	....	....
1995-96	Phoenix Roadrunners	IHL	79	29	38	67	....	....	....	72	....	....	....	....	....	....	....	....	....	....	4	2	2	4	2	....	....	....
1996-97	**Los Angeles Kings**	**NHL**	**26**	**4**	**9**	**13**	**4**	**8**	**12**	**6**	**1**	**0**	**0**	**42**	**9.5**	**18**	**4**	**20**	**0**	**–6**	....	....	....	....	....	....	....	....
	Phoenix Roadrunners	IHL	46	16	21	37	....	....	....	26	....	....	....	....	....	....	....	....	....	....	....	....	....	....	....	....	....	....
1997-98	Springfield Falcons	AHL	66	23	30	53	....	....	....	38	....	....	....	....	....	....	....	....	....	....	4	1	1	2	0	....	....	....
1998-99	Cincinnati Cyclones	IHL	76	29	34	63	....	....	....	57	....	....	....	....	....	....	....	....	....	....	3	1	1	2	0	....	....	....
99-2000	**Tampa Bay Lightning**	**NHL**	**5**	**0**	**0**	**0**	**0**	**0**	**0**	**2**	**0**	**0**	**0**	**2**	**0.0**	**0**	**0**	**1**	**0**	**–1**	....	....	....	....	....	....	....	....
	Detroit Vipers	IHL	46	11	25	36	....	....	....	42	....	....	....	....	....	....	....	....	....	....	....	....	....	....	....	....	....	....
	Quebec Citadelles	AHL	5	0	2	2	....	....	....	2	....	....	....	....	....	....	....	....	....	....	....	....	....	....	....	....	....	....
	Grand Rapids Griffins	IHL	2	0	0	0	....	....	....	0	....	....	....	....	....	....	....	....	....	....	....	....	....	....	....	....	....	....
	NHL Totals		**32**	**5**	**9**	**14**	**6**	**8**	**14**	**8**	**1**	**0**	**0**	**45**	**11.1**	**19**	**4**	**21**	**0**		....	....	....	....	....	....	....	....

OHL First All-Star Team (1994)

Signed as a free agent by **Tampa Bay**, July 8, 1999. Traded to **Ottawa** by **Tampa Bay** for future considerations, March 8, 2000.

• SHINSKE, Rick

Richard Charles C – L. 5'11", 165 lbs. b: Weyburn, Sask., 5/31/1955. California's 7th, 111th overall, in 1975.

Season	Club	League	GP	G	A	Pts	AG	AA	APts	PIM	PP	SH	GW	S	%	TGF	PGF	TGA	PGA	+/–	GP	G	A	Pts	PIM	PP	SH	GW
1971-72	Kamloops Blazers	BCJHL	48	3	9	12	....	....	....	74	....	....	....	....	....	....	....	....	....	....	....	....	....	....	....	....	....	....
1972-73	Kamloops Blazers	BCJHL	61	28	*90	*118	....	....	....	97	....	....	....	....	....	....	....	....	....	....	....	....	....	....	....	....	....	....
	Calgary Centennials	WHL	1	0	0	0	....	....	....	0	....	....	....	....	....	....	....	....	....	....	....	....	....	....	....	....	....	....
1973-74	Calgary Centennials	WHL	67	12	43	55	....	....	....	18	....	....	....	....	....	....	....	....	....	....	13	1	8	9	4	....	....	....
1974-75	Calgary Centennials	WHL	17	3	13	16	....	....	....	18	....	....	....	....	....	....	....	....	....	....	....	....	....	....	....	....	....	....
	New Westminster Bruins	WHL	48	20	44	64	....	....	....	54	....	....	....	....	....	....	....	....	....	....	18	7	11	18	18	....	....	....
	New Westminster Bruins	Mem-Cup	3	2	0	2	....	....	....	2	....	....	....	....	....	....	....	....	....	....	....	....	....	....	....	....	....	....
1975-76	New Westminster Bruins	WHL	70	52	91	143	....	....	....	86	....	....	....	....	....	....	....	....	....	....	17	7	23	30	26	....	....	....
	Salt Lake Golden Eagles	CHL	4	0	2	2	....	....	....	0	....	....	....	....	....	....	....	....	....	....	....	....	....	....	....	....	....	....
	New Westminster Bruins	Mem-Cup	4	2	7	*9	....	....	....	2	....	....	....	....	....	....	....	....	....	....	....	....	....	....	....	....	....	....
1976-77	**Cleveland Barons**	**NHL**	**5**	**0**	**0**	**0**	**0**	**0**	**0**	**2**	**0**	**0**	**0**	**3**	**0.0**	**1**	**1**	**5**	**1**	**–4**	....	....	....	....	....	....	....	....
	Salt Lake Golden Eagles	CHL	70	22	48	70	....	....	....	18	....	....	....	....	....	....	....	....	....	....	....	....	....	....	....	....	....	....
1977-78	**Cleveland Barons**	**NHL**	**47**	**5**	**12**	**17**	**5**	**9**	**14**	**6**	**1**	**0**	**1**	**40**	**12.5**	**21**	**3**	**30**	**0**	**–12**	....	....	....	....	....	....	....	....
	Phoenix Roadrunners	CHL	14	3	8	11	....	....	....	0	....	....	....	....	....	....	....	....	....	....	....	....	....	....	....	....	....	....
	Binghamton Dusters	AHL	17	8	9	17	....	....	....	2	....	....	....	....	....	....	....	....	....	....	....	....	....	....	....	....	....	....
1978-79	**St. Louis Blues**	**NHL**	**11**	**0**	**4**	**4**	**0**	**3**	**3**	**2**	**0**	**0**	**0**	**7**	**0.0**	**6**	**1**	**8**	**0**	**–3**	....	....	....	....	....	....	....	....
	Salt Lake Golden Eagles	CHL	66	22	*66	*88	....	....	....	31	....	....	....	....	....	....	....	....	....	....	10	3	7	10	6	....	....	....
1979-80	Adirondack Red Wings	AHL	78	22	58	80	....	....	....	20	....	....	....	....	....	....	....	....	....	....	5	0	3	3	0	....	....	....
1980-81	Adirondack Red Wings	AHL	46	20	35	55	....	....	....	46	....	....	....	....	....	....	....	....	....	....	....	....	....	....	....	....	....	....
1981-82	Adirondack Red Wings	AHL	35	10	23	33	....	....	....	0	....	....	....	....	....	....	....	....	....	....	5	2	4	6	0	....	....	....
1982-83	New Haven Nighthawks	AHL	45	10	27	37	....	....	....	12	....	....	....	....	....	....	....	....	....	....	12	3	6	9	2	....	....	....
	NHL Totals		**63**	**5**	**16**	**21**	**5**	**12**	**17**	**10**	**1**	**0**	**1**	**50**	**10.0**	**28**	**5**	**43**	**1**		....	....	....	....	....	....	....	....

Won George Parsons Trophy (Memorial Cup Tournament Most Sportsmanlike Player) (1976) • CHL First All-Star Team (1979)

Rights transferred to **Cleveland** after **California** franchise relocated, August 26, 1976. Claimed by **Minnesota** in **Cleveland-Minnesota** Dispersal Draft, June 15, 1978. Claimed on waivers by **St. Louis** from **Minnesota**, August 12, 1978. Signed as a free agent by **Detroit**, September, 1979.

• SHIRES, Jim

James Arthur LW – L. 6', 180 lbs. b: Edmonton, Alta., 11/15/1945.

Season	Club	League	GP	G	A	Pts	AG	AA	APts	PIM	PP	SH	GW	S	%	TGF	PGF	TGA	PGA	+/–	GP	G	A	Pts	PIM	PP	SH	GW
1963-64	Edmonton Oil Kings	CAHL	2	0	0	0	....	....	....	4	....	....	....	....	....	....	....	....	....	....	....	....	....	....	....	....	....	....
1964-65	University of Denver	WCHA	DID NOT PLAY – FRESHMAN																									
1965-66	University of Denver	WCHA	26	8	10	18	....	....	....	18	....	....	....	....	....	....	....	....	....	....	....	....	....	....	....	....	....	....
1966-67	University of Denver	WCHA	30	8	19	27	....	....	....	39	....	....	....	....	....	....	....	....	....	....	....	....	....	....	....	....	....	....
1967-68	University of Denver	WCHA	34	15	23	38	....	....	....	43	....	....	....	....	....	....	....	....	....	....	....	....	....	....	....	....	....	....
1968-69	Omaha Knights	CHL	9	0	2	2	....	....	....	4	....	....	....	....	....	....	....	....	....	....	....	....	....	....	....	....	....	....
	Denver Spurs	WHL	20	2	2	4	....	....	....	6	....	....	....	....	....	....	....	....	....	....	....	....	....	....	....	....	....	....
	Amarillo Wranglers	CHL	34	10	18	28	....	....	....	43	....	....	....	....	....	....	....	....	....	....	....	....	....	....	....	....	....	....
1969-70	Fort Worth Wings	CHL	69	16	18	34	....	....	....	61	....	....	....	....	....	....	....	....	....	....	7	1	1	2	21	....	....	....
1970-71	**Detroit Red Wings**	**NHL**	**20**	**2**	**1**	**3**	**2**	**1**	**3**	**22**	**1**	**0**	**0**	**22**	**9.1**	**4**	**1**	**6**	**0**	**–3**	....	....	....	....	....	....	....	....
	Fort Worth Wings	CHL	48	13	25	38	....	....	....	97	....	....	....	....	....	....	....	....	....	....	4	0	0	0	2	....	....	....
1971-72	**St. Louis Blues**	**NHL**	**18**	**0**	**3**	**3**	**0**	**3**	**3**	**8**	**0**	**0**	**0**	**14**	**0.0**	**3**	**1**	**16**	**1**	**–13**	....	....	....	....	....	....	....	....
	Denver Spurs	WHL	42	18	27	45	....	....	....	82	....	....	....	....	....	....	....	....	....	....	9	2	3	5	15	....	....	....
1972-73	Denver Spurs	WHL	32	10	7	17	....	....	....	45	....	....	....	....	....	....	....	....	....	....	....	....	....	....	....	....	....	....
	Pittsburgh Penguins	**NHL**	**18**	**1**	**2**	**3**	**1**	**2**	**3**	**2**	**0**	**0**	**0**	**22**	**4.5**	**6**	**0**	**14**	**0**	**–8**	....	....	....	....	....	....	....	....
1973-74	San Diego Gulls	WHL	68	26	34	60	....	....	....	44	....	....	....	....	....	....	....	....	....	....	4	2	2	4	0	....	....	....
1974-75	Fort Wayne Komets	IHL	21	3	9	12	....	....	....	12	....	....	....	....	....	....	....	....	....	....	....	....	....	....	....	....	....	....
	NHL Totals		**56**	**3**	**6**	**9**	**3**	**6**	**9**	**32**	**1**	**0**	**0**	**58**	**5.2**	**13**	**2**	**36**	**1**		....	....	....	....	....	....	....	....

Traded to **St. Louis** by **Detroit** for Rick Sentes, May 12, 1971. Traded to **Pittsburgh** by **St. Louis** for Joe Noris, January 8, 1973.

• SHMYR, Paul

D – L. 5'11", 170 lbs. b: Cudworth, Sask., 1/18/1946.

Season	Club	League	GP	G	A	Pts	AG	AA	APts	PIM	PP	SH	GW	S	%	TGF	PGF	TGA	PGA	+/–	GP	G	A	Pts	PIM	PP	SH	GW
1965-66	New Westmonster Royals	BCJHL	STATISTICS NOT AVAILABLE																									
	New Westmonster Royals	Mem-Cup	4	2	0	2	....	....	....	9	....	....	....	....	....	....	....	....	....	....	....	....	....	....	....	....	....	....
1966-67	New Westmonster Royals	BCJHL	STATISTICS NOT AVAILABLE																									
	Vancouver Canucks	WHL	1	0	0	0	....	....	....	0	....	....	....	....	....	....	....	....	....	....	....	....	....	....	....	....	....	....
	Fort Wayne Komets	IHL	70	3	18	21	....	....	....	89	....	....	....	....	....	....	....	....	....	....	11	3	3	6	19	....	....	....
1967-68	Dallas Black Hawks	CPHL	70	5	15	20	....	....	....	73	....	....	....	....	....	....	....	....	....	....	5	0	0	0	0	....	....	....
1968-69	**Chicago Black Hawks**	**NHL**	**3**	**1**	**0**	**1**	**1**	**0**	**1**	**8**	**0**	**0**	**0**	**5**	**20.0**	**4**	**0**	**4**	**0**	**0**	....	....	....	....	....	....	....	....
	Dallas Black Hawks	CHL	69	7	39	46	....	....	....	118	....	....	....	....	....	....	....	....	....	....	11	4	12	16	17	....	....	....
	Portland Buckaroos	WHL	....	....	....	....	....	....	....	....	....	....	....	....	....	....	....	....	....	....	1	0	1	1	0	....	....	....
1969-70	**Chicago Black Hawks**	**NHL**	**24**	**0**	**4**	**4**	**0**	**4**	**4**	**26**	**0**	**0**	**0**	**13**	**0.0**	**18**	**1**	**8**	**2**	**11**	**8**	**1**	**2**	**3**	**0**	**0**	**0**	**0**
	Dallas Black Hawks	CHL	48	3	21	24	....	....	....	88	....	....	....	....	....	....	....	....	....	....	....	....	....	....	....	....	....	....
1970-71	**Chicago Black Hawks**	**NHL**	**57**	**1**	**12**	**13**	**1**	**10**	**11**	**41**	**0**	**0**	**1**	**35**	**2.9**	**28**	**0**	**34**	**9**	**3**	**9**	**0**	**0**	**0**	**17**	**0**	**0**	**0**
1971-72	**California Golden Seals**	**NHL**	**69**	**6**	**21**	**27**	**6**	**18**	**24**	**156**	**0**	**0**	**0**	**82**	**7.3**	**81**	**3**	**127**	**22**	**–27**	....	....	....	....	....	....	....	....
1972-73	Cleveland Crusaders	WHA	73	5	43	48	....	....	....	169	....	....	....	....	....	....	....	....	....	....	8	1	3	4	19	....	....	....
1973-74	Cleveland Crusaders	WHA	78	13	31	44	....	....	....	165	....	....	....	....	....	....	....	....	....	....	5	0	4	4	31	....	....	....
1974-75	Team Canada	Summit-74	7	0	2	2	....	....	....	6	....	....	....	....	....	....	....	....	....	....	....	....	....	....	....	....	....	....
	Cleveland Crusaders	WHA	49	7	14	21	....	....	....	103	....	....	....	....	....	....	....	....	....	....	5	2	1	3	15	....	....	....
1975-76	Cleveland Crusaders	WHA	70	6	44	50	....	....	....	101	....	....	....	....	....	....	....	....	....	....	....	....	....	....	....	....	....	....
1976-77	San Diego Mariners	WHA	81	13	37	50	....	....	....	103	....	....	....	....	....	....	....	....	....	....	7	0	2	2	8	....	....	....
1977-78	Edmonton Oilers	WHA	80	9	40	49	....	....	....	100	....	....	....	....	....	....	....	....	....	....	5	1	3	4	11	....	....	....
1978-79	Edmonton Oilers	WHA	80	8	39	47	....	....	....	119	....	....	....	....	....	....	....	....	....	....	13	1	5	6	23	....	....	....
1979-80	**Minnesota North Stars**	**NHL**	**63**	**3**	**15**	**18**	**3**	**11**	**14**	**84**	**0**	**0**	**1**	**82**	**3.7**	**72**	**1**	**56**	**10**	**25**	**14**	**2**	**1**	**3**	**23**	**1**	**0**	**1**

			REGULAR SEASON																		PLAYOFFS							
Season	Club	League	GP	G	A	Pts	AG	AA	APts	PIM	PP	SH	GW	S	%	TGF	PGF	TGA	PGA	+/–	GP	G	A	Pts	PIM	PP	SH	GW
1980-81	Minnesota North Stars	DN-Cup	3	0	0	0	....	....	....	2	....	....	....	....	....	....	....	....	....	....	....	....	....	....	....	....	....	....
	Minnesota North Stars	**NHL**	**61**	**1**	**9**	**10**	**1**	**6**	**7**	**79**	**0**	**0**	**0**	**62**	**1.6**	**49**	**2**	**63**	**20**	**4**	**3**	**0**	**0**	**0**	**4**	**0**	**0**	**0**
1981-82	**Hartford Whalers**	**NHL**	**66**	**1**	**11**	**12**	**1**	**7**	**8**	**134**	**0**	**0**	**0**	**44**	**2.3**	**62**	**6**	**90**	**23**	**–11**	....	....	....	....	....	....	....	....
	NHL Totals		**343**	**13**	**72**	**85**	**13**	**56**	**69**	**528**	**0**	**0**	**2**	**323**	**4.0**	**314**	**13**	**382**	**86**		**34**	**3**	**3**	**6**	**44**	**1**	**0**	**1**
	Other Major League Totals		511	61	248	309	....	....	....	860	....	....	....	....	....	....	....	....	....	....	43	5	18	23	107	....	....	....

WHA First All-Star Team (1973, 1974, 1976) • Won Dennis A. Murphy Trophy (WHA Top Defenseman) (1976) • WHA Second All-Star Team (1979)

Traded to **Chicago** by **NY Rangers** for Camille Henry, August 17, 1967. Traded to **California** by **Chicago** with Gilles Marotte for Gerry Desjardins, October 18, 1971. Selected by **Miami-Philadelphia** (WHA) in 1972 WHA General Player Draft, February 12, 1972. WHA rights traded to **Cleveland** (WHA) by **Philadelphia** (WHA) for future considerations, Spetember, 1972. Traded to **San Diego** (WHA) by **Minnesota** (WHA) with Gerry Pinder for Ray Adduono, Bob Wall and cash, September, 1976. Signed as a free agent by **Edmonton** (WHA) after **San Diego** (WHA) franchise folded, August, 1977. Claimed by **Minnesota** in **Cleveland-Minnesota** Dispersal Draft, June 15, 1978. Reclaimed by **Minnesota** from **Edmonton** prior to Expansion Draft, June 9, 1979. Signed as a free agent by **Hartford**, October, 1981.

• SHOEBOTTOM, Bruce

Bruce William D – L. 6'2", 200 lbs. b: Windsor, Ont., 8/20/1965. Los Angeles' 1st, 47th overall, in 1983.

Season	Club	League	GP	G	A	Pts	AG	AA	APts	PIM	PP	SH	GW	S	%	TGF	PGF	TGA	PGA	+/–	GP	G	A	Pts	PIM	PP	SH	GW
1980-81	Toronto Young Nationals	MTHL	40	10	32	42	....	....	....	....	....	....	....	....	....	....	....	....	....	....	....	....	....	....	....	....	....	....
1981-82	Peterborough Petes	OHL	51	0	4	4	....	....	....	67	....	....	....	....	....	....	....	....	....	....	....	....	....	....	....	....	....	....
1982-83	Peterborough Petes	OHL	34	2	10	12	....	....	....	106	....	....	....	....	....	....	....	....	....	....	....	....	....	....	....	....	....	....
1983-84	Peterborough Petes	OHL	16	0	5	5	....	....	....	73	....	....	....	....	....	....	....	....	....	....	....	....	....	....	....	....	....	....
1984-85	Peterborough Petes	OHL	60	2	15	17	....	....	....	143	....	....	....	....	....	....	....	....	....	....	17	0	4	4	26	....	....	....
1985-86	New Haven Nighthawks	AHL	6	2	0	2	....	....	....	12	....	....	....	....	....	....	....	....	....	....	....	....	....	....	....	....	....	....
	Binghamton Whalers	AHL	62	7	5	12	....	....	....	249	....	....	....	....	....	....	....	....	....	....	....	....	....	....	....	....	....	....
1986-87	Fort Wayne Komets	IHL	75	2	10	12	....	....	....	309	....	....	....	....	....	....	....	....	....	....	10	0	0	0	31	....	....	....
1987-88	**Boston Bruins**	**NHL**	**3**	**0**	**1**	**1**	**0**	**1**	**1**	**0**	**0**	**0**	**0**	**2**	**0.0**	**1**	**0**	**4**	**0**	**–3**	**4**	**1**	**0**	**1**	**42**	**0**	**0**	**1**
	Maine Mariners	AHL	70	2	12	14	....	....	....	338	....	....	....	....	....	....	....	....	....	....	....	....	....	....	....	....	....	....
1988-89	**Boston Bruins**	**NHL**	**29**	**1**	**3**	**4**	**1**	**2**	**3**	**44**	**0**	**0**	**0**	**19**	**5.3**	**13**	**0**	**8**	**0**	**5**	**10**	**0**	**2**	**2**	**35**	**0**	**0**	**0**
	Maine Mariners	AHL	44	0	8	8	....	....	....	265	....	....	....	....	....	....	....	....	....	....	....	....	....	....	....	....	....	....
1989-90	**Boston Bruins**	**NHL**	**2**	**0**	**0**	**0**	**0**	**0**	**0**	**4**	**0**	**0**	**0**	**3**	**0.0**	**0**	**0**	**0**	**0**	**0**	....	....	....	....	....	....	....	....
	Maine Mariners	AHL	66	3	11	14	....	....	....	228	....	....	....	....	....	....	....	....	....	....	....	....	....	....	....	....	....	....
1990-91	**Boston Bruins**	**NHL**	**1**	**0**	**0**	**0**	**0**	**0**	**0**	**5**	**0**	**0**	**0**	**0**	**0.0**	**0**	**0**	**1**	**0**	**–1**	....	....	....	....	....	....	....	....
	Maine Mariners	AHL	71	2	8	10	....	....	....	238	....	....	....	....	....	....	....	....	....	....	1	0	0	0	14	....	....	....
1991-92	Peoria Rivermen	IHL	79	4	12	16	....	....	....	234	....	....	....	....	....	....	....	....	....	....	10	0	0	0	33	....	....	....
1992-93	Rochester Americans	AHL	65	7	5	12	....	....	....	253	....	....	....	....	....	....	....	....	....	....	14	0	0	0	19	....	....	....
1993-94	Oklahoma City Blazers	CHL	43	4	11	15	....	....	....	236	....	....	....	....	....	....	....	....	....	....	1	0	0	0	14	....	....	....
1994-95	Rochester Americans	AHL	1	0	0	0	....	....	....	0	....	....	....	....	....	....	....	....	....	....	....	....	....	....	....	....	....	....
1995-96	San Diego Gulls	WCHL	22	1	7	8	....	....	....	102	....	....	....	....	....	....	....	....	....	....	9	0	2	2	17	....	....	....
1996-97	San Diego Gulls	WCHL	38	6	6	12	....	....	....	288	....	....	....	....	....	....	....	....	....	....	2	0	0	0	24	....	....	....
1997-98	Austin Ice-Bats	WPHL	9	0	4	4	....	....	....	37	....	....	....	....	....	....	....	....	....	....	4	0	0	0	14	....	....	....
	NHL Totals		**35**	**1**	**4**	**5**	**1**	**3**	**4**	**53**	**0**	**0**	**0**	**24**	**4.2**	**14**	**0**	**13**	**0**		**14**	**1**	**2**	**3**	**77**	**0**	**0**	**1**

Traded to **Washington** by **LA Kings** for Bryan Erickson, October 31, 1985. Signed as a free agent by **Boston**, July 20, 1987.

• SHORT, Steve

Steven Andrew LW – L. 6'2", 210 lbs. b: Roseville, MN, 4/6/1954. Philadelphia's 7th, 142nd overall, in 1974.

Season	Club	League	GP	G	A	Pts	AG	AA	APts	PIM	PP	SH	GW	S	%	TGF	PGF	TGA	PGA	+/–	GP	G	A	Pts	PIM	PP	SH	GW
1973-74	Minnesota Jr. North Stars	MWJHL	54	28	47	75	....	....	....	103	....	....	....	....	....	....	....	....	....	....	....	....	....	....	....	....	....	....
	United States	WJC-A	5	1	2	3	....	....	....	14	....	....	....	....	....	....	....	....	....	....	....	....	....	....	....	....	....	....
1974-75	Philadelphia Firebirds	NAHL	12	6	1	7	....	....	....	25	....	....	....	....	....	....	....	....	....	....	....	....	....	....	....	....	....	....
	Richmond Robins	AHL	43	5	11	16	....	....	....	106	....	....	....	....	....	....	....	....	....	....	5	0	0	0	12	....	....	....
1975-76	Richmond Robins	AHL	74	5	14	19	....	....	....	*302	....	....	....	....	....	....	....	....	....	....	8	1	0	1	15	....	....	....
1976-77	Springfield Indians	AHL	24	0	3	3	....	....	....	72	....	....	....	....	....	....	....	....	....	....	....	....	....	....	....	....	....	....
	Fort Worth Texans	CHL	48	5	9	14	....	....	....	135	....	....	....	....	....	....	....	....	....	....	6	2	1	3	*33	....	....	....
1977-78	**Los Angeles Kings**	**NHL**	**5**	**0**	**0**	**0**	**0**	**0**	**0**	**2**	**0**	**0**	**0**	**1**	**0.0**	**1**	**0**	**6**	**0**	**–5**	....	....	....	....	....	....	....	....
	Springfield Indians	AHL	67	2	20	22	....	....	....	236	....	....	....	....	....	....	....	....	....	....	4	0	0	0	0	....	....	....
1978-79	**Detroit Red Wings**	**NHL**	**1**	**0**	**0**	**0**	**0**	**0**	**0**	**0**	**0**	**0**	**0**	**1**	**0.0**	**0**	**0**	**0**	**0**	**0**	....	....	....	....	....	....	....	....
	Kansas City Red Wings	CHL	51	3	11	14	....	....	....	*216	....	....	....	....	....	....	....	....	....	....	4	0	2	2	26	....	....	....
1979-80	Adirondack Red Wings	AHL	66	1	8	9	....	....	....	167	....	....	....	....	....	....	....	....	....	....	3	0	0	0	6	....	....	....
1980-81	Adirondack Red Wings	AHL	63	2	7	9	....	....	....	75	....	....	....	....	....	....	....	....	....	....	16	0	1	1	20	....	....	....
1981-82	Kalamazoo Wings	IHL	1	0	0	0	....	....	....	2	....	....	....	....	....	....	....	....	....	....	....	....	....	....	....	....	....	....
	NHL Totals		**6**	**0**	**0**	**0**	**0**	**0**	**0**	**2**	**0**	**0**	**0**	**2**	**0.0**	**1**	**0**	**6**	**0**		....	....	....	....	....	....	....	....

Traded to **LA Kings** by **Philadelphia** for future considerations (Paul Evans, November 3, 1977), June 17, 1977. Traded to **Detroit** by **LA Kings** for the rights to Steve Carlson, December 6, 1978.

• SHUCHUK, Gary

Gary R. RW – R. 5'11", 190 lbs. b: Edmonton, Alta., 2/17/1967. Detroit's 1st, 22nd overall, in 1988 Supplemental Draft.

Season	Club	League	GP	G	A	Pts	AG	AA	APts	PIM	PP	SH	GW	S	%	TGF	PGF	TGA	PGA	+/–	GP	G	A	Pts	PIM	PP	SH	GW
1985-86	St. Albert Saints	AJHL	STATISTICS NOT AVAILABLE																									
1986-87	University of Wisconsin	WCHA	42	19	11	30	....	....	....	72	....	....	....	....	....	....	....	....	....	....	....	....	....	....	....	....	....	....
1987-88	University of Wisconsin	WCHA	44	7	22	29	....	....	....	70	....	....	....	....	....	....	....	....	....	....	....	....	....	....	....	....	....	....
1988-89	University of Wisconsin	WCHA	46	18	19	37	....	....	....	102	....	....	....	....	....	....	....	....	....	....	....	....	....	....	....	....	....	....
1989-90	University of Wisconsin	WCHA	45	*41	39	*80	....	....	....	70	....	....	....	....	....	....	....	....	....	....	....	....	....	....	....	....	....	....
1990-91	**Detroit Red Wings**	**NHL**	**6**	**1**	**2**	**3**	**1**	**2**	**3**	**6**	**0**	**0**	**0**	**8**	**12.5**	**4**	**0**	**4**	**1**	**1**	**3**	**0**	**0**	**0**	**0**	**0**	**0**	**0**
	Adirondack Red Wings	AHL	59	23	24	47	....	....	....	32	....	....	....	....	....	....	....	....	....	....	....	....	....	....	....	....	....	....
1991-92	Adirondack Red Wings	AHL	79	32	48	80	....	....	....	48	....	....	....	....	....	....	....	....	....	....	19	4	9	13	18	....	....	....
1992-93	Adirondack Red Wings	AHL	47	24	53	77	....	....	....	66	....	....	....	....	....	....	....	....	....	....	....	....	....	....	....	....	....	....
	Los Angeles Kings	**NHL**	**25**	**2**	**4**	**6**	**2**	**3**	**5**	**16**	**0**	**0**	**0**	**24**	**8.3**	**11**	**1**	**11**	**1**	**0**	**17**	**2**	**2**	**4**	**12**	**0**	**0**	**1**
1993-94	**Los Angeles Kings**	**NHL**	**56**	**3**	**4**	**7**	**3**	**3**	**6**	**30**	**0**	**0**	**1**	**55**	**5.5**	**12**	**0**	**33**	**13**	**–8**	....	....	....	....	....	....	....	....
1994-95	**Los Angeles Kings**	**NHL**	**22**	**3**	**6**	**9**	**5**	**9**	**14**	**6**	**0**	**0**	**0**	**16**	**18.8**	**11**	**0**	**16**	**3**	**–2**	....	....	....	....	....	....	....	....
	Phoenix Roadrunners	IHL	13	8	7	15	....	....	....	12	....	....	....	....	....	....	....	....	....	....	....	....	....	....	....	....	....	....
1995-96	**Los Angeles Kings**	**NHL**	**33**	**4**	**10**	**14**	**4**	**8**	**12**	**12**	**0**	**0**	**0**	**22**	**18.2**	**23**	**1**	**20**	**1**	**3**	....	....	....	....	....	....	....	....
	Phoenix Roadrunners	IHL	33	8	21	29	....	....	....	76	....	....	....	....	....	....	....	....	....	....	4	1	0	1	4	....	....	....
1996-97	Houston Aeros	IHL	55	18	23	41	....	....	....	48	....	....	....	....	....	....	....	....	....	....	13	5	2	7	18	....	....	....
1997-98	SC Herisau	Switz.	40	15	33	48	....	....	....	60	....	....	....	....	....	....	....	....	....	....	....	....	....	....	....	....	....	....
1998-99	KAC Klagenfurt	Alpenliga	31	15	27	42	....	....	....	89	....	....	....	....	....	....	....	....	....	....	....	....	....	....	....	....	....	....
	KAC Klagenfurt	Austria	21	5	9	14	....	....	....	30	....	....	....	....	....	....	....	....	....	....	....	....	....	....	....	....	....	....
99-2000	Orlando Solar Bears	IHL	71	16	33	49	....	....	....	94	....	....	....	....	....	....	....	....	....	....	6	1	1	2	12	....	....	....
	NHL Totals		**142**	**13**	**26**	**39**	**15**	**25**	**40**	**70**	**0**	**0**	**1**	**125**	**10.4**	**61**	**2**	**84**	**19**		**20**	**2**	**2**	**4**	**12**	**0**	**0**	**1**

WCHA First All-Star Team (1990) • NCAA West First All-American Team (1990)

Traded to **LA Kings** by **Detroit** with Jimmy Carson and Marc Potvin for Paul Coffey, Sylvain Couturier and Jim Hiller, January 29, 1993. Signed as a free agent by **Houston** (IHL), September 14, 1996. Signed as a free agent by **Orlando** (IHL), October 29, 1999.

• SHUDRA, Ron

D – L. 6'2", 192 lbs. b: Winnipeg, Man., 11/28/1967. Edmonton's 3rd, 63rd overall, in 1986.

Season	Club	League	GP	G	A	Pts	AG	AA	APts	PIM	PP	SH	GW	S	%	TGF	PGF	TGA	PGA	+/–	GP	G	A	Pts	PIM	PP	SH	GW
1984-85	Red Deer Rustlers	AJHL	57	14	57	71	....	....	....	70	....	....	....	....	....	....	....	....	....	....	....	....	....	....	....	....	....	....
1985-86	Kamloops Blazers	WHL	72	10	40	50	....	....	....	81	....	....	....	....	....	....	....	....	....	....	16	1	11	12	11	....	....	....
	Kamloops Blazers	Mem-Cup	5	1	1	2	....	....	....	0	....	....	....	....	....	....	....	....	....	....	....	....	....	....	....	....	....	....
1986-87	Kamloops Blazers	WHL	71	49	70	119	....	....	....	68	....	....	....	....	....	....	....	....	....	....	11	7	3	10	10	....	....	....
1987-88	**Edmonton Oilers**	**NHL**	**10**	**0**	**5**	**5**	**0**	**4**	**4**	**6**	**0**	**0**	**0**	**8**	**0.0**	**8**	**0**	**3**	**0**	**5**	....	....	....	....	....	....	....	....
	Nova Scotia Oilers	AHL	49	7	15	22	....	....	....	21	....	....	....	....	....	....	....	....	....	....	....	....	....	....	....	....	....	....
1988-89	Cape Breton Oilers	AHL	5	0	0	0	....	....	....	0	....	....	....	....	....	....	....	....	....	....	....	....	....	....	....	....	....	....
	Denver Rangers	IHL	64	11	14	25	....	....	....	44	....	....	....	....	....	....	....	....	....	....	2	0	0	0	0	....	....	....
1989-90	Fort Wayne Komets	IHL	67	11	16	27	....	....	....	48	....	....	....	....	....	....	....	....	....	....	2	0	0	0	0	....	....	....
1990-91	Solihull Barons	Aut-Cup	3	1	0	1	....	....	....	2	....	....	....	....	....	....	....	....	....	....	....	....	....	....	....	....	....	....
	Solihull Barons	Britain	36	24	53	77	....	....	....	70	....	....	....	....	....	....	....	....	....	....	6	7	9	16	10	....	....	....
1991-92	Solihull Barons	Aut-Cup	6	7	6	13	....	....	....	2	....	....	....	....	....	....	....	....	....	....	....	....	....	....	....	....	....	....
	Sheffield Steelers	Britain-2	32	78	70	148	....	....	....	42	....	....	....	....	....	....	....	....	....	....	6	15	14	29	4	....	....	....

			REGULAR SEASON																		PLAYOFFS							
Season	Club	League	GP	G	A	Pts	AG	AA	APts	PIM	PP	SH	GW	S	%	TGF	PGF	TGA	PGA	+/–	GP	G	A	Pts	PIM	PP	SH	GW
1992-93	Sheffield Steelers	BH-Cup	8	6	6	12				14																		
	Sheffield Steelers	Britain	26	32	46	78				36																		
1993-94	Sheffield Steelers	BH-Cup	6	8	11	19				8																		
	Sheffield Steelers	Britain	34	31	48	79				69											8	8	16	24	6			
1994-95	Sheffield Steelers	BH-Cup	12	10	8	18				33																		
	Sheffield Steelers	Britain	43	25	38	63				83											8	5	8	13	2			
1995-96	Sheffield Steelers	BH-Cup	13	13	16	29				10																		
	Sheffield Steelers	Britain	36	23	31	54				56											8	2	4	6	2			
1996-97	Sheffield Steelers	BH-Cup	10	2	5	7				8																		
	Sheffield Steelers	Britain	41	13	16	29				12											8	3	1	4	4			
1997-98	Sheffield Steelers	BH-Cup	12	1	6	7				6																		
	Sheffield Steelers	Britain	38	8	16	24				18											9	1	2	3	0			
1998-99	Sheffield Steelers	BH-Cup	10	1	3	4				4																		
	Sheffield Steelers	Britain	11	0	1	1				2											6	2	1	3	2			
99-2000	Hull Thunder	Britain-2	35	18	32	50				26											6	2	6	8	2			
	NHL Totals		**10**	**0**	**5**	**5**	**0**	**4**	**4**	**6**	**0**	**0**	**0**	**8**	**0.0**	**8**	**0**	**3**	**0**									

WHL West Second All-Star Team (1986, 1987) • Memorial Cup All-Star Team (1986)

Traded to **NY Rangers** by **Edmonton** for Jeff Crossman, October 27, 1988.

• SHUTT, Steve

Stephen John LW – L. 5'11", 185 lbs. b: Toronto, Ont., 7/1/1952. Montreal's 1st, 4th overall, in 1972. **HHOF**

Season	Club	League	GP	G	A	Pts	AG	AA	APts	PIM	PP	SH	GW	S	%	TGF	PGF	TGA	PGA	+/–	GP	G	A	Pts	PIM	PP	SH	GW
1968-69	North York Rangers	OHA-B	17	10	17	27																						
	Toronto Marlboros	OMJHL																			5	1	3	4	2			
1969-70	Toronto Marlboros	OMJHL	49	11	14	25				93											18	10	9	19	13			
1970-71	Toronto Marlboros	OMJHL	62	70	53	123				85											13	11	11	22	20			
1971-72	Toronto Marlboros	OMJHL	58	*63	49	112				60											10	8	6	14	12			
1972-73♦	**Montreal Canadiens**	**NHL**	**50**	**8**	**8**	**16**	**7**	**6**	**13**	**24**	**1**	**0**	**2**	**55**	**14.5**	**24**	**2**	**17**	**0**	**5**	**1**	**0**	**0**	**0**	**0**	**0**	**0**	**0**
	Nova Scotia Voyageurs	AHL	6	4	1	5				2																		
1973-74	**Montreal Canadiens**	**NHL**	**70**	**15**	**20**	**35**	**14**	**16**	**30**	**17**	**3**	**0**	**1**	**131**	**11.5**	**52**	**11**	**22**	**0**	**19**	**6**	**5**	**3**	**8**	**9**	**1**	**0**	**0**
1974-75	**Montreal Canadiens**	**NHL**	**77**	**30**	**35**	**65**	**26**	**26**	**52**	**40**	**3**	**0**	**5**	**165**	**18.2**	**106**	**17**	**49**	**0**	**40**	**9**	**1**	**6**	**7**	**4**	**0**	**0**	**0**
1975-76♦	**Montreal Canadiens**	**NHL**	**80**	**45**	**34**	**79**	**40**	**25**	**65**	**47**	**7**	**0**	**7**	**223**	**20.2**	**128**	**22**	**36**	**3**	**73**	**13**	**7**	**8**	**15**	**2**	**3**	**0**	**0**
1976-77	Canada	Can-Cup	6	1	2	3				8																		
♦	**Montreal Canadiens**	**NHL**	**80**	***60**	**45**	**105**	**54**	**35**	**89**	**28**	**8**	**0**	**9**	**294**	**20.4**	**159**	**32**	**39**	**0**	**88**	**14**	**8**	**10**	**18**	**2**	**2**	**0**	**3**
1977-78♦	**Montreal Canadiens**	**NHL**	**80**	**49**	**37**	**86**	**45**	**29**	**74**	**24**	**16**	**0**	**7**	**243**	**20.2**	**145**	**42**	**47**	**0**	**56**	**15**	**9**	**8**	**17**	**20**	**3**	**0**	**0**
1978-79♦	**Montreal Canadiens**	**NHL**	**72**	**37**	**40**	**77**	**32**	**29**	**61**	**31**	**10**	**0**	**6**	**192**	**19.3**	**109**	**27**	**45**	**0**	**37**	**11**	**4**	**7**	**11**	**6**	**1**	**0**	**0**
	NHL All-Stars	Chal-Cup	2	0	1	1				0																		
1979-80	**Montreal Canadiens**	**NHL**	**77**	**47**	**42**	**89**	**40**	**31**	**71**	**34**	**17**	**0**	**4**	**224**	**21.0**	**149**	**42**	**62**	**0**	**45**	**10**	**6**	**3**	**9**	**6**	**2**	**0**	**2**
1980-81	**Montreal Canadiens**	**NHL**	**77**	**35**	**38**	**73**	**27**	**25**	**52**	**51**	**7**	**0**	**3**	**232**	**15.1**	**115**	**35**	**50**	**0**	**30**	**3**	**2**	**1**	**3**	**4**	**0**	**0**	**0**
1981-82	**Montreal Canadiens**	**NHL**	**57**	**31**	**24**	**55**	**24**	**16**	**40**	**40**	**5**	**0**	**3**	**154**	**20.1**	**77**	**16**	**37**	**0**	**24**								
1982-83	**Montreal Canadiens**	**NHL**	**78**	**35**	**22**	**57**	**29**	**15**	**44**	**26**	**8**	**0**	**0**	**202**	**17.3**	**85**	**28**	**49**	**0**	**8**	**3**	**1**	**0**	**1**	**0**	**0**	**0**	**0**
1983-84	**Montreal Canadiens**	**NHL**	**63**	**14**	**23**	**37**	**11**	**16**	**27**	**29**	**4**	**0**	**2**	**146**	**9.6**	**50**	**16**	**52**	**0**	**–18**	**11**	**7**	**2**	**9**	**8**	**2**	**0**	**0**
1984-85	**Montreal Canadiens**	**NHL**	**10**	**2**	**0**	**2**	**2**	**0**	**2**	**9**	**1**	**0**	**0**	**17**	**11.8**	**7**	**3**	**2**	**0**	**2**								
	Los Angeles Kings	**NHL**	**59**	**16**	**25**	**41**	**13**	**17**	**30**	**10**	**5**	**0**	**1**	**127**	**12.6**	**58**	**18**	**56**	**0**	**–16**	**3**	**0**	**0**	**0**	**4**	**0**	**0**	**0**
	NHL Totals		**930**	**424**	**393**	**817**	**364**	**286**	**650**	**410**	**95**	**0**	**50**	**2405**	**17.6**	**1264**	**311**	**563**	**3**		**99**	**50**	**48**	**98**	**65**	**14**	**0**	**5**

OHA-Jr. Second All-Star Team (1971) • OMJHL First All-Star Team (1972) • NHL First All-Star Team (1977) • NHL Second All-Star Team (1978, 1980) • Played in NHL All-Star Game (1976, 1978, 1981)

Traded to **LA Kings** by **Montreal** for future considerations, November 19, 1984. Claimed on waivers by **Montreal** from **LA Kings**, June 18, 1985.

• SILK, Dave

RW – R. 5'11", 190 lbs. b: Scituate, MA, 1/1/1958. NY Rangers' 4th, 59th overall, in 1978.

Season	Club	League	GP	G	A	Pts	AG	AA	APts	PIM	PP	SH	GW	S	%	TGF	PGF	TGA	PGA	+/–	GP	G	A	Pts	PIM	PP	SH	GW
1975-76	Thayer Academy	Hi-School	STATISTICS NOT AVAILABLE																									
1976-77	Boston University	ECAC	34	35	30	65				50																		
1977-78	Boston University	ECAC	28	27	31	58				57																		
1978-79	Boston University	ECAC	23	8	12	20				20																		
1979-80	United States	Nat-Team	56	12	36	48				32																		
	United States	Olympics	7	2	3	5				0																		
	New York Rangers	**NHL**	**2**	**0**	**0**	**0**	**0**	**0**	**0**	**0**	**0**	**0**	**0**	**4**	**0.0**	**1**	**0**	**0**	**0**	**1**								
	New Haven Nighthawks	AHL	11	1	9	10				0											9	1	2	3	12			
1980-81	**New York Rangers**	**NHL**	**59**	**14**	**12**	**26**	**11**	**8**	**19**	**58**	**2**	**0**	**1**	**124**	**11.3**	**38**	**9**	**58**	**5**	**–24**								
	New Haven Nighthawks	AHL	12	0	4	4				34											3	0	0	0	0			
1981-82	New York Rangers	DN-Cup	4	0	2	2																						
	New York Rangers	**NHL**	**64**	**15**	**20**	**35**	**12**	**13**	**25**	**39**	**1**	**0**	**0**	**111**	**13.5**	**57**	**12**	**29**	**1**	**17**	**9**	**2**	**4**	**6**	**4**	**0**	**0**	**1**
1982-83	**New York Rangers**	**NHL**	**16**	**1**	**1**	**2**	**1**	**1**	**2**	**15**	**0**	**0**	**0**	**10**	**10.0**	**3**	**1**	**5**	**0**	**–3**								
	Tulsa Oilers	CHL	40	28	29	57				67																		
	Binghamton Whalers	AHL	9	1	2	3				29																		
1983-84	**Boston Bruins**	**NHL**	**35**	**13**	**17**	**30**	**10**	**12**	**22**	**64**	**5**	**0**	**1**	**62**	**21.0**	**42**	**15**	**16**	**0**	**11**	**3**	**0**	**0**	**0**	**7**	**0**	**0**	**0**
	Hershey Bears	AHL	15	11	10	21				22																		
1984-85	**Boston Bruins**	**NHL**	**29**	**7**	**5**	**12**	**6**	**3**	**9**	**22**	**0**	**0**	**0**	**40**	**17.5**	**20**	**7**	**11**	**1**	**3**								
	Detroit Red Wings	**NHL**	**12**	**2**	**0**	**2**	**2**	**0**	**2**	**10**	**0**	**0**	**0**	**7**	**28.6**	**2**	**1**	**8**	**1**	**–6**								
1985-86	**Winnipeg Jets**	**NHL**	**32**	**2**	**4**	**6**	**2**	**3**	**5**	**63**	**0**	**0**	**1**	**30**	**6.7**	**10**	**0**	**19**	**13**	**–6**	**1**	**0**	**0**	**0**	**2**	**0**	**0**	**0**
	Sherbrooke Canadiens	AHL	18	5	14	19				18																		
1986-87	Mannheimer ERC	Germany	26	13	23	36				52											10	2	8	10	16			
1987-88	Mannheimer ERC	Germany	29	23	17	40				46											8	5	6	11	12			
1988-89	Mannheimer ERC	Germany	36	25	30	55				49											9	7	4	11	21			
1989-90	BSC Preussen Berlin	Germany	35	25	34	59				49											5	4	5	9	4			
1990-91	BSC Preussen Berlin	Germany	40	28	23	51				59											10	5	4	9	4			
	NHL Totals		**249**	**54**	**59**	**113**	**44**	**40**	**84**	**271**	**8**	**0**	**3**	**388**	**13.9**	**173**	**45**	**146**	**21**		**13**	**2**	**4**	**6**	**13**	**0**	**0**	**1**

NCAA Championship All-Tournament Team (1977, 1978) • ECAC Second All-Star Team (1978)

Traded to **Boston** by **NY Rangers** for Dave Barr, October 5, 1983. Claimed on waivers by **Detroit** from **Boston**, December 21, 1984. Signed as a free agent by **Winnipeg**, September 30, 1985.

• SILLINGER, Mike

Michael C – R. 5'10", 190 lbs. b: Regina, Sask., 6/29/1971. Detroit's 1st, 11th overall, in 1989.

Season	Club	League	GP	G	A	Pts	AG	AA	APts	PIM	PP	SH	GW	S	%	TGF	PGF	TGA	PGA	+/–	GP	G	A	Pts	PIM	PP	SH	GW
1986-87	Regina Kings	SAHA	31	83	51	134																						
1987-88	Regina Pats	WHL	67	18	25	43				17											4	2	2	4	0			
1988-89	Regina Pats	WHL	72	53	78	131				52																		
1989-90	Regina Pats	WHL	70	57	72	129				41											11	12	10	22	2			
	Adirondack Red Wings	AHL																			1	0	0	0	0			
1990-91	Regina Pats	WHL	57	50	66	116				42											8	6	9	15	4			
	Canada	WJC-A	7	4	2	6				2																		
	Detroit Red Wings	**NHL**	**3**	**0**	**1**	**1**	**0**	**1**	**1**	**0**	**0**	**0**	**0**	**6**	**0.0**	**1**	**0**	**3**	**0**	**–2**	**3**	**0**	**1**	**1**	**0**	**0**	**0**	**0**
1991-92	Adirondack Red Wings	AHL	64	25	41	66				26											15	9	*19	*28	12			
	Detroit Red Wings	**NHL**																			**8**	**2**	**2**	**4**	**2**	**0**	**0**	**0**
1992-93	**Detroit Red Wings**	**NHL**	**51**	**4**	**17**	**21**	**3**	**12**	**15**	**16**	**0**	**0**	**0**	**47**	**8.5**	**29**	**0**	**50**	**21**	**0**								
	Adirondack Red Wings	AHL	15	10	20	30				31											11	5	13	18	10			
1993-94	**Detroit Red Wings**	**NHL**	**62**	**8**	**21**	**29**	**7**	**16**	**23**	**10**	**0**	**1**	**1**	**91**	**8.8**	**41**	**7**	**45**	**13**	**2**								
1994-95	WEV Wien	Austria	13	13	14	27				10																		
	Detroit Red Wings	**NHL**	**13**	**2**	**6**	**8**	**4**	**9**	**13**	**2**	**0**	**0**	**0**	**11**	**18.2**	**9**	**2**	**4**	**0**	**3**								
	Mighty Ducks of Anaheim	**NHL**	**15**	**2**	**5**	**7**	**4**	**7**	**11**	**6**	**2**	**0**	**0**	**28**	**7.1**	**16**	**8**	**8**	**1**	**1**								
1995-96	**Mighty Ducks of Anaheim**	**NHL**	**62**	**13**	**21**	**34**	**13**	**17**	**30**	**32**	**7**	**0**	**2**	**143**	**9.1**	**52**	**29**	**48**	**5**	**–20**								
	Vancouver Canucks	**NHL**	**12**	**1**	**3**	**4**	**1**	**2**	**3**	**6**	**0**	**1**	**0**	**16**	**6.3**	**5**	**0**	**5**	**2**	**2**	**6**	**0**	**0**	**0**	**2**	**0**	**0**	**0**
1996-97	**Vancouver Canucks**	**NHL**	**78**	**17**	**20**	**37**	**18**	**18**	**36**	**25**	**3**	**3**	**2**	**112**	**15.2**	**53**	**5**	**80**	**29**	**–3**								

Season	Club	League	GP	G	A	Pts	AG	AA	APts	PIM	PP	SH	GW	S	%	TGF	PGF	TGA	PGA	+/–	GP	G	A	Pts	PIM	PP	SH	GW
			REGULAR SEASON																		PLAYOFFS							
1997-98	**Vancouver Canucks**	**NHL**	**48**	**10**	**9**	**19**	**12**	**9**	**21**	**34**	**1**	**2**	**1**	**56**	**17.9**	**25**	**3**	**41**	**5**	**–14**	....	....	....	....	....	....	....	....
	Philadelphia Flyers	**NHL**	**27**	**11**	**11**	**22**	**13**	**11**	**24**	**16**	**1**	**2**	**0**	**40**	**27.5**	**28**	**9**	**21**	**5**	**3**	**3**	**1**	**0**	**1**	**0**	**0**	**0**	**0**
1998-99	**Philadelphia Flyers**	**NHL**	**25**	**0**	**3**	**3**	**0**	**3**	**3**	**8**	**0**	**0**	**0**	**23**	**0.0**	**3**	**0**	**12**	**0**	**–9**	....	....	....	....	....	....	....	....
	Tampa Bay Lightning	**NHL**	**54**	**8**	**2**	**10**	**9**	**2**	**11**	**28**	**0**	**2**	**0**	**69**	**11.6**	**17**	**1**	**45**	**9**	**–20**	....	....	....	....	....	....	....	....
99-2000	**Tampa Bay Lightning**	**NHL**	**67**	**19**	**25**	**44**	**21**	**23**	**44**	**86**	**6**	**3**	**1**	**126**	**15.1**	**57**	**18**	**91**	**23**	**–29**	....	....	....	....	....	....	....	....
	Florida Panthers	**NHL**	**13**	**4**	**4**	**8**	**4**	**4**	**8**	**16**	**2**	**0**	**1**	**20**	**20.0**	**15**	**6**	**13**	**3**	**–1**	**4**	**2**	**1**	**3**	**2**	**0**	**0**	**0**
	Canada	WC-A	9	3	0	3	....	....	....	4	....	....	....	....	....	....	....	....	....	....	....	....	....	....	....	....	....	....
	NHL Totals		**530**	**99**	**148**	**247**	**109**	**134**	**243**	**285**	**22**	**14**	**8**	**788**	**12.6**	**351**	**88**	**466**	**116**		**24**	**5**	**4**	**9**	**6**	**0**	**0**	**0**

WHL East Second All-Star Team (1990) • WHL East First All-Star Team (1991)

Traded to **Anaheim** by **Detroit** with Jason York for Stu Grimson, Mark Ferner and Anaheim's 6th round choice (Magnus Nilsson) in 1996 Entry Draft, April 4, 1995. Traded to **Vancouver** by **Anaheim** for Roman Oksiuta, March 15, 1996. Traded to **Philadelphia** by **Vancouver** for Philadelphia's 5th round choice (traded back to Philadelphia — Philadelphia selected Garrett Prosofsky) in 1998 Entry Draft, February 5, 1998. Traded to **Tampa Bay** by **Philadelphia** with Chris Gratton for Mikael Renberg and Daymond Langkow, December 12, 1998. Traded to **Florida** by **Tampa Bay** for Ryan Johnson and Dwayne Hay, March 14, 2000.

• SILTALA, Mike

Michael RW – R. 5'9", 170 lbs. b: Toronto, Ont., 8/5/1963. Washington's 4th, 89th overall, in 1981.

Season	Club	League	GP	G	A	Pts	AG	AA	APts	PIM	PP	SH	GW	S	%	TGF	PGF	TGA	PGA	+/–	GP	G	A	Pts	PIM	PP	SH	GW
1979-80	Sault Ste. Marie Rangers	NOJHA	57	78	83	161	....	....	....	....	....	....	....	....	....	....	....	....	....	....	....	....	....	....	....	....	....	....
1980-81	Kingston Canadians	OMJHL	63	18	22	40	....	....	....	23	....	....	....	....	....	....	....	....	....	....	14	5	6	11	20	....	....	....
1981-82	Kingston Canadians	OHL	59	38	49	87	....	....	....	70	....	....	....	....	....	....	....	....	....	....	4	2	3	5	9	....	....	....
	Washington Capitals	**NHL**	**3**	**1**	**0**	**1**	**1**	**0**	**1**	**2**	**0**	**0**	**0**	**2**	**50.0**	**2**	**0**	**3**	**0**	**–1**	....	....	....	....	....	....	....	....
1982-83	Kingston Canadians	OHL	50	53	61	114	....	....	....	45	....	....	....	....	....	....	....	....	....	....	....	....	....	....	....	....	....	....
	Hershey Bears	AHL	9	0	3	3	....	....	....	2	....	....	....	....	....	....	....	....	....	....	....	....	....	....	....	....	....	....
1983-84	Hershey Bears	AHL	50	15	17	32	....	....	....	29	....	....	....	....	....	....	....	....	....	....	....	....	....	....	....	....	....	....
1984-85	Binghamton Whalers	AHL	75	42	36	78	....	....	....	53	....	....	....	....	....	....	....	....	....	....	5	5	5	10	0	....	....	....
1985-86	Binghamton Whalers	AHL	50	25	22	47	....	....	....	36	....	....	....	....	....	....	....	....	....	....	2	3	0	3	0	....	....	....
1986-87	**New York Rangers**	**NHL**	**1**	**0**	**0**	**0**	**0**	**0**	**0**	**0**	**0**	**0**	**0**	**0**	**0.0**	**1**	**0**	**0**	**0**	**1**	....	....	....	....	....	....	....	....
	New Haven Nighthawks	AHL	17	13	6	19	....	....	....	20	....	....	....	....	....	....	....	....	....	....	....	....	....	....	....	....	....	....
1987-88	**New York Rangers**	**NHL**	**3**	**0**	**0**	**0**	**0**	**0**	**0**	**0**	**0**	**0**	**0**	**3**	**0.0**	**1**	**0**	**1**	**0**	**0**	....	....	....	....	....	....	....	....
	New Haven Nighthawks	AHL	32	17	20	37	....	....	....	8	....	....	....	....	....	....	....	....	....	....	....	....	....	....	....	....	....	....
	Colorado Rangers	IHL	38	22	28	50	....	....	....	28	....	....	....	....	....	....	....	....	....	....	....	....	....	....	....	....	....	....
1988-89	Schwenninger ERC	Germany	26	15	20	35	....	....	....	22	....	....	....	....	....	....	....	....	....	....	3	1	0	1	2	....	....	....
	NHL Totals		**7**	**1**	**0**	**1**	**1**	**0**	**1**	**2**	**0**	**0**	**0**	**5**	**20.0**	**4**	**0**	**4**	**0**		....	....	....	....	....	....	....	....

OHL First All-Star Team (1983) • AHL Second All-Star Team (1985)

Signed as a free agent by **NY Rangers**, August 15, 1986. Traded to **LA Kings** by **NY Rangers** with Gord Walker for Joe Paterson, January 21, 1988.

• SILTANEN, Risto

"The Incredible Hulk" D – R. 5'9", 158 lbs. b: Tampere, Finland, 10/31/1958. St. Louis' 13th, 173rd overall, in 1978.

Season	Club	League	GP	G	A	Pts	AG	AA	APts	PIM	PP	SH	GW	S	%	TGF	PGF	TGA	PGA	+/–	GP	G	A	Pts	PIM	PP	SH	GW
1975-76	Finland	EJC-A	4	3	0	3	....	....	....	0	....	....	....	....	....	....	....	....	....	....	....	....	....	....	....	....	....	....
1976-77	Ilves Tampere	Finland	36	10	7	17	....	....	....	28	....	....	....	....	....	....	....	....	....	....	....	....	....	....	....	....	....	....
	Finland	WJC-A	7	4	2	6	....	....	....	8	....	....	....	....	....	....	....	....	....	....	....	....	....	....	....	....	....	....
	Finland	WEC-A	10	1	1	2	....	....	....	6	....	....	....	....	....	....	....	....	....	....	....	....	....	....	....	....	....	....
1977-78	Ilves Tampere	Finland	36	7	8	15	....	....	....	42	....	....	....	....	....	....	....	....	....	....	7	1	1	2	10	....	....	....
	Finland	WJC-A	4	0	3	3	....	....	....	4	....	....	....	....	....	....	....	....	....	....	....	....	....	....	....	....	....	....
	Finland	WEC-A	10	0	2	2	....	....	....	6	....	....	....	....	....	....	....	....	....	....	....	....	....	....	....	....	....	....
1978-79	Ilves Tampere	Finland	34	13	8	21	....	....	....	44	....	....	....	....	....	....	....	....	....	....	....	....	....	....	....	....	....	....
	Finland	Nat-Team	11	2	0	2	....	....	....	6	....	....	....	....	....	....	....	....	....	....	....	....	....	....	....	....	....	....
	Edmonton Oilers	WHA	20	3	4	7	....	....	....	4	....	....	....	....	....	....	....	....	....	....	11	0	9	9	4	....	....	....
1979-80	**Edmonton Oilers**	**NHL**	**64**	**6**	**29**	**35**	**5**	**21**	**26**	**26**	**1**	**0**	**0**	**116**	**5.2**	**95**	**34**	**70**	**0**	**–9**	**2**	**0**	**0**	**0**	**2**	**0**	**0**	**0**
1980-81	**Edmonton Oilers**	**NHL**	**79**	**17**	**36**	**53**	**13**	**24**	**37**	**54**	**7**	**1**	**3**	**209**	**8.1**	**143**	**60**	**107**	**29**	**5**	**9**	**2**	**0**	**2**	**8**	**2**	**0**	**1**
1981-82	Finland	Can-Cup	5	1	1	2	....	....	....	6	....	....	....	....	....	....	....	....	....	....	....	....	....	....	....	....	....	....
	Edmonton Oilers	**NHL**	**63**	**15**	**48**	**63**	**12**	**32**	**44**	**26**	**6**	**0**	**1**	**143**	**10.5**	**126**	**52**	**71**	**10**	**13**	**5**	**3**	**2**	**5**	**10**	**1**	**0**	**0**
1982-83	**Hartford Whalers**	**NHL**	**74**	**5**	**25**	**30**	**4**	**17**	**21**	**28**	**3**	**0**	**0**	**155**	**3.2**	**99**	**26**	**141**	**29**	**–39**	....	....	....	....	....	....	....	....
	Finland	WEC-A	6	0	1	1	....	....	....	8	....	....	....	....	....	....	....	....	....	....	....	....	....	....	....	....	....	....
1983-84	**Hartford Whalers**	**NHL**	**75**	**15**	**38**	**53**	**12**	**26**	**38**	**34**	**12**	**0**	**0**	**163**	**9.2**	**127**	**57**	**98**	**7**	**–21**	....	....	....	....	....	....	....	....
1984-85	**Hartford Whalers**	**NHL**	**76**	**12**	**33**	**45**	**10**	**22**	**32**	**30**	**8**	**0**	**2**	**174**	**6.9**	**126**	**61**	**93**	**4**	**–24**	....	....	....	....	....	....	....	....
1985-86	**Hartford Whalers**	**NHL**	**52**	**8**	**22**	**30**	**6**	**15**	**21**	**30**	**6**	**0**	**1**	**126**	**6.3**	**92**	**47**	**44**	**1**	**2**	....	....	....	....	....	....	....	....
	Quebec Nordiques	**NHL**	**13**	**2**	**5**	**7**	**2**	**3**	**5**	**6**	**2**	**0**	**0**	**53**	**3.8**	**24**	**10**	**18**	**3**	**–1**	**3**	**0**	**1**	**1**	**2**	**0**	**0**	**0**
1986-87	**Quebec Nordiques**	**NHL**	**66**	**10**	**29**	**39**	**9**	**21**	**30**	**32**	**8**	**0**	**1**	**130**	**7.7**	**91**	**57**	**36**	**0**	**–2**	**13**	**1**	**9**	**10**	**8**	**1**	**0**	**0**
	Fredericton Express	AHL	6	2	4	6	....	....	....	6	....	....	....	....	....	....	....	....	....	....	....	....	....	....	....	....	....	....
1987-88	SC Bern	Switz.	38	13	13	26	....	....	....	....	....	....	....	....	....	....	....	....	....	....	....	....	....	....	....	....	....	....
1988-89	Ilves Tampere	Finland	43	19	20	39	....	....	....	32	....	....	....	....	....	....	....	....	....	....	5	2	1	3	6	....	....	....
1989-90	Ilves Tampere	Finland	44	16	17	33	....	....	....	40	....	....	....	....	....	....	....	....	....	....	9	2	6	8	4	....	....	....
1990-91	Ilves Tampere	Finland	37	11	13	24	....	....	....	32	....	....	....	....	....	....	....	....	....	....	....	....	....	....	....	....	....	....
1991-92	Ilves Tampere	Finland	44	4	9	13	....	....	....	22	....	....	....	....	....	....	....	....	....	....	....	....	....	....	....	....	....	....
1992-93	TuTo Turku	Finland-2	43	17	21	38	....	....	....	110	....	....	....	....	....	....	....	....	....	....	6	0	0	0	8	....	....	....
1993-94	TuTo Turku	Finland-2	46	12	23	35	....	....	....	44	....	....	....	....	....	....	....	....	....	....	5	1	1	2	2	....	....	....
1994-95	TPS Turku	Finland	44	10	14	24	....	....	....	52	....	....	....	....	....	....	....	....	....	....	....	....	....	....	....	....	....	....
1995-96	TPS Turku	Finland	45	6	6	12	....	....	....	44	....	....	....	....	....	....	....	....	....	....	....	....	....	....	....	....	....	....
1996-97	SC Bietigheim-Bissingen	Germany-3	49	13	35	48	....	....	....	28	....	....	....	....	....	....	....	....	....	....	....	....	....	....	....	....	....	....
	NHL Totals		**562**	**90**	**265**	**355**	**73**	**181**	**254**	**266**	**53**	**1**	**8**	**1269**	**7.1**	**923**	**404**	**678**	**83**		**32**	**6**	**12**	**18**	**30**	**4**	**0**	**1**
	Other Major League Totals		20	3	4	7	....	....	....	4	....	....	....	....	....	....	....	....	....	....	11	0	9	9	4	....	....	....

WJC-A All-Star Team (1977, 1978) • Finnish First All-Star Team (1977, 1989, 1990) • Finnish Rookie of the Year (1977)

Signed as a free agent by **Edmonton** (WHA), June, 1978. Reclaimed by **St. Louis** from **Edmonton** prior to Expansion Draft, June 9, 1979. Traded to **Edmonton** by **St. Louis** with Tom Roulston for Joe Micheletti, August 7, 1979. Traded to **Hartford** by **Edmonton** with the rights to Brent Loney for Ken Linseman and Don Nachbaur, August 19, 1982. Traded to **Quebec** by **Hartford** for John Anderson, March 8, 1986.

• SIM, Jonathan

C – L. 5'10", 184 lbs. b: New Glasgow, N.S., 9/29/1977. Dallas' 2nd, 70th overall, in 1996.

Season	Club	League	GP	G	A	Pts	AG	AA	APts	PIM	PP	SH	GW	S	%	TGF	PGF	TGA	PGA	+/–	GP	G	A	Pts	PIM	PP	SH	GW
1994-95	Laval Titan	QMJHL	9	0	1	1	....	....	....	6	....	....	....	....	....	....	....	....	....	....	....	....	....	....	....	....	....	....
	Sarnia Sting	OHL	25	9	12	21	....	....	....	19	....	....	....	....	....	....	....	....	....	....	4	3	2	5	2	....	....	....
1995-96	Sarnia Sting	OHL	63	56	46	102	....	....	....	130	....	....	....	....	....	....	....	....	....	....	10	8	7	15	26	....	....	....
1996-97	Sarnia Sting	OHL	64	*56	39	95	....	....	....	109	....	....	....	....	....	....	....	....	....	....	12	9	5	14	32	....	....	....
1997-98	Sarnia Sting	OHL	59	44	50	94	....	....	....	95	....	....	....	....	....	....	....	....	....	....	5	1	4	5	14	....	....	....
1998-99♦	**Dallas Stars**	**NHL**	**7**	**1**	**0**	**1**	**1**	**0**	**1**	**12**	**0**	**0**	**0**	**8**	**12.5**	**3**	**0**	**2**	**0**	**1**	**4**	**0**	**0**	**0**	**0**	**0**	**0**	**0**
	Michigan K-Wings	IHL	68	24	27	51	....	....	....	91	....	....	....	....	....	....	....	....	....	....	5	3	1	4	18	....	....	....
99-2000	Michigan K-Wings	IHL	35	14	16	30	....	....	....	65	....	....	....	....	....	....	....	....	....	....	....	....	....	....	....	....	....	....
	Dallas Stars	**NHL**	**25**	**5**	**3**	**8**	**6**	**3**	**9**	**10**	**2**	**0**	**1**	**44**	**11.4**	**13**	**4**	**5**	**0**	**4**	**7**	**1**	**0**	**1**	**6**	**0**	**0**	**0**
	NHL Totals		**32**	**6**	**3**	**9**	**7**	**3**	**10**	**22**	**2**	**0**	**1**	**52**	**11.5**	**16**	**4**	**7**	**0**		**11**	**1**	**0**	**1**	**6**	**0**	**0**	**0**

OHL Second All-Star Team (1998) • Claimed on waivers by **Sarnia** (OHL) from **Laval** (QMJHL), January 25, 1995.

• SIM, Trevor

Trevor B. RW – L. 6'2", 192 lbs. b: Calgary, Alta., 6/9/1970. Edmonton's 3rd, 53rd overall, in 1988.

Season	Club	League	GP	G	A	Pts	AG	AA	APts	PIM	PP	SH	GW	S	%	TGF	PGF	TGA	PGA	+/–	GP	G	A	Pts	PIM	PP	SH	GW
1986-87	Calgary Spurs	AJHL	57	38	50	88	....	....	....	48	....	....	....	....	....	....	....	....	....	....	....	....	....	....	....	....	....	....
	Seattle Thunderbirds	WHL	4	2	0	2	....	....	....	0	....	....	....	....	....	....	....	....	....	....	....	....	....	....	....	....	....	....
1987-88	Seattle Thunderbirds	WHL	67	17	18	35	....	....	....	87	....	....	....	....	....	....	....	....	....	....	....	....	....	....	....	....	....	....
1988-89	Regina Pats	WHL	21	4	8	12	....	....	....	48	....	....	....	....	....	....	....	....	....	....	....	....	....	....	....	....	....	....
	Swift Current Broncos	WHL	42	16	19	35	....	....	....	69	....	....	....	....	....	....	....	....	....	....	11	10	6	16	20	....	....	....
	Swift Current Broncos	Mem-Cup	5	2	2	4	....	....	....	4	....	....	....	....	....	....	....	....	....	....	....	....	....	....	....	....	....	....
1989-90	Swift Current Broncos	WHL	6	3	2	5	....	....	....	21	....	....	....	....	....	....	....	....	....	....	....	....	....	....	....	....	....	....
	Kamloops Blazers	WHL	43	27	35	62	....	....	....	53	....	....	....	....	....	....	....	....	....	....	17	3	13	16	28	....	....	....
	Edmonton Oilers	**NHL**	**3**	**0**	**1**	**1**	**0**	**1**	**1**	**2**	**0**	**0**	**0**	**0**	**0.0**	**1**	**0**	**1**	**0**	**0**	....	....	....	....	....	....	....	....
	Kamloops Blazers	Mem-Cup	2	1	0	1	....	....	....	6	....	....	....	....	....	....	....	....	....	....	....	....	....	....	....	....	....	....

Season	Club	League	GP	G	A	Pts	AG	AA	APts	PIM	PP	SH	GW	S	%	TGF	PGF	TGA	PGA	+/–	GP	G	A	Pts	PIM	PP	SH	GW
			REGULAR SEASON																		PLAYOFFS							
1990-91	Cape Breton Oilers	AHL	62	20	9	29				39											2	0	0	0	0			
1991-92	Cape Breton Oilers	AHL	2	0	1	1				0																		
	Winston-Salem Thunderbirds	ECHL	53	25	29	54				110											5	7	2	9	4			
1992-93	Canada	Nat-Team	53	24	19	43				49																		
1993-94	Milwaukee Admirals	IHL	32	7	13	20				10											4	1	0	1	0			
1994-95	Syracuse Crunch	AHL	3	2	0	2				0																		
	Milwaukee Admirals	IHL	37	9	10	19				26											7	1	2	3	4			
1995-96	HC Asiago	Italy	7	1	4	5				12																		
	Canada	Nat-Team	3	0	0	0				0																		
	Milwaukee Admirals	IHL	7	0	0	0				0																		
	Raleigh IceCaps	ECHL	28	11	17	28				26											4	0	0	0	0			
1996-97	Orlando Solar Bears	IHL	58	9	21	30				32											2	0	1	1	0			
1997-98	New Orleans Brass	ECHL	13	4	11	15				23											4	0	3	3	2			
	Orlando Solar Bears	IHL	36	8	3	11				17																		
1998-99	Charlotte Checkers	ECHL	9	3	5	8				12																		
	NHL Totals		**3**	**0**	**1**	**1**	**0**	**1**	**1**	**2**	**0**	**0**	**0**	**0**	**0.0**	**1**	**0**	**1**	**0**									

• SIMARD, Martin

RW – R. 6'1", 215 lbs. b: Montreal, Que., 6/25/1966.

Season	Club	League	GP	G	A	Pts	AG	AA	APts	PIM	PP	SH	GW	S	%	TGF	PGF	TGA	PGA	+/–	GP	G	A	Pts	PIM	PP	SH	GW
1983-84	Quebec Remparts	QMJHL	59	6	10	16				26											4	0	0	0	0			
1984-85	Granby Bisons	QMJHL	58	22	31	53				78											8	3	7	10	21			
1985-86	Granby Bisons	QMJHL	54	32	28	60				129																		
	Hull Olympiques	QMJHL	14	8	8	16				55											14	8	19	27	19			
	Hull Olympiques	Mem-Cup	5	0	1	1				0																		
1986-87	Granby Bisons	QMJHL	41	30	47	77				105											8	3	7	10	21			
1987-88	Salt Lake Golden Eagles	IHL	82	8	23	31				281											19	6	3	9	100			
1988-89	Salt Lake Golden Eagles	IHL	71	13	15	28				221											14	4	0	4	45			
1989-90	Salt Lake Golden Eagles	IHL	59	22	23	45				151											11	5	8	13	12			
1990-91	**Calgary Flames**	**NHL**	**16**	**0**	**2**	**2**	**0**	**2**	**2**	**53**	**0**	**0**	**0**	**7**	**0.0**	**5**	**0**	**5**	**0**	**0**								
	Salt Lake Golden Eagles	IHL	54	24	25	49				113											4	3	0	3	20			
1991-92	**Calgary Flames**	**NHL**	**21**	**1**	**3**	**4**	**1**	**2**	**3**	**119**	**1**	**0**	**0**	**11**	**9.1**	**7**	**1**	**10**	**0**	**–4**								
	Salt Lake Golden Eagles	IHL	11	3	7	10				51																		
	Halifax Citadels	AHL	10	5	3	8				26																		
1992-93	**Tampa Bay Lightning**	**NHL**	**7**	**0**	**0**	**0**	**0**	**0**	**0**	**11**	**0**	**0**	**0**	**1**	**0.0**	**1**	**0**	**2**	**0**	**–1**								
	Atlanta Knights	IHL	19	5	5	10				77																		
	Halifax Citadels	AHL	13	3	4	7				17																		
1993-94	Cornwall Aces	AHL	57	10	10	20				152											7	3	1	4	7			
1994-95	Milwaukee Admirals	IHL	57	7	5	12				100											5	0	0	0	2			
1995-96	Providence Bruins	AHL	69	13	25	38				137											4	1	1	2	6			
1996-97	Providence Bruins	AHL	69	13	25	38				137											9	1	0	1	10			
1997-98	Springfield Falcons	AHL	35	9	5	14				89																		
	NHL Totals		**44**	**1**	**5**	**6**	**1**	**4**	**5**	**183**	**1**	**0**	**0**	**19**	**5.3**	**13**	**1**	**17**	**0**									

Signed as a free agent by **Calgary**, May 19, 1987. Traded to **Quebec** by **Calgary** for Greg Smyth, March 10, 1992. Traded to **Tampa Bay** by **Quebec** to complete transaction that sent Tim Hunter to Quebec (June 19, 1992), September 14, 1992. Traded to **Quebec** by **Tampa Bay** with Steve Tuttle and Michel Mongeau for Herb Ragglan, February 12, 1993. Signed as a free agent by **Phoenix**, August 6, 1997.

• SIMMER, Charlie

Charles Robert "Chaz" LW – L. 6'3", 210 lbs. b: Terrace Bay, Ont., 3/20/1954. California's 4th, 39th overall, in 1974.

Season	Club	League	GP	G	A	Pts	AG	AA	APts	PIM	PP	SH	GW	S	%	TGF	PGF	TGA	PGA	+/–	GP	G	A	Pts	PIM	PP	SH	GW
1971-72	Kenora Muskies	MJHL	45	14	31	45				77																		
1972-73	Kenora Muskies	MJHL	48	43	*68	*111				57																		
1973-74	Sault Ste. Marie Greyhounds	OMJHL	70	45	54	99				137																		
1974-75	**California Golden Seals**	**NHL**	**35**	**8**	**13**	**21**	**7**	**10**	**17**	**26**	**2**	**0**	**0**	**46**	**17.4**	**28**	**8**	**24**	**2**	**–2**								
	Salt Lake Golden Eagles	CHL	47	12	29	41				86																		
1975-76	**California Golden Seals**	**NHL**	**21**	**1**	**1**	**2**	**1**	**1**	**2**	**22**	**1**	**0**	**0**	**12**	**8.3**	**4**	**2**	**15**	**4**	**–9**								
	Salt Lake Golden Eagles	CHL	42	23	16	39				96																		
1976-77	**Cleveland Barons**	**NHL**	**24**	**2**	**0**	**2**	**2**	**0**	**2**	**16**	**1**	**0**	**0**	**42**	**4.8**	**8**	**4**	**21**	**6**	**–11**								
	Salt Lake Golden Eagles	CHL	51	32	30	62				37																		
1977-78	**Los Angeles Kings**	**NHL**	**3**	**0**	**0**	**0**	**0**	**0**	**0**	**2**	**0**	**0**	**0**	**4**	**0.0**	**0**	**0**	**0**	**0**	**0**								
	Springfield Indians	AHL	75	42	41	83				100											4	0	1	1	5			
1978-79	**Los Angeles Kings**	**NHL**	**38**	**21**	**27**	**48**	**18**	**20**	**38**	**16**	**8**	**0**	**0**	**112**	**18.8**	**76**	**31**	**37**	**1**	**9**	**2**	**1**	**0**	**1**	**2**	**1**	**0**	**0**
	Springfield Indians	AHL	39	13	23	36				33																		
1979-80	**Los Angeles Kings**	**NHL**	**64**	***56**	**45**	**101**	**48**	**33**	**81**	**65**	**21**	**0**	**8**	**213**	**26.3**	**146**	**56**	**44**	**1**	**47**	**3**	**2**	**0**	**2**	**0**	**1**	**0**	**0**
1980-81	**Los Angeles Kings**	**NHL**	**65**	**56**	**49**	**105**	**44**	**33**	**77**	**62**	**23**	**0**	**9**	**171**	**32.7**	**152**	**62**	**59**	**0**	**31**								
1981-82	**Los Angeles Kings**	**NHL**	**50**	**15**	**24**	**39**	**12**	**16**	**28**	**42**	**3**	**0**	**2**	**88**	**17.0**	**69**	**29**	**52**	**5**	**–7**	**10**	**4**	**7**	**11**	**22**	**1**	**0**	**1**
1982-83	**Los Angeles Kings**	**NHL**	**80**	**29**	**51**	**80**	**24**	**35**	**59**	**51**	**11**	**1**	**1**	**183**	**15.8**	**128**	**53**	**89**	**14**	**0**								
	Canada	WEC-A	10	2	3	5				8																		
1983-84	**Los Angeles Kings**	**NHL**	**79**	**44**	**48**	**92**	**35**	**33**	**68**	**78**	**13**	**1**	**4**	**188**	**23.4**	**125**	**41**	**79**	**2**	**7**								
1984-85	**Los Angeles Kings**	**NHL**	**5**	**1**	**0**	**1**	**1**	**0**	**1**	**4**	**0**	**0**	**0**	**8**	**12.5**	**1**	**0**	**5**	**0**	**–4**								
	Boston Bruins	**NHL**	**63**	**33**	**30**	**63**	**27**	**20**	**47**	**35**	**12**	**0**	**5**	**128**	**25.8**	**90**	**33**	**44**	**1**	**14**	**5**	**2**	**2**	**4**	**2**	**0**	**0**	**0**
1985-86	**Boston Bruins**	**NHL**	**55**	**36**	**24**	**60**	**29**	**16**	**45**	**42**	**14**	**0**	**5**	**141**	**25.5**	**92**	**45**	**35**	**0**	**12**	**3**	**0**	**0**	**0**	**4**	**0**	**0**	**0**
1986-87	**Boston Bruins**	**NHL**	**80**	**29**	**40**	**69**	**25**	**29**	**54**	**59**	**11**	**0**	**4**	**137**	**21.2**	**117**	**38**	**59**	**0**	**20**	**1**	**0**	**0**	**0**	**2**	**0**	**0**	**0**
1987-88	**Pittsburgh Penguins**	**NHL**	**50**	**11**	**17**	**28**	**9**	**12**	**21**	**24**	**5**	**0**	**3**	**58**	**19.0**	**54**	**26**	**22**	**0**	**6**								
1988-89	EHC Frankfurt	Germany	36	19	32	51				68											4	1	2	3	13			
1989-90			DID NOT PLAY																									
1990-91	San Diego Gulls	IHL	43	16	7	23				63																		
1991-92	San Diego Gulls	IHL	1	0	0	0				0																		
	NHL Totals		**712**	**342**	**369**	**711**	**282**	**258**	**540**	**544**	**125**	**2**	**41**	**1531**	**22.3**	**1090**	**428**	**585**	**36**		**24**	**9**	**9**	**18**	**32**	**3**	**0**	**1**

MJHL First All-Star Team (1973) • CHL Second All-Star Team (1977) • AHL Second All-Star Team (1978) • NHL First All-Star Team (1980, 1981) • Won Bill Masterton Trophy (1986) • Played in NHL All-Star Game (1981, 1984)

Transferred to **Cleveland** after **California** franchise relocated, August 26, 1976. Signed as a free agent by **LA Kings**, August 8, 1977. Traded to **Boston** by **LA Kings** for Boston's 1st round choice (Dan Gratton) in 1985 Entry Draft, October 24, 1984. Claimed by **Pittsburgh** from **Boston** in Waiver Draft, October 5, 1987.

• SIMMONS, Al

Allan Kenneth D – R. 6', 170 lbs. b: Winnipeg, Man., 9/25/1951. California's 6th, 85th overall, in 1971.

Season	Club	League	GP	G	A	Pts	AG	AA	APts	PIM	PP	SH	GW	S	%	TGF	PGF	TGA	PGA	+/–	GP	G	A	Pts	PIM	PP	SH	GW
1970-71	Winnipeg Jets	WCJHL	65	14	39	53				89											12	3	4	7	22			
1971-72	**California Golden Seals**	**NHL**	**1**	**0**	**0**	**0**	**0**	**0**	**0**	**0**	**0**	**0**	**0**	**4**	**0.0**	**3**	**0**	**4**	**0**	**–1**								
	Columbus Seals	IHL	60	2	12	14				26																		
1972-73	Salt Lake Golden Eagles	WHL	72	19	22	41				50											9	1	4	5	6			
1973-74	**Boston Bruins**	**NHL**	**3**	**0**	**0**	**0**	**0**	**0**	**0**	**0**	**0**	**0**	**0**	**1**	**0.0**	**0**	**0**	**1**	**0**	**–1**	**1**	**0**	**0**	**0**	**0**	**0**	**0**	**0**
	Boston Braves	AHL	75	5	32	37				41																		
1974-75	Rochester Americans	AHL	68	7	36	43				60											12	2	5	7	13			
1975-76	**Boston Bruins**	**NHL**	**7**	**0**	**1**	**1**	**0**	**1**	**1**	**21**	**0**	**0**	**0**	**6**	**0.0**	**6**	**0**	**9**	**3**	**0**								
	Rochester Americans	AHL	5	0	5	5				13																		
	Providence Reds	AHL	56	2	25	27				48											3	0	2	2	0			
	NHL Totals		**11**	**0**	**1**	**1**	**0**	**1**	**1**	**21**	**0**	**0**	**0**	**11**	**0.0**	**9**	**0**	**14**	**3**		**1**	**0**	**0**	**0**	**0**	**0**	**0**	**0**

AHL Second All-Star Team (1976)

Claimed by **San Diego** (WHL) from **California** in Reverse Draft, June 13, 1973. Traded to **Boston** by **San Diego** for cash, February 7, 1974. Traded to **NY Rangers** by **Boston** for cash, November 14, 1975.

• SIMON, Chris

LW – L. 6'4", 235 lbs. b: Wawa, Ont., 1/30/1972. Philadelphia's 2nd, 25th overall, in 1990.

			REGULAR SEASON																		PLAYOFFS							
Season	Club	League	GP	G	A	Pts	AG	AA	APts	PIM	PP	SH	GW	S	%	TGF	PGF	TGA	PGA	+/-	GP	G	A	Pts	PIM	PP	SH	GW
1986-87	Wawa Midget Flyers	OMHA	36	12	20	32	....	....	....	108	....	....	....	....	....	....	....	....	....	....	....	....	....	....	....	....	....	....
1987-88	Sault Ste. Marie Thunderbirds	OMHA	55	42	36	78	....	....	....	172	....	....	....	....	....	....	....	....	....	....	....	....	....	....	....	....	....	....
1988-89	Ottawa 67's	OHL	36	4	2	6	....	....	....	31	....	....	....	....	....	....	....	....	....	....	....	....	....	....	....	....	....	....
1989-90	Ottawa 67's	OHL	57	36	38	74	....	....	....	146	....	....	....	....	....	....	....	....	....	....	3	2	1	3	4	....	....	....
1990-91	Ottawa 67's	OHL	20	16	6	22	....	....	....	69	....	....	....	....	....	....	....	....	....	....	17	5	9	14	59	....	....	....
1991-92	Ottawa 67's	OHL	2	1	1	2	....	....	....	24	....	....	....	....	....	....	....	....	....	....	....	....	....	....	....	....	....	....
	Sault Ste. Marie Greyhounds	OHL	31	19	25	44	....	....	....	143	....	....	....	....	....	....	....	....	....	....	11	5	8	13	49	....	....	....
	Sault Ste. Marie Greyhounds	Mem-Cup	4	3	3	6	....	....	....	14	....	....	....	....	....	....	....	....	....	....	....	....	....	....	....	....	....	....
1992-93	**Quebec Nordiques**	**NHL**	**16**	**1**	**1**	**2**	**1**	**1**	**2**	**67**	**0**	**0**	**1**	**15**	**6.7**	**6**	**0**	**8**	**0**	**–2**	**5**	**0**	**0**	**0**	**26**	**0**	**0**	**0**
	Halifax Citadels	AHL	36	12	6	18	....	....	....	131	....	....	....	....	....	....	....	....	....	....	....	....	....	....	....	....	....	....
1993-94	**Quebec Nordiques**	**NHL**	**37**	**4**	**4**	**8**	**4**	**3**	**7**	**132**	**0**	**0**	**1**	**39**	**10.3**	**16**	**2**	**16**	**0**	**–2**	....	....	....	....	....	....	....	....
1994-95	**Quebec Nordiques**	**NHL**	**29**	**3**	**9**	**12**	**5**	**13**	**18**	**106**	**0**	**0**	**0**	**33**	**9.1**	**20**	**1**	**6**	**1**	**14**	**6**	**1**	**1**	**2**	**19**	**0**	**0**	**1**
1995-96 ♦	**Colorado Avalanche**	**NHL**	**64**	**16**	**18**	**34**	**16**	**15**	**31**	**250**	**4**	**0**	**1**	**105**	**15.2**	**51**	**11**	**30**	**0**	**10**	**12**	**1**	**2**	**3**	**11**	**0**	**0**	**0**
1996-97	**Washington Capitals**	**NHL**	**42**	**9**	**13**	**22**	**10**	**12**	**22**	**165**	**3**	**0**	**1**	**89**	**10.1**	**37**	**7**	**32**	**1**	**–1**	....	....	....	....	....	....	....	....
1997-98	**Washington Capitals**	**NHL**	**28**	**7**	**10**	**17**	**8**	**10**	**18**	**38**	**4**	**0**	**1**	**71**	**9.9**	**34**	**15**	**20**	**0**	**–1**	**18**	**1**	**0**	**1**	**26**	**0**	**0**	**0**
1998-99	**Washington Capitals**	**NHL**	**23**	**3**	**7**	**10**	**4**	**7**	**11**	**48**	**0**	**0**	**0**	**29**	**10.3**	**12**	**1**	**15**	**0**	**–4**	....	....	....	....	....	....	....	....
99-2000	**Washington Capitals**	**NHL**	**75**	**29**	**20**	**49**	**33**	**19**	**52**	**146**	**7**	**0**	**5**	**201**	**14.4**	**72**	**21**	**41**	**1**	**11**	**4**	**2**	**0**	**2**	**24**	**0**	**0**	**0**
	NHL Totals		**314**	**72**	**82**	**154**	**81**	**80**	**161**	**952**	**18**	**0**	**10**	**582**	**12.4**	**248**	**58**	**168**	**3**		**45**	**5**	**3**	**8**	**106**	**0**	**0**	**1**

• Missed majority of 1990-91 season recovering from shoulder surgery, October, 1990. Traded to **Quebec** by **Philadelphia** with Philadelphia's 1st round choice (later traded to Toronto — later traded to Washington — Washington selected Nolan Baumgartner) in 1994 Entry Draft to complete transaction that sent Eric Lindros to Philadelphia (June 30, 1992), July 21, 1992. Transferred to **Colorado** after **Quebec** franchise relocated, June 21, 1995. Traded to **Washington** by **Colorado** with Curtis Leschyshyn for Keith Jones and Washington's 1st (Scott Parker) and 4th (later traded back to Washington — Washington selected Krys Barch) round choices in 1998 Entry Draft, November 2, 1996.

• SIMON, Jason

LW – L. 6'1", 210 lbs. b: Sarnia, Ont., 3/21/1969. New Jersey's 9th, 215th overall, in 1989.

Season	Club	League	GP	G	A	Pts	AG	AA	APts	PIM	PP	SH	GW	S	%	TGF	PGF	TGA	PGA	+/-	GP	G	A	Pts	PIM	PP	SH	GW
1985-86	Chatham Maroons	OJHL-B	32	5	19	24	....	....	....	118	....	....	....	....	....	....	....	....	....	....	....	....	....	....	....	....	....	....
1986-87	London Knights	OHL	33	1	2	3	....	....	....	33	....	....	....	....	....	....	....	....	....	....	....	....	....	....	....	....	....	....
	Sudbury Wolves	OHL	26	2	3	5	....	....	....	50	....	....	....	....	....	....	....	....	....	....	....	....	....	....	....	....	....	....
1987-88	Sudbury Wolves	OHL	26	5	7	12	....	....	....	35	....	....	....	....	....	....	....	....	....	....	....	....	....	....	....	....	....	....
	Hamilton Steelhawks	OHL	29	5	13	18	....	....	....	124	....	....	....	....	....	....	....	....	....	....	11	0	2	2	15	....	....	....
1988-89	Kingston Raiders	OHL	17	7	12	19	....	....	....	58	....	....	....	....	....	....	....	....	....	....	....	....	....	....	....	....	....	....
	Windsor Spitfires	OHL	45	16	27	43	....	....	....	135	....	....	....	....	....	....	....	....	....	....	4	1	4	5	13	....	....	....
1989-90	Utica Devils	AHL	16	3	4	7	....	....	....	28	....	....	....	....	....	....	....	....	....	....	2	0	0	0	12	....	....	....
	Nashville Knights	ECHL	13	4	3	7	....	....	....	81	....	....	....	....	....	....	....	....	....	....	5	1	3	4	17	....	....	....
1990-91	Utica Devils	AHL	50	2	12	14	....	....	....	189	....	....	....	....	....	....	....	....	....	....	....	....	....	....	....	....	....	....
	Johnstown Chiefs	ECHL	22	11	9	20	....	....	....	55	....	....	....	....	....	....	....	....	....	....	....	....	....	....	....	....	....	....
1991-92	Utica Devils	AHL	1	0	0	0	....	....	....	12	....	....	....	....	....	....	....	....	....	....	....	....	....	....	....	....	....	....
	San Diego Gulls	IHL	13	1	4	5	....	....	....	45	....	....	....	....	....	....	....	....	....	....	3	0	1	1	9	....	....	....
1992-93	Detroit Falcons	ColHL	11	7	13	20	....	....	....	38	....	....	....	....	....	....	....	....	....	....	....	....	....	....	....	....	....	....
	Flint Generals	ColHL	44	17	32	49	....	....	....	202	....	....	....	....	....	....	....	....	....	....	....	....	....	....	....	....	....	....
1993-94	Salt Lake Golden Eagles	IHL	50	7	7	14	....	....	....	*323	....	....	....	....	....	....	....	....	....	....	....	....	....	....	....	....	....	....
	New York Islanders	**NHL**	**4**	**0**	**0**	**0**	**0**	**0**	**0**	**34**	**0**	**0**	**0**	**0**	**0.0**	**0**	**0**	**0**	**0**	**0**								
	Detroit Falcons	ColHL	13	9	16	25	....	....	....	87	....	....	....	....	....	....	....	....	....	....	....	....	....	....	....	....	....	....
1994-95	Denver Grizzlies	IHL	61	3	6	9	....	....	....	300	....	....	....	....	....	....	....	....	....	....	1	0	0	0	12	....	....	....
1995-96	Springfield Falcons	AHL	18	2	2	4	....	....	....	90	....	....	....	....	....	....	....	....	....	....	7	1	0	1	26	....	....	....
1996-97	**Phoenix Coyotes**	**NHL**	**1**	**0**	**0**	**0**	**0**	**0**	**0**	**0**	**0**	**0**	**0**	**0**	**0.0**	**0**	**0**	**1**	**0**	**–1**	....	....	....	....	....	....	....	....
	Las Vegas Thunder	IHL	64	4	3	7	....	....	....	402	....	....	....	....	....	....	....	....	....	....	3	0	0	0	0	....	....	....
1997-98	Hershey Bears	AHL	26	0	1	1	....	....	....	170	....	....	....	....	....	....	....	....	....	....	....	....	....	....	....	....	....	....
	Quebec Rafales	IHL	30	6	3	9	....	....	....	127	....	....	....	....	....	....	....	....	....	....	....	....	....	....	....	....	....	....
1998-99	Colorado Gold Kings	WCHL	60	16	23	39	....	....	....	419	....	....	....	....	....	....	....	....	....	....	3	1	1	2	17	....	....	....
99-2000	Port Huron Border Cats	UHL	45	21	22	43	....	....	....	118	....	....	....	....	....	....	....	....	....	....	....	....	....	....	....	....	....	....
	Louisville Panthers	AHL	11	1	0	1	....	....	....	28	....	....	....	....	....	....	....	....	....	....	....	....	....	....	....	....	....	....
	NHL Totals		**5**	**0**	**0**	**0**	**0**	**0**	**0**	**34**	**0**	**0**	**0**	**0**	**0.0**	**0**	**0**	**1**	**0**									

Signed as a free agent by **NY Islanders**, January 6, 1994. Signed as a free agent by **Winnipeg**, August 9, 1995. Transferred to **Phoenix** after **Winnipeg** franchise relocated, July 1, 1996. Signed as a free agent by **Colorado**, August 22, 1997.

• SIMON, Todd

C – R. 5'10", 188 lbs. b: Toronto, Ont., 4/21/1972. Buffalo's 10th, 203rd overall, in 1992.

Season	Club	League	GP	G	A	Pts	AG	AA	APts	PIM	PP	SH	GW	S	%	TGF	PGF	TGA	PGA	+/-	GP	G	A	Pts	PIM	PP	SH	GW
1988-89	Don Mills Flyers	MTHL	49	36	48	84	....	....	....	36	....	....	....	....	....	....	....	....	....	....	....	....	....	....	....	....	....	....
1989-90	Port Colborne Schooners	OJHL-B	45	40	43	83	....	....	....	120	....	....	....	....	....	....	....	....	....	....	....	....	....	....	....	....	....	....
	Niagara Falls Thunder	OHL	9	0	1	1	....	....	....	2	....	....	....	....	....	....	....	....	....	....	11	3	1	4	2	....	....	....
1990-91	Niagara Falls Thunder	OHL	65	51	74	125	....	....	....	35	....	....	....	....	....	....	....	....	....	....	14	7	8	15	12	....	....	....
1991-92	Niagara Falls Thunder	OHL	66	53	93	*146	....	....	....	72	....	....	....	....	....	....	....	....	....	....	17	17	24	*41	36	....	....	....
1992-93	Rochester Americans	AHL	67	27	66	93	....	....	....	54	....	....	....	....	....	....	....	....	....	....	12	3	14	17	15	....	....	....
1993-94	**Buffalo Sabres**	**NHL**	**15**	**0**	**1**	**1**	**0**	**1**	**1**	**0**	**0**	**0**	**0**	**14**	**0.0**	**3**	**2**	**4**	**0**	**–3**	**5**	**1**	**0**	**1**	**0**	**1**	**0**	**1**
	Rochester Americans	AHL	55	33	52	85	....	....	....	79	....	....	....	....	....	....	....	....	....	....	....	....	....	....	....	....	....	....
1994-95	Rochester Americans	AHL	69	25	65	90	....	....	....	78	....	....	....	....	....	....	....	....	....	....	5	0	2	2	21	....	....	....
1995-96	Las Vegas Thunder	IHL	52	26	48	74	....	....	....	48	....	....	....	....	....	....	....	....	....	....	....	....	....	....	....	....	....	....
	Detroit Vipers	IHL	29	19	16	35	....	....	....	20	....	....	....	....	....	....	....	....	....	....	12	2	12	14	6	....	....	....
1996-97	Detroit Vipers	IHL	80	21	51	72	....	....	....	46	....	....	....	....	....	....	....	....	....	....	18	4	6	10	12	....	....	....
1997-98	Cincinnati Cyclones	IHL	81	33	72	105	....	....	....	115	....	....	....	....	....	....	....	....	....	....	9	2	4	6	12	....	....	....
1998-99	Cincinnati Cyclones	IHL	81	26	61	87	....	....	....	72	....	....	....	....	....	....	....	....	....	....	3	1	1	2	12	....	....	....
99-2000	Cincinnati Cyclones	IHL	71	19	48	67	....	....	....	58	....	....	....	....	....	....	....	....	....	....	11	2	6	8	23	....	....	....
	NHL Totals		**15**	**0**	**1**	**1**	**0**	**1**	**1**	**0**	**0**	**0**	**0**	**14**	**0.0**	**3**	**2**	**4**	**0**		**5**	**1**	**0**	**1**	**0**	**1**	**0**	**1**

OHL First All-Star Team (1992) • Canadian Major Junior First All-Star Team (1992) • IHL First All-Star Team (1996)

Signed as a free agent by **Carolina**, August 31, 1999.

• SIMONETTI, Frank

Frank J. D – R. 6'1", 190 lbs. b: Melrose, MA, 9/11/1962.

Season	Club	League	GP	G	A	Pts	AG	AA	APts	PIM	PP	SH	GW	S	%	TGF	PGF	TGA	PGA	+/-	GP	G	A	Pts	PIM	PP	SH	GW
1980-1983	Norwich University	ECAC-2	STATISTICS NOT AVAILABLE																									
1983-84	Norwich University	ECAC-2	18	9	19	28	....	....	....	32	....	....	....	....	....	....	....	....	....	....	....	....	....	....	....	....	....	....
1984-85	**Boston Bruins**	**NHL**	**43**	**1**	**5**	**6**	**1**	**3**	**4**	**26**	**0**	**0**	**0**	**36**	**2.8**	**32**	**2**	**35**	**4**	**–1**	**5**	**0**	**1**	**1**	**2**	**0**	**0**	**0**
	Hershey Bears	AHL	31	0	6	6	....	....	....	14	....	....	....	....	....	....	....	....	....	....	....	....	....	....	....	....	....	....
1985-86	**Boston Bruins**	**NHL**	**17**	**1**	**0**	**1**	**1**	**0**	**1**	**14**	**0**	**0**	**0**	**8**	**12.5**	**7**	**0**	**10**	**2**	**–1**	**3**	**0**	**0**	**0**	**0**	**0**	**0**	**0**
	Moncton Golden Flames	AHL	5	0	0	0	....	....	....	2	....	....	....	....	....	....	....	....	....	....	....	....	....	....	....	....	....	....
1986-87	**Boston Bruins**	**NHL**	**25**	**1**	**0**	**1**	**1**	**0**	**1**	**17**	**0**	**0**	**0**	**11**	**9.1**	**10**	**0**	**18**	**2**	**–6**	**4**	**0**	**0**	**0**	**6**	**0**	**0**	**0**
	Moncton Golden Flames	AHL	7	0	1	1	....	....	....	6	....	....	....	....	....	....	....	....	....	....	....	....	....	....	....	....	....	....
1987-88	**Boston Bruins**	**NHL**	**30**	**2**	**3**	**5**	**2**	**2**	**4**	**19**	**0**	**0**	**1**	**20**	**10.0**	**13**	**0**	**13**	**1**	**1**	....	....	....	....	....	....	....	....
	Maine Mariners	AHL	7	0	1	1	....	....	....	4	....	....	....	....	....	....	....	....	....	....	2	0	0	0	2	....	....	....
	NHL Totals		**115**	**5**	**8**	**13**	**5**	**5**	**10**	**76**	**0**	**0**	**1**	**75**	**6.7**	**62**	**2**	**76**	**9**		**12**	**0**	**1**	**1**	**8**	**0**	**0**	**0**

NCAA (College Div.) East All-American Team (1984)

Signed as a free agent by **Boston**, October 4, 1984.

• SIMPSON, Bobby

Robert Sam LW – L. 6', 190 lbs. b: Caughnawaga, Que., 11/17/1956. Atlanta's 3rd, 28th overall, in 1976.

Season	Club	League	GP	G	A	Pts	AG	AA	APts	PIM	PP	SH	GW	S	%	TGF	PGF	TGA	PGA	+/-	GP	G	A	Pts	PIM	PP	SH	GW
1973-74	Sherbrooke Beavers	QMJHL	64	6	21	27	....	....	....	138	....	....	....	....	....	....	....	....	....	....	....	....	....	....	....	....	....	....
1974-75	Sherbrooke Beavers	QMJHL	69	38	47	85	....	....	....	146	....	....	....	....	....	....	....	....	....	....	13	10	12	22	26	....	....	....
	Sherbrooke Beavers	Mem-Cup	3	4	1	5	....	....	....	6	....	....	....	....	....	....	....	....	....	....	....	....	....	....	....	....	....	....
1975-76	Sherbrooke Beavers	QMJHL	68	56	77	133	....	....	....	126	....	....	....	....	....	....	....	....	....	....	17	11	14	25	19	....	....	....
1976-77	**Atlanta Flames**	**NHL**	**72**	**13**	**10**	**23**	**12**	**8**	**20**	**45**	**0**	**0**	**2**	**118**	**11.0**	**42**	**3**	**37**	**0**	**2**	**2**	**0**	**1**	**1**	**0**	**0**	**0**	**0**

			REGULAR SEASON																		PLAYOFFS							
Season	Club	League	GP	G	A	Pts	AG	AA	APts	PIM	PP	SH	GW	S	%	TGF	PGF	TGA	PGA	+/–	GP	G	A	Pts	PIM	PP	SH	GW
1977-78	**Atlanta Flames**	**NHL**	**55**	**10**	**8**	**18**	**9**	**6**	**15**	**49**	**0**	**0**	**1**	**91**	**11.0**	**31**	**1**	**30**	**0**	**0**	**2**	**0**	**0**	**0**	**2**	**0**	**0**	**0**
	Tulsa Oilers	CHL	14	8	8	16	....	....	....	34	....	....	....	....	....	....	....	....	....	....	....	....	....	....	....	....	....	....
1978-79	Tulsa Oilers	CHL	49	14	19	33	....	....	....	38	....	....	....	....	....	....	....	....	....	....	....	....	....	....	....	....	....	....
1979-80	**St. Louis Blues**	**NHL**	**18**	**2**	**2**	**4**	**2**	**1**	**3**	**0**	**0**	**0**	**0**	**20**	**10.0**	**7**	**1**	**8**	**0**	**–2**	....	....	....	....	....	....	....	....
	Salt Lake Golden Eagles	CHL	41	19	12	31	....	....	....	58	....	....	....	....	....	....	....	....	....	....	12	4	5	9	9	....	....	....
1980-81	Salt Lake Golden Eagles	CHL	8	2	1	3	....	....	....	4	....	....	....	....	....	....	....	....	....	....	....	....	....	....	....	....	....	....
	Muskegon Mohawks	IHL	42	17	26	43	....	....	....	42	....	....	....	....	....	....	....	....	....	....	3	2	1	3	0	....	....	....
1981-82	**Pittsburgh Penguins**	**NHL**	**26**	**9**	**9**	**18**	**7**	**6**	**13**	**4**	**0**	**0**	**1**	**37**	**24.3**	**25**	**0**	**28**	**0**	**–3**	**2**	**0**	**0**	**0**	**0**	**0**	**0**	**0**
	Erie Blades	AHL	48	25	23	48	....	....	....	45	....	....	....	....	....	....	....	....	....	....	....	....	....	....	....	....	....	....
1982-83	**Pittsburgh Penguins**	**NHL**	**4**	**1**	**0**	**1**	**1**	**0**	**1**	**0**	**0**	**0**	**0**	**3**	**33.3**	**1**	**0**	**2**	**0**	**–1**	....	....	....	....	....	....	....	....
	Baltimore Skipjacks	AHL	61	24	27	51	....	....	....	24	....	....	....	....	....	....	....	....	....	....	....	....	....	....	....	....	....	....
1983-84	Baltimore Skipjacks	AHL	71	16	16	32	....	....	....	36	....	....	....	....	....	....	....	....	....	....	10	7	5	12	8	....	....	....
1984-85	Indianapolis Checkers	IHL	55	16	24	40	....	....	....	65	....	....	....	....	....	....	....	....	....	....	....	....	....	....	....	....	....	....
	Salt Lake Golden Eagles	IHL	28	7	11	18	....	....	....	25	....	....	....	....	....	....	....	....	....	....	7	1	0	1	19	....	....	....
1985-86	Salt Lake Golden Eagles	IHL	74	6	38	44	....	....	....	37	....	....	....	....	....	....	....	....	....	....	5	2	3	5	8	....	....	....
1986-87	Salt Lake Golden Eagles	IHL	9	2	3	5	....	....	....	12	....	....	....	....	....	....	....	....	....	....	....	....	....	....	....	....	....	....
	Peoria Rivermen	IHL	58	14	29	43	....	....	....	32	....	....	....	....	....	....	....	....	....	....	....	....	....	....	....	....	....	....
	NHL Totals		**175**	**35**	**29**	**64**	**31**	**21**	**52**	**98**	**0**	**0**	**4**	**269**	**13.0**	**106**	**5**	**105**	**0**		**6**	**0**	**1**	**1**	**2**	**0**	**0**	**0**

Traded to **St. Louis** by **Atlanta** for Curt Bennett, May 24, 1979. Claimed by **St. Louis** as a fill-in during Expansion Draft, June 13, 1979. Signed as a free agent by **Pittsburgh**, October 1, 1981.

• SIMPSON, Craig

Craig Andrew LW – R. 6'2", 195 lbs. b: London, Ont., 2/15/1967. Pittsburgh's 1st, 2nd overall, in 1985.

Season	Club	League	GP	G	A	Pts	AG	AA	APts	PIM	PP	SH	GW	S	%	TGF	PGF	TGA	PGA	+/–	GP	G	A	Pts	PIM	PP	SH	GW
1982-83	London Diamonds	OJHL-B	42	*47	*64	*111	....	....	....	68	....	....	....	....	....	....	....	....	....	....	....	....	....	....	....	....	....	....
1983-84	Michigan State Spartans	CCHA	46	14	43	57	....	....	....	38	....	....	....	....	....	....	....	....	....	....	....	....	....	....	....	....	....	....
1984-85	Michigan State Spartans	CCHA	42	31	53	84	....	....	....	33	....	....	....	....	....	....	....	....	....	....	....	....	....	....	....	....	....	....
1985-86	**Pittsburgh Penguins**	**NHL**	**76**	**11**	**17**	**28**	**9**	**11**	**20**	**49**	**2**	**1**	**0**	**74**	**14.9**	**46**	**13**	**32**	**0**	**1**	....	....	....	....	....	....	....	....
1986-87	**Pittsburgh Penguins**	**NHL**	**72**	**26**	**25**	**51**	**22**	**18**	**40**	**57**	**7**	**0**	**3**	**133**	**19.5**	**87**	**21**	**55**	**0**	**11**	....	....	....	....	....	....	....	....
1987-88	**Pittsburgh Penguins**	**NHL**	**21**	**13**	**13**	**26**	**11**	**9**	**20**	**34**	**4**	**0**	**3**	**59**	**22.0**	**34**	**10**	**23**	**4**	**5**	....	....	....	....	....	....	....	....
♦	**Edmonton Oilers**	**NHL**	**59**	**43**	**21**	**64**	**37**	**15**	**52**	**43**	**18**	**0**	**5**	**118**	**36.4**	**104**	**41**	**49**	**1**	**15**	**19**	**13**	**6**	**19**	**26**	**3**	**0**	**3**
1988-89	**Edmonton Oilers**	**NHL**	**66**	**35**	**41**	**76**	**30**	**29**	**59**	**80**	**17**	**0**	**4**	**121**	**28.9**	**102**	**44**	**62**	**1**	**–3**	**7**	**2**	**0**	**2**	**10**	**1**	**0**	**1**
1989-90♦	**Edmonton Oilers**	**NHL**	**80**	**29**	**32**	**61**	**25**	**23**	**48**	**180**	**7**	**0**	**2**	**129**	**22.5**	**94**	**33**	**65**	**2**	**–2**	**22**	***16**	**15**	***31**	**8**	**6**	**0**	**3**
1990-91	**Edmonton Oilers**	**NHL**	**75**	**30**	**27**	**57**	**28**	**21**	**49**	**66**	**15**	**0**	**5**	**143**	**21.0**	**83**	**37**	**54**	**0**	**–8**	**18**	**5**	**11**	**16**	**12**	**1**	**0**	**0**
1991-92	**Edmonton Oilers**	**NHL**	**79**	**24**	**37**	**61**	**22**	**28**	**50**	**80**	**6**	**0**	**2**	**128**	**18.8**	**101**	**34**	**60**	**1**	**8**	**1**	**0**	**0**	**0**	**0**	**0**	**0**	**0**
1992-93	**Edmonton Oilers**	**NHL**	**60**	**24**	**22**	**46**	**20**	**15**	**35**	**36**	**12**	**0**	**3**	**91**	**26.4**	**70**	**36**	**49**	**1**	**–14**	....	....	....	....	....	....	....	....
1993-94	**Buffalo Sabres**	**NHL**	**22**	**8**	**8**	**16**	**7**	**6**	**13**	**8**	**2**	**0**	**2**	**28**	**28.6**	**25**	**10**	**18**	**0**	**–3**	....	....	....	....	....	....	....	....
1994-95	**Buffalo Sabres**	**NHL**	**24**	**4**	**7**	**11**	**7**	**10**	**17**	**26**	**1**	**0**	**0**	**20**	**20.0**	**13**	**6**	**12**	**0**	**–5**	....	....	....	....	....	....	....	....
	NHL Totals		**634**	**247**	**250**	**497**	**218**	**185**	**403**	**659**	**91**	**1**	**29**	**1044**	**23.7**	**759**	**285**	**479**	**10**		**67**	**36**	**32**	**68**	**56**	**11**	**0**	**7**

CCHA First All-Star Team (1985) • NCAA West First All-American Team (1985)

Traded to **Edmonton** by **Pittsburgh** with Dave Hannan, Moe Mantha and Chris Joseph for Paul Coffey, Dave Hunter and Wayne Van Dorp, November 24, 1987. Traded to **Buffalo** by **Edmonton** for Jozef Cierny and Buffalo's 4th round choice (Jussi Tarvainen) in 1994 Entry Draft, September 1, 1993. • Suffered eventual career-ending back injury in game vs. Tampa Bay, December 1, 1993.

• SIMPSON, Reid

LW – L. 6'2", 220 lbs. b: Flin Flon, Man., 5/21/1969. Philadelphia's 3rd, 72nd overall, in 1989.

Season	Club	League	GP	G	A	Pts	AG	AA	APts	PIM	PP	SH	GW	S	%	TGF	PGF	TGA	PGA	+/–	GP	G	A	Pts	PIM	PP	SH	GW
1984-85	Flin Flon Midget Bombers	MAHA	50	60	70	130	....	....	....	100	....	....	....	....	....	....	....	....	....	....	....	....	....	....	....	....	....	....
1985-86	Flin Flon Bombers	MJHL	40	20	21	41	....	....	....	200	....	....	....	....	....	....	....	....	....	....	....	....	....	....	....	....	....	....
	New Westminster Bruins	WHL	2	0	0	0	....	....	....	0	....	....	....	....	....	....	....	....	....	....	....	....	....	....	....	....	....	....
1986-87	Prince Albert Raiders	WHL	47	3	8	11	....	....	....	105	....	....	....	....	....	....	....	....	....	....	8	2	3	5	13	....	....	....
1987-88	Prince Albert Raiders	WHL	72	13	14	27	....	....	....	164	....	....	....	....	....	....	....	....	....	....	10	1	0	1	43	....	....	....
1988-89	Prince Albert Raiders	WHL	59	26	29	55	....	....	....	264	....	....	....	....	....	....	....	....	....	....	4	2	1	3	30	....	....	....
1989-90	Prince Albert Raiders	WHL	29	15	17	32	....	....	....	121	....	....	....	....	....	....	....	....	....	....	14	4	7	11	34	....	....	....
	Hershey Bears	AHL	28	2	2	4	....	....	....	175	....	....	....	....	....	....	....	....	....	....	....	....	....	....	....	....	....	....
1990-91	Hershey Bears	AHL	54	9	15	24	....	....	....	183	....	....	....	....	....	....	....	....	....	....	1	0	0	0	0	....	....	....
1991-92	**Philadelphia Flyers**	**NHL**	**1**	**0**	**0**	**0**	**0**	**0**	**0**	**0**	**0**	**0**	**0**	**0**	**0.0**	**0**	**0**	**0**	**0**	**0**	....	....	....	....	....	....	....	....
	Hershey Bears	AHL	60	11	7	18	....	....	....	145	....	....	....	....	....	....	....	....	....	....	....	....	....	....	....	....	....	....
1992-93	**Minnesota North Stars**	**NHL**	**1**	**0**	**0**	**0**	**0**	**0**	**0**	**5**	**0**	**0**	**0**	**0**	**0.0**	**0**	**0**	**0**	**0**	**0**	....	....	....	....	....	....	....	....
	Kalamazoo Wings	IHL	45	5	5	10	....	....	....	193	....	....	....	....	....	....	....	....	....	....	....	....	....	....	....	....	....	....
1993-94	Kalamazoo Wings	IHL	5	0	0	0	....	....	....	16	....	....	....	....	....	....	....	....	....	....	....	....	....	....	....	....	....	....
	Albany River Rats	AHL	37	9	5	14	....	....	....	135	....	....	....	....	....	....	....	....	....	....	5	1	1	2	18	....	....	....
1994-95	Albany River Rats	AHL	70	18	25	43	....	....	....	268	....	....	....	....	....	....	....	....	....	....	14	1	8	9	13	....	....	....
	New Jersey Devils	**NHL**	**9**	**0**	**0**	**0**	**0**	**0**	**0**	**27**	**0**	**0**	**0**	**5**	**0.0**	**1**	**0**	**2**	**0**	**–1**	....	....	....	....	....	....	....	....
1995-96	**New Jersey Devils**	**NHL**	**23**	**1**	**5**	**6**	**1**	**4**	**5**	**79**	**0**	**0**	**0**	**8**	**12.5**	**7**	**0**	**5**	**0**	**2**	....	....	....	....	....	....	....	....
	Albany River Rats	AHL	6	1	3	4	....	....	....	17	....	....	....	....	....	....	....	....	....	....	....	....	....	....	....	....	....	....
1996-97	**New Jersey Devils**	**NHL**	**27**	**0**	**4**	**4**	**0**	**4**	**4**	**60**	**0**	**0**	**0**	**17**	**0.0**	**6**	**1**	**5**	**0**	**0**	**5**	**0**	**0**	**0**	**29**	**0**	**0**	**0**
	Albany River Rats	AHL	3	0	0	0	....	....	....	10	....	....	....	....	....	....	....	....	....	....	....	....	....	....	....	....	....	....
1997-98	**New Jersey Devils**	**NHL**	**6**	**0**	**0**	**0**	**0**	**0**	**0**	**16**	**0**	**0**	**0**	**5**	**0.0**	**2**	**0**	**4**	**0**	**–2**	....	....	....	....	....	....	....	....
	Chicago Blackhawks	**NHL**	**38**	**3**	**2**	**5**	**4**	**2**	**6**	**102**	**1**	**0**	**0**	**19**	**15.8**	**7**	**2**	**6**	**0**	**–1**	....	....	....	....	....	....	....	....
1998-99	**Chicago Blackhawks**	**NHL**	**53**	**5**	**4**	**9**	**6**	**4**	**10**	**145**	**1**	**0**	**0**	**23**	**21.7**	**12**	**1**	**9**	**0**	**2**	....	....	....	....	....	....	....	....
99-2000	Cleveland Lumberjacks	IHL	12	2	2	4	....	....	....	56	....	....	....	....	....	....	....	....	....	....	....	....	....	....	....	....	....	....
	Tampa Bay Lightning	**NHL**	**26**	**1**	**0**	**1**	**1**	**0**	**1**	**103**	**0**	**0**	**0**	**13**	**7.7**	**3**	**0**	**6**	**0**	**–3**	....	....	....	....	....	....	....	....
	NHL Totals		**184**	**10**	**15**	**25**	**12**	**14**	**26**	**537**	**2**	**0**	**0**	**90**	**11.1**	**38**	**4**	**37**	**0**		**5**	**0**	**0**	**0**	**29**	**0**	**0**	**0**

Signed as a free agent by **Minnesota**, December 14, 1992. Transferred to **Dallas** after **Minnesota** franchise relocated, June 9, 1993. Traded to **New Jersey** by **Dallas** with Roy Mitchell for future considerations, March 21, 1994. Traded to **Chicago** by **New Jersey** for Chicago's 4th round choice (Mikko Jokela) in 1998 Entry Draft and future considerations, January 8, 1998. Traded to **Tampa Bay** by **Chicago** with Bryan Muir for Michael Nylander, November 12, 1999. • Missed remainder of 1999-2000 season recovering from jaw injury suffered in game vs. NY Islanders, January 13, 2000.

• SIMPSON, Todd

Todd W. D – L. 6'3", 215 lbs. b: North Vancouver, B.C., 5/28/1973.

Season	Club	League	GP	G	A	Pts	AG	AA	APts	PIM	PP	SH	GW	S	%	TGF	PGF	TGA	PGA	+/–	GP	G	A	Pts	PIM	PP	SH	GW
1990-91	Fort Saskatchewan Traders	AJHL	STATISTICS NOT AVAILABLE																									
1991-92	Brown University	ECAC	18	1	4	5	....	....	....	38	....	....	....	....	....	....	....	....	....	....	....	....	....	....	....	....	....	....
1992-93	Tri-City Americans	WHL	69	5	18	23	....	....	....	196	....	....	....	....	....	....	....	....	....	....	4	0	0	0	13	....	....	....
1993-94	Tri-City Americans	WHL	12	2	3	5	....	....	....	32	....	....	....	....	....	....	....	....	....	....	....	....	....	....	....	....	....	....
	Saskatoon Blades	WHL	51	7	19	26	....	....	....	175	....	....	....	....	....	....	....	....	....	....	16	1	5	6	42	....	....	....
1994-95	Saint John Flames	AHL	80	3	10	13	....	....	....	321	....	....	....	....	....	....	....	....	....	....	5	0	0	0	4	....	....	....
1995-96	**Calgary Flames**	**NHL**	**6**	**0**	**0**	**0**	**0**	**0**	**0**	**32**	**0**	**0**	**0**	**3**	**0.0**	**1**	**0**	**1**	**0**	**0**	....	....	....	....	....	....	....	....
	Saint John Flames	AHL	66	4	13	17	....	....	....	277	....	....	....	....	....	....	....	....	....	....	16	2	3	5	32	....	....	....
1996-97	**Calgary Flames**	**NHL**	**82**	**1**	**13**	**14**	**1**	**12**	**13**	**208**	**0**	**0**	**0**	**85**	**1.2**	**51**	**0**	**91**	**26**	**–14**	....	....	....	....	....	....	....	....
1997-98	**Calgary Flames**	**NHL**	**53**	**1**	**5**	**6**	**1**	**5**	**6**	**109**	**0**	**0**	**1**	**51**	**2.0**	**38**	**1**	**64**	**17**	**–10**	....	....	....	....	....	....	....	....
1998-99	**Calgary Flames**	**NHL**	**73**	**2**	**8**	**10**	**2**	**8**	**10**	**151**	**0**	**0**	**0**	**52**	**3.8**	**57**	**0**	**76**	**37**	**18**	....	....	....	....	....	....	....	....
99-2000	**Florida Panthers**	**NHL**	**82**	**1**	**6**	**7**	**1**	**6**	**7**	**202**	**0**	**0**	**0**	**50**	**2.0**	**49**	**0**	**58**	**14**	**5**	**4**	**0**	**0**	**0**	**4**	**0**	**0**	**0**
	NHL Totals		**296**	**5**	**32**	**37**	**5**	**31**	**36**	**702**	**0**	**0**	**1**	**241**	**2.1**	**196**	**1**	**290**	**94**		**4**	**0**	**0**	**0**	**4**	**0**	**0**	**0**

Signed as free agent by **Calgary**, July 6, 1994. Traded to **Florida** by **Calgary** for Bill Lindsay, September 30, 1999.

• SIMS, Al

Allan Eugene D – L. 6', 182 lbs. b: Toronto, Ont., 4/18/1953. Boston's 4th, 47th overall, in 1973.

Season	Club	League	GP	G	A	Pts	AG	AA	APts	PIM	PP	SH	GW	S	%	TGF	PGF	TGA	PGA	+/–	GP	G	A	Pts	PIM	PP	SH	GW
1971-72	Cornwall Royals	QMJHL	58	6	24	30	....	....	....	65	....	....	....	....	....	....	....	....	....	....	16	2	9	11	15	....	....	....
	Cornwall Royals	Mem-Cup	3	0	0	0	....	....	....	2	....	....	....	....	....	....	....	....	....	....	....	....	....	....	....	....	....	....
1972-73	Cornwall Royals	QMJHL	62	13	62	75	....	....	....	54	....	....	....	....	....	....	....	....	....	....	12	2	5	7	8	....	....	....
1973-74	**Boston Bruins**	**NHL**	**76**	**3**	**9**	**12**	**3**	**7**	**10**	**22**	**0**	**0**	**1**	**111**	**2.7**	**116**	**1**	**69**	**18**	**64**	**16**	**0**	**0**	**0**	**12**	**0**	**0**	**0**
1974-75	**Boston Bruins**	**NHL**	**75**	**4**	**8**	**12**	**3**	**6**	**9**	**73**	**0**	**0**	**0**	**102**	**3.9**	**97**	**3**	**85**	**20**	**29**	....	....	....	....	....	....	....	....
1975-76	**Boston Bruins**	**NHL**	**48**	**4**	**3**	**7**	**3**	**2**	**5**	**43**	**0**	**0**	**0**	**61**	**6.6**	**41**	**5**	**47**	**17**	**6**	**1**	**0**	**0**	**0**	**0**	**0**	**0**	**0**
	Rochester Americans	AHL	21	4	5	9	....	....	....	12	....	....	....	....	....	....	....	....	....	....	7	1	4	5	11	....	....	....

Season	Club	League	GP	G	A	Pts	AG	AA	APts	PIM	PP	SH	GW	S	%	TGF	PGF	TGA	PGA	+/–	GP	G	A	Pts	PIM	PP	SH	GW
			REGULAR SEASON																		PLAYOFFS							
1976-77	Boston Bruins	NHL	1	0	0	0	0	0	0	0	0	0	0	1	0.0	1	0	0	0	1	2	0	0	0	0	0	0	0
	Rochester Americans	AHL	80	10	32	42				42											12	2	9	11	12			
1977-78	Boston Bruins	NHL	43	2	8	10	2	6	8	6	0	0	1	55	3.6	28	0	20	3	11	8	0	0	0	0	0	0	0
	Rochester Americans	AHL	31	6	13	19				12																		
1978-79	Boston Bruins	NHL	67	9	20	29	8	14	22	28	0	0	2	128	7.0	91	16	92	39	22	11	0	2	2	0	0	0	0
	Rochester Americans	AHL	3	0	1	1				4																		
1979-80	Hartford Whalers	NHL	76	10	31	41	8	23	31	30	2	0	1	141	7.1	125	19	131	34	9	3	0	0	0	2	0	0	0
1980-81	Hartford Whalers	NHL	80	16	36	52	12	24	36	68	5	0	1	182	8.8	133	40	153	40	–20								
1981-82	Los Angeles Kings	NHL	8	1	1	2	1	1	2	16	0	0	0	14	7.1	11	0	18	4	–3								
	New Haven Nighthawks	AHL	51	4	27	31				53																		
1982-83	Los Angeles Kings	NHL	1	0	0	0	0	0	0	0	0	0	0	1	0.0	0	0	0	0	0								
	New Haven Nighthawks	AHL	76	18	50	68				46											12	3	3	6	10			
1983-84	HC Geneve-Servette	Switz-2	STATISTICS NOT AVAILABLE																									
1984-85	EV Landshut	Germany	16	8	12	20				28											4	0	4	4	8			
	New Haven Nighthawks	AHL	13	3	6	9				2																		
1985-86	BSC Preussen Berlin	Germany-2	17	7	11	18				29																		
1986-87	Fife Flyers	Britain	36	52	86	138				95											5	6	11	17	0			
1987-88	Fife Flyers	Britain	30	33	42	75				51											6	5	11	16	2			
1988-89	Fort Wayne Komets	IHL	61	7	30	37				32											6	2	2	4	2			
1989-1993	Fort Wayne Komets	IHL	DID NOT PLAY – COACHING																									
1993-1996	Mighty Ducks of Anaheim	NHL	DID NOT PLAY – ASSISTANT COACH																									
1996-1997	San Jose Sharks	NHL	DID NOT PLAY – COACHING																									
1997-2000	Milwaukee Admirals	IHL	DID NOT PLAY – COACHING																									
	NHL Totals		475	49	116	165	40	83	123	286	7	0	6	796	6.2	643	84	615	175		41	0	2	2	14	0	0	0

QMJHL First All-Star Team (1973) • AHL Second All-Star Team (1977, 1983)

Claimed by **Hartford** from **Boston** in Expansion Draft, June 13, 1979. Claimed by **LA Kings** from **Hartford** in Waiver Draft, October 5, 1981.

• SINISALO, Ilkka

Ilkka Antero Jouko RW – L. 6′, 185 lbs. b: Hauho, Finland, 7/10/1958.

Season	Club	League	GP	G	A	Pts	AG	AA	APts	PIM	PP	SH	GW	S	%	TGF	PGF	TGA	PGA	+/–	GP	G	A	Pts	PIM	PP	SH	GW
1977-78	HIFK Helsinki	Finland	36	9	3	12				18																		
	Finland	WJC-A	6	1	7	8				4																		
1978-79	HIFK Helsinki	Finland	30	6	4	10				16											6	4	1	5	2			
1979-80	HIFK Helsinki	Finland	35	16	9	25				16											7	1	3	4	4			
1980-81	HIFK Helsinki	Finland	36	27	17	44				14											6	5	3	8	4			
	Finland	WEC-A	6	0	1	1				4																		
1981-82	Finland	Can-Cup	5	1	0	1				6																		
	Philadelphia Flyers	NHL	66	15	22	37	12	15	27	22	1	0	0	87	17.2	51	10	23	0	18	4	0	2	2	0	0	0	0
	Finland	WEC-A	5	1	1	2				6																		
1982-83	Philadelphia Flyers	NHL	61	21	29	50	17	20	37	16	3	0	0	126	16.7	65	10	39	2	18	3	1	1	2	0	0	0	0
	Finland	WEC-A	8	0	2	2				4																		
1983-84	Philadelphia Flyers	NHL	73	29	17	46	23	12	35	29	2	3	4	165	17.6	70	7	53	12	22	2	2	0	2	0	1	0	0
1984-85	Philadelphia Flyers	NHL	70	36	37	73	29	25	54	16	7	1	8	166	21.7	105	33	54	14	32	19	6	1	7	0	2	0	3
1985-86	Philadelphia Flyers	NHL	74	39	37	76	31	25	56	31	19	1	7	187	20.9	104	46	55	14	17	5	2	2	4	2	0	0	0
1986-87	Philadelphia Flyers	NHL	42	10	21	31	9	15	24	8	3	1	1	80	12.5	52	17	26	5	14	18	5	1	6	4	0	0	1
1987-88	Philadelphia Flyers	NHL	68	25	17	42	21	12	33	30	6	2	4	148	16.9	71	24	61	16	2	7	4	2	6	0	1	0	0
1988-89	Philadelphia Flyers	NHL	13	1	6	7	1	4	5	2	0	0	0	15	6.7	13	1	10	4	6	8	1	1	2	0	0	1	1
1989-90	Philadelphia Flyers	NHL	59	23	23	46	20	16	36	26	4	3	4	102	22.5	66	12	58	10	6								
1990-91	Minnesota North Stars	Fr-Tour	3	1	1	2				2																		
	Minnesota North Stars	NHL	46	5	12	17	5	9	14	24	1	1	1	68	7.4	27	4	39	6	–10								
	Los Angeles Kings	NHL	7	0	0	0	0	0	0	2	0	0	0	4	0.0	6	0	2	0	4	2	0	1	1	0	0	0	0
1991-92	Los Angeles Kings	NHL	3	0	1	1	0	1	1	2	0	0	0	3	0.0	3	0	3	0	0								
	Phoenix Roadrunners	IHL	42	19	21	40				32																		
1992-93	HPK Hameelinna	Finland	46	13	16	29				55											12	2	3	5	8			
1993-94	Karput Oulu	Finland-2	28	27	15	42				20																		
	Ilves Tampere	Finland	12	1	6	7				10											4	1	0	1	6			
1994-95	Ilves Tampere	Finland	30	2	7	9				45																		
	Kiekoo Espoo	Finland	16	7	7	14				6											4	0	3	3	4			
1995-96	Kiekoo Espoo	Finland	44	7	12	19				36																		
	NHL Totals		582	204	222	426	168	154	322	208	46	12	29	1151	17.7	633	164	423	83		68	21	11	32	6	4	1	5

Signed as a free agent by **Philadelphia**, February 14, 1981. Signed as a free agent by **Minnesota**, July 3, 1990. Traded to **LA Kings** by **Minnesota** for LA Kings' 8th round choice (Michael Burkett) in 1991 Entry Draft, March 5, 1991.

• SIREN, Ville

D – L. 6′2″, 191 lbs. b: Tampere, Finland, 2/11/1964. Hartford's 3rd, 23rd overall, in 1983.

Season	Club	League	GP	G	A	Pts	AG	AA	APts	PIM	PP	SH	GW	S	%	TGF	PGF	TGA	PGA	+/–	GP	G	A	Pts	PIM	PP	SH	GW
1981-82	Ilves Tampere	Finland-Jr.	30	13	12	25				40																		
1982-83	Ilves Tampere	Finland	29	3	2	5				42											8	1	3	4	8			
	Finland	WJC-A	7	1	1	2				6																		
1983-84	Ilves Tampere	Finland	36	1	10	11				40											2	0	0	0	2			
	Finland	WJC-A	6	0	2	2				4																		
	Finland	Olympics	6	0	1	1				2																		
1984-85	Ilves Tampere	Finland	36	11	13	24				24											9	0	2	2	10			
	Finland	WEC-A	5	0	0	0				8																		
1985-86	Pittsburgh Penguins	NHL	60	4	8	12	3	5	8	32	1	0	0	58	6.9	55	11	59	7	–8								
1986-87	Pittsburgh Penguins	NHL	69	5	17	22	4	12	16	50	1	0	0	84	6.0	102	22	87	15	8								
1987-88	Finland	Can-Cup	5	0	0	0				6																		
	Pittsburgh Penguins	NHL	58	1	20	21	1	14	15	62	0	0	0	53	1.9	87	20	78	25	14								
1988-89	Pittsburgh Penguins	NHL	12	1	0	1	1	0	1	14	0	0	0	11	9.1	9	0	9	0	0								
	Minnesota North Stars	NHL	38	2	10	12	2	7	9	58	0	0	0	39	5.1	47	17	32	2	0	4	0	0	0	4	0	0	0
1989-90	Minnesota North Stars	NHL	53	1	13	14	1	9	10	60	0	0	0	53	1.9	62	14	51	4	1	3	0	0	0	2	0	0	0
1990-91	HPK Hameenlina	Finland	44	4	9	13				90											8	1	1	2	37			
	Finland	WEC-A	10	2	2	4				16																		
1991-92	Finland	Can-Cup	6	0	1	1				15																		
	Ilves Tampere	Finland	43	8	14	22				88																		
	Finland	Olympics	8	0	2	2				16																		
1992-93	Lulea IF	Sweden	37	4	11	15				84											11	0	0	0	*22			
	Finland	WC-A	6	0	0	0				6																		
1993-94	Lulea IF	Sweden	40	4	11	15				65																		
1994-95	Vasteras IK	Sweden	37	1	4	5				44											4	0	1	1	4			
1995-96	SC Bern	Switz-2	6	1	0	1				6											11	3	7	10	18			
1996-97	SC Bern	Switz.	42	10	11	21				72											12	1	5	6	*47			
	SC Bern	EuroHL	6	1	2	3				8																		
1997-98	SC Bern	Switz.	36	3	9	12				96											7	1	4	5	26			
	SC Bern	EuroHL	6	1	3	4				10																		
	SG Cortina-Milano	Italy																			2	1	2	3	0			
1998-99	HIFK Helsinki	Finland	34	3	2	5				42											11	0	0	0	12			
	HIFK Helsinki	EuroHL	2	0	0	0				0											4	0	0	0	0			
	NHL Totals		290	14	68	82	12	47	59	276	2	0	0	298	4.7	362	84	316	53		7	0	0	0	6	0	0	0

Rights traded to **Pittsburgh** by **Hartford** for Pat Boutette, November 16, 1984. Traded to **Minnesota** by **Pittsburgh** with Steve Gotaas for Gord Dineen and Scott Bjugstad, December 17, 1988.

• SIROIS, Bob

RW – L. 6', 178 lbs. b: Montreal, Que., 2/6/1954. Philadelphia's 2nd, 53rd overall, in 1974.

Season	Club	League	REGULAR SEASON GP	G	A	Pts	AG	AA	APts	PIM	PP	SH	GW	S	%	TGF	PGF	TGA	PGA	+/-	PLAYOFFS GP	G	A	Pts	PIM	PP	SH	GW
1970-71	Rosemount Nationale	QJHL	59	24	30	54	....	....	....	37	....	....	....	....	....	....	....	....	....	....	....	....	....	....	....	....	....	....
1971-72	Laval Nationale	QMJHL	59	20	44	64	....	....	....	58	....	....	....	....	....	....	....	....	....	....	....	....	....	....	....	....	....	....
1972-73	Laval Nationale	QMJHL	6	5	3	8	....	....	....	6	....	....	....	....	....	....	....	....	....	....	....	....	....	....	....	....	....	....
	Montreal Red-White-Blue	QMJHL	57	46	51	97	....	....	....	55	....	....	....	....	....	....	....	....	....	....	....	....	....	....	....	....	....	....
1973-74	Montreal Red-White-Blue	QMJHL	67	72	81	153	....	....	....	77	....	....	....	....	....	....	....	....	....	....	....	....	....	....	....	....	....	....
1974-75	**Philadelphia Flyers**	**NHL**	**3**	**1**	**0**	**1**	**1**	**0**	**1**	**4**	**0**	**0**	**0**	**3**	**33.3**	**1**	**0**	**0**	**0**	**1**	....	....	....	....	....	....	....	....
	Richmond Robins	AHL	53	26	23	49	....	....	....	38	....	....	....	....	....	....	....	....	....	....	....	....	....	....	....	....	....	....
1975-76	**Philadelphia Flyers**	**NHL**	**1**	**0**	**0**	**0**	**0**	**0**	**0**	**0**	**0**	**0**	**0**	**0**	**0.0**	**0**	**0**	**0**	**0**	**0**	....	....	....	....	....	....	....	....
	Richmond Robins	AHL	26	14	18	32	....	....	....	10	....	....	....	....	....	....	....	....	....	....	....	....	....	....	....	....	....	....
	Washington Capitals	**NHL**	**43**	**10**	**19**	**29**	**9**	**14**	**23**	**6**	**4**	**0**	**0**	**109**	**9.2**	**34**	**12**	**55**	**0**	**–33**	....	....	....	....	....	....	....	....
1976-77	**Washington Capitals**	**NHL**	**45**	**13**	**22**	**35**	**12**	**17**	**29**	**2**	**1**	**0**	**1**	**100**	**13.0**	**43**	**5**	**38**	**1**	**1**	....	....	....	....	....	....	....	....
1977-78	**Washington Capitals**	**NHL**	**72**	**24**	**37**	**61**	**22**	**29**	**51**	**6**	**5**	**0**	**1**	**189**	**12.7**	**92**	**25**	**83**	**5**	**–11**	....	....	....	....	....	....	....	....
1978-79	**Washington Capitals**	**NHL**	**73**	**29**	**25**	**54**	**25**	**18**	**43**	**6**	**9**	**0**	**3**	**207**	**14.0**	**86**	**29**	**72**	**9**	**–6**	....	....	....	....	....	....	....	....
1979-80	**Washington Capitals**	**NHL**	**49**	**15**	**17**	**32**	**13**	**12**	**25**	**18**	**4**	**1**	**2**	**110**	**13.6**	**46**	**15**	**46**	**10**	**–5**	....	....	....	....	....	....	....	....
	Hershey Bears	AHL	2	1	1	2	....	....	....	0	....	....	....	....	....	....	....	....	....	....	....	....	....	....	....	....	....	....
1980-81	HC Lausanne	Switz.	STATISTICS NOT AVAILABLE																									
1981-82	Hershey Bears	AHL	13	2	6	8	....	....	....	0	....	....	....	....	....	....	....	....	....	....	....	....	....	....	....	....	....	....
	NHL Totals		**286**	**92**	**120**	**212**	**82**	**90**	**172**	**42**	**23**	**1**	**7**	**718**	**12.8**	**302**	**86**	**294**	**25**		....	....	....	....	....	....	....	....

Played in NHL All-Star Game (1978)

Traded to **Washington** by **Philadelphia** for future considerations (John Paddock, September 1, 1976), December 15, 1975.

• SITTLER, Darryl

Darryl Glen C – L. 6', 190 lbs. b: Kitchener, Ont., 9/18/1950. Toronto's 1st, 8th overall, in 1970. **HHOF**

Season	Club	League	REGULAR SEASON GP	G	A	Pts	AG	AA	APts	PIM	PP	SH	GW	S	%	TGF	PGF	TGA	PGA	+/-	PLAYOFFS GP	G	A	Pts	PIM	PP	SH	GW
1966-67	Elmira Sugar Kings	OHA-C	STATISTICS NOT AVAILABLE																									
1967-68	London Nationals/Knights	OHA-Jr.	54	22	41	63	....	....	....	84	....	....	....	....	....	....	....	....	....	....	5	5	2	7	6	....	....	....
1968-69	London Knights	OHA-Jr.	53	34	65	99	....	....	....	90	....	....	....	....	....	....	....	....	....	....	6	2	5	7	11	....	....	....
1969-70	London Knights	OHA-Jr.	54	42	48	90	....	....	....	126	....	....	....	....	....	....	....	....	....	....	12	4	12	16	32	....	....	....
1970-71	**Toronto Maple Leafs**	**NHL**	**49**	**10**	**8**	**18**	**10**	**7**	**17**	**37**	**3**	**0**	**3**	**131**	**7.6**	**31**	**7**	**23**	**2**	**3**	**6**	**2**	**1**	**3**	**31**	**1**	**0**	**0**
1971-72	**Toronto Maple Leafs**	**NHL**	**74**	**15**	**17**	**32**	**15**	**15**	**30**	**44**	**1**	**0**	**4**	**174**	**8.6**	**46**	**5**	**48**	**3**	**–4**	**3**	**0**	**0**	**0**	**2**	**0**	**0**	**0**
1972-73	**Toronto Maple Leafs**	**NHL**	**78**	**29**	**48**	**77**	**27**	**38**	**65**	**69**	**8**	**0**	**1**	**331**	**8.8**	**102**	**26**	**102**	**15**	**–11**	....	....	....	....	....	....	....	....
1973-74	**Toronto Maple Leafs**	**NHL**	**78**	**38**	**46**	**84**	**37**	**38**	**75**	**55**	**11**	**0**	**6**	**270**	**14.1**	**112**	**28**	**72**	**0**	**12**	**4**	**2**	**1**	**3**	**6**	**1**	**0**	**0**
1974-75	**Toronto Maple Leafs**	**NHL**	**72**	**36**	**44**	**80**	**32**	**33**	**65**	**47**	**12**	**1**	**2**	**273**	**13.2**	**107**	**39**	**93**	**15**	**–10**	**7**	**2**	**1**	**3**	**15**	**1**	**0**	**0**
1975-76	**Toronto Maple Leafs**	**NHL**	**79**	**41**	**59**	**100**	**36**	**44**	**80**	**90**	**11**	**1**	**2**	**346**	**11.8**	**129**	**35**	**111**	**29**	**12**	**10**	**5**	**7**	**12**	**19**	**2**	**0**	**1**
1976-77	Canada	Can-Cup	7	4	2	6	....	....	....	4	....	....	....	....	....	....	....	....	....	....	....	....	....	....	....	....	....	....
	Toronto Maple Leafs	**NHL**	**73**	**38**	**52**	**90**	**34**	**40**	**74**	**89**	**12**	**1**	**5**	**307**	**12.4**	**124**	**42**	**92**	**18**	**8**	**9**	**5**	**16**	**21**	**4**	**3**	**0**	**0**
1977-78	**Toronto Maple Leafs**	**NHL**	**80**	**45**	**72**	**117**	**41**	**56**	**97**	**100**	**14**	**0**	**8**	**311**	**14.5**	**141**	**41**	**69**	**3**	**34**	**13**	**3**	**8**	**11**	**12**	**2**	**0**	**0**
1978-79	**Toronto Maple Leafs**	**NHL**	**70**	**36**	**51**	**87**	**31**	**37**	**68**	**69**	**12**	**0**	**4**	**290**	**12.4**	**122**	**41**	**80**	**8**	**9**	**6**	**5**	**4**	**9**	**17**	**2**	**0**	**0**
	NHL All-Stars	Chal--Cup	3	0	1	1	....	....	....	0	....	....	....	....	....	....	....	....	....	....	....	....	....	....	....	....	....	....
1979-80	**Toronto Maple Leafs**	**NHL**	**73**	**40**	**57**	**97**	**34**	**42**	**76**	**62**	**17**	**1**	**5**	**315**	**12.7**	**130**	**43**	**97**	**13**	**3**	**3**	**1**	**2**	**3**	**10**	**1**	**0**	**0**
1980-81	**Toronto Maple Leafs**	**NHL**	**80**	**43**	**53**	**96**	**34**	**35**	**69**	**77**	**14**	**2**	**2**	**267**	**16.1**	**142**	**52**	**120**	**22**	**–8**	**3**	**0**	**0**	**0**	**4**	**0**	**0**	**0**
1981-82	**Toronto Maple Leafs**	**NHL**	**38**	**18**	**20**	**38**	**14**	**13**	**27**	**24**	**5**	**2**	**0**	**127**	**14.2**	**52**	**19**	**59**	**12**	**–14**	....	....	....	....	....	....	....	....
	Philadelphia Flyers	**NHL**	**35**	**14**	**18**	**32**	**11**	**12**	**23**	**50**	**5**	**1**	**2**	**114**	**12.3**	**44**	**9**	**59**	**23**	**–1**	**4**	**3**	**1**	**4**	**6**	**1**	**0**	**0**
	Canada	WEC-A	10	4	3	7	....	....	....	2	....	....	....	....	....	....	....	....	....	....	....	....	....	....	....	....	....	....
1982-83	**Philadelphia Flyers**	**NHL**	**80**	**43**	**40**	**83**	**35**	**28**	**63**	**60**	**10**	**0**	**8**	**231**	**18.6**	**111**	**30**	**66**	**2**	**17**	**3**	**1**	**0**	**1**	**4**	**0**	**0**	**0**
	Canada	WEC-A	10	3	1	4	....	....	....	12	....	....	....	....	....	....	....	....	....	....	....	....	....	....	....	....	....	....
1983-84	**Philadelphia Flyers**	**NHL**	**76**	**27**	**36**	**63**	**22**	**25**	**47**	**38**	**11**	**1**	**3**	**212**	**12.7**	**90**	**26**	**64**	**13**	**13**	**3**	**0**	**2**	**2**	**7**	**0**	**0**	**0**
1984-85	**Detroit Red Wings**	**NHL**	**61**	**11**	**16**	**27**	**9**	**11**	**20**	**37**	**4**	**0**	**2**	**113**	**9.7**	**49**	**11**	**57**	**9**	**–10**	**2**	**0**	**2**	**2**	**0**	**0**	**0**	**0**
	NHL Totals		**1096**	**484**	**637**	**1121**	**422**	**474**	**896**	**948**	**150**	**10**	**57**	**3812**	**12.7**	**1532**	**454**	**1212**	**187**		**76**	**29**	**45**	**74**	**137**	**14**	**0**	**1**

OHA-Jr. Second All-Star Team (1969) • Canada Cup All-Star Team (1976) • NHL Second All-Star Team (1978) • Played in NHL All-Star Game (1975, 1978, 1980, 1983)

Traded to **Philadelphia** by **Toronto** for Rich Costello, Hartford's 2nd round choice (previously acquired, Toronto selected Peter Ihnacak) in 1982 Entry Draft and future considerations (Ken Strong), January 20, 1982. Traded to **Detroit** by **Philadelphia** for Murray Craven and Joe Paterson, October 10, 1984.

• SJOBERG, Lars-Erik

D – L. 5'8", 179 lbs. b: Falun, Sweden, 4/5/1944.

Season	Club	League	REGULAR SEASON GP	G	A	Pts	AG	AA	APts	PIM	PP	SH	GW	S	%	TGF	PGF	TGA	PGA	+/-	PLAYOFFS GP	G	A	Pts	PIM	PP	SH	GW
1962-63	Leksands IF	Sweden	6	1	0	1	....	....	....	0	....	....	....	....	....	....	....	....	....	....	....	....	....	....	....	....	....	....
1963-64	Leksands IF	Sweden	14	0	2	2	....	....	....	2	....	....	....	....	....	....	....	....	....	....	7	1	1	2	0	....	....	....
1964-65	Leksands IF	Sweden	14	1	2	3	....	....	....	2	....	....	....	....	....	....	....	....	....	....	14	0	1	1	4	....	....	....
1965-66	Djurgardens IF Stockholm	Sweden	20	1	3	4	....	....	....	0	....	....	....	....	....	....	....	....	....	....	3	0	1	1	0	....	....	....
1966-67	Djurgardens IF Stockholm	Sweden	21	4	7	11	....	....	....	2	....	....	....	....	....	....	....	....	....	....	3	0	1	1	0	....	....	....
1967-68	Leksands IF	Sweden	21	3	3	6	....	....	....	....	....	....	....	....	....	....	....	....	....	....	7	1	3	4	2	....	....	....
	Sweden	Olympics	7	0	0	0	....	....	....	4	....	....	....	....	....	....	....	....	....	....	....	....	....	....	....	....	....	....
1968-69	Leksands IF	Sweden	19	6	2	8	....	....	....	4	....	....	....	....	....	....	....	....	....	....	7	0	1	1	0	....	....	....
	Sweden	WEC-A	9	3	2	5	....	....	....	2	....	....	....	....	....	....	....	....	....	....	....	....	....	....	....	....	....	....
1969-70	Vastra Frolunda	Sweden	14	2	1	3	....	....	....	10	....	....	....	....	....	....	....	....	....	....	....	....	....	....	....	....	....	....
	Sweden	WEC-A	10	1	1	2	....	....	....	0	....	....	....	....	....	....	....	....	....	....	....	....	....	....	....	....	....	....
1970-71	Vastra Frolunda	Sweden	13	8	4	12	....	....	....	6	....	....	....	....	....	....	....	....	....	....	....	....	....	....	....	....	....	....
1971-72	Vastra Frolunda	Sweden	27	4	11	15	....	....	....	4	....	....	....	....	....	....	....	....	....	....	....	....	....	....	....	....	....	....
	Sweden	Olympics	6	1	1	2	....	....	....	2	....	....	....	....	....	....	....	....	....	....	....	....	....	....	....	....	....	....
	Sweden	WEC-A	10	1	1	2	....	....	....	0	....	....	....	....	....	....	....	....	....	....	....	....	....	....	....	....	....	....
1972-73	Vastra Frolunda	Sweden	14	1	6	7	....	....	....	0	....	....	....	....	....	....	....	....	....	....	....	....	....	....	....	....	....	....
	Sweden	WEC-A	10	1	2	3	....	....	....	2	....	....	....	....	....	....	....	....	....	....	....	....	....	....	....	....	....	....
1973-74	Vastra Frolunda	Sweden	41	4	35	39	....	....	....	21	....	....	....	....	....	....	....	....	....	....	....	....	....	....	....	....	....	....
	Sweden	WEC-A	9	1	0	1	....	....	....	2	....	....	....	....	....	....	....	....	....	....	....	....	....	....	....	....	....	....
1974-75	Winnipeg Jets	WHA	75	7	53	60	....	....	....	30	....	....	....	....	....	....	....	....	....	....	....	....	....	....	....	....	....	....
1975-76	Winnipeg Jets	WHA	81	5	36	41	....	....	....	12	....	....	....	....	....	....	....	....	....	....	13	0	5	5	12	....	....	....
1976-77	Sweden	Can-Cup	5	0	3	3	....	....	....	6	....	....	....	....	....	....	....	....	....	....	....	....	....	....	....	....	....	....
	Winnipeg Jets	WHA	52	2	38	40	....	....	....	31	....	....	....	....	....	....	....	....	....	....	20	0	6	6	22	....	....	....
1977-78	Winnipeg Jets	WHA	78	11	39	50	....	....	....	72	....	....	....	....	....	....	....	....	....	....	9	0	9	9	4	....	....	....
1978-79	Winnipeg Jets	WHA	9	0	3	3	....	....	....	2	....	....	....	....	....	....	....	....	....	....	10	1	2	3	4	....	....	....
1979-80	**Winnipeg Jets**	**NHL**	**79**	**7**	**27**	**34**	**6**	**20**	**26**	**48**	**3**	**1**	**0**	**145**	**4.8**	**87**	**21**	**137**	**36**	**–35**	....	....	....	....	....	....	....	....
	NHL Totals		**79**	**7**	**27**	**34**	**6**	**20**	**26**	**48**	**3**	**1**	**0**	**145**	**4.8**	**87**	**21**	**137**	**36**		....	....	....	....	....	....	....	....
	Other Major League Totals		295	25	169	194	....	....	....	147	....	....	....	....	....	....	....	....	....	....	52	1	22	23	42	....	....	....

Swedish Player of the Year (1969) • WEC-A All-Star Team (1974) • Named Best Defenseman at WEC-A (1974) • WHA First All-Star Team (1978) • Won Dennis A. Murphy Trophy (WHA Top Defenseman) (1978)

Signed as a free agent by **Winnipeg** (WHA), May 23, 1974. Rights retained by **Winnipeg** prior to Expansion Draft, June 9, 1979.

• SJODIN, Tommy

Tommy S. D – R. 5'11", 190 lbs. b: Timra, Sweden, 8/13/1965. Minnesota's 10th, 237th overall, in 1985.

Season	Club	League	REGULAR SEASON GP	G	A	Pts	AG	AA	APts	PIM	PP	SH	GW	S	%	TGF	PGF	TGA	PGA	+/-	PLAYOFFS GP	G	A	Pts	PIM	PP	SH	GW
1983-84	Timra IF	Sweden-2	16	4	4	8	....	....	....	6	....	....	....	....	....	....	....	....	....	....	6	0	0	0	4	....	....	....
1984-85	Timra IF	Sweden-2	23	8	11	19	....	....	....	14	....	....	....	....	....	....	....	....	....	....	....	....	....	....	....	....	....	....
1985-86	Timra IF	Sweden-2	32	13	12	25	....	....	....	40	....	....	....	....	....	....	....	....	....	....	....	....	....	....	....	....	....	....
1986-87	Brynas IF Gavle	Sweden	29	0	4	4	....	....	....	24	....	....	....	....	....	....	....	....	....	....	....	....	....	....	....	....	....	....
1987-88	Brynas IF Gavle	Sweden	40	6	9	15	....	....	....	28	....	....	....	....	....	....	....	....	....	....	....	....	....	....	....	....	....	....
1988-89	Brynas IF Gavle	Sweden	40	8	11	19	....	....	....	52	....	....	....	....	....	....	....	....	....	....	5	1	0	1	6	....	....	....
1989-90	Brynas IF Gavle	Sweden	40	14	14	28	....	....	....	46	....	....	....	....	....	....	....	....	....	....	5	0	0	0	2	....	....	....
1990-91	Brynas IF Gavle	Sweden	38	12	17	29	....	....	....	77	....	....	....	....	....	....	....	....	....	....	2	0	1	1	2	....	....	....
1991-92	Brynas IF Gavle	Sweden	40	6	16	22	....	....	....	46	....	....	....	....	....	....	....	....	....	....	5	0	3	3	4	....	....	....
	Sweden	Olympics	8	4	1	5	....	....	....	2	....	....	....	....	....	....	....	....	....	....	....	....	....	....	....	....	....	....
	Sweden	WC-A	8	0	1	1	....	....	....	6	....	....	....	....	....	....	....	....	....	....	....	....	....	....	....	....	....	....
1992-93	**Minnesota North Stars**	**NHL**	**77**	**7**	**29**	**36**	**6**	**20**	**26**	**30**	**5**	**0**	**1**	**175**	**4.0**	**90**	**70**	**45**	**0**	**–25**	....	....	....	....	....	....	....	....

			REGULAR SEASON																		PLAYOFFS							
Season	Club	League	GP	G	A	Pts	AG	AA	APts	PIM	PP	SH	GW	S	%	TGF	PGF	TGA	PGA	+/–	GP	G	A	Pts	PIM	PP	SH	GW
1993-94	**Dallas Stars**	**NHL**	**7**	**0**	**2**	**2**	**0**	**2**	**2**	**4**	**0**	**0**	**0**	**8**	**0.0**	**6**	**4**	**3**	**0**	**–1**	....	....	....	....	....	....	....	....
	Kalamazoo Wings	IHL	38	12	32	44	....	....	....	22	....	....	....	....	....	....	....	....	....	....	....	....	....	....	....	....	....	....
	Quebec Nordiques	**NHL**	**22**	**1**	**9**	**10**	**1**	**7**	**8**	**18**	**1**	**0**	**0**	**46**	**2.2**	**26**	**10**	**11**	**0**	**5**	....	....	....	....	....	....	....	....
	Sweden	WC-A	8	0	0	0	....	....	....	6	....	....	....	....	....	....	....	....	....	....	....	....	....	....	....	....	....	....
1994-95	HC Lugano	Switz.	36	17	27	44	....	....	....	36	....	....	....	....	....	....	....	....	....	....	5	3	2	5	2	....	....	....
	Sweden	WC-A	8	2	3	5	....	....	....	6	....	....	....	....	....	....	....	....	....	....	....	....	....	....	....	....	....	....
1995-96	HC Lugano	Switz.	30	3	21	24	....	....	....	26	....	....	....	....	....	....	....	....	....	....	4	2	2	4	2	....	....	....
	Sweden	WC-A	6	1	1	2	....	....	....	0	....	....	....	....	....	....	....	....	....	....	....	....	....	....	....	....	....	....
1996-97	HC Bolzano	Italy	6	2	2	4	....	....	....	0	....	....	....	....	....	....	....	....	....	....	....	....	....	....	....	....	....	....
	HC Lugano	Switz.	45	23	28	51	....	....	....	55	....	....	....	....	....	....	....	....	....	....	8	2	4	6	2	....	....	....
1997-98	HC Lugano	Switz.	29	12	19	31	....	....	....	36	....	....	....	....	....	....	....	....	....	....	7	4	1	5	0	....	....	....
1998-99	EHC Kloten	Switz.	33	6	19	25	....	....	....	22	....	....	....	....	....	....	....	....	....	....	8	1	2	3	6	....	....	....
99-2000	Brynas IF Gavle	Sweden	50	8	14	22	....	....	....	44	....	....	....	....	....	....	....	....	....	....	11	0	5	5	10	....	....	....
	Brynas IF Gavle	EuroHL	6	1	1	2	....	....	....	4	....	....	....	....	....	....	....	....	....	....	....	....	....	....	....	....	....	....
	NHL Totals		**106**	**8**	**40**	**48**	**7**	**29**	**36**	**52**	**6**	**0**	**1**	**229**	**3.5**	**122**	**84**	**59**	**0**		....	....	....	....	....	....	....	....

Swedish World All-Star Team (1992, 1995) • Swedish Player of the Year (1992) • WC-A All-Star Team (1995)

Transferred to **Dallas** after **Minnesota** franchise relocated, June 9, 1993. Traded to **Quebec** by **Dallas** with Dallas' 3rd round choice (Chris Drury) in 1994 Entry Draft for the rights to Manny Fernandez, February 13, 1994.

• SKAARE, Bjorn

C – L. 6', 180 lbs. b: Oslo, Norway, 10/29/1958 d: 1989. Detroit's 6th, 62nd overall, in 1978.

Season	Club	League	GP	G	A	Pts	AG	AA	APts	PIM	PP	SH	GW	S	%	TGF	PGF	TGA	PGA	+/–	GP	G	A	Pts	PIM	PP	SH	GW
1976-77	Farjestads BK Karlstad	Sweden-Jr.	40	21	20	41	....	....	....	8	....	....	....	....	....	....	....	....	....	....	....	....	....	....	....	....	....	....
	Farjestads BK Karlstad	Sweden	9	1	0	1	....	....	....	2	....	....	....	....	....	....	....	....	....	....	....	....	....	....	....	....	....	....
1977-78	Ottawa 67's	OMJHL	38	12	30	42	....	....	....	72	....	....	....	....	....	....	....	....	....	....	13	3	9	12	13	....	....	....
1978-79	**Detroit Red Wings**	**NHL**	**1**	**0**	**0**	**0**	**0**	**0**	**0**	**0**	**0**	**0**	**0**	**1**	**0.0**	**0**	**0**	**0**	**0**	**0**	....	....	....	....	....	....	....	....
	Kansas City Red Wings	CHL	37	8	26	34	....	....	....	18	....	....	....	....	....	....	....	....	....	....	....	....	....	....	....	....	....	....
	Norway	WC-B	4	2	2	4	....	....	....	8	....	....	....	....	....	....	....	....	....	....	....	....	....	....	....	....	....	....
1979-80	Furuset IF Oslo	Norway-2	27	23	23	46	....	....	....	....	....	....	....	....	....	....	....	....	....	....	....	....	....	....	....	....	....	....
1980-81	Furuset IF Oslo	Norway	33	*38	*34	*72	....	....	....	49	....	....	....	....	....	....	....	....	....	....	....	....	....	....	....	....	....	....
	Norway	WC-B	6	1	2	3	....	....	....	2	....	....	....	....	....	....	....	....	....	....	....	....	....	....	....	....	....	....
1981-82	KAC Klagenfurt	Austria	28	27	31	58	....	....	....	....	....	....	....	....	....	....	....	....	....	....	10	11	7	18	....	....	....	....
1982-83	Furuset IF Oslo	Norway	STATISTICS NOT AVAILABLE																									
1983-84	Furuset IF Oslo	Norway	23	26	28	54	....	....	....	24	....	....	....	....	....	....	....	....	....	....	4	1	2	3	....	....	....	....
	Tulsa Oilers	CHL	2	1	1	2	....	....	....	5	....	....	....	....	....	....	....	....	....	....	9	2	7	9	2	....	....	....
	Norway	Olympics	5	0	4	4	....	....	....	4	....	....	....	....	....	....	....	....	....	....	....	....	....	....	....	....	....	....
1984-85	Furuset IF Oslo	Norway	35	32	35	67	....	....	....	35	....	....	....	....	....	....	....	....	....	....	....	....	....	....	....	....	....	....
1985-86	SK Djerv-Bergen	Norway	STATISTICS NOT AVAILABLE																									
1986-87	SK Djerv-Bergen	Norway	27	22	26	48	....	....	....	16	....	....	....	....	....	....	....	....	....	....	....	....	....	....	....	....	....	....
	NHL Totals		**1**	**0**	**0**	**0**	**0**	**0**	**0**	**0**	**0**	**0**	**0**	**1**	**0.0**	**0**	**0**	**0**	**0**		....	....	....	....	....	....	....	....

Norwegian Elite League All-Star Team (1980, 1981, 1983, 1984) • Died of injuries suffered in automobile accident, 1989.

• SKALDE, Jarrod

Jarrod Janis C – L. 6', 185 lbs. b: Niagara Falls, Ont., 2/26/1971. New Jersey's 3rd, 26th overall, in 1989.

Season	Club	League	GP	G	A	Pts	AG	AA	APts	PIM	PP	SH	GW	S	%	TGF	PGF	TGA	PGA	+/–	GP	G	A	Pts	PIM	PP	SH	GW
1986-87	Fort Erie Meteors	OJHL-B	41	27	34	61	....	....	....	36	....	....	....	....	....	....	....	....	....	....	....	....	....	....	....	....	....	....
1987-88	Oshawa Generals	OHL	60	12	16	28	....	....	....	24	....	....	....	....	....	....	....	....	....	....	7	2	1	3	2	....	....	....
1988-89	Oshawa Generals	OHL	65	38	38	76	....	....	....	36	....	....	....	....	....	....	....	....	....	....	6	1	5	6	2	....	....	....
1989-90	Oshawa Generals	OHL	62	40	52	92	....	....	....	66	....	....	....	....	....	....	....	....	....	....	17	10	7	17	6	....	....	....
	Oshawa Generals	Mem-Cup	4	2	3	5	....	....	....	2	....	....	....	....	....	....	....	....	....	....	....	....	....	....	....	....	....	....
1990-91	Oshawa Generals	OHL	15	8	14	22	....	....	....	14	....	....	....	....	....	....	....	....	....	....	....	....	....	....	....	....	....	....
	Belleville Bulls	OHL	40	30	52	82	....	....	....	21	....	....	....	....	....	....	....	....	....	....	6	9	6	15	10	....	....	....
	New Jersey Devils	**NHL**	**1**	**0**	**1**	**1**	**0**	**1**	**1**	**0**	**0**	**0**	**0**	**2**	**0.0**	**1**	**0**	**1**	**0**	**0**	....	....	....	....	....	....	....	....
	Utica Devils	AHL	3	3	2	5	....	....	....	0	....	....	....	....	....	....	....	....	....	....	....	....	....	....	....	....	....	....
1991-92	**New Jersey Devils**	**NHL**	**15**	**2**	**4**	**6**	**2**	**3**	**5**	**4**	**0**	**0**	**2**	**25**	**8.0**	**8**	**0**	**9**	**0**	**–1**	....	....	....	....	....	....	....	....
	Utica Devils	AHL	62	20	20	40	....	....	....	56	....	....	....	....	....	....	....	....	....	....	4	3	1	4	8	....	....	....
1992-93	**New Jersey Devils**	**NHL**	**11**	**0**	**2**	**2**	**0**	**1**	**1**	**4**	**0**	**0**	**0**	**11**	**0.0**	**4**	**0**	**15**	**8**	**–3**	....	....	....	....	....	....	....	....
	Utica Devils	AHL	59	21	39	60	....	....	....	76	....	....	....	....	....	....	....	....	....	....	5	0	2	2	19	....	....	....
	Cincinnati Cyclones	IHL	4	1	2	3	....	....	....	4	....	....	....	....	....	....	....	....	....	....	....	....	....	....	....	....	....	....
1993-94	**Mighty Ducks of Anaheim**	**NHL**	**20**	**5**	**4**	**9**	**5**	**3**	**8**	**10**	**2**	**0**	**2**	**25**	**20.0**	**17**	**6**	**14**	**0**	**–3**	....	....	....	....	....	....	....	....
	San Diego Gulls	IHL	57	25	38	63	....	....	....	79	....	....	....	....	....	....	....	....	....	....	9	3	12	15	10	....	....	....
1994-95	Las Vegas Thunder	IHL	74	34	41	75	....	....	....	103	....	....	....	....	....	....	....	....	....	....	9	2	4	6	8	....	....	....
1995-96	Baltimore Bandits	AHL	11	2	6	8	....	....	....	55	....	....	....	....	....	....	....	....	....	....	....	....	....	....	....	....	....	....
	Calgary Flames	**NHL**	**1**	**0**	**0**	**0**	**0**	**0**	**0**	**0**	**0**	**0**	**0**	**0**	**0.0**	**0**	**0**	**0**	**0**	**0**	....	....	....	....	....	....	....	....
	Saint John Flames	AHL	68	27	40	67	....	....	....	98	....	....	....	....	....	....	....	....	....	....	16	4	9	13	6	....	....	....
1996-97	Saint John Flames	AHL	65	32	36	68	....	....	....	94	....	....	....	....	....	....	....	....	....	....	3	0	0	0	14	....	....	....
1997-98	**San Jose Sharks**	**NHL**	**22**	**4**	**6**	**10**	**5**	**6**	**11**	**14**	**0**	**0**	**0**	**30**	**13.3**	**15**	**2**	**15**	**0**	**–2**	....	....	....	....	....	....	....	....
	Kentucky Thoroughblades	AHL	6	2	6	8	....	....	....	10	....	....	....	....	....	....	....	....	....	....	....	....	....	....	....	....	....	....
	Chicago Blackhawks	**NHL**	**4**	**0**	**1**	**1**	**0**	**1**	**1**	**2**	**0**	**0**	**0**	**4**	**0.0**	....	....	....	....	**0**	....	....	....	....	....	....	....	....
	Indianapolis Ice	IHL	2	0	2	2	....	....	....	0	....	....	....	....	....	....	....	....	....	....	....	....	....	....	....	....	....	....
	Dallas Stars	**NHL**	**1**	**0**	**0**	**0**	**0**	**0**	**0**	**0**	**0**	**0**	**0**	**0**	**0.0**	**0**	**0**	**0**	**0**	**0**	....	....	....	....	....	....	....	....
	Chicago Blackhawks	**NHL**	**3**	**0**	**0**	**0**	**0**	**0**	**0**	**2**	**0**	**0**	**0**	**0**	**0.0**	....	....	....	....	**0**	....	....	....	....	....	....	....	....
	Kentucky Thoroughblades	AHL	17	3	9	12	....	....	....	38	....	....	....	....	....	....	....	....	....	....	3	3	0	3	6	....	....	....
1998-99	**San Jose Sharks**	**NHL**	**17**	**1**	**1**	**2**	**1**	**1**	**2**	**4**	**0**	**0**	**0**	**17**	**5.9**	**4**	**2**	**8**	**0**	**–6**	....	....	....	....	....	....	....	....
	Kentucky Thoroughblades	AHL	54	17	40	57	....	....	....	75	....	....	....	....	....	....	....	....	....	....	12	4	5	9	16	....	....	....
99-2000	Utah Grizzlies	IHL	77	25	54	79	....	....	....	98	....	....	....	....	....	....	....	....	....	....	5	0	1	1	10	....	....	....
	NHL Totals		**95**	**12**	**19**	**31**	**13**	**16**	**29**	**40**	**2**	**0**	**4**	**114**	**10.5**	**49**	**10**	**62**	**8**		....	....	....	....	....	....	....	....

OHL Second All-Star Team (1991) • IHL First All-Star Team (2000)

Claimed by **Anaheim** from **New Jersey** in Expansion Draft, June 24, 1993. Traded to **Calgary** by **Anaheim** for Bobby Marshall, October 30, 1995. Signed as a free agent by **San Jose**, August 14, 1997. Claimed on waivers by **Chicago** from **San Jose**, January 8, 1998. Claimed on waivers by **San Jose** from **Chicago**, January 23, 1998. Claimed on waivers by **Dallas** from **San Jose**, January 27, 1998. Claimed on waivers by **Chicago** from **Dallas**, February 10, 1998. Claimed on waivers by **San Jose** from **Chicago**, March 6, 1998.

• SKARDA, Randy

Randall J. D – R. 6'1", 205 lbs. b: St. Paul, MN, 5/5/1968. St. Louis' 8th, 157th overall, in 1986.

Season	Club	League	GP	G	A	Pts	AG	AA	APts	PIM	PP	SH	GW	S	%	TGF	PGF	TGA	PGA	+/–	GP	G	A	Pts	PIM	PP	SH	GW
1984-85	St. Thomas Academy	Hi-School	23	14	42	56	....	....	....	....	....	....	....	....	....	....	....	....	....	....	....	....	....	....	....	....	....	....
1985-86	St. Thomas Academy	Hi-School	23	15	27	42	....	....	....	....	....	....	....	....	....	....	....	....	....	....	....	....	....	....	....	....	....	....
1986-87	University of Minnesota	WCHA	43	3	10	13	....	....	....	77	....	....	....	....	....	....	....	....	....	....	....	....	....	....	....	....	....	....
1987-88	University of Minnesota	WCHA	42	19	26	45	....	....	....	102	....	....	....	....	....	....	....	....	....	....	....	....	....	....	....	....	....	....
	United States	WJC-A	6	1	2	3	....	....	....	26	....	....	....	....	....	....	....	....	....	....	....	....	....	....	....	....	....	....
1988-89	University of Minnesota	WCHA	43	6	24	30	....	....	....	91	....	....	....	....	....	....	....	....	....	....	....	....	....	....	....	....	....	....
1989-90	**St. Louis Blues**	**NHL**	**25**	**0**	**5**	**5**	**0**	**4**	**4**	**11**	**0**	**0**	**0**	**8**	**0.0**	**20**	**1**	**17**	**0**	**2**	....	....	....	....	....	....	....	....
	Peoria Rivermen	IHL	38	7	17	24	....	....	....	40	....	....	....	....	....	....	....	....	....	....	4	0	0	0	0	....	....	....
1990-91	Peoria Rivermen	IHL	78	8	34	42	....	....	....	126	....	....	....	....	....	....	....	....	....	....	19	3	5	8	22	....	....	....
1991-92	**St. Louis Blues**	**NHL**	**1**	**0**	**0**	**0**	**0**	**0**	**0**	**0**	**0**	**0**	**0**	**0**	**0.0**	**0**	**0**	**0**	**0**	**0**	....	....	....	....	....	....	....	....
	Peoria Rivermen	IHL	57	8	24	32	....	....	....	64	....	....	....	....	....	....	....	....	....	....	7	0	0	0	14	....	....	....
1992-93	Milwaukee Admirals	IHL	54	3	9	12	....	....	....	104	....	....	....	....	....	....	....	....	....	....	....	....	....	....	....	....	....	....
1993-94	P.E.I. Senators	AHL	20	1	3	4	....	....	....	14	....	....	....	....	....	....	....	....	....	....	....	....	....	....	....	....	....	....
	Hershey Bears	AHL	4	0	2	2	....	....	....	0	....	....	....	....	....	....	....	....	....	....	....	....	....	....	....	....	....	....
	Johnstown Chiefs	ECHL	9	1	6	7	....	....	....	6	....	....	....	....	....	....	....	....	....	....	....	....	....	....	....	....	....	....
	NHL Totals		**26**	**0**	**5**	**5**	**0**	**4**	**4**	**11**	**0**	**0**	**0**	**8**	**0.0**	**20**	**1**	**17**	**0**		....	....	....	....	....	....	....	....

WCHA First All-Star Team (1988) • NCAA West Second All-American Team (1988) • WCHA First All-Star Team (1988)

• Played w/ RHI's Minnesota Artic Blast in 1994 (21-18-59-77-109) and 1996 (22-13-46-59-60).

• SKINNER, Larry

Larry Foster C – L. 5'11", 180 lbs. b: Vancouver, B.C., 4/21/1956. Kansas City's 4th, 92nd overall, in 1976.

Season	Club	League	GP	G	A	Pts	AG	AA	APts	PIM	PP	SH	GW	S	%	TGF	PGF	TGA	PGA	+/-	GP	G	A	Pts	PIM	PP	SH	GW
			REGULAR SEASON																		PLAYOFFS							
1972-73	Nepean Raiders	OJHL	55	23	35	58	....	....	....	....	....	....	....	....	....	....	....	....	....	....	....	....	....	....	....	....	....	....
1973-74	Nepean Raiders	OJHL	55	22	34	56	....	....	....	15	....	....	....	....	....	....	....	....	....	....	....	....	....	....	....	....	....	....
1974-75	Winnipeg Jets	WCJHL	70	33	62	95	....	....	....	17	....	....	....	....	....	....	....	....	....	....	....	....	....	....	....	....	....	....
1975-76	Ottawa 67's	OMJHL	58	37	78	115	....	....	....	8	....	....	....	....	....	....	....	....	....	....	12	8	8	16	8	....	....	....
1976-77	**Colorado Rockies**	**NHL**	**19**	**4**	**5**	**9**	**4**	**4**	**8**	**6**	**3**	**0**	**0**	**40**	**10.0**	**11**	**7**	**21**	**4**	**–13**	....	....	....	....	....	....	....	....
	Rhode Island Reds	AHL	46	22	34	56	....	....	....	11	....	....	....	....	....	....	....	....	....	....	....	....	....	....	....	....	....	....
1977-78	**Colorado Rockies**	**NHL**	**14**	**3**	**5**	**8**	**3**	**4**	**7**	**0**	**1**	**0**	**0**	**28**	**10.7**	**12**	**2**	**8**	**0**	**2**	**2**	**0**	**0**	**0**	**0**	**0**	**0**	**0**
	Phoenix Roadrunners	CHL	20	4	6	10	....	....	....	9	....	....	....	....	....	....	....	....	....	....	....	....	....	....	....	....	....	....
	Hampton Gulls	AHL	15	7	9	16	....	....	....	6	....	....	....	....	....	....	....	....	....	....	....	....	....	....	....	....	....	....
	Springfield Indians	AHL	14	1	5	6	....	....	....	2	....	....	....	....	....	....	....	....	....	....	....	....	....	....	....	....	....	....
1978-79	**Colorado Rockies**	**NHL**	**12**	**3**	**2**	**5**	**3**	**1**	**4**	**2**	**1**	**0**	**0**	**13**	**23.1**	**9**	**4**	**10**	**0**	**–5**	....	....	....	....	....	....	....	....
	Philadelphia Firebirds	AHL	67	34	33	67	....	....	....	34	....	....	....	....	....	....	....	....	....	....	....	....	....	....	....	....	....	....
1979-80	**Colorado Rockies**	**NHL**	**2**	**0**	**0**	**0**	**0**	**0**	**0**	**0**	**0**	**0**	**0**	**2**	**0.0**	**0**	**0**	**2**	**0**	**–2**	....	....	....	....	....	....	....	....
	Fort Worth Texans	CHL	10	5	7	12	....	....	....	8	....	....	....	....	....	....	....	....	....	....	....	....	....	....	....	....	....	....
	New Haven Nighthawks	AHL	63	18	53	71	....	....	....	38	....	....	....	....	....	....	....	....	....	....	10	5	10	15	0	....	....	....
1980-81	Springfield Indians	AHL	48	21	40	61	....	....	....	36	....	....	....	....	....	....	....	....	....	....	7	3	8	11	4	....	....	....
1981-82	Hershey Bears	AHL	18	5	14	19	....	....	....	2	....	....	....	....	....	....	....	....	....	....	5	2	7	9	0	....	....	....
	IEV Innsbruck	Austria	28	21	28	49	....	....	....	....	....	....	....	....	....	....	....	....	....	....	....	....	....	....	....	....	....	....
1982-83	IEV Innsbruck	Austria	28	26	30	56	....	....	....	....	....	....	....	....	....	....	....	....	....	....	....	....	....	....	....	....	....	....
	Hershey Bears	AHL	14	8	9	17	....	....	....	2	....	....	....	....	....	....	....	....	....	....	4	1	0	1	0	....	....	....
1983-84	Paris Francais Volants	France-2	STATISTICS NOT AVAILABLE																									
1984-85	Paris Francais Volants	France	25	*44	16	60	....	....	....	....	....	....	....	....	....	....	....	....	....	....	....	....	....	....	....	....	....	....
1985-86	Paris Francais Volants	France-2	32	32	41	73	....	....	....	....	....	....	....	....	....	....	....	....	....	....	....	....	....	....	....	....	....	....
1986-87	Paris Francais Volants	France	25	50	35	85	....	....	....	....	....	....	....	....	....	....	....	....	....	....	....	....	....	....	....	....	....	....
1987-88	Paris Francais Volants	France	25	30	23	53	....	....	....	38	....	....	....	....	....	....	....	....	....	....	....	....	....	....	....	....	....	....
	NHL Totals		**47**	**10**	**12**	**22**	**10**	**9**	**19**	**8**	**5**	**0**	**0**	**83**	**12.0**	**32**	**13**	**41**	**4**		**2**	**0**	**0**	**0**	**0**	**0**	**0**	**0**

Transferred to **Colorado** after **Kansas City** franchise relocated, July 15, 1977. Selected by **Colorado** as a fill-in during Expansion Draft, June 13, 1979. Traded to **New Haven** (AHL) by **Colorado** with Dennis Owchar for Bobby Sheehan, May 12, 1979.

• SKOPINTSEV, Andrei

D – R. 6', 185 lbs. b: Elekrostal, USSR, 9/28/1971. Tampa Bay's 7th, 153rd overall, in 1997.

Season	Club	League	GP	G	A	Pts	AG	AA	APts	PIM	PP	SH	GW	S	%	TGF	PGF	TGA	PGA	+/-	GP	G	A	Pts	PIM	PP	SH	GW
1989-90	Krylja Sovetov Moscow	USSR	20	0	0	0	....	....	....	10	....	....	....	....	....	....	....	....	....	....	....	....	....	....	....	....	....	....
1990-91	Krylja Sovetov Moscow	USSR	16	0	1	1	....	....	....	2	....	....	....	....	....	....	....	....	....	....	....	....	....	....	....	....	....	....
1991-92	Krylja Sovetov Moscow	CIS	36	1	1	2	....	....	....	14	....	....	....	....	....	....	....	....	....	....	....	....	....	....	....	....	....	....
1992-93	Krylja Sovetov Moscow	CIS	12	1	0	1	....	....	....	4	....	....	....	....	....	....	....	....	....	....	7	1	0	1	2	....	....	....
1993-94	Krylja Sovetov Moscow	CIS	43	4	8	12	....	....	....	14	....	....	....	....	....	....	....	....	....	....	3	1	0	1	0	....	....	....
1994-95	Krylja Sovetov Moscow	CIS	52	8	12	20	....	....	....	55	....	....	....	....	....	....	....	....	....	....	4	1	1	2	0	....	....	....
	Russia	WC-A	6	1	1	2	....	....	....	0	....	....	....	....	....	....	....	....	....	....	....	....	....	....	....	....	....	....
1995-96	Augsburger Panther	Germany	46	10	20	30	....	....	....	32	....	....	....	....	....	....	....	....	....	....	7	3	2	5	22	....	....	....
	Russia	WC-A	7	2	1	3	....	....	....	2	....	....	....	....	....	....	....	....	....	....	....	....	....	....	....	....	....	....
1996-97	TPS Turku	Finland	46	3	6	9	....	....	....	80	....	....	....	....	....	....	....	....	....	....	10	1	1	2	4	....	....	....
	TPS Turku	EuroHL	5	0	1	1	....	....	....	4	....	....	....	....	....	....	....	....	....	....	....	....	....	....	....	....	....	....
	Russia	WC-A	9	1	0	1	....	....	....	4	....	....	....	....	....	....	....	....	....	....	....	....	....	....	....	....	....	....
1997-98	TPS Turku	Finland	48	2	9	11	....	....	....	8	....	....	....	....	....	....	....	....	....	....	4	0	1	1	4	....	....	....
	TPS Turku	EuroHL	5	0	1	1	....	....	....	4	....	....	....	....	....	....	....	....	....	....	....	....	....	....	....	....	....	....
	Russia	WC-A	6	1	0	1	....	....	....	2	....	....	....	....	....	....	....	....	....	....	....	....	....	....	....	....	....	....
1998-99	**Tampa Bay Lightning**	**NHL**	**19**	**1**	**1**	**2**	**1**	**1**	**2**	**10**	**0**	**0**	**0**	**17**	**5.9**	**13**	**2**	**12**	**2**	**1**	....	....	....	....	....	....	....	....
	Cleveland Lumberjacks	IHL	19	3	2	5	....	....	....	8	....	....	....	....	....	....	....	....	....	....	....	....	....	....	....	....	....	....
99-2000	**Tampa Bay Lightning**	**NHL**	**4**	**0**	**0**	**0**	**0**	**0**	**0**	**6**	**0**	**0**	**0**	**0**	**0.0**	**2**	**0**	**8**	**2**	**–4**	....	....	....	....	....	....	....	....
	Detroit Vipers	IHL	51	4	15	19	....	....	....	44	....	....	....	....	....	....	....	....	....	....	....	....	....	....	....	....	....	....
	NHL Totals		**23**	**1**	**1**	**2**	**1**	**1**	**2**	**16**	**0**	**0**	**0**	**17**	**5.9**	**15**	**2**	**20**	**4**		....	....	....	....	....	....	....	....

• SKOULA, Martin

D – L. 6'3", 218 lbs. b: Litomerice, Czech., 10/28/1979. Colorado's 2nd, 17th overall, in 1998.

Season	Club	League	GP	G	A	Pts	AG	AA	APts	PIM	PP	SH	GW	S	%	TGF	PGF	TGA	PGA	+/-	GP	G	A	Pts	PIM	PP	SH	GW
1995-96	HC Chemopetrol Litvinov	Czech-Jr.	38	0	4	4	....	....	....	....	....	....	....	....	....	....	....	....	....	....	....	....	....	....	....	....	....	....
	HC Chemopetrol Litvinov	Czech-Rep	....	....	....	....	....	....	....	....	....	....	....	....	....	....	....	....	....	....	1	0	0	0	0	....	....	....
1996-97	HC Chemopetrol Litvinov	Czech-Jr.	38	2	9	11	....	....	....	....	....	....	....	....	....	....	....	....	....	....	....	....	....	....	....	....	....	....
	HC Chemopetrol Litvinov	Czech-Rep	1	0	0	0	....	....	....	0	....	....	....	....	....	....	....	....	....	....	....	....	....	....	....	....	....	....
1997-98	Barrie Colts	OHL	66	8	36	44	....	....	....	36	....	....	....	....	....	....	....	....	....	....	6	1	3	4	4	....	....	....
1998-99	Barrie Colts	OHL	67	13	46	59	....	....	....	46	....	....	....	....	....	....	....	....	....	....	12	3	10	13	13	....	....	....
	Hershey Bears	AHL	....	....	....	....	....	....	....	....	....	....	....	....	....	....	....	....	....	....	1	0	0	0	0	....	....	....
99-2000	**Colorado Avalanche**	**NHL**	**80**	**3**	**13**	**16**	**3**	**12**	**15**	**20**	**2**	**0**	**0**	**66**	**4.5**	**61**	**7**	**50**	**1**	**5**	**17**	**0**	**2**	**2**	**4**	**0**	**0**	**0**
	NHL Totals		**80**	**3**	**13**	**16**	**3**	**12**	**15**	**20**	**2**	**0**	**0**	**66**	**4.5**	**61**	**7**	**50**	**1**		**17**	**0**	**2**	**2**	**4**	**0**	**0**	**0**

OHL Second All-Star Team (1999)

• SKRASTINS, Karlis

D – L. 6'1", 196 lbs. b: Riga, USSR, 7/9/1974. Nashville's 8th, 230th overall, in 1998.

Season	Club	League	GP	G	A	Pts	AG	AA	APts	PIM	PP	SH	GW	S	%	TGF	PGF	TGA	PGA	+/-	GP	G	A	Pts	PIM	PP	SH	GW
1992-93	Pardaugava Riga	CIS	40	3	5	8	....	....	....	16	....	....	....	....	....	....	....	....	....	....	2	0	0	0	0	....	....	....
1993-94	Pardaugava Riga	CIS	42	7	5	12	....	....	....	18	....	....	....	....	....	....	....	....	....	....	2	1	0	1	4	....	....	....
1994-95	Pardaugava Riga	CIS	52	4	14	18	....	....	....	69	....	....	....	....	....	....	....	....	....	....	....	....	....	....	....	....	....	....
1995-96	TPS Turku	Finland	50	4	11	15	....	....	....	32	....	....	....	....	....	....	....	....	....	....	11	2	2	4	10	....	....	....
1996-97	TPS Turku	Finland	50	2	8	10	....	....	....	20	....	....	....	....	....	....	....	....	....	....	12	0	4	4	2	....	....	....
	TPS Turku	EuroHL	6	0	1	1	....	....	....	4	....	....	....	....	....	....	....	....	....	....	4	0	0	0	14	....	....	....
1997-98	TPS Turku	Finland	48	4	15	19	....	....	....	67	....	....	....	....	....	....	....	....	....	....	4	0	0	0	0	....	....	....
	TPS Turku	EuroHL	6	0	1	1	....	....	....	6	....	....	....	....	....	....	....	....	....	....	....	....	....	....	....	....	....	....
1998-99	**Nashville Predators**	**NHL**	**2**	**0**	**1**	**1**	**0**	**1**	**1**	**0**	**0**	**0**	**0**	**0**	**0.0**	**1**	**0**	**1**	**0**	**0**	....	....	....	....	....	....	....	....
	Milwaukee Admirals	IHL	75	8	36	44	....	....	....	47	....	....	....	....	....	....	....	....	....	....	2	0	1	1	2	....	....	....
	Latvia	WC-A	6	1	1	2	....	....	....	6	....	....	....	....	....	....	....	....	....	....	....	....	....	....	....	....	....	....
99-2000	**Nashville Predators**	**NHL**	**59**	**5**	**6**	**11**	**6**	**6**	**12**	**20**	**1**	**0**	**2**	**51**	**9.8**	**45**	**2**	**68**	**18**	**–7**	....	....	....	....	....	....	....	....
	Milwaukee Admirals	IHL	19	3	8	11	....	....	....	10	....	....	....	....	....	....	....	....	....	....	....	....	....	....	....	....	....	....
	Latvia	WC-A	7	1	2	3	....	....	....	4	....	....	....	....	....	....	....	....	....	....	....	....	....	....	....	....	....	....
	NHL Totals		**61**	**5**	**7**	**12**	**6**	**7**	**13**	**20**	**1**	**0**	**2**	**51**	**9.8**	**46**	**2**	**69**	**18**		....	....	....	....	....	....	....	....

• SKRBEK, Pavel

D – L. 6'3", 212 lbs. b: Kladno, Czech., 8/9/1978. Pittsburgh's 2nd, 28th overall, in 1996.

Season	Club	League	GP	G	A	Pts	AG	AA	APts	PIM	PP	SH	GW	S	%	TGF	PGF	TGA	PGA	+/-	GP	G	A	Pts	PIM	PP	SH	GW
1994-95	Poldi Kladno-Jr.	Czech-Rep	29	7	6	13	....	....	....	....	....	....	....	....	....	....	....	....	....	....	....	....	....	....	....	....	....	....
1995-96	Poldi Kladno-Jr.	Czech-Rep	29	10	12	22	....	....	....	....	....	....	....	....	....	....	....	....	....	....	....	....	....	....	....	....	....	....
	Poldi Kladno	Czech-Rep	13	0	1	1	....	....	....	....	....	....	....	....	....	....	....	....	....	....	5	0	0	0	....	....	....	....
1996-97	Poldi Kladno	Czech-Rep	35	1	5	6	....	....	....	26	....	....	....	....	....	....	....	....	....	....	3	0	0	0	4	....	....	....
1997-98	Poldi Kladno	Czech-Rep	47	4	10	14	....	....	....	126	....	....	....	....	....	....	....	....	....	....	....	....	....	....	....	....	....	....
	Czech-Republic	WJC-A	7	2	4	6	....	....	....	8	....	....	....	....	....	....	....	....	....	....	....	....	....	....	....	....	....	....
1998-99	**Pittsburgh Penguins**	**NHL**	**4**	**0**	**0**	**0**	**0**	**0**	**0**	**2**	**0**	**0**	**0**	**1**	**0.0**	**4**	**0**	**2**	**0**	**2**	....	....	....	....	....	....	....	....
	Syracuse Crunch	AHL	64	6	16	22	....	....	....	38	....	....	....	....	....	....	....	....	....	....	....	....	....	....	....	....	....	....
99-2000	Wilkes-Barre Penguins	AHL	51	7	16	23	....	....	....	50	....	....	....	....	....	....	....	....	....	....	....	....	....	....	....	....	....	....
	Milwaukee Admirals	IHL	6	0	0	0	....	....	....	0	....	....	....	....	....	....	....	....	....	....	....	....	....	....	....	....	....	....
	NHL Totals		**4**	**0**	**0**	**0**	**0**	**0**	**0**	**2**	**0**	**0**	**0**	**1**	**0.0**	**4**	**0**	**2**	**0**									

Traded to **Nashville** by **Pittsburgh** for Bob Boughner, March 13, 2000.

• SKRIKO, Petri

Petri K. LW – L. 5'10", 175 lbs. b: Lappeenranta, Finland, 3/12/1962. Vancouver's 7th, 157th overall, in 1981.

			REGULAR SEASON																		PLAYOFFS							
Season	Club	League	GP	G	A	Pts	AG	AA	APts	PIM	PP	SH	GW	S	%	TGF	PGF	TGA	PGA	+/–	GP	G	A	Pts	PIM	PP	SH	GW
1979-80	SaiPa Lappeenranta	Finland-2	36	25	20	45	....	....	....	8	....	....	....	....	....	....	....	....	....	....	....	....	....	....	....	....	....	....
1980-81	SaiPa Lappeenranta	Finland	36	20	13	33	....	....	....	14	....	....	....	....	....	....	....	....	....	....	....	....	....	....	....	....	....	....
	Finland	WJC-A	5	3	3	6	....	....	....	10	....	....	....	....	....	....	....	....	....	....	....	....	....	....	....	....	....	....
1981-82	SaiPa Lappeenranta	Finland	33	19	27	46	....	....	....	24	....	....	....	....	....	....	....	....	....	....	....	....	....	....	....	....	....	....
	Finland	WJC-A	7	*8	7	15	....	....	....	4	....	....	....	....	....	....	....	....	....	....	....	....	....	....	....	....	....	....
1982-83	SaiPa Lappeenranta	Finland	36	23	12	35	....	....	....	12	....	....	....	....	....	....	....	....	....	....	....	....	....	....	....	....	....	....
	Finland	WEC-A	10	4	2	6	....	....	....	6	....	....	....	....	....	....	....	....	....	....	....	....	....	....	....	....	....	....
1983-84	SaiPa Lappeenranta	Finland	32	25	26	51	....	....	....	13	....	....	....	....	....	....	....	....	....	....	....	....	....	....	....	....	....	....
	Finland	Olympics	6	6	4	10	....	....	....	8	....	....	....	....	....	....	....	....	....	....	....	....	....	....	....	....	....	....
1984-85	**Vancouver Canucks**	**NHL**	**72**	**21**	**14**	**35**	**17**	**10**	**27**	**10**	**3**	**0**	**2**	**154**	**13.6**	**51**	**9**	**70**	**2**	**–26**	....	....	....	....	....	....	....	....
	Finland	WEC-A	10	2	2	4	....	....	....	0	....	....	....	....	....	....	....	....	....	....	....	....	....	....	....	....	....	....
1985-86	**Vancouver Canucks**	**NHL**	**80**	**38**	**40**	**78**	**30**	**27**	**57**	**34**	**12**	**1**	**2**	**192**	**19.8**	**117**	**44**	**121**	**31**	**–17**	**3**	**0**	**0**	**0**	**0**	**0**	**0**	**0**
1986-87	**Vancouver Canucks**	**NHL**	**76**	**33**	**41**	**74**	**29**	**30**	**59**	**44**	**10**	**6**	**4**	**224**	**14.7**	**108**	**35**	**100**	**23**	**–4**	....	....	....	....	....	....	....	....
	Finland	WEC-A	10	1	1	2	....	....	....	2	....	....	....	....	....	....	....	....	....	....	....	....	....	....	....	....	....	....
1987-88	Finland	Can-Cup	5	0	1	1	....	....	....	2	....	....	....	....	....	....	....	....	....	....	....	....	....	....	....	....	....	....
	Vancouver Canucks	**NHL**	**73**	**30**	**34**	**64**	**26**	**24**	**50**	**32**	**10**	**2**	**2**	**172**	**17.4**	**92**	**32**	**89**	**17**	**–12**	....	....	....	....	....	....	....	....
1988-89	**Vancouver Canucks**	**NHL**	**74**	**30**	**36**	**66**	**25**	**25**	**50**	**57**	**9**	**0**	**5**	**204**	**14.7**	**93**	**38**	**72**	**14**	**–3**	**7**	**1**	**5**	**6**	**0**	**0**	**0**	**0**
1989-90	**Vancouver Canucks**	**NHL**	**77**	**15**	**33**	**48**	**13**	**24**	**37**	**36**	**3**	**1**	**2**	**172**	**8.7**	**77**	**26**	**99**	**27**	**–21**	....	....	....	....	....	....	....	....
1990-91	**Vancouver Canucks**	**NHL**	**20**	**4**	**4**	**8**	**4**	**3**	**7**	**8**	**0**	**1**	**2**	**47**	**8.5**	**12**	**4**	**22**	**5**	**–9**	....	....	....	....	....	....	....	....
	Boston Bruins	**NHL**	**28**	**5**	**14**	**19**	**5**	**11**	**16**	**9**	**1**	**0**	**3**	**73**	**6.8**	**36**	**11**	**23**	**2**	**4**	**18**	**4**	**4**	**8**	**4**	**3**	**0**	**0**
1991-92	Finland	Can-Cup	6	3	2	5	....	....	....	2	....	....	....	....	....	....	....	....	....	....	....	....	....	....	....	....	....	....
	Boston Bruins	**NHL**	**9**	**1**	**0**	**1**	**1**	**0**	**1**	**6**	**1**	**0**	**0**	**20**	**5.0**	**4**	**3**	**4**	**0**	**–3**	....	....	....	....	....	....	....	....
	Winnipeg Jets	**NHL**	**15**	**2**	**3**	**5**	**2**	**2**	**4**	**4**	**0**	**0**	**0**	**27**	**7.4**	**12**	**3**	**10**	**0**	**–1**	....	....	....	....	....	....	....	....
	Finland	Olympics	8	1	4	5	....	....	....	4	....	....	....	....	....	....	....	....	....	....	....	....	....	....	....	....	....	....
1992-93	**San Jose Sharks**	**NHL**	**17**	**4**	**3**	**7**	**3**	**2**	**5**	**6**	**2**	**1**	**0**	**35**	**11.4**	**9**	**4**	**17**	**4**	**–8**	....	....	....	....	....	....	....	....
	Kiekko-Espoo	Finland	18	5	4	9	....	....	....	8	....	....	....	....	....	....	....	....	....	....	....	....	....	....	....	....	....	....
1993-94	Herning IK	Denmark	28	30	39	69	....	....	....	....	....	....	....	....	....	....	....	....	....	....	7	7	1	8	....	....	....	....
1994-95	Herning IK	Denmark	28	34	49	83	....	....	....	....	....	....	....	....	....	....	....	....	....	....	7	7	8	15	....	....	....	....
1995-96	Herning IK	Denmark	39	40	*55	95	....	....	....	30	....	....	....	....	....	....	....	....	....	....	....	....	....	....	....	....	....	....
1996-97	Herning IK	Denmark	48	49	60	109	....	....	....	57	....	....	....	....	....	....	....	....	....	....	....	....	....	....	....	....	....	....
1997-98	Herning IK	Denmark	48	38	58	96	....	....	....	....	....	....	....	....	....	....	....	....	....	....	....	....	....	....	....	....	....	....
1998-99	Herning IK	Denmark	42	26	43	69	....	....	....	....	....	....	....	....	....	....	....	....	....	....	....	....	....	....	....	....	....	....
	NHL Totals		**541**	**183**	**222**	**405**	**155**	**158**	**313**	**246**	**51**	**12**	**22**	**1320**	**13.9**	**611**	**209**	**627**	**125**		**28**	**5**	**9**	**14**	**4**	**3**	**0**	**0**

Finnish Rookie of the Year (1981) • WJC-A All-Star Team (1982) • Named Best Forward at WJC-A (1982) • Finnish First All-Star Team (1984)

Traded to **Boston** by **Vancouver** for Boston's 2nd round choice (Mike Peca) in 1992 Entry Draft, January 16, 1991. Traded to **Winnipeg** by **Boston** for Brent Ashton, October 29, 1991. Signed as a free agent by **San Jose**, August 27, 1992.

• SKRUDLAND, Brian

Brian N. C – L. 6', 195 lbs. b: Peace River, Alta., 7/31/1963.

Season	Club	League	GP	G	A	Pts	AG	AA	APts	PIM	PP	SH	GW	S	%	TGF	PGF	TGA	PGA	+/–	GP	G	A	Pts	PIM	PP	SH	GW
1979-80	Saskatoon Contacts	SAHA	STATISTICS NOT AVAILABLE																									
1980-81	Saskatoon Blades	WHL	66	15	27	42	....	....	....	97	....	....	....	....	....	....	....	....	....	....	....	....	....	....	....	....	....	....
1981-82	Saskatoon Blades	WHL	71	27	29	56	....	....	....	135	....	....	....	....	....	....	....	....	....	....	5	0	1	1	2	....	....	....
1982-83	Saskatoon Blades	WHL	71	35	59	94	....	....	....	42	....	....	....	....	....	....	....	....	....	....	6	1	3	4	19	....	....	....
1983-84	Nova Scotia Voyageurs	AHL	56	13	12	25	....	....	....	55	....	....	....	....	....	....	....	....	....	....	12	2	8	10	14	....	....	....
1984-85	Sherbrooke Canadiens	AHL	70	22	28	50	....	....	....	109	....	....	....	....	....	....	....	....	....	....	17	9	8	17	23	....	....	....
1985-86♦	**Montreal Canadiens**	**NHL**	**65**	**9**	**13**	**22**	**7**	**9**	**16**	**57**	**0**	**2**	**0**	**62**	**14.5**	**30**	**0**	**33**	**6**	**3**	**20**	**2**	**4**	**6**	**76**	**0**	**0**	**1**
1986-87	**Montreal Canadiens**	**NHL**	**79**	**11**	**17**	**28**	**9**	**12**	**21**	**107**	**0**	**1**	**0**	**72**	**15.3**	**54**	**1**	**57**	**22**	**18**	**14**	**1**	**5**	**6**	**29**	**0**	**0**	**0**
1987-88	**Montreal Canadiens**	**NHL**	**79**	**12**	**24**	**36**	**10**	**17**	**27**	**112**	**0**	**1**	**3**	**96**	**12.5**	**55**	**0**	**60**	**19**	**14**	**11**	**1**	**5**	**6**	**24**	**0**	**0**	**0**
1988-89	**Montreal Canadiens**	**NHL**	**71**	**12**	**29**	**41**	**10**	**21**	**31**	**84**	**1**	**1**	**5**	**98**	**12.2**	**60**	**3**	**53**	**18**	**22**	**21**	**3**	**7**	**10**	**40**	**0**	**0**	**0**
1989-90	**Montreal Canadiens**	**NHL**	**59**	**11**	**31**	**42**	**9**	**22**	**31**	**56**	**4**	**0**	**1**	**70**	**15.7**	**65**	**15**	**40**	**11**	**21**	**11**	**3**	**5**	**8**	**30**	**0**	**0**	**1**
1990-91	Montreal Canadiens	Fr-Tour	4	0	0	0	....	....	....	12	....	....	....	....	....	....	....	....	....	....	....	....	....	....	....	....	....	....
	Montreal Canadiens	**NHL**	**57**	**15**	**19**	**34**	**14**	**14**	**28**	**85**	**1**	**1**	**2**	**71**	**21.1**	**48**	**5**	**44**	**13**	**12**	**13**	**3**	**10**	**13**	**42**	**1**	**0**	**0**
1991-92	**Montreal Canadiens**	**NHL**	**42**	**3**	**3**	**6**	**3**	**2**	**5**	**36**	**0**	**0**	**1**	**51**	**5.9**	**14**	**0**	**29**	**11**	**–4**	**11**	**1**	**1**	**2**	**20**	**0**	**0**	**0**
1992-93	**Montreal Canadiens**	**NHL**	**23**	**5**	**3**	**8**	**4**	**2**	**6**	**55**	**0**	**2**	**1**	**29**	**17.2**	**9**	**0**	**13**	**5**	**1**	....	....	....	....	....	....	....	....
	Calgary Flames	**NHL**	**16**	**2**	**4**	**6**	**2**	**3**	**5**	**10**	**0**	**0**	**0**	**22**	**9.1**	**9**	**0**	**11**	**5**	**3**	**6**	**0**	**3**	**3**	**12**	**0**	**0**	**0**
1993-94	**Florida Panthers**	**NHL**	**79**	**15**	**25**	**40**	**14**	**19**	**33**	**136**	**0**	**2**	**1**	**110**	**13.6**	**49**	**1**	**67**	**32**	**13**	....	....	....	....	....	....	....	....
1994-95	**Florida Panthers**	**NHL**	**47**	**5**	**9**	**14**	**9**	**13**	**22**	**88**	**1**	**0**	**0**	**44**	**11.4**	**24**	**1**	**36**	**13**	**0**	....	....	....	....	....	....	....	....
1995-96	**Florida Panthers**	**NHL**	**79**	**7**	**20**	**27**	**7**	**16**	**23**	**129**	**0**	**1**	**1**	**90**	**7.8**	**47**	**1**	**65**	**25**	**6**	**21**	**1**	**3**	**4**	**18**	**0**	**0**	**0**
1996-97	**Florida Panthers**	**NHL**	**51**	**5**	**13**	**18**	**5**	**12**	**17**	**48**	**0**	**0**	**2**	**57**	**8.8**	**22**	**0**	**33**	**15**	**4**	....	....	....	....	....	....	....	....
1997-98	**New York Rangers**	**NHL**	**59**	**5**	**6**	**11**	**6**	**6**	**12**	**39**	**0**	**0**	**1**	**42**	**11.9**	**13**	**0**	**31**	**14**	**–4**	....	....	....	....	....	....	....	....
	Dallas Stars	**NHL**	**13**	**2**	**0**	**2**	**2**	**0**	**2**	**10**	**0**	**0**	**0**	**13**	**15.4**	**2**	**0**	**7**	**3**	**–2**	**17**	**0**	**1**	**1**	**16**	**0**	**0**	**0**
1998-99♦	**Dallas Stars**	**NHL**	**40**	**4**	**1**	**5**	**5**	**1**	**6**	**33**	**0**	**0**	**1**	**33**	**12.1**	**8**	**0**	**9**	**3**	**2**	**19**	**0**	**2**	**2**	**16**	**0**	**0**	**0**
99-2000	**Dallas Stars**	**NHL**	**22**	**1**	**2**	**3**	**1**	**2**	**3**	**22**	**0**	**0**	**0**	**16**	**6.3**	**4**	**0**	**5**	**1**	**0**	....	....	....	....	....	....	....	....
	NHL Totals		**881**	**124**	**219**	**343**	**117**	**171**	**288**	**1107**	**7**	**11**	**19**	**976**	**12.7**	**513**	**27**	**593**	**216**		**164**	**15**	**46**	**61**	**323**	**1**	**0**	**2**

Won Jack A. Butterfield Trophy (Playoff MVP - AHL) (1985)

Signed as a free agent by **Montreal**, September 13, 1983. Traded to **Calgary** by **Montreal** for Gary Leeman, January 28, 1993. Claimed by **Florida** from **Çalgary** in Expansion Draft, June 24, 1993. Signed as a free agent by **NY Rangers**, August 21, 1997. Traded to **Dallas** by **NY Rangers** with Mike Keane and NY Rangers' 6th round choice (Pavel Patera) in 1998 Entry Draft for Todd Harvey, Bob Errey and Dallas' 4th round choice (Boyd Kane) in 1998 Entry Draft, March 24, 1998. • Missed majority of 1999-2000 season recovering from rib injury originally suffered in game vs. Anaheim, October 8, 1999.

• SLANEY, John

D – L. 6', 185 lbs. b: St. John's, Nfld., 2/7/1972. Washington's 1st, 9th overall, in 1990.

Season	Club	League	GP	G	A	Pts	AG	AA	APts	PIM	PP	SH	GW	S	%	TGF	PGF	TGA	PGA	+/–	GP	G	A	Pts	PIM	PP	SH	GW
1987-88	St. John's Midget Capitals	NFAHA	65	41	69	110	....	....	....	70	....	....	....	....	....	....	....	....	....	....	....	....	....	....	....	....	....	....
1988-89	Cornwall Royals	OHL	66	16	43	59	....	....	....	23	....	....	....	....	....	....	....	....	....	....	18	8	16	24	10	....	....	....
1989-90	Cornwall Royals	OHL	64	38	59	97	....	....	....	68	....	....	....	....	....	....	....	....	....	....	6	0	8	8	11	....	....	....
1990-91	Cornwall Royals	OHL	34	21	25	46	....	....	....	28	....	....	....	....	....	....	....	....	....	....	....	....	....	....	....	....	....	....
	Canada	WJC-A	7	1	2	3	....	....	....	6	....	....	....	....	....	....	....	....	....	....	....	....	....	....	....	....	....	....
1991-92	Cornwall Royals	OHL	34	19	41	60	....	....	....	43	....	....	....	....	....	....	....	....	....	....	6	3	8	11	0	....	....	....
	Canada	WJC-A	7	1	3	4	....	....	....	6	....	....	....	....	....	....	....	....	....	....	....	....	....	....	....	....	....	....
	Baltimore Skipjacks	AHL	6	2	4	6	....	....	....	0	....	....	....	....	....	....	....	....	....	....	....	....	....	....	....	....	....	....
1992-93	Baltimore Skipjacks	AHL	79	20	46	66	....	....	....	60	....	....	....	....	....	....	....	....	....	....	7	0	7	7	8	....	....	....
1993-94	**Washington Capitals**	**NHL**	**47**	**7**	**9**	**16**	**6**	**7**	**13**	**27**	**3**	**0**	**1**	**70**	**10.0**	**43**	**8**	**36**	**4**	**3**	**11**	**1**	**1**	**2**	**2**	**1**	**0**	**0**
	Portland Pirates	AHL	29	14	13	27	....	....	....	17	....	....	....	....	....	....	....	....	....	....	....	....	....	....	....	....	....	....
1994-95	**Washington Capitals**	**NHL**	**16**	**0**	**3**	**3**	**0**	**4**	**4**	**6**	**0**	**0**	**0**	**21**	**0.0**	**8**	**4**	**7**	**0**	**–3**	....	....	....	....	....	....	....	....
	Portland Pirates	AHL	8	3	10	13	....	....	....	4	....	....	....	....	....	....	....	....	....	....	7	1	3	4	4	....	....	....
1995-96	**Colorado Avalanche**	**NHL**	**7**	**0**	**3**	**3**	**0**	**2**	**2**	**4**	**0**	**0**	**0**	**12**	**0.0**	**9**	**2**	**6**	**1**	**2**	....	....	....	....	....	....	....	....
	Cornwall Aces	AHL	5	0	4	4	....	....	....	2	....	....	....	....	....	....	....	....	....	....	....	....	....	....	....	....	....	....
	Los Angeles Kings	**NHL**	**31**	**6**	**11**	**17**	**6**	**9**	**15**	**10**	**3**	**1**	**0**	**63**	**9.5**	**45**	**16**	**26**	**2**	**5**	....	....	....	....	....	....	....	....
1996-97	**Los Angeles Kings**	**NHL**	**32**	**3**	**11**	**14**	**3**	**10**	**13**	**4**	**1**	**0**	**1**	**60**	**5.0**	**35**	**10**	**38**	**3**	**–10**	....	....	....	....	....	....	....	....
	Phoenix Roadrunners	IHL	35	9	25	34	....	....	....	8	....	....	....	....	....	....	....	....	....	....	....	....	....	....	....	....	....	....
1997-98	**Phoenix Coyotes**	**NHL**	**55**	**3**	**14**	**17**	**4**	**14**	**18**	**24**	**1**	**0**	**1**	**74**	**4.1**	**46**	**15**	**42**	**8**	**–3**	....	....	....	....	....	....	....	....
	Las Vegas Thunder	IHL	5	2	2	4	....	....	....	10	....	....	....	....	....	....	....	....	....	....	....	....	....	....	....	....	....	....

			REGULAR SEASON																		PLAYOFFS							
Season	Club	League	GP	G	A	Pts	AG	AA	APts	PIM	PP	SH	GW	S	%	TGF	PGF	TGA	PGA	+/–	GP	G	A	Pts	PIM	PP	SH	GW
1998-99	**Nashville Predators**	**NHL**	**46**	**2**	**12**	**14**	**2**	**12**	**14**	**14**	**0**	**0**	**1**	**84**	**2.4**	**41**	**17**	**49**	**13**	**–12**	....	....	....	....	....	....	....	....
	Milwaukee Admirals	IHL	7	0	1	1	....	....	....	0	....	....	....	....	....	....	....	....	....	....	....	....	....	....	....	....	....	....
99-2000	**Pittsburgh Penguins**	**NHL**	**29**	**1**	**4**	**5**	**1**	**4**	**5**	**10**	**1**	**0**	**0**	**27**	**3.7**	**14**	**7**	**17**	**0**	**–10**	**2**	**1**	**0**	**1**	**2**	**1**	**0**	**0**
	Wilkes-Barre Penguins	AHL	49	30	30	60	....	....	....	25	....	....	....	....	....	....	....	....	....	....	....	....	....	....	....	....	....	....
	NHL Totals		**263**	**22**	**67**	**89**	**22**	**62**	**84**	**99**	**9**	**1**	**4**	**411**	**5.4**	**241**	**79**	**221**	**31**		**13**	**2**	**1**	**3**	**4**	**2**	**0**	**0**

OHL First All-Star Team (1990) • Canadian Major Junior Defenseman of the Year (1990) • OHL Second All-Star Team (1991)

Traded to **Colorado** by **Washington** for Philadelphia's 3rd round choice (previously acquired, Washington selected Shawn McNeil) in 1996 Entry Draft, July 12, 1995. Traded to **LA Kings** by **Colorado** for Winnipeg's 6th round choice (previously acquired, Colorado selected Brian Willsie) in 1996 Entry Draft, December 28, 1995. Signed as a free agent by **Phoenix**, August 19, 1997. Claimed by **Nashville** from **Phoenix** in Expansion Draft, June 26, 1998.

• SLEGR, Jiri

D – L. 6', 207 lbs. b: Jihlava, Czech., 5/30/1971. Vancouver's 3rd, 23rd overall, in 1990.

Season	Club	League	GP	G	A	Pts	AG	AA	APts	PIM	PP	SH	GW	S	%	TGF	PGF	TGA	PGA	+/–	GP	G	A	Pts	PIM	PP	SH	GW
1987-88	CHZ Litvinov	Czech.	4	1	1	2	....	....	....	0	....	....	....	....	....	....	....	....	....	....	....	....	....	....	....	....	....	....
1988-89	CHZ Litvinov	Czech.	8	0	0	0	....	....	....	4	....	....	....	....	....	....	....	....	....	....	....	....	....	....	....	....	....	....
	Czechoslovakia	EJC-A	6	3	1	4	....	....	....	4	....	....	....	....	....	....	....	....	....	....	....	....	....	....	....	....	....	....
1989-90	CHZ Litvinov	Czech.	51	4	15	19	....	....	....	....	....	....	....	....	....	....	....	....	....	....	....	....	....	....	....	....	....	....
	Czechoslovakia	WJC-A	7	3	4	7	....	....	....	18	....	....	....	....	....	....	....	....	....	....	....	....	....	....	....	....	....	....
1990-91	CHZ Litvinov	Czech.	47	11	36	47	....	....	....	26	....	....	....	....	....	....	....	....	....	....	....	....	....	....	....	....	....	....
	Czechoslovakia	WJC-A	7	0	9	9	....	....	....	14	....	....	....	....	....	....	....	....	....	....	....	....	....	....	....	....	....	....
	Czechoslovakia	WEC-A	9	2	1	3	....	....	....	32	....	....	....	....	....	....	....	....	....	....	....	....	....	....	....	....	....	....
1991-92	Czechoslovakia	Can-Cup	5	0	1	1	....	....	....	25	....	....	....	....	....	....	....	....	....	....	....	....	....	....	....	....	....	....
	CHZ Litvinov	Czech.	42	9	23	32	....	....	....	38	....	....	....	....	....	....	....	....	....	....	....	....	....	....	....	....	....	....
	Czechoslovakia	Olympics	8	1	1	2	....	....	....	14	....	....	....	....	....	....	....	....	....	....	....	....	....	....	....	....	....	....
1992-93	**Vancouver Canucks**	**NHL**	**41**	**4**	**22**	**26**	**3**	**15**	**18**	**109**	**2**	**0**	**0**	**89**	**4.5**	**61**	**16**	**43**	**14**	**16**	**5**	**0**	**3**	**3**	**4**	**0**	**0**	**0**
	Hamilton Canucks	AHL	21	4	14	18	....	....	....	42	....	....	....	....	....	....	....	....	....	....	....	....	....	....	....	....	....	....
1993-94	**Vancouver Canucks**	**NHL**	**78**	**5**	**33**	**38**	**5**	**26**	**31**	**86**	**1**	**0**	**0**	**160**	**3.1**	**86**	**31**	**61**	**6**	**0**	....	....	....	....	....	....	....	....
1994-95	HC Chemopetrol Litvinov	Czech-Rep	11	3	10	13	....	....	....	80	....	....	....	....	....	....	....	....	....	....	....	....	....	....	....	....	....	....
	Vancouver Canucks	**NHL**	**19**	**1**	**5**	**6**	**2**	**7**	**9**	**32**	**0**	**0**	**1**	**42**	**2.4**	**21**	**4**	**17**	**0**	**0**	....	....	....	....	....	....	....	....
	Edmonton Oilers	**NHL**	**12**	**1**	**5**	**6**	**2**	**7**	**9**	**14**	**1**	**0**	**0**	**27**	**3.7**	**12**	**4**	**17**	**4**	**–5**	....	....	....	....	....	....	....	....
1995-96	**Edmonton Oilers**	**NHL**	**57**	**4**	**13**	**17**	**4**	**11**	**15**	**74**	**0**	**1**	**1**	**91**	**4.4**	**50**	**8**	**56**	**13**	**–1**	....	....	....	....	....	....	....	....
	Cape Breton Oilers	AHL	4	1	2	3	....	....	....	4	....	....	....	....	....	....	....	....	....	....	....	....	....	....	....	....	....	....
1996-97	Czech-Republic	W-Cup	3	0	0	0	....	....	....	6	....	....	....	....	....	....	....	....	....	....	....	....	....	....	....	....	....	....
	HC Chemopetrol Litvinov	Czech-Rep	1	0	0	0	....	....	....	0	....	....	....	....	....	....	....	....	....	....	....	....	....	....	....	....	....	....
	Sodertalje SK	Sweden	30	4	14	18	....	....	....	62	....	....	....	....	....	....	....	....	....	....	....	....	....	....	....	....	....	....
	Sodertalje SK	Sweden-Q	10	4	2	6	....	....	....	32	....	....	....	....	....	....	....	....	....	....	....	....	....	....	....	....	....	....
	Czech-Republic	WC-A	8	1	1	2	....	....	....	35	....	....	....	....	....	....	....	....	....	....	....	....	....	....	....	....	....	....
1997-98	**Pittsburgh Penguins**	**NHL**	**73**	**5**	**12**	**17**	**6**	**12**	**18**	**109**	**1**	**1**	**0**	**131**	**3.8**	**62**	**9**	**53**	**10**	**10**	**6**	**0**	**4**	**4**	**2**	**0**	**0**	**0**
	Czech-Republic	Olympics	6	1	0	1	....	....	....	8	....	....	....	....	....	....	....	....	....	....	....	....	....	....	....	....	....	....
	Czech-Republic	WC-A	6	0	1	1	....	....	....	20	....	....	....	....	....	....	....	....	....	....	....	....	....	....	....	....	....	....
1998-99	**Pittsburgh Penguins**	**NHL**	**63**	**3**	**20**	**23**	**4**	**19**	**23**	**86**	**1**	**0**	**0**	**91**	**3.3**	**57**	**1**	**60**	**17**	**13**	**13**	**1**	**3**	**4**	**12**	**0**	**0**	**1**
99-2000	**Pittsburgh Penguins**	**NHL**	**74**	**11**	**20**	**31**	**12**	**19**	**31**	**82**	**0**	**0**	**2**	**144**	**7.6**	**89**	**11**	**82**	**24**	**20**	**10**	**2**	**3**	**5**	**19**	**0**	**0**	**1**
	NHL Totals		**417**	**34**	**130**	**164**	**38**	**116**	**154**	**592**	**6**	**2**	**4**	**775**	**4.4**	**438**	**84**	**389**	**88**		**34**	**3**	**13**	**16**	**37**	**0**	**0**	**2**

• Son of Jiri Bubla • WJC-A All-Star Team (1990) • Named Best Defenseman at WJC-A (1991) • Czechoslovakian First All-Star Team (1991)

Traded to **Edmonton** by **Vancouver** for Roman Oksiuta, April 7, 1995. Traded to **Pittsburgh** by **Edmonton** for Pittsburgh's 3rd round choice (later traded to New Jersey — New Jersey selected Brian Gionta) in 1998 Entry Draft, August 12, 1997.

• SLEIGHER, Louis

RW – R. 5'11", 200 lbs. b: Nouvelle, Que., 10/23/1958. Montreal's 24th, 233rd overall, in 1978.

Season	Club	League	GP	G	A	Pts	AG	AA	APts	PIM	PP	SH	GW	S	%	TGF	PGF	TGA	PGA	+/–	GP	G	A	Pts	PIM	PP	SH	GW
1976-77	Chicoutimi Sagueneens	QMJHL	70	53	48	101	....	....	....	49	....	....	....	....	....	....	....	....	....	....	8	5	3	8	9	....	....	....
1977-78	Chicoutimi Sagueneens	QMJHL	71	65	54	119	....	....	....	125	....	....	....	....	....	....	....	....	....	....	....	....	....	....	....	....	....	....
1978-79	Birmingham Bulls	WHA	62	26	12	38	....	....	....	46	....	....	....	....	....	....	....	....	....	....	....	....	....	....	....	....	....	....
1979-80	**Quebec Nordiques**	**NHL**	**2**	**0**	**1**	**1**	**0**	**1**	**1**	**0**	**0**	**0**	**0**	**0**	**0.0**	**1**	**0**	**0**	**0**	**1**	....	....	....	....	....	....	....	....
	Syracuse Firebirds	AHL	58	28	15	43	....	....	....	37	....	....	....	....	....	....	....	....	....	....	1	0	1	1	15	....	....	....
1980-81	Erie Blades	EHL	50	39	29	68	....	....	....	129	....	....	....	....	....	....	....	....	....	....	8	6	4	10	12	....	....	....
1981-82	**Quebec Nordiques**	**NHL**	**8**	**0**	**0**	**0**	**0**	**0**	**0**	**0**	**0**	**0**	**0**	**3**	**0.0**	**1**	**0**	**4**	**1**	**–2**	....	....	....	....	....	....	....	....
	Fredericton Express	AHL	59	32	34	66	....	....	....	37	....	....	....	....	....	....	....	....	....	....	....	....	....	....	....	....	....	....
1982-83	**Quebec Nordiques**	**NHL**	**51**	**14**	**10**	**24**	**11**	**7**	**18**	**49**	**0**	**0**	**1**	**55**	**25.5**	**31**	**0**	**31**	**8**	**8**	**4**	**0**	**0**	**0**	**4**	**0**	**0**	**0**
	Fredericton Express	AHL	12	8	2	10	....	....	....	9	....	....	....	....	....	....	....	....	....	....	....	....	....	....	....	....	....	....
1983-84	**Quebec Nordiques**	**NHL**	**44**	**15**	**19**	**34**	**12**	**13**	**25**	**32**	**3**	**1**	**1**	**74**	**20.3**	**56**	**8**	**25**	**0**	**23**	**7**	**1**	**1**	**2**	**42**	**0**	**0**	**0**
1984-85	**Quebec Nordiques**	**NHL**	**6**	**1**	**2**	**3**	**1**	**1**	**2**	**0**	**0**	**0**	**1**	**12**	**8.3**	**3**	**0**	**4**	**0**	**–1**	....	....	....	....	....	....	....	....
	Boston Bruins	**NHL**	**70**	**12**	**19**	**31**	**10**	**13**	**23**	**45**	**0**	**0**	**2**	**102**	**11.8**	**41**	**1**	**44**	**2**	**–2**	**5**	**0**	**0**	**0**	**4**	**0**	**0**	**0**
1985-86	**Boston Bruins**	**NHL**	**13**	**4**	**2**	**6**	**3**	**1**	**4**	**20**	**0**	**0**	**1**	**18**	**22.2**	**7**	**2**	**9**	**0**	**–4**	**1**	**0**	**0**	**0**	**14**	**0**	**0**	**0**
1986-87	**Boston Bruins**	**NHL**	DID NOT PLAY – INJURED																									
	NHL Totals		**194**	**46**	**53**	**99**	**37**	**36**	**73**	**146**	**3**	**1**	**6**	**264**	**17.4**	**140**	**11**	**117**	**11**		**17**	**1**	**1**	**2**	**64**	**0**	**0**	**0**
	Other Major League Totals		62	26	12	38	....	....	....	46	....	....	....	....	....	....	....	....	....	....	....	....	....	....	....	....	....	....

Signed as an underage free agent by **Birmingham** (WHA), September, 1978. Signed as a free agent by **Quebec**, September 11, 1980. Traded to **Boston** by **Quebec** for Luc Dufour and Boston's 4th round choice (Peter Massey) in 1985 Entry Draft, October 25, 1984. • Suffered eventual career-ending groin injury in game vs. Vancouver, October 16, 1985. • Officially announced retirement, September 1, 1987.

• SLOAN, Blake

RW – R. 5'10", 196 lbs. b: Park Ridge, IL, 7/27/1975.

Season	Club	League	GP	G	A	Pts	AG	AA	APts	PIM	PP	SH	GW	S	%	TGF	PGF	TGA	PGA	+/–	GP	G	A	Pts	PIM	PP	SH	GW
1992-93	Tabor Academy Seawolves	Hi-School	33	7	15	22	....	....	....	....	....	....	....	....	....	....	....	....	....	....	....	....	....	....	....	....	....	....
	Boston Jr. Bruins	MBAHL	20	10	31	41	....	....	....	....	....	....	....	....	....	....	....	....	....	....	....	....	....	....	....	....	....	....
1993-94	University of Michigan	CCHA	38	2	4	6	....	....	....	48	....	....	....	....	....	....	....	....	....	....	....	....	....	....	....	....	....	....
1994-95	University of Michigan	CCHA	39	2	15	17	....	....	....	60	....	....	....	....	....	....	....	....	....	....	....	....	....	....	....	....	....	....
1995-96	University of Michigan	CCHA	41	6	24	30	....	....	....	55	....	....	....	....	....	....	....	....	....	....	....	....	....	....	....	....	....	....
1996-97	University of Michigan	CCHA	41	2	15	17	....	....	....	52	....	....	....	....	....	....	....	....	....	....	....	....	....	....	....	....	....	....
1997-98	Houston Aeros	IHL	70	2	13	15	....	....	....	86	....	....	....	....	....	....	....	....	....	....	2	0	0	0	0	....	....	....
1998-99♦	**Dallas Stars**	**NHL**	**14**	**0**	**0**	**0**	**0**	**0**	**0**	**10**	**0**	**0**	**0**	**7**	**0.0**	**0**	**0**	**1**	**0**	**–1**	**19**	**0**	**2**	**2**	**8**	**0**	**0**	**0**
	Houston Aeros	IHL	62	8	10	18	....	....	....	76	....	....	....	....	....	....	....	....	....	....	....	....	....	....	....	....	....	....
99-2000	**Dallas Stars**	**NHL**	**67**	**4**	**13**	**17**	**4**	**12**	**16**	**50**	**0**	**0**	**1**	**78**	**5.1**	**31**	**2**	**24**	**6**	**11**	**16**	**0**	**0**	**0**	**12**	**0**	**0**	**0**
	NHL Totals		**81**	**4**	**13**	**17**	**4**	**12**	**16**	**60**	**0**	**0**	**1**	**85**	**4.7**	**31**	**2**	**25**	**6**		**35**	**0**	**2**	**2**	**20**	**0**	**0**	**0**

Signed as a free agent by **Dallas**, March 10, 1998.

• SLY, Darryl

Darryl Hayward D – R. 5'11", 185 lbs. b: Collingwood, Ont., 4/3/1939.

Season	Club	League	GP	G	A	Pts	AG	AA	APts	PIM	PP	SH	GW	S	%	TGF	PGF	TGA	PGA	+/–	GP	G	A	Pts	PIM	PP	SH	GW
1956-57	St. Michael's Majors	OHA-Jr.	46	7	7	14	....	....	....	35	....	....	....	....	....	....	....	....	....	....	1	0	0	0	4	....	....	....
1957-58	St. Michael's Majors	OHA-Jr.	52	19	20	39	....	....	....	64	....	....	....	....	....	....	....	....	....	....	9	2	4	6	12	....	....	....
1958-59	St. Michael's Majors	OHA-Jr.	48	8	16	24	....	....	....	58	....	....	....	....	....	....	....	....	....	....	15	0	3	3	42	....	....	....
	Kitchener-Waterloo Dutchmen	OHA-Sr.	1	0	0	0	....	....	....	0	....	....	....	....	....	....	....	....	....	....	....	....	....	....	....	....	....	....
1959-60	Kitchener-Waterloo Dutchmen	OHA-Sr.	47	4	8	12	....	....	....	63	....	....	....	....	....	....	....	....	....	....	8	1	1	2	14	....	....	....
	Canada	Olympics	7	1	1	2	....	....	....	9	....	....	....	....	....	....	....	....	....	....	....	....	....	....	....	....	....	....
1960-61	Galt Terriers	OHA-Sr.	12	5	9	14	....	....	....	12	....	....	....	....	....	....	....	....	....	....	15	7	8	15	24	....	....	....
	Trail Smoke Eaters	WIHL	13	7	12	19	....	....	....	....	....	....	....	....	....	....	....	....	....	....	....	....	....	....	....	....	....	....
	Canada	Nat-Team	18	12	6	18	....	....	....	*46	....	....	....	....	....	....	....	....	....	....	....	....	....	....	....	....	....	....
	Canada	WEC-A	7	4	2	6	....	....	....	6	....	....	....	....	....	....	....	....	....	....	....	....	....	....	....	....	....	....
	Rochester Americans	AHL	2	0	0	0	....	....	....	0	....	....	....	....	....	....	....	....	....	....	....	....	....	....	....	....	....	....
	Galt Terriers	Al-Cup	12	4	6	10	....	....	....	22	....	....	....	....	....	....	....	....	....	....	....	....	....	....	....	....	....	....
1961-62	Rochester Americans	AHL	70	8	16	24	....	....	....	50	....	....	....	....	....	....	....	....	....	....	2	0	0	0	0	....	....	....
1962-63	Rochester Americans	AHL	70	4	14	18	....	....	....	52	....	....	....	....	....	....	....	....	....	....	2	0	0	0	7	....	....	....
1963-64	Rochester Americans	AHL	72	16	16	32	....	....	....	41	....	....	....	....	....	....	....	....	....	....	2	0	0	0	0	....	....	....
1964-65	Rochester Americans	AHL	72	3	18	21	....	....	....	56	....	....	....	....	....	....	....	....	....	....	10	1	2	3	8	....	....	....

			REGULAR SEASON																		PLAYOFFS							
Season	Club	League	GP	G	A	Pts	AG	AA	APts	PIM	PP	SH	GW	S	%	TGF	PGF	TGA	PGA	+/–	GP	G	A	Pts	PIM	PP	SH	GW
1965-66	**Toronto Maple Leafs**	**NHL**	**2**	**0**	**0**	**0**	**0**	**0**	**0**	**0**	....	....	....	....	....	....	....	....	....	....	....	....	....	....	....	....	....	....
	Rochester Americans	AHL	67	5	15	20	....	....	....	49	....	....	....	....	....	....	....	....	....	....	12	2	2	4	12	....	....	....
1966-67	Rochester Americans	AHL	72	8	25	33	....	....	....	56	....	....	....	....	....	....	....	....	....	....	13	1	0	1	14	....	....	....
1967-68	**Toronto Maple Leafs**	**NHL**	**17**	**0**	**0**	**0**	**0**	**0**	**0**	**4**	**0**	**0**	**0**	**2**	**0.0**	**0**	**0**	**5**	**4**	**–1**	....	....	....	....	....	....	....	....
	Rochester Americans	AHL	52	3	22	25	....	....	....	36	....	....	....	....	....	....	....	....	....	....	11	1	6	7	12	....	....	....
1968-69	Vancouver Canucks	WHL	74	6	16	22	....	....	....	45	....	....	....	....	....	....	....	....	....	....	8	0	1	1	8	....	....	....
1969-70	**Minnesota North Stars**	**NHL**	**29**	**1**	**0**	**1**	**1**	**0**	**1**	**6**	**0**	**0**	**0**	**20**	**5.0**	**15**	**2**	**25**	**7**	**–5**	....	....	....	....	....	....	....	....
	Iowa Stars	CHL	10	0	8	8	....	....	....	2	....	....	....	....	....	....	....	....	....	....	11	1	8	9	8	....	....	....
1970-71	**Vancouver Canucks**	**NHL**	**31**	**0**	**2**	**2**	**0**	**2**	**2**	**10**	**0**	**0**	**0**	**13**	**0.0**	**12**	**2**	**22**	**11**	**–1**	....	....	....	....	....	....	....	....
	Rochester Americans	AHL	37	3	4	7	....	....	....	28	....	....	....	....	....	....	....	....	....	....	....	....	....	....	....	....	....	....
1971-72	Barrie Flyers	OHA-Sr.	33	7	17	24	....	....	....	32	....	....	....	....	....	....	....	....	....	....	16	1	10	11	16	....	....	....
1972-73	Barrie Flyers	OHA-Sr.	41	3	19	22	....	....	....	42	....	....	....	....	....	....	....	....	....	....	....	....	....	....	....	....	....	....
	Rochester Americans	AHL	1	1	2	3	....	....	....	0	....	....	....	....	....	....	....	....	....	....	....	....	....	....	....	....	....	....
1973-74	Barrie Flyers	OHA-Sr.	31	3	12	15	....	....	....	15	....	....	....	....	....	....	....	....	....	....	....	....	....	....	....	....	....	....
	Rochester Americans	AHL	1	0	0	0	....	....	....	2	....	....	....	....	....	....	....	....	....	....	....	....	....	....	....	....	....	....
1974-75	Barrie Flyers	OHA-Sr.	40	4	10	14	....	....	....	28	....	....	....	....	....	....	....	....	....	....	....	....	....	....	....	....	....	....
1975-76	Barrie Flyers	OHA-Sr.	44	4	16	20	....	....	....	24	....	....	....	....	....	....	....	....	....	....	....	....	....	....	....	....	....	....
1976-77	Barrie Flyers	OHA-Sr.	34	1	10	11	....	....	....	26	....	....	....	....	....	....	....	....	....	....	....	....	....	....	....	....	....	....
1977-78	Barrie Flyers	OHA-Sr.	38	0	5	5	....	....	....	16	....	....	....	....	....	....	....	....	....	....	....	....	....	....	....	....	....	....
	NHL Totals		**79**	**1**	**2**	**3**	**1**	**2**	**3**	**20**	....	....	....	....	....	....	....	....	....	....	....	....	....	....	....	....	....	....

OHA-Jr. Second All-Star Team (1959) • WEC-A All-Star Team (1961) • WHL Second All-Star Team (1969) • OHA-Sr. First All-Star Team (1972, 1973, 1974)

Signed as a free agent by **Toronto**, June 5, 1961. Rights transferred to **Vancouver** (WHL) after WHL club purchased **Rochester** (AHL) franchise, August 13, 1968. Claimed by **Minnesota** from **Vancouver** (WHL) in Inter-League Draft, June 10, 1969. Claimed by **Vancouver** from **Minnesota** in Expansion Draft, June 10, 1970.

• SMAIL, Doug

Douglas Dean LW – L. 5'9", 175 lbs. b: Moose Jaw, Sask., 9/2/1957.

Season	Club	League	GP	G	A	Pts	AG	AA	APts	PIM	PP	SH	GW	S	%	TGF	PGF	TGA	PGA	+/–	GP	G	A	Pts	PIM	PP	SH	GW
1975-76	Moose Jaw Canucks	SJHL	58	47	40	87	....	....	....	....	....	....	....	....	....	....	....	....	....	....	....	....	....	....	....	....	....	....
1976-77	Moose Jaw Canucks	SJHL	56	45	61	106	....	....	....	....	....	....	....	....	....	....	....	....	....	....	....	....	....	....	....	....	....	....
1977-78	University of North Dakota	WCHA	38	22	28	50	....	....	....	52	....	....	....	....	....	....	....	....	....	....	....	....	....	....	....	....	....	....
1978-79	University of North Dakota	WCHA	35	24	34	58	....	....	....	46	....	....	....	....	....	....	....	....	....	....	....	....	....	....	....	....	....	....
1979-80	University of North Dakota	WCHA	40	43	44	87	....	....	....	70	....	....	....	....	....	....	....	....	....	....	....	....	....	....	....	....	....	....
1980-81	**Winnipeg Jets**	**NHL**	**30**	**10**	**8**	**18**	**8**	**5**	**13**	**45**	**1**	**3**	**1**	**58**	**17.2**	**24**	**1**	**39**	**9**	**–7**	....	....	....	....	....	....	....	....
1981-82	**Winnipeg Jets**	**NHL**	**72**	**17**	**18**	**35**	**13**	**12**	**25**	**55**	**2**	**1**	**1**	**97**	**17.5**	**50**	**3**	**88**	**19**	**–22**	**4**	**0**	**0**	**0**	**0**	**0**	**0**	**0**
1982-83	**Winnipeg Jets**	**NHL**	**80**	**15**	**29**	**44**	**12**	**20**	**32**	**32**	**0**	**3**	**3**	**113**	**13.3**	**61**	**0**	**94**	**33**	**0**	**3**	**0**	**0**	**0**	**6**	**0**	**0**	**0**
1983-84	**Winnipeg Jets**	**NHL**	**66**	**20**	**17**	**37**	**16**	**12**	**28**	**62**	**1**	**4**	**2**	**122**	**16.4**	**49**	**2**	**69**	**17**	**–5**	**3**	**0**	**1**	**1**	**7**	**0**	**0**	**0**
1984-85	**Winnipeg Jets**	**NHL**	**80**	**31**	**35**	**66**	**25**	**24**	**49**	**45**	**0**	**3**	**5**	**154**	**20.1**	**94**	**8**	**101**	**27**	**12**	**8**	**2**	**1**	**3**	**4**	**0**	**1**	**0**
1985-86	**Winnipeg Jets**	**NHL**	**73**	**16**	**26**	**42**	**13**	**17**	**30**	**32**	**1**	**3**	**4**	**150**	**10.7**	**61**	**5**	**97**	**31**	**–10**	**3**	**1**	**0**	**1**	**0**	**0**	**0**	**0**
1986-87	**Winnipeg Jets**	**NHL**	**78**	**25**	**18**	**43**	**22**	**13**	**35**	**36**	**0**	**2**	**4**	**132**	**18.9**	**66**	**2**	**66**	**20**	**18**	**10**	**4**	**0**	**4**	**10**	**0**	**1**	**0**
1987-88	**Winnipeg Jets**	**NHL**	**71**	**15**	**16**	**31**	**13**	**11**	**24**	**34**	**0**	**3**	**5**	**110**	**13.6**	**43**	**0**	**70**	**32**	**5**	**5**	**1**	**0**	**1**	**22**	**0**	**0**	**0**
1988-89	**Winnipeg Jets**	**NHL**	**47**	**14**	**15**	**29**	**12**	**11**	**23**	**52**	**0**	**2**	**0**	**68**	**20.6**	**42**	**0**	**44**	**14**	**12**	....	....	....	....	....	....	....	....
1989-90	**Winnipeg Jets**	**NHL**	**79**	**25**	**24**	**49**	**21**	**17**	**38**	**63**	**1**	**1**	**6**	**165**	**15.2**	**78**	**7**	**72**	**16**	**15**	**5**	**1**	**0**	**1**	**0**	**0**	**0**	**0**
1990-91	**Winnipeg Jets**	**NHL**	**15**	**1**	**2**	**3**	**1**	**2**	**3**	**10**	**0**	**0**	**0**	**18**	**5.6**	**4**	**1**	**13**	**4**	**–6**	....	....	....	....	....	....	....	....
	Minnesota North Stars	**NHL**	**57**	**7**	**13**	**20**	**6**	**10**	**16**	**38**	**0**	**2**	**0**	**89**	**7.9**	**25**	**0**	**39**	**12**	**–2**	**1**	**0**	**0**	**0**	**0**	**0**	**0**	**0**
1991-92	**Quebec Nordiques**	**NHL**	**46**	**10**	**18**	**28**	**9**	**14**	**23**	**47**	**0**	**1**	**1**	**72**	**13.9**	**35**	**3**	**63**	**20**	**–11**	....	....	....	....	....	....	....	....
1992-93	**Ottawa Senators**	**NHL**	**51**	**4**	**10**	**14**	**3**	**7**	**10**	**51**	**0**	**0**	**0**	**73**	**5.5**	**19**	**0**	**78**	**25**	**–34**	....	....	....	....	....	....	....	....
	San Diego Gulls	IHL	9	2	1	3	....	....	....	20	....	....	....	....	....	....	....	....	....	....	9	3	2	5	20	....	....	....
1993-94	Fife Flyers	BH-Cup	5	3	6	9	....	....	....	40	....	....	....	....	....	....	....	....	....	....	....	....	....	....	....	....	....	....
	Fife Flyers	Britain	41	62	80	142	....	....	....	66	....	....	....	....	....	....	....	....	....	....	7	9	9	18	8	....	....	....
1994-95	Cardiff Devils	Britain	3	2	5	7	....	....	....	2	....	....	....	....	....	....	....	....	....	....	....	....	....	....	....	....	....	....
	Fife Flyers	Britain	15	20	9	29	....	....	....	26	....	....	....	....	....	....	....	....	....	....	6	5	9	14	12	....	....	....
1995-96	Cardiff Devils	Britain	16	12	14	26	....	....	....	14	....	....	....	....	....	....	....	....	....	....	6	3	5	8	10	....	....	....
	NHL Totals		**845**	**210**	**249**	**459**	**174**	**175**	**349**	**602**	**6**	**28**	**32**	**1421**	**14.8**	**651**	**32**	**933**	**279**		**42**	**9**	**2**	**11**	**49**	**0**	**2**	**0**

NCAA Championship All-Tournament Team (1980) • NCAA Championship Tournament MVP (1980) • Played in NHL All-Star Game (1990)

Signed as a free agent by **Winnipeg**, May 22, 1980. • Missed majority of 1980-81 season recovering from jaw injury suffered in game vs. Hartford, January 10, 1981. Traded to **Minnesota** by **Winnipeg** for Don Barber, November 7, 1990. Signed as a free agent by **Quebec**, August 30, 1991. Signed as a free agent by **Ottawa**, August 30, 1992.

• SMEDSMO, Dale

Dale Darwin LW – L. 6'1", 195 lbs. b: Roseau, MN, 4/23/1951. Toronto's 7th, 93rd overall, in 1971.

Season	Club	League	GP	G	A	Pts	AG	AA	APts	PIM	PP	SH	GW	S	%	TGF	PGF	TGA	PGA	+/–	GP	G	A	Pts	PIM	PP	SH	GW
1969-70	Roseau Rams	Hi-School	STATISTICS NOT AVAILABLE																									
1970-71	Bemidji State Beavers	NAIA	24	16	5	21	....	....	....	52	....	....	....	....	....	....	....	....	....	....	....	....	....	....	....	....	....	....
1971-72	Bemidji State Beavers	NAIA	STATISTICS NOT AVAILABLE																									
	Tulsa Oilers	CHL	6	0	2	2	....	....	....	0	....	....	....	....	....	....	....	....	....	....	....	....	....	....	....	....	....	....
1972-73	**Toronto Maple Leafs**	**NHL**	**4**	**0**	**0**	**0**	**0**	**0**	**0**	**0**	**0**	**0**	**0**	**2**	**0.0**	**0**	**0**	**0**	**0**	**0**	....	....	....	....	....	....	....	....
	Tulsa Oilers	CHL	64	12	18	30	....	....	....	185	....	....	....	....	....	....	....	....	....	....	....	....	....	....	....	....	....	....
1973-74	Tulsa Oilers	CHL	63	11	15	26	....	....	....	214	....	....	....	....	....	....	....	....	....	....	....	....	....	....	....	....	....	....
1974-75	Saginaw Gears	IHL	12	4	1	5	....	....	....	39	....	....	....	....	....	....	....	....	....	....	....	....	....	....	....	....	....	....
	Hampton Gulls	SHL	33	12	5	17	....	....	....	134	....	....	....	....	....	....	....	....	....	....	....	....	....	....	....	....	....	....
	Oklahoma City Blazers	CHL	20	3	3	6	....	....	....	51	....	....	....	....	....	....	....	....	....	....	5	0	0	0	14	....	....	....
1975-76	Cincinnati Stingers	WHA	66	8	14	22	....	....	....	187	....	....	....	....	....	....	....	....	....	....	....	....	....	....	....	....	....	....
1976-77	Hampton Gulls	SHL	14	1	7	8	....	....	....	47	....	....	....	....	....	....	....	....	....	....	....	....	....	....	....	....	....	....
	New England Whalers	WHA	15	2	0	2	....	....	....	54	....	....	....	....	....	....	....	....	....	....	....	....	....	....	....	....	....	....
	Rhode Island Reds	AHL	2	0	0	0	....	....	....	5	....	....	....	....	....	....	....	....	....	....	....	....	....	....	....	....	....	....
	Binghamton Dusters	NAHL	2	1	1	2	....	....	....	2	....	....	....	....	....	....	....	....	....	....	....	....	....	....	....	....	....	....
	Cincinnati Stingers	WHA	23	0	5	5	....	....	....	43	....	....	....	....	....	....	....	....	....	....	2	0	1	1	0	....	....	....
1977-78	Indianapolis Racers	WHA	6	0	3	3	....	....	....	7	....	....	....	....	....	....	....	....	....	....	....	....	....	....	....	....	....	....
	Long Beach Sharks-Rockets	PHL	40	16	32	48	....	....	....	*162	....	....	....	....	....	....	....	....	....	....	....	....	....	....	....	....	....	....
1978-79	Tucson Rustlers	PHL	55	15	24	39	....	....	....	*144	....	....	....	....	....	....	....	....	....	....	....	....	....	....	....	....	....	....
	Los Angeles Blades	PHL	2	0	0	0	....	....	....	*16	....	....	....	....	....	....	....	....	....	....	....	....	....	....	....	....	....	....
	NHL Totals		**4**	**0**	**0**	**0**	**0**	**0**	**0**	**0**	**0**	**0**	**0**	**2**	**0.0**	**0**	**0**	**0**	**0**		....	....	....	....	....	....	....	....
	Other Major League Totals		110	10	22	32	....	....	....	291	....	....	....	....	....	....	....	....	....	....	2	0	1	1	0	....	....	....

Selected by **Minnesota** (WHA) in 1972 WHA General Player Draft, February 12, 1972. WHA rights claimed on waivers by **Cincinnati** (WHA) from **Minnesota** (WHA), September, 1975. Traded to **New England** (WHA) by **Cincinnatti** (WHA) for cash, November, 1976. Traded to **Cincinnatti** (WHA) by **New England** (WHA) for future considerations, February, 1977. Signed as a free agent by **Indianapolis** (WHA), March, 1978.

• SMEHLIK, Richard

D – L. 6'3", 222 lbs. b: Ostrava, Czech., 1/23/1970. Buffalo's 3rd, 97th overall, in 1990.

Season	Club	League	GP	G	A	Pts	AG	AA	APts	PIM	PP	SH	GW	S	%	TGF	PGF	TGA	PGA	+/–	GP	G	A	Pts	PIM	PP	SH	GW
1987-88	TJ Vitkovice	Czech-Jr.	STATISTICS NOT AVAILABLE																									
	Czechoslovakia	EJC-A	5	1	1	2	....	....	....	4	....	....	....	....	....	....	....	....	....	....	....	....	....	....	....	....	....	....
1988-89	TJ Vitkovice	Czech.	38	2	5	7	....	....	....	12	....	....	....	....	....	....	....	....	....	....	....	....	....	....	....	....	....	....
1989-90	TJ Vitkovice	Czech.	44	4	3	7	....	....	....	....	....	....	....	....	....	....	....	....	....	....	7	1	1	2	....	....	....	....
	Czechoslovakia	WJC-A	7	0	1	1	....	....	....	4	....	....	....	....	....	....	....	....	....	....	....	....	....	....	....	....	....	....
1990-91	Dukla Jihlava	Czech.	58	4	3	7	....	....	....	22	....	....	....	....	....	....	....	....	....	....	....	....	....	....	....	....	....	....
	Czechoslovakia	WEC-A	8	1	2	3	....	....	....	8	....	....	....	....	....	....	....	....	....	....	....	....	....	....	....	....	....	....
1991-92	Czechoslovakia	Can-Cup	5	0	1	1	....	....	....	2	....	....	....	....	....	....	....	....	....	....	....	....	....	....	....	....	....	....
	TJ Vitkovice	Czech.	47	9	10	19	....	....	....	42	....	....	....	....	....	....	....	....	....	....	....	....	....	....	....	....	....	....
	Czechoslovakia	Olympics	8	0	1	1	....	....	....	2	....	....	....	....	....	....	....	....	....	....	....	....	....	....	....	....	....	....
	Czechoslovakia	WC-A	8	0	0	0	....	....	....	4	....	....	....	....	....	....	....	....	....	....	....	....	....	....	....	....	....	....
1992-93	**Buffalo Sabres**	**NHL**	**80**	**4**	**27**	**31**	**3**	**19**	**22**	**59**	**0**	**0**	**0**	**82**	**4.9**	**86**	**4**	**115**	**42**	**9**	**8**	**0**	**4**	**4**	**2**	**0**	**0**	**0**
1993-94	**Buffalo Sabres**	**NHL**	**84**	**14**	**27**	**41**	**13**	**21**	**34**	**69**	**3**	**3**	**1**	**106**	**13.2**	**107**	**27**	**86**	**28**	**22**	**7**	**0**	**2**	**2**	**10**	**0**	**0**	**0**
1994-95	HC Vitkovice	Czech-Rep	13	5	2	7	....	....	....	12	....	....	....	....	....	....	....	....	....	....	....	....	....	....	....	....	....	....
	Buffalo Sabres	**NHL**	**39**	**4**	**7**	**11**	**7**	**10**	**17**	**46**	**0**	**1**	**1**	**49**	**8.2**	**46**	**7**	**49**	**15**	**5**	**5**	**0**	**0**	**0**	**2**	**0**	**0**	**0**
1995-96	**Buffalo Sabres**	**NHL**	DID NOT PLAY – INJURED																									

			REGULAR SEASON																		PLAYOFFS							
Season	**Club**	**League**	**GP**	**G**	**A**	**Pts**	**AG**	**AA**	**APts**	**PIM**	**PP**	**SH**	**GW**	**S**	**%**	**TGF**	**PGF**	**TGA**	**PGA**	**+/–**	**GP**	**G**	**A**	**Pts**	**PIM**	**PP**	**SH**	**GW**
1996-97	**Buffalo Sabres**	**NHL**	**62**	**11**	**19**	**30**	**12**	**17**	**29**	**43**	**2**	**0**	**1**	**100**	**11.0**	**76**	**14**	**59**	**16**	**19**	**12**	**0**	**2**	**2**	**4**	**0**	**0**	**0**
1997-98	**Buffalo Sabres**	**NHL**	**72**	**3**	**17**	**20**	**4**	**17**	**21**	**62**	**0**	**1**	**0**	**90**	**3.3**	**68**	**12**	**75**	**30**	**11**	**15**	**0**	**2**	**2**	**6**	**0**	**0**	**0**
	Czech-Republic	Olympics	6	0	1	1	....	....	....	4	....	....	....	....	....	....	....	....	....	....	....	....	....	....	....	....	....	....
1998-99	**Buffalo Sabres**	**NHL**	**72**	**3**	**11**	**14**	**4**	**11**	**15**	**44**	**0**	**0**	**0**	**61**	**4.9**	**38**	**4**	**70**	**27**	**–9**	**21**	**0**	**3**	**3**	**10**	**0**	**0**	**0**
99-2000	**Buffalo Sabres**	**NHL**	**64**	**2**	**9**	**11**	**2**	**8**	**10**	**50**	**0**	**0**	**0**	**67**	**3.0**	**55**	**2**	**54**	**14**	**13**	**5**	**1**	**0**	**1**	**0**	**0**	**0**	**0**
	NHL Totals		**473**	**41**	**117**	**158**	**45**	**103**	**148**	**373**	**5**	**5**	**3**	**555**	**7.4**	**476**	**70**	**508**	**172**		**73**	**1**	**13**	**14**	**34**	**0**	**0**	**0**

• Missed entire 1995-96 season recovering from knee surgery, August 11, 1995.

• SMITH, Barry

Barry Edward C – L. 5′11″, 178 lbs. b: Surrey, B.C., 4/25/1955. Boston's 2nd, 32nd overall, in 1975.

Season	Club	League	GP	G	A	Pts	AG	AA	APts	PIM	PP	SH	GW	S	%	TGF	PGF	TGA	PGA	+/–	GP	G	A	Pts	PIM	PP	SH	GW
1970-71	South Surrey Eagles	BCAHA	STATISTICS NOT AVAILABLE																									
1971-72	Vancouver Nats	WCJHL	41	9	15	24	....	....	....	39	....	....	....	....	....	....	....	....	....	....	....	....	....	....	....	....	....	....
	New Westminster Bruins	WCJHL	9	4	2	6	....	....	....	10	....	....	....	....	....	....	....	....	....	....	....	....	....	....	....	....	....	....
1972-73	Vancouver Nats	WCJHL	30	5	6	11	....	....	....	13	....	....	....	....	....	....	....	....	....	....	....	....	....	....	....	....	....	....
	New Westminster Bruins	WCJHL	32	5	6	11	....	....	....	46	....	....	....	....	....	....	....	....	....	....	5	0	0	0	0	....	....	....
1973-74	New Westminster Bruins	WCJHL	65	8	10	18	....	....	....	61	....	....	....	....	....	....	....	....	....	....	11	2	1	3	12	....	....	....
1974-75	New Westminster Bruins	WCJHL	65	19	24	43	....	....	....	50	....	....	....	....	....	....	....	....	....	....	18	7	6	13	14	....	....	....
	Canada	WJC-A	5	1	2	3	....	....	....	2	....	....	....	....	....	....	....	....	....	....	....	....	....	....	....	....	....	....
	New Westminster Bruins	Mem-Cup	3	1	2	3	....	....	....	0	....	....	....	....	....	....	....	....	....	....	....	....	....	....	....	....	....	....
1975-76	**Boston Bruins**	**NHL**	**19**	**1**	**0**	**1**	**1**	**0**	**1**	**2**	**0**	**0**	**0**	**8**	**12.5**	**2**	**0**	**10**	**3**	**–5**	....	....	....	....	....	....	....	....
	Rochester Americans	AHL	50	14	22	36	....	....	....	14	....	....	....	....	....	....	....	....	....	....	7	4	4	8	5	....	....	....
1976-77	Rochester Americans	AHL	79	9	13	22	....	....	....	16	....	....	....	....	....	....	....	....	....	....	12	3	2	5	4	....	....	....
1977-78	Rochester Americans	AHL	81	16	16	32	....	....	....	22	....	....	....	....	....	....	....	....	....	....	6	2	1	3	0	....	....	....
1978-79	Rochester Americans	AHL	80	23	43	66	....	....	....	46	....	....	....	....	....	....	....	....	....	....	....	....	....	....	....	....	....	....
1979-80	**Colorado Rockies**	**NHL**	**33**	**2**	**3**	**5**	**2**	**2**	**4**	**4**	**0**	**1**	**0**	**21**	**9.5**	**8**	**0**	**33**	**14**	**–11**	....	....	....	....	....	....	....	....
	Rochester Americans	AHL	35	3	7	10	....	....	....	14	....	....	....	....	....	....	....	....	....	....	....	....	....	....	....	....	....	....
	Birmingham Bulls	CHL	13	2	0	2	....	....	....	43	....	....	....	....	....	....	....	....	....	....	4	1	1	2	0	....	....	....
1980-81	**Colorado Rockies**	**NHL**	**62**	**4**	**4**	**8**	**3**	**3**	**6**	**4**	**0**	**0**	**0**	**38**	**10.5**	**20**	**0**	**56**	**34**	**–2**	....	....	....	....	....	....	....	....
	Fort Worth Texans	CHL	14	2	5	7	....	....	....	14	....	....	....	....	....	....	....	....	....	....	....	....	....	....	....	....	....	....
1981-82			OUT OF HOCKEY – RETIRED																									
1982-1987	Rochester Jr. Americans	NAJHL	DID NOT PLAY – COACHING																									
1987-1992	Rochester Monarchs	NAJHL	DID NOT PLAY – COACHING																									
1992-1998	Knoxville Cherokees	ECHL	DID NOT PLAY – COACHING																									
1998-1999	Adirondack IceHawks	UHL	DID NOT PLAY – ASSISTANT COACH																									
1999-2000	Syracuse Crunch	AHL	DID NOT PLAY – ASSISTANT COACH																									
	NHL Totals		**114**	**7**	**7**	**14**	**6**	**5**	**11**	**10**	**0**	**1**	**0**	**67**	**10.4**	**30**	**0**	**99**	**51**		....	....	....	....	....	....	....	....

Memorial Cup All-Star Team (1975) • Won Stafford Smythe Memorial Trophy (Memorial Cup Tournament MVP) (1975)

Signed as a free agent by **Colorado**, September 14, 1979.

• SMITH, Bobby

Robert David C – L. 6′4″, 210 lbs. b: North Sydney, N.S., 2/12/1958. Minnesota's 1st, 1st overall, in 1978.

Season	Club	League	GP	G	A	Pts	AG	AA	APts	PIM	PP	SH	GW	S	%	TGF	PGF	TGA	PGA	+/–	GP	G	A	Pts	PIM	PP	SH	GW
1974-75	Ottawa Golden Knights	OMHA	58	74	64	138	....	....	....	....	....	....	....	....	....	....	....	....	....	....	....	....	....	....	....	....	....	....
1975-76	Ottawa 67's	OMJHL	62	24	34	58	....	....	....	21	....	....	....	....	....	....	....	....	....	....	12	2	1	3	4	....	....	....
1976-77	Ottawa 67's	OMJHL	64	*65	70	135	....	....	....	52	....	....	....	....	....	....	....	....	....	....	19	*16	16	*32	29	....	....	....
	Ottawa 67's	Mem-Cup	....	....	....	....	....	....	....	....	....	....	....	....	....	....	....	....	....	....	....	....	....	....	....	....	....	....
1977-78	Ottawa 67's	OMJHL	61	69	*123	*192	....	....	....	44	....	....	....	....	....	....	....	....	....	....	16	*15	15	*30	10	....	....	....
	Canada	WJC-A	3	1	4	5	....	....	....	0	....	....	....	....	....	....	....	....	....	....	....	....	....	....	....	....	....	....
1978-79	**Minnesota North Stars**	**NHL**	**80**	**30**	**44**	**74**	**26**	**32**	**58**	**39**	**9**	**0**	**4**	**244**	**12.3**	**92**	**30**	**71**	**1**	**–8**	....	....	....	....	....	....	....	....
	Canada	WEC-A	8	5	3	8	....	....	....	0	....	....	....	....	....	....	....	....	....	....	....	....	....	....	....	....	....	....
1979-80	**Minnesota North Stars**	**NHL**	**61**	**27**	**56**	**83**	**23**	**41**	**64**	**24**	**9**	**0**	**3**	**223**	**12.1**	**107**	**35**	**56**	**0**	**16**	**15**	**1**	**13**	**14**	**9**	**1**	**0**	**0**
1980-81	Minnesota North Stars	DN-Cup	2	0	0	0	....	....	....	2	....	....	....	....	....	....	....	....	....	....	....	....	....	....	....	....	....	....
	Minnesota North Stars	**NHL**	**78**	**29**	**64**	**93**	**23**	**43**	**66**	**73**	**13**	**0**	**7**	**242**	**12.0**	**125**	**56**	**68**	**0**	**1**	**19**	**8**	**17**	**25**	**13**	**2**	**0**	**0**
1981-82	**Minnesota North Stars**	**NHL**	**80**	**43**	**71**	**114**	**34**	**47**	**81**	**82**	**20**	**0**	**4**	**261**	**16.5**	**149**	**57**	**82**	**0**	**10**	**4**	**2**	**4**	**6**	**5**	**0**	**0**	**0**
	Canada	WEC-A	10	1	5	6	....	....	....	0	....	....	....	....	....	....	....	....	....	....	....	....	....	....	....	....	....	....
1982-83	**Minnesota North Stars**	**NHL**	**77**	**24**	**53**	**77**	**20**	**37**	**57**	**81**	**12**	**0**	**3**	**190**	**12.6**	**107**	**50**	**78**	**1**	**–20**	**9**	**6**	**4**	**10**	**17**	**3**	**0**	**2**
1983-84	**Minnesota North Stars**	**NHL**	**10**	**3**	**6**	**9**	**2**	**4**	**6**	**9**	**1**	**0**	**0**	**21**	**14.3**	**12**	**5**	**9**	**1**	**–1**	....	....	....	....	....	....	....	....
	Montreal Canadiens	**NHL**	**70**	**26**	**37**	**63**	**21**	**25**	**46**	**62**	**6**	**1**	**3**	**179**	**14.5**	**88**	**30**	**69**	**4**	**–7**	**15**	**2**	**7**	**9**	**8**	**1**	**0**	**1**
1984-85	**Montreal Canadiens**	**NHL**	**65**	**16**	**40**	**56**	**13**	**27**	**40**	**59**	**8**	**0**	**1**	**146**	**11.0**	**72**	**37**	**45**	**1**	**–9**	**12**	**5**	**6**	**11**	**30**	**3**	**0**	**1**
1985-86♦	**Montreal Canadiens**	**NHL**	**79**	**31**	**55**	**86**	**25**	**37**	**62**	**55**	**5**	**0**	**7**	**202**	**15.3**	**121**	**40**	**77**	**6**	**10**	**20**	**7**	**8**	**15**	**22**	**3**	**0**	**3**
1986-87	**Montreal Canadiens**	**NHL**	**80**	**28**	**47**	**75**	**24**	**34**	**58**	**72**	**11**	**0**	**7**	**197**	**14.2**	**117**	**48**	**63**	**0**	**6**	**17**	**9**	**9**	**18**	**19**	**2**	**0**	**0**
1987-88	**Montreal Canadiens**	**NHL**	**78**	**27**	**66**	**93**	**23**	**47**	**70**	**78**	**8**	**0**	**4**	**198**	**13.6**	**119**	**47**	**62**	**3**	**13**	**11**	**3**	**4**	**7**	**8**	**1**	**0**	**0**
1988-89	**Montreal Canadiens**	**NHL**	**80**	**32**	**51**	**83**	**27**	**36**	**63**	**69**	**6**	**0**	**3**	**195**	**16.4**	**115**	**46**	**44**	**0**	**25**	**21**	**11**	**8**	**19**	**46**	**5**	**0**	**1**
1989-90	**Montreal Canadiens**	**NHL**	**53**	**12**	**14**	**26**	**10**	**10**	**20**	**35**	**4**	**0**	**2**	**102**	**11.8**	**40**	**10**	**34**	**0**	**–4**	**11**	**1**	**4**	**5**	**6**	**0**	**0**	**0**
1990-91	Minnesota North Stars	Fr-Tour	3	0	1	1	....	....	....	0	....	....	....	....	....	....	....	....	....	....	....	....	....	....	....	....	....	....
	Minnesota North Stars	**NHL**	**73**	**15**	**31**	**46**	**14**	**24**	**38**	**60**	**7**	**0**	**2**	**121**	**12.4**	**65**	**25**	**55**	**6**	**–9**	**23**	**8**	**8**	**16**	**56**	**2**	**0**	**5**
1991-92	**Minnesota North Stars**	**NHL**	**68**	**9**	**37**	**46**	**8**	**28**	**36**	**109**	**3**	**0**	**1**	**129**	**7.0**	**60**	**26**	**58**	**0**	**–24**	**7**	**1**	**4**	**5**	**6**	**1**	**0**	**0**
1992-93	**Minnesota North Stars**	**NHL**	**45**	**5**	**7**	**12**	**4**	**5**	**9**	**10**	**3**	**0**	**0**	**53**	**9.4**	**19**	**7**	**21**	**0**	**–9**	....	....	....	....	....	....	....	....
	NHL Totals		**1077**	**357**	**679**	**1036**	**297**	**477**	**774**	**917**	**125**	**1**	**51**	**2703**	**13.2**	**1408**	**549**	**892**	**23**		**184**	**64**	**96**	**160**	**245**	**24**	**0**	**13**

OMJHL Second All-Star Team (1976, 1977) • Memorial Cup All-Star Team (1977) • Won George Parsons Trophy (Memorial Cup Tournament Most Sportsmanlike Player) (1977) • OMJHL First All-Star Team (1978) • Canadian Major Junior Player of the Year (1978) • Won Calder Memorial Trophy (1979) • Played in NHL All-Star Game (1981, 1982, 1989, 1991)

Traded to **Montreal** by **Minnesota** for Keith Acton, Mark Napier and Toronto's 3rd round choice (previously acquired, Minnesota selected Ken Hodge Jr.) in 1984 Entry Draft, October 28, 1983. Traded to **Minnesota** by **Montreal** for Minnesota's 4th round choice (Louis Bernard) in 1992 Entry Draft, August 7, 1990.

• SMITH, Brad

Brad Allan "Motor City Smitty" RW – R. 6′1″, 195 lbs. b: Windsor, Ont., 4/13/1958. Vancouver's 5th, 57th overall, in 1978.

Season	Club	League	GP	G	A	Pts	AG	AA	APts	PIM	PP	SH	GW	S	%	TGF	PGF	TGA	PGA	+/–	GP	G	A	Pts	PIM	PP	SH	GW
1974-75	Belle River Canadians	OHA-B	66	37	53	90	....	....	....	165	....	....	....	....	....	....	....	....	....	....	....	....	....	....	....	....	....	....
1975-76	Windsor Spitfires	OMJHL	4	4	2	6	....	....	....	4	....	....	....	....	....	....	....	....	....	....	....	....	....	....	....	....	....	....
1976-77	Windsor Spitfires	OMJHL	66	37	53	90	....	....	....	154	....	....	....	....	....	....	....	....	....	....	9	4	10	14	30	....	....	....
1977-78	Windsor Spitfires	OMJHL	20	8	26	34	....	....	....	39	....	....	....	....	....	....	....	....	....	....	....	....	....	....	....	....	....	....
	Sudbury Wolves	OMJHL	46	21	21	42	....	....	....	183	....	....	....	....	....	....	....	....	....	....	....	....	....	....	....	....	....	....
	Kalamazoo Wings	IHL	....	....	....	....	....	....	....	....	....	....	....	....	....	....	....	....	....	....	3	0	1	1	15	....	....	....
1978-79	**Vancouver Canucks**	**NHL**	**2**	**0**	**0**	**0**	**0**	**0**	**0**	**2**	**0**	**0**	**0**	**0**	**0.0**	**0**	**0**	**3**	**0**	**–3**	....	....	....	....	....	....	....	....
	Dallas Black Hawks	CHL	60	17	18	35	....	....	....	143	....	....	....	....	....	....	....	....	....	....	9	1	3	4	22	....	....	....
1979-80	**Vancouver Canucks**	**NHL**	**19**	**1**	**3**	**4**	**1**	**2**	**3**	**50**	**0**	**0**	**0**	**14**	**7.1**	**9**	**0**	**13**	**0**	**–4**	....	....	....	....	....	....	....	....
	Atlanta Flames	**NHL**	**4**	**0**	**0**	**0**	**0**	**0**	**0**	**4**	**0**	**0**	**0**	**0**	**0.0**	**2**	**0**	**1**	**0**	**1**	....	....	....	....	....	....	....	....
	Dallas Black Hawks	CHL	51	26	16	42	....	....	....	138	....	....	....	....	....	....	....	....	....	....	....	....	....	....	....	....	....	....
1980-81	**Calgary Flames**	**NHL**	**45**	**7**	**4**	**11**	**5**	**3**	**8**	**65**	**1**	**0**	**1**	**51**	**13.7**	**16**	**2**	**22**	**0**	**–8**	....	....	....	....	....	....	....	....
	Birmingham Bulls	CHL	10	5	6	11	....	....	....	13	....	....	....	....	....	....	....	....	....	....	....	....	....	....	....	....	....	....
	Detroit Red Wings	**NHL**	**20**	**5**	**2**	**7**	**4**	**1**	**5**	**93**	**0**	**0**	**0**	**31**	**16.1**	**10**	**2**	**21**	**1**	**–12**	....	....	....	....	....	....	....	....
1981-82	**Detroit Red Wings**	**NHL**	**33**	**2**	**0**	**2**	**2**	**0**	**2**	**80**	**0**	**0**	**1**	**25**	**8.0**	**4**	**0**	**11**	**0**	**–7**	....	....	....	....	....	....	....	....
	Adirondack Red Wings	AHL	34	10	5	15	....	....	....	126	....	....	....	....	....	....	....	....	....	....	5	0	0	0	8	....	....	....
1982-83	**Detroit Red Wings**	**NHL**	**1**	**0**	**0**	**0**	**0**	**0**	**0**	**0**	**0**	**0**	**0**	**0**	**0.0**	**0**	**0**	**1**	**0**	**–1**	....	....	....	....	....	....	....	....
	Adirondack Red Wings	AHL	74	20	30	50	....	....	....	132	....	....	....	....	....	....	....	....	....	....	6	1	1	2	10	....	....	....
1983-84	**Detroit Red Wings**	**NHL**	**8**	**2**	**1**	**3**	**2**	**1**	**3**	**36**	**0**	**0**	**0**	**10**	**20.0**	**3**	**0**	**5**	**0**	**–2**	....	....	....	....	....	....	....	....
	Adirondack Red Wings	AHL	46	15	29	44	....	....	....	128	....	....	....	....	....	....	....	....	....	....	7	1	1	2	26	....	....	....
1984-85	**Detroit Red Wings**	**NHL**	**1**	**1**	**0**	**1**	**1**	**0**	**1**	**5**	**0**	**0**	**0**	**4**	**25.0**	**1**	**0**	**1**	**0**	**0**	**3**	**0**	**1**	**1**	**5**	**0**	**0**	**0**
	Adirondack Red Wings	AHL	75	33	39	72	....	....	....	89	....	....	....	....	....	....	....	....	....	....	....	....	....	....	....	....	....	....

			REGULAR SEASON																		PLAYOFFS							
Season	**Club**	**League**	**GP**	**G**	**A**	**Pts**	**AG**	**AA**	**APts**	**PIM**	**PP**	**SH**	**GW**	**S**	**%**	**TGF**	**PGF**	**TGA**	**PGA**	**+/–**	**GP**	**G**	**A**	**Pts**	**PIM**	**PP**	**SH**	**GW**
1985-86	**Toronto Maple Leafs**	**NHL**	**42**	**5**	**17**	**22**	**4**	**11**	**15**	**84**	**0**	**0**	**0**	**46**	**10.9**	**41**	**3**	**46**	**0**	**–8**	**6**	**2**	**1**	**3**	**20**	**1**	**0**	**0**
	St. Catharines Saints	AHL	31	13	29	42	....	....	....	79	....	....	....	....	....	....	....	....	....	....	....	....	....	....	....	....	....	....
1986-87	**Toronto Maple Leafs**	**NHL**	**47**	**5**	**7**	**12**	**4**	**5**	**9**	**172**	**0**	**0**	**2**	**45**	**11.1**	**25**	**1**	**9**	**0**	**15**	**11**	**1**	**1**	**2**	**24**	**0**	**0**	**1**
	NHL Totals		**222**	**28**	**34**	**62**	**23**	**23**	**46**	**591**	**1**	**0**	**4**	**226**	**12.4**	**111**	**8**	**133**	**1**		**20**	**3**	**3**	**6**	**49**	**1**	**0**	**1**

Traded to **Atlanta** by **Vancouver** with Don Lever for Ivan Boldirev and Darcy Rota, February 8, 1980. Transferred to **Calgary** after **Atlanta** franchise relocated, June 24, 1980. Traded to **Detroit** by **Calgary** for future considerations (Rick Vasko, May 28, 1981), February 24, 1981. Signed as a free agent by **Toronto**, July 2, 1985.

• SMITH, Brandon

Brandon Stuart D – L. 6'1", 196 lbs. b: Hazelton, B.C., 2/25/1973.

Season	Club	League	GP	G	A	Pts	AG	AA	APts	PIM	PP	SH	GW	S	%	TGF	PGF	TGA	PGA	+/–	GP	G	A	Pts	PIM	PP	SH	GW
1989-90	Portland Winter Hawks	WHL	59	2	17	19	....	....	....	16	....	....	....	....	....	....	....	....	....	....	....	....	....	....	....	....	....	....
1990-91	Portland Winter Hawks	WHL	17	8	5	13	....	....	....	8	....	....	....	....	....	....	....	....	....	....	....	....	....	....	....	....	....	....
1991-92	Portland Winter Hawks	WHL	70	12	32	44	....	....	....	63	....	....	....	....	....	....	....	....	....	....	....	....	....	....	....	....	....	....
1992-93	Portland Winter Hawks	WHL	72	20	54	74	....	....	....	38	....	....	....	....	....	....	....	....	....	....	16	4	9	13	6	....	....	....
1993-94	Portland Winter Hawks	WHL	72	19	63	82	....	....	....	47	....	....	....	....	....	....	....	....	....	....	10	2	10	12	8	....	....	....
1994-95	Dayton Bombers	ECHL	60	16	49	65	....	....	....	57	....	....	....	....	....	....	....	....	....	....	4	2	3	5	0	....	....	....
	Minnesota Moose	IHL	1	0	0	0	....	....	....	0	....	....	....	....	....	....	....	....	....	....	....	....	....	....	....	....	....	....
	Adirondack Red Wings	AHL	14	1	2	3	....	....	....	7	....	....	....	....	....	....	....	....	....	....	3	0	0	0	2	....	....	....
1995-96	Adirondack Red Wings	AHL	48	4	13	17	....	....	....	22	....	....	....	....	....	....	....	....	....	....	3	0	1	1	2	....	....	....
1996-97	Adirondack Red Wings	AHL	80	8	26	34	....	....	....	30	....	....	....	....	....	....	....	....	....	....	4	0	0	0	0	....	....	....
1997-98	Adirondack Red Wings	AHL	64	9	27	36	....	....	....	26	....	....	....	....	....	....	....	....	....	....	1	0	1	1	0	....	....	....
1998-99	**Boston Bruins**	**NHL**	**5**	**0**	**0**	**0**	**0**	**0**	**0**	**0**	**0**	**0**	**0**	**2**	**0.0**	**3**	**0**	**1**	**0**	**2**	....	....	....	....	....	....	....	....
	Providence Bruins	AHL	72	16	46	62	....	....	....	32	....	....	....	....	....	....	....	....	....	....	19	1	9	10	12	....	....	....
99-2000	**Boston Bruins**	**NHL**	**22**	**2**	**4**	**6**	**2**	**4**	**6**	**10**	**0**	**0**	**0**	**24**	**8.3**	**18**	**2**	**23**	**3**	**–4**	....	....	....	....	....	....	....	....
	Providence Bruins	AHL	55	8	30	38	....	....	....	20	....	....	....	....	....	....	....	....	....	....	14	1	11	12	2	....	....	....
	NHL Totals		**27**	**2**	**4**	**6**	**2**	**4**	**6**	**10**	**0**	**0**	**0**	**26**	**7.7**	**21**	**2**	**24**	**3**		....	....	....	....	....	....	....	....

WHL West Second All-Star Team (1993, 1994) • ECHL First All-Star Team (1995) • Top Defenseman - ECHL (1995) • AHL First All-Star Team (1999)

Signed as a free agent by **Detroit**, July 22, 1997. Signed as a free agent by **Boston**, August 5, 1998.

• SMITH, Brian

Brian Desmond LW – R. 5'11", 170 lbs. b: Ottawa, Ont., 9/6/1940 d: 8/2/1995.

Season	Club	League	GP	G	A	Pts	AG	AA	APts	PIM	PP	SH	GW	S	%	TGF	PGF	TGA	PGA	+/–	GP	G	A	Pts	PIM	PP	SH	GW
1959-60	Brockville Jr. Canadiens	OVJHL	STATISTICS NOT AVAILABLE																									
	Brockville Jr. Canadiens	Mem-Cup	13	1	2	3	....	....	....	7	....	....	....	....	....	....	....	....	....	....	....	....	....	....	....	....	....	....
1960-61	Hull Canadiens	IPSHL	STATISTICS NOT AVAILABLE																									
	Montreal Royals	EPHL	1	0	0	0	....	....	....	0	....	....	....	....	....	....	....	....	....	....	....	....	....	....	....	....	....	....
	Hull-Ottawa Canadiens	EPHL	2	0	1	1	....	....	....	0	....	....	....	....	....	....	....	....	....	....	5	1	0	1	0	....	....	....
	Hull Canadiens	Al-Cup	3	1	0	1	....	....	....	9	....	....	....	....	....	....	....	....	....	....	....	....	....	....	....	....	....	....
1961-62	Hull-Ottawa Canadiens	EPHL	59	16	15	31	....	....	....	35	....	....	....	....	....	....	....	....	....	....	8	4	3	7	2	....	....	....
1962-63	Hull-Ottawa Canadiens	EPHL	72	24	34	58	....	....	....	40	....	....	....	....	....	....	....	....	....	....	3	0	0	0	0	....	....	....
1963-64	Springfield Indians	AHL	DID NOT PLAY – SUSPENDED																									
1964-65	Springfield Indians	AHL	70	22	12	34	....	....	....	32	....	....	....	....	....	....	....	....	....	....	....	....	....	....	....	....	....	....
1965-66	Springfield Indians	AHL	69	20	18	38	....	....	....	15	....	....	....	....	....	....	....	....	....	....	6	0	2	2	4	....	....	....
1966-67	Springfield Indians	AHL	68	30	31	61	....	....	....	15	....	....	....	....	....	....	....	....	....	....	....	....	....	....	....	....	....	....
1967-68	**Los Angeles Kings**	**NHL**	**58**	**10**	**9**	**19**	**12**	**9**	**21**	**33**	**1**	**0**	**3**	**92**	**10.9**	**33**	**5**	**32**	**2**	**–2**	**7**	**0**	**0**	**0**	**0**	**0**	**0**	**0**
1968-69	**Minnesota North Stars**	**NHL**	**9**	**0**	**1**	**1**	**0**	**1**	**1**	**0**	**0**	**0**	**0**	**14**	**0.0**	**1**	**1**	**7**	**0**	**–7**	....	....	....	....	....	....	....	....
	Memphis South Stars	CHL	21	5	7	12	....	....	....	11	....	....	....	....	....	....	....	....	....	....	....	....	....	....	....	....	....	....
	Phoenix Roadrunners	WHL	21	1	3	4	....	....	....	0	....	....	....	....	....	....	....	....	....	....	....	....	....	....	....	....	....	....
1969-70	Denver Spurs	WHL	60	17	25	42	....	....	....	15	....	....	....	....	....	....	....	....	....	....	....	....	....	....	....	....	....	....
1970-71			OUT OF HOCKEY – RETIRED																									
1971-72			OUT OF HOCKEY – RETIRED																									
1972-73	Houston Aeros	WHA	48	7	6	13	....	....	....	19	....	....	....	....	....	....	....	....	....	....	10	0	2	2	0	....	....	....
	NHL Totals		**67**	**10**	**10**	**20**	**12**	**10**	**22**	**33**	**1**	**0**	**3**	**106**	**9.4**	**34**	**6**	**39**	**2**		**7**	**0**	**0**	**0**	**0**	**0**	**0**	**0**
	Other Major League Totals		48	7	6	13	....	....	....	19	....	....	....	....	....	....	....	....	....	....	10	0	2	2	0	....	....	....

• Son of Des • Brother of Gary

Traded to **Springfield** (AHL) by **Montreal** with Wayne Boddy, Fred Hilts, Lorne O'Donnell and John Rodger for Terry Gray, Bruce Cline, Wayne Larkin, John Chasczewski, Ted Harris and the loan of Gary Bergman, June, 1963. • Suspended for entire 1963-64 season for refusing to report to **Springfield** (AHL), September, 1963. NHL rights transferred to **LA Kings** after NHL club purchased **Springfield** (AHL) franchise, May, 1967. Traded to **Montreal** by **LA Kings** with Yves Locas for Larry Cahan, July 1, 1968. Traded to **Minnesota** by **Montreal** for cash, November 15, 1968. Traded to **Phoenix** (WHL) by **Minnesota** with Milan Marcetta for Tom Polanic, February 11, 1969. Signed as a free agent by **Houston** (WHA), September, 1972.

• SMITH, D.J.

D.J. Denis D – L. 6'1", 200 lbs. b: Windsor, Ont., 5/13/1977. NY Islanders' 3rd, 41st overall, in 1995.

Season	Club	League	GP	G	A	Pts	AG	AA	APts	PIM	PP	SH	GW	S	%	TGF	PGF	TGA	PGA	+/–	GP	G	A	Pts	PIM	PP	SH	GW
1992-93	Belle River Canadians	OJHL-C	40	5	18	23	....	....	....	39	....	....	....	....	....	....	....	....	....	....	....	....	....	....	....	....	....	....
	Windsor Bulldogs	OJHL-B	1	0	0	0	....	....	....	0	....	....	....	....	....	....	....	....	....	....	....	....	....	....	....	....	....	....
1993-94	Windsor Bulldogs	OJHL-B	51	8	34	42	....	....	....	267	....	....	....	....	....	....	....	....	....	....	....	....	....	....	....	....	....	....
1994-95	Windsor Spitfires	OHL	61	4	13	17	....	....	....	201	....	....	....	....	....	....	....	....	....	....	10	1	3	4	41	....	....	....
1995-96	Windsor Spitfires	OHL	64	14	45	59	....	....	....	260	....	....	....	....	....	....	....	....	....	....	7	1	7	8	23	....	....	....
	St. John's Maple Leafs	AHL	1	0	0	0	....	....	....	0	....	....	....	....	....	....	....	....	....	....	....	....	....	....	....	....	....	....
1996-97	Windsor Spitfires	OHL	63	15	52	67	....	....	....	190	....	....	....	....	....	....	....	....	....	....	5	1	7	8	11	....	....	....
	Toronto Maple Leafs	**NHL**	**8**	**0**	**1**	**1**	**0**	**1**	**1**	**7**	**0**	**0**	**0**	**4**	**0.0**	**2**	**0**	**8**	**1**	**–5**	....	....	....	....	....	....	....	....
	St. John's Maple Leafs	AHL	....	....	....	....	....	....	....	....	....	....	....	....	....	....	....	....	....	....	1	0	0	0	0	....	....	....
1997-98	St. John's Maple Leafs	AHL	65	4	11	15	....	....	....	237	....	....	....	....	....	....	....	....	....	....	4	0	0	0	4	....	....	....
1998-99	St. John's Maple Leafs	AHL	79	7	28	35	....	....	....	216	....	....	....	....	....	....	....	....	....	....	5	0	1	1	0	....	....	....
99-2000	**Toronto Maple Leafs**	**NHL**	**3**	**0**	**0**	**0**	**0**	**0**	**0**	**5**	**0**	**0**	**0**	**2**	**0.0**	**1**	**0**	**2**	**0**	**–1**	....	....	....	....	....	....	....	....
	St. John's Maple Leafs	AHL	74	6	22	28	....	....	....	197	....	....	....	....	....	....	....	....	....	....	....	....	....	....	....	....	....	....
	NHL Totals		**11**	**0**	**1**	**1**	**0**	**1**	**1**	**12**	**0**	**0**	**0**	**6**	**0.0**	**3**	**0**	**10**	**1**		....	....	....	....	....	....	....	....

OHL Second All-Star Team (1997)

Traded to **Toronto** by **NY Islanders** with Wendel Clark and Mathieu Schneider for Darby Hendrickson, Sean Haggerty, Kenny Jonsson and Toronto's 1st round choice (Roberto Luongo) in 1997 Entry Draft, March 13, 1996.

• SMITH, Dallas

Dallas Earl D – L. 5'11", 180 lbs. b: Hamiota, Man., 10/10/1941.

Season	Club	League	GP	G	A	Pts	AG	AA	APts	PIM	PP	SH	GW	S	%	TGF	PGF	TGA	PGA	+/–	GP	G	A	Pts	PIM	PP	SH	GW
1958-59	Estevan Bruins	SJHL	47	5	15	20	....	....	....	41	....	....	....	....	....	....	....	....	....	....	14	4	2	6	26	....	....	....
1959-60	Estevan Bruins	SJHL	59	12	33	45	....	....	....	102	....	....	....	....	....	....	....	....	....	....	....	....	....	....	....	....	....	....
	Boston Bruins	**NHL**	**5**	**1**	**1**	**2**	**1**	**1**	**2**	**0**	....	....	....	....	....	....	....	....	....	....	....	....	....	....	....	....	....	....
1960-61	**Boston Bruins**	**NHL**	**70**	**1**	**9**	**10**	**1**	**9**	**10**	**79**	....	....	....	....	....	....	....	....	....	....	....	....	....	....	....	....	....	....
1961-62	**Boston Bruins**	**NHL**	**7**	**0**	**0**	**0**	**0**	**0**	**0**	**10**	....	....	....	....	....	....	....	....	....	....	....	....	....	....	....	....	....	....
	Hull-Ottawa Canadiens	EPHL	3	0	0	0	....	....	....	0	....	....	....	....	....	....	....	....	....	....	....	....	....	....	....	....	....	....
	Pittsburgh Hornets	AHL	55	1	12	13	....	....	....	93	....	....	....	....	....	....	....	....	....	....	....	....	....	....	....	....	....	....
1962-63	Portland Buckaroos	WHL	68	4	18	22	....	....	....	64	....	....	....	....	....	....	....	....	....	....	7	1	2	3	14	....	....	....
1963-64	Portland Buckaroos	WHL	64	4	14	18	....	....	....	57	....	....	....	....	....	....	....	....	....	....	5	1	0	1	6	....	....	....
1964-65	San Francisco Seals	WHL	70	14	16	30	....	....	....	79	....	....	....	....	....	....	....	....	....	....	....	....	....	....	....	....	....	....
1965-66	**Boston Bruins**	**NHL**	**2**	**0**	**0**	**0**	**0**	**0**	**0**	**2**	....	....	....	....	....	....	....	....	....	....	....	....	....	....	....	....	....	....
	Oklahoma City Blazers	CPHL	69	5	23	28	....	....	....	52	....	....	....	....	....	....	....	....	....	....	9	0	5	5	10	....	....	....
1966-67	**Boston Bruins**	**NHL**	**33**	**0**	**1**	**1**	**0**	**1**	**1**	**24**	....	....	....	....	....	....	....	....	....	....	....	....	....	....	....	....	....	....
	Oklahoma City Blazers	CPHL	29	3	9	12	....	....	....	44	....	....	....	....	....	....	....	....	....	....	11	2	0	2	20	....	....	....
1967-68	**Boston Bruins**	**NHL**	**74**	**4**	**23**	**27**	**5**	**23**	**28**	**65**	**0**	**0**	**1**	**159**	**2.5**	**114**	**5**	**98**	**22**	**33**	**4**	**0**	**2**	**2**	**0**	**0**	**0**	**0**
1968-69	**Boston Bruins**	**NHL**	**75**	**4**	**24**	**28**	**4**	**21**	**25**	**74**	**0**	**1**	**0**	**131**	**3.1**	**121**	**2**	**108**	**33**	**44**	**10**	**0**	**3**	**3**	**16**	**0**	**0**	**0**
1969-70♦	**Boston Bruins**	**NHL**	**75**	**7**	**17**	**24**	**8**	**16**	**24**	**119**	**1**	**1**	**1**	**160**	**4.4**	**79**	**1**	**109**	**40**	**9**	**14**	**0**	**3**	**3**	**19**	**0**	**0**	**0**
1970-71	**Boston Bruins**	**NHL**	**73**	**7**	**38**	**45**	**7**	**32**	**39**	**68**	**0**	**2**	**1**	**159**	**4.4**	**154**	**4**	**84**	**28**	**94**	**7**	**0**	**3**	**3**	**26**	**0**	**0**	**0**
1971-72♦	**Boston Bruins**	**NHL**	**78**	**8**	**22**	**30**	**8**	**19**	**27**	**132**	**0**	**1**	**1**	**111**	**7.2**	**119**	**2**	**107**	**24**	**34**	**15**	**0**	**4**	**4**	**22**	**0**	**0**	**0**
1972-73	**Boston Bruins**	**NHL**	**78**	**4**	**27**	**31**	**4**	**21**	**25**	**72**	**0**	**0**	**0**	**130**	**3.1**	**118**	**3**	**101**	**24**	**38**	**5**	**0**	**2**	**2**	**2**	**0**	**0**	**0**
1973-74	**Boston Bruins**	**NHL**	**77**	**6**	**21**	**27**	**6**	**17**	**23**	**64**	**0**	**0**	**0**	**112**	**5.4**	**98**	**0**	**91**	**19**	**26**	**16**	**1**	**7**	**8**	**20**	**0**	**0**	**0**
1974-75	**Boston Bruins**	**NHL**	**79**	**3**	**20**	**23**	**3**	**15**	**18**	**84**	**0**	**0**	**1**	**146**	**2.1**	**104**	**1**	**99**	**26**	**30**	**3**	**0**	**2**	**2**	**4**	**0**	**0**	**0**

			REGULAR SEASON																	PLAYOFFS							
Season	Club	League	GP	G	A	Pts	AG	AA	APts	PIM	PP	SH	GW	S	%	TGF	PGF	TGA	PGA	+/–	GP	G	A	Pts	PIM	PP	SH	GW
1975-76	**Boston Bruins**	**NHL**	**77**	**7**	**25**	**32**	**6**	**19**	**25**	**103**	**0**	**0**	**0**	**125**	**5.6**	**128**	**5**	**110**	**29**	**42**	**11**	**2**	**2**	**4**	**19**	**0**	**0**	**1**
1976-77	**Boston Bruins**	**NHL**	**58**	**2**	**20**	**22**	**2**	**15**	**17**	**40**	**0**	**0**	**0**	**66**	**3.0**	**81**	**2**	**75**	**12**	**16**	....	....	....	....	....	....	....	....
	Canada	WEC-A	10	0	2	2	....	....	....	4	....	....	....	....	....	....	....	....	....	....	....	....	....	....	....	....	....	....
1977-78	**New York Rangers**	**NHL**	**29**	**1**	**4**	**5**	**1**	**3**	**4**	**23**	**0**	**0**	**0**	**35**	**2.9**	**21**	**1**	**37**	**6**	**–11**	**1**	**0**	**1**	**1**	**0**	**0**	**0**	**0**
	NHL Totals		**890**	**55**	**252**	**307**	**56**	**212**	**268**	**959**	....	....	....	....	....	....	....	....	....	....	**86**	**3**	**29**	**32**	**128**	....	....	....

CPHL Second All-Star Team (1966) • NHL Plus/Minus Leader (1968) • Played in NHL All-Star Game (1971, 1972, 1973, 1974)

Loaned to **Montreal** (Hull-Ottawa-EPHL) by **Boston** with loan of Bob Armstrong and cash for Wayne Connelly, October 26, 1961. Loaned to **San Francisco** (WHL) by **Boston** for 1964-65 season to complete transaction that sent Cliff Pennington to Boston (December 17, 1963), July 8, 1964. Signed as a free agent by **NY Rangers**, December 19, 1977.

• SMITH, Dan

D – L. 6'2", 195 lbs. b: Fernie, B.C., 10/19/1976. Colorado's 7th, 181st overall, in 1995.

Season	Club	League	GP	G	A	Pts	AG	AA	APts	PIM	PP	SH	GW	S	%	TGF	PGF	TGA	PGA	+/–	GP	G	A	Pts	PIM	PP	SH	GW
1993-94	Fernie Ghostriders	RMJHL	STATISTICS NOT AVAILABLE																									
1994-95	University of British Columbia	CWUAA	28	1	3	4	....	....	....	26	....	....	....	....	....	....	....	....	....	....	....	....	....	....	....	....	....	....
1995-96	Tri-City Americans	WHL	58	1	21	22	....	....	....	70	....	....	....	....	....	....	....	....	....	....	11	1	3	4	14	....	....	....
1996-97	Tri-City Americans	WHL	72	5	19	24	....	....	....	174	....	....	....	....	....	....	....	....	....	....	....	....	....	....	....	....	....	....
	Hershey Bears	AHL	8	0	1	1	....	....	....	6	....	....	....	....	....	....	....	....	....	....	15	0	1	1	25	....	....	....
1997-98	Hershey Bears	AHL	50	1	2	3	....	....	....	71	....	....	....	....	....	....	....	....	....	....	6	0	0	0	4	....	....	....
1998-99	**Colorado Avalanche**	**NHL**	**12**	**0**	**0**	**0**	**0**	**0**	**0**	**9**	**0**	**0**	**0**	**6**	**0.0**	**6**	**0**	**2**	**1**	**5**	....	....	....	....	....	....	....	....
	Hershey Bears	AHL	54	5	7	12	....	....	....	72	....	....	....	....	....	....	....	....	....	....	5	0	1	1	0	....	....	....
99-2000	**Colorado Avalanche**	**NHL**	**3**	**0**	**0**	**0**	**0**	**0**	**0**	**0**	**0**	**0**	**0**	**0**	**0.0**	**3**	**0**	**1**	**0**	**2**	....	....	....	....	....	....	....	....
	Hershey Bears	AHL	49	7	15	22	....	....	....	56	....	....	....	....	....	....	....	....	....	....	....	....	....	....	....	....	....	....
	NHL Totals		**15**	**0**	**0**	**0**	**0**	**0**	**0**	**9**	**0**	**0**	**0**	**6**	**0.0**	**9**	**0**	**3**	**1**		....	....	....	....	....	....	....	....

• SMITH, Dennis

Dennis D.J. D – L. 5'11", 190 lbs. b: Detroit, MI, 7/27/1964.

Season	Club	League	GP	G	A	Pts	AG	AA	APts	PIM	PP	SH	GW	S	%	TGF	PGF	TGA	PGA	+/–	GP	G	A	Pts	PIM	PP	SH	GW
1980-81	Taylor Michigan Midgets	MNHL	37	25	40	65	....	....	....	....	....	....	....	....	....	....	....	....	....	....	....	....	....	....	....	....	....	....
1981-82	Kingston Canadians	OHL	48	2	24	26	....	....	....	84	....	....	....	....	....	....	....	....	....	....	4	0	2	2	0	....	....	....
1982-83	Kingston Canadians	OHL	58	6	30	36	....	....	....	100	....	....	....	....	....	....	....	....	....	....	....	....	....	....	....	....	....	....
1983-84	Kingston Canadians	OHL	62	10	41	51	....	....	....	165	....	....	....	....	....	....	....	....	....	....	....	....	....	....	....	....	....	....
	Erie Golden Blades	ACHL	2	1	1	2	....	....	....	2	....	....	....	....	....	....	....	....	....	....	9	2	4	6	8	....	....	....
1984-85	Osby IF	Sweden-2	30	15	15	30	....	....	....	74	....	....	....	....	....	....	....	....	....	....	....	....	....	....	....	....	....	....
	Erie Golden Blades	ACHL	19	5	20	25	....	....	....	67	....	....	....	....	....	....	....	....	....	....	12	1	4	5	52	....	....	....
1985-86	Peoria Rivermen	IHL	70	5	15	20	....	....	....	102	....	....	....	....	....	....	....	....	....	....	10	0	2	2	18	....	....	....
1986-87	Adirondack Red Wings	AHL	64	4	24	28	....	....	....	120	....	....	....	....	....	....	....	....	....	....	6	0	0	0	8	....	....	....
1987-88	Adirondack Red Wings	AHL	75	6	24	30	....	....	....	213	....	....	....	....	....	....	....	....	....	....	11	2	2	4	47	....	....	....
1988-89	Adirondack Red Wings	AHL	75	5	35	40	....	....	....	176	....	....	....	....	....	....	....	....	....	....	17	1	6	7	47	....	....	....
1989-90	**Washington Capitals**	**NHL**	**4**	**0**	**0**	**0**	**0**	**0**	**0**	**0**	**0**	**0**	**0**	**0**	**0.0**	**2**	**0**	**2**	**0**	**0**	....	....	....	....	....	....	....	....
	Baltimore Skipjacks	AHL	74	8	25	33	....	....	....	103	....	....	....	....	....	....	....	....	....	....	12	0	3	3	65	....	....	....
1990-91	**Los Angeles Kings**	**NHL**	**4**	**0**	**0**	**0**	**0**	**0**	**0**	**4**	**0**	**0**	**0**	**1**	**0.0**	**5**	**1**	**2**	**1**	**3**	....	....	....	....	....	....	....	....
	New Haven Nighthawks	AHL	61	7	25	32	....	....	....	148	....	....	....	....	....	....	....	....	....	....	....	....	....	....	....	....	....	....
1991-92	Maine Mariners	AHL	59	2	32	34	....	....	....	63	....	....	....	....	....	....	....	....	....	....	....	....	....	....	....	....	....	....
	Baltimore Skipjacks	AHL	17	1	4	5	....	....	....	23	....	....	....	....	....	....	....	....	....	....	....	....	....	....	....	....	....	....
1992-93	VEU Feldkirch	Austria	25	7	19	26	....	....	....	....	....	....	....	....	....	....	....	....	....	....	....	....	....	....	....	....	....	....
1993-94	Providence Bruins	AHL	58	2	22	24	....	....	....	89	....	....	....	....	....	....	....	....	....	....	....	....	....	....	....	....	....	....
1994-95	Detroit Vipers	IHL	8	2	0	2	....	....	....	12	....	....	....	....	....	....	....	....	....	....	....	....	....	....	....	....	....	....
	Kalamazoo Wings	IHL	31	2	1	3	....	....	....	41	....	....	....	....	....	....	....	....	....	....	13	0	2	2	33	....	....	....
1995-96	Michigan K-Wings	IHL	49	0	10	10	....	....	....	62	....	....	....	....	....	....	....	....	....	....	10	0	0	0	6	....	....	....
1996-97	Michigan K-Wings	IHL	62	2	7	9	....	....	....	60	....	....	....	....	....	....	....	....	....	....	3	0	0	0	6	....	....	....
	NHL Totals		**8**	**0**	**0**	**0**	**0**	**0**	**0**	**4**	**0**	**0**	**0**	**1**	**0.0**	**7**	**1**	**4**	**1**		....	....	....	....	....	....	....	....

AHL Second All-Star Team (1990)

Signed as a free agent by **Detroit**, December 2, 1986. Signed as a free agent by **Washington**, July 25, 1989. Signed as a free agent by **LA Kings**, September 28, 1990. Signed as a free agent by **Boston**, August 2, 1991. Traded to **Washington** by **Boston** with John Byce for Brent Hughes and cash, February 24, 1992.

• SMITH, Derek

Derek Robert C/LW – L. 5'11", 180 lbs. b: Quebec City, Que., 7/31/1954. Buffalo's 10th, 168th overall, in 1974.

Season	Club	League	GP	G	A	Pts	AG	AA	APts	PIM	PP	SH	GW	S	%	TGF	PGF	TGA	PGA	+/–	GP	G	A	Pts	PIM	PP	SH	GW
1970-71	Ottawa Jr. Senators	OJHL	STATISTICS NOT AVAILABLE																									
1971-72	Ottawa 67's	OMJHL	53	6	11	17	....	....	....	10	....	....	....	....	....	....	....	....	....	....	18	2	4	6	22	....	....	....
1972-73	Ottawa 67's	OMJHL	63	52	46	98	....	....	....	32	....	....	....	....	....	....	....	....	....	....	9	3	4	7	6	....	....	....
1973-74	Ottawa 67's	OMJHL	69	47	45	92	....	....	....	40	....	....	....	....	....	....	....	....	....	....	7	0	5	5	0	....	....	....
1974-75	Charlotte Checkers	SHL	4	4	3	7	....	....	....	0	....	....	....	....	....	....	....	....	....	....	....	....	....	....	....	....	....	....
	Hershey Bears	AHL	64	11	16	27	....	....	....	10	....	....	....	....	....	....	....	....	....	....	11	7	3	10	0	....	....	....
1975-76	Hershey Bears	AHL	67	28	32	60	....	....	....	14	....	....	....	....	....	....	....	....	....	....	10	4	5	9	4	....	....	....
	Buffalo Sabres	**NHL**	....	....	....	....	....	....	....	....	....	....	....	....	....	....	....	....	....	....	**1**	**0**	**0**	**0**	**0**	**0**	**0**	**0**
1976-77	**Buffalo Sabres**	**NHL**	**5**	**0**	**0**	**0**	**0**	**0**	**0**	**0**	**0**	**0**	**0**	**0**	**0.0**	**0**	**0**	**1**	**0**	**–1**	....	....	....	....	....	....	....	....
	Hershey Bears	AHL	65	31	31	62	....	....	....	20	....	....	....	....	....	....	....	....	....	....	6	3	1	4	2	....	....	....
1977-78	**Buffalo Sabres**	**NHL**	**36**	**3**	**3**	**6**	**3**	**2**	**5**	**0**	**0**	**0**	**0**	**25**	**12.0**	**9**	**1**	**12**	**0**	**–4**	**8**	**3**	**3**	**6**	**7**	**0**	**0**	**0**
	Hershey Bears	AHL	5	2	2	4	....	....	....	2	....	....	....	....	....	....	....	....	....	....	....	....	....	....	....	....	....	....
1978-79	**Buffalo Sabres**	**NHL**	**43**	**14**	**12**	**26**	**12**	**9**	**21**	**8**	**3**	**0**	**0**	**85**	**16.5**	**35**	**9**	**32**	**1**	**–5**	....	....	....	....	....	....	....	....
1979-80	**Buffalo Sabres**	**NHL**	**79**	**24**	**39**	**63**	**20**	**28**	**48**	**16**	**8**	**0**	**3**	**137**	**17.5**	**102**	**33**	**36**	**0**	**33**	**13**	**5**	**7**	**12**	**4**	**3**	**0**	**1**
1980-81	**Buffalo Sabres**	**NHL**	**69**	**21**	**43**	**64**	**16**	**29**	**45**	**12**	**11**	**0**	**2**	**166**	**12.7**	**99**	**41**	**44**	**0**	**14**	**8**	**1**	**4**	**5**	**2**	**1**	**0**	**0**
1981-82	**Buffalo Sabres**	**NHL**	**12**	**3**	**1**	**4**	**2**	**1**	**3**	**2**	**0**	**0**	**0**	**15**	**20.0**	**9**	**2**	**8**	**1**	**0**	....	....	....	....	....	....	....	....
	Detroit Red Wings	**NHL**	**49**	**6**	**14**	**20**	**5**	**9**	**14**	**10**	**0**	**0**	**0**	**82**	**7.3**	**34**	**5**	**36**	**3**	**–4**	....	....	....	....	....	....	....	....
1982-83	**Detroit Red Wings**	**NHL**	**42**	**7**	**4**	**11**	**6**	**3**	**9**	**12**	**1**	**0**	**0**	**50**	**14.0**	**24**	**2**	**31**	**2**	**–7**	....	....	....	....	....	....	....	....
	Adirondack Red Wings	AHL	11	6	4	10	....	....	....	2	....	....	....	....	....	....	....	....	....	....	6	1	2	3	0	....	....	....
1983-84	Adirondack Red Wings	AHL	61	16	29	45	....	....	....	10	....	....	....	....	....	....	....	....	....	....	10	1	0	0	0	....	....	....
	NHL Totals		**335**	**78**	**116**	**194**	**64**	**81**	**145**	**60**	**23**	**0**	**5**	**560**	**13.9**	**312**	**93**	**200**	**7**		**30**	**9**	**14**	**23**	**13**	**4**	**0**	**1**

Traded to **Detroit** by **Buffalo** with Danny Gare and Jim Schoenfeld for Mike Foligno, Dale McCourt and Brent Peterson, December 2, 1981.

• SMITH, Derrick

LW – L. 6'2", 215 lbs. b: Scarborough, Ont., 1/22/1965. Philadelphia's 2nd, 44th overall, in 1983.

Season	Club	League	GP	G	A	Pts	AG	AA	APts	PIM	PP	SH	GW	S	%	TGF	PGF	TGA	PGA	+/–	GP	G	A	Pts	PIM	PP	SH	GW
1981-82	Wexford Raiders	OJHL-B	45	35	47	82	....	....	....	40	....	....	....	....	....	....	....	....	....	....	....	....	....	....	....	....	....	....
1982-83	Peterborough Petes	OHL	70	16	19	35	....	....	....	47	....	....	....	....	....	....	....	....	....	....	....	....	....	....	....	....	....	....
1983-84	Peterborough Petes	OHL	70	30	36	66	....	....	....	31	....	....	....	....	....	....	....	....	....	....	8	4	4	8	7	....	....	....
1984-85	**Philadelphia Flyers**	**NHL**	**77**	**17**	**22**	**39**	**14**	**15**	**29**	**31**	**0**	**1**	**4**	**140**	**12.1**	**60**	**2**	**38**	**8**	**28**	**19**	**2**	**5**	**7**	**16**	**0**	**0**	**0**
1985-86	**Philadelphia Flyers**	**NHL**	**69**	**6**	**6**	**12**	**5**	**4**	**9**	**57**	**0**	**0**	**2**	**108**	**5.6**	**38**	**0**	**25**	**1**	**14**	**4**	**0**	**0**	**0**	**10**	**0**	**0**	**0**
1986-87	**Philadelphia Flyers**	**NHL**	**71**	**11**	**21**	**32**	**9**	**15**	**24**	**34**	**0**	**0**	**0**	**150**	**7.3**	**51**	**0**	**60**	**5**	**–4**	**26**	**6**	**4**	**10**	**26**	**0**	**0**	**1**
1987-88	**Philadelphia Flyers**	**NHL**	**76**	**16**	**8**	**24**	**14**	**6**	**20**	**104**	**0**	**0**	**1**	**155**	**10.3**	**40**	**0**	**71**	**11**	**–20**	**7**	**0**	**0**	**0**	**6**	**0**	**0**	**0**
1988-89	**Philadelphia Flyers**	**NHL**	**74**	**16**	**14**	**30**	**14**	**10**	**24**	**43**	**0**	**1**	**3**	**115**	**13.9**	**45**	**0**	**66**	**17**	**–4**	**19**	**5**	**2**	**7**	**12**	**0**	**2**	**1**
1989-90	**Philadelphia Flyers**	**NHL**	**55**	**3**	**6**	**9**	**3**	**4**	**7**	**32**	**0**	**0**	**0**	**72**	**4.2**	**22**	**0**	**47**	**10**	**–15**	....	....	....	....	....	....	....	....
1990-91	**Philadelphia Flyers**	**NHL**	**72**	**11**	**10**	**21**	**10**	**8**	**18**	**37**	**0**	**1**	**2**	**100**	**11.0**	**32**	**1**	**44**	**13**	**0**	....	....	....	....	....	....	....	....
1991-92	**Minnesota North Stars**	**NHL**	**33**	**2**	**4**	**6**	**2**	**3**	**5**	**33**	**0**	**0**	**0**	**29**	**6.9**	**9**	**0**	**26**	**9**	**–8**	**7**	**1**	**0**	**1**	**9**	**0**	**0**	**1**
	Kalamazoo Wings	IHL	6	1	5	6	....	....	....	4	....	....	....	....	....	....	....	....	....	....	....	....	....	....	....	....	....	....
1992-93	**Minnesota North Stars**	**NHL**	**9**	**0**	**1**	**1**	**0**	**1**	**1**	**2**	**0**	**0**	**0**	**3**	**0.0**	**1**	**0**	**3**	**0**	**–2**	....	....	....	....	....	....	....	....
	Kalamazoo Wings	IHL	52	22	13	35	....	....	....	43	....	....	....	....	....	....	....	....	....	....	....	....	....	....	....	....	....	....
1993-94	**Dallas Stars**	**NHL**	**1**	**0**	**0**	**0**	**0**	**0**	**0**	**0**	**0**	**0**	**0**	**1**	**0.0**	**0**	**0**	**1**	**0**	**–1**	....	....	....	....	....	....	....	....
	Kalamazoo Wings	IHL	77	44	37	81	....	....	....	90	....	....	....	....	....	....	....	....	....	....	5	0	0	0	18	....	....	....
1994-95	Kalamazoo Wings	IHL	68	30	21	51	....	....	....	103	....	....	....	....	....	....	....	....	....	....	16	3	8	11	8	....	....	....
1995-96	Michigan K-Wings	IHL	69	15	26	41	....	....	....	79	....	....	....	....	....	....	....	....	....	....	10	4	3	7	16	....	....	....
1996-97	Michigan K-Wings	IHL	68	8	21	29	....	....	....	55	....	....	....	....	....	....	....	....	....	....	4	1	0	1	16	....	....	....

Season	Club	League	GP	G	A	Pts	AG	AA	APts	PIM	PP	SH	GW	S	%	TGF	PGF	TGA	PGA	+/-	GP	G	A	Pts	PIM	PP	SH	GW
			REGULAR SEASON																		PLAYOFFS							
1997-98	Michigan K-Wings	IHL	64	15	26	41	....	....	....	39	....	....	....	....	....	....	....	....	....	....	4	1	1	2	2	....	....	....
1998-99	Baton Rouge Kingfish	ECHL	6	3	7	10	....	....	....	9	....	....	....	....	....	....	....	....	....	....	6	0	0	0	0	....	....	....
99-2000	Wheeling Nailers	ECHL	66	18	29	47	....	....	....	139	....	....	....	....	....	....	....	....	....	....	....	....	....	....	....	....	....	....
	NHL Totals		**537**	**82**	**92**	**174**	**71**	**66**	**137**	**373**	**0**	**3**	**12**	**873**	**9.4**	**298**	**3**	**381**	**74**		**82**	**14**	**11**	**25**	**79**	**0**	**2**	**3**

IHL Second All-Star Team (1994)

Claimed on waivers by **Minnesota** from **Philadelphia**, October 26, 1991. Transferred to **Dallas** after **Minnesota** franchise relocated, June 9, 1993. Signed as a free agent by **Baton Rouge** (ECHL), March 23, 1999.

• SMITH, Doug

Douglas Eric C – R. 5'11", 186 lbs. b: Ottawa, Ont., 5/17/1963. Los Angeles' 1st, 2nd overall, in 1981.

Season	Club	League	GP	G	A	Pts	AG	AA	APts	PIM	PP	SH	GW	S	%	TGF	PGF	TGA	PGA	+/-	GP	G	A	Pts	PIM	PP	SH	GW
1978-79	Nepean Raiders	OJHL	24	24	17	41	....	....	....	18	....	....	....	....	....	....	....	....	....	....	....	....	....	....	....	....	....	....
1979-80	Ottawa 67's	OMJHL	64	23	34	57	....	....	....	45	....	....	....	....	....	....	....	....	....	....	11	2	0	2	33	....	....	....
1980-81	Ottawa 67's	OMJHL	54	45	56	101	....	....	....	61	....	....	....	....	....	....	....	....	....	....	7	5	6	11	13	....	....	....
1981-82	Ottawa 67's	OHL	1	1	2	3	....	....	....	17	....	....	....	....	....	....	....	....	....	....	....	....	....	....	....	....	....	....
	Los Angeles Kings	**NHL**	**80**	**16**	**14**	**30**	**13**	**9**	**22**	**64**	**1**	**0**	**1**	**141**	**11.3**	**53**	**3**	**78**	**15**	**–13**	**10**	**3**	**2**	**5**	**11**	**1**	**0**	**0**
1982-83	**Los Angeles Kings**	**NHL**	**42**	**11**	**11**	**22**	**9**	**8**	**17**	**12**	**1**	**0**	**1**	**87**	**12.6**	**27**	**5**	**38**	**2**	**–14**	....	....	....	....	....	....	....	....
1983-84	**Los Angeles Kings**	**NHL**	**72**	**16**	**20**	**36**	**13**	**14**	**27**	**28**	**6**	**0**	**0**	**146**	**11.0**	**50**	**12**	**76**	**5**	**–33**	....	....	....	....	....	....	....	....
1984-85	**Los Angeles Kings**	**NHL**	**62**	**21**	**20**	**41**	**17**	**14**	**31**	**58**	**3**	**1**	**1**	**146**	**14.4**	**54**	**12**	**69**	**12**	**–15**	**3**	**1**	**0**	**1**	**4**	**0**	**0**	**0**
1985-86	**Los Angeles Kings**	**NHL**	**48**	**8**	**9**	**17**	**6**	**6**	**12**	**56**	**1**	**1**	**0**	**115**	**7.0**	**32**	**5**	**90**	**34**	**–29**	....	....	....	....	....	....	....	....
	Buffalo Sabres	**NHL**	**30**	**10**	**11**	**21**	**8**	**7**	**15**	**73**	**3**	**1**	**3**	**72**	**13.9**	**33**	**9**	**26**	**4**	**2**	....	....	....	....	....	....	....	....
1986-87	**Buffalo Sabres**	**NHL**	**62**	**16**	**24**	**40**	**14**	**17**	**31**	**106**	**7**	**0**	**2**	**158**	**10.1**	**61**	**28**	**73**	**20**	**–20**	....	....	....	....	....	....	....	....
	Rochester Americans	AHL	15	5	6	11	....	....	....	35	....	....	....	....	....	....	....	....	....	....	....	....	....	....	....	....	....	....
1987-88	**Buffalo Sabres**	**NHL**	**70**	**9**	**19**	**28**	**8**	**14**	**22**	**117**	**1**	**0**	**0**	**136**	**6.6**	**47**	**9**	**78**	**30**	**–10**	**1**	**0**	**0**	**0**	**0**	**0**	**0**	**0**
1988-89	**Edmonton Oilers**	**NHL**	**19**	**1**	**1**	**2**	**1**	**1**	**2**	**9**	**0**	**0**	**0**	**15**	**6.7**	**6**	**0**	**8**	**1**	**–1**	....	....	....	....	....	....	....	....
	Cape Breton Oilers	AHL	24	11	11	22	....	....	....	69	....	....	....	....	....	....	....	....	....	....	....	....	....	....	....	....	....	....
	Vancouver Canucks	**NHL**	**10**	**3**	**4**	**7**	**3**	**3**	**6**	**4**	**1**	**0**	**1**	**12**	**25.0**	**8**	**2**	**5**	**2**	**3**	**4**	**0**	**0**	**0**	**6**	**0**	**0**	**0**
1989-90	**Vancouver Canucks**	**NHL**	**30**	**3**	**4**	**7**	**3**	**3**	**6**	**72**	**0**	**1**	**0**	**40**	**7.5**	**18**	**3**	**22**	**8**	**1**	....	....	....	....	....	....	....	....
	Pittsburgh Penguins	**NHL**	**10**	**1**	**1**	**2**	**1**	**1**	**2**	**25**	**0**	**0**	**0**	**11**	**9.1**	**2**	**0**	**5**	**1**	**–2**	....	....	....	....	....	....	....	....
1990-91	EC Graz	Austria	42	33	36	69	....	....	....	*200	....	....	....	....	....	....	....	....	....	....	....	....	....	....	....	....	....	....
1991-92	EC Graz	Austria	30	15	13	28	....	....	....	....	....	....	....	....	....	....	....	....	....	....	....	....	....	....	....	....	....	....
	NHL Totals		**535**	**115**	**138**	**253**	**96**	**97**	**193**	**624**	**24**	**4**	**9**	**1079**	**10.7**	**391**	**88**	**568**	**134**		**18**	**4**	**2**	**6**	**21**	**1**	**0**	**0**

Traded to **Buffalo** by **LA Kings** with Brian Engblom for Sean McKenna, Larry Playfair and Ken Baumgartner, January 30, 1986. Claimed by **Edmonton** from **Buffalo** in NHL Waiver Draft, October 3, 1988. Traded to **Vancouver** by **Edmonton** with Greg C. Adams for John LeBlanc and Vancouver's 5th round choice (Peter White) in 1989 Entry Draft, March 7, 1989. Traded to **Pittsburgh** by **Vancouver** for cash, February 26, 1990.

• SMITH, Floyd

Floyd Robert Donald RW – R. 5'10", 180 lbs. b: Perth, Ont., 5/16/1935.

Season	Club	League	GP	G	A	Pts	AG	AA	APts	PIM	PP	SH	GW	S	%	TGF	PGF	TGA	PGA	+/-	GP	G	A	Pts	PIM	PP	SH	GW
1952-53	Galt Black Hawks	OHA-Jr.	6	0	1	1	....	....	....	0	....	....	....	....	....	....	....	....	....	....	....	....	....	....	....	....	....	....
	Inkerman Rockets	OVHL	STATISTICS NOT AVAILABLE																									
1953-54	Ottawa Eastviews	OCJHL	STATISTICS NOT AVAILABLE																									
	Ottawa Eastviews	Mem-Cup	12	8	9	17	....	....	....	0	....	....	....	....	....	....	....	....	....	....	....	....	....	....	....	....	....	....
1954-55	Galt Black Hawks	OHA-Jr.	46	29	40	69	....	....	....	60	....	....	....	....	....	....	....	....	....	....	4	1	4	5	0	....	....	....
	Boston Bruins	**NHL**	**3**	**0**	**1**	**1**	**0**	**1**	**1**	**0**	....	....	....	....	....	....	....	....	....	....	....	....	....	....	....	....	....	....
1955-56	Hershey Bears	AHL	49	10	19	29	....	....	....	31	....	....	....	....	....	....	....	....	....	....	....	....	....	....	....	....	....	....
1956-57	**Boston Bruins**	**NHL**	**23**	**0**	**0**	**0**	**0**	**0**	**0**	**6**	....	....	....	....	....	....	....	....	....	....	....	....	....	....	....	....	....	....
	Hershey Bears	AHL	41	12	25	37	....	....	....	32	....	....	....	....	....	....	....	....	....	....	6	0	1	1	8	....	....	....
1957-58	Springfield Indians	AHL	70	25	50	75	....	....	....	60	....	....	....	....	....	....	....	....	....	....	13	2	11	13	4	....	....	....
1958-59	Springfield Indians	AHL	68	25	32	57	....	....	....	34	....	....	....	....	....	....	....	....	....	....	....	....	....	....	....	....	....	....
1959-60	Springfield Indians	AHL	71	31	51	82	....	....	....	26	....	....	....	....	....	....	....	....	....	....	10	1	5	6	10	....	....	....
1960-61	**New York Rangers**	**NHL**	**29**	**5**	**9**	**14**	**6**	**9**	**15**	**0**	....	....	....	....	....	....	....	....	....	....	....	....	....	....	....	....	....	....
	Springfield Indians	AHL	40	19	27	46	....	....	....	26	....	....	....	....	....	....	....	....	....	....	....	....	....	....	....	....	....	....
1961-62	Springfield Indians	AHL	69	*41	36	77	....	....	....	19	....	....	....	....	....	....	....	....	....	....	11	0	4	4	2	....	....	....
1962-63	**Detroit Red Wings**	**NHL**	**51**	**9**	**17**	**26**	**10**	**17**	**27**	**10**	....	....	....	....	....	....	....	....	....	....	**11**	**2**	**3**	**5**	**4**	**0**	**0**	**0**
	Pittsburgh Hornets	AHL	16	8	7	15	....	....	....	6	....	....	....	....	....	....	....	....	....	....	....	....	....	....	....	....	....	....
1963-64	**Detroit Red Wings**	**NHL**	**52**	**18**	**13**	**31**	**22**	**14**	**36**	**22**	....	....	....	....	....	....	....	....	....	....	**14**	**4**	**3**	**7**	**4**	**2**	**0**	**0**
	Pittsburgh Hornets	AHL	21	14	17	31	....	....	....	14	....	....	....	....	....	....	....	....	....	....	....	....	....	....	....	....	....	....
1964-65	**Detroit Red Wings**	**NHL**	**67**	**16**	**29**	**45**	**19**	**30**	**49**	**44**	....	....	....	....	....	....	....	....	....	....	**7**	**1**	**3**	**4**	**4**	**0**	**0**	**0**
1965-66	**Detroit Red Wings**	**NHL**	**66**	**21**	**28**	**49**	**24**	**27**	**51**	**20**	....	....	....	....	....	....	....	....	....	....	**12**	**5**	**2**	**7**	**4**	**2**	**0**	**1**
1966-67	**Detroit Red Wings**	**NHL**	**54**	**11**	**14**	**25**	**13**	**14**	**27**	**8**	....	....	....	....	....	....	....	....	....	....	....	....	....	....	....	....	....	....
	Pittsburgh Hornets	AHL	13	5	9	14	....	....	....	10	....	....	....	....	....	....	....	....	....	....	....	....	....	....	....	....	....	....
1967-68	**Detroit Red Wings**	**NHL**	**57**	**18**	**21**	**39**	**21**	**21**	**42**	**14**	**5**	**1**	**2**	**132**	**13.6**	**59**	**15**	**42**	**2**	**4**	....	....	....	....	....	....	....	....
	Toronto Maple Leafs	**NHL**	**6**	**6**	**1**	**7**	**7**	**1**	**8**	**0**	**1**	**0**	**1**	**19**	**31.6**	**13**	**2**	**4**	**0**	**7**	....	....	....	....	....	....	....	....
1968-69	**Toronto Maple Leafs**	**NHL**	**64**	**15**	**19**	**34**	**16**	**17**	**33**	**22**	**2**	**0**	**2**	**120**	**12.5**	**61**	**14**	**38**	**5**	**14**	**4**	**0**	**0**	**0**	**0**	**0**	**0**	**0**
1969-70	**Toronto Maple Leafs**	**NHL**	**61**	**4**	**14**	**18**	**4**	**13**	**17**	**13**	**0**	**0**	**0**	**73**	**5.5**	**30**	**4**	**31**	**2**	**–3**	....	....	....	....	....	....	....	....
1970-71	**Buffalo Sabres**	**NHL**	**77**	**6**	**11**	**17**	**6**	**9**	**15**	**46**	**0**	**2**	**0**	**80**	**7.5**	**32**	**5**	**65**	**26**	**–12**	....	....	....	....	....	....	....	....
1971-72	**Buffalo Sabres**	**NHL**	**6**	**0**	**1**	**1**	**0**	**1**	**1**	**2**	**0**	**0**	**0**	**1**	**0.0**	**0**	**0**	**5**	**1**	**–4**	....	....	....	....	....	....	....	....
	NHL Totals		**616**	**129**	**178**	**307**	**148**	**174**	**322**	**207**	....	....	....	....	....	....	....	....	....		**48**	**12**	**11**	**23**	**16**	....	....	....

AHL Second All-Star Team (1960, 1962)

Signed to a three-game amateur tryout contract by **Boston** during 1954-55 season. Signed as a free agent by **Boston**, August 23, 1955. Traded to **Springfield** (AHL) by **Boston** to complete transaction that sent Don Simmons to Boston (January 22, 1957), June, 1957. Claimed by **Detroit** from **NY Rangers** in Intra-League Draft, June 5, 1962. Traded to **Toronto** by **Detroit** with Norm Ullman, Paul Henderson and Doug Barrie for Frank Mahovlich, Pete Stemkowski, Garry Unger and the rights to Carl Brewer, March 3, 1968. Traded to **Buffalo** by **Toronto** with Brent Imlach for cash, August 31, 1970.

• SMITH, Geoff

Geoffrey Arthur D – L. 6'3", 194 lbs. b: Edmonton, Alta., 3/7/1969. Edmonton's 3rd, 63rd overall, in 1987.

Season	Club	League	GP	G	A	Pts	AG	AA	APts	PIM	PP	SH	GW	S	%	TGF	PGF	TGA	PGA	+/-	GP	G	A	Pts	PIM	PP	SH	GW
1985-86	Edmonton Maple Leafs	AAHA	41	9	21	30	....	....	....	58	....	....	....	....	....	....	....	....	....	....	....	....	....	....	....	....	....	....
	Edmonton Carnwood Wireline	AAHA	STATISTICS NOT AVAILABLE																									
1986-87	St. Albert Saints	AJHL	57	7	28	35	....	....	....	101	....	....	....	....	....	....	....	....	....	....	....	....	....	....	....	....	....	....
1987-88	University of North Dakota	WCHA	42	4	12	16	....	....	....	34	....	....	....	....	....	....	....	....	....	....	....	....	....	....	....	....	....	....
1988-89	University of North Dakota	WCHA	9	0	1	1	....	....	....	8	....	....	....	....	....	....	....	....	....	....	....	....	....	....	....	....	....	....
	Canada	WJC-A	7	0	1	1	....	....	....	4	....	....	....	....	....	....	....	....	....	....	....	....	....	....	....	....	....	....
	Kamloops Blazers	WHL	32	4	31	35	....	....	....	29	....	....	....	....	....	....	....	....	....	....	6	1	3	4	12	....	....	....
1989-90♦	**Edmonton Oilers**	**NHL**	**74**	**4**	**11**	**15**	**3**	**8**	**11**	**52**	**1**	**0**	**0**	**66**	**6.1**	**77**	**13**	**72**	**21**	**13**	**3**	**0**	**0**	**0**	**0**	**0**	**0**	**0**
1990-91	**Edmonton Oilers**	**NHL**	**59**	**1**	**12**	**13**	**1**	**9**	**10**	**55**	**0**	**0**	**0**	**66**	**1.5**	**57**	**6**	**55**	**17**	**13**	**4**	**0**	**0**	**0**	**0**	**0**	**0**	**0**
1991-92	**Edmonton Oilers**	**NHL**	**74**	**2**	**16**	**18**	**2**	**12**	**14**	**43**	**0**	**0**	**0**	**61**	**3.3**	**74**	**12**	**101**	**34**	**–5**	**5**	**0**	**1**	**1**	**6**	**0**	**0**	**0**
1992-93	**Edmonton Oilers**	**NHL**	**78**	**4**	**14**	**18**	**3**	**10**	**13**	**30**	**0**	**1**	**0**	**67**	**6.0**	**50**	**4**	**100**	**43**	**–11**	....	....	....	....	....	....	....	....
	Canada	WC-A	8	0	0	0	....	....	....	4	....	....	....	....	....	....	....	....	....	....	....	....	....	....	....	....	....	....
1993-94	**Edmonton Oilers**	**NHL**	**21**	**0**	**3**	**3**	**0**	**2**	**2**	**12**	**0**	**0**	**0**	**23**	**0.0**	**17**	**3**	**34**	**10**	**–10**	....	....	....	....	....	....	....	....
	Florida Panthers	**NHL**	**56**	**1**	**5**	**6**	**1**	**4**	**5**	**38**	**0**	**0**	**0**	**44**	**2.3**	**40**	**1**	**62**	**20**	**–3**	....	....	....	....	....	....	....	....
1994-95	**Florida Panthers**	**NHL**	**47**	**2**	**4**	**6**	**4**	**6**	**10**	**22**	**0**	**0**	**0**	**40**	**5.0**	**24**	**1**	**49**	**21**	**–5**	....	....	....	....	....	....	....	....
1995-96	**Florida Panthers**	**NHL**	**31**	**3**	**7**	**10**	**3**	**6**	**9**	**20**	**2**	**0**	**0**	**34**	**8.8**	**24**	**3**	**40**	**15**	**–4**	**1**	**0**	**0**	**0**	**2**	**0**	**0**	**0**
1996-97	**Florida Panthers**	**NHL**	**3**	**0**	**0**	**0**	**0**	**0**	**0**	**2**	**0**	**0**	**0**	**2**	**0.0**	**2**	**1**	**0**	**0**	**1**	....	....	....	....	....	....	....	....
	Carolina Monarchs	AHL	27	3	4	7	....	....	....	20	....	....	....	....	....	....	....	....	....	....	....	....	....	....	....	....	....	....
1997-98	**New York Rangers**	**NHL**	**15**	**1**	**1**	**2**	**1**	**1**	**2**	**6**	**1**	**0**	**0**	**11**	**9.1**	**7**	**1**	**15**	**5**	**–4**	....	....	....	....	....	....	....	....
	Hartford Wolf Pack	AHL	59	1	12	13	....	....	....	34	....	....	....	....	....	....	....	....	....	....	....	....	....	....	....	....	....	....

			REGULAR SEASON																		PLAYOFFS							
Season	Club	League	GP	G	A	Pts	AG	AA	APts	PIM	PP	SH	GW	S	%	TGF	PGF	TGA	PGA	+/-	GP	G	A	Pts	PIM	PP	SH	GW
1998-99	**New York Rangers**	**NHL**	4	0	0	0	0	0	0	2	0	0	0	0	0.0	0	0	6	1	–5	....	....	....	....	....	....	....	....
	Hartford Wolf Pack	AHL	9	1	4	5	....	....	....	10	....	....	....	....	....	....	....	....	....	....	....	....	....	....	....	....	....	....
	Cincinnati Cyclones	IHL	31	3	3	6	....	....	....	20	....	....	....	....	....	....	....	....	....	....	....	....	....	....	....	....	....	....
	Worcester IceCats	AHL	25	1	3	4	....	....	....	16	....	....	....	....	....	....	....	....	....	....	4	0	0	0	4	....	....	....
	NHL Totals		462	18	73	91	18	58	76	282	4	1	0	414	4.3	372	45	534	187		13	0	1	1	8	0	0	0

WHL West Second All-Star Team (1989) • NHL All-Rookie Team (1990)

Traded to **Florida** by **Edmonton** with Edmonton's 4th round choice (David Nemirovsky) in 1994 Entry Draft for Florida's 3rd round choice (Corey Neilson) in 1994 Entry Draft and St. Louis' 6th round choice (previously acquired by Florida - later traded to Winnipeg - Winnipeg selected Chris Kibermanis) in 1994 Entry Draft, December 6, 1993. Signed as a free agent by **NY Rangers**, September 29, 1997. Traded to **St. Louis** by **NY Rangers** with Jeff Finley for future considerations (Chris Kenady, February 22, 1999), February 13, 1999.

• SMITH, Gord

Gordon John D – L. 5'10", 175 lbs. b: Perth, Ont., 11/17/1949.

Season	Club	League	GP	G	A	Pts	AG	AA	APts	PIM	PP	SH	GW	S	%	TGF	PGF	TGA	PGA	+/-	GP	G	A	Pts	PIM	PP	SH	GW
1967-68	Brockville Braves	OHA-B	STATISTICS NOT AVAILABLE																									
1968-69	Cornwall Royals	MMJHL	STATISTICS NOT AVAILABLE																									
1969-70	New Haven Blades	EHL	72	4	20	24	....	....	....	92	....	....	....	....	....	....	....	....	....	....	11	0	3	3	36	....	....	....
	Omaha Knights	CHL	....	....	....	....	....	....	....	....	....	....	....	....	....	....	....	....	....	....	5	0	0	0	8	....	....	....
1970-71	New Haven Blades	EHL	73	7	24	31	....	....	....	253	....	....	....	....	....	....	....	....	....	....	14	1	5	6	66	....	....	....
1971-72	New Haven Blades	EHL	74	3	33	36	....	....	....	188	....	....	....	....	....	....	....	....	....	....	7	1	5	6	18	....	....	....
1972-73	Springfield Kings	AHL	72	3	29	32	....	....	....	134	....	....	....	....	....	....	....	....	....	....	....	....	....	....	....	....	....	....
1973-74	Springfield Kings	AHL	75	13	54	67	....	....	....	118	....	....	....	....	....	....	....	....	....	....	....	....	....	....	....	....	....	....
1974-75	**Washington Capitals**	**NHL**	63	3	8	11	3	6	9	56	2	0	0	54	5.6	49	7	125	27	–56	....	....	....	....	....	....	....	....
	Richmond Robins	AHL	15	1	4	5	....	....	....	23	....	....	....	....	....	....	....	....	....	....	....	....	....	....	....	....	....	....
1975-76	**Washington Capitals**	**NHL**	25	1	2	3	1	1	2	28	1	0	0	10	10.0	17	2	44	7	–22	....	....	....	....	....	....	....	....
	Richmond Robins	AHL	50	2	13	15	....	....	....	80	....	....	....	....	....	....	....	....	....	....	8	0	4	4	28	....	....	....
1976-77	**Washington Capitals**	**NHL**	79	1	12	13	1	9	10	92	1	0	0	72	1.4	63	5	112	27	–27	....	....	....	....	....	....	....	....
1977-78	**Washington Capitals**	**NHL**	80	4	7	11	4	5	9	78	0	0	1	57	7.0	55	2	98	25	–20	....	....	....	....	....	....	....	....
1978-79	**Washington Capitals**	**NHL**	39	0	1	1	0	1	1	22	0	0	0	11	0.0	22	1	42	14	–7	....	....	....	....	....	....	....	....
	Hershey Bears	AHL	33	1	16	17	....	....	....	54	....	....	....	....	....	....	....	....	....	....	4	0	2	2	6	....	....	....
1979-80	**Winnipeg Jets**	**NHL**	13	0	0	0	0	0	0	8	0	0	0	3	0.0	3	0	11	3	–5	....	....	....	....	....	....	....	....
	Tulsa Oilers	CHL	64	5	16	21	....	....	....	55	....	....	....	....	....	....	....	....	....	....	3	0	0	0	2	....	....	....
1980-81	New Haven Nighthawks	AHL	58	1	11	12	....	....	....	94	....	....	....	....	....	....	....	....	....	....	4	0	0	0	2	....	....	....
1981-82	Springfield Indians	AHL	80	4	12	16	....	....	....	80	....	....	....	....	....	....	....	....	....	....	....	....	....	....	....	....	....	....
1982-83	Maine Mariners	AHL	35	0	8	8	....	....	....	49	....	....	....	....	....	....	....	....	....	....	17	0	3	3	21	....	....	....
	NHL Totals		299	9	30	39	9	22	31	284	4	0	1	207	4.3	209	17	432	103		....	....	....	....	....	....	....	....

• Brother of Billy • EHL North First All-Star Team (1971, 1972) • AHL First All-Star Team (1974) • Won Eddie Shore Award (Outstanding Defenseman - AHL) (1974) • AHL Second All-Star Team (1976) • CHL Second All-Star Team (1980)

Signed as a free agent by **LA Kings**, May 22, 1970. Claimed by **Washington** from **LA Kings** in Expansion Draft, June 12, 1974. Claimed by **Winnipeg** from **Washington** in Expansion Draft, June 13, 1979. Traded to **NY Rangers** by **Winnipeg** for cash, August 6, 1980.

• SMITH, Greg

Gregory James D – L. 6', 195 lbs. b: Ponoka, Alta., 7/8/1955. California's 4th, 57th overall, in 1975.

Season	Club	League	GP	G	A	Pts	AG	AA	APts	PIM	PP	SH	GW	S	%	TGF	PGF	TGA	PGA	+/-	GP	G	A	Pts	PIM	PP	SH	GW
1973-74	Colorado College	WCHA	31	7	13	20	....	....	....	80	....	....	....	....	....	....	....	....	....	....	....	....	....	....	....	....	....	....
1974-75	Colorado College	WCHA	36	10	24	34	....	....	....	75	....	....	....	....	....	....	....	....	....	....	....	....	....	....	....	....	....	....
1975-76	Colorado College	WCHA	34	18	19	37	....	....	....	123	....	....	....	....	....	....	....	....	....	....	....	....	....	....	....	....	....	....
	California Golden Seals	**NHL**	1	0	1	1	0	1	1	2	0	0	0	1	0.0	1	1	1	0	–1	....	....	....	....	....	....	....	....
	Salt Lake Golden Eagles	CHL	5	0	2	2	....	....	....	2	....	....	....	....	....	....	....	....	....	....	5	1	2	3	4	....	....	....
1976-77	**Cleveland Barons**	**NHL**	74	9	17	26	8	13	21	65	4	0	2	128	7.0	64	21	86	12	–31	....	....	....	....	....	....	....	....
	Canada	WEC-A	10	1	1	2	....	....	....	4	....	....	....	....	....	....	....	....	....	....	....	....	....	....	....	....	....	....
1977-78	**Cleveland Barons**	**NHL**	80	7	30	37	6	23	29	92	2	0	0	148	4.7	119	24	158	37	–26	....	....	....	....	....	....	....	....
1978-79	**Minnesota North Stars**	**NHL**	80	5	27	32	4	20	24	147	1	0	1	193	2.6	99	14	127	21	–21	....	....	....	....	....	....	....	....
	Canada	WEC-A	5	0	0	0	....	....	....	12	....	....	....	....	....	....	....	....	....	....	....	....	....	....	....	....	....	....
1979-80	**Minnesota North Stars**	**NHL**	55	5	13	18	4	9	13	103	1	1	1	91	5.5	63	10	62	8	–1	12	0	1	1	9	0	0	0
1980-81	**Minnesota North Stars**	**NHL**	74	5	21	26	4	14	18	126	1	0	1	99	5.1	83	8	96	28	7	19	1	5	6	39	0	1	0
1981-82	**Detroit Red Wings**	**NHL**	69	10	22	32	8	15	23	79	2	0	1	154	6.5	99	10	143	32	–22	....	....	....	....	....	....	....	....
1982-83	**Detroit Red Wings**	**NHL**	73	4	26	30	3	18	21	79	0	0	0	92	4.3	100	4	123	34	7	....	....	....	....	....	....	....	....
1983-84	**Detroit Red Wings**	**NHL**	75	3	20	23	2	14	16	108	0	0	1	63	4.8	83	2	100	25	6	4	1	0	1	8	0	0	0
1984-85	**Detroit Red Wings**	**NHL**	73	2	18	20	2	12	14	117	0	0	0	54	3.7	61	4	115	32	–26	3	0	0	0	7	0	0	0
1985-86	**Detroit Red Wings**	**NHL**	62	5	19	24	4	13	17	84	0	0	0	53	9.4	55	8	100	39	–14	....	....	....	....	....	....	....	....
	Washington Capitals	**NHL**	14	0	3	3	0	2	2	10	0	0	0	6	0.0	13	1	13	4	3	9	2	1	3	9	0	1	0
1986-87	**Washington Capitals**	**NHL**	45	0	9	9	0	7	7	31	0	0	0	30	0.0	32	3	43	8	–6	7	0	0	0	11	0	0	0
1987-88	**Washington Capitals**	**NHL**	54	1	6	7	1	4	5	67	0	0	0	31	3.2	36	1	42	12	5	9	0	0	0	23	0	0	0
	NHL Totals		829	56	232	288	46	165	211	1110	11	1	7	1143	4.9	908	111	1209	292		63	4	7	11	106	0	2	0

Signed as a free agent by **California**, March, 1975. Transferred to **Cleveland** after **California** franchise relocated, August 26, 1976. Protected by **Minnesota** prior to **Cleveland-Minnesota** Dispersal Draft, June 15, 1978. Traded to **Detroit** by **Minnesota** with the rights to Don Murdoch and Minnesota's 1st round choice (Murray Craven) in 1982 Entry Draft for Detroit's 1st round choice (Brian Bellows) in 1982 Entry Draft, August 21, 1981. Traded to **Washington** by **Detroit** with John Barrett for Darren Veitch, March 10, 1986.

• SMITH, Jason

Jason Matthew D – R. 6'3", 210 lbs. b: Calgary, Alta., 11/2/1973. New Jersey's 1st, 18th overall, in 1992.

Season	Club	League	GP	G	A	Pts	AG	AA	APts	PIM	PP	SH	GW	S	%	TGF	PGF	TGA	PGA	+/-	GP	G	A	Pts	PIM	PP	SH	GW
1990-91	Calgary Canucks	AJHL	45	3	15	18	....	....	....	69	....	....	....	....	....	....	....	....	....	....	....	....	....	....	....	....	....	....
	Regina Pats	WHL	2	0	0	0	....	....	....	7	....	....	....	....	....	....	....	....	....	....	4	0	0	0	2	....	....	....
1991-92	Regina Pats	WHL	62	9	29	38	....	....	....	138	....	....	....	....	....	....	....	....	....	....	....	....	....	....	....	....	....	....
1992-93	Regina Pats	WHL	64	14	52	66	....	....	....	175	....	....	....	....	....	....	....	....	....	....	13	4	8	12	39	....	....	....
	Canada	WJC-A	7	1	3	4	....	....	....	10	....	....	....	....	....	....	....	....	....	....	....	....	....	....	....	....	....	....
	Utica Devils	AHL	....	....	....	....	....	....	....	....	....	....	....	....	....	....	....	....	....	....	1	0	0	0	2	....	....	....
1993-94	**New Jersey Devils**	**NHL**	41	0	5	5	0	4	4	43	0	0	0	47	0.0	24	1	20	4	7	6	0	0	0	7	0	0	0
	Albany River Rats	AHL	20	6	3	9	....	....	....	31	....	....	....	....	....	....	....	....	....	....	....	....	....	....	....	....	....	....
1994-95	**New Jersey Devils**	**NHL**	2	0	0	0	0	0	0	0	0	0	0	5	0.0	1	0	4	0	–3	....	....	....	....	....	....	....	....
	Albany River Rats	AHL	7	0	2	2	....	....	....	15	....	....	....	....	....	....	....	....	....	....	11	2	2	4	19	....	....	....
1995-96	**New Jersey Devils**	**NHL**	64	2	1	3	2	1	3	86	0	0	0	52	3.8	41	0	36	0	5	....	....	....	....	....	....	....	....
1996-97	**New Jersey Devils**	**NHL**	57	1	2	3	1	2	3	38	0	0	0	48	2.1	28	1	35	0	–8	....	....	....	....	....	....	....	....
	Toronto Maple Leafs	**NHL**	21	0	5	5	0	4	4	16	0	0	0	26	0.0	15	0	24	5	–4	....	....	....	....	....	....	....	....
1997-98	**Toronto Maple Leafs**	**NHL**	81	3	13	16	4	13	17	100	0	0	0	97	3.1	57	0	90	28	–5	....	....	....	....	....	....	....	....
1998-99	**Toronto Maple Leafs**	**NHL**	60	2	11	13	2	11	13	40	0	0	0	53	3.8	41	1	68	19	–9	....	....	....	....	....	....	....	....
	Edmonton Oilers	**NHL**	12	1	1	2	1	1	2	11	0	0	0	15	6.7	9	0	13	4	0	4	0	1	1	4	0	0	0
99-2000	**Edmonton Oilers**	**NHL**	80	3	11	14	3	10	13	60	0	0	1	96	3.1	63	0	83	36	16	5	0	1	1	4	0	0	0
	NHL Totals		418	12	49	61	13	46	59	394	0	0	1	439	2.7	279	3	373	96		15	0	2	2	15	0	0	0

WHL East First All-Star Team (1993) • Canadian Major Junior First All-Star Team (1993)

Traded to **Toronto** by **New Jersey** with Steve Sullivan and the rights to Alyn McCauley for Doug Gilmour, Dave Ellett and New Jersey's 4th round choice (previously acquired — New Jersey selected Andre Lakps) in 1999 Entry Draft, February 25, 1997. Traded to **Edmonton** by **Toronto** for Edmonton's 4th round choice (Jonathon Zion) in 1999 Entry Draft and 2nd round choice (Kris Vernarsky) in 2000 Entry Draft, March 23, 1999.

• SMITH, Randy

C – L. 6'4", 200 lbs. b: Saskatoon, Sask., 7/7/1965. St. Louis' 5th, 88th overall, in 1973.

Season	Club	League	GP	G	A	Pts	AG	AA	APts	PIM	PP	SH	GW	S	%	TGF	PGF	TGA	PGA	+/-	GP	G	A	Pts	PIM	PP	SH	GW
1981-82	Saskatoon Contacts	SAHA	STATISTICS NOT AVAILABLE																									
1982-83	Battleford Barons	SJHL	65	25	20	45	....	....	....	141	....	....	....	....	....	....	....	....	....	....	....	....	....	....	....	....	....	....
1983-84	Saskatoon Blades	WHL	69	19	21	40	....	....	....	53	....	....	....	....	....	....	....	....	....	....	....	....	....	....	....	....	....	....
1984-85	Saskatoon Blades	WHL	25	6	16	22	....	....	....	9	....	....	....	....	....	....	....	....	....	....	....	....	....	....	....	....	....	....
	Calgary Wranglers	WHL	46	28	35	63	....	....	....	17	....	....	....	....	....	....	....	....	....	....	8	4	3	7	0	....	....	....
1985-86	Saskatoon Blades	WHL	70	60	86	146	....	....	....	44	....	....	....	....	....	....	....	....	....	....	9	4	9	13	4	....	....	....
	Minnesota North Stars	**NHL**	1	0	0	0	0	0	0	0	0	0	0	0	0.0	0	0	0	0	0	....	....	....	....	....	....	....	....
1986-87	**Minnesota North Stars**	**NHL**	2	0	0	0	0	0	0	0	0	0	0	0	0.0	1	1	2	0	–2	....	....	....	....	....	....	....	....
	Springfield Indians	AHL	75	20	44	64	....	....	....	24	....	....	....	....	....	....	....	....	....	....	....	....	....	....	....	....	....	....

Season	Club	League	REGULAR SEASON																		PLAYOFFS							
			GP	G	A	Pts	AG	AA	APts	PIM	PP	SH	GW	S	%	TGF	PGF	TGA	PGA	+/–	GP	G	A	Pts	PIM	PP	SH	GW
1987-88	Kalamazoo Wings	IHL	77	13	43	56				54											6	0	8	8	2			
1988-89	Maine Mariners	AHL	33	9	16	25				34																		
	Kalamazoo Wings	IHL	23	4	9	13				2																		
1989-90	Kalamazoo Wings	IHL	8	1	2	3				12																		
	Salt Lake Golden Eagles	IHL	30	5	6	11				10											3	0	0	0	0			
1990-91	Canada	Nat-Team	58	17	39	56				42																		
	Canada	WEC-A	10	0	0	0				8																		
1991-92	EHC Biel-Bienne	Switz-2	7	1	5	6				26																		
	Canada	Nat-Team	59	20	25	45				24																		
	Canada	Olympics	8	1	7	8				4																		
	Canada	WC-A	6	1	0	1				4																		
1992-93	KAC Klagenfurt	Austria	39	26	18	44																						
1993-94	Las Vegas Thunder	IHL	53	7	7	14				78																		
1994-95	Peterborough Pirates	BH-Cup	8	10	13	23				10																		
	Peterborough Pirates	Britain	44	82	84	166				67											6	12	9	21	14			
1995-96	Cardiff Devils	BH-Cup	10	22	19	41				4																		
	Cardiff Devils	Britain	36	51	49	100				38											6	4	2	6	20			
1996-97	Cardiff Devils	BH-Cup	6	3	3	6				4																		
	Cardiff Devils	Britain	DID NOT PLAY – INJURED																									
1997-98	Newcastle Cobras	BH-Cup	10	7	4	11				6																		
	Newcastle Cobras	Britain	40	9	18	27				32											6	2	5	7	2			
1998-99	Peterborough Pirates	Britain-2	29	30	44	74				22											5	1	5	6	8			
99-2000	Peterborough Pirates	BH-Cup	11	9	17	26				25																		
	Peterborough Pirates	Britain-2	36	43	44	87				30											8	9	10	19	24			
	NHL Totals		**3**	**0**	**0**	**0**	**0**	**0**	**0**	**0**	**0**	**0**	**0**	**0**	**0.0**	**1**	**1**	**2**	**0**									

WHL East Second All-Star Team (1986)

Signed as a free agent by **Minnesota**, May 12, 1986. • Missed majority of 1996-97 season recovering from back surgery, October, 1996. • Played w/ RHI's St. Louis Vipers in 1994 (22-29-30-59-72) and 1995 (19-27-27-54-90).

• SMITH, Rick

Richard Allan D – L. 5′11″, 190 lbs. b: Kingston, Ont., 6/29/1948. Boston's 2nd, 7th overall, in 1966.

Season	Club	League	GP	G	A	Pts	AG	AA	APts	PIM	PP	SH	GW	S	%	TGF	PGF	TGA	PGA	+/–	GP	G	A	Pts	PIM	PP	SH	GW
1965-66	Hamilton Red Wings	OHA-Jr.	47	2	16	18				60											5	1	1	2	6			
1966-67	Hamilton Red Wings	OHA-Jr.	48	2	17	19				74											17	4	14	18	35			
1967-68	Hamilton Red Wings	OHA-Jr.	49	5	36	41				123											11	2	9	11	33			
1968-69	**Boston Bruins**	**NHL**	48	0	5	5	0	4	4	29	0	0	0	28	0.0	34	0	22	2	14	9	0	0	0	6	0	0	0
	Oklahoma City Blazers	CHL	19	5	10	15				37																		
1969-70♦	**Boston Bruins**	**NHL**	69	2	8	10	2	7	9	65	0	0	1	94	2.1	62	2	66	18	12	14	1	3	4	17	0	0	0
1970-71	**Boston Bruins**	**NHL**	67	4	19	23	4	16	20	44	0	0	1	79	5.1	63	0	48	15	30	6	0	0	0	0	0	0	0
1971-72	**Boston Bruins**	**NHL**	61	2	12	14	2	10	12	46	0	0	0	81	2.5	90	2	56	21	53								
	California Golden Seals	**NHL**	17	1	4	5	1	3	4	26	0	0	0	23	4.3	16	0	38	5	–17								
1972-73	**California Golden Seals**	**NHL**	64	9	24	33	8	19	27	77	3	0	0	126	7.1	95	25	141	28	–43								
1973-74	Minnesota Fighting Saints	WHA	71	10	28	38				98											11	0	1	1	22			
1974-75	Team Canada	Summit-74	7	0	0	0				12																		
	Minnesota Fighting Saints	WHA	78	9	29	38				112											12	2	7	9	6			
1975-76	Minnesota Fighting Saints	WHA	51	1	32	33				50																		
	St. Louis Blues	**NHL**	24	1	7	8	1	5	6	18	0	0	0	32	3.1	28	5	35	14	2	3	0	1	1	4	0	0	0
1976-77	**St. Louis Blues**	**NHL**	18	0	1	1	0	1	1	6	0	0	0	11	0.0	11	0	21	7	–3								
	Kansas City Blues	CHL	7	1	6	7				11																		
	Boston Bruins	**NHL**	46	6	16	22	5	12	17	30	0	0	0	72	8.3	70	1	55	9	23	14	0	9	9	14	0	0	0
1977-78	**Boston Bruins**	**NHL**	79	7	29	36	6	22	28	69	0	0	0	116	6.0	140	8	87	25	70	15	1	5	6	18	0	0	0
1978-79	**Boston Bruins**	**NHL**	65	7	18	25	6	13	19	46	0	0	1	78	9.0	83	0	78	15	20	11	0	4	4	12	0	0	0
1979-80	**Boston Bruins**	**NHL**	78	8	18	26	7	13	20	62	0	0	2	85	9.4	78	0	76	20	22	6	1	1	2	2	0	0	0
1980-81	**Detroit Red Wings**	**NHL**	11	0	2	2	0	1	1	6	0	0	0	7	0.0	5	0	11	1	–5								
	Washington Capitals	**NHL**	40	5	4	9	4	3	7	36	2	0	2	35	14.3	44	7	43	13	7								
	NHL Totals		**687**	**52**	**167**	**219**	**46**	**129**	**175**	**560**	**5**	**0**	**7**	**867**	**6.0**	**819**	**50**	**777**	**193**		**78**	**3**	**23**	**26**	**73**	**0**	**0**	**0**
	Other Major League Totals		200	20	89	109				260											23	2	8	10	28			

OHA-Jr. Second All-Star Team (1967, 1968)

Traded to **California** by **Boston** with Reggie Leach and Bob Stewart for Carol Vadnais and Don O'Donoghue, February 23, 1972. Selected by **Miami-Philadelphia** (WHA) in 1972 WHA General Player Draft, February 12, 1972. WHA rights traded to **Minnesota** (WHA) by **Philadelphia** (WHA) for Bill Young, cash and future considerations, May, 1972. Traded to **St. Louis** by **California** for cash, October 22, 1975. Traded to **Boston** by **St. Louis** for Joe Zanussi, December 20, 1976. Claimed by **Detroit** from **Boston** in Waiver Draft, October 10, 1980. Claimed on waivers by **Washington** from **Detroit**, November 7, 1980.

• SMITH, Ron

Ronald Robert D – R. 6′, 185 lbs. b: Port Hope, Ont., 11/19/1952. NY Islanders' 4th, 49th overall, in 1972.

Season	Club	League	GP	G	A	Pts	AG	AA	APts	PIM	PP	SH	GW	S	%	TGF	PGF	TGA	PGA	+/–	GP	G	A	Pts	PIM	PP	SH	GW
1969-70	St. Catharines Black Hawks	OHA-Jr.	15	0	0	0				24																		
1970-71	Sorel Eperviers	QJHL	42	4	12	16				152											2	0	2	2	2			
1971-72	Cornwall Royals	QMJHL	56	8	27	35				55											16	4	3	7	24			
	Cornwall Royals	Mem-Cup	3	0	0	0				16																		
1972-73	**New York Islanders**	**NHL**	11	1	1	2	1	1	2	14	0	0	0	10	10.0	4	0	12	0	–8								
	New Haven Nighthawks	AHL	53	6	11	17				83																		
1973-74	Fort Worth Wings	CHL	72	1	16	17				103											5	1	1	2	2			
1974-75	Fort Worth Texans	CHL	75	6	19	25				97																		
1975-76	Bodens HC	Sweden-2	24	6	7	13				69																		
1976-77	Erie Blades	NAHL	8	0	2	2				0																		
1977-78	Guelph Platers	OJHL	DID NOT PLAY – COACHING																									
	NHL Totals		**11**	**1**	**1**	**2**	**1**	**1**	**2**	**14**	**0**	**0**	**0**	**10**	**10.0**	**4**	**0**	**12**	**0**									

QMJHL First All-Star Team (1972)

• SMITH, Steve

Steve James Stephen D – L. 6′4″, 215 lbs. b: Glasgow, Scotland, 4/30/1963. Edmonton's 5th, 111th overall, in 1981.

Season	Club	League	GP	G	A	Pts	AG	AA	APts	PIM	PP	SH	GW	S	%	TGF	PGF	TGA	PGA	+/–	GP	G	A	Pts	PIM	PP	SH	GW
1979-80	Fergus Green Machine	OHA-D	23	10	14	24				40																		
1980-81	London Knights	OMJHL	62	4	12	16				141																		
1981-82	London Knights	OHL	58	10	36	46				207											4	1	2	3	13			
1982-83	London Knights	OHL	50	6	35	41				133											3	1	0	1	10			
	Moncton Alpines	AHL	2	0	0	0				0																		
1983-84	Brantford Alexanders	OHL	7	1	1	2				0																		
	Moncton Alpines	AHL	64	1	8	9				176																		
1984-85	**Edmonton Oilers**	**NHL**	2	0	0	0	0	0	0	2	0	0	0	3	0.0	1	0	3	0	–2								
	Nova Scotia Voyageurs	AHL	68	2	28	30				161											5	0	3	3	40			
1985-86	**Edmonton Oilers**	**NHL**	55	4	20	24	3	13	16	166	1	0	1	74	5.4	71	8	40	7	30	6	0	1	1	14	0	0	0
	Nova Scotia Oilers	AHL	4	0	2	2				11																		
1986-87♦	**Edmonton Oilers**	**NHL**	62	7	15	22	6	11	17	165	2	0	1	71	9.9	71	8	66	14	11	15	1	3	4	45	0	0	0
1987-88♦	**Edmonton Oilers**	**NHL**	79	12	43	55	10	31	41	286	5	0	1	116	10.3	140	37	97	34	40	19	1	11	12	55	1	0	0
1988-89	**Edmonton Oilers**	**NHL**	35	3	19	22	3	13	16	97	0	0	0	47	6.4	52	17	44	14	5	7	2	2	4	20	0	0	1
1989-90♦	**Edmonton Oilers**	**NHL**	75	7	34	41	6	24	30	171	3	0	1	125	5.6	125	52	86	19	6	22	5	10	15	37	0	1	1
1990-91	**Edmonton Oilers**	**NHL**	77	13	41	54	12	31	43	193	4	0	2	114	11.4	121	38	101	32	14	18	1	2	3	45	1	0	0
1991-92	Canada	Can-Cup	8	0	1	1				30																		
	Chicago Blackhawks	**NHL**	76	9	21	30	8	16	24	304	3	0	1	153	5.9	122	40	89	30	23	18	1	11	12	16	1	0	0
1992-93	**Chicago Blackhawks**	**NHL**	78	10	47	57	8	32	40	214	7	1	2	212	4.7	142	66	108	44	12	4	0	0	0	10	0	0	0
1993-94	**Chicago Blackhawks**	**NHL**	57	5	22	27	5	17	22	174	1	0	1	89	5.6	71	21	76	21	–5								
1994-95	**Chicago Blackhawks**	**NHL**	48	1	12	13	2	18	20	128	0	0	0	43	2.3	47	9	50	18	6	16	0	1	1	26	0	0	0
1995-96	**Chicago Blackhawks**	**NHL**	37	0	9	9	0	7	7	71	0	0	0	17	0.0	39	4	40	17	12	6	0	0	0	16	0	0	0

			REGULAR SEASON																			PLAYOFFS							
Season	**Club**	**League**	**GP**	**G**	**A**	**Pts**	**AG**	**AA**	**APts**	**PIM**	**PP**	**SH**	**GW**	**S**	**%**	**TGF**	**PGF**	**TGA**	**PGA**	**+/–**	**GP**	**G**	**A**	**Pts**	**PIM**	**PP**	**SH**	**GW**
1996-97	**Chicago Blackhawks**	**NHL**	**21**	**0**	**0**	**0**	**0**	**0**	**0**	**29**	**0**	**0**	**0**	**7**	**0.0**	**15**	**0**	**17**	**6**	**4**	**3**	**0**	**0**	**0**	**4**	**0**	**0**	**0**
1997-98	**Calgary Flames**	**NHL**	DID NOT PLAY – ASSISTANT COACH																									
1998-99	**Calgary Flames**	**NHL**	**69**	**1**	**14**	**15**	**1**	**13**	**14**	**80**	**0**	**0**	**0**	**42**	**2.4**	**55**	**3**	**82**	**33**	**3**	....	....	....	....	....	....	....	....
99-2000	**Calgary Flames**	**NHL**	**20**	**0**	**4**	**4**	**0**	**4**	**4**	**42**	**0**	**0**	**0**	**10**	**0.0**	**11**	**0**	**32**	**8**	**–13**	....	....	....	....	....	....	....	....
	NHL Totals		**791**	**72**	**301**	**373**	**64**	**230**	**294**	**2122**	**26**	**1**	**10**	**1123**	**6.4**	**1083**	**303**	**931**	**297**		**134**	**11**	**41**	**52**	**288**	**3**	**1**	**2**

Played in NHL All-Star Game (1991)

Traded to **Chicago** by **Edmonton** for Dave Manson and Chicago's 3rd round choice (Kirk Maltby) in 1992 Entry Draft, October 2, 1991. Signed as a free agent by **Calgary**, August 17, 1998.
• Missed remainder of 1999-2000 season recovering from neck injury suffered in game vs. Los Angeles, January 12, 2000.

• SMITH, Steve

D – L. 5'9", 215 lbs. b: Trenton, Ont., 4/4/1963. Philadelphia's 1st, 16th overall, in 1981.

Season	Club	League	GP	G	A	Pts	AG	AA	APts	PIM	PP	SH	GW	S	%	TGF	PGF	TGA	PGA	+/–	GP	G	A	Pts	PIM	PP	SH	GW
1979-80	Belleville Bobcats	OHA-B	41	8	25	33	....	....	....	105	....	....	....	....	....	....	....	....	....	....	....	....	....	....	....	....	....	....
	Peterborough Petes	OMJHL	5	0	3	3	....	....	....	0	....	....	....	....	....	....	....	....	....	....	....	....	....	....	....	....	....	....
	Peterborough Petes	Mem-Cup	4	2	1	3	....	....	....	8	....	....	....	....	....	....	....	....	....	....	....	....	....	....	....	....	....	....
1980-81	Sault Ste. Marie Greyhounds	OMJHL	61	3	37	40	....	....	....	143	....	....	....	....	....	....	....	....	....	....	19	0	6	6	60	....	....	....
1981-82	Sault Ste. Marie Greyhounds	OHL	50	7	20	27	....	....	....	179	....	....	....	....	....	....	....	....	....	....	12	0	2	2	23	....	....	....
	Philadelphia Flyers	**NHL**	**8**	**0**	**1**	**1**	**0**	**1**	**1**	**0**	**0**	**0**	**0**	**9**	**0.0**	**2**	**0**	**7**	**3**	**–2**	....	....	....	....	....	....	....	....
1982-83	Sault Ste. Marie Greyhounds	OHL	55	11	33	44	....	....	....	139	....	....	....	....	....	....	....	....	....	....	16	0	8	8	28	....	....	....
1983-84	Springfield Indians	AHL	70	4	25	29	....	....	....	77	....	....	....	....	....	....	....	....	....	....	4	0	0	0	0	....	....	....
1984-85	**Philadelphia Flyers**	**NHL**	**2**	**0**	**0**	**0**	**0**	**0**	**0**	**7**	**0**	**0**	**0**	**0**	**0.0**	**3**	**1**	**0**	**0**	**2**	....	....	....	....	....	....	....	....
	Hershey Bears	AHL	65	10	20	30	....	....	....	83	....	....	....	....	....	....	....	....	....	....	....	....	....	....	....	....	....	....
1985-86	**Philadelphia Flyers**	**NHL**	**2**	**0**	**0**	**0**	**0**	**0**	**0**	**2**	....	....	....	....	....	....	....	....	....	....	....	....	....	....	....	....	....	....
	Hershey Bears	AHL	49	1	11	12	....	....	....	96	....	....	....	....	....	....	....	....	....	....	16	2	4	6	43	....	....	....
1986-87	**Philadelphia Flyers**	**NHL**	**2**	**0**	**0**	**0**	**0**	**0**	**0**	**6**	**0**	**0**	**0**	**1**	**0.0**	**0**	**0**	**2**	**0**	**–2**	....	....	....	....	....	....	....	....
	Hershey Bears	AHL	66	11	26	37	....	....	....	191	....	....	....	....	....	....	....	....	....	....	5	0	2	2	8	....	....	....
1987-88	**Philadelphia Flyers**	**NHL**	**1**	**0**	**0**	**0**	**0**	**0**	**0**	**0**	....	....	....	....	....	....	....	....	....	....	....	....	....	....	....	....	....	....
	Hershey Bears	AHL	66	10	19	29	....	....	....	132	....	....	....	....	....	....	....	....	....	....	12	2	10	12	35	....	....	....
1988-89	**Buffalo Sabres**	**NHL**	**3**	**0**	**0**	**0**	**0**	**0**	**0**	**0**	**0**	**0**	**0**	**2**	**0.0**	**2**	**0**	**2**	**0**	**0**	....	....	....	....	....	....	....	....
	Rochester Americans	AHL	48	2	12	14	....	....	....	79	....	....	....	....	....	....	....	....	....	....	....	....	....	....	....	....	....	....
1989-90	Rochester Americans	AHL	42	3	15	18	....	....	....	107	....	....	....	....	....	....	....	....	....	....	17	0	5	5	27	....	....	....
1990-91	Rochester Americans	AHL	37	2	4	6	....	....	....	74	....	....	....	....	....	....	....	....	....	....	5	0	0	0	4	....	....	....
1991-92	Rochester Americans	AHL	3	1	0	1	....	....	....	0	....	....	....	....	....	....	....	....	....	....	....	....	....	....	....	....	....	....
	EK Zell-am-Zee	Austria	28	11	6	17	....	....	....	....	....	....	....	....	....	....	....	....	....	....	....	....	....	....	....	....	....	....
1992-93	SG Brunico	Alpenliga	30	12	24	36	....	....	....	20	....	....	....	....	....	....	....	....	....	....	....	....	....	....	....	....	....	....
	SG Brunico	Italy	16	6	21	27	....	....	....	4	....	....	....	....	....	....	....	....	....	....	4	10	.6	16	0	....	....	....
	NHL Totals		**18**	**0**	**1**	**1**	**0**	**1**	**1**	**15**	**0**	**0**	**0**	**12**	**0.0**	**7**	**1**	**11**	**3**		....	....	....	....	....	....	....	....

OHL Second All-Star Team (1981,1982, 1983)

Claimed by **Buffalo** from **Philadelphia** in Waiver Draft, October 3, 1988.

• SMITH, Stu

Stuart Gordon D – R. 6'1", 205 lbs. b: Toronto, Ont., 3/17/1960. Hartford's 2nd, 39th overall, in 1979.

Season	Club	League	GP	G	A	Pts	AG	AA	APts	PIM	PP	SH	GW	S	%	TGF	PGF	TGA	PGA	+/–	GP	G	A	Pts	PIM	PP	SH	GW
1976-77	Seneca Sailors	OHA-B	66	10	42	52	....	....	....	230	....	....	....	....	....	....	....	....	....	....	....	....	....	....	....	....	....	....
1977-78	Peterborough Petes	OMJHL	67	1	18	19	....	....	....	112	....	....	....	....	....	....	....	....	....	....	21	0	3	3	40	....	....	....
	Peterborough Petes	Mem-Cup	5	1	1	2	....	....	....	8	....	....	....	....	....	....	....	....	....	....	....	....	....	....	....	....	....	....
1978-79	Peterborough Petes	OMJHL	64	5	35	40	....	....	....	172	....	....	....	....	....	....	....	....	....	....	19	2	7	9	56	....	....	....
	Peterborough Petes	Mem-Cup	5	1	2	3	....	....	....	2	....	....	....	....	....	....	....	....	....	....	....	....	....	....	....	....	....	....
1979-80	Peterborough Petes	OMJHL	62	12	40	52	....	....	....	119	....	....	....	....	....	....	....	....	....	....	14	1	13	14	16	....	....	....
	Canada	WJC-A	5	0	1	1	....	....	....	10	....	....	....	....	....	....	....	....	....	....	....	....	....	....	....	....	....	....
	Hartford Whalers	**NHL**	**4**	**0**	**0**	**0**	**0**	**0**	**0**	**0**	**0**	**0**	**0**	**3**	**0.0**	**4**	**0**	**5**	**0**	**–1**	....	....	....	....	....	....	....	....
	Peterborough Petes	Mem-Cup	5	0	2	2	....	....	....	*23	....	....	....	....	....	....	....	....	....	....	....	....	....	....	....	....	....	....
1980-81	**Hartford Whalers**	**NHL**	**38**	**1**	**7**	**8**	**1**	**5**	**6**	**55**	**0**	**0**	**0**	**34**	**2.9**	**35**	**2**	**61**	**14**	**–14**	....	....	....	....	....	....	....	....
	Binghamton Whalers	AHL	42	3	9	12	....	....	....	63	....	....	....	....	....	....	....	....	....	....	....	....	....	....	....	....	....	....
1981-82	**Hartford Whalers**	**NHL**	**17**	**0**	**3**	**3**	**0**	**2**	**2**	**15**	**0**	**0**	**0**	**14**	**0.0**	**8**	**0**	**21**	**6**	**–7**	....	....	....	....	....	....	....	....
	Binghamton Whalers	AHL	61	4	21	25	....	....	....	121	....	....	....	....	....	....	....	....	....	....	15	2	7	9	22	....	....	....
1982-83	**Hartford Whalers**	**NHL**	**18**	**1**	**0**	**1**	**1**	**0**	**1**	**25**	**0**	**0**	**0**	**21**	**4.8**	**12**	**1**	**34**	**7**	**–16**	....	....	....	....	....	....	....	....
	Binghamton Whalers	AHL	50	3	8	11	....	....	....	97	....	....	....	....	....	....	....	....	....	....	5	0	1	1	12	....	....	....
1983-84	Binghamton Whalers	AHL	54	3	22	25	....	....	....	95	....	....	....	....	....	....	....	....	....	....	....	....	....	....	....	....	....	....
1984-85	New Haven Nighthawks	AHL	79	4	17	21	....	....	....	87	....	....	....	....	....	....	....	....	....	....	....	....	....	....	....	....	....	....
	NHL Totals		**77**	**2**	**10**	**12**	**2**	**7**	**9**	**95**	**0**	**0**	**0**	**72**	**2.8**	**59**	**3**	**121**	**27**		....	....	....	....	....	....	....	....

Signed as a free agent by **LA Kings**, November 8, 1984.

• SMITH, Vern

D – L. 6'1", 190 lbs. b: Winnipeg, Man., 5/30/1964. NY Islanders' 2nd, 42nd overall, in 1982.

Season	Club	League	GP	G	A	Pts	AG	AA	APts	PIM	PP	SH	GW	S	%	TGF	PGF	TGA	PGA	+/–	GP	G	A	Pts	PIM	PP	SH	GW
1980-81	Lethbridge Y's Men	AAHA	STATISTICS NOT AVAILABLE																									
1981-82	Lethbridge Broncos	WHL	72	5	38	43	....	....	....	73	....	....	....	....	....	....	....	....	....	....	12	0	2	2	8	....	....	....
1982-83	Lethbridge Broncos	WHL	30	2	10	12	....	....	....	54	....	....	....	....	....	....	....	....	....	....	....	....	....	....	....	....	....	....
	Nanaimo Islanders	WHL	42	6	21	27	....	....	....	62	....	....	....	....	....	....	....	....	....	....	....	....	....	....	....	....	....	....
1983-84	New Westminster Bruins	WHL	69	13	44	57	....	....	....	94	....	....	....	....	....	....	....	....	....	....	9	6	6	12	12	....	....	....
1984-85	**New York Islanders**	**NHL**	**1**	**0**	**0**	**0**	**0**	**0**	**0**	**0**	**0**	**0**	**0**	**0**	**0.0**	**1**	**0**	**1**	**0**	**0**	....	....	....	....	....	....	....	....
	Springfield Indians	AHL	76	6	20	26	....	....	....	115	....	....	....	....	....	....	....	....	....	....	4	0	2	2	9	....	....	....
1985-86	Springfield Indians	AHL	55	3	11	14	....	....	....	83	....	....	....	....	....	....	....	....	....	....	....	....	....	....	....	....	....	....
1986-87	Springfield Indians	AHL	41	1	10	11	....	....	....	58	....	....	....	....	....	....	....	....	....	....	....	....	....	....	....	....	....	....
1987-88	Springfield Indians	AHL	64	5	22	27	....	....	....	78	....	....	....	....	....	....	....	....	....	....	....	....	....	....	....	....	....	....
1988-89	Springfield Indians	AHL	80	3	26	29	....	....	....	121	....	....	....	....	....	....	....	....	....	....	....	....	....	....	....	....	....	....
1989-90	Phoenix Roadrunners	IHL	48	4	19	23	....	....	....	37	....	....	....	....	....	....	....	....	....	....	....	....	....	....	....	....	....	....
	Binghamton Whalers	AHL	17	3	2	5	....	....	....	14	....	....	....	....	....	....	....	....	....	....	....	....	....	....	....	....	....	....
1990-91	New Haven Nighthawks	AHL	9	0	1	1	....	....	....	2	....	....	....	....	....	....	....	....	....	....	....	....	....	....	....	....	....	....
	Albany Choppers	IHL	46	5	15	20	....	....	....	48	....	....	....	....	....	....	....	....	....	....	....	....	....	....	....	....	....	....
1991-92	Phoenix Roadrunners	IHL	16	1	2	3	....	....	....	25	....	....	....	....	....	....	....	....	....	....	....	....	....	....	....	....	....	....
	New Haven Nighthawks	AHL	4	0	0	0	....	....	....	5	....	....	....	....	....	....	....	....	....	....	....	....	....	....	....	....	....	....
	Capital District Islanders	AHL	17	1	5	6	....	....	....	6	....	....	....	....	....	....	....	....	....	....	....	....	....	....	....	....	....	....
	Erie Panthers	ECHL	8	3	5	8	....	....	....	6	....	....	....	....	....	....	....	....	....	....	....	....	....	....	....	....	....	....
	NHL Totals		**1**	**0**	**0**	**0**	**0**	**0**	**0**	**0**	**0**	**0**	**0**	**0**	**0.0**	**1**	**0**	**1**	**0**		....	....	....	....	....	....	....	....

• SMITH, Wyatt

C – L. 5'11", 198 lbs. b: Thief River Falls, MN, 2/13/1977. Phoenix's 6th, 233rd overall, in 1997.

Season	Club	League	GP	G	A	Pts	AG	AA	APts	PIM	PP	SH	GW	S	%	TGF	PGF	TGA	PGA	+/–	GP	G	A	Pts	PIM	PP	SH	GW
1994-95	Warroad Warriors	Hi-School	28	29	31	60	....	....	....	28	....	....	....	....	....	....	....	....	....	....	....	....	....	....	....	....	....	....
1995-96	University of Minnesota	WCHA	32	4	5	9	....	....	....	32	....	....	....	....	....	....	....	....	....	....	....	....	....	....	....	....	....	....
1996-97	University of Minnesota	WCHA	38	16	14	30	....	....	....	44	....	....	....	....	....	....	....	....	....	....	....	....	....	....	....	....	....	....
1997-98	University of Minnesota	WCHA	39	24	23	47	....	....	....	62	....	....	....	....	....	....	....	....	....	....	....	....	....	....	....	....	....	....
1998-99	University of Minnesota	WCHA	43	23	20	43	....	....	....	37	....	....	....	....	....	....	....	....	....	....	....	....	....	....	....	....	....	....
99-2000	**Phoenix Coyotes**	**NHL**	**2**	**0**	**0**	**0**	**0**	**0**	**0**	**0**	**0**	**0**	**0**	**0**	**0.0**	**0**	**0**	**2**	**0**	**–2**	....	....	....	....	....	....	....	....
	Springfield Falcons	AHL	60	14	26	40	....	....	....	26	....	....	....	....	....	....	....	....	....	....	5	2	3	5	13	....	....	....
	NHL Totals		**2**	**0**	**0**	**0**	**0**	**0**	**0**	**0**	**0**	**0**	**0**	**0**	**0.0**	**0**	**0**	**2**	**0**		....	....	....	....	....	....	....	....

• SMOLINSKI, Bryan

C/RW – R. 6'1", 208 lbs. b: Toledo, OH, 12/27/1971. Boston's 1st, 21st overall, in 1990.

Season	Club	League	GP	G	A	Pts	AG	AA	APts	PIM	PP	SH	GW	S	%	TGF	PGF	TGA	PGA	+/–	GP	G	A	Pts	PIM	PP	SH	GW
1987-88	Detroit Little Ceasars	MNHL	80	43	77	120	....	....	....	....	....	....	....	....	....	....	....	....	....	....	....	....	....	....	....	....	....	....
1988-89	Stratford Cullitons	OJHL-B	46	32	62	94	....	....	....	132	....	....	....	....	....	....	....	....	....	....	....	....	....	....	....	....	....	....
1989-90	Michigan State Spartans	CCHA	35	9	13	22	....	....	....	34	....	....	....	....	....	....	....	....	....	....	....	....	....	....	....	....	....	....
	United States	WJC-A	7	2	3	5	....	....	....	8	....	....	....	....	....	....	....	....	....	....	....	....	....	....	....	....	....	....
1990-91	Michigan State Spartans	CCHA	35	9	12	21	....	....	....	24	....	....	....	....	....	....	....	....	....	....	....	....	....	....	....	....	....	....

			REGULAR SEASON																		PLAYOFFS							
Season	Club	League	GP	G	A	Pts	AG	AA	APts	PIM	PP	SH	GW	S	%	TGF	PGF	TGA	PGA	+/-	GP	G	A	Pts	PIM	PP	SH	GW
1991-92	Michigan State Spartans	CCHA	41	28	33	61	....	....	....	55	....	....	....	....	....	....	....	....	....	....	....	....	....	....	....	....	....	....
1992-93	Michigan State Spartans	CCHA	40	31	37	*68	....	....	....	93	....	....	....	....	....	....	....	....	....	....	....	....	....	....	....	....	....	....
	Boston Bruins	NHL	9	1	3	4	1	2	3	0	0	0	0	10	10.0	5	1	1	0	3	4	1	0	1	2	0	0	0
1993-94	Boston Bruins	NHL	83	31	20	51	29	16	45	82	4	3	5	179	17.3	69	14	60	9	4	13	5	4	9	4	2	0	0
1994-95	Boston Bruins	NHL	44	18	13	31	32	19	51	31	6	0	5	121	14.9	40	13	35	5	–3	5	0	1	1	4	0	0	0
1995-96	Pittsburgh Penguins	NHL	81	24	40	64	24	33	57	69	8	2	1	229	10.5	94	24	85	21	6	18	5	4	9	10	0	0	1
1996-97	United States	W-Cup	6	0	5	5	....	....	....	0	....	....	....	....	....	....	....	....	....	....	....	....	....	....	....	....	....	....
	Detroit Vipers	IHL	6	5	7	12	....	....	....	10	....	....	....	....	....	....	....	....	....	....	....	....	....	....	....	....	....	....
	New York Islanders	NHL	64	28	28	56	30	25	55	25	9	0	1	183	15.3	78	21	49	1	9	....	....	....	....	....	....	....	....
1997-98	New York Islanders	NHL	81	13	30	43	15	29	44	34	3	0	4	203	6.4	68	21	66	3	–16	....	....	....	....	....	....	....	....
	United States	WC-A	6	3	1	4	....	....	....	10	....	....	....	....	....	....	....	....	....	....	....	....	....	....	....	....	....	....
1998-99	New York Islanders	NHL	82	16	24	40	19	23	42	49	7	0	3	223	7.2	74	31	54	4	–7	....	....	....	....	....	....	....	....
	United States	WC-A	6	3	3	6	....	....	....	8	....	....	....	....	....	....	....	....	....	....	....	....	....	....	....	....	....	....
99-2000	Los Angeles Kings	NHL	79	20	36	56	22	33	55	48	2	0	0	160	12.5	77	21	73	19	2	4	0	0	0	2	0	0	0
	NHL Totals		523	151	194	345	172	180	352	338	39	5	19	1308	11.5	505	146	423	62		44	11	9	20	22	2	0	1

CCHA First All-Star Team (1993) • NCAA West First All-American Team (1993)

Traded to **Pittsburgh** by **Boston** with Glen Murray and Boston's 3rd round choice (Boyd Kane) in 1996 Entry Draft for Kevin Stevens and Shawn McEachern, August 2, 1995. Traded to **NY Islanders** by **Pittsburgh** for Darius Kasparaitis and Andreas Johansson, November 17, 1996. Traded to **LA Kings** by **NY Islanders** with Zigmund Palffy, Marcel Cousineau and New Jersey's 4th round choice (previously acquired, LA Kings selected Daniel Johanssen) in 1999 Entry Draft for Olli Jokinen, Josh Green, Mathieu Biron and LA Kings' 1st round choice (Taylor Pyatt) in 1999 Entry Draft, June 20, 1999.

• SMRKE, John

LW – L. 5'11", 205 lbs. b: Chicoutimi, Que., 2/25/1956. St. Louis' 3rd, 25th overall, in 1976.

Season	Club	League	GP	G	A	Pts	AG	AA	APts	PIM	PP	SH	GW	S	%	TGF	PGF	TGA	PGA	+/-	GP	G	A	Pts	PIM	PP	SH	GW
1973-74	Toronto Marlboros	OMJHL	70	23	28	51	....	....	....	18	....	....	....	....	....	....	....	....	....	....	....	....	....	....	....	....	....	....
1974-75	Toronto Marlboros	OMJHL	61	43	54	97	....	....	....	39	....	....	....	....	....	....	....	....	....	....	23	13	9	22	16	....	....	....
	Toronto Marlboros	Mem-Cup	4	3	3	6	....	....	....	0	....	....	....	....	....	....	....	....	....	....	....	....	....	....	....	....	....	....
1975-76	Toronto Marlboros	OMJHL	64	39	46	85	....	....	....	32	....	....	....	....	....	....	....	....	....	....	10	7	6	13	9	....	....	....
1976-77	Kansas City Blues	CHL	70	25	26	51	....	....	....	8	....	....	....	....	....	....	....	....	....	....	5	2	0	2	2	....	....	....
1977-78	St. Louis Blues	NHL	18	2	4	6	2	3	5	11	0	0	0	20	10.0	11	3	15	0	–7	....	....	....	....	....	....	....	....
	Salt Lake Golden Eagles	CHL	60	25	45	70	....	....	....	21	....	....	....	....	....	....	....	....	....	....	6	4	2	6	2	....	....	....
1978-79	St. Louis Blues	NHL	55	6	8	14	5	6	11	20	0	1	0	72	8.3	21	0	63	18	–24	....	....	....	....	....	....	....	....
	Salt Lake Golden Eagles	CHL	11	5	7	12	....	....	....	0	....	....	....	....	....	....	....	....	....	....	....	....	....	....	....	....	....	....
1979-80	Quebec Nordiques	NHL	30	3	5	8	3	4	7	2	0	0	0	32	9.4	17	0	18	4	3	....	....	....	....	....	....	....	....
	Syracuse Firebirds	AHL	18	5	5	10	....	....	....	2	....	....	....	....	....	....	....	....	....	....	4	1	0	1	2	....	....	....
1980-81	Binghamton Whalers	AHL	9	1	2	3	....	....	....	0	....	....	....	....	....	....	....	....	....	....	....	....	....	....	....	....	....	....
	Houston Apollos	CHL	33	7	4	11	....	....	....	16	....	....	....	....	....	....	....	....	....	....	....	....	....	....	....	....	....	....
1981-82	Cincinnati Tigers	CHL	45	6	7	13	....	....	....	4	....	....	....	....	....	....	....	....	....	....	4	0	0	0	25	....	....	....
1982-83	HC Selva	Italy-2	STATISTICS NOT AVAILABLE																									
1983-84	HC Selva	Italy-2	20	38	55	83	....	....	....	10	....	....	....	....	....	....	....	....	....	....	4	10	6	16	0	....	....	....
1984-85	HC Auronzo	Italy	25	29	22	51	....	....	....	12	....	....	....	....	....	....	....	....	....	....	2	5	2	7	0	....	....	....
1985-86	Campbellton Tigers	RHL	40	37	57	94	....	....	....	31	....	....	....	....	....	....	....	....	....	....	6	2	9	11	....	....	....	....
	NHL Totals		103	11	17	28	10	13	23	33	0	1	0	124	8.9	49	3	96	22		....	....	....	....	....	....	....	....

• Son of Stan • Won George Parsons Trophy (Memorial Cup Tournament Most Sportsmanlike Player) (1975)

Claimed by **Quebec** from **St. Louis** in Expansion Draft, June 13, 1979.

• SMYL, Stan

Stanley Phillip "Steamer" RW – R. 5'8", 185 lbs. b: Glendon, Alta., 1/28/1958. Vancouver's 3rd, 40th overall, in 1978.

Season	Club	League	GP	G	A	Pts	AG	AA	APts	PIM	PP	SH	GW	S	%	TGF	PGF	TGA	PGA	+/-	GP	G	A	Pts	PIM	PP	SH	GW
1974-75	Bellingham Blazers	BCJHL	48	29	33	62	....	....	....	115	....	....	....	....	....	....	....	....	....	....	25	13	22	33	15	....	....	....
	New Westminster Bruins	WCJHL	....	....	....	....	....	....	....	....	....	....	....	....	....	....	....	....	....	....	3	0	0	0	15	....	....	....
1975-76	New Westminster Bruins	WCJHL	72	32	42	74	....	....	....	169	....	....	....	....	....	....	....	....	....	....	19	8	6	14	58	....	....	....
	New Westminster Bruins	Mem-Cup	4	*5	1	6	....	....	....	21	....	....	....	....	....	....	....	....	....	....	....	....	....	....	....	....	....	....
1976-77	New Westminster Bruins	WCJHL	72	35	31	66	....	....	....	200	....	....	....	....	....	....	....	....	....	....	13	6	7	13	51	....	....	....
	New Westminster Bruins	Mem-Cup	3	0	0	0	....	....	....	6	....	....	....	....	....	....	....	....	....	....	....	....	....	....	....	....	....	....
1977-78	New Westminster Bruins	WCJHL	53	29	47	76	....	....	....	211	....	....	....	....	....	....	....	....	....	....	20	14	21	35	43	....	....	....
	Canada	WJC-A	6	1	1	2	....	....	....	6	....	....	....	....	....	....	....	....	....	....	....	....	....	....	....	....	....	....
	New Westminster Bruins	Mem-Cup	5	4	*10	*14	....	....	....	0	....	....	....	....	....	....	....	....	....	....	....	....	....	....	....	....	....	....
1978-79	Vancouver Canucks	NHL	62	14	24	38	12	17	29	89	4	0	0	122	11.5	62	24	44	0	–6	2	1	1	2	0	0	0	0
	Dallas Black Hawks	CHL	3	1	1	2	....	....	....	9	....	....	....	....	....	....	....	....	....	....	....	....	....	....	....	....	....	....
1979-80	Vancouver Canucks	NHL	77	31	47	78	26	34	60	204	11	0	3	182	17.0	107	29	53	3	28	4	0	2	2	14	0	0	0
1980-81	Vancouver Canucks	NHL	80	25	38	63	19	25	44	171	6	1	2	209	12.0	92	32	72	4	–8	3	1	2	3	0	0	0	0
1981-82	Vancouver Canucks	NHL	80	34	44	78	27	29	56	144	10	2	5	222	15.3	126	40	96	28	18	17	9	9	18	25	1	0	1
1982-83	Vancouver Canucks	NHL	74	38	50	88	31	35	66	114	15	1	2	215	17.7	124	52	85	7	–6	4	3	2	5	12	1	0	1
1983-84	Vancouver Canucks	NHL	80	24	43	67	19	29	48	136	8	0	4	205	11.7	106	40	106	19	–21	4	2	1	3	4	0	0	0
1984-85	Vancouver Canucks	NHL	80	27	37	64	22	25	47	100	6	2	1	182	14.8	95	25	111	23	–18	....	....	....	....	....	....	....	....
	Canada	WEC-A	10	1	1	2	....	....	....	6	....	....	....	....	....	....	....	....	....	....	....	....	....	....	....	....	....	....
1985-86	Vancouver Canucks	NHL	73	27	35	62	22	24	46	144	3	4	1	165	16.4	90	23	117	30	–20	....	....	....	....	....	....	....	....
1986-87	Vancouver Canucks	NHL	66	20	23	43	17	17	34	84	5	2	2	113	17.7	78	30	85	17	–20	....	....	....	....	....	....	....	....
1987-88	Vancouver Canucks	NHL	57	12	25	37	10	18	28	110	5	1	0	96	12.5	58	18	53	8	–5	....	....	....	....	....	....	....	....
1988-89	Vancouver Canucks	NHL	75	7	18	25	6	13	19	102	1	0	0	89	7.9	47	8	45	6	0	7	0	0	0	9	0	0	0
1989-90	Vancouver Canucks	NHL	47	1	15	16	1	11	12	71	0	0	0	58	1.7	29	5	45	7	–14	....	....	....	....	....	....	....	....
1990-91	Vancouver Canucks	NHL	45	2	12	14	2	9	11	87	0	0	0	45	4.4	21	1	26	1	–5	....	....	....	....	....	....	....	....
1991-1999	Vancouver Canucks	NHL	DID NOT PLAY – ASSISTANT COACH																									
1999-2000	Syracuse Crunch	AHL	DID NOT PLAY – COACHING																									
	NHL Totals		896	262	411	673	214	286	500	1556	74	13	20	1903	13.8	1035	327	938	153		41	16	17	33	64	2	0	2

Memorial Cup All-Star Team (1978) • Won Stafford Smythe Memorial Trophy (Memorial Cup Tournament MVP) (1978)

• SMYTH, Brad

Brad A. RW – R. 6', 200 lbs. b: Ottawa, Ont., 3/13/1973.

Season	Club	League	GP	G	A	Pts	AG	AA	APts	PIM	PP	SH	GW	S	%	TGF	PGF	TGA	PGA	+/-	GP	G	A	Pts	PIM	PP	SH	GW
1989-90	Nepean Midget Raiders	OMHA	55	53	36	89	....	....	....	105	....	....	....	....	....	....	....	....	....	....	....	....	....	....	....	....	....	....
1990-91	London Knights	OHL	29	2	6	8	....	....	....	22	....	....	....	....	....	....	....	....	....	....	....	....	....	....	....	....	....	....
1991-92	London Knights	OHL	58	17	18	35	....	....	....	93	....	....	....	....	....	....	....	....	....	....	10	2	0	2	8	....	....	....
1992-93	London Knights	OHL	66	54	55	109	....	....	....	118	....	....	....	....	....	....	....	....	....	....	12	7	8	15	25	....	....	....
1993-94	Cincinnati Cyclones	IHL	30	7	3	10	....	....	....	54	....	....	....	....	....	....	....	....	....	....	....	....	....	....	....	....	....	....
	Birmingham Bulls	ECHL	29	26	30	56	....	....	....	38	....	....	....	....	....	....	....	....	....	....	10	8	8	16	19	....	....	....
1994-95	Springfield Falcons	AHL	3	0	0	0	....	....	....	7	....	....	....	....	....	....	....	....	....	....	....	....	....	....	....	....	....	....
	Birmingham Bulls	ECHL	36	33	35	68	....	....	....	52	....	....	....	....	....	....	....	....	....	....	3	5	2	7	0	....	....	....
	Cincinnati Cyclones	IHL	26	2	11	13	....	....	....	34	....	....	....	....	....	....	....	....	....	....	1	0	0	0	2	....	....	....
1995-96	Florida Panthers	NHL	7	1	1	2	1	1	2	4	1	0	0	12	8.3	3	3	3	0	–3	....	....	....	....	....	....	....	....
	Carolina Monarchs	AHL	68	*68	58	*126	....	....	....	80	....	....	....	....	....	....	....	....	....	....	....	....	....	....	....	....	....	....
1996-97	Florida Panthers	NHL	8	1	0	1	1	0	1	2	0	0	0	10	10.0	1	0	4	0	–3	....	....	....	....	....	....	....	....
	Los Angeles Kings	NHL	44	8	8	16	8	7	15	74	0	0	1	74	10.8	24	5	26	0	–7	....	....	....	....	....	....	....	....
	Phoenix Roadrunners	IHL	3	5	2	7	....	....	....	0	....	....	....	....	....	....	....	....	....	....	....	....	....	....	....	....	....	....
1997-98	Los Angeles Kings	NHL	9	1	3	4	1	3	4	4	0	0	0	12	8.3	5	3	3	0	–1	....	....	....	....	....	....	....	....
	New York Rangers	NHL	1	0	0	0	0	0	0	0	0	0	0	1	0.0	0	0	0	0	0	....	....	....	....	....	....	....	....
	Hartford Wolf Pack	AHL	57	29	33	62	....	....	....	79	....	....	....	....	....	....	....	....	....	....	15	12	8	20	11	....	....	....

			REGULAR SEASON																		PLAYOFFS							
Season	Club	League	GP	G	A	Pts	AG	AA	APts	PIM	PP	SH	GW	S	%	TGF	PGF	TGA	PGA	+/–	GP	G	A	Pts	PIM	PP	SH	GW
1998-99	**Nashville Predators**	**NHL**	3	0	0	0	0	0	0	6	0	0	0	5	0.0	2	1	2	0	–1	....	....	....	....	....	....	....	....
	Milwaukee Admirals	IHL	34	11	16	27	....	....	....	21	....	....	....	....	....	....	....	....	....	....	....	....	....	....	....	....	....	....
	Hartford Wolf Pack	AHL	36	25	19	44	....	....	....	48	....	....	....	....	....	....	....	....	....	....	7	6	0	6	14	....	....	....
99-2000	Hartford Wolf Pack	AHL	80	39	37	76	....	....	....	62	....	....	....	....	....	....	....	....	....	....	23	*13	10	23	8	....	....	....
	NHL Totals		72	11	12	23	11	11	22	90	1	0	1	114	9.6	35	12	38	0		....	....	....	....	....	....	....	....

AHL First All-Star Team (1996) • Won John B. Sollenberger Trophy (Top Scorer — AHL) (1996) • Won Les Cunningham Award (MVP - AHL) (1996)

Signed as a free agent by **Florida**, October 4, 1993. Traded to **LA Kings** by **Florida** for LA Kings' 3rd round choice (Vratislav Czech) in 1997 Entry Draft, November 28, 1996. • Played w/ RHI's Ottawa Loggers 1996 (21-20-23-43-24). Traded to **NY Rangers** by **LA Kings** for future considerations, November 14, 1997. Signed as a free agent by **Nashville**, July 16, 1998. Traded to **NY Rangers** by **Nashville** for future considerations, May 3, 1999.

• SMYTH, Greg

D – R. 6'3", 212 lbs. b: Oakville, Ont., 4/23/1966. Philadelphia's 1st, 22nd overall, in 1984.

Season	Club	League	GP	G	A	Pts	AG	AA	APts	PIM	PP	SH	GW	S	%	TGF	PGF	TGA	PGA	+/–	GP	G	A	Pts	PIM	PP	SH	GW
1981-82	Mississagua Reps	MTHL	STATISTICS NOT AVAILABLE																									
1982-83	Wexford Raiders	OJHL	54	11	32	43	....	....	....	132	....	....	....	....	....	....	....	....	....	....	....	....	....	....	....	....	....	....
1983-84	London Knights	OHL	64	4	21	25	....	....	....	252	....	....	....	....	....	....	....	....	....	....	6	1	0	1	24	....	....	....
1984-85	London Knights	OHL	47	7	16	23	....	....	....	188	....	....	....	....	....	....	....	....	....	....	8	2	2	4	27	....	....	....
1985-86	London Knights	OHL	46	12	42	54	....	....	....	199	....	....	....	....	....	....	....	....	....	....	4	1	2	3	28	....	....	....
	Hershey Bears	AHL	2	0	1	1	....	....	....	5	....	....	....	....	....	....	....	....	....	....	8	0	0	0	60	....	....	....
1986-87	**Philadelphia Flyers**	**NHL**	1	0	0	0	0	0	0	0	....	....	....	....	....	....	....	....	....	....	1	0	0	0	2	0	0	0
	Hershey Bears	AHL	35	0	2	2	....	....	....	158	....	....	....	....	....	....	....	....	....	....	2	0	0	0	19	....	....	....
1987-88	**Philadelphia Flyers**	**NHL**	48	1	6	7	1	4	5	192	0	0	0	29	3.4	34	0	48	12	–2	5	0	0	0	38	0	0	0
	Hershey Bears	AHL	21	0	10	10	....	....	....	102	....	....	....	....	....	....	....	....	....	....	....	....	....	....	....	....	....	....
1988-89	**Quebec Nordiques**	**NHL**	10	0	1	1	0	1	1	70	0	0	0	3	0.0	2	0	11	0	–9	....	....	....	....	....	....	....	....
	Halifax Citadels	AHL	43	3	9	12	....	....	....	310	....	....	....	....	....	....	....	....	....	....	4	0	1	1	35	....	....	....
1989-90	**Quebec Nordiques**	**NHL**	13	0	0	0	0	0	0	57	0	0	0	4	0.0	3	0	12	1	–8	....	....	....	....	....	....	....	....
	Halifax Citadels	AHL	49	5	14	19	....	....	....	235	....	....	....	....	....	....	....	....	....	....	6	1	0	1	52	....	....	....
1990-91	**Quebec Nordiques**	**NHL**	1	0	0	0	0	0	0	0	0	0	0	0	0.0	0	0	0	0	0	....	....	....	....	....	....	....	....
	Halifax Citadels	AHL	56	6	23	29	....	....	....	340	....	....	....	....	....	....	....	....	....	....	....	....	....	....	....	....	....	....
1991-92	**Quebec Nordiques**	**NHL**	29	0	2	2	0	2	2	138	0	0	0	24	0.0	12	1	23	2	–10	....	....	....	....	....	....	....	....
	Halifax Citadels	AHL	9	1	3	4	....	....	....	35	....	....	....	....	....	....	....	....	....	....	....	....	....	....	....	....	....	....
	Calgary Flames	**NHL**	7	1	1	2	1	1	2	15	0	0	0	10	10.0	10	0	6	3	7	....	....	....	....	....	....	....	....
1992-93	**Calgary Flames**	**NHL**	35	1	2	3	1	1	2	95	1	0	0	14	7.1	15	1	13	1	2	....	....	....	....	....	....	....	....
	Salt Lake Golden Eagles	IHL	5	0	1	1	....	....	....	31	....	....	....	....	....	....	....	....	....	....	....	....	....	....	....	....	....	....
1993-94	**Florida Panthers**	**NHL**	12	1	0	1	1	0	1	37	0	0	0	4	25.0	2	0	2	0	0	....	....	....	....	....	....	....	....
	Toronto Maple Leafs	**NHL**	11	0	1	1	0	1	1	38	0	0	0	3	0.0	3	0	5	0	–2	....	....	....	....	....	....	....	....
	Chicago Blackhawks	**NHL**	38	0	0	0	0	0	0	108	0	0	0	29	0.0	19	2	22	3	–2	6	0	0	0	0	0	0	0
1994-95	**Chicago Blackhawks**	**NHL**	22	0	3	3	0	4	4	33	0	0	0	10	0.0	7	0	5	0	2	....	....	....	....	....	....	....	....
	Indianapolis Ice	IHL	2	0	0	0	....	....	....	0	....	....	....	....	....	....	....	....	....	....	....	....	....	....	....	....	....	....
1995-96	Chicago Wolves	IHL	15	1	3	4	....	....	....	53	....	....	....	....	....	....	....	....	....	....	....	....	....	....	....	....	....	....
	Los Angeles Ice Dogs	IHL	41	2	7	9	....	....	....	231	....	....	....	....	....	....	....	....	....	....	....	....	....	....	....	....	....	....
1996-97	**Toronto Maple Leafs**	**NHL**	2	0	0	0	0	0	0	0	0	0	0	1	0.0	0	0	1	1	0	....	....	....	....	....	....	....	....
	St. John's Maple Leafs	AHL	43	2	4	6	....	....	....	273	....	....	....	....	....	....	....	....	....	....	5	0	1	1	14	....	....	....
1997-98	St. John's Maple Leafs	AHL	63	5	6	11	....	....	....	353	....	....	....	....	....	....	....	....	....	....	4	0	1	1	6	....	....	....
1998-99	St. John's Maple Leafs	AHL	40	0	7	7	....	....	....	159	....	....	....	....	....	....	....	....	....	....	5	0	1	1	19	....	....	....
99-2000	St. John's Maple Leafs	AHL	DID NOT PLAY – ASSISTANT COACH																									
	London Knights	Britain	9	0	0	0	....	....	....	42	....	....	....	....	....	....	....	....	....	....	....	....	....	....	....	....	....	....
	NHL Totals		229	4	16	20	4	14	18	783	1	0	0	131	3.1	107	4	148	23		12	0	0	0	40	0	0	0

OHL Second All-Star Team (1986)

Traded to **Quebec** by **Philadelphia** with Philadelphia's 3rd round choice (John Tanner) in the 1989 Entry Draft for Terry Carkner, July 25, 1988. Traded to **Calgary** by **Quebec** for Martin Simard, March 10, 1992. Signed as a free agent by **Florida**, August 10, 1993. Traded to **Toronto** by **Florida** for cash, December 7, 1993. Claimed on waivers by **Chicago** from **Toronto**, January 8, 1994. Signed as a free agent by **Toronto**, August 22, 1996. • Named Assistant Coach of **St. John's** (AHL), August 20, 1999. • Resigned as Assistant Coach of **St. John's** (AHL), October 22, 1999.

• SMYTH, Kevin

Kevin J. LW – L. 6'2", 217 lbs. b: Banff, Alta., 11/22/1973. Hartford's 4th, 79th overall, in 1992.

Season	Club	League	GP	G	A	Pts	AG	AA	APts	PIM	PP	SH	GW	S	%	TGF	PGF	TGA	PGA	+/–	GP	G	A	Pts	PIM	PP	SH	GW
1989-90	Caronport Cougars	SAHA	18	20	37	57	....	....	....	15	....	....	....	....	....	....	....	....	....	....	....	....	....	....	....	....	....	....
1990-91	Moose Jaw Warriors	WHL	66	30	45	75	....	....	....	96	....	....	....	....	....	....	....	....	....	....	6	1	1	2	0	....	....	....
1991-92	Moose Jaw Warriors	WHL	71	30	55	85	....	....	....	84	....	....	....	....	....	....	....	....	....	....	4	1	3	4	6	....	....	....
1992-93	Moose Jaw Warriors	WHL	64	44	38	82	....	....	....	111	....	....	....	....	....	....	....	....	....	....	....	....	....	....	....	....	....	....
1993-94	**Hartford Whalers**	**NHL**	21	3	2	5	3	2	5	10	0	0	0	8	37.5	7	1	7	0	–1	....	....	....	....	....	....	....	....
	Springfield Indians	AHL	42	22	27	49	....	....	....	72	....	....	....	....	....	....	....	....	....	....	6	4	5	9	0	....	....	....
1994-95	Springfield Falcons	AHL	57	17	22	39	....	....	....	72	....	....	....	....	....	....	....	....	....	....	....	....	....	....	....	....	....	....
	Hartford Whalers	**NHL**	16	1	5	6	2	7	9	13	0	0	0	20	5.0	9	1	11	0	–3	....	....	....	....	....	....	....	....
1995-96	**Hartford Whalers**	**NHL**	21	2	1	3	2	1	3	8	1	0	0	27	7.4	5	1	9	0	–5	....	....	....	....	....	....	....	....
	Springfield Falcons	AHL	47	15	33	48	....	....	....	87	....	....	....	....	....	....	....	....	....	....	10	5	5	10	8	....	....	....
1996-97	Orlando Solar Bears	IHL	38	14	17	31	....	....	....	49	....	....	....	....	....	....	....	....	....	....	10	1	2	3	6	....	....	....
1997-98	Orlando Solar Bears	IHL	43	10	5	15	....	....	....	59	....	....	....	....	....	....	....	....	....	....	1	0	0	0	2	....	....	....
1998-99	Las Vegas Thunder	IHL	1	0	0	0	....	....	....	0	....	....	....	....	....	....	....	....	....	....	....	....	....	....	....	....	....	....
	Tacoma Sabercats	WCHL	42	25	21	46	....	....	....	83	....	....	....	....	....	....	....	....	....	....	11	7	13	20	10	....	....	....
	NHL Totals		58	6	8	14	7	10	17	31	1	0	0	55	10.9	21	3	27	0		....	....	....	....	....	....	....	....

• Brother of Ryan

Rights transferred to **Carolina** after **Hartford** franchise relocated, June 25, 1997. • Suffered NHL career-ending eye injury in game vs. Indianapolis (IHL), December 28, 1996.

• SMYTH, Ryan

LW – L. 6'1", 195 lbs. b: Banff, Alta., 2/21/1976. Edmonton's 2nd, 6th overall, in 1994.

Season	Club	League	GP	G	A	Pts	AG	AA	APts	PIM	PP	SH	GW	S	%	TGF	PGF	TGA	PGA	+/–	GP	G	A	Pts	PIM	PP	SH	GW
1990-91	Banff Bantam Blazers	AAHA	25	100	50	150	....	....	....	....	....	....	....	....	....	....	....	....	....	....	....	....	....	....	....	....	....	....
	Lethbridge Y's Men	AMHL	34	8	21	29	....	....	....	....	....	....	....	....	....	....	....	....	....	....	....	....	....	....	....	....	....	....
1991-92	Caronport Cougars	SAHA	35	55	61	116	....	....	....	98	....	....	....	....	....	....	....	....	....	....	....	....	....	....	....	....	....	....
	Moose Jaw Warriors	WHL	2	0	0	0	....	....	....	0	....	....	....	....	....	....	....	....	....	....	....	....	....	....	....	....	....	....
1992-93	Moose Jaw Warriors	WHL	64	19	14	33	....	....	....	59	....	....	....	....	....	....	....	....	....	....	....	....	....	....	....	....	....	....
1993-94	Moose Jaw Warriors	WHL	72	50	55	105	....	....	....	88	....	....	....	....	....	....	....	....	....	....	....	....	....	....	....	....	....	....
1994-95	Moose Jaw Warriors	WHL	50	41	45	86	....	....	....	66	....	....	....	....	....	....	....	....	....	....	10	6	9	15	22	....	....	....
	Canada	WJC-A	7	2	5	7	....	....	....	4	....	....	....	....	....	....	....	....	....	....	....	....	....	....	....	....	....	....
	Edmonton Oilers	**NHL**	3	0	0	0	0	0	0	0	0	0	0	2	0.0	0	0	1	0	–1	....	....	....	....	....	....	....	....
1995-96	**Edmonton Oilers**	**NHL**	48	2	9	11	2	7	9	28	1	0	0	65	3.1	18	1	27	0	–10	....	....	....	....	....	....	....	....
	Cape Breton Oilers	AHL	9	6	5	11	....	....	....	4	....	....	....	....	....	....	....	....	....	....	....	....	....	....	....	....	....	....
1996-97	**Edmonton Oilers**	**NHL**	82	39	22	61	41	20	61	76	20	0	4	265	14.7	92	40	62	3	–7	12	5	5	10	12	1	0	2
1997-98	**Edmonton Oilers**	**NHL**	65	20	13	33	23	13	36	44	10	0	2	205	9.8	51	29	46	0	–24	12	1	3	4	16	1	0	0
1998-99	**Edmonton Oilers**	**NHL**	71	13	18	31	15	17	32	62	6	0	2	161	8.1	58	26	32	0	0	3	3	0	3	0	2	0	0
	Canada	WC-A	10	0	2	2	....	....	....	12	....	....	....	....	....	....	....	....	....	....	....	....	....	....	....	....	....	....
99-2000	**Edmonton Oilers**	**NHL**	82	28	26	54	32	24	56	58	11	0	4	238	11.8	87	32	69	12	–2	5	1	0	1	6	0	1	0
	Canada	WC-A	9	3	6	9	....	....	....	0	....	....	....	....	....	....	....	....	....	....	....	....	....	....	....	....	....	....
	NHL Totals		351	102	88	190	113	81	194	268	48	0	12	936	10.9	306	128	237	15		32	10	8	18	34	4	1	2

• Brother of Kevin • WHL East Second All-Star Team (1995)

• SNELL, Chris

D – L. 5'11", 200 lbs. b: Regina, Sask., 5/12/1971. Buffalo's 8th, 145th overall, in 1991.

Season	Club	League	GP	G	A	Pts	AG	AA	APts	PIM	PP	SH	GW	S	%	TGF	PGF	TGA	PGA	+/–	GP	G	A	Pts	PIM	PP	SH	GW
1987-88	Oshawa Midget Generals	OMHA	79	21	67	88	....	....	....	113	....	....	....	....	....	....	....	....	....	....	....	....	....	....	....	....	....	....
1988-89	Ottawa 67's	OHL	66	11	48	59	....	....	....	16	....	....	....	....	....	....	....	....	....	....	....	....	....	....	....	....	....	....
1989-90	Ottawa 67's	OHL	63	18	62	80	....	....	....	36	....	....	....	....	....	....	....	....	....	....	3	2	4	6	4	....	....	....
1990-91	Ottawa 67's	OHL	54	23	59	82	....	....	....	58	....	....	....	....	....	....	....	....	....	....	17	3	14	17	8	....	....	....
	Canada	WJC-A	7	0	4	4	....	....	....	0																		

Season	Club	League	GP	G	A	Pts	AG	AA	APts	PIM	PP	SH	GW	S	%	TGF	PGF	TGA	PGA	+/–	GP	G	A	Pts	PIM	PP	SH	GW
			REGULAR SEASON																		PLAYOFFS							
1991-92	Rochester Americans	AHL	65	5	27	32	....	....	....	66	....	....	....	....	....	....	....	....	....	....	10	2	1	3	6	....	....	....
1992-93	Rochester Americans	AHL	76	14	57	71	....	....	....	83	....	....	....	....	....	....	....	....	....	....	17	5	8	13	39	....	....	....
1993-94	**Toronto Maple Leafs**	**NHL**	**2**	**0**	**0**	**0**	**0**	**0**	**0**	**2**	**0**	**0**	**0**	**4**	**0.0**	**0**	**0**	**1**	**0**	**–1**	....	....	....	....	....	....	....	....
	St. John's Maple Leafs	AHL	75	22	74	96	....	....	....	92	....	....	....	....	....	....	....	....	....	....	11	1	15	16	10	....	....	....
1994-95	Phoenix Roadrunners	IHL	57	15	49	64	....	....	....	122	....	....	....	....	....	....	....	....	....	....	....	....	....	....	....	....	....	....
	Los Angeles Kings	**NHL**	**32**	**2**	**7**	**9**	**4**	**10**	**14**	**22**	**0**	**2**	**0**	**45**	**4.4**	**20**	**8**	**25**	**6**	**–7**	....	....	....	....	....	....	....	....
1995-96	Phoenix Roadrunners	IHL	40	9	22	31	....	....	....	113	....	....	....	....	....	....	....	....	....	....	....	....	....	....	....	....	....	....
	Binghamton Rangers	AHL	32	7	25	32	....	....	....	48	....	....	....	....	....	....	....	....	....	....	4	2	2	4	6	....	....	....
1996-97	Indianapolis Ice	IHL	73	22	45	67	....	....	....	130	....	....	....	....	....	....	....	....	....	....	2	0	0	0	2	....	....	....
1997-98	Frankfurt Lions	Germany	44	13	23	36	....	....	....	161	....	....	....	....	....	....	....	....	....	....	7	3	2	5	22	....	....	....
1998-99	Frankfurt Lions	Germany	49	22	29	51	....	....	....	157	....	....	....	....	....	....	....	....	....	....	8	2	4	6	6	....	....	....
	Frankfurt Lions	EuroHL	6	1	4	5	....	....	....	55	....	....	....	....	....	....	....	....	....	....	....	....	....	....	....	....	....	....
99-2000	Frankfurt Lions	Germany	50	5	19	24	....	....	....	117	....	....	....	....	....	....	....	....	....	....	....	....	....	....	....	....	....	....
	NHL Totals		**34**	**2**	**7**	**9**	**4**	**10**	**14**	**24**	**0**	**2**	**0**	**49**	**4.1**	**20**	**8**	**26**	**6**		....	....	....	....	....	....	....	....

OHL First All-Star Team (1990, 1991) • AHL First All-Star Team (1994) • Eddie Shore Award (Top Defenseman - AHL) (1994) • IHL First All-Star Team (1995) • IHL Second All-Star Team (1997)

Signed as a free agent by **Toronto**, August 3, 1993. Traded to **LA Kings** by **Toronto** with Eric Lacroix and Toronto's 4th round choice (Eric Belanger) in 1996 Entry Draft for Dixon Ward, Guy Leveque and Kelly Fairchild, October 3, 1994. Traded to **NY Rangers** by **LA Kings** for Steve Larouche, January 14, 1996. Signed as a free agent by **Chicago**, August 16, 1996.

• SNELL, Ron

Ronald Wayne RW – R. 5'10", 158 lbs. b: Regina, Sask., 8/11/1948. Pittsburgh's 2nd, 14th overall, in 1968.

Season	Club	League	GP	G	A	Pts	AG	AA	APts	PIM	PP	SH	GW	S	%	TGF	PGF	TGA	PGA	+/–	GP	G	A	Pts	PIM	PP	SH	GW
1966-67	Regina Pats	CMJHL	56	24	29	53	....	....	....	43	....	....	....	....	....	....	....	....	....	....	16	11	6	17	4	....	....	....
1967-68	Regina Pats	WCJHL	60	56	55	111	....	....	....	86	....	....	....	....	....	....	....	....	....	....	4	3	4	7	0	....	....	....
1968-69	**Pittsburgh Penguins**	**NHL**	**4**	**3**	**1**	**4**	**3**	**1**	**4**	**6**	**2**	**0**	**1**	**9**	**33.3**	**6**	**2**	**0**	**0**	**4**	....	....	....	....	....	....	....	....
	Amarillo Wranglers	CHL	69	26	19	45	....	....	....	43	....	....	....	....	....	....	....	....	....	....	....	....	....	....	....	....	....	....
1969-70	**Pittsburgh Penguins**	**NHL**	**3**	**0**	**1**	**1**	**0**	**1**	**1**	**0**	**0**	**0**	**0**	**3**	**0.0**	**1**	**0**	**3**	**0**	**–2**	....	....	....	....	....	....	....	....
	Baltimore Clippers	AHL	68	24	29	53	....	....	....	40	....	....	....	....	....	....	....	....	....	....	5	0	0	0	2	....	....	....
1970-71	Amarillo Wranglers	CHL	72	25	22	47	....	....	....	69	....	....	....	....	....	....	....	....	....	....	....	....	....	....	....	....	....	....
1971-72	Hershey Bears	AHL	76	22	31	53	....	....	....	29	....	....	....	....	....	....	....	....	....	....	4	0	1	1	12	....	....	....
1972-73	Hershey Bears	AHL	75	33	38	71	....	....	....	90	....	....	....	....	....	....	....	....	....	....	7	1	5	6	4	....	....	....
1973-74	Winnipeg Jets	WHA	70	24	25	49	....	....	....	32	....	....	....	....	....	....	....	....	....	....	4	0	0	0	0	....	....	....
1974-75	Winnipeg Jets	WHA	20	0	0	0	....	....	....	8	....	....	....	....	....	....	....	....	....	....	....	....	....	....	....	....	....	....
	Cape Cod Codders	NAHL	25	17	12	29	....	....	....	49	....	....	....	....	....	....	....	....	....	....	....	....	....	....	....	....	....	....
1975-76	Cape Cod Codders	NAHL	33	26	26	52	....	....	....	24	....	....	....	....	....	....	....	....	....	....	....	....	....	....	....	....	....	....
	Buffalo Norsemen	NAHL	3	1	2	3	....	....	....	2	....	....	....	....	....	....	....	....	....	....	....	....	....	....	....	....	....	....
	Rochester Americans	AHL	37	10	12	22	....	....	....	13	....	....	....	....	....	....	....	....	....	....	2	0	0	0	6	....	....	....
	NHL Totals		**7**	**3**	**2**	**5**	**3**	**2**	**5**	**6**	**2**	**0**	**1**	**12**	**25.0**	**7**	**2**	**3**	**0**		....	....	....	....	....	....	....	....
	Other Major League Totals		90	24	25	49	....	....	....	40	....	....	....	....	....	....	....	....	....	....	4	0	0	0	0	....	....	....

Selected by **Winnipeg** (WHA) in 1972 WHA General Player Draft, February 12, 1972. Traded to **Hershey** (AHL) by **Pittsburgh** for cash, June, 1973.

• SNELL, Ted

Harold Edward RW – R. 5'9", 190 lbs. b: Ottawa, Ont., 5/28/1946.

Season	Club	League	GP	G	A	Pts	AG	AA	APts	PIM	PP	SH	GW	S	%	TGF	PGF	TGA	PGA	+/–	GP	G	A	Pts	PIM	PP	SH	GW
1962-63	Niagara Falls Flyers	OHA-Jr.	50	20	20	40	....	....	....	17	....	....	....	....	....	....	....	....	....	....	9	0	3	3	2	....	....	....
	Niagara Falls Flyers	Mem-Cup	17	7	6	13	....	....	....	4	....	....	....	....	....	....	....	....	....	....	....	....	....	....	....	....	....	....
1963-64	Niagara Falls Flyers	OHA-Jr.	56	13	27	40	....	....	....	43	....	....	....	....	....	....	....	....	....	....	4	0	1	1	12	....	....	....
1964-65	Niagara Falls Flyers	OHA-Jr.	56	26	23	49	....	....	....	26	....	....	....	....	....	....	....	....	....	....	11	3	7	10	10	....	....	....
	Niagara Falls Flyers	Mem-Cup	13	4	14	18	....	....	....	8	....	....	....	....	....	....	....	....	....	....	....	....	....	....	....	....	....	....
1965-66	Niagara Falls Flyers	OHA-Jr.	47	18	25	43	....	....	....	73	....	....	....	....	....	....	....	....	....	....	6	2	1	3	4	....	....	....
	Hershey Bears	AHL	4	1	0	1	....	....	....	2	....	....	....	....	....	....	....	....	....	....	....	....	....	....	....	....	....	....
	Oklahoma City Blazers	CHL	....	....	....	....	....	....	....	....	....	....	....	....	....	....	....	....	....	....	1	0	0	0	0	....	....	....
1966-67	Hershey Bears	AHL	34	4	8	12	....	....	....	4	....	....	....	....	....	....	....	....	....	....	1	0	0	0	0	....	....	....
1967-68	Hershey Bears	AHL	67	11	29	40	....	....	....	23	....	....	....	....	....	....	....	....	....	....	5	0	0	0	0	....	....	....
1968-69	Phoenix Roadrunners	WHL	54	6	9	15	....	....	....	25	....	....	....	....	....	....	....	....	....	....	....	....	....	....	....	....	....	....
	Hershey Bears	AHL	20	4	5	9	....	....	....	4	....	....	....	....	....	....	....	....	....	....	11	4	5	9	2	....	....	....
1969-70	Hershey Bears	AHL	58	12	23	35	....	....	....	24	....	....	....	....	....	....	....	....	....	....	7	3	4	7	0	....	....	....
1970-71	Hershey Bears	AHL	72	12	28	40	....	....	....	13	....	....	....	....	....	....	....	....	....	....	4	1	0	1	0	....	....	....
1971-72	Hershey Bears	AHL	68	12	18	30	....	....	....	4	....	....	....	....	....	....	....	....	....	....	4	0	0	0	2	....	....	....
1972-73	Hershey Bears	AHL	72	29	35	64	....	....	....	23	....	....	....	....	....	....	....	....	....	....	6	0	3	3	0	....	....	....
1973-74	**Pittsburgh Penguins**	**NHL**	**55**	**4**	**12**	**16**	**4**	**10**	**14**	**8**	**0**	**0**	**0**	**64**	**6.3**	**19**	**1**	**62**	**22**	**–22**	....	....	....	....	....	....	....	....
1974-75	**Kansas City Scouts**	**NHL**	**29**	**3**	**2**	**5**	**3**	**1**	**4**	**8**	**0**	**1**	**0**	**25**	**12.0**	**9**	**0**	**37**	**20**	**–8**	....	....	....	....	....	....	....	....
	Detroit Red Wings	**NHL**	**20**	**0**	**4**	**4**	**0**	**3**	**3**	**6**	**0**	**0**	**0**	**12**	**0.0**	**12**	**5**	**17**	**0**	**–10**	....	....	....	....	....	....	....	....
	Virginia Wings	AHL	24	5	3	8	....	....	....	17	....	....	....	....	....	....	....	....	....	....	5	1	0	1	0	....	....	....
1975-76	Hershey Bears	AHL	74	4	15	19	....	....	....	24	....	....	....	....	....	....	....	....	....	....	10	0	0	0	0	....	....	....
	NHL Totals		**104**	**7**	**18**	**25**	**7**	**14**	**21**	**22**	**0**	**1**	**0**	**101**	**6.9**	**40**	**6**	**116**	**42**		....	....	....	....	....	....	....	....

Claimed by **Springfield** (AHL) from **Boston** in Reverse Draft, June 13, 1968. Traded to **Phoenix** (WHL) by **Springfield** (AHL) for cash, June, 1968. Traded to **Hershey** (AHL) by **Phoenix** (WHL) for cash, October, 1969. Signed as a free agent by **Pittsburgh**, October, 1973. Claimed by **Kansas City** from **Pittsburgh** in Expansion Draft, June 12, 1974. Traded to **Detroit** by **Kansas City** with Bart Crashley and Larry Giroux for Guy Charron and Claude Houde, December 14, 1974.

• SNEPSTS, Harold

Harold John D – L. 6'3", 210 lbs. b: Edmonton, Alta., 10/24/1954. Vancouver's 3rd, 59th overall, in 1974.

Season	Club	League	GP	G	A	Pts	AG	AA	APts	PIM	PP	SH	GW	S	%	TGF	PGF	TGA	PGA	+/–	GP	G	A	Pts	PIM	PP	SH	GW
1972-73	Edmonton Oil Kings	WCJHL	68	2	24	26	....	....	....	155	....	....	....	....	....	....	....	....	....	....	11	0	1	1	54	....	....	....
1973-74	Edmonton Oil Kings	WCJHL	68	8	41	49	....	....	....	239	....	....	....	....	....	....	....	....	....	....	....	....	....	....	....	....	....	....
1974-75	**Vancouver Canucks**	**NHL**	**27**	**1**	**2**	**3**	**1**	**1**	**2**	**30**	**0**	**1**	**0**	**18**	**5.6**	**14**	**2**	**16**	**4**	**0**	....	....	....	....	....	....	....	....
	Seattle Totems	CHL	19	1	6	7	....	....	....	58	....	....	....	....	....	....	....	....	....	....	....	....	....	....	....	....	....	....
1975-76	**Vancouver Canucks**	**NHL**	**78**	**3**	**15**	**18**	**3**	**11**	**14**	**125**	**0**	**0**	**1**	**74**	**4.1**	**80**	**4**	**93**	**27**	**10**	**2**	**0**	**0**	**0**	**4**	**0**	**0**	**0**
1976-77	**Vancouver Canucks**	**NHL**	**79**	**4**	**18**	**22**	**4**	**14**	**18**	**149**	**0**	**0**	**1**	**101**	**4.0**	**85**	**2**	**112**	**24**	**–5**	....	....	....	....	....	....	....	....
1977-78	**Vancouver Canucks**	**NHL**	**75**	**4**	**16**	**20**	**4**	**12**	**16**	**118**	**0**	**0**	**0**	**95**	**4.2**	**71**	**0**	**115**	**28**	**–16**	....	....	....	....	....	....	....	....
1978-79	**Vancouver Canucks**	**NHL**	**76**	**7**	**24**	**31**	**6**	**17**	**23**	**130**	**4**	**0**	**0**	**115**	**6.1**	**84**	**20**	**123**	**32**	**–27**	**3**	**0**	**0**	**0**	**0**	**0**	**0**	**0**
1979-80	**Vancouver Canucks**	**NHL**	**79**	**3**	**20**	**23**	**3**	**15**	**18**	**202**	**0**	**0**	**0**	**103**	**2.9**	**90**	**6**	**111**	**34**	**7**	**4**	**0**	**2**	**2**	**8**	**0**	**0**	**0**
1980-81	**Vancouver Canucks**	**NHL**	**76**	**3**	**16**	**19**	**2**	**11**	**13**	**212**	**0**	**0**	**1**	**77**	**3.9**	**79**	**2**	**126**	**52**	**3**	**3**	**0**	**0**	**0**	**8**	**0**	**0**	**0**
1981-82	**Vancouver Canucks**	**NHL**	**68**	**3**	**14**	**17**	**2**	**9**	**11**	**153**	**0**	**0**	**0**	**69**	**4.3**	**89**	**0**	**101**	**34**	**22**	**17**	**0**	**4**	**4**	**50**	**0**	**0**	**0**
1982-83	**Vancouver Canucks**	**NHL**	**46**	**2**	**8**	**10**	**2**	**6**	**8**	**80**	**0**	**1**	**1**	**40**	**5.0**	**31**	**0**	**71**	**23**	**–17**	**4**	**1**	**1**	**2**	**8**	**0**	**0**	**0**
1983-84	**Vancouver Canucks**	**NHL**	**79**	**4**	**16**	**20**	**3**	**11**	**14**	**152**	**0**	**0**	**0**	**77**	**5.2**	**59**	**0**	**119**	**41**	**–19**	**4**	**0**	**1**	**1**	**15**	**0**	**0**	**0**
1984-85	**Minnesota North Stars**	**NHL**	**71**	**0**	**7**	**7**	**0**	**5**	**5**	**232**	**0**	**0**	**0**	**50**	**0.0**	**44**	**1**	**90**	**28**	**–19**	**9**	**0**	**0**	**0**	**24**	**0**	**0**	**0**
1985-86	**Detroit Red Wings**	**NHL**	**35**	**0**	**6**	**6**	**0**	**4**	**4**	**75**	**0**	**0**	**0**	**12**	**0.0**	**20**	**0**	**43**	**16**	**–7**	....	....	....	....	....	....	....	....
1986-87	**Detroit Red Wings**	**NHL**	**54**	**1**	**13**	**14**	**1**	**9**	**10**	**129**	**0**	**0**	**0**	**38**	**2.6**	**46**	**0**	**56**	**17**	**7**	**11**	**0**	**2**	**2**	**18**	**0**	**0**	**0**
1987-88	**Detroit Red Wings**	**NHL**	**31**	**1**	**4**	**5**	**1**	**3**	**4**	**67**	**0**	**0**	**0**	**20**	**5.0**	**27**	**0**	**29**	**5**	**3**	**10**	**0**	**0**	**0**	**40**	**0**	**0**	**0**
	Adirondack Red Wings	AHL	3	0	2	2	....	....	....	14	....	....	....	....	....	....	....	....	....	....	....	....	....	....	....	....	....	....
1988-89	**Vancouver Canucks**	**NHL**	**59**	**0**	**8**	**8**	**0**	**6**	**6**	**69**	**0**	**0**	**0**	**27**	**0.0**	**21**	**0**	**54**	**30**	**–3**	**7**	**0**	**1**	**1**	**6**	**0**	**0**	**0**
1989-90	**Vancouver Canucks**	**NHL**	**39**	**1**	**3**	**4**	**1**	**2**	**3**	**26**	**1**	**0**	**1**	**13**	**7.7**	**16**	**1**	**39**	**27**	**3**	....	....	....	....	....	....	....	....
	St. Louis Blues	**NHL**	**7**	**0**	**1**	**1**	**0**	**1**	**1**	**10**	**0**	**0**	**0**	**2**	**0.0**	**3**	**0**	**10**	**3**	**–4**	**11**	**0**	**3**	**3**	**38**	**0**	**0**	**0**
1990-91	**St. Louis Blues**	**NHL**	**54**	**1**	**4**	**5**	**1**	**3**	**4**	**50**	**0**	**0**	**1**	**33**	**3.0**	**37**	**0**	**48**	**14**	**3**	**8**	**0**	**0**	**0**	**12**	**0**	**0**	**0**
	NHL Totals		**1033**	**38**	**195**	**233**	**34**	**140**	**174**	**2009**	**5**	**2**	**6**	**964**	**3.9**	**896**	**38**	**1356**	**439**		**93**	**1**	**14**	**15**	**231**	**0**	**0**	**0**

Played in NHL All-Star Game (1977, 1982)

Traded to **Minnesota** by **Vancouver** for Al MacAdam, June 21, 1984. Signed as a free agent by **Detroit**, July 31, 1985. Signed as a free agent by **Vancouver**, October 6, 1988. Traded to **St. Louis** by **Vancouver** with Rich Sutter and St. Louis' 2nd round choice (Craig Johnson) in 1990 Entry Draft for Adrien Plavsic, Montreal's 1st round choice (previously acquired, Vancouver selected Shawn Antoski) in 1990 Entry Draft and St. Louis' 2nd round choice (later traded to Montreal — Montreal selected Craig Darby) in 1991 Entry Draft, March 6, 1990.

• SNOW, Sandy William Alexander RW – R. 6', 175 lbs. b: Glace Bay, N.S., 11/11/1946.

Season	Club	League	GP	G	A	Pts	AG	AA	APts	PIM	PP	SH	GW	S	%	TGF	PGF	TGA	PGA	+/–	GP	G	A	Pts	PIM	PP	SH	GW
			REGULAR SEASON																		PLAYOFFS							
1963-64	Hamilton Red Wings	OHA-Jr.	41	11	15	26				17																		
1964-65	Weyburn Red Wings	SJHL	49	46	30	76				35											15	*13	10	23	24			
1965-66	Hamilton Red Wings	OHA-Jr.	46	22	25	47				64											5	2	0	2	0			
	Memphis Wings	CPHL	4	0	1	1				0																		
1966-67	Hamilton Red Wings	OHA-Jr.	48	13	20	33				52											8	1	1	2	8			
1967-68	Fort Worth Wings	CPHL	56	13	13	26				17											11	1	2	3	4			
1968-69	**Detroit Red Wings**	**NHL**	**3**	**0**	**0**	**0**	**0**	**0**	**0**	**2**	**0**	**0**	**0**	**1**	**0.0**	**0**	**0**	**0**	**0**	**0**								
	Fort Worth Wings	CHL	60	13	21	34				19																		
1969-70	Phoenix Roadrunners	WHL	72	17	14	31				10																		
1970-71	Phoenix Roadrunners	WHL	11	1	0	1				5																		
	Kansas City Blues	CHL	12	2	4	6				2																		
	Flint Generals	IHL	26	7	23	30				4											7	3	4	7	0			
1971-72	Flint Generals	IHL	55	30	27	57				8											4	0	2	2	0			
1972-73	Flint Generals	IHL	63	28	35	63				12											2	1	0	1	0			
1973-74	Brantford Forresters	OHA-Sr.	9	3	2	5				0																		
	NHL Totals		**3**	**0**	**0**	**0**	**0**	**0**	**0**	**2**	**0**	**0**	**0**	**1**	**0.0**	**0**	**0**	**0**	**0**									

Traded to **NY Rangers** by **Detroit** with Terry Sawchuk for Larry Jeffrey, June 17, 1969. Traded to **Phoenix** (WHL) by **NY Rangers** with Don Caley for Peter McDuffe, July 3, 1969. Traded to **Kansas City** (CHL) by **Phoenix** (WHL) for cash, December, 1970.

• SNUGGERUD, Dave David W. RW – L. 6', 190 lbs. b: Minnetonka, MN, 6/20/1966. Buffalo's 1st, 1st overall, in 1987 Supplemental Draft.

Season	Club	League	GP	G	A	Pts	AG	AA	APts	PIM	PP	SH	GW	S	%	TGF	PGF	TGA	PGA	+/–	GP	G	A	Pts	PIM	PP	SH	GW
1983-84	Hopkins Royals	Hi-School	17	10	19	29				30																		
1984-85	Minnesota Jr. North Stars	USHL	48	38	35	73				26																		
1985-86	University of Minnesota	WCHA	42	14	18	32				47																		
1986-87	University of Minnesota	WCHA	39	30	29	59				38																		
1987-88	United States	Nat-Team	51	14	21	35				26																		
	United States	Olympics	6	3	2	5				4																		
1988-89	University of Minnesota	WCHA	45	29	20	49				39																		
	United States	WEC-A	10	4	1	5				2																		
1989-90	**Buffalo Sabres**	**NHL**	**80**	**14**	**16**	**30**	**12**	**11**	**23**	**41**	**1**	**2**	**2**	**120**	**11.7**	**53**	**4**	**69**	**28**	**8**	**6**	**0**	**0**	**0**	**2**	**0**	**0**	**0**
1990-91	**Buffalo Sabres**	**NHL**	**80**	**9**	**15**	**24**	**8**	**11**	**19**	**32**	**0**	**4**	**2**	**128**	**7.0**	**46**	**2**	**91**	**34**	**–13**	**6**	**1**	**3**	**4**	**4**	**0**	**1**	**0**
1991-92	**Buffalo Sabres**	**NHL**	**55**	**3**	**15**	**18**	**3**	**11**	**14**	**36**	**0**	**0**	**0**	**75**	**4.0**	**28**	**3**	**53**	**25**	**–3**								
	San Jose Sharks	**NHL**	**11**	**0**	**1**	**1**	**0**	**1**	**1**	**4**	**0**	**0**	**0**	**19**	**0.0**	**3**	**0**	**20**	**5**	**–12**								
1992-93	**San Jose Sharks**	**NHL**	**25**	**4**	**5**	**9**	**3**	**3**	**6**	**14**	**0**	**1**	**1**	**51**	**7.8**	**13**	**0**	**32**	**16**	**–3**								
	Philadelphia Flyers	**NHL**	**14**	**0**	**2**	**2**	**0**	**1**	**1**	**0**	**0**	**0**	**0**	**10**	**0.0**	**2**	**0**	**3**	**1**	**0**								
1993-94			OUT OF HOCKEY – RETIRED																									
1994-95	Minnesota Moose	IHL	72	25	23	48				57											3	0	1	1	2			
1995-2000	Chaska Hawks	Hi-School	DID NOT PLAY – COACHING																									
	NHL Totals		**265**	**30**	**54**	**84**	**26**	**38**	**64**	**127**	**1**	**7**	**5**	**403**	**7.4**	**145**	**9**	**268**	**109**		**12**	**1**	**3**	**4**	**6**	**0**	**1**	**0**

WCHA Second All-Star Team (1989)

Traded to **San Jose** by **Buffalo** for Wayne Presley, March 9, 1992. Traded to **Philadelphia** by **San Jose** for Mark Pederson and future considerations, December 19, 1992. • Officially announced retirement and returned to University of Minnesota to complete BBA degree, September, 1993.

• SOBCHUK, Dennis Dennis James C – L. 6'2", 176 lbs. b: Lang, Sask., 1/12/1954. Philadelphia's 4th, 89th overall, in 1974.

Season	Club	League	GP	G	A	Pts	AG	AA	APts	PIM	PP	SH	GW	S	%	TGF	PGF	TGA	PGA	+/–	GP	G	A	Pts	PIM	PP	SH	GW
1970-71	Weyburn Red Wings	SJHL	STATISTICS NOT AVAILABLE																									
	Estevan Bruins	WCJHL	8	1	1	2				14																		
1971-72	Regina Pats	WCJHL	68	56	67	123				115											15	9	*18	*27	50			
1972-73	Regina Pats	WCJHL	66	67	80	147				128											4	3	3	6	28			
1973-74	Regina Pats	WCJHL	66	68	78	146				78											16	10	21	*31	20			
	Regina Pats	Mem-Cup	3	3	4	7				11																		
1974-75	Phoenix Roadrunners	WHA	78	32	45	77				36											5	4	1	5	2			
1975-76	Cincinnati Stingers	WHA	79	32	40	72				74																		
1976-77	Cincinnati Stingers	WHA	81	44	52	96				38											3	0	1	1	2			
1977-78	Cincinnati Stingers	WHA	23	5	9	14				22																		
	Edmonton Oilers	WHA	13	6	3	9				4											5	1	0	1	4			
1978-79	Edmonton Oilers	WHA	74	26	37	63				31											12	6	6	12	4			
1979-80	**Detroit Red Wings**	**NHL**	**33**	**4**	**6**	**10**	**3**	**4**	**7**	**0**	**0**	**0**	**0**	**47**	**8.5**	**13**	**3**	**21**	**0**	**–11**								
	Adirondack Red Wings	AHL	15	6	4	10				6											4	0	1	1	0			
1980-81	Birmingham Bulls	CHL	5	1	3	4				0																		
	EV Zug	Switz-2	STATISTICS NOT AVAILABLE																									
1981-82	IEV Innsbruck	Austria	STATISTICS NOT AVAILABLE																									
1982-83	Moncton Alpines	AHL	20	5	12	17				0																		
	Fredericton Express	AHL	29	12	17	29				2											12	8	4	12	10			
	Quebec Nordiques	**NHL**	**2**	**1**	**0**	**1**	**1**	**0**	**1**	**2**	**0**	**0**	**0**	**2**	**50.0**	**1**	**0**	**0**	**0**	**1**								
1983-84	IEV Innsbruck	Austria-2	STATISTICS NOT AVAILABLE																									
	NHL Totals		**35**	**5**	**6**	**11**	**4**	**4**	**8**	**2**	**0**	**0**	**0**	**49**	**10.2**	**14**	**3**	**21**	**0**									
	Other Major League Totals		348	145	186	331				205											25	11	8	19	12			

• Brother of Gene • WCJHL Second All-Star Team (1972) • WCJHL First All-Star Team (1974)

Signed as a free agent by **Cincinnati** (WHA), April, 1973. Loaned to **Phoenix** (WHA) by **Cincinnati** (WHA) for 1974-75 season, June, 1974. Traded to **Edmonton** (WHA) by **Cincinnati** (WHA) for the rights to Dave Debol and draft choices (later voided), December, 1977. Reclaimed by **Philadelphia** from **Edmonton** prior to Expansion Draft, June 9, 1979. Traded to **Detroit** by **Philadelphia** for Detroit's 5th round choice (Dave Michayluk) in 1981 Entry Draft, September 4, 1979. Signed as a free agent by **Quebec**, March 7, 1982. • Only combined totals (51-42-53-95-40) available for IEV Innsbruck (Austria) in 1981-82 and 1983-84 seasons.

• SOBCHUK, Gene Eugene LW/C – L. 5'9", 160 lbs. b: Lang, Sask., 2/19/1951. NY Rangers' 10th, 109th overall, in 1971.

Season	Club	League	GP	G	A	Pts	AG	AA	APts	PIM	PP	SH	GW	S	%	TGF	PGF	TGA	PGA	+/–	GP	G	A	Pts	PIM	PP	SH	GW
1969-70	Weyburn Red Wings	SJHL	45	22	*36	58				28																		
	Weyburn Red Wings	Mem-Cup	22	6	14	20				15																		
1970-71	Regina Pats	WCJHL	66	17	37	54				74											6	3	2	5	2			
1971-72	Des Moines Oak Leafs	IHL	56	16	18	34				16																		
1972-73	Rochester Americans	AHL	58	22	16	38				29											6	1	4	5	4			
1973-74	**Vancouver Canucks**	**NHL**	**1**	**0**	**0**	**0**	**0**	**0**	**0**	**0**	**0**	**0**	**0**	**0**	**0.0**	**0**	**0**	**0**	**0**	**0**								
	Seattle Totems	WHL	55	15	19	34				30																		
	Virginia Wings	AHL	18	12	5	17				14																		
1974-75	Phoenix Roadrunners	WHA	3	1	0	1				0																		
	Tulsa Oilers	CHL	73	35	28	63				65											2	1	0	1	2			
1975-76	Cincinnati Stingers	WHA	78	23	19	42				37																		
1976-77	Oklahoma City Blazers	CHL	29	4	11	15				6																		
	Springfield Indians	AHL	3	1	0	1				0																		
1977-78	Hampton Gulls	AHL	37	3	5	8				2																		
1978-79			OUT OF HOCKEY – RETIRED																									
1979-1983	Lang Knights	SAHA-I	STATISTICS NOT AVAILABLE																									
1983-1984	Milestone Flyers	SAHA-I	STATISTICS NOT AVAILABLE																									
	NHL Totals		**1**	**0**	**0**	**0**	**0**	**0**	**0**	**0**	**0**	**0**	**0**	**0**	**0.0**	**0**	**0**	**0**	**0**									
	Other Major League Totals		81	24	19	43				37																		

• Brother of Dennis

Selected by **LA Sharks** (WHA) in 1972 WHA General Player Draft, February 12, 1972. Claimed by **Vancouver** (Seattle-WHL) from **Vancouver** in Reverse Draft, June, 1973. Traded to **Detroit** (Virginia-AHL) by **Seattle** (WHL) for Ken Murray, February 18, 1974. Claimed by **Cincinnati** (WHA) from **LA Sharks** (WHA) prior to WHA Expansion Draft, June, 1974. Loaned to **Phoenix** (WHA) by **Cincinnati** (WHA) for 1974-75 season, June, 1974.

• SOLHEIM, Ken

Ken Lawrence LW – L. 6'3", 210 lbs. b: Hythe, Alta., 3/27/1961. Chicago's 4th, 30th overall, in 1980.

			REGULAR SEASON																		PLAYOFFS							
Season	Club	League	GP	G	A	Pts	AG	AA	APts	PIM	PP	SH	GW	S	%	TGF	PGF	TGA	PGA	+/–	GP	G	A	Pts	PIM	PP	SH	GW
1977-78	St. Albert Saints	AJHL	60	26	16	42	....	....	....	31	....	....	....	....	....	....	....	....	....	....	....	....	....	....	....	....	....	....
	Medicine Hat Tigers	WCJHL	....	....	....	....	....	....	....	....	....	....	....	....	....	....	....	....	....	....	7	0	0	0	0	....	....	....
1978-79	St. Albert Saints	AJHL	60	47	42	89	....	....	....	91	....	....	....	....	....	....	....	....	....	....	....	....	....	....	....	....	....	....
1979-80	Medicine Hat Tigers	WHL	72	54	33	87	....	....	....	50	....	....	....	....	....	....	....	....	....	....	13	1	6	7	16	....	....	....
1980-81	Medicine Hat Tigers	WHL	64	*68	43	111	....	....	....	87	....	....	....	....	....	....	....	....	....	....	5	5	4	9	2	....	....	....
	Chicago Black Hawks	**NHL**	**5**	**2**	**0**	**2**	**2**	**0**	**2**	**0**	**0**	**0**	**0**	**8**	**25.0**	**2**	**0**	**5**	**0**	**–3**	....	....	....	....	....	....	....	....
	Minnesota North Stars	**NHL**	**5**	**2**	**1**	**3**	**2**	**1**	**3**	**0**	**0**	**0**	**0**	**9**	**22.2**	**4**	**0**	**1**	**0**	**3**	**2**	**1**	**0**	**1**	**0**	**0**	**0**	**0**
1981-82	**Minnesota North Stars**	**NHL**	**29**	**4**	**5**	**9**	**3**	**3**	**6**	**4**	**2**	**0**	**2**	**46**	**8.7**	**17**	**3**	**22**	**0**	**–8**	**1**	**0**	**1**	**1**	**2**	**0**	**0**	**0**
	Nashville South Stars	CHL	44	23	18	41	....	....	....	40	....	....	....	....	....	....	....	....	....	....	....	....	....	....	....	....	....	....
1982-83	**Minnesota North Stars**	**NHL**	**25**	**2**	**4**	**6**	**2**	**3**	**5**	**4**	**0**	**0**	**1**	**34**	**5.9**	**11**	**0**	**10**	**0**	**1**	....	....	....	....	....	....	....	....
	Detroit Red Wings	**NHL**	**10**	**0**	**0**	**0**	**0**	**0**	**0**	**2**	**0**	**0**	**0**	**5**	**0.0**	**0**	**0**	**2**	**0**	**–2**	....	....	....	....	....	....	....	....
	Birmingham South Stars	CHL	22	14	3	17	....	....	....	4	....	....	....	....	....	....	....	....	....	....	....	....	....	....	....	....	....	....
1983-84	Adirondack Red Wings	AHL	61	24	20	44	....	....	....	13	....	....	....	....	....	....	....	....	....	....	7	1	1	2	0	....	....	....
1984-85	**Minnesota North Stars**	**NHL**	**55**	**8**	**10**	**18**	**6**	**7**	**13**	**19**	**4**	**0**	**1**	**87**	**9.2**	**33**	**17**	**32**	**1**	**–15**	....	....	....	....	....	....	....	....
	Springfield Indians	AHL	17	6	8	14	....	....	....	0	....	....	....	....	....	....	....	....	....	....	4	2	0	2	2	....	....	....
1985-86	**Edmonton Oilers**	**NHL**	**6**	**1**	**0**	**1**	**1**	**0**	**1**	**5**	**0**	**0**	**0**	**8**	**12.5**	**4**	**0**	**6**	**0**	**–2**	....	....	....	....	....	....	....	....
	Nova Scotia Oilers	AHL	71	19	27	46	....	....	....	45	....	....	....	....	....	....	....	....	....	....	....	....	....	....	....	....	....	....
	NHL Totals		**135**	**19**	**20**	**39**	**16**	**14**	**30**	**34**	**6**	**0**	**4**	**197**	**9.6**	**71**	**20**	**78**	**1**		**3**	**1**	**1**	**2**	**2**	**0**	**0**	**0**

WHL All-Star Team (1981)

Traded to **Minnesota** by **Chicago** with Chicago's 2nd round choice (Tom Hirsch) in 1981 Entry Draft for Glen Sharpley, December 29, 1980. Traded to **Detroit** by **Minnesota** for future considerations, March 8, 1983. Traded to **Minnesota** by **Detroit** for future considerations, September 20, 1984. Signed as a free agent by **Edmonton**, August 15, 1985.

• SOMMER, Roy

LW/C – L. 6', 185 lbs. b: Oakland, CA, 4/5/1957. Toronto's 7th, 101st overall, in 1977.

			REGULAR SEASON																		PLAYOFFS							
Season	Club	League	GP	G	A	Pts	AG	AA	APts	PIM	PP	SH	GW	S	%	TGF	PGF	TGA	PGA	+/–	GP	G	A	Pts	PIM	PP	SH	GW
1973-74	Slyline High School	Hi-School	STATISTICS NOT AVAILABLE																									
1974-75	Spruce Grove Mets	AJHL	85	20	21	41	....	....	....	200	....	....	....	....	....	....	....	....	....	....	....	....	....	....	....	....	....	....
	Edmonton Oil Kings	WHL	1	0	0	0	....	....	....	5	....	....	....	....	....	....	....	....	....	....	....	....	....	....	....	....	....	....
	Spruce Grove Mets	Cen-Cup	STATISTICS NOT AVAILABLE																									
1975-76	Calgary Centennials	WCJHL	70	13	24	37	....	....	....	155	....	....	....	....	....	....	....	....	....	....	....	....	....	....	....	....	....	....
1976-77	Calgary Centennials	WCJHL	50	16	22	38	....	....	....	111	....	....	....	....	....	....	....	....	....	....	9	5	9	14	8	....	....	....
1977-78	Saginaw Gears	IHL	12	2	3	5	....	....	....	2	....	....	....	....	....	....	....	....	....	....	....	....	....	....	....	....	....	....
	Grand Rapids Owls	IHL	45	20	18	38	....	....	....	67	....	....	....	....	....	....	....	....	....	....	....	....	....	....	....	....	....	....
1978-79	Spokane Flyers	PHL	45	19	30	49	....	....	....	196	....	....	....	....	....	....	....	....	....	....	....	....	....	....	....	....	....	....
1979-80	Grand Rapids Owls	IHL	9	1	4	5	....	....	....	32	....	....	....	....	....	....	....	....	....	....	....	....	....	....	....	....	....	....
	Houston Apollos	CHL	69	24	31	55	....	....	....	246	....	....	....	....	....	....	....	....	....	....	6	2	2	4	8	....	....	....
1980-81	**Edmonton Oilers**	**NHL**	**3**	**1**	**0**	**1**	**1**	**0**	**1**	**7**	**0**	**0**	**0**	**1**	**100.0**	**1**	**0**	**1**	**0**	**0**	....	....	....	....	....	....	....	....
	Wichita Wind	CHL	57	13	22	35	....	....	....	212	....	....	....	....	....	....	....	....	....	....	14	3	2	5	61	....	....	....
1981-82	Wichita Wind	CHL	76	17	28	45	....	....	....	193	....	....	....	....	....	....	....	....	....	....	....	....	....	....	....	....	....	....
1982-83	Wichita Wind	CHL	73	22	39	61	....	....	....	130	....	....	....	....	....	....	....	....	....	....	....	....	....	....	....	....	....	....
1983-84	Maine Mariners	AHL	67	7	10	17	....	....	....	202	....	....	....	....	....	....	....	....	....	....	14	6	1	7	24	....	....	....
1984-85	Maine Mariners	AHL	80	12	13	25	....	....	....	175	....	....	....	....	....	....	....	....	....	....	11	4	2	6	27	....	....	....
1985-86	Indianapolis Checkers	IHL	37	9	10	19	....	....	....	118	....	....	....	....	....	....	....	....	....	....	....	....	....	....	....	....	....	....
	Muskegon Lumberjacks	IHL	27	5	8	13	....	....	....	109	....	....	....	....	....	....	....	....	....	....	12	2	4	6	*92	....	....	....
1986-87	Muskegon Lumberjacks	IHL	65	14	13	27	....	....	....	219	....	....	....	....	....	....	....	....	....	....	15	3	3	6	44	....	....	....
1987-1990	University of Maine	H-East	DID NOT PLAY																									
1990-1991	Indiana State University	ACHA	DID NOT PLAY																									
1991-1996	Richmond Renegades	ECHL	DID NOT PLAY – COACHING																									
1996-1998	**San Jose Sharks**	**NHL**	DID NOT PLAY – ASSISTANT COACH																									
1998-2000	Kentucky Thoroughblades	AHL	DID NOT PLAY – COACHING																									
	NHL Totals		**3**	**1**	**0**	**1**	**1**	**0**	**1**	**7**	**0**	**0**	**0**	**1**	**100.0**	**1**	**0**	**1**	**0**		....	....	....	....	....	....	....	....

Signed as a free agent by **Edmonton**, January 1, 1980. Signed as a free agent by **New Jersey**, September 25, 1982. • Attended University of Maine and Indiana State University, 1987-1991.

• SONGIN, Tom

Thomas David RW – R. 6'3", 195 lbs. b: Norwood, MA, 12/20/1953.

			REGULAR SEASON																		PLAYOFFS							
Season	Club	League	GP	G	A	Pts	AG	AA	APts	PIM	PP	SH	GW	S	%	TGF	PGF	TGA	PGA	+/–	GP	G	A	Pts	PIM	PP	SH	GW
1971-72	Mount St. Charles Mounties	Hi-School	STATISTICS NOT AVAILABLE																									
1972-73	Northwood Huskies	Hi-School	STATISTICS NOT AVAILABLE																									
1973-74	Boston College	ECAC	5	0	1	1	....	....	....	4	....	....	....	....	....	....	....	....	....	....	....	....	....	....	....	....	....	....
1974-75	Boston College	ECAC	28	13	27	40	....	....	....	44	....	....	....	....	....	....	....	....	....	....	....	....	....	....	....	....	....	....
1975-76	Boston College	ECAC	22	9	7	16	....	....	....	24	....	....	....	....	....	....	....	....	....	....	....	....	....	....	....	....	....	....
1976-77	Boston College	ECAC	27	7	7	14	....	....	....	24	....	....	....	....	....	....	....	....	....	....	....	....	....	....	....	....	....	....
1977-78	Long Beach Sharks-Rockets	PHL	42	25	25	50	....	....	....	66	....	....	....	....	....	....	....	....	....	....	....	....	....	....	....	....	....	....
1978-79	**Boston Bruins**	**NHL**	**17**	**3**	**1**	**4**	**3**	**1**	**4**	**0**	**1**	**0**	**0**	**16**	**18.8**	**5**	**2**	**6**	**0**	**–3**	....	....	....	....	....	....	....	....
	Rochester Americans	AHL	59	21	38	59	....	....	....	92	....	....	....	....	....	....	....	....	....	....	....	....	....	....	....	....	....	....
1979-80	**Boston Bruins**	**NHL**	**17**	**1**	**3**	**4**	**1**	**2**	**3**	**16**	**0**	**0**	**0**	**14**	**7.1**	**5**	**0**	**5**	**0**	**0**	....	....	....	....	....	....	....	....
	Binghamton Dusters	AHL	63	24	39	63	....	....	....	36	....	....	....	....	....	....	....	....	....	....	....	....	....	....	....	....	....	....
1980-81	**Boston Bruins**	**NHL**	**9**	**1**	**1**	**2**	**1**	**1**	**2**	**6**	**0**	**0**	**1**	**10**	**10.0**	**5**	**1**	**4**	**0**	**0**	....	....	....	....	....	....	....	....
	Springfield Indians	AHL	57	26	32	58	....	....	....	68	....	....	....	....	....	....	....	....	....	....	2	0	1	1	24	....	....	....
1981-82	Erie Blades	AHL	53	10	26	36	....	....	....	10	....	....	....	....	....	....	....	....	....	....	....	....	....	....	....	....	....	....
1982-83	Birmingham South Stars	CHL	5	0	1	1	....	....	....	2	....	....	....	....	....	....	....	....	....	....	....	....	....	....	....	....	....	....
	NHL Totals		**43**	**5**	**5**	**10**	**5**	**4**	**9**	**22**	**1**	**0**	**1**	**40**	**12.5**	**15**	**3**	**15**	**0**		....	....	....	....	....	....	....	....

PHL Second All-Star Team (1978)

Signed as a free agent by **Boston**, October 10, 1978.

• SONNENBERG, Martin

Martin Lee LW – L. 6', 184 lbs. b: Wetaskiwin, Alta., 1/23/1978.

			REGULAR SEASON																		PLAYOFFS							
Season	Club	League	GP	G	A	Pts	AG	AA	APts	PIM	PP	SH	GW	S	%	TGF	PGF	TGA	PGA	+/–	GP	G	A	Pts	PIM	PP	SH	GW
1995-96	Saskatoon Blades	WHL	58	8	7	15	....	....	....	24	....	....	....	....	....	....	....	....	....	....	3	0	0	0	2	....	....	....
1996-97	Saskatoon Blades	WHL	72	38	26	64	....	....	....	79	....	....	....	....	....	....	....	....	....	....	....	....	....	....	....	....	....	....
1997-98	Saskatoon Blades	WHL	72	40	52	92	....	....	....	87	....	....	....	....	....	....	....	....	....	....	6	1	3	4	9	....	....	....
1998-99	**Pittsburgh Penguins**	**NHL**	**44**	**1**	**1**	**2**	**1**	**1**	**2**	**19**	**0**	**0**	**0**	**12**	**8.3**	**3**	**1**	**4**	**0**	**–2**	**7**	**0**	**0**	**0**	**0**	**0**	**0**	**0**
	Syracuse Crunch	AHL	36	15	9	24	....	....	....	31	....	....	....	....	....	....	....	....	....	....	....	....	....	....	....	....	....	....
99-2000	**Pittsburgh Penguins**	**NHL**	**14**	**1**	**2**	**3**	**1**	**2**	**3**	**0**	**1**	**0**	**0**	**19**	**5.3**	**6**	**1**	**7**	**2**	**0**	....	....	....	....	....	....	....	....
	Wilkes-Barre Penguins	AHL	62	20	33	53	....	....	....	109	....	....	....	....	....	....	....	....	....	....	....	....	....	....	....	....	....	....
	NHL Totals		**58**	**2**	**3**	**5**	**2**	**3**	**5**	**19**	**1**	**0**	**0**	**31**	**6.5**	**9**	**2**	**11**	**2**		**7**	**0**	**0**	**0**	**0**	**0**	**0**	**0**

Signed as a free agent by **Pittsburgh**, October 9, 1998.

• SOPEL, Brent

D – R. 6'1", 205 lbs. b: Calgary, Alta., 1/7/1977. Vancouver's 6th, 144th overall, in 1995.

			REGULAR SEASON																		PLAYOFFS							
Season	Club	League	GP	G	A	Pts	AG	AA	APts	PIM	PP	SH	GW	S	%	TGF	PGF	TGA	PGA	+/–	GP	G	A	Pts	PIM	PP	SH	GW
1992-93	Saskatoon Legionaires	SAHA	36	7	17	24	....	....	....	95	....	....	....	....	....	....	....	....	....	....	....	....	....	....	....	....	....	....
1993-94	Saskatoon Legionaires	SAHA	34	9	30	39	....	....	....	180	....	....	....	....	....	....	....	....	....	....	....	....	....	....	....	....	....	....
	Saskatoon Blades	WHL	11	2	2	4	....	....	....	2	....	....	....	....	....	....	....	....	....	....	....	....	....	....	....	....	....	....
1994-95	Saskatoon Blades	WHL	22	1	10	11	....	....	....	31	....	....	....	....	....	....	....	....	....	....	....	....	....	....	....	....	....	....
	Swift Current Broncos	WHL	41	4	19	23	....	....	....	50	....	....	....	....	....	....	....	....	....	....	3	0	3	3	0	....	....	....
1995-96	Swift Current Broncos	WHL	71	13	48	61	....	....	....	87	....	....	....	....	....	....	....	....	....	....	6	1	2	3	4	....	....	....
	Syracuse Crunch	AHL	1	0	0	0	....	....	....	0	....	....	....	....	....	....	....	....	....	....	....	....	....	....	....	....	....	....
1996-97	Swift Current Broncos	WHL	62	15	41	56	....	....	....	109	....	....	....	....	....	....	....	....	....	....	10	5	11	16	32	....	....	....
	Syracuse Crunch	AHL	2	0	0	0	....	....	....	0	....	....	....	....	....	....	....	....	....	....	3	0	0	0	0	....	....	....
1997-98	Syracuse Crunch	AHL	76	10	33	43	....	....	....	70	....	....	....	....	....	....	....	....	....	....	5	0	7	7	12	....	....	....

Season	Club	League	REGULAR SEASON GP	G	A	Pts	AG	AA	APts	PIM	PP	SH	GW	S	%	TGF	PGF	TGA	PGA	+/–	PLAYOFFS GP	G	A	Pts	PIM	PP	SH	GW
1998-99	**Vancouver Canucks**	**NHL**	**5**	**1**	**0**	**1**	**1**	**0**	**1**	**4**	**1**	**0**	**0**	**5**	**20.0**	**1**	**1**	**1**	**0**	**–1**	....	....	....	....	....	....	....	....
	Syracuse Crunch	AHL	53	10	21	31	....	....	....	59	....	....	....	....	....	....	....	....	....	....	....	....	....	....	....	....	....	....
99-2000	**Vancouver Canucks**	**NHL**	**18**	**2**	**4**	**6**	**2**	**4**	**6**	**12**	**0**	**0**	**1**	**11**	**18.2**	**13**	**0**	**4**	**0**	**9**	....	....	....	....	....	....	....	....
	Syracuse Crunch	AHL	50	6	25	31	....	....	....	67	....	....	....	....	....	....	....	....	....	....	4	0	2	2	8	....	....	....
	NHL Totals		**23**	**3**	**4**	**7**	**3**	**4**	**7**	**16**	**1**	**0**	**1**	**16**	**18.8**	**14**	**1**	**5**	**0**		....	....	....	....	....	....	....	....

• SOROCHAN, Lee

D – L. 5′11″, 210 lbs. b: Edmonton, Alta., 9/9/1975. NY Rangers' 2nd, 34th overall, in 1993.

Season	Club	League	GP	G	A	Pts	AG	AA	APts	PIM	PP	SH	GW	S	%	TGF	PGF	TGA	PGA	+/–	GP	G	A	Pts	PIM	PP	SH	GW
1990-91	Sherwood Park Crusaders	AAHA	34	10	17	27	....	....	....	46	....	....	....	....	....	....	....	....	....	....	....	....	....	....	....	....	....	....
1991-92	Lethbridge Hurricanes	WHL	67	2	9	11	....	....	....	105	....	....	....	....	....	....	....	....	....	....	5	0	2	2	6	....	....	....
1992-93	Lethbridge Hurricanes	WHL	69	8	32	40	....	....	....	208	....	....	....	....	....	....	....	....	....	....	4	0	1	1	12	....	....	....
1993-94	Lethbridge Hurricanes	WHL	46	5	27	32	....	....	....	123	....	....	....	....	....	....	....	....	....	....	9	4	3	7	16	....	....	....
1994-95	Lethbridge Hurricanes	WHL	29	4	15	19	....	....	....	93	....	....	....	....	....	....	....	....	....	....	....	....	....	....	....	....	....	....
	Saskatoon Blades	WHL	24	5	13	18	....	....	....	63	....	....	....	....	....	....	....	....	....	....	10	3	6	9	34	....	....	....
	Binghamton Rangers	AHL	....	....	....	....	....	....	....	....	....	....	....	....	....	....	....	....	....	....	8	0	0	0	11	....	....	....
	Canada	WJC-A	7	0	1	1	....	....	....	6	....	....	....	....	....	....	....	....	....	....	....	....	....	....	....	....	....	....
1995-96	Binghamton Rangers	AHL	45	2	8	10	....	....	....	26	....	....	....	....	....	....	....	....	....	....	1	0	0	0	0	....	....	....
1996-97	Binghamton Rangers	AHL	77	4	27	31	....	....	....	160	....	....	....	....	....	....	....	....	....	....	4	0	2	2	18	....	....	....
1997-98	Hartford Wolf Pack	AHL	73	7	11	18	....	....	....	197	....	....	....	....	....	....	....	....	....	....	13	0	2	2	51	....	....	....
1998-99	Fort Wayne Komets	IHL	45	0	10	10	....	....	....	204	....	....	....	....	....	....	....	....	....	....	....	....	....	....	....	....	....	....
	Hartford Wolf Pack	AHL	16	0	2	2	....	....	....	33	....	....	....	....	....	....	....	....	....	....	....	....	....	....	....	....	....	....
	Calgary Flames	**NHL**	**2**	**0**	**0**	**0**	**0**	**0**	**0**	**0**	**0**	**0**	**0**	**5**	**0.0**	**0**	**0**	**3**	**0**	**–3**	....	....	....	....	....	....	....	....
	Saint John Flames	AHL	3	1	3	4	....	....	....	4	....	....	....	....	....	....	....	....	....	....	7	3	3	6	29	....	....	....
99-2000	**Calgary Flames**	**NHL**	**1**	**0**	**0**	**0**	**0**	**0**	**0**	**0**	**0**	**0**	**0**	**0**	**0.0**	**0**	**0**	**0**	**0**	**0**	....	....	....	....	....	....	....	....
	Saint John Flames	AHL	60	4	37	41	....	....	....	124	....	....	....	....	....	....	....	....	....	....	3	2	1	3	12	....	....	....
	NHL Totals		**3**	**0**	**0**	**0**	**0**	**0**	**0**	**0**	**0**	**0**	**0**	**5**	**0.0**	**0**	**0**	**3**	**0**		....	....	....	....	....	....	....	....

Traded to **Calgary** by **NY Rangers** for Chris O'Sullivan, March 23, 1999.

• SOURAY, Sheldon

D – L. 6′4″, 230 lbs. b: Elk Point, Alta., 7/13/1976. New Jersey's 3rd, 71st overall, in 1994.

Season	Club	League	GP	G	A	Pts	AG	AA	APts	PIM	PP	SH	GW	S	%	TGF	PGF	TGA	PGA	+/–	GP	G	A	Pts	PIM	PP	SH	GW
1990-91	Bonneyville Sabres	AAHA	30	15	20	35	....	....	....	100	....	....	....	....	....	....	....	....	....	....	....	....	....	....	....	....	....	....
1991-92	Quesnel Midget Millionaires	BCAHA	20	5	15	20	....	....	....	200	....	....	....	....	....	....	....	....	....	....	....	....	....	....	....	....	....	....
	Alberta Cycle	AAHA	11	0	5	5	....	....	....	87	....	....	....	....	....	....	....	....	....	....	....	....	....	....	....	....	....	....
1992-93	Fort Saskatchewan Traders	AJHL	35	0	12	12	....	....	....	125	....	....	....	....	....	....	....	....	....	....	....	....	....	....	....	....	....	....
	Tri-City Americans	WHL	2	0	0	0	....	....	....	0	....	....	....	....	....	....	....	....	....	....	....	....	....	....	....	....	....	....
1993-94	Tri-City Americans	WHL	42	3	6	9	....	....	....	122	....	....	....	....	....	....	....	....	....	....	....	....	....	....	....	....	....	....
1994-95	Tri-City Americans	WHL	40	2	24	26	....	....	....	140	....	....	....	....	....	....	....	....	....	....	....	....	....	....	....	....	....	....
	Prince George Cougars	WHL	11	2	3	5	....	....	....	23	....	....	....	....	....	....	....	....	....	....	....	....	....	....	....	....	....	....
	Albany River Rats	AHL	7	0	2	2	....	....	....	8	....	....	....	....	....	....	....	....	....	....	....	....	....	....	....	....	....	....
1995-96	Prince George Cougars	WHL	32	9	18	27	....	....	....	91	....	....	....	....	....	....	....	....	....	....	....	....	....	....	....	....	....	....
	Kelowna Rockets	WHL	27	7	20	27	....	....	....	94	....	....	....	....	....	....	....	....	....	....	6	0	5	5	2	....	....	....
	Albany River Rats	AHL	6	0	2	2	....	....	....	12	....	....	....	....	....	....	....	....	....	....	4	0	1	1	4	....	....	....
1996-97	Albany River Rats	AHL	70	2	11	13	....	....	....	160	....	....	....	....	....	....	....	....	....	....	16	2	3	5	47	....	....	....
1997-98	**New Jersey Devils**	**NHL**	**60**	**3**	**7**	**10**	**4**	**7**	**11**	**85**	**0**	**0**	**1**	**74**	**4.1**	**39**	**4**	**20**	**3**	**18**	**3**	**0**	**1**	**1**	**2**	**0**	**0**	**0**
	Albany River Rats	AHL	6	0	0	0	....	....	....	8	....	....	....	....	....	....	....	....	....	....	....	....	....	....	....	....	....	....
1998-99	**New Jersey Devils**	**NHL**	**70**	**1**	**7**	**8**	**1**	**7**	**8**	**110**	**0**	**0**	**0**	**101**	**1.0**	**44**	**6**	**37**	**4**	**5**	**2**	**0**	**1**	**1**	**0**	**0**	**0**	**0**
99-2000	**New Jersey Devils**	**NHL**	**52**	**0**	**8**	**8**	**0**	**7**	**7**	**70**	**0**	**0**	**0**	**74**	**0.0**	**29**	**3**	**36**	**4**	**–6**	....	....	....	....	....	....	....	....
	Montreal Canadiens	**NHL**	**19**	**3**	**0**	**3**	**3**	**0**	**3**	**44**	**0**	**0**	**0**	**39**	**7.7**	**17**	**0**	**13**	**3**	**7**	....	....	....	....	....	....	....	....
	NHL Totals		**201**	**7**	**22**	**29**	**8**	**21**	**29**	**309**	**0**	**0**	**1**	**288**	**2.4**	**129**	**13**	**106**	**14**		**5**	**0**	**2**	**2**	**2**	**0**	**0**	**0**

WHL West Second All-Star Team (1996)

Traded to **Montreal** by **New Jersey** with Josh DeWolf and New Jersey's 2nd round choice in 2001 Entry Draft for Vladimir Malakhov, March 1, 2000.

• SPACEK, Jaroslav

D – L. 5′11″, 198 lbs. b: Rokycany, Czech., 2/11/1974. Florida's 5th, 117th overall, in 1998.

Season	Club	League	GP	G	A	Pts	AG	AA	APts	PIM	PP	SH	GW	S	%	TGF	PGF	TGA	PGA	+/–	GP	G	A	Pts	PIM	PP	SH	GW
1992-93	Skoda Plzen	Czech.	16	1	3	4	....	....	....	....	....	....	....	....	....	....	....	....	....	....	....	....	....	....	....	....	....	....
1993-94	Skoda Plzen	Czech-Rep	34	2	6	8	....	....	....	....	....	....	....	....	....	....	....	....	....	....	....	....	....	....	....	....	....	....
1994-95	ZKZ Plzen	Czech-Rep	38	4	8	12	....	....	....	14	....	....	....	....	....	....	....	....	....	....	3	1	0	1	2	....	....	....
1995-96	ZKZ Plzen	Czech-Rep	40	3	10	13	....	....	....	42	....	....	....	....	....	....	....	....	....	....	3	0	1	1	4	....	....	....
1996-97	ZKZ Plzen	Czech-Rep	52	9	29	38	....	....	....	44	....	....	....	....	....	....	....	....	....	....	....	....	....	....	....	....	....	....
1997-98	Farjestads BK Karlstad	Sweden	45	10	16	26	....	....	....	63	....	....	....	....	....	....	....	....	....	....	12	2	5	7	14	....	....	....
	Farjestads BK Karlstad	EuroHL	6	2	3	5	....	....	....	2	....	....	....	....	....	....	....	....	....	....	....	....	....	....	....	....	....	....
1998-99	**Florida Panthers**	**NHL**	**63**	**3**	**12**	**15**	**4**	**12**	**16**	**28**	**2**	**1**	**0**	**92**	**3.3**	**64**	**15**	**51**	**17**	**15**	....	....	....	....	....	....	....	....
	Beast of New Haven	AHL	14	4	8	12	....	....	....	15	....	....	....	....	....	....	....	....	....	....	....	....	....	....	....	....	....	....
	Czech-Republic	WC-A	12	1	5	6	....	....	....	8	....	....	....	....	....	....	....	....	....	....	....	....	....	....	....	....	....	....
99-2000	**Florida Panthers**	**NHL**	**82**	**10**	**26**	**36**	**11**	**24**	**35**	**53**	**4**	**0**	**1**	**111**	**9.0**	**94**	**29**	**77**	**19**	**7**	**4**	**0**	**0**	**0**	**0**	**0**	**0**	**0**
	NHL Totals		**145**	**13**	**38**	**51**	**15**	**36**	**51**	**81**	**6**	**1**	**1**	**203**	**6.4**	**158**	**44**	**128**	**36**		**4**	**0**	**0**	**0**	**0**	**0**	**0**	**0**

• SPECK, Fred

Frederick Edmondstone C – L. 5′9″, 160 lbs. b: Thorold, Ont., 7/22/1947.

Season	Club	League	GP	G	A	Pts	AG	AA	APts	PIM	PP	SH	GW	S	%	TGF	PGF	TGA	PGA	+/–	GP	G	A	Pts	PIM	PP	SH	GW
1962-63	Hamilton Red Wings	OHA-Jr.	1	0	0	0	....	....	....	0	....	....	....	....	....	....	....	....	....	....	....	....	....	....	....	....	....	....
1963-64	Hamilton Red Wings	OHA-Jr.	17	2	6	8	....	....	....	20	....	....	....	....	....	....	....	....	....	....	....	....	....	....	....	....	....	....
1964-65	Hamilton Red Wings	OHA-Jr.	41	16	18	34	....	....	....	108	....	....	....	....	....	....	....	....	....	....	....	....	....	....	....	....	....	....
1965-66	Hamilton Red Wings	OHA-Jr.	48	20	37	57	....	....	....	123	....	....	....	....	....	....	....	....	....	....	5	1	2	3	8	....	....	....
1966-67	Hamilton Red Wings	OHA-Jr.	39	23	32	55	....	....	....	67	....	....	....	....	....	....	....	....	....	....	13	4	6	10	14	....	....	....
1967-68	Hamilton Red Wings	OHA-Jr.	52	31	54	85	....	....	....	115	....	....	....	....	....	....	....	....	....	....	11	6	8	14	15	....	....	....
	Fort Worth Wings	CPHL	1	1	1	2	....	....	....	2	....	....	....	....	....	....	....	....	....	....	3	1	3	4	4	....	....	....
1968-69	**Detroit Red Wings**	**NHL**	**5**	**0**	**0**	**0**	**0**	**0**	**0**	**2**	**0**	**0**	**0**	**6**	**0.0**	**0**	**0**	**0**	**0**	**0**	....	....	....	....	....	....	....	....
	Fort Worth Wings	CHL	63	21	24	45	....	....	....	26	....	....	....	....	....	....	....	....	....	....	....	....	....	....	....	....	....	....
1969-70	**Detroit Red Wings**	**NHL**	**5**	**0**	**0**	**0**	**0**	**0**	**0**	**0**	**0**	**0**	**0**	**8**	**0.0**	**0**	**0**	**2**	**0**	**–2**	....	....	....	....	....	....	....	....
	Fort Worth Wings	CHL	67	30	46	76	....	....	....	47	....	....	....	....	....	....	....	....	....	....	7	0	3	3	7	....	....	....
	San Diego Gulls	WHL	....	....	....	....	....	....	....	....	....	....	....	....	....	....	....	....	....	....	2	0	0	0	0	....	....	....
1970-71	Baltimore Clippers	AHL	72	31	*61	*92	....	....	....	40	....	....	....	....	....	....	....	....	....	....	6	4	5	9	4	....	....	....
1971-72	**Vancouver Canucks**	**NHL**	**18**	**1**	**2**	**3**	**1**	**2**	**3**	**0**	**0**	**0**	**0**	**23**	**4.3**	**3**	**0**	**18**	**0**	**–15**	....	....	....	....	....	....	....	....
	Seattle Totems	WHL	6	3	3	6	....	....	....	0	....	....	....	....	....	....	....	....	....	....	....	....	....	....	....	....	....	....
	Cleveland Barons	AHL	27	6	8	14	....	....	....	21	....	....	....	....	....	....	....	....	....	....	6	0	1	1	6	....	....	....
1972-73	Minnesota Fighting Saints	WHA	47	13	16	29	....	....	....	52	....	....	....	....	....	....	....	....	....	....	....	....	....	....	....	....	....	....
	Los Angeles Sharks	WHA	28	3	13	16	....	....	....	22	....	....	....	....	....	....	....	....	....	....	6	3	2	5	2	....	....	....
1973-74	Los Angeles Sharks	WHA	18	2	5	7	....	....	....	4	....	....	....	....	....	....	....	....	....	....	....	....	....	....	....	....	....	....
	Greensboro Generals	SHL	8	1	3	4	....	....	....	19	....	....	....	....	....	....	....	....	....	....	....	....	....	....	....	....	....	....
1974-75	Michigan-Baltimore Stags	WHA	30	4	8	12	....	....	....	18	....	....	....	....	....	....	....	....	....	....	....	....	....	....	....	....	....	....
	Syracuse Blazers	NAHL	17	11	23	34	....	....	....	16	....	....	....	....	....	....	....	....	....	....	....	....	....	....	....	....	....	....
1975-76	Baltimore Clippers	AHL	76	23	52	75	....	....	....	93	....	....	....	....	....	....	....	....	....	....	....	....	....	....	....	....	....	....
1976-77	Brantford Alexanders	OHA-Sr.	27	16	21	37	....	....	....	29	....	....	....	....	....	....	....	....	....	....	....	....	....	....	....	....	....	....
1977-78	Brantford Forresters	OHA-Sr.	38	17	35	52	....	....	....	57	....	....	....	....	....	....	....	....	....	....	....	....	....	....	....	....	....	....
	NHL Totals		**28**	**1**	**2**	**3**	**1**	**2**	**3**	**2**	**0**	**0**	**0**	**37**	**2.7**	**3**	**0**	**20**	**0**		....	....	....	....	....	....	....	....
	Other Major League Totals		123	22	42	64	....	....	....	96	....	....	....	....	....	....	....	....	....	....	6	3	2	5	2	....	....	....

AHL First All-Star Team (1971) • Won Dudley "Red" Garrett Memorial Award (Top Rookie - AHL) (1971) • Won John B. Sollenberger Trophy (Top Scorer - AHL) (1971) • Won Les Cunningham Award (MVP - AHL) (1971)

Claimed by **Vancouver** from **Detroit** in Intra-League Draft, June 8, 1971. Selected by **Minnesota** (WHA) in 1972 WHA General Player Draft, February 12, 1972. Traded to **Minnesota** by **Vancouver** for cash, August, 1972. Traded to **LA Sharks** (WHA) by **Minnesota** (WHA) for Bill Young, February, 1973. Transferred to **Michigan** (WHA) after **LA Sharks** (WHA) franchise relocated, April 11, 1974.

• **SPEER, Bill** Francis William D – L. 5'11", 205 lbs. b: Lindsay, Ont., 3/20/1942.

Season	Club	League	GP	G	A	Pts	AG	AA	APts	PIM	PP	SH	GW	S	%	TGF	PGF	TGA	PGA	+/–	GP	G	A	Pts	PIM	PP	SH	GW
			REGULAR SEASON																		PLAYOFFS							
1959-60	St. Catharines Teepees	OHA-Jr.	43	1	6	7				53											16	0	1	1	10			
	St. Catharines Teepees	Mem-Cup	14	4	0	4				0																		
1960-61	St. Catharines Teepees	OHA-Jr.	42	5	22	27				70											6	0	2	2	8			
1961-62	St. Catharines Teepees	OHA-Jr.	38	6	24	30				96											6	0	0	0	8			
	Sault Ste. Marie Thunderbirds	EPHL	4	0	0	0				2																		
1962-63	Knoxville Knights	EHL	68	10	44	54				46											5	1	0	1	4			
1963-64	Springfield Indians	AHL	28	2	4	6				10																		
1964-65	Cleveland Barons	AHL	71	4	16	20				54																		
1965-66	Cleveland Barons	AHL	70	3	16	19				36											12	2	2	4	6			
1966-67	Buffalo Bisons	AHL	64	6	25	31				52																		
1967-68	**Pittsburgh Penguins**	**NHL**	**68**	**3**	**13**	**16**	**3**	**13**	**16**	**44**	**1**	**0**	**0**	**101**	**3.0**	**56**	**11**	**70**	**11**	**–14**								
	Baltimore Clippers	AHL	5	0	5	5				8																		
1968-69	**Pittsburgh Penguins**	**NHL**	**34**	**1**	**4**	**5**	**1**	**4**	**5**	**27**	**1**	**0**	**1**	**43**	**2.3**	**23**	**4**	**44**	**9**	**–16**								
	Baltimore Clippers	AHL	13	1	4	5				21																		
	Amarillo Wranglers	CHL	7	1	1	2				14																		
1969-70♦	**Boston Bruins**	**NHL**	**27**	**1**	**3**	**4**	**1**	**3**	**4**	**4**	**0**	**0**	**0**	**5**	**20.0**	**16**	**1**	**15**	**6**	**6**	**8**	**1**	**0**	**1**	**4**	**0**	**0**	**0**
	Salt Lake Golden Eagles	WHL	19	1	3	4				47																		
1970-71	**Boston Bruins**	**NHL**	**1**	**0**	**0**	**0**	**0**	**0**	**0**	**4**	**0**	**0**	**0**	**0**	**0.0**	**0**	**0**	**0**	**0**	**0**								
	Hershey Bears	AHL	27	2	6	8				42																		
	Providence Reds	AHL	25	3	19	22				35											10	1	6	7	6			
1971-72	Boston Braves	AHL	7	0	0	0				2																		
	Providence Reds	AHL	52	5	27	32				36											5	2	2	4	8			
1972-73	New York Raiders	WHA	69	3	23	26				40																		
1973-74	New York-Jersey Knights	WHA	66	1	3	4				30																		
1974-75	Orillia Terriers	OHA-Sr.	13	0	11	11				18																		
	NHL Totals		**130**	**5**	**20**	**25**	**5**	**20**	**25**	**79**	**2**	**0**	**1**	**149**	**3.4**	**95**	**16**	**129**	**26**		**8**	**1**	**0**	**1**	**4**	**0**	**0**	**0**
	Other Major League Totals		135	4	26	30				70																		

Traded to **Cleveland** (AHL) by **Springfield** (AHL) for Pete Shearer, September, 1964. Traded to **Pittsburgh** by **Cleveland** (AHL) for cash, August 11, 1966. Loaned to **Buffalo** (AHL) by **Pittsburgh** for 1966-67 season, October, 1966. Claimed by **Boston** from **Pittsburgh** in Intra-League Draft, June 11, 1969. Traded to **Providence** (AHL) by **Boston** for cash, February, 1971. Selected by **NY Raiders** (WHA) in 1972 WHA General Player Draft, February 12, 1972. Claimed by **NY Islanders** from **Providence** (AHL) in Inter-League Draft, June, 1972.

• **SPEERS, Ted** RW – R. 5'11", 200 lbs. b: Ann Arbor, MI, 1/28/1961.

Season	Club	League	GP	G	A	Pts	AG	AA	APts	PIM	PP	SH	GW	S	%	TGF	PGF	TGA	PGA	+/–	GP	G	A	Pts	PIM	PP	SH	GW
1979-80	University of Michigan	WCHA	30	13	16	29				16																		
1980-81	University of Michigan	WCHA	39	22	23	45				20																		
1981-82	University of Michigan	CCHA	38	23	16	39				46																		
1982-83	University of Michigan	CCHA	36	18	41	59				40																		
1983-84	Adirondack Red Wings	AHL	79	15	25	40				27											7	2	1	3	9			
1984-85	Adirondack Red Wings	AHL	80	22	31	53				40																		
1985-86	**Detroit Red Wings**	**NHL**	**4**	**1**	**1**	**2**	**1**	**1**	**2**	**0**	**0**	**0**	**0**	**6**	**16.7**	**4**	**0**	**4**	**2**	**2**								
	Adirondack Red Wings	AHL	74	32	35	67				20											15	7	5	12	9			
1986-87	Adirondack Red Wings	AHL	80	24	37	61				39											11	2	0	2	4			
	NHL Totals		**4**	**1**	**1**	**2**	**1**	**1**	**2**	**0**	**0**	**0**	**0**	**6**	**16.7**	**4**	**0**	**4**	**2**									

CCHA First All-Star Team (1983)

Signed as a free agent by **Detroit**, September, 1983.

• **SPENCER, Brian** Brian Roy "Spinner" LW – L. 5'11", 185 lbs. b: Fort St. James, B.C., 9/3/1949 d: 6/3/1988. Toronto's 5th, 55th overall, in 1969.

Season	Club	League	GP	G	A	Pts	AG	AA	APts	PIM	PP	SH	GW	S	%	TGF	PGF	TGA	PGA	+/–	GP	G	A	Pts	PIM	PP	SH	GW
1966-67	Estevan Bruins	SJHL	STATISTICS NOT AVAILABLE																									
1967-68	Regina Pats	WCJHL	23	1	2	3				12																		
	Calgary Centennials	WCJHL	34	13	10	23				27																		
1968-69	Estevan-Swift Current	WCJHL	53	19	29	48				120											4	3	1	4	14			
1969-70	**Toronto Maple Leafs**	**NHL**	**9**	**0**	**0**	**0**	**0**	**0**	**0**	**12**	**0**	**0**	**0**	**8**	**0.0**	**1**	**0**	**5**	**0**	**–4**								
	Tulsa Oilers	CHL	66	13	19	32				186																		
1970-71	**Toronto Maple Leafs**	**NHL**	**50**	**9**	**15**	**24**	**9**	**13**	**22**	**115**	**3**	**0**	**1**	**61**	**14.8**	**38**	**10**	**26**	**0**	**2**	**6**	**0**	**1**	**1**	**17**	**0**	**0**	**0**
	Tulsa Oilers	CHL	23	6	8	14				103																		
1971-72	**Toronto Maple Leafs**	**NHL**	**36**	**1**	**5**	**6**	**1**	**4**	**5**	**65**	**0**	**0**	**0**	**31**	**3.2**	**16**	**1**	**13**	**0**	**2**								
	Tulsa Oilers	CHL	20	7	7	14				115																		
1972-73	**New York Islanders**	**NHL**	**78**	**14**	**24**	**38**	**13**	**19**	**32**	**90**	**0**	**0**	**2**	**163**	**8.6**	**52**	**6**	**94**	**1**	**–47**								
1973-74	**New York Islanders**	**NHL**	**54**	**5**	**16**	**21**	**5**	**13**	**18**	**65**	**0**	**0**	**0**	**114**	**4.4**	**29**	**5**	**42**	**2**	**–16**								
	Buffalo Sabres	**NHL**	**13**	**3**	**2**	**5**	**3**	**2**	**5**	**4**	**1**	**0**	**0**	**21**	**14.3**	**6**	**1**	**8**	**0**	**–3**								
1974-75	**Buffalo Sabres**	**NHL**	**73**	**12**	**29**	**41**	**10**	**22**	**32**	**77**	**1**	**0**	**1**	**126**	**9.5**	**65**	**6**	**42**	**0**	**17**	**16**	**0**	**4**	**4**	**8**	**0**	**0**	**0**
1975-76	**Buffalo Sabres**	**NHL**	**77**	**13**	**26**	**39**	**11**	**19**	**30**	**70**	**0**	**0**	**1**	**84**	**15.5**	**57**	**1**	**42**	**0**	**14**	**9**	**1**	**0**	**1**	**4**	**0**	**0**	**0**
1976-77	**Buffalo Sabres**	**NHL**	**77**	**14**	**15**	**29**	**13**	**12**	**25**	**55**	**1**	**0**	**2**	**78**	**17.9**	**44**	**4**	**40**	**0**	**0**	**6**	**0**	**0**	**0**	**0**	**0**	**0**	**0**
1977-78	**Pittsburgh Penguins**	**NHL**	**79**	**9**	**11**	**20**	**8**	**8**	**16**	**81**	**0**	**0**	**1**	**101**	**8.9**	**37**	**2**	**54**	**1**	**–18**								
1978-79	**Pittsburgh Penguins**	**NHL**	**7**	**0**	**0**	**0**	**0**	**0**	**0**	**0**	**0**	**0**	**0**	**2**	**0.0**	**0**	**0**	**0**	**0**	**0**								
	Binghamton Dusters	AHL	39	5	9	14				58																		
1979-80	Springfield Indians	AHL	9	1	1	2				0																		
	Hershey Bears	AHL	30	0	4	4				23																		
	NHL Totals		**553**	**80**	**143**	**223**	**73**	**112**	**185**	**634**	**6**	**0**	**8**	**789**	**10.1**	**345**	**36**	**366**	**4**		**37**	**1**	**5**	**6**	**29**	**0**	**0**	**0**

Claimed by **NY Islanders** from **Toronto** in Expansion Draft, June 6, 1972. Traded to **Buffalo** by **NY Islanders** for Doug Rombough, March 10, 1974. Traded to **Pittsburgh** by **Buffalo** for Ron Schock, September 20, 1977.

• **SPENCER, Irv** Irvin James D – L. 5'10", 180 lbs. b: Sudbury, Ont., 12/4/1937.

Season	Club	League	GP	G	A	Pts	AG	AA	APts	PIM	PP	SH	GW	S	%	TGF	PGF	TGA	PGA	+/–	GP	G	A	Pts	PIM	PP	SH	GW
1953-54	Gatchell Hardware	NOHA	STATISTICS NOT AVAILABLE																									
1954-55	Kitchener Canucks	OHA-Jr.	49	10	9	19				65																		
1955-56	Kitchener Canucks	OHA-Jr.	48	4	9	13				36																		
1956-57	Peterborough Petes	OHA-Jr.	45	6	26	32				68											8	1	0	1	16			
	Hull-Ottawa Canadiens	QHL	8	1	2	3				2																		
1957-58	Peterborough Petes	OHA-Jr.	52	8	31	39				76											5	3	1	4	8			
	Montreal Royals	QHL	3	0	1	1				2																		
1958-59	Montreal Royals	QHL	45	6	12	18				55											8	1	2	3	8			
1959-60	**New York Rangers**	**NHL**	**32**	**1**	**2**	**3**	**1**	**2**	**3**	**20**																		
	Trois-Rivieres Lions	EPHL	18	3	4	7				8																		
	Springfield Indians	AHL	14	0	5	5				12																		
1960-61	**New York Rangers**	**NHL**	**56**	**1**	**8**	**9**	**1**	**8**	**9**	**30**																		
1961-62	**New York Rangers**	**NHL**	**43**	**2**	**10**	**12**	**2**	**10**	**12**	**31**											**1**	**0**	**0**	**0**	**2**	**0**	**0**	**0**
1962-63	**Boston Bruins**	**NHL**	**69**	**5**	**17**	**22**	**6**	**17**	**23**	**34**																		
1963-64	**Detroit Red Wings**	**NHL**	**25**	**3**	**0**	**3**	**4**	**0**	**4**	**8**											**11**	**0**	**0**	**0**	**0**	**0**	**0**	**0**
	Cincinnati Wings	CPHL	23	3	8	11				34																		
	Pittsburgh Hornets	AHL	18	5	8	13				2																		
1964-65	Pittsburgh Hornets	AHL	72	18	22	40				45											4	0	0	0	0			
	Detroit Red Wings	**NHL**																			**1**	**0**	**0**	**0**	**4**	**0**	**0**	**0**
1965-66	Memphis Wings	CPHL	54	12	21	33				14																		
	Pittsburgh Hornets	AHL	19	4	11	15				26																		
	Detroit Red Wings	**NHL**																			**3**	**0**	**0**	**0**	**2**	**0**	**0**	**0**
1966-67	Pittsburgh Hornets	AHL	2	0	1	1				0																		
	Memphis Wings	CPHL	30	2	6	8				8											7	0	5	5	4			
1967-68	**Detroit Red Wings**	**NHL**	**5**	**0**	**1**	**1**	**0**	**1**	**1**	**4**	**0**	**0**	**0**	**7**	**0.0**	**5**	**1**	**7**	**2**	**–1**								
	Fort Worth Wings	CPHL	55	7	31	38				42											13	3	3	6	12			

			REGULAR SEASON																		PLAYOFFS							
Season	Club	League	GP	G	A	Pts	AG	AA	APts	PIM	PP	SH	GW	S	%	TGF	PGF	TGA	PGA	+/–	GP	G	A	Pts	PIM	PP	SH	GW
1968-69	Fort Worth Wings	CHL	49	7	18	25	....	....	....	24	....	....	....	....	....	....	....	....	....	....	....	....	....	....	....	....	....	....
1969-70	San Diego Gulls	WHL	62	13	25	38	....	....	....	26	....	....	....	....	....	....	....	....	....	....	6	0	3	3	8	....	....	....
1970-71	San Diego Gulls	WHL	45	2	15	17	....	....	....	24	....	....	....	....	....	....	....	....	....	....	6	2	0	2	19	....	....	....
1971-72	Fort Worth Wings	CHL	1	0	0	0	....	....	....	0	....	....	....	....	....	....	....	....	....	....	....	....	....	....	....	....	....	....
1972-73	Philadelphia Blazers	WHA	54	2	27	29	....	....	....	43	....	....	....	....	....	....	....	....	....	....	....	....	....	....	....	....	....	....
	Rhode Island Eagles	EHL	11	3	3	6	....	....	....	4	....	....	....	....	....	....	....	....	....	....	....	....	....	....	....	....	....	....
1973-74	Vancouver Blazers	WHA	19	0	1	1	....	....	....	6	....	....	....	....	....	....	....	....	....	....	....	....	....	....	....	....	....	....
	NHL Totals		**230**	**12**	**38**	**50**	**14**	**38**	**52**	**127**	....	....	....	....	....	....	....	....	....	....	**16**	**0**	**0**	**0**	**8**	....	....	....
	Other Major League Totals		73	2	28	30	....	....	....	49	....	....	....	....	....	....	....	....	....	....	....	....	....	....	....	....	....	....

CPHL First All-Star Team (1968)

Claimed by **NY Rangers** from **Montreal** in Intra-League Draft, June 10, 1959. Claimed by **Boston** from **NY Rangers** in Intra-League Draft, June 4, 1962. Claimed by **Detroit** from **Boston** in Intra-League Draft, June 4, 1963. Traded to **San Diego** (WHL) by **Detroit** for cash, June 12, 1970. Traded to **Detroit** by **San Diego** (WHL) for cash, May, 1971. Claimed by **Vancouver** from **Tidewater** (AHL) in Inter-League Draft, June 7, 1971. Traded to **Detroit** by **Vancouver** with Bob Dillabough for Gary Bredin and John Cunniff, June 8, 1971. Signed as a free agent by **Philadelphia** (WHA), June, 1972. Transferred to **Vancouver** (WHA) after **Philadelphia** (WHA) franchise relocated, May, 1973.

• SPRING, Corey

RW – R. 6′4″, 214 lbs. b: Cranbrook, B.C., 5/31/1971.

Season	Club	League	GP	G	A	Pts	AG	AA	APts	PIM	PP	SH	GW	S	%	TGF	PGF	TGA	PGA	+/–	GP	G	A	Pts	PIM	PP	SH	GW
1990-91	Vernon Lakers	BCJHL	60	43	43	86	....	....	....	104	....	....	....	....	....	....	....	....	....	....	....	....	....	....	....	....	....	....
	Vernon Lakers	Cen-Cup	6	4	2	6	....	....	....	2	....	....	....	....	....	....	....	....	....	....	....	....	....	....	....	....	....	....
1991-92	University of Alaska-Fairbanks	NCAA	35	3	8	11	....	....	....	30	....	....	....	....	....	....	....	....	....	....	....	....	....	....	....	....	....	....
1992-93	University of Alaska-Fairbanks	CCHA	28	5	5	10	....	....	....	20	....	....	....	....	....	....	....	....	....	....	....	....	....	....	....	....	....	....
1993-94	University of Alaska-Fairbanks	CCHA	38	19	18	37	....	....	....	34	....	....	....	....	....	....	....	....	....	....	....	....	....	....	....	....	....	....
1994-95	University of Alaska-Fairbanks	CCHA	33	18	14	32	....	....	....	56	....	....	....	....	....	....	....	....	....	....	....	....	....	....	....	....	....	....
1995-96	Atlanta Knights	IHL	73	14	14	28	....	....	....	104	....	....	....	....	....	....	....	....	....	....	2	0	0	0	0	....	....	....
1996-97	Adirondack Red Wings	AHL	69	20	26	46	....	....	....	118	....	....	....	....	....	....	....	....	....	....	4	0	0	0	14	....	....	....
1997-98	**Tampa Bay Lightning**	**NHL**	**8**	**1**	**0**	**1**	**1**	**0**	**1**	**10**	**0**	**0**	**0**	**12**	**8.3**	**1**	**0**	**2**	**0**	**–1**	....	....	....	....	....	....	....	....
	Adirondack Red Wings	AHL	57	19	25	44	....	....	....	120	....	....	....	....	....	....	....	....	....	....	3	0	0	0	6	....	....	....
1998-99	**Tampa Bay Lighning**	**NHL**	**8**	**0**	**1**	**1**	**0**	**1**	**1**	**2**	**0**	**0**	**0**	**6**	**0.0**	**1**	**0**	**1**	**0**	**0**	....	....	....	....	....	....	....	....
	Cleveland Lumberjacks	IHL	48	18	10	28	....	....	....	98	....	....	....	....	....	....	....	....	....	....	....	....	....	....	....	....	....	....
99-2000	Detroit Vipers	IHL	22	5	4	9	....	....	....	48	....	....	....	....	....	....	....	....	....	....	....	....	....	....	....	....	....	....
	Manitoba Moose	IHL	8	2	2	4	....	....	....	8	....	....	....	....	....	....	....	....	....	....	....	....	....	....	....	....	....	....
	Augsburger Panther	Germany	7	2	0	2	....	....	....	10	....	....	....	....	....	....	....	....	....	....	....	....	....	....	....	....	....	....
	NHL Totals		**16**	**1**	**1**	**2**	**1**	**1**	**2**	**12**	**0**	**0**	**0**	**18**	**5.6**	**2**	**0**	**3**	**0**		....	....	....	....	....	....	....	....

Signed as a free agent by **Tampa Bay**, July 24, 1995.

• SPRING, Don

Donald Neil D – L. 5′11″, 195 lbs. b: Maracaibo, Venezuela, 6/15/1959.

Season	Club	League	GP	G	A	Pts	AG	AA	APts	PIM	PP	SH	GW	S	%	TGF	PGF	TGA	PGA	+/–	GP	G	A	Pts	PIM	PP	SH	GW
1976-77	University of Alberta	CWUAA	34	1	6	7	....	....	....	24	....	....	....	....	....	....	....	....	....	....	....	....	....	....	....	....	....	....
1977-78	University of Alberta	CWUAA	30	6	14	20	....	....	....	12	....	....	....	....	....	....	....	....	....	....	....	....	....	....	....	....	....	....
1978-79	University of Alberta	CWUAA	42	7	29	36	....	....	....	27	....	....	....	....	....	....	....	....	....	....	....	....	....	....	....	....	....	....
1979-80	Canada	Nat-Team	51	1	23	24	....	....	....	20	....	....	....	....	....	....	....	....	....	....	....	....	....	....	....	....	....	....
	Canada	Olympics	6	0	1	1	....	....	....	0	....	....	....	....	....	....	....	....	....	....	....	....	....	....	....	....	....	....
1980-81	**Winnipeg Jets**	**NHL**	**80**	**1**	**18**	**19**	**1**	**12**	**13**	**18**	**0**	**0**	**0**	**51**	**2.0**	**67**	**1**	**139**	**33**	**–40**	....	....	....	....	....	....	....	....
1981-82	**Winnipeg Jets**	**NHL**	**78**	**0**	**16**	**16**	**0**	**11**	**11**	**21**	**0**	**0**	**0**	**67**	**0.0**	**71**	**1**	**105**	**22**	**–13**	**4**	**0**	**0**	**0**	**4**	**0**	**0**	**0**
1982-83	**Winnipeg Jets**	**NHL**	**80**	**0**	**16**	**16**	**0**	**11**	**11**	**37**	**0**	**0**	**0**	**50**	**0.0**	**80**	**0**	**103**	**23**	**0**	**2**	**0**	**0**	**0**	**6**	**0**	**0**	**0**
1983-84	**Winnipeg Jets**	**NHL**	**21**	**0**	**4**	**4**	**0**	**3**	**3**	**4**	**0**	**0**	**0**	**10**	**0.0**	**16**	**0**	**28**	**7**	**–5**	....	....	....	....	....	....	....	....
	Sherbrooke Jets	AHL	50	0	17	17	....	....	....	21	....	....	....	....	....	....	....	....	....	....	....	....	....	....	....	....	....	....
1984-85	ESC Essen-West	Germany	36	8	19	27	....	....	....	32	....	....	....	....	....	....	....	....	....	....	18	3	13	16	12	....	....	....
	NHL Totals		**259**	**1**	**54**	**55**	**1**	**37**	**38**	**80**	**0**	**0**	**0**	**178**	**0.6**	**234**	**2**	**375**	**85**		**6**	**0**	**0**	**0**	**10**	**0**	**0**	**0**

Signed as a free agent by **Winnipeg**, May 22, 1980.

• SPRING, Frank

Franklin Patrick RW – R. 6′3″, 216 lbs. b: Cranbrook, B.C., 10/19/1949. Boston's 2nd, 4th overall, in 1969.

Season	Club	League	GP	G	A	Pts	AG	AA	APts	PIM	PP	SH	GW	S	%	TGF	PGF	TGA	PGA	+/–	GP	G	A	Pts	PIM	PP	SH	GW
1967-68	Edmonton Oil Kings	WCJHL	57	24	27	51	....	....	....	85	....	....	....	....	....	....	....	....	....	....	13	3	4	7	12	....	....	....
1968-69	Edmonton Oil Kings	WCJHL	41	9	16	25	....	....	....	60	....	....	....	....	....	....	....	....	....	....	17	10	2	12	16	....	....	....
1969-70	**Boston Bruins**	**NHL**	**1**	**0**	**0**	**0**	**0**	**0**	**0**	**0**	**0**	**0**	**0**	**0**	**0.0**	**0**	**0**	**0**	**0**	**0**	....	....	....	....	....	....	....	....
	Oklahoma City Blazers	CHL	62	17	22	39	....	....	....	55	....	....	....	....	....	....	....	....	....	....	....	....	....	....	....	....	....	....
1970-71	Hershey Bears	AHL	43	12	12	24	....	....	....	32	....	....	....	....	....	....	....	....	....	....	....	....	....	....	....	....	....	....
1971-72	Richmond Robins	AHL	75	12	19	31	....	....	....	61	....	....	....	....	....	....	....	....	....	....	....	....	....	....	....	....	....	....
1972-73	Richmond Robins	AHL	70	12	19	31	....	....	....	96	....	....	....	....	....	....	....	....	....	....	4	1	1	2	6	....	....	....
1973-74	**St. Louis Blues**	**NHL**	**2**	**0**	**0**	**0**	**0**	**0**	**0**	**0**	**0**	**0**	**0**	**2**	**0.0**	**0**	**0**	**0**	**0**	**0**	....	....	....	....	....	....	....	....
	Denver Spurs	WHL	47	17	11	28	....	....	....	41	....	....	....	....	....	....	....	....	....	....	....	....	....	....	....	....	....	....
	Richmond Robins	AHL	18	0	5	5	....	....	....	25	....	....	....	....	....	....	....	....	....	....	....	....	....	....	....	....	....	....
1974-75	**St. Louis Blues**	**NHL**	**3**	**0**	**0**	**0**	**0**	**0**	**0**	**0**	**0**	**0**	**0**	**3**	**0.0**	**1**	**0**	**2**	**0**	**–1**	....	....	....	....	....	....	....	....
	Denver Spurs	CHL	31	19	9	28	....	....	....	27	....	....	....	....	....	....	....	....	....	....	....	....	....	....	....	....	....	....
	California Golden Seals	**NHL**	**28**	**3**	**8**	**11**	**3**	**6**	**9**	**6**	**1**	**0**	**0**	**43**	**7.0**	**16**	**3**	**12**	**0**	**1**	....	....	....	....	....	....	....	....
1975-76	**California Golden Seals**	**NHL**	**1**	**0**	**2**	**2**	**0**	**1**	**1**	**0**	**0**	**0**	**0**	**1**	**0.0**	**2**	**1**	**0**	**0**	**1**	....	....	....	....	....	....	....	....
	Salt Lake Golden Eagles	CHL	75	*44	29	73	....	....	....	50	....	....	....	....	....	....	....	....	....	....	5	0	0	0	8	....	....	....
1976-77	**Cleveland Barons**	**NHL**	**26**	**11**	**10**	**21**	**10**	**8**	**18**	**6**	**5**	**0**	**0**	**49**	**22.4**	**26**	**12**	**22**	**0**	**–8**	....	....	....	....	....	....	....	....
	Salt Lake Golden Eagles	CHL	19	8	10	18	....	....	....	12	....	....	....	....	....	....	....	....	....	....	....	....	....	....	....	....	....	....
1977-78	Indianapolis Racers	WHA	13	2	4	6	....	....	....	2	....	....	....	....	....	....	....	....	....	....	....	....	....	....	....	....	....	....
	New Haven Nighthawks	AHL	45	14	11	25	....	....	....	35	....	....	....	....	....	....	....	....	....	....	13	2	4	6	0	....	....	....
	NHL Totals		**61**	**14**	**20**	**34**	**13**	**15**	**28**	**12**	**6**	**0**	**0**	**98**	**14.3**	**45**	**16**	**36**	**0**		....	....	....	....	....	....	....	....
	Other Major League Totals		13	2	4	6	....	....	....	2	....	....	....	....	....	....	....	....	....	....	....	....	....	....	....	....	....	....

CHL Second All-Star Team (1976)

Claimed by **Philadelphia** from **Boston** in Intra-League Draft, June 8, 1971. Selected by **Chicago** (WHA) in 1972 WHA General Player Draft, February 12, 1972. Traded to **St. Louis** by **Philadelphia** for Ray Schultz, December, 1973. Traded to **California** by **St. Louis** for Bruce Affleck, January 9, 1975. Transferred to **Cleveland** after **California** franchise relocated, August 26, 1976. Signed as a free agent by **Indianapolis** (WHA), September, 1977. Traded to **NY Rangers** by **Indianapolis** (WHA) for Bill Goldsworthy, December, 1977.

• SPRUCE, Andy

Andrew William LW – L. 5′11″, 178 lbs. b: London, Ont., 4/17/1954. Vancouver's 5th, 95th overall, in 1974.

Season	Club	League	GP	G	A	Pts	AG	AA	APts	PIM	PP	SH	GW	S	%	TGF	PGF	TGA	PGA	+/–	GP	G	A	Pts	PIM	PP	SH	GW
1971-72	London Knights	OMJHL	33	1	9	10	....	....	....	17	....	....	....	....	....	....	....	....	....	....	7	0	1	1	5	....	....	....
1972-73	London Knights	OMJHL	63	34	69	103	....	....	....	69	....	....	....	....	....	....	....	....	....	....	....	....	....	....	....	....	....	....
1973-74	London Knights	OMJHL	39	12	39	51	....	....	....	89	....	....	....	....	....	....	....	....	....	....	....	....	....	....	....	....	....	....
1974-75	Seattle Totems	CHL	65	17	31	48	....	....	....	104	....	....	....	....	....	....	....	....	....	....	....	....	....	....	....	....	....	....
1975-76	Tulsa Oilers	CHL	75	29	46	75	....	....	....	100	....	....	....	....	....	....	....	....	....	....	9	1	7	8	8	....	....	....
1976-77	**Vancouver Canucks**	**NHL**	**51**	**9**	**6**	**15**	**8**	**5**	**13**	**37**	**2**	**0**	**0**	**54**	**16.7**	**21**	**4**	**39**	**2**	**–20**	....	....	....	....	....	....	....	....
	Tulsa Oilers	CHL	20	6	14	20	....	....	....	35	....	....	....	....	....	....	....	....	....	....	9	3	6	*9	21	....	....	....
1977-78	**Colorado Rockies**	**NHL**	**74**	**19**	**21**	**40**	**17**	**16**	**33**	**43**	**3**	**0**	**1**	**119**	**16.0**	**68**	**10**	**77**	**12**	**–7**	**2**	**0**	**2**	**2**	**0**	**0**	**0**	**0**
1978-79	**Colorado Rockies**	**NHL**	**47**	**3**	**15**	**18**	**3**	**11**	**14**	**31**	**0**	**0**	**0**	**57**	**5.3**	**35**	**12**	**42**	**1**	**–18**	....	....	....	....	....	....	....	....
1979-80	Fort Worth Texans	CHL	77	31	41	72	....	....	....	97	....	....	....	....	....	....	....	....	....	....	15	8	6	14	10	....	....	....
1980-81	Springfield Indians	AHL	79	15	38	53	....	....	....	108	....	....	....	....	....	....	....	....	....	....	7	2	3	5	17	....	....	....
1981-82	Erie Blades	AHL	76	8	17	25	....	....	....	95	....	....	....	....	....	....	....	....	....	....	....	....	....	....	....	....	....	....
	NHL Totals		**172**	**31**	**42**	**73**	**28**	**32**	**60**	**111**	**5**	**0**	**1**	**230**	**13.5**	**124**	**26**	**158**	**15**		**2**	**0**	**2**	**2**	**0**	**0**	**0**	**0**

Signed as a free agent by **Colorado**, October 5, 1977.

• SRSEN, Tomas

RW – L. 5′11″, 180 lbs. b: Olomouc, Czech., 8/25/1966. Edmonton's 7th, 147th overall, in 1987.

Season	Club	League	GP	G	A	Pts	AG	AA	APts	PIM	PP	SH	GW	S	%	TGF	PGF	TGA	PGA	+/–	GP	G	A	Pts	PIM	PP	SH	GW
1984-85	HC Olomouc	Czech-2	31	14	8	22	....	....	....	20	....	....	....	....	....	....	....	....	....	....	....	....	....	....	....	....	....	....
1985-86	Zetor Brno	Czech.	40	6	5	11	....	....	....	44	....	....	....	....	....	....	....	....	....	....	....	....	....	....	....	....	....	....
	Czechoslovakia	WJC-A	7	0	2	2	....	....	....	6	....	....	....	....	....	....	....	....	....	....	....	....	....	....	....	....	....	....
1986-87	Zetor Brno	Czech.	40	15	8	23	....	....	....	44	....	....	....	....	....	....	....	....	....	....	....	....	....	....	....	....	....	....

			REGULAR SEASON																		PLAYOFFS							
Season	Club	League	GP	G	A	Pts	AG	AA	APts	PIM	PP	SH	GW	S	%	TGF	PGF	TGA	PGA	+/–	GP	G	A	Pts	PIM	PP	SH	GW
1987-88	Zetor Brno	Czech.	45	24	8	32	....	....	....	114	....	....	....	....	....	....	....	....	....	....	....	....	....	....	....	....	....	....
1988-89	Dukla Jihlava	Czech.	42	19	11	30	....	....	....	48	....	....	....	....	....	....	....	....	....	....	....	....	....	....	....	....	....	....
1989-90	Dukla Jihlava	Czech.	25	5	10	15	....	....	....	....	....	....	....	....	....	....	....	....	....	....	....	....	....	....	....	....	....	....
	Zetor Brno	Czech.	5	3	5	8	....	....	....	....	....	....	....	....	....	....	....	....	....	....	....	....	....	....	....	....	....	....
1990-91	**Edmonton Oilers**	**NHL**	**2**	**0**	**0**	**0**	**0**	**0**	**0**	**0**	**0**	**0**	**0**	**2**	**0.0**	**0**	**0**	**0**	**0**	**0**	....	....	....	....	....	....	....	....
	Cape Breton Oilers	AHL	72	32	26	58	....	....	....	100	....	....	....	....	....	....	....	....	....	....	4	3	1	4	6	....	....	....
1991-92	Cape Breton Oilers	AHL	68	19	27	46	....	....	....	79	....	....	....	....	....	....	....	....	....	....	5	2	2	4	4	....	....	....
1992-93	Leksands IF	Sweden	39	20	6	26	....	....	....	48	....	....	....	....	....	....	....	....	....	....	2	1	1	2	2	....	....	....
1993-94	Rogle BK Angelholm	Sweden	40	*28	13	41	....	....	....	72	....	....	....	....	....	....	....	....	....	....	....	....	....	....	....	....	....	....
	Czech-Republic	Olympics	8	2	3	5	....	....	....	8	....	....	....	....	....	....	....	....	....	....	....	....	....	....	....	....	....	....
	Czech-Republic	WC-A	6	1	1	2	....	....	....	2	....	....	....	....	....	....	....	....	....	....	....	....	....	....	....	....	....	....
1994-95	Rogle BK Angelholm	Sweden	16	3	1	4	....	....	....	30	....	....	....	....	....	....	....	....	....	....	....	....	....	....	....	....	....	....
	HC Petra Vsetin	Czech-Rep	24	9	18	27	....	....	....	....	....	....	....	....	....	....	....	....	....	....	11	6	3	9	....	....	....	....
	Czech-Republic	WC-A	8	1	1	2	....	....	....	6	....	....	....	....	....	....	....	....	....	....	....	....	....	....	....	....	....	....
1995-96	HC Petra Vsetin	Czech-Rep	31	8	18	26	....	....	....	....	....	....	....	....	....	....	....	....	....	....	12	4	5	9	....	....	....	....
1996-97	HC Petra Vsetin	Czech-Rep	52	16	36	52	....	....	....	92	....	....	....	....	....	....	....	....	....	....	10	7	*10	*17	38	....	....	....
1997-98	HC Petra Vsetin	EuroHL	10	3	6	9	....	....	....	12	....	....	....	....	....	....	....	....	....	....	....	....	....	....	....	....	....	....
	HC Petra Vsetin	Czech-Rep	50	13	31	44	....	....	....	107	....	....	....	....	....	....	....	....	....	....	10	5	3	8	20	....	....	....
1998-99	HC Petra Vsetin	Czech-Rep	48	9	27	36	....	....	....	81	....	....	....	....	....	....	....	....	....	....	10	5	2	7	....	....	....	....
99-2000	Moskitos Essen	Germany	67	21	21	42	....	....	....	92	....	....	....	....	....	....	....	....	....	....	....	....	....	....	....	....	....	....
	NHL Totals		**2**	**0**	**0**	**0**	**0**	**0**	**0**	**0**	**0**	**0**	**0**	**2**	**0.0**	**0**	**0**	**0**	**0**		....	....	....	....	....	....	....	....

• STACKHOUSE, Ron

Ronald Lorne D – R. 6'3", 210 lbs. b: Haliburton, Ont., 8/26/1949. Oakland's 2nd, 18th overall, in 1969.

Season	Club	League	GP	G	A	Pts	AG	AA	APts	PIM	PP	SH	GW	S	%	TGF	PGF	TGA	PGA	+/–	GP	G	A	Pts	PIM	PP	SH	GW
1965-1967	Haliburton Hawks	OHA-D	STATISTICS NOT AVAILABLE																									
1967-68	Peterborough Petes	OHA-Jr.	49	13	9	22	....	....	....	88	....	....	....	....	....	....	....	....	....	....	5	0	3	3	20	....	....	....
1968-69	Peterborough Petes	OHA-Jr.	54	15	31	46	....	....	....	52	....	....	....	....	....	....	....	....	....	....	10	6	4	10	14	....	....	....
1969-70	Providence Reds	AHL	65	1	5	6	....	....	....	37	....	....	....	....	....	....	....	....	....	....	....	....	....	....	....	....	....	....
	Seattle Totems	WHL	....	....	....	....	....	....	....	....	....	....	....	....	....	....	....	....	....	....	5	0	0	0	0	....	....	....
1970-71	**California Golden Seals**	**NHL**	**78**	**8**	**24**	**32**	**8**	**20**	**28**	**73**	**3**	**0**	**2**	**135**	**5.9**	**109**	**28**	**140**	**31**	**–28**	....	....	....	....	....	....	....	....
1971-72	**California Golden Seals**	**NHL**	**5**	**1**	**3**	**4**	**1**	**3**	**4**	**6**	**0**	**0**	**0**	**13**	**7.7**	**9**	**1**	**12**	**4**	**0**	....	....	....	....	....	....	....	....
	Detroit Red Wings	**NHL**	**74**	**5**	**25**	**30**	**5**	**22**	**27**	**83**	**1**	**0**	**0**	**117**	**4.3**	**103**	**18**	**113**	**20**	**–8**	....	....	....	....	....	....	....	....
1972-73	**Detroit Red Wings**	**NHL**	**78**	**5**	**29**	**34**	**5**	**23**	**28**	**82**	**0**	**0**	**0**	**129**	**3.9**	**109**	**8**	**102**	**23**	**22**	....	....	....	....	....	....	....	....
1973-74	**Detroit Red Wings**	**NHL**	**33**	**2**	**14**	**16**	**2**	**12**	**14**	**33**	**0**	**0**	**0**	**46**	**4.3**	**57**	**10**	**49**	**3**	**1**	....	....	....	....	....	....	....	....
	Pittsburgh Penguins	**NHL**	**36**	**4**	**15**	**19**	**4**	**12**	**16**	**33**	**0**	**0**	**1**	**67**	**6.0**	**50**	**7**	**41**	**10**	**12**	....	....	....	....	....	....	....	....
1974-75	**Pittsburgh Penguins**	**NHL**	**72**	**15**	**45**	**60**	**13**	**34**	**47**	**52**	**6**	**1**	**0**	**152**	**9.9**	**135**	**46**	**102**	**26**	**13**	**9**	**2**	**6**	**8**	**10**	**1**	**0**	**0**
1975-76	**Pittsburgh Penguins**	**NHL**	**80**	**11**	**60**	**71**	**10**	**45**	**55**	**76**	**1**	**0**	**2**	**228**	**4.8**	**162**	**50**	**120**	**27**	**19**	**3**	**0**	**0**	**0**	**0**	**0**	**0**	**0**
1976-77	**Pittsburgh Penguins**	**NHL**	**80**	**7**	**34**	**41**	**6**	**26**	**32**	**72**	**3**	**1**	**0**	**219**	**3.2**	**136**	**34**	**118**	**27**	**11**	**3**	**2**	**1**	**3**	**0**	**0**	**0**	**0**
1977-78	**Pittsburgh Penguins**	**NHL**	**50**	**5**	**15**	**20**	**5**	**12**	**17**	**36**	**3**	**0**	**1**	**115**	**4.3**	**68**	**15**	**87**	**18**	**–16**	....	....	....	....	....	....	....	....
1978-79	**Pittsburgh Penguins**	**NHL**	**75**	**10**	**33**	**43**	**9**	**24**	**33**	**54**	**3**	**1**	**1**	**173**	**5.8**	**123**	**25**	**99**	**22**	**21**	**7**	**0**	**0**	**0**	**4**	**0**	**0**	**0**
1979-80	**Pittsburgh Penguins**	**NHL**	**78**	**6**	**27**	**33**	**5**	**20**	**25**	**36**	**2**	**0**	**1**	**166**	**3.6**	**116**	**17**	**123**	**40**	**16**	**5**	**1**	**0**	**1**	**18**	**1**	**0**	**0**
1980-81	**Pittsburgh Penguins**	**NHL**	**74**	**6**	**29**	**35**	**5**	**19**	**24**	**86**	**2**	**0**	**1**	**127**	**4.7**	**111**	**29**	**136**	**43**	**–11**	**4**	**0**	**1**	**1**	**6**	**0**	**0**	**0**
1981-82	**Pittsburgh Penguins**	**NHL**	**76**	**2**	**19**	**21**	**2**	**13**	**15**	**102**	**0**	**0**	**0**	**95**	**2.1**	**91**	**14**	**134**	**46**	**–11**	**1**	**0**	**0**	**0**	**0**	**0**	**0**	**0**
	NHL Totals		**889**	**87**	**372**	**459**	**80**	**285**	**365**	**824**	**24**	**3**	**9**	**1782**	**4.9**	**1379**	**302**	**1376**	**340**		**32**	**5**	**8**	**13**	**38**	**2**	**0**	**0**

OHA-Jr. Second All-Star Team (1969) • Played in NHL All-Star Game (1980)

Traded to **Detroit** by **California** for Tom Webster, October 22, 1971. Traded to **Pittsburgh** by **Detroit** for Jack Lynch and Jim Rutherford, January 17, 1974.

• STAIOS, Steve

D/RW – R. 6'1", 200 lbs. b: Hamilton, Ont., 7/28/1973. St. Louis' 1st, 27th overall, in 1991.

Season	Club	League	GP	G	A	Pts	AG	AA	APts	PIM	PP	SH	GW	S	%	TGF	PGF	TGA	PGA	+/–	GP	G	A	Pts	PIM	PP	SH	GW
1988-89	Hamilton Huskies	OMHA	58	13	39	52	....	....	....	78	....	....	....	....	....	....	....	....	....	....	....	....	....	....	....	....	....	....
1989-90	Hamilton Kilty B's	OJHL-B	40	9	27	36	....	....	....	66	....	....	....	....	....	....	....	....	....	....	....	....	....	....	....	....	....	....
1990-91	Niagara Falls Thunder	OHL	66	17	29	46	....	....	....	115	....	....	....	....	....	....	....	....	....	....	12	2	3	5	10	....	....	....
1991-92	Niagara Falls Thunder	OHL	65	11	42	53	....	....	....	122	....	....	....	....	....	....	....	....	....	....	17	7	8	15	27	....	....	....
1992-93	Niagara Falls Thunder	OHL	12	4	14	18	....	....	....	30	....	....	....	....	....	....	....	....	....	....	....	....	....	....	....	....	....	....
	Sudbury Wolves	OHL	53	13	44	57	....	....	....	67	....	....	....	....	....	....	....	....	....	....	11	5	6	11	22	....	....	....
1993-94	Peoria Rivermen	IHL	38	3	9	12	....	....	....	42	....	....	....	....	....	....	....	....	....	....	....	....	....	....	....	....	....	....
1994-95	Peoria Rivermen	IHL	60	3	13	16	....	....	....	64	....	....	....	....	....	....	....	....	....	....	6	0	0	0	10	....	....	....
1995-96	Peoria Rivermen	IHL	6	0	1	1	....	....	....	14	....	....	....	....	....	....	....	....	....	....	....	....	....	....	....	....	....	....
	Worcester IceCats	AHL	57	1	11	12	....	....	....	114	....	....	....	....	....	....	....	....	....	....	....	....	....	....	....	....	....	....
	Boston Bruins	**NHL**	**12**	**0**	**0**	**0**	**0**	**0**	**0**	**4**	**0**	**0**	**0**	**4**	**0.0**	**0**	**0**	**5**	**0**	**–5**	**3**	**0**	**0**	**0**	**0**	**0**	**0**	**0**
	Providence Bruins	AHL	7	1	4	5	....	....	....	8	....	....	....	....	....	....	....	....	....	....	....	....	....	....	....	....	....	....
1996-97	**Boston Bruins**	**NHL**	**54**	**3**	**8**	**11**	**3**	**7**	**10**	**71**	**0**	**0**	**0**	**56**	**5.4**	**28**	**1**	**58**	**5**	**–26**	....	....	....	....	....	....	....	....
	Vancouver Canucks	**NHL**	**9**	**0**	**6**	**6**	**0**	**5**	**5**	**20**	**0**	**0**	**0**	**10**	**0.0**	**7**	**0**	**6**	**1**	**2**	....	....	....	....	....	....	....	....
1997-98	**Vancouver Canucks**	**NHL**	**77**	**3**	**4**	**7**	**4**	**4**	**8**	**134**	**0**	**0**	**1**	**45**	**6.7**	**29**	**0**	**35**	**3**	**–3**	....	....	....	....	....	....	....	....
1998-99	**Vancouver Canucks**	**NHL**	**57**	**0**	**2**	**2**	**0**	**2**	**2**	**54**	**0**	**0**	**0**	**33**	**0.0**	**5**	**0**	**18**	**1**	**–12**	....	....	....	....	....	....	....	....
99-2000	**Atlanta Thrashers**	**NHL**	**27**	**2**	**3**	**5**	**2**	**3**	**5**	**66**	**0**	**0**	**0**	**38**	**5.3**	**14**	**3**	**21**	**5**	**–5**	....	....	....	....	....	....	....	....
	NHL Totals		**236**	**8**	**23**	**31**	**9**	**21**	**30**	**349**	**0**	**0**	**1**	**186**	**4.3**	**83**	**4**	**143**	**15**		**3**	**0**	**0**	**0**	**0**	**0**	**0**	**0**

Traded to **Boston** by **St. Louis** with Kevin Sawyer for Steve Leach, March 8, 1996. Claimed on waivers by **Vancouver** from **Boston**, March 18, 1997. Claimed by **Atlanta** from **Vancouver** in Expansion Draft, June 25, 1999. • Missed majority of 1999-2000 season recovering from knee injury originally suffered in game vs. Colorado, October 23, 1999. Traded to **New Jersey** by **Atlanta** for New Jersey's 9th round choice (Simon Gamache) in 2000 Entry Draft, June 12, 2000. Traded to **Atlanta** by **New Jersey** for future considerations, July 10, 2000.

• STAJDUHAR, Nick

D – L. 6'3", 200 lbs. b: Kitchener, Ont., 12/6/1974. Edmonton's 2nd, 16th overall, in 1993.

Season	Club	League	GP	G	A	Pts	AG	AA	APts	PIM	PP	SH	GW	S	%	TGF	PGF	TGA	PGA	+/–	GP	G	A	Pts	PIM	PP	SH	GW
1989-90	Kitchener Greenshirts	OMHA	74	13	38	51	....	....	....	90	....	....	....	....	....	....	....	....	....	....	....	....	....	....	....	....	....	....
1990-91	London Knights	OHL	66	3	12	15	....	....	....	51	....	....	....	....	....	....	....	....	....	....	7	0	0	0	2	....	....	....
1991-92	London Knights	OHL	66	6	15	21	....	....	....	62	....	....	....	....	....	....	....	....	....	....	10	1	4	5	10	....	....	....
1992-93	London Knights	OHL	49	15	45	60	....	....	....	58	....	....	....	....	....	....	....	....	....	....	12	4	11	15	10	....	....	....
1993-94	London Knights	OHL	52	34	52	86	....	....	....	58	....	....	....	....	....	....	....	....	....	....	5	0	2	2	8	....	....	....
	Canada	WJC-A	7	1	4	5	....	....	....	8	....	....	....	....	....	....	....	....	....	....	....	....	....	....	....	....	....	....
1994-95	Cape Breton Oilers	AHL	54	12	26	38	....	....	....	55	....	....	....	....	....	....	....	....	....	....	....	....	....	....	....	....	....	....
1995-96	Canada	Nat-Team	46	7	21	28	....	....	....	60	....	....	....	....	....	....	....	....	....	....	....	....	....	....	....	....	....	....
	Edmonton Oilers	**NHL**	**2**	**0**	**0**	**0**	**0**	**0**	**0**	**4**	**0**	**0**	**0**	**1**	**0.0**	**2**	**0**	**0**	**0**	**2**	....	....	....	....	....	....	....	....
	Cape Breton Oilers	AHL	8	2	0	2	....	....	....	11	....	....	....	....	....	....	....	....	....	....	....	....	....	....	....	....	....	....
1996-97	Hamilton Bulldogs	AHL	11	1	2	3	....	....	....	2	....	....	....	....	....	....	....	....	....	....	....	....	....	....	....	....	....	....
	Quebec Rafales	IHL	7	1	3	4	....	....	....	2	....	....	....	....	....	....	....	....	....	....	....	....	....	....	....	....	....	....
	Pensacola Ice Pilots	ECHL	30	9	15	24	....	....	....	32	....	....	....	....	....	....	....	....	....	....	12	1	6	7	34	....	....	....
1997-98	Cincinnati Mighty Ducks	AHL	13	0	0	0	....	....	....	12	....	....	....	....	....	....	....	....	....	....	....	....	....	....	....	....	....	....
	Fort Wayne Komets	IHL	15	2	0	2	....	....	....	27	....	....	....	....	....	....	....	....	....	....	....	....	....	....	....	....	....	....
	Pensacola Ice Pilots	ECHL	19	4	8	12	....	....	....	36	....	....	....	....	....	....	....	....	....	....	19	5	21	26	10	....	....	....
1998-99	Pensacola Ice Pilots	ECHL	33	7	18	25	....	....	....	66	....	....	....	....	....	....	....	....	....	....	....	....	....	....	....	....	....	....
	Louisiana IceGators	ECHL	30	5	18	23	....	....	....	26	....	....	....	....	....	....	....	....	....	....	5	1	1	2	10	....	....	....
99-2000	Flint Generals	UHL	67	22	49	71	....	....	....	106	....	....	....	....	....	....	....	....	....	....	15	5	*21	*26	24	....	....	....
	NHL Totals		**2**	**0**	**0**	**0**	**0**	**0**	**0**	**4**	**0**	**0**	**0**	**1**	**0.0**	**2**	**0**	**0**	**0**		....	....	....	....	....	....	....	....

OHL First All-Star Team (1994) • UHL Second All-Star Team (2000) • Named UHL Playoff MVP (2000)

• STAMLER, Lorne

Lorne Joseph Alexander LW – L. 6', 190 lbs. b: Winnipeg, Man., 8/9/1951. Los Angeles' 7th, 103rd overall, in 1971.

Season	Club	League	GP	G	A	Pts	AG	AA	APts	PIM	PP	SH	GW	S	%	TGF	PGF	TGA	PGA	+/–	GP	G	A	Pts	PIM	PP	SH	GW
1968-69	Toronto Marlboros	OHA-Jr.	25	2	3	5	....	....	....	14	....	....	....	....	....	....	....	....	....	....	1	0	0	0	0	....	....	....
1969-70	Toronto Marlboros	OHA-Jr.	51	6	12	18	....	....	....	32	....	....	....	....	....	....	....	....	....	....	18	4	7	11	24	....	....	....
1970-71	Michigan Tech Huskies	WCHA	32	8	5	13	....	....	....	8	....	....	....	....	....	....	....	....	....	....	....	....	....	....	....	....	....	....
1971-72	Michigan Tech Huskies	WCHA	32	20	12	32	....	....	....	20	....	....	....	....	....	....	....	....	....	....	....	....	....	....	....	....	....	....
1972-73	Michigan Tech Huskies	WCHA	37	11	17	28	....	....	....	22	....	....	....	....	....	....	....	....	....	....	....	....	....	....	....	....	....	....
1973-74	Michigan Tech Huskies	WCHA	39	26	30	56	....	....	....	36	....	....	....	....	....	....	....	....	....	....	....	....	....	....	....	....	....	....

			REGULAR SEASON																		PLAYOFFS							
Season	Club	League	GP	G	A	Pts	AG	AA	APts	PIM	PP	SH	GW	S	%	TGF	PGF	TGA	PGA	+/–	GP	G	A	Pts	PIM	PP	SH	GW
1974-75	Springfield Indians	AHL	43	16	9	25	....	....	....	5	....	....	....	....	....	....	....	....	....	....	17	5	8	13	8	....	....	....
1975-76	Fort Worth Texans	CHL	76	33	33	66	....	....	....	12	....	....	....	....	....	....	....	....	....	....	....	....	....	....	....	....	....	....
1976-77	**Los Angeles Kings**	**NHL**	**7**	**2**	**1**	**3**	**2**	**1**	**3**	**2**	**0**	**0**	**0**	**8**	**25.0**	**3**	**0**	**3**	**0**	**0**	....	....	....	....	....	....	....	....
	Fort Worth Texans	CHL	48	19	21	40	....	....	....	12	....	....	....	....	....	....	....	....	....	....	5	*4	2	6	0	....	....	....
1977-78	**Los Angeles Kings**	**NHL**	**2**	**0**	**0**	**0**	**0**	**0**	**0**	**0**	**0**	**0**	**0**	**1**	**0.0**	**0**	**0**	**0**	**0**	**0**	....	....	....	....	....	....	....	....
	Springfield Indians	AHL	70	18	34	52	....	....	....	4	....	....	....	....	....	....	....	....	....	....	....	....	....	....	....	....	....	....
1978-79	**Toronto Maple Leafs**	**NHL**	**45**	**4**	**3**	**7**	**3**	**2**	**5**	**2**	**0**	**0**	**1**	**31**	**12.9**	**9**	**1**	**27**	**13**	**–6**	....	....	....	....	....	....	....	....
	New Brunswick Hawks	AHL	14	9	1	10	....	....	....	4	....	....	....	....	....	....	....	....	....	....	5	2	1	3	9	....	....	....
1979-80	**Winnipeg Jets**	**NHL**	**62**	**8**	**7**	**15**	**7**	**5**	**12**	**12**	**0**	**0**	**0**	**89**	**9.0**	**23**	**0**	**59**	**7**	**–29**	....	....	....	....	....	....	....	....
	Tulsa Oilers	CHL	6	8	3	11	....	....	....	0	....	....	....	....	....	....	....	....	....	....	....	....	....	....	....	....	....	....
1980-81	Indianapolis Checkers	CHL	42	7	6	13	....	....	....	25	....	....	....	....	....	....	....	....	....	....	....	....	....	....	....	....	....	....
1981-82	Indianapolis Checkers	CHL	53	5	7	12	....	....	....	8	....	....	....	....	....	....	....	....	....	....	13	4	2	6	0	....	....	....
1982-83	Indianapolis Checkers	CHL	38	4	4	8	....	....	....	0	....	....	....	....	....	....	....	....	....	....	13	2	0	2	0	....	....	....
1983-84	Indianapolis Checkers	CHL	15	3	2	5	....	....	....	0	....	....	....	....	....	....	....	....	....	....	....	....	....	....	....	....	....	....
	NHL Totals		**116**	**14**	**11**	**25**	**12**	**8**	**20**	**16**	**0**	**0**	**1**	**129**	**10.9**	**35**	**1**	**89**	**20**		....	....	....	....	....	....	....	....

WCHA Second All-Star Team (1974)

Traded to **Toronto** by **LA Kings** with Dave Hutchison for Brian Glennie, Scott Garland, Kurt Walker and Toronto's 2nd round choice (Mark Hardy) in 1979 Entry Draft, June 14, 1978. Claimed by **Winnipeg** from **Toronto** in Expansion Draft, June 13, 1979. Signed as a free agent by **NY Islanders**, October 8, 1980.

• STANDING, George

George Michael RW – R. 5'10", 190 lbs. b: Toronto, Ont., 8/3/1941.

Season	Club	League	GP	G	A	Pts	AG	AA	APts	PIM	PP	SH	GW	S	%	TGF	PGF	TGA	PGA	+/–	GP	G	A	Pts	PIM	PP	SH	GW
1957-58	Toronto Midget Marlboros	OMHA	STATISTICS NOT AVAILABLE																									
	Toronto Marlboros	OHA-Jr.	2	1	0	1	....	....	....	0	....	....	....	....	....	....	....	....	....	....	....	....	....	....	....	....	....	....
1958-59	Weston Dukes	OHA-B	STATISTICS NOT AVAILABLE																									
	Toronto Marlboros	OHA-Jr.	26	1	2	3	....	....	....	18	....	....	....	....	....	....	....	....	....	....	....	....	....	....	....	....	....	....
1959-60	Toronto Marlboros	OHA-Jr.	45	1	1	2	....	....	....	4	....	....	....	....	....	....	....	....	....	....	4	0	0	0	0	....	....	....
1960-61	Toronto Marlboros	OHA-Jr.	48	18	24	42	....	....	....	69	....	....	....	....	....	....	....	....	....	....	....	....	....	....	....	....	....	....
1961-62	Guelph Royals	OHA-Jr.	10	5	5	10	....	....	....	18	....	....	....	....	....	....	....	....	....	....	....	....	....	....	....	....	....	....
	St. Catharines Teepees	OHA-Jr.	39	17	19	36	....	....	....	25	....	....	....	....	....	....	....	....	....	....	6	0	2	2	20	....	....	....
	North Bay Trappers	EPHL	1	0	0	0	....	....	....	2	....	....	....	....	....	....	....	....	....	....	....	....	....	....	....	....	....	....
1962-63			DID NOT PLAY																									
1963-64	Nashville Dixie Flyers	EHL	72	20	33	53	....	....	....	39	....	....	....	....	....	....	....	....	....	....	3	0	0	0	0	....	....	....
1964-65	Nashville Dixie Flyers	EHL	67	54	34	88	....	....	....	79	....	....	....	....	....	....	....	....	....	....	13	4	10	14	4	....	....	....
1965-66	Nashville Dixie Flyers	EHL	72	30	36	66	....	....	....	36	....	....	....	....	....	....	....	....	....	....	11	4	5	9	4	....	....	....
1966-67	Nashville Dixie Flyers	EHL	72	47	40	87	....	....	....	46	....	....	....	....	....	....	....	....	....	....	14	*14	8	*22	4	....	....	....
1967-68	**Minnesota North Stars**	**NHL**	**2**	**0**	**0**	**0**	**0**	**0**	**0**	**0**	**0**	**0**	**0**	**1**	**0.0**	**1**	**1**	**1**	**0**	**–1**	....	....	....	....	....	....	....	....
	Memphis South Stars	CPHL	63	20	15	35	....	....	....	34	....	....	....	....	....	....	....	....	....	....	3	0	3	3	0	....	....	....
1968-69	Memphis South Stars	CHL	13	3	3	6	....	....	....	14	....	....	....	....	....	....	....	....	....	....	....	....	....	....	....	....	....	....
	Jacksonville Rockets	EHL	36	15	20	35	....	....	....	6	....	....	....	....	....	....	....	....	....	....	4	1	2	3	0	....	....	....
1969-70	Nashville Dixie Flyers	EHL	74	30	45	75	....	....	....	35	....	....	....	....	....	....	....	....	....	....	....	....	....	....	....	....	....	....
1970-71	Nashville Dixie Flyers	EHL	36	10	15	25	....	....	....	7	....	....	....	....	....	....	....	....	....	....	4	1	2	3	0	....	....	....
1971-72	St. Petersburg Suns	EHL	15	3	7	10	....	....	....	6	....	....	....	....	....	....	....	....	....	....	....	....	....	....	....	....	....	....
	NHL Totals		**2**	**0**	**0**	**0**	**0**	**0**	**0**	**0**	**0**	**0**	**0**	**1**	**0.0**	**1**	**1**	**1**	**0**		....	....	....	....	....	....	....	....

EHL South First All-Star Team (1965) • EHL South Second All-Star Team (1967)

• Missed majority of 1958-59 season recovering from wrist injury, December, 1958. Signed as a free agent by **Minnesota**, September, 1967.

• STANFIELD, Fred

Frederick William LW – L. 5'10", 185 lbs. b: Toronto, Ont., 5/4/1944.

Season	Club	League	GP	G	A	Pts	AG	AA	APts	PIM	PP	SH	GW	S	%	TGF	PGF	TGA	PGA	+/–	GP	G	A	Pts	PIM	PP	SH	GW
1960-61	Mississagua Reps	MTHL	STATISTICS NOT AVAILABLE																									
1961-62	St. Catharines Teepees	OHA-Jr.	49	11	15	26	....	....	....	19	....	....	....	....	....	....	....	....	....	....	6	0	0	0	2	....	....	....
1962-63	St. Catharines Teepees	OHA-Jr.	48	28	39	67	....	....	....	25	....	....	....	....	....	....	....	....	....	....	....	....	....	....	....	....	....	....
1963-64	St. Catharines Black Hawks	OHA-Jr.	56	34	75	109	....	....	....	29	....	....	....	....	....	....	....	....	....	....	13	15	12	27	4	....	....	....
1964-65	**Chicago Black Hawks**	**NHL**	**58**	**7**	**10**	**17**	**8**	**10**	**18**	**14**	....	....	....	....	....	....	....	....	....	....	**14**	**2**	**1**	**3**	**2**	**0**	**0**	**0**
1965-66	**Chicago Black Hawks**	**NHL**	**39**	**2**	**2**	**4**	**2**	**2**	**4**	**2**	....	....	....	....	....	....	....	....	....	....	**5**	**0**	**0**	**0**	**2**	**0**	**0**	**0**
	St. Louis Braves	CPHL	24	7	11	18	....	....	....	2	....	....	....	....	....	....	....	....	....	....	....	....	....	....	....	....	....	....
1966-67	**Chicago Black Hawks**	**NHL**	**10**	**1**	**0**	**1**	**1**	**0**	**1**	**0**	....	....	....	....	....	....	....	....	....	....	**1**	**0**	**0**	**0**	**0**	**0**	**0**	**0**
	St. Louis Braves	CPHL	37	20	21	41	....	....	....	10	....	....	....	....	....	....	....	....	....	....	....	....	....	....	....	....	....	....
1967-68	**Boston Bruins**	**NHL**	**73**	**20**	**44**	**64**	**23**	**44**	**67**	**10**	**3**	**0**	**1**	**215**	**9.3**	**95**	**30**	**57**	**1**	**9**	**4**	**0**	**1**	**1**	**0**	**0**	**0**	**0**
1968-69	**Boston Bruins**	**NHL**	**71**	**25**	**29**	**54**	**27**	**26**	**53**	**22**	**6**	**0**	**1**	**199**	**12.6**	**80**	**26**	**63**	**5**	**–4**	**10**	**2**	**2**	**4**	**0**	**1**	**0**	**0**
1969-70♦	**Boston Bruins**	**NHL**	**73**	**23**	**35**	**58**	**25**	**33**	**58**	**14**	**13**	**0**	**3**	**254**	**9.1**	**107**	**63**	**50**	**13**	**7**	**14**	**4**	**12**	**16**	**6**	**2**	**0**	**0**
1970-71	**Boston Bruins**	**NHL**	**75**	**24**	**52**	**76**	**24**	**44**	**68**	**12**	**8**	**0**	**3**	**267**	**9.0**	**153**	**74**	**48**	**1**	**32**	**7**	**3**	**4**	**7**	**0**	**1**	**0**	**0**
1971-72♦	**Boston Bruins**	**NHL**	**78**	**23**	**56**	**79**	**23**	**49**	**72**	**12**	**5**	**1**	**4**	**168**	**13.7**	**112**	**48**	**45**	**1**	**20**	**15**	**7**	**9**	**16**	**0**	**1**	**0**	**0**
1972-73	**Boston Bruins**	**NHL**	**78**	**20**	**58**	**78**	**19**	**46**	**65**	**10**	**7**	**0**	**2**	**214**	**9.3**	**142**	**63**	**68**	**1**	**12**	**5**	**1**	**1**	**2**	**0**	**0**	**0**	**0**
1973-74	**Minnesota North Stars**	**NHL**	**71**	**16**	**28**	**44**	**15**	**23**	**38**	**10**	**3**	**0**	**2**	**218**	**7.3**	**73**	**24**	**69**	**6**	**–14**	....	....	....	....	....	....	....	....
1974-75	**Minnesota North Stars**	**NHL**	**40**	**8**	**18**	**26**	**7**	**13**	**20**	**12**	**2**	**0**	**1**	**107**	**7.5**	**40**	**22**	**35**	**3**	**–14**	....	....	....	....	....	....	....	....
	Buffalo Sabres	**NHL**	**32**	**12**	**21**	**33**	**10**	**16**	**26**	**4**	**6**	**0**	**2**	**77**	**15.6**	**54**	**27**	**20**	**2**	**9**	**17**	**2**	**4**	**6**	**0**	**0**	**0**	**0**
1975-76	**Buffalo Sabres**	**NHL**	**80**	**18**	**30**	**48**	**16**	**22**	**38**	**4**	**2**	**1**	**3**	**112**	**16.1**	**78**	**28**	**60**	**15**	**5**	**9**	**0**	**1**	**1**	**0**	**0**	**0**	**0**
1976-77	**Buffalo Sabres**	**NHL**	**79**	**9**	**14**	**23**	**8**	**11**	**19**	**6**	**2**	**0**	**2**	**69**	**13.0**	**37**	**19**	**20**	**0**	**–2**	**5**	**0**	**0**	**0**	**0**	**0**	**0**	**0**
1977-78	**Buffalo Sabres**	**NHL**	**57**	**3**	**8**	**11**	**3**	**6**	**9**	**2**	**0**	**0**	**0**	**38**	**7.9**	**21**	**12**	**21**	**4**	**–8**	....	....	....	....	....	....	....	....
1978-79	Hershey Bears	AHL	50	19	41	60	....	....	....	4	....	....	....	....	....	....	....	....	....	....	....	....	....	....	....	....	....	....
	NHL Totals		**914**	**211**	**405**	**616**	**211**	**345**	**556**	**134**	....	....	....	....	....	....	....	....	....	....	**106**	**21**	**35**	**56**	**10**	....	....	....

• Brother of Jack and Jim

Traded to **Boston** by **Chicago** with Phil Esposito and Ken Hodge for Gilles Marotte, Pit Martin and Jack Norris, May 15, 1967. Traded to **Minnesota** by **Boston** for Gilles Gilbert, May 22, 1973. Traded to **Buffalo** by **Minnesota** for Norm Gratton and Buffalo's 3rd round choice (Ron Zanussi) in 1976 Amateur Draft, January 27, 1975.

• STANFIELD, Jim

James Boviard C/RW – L. 5'10", 160 lbs. b: Toronto, Ont., 1/1/1947.

Season	Club	League	GP	G	A	Pts	AG	AA	APts	PIM	PP	SH	GW	S	%	TGF	PGF	TGA	PGA	+/–	GP	G	A	Pts	PIM	PP	SH	GW
1964-65	St. Catharines Black Hawks	OHA-Jr.	3	0	1	1	....	....	....	0	....	....	....	....	....	....	....	....	....	....	....	....	....	....	....	....	....	....
1965-66	St. Catharines Black Hawks	OHA-Jr.	45	7	10	17	....	....	....	42	....	....	....	....	....	....	....	....	....	....	2	0	0	0	4	....	....	....
1966-67	London Nationals	OHA-Jr.	45	32	19	51	....	....	....	53	....	....	....	....	....	....	....	....	....	....	6	6	2	8	0	....	....	....
1967-68	Dallas Black Hawks	CPHL	24	5	5	10	....	....	....	6	....	....	....	....	....	....	....	....	....	....	....	....	....	....	....	....	....	....
1968-69	Dallas Black Hawks	CHL	66	24	15	39	....	....	....	16	....	....	....	....	....	....	....	....	....	....	11	5	3	8	2	....	....	....
1969-70	**Los Angeles Kings**	**NHL**	**1**	**0**	**0**	**0**	**0**	**0**	**0**	**0**	**0**	**0**	**0**	**0**	**0.0**	**0**	**0**	**0**	**0**	**0**	....	....	....	....	....	....	....	....
	Dallas Black Hawks	CHL	55	18	11	29	....	....	....	8	....	....	....	....	....	....	....	....	....	....	....	....	....	....	....	....	....	....
	Springfield Kings	AHL	18	11	5	16	....	....	....	2	....	....	....	....	....	....	....	....	....	....	14	*8	9	*17	2	....	....	....
1970-71	**Los Angeles Kings**	**NHL**	**2**	**0**	**0**	**0**	**0**	**0**	**0**	**0**	**0**	**0**	**0**	**8**	**0.0**	**2**	**1**	**0**	**0**	**1**	....	....	....	....	....	....	....	....
	Springfield Kings	AHL	45	7	19	26	....	....	....	22	....	....	....	....	....	....	....	....	....	....	11	1	0	1	6	....	....	....
1971-72	**Los Angeles Kings**	**NHL**	**4**	**0**	**1**	**1**	**0**	**1**	**1**	**0**	**0**	**0**	**0**	**7**	**0.0**	**0**	**0**	**1**	**0**	**–1**	....	....	....	....	....	....	....	....
	Springfield Kings	AHL	64	30	26	56	....	....	....	11	....	....	....	....	....	....	....	....	....	....	3	0	0	0	0	....	....	....
1972-73	San Diego Gulls	WHL	21	9	14	23	....	....	....	4	....	....	....	....	....	....	....	....	....	....	....	....	....	....	....	....	....	....
	Portland Buckaroos	WHL	47	15	8	23	....	....	....	7	....	....	....	....	....	....	....	....	....	....	....	....	....	....	....	....	....	....
1973-74	San Diego Gulls	WHL	32	4	14	18	....	....	....	2	....	....	....	....	....	....	....	....	....	....	....	....	....	....	....	....	....	....
	Denver Spurs	WHL	35	15	21	36	....	....	....	4	....	....	....	....	....	....	....	....	....	....	....	....	....	....	....	....	....	....
1974-75	Spokane Jets	WIHL	47	45	57	*102	....	....	....	6	....	....	....	....	....	....	....	....	....	....	....	....	....	....	....	....	....	....

			REGULAR SEASON																		PLAYOFFS							
Season	Club	League	GP	G	A	Pts	AG	AA	APts	PIM	PP	SH	GW	S	%	TGF	PGF	TGA	PGA	+/–	GP	G	A	Pts	PIM	PP	SH	GW
1975-76	Spokane Jets	WHL	33	33	21	54	....	....	....	2	....	....	....	....	....	....	....	....	....	....	....	....	....	....	....	....	....	....
	Buffalo Norsemen	NAHL	27	10	19	29	....	....	....	0	....	....	....	....	....	....	....	....	....	....	4	1	1	2	0	....	....	....
1976-77	Spokane Flyers	WHL	56	10	16	26	....	....	....	4	....	....	....	....	....	....	....	....	....	....	....	....	....	....	....	....	....	....
	NHL Totals		**7**	**0**	**1**	**1**	**0**	**1**	**1**	**0**	**0**	**0**	**0**	**15**	**0.0**	**2**	**1**	**1**	**0**		....	....	....	....	....	....	....	....

• Brother of Fred and Jack

Traded to **LA Kings** by **Chicago** with Gilles Marotte and Denis Dejordy for Bryan Campbell, Bill White and Gerry Desjardins, February 20, 1970. Traded to **Portland** (WHL) by **LA Kings** with Mike Keeler and Glen Toner for John VanHorlick, December, 1972. Traded to **Philadelphia** by **Portland** (WHL) for cash, May, 1973. Traded to **San Diego** (WHL) by **Philadelphia** with Tom Trevelyan, Bob Currier and Bob Hurlburt for Bruce Cowick, May 25, 1973. Traded to **St. Louis** (Denver-WHL) by **San Diego** (WHL) for Bernie MacNeil, January 16, 1974.

• STANKIEWICZ, Myron

LW – L. 5'11", 185 lbs. b: Kitchener, Ont., 12/4/1935.

Season	Club	League	GP	G	A	Pts	AG	AA	APts	PIM	PP	SH	GW	S	%	TGF	PGF	TGA	PGA	+/–	GP	G	A	Pts	PIM	PP	SH	GW
1952-53	Kitchener Greenshirts	OHA-Jr.	18	0	3	3	....	....	....	2	....	....	....	....	....	....	....	....	....	....	....	....	....	....	....	....	....	....
1953-54	Barrie Flyers	OHA-Jr.	19	0	6	6	....	....	....	0	....	....	....	....	....	....	....	....	....	....	....	....	....	....	....	....	....	....
1954-55	Kitchener–Galt Kists	OHA-Jr.	40	8	10	18	....	....	....	52	....	....	....	....	....	....	....	....	....	....	4	0	0	0	9	....	....	....
1955-56	Toledo–Indianapolis Chiefs	IHL	54	16	10	26	....	....	....	76	....	....	....	....	....	....	....	....	....	....	....	....	....	....	....	....	....	....
1956-57	Toledo–Indianapolis Chiefs	IHL	58	16	16	32	....	....	....	52	....	....	....	....	....	....	....	....	....	....	6	0	0	0	4	....	....	....
1957-58	Indianapolis Chiefs	IHL	63	25	36	61	....	....	....	58	....	....	....	....	....	....	....	....	....	....	11	2	4	6	12	....	....	....
1958-59	Edmonton Flyers	WHL	35	4	11	15	....	....	....	19	....	....	....	....	....	....	....	....	....	....	....	....	....	....	....	....	....	....
	Quebec Aces	QHL	20	4	2	6	....	....	....	6	....	....	....	....	....	....	....	....	....	....	....	....	....	....	....	....	....	....
1959-60	Quebec Aces	AHL	62	10	11	21	....	....	....	66	....	....	....	....	....	....	....	....	....	....	....	....	....	....	....	....	....	....
1960-61	Sudbury Wolves	EPHL	37	9	10	19	....	....	....	27	....	....	....	....	....	....	....	....	....	....	....	....	....	....	....	....	....	....
	Hershey Bears	AHL	33	2	11	13	....	....	....	39	....	....	....	....	....	....	....	....	....	....	....	....	....	....	....	....	....	....
1961-62	Hershey Bears	AHL	70	20	33	53	....	....	....	66	....	....	....	....	....	....	....	....	....	....	7	2	2	4	4	....	....	....
1962-63	Hershey Bears	AHL	68	21	43	64	....	....	....	30	....	....	....	....	....	....	....	....	....	....	15	3	4	7	21	....	....	....
1963-64	Hershey Bears	AHL	72	25	41	66	....	....	....	65	....	....	....	....	....	....	....	....	....	....	6	1	1	2	21	....	....	....
1964-65	Hershey Bears	AHL	72	28	36	64	....	....	....	59	....	....	....	....	....	....	....	....	....	....	15	2	6	8	16	....	....	....
1965-66	Hershey Bears	AHL	72	28	30	58	....	....	....	53	....	....	....	....	....	....	....	....	....	....	3	1	0	1	2	....	....	....
1966-67	Hershey Bears	AHL	70	8	23	31	....	....	....	42	....	....	....	....	....	....	....	....	....	....	4	1	0	1	5	....	....	....
1967-68	Hershey Bears	AHL	65	23	27	50	....	....	....	49	....	....	....	....	....	....	....	....	....	....	1	0	0	0	0	....	....	....
1968-69	**St. Louis Blues**	**NHL**	**16**	**0**	**2**	**2**	**0**	**2**	**2**	**11**	**0**	**0**	**0**	**17**	**0.0**	**6**	**0**	**8**	**0**	**–2**	....	....	....	....	....	....	....	....
	Omaha Knights	CHL	5	1	2	3	....	....	....	8	....	....	....	....	....	....	....	....	....	....	....	....	....	....	....	....	....	....
	Philadelphia Flyers	**NHL**	**19**	**0**	**5**	**5**	**0**	**4**	**4**	**25**	**0**	**0**	**0**	**43**	**0.0**	**7**	**0**	**18**	**0**	**–11**	**1**	**0**	**0**	**0**	**0**	**0**	**0**	**0**
	Quebec Aces	AHL	15	6	6	12	....	....	....	5	....	....	....	....	....	....	....	....	....	....	15	5	8	13	10	....	....	....
	NHL Totals		**35**	**0**	**7**	**7**	**0**	**6**	**6**	**36**	**0**	**0**	**0**	**60**	**0.0**	**13**	**0**	**26**	**0**		**1**	**0**	**0**	**0**	**0**	**0**	**0**	**0**

• Brother of Ed

Traded to **Quebec** (QHL) by **Detroit** (Edmonton-WHL) for Roger Dejordy, January, 1959. Traded to **Hershey** (AHL) by **Quebec** (AHL) with Al Millar for Claude Dufour, June, 1960. Claimed by **St. Louis** from **Hershey** (AHL) in Inter-League Draft, June 11, 1968. Traded to **LA Kings** by **St. Louis** for Terry Gray, June 11, 1968. Claimed by **St. Louis** from **LA Kings** in Intra-League Draft, June 12, 1968. Claimed on waivers by **Philadelphia** from **St. Louis**, January 16, 1969.

• STANLEY, Allan

Allan Herbert "Snowshoes" D – L. 6'1", 170 lbs. b: Timmins, Ont., 3/1/1926. **HHOF**

Season	Club	League	GP	G	A	Pts	AG	AA	APts	PIM	PP	SH	GW	S	%	TGF	PGF	TGA	PGA	+/–	GP	G	A	Pts	PIM	PP	SH	GW
1942-43	Holman Pluggers	NOHA	STATISTICS NOT AVAILABLE																									
1943-44	Boston Olympics	EAHL	40	10	32	42	....	....	....	10	....	....	....	....	....	....	....	....	....	....	....	....	....	....	....	....	....	....
1944-45	Porcupine Combines	NOJHA	....	5	4	9	....	....	....	7	....	....	....	....	....	....	....	....	....	....	....	....	....	....	....	....	....	....
1945-46	Boston Olympics	EAHL	30	8	15	23	....	....	....	35	....	....	....	....	....	....	....	....	....	....	....	....	....	....	....	....	....	....
1946-47	Providence Reds	AHL	54	8	13	21	....	....	....	32	....	....	....	....	....	....	....	....	....	....	....	....	....	....	....	....	....	....
1947-48	Boston Olympics	QSHL	1	0	0	0	....	....	....	0	....	....	....	....	....	....	....	....	....	....	....	....	....	....	....	....	....	....
	Providence Reds	AHL	68	9	32	41	....	....	....	81	....	....	....	....	....	....	....	....	....	....	5	0	0	0	4	....	....	....
1948-49	Providence Reds	AHL	23	7	16	23	....	....	....	24	....	....	....	....	....	....	....	....	....	....	....	....	....	....	....	....	....	....
	New York Rangers	**NHL**	**40**	**2**	**8**	**10**	**3**	**11**	**14**	**22**	....	....	....	....	....	....	....	....	....	....	....	....	....	....	....	....	....	....
1949-50	**New York Rangers**	**NHL**	**55**	**4**	**4**	**8**	**5**	**5**	**10**	**58**	....	....	....	....	....	....	....	....	....	....	**12**	**2**	**5**	**7**	**10**	....	....	....
1950-51	**New York Rangers**	**NHL**	**70**	**7**	**14**	**21**	**9**	**17**	**26**	**75**	....	....	....	....	....	....	....	....	....	....	....	....	....	....	....	....	....	....
1951-52	**New York Rangers**	**NHL**	**50**	**5**	**14**	**19**	**7**	**17**	**24**	**52**	....	....	....	....	....	....	....	....	....	....	....	....	....	....	....	....	....	....
1952-53	**New York Rangers**	**NHL**	**70**	**5**	**12**	**17**	**7**	**14**	**21**	**52**	....	....	....	....	....	....	....	....	....	....	....	....	....	....	....	....	....	....
1953-54	**New York Rangers**	**NHL**	**10**	**0**	**2**	**2**	**0**	**2**	**2**	**11**	....	....	....	....	....	....	....	....	....	....	....	....	....	....	....	....	....	....
	Vancouver Canucks	WHL	47	6	30	36	....	....	....	43	....	....	....	....	....	....	....	....	....	....	13	2	5	7	10	....	....	....
1954-55	**New York Rangers**	**NHL**	**12**	**0**	**1**	**1**	**0**	**1**	**1**	**2**	....	....	....	....	....	....	....	....	....	....	....	....	....	....	....	....	....	....
	Chicago Black Hawks	**NHL**	**52**	**10**	**15**	**25**	**13**	**17**	**30**	**22**	....	....	....	....	....	....	....	....	....	....	....	....	....	....	....	....	....	....
1955-56	**Chicago Black Hawks**	**NHL**	**59**	**4**	**14**	**18**	**5**	**17**	**22**	**70**	....	....	....	....	....	....	....	....	....	....	....	....	....	....	....	....	....	....
1956-57	**Boston Bruins**	**NHL**	**60**	**6**	**25**	**31**	**8**	**28**	**36**	**45**	....	....	....	....	....	....	....	....	....	....	....	....	....	....	....	....	....	....
1957-58	**Boston Bruins**	**NHL**	**69**	**6**	**25**	**31**	**7**	**26**	**33**	**37**	....	....	....	....	....	....	....	....	....	....	**12**	**1**	**3**	**4**	**6**	....	....	....
1958-59	**Toronto Maple Leafs**	**NHL**	**70**	**1**	**22**	**23**	**1**	**22**	**23**	**47**	....	....	....	....	....	....	....	....	....	....	**12**	**0**	**3**	**3**	**2**	....	....	....
1959-60	**Toronto Maple Leafs**	**NHL**	**64**	**10**	**23**	**33**	**12**	**22**	**34**	**22**	....	....	....	....	....	....	....	....	....	....	**10**	**2**	**3**	**5**	**2**	....	....	....
1960-61	**Toronto Maple Leafs**	**NHL**	**68**	**9**	**25**	**34**	**10**	**24**	**34**	**42**	....	....	....	....	....	....	....	....	....	....	**5**	**0**	**3**	**3**	**0**	....	....	....
1961-62♦	**Toronto Maple Leafs**	**NHL**	**60**	**9**	**26**	**35**	**10**	**25**	**35**	**24**	....	....	....	....	....	....	....	....	....	....	**12**	**0**	**3**	**3**	**6**	....	....	....
1962-63♦	**Toronto Maple Leafs**	**NHL**	**61**	**4**	**15**	**19**	**5**	**15**	**20**	**22**	....	....	....	....	....	....	....	....	....	....	**10**	**1**	**6**	**7**	**8**	....	....	....
1963-64♦	**Toronto Maple Leafs**	**NHL**	**70**	**6**	**21**	**27**	**7**	**22**	**29**	**60**	....	....	....	....	....	....	....	....	....	....	**14**	**1**	**6**	**7**	**20**	....	....	....
1964-65	**Toronto Maple Leafs**	**NHL**	**64**	**2**	**15**	**17**	**2**	**15**	**17**	**30**	....	....	....	....	....	....	....	....	....	....	**6**	**0**	**1**	**1**	**12**	....	....	....
1965-66	**Toronto Maple Leafs**	**NHL**	**59**	**4**	**14**	**18**	**4**	**13**	**17**	**35**	....	....	....	....	....	....	....	....	....	....	**1**	**0**	**0**	**0**	**0**	....	....	....
1966-67♦	**Toronto Maple Leafs**	**NHL**	**53**	**1**	**12**	**13**	**1**	**12**	**13**	**20**	....	....	....	....	....	....	....	....	....	....	**12**	**0**	**2**	**2**	**10**	....	....	....
1967-68	**Toronto Maple Leafs**	**NHL**	**64**	**1**	**13**	**14**	**1**	**13**	**14**	**16**	**0**	**0**	**0**	**61**	**1.6**	**62**	**0**	**63**	**7**	**6**	....	....	....	....	....	....	....	....
1968-69	**Philadelphia Flyers**	**NHL**	**64**	**4**	**13**	**17**	**4**	**12**	**16**	**28**	**2**	**0**	**0**	**75**	**5.3**	**62**	**29**	**49**	**12**	**–4**	**3**	**0**	**1**	**1**	**4**	**0**	**0**	**0**
	NHL Totals		**1244**	**100**	**333**	**433**	**121**	**350**	**471**	**792**	....	....	....	....	....	....	....	....	....	....	**109**	**7**	**36**	**43**	**80**	....	....	....

EAHL First All-Star Team (1944) • WHL First All-Star Team (1954) • NHL Second All-Star Team (1960, 1961, 1966) • Played in NHL All-Star Game (1955, 1957, 1960, 1962, 1963, 1967, 1968)

Traded to **NY Rangers** by **Providence** (AHL) for Eddie Kullman, Elwyn Morris, cash and future considerations (Buck Davies, June, 1949), December 9, 1948. Traded to **Chicago** by **NY Rangers** with Nick Mickoski and Rich Lamoureux for Bill Gadsby and Pete Conacher, November 23, 1954. Traded to **Boston** by **Chicago** for cash, October 8, 1956. Traded to **Toronto** by **Boston** for Jim Morrison, October 8, 1958. Claimed by **Philadelphia** (Quebec-AHL) from **Toronto** in Reverse Draft, June 13, 1968.

• STANLEY, Daryl

D/LW – L. 6'2", 200 lbs. b: Winnipeg, Man., 12/2/1962.

Season	Club	League	GP	G	A	Pts	AG	AA	APts	PIM	PP	SH	GW	S	%	TGF	PGF	TGA	PGA	+/–	GP	G	A	Pts	PIM	PP	SH	GW
1978-79	Revelstoke Bruins	BCJHL	46	12	11	23	....	....	....	117	....	....	....	....	....	....	....	....	....	....	....	....	....	....	....	....	....	....
1979-80	New Westminster Bruins	WHL	64	2	12	14	....	....	....	110	....	....	....	....	....	....	....	....	....	....	....	....	....	....	....	....	....	....
1980-81	New Westminster Bruins	WHL	66	7	27	34	....	....	....	127	....	....	....	....	....	....	....	....	....	....	....	....	....	....	....	....	....	....
1981-82	Saskatoon Blades	WHL	65	7	25	32	....	....	....	175	....	....	....	....	....	....	....	....	....	....	5	1	1	2	14	....	....	....
	Maine Mariners	AHL	....	....	....	....	....	....	....	....	....	....	....	....	....	....	....	....	....	....	2	0	2	2	2	....	....	....
1982-83	Maine Mariners	AHL	44	2	5	7	....	....	....	95	....	....	....	....	....	....	....	....	....	....	2	0	0	0	0	....	....	....
	Toledo Goaldiggers	IHL	5	0	2	2	....	....	....	2	....	....	....	....	....	....	....	....	....	....	....	....	....	....	....	....	....	....
1983-84	**Philadelphia Flyers**	**NHL**	**23**	**1**	**4**	**5**	**1**	**3**	**4**	**71**	**0**	**0**	**1**	**14**	**7.1**	**23**	**0**	**22**	**3**	**4**	**3**	**0**	**0**	**0**	**19**	**0**	**0**	**0**
	Springfield Indians	AHL	51	4	10	14	....	....	....	122	....	....	....	....	....	....	....	....	....	....	....	....	....	....	....	....	....	....
1984-85	Hershey Bears	AHL	24	0	7	7	....	....	....	33	....	....	....	....	....	....	....	....	....	....	....	....	....	....	....	....	....	....
1985-86	**Philadelphia Flyers**	**NHL**	**33**	**0**	**2**	**2**	**0**	**1**	**1**	**69**	**0**	**0**	**0**	**7**	**0.0**	**6**	**0**	**12**	**1**	**–5**	**1**	**0**	**0**	**0**	**2**	**0**	**0**	**0**
	Hershey Bears	AHL	27	0	4	4	....	....	....	88	....	....	....	....	....	....	....	....	....	....	....	....	....	....	....	....	....	....
1986-87	**Philadelphia Flyers**	**NHL**	**33**	**1**	**2**	**3**	**1**	**1**	**2**	**76**	**0**	**0**	**1**	**22**	**4.5**	**15**	**0**	**11**	**2**	**6**	**13**	**0**	**0**	**0**	**9**	**0**	**0**	**0**
1987-88	**Vancouver Canucks**	**NHL**	**57**	**2**	**7**	**9**	**2**	**5**	**7**	**151**	**0**	**0**	**0**	**27**	**7.4**	**36**	**1**	**65**	**18**	**–12**	....	....	....	....	....	....	....	....
1988-89	**Vancouver Canucks**	**NHL**	**20**	**3**	**1**	**4**	**3**	**1**	**4**	**14**	**0**	**0**	**1**	**12**	**25.0**	**6**	**0**	**3**	**0**	**3**	....	....	....	....	....	....	....	....
1989-90	**Vancouver Canucks**	**NHL**	**23**	**1**	**1**	**2**	**1**	**1**	**2**	**27**	**0**	**0**	**1**	**7**	**14.3**	**7**	**0**	**9**	**0**	**–2**	....	....	....	....	....	....	....	....
	NHL Totals		**189**	**8**	**17**	**25**	**8**	**12**	**20**	**408**	**0**	**0**	**4**	**89**	**9.0**	**93**	**1**	**122**	**24**		**17**	**0**	**0**	**0**	**30**	**0**	**0**	**0**

Signed as a free agent by **Philadelphia**, October 9, 1981. Traded to **Vancouver** by **Philadelphia** with Darren Jensen for Wendell Young and Vancouver's 3rd round choice (Kimbi Daniels) in 1980 Entry Draft, August 31, 1987.

• STANTON, Paul D – R. 6'1", 195 lbs. b: Boston, MA, 6/22/1967. Pittsburgh's 8th, 149th overall, in 1985.

			REGULAR SEASON																		PLAYOFFS							
Season	Club	League	GP	G	A	Pts	AG	AA	APts	PIM	PP	SH	GW	S	%	TGF	PGF	TGA	PGA	+/-	GP	G	A	Pts	PIM	PP	SH	GW
1983-84	Catholic Memorial Knights	Hi-School	20	15	20	35																						
1984-85	Catholic Memorial Knights	Hi-School	20	16	21	37				17																		
1985-86	University of Wisconsin	WCHA	36	4	6	10				16																		
1986-87	University of Wisconsin	WCHA	41	5	17	22				70																		
1987-88	University of Wisconsin	WCHA	45	9	38	47				98																		
1988-89	University of Wisconsin	WCHA	45	7	29	36				126																		
1989-90	Muskegon Lumberjacks	IHL	77	5	27	32				61											15	2	4	6	21			
1990-91♦	**Pittsburgh Penguins**	**NHL**	**75**	**5**	**18**	**23**	**5**	**14**	**19**	**40**	**1**	**0**	**1**	**72**	**6.9**	**78**	**7**	**91**	**31**	**11**	**22**	**1**	**2**	**3**	**24**	**0**	**0**	**0**
1991-92♦	**Pittsburgh Penguins**	**NHL**	**54**	**2**	**8**	**10**	**2**	**6**	**8**	**62**	**0**	**0**	**0**	**70**	**2.9**	**45**	**8**	**56**	**11**	**–8**	**21**	**1**	**7**	**8**	**42**	**0**	**0**	**0**
1992-93	**Pittsburgh Penguins**	**NHL**	**77**	**4**	**12**	**16**	**3**	**8**	**11**	**97**	**2**	**0**	**1**	**106**	**3.8**	**81**	**15**	**72**	**13**	**7**	**1**	**0**	**1**	**1**	**0**	**0**	**0**	**0**
1993-94	**Boston Bruins**	**NHL**	**71**	**3**	**7**	**10**	**3**	**5**	**8**	**54**	**1**	**0**	**1**	**136**	**2.2**	**56**	**11**	**60**	**8**	**–7**								
1994-95	Providence Bruins	AHL	8	4	4	8				4																		
	New York Islanders	**NHL**	**18**	**0**	**4**	**4**	**0**	**6**	**6**	**9**	**0**	**0**	**0**	**28**	**0.0**	**11**	**5**	**13**	**1**	**–6**								
	Denver Grizzlies	IHL	11	2	6	8				15																		
	United States	WC-A	6	2	1	3				4																		
1995-96	Adler Mannheim	Germany	47	12	24	36				88											9	2	5	7	8			
	United States	WC-A	7	0	0	0				4																		
1996-97	Adler Mannheim	Germany	50	5	26	31				64											9	2	4	6	26			
1997-98	Adler Mannheim	Germany	47	10	25	35				72											10	4	6	10	22			
	Adler Mannheim	EuroHL	5	3	0	3				31																		
	United States	WC-A	5	0	0	0				0																		
1998-99	Adler Mannheim	Germany	38	6	16	22				50											12	2	7	9	22			
	Adler Mannheim	EuroHL	2	1	1	2				2											4	0	2	2	2			
99-2000	Adler Mannheim	Germany	56	2	19	21				77											4	0	1	1	37			
	Adler Mannheim	EuroHL	5	0	0	0				38																		
	NHL Totals		**295**	**14**	**49**	**63**	**13**	**39**	**52**	**262**	**4**	**0**	**3**	**412**	**3.4**	**271**	**46**	**292**	**64**		**44**	**2**	**10**	**12**	**66**	**0**	**0**	**0**

WCHA Second All-Star Team (1988) • NCAA West First All-American Team (1988) • WCHA First All-Star Team (1989)

Traded to **Boston** by **Pittsburgh** for Boston's 3rd round choice (Greg Crozier) in 1994 Entry Draft, October 8, 1993. Traded to **NY Islanders** by **Boston** for NY Islanders' 8th round choice (later traded to Ottawa — Ottawa selected Ray Schultz) in 1995 Entry Draft, February 10, 1995.

• STAPLETON, Brian Brian Gregory RW – R. 6'2", 190 lbs. b: Fort Erie, Ont., 12/25/1951.

Season	Club	League	GP	G	A	Pts	AG	AA	APts	PIM	PP	SH	GW	S	%	TGF	PGF	TGA	PGA	+/-	GP	G	A	Pts	PIM	PP	SH	GW
1971-72	Brown University	ECAC	25	4	9	13				23																		
1972-73	Brown University	ECAC	25	12	12	24				54																		
1973-74	Brown University	ECAC	23	8	18	26				40																		
1974-75	Dayton–Fort Wayne	IHL	69	14	19	33				66											14	2	2	4	4			
1975-76	**Washington Capitals**	**NHL**	**1**	**0**	**0**	**0**	**0**	**0**	**0**	**0**	**0**	**0**	**0**	**0**	**0.0**	**0**	**0**	**2**	**0**	**–2**								
	Dayton Gems	IHL	74	26	34	60				69											15	7	8	15	4			
1976-77	Dayton Gems	IHL	68	20	46	66				21											4	2	0	2	0			
	NHL Totals		**1**	**0**	**0**	**0**	**0**	**0**	**0**	**0**	**0**	**0**	**0**	**0**	**0.0**	**0**	**0**	**2**	**0**									

Traded to **Fort Wayne** (IHL) by **Dayton** (IHL) with Herb Howdle for Chick Balon, January, 1975. Signed as a free agent by **Washington** to three-game tryout contract, October, 1975.

• STAPLETON, Mike C – R. 5'10", 183 lbs. b: Sarnia, Ont., 5/5/1966. Chicago's 7th, 132nd overall, in 1984.

Season	Club	League	GP	G	A	Pts	AG	AA	APts	PIM	PP	SH	GW	S	%	TGF	PGF	TGA	PGA	+/-	GP	G	A	Pts	PIM	PP	SH	GW
1982-83	Strathroy Rockets	OJHL-B	40	39	38	77				99																		
1983-84	Cornwall Royals	OHL	70	24	45	69				94											3	1	2	3	4			
1984-85	Cornwall Royals	OHL	56	41	44	85				68											9	2	4	6	23			
1985-86	Cornwall Royals	OHL	56	39	64	103				74											6	2	3	5	2			
	Canada	WJC-A	7	3	3	6				6																		
1986-87	Canada	Nat-Team	21	2	4	6				4																		
	Chicago Blackhawks	**NHL**	**39**	**3**	**6**	**9**	**3**	**4**	**7**	**6**	**0**	**0**	**0**	**54**	**5.6**	**17**	**0**	**32**	**6**	**–9**	**4**	**0**	**0**	**0**	**2**	**0**	**0**	**0**
1987-88	**Chicago Blackhawks**	**NHL**	**53**	**2**	**9**	**11**	**2**	**6**	**8**	**59**	**0**	**0**	**1**	**50**	**4.0**	**19**	**8**	**39**	**18**	**–10**								
	Saginaw Hawks	IHL	31	11	19	30				52											10	5	6	11	10			
1988-89	**Chicago Blackhawks**	**NHL**	**7**	**0**	**1**	**1**	**0**	**1**	**1**	**7**	**0**	**0**	**0**	**6**	**0.0**	**2**	**0**	**3**	**0**	**–1**								
	Saginaw Hawks	IHL	69	21	47	68				162											6	1	3	4	4			
1989-90	Arvika IF	Sweden-3	30	15	18	33																						
	Indianapolis Ice	IHL	16	5	10	15				6											13	9	10	19	38			
1990-91	**Chicago Blackhawks**	**NHL**	**7**	**0**	**1**	**1**	**0**	**1**	**1**	**2**	**0**	**0**	**0**	**6**	**0.0**	**1**	**0**	**1**	**0**	**0**								
	Indianapolis Ice	IHL	75	29	52	81				76											7	1	4	5	0			
1991-92	**Chicago Blackhawks**	**NHL**	**19**	**4**	**4**	**8**	**4**	**3**	**7**	**8**	**1**	**0**	**0**	**32**	**12.5**	**9**	**2**	**9**	**2**	**0**								
	Indianapolis Ice	IHL	59	18	40	58				65																		
1992-93	**Pittsburgh Penguins**	**NHL**	**78**	**4**	**9**	**13**	**3**	**6**	**9**	**10**	**0**	**1**	**1**	**78**	**5.1**	**20**	**6**	**35**	**13**	**–8**	**4**	**0**	**0**	**0**	**0**	**0**	**0**	**0**
1993-94	**Pittsburgh Penguins**	**NHL**	**58**	**7**	**4**	**11**	**6**	**3**	**9**	**18**	**3**	**0**	**0**	**59**	**11.9**	**17**	**8**	**29**	**16**	**–4**								
	Edmonton Oilers	**NHL**	**23**	**5**	**9**	**14**	**5**	**7**	**12**	**28**	**1**	**0**	**0**	**43**	**11.6**	**20**	**5**	**17**	**1**	**–1**								
1994-95	**Edmonton Oilers**	**NHL**	**46**	**6**	**11**	**17**	**11**	**16**	**27**	**21**	**3**	**0**	**2**	**59**	**10.2**	**27**	**9**	**36**	**6**	**–12**								
1995-96	**Winnipeg Jets**	**NHL**	**58**	**10**	**14**	**24**	**10**	**11**	**21**	**37**	**3**	**1**	**0**	**91**	**11.0**	**43**	**10**	**54**	**17**	**–4**	**6**	**0**	**0**	**0**	**21**	**0**	**0**	**0**
1996-97	**Phoenix Coyotes**	**NHL**	**55**	**4**	**11**	**15**	**4**	**10**	**14**	**36**	**2**	**0**	**1**	**74**	**5.4**	**23**	**9**	**29**	**11**	**–4**	**7**	**0**	**0**	**0**	**14**	**0**	**0**	**0**
1997-98	**Phoenix Coyotes**	**NHL**	**64**	**5**	**5**	**10**	**6**	**5**	**11**	**36**	**1**	**1**	**1**	**69**	**7.2**	**20**	**5**	**30**	**11**	**–4**	**6**	**0**	**0**	**0**	**2**	**0**	**0**	**0**
1998-99	**Phoenix Coyotes**	**NHL**	**76**	**9**	**9**	**18**	**11**	**9**	**20**	**34**	**0**	**2**	**2**	**106**	**8.5**	**24**	**3**	**53**	**25**	**–6**	**7**	**1**	**0**	**1**	**0**	**0**	**0**	**0**
99-2000	**Atlanta Thrashers**	**NHL**	**62**	**10**	**12**	**22**	**11**	**11**	**22**	**30**	**4**	**0**	**1**	**146**	**6.8**	**32**	**13**	**69**	**21**	**–29**								
	NHL Totals		**645**	**69**	**105**	**174**	**76**	**93**	**169**	**332**	**18**	**5**	**9**	**873**	**7.9**	**274**	**78**	**436**	**147**		**34**	**1**	**0**	**1**	**39**	**0**	**0**	**0**

• Son of Pat

Signed as a free agent by **Pittsburgh**, September 30, 1992. Claimed on waivers by **Edmonton** from **Pittsburgh**, February 19, 1994. Signed as a free agent by **Winnipeg**, August 18, 1995. Transferred to **Phoenix** after **Winnipeg** franchise relocated, July 1, 1996. Claimed by **Atlanta** from **Phoenix** in Expansion Draft, June 25, 1999. Signed as a free agent by **NY Islanders**, July 3, 2000.

• STAPLETON, Pat Patrick James D – L. 5'8", 180 lbs. b: Sarnia, Ont., 7/4/1940.

Season	Club	League	GP	G	A	Pts	AG	AA	APts	PIM	PP	SH	GW	S	%	TGF	PGF	TGA	PGA	+/-	GP	G	A	Pts	PIM	PP	SH	GW
1957-58	Sarnia Legionaires	OHA-B	48	14	31	45				24																		
1958-59	St. Catharines Teepees	OHA-Jr.	49	10	26	36				18											7	0	0	0	6			
1959-60	St. Catharines Teepees	OHA-Jr.	47	12	35	47				83											17	5	12	17	32			
	Buffalo Bisons	AHL	1	0	0	0				2																		
	St. Catharines Teepees	Mem-Cup	14	5	9	14				37																		
1960-61	Sault Ste. Marie Thunderbirds	EPHL	59	5	43	48				22											12	1	8	9	2			
1961-62	**Boston Bruins**	**NHL**	**69**	**2**	**5**	**7**	**2**	**5**	**7**	**42**																		
1962-63	**Boston Bruins**	**NHL**	**21**	**0**	**3**	**3**	**0**	**3**	**3**	**8**																		
	Kingston Frontenacs	EPHL	49	10	26	36				92											5	4	2	6	12			
1963-64	Portland Buckaroos	WHL	70	5	44	49				80											5	1	6	7	0			
1964-65	Portland Buckaroos	WHL	70	29	57	86				61											10	3	4	7	16			
1965-66	**Chicago Black Hawks**	**NHL**	**55**	**4**	**30**	**34**	**4**	**29**	**33**	**52**											**6**	**2**	**3**	**5**	**4**	**1**	**0**	**0**
	St. Louis Braves	CPHL	14	2	4	6				6																		
1966-67	**Chicago Black Hawks**	**NHL**	**70**	**3**	**31**	**34**	**3**	**30**	**33**	**54**											**6**	**1**	**1**	**2**	**12**	**0**	**0**	**0**
1967-68	**Chicago Black Hawks**	**NHL**	**67**	**4**	**34**	**38**	**5**	**34**	**39**	**34**	**0**	**0**	**0**	**38**	**10.5**	**98**	**12**	**90**	**8**	**4**	**11**	**0**	**4**	**4**	**4**	**0**	**0**	**0**
1968-69	**Chicago Black Hawks**	**NHL**	**75**	**6**	**50**	**56**	**6**	**45**	**51**	**44**	**0**	**0**	**0**	**112**	**5.4**	**160**	**41**	**124**	**28**	**23**								
1969-70	**Chicago Black Hawks**	**NHL**	**49**	**4**	**38**	**42**	**4**	**36**	**40**	**28**	**1**	**0**	**1**	**106**	**3.8**	**97**	**24**	**63**	**8**	**18**								
1970-71	**Chicago Black Hawks**	**NHL**	**76**	**7**	**44**	**51**	**7**	**37**	**44**	**30**	**4**	**0**	**0**	**130**	**5.4**	**161**	**44**	**84**	**16**	**49**	**18**	**3**	**14**	**17**	**4**	**1**	**1**	**0**
1971-72	**Chicago Black Hawks**	**NHL**	**78**	**3**	**38**	**41**	**3**	**33**	**36**	**47**	**2**	**0**	**2**	**133**	**2.3**	**150**	**41**	**89**	**21**	**41**	**8**	**2**	**2**	**4**	**4**	**2**	**0**	**0**
1972-73	Team Canada	Summit-72	7	0	0	0				6																		
	Chicago Black Hawks	**NHL**	**75**	**10**	**21**	**31**	**9**	**17**	**26**	**14**	**2**	**0**	**2**	**128**	**7.8**	**112**	**26**	**89**	**22**	**19**	**16**	**2**	***15**	**17**	**10**	**1**	**0**	**0**
1973-74	Chicago Cougars	WHA	78	6	52	58				44											12	0	13	13	36			

Season	Club	League	GP	G	A	Pts	AG	AA	APts	PIM	PP	SH	GW	S	%	TGF	PGF	TGA	PGA	+/–	GP	G	A	Pts	PIM	PP	SH	GW
			REGULAR SEASON																		PLAYOFFS							
1974-75	Team Canada	Summit-74	8	0	3	3				12																		
	Chicago Cougars	WHA	68	4	30	34				38																		
1975-76	Indianapolis Racers	WHA	80	5	40	45				48											7	0	2	2	2			
1976-77	Indianapolis Racers	WHA	81	8	45	53				29											9	2	6	8	0			
1977-78	Cincinnati Stingers	WHA	65	4	45	49				28																		
	NHL Totals		**635**	**43**	**294**	**337**	**43**	**269**	**312**	**353**											**65**	**10**	**39**	**49**	**38**			
	Other Major League Totals		372	27	212	239				187											28	2	21	23	38			

• Father of Mike • OHA-Jr. First All-Star Team (1959, 1960) • EPHL Second All-Star Team (1961) • EPHL First All-Star Team (1963) • WHL Second All-Star Team (1964) • WHL First All-Star Team (1965) • Won Hal Laycoe Cup (WHL Top Defenseman) (1965) • NHL Second All-Star Team (1966, 1971, 1972) • WHA First All-Star Team (1974) • Won Dennis A. Murphy Trophy (WHA Top Defenseman) (1974) • WHA Second All-Star Team (1976) • Played in NHL All-Star Game (1967, 1969, 1971, 1972)

Claimed by **Boston** from **Chicago** in Intra-League Draft, June 13, 1961. Traded to **Toronto** by **Boston** with Orland Kurtenbach and Andy Hebenton for Ron Stewart, June 8, 1965. Claimed by **Chicago** from **Toronto** in Intra-League Draft, June 9, 1965. Selected by **LA Sharks** (WHA) in 1972 WHA General Player Draft, February 12, 1972. WHA rights traded to **Chicago** (WHA) by **LA Sharks** (WHA) for cash, September, 1973. Selected by **Indianapolis** (WHA) from **Chicago** (WHA) in WHA Dispersal Draft, May 19, 1975. WHA rights transferred to **Cincinnati** (WHA) in Special Dispersal Auction after **Indianapolis** (WHA) refused to honour his contract, November, 1977.

• STARIKOV, Sergei

D – L. 5'10", 225 lbs. b: Chelyabinsk, Soviet Union, 12/4/1958. New Jersey's 7th, 152nd overall, in 1989.

Season	Club	League	GP	G	A	Pts	AG	AA	APts	PIM	PP	SH	GW	S	%	TGF	PGF	TGA	PGA	+/–	GP	G	A	Pts	PIM	PP	SH	GW
1975-76	Traktor Chelyabinsk	USSR-2	STATISTICS NOT AVAILABLE																									
	Soviet Union	EJC-A	4	0	0	0				6																		
1976-77	Traktor Chelyabinsk	USSR	35	2	4	6				28																		
	Soviet Union	WJC-A	7	1	2	3				8																		
1977-78	Traktor Chelyabinsk	USSR	36	3	5	8				26																		
	Soviet Union	WJC-A	7	1	5	6				2																		
1978-79	Traktor Chelyabinsk	USSR	44	6	8	14				34																		
	USSR	Chal-Cup	3	0	1	1				0																		
	Kralja Moscow Sovetov	Super-S	4	1	3	4				4																		
	Soviet Union	WEC-A	1	0	1	1				2																		
1979-80	CSKA Moscow	USSR	39	10	8	18				14																		
	CSKA Moscow	Super-S	5	0	2	2				0																		
	Soviet Union	Olympics	7	1	6	7				0																		
1980-81	CSKA Moscow	USSR	49	4	8	12				26																		
1981-82	CSKA Moscow	USSR	40	1	4	5				14																		
1982-83	CSKA Moscow	USSR	44	6	14	20				14																		
	USSR	Super-S	5	1	0	1				2																		
	Soviet Union	WEC-A	10	1	4	5				0																		
1983-84	CSKA Moscow	USSR	44	11	7	18				20																		
	Soviet Union	Olympics	7	1	1	2				2																		
1984-85	Soviet Union	Can-Cup	6	0	3	3				2																		
	CSKA Moscow	USSR	40	3	10	13				12																		
	Soviet Union	WEC-A	10	0	4	4				2																		
1985-86	CSKA Moscow	USSR	37	3	2	5				6																		
	CSKA Moscow	Super-S	6	0	0	0				0																		
	Soviet Union	WEC-A	10	0	2	2				0																		
1986-87	CSKA Moscow	USSR	34	4	2	6				8																		
	USSR	RV-87	2	0	1	1				0																		
	Soviet Union	WEC-A	10	4	2	6				8																		
1987-88	CSKA Moscow	USSR	38	2	11	13				12																		
	Soviet Union	Olympics	5	0	2	2				4																		
1988-89	CSKA Moscow	USSR	30	3	3	6				4																		
	CSKA Moscow	Super-S	5	0	2	2				2																		
1989-90	**New Jersey Devils**	**NHL**	**16**	**0**	**1**	**1**	**0**	**1**	**1**	**8**	**0**	**0**	**0**	**6**	**0.0**	**11**	**0**	**26**	**7**	**–8**								
	Utica Devils	AHL	43	8	11	19				14											4	0	3	3	0			
1990-91	Utica Devils	AHL	51	2	7	9				26																		
1991-92	San Diego Gulls	IHL	70	7	31	38				42											4	0	0	0	0			
1992-93	San Diego Gulls	IHL	42	0	9	9				12																		
	NHL Totals		**16**	**0**	**1**	**1**	**0**	**1**	**1**	**8**	**0**	**0**	**0**	**6**	**0.0**	**11**	**0**	**26**	**7**									

• STASTNY, Anton

LW – L. 6', 188 lbs. b: Bratislava, Czech., 8/5/1959. Quebec's 4th, 83rd overall, in 1979.

Season	Club	League	GP	G	A	Pts	AG	AA	APts	PIM	PP	SH	GW	S	%	TGF	PGF	TGA	PGA	+/–	GP	G	A	Pts	PIM	PP	SH	GW
1976-77	Czechoslovakia	EJC-A	6	6	2	8				0																		
1977-78	Slovan Bratislava	Czech.	44	19	17	36				22																		
	Czechoslovakia	WJC-A	6	4	2	6				4																		
1978-79	Slovan Bratislava	Czech.	44	32	19	51				38																		
	Czechoslovakia	WJC-A	6	3	4	7				6																		
	Czechoslovakia	WEC-A	8	5	1	6				2																		
1979-80	Slovan Bratislava	Czech.	40	30	30	60				33																		
	Czechoslovakia	Olympics	6	4	4	8				2																		
1980-81	**Quebec Nordiques**	**NHL**	**80**	**39**	**46**	**85**	**30**	**31**	**61**	**12**	**12**	**0**	**4**	**177**	**22.0**	**123**	**39**	**80**	**0**	**4**	**5**	**4**	**3**	**7**	**2**	**2**	**0**	**0**
1981-82	**Quebec Nordiques**	**NHL**	**68**	**26**	**46**	**72**	**21**	**31**	**52**	**16**	**10**	**0**	**4**	**135**	**19.3**	**107**	**43**	**94**	**1**	**–29**	**16**	**5**	**10**	**15**	**10**	**3**	**0**	**0**
1982-83	**Quebec Nordiques**	**NHL**	**79**	**32**	**60**	**92**	**26**	**42**	**68**	**25**	**10**	**0**	**7**	**169**	**18.9**	**136**	**40**	**71**	**0**	**25**	**4**	**2**	**2**	**4**	**0**	**0**	**0**	**0**
1983-84	**Quebec Nordiques**	**NHL**	**69**	**25**	**37**	**62**	**20**	**25**	**45**	**14**	**7**	**0**	**0**	**145**	**17.2**	**106**	**37**	**57**	**0**	**12**	**9**	**2**	**5**	**7**	**7**	**0**	**0**	**0**
1984-85	**Quebec Nordiques**	**NHL**	**79**	**38**	**42**	**80**	**31**	**29**	**60**	**30**	**9**	**0**	**3**	**176**	**21.6**	**119**	**29**	**73**	**1**	**18**	**16**	**3**	**3**	**6**	**6**	**1**	**0**	**1**
1985-86	**Quebec Nordiques**	**NHL**	**74**	**31**	**43**	**74**	**25**	**29**	**54**	**19**	**8**	**0**	**4**	**163**	**19.0**	**107**	**31**	**68**	**0**	**8**	**3**	**1**	**1**	**2**	**0**	**0**	**0**	**0**
1986-87	**Quebec Nordiques**	**NHL**	**77**	**27**	**35**	**62**	**23**	**25**	**48**	**8**	**6**	**0**	**5**	**172**	**15.7**	**81**	**23**	**55**	**0**	**3**	**13**	**3**	**8**	**11**	**6**	**0**	**0**	**0**
1987-88	**Quebec Nordiques**	**NHL**	**69**	**27**	**45**	**72**	**23**	**32**	**55**	**14**	**15**	**0**	**4**	**177**	**15.3**	**108**	**62**	**55**	**0**	**–9**								
1988-89	**Quebec Nordiques**	**NHL**	**55**	**7**	**30**	**37**	**6**	**21**	**27**	**12**	**3**	**0**	**0**	**84**	**8.3**	**58**	**26**	**52**	**1**	**–19**								
	Halifax Citadels	AHL	16	9	5	14				4																		
1989-90	HC Fribourg	Switz.	36	25	22	47															3	3	4	7				
1990-91	EHC Olten	Switz.	36	26	14	40															10	10	16	26				
1991-92	EHC Olten	Switz.	33	20	19	39				66																		
1992-93			DID NOT PLAY																									
1993-94	Slovan Bratislava	Czech-Rep	11	6	8	14				2																		
	NHL Totals		**650**	**252**	**384**	**636**	**205**	**265**	**470**	**150**	**80**	**0**	**31**	**1398**	**18.0**	**945**	**330**	**605**	**3**		**66**	**20**	**32**	**52**	**31**	**6**	**0**	**1**

• Brother of Peter and Marian • WJC-A All-Star Team (1978) • Czech Elite League First All-Star Team (1979)

Re-entered NHL draft. Originally Philadelphia's 19th choice, 198th overall, in 1978 Amateur Draft.

• STASTNY, Marian

RW – L. 5'10", 195 lbs. b: Bratislava, Czech., 1/8/1953.

Season	Club	League	GP	G	A	Pts	AG	AA	APts	PIM	PP	SH	GW	S	%	TGF	PGF	TGA	PGA	+/–	GP	G	A	Pts	PIM	PP	SH	GW
1970-71	Slovan Bratislava	Czech.	STATISTICS NOT AVAILABLE																									
1971-72	Slovan Bratislava	Czech.	....	17	11	28																						
1972-73	Slovan Bratislava	Czech.	STATISTICS NOT AVAILABLE																									
1973-74	Slovan Bratislava	Czech.	....	14	7	21																						
1974-75	Slovan Bratislava	Czech.	44	36	27	63				57																		
	Czechoslovakia	WEC-A	5	3	1	4				0																		
1975-76	Slovan Bratislava	Czech.	31	17	11	28				53																		
	Czechoslovakia	WEC-A	8	2	4	6				2																		
1976-77	Czechoslovakia	Can-Cup	7	1	4	5				2																		
	Slovan Bratislava	Czech.	44	28	24	52																						
	Czechoslovakia	WEC-A	10	7	4	11				2																		
1977-78	Slovan Bratislava	Czech.	44	33	23	56				58																		
	Czechoslovakia	WEC-A	9	4	5	9				4																		
1978-79	Slovan Bratislava	Czech.	40	39	*35	*74				22											14	12	8	20				
	Czechoslovakia	WEC-A	8	0	5	5				2																		

			REGULAR SEASON																		PLAYOFFS							
Season	Club	League	GP	G	A	Pts	AG	AA	APts	PIM	PP	SH	GW	S	%	TGF	PGF	TGA	PGA	+/-	GP	G	A	Pts	PIM	PP	SH	GW
1979-80	Dukla Trenchin	Czech.	14	8	6	14	....	....	....	0	....	....	....	....	....	....	....	....	....	....	....	....	....	....	....	....	....	....
	Slovan Bratislava	Czech.	21	20	15	35	....	....	....	16	....	....	....	....	....	....	....	....	....	....	19	10	11	21	6	....	....	....
	Czechoslovakia	Olympics	6	5	6	11	....	....	....	4	....	....	....	....	....	....	....	....	....	....	....	....	....	....	....	....	....	....
1980-81			DID NOT PLAY																									
1981-82	**Quebec Nordiques**	**NHL**	**74**	**35**	**54**	**89**	**28**	**36**	**64**	**27**	**13**	**0**	**3**	**176**	**19.9**	**124**	**39**	**89**	**4**	**0**	**16**	**3**	**14**	**17**	**5**	**1**	**0**	**0**
1982-83	**Quebec Nordiques**	**NHL**	**60**	**36**	**43**	**79**	**30**	**30**	**60**	**32**	**13**	**0**	**3**	**169**	**21.3**	**107**	**34**	**53**	**0**	**20**	**2**	**0**	**0**	**0**	**0**	**0**	**0**	**0**
1983-84	**Quebec Nordiques**	**NHL**	**68**	**20**	**32**	**52**	**16**	**22**	**38**	**26**	**4**	**0**	**5**	**113**	**17.7**	**80**	**20**	**59**	**0**	**1**	**9**	**2**	**3**	**5**	**2**	**0**	**0**	**1**
1984-85	**Quebec Nordiques**	**NHL**	**50**	**7**	**14**	**21**	**6**	**10**	**16**	**4**	**0**	**0**	**1**	**45**	**15.6**	**32**	**3**	**28**	**0**	**1**	**2**	**0**	**0**	**0**	**0**	**0**	**0**	**0**
1985-86	**Toronto Maple Leafs**	**NHL**	**70**	**23**	**30**	**53**	**18**	**20**	**38**	**21**	**7**	**0**	**0**	**132**	**17.4**	**87**	**24**	**71**	**2**	**–6**	**3**	**0**	**0**	**0**	**0**	**0**	**0**	**0**
1986-87	HC Sierre	Switz.	27	23	19	42	....	....	....	24	....	....	....	....	....	....	....	....	....	....	....	....	....	....	....	....	....	....
	NHL Totals		**322**	**121**	**173**	**294**	**98**	**118**	**216**	**110**	**37**	**0**	**12**	**635**	**19.1**	**430**	**120**	**300**	**6**		**32**	**5**	**17**	**22**	**7**	**1**	**0**	**1**

• Brother of Peter and Anton • Czech Eliet League All-Star Team (1978, 1979) • Played in NHL All-Star Game (1983)

• Scored total of 236 goals in 369 Czech Elite League games. • Did not play during 1980-81 season preparing to defect to North America in June, 1981. Signed as a free agent by **Quebec**, August 26, 1980. Signed as a free agent by **Toronto**, August 12, 1985.

• STASTNY, Peter

C – L. 6'1", 200 lbs. b: Bratislava, Czech., 9/18/1956. **HHOF**

Season	Club	League	GP	G	A	Pts	AG	AA	APts	PIM	PP	SH	GW	S	%	TGF	PGF	TGA	PGA	+/-	GP	G	A	Pts	PIM	PP	SH	GW
1974-75	Slovan Bratislava	Czech-Jr.	STATISTICS NOT AVAILABLE																									
	Czechoslovakia	WJC-A	....	4	0	4	....	....	....	....	....	....	....	....	....	....	....	....	....	....	....	....	....	....	....	....	....	....
	Czechoslovakia	EJC-A	5	3	1	4	....	....	....	4	....	....	....	....	....	....	....	....	....	....	....	....	....	....	....	....	....	....
1975-76	Slovan Bratislava	Czech.	32	19	9	28	....	....	....	....	....	....	....	....	....	....	....	....	....	....	....	....	....	....	....	....	....	....
	Czechoslovakia	WJC-A	4	1	1	2	....	....	....	0	....	....	....	....	....	....	....	....	....	....	....	....	....	....	....	....	....	....
	Czechoslovakia	WEC-A	9	8	4	12	....	....	....	0	....	....	....	....	....	....	....	....	....	....	....	....	....	....	....	....	....	....
1976-77	Czechoslovakia	Can-Cup	7	0	4	4	....	....	....	2	....	....	....	....	....	....	....	....	....	....	....	....	....	....	....	....	....	....
	Slovan Bratislava	Czech.	44	25	27	52	....	....	....	....	....	....	....	....	....	....	....	....	....	....	....	....	....	....	....	....	....	....
	Czechoslovakia	WEC-A	10	3	5	8	....	....	....	0	....	....	....	....	....	....	....	....	....	....	....	....	....	....	....	....	....	....
1977-78	Slovan Bratislava	Czech.	42	29	24	53	....	....	....	28	....	....	....	....	....	....	....	....	....	....	....	....	....	....	....	....	....	....
	Czechoslovakia	WEC-A	10	5	6	11	....	....	....	7	....	....	....	....	....	....	....	....	....	....	....	....	....	....	....	....	....	....
1978-79	Slovan Bratislava	Czech.	39	32	23	55	....	....	....	21	....	....	....	....	....	....	....	....	....	....	....	....	....	....	....	....	....	....
	Czechoslovakia	WEC-A	8	2	3	5	....	....	....	6	....	....	....	....	....	....	....	....	....	....	....	....	....	....	....	....	....	....
1979-80	Slovan Bratislava	Czech.	41	26	26	52	....	....	....	58	....	....	....	....	....	....	....	....	....	....	....	....	....	....	....	....	....	....
	Czechoslovakia	Olympics	6	7	7	14	....	....	....	6	....	....	....	....	....	....	....	....	....	....	....	....	....	....	....	....	....	....
1980-81	**Quebec Nordiques**	**NHL**	**77**	**39**	**70**	**109**	**30**	**47**	**77**	**37**	**11**	**2**	**4**	**232**	**16.8**	**147**	**49**	**99**	**12**	**11**	**5**	**2**	**8**	**10**	**7**	**1**	**0**	**0**
1981-82	**Quebec Nordiques**	**NHL**	**80**	**46**	**93**	**139**	**36**	**62**	**98**	**91**	**16**	**3**	**3**	**227**	**20.3**	**173**	**65**	**125**	**7**	**–10**	**12**	**7**	**11**	**18**	**10**	**4**	**0**	**1**
1982-83	**Quebec Nordiques**	**NHL**	**75**	**47**	**77**	**124**	**39**	**54**	**93**	**78**	**5**	**0**	**4**	**201**	**23.4**	**153**	**40**	**93**	**8**	**28**	**4**	**3**	**2**	**5**	**10**	**1**	**0**	**0**
1983-84	**Quebec Nordiques**	**NHL**	**80**	**46**	**73**	**119**	**37**	**50**	**87**	**73**	**11**	**0**	**4**	**189**	**24.3**	**156**	**43**	**97**	**6**	**22**	**9**	**2**	**7**	**9**	**31**	**2**	**0**	**0**
1984-85	Canada	Can-Cup	8	1	2	3	....	....	....	0	....	....	....	....	....	....	....	....	....	....	....	....	....	....	....	....	....	....
	Quebec Nordiques	**NHL**	**75**	**32**	**68**	**100**	**26**	**46**	**72**	**95**	**7**	**1**	**9**	**207**	**15.5**	**140**	**40**	**81**	**4**	**23**	**18**	**4**	**19**	**23**	**24**	**1**	**0**	**2**
1985-86	**Quebec Nordiques**	**NHL**	**76**	**41**	**81**	**122**	**33**	**55**	**88**	**60**	**15**	**0**	**8**	**207**	**19.8**	**167**	**77**	**92**	**4**	**2**	**3**	**0**	**1**	**1**	**2**	**0**	**0**	**0**
1986-87	**Quebec Nordiques**	**NHL**	**64**	**24**	**53**	**77**	**21**	**39**	**60**	**43**	**12**	**0**	**4**	**157**	**15.3**	**112**	**51**	**83**	**1**	**–21**	**13**	**6**	**9**	**15**	**12**	**2**	**1**	**1**
1987-88	**Quebec Nordiques**	**NHL**	**76**	**46**	**65**	**111**	**39**	**47**	**86**	**69**	**20**	**0**	**2**	**199**	**23.1**	**146**	**78**	**77**	**11**	**2**	....	....	....	....	....	....	....	....
1988-89	**Quebec Nordiques**	**NHL**	**72**	**35**	**50**	**85**	**30**	**35**	**65**	**117**	**13**	**0**	**5**	**195**	**17.9**	**114**	**54**	**94**	**11**	**–23**	....	....	....	....	....	....	....	....
1989-90	**Quebec Nordiques**	**NHL**	**62**	**24**	**38**	**62**	**21**	**27**	**48**	**24**	**10**	**0**	**0**	**131**	**18.3**	**83**	**39**	**97**	**8**	**–45**	....	....	....	....	....	....	....	....
	New Jersey Devils	**NHL**	**12**	**5**	**6**	**11**	**4**	**4**	**8**	**16**	**2**	**0**	**1**	**25**	**20.0**	**15**	**8**	**9**	**1**	**–1**	**6**	**3**	**2**	**5**	**2**	**1**	**0**	**1**
1990-91	**New Jersey Devils**	**NHL**	**77**	**18**	**42**	**60**	**16**	**32**	**48**	**53**	**4**	**0**	**3**	**117**	**15.4**	**92**	**39**	**53**	**0**	**0**	**7**	**3**	**4**	**7**	**2**	**1**	**0**	**2**
1991-92	**New Jersey Devils**	**NHL**	**66**	**24**	**38**	**62**	**22**	**29**	**51**	**42**	**10**	**1**	**3**	**142**	**16.9**	**102**	**35**	**63**	**2**	**6**	**7**	**3**	**7**	**10**	**19**	**0**	**0**	**0**
1992-93	**New Jersey Devils**	**NHL**	**62**	**17**	**23**	**40**	**14**	**16**	**30**	**22**	**7**	**0**	**3**	**106**	**16.0**	**70**	**34**	**45**	**4**	**–5**	**5**	**0**	**2**	**2**	**2**	**0**	**0**	**0**
1993-94	Slovan Bratislava	Slovakia	4	0	4	4	....	....	....	0	....	....	....	....	....	....	....	....	....	....	....	....	....	....	....	....	....	....
	Slovakia	Olympics	8	5	4	9	....	....	....	9	....	....	....	....	....	....	....	....	....	....	....	....	....	....	....	....	....	....
	St. Louis Blues	**NHL**	**17**	**5**	**11**	**16**	**5**	**9**	**14**	**4**	**2**	**0**	**1**	**30**	**16.7**	**20**	**12**	**10**	**0**	**–2**	**4**	**0**	**0**	**0**	**2**	**0**	**0**	**0**
1994-95	**St. Louis Blues**	**NHL**	**6**	**1**	**1**	**2**	**2**	**1**	**3**	**0**	**0**	**0**	**0**	**9**	**11.1**	**3**	**0**	**2**	**0**	**1**	....	....	....	....	....	....	....	....
	Slovakia	WC-B	6	8	8	16	....	....	....	0	....	....	....	....	....	....	....	....	....	....	....	....	....	....	....	....	....	....
	NHL Totals		**977**	**450**	**789**	**1239**	**375**	**553**	**928**	**824**	**145**	**7**	**54**	**2374**	**19.0**	**1693**	**664**	**1120**	**79**		**93**	**33**	**72**	**105**	**123**	**13**	**1**	**7**

• Brother of Marian and Anton • Czech Elite League All-Star Team (1979, 1980) • Czechoslovakian Player of the Year (1980) • Won Calder Memorial Trophy (1981) • WC-B All-Star Team (1995) • Named Best Forward at WC-B (1995) • Played in NHL All-Star Game (1981, 1982, 1983, 1984, 1986, 1988)

Signed as a free agent by **Quebec**, August 26, 1980. Traded to **New Jersey** by **Quebec** for Craig Wolanin and future considerations (Randy Velischek, August 13, 1990), March 6, 1990. Signed as a free agent by **St. Louis**, March 9, 1994.

• STASZAK, Ray

RW – R. 6', 200 lbs. b: Philadelphia, PA, 12/1/1962.

Season	Club	League	GP	G	A	Pts	AG	AA	APts	PIM	PP	SH	GW	S	%	TGF	PGF	TGA	PGA	+/-	GP	G	A	Pts	PIM	PP	SH	GW
1981-82	Bucks County Pioneers	MWJHL	45	20	23	43	....	....	....	....	....	....	....	....	....	....	....	....	....	....	....	....	....	....	....	....	....	....
1982-83	Austin Mavericks	USHL	30	18	13	31	....	....	....	....	....	....	....	....	....	....	....	....	....	....	....	....	....	....	....	....	....	....
1983-84	University of Illinois-Chicago	CCHA	31	15	17	32	....	....	....	42	....	....	....	....	....	....	....	....	....	....	....	....	....	....	....	....	....	....
1984-85	University of Illinois-Chicago	CCHA	38	37	35	72	....	....	....	98	....	....	....	....	....	....	....	....	....	....	....	....	....	....	....	....	....	....
1985-86	**Detroit Red Wings**	**NHL**	**4**	**0**	**1**	**1**	**0**	**1**	**1**	**7**	**0**	**0**	**0**	**5**	**0.0**	**2**	**0**	**8**	**3**	**–3**	....	....	....	....	....	....	....	....
	Adirondack Red Wings	AHL	26	13	8	21	....	....	....	41	....	....	....	....	....	....	....	....	....	....	16	2	3	5	70	....	....	....
	NHL Totals		**4**	**0**	**1**	**1**	**0**	**1**	**1**	**7**	**0**	**0**	**0**	**5**	**0.0**	**2**	**0**	**8**	**3**		....	....	....	....	....	....	....	....

CCHA First All-Star Team (1985) • NCAA West Second All-American Team (1985)

Signed as a free agent by **Detroit**, July 31, 1985. • Suffered eventual career-ending groin injury in game vs. Minnesota, December 11, 1985.

• STEEN, Anders

Anders Henry C – L. 6'1", 204 lbs. b: Nykoping, Sweden, 4/28/1955.

Season	Club	League	GP	G	A	Pts	AG	AA	APts	PIM	PP	SH	GW	S	%	TGF	PGF	TGA	PGA	+/-	GP	G	A	Pts	PIM	PP	SH	GW
1970-71	Nykopings BIS	Sweden-3	2	0	0	0	....	....	....	0	....	....	....	....	....	....	....	....	....	....	....	....	....	....	....	....	....	....
1971-72	Nykopings BIS	Sweden-3	17	10	4	14	....	....	....	....	....	....	....	....	....	....	....	....	....	....	....	....	....	....	....	....	....	....
1972-73	Nykopings BIS	Sweden-3	16	10	10	20	....	....	....	....	....	....	....	....	....	....	....	....	....	....	....	....	....	....	....	....	....	....
1973-74	Nykopings BIS	Sweden-3	12	10	5	15	....	....	....	....	....	....	....	....	....	....	....	....	....	....	....	....	....	....	....	....	....	....
	Sweden	EJC-A	5	4	1	5	....	....	....	6	....	....	....	....	....	....	....	....	....	....	....	....	....	....	....	....	....	....
1974-75	Farjestads BK Karlstad	Sweden	13	1	1	2	....	....	....	0	....	....	....	....	....	....	....	....	....	....	....	....	....	....	....	....	....	....
	Sweden	WJC-A	5	1	1	2	....	....	....	....	....	....	....	....	....	....	....	....	....	....	....	....	....	....	....	....	....	....
1975-76	Farjestads BK Karlstad	Sweden	32	21	7	28	....	....	....	8	....	....	....	....	....	....	....	....	....	....	....	1	0	1	2	....	....	....
1976-77	Farjestads BK Karlstad	Sweden	32	17	20	37	....	....	....	17	....	....	....	....	....	....	....	....	....	....	5	2	0	2	2	....	....	....
1977-78	Farjestads BK Karlstad	Sweden	35	22	12	34	....	....	....	35	....	....	....	....	....	....	....	....	....	....	....	....	....	....	....	....	....	....
1978-79	Farjestads BK Karlstad	Sweden	35	18	16	34	....	....	....	42	....	....	....	....	....	....	....	....	....	....	....	1	0	1	0	....	....	....
1979-80	Farjestads BK Karlstad	Sweden	36	*29	16	*45	....	....	....	46	....	....	....	....	....	....	....	....	....	....	....	....	....	....	....	....	....	....
1980-81	**Winnipeg Jets**	**NHL**	**42**	**5**	**11**	**16**	**4**	**7**	**11**	**22**	**3**	**0**	**1**	**57**	**8.8**	**18**	**7**	**35**	**2**	**–22**	....	....	....	....	....	....	....	....
	Tulsa Oilers	CHL	21	11	14	25	....	....	....	28	....	....	....	....	....	....	....	....	....	....	7	0	4	4	10	....	....	....
1981-82	Farjestads BK Karlstad	Sweden	30	14	5	19	....	....	....	34	....	....	....	....	....	....	....	....	....	....	2	1	1	2	4	....	....	....
1982-83	Farjestads BK Karlstad	Sweden	23	9	9	18	....	....	....	20	....	....	....	....	....	....	....	....	....	....	4	0	1	1	2	....	....	....
1983-84	Farjestads BK Karlstad	Sweden	11	1	0	1	....	....	....	0	....	....	....	....	....	....	....	....	....	....	....	....	....	....	....	....	....	....
	NHL Totals		**42**	**5**	**11**	**16**	**4**	**7**	**11**	**22**	**3**	**0**	**1**	**57**	**8.8**	**18**	**7**	**35**	**2**		....	....	....	....	....	....	....	....

Signed as a free agent by **Winnipeg**, March 26, 1980.

• STEEN, Thomas

C – L. 5'11", 190 lbs. b: Grums, Sweden, 6/8/1960. Winnipeg's 5th, 103rd overall, in 1979.

Season	Club	League	GP	G	A	Pts	AG	AA	APts	PIM	PP	SH	GW	S	%	TGF	PGF	TGA	PGA	+/-	GP	G	A	Pts	PIM	PP	SH	GW
1975-76	Grums IK	Sweden-2	21	4	5	9	....	....	....	....	....	....	....	....	....	....	....	....	....	....	....	....	....	....	....	....	....	....
1976-77	Leksands IF	Sweden	2	1	1	2	....	....	....	2	....	....	....	....	....	....	....	....	....	....	....	....	....	....	....	....	....	....
	Sweden	EJC-A	6	5	3	8	....	....	....	6	....	....	....	....	....	....	....	....	....	....	....	....	....	....	....	....	....	....
1977-78	Leksands IF	Sweden	35	5	6	11	....	....	....	30	....	....	....	....	....	....	....	....	....	....	....	....	....	....	....	....	....	....
	Sweden	WJC-A	7	3	3	6	....	....	....	4	....	....	....	....	....	....	....	....	....	....	....	....	....	....	....	....	....	....
1978-79	Leksands IF	Sweden	23	13	4	17	....	....	....	35	....	....	....	....	....	....	....	....	....	....	2	0	0	0	0	....	....	....
	Sweden	WJC-A	6	5	1	6	....	....	....	6	....	....	....	....	....	....	....	....	....	....	....	....	....	....	....	....	....	....

			REGULAR SEASON																		PLAYOFFS							
Season	Club	League	GP	G	A	Pts	AG	AA	APts	PIM	PP	SH	GW	S	%	TGF	PGF	TGA	PGA	+/–	GP	G	A	Pts	PIM	PP	SH	GW
1979-80	Leksands IF	Sweden	18	7	7	14	....	....	....	14	....	....	....	....	....	....	....	....	....	....	2	0	0	0	6	....	....	....
	Sweden	WJC-A	5	2	4	6	....	....	....	12	....	....	....	....	....	....	....	....	....	....	....	....	....	....	....	....	....	....
1980-81	Farjestads BK Karlstad	Sweden	32	16	23	39	....	....	....	30	....	....	....	....	....	....	....	....	....	....	7	4	2	6	8	....	....	....
	Sweden	WEC-A	8	1	3	4	....	....	....	6	....	....	....	....	....	....	....	....	....	....	....	....	....	....	....	....	....	....
1981-82	Sweden	Can-Cup	3	0	0	0	....	....	....	2	....	....	....	....	....	....	....	....	....	....	....	....	....	....	....	....	....	....
	Winnipeg Jets	**NHL**	73	15	29	44	12	19	31	42	4	0	1	133	11.3	78	16	46	0	16	4	0	4	4	2	0	0	0
1982-83	**Winnipeg Jets**	**NHL**	75	26	33	59	21	23	44	60	5	0	3	156	16.7	82	12	81	5	–6	3	0	2	2	0	0	0	0
1983-84	**Winnipeg Jets**	**NHL**	78	20	45	65	16	31	47	69	5	3	2	181	11.0	85	25	93	28	–5	3	0	1	1	9	0	0	0
1984-85	Sweden	Can-Cup	8	7	1	8	....	....	....	4	....	....	....	....	....	....	....	....	....	....	....	....	....	....	....	....	....	....
	Winnipeg Jets	**NHL**	79	30	54	84	24	37	61	80	7	2	4	238	12.6	118	37	108	26	–1	8	2	3	5	17	2	0	0
1985-86	**Winnipeg Jets**	**NHL**	78	17	47	64	14	32	46	76	2	3	1	195	8.7	94	31	129	37	–29	3	1	1	2	4	0	1	0
	Sweden	WEC-A	8	8	3	11	....	....	....	16	....	....	....	....	....	....	....	....	....	....	....	....	....	....	....	....	....	....
1986-87	**Winnipeg Jets**	**NHL**	75	17	33	50	15	24	39	59	3	3	1	143	11.9	88	23	76	18	7	10	3	4	7	8	0	1	1
1987-88	**Winnipeg Jets**	**NHL**	76	16	38	54	14	27	41	53	3	1	1	167	9.6	91	35	100	33	–11	5	1	5	6	2	1	0	0
1988-89	**Winnipeg Jets**	**NHL**	80	27	61	88	23	43	66	80	9	1	2	173	15.6	125	39	113	41	14	....	....	....	....	....	....	....	....
	Sweden	WEC-A	10	2	4	6	....	....	....	10	....	....	....	....	....	....	....	....	....	....	....	....	....	....	....	....	....	....
1989-90	**Winnipeg Jets**	**NHL**	53	18	48	66	15	34	49	35	5	0	3	129	14.0	84	32	60	10	2	7	2	5	7	16	1	0	0
1990-91	**Winnipeg Jets**	**NHL**	58	19	48	67	17	37	54	49	7	0	3	125	15.2	91	42	54	2	–3	....	....	....	....	....	....	....	....
1991-92	Sweden	Can-Cup	6	0	3	3	....	....	....	11	....	....	....	....	....	....	....	....	....	....	....	....	....	....	....	....	....	....
	Winnipeg Jets	**NHL**	38	13	25	38	12	19	31	29	10	0	0	75	17.3	60	28	29	2	5	7	2	4	6	2	2	0	0
1992-93	**Winnipeg Jets**	**NHL**	80	22	50	72	18	34	52	75	6	0	6	150	14.7	102	45	68	3	–8	6	1	3	4	2	1	0	0
1993-94	**Winnipeg Jets**	**NHL**	76	19	32	51	18	25	43	32	6	0	1	137	13.9	80	33	100	15	–38	....	....	....	....	....	....	....	....
1994-95	**Winnipeg Jets**	**NHL**	31	5	10	15	9	15	24	14	2	0	0	32	15.6	20	7	26	0	–13	....	....	....	....	....	....	....	....
1995-96	Frankfurt Lions	Germany	4	1	0	1	....	....	....	2	....	....	....	....	....	....	....	....	....	....	3	0	1	1	6	....	....	....
1996-97	Eisbaren Berlin	Germany	49	15	18	33	....	....	....	48	....	....	....	....	....	....	....	....	....	....	8	0	2	2	27	....	....	....
1997-98	Eisbaren Berlin	Germany	43	4	7	11	....	....	....	20	....	....	....	....	....	....	....	....	....	....	10	3	4	7	10	....	....	....
1998-99	Eisbaren Berlin	Germany	40	7	15	22	....	....	....	28	....	....	....	....	....	....	....	....	....	....	8	1	5	6	2	....	....	....
	Eisbaren Berlin	EuroHL	5	1	2	3	....	....	....	2	....	....	....	....	....	....	....	....	....	....	6	0	2	2	0	....	....	....
	NHL Totals		**950**	**264**	**553**	**817**	**228**	**400**	**628**	**753**	**74**	**13**	**28**	**2034**	**13.0**	**1198**	**405**	**1083**	**220**		**56**	**12**	**32**	**44**	**62**	**7**	**2**	**1**

WJC-A All-Star Team (1979) • Swedish World All-Star Team (1981, 1985, 1986)

• STEFAN, Patrik

C – L. 6'3", 205 lbs. b: Pribram, Czech., 9/16/1980. Atlanta's 1st, 1st overall, in 1999.

Season	Club	League	GP	G	A	Pts	AG	AA	APts	PIM	PP	SH	GW	S	%	TGF	PGF	TGA	PGA	+/–	GP	G	A	Pts	PIM	PP	SH	GW
1996-97	HC Sparta Praha	Czech-Rep.	5	0	1	1	....	....	....	2	....	....	....	....	....	....	....	....	....	....	7	1	0	1	0	....	....	....
1997-98	HC Sparta Praha	Czech-Rep.	27	2	6	8	....	....	....	16	....	....	....	....	....	....	....	....	....	....	....	....	....	....	....	....	....	....
	Long Beach Ice Dogs	IHL	25	5	10	15	....	....	....	10	....	....	....	....	....	....	....	....	....	....	10	1	1	2	2	....	....	....
1998-99	Long Beach Ice Dogs	IHL	33	11	24	35	....	....	....	26	....	....	....	....	....	....	....	....	....	....	....	....	....	....	....	....	....	....
99-2000	**Atlanta Thrashers**	**NHL**	72	5	20	25	6	19	25	30	1	0	0	117	4.3	43	11	60	8	–20	....	....	....	....	....	....	....	....
	NHL Totals		**72**	**5**	**20**	**25**	**6**	**19**	**25**	**30**	**1**	**0**	**0**	**117**	**4.3**	**43**	**11**	**60**	**8**		....	....	....	....	....	....	....	....

• STEFANIW, Morris

Morris Alexander C – L. 5'11", 170 lbs. b: North Battleford, Sask., 1/10/1948.

Season	Club	League	GP	G	A	Pts	AG	AA	APts	PIM	PP	SH	GW	S	%	TGF	PGF	TGA	PGA	+/–	GP	G	A	Pts	PIM	PP	SH	GW
1964-65	Estevan Bruins	SJHL	54	52	44	96	....	....	....	64	....	....	....	....	....	....	....	....	....	....	6	4	2	6	10	....	....	....
1965-66	Estevan Bruins	SJHL	60	52	66	118	....	....	....	51	....	....	....	....	....	....	....	....	....	....	12	7	12	19	18	....	....	....
	Estevan Bruins	Mem-Cup	13	4	*14	18	....	....	....	8	....	....	....	....	....	....	....	....	....	....	....	....	....	....	....	....	....	....
1966-67	Estevan Bruins	CMJHL	55	36	58	94	....	....	....	28	....	....	....	....	....	....	....	....	....	....	13	2	10	12	4	....	....	....
1967-68	Oklahoma City Blazers	CPHL	37	11	15	26	....	....	....	11	....	....	....	....	....	....	....	....	....	....	....	....	....	....	....	....	....	....
	Phoenix Roadrunners	WHL	17	8	0	8	....	....	....	2	....	....	....	....	....	....	....	....	....	....	4	0	0	0	2	....	....	....
1968-69	Phoenix Roadrunners	WHL	68	12	15	27	....	....	....	50	....	....	....	....	....	....	....	....	....	....	....	....	....	....	....	....	....	....
1969-70	Phoenix Roadrunners	WHL	72	7	22	29	....	....	....	33	....	....	....	....	....	....	....	....	....	....	....	....	....	....	....	....	....	....
1970-71	Omaha Knights	CHL	70	19	41	60	....	....	....	98	....	....	....	....	....	....	....	....	....	....	11	*7	9	16	6	....	....	....
1971-72	Providence Reds	AHL	70	11	20	31	....	....	....	16	....	....	....	....	....	....	....	....	....	....	5	3	3	6	12	....	....	....
1972-73	**Atlanta Flames**	**NHL**	13	1	1	2	1	1	2	2	0	1	0	16	6.3	3	1	12	7	–3	....	....	....	....	....	....	....	....
	Nova Scotia Voyageurs	AHL	64	30	*71	101	....	....	....	80	....	....	....	....	....	....	....	....	....	....	13	8	*17	*25	12	....	....	....
1973-74	Nova Scotia Voyageurs	AHL	27	3	12	15	....	....	....	42	....	....	....	....	....	....	....	....	....	....	....	....	....	....	....	....	....	....
	Albuquerque 6-Guns	CHL	41	7	22	29	....	....	....	24	....	....	....	....	....	....	....	....	....	....	....	....	....	....	....	....	....	....
1974-75	Baltimore Clippers	AHL	46	11	18	29	....	....	....	50	....	....	....	....	....	....	....	....	....	....	....	....	....	....	....	....	....	....
	Johnstown Jets	NAHL	17	1	5	6	....	....	....	6	....	....	....	....	....	....	....	....	....	....	....	....	....	....	....	....	....	....
1975-76	Baltimore Clippers	AHL	76	7	39	46	....	....	....	48	....	....	....	....	....	....	....	....	....	....	....	....	....	....	....	....	....	....
	NHL Totals		**13**	**1**	**1**	**2**	**1**	**1**	**2**	**2**	**0**	**1**	**0**	**16**	**6.3**	**3**	**1**	**12**	**7**		....	....	....	....	....	....	....	....

CMJHL First All-Star Team (1967) • AHL Second All-Star Team (1973)

Traded to **Phoenix** (WHL) by **Boston** for cash, February, 1969. Traded to **NY Rangers** by **Phoenix** (WHL) for cash, October, 1970. Claimed by **Atlanta** from **NY Rangers** in Expansion Draft, June 6, 1972. Traded to **Kansas City** by **Atlanta** for cash, September 17, 1974.

• STEFANSKI, Bud

Edward Stanley Michael C – L. 5'10", 170 lbs. b: South Porcupine, Ont., 4/28/1955. NY Rangers' 9th, 154th overall, in 1975.

Season	Club	League	GP	G	A	Pts	AG	AA	APts	PIM	PP	SH	GW	S	%	TGF	PGF	TGA	PGA	+/–	GP	G	A	Pts	PIM	PP	SH	GW
1973-74	Oshawa Generals	OMJHL	67	25	32	57	....	....	....	22	....	....	....	....	....	....	....	....	....	....	....	....	....	....	....	....	....	....
1974-75	Oshawa Generals	OMJHL	61	18	48	66	....	....	....	35	....	....	....	....	....	....	....	....	....	....	5	2	2	4	14	....	....	....
1975-76	Port Huron Flags	IHL	71	26	30	56	....	....	....	59	....	....	....	....	....	....	....	....	....	....	15	4	4	8	16	....	....	....
1976-77	Port Huron Flags	IHL	77	49	54	103	....	....	....	61	....	....	....	....	....	....	....	....	....	....	....	....	....	....	....	....	....	....
	New Haven Nighthawks	AHL	....	....	....	....	....	....	....	....	....	....	....	....	....	....	....	....	....	....	2	1	0	1	0	....	....	....
1977-78	**New York Rangers**	**NHL**	1	0	0	0	0	0	0	0	0	0	0	1	0.0	0	0	1	0	–1	....	....	....	....	....	....	....	....
	New Haven Nighthawks	AHL	79	27	37	64	....	....	....	61	....	....	....	....	....	....	....	....	....	....	15	5	4	9	6	....	....	....
1978-79	New Haven Nighthawks	AHL	51	18	40	58	....	....	....	71	....	....	....	....	....	....	....	....	....	....	10	3	7	10	21	....	....	....
1979-80	Tulsa Oilers	CHL	71	19	44	63	....	....	....	61	....	....	....	....	....	....	....	....	....	....	3	0	0	0	9	....	....	....
1980-81	VSV Villach	Austria	34	32	40	72	....	....	....	71	....	....	....	....	....	....	....	....	....	....	....	....	....	....	....	....	....	....
	New Haven Nighthawks	AHL	20	9	18	27	....	....	....	46	....	....	....	....	....	....	....	....	....	....	4	0	1	1	8	....	....	....
1981-82	VSV Villach	Austria	28	23	46	69	....	....	....	....	....	....	....	....	....	....	....	....	....	....	10	9	17	26	....	....	....	....
	New Haven Nighthawks	AHL	16	6	5	11	....	....	....	24	....	....	....	....	....	....	....	....	....	....	4	2	1	3	11	....	....	....
1982-83	Springfield Indians	AHL	80	30	40	70	....	....	....	65	....	....	....	....	....	....	....	....	....	....	....	....	....	....	....	....	....	....
1983-84	Maine Mariners	AHL	57	26	24	50	....	....	....	47	....	....	....	....	....	....	....	....	....	....	17	*12	9	21	16	....	....	....
1984-85	Maine Mariners	AHL	75	19	34	53	....	....	....	67	....	....	....	....	....	....	....	....	....	....	11	1	7	8	12	....	....	....
1985-86	Maine Mariners	AHL	68	32	39	71	....	....	....	70	....	....	....	....	....	....	....	....	....	....	2	0	0	0	6	....	....	....
1986-87	Maine Mariners	AHL	29	9	12	21	....	....	....	34	....	....	....	....	....	....	....	....	....	....	....	....	....	....	....	....	....	....
	NHL Totals		**1**	**0**	**0**	**0**	**0**	**0**	**0**	**0**	**0**	**0**	**0**	**1**	**0.0**	**0**	**0**	**1**	**0**		....	....	....	....	....	....	....	....

Won Jack A. Butterfield Trophy (Playoff MVP - AHL) (1984)

Traded to **Winnipeg** by **NY Rangers** for cash and future considerations, October 12, 1979.

• STEMKOWSKI, Pete

Peter David "Stemmer" C – L. 6'1", 196 lbs. b: Winnipeg, Man., 8/25/1943.

Season	Club	League	GP	G	A	Pts	AG	AA	APts	PIM	PP	SH	GW	S	%	TGF	PGF	TGA	PGA	+/–	GP	G	A	Pts	PIM	PP	SH	GW
1960-61	Winnipeg Monarchs	MJHL	31	22	16	38	....	....	....	29	....	....	....	....	....	....	....	....	....	....	....	....	....	....	....	....	....	....
1961-62	Winnipeg Monarchs	MJHL	40	31	34	65	....	....	....	100	....	....	....	....	....	....	....	....	....	....	8	3	7	10	22	....	....	....
1962-63	Winnipeg Monarchs	MJHL	5	6	3	9	....	....	....	8	....	....	....	....	....	....	....	....	....	....	....	....	....	....	....	....	....	....
	Toronto Marlboros	OHA-Jr.	23	16	27	43	....	....	....	44	....	....	....	....	....	....	....	....	....	....	11	7	17	24	26	....	....	....
1963-64	Toronto Marlboros	OHA-Jr.	51	42	61	103	....	....	....	89	....	....	....	....	....	....	....	....	....	....	9	5	9	14	8	....	....	....
	Toronto Maple Leafs	**NHL**	1	0	0	0	0	0	0	2	....	....	....	....	....	....	....	....	....	....	....	....	....	....	....	....	....	....
	Rochester Americans	AHL	3	1	1	2	....	....	....	0	....	....	....	....	....	....	....	....	....	....	....	....	....	....	....	....	....	....
	Toronto Marlboros	Mem-Cup	12	14	15	29	....	....	....	6	....	....	....	....	....	....	....	....	....	....	....	....	....	....	....	....	....	....
1964-65	**Toronto Maple Leafs**	**NHL**	36	5	15	20	6	15	21	33	....	....	....	....	....	....	....	....	....	....	6	0	3	3	7	0	0	0
	Rochester Americans	AHL	35	17	22	39	....	....	....	52	....	....	....	....	....	....	....	....	....	....	....	....	....	....	....	....	....	....
1965-66	**Toronto Maple Leafs**	**NHL**	56	4	12	16	4	11	15	55	....	....	....	....	....	....	....	....	....	....	4	0	0	0	26	0	0	0
	Rochester Americans	AHL	7	5	5	10	....	....	....	8	....	....	....	....	....	....	....	....	....	....	....	....	....	....	....	....	....	....

			REGULAR SEASON																		PLAYOFFS							
Season	Club	League	GP	G	A	Pts	AG	AA	APts	PIM	PP	SH	GW	S	%	TGF	PGF	TGA	PGA	+/–	GP	G	A	Pts	PIM	PP	SH	GW
1966-67♦	**Toronto Maple Leafs**	**NHL**	**68**	**13**	**22**	**35**	**15**	**21**	**36**	**75**	....	....	....	....	....	....	....	....	....	....	**12**	**5**	**7**	**12**	**20**	**2**	**0**	**2**
1967-68	**Toronto Maple Leafs**	**NHL**	**60**	**7**	**15**	**22**	**8**	**15**	**23**	**82**	**0**	**0**	**1**	**141**	**5.0**	**28**	**3**	**30**	**0**	**–5**	....	....	....	....	....	....	....	....
	Detroit Red Wings	**NHL**	**13**	**3**	**6**	**9**	**3**	**6**	**9**	**4**	**0**	**0**	**0**	**38**	**7.9**	**13**	**0**	**20**	**3**	**–4**	....	....	....	....	....	....	....	....
1968-69	**Detroit Red Wings**	**NHL**	**71**	**21**	**31**	**52**	**22**	**28**	**50**	**81**	**3**	**2**	**4**	**209**	**10.0**	**65**	**9**	**75**	**20**	**1**	....	....	....	....	....	....	....	....
1969-70	**Detroit Red Wings**	**NHL**	**76**	**25**	**24**	**49**	**27**	**22**	**49**	**114**	**4**	**1**	**6**	**268**	**9.3**	**75**	**16**	**68**	**22**	**13**	**4**	**1**	**1**	**2**	**6**	**0**	**0**	**1**
1970-71	**Detroit Red Wings**	**NHL**	**10**	**2**	**2**	**4**	**2**	**2**	**4**	**8**	**1**	**0**	**0**	**31**	**6.5**	**8**	**3**	**10**	**4**	**–1**	....	....	....	....	....	....	....	....
	New York Rangers	**NHL**	**68**	**16**	**29**	**45**	**16**	**24**	**40**	**61**	**4**	**0**	**2**	**244**	**6.6**	**63**	**10**	**46**	**9**	**16**	**13**	**3**	**2**	**5**	**6**	**0**	**0**	**2**
1971-72	**New York Rangers**	**NHL**	**59**	**11**	**17**	**28**	**11**	**15**	**26**	**53**	**1**	**0**	**1**	**159**	**6.9**	**40**	**5**	**35**	**2**	**2**	**16**	**4**	**8**	**12**	**18**	**0**	**0**	**1**
1972-73	**New York Rangers**	**NHL**	**78**	**22**	**37**	**59**	**21**	**29**	**50**	**71**	**2**	**0**	**1**	**200**	**11.0**	**78**	**10**	**47**	**7**	**28**	**10**	**4**	**2**	**6**	**6**	**1**	**0**	**1**
1973-74	**New York Rangers**	**NHL**	**78**	**25**	**45**	**70**	**24**	**37**	**61**	**74**	**2**	**0**	**2**	**232**	**10.8**	**89**	**8**	**97**	**19**	**3**	**13**	**6**	**6**	**12**	**35**	**1**	**0**	**0**
1974-75	**New York Rangers**	**NHL**	**77**	**24**	**35**	**59**	**21**	**26**	**47**	**63**	**3**	**0**	**0**	**159**	**15.1**	**78**	**10**	**86**	**15**	**–3**	**3**	**1**	**0**	**1**	**10**	**0**	**0**	**0**
1975-76	**New York Rangers**	**NHL**	**75**	**13**	**28**	**41**	**11**	**21**	**32**	**49**	**1**	**0**	**2**	**126**	**10.3**	**50**	**4**	**73**	**20**	**–7**	....	....	....	....	....	....	....	....
1976-77	**New York Rangers**	**NHL**	**61**	**2**	**13**	**15**	**2**	**10**	**12**	**8**	**0**	**1**	**0**	**56**	**3.6**	**22**	**1**	**60**	**25**	**–14**	....	....	....	....	....	....	....	....
1977-78	**Los Angeles Kings**	**NHL**	**80**	**13**	**18**	**31**	**12**	**14**	**26**	**33**	**0**	**0**	**2**	**134**	**9.7**	**35**	**1**	**47**	**14**	**1**	**2**	**1**	**0**	**1**	**2**	**0**	**0**	**0**
1978-79	Springfield Indians	AHL	24	3	12	15	....	....	....	8	....	....	....	....	....	....	....	....	....	....	....	....	....	....	....	....	....	....
	NHL Totals		**967**	**206**	**349**	**555**	**205**	**296**	**501**	**866**	....	....	....	....	....	....	....	....	....	....	**83**	**25**	**29**	**54**	**136**	....	....	....

Played in NHL All-Star Game (1968)

Traded to **Detroit** by **Toronto** with Frank Mahovlich, Garry Unger and rights to Carl Brewer for Norm Ullman, Paul Henderson, Floyd Smith and Doug Barrie, March 3, 1968. Traded to **NY Rangers** by **Detroit** for Larry Brown, October 31, 1970. Signed as a free agent by **LA Kings**, August 31, 1977.

• STENLUND, Vern

Kenneth Vern C – L. 6'1", 178 lbs. b: Thunder Bay, Ont., 4/11/1956. California's 2nd, 23rd overall, in 1976.

Season	Club	League	GP	G	A	Pts	AG	AA	APts	PIM	PP	SH	GW	S	%	TGF	PGF	TGA	PGA	+/–	GP	G	A	Pts	PIM	PP	SH	GW
1972-73	Chatham Maroons	OHA-B	40	28	36	64	....	....	....	11	....	....	....	....	....	....	....	....	....	....	....	....	....	....	....	....	....	....
1973-74	London Knights	OMJHL	66	17	27	44	....	....	....	16	....	....	....	....	....	....	....	....	....	....	....	....	....	....	....	....	....	....
1974-75	London Knights	OMJHL	70	23	37	60	....	....	....	20	....	....	....	....	....	....	....	....	....	....	....	....	....	....	....	....	....	....
1975-76	London Knights	OMJHL	64	44	75	119	....	....	....	24	....	....	....	....	....	....	....	....	....	....	....	....	....	....	....	....	....	....
1976-77	**Cleveland Barons**	**NHL**	**4**	**0**	**0**	**0**	**0**	**0**	**0**	**0**	**0**	**0**	**0**	**1**	**0.0**	**0**	**0**	**3**	**0**	**–3**	....	....	....	....	....	....	....	....
	Salt Lake Golden Eagles	CHL	67	13	17	30	....	....	....	10	....	....	....	....	....	....	....	....	....	....	....	....	....	....	....	....	....	....
1977-78	Phoenix Roadrunners	CHL	19	0	7	7	....	....	....	0	....	....	....	....	....	....	....	....	....	....	....	....	....	....	....	....	....	....
1978-79			DID NOT PLAY																									
1979-80			DID NOT PLAY																									
1980-81	SK Bergen	Norway	36	36	28	64	....	....	....	45	....	....	....	....	....	....	....	....	....	....	....	....	....	....	....	....	....	....
1981-82	London Southwest	OMHA	DID NOT PLAY – COACHING																									
	NHL Totals		**4**	**0**	**0**	**0**	**0**	**0**	**0**	**0**	**0**	**0**	**0**	**1**	**0.0**	**0**	**0**	**3**	**0**		....	....	....	....	....	....	....	....

Transferred to **Cleveland** after **California** franchise relocated, August 26, 1976.

• STEPHENSON, Bob

Robert RW – R. 6'1", 187 lbs. b: Saskatoon, Sask., 2/1/1954.

Season	Club	League	GP	G	A	Pts	AG	AA	APts	PIM	PP	SH	GW	S	%	TGF	PGF	TGA	PGA	+/–	GP	G	A	Pts	PIM	PP	SH	GW
1974-75	St. Francis Xavier X-Men	AUAA	18	*21	24	45	....	....	....	67	....	....	....	....	....	....	....	....	....	....	....	....	....	....	....	....	....	....
1975-76	St. Francis Xavier X-Men	AUAA	16	*22	16	38	....	....	....	38	....	....	....	....	....	....	....	....	....	....	....	....	....	....	....	....	....	....
1976-77	St. Francis Xavier X-Men	AUAA	19	20	23	43	....	....	....	39	....	....	....	....	....	....	....	....	....	....	....	....	....	....	....	....	....	....
1977-78	Birmingham Bulls	WHA	39	7	6	13	....	....	....	33	....	....	....	....	....	....	....	....	....	....	....	....	....	....	....	....	....	....
	Hampton Gulls	AHL	1	0	0	0	....	....	....	0	....	....	....	....	....	....	....	....	....	....	....	....	....	....	....	....	....	....
	Flint Generals	IHL	6	2	5	7	....	....	....	7	....	....	....	....	....	....	....	....	....	....	....	....	....	....	....	....	....	....
	Tulsa Oilers	CHL	9	1	1	2	....	....	....	7	....	....	....	....	....	....	....	....	....	....	....	....	....	....	....	....	....	....
1978-79	Birmingham Bulls	WHA	78	23	24	47	....	....	....	72	....	....	....	....	....	....	....	....	....	....	....	....	....	....	....	....	....	....
1979-80	**Hartford Whalers**	**NHL**	**4**	**0**	**1**	**1**	**0**	**1**	**1**	**0**	**0**	**0**	**0**	**3**	**0.0**	**4**	**0**	**2**	**0**	**2**	....	....	....	....	....	....	....	....
	Springfield Indians	AHL	28	10	18	28	....	....	....	40	....	....	....	....	....	....	....	....	....	....	....	....	....	....	....	....	....	....
	Toronto Maple Leafs	**NHL**	**14**	**2**	**2**	**4**	**2**	**1**	**3**	**4**	**0**	**0**	**0**	**10**	**20.0**	**5**	**0**	**13**	**1**	**–7**	....	....	....	....	....	....	....	....
	New Brunswick Hawks	AHL	10	6	2	8	....	....	....	4	....	....	....	....	....	....	....	....	....	....	12	2	1	3	0	....	....	....
1980-81	Springfield Indians	AHL	27	5	2	7	....	....	....	43	....	....	....	....	....	....	....	....	....	....	....	....	....	....	....	....	....	....
	NHL Totals		**18**	**2**	**3**	**5**	**2**	**2**	**4**	**4**	**0**	**0**	**0**	**13**	**15.4**	**9**	**0**	**15**	**1**		....	....	....	....	....	....	....	....
	Other Major League Totals		117	30	30	60	....	....	....	105	....	....	....	....	....	....	....	....	....	....	....	....	....	....	....	....	....	....

AUAA First All-Star Team (1976, 1977)

Signed as a free agent by **Birmingham** (WHA), September, 1977. Claimed by **Hartford** from **Birmingham** (WHA) in WHA Dispersal Draft, June, 1979. Traded to **Toronto** by **Hartford** for Pat Boutette, December 24, 1979.

• STERN, Ron

Ronald RW – R. 6', 200 lbs. b: Ste. Agathe, Que., 1/11/1967. Vancouver's 3rd, 70th overall, in 1986.

Season	Club	League	GP	G	A	Pts	AG	AA	APts	PIM	PP	SH	GW	S	%	TGF	PGF	TGA	PGA	+/–	GP	G	A	Pts	PIM	PP	SH	GW
1983-84	Laurentides-Pionniers	QAAA	39	6	6	12	....	....	....	....	....	....	....	....	....	....	....	....	....	....	....	....	....	....	....	....	....	....
1984-85	Longueuil Chevaliers	QMJHL	67	6	14	20	....	....	....	176	....	....	....	....	....	....	....	....	....	....	....	....	....	....	....	....	....	....
1985-86	Longueuil Chevaliers	QMJHL	70	39	33	72	....	....	....	317	....	....	....	....	....	....	....	....	....	....	....	....	....	....	....	....	....	....
1986-87	Longueuil Chevaliers	QMJHL	56	32	39	71	....	....	....	266	....	....	....	....	....	....	....	....	....	....	19	11	9	20	55	....	....	....
	Longueuil Chevaliers	Mem-Cup	4	1	0	1	....	....	....	*69	....	....	....	....	....	....	....	....	....	....	....	....	....	....	....	....	....	....
1987-88	**Vancouver Canucks**	**NHL**	**15**	**0**	**0**	**0**	**0**	**0**	**0**	**52**	**0**	**0**	**0**	**7**	**0.0**	**0**	**0**	**7**	**0**	**–7**	....	....	....	....	....	....	....	....
	Fredericton Express	AHL	2	1	0	1	....	....	....	4	....	....	....	....	....	....	....	....	....	....	....	....	....	....	....	....	....	....
	Flint Spirits	IHL	55	14	19	33	....	....	....	294	....	....	....	....	....	....	....	....	....	....	16	8	8	16	94	....	....	....
1988-89	**Vancouver Canucks**	**NHL**	**17**	**1**	**0**	**1**	**1**	**0**	**1**	**49**	**0**	**0**	**0**	**13**	**7.7**	**2**	**0**	**8**	**0**	**–6**	**3**	**0**	**1**	**1**	**17**	**0**	**0**	**0**
	Milwaukee Admirals	IHL	45	19	23	42	....	....	....	280	....	....	....	....	....	....	....	....	....	....	5	1	0	1	11	....	....	....
1989-90	**Vancouver Canucks**	**NHL**	**34**	**2**	**3**	**5**	**2**	**2**	**4**	**208**	**0**	**0**	**0**	**27**	**7.4**	**9**	**0**	**26**	**0**	**–17**	....	....	....	....	....	....	....	....
	Milwaukee Admirals	IHL	26	8	9	17	....	....	....	165	....	....	....	....	....	....	....	....	....	....	....	....	....	....	....	....	....	....
1990-91	**Vancouver Canucks**	**NHL**	**31**	**2**	**3**	**5**	**2**	**2**	**4**	**171**	**0**	**0**	**0**	**30**	**6.7**	**8**	**1**	**21**	**0**	**–14**	....	....	....	....	....	....	....	....
	Milwaukee Admirals	IHL	7	2	2	4	....	....	....	81	....	....	....	....	....	....	....	....	....	....	....	....	....	....	....	....	....	....
	Calgary Flames	**NHL**	**13**	**1**	**3**	**4**	**1**	**2**	**3**	**69**	**0**	**0**	**0**	**15**	**6.7**	**5**	**0**	**5**	**0**	**0**	**7**	**1**	**3**	**4**	**14**	**0**	**0**	**0**
1991-92	**Calgary Flames**	**NHL**	**72**	**13**	**9**	**22**	**12**	**7**	**19**	**338**	**0**	**1**	**1**	**96**	**13.5**	**35**	**0**	**47**	**12**	**0**	....	....	....	....	....	....	....	....
1992-93	**Calgary Flames**	**NHL**	**70**	**10**	**15**	**25**	**8**	**10**	**18**	**207**	**0**	**0**	**1**	**82**	**12.2**	**34**	**0**	**34**	**4**	**4**	**6**	**0**	**0**	**0**	**43**	**0**	**0**	**0**
1993-94	**Calgary Flames**	**NHL**	**71**	**9**	**20**	**29**	**8**	**16**	**24**	**243**	**0**	**1**	**3**	**105**	**8.6**	**43**	**0**	**39**	**2**	**6**	**7**	**2**	**0**	**2**	**12**	**0**	**0**	**0**
1994-95	**Calgary Flames**	**NHL**	**39**	**9**	**4**	**13**	**16**	**6**	**22**	**163**	**1**	**0**	**0**	**69**	**13.0**	**24**	**1**	**27**	**8**	**4**	**7**	**3**	**1**	**4**	**8**	**1**	**1**	**0**
1995-96	**Calgary Flames**	**NHL**	**52**	**10**	**5**	**15**	**10**	**4**	**14**	**111**	**0**	**0**	**1**	**64**	**15.6**	**29**	**4**	**35**	**12**	**2**	**4**	**0**	**2**	**2**	**8**	**0**	**0**	**0**
1996-97	**Calgary Flames**	**NHL**	**79**	**7**	**10**	**17**	**7**	**9**	**16**	**157**	**0**	**1**	**1**	**98**	**7.1**	**25**	**0**	**44**	**15**	**–4**	....	....	....	....	....	....	....	....
1997-98	**Calgary Flames**	**NHL**	DID NOT PLAY – INJURED																									
1998-99	**San Jose Sharks**	**NHL**	**78**	**7**	**9**	**16**	**8**	**9**	**17**	**158**	**1**	**0**	**2**	**94**	**7.4**	**28**	**1**	**31**	**1**	**–3**	**6**	**0**	**0**	**0**	**6**	**0**	**0**	**0**
99-2000	**San Jose Sharks**	**NHL**	**67**	**4**	**5**	**9**	**4**	**5**	**9**	**151**	**0**	**0**	**0**	**63**	**6.3**	**13**	**0**	**22**	**0**	**–9**	**3**	**1**	**0**	**1**	**11**	**0**	**0**	**0**
	NHL Totals		**638**	**75**	**86**	**161**	**79**	**72**	**151**	**2077**	**2**	**3**	**9**	**763**	**9.8**	**255**	**7**	**346**	**54**		**43**	**7**	**7**	**14**	**119**	**1**	**1**	**0**

Traded to **Calgary** by **Vancouver** with Kevan Guy for Dana Murzyn, March 5, 1991. • Missed entire 1997-98 season recovering from knee surgery, October, 1997. Signed as a free agent by **San Jose**, August 25, 1998.

• STEVENS, John

John A. D – L. 6'1", 195 lbs. b: Campbellton, N.B., 5/4/1966. Philadelphia's 5th, 47th overall, in 1984.

Season	Club	League	GP	G	A	Pts	AG	AA	APts	PIM	PP	SH	GW	S	%	TGF	PGF	TGA	PGA	+/–	GP	G	A	Pts	PIM	PP	SH	GW
1982-83	Newmarket Flyers	OJHL	48	2	9	11	....	....	....	111	....	....	....	....	....	....	....	....	....	....	....	....	....	....	....	....	....	....
1983-84	Oshawa Generals	OHL	70	1	10	11	....	....	....	71	....	....	....	....	....	....	....	....	....	....	7	0	1	1	6	....	....	....
1984-85	Oshawa Generals	OHL	44	2	10	12	....	....	....	61	....	....	....	....	....	....	....	....	....	....	5	0	2	2	4	....	....	....
	Hershey Bears	AHL	3	0	0	0	....	....	....	0	....	....	....	....	....	....	....	....	....	....	....	....	....	....	....	....	....	....
1985-86	Oshawa Generals	OHL	65	1	7	8	....	....	....	146	....	....	....	....	....	....	....	....	....	....	6	0	2	2	14	....	....	....
	Kalamazoo Wings	IHL	6	0	1	1	....	....	....	8	....	....	....	....	....	....	....	....	....	....	6	0	3	3	9	....	....	....
1986-87	**Philadelphia Flyers**	**NHL**	**6**	**0**	**2**	**2**	**0**	**1**	**1**	**14**	**0**	**0**	**0**	**2**	**0.0**	**6**	**1**	**5**	**0**	**0**	....	....	....	....	....	....	....	....
	Hershey Bears	AHL	63	1	15	16	....	....	....	131	....	....	....	....	....	....	....	....	....	....	3	0	0	0	7	....	....	....
1987-88	**Philadelphia Flyers**	**NHL**	**3**	**0**	**0**	**0**	**0**	**0**	**0**	**0**	**0**	**0**	**0**	**0**	**0.0**	**1**	**0**	**2**	**0**	**–1**	....	....	....	....	....	....	....	....
	Hershey Bears	AHL	59	1	15	16	....	....	....	108	....	....	....	....	....	....	....	....	....	....	....	....	....	....	....	....	....	....
1988-89	Hershey Bears	AHL	78	3	13	16	....	....	....	129	....	....	....	....	....	....	....	....	....	....	12	1	1	2	29	....	....	....
1989-90	Hershey Bears	AHL	79	3	10	13	....	....	....	193	....	....	....	....	....	....	....	....	....	....	....	....	....	....	....	....	....	....

			REGULAR SEASON																		PLAYOFFS							
Season	Club	League	GP	G	A	Pts	AG	AA	APts	PIM	PP	SH	GW	S	%	TGF	PGF	TGA	PGA	+/–	GP	G	A	Pts	PIM	PP	SH	GW
1990-91	**Hartford Whalers**	**NHL**	**14**	**0**	**1**	**1**	**0**	**1**	**1**	**11**	**0**	**0**	**0**	**7**	**0.0**	**6**	**0**	**10**	**4**	**0**	....	....	....	....	....	....	....	....
	Springfield Indians	AHL	65	0	12	12	....	....	....	139	....	....	....	....	....	....	....	....	....	....	18	0	6	6	35	....	....	....
1991-92	**Hartford Whalers**	**NHL**	**21**	**0**	**4**	**4**	**0**	**3**	**3**	**19**	**0**	**0**	**0**	**13**	**0.0**	**19**	**3**	**24**	**4**	**–4**	....	....	....	....	....	....	....	....
	Springfield Indians	AHL	45	1	12	13	....	....	....	73	....	....	....	....	....	....	....	....	....	....	11	1	3	4	27	....	....	....
1992-93	Springfield Indians	AHL	74	1	19	20	....	....	....	111	....	....	....	....	....	....	....	....	....	....	15	0	1	1	18	....	....	....
1993-94	**Hartford Whalers**	**NHL**	**9**	**0**	**3**	**3**	**0**	**2**	**2**	**4**	**0**	**0**	**0**	**3**	**0.0**	**9**	**0**	**5**	**0**	**4**	....	....	....	....	....	....	....	....
	Springfield Indians	AHL	71	3	9	12	....	....	....	85	....	....	....	....	....	....	....	....	....	....	3	0	0	0	0	....	....	....
1994-95	Springfield Falcons	AHL	79	5	15	20	....	....	....	122	....	....	....	....	....	....	....	....	....	....	....	....	....	....	....	....	....	....
1995-96	Springfield Falcons	AHL	69	0	19	19	....	....	....	95	....	....	....	....	....	....	....	....	....	....	10	0	1	1	31	....	....	....
1996-97	Philadelphia Phantoms	AHL	74	2	18	20	....	....	....	116	....	....	....	....	....	....	....	....	....	....	10	0	2	2	8	....	....	....
1997-98	Philadelphia Phantoms	AHL	50	1	9	10	....	....	....	76	....	....	....	....	....	....	....	....	....	....	20	0	6	6	44	....	....	....
1998-99	Philadelphia Phantoms	AHL	25	0	1	1	....	....	....	19	....	....	....	....	....	....	....	....	....	....	....	....	....	....	....	....	....	....
1999-2000	Philadelphia Phantoms	AHL	DID NOT PLAY – ASSISTANT COACH																									
	NHL Totals		**53**	**0**	**10**	**10**	**0**	**7**	**7**	**48**	**0**	**0**	**0**	**25**	**0.0**	**41**	**4**	**46**	**8**		....	....	....	....	....	....	....	....

Signed as a free agent by **Hartford**, July 30, 1990. Signed as a free agent by **Philadelphia**, August 6, 1996. • Suffered career-ending eye injury in game vs. Kentucky (AHL), December 13, 1998. • Named Head Coach of **Philadelphia Phantoms** (AHL), July 6, 2000.

• STEVENS, Kevin

LW – L. 6'3", 230 lbs. b: Brockton, MA, 4/15/1965. Los Angeles' 6th, 112th overall, in 1983.

Season	Club	League	GP	G	A	Pts	AG	AA	APts	PIM	PP	SH	GW	S	%	TGF	PGF	TGA	PGA	+/–	GP	G	A	Pts	PIM	PP	SH	GW
1982-83	Silver Lake Lakers	Hi-School	18	24	27	51	....	....	....	....	....	....	....	....	....	....	....	....	....	....	....	....	....	....	....	....	....	....
1983-84	Boston College	ECAC	37	6	14	20	....	....	....	36	....	....	....	....	....	....	....	....	....	....	....	....	....	....	....	....	....	....
1984-85	Boston College	H-East	40	13	23	36	....	....	....	36	....	....	....	....	....	....	....	....	....	....	....	....	....	....	....	....	....	....
1985-86	Boston College	H-East	42	17	27	44	....	....	....	56	....	....	....	....	....	....	....	....	....	....	....	....	....	....	....	....	....	....
1986-87	Boston College	H-East	39	35	35	70	....	....	....	54	....	....	....	....	....	....	....	....	....	....	....	....	....	....	....	....	....	....
	United States	WEC-A	8	1	1	2	....	....	....	10	....	....	....	....	....	....	....	....	....	....	....	....	....	....	....	....	....	....
1987-88	United States	Nat-Team	44	22	23	45	....	....	....	52	....	....	....	....	....	....	....	....	....	....	....	....	....	....	....	....	....	....
	United States	Olympics	5	1	3	4	....	....	....	2	....	....	....	....	....	....	....	....	....	....	....	....	....	....	....	....	....	....
	Pittsburgh Penguins	**NHL**	**16**	**5**	**2**	**7**	**4**	**1**	**5**	**8**	**2**	**0**	**0**	**22**	**22.7**	**18**	**8**	**16**	**0**	**–6**	....	....	....	....	....	....	....	....
1988-89	**Pittsburgh Penguins**	**NHL**	**24**	**12**	**3**	**15**	**10**	**2**	**12**	**19**	**4**	**0**	**3**	**52**	**23.1**	**22**	**7**	**23**	**0**	**–8**	**11**	**3**	**7**	**10**	**16**	**0**	**0**	**0**
	Muskegon Lumberjacks	IHL	45	24	41	65	....	....	....	113	....	....	....	....	....	....	....	....	....	....	....	....	....	....	....	....	....	....
1989-90	**Pittsburgh Penguins**	**NHL**	**76**	**29**	**41**	**70**	**25**	**29**	**54**	**171**	**12**	**0**	**1**	**179**	**16.2**	**109**	**38**	**92**	**8**	**–13**	....	....	....	....	....	....	....	....
	United States	WEC-A	10	5	2	7	....	....	....	18	....	....	....	....	....	....	....	....	....	....	....	....	....	....	....	....	....	....
1990-91 ♦	**Pittsburgh Penguins**	**NHL**	**80**	**40**	**46**	**86**	**37**	**35**	**72**	**133**	**18**	**0**	**6**	**253**	**15.8**	**143**	**60**	**86**	**2**	**–1**	**24**	***17**	**16**	**33**	**53**	**7**	**0**	**4**
1991-92 ♦	**Pittsburgh Penguins**	**NHL**	**80**	**54**	**69**	**123**	**49**	**52**	**101**	**254**	**19**	**0**	**4**	**325**	**16.6**	**175**	**69**	**99**	**1**	**8**	**21**	**13**	**15**	**28**	**28**	**4**	**0**	**3**
1992-93	**Pittsburgh Penguins**	**NHL**	**72**	**55**	**56**	**111**	**46**	**39**	**85**	**177**	**26**	**0**	**5**	**326**	**16.9**	**166**	**70**	**80**	**1**	**17**	**12**	**5**	**11**	**16**	**22**	**4**	**0**	**0**
1993-94	**Pittsburgh Penguins**	**NHL**	**83**	**41**	**47**	**88**	**38**	**37**	**75**	**155**	**21**	**0**	**4**	**284**	**14.4**	**138**	**69**	**94**	**1**	**–24**	**6**	**1**	**1**	**2**	**10**	**0**	**0**	**0**
1994-95	**Pittsburgh Penguins**	**NHL**	**27**	**15**	**12**	**27**	**27**	**18**	**45**	**51**	**6**	**0**	**4**	**80**	**18.8**	**33**	**13**	**20**	**0**	**0**	**12**	**4**	**7**	**11**	**21**	**3**	**0**	**1**
1995-96	**Boston Bruins**	**NHL**	**41**	**10**	**13**	**23**	**10**	**11**	**21**	**49**	**3**	**0**	**1**	**101**	**9.9**	**53**	**19**	**33**	**0**	**1**	....	....	....	....	....	....	....	....
	Los Angeles Kings	**NHL**	**20**	**3**	**10**	**13**	**3**	**8**	**11**	**22**	**3**	**0**	**0**	**69**	**4.3**	**17**	**9**	**19**	**0**	**–11**	....	....	....	....	....	....	....	....
	United States	WC-A	8	4	3	7	....	....	....	12	....	....	....	....	....	....	....	....	....	....	....	....	....	....	....	....	....	....
1996-97	**Los Angeles Kings**	**NHL**	**69**	**14**	**20**	**34**	**15**	**18**	**33**	**96**	**4**	**0**	**1**	**175**	**8.0**	**68**	**21**	**74**	**0**	**–27**	....	....	....	....	....	....	....	....
1997-98	**New York Rangers**	**NHL**	**80**	**14**	**27**	**41**	**16**	**26**	**42**	**130**	**5**	**0**	**3**	**144**	**9.7**	**60**	**17**	**50**	**0**	**–7**	....	....	....	....	....	....	....	....
1998-99	**New York Rangers**	**NHL**	**81**	**23**	**20**	**43**	**27**	**19**	**46**	**64**	**8**	**0**	**3**	**136**	**16.9**	**62**	**19**	**54**	**1**	**–10**	....	....	....	....	....	....	....	....
99-2000	**New York Rangers**	**NHL**	**38**	**3**	**5**	**8**	**3**	**5**	**8**	**43**	**1**	**0**	**0**	**44**	**6.8**	**14**	**1**	**21**	**1**	**–7**	....	....	....	....	....	....	....	....
	NHL Totals		**787**	**318**	**371**	**689**	**310**	**300**	**610**	**1372**	**132**	**0**	**35**	**2190**	**14.5**	**1078**	**420**	**761**	**15**		**86**	**43**	**57**	**100**	**150**	**18**	**0**	**8**

Hockey East First All-Star Team (1987) • NCAA East Second All-American Team (1987) • NHL Second All-Star Team (1991, 1993) • NHL First All-Star Team (1992) • Played in NHL All-Star Game (1991, 1992, 1993)

Rights traded to **Pittsburgh** by **LA Kings** for Anders Hakansson, September 9, 1983. Traded to **Boston** by **Pittsburgh** with Shawn McEachern for Glen Murray, Bryan Smolinski and Boston's 3rd round choice (Boyd Kane) in 1996 Entry Draft, August 2, 1995. Traded to **LA Kings** by **Boston** for Rick Tocchet, January 25, 1996. Traded to **NY Rangers** by **LA Kings** for Luc Robitaille, August 28, 1997. • Missed majority of 1999-2000 season after entering NHL/NHLPA substance abuse program, January 23, 2000. Signed as a free agent by **Philadelphia**, July 7, 2000.

• STEVENS, Mike

LW – L. 6', 202 lbs. b: Kitchener, Ont., 12/30/1965. Vancouver's 5th, 58th overall, in 1984.

Season	Club	League	GP	G	A	Pts	AG	AA	APts	PIM	PP	SH	GW	S	%	TGF	PGF	TGA	PGA	+/–	GP	G	A	Pts	PIM	PP	SH	GW
1982-83	Kitchener Ranger B's	OJHL-B	29	5	18	23	....	....	....	86	....	....	....	....	....	....	....	....	....	....	....	....	....	....	....	....	....	....
	Kitchener Rangers	OHL	13	0	4	4	....	....	....	16	....	....	....	....	....	....	....	....	....	....	12	0	1	1	9	....	....	....
1983-84	Kitchener Rangers	OHL	66	19	21	40	....	....	....	109	....	....	....	....	....	....	....	....	....	....	16	10	7	17	40	....	....	....
	Kitchener Rangers	Mem-Cup	4	1	6	7	....	....	....	13	....	....	....	....	....	....	....	....	....	....	....	....	....	....	....	....	....	....
1984-85	Kitchener Rangers	OHL	37	17	18	35	....	....	....	121	....	....	....	....	....	....	....	....	....	....	4	1	1	2	8	....	....	....
	Vancouver Canucks	**NHL**	**6**	**0**	**3**	**3**	**0**	**2**	**2**	**6**	**0**	**0**	**0**	**10**	**0.0**	**3**	**0**	**5**	**0**	**–2**	....	....	....	....	....	....	....	....
1985-86	Fredericton Express	AHL	79	12	19	31	....	....	....	208	....	....	....	....	....	....	....	....	....	....	6	1	1	2	35	....	....	....
1986-87	Fredericton Express	AHL	71	7	18	25	....	....	....	258	....	....	....	....	....	....	....	....	....	....	....	....	....	....	....	....	....	....
1987-88	**Boston Bruins**	**NHL**	**7**	**0**	**1**	**1**	**0**	**1**	**1**	**9**	**0**	**0**	**0**	**5**	**0.0**	**1**	**0**	**1**	**0**	**0**	....	....	....	....	....	....	....	....
	Maine Mariners	AHL	63	30	25	55	....	....	....	265	....	....	....	....	....	....	....	....	....	....	7	1	2	3	37	....	....	....
1988-89	**New York Islanders**	**NHL**	**9**	**1**	**0**	**1**	**1**	**0**	**1**	**14**	**0**	**0**	**0**	**9**	**11.1**	**2**	**0**	**3**	**0**	**–1**	....	....	....	....	....	....	....	....
	Springfield Indians	AHL	42	17	13	30	....	....	....	120	....	....	....	....	....	....	....	....	....	....	....	....	....	....	....	....	....	....
1989-90	Springfield Indians	AHL	28	12	10	22	....	....	....	75	....	....	....	....	....	....	....	....	....	....	....	....	....	....	....	....	....	....
	Toronto Maple Leafs	**NHL**	**1**	**0**	**0**	**0**	**0**	**0**	**0**	**0**	**0**	**0**	**0**	**2**	**0.0**	**0**	**0**	**0**	**0**	**0**	....	....	....	....	....	....	....	....
	Newmarket Saints	AHL	46	16	28	44	....	....	....	86	....	....	....	....	....	....	....	....	....	....	....	....	....	....	....	....	....	....
1990-91	Newmarket Saints	AHL	68	24	23	47	....	....	....	229	....	....	....	....	....	....	....	....	....	....	....	....	....	....	....	....	....	....
1991-92	St. John's Maple Leafs	AHL	30	13	11	24	....	....	....	65	....	....	....	....	....	....	....	....	....	....	....	....	....	....	....	....	....	....
	Binghamton Rangers	AHL	44	15	15	30	....	....	....	87	....	....	....	....	....	....	....	....	....	....	11	7	6	13	45	....	....	....
1992-93	Binghamton Rangers	AHL	68	31	61	92	....	....	....	230	....	....	....	....	....	....	....	....	....	....	14	5	5	10	63	....	....	....
1993-94	Saint John Flames	AHL	79	20	37	57	....	....	....	293	....	....	....	....	....	....	....	....	....	....	6	1	3	4	34	....	....	....
1994-95	Cincinnati Cyclones	IHL	80	34	43	77	....	....	....	274	....	....	....	....	....	....	....	....	....	....	10	6	3	9	16	....	....	....
1995-96	Cleveland Lumberjacks	IHL	81	31	43	74	....	....	....	252	....	....	....	....	....	....	....	....	....	....	3	1	0	1	8	....	....	....
1996-97	Cleveland Lumberjacks	IHL	6	1	4	5	....	....	....	32	....	....	....	....	....	....	....	....	....	....	....	....	....	....	....	....	....	....
	Manitoba Moose	IHL	22	8	4	12	....	....	....	54	....	....	....	....	....	....	....	....	....	....	....	....	....	....	....	....	....	....
	Cincinnati Cyclones	IHL	46	16	18	34	....	....	....	140	....	....	....	....	....	....	....	....	....	....	3	0	2	2	8	....	....	....
1997-98	Schwenningen Wild Wings	Germany	50	18	32	50	....	....	....	197	....	....	....	....	....	....	....	....	....	....	....	....	....	....	....	....	....	....
1998-99	Adler Mannheim	Germany	44	8	12	20	....	....	....	233	....	....	....	....	....	....	....	....	....	....	11	4	4	8	49	....	....	....
	Adler Mannheim	EuroHL	4	1	0	1	....	....	....	4	....	....	....	....	....	....	....	....	....	....	4	0	0	0	12	....	....	....
99-2000	Adler Mannheim	Germany	48	17	16	33	....	....	....	126	....	....	....	....	....	....	....	....	....	....	5	1	0	1	42	....	....	....
	Adler Mannheim	EuroHL	4	1	1	2	....	....	....	4	....	....	....	....	....	....	....	....	....	....	....	....	....	....	....	....	....	....
	NHL Totals		**23**	**1**	**4**	**5**	**1**	**3**	**4**	**29**	**0**	**0**	**0**	**26**	**3.8**	**6**	**0**	**9**	**0**		....	....	....	....	....	....	....	....

• Brother of Scott

Traded to **Boston** by **Vancouver** for cash, October 6, 1987. Signed as a free agent by **NY Islanders**, August 20, 1988. Traded to **Toronto** by **NY Islanders** with Gilles Thibaudeau for Jack Capuano, Paul Gagne and Derek Laxdal, December 20, 1989. Traded to **NY Rangers** by **Toronto** for Guy Larose, December 26, 1991. Signed as a free agent by **Calgary**, August 10, 1993.

• STEVENS, Scott

D – L. 6'1", 215 lbs. b: Kitchener, Ont., 4/1/1964. Washington's 1st, 5th overall, in 1982.

Season	Club	League	GP	G	A	Pts	AG	AA	APts	PIM	PP	SH	GW	S	%	TGF	PGF	TGA	PGA	+/–	GP	G	A	Pts	PIM	PP	SH	GW
1980-81	Kitchener Ranger B'S	OHA-B	39	7	33	40	....	....	....	82	....	....	....	....	....	....	....	....	....	....	....	....	....	....	....	....	....	....
	Kitchener Rangers	OMJHL	1	0	0	0	....	....	....	0	....	....	....	....	....	....	....	....	....	....	....	....	....	....	....	....	....	....
1981-82	Kitchener Rangers	OHL	68	6	36	42	....	....	....	158	....	....	....	....	....	....	....	....	....	....	15	1	10	11	71	....	....	....
	Kitchener Rangers	Mem-Cup	5	0	2	2	....	....	....	11	....	....	....	....	....	....	....	....	....	....	....	....	....	....	....	....	....	....
1982-83	**Washington Capitals**	**NHL**	**77**	**9**	**16**	**25**	**7**	**11**	**18**	**195**	**0**	**0**	**0**	**121**	**7.4**	**91**	**3**	**81**	**7**	**14**	**4**	**1**	**0**	**1**	**26**	**0**	**0**	**0**
	Canada	WEC-A	10	0	2	2	....	....	....	8	....	....	....	....	....	....	....	....	....	....	....	....	....	....	....	....	....	....
1983-84	**Washington Capitals**	**NHL**	**78**	**13**	**32**	**45**	**10**	**22**	**32**	**201**	**7**	**0**	**2**	**155**	**8.4**	**128**	**29**	**87**	**14**	**26**	**8**	**1**	**8**	**9**	**21**	**1**	**0**	**0**
1984-85	**Washington Capitals**	**NHL**	**80**	**21**	**44**	**65**	**17**	**30**	**47**	**221**	**16**	**0**	**5**	**170**	**12.4**	**147**	**50**	**109**	**31**	**19**	**5**	**0**	**1**	**1**	**20**	**0**	**0**	**0**
	Canada	WEC-A	8	1	2	3	....	....	....	6	....	....	....	....	....	....	....	....	....	....	....	....	....	....	....	....	....	....
1985-86	**Washington Capitals**	**NHL**	**73**	**15**	**38**	**53**	**12**	**26**	**38**	**165**	**3**	**0**	**2**	**121**	**12.4**	**133**	**35**	**122**	**24**	**0**	**9**	**3**	**8**	**11**	**12**	**2**	**0**	**2**
1986-87	**Washington Capitals**	**NHL**	**77**	**10**	**51**	**61**	**9**	**37**	**46**	**283**	**2**	**0**	**0**	**165**	**6.1**	**150**	**45**	**115**	**23**	**13**	**7**	**0**	**5**	**5**	**19**	**0**	**0**	**0**
	Canada	WEC-A	2	0	1	1	....	....	....	2	....	....	....	....	....	....	....	....	....	....	....	....	....	....	....	....	....	....

			REGULAR SEASON																		PLAYOFFS							
Season	Club	League	GP	G	A	Pts	AG	AA	APts	PIM	PP	SH	GW	S	%	TGF	PGF	TGA	PGA	+/–	GP	G	A	Pts	PIM	PP	SH	GW
1987-88	Washington Capitals	NHL	80	12	60	72	10	43	53	184	5	1	2	231	5.2	158	62	124	42	14	13	1	11	12	46	0	0	0
1988-89	Washington Capitals	NHL	80	7	61	68	6	43	49	225	6	0	3	195	3.6	163	66	134	38	1	6	1	4	5	11	0	0	0
	Canada	WEC-A	7	2	1	3	....	....	....	2	....	....	....	....	....	....	....	....	....	....	....	....	....	....	....	....	....	....
1989-90	Washington Capitals	Fr-Tour	4	1	4	5	....	....	....	15	....	....	....	....	....	....	....	....	....	....	....	....	....	....	....	....	....	....
	Washington Capitals	NHL	56	11	29	40	9	21	30	154	7	0	0	143	7.7	99	34	87	23	1	15	2	7	9	25	1	0	0
1990-91	St. Louis Blues	NHL	78	5	44	49	5	34	39	150	1	0	1	160	3.1	142	37	117	35	23	13	0	3	3	36	0	0	0
1991-92	Canada	Can-Cup	8	1	0	1	....	....	....	4	....	....	....	....	....	....	....	....	....	....	....	....	....	....	....	....	....	....
	New Jersey Devils	NHL	68	17	42	59	15	32	47	124	7	1	2	156	10.9	120	28	87	19	24	7	2	1	3	29	2	0	1
1992-93	New Jersey Devils	NHL	81	12	45	57	10	31	41	120	8	0	1	146	8.2	128	39	125	50	14	5	2	2	4	10	1	0	0
1993-94	New Jersey Devils	NHL	83	18	60	78	17	47	64	112	5	1	4	215	8.4	153	38	93	31	53	20	2	9	11	42	2	0	1
1994-95♦	New Jersey Devils	NHL	48	2	20	22	4	30	34	56	1	0	1	111	1.8	54	10	56	16	4	20	1	7	8	24	0	0	1
1995-96	New Jersey Devils	NHL	82	5	23	28	5	19	24	100	2	1	1	174	2.9	80	17	86	30	7	....	....	....	....	....	....	....	....
1996-97	Canada	W-Cup	8	0	2	2	....	....	....	4	....	....	....	....	....	....	....	....	....	....	....	....	....	....	....	....	....	....
	New Jersey Devils	NHL	79	5	19	24	5	17	22	70	0	0	1	166	3.0	92	12	69	15	26	10	0	4	4	2	0	0	0
1997-98	New Jersey Devils	NHL	80	4	22	26	5	22	27	80	1	0	1	94	4.3	62	2	71	30	19	6	1	0	1	8	0	0	0
	Canada	Olympics	6	0	0	0	....	....	....	2	....	....	....	....	....	....	....	....	....	....	....	....	....	....	....	....	....	....
1998-99	New Jersey Devils	NHL	75	5	22	27	6	21	27	64	0	0	1	111	4.5	75	1	78	33	29	7	2	1	3	10	2	0	0
99-2000♦	New Jersey Devils	NHL	78	8	21	29	9	19	28	103	0	1	1	133	6.0	87	5	84	32	30	23	3	8	11	6	0	0	2
	NHL Totals		1353	179	649	828	161	505	666	2607	71	5	28	2767	6.5	2062	513	1725	493		178	22	79	101	347	11	0	7

• Brother of Mike • NHL All-Rookie Team (1983) • NHL First All-Star Team (1988, 1994) • NHL Second All-Star Team (1992, 1997) • Won Alka-Seltzer Plus Award (1994) • Played in NHL All-Star Game (1985, 1989, 1991, 1992, 1993, 1994, 1996, 1997, 1998, 1999, 2000)

Signed as a free agent by **St. Louis**, July 16, 1990. Transferred to **New Jersey** from **St. Louis** as compensation for St. Louis' signing of free agent Brendan Shanahan, September 3, 1991.

• STEVENSON, Jeremy

LW – L. 6'2", 220 lbs. b: San Bernadino, CA, 7/28/1974. Anaheim's 10th, 262nd overall, in 1994.

Season	Club	League	GP	G	A	Pts	AG	AA	APts	PIM	PP	SH	GW	S	%	TGF	PGF	TGA	PGA	+/–	GP	G	A	Pts	PIM	PP	SH	GW
1989-90	Elliot Lake Vikings	NOHA	61	39	26	65	....	....	....	203	....	....	....	....	....	....	....	....	....	....	....	....	....	....	....	....	....	....
1990-91	Cornwall Royals	OHL	58	13	20	33	....	....	....	124	....	....	....	....	....	....	....	....	....	....	....	....	....	....	....	....	....	....
1991-92	Cornwall Royals	OHL	63	15	23	38	....	....	....	176	....	....	....	....	....	....	....	....	....	....	6	3	1	4	4	....	....	....
1992-93	Newmarket Royals	OHL	54	28	28	56	....	....	....	144	....	....	....	....	....	....	....	....	....	....	5	5	1	6	28	....	....	....
1993-94	Newmarket Royals	OHL	9	2	4	6	....	....	....	27	....	....	....	....	....	....	....	....	....	....	....	....	....	....	....	....	....	....
	Sault Ste. Marie Greyhounds	OHL	48	18	19	37	....	....	....	183	....	....	....	....	....	....	....	....	....	....	14	1	1	2	23	....	....	....
1994-95	Greensboro Monarchs	ECHL	43	14	13	27	....	....	....	231	....	....	....	....	....	....	....	....	....	....	17	6	11	17	64	....	....	....
1995-96	Mighty Ducks of Anaheim	NHL	3	0	1	1	0	1	1	12	0	0	0	1	0.0	1	0	0	0	1	....	....	....	....	....	....	....	....
	Baltimore Bandits	AHL	60	11	10	21	....	....	....	295	....	....	....	....	....	....	....	....	....	....	12	4	2	6	23	....	....	....
1996-97	Mighty Ducks of Anaheim	NHL	5	0	0	0	0	0	0	14	0	0	0	1	0.0	0	0	1	0	–1	....	....	....	....	....	....	....	....
	Baltimore Bandits	AHL	25	8	8	16	....	....	....	125	....	....	....	....	....	....	....	....	....	....	3	0	0	0	8	....	....	....
1997-98	Mighty Ducks of Anaheim	NHL	45	3	5	8	4	5	9	101	0	0	1	43	7.0	11	0	15	0	–4	....	....	....	....	....	....	....	....
	Cincinnati Mighty Ducks	AHL	10	5	0	5	....	....	....	34	....	....	....	....	....	....	....	....	....	....	....	....	....	....	....	....	....	....
1998-99	Cincinnati Mighty Ducks	AHL	22	4	4	8	....	....	....	83	....	....	....	....	....	....	....	....	....	....	3	1	0	1	2	....	....	....
99-2000	Mighty Ducks of Anaheim	NHL	3	0	0	0	0	0	0	7	0	0	0	2	0.0	0	0	1	0	–1	....	....	....	....	....	....	....	....
	Cincinnati Mighty Ducks	AHL	41	11	14	25	....	....	....	100	....	....	....	....	....	....	....	....	....	....	....	....	....	....	....	....	....	....
	NHL Totals		56	3	6	9	4	6	10	134	0	0	1	47	6.4	12	0	17	0		....	....	....	....	....	....	....	....

• Re-entered NHL draft. Originally Winnipeg's 3rd choice, 60th overall, in 1992 Entry Draft.

• STEVENSON, Shayne

Shayne T. RW – R. 6'1", 190 lbs. b: Newmarket, Ont., 10/26/1970. Boston's 1st, 17th overall, in 1989.

Season	Club	League	GP	G	A	Pts	AG	AA	APts	PIM	PP	SH	GW	S	%	TGF	PGF	TGA	PGA	+/–	GP	G	A	Pts	PIM	PP	SH	GW
1985-86	Barrie Colts	OJHL-B	38	14	23	37	....	....	....	75	....	....	....	....	....	....	....	....	....	....	....	....	....	....	....	....	....	....
	Orillia Travelways	OJHL	1	0	0	0	....	....	....	0	....	....	....	....	....	....	....	....	....	....	....	....	....	....	....	....	....	....
1986-87	London Knights	OHL	61	7	15	22	....	....	....	56	....	....	....	....	....	....	....	....	....	....	....	....	....	....	....	....	....	....
1987-88	London Knights	OHL	36	14	25	39	....	....	....	56	....	....	....	....	....	....	....	....	....	....	....	....	....	....	....	....	....	....
	Kitchener Rangers	OHL	30	10	25	35	....	....	....	48	....	....	....	....	....	....	....	....	....	....	4	1	1	2	4	....	....	....
1988-89	Kitchener Rangers	OHL	56	25	51	76	....	....	....	86	....	....	....	....	....	....	....	....	....	....	5	2	3	5	4	....	....	....
1989-90	Kitchener Rangers	OHL	56	28	61	89	....	....	....	225	....	....	....	....	....	....	....	....	....	....	17	16	21	*37	31	....	....	....
	Kitchener Rangers	Mem-Cup	5	4	7	*11	....	....	....	4	....	....	....	....	....	....	....	....	....	....	....	....	....	....	....	....	....	....
1990-91	Boston Bruins	NHL	14	0	0	0	0	0	0	26	0	0	0	8	0.0	3	0	7	0	–4	....	....	....	....	....	....	....	....
	Maine Mariners	AHL	58	22	28	50	....	....	....	112	....	....	....	....	....	....	....	....	....	....	....	....	....	....	....	....	....	....
1991-92	Boston Bruins	NHL	5	0	1	1	0	1	1	2	0	0	0	3	0.0	2	0	1	0	1	....	....	....	....	....	....	....	....
	Maine Mariners	AHL	54	10	23	33	....	....	....	150	....	....	....	....	....	....	....	....	....	....	....	....	....	....	....	....	....	....
1992-93	Tampa Bay Lightning	NHL	8	0	1	1	0	1	1	7	0	0	0	4	0.0	1	0	6	0	–5	....	....	....	....	....	....	....	....
	Atlanta Knights	IHL	53	17	17	34	....	....	....	160	....	....	....	....	....	....	....	....	....	....	6	0	2	2	21	....	....	....
1993-94	Brunico HC	Alpenliga	16	8	15	23	....	....	....	66	....	....	....	....	....	....	....	....	....	....	....	....	....	....	....	....	....	....
	Fort Wayne Komets	IHL	22	3	5	8	....	....	....	116	....	....	....	....	....	....	....	....	....	....	....	....	....	....	....	....	....	....
	Muskegon Fury	ColHL	1	2	0	2	....	....	....	0	....	....	....	....	....	....	....	....	....	....	....	....	....	....	....	....	....	....
	St. Thomas Wildcats	ColHL	6	3	3	6	....	....	....	15	....	....	....	....	....	....	....	....	....	....	2	0	2	2	9	....	....	....
1994-95	Utica Blizzard	ColHL	43	17	40	57	....	....	....	37	....	....	....	....	....	....	....	....	....	....	6	0	3	3	14	....	....	....
1995-96	Utica Blizzard	ColHL	27	11	21	32	....	....	....	72	....	....	....	....	....	....	....	....	....	....	....	....	....	....	....	....	....	....
1996-97	Utica Blizzard	ColHL	10	2	6	8	....	....	....	18	....	....	....	....	....	....	....	....	....	....	....	....	....	....	....	....	....	....
	Saginaw Lumber Kings	ColHL	17	2	23	25	....	....	....	30	....	....	....	....	....	....	....	....	....	....	....	....	....	....	....	....	....	....
	Brantford Smoke	ColHL	10	3	9	12	....	....	....	25	....	....	....	....	....	....	....	....	....	....	6	3	5	8	24	....	....	....
1997-98	Port Huron Border Cats	UHL	18	8	9	17	....	....	....	27	....	....	....	....	....	....	....	....	....	....	3	2	0	2	4	....	....	....
1998-99	San Angelo Outlaws	WPHL	48	28	28	56	....	....	....	41	....	....	....	....	....	....	....	....	....	....	13	7	8	15	51	....	....	....
99-2000	Ayr Scottish Eagles	Britain	7	2	7	9	....	....	....	24	....	....	....	....	....	....	....	....	....	....	7	2	2	4	29	....	....	....
	NHL Totals		27	0	2	2	0	2	2	35	0	0	0	15	0.0	6	0	14	0		....	....	....	....	....	....	....	....

Claimed by **Tampa Bay** from **Boston** in Expansion Draft, June 18, 1992. • Played w/ MRHL's Port Huron Americans (9-11-7-18-4) and Toronto Torpedos (5-7-2-9-7) in 1998. Signed as a free agent by **Ayr Eagles** (Britain), January 13, 2000.

• STEVENSON, Turner

Turner L. RW – R. 6'3", 226 lbs. b: Prince George, B.C., 5/18/1972. Montreal's 1st, 12th overall, in 1990.

Season	Club	League	GP	G	A	Pts	AG	AA	APts	PIM	PP	SH	GW	S	%	TGF	PGF	TGA	PGA	+/–	GP	G	A	Pts	PIM	PP	SH	GW
1987-88	Prince George Bantam Kings	BCAHA	53	45	46	91	....	....	....	127	....	....	....	....	....	....	....	....	....	....	....	....	....	....	....	....	....	....
1988-89	Seattle Thunderbirds	WHL	69	15	12	27	....	....	....	84	....	....	....	....	....	....	....	....	....	....	....	....	....	....	....	....	....	....
1989-90	Seattle Thunderbirds	WHL	62	29	32	61	....	....	....	276	....	....	....	....	....	....	....	....	....	....	13	3	2	5	35	....	....	....
1990-91	Seattle Thunderbirds	WHL	57	36	27	63	....	....	....	222	....	....	....	....	....	....	....	....	....	....	6	1	5	6	15	....	....	....
	Fredericton Canadiens	AHL	....	....	....	....	....	....	....	....	....	....	....	....	....	....	....	....	....	....	4	0	0	0	5	....	....	....
1991-92	Seattle Thunderbirds	WHL	58	20	32	52	....	....	....	264	....	....	....	....	....	....	....	....	....	....	15	9	3	12	55	....	....	....
	Canada	WJC-A	7	0	2	2	....	....	....	14	....	....	....	....	....	....	....	....	....	....	....	....	....	....	....	....	....	....
	Seattle Thunderbirds	Mem-Cup	4	2	0	2	....	....	....	*18	....	....	....	....	....	....	....	....	....	....	....	....	....	....	....	....	....	....
1992-93	Montreal Canadiens	NHL	1	0	0	0	0	0	0	0	0	0	0	1	0.0	0	0	1	0	–1	....	....	....	....	....	....	....	....
	Fredericton Canadiens	AHL	79	25	34	59	....	....	....	102	....	....	....	....	....	....	....	....	....	....	5	2	3	5	11	....	....	....
1993-94	Montreal Canadiens	NHL	2	0	0	0	0	0	0	2	0	0	0	0	0.0	0	0	2	0	–2	3	0	2	2	0	0	0	0
	Fredericton Canadiens	AHL	66	19	28	47	....	....	....	155	....	....	....	....	....	....	....	....	....	....	....	....	....	....	....	....	....	....
1994-95	Fredericton Canadiens	AHL	37	12	12	24	....	....	....	109	....	....	....	....	....	....	....	....	....	....	....	....	....	....	....	....	....	....
	Montreal Canadiens	NHL	41	6	1	7	11	1	12	86	0	0	1	35	17.1	10	0	11	1	0	....	....	....	....	....	....	....	....
1995-96	Montreal Canadiens	NHL	80	9	16	25	9	13	22	167	0	0	2	101	8.9	39	2	39	0	–2	6	0	1	1	2	0	0	0
1996-97	Montreal Canadiens	NHL	65	8	13	21	8	12	20	97	1	0	0	76	10.5	29	2	41	0	–14	5	1	1	2	2	0	0	0
1997-98	Montreal Canadiens	NHL	63	4	6	10	5	6	11	110	1	0	0	43	9.3	13	1	20	0	–8	10	3	4	7	12	0	0	0
1998-99	Montreal Canadiens	NHL	69	10	17	27	12	16	28	88	0	0	2	102	9.8	38	2	31	1	6	....	....	....	....	....	....	....	....
99-2000	Montreal Canadiens	NHL	64	8	13	21	9	12	21	61	0	0	2	94	8.5	33	2	32	0	–1	....	....	....	....	....	....	....	....
	NHL Totals		385	45	66	111	54	60	114	611	2	0	7	452	10.0	162	9	177	2		24	4	8	12	16	0	0	0

WHL West First All-Star Team (1992) • Memorial Cup All-Star Team (1992).

Selected by **Columbus** from **Montreal** in Expansion Draft, June 23, 2000. Traded to **New Jersey** by **Columbus** to complete transaction that sent Krzysztof Oliwa to **Columbus** (June 12, 2000), June 23, 2000.

• STEWART, Allan

LW – L. 6', 195 lbs. b: Fort St. John, B.C., 1/31/1964. New Jersey's 9th, 213th overall, in 1983.

			REGULAR SEASON																		PLAYOFFS							
Season	Club	League	GP	G	A	Pts	AG	AA	APts	PIM	PP	SH	GW	S	%	TGF	PGF	TGA	PGA	+/–	GP	G	A	Pts	PIM	PP	SH	GW
1981-82	Prince Albert Midget Raiders	SAHA	46	9	25	34	....	....	....	53	....	....	....	....	....	....	....	....	....	....	....	....	....	....	....	....	....	....
1982-83	Prince Albert Raiders	WHL	70	25	34	59	....	....	....	272	....	....	....	....	....	....	....	....	....	....	....	....	....	....	....	....	....	....
1983-84	Prince Albert Raiders	WHL	67	44	39	83	....	....	....	216	....	....	....	....	....	....	....	....	....	....	5	1	2	3	29	....	....	....
	Maine Mariners	AHL	....	....	....	....	....	....	....	....	....	....	....	....	....	....	....	....	....	....	3	0	0	0	0	....	....	....
1984-85	Maine Mariners	AHL	75	8	11	19	....	....	....	241	....	....	....	....	....	....	....	....	....	....	11	1	2	3	58	....	....	....
1985-86	**New Jersey Devils**	**NHL**	**4**	**0**	**0**	**0**	**0**	**0**	**0**	**21**	**0**	**0**	**0**	**0**	**0.0**	**0**	**0**	**1**	**0**	**–1**	....	....	....	....	....	....	....	....
	Maine Mariners	AHL	58	7	12	19	....	....	....	181	....	....	....	....	....	....	....	....	....	....	....	....	....	....	....	....	....	....
1986-87	**New Jersey Devils**	**NHL**	**7**	**1**	**0**	**1**	**1**	**0**	**1**	**26**	**0**	**0**	**0**	**8**	**12.5**	**3**	**0**	**9**	**2**	**–4**	....	....	....	....	....	....	....	....
	Maine Mariners	AHL	74	14	24	38	....	....	....	143	....	....	....	....	....	....	....	....	....	....	....	....	....	....	....	....	....	....
1987-88	**New Jersey Devils**	**NHL**	**1**	**0**	**0**	**0**	**0**	**0**	**0**	**0**	**0**	**0**	**0**	**0**	**0.0**	**2**	**0**	**0**	**0**	**2**	....	....	....	....	....	....	....	....
	Utica Devils	AHL	49	8	17	25	....	....	....	129	....	....	....	....	....	....	....	....	....	....	....	....	....	....	....	....	....	....
1988-89	**New Jersey Devils**	**NHL**	**6**	**0**	**2**	**2**	**0**	**1**	**1**	**15**	**0**	**0**	**0**	**4**	**0.0**	**2**	**0**	**4**	**0**	**–2**	....	....	....	....	....	....	....	....
	Utica Devils	AHL	72	9	23	32	....	....	....	110	....	....	....	....	....	....	....	....	....	....	5	1	0	1	4	....	....	....
1989-90	Utica Devils	AHL	1	0	0	0	....	....	....	0	....	....	....	....	....	....	....	....	....	....	1	0	0	0	11	....	....	....
1990-91	**New Jersey Devils**	**NHL**	**41**	**5**	**2**	**7**	**5**	**2**	**7**	**159**	**0**	**0**	**0**	**33**	**15.2**	**16**	**0**	**32**	**10**	**–6**	....	....	....	....	....	....	....	....
	Utica Devils	AHL	9	2	0	2	....	....	....	9	....	....	....	....	....	....	....	....	....	....	....	....	....	....	....	....	....	....
1991-92	**New Jersey Devils**	**NHL**	**1**	**0**	**0**	**0**	**0**	**0**	**0**	**5**	**0**	**0**	**0**	**0**	**0.0**	**0**	**0**	**0**	**0**	**0**	....	....	....	....	....	....	....	....
	Boston Bruins	**NHL**	**4**	**0**	**0**	**0**	**0**	**0**	**0**	**17**	**0**	**0**	**0**	**1**	**0.0**	**0**	**0**	**1**	**0**	**–1**	....	....	....	....	....	....	....	....
1992-93	Moncton Hawks	AHL	45	3	8	11	....	....	....	118	....	....	....	....	....	....	....	....	....	....	2	1	0	1	20	....	....	....
	NHL Totals		**64**	**6**	**4**	**10**	**6**	**3**	**9**	**243**	**0**	**0**	**0**	**46**	**13.0**	**23**	**0**	**47**	**12**		....	....	....	....	....	....	....	....

• Missed majority of 1991-92 season recovering from knee injury suffered in training camp that required surgery, October 21, 1991. Traded to **Boston** by **New Jersey** for future considerations, October 16, 1991. Signed as a free agent by **Winnipeg**, October 5, 1992.

• STEWART, Bill

William Donald D – R. 6'2", 190 lbs. b: Toronto, Ont., 10/6/1957. Buffalo's 3rd, 68th overall, in 1977.

Season	Club	League	GP	G	A	Pts	AG	AA	APts	PIM	PP	SH	GW	S	%	TGF	PGF	TGA	PGA	+/–	GP	G	A	Pts	PIM	PP	SH	GW
1973-74	Dixie Beehives	OHA-B	41	9	24	33	....	....	....	38	....	....	....	....	....	....	....	....	....	....	....	....	....	....	....	....	....	....
1974-75	Kitchener Rangers	OMJHL	55	6	15	21	....	....	....	70	....	....	....	....	....	....	....	....	....	....	....	....	....	....	....	....	....	....
1975-76	Kitchener Rangers	OMJHL	4	1	3	4	....	....	....	4	....	....	....	....	....	....	....	....	....	....	....	....	....	....	....	....	....	....
	St. Catharines Black Hawks	OMJHL	48	9	31	40	....	....	....	57	....	....	....	....	....	....	....	....	....	....	4	0	3	3	8	....	....	....
1976-77	Niagara Falls Black Hawks	OMJHL	59	18	37	55	....	....	....	202	....	....	....	....	....	....	....	....	....	....	....	....	....	....	....	....	....	....
1977-78	**Buffalo Sabres**	**NHL**	**13**	**2**	**0**	**2**	**2**	**0**	**2**	**15**	**0**	**0**	**1**	**12**	**16.7**	**6**	**0**	**5**	**0**	**1**	**8**	**0**	**2**	**2**	**0**	**0**	**0**	**0**
	Hershey Bears	AHL	54	6	18	24	....	....	....	92	....	....	....	....	....	....	....	....	....	....	....	....	....	....	....	....	....	....
1978-79	**Buffalo Sabres**	**NHL**	**68**	**1**	**17**	**18**	**1**	**12**	**13**	**101**	**0**	**0**	**0**	**87**	**1.1**	**76**	**4**	**80**	**13**	**5**	**1**	**0**	**1**	**1**	**0**	**0**	**0**	**0**
1979-80	Rochester Americans	AHL	63	12	28	40	....	....	....	189	....	....	....	....	....	....	....	....	....	....	4	1	2	3	42	....	....	....
1980-81	Rochester Americans	AHL	6	1	6	7	....	....	....	12	....	....	....	....	....	....	....	....	....	....	....	....	....	....	....	....	....	....
	St. Louis Blues	**NHL**	**60**	**2**	**21**	**23**	**2**	**14**	**16**	**114**	**0**	**0**	**0**	**62**	**3.2**	**84**	**3**	**76**	**14**	**19**	**4**	**1**	**0**	**1**	**11**	**0**	**0**	**0**
	Salt Lake Golden Eagles	CHL	2	0	0	0	....	....	....	2	....	....	....	....	....	....	....	....	....	....	....	....	....	....	....	....	....	....
1981-82	**St. Louis Blues**	**NHL**	**22**	**0**	**5**	**5**	**0**	**3**	**3**	**25**	**0**	**0**	**0**	**21**	**0.0**	**21**	**1**	**29**	**4**	**–5**	....	....	....	....	....	....	....	....
	Salt Lake Golden Eagles	CHL	40	2	12	14	....	....	....	93	....	....	....	....	....	....	....	....	....	....	10	0	6	6	12	....	....	....
1982-83	**St. Louis Blues**	**NHL**	**7**	**0**	**0**	**0**	**0**	**0**	**0**	**8**	**0**	**0**	**0**	**5**	**0.0**	**3**	**0**	**7**	**3**	**–1**	....	....	....	....	....	....	....	....
	Salt Lake Golden Eagles	CHL	62	10	42	52	....	....	....	143	....	....	....	....	....	....	....	....	....	....	5	1	4	5	8	....	....	....
1983-84	**Toronto Maple Leafs**	**NHL**	**56**	**2**	**17**	**19**	**2**	**12**	**14**	**116**	**0**	**0**	**0**	**42**	**4.8**	**61**	**2**	**86**	**26**	**–1**	....	....	....	....	....	....	....	....
1984-85	**Toronto Maple Leafs**	**NHL**	**27**	**0**	**2**	**2**	**0**	**1**	**1**	**32**	**0**	**0**	**0**	**9**	**0.0**	**21**	**0**	**28**	**4**	**–3**	....	....	....	....	....	....	....	....
	St. Catharines Saints	AHL	12	2	5	7	....	....	....	11	....	....	....	....	....	....	....	....	....	....	....	....	....	....	....	....	....	....
1985-86	**Minnesota North Stars**	**NHL**	**8**	**0**	**2**	**2**	**0**	**1**	**1**	**13**	**0**	**0**	**0**	**3**	**0.0**	**7**	**0**	**6**	**1**	**2**	....	....	....	....	....	....	....	....
	Springfield Indians	AHL	59	7	19	26	....	....	....	135	....	....	....	....	....	....	....	....	....	....	....	....	....	....	....	....	....	....
1986-87	SG Brunico	Italy	40	20	21	41	....	....	....	91	....	....	....	....	....	....	....	....	....	....	....	....	....	....	....	....	....	....
1987-88	SG Brunico	Italy	34	8	35	43	....	....	....	62	....	....	....	....	....	....	....	....	....	....	....	....	....	....	....	....	....	....
1988-89	HC Milano Saima	Italy	18	4	11	15	....	....	....	24	....	....	....	....	....	....	....	....	....	....	....	....	....	....	....	....	....	....
1989-90	HC Milano Alaska	Italy-2	STATISTICS NOT AVAILABLE																									
1990-91	HC Milano Saima	Italy	34	11	33	44	....	....	....	52	....	....	....	....	....	....	....	....	....	....	10	0	9	9	10	....	....	....
1991-92	HC Milano Saima	Alpenliga	20	2	6	8	....	....	....	64	....	....	....	....	....	....	....	....	....	....	....	....	....	....	....	....	....	....
	HC Milano Saima	Italy	17	3	16	19	....	....	....	8	....	....	....	....	....	....	....	....	....	....	12	0	6	6	20	....	....	....
	Italy	Olympics	7	0	3	3	....	....	....	12	....	....	....	....	....	....	....	....	....	....	....	....	....	....	....	....	....	....
	Italy	WEC-A	5	0	0	0	....	....	....	6	....	....	....	....	....	....	....	....	....	....	....	....	....	....	....	....	....	....
1992-93	HC Milano Saima	Alpenliga	32	0	9	9	....	....	....	0	....	....	....	....	....	....	....	....	....	....	....	....	....	....	....	....	....	....
	HC Milano Saima	Italy	12	2	4	6	....	....	....	26	....	....	....	....	....	....	....	....	....	....	11	1	4	5	28	....	....	....
	Italy	WEC-A	6	0	0	0	....	....	....	4	....	....	....	....	....	....	....	....	....	....	....	....	....	....	....	....	....	....
1993-94	HC Gardena-Groden	Alpenliga	27	5	12	17	....	....	....	21	....	....	....	....	....	....	....	....	....	....	....	....	....	....	....	....	....	....
	HC Gardena-Groden	Italy	17	3	7	10	....	....	....	17	....	....	....	....	....	....	....	....	....	....	2	0	0	0	0	....	....	....
	Italy	Olympics	6	0	0	0	....	....	....	0	....	....	....	....	....	....	....	....	....	....	....	....	....	....	....	....	....	....
1994-95	HC Courmaosta	EuroHL	17	4	7	11	....	....	....	18	....	....	....	....	....	....	....	....	....	....	....	....	....	....	....	....	....	....
	HC Courmaosta	Italy	31	1	13	14	....	....	....	68	....	....	....	....	....	....	....	....	....	....	5	1	2	3	2	....	....	....
1995-1996	Muskegon Fury	ColHL	DID NOT PLAY – COACHING																									
1996-1997	Oshawa Generals	OHL	DID NOT PLAY – COACHING																									
1997-1998	Saint John Flames	AHL	DID NOT PLAY – COACHING																									
1998-1999	**New York Islanders**	**NHL**	DID NOT PLAY – ASSISTANT COACH																									
	New York Islanders	**NHL**	DID NOT PLAY – COACHING																									
1999-2000	Barrie Colts	OHL	DID NOT PLAY – COACHING																									
	NHL Totals		**261**	**7**	**64**	**71**	**7**	**43**	**50**	**424**	**0**	**0**	**1**	**241**	**2.9**	**279**	**10**	**317**	**65**		**13**	**1**	**3**	**4**	**11**	**0**	**0**	**0**

Claimed by **Buffalo** as a fill-in during Expansion Draft, June 13, 1979. Traded to **St. Louis** by **Buffalo** for Bob Hess and St. Louis' 4th round choice (Anders Wickberg) in 1981 Entry Draft, October 30, 1980. Signed as a free agent by **Toronto**, September 10, 1983. Signed as a free agent by **Minnesota**, September 15, 1985.

• STEWART, Blair

Blair James C – R. 5'11", 185 lbs. b: Winnipeg, Man., 3/15/1953. Detroit's 5th, 75th overall, in 1973.

Season	Club	League	GP	G	A	Pts	AG	AA	APts	PIM	PP	SH	GW	S	%	TGF	PGF	TGA	PGA	+/–	GP	G	A	Pts	PIM	PP	SH	GW
1971-72	Winnipeg Jets	WCJHL	44	8	10	18	....	....	....	112	....	....	....	....	....	....	....	....	....	....	....	....	....	....	....	....	....	....
1972-73	Winnipeg Jets	WCJHL	68	24	36	60	....	....	....	151	....	....	....	....	....	....	....	....	....	....	....	....	....	....	....	....	....	....
1973-74	**Detroit Red Wings**	**NHL**	**17**	**0**	**4**	**4**	**0**	**3**	**3**	**16**	**0**	**0**	**0**	**22**	**0.0**	**8**	**0**	**14**	**0**	**–6**	....	....	....	....	....	....	....	....
	Virginia Wings	AHL	54	9	13	22	....	....	....	99	....	....	....	....	....	....	....	....	....	....	....	....	....	....	....	....	....	....
1974-75	Virginia Wings	AHL	26	7	10	17	....	....	....	93	....	....	....	....	....	....	....	....	....	....	....	....	....	....	....	....	....	....
	Detroit Red Wings	**NHL**	**19**	**0**	**5**	**5**	**0**	**4**	**4**	**38**	**0**	**0**	**0**	**31**	**0.0**	**9**	**1**	**13**	**0**	**–5**	....	....	....	....	....	....	....	....
	Washington Capitals	**NHL**	**2**	**1**	**0**	**1**	**1**	**0**	**1**	**2**	**0**	**0**	**0**	**4**	**25.0**	**1**	**0**	**3**	**0**	**–2**	....	....	....	....	....	....	....	....
1975-76	**Washington Capitals**	**NHL**	**74**	**13**	**14**	**27**	**11**	**10**	**21**	**113**	**0**	**0**	**0**	**88**	**14.8**	**44**	**6**	**100**	**9**	**–53**	....	....	....	....	....	....	....	....
1976-77	**Washington Capitals**	**NHL**	**34**	**5**	**2**	**7**	**4**	**2**	**6**	**85**	**0**	**0**	**0**	**41**	**12.2**	**14**	**0**	**21**	**1**	**–6**	....	....	....	....	....	....	....	....
	Springfield Indians	AHL	4	1	3	4	....	....	....	11	....	....	....	....	....	....	....	....	....	....	....	....	....	....	....	....	....	....
1977-78	**Washington Capitals**	**NHL**	**8**	**0**	**1**	**1**	**0**	**1**	**1**	**9**	**0**	**0**	**0**	**4**	**0.0**	**2**	**0**	**5**	**0**	**–3**	....	....	....	....	....	....	....	....
	Hershey Bears	AHL	20	9	9	18	....	....	....	46	....	....	....	....	....	....	....	....	....	....	....	....	....	....	....	....	....	....
1978-79	**Washington Capitals**	**NHL**	**45**	**7**	**12**	**19**	**6**	**9**	**15**	**48**	**0**	**0**	**0**	**56**	**12.5**	**34**	**1**	**33**	**1**	**1**	....	....	....	....	....	....	....	....
	Hershey Bears	AHL	23	16	8	24	....	....	....	49	....	....	....	....	....	....	....	....	....	....	....	....	....	....	....	....	....	....
1979-80	**Quebec Nordiques**	**NHL**	**30**	**8**	**6**	**14**	**7**	**4**	**11**	**15**	**0**	**1**	**2**	**53**	**15.1**	**22**	**4**	**24**	**8**	**2**	....	....	....	....	....	....	....	....
	Syracuse Firebirds	AHL	20	9	10	19	....	....	....	35	....	....	....	....	....	....	....	....	....	....	4	1	1	2	27	....	....	....
1980-81	Houston Apollos	CHL	9	1	0	1	....	....	....	24	....	....	....	....	....	....	....	....	....	....	....	....	....	....	....	....	....	....
	Fort Worth Texans	CHL	38	12	9	21	....	....	....	48	....	....	....	....	....	....	....	....	....	....	5	1	2	3	18	....	....	....
	NHL Totals		**229**	**34**	**44**	**78**	**29**	**33**	**62**	**326**	**0**	**1**	**2**	**299**	**11.4**	**134**	**12**	**213**	**19**		....	....	....	....	....	....	....	....

Traded to **Washington** by **Detroit** for Mike Bloom, March 9, 1975. Claimed by **Quebec** from **Washington** in Expansion Draft, June 13, 1979.

• STEWART, Bob

Robert Harold D – L. 6'1", 206 lbs. b: Charlottetown, P.E.I., 11/10/1950. Boston's 4th, 13th overall, in 1970.

Season	Club	League	GP	G	A	Pts	AG	AA	APts	PIM	PP	SH	GW	S	%	TGF	PGF	TGA	PGA	+/–	GP	G	A	Pts	PIM	PP	SH	GW
1967-68	Oshawa Generals	OHA-Jr.	50	2	11	13	....	....	....	172	....	....	....	....	....	....	....	....	....	....	....	....	....	....	....	....	....	....
1968-69	Oshawa Generals	OHA-Jr.	52	7	32	39	....	....	....	226	....	....	....	....	....	....	....	....	....	....	....	....	....	....	....	....	....	....
1969-70	Oshawa Generals	OHA-Jr.	44	11	24	35	....	....	....	159	....	....	....	....	....	....	....	....	....	....	6	1	3	4	12	....	....	....

			REGULAR SEASON																		PLAYOFFS							
Season	**Club**	**League**	**GP**	**G**	**A**	**Pts**	**AG**	**AA**	**APts**	**PIM**	**PP**	**SH**	**GW**	**S**	**%**	**TGF**	**PGF**	**TGA**	**PGA**	**+/–**	**GP**	**G**	**A**	**Pts**	**PIM**	**PP**	**SH**	**GW**
1970-71	Oklahoma City Blazers	CHL	61	6	16	22	....	....	....	270	....	....	....	....	....	....	....	....	....	....	5	0	1	1	23	....	....	....
1971-72	**Boston Bruins**	**NHL**	**8**	**0**	**0**	**0**	**0**	**0**	**0**	**15**	**0**	**0**	**0**	**0**	**0.0**	**5**	**0**	**2**	**0**	**3**	....	....	....	....	....	....	....	....
	Oklahoma City Blazers	CHL	10	1	3	4	....	....	....	34	....	....	....	....	....	....	....	....	....	....	....	....	....	....	....	....	....	....
	Boston Braves	AHL	39	1	7	8	....	....	....	102	....	....	....	....	....	....	....	....	....	....	....	....	....	....	....	....	....	....
	California Golden Seals	**NHL**	**16**	**1**	**2**	**3**	**1**	**2**	**3**	**44**	**0**	**0**	**0**	**18**	**5.6**	**13**	**0**	**27**	**3**	**–11**	....	....	....	....	....	....	....	....
1972-73	**California Golden Seals**	**NHL**	**63**	**4**	**17**	**21**	**4**	**13**	**17**	**181**	**0**	**0**	**0**	**95**	**4.2**	**68**	**1**	**139**	**26**	**–46**	....	....	....	....	....	....	....	....
1973-74	**California Golden Seals**	**NHL**	**47**	**2**	**5**	**7**	**2**	**4**	**6**	**69**	**1**	**0**	**0**	**42**	**4.8**	**38**	**4**	**91**	**15**	**–42**	....	....	....	....	....	....	....	....
1974-75	**California Golden Seals**	**NHL**	**67**	**5**	**12**	**17**	**4**	**9**	**13**	**93**	**0**	**0**	**1**	**87**	**5.7**	**71**	**2**	**122**	**35**	**–18**	....	....	....	....	....	....	....	....
1975-76	**California Golden Seals**	**NHL**	**76**	**4**	**17**	**21**	**3**	**13**	**16**	**112**	**2**	**0**	**0**	**67**	**6.0**	**71**	**13**	**122**	**30**	**–34**	....	....	....	....	....	....	....	....
1976-77	**Cleveland Barons**	**NHL**	**73**	**1**	**12**	**13**	**1**	**9**	**10**	**108**	**0**	**0**	**0**	**69**	**1.4**	**67**	**2**	**119**	**23**	**–31**	....	....	....	....	....	....	....	....
1977-78	**Cleveland Barons**	**NHL**	**72**	**2**	**15**	**17**	**2**	**12**	**14**	**84**	**0**	**0**	**0**	**57**	**3.5**	**80**	**3**	**131**	**29**	**–25**	....	....	....	....	....	....	....	....
1978-79	**St. Louis Blues**	**NHL**	**78**	**5**	**13**	**18**	**4**	**9**	**13**	**47**	**1**	**0**	**0**	**57**	**8.8**	**76**	**2**	**149**	**47**	**–28**	....	....	....	....	....	....	....	....
1979-80	**St. Louis Blues**	**NHL**	**10**	**0**	**1**	**1**	**0**	**1**	**1**	**4**	**0**	**0**	**0**	**7**	**0.0**	**7**	**0**	**9**	**1**	**–1**	....	....	....	....	....	....	....	....
	Pittsburgh Penguins	**NHL**	**65**	**3**	**7**	**10**	**3**	**5**	**8**	**52**	**0**	**0**	**0**	**53**	**5.7**	**57**	**3**	**99**	**18**	**–27**	**5**	**1**	**1**	**2**	**2**	**0**	**0**	**0**
	NHL Totals		**575**	**27**	**101**	**128**	**24**	**77**	**101**	**809**	**4**	**0**	**1**	**552**	**4.9**	**553**	**30**	**1010**	**227**		**5**	**1**	**1**	**2**	**2**	**0**	**0**	**0**

OHA-Jr. First All-Star Team (1970)

Traded to **California** by **Boston** with Reggie Leach and Rick Smith for Carol Vadnais and Don O'Donoghue, February 23, 1972. Transferred to **Cleveland** after **California** franchise relocated, August 26, 1976. Claimed as a fill-in by **Minnesota** during **Cleveland-Minnesota** Dispersal Draft, June 15, 1978. Traded to **St. Louis** by **Minnesota** for St. Louis' 2nd round choice (Jali Wahlsten) in 1981 Entry Draft and future considerations, June 15, 1978. Traded to **Pittsburgh** by **St. Louis** for Blair Chapman, November 13, 1979.

• STEWART, Cam

Cameron LW – L. 5'11", 196 lbs. b: Kitchener, Ont., 9/18/1971. Boston's 2nd, 63rd overall, in 1990.

Season	Club	League	GP	G	A	Pts	AG	AA	APts	PIM	PP	SH	GW	S	%	TGF	PGF	TGA	PGA	+/–	GP	G	A	Pts	PIM	PP	SH	GW
1987-88	Woolrich Major Midgets	OMHA	21	25	32	57	....	....	....	65	....	....	....	....	....	....	....	....	....	....	....	....	....	....	....	....	....	....
1988-89	Elmira Sugar Kings	OJHL-B	43	38	50	88	....	....	....	138	....	....	....	....	....	....	....	....	....	....	....	....	....	....	....	....	....	....
1989-90	Elmira Sugar Kings	OJHL-B	46	43	95	138	....	....	....	174	....	....	....	....	....	....	....	....	....	....	....	....	....	....	....	....	....	....
1990-91	University of Michigan	CCHA	44	8	24	32	....	....	....	122	....	....	....	....	....	....	....	....	....	....	....	....	....	....	....	....	....	....
1991-92	University of Michigan	CCHA	44	13	15	28	....	....	....	106	....	....	....	....	....	....	....	....	....	....	....	....	....	....	....	....	....	....
1992-93	University of Michigan	CCHA	39	20	39	59	....	....	....	69	....	....	....	....	....	....	....	....	....	....	....	....	....	....	....	....	....	....
1993-94	**Boston Bruins**	**NHL**	**57**	**3**	**6**	**9**	**3**	**5**	**8**	**66**	**0**	**0**	**1**	**55**	**5.5**	**19**	**0**	**29**	**4**	**–6**	**8**	**0**	**3**	**3**	**7**	**0**	**0**	**0**
	Providence Bruins	AHL	14	3	2	5	....	....	....	5	....	....	....	....	....	....	....	....	....	....	....	....	....	....	....	....	....	....
1994-95	**Boston Bruins**	**NHL**	**5**	**0**	**0**	**0**	**0**	**0**	**0**	**2**	**0**	**0**	**0**	**2**	**0.0**	**1**	**0**	**2**	**1**	**0**	....	....	....	....	....	....	....	....
	Providence Bruins	AHL	31	13	11	24	....	....	....	38	....	....	....	....	....	....	....	....	....	....	9	2	5	7	0	....	....	....
1995-96	**Boston Bruins**	**NHL**	**6**	**0**	**0**	**0**	**0**	**0**	**0**	**0**	**0**	**0**	**0**	**2**	**0.0**	**0**	**0**	**2**	**0**	**–2**	**5**	**1**	**0**	**1**	**2**	**0**	**0**	**0**
	Providence Bruins	AHL	54	17	25	42	....	....	....	39	....	....	....	....	....	....	....	....	....	....	....	....	....	....	....	....	....	....
1996-97	**Boston Bruins**	**NHL**	**15**	**0**	**1**	**1**	**0**	**1**	**1**	**4**	**0**	**0**	**0**	**21**	**0.0**	**3**	**0**	**5**	**0**	**–2**	....	....	....	....	....	....	....	....
	Providence Bruins	AHL	18	4	3	7	....	....	....	37	....	....	....	....	....	....	....	....	....	....	....	....	....	....	....	....	....	....
	Cincinnati Cyclones	IHL	7	3	2	5	....	....	....	8	....	....	....	....	....	....	....	....	....	....	1	0	0	0	0	....	....	....
1997-98	Houston Aeros	IHL	63	18	27	45	....	....	....	51	....	....	....	....	....	....	....	....	....	....	4	0	1	1	18	....	....	....
1998-99	Houston Aeros	IHL	61	36	26	62	....	....	....	75	....	....	....	....	....	....	....	....	....	....	19	10	5	15	26	....	....	....
99-2000	**Florida Panthers**	**NHL**	**65**	**9**	**7**	**16**	**10**	**6**	**16**	**30**	**0**	**0**	**3**	**52**	**17.3**	**23**	**1**	**26**	**2**	**–2**	....	....	....	....	....	....	....	....
	NHL Totals		**148**	**12**	**14**	**26**	**13**	**12**	**25**	**102**	**0**	**0**	**4**	**132**	**9.1**	**46**	**1**	**64**	**7**		**13**	**1**	**3**	**4**	**9**	**0**	**0**	**0**

Signed as a free agent by **Florida**, July 21, 1999. Selected by **Minnesota** from **Florida** in Expansion Draft, June 23, 2000.

• STEWART, John

John Alexander LW – L. 6', 180 lbs. b: Eriksdale, Man., 5/16/1950. Pittsburgh's 2nd, 21st overall, in 1970.

Season	Club	League	GP	G	A	Pts	AG	AA	APts	PIM	PP	SH	GW	S	%	TGF	PGF	TGA	PGA	+/–	GP	G	A	Pts	PIM	PP	SH	GW
1967-68	Winnipeg Jets	WCJHL	24	7	8	15	....	....	....	33	....	....	....	....	....	....	....	....	....	....	4	0	0	0	0	....	....	....
1968-69	Winnipeg Jets	WCJHL	4	3	1	4	....	....	....	5	....	....	....	....	....	....	....	....	....	....	....	....	....	....	....	....	....	....
	Sorel Black Hawks	MMJHL	STATISTICS NOT AVAILABLE																									
	Sorel Black Hawks	Mem-Cup	....	....	....	....	....	....	....	....	....	....	....	....	....	....	....	....	....	....	....	....	....	....	....	....	....	....
1969-70	Flin Flon Bombers	WCJHL	25	10	13	23	....	....	....	71	....	....	....	....	....	....	....	....	....	....	17	10	16	26	28	....	....	....
1970-71	**Pittsburgh Penguins**	**NHL**	**15**	**2**	**1**	**3**	**2**	**1**	**3**	**9**	**1**	**0**	**0**	**25**	**8.0**	**8**	**4**	**13**	**0**	**–9**	....	....	....	....	....	....	....	....
	Amarillo Wranglers	CHL	57	19	15	34	....	....	....	92	....	....	....	....	....	....	....	....	....	....	....	....	....	....	....	....	....	....
1971-72	**Pittsburgh Penguins**	**NHL**	**25**	**2**	**8**	**10**	**2**	**7**	**9**	**23**	**0**	**0**	**0**	**33**	**6.1**	**16**	**3**	**19**	**0**	**–6**	....	....	....	....	....	....	....	....
	Hershey Bears	AHL	46	10	17	27	....	....	....	32	....	....	....	....	....	....	....	....	....	....	4	1	2	3	4	....	....	....
1972-73	**Atlanta Flames**	**NHL**	**68**	**17**	**17**	**34**	**16**	**13**	**29**	**30**	**2**	**0**	**3**	**168**	**10.1**	**53**	**16**	**47**	**1**	**–9**	....	....	....	....	....	....	....	....
	Nova Scotia Voyageurs	AHL	5	3	3	6	....	....	....	7	....	....	....	....	....	....	....	....	....	....	....	....	....	....	....	....	....	....
1973-74	**Atlanta Flames**	**NHL**	**74**	**18**	**15**	**33**	**17**	**12**	**29**	**41**	**3**	**0**	**3**	**143**	**12.6**	**53**	**7**	**43**	**0**	**3**	**4**	**0**	**0**	**0**	**10**	**0**	**0**	**0**
1974-75	**California Golden Seals**	**NHL**	**76**	**19**	**19**	**38**	**17**	**14**	**31**	**55**	**2**	**0**	**2**	**191**	**9.9**	**62**	**15**	**95**	**6**	**–42**	....	....	....	....	....	....	....	....
1975-76	Cleveland Crusaders	WHA	79	12	21	33	....	....	....	42	....	....	....	....	....	....	....	....	....	....	3	0	0	0	2	....	....	....
1976-77	Minnesota Fighting Saints	WHA	15	3	3	6	....	....	....	2	....	....	....	....	....	....	....	....	....	....	....	....	....	....	....	....	....	....
	Birmingham Bulls	WHA	1	0	0	0	....	....	....	0	....	....	....	....	....	....	....	....	....	....	....	....	....	....	....	....	....	....
1977-78	Philadelphia Firebirds	AHL	70	23	15	38	....	....	....	90	....	....	....	....	....	....	....	....	....	....	4	1	3	4	2	....	....	....
	NHL Totals		**258**	**58**	**60**	**118**	**54**	**47**	**101**	**158**	**8**	**0**	**8**	**560**	**10.4**	**192**	**45**	**217**	**7**		**4**	**0**	**0**	**0**	**10**	**0**	**0**	**0**
	Other Major League Totals		95	15	24	39	....	....	....	44	....	....	....	....	....	....	....	....	....	....	3	0	0	0	2	....	....	....

Selected by **Alberta** (WHA) in 1972 WHA General Player Draft, February 12, 1972. Claimed by **Atlanta** from **Pittsburgh** in Expansion Draft, June 6, 1972. Traded to **California** by **Atlanta** for Hilliard Graves, July 18, 1974. WHA rights traded to **Cleveland** (WHA) by **Edmonton** (WHA) for future considerations, June, 1975. Transferred to **Minnesota** (WHA) after **Cleveland** (WHA) franchise relocated, July, 1976. Signed as a free agent by **Birmingham** (WHA) after **Minnesota** (WHA) franchise folded, January, 1977.

• STEWART, John

John Christopher "J.C." C – L. 6', 180 lbs. b: Toronto, Ont., 1/2/1954. Montreal's 11th, 105th overall, in 1974.

Season	Club	League	GP	G	A	Pts	AG	AA	APts	PIM	PP	SH	GW	S	%	TGF	PGF	TGA	PGA	+/–	GP	G	A	Pts	PIM	PP	SH	GW
1971-72	Markham Waxers	OHA-B	STATISTICS NOT AVAILABLE																									
1972-73	Bowling Green University	CCHA	35	20	31	51	....	....	....	26	....	....	....	....	....	....	....	....	....	....	....	....	....	....	....	....	....	....
1973-74	Bowling Green University	CCHA	39	27	43	70	....	....	....	50	....	....	....	....	....	....	....	....	....	....	....	....	....	....	....	....	....	....
1974-75	Cleveland Crusaders	WHA	59	4	7	11	....	....	....	8	....	....	....	....	....	....	....	....	....	....	1	0	0	0	0	....	....	....
	Cape Cod Codders	NAHL	13	5	11	16	....	....	....	14	....	....	....	....	....	....	....	....	....	....	....	....	....	....	....	....	....	....
1975-76	Cleveland Crusaders	WHA	42	2	9	11	....	....	....	15	....	....	....	....	....	....	....	....	....	....	....	....	....	....	....	....	....	....
	Syracuse Blazers	NAHL	23	11	17	28	....	....	....	29	....	....	....	....	....	....	....	....	....	....	....	....	....	....	....	....	....	....
1976-77	Birmingham Bulls	WHA	52	17	24	41	....	....	....	33	....	....	....	....	....	....	....	....	....	....	....	....	....	....	....	....	....	....
	Syracuse Blazers	NAHL	18	18	36	54	....	....	....	4	....	....	....	....	....	....	....	....	....	....	....	....	....	....	....	....	....	....
1977-78	Birmingham Bulls	WHA	48	13	26	39	....	....	....	52	....	....	....	....	....	....	....	....	....	....	5	1	1	2	6	....	....	....
	Philadelphia Firebirds	AHL	24	11	13	24	....	....	....	44	....	....	....	....	....	....	....	....	....	....	....	....	....	....	....	....	....	....
1978-79	Birmingham Bulls	WHA	71	24	26	50	....	....	....	108	....	....	....	....	....	....	....	....	....	....	....	....	....	....	....	....	....	....
1979-80	**Quebec Nordiques**	**NHL**	**2**	**0**	**0**	**0**	**0**	**0**	**0**	**0**	**0**	**0**	**0**	**4**	**0.0**	**0**	**0**	**2**	**0**	**–2**	....	....	....	....	....	....	....	....
	Syracuse Firebirds	AHL	71	28	40	68	....	....	....	59	....	....	....	....	....	....	....	....	....	....	2	0	0	0	0	....	....	....
1980-81	Birmingham Bulls	CHL	57	22	33	55	....	....	....	57	....	....	....	....	....	....	....	....	....	....	....	....	....	....	....	....	....	....
	Binghamton Whalers	AHL	18	10	10	20	....	....	....	29	....	....	....	....	....	....	....	....	....	....	6	4	2	6	2	....	....	....
1981-82	EHC Eisbaren Berlin	Germany	35	12	17	29	....	....	....	46	....	....	....	....	....	....	....	....	....	....	....	....	....	....	....	....	....	....
	NHL Totals		**2**	**0**	**0**	**0**	**0**	**0**	**0**	**0**	**0**	**0**	**0**	**4**	**0.0**	**0**	**0**	**2**	**0**		....	....	....	....	....	....	....	....
	Other Major League Totals		272	60	92	152	....	....	....	216	....	....	....	....	....	....	....	....	....	....	6	1	1	2	6	....	....	....

CCHA Second All-Star Team (1974)

Selected by **Cleveland** (WHA) in 1973 WHA Amateur Draft, May, 1974. Transferred to **Minnesota** (WHA) after **Cleveland** (WHA) franchise relocated, July, 1976. Signed as a free agent by **Birmingham** (WHA) after **Minnesota** (WHA) franchise folded, January, 1977. Claimed by **Quebec** from **Birmingham** (WHA) in WHA Dispersal Draft, June 9, 1979. Signed as a free agent by **Calgary**, August, 1980. Traded to **Hartford** by **Calgary** for future considerations, February, 1981.

• STEWART, Paul

Paul George LW/D – L. 6'1", 205 lbs. b: Boston, MA, 3/21/1954.

Season	Club	League	GP	G	A	Pts	AG	AA	APts	PIM	PP	SH	GW	S	%	TGF	PGF	TGA	PGA	+/–	GP	G	A	Pts	PIM	PP	SH	GW
1975-76	Binghamton Dusters	NAHL	46	3	4	7	....	....	....	273	....	....	....	....	....	....	....	....	....	....	....	....	....	....	....	....	....	....
1976-77	Edmonton Oilers	WHA	2	0	0	0	....	....	....	2	....	....	....	....	....	....	....	....	....	....	....	....	....	....	....	....	....	....
	New Haven Nighthawks	AHL	1	0	0	0	....	....	....	6	....	....	....	....	....	....	....	....	....	....	....	....	....	....	....	....	....	....
	Binghamton Dusters	NAHL	60	4	13	17	....	....	....	232	....	....	....	....	....	....	....	....	....	....	10	1	1	32	35	....	....	....
1977-78	Cincinnati Stingers	WHA	40	1	5	6	....	....	....	241	....	....	....	....	....	....	....	....	....	....	....	....	....	....	....	....	....	....
	Binghamton Dusters	AHL	21	5	2	7	....	....	....	69	....	....	....	....	....	....	....	....	....	....	....	....	....	....	....	....	....	....

			REGULAR SEASON																		PLAYOFFS							
Season	Club	League	GP	G	A	Pts	AG	AA	APts	PIM	PP	SH	GW	S	%	TGF	PGF	TGA	PGA	+/-	GP	G	A	Pts	PIM	PP	SH	GW
1978-79	Cape Cod Freedoms	NEHL	18	2	3	5	....	....	....	33	....	....	....	....	....	....	....	....	....	....	....	....	....	....	....	....	....	....
	Binghamton Dusters	AHL	7	1	2	3	....	....	....	40	....	....	....	....	....	....	....	....	....	....	....	....	....	....	....	....	....	....
	Philadelphia Firebirds	AHL	16	2	0	2	....	....	....	92	....	....	....	....	....	....	....	....	....	....	....	....	....	....	....	....	....	....
	Cincinnati Stingers	WHA	23	2	1	3	....	....	....	45	....	....	....	....	....	....	....	....	....	....	....	3	0	0	0	0	....	....	....
1979-80	**Quebec Nordiques**	**NHL**	**21**	**2**	**0**	**2**	**2**	**0**	**2**	**74**	**0**	**0**	**0**	**9**	**22.2**	**7**	**0**	**8**	**0**	**–1**	....	....	....	....	....	....	....	....
	Cincinnati Stingers	CHL	20	1	2	3	....	....	....	79	....	....	....	....	....	....	....	....	....	....	....	....	....	....	....	....	....	....
	Birmingham Bulls	CHL	10	0	0	0	....	....	....	56	....	....	....	....	....	....	....	....	....	....	....	....	....	....	....	....	....	....
1980-81	Binghamton Dusters	AHL	15	2	1	3	....	....	....	59	....	....	....	....	....	....	....	....	....	....	....	....	....	....	....	....	....	....
1981-82	Cape Cod Buccaneers	ACHL	5	0	2	2	....	....	....	20	....	....	....	....	....	....	....	....	....	....	....	....	....	....	....	....	....	....
1982-83	Mohawk Valley Stars	ACHL	....	....	....	....	....	....	....	....	....	....	....	....	....	....	....	....	....	....	....	2	0	0	0	2	....	....	....
	NHL Totals		**21**	**2**	**0**	**2**	**2**	**0**	**2**	**74**	**0**	**0**	**0**	**9**	**22.2**	**7**	**0**	**8**	**0**		....	....	....	....	....	....	....	....
	Other Major League Totals		65	3	6	9	....	....	....	288	....	....	....	....	....	....	....	....	....	....	....	3	0	0	0	0	....	....	....

Signed as a free agent by **Edmonton** (WHA), October, 1976. Signed as a free agent by **Cincinnati** (WHA), December, 1977. Claimed by **Quebec** from **Cincinnati** (WHA) in WHA Dispersal Draft, June 9, 1979.

• STEWART, Ralph

Ralph Donald C – L. 6'1", 190 lbs. b: Fort William, Ont., 12/2/1948. **USHOF**

Season	Club	League	GP	G	A	Pts	AG	AA	APts	PIM	PP	SH	GW	S	%	TGF	PGF	TGA	PGA	+/-	GP	G	A	Pts	PIM	PP	SH	GW
1962-63	Fort William Canadiens	TBJHL	....	....	....	....	....	....	....	....	....	....	....	....	....	....	....	....	....	....	5	1	1	2	0	....	....	....
1963-64	Fort William Canadiens	TBJHL	20	4	5	9	....	....	....	6	....	....	....	....	....	....	....	....	....	....	....	12	8	5	13	8	....	....	....
1964-65	Fort William Canadiens	TBJHL	24	13	18	31	....	....	....	38	....	....	....	....	....	....	....	....	....	....	....	....	....	....	....	....	....	....	....
	Port Arthur North Stars	Mem-Cup	4	4	0	4	....	....	....	6	....	....	....	....	....	....	....	....	....	....	....	....	....	....	....	....	....	....	....
1965-66	Montreal Jr. Canadiens	OHA-Jr.	46	7	9	16	....	....	....	28	....	....	....	....	....	....	....	....	....	....	....	10	0	0	0	2	....	....	....
1966-67	Montreal Jr. Canadiens	OHA-Jr.	48	6	23	29	....	....	....	49	....	....	....	....	....	....	....	....	....	....	....	6	4	1	5	0	....	....	....
1967-68	Montreal Jr. Canadiens	OHA-Jr.	43	17	31	48	....	....	....	28	....	....	....	....	....	....	....	....	....	....	....	11	5	4	9	8	....	....	....
1968-69	Vancouver Canucks	WHL	6	0	1	1	....	....	....	0	....	....	....	....	....	....	....	....	....	....	....	....	....	....	....	....	....	....	....
	Houston Apollos	CHL	44	10	17	27	....	....	....	10	....	....	....	....	....	....	....	....	....	....	....	3	0	0	0	0	....	....	....
1969-70	Kansas City Blues	CHL	72	21	21	42	....	....	....	37	....	....	....	....	....	....	....	....	....	....	....	....	....	....	....	....	....	....	....
1970-71	**Vancouver Canucks**	**NHL**	**3**	**0**	**1**	**1**	**0**	**1**	**1**	**0**	**0**	**0**	**0**	**2**	**0.0**	**2**	**1**	**2**	**0**	**–1**	....	....	....	....	....	....	....	....
	Rochester Americans	AHL	66	27	16	43	....	....	....	14	....	....	....	....	....	....	....	....	....	....	....	....	....	....	....	....	....	....	....
1971-72	Seattle Totems	WHL	16	2	6	8	....	....	....	4	....	....	....	....	....	....	....	....	....	....	....	....	....	....	....	....	....	....	....
	Tidewater Red Wings	AHL	20	3	8	11	....	....	....	8	....	....	....	....	....	....	....	....	....	....	....	....	....	....	....	....	....	....	....
	Fort Worth Wings	CHL	38	21	36	57	....	....	....	23	....	....	....	....	....	....	....	....	....	....	....	7	6	6	12	6	....	....	....
1972-73	Fort Worth Wings	CHL	39	29	36	65	....	....	....	23	....	....	....	....	....	....	....	....	....	....	....	....	....	....	....	....	....	....	....
	New York Islanders	**NHL**	**31**	**4**	**10**	**14**	**4**	**8**	**12**	**4**	**0**	**0**	**0**	**68**	**5.9**	**21**	**2**	**30**	**0**	**–11**	....	....	....	....	....	....	....	....
1973-74	**New York Islanders**	**NHL**	**67**	**23**	**20**	**43**	**22**	**16**	**38**	**6**	**2**	**5**	**2**	**178**	**12.9**	**54**	**11**	**69**	**19**	**–7**	....	....	....	....	....	....	....	....
1974-75	**New York Islanders**	**NHL**	**70**	**16**	**24**	**40**	**14**	**18**	**32**	**12**	**6**	**1**	**2**	**145**	**11.0**	**55**	**18**	**58**	**12**	**–9**	**13**	**3**	**3**	**6**	**2**	**1**	**0**	**0**
1975-76	**New York Islanders**	**NHL**	**31**	**6**	**7**	**13**	**5**	**5**	**10**	**2**	**0**	**1**	**1**	**28**	**21.4**	**19**	**1**	**16**	**1**	**3**	**6**	**1**	**1**	**2**	**0**	**1**	**0**	**0**
	Fort Worth Texans	CHL	3	2	5	7	....	....	....	2	....	....	....	....	....	....	....	....	....	....	....	....	....	....	....	....	....	....	....
1976-77	**Vancouver Canucks**	**NHL**	**34**	**6**	**8**	**14**	**5**	**6**	**11**	**4**	**0**	**0**	**1**	**54**	**11.1**	**23**	**1**	**26**	**7**	**3**	....	....	....	....	....	....	....	....
	Tulsa Oilers	CHL	43	24	26	50	....	....	....	14	....	....	....	....	....	....	....	....	....	....	....	....	....	....	....	....	....	....	....
1977-78	**Vancouver Canucks**	**NHL**	**16**	**2**	**3**	**5**	**2**	**2**	**4**	**0**	**1**	**0**	**0**	**28**	**7.1**	**5**	**1**	**15**	**1**	**–10**	....	....	....	....	....	....	....	....
	Tulsa Oilers	CHL	50	16	29	45	....	....	....	12	....	....	....	....	....	....	....	....	....	....	....	7	6	3	9	0	....	....	....
1978-79	Fort Worth Texans	CHL	76	15	33	48	....	....	....	8	....	....	....	....	....	....	....	....	....	....	....	5	0	0	0	4	....	....	....
1979-80	Thunder Bay Twins	CASH	STATISTICS NOT AVAILABLE																									
	NHL Totals		**252**	**57**	**73**	**130**	**52**	**56**	**108**	**28**	**9**	**7**	**6**	**503**	**11.3**	**179**	**35**	**216**	**40**		**19**	**4**	**4**	**8**	**2**	**2**	**0**	**0**

• Regular season totals for **Fort William** during 1962-63 season are unavailable. Loaned to **Vancouver** (WHL) by **Montreal** for cash, September 27, 1968. Claimed by **Vancouver** from **Montreal** in Expansion Draft, June 10, 1970. Traded to **Detroit** by **Vancouver** for Jim Niekamp, March 6, 1972. Traded to **NY Islanders** by **Detroit** with Bob Cook for Ken Murray and Brian Lavender, January 17, 1973. Traded to **Vancouver** by **NY Islanders** with Dave Fortier for cash, October 6, 1976.

• STEWART, Ron

Ronald George "Stew" RW – R. 6'1", 197 lbs. b: Calgary, Alta., 7/11/1932.

Season	Club	League	GP	G	A	Pts	AG	AA	APts	PIM	PP	SH	GW	S	%	TGF	PGF	TGA	PGA	+/-	GP	G	A	Pts	PIM	PP	SH	GW
1949-50	Toronto Marlboros	OHA-Jr.	30	2	5	7	....	....	....	41	....	....	....	....	....	....	....	....	....	....	5	0	1	1	8	....	....	....
1950-51	Toronto Marlboros	OHA-Jr.	53	22	23	45	....	....	....	49	....	....	....	....	....	....	....	....	....	....	13	6	8	14	31	....	....	....
1951-52	Toronto Marlboros	OHA-Jr.	21	9	10	19	....	....	....	57	....	....	....	....	....	....	....	....	....	....	....	....	....	....	....	....	....	....
	Barrie Flyers	OHA-Jr.	29	13	18	31	....	....	....	43	....	....	....	....	....	....	....	....	....	....	....	....	....	....	....	....	....	....
	Guelph Biltmores	OHA-Jr.	....	....	....	....	....	....	....	....	....	....	....	....	....	....	....	....	....	....	11	7	7	14	4	....	....	....
	Guelph Biltmores	Mem-Cup	12	10	7	17	....	....	....	10	....	....	....	....	....	....	....	....	....	....	....	....	....	....	....	....	....	....
1952-53	**Toronto Maple Leafs**	**NHL**	**70**	**13**	**22**	**35**	**17**	**27**	**44**	**29**	....	....	....	....	....	....	....	....	....	....	....	....	....	....	....	....	....	....
1953-54	**Toronto Maple Leafs**	**NHL**	**70**	**14**	**11**	**25**	**19**	**13**	**32**	**72**	....	....	....	....	....	....	....	....	....	....	**5**	**0**	**1**	**1**	**10**	....	....	....
1954-55	**Toronto Maple Leafs**	**NHL**	**53**	**14**	**5**	**19**	**18**	**6**	**24**	**20**	....	....	....	....	....	....	....	....	....	....	**4**	**0**	**0**	**0**	**2**	....	....	....
1955-56	**Toronto Maple Leafs**	**NHL**	**69**	**13**	**14**	**27**	**18**	**17**	**35**	**35**	....	....	....	....	....	....	....	....	....	....	**5**	**1**	**1**	**2**	**2**	....	....	....
1956-57	**Toronto Maple Leafs**	**NHL**	**65**	**15**	**20**	**35**	**19**	**22**	**41**	**28**	....	....	....	....	....	....	....	....	....	....	....	....	....	....	....	....	....	....
1957-58	**Toronto Maple Leafs**	**NHL**	**70**	**15**	**24**	**39**	**18**	**25**	**43**	**51**	....	....	....	....	....	....	....	....	....	....	....	....	....	....	....	....	....	....
1958-59	**Toronto Maple Leafs**	**NHL**	**70**	**21**	**13**	**34**	**25**	**13**	**38**	**23**	....	....	....	....	....	....	....	....	....	....	**12**	**3**	**3**	**6**	**6**	....	....	....
1959-60	**Toronto Maple Leafs**	**NHL**	**67**	**14**	**20**	**34**	**16**	**19**	**35**	**28**	....	....	....	....	....	....	....	....	....	....	**10**	**0**	**2**	**2**	**2**	....	....	....
1960-61	**Toronto Maple Leafs**	**NHL**	**51**	**13**	**12**	**25**	**15**	**12**	**27**	**8**	....	....	....	....	....	....	....	....	....	....	**5**	**1**	**0**	**1**	**2**	....	....	....
1961-62♦	**Toronto Maple Leafs**	**NHL**	**60**	**8**	**9**	**17**	**9**	**9**	**18**	**14**	....	....	....	....	....	....	....	....	....	....	**11**	**1**	**6**	**7**	**4**	....	....	....
1962-63♦	**Toronto Maple Leafs**	**NHL**	**63**	**16**	**16**	**32**	**19**	**16**	**35**	**26**	....	....	....	....	....	....	....	....	....	....	**10**	**4**	**0**	**4**	**2**	....	....	....
1963-64♦	**Toronto Maple Leafs**	**NHL**	**65**	**14**	**5**	**19**	**17**	**5**	**22**	**46**	....	....	....	....	....	....	....	....	....	....	**14**	**0**	**4**	**4**	**24**	....	....	....
1964-65	**Toronto Maple Leafs**	**NHL**	**65**	**16**	**11**	**27**	**19**	**11**	**30**	**33**	....	....	....	....	....	....	....	....	....	....	**6**	**0**	**1**	**1**	**2**	....	....	....
1965-66	**Boston Bruins**	**NHL**	**70**	**20**	**16**	**36**	**23**	**15**	**38**	**17**	....	....	....	....	....	....	....	....	....	....	....	....	....	....	....	....	....	....
1966-67	**Boston Bruins**	**NHL**	**56**	**14**	**10**	**24**	**16**	**10**	**26**	**31**	....	....	....	....	....	....	....	....	....	....	....	....	....	....	....	....	....	....
1967-68	**St. Louis Blues**	**NHL**	**19**	**7**	**5**	**12**	**8**	**5**	**13**	**11**	**1**	**1**	**2**	**69**	**10.1**	**17**	**7**	**22**	**5**	**–7**	....	....	....	....	....	....	....	....
	New York Rangers	**NHL**	**55**	**7**	**7**	**14**	**8**	**7**	**15**	**19**	**0**	**0**	**1**	**101**	**6.9**	**32**	**5**	**44**	**13**	**–4**	**6**	**1**	**1**	**2**	**2**	**0**	**0**	**0**
1968-69	**New York Rangers**	**NHL**	**75**	**18**	**11**	**29**	**19**	**10**	**29**	**20**	**1**	**2**	**5**	**184**	**9.8**	**41**	**3**	**68**	**19**	**–11**	**4**	**0**	**1**	**1**	**0**	**0**	**0**	**0**
1969-70	**New York Rangers**	**NHL**	**76**	**14**	**10**	**24**	**15**	**9**	**24**	**14**	**1**	**4**	**5**	**109**	**12.8**	**35**	**4**	**45**	**21**	**7**	**6**	**0**	**0**	**0**	**2**	**0**	**0**	**0**
1970-71	**New York Rangers**	**NHL**	**76**	**5**	**6**	**11**	**5**	**5**	**10**	**19**	**0**	**2**	**1**	**52**	**9.6**	**19**	**2**	**30**	**22**	**9**	**13**	**1**	**0**	**1**	**0**	**0**	**1**	**0**
1971-72	Providence Reds	AHL	18	6	5	11	....	....	....	2	....	....	....	....	....	....	....	....	....	....	....	....	....	....	....	....	....	....
	Vancouver Canucks	**NHL**	**42**	**3**	**1**	**4**	**3**	**1**	**4**	**10**	**0**	**0**	**0**	**19**	**15.8**	**8**	**0**	**34**	**23**	**–3**	....	....	....	....	....	....	....	....
	New York Rangers	**NHL**	**13**	**0**	**2**	**2**	**0**	**2**	**2**	**2**	**0**	**0**	**0**	**10**	**0.0**	**3**	**1**	**10**	**2**	**–6**	**8**	**2**	**1**	**3**	**0**	**0**	**0**	**0**
1972-73	**New York Rangers**	**NHL**	**11**	**0**	**1**	**1**	**0**	**1**	**1**	**0**	**0**	**0**	**0**	**8**	**0.0**	**2**	**0**	**3**	**1**	**0**	....	....	....	....	....	....	....	....
	New York Islanders	**NHL**	**22**	**2**	**2**	**4**	**2**	**2**	**4**	**4**	**2**	**0**	**0**	**11**	**18.2**	**10**	**4**	**34**	**11**	**–17**	....	....	....	....	....	....	....	....
	NHL Totals		**1353**	**276**	**253**	**529**	**328**	**262**	**590**	**560**	....	....	....	....	....	....	....	....	....	....	**119**	**14**	**21**	**35**	**60**	....	....	....

Played in NHL All-Star Game (1955, 1962, 1963, 1964)

Traded to **Boston** by **Toronto** for Orland Kurtenbach, Andy Hebenton and Pat Stapleton, June 8, 1965. Claimed by **St. Louis** from **Boston** in Expansion Draft, June 6, 1967. Traded to **NY Rangers** by **St. Louis** with Ron Attwell for Red Berenson and Barclay Plager, November 29, 1967. Traded to **Vancouver** by **NY Rangers** with Dave Balon and Wayne Connelly for Gary Doak and Jim Wiste, November 16, 1971. Traded to **NY Rangers** (Providence-AHL) by **Vancouver** (Rochester-AHL) for the loan of Mike McMahon for the remainder of the 1971-72 season, March 5, 1972. Traded to **NY Islanders** by **NY Rangers** for cash, November 14, 1972.

• STEWART, Ryan

C – R. 6'1", 175 lbs. b: Houston, B.C., 6/1/1967. Winnipeg's 1st, 18th overall, in 1985.

Season	Club	League	GP	G	A	Pts	AG	AA	APts	PIM	PP	SH	GW	S	%	TGF	PGF	TGA	PGA	+/-	GP	G	A	Pts	PIM	PP	SH	GW
1982-83	Kelowna Hawks	BCAHA	STATISTICS NOT AVAILABLE																									
1983-84	Kamloops Jr. Oilers	WHL	69	31	38	69	....	....	....	88	....	....	....	....	....	....	....	....	....	....	16	7	7	14	19	....	....	....
	Kamloops Jr. Oilers	Mem-Cup	4	1	1	2	....	....	....	9	....	....	....	....	....	....	....	....	....	....	....	....	....	....	....	....	....	....
1984-85	Kamloops Blazers	WHL	54	33	37	70	....	....	....	92	....	....	....	....	....	....	....	....	....	....	11	6	6	12	34	....	....	....
1985-86	Kamloops Blazers	WHL	10	7	11	18	....	....	....	27	....	....	....	....	....	....	....	....	....	....	....	....	....	....	....	....	....	....
	Prince Albert Raiders	WHL	52	45	33	78	....	....	....	55	....	....	....	....	....	....	....	....	....	....	15	7	8	15	21	....	....	....
	Winnipeg Jets	**NHL**	**3**	**1**	**0**	**1**	**1**	**0**	**1**	**0**	**0**	**0**	**0**	**5**	**20.0**	**1**	**0**	**1**	**0**	**0**	....	....	....	....	....	....	....	....
1986-87	Brandon Wheat Kings	WHL	15	7	9	16	....	....	....	15	....	....	....	....	....	....	....	....	....	....	....	....	....	....	....	....	....	....
	Portland Winter Hawks	WHL	7	5	2	7	....	....	....	12	....	....	....	....	....	....	....	....	....	....	17	7	11	18	34	....	....	....
1987-88	Moncton Hawks	AHL	48	5	18	23	....	....	....	83	....	....	....	....	....	....	....	....	....	....	....	....	....	....	....	....	....	....
1988-89	Maine Mariners	AHL	7	1	0	1	....	....	....	7	....	....	....	....	....	....	....	....	....	....	....	....	....	....	....	....	....	....
	Moncton Hawks	AHL	1	0	0	0	....	....	....	0	....	....	....	....	....	....	....	....	....	....	....	....	....	....	....	....	....	....

			REGULAR SEASON																		PLAYOFFS							
Season	Club	League	GP	G	A	Pts	AG	AA	APts	PIM	PP	SH	GW	S	%	TGF	PGF	TGA	PGA	+/–	GP	G	A	Pts	PIM	PP	SH	GW
1989-90			STATISTICS NOT AVAILABLE																									
1990-91	Albany Choppers	IHL	1	0	0	0	....	....	....	10	....	....	....	....	....	....	....	....	....	....	....	....	....	....	....	....	....	....
1991-92	Swindon Wildcats	Aut-Cup	6	13	15	28	....	....	....	26	....	....	....	....	....	....	....	....	....	....	....	....	....	....	....	....	....	....
	Swindon Wildcats	Britain-2	34	79	65	144	....	....	....	....	....	....	....	....	....	....	....	....	....	....	6	20	13	33	10	....	....	....
1992-93	Swindon Wildcats	Aut-Cup	11	18	13	31	....	....	....	40	....	....	....	....	....	....	....	....	....	....	....	....	....	....	....	....	....	....
	Swindon Wildcats	Britain-2	31	71	57	128	....	....	....	66	....	....	....	....	....	....	....	....	....	....	6	8	5	13	6	....	....	....
	NHL Totals		**3**	**1**	**0**	**1**	**1**	**0**	**1**	**0**	**0**	**0**	**0**	**5**	**20.0**	**1**	**0**	**1**	**0**		....	....	....	....	....	....	....	....

• STIENBURG, Trevor

RW – R. 6'1", 200 lbs. b: Kingston, Ont., 5/13/1966. Quebec's 1st, 15th overall, in 1984.

Season	Club	League	GP	G	A	Pts	AG	AA	APts	PIM	PP	SH	GW	S	%	TGF	PGF	TGA	PGA	+/–	GP	G	A	Pts	PIM	PP	SH	GW
1982-83	Brockville Braves	OJHL-B	47	39	30	69	....	....	....	182	....	....	....	....	....	....	....	....	....	....	....	....	....	....	....	....	....	....
1983-84	Guelph Platers	OHL	65	33	18	51	....	....	....	104	....	....	....	....	....	....	....	....	....	....	....	....	....	....	....	....	....	....
1984-85	Guelph Platers	OHL	18	7	12	19	....	....	....	38	....	....	....	....	....	....	....	....	....	....	....	....	....	....	....	....	....	....
	London Knights	OHL	22	9	11	20	....	....	....	45	....	....	....	....	....	....	....	....	....	....	8	1	3	4	22	....	....	....
1985-86	**Quebec Nordiques**	**NHL**	**2**	**1**	**0**	**1**	**1**	**0**	**1**	**0**	**0**	**0**	**0**	**6**	**16.7**	**2**	**0**	**2**	**0**	**0**	**1**	**0**	**0**	**0**	**0**	**0**	**0**	**0**
	London Knights	OHL	31	12	18	30	....	....	....	88	....	....	....	....	....	....	....	....	....	....	5	0	0	0	20	....	....	....
1986-87	**Quebec Nordiques**	**NHL**	**6**	**1**	**0**	**1**	**1**	**0**	**1**	**12**	**0**	**0**	**1**	**6**	**16.7**	**1**	**0**	**1**	**0**	**0**	....	....	....	....	....	....	....	....
	Fredericton Express	AHL	48	14	12	26	....	....	....	123	....	....	....	....	....	....	....	....	....	....	....	....	....	....	....	....	....	....
1987-88	**Quebec Nordiques**	**NHL**	**8**	**0**	**1**	**1**	**0**	**1**	**1**	**24**	**0**	**0**	**0**	**3**	**0.0**	**1**	**0**	**2**	**0**	**–1**	....	....	....	....	....	....	....	....
	Fredericton Express	AHL	55	12	24	36	....	....	....	279	....	....	....	....	....	....	....	....	....	....	13	3	3	6	115	....	....	....
1988-89	**Quebec Nordiques**	**NHL**	**55**	**6**	**3**	**9**	**5**	**2**	**7**	**125**	**1**	**0**	**0**	**65**	**9.2**	**17**	**3**	**31**	**0**	**–17**	....	....	....	....	....	....	....	....
1989-90	Halifax Citadels	AHL	11	3	3	6	....	....	....	36	....	....	....	....	....	....	....	....	....	....	....	....	....	....	....	....	....	....
1990-91	Halifax Citadels	AHL	41	16	7	23	....	....	....	190	....	....	....	....	....	....	....	....	....	....	....	....	....	....	....	....	....	....
1991-92	New Haven Nighthawks	AHL	66	17	22	39	....	....	....	201	....	....	....	....	....	....	....	....	....	....	1	0	0	0	2	....	....	....
1992-93	Springfield Indians	AHL	65	14	20	34	....	....	....	244	....	....	....	....	....	....	....	....	....	....	10	0	0	0	31	....	....	....
1993-94	Springfield Indians	AHL	47	4	10	14	....	....	....	134	....	....	....	....	....	....	....	....	....	....	....	....	....	....	....	....	....	....
	NHL Totals		**71**	**8**	**4**	**12**	**7**	**3**	**10**	**161**	**1**	**0**	**1**	**80**	**10.0**	**21**	**3**	**36**	**0**		**1**	**0**	**0**	**0**	**0**	**0**	**0**	**0**

Signed as a free agent by **Hartford**, July 21, 1992.

• STILES, Tony

D – L. 5'11", 200 lbs. b: Carstairs, Alta., 8/12/1959.

Season	Club	League	GP	G	A	Pts	AG	AA	APts	PIM	PP	SH	GW	S	%	TGF	PGF	TGA	PGA	+/–	GP	G	A	Pts	PIM	PP	SH	GW
1977-78	Calgary Canucks	AJHL	59	7	29	36	....	....	....	73	....	....	....	....	....	....	....	....	....	....	....	....	....	....	....	....	....	....
1978-79	Michigan Tech Huskies	WCHA	32	8	9	17	....	....	....	31	....	....	....	....	....	....	....	....	....	....	....	....	....	....	....	....	....	....
1979-80	Michigan Tech Huskies	WCHA	29	1	12	13	....	....	....	34	....	....	....	....	....	....	....	....	....	....	....	....	....	....	....	....	....	....
1980-81	Michigan Tech Huskies	WCHA	44	10	20	30	....	....	....	58	....	....	....	....	....	....	....	....	....	....	....	....	....	....	....	....	....	....
1981-82	Michigan Tech Huskies	WCHA	38	7	14	21	....	....	....	26	....	....	....	....	....	....	....	....	....	....	....	....	....	....	....	....	....	....
1982-83	Colorado Flames	CHL	58	2	7	9	....	....	....	53	....	....	....	....	....	....	....	....	....	....	1	0	0	0	0	....	....	....
1983-84	**Calgary Flames**	**NHL**	**30**	**2**	**7**	**9**	**2**	**5**	**7**	**20**	**0**	**0**	**0**	**19**	**10.5**	**34**	**0**	**24**	**4**	**14**	....	....	....	....	....	....	....	....
	Colorado Flames	CHL	39	3	18	21	....	....	....	24	....	....	....	....	....	....	....	....	....	....	1	0	0	0	0	....	....	....
1984-85	Moncton Golden Flames	AHL	79	5	9	14	....	....	....	46	....	....	....	....	....	....	....	....	....	....	....	....	....	....	....	....	....	....
1985-86	Moncton Golden Flames	AHL	20	0	2	2	....	....	....	18	....	....	....	....	....	....	....	....	....	....	....	....	....	....	....	....	....	....
	Fredericton Express	AHL	9	0	1	1	....	....	....	9	....	....	....	....	....	....	....	....	....	....	....	....	....	....	....	....	....	....
	Canada	Nat-Team	11	1	1	2	....	....	....	6	....	....	....	....	....	....	....	....	....	....	....	....	....	....	....	....	....	....
1986-87	Canada	Nat-Team	70	4	18	22	....	....	....	58	....	....	....	....	....	....	....	....	....	....	....	....	....	....	....	....	....	....
1987-88	Canada	Nat-Team	58	0	8	8	....	....	....	44	....	....	....	....	....	....	....	....	....	....	....	....	....	....	....	....	....	....
	Canada	Olympics	5	0	0	0	....	....	....	0	....	....	....	....	....	....	....	....	....	....	....	....	....	....	....	....	....	....
1988-89	EC Bad Tolz	Germany-2	35	18	33	51	....	....	....	48	....	....	....	....	....	....	....	....	....	....	....	....	....	....	....	....	....	....
1989-90	EC Bad Tolz	Germany-2	47	16	33	49	....	....	....	28	....	....	....	....	....	....	....	....	....	....	....	....	....	....	....	....	....	....
	NHL Totals		**30**	**2**	**7**	**9**	**2**	**5**	**7**	**20**	**0**	**0**	**0**	**19**	**10.5**	**34**	**0**	**24**	**4**		....	....	....	....	....	....	....	....

Signed as a free agent by **Calgary**, September 17, 1982. Traded to **Quebec** by **Calgary** for Tom Thornbury, January 16, 1986.

• STILLMAN, Cory

C – L. 6', 194 lbs. b: Peterborough, Ont., 12/20/1973. Calgary's 1st, 6th overall, in 1992.

Season	Club	League	GP	G	A	Pts	AG	AA	APts	PIM	PP	SH	GW	S	%	TGF	PGF	TGA	PGA	+/–	GP	G	A	Pts	PIM	PP	SH	GW
1989-90	Peterborough Roadrunners	OJHL-B	41	30	*54	84	....	....	....	76	....	....	....	....	....	....	....	....	....	....	....	....	....	....	....	....	....	....
1990-91	Windsor Spitfires	OHL	64	31	70	101	....	....	....	31	....	....	....	....	....	....	....	....	....	....	11	3	6	9	8	....	....	....
1991-92	Windsor Spitfires	OHL	53	29	61	90	....	....	....	59	....	....	....	....	....	....	....	....	....	....	7	2	4	6	8	....	....	....
1992-93	Peterborough Petes	OHL	61	25	55	80	....	....	....	55	....	....	....	....	....	....	....	....	....	....	18	3	8	11	18	....	....	....
	Canada	Nat-Team	1	0	0	0	....	....	....	0	....	....	....	....	....	....	....	....	....	....	....	....	....	....	....	....	....	....
	Peterborough Petes	Mem-Cup	4	0	2	2	....	....	....	4	....	....	....	....	....	....	....	....	....	....	....	....	....	....	....	....	....	....
1993-94	Saint John Flames	AHL	79	35	48	83	....	....	....	52	....	....	....	....	....	....	....	....	....	....	7	2	4	6	16	....	....	....
1994-95	Saint John Flames	AHL	63	28	53	81	....	....	....	70	....	....	....	....	....	....	....	....	....	....	5	0	2	2	2	....	....	....
	Calgary Flames	**NHL**	**10**	**0**	**2**	**2**	**0**	**3**	**3**	**2**	**0**	**0**	**0**	**7**	**0.0**	**3**	**1**	**1**	**0**	**1**	....	....	....	....	....	....	....	....
1995-96	**Calgary Flames**	**NHL**	**74**	**16**	**19**	**35**	**16**	**16**	**32**	**41**	**4**	**1**	**3**	**132**	**12.1**	**56**	**29**	**38**	**6**	**–5**	**2**	**1**	**1**	**2**	**0**	**0**	**0**	**0**
1996-97	**Calgary Flames**	**NHL**	**58**	**6**	**20**	**26**	**6**	**18**	**24**	**14**	**2**	**0**	**0**	**112**	**5.4**	**41**	**19**	**28**	**0**	**–6**	....	....	....	....	....	....	....	....
1997-98	**Calgary Flames**	**NHL**	**72**	**27**	**22**	**49**	**32**	**22**	**54**	**40**	**9**	**4**	**1**	**178**	**15.2**	**65**	**23**	**67**	**16**	**–9**	....	....	....	....	....	....	....	....
1998-99	**Calgary Flames**	**NHL**	**76**	**27**	**30**	**57**	**32**	**29**	**61**	**38**	**9**	**3**	**5**	**175**	**15.4**	**77**	**31**	**51**	**12**	**7**	....	....	....	....	....	....	....	....
	Canada	WC-A	10	4	4	8	....	....	....	14	....	....	....	....	....	....	....	....	....	....	....	....	....	....	....	....	....	....
99-2000	**Calgary Flames**	**NHL**	**37**	**12**	**9**	**21**	**13**	**8**	**21**	**12**	**6**	**0**	**3**	**59**	**20.3**	**27**	**12**	**35**	**11**	**–9**	....	....	....	....	....	....	....	....
	NHL Totals		**327**	**88**	**102**	**190**	**99**	**96**	**195**	**147**	**30**	**8**	**12**	**663**	**13.3**	**269**	**115**	**220**	**45**		**2**	**1**	**1**	**2**	**0**	**0**	**0**	**0**

• Missed remainder of 1999-2000 season recovering from shoulder injury suffered in game vs. Philadelphia, December 27, 1999.

• STOCK, P.J.

Philip Joseph LW – L. 5'10", 190 lbs. b: Victoriaville, Que., 5/26/1975.

Season	Club	League	GP	G	A	Pts	AG	AA	APts	PIM	PP	SH	GW	S	%	TGF	PGF	TGA	PGA	+/–	GP	G	A	Pts	PIM	PP	SH	GW
1994-95	Victoriaville Tigres	QMJHL	70	9	46	55	....	....	....	386	....	....	....	....	....	....	....	....	....	....	4	0	0	0	60	....	....	....
1995-96	Victoriaville Tigres	QMJHL	67	19	43	62	....	....	....	432	....	....	....	....	....	....	....	....	....	....	12	5	4	9	79	....	....	....
1996-97	St. Francis Xavier X-Men	AUAA	27	11	20	31	....	....	....	110	....	....	....	....	....	....	....	....	....	....	3	0	4	4	14	....	....	....
1997-98	Hartford Wolf Pack	AHL	41	8	8	16	....	....	....	202	....	....	....	....	....	....	....	....	....	....	11	1	3	4	79	....	....	....
	New York Rangers	**NHL**	**38**	**2**	**3**	**5**	**2**	**3**	**5**	**114**	**0**	**0**	**1**	**9**	**22.2**	....	....	....	....	**4**	....	....	....	....	....	....	....	....
1998-99	**New York Rangers**	**NHL**	**5**	**0**	**0**	**0**	**0**	**0**	**0**	**6**	**0**	**0**	**0**	**0**	**0.0**	**0**	**0**	**1**	**0**	**–1**	....	....	....	....	....	....	....	....
	Hartford Wolf Pack	AHL	55	4	14	18	....	....	....	250	....	....	....	....	....	....	....	....	....	....	6	0	1	1	35	....	....	....
99-2000	**New York Rangers**	**NHL**	**11**	**0**	**1**	**1**	**0**	**1**	**1**	**11**	**0**	**0**	**0**	**2**	**0.0**	**2**	**0**	**1**	**0**	**1**	....	....	....	....	....	....	....	....
	Hartford Wolf Pack	AHL	64	13	23	36	....	....	....	290	....	....	....	....	....	....	....	....	....	....	23	1	11	12	69	....	....	....
	NHL Totals		**54**	**2**	**4**	**6**	**2**	**4**	**6**	**131**	**0**	**0**	**1**	**11**	**18.2**	**2**	**0**	**2**	**0**		....	....	....	....	....	....	....	....

Signed as a free agent by **NY Rangers**, November 18, 1997. Signed as a free agent by **Montreal**, July 7, 2000.

• STOJANOV, Alek

RW – L. 6'4", 225 lbs. b: Windsor, Ont., 4/25/1973. Vancouver's 1st, 7th overall, in 1991.

Season	Club	League	GP	G	A	Pts	AG	AA	APts	PIM	PP	SH	GW	S	%	TGF	PGF	TGA	PGA	+/–	GP	G	A	Pts	PIM	PP	SH	GW
1988-89	Windsor Riversides	OMHA	26	19	15	34	....	....	....	53	....	....	....	....	....	....	....	....	....	....	....	....	....	....	....	....	....	....
	Belle River Canadians	OJHL-C	7	3	2	5	....	....	....	42	....	....	....	....	....	....	....	....	....	....	....	....	....	....	....	....	....	....
	Amherstburg Vikings	OJHL-C	1	0	0	0	....	....	....	2	....	....	....	....	....	....	....	....	....	....	....	....	....	....	....	....	....	....
1989-90	Dukes of Hamilton	OHL	37	4	4	8	....	....	....	91	....	....	....	....	....	....	....	....	....	....	....	....	....	....	....	....	....	....
1990-91	Dukes of Hamilton	OHL	62	25	20	45	....	....	....	181	....	....	....	....	....	....	....	....	....	....	4	1	1	2	14	....	....	....
1991-92	Guelph Storm	OHL	33	12	15	27	....	....	....	91	....	....	....	....	....	....	....	....	....	....	....	....	....	....	....	....	....	....
1992-93	Guelph Storm	OHL	36	27	28	55	....	....	....	62	....	....	....	....	....	....	....	....	....	....	....	....	....	....	....	....	....	....
	Newmarket Royals	OHL	14	9	7	16	....	....	....	26	....	....	....	....	....	....	....	....	....	....	7	1	3	4	26	....	....	....
	Hamilton Canucks	AHL	4	4	0	4	....	....	....	0	....	....	....	....	....	....	....	....	....	....	....	....	....	....	....	....	....	....
1993-94	Hamilton Canucks	AHL	4	0	1	1	....	....	....	5	....	....	....	....	....	....	....	....	....	....	....	....	....	....	....	....	....	....
1994-95	Syracuse Crunch	AHL	73	18	12	30	....	....	....	270	....	....	....	....	....	....	....	....	....	....	....	....	....	....	....	....	....	....
	Vancouver Canucks	**NHL**	**4**	**0**	**0**	**0**	**0**	**0**	**0**	**13**	**0**	**0**	**0**	**1**	**0.0**	**0**	**0**	**2**	**0**	**–2**	**5**	**0**	**0**	**0**	**2**	**0**	**0**	**0**
1995-96	**Vancouver Canucks**	**NHL**	**58**	**0**	**1**	**1**	**0**	**1**	**1**	**123**	**0**	**0**	**0**	**16**	**0.0**	**7**	**0**	**19**	**0**	**–12**	....	....	....	....	....	....	....	....
	Pittsburgh Penguins	**NHL**	**10**	**1**	**0**	**1**	**1**	**0**	**1**	**7**	**0**	**0**	**0**	**4**	**25.0**	**1**	**0**	**2**	**0**	**–1**	**9**	**0**	**0**	**0**	**19**	**0**	**0**	**0**
1996-97	**Pittsburgh Penguins**	**NHL**	**35**	**1**	**4**	**5**	**1**	**4**	**5**	**79**	**0**	**0**	**0**	**11**	**9.1**	**8**	**0**	**5**	**0**	**3**	....	....	....	....	....	....	....	....
1997-98	Syracuse Crunch	AHL	41	5	4	9	....	....	....	215	....	....	....	....	....	....	....	....	....	....	3	1	0	1	4	....	....	....

			REGULAR SEASON																		PLAYOFFS							
Season	Club	League	GP	G	A	Pts	AG	AA	APts	PIM	PP	SH	GW	S	%	TGF	PGF	TGA	PGA	+/–	GP	G	A	Pts	PIM	PP	SH	GW
1998-99	Hamilton Bulldogs	AHL	12	0	1	1				35																		
	Milwaukee Admirals	IHL	13	0	1	1				58																		
	Detroit Vipers	IHL	27	1	3	4				91																		
99-2000	Detroit Vipers	IHL	43	4	10	14				135																		
	NHL Totals		**107**	**2**	**5**	**7**	**2**	**5**	**7**	**222**	**0**	**0**	**0**	**32**	**6.3**	**16**	**0**	**28**	**0**		**14**	**0**	**0**	**0**	**21**	**0**	**0**	**0**

Traded to **Pittsburgh** by **Vancouver** for Markus Naslund, March 20, 1996.

• STOLTZ, Roland

Roland Stig RW – R. 6'1", 191 lbs. b: Oeverkalix, Sweden, 8/15/1954.

Season	Club	League	GP	G	A	Pts	AG	AA	APts	PIM	PP	SH	GW	S	%	TGF	PGF	TGA	PGA	+/–	GP	G	A	Pts	PIM	PP	SH	GW
1971-72	Overkalix IF	Sweden-3	15	12	3	15																						
1972-73	IFK Lulea	Sweden-2	17	11		11																						
1973-74	IFK Lulea	Sweden-2	24	26		26																						
1974-75	IFK Lulea	Sweden-2	STATISTICS NOT AVAILABLE																									
1975-76	Skelleftea AIK	Sweden	32	15	10	25				8											3	0	1	1	2			
1976-77	Skelleftea AIK	Sweden	32	12	5	17				16																		
1977-78	Skelleftea AIK	Sweden	34	13	13	26				14											5	0	1	1	2			
1978-79	Skelleftea AIK	Sweden	36	16	12	28				26																		
	Skelleftea AIK	Sweden-Q	4	2	5	7				4																		
1979-80	Skelleftea AIK	Sweden	36	15	9	24				44																		
1980-81	Skelleftea AIK	Sweden	35	18	19	37				34											3	0	0	0	0			
1981-82	Djurgardens IF Stockholm	DN-Cup	4	0	2	2				0																		
	Washington Capitals	**NHL**	**14**	**2**	**2**	**4**	**2**	**1**	**3**	**14**	**0**	**0**	**0**	**6**	**33.3**	**7**	**2**	**12**	**4**	**–3**								
	Skelleftea AIK	Sweden	20	7	7	14				24																		
1982-83	Skelleftea AIK	Sweden	31	4	8	12				26																		
1983-84	Skelleftea AIK	Sweden	35	8	22	30				36																		
1984-85	Skelleftea AIK	Sweden	36	17	17	34				36																		
1985-86	Skelleftea AIK	Sweden-2	30	15	23	38				28																		
1986-87	Skelleftea AIK	Sweden	34	7	11	18				38																		
1987-88	Mala IF	Sweden-3	23	19	23	42																						
1988-89	Mala IF	Sweden-3	1	2	2	4				0																		
	NHL Totals		**14**	**2**	**2**	**4**	**2**	**1**	**3**	**14**	**0**	**0**	**0**	**6**	**33.3**	**7**	**2**	**12**	**4**									

• Only goals and games played totals available for IFK Lulea in 1972-73 and 1973-74 seasons. Signed as a free agent by **Washington**, June 5, 1981.

• STONE, Steve

Stephen George RW – R. 5'8", 170 lbs. b: Toronto, Ont., 9/26/1952. Vancouver's 9th, 131st overall, in 1972.

Season	Club	League	GP	G	A	Pts	AG	AA	APts	PIM	PP	SH	GW	S	%	TGF	PGF	TGA	PGA	+/–	GP	G	A	Pts	PIM	PP	SH	GW
1970-71	Niagara Falls Flyers	OHA-Jr.	57	18	35	53				36																		
1971-72	Niagara Falls Flyers	OMJHL	62	30	62	92				25											6	1	5	6	7			
1972-73	Des Moines Capitols	IHL	74	35	49	84				10											3	2	0	2	0			
1973-74	**Vancouver Canucks**	**NHL**	**2**	**0**	**0**	**0**	**0**	**0**	**0**	**0**	**0**	**0**	**0**	**1**	**0.0**	**0**	**0**	**2**	**0**	**–2**								
	Seattle Totems	WHL	77	23	32	55				28																		
1974-75	Des Moines Oak Leafs	IHL	72	12	14	26				67																		
1975-76	Port Huron Flags	IHL	78	19	42	61				47											15	4	3	7	9			
1976-77	Port Huron Flags	IHL	2	0	1	1				0																		
	NHL Totals		**2**	**0**	**0**	**0**	**0**	**0**	**0**	**0**	**0**	**0**	**0**	**1**	**0.0**	**0**	**0**	**2**	**0**									

Claimed on waivers by **Port Huron** (IHL) from **Des Moines** (IHL), July, 1975.

• STORM, Jim

James David LW – L. 6'2", 200 lbs. b: Milford, MI, 2/5/1971. Hartford's 5th, 75th overall, in 1991.

Season	Club	League	GP	G	A	Pts	AG	AA	APts	PIM	PP	SH	GW	S	%	TGF	PGF	TGA	PGA	+/–	GP	G	A	Pts	PIM	PP	SH	GW
1988-89	Detroit Compuware	NAJHL	60	30	45	75				50																		
1989-90	Detroit Compuware	NAJHL	55	38	73	111				58																		
1990-91	Michigan Tech Huskies	WCHA	36	16	18	34				46																		
	United States	WJC-A	7	3	4	7				0																		
1991-92	Michigan Tech Huskies	WCHA	39	25	33	58				12																		
1992-93	Michigan Tech Huskies	WCHA	33	22	32	54				30																		
1993-94	**Hartford Whalers**	**NHL**	**68**	**6**	**10**	**16**	**6**	**8**	**14**	**27**	**1**	**0**	**0**	**84**	**7.1**	**34**	**1**	**35**	**6**	**4**								
	United States	Nat-Team	28	8	12	20				14																		
1994-95	**Hartford Whalers**	**NHL**	**6**	**0**	**3**	**3**	**0**	**4**	**4**	**0**	**0**	**0**	**0**	**3**	**0.0**	**3**	**0**	**1**	**0**	**2**								
	Springfield Falcons	AHL	33	11	11	22				29																		
1995-96	**Dallas Stars**	**NHL**	**10**	**1**	**2**	**3**	**1**	**2**	**3**	**17**	**0**	**0**	**1**	**11**	**9.1**	**3**	**1**	**3**	**0**	**–1**								
	Michigan K-Wings	IHL	60	18	33	51				27											10	4	8	12	2			
1996-97	Michigan K-Wings	IHL	75	25	24	49				27											4	0	1	1	4			
1997-98	Utah Grizzlies	IHL	5	0	0	0				2																		
	NHL Totals		**84**	**7**	**15**	**22**	**7**	**14**	**21**	**44**	**1**	**0**	**1**	**98**	**7.1**	**40**	**2**	**39**	**6**									

Signed as a free agent by **Dallas**, September 13, 1995. Signed as a free agent by **NY Islanders**, July 21, 1997.

• STOTHERS, Mike

Michael Patrick D – L. 6'4", 212 lbs. b: Toronto, Ont., 2/22/1962. Philadelphia's 1st, 21st overall, in 1980.

Season	Club	League	GP	G	A	Pts	AG	AA	APts	PIM	PP	SH	GW	S	%	TGF	PGF	TGA	PGA	+/–	GP	G	A	Pts	PIM	PP	SH	GW
1978-79	St. Michael's Buzzers	OHA-B	40	15	35	50																						
1979-80	Kingston Canadians	OMJHL	66	4	23	27				137											3	1	1	2	26			
1980-81	Kingston Canadians	OMJHL	66	4	22	26				237											14	0	3	3	27			
1981-82	Kingston Canadians	OHL	61	1	20	21				203											4	0	1	1	8			
	Maine Mariners	AHL	5	0	0	0				4											1	0	0	0	0			
1982-83	Maine Mariners	AHL	80	2	16	18				139											12	0	0	0	21			
1983-84	Maine Mariners	AHL	61	2	10	12				109											17	0	1	1	34			
1984-85	**Philadelphia Flyers**	**NHL**	**1**	**0**	**0**	**0**	**0**	**0**	**0**	**0**	**0**	**0**	**0**	**0**	**0.0**	**0**	**0**	**1**	**0**	**–1**								
	Hershey Bears	AHL	60	8	18	26				142																		
1985-86	**Philadelphia Flyers**	**NHL**	**6**	**0**	**1**	**1**	**0**	**1**	**1**	**6**	**0**	**0**	**0**	**1**	**0.0**	**3**	**1**	**1**	**0**	**1**	**3**	**0**	**0**	**0**	**4**	**0**	**0**	**0**
	Hershey Bears	AHL	66	4	9	13				221											13	0	3	3	88			
1986-87	**Philadelphia Flyers**	**NHL**	**2**	**0**	**0**	**0**	**0**	**0**	**0**	**4**	**0**	**0**	**0**	**2**	**0.0**	**1**	**0**	**1**	**0**	**0**	**2**	**0**	**0**	**0**	**7**	**0**	**0**	**0**
	Hershey Bears	AHL	75	5	11	16				283											5	0	0	0	10			
1987-88	**Philadelphia Flyers**	**NHL**	**3**	**0**	**0**	**0**	**0**	**0**	**0**	**13**	**0**	**0**	**0**	**0**	**0.0**	**0**	**0**	**2**	**1**	**–1**								
	Hershey Bears	AHL	13	3	2	5				55																		
	Toronto Maple Leafs	**NHL**	**18**	**0**	**1**	**1**	**0**	**1**	**1**	**42**	**0**	**0**	**0**	**0**	**0.0**	**3**	**0**	**10**	**1**	**–6**								
	Newmarket Saints	AHL	38	1	9	10				69																		
1988-89	Hershey Bears	AHL	76	4	11	15				262											9	0	2	2	29			
1989-90	Hershey Bears	AHL	56	1	6	7				170																		
1990-91	Hershey Bears	AHL	72	5	6	11				234											7	0	1	1	9			
1991-92	Hershey Bears	AHL	70	3	8	11				152											6	0	1	1	6			
1992-1996	Hershey Bears	AHL	DID NOT PLAY – ASSISTANT COACH																									
1996-1999	Philadelphia Phantoms	AHL	DID NOT PLAY – ASSISTANT COACH																									
	NHL Totals		**30**	**0**	**2**	**2**	**0**	**2**	**2**	**65**	**0**	**0**	**0**	**3**	**0.0**	**7**	**1**	**15**	**2**		**5**	**0**	**0**	**0**	**11**	**0**	**0**	**0**

Traded to **Toronto** by **Philadelphia** for future considerations, December 4, 1987. Traded to **Philadelphia** by **Toronto** for Bill Root, June 21, 1988. • Served as interim Assistant Coach for **Philadelphia Flyers**, January 27 to May 2, 1999 and February 20 to May 26, 2000. • Named Assistant Coach of **Philadelphia Flyers**, June 13, 2000.

• STOUGHTON, Blaine

Blaine A. "Stash" RW – R. 5'11", 185 lbs. b: Gilbert Plains, Man., 3/13/1953. Pittsburgh's 1st, 7th overall, in 1973.

Season	Club	League	GP	G	A	Pts	AG	AA	APts	PIM	PP	SH	GW	S	%	TGF	PGF	TGA	PGA	+/–	GP	G	A	Pts	PIM	PP	SH	GW
1968-69	Dauphin Kings	MJHL	STATISTICS NOT AVAILABLE																									
	Dauphin Kings	Mem-Cup	1	0	0	0				7																		
1969-70	Flin Flon Bombers	WCJHL	59	19	20	39				181											17	4	2	6	69			
1970-71	Flin Flon Bombers	WCJHL	35	26	24	50				96											17	13	13	26	61			
1971-72	Flin Flon Bombers	WCJHL	68	*60	66	126				121											7	4	6	10	27			
1972-73	Flin Flon Bombers	WCJHL	66	58	60	118				86											9	9	5	14	18			

			REGULAR SEASON																		PLAYOFFS							
Season	Club	League	GP	G	A	Pts	AG	AA	APts	PIM	PP	SH	GW	S	%	TGF	PGF	TGA	PGA	+/-	GP	G	A	Pts	PIM	PP	SH	GW
1973-74	Pittsburgh Penguins	NHL	34	5	6	11	5	5	10	8	0	0	0	52	9.6	18	0	31	1	-12	....	....	....	....	....	....	....	....
	Hershey Bears	AHL	47	23	17	40	....	....	....	35	....	....	....	....	....	....	....	....	....	....	....	....	....	....	....	....	....	....
1974-75	Toronto Maple Leafs	NHL	78	23	14	37	20	10	30	24	4	0	1	161	14.3	63	12	69	11	-7	7	4	2	6	2	1	0	1
1975-76	Toronto Maple Leafs	NHL	43	6	11	17	5	8	13	8	1	0	0	60	10.0	29	5	28	2	-2	....	....	....	....	....	....	....	....
	Oklahoma City Blazers	CHL	30	14	22	36	....	....	....	24	....	....	....	....	....	....	....	....	....	....	4	0	0	0	2	....	....	....
1976-77	Cincinnati Stingers	WHA	81	52	52	104	....	....	....	39	....	....	....	....	....	....	....	....	....	....	4	0	3	3	2	....	....	....
1977-78	Cincinnati Stingers	WHA	30	6	13	19	....	....	....	36	....	....	....	....	....	....	....	....	....	....	....	....	....	....	....	....	....	....
	Indianapolis Racers	WHA	47	13	13	26	....	....	....	28	....	....	....	....	....	....	....	....	....	....	....	....	....	....	....	....	....	....
1978-79	Indianapolis Racers	WHA	25	9	9	18	....	....	....	16	....	....	....	....	....	....	....	....	....	....	....	....	....	....	....	....	....	....
	New England Whalers	WHA	36	9	3	12	....	....	....	2	....	....	....	....	....	....	....	....	....	....	7	4	3	7	4	....	....	....
1979-80	Hartford Whalers	NHL	80	*56	44	100	48	32	80	16	16	2	9	234	23.9	134	31	104	10	9	1	0	0	0	0	0	0	0
1980-81	Hartford Whalers	NHL	71	43	30	73	34	20	54	56	10	2	6	212	20.3	114	33	115	17	-17	....	....	....	....	....	....	....	....
1981-82	Hartford Whalers	NHL	80	52	39	91	41	26	67	57	13	1	4	266	19.5	129	51	102	7	-17	....	....	....	....	....	....	....	....
1982-83	Hartford Whalers	NHL	72	45	31	76	37	21	58	27	10	0	8	207	21.7	108	31	103	3	-23	....	....	....	....	....	....	....	....
1983-84	Hartford Whalers	NHL	54	23	14	37	18	10	28	4	7	0	2	103	22.3	57	24	46	0	-13	....	....	....	....	....	....	....	....
	New York Rangers	NHL	14	5	2	7	4	1	5	4	1	0	1	27	18.5	9	4	17	0	-12	....	....	....	....	....	....	....	....
1984-85	New Haven Nighthawks	AHL	60	20	25	45	....	....	....	35	....	....	....	....	....	....	....	....	....	....	....	....	....	....	....	....	....	....
1986-87			DID NOT PLAY																									
1987-88	HC Asiago	Italy	15	10	16	26	....	....	....	2	....	....	....	....	....	....	....	....	....	....	....	....	....	....	....	....	....	....
	NHL Totals		526	258	191	449	212	133	345	204	62	5	31	1322	19.5	661	191	615	51		8	4	2	6	2	1	0	1
	Other Major League Totals		219	89	90	179	....	....	....	121	....	....	....	....	....	....	....	....	....	....	11	4	6	10	6	....	....	....

WCJHL All-Star Team (1972) • Played in NHL All-Star Game (1982)

Selected by **Quebec** (WHA) in 1973 WHA Amateur Draft, June, 1973. Traded to **Toronto** by **Pittsburgh** with future considerations for Rick Kehoe, September 13, 1974. WHA rights claimed by **Cincinnati** (WHA) from **Quebec** (WHA) prior to WHA Expansion Draft, June, 1975. Traded to **Indianapolis** (WHA) by **Cincinnati** (WHA) with Gilles Marotte for Bryon Baltimore and Hugh Harris, January, 1978. Traded to **New England** (WHA) by **Indianapolis** (WHA) with Dave Inkpen for cash, December, 1978. Claimed by **Hartford** from **Toronto** in Expansion Draft, June 13, 1979. Traded to **NY Rangers** by **Hartford** for Scot Kleinendorst, February 27, 1984.

• STOYANOVICH, Steve

C – R. 6'2", 205 lbs. b: London, Ont., 5/2/1957. NY Islanders' 5th, 69th overall, in 1977.

Season	Club	League	GP	G	A	Pts	AG	AA	APts	PIM	PP	SH	GW	S	%	TGF	PGF	TGA	PGA	+/-	GP	G	A	Pts	PIM	PP	SH	GW
1975-76	Sir Frederick Banting High	Hi-School	60	70	60	130	....	....	....	....	....	....	....	....	....	....	....	....	....	....	....	....	....	....	....	....	....	....
1976-77	Oak Ridge Acres High School	Hi-School	30	20	30	50	....	....	....	....	....	....	....	....	....	....	....	....	....	....	....	....	....	....	....	....	....	....
1977-78	RPI Engineers	ECAC	28	22	30	52	....	....	....	24	....	....	....	....	....	....	....	....	....	....	....	....	....	....	....	....	....	....
1978-79	RPI Engineers	ECAC	28	17	30	47	....	....	....	32	....	....	....	....	....	....	....	....	....	....	....	....	....	....	....	....	....	....
1979-80	RPI Engineers	ECAC	17	9	15	24	....	....	....	16	....	....	....	....	....	....	....	....	....	....	....	....	....	....	....	....	....	....
1980-81	RPI Engineers	ECAC	DID NOT PLAY – ACADEMICALLY INELIGIBLE																									
1981-82	Indianapolis Checkers	CHL	80	42	30	72	....	....	....	55	....	....	....	....	....	....	....	....	....	....	13	7	8	15	20	....	....	....
1982-83	Indianapolis Checkers	CHL	79	41	43	84	....	....	....	65	....	....	....	....	....	....	....	....	....	....	13	6	3	9	4	....	....	....
1983-84	Hartford Whalers	NHL	23	3	5	8	2	3	5	11	0	0	1	60	5.0	13	2	12	0	-1	....	....	....	....	....	....	....	....
	Binghamton Whalers	AHL	21	11	8	19	....	....	....	0	....	....	....	....	....	....	....	....	....	....	....	....	....	....	....	....	....	....
1984-85	HC Gardena-Groden	Italy	26	31	35	66	....	....	....	28	....	....	....	....	....	....	....	....	....	....	8	14	6	20	16	....	....	....
1985-86	HC Gardena-Groden	Italy	36	53	35	88	....	....	....	52	....	....	....	....	....	....	....	....	....	....	4	8	5	13	8	....	....	....
1986-87	HC Fiemme	Italy-2	STATISTICS NOT AVAILABLE																									
1987-88	HC Fiemme	Italy	35	37	47	84	....	....	....	79	....	....	....	....	....	....	....	....	....	....	....	....	....	....	....	....	....	....
1988-89	HC Alleghe	Italy	12	10	14	24	....	....	....	16	....	....	....	....	....	....	....	....	....	....	....	....	....	....	....	....	....	....
	NHL Totals		23	3	5	8	2	3	5	11	0	0	1	60	5.0	13	2	12	0		....	....	....	....	....	....	....	....

CHL First All-Star Team (1983)

Traded to **Hartford** by **NY Islanders** for Hartford's 5th round choice (Tommy Hedlund) in 1985 Entry Draft, August 19, 1983.

• STRAKA, Martin

Martin J. C – L. 5'10", 175 lbs. b: Plzen, Czech., 9/3/1972. Pittsburgh's 1st, 19th overall, in 1992.

Season	Club	League	GP	G	A	Pts	AG	AA	APts	PIM	PP	SH	GW	S	%	TGF	PGF	TGA	PGA	+/-	GP	G	A	Pts	PIM	PP	SH	GW
1989-90	Skoda Plzen	Czech.	1	0	3	3	....	....	....	....	....	....	....	....	....	....	....	....	....	....	....	....	....	....	....	....	....	....
	Czechoslovakia	EJC-A	6	4	2	6	....	....	....	2	....	....	....	....	....	....	....	....	....	....	....	....	....	....	....	....	....	....
1990-91	Skoda Plzen	Czech.	47	7	24	31	....	....	....	6	....	....	....	....	....	....	....	....	....	....	....	....	....	....	....	....	....	....
	Czechoslovakia	WJC-A	6	1	5	6	....	....	....	0	....	....	....	....	....	....	....	....	....	....	....	....	....	....	....	....	....	....
1991-92	Skoda Plzen	Czech.	50	27	28	55	....	....	....	20	....	....	....	....	....	....	....	....	....	....	....	....	....	....	....	....	....	....
	Czechoslovakia	WJC-A	7	2	6	8	....	....	....	4	....	....	....	....	....	....	....	....	....	....	....	....	....	....	....	....	....	....
1992-93	Pittsburgh Penguins	NHL	42	3	13	16	2	9	11	29	0	0	1	28	10.7	21	4	15	0	2	11	2	1	3	2	0	0	0
	Cleveland Lumberjacks	IHL	4	4	3	7	....	....	....	0	....	....	....	....	....	....	....	....	....	....	....	....	....	....	....	....	....	....
1993-94	Pittsburgh Penguins	NHL	84	30	34	64	28	26	54	24	2	0	6	130	23.1	98	7	70	3	24	6	1	0	1	2	0	0	0
	Czech-Republic	WC-A	3	1	0	1	....	....	....	4	....	....	....	....	....	....	....	....	....	....	....	....	....	....	....	....	....	....
1994-95	ZKZ Plzen	Czech-Rep	19	10	11	21	....	....	....	18	....	....	....	....	....	....	....	....	....	....	....	....	....	....	....	....	....	....
	Pittsburgh Penguins	NHL	31	4	12	16	7	18	25	16	0	0	0	36	11.1	26	5	22	1	0	....	....	....	....	....	....	....	....
	Ottawa Senators	NHL	6	1	1	2	2	1	3	0	0	0	0	13	7.7	4	2	3	0	-1	....	....	....	....	....	....	....	....
1995-96	Ottawa Senators	NHL	43	9	16	25	9	13	22	29	5	0	1	63	14.3	36	14	38	2	-14	....	....	....	....	....	....	....	....
	New York Islanders	NHL	22	2	10	12	2	8	10	6	0	0	0	18	11.1	21	6	21	0	-6	....	....	....	....	....	....	....	....
	Florida Panthers	NHL	12	2	4	6	2	3	5	6	1	0	0	17	11.8	9	2	6	0	1	13	2	2	4	2	0	0	0
1996-97	Czech-Republic	W-Cup	1	0	0	0	....	....	....	0	....	....	....	....	....	....	....	....	....	....	....	....	....	....	....	....	....	....
	Florida Panthers	NHL	55	7	22	29	7	20	27	12	2	0	1	94	7.4	50	15	26	0	9	4	0	0	0	0	0	0	0
1997-98	Pittsburgh Penguins	NHL	75	19	23	42	22	23	45	28	4	3	4	117	16.2	57	13	59	14	-1	6	2	0	2	2	0	1	0
	Czech-Republic	Olympics	6	1	2	3	....	....	....	0	....	....	....	....	....	....	....	....	....	....	....	....	....	....	....	....	....	....
1998-99	Pittsburgh Penguins	NHL	80	35	48	83	41	46	87	26	5	4	4	177	19.8	128	47	92	23	12	13	6	9	15	6	1	0	0
99-2000	Pittsburgh Penguins	NHL	71	20	39	59	22	36	58	26	3	1	2	146	13.7	101	34	62	19	24	11	3	9	12	10	1	0	0
	NHL Totals		521	132	222	354	144	203	347	202	22	8	19	839	15.7	551	149	414	62		64	16	21	37	24	2	1	0

Czechoslovakian First All-Star Team (1992) • Played in NHL All-Star Game (1999)

Traded to **Ottawa** by **Pittsburgh** for Troy Murray and Norm Maciver, April 7, 1995. Traded to **NY Islanders** by **Ottawa** with Don Beaupre and Bryan Berard for Damian Rhodes and Wade Redden, January 23, 1996. Claimed on waivers by **Florida** from **NY Islanders**, March 15, 1996. Signed as a free agent by **Pittsburgh**, August 6, 1997.

• STRATTON, Art

Arthur C/LW – L. 5'11", 170 lbs. b: Winnipeg, Man., 10/8/1935.

Season	Club	League	GP	G	A	Pts	AG	AA	APts	PIM	PP	SH	GW	S	%	TGF	PGF	TGA	PGA	+/-	GP	G	A	Pts	PIM	PP	SH	GW
1953-54	Winnipeg Barons	MJHL	36	17	28	45	....	....	....	39	....	....	....	....	....	....	....	....	....	....	6	0	5	5	0	....	....	....
1954-55	Winnipeg Barons	MJHL	32	*50	26	*76	....	....	....	39	....	....	....	....	....	....	....	....	....	....	5	3	3	6	0	....	....	....
	Warroad Lakers	OMSHL	STATISTICS NOT AVAILABLE																									
1955-56	St. Catharines Teepees	OHA-Jr.	48	37	42	79	....	....	....	49	....	....	....	....	....	....	....	....	....	....	6	1	3	4	17	....	....	....
	Cleveland Barons	AHL	1	0	0	0	....	....	....	0	....	....	....	....	....	....	....	....	....	....	1	0	1	1	2	....	....	....
1956-57	North Bay Trappers	NOHA	60	29	34	63	....	....	....	23	....	....	....	....	....	....	....	....	....	....	13	5	8	13	12	....	....	....
1957-58	Winnipeg Warriors	WHL	70	23	53	76	....	....	....	12	....	....	....	....	....	....	....	....	....	....	7	4	1	5	4	....	....	....
1958-59	Cleveland Barons	AHL	62	29	47	76	....	....	....	40	....	....	....	....	....	....	....	....	....	....	7	1	3	4	2	....	....	....
1959-60	New York Rangers	NHL	18	2	5	7	2	5	7	2	....	....	....	....	....	....	....	....	....	....	....	....	....	....	....	....	....	....
	Springfield Indians	AHL	46	12	44	56	....	....	....	29	....	....	....	....	....	....	....	....	....	....	....	....	....	....	....	....	....	....
1960-61	Springfield Indians	AHL	48	16	41	57	....	....	....	16	....	....	....	....	....	....	....	....	....	....	....	....	....	....	....	....	....	....
	Kitchener-Waterloo Beavers	EPHL	16	7	5	12	....	....	....	4	....	....	....	....	....	....	....	....	....	....	7	0	2	2	0	....	....	....
1961-62	Buffalo Bisons	AHL	63	15	24	39	....	....	....	52	....	....	....	....	....	....	....	....	....	....	6	1	3	4	2	....	....	....
1962-63	Buffalo Bisons	AHL	70	20	*70	90	....	....	....	18	....	....	....	....	....	....	....	....	....	....	13	4	*15	19	2	....	....	....
1963-64	Detroit Red Wings	NHL	5	0	3	3	0	3	3	2	....	....	....	....	....	....	....	....	....	....	....	....	....	....	....	....	....	....
	Pittsburgh Hornets	AHL	66	17	*65	82	....	....	....	29	....	....	....	....	....	....	....	....	....	....	5	0	2	2	4	....	....	....
1964-65	Buffalo Bisons	AHL	71	25	*84	*109	....	....	....	32	....	....	....	....	....	....	....	....	....	....	9	1	5	6	4	....	....	....
1965-66	Chicago Black Hawks	NHL	2	0	0	0	0	0	0	0	....	....	....	....	....	....	....	....	....	....	....	....	....	....	....	....	....	....
	St. Louis Braves	CPHL	66	28	*66	*94	....	....	....	14	....	....	....	....	....	....	....	....	....	....	5	0	1	1	2	....	....	....
1966-67	St. Louis Braves	CPHL	67	34	56	*90	....	....	....	46	....	....	....	....	....	....	....	....	....	....	....	....	....	....	....	....	....	....
1967-68	Pittsburgh Penguins	NHL	58	16	21	37	19	21	40	16	5	0	2	105	15.2	44	10	42	2	-6	....	....	....	....	....	....	....	....
	Philadelphia Flyers	NHL	12	0	4	4	0	4	4	4	0	0	0	18	0.0	5	3	6	0	-4	5	0	0	0	0	0	0	0
1968-69	Seattle Totems	WHL	66	15	44	59	....	....	....	58	....	....	....	....	....	....	....	....	....	....	4	0	0	0	4	....	....	....

			REGULAR SEASON																		PLAYOFFS							
Season	Club	League	GP	G	A	Pts	AG	AA	APts	PIM	PP	SH	GW	S	%	TGF	PGF	TGA	PGA	+/–	GP	G	A	Pts	PIM	PP	SH	GW
1969-70	Seattle Totems	WHL	59	24	55	79	....	....	....	22	....	....	....	....	....	....	....	....	....	....	....	....	....	....	....	....	....	....
1970-71	Seattle Totems	WHL	71	17	31	48	....	....	....	40	....	....	....	....	....	....	....	....	....	....	....	....	....	....	....	....	....	....
1971-72	Seattle Totems	WHL	11	1	6	7	....	....	....	6	....	....	....	....	....	....	....	....	....	....	....	....	....	....	....	....	....	....
	Tidewater Red Wings	AHL	61	15	41	56	....	....	....	54	....	....	....	....	....	....	....	....	....	....	....	....	....	....	....	....	....	....
1972-73	Tidewater Red Wings	AHL	76	30	50	80	....	....	....	32	....	....	....	....	....	....	....	....	....	....	12	4	4	8	0	....	....	....
1973-74	Rochester Americans	AHL	76	24	*71	95	....	....	....	118	....	....	....	....	....	....	....	....	....	....	6	2	6	8	4	....	....	....
1974-75	Richmond Robins	AHL	29	8	18	26	....	....	....	10	....	....	....	....	....	....	....	....	....	....	7	1	2	3	10	....	....	....
1975-76	Hampton Gulls	SHL	70	14	64	78	....	....	....	112	....	....	....	....	....	....	....	....	....	....	9	2	3	5	2	....	....	....
	NHL Totals		**95**	**18**	**33**	**51**	**21**	**33**	**54**	**24**	....	....	....	....	....	....	....	....	....	....	**5**	**0**	**0**	**0**	**0**	....	....	....

NOHA Rookie of the Year (1957) • Won WHL Prairie Division Rookie of the Year Award (1958) • AHL First All-Star Team (1963, 1964, 1965) • Won Les Cunningham Award (MVP - AHL) (1965, 1974) • Won John B. Sollenberger Trophy (Top Scorer - AHL) (1965) • CPHL First All-Star Team (1966, 1967) • Won Tommy Ivan Trophy (MVP - CPHL) (1966, 1967) • AHL Second All-Star Team (1974) • SHL Second All-Star Team (1976) • Named SHL's MVP (1976)

Traded to **NY Rangers** by **Cleveland** (AHL) for Aldo Guidolin and Ed Hoekstra with NY Rangers holding right of recall, June, 1959. Traded to **Chicago** (Buffalo-AHL) by **NY Rangers** for cash, September, 1961. Claimed by **Detroit** from **Chicago** (Buffalo-AHL) in Inter-League Draft, June 4, 1963. Traded to **Chicago** by **Detroit** with Ian Cushenan and John Miszuk for Ron Murphy and Aut Erickson, June 9, 1964. Claimed by **Pittsburgh** from **Chicago** in Expansion Draft, June 6, 1967. Traded to **Philadelphia** by **Pittsburgh** for Wayne Hicks, February 27, 1968. Traded to **Seattle** (WHL) by **Philadelphia** with John Hanna to complete transaction that sent Earl Heiskala to Philadelphia (May 19, 1968), June, 1968. Traded to **Detroit** by **Seattle** (WHL) for Bob Sneddon, November, 1971. Claimed by **Rochester** (AHL) from **Detroit** in Reverse Draft, June, 1973.

• STRONG, Ken

LW – L. 5'11", 185 lbs. b: Toronto, Ont., 5/9/1963. Philadelphia's 4th, 58th overall, in 1981.

Season	Club	League	GP	G	A	Pts	AG	AA	APts	PIM	PP	SH	GW	S	%	TGF	PGF	TGA	PGA	+/–	GP	G	A	Pts	PIM	PP	SH	GW
1979-80	Mississagua Reps	MTHL	STATISTICS NOT AVAILABLE																									
	Streetsville Derbys	OJHL-B	36	21	24	45	....	....	....	125	....	....	....	....	....	....	....	....	....	....	....	....	....	....	....	....	....	....
1980-81	Peterborough Petes	OMJHL	64	17	36	53	....	....	....	52	....	....	....	....	....	....	....	....	....	....	5	2	1	3	18	....	....	....
1981-82	Peterborough Petes	OHL	42	21	22	43	....	....	....	69	....	....	....	....	....	....	....	....	....	....	9	8	11	19	23	....	....	....
1982-83	Peterborough Petes	OHL	57	41	48	89	....	....	....	80	....	....	....	....	....	....	....	....	....	....	4	2	2	4	4	....	....	....
	Toronto Maple Leafs	**NHL**	**2**	**0**	**0**	**0**	**0**	**0**	**0**	**0**	**0**	**0**	**0**	**2**	**0.0**	**0**	**0**	**0**	**0**	**0**	....	....	....	....	....	....	....	....
1983-84	**Toronto Maple Leafs**	**NHL**	**2**	**0**	**2**	**2**	**0**	**1**	**1**	**2**	**0**	**0**	**0**	**3**	**0.0**	**2**	**0**	**4**	**2**	**0**	....	....	....	....	....	....	....	....
	St. Catharines Saints	AHL	78	27	45	72	....	....	....	78	....	....	....	....	....	....	....	....	....	....	7	3	3	6	4	....	....	....
1984-85	**Toronto Maple Leafs**	**NHL**	**11**	**2**	**0**	**2**	**2**	**0**	**2**	**4**	**0**	**0**	**0**	**19**	**10.5**	**3**	**0**	**8**	**2**	**–3**	....	....	....	....	....	....	....	....
	St. Catharines Saints	AHL	45	15	19	34	....	....	....	41	....	....	....	....	....	....	....	....	....	....	....	....	....	....	....	....	....	....
1985-86	St. Catharines Saints	AHL	33	16	25	41	....	....	....	14	....	....	....	....	....	....	....	....	....	....	3	0	1	1	0	....	....	....
1986-87	Adirondack Red Wings	AHL	31	7	13	20	....	....	....	18	....	....	....	....	....	....	....	....	....	....	11	6	7	13	12	....	....	....
	EHC Chur	Switz.	....	9	5	14	....	....	....	....	....	....	....	....	....	....	....	....	....	....	....	....	....	....	....	....	....	....
1987-88	VSV Villach	Austria	22	29	25	54	....	....	....	....	....	....	....	....	....	....	....	....	....	....	....	....	....	....	....	....	....	....
1988-89	VSV Villach	Austria	46	42	*57	*99	....	....	....	....	....	....	....	....	....	....	....	....	....	....	....	....	....	....	....	....	....	....
1989-90	VSV Villach	Austria	37	32	45	77	....	....	....	52	....	....	....	....	....	....	....	....	....	....	....	....	....	....	....	....	....	....
1990-91	VSV Villach	Austria	43	*40	42	82	....	....	....	111	....	....	....	....	....	....	....	....	....	....	....	....	....	....	....	....	....	....
1991-92	VSV Villach	Alpenliga	18	18	13	31	....	....	....	20	....	....	....	....	....	....	....	....	....	....	....	....	....	....	....	....	....	....
	VSV Villach	Austria	18	18	13	31	....	....	....	27	....	....	....	....	....	....	....	....	....	....	26	30	28	58	57	....	....	....
	Austria	WC-B	2	4	4	8	....	....	....	0	....	....	....	....	....	....	....	....	....	....	....	....	....	....	....	....	....	....
1992-93	VSV Villach	Alpenliga	24	17	23	40	....	....	....	26	....	....	....	....	....	....	....	....	....	....	....	....	....	....	....	....	....	....
	VSV Villach	Austria	....	....	....	....	....	....	....	....	....	....	....	....	....	....	....	....	....	....	22	17	11	28	12	....	....	....
1993-94	VSV Villach	Alpenliga	25	20	21	41	....	....	....	18	....	....	....	....	....	....	....	....	....	....	....	....	....	....	....	....	....	....
	VSV Villach	Austria	....	....	....	....	....	....	....	....	....	....	....	....	....	....	....	....	....	....	23	13	21	34	....	....	....	....
	Austria	Olympics	7	3	1	4	....	....	....	12	....	....	....	....	....	....	....	....	....	....	....	....	....	....	....	....	....	....
	Austria	WC-A	6	2	0	2	....	....	....	8	....	....	....	....	....	....	....	....	....	....	....	....	....	....	....	....	....	....
1994-95	HC Gardena-Groden	EuroHL	8	2	5	7	....	....	....	8	....	....	....	....	....	....	....	....	....	....	....	....	....	....	....	....	....	....
	HC Gardena-Groden	Italy	28	15	24	39	....	....	....	26	....	....	....	....	....	....	....	....	....	....	....	....	....	....	....	....	....	....
	Austria	WC-A	7	0	1	1	....	....	....	4	....	....	....	....	....	....	....	....	....	....	....	....	....	....	....	....	....	....
1995-96	VSV Villach	Alpenliga	10	12	7	19	....	....	....	34	....	....	....	....	....	....	....	....	....	....	....	....	....	....	....	....	....	....
	VSV Villach	Austria	33	23	23	46	....	....	....	65	....	....	....	....	....	....	....	....	....	....	....	....	....	....	....	....	....	....
1996-97	EC Kafenberg	Alpenliga	35	21	14	35	....	....	....	52	....	....	....	....	....	....	....	....	....	....	....	....	....	....	....	....	....	....
	EC Kafenberg	Austria	43	25	17	42	....	....	....	70	....	....	....	....	....	....	....	....	....	....	....	....	....	....	....	....	....	....
	NHL Totals		**15**	**2**	**2**	**4**	**2**	**1**	**3**	**6**	**0**	**0**	**0**	**24**	**8.3**	**5**	**0**	**12**	**4**		....	....	....	....	....	....	....	....

Traded to **Toronto** by **Philadelphia** to complete transaction that sent Darryl Sittler to Philadelphia, January 20, 1982.

• STRUCH, David

C – L. 5'10", 180 lbs. b: Flin Flon, Man., 2/11/1971. Calgary's 11th, 195th overall, in 1991.

Season	Club	League	GP	G	A	Pts	AG	AA	APts	PIM	PP	SH	GW	S	%	TGF	PGF	TGA	PGA	+/–	GP	G	A	Pts	PIM	PP	SH	GW
1988-89	Saskatoon Blades	WHL	66	20	31	51	....	....	....	18	....	....	....	....	....	....	....	....	....	....	8	2	3	5	6	....	....	....
	Saskatoon Blades	Mem-Cup	4	0	1	1	....	....	....	4	....	....	....	....	....	....	....	....	....	....	....	....	....	....	....	....	....	....
1989-90	Saskatoon Blades	WHL	68	40	37	77	....	....	....	67	....	....	....	....	....	....	....	....	....	....	10	8	5	13	6	....	....	....
1990-91	Saskatoon Blades	WHL	72	45	57	102	....	....	....	69	....	....	....	....	....	....	....	....	....	....	....	....	....	....	....	....	....	....
1991-92	Saskatoon Blades	WHL	47	29	26	55	....	....	....	34	....	....	....	....	....	....	....	....	....	....	22	8	15	23	26	....	....	....
	Salt Lake Golden Eagles	IHL	12	4	1	5	....	....	....	8	....	....	....	....	....	....	....	....	....	....	....	....	....	....	....	....	....	....
1992-93	Salt Lake Golden Eagles	IHL	78	20	22	42	....	....	....	73	....	....	....	....	....	....	....	....	....	....	....	....	....	....	....	....	....	....
1993-94	**Calgary Flames**	**NHL**	**4**	**0**	**0**	**0**	**0**	**0**	**0**	**4**	**0**	**0**	**0**	**3**	**0.0**	**2**	**0**	**4**	**0**	**–2**	....	....	....	....	....	....	....	....
	Saint John Flames	AHL	58	18	25	43	....	....	....	87	....	....	....	....	....	....	....	....	....	....	7	0	1	1	4	....	....	....
1994-95	Saint John Flames	AHL	7	0	1	1	....	....	....	4	....	....	....	....	....	....	....	....	....	....	....	....	....	....	....	....	....	....
1995-96	Saint John Flames	AHL	45	10	15	25	....	....	....	57	....	....	....	....	....	....	....	....	....	....	3	0	1	1	4	....	....	....
1996-97	Waco Wizards	WPHL	11	4	7	11	....	....	....	0	....	....	....	....	....	....	....	....	....	....	....	....	....	....	....	....	....	....
	EC Graz	Austria	26	6	16	22	....	....	....	18	....	....	....	....	....	....	....	....	....	....	....	....	....	....	....	....	....	....
1997-98	SG Cortina-Milano	Italy	44	24	37	61	....	....	....	34	....	....	....	....	....	....	....	....	....	....	....	....	....	....	....	....	....	....
1998-99	SG Cortina-Milano	Alpenliga	30	9	10	19	....	....	....	38	....	....	....	....	....	....	....	....	....	....	....	....	....	....	....	....	....	....
	SG Cortina-Milano	Italy	24	7	4	11	....	....	....	16	....	....	....	....	....	....	....	....	....	....	....	....	....	....	....	....	....	....
99-2000	Nottingham Panthers	BH-Cup	9	3	6	9	....	....	....	8	....	....	....	....	....	....	....	....	....	....	....	....	....	....	....	....	....	....
	Nottingham Panthers	Britain	42	8	16	24	....	....	....	22	....	....	....	....	....	....	....	....	....	....	6	1	0	1	0	....	....	....
	NHL Totals		**4**	**0**	**0**	**0**	**0**	**0**	**0**	**4**	**0**	**0**	**0**	**3**	**0.0**	**2**	**0**	**4**	**0**		....	....	....	....	....	....	....	....

• STRUDWICK, Jason

D – L. 6'3", 215 lbs. b: Edmonton, Alta., 7/17/1975. NY Islanders' 3rd, 63rd overall, in 1994.

Season	Club	League	GP	G	A	Pts	AG	AA	APts	PIM	PP	SH	GW	S	%	TGF	PGF	TGA	PGA	+/–	GP	G	A	Pts	PIM	PP	SH	GW
1991-92	Edmonton Pat Canadians	AAHA	35	3	8	11	....	....	....	67	....	....	....	....	....	....	....	....	....	....	....	....	....	....	....	....	....	....
1992-93	Edmonton Legionaires	AAHA	33	8	20	28	....	....	....	135	....	....	....	....	....	....	....	....	....	....	....	....	....	....	....	....	....	....
1993-94	Kamloops Blazers	WHL	61	6	8	14	....	....	....	118	....	....	....	....	....	....	....	....	....	....	19	0	4	4	24	....	....	....
	Kamloops Blazers	Mem-Cup	4	0	0	0	....	....	....	4	....	....	....	....	....	....	....	....	....	....	....	....	....	....	....	....	....	....
1994-95	Kamloops Blazers	WHL	72	3	11	14	....	....	....	183	....	....	....	....	....	....	....	....	....	....	21	1	1	2	39	....	....	....
	Kamloops Blazers	Mem-Cup	4	0	1	1	....	....	....	8	....	....	....	....	....	....	....	....	....	....	....	....	....	....	....	....	....	....
1995-96	**New York Islanders**	**NHL**	**1**	**0**	**0**	**0**	**0**	**0**	**0**	**7**	**0**	**0**	**0**	**0**	**0.0**	**0**	**0**	**0**	**0**	**0**	....	....	....	....	....	....	....	....
	Worcester IceCats	AHL	60	2	7	9	....	....	....	119	....	....	....	....	....	....	....	....	....	....	4	0	1	1	0	....	....	....
1996-97	Kentucky Thoroughblades	AHL	80	1	9	10	....	....	....	198	....	....	....	....	....	....	....	....	....	....	4	0	0	0	0	....	....	....
1997-98	**New York Islanders**	**NHL**	**17**	**0**	**1**	**1**	**0**	**1**	**1**	**36**	**0**	**0**	**0**	**3**	**0.0**	**4**	**0**	**3**	**0**	**1**	....	....	....	....	....	....	....	....
	Kentucky Thoroughblades	AHL	39	3	1	4	....	....	....	87	....	....	....	....	....	....	....	....	....	....	....	....	....	....	....	....	....	....
	Vancouver Canucks	**NHL**	**11**	**0**	**1**	**1**	**0**	**1**	**1**	**29**	**0**	**0**	**0**	**5**	**0.0**	**4**	**0**	**11**	**4**	**–3**	....	....	....	....	....	....	....	....
	Syracuse Crunch	AHL	....	....	....	....	....	....	....	....	....	....	....	....	....	....	....	....	....	....	3	0	0	0	6	....	....	....
1998-99	**Vancouver Canucks**	**NHL**	**65**	**0**	**3**	**3**	**0**	**3**	**3**	**114**	**0**	**0**	**0**	**25**	**0.0**	**17**	**1**	**42**	**7**	**–19**	....	....	....	....	....	....	....	....
99-2000	**Vancouver Canucks**	**NHL**	**63**	**1**	**3**	**4**	**1**	**3**	**4**	**64**	**0**	**0**	**0**	**18**	**5.6**	**30**	**0**	**59**	**16**	**–13**	....	....	....	....	....	....	....	....
	NHL Totals		**157**	**1**	**8**	**9**	**1**	**8**	**9**	**250**	**0**	**0**	**0**	**51**	**2.0**	**55**	**1**	**115**	**27**		....	....	....	....	....	....	....	....

Traded to **Vancouver** by **NY Islanders** for Gino Odjick, March 23, 1998.

			REGULAR SEASON																		PLAYOFFS							
Season	Club	League	GP	G	A	Pts	AG	AA	APts	PIM	PP	SH	GW	S	%	TGF	PGF	TGA	PGA	+/–	GP	G	A	Pts	PIM	PP	SH	GW

• STRUEBY, Todd

Todd Kenneth LW – L. 6'1", 185 lbs. b: Lannigan, Sask., 6/15/1963. Edmonton's 2nd, 29th overall, in 1981.

Season	Club	League	GP	G	A	Pts	AG	AA	APts	PIM	PP	SH	GW	S	%	TGF	PGF	TGA	PGA	+/–	GP	G	A	Pts	PIM	PP	SH	GW
1979-80	Notre Damet Midget Hounds	SAHA	58	44	61	105				112																		
1980-81	Regina Pats	WHL	71	18	27	45				99											11	3	6	9	19			
1981-82	Saskatoon Blades	WHL	61	60	58	118				160											5	2	2	4	6			
	Canada	WJC-A	7	0	5	5				4																		
	Edmonton Oilers	NHL	3	0	0	0	0	0	0	0	0	0	0	1	0.0	0	0	0	0	0								
1982-83	Saskatoon Blades	WHL	65	40	70	110				119											6	3	3	6	19			
	Edmonton Oilers	NHL	1	0	0	0	0	0	0	0	0	0	0	1	0.0	0	0	2	0	–2								
1983-84	Edmonton Oilers	NHL	1	0	1	1	0	1	1	2	0	0	0	1	0.0	2	0	0	0	2								
	Moncton Alpines	AHL	72	17	25	42				38																		
1984-85	Nova Scotia Voyageurs	AHL	38	2	3	5				29																		
	Muskegon Mohawks	IHL	27	19	12	31				55											17	4	10	14	27			
1985-86	Muskegon Lumberjacks	IHL	58	25	40	65				191											14	7	5	12	51			
1986-87	Muskegon Lumberjacks	IHL	82	28	41	69				208											13	4	6	10	53			
1987-88	Fort Wayne Komets	IHL	68	29	27	56				211											4	0	0	0	14			
1988-89	Canada	Nat-Team	61	18	20	38				112																		
1989-90	EHC Freiburg	Germany	25	13	12	25				76											15	12	9	21	*50			
	Canada	Nat-Team	15	12	3	15				35																		
1990-91	EHC Freiburg	Germany	7	0	3	3				10																		
	Canada	Nat-Team	31	12	13	25				49																		
1991-92	Salt Lake Golden Eagles	IHL	61	15	16	31				72											3	1	0	1	6			
1992-93	REV Bremerhaven	Germany-3	28	35	28	63																						
	Canada	Nat-Team	4	3	1	4				0																		
1993-1999			OUT OF HOCKEY – RETIRED																									
99-2000	Regina Crestview Rangers	X-Games	2	1	1	2				4																		
	Regina Crestview Rangers	Al-Cup	3	0	1	1				8																		
	NHL Totals		5	0	1	1	0	1	1	2	0	0	0	3	0.0	2	0	2	0									

WHL First All-Star Team (1982) • WHL Second All-Star Team (1983)

Traded to **NY Rangers** by **Edmonton** with Larry Melnyk for Mike Rogers, December 20, 1985.

• STUART, Brad

Brad William D – L. 6'2", 210 lbs. b: Rocky Mountain House, Alta., 11/6/1979. San Jose's 1st, 3rd overall, in 1998.

Season	Club	League	GP	G	A	Pts	AG	AA	APts	PIM	PP	SH	GW	S	%	TGF	PGF	TGA	PGA	+/–	GP	G	A	Pts	PIM	PP	SH	GW
1995-96	Red Deer Chiefs	AAHA	35	12	25	37				83																		
	Regina Pats	WHL	3	0	0	0				0																		
1996-97	Regina Pats	WHL	57	7	36	43				58											5	0	4	4	14			
1997-98	Regina Pats	WHL	72	20	45	65				82											9	3	4	7	10			
1998-99	Regina Pats	WHL	29	10	19	29				43																		
	Canada	WJC-A	7	0	1	1				2																		
	Calgary Hitmen	WHL	30	11	22	33				26											21	8	15	23	59			
	Calgary Hitmen	Mem-Cup	2	0	2	2				8																		
99-2000	San Jose Sharks	NHL	82	10	26	36	11	24	35	32	5	1	3	133	7.5	94	34	72	15	3	12	1	0	1	6	1	0	0
	NHL Totals		82	10	26	36	11	24	35	32	5	1	3	133	7.5	94	34	72	15		12	1	0	1	6	1	0	0

WHL East Second All-Star Team (1998) • WHL East First All-Star Team (1999) • Canadian Major Junior First All-Star Team (1999) • Canadian Major Junior Defenseman of the Year (1999) • NHL All-Rookie Team (2000)

• STUMPEL, Jozef

"Stumpy" C – R. 6'3", 225 lbs. b: Nitra, Czech., 7/20/1972. Boston's 2nd, 40th overall, in 1991.

Season	Club	League	GP	G	A	Pts	AG	AA	APts	PIM	PP	SH	GW	S	%	TGF	PGF	TGA	PGA	+/–	GP	G	A	Pts	PIM	PP	SH	GW
1989-90	AC Nitra	Czech-2	38	12	11	23																						
	Czechoslovakia	EJC-A	6	1	3	4				4																		
1990-91	AC Nitra	Czech.	49	23	22	45				14																		
	Czechoslovakia	WJC-A	7	4	4	8				2																		
1991-92	Kolner EC	Germany	33	19	18	37				35											4	1	1	2	0			
	Boston Bruins	NHL	4	1	0	1	1	0	1	0	0	0	0	3	33.3	2	0	1	0	1								
1992-93	Boston Bruins	NHL	13	1	3	4	1	2	3	4	0	0	0	8	12.5	4	0	7	0	–3								
	Providence Bruins	AHL	56	31	61	92				26											6	4	4	8	0			
1993-94	Boston Bruins	NHL	59	8	15	23	7	12	19	14	0	0	1	62	12.9	30	8	19	1	4	13	1	7	8	4	0	0	0
	Providence Bruins	AHL	17	5	12	17				4																		
1994-95	Kolner EC	Germany	25	16	23	39				18																		
	Boston Bruins	NHL	44	5	13	18	9	19	28	8	1	0	2	46	10.9	34	10	22	2	4	5	0	0	0	0	0	0	0
1995-96	Boston Bruins	NHL	76	18	36	54	18	30	48	14	5	0	2	158	11.4	75	30	53	0	–8	5	1	2	3	0	0	0	0
1996-97	Slovakia	W-Cup	3	0	0	0				0																		
	Boston Bruins	NHL	78	21	55	76	22	49	71	14	6	0	1	168	12.5	95	29	89	1	–22								
	Slovakia	WC-A	8	2	1	3				4																		
1997-98	Los Angeles Kings	NHL	77	21	58	79	25	57	82	53	4	0	2	162	13.0	99	31	64	13	17	4	1	2	3	2	0	0	0
	Slovakia	WC-A	4	1	2	3				6																		
1998-99	Los Angeles Kings	NHL	64	13	21	34	15	20	35	10	1	0	1	131	9.9	49	15	69	17	–18								
99-2000	Los Angeles Kings	NHL	57	17	41	58	19	38	57	10	3	0	7	126	13.5	93	34	38	2	23	4	0	4	4	8	0	0	0
	NHL Totals		472	105	242	347	117	227	344	127	20	0	16	864	12.2	481	157	362	36		31	3	15	18	14	0	0	0

Traded to **LA Kings** by **Boston** with Sandy Moger and Boston's 4th round choice (later traded to New Jersey — New Jersey selected Pierre Dagenais) in 1998 Entry Draft for Dimitri Kristich and Byron Dafoe, August 29, 1997.

• STUMPF, Bob

RW/D – R. 6'1", 195 lbs. b: Milo, Alta., 4/25/1953. Philadelphia's 3rd, 40th overall, in 1973.

Season	Club	League	GP	G	A	Pts	AG	AA	APts	PIM	PP	SH	GW	S	%	TGF	PGF	TGA	PGA	+/–	GP	G	A	Pts	PIM	PP	SH	GW
1968-69	Red Deer Rustlers	AJHL	....	1	8	9				11																		
1969-70	Red Deer Rustlers	AJHL	37	13	16	29				138																		
1970-71	Estevan Bruins	WCJHL	64	3	28	31				174											4	1	1	2	0			
1971-72	New Westminster Bruins	WCJHL	66	7	43	50				226											5	0	3	3	4			
1972-73	New Westminster Bruins	WCJHL	46	19	43	62				93											3	4	2	6	28			
1973-74	Richmond Robins	AHL	6	0	4	4				6																		
	Denver Spurs	WHL	67	18	20	38				85																		
1974-75	Denver Spurs	CHL	34	3	14	17				72																		
	St. Louis Blues	NHL	7	1	1	2	1	1	2	16	0	0	0	8	12.5	8	0	11	5	2								
	Pittsburgh Penguins	NHL	3	0	0	0	0	0	0	4	0	0	0	1	0.0	1	0	5	0	–4								
	Hershey Bears	AHL	17	2	4	6				18																		
1975-76	Hershey Bears	AHL	69	2	22	24				128											10	1	2	3	4			
	NHL Totals		10	1	1	2	1	1	2	20	0	0	0	9	11.1	9	0	16	5									

Traded to **St. Louis** by **Philadelphia** for George Pesut, November, 1973. Traded to **Pittsburgh** by **St. Louis** for Bernie Lukowich, January 20, 1975.

• STURGEON, Peter

LW – L. 6'2", 198 lbs. b: Whitehorse, Yukon, 2/12/1954. Boston's 3rd, 36th overall, in 1974.

Season	Club	League	GP	G	A	Pts	AG	AA	APts	PIM	PP	SH	GW	S	%	TGF	PGF	TGA	PGA	+/–	GP	G	A	Pts	PIM	PP	SH	GW
1971-72	Chatham Maroons	OHA-B	STATISTICS NOT AVAILABLE																									
	Kitchener Rangers	OMJHL	26	1	5	6				8											2	1	0	1	0			
1972-73	Chatham Maroons	OHA-B	48	41	33	74				44																		
	Kitchener Rangers	OMJHL	5	1	1	2				0																		
1973-74	Kitchener Rangers	OMJHL	70	39	48	87				42																		
1974-75	Rochester Americans	AHL	32	6	11	17				19																		
1975-76	Baltimore Clippers	AHL	4	0	1	1				7																		
	Rochester Americans	AHL	1	0	0	0				0																		
	Binghamton Dusters	NAHL	67	18	15	33				62																		
1976-77	Columbus Owls	IHL	48	16	13	29				55											7	1	1	2	24			

			REGULAR SEASON																		PLAYOFFS							
Season	Club	League	GP	G	A	Pts	AG	AA	APts	PIM	PP	SH	GW	S	%	TGF	PGF	TGA	PGA	+/–	GP	G	A	Pts	PIM	PP	SH	GW
1977-78	Rochester Americans	AHL	12	0	1	1	....	....	....	21	....	....	....	....	....	....	....	....	....	....	....	....	....	....	....	....	....	....
	Dayton-Grand Rapids	IHL	6	2	1	3	....	....	....	24	....	....	....	....	....	....	....	....	....	....	....	....	....	....	....	....	....	....
	Phoenix Roadrunners	PHL	42	12	14	26	....	....	....	13	....	....	....	....	....	....	....	....	....	....	....	....	....	....	....	....	....	....
1978-79	Grand Rapids Owls	IHL	6	2	1	3	....	....	....	34	....	....	....	....	....	....	....	....	....	....	....	....	....	....	....	....	....	....
1979-80	**Colorado Rockies**	**NHL**	**2**	**0**	**0**	**0**	**0**	**0**	**0**	**0**	**0**	**0**	**0**	**1**	**0.0**	**0**	**0**	**0**	**0**	**0**	....	....	....	....	....	....	....	....
	Fort Worth Texans	CHL	22	8	12	20	....	....	....	10	....	....	....	....	....	....	....	....	....	....	15	2	6	8	6	....	....	....
1980-81	**Colorado Rockies**	**NHL**	**4**	**0**	**1**	**1**	**0**	**1**	**1**	**2**	**0**	**0**	**0**	**4**	**0.0**	**1**	**0**	**1**	**0**	**0**	....	....	....	....	....	....	....	....
	Fort Worth Texans	CHL	52	5	14	19	....	....	....	21	....	....	....	....	....	....	....	....	....	....	....	....	....	....	....	....	....	....
1981-82	Georgetown Raiders	OHA-Sr.	34	36	55	91	....	....	....	....	....	....	....	....	....	....	....	....	....	....	....	....	....	....	....	....	....	....
	NHL Totals		**6**	**0**	**1**	**1**	**0**	**1**	**1**	**2**	**0**	**0**	**0**	**5**	**0.0**	**1**	**0**	**1**	**0**		....	....	....	....	....	....	....	....

Signed as a free agent by **Colorado**, July 10, 1979.

• STURM, Marco

Marco Johann C – L. 6', 195 lbs. b: Dingolfing, Germany, 9/8/1978. San Jose's 2nd, 21st overall, in 1996.

Season	Club	League	GP	G	A	Pts	AG	AA	APts	PIM	PP	SH	GW	S	%	TGF	PGF	TGA	PGA	+/–	GP	G	A	Pts	PIM	PP	SH	GW
1994-95	EV Landshut	German-Jr.	STATISTICS NOT AVAILABLE																									
	Germany	WJC-A	7	0	0	0	....	....	....	6	....	....	....	....	....	....	....	....	....	....	....	....	....	....	....	....	....	....
	Germany	EJC-A	5	2	3	5	....	....	....	2	....	....	....	....	....	....	....	....	....	....	....	....	....	....	....	....	....	....
1995-96	EV Landshut	Germany	47	12	20	32	....	....	....	50	....	....	....	....	....	....	....	....	....	....	11	1	3	4	18	....	....	....
	Germany	WJC-A	6	4	6	10	....	....	....	51	....	....	....	....	....	....	....	....	....	....	....	....	....	....	....	....	....	....
	Germany	EJC-A	5	5	6	11	....	....	....	8	....	....	....	....	....	....	....	....	....	....	....	....	....	....	....	....	....	....
1996-97	EV Landshut	Germany	46	16	27	43	....	....	....	40	....	....	....	....	....	....	....	....	....	....	7	1	4	5	6	....	....	....
	Germany	WC-A	8	1	1	2	....	....	....	4	....	....	....	....	....	....	....	....	....	....	....	....	....	....	....	....	....	....
1997-98	**San Jose Sharks**	**NHL**	**74**	**10**	**20**	**30**	**12**	**20**	**32**	**40**	**2**	**0**	**3**	**118**	**8.5**	**52**	**16**	**44**	**6**	**–2**	**2**	**0**	**0**	**0**	**0**	**0**	**0**	**0**
	Germany	Olympics	2	0	0	0	....	....	....	0	....	....	....	....	....	....	....	....	....	....	....	....	....	....	....	....	....	....
1998-99	**San Jose Sharks**	**NHL**	**78**	**16**	**22**	**38**	**19**	**21**	**40**	**52**	**3**	**2**	**3**	**140**	**11.4**	**51**	**15**	**49**	**20**	**7**	**6**	**2**	**2**	**4**	**4**	**0**	**0**	**1**
99-2000	**San Jose Sharks**	**NHL**	**74**	**12**	**15**	**27**	**13**	**14**	**27**	**22**	**2**	**4**	**3**	**120**	**10.0**	**40**	**4**	**42**	**10**	**4**	**12**	**1**	**3**	**4**	**6**	**0**	**0**	**0**
	NHL Totals		**226**	**38**	**57**	**95**	**44**	**55**	**99**	**114**	**7**	**6**	**9**	**378**	**10.1**	**143**	**35**	**135**	**36**		**20**	**3**	**5**	**8**	**10**	**0**	**0**	**1**

Played in NHL All-Star Game (1999)

• SUCHY, Radoslav

D – L. 6'1", 185 lbs. b: Kezmarok, Czech., 4/7/1976.

Season	Club	League	GP	G	A	Pts	AG	AA	APts	PIM	PP	SH	GW	S	%	TGF	PGF	TGA	PGA	+/–	GP	G	A	Pts	PIM	PP	SH	GW
1993-94	SKP Poprad	Slovakia-Jr.	30	11	12	23	....	....	....	16	....	....	....	....	....	....	....	....	....	....	....	....	....	....	....	....	....	....
	SKP Poprad	Slovakia	3	0	0	0	....	....	....	0	....	....	....	....	....	....	....	....	....	....	....	....	....	....	....	....	....	....
1994-95	Sherbrooke Faucons	QMJHL	69	12	32	44	....	....	....	30	....	....	....	....	....	....	....	....	....	....	7	0	3	3	2	....	....	....
1995-96	Sherbrooke Faucons	QMJHL	68	15	53	68	....	....	....	68	....	....	....	....	....	....	....	....	....	....	7	0	3	3	2	....	....	....
1996-97	Sherbrooke Faucons	QMJHL	32	6	34	40	....	....	....	14	....	....	....	....	....	....	....	....	....	....	....	....	....	....	....	....	....	....
	Chicoutimi Sagueneens	QMJHL	28	5	24	29	....	....	....	26	....	....	....	....	....	....	....	....	....	....	19	6	15	21	12	....	....	....
1997-98	Las Vegas Thunder	IHL	26	1	4	5	....	....	....	10	....	....	....	....	....	....	....	....	....	....	....	....	....	....	....	....	....	....
	Springfield Falcons	AHL	41	6	15	21	....	....	....	16	....	....	....	....	....	....	....	....	....	....	4	0	1	1	2	....	....	....
1998-99	Springfield Falcons	AHL	69	4	32	36	....	....	....	10	....	....	....	....	....	....	....	....	....	....	3	0	1	1	0	....	....	....
99-2000	**Phoenix Coyotes**	**NHL**	**60**	**0**	**6**	**6**	**0**	**6**	**6**	**16**	**0**	**0**	**0**	**36**	**0.0**	**33**	**1**	**33**	**3**	**2**	**5**	**0**	**1**	**1**	**0**	**0**	**0**	**0**
	Springfield Falcons	AHL	2	0	1	1	....	....	....	0	....	....	....	....	....	....	....	....	....	....	....	....	....	....	....	....	....	....
	Slovakia	WC-A	8	0	5	5	....	....	....	0	....	....	....	....	....	....	....	....	....	....	....	....	....	....	....	....	....	....
	NHL Totals		**60**	**0**	**6**	**6**	**0**	**6**	**6**	**16**	**0**	**0**	**0**	**36**	**0.0**	**33**	**1**	**33**	**3**		**5**	**0**	**1**	**1**	**0**	**0**	**0**	**0**

QMJHL Second All-Star Team (1997) • Won George Parsons Trophy (Memorial Cup Tournament Most Sportsmanlike Player) (1997)
Signed as a free agent by **Phoenix**, September 26, 1997.

• SUIKKANEN, Kai

D – L. 6'2", 205 lbs. b: Parkano, Finland, 6/29/1959.

Season	Club	League	GP	G	A	Pts	AG	AA	APts	PIM	PP	SH	GW	S	%	TGF	PGF	TGA	PGA	+/–	GP	G	A	Pts	PIM	PP	SH	GW
1977-78	Karpat Oulu	Finland	35	21	6	27	....	....	....	19	....	....	....	....	....	....	....	....	....	....	....	....	....	....	....	....	....	....
	Finland	WJC-A	6	5	3	8	....	....	....	9	....	....	....	....	....	....	....	....	....	....	....	....	....	....	....	....	....	....
1978-79	Karpat Oulu	Finland	36	16	6	22	....	....	....	65	....	....	....	....	....	....	....	....	....	....	....	....	....	....	....	....	....	....
	Finland	WJC-A	6	1	2	3	....	....	....	0	....	....	....	....	....	....	....	....	....	....	....	....	....	....	....	....	....	....
1979-80	Karpat Oulu	Finland	36	21	17	38	....	....	....	18	....	....	....	....	....	....	....	....	....	....	6	0	3	3	6	....	....	....
1980-81	Karpat Oulu	Finland	33	20	11	31	....	....	....	60	....	....	....	....	....	....	....	....	....	....	11	5	2	7	32	....	....	....
1981-82	**Buffalo Sabres**	**NHL**	**1**	**0**	**0**	**0**	**0**	**0**	**0**	**0**	**0**	**0**	**0**	**0**	**0.0**	**0**	**0**	**1**	**0**	**–1**	....	....	....	....	....	....	....	....
	Rochester Americans	AHL	71	34	33	67	....	....	....	32	....	....	....	....	....	....	....	....	....	....	9	4	2	6	4	....	....	....
1982-83	**Buffalo Sabres**	**NHL**	**1**	**0**	**0**	**0**	**0**	**0**	**0**	**0**	**0**	**0**	**0**	**1**	**0.0**	**1**	**0**	**0**	**0**	**1**	....	....	....	....	....	....	....	....
	Rochester Americans	AHL	66	33	44	77	....	....	....	65	....	....	....	....	....	....	....	....	....	....	16	7	7	14	21	....	....	....
1983-84	Rochester Americans	AHL	15	7	10	17	....	....	....	2	....	....	....	....	....	....	....	....	....	....	....	....	....	....	....	....	....	....
	Karpat Oulu	Finland	23	9	4	13	....	....	....	20	....	....	....	....	....	....	....	....	....	....	10	6	4	10	8	....	....	....
1984-85	Karpat Oulu	Finland	22	8	6	14	....	....	....	47	....	....	....	....	....	....	....	....	....	....	7	2	3	5	4	....	....	....
1985-86	Karpat Oulu	Finland	33	26	10	36	....	....	....	34	....	....	....	....	....	....	....	....	....	....	4	0	0	0	24	....	....	....
	Finland	WEC-A	10	0	3	3	....	....	....	4	....	....	....	....	....	....	....	....	....	....	....	....	....	....	....	....	....	....
1986-87	Karpat Oulu	Finland	44	24	25	49	....	....	....	30	....	....	....	....	....	....	....	....	....	....	9	*7	1	8	6	....	....	....
1987-88	Karpat Oulu	Finland	26	17	14	31	....	....	....	25	....	....	....	....	....	....	....	....	....	....	....	....	....	....	....	....	....	....
	Finland	Olympics	8	1	0	1	....	....	....	4	....	....	....	....	....	....	....	....	....	....	....	....	....	....	....	....	....	....
1988-89	Karpat Oulu	Finland	33	13	10	23	....	....	....	16	....	....	....	....	....	....	....	....	....	....	....	....	....	....	....	....	....	....
1989-90	Karpat Oulu	Finland-2	35	17	24	41	....	....	....	31	....	....	....	....	....	....	....	....	....	....	....	....	....	....	....	....	....	....
1990-91	TPS Turku	Finland	41	4	3	7	....	....	....	6	....	....	....	....	....	....	....	....	....	....	9	1	1	2	2	....	....	....
	NHL Totals		**2**	**0**	**0**	**0**	**0**	**0**	**0**	**0**	**0**	**0**	**0**	**1**	**0.0**	**1**	**0**	**1**	**0**		....	....	....	....	....	....	....	....

Signed as a free agent by **Buffalo**, August 31, 1981.

• SULLIMAN, Doug

Simon Douglas RW – L. 6'2", 210 lbs. b: Glace Bay, N.S., 8/29/1959. NY Rangers' 1st, 13th overall, in 1979.

Season	Club	League	GP	G	A	Pts	AG	AA	APts	PIM	PP	SH	GW	S	%	TGF	PGF	TGA	PGA	+/–	GP	G	A	Pts	PIM	PP	SH	GW
1975-76	Glace Bay Metros	NSAHA	35	44	53	97	....	....	....	42	....	....	....	....	....	....	....	....	....	....	....	....	....	....	....	....	....	....
1976-77	Kitchener Rangers	OMJHL	65	30	41	71	....	....	....	123	....	....	....	....	....	....	....	....	....	....	3	0	2	2	2	....	....	....
1977-78	Kitchener Rangers	OMJHL	68	50	39	89	....	....	....	87	....	....	....	....	....	....	....	....	....	....	9	5	7	12	24	....	....	....
1978-79	Kitchener Rangers	OMJHL	68	38	77	115	....	....	....	88	....	....	....	....	....	....	....	....	....	....	10	5	7	12	7	....	....	....
1979-80	**New York Rangers**	**NHL**	**31**	**4**	**7**	**11**	**3**	**5**	**8**	**2**	**1**	**0**	**0**	**26**	**15.4**	**23**	**5**	**18**	**0**	**0**	....	....	....	....	....	....	....	....
	New Haven Nighthawks	AHL	31	9	7	16	....	....	....	9	....	....	....	....	....	....	....	....	....	....	....	....	....	....	....	....	....	....
1980-81	**New York Rangers**	**NHL**	**32**	**4**	**1**	**5**	**3**	**1**	**4**	**32**	**0**	**0**	**0**	**56**	**7.1**	**11**	**0**	**24**	**4**	**–9**	**3**	**1**	**0**	**1**	**0**	**0**	**0**	**0**
	New Haven Nighthawks	AHL	45	10	16	26	....	....	....	18	....	....	....	....	....	....	....	....	....	....	1	0	0	0	0	....	....	....
1981-82	**Hartford Whalers**	**NHL**	**77**	**29**	**40**	**69**	**23**	**27**	**50**	**39**	**5**	**0**	**4**	**195**	**14.9**	**106**	**34**	**113**	**28**	**–13**	....	....	....	....	....	....	....	....
1982-83	**Hartford Whalers**	**NHL**	**77**	**22**	**19**	**41**	**18**	**13**	**31**	**14**	**8**	**0**	**0**	**162**	**13.6**	**73**	**23**	**126**	**19**	**–57**	....	....	....	....	....	....	....	....
1983-84	**Hartford Whalers**	**NHL**	**67**	**6**	**13**	**19**	**5**	**9**	**14**	**20**	**0**	**0**	**0**	**130**	**4.6**	**32**	**1**	**58**	**16**	**–11**	....	....	....	....	....	....	....	....
1984-85	**New Jersey Devils**	**NHL**	**57**	**22**	**16**	**38**	**18**	**11**	**29**	**4**	**6**	**0**	**1**	**112**	**19.6**	**59**	**21**	**50**	**1**	**–11**	....	....	....	....	....	....	....	....
1985-86	**New Jersey Devils**	**NHL**	**73**	**21**	**22**	**43**	**17**	**15**	**32**	**20**	**6**	**1**	**5**	**139**	**15.1**	**65**	**16**	**80**	**21**	**–10**	....	....	....	....	....	....	....	....
1986-87	**New Jersey Devils**	**NHL**	**78**	**27**	**26**	**53**	**23**	**19**	**42**	**14**	**4**	**1**	**4**	**148**	**18.2**	**76**	**18**	**109**	**34**	**–17**	....	....	....	....	....	....	....	....
1987-88	**New Jersey Devils**	**NHL**	**59**	**16**	**14**	**30**	**14**	**10**	**24**	**22**	**8**	**1**	**0**	**89**	**18.0**	**44**	**18**	**40**	**6**	**–8**	**9**	**0**	**3**	**3**	**2**	**0**	**0**	**0**
1988-89	**Philadelphia Flyers**	**NHL**	**52**	**6**	**6**	**12**	**5**	**4**	**9**	**8**	**0**	**1**	**1**	**52**	**11.5**	**20**	**0**	**38**	**10**	**–8**	**4**	**0**	**0**	**0**	**0**	**0**	**0**	**0**
1989-90	**Philadelphia Flyers**	**NHL**	**28**	**3**	**4**	**7**	**3**	**3**	**6**	**0**	**0**	**0**	**0**	**28**	**10.7**	**13**	**0**	**9**	**0**	**4**	....	....	....	....	....	....	....	....
	NHL Totals		**631**	**160**	**168**	**328**	**132**	**117**	**249**	**175**	**38**	**4**	**15**	**1137**	**14.1**	**522**	**136**	**665**	**139**		**16**	**1**	**3**	**4**	**2**	**0**	**0**	**0**

Traded to **Hartford** by **NY Rangers** with Chris Kotsopoulos and Gerry McDonald for Mike Rogers and Hartford's 10th round choice (Simo Saarinen) in 1982 Entry Draft, October 2, 1981. Signed as a free agent by **New Jersey**, July 11, 1984. Claimed by **Philadelphia** from **New Jersey** in Waiver Draft, October 3, 1988.

• SULLIVAN, Bob

LW – R. 6', 210 lbs. b: Noranda, Que., 11/29/1957. NY Rangers' 8th, 116th overall, in 1977.

Season	Club	League	GP	G	A	Pts	AG	AA	APts	PIM	PP	SH	GW	S	%	TGF	PGF	TGA	PGA	+/–	GP	G	A	Pts	PIM	PP	SH	GW
1974-75	St-Jerome Alouettes	QMJHL	56	29	47	76	....	....	....	31	....	....	....	....	....	....	....	....	....	....	....	....	....	....	....	....	....	....
1975-76	Chicoutimi Sagueneens	QMJHL	68	20	22	42	....	....	....	34	....	....	....	....	....	....	....	....	....	....	5	4	2	6	0	....	....	....
1976-77	Chicoutimi Sagueneens	QMJHL	71	45	65	110	....	....	....	80	....	....	....	....	....	....	....	....	....	....	8	3	7	10	13	....	....	....

Season	Club	League	REGULAR SEASON																		PLAYOFFS							
			GP	G	A	Pts	AG	AA	APts	PIM	PP	SH	GW	S	%	TGF	PGF	TGA	PGA	+/–	GP	G	A	Pts	PIM	PP	SH	GW
1977-78	Dalhousie University	AUAA	5	5	1	6	....	....	....	....	....	....	....	....	....	....	....	....	....	....	....	....	....	....	....	....	....	....
	New Haven Nighthawks	AHL	2	0	0	0	....	....	....	0	....	....	....	....	....	....	....	....	....	....	....	....	....	....	....	....	....	....
	Toledo Goaldiggers	IHL	65	27	27	54	....	....	....	60	....	....	....	....	....	....	....	....	....	....	17	3	9	12	16	....	....	....
1978-79	Toledo Goaldiggers	IHL	1	0	1	1	....	....	....	0	....	....	....	....	....	....	....	....	....	....	....	....	....	....	....	....	....	....
	Los Angeles Blades	PHL	21	7	14	21	....	....	....	42	....	....	....	....	....	....	....	....	....	....	....	....	....	....	....	....	....	....
1979-80	Toledo Goaldiggers	IHL	56	30	26	56	....	....	....	68	....	....	....	....	....	....	....	....	....	....	4	0	4	4	6	....	....	....
1980-81	Toledo Goaldiggers	IHL	79	32	52	84	....	....	....	69	....	....	....	....	....	....	....	....	....	....	....	....	....	....	....	....	....	....
1981-82	Binghamton Whalers	AHL	74	47	43	90	....	....	....	44	....	....	....	....	....	....	....	....	....	....	....	....	....	....	....	....	....	....
1982-83	**Hartford Whalers**	**NHL**	**62**	**18**	**19**	**37**	**15**	**13**	**28**	**18**	**5**	**0**	**0**	**93**	**19.4**	**47**	**8**	**56**	**0**	**–17**	....	....	....	....	....	....	....	....
	Binghamton Whalers	AHL	18	18	14	32	....	....	....	2	....	....	....	....	....	....	....	....	....	....	....	....	....	....	....	....	....	....
1983-84	Binghamton Whalers	AHL	76	33	47	80	....	....	....	48	....	....	....	....	....	....	....	....	....	....	....	....	....	....	....	....	....	....
1984-85	HC Bolzano	Italy	26	*47	40	87	....	....	....	28	....	....	....	....	....	....	....	....	....	....	9	*17	6	23	6	....	....	....
1985-86	HC Bolzano	Italy	36	54	53	107	....	....	....	76	....	....	....	....	....	....	....	....	....	....	7	8	11	19	6	....	....	....
1986-87	BSC Preussen Berlin	Germany-2	STATISTICS NOT AVAILABLE																									
1987-88	HC Asiago	Italy	21	25	21	46	....	....	....	29	....	....	....	....	....	....	....	....	....	....	7	5	12	17	9	....	....	....
	EHC Lustenau	Austria	11	13	4	17	....	....	....	12	....	....	....	....	....	....	....	....	....	....	....	....	....	....	....	....	....	....
1988-89	SIJ Rotterdam	Holland	STATISTICS NOT AVAILABLE																									
	NHL Totals		**62**	**18**	**19**	**37**	**15**	**13**	**28**	**18**	**5**	**0**	**0**	**93**	**19.4**	**47**	**8**	**56**	**0**		....	....	....	....	....	....	....	....

AHL First All-Star Team (1982) • Won Dudley "Red" Garrett Memorial Award (Top Rookie - AHL) (1982)

Signed as a free agent by **Hartford**, August 24, 1982.

• SULLIVAN, Brian

Brian Scott RW – R. 6'4", 195 lbs. b: South Windsor, CT, 4/23/1969. New Jersey's 3rd, 65th overall, in 1987.

Season	Club	League	GP	G	A	Pts	AG	AA	APts	PIM	PP	SH	GW	S	%	TGF	PGF	TGA	PGA	+/–	GP	G	A	Pts	PIM	PP	SH	GW
1983-84	South Windsor High School	Hi-School	21	15	11	26	....	....	....	....	....	....	....	....	....	....	....	....	....	....	....	....	....	....	....	....	....	....
1984-85	South Windsor High School	Hi-School	20	24	19	43	....	....	....	....	....	....	....	....	....	....	....	....	....	....	....	....	....	....	....	....	....	....
1985-86	South Windsor High School	Hi-School	22	39	50	89	....	....	....	....	....	....	....	....	....	....	....	....	....	....	....	....	....	....	....	....	....	....
1986-87	Springfield Jr. Blues	NEJHL	50	30	35	65	....	....	....	....	....	....	....	....	....	....	....	....	....	....	....	....	....	....	....	....	....	....
1987-88	Northeastern University	H-East	37	20	12	32	....	....	....	18	....	....	....	....	....	....	....	....	....	....	....	....	....	....	....	....	....	....
1988-89	Northeastern University	H-East	34	13	14	27	....	....	....	65	....	....	....	....	....	....	....	....	....	....	....	....	....	....	....	....	....	....
1989-90	Northeastern University	H-East	34	24	21	45	....	....	....	72	....	....	....	....	....	....	....	....	....	....	....	....	....	....	....	....	....	....
1990-91	Northeastern University	H-East	32	17	23	40	....	....	....	75	....	....	....	....	....	....	....	....	....	....	....	....	....	....	....	....	....	....
1991-92	Utica Devils	AHL	70	23	24	47	....	....	....	58	....	....	....	....	....	....	....	....	....	....	4	0	4	4	6	....	....	....
1992-93	**New Jersey Devils**	**NHL**	**2**	**0**	**1**	**1**	**0**	**1**	**1**	**0**	**0**	**0**	**0**	**2**	**0.0**	**1**	**0**	**2**	**0**	**–1**	....	....	....	....	....	....	....	....
	Utica Devils	AHL	75	30	27	57	....	....	....	88	....	....	....	....	....	....	....	....	....	....	5	0	0	0	12	....	....	....
1993-94	Albany River Rats	AHL	77	31	30	61	....	....	....	140	....	....	....	....	....	....	....	....	....	....	5	1	1	2	18	....	....	....
1994-95	San Diego Gulls	IHL	74	24	23	47	....	....	....	97	....	....	....	....	....	....	....	....	....	....	5	0	1	1	7	....	....	....
1995-96	HC Fassa	Italy	29	15	18	33	....	....	....	81	....	....	....	....	....	....	....	....	....	....	3	0	1	1	10	....	....	....
1996-97	San Antonio Dragons	IHL	77	22	24	46	....	....	....	115	....	....	....	....	....	....	....	....	....	....	9	1	2	3	11	....	....	....
1997-98	Grand Rapids Griffins	IHL	54	12	7	19	....	....	....	49	....	....	....	....	....	....	....	....	....	....	....	....	....	....	....	....	....	....
	Springfield Falcons	AHL	11	2	4	6	....	....	....	29	....	....	....	....	....	....	....	....	....	....	1	0	0	0	0	....	....	....
1998-99	Houston Aeros	IHL	53	9	7	16	....	....	....	32	....	....	....	....	....	....	....	....	....	....	....	....	....	....	....	....	....	....
	Kansas City Blades	IHL	2	0	0	0	....	....	....	0	....	....	....	....	....	....	....	....	....	....	....	....	....	....	....	....	....	....
99-2000	Cincinnati Cyclones	IHL	DID NOT PLAY – FRONT OFFICE STAFF																									
	NHL Totals		**2**	**0**	**1**	**1**	**0**	**1**	**1**	**0**	**0**	**0**	**0**	**2**	**0.0**	**1**	**0**	**2**	**0**		....	....	....	....	....	....	....	....

Signed as a free agent by **Anaheim**, August 31, 1994. Claimed on waivers by **Kansas City** (IHL) from **Houston** (IHL), March 22, 1999.

• SULLIVAN, Mike

Michael Barry C – L. 6'2", 190 lbs. b: Marshfield, MA, 2/27/1968. NY Rangers' 4th, 69th overall, in 1987.

Season	Club	League	GP	G	A	Pts	AG	AA	APts	PIM	PP	SH	GW	S	%	TGF	PGF	TGA	PGA	+/–	GP	G	A	Pts	PIM	PP	SH	GW
1985-86	Boston College Prep School	Hi-School	22	26	33	59	....	....	....	....	....	....	....	....	....	....	....	....	....	....	....	....	....	....	....	....	....	....
1986-87	Boston University	H-East	37	13	18	31	....	....	....	18	....	....	....	....	....	....	....	....	....	....	....	....	....	....	....	....	....	....
1987-88	Boston University	H-East	30	18	22	40	....	....	....	30	....	....	....	....	....	....	....	....	....	....	....	....	....	....	....	....	....	....
	United States	WJC-A	6	0	2	2	....	....	....	14	....	....	....	....	....	....	....	....	....	....	....	....	....	....	....	....	....	....
1988-89	Boston University	H-East	36	19	17	36	....	....	....	30	....	....	....	....	....	....	....	....	....	....	....	....	....	....	....	....	....	....
1989-90	Boston University	H-East	38	11	20	31	....	....	....	26	....	....	....	....	....	....	....	....	....	....	....	....	....	....	....	....	....	....
1990-91	San Diego Gulls	IHL	74	12	23	35	....	....	....	27	....	....	....	....	....	....	....	....	....	....	....	....	....	....	....	....	....	....
1991-92	**San Jose Sharks**	**NHL**	**64**	**8**	**11**	**19**	**7**	**8**	**15**	**15**	**1**	**0**	**1**	**72**	**11.1**	**38**	**10**	**54**	**8**	**–18**	....	....	....	....	....	....	....	....
	Kansas City Blades	IHL	10	2	8	10	....	....	....	8	....	....	....	....	....	....	....	....	....	....	....	....	....	....	....	....	....	....
1992-93	**San Jose Sharks**	**NHL**	**81**	**6**	**8**	**14**	**5**	**5**	**10**	**30**	**0**	**2**	**0**	**95**	**6.3**	**33**	**2**	**113**	**40**	**–42**	....	....	....	....	....	....	....	....
1993-94	**San Jose Sharks**	**NHL**	**26**	**2**	**2**	**4**	**2**	**2**	**4**	**4**	**0**	**2**	**1**	**21**	**9.5**	**8**	**0**	**21**	**10**	**–3**	....	....	....	....	....	....	....	....
	Kansas City Blades	IHL	6	3	3	6	....	....	....	0	....	....	....	....	....	....	....	....	....	....	....	....	....	....	....	....	....	....
	Calgary Flames	**NHL**	**19**	**2**	**3**	**5**	**2**	**2**	**4**	**6**	**0**	**2**	**0**	**27**	**7.4**	**6**	**0**	**5**	**1**	**2**	**7**	**1**	**1**	**2**	**8**	**0**	**1**	**0**
	Saint John Flames	AHL	5	2	0	2	....	....	....	4	....	....	....	....	....	....	....	....	....	....	....	....	....	....	....	....	....	....
1994-95	**Calgary Flames**	**NHL**	**38**	**4**	**7**	**11**	**7**	**10**	**17**	**14**	**0**	**0**	**2**	**31**	**12.9**	**19**	**0**	**28**	**7**	**–2**	**7**	**3**	**5**	**8**	**2**	**0**	**1**	**1**
1995-96	**Calgary Flames**	**NHL**	**81**	**9**	**12**	**21**	**9**	**10**	**19**	**24**	**0**	**1**	**1**	**106**	**8.5**	**30**	**0**	**69**	**33**	**–6**	**4**	**0**	**0**	**0**	**0**	**0**	**0**	**0**
1996-97	**Calgary Flames**	**NHL**	**67**	**5**	**6**	**11**	**5**	**5**	**10**	**10**	**0**	**3**	**2**	**64**	**7.8**	**17**	**0**	**45**	**17**	**–11**	....	....	....	....	....	....	....	....
	United States	WC-A	8	1	2	3	....	....	....	2	....	....	....	....	....	....	....	....	....	....	....	....	....	....	....	....	....	....
1997-98	**Boston Bruins**	**NHL**	**77**	**5**	**13**	**18**	**6**	**13**	**19**	**34**	**0**	**0**	**2**	**83**	**6.0**	**32**	**1**	**45**	**13**	**–1**	**6**	**0**	**1**	**1**	**2**	**0**	**0**	**0**
1998-99	**Phoenix Coyotes**	**NHL**	**63**	**2**	**4**	**6**	**2**	**4**	**6**	**24**	**0**	**1**	**1**	**66**	**3.0**	**9**	**0**	**34**	**14**	**–11**	**5**	**0**	**0**	**0**	**2**	**0**	**0**	**0**
99-2000	**Phoenix Coyotes**	**NHL**	**79**	**5**	**10**	**15**	**6**	**9**	**15**	**10**	**0**	**2**	**1**	**59**	**8.5**	**23**	**0**	**54**	**27**	**–4**	**5**	**0**	**1**	**1**	**0**	**0**	**0**	**0**
	NHL Totals		**595**	**48**	**76**	**124**	**51**	**68**	**119**	**171**	**1**	**13**	**11**	**624**	**7.7**	**215**	**13**	**468**	**170**		**34**	**4**	**8**	**12**	**14**	**0**	**2**	**1**

Rights traded to **Minnesota** by **NY Rangers** with Mark Tinordi, Paul Jerrard, the rights to Bret Barnett and LA Kings' 3rd round choice (previously acquired, Minnesota selected Murray Garbutt) in 1989 Entry Draft for Brian Lawton, Igor Liba and the rights to Eric Bennett, October 11, 1988. Signed as a free agent by **San Jose**, August 9, 1991. Claimed on waivers by **Calgary** from **San Jose**, January 6, 1994. Traded to **Boston** by **Calgary** for Boston's 7th round choice (Radek Duda) in 1998 Entry Draft, June 21, 1997. Claimed by **Nashville** from **Boston** in Expansion Draft, June 26, 1998. Traded to **Phoenix** by **Nashville** for Phoenix's 7th round choice in 1999 Entry Draft, June 30, 1998.

• SULLIVAN, Peter

Peter Gerald "Silky" C – R. 5'9", 165 lbs. b: Toronto, Ont., 7/25/1951. Montreal's 12th, 95th overall, in 1971.

Season	Club	League	GP	G	A	Pts	AG	AA	APts	PIM	PP	SH	GW	S	%	TGF	PGF	TGA	PGA	+/–	GP	G	A	Pts	PIM	PP	SH	GW
1967-68	St. Michael's Midget Majors	MTHL	STATISTICS NOT AVAILABLE																									
1968-69	St. Michael's Buzzers	OHA-B	STATISTICS NOT AVAILABLE																									
	Peterborough Petes	OHA-Jr.	4	1	0	1	....	....	....	0	....	....	....	....	....	....	....	....	....	....	....	....	....	....	....	....	....	....
1969-70	Oshawa Generals	OHA-Jr.	52	40	30	70	....	....	....	16	....	....	....	....	....	....	....	....	....	....	6	3	2	5	0	....	....	....
1970-71	Oshawa Generals	OHA-Jr.	61	29	23	52	....	....	....	26	....	....	....	....	....	....	....	....	....	....	....	....	....	....	....	....	....	....
1971-72	Mount Royal College	AJHL	26	14	19	33	....	....	....	4	....	....	....	....	....	....	....	....	....	....	....	....	....	....	....	....	....	....
	St. Petersburg Suns	EHL	5	2	1	3	....	....	....	0	....	....	....	....	....	....	....	....	....	....	....	....	....	....	....	....	....	....
	Muskegon Mohawks	IHL	1	0	0	0	....	....	....	0	....	....	....	....	....	....	....	....	....	....	....	....	....	....	....	....	....	....
1972-73	Nova Scotia Voyageurs	AHL	39	10	14	24	....	....	....	8	....	....	....	....	....	....	....	....	....	....	13	1	0	1	2	....	....	....
1973-74	Nova Scotia Voyageurs	AHL	74	30	40	70	....	....	....	22	....	....	....	....	....	....	....	....	....	....	6	5	4	9	2	....	....	....
1974-75	Nova Scotia Voyageurs	AHL	75	*44	60	104	....	....	....	48	....	....	....	....	....	....	....	....	....	....	6	2	6	8	5	....	....	....
1975-76	Winnipeg Jets	WHA	78	32	39	71	....	....	....	22	....	....	....	....	....	....	....	....	....	....	13	6	7	13	0	....	....	....
1976-77	Winnipeg Jets	WHA	78	31	52	83	....	....	....	18	....	....	....	....	....	....	....	....	....	....	20	7	12	19	2	....	....	....
1977-78	Winnipeg Jets	WHA	77	16	39	55	....	....	....	43	....	....	....	....	....	....	....	....	....	....	9	3	4	7	4	....	....	....
1978-79	Winnipeg Jets	WHA	80	46	40	86	....	....	....	24	....	....	....	....	....	....	....	....	....	....	10	5	9	14	2	....	....	....
1979-80	**Winnipeg Jets**	**NHL**	**79**	**24**	**35**	**59**	**20**	**26**	**46**	**20**	**5**	**0**	**3**	**166**	**14.5**	**84**	**34**	**98**	**3**	**–45**	....	....	....	....	....	....	....	....
1980-81	**Winnipeg Jets**	**NHL**	**47**	**4**	**19**	**23**	**3**	**13**	**16**	**20**	**2**	**0**	**0**	**42**	**9.5**	**33**	**16**	**37**	**3**	**–17**	....	....	....	....	....	....	....	....
1981-82	HC Langnau	Switz.	36	37	24	61	....	....	....	....	....	....	....	....	....	....	....	....	....	....	....	....	....	....	....	....	....	....
	Wichita Wind	CHL	15	12	11	23	....	....	....	0	....	....	....	....	....	....	....	....	....	....	7	5	2	7	0	....	....	....
1982-83	HC Langnau	Switz.	38	31	33	64	....	....	....	....	....	....	....	....	....	....	....	....	....	....	....	....	....	....	....	....	....	....
1983-84	SC Bern	Switz-2	38	46	39	85	....	....	....	....	....	....	....	....	....	....	....	....	....	....	....	....	....	....	....	....	....	....

Season	Club	League	GP	G	A	Pts	AG	AA	APts	PIM	PP	SH	GW	S	%	TGF	PGF	TGA	PGA	+/–	GP	G	A	Pts	PIM	PP	SH	GW
			REGULAR SEASON																		PLAYOFFS							
1984-85	HC Langnau	Switz.	38	53	29	82																						
	Moncton Golden Flames	AHL	5	2	3	5				0																		
1985-86	HC Langnau	Switz.	36	34	27	61																						
1986-87	HC Geneve-Servette	Switz-2	STATISTICS NOT AVAILABLE																									
	NHL Totals		**126**	**28**	**54**	**82**	**23**	**39**	**62**	**40**	**7**	**0**	**3**	**208**	**13.5**	**117**	**50**	**135**	**6**									
	Other Major League Totals		313	125	170	295				107											52	21	32	53	8			

• Brother of Frank • AHL Second All-Star Team (1975)

Signed as a free agent by **Winnipeg** (WHA), August, 1975. Rights retained by **Winnipeg** prior to Expansion Draft, June 9, 1979. Signed as a free agent by **Moncton** (AHL), March 5, 1985.

• SULLIVAN, Steve

Stephen H. C – R. 5'9", 160 lbs. b: Timmins, Ont., 7/6/1974. New Jersey's 10th, 233rd overall, in 1994.

Season	Club	League	GP	G	A	Pts	AG	AA	APts	PIM	PP	SH	GW	S	%	TGF	PGF	TGA	PGA	+/–	GP	G	A	Pts	PIM	PP	SH	GW
1991-92	Timmins Golden Bears	NOJHL	47	66	55	121				141																		
1992-93	Sault Ste. Marie Greyhounds	OHL	62	36	27	63				44											16	3	8	11	18			
	Sault Ste. Marie Greyhounds	Mem-Cup	4	1	0	1				4																		
1993-94	Sault Ste. Marie Greyhounds	OHL	63	51	62	113				82											14	9	16	25	22			
1994-95	Albany River Rats	AHL	75	31	50	81				124											14	4	7	11	10			
1995-96	**New Jersey Devils**	**NHL**	**16**	**5**	**4**	**9**	**5**	**3**	**8**	**8**	**2**	**0**	**1**	**23**	**21.7**	**18**	**8**	**7**	**0**	**3**								
	Albany River Rats	AHL	53	33	42	75				127											4	3	0	3	6			
1996-97	**New Jersey Devils**	**NHL**	**33**	**8**	**14**	**22**	**8**	**12**	**20**	**14**	**2**	**0**	**2**	**63**	**12.7**	**30**	**9**	**12**	**0**	**9**								
	Albany River Rats	AHL	15	8	7	15				16																		
	Toronto Maple Leafs	**NHL**	**21**	**5**	**11**	**16**	**5**	**10**	**15**	**23**	**1**	**0**	**1**	**45**	**11.1**	**22**	**6**	**11**	**0**	**5**								
1997-98	**Toronto Maple Leafs**	**NHL**	**63**	**10**	**18**	**28**	**12**	**18**	**30**	**40**	**1**	**0**	**1**	**112**	**8.9**	**44**	**9**	**44**	**1**	**–8**								
1998-99	**Toronto Maple Leafs**	**NHL**	**63**	**20**	**20**	**40**	**23**	**19**	**42**	**28**	**4**	**0**	**5**	**110**	**18.2**	**53**	**16**	**26**	**1**	**12**	**13**	**3**	**3**	**6**	**14**	**2**	**0**	**0**
99-2000	**Toronto Maple Leafs**	**NHL**	**7**	**0**	**1**	**1**	**0**	**1**	**1**	**4**	**0**	**0**	**0**	**11**	**0.0**	**1**	**0**	**2**	**0**	**–1**								
	Chicago Blackhawks	**NHL**	**73**	**22**	**42**	**64**	**25**	**39**	**64**	**52**	**2**	**1**	**6**	**169**	**13.0**	**85**	**22**	**57**	**14**	**20**								
	Canada	WC-A	9	4	1	5				14																		
	NHL Totals		**276**	**70**	**110**	**180**	**78**	**102**	**180**	**169**	**12**	**1**	**16**	**533**	**13.1**	**253**	**70**	**159**	**16**		**13**	**3**	**3**	**6**	**14**	**2**	**0**	**0**

AHL First All-Star Team (1996)

Traded to **Toronto** by **New Jersey** with Jason Smith and the rights to Alyn McCauley for Doug Gilmour, Dave Ellett and New Jersey's 3rd round choice (previously acquired, New Jersey selected Andre Lakos) in 1999 Entry Draft, February 25, 1997. Claimed on waivers by **Chicago** from **Toronto**, October 23, 1999.

• SUMMANEN, Raimo

LW – L. 5'11", 185 lbs. b: Jyvaskyla, Finland, 3/2/1962. Edmonton's 6th, 125th overall, in 1982.

Season	Club	League	GP	G	A	Pts	AG	AA	APts	PIM	PP	SH	GW	S	%	TGF	PGF	TGA	PGA	+/–	GP	G	A	Pts	PIM	PP	SH	GW
1979-80	JyP-HT Jyvaskyla	Finland-2	31	22	12	34				16																		
1980-81	JyP-HT Jyvaskyla	Finland-Jr.	9	13	11	24				4																		
	JyP-HT Jyvaskyla	Finland-2	35	15	18	33				24																		
1981-82	Kiekko-Reipas	Finland	36	15	6	21				17											2	2	0	2	0			
	Finland	WJC-A	7	7	9	*16				0																		
1982-83	Ilves Tampere	Finland	36	*45	15	60				36											8	7	3	10	2			
	Finland	WEC-A	9	0	3	3				0																		
1983-84	Ilves Tampere	Finland	37	28	19	47				26																		
	Finland	Olympics	6	4	6	10				4																		
	♦ **Edmonton Oilers**	**NHL**	**2**	**1**	**4**	**5**	**1**	**3**	**4**	**2**	**0**	**0**	**0**	**3**	**33.3**	**7**	**1**	**2**	**0**	**4**	**5**	**1**	**4**	**5**	**0**	**0**	**0**	**0**
1984-85	**Edmonton Oilers**	**NHL**	**9**	**0**	**4**	**4**	**0**	**3**	**3**	**0**	**0**	**0**	**0**	**5**	**0.0**	**7**	**1**	**7**	**0**	**–1**								
	Nova Scotia Voyageurs	AHL	66	20	33	53				2											5	1	2	3	0			
1985-86	**Edmonton Oilers**	**NHL**	**73**	**19**	**18**	**37**	**15**	**12**	**27**	**16**	**1**	**0**	**4**	**83**	**22.9**	**58**	**4**	**47**	**0**	**7**	**5**	**1**	**1**	**2**	**0**	**0**	**0**	**0**
1986-87	**Edmonton Oilers**	**NHL**	**48**	**10**	**7**	**17**	**9**	**5**	**14**	**15**	**0**	**0**	**0**	**55**	**18.2**	**26**	**1**	**26**	**0**	**–1**								
	Vancouver Canucks	**NHL**	**10**	**4**	**4**	**8**	**3**	**3**	**6**	**0**	**1**	**0**	**0**	**18**	**22.2**	**11**	**4**	**8**	**0**	**–1**								
	Finland	WEC-A	10	2	0	2				2																		
1987-88	Finland	Can-Cup	5	1	1	2				0																		
	Vancouver Canucks	**NHL**	**9**	**2**	**3**	**5**	**2**	**2**	**4**	**2**	**0**	**0**	**0**	**11**	**18.2**	**7**	**1**	**10**	**0**	**–4**								
	Fredericton Express	AHL	20	7	15	22				38																		
	Flint Spirits	IHL	7	1	1	2				0																		
1988-89	Ilves Tampere	Finland	44	35	46	*81				22											5	4	3	7	6			
1989-90	Ilves Tampere	Finland	40	39	31	70				42											9	3	4	7	8			
	Finland	WEC-A	10	5	3	8				10																		
1990-91	Ilves Tampere	Finland	39	25	30	55				67											8	*6	2	8	20			
	Finland	WEC-A	10	1	1	2				6																		
1991-92	Finland	Can-Cup	6	0	1	1				0																		
	Ilves Tampere	Finland	26	13	9	22				94																		
	Finland	Olympics	8	2	0	2				6																		
1992-93	TPS Turku	Finland	47	17	20	37				50																		
1993-94	Jokerit Helsinki	Finland	25	9	3	12				44																		
	SC Bern	Switz.	10	6	13	19				24																		
1994-95	TPS Turku	Finland	47	23	26	49				53											12	7	4	11	29			
	Finland	WC-A	8	1	1	2				0																		
	NHL Totals		**151**	**36**	**40**	**76**	**30**	**28**	**58**	**35**	**2**	**0**	**4**	**175**	**20.6**	**116**	**12**	**100**	**0**		**10**	**2**	**5**	**7**	**0**	**0**	**0**	**0**

Finnish First All-Star Team (1983, 1984, 1989, 1990)

Traded to **Vancouver** by **Edmonton** for Moe Lemay, March 10, 1987.

• SUNDBLAD, Niklas

RW – R. 6'1", 200 lbs. b: Stockholm, Sweden, 1/3/1973. Calgary's 1st, 19th overall, in 1991.

Season	Club	League	GP	G	A	Pts	AG	AA	APts	PIM	PP	SH	GW	S	%	TGF	PGF	TGA	PGA	+/–	GP	G	A	Pts	PIM	PP	SH	GW
1989-90	AIK Solna Stockholm	Sweden-Jr.	STATISTICS NOT AVAILABLE																									
	Sweden	EJC-A	6	3	5	8				20																		
1990-91	AIK Solna Stockholm	Sweden	39	1	3	4				14																		
1991-92	AIK Solna Stockholm	Sweden	33	9	2	11				20											3	3	1	4	0			
	Sweden	WJC-A	7	2	3	5				10																		
1992-93	AIK Solna Stockholm	Sweden	22	5	4	9				56																		
	Sweden	WJC-A	7	0	3	3				10																		
1993-94	Saint John Flames	AHL	76	13	19	32				75											4	1	1	2	2			
1994-95	Saint John Flames	AHL	72	9	5	14				151											2	0	0	0	6			
1995-96	**Calgary Flames**	**NHL**	**2**	**0**	**0**	**0**	**0**	**0**	**0**	**0**	**0**	**0**	**0**	**3**	**0.0**	**0**	**0**	**0**	**0**	**0**								
	Saint John Flames	AHL	74	16	20	36				66											16	0	4	4	14			
1996-97	TPS Turku	Finland	50	15	21	36				93											11	2	2	4	24			
	TPS Turku	EuroHL	6	2	4	6				10											4	1	5	6	2			
	Sweden	WC-A	11	2	1	3				22																		
1997-98	TPS Turku	Finland	47	17	16	33				68											4	0	0	0	6			
	TPS Turku	EuroHL	6	2	1	3				31																		
1998-99	Malmo IF	Sweden	43	21	12	33				104											8	1	1	2	12			
99-2000	Malmo IF	Sweden	47	22	10	32				75											6	2	2	4	6			
	NHL Totals		**2**	**0**	**0**	**0**	**0**	**0**	**0**	**0**	**0**	**0**	**0**	**3**	**0.0**	**0**	**0**	**0**	**0**									

• SUNDIN, Mats

Mats Johan C/RW – R. 6'4", 228 lbs. b: Bromma, Sweden, 2/13/1971. Quebec's 1st, 1st overall, in 1989.

Season	Club	League	GP	G	A	Pts	AG	AA	APts	PIM	PP	SH	GW	S	%	TGF	PGF	TGA	PGA	+/–	GP	G	A	Pts	PIM	PP	SH	GW
1988-89	Nacka IK	Sweden-2	25	10	8	18				18																		
1989-90	Djurgardens IF Stockholm	Sweden	34	10	8	18				16											8	7	0	7	4			
	Sweden	WJC-A	7	5	2	7				6																		
	Sweden	WEC-A	4	0	0	0				0																		
1990-91	**Quebec Nordiques**	**NHL**	**80**	**23**	**36**	**59**	**21**	**27**	**48**	**58**	**4**	**0**	**0**	**155**	**14.8**	**90**	**27**	**90**	**3**	**–24**								
	Sweden	WEC-A	10	7	5	12				12																		

Season	Club	League	GP	G	A	Pts	AG	AA	APts	PIM	PP	SH	GW	S	%	TGF	PGF	TGA	PGA	+/–	GP	G	A	Pts	PIM	PP	SH	GW
			REGULAR SEASON																		PLAYOFFS							
1991-92	Sweden	Can-Cup	6	2	4	6	....	....	....	16	....	....	....	....	....	....	....	....	....	....	....	....	....	....	....	....	....	....
	Quebec Nordiques	**NHL**	**80**	**33**	**43**	**76**	**30**	**33**	**63**	**103**	**8**	**2**	**2**	**231**	**14.3**	**106**	**36**	**104**	**15**	**–19**	....	....	....	....	....	....	....	....
	Sweden	WC-A	8	2	6	8	....	....	....	8	....	....	....	....	....	....	....	....	....	....	....	....	....	....	....	....	....	....
1992-93	**Quebec Nordiques**	**NHL**	**80**	**47**	**67**	**114**	**39**	**46**	**85**	**96**	**13**	**4**	**9**	**215**	**21.9**	**154**	**70**	**89**	**26**	**21**	**6**	**3**	**1**	**4**	**6**	**1**	**0**	**0**
1993-94	**Quebec Nordiques**	**NHL**	**84**	**32**	**53**	**85**	**30**	**41**	**71**	**60**	**6**	**2**	**4**	**226**	**14.2**	**114**	**39**	**100**	**26**	**1**	....	....	....	....	....	....	....	....
	Sweden	WC-A	8	5	9	14	....	....	....	4	....	....	....	....	....	....	....	....	....	....	....	....	....	....	....	....	....	....
1994-95	Djurgardens IF Stockholm	Sweden	12	7	2	9	....	....	....	14	....	....	....	....	....	....	....	....	....	....	....	....	....	....	....	....	....	....
	Toronto Maple Leafs	**NHL**	**47**	**23**	**24**	**47**	**41**	**35**	**76**	**14**	**9**	**0**	**4**	**173**	**13.3**	**58**	**24**	**44**	**5**	**–5**	**7**	**5**	**4**	**9**	**4**	**2**	**0**	**1**
1995-96	**Toronto Maple Leafs**	**NHL**	**76**	**33**	**50**	**83**	**32**	**41**	**73**	**46**	**7**	**6**	**7**	**301**	**11.0**	**111**	**47**	**73**	**17**	**8**	**6**	**3**	**1**	**4**	**4**	**2**	**0**	**1**
1996-97	Sweden	W-Cup	4	4	3	7	....	....	....	4	....	....	....	....	....	....	....	....	....	....	....	....	....	....	....	....	....	....
	Toronto Maple Leafs	**NHL**	**82**	**41**	**53**	**94**	**44**	**47**	**91**	**59**	**7**	**4**	**8**	**281**	**14.6**	**125**	**35**	**103**	**19**	**6**	....	....	....	....	....	....	....	....
1997-98	**Toronto Maple Leafs**	**NHL**	**82**	**33**	**41**	**74**	**39**	**40**	**79**	**49**	**9**	**1**	**5**	**219**	**15.1**	**96**	**31**	**88**	**20**	**–3**	....	....	....	....	....	....	....	....
	Sweden	Olympics	4	3	0	3	....	....	....	4	....	....	....	....	....	....	....	....	....	....	....	....	....	....	....	....	....	....
	Sweden	WC-A	10	5	6	11	....	....	....	6	....	....	....	....	....	....	....	....	....	....	....	....	....	....	....	....	....	....
1998-99	**Toronto Maple Leafs**	**NHL**	**82**	**31**	**52**	**83**	**36**	**50**	**86**	**58**	**4**	**0**	**6**	**209**	**14.8**	**115**	**30**	**79**	**16**	**22**	**17**	**8**	**8**	**16**	**16**	**3**	**0**	**2**
99-2000	**Toronto Maple Leafs**	**NHL**	**73**	**32**	**41**	**73**	**36**	**38**	**74**	**46**	**10**	**2**	**7**	**184**	**17.4**	**104**	**30**	**69**	**11**	**16**	**12**	**3**	**5**	**8**	**10**	**0**	**0**	**1**
	NHL Totals		**766**	**328**	**460**	**788**	**348**	**398**	**746**	**589**	**77**	**21**	**52**	**2194**	**14.9**	**1073**	**369**	**839**	**158**		**48**	**22**	**19**	**41**	**40**	**8**	**0**	**5**

Swedish World All-Star Team (1991, 1992, 1994, 1997) • Canada Cup All-Star Team (1991) • WC-A All-Star Team (1992) • Named Best Forward at WC-A (1992) • World Cup All-Star Team (1996) • Played in NHL All-Star Game (1996, 1997, 1998, 1999, 2000)

Traded to **Toronto** by **Quebec** with Garth Butcher, Todd Warriner and Philadelphia's 1st round choice (previously acquired by Quebec — later traded to Washington — Washington selected Nolan Baumgartner) in 1994 Entry Draft for Wendel Clark, Sylvain Lefebvre, Landon Wilson and Toronto's 1st round choice (Jeffrey Kealty) in 1994 Entry Draft, June 28, 1994.

• SUNDIN, Ronnie

D – L. 6'1", 220 lbs. b: Ludvika, Sweden, 10/3/1970. NY Rangers' 8th, 237th overall, in 1996.

Season	Club	League	GP	G	A	Pts	AG	AA	APts	PIM	PP	SH	GW	S	%	TGF	PGF	TGA	PGA	+/–	GP	G	A	Pts	PIM	PP	SH	GW
1986-87	Ludvika HC	Sweden-3	4	0	0	0	....	....	....	0	....	....	....	....	....	....	....	....	....	....	....	....	....	....	....	....	....	....
1987-88	Ludvika HC	Sweden-3	31	0	4	4	....	....	....	....	....	....	....	....	....	....	....	....	....	....	....	....	....	....	....	....	....	....
1988-89	Mora IK	Sweden-2	28	2	4	6	....	....	....	16	....	....	....	....	....	....	....	....	....	....	3	0	2	2	0	....	....	....
1989-90	Mora IK	Sweden-2	34	3	4	7	....	....	....	26	....	....	....	....	....	....	....	....	....	....	....	....	....	....	....	....	....	....
1990-91	Mora IK	Sweden-2	32	4	8	12	....	....	....	16	....	....	....	....	....	....	....	....	....	....	2	0	0	0	0	....	....	....
1991-92	Mora IK	Sweden-2	35	2	5	7	....	....	....	18	....	....	....	....	....	....	....	....	....	....	2	0	0	0	0	....	....	....
1992-93	Vastra Frolunda	Sweden	17	2	3	5	....	....	....	12	....	....	....	....	....	....	....	....	....	....	....	....	....	....	....	....	....	....
1993-94	Vastra Frolunda	Sweden	38	0	9	9	....	....	....	42	....	....	....	....	....	....	....	....	....	....	4	0	0	0	0	....	....	....
1994-95	Vastra Frolunda	Sweden	11	3	4	7	....	....	....	6	....	....	....	....	....	....	....	....	....	....	....	....	....	....	....	....	....	....
1995-96	Vastra Frolunda	Sweden	40	3	6	9	....	....	....	18	....	....	....	....	....	....	....	....	....	....	13	1	4	5	10	....	....	....
	Sweden	WC-A	1	0	0	0	....	....	....	0	....	....	....	....	....	....	....	....	....	....	....	....	....	....	....	....	....	....
1996-97	Vastra Frolunda	Sweden	47	3	14	17	....	....	....	24	....	....	....	....	....	....	....	....	....	....	3	1	0	1	2	....	....	....
	Vastra Frolunda	EuroHL	3	1	1	2	....	....	....	0	....	....	....	....	....	....	....	....	....	....	4	0	2	2	0	....	....	....
	Sweden	WC-A	8	0	0	0	....	....	....	0	....	....	....	....	....	....	....	....	....	....	....	....	....	....	....	....	....	....
1997-98	**New York Rangers**	**NHL**	**1**	**0**	**0**	**0**	**0**	**0**	**0**	**0**	**0**	**0**	**0**	**0**	**0.0**	**0**	**0**	**0**	**0**	**0**	....	....	....	....	....	....	....	....
	Hartford Wolf Pack	AHL	67	3	19	22	....	....	....	59	....	....	....	....	....	....	....	....	....	....	14	2	5	7	15	....	....	....
1998-99	Vastra Frolunda	Sweden	50	5	3	8	....	....	....	26	....	....	....	....	....	....	....	....	....	....	4	0	1	1	2	....	....	....
99-2000	Vastra Frolunda	Sweden	49	5	5	10	....	....	....	40	....	....	....	....	....	....	....	....	....	....	5	1	1	2	4	....	....	....
	NHL Totals		**1**	**0**	**0**	**0**	**0**	**0**	**0**	**0**	**0**	**0**	**0**	**0**	**0.0**	**0**	**0**	**0**	**0**		....	....	....	....	....	....	....	....

• SUNDSTROM, Niklas

LW – L. 6', 185 lbs. b: Ornskoldsvik, Sweden, 6/6/1975. NY Rangers' 1st, 8th overall, in 1993.

Season	Club	League	GP	G	A	Pts	AG	AA	APts	PIM	PP	SH	GW	S	%	TGF	PGF	TGA	PGA	+/–	GP	G	A	Pts	PIM	PP	SH	GW
1991-92	MoDo AIK	Sweden	9	1	3	4	....	....	....	0	....	....	....	....	....	....	....	....	....	....	....	....	....	....	....	....	....	....
	Sweden	EJC-A	6	1	0	1	....	....	....	6	....	....	....	....	....	....	....	....	....	....	....	....	....	....	....	....	....	....
1992-93	MoDo AIK	Sweden-Jr.	2	3	1	4	....	....	....	0	....	....	....	....	....	....	....	....	....	....	....	....	....	....	....	....	....	....
	MoDo AIK	Sweden	40	7	11	18	....	....	....	18	....	....	....	....	....	....	....	....	....	....	3	0	0	0	0	....	....	....
	Sweden	WJC-A	7	10	4	14	....	....	....	0	....	....	....	....	....	....	....	....	....	....	....	....	....	....	....	....	....	....
	Sweden	EJC-A	5	4	9	13	....	....	....	10	....	....	....	....	....	....	....	....	....	....	....	....	....	....	....	....	....	....
1993-94	MoDo AIK	Sweden-Jr.	3	3	4	7	....	....	....	2	....	....	....	....	....	....	....	....	....	....	....	....	....	....	....	....	....	....
	MoDo AIK	Sweden	37	7	12	19	....	....	....	28	....	....	....	....	....	....	....	....	....	....	11	4	3	7	2	....	....	....
	Sweden	WJC-A	7	4	7	*11	....	....	....	10	....	....	....	....	....	....	....	....	....	....	....	....	....	....	....	....	....	....
1994-95	MoDo Hockey	Sweden	33	8	13	21	....	....	....	30	....	....	....	....	....	....	....	....	....	....	....	....	....	....	....	....	....	....
	Sweden	WJC-A	7	4	4	8	....	....	....	8	....	....	....	....	....	....	....	....	....	....	....	....	....	....	....	....	....	....
1995-96	**New York Rangers**	**NHL**	**82**	**9**	**12**	**21**	**9**	**10**	**19**	**14**	**1**	**1**	**2**	**90**	**10.0**	**34**	**1**	**59**	**28**	**2**	**11**	**4**	**3**	**7**	**4**	**1**	**0**	**0**
1996-97	Sweden	W-Cup	4	2	2	4	....	....	....	0	....	....	....	....	....	....	....	....	....	....	....	....	....	....	....	....	....	....
	New York Rangers	**NHL**	**82**	**24**	**28**	**52**	**25**	**25**	**50**	**20**	**5**	**1**	**4**	**132**	**18.2**	**87**	**14**	**78**	**28**	**23**	**9**	**0**	**5**	**5**	**2**	**0**	**0**	**0**
1997-98	**New York Rangers**	**NHL**	**70**	**19**	**28**	**47**	**22**	**27**	**49**	**24**	**4**	**0**	**1**	**115**	**16.5**	**70**	**18**	**69**	**17**	**0**	....	....	....	....	....	....	....	....
	Sweden	Olympics	4	1	1	2	....	....	....	2	....	....	....	....	....	....	....	....	....	....	....	....	....	....	....	....	....	....
	Sweden	WC-A	10	1	5	6	....	....	....	8	....	....	....	....	....	....	....	....	....	....	....	....	....	....	....	....	....	....
1998-99	**New York Rangers**	**NHL**	**81**	**13**	**30**	**43**	**15**	**29**	**44**	**20**	**1**	**2**	**3**	**89**	**14.6**	**60**	**9**	**71**	**18**	**–2**	....	....	....	....	....	....	....	....
	Sweden	WC-A	8	5	2	7	....	....	....	4	....	....	....	....	....	....	....	....	....	....	....	....	....	....	....	....	....	....
99-2000	**San Jose Sharks**	**NHL**	**79**	**12**	**25**	**37**	**13**	**23**	**36**	**22**	**2**	**1**	**2**	**90**	**13.3**	**53**	**8**	**44**	**8**	**9**	**12**	**0**	**2**	**2**	**2**	**0**	**0**	**0**
	NHL Totals		**394**	**77**	**123**	**200**	**84**	**114**	**198**	**100**	**13**	**5**	**12**	**516**	**14.9**	**304**	**50**	**321**	**99**		**32**	**4**	**10**	**14**	**8**	**1**	**0**	**0**

EJC-A All-Star Team (1993) • WJC-A All-Star Team (1994) • Named Best Forward at WJC-A (1994)

Traded to **Tampa Bay** by **NY Rangers** with Dan Cloutier and NY Rangers' 1st (Nikita Alexeev) and 3rd (later traded to San Jose - later traded to Chicago - Chicago selected Igor Radulov) round choices in 2000 Entry Draft for Chicago's 1st round choice (previously acquired, NY Rangers selected Pavel Brendl) in 1999 Entry Draft, June 26, 1999. Traded to **San Jose** by **Tampa Bay** with NY Rangers' 3rd round choice (previously acquired, later traded to Chicago - Chicago selected Igor Radulov) in 2000 Entry Draft for Bill Houlder, Andrei Zyuzin, Shawn Burr and Steve Guolla, August 4, 1999.

• SUNDSTROM, Patrik

C – L. 6'1", 200 lbs. b: Skelleftea, Sweden, 12/14/1961. Vancouver's 8th, 175th overall, in 1980.

Season	Club	League	GP	G	A	Pts	AG	AA	APts	PIM	PP	SH	GW	S	%	TGF	PGF	TGA	PGA	+/–	GP	G	A	Pts	PIM	PP	SH	GW
1978-79	IF Bjorkloven	Sweden	1	0	0	0	....	....	....	0	....	....	....	....	....	....	....	....	....	....	....	....	....	....	....	....	....	....
1979-80	IF Bjorkloven	Sweden	26	5	7	12	....	....	....	20	....	....	....	....	....	....	....	....	....	....	3	1	0	1	4	....	....	....
	Sweden	WJC-A	5	0	1	1	....	....	....	4	....	....	....	....	....	....	....	....	....	....	....	....	....	....	....	....	....	....
1980-81	IF Bjorkloven	Sweden	36	10	18	28	....	....	....	30	....	....	....	....	....	....	....	....	....	....	....	....	....	....	....	....	....	....
	Sweden	WJC-A	5	7	0	7	....	....	....	8	....	....	....	....	....	....	....	....	....	....	....	....	....	....	....	....	....	....
	Sweden	WEC-A	7	4	0	4	....	....	....	2	....	....	....	....	....	....	....	....	....	....	....	....	....	....	....	....	....	....
1981-82	Sweden	Can-Cup	5	0	2	2	....	....	....	4	....	....	....	....	....	....	....	....	....	....	....	....	....	....	....	....	....	....
	IF Bjorkloven	Sweden	36	22	13	35	....	....	....	38	....	....	....	....	....	....	....	....	....	....	7	3	4	7	6	....	....	....
	Sweden	WEC-A	10	5	2	7	....	....	....	8	....	....	....	....	....	....	....	....	....	....	....	....	....	....	....	....	....	....
1982-83	**Vancouver Canucks**	**NHL**	**74**	**23**	**23**	**46**	**19**	**16**	**35**	**30**	**6**	**0**	**5**	**156**	**14.7**	**72**	**26**	**77**	**11**	**–20**	**4**	**0**	**0**	**0**	**2**	**0**	**0**	**0**
1983-84	**Vancouver Canucks**	**NHL**	**78**	**38**	**53**	**91**	**31**	**36**	**67**	**37**	**7**	**0**	**7**	**216**	**17.6**	**129**	**48**	**102**	**10**	**–11**	**4**	**0**	**1**	**1**	**7**	**0**	**0**	**0**
1984-85	Sweden	Can-Cup	8	1	6	7	....	....	....	6	....	....	....	....	....	....	....	....	....	....	....	....	....	....	....	....	....	....
	Vancouver Canucks	**NHL**	**71**	**25**	**43**	**68**	**20**	**29**	**49**	**46**	**5**	**0**	**2**	**186**	**13.4**	**98**	**28**	**102**	**15**	**–17**	....	....	....	....	....	....	....	....
1985-86	**Vancouver Canucks**	**NHL**	**79**	**18**	**48**	**66**	**14**	**32**	**46**	**28**	**6**	**1**	**0**	**155**	**11.6**	**100**	**39**	**81**	**12**	**–8**	**3**	**1**	**0**	**1**	**0**	**1**	**0**	**0**
1986-87	**Vancouver Canucks**	**NHL**	**72**	**29**	**42**	**71**	**25**	**31**	**56**	**40**	**12**	**1**	**0**	**141**	**20.6**	**102**	**30**	**84**	**21**	**9**	....	....	....	....	....	....	....	....
1987-88	**New Jersey Devils**	**NHL**	**78**	**15**	**36**	**51**	**13**	**26**	**39**	**42**	**9**	**1**	**4**	**126**	**11.9**	**77**	**34**	**100**	**41**	**–16**	**18**	**7**	**13**	**20**	**14**	**3**	**0**	**1**
1988-89	**New Jersey Devils**	**NHL**	**65**	**28**	**41**	**69**	**24**	**29**	**53**	**36**	**12**	**1**	**4**	**156**	**17.9**	**110**	**43**	**82**	**37**	**22**	....	....	....	....	....	....	....	....
1989-90	**New Jersey Devils**	**NHL**	**74**	**27**	**49**	**76**	**23**	**35**	**58**	**34**	**8**	**1**	**0**	**142**	**19.0**	**116**	**33**	**94**	**26**	**15**	**6**	**1**	**3**	**4**	**2**	**0**	**0**	**0**
1990-91	**New Jersey Devils**	**NHL**	**71**	**15**	**31**	**46**	**14**	**24**	**38**	**48**	**4**	**1**	**1**	**96**	**15.6**	**78**	**24**	**68**	**21**	**7**	**2**	**0**	**0**	**0**	**0**	**0**	**0**	**0**
1991-92	**New Jersey Devils**	**NHL**	**17**	**1**	**3**	**4**	**1**	**2**	**3**	**8**	**1**	**0**	**0**	**16**	**6.3**	**8**	**2**	**12**	**1**	**–5**	....	....	....	....	....	....	....	....
	Utica Devils	AHL	1	0	0	0	....	....	....	0	....	....	....	....	....	....	....	....	....	....	....	....	....	....	....	....	....	....
1992-93	IF Bjorkloven	Sweden-2	36	16	21	37	....	....	....	46	....	....	....	....	....	....	....	....	....	....	9	3	5	8	10	....	....	....
	NHL Totals		**679**	**219**	**369**	**588**	**184**	**260**	**444**	**349**	**70**	**6**	**19**	**1390**	**15.8**	**890**	**307**	**802**	**195**		**37**	**9**	**17**	**26**	**25**	**4**	**0**	**1**

• Brother of Peter • WJC-A All-Star Team (1981) • Named Best Forward at WJC-A (1981) • Swedish World All-Star Team (1982) • Swedish Player of the Year (1982)

Traded to **New Jersey** by **Vancouver** with Vancouver's 2nd (Jeff Christian) and 4th (Matt Ruchty) round choices in 1988 Entry Draft for Kirk McLean, Greg Adams and New Jersey's 2nd round choice (Leif Rohlin) in 1988 Entry Draft, September 15, 1987.

• SUNDSTROM, Peter

LW – L. 6', 180 lbs. b: Skelleftea, Sweden, 12/14/1961. NY Rangers' 3rd, 50th overall, in 1981.

			REGULAR SEASON																		PLAYOFFS							
Season	Club	League	GP	G	A	Pts	AG	AA	APts	PIM	PP	SH	GW	S	%	TGF	PGF	TGA	PGA	+/–	GP	G	A	Pts	PIM	PP	SH	GW
1978-79	IF Bjorkloven	Sweden	1	0	0	0	....	....	....	0	....	....	....	....	....	....	....	....	....	....	....	....	....	....	....	....	....	....
1979-80	IF Bjorkloven	Sweden	8	0	0	0	....	....	....	4	....	....	....	....	....	....	....	....	....	....	....	....	....	....	....	....	....	....
1980-81	IF Bjorkloven	Sweden	29	7	2	9	....	....	....	8	....	....	....	....	....	....	....	....	....	....	....	....	....	....	....	....	....	....
	Sweden	WJC-A	5	2	3	5	....	....	....	4	....	....	....	....	....	....	....	....	....	....	....	....	....	....	....	....	....	....
1981-82	IF Bjorkloven	Sweden	35	10	14	24	....	....	....	18	....	....	....	....	....	....	....	....	....	....	7	2	1	3	0	....	....	....
	Sweden	WEC-A	8	3	1	4	....	....	....	2	....	....	....	....	....	....	....	....	....	....	....	....	....	....	....	....	....	....
1982-83	IF Bjorkloven	Sweden	33	14	11	25	....	....	....	26	....	....	....	....	....	....	....	....	....	....	3	2	0	2	4	....	....	....
	Sweden	WEC-A	10	3	3	6	....	....	....	4	....	....	....	....	....	....	....	....	....	....	....	....	....	....	....	....	....	....
1983-84	**New York Rangers**	**NHL**	**77**	**22**	**22**	**44**	**18**	**15**	**33**	**24**	**0**	**2**	**4**	**153**	**14.4**	**68**	**3**	**72**	**10**	**3**	**5**	**1**	**3**	**4**	**0**	**1**	**0**	**0**
1984-85	Sweden	Can-Cup	8	2	2	4	....	....	....	8	....	....	....	....	....	....	....	....	....	....	....	....	....	....	....	....	....	....
	New York Rangers	**NHL**	**76**	**18**	**25**	**43**	**15**	**17**	**32**	**34**	**0**	**2**	**2**	**157**	**11.5**	**60**	**0**	**110**	**24**	**–26**	**3**	**0**	**0**	**0**	**0**	**0**	**0**	**0**
1985-86	**New York Rangers**	**NHL**	**53**	**8**	**15**	**23**	**6**	**10**	**16**	**12**	**0**	**0**	**1**	**63**	**12.7**	**30**	**0**	**25**	**2**	**7**	**1**	**0**	**0**	**0**	**2**	**0**	**0**	**0**
	New Haven Nighthawks	AHL	8	3	6	9	....	....	....	4	....	....	....	....	....	....	....	....	....	....	....	....	....	....	....	....	....	....
1986-87	IF Bjorkloven	Sweden	36	22	16	38	....	....	....	44	....	....	....	....	....	....	....	....	....	....	6	2	*5	7	8	....	....	....
	Sweden	WEC-A	10	1	1	2	....	....	....	8	....	....	....	....	....	....	....	....	....	....	....	....	....	....	....	....	....	....
1987-88	**Washington Capitals**	**NHL**	**76**	**8**	**17**	**25**	**7**	**12**	**19**	**34**	**0**	**1**	**1**	**89**	**9.0**	**35**	**0**	**54**	**17**	**–2**	**14**	**2**	**0**	**2**	**6**	**0**	**1**	**1**
1988-89	**Washington Capitals**	**NHL**	**35**	**4**	**2**	**6**	**3**	**1**	**4**	**12**	**0**	**0**	**0**	**39**	**10.3**	**11**	**0**	**23**	**7**	**–5**	....	....	....	....	....	....	....	....
1989-90	**New Jersey Devils**	**NHL**	**21**	**1**	**2**	**3**	**1**	**1**	**2**	**4**	**0**	**0**	**0**	**16**	**6.3**	**9**	**0**	**12**	**4**	**1**	....	....	....	....	....	....	....	....
	Utica Devils	AHL	31	11	18	29	....	....	....	6	....	....	....	....	....	....	....	....	....	....	5	4	1	5	0	....	....	....
1990-91	Malmo IF	Sweden	40	12	19	31	....	....	....	50	....	....	....	....	....	....	....	....	....	....	2	1	0	1	4	....	....	....
1991-92	Malmo IF	Sweden	40	10	17	27	....	....	....	36	....	....	....	....	....	....	....	....	....	....	10	*5	6	*11	2	....	....	....
1992-93	Malmo IF	Sweden	40	11	15	26	....	....	....	36	....	....	....	....	....	....	....	....	....	....	6	1	0	1	18	....	....	....
1993-94	Malmo IF	Sweden	40	4	14	18	....	....	....	28	....	....	....	....	....	....	....	....	....	....	11	5	2	7	8	....	....	....
1994-95	Malmo IF	Sweden	40	9	13	22	....	....	....	30	....	....	....	....	....	....	....	....	....	....	9	1	4	5	2	....	....	....
	NHL Totals		**338**	**61**	**83**	**144**	**50**	**56**	**106**	**120**	**0**	**5**	**8**	**517**	**11.8**	**213**	**3**	**296**	**64**		**23**	**3**	**3**	**6**	**8**	**1**	**1**	**1**

• Brother of Patrik

Traded to **Washington** by **NY Rangers** for Washington's 5th round choice (Martin Bergeron) in 1988 Entry Draft, August 27, 1987. Traded to **New Jersey** by **Washington** for New Jersey's 10th round choice (Rob Leask) in 1991 Entry Draft, June 19, 1989.

• SUTER, Gary

Gary Lee D – L. 6', 205 lbs. b: Madison, WI, 6/24/1964. Calgary's 9th, 180th overall, in 1984.

Season	Club	League	GP	G	A	Pts	AG	AA	APts	PIM	PP	SH	GW	S	%	TGF	PGF	TGA	PGA	+/–	GP	G	A	Pts	PIM	PP	SH	GW
1981-82	Culver Academy Eagles	Hi-School	STATISTICS NOT AVAILABLE																									
	Dubuque Fighting Saints	USHL	18	3	4	7	....	....	....	32	....	....	....	....	....	....	....	....	....	....	....	....	....	....	....	....	....	....
1982-83	Dubuque Fighting Saints	USHL	41	9	30	39	....	....	....	112	....	....	....	....	....	....	....	....	....	....	....	....	....	....	....	....	....	....
1983-84	University of Wisconsin	WCHA	35	4	18	22	....	....	....	32	....	....	....	....	....	....	....	....	....	....	....	....	....	....	....	....	....	....
	United States	WJC-A	7	1	1	2	....	....	....	12	....	....	....	....	....	....	....	....	....	....	....	....	....	....	....	....	....	....
1984-85	University of Wisconsin	WCHA	39	12	39	51	....	....	....	110	....	....	....	....	....	....	....	....	....	....	....	....	....	....	....	....	....	....
	United States	WEC-A	10	1	2	3	....	....	....	22	....	....	....	....	....	....	....	....	....	....	....	....	....	....	....	....	....	....
1985-86	**Calgary Flames**	**NHL**	**80**	**18**	**50**	**68**	**14**	**34**	**48**	**141**	**9**	**0**	**4**	**195**	**9.2**	**156**	**69**	**106**	**30**	**11**	**10**	**2**	**8**	**10**	**8**	**0**	**0**	**1**
1986-87	**Calgary Flames**	**NHL**	**68**	**9**	**40**	**49**	**8**	**29**	**37**	**70**	**4**	**0**	**0**	**152**	**5.9**	**106**	**51**	**85**	**20**	**–10**	**6**	**0**	**3**	**3**	**10**	**0**	**0**	**0**
1987-88	United States	Can-Cup	5	0	3	3	....	....	....	9	....	....	....	....	....	....	....	....	....	....	....	....	....	....	....	....	....	....
	Calgary Flames	**NHL**	**75**	**21**	**70**	**91**	**18**	**50**	**68**	**124**	**6**	**1**	**3**	**204**	**10.3**	**186**	**79**	**100**	**32**	**39**	**9**	**1**	**9**	**10**	**6**	**0**	**1**	**0**
1988-89♦	**Calgary Flames**	**NHL**	**63**	**13**	**49**	**62**	**11**	**35**	**46**	**78**	**8**	**0**	**1**	**216**	**6.0**	**141**	**71**	**60**	**16**	**26**	**5**	**0**	**3**	**3**	**10**	**0**	**0**	**0**
1989-90	Calgary Flames	Fr-Tour	4	0	1	1	....	....	....	2	....	....	....	....	....	....	....	....	....	....	....	....	....	....	....	....	....	....
	Calgary Flames	**NHL**	**76**	**16**	**60**	**76**	**14**	**43**	**57**	**97**	**5**	**0**	**1**	**211**	**7.6**	**160**	**82**	**83**	**9**	**4**	**6**	**0**	**1**	**1**	**14**	**0**	**0**	**0**
1990-91	**Calgary Flames**	**NHL**	**79**	**12**	**58**	**70**	**11**	**44**	**55**	**102**	**6**	**0**	**1**	**258**	**4.7**	**164**	**78**	**78**	**18**	**26**	**7**	**1**	**6**	**7**	**12**	**1**	**0**	**0**
1991-92	United States	Can-Cup	8	1	3	4	....	....	....	4	....	....	....	....	....	....	....	....	....	....	....	....	....	....	....	....	....	....
	Calgary Flames	**NHL**	**70**	**12**	**43**	**55**	**11**	**33**	**44**	**128**	**4**	**0**	**0**	**189**	**6.3**	**139**	**64**	**103**	**29**	**1**	....	....	....	....	....	....	....	....
	United States	WC-A	6	0	1	1	....	....	....	6	....	....	....	....	....	....	....	....	....	....	....	....	....	....	....	....	....	....
1992-93	**Calgary Flames**	**NHL**	**81**	**23**	**58**	**81**	**19**	**40**	**59**	**112**	**10**	**1**	**2**	**263**	**8.7**	**161**	**70**	**125**	**33**	**–1**	**6**	**2**	**3**	**5**	**8**	**0**	**1**	**0**
1993-94	**Calgary Flames**	**NHL**	**25**	**4**	**9**	**13**	**4**	**7**	**11**	**20**	**2**	**1**	**0**	**51**	**7.8**	**26**	**11**	**24**	**6**	**–3**	....	....	....	....	....	....	....	....
	Chicago Blackhawks	**NHL**	**16**	**2**	**3**	**5**	**2**	**2**	**4**	**18**	**2**	**0**	**0**	**35**	**5.7**	**25**	**15**	**34**	**15**	**–9**	**6**	**3**	**2**	**5**	**6**	**2**	**0**	**0**
1994-95	**Chicago Blackhawks**	**NHL**	**48**	**10**	**27**	**37**	**18**	**40**	**58**	**42**	**5**	**0**	**0**	**144**	**6.9**	**89**	**43**	**43**	**11**	**14**	**12**	**2**	**5**	**7**	**10**	**1**	**0**	**0**
1995-96	**Chicago Blackhawks**	**NHL**	**82**	**20**	**47**	**67**	**20**	**39**	**59**	**80**	**12**	**2**	**4**	**242**	**8.3**	**137**	**58**	**103**	**27**	**3**	**10**	**3**	**3**	**6**	**8**	**2**	**0**	**1**
1996-97	United States	W-Cup	6	0	2	2	....	....	....	6	....	....	....	....	....	....	....	....	....	....	....	....	....	....	....	....	....	....
	Chicago Blackhawks	**NHL**	**82**	**7**	**21**	**28**	**7**	**19**	**26**	**70**	**3**	**0**	**0**	**225**	**3.1**	**98**	**35**	**83**	**16**	**–4**	**6**	**1**	**4**	**5**	**8**	**0**	**0**	**0**
1997-98	**Chicago Blackhawks**	**NHL**	**73**	**14**	**28**	**42**	**16**	**27**	**43**	**74**	**5**	**2**	**0**	**199**	**7.0**	**78**	**32**	**62**	**17**	**1**	....	....	....	....	....	....	....	....
	United States	Olympics	4	0	0	0	....	....	....	2	....	....	....	....	....	....	....	....	....	....	....	....	....	....	....	....	....	....
1998-99	**San Jose Sharks**	**NHL**	**1**	**0**	**0**	**0**	**0**	**0**	**0**	**0**	**0**	**0**	**0**	**1**	**0.0**	**0**	**0**	**1**	**1**	**0**	....	....	....	....	....	....	....	....
99-2000	**San Jose Sharks**	**NHL**	**76**	**6**	**28**	**34**	**7**	**26**	**33**	**52**	**2**	**1**	**0**	**175**	**3.4**	**105**	**44**	**83**	**29**	**7**	**12**	**2**	**5**	**7**	**12**	**1**	**0**	**1**
	NHL Totals		**995**	**187**	**591**	**778**	**180**	**468**	**648**	**1208**	**83**	**8**	**16**	**2760**	**6.8**	**1771**	**802**	**1173**	**309**		**95**	**17**	**52**	**69**	**112**	**7**	**2**	**3**

Won Calder Memorial Trophy (1986) • NHL All-Rookie Team (1986) • NHL Second All-Star Team (1988) • Played in NHL All-Star Game (1986, 1988, 1989, 1991)

Traded to **Hartford** by **Calgary** with Paul Ranheim and Ted Drury for James Patrick, Zarley Zalapski and Michael Nylander, March 10, 1994. Traded to **Chicago** by **Hartford** with Randy Cunneyworth and Hartford's 3rd round choice (later traded to Vancouver - Vancouver selected Larry Courville) in 1995 Entry Draft for Frantisek Kucera and Jocelyn Lemieux, March 11, 1994. Signed as a free agent by **San Jose**, July 1, 1998. • Missed remainder of 1998-99 season recovering from tricep muscle injury suffered in game vs. Dallas, October 24, 1998.

• SUTHERLAND, Bill

William Fraser C – L. 5'10", 160 lbs. b: Regina, Sask., 11/10/1934.

Season	Club	League	GP	G	A	Pts	AG	AA	APts	PIM	PP	SH	GW	S	%	TGF	PGF	TGA	PGA	+/–	GP	G	A	Pts	PIM	PP	SH	GW
1952-53	St. Boniface Midget Canadiens	MAHA	STATISTICS NOT AVAILABLE																									
	St. Boniface Canadiens	MJHL	1	0	1	1	....	....	....	0	....	....	....	....	....	....	....	....	....	....	....	....	....	....	....	....	....	....
1953-54	St. Boniface Canadiens	MJHL	25	25	18	43	....	....	....	42	....	....	....	....	....	....	....	....	....	....	10	*5	*12	*17	14	....	....	....
	St. Boniface Canadiens	Mem-Cup	8	*6	*6	*12	....	....	....	10	....	....	....	....	....	....	....	....	....	....	....	....	....	....	....	....	....	....
1954-55	St. Boniface Canadiens	MJHL	25	25	35	60	....	....	....	33	....	....	....	....	....	....	....	....	....	....	....	....	....	....	....	....	....	....
1955-56	Cincinnati Mohawks	IHL	53	25	31	56	....	....	....	24	....	....	....	....	....	....	....	....	....	....	....	....	....	....	....	....	....	....
1956-57	Cincinnati Mohawks	IHL	58	27	26	53	....	....	....	30	....	....	....	....	....	....	....	....	....	....	7	1	1	2	4	....	....	....
1957-58	Cincinnati Mohawks	IHL	60	*55	39	94	....	....	....	43	....	....	....	....	....	....	....	....	....	....	....	....	....	....	....	....	....	....
	Shawinigan Cataracts	QHL	2	0	1	1	....	....	....	0	....	....	....	....	....	....	....	....	....	....	....	....	....	....	....	....	....	....
1958-59	Rochester Americans	AHL	1	0	0	0	....	....	....	0	....	....	....	....	....	....	....	....	....	....	....	....	....	....	....	....	....	....
	Montreal Royals	QHL	47	27	16	43	....	....	....	32	....	....	....	....	....	....	....	....	....	....	7	*7	3	*10	13	....	....	....
1959-60	Montreal Royals	EPHL	65	35	40	75	....	....	....	40	....	....	....	....	....	....	....	....	....	....	14	3	7	10	13	....	....	....
1960-61	Cleveland Barons	AHL	58	19	14	33	....	....	....	30	....	....	....	....	....	....	....	....	....	....	4	0	0	0	12	....	....	....
1961-62	Cleveland Barons	AHL	70	20	28	48	....	....	....	49	....	....	....	....	....	....	....	....	....	....	6	0	2	2	4	....	....	....
1962-63	Quebec Aces	AHL	45	21	17	38	....	....	....	22	....	....	....	....	....	....	....	....	....	....	....	....	....	....	....	....	....	....
	Montreal Canadiens	**NHL**	....	....	....	....	....	....	....	....	....	....	....	....	....	....	....	....	....	....	**2**	**0**	**0**	**0**	**0**	**0**	**0**	**0**
1963-64	Quebec Aces	AHL	49	22	33	55	....	....	....	32	....	....	....	....	....	....	....	....	....	....	9	2	7	9	22	....	....	....
1964-65	Quebec Aces	AHL	58	25	35	60	....	....	....	50	....	....	....	....	....	....	....	....	....	....	5	3	2	5	6	....	....	....
1965-66	Quebec Aces	AHL	48	24	25	49	....	....	....	24	....	....	....	....	....	....	....	....	....	....	6	3	3	6	2	....	....	....
1966-67	Quebec Aces	AHL	67	40	38	78	....	....	....	27	....	....	....	....	....	....	....	....	....	....	5	3	4	7	4	....	....	....
1967-68	**Philadelphia Flyers**	**NHL**	**60**	**20**	**9**	**29**	**23**	**9**	**32**	**6**	**5**	**2**	**1**	**98**	**20.4**	**40**	**12**	**41**	**14**	**1**	**7**	**1**	**3**	**4**	**0**	**1**	**0**	**0**
1968-69	**Toronto Maple Leafs**	**NHL**	**44**	**7**	**5**	**12**	**7**	**4**	**11**	**14**	**0**	**0**	**0**	**53**	**13.2**	**19**	**1**	**23**	**2**	**–3**	....	....	....	....	....	....	....	....
	Philadelphia Flyers	**NHL**	**12**	**7**	**3**	**10**	**7**	**3**	**10**	**4**	**1**	**1**	**0**	**23**	**30.4**	**13**	**3**	**10**	**5**	**5**	**4**	**1**	**1**	**2**	**0**	**1**	**0**	**0**
1969-70	**Philadelphia Flyers**	**NHL**	**51**	**15**	**17**	**32**	**16**	**16**	**32**	**30**	**3**	**0**	**1**	**103**	**14.6**	**44**	**8**	**48**	**10**	**–2**	....	....	....	....	....	....	....	....
1970-71	**Philadelphia Flyers**	**NHL**	**1**	**0**	**0**	**0**	**0**	**0**	**0**	**0**	**0**	**0**	**0**	**0**	**0.0**	**0**	**0**	**0**	**0**	**0**	....	....	....	....	....	....	....	....
	St. Louis Blues	**NHL**	**68**	**19**	**20**	**39**	**19**	**17**	**36**	**41**	**11**	**0**	**3**	**106**	**17.9**	**68**	**24**	**31**	**0**	**13**	**1**	**0**	**0**	**0**	**0**	**0**	**0**	**0**

			REGULAR SEASON																		PLAYOFFS							
Season	**Club**	**League**	**GP**	**G**	**A**	**Pts**	**AG**	**AA**	**APts**	**PIM**	**PP**	**SH**	**GW**	**S**	**%**	**TGF**	**PGF**	**TGA**	**PGA**	**+/–**	**GP**	**G**	**A**	**Pts**	**PIM**	**PP**	**SH**	**GW**
1971-72	**St. Louis Blues**	**NHL**	**9**	**2**	**3**	**5**	**2**	**3**	**5**	**2**	**0**	**1**	**0**	**7**	**28.6**	**9**	**3**	**8**	**6**	**4**	....	....	....	....	....	....	....	....
	Detroit Red Wings	**NHL**	**5**	**0**	**1**	**1**	**0**	**1**	**1**	**2**	**0**	**0**	**0**	**3**	**0.0**	**1**	**0**	**2**	**0**	**–1**	....	....	....	....	....	....	....	....
	Tidewater Red Wings	AHL	40	6	10	16	....	....	....	26	....	....	....	....	....	....	....	....	....	....	....	....	....	....	....	....	....	....
1972-73	Winnipeg Jets	WHA	48	6	16	22	....	....	....	34	....	....	....	....	....	....	....	....	....	....	14	5	9	14	9	....	....	....
1973-74	Winnipeg Jets	WHA	12	4	5	9	....	....	....	6	....	....	....	....	....	....	....	....	....	....	4	0	0	0	4	....	....	....
	NHL Totals		**250**	**70**	**58**	**128**	**74**	**53**	**127**	**99**	....	....	....	....	....	....	....	....	....	....	**14**	**2**	**4**	**6**	**0**	....	....	....
	Other Major League Totals		60	10	21	31	....	....	....	40	....	....	....	....	....	....	....	....	....	....	18	5	9	14	13	....	....	....

IHL Second All-Star Team (1958)

Traded to **Quebec** (AHL) by **Montreal** for cash, July, 1962. NHL rights transferred to **Philadelphia** after NHL club purchased **Quebec** (AHL) franchise, May 8, 1967. Claimed by **Minnesota** from **Philadelphia** in Intra-League Draft, June 12, 1968. Claimed by **Toronto** from **Minnesota** in Intra-League Draft, June 12, 1968. Traded to **Philadelphia** by **Toronto** with Mike Byers and Gerry Meehan for Brit Selby and Forbes Kennedy, March 2, 1969. Claimed on waivers by **Buffalo** from **Philadelphia**, October 19, 1970. Traded to **St. Louis** by **Buffalo** for cash, October 19, 1970. Traded to **Detroit** by **St. Louis** for cash, November 9, 1971. Selected by **Winnipeg** (WHA) in 1972 WHA General Player Draft, February 12, 1972.

• SUTTER, Brent

Brent C. "Pup" C – R. 6', 188 lbs. b: Viking, Alta., 6/10/1962. NY Islanders' 1st, 17th overall, in 1980.

Season	Club	League	GP	G	A	Pts	AG	AA	APts	PIM	PP	SH	GW	S	%	TGF	PGF	TGA	PGA	+/–	GP	G	A	Pts	PIM	PP	SH	GW
1977-78	Red Deer Rustlers	AJHL	60	12	18	30	....	....	....	33	....	....	....	....	....	....	....	....	....	....	....	....	....	....	....	....	....	....
1978-79	Red Deer Rustlers	AJHL	60	42	42	84	....	....	....	79	....	....	....	....	....	....	....	....	....	....	....	....	....	....	....	....	....	....
1979-80	Red Deer Rustlers	AJHL	59	70	101	171	....	....	....	....	....	....	....	....	....	....	....	....	....	....	....	....	....	....	....	....	....	....
	Lethbridge Broncos	WHL	5	1	0	1	....	....	....	2	....	....	....	....	....	....	....	....	....	....	....	....	....	....	....	....	....	....
	Red Deer Rustlers	Cen-Cup	STATISTICS NOT AVAILABLE																									
1980-81	Lethbridge Broncos	WHL	68	54	54	108	....	....	....	116	....	....	....	....	....	....	....	....	....	....	9	6	4	10	51	....	....	....
	New York Islanders	**NHL**	**3**	**2**	**2**	**4**	**2**	**1**	**3**	**0**	**0**	**0**	**1**	**2**	**100.0**	**4**	**1**	**1**	**0**	**2**	....	....	....	....	....	....	....	....
1981-82	Lethbridge Broncos	WHL	34	46	34	80	....	....	....	162	....	....	....	....	....	....	....	....	....	....	....	....	....	....	....	....	....	....
♦	**New York Islanders**	**NHL**	**43**	**21**	**22**	**43**	**17**	**15**	**32**	**114**	**3**	**0**	**1**	**93**	**22.6**	**59**	**15**	**16**	**0**	**28**	**19**	**2**	**6**	**8**	**36**	**0**	**0**	**0**
1982-83♦	**New York Islanders**	**NHL**	**80**	**21**	**19**	**40**	**17**	**13**	**30**	**128**	**1**	**0**	**3**	**149**	**14.1**	**58**	**6**	**39**	**1**	**14**	**20**	**10**	**11**	**21**	**26**	**3**	**0**	**0**
1983-84	**New York Islanders**	**NHL**	**69**	**34**	**15**	**49**	**27**	**10**	**37**	**69**	**7**	**0**	**6**	**154**	**22.1**	**73**	**16**	**61**	**8**	**4**	**20**	**4**	**10**	**14**	**18**	**0**	**1**	**3**
1984-85	Canada	Can-Cup	8	2	2	4	....	....	....	10	....	....	....	....	....	....	....	....	....	....	....	....	....	....	....	....	....	....
	New York Islanders	**NHL**	**72**	**42**	**60**	**102**	**34**	**41**	**75**	**51**	**12**	**0**	**4**	**194**	**21.6**	**145**	**40**	**85**	**22**	**42**	**10**	**3**	**3**	**6**	**14**	**1**	**0**	**2**
1985-86	**New York Islanders**	**NHL**	**61**	**24**	**31**	**55**	**19**	**21**	**40**	**74**	**10**	**0**	**2**	**135**	**17.8**	**75**	**24**	**60**	**20**	**11**	**3**	**0**	**1**	**1**	**2**	**0**	**0**	**0**
	Canada	WEC-A	8	4	7	11	....	....	....	8	....	....	....	....	....	....	....	....	....	....	....	....	....	....	....	....	....	....
1986-87	**New York Islanders**	**NHL**	**69**	**27**	**36**	**63**	**23**	**26**	**49**	**73**	**6**	**3**	**8**	**177**	**15.3**	**93**	**32**	**63**	**25**	**23**	**5**	**1**	**0**	**1**	**4**	**1**	**0**	**0**
1987-88	Canada	Can-Cup	9	1	3	4	....	....	....	6	....	....	....	....	....	....	....	....	....	....	....	....	....	....	....	....	....	....
	New York Islanders	**NHL**	**70**	**29**	**31**	**60**	**25**	**22**	**47**	**55**	**11**	**2**	**2**	**162**	**17.9**	**87**	**33**	**74**	**33**	**13**	**6**	**2**	**1**	**3**	**18**	**0**	**1**	**1**
1988-89	**New York Islanders**	**NHL**	**77**	**29**	**34**	**63**	**25**	**24**	**49**	**77**	**17**	**2**	**2**	**187**	**15.5**	**95**	**46**	**94**	**33**	**–12**	....	....	....	....	....	....	....	....
1989-90	**New York Islanders**	**NHL**	**67**	**33**	**35**	**68**	**28**	**25**	**53**	**65**	**17**	**3**	**3**	**198**	**16.7**	**97**	**42**	**76**	**30**	**9**	**5**	**2**	**3**	**5**	**2**	**2**	**0**	**1**
1990-91	**New York Islanders**	**NHL**	**75**	**21**	**32**	**53**	**19**	**24**	**43**	**49**	**6**	**2**	**4**	**186**	**11.3**	**85**	**32**	**91**	**30**	**–8**	....	....	....	....	....	....	....	....
1991-92	Canada	Can-Cup	8	3	1	4	....	....	....	6	....	....	....	....	....	....	....	....	....	....	....	....	....	....	....	....	....	....
	Chicago Blackhawks	**NHL**	**61**	**18**	**32**	**50**	**16**	**24**	**40**	**30**	**7**	**1**	**2**	**185**	**9.7**	**72**	**33**	**56**	**12**	**–5**	**18**	**3**	**5**	**8**	**22**	**1**	**0**	**1**
	New York Islanders	**NHL**	**8**	**4**	**6**	**10**	**4**	**5**	**9**	**6**	**1**	**0**	**1**	**21**	**19.0**	**14**	**6**	**13**	**0**	**–5**	....	....	....	....	....	....	....	....
1992-93	**Chicago Blackhawks**	**NHL**	**65**	**20**	**34**	**54**	**17**	**23**	**40**	**67**	**8**	**2**	**3**	**151**	**13.2**	**84**	**44**	**53**	**23**	**10**	**4**	**1**	**1**	**2**	**4**	**0**	**0**	**0**
1993-94	**Chicago Blackhawks**	**NHL**	**73**	**9**	**29**	**38**	**8**	**22**	**30**	**43**	**3**	**2**	**0**	**127**	**7.1**	**60**	**13**	**60**	**30**	**17**	**6**	**0**	**0**	**0**	**2**	**0**	**0**	**0**
1994-95	**Chicago Blackhawks**	**NHL**	**47**	**7**	**8**	**15**	**12**	**12**	**24**	**51**	**1**	**0**	**1**	**65**	**10.8**	**27**	**3**	**32**	**14**	**6**	**16**	**1**	**2**	**3**	**4**	**0**	**0**	**0**
1995-96	**Chicago Blackhawks**	**NHL**	**80**	**13**	**27**	**40**	**13**	**22**	**35**	**56**	**0**	**0**	**3**	**102**	**12.7**	**52**	**1**	**66**	**29**	**14**	**10**	**1**	**1**	**2**	**6**	**0**	**0**	**0**
1996-97	**Chicago Blackhawks**	**NHL**	**39**	**7**	**7**	**14**	**7**	**6**	**13**	**18**	**0**	**0**	**1**	**62**	**11.3**	**27**	**0**	**23**	**6**	**10**	**2**	**0**	**0**	**0**	**6**	**0**	**0**	**0**
1997-98	**Chicago Blackhawks**	**NHL**	**52**	**2**	**6**	**8**	**2**	**6**	**8**	**28**	**0**	**1**	**0**	**43**	**4.7**	**12**	**1**	**27**	**10**	**–6**	....	....	....	....	....	....	....	....
	NHL Totals		**1111**	**363**	**466**	**829**	**315**	**342**	**657**	**1054**	**110**	**18**	**47**	**2393**	**15.2**	**1219**	**388**	**990**	**326**		**144**	**30**	**44**	**74**	**164**	**8**	**2**	**8**

• Brother of Brian, Darryl, Duane, Rich and Ron • Played in NHL All-Star Game (1985)

Traded to **Chicago** by **NY Islanders** with Brad Lauer for Adam Creighton and Steve Thomas, October 25, 1991.

• SUTTER, Brian

Brian Louis Allen LW – L. 5'11", 173 lbs. b: Viking, Alta., 10/7/1956. St. Louis' 2nd, 20th overall, in 1976.

Season	Club	League	GP	G	A	Pts	AG	AA	APts	PIM	PP	SH	GW	S	%	TGF	PGF	TGA	PGA	+/–	GP	G	A	Pts	PIM	PP	SH	GW
1972-73	Red Deer Rustlers	AJHL	51	27	40	67	....	....	....	54	....	....	....	....	....	....	....	....	....	....	....	....	....	....	....	....	....	....
1973-74	Red Deer Rustlers	AJHL	59	42	54	96	....	....	....	139	....	....	....	....	....	....	....	....	....	....	....	....	....	....	....	....	....	....
1974-75	Lethbridge Broncos	WCJHL	53	34	47	81	....	....	....	134	....	....	....	....	....	....	....	....	....	....	6	0	1	1	39	....	....	....
	Canada	WJC-A	5	1	4	5	....	....	....	2	....	....	....	....	....	....	....	....	....	....	....	....	....	....	....	....	....	....
1975-76	Lethbridge Broncos	WCJHL	72	36	56	92	....	....	....	233	....	....	....	....	....	....	....	....	....	....	7	3	4	7	45	....	....	....
1976-77	**St. Louis Blues**	**NHL**	**35**	**4**	**10**	**14**	**4**	**8**	**12**	**82**	**0**	**0**	**0**	**49**	**8.2**	**26**	**7**	**27**	**0**	**–8**	**4**	**1**	**0**	**1**	**14**	**0**	**0**	**0**
	Kansas City Blues	CHL	38	15	23	38	....	....	....	47	....	....	....	....	....	....	....	....	....	....	....	....	....	....	....	....	....	....
1977-78	**St. Louis Blues**	**NHL**	**78**	**9**	**13**	**22**	**8**	**10**	**18**	**123**	**4**	**0**	**1**	**98**	**9.2**	**42**	**10**	**71**	**1**	**–38**	....	....	....	....	....	....	....	....
1978-79	**St. Louis Blues**	**NHL**	**77**	**41**	**39**	**80**	**35**	**28**	**63**	**165**	**12**	**0**	**3**	**177**	**23.2**	**118**	**39**	**81**	**0**	**–2**	....	....	....	....	....	....	....	....
1979-80	**St. Louis Blues**	**NHL**	**71**	**23**	**35**	**58**	**20**	**26**	**46**	**156**	**6**	**0**	**1**	**173**	**13.3**	**101**	**30**	**68**	**0**	**3**	**3**	**0**	**0**	**0**	**4**	**0**	**0**	**0**
1980-81	**St. Louis Blues**	**NHL**	**78**	**35**	**34**	**69**	**27**	**23**	**50**	**232**	**17**	**0**	**4**	**203**	**17.2**	**114**	**41**	**63**	**2**	**12**	**11**	**6**	**3**	**9**	**77**	**3**	**0**	**0**
1981-82	**St. Louis Blues**	**NHL**	**74**	**39**	**36**	**75**	**31**	**24**	**55**	**239**	**14**	**0**	**3**	**195**	**20.0**	**108**	**38**	**74**	**2**	**–2**	**10**	**8**	**6**	**14**	**49**	**0**	**0**	**1**
1982-83	**St. Louis Blues**	**NHL**	**79**	**46**	**30**	**76**	**38**	**21**	**59**	**254**	**11**	**0**	**4**	**204**	**22.5**	**115**	**38**	**79**	**2**	**0**	**4**	**2**	**1**	**3**	**10**	**2**	**0**	**0**
1983-84	**St. Louis Blues**	**NHL**	**76**	**32**	**51**	**83**	**26**	**35**	**61**	**162**	**14**	**2**	**3**	**193**	**16.6**	**126**	**51**	**103**	**22**	**–6**	**11**	**1**	**5**	**6**	**22**	**1**	**0**	**0**
1984-85	**St. Louis Blues**	**NHL**	**77**	**37**	**37**	**74**	**30**	**25**	**55**	**121**	**14**	**0**	**7**	**181**	**20.4**	**108**	**36**	**81**	**20**	**11**	**3**	**2**	**1**	**3**	**2**	**2**	**0**	**0**
1985-86	**St. Louis Blues**	**NHL**	**44**	**19**	**23**	**42**	**15**	**15**	**30**	**87**	**8**	**0**	**1**	**92**	**20.7**	**61**	**23**	**59**	**9**	**–12**	**9**	**1**	**2**	**3**	**22**	**0**	**0**	**0**
1986-87	**St. Louis Blues**	**NHL**	**14**	**3**	**3**	**6**	**3**	**2**	**5**	**18**	**3**	**0**	**0**	**22**	**13.6**	**13**	**7**	**11**	**0**	**–5**	....	....	....	....	....	....	....	....
1987-88	**St. Louis Blues**	**NHL**	**76**	**15**	**22**	**37**	**13**	**16**	**29**	**147**	**4**	**1**	**2**	**99**	**15.2**	**55**	**14**	**89**	**32**	**–16**	**10**	**0**	**3**	**3**	**49**	**0**	**0**	**0**
1988-1992	**St. Louis Blues**	**NHL**	DID NOT PLAY – COACHING																									
1992-1995	**Boston Bruins**	**NHL**	DID NOT PLAY – COACHING																									
1995-1997			OUT OF HOCKEY – RETIRED																									
1997-2000	**Calgary Flames**	**NHL**	DID NOT PLAY – COACHING																									
	NHL Totals		**779**	**303**	**333**	**636**	**250**	**233**	**483**	**1786**	**107**	**3**	**29**	**1686**	**18.0**	**987**	**334**	**806**	**90**		**65**	**21**	**21**	**42**	**249**	**8**	**0**	**1**

• Brother of Brent, Darryl, Duane, Rich and Ron • Won Jack Adams Award (1991) • Played in NHL All-Star Game (1982, 1983, 1985)

• SUTTER, Darryl

Darryl John LW – L. 5'11", 176 lbs. b: Viking, Alta., 8/19/1958. Chicago's 11th, 179th overall, in 1978.

Season	Club	League	GP	G	A	Pts	AG	AA	APts	PIM	PP	SH	GW	S	%	TGF	PGF	TGA	PGA	+/–	GP	G	A	Pts	PIM	PP	SH	GW
1974-75	Red Deer Rustlers	AJHL	60	16	20	36	....	....	....	43	....	....	....	....	....	....	....	....	....	....	....	....	....	....	....	....	....	....
1975-76	Red Deer Rustlers	AJHL	60	43	93	136	....	....	....	82	....	....	....	....	....	....	....	....	....	....	....	....	....	....	....	....	....	....
1976-77	Red Deer Rustlers	AJHL	56	55	*78	*133	....	....	....	131	....	....	....	....	....	....	....	....	....	....	....	....	....	....	....	....	....	....
	Lethbridge Broncos	WCJHL	1	1	0	1	....	....	....	0	....	....	....	....	....	....	....	....	....	....	15	3	7	10	13	....	....	....
1977-78	Lethbridge Broncos	WCJHL	68	33	48	81	....	....	....	119	....	....	....	....	....	....	....	....	....	....	8	4	9	13	2	....	....	....
1978-79	Iwakura Tomakomai	Japan	20	*28	*13	*41	....	....	....	....	....	....	....	....	....	....	....	....	....	....	....	....	....	....	....	....	....	....
	New Brunswick Hawks	AHL	19	7	6	13	....	....	....	6	....	....	....	....	....	....	....	....	....	....	5	1	2	3	0	....	....	....
1979-80	**Chicago Black Hawks**	**NHL**	**8**	**2**	**0**	**2**	**2**	**0**	**2**	**2**	**0**	**0**	**0**	**3**	**66.7**	**2**	**0**	**1**	**0**	**1**	**7**	**3**	**1**	**4**	**2**	**2**	**0**	**1**
	New Brunswick Hawks	AHL	69	35	31	66	....	....	....	69	....	....	....	....	....	....	....	....	....	....	12	6	6	12	8	....	....	....
1980-81	**Chicago Black Hawks**	**NHL**	**76**	**40**	**22**	**62**	**31**	**15**	**46**	**86**	**14**	**0**	**4**	**179**	**22.3**	**98**	**28**	**86**	**15**	**–1**	**3**	**3**	**1**	**4**	**2**	**1**	**0**	**0**
1981-82	**Chicago Black Hawks**	**NHL**	**40**	**23**	**12**	**35**	**18**	**8**	**26**	**31**	**4**	**3**	**0**	**102**	**22.5**	**53**	**13**	**46**	**6**	**0**	**3**	**0**	**1**	**1**	**2**	**0**	**0**	**0**
1982-83	**Chicago Black Hawks**	**NHL**	**80**	**31**	**30**	**61**	**25**	**21**	**46**	**53**	**10**	**0**	**5**	**169**	**18.3**	**96**	**26**	**55**	**3**	**18**	**13**	**4**	**6**	**10**	**8**	**0**	**0**	**0**
1983-84	**Chicago Black Hawks**	**NHL**	**59**	**20**	**20**	**40**	**16**	**14**	**30**	**44**	**8**	**0**	**4**	**135**	**14.8**	**63**	**23**	**60**	**2**	**–18**	**5**	**1**	**1**	**2**	**0**	**0**	**0**	**0**
1984-85	**Chicago Black Hawks**	**NHL**	**49**	**20**	**18**	**38**	**16**	**12**	**28**	**12**	**2**	**0**	**2**	**90**	**22.2**	**56**	**12**	**36**	**0**	**8**	**15**	**12**	**7**	**19**	**12**	**2**	**0**	**4**
1985-86	**Chicago Black Hawks**	**NHL**	**50**	**17**	**10**	**27**	**14**	**7**	**21**	**44**	**3**	**0**	**2**	**89**	**19.1**	**41**	**7**	**49**	**0**	**–15**	**3**	**1**	**2**	**3**	**0**	**1**	**0**	**0**
1986-87	**Chicago Blackhawks**	**NHL**	**44**	**8**	**6**	**14**	**7**	**4**	**11**	**16**	**1**	**0**	**0**	**62**	**12.9**	**21**	**1**	**23**	**0**	**–3**	**2**	**0**	**0**	**0**	**0**	**0**	**0**	**0**
1987-1988	**Chicago Blackhawks**	**NHL**	DID NOT PLAY – ASSISTANT COACH																									
1988-1989	Saginaw Hawks	IHL	DID NOT PLAY – COACHING																									
1989-1990	Indianapolis Ice	IHL	DID NOT PLAY – COACHING																									
1990-1992	**Chicago Blackhawks**	**NHL**	DID NOT PLAY – ASSISTANT COACH																									

Season	Club	League	GP	G	A	Pts	AG	AA	APts	PIM	PP	SH	GW	S	%	TGF	PGF	TGA	PGA	+/-	GP	G	A	Pts	PIM	PP	SH	GW
			REGULAR SEASON																		PLAYOFFS							
1992-1995	**Chicago Blackhawks**	**NHL**	DID NOT PLAY – COACHING																									
1995-1997	**Chicago Blackhawks**	**NHL**	DID NOT PLAY – ASSISTANT GENERAL MANAGER																									
1997-2000	**San Jose Sharks**	**NHL**	DID NOT PLAY – COACHING																									
	NHL Totals		**406**	**161**	**118**	**279**	**129**	**81**	**210**	**288**	**42**	**3**	**17**	**829**	**19.4**	**430**	**110**	**356**	**26**		**51**	**24**	**19**	**43**	**26**	**6**	**0**	**5**

• Brother of Brian, Brent, Duane, Rich and Ron • AJHL First All-Star Team (1977) • AJHL MVP (1977) • AHL Second All-Star Team (1980) • Won Dudley "Red" Garrett Memorial Award (Top Rookie - AHL) (1980)

• SUTTER, Duane

Duane Calvin "Dog" RW – R. 6'1", 185 lbs. b: Viking, Alta., 3/16/1960. NY Islanders' 1st, 17th overall, in 1979.

Season	Club	League	GP	G	A	Pts	AG	AA	APts	PIM	PP	SH	GW	S	%	TGF	PGF	TGA	PGA	+/-	GP	G	A	Pts	PIM	PP	SH	GW
1976-77	Red Deer Rustlers	AJHL	60	9	26	35	....	....	....	76	....	....	....	....	....	....	....	....	....	....	....	....	....	....	....	....	....	....
	Lethbridge Broncos	WCJHL	1	0	1	1	....	....	....	2	....	....	....	....	....	....	....	....	....	....	8	0	1	1	15	....	....	....
1977-78	Red Deer Rustlers	AJHL	59	47	53	100	....	....	....	218	....	....	....	....	....	....	....	....	....	....	....	....	....	....	....	....	....	....
	Lethbridge Broncos	WCJHL	5	1	5	6	....	....	....	19	....	....	....	....	....	....	....	....	....	....	8	1	4	5	10	....	....	....
1978-79	Lethbridge Broncos	WHL	71	50	75	125	....	....	....	212	....	....	....	....	....	....	....	....	....	....	19	11	12	23	43	....	....	....
1979-80	Lethbridge Broncos	WHL	21	18	16	34	....	....	....	74	....	....	....	....	....	....	....	....	....	....	....	....	....	....	....	....	....	....
♦	**New York Islanders**	**NHL**	**56**	**15**	**9**	**24**	**13**	**7**	**20**	**55**	**0**	**0**	**1**	**75**	**20.0**	**32**	**2**	**25**	**0**	**5**	**21**	**3**	**7**	**10**	**74**	**0**	**0**	**0**
1980-81 ♦	**New York Islanders**	**NHL**	**23**	**7**	**11**	**18**	**5**	**7**	**12**	**26**	**1**	**0**	**1**	**48**	**14.6**	**19**	**4**	**23**	**0**	**–8**	**12**	**3**	**1**	**4**	**10**	**0**	**0**	**0**
1981-82 ♦	**New York Islanders**	**NHL**	**77**	**18**	**35**	**53**	**14**	**23**	**37**	**100**	**4**	**0**	**0**	**140**	**12.9**	**81**	**14**	**45**	**1**	**23**	**19**	**5**	**5**	**10**	**57**	**0**	**0**	**2**
1982-83 ♦	**New York Islanders**	**NHL**	**75**	**13**	**19**	**32**	**11**	**13**	**24**	**118**	**1**	**0**	**2**	**122**	**10.7**	**47**	**5**	**35**	**1**	**8**	**20**	**9**	**12**	**21**	**43**	**2**	**0**	**1**
1983-84	**New York Islanders**	**NHL**	**78**	**17**	**23**	**40**	**14**	**16**	**30**	**94**	**2**	**0**	**1**	**137**	**12.4**	**62**	**8**	**52**	**0**	**2**	**21**	**1**	**3**	**4**	**48**	**0**	**0**	**0**
1984-85	**New York Islanders**	**NHL**	**78**	**17**	**24**	**41**	**14**	**16**	**30**	**174**	**1**	**0**	**1**	**125**	**13.6**	**58**	**8**	**62**	**0**	**–12**	**10**	**0**	**2**	**2**	**47**	**0**	**0**	**0**
1985-86	**New York Islanders**	**NHL**	**80**	**20**	**33**	**53**	**16**	**22**	**38**	**157**	**4**	**0**	**1**	**151**	**13.2**	**87**	**18**	**57**	**3**	**15**	**3**	**0**	**0**	**0**	**16**	**0**	**0**	**0**
1986-87	**New York Islanders**	**NHL**	**80**	**14**	**17**	**31**	**12**	**12**	**24**	**169**	**1**	**0**	**1**	**152**	**9.2**	**57**	**9**	**56**	**9**	**1**	**14**	**1**	**0**	**1**	**26**	**0**	**0**	**0**
1987-88	**Chicago Blackhawks**	**NHL**	**37**	**7**	**9**	**16**	**6**	**6**	**12**	**70**	**3**	**0**	**0**	**74**	**9.5**	**36**	**9**	**39**	**14**	**2**	**5**	**0**	**0**	**0**	**21**	**0**	**0**	**0**
1988-89	**Chicago Blackhawks**	**NHL**	**75**	**7**	**9**	**16**	**6**	**6**	**12**	**214**	**0**	**0**	**1**	**83**	**8.4**	**23**	**0**	**35**	**1**	**–11**	**16**	**3**	**1**	**4**	**15**	**0**	**0**	**2**
1989-90	**Chicago Blackhawks**	**NHL**	**72**	**4**	**14**	**18**	**3**	**10**	**13**	**156**	**0**	**0**	**1**	**70**	**5.7**	**26**	**1**	**27**	**0**	**–2**	**20**	**1**	**1**	**2**	**48**	**0**	**0**	**0**
	NHL Totals		**731**	**139**	**203**	**342**	**114**	**138**	**252**	**1333**	**17**	**0**	**10**	**1177**	**11.8**	**528**	**78**	**456**	**29**		**161**	**26**	**32**	**58**	**405**	**2**	**0**	**5**

Brother of Brian, Darryl, Brent, Rich and Ron • Traded to **Chicago** by **NY Islanders** for Chicago's 2nd round choice (Wayne Doucet) in 1988 Entry Draft, September 9, 1987.

• SUTTER, Rich

Richard G. RW – R. 5'11", 188 lbs. b: Viking, Alta., 12/2/1963. Pittsburgh's 1st, 10th overall, in 1982.

Season	Club	League	GP	G	A	Pts	AG	AA	APts	PIM	PP	SH	GW	S	%	TGF	PGF	TGA	PGA	+/-	GP	G	A	Pts	PIM	PP	SH	GW
1979-80	Red Deer Rustlers	AJHL	60	13	19	32	....	....	....	157	....	....	....	....	....	....	....	....	....	....	....	....	....	....	....	....	....	....
	Red Deer Rustlers	Cen-Cup	STATISTICS NOT AVAILABLE																									
1980-81	Lethbridge Broncos	WHL	72	23	18	41	....	....	....	255	....	....	....	....	....	....	....	....	....	....	9	3	1	4	35	....	....	....
1981-82	Lethbridge Broncos	WHL	57	38	31	69	....	....	....	263	....	....	....	....	....	....	....	....	....	....	12	3	3	6	55	....	....	....
1982-83	Lethbridge Broncos	WHL	64	37	30	67	....	....	....	200	....	....	....	....	....	....	....	....	....	....	17	14	9	23	43	....	....	....
	Pittsburgh Penguins	**NHL**	**4**	**0**	**0**	**0**	**0**	**0**	**0**	**0**	**0**	**0**	**0**	**3**	**0.0**	**1**	**0**	**3**	**0**	**–2**	....	....	....	....	....	....	....	....
	Lethbridge Broncos	Mem-Cup	3	4	2	6	....	....	....	2	....	....	....	....	....	....	....	....	....	....	....	....	....	....	....	....	....	....
1983-84	**Pittsburgh Penguins**	**NHL**	**5**	**0**	**0**	**0**	**0**	**0**	**0**	**0**	**0**	**0**	**0**	**2**	**0.0**	**0**	**0**	**2**	**0**	**–2**	....	....	....	....	....	....	....	....
	Baltimore Skipjacks	AHL	2	0	1	1	....	....	....	0	....	....	....	....	....	....	....	....	....	....	....	....	....	....	....	....	....	....
	Philadelphia Flyers	**NHL**	**70**	**16**	**12**	**28**	**13**	**8**	**21**	**93**	**2**	**0**	**1**	**133**	**12.0**	**46**	**3**	**33**	**0**	**10**	**3**	**0**	**0**	**0**	**15**	**0**	**0**	**0**
1984-85	**Philadelphia Flyers**	**NHL**	**56**	**6**	**10**	**16**	**5**	**7**	**12**	**89**	**0**	**0**	**0**	**62**	**9.7**	**25**	**0**	**28**	**3**	**0**	**11**	**3**	**0**	**3**	**10**	**0**	**0**	**0**
	Hershey Bears	AHL	13	3	7	10	....	....	....	14	....	....	....	....	....	....	....	....	....	....	....	....	....	....	....	....	....	....
1985-86	**Philadelphia Flyers**	**NHL**	**78**	**14**	**25**	**39**	**11**	**17**	**28**	**199**	**0**	**0**	**2**	**124**	**11.3**	**58**	**1**	**35**	**6**	**28**	**5**	**2**	**0**	**2**	**19**	**0**	**0**	**0**
1986-87	**Vancouver Canucks**	**NHL**	**74**	**20**	**22**	**42**	**17**	**16**	**33**	**113**	**3**	**0**	**2**	**166**	**12.0**	**62**	**13**	**74**	**8**	**–17**	....	....	....	....	....	....	....	....
1987-88	**Vancouver Canucks**	**NHL**	**80**	**15**	**15**	**30**	**13**	**11**	**24**	**165**	**2**	**1**	**2**	**132**	**11.4**	**50**	**6**	**69**	**21**	**–4**	....	....	....	....	....	....	....	....
1988-89	**Vancouver Canucks**	**NHL**	**75**	**17**	**15**	**32**	**14**	**11**	**25**	**122**	**1**	**3**	**4**	**125**	**13.6**	**49**	**5**	**69**	**28**	**3**	**7**	**2**	**1**	**3**	**12**	**0**	**0**	**0**
1989-90	**Vancouver Canucks**	**NHL**	**62**	**9**	**9**	**18**	**8**	**6**	**14**	**133**	**0**	**1**	**1**	**100**	**9.0**	**32**	**0**	**55**	**22**	**–1**	....	....	....	....	....	....	....	....
	St. Louis Blues	**NHL**	**12**	**2**	**0**	**2**	**2**	**0**	**2**	**22**	**0**	**0**	**0**	**22**	**9.1**	**5**	**0**	**9**	**2**	**–2**	**12**	**2**	**1**	**3**	**39**	**0**	**1**	**1**
1990-91	**St. Louis Blues**	**NHL**	**77**	**16**	**11**	**27**	**15**	**8**	**23**	**122**	**0**	**2**	**2**	**130**	**12.3**	**43**	**0**	**58**	**21**	**6**	**13**	**4**	**2**	**6**	**16**	**0**	**0**	**1**
1991-92	**St. Louis Blues**	**NHL**	**77**	**9**	**16**	**25**	**8**	**12**	**20**	**107**	**0**	**1**	**3**	**113**	**8.0**	**40**	**0**	**48**	**15**	**7**	**6**	**0**	**0**	**0**	**8**	**0**	**0**	**0**
1992-93	**St. Louis Blues**	**NHL**	**84**	**13**	**14**	**27**	**11**	**10**	**21**	**100**	**0**	**2**	**1**	**148**	**8.8**	**42**	**1**	**77**	**32**	**–4**	**11**	**0**	**1**	**1**	**10**	**0**	**0**	**0**
1993-94	**Chicago Blackhawks**	**NHL**	**83**	**12**	**14**	**26**	**11**	**11**	**22**	**108**	**0**	**0**	**2**	**122**	**9.8**	**36**	**2**	**47**	**5**	**–8**	**6**	**0**	**0**	**0**	**2**	**0**	**0**	**0**
1994-95	**Chicago Blackhawks**	**NHL**	**15**	**0**	**0**	**0**	**0**	**0**	**0**	**28**	**0**	**0**	**0**	**17**	**0.0**	**4**	**0**	**4**	**1**	**1**	....	....	....	....	....	....	....	....
	Tampa Bay Lightning	**NHL**	**4**	**0**	**0**	**0**	**0**	**0**	**0**	**0**	**0**	**0**	**0**	**3**	**0.0**	**0**	**0**	**0**	**0**	**0**	....	....	....	....	....	....	....	....
	Atlanta Knights	IHL	4	0	5	5	....	....	....	0	....	....	....	....	....	....	....	....	....	....	....	....	....	....	....	....	....	....
	Toronto Maple Leafs	**NHL**	**18**	**0**	**3**	**3**	**0**	**4**	**4**	**10**	**0**	**0**	**0**	**19**	**0.0**	**3**	**0**	**11**	**1**	**–7**	**4**	**0**	**0**	**0**	**2**	**0**	**0**	**0**
	NHL Totals		**874**	**149**	**166**	**315**	**128**	**121**	**249**	**1411**	**8**	**10**	**20**	**1421**	**10.5**	**496**	**31**	**622**	**165**		**78**	**13**	**5**	**18**	**133**	**0**	**1**	**2**

• Brother of Brent, Brian, Darryl, Duane, and Ron

Traded to **Philadelphia** by **Pittsburgh** with Pittsburgh's 2nd (Greg Smyth) and 3rd (David McLay) round choices in 1984 Entry Draft for Andy Brickley, Mark Taylor, Ron Flockhart and Philadelphia's 1st (Roger Belanger) and 3rd (later traded to Vancouver - Vancouver selected Mike Stevens) in 1984 Entry Draft, October 23, 1983. Traded to **Vancouver** by **Philadelphia** with Dave Richter and Vancouver's 3rd round choice (previously acquired, Vancouver selected Don Gibson) in 1986 Entry Draft for J.J. Daigneault, Vancouver's 2nd round choice (Kent Hawley) in 1986 Entry Draft and Vancouver's 5th round choice (later traded back to Vancouver–Vancouver selected Sean Fabian) in 1987 Entry Draft, June 6, 1986. Traded to **St. Louis** by **Vancouver** with Harold Snepsts and St. Louis' 2nd round choice (previously acquired, St. Louis selected Craig Johnson) in 1990 Entry Draft for Adrien Plavsic, Montreal's 1st round choice (previously acquired, Vancouver selected Shawn Antoski) in 1990 Entry Draft and St. Louis' 2nd round choice (later traded to Montreal - Montreal selected Craig Darby) in 1991 Entry Draft, March 6, 1990. Claimed by **Chicago** from **St. Louis** in Waiver Draft, October 3, 1993. Traded to **Tampa Bay** by **Chicago** with Paul Ysebaert for Jim Cummins, Tom Tilley and Jeff Buchanan, February 22, 1995. Traded to **Toronto** by **Tampa Bay** for cash, March 13, 1995.

• SUTTER, Ron

C – R. 6', 180 lbs. b: Viking, Alta., 12/2/1963. Philadelphia's 1st, 4th overall, in 1982.

Season	Club	League	GP	G	A	Pts	AG	AA	APts	PIM	PP	SH	GW	S	%	TGF	PGF	TGA	PGA	+/-	GP	G	A	Pts	PIM	PP	SH	GW
1979-80	Red Deer Rustlers	AJHL	60	12	33	45	....	....	....	44	....	....	....	....	....	....	....	....	....	....	....	....	....	....	....	....	....	....
	Red Deer Rustlers	Cen-Cup	....	....	....	....	....	....	....	....	....	....	....	....	....	....	....	....	....	....	....	....	....	....	....	....	....	....
1980-81	Lethbridge Broncos	WHL	72	13	32	45	....	....	....	152	....	....	....	....	....	....	....	....	....	....	9	2	5	7	29	....	....	....
1981-82	Lethbridge Broncos	WHL	59	38	54	92	....	....	....	207	....	....	....	....	....	....	....	....	....	....	12	6	5	11	28	....	....	....
1982-83	Lethbridge Broncos	WHL	58	35	48	83	....	....	....	98	....	....	....	....	....	....	....	....	....	....	20	*22	*19	*41	45	....	....	....
	Philadelphia Flyers	**NHL**	**10**	**1**	**1**	**2**	**1**	**1**	**2**	**9**	**0**	**0**	**1**	**4**	**25.0**	**4**	**0**	**4**	**0**	**0**	....	....	....	....	....	....	....	....
	Lethbridge Broncos	Mem-Cup	3	2	2	4	....	....	....	4	....	....	....	....	....	....	....	....	....	....	....	....	....	....	....	....	....	....
1983-84	**Philadelphia Flyers**	**NHL**	**79**	**19**	**32**	**51**	**15**	**22**	**37**	**101**	**5**	**3**	**3**	**145**	**13.1**	**76**	**20**	**71**	**19**	**4**	**3**	**0**	**0**	**0**	**22**	**0**	**0**	**0**
1984-85	**Philadelphia Flyers**	**NHL**	**73**	**16**	**29**	**45**	**13**	**20**	**33**	**94**	**2**	**0**	**5**	**140**	**11.4**	**66**	**5**	**66**	**18**	**13**	**19**	**4**	**8**	**12**	**28**	**0**	**0**	**1**
1985-86	**Philadelphia Flyers**	**NHL**	**75**	**18**	**42**	**60**	**14**	**28**	**42**	**159**	**0**	**0**	**4**	**145**	**12.4**	**75**	**3**	**62**	**16**	**26**	**5**	**0**	**2**	**2**	**10**	**0**	**0**	**0**
1986-87	**Philadelphia Flyers**	**NHL**	**39**	**10**	**17**	**27**	**9**	**12**	**21**	**69**	**0**	**0**	**0**	**68**	**14.7**	**33**	**0**	**35**	**12**	**10**	**16**	**1**	**7**	**8**	**12**	**0**	**0**	**0**
1987-88	**Philadelphia Flyers**	**NHL**	**69**	**8**	**25**	**33**	**7**	**18**	**25**	**146**	**1**	**0**	**0**	**107**	**7.5**	**43**	**1**	**78**	**27**	**–9**	**7**	**0**	**1**	**1**	**26**	**0**	**0**	**0**
1988-89	**Philadelphia Flyers**	**NHL**	**55**	**26**	**22**	**48**	**22**	**16**	**38**	**80**	**4**	**1**	**2**	**106**	**24.5**	**62**	**6**	**51**	**20**	**25**	**19**	**1**	**9**	**10**	**51**	**0**	**0**	**0**
1989-90	**Philadelphia Flyers**	**NHL**	**75**	**22**	**26**	**48**	**19**	**19**	**38**	**104**	**0**	**2**	**6**	**157**	**14.0**	**68**	**1**	**94**	**29**	**2**	....	....	....	....	....	....	....	....
	Canada	WEC-A	10	1	1	2	....	....	....	4	....	....	....	....	....	....	....	....	....	....	....	....	....	....	....	....	....	....
1990-91	**Philadelphia Flyers**	**NHL**	**80**	**17**	**28**	**45**	**16**	**21**	**37**	**92**	**2**	**0**	**1**	**149**	**11.4**	**65**	**7**	**93**	**37**	**2**	....	....	....	....	....	....	....	....
1991-92	**St. Louis Blues**	**NHL**	**68**	**19**	**27**	**46**	**17**	**20**	**37**	**91**	**5**	**4**	**1**	**106**	**17.9**	**71**	**18**	**60**	**16**	**9**	**6**	**1**	**3**	**4**	**8**	**1**	**0**	**0**
1992-93	**St. Louis Blues**	**NHL**	**59**	**12**	**15**	**27**	**10**	**10**	**20**	**99**	**4**	**0**	**3**	**90**	**13.3**	**43**	**15**	**43**	**4**	**–11**	....	....	....	....	....	....	....	....
1993-94	**St. Louis Blues**	**NHL**	**36**	**6**	**12**	**18**	**6**	**9**	**15**	**46**	**1**	**0**	**2**	**42**	**14.3**	**28**	**5**	**27**	**3**	**–1**	....	....	....	....	....	....	....	....
	Quebec Nordiques	**NHL**	**37**	**9**	**13**	**22**	**8**	**10**	**18**	**44**	**4**	**0**	**0**	**66**	**13.6**	**37**	**10**	**36**	**12**	**3**	....	....	....	....	....	....	....	....
1994-95	**New York Islanders**	**NHL**	**27**	**1**	**4**	**5**	**2**	**6**	**8**	**21**	**0**	**0**	**1**	**29**	**3.4**	**7**	**0**	**25**	**10**	**–8**	....	....	....	....	....	....	....	....
1995-96	Phoenix Roadrunners	IHL	25	6	13	19	....	....	....	28	....	....	....	....	....	....	....	....	....	....	....	....	....	....	....	....	....	....
	Boston Bruins	**NHL**	**18**	**5**	**7**	**12**	**5**	**6**	**11**	**24**	**0**	**1**	**0**	**34**	**14.7**	**20**	**0**	**15**	**5**	**10**	**5**	**0**	**0**	**0**	**8**	**0**	**0**	**0**
1996-97	**San Jose Sharks**	**NHL**	**78**	**5**	**7**	**12**	**5**	**6**	**11**	**65**	**1**	**2**	**1**	**78**	**6.4**	**22**	**1**	**46**	**17**	**–8**	....	....	....	....	....	....	....	....

			REGULAR SEASON																		PLAYOFFS							
Season	Club	League	GP	G	A	Pts	AG	AA	APts	PIM	PP	SH	GW	S	%	TGF	PGF	TGA	PGA	+/–	GP	G	A	Pts	PIM	PP	SH	GW
1997-98	**San Jose Sharks**	**NHL**	57	2	7	9	2	7	9	22	0	0	1	57	3.5	14	0	25	9	–2	6	1	0	1	14	0	0	0
1998-99	**San Jose Sharks**	**NHL**	59	3	6	9	4	6	10	40	0	0	1	67	4.5	11	1	26	8	–8	6	0	0	0	4	0	0	0
99-2000	**San Jose Sharks**	**NHL**	78	5	6	11	6	6	12	34	0	1	1	68	7.4	18	1	28	8	–3	12	0	2	2	10	0	0	0
	NHL Totals		1072	204	326	530	181	243	424	1340	29	14	33	1658	12.3	763	94	885	270		104	8	32	40	193	1	0	1

• Brother of Brent, Brian, Darryl, Duane and Rich

Traded to **St. Louis** by **Philadelphia** with Murray Baron for Dan Quinn and Rod Brind'Amour, September 22, 1991. Traded to **Quebec** by **St. Louis** with Garth Butcher and Bob Bassen for Steve Duchesne and Denis Chasse, January 23, 1994. Traded to **NY Islanders** by **Quebec** with Quebec's 1st round choice (Brett Lindros) in 1994 Entry Draft for Uwe Krupp and NY Islanders' 1st round choice (Wade Belak) in 1994 Entry Draft, June 28, 1994. Signed as a free agent by **Boston**, March 9, 1996. Signed as a free agent by **San Jose**, October 12, 1996.

• SUTTON, Andy

Andy Cameron D – L. 6'6", 245 lbs. b: Edmonton, Alta., 3/10/1975.

Season	Club	League	GP	G	A	Pts	AG	AA	APts	PIM	PP	SH	GW	S	%	TGF	PGF	TGA	PGA	+/–	GP	G	A	Pts	PIM	PP	SH	GW
1991-92	Gananoque Islanders	OJHL-B	50	20	30	50	....	....	....	....	....	....	....	....	....	....	....	....	....	....	....	....	....	....	....	....	....	....
1992-93	Gananoque Islanders	OJHL-B	50	25	27	52	....	....	....	....	....	....	....	....	....	....	....	....	....	....	....	....	....	....	....	....	....	....
1993-94	St. Michael's Buzzers	OJHL	48	17	23	40	....	....	....	161	....	....	....	....	....	....	....	....	....	....	3	0	0	0	20	....	....	....
1994-95	Michigan Tech Huskies	WCHA	19	2	1	3	....	....	....	42	....	....	....	....	....	....	....	....	....	....	....	....	....	....	....	....	....	....
1995-96	Michigan Tech Huskies	WCHA	33	2	2	4	....	....	....	58	....	....	....	....	....	....	....	....	....	....	....	....	....	....	....	....	....	....
1996-97	Michigan Tech Huskies	WCHA	32	2	7	9	....	....	....	73	....	....	....	....	....	....	....	....	....	....	....	....	....	....	....	....	....	....
1997-98	Michigan Tech Huskies	WCHA	38	16	24	40	....	....	....	97	....	....	....	....	....	....	....	....	....	....	....	....	....	....	....	....	....	....
	Kentucky Thoroughblades	AHL	7	0	0	0	....	....	....	33	....	....	....	....	....	....	....	....	....	....	....	....	....	....	....	....	....	....
1998-99	**San Jose Sharks**	**NHL**	31	0	3	3	0	3	3	65	0	0	0	24	0.0	14	2	17	1	–4	....	....	....	....	....	....	....	....
	Kentucky Thoroughblades	AHL	21	5	10	15	....	....	....	53	....	....	....	....	....	....	....	....	....	....	5	0	0	0	23	....	....	....
99-2000	**San Jose Sharks**	**NHL**	40	1	1	2	1	1	2	80	0	0	0	29	3.4	13	1	17	0	–5	....	....	....	....	....	....	....	....
	Kentucky Thoroughblades	AHL	3	0	1	1	....	....	....	0	....	....	....	....	....	....	....	....	....	....	....	....	....	....	....	....	....	....
	NHL Totals		71	1	4	5	1	4	5	145	0	0	0	53	1.9	27	3	34	1		....	....	....	....	....	....	....	....

WCHA Second All-Star Team (1998)

Signed as a free agent by **San Jose**, March 20, 1998. Traded to **Minnesota** by **San Jose** with San Jose's 7th round choice (Peter Bartos) in 2000 Entry Draft and 3rd round choice in 2001 Entry Draft for Minnesota's 8th round choice in 2001 Entry Draft and future considerations, June 12, 2000.

• SUTTON, Ken

Kenneth William D – L. 6'1", 205 lbs. b: Edmonton, Alta., 11/5/1969. Buffalo's 4th, 98th overall, in 1989.

Season	Club	League	GP	G	A	Pts	AG	AA	APts	PIM	PP	SH	GW	S	%	TGF	PGF	TGA	PGA	+/–	GP	G	A	Pts	PIM	PP	SH	GW
1987-88	Calgary Canucks	AJHL	53	13	43	56	....	....	....	228	....	....	....	....	....	....	....	....	....	....	....	....	....	....	....	....	....	....
1988-89	Saskatoon Blades	WHL	71	22	31	53	....	....	....	104	....	....	....	....	....	....	....	....	....	....	8	2	5	7	12	....	....	....
	Saskatoon Blades	Mem-Cup	4	3	2	5	....	....	....	6	....	....	....	....	....	....	....	....	....	....	....	....	....	....	....	....	....	....
1989-90	Rochester Americans	AHL	57	5	14	19	....	....	....	83	....	....	....	....	....	....	....	....	....	....	11	1	6	7	15	....	....	....
1990-91	**Buffalo Sabres**	**NHL**	15	3	6	9	3	5	8	13	2	0	0	26	11.5	25	9	15	1	2	6	0	1	1	2	0	0	0
	Rochester Americans	AHL	62	7	24	31	....	....	....	65	....	....	....	....	....	....	....	....	....	....	3	1	1	2	14	....	....	....
1991-92	**Buffalo Sabres**	**NHL**	64	2	18	20	2	14	16	71	0	0	0	81	2.5	69	14	76	26	5	7	0	2	2	4	0	0	0
1992-93	**Buffalo Sabres**	**NHL**	63	8	14	22	7	10	17	30	1	0	2	77	10.4	71	1	81	8	–3	8	3	1	4	8	0	0	0
1993-94	**Buffalo Sabres**	**NHL**	78	4	20	24	4	16	20	71	1	0	0	95	4.2	72	25	61	8	–6	4	0	0	0	2	0	0	0
1994-95	**Buffalo Sabres**	**NHL**	12	1	2	3	2	3	5	30	0	0	1	12	8.3	10	4	8	0	–2	....	....	....	....	....	....	....	....
	Edmonton Oilers	**NHL**	12	3	1	4	5	1	6	12	0	0	0	28	10.7	9	2	13	5	–1	....	....	....	....	....	....	....	....
1995-96	**Edmonton Oilers**	**NHL**	32	0	8	8	0	7	7	39	0	0	0	38	0.0	28	8	46	14	–12	....	....	....	....	....	....	....	....
	St. Louis Blues	**NHL**	6	0	0	0	0	0	0	4	0	0	0	3	0.0	1	0	2	0	–1	1	0	0	0	0	0	0	0
	Worcester IceCats	AHL	32	4	16	20	....	....	....	60	....	....	....	....	....	....	....	....	....	....	4	0	2	2	21	....	....	....
1996-97	Manitoba Moose	IHL	20	3	10	13	....	....	....	48	....	....	....	....	....	....	....	....	....	....	....	....	....	....	....	....	....	....
	Albany River Rats	AHL	61	6	13	19	....	....	....	79	....	....	....	....	....	....	....	....	....	....	16	4	8	12	55	....	....	....
1997-98	**New Jersey Devils**	**NHL**	13	0	0	0	0	0	0	6	0	0	0	5	0.0	5	0	4	0	1	....	....	....	....	....	....	....	....
	Albany River Rats	AHL	10	0	7	7	....	....	....	15	....	....	....	....	....	....	....	....	....	....	....	....	....	....	....	....	....	....
	San Jose Sharks	**NHL**	8	0	0	0	0	0	0	15	0	0	0	7	0.0	2	0	6	0	–4	....	....	....	....	....	....	....	....
1998-99	**New Jersey Devils**	**NHL**	5	1	0	1	1	0	1	0	0	0	0	5	20.0	4	0	3	0	1	....	....	....	....	....	....	....	....
	Albany River Rats	AHL	75	13	42	55	....	....	....	118	....	....	....	....	....	....	....	....	....	....	5	0	2	2	12	....	....	....
99-2000	**New Jersey Devils**	**NHL**	6	0	2	2	0	2	2	2	0	0	0	10	0.0	5	1	2	0	2	....	....	....	....	....	....	....	....
	Albany River Rats	AHL	57	5	16	21	....	....	....	129	....	....	....	....	....	....	....	....	....	....	....	....	....	....	....	....	....	....
	NHL Totals		314	22	71	93	24	58	82	293	4	0	3	387	5.7	301	64	317	62		26	3	4	7	16	0	0	0

Memorial Cup All-Star Team (1989) • AHL First All-Star Team (1999) • Won Eddie Shore Award (Outstanding Defenseman - AHL) (1999)

Traded to **Edmonton** by **Buffalo** for Scott Pearson, April 7, 1995. Traded to **St. Louis** by **Edmonton** with Igor Kravchuk for Jeff Norton and Donald Dufresne, January 4, 1996. Traded to **New Jersey** by **St. Louis** with St. Louis' 2nd round choice (Brett Clouthier) in 1999 Entry Draft for Mike Peluso and Ricard Persson, November 26, 1996. Traded to **San Jose** by **New Jersey** with John MacLean for Doug Bodger and Dody Wood, December 7, 1997. Traded to **New Jersey** by **San Jose** for future considerations, August 26, 1998. Claimed by **Washington** from **New Jersey** in Waiver Draft, September 27, 1999. Traded to **New Jersey** by **Washington** for future considerations, October 5, 1999.

• SUZOR, Mark

Mark Joseph D – L. 6'1", 212 lbs. b: Windsor, Ont., 11/5/1956. Philadelphia's 1st, 17th overall, in 1976.

Season	Club	League	GP	G	A	Pts	AG	AA	APts	PIM	PP	SH	GW	S	%	TGF	PGF	TGA	PGA	+/–	GP	G	A	Pts	PIM	PP	SH	GW
1973-74	Kingston Canadians	OMJHL	68	6	9	15	....	....	....	13	....	....	....	....	....	....	....	....	....	....	....	....	....	....	....	....	....	....
1974-75	Kingston Canadians	OMJHL	70	14	44	58	....	....	....	104	....	....	....	....	....	....	....	....	....	....	8	1	8	9	42	....	....	....
1975-76	Kingston Canadians	OMJHL	48	16	30	46	....	....	....	108	....	....	....	....	....	....	....	....	....	....	7	2	5	7	18	....	....	....
1976-77	**Philadelphia Flyers**	**NHL**	4	0	1	1	0	1	1	4	0	0	0	4	0.0	2	0	1	1	2	....	....	....	....	....	....	....	....
	Springfield Indians	AHL	74	24	25	49	....	....	....	108	....	....	....	....	....	....	....	....	....	....	....	....	....	....	....	....	....	....
1977-78	**Colorado Rockies**	**NHL**	60	4	15	19	4	12	16	56	2	0	0	89	4.5	47	12	76	6	–35	....	....	....	....	....	....	....	....
1978-79	Rochester Americans	AHL	24	4	6	10	....	....	....	16	....	....	....	....	....	....	....	....	....	....	....	....	....	....	....	....	....	....
	Saginaw Gears	IHL	29	12	12	24	....	....	....	43	....	....	....	....	....	....	....	....	....	....	....	....	....	....	....	....	....	....
	Grand Rapids Owls	IHL	2	0	2	2	....	....	....	0	....	....	....	....	....	....	....	....	....	....	....	....	....	....	....	....	....	....
	Muskegon Mohawks	IHL	16	1	5	6	....	....	....	6	....	....	....	....	....	....	....	....	....	....	....	....	....	....	....	....	....	....
1979-80	Binghamton Dusters	AHL	7	0	1	1	....	....	....	2	....	....	....	....	....	....	....	....	....	....	....	....	....	....	....	....	....	....
	Grand Rapids Owls	IHL	58	20	33	53	....	....	....	109	....	....	....	....	....	....	....	....	....	....	....	....	....	....	....	....	....	....
1980-81	Toledo Goaldiggers	IHL	8	1	2	3	....	....	....	0	....	....	....	....	....	....	....	....	....	....	....	....	....	....	....	....	....	....
	NHL Totals		64	4	16	20	4	13	17	60	2	0	0	93	4.3	49	12	77	7		....	....	....	....	....	....	....	....

Traded to **Colorado** by **Philadelphia** for Barry Dean, August 5, 1977. Traded to **Boston** by **Colorado** for Clayton Pachal, October 11, 1978.

• SVARTVADET, Per

C – L. 6'1", 190 lbs. b: Solleftea, Sweden, 5/17/1975. Dallas' 5th, 139th overall, in 1993.

Season	Club	League	GP	G	A	Pts	AG	AA	APts	PIM	PP	SH	GW	S	%	TGF	PGF	TGA	PGA	+/–	GP	G	A	Pts	PIM	PP	SH	GW
1992-93	MoDo AIK	Sweden-Jr.	14	5	10	15	....	....	....	18	....	....	....	....	....	....	....	....	....	....	....	....	....	....	....	....	....	....
	Sweden	EJC-A	6	2	6	8	....	....	....	4	....	....	....	....	....	....	....	....	....	....	....	....	....	....	....	....	....	....
	MoDo AIK	Sweden	2	0	0	0	....	....	....	0	....	....	....	....	....	....	....	....	....	....	....	....	....	....	....	....	....	....
1993-94	MoDo AIK	Sweden-Jr.	12	7	12	19	....	....	....	6	....	....	....	....	....	....	....	....	....	....	....	....	....	....	....	....	....	....
	Sweden	WJC-A	7	0	3	3	....	....	....	8	....	....	....	....	....	....	....	....	....	....	....	....	....	....	....	....	....	....
	MoDo AIK	Sweden	36	2	1	3	....	....	....	4	....	....	....	....	....	....	....	....	....	....	11	0	0	0	6	....	....	....
1994-95	MoDo Hockey	Sweden	40	6	9	15	....	....	....	31	....	....	....	....	....	....	....	....	....	....	....	....	....	....	....	....	....	....
	Sweden	WJC-A	7	2	6	8	....	....	....	2	....	....	....	....	....	....	....	....	....	....	....	....	....	....	....	....	....	....
1995-96	MoDo Hockey	Sweden	40	9	14	23	....	....	....	26	....	....	....	....	....	....	....	....	....	....	8	2	3	5	0	....	....	....
1996-97	MoDo Hockey	Sweden	50	7	18	25	....	....	....	38	....	....	....	....	....	....	....	....	....	....	....	....	....	....	....	....	....	....
	Sweden	WC-A	10	0	2	2	....	....	....	0	....	....	....	....	....	....	....	....	....	....	....	....	....	....	....	....	....	....
1997-98	MoDo Hockey	Sweden	46	6	12	18	....	....	....	28	....	....	....	....	....	....	....	....	....	....	7	3	2	5	2	....	....	....
1998-99	MoDo Hockey	Sweden	50	9	23	32	....	....	....	30	....	....	....	....	....	....	....	....	....	....	13	3	6	9	6	....	....	....
99-2000	**Atlanta Thrashers**	**NHL**	38	3	4	7	3	4	7	6	0	0	0	36	8.3	12	1	26	7	–8	....	....	....	....	....	....	....	....
	Orlando Solar Bears	IHL	27	4	6	10	....	....	....	10	....	....	....	....	....	....	....	....	....	....	5	0	1	1	0	....	....	....
	NHL Totals		38	3	4	7	3	4	7	6	0	0	0	36	8.3	12	1	26	7		....	....	....	....	....	....	....	....

Traded to **Atlanta** by **Dallas** for Ottawa's 6th round choice (previously acquired, Dallas selected Justin Cox) in 1999 Entry Draft, June 26, 1999.

• SVEHLA, Robert

D – R. 6'1", 210 lbs. b: Martin, Czech., 1/2/1969. Calgary's 4th, 78th overall, in 1992.

			REGULAR SEASON																		PLAYOFFS							
Season	Club	League	GP	G	A	Pts	AG	AA	APts	PIM	PP	SH	GW	S	%	TGF	PGF	TGA	PGA	+/–	GP	G	A	Pts	PIM	PP	SH	GW
1986-87	Czechoslovakia	EJC-A	7	2	2	4	....	....	....	2	....	....	....	....	....	....	....	....	....	....	....	....	....	....	....	....	....	....
1989-90	Dukla Trencin	Czech.	29	4	3	7	....	....	....	....	....	....	....	....	....	....	....	....	....	....	....	....	....	....	....	....	....	....
1990-91	Dukla Trencin	Czech.	52	16	9	25	....	....	....	62	....	....	....	....	....	....	....	....	....	....	....	....	....	....	....	....	....	....
1991-92	Dukla Trencin	Czech.	51	23	28	51	....	....	....	74	....	....	....	....	....	....	....	....	....	....	....	....	....	....	....	....	....	....
	Czechoslovakia	Olympics	8	2	1	3	....	....	....	8	....	....	....	....	....	....	....	....	....	....	....	....	....	....	....	....	....	....
	Czechoslovakia	WC-A	8	4	4	8	....	....	....	14	....	....	....	....	....	....	....	....	....	....	....	....	....	....	....	....	....	....
1992-93	Malmo IF	Sweden	40	19	10	29	....	....	....	86	....	....	....	....	....	....	....	....	....	....	6	0	1	1	14	....	....	....
1993-94	Malmo IF	Sweden	37	14	25	39	....	....	....	*127	....	....	....	....	....	....	....	....	....	....	10	5	1	6	23	....	....	....
	Slovakia	Olympics	8	2	4	6	....	....	....	26	....	....	....	....	....	....	....	....	....	....	....	....	....	....	....	....	....	....
1994-95	Malmo IF	Sweden	32	11	13	24	....	....	....	83	....	....	....	....	....	....	....	....	....	....	9	2	3	5	6	....	....	....
	Florida Panthers	**NHL**	**5**	**1**	**1**	**2**	**2**	**1**	**3**	**0**	**1**	**0**	**0**	**6**	**16.7**	**7**	**2**	**2**	**0**	**3**	....	....	....	....	....	....	....	....
	Slovakia	WC-B	4	0	6	6	....	....	....	10	....	....	....	....	....	....	....	....	....	....	....	....	....	....	....	....	....	....
1995-96	**Florida Panthers**	**NHL**	**81**	**8**	**49**	**57**	**8**	**40**	**48**	**94**	**7**	**0**	**0**	**146**	**5.5**	**124**	**53**	**89**	**15**	**–3**	**22**	**0**	**6**	**6**	**32**	**0**	**0**	**0**
1996-97	Slovakia	W-Cup	3	0	3	3	....	....	....	4	....	....	....	....	....	....	....	....	....	....	....	....	....	....	....	....	....	....
	Florida Panthers	**NHL**	**82**	**13**	**32**	**45**	**14**	**28**	**42**	**86**	**5**	**0**	**3**	**159**	**8.2**	**100**	**33**	**82**	**17**	**2**	**5**	**1**	**4**	**5**	**4**	**1**	**0**	**0**
1997-98	**Florida Panthers**	**NHL**	**79**	**9**	**34**	**43**	**11**	**33**	**44**	**113**	**3**	**0**	**0**	**144**	**6.3**	**109**	**41**	**107**	**36**	**–3**	....	....	....	....	....	....	....	....
	Slovakia	Olympics	2	0	1	1	....	....	....	0	....	....	....	....	....	....	....	....	....	....	....	....	....	....	....	....	....	....
	Slovakia	WC-A	6	1	1	2	....	....	....	14	....	....	....	....	....	....	....	....	....	....	....	....	....	....	....	....	....	....
1998-99	**Florida Panthers**	**NHL**	**80**	**8**	**29**	**37**	**9**	**28**	**37**	**83**	**4**	**0**	**0**	**157**	**5.1**	**96**	**36**	**102**	**29**	**–13**	....	....	....	....	....	....	....	....
99-2000	**Florida Panthers**	**NHL**	**82**	**9**	**40**	**49**	**10**	**37**	**47**	**64**	**3**	**0**	**1**	**143**	**6.3**	**122**	**40**	**82**	**23**	**23**	**4**	**0**	**1**	**1**	**4**	**0**	**0**	**0**
	NHL Totals		**409**	**48**	**185**	**233**	**54**	**167**	**221**	**440**	**23**	**0**	**4**	**755**	**6.4**	**558**	**205**	**464**	**120**		**31**	**1**	**11**	**12**	**40**	**1**	**0**	**0**

Czechoslovakian First All-Star Team (1992) • Named Best Defenseman at WC-A (1992) • WC-B All-Star Team (1995) • Played in NHL All-Star Game (1997)

Traded to **Florida** by **Calgary** with Magnus Svensson for Florida's 3rd round choice (Dmitri Vlasenkov) in 1996 Entry Draft and 4th round choice (Ryan Ready) in 1997 Entry Draft, September 29, 1994.

• SVEJKOVSKY, Jaroslav

RW – R. 6'1", 185 lbs. b: Plzen, Czech., 10/1/1976. Washington's 2nd, 17th overall, in 1996.

			REGULAR SEASON																		PLAYOFFS							
Season	Club	League	GP	G	A	Pts	AG	AA	APts	PIM	PP	SH	GW	S	%	TGF	PGF	TGA	PGA	+/–	GP	G	A	Pts	PIM	PP	SH	GW
1993-94	ZKZ Plzen	Czech-Rep	8	0	0	0	....	....	....	8	....	....	....	....	....	....	....	....	....	....	....	....	....	....	....	....	....	....
1994-95	ZKZ Plzen	Czech-Jr.	25	18	19	37	....	....	....	30	....	....	....	....	....	....	....	....	....	....	....	....	....	....	....	....	....	....
	SK Tabor	Czech-Rep	11	6	7	13	....	....	....	....	....	....	....	....	....	....	....	....	....	....	....	....	....	....	....	....	....	....
1995-96	Tri-City Americans	WHL	70	58	43	101	....	....	....	118	....	....	....	....	....	....	....	....	....	....	11	10	9	19	8	....	....	....
1996-97	**Washington Capitals**	**NHL**	**19**	**7**	**3**	**10**	**7**	**3**	**10**	**4**	**2**	**0**	**1**	**30**	**23.3**	**10**	**3**	**8**	**0**	**–1**	....	....	....	....	....	....	....	....
	Portland Pirates	AHL	54	38	28	66	....	....	....	56	....	....	....	....	....	....	....	....	....	....	5	2	0	2	6	....	....	....
1997-98	**Washington Capitals**	**NHL**	**17**	**4**	**1**	**5**	**5**	**1**	**6**	**10**	**2**	**0**	**1**	**29**	**13.8**	**8**	**4**	**9**	**0**	**–5**	**1**	**0**	**0**	**0**	**2**	**0**	**0**	**0**
	Portland Pirates	AHL	16	12	7	19	....	....	....	16	....	....	....	....	....	....	....	....	....	....	7	1	2	3	2	....	....	....
1998-99	**Washington Capitals**	**NHL**	**25**	**6**	**8**	**14**	**7**	**8**	**15**	**12**	**4**	**0**	**2**	**50**	**12.0**	**24**	**11**	**15**	**0**	**–2**	....	....	....	....	....	....	....	....
99-2000	**Washington Capitals**	**NHL**	**23**	**1**	**2**	**3**	**1**	**2**	**3**	**2**	**1**	**0**	**0**	**18**	**5.6**	**5**	**5**	**7**	**0**	**–7**	....	....	....	....	....	....	....	....
	Tampa Bay Lightning	**NHL**	**29**	**5**	**5**	**10**	**6**	**5**	**11**	**28**	**0**	**0**	**0**	**42**	**11.9**	**17**	**1**	**23**	**0**	**–7**	....	....	....	....	....	....	....	....
	NHL Totals		**113**	**23**	**19**	**42**	**26**	**19**	**45**	**56**	**9**	**0**	**4**	**169**	**13.6**	**64**	**24**	**62**	**0**		**1**	**0**	**0**	**0**	**2**	**0**	**0**	**0**

WHL West Second All-Star Team (1996) • Won Dudley "Red" Garrett Memorial Trophy (Top Rookie — AHL) (1997)

Traded to **Tampa Bay** by **Washington** for Tampa Bay's 7th round choice (later traded to LA Kings - LA Kings selected Evgeny Federov) in 2000 Entry Draft and 3rd round choice in 2001 Entry Draft, January 17, 2000.

• SVENSSON, Leif

Leif Gunnar D – L. 6'3", 190 lbs. b: Harnosand, Sweden, 7/8/1951.

			REGULAR SEASON																		PLAYOFFS							
Season	Club	League	GP	G	A	Pts	AG	AA	APts	PIM	PP	SH	GW	S	%	TGF	PGF	TGA	PGA	+/–	GP	G	A	Pts	PIM	PP	SH	GW
1970-71	Nacka IK	Sweden-2	6	2	2	4	....	....	....	6	....	....	....	....	....	....	....	....	....	....	....	....	....	....	....	....	....	....
1971-72	Nacka IK	Sweden-2	7	1	5	6	....	....	....	6	....	....	....	....	....	....	....	....	....	....	....	....	....	....	....	....	....	....
1972-73	Sodertalje SK	Sweden	4	0	0	0	....	....	....	0	....	....	....	....	....	....	....	....	....	....	14	5	1	6	14	....	....	....
1973-74	Sodertalje SK	Sweden	14	8	4	12	....	....	....	8	....	....	....	....	....	....	....	....	....	....	....	....	....	....	....	....	....	....
1974-75	Djurgardens IF Stockholm	Sweden	28	2	6	8	....	....	....	30	....	....	....	....	....	....	....	....	....	....	....	....	....	....	....	....	....	....
	Djurgardens IF Stockholm	Sweden-Q	6	0	1	1	....	....	....	6	....	....	....	....	....	....	....	....	....	....	....	....	....	....	....	....	....	....
1975-76	Djurgardens IF Stockholm	Sweden	36	5	15	20	....	....	....	48	....	....	....	....	....	....	....	....	....	....	....	....	....	....	....	....	....	....
1976-77	Djurgardens IF Stockholm	Sweden	31	7	15	22	....	....	....	....	....	....	....	....	....	....	....	....	....	....	....	....	....	....	....	....	....	....
1977-78	Djurgardens IF Stockholm	Sweden	29	2	7	9	....	....	....	34	....	....	....	....	....	....	....	....	....	....	....	....	....	....	....	....	....	....
1978-79	**Washington Capitals**	**NHL**	**74**	**2**	**29**	**31**	**2**	**21**	**23**	**28**	**0**	**0**	**0**	**72**	**2.8**	**102**	**19**	**118**	**32**	**–3**	....	....	....	....	....	....	....	....
	Sweden	WEC-A	8	0	0	0	....	....	....	6	....	....	....	....	....	....	....	....	....	....	....	....	....	....	....	....	....	....
1979-80	**Washington Capitals**	**NHL**	**47**	**4**	**11**	**15**	**3**	**8**	**11**	**21**	**0**	**0**	**0**	**41**	**9.8**	**34**	**3**	**62**	**21**	**–10**	....	....	....	....	....	....	....	....
1980-81	Djurgardens IF Stockholm	Sweden	18	1	2	3	....	....	....	20	....	....	....	....	....	....	....	....	....	....	....	....	....	....	....	....	....	....
1981-82	Djurgardens IF Stockholm	DN-Cup	4	1	1	2	....	....	....	....	....	....	....	....	....	....	....	....	....	....	....	....	....	....	....	....	....	....
	Djurgardens IF Stockholm	Sweden	18	2	3	5	....	....	....	28	....	....	....	....	....	....	....	....	....	....	....	....	....	....	....	....	....	....
	NHL Totals		**121**	**6**	**40**	**46**	**5**	**29**	**34**	**49**	**0**	**0**	**0**	**113**	**5.3**	**136**	**22**	**180**	**53**		....	....	....	....	....	....	....	....

Signed as a free agent by **Washington**, June 10, 1978.

• SVENSSON, Magnus

D – L. 5'11", 180 lbs. b: Tranas, Sweden, 3/1/1963. Calgary's 13th, 250th overall, in 1987.

			REGULAR SEASON																		PLAYOFFS							
Season	Club	League	GP	G	A	Pts	AG	AA	APts	PIM	PP	SH	GW	S	%	TGF	PGF	TGA	PGA	+/–	GP	G	A	Pts	PIM	PP	SH	GW
1980-81	Tranas AIF	Sweden-2	16	0	1	1	....	....	....	6	....	....	....	....	....	....	....	....	....	....	....	....	....	....	....	....	....	....
1981-1983	Tranas AIF	Sweden-3	STATISTICS NOT AVAILABLE																									
1983-84	Leksands IF	Sweden	35	3	8	11	....	....	....	20	....	....	....	....	....	....	....	....	....	....	....	....	....	....	....	....	....	....
1984-85	Leksands IF	Sweden	35	8	7	15	....	....	....	22	....	....	....	....	....	....	....	....	....	....	....	....	....	....	....	....	....	....
1985-86	Leksands IF	Sweden	36	6	9	15	....	....	....	62	....	....	....	....	....	....	....	....	....	....	....	....	....	....	....	....	....	....
1986-87	Leksands IF	Sweden	33	8	16	24	....	....	....	42	....	....	....	....	....	....	....	....	....	....	....	....	....	....	....	....	....	....
	Sweden	WEC-A	2	0	0	0	....	....	....	4	....	....	....	....	....	....	....	....	....	....	....	....	....	....	....	....	....	....
1987-88	Leksands IF	Sweden	40	12	11	23	....	....	....	20	....	....	....	....	....	....	....	....	....	....	3	0	0	0	8	....	....	....
1988-89	Leksands IF	Sweden	39	15	22	37	....	....	....	40	....	....	....	....	....	....	....	....	....	....	9	3	5	8	8	....	....	....
1989-90	Leksands IF	Sweden	26	11	12	23	....	....	....	60	....	....	....	....	....	....	....	....	....	....	1	0	0	0	0	....	....	....
	Sweden	WEC-A	10	2	1	3	....	....	....	8	....	....	....	....	....	....	....	....	....	....	....	....	....	....	....	....	....	....
1990-91	HC Lugano	Switz.	33	16	20	36	....	....	....	74	....	....	....	....	....	....	....	....	....	....	11	2	3	5	....	....	....	....
1991-92	Leksands IF	Sweden	22	4	10	14	....	....	....	32	....	....	....	....	....	....	....	....	....	....	....	....	....	....	....	....	....	....
	Leksands IF	Sweden-Q	18	8	8	16	....	....	....	28	....	....	....	....	....	....	....	....	....	....	11	7	4	11	22	....	....	....
1992-93	Leksands IF	Sweden	37	10	17	27	....	....	....	36	....	....	....	....	....	....	....	....	....	....	2	0	2	2	0	....	....	....
1993-94	Leksands IF	Sweden	39	13	16	29	....	....	....	22	....	....	....	....	....	....	....	....	....	....	4	3	1	4	0	....	....	....
	Sweden	Olympics	7	4	1	5	....	....	....	6	....	....	....	....	....	....	....	....	....	....	....	....	....	....	....	....	....	....
	Sweden	WC-A	8	8	1	9	....	....	....	8	....	....	....	....	....	....	....	....	....	....	....	....	....	....	....	....	....	....
1994-95	HC Davos	Switz.	35	8	25	33	....	....	....	46	....	....	....	....	....	....	....	....	....	....	5	2	2	4	8	....	....	....
	Florida Panthers	**NHL**	**19**	**2**	**5**	**7**	**4**	**7**	**11**	**10**	**1**	**0**	**0**	**41**	**4.9**	**23**	**5**	**16**	**3**	**5**	....	....	....	....	....	....	....	....
1995-96	**Florida Panthers**	**NHL**	**27**	**2**	**9**	**11**	**2**	**7**	**9**	**21**	**2**	**0**	**1**	**58**	**3.4**	**26**	**15**	**12**	**0**	**–1**	....	....	....	....	....	....	....	....
1996-97	Leksands IF	Sweden	45	8	17	25	....	....	....	62	....	....	....	....	....	....	....	....	....	....	9	1	2	3	35	....	....	....
	Sweden	WC-A	10	0	6	6	....	....	....	16	....	....	....	....	....	....	....	....	....	....	....	....	....	....	....	....	....	....
1997-98	Leksands IF	Sweden	42	2	23	25	....	....	....	52	....	....	....	....	....	....	....	....	....	....	4	0	1	1	6	....	....	....
	Leksands IF	EuroHL	6	2	2	4	....	....	....	18	....	....	....	....	....	....	....	....	....	....	....	....	....	....	....	....	....	....
1998-99	Leksands IF	Sweden	48	11	24	35	....	....	....	70	....	....	....	....	....	....	....	....	....	....	4	1	1	2	2	....	....	....
	Leksands IF	EuroHL	6	4	1	5	....	....	....	10	....	....	....	....	....	....	....	....	....	....	2	0	0	0	2	....	....	....
99-2000	SC Rapperswil-Jona	Switz.	42	7	25	32	....	....	....	44	....	....	....	....	....	....	....	....	....	....	6	1	2	3	8	....	....	....
	NHL Totals		**46**	**4**	**14**	**18**	**6**	**14**	**20**	**31**	**3**	**0**	**1**	**99**	**4.0**	**49**	**20**	**28**	**3**		....	....	....	....	....	....	....	....

Swedish World All-Star Team (1994) • WC-A All-Star Team (1994) • Named Best Defenseman at WC-A (1994)

Traded to **Florida** by **Calgary** with Robert Svehla for Florida's 3rd round choice (Dmitri Vlasenkov) in 1996 Entry Draft and cash, September 29, 1994.

• SVOBODA, Petr

D – L. 6'1", 180 lbs. b: Most, Czech., 2/14/1966. Montreal's 1st, 5th overall, in 1984.

			REGULAR SEASON																		PLAYOFFS							
Season	**Club**	**League**	**GP**	**G**	**A**	**Pts**	**AG**	**AA**	**APts**	**PIM**	**PP**	**SH**	**GW**	**S**	**%**	**TGF**	**PGF**	**TGA**	**PGA**	**+/–**	**GP**	**G**	**A**	**Pts**	**PIM**	**PP**	**SH**	**GW**
1982-83	CHZ Litvinov	Czech.	4	0	0	0	....	....	....	2	....	....	....	....	....	....	....	....	....	....	....	....	....	....	....	....	....	....
	Czechoslovakia	EJC-A	5	0	0	0	....	....	....	8	....	....	....	....	....	....	....	....	....	....	....	....	....	....	....	....	....	....
1983-84	CHZ Litvinov	Czech.	18	3	1	4	....	....	....	20	....	....	....	....	....	....	....	....	....	....	....	....	....	....	....	....	....	....
	Czechoslovakia	WJC-A	7	0	4	4	....	....	....	16	....	....	....	....	....	....	....	....	....	....	....	....	....	....	....	....	....	....
	Czechoslovakia	EJC-A	5	1	1	2	....	....	....	16	....	....	....	....	....	....	....	....	....	....	....	....	....	....	....	....	....	....
1984-85	**Montreal Canadiens**	**NHL**	**73**	**4**	**27**	**31**	**3**	**18**	**21**	**65**	**0**	**0**	**1**	**80**	**5.0**	**79**	**21**	**43**	**1**	**16**	**7**	**1**	**1**	**2**	**12**	**0**	**0**	**0**
1985-86♦	**Montreal Canadiens**	**NHL**	**73**	**1**	**18**	**19**	**1**	**12**	**13**	**93**	**0**	**0**	**0**	**63**	**1.6**	**89**	**9**	**58**	**2**	**24**	**8**	**0**	**0**	**0**	**21**	**0**	**0**	**0**
1986-87	**Montreal Canadiens**	**NHL**	**70**	**5**	**17**	**22**	**4**	**12**	**16**	**63**	**1**	**0**	**1**	**80**	**6.3**	**76**	**12**	**50**	**0**	**14**	**14**	**0**	**5**	**5**	**10**	**0**	**0**	**0**
1987-88	**Montreal Canadiens**	**NHL**	**69**	**7**	**22**	**29**	**6**	**16**	**22**	**149**	**2**	**0**	**1**	**138**	**5.1**	**113**	**16**	**57**	**6**	**46**	**10**	**0**	**5**	**5**	**12**	**0**	**0**	**0**
1988-89	**Montreal Canadiens**	**NHL**	**71**	**8**	**37**	**45**	**7**	**26**	**33**	**147**	**4**	**0**	**1**	**131**	**6.1**	**114**	**38**	**63**	**15**	**28**	**21**	**1**	**11**	**12**	**16**	**0**	**0**	**0**
1989-90	**Montreal Canadiens**	**NHL**	**60**	**5**	**31**	**36**	**4**	**22**	**26**	**98**	**2**	**0**	**2**	**90**	**5.6**	**94**	**30**	**48**	**4**	**20**	**10**	**0**	**5**	**5**	**7**	**0**	**0**	**0**
1990-91	Montreal Canadiens	Fr-Tour	3	0	0	0	....	....	....	27	....	....	....	....	....	....	....	....	....	....	....	....	....	....	....	....	....	....
	Montreal Canadiens	**NHL**	**60**	**4**	**22**	**26**	**4**	**17**	**21**	**52**	**3**	**0**	**1**	**67**	**6.0**	**72**	**20**	**66**	**19**	**5**	**2**	**0**	**1**	**1**	**2**	**0**	**0**	**0**
1991-92	**Montreal Canadiens**	**NHL**	**58**	**5**	**16**	**21**	**5**	**12**	**17**	**94**	**1**	**0**	**3**	**88**	**5.7**	**65**	**21**	**44**	**9**	**9**	....	....	....	....	....	....	....	....
	Buffalo Sabres	**NHL**	**13**	**1**	**6**	**7**	**1**	**5**	**6**	**52**	**0**	**0**	**0**	**23**	**4.3**	**15**	**12**	**21**	**10**	**–8**	**7**	**1**	**4**	**5**	**6**	**0**	**1**	**0**
1992-93	**Buffalo Sabres**	**NHL**	**40**	**2**	**24**	**26**	**2**	**17**	**19**	**59**	**1**	**0**	**1**	**61**	**3.3**	**63**	**24**	**46**	**10**	**3**	....	....	....	....	....	....	....	....
1993-94	**Buffalo Sabres**	**NHL**	**60**	**2**	**14**	**16**	**2**	**11**	**13**	**89**	**1**	**0**	**0**	**80**	**2.5**	**65**	**25**	**36**	**7**	**11**	**3**	**0**	**0**	**0**	**4**	**0**	**0**	**0**
1994-95	CHZ Chemopetrol Litvinov	Czech-Rep	8	2	0	2	....	....	....	50	....	....	....	....	....	....	....	....	....	....	....	....	....	....	....	....	....	....
	Buffalo Sabres	**NHL**	**26**	**0**	**5**	**5**	**0**	**7**	**7**	**60**	**0**	**0**	**0**	**22**	**0.0**	**16**	**6**	**22**	**7**	**–5**	....	....	....	....	....	....	....	....
	Philadelphia Flyers	**NHL**	**11**	**0**	**3**	**3**	**0**	**4**	**4**	**10**	**0**	**0**	**0**	**17**	**0.0**	**9**	**2**	**11**	**4**	**0**	**14**	**0**	**4**	**4**	**8**	**0**	**0**	**0**
1995-96	**Philadelphia Flyers**	**NHL**	**73**	**1**	**28**	**29**	**1**	**23**	**24**	**105**	**0**	**0**	**0**	**91**	**1.1**	**87**	**27**	**45**	**13**	**28**	**12**	**0**	**6**	**6**	**22**	**0**	**0**	**0**
1996-97	**Philadelphia Flyers**	**NHL**	**67**	**2**	**12**	**14**	**2**	**11**	**13**	**94**	**1**	**0**	**0**	**36**	**5.6**	**54**	**3**	**53**	**12**	**10**	**16**	**1**	**2**	**3**	**16**	**0**	**0**	**0**
1997-98	**Philadelphia Flyers**	**NHL**	**56**	**3**	**15**	**18**	**4**	**15**	**19**	**83**	**2**	**0**	**0**	**44**	**6.8**	**53**	**16**	**29**	**11**	**19**	**3**	**0**	**1**	**1**	**4**	**0**	**0**	**0**
	Czech-Republic	Olympics	6	1	1	2	....	....	....	*39	....	....	....	....	....	....	....	....	....	....	....	....	....	....	....	....	....	....
1998-99	**Philadelphia Flyers**	**NHL**	**25**	**4**	**2**	**6**	**5**	**2**	**7**	**28**	**1**	**1**	**1**	**37**	**10.8**	**21**	**3**	**15**	**2**	**5**	....	....	....	....	....	....	....	....
	Tampa Bay Lightning	**NHL**	**34**	**1**	**16**	**17**	**1**	**15**	**16**	**53**	**0**	**0**	**0**	**46**	**2.2**	**42**	**12**	**48**	**14**	**–4**	....	....	....	....	....	....	....	....
99-2000	**Tampa Bay Lightning**	**NHL**	**70**	**2**	**23**	**25**	**2**	**21**	**23**	**170**	**2**	**0**	**0**	**93**	**2.2**	**74**	**22**	**101**	**38**	**–11**	....	....	....	....	....	....	....	....
	NHL Totals		**1009**	**57**	**338**	**395**	**54**	**266**	**320**	**1564**	**21**	**1**	**12**	**1287**	**4.4**	**1201**	**319**	**856**	**184**		**127**	**4**	**45**	**49**	**140**	**0**	**1**	**0**

EJC-A All-Star Team (1983) • Named Best Defenseman at EJC-A (1983) • Played in NHL All-Star Game (2000)

Traded to **Buffalo** by **Montreal** for Kevin Haller, March 10, 1992. Traded to **Philadelphia** by **Buffalo** for Garry Galley, April 7, 1995. Traded to **Tampa Bay** by **Philadelphia** for Karl Dykhuis, December 28, 1998.

• SWAIN, Garry

Garth Frederick C – L. 5'8", 164 lbs. b: Welland, Ont., 9/11/1947. Pittsburgh's 1st, 4th overall, in 1968.

Season	**Club**	**League**	**GP**	**G**	**A**	**Pts**	**AG**	**AA**	**APts**	**PIM**	**PP**	**SH**	**GW**	**S**	**%**	**TGF**	**PGF**	**TGA**	**PGA**	**+/–**	**GP**	**G**	**A**	**Pts**	**PIM**	**PP**	**SH**	**GW**
1966-67	Niagara Falls Flyers	OHA-Jr.	48	10	19	29	....	....	....	51	....	....	....	....	....	....	....	....	....	....	13	3	6	9	2	....	....	....
1967-68	Niagara Falls Flyers	OHA-Jr.	54	41	62	103	....	....	....	79	....	....	....	....	....	....	....	....	....	....	19	9	16	25	35	....	....	....
	Niagara Falls Flyers	Mem-Cup	10	9	5	14	....	....	....	10	....	....	....	....	....	....	....	....	....	....	....	....	....	....	....	....	....	....
1968-69	**Pittsburgh Penguins**	**NHL**	**9**	**1**	**1**	**2**	**1**	**1**	**2**	**0**	**0**	**0**	**0**	**17**	**5.9**	**2**	**0**	**4**	**1**	**–1**	....	....	....	....	....	....	....	....
	Amarillo Wranglers	CHL	69	20	27	47	....	....	....	51	....	....	....	....	....	....	....	....	....	....	....	....	....	....	....	....	....	....
1969-70	Baltimore Clippers	AHL	72	4	9	13	....	....	....	26	....	....	....	....	....	....	....	....	....	....	5	0	0	0	2	....	....	....
1970-71	Amarillo Wranglers	CHL	71	17	31	48	....	....	....	87	....	....	....	....	....	....	....	....	....	....	....	....	....	....	....	....	....	....
1971-72	Fort Wayne Komets	IHL	60	26	26	52	....	....	....	60	....	....	....	....	....	....	....	....	....	....	8	0	4	4	16	....	....	....
1972-73	Baltimore Clippers	AHL	76	14	24	38	....	....	....	69	....	....	....	....	....	....	....	....	....	....	....	....	....	....	....	....	....	....
1973-74	Baltimore Clippers	AHL	12	2	7	9	....	....	....	10	....	....	....	....	....	....	....	....	....	....	9	5	4	9	18	....	....	....
	Charlotte Checkers	SHL	68	34	*64	*98	....	....	....	84	....	....	....	....	....	....	....	....	....	....	....	....	....	....	....	....	....	....
1974-75	New England Whalers	WHA	66	7	15	22	....	....	....	18	....	....	....	....	....	....	....	....	....	....	6	0	3	3	41	....	....	....
1975-76	New England Whalers	WHA	79	10	16	26	....	....	....	46	....	....	....	....	....	....	....	....	....	....	17	3	2	5	15	....	....	....
1976-77	New England Whalers	WHA	26	5	2	7	....	....	....	6	....	....	....	....	....	....	....	....	....	....	2	0	0	0	0	....	....	....
	Rhode Island Reds	AHL	17	1	6	7	....	....	....	19	....	....	....	....	....	....	....	....	....	....	....	....	....	....	....	....	....	....
	NHL Totals		**9**	**1**	**1**	**2**	**1**	**1**	**2**	**0**	**0**	**0**	**0**	**17**	**5.9**	**2**	**0**	**4**	**1**		....	....	....	....	....	....	....	....
	Other Major League Totals		171	22	33	55	....	....	....	70	....	....	....	....	....	....	....	....	....	....	25	3	5	8	56	....	....	....

SHL Second All-Star Team (1974)

Selected by **Calgary-Cleveland** (WHA) in 1972 WHA General Player Draft, February 12, 1972. WHA rights traded to **New England** (WHA) by **Cleveland** (WHA) for future considerations, September, 1974.

• SWARBRICK, George

George Raymond RW – R. 5'10", 175 lbs. b: Moose Jaw, Sask., 2/16/1942.

Season	**Club**	**League**	**GP**	**G**	**A**	**Pts**	**AG**	**AA**	**APts**	**PIM**	**PP**	**SH**	**GW**	**S**	**%**	**TGF**	**PGF**	**TGA**	**PGA**	**+/–**	**GP**	**G**	**A**	**Pts**	**PIM**	**PP**	**SH**	**GW**
1959-60	Moose Jaw Canucks	SJHL	59	17	13	30	....	....	....	48	....	....	....	....	....	....	....	....	....	....	....	....	....	....	....	....	....	....
1960-61	Moose Jaw Canucks	SJHL	50	17	17	34	....	....	....	94	....	....	....	....	....	....	....	....	....	....	6	1	3	4	6	....	....	....
	Victoria Cougars	WHL	3	0	0	0	....	....	....	0	....	....	....	....	....	....	....	....	....	....	....	....	....	....	....	....	....	....
	Moose Jaw Canucks	Mem-Cup	4	0	1	1	....	....	....	5	....	....	....	....	....	....	....	....	....	....	....	....	....	....	....	....	....	....
1961-62	Moose Jaw Canucks	SJHL	55	40	36	76	....	....	....	75	....	....	....	....	....	....	....	....	....	....	....	....	....	....	....	....	....	....
1962-63	Moose Jaw Pla-Mors	SSHL	38	29	28	57	....	....	....	92	....	....	....	....	....	....	....	....	....	....	5	5	2	7	11	....	....	....
1963-64	Canada	Nat-Team	STATISTICS NOT AVAILABLE																									
	Canada	Olympics	7	3	3	6	....	....	....	2	....	....	....	....	....	....	....	....	....	....	....	....	....	....	....	....	....	....
	Moose Jaw Pla-Mors	SSHL	....	....	....	....	....	....	....	....	....	....	....	....	....	....	....	....	....	....	5	7	8	15	23	....	....	....
1964-65	San Francisco Seals	WHL	70	22	22	44	....	....	....	66	....	....	....	....	....	....	....	....	....	....	....	....	....	....	....	....	....	....
1965-66	San Francisco Seals	WHL	71	20	21	41	....	....	....	89	....	....	....	....	....	....	....	....	....	....	7	2	3	5	8	....	....	....
1966-67	California Seals	WHL	71	31	22	53	....	....	....	75	....	....	....	....	....	....	....	....	....	....	6	1	3	4	16	....	....	....
1967-68	**Oakland Seals**	**NHL**	**49**	**13**	**5**	**18**	**15**	**5**	**20**	**62**	**3**	**1**	**2**	**86**	**15.1**	**28**	**7**	**38**	**0**	**–17**	....	....	....	....	....	....	....	....
1968-69	**Oakland Seals**	**NHL**	**50**	**3**	**13**	**16**	**3**	**12**	**15**	**75**	**1**	**0**	**1**	**121**	**2.5**	**27**	**6**	**38**	**4**	**–13**	....	....	....	....	....	....	....	....
	Pittsburgh Penguins	**NHL**	**19**	**1**	**6**	**7**	**1**	**5**	**6**	**28**	**0**	**0**	**0**	**27**	**3.7**	**9**	**2**	**12**	**1**	**–4**	....	....	....	....	....	....	....	....
1969-70	**Pittsburgh Penguins**	**NHL**	**12**	**0**	**1**	**1**	**0**	**1**	**1**	**8**	**0**	**0**	**0**	**38**	**0.0**	**5**	**0**	**5**	**0**	**0**	....	....	....	....	....	....	....	....
	Baltimore Clippers	AHL	56	19	22	41	....	....	....	81	....	....	....	....	....	....	....	....	....	....	4	0	3	3	8	....	....	....
1970-71	**Philadelphia Flyers**	**NHL**	**2**	**0**	**0**	**0**	**0**	**0**	**0**	**0**	**0**	**0**	**0**	**4**	**0.0**	**2**	**2**	**2**	**0**	**–2**	....	....	....	....	....	....	....	....
	Baltimore Clippers	AHL	34	4	7	11	....	....	....	54	....	....	....	....	....	....	....	....	....	....	....	....	....	....	....	....	....	....
	Hershey Bears	AHL	24	10	8	18	....	....	....	56	....	....	....	....	....	....	....	....	....	....	4	0	2	2	6	....	....	....
1971-72	San Diego Gulls	WHL	54	25	19	44	....	....	....	105	....	....	....	....	....	....	....	....	....	....	4	0	0	0	7	....	....	....
1972-73	San Diego Gulls	WHL	64	13	23	36	....	....	....	115	....	....	....	....	....	....	....	....	....	....	6	1	2	3	22	....	....	....
1973-74	Omaha Knights	CHL	65	23	30	53	....	....	....	89	....	....	....	....	....	....	....	....	....	....	5	2	2	4	20	....	....	....
1974-75	Long Island Cougars	NAHL	68	31	47	78	....	....	....	171	....	....	....	....	....	....	....	....	....	....	10	6	5	11	....	....	....	....
1975-76	Erie Blades	NAHL	27	10	9	19	....	....	....	46	....	....	....	....	....	....	....	....	....	....	5	3	2	5	13	....	....	....
1976-77	Philadelphia Firebirds	NAHL	74	32	27	59	....	....	....	91	....	....	....	....	....	....	....	....	....	....	4	1	2	3	6	....	....	....
	NHL Totals		**132**	**17**	**25**	**42**	**19**	**23**	**42**	**173**	**4**	**1**	**3**	**276**	**6.2**	**71**	**17**	**95**	**5**		....	....	....	....	....	....	....	....

Won WHL Rookie of the Year Award (1965)

NHL rights transferred to **California** after owners of **San Francisco** (WHL) franchise awarded NHL expansion team, April 5, 1966. Traded to **Pittsburgh** by **Oakland** with Bryan Watson and Tracy Pratt for Earl Ingarfield, Gene Ubriaco and Dick Mattiussi, January 30, 1969. Traded to **Philadelphia** by **Pittsburgh** for Terry Ball, June 11, 1970. Signed as a free agent by **Atlanta** (Omaha-CHL), October 30, 1973. Traded to **Syracuse** (AHL) by **Atlanta** for cash, August, 1974.

• SWEENEY, Bob

Robert C/RW – R. 6'3", 200 lbs. b: Concord, MA, 1/25/1964. Boston's 6th, 123rd overall, in 1982.

Season	**Club**	**League**	**GP**	**G**	**A**	**Pts**	**AG**	**AA**	**APts**	**PIM**	**PP**	**SH**	**GW**	**S**	**%**	**TGF**	**PGF**	**TGA**	**PGA**	**+/–**	**GP**	**G**	**A**	**Pts**	**PIM**	**PP**	**SH**	**GW**
1981-82	Acton-Boxborough Rams	Hi-School	STATISTICS NOT AVAILABLE																									
1982-83	Boston College	ECAC	30	17	11	28	....	....	....	10	....	....	....	....	....	....	....	....	....	....	....	....	....	....	....	....	....	....
1983-84	Boston College	ECAC	23	14	7	21	....	....	....	10	....	....	....	....	....	....	....	....	....	....	....	....	....	....	....	....	....	....
1984-85	Boston College	H-East	44	32	32	64	....	....	....	43	....	....	....	....	....	....	....	....	....	....	....	....	....	....	....	....	....	....
1985-86	Boston College	H-East	41	15	24	39	....	....	....	52	....	....	....	....	....	....	....	....	....	....	....	....	....	....	....	....	....	....
1986-87	**Boston Bruins**	**NHL**	**14**	**2**	**4**	**6**	**2**	**3**	**5**	**21**	**0**	**0**	**0**	**13**	**15.4**	**8**	**2**	**11**	**0**	**–5**	**3**	**0**	**0**	**0**	**0**	**0**	**0**	**0**
	Moncton Golden Flames	AHL	58	29	26	55	....	....	....	81	....	....	....	....	....	....	....	....	....	....	4	0	2	2	13	....	....	....
1987-88	**Boston Bruins**	**NHL**	**80**	**22**	**23**	**45**	**19**	**16**	**35**	**73**	**6**	**0**	**7**	**118**	**18.6**	**72**	**19**	**42**	**0**	**11**	**23**	**6**	**8**	**14**	**66**	**1**	**1**	**1**
1988-89	**Boston Bruins**	**NHL**	**75**	**14**	**14**	**28**	**12**	**10**	**22**	**99**	**2**	**1**	**3**	**117**	**12.0**	**50**	**15**	**65**	**11**	**–19**	**10**	**2**	**4**	**6**	**19**	**0**	**0**	**0**

			REGULAR SEASON																		PLAYOFFS							
Season	Club	League	GP	G	A	Pts	AG	AA	APts	PIM	PP	SH	GW	S	%	TGF	PGF	TGA	PGA	+/-	GP	G	A	Pts	PIM	PP	SH	GW
1989-90	Boston Bruins	NHL	70	22	24	46	19	17	36	93	5	2	6	147	15.0	70	19	64	15	2	20	0	2	2	30	0	0	0
1990-91	Boston Bruins	NHL	80	15	33	48	14	25	39	115	0	1	2	116	12.9	71	6	71	18	12	17	4	2	6	45	0	0	1
1991-92	Boston Bruins	NHL	63	6	14	20	5	11	16	103	0	1	1	70	8.6	35	6	60	22	-9	14	1	0	1	25	0	1	0
	Maine Mariners	AHL	1	1	0	1				0																		
1992-93	Buffalo Sabres	NHL	80	21	26	47	17	18	35	118	4	3	3	120	17.5	80	20	90	32	2	8	2	2	4	8	0	0	1
1993-94	Buffalo Sabres	NHL	60	11	14	25	10	11	21	94	3	3	1	76	14.5	35	5	41	14	3	1	0	0	0	0	0	0	0
1994-95	Buffalo Sabres	NHL	45	5	4	9	9	6	15	18	1	2	0	47	10.6	21	7	26	6	-6	5	0	0	0	4	0	0	0
1995-96	New York Islanders	NHL	66	6	6	12	6	5	11	59	0	1	1	54	11.1	18	0	68	27	-23								
	Calgary Flames	NHL	6	1	1	2	1	1	2	6	0	0	0	8	12.5	6	1	2	0	3	2	0	0	0	0	0	0	0
1996-97	Quebec Rafales	IHL	69	10	21	31				120											9	2	0	2	8			
1997-98	Revier Lowen	Germany	27	9	4	13				77																		
	Frankfurt Lions	Germany	20	7	8	15				32											7	1	3	4	6			
1998-99	Frankfurt Lions	Germany	46	6	21	27				30											1	0	1	1	8			
	Frankfurt Lions	EuroHL	5	1	0	1				4																		
	United States	WC-Q	3	1	1	2				0																		
99-2000	Munich Barons	Germany	37	9	21	30				63											12	3	5	8	20			
	NHL Totals		639	125	163	288	114	123	237	799	21	14	24	886	14.1	466	100	540	145		103	15	18	33	197	1	2	3

Hockey East Second All-Star Team (1985)

Claimed on waivers by **Buffalo** from **Boston**, October 9, 1992. Claimed by **NY Islanders** from **Buffalo** in NHL Waiver Draft, October 2, 1995. Traded to **Calgary** by **NY Islanders** for Pat Conacher and Calgary's 6th round choice (later traded back to Calgary - Calgary selected Ilja Demidov) in 1997 Entry Draft, March 20, 1996.

• SWEENEY, Don

Donald Clarke D – L. 5'10", 184 lbs. b: St. Stephen, N.B., 8/17/1966. Boston's 8th, 166th overall, in 1984.

Season	Club	League	GP	G	A	Pts	AG	AA	APts	PIM	PP	SH	GW	S	%	TGF	PGF	TGA	PGA	+/-	GP	G	A	Pts	PIM	PP	SH	GW
1982-83	Saint John Beavers	NBAHA	STATISTICS NOT AVAILABLE																									
1983-84	St. Paul's High School	Hi-School	22	33	26	59																						
1984-85	Harvard University	ECAC	29	3	7	10				30																		
1985-86	Harvard University	ECAC	31	4	5	9				12																		
1986-87	Harvard University	ECAC	34	7	4	11				22																		
1987-88	Harvard University	ECAC	30	6	23	29				37																		
	Maine Mariners	AHL																			6	1	3	4	0			
1988-89	Boston Bruins	NHL	36	3	5	8	3	4	7	20	0	0	0	35	8.6	23	1	38	10	-6								
	Maine Mariners	AHL	42	8	17	25				24																		
1989-90	Boston Bruins	NHL	58	3	5	8	3	4	7	58	0	0	0	49	6.1	41	0	41	11	11	21	1	5	6	18	1	0	0
	Maine Mariners	AHL	11	0	8	8				8																		
1990-91	Boston Bruins	NHL	77	8	13	21	7	10	17	67	0	1	3	102	7.8	67	1	89	25	2	19	3	0	3	25	0	0	0
1991-92	Boston Bruins	NHL	75	3	11	14	3	8	11	74	0	0	1	92	3.3	50	0	97	38	-9	15	0	0	0	10	0	0	0
1992-93	Boston Bruins	NHL	84	7	27	34	6	19	25	68	0	1	0	107	6.5	94	0	88	28	34	4	0	0	0	4	0	0	0
1993-94	Boston Bruins	NHL	75	6	15	21	6	12	18	50	1	2	2	136	4.4	85	3	83	30	29	12	2	1	3	4	0	0	1
1994-95	Boston Bruins	NHL	47	3	19	22	5	28	33	24	1	0	2	102	2.9	65	20	51	12	6	5	0	0	0	4	0	0	0
1995-96	Boston Bruins	NHL	77	4	24	28	4	20	24	42	2	0	3	142	2.8	98	20	111	29	-4	5	0	2	2	6	0	0	0
1996-97	Boston Bruins	NHL	82	3	23	26	3	20	23	39	0	0	0	113	2.7	92	12	115	30	-5								
	Canada	WC-A	11	1	3	4				6																		
1997-98	Boston Bruins	NHL	59	1	15	16	1	15	16	24	0	0	0	55	1.8	53	2	46	7	12								
1998-99	Boston Bruins	NHL	81	2	10	12	2	10	12	64	0	0	0	79	2.5	56	3	48	9	14	11	3	0	3	6	1	0	0
99-2000	Boston Bruins	NHL	81	1	13	14	1	12	13	48	0	0	0	82	1.2	55	4	87	22	-14								
	NHL Totals		832	44	180	224	44	162	206	578	4	4	11	1094	4.0	779	66	894	251		92	9	8	17	77	2	0	1

NCAA East All-American Team (1988) • ECAC First All-Star Team (1988)

• SWEENEY, Tim

LW – L. 5'11", 185 lbs. b: Boston, MA, 4/12/1967. Calgary's 7th, 122nd overall, in 1985.

Season	Club	League	GP	G	A	Pts	AG	AA	APts	PIM	PP	SH	GW	S	%	TGF	PGF	TGA	PGA	+/-	GP	G	A	Pts	PIM	PP	SH	GW
1982-83	Madison Capitols	USHL	STATISTICS NOT AVAILABLE																									
1983-84	Weymouth-North Maroons	Hi-School	23	33	26	59																						
1984-85	Weymouth-North Maroons	Hi-School	22	32	56	88																						
1985-86	Boston College	H-East	32	8	4	12				8																		
1986-87	Boston College	H-East	38	31	18	49				28																		
1987-88	Boston College	H-East	18	9	11	20				18																		
1988-89	Boston College	H-East	39	29	44	73				26																		
1989-90	Salt Lake Golden Eagles	IHL	81	46	51	97				32											11	5	4	9	4			
1990-91	Calgary Flames	NHL	42	7	9	16	6	7	13	8	0	0	4	40	17.5	24	1	33	11	1								
	Salt Lake Golden Eagles	IHL	31	19	16	35				8											4	3	3	6	0			
1991-92	United States	Nat-Team	21	9	11	20				10																		
	United States	Olympics	8	3	4	7				6																		
	Calgary Flames	NHL	11	1	2	3	1	2	3	4	0	0	1	16	6.3	4	0	9	5	0								
1992-93	Boston Bruins	NHL	14	1	7	8	1	5	6	6	0	0	0	15	6.7	10	0	9	0	1	3	0	0	0	0	0	0	0
	Providence Bruins	AHL	60	41	55	96				32											3	2	2	4	0			
1993-94	Mighty Ducks of Anaheim	NHL	78	16	27	43	15	21	36	49	6	1	2	114	14.0	62	18	50	9	3								
	United States	WC-A	8	3	2	5				0																		
1994-95	Mighty Ducks of Anaheim	NHL	13	1	1	2	2	1	3	2	0	0	0	11	9.1	6	0	16	7	-3								
	Providence Bruins	AHL	2	2	2	4				0											13	8	*17	*25	6			
1995-96	Boston Bruins	NHL	41	8	8	16	8	7	15	14	1	0	2	47	17.0	20	4	22	10	4	1	0	0	0	2	0	0	0
	Providence Bruins	AHL	34	17	22	39				12																		
1996-97	Boston Bruins	NHL	36	10	11	21	11	10	21	14	2	0	2	65	15.4	34	6	34	6	0								
	Providence Bruins	AHL	23	11	22	33				6																		
1997-98	New York Rangers	NHL	56	11	18	29	13	18	31	26	2	0	1	75	14.7	42	11	25	1	7								
	Hartford Wolf Pack	AHL	7	2	6	8				8																		
1998-99	Providence Bruins	AHL	2	0	0	0				0																		
	NHL Totals		291	55	83	138	57	71	128	123	11	1	12	383	14.4	202	40	198	49		4	0	0	0	2	0	0	0

Hockey East First All-Star Team (1989) • NCAA East Second All-American Team (1989) • IHL Second All-Star Team (1990) • AHL Second All-Star Team (1993)

Signed as a free agent by **Boston**, September 16, 1992. Claimed by **Anaheim** from **Boston** in Expansion Draft, June 24, 1993. Signed as a free agent by **Boston**, August 9, 1995. Signed as a free agent by **NY Rangers**, September 15, 1997. Signed as a free agent by **Providence** (AHL), October 3, 1998. • Officially announced retirement, October 11, 1998.

• SYDOR, Darryl

Darryl M. D – L. 6'1", 205 lbs. b: Edmonton, Alta., 5/13/1972. Los Angeles' 1st, 7th overall, in 1990.

Season	Club	League	GP	G	A	Pts	AG	AA	APts	PIM	PP	SH	GW	S	%	TGF	PGF	TGA	PGA	+/-	GP	G	A	Pts	PIM	PP	SH	GW
1985-86	Genstar Cement	AAHA	34	20	17	37				60																		
1986-87	Genstar Cement	AAHA	36	15	20	35				60																		
1987-88	Edmonton Mets	AAHA	38	10	11	21				54																		
1988-89	Kamloops Blazers	WHL	65	12	14	26				86											15	1	4	5	19			
1989-90	Kamloops Blazers	WHL	67	29	66	95				129											17	2	9	11	28			
	Kamloops Blazers	Mem-Cup	3	4	0	4				2																		
1990-91	Kamloops Blazers	WHL	66	27	78	105				88											12	3	*22	25	10			
1991-92	Kamloops Blazers	WHL	29	9	39	48				33											17	3	15	18	18			
	Canada	WJC-A	7	3	1	4				4																		
	Los Angeles Kings	NHL	18	1	5	6	1	4	5	22	0	0	0	18	5.6	17	5	15	0	-3								
	Kamloops Blazers	Mem-Cup	5	0	2	2				6																		
1992-93	Los Angeles Kings	NHL	80	6	23	29	5	16	21	63	0	0	1	112	5.4	81	15	100	32	-2	24	3	8	11	16	2	0	0
1993-94	Los Angeles Kings	NHL	84	8	27	35	7	21	28	94	1	0	0	146	5.5	81	19	93	22	-9								
	Canada	WC-A	8	0	1	1				4																		
1994-95	Los Angeles Kings	NHL	48	4	19	23	7	28	35	36	3	0	0	96	4.2	61	8	76	21	-2								
1995-96	Los Angeles Kings	NHL	58	1	11	12	1	9	10	34	1	0	0	84	1.2	59	12	82	24	-11								
	Dallas Stars	NHL	26	2	6	8	2	5	7	41	1	0	0	33	6.1	17	5	13	0	-1								
	Canada	WC-A	8	0	1	1				0																		
1996-97	Dallas Stars	NHL	82	8	40	48	8	36	44	51	2	0	2	142	5.6	108	33	39	1	37	7	0	2	2	0	0	0	0

			REGULAR SEASON																		PLAYOFFS							
Season	Club	League	GP	G	A	Pts	AG	AA	APts	PIM	PP	SH	GW	S	%	TGF	PGF	TGA	PGA	+/-	GP	G	A	Pts	PIM	PP	SH	GW
1997-98	Dallas Stars	NHL	79	11	35	46	13	34	47	51	4	1	1	166	6.6	109	54	45	7	17	17	0	5	5	14	0	0	0
1998-99♦	Dallas Stars	NHL	74	14	34	48	16	33	49	50	9	0	2	163	8.6	94	55	52	12	–1	23	3	9	12	16	1	0	1
99-2000	Dallas Stars	NHL	74	8	26	34	9	24	33	32	5	0	1	132	6.1	90	33	58	7	6	23	1	6	7	6	0	0	0
	NHL Totals		623	63	226	289	69	210	279	474	26	1	7	1092	5.8	717	239	573	126		94	7	30	37	52	3	0	1

WHL West First All-Star Team (1990, 1991, 1992) • Played in NHL All-Star Game (1998, 1999)

Traded to **Dallas** by **LA Kings** with LA Kings' 5th round choice (Ryan Christie) in 1996 Entry Draft for Shane Churla and Doug Zmolek, February 17, 1996.

• SYKES, Bob

Robert John William LW – L. 6', 200 lbs. b: Sudbury, Ont., 9/26/1951. Toronto's 5th, 65th overall, in 1971.

Season	Club	League	GP	G	A	Pts	AG	AA	APts	PIM	PP	SH	GW	S	%	TGF	PGF	TGA	PGA	+/-	GP	G	A	Pts	PIM	PP	SH	GW
1969-70	Sudbury Wolves	NOJHA	45	18	23	41	....	....	....	79	....	....	....	....	....	....	....	....	....	....	....	....	....	....	....	....	....	....
1970-71	Sudbury Wolves	NOJHA	48	48	59	107	....	....	....	26	....	....	....	....	....	....	....	....	....	....	....	....	....	....	....	....	....	....
1971-72	St. Louis University	CCHA	32	16	23	39	....	....	....	22	....	....	....	....	....	....	....	....	....	....	....	....	....	....	....	....	....	....
1972-73	St. Louis University	CCHA	15	17	22	39	....	....	....	16	....	....	....	....	....	....	....	....	....	....	....	....	....	....	....	....	....	....
1973-74	Oklahoma City Blazers	CHL	50	13	11	24	....	....	....	19	....	....	....	....	....	....	....	....	....	....	8	2	1	3	2	....	....	....
1974-75	Toronto Maple Leafs	NHL	2	0	0	0	0	0	0	0	0	0	0	1	0.0	0	0	2	0	–2	....	....	....	....	....	....	....	....
	Oklahoma City Blazers	CHL	73	30	21	51	....	....	....	24	....	....	....	....	....	....	....	....	....	....	5	1	2	3	0	....	....	....
1975-76	Oklahoma City Blazers	CHL	52	17	6	23	....	....	....	44	....	....	....	....	....	....	....	....	....	....	....	....	....	....	....	....	....	....
	Saginaw Gears	IHL	1	0	3	3	....	....	....	0	....	....	....	....	....	....	....	....	....	....	....	....	....	....	....	....	....	....
1976-77	Orillia Terriers	OHA-Sr.	10	2	1	3	....	....	....	11	....	....	....	....	....	....	....	....	....	....	....	....	....	....	....	....	....	....
	NHL Totals		2	0	0	0	0	0	0	0	0	0	0	1	0.0	0	0	2	0		....	....	....	....	....	....	....	....

• SYKES, Phil

Phillip Maxwell "Psycho" LW – L. 6', 175 lbs. b: Dawson Creek, B.C., 3/18/1959.

Season	Club	League	GP	G	A	Pts	AG	AA	APts	PIM	PP	SH	GW	S	%	TGF	PGF	TGA	PGA	+/-	GP	G	A	Pts	PIM	PP	SH	GW
1978-79	University of North Dakota	WCHA	41	9	5	14	....	....	....	16	....	....	....	....	....	....	....	....	....	....	....	....	....	....	....	....	....	....
1979-80	University of North Dakota	WCHA	37	22	27	49	....	....	....	34	....	....	....	....	....	....	....	....	....	....	....	....	....	....	....	....	....	....
1980-81	University of North Dakota	WCHA	38	28	34	62	....	....	....	22	....	....	....	....	....	....	....	....	....	....	....	....	....	....	....	....	....	....
1981-82	University of North Dakota	WCHA	37	22	27	49	....	....	....	34	....	....	....	....	....	....	....	....	....	....	....	....	....	....	....	....	....	....
1982-83	Los Angeles Kings	NHL	7	2	0	2	2	0	2	2	0	0	0	5	40.0	3	0	2	0	1	....	....	....	....	....	....	....	....
	New Haven Nighthawks	AHL	71	19	26	45	....	....	....	111	....	....	....	....	....	....	....	....	....	....	12	2	2	4	21	....	....	....
1983-84	Los Angeles Kings	NHL	3	0	0	0	0	0	0	2	0	0	0	2	0.0	0	0	1	0	–1	....	....	....	....	....	....	....	....
	New Haven Nighthawks	AHL	77	29	37	66	....	....	....	101	....	....	....	....	....	....	....	....	....	....	....	....	....	....	....	....	....	....
1984-85	Los Angeles Kings	NHL	79	17	15	32	14	10	24	38	1	2	2	96	17.7	49	3	78	14	–18	3	0	1	1	4	0	0	0
1985-86	Los Angeles Kings	NHL	76	20	24	44	16	16	32	97	1	2	4	132	15.2	61	10	125	48	–26	....	....	....	....	....	....	....	....
	Canada	WEC-A	9	0	0	0	....	....	....	4	....	....	....	....	....	....	....	....	....	....	....	....	....	....	....	....	....	....
1986-87	Los Angeles Kings	NHL	58	6	15	21	5	11	16	133	0	1	0	62	9.7	31	1	51	31	10	5	0	1	1	8	0	0	0
1987-88	Los Angeles Kings	NHL	40	9	12	21	8	9	17	82	3	1	0	61	14.8	36	6	31	6	5	4	0	0	0	0	0	0	0
1988-89	Los Angeles Kings	NHL	23	0	1	1	0	1	1	8	0	0	0	5	0.0	4	0	7	0	–3	3	0	0	0	8	0	0	0
	New Haven Nighthawks	AHL	34	9	17	26	....	....	....	23	....	....	....	....	....	....	....	....	....	....	....	....	....	....	....	....	....	....
1989-90	New Haven Nighthawks	AHL	25	3	12	15	....	....	....	32	....	....	....	....	....	....	....	....	....	....	....	....	....	....	....	....	....	....
	Winnipeg Jets	NHL	48	9	6	15	8	4	12	26	0	1	0	50	18.0	22	0	38	8	–8	4	0	0	0	0	0	0	0
	Moncton Hawks	AHL	5	0	1	1	....	....	....	20	....	....	....	....	....	....	....	....	....	....	....	....	....	....	....	....	....	....
1990-91	Winnipeg Jets	NHL	70	12	10	22	11	8	19	59	0	2	0	65	18.5	40	0	63	14	–9	....	....	....	....	....	....	....	....
1991-92	Winnipeg Jets	NHL	52	4	2	6	4	2	6	72	0	0	2	34	11.8	11	0	41	18	–12	7	0	1	1	9	0	0	0
	NHL Totals		456	79	85	164	68	61	129	519	5	9	8	512	15.4	257	20	437	139		26	0	3	3	29	0	0	0

NCAA Championship All-Tournament Team (1980, 1982) • WCHA First All-Star Team (1982) • NCAA Championship Tournament MVP (1982)

Signed as a free agent by **LA Kings**, April 5, 1982. Traded to **Winnipeg** by **LA Kings** for Brad Jones, December 1, 1989.

• SYKORA, Michal

D – L. 6'5", 225 lbs. b: Pardubice, Czech., 7/5/1973. San Jose's 6th, 123rd overall, in 1992.

Season	Club	League	GP	G	A	Pts	AG	AA	APts	PIM	PP	SH	GW	S	%	TGF	PGF	TGA	PGA	+/-	GP	G	A	Pts	PIM	PP	SH	GW
1990-91	HC Tesla	Czech-Jr.	40	17	26	43	....	....	....	45	....	....	....	....	....	....	....	....	....	....	....	....	....	....	....	....	....	....
	HC Pardubice	Czech.	2	0	0	0	....	....	....	....	....	....	....	....	....	....	....	....	....	....	....	....	....	....	....	....	....	....
	Czechoslovakia	EJC-A	5	0	0	0	....	....	....	0	....	....	....	....	....	....	....	....	....	....	....	....	....	....	....	....	....	....
1991-92	Tacoma Rockets	WHL	61	13	23	36	....	....	....	46	....	....	....	....	....	....	....	....	....	....	4	0	2	2	2	....	....	....
1992-93	Tacoma Rockets	WHL	70	23	50	73	....	....	....	73	....	....	....	....	....	....	....	....	....	....	7	4	8	12	2	....	....	....
1993-94	San Jose Sharks	NHL	22	1	4	5	1	3	4	14	0	0	0	22	4.5	13	1	23	7	–4	....	....	....	....	....	....	....	....
	Kansas City Blades	IHL	47	5	11	16	....	....	....	30	....	....	....	....	....	....	....	....	....	....	....	....	....	....	....	....	....	....
1994-95	Kansas City Blades	IHL	36	1	10	11	....	....	....	30	....	....	....	....	....	....	....	....	....	....	....	....	....	....	....	....	....	....
	San Jose Sharks	NHL	16	0	4	4	0	6	6	10	0	0	0	6	0.0	11	0	12	7	6	....	....	....	....	....	....	....	....
1995-96	San Jose Sharks	NHL	79	4	16	20	4	13	17	54	1	0	0	80	5.0	69	1	123	41	–14	....	....	....	....	....	....	....	....
	Czech-Republic	WC-A	8	0	1	1	....	....	....	6	....	....	....	....	....	....	....	....	....	....	....	....	....	....	....	....	....	....
1996-97	Czech-Republic	W-Cup	2	0	0	0	....	....	....	2	....	....	....	....	....	....	....	....	....	....	....	....	....	....	....	....	....	....
	San Jose Sharks	NHL	35	2	5	7	2	4	6	59	1	0	0	39	5.1	26	3	29	6	0	....	....	....	....	....	....	....	....
	Chicago Blackhawks	NHL	28	1	9	10	1	8	9	10	0	0	0	38	2.6	18	3	11	0	4	1	0	0	0	0	0	0	0
1997-98	Chicago Blackhawks	NHL	28	1	3	4	1	3	4	12	0	0	0	35	2.9	12	5	17	0	–10	....	....	....	....	....	....	....	....
	Indianapolis Ice	IHL	6	0	0	0	....	....	....	4	....	....	....	....	....	....	....	....	....	....	....	....	....	....	....	....	....	....
	HC Pardubice	Czech-Rep	1	1	0	1	....	....	....	2	....	....	....	....	....	....	....	....	....	....	....	....	....	....	....	....	....	....
1998-99	HC Sparta Praha	Czech-Rep	26	4	9	13	....	....	....	38	....	....	....	....	....	....	....	....	....	....	8	2	0	2	....	....	....	....
	HC Sparta Praha	EuroHL	2	2	2	4	....	....	....	4	....	....	....	....	....	....	....	....	....	....	2	2	2	4	0	....	....	....
	Tampa Bay Lighning	NHL	10	1	2	3	1	2	3	0	0	0	1	24	4.2	7	3	13	2	–7	....	....	....	....	....	....	....	....
99-2000	HC Sparta Praha	Czech-Rep	48	11	14	25	....	....	....	89	....	....	....	....	....	....	....	....	....	....	9	5	3	8	8	....	....	....
	HC Sparta Praha	EuroHL	4	2	0	2	....	....	....	6	....	....	....	....	....	....	....	....	....	....	4	0	0	0	6	....	....	....
	Czech-Republic	WC-A	9	5	3	8	....	....	....	16	....	....	....	....	....	....	....	....	....	....	....	....	....	....	....	....	....	....
	NHL Totals		218	10	43	53	10	39	49	159	2	0	1	244	4.1	156	16	228	63		1	0	0	0	0	0	0	0

WHL West First All-Star Team (1993) • WC-A All-Star Team (1996) • WC-A All-Star Team (2000)

Traded to **Chicago** by **San Jose** with Chris Terreri and Ulf Dahlen for Ed Belfour, January 25, 1997. Traded to **Tampa Bay** by **Chicago** for Mark Fitzpatrick and Tampa Bay's 4th round choice (later traded to Montreal - Montreal selected Chris Dyment) in 1999 Entry Draft, July 17, 1998. Signed as a free agent by **Philadelphia**, July 6, 2000.

• SYKORA, Petr

C – L. 6', 190 lbs. b: Plzen, Czech., 11/19/1976. New Jersey's 1st, 18th overall, in 1995.

Season	Club	League	GP	G	A	Pts	AG	AA	APts	PIM	PP	SH	GW	S	%	TGF	PGF	TGA	PGA	+/-	GP	G	A	Pts	PIM	PP	SH	GW
1991-92	Skoda Plzen	Czech-Jr.	30	50	50	100	....	....	....	....	....	....	....	....	....	....	....	....	....	....	....	....	....	....	....	....	....	....
1992-93	Skoda Plzen	Czech.	19	12	5	17	....	....	....	....	....	....	....	....	....	....	....	....	....	....	....	....	....	....	....	....	....	....
1993-94	Skoda Plzen	Czech-Rep	37	10	16	26	....	....	....	....	....	....	....	....	....	....	....	....	....	....	4	0	1	1	....	....	....	....
	Czech-Republic	WJC-A	7	6	2	8	....	....	....	6	....	....	....	....	....	....	....	....	....	....	....	....	....	....	....	....	....	....
	Cleveland Lumberjacks	IHL	13	4	5	9	....	....	....	8	....	....	....	....	....	....	....	....	....	....	....	....	....	....	....	....	....	....
1994-95	Detroit Vipers	IHL	29	12	17	29	....	....	....	16	....	....	....	....	....	....	....	....	....	....	....	....	....	....	....	....	....	....
	Czech-Republic	WJC-A	3	0	0	0	....	....	....	0	....	....	....	....	....	....	....	....	....	....	....	....	....	....	....	....	....	....
1995-96	New Jersey Devils	NHL	63	18	24	42	18	20	38	32	8	0	3	128	14.1	62	25	30	0	7	....	....	....	....	....	....	....	....
	Albany River Rats	AHL	5	4	1	5	....	....	....	0	....	....	....	....	....	....	....	....	....	....	....	....	....	....	....	....	....	....
1996-97	Czech-Republic	W-Cup	2	0	1	1	....	....	....	0	....	....	....	....	....	....	....	....	....	....	....	....	....	....	....	....	....	....
	New Jersey Devils	NHL	19	1	2	3	1	2	3	4	0	0	0	26	3.8	8	3	13	0	–8	2	0	0	0	2	0	0	0
	Albany River Rats	AHL	43	20	25	45	....	....	....	48	....	....	....	....	....	....	....	....	....	....	4	1	4	5	2	....	....	....
1997-98	New Jersey Devils	NHL	58	16	20	36	19	20	39	22	3	1	4	130	12.3	50	22	33	5	0	2	0	0	0	0	0	0	0
	Albany River Rats	AHL	2	4	1	5	....	....	....	0	....	....	....	....	....	....	....	....	....	....	....	....	....	....	....	....	....	....
	Czech-Republic	WC-A	6	0	2	2	....	....	....	2	....	....	....	....	....	....	....	....	....	....	....	....	....	....	....	....	....	....
1998-99	New Jersey Devils	NHL	80	29	43	72	34	42	76	22	15	0	7	222	13.1	94	36	44	2	16	7	3	3	6	4	0	0	1
	Czech-Republic	WC-A	8	1	5	6	....	....	....	14	....	....	....	....	....	....	....	....	....	....	....	....	....	....	....	....	....	....
99-2000♦	New Jersey Devils	NHL	79	25	43	68	28	40	68	26	5	1	4	222	11.3	....	....	....	....	24	23	9	8	17	10	1	0	3
	NHL Totals		299	89	132	221	100	124	224	106	31	2	18	728	12.2	214	86	120	7		34	12	11	23	16	1	0	4

NHL All-Rookie Team (1996)

• SYKORA, Petr
C – R. 6'2", 180 lbs. b: Pardubice, Czech., 12/21/1978. Detroit's 2nd, 76th overall, in 1997.

Season	Club	League	GP	G	A	Pts	AG	AA	APts	PIM	PP	SH	GW	S	%	TGF	PGF	TGA	PGA	+/-	GP	G	A	Pts	PIM	PP	SH	GW
			REGULAR SEASON																		PLAYOFFS							
1994-95	HC Pardubice-Jr.	Czech-Rep	38	35	33	68	....	....	....	....	....	....	....	....	....	....	....	....	....	....	....	....	....	....	....	....	....	....
1995-96	HC Pardubice-Jr.	Czech-Rep	16	26	17	43	....	....	....	....	....	....	....	....	....	....	....	....	....	....	....	....	....	....	....	....	....	....
1996-97	HC Pardubice-Jr.	Czech-Rep	12	14	4	18	....	....	....	....	....	....	....	....	....	....	....	....	....	....	....	....	....	....	....	....	....	....
	HC Pardubice	Czech-Rep	29	1	3	4	....	....	....	4	....	....	....	....	....	....	....	....	....	....	....	....	....	....	....	....	....	....
1997-98	HC Pardubice	Czech-Rep	39	4	5	9	....	....	....	8	....	....	....	....	....	....	....	....	....	....	3	0	0	0	....	....	....	....
1998-99	**Nashville Predators**	**NHL**	**2**	**0**	**0**	**0**	**0**	**0**	**0**	**0**	**0**	**0**	**0**	**2**	**0.0**	**0**	**0**	**1**	**0**	**–1**	....	....	....	....	....	....	....	....
	Milwaukee Admirals	IHL	73	14	15	29	....	....	....	50	....	....	....	....	....	....	....	....	....	....	2	1	1	2	0	....	....	....
99-2000	Milwaukee Admirals	IHL	3	0	1	1	....	....	....	2	....	....	....	....	....	....	....	....	....	....	....	....	....	....	....	....	....	....
	HC Pardubice	Czech-Rep	36	7	13	20	....	....	....	49	....	....	....	....	....	....	....	....	....	....	3	0	0	0	2	....	....	....
	NHL Totals		**2**	**0**	**0**	**0**	**0**	**0**	**0**	**0**	**0**	**0**	**0**	**2**	**0.0**	**0**	**0**	**1**	**0**		....	....	....	....	....	....	....	....

Traded to **Nashville** by **Detroit** with Detroit's 3rd round choice (later traded to Edmonton - Edmonton selected Mike Comrie) in 1999 Entry Draft and future considerations (Detroit's compensatory 4th round choice (Alexander Krevsun) in 1999 Entry Draft) for Doug Brown, July 14, 1998.

• SYLVESTER, Dean
RW – R. 6'2", 210 lbs. b: Hanson, MA, 12/30/1972.

Season	Club	League	GP	G	A	Pts	AG	AA	APts	PIM	PP	SH	GW	S	%	TGF	PGF	TGA	PGA	+/-	GP	G	A	Pts	PIM	PP	SH	GW
1990-91	Boston College Prep School	Hi-School	18	19	13	32	....	....	....	....	....	....	....	....	....	....	....	....	....	....	....	....	....	....	....	....	....	....
1991-92	Kent State University	NCAA	31	7	21	28	....	....	....	10	....	....	....	....	....	....	....	....	....	....	....	....	....	....	....	....	....	....
1992-93	Kent State University	NCAA	38	33	20	53	....	....	....	28	....	....	....	....	....	....	....	....	....	....	....	....	....	....	....	....	....	....
1993-94	Kent State University	NCAA	39	22	24	46	....	....	....	28	....	....	....	....	....	....	....	....	....	....	....	....	....	....	....	....	....	....
1994-95	Michigan State Spartans	CCHA	40	15	15	30	....	....	....	38	....	....	....	....	....	....	....	....	....	....	....	....	....	....	....	....	....	....
1995-96	Mobile Mysticks	ECHL	44	24	27	51	....	....	....	35	....	....	....	....	....	....	....	....	....	....	....	....	....	....	....	....	....	....
	Kansas City Blades	IHL	36	11	10	21	....	....	....	15	....	....	....	....	....	....	....	....	....	....	4	0	0	0	2	....	....	....
1996-97	Kansas City Blades	IHL	77	23	22	45	....	....	....	47	....	....	....	....	....	....	....	....	....	....	3	1	1	2	0	....	....	....
1997-98	Kansas City Blades	IHL	77	33	20	53	....	....	....	63	....	....	....	....	....	....	....	....	....	....	11	5	2	7	4	....	....	....
1998-99	**Buffalo Sabres**	**NHL**	**1**	**0**	**0**	**0**	**0**	**0**	**0**	**0**	**0**	**0**	**0**	**1**	**0.0**	**0**	**0**	**1**	**0**	**–1**	**4**	**0**	**0**	**0**	**0**	**0**	**0**	**0**
	Rochester Americans	AHL	76	35	30	65	....	....	....	46	....	....	....	....	....	....	....	....	....	....	18	*12	5	17	8	....	....	....
99-2000	**Atlanta Thrashers**	**NHL**	**52**	**16**	**10**	**26**	**18**	**9**	**27**	**24**	**1**	**0**	**2**	**98**	**16.3**	**32**	**5**	**50**	**9**	**–14**	....	....	....	....	....	....	....	....
	Orlando Solar Bears	IHL	16	4	3	7	....	....	....	43	....	....	....	....	....	....	....	....	....	....	....	....	....	....	....	....	....	....
	NHL Totals		**53**	**16**	**10**	**26**	**18**	**9**	**27**	**24**	**1**	**0**	**2**	**99**	**16.2**	**32**	**5**	**51**	**9**		**4**	**0**	**0**	**0**	**0**	**0**	**0**	**0**

Signed as a free agent by **Buffalo**, October 1, 1998. Traded to **Atlanta** by **Buffalo** for future considerations, June 25, 1999.

• SZURA, Joe
Joseph Boleslaw C – L. 6'3", 185 lbs. b: Fort William, Ont., 12/18/1938.

Season	Club	League	GP	G	A	Pts	AG	AA	APts	PIM	PP	SH	GW	S	%	TGF	PGF	TGA	PGA	+/-	GP	G	A	Pts	PIM	PP	SH	GW
1956-57	Fort William Canadiens	TBJHL	30	27	*36	*63	....	....	....	14	....	....	....	....	....	....	....	....	....	....	8	3	4	7	0	....	....	....
	Fort William Canadiens	Mem-Cup	10	2	2	4	....	....	....	2	....	....	....	....	....	....	....	....	....	....	....	....	....	....	....	....	....	....
1957-58	Fort William Canadiens	TBJHL	30	10	21	31	....	....	....	2	....	....	....	....	....	....	....	....	....	....	4	1	5	6	0	....	....	....
	Fort William Canadiens	Mem-Cup	5	2	3	5	....	....	....	0	....	....	....	....	....	....	....	....	....	....	....	....	....	....	....	....	....	....
1958-59	Fort William Canadiens	TBJHL	30	13	27	*40	....	....	....	20	....	....	....	....	....	....	....	....	....	....	....	....	....	....	....	....	....	....
1959-60	Montreal Royals	EPHL	14	2	3	5	....	....	....	4	....	....	....	....	....	....	....	....	....	....	6	0	1	1	0	....	....	....
	Hull-Ottawa Canadiens	EPHL	26	5	8	13	....	....	....	4	....	....	....	....	....	....	....	....	....	....	....	....	....	....	....	....	....	....
1960-61	Montreal–Hull-Ottawa	EPHL	65	10	24	34	....	....	....	20	....	....	....	....	....	....	....	....	....	....	....	....	....	....	....	....	....	....
1961-62	North Bay Trappers	EPHL	68	27	35	62	....	....	....	24	....	....	....	....	....	....	....	....	....	....	....	....	....	....	....	....	....	....
1962-63	Cleveland Barons	AHL	72	15	29	44	....	....	....	20	....	....	....	....	....	....	....	....	....	....	7	1	1	2	2	....	....	....
1963-64	Cleveland Barons	AHL	72	23	44	67	....	....	....	33	....	....	....	....	....	....	....	....	....	....	9	*13	6	*19	2	....	....	....
1964-65	Cleveland Barons	AHL	67	29	30	59	....	....	....	26	....	....	....	....	....	....	....	....	....	....	....	....	....	....	....	....	....	....
1965-66	Cleveland Barons	AHL	72	46	30	76	....	....	....	22	....	....	....	....	....	....	....	....	....	....	12	1	4	5	8	....	....	....
1966-67	Cleveland Barons	AHL	68	27	42	69	....	....	....	32	....	....	....	....	....	....	....	....	....	....	3	0	0	0	4	....	....	....
1967-68	**Oakland Seals**	**NHL**	**20**	**1**	**3**	**4**	**1**	**3**	**4**	**10**	**0**	**0**	**0**	**18**	**5.6**	**9**	**1**	**12**	**0**	**–4**	....	....	....	....	....	....	....	....
	Buffalo Bisons	AHL	43	13	22	35	....	....	....	16	....	....	....	....	....	....	....	....	....	....	5	3	1	4	2	....	....	....
1968-69	**Oakland Seals**	**NHL**	**70**	**9**	**12**	**21**	**9**	**11**	**20**	**20**	**0**	**0**	**1**	**102**	**8.8**	**40**	**4**	**42**	**1**	**–5**	**7**	**2**	**3**	**5**	**2**	**1**	**0**	**0**
1969-70	Providence Reds	AHL	72	21	46	67	....	....	....	23	....	....	....	....	....	....	....	....	....	....	....	....	....	....	....	....	....	....
1970-71	Providence Reds	AHL	70	21	53	74	....	....	....	39	....	....	....	....	....	....	....	....	....	....	10	5	6	11	23	....	....	....
1971-72	Baltimore Clippers	AHL	73	38	38	76	....	....	....	20	....	....	....	....	....	....	....	....	....	....	18	1	10	11	12	....	....	....
1972-73	Los Angeles Sharks	WHA	72	13	32	45	....	....	....	25	....	....	....	....	....	....	....	....	....	....	2	0	0	0	0	....	....	....
1973-74	Houston Aeros	WHA	42	8	7	15	....	....	....	4	....	....	....	....	....	....	....	....	....	....	10	0	0	0	0	....	....	....
1974-75	Cape Cod Codders	NAHL	10	3	2	5	....	....	....	0	....	....	....	....	....	....	....	....	....	....	....	....	....	....	....	....	....	....
	NHL Totals		**90**	**10**	**15**	**25**	**10**	**14**	**24**	**30**	**0**	**0**	**1**	**120**	**8.3**	**49**	**5**	**54**	**1**		**7**	**2**	**3**	**5**	**2**	**1**	**0**	**0**
	Other Major League Totals		114	21	39	60	....	....	....	29	....	....	....	....	....	....	....	....	....	....	12	0	0	0	0	....	....	....

AHL First All-Star Team (1966)

Claimed by **Oakland** from **Montreal** in Expansion Draft, June 6, 1967. Selected by **LA Sharks** (WHA) in 1972 WHA General Player Draft, February 12, 1972. Traded to **Houston** (WHA) by **LA Sharks** (WHA) for Brian McDonald, September, 1973.

• TAFT, John
John Philip D – L. 6'2", 185 lbs. b: Minneapolis, MN, 3/8/1954. Detroit's 5th, 81st overall, in 1974.

Season	Club	League	GP	G	A	Pts	AG	AA	APts	PIM	PP	SH	GW	S	%	TGF	PGF	TGA	PGA	+/-	GP	G	A	Pts	PIM	PP	SH	GW
1971-72	Southwest High School	Hi-School	STATISTICS NOT AVAILABLE																									
1972-73	University of Wisconsin	WCHA	40	9	18	27	....	....	....	28	....	....	....	....	....	....	....	....	....	....	....	....	....	....	....	....	....	....
	United States	WEC-B	7	0	0	0	....	....	....	0	....	....	....	....	....	....	....	....	....	....	....	....	....	....	....	....	....	....
1973-74	University of Wisconsin	WCHA	36	1	17	18	....	....	....	20	....	....	....	....	....	....	....	....	....	....	....	....	....	....	....	....	....	....
1974-75	University of Wisconsin	WCHA	11	11	17	28	....	....	....	22	....	....	....	....	....	....	....	....	....	....	....	....	....	....	....	....	....	....
	United States	Nat-Team	18	1	4	5	....	....	....	....	....	....	....	....	....	....	....	....	....	....	....	....	....	....	....	....	....	....
	United States	WEC-A	10	1	2	3	....	....	....	4	....	....	....	....	....	....	....	....	....	....	....	....	....	....	....	....	....	....
1975-76	United States	Nat-Team	51	9	34	43	....	....	....	66	....	....	....	....	....	....	....	....	....	....	....	....	....	....	....	....	....	....
	United States	Olympics	6	1	2	3	....	....	....	8	....	....	....	....	....	....	....	....	....	....	....	....	....	....	....	....	....	....
1976-77	University of Wisconsin	WCHA	42	15	43	58	....	....	....	41	....	....	....	....	....	....	....	....	....	....	....	....	....	....	....	....	....	....
1977-78	Kansas City Red Wings	CHL	71	5	22	27	....	....	....	25	....	....	....	....	....	....	....	....	....	....	....	....	....	....	....	....	....	....
1978-79	**Detroit Red Wings**	**NHL**	**15**	**0**	**2**	**2**	**0**	**1**	**1**	**4**	**0**	**0**	**0**	**13**	**0.0**	**14**	**0**	**13**	**1**	**2**	....	....	....	....	....	....	....	....
	Kansas City Red Wings	CHL	61	8	24	32	....	....	....	48	....	....	....	....	....	....	....	....	....	....	4	0	2	2	0	....	....	....
1979-80	Adirondack Red Wings	AHL	47	1	7	8	....	....	....	25	....	....	....	....	....	....	....	....	....	....	....	....	....	....	....	....	....	....
1980-81	Salt Lake Golden Eagles	CHL	68	8	19	27	....	....	....	68	....	....	....	....	....	....	....	....	....	....	17	1	2	3	33	....	....	....
1981-82	Salt Lake Golden Eagles	CHL	70	6	16	22	....	....	....	46	....	....	....	....	....	....	....	....	....	....	1	0	0	0	0	....	....	....
1982-83	Salt Lake Golden Eagles	CHL	77	5	25	30	....	....	....	65	....	....	....	....	....	....	....	....	....	....	6	0	0	0	8	....	....	....
	NHL Totals		**15**	**0**	**2**	**2**	**0**	**1**	**1**	**4**	**0**	**0**	**0**	**13**	**0.0**	**14**	**0**	**13**	**1**		....	....	....	....	....	....	....	....

NCAA Championship All-Tournament Team (1973, 1977) • WEC-B All-Star Team (1974) • WCHA Second All-Star Team (1977)

Signed as a free agent by **St. Louis**, July 14, 1980.

• TAGLIANETTI, Peter
Peter A. D – L. 6'2", 195 lbs. b: Framingham, MA, 8/15/1963. Winnipeg's 4th, 43rd overall, in 1983.

Season	Club	League	GP	G	A	Pts	AG	AA	APts	PIM	PP	SH	GW	S	%	TGF	PGF	TGA	PGA	+/-	GP	G	A	Pts	PIM	PP	SH	GW
1980-81	Framingham South High	Hi-School	STATISTICS NOT AVAILABLE																									
1981-82	Providence College	ECAC	2	0	0	0	....	....	....	2	....	....	....	....	....	....	....	....	....	....	....	....	....	....	....	....	....	....
1982-83	Providence College	ECAC	43	4	17	21	....	....	....	68	....	....	....	....	....	....	....	....	....	....	....	....	....	....	....	....	....	....
1983-84	Providence College	ECAC	30	4	25	29	....	....	....	68	....	....	....	....	....	....	....	....	....	....	....	....	....	....	....	....	....	....
1984-85	Providence College	H-East	35	6	18	24	....	....	....	32	....	....	....	....	....	....	....	....	....	....	....	....	....	....	....	....	....	....
	Winnipeg Jets	**NHL**	**1**	**0**	**0**	**0**	**0**	**0**	**0**	**0**	**0**	**0**	**0**	**2**	**0.0**	**2**	**1**	**1**	**1**	**1**	**1**	**0**	**0**	**0**	**0**	**0**	**0**	**0**
1985-86	**Winnipeg Jets**	**NHL**	**18**	**0**	**0**	**0**	**0**	**0**	**0**	**48**	**0**	**0**	**0**	**8**	**0.0**	**9**	**0**	**14**	**4**	**–1**	**3**	**0**	**0**	**0**	**2**	**0**	**0**	**0**
	Sherbrooke Canadiens	AHL	24	1	8	9	....	....	....	75	....	....	....	....	....	....	....	....	....	....	....	....	....	....	....	....	....	....
1986-87	**Winnipeg Jets**	**NHL**	**3**	**0**	**0**	**0**	**0**	**0**	**0**	**12**	**0**	**0**	**0**	**2**	**0.0**	**2**	**0**	**6**	**0**	**–4**	....	....	....	....	....	....	....	....
	Sherbrooke Canadiens	AHL	54	5	14	19	....	....	....	104	....	....	....	....	....	....	....	....	....	....	10	2	5	7	25	....	....	....
1987-88	**Winnipeg Jets**	**NHL**	**70**	**6**	**17**	**23**	**5**	**12**	**17**	**182**	**2**	**0**	**1**	**92**	**6.5**	**66**	**26**	**72**	**19**	**–13**	**5**	**1**	**1**	**2**	**12**	**0**	**0**	**0**
1988-89	**Winnipeg Jets**	**NHL**	**66**	**1**	**14**	**15**	**1**	**10**	**11**	**226**	**1**	**0**	**0**	**72**	**1.4**	**62**	**3**	**115**	**33**	**–23**	....	....	....	....	....	....	....	....

			REGULAR SEASON																		PLAYOFFS							
Season	Club	League	GP	G	A	Pts	AG	AA	APts	PIM	PP	SH	GW	S	%	TGF	PGF	TGA	PGA	+/–	GP	G	A	Pts	PIM	PP	SH	GW
1989-90	**Winnipeg Jets**	**NHL**	**49**	**3**	**6**	**9**	**3**	**4**	**7**	**136**	**0**	**0**	**1**	**57**	**5.3**	**51**	**1**	**42**	**12**	**20**	**5**	**0**	**0**	**0**	**6**	**0**	**0**	**0**
	Moncton Hawks	AHL	3	0	2	2	....	....	....	2	....	....	....	....	....	....	....	....	....	....	....	....	....	....	....	....	....	....
1990-91	**Minnesota North Stars**	**NHL**	**16**	**0**	**1**	**1**	**0**	**1**	**1**	**14**	**0**	**0**	**0**	**15**	**0.0**	**16**	**2**	**20**	**6**	**0**	....	....	....	....	....	....	....	....
♦	**Pittsburgh Penguins**	**NHL**	**39**	**3**	**8**	**11**	**3**	**6**	**9**	**93**	**0**	**0**	**0**	**25**	**12.0**	**51**	**0**	**50**	**15**	**16**	**19**	**0**	**3**	**3**	**49**	**0**	**0**	**0**
1991-92♦	**Pittsburgh Penguins**	**NHL**	**44**	**1**	**3**	**4**	**1**	**2**	**3**	**57**	**0**	**0**	**0**	**23**	**4.3**	**37**	**0**	**49**	**19**	**7**	....	....	....	....	....	....	....	....
1992-93	**Tampa Bay Lightning**	**NHL**	**61**	**1**	**8**	**9**	**1**	**5**	**6**	**150**	**0**	**0**	**0**	**60**	**1.7**	**48**	**0**	**76**	**36**	**8**	....	....	....	....	....	....	....	....
	Pittsburgh Penguins	**NHL**	**11**	**1**	**4**	**5**	**1**	**3**	**4**	**34**	**0**	**0**	**0**	**18**	**5.6**	**15**	**0**	**12**	**1**	**4**	**11**	**1**	**2**	**3**	**16**	**0**	**0**	**0**
1993-94	**Pittsburgh Penguins**	**NHL**	**60**	**2**	**12**	**14**	**2**	**9**	**11**	**142**	**0**	**0**	**0**	**57**	**3.5**	**45**	**0**	**54**	**14**	**5**	**5**	**0**	**2**	**2**	**16**	**0**	**0**	**0**
1994-95	**Pittsburgh Penguins**	**NHL**	**13**	**0**	**1**	**1**	**0**	**1**	**1**	**12**	**0**	**0**	**0**	**5**	**0.0**	**14**	**0**	**15**	**2**	**1**	**4**	**0**	**0**	**0**	**2**	**0**	**0**	**0**
	Cleveland Lumberjacks	IHL	3	0	1	1	....	....	....	7	....	....	....	....	....	....	....	....	....	....	4	0	0	0	19	....	....	....
1995-96	Providence Bruins	AHL	34	0	6	6	....	....	....	44	....	....	....	....	....	....	....	....	....	....	....	....	....	....	....	....	....	....
	NHL Totals		**451**	**18**	**74**	**92**	**17**	**53**	**70**	**1106**	**3**	**0**	**2**	**436**	**4.1**	**418**	**33**	**526**	**162**		**53**	**2**	**8**	**10**	**103**	**0**	**0**	**0**

ECAC Second All-Star Team (1984) • Hockey East First All-Star Team (1985)

Traded to **Minnesota** by **Winnipeg** for future considerations, September 30, 1990. Traded to **Pittsburgh** by **Minnesota** with Larry Murphy for Chris Dahlquist and Jim Johnson, December 11, 1990. Claimed by **Tampa Bay** from **Pittsburgh** in Expansion Draft, June 18, 1992. Traded to **Pittsburgh** by **Tampa Bay** for Pittsburgh's 3rd round choice (later traded to Florida - Florida selected Steve Washburn) in 1993 Entry Draft, March 22, 1993. Signed as a free agent by **Boston**, August 9, 1995.

• TALAFOUS, Dean

Dean Charles RW – R. 6'4", 180 lbs. b: Duluth, MN, 8/25/1953. Atlanta's 4th, 53rd overall, in 1973.

Season	Club	League	GP	G	A	Pts	AG	AA	APts	PIM	PP	SH	GW	S	%	TGF	PGF	TGA	PGA	+/–	GP	G	A	Pts	PIM	PP	SH	GW
1971-72	University of Wisconsin	WCHA	37	10	24	34	....	....	....	42	....	....	....	....	....	....	....	....	....	....	....	....	....	....	....	....	....	....
1972-73	University of Wisconsin	WCHA	38	18	31	49	....	....	....	34	....	....	....	....	....	....	....	....	....	....	....	....	....	....	....	....	....	....
	United States	WEC-B	7	2	8	10	....	....	....	....	....	....	....	....	....	....	....	....	....	....	....	....	....	....	....	....	....	....
1973-74	University of Wisconsin	WCHA	34	17	29	46	....	....	....	29	....	....	....	....	....	....	....	....	....	....	....	....	....	....	....	....	....	....
1974-75	**Atlanta Flames**	**NHL**	**18**	**1**	**4**	**5**	**1**	**3**	**4**	**13**	**0**	**0**	**0**	**22**	**4.5**	**13**	**3**	**17**	**0**	**–7**	....	....	....	....	....	....	....	....
	Omaha Knights	CHL	11	3	5	8	....	....	....	10	....	....	....	....	....	....	....	....	....	....	....	....	....	....	....	....	....	....
	Minnesota North Stars	**NHL**	**43**	**8**	**17**	**25**	**7**	**13**	**20**	**6**	**0**	**0**	**2**	**68**	**11.8**	**36**	**8**	**46**	**1**	**–17**	....	....	....	....	....	....	....	....
1975-76	**Minnesota North Stars**	**NHL**	**79**	**18**	**30**	**48**	**16**	**22**	**38**	**18**	**4**	**1**	**2**	**137**	**13.1**	**78**	**23**	**67**	**0**	**–12**	....	....	....	....	....	....	....	....
1976-77	United States	Can-Cup	5	2	2	4	....	....	....	8	....	....	....	....	....	....	....	....	....	....	....	....	....	....	....	....	....	....
	Minnesota North Stars	**NHL**	**80**	**22**	**27**	**49**	**20**	**21**	**41**	**10**	**9**	**0**	**2**	**185**	**11.9**	**87**	**44**	**72**	**0**	**–29**	**2**	**0**	**0**	**0**	**0**	**0**	**0**	**0**
1977-78	**Minnesota North Stars**	**NHL**	**75**	**13**	**16**	**29**	**12**	**12**	**24**	**25**	**2**	**0**	**2**	**80**	**16.3**	**51**	**13**	**55**	**1**	**–16**	....	....	....	....	....	....	....	....
1978-79	**New York Rangers**	**NHL**	**68**	**13**	**16**	**29**	**11**	**12**	**23**	**29**	**2**	**2**	**3**	**88**	**14.8**	**45**	**6**	**53**	**19**	**5**	....	....	....	....	....	....	....	....
1979-80	**New York Rangers**	**NHL**	**55**	**10**	**20**	**30**	**8**	**15**	**23**	**26**	**4**	**0**	**0**	**69**	**14.5**	**49**	**15**	**44**	**11**	**1**	**5**	**1**	**2**	**3**	**9**	**1**	**0**	**0**
1980-81	**New York Rangers**	**NHL**	**50**	**13**	**17**	**30**	**10**	**11**	**21**	**28**	**1**	**2**	**0**	**73**	**17.8**	**45**	**4**	**49**	**10**	**2**	**14**	**3**	**5**	**8**	**2**	**0**	**0**	**0**
1981-82	United States	Can-Cup	6	3	2	5	....	....	....	0	....	....	....	....	....	....	....	....	....	....	....	....	....	....	....	....	....	....
	New York Rangers	DN-Cup	4	2	0	2	....	....	....	....	....	....	....	....	....	....	....	....	....	....	....	....	....	....	....	....	....	....
	New York Rangers	**NHL**	**29**	**6**	**7**	**13**	**5**	**5**	**10**	**8**	**1**	**0**	**2**	**33**	**18.2**	**21**	**3**	**25**	**4**	**–3**	....	....	....	....	....	....	....	....
1982-1984			OUT OF HOCKEY – RETIRED																									
1984-1985	St. Paul Jr. Stars	USHL	DID NOT PLAY – COACHING																									
1985-1990	University of Minnesota	WCHA	DID NOT PLAY – ASSISTANT COACH																									
1990-1996	U. of Wisconsin-River Falls	NCAA-3	DID NOT PLAY – COACHING																									
1996-2000	U. of Alaska-Anchorage	WCHA	DID NOT PLAY – COACHING																									
	NHL Totals		**497**	**104**	**154**	**258**	**90**	**114**	**204**	**163**	**23**	**5**	**13**	**755**	**13.8**	**425**	**119**	**428**	**46**		**21**	**4**	**7**	**11**	**11**	**1**	**0**	**0**

NCAA Championship All-Tournament Team (1973) • NCAA Championship Tournament MVP (1973)

Traded to **Minnesota** by **Atlanta** with Dwight Bialowas for Barry Gibbs, January 3, 1975. Signed as a free agent by **NY Rangers**, July 17, 1978. • Officially announced retirement, December 30, 1981.

• TALAKOSKI, Ron

RW – R. 6'3", 220 lbs. b: Thunder Bay, Ont., 6/1/1962.

Season	Club	League	GP	G	A	Pts	AG	AA	APts	PIM	PP	SH	GW	S	%	TGF	PGF	TGA	PGA	+/–	GP	G	A	Pts	PIM	PP	SH	GW
1979-80	Thunder Bay North Stars	TBJHL	34	20	24	44	....	....	....	24	....	....	....	....	....	....	....	....	....	....	....	....	....	....	....	....	....	....
1980-81	Thunder Bay North Stars	TBJHL	STATISTICS NOT AVAILABLE																									
1981-82	University of Manitoba	GPAC	STATISTICS NOT AVAILABLE																									
1982-83	University of Manitoba	GPAC	31	12	11	23	....	....	....	51	....	....	....	....	....	....	....	....	....	....	....	....	....	....	....	....	....	....
1983-84	University of Manitoba	GPAC	DID NOT PLAY																									
1984-85	University of Manitoba	GPAC	11	4	4	8	....	....	....	77	....	....	....	....	....	....	....	....	....	....	....	....	....	....	....	....	....	....
1985-86	University of Manitoba	GPAC	DID NOT PLAY																									
1986-87	**New York Rangers**	**NHL**	**3**	**0**	**0**	**0**	**0**	**0**	**0**	**21**	**0**	**0**	**0**	**1**	**0.0**	**2**	**0**	**1**	**0**	**1**	....	....	....	....	....	....	....	....
	New Haven Nighthawks	AHL	26	2	2	4	....	....	....	58	....	....	....	....	....	....	....	....	....	....	1	0	0	0	0	....	....	....
	Flint Spirits	IHL	3	2	1	3	....	....	....	12	....	....	....	....	....	....	....	....	....	....	....	....	....	....	....	....	....	....
1987-88	**New York Rangers**	**NHL**	**6**	**0**	**1**	**1**	**0**	**1**	**1**	**12**	**0**	**0**	**0**	**6**	**0.0**	**3**	**0**	**3**	**0**	**0**	....	....	....	....	....	....	....	....
	Colorado Rangers	IHL	62	24	19	43	....	....	....	104	....	....	....	....	....	....	....	....	....	....	10	1	4	5	17	....	....	....
1988-1993	Thunder Bay Twins	CASH	STATISTICS NOT AVAILABLE																									
1993-94	Thunder Bay Senators	ColHL	43	19	20	39	....	....	....	51	....	....	....	....	....	....	....	....	....	....	9	7	3	10	0	....	....	....
1994-95			OUT OF HOCKEY – RETIRED																									
1995-96	Thunder Bay Senators	ColHL	8	1	1	2	....	....	....	13	....	....	....	....	....	....	....	....	....	....	15	2	1	3	8	....	....	....
	NHL Totals		**9**	**0**	**1**	**1**	**0**	**1**	**1**	**33**	**0**	**0**	**0**	**7**	**0.0**	**5**	**0**	**4**	**0**		....	....	....	....	....	....	....	....

• Played college football instead of hockey in 1983-84 and 1985-86 seasons. Signed as a free agent by **NY Rangers**, October 3, 1986.

• TALBOT, Jean-Guy

D – L. 5'11", 170 lbs. b: Cap de La Madeliene, Que., 7/11/1932.

Season	Club	League	GP	G	A	Pts	AG	AA	APts	PIM	PP	SH	GW	S	%	TGF	PGF	TGA	PGA	+/–	GP	G	A	Pts	PIM	PP	SH	GW
1949-50	Trois-Rivieres Reds	QJHL	36	3	4	7	....	....	....	79	....	....	....	....	....	....	....	....	....	....	9	0	3	3	12	....	....	....
1950-51	Trois-Rivieres Reds	QJHL	44	7	22	29	....	....	....	*136	....	....	....	....	....	....	....	....	....	....	8	0	1	1	18	....	....	....
	Shawinigan Cataracts	QSHL	1	0	0	0	....	....	....	0	....	....	....	....	....	....	....	....	....	....	....	....	....	....	....	....	....	....
1951-52	Trois-Rivieres Reds	QJHL	43	12	36	48	....	....	....	132	....	....	....	....	....	....	....	....	....	....	4	1	0	1	12	....	....	....
1952-53	Quebec Aces	QSHL	24	2	4	6	....	....	....	33	....	....	....	....	....	....	....	....	....	....	....	....	....	....	....	....	....	....
1953-54	Quebec Aces	QHL	67	9	11	20	....	....	....	58	....	....	....	....	....	....	....	....	....	....	16	0	2	2	12	....	....	....
	Quebec Aces	Ed-Cup	7	2	0	2	....	....	....	2	....	....	....	....	....	....	....	....	....	....	....	....	....	....	....	....	....	....
1954-55	**Montreal Canadiens**	**NHL**	**3**	**0**	**1**	**1**	**0**	**1**	**1**	**0**	....	....	....	....	....	....	....	....	....	....	....	....	....	....	....	....	....	....
	Shawinigan Cataracts	QHL	59	6	28	34	....	....	....	82	....	....	....	....	....	....	....	....	....	....	13	2	5	7	14	....	....	....
	Shawinigan Cataracts	Ed-Cup	7	0	2	2	....	....	....	6	....	....	....	....	....	....	....	....	....	....	....	....	....	....	....	....	....	....
1955-56♦	**Montreal Canadiens**	**NHL**	**66**	**1**	**13**	**14**	**1**	**15**	**16**	**80**	....	....	....	....	....	....	....	....	....	....	**9**	**0**	**2**	**2**	**4**	**0**	**0**	**0**
1956-57♦	**Montreal Canadiens**	**NHL**	**59**	**0**	**13**	**13**	**0**	**14**	**14**	**70**	....	....	....	....	....	....	....	....	....	....	**10**	**0**	**2**	**2**	**10**	**0**	**0**	**0**
1957-58♦	**Montreal Canadiens**	**NHL**	**55**	**4**	**15**	**19**	**5**	**15**	**20**	**65**	....	....	....	....	....	....	....	....	....	....	**10**	**0**	**3**	**3**	**12**	**0**	**0**	**0**
1958-59♦	**Montreal Canadiens**	**NHL**	**69**	**4**	**17**	**21**	**5**	**17**	**22**	**77**	....	....	....	....	....	....	....	....	....	....	**11**	**0**	**1**	**1**	**10**	**0**	**0**	**0**
1959-60♦	**Montreal Canadiens**	**NHL**	**69**	**1**	**14**	**15**	**1**	**14**	**15**	**60**	....	....	....	....	....	....	....	....	....	....	**8**	**1**	**1**	**2**	**8**	**0**	**0**	**0**
1960-61	**Montreal Canadiens**	**NHL**	**70**	**5**	**26**	**31**	**6**	**25**	**31**	**143**	....	....	....	....	....	....	....	....	....	....	**6**	**1**	**1**	**2**	**10**	**1**	**0**	**0**
1961-62	**Montreal Canadiens**	**NHL**	**70**	**5**	**42**	**47**	**6**	**41**	**47**	**90**	....	....	....	....	....	....	....	....	....	....	**6**	**1**	**1**	**2**	**10**	**0**	**0**	**0**
1962-63	**Montreal Canadiens**	**NHL**	**70**	**3**	**22**	**25**	**3**	**22**	**25**	**51**	....	....	....	....	....	....	....	....	....	....	**5**	**0**	**0**	**0**	**8**	**0**	**0**	**0**
1963-64	**Montreal Canadiens**	**NHL**	**66**	**1**	**13**	**14**	**1**	**14**	**15**	**83**	....	....	....	....	....	....	....	....	....	....	**7**	**0**	**2**	**2**	**10**	**0**	**0**	**0**
1964-65♦	**Montreal Canadiens**	**NHL**	**67**	**8**	**14**	**22**	**10**	**14**	**24**	**64**	....	....	....	....	....	....	....	....	....	....	**13**	**0**	**1**	**1**	**22**	**0**	**0**	**0**
1965-66♦	**Montreal Canadiens**	**NHL**	**59**	**1**	**14**	**15**	**1**	**13**	**14**	**50**	....	....	....	....	....	....	....	....	....	....	**10**	**0**	**2**	**2**	**8**	**0**	**0**	**0**
1966-67	**Montreal Canadiens**	**NHL**	**68**	**3**	**5**	**8**	**3**	**5**	**8**	**51**	....	....	....	....	....	....	....	....	....	....	**10**	**0**	**0**	**0**	**0**	**0**	**0**	**0**
1967-68	**Minnesota North Stars**	**NHL**	**4**	**0**	**0**	**0**	**0**	**0**	**0**	**4**	**0**	**0**	**0**	**7**	**0.0**	**2**	**0**	**9**	**1**	**–6**	....	....	....	....	....	....	....	....
	Detroit Red Wings	**NHL**	**32**	**0**	**3**	**3**	**0**	**3**	**3**	**10**	**0**	**0**	**0**	**11**	**0.0**	**13**	**0**	**26**	**13**	**0**	....	....	....	....	....	....	....	....
	St. Louis Blues	**NHL**	**23**	**0**	**4**	**4**	**0**	**4**	**4**	**2**	**0**	**0**	**0**	**29**	**0.0**	**19**	**1**	**21**	**6**	**3**	**17**	**0**	**2**	**2**	**8**	**0**	**0**	**0**
1968-69	**St. Louis Blues**	**NHL**	**69**	**5**	**4**	**9**	**5**	**4**	**9**	**24**	**0**	**0**	**1**	**67**	**7.5**	**41**	**2**	**49**	**19**	**9**	**12**	**0**	**2**	**2**	**6**	**0**	**0**	**0**

			REGULAR SEASON																		PLAYOFFS							
Season	Club	League	GP	G	A	Pts	AG	AA	APts	PIM	PP	SH	GW	S	%	TGF	PGF	TGA	PGA	+/–	GP	G	A	Pts	PIM	PP	SH	GW
1969-70	**St. Louis Blues**	**NHL**	**75**	**2**	**15**	**17**	**2**	**14**	**16**	**40**	**0**	**1**	**0**	**60**	**3.3**	**62**	**7**	**46**	**9**	**18**	**16**	**1**	**6**	**7**	**16**	**0**	**0**	**0**
1970-71	**St. Louis Blues**	**NHL**	**5**	**0**	**0**	**0**	**0**	**0**	**0**	**6**	**0**	**0**	**0**	**3**	**0.0**	**1**	**0**	**4**	**0**	**–3**								
	Buffalo Sabres	**NHL**	**57**	**0**	**7**	**7**	**0**	**6**	**6**	**36**	**0**	**0**	**0**	**41**	**0.0**	**41**	**2**	**73**	**14**	**–20**								
	NHL Totals		**1056**	**43**	**242**	**285**	**49**	**241**	**290**	**1006**											**150**	**4**	**26**	**30**	**142**			

QHL First All-Star Team (1955) • NHL First All-Star Team (1962) • Played in NHL All-Star Game (1956, 1957, 1958, 1960, 1962, 1965, 1967)

Claimed by **Minnesota** from **Montreal** in Expansion Draft, June 6, 1967. Traded to **Detroit** by **Minnesota** with Dave Richardson for Bob McCord and Duke Harris, October 19, 1967. Claimed on waivers by **St. Louis** from **Detroit**, January 13, 1968. Traded to **Buffalo** by **St. Louis** with Larry Keenan for Bob Baun, November 4, 1970.

• TALLON, Dale

Michael Dale Lee D – L. 6'1", 195 lbs. b: Noranda, Que., 10/19/1950. Vancouver's 1st, 2nd overall, in 1970.

Season	Club	League	GP	G	A	Pts	AG	AA	APts	PIM	PP	SH	GW	S	%	TGF	PGF	TGA	PGA	+/–	GP	G	A	Pts	PIM	PP	SH	GW
1967-68	Oshawa Generals	OHA-Jr.	50	12	31	43				88																		
1968-69	Toronto Marlboros	OHA-Jr.	48	17	32	49				80											6	6	2	8	8			
1969-70	Toronto Marlboros	OHA-Jr.	54	39	40	79				128											18	12	17	29	13			
1970-71	**Vancouver Canucks**	**NHL**	**78**	**14**	**42**	**56**	**14**	**35**	**49**	**58**	**5**	**0**	**1**	**232**	**6.0**	**134**	**48**	**124**	**13**	**–25**								
1971-72	**Vancouver Canucks**	**NHL**	**69**	**17**	**27**	**44**	**17**	**23**	**40**	**78**	**11**	**0**	**1**	**240**	**7.1**	**84**	**27**	**92**	**11**	**–24**								
1972-73	Team Canada	Summit-72	DID NOT PLAY																									
	Vancouver Canucks	**NHL**	**75**	**13**	**24**	**37**	**12**	**19**	**31**	**83**	**5**	**0**	**1**	**170**	**7.6**	**102**	**29**	**128**	**25**	**–30**								
1973-74	**Chicago Black Hawks**	**NHL**	**65**	**15**	**19**	**34**	**14**	**16**	**30**	**36**	**3**	**0**	**3**	**98**	**15.3**	**43**	**8**	**24**	**1**	**12**	**11**	**1**	**3**	**4**	**29**	**1**	**0**	**0**
1974-75	**Chicago Black Hawks**	**NHL**	**35**	**5**	**10**	**15**	**4**	**7**	**11**	**28**	**0**	**0**	**0**	**34**	**14.7**	**25**	**6**	**18**	**3**	**4**	**8**	**1**	**3**	**4**	**4**	**0**	**0**	**0**
	Dallas Black Hawks	CHL	7	1	4	5				14																		
1975-76	**Chicago Black Hawks**	**NHL**	**80**	**15**	**47**	**62**	**13**	**35**	**48**	**101**	**7**	**1**	**5**	**161**	**9.3**	**141**	**49**	**130**	**27**	**–11**	**4**	**0**	**1**	**1**	**8**	**0**	**0**	**0**
1976-77	**Chicago Black Hawks**	**NHL**	**70**	**5**	**16**	**21**	**4**	**12**	**16**	**65**	**1**	**0**	**0**	**107**	**4.7**	**74**	**15**	**101**	**21**	**–21**	**2**	**0**	**1**	**1**	**0**	**0**	**0**	**0**
1977-78	**Chicago Black Hawks**	**NHL**	**75**	**4**	**20**	**24**	**4**	**15**	**19**	**66**	**2**	**1**	**2**	**93**	**4.3**	**61**	**4**	**70**	**16**	**3**	**4**	**0**	**2**	**2**	**0**	**0**	**0**	**0**
1978-79	**Pittsburgh Penguins**	**NHL**	**63**	**5**	**24**	**29**	**4**	**17**	**21**	**35**	**2**	**0**	**3**	**91**	**5.5**	**83**	**18**	**101**	**21**	**–15**								
1979-80	**Pittsburgh Penguins**	**NHL**	**32**	**5**	**9**	**14**	**4**	**7**	**11**	**18**	**4**	**0**	**1**	**46**	**10.9**	**25**	**12**	**24**	**7**	**–4**	**4**	**0**	**0**	**0**	**4**	**0**	**0**	**0**
	Syracuse Firebirds	AHL	6	0	1	1				4																		
	NHL Totals		**642**	**98**	**238**	**336**	**90**	**186**	**276**	**568**	**40**	**2**	**17**	**1272**	**7.7**	**772**	**216**	**812**	**145**		**33**	**2**	**10**	**12**	**45**	**1**	**0**	**0**

Played in NHL All-Star Game (1971, 1972)

Traded to **Chicago** by **Vancouver** for Jerry Korab and Gary Smith, May 14, 1973. Traded to **Pittsburgh** by **Chicago** for Pittsburgh's 2nd round choice (Ken Solheim) in 1980 Entry Draft, October 9, 1978. Claimed by **Pittsburgh** as a fill-in during Expansion Draft, June 13, 1979.

• TAMBELLINI, Steve

Steven Anthony C – L. 6', 190 lbs. b: Trail, B.C., 5/14/1958. NY Islanders' 1st, 15th overall, in 1978.

Season	Club	League	GP	G	A	Pts	AG	AA	APts	PIM	PP	SH	GW	S	%	TGF	PGF	TGA	PGA	+/–	GP	G	A	Pts	PIM	PP	SH	GW
1974-75	Trail Smoke Eaters	BCJBL	33	52	53	105				30																		
1975-76	Lethbridge Broncos	WCJHL	72	38	59	97				42											7	3	6	9	2			
1976-77	Lethbridge Broncos	WCJHL	55	42	42	84				23											15	10	11	21	0			
1977-78	Lethbridge Broncos	WCJHL	66	75	80	155				32											8	10	5	15	5			
	Canada	WJC-A	6	2	2	4				0																		
1978-79	**New York Islanders**	**NHL**	**1**	**0**	**0**	**0**	**0**	**0**	**0**	**0**	**0**	**0**	**0**	**3**	**0.0**	**0**	**0**	**1**	**0**	**–1**								
	Fort Worth Texans	CHL	73	25	27	52				32											5	0	1	1	0			
1979-80♦	**New York Islanders**	**NHL**	**45**	**5**	**8**	**13**	**4**	**6**	**10**	**4**	**0**	**0**	**0**	**63**	**7.9**	**21**	**1**	**21**	**0**	**–1**								
1980-81	**New York Islanders**	**NHL**	**61**	**19**	**17**	**36**	**15**	**11**	**26**	**17**	**2**	**0**	**4**	**112**	**17.0**	**49**	**11**	**51**	**1**	**–12**								
	Colorado Rockies	**NHL**	**13**	**6**	**12**	**18**	**5**	**8**	**13**	**2**	**2**	**0**	**1**	**33**	**18.2**	**22**	**7**	**16**	**0**	**–1**								
	Canada	WEC-A	8	0	3	3				4																		
1981-82	**Colorado Rockies**	**NHL**	**79**	**29**	**30**	**59**	**23**	**20**	**43**	**14**	**9**	**0**	**0**	**185**	**15.7**	**83**	**24**	**93**	**1**	**–33**								
1982-83	**New Jersey Devils**	**NHL**	**73**	**25**	**18**	**43**	**20**	**12**	**32**	**14**	**6**	**1**	**4**	**153**	**16.3**	**67**	**19**	**82**	**7**	**–27**								
1983-84	**Calgary Flames**	**NHL**	**73**	**15**	**10**	**25**	**12**	**7**	**19**	**16**	**1**	**0**	**2**	**99**	**15.2**	**40**	**1**	**47**	**0**	**–8**	**2**	**0**	**1**	**1**	**0**	**0**	**0**	**0**
1984-85	**Calgary Flames**	**NHL**	**47**	**19**	**10**	**29**	**15**	**7**	**22**	**4**	**1**	**2**	**2**	**103**	**18.4**	**39**	**1**	**40**	**10**	**8**								
	Moncton Golden Flames	AHL	7	2	5	7				0																		
1985-86	**Vancouver Canucks**	**NHL**	**48**	**15**	**15**	**30**	**12**	**10**	**22**	**12**	**6**	**0**	**2**	**89**	**16.9**	**36**	**14**	**40**	**0**	**–18**								
1986-87	**Vancouver Canucks**	**NHL**	**72**	**16**	**20**	**36**	**14**	**15**	**29**	**14**	**9**	**0**	**0**	**162**	**9.9**	**67**	**49**	**41**	**1**	**–22**								
1987-88	**Vancouver Canucks**	**NHL**	**41**	**11**	**10**	**21**	**9**	**7**	**16**	**8**	**3**	**1**	**1**	**91**	**12.1**	**32**	**15**	**39**	**5**	**–17**								
	Canada	Nat-Team	2	1	0	1				0																		
	Canada	Olympics	8	1	3	4				2																		
1988-89	ZSC Zurich	Switz-2	10	4	8	12																						
1989-90	VSV Villach	Austria	38	44	37	81				34																		
	NHL Totals		**553**	**160**	**150**	**310**	**129**	**103**	**232**	**105**	**39**	**4**	**16**	**1093**	**14.6**	**456**	**142**	**471**	**25**		**2**	**0**	**1**	**1**	**0**	**0**	**0**	**0**

Traded to **Colorado** by **NY Islanders** with Glenn Resch for Mike McEwen and Jari Kaarela, March 10, 1981. Transferred to **New Jersey** after **Colorado** franchise relocated, June 30, 1982. Traded to **Calgary** by **New Jersey** with Joel Quenneville for Mel Bridgman and Phil Russell, June 20, 1983. Signed as a free agent by **Vancouver**, August 28, 1985.

• TAMER, Chris

D – L. 6'2", 215 lbs. b: Dearborn, MI, 11/17/1970. Pittsburgh's 3rd, 68th overall, in 1990.

Season	Club	League	GP	G	A	Pts	AG	AA	APts	PIM	PP	SH	GW	S	%	TGF	PGF	TGA	PGA	+/–	GP	G	A	Pts	PIM	PP	SH	GW
1987-88	Redford Royals	NAJHL	40	10	20	30				217																		
1988-89	Redford Royals	NAJHL	31	6	13	19				79																		
1989-90	University of Michigan	CCHA	42	2	7	9				147																		
1990-91	University of Michigan	CCHA	45	8	19	27				130																		
1991-92	University of Michigan	CCHA	43	4	15	19				125																		
1992-93	University of Michigan	CCHA	39	5	18	23				113																		
1993-94	**Pittsburgh Penguins**	**NHL**	**12**	**0**	**0**	**0**	**0**	**0**	**0**	**9**	**0**	**0**	**0**	**10**	**0.0**	**7**	**0**	**5**	**1**	**3**	**5**	**0**	**0**	**0**	**2**	**0**	**0**	**0**
	Cleveland Lumberjacks	IHL	53	1	2	3				160																		
1994-95	Cleveland Lumberjacks	IHL	48	4	10	14				204																		
	Pittsburgh Penguins	**NHL**	**36**	**2**	**0**	**2**	**4**	**0**	**4**	**82**	**0**	**0**	**0**	**26**	**7.7**	**18**	**0**	**22**	**4**	**0**	**4**	**0**	**0**	**0**	**18**	**0**	**0**	**0**
1995-96	**Pittsburgh Penguins**	**NHL**	**70**	**4**	**10**	**14**	**4**	**8**	**12**	**153**	**0**	**0**	**1**	**75**	**5.3**	**82**	**2**	**89**	**29**	**20**	**18**	**0**	**7**	**7**	**24**	**0**	**0**	**0**
1996-97	**Pittsburgh Penguins**	**NHL**	**45**	**2**	**4**	**6**	**2**	**4**	**6**	**131**	**0**	**1**	**0**	**56**	**3.6**	**26**	**0**	**61**	**10**	**–25**	**4**	**0**	**0**	**0**	**4**	**0**	**0**	**0**
1997-98	**Pittsburgh Penguins**	**NHL**	**79**	**0**	**7**	**7**	**0**	**7**	**7**	**181**	**0**	**0**	**0**	**55**	**0.0**	**36**	**1**	**45**	**14**	**4**	**6**	**0**	**1**	**1**	**4**	**0**	**0**	**0**
1998-99	**Pittsburgh Penguins**	**NHL**	**11**	**0**	**0**	**0**	**0**	**0**	**0**	**32**	**0**	**0**	**0**	**2**	**0.0**	**0**	**0**	**5**	**3**	**–2**								
	New York Rangers	**NHL**	**52**	**1**	**5**	**6**	**1**	**5**	**6**	**92**	**0**	**0**	**1**	**46**	**2.2**	**23**	**0**	**38**	**3**	**–12**								
	United States	WC-A	6	1	0	1				8																		
99-2000	**Atlanta Thrashers**	**NHL**	**69**	**2**	**8**	**10**	**2**	**7**	**9**	**91**	**0**	**0**	**0**	**61**	**3.3**	**32**	**1**	**80**	**17**	**–32**								
	NHL Totals		**374**	**11**	**34**	**45**	**13**	**31**	**44**	**771**	**0**	**1**	**2**	**331**	**3.3**	**224**	**4**	**345**	**81**		**37**	**0**	**8**	**8**	**52**	**0**	**0**	**0**

Traded to **NY Rangers** by **Pittsburgh** with Petr Nedved and Sean Pronger for Alexei Kovalev and Harry York, November 25, 1998. Claimed by **Atlanta** from **NY Rangers** in Expansion Draft, June 25, 1999.

• TANABE, David

D – R. 6'1", 190 lbs. b: Minneapolis, MN, 7/19/1980. Carolina's 1st, 16th overall, in 1999.

Season	Club	League	GP	G	A	Pts	AG	AA	APts	PIM	PP	SH	GW	S	%	TGF	PGF	TGA	PGA	+/–	GP	G	A	Pts	PIM	PP	SH	GW
1996-97	Hill-Murray Pioneers	Hi-School	28	12	14	26																						
1997-98	Team USA	Under-18	73	8	21	29				96																		
1998-99	University of Wisconsin	WCHA	35	10	12	22				44																		
	United States	WJC-A	6	0	1	1				4																		
99-2000	**Carolina Hurricanes**	**NHL**	**31**	**4**	**0**	**4**	**4**	**0**	**4**	**14**	**3**	**0**	**0**	**28**	**14.3**	**18**	**9**	**13**	**0**	**–4**								
	Cincinnati Cyclones	IHL	32	0	13	13				14											11	1	4	5	6			
	NHL Totals		**31**	**4**	**0**	**4**	**4**	**0**	**4**	**14**	**3**	**0**	**0**	**28**	**14.3**	**18**	**9**	**13**	**0**									

• TANCILL, Chris

Christopher W. C – L. 5'10", 185 lbs. b: Livonia, MI, 2/7/1968. Hartford's 1st, 15th overall, in 1989 Supplemental Draft.

Season	Club	League	GP	G	A	Pts	AG	AA	APts	PIM	PP	SH	GW	S	%	TGF	PGF	TGA	PGA	+/–	GP	G	A	Pts	PIM	PP	SH	GW
1984-85	St. Clair Shores Falcons	NAJHL	45	51	99	150																						
1986-87	University of Wisconsin	WCHA	40	9	23	32				26																		
1987-88	University of Wisconsin	WCHA	44	13	14	27				48																		
1988-89	University of Wisconsin	WCHA	44	20	23	43				50																		
1989-90	University of Wisconsin	WCHA	45	39	32	71				44																		
1990-91	**Hartford Whalers**	**NHL**	**9**	**1**	**1**	**2**	**1**	**1**	**2**	**4**	**0**	**1**	**0**	**6**	**16.7**	**5**	**0**	**3**	**0**	**2**								
	Springfield Indians	AHL	72	37	35	72				46											17	8	4	12	32			

			REGULAR SEASON																		PLAYOFFS							
Season	Club	League	GP	G	A	Pts	AG	AA	APts	PIM	PP	SH	GW	S	%	TGF	PGF	TGA	PGA	+/–	GP	G	A	Pts	PIM	PP	SH	GW
1991-92	**Hartford Whalers**	**NHL**	**10**	**0**	**0**	**0**	**0**	**0**	**0**	**2**	**0**	**0**	**0**	**13**	**0.0**	**3**	**0**	**9**	**0**	**–6**	....	....	....	....	....	....	....	....
	Springfield Indians	AHL	17	12	7	19	....	....	....	20	....	....	....	....	....	....	....	....	....	....	....	....	....	....	....	....	....	....
	Detroit Red Wings	**NHL**	**1**	**0**	**0**	**0**	**0**	**0**	**0**	**0**	**0**	**0**	**0**	**0**	**0.0**	**0**	**0**	**0**	**0**	**0**	....	....	....	....	....	....	....	....
	Adirondack Red Wings	AHL	50	36	34	70	....	....	....	42	....	....	....	....	....	....	....	....	....	....	19	7	9	16	31	....	....	....
1992-93	**Detroit Red Wings**	**NHL**	**4**	**1**	**0**	**1**	**1**	**0**	**1**	**2**	**0**	**0**	**0**	**3**	**33.3**	**1**	**0**	**4**	**1**	**–2**	....	....	....	....	....	....	....	....
	Adirondack Red Wings	AHL	68	*59	43	102	....	....	....	62	....	....	....	....	....	....	....	....	....	....	10	7	7	14	10	....	....	....
1993-94	**Dallas Stars**	**NHL**	**12**	**1**	**3**	**4**	**1**	**2**	**3**	**8**	**0**	**0**	**0**	**18**	**5.6**	**9**	**5**	**11**	**0**	**–7**	....	....	....	....	....	....	....	....
	Kalamazoo Wings	IHL	60	41	54	95	....	....	....	55	....	....	....	....	....	....	....	....	....	....	5	0	2	2	8	....	....	....
1994-95	Kansas City Blades	IHL	64	31	28	59	....	....	....	40	....	....	....	....	....	....	....	....	....	....	....	....	....	....	....	....	....	....
	San Jose Sharks	**NHL**	**26**	**3**	**11**	**14**	**5**	**16**	**21**	**10**	**0**	**1**	**0**	**39**	**7.7**	**15**	**0**	**19**	**5**	**1**	**11**	**1**	**1**	**2**	**8**	**0**	**0**	**0**
1995-96	**San Jose Sharks**	**NHL**	**45**	**7**	**16**	**23**	**7**	**13**	**20**	**20**	**0**	**1**	**0**	**93**	**7.5**	**30**	**2**	**55**	**15**	**–12**	....	....	....	....	....	....	....	....
	Kansas City Blades	IHL	27	12	16	28	....	....	....	18	....	....	....	....	....	....	....	....	....	....	....	....	....	....	....	....	....	....
	United States	WC-A	7	5	2	7	....	....	....	10	....	....	....	....	....	....	....	....	....	....	....	....	....	....	....	....	....	....
1996-97	**San Jose Sharks**	**NHL**	**25**	**4**	**0**	**4**	**4**	**0**	**4**	**8**	**1**	**0**	**0**	**20**	**20.0**	**5**	**1**	**10**	**1**	**–5**	....	....	....	....	....	....	....	....
	Kentucky Thoroughblades	AHL	42	19	26	45	....	....	....	31	....	....	....	....	....	....	....	....	....	....	4	2	0	2	2	....	....	....
	United States	WC-A	8	2	3	5	....	....	....	2	....	....	....	....	....	....	....	....	....	....	....	....	....	....	....	....	....	....
1997-98	**Dallas Stars**	**NHL**	**2**	**0**	**1**	**1**	**0**	**1**	**1**	**0**	**0**	**0**	**0**	**1**	**0.0**	**1**	**0**	**2**	**0**	**–1**	....	....	....	....	....	....	....	....
	Michigan K-Wings	IHL	70	30	39	69	....	....	....	86	....	....	....	....	....	....	....	....	....	....	4	3	0	3	14	....	....	....
1998-99	EHC Kloten	Switz.	42	19	30	49	....	....	....	46	....	....	....	....	....	....	....	....	....	....	12	4	2	6	16	....	....	....
99-2000	EV Zug	Switz.	45	*25	26	51	....	....	....	56	....	....	....	....	....	....	....	....	....	....	11	6	4	10	10	....	....	....
	United States	WC-A	7	1	2	3	....	....	....	2	....	....	....	....	....	....	....	....	....	....	....	....	....	....	....	....	....	....
	NHL Totals		**134**	**17**	**32**	**49**	**19**	**33**	**52**	**54**	**1**	**3**	**0**	**193**	**8.8**	**69**	**8**	**113**	**22**		**11**	**1**	**1**	**2**	**8**	**0**	**0**	**0**

NCAA Championship All-Tournament Team (1990) • NCAA Championship Tournament MVP (1990) • AHL First All-Star Team (1992, 1993)

Traded to **Detroit** by **Hartford** for Daniel Shank, December 18, 1991. Signed as a free agent by **Dallas**, August 28, 1993. Signed as a free agent by **San Jose**, August 24, 1994. Signed as a free agent by **Dallas**, August 6, 1997.

• TANGUAY, Alex

C – L. 6', 190 lbs. b: Ste-Justine, Que., 11/21/1979. Colorado's 1st, 12th overall, in 1998.

Season	Club	League	GP	G	A	Pts	AG	AA	APts	PIM	PP	SH	GW	S	%	TGF	PGF	TGA	PGA	+/–	GP	G	A	Pts	PIM	PP	SH	GW
1994-95	Beauce-Amiante	QAAA	STATISTICS NOT AVAILABLE																									
1995-96	Cap-de-Madelaine Canadiens	QAAA	44	29	34	63	....	....	....	64	....	....	....	....	....	....	....	....	....	....	....	....	....	....	....	....	....	....
1996-97	Halifax Mooseheads	QMJHL	70	27	41	68	....	....	....	60	....	....	....	....	....	....	....	....	....	....	12	5	8	13	8	....	....	....
1997-98	Halifax Mooseheads	QMJHL	51	47	38	85	....	....	....	32	....	....	....	....	....	....	....	....	....	....	5	7	6	13	4	....	....	....
1998-99	Halifax Mooseheads	QMJHL	31	27	34	61	....	....	....	30	....	....	....	....	....	....	....	....	....	....	5	1	2	3	2	....	....	....
	Hershey Bears	AHL	5	1	2	3	....	....	....	2	....	....	....	....	....	....	....	....	....	....	5	0	2	2	0	....	....	....
99-2000	**Colorado Avalanche**	**NHL**	**76**	**17**	**34**	**51**	**19**	**32**	**51**	**22**	**5**	**0**	**3**	**74**	**23.0**	**76**	**19**	**51**	**0**	**6**	**17**	**2**	**1**	**3**	**2**	**1**	**0**	**1**
	NHL Totals		**76**	**17**	**34**	**51**	**19**	**32**	**51**	**22**	**5**	**0**	**3**	**74**	**23.0**	**76**	**19**	**51**	**0**		**17**	**2**	**1**	**3**	**2**	**1**	**0**	**1**

• TANGUAY, Christian

RW – R. 5'10", 190 lbs. b: Beauport, Que., 8/4/1962. Quebec's 7th, 171st overall, in 1980.

Season	Club	League	GP	G	A	Pts	AG	AA	APts	PIM	PP	SH	GW	S	%	TGF	PGF	TGA	PGA	+/–	GP	G	A	Pts	PIM	PP	SH	GW
1979-80	Trois-Rivieres Draveurs	QMJHL	65	24	20	44	....	....	....	39	....	....	....	....	....	....	....	....	....	....	7	3	2	5	6	....	....	....
1980-81	Trois-Rivieres Draveurs	QMJHL	72	45	39	84	....	....	....	34	....	....	....	....	....	....	....	....	....	....	19	12	8	20	27	....	....	....
1981-82	Trois-Rivieres Draveurs	QMJHL	59	52	55	107	....	....	....	27	....	....	....	....	....	....	....	....	....	....	24	16	13	29	11	....	....	....
	Quebec Nordiques	**NHL**	**2**	**0**	**0**	**0**	**0**	**0**	**0**	**0**	**0**	**0**	**0**	**0**	**0.0**	**0**	**0**	**0**	**0**	**0**	....	....	....	....	....	....	....	....
1982-83	Fredericton Express	AHL	48	6	7	13	....	....	....	4	....	....	....	....	....	....	....	....	....	....	....	....	....	....	....	....	....	....
	Milwaukee Admirals	IHL	14	8	11	19	....	....	....	6	....	....	....	....	....	....	....	....	....	....	....	....	....	....	....	....	....	....
1983-84	Fredericton Express	AHL	3	2	0	2	....	....	....	0	....	....	....	....	....	....	....	....	....	....	....	....	....	....	....	....	....	....
	Milwaukee Admirals	IHL	74	44	50	94	....	....	....	23	....	....	....	....	....	....	....	....	....	....	4	0	2	2	0	....	....	....
1984-85	Muskegon Mohawks	IHL	19	1	8	9	....	....	....	9	....	....	....	....	....	....	....	....	....	....	....	....	....	....	....	....	....	....
	Rimouski Mariners	RHL	6	10	8	18	....	....	....	....	....	....	....	....	....	....	....	....	....	....	....	....	....	....	....	....	....	....
1985-86	HC Auronzo	Italy	24	35	49	84	....	....	....	10	....	....	....	....	....	....	....	....	....	....	4	2	1	3	2	....	....	....
	Rimouski Mariners	RHL	8	12	10	22	....	....	....	4	....	....	....	....	....	....	....	....	....	....	....	....	....	....	....	....	....	....
1986-87	Riviere-du-Loup 3 L's	RHL	29	37	29	66	....	....	....	4	....	....	....	....	....	....	....	....	....	....	12	*12	12	*24	....	....	....	....
	Milwaukee Admirals	IHL	3	0	0	0	....	....	....	0	....	....	....	....	....	....	....	....	....	....	....	....	....	....	....	....	....	....
1987-88	Chomedy Chibucto	QSAAL	STATISTICS NOT AVAILABLE																									
1988-89	Chandler Gaillard	QSAAL	STATISTICS NOT AVAILABLE																									
1989-90	HC Chamonix	France-2	28	33	27	60	....	....	....	52	....	....	....	....	....	....	....	....	....	....	....	....	....	....	....	....	....	....
1990-1997			OUT OF HOCKEY – RETIRED																									
1997-98	St-Gabriel Blizzard	QSPHL	6	1	6	7	....	....	....	0	....	....	....	....	....	....	....	....	....	....	....	....	....	....	....	....	....	....
	NHL Totals		**2**	**0**	**0**	**0**	**0**	**0**	**0**	**0**	**0**	**0**	**0**	**0**	**0.0**	**0**	**0**	**0**	**0**		....	....	....	....	....	....	....	....

IHL Second All-Star Team (1984)

• TANNAHILL, Don

Donald Andrew LW – L. 5'11", 178 lbs. b: Penetanguishene, Ont., 2/21/1949. Boston's 1st, 3rd overall, in 1969.

Season	Club	League	GP	G	A	Pts	AG	AA	APts	PIM	PP	SH	GW	S	%	TGF	PGF	TGA	PGA	+/–	GP	G	A	Pts	PIM	PP	SH	GW
1966-67	Niagara Falls Flyers	OHA-Jr.	45	8	13	21	....	....	....	15	....	....	....	....	....	....	....	....	....	....	13	0	4	4	0	....	....	....
1967-68	Niagara Falls Flyers	OHA-Jr.	54	29	49	78	....	....	....	30	....	....	....	....	....	....	....	....	....	....	18	7	11	18	18	....	....	....
	Niagara Falls Flyers	Mem-Cup	10	5	8	13	....	....	....	*20	....	....	....	....	....	....	....	....	....	....	....	....	....	....	....	....	....	....
1968-69	Niagara Falls Flyers	OHA-Jr.	54	48	41	89	....	....	....	131	....	....	....	....	....	....	....	....	....	....	14	17	6	23	10	....	....	....
1969-70	Oklahoma City Blazers	CHL	27	10	12	22	....	....	....	14	....	....	....	....	....	....	....	....	....	....	....	....	....	....	....	....	....	....
1970-71	Oklahoma City Blazers	CHL	69	27	36	63	....	....	....	22	....	....	....	....	....	....	....	....	....	....	5	2	2	4	0	....	....	....
1971-72	Boston Braves	AHL	76	30	44	74	....	....	....	23	....	....	....	....	....	....	....	....	....	....	9	5	1	6	2	....	....	....
1972-73	**Vancouver Canucks**	**NHL**	**78**	**22**	**21**	**43**	**21**	**17**	**38**	**21**	**2**	**1**	**3**	**186**	**11.8**	**68**	**10**	**95**	**8**	**–29**	....	....	....	....	....	....	....	....
1973-74	**Vancouver Canucks**	**NHL**	**33**	**8**	**12**	**20**	**8**	**10**	**18**	**4**	**0**	**0**	**1**	**43**	**18.6**	**29**	**5**	**23**	**0**	**1**	....	....	....	....	....	....	....	....
1974-75	Minnesota Fighting Saints	WHA	72	23	30	53	....	....	....	20	....	....	....	....	....	....	....	....	....	....	10	2	4	6	0	....	....	....
1975-76	Calgary Cowboys	WHA	78	25	24	49	....	....	....	10	....	....	....	....	....	....	....	....	....	....	10	2	5	7	8	....	....	....
1976-77	Calgary Cowboys	WHA	72	10	22	32	....	....	....	4	....	....	....	....	....	....	....	....	....	....	....	....	....	....	....	....	....	....
1977-78	Salt Lake Golden Eagles	CHL	7	3	3	6	....	....	....	0	....	....	....	....	....	....	....	....	....	....	....	....	....	....	....	....	....	....
	Barrie Flyers	OHA-Sr.	23	10	16	26	....	....	....	0	....	....	....	....	....	....	....	....	....	....	....	....	....	....	....	....	....	....
	NHL Totals		**111**	**30**	**33**	**63**	**29**	**27**	**56**	**25**	**2**	**1**	**4**	**229**	**13.1**	**97**	**15**	**118**	**8**		....	....	....	....	....	....	....	....
	Other Major League Totals		222	58	76	134	....	....	....	34	....	....	....	....	....	....	....	....	....	....	20	4	9	13	8	....	....	....

OHA-Jr. Second All-Star Team (1969) • AHL Second All-Star Team (1972)

Selected by **Chicago** (WHA) in 1972 WHA General Player Draft, February 12, 1972. Claimed by **Vancouver** from **Boston** in Intra-League Draft, June 5, 1972. WHA rights traded to **Minnesota** (WHA) by **Chicago** (WHA) for future considerations, June, 1974. Traded to **Calgary** (WHA) by **Minnesota** (WHA) with George Morrison and the rights to Wally Olds and Joe Micheletti for John McKenzie and cash, September, 1975. Traded to **Edmonton** (WHA) by **Calgary** (WHA) for cash, August, 1977.

• TANTI, Tony

RW – L. 5'9", 180 lbs. b: Toronto, Ont., 9/7/1963. Chicago's 1st, 12th overall, in 1981.

Season	Club	League	GP	G	A	Pts	AG	AA	APts	PIM	PP	SH	GW	S	%	TGF	PGF	TGA	PGA	+/–	GP	G	A	Pts	PIM	PP	SH	GW
1978-79	Mississauga Reps	MTHL	STATISTICS NOT AVAILABLE																									
1979-80	St. Michael's Buzzers	OHA-B	37	31	27	58	....	....	....	67	....	....	....	....	....	....	....	....	....	....	....	....	....	....	....	....	....	....
1980-81	Oshawa Generals	OMJHL	67	81	69	150	....	....	....	197	....	....	....	....	....	....	....	....	....	....	11	7	8	15	41	....	....	....
1981-82	Oshawa Generals	OHL	57	62	64	126	....	....	....	138	....	....	....	....	....	....	....	....	....	....	12	14	12	26	15	....	....	....
	Chicago Black Hawks	**NHL**	**2**	**0**	**0**	**0**	**0**	**0**	**0**	**0**	**0**	**0**	**0**	**0**	**0.0**	**1**	**0**	**1**	**0**	**0**	....	....	....	....	....	....	....	....
1982-83	Oshawa Generals	OHL	30	34	28	62	....	....	....	35	....	....	....	....	....	....	....	....	....	....	....	....	....	....	....	....	....	....
	Chicago Black Hawks	**NHL**	**1**	**1**	**0**	**1**	**1**	**0**	**1**	**0**	**0**	**0**	**0**	**5**	**20.0**	**1**	**0**	**1**	**0**	**0**	....	....	....	....	....	....	....	....
	Vancouver Canucks	**NHL**	**39**	**8**	**8**	**16**	**7**	**6**	**13**	**16**	**4**	**0**	**0**	**81**	**9.9**	**30**	**10**	**29**	**0**	**–9**	**4**	**0**	**1**	**1**	**0**	**0**	**0**	**0**
1983-84	**Vancouver Canucks**	**NHL**	**79**	**45**	**41**	**86**	**36**	**28**	**64**	**50**	**19**	**1**	**6**	**247**	**18.2**	**123**	**48**	**95**	**8**	**–12**	**4**	**1**	**2**	**3**	**0**	**0**	**0**	**0**
	Canada	WJC-A	7	0	4	4	....	....	....	0	....	....	....	....	....	....	....	....	....	....	....	....	....	....	....	....	....	....
1984-85	**Vancouver Canucks**	**NHL**	**68**	**39**	**20**	**59**	**32**	**14**	**46**	**45**	**14**	**0**	**4**	**212**	**18.4**	**90**	**29**	**95**	**13**	**–21**	....	....	....	....	....	....	....	....
	Canada	WEC-A	10	5	2	7	....	....	....	12	....	....	....	....	....	....	....	....	....	....	....	....	....	....	....	....	....	....
1985-86	**Vancouver Canucks**	**NHL**	**77**	**39**	**33**	**72**	**31**	**22**	**53**	**85**	**17**	**0**	**5**	**213**	**18.3**	**114**	**53**	**73**	**4**	**–8**	**3**	**0**	**1**	**1**	**11**	**0**	**0**	**0**
	Canada	WEC-A	8	5	3	8	....	....	....	22	....	....	....	....	....	....	....	....	....	....	....	....	....	....	....	....	....	....
1986-87	**Vancouver Canucks**	**NHL**	**77**	**41**	**38**	**79**	**35**	**28**	**63**	**84**	**15**	**0**	**7**	**242**	**16.9**	**113**	**40**	**75**	**7**	**5**	....	....	....	....	....	....	....	....
	Canada	WEC-A	10	6	2	8	....	....	....	6	....	....	....	....	....	....	....	....	....	....	....	....	....	....	....	....	....	....

Season	Club	League	GP	G	A	Pts	AG	AA	APts	PIM	PP	SH	GW	S	%	TGF	PGF	TGA	PGA	+/-	GP	G	A	Pts	PIM	PP	SH	GW
			REGULAR SEASON																		PLAYOFFS							
1987-88	**Vancouver Canucks**	**NHL**	73	40	37	77	34	26	60	90	20	0	4	202	19.8	114	45	83	13	–1	....	....	....	....	....	....	....	....
1988-89	**Vancouver Canucks**	**NHL**	77	24	25	49	20	18	38	69	8	0	3	211	11.4	75	32	60	7	–10	7	0	5	5	4	0	0	0
1989-90	**Vancouver Canucks**	**NHL**	41	14	18	32	12	13	25	50	5	0	0	103	13.6	48	17	35	5	1	....	....	....	....	....	....	....	....
	Pittsburgh Penguins	**NHL**	37	14	18	32	12	13	25	22	7	0	0	89	15.7	51	22	41	1	–11	....	....	....	....	....	....	....	....
1990-91	**Pittsburgh Penguins**	**NHL**	46	6	12	18	5	9	14	44	3	0	0	74	8.1	37	14	22	0	1	....	....	....	....	....	....	....	....
	Buffalo Sabres	**NHL**	10	1	7	8	1	5	6	6	0	0	0	19	5.3	11	4	5	0	2	5	2	0	2	8	1	0	0
1991-92	**Buffalo Sabres**	**NHL**	70	15	16	31	14	12	26	100	6	1	0	133	11.3	52	18	55	17	–4	7	0	3	3	4	0	0	0
1992-93	BSC Preussen Berlin	Germany	34	14	17	31	....	....	....	73	....	....	....	....	....	....	....	....	....	....	....	....	....	....	....	....	....	....
1993-94	BSC Preussen Berlin	Germany	43	19	24	43	....	....	....	50	....	....	....	....	....	....	....	....	....	....	....	....	....	....	....	....	....	....
1994-95	BSC Preussen Berlin	Germany	42	25	33	58	....	....	....	114	....	....	....	....	....	....	....	....	....	....	9	2	2	4	8	....	....	....
1995-96	Berlin Devils	Germany	43	32	28	60	....	....	....	56	....	....	....	....	....	....	....	....	....	....	11	9	5	14	16	....	....	....
1996-97	Berlin Capitals	Germany	43	14	25	39	....	....	....	42	....	....	....	....	....	....	....	....	....	....	4	0	2	2	6	....	....	....
	Berlin Capitals	EuroHL	5	0	0	0	....	....	....	12	....	....	....	....	....	....	....	....	....	....	....	....	....	....	....	....	....	....
1997-98	Berlin Capitals	Germany	41	6	24	30	....	....	....	84	....	....	....	....	....	....	....	....	....	....	....	....	....	....	....	....	....	....
	NHL Totals		**697**	**287**	**273**	**560**	**240**	**194**	**434**	**661**	**118**	**2**	**29**	**1831**	**15.7**	**860**	**332**	**670**	**75**		**30**	**3**	**12**	**15**	**27**	**1**	**0**	**0**

OHA-Jr. First All-Star Team (1981) • OHL Second All-Star Team (1982) • Played in NHL All-Star Game (1986)

Traded to **Vancouver** by **Chicago** for Curt Fraser, January 6, 1983. Traded to **Pittsburgh** by **Vancouver** with Rod Buskas and Barry Pederson for Dave Capuano, Andrew McBain and Dan Quinn, January 8, 1990. Traded to **Buffalo** by **Pittsburgh** for Ken Priestlay, March 5, 1991.

• TARDIF, Marc

LW – L. 6', 195 lbs. b: Granby, Que., 6/12/1949. Montreal's 2nd, 2nd overall, in 1969.

Season	Club	League	GP	G	A	Pts	AG	AA	APts	PIM	PP	SH	GW	S	%	TGF	PGF	TGA	PGA	+/-	GP	G	A	Pts	PIM	PP	SH	GW
1966-67	Thetford Mines Canadiens	QJHL	40	36	44	80	....	....	....	89	....	....	....	....	....	....	....	....	....	....	11	13	13	26	2	....	....	....
	Thetford Mines Canadiens	Mem-Cup	19	11	14	25	....	....	....	42	....	....	....	....	....	....	....	....	....	....	....	....	....	....	....	....	....	....
1967-68	Montreal Jr. Canadiens	OHA-Jr.	54	32	34	66	....	....	....	62	....	....	....	....	....	....	....	....	....	....	11	3	9	12	18	....	....	....
1968-69	Montreal Jr. Canadiens	OHA-Jr.	51	31	41	72	....	....	....	121	....	....	....	....	....	....	....	....	....	....	14	19	12	31	60	....	....	....
	Montreal Jr. Canadiens	Mem-Cup	7	6	9	*15	....	....	....	16	....	....	....	....	....	....	....	....	....	....	....	....	....	....	....	....	....	....
1969-70	**Montreal Canadiens**	**NHL**	18	3	2	5	3	2	5	27	1	0	0	25	12.0	10	4	6	0	0	....	....	....	....	....	....	....	....
	Montreal Voyageurs	AHL	45	27	31	58	....	....	....	70	....	....	....	....	....	....	....	....	....	....	8	3	6	9	29	....	....	....
1970-71♦	**Montreal Canadiens**	**NHL**	76	19	30	49	19	25	44	133	4	0	2	144	13.2	77	21	34	3	25	20	3	1	4	40	0	0	0
1971-72	**Montreal Canadiens**	**NHL**	75	31	22	53	31	19	50	81	9	0	4	203	15.3	83	27	43	2	15	6	2	3	5	9	0	0	1
1972-73♦	**Montreal Canadiens**	**NHL**	76	25	25	50	23	20	43	48	3	0	4	152	16.4	71	21	32	0	18	14	6	6	12	6	2	0	2
1973-74	Los Angeles Sharks	WHA	75	40	30	70	....	....	....	47	....	....	....	....	....	....	....	....	....	....	....	....	....	....	....	....	....	....
1974-75	Team Canada	Summit-74	5	0	2	2	....	....	....	10	....	....	....	....	....	....	....	....	....	....	....	....	....	....	....	....	....	....
	Michigan Stags	WHA	23	12	5	17	....	....	....	9	....	....	....	....	....	....	....	....	....	....	....	....	....	....	....	....	....	....
	Quebec Nordiques	WHA	53	38	34	72	....	....	....	70	....	....	....	....	....	....	....	....	....	....	15	*10	11	21	10	....	....	....
1975-76	Quebec Nordiques	WHA	81	*71	*77	*148	....	....	....	79	....	....	....	....	....	....	....	....	....	....	2	1	0	1	2	....	....	....
1976-77	Quebec Nordiques	WHA	62	49	60	109	....	....	....	65	....	....	....	....	....	....	....	....	....	....	12	4	10	14	8	....	....	....
1977-78	Quebec Nordiques	WHA	78	*65	*89	*154	....	....	....	50	....	....	....	....	....	....	....	....	....	....	11	6	9	15	11	....	....	....
1978-79	Quebec Nordiques	WHA	74	41	55	96	....	....	....	98	....	....	....	....	....	....	....	....	....	....	4	6	2	8	4	....	....	....
1979-80	**Quebec Nordiques**	**NHL**	58	33	35	68	28	26	54	30	9	0	4	229	14.4	87	26	75	1	–13	....	....	....	....	....	....	....	....
1980-81	**Quebec Nordiques**	**NHL**	63	23	31	54	18	21	39	35	11	0	3	144	16.0	74	32	46	0	–4	5	1	3	4	2	0	0	0
1981-82	**Quebec Nordiques**	**NHL**	75	39	31	70	31	21	52	55	14	0	3	166	23.5	107	51	71	0	–15	13	1	2	3	16	0	0	0
1982-83	**Quebec Nordiques**	**NHL**	76	21	31	52	17	21	38	34	4	0	3	116	18.1	78	28	50	0	0	4	0	0	0	2	0	0	0
	NHL Totals		**517**	**194**	**207**	**401**	**170**	**155**	**325**	**443**	**55**	**0**	**23**	**1179**	**16.5**	**587**	**210**	**357**	**6**		**62**	**13**	**15**	**28**	**75**	**2**	**0**	**3**
	Other Major League Totals		446	316	350	666				418											44	27	32	59	35			

OHA-Jr. First All-Star Team (1969) • WHA Second All-Star Team (1975) • WHA First All-Star Team (1976, 1977, 1978) • Won W. D. (Bill) Hunter Trophy (WHA Scoring Leader) (1976, 1978) • Won Gary Davidson Trophy (WHA MVP) (1976, 1978) • Played in NHL All-Star Game (1982)

Selected by **LA Sharks** (WHA) in 1972 WHA General Player Draft, February 12, 1972. Transferred to **Michigan** (WHA) after **LA Sharks** (WHA) franchise relocated, April 11, 1974. Traded to **Quebec** (WHA) by **Michigan** (WHA) with Steve Sutherland for Alain Caron, Pierre Guite and Michel Rouleau, December, 1974. Claimed by **Quebec** from **Montreal** in Expansion Draft, June 13, 1979.

• TARDIF, Patrice

C – L. 6'2", 202 lbs. b: Thetford Mines, Que., 10/30/1970. St. Louis' 2nd, 54th overall, in 1990.

Season	Club	League	GP	G	A	Pts	AG	AA	APts	PIM	PP	SH	GW	S	%	TGF	PGF	TGA	PGA	+/-	GP	G	A	Pts	PIM	PP	SH	GW
1988-89	Black Lake Miners	QJHL-B	32	37	33	70	....	....	....	....	....	....	....	....	....	....	....	....	....	....	....	....	....	....	....	....	....	....
1989-90	Lennoxville Junior College	QCAA	27	58	36	94	....	....	....	36	....	....	....	....	....	....	....	....	....	....	....	....	....	....	....	....	....	....
1990-91	University of Maine	H-East	36	13	12	25	....	....	....	18	....	....	....	....	....	....	....	....	....	....	....	....	....	....	....	....	....	....
1991-92	University of Maine	H-East	31	18	20	38	....	....	....	14	....	....	....	....	....	....	....	....	....	....	....	....	....	....	....	....	....	....
1992-93	University of Maine	H-East	45	23	25	48	....	....	....	22	....	....	....	....	....	....	....	....	....	....	....	....	....	....	....	....	....	....
1993-94	University of Maine	H-East	34	18	15	33	....	....	....	42	....	....	....	....	....	....	....	....	....	....	....	....	....	....	....	....	....	....
	Peoria Rivermen	IHL	11	4	4	8	....	....	....	21	....	....	....	....	....	....	....	....	....	....	4	2	0	2	4	....	....	....
1994-95	Peoria Rivermen	IHL	53	27	18	45	....	....	....	83	....	....	....	....	....	....	....	....	....	....	....	....	....	....	....	....	....	....
	St. Louis Blues	**NHL**	27	3	10	13	5	15	20	29	1	0	0	46	6.5	20	6	11	1	4	....	....	....	....	....	....	....	....
1995-96	**St. Louis Blues**	**NHL**	23	3	0	3	3	0	3	12	0	0	1	21	14.3	4	1	5	0	–2	....	....	....	....	....	....	....	....
	Worcester IceCats	AHL	30	13	13	26	....	....	....	69	....	....	....	....	....	....	....	....	....	....	....	....	....	....	....	....	....	....
	Los Angeles Kings	**NHL**	15	1	1	2	1	1	2	37	1	0	0	29	3.4	4	3	10	0	–9	....	....	....	....	....	....	....	....
1996-97	Phoenix Roadrunners	IHL	9	0	3	3	....	....	....	13	....	....	....	....	....	....	....	....	....	....	....	....	....	....	....	....	....	....
	Detroit Vipers	IHL	66	24	23	47	....	....	....	70	....	....	....	....	....	....	....	....	....	....	11	0	1	1	8	....	....	....
1997-98	Rochester Americans	AHL	41	13	13	26	....	....	....	68	....	....	....	....	....	....	....	....	....	....	....	....	....	....	....	....	....	....
	Detroit Vipers	IHL	28	10	9	19	....	....	....	24	....	....	....	....	....	....	....	....	....	....	15	3	7	10	14	....	....	....
1998-99	Manitoba Moose	IHL	63	21	35	56	....	....	....	88	....	....	....	....	....	....	....	....	....	....	5	1	2	3	0	....	....	....
99-2000	Manitoba Moose	IHL	50	12	18	30	....	....	....	70	....	....	....	....	....	....	....	....	....	....	....	....	....	....	....	....	....	....
	Quebec Citadelles	AHL	18	9	10	19	....	....	....	23	....	....	....	....	....	....	....	....	....	....	3	1	1	2	8	....	....	....
	NHL Totals		**65**	**7**	**11**	**18**	**9**	**16**	**25**	**78**	**2**	**0**	**1**	**96**	**7.3**	**28**	**10**	**26**	**1**		....	....	....	....	....	....	....	....

Traded to **LA Kings** by **St. Louis** with Craig Johnson, Roman Vopat, St. Louis' 5th round choice (Peter Hogan) in 1996 Entry Draft and 1st round choice (Matt Zultek) in 1997 Entry Draft for Wayne Gretzky, February 27, 1996. Signed as a free agent by **Buffalo**, September 9, 1997. Signed as a free agent by **Manitoba** (IHL), August 31, 1998. Loaned to **Quebec** (AHL) by **Manitoba** (IHL) for loan of Barry Richter, March 3, 2000.

• TATARINOV, Mikhail

D – L. 5'10", 195 lbs. b: Angarsk, USSR, 7/16/1966. Washington's 10th, 225th overall, in 1984.

Season	Club	League	GP	G	A	Pts	AG	AA	APts	PIM	PP	SH	GW	S	%	TGF	PGF	TGA	PGA	+/-	GP	G	A	Pts	PIM	PP	SH	GW
1983-84	Sokol Kiev	USSR	38	7	3	10	....	....	....	46	....	....	....	....	....	....	....	....	....	....	....	....	....	....	....	....	....	....
	Soviet Union	WJC-A	7	1	2	3	....	....	....	0	....	....	....	....	....	....	....	....	....	....	....	....	....	....	....	....	....	....
	Soviet Union	EJC-A	5	3	1	4	....	....	....	18	....	....	....	....	....	....	....	....	....	....	....	....	....	....	....	....	....	....
1984-85	Sokol Kiev	USSR	34	3	6	9	....	....	....	54	....	....	....	....	....	....	....	....	....	....	....	....	....	....	....	....	....	....
	Soviet Union	WJC-A	5	1	2	3	....	....	....	6	....	....	....	....	....	....	....	....	....	....	....	....	....	....	....	....	....	....
1985-86	Sokol Kiev	USSR	37	7	5	12	....	....	....	41	....	....	....	....	....	....	....	....	....	....	....	....	....	....	....	....	....	....
	Soviet Union	WJC-A	7	2	5	7	....	....	....	16	....	....	....	....	....	....	....	....	....	....	....	....	....	....	....	....	....	....
1986-87	Dynamo Moscow	USSR	40	10	8	18	....	....	....	43	....	....	....	....	....	....	....	....	....	....	....	....	....	....	....	....	....	....
	USSR	RV-87	2	0	1	1	....	....	....	0	....	....	....	....	....	....	....	....	....	....	....	....	....	....	....	....	....	....
1987-88	Dynamo Moscow	USSR	30	2	2	4	....	....	....	8	....	....	....	....	....	....	....	....	....	....	....	....	....	....	....	....	....	....
1988-89	Dynamo Moscow	USSR	4	1	0	1	....	....	....	2	....	....	....	....	....	....	....	....	....	....	....	....	....	....	....	....	....	....
1989-90	Dynamo Moscow	Fr-Tour	1	1	2	3	....	....	....	0	....	....	....	....	....	....	....	....	....	....	....	....	....	....	....	....	....	....
	Dynamo Moscow	USSR	44	11	10	21	....	....	....	34	....	....	....	....	....	....	....	....	....	....	....	....	....	....	....	....	....	....
	Dynamo Moscow	Super-S	5	0	1	1	....	....	....	0	....	....	....	....	....	....	....	....	....	....	....	....	....	....	....	....	....	....
	Soviet Union	WEC-A	10	3	8	11	....	....	....	20	....	....	....	....	....	....	....	....	....	....	....	....	....	....	....	....	....	....
1990-91	Dynamo Moscow	Fr-Tour	1	0	0	0	....	....	....	2	....	....	....	....	....	....	....	....	....	....	....	....	....	....	....	....	....	....
	Dynamo Moscow	USSR	11	5	4	9	....	....	....	6	....	....	....	....	....	....	....	....	....	....	....	....	....	....	....	....	....	....
	Washington Capitals	**NHL**	65	8	15	23	7	11	18	82	3	1	1	145	5.5	75	24	58	3	–4	....	....	....	....	....	....	....	....
1991-92	Soviet Union	Can-Cup	5	0	1	1	....	....	....	17	....	....	....	....	....	....	....	....	....	....	....	....	....	....	....	....	....	....
	Quebec Nordiques	**NHL**	66	11	27	38	10	20	30	72	5	0	1	191	5.8	104	32	88	24	8	....	....	....	....	....	....	....	....

			REGULAR SEASON																		PLAYOFFS							
Season	Club	League	GP	G	A	Pts	AG	AA	APts	PIM	PP	SH	GW	S	%	TGF	PGF	TGA	PGA	+/-	GP	G	A	Pts	PIM	PP	SH	GW
1992-93	**Quebec Nordiques**	**NHL**	**28**	**2**	**6**	**8**	**2**	**4**	**6**	**28**	**1**	**0**	**0**	**46**	**4.3**	**34**	**13**	**22**	**7**	**6**								
1993-94	**Boston Bruins**	**NHL**	**2**	**0**	**0**	**0**	**0**	**0**	**0**	**2**	**0**	**0**	**0**	**4**	**0.0**	**2**	**2**	**0**	**0**	**0**								
	Providence Bruins	AHL	3	0	3	3				0																		
	NHL Totals		**161**	**21**	**48**	**69**	**19**	**35**	**54**	**184**	**9**	**1**	**2**	**386**	**5.4**	**215**	**71**	**168**	**34**									

Named Best Defenseman at EJC-A (1984) • WJC-A All-Star Team (1985, 1986) • Named Best Defenseman at WJC-A (1986) • USSR First All-Star Team (1990) • WEC-A All-Star Team (1990) • Named Best Defenseman at WEC-A (1990)

Traded to **Quebec** by **Washington** for Toronto's 2nd round choice (previously acquired, Washington selected Eric Lavigne) in 1991 Entry Draft, June 22, 1991. Signed as a free agent by **Boston**, July 30, 1993.

• TAYLOR, Chris

C – L. 6', 189 lbs. b: Stratford, Ont., 3/6/1972. NY Islanders' 2nd, 27th overall, in 1990.

Season	Club	League	GP	G	A	Pts	AG	AA	APts	PIM	PP	SH	GW	S	%	TGF	PGF	TGA	PGA	+/-	GP	G	A	Pts	PIM	PP	SH	GW
1987-88	Stratford Cullitons	OJHL-B	52	28	37	65				112																		
1988-89	London Knights	OHL	62	7	16	23				52											15	0	2	2	15			
1989-90	London Knights	OHL	66	45	60	105				60											6	3	2	5	6			
1990-91	London Knights	OHL	65	50	78	128				50											7	4	8	12	6			
1991-92	London Knights	OHL	66	48	74	122				57											10	8	16	24	9			
1992-93	Capital District Islanders	AHL	77	19	43	62				32											4	0	1	1	2			
1993-94	Salt Lake Golden Eagles	IHL	79	21	20	41				38																		
1994-95	Denver Grizzlies	IHL	78	38	48	86				47											14	7	6	13	10			
	New York Islanders	**NHL**	**10**	**0**	**3**	**3**	**0**	**4**	**4**	**2**	**0**	**0**	**0**	**13**	**0.0**	**8**	**4**	**5**	**2**	**1**								
1995-96	**New York Islanders**	**NHL**	**11**	**0**	**1**	**1**	**0**	**1**	**1**	**2**	**0**	**0**	**0**	**4**	**0.0**	**3**	**0**	**2**	**0**	**1**								
	Utah Grizzlies	IHL	50	18	23	41				60											22	5	11	16	26			
1996-97	**New York Islanders**	**NHL**	**1**	**0**	**0**	**0**	**0**	**0**	**0**	**0**	**0**	**0**	**0**	**1**	**0.0**	**0**	**0**	**0**	**0**	**0**								
	Utah Grizzlies	IHL	71	27	40	67				24											7	1	2	3	0			
1997-98	Utah Grizzlies	IHL	79	28	56	84				66											4	0	2	2	6			
1998-99	**Boston Bruins**	**NHL**	**37**	**3**	**5**	**8**	**4**	**5**	**9**	**12**	**0**	**1**	**0**	**60**	**5.0**	**11**	**1**	**24**	**11**	**-3**								
	Providence Bruins	AHL	21	6	11	17				6																		
	Las Vegas Thunder	IHL	14	3	12	15				2																		
99-2000	**Buffalo Sabres**	**NHL**	**11**	**1**	**1**	**2**	**1**	**1**	**2**	**2**	**0**	**0**	**0**	**15**	**6.7**	**3**	**0**	**6**	**1**	**-2**	**2**	**0**	**0**	**0**	**2**	**0**	**0**	**0**
	Rochester Americans	AHL	49	21	28	49				21																		
	NHL Totals		**70**	**4**	**10**	**14**	**5**	**11**	**16**	**18**	**0**	**1**	**0**	**93**	**4.3**	**25**	**5**	**37**	**14**		**2**	**0**	**0**	**0**	**2**	**0**	**0**	**0**

• Brother of Tim • Signed as a free agent by **LA Kings**, July 25, 1997. Signed as a free agent by **Boston**, August 5, 1998. Signed as a free agent by **Buffalo**, August 13, 1999.

• TAYLOR, Dave

David Andrew "Stitch" RW – R. 6', 190 lbs. b: Levack, Ont., 12/4/1955. Los Angeles' 14th, 210th overall, in 1975.

Season	Club	League	GP	G	A	Pts	AG	AA	APts	PIM	PP	SH	GW	S	%	TGF	PGF	TGA	PGA	+/-	GP	G	A	Pts	PIM	PP	SH	GW
1973-74	Levack Huskies	NOJHA	45	67	76	*143																						
1974-75	Clarkson College	ECAC	32	20	34	54																						
1975-76	Clarkson College	ECAC	31	26	33	59																						
1976-77	Clarkson College	ECAC	34	*41	*67	*108																						
	Fort Worth Texans	CHL	7	2	4	6				6																		
1977-78	**Los Angeles Kings**	**NHL**	**64**	**22**	**21**	**43**	**20**	**16**	**36**	**47**	**4**	**0**	**3**	**122**	**18.0**	**58**	**11**	**34**	**1**	**14**	**2**	**0**	**0**	**0**	**5**	**0**	**0**	**0**
1978-79	**Los Angeles Kings**	**NHL**	**78**	**43**	**48**	**91**	**37**	**35**	**72**	**124**	**13**	**0**	**4**	**238**	**18.1**	**133**	**45**	**66**	**5**	**27**	**2**	**0**	**0**	**0**	**2**	**0**	**0**	**0**
1979-80	**Los Angeles Kings**	**NHL**	**61**	**37**	**53**	**90**	**32**	**39**	**71**	**72**	**12**	**0**	**7**	**170**	**21.8**	**132**	**48**	**48**	**3**	**39**	**4**	**2**	**1**	**3**	**4**	**0**	**0**	**0**
1980-81	**Los Angeles Kings**	**NHL**	**72**	**47**	**65**	**112**	**37**	**43**	**80**	**130**	**13**	**0**	**3**	**206**	**22.8**	**165**	**62**	**56**	**0**	**47**	**4**	**2**	**2**	**4**	**10**	**1**	**0**	**0**
1981-82	**Los Angeles Kings**	**NHL**	**78**	**39**	**67**	**106**	**31**	**45**	**76**	**130**	**13**	**0**	**3**	**232**	**16.8**	**149**	**56**	**101**	**4**	**-4**	**10**	**4**	**6**	**10**	**20**	**3**	**0**	**0**
1982-83	**Los Angeles Kings**	**NHL**	**46**	**21**	**37**	**58**	**17**	**26**	**43**	**76**	**6**	**0**	**1**	**117**	**17.9**	**86**	**36**	**46**	**0**	**4**								
	Canada	WEC-A	10	1	4	5				4																		
1983-84	**Los Angeles Kings**	**NHL**	**63**	**20**	**49**	**69**	**16**	**33**	**49**	**91**	**6**	**0**	**2**	**150**	**13.3**	**99**	**32**	**75**	**5**	**-3**								
1984-85	**Los Angeles Kings**	**NHL**	**79**	**41**	**51**	**92**	**33**	**35**	**68**	**132**	**11**	**2**	**6**	**175**	**23.4**	**140**	**55**	**81**	**9**	**13**	**3**	**2**	**2**	**4**	**8**	**0**	**0**	**0**
	Canada	WEC-A	10	3	2	5				4																		
1985-86	**Los Angeles Kings**	**NHL**	**76**	**33**	**38**	**71**	**26**	**26**	**52**	**110**	**11**	**0**	**1**	**203**	**16.3**	**111**	**38**	**99**	**10**	**-16**								
	Canada	WEC-A	10	3	4	7				12																		
1986-87	**Los Angeles Kings**	**NHL**	**67**	**18**	**44**	**62**	**16**	**32**	**48**	**84**	**9**	**1**	**3**	**115**	**15.7**	**91**	**38**	**70**	**17**	**0**	**5**	**2**	**3**	**5**	**6**	**1**	**0**	**0**
1987-88	**Los Angeles Kings**	**NHL**	**68**	**26**	**41**	**67**	**22**	**29**	**51**	**129**	**9**	**0**	**2**	**149**	**17.4**	**114**	**51**	**69**	**2**	**-4**	**5**	**3**	**3**	**6**	**6**	**2**	**0**	**0**
1988-89	**Los Angeles Kings**	**NHL**	**70**	**26**	**37**	**63**	**22**	**26**	**48**	**80**	**7**	**0**	**4**	**141**	**18.4**	**101**	**30**	**61**	**0**	**10**	**11**	**1**	**5**	**6**	**19**	**1**	**0**	**0**
1989-90	**Los Angeles Kings**	**NHL**	**58**	**15**	**26**	**41**	**13**	**19**	**32**	**96**	**2**	**0**	**1**	**100**	**15.0**	**65**	**9**	**39**	**0**	**17**	**6**	**4**	**4**	**8**	**2**	**2**	**0**	**0**
1990-91	**Los Angeles Kings**	**NHL**	**73**	**23**	**30**	**53**	**21**	**23**	**44**	**148**	**6**	**0**	**2**	**122**	**18.9**	**81**	**14**	**40**	**0**	**27**	**12**	**2**	**1**	**3**	**12**	**0**	**0**	**1**
1991-92	**Los Angeles Kings**	**NHL**	**77**	**10**	**19**	**29**	**9**	**14**	**23**	**63**	**0**	**0**	**2**	**81**	**12.3**	**45**	**2**	**33**	**0**	**10**	**6**	**1**	**1**	**2**	**20**	**0**	**0**	**0**
1992-93	**Los Angeles Kings**	**NHL**	**48**	**6**	**9**	**15**	**5**	**6**	**11**	**49**	**1**	**0**	**1**	**53**	**11.3**	**22**	**3**	**37**	**19**	**1**	**22**	**3**	**5**	**8**	**31**	**0**	**2**	**0**
1993-94	**Los Angeles Kings**	**NHL**	**33**	**4**	**3**	**7**	**4**	**2**	**6**	**28**	**0**	**1**	**2**	**39**	**10.3**	**15**	**0**	**27**	**11**	**-1**								
	NHL Totals		**1111**	**431**	**638**	**1069**	**361**	**449**	**810**	**1589**	**123**	**4**	**47**	**2413**	**17.9**	**1607**	**530**	**982**	**86**		**92**	**26**	**33**	**59**	**145**	**10**	**2**	**1**

ECAC First All Star Team (1977) • NCAA East First All-American Team (1977) • NHL Second All-Star Team (1981) • Won Bill Masterton Memorial Trophy (1991) • Won King Clancy Memorial Trophy (1991) • Played in NHL All-Star Game (1981, 1982, 1986, 1994)

Selected by **Houston** (WHA) in WHA Amateur Draft, June, 1974. Rights traded to **Cincinnati** (WHA) by **Houston** (WHA) with Craig Norwich for John Hughes, May, 1977.

• TAYLOR, Mark

C – L. 6', 190 lbs. b: Vancouver, B.C., 1/26/1958. Philadelphia's 9th, 100th overall, in 1978.

Season	Club	League	GP	G	A	Pts	AG	AA	APts	PIM	PP	SH	GW	S	%	TGF	PGF	TGA	PGA	+/-	GP	G	A	Pts	PIM	PP	SH	GW
1975-76	Langley Lords	BCJHL	63	49	79	128				48																		
1976-77	University of North Dakota	WCHA	31	16	19	35				20																		
1977-78	University of North Dakota	WCHA	37	18	22	40				28																		
1978-79	University of North Dakota	WCHA	42	24	59	83				28																		
1979-80	University of North Dakota	WCHA	40	33	59	92				30																		
1980-81	Maine Mariners	AHL	79	19	50	69				56											20	5	16	*21	20			
1981-82	**Philadelphia Flyers**	**NHL**	**2**	**0**	**0**	**0**	**0**	**0**	**0**	**0**	**0**	**0**	**0**	**1**	**0.0**	**0**	**0**	**1**	**0**	**-1**								
	Maine Mariners	AHL	75	32	48	80				42											4	2	3	5	4			
1982-83	**Philadelphia Flyers**	**NHL**	**61**	**8**	**25**	**33**	**7**	**17**	**24**	**24**	**0**	**1**	**3**	**73**	**11.0**	**51**	**7**	**39**	**20**	**25**	**3**	**0**	**0**	**0**	**0**	**0**	**0**	**0**
1983-84	**Philadelphia Flyers**	**NHL**	**1**	**0**	**0**	**0**	**0**	**0**	**0**	**0**	**0**	**0**	**0**	**0**	**0.0**	**0**	**0**	**0**	**0**	**0**								
	Pittsburgh Penguins	**NHL**	**59**	**24**	**31**	**55**	**19**	**21**	**40**	**24**	**9**	**1**	**1**	**107**	**22.4**	**84**	**30**	**95**	**21**	**-20**								
1984-85	**Pittsburgh Penguins**	**NHL**	**47**	**7**	**10**	**17**	**6**	**7**	**13**	**19**	**0**	**1**	**1**	**46**	**15.2**	**24**	**1**	**39**	**9**	**-7**								
	Washington Capitals	**NHL**	**9**	**1**	**1**	**2**	**1**	**1**	**2**	**2**	**0**	**0**	**0**	**10**	**10.0**	**4**	**1**	**4**	**0**	**-1**								
1985-86	**Washington Capitals**	**NHL**	**30**	**2**	**1**	**3**	**2**	**1**	**3**	**4**	**0**	**0**	**0**	**23**	**8.7**	**7**	**0**	**13**	**2**	**-4**	**3**	**0**	**0**	**0**	**0**	**0**	**0**	**0**
	Binghamton Whalers	AHL	43	19	38	57				27																		
1986-87	Binghamton Whalers	AHL	67	16	37	53				40											13	2	6	8	9			
1987-88	SC Uzwil	Switz-2	28	24	43	67																						
1988-89	SC Uzwil	Switz-2	STATISTICS NOT AVAILABLE																									
1989-90	Canada	Nat-Team	1	0	0	0				0																		
1990-91			STATISTICS NOT AVAILABLE																									
1991-92	HC Bolzano	Italy	5	1	4	5				0																		
	ECD Sauerland	Germany-2	32	23	52	75				28											8	4	19	23	10			
	NHL Totals		**209**	**42**	**68**	**110**	**35**	**47**	**82**	**73**	**9**	**3**	**5**	**260**	**16.2**	**170**	**39**	**191**	**52**		**6**	**0**	**0**	**0**	**0**	**0**	**0**	**0**

NCAA Championship All-Tournament Team (1979) • WCHA First All-Star Team (1980) • NCAA West First All-American Team (1980)

Traded to **Pittsburgh** by **Philadelphia** with Ron Flockhart, Andy Brickley and Philadelphia's 1st (Roger Belanger) and 3rd (later traded to Vancouver - Vancouver selected Mike Stevens) round choices in 1984 Entry Draft for Ron Sutter and Pittsburgh's 2nd (Greg Smyth) and 3rd (David McLay) round choices in 1984 Entry Draft, October 23, 1983. Traded to **Washington** by **Pittsburgh** for Jim McGeough, March 12, 1985.

• TAYLOR, Ted

Edward Wray LW – L. 6', 175 lbs. b: Oak Lake, Man., 2/25/1942.

Season	Club	League	GP	G	A	Pts	AG	AA	APts	PIM	PP	SH	GW	S	%	TGF	PGF	TGA	PGA	+/-	GP	G	A	Pts	PIM	PP	SH	GW
1959-60	Brandon Wheat Kings	MJHL	32	14	12	26				54											11	2	*7	9	2			
	Brandon Wheat Kings	Mem-Cup	11	2	9	11				8																		
1960-61	Brandon Wheat Kings	MJHL	32	28	30	58				53											9	5	5	10	18			
	Vancouver Canucks	WHL	1	0	0	0				0																		

			REGULAR SEASON																		PLAYOFFS							
Season	**Club**	**League**	**GP**	**G**	**A**	**Pts**	**AG**	**AA**	**APts**	**PIM**	**PP**	**SH**	**GW**	**S**	**%**	**TGF**	**PGF**	**TGA**	**PGA**	**+/–**	**GP**	**G**	**A**	**Pts**	**PIM**	**PP**	**SH**	**GW**
1961-62	Brandon Wheat Kings	MJHL	40	28	32	60	....	....	....	72	....	....	....	....	....	....	....	....	....	....	9	6	4	10	13	....	....	....
	Brandon Wheat Kings	Mem-Cup	11	8	5	13	....	....	....	*27	....	....	....	....	....	....	....	....	....	....	....	....	....	....	....	....	....	....
1962-63	Sudbury Wolves	EPHL	56	22	23	45	....	....	....	76	....	....	....	....	....	....	....	....	....	....	....	....	....	....	....	....	....	....
	Baltimore Clippers	AHL	14	5	7	12	....	....	....	17	....	....	....	....	....	....	....	....	....	....	3	0	0	0	4	....	....	....
1963-64	Baltimore Clippers	AHL	6	0	2	2	....	....	....	6	....	....	....	....	....	....	....	....	....	....	....	....	....	....	....	....	....	....
	St. Paul Rangers	CPHL	59	18	30	48	....	....	....	97	....	....	....	....	....	....	....	....	....	....	11	2	2	4	4	....	....	....
1964-65	**New York Rangers**	**NHL**	**4**	**0**	**0**	**0**	**0**	**0**	**0**	**4**	....	....	....	....	....	....	....	....	....	....	....	....	....	....	....	....	....	....
	Baltimore Clippers	AHL	68	25	28	53	....	....	....	74	....	....	....	....	....	....	....	....	....	....	3	0	0	0	4	....	....	....
1965-66	**New York Rangers**	**NHL**	**4**	**0**	**1**	**1**	**0**	**1**	**1**	**2**	....	....	....	....	....	....	....	....	....	....	....	....	....	....	....	....	....	....
	Baltimore Clippers	AHL	62	21	30	51	....	....	....	98	....	....	....	....	....	....	....	....	....	....	....	....	....	....	....	....	....	....
1966-67	**Detroit Red Wings**	**NHL**	**2**	**0**	**0**	**0**	**0**	**0**	**0**	**0**	....	....	....	....	....	....	....	....	....	....	....	....	....	....	....	....	....	....
	Pittsburgh Hornets	AHL	69	20	38	58	....	....	....	91	....	....	....	....	....	....	....	....	....	....	9	3	2	5	8	....	....	....
1967-68	**Minnesota North Stars**	**NHL**	**31**	**3**	**5**	**8**	**3**	**5**	**8**	**34**	**1**	**0**	**0**	**67**	**4.5**	**14**	**2**	**21**	**2**	**–7**	....	....	....	....	....	....	....	....
	Rochester Americans	AHL	37	14	16	30	....	....	....	54	....	....	....	....	....	....	....	....	....	....	11	5	5	10	29	....	....	....
1968-69	Vancouver Canucks	WHL	64	15	29	44	....	....	....	121	....	....	....	....	....	....	....	....	....	....	8	1	4	5	4	....	....	....
1969-70	Vancouver Canucks	WHL	66	36	35	71	....	....	....	97	....	....	....	....	....	....	....	....	....	....	11	9	8	17	46	....	....	....
1970-71	**Vancouver Canucks**	**NHL**	**56**	**11**	**16**	**27**	**11**	**13**	**24**	**53**	**1**	**1**	**1**	**82**	**13.4**	**39**	**3**	**61**	**16**	**–9**	....	....	....	....	....	....	....	....
1971-72	**Vancouver Canucks**	**NHL**	**69**	**9**	**13**	**22**	**9**	**11**	**20**	**88**	**0**	**0**	**0**	**82**	**11.0**	**32**	**0**	**55**	**3**	**–20**	....	....	....	....	....	....	....	....
1972-73	Houston Aeros	WHA	72	34	42	76	....	....	....	101	....	....	....	....	....	....	....	....	....	....	10	3	1	4	10	....	....	....
1973-74	Houston Aeros	WHA	75	21	23	44	....	....	....	143	....	....	....	....	....	....	....	....	....	....	14	4	8	12	60	....	....	....
1974-75	Houston Aeros	WHA	73	26	27	53	....	....	....	130	....	....	....	....	....	....	....	....	....	....	11	2	5	7	22	....	....	....
1975-76	Houston Aeros	WHA	68	15	26	41	....	....	....	88	....	....	....	....	....	....	....	....	....	....	11	2	2	4	17	....	....	....
1976-77	Houston Aeros	WHA	78	16	35	51	....	....	....	90	....	....	....	....	....	....	....	....	....	....	11	4	4	8	28	....	....	....
1977-78	Houston Aeros	WHA	54	11	11	22	....	....	....	46	....	....	....	....	....	....	....	....	....	....	6	3	1	4	10	....	....	....
	NHL Totals		**166**	**23**	**35**	**58**	**23**	**30**	**53**	**181**	....	....	....	....	....	....	....	....	....	....	....	....	....	....	....	....	....	....
	Other Major League Totals		420	123	164	287	....	....	....	598	....	....	....	....	....	....	....	....	....	....	63	18	21	39	147	....	....	....

Traded to **Montreal** by **NY Rangers** with Garry Peters for Red Berenson, June 13, 1966. Claimed by **Detroit** from **Montreal** in Intra-League Draft, June 15, 1966. Claimed by **Minnesota** from **Detroit** in Expansion Draft, June 6, 1967. Traded to **Toronto** (Rochester-AHL) by **Minnesota** with Duke Harris, Murray Hall, Len Lunde, Don Johns and the loan of Carl Wetzel for Milan Marcetta and Jean-Paul Parise, December 23, 1967. Rights transferred to **Vancouver** (WHL) after WHL club purchased **Rochester** (AHL) franchise, August 13, 1968. NHL rights transferred to **Vancouver** after NHL club purchased **Vancouver** (WHL) franchise, December 19, 1969. Selected by **Dayton-Houston** (WHA) in 1972 WHA General Player Draft, February 12, 1972. Claimed by **NY Islanders** from **Vancouver** in Expansion Draft, June 6, 1972.

• TAYLOR, Tim

"The Toolman" C – L. 6'1", 185 lbs. b: Stratford, Ont., 2/6/1969. Washington's 2nd, 36th overall, in 1988.

Season	Club	League	GP	G	A	Pts	AG	AA	APts	PIM	PP	SH	GW	S	%	TGF	PGF	TGA	PGA	+/–	GP	G	A	Pts	PIM	PP	SH	GW
1985-86	Stratford Midget Cullitans	OMHA	STATISTICS NOT AVAILABLE																									
	Stratford Cullitons	OJHL-B	1	0	0	0	....	....	....	0	....	....	....	....	....	....	....	....	....	....	....	....	....	....	....	....	....	....
1986-87	Stratford Cullitons	OJHL-B	31	25	26	51	....	....	....	51	....	....	....	....	....	....	....	....	....	....	....	....	....	....	....	....	....	....
	London Knights	OHL	34	7	9	16	....	....	....	11	....	....	....	....	....	....	....	....	....	....	....	....	....	....	....	....	....	....
1987-88	London Knights	OHL	64	46	50	96	....	....	....	66	....	....	....	....	....	....	....	....	....	....	12	9	9	18	26	....	....	....
1988-89	London Knights	OHL	61	34	80	114	....	....	....	93	....	....	....	....	....	....	....	....	....	....	21	*21	25	*46	58	....	....	....
1989-90	Baltimore Skipjacks	AHL	79	31	36	67	....	....	....	124	....	....	....	....	....	....	....	....	....	....	9	2	2	4	13	....	....	....
1990-91	Baltimore Skipjacks	AHL	79	25	42	67	....	....	....	75	....	....	....	....	....	....	....	....	....	....	5	0	1	1	4	....	....	....
1991-92	Baltimore Skipjacks	AHL	65	9	18	27	....	....	....	131	....	....	....	....	....	....	....	....	....	....	....	....	....	....	....	....	....	....
1992-93	Baltimore Skipjacks	AHL	41	15	16	31	....	....	....	49	....	....	....	....	....	....	....	....	....	....	....	....	....	....	....	....	....	....
	Hamilton Canucks	AHL	36	15	22	37	....	....	....	37	....	....	....	....	....	....	....	....	....	....	....	....	....	....	....	....	....	....
1993-94	**Detroit Red Wings**	**NHL**	**1**	**1**	**0**	**1**	**1**	**0**	**1**	**0**	**0**	**0**	**0**	**4**	**25.0**	**1**	**0**	**2**	**0**	**–1**	....	....	....	....	....	....	....	....
	Adirondack Red Wings	AHL	79	36	*81	*117	....	....	....	86	....	....	....	....	....	....	....	....	....	....	12	2	10	12	12	....	....	....
1994-95	**Detroit Red Wings**	**NHL**	**22**	**0**	**4**	**4**	**0**	**6**	**6**	**16**	**0**	**0**	**0**	**21**	**0.0**	**10**	**3**	**4**	**0**	**3**	**6**	**0**	**1**	**1**	**12**	**0**	**0**	**0**
1995-96	**Detroit Red Wings**	**NHL**	**72**	**11**	**14**	**25**	**11**	**11**	**22**	**39**	**1**	**1**	**4**	**81**	**13.6**	**32**	**3**	**20**	**2**	**11**	**18**	**0**	**4**	**4**	**4**	**0**	**0**	**0**
1996-97♦	**Detroit Red Wings**	**NHL**	**44**	**3**	**4**	**7**	**3**	**4**	**7**	**52**	**0**	**1**	**0**	**44**	**6.8**	**17**	**3**	**26**	**6**	**–6**	**2**	**0**	**0**	**0**	**0**	**0**	**0**	**0**
1997-98	**Boston Bruins**	**NHL**	**79**	**20**	**11**	**31**	**23**	**11**	**34**	**57**	**1**	**3**	**0**	**127**	**15.7**	**44**	**7**	**73**	**20**	**–16**	**6**	**0**	**0**	**0**	**10**	**0**	**0**	**0**
1998-99	**Boston Bruins**	**NHL**	**49**	**4**	**7**	**11**	**5**	**7**	**12**	**55**	**0**	**0**	**1**	**76**	**5.3**	**18**	**4**	**28**	**4**	**–10**	**12**	**0**	**3**	**3**	**8**	**0**	**0**	**0**
99-2000	**New York Rangers**	**NHL**	**76**	**9**	**11**	**20**	**10**	**10**	**20**	**72**	**0**	**0**	**2**	**79**	**11.4**	**34**	**3**	**51**	**16**	**–4**	....	....	....	....	....	....	....	....
	NHL Totals		**343**	**48**	**51**	**99**	**53**	**49**	**102**	**291**	**2**	**5**	**7**	**432**	**11.1**	**156**	**23**	**204**	**48**		**44**	**0**	**8**	**8**	**34**	**0**	**0**	**0**

• Brother of Chris • AHL First All-Star Team (1994) • Won John B. Sollenberger Trophy (Top Scorer - AHL) (1994)

Traded to **Vancouver** by **Washington** for Eric Murano, January 29, 1993. Signed as a free agent by **Detroit**, July 28, 1993. Claimed by **Boston** from **Detroit** in NHL Waiver Draft, September 28, 1998. Signed as a free agent by **NY Rangers**, July 30, 1999.

• TEAL, Jeff

Jefferson Bradley RW – L. 6'3", 205 lbs. b: Edina, MN, 5/30/1960. Montreal's 6th, 82nd overall, in 1980.

Season	Club	League	GP	G	A	Pts	AG	AA	APts	PIM	PP	SH	GW	S	%	TGF	PGF	TGA	PGA	+/–	GP	G	A	Pts	PIM	PP	SH	GW
1978-79	John Marshall Rockets	Hi-School	STATISTICS NOT AVAILABLE																									
1979-80	University of Minnesota	WCHA	37	10	15	25	....	....	....	30	....	....	....	....	....	....	....	....	....	....	....	....	....	....	....	....	....	....
1980-81	University of Minnesota	WCHA	45	15	9	24	....	....	....	38	....	....	....	....	....	....	....	....	....	....	....	....	....	....	....	....	....	....
1981-82	University of Minnesota	WCHA	37	13	9	22	....	....	....	36	....	....	....	....	....	....	....	....	....	....	....	....	....	....	....	....	....	....
	Nova Scotia Voyageurs	AHL	7	0	1	1	....	....	....	0	....	....	....	....	....	....	....	....	....	....	6	1	1	2	2	....	....	....
1982-83	Nova Scotia Voyageurs	AHL	76	8	20	28	....	....	....	14	....	....	....	....	....	....	....	....	....	....	7	0	1	1	2	....	....	....
1983-84	Nova Scotia Voyageurs	AHL	15	8	4	12	....	....	....	2	....	....	....	....	....	....	....	....	....	....	....	....	....	....	....	....	....	....
1984-85	**Montreal Canadiens**	**NHL**	**6**	**0**	**1**	**1**	**0**	**1**	**1**	**0**	**0**	**0**	**0**	**4**	**0.0**	**1**	**0**	**1**	**0**	**0**	....	....	....	....	....	....	....	....
	Sherbrooke Canadiens	AHL	69	18	24	42	....	....	....	16	....	....	....	....	....	....	....	....	....	....	17	4	8	12	8	....	....	....
	NHL Totals		**6**	**0**	**1**	**1**	**0**	**1**	**1**	**0**	**0**	**0**	**0**	**4**	**0.0**	**1**	**0**	**1**	**0**		....	....	....	....	....	....	....	....

• Missed majority of 1983-84 season recovering from leg injury suffered in game vs. New Haven (AHL), November 4, 1983.

• TEAL, Vic

"Skeeter" RW – R. 6'1", 160 lbs. b: St. Catharines, Ont., 8/10/1949. St. Louis' 3rd, 42nd overall, in 1969.

Season	Club	League	GP	G	A	Pts	AG	AA	APts	PIM	PP	SH	GW	S	%	TGF	PGF	TGA	PGA	+/–	GP	G	A	Pts	PIM	PP	SH	GW
1965-66	St. Catharines Falcons	OHA-B	30	34	25	59	....	....	....	....	....	....	....	....	....	....	....	....	....	....	7	13	9	22	....	....	....	....
	St. Catharines Black Hawks	OHA-Jr.	....	....	....	....	....	....	....	....	....	....	....	....	....	....	....	....	....	....	4	0	0	0	0	....	....	....
1966-67	St. Catharines Black Hawks	OHA-Jr.	47	15	15	30	....	....	....	4	....	....	....	....	....	....	....	....	....	....	6	1	0	1	2	....	....	....
1967-68	St. Catharines Black Hawks	OHA-Jr.	54	34	29	63	....	....	....	29	....	....	....	....	....	....	....	....	....	....	5	1	5	6	0	....	....	....
1968-69	St. Catharines Black Hawks	OHA-Jr.	51	30	53	83	....	....	....	55	....	....	....	....	....	....	....	....	....	....	18	8	18	26	11	....	....	....
1969-70	Kansas City Blues	CHL	58	8	13	21	....	....	....	28	....	....	....	....	....	....	....	....	....	....	....	....	....	....	....	....	....	....
1970-71			REINSTATED AS AN AMATEUR																									
1971-72	Galt Terriers	OHA-Sr.	36	36	27	63	....	....	....	11	....	....	....	....	....	....	....	....	....	....	....	....	....	....	....	....	....	....
1972-73	New Haven Nighthawks	AHL	69	18	34	52	....	....	....	6	....	....	....	....	....	....	....	....	....	....	....	....	....	....	....	....	....	....
1973-74	**New York Islanders**	**NHL**	**1**	**0**	**0**	**0**	**0**	**0**	**0**	**0**	**0**	**0**	**0**	**4**	**0.0**	**0**	**0**	**0**	**1**	**1**	....	....	....	....	....	....	....	....
	Fort Worth Wings	CHL	72	33	43	76	....	....	....	8	....	....	....	....	....	....	....	....	....	....	5	0	1	1	0	....	....	....
1974-75	Fort Worth Texans	CHL	69	27	29	56	....	....	....	20	....	....	....	....	....	....	....	....	....	....	....	....	....	....	....	....	....	....
1975-76	Erie Blades	NAHL	63	36	27	63	....	....	....	4	....	....	....	....	....	....	....	....	....	....	2	0	2	2	0	....	....	....
1976-77	Cambridge Hornets	OHA-Sr.	12	14	7	21	....	....	....	0	....	....	....	....	....	....	....	....	....	....	....	....	....	....	....	....	....	....
	NHL Totals		**1**	**0**	**0**	**0**	**0**	**0**	**0**	**0**	**0**	**0**	**0**	**4**	**0.0**	**0**	**0**	**0**	**1**		....	....	....	....	....	....	....	....

• Brother of Allan (Skip) • CHL Second All-Star Team (1974)

Signed as a free agent by **NY Islanders**, September 29, 1973.

• TEBBUTT, Greg

D – L. 6'3", 215 lbs. b: North Vancouver, B.C., 5/11/1957. Minnesota's 7th, 130th overall, in 1977.

Season	Club	League	GP	G	A	Pts	AG	AA	APts	PIM	PP	SH	GW	S	%	TGF	PGF	TGA	PGA	+/–	GP	G	A	Pts	PIM	PP	SH	GW
1974-75	Nor-West Caps	BCJHL	STATISTICS NOT AVAILABLE																									
1975-76	Victoria Cougars	WCJHL	51	3	4	7	....	....	....	217	....	....	....	....	....	....	....	....	....	....	15	2	0	2	43	....	....	....
1976-77	Victoria Cougars	WCJHL	29	7	12	19	....	....	....	98	....	....	....	....	....	....	....	....	....	....	....	....	....	....	....	....	....	....
	Regina Pats	WCJHL	40	8	17	25	....	....	....	138	....	....	....	....	....	....	....	....	....	....	....	....	....	....	....	....	....	....
1977-78	Flin Flon Bombers	WCJHL	55	28	46	74	....	....	....	270	....	....	....	....	....	....	....	....	....	....	15	11	17	28	45	....	....	....
1978-79	Binghamton Dusters	AHL	33	8	9	17	....	....	....	50	....	....	....	....	....	....	....	....	....	....	....	....	....	....	....	....	....	....
	Birmingham Bulls	WHA	38	2	5	7	....	....	....	83	....	....	....	....	....	....	....	....	....	....	....	....	....	....	....	....	....	....

			REGULAR SEASON																		PLAYOFFS							
Season	Club	League	GP	G	A	Pts	AG	AA	APts	PIM	PP	SH	GW	S	%	TGF	PGF	TGA	PGA	+/–	GP	G	A	Pts	PIM	PP	SH	GW
1979-80	**Quebec Nordiques**	**NHL**	2	0	1	1	0	1	1	4	0	0	0	0	0.0	1	0	2	0	–1	....	....	....	....	....	....	....	....
	Syracuse Firebirds	AHL	14	2	3	5	....	....	....	35	....	....	....	....	....	....	....	....	....	....	....	....	....	....	....	....	....	....
	Erie Blades	EHL	48	20	53	73	....	....	....	138	....	....	....	....	....	....	....	....	....	....	9	*11	*12	*23	32	....	....	....
1980-81	Erie Blades	EHL	35	16	37	53	....	....	....	93	....	....	....	....	....	....	....	....	....	....	8	0	*12	12	28	....	....	....
1981-82	Fort Wayne Komets	IHL	49	13	34	47	....	....	....	148	....	....	....	....	....	....	....	....	....	....	9	3	1	4	16	....	....	....
1982-83	Baltimore Skipjacks	AHL	80	28	56	84	....	....	....	140	....	....	....	....	....	....	....	....	....	....	....	....	....	....	....	....	....	....
1983-84	**Pittsburgh Penguins**	**NHL**	24	0	2	2	0	1	1	31	0	0	0	38	0.0	18	2	47	5	–26	....	....	....	....	....	....	....	....
	Baltimore Skipjacks	AHL	44	12	42	54	....	....	....	125	....	....	....	....	....	....	....	....	....	....	10	0	6	6	20	....	....	....
1984-85	Baltimore Skipjacks	AHL	2	0	0	0	....	....	....	4	....	....	....	....	....	....	....	....	....	....	....	....	....	....	....	....	....	....
	Muskegon Mohawks	IHL	73	23	55	78	....	....	....	220	....	....	....	....	....	....	....	....	....	....	17	3	9	12	87	....	....	....
1985-86	Milwaukee Admirals	IHL	77	20	49	69	....	....	....	226	....	....	....	....	....	....	....	....	....	....	5	0	3	3	8	....	....	....
1986-87	Saginaw Generals	IHL	81	27	59	86	....	....	....	215	....	....	....	....	....	....	....	....	....	....	8	6	5	11	34	....	....	....
1987-88	Baltimore Skipjacks	AHL	24	1	14	15	....	....	....	72	....	....	....	....	....	....	....	....	....	....	....	....	....	....	....	....	....	....
	NHL Totals		26	0	3	3	0	2	2	35	0	0	0	38	0.0	19	2	49	5		....	....	....	....	....	....	....	....
	Other Major League Totals		38	2	5	7	....	....	....	83	....	....	....	....	....	....	....	....	....	....	....	....	....	....	....	....	....	....

EHL Second All-Star Team (1980) • AHL First All-Star Team (1983) • Won Eddie Shore Award (Outstanding Defenseman - AHL) (1983) • IHL Second All-Star Team (1985) • IHL First All-Star Team (1987)

Selected by **Birmingham** (WHA) in 1977 WHA Amateur Draft, June, 1977. Reclaimed by **Minnesota** from **Birmingham** (WHA) prior to Expansion Draft, June 9, 1979. Claimed by **Quebec** from **Minnesota** on waivers, August 13, 1979. Signed as a free agent by **Pittsburgh**, July 22, 1983.

• TEPPER, Stephen

RW – R. 6'4", 215 lbs. b: Santa Ana, CA, 3/10/1969. Chicago's 7th, 134th overall, in 1987.

1985-86	Westboro High School	Hi-School	24	18	26	44	....	....	....	....	....	....	....	....	....	....	....	....	....	....	....	....	....	....	....	....	....	....
1986-87	Westboro High School	Hi-School	25	34	18	52	....	....	....	....	....	....	....	....	....	....	....	....	....	....	....	....	....	....	....	....	....	....
1987-88	Westboro High School	Hi-School	24	39	24	63	....	....	....	....	....	....	....	....	....	....	....	....	....	....	....	....	....	....	....	....	....	....
1988-89	University of Maine	H-East	26	3	9	12	....	....	....	32	....	....	....	....	....	....	....	....	....	....	....	....	....	....	....	....	....	....
1989-90	University of Maine	H-East	41	10	6	16	....	....	....	68	....	....	....	....	....	....	....	....	....	....	....	....	....	....	....	....	....	....
1990-91	University of Maine	H-East	38	6	11	17	....	....	....	58	....	....	....	....	....	....	....	....	....	....	....	....	....	....	....	....	....	....
1991-92	University of Maine	H-East	16	0	3	3	....	....	....	20	....	....	....	....	....	....	....	....	....	....	....	....	....	....	....	....	....	....
1992-93	**Chicago Blackhawks**	**NHL**	1	0	0	0	0	0	0	0	0	0	0	0	0.0	0	0	0	0	0	....	....	....	....	....	....	....	....
	Indianapolis Ice	IHL	12	0	1	1	....	....	....	40	....	....	....	....	....	....	....	....	....	....	....	....	....	....	....	....	....	....
	Kansas City Blades	IHL	32	4	10	14	....	....	....	51	....	....	....	....	....	....	....	....	....	....	4	0	1	1	6	....	....	....
1993-94	Fort Worth Fire	CHL	25	23	11	34	....	....	....	54	....	....	....	....	....	....	....	....	....	....	....	....	....	....	....	....	....	....
	Roanoke Express	ECHL	9	2	2	4	....	....	....	33	....	....	....	....	....	....	....	....	....	....	....	....	....	....	....	....	....	....
	Kansas City Blades	IHL	23	1	3	4	....	....	....	52	....	....	....	....	....	....	....	....	....	....	....	....	....	....	....	....	....	....
1994-95	Fort Worth Fire	CHL	35	26	22	48	....	....	....	63	....	....	....	....	....	....	....	....	....	....	....	....	....	....	....	....	....	....
	Cape Breton Oilers	AHL	26	1	4	5	....	....	....	16	....	....	....	....	....	....	....	....	....	....	....	....	....	....	....	....	....	....
1995-96	Cape Breton Oilers	AHL	52	8	14	22	....	....	....	74	....	....	....	....	....	....	....	....	....	....	....	....	....	....	....	....	....	....
1996-2000	Worcester IceCats	AHL	DID NOT PLAY – FRONT OFFICE STAFF																									
	NHL Totals		1	0	0	0	0	0	0	0	0	0	0	0	0.0	0	0	0	0		....	....	....	....	....	....	....	....

• TERBENCHE, Paul

Paul Frederick D – L. 5'10", 170 lbs. b: Port Hope, Ont., 9/16/1945.

1963-64	Milton-Ingersoll Aces	OHA-B	STATISTICS NOT AVAILABLE																									
1964-65	St. Catharines Black Hawks	OHA-Jr.	56	3	23	26	....	....	....	63	....	....	....	....	....	....	....	....	....	....	5	0	0	0	4	....	....	....
1965-66	St. Catharines Black Hawks	OHA-Jr.	48	5	31	36	....	....	....	26	....	....	....	....	....	....	....	....	....	....	7	1	4	5	2	....	....	....
	St. Louis Braves	CPHL	2	0	0	0	....	....	....	0	....	....	....	....	....	....	....	....	....	....	5	0	2	2	0	....	....	....
1966-67	St. Louis Braves	CPHL	63	4	14	18	....	....	....	39	....	....	....	....	....	....	....	....	....	....	....	....	....	....	....	....	....	....
1967-68	**Chicago Black Hawks**	**NHL**	68	3	7	10	3	7	10	8	0	0	1	65	4.6	22	2	35	4	–11	6	0	0	0	0	0	0	0
1968-69	Dallas Black Hawks	CHL	26	0	4	4	....	....	....	2	....	....	....	....	....	....	....	....	....	....	11	0	3	3	2	....	....	....
1969-70	Portland Buckaroos	WHL	66	5	15	20	....	....	....	8	....	....	....	....	....	....	....	....	....	....	3	0	0	0	0	....	....	....
1970-71	**Buffalo Sabres**	**NHL**	3	0	0	0	0	0	0	2	0	0	0	1	0.0	0	0	3	0	–3	....	....	....	....	....	....	....	....
	Salt Lake Golden Eagles	WHL	51	4	20	24	....	....	....	16	....	....	....	....	....	....	....	....	....	....	....	....	....	....	....	....	....	....
1971-72	**Buffalo Sabres**	**NHL**	9	0	0	0	0	0	0	2	0	0	0	7	0.0	0	0	16	3	–13	....	....	....	....	....	....	....	....
	Salt Lake Golden Eagles	WHL	64	1	31	32	....	....	....	10	....	....	....	....	....	....	....	....	....	....	....	....	....	....	....	....	....	....
1972-73	**Buffalo Sabres**	**NHL**	42	0	7	7	0	6	6	8	0	0	0	20	0.0	32	0	32	7	7	6	0	0	0	0	0	0	0
1973-74	**Buffalo Sabres**	**NHL**	67	2	12	14	2	10	12	8	0	0	0	42	4.8	49	6	47	7	3	....	....	....	....	....	....	....	....
1974-75	Vancouver Blazers	WHA	60	3	14	17	....	....	....	10	....	....	....	....	....	....	....	....	....	....	....	....	....	....	....	....	....	....
1975-76	Calgary Cowboys	WHA	58	2	4	6	....	....	....	22	....	....	....	....	....	....	....	....	....	....	10	0	6	6	6	....	....	....
1976-77	Calgary Cowboys	WHA	80	9	24	33	....	....	....	30	....	....	....	....	....	....	....	....	....	....	....	....	....	....	....	....	....	....
1977-78	Birmingham Bulls	WHA	11	1	0	1	....	....	....	0	....	....	....	....	....	....	....	....	....	....	....	....	....	....	....	....	....	....
	Hampton Gulls	AHL	26	0	9	9	....	....	....	11	....	....	....	....	....	....	....	....	....	....	....	....	....	....	....	....	....	....
	Springfield Indians	AHL	8	0	5	5	....	....	....	4	....	....	....	....	....	....	....	....	....	....	....	....	....	....	....	....	....	....
	Houston Aeros	WHA	....	....	....	....	....	....	....	....	....	....	....	....	....	....	....	....	....	....	6	1	1	2	0	....	....	....
1978-79	Winnipeg Jets	WHA	68	3	22	25	....	....	....	12	....	....	....	....	....	....	....	....	....	....	10	1	1	2	4	....	....	....
1979-80	Birmingham Bulls	CHL	63	3	14	17	....	....	....	20	....	....	....	....	....	....	....	....	....	....	4	0	2	2	2	....	....	....
1980-81	Birmingham Bulls	CHL	41	2	2	4	....	....	....	26	....	....	....	....	....	....	....	....	....	....	....	....	....	....	....	....	....	....
	NHL Totals		189	5	26	31	5	23	28	28	0	0	1	135	3.7	103	8	133	21		12	0	0	0	0	0	0	0
	Other Major League Totals		277	18	64	82	....	....	....	74	....	....	....	....	....	....	....	....	....	....	26	2	8	10	10	....	....	....

Claimed by **Buffalo** from **Chicago** in Expansion Draft, June, 1970. Selected by **Dayton-Houston** in 1972 WHA General Player Draft, February 12, 1972. Claimed by **Kansas City** from **Buffalo** in Expansion Draft, June, 1974. Signed as a free agent by **Vancouver** (WHA), July, 1974. Transferred to **Calgary** (WHA) after **Vancouver** (WHA) franchise relocated, June, 1975. Signed as a free agent by **Birmingham** (WHA) after **Calgary** (WHA) franchise folded, May, 1977. Traded to **Houston** (WHA) by **Birmingham** (WHA) for future considerations, February, 1978. Traded to **Winnipeg** (WHA) by **Houston** (WHA) for cash, July, 1978. Retained by **Winnipeg** prior to Expansion Draft, June 9, 1979. Traded to **Atlanta** by **Winnipeg** for future considerations, August, 1979.

• TERRION, Greg

Gregory Patrick "Tubby" LW – L. 5'11", 190 lbs. b: Marmora, Ont., 5/2/1960. Los Angeles' 3rd, 33rd overall, in 1980.

1976-77	Belleville Bulls	OHA-B	20	15	17	32	....	....	....	....	....	....	....	....	....	....	....	....	....	....	....	....	....	....	....	....	....	....
1977-78	Hamilton Fincups	OMJHL	64	11	30	41	....	....	....	43	....	....	....	....	....	....	....	....	....	....	20	4	5	9	26	....	....	....
1978-79	Brantford Alexanders	OMJHL	59	27	28	55	....	....	....	48	....	....	....	....	....	....	....	....	....	....	....	....	....	....	....	....	....	....
1979-80	Brantford Alexanders	OMJHL	67	44	78	122	....	....	....	13	....	....	....	....	....	....	....	....	....	....	11	4	7	11	12	....	....	....
1980-81	**Los Angeles Kings**	**NHL**	73	12	25	37	9	17	26	99	2	0	2	92	13.0	48	9	46	6	–1	3	1	0	1	4	1	0	0
1981-82	**Los Angeles Kings**	**NHL**	61	15	22	37	12	15	27	23	1	0	3	106	14.2	61	15	67	9	–12	....	....	....	....	....	....	....	....
1982-83	**Toronto Maple Leafs**	**NHL**	74	16	16	32	13	11	24	59	0	3	1	73	21.9	50	2	82	31	–3	4	1	2	3	2	0	0	0
	New Haven Nighthawks	AHL	4	0	1	1	....	....	....	7	....	....	....	....	....	....	....	....	....	....	....	....	....	....	....	....	....	....
1983-84	**Toronto Maple Leafs**	**NHL**	79	15	24	39	12	16	28	36	0	2	2	92	16.3	63	3	109	43	–6	....	....	....	....	....	....	....	....
1984-85	**Toronto Maple Leafs**	**NHL**	72	14	17	31	11	12	23	20	1	4	0	91	15.4	46	4	101	44	–15	....	....	....	....	....	....	....	....
1985-86	**Toronto Maple Leafs**	**NHL**	76	10	22	32	8	15	23	31	0	2	1	105	9.5	46	0	77	26	–5	10	0	3	3	17	0	0	0
1986-87	**Toronto Maple Leafs**	**NHL**	67	7	8	15	6	6	12	6	0	2	0	55	12.7	27	0	59	27	–5	13	0	2	2	14	0	0	0
1987-88	**Toronto Maple Leafs**	**NHL**	59	4	16	20	3	11	14	65	1	0	1	57	7.0	30	1	57	22	–6	5	0	2	2	4	0	0	0
	Newmarket Saints	AHL	4	1	3	4	....	....	....	6	....	....	....	....	....	....	....	....	....	....	....	....	....	....	....	....	....	....
1988-89	Newmarket Saints	AHL	60	15	34	49	....	....	....	64	....	....	....	....	....	....	....	....	....	....	4	0	1	1	2	....	....	....
	NHL Totals		561	93	150	243	74	103	177	339	5	13	10	671	13.9	371	34	598	208		35	2	9	11	41	1	0	0

Traded to **Toronto** by **LA Kings** for Toronto's 4th round choice (later traded to Detroit — Detroit selected David Korol) in 1983 Entry Draft, October 19, 1982.

• TERRY, Bill

William Charles C – R. 5'8", 175 lbs. b: Toronto, Ont., 7/13/1961.

1976-77	Wexford Raiders	MTHL	STATISTICS NOT AVAILABLE																									
1978-79	Sault Ste. Marie Greyhounds	OMJHL	68	28	21	49	....	....	....	85	....	....	....	....	....	....	....	....	....	....	....	....	....	....	....	....	....	....
1979-80	Sault Ste. Marie Greyhounds	OMJHL	68	21	34	55	....	....	....	64	....	....	....	....	....	....	....	....	....	....	....	....	....	....	....	....	....	....
1980-81	Michigan Tech Huskies	WCHA	40	23	19	42	....	....	....	12	....	....	....	....	....	....	....	....	....	....	....	....	....	....	....	....	....	....
1981-82	Michigan Tech Huskies	CCHA	35	26	24	50	....	....	....	37	....	....	....	....	....	....	....	....	....	....	....	....	....	....	....	....	....	....
1982-83	Michigan Tech Huskies	CCHA	37	19	29	48	....	....	....	37	....	....	....	....	....	....	....	....	....	....	....	....	....	....	....	....	....	....

Season	Club	League	GP	G	A	Pts	AG	AA	APts	PIM	PP	SH	GW	S	%	TGF	PGF	TGA	PGA	+/–	GP	G	A	Pts	PIM	PP	SH	GW
			REGULAR SEASON																		PLAYOFFS							
1983-84	Michigan Tech Huskies	CCHA	40	23	17	40	....	....	....	40	....	....	....	....	....	....	....	....	....	....	....	....	....	....	....	....	....	....
	Toledo Goaldiggers	IHL	3	2	2	4	....	....	....	4	....	....	....	....	....	....	....	....	....	....	....	....	....	....	....	....	....	....
1984-85	Augsburger EV	Germany-2	STATISTICS NOT AVAILABLE																									
1985-86	Kalamazoo Wings	IHL	78	43	66	109	....	....	....	28	....	....	....	....	....	....	....	....	....	....	6	6	4	10	8	....	....	....
1986-87	Kalamazoo Wings	IHL	27	11	22	33	....	....	....	8	....	....	....	....	....	....	....	....	....	....	....	....	....	....	....	....	....	....
1987-88	**Minnesota North Stars**	**NHL**	**5**	**0**	**0**	**0**	**0**	**0**	**0**	**0**	**0**	**0**	**0**	**3**	**0.0**	**0**	**0**	**4**	**0**	**–4**	....	....	....	....	....	....	....	....
	Kalamazoo Wings	IHL	77	31	54	85	....	....	....	75	....	....	....	....	....	....	....	....	....	....	7	5	5	10	6	....	....	....
1988-89	HC Ajoie	Switz.	36	9	5	14	....	....	....	....	....	....	....	....	....	....	....	....	....	....	10	10	*15	25	....	....	....	....
1989-90	SC Herisau	Switz-2	36	42	35	77	....	....	....	....	....	....	....	....	....	....	....	....	....	....	10	5	11	16	....	....	....	....
	NHL Totals		**5**	**0**	**0**	**0**	**0**	**0**	**0**	**0**	**0**	**0**	**0**	**3**	**0.0**	**0**	**0**	**4**	**0**		....	....	....	....	....	....	....	....

IHL Second All-Star Team (1986)

Signed as a free agent by **Detroit**, September, 1986. Signed as a free agent by **Minnesota**, September, 1987.

• TERTYSHNY, Dimitri

D – L. 6'1", 176 lbs. b: Chelyabinsk, USSR, 12/26/1976 d: 7/23/1999. Philadelphia's 4th, 132nd overall, in 1995.

Season	Club	League	GP	G	A	Pts	AG	AA	APts	PIM	PP	SH	GW	S	%	TGF	PGF	TGA	PGA	+/–	GP	G	A	Pts	PIM	PP	SH	GW
1994-95	Traktor Chelyabinsk	CIS	38	0	3	3	....	....	....	14	....	....	....	....	....	....	....	....	....	....	1	0	0	0	0	....	....	....
1995-96	Traktor Chelyabinsk	CIS	44	1	5	6	....	....	....	50	....	....	....	....	....	....	....	....	....	....	....	....	....	....	....	....	....	....
1996-97	Traktor Chelyabinsk	Russia	40	2	5	7	....	....	....	32	....	....	....	....	....	....	....	....	....	....	2	0	0	0	2	....	....	....
1997-98	Traktor Chelyabinsk	Russia	46	3	7	10	....	....	....	18	....	....	....	....	....	....	....	....	....	....	....	....	....	....	....	....	....	....
1998-99	**Philadelphia Flyers**	**NHL**	**62**	**2**	**8**	**10**	**2**	**8**	**10**	**30**	**1**	**0**	**0**	**68**	**2.9**	**47**	**12**	**42**	**6**	**–1**	**1**	**0**	**0**	**0**	**0**	**0**	**0**	**0**
	NHL Totals		**62**	**2**	**8**	**10**	**2**	**8**	**10**	**30**	**1**	**0**	**0**	**68**	**2.9**	**47**	**12**	**42**	**6**		**1**	**0**	**0**	**0**	**0**	**0**	**0**	**0**

• Died of injuries suffered in motor-boat accident, July 23, 1999.

• TEZIKOV, Alexei

D – L. 6'1", 208 lbs. b: Togliatti, USSR, 6/22/1978. Buffalo's 7th, 115th overall, in 1996.

Season	Club	League	GP	G	A	Pts	AG	AA	APts	PIM	PP	SH	GW	S	%	TGF	PGF	TGA	PGA	+/–	GP	G	A	Pts	PIM	PP	SH	GW
1995-96	Lada Togliatti	CIS	14	0	0	0	....	....	....	8	....	....	....	....	....	....	....	....	....	....	....	....	....	....	....	....	....	....
1996-97	Lada Togliatti	Russia	7	0	0	0	....	....	....	4	....	....	....	....	....	....	....	....	....	....	....	....	....	....	....	....	....	....
	Torpedo Nizhny	Russia	5	0	2	2	....	....	....	2	....	....	....	....	....	....	....	....	....	....	....	....	....	....	....	....	....	....
1997-98	Moncton Wildcats	QMJHL	60	15	33	48	....	....	....	144	....	....	....	....	....	....	....	....	....	....	10	3	8	11	20	....	....	....
	Russia	WJC-A	7	0	3	3	....	....	....	6	....	....	....	....	....	....	....	....	....	....	....	....	....	....	....	....	....	....
1998-99	Moncton Wildcats	QMJHL	25	9	21	30	....	....	....	52	....	....	....	....	....	....	....	....	....	....	....	....	....	....	....	....	....	....
	Rochester Americans	AHL	31	3	7	10	....	....	....	41	....	....	....	....	....	....	....	....	....	....	....	....	....	....	....	....	....	....
	Washington Capitals	**NHL**	**5**	**0**	**0**	**0**	**0**	**0**	**0**	**0**	**0**	**0**	**0**	**4**	**0.0**	**2**	**0**	**3**	**0**	**–1**	....	....	....	....	....	....	....	....
	Cincinnati Cyclones	IHL	5	0	0	0	....	....	....	2	....	....	....	....	....	....	....	....	....	....	3	0	0	0	10	....	....	....
99-2000	**Washington Capitals**	**NHL**	**23**	**1**	**1**	**2**	**1**	**1**	**2**	**2**	**1**	**0**	**1**	**18**	**5.6**	**8**	**2**	**8**	**0**	**–2**	....	....	....	....	....	....	....	....
	Portland Pirates	AHL	53	6	9	15	....	....	....	70	....	....	....	....	....	....	....	....	....	....	....	....	....	....	....	....	....	....
	NHL Totals		**28**	**1**	**1**	**2**	**1**	**1**	**2**	**2**	**1**	**0**	**1**	**22**	**4.5**	**10**	**2**	**11**	**0**		....	....	....	....	....	....	....	....

QMJHL Second All-Star Team (1998)

Traded to **Washington** by **Buffalo** with Buffalo's 4th round compensatory choice (later traded to Calgary - Calgary selected Levente Szuper) in 2000 Entry Draft for Joe Juneau and Washington's 3rd round choice (Tim Preston) in 1999 Entry Draft, March 22, 1999.

• THEBERGE, Greg

Greg Ray D – R. 5'10", 185 lbs. b: Peterborough, Ont., 9/3/1959. Washington's 5th, 109th overall, in 1979.

Season	Club	League	GP	G	A	Pts	AG	AA	APts	PIM	PP	SH	GW	S	%	TGF	PGF	TGA	PGA	+/–	GP	G	A	Pts	PIM	PP	SH	GW
1975-76	Wexford Raiders	OJHL	36	15	19	34	....	....	....	40	....	....	....	....	....	....	....	....	....	....	....	....	....	....	....	....	....	....
1976-77	Peterborough Petes	OMJHL	65	10	22	32	....	....	....	47	....	....	....	....	....	....	....	....	....	....	4	1	1	2	0	....	....	....
1977-78	Peterborough Petes	OMJHL	66	13	54	67	....	....	....	88	....	....	....	....	....	....	....	....	....	....	19	3	12	15	18	....	....	....
	Peterborough Petes	Mem-Cup	5	3	0	3	....	....	....	4	....	....	....	....	....	....	....	....	....	....	....	....	....	....	....	....	....	....
1978-79	Peterborough Petes	OMJHL	63	20	60	80	....	....	....	90	....	....	....	....	....	....	....	....	....	....	19	8	9	17	40	....	....	....
	Peterborough Petes	Mem-Cup	5	0	0	0	....	....	....	2	....	....	....	....	....	....	....	....	....	....	....	....	....	....	....	....	....	....
1979-80	**Washington Capitals**	**NHL**	**12**	**0**	**1**	**1**	**0**	**1**	**1**	**0**	**0**	**0**	**0**	**21**	**0.0**	**9**	**5**	**7**	**0**	**–3**	....	....	....	....	....	....	....	....
	Hershey Bears	AHL	58	7	22	29	....	....	....	31	....	....	....	....	....	....	....	....	....	....	16	5	6	11	18	....	....	....
1980-81	**Washington Capitals**	**NHL**	**1**	**1**	**0**	**1**	**1**	**0**	**1**	**0**	**0**	**0**	**0**	**1**	**100.0**	**1**	**0**	**3**	**0**	**–2**	....	....	....	....	....	....	....	....
	Hershey Bears	AHL	78	12	53	65	....	....	....	117	....	....	....	....	....	....	....	....	....	....	10	0	4	4	12	....	....	....
1981-82	**Washington Capitals**	**NHL**	**57**	**5**	**32**	**37**	**4**	**21**	**25**	**49**	**2**	**0**	**0**	**150**	**3.3**	**90**	**29**	**71**	**2**	**–8**	....	....	....	....	....	....	....	....
1982-83	**Washington Capitals**	**NHL**	**70**	**8**	**28**	**36**	**7**	**19**	**26**	**20**	**7**	**0**	**1**	**136**	**5.9**	**90**	**53**	**40**	**0**	**–3**	**4**	**0**	**1**	**1**	**0**	**0**	**0**	**0**
	Hershey Bears	AHL	6	1	5	6	....	....	....	2	....	....	....	....	....	....	....	....	....	....	....	....	....	....	....	....	....	....
1983-84	**Washington Capitals**	**NHL**	**13**	**1**	**2**	**3**	**1**	**1**	**2**	**4**	**1**	**0**	**0**	**19**	**5.3**	**7**	**5**	**6**	**0**	**–4**	....	....	....	....	....	....	....	....
	Hershey Bears	AHL	41	3	27	30	....	....	....	25	....	....	....	....	....	....	....	....	....	....	....	....	....	....	....	....	....	....
1984-85	EHC Olten	Switz-2	14	8	11	19	....	....	....	....	....	....	....	....	....	....	....	....	....	....	....	....	....	....	....	....	....	....
1985-86	EV Zug	Switz-2	STATISTICS NOT AVAILABLE																									
1986-87	Augsburger EV	Germany-2	16	8	23	31	....	....	....	18	....	....	....	....	....	....	....	....	....	....	....	....	....	....	....	....	....	....
	NHL Totals		**153**	**15**	**63**	**78**	**13**	**42**	**55**	**73**	**10**	**0**	**1**	**327**	**4.6**	**197**	**92**	**127**	**2**		**4**	**0**	**1**	**1**	**0**	**0**	**0**	**0**

OHA First All-Star Team (1979) • AHL Second All-Star Team (1981)

• THELIN, Mats

D – L. 5'10", 185 lbs. b: Stockholm, Sweden, 3/30/1961. Boston's 6th, 140th overall, in 1981.

Season	Club	League	GP	G	A	Pts	AG	AA	APts	PIM	PP	SH	GW	S	%	TGF	PGF	TGA	PGA	+/–	GP	G	A	Pts	PIM	PP	SH	GW
1980-81	AIK Solna Stockholm	Sweden	9	0	0	0	....	....	....	4	....	....	....	....	....	....	....	....	....	....	5	0	0	0	6	....	....	....
1981-82	AIK Solna Stockholm	DN-Cup	4	0	1	1	....	....	....	....	....	....	....	....	....	....	....	....	....	....	....	....	....	....	....	....	....	....
	AIK Solna Stockholm	Sweden-2	36	2	2	4	....	....	....	28	....	....	....	....	....	....	....	....	....	....	7	0	1	1	16	....	....	....
	Sweden	WEC-A	10	0	0	0	....	....	....	8	....	....	....	....	....	....	....	....	....	....	....	....	....	....	....	....	....	....
1982-83	AIK Solna Stockholm	Sweden	28	6	4	10	....	....	....	50	....	....	....	....	....	....	....	....	....	....	3	1	1	2	4	....	....	....
	Sweden	WEC-A	5	0	3	3	....	....	....	4	....	....	....	....	....	....	....	....	....	....	....	....	....	....	....	....	....	....
1983-84	AIK Solna Stockholm	Sweden	16	4	1	5	....	....	....	20	....	....	....	....	....	....	....	....	....	....	....	....	....	....	....	....	....	....
	Sweden	Olympics	7	0	1	1	....	....	....	4	....	....	....	....	....	....	....	....	....	....	....	....	....	....	....	....	....	....
1984-85	Sweden	Can-Cup	8	1	3	4	....	....	....	14	....	....	....	....	....	....	....	....	....	....	....	....	....	....	....	....	....	....
	Boston Bruins	**NHL**	**73**	**5**	**13**	**18**	**4**	**9**	**13**	**9**	**0**	**0**	**2**	**91**	**5.5**	**82**	**7**	**81**	**15**	**9**	**5**	**0**	**0**	**0**	**6**	**0**	**0**	**0**
1985-86	**Boston Bruins**	**NHL**	**31**	**2**	**3**	**5**	**2**	**2**	**4**	**29**	**1**	**0**	**0**	**29**	**6.9**	**28**	**1**	**41**	**17**	**3**	....	....	....	....	....	....	....	....
	Moncton Golden Flames	AHL	2	0	1	1	....	....	....	0	....	....	....	....	....	....	....	....	....	....	....	....	....	....	....	....	....	....
1986-87	**Boston Bruins**	**NHL**	**59**	**1**	**3**	**4**	**1**	**2**	**3**	**69**	**0**	**0**	**0**	**39**	**2.6**	**33**	**0**	**43**	**2**	**–8**	....	....	....	....	....	....	....	....
1987-88	AIK Solna Stockholm	Sweden	39	2	8	10	....	....	....	56	....	....	....	....	....	....	....	....	....	....	1	0	0	0	0	....	....	....
1988-89	AIK Solna Stockholm	Sweden	38	6	16	22	....	....	....	62	....	....	....	....	....	....	....	....	....	....	2	0	2	2	0	....	....	....
1989-90	AIK Solna Stockholm	Sweden	15	3	4	7	....	....	....	20	....	....	....	....	....	....	....	....	....	....	2	0	0	0	2	....	....	....
1990-91	AIK Solna Stockholm	Sweden	37	1	3	4	....	....	....	54	....	....	....	....	....	....	....	....	....	....	....	....	....	....	....	....	....	....
1991-92	AIK Solna Stockholm	Sweden	36	0	5	5	....	....	....	79	....	....	....	....	....	....	....	....	....	....	3	0	0	0	2	....	....	....
1992-93	AIK Solna Stockholm	Sweden	22	0	3	3	....	....	....	22	....	....	....	....	....	....	....	....	....	....	....	....	....	....	....	....	....	....
1993-94	AIK Solna Stockholm	Sweden-2	38	8	9	17	....	....	....	46	....	....	....	....	....	....	....	....	....	....	9	0	2	2	12	....	....	....
	NHL Totals		**163**	**8**	**19**	**27**	**7**	**13**	**20**	**107**	**1**	**0**	**2**	**159**	**5.0**	**143**	**8**	**165**	**34**		**5**	**0**	**0**	**0**	**6**	**0**	**0**	**0**

• THELVEN, Michael

D – R. 5'11", 185 lbs. b: Stockholm, Sweden, 1/7/1961. Boston's 8th, 186th overall, in 1980.

Season	Club	League	GP	G	A	Pts	AG	AA	APts	PIM	PP	SH	GW	S	%	TGF	PGF	TGA	PGA	+/–	GP	G	A	Pts	PIM	PP	SH	GW
1978-79	Djurgardens IF Stockholm	Sweden	10	0	1	1	....	....	....	8	....	....	....	....	....	....	....	....	....	....	....	....	....	....	....	....	....	....
1979-80	Djurgardens IF Stockholm	Sweden-Jr.	STATISTICS NOT AVAILABLE																									
1980-81	Djurgardens IF Stockholm	DN-Cup	3	0	0	0	....	....	....	0	....	....	....	....	....	....	....	....	....	....	....	....	....	....	....	....	....	....
	Djurgardens IF Stockholm	Sweden	28	2	4	6	....	....	....	38	....	....	....	....	....	....	....	....	....	....	....	....	....	....	....	....	....	....
	Sweden	WJC-A	5	2	1	3	....	....	....	4	....	....	....	....	....	....	....	....	....	....	....	....	....	....	....	....	....	....
1981-82	Djurgardens IF Stockholm	DN-Cup	4	0	1	....	....	....	....	....	....	....	....	....	....	....	....	....	....	....	....	....	....	....	....	....	....	....
	Djurgardens IF Stockholm	Sweden	34	5	3	8	....	....	....	53	....	....	....	....	....	....	....	....	....	....	6	2	1	3	2	....	....	....
1982-83	Djurgardens IF Stockholm	Sweden	30	3	14	17	....	....	....	50	....	....	....	....	....	....	....	....	....	....	7	1	2	3	12	....	....	....
1983-84	Djurgardens IF Stockholm	Sweden	27	6	7	13	....	....	....	51	....	....	....	....	....	....	....	....	....	....	5	1	1	2	6	....	....	....
	Sweden	Olympics	4	1	3	4	....	....	....	4	....	....	....	....	....	....	....	....	....	....	....	....	....	....	....	....	....	....

			REGULAR SEASON																		PLAYOFFS							
Season	Club	League	GP	G	A	Pts	AG	AA	APts	PIM	PP	SH	GW	S	%	TGF	PGF	TGA	PGA	+/–	GP	G	A	Pts	PIM	PP	SH	GW
1984-85	Sweden	Can-Cup	8	0	3	3				14																		
	Djurgardens IF Stockholm	Sweden	33	8	13	21				54											8	0	2	2	2			
	Sweden	WEC-A	10	0	2	2				10																		
1985-86	**Boston Bruins**	**NHL**	60	6	20	26	5	13	18	48	1	0	0	108	5.6	77	21	73	24	7	3	0	0	0	0	0	0	0
1986-87	**Boston Bruins**	**NHL**	34	5	15	20	4	11	15	18	3	0	0	60	8.3	47	12	38	1	–2								
1987-88	Sweden	Can-Cup	6	0	3	3				10																		
	Boston Bruins	**NHL**	67	6	25	31	5	18	23	57	1	0	1	106	5.7	74	17	61	16	12	21	3	3	6	26	1	0	0
1988-89	**Boston Bruins**	**NHL**	40	3	18	21	3	13	16	71	1	1	0	68	4.4	57	19	42	14	10	10	1	7	8	8	0	0	1
1989-90	**Boston Bruins**	**NHL**	6	0	2	2	0	1	1	23	0	0	0	8	0.0	5	0	2	0	3								
	NHL Totals		207	20	80	100	17	56	73	217	6	1	1	350	5.7	260	69	216	55		34	4	10	14	34	1	0	1

Swedish World All-Star Team (1984, 1985)

• THERIEN, Chris

Chris B. D – L. 6′4″, 230 lbs. b: Ottawa, Ont., 12/14/1971. Philadelphia's 7th, 47th overall, in 1990.

Season	Club	League	GP	G	A	Pts	AG	AA	APts	PIM	PP	SH	GW	S	%	TGF	PGF	TGA	PGA	+/–	GP	G	A	Pts	PIM	PP	SH	GW
1988-89	Ottawa Jr. Senators	OJHL	8	3	1	4				22																		
1989-90	Ottawa Jr. Senators	OJHL	3	0	2	2				2																		
	Northwood Huskies	Hi-School	31	35	37	72				54																		
1990-91	Providence College	H-East	36	4	18	22				36																		
1991-92	Providence College	H-East	36	16	25	41				38																		
1992-93	Providence College	H-East	33	8	11	19				52																		
	Canada	Nat-Team	8	1	4	5				8																		
1993-94	Canada	Nat-Team	59	7	15	22				46																		
	Canada	Olympics	4	0	0	0				4																		
	Hershey Bears	AHL	6	0	0	0				2																		
1994-95	Hershey Bears	AHL	34	3	13	16				27																		
	Philadelphia Flyers	**NHL**	48	3	10	13	5	15	20	38	1	0	0	53	5.7	44	5	37	6	8	15	0	0	0	10	0	0	0
1995-96	**Philadelphia Flyers**	**NHL**	82	6	17	23	6	14	20	89	3	0	1	123	4.9	75	10	61	12	16	12	0	0	0	18	0	0	0
1996-97	**Philadelphia Flyers**	**NHL**	71	2	22	24	2	20	22	64	0	0	0	107	1.9	71	8	52	16	27	19	1	6	7	6	0	0	1
1997-98	**Philadelphia Flyers**	**NHL**	78	3	16	19	4	16	20	80	1	0	1	102	2.9	68	12	71	20	5	5	0	1	1	4	0	0	0
1998-99	**Philadelphia Flyers**	**NHL**	74	3	15	18	4	14	18	48	1	0	0	115	2.6	65	1	66	18	16	6	0	0	0	6	0	0	0
99-2000	**Philadelphia Flyers**	**NHL**	80	4	9	13	4	8	12	66	1	0	1	126	3.2	66	3	67	15	11	18	0	1	1	12	0	0	0
	NHL Totals		433	21	89	110	25	87	112	385	7	0	3	626	3.4	389	39	354	87		75	1	8	9	56	0	0	1

Hockey East Second All-Star Team (1993) • NHL All-Rookie Team (1995)

• THERRIEN, Gaston

D – R. 5′10″, 185 lbs. b: Montreal, Que., 5/27/1960. Quebec's 5th, 129th overall, in 1980.

Season	Club	League	GP	G	A	Pts	AG	AA	APts	PIM	PP	SH	GW	S	%	TGF	PGF	TGA	PGA	+/–	GP	G	A	Pts	PIM	PP	SH	GW
1976-77	Cap-de-la-Madelein Barons	QJHL	60	30	37	67																						
1977-78	Quebec Remparts	QMJHL	72	17	60	77				73																		
1978-79	Quebec Remparts	QMJHL	65	10	52	62				126											6	1	5	6	24			
1979-80	Quebec Remparts	QMJHL	71	39	86	125				152											3	1	2	3	6			
1980-81	**Quebec Nordiques**	**NHL**	3	0	1	1	0	1	1	2	0	0	0	10	0.0	4	1	4	0	–1								
	Rochester Americans	AHL	18	2	10	12				6																		
	HC Villard-de-Lans	France	STATISTICS NOT AVAILABLE																									
1981-82	**Quebec Nordiques**	**NHL**	14	0	7	7	0	5	5	6	0	0	0	15	0.0	17	4	11	0	2	9	0	1	1	4	0	0	0
	Fredericton Express	AHL	61	11	42	53				79																		
1982-83	**Quebec Nordiques**	**NHL**	5	0	0	0	0	0	0	4	0	0	0	5	0.0	1	1	4	0	–4								
	Fredericton Express	AHL	41	3	10	13				60																		
	Erie Blades	ACHL	3	1	4	5				0																		
1983-84	HC Villard-de-Lans	France	36	47	24	71																						
1984-85	SC Bern	Switz-2	STATISTICS NOT AVAILABLE																									
1985-86	SC Bern	Switz-2	STATISTICS NOT AVAILABLE																									
1986-87	HC Villard-de-Lans	France	29	36	48	84																						
1987-88	HC Villard-de-Lans	France	28	18	31	49				45																		
1988-89	HC Villard-de-Lans	France	37	25	31	56				50											2	1	2	3	6			
1989-90	HC Villard-de-Lans	France	33	12	17	29				75																		
1990-91	ASG Tours	France	22	9	20	29				24											3	1	0	1	8			
1991-92	HC Viry	France	12	7	11	18				28											16	10	10	20	14			
	NHL Totals		22	0	8	8	0	6	6	12	0	0	0	30	0.0	22	6	19	0		9	0	1	1	4	0	0	0

QMJHL First All-Star Team (1980)

• THIBAUDEAU, Gilles

C – L. 5′10″, 165 lbs. b: Montreal, Que., 3/4/1963.

Season	Club	League	GP	G	A	Pts	AG	AA	APts	PIM	PP	SH	GW	S	%	TGF	PGF	TGA	PGA	+/–	GP	G	A	Pts	PIM	PP	SH	GW
1983-84	St-Antoine Saints	QJHL-B	38	63	77	140				146																		
1984-85	Sherbrooke Canadiens	AHL	7	2	4	6				2																		
	Flint Generals	IHL	71	52	45	97				81											7	3	1	4	18			
1985-86	Sherbrooke Canadiens	AHL	61	15	23	38				20																		
1986-87	**Montreal Canadiens**	**NHL**	9	1	3	4	1	2	3	0	0	0	0	10	10.0	6	0	1	0	5								
	Sherbrooke Canadiens	AHL	62	27	40	67				26																		
1987-88	**Montreal Canadiens**	**NHL**	17	5	6	11	4	4	8	0	2	0	1	25	20.0	16	5	5	0	6	8	3	3	6	2	1	0	0
	Sherbrooke Canadiens	AHL	59	39	57	96				45																		
1988-89	**Montreal Canadiens**	**NHL**	32	6	6	12	5	4	9	6	1	0	0	42	14.3	25	6	14	0	5								
1989-90	**New York Islanders**	**NHL**	20	4	4	8	3	3	6	17	0	0	0	23	17.4	11	1	8	0	2								
	Springfield Indians	AHL	6	5	8	13				0																		
	Toronto Maple Leafs	**NHL**	21	7	11	18	6	8	14	13	3	0	2	44	15.9	31	13	12	0	6								
	Newmarket Saints	AHL	10	7	13	20				4																		
1990-91	**Toronto Maple Leafs**	**NHL**	20	2	7	9	2	5	7	4	0	0	0	36	5.6	19	3	26	3	–7								
	Newmarket Saints	AHL	60	34	37	71				28																		
1991-92	HC Lugano	Switz.	33	29	17	46				12											4	6	3	9	2			
1992-93	HC Davos	Switz-2	36	*51	25	76				18											7	7	4	11	6			
1993-94	HC Davos	Switz-2	36	32	15	47				8											4	2	0	2	6			
1994-95	HC Davos	Switz.	36	17	20	37				24											5	5	4	9	0			
	Canada	Nat-Team	3	1	1	2				0																		
1995-96	SC Rapperswil-Jona	Switz.	36	26	27	53				12											4	4	1	5	4			
1996-97	SC Rapperswil-Jona	Switz.	45	25	16	41				26											3	0	1	1	25			
1997-98	SC Rapperswil-Jona	Switz.	40	18	29	47				32											7	6	3	9	2			
1998-99	HC Sierre	Switz-2	35	21	25	46				26											3	2	1	3	2			
99-2000	HC Sierre	Switz-2	35	23	19	42				40																		
	NHL Totals		119	25	37	62	21	26	47	40	6	0	3	180	13.9	108	28	66	3		8	3	3	6	2	1	0	0

IHL Second All-Star Team (1985) • Won Garry F. Longman Memorial Trophy (Top Rookie - IHL) (1985)

Signed as a free agent by **Montreal**, October 9, 1984. Signed as a free agent by **NY Islanders**, September, 1989. Traded to **Toronto** by **NY Islanders** with Mike Stevens for Jack Capuano, Paul Gagne and Derek Laxdal, December 20, 1989.

• THIFFAULT, Leo

Leo Edmond LW – L. 5′10″, 175 lbs. b: Drummondville, Que., 12/16/1944.

Season	Club	League	GP	G	A	Pts	AG	AA	APts	PIM	PP	SH	GW	S	%	TGF	PGF	TGA	PGA	+/–	GP	G	A	Pts	PIM	PP	SH	GW
1961-62	Montreal Nationale	MMJHL	STATISTICS NOT AVAILABLE																									
	Montreal Nationale	Mem-Cup	2	0	0	0				8																		
1962-63	Montreal Jr. Canadiens	OHA-Jr.	50	9	9	18				64											10	1	1	2	2			
1963-64	Montreal Jr. Canadiens	OHA-Jr.	55	23	38	61				44											17	7	12	19	22			
1964-65	Peterborough Petes	OHA-Jr.	56	33	52	85				52											12	4	10	14	8			
	Quebec Aces	AHL	2	0	0	0				0																		
1965-66	Houston Apollos	CPHL	69	19	26	45				55																		

			REGULAR SEASON																		PLAYOFFS							
Season	Club	League	GP	G	A	Pts	AG	AA	APts	PIM	PP	SH	GW	S	%	TGF	PGF	TGA	PGA	+/–	GP	G	A	Pts	PIM	PP	SH	GW
1966-67	Houston Apollos	CPHL	47	7	15	22	....	....	....	37	....	....	....	....	....	....	....	....	....	....	2	0	0	0	0	....	....	....
	Cleveland Barons	AHL	5	1	1	2	....	....	....	4	....	....	....	....	....	....	....	....	....	....	....	....	....	....	....	....	....	....
1967-68	Memphis South Stars	CPHL	66	22	32	54	....	....	....	52	....	....	....	....	....	....	....	....	....	....	3	0	1	1	6	....	....	....
	Minnesota North Stars	**NHL**	....	....	....	....	....	....	....	....	....	....	....	....	....	....	....	....	....	....	**5**	**0**	**0**	**0**	**0**	**0**	**0**	**0**
1968-69	Phoenix Roadrunners	WHL	70	16	24	40	....	....	....	25	....	....	....	....	....	....	....	....	....	....	....	....	....	....	....	....	....	....
1969-1972			OUT OF HOCKEY – RETIRED																									
1972-73	Phoenix Roadrunners	WHL	70	12	35	47	....	....	....	57	....	....	....	....	....	....	....	....	....	....	5	1	0	1	5	....	....	....
1973-74	Tulsa Oilers	CHL	1	0	1	1	....	....	....	0	....	....	....	....	....	....	....	....	....	....	....	....	....	....	....	....	....	....
	Phoenix Roadrunners	WHL	35	5	6	11	....	....	....	26	....	....	....	....	....	....	....	....	....	....	2	0	0	0	0	....	....	....
	NHL Totals		....	....	....	....	....	....	....	....	....	....	....	....	....	....	....	....	....	....	**5**	**0**	**0**	**0**	**0**	**0**	**0**	**0**

Rights traded to **Minnesota** by **Montreal** with Bill Plager and the rights to Barrie Meissner for Bryan Watson, June 6, 1967. Traded to **Phoenix** (WHL) by **Minnesota** with Bob Charlebois to complete deal for Walt McKechnie (February 17, 1968), June, 1968.

• THOMAS, Reg

Reginald Kenneth LW – L. 5′10″, 185 lbs. b: Lambeth, Ont., 4/21/1953. Chicago's 2nd, 29th overall, in 1973.

Season	Club	League	GP	G	A	Pts	AG	AA	APts	PIM	PP	SH	GW	S	%	TGF	PGF	TGA	PGA	+/–	GP	G	A	Pts	PIM	PP	SH	GW
1969-70	Glanworth Selects	OMHA	STATISTICS NOT AVAILABLE																									
1970-71	London Knights	OHA-Jr.	58	35	35	70	....	....	....	29	....	....	....	....	....	....	....	....	....	....	4	2	1	3	2	....	....	....
1971-72	London Knights	OMJHL	61	49	55	104	....	....	....	38	....	....	....	....	....	....	....	....	....	....	7	5	7	12	6	....	....	....
1972-73	London Knights	OMJHL	61	52	83	135	....	....	....	41	....	....	....	....	....	....	....	....	....	....	....	....	....	....	....	....	....	....
1973-74	Los Angeles Sharks	WHA	72	14	21	35	....	....	....	22	....	....	....	....	....	....	....	....	....	....	....	....	....	....	....	....	....	....
1974-75	Michigan-Baltimore Blades	WHA	50	8	13	21	....	....	....	42	....	....	....	....	....	....	....	....	....	....	....	....	....	....	....	....	....	....
1975-76	Indianapolis Racers	WHA	80	23	17	40	....	....	....	23	....	....	....	....	....	....	....	....	....	....	7	1	0	1	4	....	....	....
1976-77	Indianapolis Racers	WHA	79	25	30	55	....	....	....	34	....	....	....	....	....	....	....	....	....	....	9	7	9	16	4	....	....	....
1977-78	Indianapolis Racers	WHA	49	15	16	31	....	....	....	44	....	....	....	....	....	....	....	....	....	....	....	....	....	....	....	....	....	....
	Cincinnati Stingers	WHA	18	4	2	6	....	....	....	12	....	....	....	....	....	....	....	....	....	....	....	....	....	....	....	....	....	....
1978-79	Cincinnati Stingers	WHA	80	32	39	71	....	....	....	22	....	....	....	....	....	....	....	....	....	....	3	1	1	2	0	....	....	....
1979-80	**Quebec Nordiques**	**NHL**	**39**	**9**	**7**	**16**	**8**	**5**	**13**	**6**	**2**	**0**	**0**	**89**	**10.1**	**24**	**4**	**28**	**3**	**–5**	....	....	....	....	....	....	....	....
	New Brunswick Hawks	AHL	31	20	20	40	....	....	....	18	....	....	....	....	....	....	....	....	....	....	....	....	....	....	....	....	....	....
1980-81	Nova Scotia Voyageurs	AHL	74	36	43	79	....	....	....	90	....	....	....	....	....	....	....	....	....	....	4	1	6	7	2	....	....	....
1981-82	Cincinnati Tigers	CHL	80	47	63	110	....	....	....	55	....	....	....	....	....	....	....	....	....	....	4	2	2	4	2	....	....	....
1982-83	St. Catharines Saints	AHL	80	35	57	92	....	....	....	22	....	....	....	....	....	....	....	....	....	....	....	....	....	....	....	....	....	....
1983-84	Montana Magic	CHL	3	0	0	0	....	....	....	0	....	....	....	....	....	....	....	....	....	....	....	....	....	....	....	....	....	....
	WAT Stadlau	Austria	28	29	33	62	....	....	....	....	....	....	....	....	....	....	....	....	....	....	10	11	7	18	....	....	....	....
1984-85	WAT Stadlau	Austria	34	24	30	54	....	....	....	20	....	....	....	....	....	....	....	....	....	....	....	....	....	....	....	....	....	....
	NHL Totals		**39**	**9**	**7**	**16**	**8**	**5**	**13**	**6**	**2**	**0**	**0**	**89**	**10.1**	**24**	**4**	**28**	**3**		....	....	....	....	....	....	....	....
	Other Major League Totals		428	121	138	259	....	....	....	199	....	....	....	....	....	....	....	....	....	....	19	9	10	19	8	....	....	....

OMJHL First All-Star Team (1973) • CHL First All-Star Team (1982) • AHL First All-Star Team (1983)

Selected by **LA Sharks** (WHA) in 1973 WHA Professional Player Draft, June, 1973. Transferred to **Michigan** (WHA) after **LA Sharks** (WHA) franchise relocated, May, 1974. Claimed by **Indianapolis** (WHA) from **Michigan-Baltimore** (WHA) in WHA Dispersal Draft, June 19, 1975. Traded to **Cincinnati** (WHA) by **Indianapolis** (WHA) with Darryl Maggs for Claude Larose and Rich Leduc, February, 1978. Claimed by **Edmonton** from **Chicago** in Expansion Draft, June 13, 1979. Traded to **Toronto** by **Edmonton** for Toronto's 6th round choice (Steve Smith) in 1981 Entry Draft, August 22, 1979. Traded to **Quebec** by **Toronto** for Dave Farrish and Terry Martin, December 13, 1979. Signed as a free agent by **Toronto**, July 21, 1981.

• THOMAS, Scott

John Scott RW – R. 6′2″, 200 lbs. b: Buffalo, NY, 1/18/1970. Buffalo's 2nd, 56th overall, in 1989.

Season	Club	League	GP	G	A	Pts	AG	AA	APts	PIM	PP	SH	GW	S	%	TGF	PGF	TGA	PGA	+/–	GP	G	A	Pts	PIM	PP	SH	GW
1987-88	Nichols High School	Hi-School	16	23	39	62	....	....	....	62	....	....	....	....	....	....	....	....	....	....	....	....	....	....	....	....	....	....
1988-89	Nichols High School	Hi-School	17	38	52	90	....	....	....	....	....	....	....	....	....	....	....	....	....	....	....	....	....	....	....	....	....	....
1989-90	Clarkson University	ECAC	34	19	13	32	....	....	....	95	....	....	....	....	....	....	....	....	....	....	....	....	....	....	....	....	....	....
1990-91	Clarkson University	ECAC	40	28	14	42	....	....	....	89	....	....	....	....	....	....	....	....	....	....	....	....	....	....	....	....	....	....
1991-92	Clarkson University	ECAC	29	22	20	42	....	....	....	57	....	....	....	....	....	....	....	....	....	....	....	....	....	....	....	....	....	....
	Rochester Americans	AHL	....	....	....	....	....	....	....	....	....	....	....	....	....	....	....	....	....	....	9	0	1	1	17	....	....	....
1992-93	**Buffalo Sabres**	**NHL**	**7**	**1**	**1**	**2**	**1**	**1**	**2**	**15**	**0**	**0**	**0**	**4**	**25.0**	**3**	**0**	**1**	**0**	**2**	....	....	....	....	....	....	....	....
	Rochester Americans	AHL	65	32	27	59	....	....	....	38	....	....	....	....	....	....	....	....	....	....	17	8	5	13	6	....	....	....
1993-94	**Buffalo Sabres**	**NHL**	**32**	**2**	**2**	**4**	**2**	**2**	**4**	**8**	**1**	**0**	**0**	**26**	**7.7**	**9**	**2**	**13**	**0**	**–6**	....	....	....	....	....	....	....	....
	Rochester Americans	AHL	11	4	5	9	....	....	....	0	....	....	....	....	....	....	....	....	....	....	....	....	....	....	....	....	....	....
1994-95	Rochester Americans	AHL	55	21	25	46	....	....	....	115	....	....	....	....	....	....	....	....	....	....	5	4	0	4	4	....	....	....
1995-96	Cincinnati Cyclones	IHL	78	32	28	60	....	....	....	54	....	....	....	....	....	....	....	....	....	....	17	*13	2	15	4	....	....	....
1996-97	Cincinnati Cyclones	IHL	71	32	29	61	....	....	....	46	....	....	....	....	....	....	....	....	....	....	3	0	0	0	0	....	....	....
1997-98	Detroit Vipers	IHL	44	11	16	27	....	....	....	18	....	....	....	....	....	....	....	....	....	....	....	....	....	....	....	....	....	....
	Manitoba Moose	IHL	26	12	4	16	....	....	....	8	....	....	....	....	....	....	....	....	....	....	3	0	1	1	2	....	....	....
1998-99	Manitoba Moose	IHL	78	45	25	70	....	....	....	32	....	....	....	....	....	....	....	....	....	....	5	3	4	7	4	....	....	....
99-2000	Long Beach Ice Dogs	IHL	52	15	16	31	....	....	....	18	....	....	....	....	....	....	....	....	....	....	6	2	1	3	6	....	....	....
	NHL Totals		**39**	**3**	**3**	**6**	**3**	**3**	**6**	**23**	**1**	**0**	**0**	**30**	**10.0**	**12**	**2**	**14**	**0**		....	....	....	....	....	....	....	....

Signed as a free agent by **LA Kings**, July 30, 1999.

• THOMAS, Steve

Stephen Anthony LW – L. 5′11″, 185 lbs. b: Stockport, England, 7/15/1963.

Season	Club	League	GP	G	A	Pts	AG	AA	APts	PIM	PP	SH	GW	S	%	TGF	PGF	TGA	PGA	+/–	GP	G	A	Pts	PIM	PP	SH	GW
1980-81	Markham Waxers	OJHL	42	22	25	47	....	....	....	76	....	....	....	....	....	....	....	....	....	....	....	....	....	....	....	....	....	....
	Toronto Marlboros	OMJHL	1	0	0	0	....	....	....	0	....	....	....	....	....	....	....	....	....	....	....	....	....	....	....	....	....	....
1981-82	Markham Waxers	OJHL	48	68	57	125	....	....	....	113	....	....	....	....	....	....	....	....	....	....	....	....	....	....	....	....	....	....
	Toronto Marlboros	OHL	1	0	0	0	....	....	....	0	....	....	....	....	....	....	....	....	....	....	....	....	....	....	....	....	....	....
1982-83	Toronto Marlboros	OHL	61	18	20	38	....	....	....	42	....	....	....	....	....	....	....	....	....	....	....	....	....	....	....	....	....	....
1983-84	Toronto Marlboros	OHL	70	51	54	105	....	....	....	77	....	....	....	....	....	....	....	....	....	....	....	....	....	....	....	....	....	....
1984-85	**Toronto Maple Leafs**	**NHL**	**18**	**1**	**1**	**2**	**1**	**1**	**2**	**2**	**0**	**0**	**0**	**26**	**3.8**	**6**	**3**	**16**	**0**	**–13**	....	....	....	....	....	....	....	....
	St. Catharines Saints	AHL	64	42	48	90	....	....	....	56	....	....	....	....	....	....	....	....	....	....	....	....	....	....	....	....	....	....
1985-86	**Toronto Maple Leafs**	**NHL**	**65**	**20**	**37**	**57**	**16**	**25**	**41**	**36**	**5**	**0**	**5**	**197**	**10.2**	**77**	**17**	**75**	**0**	**–15**	**10**	**6**	**8**	**14**	**9**	**3**	**0**	**0**
	St. Catharines Saints	AHL	19	18	14	32	....	....	....	35	....	....	....	....	....	....	....	....	....	....	....	....	....	....	....	....	....	....
1986-87	**Toronto Maple Leafs**	**NHL**	**78**	**35**	**27**	**62**	**30**	**20**	**50**	**114**	**3**	**0**	**7**	**245**	**14.3**	**91**	**16**	**78**	**0**	**–3**	**13**	**2**	**3**	**5**	**13**	**0**	**0**	**0**
1987-88	**Chicago Blackhawks**	**NHL**	**30**	**13**	**13**	**26**	**11**	**9**	**20**	**40**	**5**	**0**	**3**	**69**	**18.8**	**41**	**17**	**23**	**0**	**1**	**3**	**1**	**2**	**3**	**6**	**0**	**0**	**0**
1988-89	**Chicago Blackhawks**	**NHL**	**45**	**21**	**19**	**40**	**18**	**13**	**31**	**69**	**8**	**0**	**0**	**124**	**16.9**	**51**	**19**	**44**	**10**	**–2**	**12**	**3**	**5**	**8**	**10**	**1**	**0**	**2**
1989-90	**Chicago Blackhawks**	**NHL**	**76**	**40**	**30**	**70**	**34**	**21**	**55**	**91**	**13**	**0**	**7**	**235**	**17.0**	**97**	**29**	**71**	**0**	**–3**	**20**	**7**	**6**	**13**	**33**	**1**	**0**	**3**
1990-91	**Chicago Blackhawks**	**NHL**	**69**	**19**	**35**	**54**	**17**	**27**	**44**	**129**	**2**	**0**	**3**	**192**	**9.9**	**66**	**13**	**45**	**0**	**8**	**6**	**1**	**2**	**3**	**15**	**0**	**0**	**0**
	Canada	WEC-A	10	5	3	8	....	....	....	12	....	....	....	....	....	....	....	....	....	....	....	....	....	....	....	....	....	....
1991-92	**Chicago Blackhawks**	**NHL**	**11**	**2**	**6**	**8**	**2**	**5**	**7**	**26**	**0**	**0**	**1**	**35**	**5.7**	**11**	**3**	**15**	**4**	**–3**	....	....	....	....	....	....	....	....
	New York Islanders	**NHL**	**71**	**28**	**42**	**70**	**25**	**32**	**57**	**71**	**3**	**0**	**2**	**210**	**13.3**	**93**	**33**	**52**	**3**	**11**	....	....	....	....	....	....	....	....
	Canada	WC-A	5	2	2	4	....	....	....	4	....	....	....	....	....	....	....	....	....	....	....	....	....	....	....	....	....	....
1992-93	**New York Islanders**	**NHL**	**79**	**37**	**50**	**87**	**31**	**34**	**65**	**111**	**12**	**0**	**7**	**264**	**14.0**	**131**	**58**	**70**	**0**	**3**	**18**	**9**	**8**	**17**	**37**	**0**	**0**	**0**
1993-94	**New York Islanders**	**NHL**	**78**	**42**	**33**	**75**	**39**	**26**	**65**	**139**	**17**	**0**	**5**	**249**	**16.9**	**103**	**45**	**68**	**1**	**–9**	**4**	**1**	**0**	**1**	**8**	**1**	**0**	**0**
	Canada	WC-A	6	1	5	6	....	....	....	0	....	....	....	....	....	....	....	....	....	....	....	....	....	....	....	....	....	....
1994-95	**New York Islanders**	**NHL**	**47**	**11**	**15**	**26**	**19**	**22**	**41**	**60**	**3**	**0**	**2**	**133**	**8.3**	**33**	**13**	**34**	**0**	**–14**	....	....	....	....	....	....	....	....
1995-96	**New Jersey Devils**	**NHL**	**81**	**26**	**35**	**61**	**26**	**29**	**55**	**98**	**6**	**0**	**6**	**192**	**13.5**	**81**	**28**	**55**	**0**	**–2**	....	....	....	....	....	....	....	....
	Canada	WC-A	8	2	3	5	....	....	....	29	....	....	....	....	....	....	....	....	....	....	....	....	....	....	....	....	....	....
1996-97	**New Jersey Devils**	**NHL**	**57**	**15**	**19**	**34**	**16**	**17**	**33**	**46**	**1**	**0**	**2**	**124**	**12.1**	**48**	**10**	**29**	**0**	**9**	**10**	**1**	**1**	**2**	**18**	**0**	**0**	**0**
1997-98	**New Jersey Devils**	**NHL**	**55**	**14**	**10**	**24**	**16**	**10**	**26**	**32**	**3**	**0**	**4**	**111**	**12.6**	**38**	**9**	**25**	**0**	**4**	**6**	**0**	**3**	**3**	**2**	**0**	**0**	**0**
1998-99	**Toronto Maple Leafs**	**NHL**	**78**	**28**	**45**	**73**	**33**	**43**	**76**	**33**	**11**	**0**	**7**	**209**	**13.4**	**102**	**26**	**59**	**9**	**26**	**17**	**6**	**3**	**9**	**12**	**2**	**0**	**1**
99-2000	**Toronto Maple Leafs**	**NHL**	**81**	**26**	**37**	**63**	**29**	**34**	**63**	**68**	**9**	**0**	**9**	**151**	**17.2**	**89**	**35**	**53**	**0**	**1**	**12**	**6**	**3**	**9**	**10**	**0**	**0**	**1**
	NHL Totals		**1019**	**378**	**454**	**832**	**363**	**368**	**731**	**1165**	**101**	**0**	**70**	**2766**	**13.7**	**1158**	**374**	**812**	**27**		**131**	**43**	**44**	**87**	**173**	**8**	**0**	**7**

Won Dudley "Red" Garrett Memorial Trophy (Top Rookie - AHL) (1985) • AHL First All-Star Team (1985)

Signed as a free agent by **Toronto,** May 12, 1984. Traded to **Chicago** by **Toronto** with Rick Vaive and Bob McGill for Al Secord and Ed Olczyk, September 3, 1987. Traded to **NY Islanders** by **Chicago** with Adam Creighton for Brent Sutter and Brad Lauer, October 25, 1991. Traded to **New Jersey** by **NY Islanders** for Claude Lemieux, October 3, 1995. Signed as a free agent by **Toronto**, July 30, 1998.

• THOMLINSON, Dave

David N. LW – L. 6'1", 215 lbs. b: Edmonton, Alta., 10/22/1966. Toronto's 3rd, 43rd overall, in 1985.

			REGULAR SEASON																		PLAYOFFS							
Season	**Club**	**League**	**GP**	**G**	**A**	**Pts**	**AG**	**AA**	**APts**	**PIM**	**PP**	**SH**	**GW**	**S**	**%**	**TGF**	**PGF**	**TGA**	**PGA**	**+/–**	**GP**	**G**	**A**	**Pts**	**PIM**	**PP**	**SH**	**GW**
1982-83	Red Deer Rustlers	AJHL	STATISTICS NOT AVAILABLE																									
1983-84	Brandon Wheat Kings	WHL	41	17	12	29	....	....	....	62	....	....	....	....	....	....	....	....	....	....	12	3	2	5	24	....	....	....
1984-85	Brandon Wheat Kings	WHL	26	13	14	27	....	....	....	70	....	....	....	....	....	....	....	....	....	....	....	....	....	....	....	....	....	....
1985-86	Brandon Wheat Kings	WHL	53	25	20	45	....	....	....	116	....	....	....	....	....	....	....	....	....	....	....	....	....	....	....	....	....	....
1986-87	Brandon Wheat Kings	WHL	2	0	1	1	....	....	....	9	....	....	....	....	....	....	....	....	....	....	....	....	....	....	....	....	....	....
	Moose Jaw Warriors	WHL	70	44	36	80	....	....	....	117	....	....	....	....	....	....	....	....	....	....	9	7	3	10	19	....	....	....
1987-88	Peoria Rivermen	IHL	74	27	30	57	....	....	....	56	....	....	....	....	....	....	....	....	....	....	7	4	3	7	11	....	....	....
1988-89	Peoria Rivermen	IHL	64	27	29	56	....	....	....	154	....	....	....	....	....	....	....	....	....	....	3	0	1	1	8	....	....	....
1989-90	**St. Louis Blues**	**NHL**	**19**	**1**	**2**	**3**	**1**	**1**	**2**	**12**	**0**	**0**	**0**	**17**	**5.9**	**4**	**0**	**8**	**0**	**–4**	....	....	....	....	....	....	....	....
	Peoria Rivermen	IHL	59	27	40	67	....	....	....	87	....	....	....	....	....	....	....	....	....	....	5	1	1	2	15	....	....	....
1990-91	**St. Louis Blues**	**NHL**	**3**	**0**	**0**	**0**	**0**	**0**	**0**	**0**	**0**	**0**	**0**	**0**	**0.0**	**0**	**0**	**3**	**0**	**–3**	**9**	**3**	**1**	**4**	**4**	**1**	**0**	**1**
	Peoria Rivermen	IHL	80	53	54	107	....	....	....	107	....	....	....	....	....	....	....	....	....	....	11	6	7	13	28	....	....	....
1991-92	**Boston Bruins**	**NHL**	**12**	**0**	**1**	**1**	**0**	**1**	**1**	**17**	**0**	**0**	**0**	**12**	**0.0**	**2**	**0**	**5**	**1**	**–2**	....	....	....	....	....	....	....	....
	Maine Mariners	AHL	25	9	11	20	....	....	....	36	....	....	....	....	....	....	....	....	....	....	....	....	....	....	....	....	....	....
1992-93	Binghamton Rangers	AHL	54	25	35	60	....	....	....	61	....	....	....	....	....	....	....	....	....	....	12	2	5	7	8	....	....	....
1993-94	**Los Angeles Kings**	**NHL**	**7**	**0**	**0**	**0**	**0**	**0**	**0**	**21**	**0**	**0**	**0**	**6**	**0.0**	**0**	**0**	**6**	**0**	**–6**	....	....	....	....	....	....	....	....
	Phoenix Roadrunners	IHL	39	10	15	25	....	....	....	70	....	....	....	....	....	....	....	....	....	....	....	....	....	....	....	....	....	....
1994-95	**Los Angeles Kings**	**NHL**	**1**	**0**	**0**	**0**	**0**	**0**	**0**	**0**	**0**	**0**	**0**	**0**	**0.0**	**0**	**0**	**1**	**0**	**–1**	....	....	....	....	....	....	....	....
	Phoenix Roadrunners	IHL	77	30	40	70	....	....	....	87	....	....	....	....	....	....	....	....	....	....	9	5	3	8	8	....	....	....
1995-96	Phoenix Roadrunners	IHL	48	10	13	23	....	....	....	65	....	....	....	....	....	....	....	....	....	....	4	1	0	1	2	....	....	....
1996-97	Phoenix Roadrunners	IHL	67	16	24	40	....	....	....	40	....	....	....	....	....	....	....	....	....	....	....	....	....	....	....	....	....	....
1997-98	Manitoba Moose	IHL	28	1	4	5	....	....	....	22	....	....	....	....	....	....	....	....	....	....	....	....	....	....	....	....	....	....
	NHL Totals		**42**	**1**	**3**	**4**	**1**	**2**	**3**	**50**	**0**	**0**	**0**	**35**	**2.9**	**6**	**0**	**23**	**1**		**9**	**3**	**1**	**4**	**4**	**1**	**0**	**1**

Signed as a free agent by **St. Louis**, June 4, 1987. Signed as a free agent by **Boston**, July 30, 1991. Signed as a free agent by **NY Rangers**, September 4, 1992. Signed as a free agent by **LA Kings**, July 22, 1993.

• THOMPSON, Brent

Brent K. D – L. 6'2", 205 lbs. b: Calgary, Alta., 1/9/1971. Los Angeles' 1st, 39th overall, in 1989.

			REGULAR SEASON																		PLAYOFFS							
Season	**Club**	**League**	**GP**	**G**	**A**	**Pts**	**AG**	**AA**	**APts**	**PIM**	**PP**	**SH**	**GW**	**S**	**%**	**TGF**	**PGF**	**TGA**	**PGA**	**+/–**	**GP**	**G**	**A**	**Pts**	**PIM**	**PP**	**SH**	**GW**
1987-88	Calgary North Stars	AAHA	25	0	13	13	....	....	....	33	....	....	....	....	....	....	....	....	....	....	....	....	....	....	....	....	....	....
1988-89	Medicine Hat Tigers	WHL	72	3	10	13	....	....	....	160	....	....	....	....	....	....	....	....	....	....	3	0	0	0	2	....	....	....
1989-90	Medicine Hat Tigers	WHL	68	10	35	45	....	....	....	167	....	....	....	....	....	....	....	....	....	....	3	0	1	1	14	....	....	....
1990-91	Medicine Hat Tigers	WHL	51	5	40	45	....	....	....	87	....	....	....	....	....	....	....	....	....	....	12	1	7	8	16	....	....	....
	Phoenix Roadrunners	IHL	....	....	....	....	....	....	....	....	....	....	....	....	....	....	....	....	....	....	4	0	1	1	6	....	....	....
1991-92	**Los Angeles Kings**	**NHL**	**27**	**0**	**5**	**5**	**0**	**4**	**4**	**89**	**0**	**0**	**0**	**18**	**0.0**	**17**	**0**	**25**	**1**	**–7**	**4**	**0**	**0**	**0**	**4**	**0**	**0**	**0**
	Phoenix Roadrunners	IHL	42	4	13	17	....	....	....	139	....	....	....	....	....	....	....	....	....	....	....	....	....	....	....	....	....	....
1992-93	**Los Angeles Kings**	**NHL**	**30**	**0**	**4**	**4**	**0**	**3**	**3**	**76**	**0**	**0**	**0**	**18**	**0.0**	**17**	**0**	**26**	**5**	**–4**	....	....	....	....	....	....	....	....
	Phoenix Roadrunners	IHL	22	0	5	5	....	....	....	112	....	....	....	....	....	....	....	....	....	....	....	....	....	....	....	....	....	....
1993-94	**Los Angeles Kings**	**NHL**	**24**	**1**	**0**	**1**	**1**	**0**	**1**	**81**	**0**	**0**	**0**	**9**	**11.1**	**13**	**1**	**15**	**2**	**–1**	....	....	....	....	....	....	....	....
	Phoenix Roadrunners	IHL	26	1	11	12	....	....	....	118	....	....	....	....	....	....	....	....	....	....	....	....	....	....	....	....	....	....
1994-95	**Winnipeg Jets**	**NHL**	**29**	**0**	**0**	**0**	**0**	**0**	**0**	**78**	**0**	**0**	**0**	**16**	**0.0**	**7**	**1**	**25**	**2**	**–17**	....	....	....	....	....	....	....	....
1995-96	**Winnipeg Jets**	**NHL**	**10**	**0**	**1**	**1**	**0**	**1**	**1**	**21**	**0**	**0**	**0**	**7**	**0.0**	**6**	**0**	**10**	**2**	**–2**	....	....	....	....	....	....	....	....
	Springfield Falcons	AHL	58	2	10	12	....	....	....	203	....	....	....	....	....	....	....	....	....	....	10	1	4	5	*55	....	....	....
1996-97	**Phoenix Coyotes**	**NHL**	**1**	**0**	**0**	**0**	**0**	**0**	**0**	**7**	**0**	**0**	**0**	**0**	**0.0**	**0**	**0**	**1**	**0**	**–1**	....	....	....	....	....	....	....	....
	Springfield Falcons	AHL	64	2	15	17	....	....	....	215	....	....	....	....	....	....	....	....	....	....	17	0	2	2	31	....	....	....
	Phoenix Roadrunners	IHL	12	0	1	1	....	....	....	67	....	....	....	....	....	....	....	....	....	....	....	....	....	....	....	....	....	....
1997-98	Hartford Wolf Pack	AHL	77	4	15	19	....	....	....	308	....	....	....	....	....	....	....	....	....	....	15	0	4	4	25	....	....	....
1998-99	Hartford Wolf Pack	AHL	76	3	15	18	....	....	....	265	....	....	....	....	....	....	....	....	....	....	7	0	0	0	23	....	....	....
99-2000	Louisville Panthers	AHL	67	4	22	26	....	....	....	311	....	....	....	....	....	....	....	....	....	....	3	0	0	0	11	....	....	....
	NHL Totals		**121**	**1**	**10**	**11**	**1**	**8**	**9**	**352**	**0**	**0**	**0**	**68**	**1.5**	**60**	**2**	**102**	**12**		**4**	**0**	**0**	**0**	**4**	**0**	**0**	**0**

WHL East Second All-Star Team (1991)

Traded to **Winnipeg** by **LA Kings** with cash for the rights to Ruslan Batyrshin and Winnipeg's 2nd round choice (Marian Cisar) in 1996 Entry Draft, August 8, 1994. Transferred to **Phoenix** after **Winnipeg** franchise relocated, July 1, 1996. Signed as a free agent by **NY Rangers**, August 26, 1997. Signed as a free agent by **Florida**, July 27, 1999.

• THOMPSON, Errol

Loran Errol "Spud" LW – L. 5'9", 185 lbs. b: Summerside, P.E.I., 5/28/1950. Toronto's 2nd, 22nd overall, in 1970.

			REGULAR SEASON																		PLAYOFFS							
Season	**Club**	**League**	**GP**	**G**	**A**	**Pts**	**AG**	**AA**	**APts**	**PIM**	**PP**	**SH**	**GW**	**S**	**%**	**TGF**	**PGF**	**TGA**	**PGA**	**+/–**	**GP**	**G**	**A**	**Pts**	**PIM**	**PP**	**SH**	**GW**
1966-67	Halifax Jr. Canadians	X-Games	47	28	32	60	....	....	....	29	....	....	....	....	....	....	....	....	....	....	....	....	....	....	....	....	....	....
	Halifax Jr. Canadians	Mem-Cup	17	15	9	24	....	....	....	9	....	....	....	....	....	....	....	....	....	....	....	....	....	....	....	....	....	....
1967-68	Halifax Jr. Canadians	X-Games	45	41	40	81	....	....	....	55	....	....	....	....	....	....	....	....	....	....	....	....	....	....	....	....	....	....
	Halifax Jr. Canadians	Mem-Cup	11	6	7	13	....	....	....	12	....	....	....	....	....	....	....	....	....	....	....	....	....	....	....	....	....	....
1968-69	Halifax Jr. Canadians	MJrHL	30	11	18	29	....	....	....	25	....	....	....	....	....	....	....	....	....	....	....	....	....	....	....	....	....	....
1969-70	Charlottetown Royals	NBSHL	20	13	23	36	....	....	....	....	....	....	....	....	....	....	....	....	....	....	3	1	3	4	0	....	....	....
1970-71	**Toronto Maple Leafs**	**NHL**	**1**	**0**	**0**	**0**	**0**	**0**	**0**	**0**	**0**	**0**	**0**	**0**	**0.0**	**0**	**0**	**1**	**0**	**–1**	....	....	....	....	....	....	....	....
	Tulsa Oilers	CHL	65	15	14	29	....	....	....	37	....	....	....	....	....	....	....	....	....	....	....	....	....	....	....	....	....	....
1971-72	Tulsa Oilers	CHL	46	21	21	42	....	....	....	30	....	....	....	....	....	....	....	....	....	....	13	4	6	10	8	....	....	....
1972-73	**Toronto Maple Leafs**	**NHL**	**68**	**13**	**19**	**32**	**12**	**15**	**27**	**8**	**2**	**0**	**1**	**137**	**9.5**	**55**	**11**	**43**	**3**	**4**	....	....	....	....	....	....	....	....
1973-74	**Toronto Maple Leafs**	**NHL**	**56**	**7**	**8**	**15**	**7**	**7**	**14**	**6**	**0**	**0**	**2**	**74**	**9.5**	**25**	**1**	**31**	**9**	**2**	**2**	**0**	**1**	**1**	**0**	**0**	**0**	**0**
1974-75	**Toronto Maple Leafs**	**NHL**	**65**	**25**	**17**	**42**	**22**	**13**	**35**	**12**	**3**	**1**	**4**	**202**	**12.4**	**65**	**10**	**66**	**10**	**–1**	**6**	**0**	**0**	**0**	**9**	**0**	**0**	**0**
1975-76	**Toronto Maple Leafs**	**NHL**	**75**	**43**	**37**	**80**	**38**	**28**	**66**	**26**	**13**	**1**	**7**	**210**	**20.5**	**120**	**36**	**75**	**19**	**28**	**10**	**3**	**3**	**6**	**0**	**2**	**1**	**0**
1976-77	**Toronto Maple Leafs**	**NHL**	**41**	**21**	**16**	**37**	**19**	**12**	**31**	**8**	**8**	**1**	**2**	**109**	**19.3**	**62**	**22**	**63**	**13**	**–10**	**9**	**2**	**0**	**2**	**0**	**0**	**0**	**1**
1977-78	**Toronto Maple Leafs**	**NHL**	**59**	**17**	**22**	**39**	**15**	**17**	**32**	**10**	**4**	**1**	**2**	**132**	**12.9**	**67**	**12**	**43**	**5**	**17**	....	....	....	....	....	....	....	....
	Detroit Red Wings	**NHL**	**14**	**5**	**1**	**6**	**5**	**1**	**6**	**2**	**1**	**0**	**0**	**27**	**18.5**	**12**	**6**	**10**	**0**	**–4**	**7**	**2**	**1**	**3**	**2**	**1**	**0**	**1**
1978-79	**Detroit Red Wings**	**NHL**	**70**	**23**	**31**	**54**	**20**	**22**	**42**	**26**	**8**	**0**	**3**	**163**	**14.1**	**84**	**42**	**70**	**0**	**–28**	....	....	....	....	....	....	....	....
1979-80	**Detroit Red Wings**	**NHL**	**77**	**34**	**14**	**48**	**29**	**10**	**39**	**22**	**8**	**2**	**3**	**164**	**20.7**	**77**	**19**	**94**	**26**	**–10**	....	....	....	....	....	....	....	....
1980-81	**Detroit Red Wings**	**NHL**	**39**	**14**	**12**	**26**	**11**	**8**	**19**	**52**	**5**	**0**	**2**	**83**	**16.9**	**44**	**15**	**41**	**8**	**–4**	....	....	....	....	....	....	....	....
	Pittsburgh Penguins	**NHL**	**34**	**6**	**8**	**14**	**5**	**5**	**10**	**12**	**0**	**0**	**1**	**54**	**11.1**	**24**	**2**	**33**	**2**	**–9**	....	....	....	....	....	....	....	....
	NHL Totals		**599**	**208**	**185**	**393**	**183**	**138**	**321**	**184**	**52**	**6**	**27**	**1355**	**15.4**	**635**	**176**	**570**	**95**		**34**	**7**	**5**	**12**	**11**	**3**	**1**	**2**

Traded to **Detroit** by **Toronto** with Toronto's 1st (Brent Peterson) and 2nd (Al Jensen) round choices in 1978 Amateur Draft and Toronto's 1st round choice (Mike Blaisdell) in 1980 Entry Draft for Dan Maloney and Detroit's 2nd round choice (Craig Muni) in 1980 Entry Draft, March 13, 1978. Traded to **Pittsburgh** by **Detroit** for Gary McAdam, January 8, 1981.

• THOMPSON, Rocky

RW – R. 6'2", 205 lbs. b: Calgary, Alta., 8/8/1977. Calgary's 3rd, 72nd overall, in 1995.

			REGULAR SEASON																		PLAYOFFS							
Season	**Club**	**League**	**GP**	**G**	**A**	**Pts**	**AG**	**AA**	**APts**	**PIM**	**PP**	**SH**	**GW**	**S**	**%**	**TGF**	**PGF**	**TGA**	**PGA**	**+/–**	**GP**	**G**	**A**	**Pts**	**PIM**	**PP**	**SH**	**GW**
1992-93	Spruce Grove Mets	AAHA	65	13	50	63	....	....	....	295	....	....	....	....	....	....	....	....	....	....	....	....	....	....	....	....	....	....
1993-94	Medicine Hat Tigers	WHL	68	1	4	5	....	....	....	166	....	....	....	....	....	....	....	....	....	....	3	0	0	0	2	....	....	....
1994-95	Medicine Hat Tigers	WHL	63	1	6	7	....	....	....	220	....	....	....	....	....	....	....	....	....	....	5	0	0	0	17	....	....	....
1995-96	Medicine Hat Tigers	WHL	71	9	20	29	....	....	....	260	....	....	....	....	....	....	....	....	....	....	5	2	3	5	26	....	....	....
	Saint John Flames	AHL	4	0	0	0	....	....	....	33	....	....	....	....	....	....	....	....	....	....	....	....	....	....	....	....	....	....
1996-97	Medicine Hat Tigers	WHL	47	6	9	15	....	....	....	170	....	....	....	....	....	....	....	....	....	....	....	....	....	....	....	....	....	....
	Swift Current Broncos	WHL	22	3	5	8	....	....	....	90	....	....	....	....	....	....	....	....	....	....	10	1	2	3	22	....	....	....
1997-98	**Calgary Flames**	**NHL**	**12**	**0**	**0**	**0**	**0**	**0**	**0**	**61**	**0**	**0**	**0**	**3**	**0.0**	**1**	**0**	**1**	**0**	**0**	....	....	....	....	....	....	....	....
	Saint John Flames	AHL	51	3	0	3	....	....	....	187	....	....	....	....	....	....	....	....	....	....	18	1	1	2	47	....	....	....
1998-99	**Calgary Flames**	**NHL**	**3**	**0**	**0**	**0**	**0**	**0**	**0**	**25**	**0**	**0**	**0**	**0**	**0.0**	**0**	**0**	**0**	**0**	**0**	....	....	....	....	....	....	....	....
	Saint John Flames	AHL	27	2	2	4	....	....	....	108	....	....	....	....	....	....	....	....	....	....	....	....	....	....	....	....	....	....
99-2000	Saint John Flames	AHL	53	2	8	10	....	....	....	125	....	....	....	....	....	....	....	....	....	....	....	....	....	....	....	....	....	....
	Louisville Panthers	AHL	3	0	1	1	....	....	....	54	....	....	....	....	....	....	....	....	....	....	4	0	0	0	4	....	....	....
	NHL Totals		**15**	**0**	**0**	**0**	**0**	**0**	**0**	**86**	**0**	**0**	**0**	**3**	**0.0**	**1**	**0**	**1**	**0**		....	....	....	....	....	....	....	....

Traded to **Florida** by **Calgary** for Filip Kuba, March 16, 2000.

• THOMSON, Floyd

Floyd Harvey "White Pine" LW – L. 6', 190 lbs. b: Sudbury, Ont., 6/14/1949.

			REGULAR SEASON																		PLAYOFFS							
Season	Club	League	GP	G	A	Pts	AG	AA	APts	PIM	PP	SH	GW	S	%	TGF	PGF	TGA	PGA	+/–	GP	G	A	Pts	PIM	PP	SH	GW
1967-68	Garson Eagles	NOJHA	STATISTICS NOT AVAILABLE																									
1968-69	Garson Falcons	NOJHA	STATISTICS NOT AVAILABLE																									
1969-70	Fort Wayne Komets	IHL	69	10	19	29	....	....	....	81	....	....	....	....	....	....	....	....	....	....	3	0	1	1	0	....	....	....
1970-71	Kansas City Blues	CHL	72	15	18	33	....	....	....	73	....	....	....	....	....	....	....	....	....	....	....	....	....	....	....	....	....	....
1971-72	**St. Louis Blues**	**NHL**	**49**	**4**	**6**	**10**	**4**	**5**	**9**	**48**	**0**	**0**	**2**	**69**	**5.8**	**22**	**1**	**30**	**0**	**–9**	....	....	....	....	....	....	....	....
	Kansas City Blues	CHL	6	1	5	6	....	....	....	0	....	....	....	....	....	....	....	....	....	....	....	....	....	....	....	....	....	....
	Denver Spurs	WHL	17	6	6	12	....	....	....	8	....	....	....	....	....	....	....	....	....	....	9	2	2	4	14	....	....	....
1972-73	**St. Louis Blues**	**NHL**	**75**	**14**	**20**	**34**	**13**	**16**	**29**	**71**	**1**	**0**	**1**	**98**	**14.3**	**49**	**3**	**50**	**2**	**–2**	**5**	**0**	**1**	**1**	**2**	**0**	**0**	**0**
1973-74	**St. Louis Blues**	**NHL**	**77**	**11**	**22**	**33**	**11**	**18**	**29**	**58**	**0**	**0**	**1**	**125**	**8.8**	**46**	**2**	**63**	**0**	**–19**	....	....	....	....	....	....	....	....
1974-75	**St. Louis Blues**	**NHL**	**77**	**9**	**27**	**36**	**8**	**20**	**28**	**106**	**0**	**0**	**0**	**111**	**8.1**	**61**	**2**	**53**	**7**	**13**	**2**	**0**	**1**	**1**	**0**	**0**	**0**	**0**
1975-76	**St. Louis Blues**	**NHL**	**58**	**8**	**10**	**18**	**7**	**7**	**14**	**25**	**0**	**0**	**1**	**71**	**11.3**	**28**	**2**	**33**	**3**	**–4**	....	....	....	....	....	....	....	....
1976-77	**St. Louis Blues**	**NHL**	**58**	**7**	**8**	**15**	**6**	**6**	**12**	**11**	**0**	**1**	**2**	**46**	**15.2**	**27**	**0**	**41**	**15**	**1**	**3**	**0**	**0**	**0**	**4**	**0**	**0**	**0**
	Kansas City Blues	CHL	13	3	11	14	....	....	....	16	....	....	....	....	....	....	....	....	....	....	....	....	....	....	....	....	....	....
1977-78	**St. Louis Blues**	**NHL**	**6**	**1**	**1**	**2**	**1**	**1**	**2**	**4**	**0**	**0**	**0**	**4**	**25.0**	**2**	**0**	**5**	**0**	**–3**	....	....	....	....	....	....	....	....
	Salt Lake Golden Eagles	CHL	69	26	26	52	....	....	....	45	....	....	....	....	....	....	....	....	....	....	6	2	1	3	2	....	....	....
1978-79	Salt Lake Golden Eagles	CHL	76	41	40	81	....	....	....	96	....	....	....	....	....	....	....	....	....	....	10	5	4	9	11	....	....	....
1979-80	**St. Louis Blues**	**NHL**	**11**	**2**	**3**	**5**	**2**	**2**	**4**	**18**	**0**	**0**	**0**	**13**	**15.4**	**6**	**0**	**8**	**1**	**–1**	....	....	....	....	....	....	....	....
	Salt Lake Golden Eagles	CHL	73	23	41	64	....	....	....	49	....	....	....	....	....	....	....	....	....	....	13	6	8	14	11	....	....	....
1980-81	Salt Lake Golden Eagles	CHL	76	24	33	57	....	....	....	104	....	....	....	....	....	....	....	....	....	....	17	3	4	7	0	....	....	....
1981-82	Salt Lake Golden Eagles	CHL	74	17	28	45	....	....	....	83	....	....	....	....	....	....	....	....	....	....	9	1	0	1	4	....	....	....
	NHL Totals		**411**	**56**	**97**	**153**	**52**	**75**	**127**	**341**	**1**	**1**	**7**	**537**	**10.4**	**241**	**10**	**283**	**28**		**10**	**0**	**2**	**2**	**6**	**0**	**0**	**0**

CHL Second All-Star Team (1978) • CHL First All-Star Team (1979)

Signed as a free agent by **St. Louis**, October 1, 1970.

• THOMSON, Jim

James B. RW – R. 6'1", 220 lbs. b: Edmonton, Alta., 12/30/1965. Washington's 8th, 185th overall, in 1984.

Season	Club	League	GP	G	A	Pts	AG	AA	APts	PIM	PP	SH	GW	S	%	TGF	PGF	TGA	PGA	+/–	GP	G	A	Pts	PIM	PP	SH	GW
1980-81	Markham Waxers	OJHL	3	0	1	1	....	....	....	0	....	....	....	....	....	....	....	....	....	....	....	....	....	....	....	....	....	....
1981-82	Devon Dynamiters	AAHA	55	60	56	116	....	....	....	72	....	....	....	....	....	....	....	....	....	....	....	....	....	....	....	....	....	....
1982-83	Markham Waxers	OJHL	35	6	7	13	....	....	....	81	....	....	....	....	....	....	....	....	....	....	....	....	....	....	....	....	....	....
1983-84	Toronto Marlboros	OHL	60	10	18	28	....	....	....	68	....	....	....	....	....	....	....	....	....	....	9	1	0	1	26	....	....	....
1984-85	Toronto Marlboros	OHL	63	23	28	51	....	....	....	122	....	....	....	....	....	....	....	....	....	....	5	3	1	4	25	....	....	....
	Binghamton Whalers	AHL	4	0	0	0	....	....	....	2	....	....	....	....	....	....	....	....	....	....	....	....	....	....	....	....	....	....
1985-86	Binghamton Whalers	AHL	59	15	9	24	....	....	....	195	....	....	....	....	....	....	....	....	....	....	....	....	....	....	....	....	....	....
1986-87	**Washington Capitals**	**NHL**	**10**	**0**	**0**	**0**	**0**	**0**	**0**	**35**	**0**	**0**	**0**	**5**	**0.0**	**0**	**0**	**2**	**0**	**–2**	....	....	....	....	....	....	....	....
	Binghamton Whalers	AHL	57	13	10	23	....	....	....	360	....	....	....	....	....	....	....	....	....	....	10	0	1	1	40	....	....	....
1987-88	Binghamton Whalers	AHL	25	8	9	17	....	....	....	64	....	....	....	....	....	....	....	....	....	....	4	1	2	3	7	....	....	....
1988-89	**Washington Capitals**	**NHL**	**14**	**2**	**0**	**2**	**2**	**0**	**2**	**53**	**0**	**0**	**0**	**9**	**22.2**	**3**	**0**	**6**	**0**	**–3**	....	....	....	....	....	....	....	....
	Baltimore Skipjacks	AHL	41	25	16	41	....	....	....	129	....	....	....	....	....	....	....	....	....	....	....	....	....	....	....	....	....	....
	Hartford Whalers	**NHL**	**5**	**0**	**0**	**0**	**0**	**0**	**0**	**14**	**0**	**0**	**0**	**3**	**0.0**	**0**	**0**	**3**	**0**	**–3**	....	....	....	....	....	....	....	....
1989-90	Binghamton Whalers	AHL	8	1	2	3	....	....	....	30	....	....	....	....	....	....	....	....	....	....	....	....	....	....	....	....	....	....
	New Jersey Devils	**NHL**	**3**	**0**	**0**	**0**	**0**	**0**	**0**	**31**	**0**	**0**	**0**	**3**	**0.0**	**0**	**0**	**3**	**0**	**–3**	....	....	....	....	....	....	....	....
	Utica Devils	AHL	60	20	23	43	....	....	....	124	....	....	....	....	....	....	....	....	....	....	4	1	0	1	19	....	....	....
1990-91	**Los Angeles Kings**	**NHL**	**8**	**1**	**0**	**1**	**1**	**0**	**1**	**19**	**0**	**0**	**1**	**6**	**16.7**	**1**	**0**	**1**	**0**	**0**	....	....	....	....	....	....	....	....
	New Haven Nighthawks	AHL	27	5	8	13	....	....	....	121	....	....	....	....	....	....	....	....	....	....	....	....	....	....	....	....	....	....
1991-92	**Los Angeles Kings**	**NHL**	**45**	**1**	**2**	**3**	**1**	**2**	**3**	**162**	**0**	**0**	**0**	**24**	**4.2**	**5**	**0**	**6**	**0**	**–1**	....	....	....	....	....	....	....	....
	Phoenix Roadrunners	IHL	2	1	0	1	....	....	....	0	....	....	....	....	....	....	....	....	....	....	....	....	....	....	....	....	....	....
1992-93	**Ottawa Senators**	**NHL**	**15**	**0**	**1**	**1**	**0**	**1**	**1**	**41**	**0**	**0**	**0**	**21**	**0.0**	**1**	**0**	**12**	**0**	**–11**	....	....	....	....	....	....	....	....
	Los Angeles Kings	**NHL**	**9**	**0**	**0**	**0**	**0**	**0**	**0**	**56**	**0**	**0**	**0**	**2**	**0.0**	**1**	**0**	**2**	**0**	**–1**	**1**	**0**	**0**	**0**	**0**	**0**	**0**	**0**
	Phoenix Roadrunners	IHL	14	4	5	9	....	....	....	44	....	....	....	....	....	....	....	....	....	....	....	....	....	....	....	....	....	....
1993-94	**Mighty Ducks of Anaheim**	**NHL**	**6**	**0**	**0**	**0**	**0**	**0**	**0**	**5**	**0**	**0**	**0**	**1**	**0.0**	**0**	**0**	**0**	**0**	**0**	....	....	....	....	....	....	....	....
	NHL Totals		**115**	**4**	**3**	**7**	**4**	**3**	**7**	**416**	**0**	**0**	**1**	**74**	**5.4**	**11**	**0**	**35**	**0**		**1**	**0**	**0**	**0**	**0**	**0**	**0**	**0**

Traded to **Hartford** by **Washington** for Scot Kleinendorst, March 6, 1989. Traded to **New Jersey** by **Hartford** for Chris Cihocki, October 31, 1989. Signed as a free agent by **LA Kings**, July 2, 1990. Claimed by **Minnesota** from **LA Kings** in Expansion Draft, May 30, 1991. Traded to **LA Kings** by **Minnesota** with Randy Gilhen, Charlie Huddy and NY Rangers' 4th round choice (previously acquired, LA Kings selected Alexei Zhitnik) in 1991 Entry Draft for Todd Elik, June 22, 1991. Claimed by **Ottawa** from **LA Kings** in Expansion Draft, June 18, 1992. Traded to **LA Kings** by **Ottawa** with Marc Fortier for Bob Kudelski and Shawn McCosh, December 19, 1992. Claimed by **Anaheim** from **LA Kings** in Expansion Draft, June 24, 1993.

• THORNBURY, Tom

Thomas D – R. 5'11", 175 lbs. b: Lindsay, Ont., 3/17/1963. Pittsburgh's 2nd, 49th overall, in 1981.

Season	Club	League	GP	G	A	Pts	AG	AA	APts	PIM	PP	SH	GW	S	%	TGF	PGF	TGA	PGA	+/–	GP	G	A	Pts	PIM	PP	SH	GW
1979-80	Aurora Tigers	OJHL	44	19	30	49	....	....	....	84	....	....	....	....	....	....	....	....	....	....	....	....	....	....	....	....	....	....
1980-81	Niagara Falls Flyers	OMJHL	60	15	22	37	....	....	....	136	....	....	....	....	....	....	....	....	....	....	12	1	5	6	31	....	....	....
1981-82	Niagara Falls Flyers	OHL	43	11	22	33	....	....	....	65	....	....	....	....	....	....	....	....	....	....	1	0	0	0	2	....	....	....
1982-83	North Bay Centennials	OHL	17	6	9	15	....	....	....	30	....	....	....	....	....	....	....	....	....	....	....	....	....	....	....	....	....	....
	Cornwall Royals	OHL	50	21	35	56	....	....	....	66	....	....	....	....	....	....	....	....	....	....	8	2	4	6	8	....	....	....
1983-84	**Pittsburgh Penguins**	**NHL**	**14**	**1**	**8**	**9**	**1**	**5**	**6**	**16**	**0**	**0**	**0**	**44**	**2.3**	**16**	**9**	**26**	**0**	**–19**	....	....	....	....	....	....	....	....
	Baltimore Skipjacks	AHL	65	17	46	63	....	....	....	64	....	....	....	....	....	....	....	....	....	....	10	2	15	17	8	....	....	....
1984-85	Baltimore Skipjacks	AHL	22	4	12	16	....	....	....	21	....	....	....	....	....	....	....	....	....	....	....	....	....	....	....	....	....	....
	Fredericton Express	AHL	53	11	16	27	....	....	....	26	....	....	....	....	....	....	....	....	....	....	6	0	2	2	5	....	....	....
1985-86	Fredericton Express	AHL	24	0	15	15	....	....	....	30	....	....	....	....	....	....	....	....	....	....	....	....	....	....	....	....	....	....
	Muskegon Lumberjacks	IHL	9	0	8	8	....	....	....	8	....	....	....	....	....	....	....	....	....	....	....	....	....	....	....	....	....	....
	Moncton Golden Flames	AHL	40	6	12	18	....	....	....	38	....	....	....	....	....	....	....	....	....	....	7	0	2	2	10	....	....	....
1986-87	Canada	Nat-Team	19	0	10	10	....	....	....	22	....	....	....	....	....	....	....	....	....	....	....	....	....	....	....	....	....	....
	Kolner EC	Germany	17	8	8	16	....	....	....	26	....	....	....	....	....	....	....	....	....	....	9	2	8	10	14	....	....	....
1987-88	Kolner EC	Germany	36	6	14	20	....	....	....	56	....	....	....	....	....	....	....	....	....	....	11	4	9	13	16	....	....	....
1988-89	Kolner EC	Germany	34	15	26	41	....	....	....	36	....	....	....	....	....	....	....	....	....	....	9	1	9	10	2	....	....	....
1989-90	Kolner EC	Germany	36	12	18	30	....	....	....	38	....	....	....	....	....	....	....	....	....	....	8	2	0	2	12	....	....	....
1990-91	Kolner EC	Germany	36	11	32	43	....	....	....	67	....	....	....	....	....	....	....	....	....	....	3	0	1	1	16	....	....	....
1991-92	Kolner EC	Germany	31	14	15	29	....	....	....	62	....	....	....	....	....	....	....	....	....	....	3	0	0	0	5	....	....	....
1992-93	ESC Frankfurt	Germany-3	51	51	64	115	....	....	....	144	....	....	....	....	....	....	....	....	....	....	....	....	....	....	....	....	....	....
1993-94	ESC Frankfurt	Germany-2	39	10	8	18	....	....	....	82	....	....	....	....	....	....	....	....	....	....	....	....	....	....	....	....	....	....
1994-95	Oklahoma City Blazers	CHL	43	11	29	40	....	....	....	34	....	....	....	....	....	....	....	....	....	....	....	....	....	....	....	....	....	....
1995-96	EC Wolfsburg	Germany-2	STATISTICS NOT AVAILABLE																									
	Frankfurt Lions	Germany	5	0	1	1	....	....	....	10	....	....	....	....	....	....	....	....	....	....	3	0	1	1	0	....	....	....
	NHL Totals		**14**	**1**	**8**	**9**	**1**	**5**	**6**	**16**	**0**	**0**	**0**	**44**	**2.3**	**16**	**9**	**26**	**0**		....	....	....	....	....	....	....	....

AHL Second All-Star Team (1984)

Traded to **Quebec** by **Pittsburgh** for Brian Ford, December 6, 1984. Traded to **Calgary** by **Quebec** for Tony Stiles, Janaury 16, 1986.

• THORNTON, Joe

Joseph Eric C – L. 6'4", 225 lbs. b: London, Ont., 7/2/1979. Boston's 1st, 1st overall, in 1997.

Season	Club	League	GP	G	A	Pts	AG	AA	APts	PIM	PP	SH	GW	S	%	TGF	PGF	TGA	PGA	+/–	GP	G	A	Pts	PIM	PP	SH	GW
1993-94	Elgin-Middlesex Elks	OMHA	67	83	85	168	....	....	....	45	....	....	....	....	....	....	....	....	....	....	....	....	....	....	....	....	....	....
	St. Thomas Stars	OJHL-B	6	2	6	8	....	....	....	2	....	....	....	....	....	....	....	....	....	....	....	....	....	....	....	....	....	....
1994-95	St. Thomas Stars	OJHL-B	50	40	64	104	....	....	....	53	....	....	....	....	....	....	....	....	....	....	....	....	....	....	....	....	....	....
1995-96	Sault Ste. Marie Greyhounds	OHL	66	30	46	76	....	....	....	53	....	....	....	....	....	....	....	....	....	....	4	1	1	2	11	....	....	....
1996-97	Sault Ste. Marie Greyhounds	OHL	59	41	81	122	....	....	....	123	....	....	....	....	....	....	....	....	....	....	11	11	8	19	24	....	....	....
	Canada	WJC-A	7	2	2	4	....	....	....	0	....	....	....	....	....	....	....	....	....	....	....	....	....	....	....	....	....	....
1997-98	**Boston Bruins**	**NHL**	**55**	**3**	**4**	**7**	**4**	**4**	**8**	**19**	**0**	**0**	**1**	**33**	**9.1**	**9**	**2**	**13**	**0**	**–6**	**6**	**0**	**0**	**0**	**9**	**0**	**0**	**0**
1998-99	**Boston Bruins**	**NHL**	**81**	**16**	**25**	**41**	**19**	**24**	**43**	**69**	**7**	**0**	**1**	**128**	**12.5**	**60**	**23**	**35**	**1**	**3**	**11**	**3**	**6**	**9**	**4**	**2**	**0**	**2**
99-2000	**Boston Bruins**	**NHL**	**81**	**23**	**37**	**60**	**26**	**34**	**60**	**82**	**5**	**0**	**3**	**171**	**13.5**	**90**	**26**	**80**	**11**	**–5**	....	....	....	....	....	....	....	....
	NHL Totals		**217**	**42**	**66**	**108**	**49**	**62**	**111**	**170**	**12**	**0**	**5**	**332**	**12.7**	**159**	**51**	**128**	**12**		**17**	**3**	**6**	**9**	**13**	**2**	**0**	**2**

Canadian Major Junior Rookie of the Year (1996) • OHL Second All-Star Team (1997)

• THORNTON, Scott

Scott C. C – L. 6'3", 216 lbs. b: London, Ont., 1/9/1971. Toronto's 1st, 3rd overall, in 1989.

			REGULAR SEASON																		PLAYOFFS							
Season	Club	League	GP	G	A	Pts	AG	AA	APts	PIM	PP	SH	GW	S	%	TGF	PGF	TGA	PGA	+/–	GP	G	A	Pts	PIM	PP	SH	GW
1986-87	London Diamonds	OJHL-B	31	10	7	17				10																		
1987-88	Belleville Bulls	OHL	62	11	19	30				54											6	0	1	1	2			
1988-89	Belleville Bulls	OHL	59	28	34	62				103											5	1	1	2	6			
1989-90	Belleville Bulls	OHL	47	21	28	49				91											11	2	10	12	15			
1990-91	Belleville Bulls	OHL	3	2	1	3				2											6	0	7	7	14			
	Canada	WJC-A	7	3	1	4				0																		
	Toronto Maple Leafs	**NHL**	**33**	**1**	**3**	**4**	**1**	**2**	**3**	**30**	**0**	**0**	**0**	**31**	**3.2**	**9**	**0**	**26**	**2**	**–15**								
	Newmarket Saints	AHL	5	1	0	1				4																		
1991-92	**Edmonton Oilers**	**NHL**	**15**	**0**	**1**	**1**	**0**	**1**	**1**	**43**	**0**	**0**	**0**	**11**	**0.0**	**2**	**0**	**8**	**0**	**–6**	**1**	**0**	**0**	**0**	**0**	**0**	**0**	**0**
	Cape Breton Oilers	AHL	49	9	14	23				40											5	1	0	1	8			
1992-93	**Edmonton Oilers**	**NHL**	**9**	**0**	**1**	**1**	**0**	**1**	**1**	**0**	**0**	**0**	**0**	**7**	**0.0**	**1**	**0**	**5**	**0**	**–4**								
	Cape Breton Oilers	AHL	58	23	27	50				102											16	1	2	3	35			
1993-94	**Edmonton Oilers**	**NHL**	**61**	**4**	**7**	**11**	**4**	**5**	**9**	**104**	**0**	**0**	**0**	**65**	**6.2**	**21**	**2**	**41**	**7**	**–15**								
	Cape Breton Oilers	AHL	2	1	1	2				31																		
1994-95	**Edmonton Oilers**	**NHL**	**47**	**10**	**12**	**22**	**18**	**18**	**36**	**89**	**0**	**1**	**1**	**69**	**14.5**	**32**	**4**	**47**	**15**	**–4**								
1995-96	**Edmonton Oilers**	**NHL**	**77**	**9**	**9**	**18**	**9**	**7**	**16**	**149**	**0**	**2**	**3**	**95**	**9.5**	**27**	**2**	**76**	**26**	**–25**								
1996-97	**Montreal Canadiens**	**NHL**	**73**	**10**	**10**	**20**	**11**	**9**	**20**	**128**	**1**	**1**	**1**	**110**	**9.1**	**27**	**3**	**54**	**11**	**–19**	**5**	**1**	**0**	**1**	**2**	**0**	**0**	**0**
1997-98	**Montreal Canadiens**	**NHL**	**67**	**6**	**9**	**15**	**7**	**9**	**16**	**158**	**1**	**0**	**1**	**51**	**11.8**	**24**	**3**	**25**	**4**	**0**	**9**	**0**	**2**	**2**	**10**	**0**	**0**	**0**
1998-99	**Montreal Canadiens**	**NHL**	**47**	**7**	**4**	**11**	**8**	**4**	**12**	**87**	**1**	**0**	**1**	**56**	**12.5**	**20**	**2**	**23**	**3**	**–2**								
	Canada	WC-A	10	5	1	6				6																		
99-2000	**Montreal Canadiens**	**NHL**	**35**	**2**	**3**	**5**	**2**	**3**	**5**	**70**	**0**	**0**	**1**	**36**	**5.6**	**11**	**2**	**16**	**0**	**–7**								
	Dallas Stars	**NHL**	**30**	**6**	**3**	**9**	**7**	**3**	**10**	**38**	**1**	**0**	**0**	**47**	**12.8**	**10**	**2**	**13**	**0**	**–5**	**23**	**2**	**7**	**9**	**28**	**0**	**0**	**1**
	NHL Totals		**494**	**55**	**62**	**117**	**67**	**62**	**129**	**896**	**4**	**4**	**8**	**578**	**9.5**	**184**	**20**	**334**	**68**		**38**	**3**	**9**	**12**	**40**	**0**	**0**	**1**

Traded to **Edmonton** by **Toronto** with Vincent Damphousse, Peter Ing, Luke Richardson and cash for Grant Fuhr, Glenn Anderson and Craig Berube, September 19, 1991. Traded to **Montreal** by **Edmonton** for Andrei Kovalenko, September 6, 1996. Traded to **Dallas** by **Montreal** for Juha Lind, January 22, 2000. Signed as a free agent by **San Jose**, July 1, 2000.

• THURLBY, Tom

Thomas Newman D – L. 5'10", 175 lbs. b: Kingston, Ont., 11/9/1938.

Season	Club	League	GP	G	A	Pts	AG	AA	APts	PIM	PP	SH	GW	S	%	TGF	PGF	TGA	PGA	+/–	GP	G	A	Pts	PIM	PP	SH	GW
1955-56	Kitchener Canucks	OHA-Jr.	35	2	4	6				4											8	2	4	6	4			
1956-57	Peterborough Petes	OHA-Jr.	52	8	7	15				30																		
1957-58	Peterborough Petes	OHA-Jr.	52	7	10	17				28											5	2	0	2	8			
1958-59	Peterborough Petes	OHA-Jr.	54	9	19	28				34											19	0	3	3	18			
	Peterborough Petes	Mem-Cup	12	2	3	5				12																		
1959-60	Montreal Royals	EPHL	68	4	12	16				57											11	0	1	1	14			
1960-61	Kingston Frontenacs	EPHL	44	3	11	14				37																		
	Winnipeg–Portland	WHL	23	4	3	7				17											14	2	3	5	17			
1961-62	San Francisco Seals	WHL	70	4	17	21				36											2	0	0	0	0			
1962-63	San Francisco Seals	WHL	70	12	24	36				41											17	3	5	8	4			
1963-64	San Francisco Seals	WHL	61	7	10	17				14											11	4	6	10	12			
1964-65	San Francisco Seals	WHL	70	11	22	33				32																		
1965-66	San Francisco Seals	WHL	71	13	17	30				26											7	1	1	2	4			
1966-67	California Seals	WHL	72	10	16	26				26											6	0	0	0	2			
1967-68	Vancouver Canucks	WHL	47	4	11	15				20																		
	Oakland Seals	**NHL**	**20**	**1**	**1**	**2**	**1**	**1**	**2**	**4**	**0**	**0**	**0**	**27**	**3.7**	**5**	**3**	**8**	**0**	**–6**								
1968-69	Houston Apollos	CHL	53	3	7	10				8											3	0	0	0	0			
1969-70	Muskegon Mohawks	IHL	60	5	19	24				28											6	0	3	3	2			
1970-71			REINSTATED AS AN AMATEUR																									
1971-72	Kingston Aces	OHA-Sr.	36	5	20	25				24																		
1972-73	Kingston Aces	OHA-Sr.	31	2	9	11				20																		
	NHL Totals		**20**	**1**	**1**	**2**	**1**	**1**	**2**	**4**	**0**	**0**	**0**	**27**	**3.7**	**5**	**3**	**8**	**0**									

OHA-Sr. Second All-Star Team (1973)

Claimed by **Boston** from **Montreal** in Intra-League Draft, June 8, 1960. NHL rights transferred to **California** after owners of **San Francisco** (WHL) franchise awarded NHL expansion team, April 5, 1966. Loaned to **Vancouver** (WHL) by **Oakland** for cash, October, 1967. Traded to **Montrreal** by **Oakland** to complete transaction that sent Bryan Watson to Oakland (June 28, 1968), September, 1968. Signed as a free agent by **Muskegon** (IHL), November, 1969.

• THYER, Mario

C – L. 5'11", 170 lbs. b: Montreal, Que., 9/29/1966.

Season	Club	League	GP	G	A	Pts	AG	AA	APts	PIM	PP	SH	GW	S	%	TGF	PGF	TGA	PGA	+/–	GP	G	A	Pts	PIM	PP	SH	GW
1982-83	Montreal Concordia	QAAA	48	20	37	57																						
1983-1987	St-Laurent College	QCAAA	STATISTICS NOT AVAILABLE																									
1987-88	University of Maine	H-East	44	24	42	66				4																		
1988-89	University of Maine	H-East	9	9	7	16				0																		
1989-90	**Minnesota North Stars**	**NHL**	**5**	**0**	**0**	**0**	**0**	**0**	**0**	**0**	**0**	**0**	**0**	**4**	**0.0**	**0**	**0**	**3**	**0**	**–3**	**1**	**0**	**0**	**0**	**2**	**0**	**0**	**0**
	Kalamazoo Wings	IHL	68	19	42	61				12											10	2	6	8	4			
1990-91	Kalamazoo Wings	IHL	75	15	51	66				15											10	4	5	9	2			
1991-92	Kalamazoo Wings	IHL	46	17	28	45				0																		
	Binghamton Rangers	AHL	9	2	7	9				0											3	0	0	0	0			
1992-93	Cincinnati Cyclones	IHL	77	13	36	49				26																		
1993-94	Portland Pirates	AHL	3	0	0	0				0																		
	NHL Totals		**5**	**0**	**0**	**0**	**0**	**0**	**0**	**0**	**0**	**0**	**0**	**4**	**0.0**	**0**	**0**	**3**	**0**		**1**	**0**	**0**	**0**	**2**	**0**	**0**	**0**

Signed as a free agent by **Minnesota**, July 12, 1989. Traded to **NY Rangers** by **Minnesota** with Minnesota's 3rd round choice (Maxim Galanov) in 1993 Entry Draft for Mark Janssens, March 10, 1992. Traded to **Minnesota** by **NY Rangers** for cash, July 16, 1992. • Played w/ RHI's New England Stingers in 1994 (17-16-25-41-4).

• TICHY, Milan

D – L. 6'3", 198 lbs. b: Plzen, Czech., 9/22/1969. Chicago's 6th, 153rd overall, in 1989.

Season	Club	League	GP	G	A	Pts	AG	AA	APts	PIM	PP	SH	GW	S	%	TGF	PGF	TGA	PGA	+/–	GP	G	A	Pts	PIM	PP	SH	GW
1987-88	Skoda Plzen	Czech.	30	1	3	4				20																		
	Czechoslovakia	WJC-A	7	1	2	3				2																		
1988-89	Skoda Plzen	Czech.	36	1	12	13				44																		
1989-90	Dukla Trencin	Czech.	42	13	6	19															9	1	2	3				
1990-91	Dukla Trencin	Czech.	41	9	12	21				72																		
1991-92	Indianapolis Ice	IHL	49	6	23	29				28																		
1992-93	**Chicago Blackhawks**	**NHL**	**13**	**0**	**1**	**1**	**0**	**1**	**1**	**30**	**0**	**0**	**0**	**12**	**0.0**	**10**	**2**	**5**	**4**	**7**								
	Indianapolis Ice	IHL	49	7	32	39				62											4	0	5	5	14			
1993-94	Moncton Hawks	AHL	48	1	20	21				103											20	3	3	6	12			
1994-95	**New York Islanders**	**NHL**	**2**	**0**	**0**	**0**	**0**	**0**	**0**	**2**	**0**	**0**	**0**	**1**	**0.0**	**0**	**0**	**1**	**0**	**–1**								
	Denver Grizzlies	IHL	71	18	36	54				90											17	4	9	13	12			
1995-96	**New York Islanders**	**NHL**	**8**	**0**	**4**	**4**	**0**	**3**	**3**	**8**	**0**	**0**	**0**	**6**	**0.0**	**8**	**0**	**7**	**2**	**3**								
	Utah Grizzlies	IHL	21	1	12	13				26																		
	ZPS Zlin	Czech-Rep	8	0	3	3															4	0	0	0				
	NHL Totals		**23**	**0**	**5**	**5**	**0**	**4**	**4**	**40**	**0**	**0**	**0**	**19**	**0.0**	**18**	**2**	**13**	**6**									

WJC-A All-Star Team (1989)

Claimed by **Florida** from **Chicago** in Expansion Draft, June 24, 1993. Traded to **Winnipeg** by **Florida** for Brent Severyn, October 3, 1993. Signed as a free agent by **NY Islanders**, August 2, 1994.

• TIDEY, Alex

Alex Mansfield RW – R. 6', 182 lbs. b: Vancouver, B.C., 1/5/1955. Buffalo's 9th, 143rd overall, in 1975.

Season	Club	League	GP	G	A	Pts	AG	AA	APts	PIM	PP	SH	GW	S	%	TGF	PGF	TGA	PGA	+/–	GP	G	A	Pts	PIM	PP	SH	GW
1972-73	Vancouver Centennials	BCJHL	STATISTICS NOT AVAILABLE																									
	Vancouver Nats	WCJHL	1	0	1	1				0																		
1973-74	Kamloops Chiefs	WCJHL	64	10	12	22				52																		

			REGULAR SEASON																		PLAYOFFS							
Season	Club	League	GP	G	A	Pts	AG	AA	APts	PIM	PP	SH	GW	S	%	TGF	PGF	TGA	PGA	+/–	GP	G	A	Pts	PIM	PP	SH	GW
1974-75	Lethbridge Broncos	WCJHL	68	42	54	96	....	....	....	78	....	....	....	....	....	....	....	....	....	....	6	4	2	6	0	....	....	....
1975-76	San Diego Mariners	WHA	74	16	11	27	....	....	....	46	....	....	....	....	....	....	....	....	....	....	11	3	6	9	10	....	....	....
1976-77	**Buffalo Sabres**	**NHL**	**3**	**0**	**0**	**0**	**0**	**0**	**0**	**0**	**0**	**0**	**0**	**3**	**0.0**	**0**	**0**	**1**	**0**	**–1**	**2**	**0**	**0**	**0**	**0**	**0**	**0**	**0**
	Hershey Bears	AHL	74	25	38	63	....	....	....	55	....	....	....	....	....	....	....	....	....	....	6	1	5	6	4	....	....	....
1977-78	**Buffalo Sabres**	**NHL**	**1**	**0**	**0**	**0**	**0**	**0**	**0**	**0**	**0**	**0**	**0**	**2**	**0.0**	**0**	**0**	**1**	**0**	**–1**	....	....	....	....	....	....	....	....
	Hershey Bears	AHL	49	14	19	33	....	....	....	36	....	....	....	....	....	....	....	....	....	....	....	....	....	....	....	....	....	....
1978-79	Hershey Bears	AHL	79	31	30	61	....	....	....	60	....	....	....	....	....	....	....	....	....	....	4	1	0	1	0	....	....	....
1979-80	**Edmonton Oilers**	**NHL**	**5**	**0**	**0**	**0**	**0**	**0**	**0**	**8**	**0**	**0**	**0**	**4**	**0.0**	**0**	**0**	**3**	**0**	**–3**	....	....	....	....	....	....	....	....
	Rochester Americans	AHL	9	2	3	5	....	....	....	6	....	....	....	....	....	....	....	....	....	....	....	....	....	....	....	....	....	....
	Cincinnati Stingers	CHL	10	3	2	5	....	....	....	10	....	....	....	....	....	....	....	....	....	....	....	....	....	....	....	....	....	....
	Houston Apollos	CHL	40	20	29	49	....	....	....	29	....	....	....	....	....	....	....	....	....	....	6	5	4	9	6	....	....	....
1980-81	Houston Apollos	CHL	17	9	8	17	....	....	....	12	....	....	....	....	....	....	....	....	....	....	....	....	....	....	....	....	....	....
	Springfield Indians	AHL	30	9	7	16	....	....	....	34	....	....	....	....	....	....	....	....	....	....	5	1	1	2	0	....	....	....
	NHL Totals		**9**	**0**	**0**	**0**	**0**	**0**	**0**	**8**	**0**	**0**	**0**	**9**	**0.0**	**0**	**0**	**5**	**0**		**2**	**0**	**0**	**0**	**0**	**0**	**0**	**0**
	Other Major League Totals		74	16	11	27	....	....	....	46	....	....	....	....	....	....	....	....	....	....	11	3	6	9	10	....	....	....

Selected by **San Diego** (WHA) in 1975 WHA Amateur Draft, May, 1975. Traded to **Edmonton** by **Buffalo** for John Gould, November 13, 1979. Signed as a free agent by **LA Kings**, August, 1980.

• TIKKANEN, Esa

"The Grate One" LW – L. 6′1″, 190 lbs. b: Helsinki, Finland, 1/25/1965. Edmonton's 4th, 82nd overall, in 1983.

Season	Club	League	GP	G	A	Pts	AG	AA	APts	PIM	PP	SH	GW	S	%	TGF	PGF	TGA	PGA	+/–	GP	G	A	Pts	PIM	PP	SH	GW
1981-82	Regina Blues	SJHL	59	38	37	75	....	....	....	216	....	....	....	....	....	....	....	....	....	....	....	....	....	....	....	....	....	....
	Regina Pats	WHL	2	0	0	0	....	....	....	0	....	....	....	....	....	....	....	....	....	....	....	....	....	....	....	....	....	....
1982-83	HIFK Helsinki	Finland-Jr.	30	34	31	65	....	....	....	*104	....	....	....	....	....	....	....	....	....	....	4	4	3	7	10	....	....	....
	Finland	WJC-A	7	2	3	5	....	....	....	4	....	....	....	....	....	....	....	....	....	....	....	....	....	....	....	....	....	....
	HIFK Helsinki	Finland	....	....	....	....	....	....	....	....	....	....	....	....	....	....	....	....	....	....	1	0	0	0	2	....	....	....
	Finland	EJC-A	5	2	1	3	....	....	....	14	....	....	....	....	....	....	....	....	....	....	....	....	....	....	....	....	....	....
1983-84	HIFK Helsinki	Finland-Jr.	6	5	9	14	....	....	....	13	....	....	....	....	....	....	....	....	....	....	4	4	3	7	8	....	....	....
	Finland	WJC-A	7	8	3	11	....	....	....	12	....	....	....	....	....	....	....	....	....	....	....	....	....	....	....	....	....	....
	HIFK Helsinki	Finland	36	19	11	30	....	....	....	30	....	....	....	....	....	....	....	....	....	....	2	0	0	0	0	....	....	....
1984-85	HIFK Helsinki	Finland	36	21	33	54	....	....	....	42	....	....	....	....	....	....	....	....	....	....	....	....	....	....	....	....	....	....
	Finland	WJC-A	7	7	12	19	....	....	....	10	....	....	....	....	....	....	....	....	....	....	....	....	....	....	....	....	....	....
	Finland	WEC-A	10	4	5	9	....	....	....	12	....	....	....	....	....	....	....	....	....	....	....	....	....	....	....	....	....	....
♦	**Edmonton Oilers**	**NHL**	....	....	....	....	....	....	....	....	....	....	....	....	....	....	....	....	....	....	**3**	**0**	**0**	**0**	**2**	**0**	**0**	**0**
1985-86	**Edmonton Oilers**	**NHL**	**35**	**7**	**6**	**13**	**6**	**4**	**10**	**28**	**0**	**0**	**2**	**44**	**15.9**	**22**	**3**	**14**	**0**	**5**	**8**	**3**	**2**	**5**	**7**	**0**	**0**	**0**
	Nova Scotia Oilers	AHL	15	4	8	12	....	....	....	17	....	....	....	....	....	....	....	....	....	....	....	....	....	....	....	....	....	....
1986-87♦	**Edmonton Oilers**	**NHL**	**76**	**34**	**44**	**78**	**29**	**32**	**61**	**120**	**7**	**0**	**6**	**126**	**27.0**	**125**	**27**	**54**	**0**	**44**	**21**	**7**	**2**	**9**	**22**	**1**	**0**	**1**
	NHL All-Stars	RV-87	2	0	1	1	....	....	....	2	....	....	....	....	....	....	....	....	....	....	....	....	....	....	....	....	....	....
1987-88	Finland	Can-Cup	5	0	1	1	....	....	....	6	....	....	....	....	....	....	....	....	....	....	....	....	....	....	....	....	....	....
♦	**Edmonton Oilers**	**NHL**	**80**	**23**	**51**	**74**	**20**	**37**	**57**	**153**	**6**	**1**	**2**	**142**	**16.2**	**113**	**39**	**60**	**7**	**21**	**19**	**10**	**17**	**27**	**72**	**5**	**0**	**1**
1988-89	**Edmonton Oilers**	**NHL**	**67**	**31**	**47**	**78**	**26**	**33**	**59**	**92**	**6**	**8**	**4**	**151**	**20.5**	**109**	**37**	**79**	**17**	**10**	**7**	**1**	**3**	**4**	**12**	**0**	**0**	**0**
	Finland	WEC-A	8	4	4	8	....	....	....	14	....	....	....	....	....	....	....	....	....	....	....	....	....	....	....	....	....	....
1989-90♦	**Edmonton Oilers**	**NHL**	**79**	**30**	**33**	**63**	**26**	**24**	**50**	**161**	**6**	**4**	**6**	**199**	**15.1**	**103**	**41**	**74**	**29**	**17**	**22**	**13**	**11**	**24**	**26**	**2**	**2**	**0**
1990-91	**Edmonton Oilers**	**NHL**	**79**	**27**	**42**	**69**	**25**	**32**	**57**	**85**	**3**	**2**	**6**	**235**	**11.5**	**113**	**35**	**98**	**42**	**22**	**18**	**12**	**8**	**20**	**24**	**3**	**0**	**3**
1991-92	Finland	Can-Cup	6	2	2	4	....	....	....	6	....	....	....	....	....	....	....	....	....	....	....	....	....	....	....	....	....	....
	Edmonton Oilers	**NHL**	**40**	**12**	**16**	**28**	**11**	**12**	**23**	**44**	**6**	**2**	**1**	**117**	**10.3**	**48**	**24**	**47**	**15**	**–8**	**16**	**5**	**3**	**8**	**8**	**1**	**0**	**1**
1992-93	**Edmonton Oilers**	**NHL**	**66**	**14**	**19**	**33**	**12**	**13**	**25**	**76**	**2**	**4**	**3**	**162**	**8.6**	**64**	**24**	**75**	**24**	**–11**	....	....	....	....	....	....	....	....
	New York Rangers	**NHL**	**15**	**2**	**5**	**7**	**2**	**3**	**5**	**18**	**0**	**0**	**0**	**40**	**5.0**	**14**	**3**	**29**	**5**	**–13**	....	....	....	....	....	....	....	....
	Finland	WC-A	6	0	0	0	....	....	....	2	....	....	....	....	....	....	....	....	....	....	....	....	....	....	....	....	....	....
1993-94♦	**New York Rangers**	**NHL**	**83**	**22**	**32**	**54**	**20**	**25**	**45**	**114**	**5**	**3**	**4**	**257**	**8.6**	**93**	**35**	**69**	**16**	**5**	**23**	**4**	**4**	**8**	**34**	**0**	**0**	**1**
1994-95	HIFK Helsinki	Finland	19	2	11	13	....	....	....	16	....	....	....	....	....	....	....	....	....	....	....	....	....	....	....	....	....	....
	St. Louis Blues	**NHL**	**43**	**12**	**23**	**35**	**21**	**34**	**55**	**22**	**5**	**2**	**1**	**107**	**11.2**	**57**	**21**	**46**	**23**	**13**	**7**	**2**	**2**	**4**	**20**	**1**	**0**	**1**
1995-96	**St. Louis Blues**	**NHL**	**11**	**1**	**4**	**5**	**1**	**3**	**4**	**18**	**0**	**1**	**0**	**19**	**5.3**	**11**	**5**	**8**	**3**	**1**	....	....	....	....	....	....	....	....
	New Jersey Devils	**NHL**	**9**	**0**	**2**	**2**	**0**	**2**	**2**	**4**	**0**	**0**	**0**	**15**	**0.0**	**3**	**1**	**11**	**3**	**–6**	....	....	....	....	....	....	....	....
	Vancouver Canucks	**NHL**	**38**	**13**	**24**	**37**	**13**	**20**	**33**	**14**	**8**	**0**	**2**	**61**	**21.3**	**55**	**27**	**23**	**1**	**6**	**6**	**3**	**2**	**5**	**2**	**2**	**0**	**0**
	Finland	WC-A	1	0	0	0	....	....	....	0	....	....	....	....	....	....	....	....	....	....	....	....	....	....	....	....	....	....
1996-97	**Vancouver Canucks**	**NHL**	**62**	**12**	**15**	**27**	**13**	**13**	**26**	**66**	**4**	**1**	**2**	**103**	**11.7**	**54**	**21**	**47**	**5**	**–9**	....	....	....	....	....	....	....	....
	New York Rangers	**NHL**	**14**	**1**	**2**	**3**	**1**	**2**	**3**	**6**	**0**	**1**	**0**	**30**	**3.3**	**8**	**2**	**9**	**3**	**0**	**15**	**9**	**3**	**12**	**26**	**3**	**1**	**3**
1997-98	**Florida Panthers**	**NHL**	**28**	**1**	**8**	**9**	**1**	**8**	**9**	**16**	**0**	**0**	**0**	**34**	**2.9**	**14**	**5**	**24**	**8**	**–7**	....	....	....	....	....	....	....	....
	Finland	Olympics	6	1	1	2	....	....	....	0	....	....	....	....	....	....	....	....	....	....	....	....	....	....	....	....	....	....
	Washington Capitals	**NHL**	**20**	**2**	**10**	**12**	**2**	**10**	**12**	**2**	**1**	**0**	**2**	**33**	**6.1**	**17**	**8**	**14**	**1**	**–4**	**21**	**3**	**3**	**6**	**20**	**1**	**0**	**0**
1998-99	**New York Rangers**	**NHL**	**32**	**0**	**3**	**3**	**0**	**3**	**3**	**38**	**0**	**0**	**0**	**25**	**0.0**	**6**	**0**	**19**	**8**	**–5**	....	....	....	....	....	....	....	....
99-2000	Jokerit Helsinki	Finland	43	10	13	23	....	....	....	85	....	....	....	....	....	....	....	....	....	....	11	1	6	7	10	....	....	....
	Finland	WC-A	9	2	1	3	....	....	....	10	....	....	....	....	....	....	....	....	....	....	....	....	....	....	....	....	....	....
	NHL Totals		**877**	**244**	**386**	**630**	**229**	**310**	**539**	**1077**	**59**	**29**	**41**	**1900**	**12.8**	**1029**	**358**	**800**	**210**		**186**	**72**	**60**	**132**	**275**	**19**	**3**	**11**

WJC-A All-Star Team (1985)

Traded to **NY Rangers** by **Edmonton** for Doug Weight, March 17, 1993. Traded to **St. Louis** by **NY Rangers** with Doug Lidster for Petr Nedved, July 24, 1994. Traded to **New Jersey** by **St. Louis** for New Jersey's 3rd round choice (later traded to Colorado — Colorado selected Ville Nielnen) in 1997 Entry Draft, November 1, 1995. Traded to **Vancouver** by **New Jersey** for Vancouver's 2nd round choice (Wesley Mason) in 1996 Entry Draft, November 23, 1995. Traded to **NY Rangers** by **Vancouver** with Russ Courtnall for Sergei Nemchinov and Brian Noonan, March 8, 1997. Signed as a free agent by **Florida**, September 17, 1997. Traded to **Washington** by **Florida** for Dwayne Hay and future considerations, March 9, 1998. Signed as a free agent by **NY Rangers**, October 9, 1998.

• TILEY, Brad

Bradley Philip D – L. 6′1″, 204 lbs. b: Markdale, Ont., 7/5/1971. Boston's 4th, 84th overall, in 1991.

Season	Club	League	GP	G	A	Pts	AG	AA	APts	PIM	PP	SH	GW	S	%	TGF	PGF	TGA	PGA	+/–	GP	G	A	Pts	PIM	PP	SH	GW
1987-88	Owen Sound Greys	OJHL-B	45	18	25	43	....	....	....	69	....	....	....	....	....	....	....	....	....	....	....	....	....	....	....	....	....	....
1988-89	Sault Ste. Marie Greyhounds	OHL	50	4	11	15	....	....	....	31	....	....	....	....	....	....	....	....	....	....	....	....	....	....	....	....	....	....
1989-90	Sault Ste. Marie Greyhounds	OHL	66	9	32	41	....	....	....	47	....	....	....	....	....	....	....	....	....	....	....	....	....	....	....	....	....	....
1990-91	Sault Ste. Marie Greyhounds	OHL	66	11	55	66	....	....	....	29	....	....	....	....	....	....	....	....	....	....	14	4	15	19	12	....	....	....
	Sault Ste. Marie Greyhounds	Mem-Cup	3	0	2	2	....	....	....	15	....	....	....	....	....	....	....	....	....	....	....	....	....	....	....	....	....	....
1991-92	Maine Mariners	AHL	62	7	22	29	....	....	....	36	....	....	....	....	....	....	....	....	....	....	....	....	....	....	....	....	....	....
1992-93	Phoenix Roadrunners	IHL	46	11	27	38	....	....	....	35	....	....	....	....	....	....	....	....	....	....	....	....	....	....	....	....	....	....
	Binghamton Rangers	AHL	26	6	10	16	....	....	....	19	....	....	....	....	....	....	....	....	....	....	8	0	1	1	2	....	....	....
1993-94	Binghamton Rangers	AHL	29	6	10	16	....	....	....	6	....	....	....	....	....	....	....	....	....	....	....	....	....	....	....	....	....	....
	Phoenix Roadrunners	IHL	35	8	15	23	....	....	....	21	....	....	....	....	....	....	....	....	....	....	....	....	....	....	....	....	....	....
1994-95	Detroit Vipers	IHL	56	7	19	26	....	....	....	32	....	....	....	....	....	....	....	....	....	....	....	....	....	....	....	....	....	....
	Fort Wayne Komets	IHL	14	1	6	7	....	....	....	2	....	....	....	....	....	....	....	....	....	....	3	1	2	3	0	....	....	....
1995-96	Orlando Solar Bears	IHL	69	11	23	34	....	....	....	82	....	....	....	....	....	....	....	....	....	....	23	2	4	6	16	....	....	....
1996-97	Phoenix Roadrunners	IHL	66	8	28	36	....	....	....	34	....	....	....	....	....	....	....	....	....	....	....	....	....	....	....	....	....	....
	Long Beach Ice Dogs	IHL	3	1	0	1	....	....	....	2	....	....	....	....	....	....	....	....	....	....	....	....	....	....	....	....	....	....
1997-98	**Phoenix Coyotes**	**NHL**	**1**	**0**	**0**	**0**	**0**	**0**	**0**	**0**	....	....	....	....	....	....	....	....	....	....	....	....	....	....	....	....	....	....
	Springfield Falcons	AHL	60	10	31	41	....	....	....	36	....	....	....	....	....	....	....	....	....	....	4	0	4	4	2	....	....	....
1998-99	**Phoenix Coyotes**	**NHL**	**8**	**0**	**0**	**0**	**0**	**0**	**0**	**0**	**0**	**0**	**0**	**1**	**0.0**	**3**	**0**	**4**	**0**	**–1**	**1**	**0**	**0**	**0**	**0**	**0**	**0**	**0**
	Springfield Falcons	AHL	69	9	35	44	....	....	....	14	....	....	....	....	....	....	....	....	....	....	1	0	0	0	0	....	....	....
99-2000	Springfield Falcons	AHL	80	14	54	68	....	....	....	51	....	....	....	....	....	....	....	....	....	....	5	0	4	4	2	....	....	....
	NHL Totals		**9**	**0**	**0**	**0**	**0**	**0**	**0**	**0**	**0**	**0**	**0**	**1**	**0.0**	**3**	**0**	**4**	**0**		**1**	**0**	**0**	**0**	**0**	**0**	**0**	**0**

Memorial Cup All-Star Team (1991) • AHL First All-Star Team (2000) • Won Eddie Shore Award (Top Defenseman - AHL) (2000)

Signed as a free agent by **NY Rangers**, September 4, 1992. Traded to **LA Kings** by **NY Rangers** for LA Kings' 11th round choice (Jamie Butt) in 1994 Entry Draft, January 28, 1994. Signed as a free agent by **Phoenix**, September 4, 1997. Signed as a free agent by **Philadelphia**, July 14, 2000. • Played w/ RHI's Anaheim Bullfrogs in 1995 (17-3-11-14-19).

• **TILLEY, Tom** Thomas R. D – R. 6', 190 lbs. b: Trenton, Ont., 3/28/1965. St. Louis' 13th, 196th overall, in 1984.

			REGULAR SEASON																		PLAYOFFS							
Season	Club	League	GP	G	A	Pts	AG	AA	APts	PIM	PP	SH	GW	S	%	TGF	PGF	TGA	PGA	+/–	GP	G	A	Pts	PIM	PP	SH	GW
1982-83	Orillia Travelways	OJHL	42	6	13	19	....	....	....	77	....	....	....	....	....	....	....	....	....	....	....	....	....	....	....	....	....	....
1983-84	Orillia Travelways	OJHL	38	16	35	51	....	....	....	113	....	....	....	....	....	....	....	....	....	....	....	....	....	....	....	....	....	....
1984-85	Michigan State Spartans	CCHA	37	1	5	6	....	....	....	58	....	....	....	....	....	....	....	....	....	....	....	....	....	....	....	....	....	....
1985-86	Michigan State Spartans	CCHA	42	9	25	34	....	....	....	48	....	....	....	....	....	....	....	....	....	....	....	....	....	....	....	....	....	....
1986-87	Michigan State Spartans	CCHA	42	7	14	21	....	....	....	48	....	....	....	....	....	....	....	....	....	....	....	....	....	....	....	....	....	....
1987-88	Michigan State Spartans	CCHA	46	8	18	26	....	....	....	44	....	....	....	....	....	....	....	....	....	....	....	....	....	....	....	....	....	....
1988-89	**St. Louis Blues**	**NHL**	**70**	**1**	**22**	**23**	**1**	**16**	**17**	**47**	**0**	**0**	**0**	**77**	**1.3**	**63**	**10**	**77**	**25**	**1**	**10**	**1**	**2**	**3**	**17**	**0**	**0**	**0**
1989-90	**St. Louis Blues**	**NHL**	**34**	**0**	**5**	**5**	**0**	**4**	**4**	**6**	**0**	**0**	**0**	**19**	**0.0**	**27**	**0**	**19**	**2**	**10**	....	....	....	....	....	....	....	....
	Peoria Rivermen	IHL	22	1	8	9	....	....	....	13	....	....	....	....	....	....	....	....	....	....	....	....	....	....	....	....	....	....
1990-91	**St. Louis Blues**	**NHL**	**22**	**2**	**4**	**6**	**2**	**3**	**5**	**4**	**0**	**0**	**0**	**28**	**7.1**	**22**	**0**	**18**	**1**	**5**	....	....	....	....	....	....	....	....
	Peoria Rivermen	IHL	48	7	38	45	....	....	....	53	....	....	....	....	....	....	....	....	....	....	13	2	9	11	25	....	....	....
1991-92	HC Milano Devils	Alpenliga	20	3	12	15	....	....	....	26	....	....	....	....	....	....	....	....	....	....	....	....	....	....	....	....	....	....
	HC Milano Devils	Italy	18	7	13	20	....	....	....	12	....	....	....	....	....	....	....	....	....	....	12	5	12	17	10	....	....	....
	Canada	Nat-Team	4	0	1	1	....	....	....	0	....	....	....	....	....	....	....	....	....	....	....	....	....	....	....	....	....	....
1992-93	HC Milano Devils	Alpenliga	32	5	17	22	....	....	....	21	....	....	....	....	....	....	....	....	....	....	....	....	....	....	....	....	....	....
	HC Milano Devils	Italy	14	8	3	11	....	....	....	2	....	....	....	....	....	....	....	....	....	....	8	1	5	6	4	....	....	....
1993-94	**St. Louis Blues**	**NHL**	**48**	**1**	**7**	**8**	**1**	**5**	**6**	**32**	**0**	**0**	**0**	**41**	**2.4**	**28**	**7**	**25**	**7**	**3**	**4**	**0**	**1**	**1**	**2**	**0**	**0**	**0**
1994-95	Atlanta Knights	IHL	10	2	6	8	....	....	....	14	....	....	....	....	....	....	....	....	....	....	....	....	....	....	....	....	....	....
	Indianapolis Ice	IHL	25	2	13	15	....	....	....	19	....	....	....	....	....	....	....	....	....	....	....	....	....	....	....	....	....	....
	Canada	WC-A	8	0	0	0	....	....	....	14	....	....	....	....	....	....	....	....	....	....	....	....	....	....	....	....	....	....
1995-96	Milwaukee Admirals	IHL	80	11	68	79	....	....	....	58	....	....	....	....	....	....	....	....	....	....	4	2	2	4	4	....	....	....
1996-97	Milwaukee Admirals	IHL	25	1	10	11	....	....	....	8	....	....	....	....	....	....	....	....	....	....	3	0	1	1	0	....	....	....
1997-98	Chicago Wolves	IHL	73	9	49	58	....	....	....	49	....	....	....	....	....	....	....	....	....	....	22	2	*17	19	14	....	....	....
1998-99	Chicago Wolves	IHL	73	5	55	60	....	....	....	32	....	....	....	....	....	....	....	....	....	....	10	1	1	2	2	....	....	....
99-2000	Chicago Wolves	IHL	75	2	34	36	....	....	....	42	....	....	....	....	....	....	....	....	....	....	12	1	6	7	6	....	....	....
	NHL Totals		**174**	**4**	**38**	**42**	**4**	**28**	**32**	**89**	**0**	**0**	**0**	**165**	**2.4**	**140**	**17**	**139**	**35**		**14**	**1**	**3**	**4**	**19**	**0**	**0**	**0**

CCHA First All-Star Team (1988) • IHL Second All-Star Team (1991, 1996) • IHL Second All-Star Team (1999)

Traded to **Tampa Bay** by **St. Louis** for Adam Creighton, October 6, 1994. Traded to **Chicago** by **Tampa Bay** with Jim Cummins and Jeff Buchanan for Paul Ysebaert and Rich Sutter, February 22, 1995.

• **TIMANDER, Mattias** Erik Mattias D – L. 6'3", 210 lbs. b: Solleftea, Sweden, 4/16/1974. Boston's 7th, 208th overall, in 1992.

Season	Club	League	GP	G	A	Pts	AG	AA	APts	PIM	PP	SH	GW	S	%	TGF	PGF	TGA	PGA	+/–	GP	G	A	Pts	PIM	PP	SH	GW
1991-92	MoDo AIK	Sweden-Jr.	STATISTICS NOT AVAILABLE																									
	Sweden	EJC-A	5	0	2	2	....	....	....	2	....	....	....	....	....	....	....	....	....	....	....	....	....	....	....	....	....	....
1992-93	MoDo AIK	Sweden-Jr.	4	0	0	0	....	....	....	0	....	....	....	....	....	....	....	....	....	....	....	....	....	....	....	....	....	....
	Husums IF	Sweden-2	27	4	9	13	....	....	....	22	....	....	....	....	....	....	....	....	....	....	....	....	....	....	....	....	....	....
	MoDo AIK	Sweden	1	0	0	0	....	....	....	0	....	....	....	....	....	....	....	....	....	....	....	....	....	....	....	....	....	....
1993-94	MoDo AIK	Sweden-Jr.	3	2	2	4	....	....	....	10	....	....	....	....	....	....	....	....	....	....	....	....	....	....	....	....	....	....
	MoDo AIK	Sweden	23	2	2	4	....	....	....	6	....	....	....	....	....	....	....	....	....	....	11	2	0	2	10	....	....	....
	Sweden	WJC-A	7	0	1	1	....	....	....	0	....	....	....	....	....	....	....	....	....	....	....	....	....	....	....	....	....	....
1994-95	MoDo Hockey	Sweden	39	8	9	17	....	....	....	24	....	....	....	....	....	....	....	....	....	....	....	....	....	....	....	....	....	....
1995-96	MoDo Hockey	Sweden	37	4	10	14	....	....	....	34	....	....	....	....	....	....	....	....	....	....	7	1	1	2	8	....	....	....
1996-97	**Boston Bruins**	**NHL**	**41**	**1**	**8**	**9**	**1**	**7**	**8**	**14**	**0**	**0**	**0**	**62**	**1.6**	**38**	**8**	**43**	**4**	**–9**	....	....	....	....	....	....	....	....
	Providence Bruins	AHL	32	3	11	14	....	....	....	20	....	....	....	....	....	....	....	....	....	....	10	1	1	2	12	....	....	....
1997-98	**Boston Bruins**	**NHL**	**23**	**1**	**1**	**2**	**1**	**1**	**2**	**6**	**0**	**0**	**0**	**17**	**5.9**	**8**	**2**	**17**	**2**	**–9**	....	....	....	....	....	....	....	....
	Providence Bruins	AHL	31	3	7	10	....	....	....	25	....	....	....	....	....	....	....	....	....	....	....	....	....	....	....	....	....	....
1998-99	**Boston Bruins**	**NHL**	**22**	**0**	**6**	**6**	**0**	**6**	**6**	**10**	**0**	**0**	**0**	**22**	**0.0**	**16**	**4**	**9**	**1**	**4**	**4**	**1**	**1**	**2**	**2**	**0**	**0**	**0**
	Providence Bruins	AHL	43	2	22	24	....	....	....	24	....	....	....	....	....	....	....	....	....	....	....	....	....	....	....	....	....	....
99-2000	**Boston Bruins**	**NHL**	**60**	**0**	**8**	**8**	**0**	**7**	**7**	**22**	**0**	**0**	**0**	**39**	**0.0**	**30**	**2**	**42**	**3**	**–11**	....	....	....	....	....	....	....	....
	Hershey Bears	AHL	1	0	0	0	....	....	....	2	....	....	....	....	....	....	....	....	....	....	....	....	....	....	....	....	....	....
	NHL Totals		**146**	**2**	**23**	**25**	**2**	**21**	**23**	**52**	**0**	**0**	**0**	**140**	**1.4**	**92**	**16**	**111**	**10**		**4**	**1**	**1**	**2**	**2**	**0**	**0**	**0**

Selected by **Columbus** from **Boston** in Expansion Draft, June 23, 2000.

• **TIMONEN, Kimmo** D – L. 5'10", 187 lbs. b: Kuopio, Finland, 3/18/1975. Los Angeles' 11th, 250th overall, in 1993.

Season	Club	League	GP	G	A	Pts	AG	AA	APts	PIM	PP	SH	GW	S	%	TGF	PGF	TGA	PGA	+/–	GP	G	A	Pts	PIM	PP	SH	GW
1990-91	KalPa Kuopio	Finland-Jr.	4	0	1	1	....	....	....	2	....	....	....	....	....	....	....	....	....	....	....	....	....	....	....	....	....	....
1991-92	KalPa Kuopio	Finland-Jr.	32	7	10	17	....	....	....	4	....	....	....	....	....	....	....	....	....	....	....	....	....	....	....	....	....	....
	KalPa Kuopio	Finland	5	0	0	0	....	....	....	0	....	....	....	....	....	....	....	....	....	....	....	....	....	....	....	....	....	....
1992-93	KalPa Kuopio	Finland-Jr.	16	9	15	24	....	....	....	10	....	....	....	....	....	....	....	....	....	....	....	....	....	....	....	....	....	....
	Finland	WJC-A	7	2	0	2	....	....	....	6	....	....	....	....	....	....	....	....	....	....	....	....	....	....	....	....	....	....
	KalPa Kuopio	Finland	33	0	2	2	....	....	....	4	....	....	....	....	....	....	....	....	....	....	....	....	....	....	....	....	....	....
1993-94	KalPa Kuopio	Finland-Jr.	5	4	7	11	....	....	....	0	....	....	....	....	....	....	....	....	....	....	....	....	....	....	....	....	....	....
	KalPa Kuopio	Finland	46	6	7	13	....	....	....	55	....	....	....	....	....	....	....	....	....	....	....	....	....	....	....	....	....	....
	Finland	WJC-A	7	3	3	6	....	....	....	4	....	....	....	....	....	....	....	....	....	....	....	....	....	....	....	....	....	....
1994-95	TPS Turku	Finland-Jr.	1	0	0	0	....	....	....	0	....	....	....	....	....	....	....	....	....	....	....	....	....	....	....	....	....	....
	TPS Turku	Finland	45	3	4	7	....	....	....	10	....	....	....	....	....	....	....	....	....	....	13	0	1	1	6	....	....	....
	Finland	WJC-A	7	2	6	8	....	....	....	4	....	....	....	....	....	....	....	....	....	....	....	....	....	....	....	....	....	....
1995-96	TPS Turku	Finland	48	3	21	24	....	....	....	22	....	....	....	....	....	....	....	....	....	....	9	1	2	3	12	....	....	....
	Finland	WC-A	6	0	1	1	....	....	....	0	....	....	....	....	....	....	....	....	....	....	....	....	....	....	....	....	....	....
1996-97	TPS Turku	Finland	50	10	14	24	....	....	....	18	....	....	....	....	....	....	....	....	....	....	12	2	7	9	8	....	....	....
	Finland	W-Cup	DID NOT PLAY																									
1997-98	HIFK Helsinki	Finland	45	10	15	25	....	....	....	59	....	....	....	....	....	....	....	....	....	....	9	3	4	7	8	....	....	....
	Finland	Olympics	6	0	1	1	....	....	....	2	....	....	....	....	....	....	....	....	....	....	....	....	....	....	....	....	....	....
	Finland	WC-A	10	2	6	8	....	....	....	4	....	....	....	....	....	....	....	....	....	....	....	....	....	....	....	....	....	....
1998-99	**Nashville Predators**	**NHL**	**50**	**4**	**8**	**12**	**5**	**8**	**13**	**30**	**1**	**0**	**0**	**75**	**5.3**	**44**	**13**	**38**	**3**	**–4**	....	....	....	....	....	....	....	....
	Milwaukee Admirals	IHL	29	2	13	15	....	....	....	22	....	....	....	....	....	....	....	....	....	....	....	....	....	....	....	....	....	....
	Finland	WC-A	12	1	4	5	....	....	....	6	....	....	....	....	....	....	....	....	....	....	....	....	....	....	....	....	....	....
99-2000	**Nashville Predators**	**NHL**	**51**	**8**	**25**	**33**	**9**	**23**	**32**	**26**	**2**	**1**	**2**	**97**	**8.2**	**62**	**24**	**46**	**3**	**–5**	....	....	....	....	....	....	....	....
	NHL Totals		**101**	**12**	**33**	**45**	**14**	**31**	**45**	**56**	**3**	**1**	**2**	**172**	**7.0**	**106**	**37**	**84**	**6**		....	....	....	....	....	....	....	....

Traded to **Nashville** by **LA Kings** with Jan Vopat for future considerations, June 26, 1998.

• **TINORDI, Mark** Mark D. D – L. 6'4", 213 lbs. b: Red Deer, Alta., 5/9/1966.

Season	Club	League	GP	G	A	Pts	AG	AA	APts	PIM	PP	SH	GW	S	%	TGF	PGF	TGA	PGA	+/–	GP	G	A	Pts	PIM	PP	SH	GW
1981-82	Red Deer Optomist Chiefs	AAHA	STATISTICS NOT AVAILABLE																									
1982-83	Lethbridge Broncos	WHL	64	0	4	4	....	....	....	50	....	....	....	....	....	....	....	....	....	....	20	1	1	2	6	....	....	....
	Lethbridge Broncos	Mem-Cup	3	0	0	0	....	....	....	0	....	....	....	....	....	....	....	....	....	....	....	....	....	....	....	....	....	....
1983-84	Lethbridge Broncos	WHL	72	5	14	19	....	....	....	53	....	....	....	....	....	....	....	....	....	....	5	0	1	1	7	....	....	....
1984-85	Lethbridge Broncos	WHL	58	10	15	25	....	....	....	134	....	....	....	....	....	....	....	....	....	....	4	0	2	2	12	....	....	....
1985-86	Lethbridge Broncos	WHL	58	8	30	38	....	....	....	139	....	....	....	....	....	....	....	....	....	....	8	1	3	4	15	....	....	....
1986-87	Calgary Wranglers	WHL	61	29	37	66	....	....	....	148	....	....	....	....	....	....	....	....	....	....	....	....	....	....	....	....	....	....
	New Haven Nighthawks	AHL	2	0	0	0	....	....	....	2	....	....	....	....	....	....	....	....	....	....	2	0	0	0	0	....	....	....
1987-88	**New York Rangers**	**NHL**	**24**	**1**	**2**	**3**	**1**	**1**	**2**	**50**	**0**	**0**	**0**	**13**	**7.7**	**11**	**1**	**16**	**1**	**–5**	....	....	....	....	....	....	....	....
	Colorado Rangers	IHL	41	8	19	27	....	....	....	150	....	....	....	....	....	....	....	....	....	....	11	1	5	6	31	....	....	....
1988-89	**Minnesota North Stars**	**NHL**	**47**	**2**	**3**	**5**	**2**	**2**	**4**	**107**	**0**	**0**	**0**	**39**	**5.1**	**25**	**0**	**53**	**19**	**–9**	**5**	**0**	**0**	**0**	**0**	**0**	**0**	**0**
	Kalamazoo Wings	IHL	10	0	0	0	....	....	....	35	....	....	....	....	....	....	....	....	....	....	....	....	....	....	....	....	....	....
1989-90	**Minnesota North Stars**	**NHL**	**66**	**3**	**7**	**10**	**3**	**5**	**8**	**240**	**1**	**0**	**0**	**50**	**6.0**	**49**	**2**	**76**	**29**	**0**	**7**	**0**	**1**	**1**	**16**	**0**	**0**	**0**

			REGULAR SEASON																		PLAYOFFS							
Season	Club	League	GP	G	A	Pts	AG	AA	APts	PIM	PP	SH	GW	S	%	TGF	PGF	TGA	PGA	+/–	GP	G	A	Pts	PIM	PP	SH	GW
1990-91	Minnesota North Stars	Fr-Tour	4	0	0	0	....	....	....	24	....	....	....	....	....	....	....	....	....	....	....	....	....	....	....	....	....	....
	Minnesota North Stars	**NHL**	69	5	27	32	5	21	26	189	1	0	2	92	5.4	92	29	94	32	1	23	5	6	11	78	4	0	0
1991-92	Canada	Can-Cup	3	0	0	0	....	....	....	2	....	....	....	....	....	....	....	....	....	....	....	....	....	....	....	....	....	....
	Minnesota North Stars	**NHL**	63	4	24	28	4	18	22	179	4	0	0	93	4.3	84	32	92	27	–13	7	1	2	3	11	0	0	0
1992-93	**Minnesota North Stars**	**NHL**	69	15	27	42	12	19	31	157	7	0	2	122	12.3	110	31	118	38	–1	....	....	....	....	....	....	....	....
1993-94	**Dallas Stars**	**NHL**	61	6	18	24	6	14	20	143	1	0	0	112	5.4	80	20	79	25	6	....	....	....	....	....	....	....	....
1994-95	**Washington Capitals**	**NHL**	42	3	9	12	5	13	18	71	2	0	1	71	4.2	31	7	42	13	–5	1	0	0	0	2	0	0	0
1995-96	**Washington Capitals**	**NHL**	71	3	10	13	3	8	11	113	2	0	0	82	3.7	64	13	61	36	26	6	0	0	0	16	0	0	0
1996-97	**Washington Capitals**	**NHL**	56	2	6	8	2	5	7	118	0	0	0	53	3.8	42	1	58	20	3	....	....	....	....	....	....	....	....
1997-98	**Washington Capitals**	**NHL**	47	8	9	17	9	9	18	39	0	1	0	57	14.0	48	2	44	7	9	21	1	2	3	42	0	0	0
1998-99	**Washington Capitals**	**NHL**	48	0	6	6	0	6	6	108	0	0	0	32	0.0	31	4	50	17	–6	....	....	....	....	....	....	....	....
	NHL Totals		663	52	148	200	52	121	173	1514	18	1	5	816	6.4	667	142	783	264		70	7	11	18	165	4	0	0

Played in NHL All-Star Game (1992)

Signed as a free agent by **NY Rangers**, January 4, 1987. Traded to **Minnesota** by **NY Rangers** with Paul Jerrard, the rights to Bret Barnett and Mike Sullivan and LA Kings' 3rd round choice (previously acquired, Minnesota selected Murray Garbutt) in 1989 Entry Draft for Brian Lawton, Igor Liba and the rights to Eric Bennett, October 11, 1988. Transferred to **Dallas** after **Minnesota** franchise relocated, June 9, 1993. Traded to **Washington** by **Dallas** with Rich Mrozik for Kevin Hatcher, January 18, 1995. Claimed by **Atlanta** from **Washington** in Expansion Draft, June 25, 1999.

• TIPPETT, Dave

LW – L. 5'10", 180 lbs. b: Moosomin, Sask., 8/25/1961.

Season	Club	League	GP	G	A	Pts	AG	AA	APts	PIM	PP	SH	GW	S	%	TGF	PGF	TGA	PGA	+/–	GP	G	A	Pts	PIM	PP	SH	GW
1979-80	Prince Albert Raiders	SJHL	60	53	72	125	....	....	....	58	....	....	....	....	....	....	....	....	....	....	25	19	21	40	18	....	....	....
1980-81	Prince Albert Raiders	SJHL	60	42	68	110	....	....	....	64	....	....	....	....	....	....	....	....	....	....	24	20	25	45	22	....	....	....
	Prince Albert Raiders	Cen-Cup	STATISTICS NOT AVAILABLE																									
1981-82	University of North Dakota	WCHA	43	13	28	41	....	....	....	20	....	....	....	....	....	....	....	....	....	....	....	....	....	....	....	....	....	....
1982-83	University of North Dakota	WCHA	36	15	31	46	....	....	....	24	....	....	....	....	....	....	....	....	....	....	....	....	....	....	....	....	....	....
1983-84	Canada	Nat-Team	66	14	19	33	....	....	....	24	....	....	....	....	....	....	....	....	....	....	....	....	....	....	....	....	....	....
	Canada	Olympics	7	1	1	2	....	....	....	2	....	....	....	....	....	....	....	....	....	....	....	....	....	....	....	....	....	....
	Hartford Whalers	**NHL**	17	4	2	6	3	1	4	2	0	1	0	25	16.0	8	0	17	8	–1	....	....	....	....	....	....	....	....
1984-85	**Hartford Whalers**	**NHL**	80	7	12	19	6	8	14	12	0	0	0	98	7.1	30	3	88	37	–24	....	....	....	....	....	....	....	....
1985-86	**Hartford Whalers**	**NHL**	80	14	20	34	11	13	24	18	0	2	1	118	11.9	51	3	87	48	9	10	2	2	4	4	0	1	0
1986-87	**Hartford Whalers**	**NHL**	80	9	22	31	8	16	24	42	0	3	2	120	7.5	41	1	77	37	0	6	0	2	2	4	0	0	0
1987-88	**Hartford Whalers**	**NHL**	80	16	21	37	14	15	29	32	1	2	2	126	12.7	51	4	88	37	–4	6	0	0	0	2	0	0	0
1988-89	**Hartford Whalers**	**NHL**	80	17	24	41	14	17	31	45	1	2	1	165	10.3	75	9	120	48	–6	4	0	1	1	0	0	0	0
1989-90	**Hartford Whalers**	**NHL**	66	8	19	27	7	14	21	32	0	1	3	91	8.8	36	0	64	28	0	7	1	3	4	2	0	0	0
1990-91	**Washington Capitals**	**NHL**	61	6	9	15	5	7	12	24	0	0	2	68	8.8	31	0	56	12	–13	10	2	3	5	8	0	0	0
1991-92	**Washington Capitals**	**NHL**	30	2	10	12	2	8	10	16	0	0	0	26	7.7	14	1	18	7	2	7	0	1	1	0	0	0	0
	Canada	Nat-Team	1	0	0	0	....	....	....	4	....	....	....	....	....	....	....	....	....	....	....	....	....	....	....	....	....	....
	Canada	Olympics	7	1	2	3	....	....	....	10	....	....	....	....	....	....	....	....	....	....	....	....	....	....	....	....	....	....
1992-93	**Pittsburgh Penguins**	**NHL**	74	6	19	25	5	13	18	56	0	1	1	64	9.4	30	0	46	21	5	12	1	4	5	14	0	0	0
1993-94	**Philadelphia Flyers**	**NHL**	73	4	11	15	4	9	13	38	0	2	1	45	8.9	18	0	68	30	–20	....	....	....	....	....	....	....	....
1994-95	Houston Aeros	IHL	75	18	48	66	....	....	....	56	....	....	....	....	....	....	....	....	....	....	4	1	2	3	4	....	....	....
1995-1996	Houston Aeros	IHL	DID NOT PLAY – ASSISTANT COACH																									
1996-1999	Houston Aeros	IHL	DID NOT PLAY – COACHING																									
1999-2000	**Los Angeles Kings**	**NHL**	DID NOT PLAY – ASSISTANT COACH																									
	NHL Totals		721	93	169	262	79	121	200	317	2	14	13	946	9.8	385	21	729	313		62	6	16	22	34	0	1	0

WCHA Second All-Star Team (1983)

Signed as a free agent by **Hartford**, February 29, 1984. Traded to **Washington** by **Hartford** for Washington's 6th round choice (Jarrett Reid) in 1992 Entry Draft, September 30, 1990. Signed as a free agent by **Pittsburgh**, August 25, 1992. Signed as a free agent by **Philadelphia**, August 30, 1993.

• TITANIC, Morris

Morris S. LW – L. 6'1", 180 lbs. b: Toronto, Ont., 1/7/1953. Buffalo's 1st, 12th overall, in 1973.

Season	Club	League	GP	G	A	Pts	AG	AA	APts	PIM	PP	SH	GW	S	%	TGF	PGF	TGA	PGA	+/–	GP	G	A	Pts	PIM	PP	SH	GW
1970-71	Niagara Falls Flyers	OHA-Jr.	59	27	17	44	....	....	....	61	....	....	....	....	....	....	....	....	....	....	....	....	....	....	....	....	....	....
1971-72	Niagara Falls Flyers	OMJHL	64	29	28	57	....	....	....	105	....	....	....	....	....	....	....	....	....	....	6	1	5	6	6	....	....	....
1972-73	Sudbury Wolves	OMJHL	63	61	60	121	....	....	....	80	....	....	....	....	....	....	....	....	....	....	4	2	0	2	0	....	....	....
1973-74	Cincinnati Swords	AHL	62	31	28	59	....	....	....	47	....	....	....	....	....	....	....	....	....	....	5	4	2	6	0	....	....	....
1974-75	**Buffalo Sabres**	**NHL**	17	0	0	0	0	0	0	0	0	0	0	6	0.0	4	2	7	1	–4	....	....	....	....	....	....	....	....
	Hershey Bears	AHL	34	9	17	26	....	....	....	64	....	....	....	....	....	....	....	....	....	....	6	3	3	6	16	....	....	....
1975-76	**Buffalo Sabres**	**NHL**	2	0	0	0	0	0	0	0	0	0	0	2	0.0	1	0	0	0	1	....	....	....	....	....	....	....	....
	Hershey Bears	AHL	35	6	13	19	....	....	....	10	....	....	....	....	....	....	....	....	....	....	10	2	1	3	8	....	....	....
1976-77	**Buffalo Sabres**	**NHL**	DID NOT PLAY – INJURED																									
1977-78	Hershey Bears	AHL	69	10	20	30	....	....	....	54	....	....	....	....	....	....	....	....	....	....	....	....	....	....	....	....	....	....
1978-79	Milwaukee Admirals	IHL	75	26	44	70	....	....	....	31	....	....	....	....	....	....	....	....	....	....	8	3	1	4	0	....	....	....
1979-80	Rochester Americans	AHL	25	3	3	6	....	....	....	6	....	....	....	....	....	....	....	....	....	....	....	....	....	....	....	....	....	....
	NHL Totals		19	0	0	0	0	0	0	0	0	0	0	8	0.0	5	2	7	1		....	....	....	....	....	....	....	....

OMJHL First All-Star Team (1973) • Missed entire 1976-77 season recovering from back surgery, September, 1976.

• TITOV, German

C – L. 6'1", 201 lbs. b: Moscow, USSR, 10/16/1965. Calgary's 10th, 252nd overall, in 1993.

Season	Club	League	GP	G	A	Pts	AG	AA	APts	PIM	PP	SH	GW	S	%	TGF	PGF	TGA	PGA	+/–	GP	G	A	Pts	PIM	PP	SH	GW
1982-83	Khimik Voskresensk	USSR	16	0	4	4	....	....	....	2	....	....	....	....	....	....	....	....	....	....	....	....	....	....	....	....	....	....
1983-1986			DID NOT PLAY																									
1986-87	Khimik Voskresensk	USSR	23	1	0	1	....	....	....	10	....	....	....	....	....	....	....	....	....	....	....	....	....	....	....	....	....	....
1987-88	Khimik Voskresensk	USSR	39	6	5	11	....	....	....	10	....	....	....	....	....	....	....	....	....	....	....	....	....	....	....	....	....	....
1988-89	Khimik Voskresensk	USSR	44	10	3	13	....	....	....	24	....	....	....	....	....	....	....	....	....	....	....	....	....	....	....	....	....	....
1989-90	Khimik Voskresensk	Fr-Tour	1	0	0	0	....	....	....	0	....	....	....	....	....	....	....	....	....	....	....	....	....	....	....	....	....	....
	Khimik Voskresensk	USSR	44	6	14	20	....	....	....	19	....	....	....	....	....	....	....	....	....	....	....	....	....	....	....	....	....	....
	Khimik Voskresensk	Super-S	6	0	0	0	....	....	....	0	....	....	....	....	....	....	....	....	....	....	....	....	....	....	....	....	....	....
1990-91	Khimik Voskresensk	Fr-Tour	1	0	0	0	....	....	....	0	....	....	....	....	....	....	....	....	....	....	....	....	....	....	....	....	....	....
	Khimik Voskresensk	USSR	45	13	11	24	....	....	....	28	....	....	....	....	....	....	....	....	....	....	....	....	....	....	....	....	....	....
	Khimik Voskresensk	Super-S	7	2	5	7	....	....	....	0	....	....	....	....	....	....	....	....	....	....	....	....	....	....	....	....	....	....
1991-92	Khimik Voskresensk	CIS	42	18	13	31	....	....	....	35	....	....	....	....	....	....	....	....	....	....	....	....	....	....	....	....	....	....
1992-93	TPS Turku	Finland	47	25	19	44	....	....	....	49	....	....	....	....	....	....	....	....	....	....	12	5	12	17	10	....	....	....
	Russia	WC-A	8	4	2	6	....	....	....	0	....	....	....	....	....	....	....	....	....	....	....	....	....	....	....	....	....	....
1993-94	**Calgary Flames**	**NHL**	76	27	18	45	25	14	39	28	8	3	2	153	17.6	77	21	67	31	20	7	2	1	3	4	1	0	0
1994-95	TPS Turku	Finland	14	6	6	12	....	....	....	20	....	....	....	....	....	....	....	....	....	....	....	....	....	....	....	....	....	....
	Calgary Flames	**NHL**	40	12	12	24	21	18	39	16	3	2	3	88	13.6	35	6	33	10	6	7	5	3	8	10	0	1	0
1995-96	**Calgary Flames**	**NHL**	82	28	39	67	28	32	60	24	13	2	2	214	13.1	116	42	78	13	9	4	0	2	2	0	0	0	0
1996-97	**Calgary Flames**	**NHL**	79	22	30	52	23	27	50	36	12	0	4	192	11.5	75	32	64	9	–12	....	....	....	....	....	....	....	....
1997-98	**Calgary Flames**	**NHL**	68	18	22	40	21	22	43	38	6	1	2	133	13.5	70	15	66	10	–1	....	....	....	....	....	....	....	....
	Russia	Olympics	6	1	0	1	....	....	....	6	....	....	....	....	....	....	....	....	....	....	....	....	....	....	....	....	....	....
1998-99	**Pittsburgh Penguins**	**NHL**	72	11	45	56	13	43	56	34	3	1	3	113	9.7	92	30	57	13	18	11	3	5	8	4	0	0	0
99-2000	**Pittsburgh Penguins**	**NHL**	63	17	25	42	19	23	42	34	4	2	3	111	15.3	61	18	59	13	–3	....	....	....	....	....	....	....	....
	Edmonton Oilers	**NHL**	7	0	4	4	0	4	4	4	0	0	0	11	0.0	5	1	2	0	2	5	1	1	2	0	0	0	0
	NHL Totals		487	135	195	330	150	183	333	214	49	11	19	1015	13.3	531	165	426	99		34	11	12	23	18	1	1	0

Traded to **Pittsburgh** by **Calgary** with Todd Hlushko for Ken Wregget and Dave Roche, June 17, 1998. Traded to **Edmonton** by **Pittsburgh** for Josef Beranek, March 14, 2000. Signed as a free agent by **Anaheim**, July 1, 2000.

• TKACHUK, Keith

Keith Matthew "Walt" LW – L. 6'2", 220 lbs. b: Melrose, MA, 3/28/1972. Winnipeg's 1st, 19th overall, in 1990.

Season	Club	League	GP	G	A	Pts	AG	AA	APts	PIM	PP	SH	GW	S	%	TGF	PGF	TGA	PGA	+/–	GP	G	A	Pts	PIM	PP	SH	GW
1988-89	Malden Catholic High School	Hi-School	21	30	16	46	....	....	....	....	....	....	....	....	....	....	....	....	....	....	....	....	....	....	....	....	....	....
1989-90	Malden Catholic High School	Hi-School	6	12	14	26	....	....	....	....	....	....	....	....	....	....	....	....	....	....	....	....	....	....	....	....	....	....
1990-91	Boston University	H-East	36	17	23	40	....	....	....	70	....	....	....	....	....	....	....	....	....	....	....	....	....	....	....	....	....	....
	United States	WJC-A	7	6	3	9	....	....	....	12	....	....	....	....	....	....	....	....	....	....	....	....	....	....	....	....	....	....

			REGULAR SEASON																		PLAYOFFS							
Season	**Club**	**League**	**GP**	**G**	**A**	**Pts**	**AG**	**AA**	**APts**	**PIM**	**PP**	**SH**	**GW**	**S**	**%**	**TGF**	**PGF**	**TGA**	**PGA**	**+/–**	**GP**	**G**	**A**	**Pts**	**PIM**	**PP**	**SH**	**GW**
1991-92	United States	Nat-Team	45	10	10	20	....	....	....	141	....	....	....	....	....	....	....	....	....	....	....	....	....	....	....	....	....	....
	United States	WJC-A	7	3	4	7	....	....	....	6	....	....	....	....	....	....	....	....	....	....	....	....	....	....	....	....	....	....
	United States	Olympics	8	1	1	2	....	....	....	12	....	....	....	....	....	....	....	....	....	....	....	....	....	....	....	....	....	....
	Winnipeg Jets	**NHL**	17	3	5	8	3	4	7	28	2	0	0	22	13.6	12	5	7	0	0	7	3	0	3	30	0	0	0
1992-93	**Winnipeg Jets**	**NHL**	83	28	23	51	23	16	39	201	12	0	2	199	14.1	92	39	67	1	–13	6	4	0	4	14	1	0	0
1993-94	**Winnipeg Jets**	**NHL**	84	41	40	81	38	31	69	255	22	3	3	218	18.8	125	56	97	16	–12	....	....	....	....	....	....	....	....
1994-95	**Winnipeg Jets**	**NHL**	48	22	29	51	39	43	82	152	7	2	2	129	17.1	72	29	59	12	–4	....	....	....	....	....	....	....	....
1995-96	**Winnipeg Jets**	**NHL**	76	50	48	98	49	39	88	156	20	2	6	249	20.1	140	61	94	26	11	6	1	2	3	22	0	0	0
1996-97	United States	W-Cup	7	5	1	6	....	....	....	44	....	....	....	....	....	....	....	....	....	....	....	....	....	....	....	....	....	....
	Phoenix Coyotes	**NHL**	81	*52	34	86	55	30	85	228	9	2	7	296	17.6	121	36	96	10	–1	7	6	0	6	7	2	0	0
1997-98	**Phoenix Coyotes**	**NHL**	69	40	26	66	47	25	72	147	11	0	8	232	17.2	96	34	61	8	9	6	3	3	6	10	0	0	0
	United States	Olympics	4	0	2	2	....	....	....	6	....	....	....	....	....	....	....	....	....	....	....	....	....	....	....	....	....	....
1998-99	**Phoenix Coyotes**	**NHL**	68	36	32	68	42	31	73	151	11	2	7	258	14.0	91	24	47	2	22	7	1	3	4	13	1	0	0
99-2000	**Phoenix Coyotes**	**NHL**	50	22	21	43	25	19	44	82	5	1	1	183	12.0	68	19	45	3	7	5	1	1	2	4	1	0	0
	NHL Totals		576	294	258	552	321	238	559	1400	99	12	36	1786	16.5	817	303	573	78		44	19	9	28	100	5	0	0

NHL Second All-Star Team (1995, 1998) • Played in NHL All-Star Game (1997, 1998, 1999)

Transferred to **Phoenix** after **Winnipeg** franchise relocated, July 1, 1996.

• TKACZUK, Walt

Walter Robert C – L. 6′, 185 lbs. b: Emstedetten, Germany, 9/29/1947.

			REGULAR SEASON																		PLAYOFFS							
Season	**Club**	**League**	**GP**	**G**	**A**	**Pts**	**AG**	**AA**	**APts**	**PIM**	**PP**	**SH**	**GW**	**S**	**%**	**TGF**	**PGF**	**TGA**	**PGA**	**+/–**	**GP**	**G**	**A**	**Pts**	**PIM**	**PP**	**SH**	**GW**
1963-64	Kitchener Greenshirts	OHA-B	30	25	37	62	....	....	....	....	....	....	....	....	....	....	....	....	....	....	....	....	....	....	....	....	....	....
	Kitchener Rangers	OHA-Jr.	21	5	5	10	....	....	....	4	....	....	....	....	....	....	....	....	....	....	....	....	....	....	....	....	....	....
1964-65	Kitchener Greenshirts	OHA-B	STATISTICS NOT AVAILABLE																									
	Kitchener Rangers	OHA-Jr.	7	1	2	3	....	....	....	6	....	....	....	....	....	....	....	....	....	....	....	....	....	....	....	....	....	....
1965-66	Kitchener Rangers	OHA-Jr.	47	12	31	43	....	....	....	39	....	....	....	....	....	....	....	....	....	....	19	7	*23	30	13	....	....	....
1966-67	Kitchener Rangers	OHA-Jr.	48	23	47	70	....	....	....	85	....	....	....	....	....	....	....	....	....	....	13	6	8	14	23	....	....	....
	Omaha Knights	CPHL	....	....	....	....	....	....	....	....	....	....	....	....	....	....	....	....	....	....	3	2	0	2	2	....	....	....
1967-68	Kitchener Rangers	OHA-Jr.	52	37	56	93	....	....	....	81	....	....	....	....	....	....	....	....	....	....	19	*17	*20	*37	58	....	....	....
	New York Rangers	**NHL**	2	0	0	0	0	0	0	0	0	0	0	0	0.0	0	0	1	0	–1	....	....	....	....	....	....	....	....
1968-69	**New York Rangers**	**NHL**	71	12	24	36	13	21	34	28	0	0	1	130	9.2	43	8	46	0	–11	4	0	1	1	6	0	0	0
	Buffalo Bisons	AHL	5	2	7	9	....	....	....	9	....	....	....	....	....	....	....	....	....	....	....	....	....	....	....	....	....	....
1969-70	**New York Rangers**	**NHL**	76	27	50	77	29	47	76	38	5	0	2	203	13.3	96	18	53	1	26	6	2	1	3	17	1	0	0
1970-71	**New York Rangers**	**NHL**	77	26	49	75	26	41	67	48	5	1	4	212	12.3	97	23	58	2	18	13	1	5	6	14	0	0	1
1971-72	**New York Rangers**	**NHL**	76	24	42	66	24	36	60	65	3	2	2	231	10.4	89	15	57	17	34	16	4	6	10	35	0	0	2
1972-73	**New York Rangers**	**NHL**	76	27	39	66	25	31	56	59	6	1	7	264	10.2	106	25	67	21	35	10	7	2	9	8	1	0	1
1973-74	**New York Rangers**	**NHL**	71	21	42	63	20	35	55	58	3	3	0	218	9.6	84	21	65	17	15	13	0	5	5	22	0	0	0
1974-75	**New York Rangers**	**NHL**	62	11	25	36	10	19	29	34	2	0	1	134	8.2	65	24	56	16	1	3	1	2	3	5	0	0	0
1975-76	**New York Rangers**	**NHL**	78	8	28	36	7	21	28	56	1	0	1	142	5.6	44	4	81	31	–10	....	....	....	....	....	....	....	....
1976-77	**New York Rangers**	**NHL**	80	12	38	50	11	29	40	38	1	1	0	139	8.6	69	5	68	15	11	....	....	....	....	....	....	....	....
1977-78	**New York Rangers**	**NHL**	80	26	40	66	24	31	55	30	6	1	3	144	18.1	86	13	91	33	15	3	0	2	2	0	0	0	0
1978-79	**New York Rangers**	**NHL**	77	15	27	42	13	20	33	38	4	0	0	134	11.2	73	8	80	35	20	18	4	7	11	10	0	1	0
1979-80	**New York Rangers**	**NHL**	76	12	25	37	10	18	28	36	4	2	2	128	9.4	67	13	55	20	19	7	0	1	1	2	0	0	0
1980-81	**New York Rangers**	**NHL**	43	6	22	28	5	15	20	28	1	0	0	67	9.0	40	2	38	13	13	....	....	....	....	....	....	....	....
	NHL Totals		945	227	451	678	217	364	581	556	41	11	23	2146	10.6	959	179	816	221		93	19	32	51	119	2	1	4

OHA-Jr. Second All-Star Team (1967) • OHA-Jr. First All-Star Team (1968) • Played in NHL All-Star Game (1970)

• TOAL, Mike

Michael James C – R. 6′, 175 lbs. b: Red Deer, Alta., 3/23/1959. Edmonton's 5th, 105th overall, in 1979.

			REGULAR SEASON																		PLAYOFFS							
Season	**Club**	**League**	**GP**	**G**	**A**	**Pts**	**AG**	**AA**	**APts**	**PIM**	**PP**	**SH**	**GW**	**S**	**%**	**TGF**	**PGF**	**TGA**	**PGA**	**+/–**	**GP**	**G**	**A**	**Pts**	**PIM**	**PP**	**SH**	**GW**
1975-76	Red Deer Royals	AAHA	STATISTICS NOT AVAILABLE																									
1976-77	Victoria Cougars	WCJHL	29	6	12	18	....	....	....	25	....	....	....	....	....	....	....	....	....	....	....	....	....	....	....	....	....	....
	Calgary Centennials	WCJHL	34	10	11	21	....	....	....	11	....	....	....	....	....	....	....	....	....	....	4	0	1	1	0	....	....	....
1977-78	Billings Bighorns	WCJHL	69	30	34	64	....	....	....	48	....	....	....	....	....	....	....	....	....	....	19	5	13	18	4	....	....	....
1978-79	Portland Winter Hawks	WHL	71	38	83	121	....	....	....	32	....	....	....	....	....	....	....	....	....	....	....	....	....	....	....	....	....	....
1979-80	**Edmonton Oilers**	**NHL**	3	0	0	0	0	0	0	0	0	0	0	1	0.0	0	0	0	0	0	....	....	....	....	....	....	....	....
	Houston Apollos	CHL	76	31	45	76	....	....	....	47	....	....	....	....	....	....	....	....	....	....	6	1	0	1	2	....	....	....
1980-81	Rochester Americans	AHL	14	0	0	0	....	....	....	84	....	....	....	....	....	....	....	....	....	....	....	....	....	....	....	....	....	....
	Wichita Wind	CHL	70	16	18	34	....	....	....	63	....	....	....	....	....	....	....	....	....	....	....	....	....	....	....	....	....	....
1981-82	Wichita Wind	CHL	55	15	15	30	....	....	....	14	....	....	....	....	....	....	....	....	....	....	1	0	0	0	0	....	....	....
	NHL Totals		3	0	0	0	0	0	0	0	0	0	0	1	0.0	0	0	0	0		....	....	....	....	....	....	....	....

WHL Second All-Star Team (1979)

• TOCCHET, Rick

RW – R. 6′, 210 lbs. b: Scarborough, Ont., 4/9/1964. Philadelphia's 5th, 125th overall, in 1983.

			REGULAR SEASON																		PLAYOFFS							
Season	**Club**	**League**	**GP**	**G**	**A**	**Pts**	**AG**	**AA**	**APts**	**PIM**	**PP**	**SH**	**GW**	**S**	**%**	**TGF**	**PGF**	**TGA**	**PGA**	**+/–**	**GP**	**G**	**A**	**Pts**	**PIM**	**PP**	**SH**	**GW**
1980-81	St. Michael's Midget Buzzers	MTHL	41	28	46	74	....	....	....	....	....	....	....	....	....	....	....	....	....	....	....	....	....	....	....	....	....	....
	St. Michael's Buzzers	OHA-B	5	1	1	2	....	....	....	2	....	....	....	....	....	....	....	....	....	....	....	....	....	....	....	....	....	....
1981-82	Sault Ste. Marie Greyhounds	OHL	59	7	15	22	....	....	....	184	....	....	....	....	....	....	....	....	....	....	11	1	1	2	28	....	....	....
1982-83	Sault Ste. Marie Greyhounds	OHL	66	32	34	66	....	....	....	146	....	....	....	....	....	....	....	....	....	....	16	4	13	17	67	....	....	....
1983-84	Sault Ste. Marie Greyhounds	OHL	64	44	64	108	....	....	....	209	....	....	....	....	....	....	....	....	....	....	16	*22	14	*36	41	....	....	....
1984-85	**Philadelphia Flyers**	**NHL**	75	14	25	39	11	17	28	181	0	0	0	112	12.5	50	4	42	2	6	19	3	4	7	72	0	0	2
1985-86	**Philadelphia Flyers**	**NHL**	69	14	21	35	11	14	25	284	3	0	1	107	13.1	56	7	41	4	12	5	1	2	3	26	0	0	0
1986-87	**Philadelphia Flyers**	**NHL**	69	21	28	49	18	20	38	288	1	1	5	147	14.3	68	6	58	12	16	26	11	10	21	72	0	1	2
1987-88	Canada	Can-Cup	7	3	2	5	....	....	....	8	....	....	....	....	....	....	....	....	....	....	....	....	....	....	....	....	....	....
	Philadelphia Flyers	**NHL**	65	31	33	64	26	24	50	301	10	2	3	182	17.0	87	32	62	10	3	5	1	4	5	55	2	1	0
1988-89	**Philadelphia Flyers**	**NHL**	66	45	36	81	38	25	63	183	16	1	5	220	20.5	113	49	68	3	–1	16	6	6	12	69	2	0	1
1989-90	**Philadelphia Flyers**	**NHL**	75	37	59	96	32	42	74	196	15	1	0	269	13.8	119	43	89	17	4	....	....	....	....	....	....	....	....
	Canada	WEC-A	10	4	2	6	....	....	....	14	....	....	....	....	....	....	....	....	....	....	....	....	....	....	....	....	....	....
1990-91	**Philadelphia Flyers**	**NHL**	70	40	31	71	37	24	61	150	8	0	5	217	18.4	117	46	77	8	2	....	....	....	....	....	....	....	....
1991-92	Canada	Can-Cup	8	1	1	2	....	....	....	10	....	....	....	....	....	....	....	....	....	....	....	....	....	....	....	....	....	....
	Philadelphia Flyers	**NHL**	42	13	16	29	12	12	24	102	4	0	1	107	12.1	44	17	24	0	3	....	....	....	....	....	....	....	....
♦	**Pittsburgh Penguins**	**NHL**	19	14	16	30	13	12	25	49	4	1	1	59	23.7	42	12	22	4	12	14	6	13	19	24	3	0	1
1992-93	**Pittsburgh Penguins**	**NHL**	80	48	61	109	40	42	82	252	20	4	5	240	20.0	165	62	83	8	28	12	7	6	13	24	1	0	0
1993-94	**Pittsburgh Penguins**	**NHL**	51	14	26	40	13	20	33	134	5	1	2	150	9.3	67	28	58	4	–15	6	2	3	5	20	1	0	1
1994-95	**Los Angeles Kings**	**NHL**	36	18	17	35	32	25	57	70	7	1	3	95	18.9	54	22	41	1	–8	....	....	....	....	....	....	....	....
1995-96	**Los Angeles Kings**	**NHL**	44	13	23	36	13	19	32	117	4	0	0	100	13.0	49	14	32	0	3	....	....	....	....	....	....	....	....
	Boston Bruins	**NHL**	27	16	8	24	16	7	23	64	6	0	3	85	18.8	39	16	16	0	7	5	4	0	4	21	3	0	1
1996-97	**Boston Bruins**	**NHL**	40	16	14	30	17	12	29	67	3	0	1	120	13.3	45	11	37	0	–3	....	....	....	....	....	....	....	....
	Washington Capitals	**NHL**	13	5	5	10	5	4	9	31	1	0	1	37	13.5	15	2	13	0	0	....	....	....	....	....	....	....	....
1997-98	**Phoenix Coyotes**	**NHL**	68	26	19	45	30	19	49	157	8	0	6	161	16.1	71	29	43	2	1	6	6	2	8	25	3	0	0
1998-99	**Phoenix Coyotes**	**NHL**	81	26	30	56	31	29	60	147	6	1	5	178	14.6	85	27	53	0	5	7	0	3	3	8	0	0	0
99-2000	**Phoenix Coyotes**	**NHL**	64	12	17	29	13	16	29	67	2	0	1	107	11.2	47	7	45	0	–5	....	....	....	....	....	....	....	....
	Philadelphia Flyers	**NHL**	16	3	3	6	3	3	6	23	2	0	0	23	13.0	11	2	5	0	4	18	5	6	11	*49	2	0	1
	NHL Totals		1070	426	488	914	411	386	797	2863	125	13	48	2716	15.7	1344	436	909	75		139	52	59	111	465	17	2	9

Played in NHL All-Star Game (1989, 1990, 1991, 1993)

Traded to **Pittsburgh** by **Philadelphia** with Kjell Samuelsson, Ken Wregget and Philadelphia's 3rd round choice (Dave Roche) in 1993 Entry Draft for Mark Recchi, Brian Benning and LA Kings' 1st round choice (previously acquired, Philadelphia selected Jason Bowen) in 1992 Entry Draft, February 19, 1992 Traded to **LA Kings** by **Pittsburgh** with Pittsburgh's 2nd round choice (Pavel Rosa) in 1995 Entry Draft for Luc Robitaille, July 29, 1994. Traded to **Boston** by **LA Kings** for Kevin Stevens, January 25, 1996. Traded to **Washington** by **Boston** with Bill Ranford and Adam Oates for Jim Carey, Anson Carter, Jason Allison and Washington's 3rd round choice (Lee Goren) in 1997 Entry Draft, March 1, 1997. Signed as a free agent by **Phoenix**, July 23, 1997. Traded to **Philadelphia** by **Phoenix** for Mikael Renberg, March 8, 2000.

• TODD, Kevin

Kevin L. "Rat"   C – L. 5'10", 180 lbs.   b: Winnipeg, Man., 5/4/1968. New Jersey's 7th, 129th overall, in 1986.

			REGULAR SEASON																		PLAYOFFS							
Season	Club	League	GP	G	A	Pts	AG	AA	APts	PIM	PP	SH	GW	S	%	TGF	PGF	TGA	PGA	+/–	GP	G	A	Pts	PIM	PP	SH	GW
1984-85	Winnipeg Stars	MAHA	60	66	100	166																						
1985-86	Prince Albert Raiders	WHL	55	14	25	39				19											20	7	6	13	29			
1986-87	Prince Albert Raiders	WHL	71	39	46	85				92											8	2	5	7	17			
1987-88	Prince Albert Raiders	WHL	72	49	72	121				83											10	8	11	19	27			
1988-89	**New Jersey Devils**	**NHL**	**1**	**0**	**0**	**0**	**0**	**0**	**0**	**0**	**0**	**0**	**0**	**0**	**0.0**	**0**	**0**	**1**	**0**	**–1**								
	Utica Devils	AHL	78	26	45	71				62											4	2	0	2	6			
1989-90	Utica Devils	AHL	71	18	36	54				72											5	2	4	6	2			
1990-91	**New Jersey Devils**	**NHL**	**1**	**0**	**0**	**0**	**0**	**0**	**0**	**0**	**0**	**0**	**0**	**0**	**0.0**	**0**	**0**	**1**	**0**	**–1**	**1**	**0**	**0**	**0**	**6**	**0**	**0**	**0**
	Utica Devils	AHL	75	37	*81	*118				75																		
1991-92	**New Jersey Devils**	**NHL**	**80**	**21**	**42**	**63**	**19**	**32**	**51**	**69**	**2**	**0**	**2**	**131**	**16.0**	**88**	**21**	**60**	**1**	**8**	**7**	**3**	**2**	**5**	**8**	**1**	**0**	**0**
1992-93	**New Jersey Devils**	**NHL**	**30**	**5**	**5**	**10**	**4**	**3**	**7**	**16**	**0**	**0**	**2**	**48**	**10.4**	**21**	**4**	**24**	**3**	**–4**								
	Utica Devils	AHL	2	2	1	3				0																		
	Edmonton Oilers	**NHL**	**25**	**4**	**9**	**13**	**3**	**6**	**9**	**10**	**0**	**0**	**1**	**39**	**10.3**	**18**	**2**	**21**	**0**	**–5**								
1993-94	**Chicago Blackhawks**	**NHL**	**35**	**5**	**6**	**11**	**5**	**5**	**10**	**16**	**1**	**0**	**1**	**49**	**10.2**	**18**	**4**	**16**	**0**	**–2**								
	Los Angeles Kings	**NHL**	**12**	**3**	**8**	**11**	**3**	**6**	**9**	**8**	**3**	**0**	**0**	**16**	**18.8**	**14**	**5**	**13**	**3**	**–1**								
1994-95	**Los Angeles Kings**	**NHL**	**33**	**3**	**8**	**11**	**5**	**12**	**17**	**12**	**0**	**0**	**1**	**34**	**8.8**	**15**	**0**	**30**	**10**	**–5**								
1995-96	**Los Angeles Kings**	**NHL**	**74**	**16**	**27**	**43**	**16**	**22**	**38**	**38**	**0**	**2**	**4**	**132**	**12.1**	**51**	**4**	**72**	**31**	**6**								
1996-97	**Mighty Ducks of Anaheim**	**NHL**	**65**	**9**	**21**	**30**	**10**	**19**	**29**	**44**	**0**	**0**	**1**	**95**	**9.5**	**47**	**12**	**51**	**9**	**–7**	**4**	**0**	**0**	**0**	**2**	**0**	**0**	**0**
1997-98	**Mighty Ducks of Anaheim**	**NHL**	**27**	**4**	**7**	**11**	**5**	**7**	**12**	**12**	**3**	**0**	**1**	**30**	**13.3**	**18**	**9**	**14**	**0**	**–5**								
	Long Beach Ice Dogs	IHL	30	18	28	46				54											13	1	10	11	38			
1998-99	EV Zug	Switz.	40	9	41	50				81											5	0	2	2	2			
	EV Zug	EuroHL	4	0	0	0				31											2	1	2	3	4			
	NHL Totals		**383**	**70**	**133**	**203**	**70**	**112**	**182**	**225**	**9**	**2**	**13**	**574**	**12.2**	**290**	**61**	**303**	**57**		**12**	**3**	**2**	**5**	**16**	**1**	**0**	**0**

AHL First All-Star Team (1991) • Won John B. Sollenberger Trophy (Leading Scorer - AHL) (1991) • Won Les Cunningham Award (MVP - AHL) (1992) • NHL All-Rookie Team (1992)

Traded to **Edmonton** by **New Jersey** with Zdeno Ciger for Bernie Nicholls, January 13, 1993. Traded to **Chicago** by **Edmonton** for Adam Bennett, October 7, 1993. Traded to **LA Kings** by **Chicago** for LA Kings' 4th round choice (Steve McLaren) in 1994 Entry Draft, March 21, 1994. Signed as a free agent by **Pittsburgh**, July 10, 1996. Claimed on waivers by **Anaheim** from **Pittsburgh**, October 4, 1996.

• TOMALTY, Glenn

Glenn William "Buster"   LW – L. 6'1", 205 lbs.   b: Lachute, Que., 7/23/1954.

Season	Club	League	GP	G	A	Pts	AG	AA	APts	PIM	PP	SH	GW	S	%	TGF	PGF	TGA	PGA	+/–	GP	G	A	Pts	PIM	PP	SH	GW
1975-1977	Concordia University	QUAA	STATISTICS NOT AVAILABLE																									
1977-78	Grand Rapids Owls	IHL	3	0	0	0				5																		
1978-79	Cape Cod Freedoms	NEHL	41	24	23	47				51																		
	Utica Mohawks	NEHL	27	9	11	20				16																		
1979-80	**Winnipeg Jets**	**NHL**	**1**	**0**	**0**	**0**	**0**	**0**	**0**	**0**	**0**	**0**	**0**	**1**	**0.0**	**0**	**0**	**0**	**0**	**0**								
	Dayton Gems	IHL	61	29	32	61				86																		
	Tulsa Oilers	CHL	22	5	2	7				59											3	1	1	2	17			
1980-81	Tulsa Oilers	CHL	12	4	2	6				34																		
	Fort Wayne Komets	IHL	67	22	26	48				225											12	4	4	8	21			
1981-82	Brussels IHC	Belgium	21	34	52	86				42																		
	NHL Totals		**1**	**0**	**0**	**0**	**0**	**0**	**0**	**0**	**0**	**0**	**0**	**1**	**0.0**	**0**	**0**	**0**	**0**									

OUAA First All-Star Team (1977)

Signed as a free agent by **Winnipeg**, October 1, 1979.

• TOMLAK, Mike

Michael Richard   C/LW – L. 6'3", 205 lbs.   b: Thunder Bay, Ont., 10/17/1964. Toronto's 10th, 217th overall, in 1983.

Season	Club	League	GP	G	A	Pts	AG	AA	APts	PIM	PP	SH	GW	S	%	TGF	PGF	TGA	PGA	+/–	GP	G	A	Pts	PIM	PP	SH	GW
1980-81	Thunder Bay Kings	TBAHA	STATISTICS NOT AVAILABLE																									
1981-82	Thunder Bay North Stars	TBJHL	25	19	26	45				30																		
1982-83	Cornwall Royals	OHL	70	18	49	67				26																		
1983-84	Cornwall Royals	OHL	64	24	64	88				21																		
1984-85	Cornwall Royals	OHL	66	30	70	100				9																		
1985-86	University of Western Ontario	OUAA	38	28	20	48				45																		
	Canada	Nat-Team	3	1	1	2				0																		
1986-87	University of Western Ontario	OUAA	38	16	30	46				10																		
1987-88	University of Western Ontario	OUAA	39	24	52	76																						
1988-89	University of Western Ontario	OUAA	35	16	34	50																						
1989-90	**Hartford Whalers**	**NHL**	**70**	**7**	**14**	**21**	**6**	**10**	**16**	**48**	**1**	**1**	**2**	**64**	**10.9**	**25**	**2**	**32**	**14**	**5**	**7**	**0**	**1**	**1**	**2**	**0**	**0**	**0**
1990-91	**Hartford Whalers**	**NHL**	**64**	**8**	**8**	**16**	**7**	**6**	**13**	**55**	**0**	**1**	**0**	**69**	**11.6**	**24**	**0**	**46**	**13**	**–9**	**3**	**0**	**0**	**0**	**2**	**0**	**0**	**0**
	Springfield Indians	AHL	15	4	9	13				15																		
1991-92	**Hartford Whalers**	**NHL**	**6**	**0**	**0**	**0**	**0**	**0**	**0**	**0**	**0**	**0**	**0**	**10**	**0.0**	**0**	**0**	**5**	**3**	**–2**								
	Springfield Indians	AHL	39	16	21	37				24																		
1992-93	Springfield Indians	AHL	38	16	21	37				56											5	1	1	2	2			
1993-94	**Hartford Whalers**	**NHL**	**1**	**0**	**0**	**0**	**0**	**0**	**0**	**0**	**0**	**0**	**0**	**2**	**0.0**	**0**	**0**	**0**	**0**	**0**								
	Springfield Indians	AHL	79	44	56	100				53											4	2	5	7	4			
1994-95	Milwaukee Admirals	IHL	63	27	41	68				54											15	4	5	9	8			
1995-96	Milwaukee Admirals	IHL	82	11	32	43				68											5	0	2	2	6			
1996-97	Milwaukee Admirals	IHL	47	8	23	31				44																		
1997-98	Milwaukee Admirals	IHL	82	19	32	51				62											10	1	3	4	10			
1998-99	HK Olimpija Ljubljana	Alpenliga	31	11	20	31				46																		
	HK Olimpija Ljubljana	Slovenia	17	*13	*16	*29				12																		
	NHL Totals		**141**	**15**	**22**	**37**	**13**	**16**	**29**	**103**	**1**	**2**	**2**	**145**	**10.3**	**49**	**2**	**83**	**30**		**10**	**0**	**1**	**1**	**4**	**0**	**0**	**0**

• Signed as a free agent by **Hartford**, November 14, 1988.

• TOMLINSON, Dave

David H.   C – L. 5'11", 180 lbs.   b: North Vancouver, B.C., 5/8/1969. Toronto's 1st, 3rd overall, in 1989 Supplemental Draft.

Season	Club	League	GP	G	A	Pts	AG	AA	APts	PIM	PP	SH	GW	S	%	TGF	PGF	TGA	PGA	+/–	GP	G	A	Pts	PIM	PP	SH	GW
1985-86	Summerland Buckaroos	BCJHL	52	48	40	88				78																		
1986-87	Richmond Sockeyes	BCJHL	51	43	65	108				75																		
	Richmond Sockeyes	Cen-Cup	5	4	3	7				0																		
1987-88	Boston University	H-East	34	16	20	36				28																		
1988-89	Boston University	H-East	34	16	30	46				40																		
1989-90	Boston University	H-East	43	15	22	37				53																		
1990-91	Boston University	H-East	41	30	30	60				55																		
1991-92	**Toronto Maple Leafs**	**NHL**	**3**	**0**	**0**	**0**	**0**	**0**	**0**	**2**	**0**	**0**	**0**	**6**	**0.0**	**1**	**0**	**2**	**0**	**–1**								
	St. John's Maple Leafs	AHL	75	23	34	57				75											12	4	5	9	6			
1992-93	**Toronto Maple Leafs**	**NHL**	**3**	**0**	**0**	**0**	**0**	**0**	**0**	**2**	**0**	**0**	**0**	**1**	**0.0**	**0**	**0**	**0**	**0**	**0**								
	St. John's Maple Leafs	AHL	70	36	48	84				115											9	1	4	5	8			
1993-94	**Winnipeg Jets**	**NHL**	**31**	**1**	**3**	**4**	**1**	**2**	**3**	**24**	**0**	**0**	**0**	**29**	**3.4**	**6**	**0**	**18**	**0**	**–12**								
	Moncton Hawks	AHL	39	23	23	46				38											20	6	6	12	24			
1994-95	Cincinnati Cyclones	IHL	78	38	72	110				79											10	7	3	10	8			
	Florida Panthers	**NHL**	**5**	**0**	**0**	**0**	**0**	**0**	**0**	**0**	**0**	**0**	**0**	**0**	**0.0**	**0**	**0**	**2**	**0**	**–2**								
1995-96	Cincinnati Cyclones	IHL	81	39	57	96				127											17	4	12	16	18			
1996-97	Adler Mannheim	Germany	49	19	32	51				66											9	3	4	7	6			
1997-98	Adler Mannheim	Germany	44	20	30	50				58											10	4	*11	*15	10			
	Adler Mannheim	EuroHL	4	2	1	3				6																		

			REGULAR SEASON																		PLAYOFFS							
Season	Club	League	GP	G	A	Pts	AG	AA	APts	PIM	PP	SH	GW	S	%	TGF	PGF	TGA	PGA	+/–	GP	G	A	Pts	PIM	PP	SH	GW
1998-99	Adler Mannheim	Germany	49	12	27	39	....	....	....	74	....	....	....	....	....	....	....	....	....	....	12	7	3	10	12	....	....	....
	Adler Mannheim	EuroHL	6	3	2	5	....	....	....	4	....	....	....	....	....	....	....	....	....	....	4	1	3	4	2	....	....	....
99-2000	Adler Mannheim	Germany	56	20	30	50	....	....	....	101	....	....	....	....	....	....	....	....	....	....	5	1	2	3	6	....	....	....
	Adler Mannheim	EuroHL	5	2	1	3	....	....	....	8	....	....	....	....	....	....	....	....	....	....	....	....	....	....	....	....	....	....
	NHL Totals		**42**	**1**	**3**	**4**	**1**	**2**	**3**	**28**	**0**	**0**	**0**	**36**	**2.8**	**7**	**0**	**22**	**0**		....	....	....	....	....	....	....	....

IHL Second All-Star Team (1996)

Traded to **Florida** by **Toronto** for cash, July 30, 1993. Traded to **Winnipeg** by **Florida** for Jason Cirone, August 3, 1993. Signed as a free agent by **Florida**, June 23, 1994.

• TOMLINSON, Kirk

Kirk H. C – L. 5'10", 175 lbs. b: Toronto, Ont., 5/2/1968. Minnesota's 7th, 75th overall, in 1986.

Season	Club	League	GP	G	A	Pts	AG	AA	APts	PIM	PP	SH	GW	S	%	TGF	PGF	TGA	PGA	+/–	GP	G	A	Pts	PIM	PP	SH	GW
1983-84	Toronto Young Nationals	MTHL	STATISTICS NOT AVAILABLE																									
1984-85	New Westminster Bruins	WHL	66	9	14	23	....	....	....	48	....	....	....	....	....	....	....	....	....	....	11	1	3	4	20	....	....	....
1985-86	Hamilton Steelhawks	OHL	58	28	23	51	....	....	....	230	....	....	....	....	....	....	....	....	....	....	....	....	....	....	....	....	....	....
1986-87	Hamilton Steelhawks	OHL	65	33	37	70	....	....	....	169	....	....	....	....	....	....	....	....	....	....	9	4	6	10	28	....	....	....
1987-88	Hamilton Steelhawks	OHL	23	10	18	28	....	....	....	72	....	....	....	....	....	....	....	....	....	....	....	....	....	....	....	....	....	....
	Oshawa Generals	OHL	26	10	13	23	....	....	....	128	....	....	....	....	....	....	....	....	....	....	6	4	4	8	16	....	....	....
	Minnesota North Stars	**NHL**	**1**	**0**	**0**	**0**	**0**	**0**	**0**	**0**	**0**	**0**	**0**	**0**	**0.0**	**0**	**0**	**0**	**0**	**0**	....	....	....	....	....	....	....	....
1988-89	Kitchener Rangers	OHL	43	29	30	59	....	....	....	131	....	....	....	....	....	....	....	....	....	....	5	2	4	6	2	....	....	....
	Kalamazoo Wings	IHL	3	0	0	0	....	....	....	12	....	....	....	....	....	....	....	....	....	....	....	....	....	....	....	....	....	....
1989-90			DID NOT PLAY																									
1990-91	Nashville Knights	ECHL	57	36	47	83	....	....	....	385	....	....	....	....	....	....	....	....	....	....	8	0	2	2	62	....	....	....
	Adirondack Red Wings	AHL	8	0	2	2	....	....	....	62	....	....	....	....	....	....	....	....	....	....	2	0	0	0	5	....	....	....
1991-92	Adirondack Red Wings	AHL	54	3	12	15	....	....	....	*356	....	....	....	....	....	....	....	....	....	....	8	1	0	1	17	....	....	....
1992-93	Adirondack Red Wings	AHL	50	8	12	20	....	....	....	224	....	....	....	....	....	....	....	....	....	....	9	0	1	1	32	....	....	....
1993-94	Las Vegas Thunder	IHL	15	2	6	8	....	....	....	95	....	....	....	....	....	....	....	....	....	....	....	....	....	....	....	....	....	....
1994-95	Fort Wayne Komets	IHL	13	0	1	1	....	....	....	82	....	....	....	....	....	....	....	....	....	....	....	....	....	....	....	....	....	....
	Peoria Rivermen	IHL	41	11	9	20	....	....	....	171	....	....	....	....	....	....	....	....	....	....	9	0	1	1	17	....	....	....
1995-96	Peoria Rivermen	IHL	24	3	6	9	....	....	....	59	....	....	....	....	....	....	....	....	....	....	....	....	....	....	....	....	....	....
1996-1997			OUT OF HOCKEY – RETIRED																									
1997-1998	Quad City Mallards	UHL	DID NOT PLAY – ASSISTANT COACH																									
1998-2000	Colorado Gold Kings	WCHL	DID NOT PLAY – COACHING																									
	NHL Totals		**1**	**0**	**0**	**0**	**0**	**0**	**0**	**0**	**0**	**0**	**0**	**0**	**0.0**	**0**	**0**	**0**	**0**		....	....	....	....	....	....	....	....

• TOMS, Jeff

LW – L. 6'5", 213 lbs. b: Swift Current, Sask., 6/4/1974. New Jersey's 10th, 210th overall, in 1992.

Season	Club	League	GP	G	A	Pts	AG	AA	APts	PIM	PP	SH	GW	S	%	TGF	PGF	TGA	PGA	+/–	GP	G	A	Pts	PIM	PP	SH	GW
1990-91	Oakville Ambassadors	OMHA	58	34	47	81	....	....	....	72	....	....	....	....	....	....	....	....	....	....	....	....	....	....	....	....	....	....
1991-92	Sault Ste. Marie Greyhounds	OHL	36	9	5	14	....	....	....	0	....	....	....	....	....	....	....	....	....	....	16	0	1	1	2	....	....	....
	Sault Ste. Marie Greyhounds	Mem-Cup	2	0	0	0	....	....	....	0	....	....	....	....	....	....	....	....	....	....	....	....	....	....	....	....	....	....
1992-93	Sault Ste. Marie Greyhounds	OHL	59	16	23	39	....	....	....	20	....	....	....	....	....	....	....	....	....	....	16	4	4	8	7	....	....	....
	Sault Ste. Marie Greyhounds	Mem-Cup	4	1	4	5	....	....	....	0	....	....	....	....	....	....	....	....	....	....	....	....	....	....	....	....	....	....
1993-94	Sault Ste. Marie Greyhounds	OHL	64	52	45	97	....	....	....	19	....	....	....	....	....	....	....	....	....	....	14	11	4	15	2	....	....	....
1994-95	Atlanta Knights	IHL	40	7	8	15	....	....	....	10	....	....	....	....	....	....	....	....	....	....	4	0	0	0	4	....	....	....
1995-96	**Tampa Bay Lightning**	**NHL**	**1**	**0**	**0**	**0**	**0**	**0**	**0**	**0**	**0**	**0**	**0**	**1**	**0.0**	**0**	**0**	**0**	**0**	**0**	....	....	....	....	....	....	....	....
	Atlanta Knights	IHL	68	16	18	34	....	....	....	18	....	....	....	....	....	....	....	....	....	....	1	0	0	0	0	....	....	....
1996-97	**Tampa Bay Lightning**	**NHL**	**34**	**2**	**8**	**10**	**2**	**7**	**9**	**10**	**0**	**0**	**1**	**53**	**3.8**	**12**	**1**	**9**	**0**	**2**	....	....	....	....	....	....	....	....
	Adirondack Red Wings	AHL	37	11	16	27	....	....	....	8	....	....	....	....	....	....	....	....	....	....	4	1	2	3	0	....	....	....
1997-98	**Tampa Bay Lightning**	**NHL**	**13**	**1**	**2**	**3**	**1**	**2**	**3**	**7**	**0**	**0**	**0**	**14**	**7.1**	**4**	**0**	**11**	**1**	**–6**	....	....	....	....	....	....	....	....
	Washington Capitals	**NHL**	**33**	**3**	**4**	**7**	**4**	**4**	**8**	**8**	**0**	**0**	**1**	**55**	**5.5**	**7**	**0**	**19**	**1**	**–11**	**1**	**0**	**0**	**0**	**0**	**0**	**0**	**0**
1998-99	**Washington Capitals**	**NHL**	**21**	**1**	**5**	**6**	**1**	**5**	**6**	**2**	**0**	**0**	**0**	**30**	**3.3**	**9**	**0**	**11**	**2**	**0**	....	....	....	....	....	....	....	....
	Portland Pirates	AHL	20	3	7	10	....	....	....	8	....	....	....	....	....	....	....	....	....	....	....	....	....	....	....	....	....	....
99-2000	**Washington Capitals**	**NHL**	**20**	**1**	**2**	**3**	**1**	**2**	**3**	**4**	**0**	**0**	**1**	**18**	**5.6**	**5**	**0**	**7**	**1**	**–1**	....	....	....	....	....	....	....	....
	Portland Pirates	AHL	33	16	21	37	....	....	....	16	....	....	....	....	....	....	....	....	....	....	4	1	1	2	2	....	....	....
	NHL Totals		**122**	**8**	**21**	**29**	**9**	**20**	**29**	**31**	**0**	**0**	**3**	**171**	**4.7**	**37**	**1**	**57**	**5**		**1**	**0**	**0**	**0**	**0**	**0**	**0**	**0**

Traded to **Tampa Bay** by **New Jersey** for Vancouver's 4th round choice (previously acquired by Tampa Bay — later traded to New Jersey—later traded to Calgary — Calgary selected Ryan Duthie) in 1994 Entry Draft, May 31, 1994. Claimed by on waivers by **Washington** from **Tampa Bay**, November 19, 1997.

• TONELLI, John

John A. LW – L. 6'1", 200 lbs. b: Milton, Ont., 3/23/1957. NY Islanders' 2nd, 33rd overall, in 1977.

Season	Club	League	GP	G	A	Pts	AG	AA	APts	PIM	PP	SH	GW	S	%	TGF	PGF	TGA	PGA	+/–	GP	G	A	Pts	PIM	PP	SH	GW
1973-74	Toronto Marlboros	OMJHL	69	18	37	55	....	....	....	62	....	....	....	....	....	....	....	....	....	....	....	....	....	....	....	....	....	....
1974-75	Toronto Marlboros	OMJHL	70	49	86	135	....	....	....	85	....	....	....	....	....	....	....	....	....	....	....	....	....	....	....	....	....	....
1975-76	Houston Aeros	WHA	79	17	14	31	....	....	....	66	....	....	....	....	....	....	....	....	....	....	17	7	7	14	18	....	....	....
1976-77	Houston Aeros	WHA	80	24	31	55	....	....	....	109	....	....	....	....	....	....	....	....	....	....	11	3	4	7	12	....	....	....
1977-78	Houston Aeros	WHA	65	23	41	64	....	....	....	103	....	....	....	....	....	....	....	....	....	....	6	1	3	4	8	....	....	....
1978-79	**New York Islanders**	**NHL**	**73**	**17**	**39**	**56**	**15**	**28**	**43**	**44**	**1**	**0**	**4**	**113**	**15.0**	**88**	**12**	**47**	**0**	**29**	**10**	**1**	**6**	**7**	**0**	**0**	**0**	**0**
1979-80♦	**New York Islanders**	**NHL**	**77**	**14**	**30**	**44**	**12**	**22**	**34**	**49**	**3**	**0**	**2**	**103**	**13.6**	**68**	**10**	**52**	**2**	**8**	**21**	**7**	**9**	**16**	**18**	**0**	**0**	**0**
1980-81♦	**New York Islanders**	**NHL**	**70**	**20**	**32**	**52**	**16**	**21**	**37**	**57**	**2**	**0**	**3**	**114**	**17.5**	**72**	**15**	**49**	**0**	**8**	**16**	**5**	**8**	**13**	**16**	**0**	**0**	**2**
1981-82♦	**New York Islanders**	**NHL**	**80**	**35**	**58**	**93**	**28**	**39**	**67**	**57**	**5**	**0**	**5**	**165**	**21.2**	**139**	**29**	**67**	**5**	**48**	**19**	**6**	**10**	**16**	**18**	**1**	**0**	**1**
1982-83♦	**New York Islanders**	**NHL**	**76**	**31**	**40**	**71**	**25**	**28**	**53**	**55**	**8**	**1**	**4**	**166**	**18.7**	**110**	**27**	**58**	**5**	**30**	**20**	**7**	**11**	**18**	**20**	**0**	**0**	**2**
1983-84	**New York Islanders**	**NHL**	**73**	**27**	**40**	**67**	**22**	**27**	**49**	**66**	**5**	**1**	**7**	**105**	**25.7**	**90**	**13**	**69**	**13**	**21**	**17**	**1**	**3**	**4**	**31**	**0**	**0**	**0**
1984-85	Canada	Can-Cup	8	3	6	9	....	....	....	2	....	....	....	....	....	....	....	....	....	....	....	....	....	....	....	....	....	....
	New York Islanders	**NHL**	**80**	**42**	**58**	**100**	**34**	**40**	**74**	**95**	**8**	**1**	**3**	**197**	**21.3**	**158**	**42**	**77**	**11**	**50**	**10**	**1**	**8**	**9**	**10**	**0**	**0**	**0**
1985-86	**New York Islanders**	**NHL**	**65**	**20**	**41**	**61**	**16**	**28**	**44**	**50**	**3**	**0**	**1**	**139**	**14.4**	**94**	**22**	**66**	**16**	**22**	....	....	....	....	....	....	....	....
	Calgary Flames	**NHL**	**9**	**3**	**4**	**7**	**2**	**3**	**5**	**10**	**1**	**0**	**1**	**18**	**16.7**	**12**	**1**	**12**	**0**	**–1**	**22**	**7**	**9**	**16**	**49**	**1**	**0**	**1**
1986-87	**Calgary Flames**	**NHL**	**78**	**20**	**31**	**51**	**17**	**23**	**40**	**72**	**10**	**0**	**3**	**150**	**13.3**	**93**	**32**	**63**	**0**	**–2**	**3**	**0**	**0**	**0**	**4**	**0**	**0**	**0**
1987-88	**Calgary Flames**	**NHL**	**74**	**17**	**41**	**58**	**14**	**29**	**43**	**84**	**6**	**0**	**1**	**128**	**13.3**	**101**	**38**	**53**	**0**	**10**	**6**	**2**	**5**	**7**	**8**	**2**	**0**	**1**
1988-89	**Los Angeles Kings**	**NHL**	**77**	**31**	**33**	**64**	**26**	**23**	**49**	**110**	**1**	**1**	**3**	**156**	**19.9**	**94**	**13**	**83**	**11**	**9**	**6**	**0**	**0**	**0**	**8**	**0**	**0**	**0**
1989-90	**Los Angeles Kings**	**NHL**	**73**	**31**	**37**	**68**	**27**	**27**	**54**	**62**	**15**	**0**	**4**	**163**	**19.0**	**88**	**36**	**60**	**0**	**–8**	**10**	**1**	**2**	**3**	**6**	**0**	**0**	**0**
1990-91	**Los Angeles Kings**	**NHL**	**71**	**14**	**16**	**30**	**13**	**12**	**25**	**49**	**2**	**0**	**5**	**84**	**16.7**	**51**	**16**	**33**	**1**	**3**	**12**	**2**	**4**	**6**	**12**	**1**	**0**	**0**
1991-92	**Chicago Blackhawks**	**NHL**	**33**	**1**	**7**	**8**	**1**	**5**	**6**	**37**	**0**	**0**	**1**	**29**	**3.4**	**20**	**8**	**11**	**1**	**2**	....	....	....	....	....	....	....	....
	Quebec Nordiques	**NHL**	**19**	**2**	**4**	**6**	**2**	**3**	**5**	**14**	**2**	**0**	**0**	**16**	**12.5**	**11**	**7**	**11**	**0**	**–7**	....	....	....	....	....	....	....	....
	NHL Totals		**1028**	**325**	**511**	**836**	**270**	**358**	**628**	**911**	**72**	**4**	**47**	**1846**	**17.6**	**1289**	**321**	**811**	**65**		**172**	**40**	**75**	**115**	**200**	**5**	**0**	**7**
	Other Major League Totals		224	64	86	150	....	....	....	278	....	....	....	....	....	....	....	....	....	....	34	11	14	25	38	....	....	....

OMJHL First All-Star Team (1975) • NHL Second All-Star Team (1982, 1985) • Canada Cup All-Star Team (1984) • Named Canada Cup MVP (1984) • Played in NHL All-Star Game (1982, 1985)

Signed as an underage free agent by **Houston** (WHA), March, 1975. NHL rights reclaimed by **NY Islanders** after **Houston** (WHA) franchise folded, July 6, 1978. Traded to **Calgary** by **NY Islanders** for Richard Kromm and Steve Konroyd, March 11, 1986. Signed as a free agent by **LA Kings**, June 29, 1988. Signed as a free agent by **Chicago**, June 30, 1991. Traded to **Quebec** by **Chicago** for future considerations, February 18, 1992.

• TOOKEY, Tim

Timothy Raymond C – L. 5'11", 185 lbs. b: Edmonton, Alta., 8/29/1960. Washington's 4th, 88th overall, in 1979.

Season	Club	League	GP	G	A	Pts	AG	AA	APts	PIM	PP	SH	GW	S	%	TGF	PGF	TGA	PGA	+/–	GP	G	A	Pts	PIM	PP	SH	GW
1977-78	Portland Winter Hawks	WCJHL	72	16	15	31	....	....	....	55	....	....	....	....	....	....	....	....	....	....	8	2	2	4	5	....	....	....
1978-79	Portland Winter Hawks	WHL	56	33	47	80	....	....	....	55	....	....	....	....	....	....	....	....	....	....	25	6	14	20	6	....	....	....
1979-80	Portland Winter Hawks	WHL	70	58	83	141	....	....	....	55	....	....	....	....	....	....	....	....	....	....	8	2	5	7	4	....	....	....
1980-81	**Washington Capitals**	**NHL**	**29**	**10**	**13**	**23**	**8**	**9**	**17**	**18**	**6**	**0**	**1**	**33**	**30.3**	**27**	**17**	**23**	**7**	**–6**	....	....	....	....	....	....	....	....
	Hershey Bears	AHL	47	20	38	58	....	....	....	129	....	....	....	....	....	....	....	....	....	....	....	....	....	....	....	....	....	....
1981-82	**Washington Capitals**	**NHL**	**28**	**8**	**8**	**16**	**6**	**5**	**11**	**35**	**5**	**0**	**0**	**52**	**15.4**	**21**	**9**	**21**	**0**	**–9**	....	....	....	....	....	....	....	....
	Hershey Bears	AHL	14	4	9	13	....	....	....	10	....	....	....	....	....	....	....	....	....	....	....	....	....	....	....	....	....	....
	Fredericton Express	AHL	16	6	10	16	....	....	....	16	....	....	....	....	....	....	....	....	....	....	....	....	....	....	....	....	....	....
1982-83	**Quebec Nordiques**	**NHL**	**12**	**1**	**6**	**7**	**1**	**4**	**5**	**4**	**0**	**0**	**0**	**8**	**12.5**	**9**	**1**	**6**	**0**	**2**	....	....	....	....	....	....	....	....
	Fredericton Express	AHL	53	24	43	67	....	....	....	24	....	....	....	....	....	....	....	....	....	....	9	5	4	9	0	....	....	....
1983-84	**Pittsburgh Penguins**	**NHL**	**8**	**0**	**2**	**2**	**0**	**1**	**1**	**2**	**0**	**0**	**0**	**7**	**0.0**	**2**	**0**	**4**	**0**	**–2**	....	....	....	....	....	....	....	....
	Baltimore Skipjacks	AHL	58	16	28	44	....	....	....	25	....	....	....	....	....	....	....	....	....	....	8	1	1	2	2	....	....	....
1984-85	Baltimore Skipjacks	AHL	74	25	43	68	....	....	....	74	....	....	....	....	....	....	....	....	....	....	15	8	10	18	13	....	....	....

Season	Club	League	REGULAR SEASON GP	G	A	Pts	AG	AA	APts	PIM	PP	SH	GW	S	%	TGF	PGF	TGA	PGA	+/–	PLAYOFFS GP	G	A	Pts	PIM	PP	SH	GW
1985-86	Hershey Bears	AHL	69	35	*62	97	....	....	....	66	....	....	....	....	....	....	....	....	....	....	18	*11	8	19	10	....	....	....
1986-87	**Philadelphia Flyers**	**NHL**	**2**	**0**	**0**	**0**	**0**	**0**	**0**	**0**	**0**	**0**	**0**	**1**	**0.0**	**1**	**1**	**0**	**0**	**0**	**10**	**1**	**3**	**4**	**2**	**0**	**0**	**0**
	Hershey Bears	AHL	80	51	*73	*124	....	....	....	45	....	....	....	....	....	....	....	....	....	....	5	5	4	9	0	....	....	....
1987-88	**Los Angeles Kings**	**NHL**	**20**	**1**	**6**	**7**	**1**	**4**	**5**	**8**	**0**	**0**	**0**	**28**	**3.6**	**8**	**1**	**9**	**0**	**–2**	....	....	....	....	....	....	....	....
	New Haven Nighthawks	AHL	11	6	7	13	....	....	....	2	....	....	....	....	....	....	....	....	....	....	....	....	....	....	....	....	....	....
1988-89	**Los Angeles Kings**	**NHL**	**7**	**2**	**1**	**3**	**2**	**1**	**3**	**4**	**0**	**0**	**0**	**8**	**25.0**	**5**	**1**	**7**	**0**	**–3**	....	....	....	....	....	....	....	....
	New Haven Nighthawks	AHL	33	11	18	29	....	....	....	30	....	....	....	....	....	....	....	....	....	....	....	....	....	....	....	....	....	....
	Muskegon Lumberjacks	IHL	18	7	14	21	....	....	....	7	....	....	....	....	....	....	....	....	....	....	8	2	9	11	4	....	....	....
1989-90	Hershey Bears	AHL	42	18	22	40	....	....	....	28	....	....	....	....	....	....	....	....	....	....	....	....	....	....	....	....	....	....
1990-91	Hershey Bears	AHL	51	17	42	59	....	....	....	43	....	....	....	....	....	....	....	....	....	....	5	0	5	5	0	....	....	....
1991-92	Hershey Bears	AHL	80	36	69	105	....	....	....	63	....	....	....	....	....	....	....	....	....	....	6	4	2	6	4	....	....	....
1992-93	Hershey Bears	AHL	80	38	70	108	....	....	....	63	....	....	....	....	....	....	....	....	....	....	....	....	....	....	....	....	....	....
1993-94	Hershey Bears	AHL	66	32	57	89	....	....	....	43	....	....	....	....	....	....	....	....	....	....	11	4	9	13	8	....	....	....
1994-95	Providence Bruins	AHL	50	14	30	44	....	....	....	28	....	....	....	....	....	....	....	....	....	....	1	0	1	1	2	....	....	....
	NHL Totals		**106**	**22**	**36**	**58**	**18**	**24**	**42**	**71**	**11**	**0**	**1**	**137**	**16.1**	**73**	**30**	**70**	**7**		**10**	**1**	**3**	**4**	**2**	**0**	**0**	**0**

AHL Second All-Star Team (1986, 1992) • Won Jack A. Butterfield Trophy (Playoff MVP - AHL) (1986) • AHL First All-Star Team (1987) • Won John B. Sollenberger Trophy (Top Scorer - AHL) (1987) • Won Les Cunningham Award (MVP - AHL) (1987) • Won Fred T. Hunt Memorial Trophy (Sportsmanship - AHL) (1993)

Traded to **Quebec** by **Washington** with Washington's 7th round choice (Daniel Poudrier) in 1982 Entry Draft for Lee Norwood and Quebec's 6th round choice (Mats Kilstrom) in 1982 Entry Draft, February 1, 1982. Signed as a free agent by **Pittsburgh**, September 12, 1983. Signed as a free agent by **Philadelphia**, July 11, 1985. Claimed by **LA Kings** from **Philadelphia** in Waiver Draft, October 5, 1987. Traded to **Pittsburgh** by **LA Kings** for Pat Mayer, March 7, 1989. Signed as a free agent by **Philadelphia**, June 30, 1989.

• TOOMEY, Sean

Sean J. LW – L. 6'1", 200 lbs. b: St. Paul, MN, 6/27/1965. Minnesota's 8th, 141st overall, in 1983.

Season	Club	League	GP	G	A	Pts	AG	AA	APts	PIM	PP	SH	GW	S	%	TGF	PGF	TGA	PGA	+/–	GP	G	A	Pts	PIM	PP	SH	GW
1982-83	Cretin High Raiders	Hi-School	23	48	32	80	....	....	....	....	....	....	....	....	....	....	....	....	....	....	....	....	....	....	....	....	....	....
1983-84	University of Minnesota-Duluth	WCHA	29	3	5	8	....	....	....	8	....	....	....	....	....	....	....	....	....	....	....	....	....	....	....	....	....	....
1984-85	University of Minnesota-Duluth	WCHA	43	6	7	13	....	....	....	14	....	....	....	....	....	....	....	....	....	....	....	....	....	....	....	....	....	....
1985-86	University of Minnesota-Duluth	WCHA	33	23	11	34	....	....	....	10	....	....	....	....	....	....	....	....	....	....	....	....	....	....	....	....	....	....
1986-87	University of Minnesota-Duluth	WCHA	39	26	17	43	....	....	....	34	....	....	....	....	....	....	....	....	....	....	....	....	....	....	....	....	....	....
	Minnesota North Stars	**NHL**	**1**	**0**	**0**	**0**	**0**	**0**	**0**	**0**	**0**	**0**	**0**	**2**	**0.0**	**0**	**0**	**1**	**0**	**–1**	....	....	....	....	....	....	....	....
	Indianapolis Checkers	IHL	13	3	3	6	....	....	....	0	....	....	....	....	....	....	....	....	....	....	5	2	2	4	2	....	....	....
1987-88	Baltimore Skipjacks	AHL	49	15	18	33	....	....	....	12	....	....	....	....	....	....	....	....	....	....	....	....	....	....	....	....	....	....
	Kalamazoo Wings	IHL	23	12	5	17	....	....	....	2	....	....	....	....	....	....	....	....	....	....	4	1	3	4	0	....	....	....
1988-89	Assat Pori	Finland	34	14	13	27	....	....	....	18	....	....	....	....	....	....	....	....	....	....	....	....	....	....	....	....	....	....
	NHL Totals		**1**	**0**	**0**	**0**	**0**	**0**	**0**	**0**	**0**	**0**	**0**	**2**	**0.0**	**0**	**0**	**1**	**0**		....	....	....	....	....	....	....	....

• TOPOROWSKI, Shayne

Shayne A. RW – R. 6'2", 216 lbs. b: Paddockwood, Sask., 8/6/1975. Los Angeles' 1st, 42nd overall, in 1993.

Season	Club	League	GP	G	A	Pts	AG	AA	APts	PIM	PP	SH	GW	S	%	TGF	PGF	TGA	PGA	+/–	GP	G	A	Pts	PIM	PP	SH	GW
1990-91	Prince Albert Midget Raiders	SAHA	30	19	13	32	....	....	....	91	....	....	....	....	....	....	....	....	....	....	....	....	....	....	....	....	....	....
1991-92	Prince Albert Midget Raiders	SAHA	27	23	29	52	....	....	....	91	....	....	....	....	....	....	....	....	....	....	....	....	....	....	....	....	....	....
	Prince Albert Raiders	WHL	6	2	0	2	....	....	....	2	....	....	....	....	....	....	....	....	....	....	7	2	1	3	6	....	....	....
1992-93	Prince Albert Raiders	WHL	72	25	32	57	....	....	....	235	....	....	....	....	....	....	....	....	....	....	....	....	....	....	....	....	....	....
1993-94	Prince Albert Raiders	WHL	68	37	45	82	....	....	....	183	....	....	....	....	....	....	....	....	....	....	....	....	....	....	....	....	....	....
1994-95	Prince Albert Raiders	WHL	72	36	38	74	....	....	....	151	....	....	....	....	....	....	....	....	....	....	15	10	8	18	25	....	....	....
1995-96	St. John's Maple Leafs	AHL	72	11	26	37	....	....	....	216	....	....	....	....	....	....	....	....	....	....	4	1	1	2	4	....	....	....
1996-97	**Toronto Maple Leafs**	**NHL**	**3**	**0**	**0**	**0**	**0**	**0**	**0**	**7**	**0**	**0**	**0**	**3**	**0.0**	**0**	**0**	**0**	**0**	**0**	....	....	....	....	....	....	....	....
	St. John's Maple Leafs	AHL	72	20	17	37	....	....	....	210	....	....	....	....	....	....	....	....	....	....	11	3	2	5	16	....	....	....
1997-98	Worcester IceCats	AHL	73	9	21	30	....	....	....	128	....	....	....	....	....	....	....	....	....	....	11	5	3	8	44	....	....	....
1998-99	Worcester IceCats	AHL	75	18	29	47	....	....	....	124	....	....	....	....	....	....	....	....	....	....	4	1	0	1	6	....	....	....
99-2000	Springfield Falcons	AHL	80	27	28	55	....	....	....	191	....	....	....	....	....	....	....	....	....	....	5	0	1	1	10	....	....	....
	NHL Totals		**3**	**0**	**0**	**0**	**0**	**0**	**0**	**7**	**0**	**0**	**0**	**3**	**0.0**	**0**	**0**	**0**	**0**		....	....	....	....	....	....	....	....

Traded to **Toronto** by **LA Kings** with Dixon Ward, Guy Leveque and Kelly Fairchild for Eric Lacroix, Chris Snell and Toronto's 4th round choice (Eric Belanger) in 1996 Entry Draft, October 3, 1994. Signed as a free agent by **St. Louis**, September 9, 1997. Signed as a free agent by **Phoenix**, August 17, 1999.

• TORGAEV, Pavel

LW – L. 6'1", 187 lbs. b: Gorky, USSR, 1/25/1966. Calgary's 13th, 279th overall, in 1994.

Season	Club	League	GP	G	A	Pts	AG	AA	APts	PIM	PP	SH	GW	S	%	TGF	PGF	TGA	PGA	+/–	GP	G	A	Pts	PIM	PP	SH	GW
1982-83	Torpedo Gorky	USSR	4	0	0	0	....	....	....	0	....	....	....	....	....	....	....	....	....	....	....	....	....	....	....	....	....	....
1983-84	Torpedo Gorky	USSR	27	2	3	5	....	....	....	8	....	....	....	....	....	....	....	....	....	....	....	....	....	....	....	....	....	....
	Soviet Union	EJC-A	5	0	4	4	....	....	....	8	....	....	....	....	....	....	....	....	....	....	....	....	....	....	....	....	....	....
1984-85	Torpedo Gorky	USSR	47	11	5	16	....	....	....	52	....	....	....	....	....	....	....	....	....	....	....	....	....	....	....	....	....	....
	Soviet Union	WJC-A	7	2	2	4	....	....	....	8	....	....	....	....	....	....	....	....	....	....	....	....	....	....	....	....	....	....
1985-86	Torpedo Gorky	USSR	38	1	4	5	....	....	....	18	....	....	....	....	....	....	....	....	....	....	....	....	....	....	....	....	....	....
	Soviet Union	WJC-A	7	2	2	4	....	....	....	6	....	....	....	....	....	....	....	....	....	....	....	....	....	....	....	....	....	....
1986-87	Torpedo Gorky	USSR	40	6	9	15	....	....	....	30	....	....	....	....	....	....	....	....	....	....	....	....	....	....	....	....	....	....
1987-88	Torpedo Gorky	USSR	25	7	4	11	....	....	....	14	....	....	....	....	....	....	....	....	....	....	....	....	....	....	....	....	....	....
1988-89	Torpedo Gorky	USSR	26	6	3	9	....	....	....	17	....	....	....	....	....	....	....	....	....	....	....	....	....	....	....	....	....	....
1989-90	Torpedo Gorky	USSR	48	18	5	23	....	....	....	64	....	....	....	....	....	....	....	....	....	....	....	....	....	....	....	....	....	....
1990-91	Torpedo Nizhny	USSR	37	10	5	15	....	....	....	22	....	....	....	....	....	....	....	....	....	....	....	....	....	....	....	....	....	....
1991-92	Torpedo Nizhny	CIS	45	13	5	18	....	....	....	46	....	....	....	....	....	....	....	....	....	....	....	....	....	....	....	....	....	....
1992-93	Torpedo Nizhny	CIS	5	1	0	1	....	....	....	4	....	....	....	....	....	....	....	....	....	....	....	....	....	....	....	....	....	....
	Kiekko-Espoo	Finland 2	30	16	20	36	....	....	....	48	....	....	....	....	....	....	....	....	....	....	....	....	....	....	....	....	....	....
1993-94	TPS Turku	Finland	47	19	11	30	....	....	....	60	....	....	....	....	....	....	....	....	....	....	3	0	1	1	14	....	....	....
	Russia	Olympics	8	2	1	3	....	....	....	10	....	....	....	....	....	....	....	....	....	....	....	....	....	....	....	....	....	....
1994-95	JyP-HT Jyvaskyla	Finland	50	13	18	31	....	....	....	44	....	....	....	....	....	....	....	....	....	....	4	0	1	1	25	....	....	....
	Russia	WC-A	6	0	2	2	....	....	....	4	....	....	....	....	....	....	....	....	....	....	....	....	....	....	....	....	....	....
1995-96	**Calgary Flames**	**NHL**	**41**	**6**	**10**	**16**	**6**	**8**	**14**	**14**	**0**	**0**	**0**	**50**	**12.0**	**21**	**2**	**18**	**1**	**2**	**1**	**0**	**0**	**0**	**0**	**0**	**0**	**0**
	Saint John Flames	AHL	16	11	6	17	....	....	....	18	....	....	....	....	....	....	....	....	....	....	....	....	....	....	....	....	....	....
1996-97	HC Lugano	Switz.	34	18	21	39	....	....	....	87	....	....	....	....	....	....	....	....	....	....	8	3	3	6	10	....	....	....
1997-98	HC Davos	Switz.	38	20	27	47	....	....	....	85	....	....	....	....	....	....	....	....	....	....	17	6	9	15	14	....	....	....
1998-99	HC Fribourg-Gotteron	Switz.	26	15	11	26	....	....	....	36	....	....	....	....	....	....	....	....	....	....	....	....	....	....	....	....	....	....
99-2000	**Calgary Flames**	**NHL**	**9**	**0**	**2**	**2**	**0**	**2**	**2**	**4**	**0**	**0**	**0**	**12**	**0.0**	....	....	....	....	....	....	....	....	....	....	....	....	....
	Tampa Bay Lightning	**NHL**	**5**	**0**	**2**	**2**	**0**	**2**	**2**	**2**	**0**	**0**	**0**	**6**	**0.0**	....	....	....	....	....	....	....	....	....	....	....	....	....
	Long Beach Ice Dogs	IHL	36	8	9	17	....	....	....	47	....	....	....	....	....	....	....	....	....	....	....	....	....	....	....	....	....	....
	NHL Totals		**55**	**6**	**14**	**20**	**6**	**12**	**18**	**20**	**0**	**0**	**0**	**68**	**8.8**	**21**	**2**	**18**	**1**		**1**	**0**	**0**	**0**	**0**	**0**	**0**	**0**

Claimed on waivers by **Tampa Bay** from **Calgary**, November 26, 1999. • Suspended by **Tampa Bay** for refusing assignment to **Detroit** (IHL), December 21, 1999. Signed as a free agent by **Long Beach** (IHL) after release by **Tampa Bay**, January 2, 2000.

• TORKKI, Jari

LW – L. 5'11", 185 lbs. b: Rauma, Finland, 8/11/1965. Chicago's 6th, 119th overall, in 1983.

Season	Club	League	GP	G	A	Pts	AG	AA	APts	PIM	PP	SH	GW	S	%	TGF	PGF	TGA	PGA	+/–	GP	G	A	Pts	PIM	PP	SH	GW
1981-82	Lukko Rauma	Finland-Jr.	8	15	10	25	....	....	....	10	....	....	....	....	....	....	....	....	....	....	....	....	....	....	....	....	....	....
	Lukko Rauma	Finland	1	0	0	0	....	....	....	0	....	....	....	....	....	....	....	....	....	....	....	....	....	....	....	....	....	....
1982-83	Lukko Rauma	Finland-Jr.	7	8	6	14	....	....	....	24	....	....	....	....	....	....	....	....	....	....	....	....	....	....	....	....	....	....
	Lukko Rauma	Finland	34	13	17	30	....	....	....	34	....	....	....	....	....	....	....	....	....	....	....	....	....	....	....	....	....	....
	Finland	EJC-A	5	6	1	7	....	....	....	10	....	....	....	....	....	....	....	....	....	....	....	....	....	....	....	....	....	....
1983-84	Lukko Rauma	Finland-2	36	*41	25	66	....	....	....	70	....	....	....	....	....	....	....	....	....	....	3	5	0	5	2	....	....	....
	Finland	WJC-A	7	4	2	6	....	....	....	10	....	....	....	....	....	....	....	....	....	....	....	....	....	....	....	....	....	....
1984-85	Lukko Rauma	Finland	36	25	21	46	....	....	....	40	....	....	....	....	....	....	....	....	....	....	....	....	....	....	....	....	....	....
	Finland	WJC-A	7	5	4	9	....	....	....	8	....	....	....	....	....	....	....	....	....	....	....	....	....	....	....	....	....	....
1985-86	Lukko Rauma	Finland	32	22	18	40	....	....	....	40	....	....	....	....	....	....	....	....	....	....	....	....	....	....	....	....	....	....
1986-87	Lukko Rauma	Finland	44	27	8	35	....	....	....	42	....	....	....	....	....	....	....	....	....	....	....	....	....	....	....	....	....	....
	Finland	WEC-A	10	5	2	7	....	....	....	12	....	....	....	....	....	....	....	....	....	....	....	....	....	....	....	....	....	....
1987-88	Lukko Rauma	Finland	43	23	24	47	....	....	....	54	....	....	....	....	....	....	....	....	....	....	8	4	3	7	12	....	....	....
	Finland	Olympics	4	1	0	1	....	....	....	2	....	....	....	....	....	....	....	....	....	....	....	....	....	....	....	....	....	....

Season	Club	League	REGULAR SEASON GP	G	A	Pts	AG	AA	APts	PIM	PP	SH	GW	S	%	TGF	PGF	TGA	PGA	+/–	PLAYOFFS GP	G	A	Pts	PIM	PP	SH	GW
1988-89	**Chicago Blackhawks**	**NHL**	**4**	**1**	**0**	**1**	**1**	**0**	**1**	**0**	**1**	**0**	**0**	**2**	**50.0**	**2**	**1**	**3**	**0**	**–2**	....	....	....	....	....	....	....	....
	Saginaw Hawks	IHL	72	30	42	72	....	....	....	22	....	....	....	....	....	....	....	....	....	....	6	2	1	3	4	....	....	....
1989-90	Indianapolis Ice	IHL	66	25	29	54	....	....	....	50	....	....	....	....	....	....	....	....	....	....	11	5	2	7	8	....	....	....
1990-91	Lukko Rauma	Finland	44	23	26	49	....	....	....	52	....	....	....	....	....	....	....	....	....	....	....	....	....	....	....	....	....	....
	Lukko Rauma	Finland-Q	4	0	2	2	....	....	....	6	....	....	....	....	....	....	....	....	....	....	....	....	....	....	....	....	....	....
1991-92	Lukko Rauma	Finland	44	16	19	35	....	....	....	34	....	....	....	....	....	....	....	....	....	....	2	0	0	0	4	....	....	....
1992-93	Lukko Rauma	Finland	48	17	14	31	....	....	....	38	....	....	....	....	....	....	....	....	....	....	....	....	....	....	....	....	....	....
	Lukko Rauma	Finland	48	17	14	31	....	....	....	38	....	....	....	....	....	....	....	....	....	....	3	1	0	1	0	....	....	....
1993-94	Lukko Rauma	Finland	46	14	18	32	....	....	....	22	....	....	....	....	....	....	....	....	....	....	9	4	1	5	8	....	....	....
1994-95	Lukko Rauma	Finland	33	14	30	44	....	....	....	48	....	....	....	....	....	....	....	....	....	....	9	2	0	2	4	....	....	....
1995-96	Lukko Rauma	Finland	48	16	20	36	....	....	....	50	....	....	....	....	....	....	....	....	....	....	4	0	1	1	10	....	....	....
1996-97	Star Bulls Rosenheim	Germany	47	17	18	35	....	....	....	80	....	....	....	....	....	....	....	....	....	....	3	0	1	1	6	....	....	....
1997-98	Star Bulls Rosenheim	Germany	41	10	14	24	....	....	....	20	....	....	....	....	....	....	....	....	....	....	....	....	....	....	....	....	....	....
1998-99	HC Merano	Alpenliga	27	7	7	14	....	....	....	18	....	....	....	....	....	....	....	....	....	....	....	....	....	....	....	....	....	....
	HC Merano	Italy	16	11	12	23	....	....	....	10	....	....	....	....	....	....	....	....	....	....	9	2	3	5	4	....	....	....
99-2000	HC Milano Saima	Italy	STATISTICS NOT AVAILABLE																									
	NHL Totals		**4**	**1**	**0**	**1**	**1**	**0**	**1**	**0**	**1**	**0**	**0**	**2**	**50.0**	**2**	**1**	**3**	**0**		....	....	....	....	....	....	....	....

• TORMANEN, Antti

RW – L. 6'1", 198 lbs. b: Espoo, Finland, 9/19/1970. Ottawa's 10th, 274th overall, in 1994.

Season	Club	League	GP	G	A	Pts	AG	AA	APts	PIM	PP	SH	GW	S	%	TGF	PGF	TGA	PGA	+/–	GP	G	A	Pts	PIM	PP	SH	GW
1987-88	Kiekko-Espoo	Finland-Jr.	32	21	21	42	....	....	....	18	....	....	....	....	....	....	....	....	....	....	....	....	....	....	....	....	....	....
	Finland	EJC-A	6	0	1	1	....	....	....	4	....	....	....	....	....	....	....	....	....	....	....	....	....	....	....	....	....	....
1988-89	Kiekko-Espoo	Finland-Jr.	6	4	8	12	....	....	....	8	....	....	....	....	....	....	....	....	....	....	4	6	6	12	0	....	....	....
	Kiekko-Espoo	Finland-2	39	11	8	19	....	....	....	27	....	....	....	....	....	....	....	....	....	....	....	....	....	....	....	....	....	....
1988-99	Finland	WC-A	12	0	0	0	....	....	....	10	....	....	....	....	....	....	....	....	....	....	....	....	....	....	....	....	....	....
1989-90	Kiekko-Espoo	Finland-Jr.	8	7	7	14	....	....	....	4	....	....	....	....	....	....	....	....	....	....	5	6	6	12	4	....	....	....
	Army Sports Academy	Finland-Jr.	8	3	5	8	....	....	....	10	....	....	....	....	....	....	....	....	....	....	....	....	....	....	....	....	....	....
	Kiekko-Espoo	Finland-2	41	13	15	28	....	....	....	15	....	....	....	....	....	....	....	....	....	....	....	....	....	....	....	....	....	....
1990-91	Jokerit Helsinki	Finland-Jr.	3	4	0	4	....	....	....	4	....	....	....	....	....	....	....	....	....	....	....	....	....	....	....	....	....	....
	Jokerit Helsinki	Finland	44	12	9	21	....	....	....	70	....	....	....	....	....	....	....	....	....	....	....	....	....	....	....	....	....	....
1991-92	Jokerit Helsinki	Finland	40	18	11	29	....	....	....	18	....	....	....	....	....	....	....	....	....	....	....	....	....	....	....	....	....	....
1992-93	Vantaa HT	Finland-2	6	3	2	5	....	....	....	6	....	....	....	....	....	....	....	....	....	....	....	....	....	....	....	....	....	....
	Jokerit Helsinki	Finland	21	2	0	2	....	....	....	8	....	....	....	....	....	....	....	....	....	....	....	....	....	....	....	....	....	....
1993-94	Jokerit Helsinki	Finland	46	20	18	38	....	....	....	46	....	....	....	....	....	....	....	....	....	....	....	....	....	....	....	....	....	....
1994-95	Jokerit Helsinki	Finland	50	19	13	32	....	....	....	32	....	....	....	....	....	....	....	....	....	....	11	7	3	10	20	....	....	....
	Finland	WC-A	5	0	0	0	....	....	....	2	....	....	....	....	....	....	....	....	....	....	....	....	....	....	....	....	....	....
1995-96	**Ottawa Senators**	**NHL**	**50**	**7**	**8**	**15**	**7**	**7**	**14**	**28**	**0**	**0**	**0**	**68**	**10.3**	**21**	**1**	**35**	**0**	**–15**	....	....	....	....	....	....	....	....
	P.E.I. Senators	AHL	22	6	11	17	....	....	....	17	....	....	....	....	....	....	....	....	....	....	5	2	3	5	2	....	....	....
1996-97	Finland	W-Cup	DID NOT PLAY																									
	Jokerit Helsinki	Finland	50	18	14	32	....	....	....	54	....	....	....	....	....	....	....	....	....	....	9	3	5	8	10	....	....	....
	Jokerit Helsinki	EuroHL	6	4	2	6	....	....	....	4	....	....	....	....	....	....	....	....	....	....	2	0	0	0	2	....	....	....
	Finland	WC-A	5	0	1	1	....	....	....	2	....	....	....	....	....	....	....	....	....	....	....	....	....	....	....	....	....	....
1997-98	Jokerit Helsinki	Finland	48	20	14	34	....	....	....	37	....	....	....	....	....	....	....	....	....	....	8	3	2	5	12	....	....	....
	Jokerit Helsinki	EuroHL	6	1	5	6	....	....	....	2	....	....	....	....	....	....	....	....	....	....	....	....	....	....	....	....	....	....
	Finland	Olympics	5	0	0	0	....	....	....	0	....	....	....	....	....	....	....	....	....	....	....	....	....	....	....	....	....	....
	Finland	WC-A	10	3	2	5	....	....	....	6	....	....	....	....	....	....	....	....	....	....	....	....	....	....	....	....	....	....
1998-99	HV-71 Jonkoping	Sweden	50	14	22	36	....	....	....	50	....	....	....	....	....	....	....	....	....	....	....	....	....	....	....	....	....	....
	Finland	WC-A	12	0	0	0	....	....	....	10	....	....	....	....	....	....	....	....	....	....	....	....	....	....	....	....	....	....
99-2000	HV-71 Jonkoping	Sweden	50	18	15	33	....	....	....	76	....	....	....	....	....	....	....	....	....	....	6	2	4	6	20	....	....	....
	NHL Totals		**50**	**7**	**8**	**15**	**7**	**7**	**14**	**28**	**0**	**0**	**0**	**68**	**10.3**	**21**	**1**	**35**	**0**		....	....	....	....	....	....	....	....

• TOWNSHEND, Graeme

Graeme Scott RW – R. 6'2", 225 lbs. b: Kingston, Jamaica, 10/2/1965.

Season	Club	League	GP	G	A	Pts	AG	AA	APts	PIM	PP	SH	GW	S	%	TGF	PGF	TGA	PGA	+/–	GP	G	A	Pts	PIM	PP	SH	GW
1984-85	Mimico Monarchs	OJHL-B	35	22	22	44	....	....	....	93	....	....	....	....	....	....	....	....	....	....	25	14	11	25	....	....	....	....
1985-86	RPI Engineers	ECAC	29	1	7	8	....	....	....	52	....	....	....	....	....	....	....	....	....	....	....	....	....	....	....	....	....	....
1986-87	RPI Engineers	ECAC	29	6	1	7	....	....	....	50	....	....	....	....	....	....	....	....	....	....	....	....	....	....	....	....	....	....
1987-88	RPI Engineers	ECAC	32	6	14	20	....	....	....	64	....	....	....	....	....	....	....	....	....	....	....	....	....	....	....	....	....	....
1988-89	RPI Engineers	ECAC	31	6	16	22	....	....	....	50	....	....	....	....	....	....	....	....	....	....	....	....	....	....	....	....	....	....
	Maine Mariners	AHL	5	2	1	3	....	....	....	11	....	....	....	....	....	....	....	....	....	....	....	....	....	....	....	....	....	....
1989-90	**Boston Bruins**	**NHL**	**4**	**0**	**0**	**0**	**0**	**0**	**0**	**7**	**0**	**0**	**0**	**3**	**0.0**	**0**	**0**	**1**	**0**	**–1**	....	....	....	....	....	....	....	....
	Maine Mariners	AHL	64	15	13	28	....	....	....	162	....	....	....	....	....	....	....	....	....	....	....	....	....	....	....	....	....	....
1990-91	**Boston Bruins**	**NHL**	**18**	**2**	**5**	**7**	**2**	**4**	**6**	**12**	**0**	**0**	**0**	**10**	**20.0**	**10**	**0**	**9**	**0**	**1**	....	....	....	....	....	....	....	....
	Maine Mariners	AHL	46	16	10	26	....	....	....	119	....	....	....	....	....	....	....	....	....	....	2	2	0	2	4	....	....	....
1991-92	**New York Islanders**	**NHL**	**7**	**1**	**2**	**3**	**1**	**2**	**3**	**0**	**0**	**0**	**0**	**6**	**16.7**	**8**	**0**	**2**	**0**	**6**	....	....	....	....	....	....	....	....
	Capital District Islanders	AHL	61	14	23	37	....	....	....	94	....	....	....	....	....	....	....	....	....	....	4	0	2	2	0	....	....	....
1992-93	**New York Islanders**	**NHL**	**2**	**0**	**0**	**0**	**0**	**0**	**0**	**0**	**0**	**0**	**0**	**0**	**0.0**	**0**	**0**	**0**	**0**	**0**	....	....	....	....	....	....	....	....
	Capital District Islanders	AHL	67	29	21	50	....	....	....	45	....	....	....	....	....	....	....	....	....	....	2	0	0	0	0	....	....	....
1993-94	**Ottawa Senators**	**NHL**	**14**	**0**	**0**	**0**	**0**	**0**	**0**	**9**	**0**	**0**	**0**	**5**	**0.0**	**0**	**0**	**7**	**0**	**–7**	....	....	....	....	....	....	....	....
	P.E.I. Senators	AHL	56	16	13	29	....	....	....	107	....	....	....	....	....	....	....	....	....	....	....	....	....	....	....	....	....	....
1994-95	Houston Aeros	IHL	71	19	21	40	....	....	....	204	....	....	....	....	....	....	....	....	....	....	4	0	2	2	22	....	....	....
1995-96	Minnesota Moose	IHL	3	0	0	0	....	....	....	0	....	....	....	....	....	....	....	....	....	....	....	....	....	....	....	....	....	....
	Houston Aeros	IHL	63	21	11	32	....	....	....	97	....	....	....	....	....	....	....	....	....	....	....	....	....	....	....	....	....	....
1996-97	Houston Aeros	IHL	74	21	15	36	....	....	....	68	....	....	....	....	....	....	....	....	....	....	3	0	0	0	2	....	....	....
1997-98	Utah Grizzlies	IHL	1	0	0	0	....	....	....	0	....	....	....	....	....	....	....	....	....	....	....	....	....	....	....	....	....	....
	Houston Aeros	IHL	1	0	0	0	....	....	....	0	....	....	....	....	....	....	....	....	....	....	....	....	....	....	....	....	....	....
	Lake Charles Ice Pirates	WPHL	68	43	44	87	....	....	....	67	....	....	....	....	....	....	....	....	....	....	4	0	4	4	14	....	....	....
1998-99	Lake Charles Ice Pirates	WPHL	60	28	29	57	....	....	....	113	....	....	....	....	....	....	....	....	....	....	11	7	3	10	12	....	....	....
99-2000	Macoun Whoopee	CHL	DID NOT PLAY – COACHING																									
	NHL Totals		**45**	**3**	**7**	**10**	**3**	**6**	**9**	**28**	**0**	**0**	**0**	**24**	**12.5**	**18**	**0**	**19**	**0**		....	....	....	....	....	....	....	....

Signed as a free agent by **Boston**, May 12, 1989. Signed as a free agent by **NY Islanders**, September 3, 1991. Signed as a free agent by **Ottawa**, August 24, 1993.

• TRADER, Larry

Larry J. D – L. 6'1", 180 lbs. b: Barry's Bay, Ont., 7/7/1963. Detroit's 3rd, 86th overall, in 1981.

Season	Club	League	GP	G	A	Pts	AG	AA	APts	PIM	PP	SH	GW	S	%	TGF	PGF	TGA	PGA	+/–	GP	G	A	Pts	PIM	PP	SH	GW
1979-80	Gloucester Rangers	OJHL	50	11	22	33	....	....	....	70	....	....	....	....	....	....	....	....	....	....	....	....	....	....	....	....	....	....
1980-81	London Knights	OMJHL	68	5	23	28	....	....	....	132	....	....	....	....	....	....	....	....	....	....	....	....	....	....	....	....	....	....
1981-82	London Knights	OHL	68	19	37	56	....	....	....	161	....	....	....	....	....	....	....	....	....	....	4	0	1	1	6	....	....	....
1982-83	London Knights	OHL	39	16	28	44	....	....	....	67	....	....	....	....	....	....	....	....	....	....	3	0	1	1	6	....	....	....
	Canada	WJC-A	7	2	3	5	....	....	....	8	....	....	....	....	....	....	....	....	....	....	....	....	....	....	....	....	....	....
	Detroit Red Wings	**NHL**	**15**	**0**	**2**	**2**	**0**	**1**	**1**	**6**	**0**	**0**	**0**	**8**	**0.0**	**7**	**1**	**16**	**1**	**–9**	....	....	....	....	....	....	....	....
	Adirondack Red Wings	AHL	6	2	2	4	....	....	....	4	....	....	....	....	....	....	....	....	....	....	6	2	1	3	10	....	....	....
1983-84	Adirondack Red Wings	AHL	80	13	28	41	....	....	....	89	....	....	....	....	....	....	....	....	....	....	6	1	1	2	4	....	....	....
1984-85	**Detroit Red Wings**	**NHL**	**40**	**3**	**7**	**10**	**2**	**5**	**7**	**39**	**1**	**0**	**0**	**47**	**6.4**	**44**	**7**	**29**	**3**	**11**	**3**	**0**	**0**	**0**	**0**	**0**	**0**	**0**
	Adirondack Red Wings	AHL	6	0	4	4	....	....	....	0	....	....	....	....	....	....	....	....	....	....	....	....	....	....	....	....	....	....
1985-86	Adirondack Red Wings	AHL	64	10	46	56	....	....	....	77	....	....	....	....	....	....	....	....	....	....	17	6	*16	*22	14	....	....	....
1986-87	Canada	Nat-Team	48	4	16	20	....	....	....	56	....	....	....	....	....	....	....	....	....	....	....	....	....	....	....	....	....	....
	St. Louis Blues	**NHL**	**5**	**0**	**0**	**0**	**0**	**0**	**0**	**8**	**0**	**0**	**0**	**3**	**0.0**	**3**	**1**	**7**	**0**	**–5**	....	....	....	....	....	....	....	....
1987-88	**St. Louis Blues**	**NHL**	**1**	**0**	**0**	**0**	**0**	**0**	**0**	**2**	**0**	**0**	**0**	**1**	**0.0**	**0**	**0**	**1**	**0**	**–1**	....	....	....	....	....	....	....	....
	Montreal Canadiens	**NHL**	**30**	**2**	**4**	**6**	**2**	**3**	**5**	**19**	**1**	**0**	**0**	**18**	**11.1**	**22**	**2**	**20**	**2**	**2**	....	....	....	....	....	....	....	....
	Sherbrooke Canadiens	AHL	11	2	2	4	....	....	....	25	....	....	....	....	....	....	....	....	....	....	....	....	....	....	....	....	....	....
1988-89	Binghamton Whalers	AHL	65	11	40	51	....	....	....	72	....	....	....	....	....	....	....	....	....	....	....	....	....	....	....	....	....	....
1989-90	KAC Klagenfurt	Austria	35	12	22	34	....	....	....	79	....	....	....	....	....	....	....	....	....	....	....	....	....	....	....	....	....	....
1990-91	SG Bruneck	Italy	36	8	23	31	....	....	....	44	....	....	....	....	....	....	....	....	....	....	6	5	4	9	18	....	....	....
1991-92	SG Bruneck	Alpenliga	18	3	13	16	....	....	....	56	....	....	....	....	....	....	....	....	....	....	....	....	....	....	....	....	....	....
	SG Bruneck	Italy	18	2	12	14	....	....	....	29	....	....	....	....	....	....	....	....	....	....	3	1	4	5	2	....	....	....

			REGULAR SEASON																		PLAYOFFS							
Season	Club	League	GP	G	A	Pts	AG	AA	APts	PIM	PP	SH	GW	S	%	TGF	PGF	TGA	PGA	+/–	GP	G	A	Pts	PIM	PP	SH	GW
1992-93	SG Bruneck	Alpenliga	19	2	15	17	....	....	....	83	....	....	....	....	....	....	....	....	....	....	....	....	....	....	....	....	....	....
	EK Zell-am-Zee	Austria	4	1	1	2	....	....	....	....	....	....	....	....	....	....	....	....	....	....	....	....	....	....	....	....	....	....
	SG Bruneck	Italy	14	10	13	23	....	....	....	18	....	....	....	....	....	....	....	....	....	....	3	1	1	2	6	....	....	....
1993-94	HC Varese	Italy	4	1	3	4	....	....	....	8	....	....	....	....	....	....	....	....	....	....	3	1	0	1	32	....	....	....
	NHL Totals		**91**	**5**	**13**	**18**	**4**	**9**	**13**	**74**	**2**	**0**	**0**	**77**	**6.5**	**76**	**11**	**73**	**6**		**3**	**0**	**0**	**0**	**0**	**0**	**0**	**0**

AHL Second All-Star Team (1986)

Traded to **St. Louis** by **Detroit** for Lee Norwood, August 7, 1986. Traded to **Montreal** by **St. Louis** with St. Louis' 3rd round choice (Pierre Sevigny) in 1989 Entry Draft for Gaston Gingras and Montreal's 3rd round choice (later traded to Winnipeg — Winnipeg selected Kris Draper) in 1989 Entry Draft, October 13, 1987. Signed as a free agent by **Hartford**, August 3, 1988.

• TRAPP, Doug

LW – L. 6', 180 lbs. b: Balcarres, Sask., 11/28/1965. Buffalo's 2nd, 39th overall, in 1984.

Season	Club	League	GP	G	A	Pts	AG	AA	APts	PIM	PP	SH	GW	S	%	TGF	PGF	TGA	PGA	+/–	GP	G	A	Pts	PIM	PP	SH	GW
1981-82	Regina Blues	SJHL	43	25	28	53	....	....	....	102	....	....	....	....	....	....	....	....	....	....	....	....	....	....	....	....	....	....
1982-83	Regina Pats	WHL	71	23	28	51	....	....	....	123	....	....	....	....	....	....	....	....	....	....	5	0	2	2	18	....	....	....
1983-84	Regina Pats	WHL	59	43	50	93	....	....	....	44	....	....	....	....	....	....	....	....	....	....	23	12	12	24	38	....	....	....
1984-85	Regina Pats	WHL	72	48	60	108	....	....	....	81	....	....	....	....	....	....	....	....	....	....	8	7	7	14	2	....	....	....
1985-86	Rochester Americans	AHL	75	21	42	63	....	....	....	86	....	....	....	....	....	....	....	....	....	....	....	....	....	....	....	....	....	....
1986-87	**Buffalo Sabres**	**NHL**	**2**	**0**	**0**	**0**	**0**	**0**	**0**	**0**	**0**	**0**	**0**	**1**	**0.0**	**0**	**0**	**0**	**0**	**0**	....	....	....	....	....	....	....	....
	Rochester Americans	AHL	68	27	35	62	....	....	....	80	....	....	....	....	....	....	....	....	....	....	16	0	9	9	5	....	....	....
1987-88	Balcarres Broncos	SIHA	STATISTICS NOT AVAILABLE																									
	NHL Totals		**2**	**0**	**0**	**0**	**0**	**0**	**0**	**0**	**0**	**0**	**0**	**1**	**0.0**	**0**	**0**	**0**	**0**		....	....	....	....	....	....	....	....

WHL Second All-Star Team (1984)

• TRAVERSE, Patrick

D – L. 6'4", 200 lbs. b: Montreal, Que., 3/14/1974. Ottawa's 3rd, 50th overall, in 1992.

Season	Club	League	GP	G	A	Pts	AG	AA	APts	PIM	PP	SH	GW	S	%	TGF	PGF	TGA	PGA	+/–	GP	G	A	Pts	PIM	PP	SH	GW
1990-91	Montreal-Bourassa Canadiens	QAAA	42	4	19	23	....	....	....	10	....	....	....	....	....	....	....	....	....	....	5	0	3	3	2	....	....	....
1991-92	Shawinigan Cataractes	QMJHL	59	3	11	14	....	....	....	12	....	....	....	....	....	....	....	....	....	....	10	0	0	0	4	....	....	....
1992-93	St-Jean Lynx	QMJHL	68	6	30	36	....	....	....	24	....	....	....	....	....	....	....	....	....	....	4	0	1	1	2	....	....	....
	New Haven Senators	AHL	2	0	0	0	....	....	....	2	....	....	....	....	....	....	....	....	....	....	....	....	....	....	....	....	....	....
1993-94	St-Jean Lynx	QMJHL	66	15	37	52	....	....	....	30	....	....	....	....	....	....	....	....	....	....	5	0	4	4	4	....	....	....
	P.E.I. Senators	AHL	3	0	1	1	....	....	....	2	....	....	....	....	....	....	....	....	....	....	....	....	....	....	....	....	....	....
1994-95	P.E.I. Senators	AHL	70	5	13	18	....	....	....	19	....	....	....	....	....	....	....	....	....	....	7	0	2	2	0	....	....	....
1995-96	**Ottawa Senators**	**NHL**	**5**	**0**	**0**	**0**	**0**	**0**	**0**	**2**	**0**	**0**	**0**	**2**	**0.0**	**1**	**0**	**2**	**0**	**–1**	....	....	....	....	....	....	....	....
	P.E.I. Senators	AHL	55	4	21	25	....	....	....	32	....	....	....	....	....	....	....	....	....	....	5	1	2	3	2	....	....	....
1996-97	Worcester IceCats	AHL	24	0	4	4	....	....	....	23	....	....	....	....	....	....	....	....	....	....	....	....	....	....	....	....	....	....
	Grand Rapids Griffins	IHL	10	2	1	3	....	....	....	10	....	....	....	....	....	....	....	....	....	....	2	0	1	1	2	....	....	....
1997-98	Hershey Bears	AHL	71	14	15	29	....	....	....	67	....	....	....	....	....	....	....	....	....	....	7	1	3	4	4	....	....	....
1998-99	**Ottawa Senators**	**NHL**	**46**	**1**	**9**	**10**	**1**	**9**	**10**	**22**	**0**	**0**	**0**	**35**	**2.9**	**33**	**4**	**23**	**6**	**12**	....	....	....	....	....	....	....	....
99-2000	**Ottawa Senators**	**NHL**	**66**	**6**	**17**	**23**	**7**	**16**	**23**	**21**	**1**	**0**	**0**	**73**	**8.2**	**70**	**11**	**51**	**9**	**17**	**6**	**0**	**0**	**0**	**2**	**0**	**0**	**0**
	Canada	WC-A	8	1	0	1	....	....	....	0	....	....	....	....	....	....	....	....	....	....	....	....	....	....	....	....	....	....
	NHL Totals		**117**	**7**	**26**	**33**	**8**	**25**	**33**	**45**	**1**	**0**	**0**	**110**	**6.4**	**104**	**15**	**76**	**15**		**6**	**0**	**0**	**0**	**2**	**0**	**0**	**0**

Traded to **Anaheim** by **Ottawa** for Joel Kwiatkowski, June 12, 2000.

• TREBIL, Daniel

D – R. 6'3", 210 lbs. b: Bloomington, MN, 4/10/1974. New Jersey's 7th, 138th overall, in 1992.

Season	Club	League	GP	G	A	Pts	AG	AA	APts	PIM	PP	SH	GW	S	%	TGF	PGF	TGA	PGA	+/–	GP	G	A	Pts	PIM	PP	SH	GW
1989-90	Jefferson Jaguars	Hi-School	22	3	6	9	....	....	....	10	....	....	....	....	....	....	....	....	....	....	....	....	....	....	....	....	....	....
1990-91	Jefferson Jaguars	Hi-School	23	4	12	16	....	....	....	8	....	....	....	....	....	....	....	....	....	....	....	....	....	....	....	....	....	....
1991-92	Jefferson Jaguars	Hi-School	28	7	26	33	....	....	....	6	....	....	....	....	....	....	....	....	....	....	....	....	....	....	....	....	....	....
1992-93	University of Minnesota	WCHA	36	2	11	13	....	....	....	16	....	....	....	....	....	....	....	....	....	....	....	....	....	....	....	....	....	....
1993-94	University of Minnesota	WCHA	42	1	21	22	....	....	....	24	....	....	....	....	....	....	....	....	....	....	....	....	....	....	....	....	....	....
1994-95	University of Minnesota	WCHA	44	10	33	43	....	....	....	10	....	....	....	....	....	....	....	....	....	....	....	....	....	....	....	....	....	....
1995-96	University of Minnesota	WCHA	42	11	35	46	....	....	....	36	....	....	....	....	....	....	....	....	....	....	....	....	....	....	....	....	....	....
1996-97	**Mighty Ducks of Anaheim**	**NHL**	**29**	**3**	**3**	**6**	**3**	**3**	**6**	**23**	**0**	**0**	**0**	**30**	**10.0**	**27**	**5**	**23**	**6**	**5**	**9**	**0**	**1**	**1**	**6**	**0**	**0**	**0**
	Baltimore Bandits	AHL	49	4	20	24	....	....	....	38	....	....	....	....	....	....	....	....	....	....	....	....	....	....	....	....	....	....
1997-98	**Mighty Ducks of Anaheim**	**NHL**	**21**	**0**	**1**	**1**	**0**	**1**	**1**	**2**	**0**	**0**	**0**	**11**	**0.0**	**7**	**1**	**15**	**1**	**–8**	....	....	....	....	....	....	....	....
	Cincinnati Mighty Ducks	AHL	32	5	15	20	....	....	....	21	....	....	....	....	....	....	....	....	....	....	....	....	....	....	....	....	....	....
	United States	WC-A	4	0	0	0	....	....	....	0	....	....	....	....	....	....	....	....	....	....	....	....	....	....	....	....	....	....
1998-99	**Mighty Ducks of Anaheim**	**NHL**	**6**	**0**	**0**	**0**	**0**	**0**	**0**	**0**	**0**	**0**	**0**	**1**	**0.0**	**2**	**0**	**4**	**0**	**–2**	**1**	**0**	**0**	**0**	**2**	**0**	**0**	**0**
	Cincinnati Mighty Ducks	AHL	52	6	15	21	....	....	....	31	....	....	....	....	....	....	....	....	....	....	....	....	....	....	....	....	....	....
99-2000	Cincinnati Mighty Ducks	AHL	52	7	21	28	....	....	....	48	....	....	....	....	....	....	....	....	....	....	....	....	....	....	....	....	....	....
	Pittsburgh Penguins	**NHL**	**3**	**1**	**0**	**1**	**1**	**0**	**1**	**0**	**0**	**0**	**0**	**2**	**50.0**	**3**	**0**	**1**	**0**	**2**	....	....	....	....	....	....	....	....
	NHL Totals		**59**	**4**	**4**	**8**	**4**	**4**	**8**	**25**	**0**	**0**	**0**	**44**	**9.1**	**39**	**6**	**43**	**7**		**10**	**0**	**1**	**1**	**8**	**0**	**0**	**0**

WCHA Second All-Star Team (1996) • NCAA West Second All-American Team (1996)

Signed as a free agent by **Anaheim**, May 30, 1996. Traded to **Pittsburgh** by **Anaheim** for Pittsburgh's 5th round choice (Bill Cass) in 2000 Entry Draft, March 14, 2000.

• TREDWAY, Brock

Brock R. RW – R. 6', 180 lbs. b: Highland Creek, Ont., 6/23/1959.

Season	Club	League	GP	G	A	Pts	AG	AA	APts	PIM	PP	SH	GW	S	%	TGF	PGF	TGA	PGA	+/–	GP	G	A	Pts	PIM	PP	SH	GW
1977-78	Cornell University	ECAC	22	28	12	40	....	....	....	2	....	....	....	....	....	....	....	....	....	....	....	....	....	....	....	....	....	....
1978-79	Cornell University	ECAC	29	31	29	60	....	....	....	8	....	....	....	....	....	....	....	....	....	....	....	....	....	....	....	....	....	....
1979-80	Cornell University	ECAC	31	25	35	60	....	....	....	10	....	....	....	....	....	....	....	....	....	....	....	....	....	....	....	....	....	....
1980-81	Cornell University	ECAC	31	29	17	46	....	....	....	0	....	....	....	....	....	....	....	....	....	....	....	....	....	....	....	....	....	....
1981-82	New Haven Nighthawks	AHL	80	35	24	59	....	....	....	7	....	....	....	....	....	....	....	....	....	....	4	3	3	6	0	....	....	....
	Los Angeles Kings	**NHL**	....	....	....	....	....	....	....	....	....	....	....	....	....	....	....	....	....	....	**1**	**0**	**0**	**0**	**0**	**0**	**0**	**0**
1982-83	New Haven Nighthawks	AHL	74	15	26	41	....	....	....	9	....	....	....	....	....	....	....	....	....	....	12	1	7	8	2	....	....	....
1983-84	New Haven Nighthawks	AHL	70	21	42	63	....	....	....	4	....	....	....	....	....	....	....	....	....	....	....	....	....	....	....	....	....	....
1984-85	KAC Klagenfurt	Austria	39	19	21	40	....	....	....	20	....	....	....	....	....	....	....	....	....	....	....	....	....	....	....	....	....	....
1985-86	New Haven Nighthawks	AHL	39	2	6	8	....	....	....	0	....	....	....	....	....	....	....	....	....	....	....	....	....	....	....	....	....	....
	NHL Totals		....	....	....	....	....	....	....	....	....	....	....	....	....	....	....	....	....		**1**	**0**	**0**	**0**	**0**	**0**	**0**	**0**

ECAC Second All-Star Team (1979)

Signed as a free agent by **LA Kings**, May 11, 1981.

• TREMBLAY, Brent

Brent Francis D – L. 6'2", 192 lbs. b: North Bay, Ont., 11/1/1957. Washington's 8th, 127th overall, in 1977.

Season	Club	League	GP	G	A	Pts	AG	AA	APts	PIM	PP	SH	GW	S	%	TGF	PGF	TGA	PGA	+/–	GP	G	A	Pts	PIM	PP	SH	GW
1975-76	Hull Festivals	QMJHL	72	2	18	20	....	....	....	129	....	....	....	....	....	....	....	....	....	....	....	....	....	....	....	....	....	....
1976-77	Trois-Rivieres Draveurs	QMJHL	60	9	17	26	....	....	....	131	....	....	....	....	....	....	....	....	....	....	....	....	....	....	....	....	....	....
1977-78	Port Huron Flags	IHL	61	7	25	32	....	....	....	231	....	....	....	....	....	....	....	....	....	....	17	5	8	15	74	....	....	....
	Hershey Bears	AHL	11	0	1	1	....	....	....	15	....	....	....	....	....	....	....	....	....	....	....	....	....	....	....	....	....	....
1978-79	**Washington Capitals**	**NHL**	**1**	**0**	**0**	**0**	**0**	**0**	**0**	**0**	**0**	**0**	**0**	**1**	**0.0**	**0**	**0**	**0**	**0**	**0**	....	....	....	....	....	....	....	....
	Hershey Bears	AHL	75	2	16	18	....	....	....	109	....	....	....	....	....	....	....	....	....	....	4	0	0	0	9	....	....	....
1979-80	**Washington Capitals**	**NHL**	**9**	**1**	**0**	**1**	**1**	**0**	**1**	**6**	**0**	**0**	**0**	**6**	**16.7**	**4**	**0**	**4**	**1**	**1**	....	....	....	....	....	....	....	....
	Hershey Bears	AHL	26	2	11	13	....	....	....	54	....	....	....	....	....	....	....	....	....	....	....	....	....	....	....	....	....	....
	NHL Totals		**10**	**1**	**0**	**1**	**1**	**0**	**1**	**6**	**0**	**0**	**0**	**7**	**14.3**	**4**	**0**	**4**	**1**		....	....	....	....	....	....	....	....

QMJHL West Division Second All-Star Team (1976)

• TREMBLAY, Gilles

Joseph Jean Gilles LW – L. 5'10", 170 lbs. b: Montmorency, Que., 12/17/1938.

Season	Club	League	GP	G	A	Pts	AG	AA	APts	PIM	PP	SH	GW	S	%	TGF	PGF	TGA	PGA	+/–	GP	G	A	Pts	PIM	PP	SH	GW
1956-57	Hull-Ottawa Canadiens	OHA-Jr.	18	3	4	7	....	....	....	2	....	....	....	....	....	....	....	....	....	....	....	....	....	....	....	....	....	....
	Hull-Ottawa Canadiens	EOHL	8	0	2	2	....	....	....	2	....	....	....	....	....	....	....	....	....	....	....	....	....	....	....	....	....	....
	Hull-Ottawa Canadiens	QHL	14	2	1	3	....	....	....	0	....	....	....	....	....	....	....	....	....	....	....	....	....	....	....	....	....	....
	Hull-Ottawa Canadiens	Mem-Cup	15	5	4	9	....	....	....	4	....	....	....	....	....	....	....	....	....	....	....	....	....	....	....	....	....	....

Season	Club	League	REGULAR SEASON																		PLAYOFFS							
			GP	G	A	Pts	AG	AA	APts	PIM	PP	SH	GW	S	%	TGF	PGF	TGA	PGA	+/–	GP	G	A	Pts	PIM	PP	SH	GW
1957-58	Hull-Ottawa Canadiens	OHA-Jr.	27	15	12	27	....	....	....	6	....	....	....	....	....	....	....	....	....	....	....	....	....	....	....	....	....	....
	Hull-Ottawa Canadiens	EOHL	36	13	19	32	....	....	....	10	....	....	....	....	....	....	....	....	....	....	....	....	....	....	....	....	....	....
	Hull-Ottawa Canadiens	Mem-Cup	13	6	11	17	....	....	....	6	....	....	....	....	....	....	....	....	....	....	....	....	....	....	....	....	....	....
1958-59	Hull-Ottawa Canadiens	X-Games	STATISTICS NOT AVAILABLE																									
	Hull-Ottawa Canadiens	EOHL	3	1	0	1	....	....	....	4	....	....	....	....	....	....	....	....	....	....	3	1	0	1	0	....	....	....
	Rochester Americans	AHL	3	1	1	2	....	....	....	2	....	....	....	....	....	....	....	....	....	....	....	....	....	....	....	....	....	....
	Hull-Ottawa Canadiens	Mem-Cup	9	3	5	8	....	....	....	6	....	....	....	....	....	....	....	....	....	....	....	....	....	....	....	....	....	....
1959-60	Hull-Ottawa Canadiens	EPHL	67	32	51	83	....	....	....	45	....	....	....	....	....	....	....	....	....	....	7	4	3	7	8	....	....	....
1960-61	**Montreal Canadiens**	**NHL**	**45**	**7**	**11**	**18**	**8**	**11**	**19**	**4**	....	....	....	....	....	....	....	....	....	....	**6**	**1**	**3**	**4**	**0**	**0**	**0**	**0**
	Hull-Ottawa Canadiens	EPHL	14	9	11	20	....	....	....	12	....	....	....	....	....	....	....	....	....	....	....	....	....	....	....	....	....	....
1961-62	**Montreal Canadiens**	**NHL**	**70**	**32**	**22**	**54**	**37**	**21**	**58**	**28**	....	....	....	....	....	....	....	....	....	....	**6**	**1**	**0**	**1**	**2**	**0**	**0**	**0**
1962-63	**Montreal Canadiens**	**NHL**	**60**	**25**	**24**	**49**	**29**	**24**	**53**	**42**	....	....	....	....	....	....	....	....	....	....	**5**	**2**	**0**	**2**	**0**	**2**	**0**	**1**
1963-64	**Montreal Canadiens**	**NHL**	**61**	**22**	**15**	**37**	**27**	**16**	**43**	**21**	....	....	....	....	....	....	....	....	....	....	**2**	**0**	**0**	**0**	**0**	**0**	**0**	**0**
1964-65	**Montreal Canadiens**	**NHL**	**26**	**9**	**7**	**16**	**11**	**7**	**18**	**16**	....	....	....	....	....	....	....	....	....	....	....	....	....	....	....	....	....	....
1965-66♦	**Montreal Canadiens**	**NHL**	**70**	**27**	**21**	**48**	**31**	**20**	**51**	**24**	....	....	....	....	....	....	....	....	....	....	**10**	**4**	**5**	**9**	**0**	**3**	**0**	**1**
1966-67	**Montreal Canadiens**	**NHL**	**62**	**13**	**19**	**32**	**15**	**19**	**34**	**16**	....	....	....	....	....	....	....	....	....	....	**10**	**0**	**1**	**1**	**0**	**0**	**0**	**0**
1967-68♦	**Montreal Canadiens**	**NHL**	**71**	**23**	**28**	**51**	**27**	**28**	**55**	**8**	**7**	**1**	**2**	**215**	**10.7**	**80**	**14**	**65**	**27**	**28**	**9**	**1**	**5**	**6**	**2**	**0**	**0**	**0**
1968-69♦	**Montreal Canadiens**	**NHL**	**44**	**10**	**15**	**25**	**11**	**13**	**24**	**2**	**0**	**0**	**0**	**95**	**10.5**	**48**	**4**	**51**	**22**	**15**	....	....	....	....	....	....	....	....
	NHL Totals		**509**	**168**	**162**	**330**	**196**	**159**	**355**	**161**	....	....	....	....	....	....	....	....	....		**48**	**9**	**14**	**23**	**4**	....	....	....

Played in NHL All-Star Game (1965, 1967)

• Missed remainder of 1964-65 season recovering from leg injury suffered in game vs. Toronto, December 17, 1964.

• TREMBLAY, J.C.

Jean Claude D – L. 5′11″, 170 lbs. b: Bagotville, Que., 1/22/1939 d: 12/7/1994.

Season	Club	League	GP	G	A	Pts	AG	AA	APts	PIM	PP	SH	GW	S	%	TGF	PGF	TGA	PGA	+/–	GP	G	A	Pts	PIM	PP	SH	GW
1956-57	Port Alfred Nationale	QJHL	STATISTICS NOT AVAILABLE																									
1957-58	Hull-Ottawa Canadiens	OHA-Jr.	24	7	12	19	....	....	....	8	....	....	....	....	....	....	....	....	....	....	....	....	....	....	....	....	....	....
	Hull-Ottawa Canadiens	EOHL	34	5	17	22	....	....	....	16	....	....	....	....	....	....	....	....	....	....	....	....	....	....	....	....	....	....
	Hull-Ottawa Canadiens	Mem-Cup	13	2	5	7	....	....	....	10	....	....	....	....	....	....	....	....	....	....	....	....	....	....	....	....	....	....
1958-59	Hull-Ottawa Canadiens	X-Games	STATISTICS NOT AVAILABLE																									
	Hull-Ottawa Canadiens	EOHL	26	4	13	17	....	....	....	22	....	....	....	....	....	....	....	....	....	....	1	0	1	1	9	....	....	....
	Rochester Americans	AHL	3	0	0	0	....	....	....	0	....	....	....	....	....	....	....	....	....	....	....	....	....	....	....	....	....	....
	Hull-Ottawa Canadiens	Mem-Cup	9	4	5	9	....	....	....	12	....	....	....	....	....	....	....	....	....	....	....	....	....	....	....	....	....	....
1959-60	**Montreal Canadiens**	**NHL**	**11**	**0**	**1**	**1**	**0**	**1**	**1**	**0**	....	....	....	....	....	....	....	....	....	....	....	....	....	....	....	....	....	....
	Hull-Ottawa Canadiens	EPHL	55	25	31	56	....	....	....	55	....	....	....	....	....	....	....	....	....	....	7	1	4	5	2	....	....	....
1960-61	**Montreal Canadiens**	**NHL**	**29**	**1**	**3**	**4**	**1**	**3**	**4**	**18**	....	....	....	....	....	....	....	....	....	....	**5**	**0**	**0**	**0**	**2**	**0**	**0**	**0**
	Hull-Ottawa Canadiens	EPHL	37	7	33	40	....	....	....	28	....	....	....	....	....	....	....	....	....	....	....	....	....	....	....	....	....	....
1961-62	**Montreal Canadiens**	**NHL**	**70**	**3**	**17**	**20**	**3**	**16**	**19**	**18**	....	....	....	....	....	....	....	....	....	....	**6**	**0**	**2**	**2**	**2**	**0**	**0**	**0**
1962-63	**Montreal Canadiens**	**NHL**	**69**	**1**	**17**	**18**	**1**	**17**	**18**	**10**	....	....	....	....	....	....	....	....	....	....	**5**	**0**	**0**	**0**	**0**	**0**	**0**	**0**
1963-64	**Montreal Canadiens**	**NHL**	**70**	**5**	**16**	**21**	**6**	**17**	**23**	**24**	....	....	....	....	....	....	....	....	....	....	**7**	**2**	**1**	**3**	**9**	**0**	**1**	**0**
1964-65♦	**Montreal Canadiens**	**NHL**	**68**	**3**	**17**	**20**	**4**	**17**	**21**	**22**	....	....	....	....	....	....	....	....	....	....	**13**	**1**	***9**	**10**	**18**	**0**	**1**	**0**
1965-66♦	**Montreal Canadiens**	**NHL**	**59**	**6**	**29**	**35**	**7**	**28**	**35**	**8**	....	....	....	....	....	....	....	....	....	....	**10**	**2**	**9**	**11**	**2**	**2**	**0**	**0**
1966-67	**Montreal Canadiens**	**NHL**	**60**	**8**	**26**	**34**	**9**	**25**	**34**	**14**	....	....	....	....	....	....	....	....	....	....	**10**	**2**	**4**	**6**	**2**	**0**	**0**	**0**
1967-68♦	**Montreal Canadiens**	**NHL**	**73**	**4**	**26**	**30**	**5**	**26**	**31**	**18**	**1**	**0**	**1**	**105**	**3.8**	**116**	**29**	**88**	**29**	**28**	**13**	**3**	**6**	**9**	**2**	**0**	**1**	**1**
1968-69♦	**Montreal Canadiens**	**NHL**	**75**	**7**	**32**	**39**	**7**	**29**	**36**	**18**	**2**	**0**	**1**	**139**	**5.0**	**146**	**29**	**118**	**30**	**29**	**13**	**1**	**4**	**5**	**6**	**0**	**1**	**0**
1969-70	**Montreal Canadiens**	**NHL**	**58**	**2**	**19**	**21**	**2**	**18**	**20**	**7**	**1**	**0**	**0**	**77**	**2.6**	**72**	**21**	**55**	**9**	**5**	....	....	....	....	....	....	....	....
1970-71♦	**Montreal Canadiens**	**NHL**	**76**	**11**	**52**	**63**	**11**	**44**	**55**	**23**	**5**	**0**	**4**	**122**	**9.0**	**153**	**63**	**102**	**28**	**16**	**20**	**3**	**14**	**17**	**15**	**1**	**0**	**3**
1971-72	**Montreal Canadiens**	**NHL**	**76**	**6**	**51**	**57**	**6**	**44**	**50**	**24**	**3**	**0**	**2**	**130**	**4.6**	**167**	**51**	**91**	**27**	**52**	**6**	**0**	**2**	**2**	**0**	**0**	**0**	**0**
1972-73	Quebec Nordiques	WHA	75	14	*75	89	....	....	....	32	....	....	....	....	....	....	....	....	....	....	....	....	....	....	....	....	....	....
1973-74	Quebec Nordiques	WHA	68	9	44	53	....	....	....	10	....	....	....	....	....	....	....	....	....	....	....	....	....	....	....	....	....	....
1974-75	Team Canada	Summit-74	8	1	4	5	....	....	....	2	....	....	....	....	....	....	....	....	....	....	....	....	....	....	....	....	....	....
	Quebec Nordiques	WHA	68	16	56	72	....	....	....	18	....	....	....	....	....	....	....	....	....	....	11	0	10	10	2	....	....	....
1975-76	Quebec Nordiques	WHA	80	12	*77	89	....	....	....	16	....	....	....	....	....	....	....	....	....	....	5	0	3	3	0	....	....	....
1976-77	Quebec Nordiques	WHA	53	4	31	35	....	....	....	16	....	....	....	....	....	....	....	....	....	....	17	2	9	11	2	....	....	....
1977-78	Quebec Nordiques	WHA	54	5	37	42	....	....	....	26	....	....	....	....	....	....	....	....	....	....	1	0	1	1	0	....	....	....
1978-79	Quebec Nordiques	WHA	56	6	38	44	....	....	....	8	....	....	....	....	....	....	....	....	....	....	....	....	....	....	....	....	....	....
1979-80			OUT OF HOCKEY – RETIRED																									
1980-81	HC Geneve-Servette	Switz-2	PLAYER/COACH – STATISTICS UNAVAILABLE																									
	NHL Totals		**794**	**57**	**306**	**363**	**62**	**285**	**347**	**204**	....	....	....	....	....	....	....	....	....	....	**108**	**14**	**51**	**65**	**58**	....	....	....
	Other Major League Totals		454	66	358	424	....	....	....	126	....	....	....	....	....	....	....	....	....	....	34	2	23	25	4	....	....	....

EPHL First All-Star Team (1960) • NHL Second All-Star Team (1968) • NHL First All-Star Team (1971) • WHA First All-Star Team (1973, 1975, 1976) • Won Dennis A. Murphy Trophy (WHA Top Defenseman) (1973, 1975) • WHA Second All-Star Team (1974) • Played in NHL All-Star Game (1959, 1965, 1967, 1968, 1969, 1971, 1972)

• Hull-Ottawa (OHA-Jr.) played partial schedule against OHA-Jr. teams that counted for opposition only. Selected by **LA Sharks** (WHA) in 1972 WHA General Player Draft, February 12, 1972. Traded to **Quebec** (WHA) by **LA Sharks** (WHA) for future considerations, August, 1972.

• TREMBLAY, Mario

RW – R. 6′, 185 lbs. b: Montreal, Que., 2/9/1956. Montreal's 4th, 12th overall, in 1974.

Season	Club	League	GP	G	A	Pts	AG	AA	APts	PIM	PP	SH	GW	S	%	TGF	PGF	TGA	PGA	+/–	GP	G	A	Pts	PIM	PP	SH	GW
1972-73	Montreal Red-White-Blue	QMJHL	56	43	37	80	....	....	....	155	....	....	....	....	....	....	....	....	....	....	4	0	1	1	4	....	....	....
1973-74	Montreal Red-White-Blue	QMJHL	47	49	51	100	....	....	....	154	....	....	....	....	....	....	....	....	....	....	7	1	3	4	17	....	....	....
1974-75	**Montreal Canadiens**	**NHL**	**63**	**21**	**18**	**39**	**18**	**13**	**31**	**108**	**0**	**0**	**1**	**127**	**16.5**	**60**	**4**	**33**	**0**	**23**	**11**	**0**	**1**	**1**	**7**	**0**	**0**	**0**
	Nova Scotia Voyageurs	AHL	15	10	8	18	....	....	....	47	....	....	....	....	....	....	....	....	....	....	....	....	....	....	....	....	....	....
1975-76♦	**Montreal Canadiens**	**NHL**	**71**	**11**	**16**	**27**	**10**	**12**	**22**	**88**	**1**	**0**	**2**	**94**	**11.7**	**38**	**4**	**29**	**0**	**5**	**10**	**0**	**1**	**1**	**27**	**0**	**0**	**0**
1976-77♦	**Montreal Canadiens**	**NHL**	**74**	**18**	**28**	**46**	**16**	**22**	**38**	**61**	**4**	**0**	**3**	**139**	**12.9**	**69**	**7**	**37**	**0**	**25**	**14**	**3**	**0**	**3**	**9**	**0**	**0**	**0**
1977-78♦	**Montreal Canadiens**	**NHL**	**56**	**10**	**14**	**24**	**9**	**11**	**20**	**44**	**0**	**1**	**0**	**89**	**11.2**	**34**	**1**	**29**	**2**	**6**	**5**	**2**	**1**	**3**	**16**	**0**	**0**	**1**
1978-79♦	**Montreal Canadiens**	**NHL**	**76**	**30**	**29**	**59**	**26**	**21**	**47**	**74**	**3**	**0**	**4**	**163**	**18.4**	**78**	**6**	**55**	**6**	**23**	**13**	**3**	**4**	**7**	**13**	**0**	**0**	**1**
1979-80	**Montreal Canadiens**	**NHL**	**77**	**16**	**26**	**42**	**14**	**19**	**33**	**105**	**0**	**0**	**2**	**192**	**8.3**	**60**	**5**	**51**	**2**	**6**	**10**	**0**	**11**	**11**	**14**	**0**	**0**	**0**
1980-81	**Montreal Canadiens**	**NHL**	**77**	**25**	**38**	**63**	**19**	**25**	**44**	**123**	**4**	**1**	**4**	**254**	**9.8**	**91**	**20**	**57**	**2**	**16**	**3**	**0**	**0**	**0**	**9**	**0**	**0**	**0**
1981-82	**Montreal Canadiens**	**NHL**	**80**	**33**	**40**	**73**	**26**	**27**	**53**	**66**	**7**	**0**	**4**	**205**	**16.1**	**105**	**28**	**53**	**0**	**24**	**5**	**4**	**1**	**5**	**24**	**0**	**0**	**1**
1982-83	**Montreal Canadiens**	**NHL**	**80**	**30**	**37**	**67**	**25**	**26**	**51**	**87**	**7**	**0**	**4**	**175**	**17.1**	**101**	**20**	**52**	**0**	**29**	**3**	**0**	**1**	**1**	**7**	**0**	**0**	**0**
1983-84	**Montreal Canadiens**	**NHL**	**67**	**14**	**25**	**39**	**11**	**17**	**28**	**112**	**3**	**0**	**3**	**133**	**10.5**	**68**	**16**	**51**	**1**	**2**	**15**	**6**	**3**	**9**	**31**	**0**	**0**	**1**
1984-85	**Montreal Canadiens**	**NHL**	**75**	**31**	**35**	**66**	**25**	**24**	**49**	**120**	**14**	**0**	**6**	**193**	**16.1**	**96**	**30**	**45**	**0**	**21**	**12**	**2**	**6**	**8**	**30**	**1**	**0**	**0**
1985-86♦	**Montreal Canadiens**	**NHL**	**56**	**19**	**20**	**39**	**15**	**13**	**28**	**55**	**3**	**0**	**3**	**119**	**16.0**	**62**	**13**	**45**	**0**	**4**	....	....	....	....	....	....	....	....
	NHL Totals		**852**	**258**	**326**	**584**	**214**	**230**	**444**	**1043**	**46**	**2**	**36**	**1883**	**13.7**	**862**	**154**	**537**	**13**		**101**	**20**	**29**	**49**	**187**	**1**	**0**	**4**

• Suffered career-ending shoulder injury in game vs. Quebec, March 17, 1986.

• TREMBLAY, Yannick

D – R. 6′2″, 185 lbs. b: Pointe-aux-Trembles, Que., 11/15/1975. Toronto's 4th, 145th overall, in 1995.

Season	Club	League	GP	G	A	Pts	AG	AA	APts	PIM	PP	SH	GW	S	%	TGF	PGF	TGA	PGA	+/–	GP	G	A	Pts	PIM	PP	SH	GW
1991-92	Montreal-Bourassa	QAAA	35	2	5	7	....	....	....	55	....	....	....	....	....	....	....	....	....	....	....	....	....	....	....	....	....	....
1992-93	Montreal-Bourassa College	CEGEP	21	2	5	7	....	....	....	10	....	....	....	....	....	....	....	....	....	....	3	0	0	0	2	....	....	....
1993-94	St. Thomas University	AUAA	25	2	3	5	....	....	....	10	....	....	....	....	....	....	....	....	....	....	....	....	....	....	....	....	....	....
1994-95	Beauport Harfangs	QMJHL	70	10	32	42	....	....	....	22	....	....	....	....	....	....	....	....	....	....	17	6	8	14	6	....	....	....
1995-96	Beauport Harfangs	QMJHL	61	12	33	45	....	....	....	42	....	....	....	....	....	....	....	....	....	....	20	3	16	19	18	....	....	....
	St. John's Maple Leafs	AHL	3	0	1	1	....	....	....	0	....	....	....	....	....	....	....	....	....	....	....	....	....	....	....	....	....	....
1996-97	**Toronto Maple Leafs**	**NHL**	**5**	**0**	**0**	**0**	**0**	**0**	**0**	**0**	**0**	**0**	**0**	**2**	**0.0**	**0**	**0**	**4**	**0**	**–4**	....	....	....	....	....	....	....	....
	St. John's Maple Leafs	AHL	67	7	25	32	....	....	....	34	....	....	....	....	....	....	....	....	....	....	11	2	9	11	0	....	....	....
1997-98	**Toronto Maple Leafs**	**NHL**	**38**	**2**	**4**	**6**	**2**	**4**	**6**	**6**	**1**	**0**	**0**	**45**	**4.4**	**18**	**5**	**19**	**0**	**–6**	....	....	....	....	....	....	....	....
	St. John's Maple Leafs	AHL	17	3	7	10	....	....	....	4	....	....	....	....	....	....	....	....	....	....	4	0	1	1	5	....	....	....
1998-99	**Toronto Maple Leafs**	**NHL**	**35**	**2**	**7**	**9**	**2**	**7**	**9**	**16**	**0**	**0**	**0**	**37**	**5.4**	**31**	**5**	**27**	**1**	**0**	....	....	....	....	....	....	....	....
99-2000	**Atlanta Thrashers**	**NHL**	**75**	**10**	**21**	**31**	**11**	**19**	**30**	**22**	**4**	**1**	**2**	**139**	**7.2**	**67**	**30**	**93**	**14**	**–42**	....	....	....	....	....	....	....	....
	Canada	WC-A	9	1	1	2	....	....	....	0	....	....	....	....	....	....	....	....	....	....	....	....	....	....	....	....	....	....
	NHL Totals		**153**	**14**	**32**	**46**	**15**	**30**	**45**	**44**	**5**	**1**	**2**	**223**	**6.3**	**116**	**40**	**143**	**15**		....	....	....	....	....	....	....	....

Claimed by **Atlanta** from **Toronto** in Expansion Draft, June 25, 1999.

• TREPANIER, Pascal

D – R. 6', 205 lbs. b: Gaspe, Que., 9/4/1973.

Season	Club	League	GP	G	A	Pts	AG	AA	APts	PIM	PP	SH	GW	S	%	TGF	PGF	TGA	PGA	+/–	GP	G	A	Pts	PIM	PP	SH	GW
			REGULAR SEASON																		PLAYOFFS							
1990-91	Hull Olympiques	QMJHL	46	3	3	6	....	....	....	56	....	....	....	....	....	....	....	....	....	....	4	0	2	2	7	....	....	....
1991-92	Trois-Rivieres Draveurs	QMJHL	53	4	18	22	....	....	....	125	....	....	....	....	....	....	....	....	....	....	15	3	5	8	21	....	....	....
1992-93	Sherbrooke Faucons	QMJHL	59	15	33	48	....	....	....	130	....	....	....	....	....	....	....	....	....	....	15	5	7	12	36	....	....	....
1993-94	Sherbrooke Faucons	QMJHL	48	16	41	57	....	....	....	67	....	....	....	....	....	....	....	....	....	....	12	1	8	9	14	....	....	....
1994-95	Dayton Bombers	ECHL	36	16	28	44	....	....	....	113	....	....	....	....	....	....	....	....	....	....	9	2	4	6	20	....	....	....
	Kalamazoo Wings	IHL	14	1	2	3	....	....	....	47	....	....	....	....	....	....	....	....	....	....	....	....	....	....	....	....	....	....
	Cornwall Aces	AHL	4	0	0	0	....	....	....	9	....	....	....	....	....	....	....	....	....	....	14	2	7	9	32	....	....	....
1995-96	Cornwall Aces	AHL	70	13	20	33	....	....	....	142	....	....	....	....	....	....	....	....	....	....	8	1	2	3	24	....	....	....
1996-97	Hershey Bears	AHL	73	14	39	53	....	....	....	151	....	....	....	....	....	....	....	....	....	....	23	6	13	19	59	....	....	....
1997-98	**Colorado Avalanche**	**NHL**	**15**	**0**	**1**	**1**	**0**	**1**	**1**	**18**	**0**	**0**	**0**	**9**	**0.0**	**2**	**0**	**4**	**0**	**–2**	....	....	....	....	....	....	....	....
	Hershey Bears	AHL	43	13	18	31	....	....	....	105	....	....	....	....	....	....	....	....	....	....	7	4	2	6	8	....	....	....
1998-99	**Mighty Ducks of Anaheim**	**NHL**	**45**	**2**	**4**	**6**	**2**	**4**	**6**	**48**	**0**	**0**	**1**	**49**	**4.1**	**18**	**4**	**18**	**4**	**0**	....	....	....	....	....	....	....	....
99-2000	**Mighty Ducks of Anaheim**	**NHL**	**37**	**0**	**4**	**4**	**0**	**4**	**4**	**54**	**0**	**0**	**0**	**33**	**0.0**	**15**	**2**	**17**	**6**	**2**	....	....	....	....	....	....	....	....
	NHL Totals		**97**	**2**	**9**	**11**	**2**	**9**	**11**	**120**	**0**	**0**	**1**	**91**	**2.2**	**35**	**6**	**39**	**10**		....	....	....	....	....	....	....	....

AHL Second All-Star Team (1997)

Signed as a free agent by **Colorado**, August 30, 1995. Claimed by **Anaheim** from **Colorado** in NHL Waiver Draft, October 5, 1998.

• TRIMPER, Tim

Timothy Edward LW – L. 5'9", 184 lbs. b: Windsor, Ont., 9/28/1959. Chicago's 2nd, 28th overall, in 1979.

Season	Club	League	GP	G	A	Pts	AG	AA	APts	PIM	PP	SH	GW	S	%	TGF	PGF	TGA	PGA	+/–	GP	G	A	Pts	PIM	PP	SH	GW
1975-76	Royal York Royals	OJHL	37	2	16	18	....	....	....	47	....	....	....	....	....	....	....	....	....	....	....	....	....	....	....	....	....	....
1976-77	Peterborough Petes	OMJHL	62	14	11	25	....	....	....	95	....	....	....	....	....	....	....	....	....	....	4	0	1	1	2	....	....	....
1977-78	Peterborough Petes	OMJHL	59	26	34	60	....	....	....	73	....	....	....	....	....	....	....	....	....	....	21	8	8	16	25	....	....	....
	Peterborough Petes	Mem-Cup	5	2	5	7	....	....	....	8	....	....	....	....	....	....	....	....	....	....	....	....	....	....	....	....	....	....
1978-79	Peterborough Petes	OMJHL	66	62	46	108	....	....	....	97	....	....	....	....	....	....	....	....	....	....	17	7	24	31	25	....	....	....
	Peterborough Petes	Mem-Cup	5	3	3	6	....	....	....	8	....	....	....	....	....	....	....	....	....	....	....	....	....	....	....	....	....	....
1979-80	**Chicago Black Hawks**	**NHL**	**30**	**6**	**10**	**16**	**5**	**7**	**12**	**10**	**2**	**0**	**1**	**65**	**9.2**	**29**	**16**	**20**	**0**	**–7**	**1**	**0**	**0**	**0**	**2**	**0**	**0**	**0**
	New Brunswick Hawks	AHL	43	26	31	57	....	....	....	18	....	....	....	....	....	....	....	....	....	....	....	....	....	....	....	....	....	....
1980-81	**Winnipeg Jets**	**NHL**	**56**	**15**	**14**	**29**	**12**	**9**	**21**	**28**	**1**	**0**	**1**	**95**	**15.8**	**39**	**2**	**69**	**1**	**–31**	....	....	....	....	....	....	....	....
	New Brunswick Hawks	AHL	19	7	8	15	....	....	....	21	....	....	....	....	....	....	....	....	....	....	....	....	....	....	....	....	....	....
	Hershey Bears	AHL	47	20	38	58	....	....	....	129	....	....	....	....	....	....	....	....	....	....	....	....	....	....	....	....	....	....
1981-82	**Winnipeg Jets**	**NHL**	**74**	**8**	**8**	**16**	**6**	**5**	**11**	**100**	**0**	**1**	**0**	**68**	**11.8**	**26**	**0**	**57**	**24**	**–7**	**1**	**0**	**0**	**0**	**0**	**0**	**0**	**0**
1982-83	**Winnipeg Jets**	**NHL**	**5**	**0**	**0**	**0**	**0**	**0**	**0**	**0**	**0**	**0**	**0**	**2**	**0.0**	**0**	**0**	**5**	**3**	**–2**	....	....	....	....	....	....	....	....
	Sherbrooke Jets	AHL	68	28	38	66	....	....	....	53	....	....	....	....	....	....	....	....	....	....	....	....	....	....	....	....	....	....
1983-84	**Winnipeg Jets**	**NHL**	**5**	**0**	**0**	**0**	**0**	**0**	**0**	**0**	**0**	**0**	**0**	**1**	**0.0**	**1**	**0**	**0**	**0**	**1**	....	....	....	....	....	....	....	....
	Sherbrooke Jets	AHL	31	10	24	34	....	....	....	26	....	....	....	....	....	....	....	....	....	....	....	....	....	....	....	....	....	....
	Salt Lake Golden Eagles	IHL	35	18	27	45	....	....	....	26	....	....	....	....	....	....	....	....	....	....	5	4	3	7	9	....	....	....
1984-85	**Minnesota North Stars**	**NHL**	**20**	**1**	**4**	**5**	**1**	**3**	**4**	**15**	**0**	**0**	**0**	**28**	**3.6**	**7**	**0**	**16**	**0**	**–9**	....	....	....	....	....	....	....	....
	Springfield Indians	AHL	60	27	34	61	....	....	....	84	....	....	....	....	....	....	....	....	....	....	4	1	3	4	9	....	....	....
	NHL Totals		**190**	**30**	**36**	**66**	**24**	**24**	**48**	**153**	**3**	**1**	**2**	**259**	**11.6**	**102**	**18**	**167**	**28**		**2**	**0**	**0**	**0**	**2**	**0**	**0**	**0**

OMJHL Second All-Star Team (1979) • Memorial Cup All-Star Team (1979)

Traded to **Winnipeg** by **Chicago** with Doug Lecuyer for Peter Marsh, December 1, 1980. Traded to **Minnesota** by **Winnipeg** for Jordy Douglas, January 12, 1984.

• TRNKA, Pavel

D – L. 6'3", 200 lbs. b: Plzen, Czech., 7/27/1976. Anaheim's 5th, 106th overall, in 1994.

Season	Club	League	GP	G	A	Pts	AG	AA	APts	PIM	PP	SH	GW	S	%	TGF	PGF	TGA	PGA	+/–	GP	G	A	Pts	PIM	PP	SH	GW
1992-93	ZKZ Plzen	Czech-Jr.	STATISTICS NOT AVAILABLE																									
1993-94	ZKZ Plzen	Czech-Rep	12	0	1	1	....	....	....	....	....	....	....	....	....	....	....	....	....	....	....	....	....	....	....	....	....	....
	Czech-Republic	EJC-A	5	0	1	1	....	....	....	6	....	....	....	....	....	....	....	....	....	....	....	....	....	....	....	....	....	....
1994-95	Poldi Kladno	Czech-Rep	28	0	5	5	....	....	....	24	....	....	....	....	....	....	....	....	....	....	....	....	....	....	....	....	....	....
	ZKZ Plzen	Czech-Rep	6	0	0	0	....	....	....	0	....	....	....	....	....	....	....	....	....	....	....	....	....	....	....	....	....	....
	Czech-Republic	WJC-A	7	0	0	0	....	....	....	8	....	....	....	....	....	....	....	....	....	....	....	....	....	....	....	....	....	....
1995-96	Baltimore Bandits	AHL	69	2	6	8	....	....	....	44	....	....	....	....	....	....	....	....	....	....	6	0	0	0	2	....	....	....
1996-97	Baltimore Bandits	AHL	69	6	14	20	....	....	....	86	....	....	....	....	....	....	....	....	....	....	3	0	0	0	2	....	....	....
1997-98	**Mighty Ducks of Anaheim**	**NHL**	**48**	**3**	**4**	**7**	**4**	**4**	**8**	**40**	**1**	**0**	**0**	**46**	**6.5**	**30**	**6**	**36**	**8**	**–4**	....	....	....	....	....	....	....	....
	Cincinnati Mighty Ducks	AHL	23	3	5	8	....	....	....	28	....	....	....	....	....	....	....	....	....	....	....	....	....	....	....	....	....	....
1998-99	**Mighty Ducks of Anaheim**	**NHL**	**63**	**0**	**4**	**4**	**0**	**4**	**4**	**60**	**0**	**0**	**0**	**50**	**0.0**	**31**	**2**	**42**	**7**	**–6**	**4**	**0**	**1**	**1**	**2**	**0**	**0**	**0**
99-2000	**Mighty Ducks of Anaheim**	**NHL**	**57**	**2**	**15**	**17**	**2**	**14**	**16**	**34**	**0**	**0**	**0**	**54**	**3.7**	**53**	**3**	**53**	**15**	**12**	....	....	....	....	....	....	....	....
	NHL Totals		**168**	**5**	**23**	**28**	**6**	**22**	**28**	**134**	**1**	**0**	**0**	**150**	**3.3**	**114**	**11**	**131**	**30**		**4**	**0**	**1**	**1**	**2**	**0**	**0**	**0**

• TROTTIER, Bryan

Bryan John "Trots" C – L. 5'11", 195 lbs. b: Val Marie, Sask., 7/17/1956. NY Islanders' 2nd, 22nd overall, in 1974. **HHOF**

Season	Club	League	GP	G	A	Pts	AG	AA	APts	PIM	PP	SH	GW	S	%	TGF	PGF	TGA	PGA	+/–	GP	G	A	Pts	PIM	PP	SH	GW
1971-72	Humboldt Broncos	SJHL	STATISTICS NOT AVAILABLE																									
1972-73	Swift Current Broncos	WCJHL	67	16	29	45	....	....	....	10	....	....	....	....	....	....	....	....	....	....	....	....	....	....	....	....	....	....
1973-74	Swift Current Broncos	WCJHL	68	41	71	112	....	....	....	76	....	....	....	....	....	....	....	....	....	....	13	7	8	15	8	....	....	....
1974-75	Lethbridge Broncos	WCJHL	67	46	*98	144	....	....	....	103	....	....	....	....	....	....	....	....	....	....	6	2	5	7	14	....	....	....
	Canada	WJC-A	7	*5	2	7	....	....	....	....	....	....	....	....	....	....	....	....	....	....	....	....	....	....	....	....	....	....
1975-76	**New York Islanders**	**NHL**	**80**	**32**	**63**	**95**	**28**	**47**	**75**	**21**	**11**	**1**	**5**	**178**	**18.0**	**129**	**63**	**40**	**2**	**28**	**13**	**1**	**7**	**8**	**8**	**0**	**0**	**0**
1976-77	**New York Islanders**	**NHL**	**76**	**30**	**42**	**72**	**27**	**32**	**59**	**34**	**11**	**1**	**6**	**175**	**17.1**	**103**	**33**	**46**	**4**	**28**	**12**	**2**	**8**	**10**	**2**	**0**	**0**	**0**
1977-78	**New York Islanders**	**NHL**	**77**	**46**	***77**	**123**	**42**	**60**	**102**	**46**	**13**	**2**	**6**	**193**	**23.8**	**156**	**55**	**55**	**6**	**52**	**7**	**0**	**3**	**3**	**4**	**0**	**0**	**0**
1978-79	**New York Islanders**	**NHL**	**76**	**47**	***87**	***134**	**40**	**64**	**104**	**50**	**15**	**0**	**8**	**187**	**25.1**	**189**	**66**	**51**	**4**	**76**	**10**	**2**	**4**	**6**	**13**	**0**	**0**	**1**
	NHL All-Stars	Chal-Cup	3	1	1	2	....	....	....	2	....	....	....	....	....	....	....	....	....	....	....	....	....	....	....	....	....	....
1979-80♦	**New York Islanders**	**NHL**	**78**	**42**	**62**	**104**	**36**	**45**	**81**	**68**	**15**	**0**	**6**	**186**	**22.6**	**139**	**46**	**74**	**12**	**31**	**21**	***12**	**17**	***29**	**16**	**4**	**2**	**2**
1980-81♦	**New York Islanders**	**NHL**	**73**	**31**	**72**	**103**	**24**	**48**	**72**	**74**	**9**	**2**	**5**	**156**	**19.9**	**151**	**53**	**73**	**24**	**49**	***18**	**11**	***18**	**29**	**34**	**4**	**2**	**1**
1981-82	Canada	Can-Cup	7	3	8	11	....	....	....	6	....	....	....	....	....	....	....	....	....	....	....	....	....	....	....	....	....	....
♦	**New York Islanders**	**NHL**	**80**	**50**	**79**	**129**	**40**	**53**	**93**	**88**	**18**	**2**	**10**	**217**	**23.0**	**177**	**51**	**82**	**26**	**70**	**19**	**6**	***23**	***29**	**40**	**2**	**0**	**2**
1982-83♦	**New York Islanders**	**NHL**	**80**	**34**	**55**	**89**	**28**	**38**	**66**	**68**	**13**	**0**	**5**	**179**	**19.0**	**139**	**46**	**75**	**19**	**37**	**17**	**8**	**12**	**20**	**18**	**3**	**0**	**1**
1983-84	**New York Islanders**	**NHL**	**68**	**40**	**71**	**111**	**32**	**49**	**81**	**59**	**7**	**3**	**4**	**194**	**20.6**	**156**	**35**	**58**	**7**	**70**	**21**	**8**	**6**	**14**	**49**	**1**	**0**	**0**
1984-85	United States	Can-Cup	6	2	3	5	....	....	....	8	....	....	....	....	....	....	....	....	....	....	....	....	....	....	....	....	....	....
	New York Islanders	**NHL**	**68**	**28**	**31**	**59**	**23**	**21**	**44**	**47**	**4**	**5**	**3**	**159**	**17.6**	**95**	**21**	**88**	**19**	**5**	**10**	**4**	**2**	**6**	**8**	**1**	**0**	**1**
1985-86	**New York Islanders**	**NHL**	**78**	**37**	**59**	**96**	**30**	**40**	**70**	**72**	**5**	**1**	**3**	**185**	**20.0**	**138**	**44**	**93**	**28**	**29**	**3**	**1**	**1**	**2**	**2**	**0**	**0**	**0**
1986-87	**New York Islanders**	**NHL**	**80**	**23**	**64**	**87**	**20**	**47**	**67**	**50**	**13**	**0**	**1**	**194**	**11.9**	**126**	**54**	**95**	**26**	**3**	**14**	**8**	**5**	**13**	**12**	**3**	**0**	**2**
1987-88	**New York Islanders**	**NHL**	**77**	**30**	**52**	**82**	**26**	**37**	**63**	**48**	**15**	**0**	**3**	**176**	**17.0**	**110**	**48**	**81**	**29**	**10**	**6**	**0**	**0**	**0**	**10**	**0**	**0**	**0**
1988-89	**New York Islanders**	**NHL**	**73**	**17**	**28**	**45**	**14**	**20**	**34**	**44**	**5**	**0**	**3**	**163**	**10.4**	**79**	**25**	**102**	**41**	**–7**	....	....	....	....	....	....	....	....
1989-90	**New York Islanders**	**NHL**	**59**	**13**	**11**	**24**	**11**	**8**	**19**	**29**	**4**	**0**	**0**	**84**	**15.5**	**40**	**8**	**64**	**21**	**–11**	**4**	**1**	**0**	**1**	**4**	**0**	**0**	**0**
1990-91♦	**Pittsburgh Penguins**	**NHL**	**52**	**9**	**19**	**28**	**8**	**14**	**22**	**24**	**0**	**1**	**0**	**68**	**13.2**	**37**	**1**	**48**	**17**	**5**	**23**	**3**	**4**	**7**	**49**	**0**	**0**	**2**
1991-92♦	**Pittsburgh Penguins**	**NHL**	**63**	**11**	**18**	**29**	**10**	**14**	**24**	**54**	**3**	**1**	**0**	**102**	**10.8**	**49**	**10**	**76**	**26**	**–11**	**21**	**4**	**3**	**7**	**8**	**0**	**0**	**0**
1992-93	**New York Islanders**	**NHL**	DID NOT PLAY – ASSISTANT COACH																									
1993-94	**Pittsburgh Penguins**	**NHL**	**41**	**4**	**11**	**15**	**4**	**9**	**13**	**36**	**0**	**0**	**0**	**45**	**8.9**	**19**	**1**	**45**	**15**	**–12**	**2**	**0**	**0**	**0**	**0**	**0**	**0**	**0**
1994-1997	**Pittsburgh Penguins**	**NHL**	DID NOT PLAY – ASSISTANT COACH																									
1997-1998	Portland Pirates	AHL	DID NOT PLAY – COACHING																									
1998-2000	**Colorado Avalanche**	**NHL**	DID NOT PLAY – ASSISTANT COACH																									
	NHL Totals		**1279**	**524**	**901**	**1425**	**443**	**646**	**1089**	**912**	**161**	**19**	**68**	**2841**	**18.4**	**2032**	**660**	**1246**	**326**		**221**	**71**	**113**	**184**	**277**	**18**	**4**	**12**

• Brother of Rocky • WCJHL First All-Star Team (1975) • Won Calder Memorial Trophy (1976) • NHL First All-Star Team (1978, 1979) • NHL Plus/Minus Leader (1979) • Won Art Ross Trophy (1979) • Won Hart Trophy (1979) • Won Conn Smythe Trophy (1980) • NHL Second All-Star Team (1982, 1984) • Won Bud Man of the Year Award (1988) • Won King Clancy Memorial Trophy (1989) • Played in NHL All-Star Game (1976, 1978, 1980, 1982, 1983, 1985, 1986, 1992)

Signed as a free agent by **Pittsburgh**, July 20, 1990. Signed as a free agent by **Pittsburgh**, June 22, 1993. • Played w/ RHI's Pittsburgh Phantoms 1993-94 (9-9-13-22-2).

			REGULAR SEASON																		PLAYOFFS							
Season	Club	League	GP	G	A	Pts	AG	AA	APts	PIM	PP	SH	GW	S	%	TGF	PGF	TGA	PGA	+/–	GP	G	A	Pts	PIM	PP	SH	GW

• TROTTIER, Guy

"The Mouse" RW – R. 5'8", 165 lbs. b: Hull, Que., 4/1/1941.

Season	Club	League	GP	G	A	Pts	AG	AA	APts	PIM	PP	SH	GW	S	%	TGF	PGF	TGA	PGA	+/–	GP	G	A	Pts	PIM	PP	SH	GW
1962-63	Ottawa Montagnards	OCHL	STATISTICS NOT AVAILABLE																									
1963-64	Knoxville Knights	EHL	15	12	11	23	....	....	....	27	....	....	....	....	....	....	....	....	....	....	....	....	....	....	....	....	....	....
	Philadelphia Ramblers	EHL	12	2	5	7	....	....	....	11	....	....	....	....	....	....	....	....	....	....	....	....	....	....	....	....	....	....
	Port Huron Flags	IHL	42	19	15	34	....	....	....	52	....	....	....	....	....	....	....	....	....	....	7	1	0	1	2	....	....	....
1964-65	Dayton Gems	IHL	68	46	42	88	....	....	....	56	....	....	....	....	....	....	....	....	....	....	....	....	....	....	....	....	....	....
1965-66	Dayton Gems	IHL	66	68	64	132	....	....	....	16	....	....	....	....	....	....	....	....	....	....	11	10	9	19	21	....	....	....
1966-67	Dayton Gems	IHL	68	*71	64	135	....	....	....	23	....	....	....	....	....	....	....	....	....	....	4	0	5	5	0	....	....	....
1967-68	Buffalo Bisons	AHL	41	16	19	35	....	....	....	6	....	....	....	....	....	....	....	....	....	....	4	2	4	6	2	....	....	....
1968-69	**New York Rangers**	**NHL**	**2**	**0**	**0**	**0**	**0**	**0**	**0**	**0**	**0**	**0**	**0**	**6**	**0.0**	**0**	**0**	**0**	**0**	**0**	....	....	....	....	....	....	....	....
	Buffalo Bisons	AHL	72	*45	37	82	....	....	....	21	....	....	....	....	....	....	....	....	....	....	6	4	3	7	0	....	....	....
1969-70	Buffalo Bisons	AHL	71	*55	33	88	....	....	....	8	....	....	....	....	....	....	....	....	....	....	9	6	2	8	9	....	....	....
1970-71	**Toronto Maple Leafs**	**NHL**	**61**	**19**	**5**	**24**	**19**	**4**	**23**	**21**	**7**	**0**	**3**	**106**	**17.9**	**36**	**15**	**33**	**0**	**–12**	**5**	**0**	**0**	**0**	**0**	**0**	**0**	**0**
1971-72	**Toronto Maple Leafs**	**NHL**	**52**	**9**	**12**	**21**	**9**	**10**	**19**	**16**	**2**	**0**	**1**	**81**	**11.1**	**27**	**10**	**29**	**0**	**–12**	**4**	**1**	**0**	**1**	**16**	**0**	**0**	**0**
1972-73	Ottawa Nationals	WHA	72	26	32	58	....	....	....	25	....	....	....	....	....	....	....	....	....	....	5	1	2	3	0	....	....	....
1973-74	Toronto Toros	WHA	71	27	35	62	....	....	....	58	....	....	....	....	....	....	....	....	....	....	12	5	5	10	4	....	....	....
1974-75	Toronto Toros	WHA	6	2	2	4	....	....	....	2	....	....	....	....	....	....	....	....	....	....	....	....	....	....	....	....	....	....
	Michigan Stags	WHA	17	5	4	9	....	....	....	2	....	....	....	....	....	....	....	....	....	....	....	....	....	....	....	....	....	....
	Dayton Gems	IHL	20	12	5	17	....	....	....	6	....	....	....	....	....	....	....	....	....	....	13	4	1	5	5	....	....	....
1975-76	Buffalo Norsemen	NAHL	56	36	22	58	....	....	....	59	....	....	....	....	....	....	....	....	....	....	1	0	0	0	20	....	....	....
	NHL Totals		**115**	**28**	**17**	**45**	**28**	**14**	**42**	**37**	**9**	**0**	**4**	**193**	**14.5**	**63**	**25**	**62**	**0**		**9**	**1**	**0**	**1**	**16**	**0**	**0**	**0**
	Other Major League Totals		166	60	73	133	....	....	....	87	....	....	....	....	....	....	....	....	....	....	17	6	7	13	4	....	....	....

IHL Second All-Star Team (1965, 1966) • IHL First All-Star Team (1967) • AHL First All-Star Team (1969, 1970)

Signed as a free agent by **Knoxville** (EHL), September, 1963. Traded to **Philadelphia** (EHL) by **Knoxville** (EHL) for Chuck Stuart, November 12, 1963. Traded to **Port Huron** (IHL) by **Philadelphia** (EHL) for cash, December 28, 1963. Traded to **Dayton** (IHL) by **Port Huron** for cash, September, 1964. Signed as a free agent by **Buffalo** (AHL), September, 1967. Traded to **NY Rangers** by **Buffalo** (AHL) for cash, December, 1968. Claimed by **Toronto** from **NY Rangers** in Intra-League Draft, June 9, 1970. Selected by **Dayton-Houston** (WHA) in 1972 WHA General Player Draft, February 12, 1972. WHA rights traded to **Ottawa** (WHA) by **Houston** (WHA) for cash, June, 1972. Transferred to **Toronto** (WHA) after **Ottawa** (WHA) franchise relocated, May, 1973. Traded to **Michigan** (WHA) by **Toronto** (WHA) for Toronto's 4th round choice (Rick Bourbonnais) in 1975 WHA Amateur Draft, November, 1974.

• TROTTIER, Rocky

RW – L. 5'11", 185 lbs. b: Climax, Sask., 4/11/1964. New Jersey's 1st, 8th overall, in 1982.

Season	Club	League	GP	G	A	Pts	AG	AA	APts	PIM	PP	SH	GW	S	%	TGF	PGF	TGA	PGA	+/–	GP	G	A	Pts	PIM	PP	SH	GW
1979-80	Swift Current Legionaires	SAHA	STATISTICS NOT AVAILABLE																									
1980-81	Saskatoon Blades	WHL	34	9	15	24	....	....	....	26	....	....	....	....	....	....	....	....	....	....	....	....	....	....	....	....	....	....
	Billings Bighorns	WHL	28	2	11	13	....	....	....	41	....	....	....	....	....	....	....	....	....	....	5	0	0	0	0	....	....	....
1981-82	Billings Bighorns	WHL	28	13	21	34	....	....	....	36	....	....	....	....	....	....	....	....	....	....	....	....	....	....	....	....	....	....
1982-83	Nanaimo Islanders	WHL	34	13	22	35	....	....	....	12	....	....	....	....	....	....	....	....	....	....	....	....	....	....	....	....	....	....
	Medicine Hat Tigers	WHL	20	5	9	14	....	....	....	11	....	....	....	....	....	....	....	....	....	....	5	0	2	2	2	....	....	....
	Wichita Wind	CHL	2	0	1	1	....	....	....	0	....	....	....	....	....	....	....	....	....	....	....	....	....	....	....	....	....	....
1983-84	Medicine Hat Tigers	WHL	65	34	50	84	....	....	....	41	....	....	....	....	....	....	....	....	....	....	14	5	10	15	13	....	....	....
	New Jersey Devils	**NHL**	**5**	**1**	**1**	**2**	**1**	**1**	**2**	**0**	**0**	**0**	**0**	**2**	**50.0**	**2**	**0**	**3**	**0**	**–1**	....	....	....	....	....	....	....	....
1984-85	**New Jersey Devils**	**NHL**	**33**	**5**	**3**	**8**	**4**	**2**	**6**	**2**	**0**	**0**	**0**	**30**	**16.7**	**12**	**0**	**15**	**0**	**–3**	....	....	....	....	....	....	....	....
	Maine Mariners	AHL	34	17	16	33	....	....	....	4	....	....	....	....	....	....	....	....	....	....	10	2	0	2	15	....	....	....
1985-86	Maine Mariners	AHL	66	12	19	31	....	....	....	42	....	....	....	....	....	....	....	....	....	....	....	....	....	....	....	....	....	....
1986-87	Maine Mariners	AHL	77	9	14	23	....	....	....	41	....	....	....	....	....	....	....	....	....	....	....	....	....	....	....	....	....	....
1987-88	Rogle BK Angelholm	Sweden-2	21	8	5	13	....	....	....	10	....	....	....	....	....	....	....	....	....	....	2	0	0	0	0	....	....	....
1988-89	EV Fussen	Germany-2	33	23	31	54	....	....	....	22	....	....	....	....	....	....	....	....	....	....	....	....	....	....	....	....	....	....
1989-90	Hershey Bears	AHL	49	15	13	28	....	....	....	18	....	....	....	....	....	....	....	....	....	....	....	....	....	....	....	....	....	....
	NHL Totals		**38**	**6**	**4**	**10**	**5**	**3**	**8**	**2**	**0**	**0**	**0**	**32**	**18.8**	**14**	**0**	**18**	**0**		....	....	....	....	....	....	....	....

Brother of Bryan

• TRUDEL, Jean-Guy

Jean-Guy Andre LW – L. 6', 194 lbs. b: Sudbury, Ont., 10/10/1975.

Season	Club	League	GP	G	A	Pts	AG	AA	APts	PIM	PP	SH	GW	S	%	TGF	PGF	TGA	PGA	+/–	GP	G	A	Pts	PIM	PP	SH	GW
1991-92	Beauport Harfangs	QMJHL	35	5	7	12	....	....	....	20	....	....	....	....	....	....	....	....	....	....	....	....	....	....	....	....	....	....
1992-93	Beauport Harfangs	QMJHL	56	1	4	5	....	....	....	20	....	....	....	....	....	....	....	....	....	....	....	....	....	....	....	....	....	....
	Verdun College-Francais	QMJHL	10	1	0	1	....	....	....	0	....	....	....	....	....	....	....	....	....	....	2	0	0	0	5	....	....	....
1993-94			DID NOT PLAY																									
1994-95	Hull Olympiques	QMJHL	54	29	42	71	....	....	....	76	....	....	....	....	....	....	....	....	....	....	19	4	13	17	25	....	....	....
1995-96	Hull Olympiques	QMJHL	70	50	71	121	....	....	....	96	....	....	....	....	....	....	....	....	....	....	17	11	18	29	8	....	....	....
1996-97	Quad City Mallards	ColHL	5	8	7	15	....	....	....	4	....	....	....	....	....	....	....	....	....	....	....	....	....	....	....	....	....	....
	Chicago Wolves	IHL	6	1	2	3	....	....	....	2	....	....	....	....	....	....	....	....	....	....	....	....	....	....	....	....	....	....
	San Antonio Dragons	IHL	12	1	5	6	....	....	....	4	....	....	....	....	....	....	....	....	....	....	....	....	....	....	....	....	....	....
	Peoria Rivermen	ECHL	37	25	29	54	....	....	....	47	....	....	....	....	....	....	....	....	....	....	9	9	10	19	22	....	....	....
1997-98	Peoria Rivermen	ECHL	62	39	74	113	....	....	....	147	....	....	....	....	....	....	....	....	....	....	3	0	0	0	2	....	....	....
1998-99	Kansas City Blades	IHL	76	24	25	49	....	....	....	66	....	....	....	....	....	....	....	....	....	....	3	1	0	1	0	....	....	....
99-2000	**Phoenix Coyotes**	**NHL**	**1**	**0**	**0**	**0**	**0**	**0**	**0**	**0**	**0**	**0**	**0**	**0**	**0.0**	**0**	**0**	**1**	**0**	**–1**	....	....	....	....	....	....	....	....
	Springfield Falcons	AHL	72	34	39	73	....	....	....	80	....	....	....	....	....	....	....	....	....	....	3	0	1	1	4	....	....	....
	NHL Totals		**1**	**0**	**0**	**0**	**0**	**0**	**0**	**0**	**0**	**0**	**0**	**0**	**0.0**	**0**	**0**	**1**	**0**		....	....	....	....	....	....	....	....

• AHL Second All-Star Team (2000)

• Sat out entire 1993-94 season to regain eligibility for U.S. College scholarship. Signed as a free agent by **Phoenix**, July 17, 1999.

• TSULYGIN, Nikolai

D – R. 6'3", 210 lbs. b: Ufa, USSR, 5/29/1975. Anaheim's 2nd, 30th overall, in 1993.

Season	Club	League	GP	G	A	Pts	AG	AA	APts	PIM	PP	SH	GW	S	%	TGF	PGF	TGA	PGA	+/–	GP	G	A	Pts	PIM	PP	SH	GW
1992-93	Ufa Salavat	CIS	42	5	4	9	....	....	....	21	....	....	....	....	....	....	....	....	....	....	2	0	0	0	0	....	....	....
	Russia	WJC-A	5	0	0	0	....	....	....	2	....	....	....	....	....	....	....	....	....	....	....	....	....	....	....	....	....	....
	Russia	EJC-A	6	1	1	2	....	....	....	6	....	....	....	....	....	....	....	....	....	....	....	....	....	....	....	....	....	....
1993-94	Ufa Salavat	CIS	43	0	14	14	....	....	....	24	....	....	....	....	....	....	....	....	....	....	5	0	1	1	0	....	....	....
	Russia	WJC-A	7	1	2	3	....	....	....	12	....	....	....	....	....	....	....	....	....	....	....	....	....	....	....	....	....	....
1994-95	CSKA Moscow	CIS	16	0	0	0	....	....	....	12	....	....	....	....	....	....	....	....	....	....	....	....	....	....	....	....	....	....
	Ufa Salavat	CIS	13	2	2	4	....	....	....	10	....	....	....	....	....	....	....	....	....	....	7	0	0	0	4	....	....	....
1995-96	Baltimore Bandits	AHL	78	3	18	21	....	....	....	109	....	....	....	....	....	....	....	....	....	....	12	0	5	5	18	....	....	....
1996-97	**Mighty Ducks of Anaheim**	**NHL**	**22**	**0**	**1**	**1**	**0**	**1**	**1**	**8**	**0**	**0**	**0**	**10**	**0.0**	**5**	**0**	**10**	**0**	**–5**	....	....	....	....	....	....	....	....
	Fort Wayne Komets	IHL	5	2	1	3	....	....	....	8	....	....	....	....	....	....	....	....	....	....	....	....	....	....	....	....	....	....
	Baltimore Bandits	AHL	17	4	13	17	....	....	....	8	....	....	....	....	....	....	....	....	....	....	3	0	0	0	0	....	....	....
1997-98	Cincinnati Mighty Ducks	AHL	77	5	31	36	....	....	....	63	....	....	....	....	....	....	....	....	....	....	....	....	....	....	....	....	....	....
1998-99	Ufa Salavat	Russia	27	4	9	13	....	....	....	40	....	....	....	....	....	....	....	....	....	....	....	....	....	....	....	....	....	....
	Fort Wayne Komets	IHL	17	1	4	5	....	....	....	8	....	....	....	....	....	....	....	....	....	....	....	....	....	....	....	....	....	....
99-2000	Ak Bars Kazan	Russia	19	1	5	6	....	....	....	18	....	....	....	....	....	....	....	....	....	....	12	2	0	2	8	....	....	....
	NHL Totals		**22**	**0**	**1**	**1**	**0**	**1**	**1**	**8**	**0**	**0**	**0**	**10**	**0.0**	**5**	**0**	**10**	**0**		....	....	....	....	....	....	....	....

• TSYGUROV, Denis

D – L. 6'3", 198 lbs. b: Chelyabinsk, USSR, 2/26/1971. Buffalo's 1st, 38th overall, in 1993.

Season	Club	League	GP	G	A	Pts	AG	AA	APts	PIM	PP	SH	GW	S	%	TGF	PGF	TGA	PGA	+/–	GP	G	A	Pts	PIM	PP	SH	GW
1988-89	Traktor Chelyabinsk	USSR	8	0	0	0	....	....	....	2	....	....	....	....	....	....	....	....	....	....	....	....	....	....	....	....	....	....
1989-90	Traktor Chelyabinsk	USSR	27	0	1	1	....	....	....	18	....	....	....	....	....	....	....	....	....	....	....	....	....	....	....	....	....	....
1990-91	Traktor Chelyabinsk	USSR	26	0	1	1	....	....	....	16	....	....	....	....	....	....	....	....	....	....	....	....	....	....	....	....	....	....
1991-92	Lada Togliatti	CIS	29	3	2	5	....	....	....	6	....	....	....	....	....	....	....	....	....	....	....	....	....	....	....	....	....	....
1992-93	Lada Togliatti	CIS	37	7	13	20	....	....	....	29	....	....	....	....	....	....	....	....	....	....	10	1	1	2	6	....	....	....
1993-94	**Buffalo Sabres**	**NHL**	**8**	**0**	**0**	**0**	**0**	**0**	**0**	**8**	**0**	**0**	**0**	**3**	**0.0**	**4**	**0**	**5**	**0**	**–1**	....	....	....	....	....	....	....	....
	Rochester Americans	AHL	24	1	10	11	....	....	....	10	....	....	....	....	....	....	....	....	....	....	1	0	1	1	0	....	....	....
1994-95	Lada Togliatti	CIS	10	3	7	10	....	....	....	6	....	....	....	....	....	....	....	....	....	....	....	....	....	....	....	....	....	....
	Buffalo Sabres	**NHL**	**4**	**0**	**0**	**0**	**0**	**0**	**0**	**4**	**0**	**0**	**0**	**4**	**0.0**	**1**	**0**	**2**	**0**	**–1**	....	....	....	....	....	....	....	....
	Los Angeles Kings	**NHL**	**21**	**0**	**0**	**0**	**0**	**0**	**0**	**11**	**0**	**0**	**0**	**16**	**0.0**	**8**	**0**	**13**	**3**	**–2**	....	....	....	....	....	....	....	....

Season	Club	League	REGULAR SEASON																		PLAYOFFS							
			GP	G	A	Pts	AG	AA	APts	PIM	PP	SH	GW	S	%	TGF	PGF	TGA	PGA	+/–	GP	G	A	Pts	PIM	PP	SH	GW
1995-96	Los Angeles Kings	NHL	18	1	5	6	1	4	5	22	1	0	0	21	4.8	22	5	20	3	0	....	....	....	....	....	....	....	....
	Phoenix Roadrunners	IHL	17	1	3	4	....	....	....	10	....	....	....	....	....	....	....	....	....	....	....	....	....	....	....	....	....	....
	Lada Togliatti	CIS	3	0	0	0	....	....	....	4	....	....	....	....	....	....	....	....	....	....	....	....	....	....	....	....	....	....
1996-97	Lada Togliatti	Russia	8	2	1	3	....	....	....	0	....	....	....	....	....	....	....	....	....	....	....	....	....	....	....	....	....	....
	HC Slezan Opava	Czech-Rep	17	1	4	5	....	....	....	50	....	....	....	....	....	....	....	....	....	....	....	....	....	....	....	....	....	....
1997-98	Long Beach Ice Dogs	IHL	15	1	4	5	....	....	....	8	....	....	....	....	....	....	....	....	....	....	....	....	....	....	....	....	....	....
	Karpat Oulu	Finland-2	15	2	7	9	....	....	....	106	....	....	....	....	....	....	....	....	....	....	7	0	4	4	6	....	....	....
1998-99	Lada Togliatti	Russia	20	0	2	2	....	....	....	22	....	....	....	....	....	....	....	....	....	....	7	3	0	3	6	....	....	....
99-2000	CSK VVS Samara	Russia	2	1	0	1	....	....	....	4	....	....	....	....	....	....	....	....	....	....	....	....	....	....	....	....	....	....
	Lada Togliatti	Russia	13	3	4	7	....	....	....	24	....	....	....	....	....	....	....	....	....	....	....	....	....	....	....	....	....	....
	Neftekhimik Nizhnekamsk	Russia	17	0	2	2	....	....	....	10	....	....	....	....	....	....	....	....	....	....	....	....	....	....	....	....	....	....
	NHL Totals		51	1	5	6	1	4	5	45	1	0	0	44	2.3	35	5	40	6		....	....	....	....	....	....	....	....

Traded to **LA Kings** by **Buffalo** with Philippe Boucher and Grant Fuhr for Alexei Zhitnik, Robb Stauber, Charlie Huddy and LA Kings' 5th round choice (Marian Menhart) in 1995 Entry Draft, February 14, 1995.

• TSYPLAKOV, Vladimir

LW – L. 6'1", 210 lbs. b: Inta, USSR, 4/18/1969. Los Angeles' 4th, 59th overall, in 1995.

Season	Club	League	GP	G	A	Pts	AG	AA	APts	PIM	PP	SH	GW	S	%	TGF	PGF	TGA	PGA	+/–	GP	G	A	Pts	PIM	PP	SH	GW
1988-89	Dynamo Minsk	USSR	19	6	1	7	....	....	....	4	....	....	....	....	....	....	....	....	....	....	....	....	....	....	....	....	....	....
	Soviet Union	WJC-A	7	1	0	1	....	....	....	8	....	....	....	....	....	....	....	....	....	....	....	....	....	....	....	....	....	....
1989-90	Dynamo Minsk	USSR	47	11	6	17	....	....	....	20	....	....	....	....	....	....	....	....	....	....	....	....	....	....	....	....	....	....
1990-91	Dynamo Minsk	USSR	28	6	5	11	....	....	....	14	....	....	....	....	....	....	....	....	....	....	....	....	....	....	....	....	....	....
1991-92	Dynamo Minsk	CIS	29	10	9	19	....	....	....	16	....	....	....	....	....	....	....	....	....	....	....	....	....	....	....	....	....	....
1992-93	Detroit Falcons	ColHL	44	33	43	76	....	....	....	20	....	....	....	....	....	....	....	....	....	....	6	5	4	9	6	....	....	....
	Indianapolis Ice	IHL	11	6	7	13	....	....	....	4	....	....	....	....	....	....	....	....	....	....	5	1	1	2	2	....	....	....
1993-94	Fort Wayne Komets	IHL	63	31	32	63	....	....	....	51	....	....	....	....	....	....	....	....	....	....	14	6	8	14	16	....	....	....
1994-95	Fort Wayne Komets	IHL	79	38	40	78	....	....	....	39	....	....	....	....	....	....	....	....	....	....	4	2	4	6	2	....	....	....
1995-96	Los Angeles Kings	NHL	23	5	5	10	5	4	9	4	0	0	0	40	12.5	16	4	11	0	1	....	....	....	....	....	....	....	....
	Las Vegas Thunder	IHL	9	5	6	11	....	....	....	4	....	....	....	....	....	....	....	....	....	....	....	....	....	....	....	....	....	....
1996-97	Los Angeles Kings	NHL	67	16	23	39	17	20	37	12	1	0	2	118	13.6	57	11	38	0	8	....	....	....	....	....	....	....	....
1997-98	Los Angeles Kings	NHL	73	18	34	52	21	33	54	18	2	0	1	113	15.9	75	14	50	4	15	4	0	1	1	8	0	0	0
	Belarus	Olympics	5	1	1	2	....	....	....	2	....	....	....	....	....	....	....	....	....	....	....	....	....	....	....	....	....	....
1998-99	Los Angeles Kings	NHL	69	11	12	23	13	12	25	32	0	2	2	111	9.9	43	7	55	12	–7	....	....	....	....	....	....	....	....
	Belarus	WC-A	6	2	2	4	....	....	....	2	....	....	....	....	....	....	....	....	....	....	....	....	....	....	....	....	....	....
99-2000	Los Angeles Kings	NHL	29	6	7	13	7	6	13	4	1	0	1	30	20.0	18	1	11	0	6	....	....	....	....	....	....	....	....
	Buffalo Sabres	NHL	34	6	13	19	7	12	19	10	0	0	1	46	13.0	25	2	6	0	17	5	0	1	1	4	0	0	0
	Belarus	WC-A	5	3	2	5	....	....	....	4	....	....	....	....	....	....	....	....	....	....	....	....	....	....	....	....	....	....
	NHL Totals		295	62	94	156	70	87	157	80	4	2	7	458	13.5	234	39	171	16		9	0	2	2	12	0	0	0

ColHL First All-Star Team (1993)

Traded to **Buffalo** by **LA Kings** for Buffalo's 8th round choice (Dan Welch) in 2000 Entry Draft and future considerations, January 24, 2000.

• TUCKER, Darcy

C – L. 5'10", 179 lbs. b: Endiang, Alta., 3/15/1975. Montreal's 8th, 151st overall, in 1993.

Season	Club	League	GP	G	A	Pts	AG	AA	APts	PIM	PP	SH	GW	S	%	TGF	PGF	TGA	PGA	+/–	GP	G	A	Pts	PIM	PP	SH	GW
1990-91	Red Deer Chiefs	AAHA	47	70	90	160	....	....	....	48	....	....	....	....	....	....	....	....	....	....	....	....	....	....	....	....	....	....
1991-92	Kamloops Blazers	WHL	26	3	10	13	....	....	....	32	....	....	....	....	....	....	....	....	....	....	9	0	1	1	16	....	....	....
	Kamloops Blazers	Mem-Cup	3	0	0	0	....	....	....	0	....	....	....	....	....	....	....	....	....	....	....	....	....	....	....	....	....	....
1992-93	Kamloops Blazers	WHL	67	31	58	89	....	....	....	155	....	....	....	....	....	....	....	....	....	....	13	7	6	13	34	....	....	....
1993-94	Kamloops Blazers	WHL	66	52	88	140	....	....	....	143	....	....	....	....	....	....	....	....	....	....	19	9	*18	*27	43	....	....	....
	Kamloops Blazers	Mem-Cup	4	*6	3	*9	....	....	....	6	....	....	....	....	....	....	....	....	....	....	....	....	....	....	....	....	....	....
1994-95	Kamloops Blazers	WHL	64	64	73	137	....	....	....	94	....	....	....	....	....	....	....	....	....	....	21	*16	15	*31	19	....	....	....
	Canada	WJC-A	7	0	4	4	....	....	....	0	....	....	....	....	....	....	....	....	....	....	....	....	....	....	....	....	....	....
	Kamloops Blazers	Mem-Cup	4	2	4	6	....	....	....	4	....	....	....	....	....	....	....	....	....	....	....	....	....	....	....	....	....	....
1995-96	Montreal Canadiens	NHL	3	0	0	0	0	0	0	0	0	0	0	1	0.0	0	0	1	0	–1	....	....	....	....	....	....	....	....
	Fredericton Canadiens	AHL	74	29	64	93	....	....	....	174	....	....	....	....	....	....	....	....	....	....	7	7	3	10	14	....	....	....
1996-97	Montreal Canadiens	NHL	73	7	13	20	7	12	19	110	1	0	3	62	11.3	31	4	32	0	–5	4	0	0	0	0	0	0	0
1997-98	Montreal Canadiens	NHL	39	1	5	6	1	5	6	57	0	0	0	19	5.3	9	1	21	7	–6	....	....	....	....	....	....	....	....
	Tampa Bay Lightning	NHL	35	6	8	14	7	8	15	89	1	1	0	44	13.6	21	1	33	5	–8	....	....	....	....	....	....	....	....
1998-99	Tampa Bay Lightning	NHL	82	21	22	43	25	21	46	176	8	2	3	178	11.8	61	23	113	41	–34	....	....	....	....	....	....	....	....
99-2000	Tampa Bay Lightning	NHL	50	14	20	34	16	19	35	108	1	0	2	98	14.3	47	8	61	7	–15	....	....	....	....	....	....	....	....
	Toronto Maple Leafs	NHL	27	7	10	17	8	9	17	55	0	2	3	40	17.5	23	5	21	6	3	12	4	2	6	15	1	0	2
	NHL Totals		309	56	78	134	64	74	138	595	11	5	11	442	12.7	192	42	282	66		16	4	2	6	15	1	0	2

WHL West First All-Star Team (1994, 1995) • Canadian Major Junior First All-Star Team (1994) • Memorial Cup All-Star Team (1994, 1995) • Won Stafford Smythe Memorial Trophy (Memorial Cup Tournament MVP) (1994) • Won Dudley "Red" Garrett Memorial Trophy (Top Rookie — AHL) (1996)

Traded to **Tampa Bay** by **Montreal** with Stephane Richer and David Wilkie for Patrick Poulin, Mick Vukota and Igor Ulanov, January 15, 1998. Traded to **Toronto** by **Tampa Bay** with Tampa Bay's 4th round choice (Miguel Delisle) in 2000 Entry Draft and future considerations for Mike Johnson, Marek Posmyk, Toronto's 5th (Pavel Sedov) and 6th (Aaron Gionet) round choices in 2000 Entry Draft and future considerations, February 9, 2000.

• TUCKER, John

John G. C – R. 6', 200 lbs. b: Windsor, Ont., 9/29/1964. Buffalo's 4th, 31st overall, in 1983.

Season	Club	League	GP	G	A	Pts	AG	AA	APts	PIM	PP	SH	GW	S	%	TGF	PGF	TGA	PGA	+/–	GP	G	A	Pts	PIM	PP	SH	GW
1980-81	Windsor Legionaires	OMHA	58	107	94	201	....	....	....	....	....	....	....	....	....	....	....	....	....	....	....	....	....	....	....	....	....	....
1981-82	Kitchener Rangers	OHL	67	16	32	48	....	....	....	32	....	....	....	....	....	....	....	....	....	....	15	2	3	5	2	....	....	....
	Kitchener Rangers	Mem-Cup	5	0	0	0	....	....	....	6	....	....	....	....	....	....	....	....	....	....	....	....	....	....	....	....	....	....
1982-83	Kitchener Rangers	OHL	70	60	80	140	....	....	....	33	....	....	....	....	....	....	....	....	....	....	11	5	9	14	10	....	....	....
1983-84	Kitchener Rangers	OHL	39	40	60	100	....	....	....	25	....	....	....	....	....	....	....	....	....	....	12	12	18	30	8	....	....	....
	Buffalo Sabres	NHL	21	12	4	16	10	3	13	4	5	0	2	40	30.0	22	8	12	0	2	3	1	0	1	0	0	0	0
	Kitchener Rangers	Mem-Cup	4	2	4	6	....	....	....	0	....	....	....	....	....	....	....	....	....	....	....	....	....	....	....	....	....	....
1984-85	Buffalo Sabres	NHL	64	22	27	49	18	18	36	21	11	0	3	112	19.6	76	39	31	0	6	5	1	5	6	0	0	0	0
1985-86	Buffalo Sabres	NHL	75	31	34	65	25	23	48	39	8	0	3	146	21.2	92	37	56	1	0	....	....	....	....	....	....	....	....
1986-87	Buffalo Sabres	NHL	54	17	34	51	15	25	40	21	4	0	0	104	16.3	67	21	51	2	–3	....	....	....	....	....	....	....	....
1987-88	Buffalo Sabres	NHL	45	19	19	38	16	14	30	20	6	0	0	93	20.4	59	23	32	0	4	6	7	3	10	18	4	0	2
1988-89	Buffalo Sabres	NHL	60	13	31	44	11	22	33	31	3	0	1	94	13.8	65	22	50	2	–5	3	0	3	3	0	0	0	0
1989-90	Buffalo Sabres	NHL	8	1	2	3	1	1	2	2	1	0	0	8	12.5	4	1	7	1	–3	....	....	....	....	....	....	....	....
	Washington Capitals	NHL	38	9	19	28	8	14	22	10	1	0	1	61	14.8	51	17	23	0	11	12	1	7	8	4	0	0	0
1990-91	Buffalo Sabres	NHL	18	1	3	4	1	2	3	4	0	0	0	16	6.3	8	3	5	0	0	....	....	....	....	....	....	....	....
	New York Islanders	NHL	20	3	4	7	3	3	6	4	1	0	0	19	15.8	11	1	11	0	–1	....	....	....	....	....	....	....	....
1991-92	HC Asiago	Alpenliga	18	17	34	51	....	....	....	4	....	....	....	....	....	....	....	....	....	....	....	....	....	....	....	....	....	....
	HC Asiago	Italy	18	16	21	37	....	....	....	6	....	....	....	....	....	....	....	....	....	....	11	7	13	20	15	....	....	....
1992-93	Tampa Bay Lightning	NHL	78	17	39	56	14	27	41	69	5	1	1	179	9.5	94	35	94	23	–12	....	....	....	....	....	....	....	....
1993-94	Tampa Bay Lightning	NHL	66	17	23	40	16	18	34	28	2	0	6	126	13.5	59	9	58	17	9	....	....	....	....	....	....	....	....
1994-95	Tampa Bay Lightning	NHL	46	12	13	25	21	19	40	14	2	0	1	81	14.8	38	11	52	15	–10	....	....	....	....	....	....	....	....
1995-96	Tampa Bay Lightning	NHL	63	3	7	10	3	6	9	18	0	1	0	53	5.7	22	1	59	30	–8	2	0	0	0	2	0	0	0
1996-97	HC Milano Devils	Alpenliga	30	12	29	41	....	....	....	88	....	....	....	....	....	....	....	....	....	....	....	....	....	....	....	....	....	....
	HC Milano Devils	EuroHL	4	0	1	1	....	....	....	6	....	....	....	....	....	....	....	....	....	....	....	....	....	....	....	....	....	....
	HC Fassa	Italy	20	11	16	27	....	....	....	....	....	....	....	....	....	....	....	....	....	....	....	....	....	....	....	....	....	....
1997-98	EC Kapfenberg	Alpenliga	17	4	8	12	....	....	....	....	....	....	....	....	....	....	....	....	....	....	....	....	....	....	....	....	....	....
	Kokudo Toyko	Japan	39	27	47	74	....	....	....	53	....	....	....	....	....	....	....	....	....	....	....	....	....	....	....	....	....	....
1998-99	Kokudo Toyko	Japan	23	21	20	41	....	....	....	30	....	....	....	....	....	....	....	....	....	....	....	....	....	....	....	....	....	....
99-2000	Kokudo Toyko	Japan	24	14	22	36	....	....	....	....	....	....	....	....	....	....	....	....	....	....	4	6	3	9	12	....	....	....
	NHL Totals		656	177	259	436	162	195	357	285	49	2	18	1132	15.6	668	228	541	91		31	10	18	28	24	4	0	2

OHL First All-Star Team (1984)

Traded to **Washington** by **Buffalo** for future considerations, January 5, 1990. Traded to **Buffalo** by **Washington** for cash, July 3, 1990. Traded to **NY Islanders** by **Buffalo** for future considerations, January 21, 1991. Signed as a free agent by **Tampa Bay**, August 5, 1992.

• TUDOR, Rob

Robert Alan RW/C – R. 5'11", 188 lbs. b: Cupar, Sask., 6/30/1956. Vancouver's 5th, 98th overall, in 1976.

			REGULAR SEASON																		PLAYOFFS							
Season	Club	League	GP	G	A	Pts	AG	AA	APts	PIM	PP	SH	GW	S	%	TGF	PGF	TGA	PGA	+/–	GP	G	A	Pts	PIM	PP	SH	GW
1971-72	Dysart Blues	SIHA	STATISTICS NOT AVAILABLE																									
1972-73	Regina Pat Blues	SJHL	STATISTICS NOT AVAILABLE																									
	Regina Pats	WHL	5	0	1	1				0																		
1973-74	Regina Pats	WHL	68	17	17	34				60											16	4	2	6	17			
	Regina Pats	Mem-Cup	3	1	0	1				2																		
1974-75	Regina Pats	WHL	68	48	48	96				125											11	5	6	11	20			
1975-76	Regina Pats	WHL	72	46	60	106				228											6	6	3	9	15			
1976-77	Fort Wayne Komets	IHL	78	34	60	94				108											9	11	8	19	26			
1977-78	Tulsa Oilers	CHL	65	23	33	56				58											7	1	2	3	37			
1978-79	**Vancouver Canucks**	**NHL**	**24**	**4**	**4**	**8**	**3**	**3**	**6**	**19**	**0**	**0**	**0**	**51**	**7.8**	**12**	**1**	**12**	**1**	**0**	**2**	**0**	**0**	**0**	**0**	**0**	**0**	**0**
	Dallas Black Hawks	CHL	51	27	37	64				80																		
1979-80	**Vancouver Canucks**	**NHL**	**2**	**0**	**0**	**0**	**0**	**0**	**0**	**0**	**0**	**0**	**0**	**0**	**0.0**	**0**	**0**	**0**	**0**	**0**	**1**	**0**	**0**	**0**	**0**	**0**	**0**	**0**
	Dallas Black Hawks	CHL	74	39	41	80				177																		
1980-81	Dallas Black Hawks	CHL	79	31	32	63				155											6	0	1	1	25			
1981-82	Dallas Black Hawks	CHL	80	32	47	79				132											15	7	13	20	56			
1982-83	**St. Louis Blues**	**NHL**	**2**	**0**	**0**	**0**	**0**	**0**	**0**	**0**	**0**	**0**	**0**	**0**	**0.0**	**0**	**0**	**0**	**0**	**0**								
	Salt Lake Golden Eagles	CHL	76	37	30	67				168											6	1	4	5	2			
1983-84	Salt Lake Golden Eagles	CHL	32	10	12	22				35											5	1	2	3	21			
	Kolner EC	Germany	28	9	8	17				82																		
1984-85	Nova Scotia Voyageurs	AHL	22	6	6	12				40																		
	New Haven Nighthawks	AHL	52	9	11	20				45																		
1985-86	Dysart Blues	SAHA-I	STATISTICS NOT AVAILABLE																									
	Fort Wayne Komets	IHL	13	6	8	14				7											15	4	2	6	35			
	NHL Totals		**28**	**4**	**4**	**8**	**3**	**3**	**6**	**19**	**0**	**0**	**0**	**51**	**7.8**	**12**	**1**	**12**	**1**		**3**	**0**	**0**	**0**	**0**	**0**	**0**	**0**

CHL Second All-Star Team (1980)

Signed as a free agent by **St. Louis**, July 22, 1982.

• TUER, Allan

Allan T. D – L. 6', 190 lbs. b: North Battleford, Sask., 7/19/1963. Los Angeles' 8th, 186th overall, in 1981.

			REGULAR SEASON																		PLAYOFFS							
Season	Club	League	GP	G	A	Pts	AG	AA	APts	PIM	PP	SH	GW	S	%	TGF	PGF	TGA	PGA	+/–	GP	G	A	Pts	PIM	PP	SH	GW
1980-81	Regina Pat Blues	SJHL	STATISTICS NOT AVAILABLE																									
	Regina Pats	WHL	31	0	7	7				58											8	0	1	1	37			
1981-82	Regina Pats	WHL	63	2	18	20				*486											13	0	3	3	117			
1982-83	Regina Pats	WHL	71	3	27	30				229											5	0	0	0	37			
1983-84	New Haven Nighthawks	AHL	78	0	20	20				195																		
1984-85	New Haven Nighthawks	AHL	56	0	7	7				241																		
1985-86	**Los Angeles Kings**	**NHL**	**45**	**0**	**1**	**1**	**0**	**1**	**1**	**150**	**0**	**0**	**0**	**14**	**0.0**	**5**	**1**	**23**	**3**	**–16**								
	New Haven Nighthawks	AHL	8	1	0	1				53																		
1986-87	Nova Scotia Oilers	AHL	69	1	14	15				273											5	0	1	1	48			
1987-88	**Minnesota North Stars**	**NHL**	**6**	**1**	**0**	**1**	**1**	**0**	**1**	**29**	**0**	**0**	**0**	**1**	**100.0**	**1**	**0**	**5**	**1**	**–3**								
	Kalamazoo Wings	IHL	68	2	15	17				303											7	0	0	0	34			
1988-89	**Hartford Whalers**	**NHL**	**4**	**0**	**0**	**0**	**0**	**0**	**0**	**23**	**0**	**0**	**0**	**0**	**0.0**	**0**	**0**	**2**	**0**	**–2**								
	Binghamton Whalers	AHL	43	1	7	8				234																		
1989-90	**Hartford Whalers**	**NHL**	**2**	**0**	**0**	**0**	**0**	**0**	**0**	**6**	**0**	**0**	**0**	**0**	**0.0**	**1**	**0**	**2**	**0**	**–1**								
	Binghamton Whalers	AHL	58	3	7	10				56																		
1990-91	San Diego Gulls	IHL	60	0	5	5				305																		
1991-92	New Haven Nighthawks	AHL	68	2	10	12				199											4	0	1	1	12			
1992-93	Cincinnati Cyclones	IHL	52	1	9	10				248																		
	Cleveland Lumberjacks	IHL	13	1	4	5				29											2	0	0	0	4			
	NHL Totals		**57**	**1**	**1**	**2**	**1**	**1**	**2**	**208**	**0**	**0**	**0**	**15**	**6.7**	**7**	**1**	**32**	**4**									

Signed as a free agent by **Edmonton**, August 18, 1986. Claimed by **Minnesota** from **Edmonton** in Waiver Draft, October 5, 1987. Signed as a free agent by **Hartford**, July 12, 1988.

• TUOMAINEN, Marko

Marko J. RW – R. 6'3", 218 lbs. b: Kuopio, Finland, 4/25/1972. Edmonton's 10th, 205th overall, in 1992.

			REGULAR SEASON																		PLAYOFFS							
Season	Club	League	GP	G	A	Pts	AG	AA	APts	PIM	PP	SH	GW	S	%	TGF	PGF	TGA	PGA	+/–	GP	G	A	Pts	PIM	PP	SH	GW
1988-89	KalPa Kuopio	Finland-Jr.	7	6	6	12				4																		
1989-90	KalPa Kuopio	Finland-Jr.	36	13	24	37				30																		
	KalPa Kuopio	Finland	5	0	0	0				0																		
1990-91	KalPa Kuopio	Finland-Jr.	35	36	17	53				61																		
	KalPa Kuopio	Finland	30	2	1	3				2											8	0	0	0	6			
1991-92	Clarkson University	ECAC	28	11	12	23				32																		
	Finland	WJC-A	7	1	4	5				14																		
1992-93	Clarkson University	ECAC	35	25	30	55				26																		
1993-94	Clarkson University	ECAC	34	23	29	52				60																		
1994-95	Clarkson University	ECAC	37	23	38	61				34																		
	Edmonton Oilers	**NHL**	**4**	**0**	**0**	**0**	**0**	**0**	**0**	**0**	**0**	**0**	**0**	**5**	**0.0**	**2**	**0**	**2**	**0**	**0**								
1995-96	Cape Breton Oilers	AHL	58	25	35	60				71																		
1996-97	Hamilton Bulldogs	AHL	79	31	21	52				130											22	7	5	12	4			
1997-98	HIFK Helsinki	Finland	46	13	9	22				20											9	0	3	3	0			
	Finland	WC-A	8	0	1	1				8																		
1998-99	HIFK Helsinki	Finland	48	11	17	28				*173											11	1	3	4	12			
	HIFK Helsinki	EuroHL	6	0	1	1				8											4	3	0	3	4			
	Finland	WC-A	12	4	2	6				28																		
99-2000	**Los Angeles Kings**	**NHL**	**63**	**9**	**8**	**17**	**10**	**7**	**17**	**80**	**2**	**1**	**1**	**74**	**12.2**	**25**	**3**	**37**	**3**	**–12**	**1**	**0**	**0**	**0**	**0**	**0**	**0**	**0**
	Finland	WC-A	9	2	3	5				6																		
	NHL Totals		**67**	**9**	**8**	**17**	**10**	**7**	**17**	**80**	**2**	**1**	**1**	**79**	**11.4**	**27**	**3**	**39**	**3**		**1**	**0**	**0**	**0**	**0**	**0**	**0**	**0**

ECAC First All-Star Team (1993, 1995) • NCAA East Second All-American Team (1995)

Signed as a free agent by **Los Angeles**, June 20, 1999.

• TURCOTTE, Alfie

C – L. 5'11", 185 lbs. b: Gary, IN, 6/5/1965. Montreal's 1st, 17th overall, in 1983.

			REGULAR SEASON																		PLAYOFFS							
Season	Club	League	GP	G	A	Pts	AG	AA	APts	PIM	PP	SH	GW	S	%	TGF	PGF	TGA	PGA	+/–	GP	G	A	Pts	PIM	PP	SH	GW
1981-82	Detroit Compuware	MNHL	93	131	152	283				40																		
1982-83	Nanaimo Islanders	WHL	36	23	27	50				22																		
	Portland Winter Hawks	WHL	39	26	51	77				26											14	14	18	32	9			
	Portland Winter Hawks	Mem-Cup	4	*5	3	8				6																		
1983-84	Portland Winter Hawks	WHL	32	22	41	63				39																		
	United States	WJC-A	7	2	9	11				2																		
	Montreal Canadiens	**NHL**	**30**	**7**	**7**	**14**	**6**	**5**	**11**	**10**	**5**	**0**	**0**	**33**	**21.2**	**18**	**8**	**19**	**0**	**–9**								
1984-85	**Montreal Canadiens**	**NHL**	**53**	**8**	**16**	**24**	**6**	**11**	**17**	**35**	**3**	**0**	**1**	**59**	**13.6**	**42**	**20**	**23**	**0**	**–1**	**5**	**0**	**0**	**0**	**0**	**0**	**0**	**0**
1985-86	**Montreal Canadiens**	**NHL**	**2**	**0**	**0**	**0**	**0**	**0**	**0**	**2**	**0**	**0**	**0**	**0**	**0.0**	**0**	**0**	**0**	**0**	**0**								
	Sherbrooke Canadiens	AHL	75	29	36	65				60																		
	United States	WEC-A	9	0	2	2				8																		
1986-87	Nova Scotia Oilers	AHL	70	27	41	68				37											5	2	4	6	2			
1987-88	**Winnipeg Jets**	**NHL**	**3**	**0**	**0**	**0**	**0**	**0**	**0**	**0**	**0**	**0**	**0**	**3**	**0.0**	**1**	**0**	**5**	**0**	**–4**								
	Baltimore Skipjacks	AHL	33	21	33	54				42																		
	Moncton Hawks	AHL	25	12	25	37				18																		
	Sherbrooke Canadiens	AHL	8	3	8	11				4																		
1988-89	**Winnipeg Jets**	**NHL**	**14**	**1**	**3**	**4**	**1**	**2**	**3**	**2**	**0**	**0**	**0**	**10**	**10.0**	**7**	**1**	**12**	**0**	**–6**								
	Moncton Hawks	AHL	54	27	39	66				74											10	3	9	12	17			
1989-90	**Washington Capitals**	**NHL**	**4**	**0**	**2**	**2**	**0**	**1**	**1**	**0**	**0**	**0**	**0**	**4**	**0.0**	**3**	**1**	**2**	**0**	**0**								
	Baltimore Skipjacks	AHL	65	26	40	66				42											12	7	9	16	14			
1990-91	**Washington Capitals**	**NHL**	**6**	**1**	**1**	**2**	**1**	**1**	**2**	**0**	**0**	**0**	**1**	**8**	**12.5**	**3**	**0**	**4**	**0**	**–1**								
	Baltimore Skipjacks	AHL	65	33	52	85				20											6	3	3	6	4			

Season	Club	League	REGULAR SEASON																		PLAYOFFS							
			GP	G	A	Pts	AG	AA	APts	PIM	PP	SH	GW	S	%	TGF	PGF	TGA	PGA	+/–	GP	G	A	Pts	PIM	PP	SH	GW
1991-92	VSV Villach	Austria	45	43	*61	*104	....	....	....	....	....	....	....	....	....	....	....	....	....	....	....	....	....	....	....	....	....	....
	HC Lugano	Switz.	2	1	3	4	....	....	....	....	....	....	....	....	....	....	....	....	....	....	....	....	....	....	....	....	....	....
1992-93	VSV Villach	Austria	56	26	*75	101	....	....	....	....	....	....	....	....	....	....	....	....	....	....	....	....	....	....	....	....	....	....
1993-94	VSV Villach	Austria	51	26	*63	*89	....	....	....	....	....	....	....	....	....	....	....	....	....	....	....	....	....	....	....	....	....	....
1994-95	Frankfurt Lions	Germany	33	7	40	47	....	....	....	30	....	....	....	....	....	....	....	....	....	....	11	7	5	12	12	....	....	....
1995-96	Orlando Solar Bears	IHL	73	22	47	69	....	....	....	44	....	....	....	....	....	....	....	....	....	....	23	3	10	13	8	....	....	....
1996-97	Schwenningen Wild Wings	Germany	1	0	0	0	....	....	....	0	....	....	....	....	....	....	....	....	....	....	....	....	....	....	....	....	....	....
	HC Geneve-Servette	Switz-2	5	1	1	2	....	....	....	4	....	....	....	....	....	....	....	....	....	....	....	....	....	....	....	....	....	....
	HC Lausanne	Switz-2	45	25	45	70	....	....	....	26	....	....	....	....	....	....	....	....	....	....	....	....	....	....	....	....	....	....
1997-98	Frankfurt Lions	Germany	26	2	6	8	....	....	....	12	....	....	....	....	....	....	....	....	....	....	7	0	0	0	0	....	....	....
	Indianapolis Ice	IHL	17	5	6	11	....	....	....	26	....	....	....	....	....	....	....	....	....	....	....	....	....	....	....	....	....	....
1998-99	Arkansas Glaciercats	WPHL	2	0	0	0	....	....	....	0	....	....	....	....	....	....	....	....	....	....	....	....	....	....	....	....	....	....
	NHL Totals		**112**	**17**	**29**	**46**	**14**	**20**	**34**	**49**	**8**	**0**	**2**	**117**	**14.5**	**74**	**30**	**65**	**0**		**5**	**0**	**0**	**0**	**0**	**0**	**0**	**0**

Won Stafford Smythe Memorial Trophy (Memorial Cup Tournament MVP) (1983) • AHL Second All-Star Team (1988)

Traded to **Edmonton** by **Montreal** for future considerations, June 25, 1986. Traded to **Montreal** by **Edmonton** for cash, May 14, 1987. Traded to **Winnipeg** by **Montreal** for future considerations, January 14, 1988. Signed as a free agent by **Boston**, June 27, 1989. Traded to **Washington** by **Boston** for Mike Millar, October 2, 1989.

• TURCOTTE, Darren

C – L. 6', 182 lbs. b: Boston, MA, 5/2/1968. NY Rangers' 6th, 114th overall, in 1986.

Season	Club	League	GP	G	A	Pts	AG	AA	APts	PIM	PP	SH	GW	S	%	TGF	PGF	TGA	PGA	+/–	GP	G	A	Pts	PIM	PP	SH	GW
1983-84	North Bay Athletics	NOHA	70	61	40	101	....	....	....	28	....	....	....	....	....	....	....	....	....	....	....	....	....	....	....	....	....	....
1984-85	North Bay Centennials	OHL	62	33	32	65	....	....	....	28	....	....	....	....	....	....	....	....	....	....	8	0	2	2	0	....	....	....
1985-86	North Bay Centennials	OHL	62	35	37	72	....	....	....	35	....	....	....	....	....	....	....	....	....	....	10	3	4	7	8	....	....	....
1986-87	North Bay Centennials	OHL	55	30	48	78	....	....	....	20	....	....	....	....	....	....	....	....	....	....	18	12	8	20	6	....	....	....
	United States	WJC-A	7	6	4	10	....	....	....	8	....	....	....	....	....	....	....	....	....	....	....	....	....	....	....	....	....	....
1987-88	North Bay Centennials	OHL	32	30	33	63	....	....	....	16	....	....	....	....	....	....	....	....	....	....	4	3	0	3	4	....	....	....
	United States	WJC-A	7	2	2	4	....	....	....	6	....	....	....	....	....	....	....	....	....	....	....	....	....	....	....	....	....	....
	Colorado Rangers	IHL	8	4	3	7	....	....	....	9	....	....	....	....	....	....	....	....	....	....	6	2	6	8	8	....	....	....
1988-89	**New York Rangers**	**NHL**	**20**	**7**	**3**	**10**	**6**	**2**	**8**	**4**	**2**	**0**	**2**	**49**	**14.3**	**15**	**5**	**10**	**0**	**0**	**1**	**0**	**0**	**0**	**0**	**0**	**0**	**0**
	Denver Rangers	IHL	40	21	28	49	....	....	....	32	....	....	....	....	....	....	....	....	....	....	....	....	....	....	....	....	....	....
1989-90	**New York Rangers**	**NHL**	**76**	**32**	**34**	**66**	**28**	**24**	**52**	**32**	**10**	**1**	**4**	**205**	**15.6**	**89**	**44**	**69**	**27**	**3**	**10**	**1**	**6**	**7**	**4**	**0**	**0**	**1**
1990-91	**New York Rangers**	**NHL**	**74**	**26**	**41**	**67**	**24**	**31**	**55**	**37**	**15**	**2**	**3**	**212**	**12.3**	**94**	**47**	**94**	**42**	**–5**	**6**	**1**	**2**	**3**	**0**	**1**	**0**	**0**
1991-92	**New York Rangers**	**NHL**	**71**	**30**	**23**	**53**	**27**	**17**	**44**	**57**	**13**	**1**	**4**	**216**	**13.9**	**85**	**42**	**51**	**19**	**11**	**8**	**4**	**0**	**4**	**6**	**2**	**1**	**0**
1992-93	**New York Rangers**	**NHL**	**71**	**25**	**28**	**53**	**21**	**19**	**40**	**40**	**7**	**3**	**3**	**213**	**11.7**	**81**	**35**	**73**	**24**	**–3**	....	....	....	....	....	....	....	....
	United States	WC-A	6	2	1	3	....	....	....	0	....	....	....	....	....	....	....	....	....	....	....	....	....	....	....	....	....	....
1993-94	**New York Rangers**	**NHL**	**13**	**2**	**4**	**6**	**2**	**3**	**5**	**13**	**0**	**0**	**0**	**17**	**11.8**	**8**	**5**	**5**	**0**	**–2**	....	....	....	....	....	....	....	....
	Hartford Whalers	**NHL**	**19**	**2**	**11**	**13**	**2**	**9**	**11**	**4**	**0**	**0**	**0**	**43**	**4.7**	**21**	**8**	**29**	**5**	**–11**	....	....	....	....	....	....	....	....
1994-95	**Hartford Whalers**	**NHL**	**47**	**17**	**18**	**35**	**30**	**27**	**57**	**22**	**3**	**1**	**3**	**121**	**14.0**	**47**	**14**	**45**	**13**	**1**	....	....	....	....	....	....	....	....
1995-96	**Winnipeg Jets**	**NHL**	**59**	**16**	**16**	**32**	**16**	**13**	**29**	**26**	**2**	**0**	**2**	**134**	**11.9**	**46**	**11**	**58**	**20**	**–3**	....	....	....	....	....	....	....	....
	San Jose Sharks	**NHL**	**9**	**6**	**5**	**11**	**6**	**4**	**10**	**4**	**0**	**1**	**2**	**33**	**18.2**	**14**	**2**	**7**	**3**	**8**	....	....	....	....	....	....	....	....
1996-97	**San Jose Sharks**	**NHL**	**65**	**16**	**21**	**37**	**17**	**19**	**36**	**16**	**3**	**1**	**4**	**126**	**12.7**	**56**	**21**	**53**	**10**	**–8**	....	....	....	....	....	....	....	....
1997-98	**St. Louis Blues**	**NHL**	**62**	**12**	**6**	**18**	**14**	**6**	**20**	**26**	**3**	**0**	**1**	**75**	**16.0**	**29**	**6**	**33**	**16**	**6**	**10**	**0**	**0**	**0**	**2**	**0**	**0**	**0**
1998-99	**Nashville Predators**	**NHL**	**40**	**4**	**5**	**9**	**5**	**5**	**10**	**16**	**0**	**0**	**1**	**73**	**5.5**	**16**	**1**	**47**	**21**	**–11**	....	....	....	....	....	....	....	....
99-2000	**Nashville Predators**	**NHL**	**9**	**0**	**1**	**1**	**0**	**1**	**1**	**4**	**0**	**0**	**0**	**13**	**0.0**	**2**	**0**	**3**	**1**	**0**	....	....	....	....	....	....	....	....
	NHL Totals		**635**	**195**	**216**	**411**	**198**	**180**	**378**	**301**	**58**	**10**	**29**	**1530**	**12.7**	**603**	**241**	**577**	**201**		**35**	**6**	**8**	**14**	**12**	**3**	**1**	**1**

Played in NHL All-Star Game (1991)

Traded to **Hartford** by **NY Rangers** with James Patrick for Steve Larmer, Nick Kypreos, Barry Richter and Hartford's 6th round choice (Yuri Litvinov) in 1994 Entry Draft, November 2, 1993. Traded to **Winnipeg** by **Hartford** for Nelson Emerson, October 6, 1995. Traded to **San Jose** by **Winnipeg** with Dallas' 2nd round choice (previously acquired and later traded to Chicago — Chicago selected Remi Royer) in 1996 Entry Draft for Craig Janney, March 18, 1996. Traded to **St. Louis** by **San Jose** for Stephane Matteau, July 24, 1997. Traded to **Nashville** by **St. Louis** for future considerations, June 26, 1998. • Missed remainder of 1999-2000 season recovering from knee injury suffered in game vs. Montreal, November 18, 1999.

• TURGEON, Pierre

C – L. 6'1", 199 lbs. b: Rouyn, Que., 8/28/1969. Buffalo's 1st, 1st overall, in 1987.

Season	Club	League	GP	G	A	Pts	AG	AA	APts	PIM	PP	SH	GW	S	%	TGF	PGF	TGA	PGA	+/–	GP	G	A	Pts	PIM	PP	SH	GW
1984-85	Bourassa Angevins	QAAA	41	49	52	101	....	....	....	....	....	....	....	....	....	....	....	....	....	....	....	....	....	....	....	....	....	....
1985-86	Granby Bisons	QMJHL	69	47	67	114	....	....	....	31	....	....	....	....	....	....	....	....	....	....	....	....	....	....	....	....	....	....
	Canada	Nat-Team	11	2	4	6	....	....	....	2	....	....	....	....	....	....	....	....	....	....	....	....	....	....	....	....	....	....
1986-87	Granby Bisons	QMJHL	58	69	85	154	....	....	....	8	....	....	....	....	....	....	....	....	....	....	7	9	6	15	15	....	....	....
	Canada	WJC-A	6	3	0	3	....	....	....	2	....	....	....	....	....	....	....	....	....	....	....	....	....	....	....	....	....	....
1987-88	**Buffalo Sabres**	**NHL**	**76**	**14**	**28**	**42**	**12**	**20**	**32**	**34**	**8**	**0**	**3**	**101**	**13.9**	**68**	**28**	**48**	**0**	**–8**	**6**	**4**	**3**	**7**	**4**	**3**	**0**	**0**
1988-89	**Buffalo Sabres**	**NHL**	**80**	**34**	**54**	**88**	**29**	**38**	**67**	**26**	**19**	**0**	**5**	**182**	**18.7**	**117**	**53**	**87**	**21**	**–2**	**5**	**3**	**5**	**8**	**2**	**1**	**0**	**0**
1989-90	**Buffalo Sabres**	**NHL**	**80**	**40**	**66**	**106**	**34**	**47**	**81**	**29**	**17**	**1**	**10**	**193**	**20.7**	**140**	**61**	**86**	**17**	**10**	**6**	**2**	**4**	**6**	**2**	**0**	**0**	**1**
1990-91	**Buffalo Sabres**	**NHL**	**78**	**32**	**47**	**79**	**29**	**36**	**65**	**26**	**13**	**2**	**3**	**174**	**18.4**	**114**	**36**	**80**	**16**	**14**	**6**	**3**	**1**	**4**	**6**	**1**	**0**	**0**
1991-92	**Buffalo Sabres**	**NHL**	**8**	**2**	**6**	**8**	**2**	**5**	**7**	**4**	**0**	**0**	**0**	**14**	**14.3**	**8**	**4**	**9**	**4**	**–1**	....	....	....	....	....	....	....	....
	New York Islanders	**NHL**	**69**	**38**	**49**	**87**	**35**	**37**	**72**	**16**	**13**	**0**	**6**	**193**	**19.7**	**111**	**41**	**75**	**13**	**8**	....	....	....	....	....	....	....	....
1992-93	**New York Islanders**	**NHL**	**83**	**58**	**74**	**132**	**48**	**51**	**99**	**26**	**24**	**0**	**10**	**301**	**19.3**	**166**	**76**	**93**	**2**	**–1**	**11**	**6**	**7**	**13**	**0**	**0**	**0**	**0**
1993-94	**New York Islanders**	**NHL**	**69**	**38**	**56**	**94**	**35**	**44**	**79**	**18**	**10**	**4**	**6**	**254**	**15.0**	**120**	**46**	**76**	**16**	**14**	**4**	**0**	**1**	**1**	**0**	**0**	**0**	**0**
1994-95	**New York Islanders**	**NHL**	**34**	**13**	**14**	**27**	**23**	**21**	**44**	**10**	**3**	**2**	**2**	**93**	**14.0**	**29**	**12**	**41**	**12**	**–12**	....	....	....	....	....	....	....	....
	Montreal Canadiens	**NHL**	**15**	**11**	**9**	**20**	**19**	**13**	**32**	**4**	**2**	**0**	**2**	**67**	**16.4**	**25**	**6**	**7**	**0**	**12**	....	....	....	....	....	....	....	....
1995-96	**Montreal Canadiens**	**NHL**	**80**	**38**	**58**	**96**	**37**	**48**	**85**	**44**	**17**	**1**	**6**	**297**	**12.8**	**128**	**57**	**63**	**11**	**19**	**6**	**2**	**4**	**6**	**2**	**0**	**0**	**0**
1996-97	**Montreal Canadiens**	**NHL**	**9**	**1**	**10**	**11**	**1**	**9**	**10**	**2**	**0**	**0**	**0**	**22**	**4.5**	**19**	**9**	**6**	**0**	**4**	....	....	....	....	....	....	....	....
	St. Louis Blues	**NHL**	**69**	**25**	**49**	**74**	**26**	**44**	**70**	**12**	**5**	**0**	**7**	**194**	**12.9**	**97**	**30**	**72**	**9**	**4**	**5**	**1**	**1**	**2**	**2**	**1**	**0**	**0**
1997-98	**St. Louis Blues**	**NHL**	**60**	**22**	**46**	**68**	**26**	**45**	**71**	**24**	**6**	**0**	**4**	**140**	**15.7**	**90**	**32**	**48**	**3**	**13**	**10**	**4**	**4**	**8**	**2**	**2**	**0**	**0**
1998-99	**St. Louis Blues**	**NHL**	**67**	**31**	**34**	**65**	**36**	**33**	**69**	**36**	**10**	**0**	**5**	**193**	**16.1**	**81**	**28**	**50**	**1**	**4**	**13**	**4**	**9**	**13**	**6**	**0**	**0**	**2**
99-2000	**St. Louis Blues**	**NHL**	**52**	**26**	**40**	**66**	**29**	**37**	**66**	**8**	**8**	**0**	**3**	**139**	**18.7**	**82**	**31**	**22**	**1**	**30**	**7**	**0**	**7**	**7**	**0**	**0**	**0**	**0**
	NHL Totals		**929**	**423**	**640**	**1063**	**421**	**528**	**949**	**319**	**155**	**10**	**72**	**2557**	**16.5**	**1395**	**550**	**863**	**126**		**79**	**29**	**46**	**75**	**26**	**8**	**0**	**3**

• Brother of Sylvain • Won Lady Byng Memorial Trophy (1993) • Played in NHL All-Star Game (1990, 1993, 1994, 1996)

Traded to **NY Islanders** by **Buffalo** with Uwe Krupp, Benoit Hogue and Dave McLlwain for Pat LaFontaine, Randy Hillier, Randy Wood and NY Islanders' 4th round choice (Dean Melanson) in 1992 Entry Draft, October 25, 1991. Traded to **Montreal** by **NY Islanders** with Vladimir Malakhov for Kirk Muller, Mathieu Schneider and Craig Darby, April 5, 1995. Traded to **St. Louis** by **Montreal** with Rory Fitzpatrick and Craig Conroy for Murray Baron, Shayne Corson and St. Louis' 5th round choice (Gennady Razin) in 1997 Entry Draft, October 29, 1996.

• TURGEON, Sylvain

LW – L. 6', 200 lbs. b: Noranda, Que., 1/17/1965. Hartford's 1st, 2nd overall, in 1983.

Season	Club	League	GP	G	A	Pts	AG	AA	APts	PIM	PP	SH	GW	S	%	TGF	PGF	TGA	PGA	+/–	GP	G	A	Pts	PIM	PP	SH	GW
1980-81	Bourassa Angevins	QAAA	43	34	44	78	....	....	....	....	....	....	....	....	....	....	....	....	....	....	....	....	....	....	....	....	....	....
1981-82	Hull Olympiques	QMJHL	57	33	40	73	....	....	....	78	....	....	....	....	....	....	....	....	....	....	14	11	11	22	16	....	....	....
1982-83	Hull Olympiques	QMJHL	67	54	109	163	....	....	....	103	....	....	....	....	....	....	....	....	....	....	7	8	7	15	10	....	....	....
	Canada	WJC-A	7	4	2	6	....	....	....	8	....	....	....	....	....	....	....	....	....	....	....	....	....	....	....	....	....	....
1983-84	**Hartford Whalers**	**NHL**	**76**	**40**	**32**	**72**	**32**	**22**	**54**	**55**	**18**	**0**	**3**	**237**	**16.9**	**106**	**46**	**71**	**0**	**–11**	....	....	....	....	....	....	....	....
1984-85	**Hartford Whalers**	**NHL**	**64**	**31**	**31**	**62**	**25**	**21**	**46**	**67**	**11**	**0**	**3**	**185**	**16.8**	**95**	**42**	**63**	**0**	**–10**	....	....	....	....	....	....	....	....
1985-86	**Hartford Whalers**	**NHL**	**76**	**45**	**34**	**79**	**36**	**23**	**59**	**88**	**13**	**0**	**5**	**249**	**18.1**	**115**	**41**	**73**	**0**	**1**	**9**	**2**	**3**	**5**	**4**	**0**	**0**	**0**
1986-87	**Hartford Whalers**	**NHL**	**41**	**23**	**13**	**36**	**20**	**9**	**29**	**45**	**6**	**0**	**4**	**137**	**16.8**	**47**	**15**	**35**	**0**	**–3**	**6**	**1**	**2**	**3**	**4**	**0**	**0**	**0**
1987-88	**Hartford Whalers**	**NHL**	**71**	**23**	**26**	**49**	**20**	**19**	**39**	**71**	**13**	**0**	**3**	**247**	**9.3**	**85**	**44**	**46**	**0**	**–5**	**6**	**0**	**0**	**0**	**4**	**0**	**0**	**0**
1988-89	**Hartford Whalers**	**NHL**	**42**	**16**	**14**	**30**	**14**	**10**	**24**	**40**	**7**	**0**	**1**	**122**	**13.1**	**44**	**18**	**37**	**0**	**–11**	**4**	**0**	**2**	**2**	**4**	**0**	**0**	**0**
1989-90	**New Jersey Devils**	**NHL**	**72**	**30**	**17**	**47**	**26**	**12**	**38**	**81**	**7**	**0**	**3**	**218**	**13.8**	**77**	**20**	**65**	**0**	**–8**	**1**	**0**	**0**	**0**	**0**	**0**	**0**	**0**
1990-91	**Montreal Canadiens**	**NHL**	**19**	**5**	**7**	**12**	**5**	**5**	**10**	**20**	**1**	**0**	**1**	**41**	**12.2**	**17**	**7**	**12**	**0**	**–2**	**5**	**0**	**0**	**0**	**2**	**0**	**0**	**0**
1991-92	**Montreal Canadiens**	**NHL**	**56**	**9**	**11**	**20**	**8**	**8**	**16**	**39**	**6**	**0**	**1**	**99**	**9.1**	**42**	**26**	**21**	**1**	**–4**	**5**	**1**	**0**	**1**	**4**	**0**	**0**	**0**
1992-93	**Ottawa Senators**	**NHL**	**72**	**25**	**18**	**43**	**21**	**12**	**33**	**104**	**8**	**0**	**2**	**249**	**10.0**	**65**	**30**	**64**	**0**	**–29**	....	....	....	....	....	....	....	....
1993-94	**Ottawa Senators**	**NHL**	**47**	**11**	**15**	**26**	**10**	**12**	**22**	**52**	**7**	**0**	**2**	**116**	**9.5**	**40**	**19**	**47**	**1**	**–25**	....	....	....	....	....	....	....	....
1994-95	**Ottawa Senators**	**NHL**	**33**	**11**	**8**	**19**	**19**	**12**	**31**	**29**	**2**	**0**	**1**	**83**	**13.3**	**22**	**5**	**18**	**0**	**–1**	....	....	....	....	....	....	....	....
1995-96	Houston Aeros	IHL	65	28	31	59	....	....	....	66	....	....	....	....	....	....	....	....	....	....	....	....	....	....	....	....	....	....
1996-97	HC Bolzano	Alpenliga	23	14	11	25	....	....	....	22	....	....	....	....	....	....	....	....	....	....	....	....	....	....	....	....	....	....
	EHC Olten	Switz-2	STATISTICS NOT AVAILABLE																									
	Wedemark Scorpions	Germany	10	4	6	10	....	....	....	12	....	....	....	....	....	....	....	....	....	....	8	5	2	7	41	....	....	....

			REGULAR SEASON																		PLAYOFFS							
Season	Club	League	GP	G	A	Pts	AG	AA	APts	PIM	PP	SH	GW	S	%	TGF	PGF	TGA	PGA	+/–	GP	G	A	Pts	PIM	PP	SH	GW
1997-98	Revier Lowen	Germany	27	11	15	26				24																		
	SC Herisau	Switz.	14	9	2	11				26																		
1998-99	SC Langnau	Switz.	5	1	1	2				4																		
	Kassel Huskies	Germany	34	20	8	28				32																		
99-2000	Kassel Huskies	Germany	49	32	13	45				49											8	2	2	4	10			
	NHL Totals		**669**	**269**	**226**	**495**	**236**	**165**	**401**	**691**	**99**	**0**	**29**	**1983**	**13.6**	**755**	**313**	**552**	**2**		**36**	**4**	**7**	**11**	**22**	**0**	**0**	**0**

• Brother of Pierre • QMJHL First All-Star Team (1983) • NHL All-Rookie Team (1984) • Played in NHL All-Star Game (1986)

Traded to **New Jersey** by **Hartford** for Pat Verbeek, June 17, 1989. • Missed majority of 1990-91 season recovering from hernia surgery (August 23, 1990) and kneecap injury suffered in game vs. Chicago, February 6, 1991. Traded to **Montreal** by **New Jersey** for Claude Lemieux, September 4, 1990. Claimed by **Ottawa** from **Montreal** in Expansion Draft, June 18, 1992.

• TURNBULL, Ian

Ian Wayne "Bull" D – L. 6', 200 lbs. b: Montreal, Que., 12/22/1953. Toronto's 3rd, 15th overall, in 1973.

Season	Club	League	GP	G	A	Pts	AG	AA	APts	PIM	PP	SH	GW	S	%	TGF	PGF	TGA	PGA	+/–	GP	G	A	Pts	PIM	PP	SH	GW
1968-69	West Island Flyers	MMJHL	25	6	17	23																						
1969-70	Montreal Jr. Canadiens	OHA-Jr.	53	4	21	25				88											16	3	3	6	8			
	Montreal Jr. Canadiens	Mem-Cup	6	6	4	10				6																		
1970-71	Montreal Jr. Canadiens	OHA-Jr.	59	17	45	62				85											11	3	8	11	6			
1971-72	Montreal Jr. Canadiens	OMJHL	63	34	48	82				85																		
1972-73	Ottawa 67's	OMJHL	60	31	50	81				98											9	6	10	16	8			
1973-74	**Toronto Maple Leafs**	**NHL**	**78**	**8**	**27**	**35**	**8**	**22**	**30**	**74**	**2**	**0**	**2**	**231**	**3.5**	**101**	**23**	**88**	**22**	**12**	**4**	**0**	**0**	**0**	**8**	**0**	**0**	**0**
1974-75	**Toronto Maple Leafs**	**NHL**	**22**	**6**	**7**	**13**	**5**	**5**	**10**	**44**	**1**	**0**	**0**	**69**	**8.7**	**31**	**7**	**38**	**8**	**–6**	**7**	**0**	**2**	**2**	**4**	**0**	**0**	**0**
	Oklahoma City Blazers	CHL	8	2	1	3				15																		
1975-76	**Toronto Maple Leafs**	**NHL**	**76**	**20**	**36**	**56**	**18**	**27**	**45**	**90**	**7**	**1**	**3**	**262**	**7.6**	**153**	**48**	**118**	**37**	**24**	**10**	**2**	**9**	**11**	**29**	**1**	**0**	**0**
1976-77	**Toronto Maple Leafs**	**NHL**	**80**	**22**	**57**	**79**	**20**	**44**	**64**	**84**	**4**	**2**	**0**	**316**	**7.0**	**195**	**50**	**128**	**30**	**47**	**9**	**4**	**4**	**8**	**10**	**4**	**0**	**0**
1977-78	**Toronto Maple Leafs**	**NHL**	**77**	**14**	**47**	**61**	**13**	**36**	**49**	**77**	**3**	**1**	**3**	**241**	**5.8**	**151**	**41**	**125**	**21**	**6**	**13**	**6**	**10**	**16**	**10**	**1**	**0**	**0**
1978-79	**Toronto Maple Leafs**	**NHL**	**80**	**12**	**51**	**63**	**10**	**37**	**47**	**80**	**4**	**0**	**0**	**239**	**5.0**	**141**	**41**	**145**	**38**	**–7**	**6**	**0**	**4**	**4**	**27**	**0**	**0**	**0**
1979-80	**Toronto Maple Leafs**	**NHL**	**75**	**11**	**28**	**39**	**9**	**20**	**29**	**90**	**3**	**0**	**0**	**202**	**5.4**	**111**	**22**	**133**	**21**	**–23**	**3**	**0**	**3**	**3**	**2**	**0**	**0**	**0**
1980-81	**Toronto Maple Leafs**	**NHL**	**80**	**19**	**47**	**66**	**15**	**31**	**46**	**104**	**8**	**0**	**1**	**262**	**7.3**	**159**	**55**	**169**	**48**	**–17**	**3**	**1**	**0**	**1**	**4**	**0**	**0**	**0**
1981-82	**Toronto Maple Leafs**	**NHL**	**12**	**0**	**2**	**2**	**0**	**1**	**1**	**8**	**0**	**0**	**0**	**26**	**0.0**	**16**	**3**	**24**	**7**	**–4**								
	Los Angeles Kings	**NHL**	**42**	**11**	**15**	**26**	**9**	**10**	**19**	**81**	**1**	**0**	**1**	**120**	**9.2**	**60**	**15**	**57**	**12**	**0**								
	New Haven Nighthawks	AHL	13	1	7	8				4											3	0	0	0	0			
1982-83	**Pittsburgh Penguins**	**NHL**	**6**	**0**	**0**	**0**	**0**	**0**	**0**	**4**	**0**	**0**	**0**	**6**	**0.0**	**2**	**1**	**4**	**0**	**–3**								
	Baltimore Skipjacks	AHL	13	3	8	11				10																		
	NHL Totals		**628**	**123**	**317**	**440**	**107**	**233**	**340**	**736**	**33**	**4**	**10**	**1974**	**6.2**	**1120**	**306**	**1029**	**244**		**55**	**13**	**32**	**45**	**94**	**6**	**0**	**0**

OMJHL Second All-Star Team (1972, 1973) • Played in NHL All-Star Game (1977)

• Missed majority of 1974-75 season recovering from knee injury suffered in game vs. St. Louis, November 25, 1974. Traded to **LA Kings** by **Toronto** for Billy Harris and John Gibson, November 11, 1981. Signed as a free agent by **Pittsburgh**, October 4, 1982.

• TURNBULL, Perry

Perry John C – L. 6'2", 200 lbs. b: Bentley, Alta., 3/9/1959. St. Louis' 1st, 2nd overall, in 1979.

Season	Club	League	GP	G	A	Pts	AG	AA	APts	PIM	PP	SH	GW	S	%	TGF	PGF	TGA	PGA	+/–	GP	G	A	Pts	PIM	PP	SH	GW
1974-75	The Pas Blue Devils	AJHL	69	6	4	10				134																		
1975-76	The Pas Blue Devils	AJHL	45	27	23	50				140																		
	Calgary Centennials	WCJHL	19	6	7	13				14																		
1976-77	Calgary Centennials	WCJHL	10	8	5	13				33																		
	Portland Winter Hawks	WCJHL	58	23	30	53				249											10	2	1	3	36			
1977-78	Portland Winter Hawks	WCJHL	57	36	27	63				318											8	2	3	5	44			
1978-79	Portland Winter Hawks	WHL	70	75	43	118				191											20	10	8	18	33			
1979-80	**St. Louis Blues**	**NHL**	**80**	**16**	**19**	**35**	**14**	**14**	**28**	**124**	**3**	**0**	**1**	**139**	**11.5**	**58**	**11**	**58**	**0**	**–11**	**3**	**1**	**1**	**2**	**2**	**1**	**0**	**0**
1980-81	**St. Louis Blues**	**NHL**	**75**	**34**	**22**	**56**	**26**	**15**	**41**	**209**	**5**	**0**	**5**	**209**	**16.3**	**85**	**15**	**55**	**0**	**15**								
1981-82	**St. Louis Blues**	**NHL**	**79**	**33**	**26**	**59**	**26**	**17**	**43**	**161**	**2**	**0**	**2**	**215**	**15.3**	**83**	**13**	**87**	**2**	**–15**	**5**	**3**	**2**	**5**	**11**	**1**	**0**	**0**
1982-83	**St. Louis Blues**	**NHL**	**79**	**32**	**15**	**47**	**26**	**10**	**36**	**172**	**6**	**0**	**1**	**205**	**15.6**	**63**	**10**	**74**	**1**	**–20**	**4**	**1**	**0**	**1**	**14**	**0**	**0**	**0**
1983-84	**St. Louis Blues**	**NHL**	**32**	**14**	**8**	**22**	**11**	**5**	**16**	**81**	**1**	**0**	**0**	**84**	**16.7**	**32**	**9**	**26**	**1**	**–2**								
	Montreal Canadiens	**NHL**	**40**	**6**	**7**	**13**	**5**	**5**	**10**	**59**	**2**	**0**	**1**	**67**	**9.0**	**19**	**4**	**28**	**1**	**–12**	**9**	**1**	**2**	**3**	**10**	**0**	**0**	**0**
1984-85	**Winnipeg Jets**	**NHL**	**66**	**22**	**21**	**43**	**18**	**14**	**32**	**130**	**2**	**0**	**1**	**138**	**15.9**	**76**	**11**	**58**	**2**	**9**	**8**	**0**	**1**	**1**	**26**	**0**	**0**	**0**
1985-86	**Winnipeg Jets**	**NHL**	**80**	**20**	**31**	**51**	**16**	**21**	**37**	**183**	**6**	**0**	**2**	**168**	**11.9**	**74**	**13**	**80**	**1**	**–18**	**3**	**0**	**1**	**1**	**11**	**0**	**0**	**0**
1986-87	**Winnipeg Jets**	**NHL**	**26**	**1**	**5**	**6**	**1**	**4**	**5**	**44**	**0**	**0**	**0**	**29**	**3.4**	**12**	**3**	**11**	**0**	**–2**	**1**	**0**	**0**	**0**	**10**	**0**	**0**	**0**
1987-88	**St. Louis Blues**	**NHL**	**51**	**10**	**9**	**19**	**9**	**6**	**15**	**82**	**0**	**0**	**2**	**62**	**16.1**	**30**	**0**	**22**	**0**	**8**	**1**	**0**	**0**	**0**	**2**	**0**	**0**	**0**
	Peoria Rivermen	IHL	3	5	0	5				4																		
1988-89	HC Asiago	Italy	32	31	27	58				*131																		
1989-90	ZSC Zurich	Switz.	1	0	0	0				0																		
	HC Alleghe	Italy	34	24	29	53				68											1	1	1	2	5			
1990-91	HC Bolzano	Italy	18	14	8	22				29											10	8	3	11	41			
1991-92	EC Dorsten	Germany-3	42	55	50	105				187																		
	NHL Totals		**608**	**188**	**163**	**351**	**152**	**111**	**263**	**1245**	**27**	**0**	**15**	**1316**	**14.3**	**532**	**89**	**499**	**8**		**34**	**6**	**7**	**13**	**86**	**2**	**0**	**0**

Traded to **Montreal** by **St. Louis** for Doug Wickenheiser, Gilbert Delorme and Greg Paslawski, December 21, 1983. Traded to **Winnipeg** by **Montreal** for Lucien DeBlois, June 13, 1984. Traded to **St. Louis** by **Winnipeg** for St. Louis' 5th round choice (Ken Gernander) in 1987 Entry Draft, June 5, 1987. • Played w/ RHI's St. Louis Vipers in 1993 (13-16-10-26-57) and 1994 (13-17-14-31-59).

• TURNBULL, Randy

Randy Layne D – R. 6', 185 lbs. b: Bentley, Alta., 2/7/1962. Calgary's 6th, 97th overall, in 1980.

Season	Club	League	GP	G	A	Pts	AG	AA	APts	PIM	PP	SH	GW	S	%	TGF	PGF	TGA	PGA	+/–	GP	G	A	Pts	PIM	PP	SH	GW
1977-78	Fort Saskatchewan Traders	AJHL	47	1	3	4				172																		
1978-79	Fort Saskatchewan Traders	AJHL	51	4	30	34				367											4	0	0	0	2			
	Portland Winter Hawks	WHL	1	0	0	0				7											4	0	0	0	2			
1979-80	Portland Winter Hawks	WHL	72	4	25	29				355											8	0	1	1	50			
1980-81	Portland Winter Hawks	WHL	56	1	31	32				295											8	0	1	1	86			
1981-82	Portland Winter Hawks	WHL	69	5	19	24				430											15	1	9	10	100			
	Calgary Flames	**NHL**	**1**	**0**	**0**	**0**	**0**	**0**	**0**	**2**	**0**	**0**	**0**	**0**	**0.0**	**0**	**0**	**1**	**0**	**–1**								
	Portland Winter Hawks	Mem-Cup	4	1	1	2				6																		
1982-83	Colorado Flames	CHL	65	2	1	3				292											6	0	1	1	7			
1983-84	New Haven Nighthawks	AHL	8	0	0	0				46																		
	Peoria Prancers	IHL	73	3	18	21				213																		
1984-85	Salt Lake Golden Eagles	IHL	81	10	14	24				282											7	0	0	0	41			
1985-86	Salt Lake Golden Eagles	IHL	77	6	14	20				236											5	0	1	1	15			
1986-87	Salt Lake Golden Eagles	IHL	60	2	6	8				212											10	0	0	0	56			
1987-88	Flint Spirits	IHL	1	0	0	0				2																		
	NHL Totals		**1**	**0**	**0**	**0**	**0**	**0**	**0**	**2**	**0**	**0**	**0**	**0**	**0.0**	**0**	**0**	**1**	**0**									

• TURNER, Brad

D – R. 6'2", 205 lbs. b: Winnipeg, Man., 5/25/1968. Minnesota's 6th, 58th overall, in 1986.

Season	Club	League	GP	G	A	Pts	AG	AA	APts	PIM	PP	SH	GW	S	%	TGF	PGF	TGA	PGA	+/–	GP	G	A	Pts	PIM	PP	SH	GW
1984-85	Darien High School	Hi-School	24	32	34	66																						
1985-86	Calgary Canucks	AJHL	52	14	21	35				109																		
1986-87	University of Michigan	CCHA	40	3	10	13				40																		
1987-88	University of Michigan	CCHA	39	3	11	14				52																		
1988-89	University of Michigan	CCHA	33	3	8	11				38																		
1989-90	University of Michigan	CCHA	32	8	9	17				34																		
1990-91	Capital District Islanders	AHL	31	1	2	3				8																		
	Richmond Renegades	ECHL	40	16	25	41				31																		
1991-92	**New York Islanders**	**NHL**	**3**	**0**	**0**	**0**	**0**	**0**	**0**	**0**	**0**	**0**	**0**	**1**	**0.0**	**1**	**0**	**0**	**0**	**1**								
	Capital District Islanders	AHL	35	3	6	9				17																		
	New Haven Nighthawks	AHL	32	6	11	17				58																		
1992-93	Capital District Islanders	AHL	65	8	11	19				71											3	0	0	0	2			
1993-94	Canada	Nat-Team	30	6	9	15				21																		
	Cornwall Aces	AHL	29	3	13	16				19											4	1	1	2	4			

			REGULAR SEASON																		PLAYOFFS							
Season	**Club**	**League**	**GP**	**G**	**A**	**Pts**	**AG**	**AA**	**APts**	**PIM**	**PP**	**SH**	**GW**	**S**	**%**	**TGF**	**PGF**	**TGA**	**PGA**	**+/–**	**GP**	**G**	**A**	**Pts**	**PIM**	**PP**	**SH**	**GW**
1994-95	TuTo Turku	Finland	43	3	9	12	....	....	....	114	....	....	....	....	....	....	....	....	....	....	....	....	....	....	....	....	....	....
1995-96	WEV Wien	Austria	31	7	14	21	....	....	....	100	....	....	....	....	....	....	....	....	....	....	....	....	....	....	....	....	....	....
1996-97	Manchester Storm	Britain	21	3	8	11	....	....	....	12	....	....	....	....	....	....	....	....	....	....	6	2	0	2	4	....	....	....
1997-98	Manchester Storm	BH-Cup	14	2	2	4	....	....	....	14	....	....	....	....	....	....	....	....	....	....	....	....	....	....	....	....	....	....
	Manchester Storm	Britain	11	1	1	2	....	....	....	4	....	....	....	....	....	....	....	....	....	....	....	....	....	....	....	....	....	....
	Manchester Storm	EuroHL	5	1	3	4	....	....	....	4	....	....	....	....	....	....	....	....	....	....	....	....	....	....	....	....	....	....
	NHL Totals		**3**	**0**	**0**	**0**	**0**	**0**	**0**	**0**	**0**	**0**	**0**	**1**	**0.0**	**1**	**0**	**0**	**0**		....	....	....	....	....	....	....	....

Signed as a free agent by **NY Islanders**, June 4, 1991.

• TURNER, Dean

Dean Cameron D – L. 6'2", 215 lbs. b: Dearborn, MI, 6/22/1958. NY Rangers' 3rd, 44th overall, in 1978.

Season	Club	League	GP	G	A	Pts	AG	AA	APts	PIM	PP	SH	GW	S	%	TGF	PGF	TGA	PGA	+/–	GP	G	A	Pts	PIM	PP	SH	GW
1975-76	Detroit Little Caesars	GLJHL	50	34	34	68	....	....	....	....	....	....	....	....	....	....	....	....	....	....	....	....	....	....	....	....	....	....
1976-77	University of Michigan	WCHA	45	13	18	31	....	....	....	106	....	....	....	....	....	....	....	....	....	....	....	....	....	....	....	....	....	....
1977-78	University of Michigan	WCHA	36	5	14	19	....	....	....	88	....	....	....	....	....	....	....	....	....	....	....	....	....	....	....	....	....	....
1978-79	**New York Rangers**	**NHL**	**1**	**0**	**0**	**0**	**0**	**0**	**0**	**0**	**0**	**0**	**0**	**0**	**0.0**	**0**	**0**	**1**	**0**	**–1**	....	....	....	....	....	....	....	....
	New Haven Nighthawks	AHL	76	9	25	34	....	....	....	275	....	....	....	....	....	....	....	....	....	....	6	0	0	0	9	....	....	....
1979-80	**Colorado Rockies**	**NHL**	**27**	**1**	**0**	**1**	**1**	**0**	**1**	**51**	**0**	**0**	**0**	**24**	**4.2**	**17**	**1**	**22**	**6**	**0**	....	....	....	....	....	....	....	....
	New Haven Nighthawks	AHL	6	1	3	4	....	....	....	10	....	....	....	....	....	....	....	....	....	....	....	....	....	....	....	....	....	....
	Fort Worth Texans	CHL	39	5	23	28	....	....	....	81	....	....	....	....	....	....	....	....	....	....	15	0	5	5	39	....	....	....
1980-81	**Colorado Rockies**	**NHL**	**4**	**0**	**0**	**0**	**0**	**0**	**0**	**4**	**0**	**0**	**0**	**0**	**0.0**	**2**	**0**	**6**	**0**	**–4**	....	....	....	....	....	....	....	....
	Fort Worth Texans	CHL	44	5	9	14	....	....	....	103	....	....	....	....	....	....	....	....	....	....	....	....	....	....	....	....	....	....
	Springfield Indians	AHL	11	2	7	9	....	....	....	31	....	....	....	....	....	....	....	....	....	....	6	4	5	9	7	....	....	....
1981-82	Rochester Americans	AHL	75	8	46	54	....	....	....	155	....	....	....	....	....	....	....	....	....	....	9	0	4	4	6	....	....	....
1982-83	**Los Angeles Kings**	**NHL**	**3**	**0**	**0**	**0**	**0**	**0**	**0**	**4**	**0**	**0**	**0**	**1**	**0.0**	**1**	**0**	**1**	**0**	**0**	....	....	....	....	....	....	....	....
	New Haven Nighthawks	AHL	66	14	20	34	....	....	....	129	....	....	....	....	....	....	....	....	....	....	12	2	3	5	34	....	....	....
	NHL Totals		**35**	**1**	**0**	**1**	**1**	**0**	**1**	**59**	**0**	**0**	**0**	**25**	**4.0**	**20**	**1**	**30**	**6**		....	....	....	....	....	....	....	....

Traded to **Colorado** by **NY Rangers** with Pat Hickey, Mike McEwen, Lucien DeBlois and future considerations (Bobby Crawford, January 15, 1980) for Barry Beck, November 2, 1979. Signed as a free agent by **Buffalo**, September 24, 1981. Traded to **LA Kings** by **Buffalo** for cash, September 9, 1982.

• TUTT, Brian

D – L. 6'1", 195 lbs. b: Swalwell, Alta., 6/9/1962. Philadelphia's 6th, 126th overall, in 1980.

Season	Club	League	GP	G	A	Pts	AG	AA	APts	PIM	PP	SH	GW	S	%	TGF	PGF	TGA	PGA	+/–	GP	G	A	Pts	PIM	PP	SH	GW
1979-80	Calgary Canucks	AJHL	59	6	14	20	....	....	....	55	....	....	....	....	....	....	....	....	....	....	....	....	....	....	....	....	....	....
	Calgary Wranglers	WHL	2	0	0	0	....	....	....	2	....	....	....	....	....	....	....	....	....	....	4	0	1	1	6	....	....	....
1980-81	Calgary Wranglers	WHL	72	10	41	51	....	....	....	111	....	....	....	....	....	....	....	....	....	....	22	3	11	14	30	....	....	....
1981-82	Calgary Wranglers	WHL	40	2	16	18	....	....	....	85	....	....	....	....	....	....	....	....	....	....	9	2	2	4	22	....	....	....
1982-83	Maine Mariners	AHL	31	0	0	0	....	....	....	28	....	....	....	....	....	....	....	....	....	....	....	....	....	....	....	....	....	....
	Toledo Goaldiggers	IHL	23	5	10	15	....	....	....	26	....	....	....	....	....	....	....	....	....	....	11	1	7	8	16	....	....	....
1983-84	Springfield Indians	AHL	1	0	0	0	....	....	....	2	....	....	....	....	....	....	....	....	....	....	....	....	....	....	....	....	....	....
	Toledo Goaldiggers	IHL	82	7	44	51	....	....	....	79	....	....	....	....	....	....	....	....	....	....	13	0	6	6	16	....	....	....
1984-85	Hershey Bears	AHL	3	0	0	0	....	....	....	8	....	....	....	....	....	....	....	....	....	....	....	....	....	....	....	....	....	....
	Kalamazoo Wings	IHL	80	8	45	53	....	....	....	62	....	....	....	....	....	....	....	....	....	....	11	2	4	6	19	....	....	....
1985-86	Kalamazoo Wings	IHL	82	11	39	50	....	....	....	129	....	....	....	....	....	....	....	....	....	....	6	1	6	7	11	....	....	....
1986-87	Maine Mariners	AHL	41	6	15	21	....	....	....	19	....	....	....	....	....	....	....	....	....	....	....	....	....	....	....	....	....	....
	Kalamazoo Wings	IHL	19	2	7	9	....	....	....	10	....	....	....	....	....	....	....	....	....	....	....	....	....	....	....	....	....	....
	Canada	Nat-Team	15	0	3	3	....	....	....	18	....	....	....	....	....	....	....	....	....	....	....	....	....	....	....	....	....	....
1987-88	New Haven Nighthawks	AHL	32	1	12	13	....	....	....	33	....	....	....	....	....	....	....	....	....	....	....	....	....	....	....	....	....	....
	EHC Lustenau	Austria	24	5	12	17	....	....	....	36	....	....	....	....	....	....	....	....	....	....	....	....	....	....	....	....	....	....
1988-89	Baltimore Skipjacks	AHL	6	1	5	6	....	....	....	6	....	....	....	....	....	....	....	....	....	....	....	....	....	....	....	....	....	....
	Canada	Nat-Team	63	0	19	19	....	....	....	87	....	....	....	....	....	....	....	....	....	....	....	....	....	....	....	....	....	....
1989-90	**Washington Capitals**	**NHL**	**7**	**1**	**0**	**1**	**1**	**0**	**1**	**2**	**0**	**0**	**0**	**5**	**20.0**	**3**	**0**	**7**	**0**	**–4**	....	....	....	....	....	....	....	....
	Baltimore Skipjacks	AHL	67	2	13	15	....	....	....	80	....	....	....	....	....	....	....	....	....	....	9	1	0	1	4	....	....	....
1990-91	Canada	Nat-Team	10	4	3	7	....	....	....	14	....	....	....	....	....	....	....	....	....	....	....	....	....	....	....	....	....	....
	Furuset IF Oslo	Norway	35	13	24	37	....	....	....	100	....	....	....	....	....	....	....	....	....	....	6	3	2	5	....	....	....	....
1991-92	Furuset IF Oslo	Norway	28	7	9	16	....	....	....	96	....	....	....	....	....	....	....	....	....	....	....	....	....	....	....	....	....	....
	Canada	Nat-Team	6	0	1	1	....	....	....	6	....	....	....	....	....	....	....	....	....	....	....	....	....	....	....	....	....	....
	Canada	Olympics	8	0	0	0	....	....	....	4	....	....	....	....	....	....	....	....	....	....	....	....	....	....	....	....	....	....
	Canada	WC-A	5	0	0	0	....	....	....	8	....	....	....	....	....	....	....	....	....	....	....	....	....	....	....	....	....	....
1992-93	Ilves Tampere	Finland	46	5	18	23	....	....	....	*148	....	....	....	....	....	....	....	....	....	....	3	1	1	2	0	....	....	....
1993-94	Farjestads BK Stockholm	Sweden	21	1	3	4	....	....	....	32	....	....	....	....	....	....	....	....	....	....	....	....	....	....	....	....	....	....
	Canada	Nat-Team	12	0	0	0	....	....	....	4	....	....	....	....	....	....	....	....	....	....	....	....	....	....	....	....	....	....
1994-95	Ilves Tampere	Finland	25	1	3	4	....	....	....	42	....	....	....	....	....	....	....	....	....	....	....	....	....	....	....	....	....	....
	Canada	WC-A	7	0	0	0	....	....	....	6	....	....	....	....	....	....	....	....	....	....	....	....	....	....	....	....	....	....
1995-96	SaPKo Savonlinna	Finland-2	22	2	9	11	....	....	....	131	....	....	....	....	....	....	....	....	....	....	7	2	4	6	12	....	....	....
1996-97	Schwenningen Wild Wings	Germany	31	4	14	18	....	....	....	71	....	....	....	....	....	....	....	....	....	....	5	2	3	5	12	....	....	....
1997-98	Hannover Scorpions	Germany	49	3	14	17	....	....	....	86	....	....	....	....	....	....	....	....	....	....	4	0	1	1	8	....	....	....
1998-99	Adler Mannheim	Germany	13	2	2	4	....	....	....	10	....	....	....	....	....	....	....	....	....	....	....	....	....	....	....	....	....	....
	Hannover Scorpions	Germany	35	1	9	10	....	....	....	84	....	....	....	....	....	....	....	....	....	....	....	....	....	....	....	....	....	....
99-2000	Hannover Scorpions	Germany	45	1	6	7	....	....	....	82	....	....	....	....	....	....	....	....	....	....	....	....	....	....	....	....	....	....
	NHL Totals		**7**	**1**	**0**	**1**	**1**	**0**	**1**	**2**	**0**	**0**	**0**	**5**	**20.0**	**3**	**0**	**7**	**0**		....	....	....	....	....	....	....	....

IHL Second All-Star Team (1984, 1985)

Signed as a free agent by **Washington**, July 25, 1989.

• TUTTLE, Steve

Steve Walter RW – R. 6'1", 197 lbs. b: Vancouver, B.C., 1/5/1966. St. Louis' 8th, 113th overall, in 1984.

Season	Club	League	GP	G	A	Pts	AG	AA	APts	PIM	PP	SH	GW	S	%	TGF	PGF	TGA	PGA	+/–	GP	G	A	Pts	PIM	PP	SH	GW
1983-84	Richmond Sockeyes	BCJHL	46	46	34	80	....	....	....	22	....	....	....	....	....	....	....	....	....	....	....	....	....	....	....	....	....	....
1984-85	University of Wisconsin	WCHA	28	3	4	7	....	....	....	0	....	....	....	....	....	....	....	....	....	....	....	....	....	....	....	....	....	....
1985-86	University of Wisconsin	WCHA	32	2	10	12	....	....	....	2	....	....	....	....	....	....	....	....	....	....	....	....	....	....	....	....	....	....
1986-87	University of Wisconsin	WCHA	42	31	21	52	....	....	....	14	....	....	....	....	....	....	....	....	....	....	....	....	....	....	....	....	....	....
1987-88	University of Wisconsin	WCHA	45	27	39	66	....	....	....	18	....	....	....	....	....	....	....	....	....	....	....	....	....	....	....	....	....	....
1988-89	**St. Louis Blues**	**NHL**	**53**	**13**	**12**	**25**	**11**	**8**	**19**	**6**	**0**	**1**	**3**	**82**	**15.9**	**37**	**0**	**60**	**26**	**3**	**6**	**1**	**2**	**3**	**0**	**0**	**0**	**0**
1989-90	**St. Louis Blues**	**NHL**	**71**	**12**	**10**	**22**	**10**	**7**	**17**	**4**	**1**	**1**	**1**	**92**	**13.0**	**29**	**2**	**42**	**9**	**–6**	**5**	**0**	**1**	**1**	**2**	**0**	**0**	**0**
1990-91	**St. Louis Blues**	**NHL**	**20**	**3**	**6**	**9**	**3**	**5**	**8**	**2**	**0**	**0**	**0**	**16**	**18.8**	**14**	**1**	**12**	**1**	**2**	**6**	**0**	**3**	**3**	**0**	**0**	**0**	**0**
	Peoria Rivermen	IHL	42	24	32	56	....	....	....	8	....	....	....	....	....	....	....	....	....	....	....	....	....	....	....	....	....	....
1991-92	Peoria Rivermen	IHL	71	43	46	89	....	....	....	22	....	....	....	....	....	....	....	....	....	....	10	4	8	12	4	....	....	....
1992-93	Milwaukee Admirals	IHL	51	27	34	61	....	....	....	12	....	....	....	....	....	....	....	....	....	....	4	0	2	2	2	....	....	....
	Halifax Citadels	AHL	22	11	17	28	....	....	....	2	....	....	....	....	....	....	....	....	....	....	....	....	....	....	....	....	....	....
1993-94	Milwaukee Admirals	IHL	78	27	44	71	....	....	....	34	....	....	....	....	....	....	....	....	....	....	4	0	2	2	4	....	....	....
1994-95	Peoria Rivermen	IHL	38	14	13	27	....	....	....	14	....	....	....	....	....	....	....	....	....	....	....	....	....	....	....	....	....	....
	Milwaukee Admirals	IHL	21	3	1	4	....	....	....	8	....	....	....	....	....	....	....	....	....	....	....	....	....	....	....	....	....	....
1995-96	Milwaukee Admirals	IHL	81	32	35	67	....	....	....	36	....	....	....	....	....	....	....	....	....	....	5	1	2	3	0	....	....	....
1996-97	Milwaukee Admirals	IHL	71	25	19	44	....	....	....	20	....	....	....	....	....	....	....	....	....	....	3	1	1	2	2	....	....	....
1997-98	Milwaukee Admirals	IHL	37	7	6	13	....	....	....	26	....	....	....	....	....	....	....	....	....	....	10	3	4	7	2	....	....	....
	NHL Totals		**144**	**28**	**28**	**56**	**24**	**20**	**44**	**12**	**1**	**2**	**4**	**190**	**14.7**	**80**	**3**	**114**	**36**		**17**	**1**	**6**	**7**	**2**	**0**	**0**	**0**

ECAC Second All-Star Team (1985) • WCHA Second All-Star Team (1988) • NCAA West Second All-American Team (1988) • IHL First All-Star Team (1992)

Traded to **Tampa Bay** by **St. Louis** with Pat Jablonski, Darin Kimble, and Rob Robinson for future considerations, June 19, 1992. Traded to **Quebec** by **Tampa Bay** with Martin Simard and Michel Mongeau for Herb Raglan, February 12, 1993.

• TUZZOLINO, Tony

RW – R. 6'2", 208 lbs. b: Buffalo, NY, 10/9/1975. Quebec's 7th, 113th overall, in 1994.

Season	Club	League	GP	G	A	Pts	AG	AA	APts	PIM	PP	SH	GW	S	%	TGF	PGF	TGA	PGA	+/–	GP	G	A	Pts	PIM	PP	SH	GW
1989-90	Amherst Knights	NYAHA	29	50	95	145	....	....	....	....	....	....	....	....	....	....	....	....	....	....	....	....	....	....	....	....	....	....
1990-91	Buffalo Regals	NAJHL	55	39	47	86	....	....	....	....	....	....	....	....	....	....	....	....	....	....	....	....	....	....	....	....	....	....
1991-92	Niagara Scenics	NAJHL	45	19	27	46	....	....	....	82	....	....	....	....	....	....	....	....	....	....	....	....	....	....	....	....	....	....

			REGULAR SEASON																		PLAYOFFS							
Season	Club	League	GP	G	A	Pts	AG	AA	APts	PIM	PP	SH	GW	S	%	TGF	PGF	TGA	PGA	+/–	GP	G	A	Pts	PIM	PP	SH	GW
1992-93	Niagara Scenics	NAJHL	50	36	41	77	....	....	....	134	....	....	....	....	....	....	....	....	....	....	....	....	....	....	....	....	....	....
1993-94	Michigan State Spartans	CCHA	35	4	3	7	....	....	....	46	....	....	....	....	....	....	....	....	....	....	....	....	....	....	....	....	....	....
1994-95	Michigan State Spartans	CCHA	39	9	18	27	....	....	....	81	....	....	....	....	....	....	....	....	....	....	....	....	....	....	....	....	....	....
1995-96	Michigan State Spartans	CCHA	41	12	17	29	....	....	....	120	....	....	....	....	....	....	....	....	....	....	....	....	....	....	....	....	....	....
1996-97	Michigan State Spartans	CCHA	39	14	18	32	....	....	....	120	....	....	....	....	....	....	....	....	....	....	....	....	....	....	....	....	....	....
1997-98	Kentucky Thoroughblades	AHL	35	9	14	23	....	....	....	83	....	....	....	....	....	....	....	....	....	....	....	....	....	....	....	....	....	....
	Mighty Ducks of Anaheim	**NHL**	**1**	**0**	**0**	**0**	**0**	**0**	**0**	**2**	**0**	**0**	**0**	**0**	**0.0**	**0**	**0**	**2**	**0**	**–2**	....	....	....	....	....	....	....	....
	Cincinnati Mighty Ducks	AHL	13	3	3	6	....	....	....	6	....	....	....	....	....	....	....	....	....	....	....	....	....	....	....	....	....	....
1998-99	Cincinnati Mighty Ducks	AHL	50	4	10	14	....	....	....	55	....	....	....	....	....	....	....	....	....	....	....	....	....	....	....	....	....	....
	Cleveland Lumberjacks	IHL	15	2	4	6	....	....	....	22	....	....	....	....	....	....	....	....	....	....	....	....	....	....	....	....	....	....
99-2000	Cincinnati Mighty Ducks	AHL	15	0	3	3	....	....	....	8	....	....	....	....	....	....	....	....	....	....	....	....	....	....	....	....	....	....
	Huntington Blizzard	ECHL	20	6	13	19	....	....	....	43	....	....	....	....	....	....	....	....	....	....	....	....	....	....	....	....	....	....
	Hartford Wolf Pack	AHL	32	3	8	11	....	....	....	41	....	....	....	....	....	....	....	....	....	....	19	2	2	4	16	....	....	....
	NHL Totals		**1**	**0**	**0**	**0**	**0**	**0**	**0**	**2**	**0**	**0**	**0**	**0**	**0.0**	**0**	**0**	**2**	**0**		....	....	....	....	....	....	....	....

Rights transferred to **Colorado** after **Quebec** franchise relocated, June 21, 1995. Signed as a free agent by **NY Islanders**, April 26, 1997. Traded to **Anaheim** by **NY Islanders** with Travis Green and Doug Houda for Joe Sacco, J.J. Daigneault and Mark Janssens, February 6, 1998.

• TVERDOVSKY, Oleg

D – L. 6', 195 lbs. b: Donetsk, USSR, 5/18/1976. Anaheim's 1st, 2nd overall, in 1994.

Season	Club	League	GP	G	A	Pts	AG	AA	APts	PIM	PP	SH	GW	S	%	TGF	PGF	TGA	PGA	+/–	GP	G	A	Pts	PIM	PP	SH	GW
1992-93	Krylja Sovetov Moscow	CIS	21	0	1	1	....	....	....	6	....	....	....	....	....	....	....	....	....	....	6	0	0	0	0	....	....	....
	Russia	EJC-A	6	1	2	3	....	....	....	0	....	....	....	....	....	....	....	....	....	....	....	....	....	....	....	....	....	....
1993-94	Krylja Sovetov Moscow	CIS	46	4	10	14	....	....	....	22	....	....	....	....	....	....	....	....	....	....	3	1	0	1	2	....	....	....
	Russia	WJC-A	7	1	5	6	....	....	....	6	....	....	....	....	....	....	....	....	....	....	....	....	....	....	....	....	....	....
	Russia	EJC-A	5	1	9	10	....	....	....	22	....	....	....	....	....	....	....	....	....	....	....	....	....	....	....	....	....	....
1994-95	Brandon Wheat Kings	WHL	7	1	4	5	....	....	....	4	....	....	....	....	....	....	....	....	....	....	....	....	....	....	....	....	....	....
	Mighty Ducks of Anaheim	**NHL**	**36**	**3**	**9**	**12**	**5**	**13**	**18**	**14**	**1**	**1**	**0**	**26**	**11.5**	**32**	**7**	**35**	**4**	**–6**	....	....	....	....	....	....	....	....
1995-96	**Mighty Ducks of Anaheim**	**NHL**	**51**	**7**	**15**	**22**	**7**	**12**	**19**	**35**	**2**	**0**	**0**	**84**	**8.3**	**50**	**10**	**43**	**3**	**0**	....	....	....	....	....	....	....	....
	Winnipeg Jets	**NHL**	**31**	**0**	**8**	**8**	**0**	**7**	**7**	**6**	**0**	**0**	**0**	**35**	**0.0**	**25**	**8**	**26**	**2**	**–7**	**6**	**0**	**1**	**1**	**0**	**0**	**0**	**0**
	Russia	WC-A	3	0	1	1	....	....	....	0	....	....	....	....	....	....	....	....	....	....	....	....	....	....	....	....	....	....
1996-97	Russia	W-Cup	4	1	0	1	....	....	....	0	....	....	....	....	....	....	....	....	....	....	....	....	....	....	....	....	....	....
	Phoenix Coyotes	**NHL**	**82**	**10**	**45**	**55**	**11**	**40**	**51**	**30**	**3**	**1**	**2**	**144**	**6.9**	**121**	**46**	**96**	**16**	**–5**	**7**	**0**	**1**	**1**	**0**	**0**	**0**	**0**
1997-98	Hamilton Bulldogs	AHL	9	8	6	14	....	....	....	2	....	....	....	....	....	....	....	....	....	....	....	....	....	....	....	....	....	....
	Phoenix Coyotes	**NHL**	**46**	**7**	**12**	**19**	**8**	**12**	**20**	**12**	**4**	**0**	**1**	**83**	**8.4**	**50**	**21**	**31**	**3**	**1**	**6**	**0**	**7**	**7**	**0**	**0**	**0**	**0**
1998-99	**Phoenix Coyotes**	**NHL**	**82**	**7**	**18**	**25**	**8**	**17**	**25**	**32**	**2**	**0**	**2**	**117**	**6.0**	**80**	**13**	**68**	**12**	**11**	**6**	**0**	**2**	**2**	**6**	**0**	**0**	**0**
99-2000	**Mighty Ducks of Anaheim**	**NHL**	**82**	**15**	**36**	**51**	**17**	**33**	**50**	**30**	**5**	**0**	**5**	**153**	**9.8**	**121**	**40**	**90**	**14**	**5**	....	....	....	....	....	....	....	....
	NHL Totals		**410**	**49**	**143**	**192**	**56**	**134**	**190**	**159**	**17**	**2**	**10**	**642**	**7.6**	**479**	**145**	**389**	**54**		**25**	**0**	**11**	**11**	**6**	**0**	**0**	**0**

EJC-A All-Star Team (1994) • Played in NHL All-Star Game (1997)

Traded to **Winnipeg** by **Anaheim** with Chad Kilger and Anaheim's 3rd round choice (Per-Anton Lundstrom) in 1996 Entry Draft for Teemu Selanne, Marc Chouinard and Winnipeg's 4th round choice (later traded to Toronto — later traded to Montreal — Montreal selected Kim Staal) in 1996 Entry Draft, February 7, 1996. Transferred to **Phoenix** after **Winnipeg** franchise relocated, July 1, 1996. Traded to **Anaheim** by **Phoenix** for Travis Green and Anaheim's 1st round choice (Scott Kelman) in 1999 Entry Draft, June 26, 1999.

• TWIST, Tony

Anthony LW – L. 6'1", 220 lbs. b: Sherwood Park, Alta., 5/9/1968. St. Louis' 9th, 177th overall, in 1988.

Season	Club	League	GP	G	A	Pts	AG	AA	APts	PIM	PP	SH	GW	S	%	TGF	PGF	TGA	PGA	+/–	GP	G	A	Pts	PIM	PP	SH	GW
1984-85	Prince George Kings	BCAHA	STATISTICS NOT AVAILABLE																									
1985-86	Prince George Spruce Kings	BCJHL	42	32	20	52	....	....	....	162	....	....	....	....	....	....	....	....	....	....	....	....	....	....	....	....	....	....
1986-87	Saskatoon Blades	WHL	64	0	8	8	....	....	....	181	....	....	....	....	....	....	....	....	....	....	....	....	....	....	....	....	....	....
1987-88	Saskatoon Blades	WHL	55	1	8	9	....	....	....	226	....	....	....	....	....	....	....	....	....	....	10	1	1	2	6	....	....	....
1988-89	Peoria Rivermen	IHL	67	3	8	11	....	....	....	312	....	....	....	....	....	....	....	....	....	....	....	....	....	....	....	....	....	....
1989-90	**St. Louis Blues**	**NHL**	**28**	**0**	**0**	**0**	**0**	**0**	**0**	**124**	**0**	**0**	**0**	**2**	**0.0**	**3**	**0**	**5**	**0**	**–2**	....	....	....	....	....	....	....	....
	Peoria Rivermen	IHL	36	1	5	6	....	....	....	200	....	....	....	....	....	....	....	....	....	....	5	0	1	1	8	....	....	....
1990-91	Peoria Rivermen	IHL	38	2	10	12	....	....	....	244	....	....	....	....	....	....	....	....	....	....	....	....	....	....	....	....	....	....
	Quebec Nordiques	**NHL**	**24**	**0**	**0**	**0**	**0**	**0**	**0**	**104**	**0**	**0**	**0**	**2**	**0.0**	**1**	**0**	**5**	**0**	**–4**	....	....	....	....	....	....	....	....
1991-92	**Quebec Nordiques**	**NHL**	**44**	**0**	**1**	**1**	**0**	**1**	**1**	**164**	**0**	**0**	**0**	**9**	**0.0**	**4**	**0**	**7**	**0**	**–3**	....	....	....	....	....	....	....	....
1992-93	**Quebec Nordiques**	**NHL**	**34**	**0**	**2**	**2**	**0**	**1**	**1**	**64**	**0**	**0**	**0**	**14**	**0.0**	**4**	**0**	**4**	**0**	**0**	....	....	....	....	....	....	....	....
1993-94	**Quebec Nordiques**	**NHL**	**49**	**0**	**4**	**4**	**0**	**3**	**3**	**101**	**0**	**0**	**0**	**15**	**0.0**	**8**	**0**	**9**	**0**	**–1**	....	....	....	....	....	....	....	....
1994-95	**St. Louis Blues**	**NHL**	**28**	**3**	**0**	**3**	**5**	**0**	**5**	**89**	**0**	**0**	**1**	**8**	**37.5**	**5**	**0**	**5**	**0**	**0**	**1**	**0**	**0**	**0**	**6**	**0**	**0**	**0**
1995-96	**St. Louis Blues**	**NHL**	**51**	**3**	**2**	**5**	**3**	**2**	**5**	**100**	**0**	**0**	**1**	**12**	**25.0**	**8**	**0**	**9**	**0**	**–1**	**10**	**1**	**1**	**2**	**16**	**0**	**0**	**0**
1996-97	**St. Louis Blues**	**NHL**	**64**	**1**	**2**	**3**	**1**	**2**	**3**	**121**	**0**	**0**	**0**	**21**	**4.8**	**7**	**0**	**15**	**0**	**–8**	**6**	**0**	**0**	**0**	**0**	**0**	**0**	**0**
1997-98	**St. Louis Blues**	**NHL**	**60**	**1**	**1**	**2**	**1**	**1**	**2**	**105**	**0**	**0**	**0**	**17**	**5.9**	**7**	**1**	**11**	**1**	**–4**	....	....	....	....	....	....	....	....
1998-99	**St. Louis Blues**	**NHL**	**63**	**2**	**6**	**8**	**2**	**6**	**8**	**149**	**0**	**0**	**0**	**23**	**8.7**	**13**	**0**	**13**	**0**	**0**	**1**	**0**	**0**	**0**	**0**	**0**	**0**	**0**
99-2000	**St. Louis Blues**	**NHL**	DID NOT PLAY – INJURED																									
	NHL Totals		**445**	**10**	**18**	**28**	**12**	**16**	**28**	**1121**	**0**	**0**	**2**	**123**	**8.1**	**60**	**1**	**83**	**1**		**18**	**1**	**1**	**2**	**22**	**0**	**0**	**0**

Traded to **Quebec** by **St. Louis** with Herb Raglan and Andy Rymsha for Darin Kimble, February 4, 1991. Signed as a free agent by **St. Louis**, August 16, 1994. • Missed entire 1999-2000 season recovering from injuries suffered in motorcycle accident, July, 1999.

• UBRIACO, Gene

Eugene Stephen LW/C – L. 5'8", 157 lbs. b: Sault Ste. Marie, Ont., 12/26/1937.

Season	Club	League	GP	G	A	Pts	AG	AA	APts	PIM	PP	SH	GW	S	%	TGF	PGF	TGA	PGA	+/–	GP	G	A	Pts	PIM	PP	SH	GW
1954-55	St. Michael's Majors	OHA-Jr.	28	2	5	7	....	....	....	14	....	....	....	....	....	....	....	....	....	....	4	1	1	2	0	....	....	....
1955-56	St. Michael's Majors	OHA-Jr.	48	26	16	42	....	....	....	44	....	....	....	....	....	....	....	....	....	....	8	3	4	7	6	....	....	....
1956-57	St. Michael's Majors	OHA-Jr.	52	22	32	54	....	....	....	49	....	....	....	....	....	....	....	....	....	....	4	1	3	4	0	....	....	....
1957-58	St. Michael's Majors	OHA-Jr.	39	19	18	37	....	....	....	43	....	....	....	....	....	....	....	....	....	....	9	10	6	16	4	....	....	....
	Kitchener Dutchman	Al-Cup	2	0	1	1	....	....	....	0	....	....	....	....	....	....	....	....	....	....	....	....	....	....	....	....	....	....
1958-59	New Westminster Royals	WHL	63	19	19	38	....	....	....	33	....	....	....	....	....	....	....	....	....	....	....	....	....	....	....	....	....	....
1959-60	Sudbury Wolves	EPHL	70	30	32	62	....	....	....	40	....	....	....	....	....	....	....	....	....	....	14	2	4	6	12	....	....	....
1960-61	Sudbury Wolves	EPHL	24	4	12	16	....	....	....	27	....	....	....	....	....	....	....	....	....	....	....	....	....	....	....	....	....	....
	Rochester Americans	AHL	60	16	24	40	....	....	....	15	....	....	....	....	....	....	....	....	....	....	....	....	....	....	....	....	....	....
1961-62	Pittsburgh Hornets	AHL	44	13	12	25	....	....	....	14	....	....	....	....	....	....	....	....	....	....	....	....	....	....	....	....	....	....
1962-63	Rochester Americans	AHL	72	22	48	70	....	....	....	21	....	....	....	....	....	....	....	....	....	....	2	1	0	1	0	....	....	....
1963-64	Hershey Bears	AHL	72	13	45	58	....	....	....	36	....	....	....	....	....	....	....	....	....	....	6	5	3	8	2	....	....	....
1964-65	Hershey Bears	AHL	63	15	32	47	....	....	....	12	....	....	....	....	....	....	....	....	....	....	15	3	6	9	0	....	....	....
1965-66	Hershey Bears	AHL	72	42	44	86	....	....	....	18	....	....	....	....	....	....	....	....	....	....	3	1	1	2	0	....	....	....
1966-67	Hershey Bears	AHL	69	38	43	81	....	....	....	50	....	....	....	....	....	....	....	....	....	....	5	3	0	3	2	....	....	....
1967-68	**Pittsburgh Penguins**	**NHL**	**65**	**18**	**15**	**33**	**21**	**15**	**36**	**16**	**3**	**0**	**3**	**119**	**15.1**	**39**	**12**	**40**	**0**	**–13**	....	....	....	....	....	....	....	....
	Baltimore Clippers	AHL	6	1	4	5	....	....	....	6	....	....	....	....	....	....	....	....	....	....	....	....	....	....	....	....	....	....
1968-69	**Pittsburgh Penguins**	**NHL**	**49**	**15**	**11**	**26**	**16**	**10**	**26**	**14**	**4**	**0**	**2**	**100**	**15.0**	**38**	**11**	**27**	**0**	**0**	....	....	....	....	....	....	....	....
	Oakland Seals	**NHL**	**26**	**4**	**7**	**11**	**4**	**6**	**10**	**14**	**1**	**0**	**0**	**39**	**10.3**	**18**	**6**	**18**	**1**	**–5**	**7**	**2**	**0**	**2**	**2**	**0**	**0**	**0**
1969-70	**Oakland Seals**	**NHL**	**16**	**1**	**1**	**2**	**1**	**1**	**2**	**4**	**0**	**0**	**0**	**13**	**7.7**	**2**	**0**	**3**	**0**	**–1**	....	....	....	....	....	....	....	....
	Providence Reds	AHL	8	2	6	8	....	....	....	8	....	....	....	....	....	....	....	....	....	....	....	....	....	....	....	....	....	....
	Chicago Black Hawks	**NHL**	**21**	**1**	**1**	**2**	**1**	**1**	**2**	**2**	**0**	**0**	**0**	**7**	**14.3**	**2**	**1**	**2**	**0**	**–1**	**4**	**0**	**0**	**0**	**2**	**0**	**0**	**0**
	NHL Totals		**177**	**39**	**35**	**74**	**43**	**33**	**76**	**50**	**8**	**0**	**5**	**278**	**14.0**	**99**	**30**	**90**	**1**		**11**	**2**	**0**	**2**	**4**	**0**	**0**	**0**

AHL Second All-Star Team (1966)

Traded to **Hershey** (AHL) by **Toronto** with future considerations (Bruce Draper, September, 1964) for Les Duff, September, 1963. Traded to **Pittsburgh** by **Hershey** (AHL) for Jeannot Gilbert, October, 1967. Traded to **Oakland** by **Pittsburgh** with Earl Ingarfield and Dick Mattiussi for Bryan Watson, George Swarbrick and Tracy Pratt, January 30, 1969. Traded to **Chicago** by **Oakland** for Howie Menard, December 15, 1969.

• ULANOV, Igor

Igor S. D – L. 6'3", 211 lbs. b: Krasnokamsk, USSR, 10/1/1969. Winnipeg's 8th, 203rd overall, in 1991.

Season	Club	League	GP	G	A	Pts	AG	AA	APts	PIM	PP	SH	GW	S	%	TGF	PGF	TGA	PGA	+/–	GP	G	A	Pts	PIM	PP	SH	GW
1985-1988	Molot Perm	USSR-2	STATISTICS NOT AVAILABLE																									
1988-1990	SKA Sverdlovsk	USSR-2	STATISTICS NOT AVAILABLE																									
1990-91	Khimik Voskresensk	Fr-Tour	1	0	0	0	....	....	....	2	....	....	....	....	....	....	....	....	....	....	....	....	....	....	....	....	....	....
	Khimik Voskresensk	USSR	41	2	2	4	....	....	....	52	....	....	....	....	....	....	....	....	....	....	....	....	....	....	....	....	....	....
	Khimik Voskresensk	Super-S	6	0	1	1	....	....	....	6	....	....	....	....	....	....	....	....	....	....	....	....	....	....	....	....	....	....

Season	Club	League	GP	G	A	Pts	AG	AA	APts	PIM	PP	SH	GW	S	%	TGF	PGF	TGA	PGA	+/–	GP	G	A	Pts	PIM	PP	SH	GW
			REGULAR SEASON																		PLAYOFFS							
1991-92	Khimik Voskresensk	CIS	27	1	4	5	....	....	....	24	....	....	....	....	....	....	....	....	....	....	....	....	....	....	....	....	....	....
	Winnipeg Jets	**NHL**	**27**	**2**	**9**	**11**	**2**	**7**	**9**	**67**	**0**	**0**	**0**	**23**	**8.7**	**23**	**0**	**21**	**3**	**5**	**7**	**0**	**0**	**0**	**39**	**0**	**0**	**0**
	Moncton Hawks	AHL	3	0	1	1	....	....	....	16	....	....	....	....	....	....	....	....	....	....	....	....	....	....	....	....	....	....
1992-93	**Winnipeg Jets**	**NHL**	**56**	**2**	**14**	**16**	**2**	**10**	**12**	**124**	**0**	**0**	**0**	**26**	**7.7**	**62**	**1**	**65**	**10**	**6**	**4**	**0**	**0**	**0**	**4**	**0**	**0**	**0**
	Moncton Hawks	AHL	9	1	3	4	....	....	....	26	....	....	....	....	....	....	....	....	....	....	....	....	....	....	....	....	....	....
	Fort Wayne Komets	IHL	3	0	1	1	....	....	....	29	....	....	....	....	....	....	....	....	....	....	....	....	....	....	....	....	....	....
1993-94	**Winnipeg Jets**	**NHL**	**74**	**0**	**17**	**17**	**0**	**13**	**13**	**165**	**0**	**0**	**0**	**46**	**0.0**	**55**	**3**	**83**	**20**	**–11**	....	....	....	....	....	....	....	....
	Russia	WC-A	6	1	0	1	....	....	....	20	....	....	....	....	....	....	....	....	....	....	....	....	....	....	....	....	....	....
1994-95	**Winnipeg Jets**	**NHL**	**19**	**1**	**3**	**4**	**2**	**4**	**6**	**27**	**0**	**0**	**0**	**13**	**7.7**	**10**	**0**	**17**	**5**	**–2**	....	....	....	....	....	....	....	....
	Washington Capitals	**NHL**	**3**	**0**	**1**	**1**	**0**	**1**	**1**	**2**	**0**	**0**	**0**	**0**	**0.0**	**4**	**0**	**1**	**0**	**3**	**2**	**0**	**0**	**0**	**4**	**0**	**0**	**0**
1995-96	**Chicago Blackhawks**	**NHL**	**53**	**1**	**8**	**9**	**1**	**7**	**8**	**92**	**0**	**0**	**0**	**24**	**4.2**	**31**	**0**	**22**	**3**	**12**	....	....	....	....	....	....	....	....
	Indianapolis Ice	IHL	1	0	0	0	....	....	....	0	....	....	....	....	....	....	....	....	....	....	....	....	....	....	....	....	....	....
	Tampa Bay Lightning	**NHL**	**11**	**2**	**1**	**3**	**2**	**1**	**3**	**24**	**0**	**0**	**1**	**13**	**15.4**	**9**	**0**	**11**	**1**	**–1**	**5**	**0**	**0**	**0**	**15**	**0**	**0**	**0**
1996-97	Russia	W-Cup	1	0	0	0	....	....	....	4	....	....	....	....	....	....	....	....	....	....	....	....	....	....	....	....	....	....
	Tampa Bay Lightning	**NHL**	**59**	**1**	**7**	**8**	**1**	**6**	**7**	**108**	**0**	**0**	**0**	**56**	**1.8**	**37**	**2**	**46**	**13**	**2**	....	....	....	....	....	....	....	....
1997-98	**Tampa Bay Lightning**	**NHL**	**45**	**2**	**7**	**9**	**2**	**7**	**9**	**85**	**1**	**0**	**0**	**32**	**6.3**	**26**	**2**	**43**	**14**	**–5**	....	....	....	....	....	....	....	....
	Montreal Canadiens	**NHL**	**4**	**0**	**1**	**1**	**0**	**1**	**1**	**12**	**0**	**0**	**0**	**4**	**0.0**	**1**	**0**	**5**	**2**	**–2**	**10**	**1**	**4**	**5**	**12**	**0**	**0**	**0**
1998-99	**Montreal Canadiens**	**NHL**	**76**	**3**	**9**	**12**	**4**	**9**	**13**	**109**	**0**	**0**	**0**	**55**	**5.5**	**38**	**1**	**55**	**15**	**–3**	....	....	....	....	....	....	....	....
99-2000	**Montreal Canadiens**	**NHL**	**43**	**1**	**5**	**6**	**1**	**5**	**6**	**76**	**0**	**0**	**0**	**33**	**3.0**	**17**	**0**	**35**	**7**	**–11**	....	....	....	....	....	....	....	....
	Edmonton Oilers	**NHL**	**14**	**0**	**3**	**3**	**0**	**3**	**3**	**10**	**0**	**0**	**0**	**6**	**0.0**	**7**	**2**	**9**	**1**	**–3**	**5**	**0**	**0**	**0**	**6**	**0**	**0**	**0**
	NHL Totals		**484**	**15**	**85**	**100**	**17**	**74**	**91**	**901**	**1**	**0**	**1**	**331**	**4.5**	**320**	**11**	**413**	**94**		**33**	**1**	**4**	**5**	**80**	**0**	**0**	**0**

Traded to **Washington** by **Winnipeg** with Mike Eagles for Washington's 3rd (later traded to Dallas — Dallas selected Sergei Gusev) and 5th (Brian Elder) round choices in 1995 Entry Draft, April 7, 1995. Traded to **Chicago** by **Washington** for Chicago's 3rd round choice (Dave Weninger) in 1996 Entry Draft, October 17, 1995. Traded to **Tampa Bay** by **Chicago** with Patrick Poulin and Chicago's 2nd round choice (later traded to New Jersey — New Jersey selected Pierre Dagenais) in 1996 Entry Draft for Enrico Ciccone and Tampa Bay's 2nd round choice (Jeff Paul) in 1996 Entry Draft, March 20, 1996. Traded to **Montreal** by **Tampa Bay** with Patrick Poulin and Mick Vukota for Stephane Richer, Darcy Tucker and David Wilkie, January 15, 1998. Traded to **Edmonton** by **Montreal** with Alain Nasreddine for Christian Laflamme and Matthieu Descoteaux, March 9, 2000.

• ULLMAN, Norm

Norman Victor Alexander C – L. 5'10", 175 lbs. b: Provost, Alta., 12/26/1935. **HHOF**

Season	Club	League	GP	G	A	Pts	AG	AA	APts	PIM	PP	SH	GW	S	%	TGF	PGF	TGA	PGA	+/–	GP	G	A	Pts	PIM	PP	SH	GW
1951-52	Edmonton Oil Kings	WCJHL	1	1	0	1	....	....	....	0	....	....	....	....	....	....	....	....	....	....	1	0	0	0	0	....	....	....
1952-53	Edmonton Oil Kings	WCJHL	36	29	*47	*76	....	....	....	4	....	....	....	....	....	....	....	....	....	....	13	4	6	10	0	....	....	....
1953-54	Edmonton Oil Kings	WCJHL	36	56	45	101	....	....	....	17	....	....	....	....	....	....	....	....	....	....	10	11	*26	*37	0	....	....	....
	Edmonton Flyers	WHL	1	1	0	1	....	....	....	0	....	....	....	....	....	....	....	....	....	....	....	....	....	....	....	....	....	....
	Edmonton Oil Kings	Mem-Cup	14	12	18	30	....	....	....	14	....	....	....	....	....	....	....	....	....	....	....	....	....	....	....	....	....	....
1954-55	Edmonton Flyers	WHL	60	25	34	59	....	....	....	23	....	....	....	....	....	....	....	....	....	....	9	3	1	4	6	....	....	....
1955-56	**Detroit Red Wings**	**NHL**	**66**	**9**	**9**	**18**	**12**	**11**	**23**	**26**	....	....	....	....	....	....	....	....	....	....	**10**	**1**	**3**	**4**	**13**	....	....	....
1956-57	**Detroit Red Wings**	**NHL**	**64**	**16**	**36**	**52**	**21**	**40**	**61**	**47**	....	....	....	....	....	....	....	....	....	....	**5**	**1**	**1**	**2**	**6**	....	....	....
1957-58	**Detroit Red Wings**	**NHL**	**69**	**23**	**28**	**51**	**29**	**29**	**58**	**38**	....	....	....	....	....	....	....	....	....	....	**4**	**0**	**2**	**2**	**4**	....	....	....
1958-59	**Detroit Red Wings**	**NHL**	**69**	**22**	**36**	**58**	**26**	**37**	**63**	**42**	....	....	....	....	....	....	....	....	....	....	....	....	....	....	....	....	....	....
1959-60	**Detroit Red Wings**	**NHL**	**70**	**24**	**34**	**58**	**28**	**33**	**61**	**46**	....	....	....	....	....	....	....	....	....	....	**6**	**2**	**2**	**4**	**0**	....	....	....
1960-61	**Detroit Red Wings**	**NHL**	**70**	**28**	**42**	**70**	**32**	**41**	**73**	**34**	....	....	....	....	....	....	....	....	....	....	**11**	**0**	**4**	**4**	**4**	....	....	....
1961-62	**Detroit Red Wings**	**NHL**	**70**	**26**	**38**	**64**	**30**	**37**	**67**	**54**	....	....	....	....	....	....	....	....	....	....	....	....	....	....	....	....	....	....
1962-63	**Detroit Red Wings**	**NHL**	**70**	**26**	**30**	**56**	**30**	**30**	**60**	**53**	....	....	....	....	....	....	....	....	....	....	**11**	**4**	***12**	***16**	**14**	....	....	....
1963-64	**Detroit Red Wings**	**NHL**	**61**	**21**	**30**	**51**	**26**	**32**	**58**	**55**	....	....	....	....	....	....	....	....	....	....	**14**	**7**	**10**	**17**	**6**	....	....	....
1964-65	**Detroit Red Wings**	**NHL**	**70**	***42**	**41**	**83**	**51**	**42**	**93**	**70**	....	....	....	....	....	....	....	....	....	....	**7**	**6**	**4**	**10**	**2**	....	....	....
1965-66	**Detroit Red Wings**	**NHL**	**70**	**31**	**41**	**72**	**36**	**39**	**75**	**35**	....	....	....	....	....	....	....	....	....	....	**12**	***6**	**9**	***15**	**12**	....	....	....
1966-67	**Detroit Red Wings**	**NHL**	**68**	**26**	**44**	**70**	**30**	**43**	**73**	**26**	....	....	....	....	....	....	....	....	....	....	....	....	....	....	....	....	....	....
1967-68	**Detroit Red Wings**	**NHL**	**58**	**30**	**25**	**55**	**35**	**25**	**60**	**26**	**7**	**0**	**4**	**189**	**15.9**	**68**	**16**	**77**	**12**	**–13**	....	....	....	....	....	....	....	....
	Toronto Maple Leafs	**NHL**	**13**	**5**	**12**	**17**	**6**	**12**	**18**	**2**	**1**	**0**	**0**	**39**	**12.8**	**21**	**2**	**7**	**0**	**12**	....	....	....	....	....	....	....	....
1968-69	**Toronto Maple Leafs**	**NHL**	**75**	**35**	**42**	**77**	**37**	**38**	**75**	**41**	**13**	**0**	**2**	**247**	**14.2**	**99**	**26**	**55**	**1**	**19**	**4**	**1**	**0**	**1**	**0**	**0**	**0**	**0**
1969-70	**Toronto Maple Leafs**	**NHL**	**74**	**18**	**42**	**60**	**20**	**39**	**59**	**37**	**4**	**1**	**0**	**207**	**8.7**	**90**	**20**	**55**	**5**	**20**	....	....	....	....	....	....	....	....
1970-71	**Toronto Maple Leafs**	**NHL**	**73**	**34**	**51**	**85**	**34**	**43**	**77**	**24**	**11**	**1**	**4**	**226**	**15.0**	**104**	**29**	**66**	**5**	**14**	**6**	**0**	**2**	**2**	**2**	**0**	**0**	**0**
1971-72	**Toronto Maple Leafs**	**NHL**	**77**	**23**	**50**	**73**	**23**	**43**	**66**	**26**	**9**	**0**	**1**	**204**	**11.3**	**97**	**31**	**64**	**6**	**8**	**5**	**1**	**3**	**4**	**2**	**0**	**0**	**0**
1972-73	**Toronto Maple Leafs**	**NHL**	**65**	**20**	**35**	**55**	**19**	**28**	**47**	**10**	**3**	**0**	**1**	**174**	**11.5**	**77**	**14**	**85**	**4**	**–18**	....	....	....	....	....	....	....	....
1973-74	**Toronto Maple Leafs**	**NHL**	**78**	**22**	**47**	**69**	**21**	**39**	**60**	**12**	**4**	**0**	**2**	**178**	**12.4**	**86**	**17**	**59**	**0**	**10**	**4**	**1**	**1**	**2**	**0**	**0**	**0**	**0**
1974-75	**Toronto Maple Leafs**	**NHL**	**80**	**9**	**26**	**35**	**8**	**19**	**27**	**8**	**1**	**0**	**0**	**117**	**7.7**	**54**	**13**	**62**	**9**	**–12**	**7**	**0**	**0**	**0**	**2**	**0**	**0**	**0**
1975-76	Edmonton Oilers	WHA	77	31	56	87	....	....	....	12	....	....	....	....	....	....	....	....	....	....	4	1	3	4	2	....	....	....
1976-77	Edmonton Oilers	WHA	67	16	27	43	....	....	....	28	....	....	....	....	....	....	....	....	....	....	5	0	3	3	0	....	....	....
	NHL Totals		**1410**	**490**	**739**	**1229**	**554**	**700**	**1254**	**712**	....	....	....	....	....	....	....	....	....	....	**106**	**30**	**53**	**83**	**67**	....	....	....
	Other Major League Totals		144	47	83	130				40	....	....	....	....	....	....	....	....	....	....	9	1	6	7	2	....	....	....

NHL First All-Star Team (1965) • NHL Second All-Star Team (1967) • Played in NHL All-Star Game (1955, 1960, 1961, 1962, 1963, 1964, 1965, 1967, 1968, 1969, 1974)

Traded to **Toronto** by **Detroit** with Floyd Smith, Paul Henderson and Doug Barrie for Frank Mahovlich, Pete Stemkowski, Garry Unger and the rights to Carl Brewer, March 3, 1968. Selected by **Edmonton** (WHA) in 1972 General Player Draft, February 12, 1972.

• UNGER, Garry

Garry Douglas "Iron Man" C – L. 5'11", 170 lbs. b: Calgary, Alta., 12/7/1947.

Season	Club	League	GP	G	A	Pts	AG	AA	APts	PIM	PP	SH	GW	S	%	TGF	PGF	TGA	PGA	+/–	GP	G	A	Pts	PIM	PP	SH	GW
1964-1966	Calgary Buffaloes	AJHL	STATISTICS NOT AVAILABLE																									
1966-67	London Nationals	OHA-Jr.	48	38	35	73	....	....	....	60	....	....	....	....	....	....	....	....	....	....	6	2	5	7	27	....	....	....
	Rochester Americans	AHL	1	0	0	0	....	....	....	0	....	....	....	....	....	....	....	....	....	....	1	0	0	0	0	....	....	....
	Tulsa Oilers	CPHL	2	2	0	2	....	....	....	2	....	....	....	....	....	....	....	....	....	....	....	....	....	....	....	....	....	....
1967-68	London Nationals	OHA-Jr.	2	4	1	5	....	....	....	2	....	....	....	....	....	....	....	....	....	....	....	....	....	....	....	....	....	....
	Toronto Maple Leafs	**NHL**	**15**	**1**	**1**	**2**	**1**	**1**	**2**	**4**	**0**	**0**	**0**	**15**	**6.7**	**3**	**1**	**7**	**0**	**–5**	....	....	....	....	....	....	....	....
	Tulsa Oilers	CPHL	9	3	5	8	....	....	....	6	....	....	....	....	....	....	....	....	....	....	....	....	....	....	....	....	....	....
	Rochester Americans	AHL	5	1	3	4	....	....	....	6	....	....	....	....	....	....	....	....	....	....	....	....	....	....	....	....	....	....
	Detroit Red Wings	**NHL**	**13**	**5**	**10**	**15**	**6**	**10**	**16**	**2**	**0**	**0**	**0**	**42**	**11.9**	**20**	**3**	**13**	**0**	**4**	....	....	....	....	....	....	....	....
1968-69	**Detroit Red Wings**	**NHL**	**76**	**24**	**20**	**44**	**25**	**18**	**43**	**33**	**5**	**1**	**4**	**186**	**12.9**	**71**	**20**	**48**	**3**	**6**	....	....	....	....	....	....	....	....
1969-70	**Detroit Red Wings**	**NHL**	**76**	**42**	**24**	**66**	**46**	**22**	**68**	**67**	**12**	**0**	**4**	**234**	**17.9**	**89**	**19**	**46**	**0**	**24**	**4**	**0**	**1**	**1**	**6**	**0**	**0**	**0**
1970-71	**Detroit Red Wings**	**NHL**	**51**	**13**	**14**	**27**	**13**	**12**	**25**	**63**	**0**	**0**	**1**	**157**	**8.3**	**35**	**6**	**64**	**3**	**–32**	....	....	....	....	....	....	....	....
	St. Louis Blues	**NHL**	**28**	**15**	**14**	**29**	**15**	**12**	**27**	**41**	**7**	**0**	**3**	**122**	**12.3**	**36**	**18**	**22**	**0**	**–4**	**6**	**3**	**2**	**5**	**20**	**0**	**1**	**0**
1971-72	**St. Louis Blues**	**NHL**	**78**	**36**	**34**	**70**	**36**	**29**	**65**	**104**	**14**	**1**	**4**	**321**	**11.2**	**96**	**28**	**83**	**7**	**–8**	**11**	**4**	**5**	**9**	**35**	**2**	**0**	**1**
1972-73	**St. Louis Blues**	**NHL**	**78**	**41**	**39**	**80**	**39**	**31**	**70**	**119**	**13**	**1**	**5**	**342**	**12.0**	**103**	**34**	**69**	**7**	**7**	**5**	**1**	**2**	**3**	**2**	**0**	**0**	**0**
1973-74	**St. Louis Blues**	**NHL**	**78**	**33**	**35**	**68**	**32**	**29**	**61**	**96**	**9**	**1**	**4**	**327**	**10.1**	**93**	**36**	**83**	**9**	**–17**	....	....	....	....	....	....	....	....
1974-75	**St. Louis Blues**	**NHL**	**80**	**36**	**44**	**80**	**32**	**33**	**65**	**123**	**10**	**0**	**8**	**349**	**10.3**	**100**	**34**	**83**	**16**	**–1**	**2**	**1**	**3**	**4**	**6**	**0**	**0**	**0**
1975-76	**St. Louis Blues**	**NHL**	**80**	**39**	**44**	**83**	**34**	**33**	**67**	**95**	**13**	**0**	**3**	**357**	**10.9**	**110**	**43**	**79**	**13**	**1**	**3**	**2**	**1**	**3**	**7**	**0**	**0**	**0**
1976-77	**St. Louis Blues**	**NHL**	**80**	**30**	**27**	**57**	**27**	**21**	**48**	**56**	**7**	**0**	**5**	**235**	**12.8**	**85**	**33**	**66**	**2**	**–12**	**4**	**0**	**1**	**1**	**2**	**0**	**0**	**0**
1977-78	**St. Louis Blues**	**NHL**	**80**	**32**	**20**	**52**	**29**	**15**	**44**	**66**	**10**	**0**	**5**	**238**	**13.4**	**69**	**25**	**82**	**3**	**–35**	....	....	....	....	....	....	....	....
	Canada	WEC-A	10	0	0	0	....	....	....	30	....	....	....	....	....	....	....	....	....	....	....	....	....	....	....	....	....	....
1978-79	**St. Louis Blues**	**NHL**	**80**	**30**	**26**	**56**	**26**	**19**	**45**	**44**	**3**	**0**	**3**	**182**	**16.5**	**84**	**19**	**113**	**4**	**–44**	....	....	....	....	....	....	....	....
	Canada	WEC-A	7	2	1	3	....	....	....	12	....	....	....	....	....	....	....	....	....	....	....	....	....	....	....	....	....	....
1979-80	**Atlanta Flames**	**NHL**	**79**	**17**	**16**	**33**	**14**	**12**	**26**	**39**	**1**	**0**	**3**	**170**	**10.0**	**55**	**9**	**51**	**7**	**2**	**4**	**0**	**3**	**3**	**2**	**0**	**0**	**0**
1980-81	**Los Angeles Kings**	**NHL**	**58**	**10**	**10**	**20**	**8**	**7**	**15**	**40**	**1**	**0**	**0**	**67**	**14.9**	**29**	**3**	**43**	**0**	**–17**	....	....	....	....	....	....	....	....
	Edmonton Oilers	**NHL**	**13**	**0**	**0**	**0**	**0**	**0**	**0**	**6**	**0**	**0**	**0**	**13**	**0.0**	**1**	**1**	**9**	**0**	**–9**	**8**	**0**	**0**	**0**	**2**	**0**	**0**	**0**
1981-82	**Edmonton Oilers**	**NHL**	**46**	**7**	**13**	**20**	**6**	**9**	**15**	**69**	**0**	**0**	**2**	**62**	**11.3**	**32**	**4**	**30**	**10**	**8**	**4**	**1**	**0**	**1**	**23**	**0**	**0**	**0**
1982-83	**Edmonton Oilers**	**NHL**	**16**	**2**	**0**	**2**	**2**	**0**	**2**	**8**	**0**	**0**	**0**	**14**	**14.3**	**4**	**1**	**4**	**2**	**1**	**1**	**0**	**0**	**0**	**0**	**0**	**0**	**0**
	Moncton Alpines	AHL	8	2	3	5	....	....	....	0	....	....	....	....	....	....	....	....	....	....	....	....	....	....	....	....	....	....
1983-84			DID NOT PLAY																									
1984-85			DID NOT PLAY																									

			REGULAR SEASON																		PLAYOFFS							
Season	**Club**	**League**	**GP**	**G**	**A**	**Pts**	**AG**	**AA**	**APts**	**PIM**	**PP**	**SH**	**GW**	**S**	**%**	**TGF**	**PGF**	**TGA**	**PGA**	**+/–**	**GP**	**G**	**A**	**Pts**	**PIM**	**PP**	**SH**	**GW**
1985-86	Dundee Rockets	Britain	35	86	48	134	....	....	....	64	....	....	....	....	....	....	....	....	....	....	6	7	6	13	44	....	....	....
1986-87	Peterborough Pirates	Britain-2	30	95	*143	*238	....	....	....	58	....	....	....	....	....	....	....	....	....	....	8	17	15	32	38	....	....	....
1987-88	Peterborough Pirates	Britain	32	37	44	81	....	....	....	116	....	....	....	....	....	....	....	....	....	....	....	....	....	....	....	....	....	....
	NHL Totals		**1105**	**413**	**391**	**804**	**391**	**313**	**704**	**1075**	**105**	**4**	**54**	**3433**	**12.0**	**1115**	**337**	**995**	**86**		**52**	**12**	**18**	**30**	**105**	**2**	**1**	**1**

Played in NHL All-Star Game (1972, 1973, 1974, 1975, 1976, 1977, 1978)

Traded to **Detroit** by **Toronto** with Frank Mahovlich, Pete Stemkowski and rights to Carl Brewer for Norm Ullman, Paul Henderson, Floyd Smith and Doug Barrie, March 3, 1968. Traded to **St. Louis** by **Detroit** with Wayne Connelly for Red Berenson and Tim Eccelstone, February 6, 1971. Traded to **Atlanta** by **St. Louis** for Ed Kea, Don Laurence and Atlanta's 2nd round choice (Hakan Nordin) in 1981 Entry Draft, October 10, 1979. Transferred to **Calgary** after **Atlanta** franchise relocated, June 24, 1980. Traded to **LA Kings** by **Calgary** for Bert Wilson and Randy Holt, June 6, 1980. Traded to **Edmonton** by **LA Kings** for Edmonton's 7th round choice (Craig Hurley) in 1981 Entry Draft, March 10, 1981.

• USTORF, Stefan

C – L. 6′, 195 lbs. b: Kaufbeuren, Germany, 1/3/1974. Washington's 3rd, 53rd overall, in 1992.

Season	Club	League	GP	G	A	Pts	AG	AA	APts	PIM	PP	SH	GW	S	%	TGF	PGF	TGA	PGA	+/–	GP	G	A	Pts	PIM	PP	SH	GW
1989-90	ESV Kaufbeuren	German-Jr.	8	10	11	21	....	....	....	8	....	....	....	....	....	....	....	....	....	....	....	....	....	....	....	....	....	....
1990-91	ESV Kaufbeuren	German-Jr.	37	33	34	67	....	....	....	78	....	....	....	....	....	....	....	....	....	....	....	....	....	....	....	....	....	....
	Germany	WJC-B	7	5	5	10	....	....	....	2	....	....	....	....	....	....	....	....	....	....	....	....	....	....	....	....	....	....
1991-92	ESV Kaufbeuren	Germany	41	2	22	24	....	....	....	46	....	....	....	....	....	....	....	....	....	....	5	2	7	9	6	....	....	....
	Germany	WJC-A	5	0	2	2	....	....	....	4	....	....	....	....	....	....	....	....	....	....	....	....	....	....	....	....	....	....
	Germany	EJC-A	6	4	4	8	....	....	....	4	....	....	....	....	....	....	....	....	....	....	....	....	....	....	....	....	....	....
	Germany	WC-A	6	1	1	2	....	....	....	0	....	....	....	....	....	....	....	....	....	....	....	....	....	....	....	....	....	....
1992-93	ESV Kaufbeuren	Germany	37	14	18	32	....	....	....	32	....	....	....	....	....	....	....	....	....	....	3	1	0	1	10	....	....	....
	Germany	WC-A	4	1	1	2	....	....	....	26	....	....	....	....	....	....	....	....	....	....	....	....	....	....	....	....	....	....
1993-94	ESV Kaufbeuren	Germany	38	10	20	30	....	....	....	21	....	....	....	....	....	....	....	....	....	....	3	0	0	0	4	....	....	....
	Germany	WJC-A	7	3	1	4	....	....	....	2	....	....	....	....	....	....	....	....	....	....	....	....	....	....	....	....	....	....
	Germany	Olympics	8	1	2	3	....	....	....	2	....	....	....	....	....	....	....	....	....	....	....	....	....	....	....	....	....	....
1994-95	Portland Pirates	AHL	63	21	38	59	....	....	....	51	....	....	....	....	....	....	....	....	....	....	7	1	6	7	7	....	....	....
1995-96	**Washington Capitals**	**NHL**	**48**	**7**	**10**	**17**	**7**	**8**	**15**	**14**	**0**	**0**	**1**	**39**	**17.9**	**26**	**1**	**18**	**1**	**8**	**5**	**0**	**0**	**0**	**0**	**0**	**0**	**0**
	Portland Pirates	AHL	8	1	4	5	....	....	....	6	....	....	....	....	....	....	....	....	....	....	....	....	....	....	....	....	....	....
1996-97	Germany	W-Cup	4	0	2	2	....	....	....	2	....	....	....	....	....	....	....	....	....	....	....	....	....	....	....	....	....	....
	Washington Capitals	**NHL**	**6**	**0**	**0**	**0**	**0**	**0**	**0**	**2**	**0**	**0**	**0**	**7**	**0.0**	**0**	**0**	**3**	**0**	**–3**	....	....	....	....	....	....	....	....
	Portland Pirates	AHL	36	7	17	24	....	....	....	27	....	....	....	....	....	....	....	....	....	....	....	....	....	....	....	....	....	....
1997-98	Berlin Capitals	Germany	45	17	23	40	....	....	....	54	....	....	....	....	....	....	....	....	....	....	....	....	....	....	....	....	....	....
	Germany	Olympics	4	0	0	0	....	....	....	0	....	....	....	....	....	....	....	....	....	....	....	....	....	....	....	....	....	....
1998-99	Las Vegas Thunder	IHL	40	11	17	28	....	....	....	40	....	....	....	....	....	....	....	....	....	....	....	....	....	....	....	....	....	....
	Detroit Vipers	IHL	14	3	7	10	....	....	....	11	....	....	....	....	....	....	....	....	....	....	11	4	7	11	2	....	....	....
99-2000	Cincinnati Cyclones	IHL	79	20	34	54	....	....	....	53	....	....	....	....	....	....	....	....	....	....	11	1	4	5	10	....	....	....
	NHL Totals		**54**	**7**	**10**	**17**	**7**	**8**	**15**	**16**	**0**	**0**	**1**	**46**	**15.2**	**26**	**1**	**21**	**1**		**5**	**0**	**0**	**0**	**0**	**0**	**0**	**0**

Signed as a free agent by **Cincinnati** (IHL), September 29, 1999. Signed as a free agent by **Washington**, July 13, 2000.

• VACHON, Nick

C – L. 5′10″, 185 lbs. b: Montreal, Que., 7/20/1972. Toronto's 11th, 241st overall, in 1990.

Season	Club	League	GP	G	A	Pts	AG	AA	APts	PIM	PP	SH	GW	S	%	TGF	PGF	TGA	PGA	+/–	GP	G	A	Pts	PIM	PP	SH	GW
1989-90	Governor Dummer School	Hi-School	20	20	22	42	....	....	....	....	....	....	....	....	....	....	....	....	....	....	....	....	....	....	....	....	....	....
1990-91	Boston University	H-East	8	0	1	1	....	....	....	4	....	....	....	....	....	....	....	....	....	....	....	....	....	....	....	....	....	....
1991-92	Boston University	H-East	16	6	7	13	....	....	....	10	....	....	....	....	....	....	....	....	....	....	....	....	....	....	....	....	....	....
	Portland Winter Hawks	WHL	25	9	19	28	....	....	....	46	....	....	....	....	....	....	....	....	....	....	6	0	3	3	14	....	....	....
1992-93	Portland Winter Hawks	WHL	66	33	58	91	....	....	....	100	....	....	....	....	....	....	....	....	....	....	16	11	7	18	34	....	....	....
1993-94	Atlanta Knights	IHL	3	1	1	2	....	....	....	0	....	....	....	....	....	....	....	....	....	....	....	....	....	....	....	....	....	....
	Knoxville Cherokees	ECHL	61	29	57	86	....	....	....	139	....	....	....	....	....	....	....	....	....	....	3	0	0	0	2	....	....	....
1994-95	Phoenix Roadrunners	IHL	64	13	26	39	....	....	....	137	....	....	....	....	....	....	....	....	....	....	9	1	2	3	24	....	....	....
1995-96	Phoenix Roadrunners	IHL	73	13	17	30	....	....	....	168	....	....	....	....	....	....	....	....	....	....	1	0	0	0	2	....	....	....
1996-97	Phoenix Roadrunners	IHL	16	3	3	6	....	....	....	18	....	....	....	....	....	....	....	....	....	....	....	....	....	....	....	....	....	....
	New York Islanders	**NHL**	**1**	**0**	**0**	**0**	**0**	**0**	**0**	**0**	**0**	**0**	**0**	**0**	**0.0**	**0**	**0**	**1**	**0**	**–1**	....	....	....	....	....	....	....	....
	Utah Grizzlies	IHL	33	3	5	8	....	....	....	110	....	....	....	....	....	....	....	....	....	....	....	....	....	....	....	....	....	....
	Long Beach Ice Dogs	IHL	13	1	2	3	....	....	....	42	....	....	....	....	....	....	....	....	....	....	18	1	2	3	43	....	....	....
1997-98	Springfield Falcons	AHL	7	0	0	0	....	....	....	16	....	....	....	....	....	....	....	....	....	....	....	....	....	....	....	....	....	....
	Long Beach Ice Dogs	IHL	56	3	6	9	....	....	....	113	....	....	....	....	....	....	....	....	....	....	....	....	....	....	....	....	....	....
	NHL Totals		**1**	**0**	**0**	**0**	**0**	**0**	**0**	**0**	**0**	**0**	**0**	**0**	**0.0**	**0**	**0**	**1**	**0**		....	....	....	....	....	....	....	....

• Son of Rogie

Signed as a free agent by **LA Kings**, September 12, 1995. Traded to **NY Islanders** by **LA Kings** for Chris Marinucci, November 19, 1996. • Played w/ RHI's LA Blades in 1994 (18-16-14-30-38).

• VADNAIS, Carol

Carol Marcel D – L. 6′1″, 185 lbs. b: Montreal, Que., 9/25/1945.

Season	Club	League	GP	G	A	Pts	AG	AA	APts	PIM	PP	SH	GW	S	%	TGF	PGF	TGA	PGA	+/–	GP	G	A	Pts	PIM	PP	SH	GW
1963-64	Montreal NDG Monarchs	MMJHL	44	39	49	88	....	....	....	90	....	....	....	....	....	....	....	....	....	....	17	7	15	22	34	....	....	....
	Montreal NDG Monarchs	Mem-Cup	13	13	11	24	....	....	....	12	....	....	....	....	....	....	....	....	....	....	....	....	....	....	....	....	....	....
1964-65	Montreal Jr. Canadiens	OHA-Jr.	56	9	16	25	....	....	....	74	....	....	....	....	....	....	....	....	....	....	7	1	0	1	13	....	....	....
1965-66	Montreal Jr. Canadiens	OHA-Jr.	48	9	14	23	....	....	....	184	....	....	....	....	....	....	....	....	....	....	10	1	4	5	24	....	....	....
1966-67	**Montreal Canadiens**	**NHL**	**11**	**0**	**3**	**3**	**0**	**3**	**3**	**35**	....	....	....	....	....	....	....	....	....	....	**1**	**0**	**0**	**0**	**2**	**0**	**0**	**0**
	Houston Apollos	CPHL	21	5	5	10	....	....	....	45	....	....	....	....	....	....	....	....	....	....	....	....	....	....	....	....	....	....
1967-68♦	**Montreal Canadiens**	**NHL**	**31**	**1**	**1**	**2**	**1**	**1**	**2**	**31**	**0**	**0**	**0**	**25**	**4.0**	**14**	**2**	**18**	**4**	**–2**	**1**	**0**	**0**	**0**	**0**	**0**	**0**	**0**
	Houston Apollos	CPHL	36	5	21	26	....	....	....	178	....	....	....	....	....	....	....	....	....	....	....	....	....	....	....	....	....	....
1968-69	**Oakland Seals**	**NHL**	**76**	**15**	**27**	**42**	**16**	**24**	**40**	**151**	**4**	**0**	**4**	**274**	**5.5**	**118**	**28**	**133**	**25**	**–18**	**7**	**1**	**4**	**5**	**10**	**1**	**0**	**0**
1969-70	**Oakland Seals**	**NHL**	**76**	**24**	**20**	**44**	**26**	**19**	**45**	**212**	**7**	**0**	**0**	**245**	**9.8**	**81**	**29**	**103**	**27**	**–24**	**4**	**2**	**1**	**3**	**15**	**2**	**0**	**0**
1970-71	**California Golden Seals**	**NHL**	**42**	**10**	**16**	**26**	**10**	**13**	**23**	**91**	**3**	**1**	**3**	**146**	**6.8**	**61**	**16**	**63**	**15**	**–3**	....	....	....	....	....	....	....	....
1971-72	**California Golden Seals**	**NHL**	**52**	**14**	**20**	**34**	**14**	**17**	**31**	**106**	**7**	**0**	**2**	**139**	**10.1**	**86**	**27**	**104**	**25**	**–20**	....	....	....	....	....	....	....	....
♦	**Boston Bruins**	**NHL**	**16**	**4**	**6**	**10**	**4**	**5**	**9**	**37**	**0**	**0**	**0**	**37**	**10.8**	**36**	**3**	**41**	**10**	**2**	**15**	**0**	**2**	**2**	**43**	**0**	**0**	**0**
1972-73	**Boston Bruins**	**NHL**	**78**	**7**	**24**	**31**	**7**	**19**	**26**	**127**	**1**	**0**	**3**	**150**	**4.7**	**117**	**8**	**98**	**10**	**21**	**5**	**0**	**0**	**0**	**8**	**0**	**0**	**0**
1973-74	**Boston Bruins**	**NHL**	**78**	**16**	**43**	**59**	**15**	**36**	**51**	**123**	**6**	**0**	**1**	**187**	**8.6**	**175**	**57**	**100**	**17**	**35**	**16**	**1**	**12**	**13**	**42**	**1**	**0**	**0**
1974-75	**Boston Bruins**	**NHL**	**79**	**18**	**56**	**74**	**16**	**42**	**58**	**129**	**6**	**0**	**2**	**256**	**7.0**	**181**	**68**	**127**	**24**	**10**	**3**	**1**	**5**	**6**	**0**	**0**	**0**	**0**
1975-76	**Boston Bruins**	**NHL**	**12**	**2**	**5**	**7**	**2**	**4**	**6**	**17**	**1**	**0**	**0**	**33**	**6.1**	**23**	**8**	**23**	**9**	**1**	....	....	....	....	....	....	....	....
	New York Rangers	**NHL**	**64**	**20**	**30**	**50**	**18**	**22**	**40**	**104**	**7**	**0**	**1**	**197**	**10.2**	**145**	**49**	**143**	**30**	**–17**	....	....	....	....	....	....	....	....
1976-77	Canada	Can-Cup	DID NOT PLAY																									
	New York Rangers	**NHL**	**74**	**11**	**37**	**48**	**10**	**29**	**39**	**131**	**3**	**1**	**0**	**169**	**6.5**	**138**	**46**	**149**	**37**	**–20**	....	....	....	....	....	....	....	....
	Canada	WEC-A	10	3	1	4	....	....	....	33	....	....	....	....	....	....	....	....	....	....	....	....	....	....	....	....	....	....
1977-78	**New York Rangers**	**NHL**	**80**	**6**	**40**	**46**	**5**	**31**	**36**	**115**	**3**	**1**	**1**	**164**	**3.7**	**140**	**59**	**141**	**35**	**–25**	**3**	**0**	**2**	**2**	**16**	**0**	**0**	**0**
1978-79	**New York Rangers**	**NHL**	**77**	**8**	**37**	**45**	**7**	**27**	**34**	**86**	**4**	**1**	**1**	**149**	**5.4**	**116**	**37**	**111**	**46**	**14**	**18**	**2**	**9**	**11**	**13**	**0**	**0**	**0**
1979-80	**New York Rangers**	**NHL**	**66**	**3**	**20**	**23**	**3**	**15**	**18**	**118**	**1**	**0**	**1**	**82**	**3.7**	**86**	**15**	**97**	**25**	**–1**	**9**	**1**	**2**	**3**	**6**	**0**	**0**	**0**
1980-81	**New York Rangers**	**NHL**	**74**	**3**	**20**	**23**	**2**	**13**	**15**	**91**	**1**	**0**	**0**	**118**	**2.5**	**86**	**9**	**102**	**44**	**19**	**14**	**1**	**3**	**4**	**26**	**0**	**0**	**0**
1981-82	**New York Rangers**	**NHL**	**50**	**5**	**6**	**11**	**4**	**4**	**8**	**45**	**1**	**0**	**0**	**43**	**11.6**	**47**	**2**	**70**	**23**	**–2**	**10**	**1**	**0**	**1**	**4**	**0**	**0**	**0**
1982-83	**New Jersey Devils**	**NHL**	**51**	**2**	**7**	**9**	**2**	**5**	**7**	**64**	**1**	**0**	**0**	**33**	**6.1**	**37**	**5**	**81**	**17**	**–32**	....	....	....	....	....	....	....	....
	NHL Totals		**1087**	**169**	**418**	**587**	**162**	**329**	**491**	**1813**	....	....	....	....	....	....	....	....	....		**106**	**10**	**40**	**50**	**185**	....	....	....

Played in NHL All-Star Game (1969, 1970, 1972, 1975, 1976, 1978)

Claimed by **Oakland** from **Montreal** in Intra-League Draft, June 12, 1968. Traded to **Boston** by **California** with Don O'Donoghue for Reggie Leach, Rick Smith and Bob Stewart, February 23, 1972. Traded to **NY Rangers** by **Boston** with Phil Esposito for Brad Park, Jean Ratelle and Joe Zanussi, November 7, 1975. Claimed by **New Jersey** from **NY Rangers** in Waiver Draft, October 4, 1982.

• VAIC, Lubomir

C – L. 5′9″, 178 lbs. b: Spisska Nova Ves, Czech., 3/6/1977. Vancouver's 8th, 227th overall, in 1996.

Season	Club	League	GP	G	A	Pts	AG	AA	APts	PIM	PP	SH	GW	S	%	TGF	PGF	TGA	PGA	+/–	GP	G	A	Pts	PIM	PP	SH	GW
1993-94	SKP Poprad	Slovakia	28	10	6	16	....	....	....	10	....	....	....	....	....	....	....	....	....	....	....	....	....	....	....	....	....	....
	Slovakia	WJC-C	4	3	2	5	....	....	....	2	....	....	....	....	....	....	....	....	....	....	....	....	....	....	....	....	....	....
	Slovakia	EJC-A	6	10	6	16	....	....	....	20	....	....	....	....	....	....	....	....	....	....	....	....	....	....	....	....	....	....
1994-95	VTJ Spisska	Slovakia	19	5	4	9	....	....	....	2	....	....	....	....	....	....	....	....	....	....	....	....	....	....	....	....	....	....
	Slovakia	EJC-A	5	6	10	16	....	....	....	4	....	....	....	....	....	....	....	....	....	....	....	....	....	....	....	....	....	....

Season	Club	League	REGULAR SEASON																		PLAYOFFS							
			GP	G	A	Pts	AG	AA	APts	PIM	PP	SH	GW	S	%	TGF	PGF	TGA	PGA	+/–	GP	G	A	Pts	PIM	PP	SH	GW
1995-96	VSV Kosice	Slovakia	36	7	19	26	....	....	....	10	....	....	....	....	....	....	....	....	....	....	13	0	7	7	....	....	....	....
	Slovakia	WJC-A	6	2	4	6	....	....	....	25	....	....	....	....	....	....	....	....	....	....	....	....	....	....	....	....	....	....
1996-97	VSV Kosice	Slovakia	36	13	12	25	....	....	....	....	....	....	....	....	....	....	....	....	....	....	7	2	0	2	....	....	....	....
	Slovakia	WJC-A	6	1	7	8	....	....	....	10	....	....	....	....	....	....	....	....	....	....	....	....	....	....	....	....	....	....
1997-98	**Vancouver Canucks**	**NHL**	**5**	**1**	**1**	**2**	**1**	**1**	**2**	**2**	**0**	**0**	**0**	**8**	**12.5**	**3**	**0**	**5**	**0**	**–2**	....	....	....	....	....	....	....	....
	Syracuse Crunch	AHL	50	12	15	27	....	....	....	22	....	....	....	....	....	....	....	....	....	....	3	0	0	0	4	....	....	....
1998-99	VTJ Spisska	Slovakia	35	20	22	42	....	....	....	42	....	....	....	....	....	....	....	....	....	....	....	....	....	....	....	....	....	....
	VSV Kosice	Slovakia	....	....	....	....	....	....	....	....	....	....	....	....	....	....	....	....	....	....	11	2	3	5	8	....	....	....
99-2000	**Vancouver Canucks**	**NHL**	**4**	**0**	**0**	**0**	**0**	**0**	**0**	**0**	**0**	**0**	**0**	**2**	**0.0**	**1**	**0**	**1**	**0**	**0**	....	....	....	....	....	....	....	....
	Syracuse Crunch	AHL	63	13	29	42	....	....	....	42	....	....	....	....	....	....	....	....	....	....	4	0	3	3	8	....	....	....
	Slovakia	WC-A	9	0	3	3	....	....	....	4	....	....	....	....	....	....	....	....	....	....	....	....	....	....	....	....	....	....
	NHL Totals		**9**	**1**	**1**	**2**	**1**	**1**	**2**	**2**	**0**	**0**	**0**	**10**	**10.0**	**4**	**0**	**6**	**0**		....	....	....	....	....	....	....	....

• VAIL, Eric

Eric Douglas "Big Train"　LW – L. 6′1″, 220 lbs.　b: Timmins, Ont., 9/16/1953. Atlanta's 3rd, 21st overall, in 1973.

Season	Club	League	GP	G	A	Pts	AG	AA	APts	PIM	PP	SH	GW	S	%	TGF	PGF	TGA	PGA	+/–	GP	G	A	Pts	PIM	PP	SH	GW
1970-71	Niagara Falls Flyers	OHA-Jr.	59	18	30	48	....	....	....	76	....	....	....	....	....	....	....	....	....	....	....	....	....	....	....	....	....	....
1971-72	Niagara Falls Flyers	OMJHL	60	25	48	73	....	....	....	122	....	....	....	....	....	....	....	....	....	....	....	....	....	....	....	....	....	....
1972-73	Sault Ste. Marie Greyhounds	OMJHL	38	29	31	60	....	....	....	50	....	....	....	....	....	....	....	....	....	....	....	....	....	....	....	....	....	....
	Sudbury Wolves	OMJHL	25	19	26	45	....	....	....	30	....	....	....	....	....	....	....	....	....	....	4	1	1	2	2	....	....	....
1973-74	**Atlanta Flames**	**NHL**	**23**	**2**	**9**	**11**	**2**	**7**	**9**	**30**	**2**	**0**	**1**	**44**	**4.5**	**18**	**4**	**12**	**0**	**2**	**1**	**0**	**0**	**0**	**2**	**0**	**0**	**0**
	Omaha Knights	CHL	37	10	18	28	....	....	....	54	....	....	....	....	....	....	....	....	....	....	....	....	....	....	....	....	....	....
1974-75	**Atlanta Flames**	**NHL**	**72**	**39**	**21**	**60**	**34**	**16**	**50**	**46**	**6**	**0**	**4**	**177**	**22.0**	**79**	**24**	**56**	**2**	**1**	....	....	....	....	....	....	....	....
1975-76	**Atlanta Flames**	**NHL**	**60**	**16**	**31**	**47**	**14**	**23**	**37**	**34**	**2**	**0**	**1**	**127**	**12.6**	**75**	**21**	**49**	**2**	**7**	**2**	**0**	**0**	**0**	**0**	**0**	**0**	**0**
1976-77	**Atlanta Flames**	**NHL**	**78**	**32**	**39**	**71**	**29**	**30**	**59**	**22**	**12**	**1**	**3**	**208**	**15.4**	**107**	**26**	**76**	**4**	**9**	**3**	**1**	**3**	**4**	**0**	**0**	**0**	**1**
	Canada	WEC-A	9	4	1	5	....	....	....	18	....	....	....	....	....	....	....	....	....	....	....	....	....	....	....	....	....	....
1977-78	**Atlanta Flames**	**NHL**	**79**	**22**	**36**	**58**	**20**	**28**	**48**	**16**	**8**	**0**	**6**	**178**	**12.4**	**98**	**29**	**68**	**2**	**3**	**2**	**1**	**1**	**2**	**0**	**0**	**0**	**0**
1978-79	**Atlanta Flames**	**NHL**	**80**	**35**	**48**	**83**	**30**	**35**	**65**	**53**	**5**	**1**	**5**	**203**	**17.2**	**139**	**37**	**83**	**6**	**25**	**2**	**0**	**1**	**1**	**2**	**0**	**0**	**0**
1979-80	**Atlanta Flames**	**NHL**	**77**	**28**	**25**	**53**	**24**	**18**	**42**	**22**	**6**	**0**	**3**	**193**	**14.5**	**98**	**23**	**75**	**5**	**5**	**4**	**3**	**1**	**4**	**2**	**1**	**0**	**1**
1980-81	**Calgary Flames**	**NHL**	**64**	**28**	**36**	**64**	**22**	**24**	**46**	**23**	**12**	**0**	**6**	**164**	**17.1**	**92**	**32**	**57**	**5**	**8**	**6**	**0**	**0**	**0**	**0**	**0**	**0**	**0**
1981-82	**Calgary Flames**	**NHL**	**6**	**4**	**1**	**5**	**3**	**1**	**4**	**0**	**1**	**0**	**0**	**8**	**50.0**	**7**	**4**	**4**	**0**	**–1**	....	....	....	....	....	....	....	....
	Oklahoma City Stars	CHL	3	0	3	3	....	....	....	0	....	....	....	....	....	....	....	....	....	....	....	....	....	....	....	....	....	....
	Detroit Red Wings	**NHL**	**52**	**10**	**14**	**24**	**8**	**9**	**17**	**35**	**3**	**0**	**0**	**86**	**11.6**	**43**	**15**	**54**	**5**	**–21**	....	....	....	....	....	....	....	....
	Adirondack Red Wings	AHL	10	3	4	7	....	....	....	0	....	....	....	....	....	....	....	....	....	....	....	....	....	....	....	....	....	....
1982-83	Adirondack Red Wings	AHL	74	20	29	49	....	....	....	33	....	....	....	....	....	....	....	....	....	....	5	1	1	2	0	....	....	....
	NHL Totals		**591**	**216**	**260**	**476**	**186**	**191**	**377**	**281**	**57**	**2**	**29**	**1388**	**15.6**	**756**	**215**	**534**	**31**		**20**	**5**	**6**	**11**	**6**	**1**	**0**	**2**

Won Calder Memorial Trophy (1975) • Played in NHL All-Star Game (1977)

Transferred to **Calgary** after **Atlanta** franchise relocated, June 24, 1980. Traded to **Detroit** by **Calgary** for Gary McAdam and Detroit's 4th round choice (John Bekkers) in 1983 Entry Draft, November 10, 1981.

• VAIVE, Rick

Richard Claude "Squiddly"　RW – R. 6′1″, 198 lbs.　b: Ottawa, Ont., 5/14/1959. Vancouver's 1st, 5th overall, in 1979.

Season	Club	League	GP	G	A	Pts	AG	AA	APts	PIM	PP	SH	GW	S	%	TGF	PGF	TGA	PGA	+/–	GP	G	A	Pts	PIM	PP	SH	GW
1975-76	Colonel Gray High School	Hi-School	STATISTICS NOT AVAILABLE																									
	Charlottetown Islanders	Cen-Cup	STATISTICS NOT AVAILABLE																									
1976-77	Sherbrooke Beavers	QMJHL	67	51	59	110	....	....	....	91	....	....	....	....	....	....	....	....	....	....	18	10	13	23	78	....	....	....
1977-78	Sherbrooke Beavers	QMJHL	68	76	79	155	....	....	....	199	....	....	....	....	....	....	....	....	....	....	9	8	4	12	38	....	....	....
	Canada	WJC-A	6	3	0	3	....	....	....	4	....	....	....	....	....	....	....	....	....	....	....	....	....	....	....	....	....	....
1978-79	Birmingham Bulls	WHA	75	26	33	59	....	....	....	*248	....	....	....	....	....	....	....	....	....	....	....	....	....	....	....	....	....	....
1979-80	**Vancouver Canucks**	**NHL**	**47**	**13**	**8**	**21**	**11**	**6**	**17**	**111**	**1**	**0**	**4**	**89**	**14.6**	**29**	**2**	**39**	**0**	**–12**	....	....	....	....	....	....	....	....
	Toronto Maple Leafs	**NHL**	**22**	**9**	**7**	**16**	**8**	**5**	**13**	**77**	**2**	**0**	**1**	**55**	**16.4**	**24**	**5**	**24**	**1**	**–4**	**3**	**1**	**0**	**1**	**11**	**0**	**0**	**0**
1980-81	**Toronto Maple Leafs**	**NHL**	**75**	**33**	**29**	**62**	**26**	**19**	**45**	**229**	**8**	**2**	**1**	**195**	**16.9**	**93**	**23**	**99**	**13**	**–16**	**3**	**1**	**0**	**1**	**4**	**0**	**0**	**0**
1981-82	**Toronto Maple Leafs**	**NHL**	**77**	**54**	**35**	**89**	**43**	**23**	**66**	**157**	**12**	**5**	**6**	**267**	**20.2**	**119**	**29**	**106**	**28**	**12**	....	....	....	....	....	....	....	....
	Canada	WEC-A	9	3	1	4	....	....	....	12	....	....	....	....	....	....	....	....	....	....	....	....	....	....	....	....	....	....
1982-83	**Toronto Maple Leafs**	**NHL**	**78**	**51**	**28**	**79**	**42**	**19**	**61**	**105**	**18**	**3**	**8**	**296**	**17.2**	**121**	**47**	**109**	**22**	**–13**	**4**	**2**	**5**	**7**	**6**	**0**	**0**	**0**
1983-84	**Toronto Maple Leafs**	**NHL**	**76**	**52**	**41**	**93**	**42**	**28**	**70**	**114**	**17**	**0**	**6**	**261**	**19.9**	**135**	**55**	**96**	**4**	**–12**	....	....	....	....	....	....	....	....
1984-85	**Toronto Maple Leafs**	**NHL**	**72**	**35**	**33**	**68**	**29**	**22**	**51**	**112**	**13**	**0**	**2**	**258**	**13.6**	**109**	**42**	**95**	**2**	**–26**	....	....	....	....	....	....	....	....
	Canada	WEC-A	10	6	2	8	....	....	....	16	....	....	....	....	....	....	....	....	....	....	....	....	....	....	....	....	....	....
1985-86	**Toronto Maple Leafs**	**NHL**	**61**	**33**	**31**	**64**	**26**	**21**	**47**	**85**	**12**	**0**	**1**	**225**	**14.7**	**86**	**28**	**88**	**11**	**–19**	**9**	**6**	**2**	**8**	**9**	**3**	**0**	**0**
1986-87	**Toronto Maple Leafs**	**NHL**	**73**	**32**	**34**	**66**	**28**	**25**	**53**	**61**	**8**	**1**	**6**	**214**	**15.0**	**109**	**31**	**70**	**4**	**12**	**13**	**4**	**2**	**6**	**23**	**1**	**0**	**0**
1987-88	**Chicago Blackhawks**	**NHL**	**76**	**43**	**26**	**69**	**37**	**19**	**56**	**108**	**19**	**0**	**6**	**229**	**18.8**	**119**	**62**	**77**	**0**	**–20**	**5**	**6**	**2**	**8**	**38**	**5**	**0**	**0**
1988-89	**Chicago Blackhawks**	**NHL**	**30**	**12**	**13**	**25**	**10**	**9**	**19**	**60**	**9**	**0**	**1**	**57**	**21.1**	**45**	**29**	**22**	**1**	**–5**	....	....	....	....	....	....	....	....
	Buffalo Sabres	**NHL**	**28**	**19**	**13**	**32**	**16**	**9**	**25**	**64**	**7**	**0**	**3**	**81**	**23.5**	**46**	**21**	**19**	**1**	**7**	**5**	**2**	**1**	**3**	**8**	**2**	**0**	**0**
1989-90	**Buffalo Sabres**	**NHL**	**70**	**29**	**19**	**48**	**25**	**14**	**39**	**74**	**8**	**0**	**4**	**195**	**14.9**	**102**	**50**	**43**	**0**	**9**	**6**	**4**	**2**	**6**	**6**	**4**	**0**	**1**
1990-91	**Buffalo Sabres**	**NHL**	**71**	**25**	**27**	**52**	**23**	**21**	**44**	**74**	**9**	**0**	**3**	**155**	**16.1**	**75**	**29**	**35**	**0**	**11**	**6**	**1**	**2**	**3**	**6**	**1**	**0**	**0**
1991-92	**Buffalo Sabres**	**NHL**	**20**	**1**	**3**	**4**	**1**	**2**	**3**	**14**	**0**	**0**	**0**	**25**	**4.0**	**10**	**3**	**9**	**0**	**–2**	....	....	....	....	....	....	....	....
	Rochester Americans	AHL	12	4	9	13	....	....	....	4	....	....	....	....	....	....	....	....	....	....	16	4	4	8	10	....	....	....
1992-93	Hamilton Canucks	AHL	38	16	15	31	....	....	....	34	....	....	....	....	....	....	....	....	....	....	....	....	....	....	....	....	....	....
1993-1998	South Carolina Stingrays	ECHL	DID NOT PLAY – COACHING																									
1998-2000	Saint John Flames	AHL	DID NOT PLAY – COACHING																									
	NHL Totals		**876**	**441**	**347**	**788**	**367**	**242**	**609**	**1445**	**143**	**11**	**52**	**2602**	**16.9**	**1222**	**456**	**931**	**87**		**54**	**27**	**16**	**43**	**111**	**16**	**0**	**1**
	Other Major League Totals		75	26	33	59	....	....	....	248	....	....	....	....	....	....	....	....	....	....	....	....	....	....	....	....	....	....

Played in NHL All-Star Game (1982, 1983, 1984)

Signed as an underage free agent by **Birmingham** (WHA), May, 1978. Traded to **Toronto** by **Vancouver** with Bill Derlago for Tiger Williams and Jerry Butler, February 18, 1980. Traded to **Chicago** by **Toronto** with Steve Thomas and Bob McGill for Al Secord and Ed Olczyk, September 3, 1987. Traded to **Buffalo** by **Chicago** for Adam Creighton, December 26, 1988. Signed as a free agent by **Vancouver**, September 2, 1992. • Named Head Coach of **Mississauga** (OHL), July 20, 2000.

• VALENTINE, Chris

Christopher William　C – R. 6′, 190 lbs.　b: Belleville, Ont., 12/6/1961. Washington's 10th, 194th overall, in 1981.

Season	Club	League	GP	G	A	Pts	AG	AA	APts	PIM	PP	SH	GW	S	%	TGF	PGF	TGA	PGA	+/–	GP	G	A	Pts	PIM	PP	SH	GW
1977-78	Lac St-Louis Lions	QAAA	39	41	61	102	....	....	....	....	....	....	....	....	....	....	....	....	....	....	....	....	....	....	....	....	....	....
1978-79	St. Louis University	WCHA	34	27	44	71	....	....	....	52	....	....	....	....	....	....	....	....	....	....	....	....	....	....	....	....	....	....
1979-80	Sorel Black Hawks	QMJHL	72	48	80	128	....	....	....	76	....	....	....	....	....	....	....	....	....	....	....	....	....	....	....	....	....	....
1980-81	Sorel Black Hawks	QMJHL	72	65	77	142	....	....	....	176	....	....	....	....	....	....	....	....	....	....	7	5	5	10	8	....	....	....
1981-82	**Washington Capitals**	**NHL**	**60**	**30**	**37**	**67**	**24**	**25**	**49**	**92**	**18**	**0**	**5**	**154**	**19.5**	**97**	**52**	**62**	**2**	**–15**	....	....	....	....	....	....	....	....
	Hershey Bears	AHL	19	12	9	21	....	....	....	69	....	....	....	....	....	....	....	....	....	....	....	....	....	....	....	....	....	....
1982-83	**Washington Capitals**	**NHL**	**23**	**7**	**10**	**17**	**6**	**7**	**13**	**14**	**1**	**0**	**1**	**24**	**29.2**	**23**	**9**	**16**	**0**	**–2**	**2**	**0**	**0**	**0**	**4**	**0**	**0**	**0**
	Hershey Bears	AHL	51	31	38	69	....	....	....	66	....	....	....	....	....	....	....	....	....	....	....	....	....	....	....	....	....	....
1983-84	**Washington Capitals**	**NHL**	**22**	**6**	**5**	**11**	**5**	**3**	**8**	**21**	**2**	**0**	**1**	**33**	**18.2**	**14**	**5**	**17**	**0**	**–8**	....	....	....	....	....	....	....	....
	Hershey Bears	AHL	47	15	44	59	....	....	....	41	....	....	....	....	....	....	....	....	....	....	....	....	....	....	....	....	....	....
1984-85	Dusseldorfer EG	Germany-2	36	*37	42	*79	....	....	....	74	....	....	....	....	....	....	....	....	....	....	4	1	3	4	24	....	....	....
1985-86	Dusseldorfer EG	Germany-2	36	27	52	*79	....	....	....	*79	....	....	....	....	....	....	....	....	....	....	9	9	*15	*24	19	....	....	....
1986-87	Dusseldorfer EG	Germany-2	36	24	*39	*63	....	....	....	71	....	....	....	....	....	....	....	....	....	....	8	4	11	15	....	....	....	....
1987-88	Dusseldorfer EG	Germany-2	32	30	36	66	....	....	....	40	....	....	....	....	....	....	....	....	....	....	10	4	14	18	23	....	....	....
1988-89	Dusseldorfer EG	Germany-2	36	27	47	74	....	....	....	34	....	....	....	....	....	....	....	....	....	....	11	4	10	14	27	....	....	....
1989-90	Dusseldorfer EG	Germany-2	36	27	*39	66	....	....	....	35	....	....	....	....	....	....	....	....	....	....	11	5	10	15	22	....	....	....
1990-91	Dusseldorfer EG	Germany-2	42	22	52	74	....	....	....	76	....	....	....	....	....	....	....	....	....	....	12	8	13	21	8	....	....	....
1991-92	Dusseldorfer EG	Germany-2	44	32	49	81	....	....	....	56	....	....	....	....	....	....	....	....	....	....	10	10	8	18	16	....	....	....
1992-93	Dusseldorfer EG	Germany-2	44	26	*44	*70	....	....	....	56	....	....	....	....	....	....	....	....	....	....	....	....	....	....	....	....	....	....
1993-94	Dusseldorfer EG	Germany-2	43	19	*40	59	....	....	....	52	....	....	....	....	....	....	....	....	....	....	....	....	....	....	....	....	....	....
1994-95	Dusseldorfer EG	Germany	42	16	34	50	....	....	....	102	....	....	....	....	....	....	....	....	....	....	10	10	7	17	16	....	....	....
1995-96	Dusseldorfer EG	Germany	26	9	8	17	....	....	....	22	....	....	....	....	....	....	....	....	....	....	12	5	10	15	30	....	....	....
	NHL Totals		**105**	**43**	**52**	**95**	**35**	**35**	**70**	**127**	**21**	**0**	**7**	**211**	**20.4**	**134**	**66**	**95**	**2**		**2**	**0**	**0**	**0**	**4**	**0**	**0**	**0**

CCHA Second All-Star Team (1979)

• VALICEVIC, Robert

RW – R. 6'2", 197 lbs. b: Detroit, MI, 1/6/1971. NY Islanders' 6th, 114th overall, in 1991.

Season	Club	League	GP	G	A	Pts	AG	AA	APts	PIM	PP	SH	GW	S	%	TGF	PGF	TGA	PGA	+/-	Playoffs GP	G	A	Pts	PIM	PP	SH	GW
1990-91	Detroit Compuware	NAJHL	39	31	44	75	....	....	....	54	....	....	....	....	....	....	....	....	....	....	....	....	....	....	....	....	....	....
1991-92	Lake Superior State	CCHA	32	8	4	12	....	....	....	12	....	....	....	....	....	....	....	....	....	....	....	....	....	....	....	....	....	....
1992-93	Lake Superior State	CCHA	43	21	20	41	....	....	....	28	....	....	....	....	....	....	....	....	....	....	....	....	....	....	....	....	....	....
1993-94	Lake Superior State	CCHA	45	18	20	38	....	....	....	46	....	....	....	....	....	....	....	....	....	....	....	....	....	....	....	....	....	....
1994-95	Lake Superior State	CCHA	37	10	21	31	....	....	....	40	....	....	....	....	....	....	....	....	....	....	....	....	....	....	....	....	....	....
1995-96	Louisiana Ice Gators	ECHL	60	42	20	62	....	....	....	85	....	....	....	....	....	....	....	....	....	....	....	5	2	3	5	8	....	....	....
	Springfield Falcons	AHL	2	0	0	0	....	....	....	2	....	....	....	....	....	....	....	....	....	....	....	....	....	....	....	....	....	....
1996-97	Louisiana Ice Gators	ECHL	8	7	2	9	....	....	....	21	....	....	....	....	....	....	....	....	....	....	....	....	....	....	....	....	....	....
	Houston Aeros	IHL	58	11	12	23	....	....	....	42	....	....	....	....	....	....	....	....	....	....	....	12	1	3	4	11	....	....	....
1997-98	Houston Aeros	IHL	72	29	28	57	....	....	....	47	....	....	....	....	....	....	....	....	....	....	....	4	2	0	2	2	....	....	....
1998-99	**Nashville Predators**	**NHL**	**19**	**4**	**2**	**6**	**5**	**2**	**7**	**2**	**0**	**0**	**2**	**23**	**17.4**	**10**	**0**	**7**	**1**	**4**	....	....	....	....	....	....	....	....
	Houston Aeros	IHL	57	16	33	49	....	....	....	62	....	....	....	....	....	....	....	....	....	....	....	19	7	10	17	8	....	....	....
99-2000	**Nashville Predators**	**NHL**	**80**	**14**	**11**	**25**	**16**	**10**	**26**	**21**	**2**	**1**	**3**	**113**	**12.4**	**36**	**8**	**56**	**17**	**-11**	....	....	....	....	....	....	....	....
	NHL Totals		**99**	**18**	**13**	**31**	**21**	**12**	**33**	**23**	**2**	**1**	**5**	**136**	**13.2**	**46**	**8**	**63**	**18**		....	....	....	....	....	....	....	....

Signed as a free agent by **Nashville**, May 28, 1998.

• VALIQUETTE, Jack

John Jack Joseph C – L. 6'2", 195 lbs. b: St. Thomas, Ont., 3/18/1954. Toronto's 1st, 13th overall, in 1974.

Season	Club	League	GP	G	A	Pts	AG	AA	APts	PIM	PP	SH	GW	S	%	TGF	PGF	TGA	PGA	+/-	Playoffs GP	G	A	Pts	PIM	PP	SH	GW
1970-71	Alymer Aces	QAAA	STATISTICS NOT AVAILABLE																									
1971-72	Laurentian University	OUAA	3	0	3	3	....	....	....	6	....	....	....	....	....	....	....	....	....	....	....	....	....	....	....	....	....	....
1972-73	St. Marys Lincolns	OHA-B	42	47	41	88	....	....	....	25	....	....	....	....	....	....	....	....	....	....	....	....	....	....	....	....	....	....
1973-74	Sault Ste. Marie Greyhounds	OMJHL	69	*63	72	*135	....	....	....	38	....	....	....	....	....	....	....	....	....	....	....	....	....	....	....	....	....	....
1974-75	**Toronto Maple Leafs**	**NHL**	**1**	**0**	**0**	**0**	**0**	**0**	**0**	**0**	**0**	**0**	**0**	**1**	**0.0**	**0**	**0**	**4**	**0**	**-4**	....	....	....	....	....	....	....	....
	Oklahoma City Blazers	CHL	76	22	51	73	....	....	....	52	....	....	....	....	....	....	....	....	....	....	....	5	0	1	1	0	....	....	....
1975-76	**Toronto Maple Leafs**	**NHL**	**45**	**10**	**23**	**33**	**9**	**17**	**26**	**30**	**1**	**1**	**1**	**111**	**9.0**	**44**	**10**	**46**	**4**	**-8**	**10**	**2**	**3**	**5**	**2**	**0**	**0**	**0**
	Oklahoma City Blazers	CHL	32	15	8	23	....	....	....	25	....	....	....	....	....	....	....	....	....	....	....	....	....	....	....	....	....	....
1976-77	**Toronto Maple Leafs**	**NHL**	**66**	**15**	**30**	**45**	**13**	**23**	**36**	**7**	**0**	**3**	**1**	**121**	**12.4**	**59**	**2**	**73**	**21**	**5**	....	....	....	....	....	....	....	....
1977-78	**Toronto Maple Leafs**	**NHL**	**60**	**8**	**13**	**21**	**7**	**10**	**17**	**15**	**3**	**0**	**2**	**49**	**16.3**	**35**	**9**	**26**	**2**	**2**	**13**	**1**	**3**	**4**	**2**	**1**	**0**	**0**
	Tulsa Oilers	CHL	7	7	5	12	....	....	....	2	....	....	....	....	....	....	....	....	....	....	....	....	....	....	....	....	....	....
1978-79	**Colorado Rockies**	**NHL**	**76**	**23**	**34**	**57**	**20**	**25**	**45**	**12**	**8**	**2**	**3**	**159**	**14.5**	**84**	**30**	**114**	**18**	**-42**	....	....	....	....	....	....	....	....
1979-80	**Colorado Rockies**	**NHL**	**77**	**25**	**25**	**50**	**21**	**18**	**39**	**8**	**6**	**0**	**2**	**157**	**15.9**	**88**	**28**	**75**	**8**	**-7**	....	....	....	....	....	....	....	....
1980-81	**Colorado Rockies**	**NHL**	**25**	**3**	**9**	**12**	**2**	**6**	**8**	**7**	**0**	**0**	**0**	**28**	**10.7**	**19**	**6**	**28**	**3**	**-12**	....	....	....	....	....	....	....	....
	Fort Worth Texans	CHL	37	18	18	36	....	....	....	4	....	....	....	....	....	....	....	....	....	....	....	....	....	....	....	....	....	....
	NHL Totals		**350**	**84**	**134**	**218**	**72**	**99**	**171**	**79**	**18**	**6**	**9**	**626**	**13.4**	**329**	**85**	**366**	**56**		**23**	**3**	**6**	**9**	**4**	**1**	**0**	**0**

Traded to **Colorado** by **Toronto** for Colorado's 2nd round choice (Gary Yaremchuk) in 1981 Entry Draft, October 19, 1978.

• VALK, Garry

LW – L. 6'1", 205 lbs. b: Edmonton, Alta., 11/27/1967. Vancouver's 5th, 108th overall, in 1987.

Season	Club	League	GP	G	A	Pts	AG	AA	APts	PIM	PP	SH	GW	S	%	TGF	PGF	TGA	PGA	+/-	Playoffs GP	G	A	Pts	PIM	PP	SH	GW
1984-85	Sherwood Park Crusaders	AJHL	55	20	22	42	....	....	....	46	....	....	....	....	....	....	....	....	....	....	....	....	....	....	....	....	....	....
1985-86	Sherwood Park Crusaders	AJHL	40	20	26	46	....	....	....	116	....	....	....	....	....	....	....	....	....	....	....	....	....	....	....	....	....	....
1986-87	Sherwood Park Crusaders	AJHL	59	42	44	86	....	....	....	204	....	....	....	....	....	....	....	....	....	....	....	....	....	....	....	....	....	....
1987-88	University of North Dakota	WCHA	38	23	12	35	....	....	....	64	....	....	....	....	....	....	....	....	....	....	....	....	....	....	....	....	....	....
1988-89	University of North Dakota	WCHA	40	14	17	31	....	....	....	71	....	....	....	....	....	....	....	....	....	....	....	....	....	....	....	....	....	....
1989-90	University of North Dakota	WCHA	43	22	17	39	....	....	....	92	....	....	....	....	....	....	....	....	....	....	....	....	....	....	....	....	....	....
1990-91	**Vancouver Canucks**	**NHL**	**59**	**10**	**11**	**21**	**9**	**8**	**17**	**67**	**1**	**0**	**1**	**90**	**11.1**	**37**	**12**	**51**	**3**	**-23**	**5**	**0**	**0**	**0**	**20**	**0**	**0**	**0**
	Milwaukee Admirals	IHL	10	12	4	16	....	....	....	13	....	....	....	....	....	....	....	....	....	....	....	3	0	0	0	2	....	....	....
1991-92	**Vancouver Canucks**	**NHL**	**65**	**8**	**17**	**25**	**7**	**13**	**20**	**56**	**2**	**1**	**2**	**93**	**8.6**	**41**	**7**	**49**	**18**	**3**	**4**	**0**	**0**	**0**	**5**	**0**	**0**	**0**
1992-93	**Vancouver Canucks**	**NHL**	**48**	**6**	**7**	**13**	**5**	**5**	**10**	**77**	**0**	**0**	**2**	**46**	**13.0**	**20**	**0**	**28**	**14**	**6**	**7**	**0**	**1**	**1**	**12**	**0**	**0**	**0**
	Hamilton Canucks	AHL	7	3	6	9	....	....	....	6	....	....	....	....	....	....	....	....	....	....	....	....	....	....	....	....	....	....
1993-94	**Mighty Ducks of Anaheim**	**NHL**	**78**	**18**	**27**	**45**	**17**	**21**	**38**	**100**	**4**	**1**	**5**	**165**	**10.9**	**68**	**15**	**72**	**27**	**8**	....	....	....	....	....	....	....	....
1994-95	**Mighty Ducks of Anaheim**	**NHL**	**36**	**3**	**6**	**9**	**5**	**9**	**14**	**34**	**0**	**0**	**0**	**53**	**5.7**	**17**	**2**	**26**	**7**	**-4**	....	....	....	....	....	....	....	....
1995-96	**Mighty Ducks of Anaheim**	**NHL**	**79**	**12**	**12**	**24**	**12**	**10**	**22**	**125**	**1**	**1**	**2**	**108**	**11.1**	**39**	**5**	**55**	**29**	**8**	....	....	....	....	....	....	....	....
1996-97	**Mighty Ducks of Anaheim**	**NHL**	**53**	**7**	**7**	**14**	**7**	**6**	**13**	**53**	**0**	**0**	**1**	**68**	**10.3**	**22**	**0**	**30**	**6**	**-2**	....	....	....	....	....	....	....	....
	Pittsburgh Penguins	**NHL**	**17**	**3**	**4**	**7**	**3**	**4**	**7**	**25**	**0**	**0**	**0**	**32**	**9.4**	**8**	**2**	**14**	**2**	**-6**	....	....	....	....	....	....	....	....
1997-98	**Pittsburgh Penguins**	**NHL**	**39**	**2**	**1**	**3**	**2**	**1**	**3**	**33**	**0**	**0**	**0**	**32**	**6.3**	**4**	**0**	**9**	**2**	**-3**	....	....	....	....	....	....	....	....
1998-99	**Toronto Maple Leafs**	**NHL**	**77**	**8**	**21**	**29**	**9**	**20**	**29**	**53**	**1**	**0**	**0**	**93**	**8.6**	**51**	**6**	**55**	**18**	**8**	**17**	**3**	**4**	**7**	**22**	**0**	**0**	**1**
99-2000	**Toronto Maple Leafs**	**NHL**	**73**	**10**	**14**	**24**	**11**	**13**	**24**	**44**	**0**	**1**	**1**	**91**	**11.0**	**34**	**3**	**48**	**15**	**-2**	**12**	**1**	**2**	**3**	**14**	**0**	**0**	**0**
	NHL Totals		**624**	**87**	**127**	**214**	**87**	**110**	**197**	**667**	**9**	**4**	**14**	**871**	**10.0**	**341**	**52**	**437**	**141**		**45**	**4**	**7**	**11**	**73**	**0**	**0**	**1**

Claimed by **Anaheim** from **Vancouver** in NHL Waiver Draft, October 3, 1993. Traded to **Pittsburgh** by **Anaheim** for Jean-Jacques Daigneault, February 21, 1997. Signed as a free agent by **Toronto**, October 8, 1998.

• VALLIS, Lindsay

Lindsay G. D – R. 6'3", 207 lbs. b: Winnipeg, Man., 1/12/1971. Montreal's 1st, 13th overall, in 1989.

Season	Club	League	GP	G	A	Pts	AG	AA	APts	PIM	PP	SH	GW	S	%	TGF	PGF	TGA	PGA	+/-	Playoffs GP	G	A	Pts	PIM	PP	SH	GW
1986-87	Winnipeg Mavericks	MAHA	59	16	49	65	....	....	....	95	....	....	....	....	....	....	....	....	....	....	....	....	....	....	....	....	....	....
1987-88	Seattle Thunderbirds	WHL	68	31	45	76	....	....	....	65	....	....	....	....	....	....	....	....	....	....	....	....	....	....	....	....	....	....
1988-89	Seattle Thunderbirds	WHL	63	21	32	53	....	....	....	48	....	....	....	....	....	....	....	....	....	....	....	....	....	....	....	....	....	....
1989-90	Seattle Thunderbirds	WHL	65	34	43	77	....	....	....	68	....	....	....	....	....	....	....	....	....	....	....	13	6	5	11	14	....	....	....
1990-91	Seattle Thunderbirds	WHL	72	41	38	79	....	....	....	119	....	....	....	....	....	....	....	....	....	....	....	6	1	3	4	17	....	....	....
	Fredericton Canadiens	AHL	....	....	....	....	....	....	....	....	....	....	....	....	....	....	....	....	....	....	....	7	0	0	0	6	....	....	....
1991-92	Fredericton Canadiens	AHL	71	10	19	29	....	....	....	84	....	....	....	....	....	....	....	....	....	....	....	4	0	1	1	7	....	....	....
1992-93	Fredericton Canadiens	AHL	65	18	16	34	....	....	....	38	....	....	....	....	....	....	....	....	....	....	....	5	0	2	2	10	....	....	....
1993-94	**Montreal Canadiens**	**NHL**	**1**	**0**	**0**	**0**	**0**	**0**	**0**	**0**	**0**	**0**	**0**	**0**	**0.0**	**0**	**0**	**0**	**0**	**0**	....	....	....	....	....	....	....	....
	Fredericton Canadiens	AHL	75	9	30	39	....	....	....	103	....	....	....	....	....	....	....	....	....	....	....	....	....	....	....	....	....	....
1994-95	Worcester IceCats	AHL	14	0	7	7	....	....	....	28	....	....	....	....	....	....	....	....	....	....	....	....	....	....	....	....	....	....
1995-96	Worcester IceCats	AHL	65	9	19	28	....	....	....	81	....	....	....	....	....	....	....	....	....	....	....	4	0	2	2	4	....	....	....
1996-97	Bakersfield Fog	WCHL	58	26	65	91	....	....	....	82	....	....	....	....	....	....	....	....	....	....	....	4	0	3	3	0	....	....	....
1997-98	Bakersfield Fog	WCHL	41	21	24	45	....	....	....	34	....	....	....	....	....	....	....	....	....	....	....	4	1	2	3	26	....	....	....
1998-99	Hershey Bears	AHL	4	1	0	1	....	....	....	0	....	....	....	....	....	....	....	....	....	....	....	....	....	....	....	....	....	....
	Asheville Smoke	UHL	66	27	73	100	....	....	....	46	....	....	....	....	....	....	....	....	....	....	....	4	3	0	3	0	....	....	....
99-2000	Asheville Smoke	UHL	69	24	52	76	....	....	....	54	....	....	....	....	....	....	....	....	....	....	....	2	0	1	1	2	....	....	....
	NHL Totals		**1**	**0**	**0**	**0**	**0**	**0**	**0**	**0**	**0**	**0**	**0**	**0**	**0.0**	**0**	**0**	**0**	**0**		....	....	....	....	....	....	....	....

WCHL Second All-Star Team (1997)

• VAN ALLEN, Shaun

C – L. 6'1", 204 lbs. b: Calgary, Alta., 8/29/1967. Edmonton's 5th, 105th overall, in 1987.

Season	Club	League	GP	G	A	Pts	AG	AA	APts	PIM	PP	SH	GW	S	%	TGF	PGF	TGA	PGA	+/-	Playoffs GP	G	A	Pts	PIM	PP	SH	GW
1984-85	Swift Current Indians	SJHL	61	12	20	32	....	....	....	136	....	....	....	....	....	....	....	....	....	....	....	....	....	....	....	....	....	....
1985-86	Saskatoon Blades	WHL	55	12	11	23	....	....	....	43	....	....	....	....	....	....	....	....	....	....	....	13	4	8	12	28	....	....	....
1986-87	Saskatoon Blades	WHL	72	38	59	97	....	....	....	116	....	....	....	....	....	....	....	....	....	....	....	11	4	6	10	24	....	....	....
1987-88	Milwaukee Admirals	IHL	40	14	28	42	....	....	....	34	....	....	....	....	....	....	....	....	....	....	....	....	....	....	....	....	....	....
	Nova Scotia Oilers	AHL	19	4	10	14	....	....	....	17	....	....	....	....	....	....	....	....	....	....	....	4	1	1	2	4	....	....	....
1988-89	Cape Breton Oilers	AHL	76	32	42	74	....	....	....	81	....	....	....	....	....	....	....	....	....	....	....	....	....	....	....	....	....	....
1989-90	Cape Breton Oilers	AHL	61	25	44	69	....	....	....	83	....	....	....	....	....	....	....	....	....	....	....	4	0	2	2	8	....	....	....
1990-91	**Edmonton Oilers**	**NHL**	**2**	**0**	**0**	**0**	**0**	**0**	**0**	**0**	**0**	**0**	**0**	**0**	**0.0**	**0**	**0**	**0**	**0**	**0**	....	....	....	....	....	....	....	....
	Cape Breton Oilers	AHL	76	25	75	100	....	....	....	182	....	....	....	....	....	....	....	....	....	....	....	4	0	1	1	8	....	....	....
1991-92	Cape Breton Oilers	AHL	77	29	*84	*113	....	....	....	80	....	....	....	....	....	....	....	....	....	....	....	5	3	7	10	14	....	....	....
1992-93	**Edmonton Oilers**	**NHL**	**21**	**1**	**4**	**5**	**1**	**3**	**4**	**6**	**0**	**0**	**0**	**19**	**5.3**	**8**	**4**	**6**	**0**	**-2**	....	....	....	....	....	....	....	....
	Cape Breton Oilers	AHL	43	14	62	76	....	....	....	68	....	....	....	....	....	....	....	....	....	....	....	15	8	9	17	18	....	....	....
1993-94	**Mighty Ducks of Anaheim**	**NHL**	**80**	**8**	**25**	**33**	**7**	**19**	**26**	**64**	**2**	**2**	**1**	**104**	**7.7**	**58**	**15**	**52**	**9**	**0**	....	....	....	....	....	....	....	....
1994-95	**Mighty Ducks of Anaheim**	**NHL**	**45**	**8**	**21**	**29**	**14**	**31**	**45**	**32**	**1**	**1**	**1**	**68**	**11.8**	**37**	**10**	**45**	**14**	**-4**	....	....	....	....	....	....	....	....
1995-96	**Mighty Ducks of Anaheim**	**NHL**	**49**	**8**	**17**	**25**	**8**	**14**	**22**	**41**	**0**	**0**	**2**	**78**	**10.3**	**44**	**8**	**34**	**11**	**13**	....	....	....	....	....	....	....	....
1996-97	**Ottawa Senators**	**NHL**	**80**	**11**	**14**	**25**	**12**	**12**	**24**	**35**	**1**	**1**	**2**	**123**	**8.9**	**36**	**3**	**48**	**7**	**-8**	**7**	**0**	**1**	**1**	**4**	**0**	**0**	**0**

			REGULAR SEASON																		PLAYOFFS							
Season	Club	League	GP	G	A	Pts	AG	AA	APts	PIM	PP	SH	GW	S	%	TGF	PGF	TGA	PGA	+/-	GP	G	A	Pts	PIM	PP	SH	GW
1997-98	**Ottawa Senators**	**NHL**	80	4	15	19	5	15	20	48	0	0	0	104	3.8	31	2	47	22	4	11	0	1	1	10	0	0	0
1998-99	**Ottawa Senators**	**NHL**	79	6	11	17	7	11	18	30	0	1	0	47	12.8	23	0	32	12	3	4	0	0	0	0	0	0	0
99-2000	**Ottawa Senators**	**NHL**	75	9	19	28	10	18	28	37	0	2	4	75	12.0	46	1	41	16	20	6	0	1	1	9	0	0	0
	NHL Totals		511	55	126	181	64	123	187	293	4	7	10	618	8.9	283	43	305	91		28	0	3	3	23	0	0	0

AHL Second All-Star Team (1991) • AHL First All-Star Team (1992) • Won John B. Sollenberger Trophy (Top Scorer - AHL) (1992)

Signed as a free agent by **Anaheim**, July 22, 1993. Traded to **Ottawa** by **Anaheim** with Jason York for Ted Drury and the rights to Marc Moro, October 1, 1996. Signed as a free agent by **Dallas**, July 12, 2000.

• VAN BOXMEER, John

John Martin "Boxy" D – R. 6', 190 lbs. b: Petrolia, Ont., 11/20/1952. Montreal's 4th, 14th overall, in 1972.

Season	Club	League	GP	G	A	Pts	AG	AA	APts	PIM	PP	SH	GW	S	%	TGF	PGF	TGA	PGA	+/-	GP	G	A	Pts	PIM	PP	SH	GW
1970-71	Petrolia Jr. Cees	OHA-C	STATISTICS NOT AVAILABLE																									
1971-72	Guelph CMC's	OJHL	56	30	42	72	....	....	....	160	....	....	....	....	....	....	....	....	....	....	....	....	....	....	....	....	....	....
1972-73	Nova Scotia Voyageurs	AHL	76	5	29	34	....	....	....	139	....	....	....	....	....	....	....	....	....	....	13	1	6	7	26	....	....	....
1973-74	**Montreal Canadiens**	**NHL**	20	1	4	5	1	3	4	18	1	0	0	12	8.3	9	1	12	1	-3	1	0	0	0	0	0	0	0
	Nova Scotia Voyageurs	AHL	47	8	20	28	....	....	....	78	....	....	....	....	....	....	....	....	....	....	....	....	....	....	....	....	....	....
1974-75	**Montreal Canadiens**	**NHL**	9	0	2	2	0	1	1	0	0	0	0	10	0.0	3	0	4	0	-1	....	....	....	....	....	....	....	....
	Nova Scotia Voyageurs	AHL	43	4	15	19	....	....	....	68	....	....	....	....	....	....	....	....	....	....	6	1	3	4	9	....	....	....
1975-76♦	**Montreal Canadiens**	**NHL**	46	6	11	17	5	8	13	31	0	0	1	88	6.8	41	5	19	0	17	....	....	....	....	....	....	....	....
1976-77	**Montreal Canadiens**	**NHL**	4	0	1	1	0	1	1	0	0	0	0	5	0.0	3	1	1	0	1	....	....	....	....	....	....	....	....
	Colorado Rockies	**NHL**	41	2	11	13	2	8	10	32	0	0	0	88	2.3	39	15	50	6	-20	....	....	....	....	....	....	....	....
1977-78	**Colorado Rockies**	**NHL**	80	12	42	54	11	33	44	87	5	0	0	262	4.6	129	41	124	24	-12	2	0	1	1	2	0	0	0
1978-79	**Colorado Rockies**	**NHL**	76	9	34	43	8	25	33	46	4	0	0	189	4.8	106	36	119	23	-26	....	....	....	....	....	....	....	....
1979-80	**Buffalo Sabres**	**NHL**	80	11	40	51	9	29	38	55	4	0	1	198	5.6	138	40	63	5	40	14	3	5	8	12	2	0	2
1980-81	**Buffalo Sabres**	**NHL**	80	18	51	69	14	34	48	69	6	1	2	258	7.0	139	52	96	7	-2	8	1	8	9	7	0	0	0
1981-82	**Buffalo Sabres**	**NHL**	69	14	54	68	11	36	47	62	3	0	1	120	11.7	82	32	34	4	20	4	0	1	1	6	0	0	0
	Canada	WEC-A	8	2	0	2	....	....	....	8	....	....	....	....	....	....	....	....	....	....	....	....	....	....	....	....	....	....
1982-83	**Buffalo Sabres**	**NHL**	65	6	21	27	5	15	20	53	1	0	1	144	4.2	89	20	69	7	7	9	1	0	1	10	1	0	0
1983-84	**Quebec Nordiques**	**NHL**	18	5	3	8	4	2	6	12	4	0	0	33	15.2	34	15	25	5	-1	....	....	....	....	....	....	....	....
	Fredericton Express	AHL	45	10	34	44	....	....	....	48	....	....	....	....	....	....	....	....	....	....	7	2	5	7	8	....	....	....
1984-85	Rochester Americans	AHL	2	0	0	0	....	....	....	2	....	....	....	....	....	....	....	....	....	....	....	....	....	....	....	....	....	....
1985-1995	Rochester Americans	AHL	DID NOT PLAY – COACHING																									
1995-2000	Long Beach Ice Dogs	IHL	DID NOT PLAY – COACHING																									
	NHL Totals		588	84	274	358	70	195	265	465	28	1	6	1407	6.0	812	258	616	82		38	5	15	20	37	3	0	2

OJHL First All-Star Team (1972)

Traded to **Colorado** by **Montreal** for Colorado's 3rd round choice (Craig Levie) in 1979 Entry Draft and cash, November 24, 1976. Traded to **Buffalo** by **Colorado** for Rene Robert, October 5, 1979. Claimed by **Quebec** from **Buffalo** in Waiver Draft, October 3, 1983.

• VANDENBUSSCHE, Ryan

RW – R. 6', 200 lbs. b: Simcoe, Ont., 2/28/1973. Toronto's 9th, 173rd overall, in 1992.

Season	Club	League	GP	G	A	Pts	AG	AA	APts	PIM	PP	SH	GW	S	%	TGF	PGF	TGA	PGA	+/-	GP	G	A	Pts	PIM	PP	SH	GW
1988-89	Delhi Flames	OJHL-D	3	1	1	2	....	....	....	2	....	....	....	....	....	....	....	....	....	....	....	....	....	....	....	....	....	....
1989-90	Norwich Merchants	OJHL-C	21	12	10	22	....	....	....	146	....	....	....	....	....	....	....	....	....	....	....	....	....	....	....	....	....	....
	Tillsonburg Titans	OJHL-B	24	0	5	5	....	....	....	113	....	....	....	....	....	....	....	....	....	....	....	....	....	....	....	....	....	....
1990-91	Massena Americans	OJHL	10	2	3	5	....	....	....	46	....	....	....	....	....	....	....	....	....	....	....	....	....	....	....	....	....	....
	Cornwall Royals	OHL	49	3	8	11	....	....	....	139	....	....	....	....	....	....	....	....	....	....	....	....	....	....	....	....	....	....
1991-92	Cornwall Royals	OHL	61	13	15	28	....	....	....	232	....	....	....	....	....	....	....	....	....	....	6	0	2	2	9	....	....	....
1992-93	Newmarket Royals	OHL	30	15	12	27	....	....	....	161	....	....	....	....	....	....	....	....	....	....	....	....	....	....	....	....	....	....
	Guelph Storm	OHL	29	3	14	17	....	....	....	99	....	....	....	....	....	....	....	....	....	....	5	1	3	4	13	....	....	....
	St. John's Maple Leafs	AHL	1	0	0	0	....	....	....	0	....	....	....	....	....	....	....	....	....	....	....	....	....	....	....	....	....	....
1993-94	St. John's Maple Leafs	AHL	44	4	10	14	....	....	....	124	....	....	....	....	....	....	....	....	....	....	....	....	....	....	....	....	....	....
	Springfield Indians	AHL	9	1	2	3	....	....	....	29	....	....	....	....	....	....	....	....	....	....	5	0	0	0	16	....	....	....
1994-95	St. John's Maple Leafs	AHL	53	2	13	15	....	....	....	239	....	....	....	....	....	....	....	....	....	....	3	0	0	0	17	....	....	....
1995-96	Binghamton Rangers	AHL	68	3	17	20	....	....	....	240	....	....	....	....	....	....	....	....	....	....	4	0	0	0	9	....	....	....
1996-97	**New York Rangers**	**NHL**	11	1	0	1	1	0	1	30	0	0	0	4	25.0	1	0	3	0	-2	....	....	....	....	....	....	....	....
	Binghamton Rangers	AHL	38	8	11	19	....	....	....	133	....	....	....	....	....	....	....	....	....	....	....	....	....	....	....	....	....	....
1997-98	**New York Rangers**	**NHL**	16	1	0	1	1	0	1	38	0	0	0	2	50.0	1	0	3	0	-2	....	....	....	....	....	....	....	....
	Hartford Wolf Pack	AHL	15	2	0	2	....	....	....	45	....	....	....	....	....	....	....	....	....	....	....	....	....	....	....	....	....	....
	Chicago Blackhawks	**NHL**	4	0	1	1	0	1	1	5	0	0	0	0	0.0	1	0	1	0	0	....	....	....	....	....	....	....	....
	Indianapolis Ice	IHL	3	1	1	2	....	....	....	4	....	....	....	....	....	....	....	....	....	....	....	....	....	....	....	....	....	....
1998-99	**Chicago Blackhawks**	**NHL**	6	0	0	0	0	0	0	17	0	0	0	3	0.0	1	0	1	0	0	....	....	....	....	....	....	....	....
	Indianapolis Ice	IHL	34	3	10	13	....	....	....	130	....	....	....	....	....	....	....	....	....	....	....	....	....	....	....	....	....	....
	Portland Pirates	AHL	37	4	1	5	....	....	....	119	....	....	....	....	....	....	....	....	....	....	....	....	....	....	....	....	....	....
99-2000	**Chicago Blackhawks**	**NHL**	52	0	1	1	0	1	1	143	0	0	0	19	0.0	8	2	10	1	-3	....	....	....	....	....	....	....	....
	NHL Totals		89	2	2	4	2	2	4	233	0	0	0	28	7.1	12	2	18	1		....	....	....	....	....	....	....	....

Signed as a free agent by **NY Rangers**, August 22, 1995. Traded to **Chicago** by **NY Rangers** for Ryan Risidore, March 24, 1998.

• VAN DORP, Wayne

LW – L. 6'4", 225 lbs. b: Vancouver, B.C., 5/19/1961.

Season	Club	League	GP	G	A	Pts	AG	AA	APts	PIM	PP	SH	GW	S	%	TGF	PGF	TGA	PGA	+/-	GP	G	A	Pts	PIM	PP	SH	GW
1978-79	Bellingham Blazers	BCJHL	26	12	10	22	....	....	....	106	....	....	....	....	....	....	....	....	....	....	....	....	....	....	....	....	....	....
1979-80	Seattle Breakers	WHL	68	8	13	21	....	....	....	195	....	....	....	....	....	....	....	....	....	....	12	3	1	4	33	....	....	....
1980-81	Seattle Breakers	WHL	63	22	30	52	....	....	....	242	....	....	....	....	....	....	....	....	....	....	5	1	0	1	10	....	....	....
1981-82	SIJ Feenstra	Holland	22	11	7	18	....	....	....	44	....	....	....	....	....	....	....	....	....	....	12	1	4	5	34	....	....	....
1982-83	SIJ Feenstra	Holland	23	7	12	19	....	....	....	40	....	....	....	....	....	....	....	....	....	....	15	4	5	9	20	....	....	....
1983-84	Erie Blades	ACHL	45	19	18	37	....	....	....	202	....	....	....	....	....	....	....	....	....	....	8	1	2	3	46	....	....	....
1984-85	GIJS Groningen	Holland	29	38	46	84	....	....	....	112	....	....	....	....	....	....	....	....	....	....	6	6	2	8	23	....	....	....
	Erie Blades	ACHL	7	9	8	17	....	....	....	21	....	....	....	....	....	....	....	....	....	....	10	0	2	2	62	....	....	....
1985-86	GIJS Groningen	Holland	29	19	24	43	....	....	....	81	....	....	....	....	....	....	....	....	....	....	8	9	*12	21	6	....	....	....
	Holland	WEC-B	7	0	0	0	....	....	....	0	....	....	....	....	....	....	....	....	....	....	....	....	....	....	....	....	....	....
1986-87	Rochester Americans	AHL	47	7	3	10	....	....	....	192	....	....	....	....	....	....	....	....	....	....	....	....	....	....	....	....	....	....
♦	**Edmonton Oilers**	**NHL**	3	0	0	0	0	0	0	25	0	0	0	3	0.0	0	0	1	0	-1	3	0	0	0	2	0	0	0
	Nova Scotia Oilers	AHL	11	2	3	5	....	....	....	37	....	....	....	....	....	....	....	....	....	....	5	0	0	0	56	....	....	....
1987-88	**Pittsburgh Penguins**	**NHL**	25	1	3	4	1	2	3	75	0	0	0	15	6.7	7	0	5	0	2	....	....	....	....	....	....	....	....
	Nova Scotia Oilers	AHL	12	2	2	4	....	....	....	87	....	....	....	....	....	....	....	....	....	....	....	....	....	....	....	....	....	....
1988-89	Rochester Americans	AHL	28	3	6	9	....	....	....	202	....	....	....	....	....	....	....	....	....	....	....	....	....	....	....	....	....	....
	Saginaw Hawks	IHL	11	4	3	7	....	....	....	60	....	....	....	....	....	....	....	....	....	....	....	....	....	....	....	....	....	....
	Chicago Blackhawks	**NHL**	8	0	0	0	0	0	0	23	0	0	0	4	0.0	3	0	2	0	1	16	0	1	1	17	0	0	0
1989-90	**Chicago Blackhawks**	**NHL**	61	7	4	11	6	3	9	303	0	0	1	38	18.4	23	0	26	0	-3	8	0	0	0	23	0	0	0
1990-91	**Quebec Nordiques**	**NHL**	4	1	0	1	1	0	1	30	0	0	0	2	50.0	1	0	0	0	1	....	....	....	....	....	....	....	....
1991-92	**Quebec Nordiques**	**NHL**	24	3	5	8	3	4	7	109	0	0	0	19	15.8	9	1	3	0	5	....	....	....	....	....	....	....	....
	Halifax Citadels	AHL	15	5	5	10	....	....	....	54	....	....	....	....	....	....	....	....	....	....	....	....	....	....	....	....	....	....
1992-93	HC Fiemme	Alpenliga	14	5	12	17	....	....	....	62	....	....	....	....	....	....	....	....	....	....	....	....	....	....	....	....	....	....
	HC Fiemme	Italy	9	1	1	2	....	....	....	24	....	....	....	....	....	....	....	....	....	....	....	....	....	....	....	....	....	....
	Milwaukee Admirals	IHL	19	1	4	5	....	....	....	57	....	....	....	....	....	....	....	....	....	....	....	....	....	....	....	....	....	....
1993-94	Los Angeles Jets	SCSHL	STATISTICS NOT AVAILABLE																									
1994-95	Los Angeles Bandits	SCSHL	STATISTICS NOT AVAILABLE																									
	NHL Totals		125	12	12	24	11	9	20	565	0	0	1	81	14.8	43	1	37	0		27	0	1	1	42	0	0	0

Signed as a free agent by **Buffalo**, October, 1986. Traded to **Edmonton** by **Buffalo** with Normand Lacombe and Buffalo's 4th round choice (Peter Ericksson) in 1987 Entry Draft for Lee Fogolin, Mark Napier and Edmonton's 4th round choice (John Bradley) in 1987 Entry Draft, March 6, 1987. Traded to **Pittsburgh** by **Edmonton** with Paul Coffey and Dave Hunter for Craig Simpson, Dave Hannan, Moe Mantha and Chris Joseph, November 24, 1987. Traded to **Buffalo** by **Pittsburgh** for future considerations, September 30, 1988. Traded to **Chicago** by **Buffalo** for Chicago's 7th round choice (Viktor Gordijuk) in 1990 Entry Draft, February 16, 1989. Claimed by **Quebec** from **Chicago** in Waiver Draft, October 1, 1990. • Missed remainder of 1990-91 season recovering from shoulder injury originally suffered in training camp and re-injured in game vs. Hartford, November 21, 1990.

			REGULAR SEASON																			PLAYOFFS							
Season	**Club**	**League**	**GP**	**G**	**A**	**Pts**	**AG**	**AA**	**APts**	**PIM**	**PP**	**SH**	**GW**	**S**	**%**	**TGF**	**PGF**	**TGA**	**PGA**	**+/–**	**GP**	**G**	**A**	**Pts**	**PIM**	**PP**	**SH**	**GW**

• VAN DRUNEN, David

D – R. 6', 204 lbs. b: Sherwood Park, Alta., 1/31/1976.

Season	Club	League	GP	G	A	Pts	AG	AA	APts	PIM	PP	SH	GW	S	%	TGF	PGF	TGA	PGA	+/–	GP	G	A	Pts	PIM	PP	SH	GW
1992-93	Sherwood Park Kings	AAHA	32	3	16	19	....	....	....	114	....	....	....	....	....	....	....	....	....	....	....	....	....	....	....	....	....	....
1993-94	Prince Albert Raiders	WHL	63	3	10	13	....	....	....	95	....	....	....	....	....	....	....	....	....	....	....	....	....	....	....	....	....	....
1994-95	Prince Albert Raiders	WHL	71	2	14	16	....	....	....	132	....	....	....	....	....	....	....	....	....	....	15	3	4	7	36	....	....	....
1995-96	Prince Albert Raiders	WHL	70	10	23	33	....	....	....	172	....	....	....	....	....	....	....	....	....	....	18	1	5	6	37	....	....	....
1996-97	Prince Albert Raiders	WHL	72	18	47	65	....	....	....	218	....	....	....	....	....	....	....	....	....	....	4	0	4	4	24	....	....	....
1997-98	Hershey Bears	AHL	5	0	0	0	....	....	....	2	....	....	....	....	....	....	....	....	....	....	....	....	....	....	....	....	....	....
	Portland Pirates	AHL	4	0	0	0	....	....	....	2	....	....	....	....	....	....	....	....	....	....	....	....	....	....	....	....	....	....
	Baton Rouge Kingfish	ECHL	59	8	22	30	....	....	....	107	....	....	....	....	....	....	....	....	....	....	....	....	....	....	....	....	....	....
1998-99	Saginaw Gears	UHL	63	5	17	22	....	....	....	107	....	....	....	....	....	....	....	....	....	....	....	....	....	....	....	....	....	....
	Cincinnati Cyclones	IHL	1	0	0	0	....	....	....	0	....	....	....	....	....	....	....	....	....	....	....	....	....	....	....	....	....	....
	Dayton Bombers	ECHL	9	2	4	6	....	....	....	12	....	....	....	....	....	....	....	....	....	....	4	0	0	0	12	....	....	....
99-2000	**Ottawa Senators**	**NHL**	**1**	**0**	**0**	**0**	**0**	**0**	**0**	**0**	**0**	**0**	**0**	**0**	**0.0**	**0**	**0**	**0**	**0**	**0**	....	....	....	....	....	....	....	....
	Grand Rapids Griffins	IHL	36	0	6	6	....	....	....	76	....	....	....	....	....	....	....	....	....	....	1	0	0	0	2	....	....	....
	Mobile Mysticks	ECHL	29	1	9	10	....	....	....	78	....	....	....	....	....	....	....	....	....	....	5	1	1	2	14	....	....	....
	NHL Totals		**1**	**0**	**0**	**0**	**0**	**0**	**0**	**0**	**0**	**0**	**0**	**0**	**0.0**	**0**	**0**	**0**	**0**		....	....	....	....	....	....	....	....

WHL East Second All-Star Team (1997)

Signed as a free agent by **Ottawa**, May 2, 1997.

• VAN IMPE, Darren

Darren Cyril D – L. 6'1", 205 lbs. b: Saskatoon, Sask., 5/18/1973. NY Islanders' 7th, 170th overall, in 1993.

Season	Club	League	GP	G	A	Pts	AG	AA	APts	PIM	PP	SH	GW	S	%	TGF	PGF	TGA	PGA	+/–	GP	G	A	Pts	PIM	PP	SH	GW
1989-90	Prince Albert Midget Raiders	AAHA	32	16	31	47	....	....	....	100	....	....	....	....	....	....	....	....	....	....	....	....	....	....	....	....	....	....
	Prince Albert Raiders	WHL	1	0	1	1	....	....	....	0	....	....	....	....	....	....	....	....	....	....	....	....	....	....	....	....	....	....
1990-91	Prince Albert Raiders	WHL	70	15	45	60	....	....	....	57	....	....	....	....	....	....	....	....	....	....	3	1	1	2	2	....	....	....
1991-92	Prince Albert Raiders	WHL	69	9	37	46	....	....	....	89	....	....	....	....	....	....	....	....	....	....	8	1	5	6	10	....	....	....
1992-93	Red Deer Rebels	WHL	54	23	47	70	....	....	....	118	....	....	....	....	....	....	....	....	....	....	4	2	5	7	16	....	....	....
1993-94	Red Deer Rebels	WHL	58	20	64	84	....	....	....	125	....	....	....	....	....	....	....	....	....	....	4	2	4	6	6	....	....	....
1994-95	San Diego Gulls	IHL	76	6	17	23	....	....	....	74	....	....	....	....	....	....	....	....	....	....	5	0	0	0	0	....	....	....
	Mighty Ducks of Anaheim	**NHL**	**1**	**0**	**1**	**1**	**0**	**1**	**1**	**4**	**0**	**0**	**0**	**0**	**0.0**	**1**	**0**	**1**	**0**	**0**	....	....	....	....	....	....	....	....
1995-96	**Mighty Ducks of Anaheim**	**NHL**	**16**	**1**	**2**	**3**	**1**	**2**	**3**	**14**	**0**	**0**	**1**	**13**	**7.7**	**12**	**1**	**6**	**3**	**8**	....	....	....	....	....	....	....	....
	Baltimore Bandits	AHL	63	11	47	58	....	....	....	79	....	....	....	....	....	....	....	....	....	....	....	....	....	....	....	....	....	....
1996-97	**Mighty Ducks of Anaheim**	**NHL**	**74**	**4**	**19**	**23**	**4**	**17**	**21**	**90**	**2**	**0**	**0**	**107**	**3.7**	**67**	**15**	**51**	**2**	**3**	**9**	**0**	**2**	**2**	**16**	**0**	**0**	**0**
1997-98	**Mighty Ducks of Anaheim**	**NHL**	**19**	**1**	**3**	**4**	**1**	**3**	**4**	**4**	**0**	**0**	**0**	**21**	**4.8**	**8**	**2**	**16**	**0**	**–10**	....	....	....	....	....	....	....	....
	Boston Bruins	**NHL**	**50**	**2**	**8**	**10**	**2**	**8**	**10**	**36**	**2**	**0**	**0**	**50**	**4.0**	**37**	**9**	**25**	**1**	**4**	**6**	**2**	**1**	**3**	**0**	**1**	**0**	**1**
1998-99	**Boston Bruins**	**NHL**	**60**	**5**	**15**	**20**	**6**	**14**	**20**	**66**	**4**	**0**	**0**	**92**	**5.4**	**57**	**25**	**38**	**1**	**–5**	**11**	**1**	**2**	**3**	**4**	**1**	**0**	**0**
99-2000	**Boston Bruins**	**NHL**	**79**	**5**	**23**	**28**	**6**	**21**	**27**	**73**	**4**	**0**	**0**	**97**	**5.2**	**74**	**34**	**69**	**10**	**–19**	....	....	....	....	....	....	....	....
	NHL Totals		**299**	**18**	**71**	**89**	**20**	**66**	**86**	**287**	**12**	**0**	**1**	**380**	**4.7**	**256**	**86**	**206**	**17**		**26**	**3**	**5**	**8**	**20**	**2**	**0**	**1**

WHL East First All-Star Team (1993, 1994)

Traded to **Anaheim** by **NY Islanders** for Anaheim's 8th round choice (Mike Broda) in 1995 Entry Draft, August 31, 1994. Claimed on waivers by **Boston** from **Anaheim**, November 26, 1997.

• VAN IMPE, Ed

Edward Charles D – L. 5'10", 205 lbs. b: Saskatoon, Sask., 5/27/1940.

Season	Club	League	GP	G	A	Pts	AG	AA	APts	PIM	PP	SH	GW	S	%	TGF	PGF	TGA	PGA	+/–	GP	G	A	Pts	PIM	PP	SH	GW
1955-56	Riversdale Raiders	SAHA	STATISTICS NOT AVAILABLE																									
1956-57	Riversdale Raiders	SAHA	STATISTICS NOT AVAILABLE																									
	Saskatoon Jr. Quakers	SJHL	2	0	0	0	....	....	....	0	....	....	....	....	....	....	....	....	....	....	....	....	....	....	....	....	....	....
1957-58	Saskatoon Jr. Quakers	SJHL	49	2	2	4	....	....	....	58	....	....	....	....	....	....	....	....	....	....	....	....	....	....	....	....	....	....
1958-59	Saskatoon Jr. Quakers	SJHL	48	0	23	23	....	....	....	*150	....	....	....	....	....	....	....	....	....	....	5	0	2	2	24	....	....	....
1959-60	Saskatoon Jr. Quakers	SJHL	58	11	42	53	....	....	....	136	....	....	....	....	....	....	....	....	....	....	7	1	2	3	4	....	....	....
	Saskatoon Quakers	Al-Cup	6	1	0	1	....	....	....	6	....	....	....	....	....	....	....	....	....	....	....	....	....	....	....	....	....	....
1960-61	Calgary Stampeders	WHL	66	4	15	19	....	....	....	123	....	....	....	....	....	....	....	....	....	....	5	0	2	2	16	....	....	....
1961-62	Buffalo Bisons	AHL	70	0	19	19	....	....	....	172	....	....	....	....	....	....	....	....	....	....	11	0	1	1	*25	....	....	....
1962-63	Buffalo Bisons	AHL	65	3	12	15	....	....	....	*196	....	....	....	....	....	....	....	....	....	....	13	1	4	5	34	....	....	....
1963-64	Buffalo Bisons	AHL	70	4	22	26	....	....	....	*193	....	....	....	....	....	....	....	....	....	....	....	....	....	....	....	....	....	....
1964-65	Buffalo Bisons	AHL	72	5	6	11	....	....	....	197	....	....	....	....	....	....	....	....	....	....	9	0	0	0	26	....	....	....
1965-66	Buffalo Bisons	AHL	70	9	28	37	....	....	....	153	....	....	....	....	....	....	....	....	....	....	....	....	....	....	....	....	....	....
1966-67	**Chicago Black Hawks**	**NHL**	**61**	**8**	**11**	**19**	**9**	**11**	**20**	**111**	....	....	....	....	....	....	....	....	....	....	**6**	**0**	**0**	**0**	**8**	**0**	**0**	**0**
1967-68	**Philadelphia Flyers**	**NHL**	**67**	**4**	**13**	**17**	**5**	**13**	**18**	**141**	**4**	**0**	**1**	**129**	**3.1**	**66**	**16**	**70**	**15**	**–5**	**7**	**0**	**4**	**4**	**11**	**0**	**0**	**0**
1968-69	**Philadelphia Flyers**	**NHL**	**68**	**7**	**12**	**19**	**7**	**11**	**18**	**112**	**1**	**0**	**0**	**118**	**5.9**	**66**	**13**	**81**	**15**	**–13**	**1**	**0**	**0**	**0**	**17**	**0**	**0**	**0**
1969-70	**Philadelphia Flyers**	**NHL**	**65**	**0**	**10**	**10**	**0**	**9**	**9**	**117**	**0**	**0**	**0**	**81**	**0.0**	**52**	**1**	**74**	**22**	**–1**	....	....	....	....	....	....	....	....
1970-71	**Philadelphia Flyers**	**NHL**	**77**	**0**	**11**	**11**	**0**	**9**	**9**	**80**	**0**	**0**	**0**	**70**	**0.0**	**46**	**2**	**77**	**20**	**–13**	**4**	**0**	**1**	**1**	**8**	**0**	**0**	**0**
1971-72	**Philadelphia Flyers**	**NHL**	**73**	**4**	**9**	**13**	**4**	**8**	**12**	**78**	**0**	**0**	**0**	**110**	**3.6**	**62**	**1**	**95**	**26**	**–8**	....	....	....	....	....	....	....	....
1972-73	**Philadelphia Flyers**	**NHL**	**72**	**1**	**11**	**12**	**1**	**9**	**10**	**76**	**0**	**0**	**0**	**66**	**1.5**	**81**	**2**	**97**	**40**	**22**	**11**	**0**	**0**	**0**	**16**	**0**	**0**	**0**
1973-74♦	**Philadelphia Flyers**	**NHL**	**77**	**2**	**16**	**18**	**2**	**13**	**15**	**119**	**0**	**0**	**1**	**76**	**2.6**	**74**	**1**	**64**	**22**	**31**	**17**	**1**	**2**	**3**	**41**	**0**	**0**	**0**
1974-75♦	**Philadelphia Flyers**	**NHL**	**78**	**1**	**17**	**18**	**1**	**13**	**14**	**109**	**0**	**0**	**0**	**57**	**1.8**	**71**	**3**	**68**	**39**	**39**	**17**	**0**	**4**	**4**	**28**	**0**	**0**	**0**
1975-76	**Philadelphia Flyers**	**NHL**	**40**	**0**	**8**	**8**	**0**	**6**	**6**	**60**	**0**	**0**	**0**	**15**	**0.0**	**39**	**0**	**43**	**20**	**16**	....	....	....	....	....	....	....	....
	Pittsburgh Penguins	**NHL**	**12**	**0**	**5**	**5**	**0**	**4**	**4**	**16**	**0**	**0**	**0**	**7**	**0.0**	**17**	**0**	**16**	**3**	**4**	**3**	**0**	**1**	**1**	**2**	**0**	**0**	**0**
1976-77	**Pittsburgh Penguins**	**NHL**	**10**	**0**	**3**	**3**	**0**	**2**	**2**	**6**	**0**	**0**	**0**	**3**	**0.0**	**5**	**0**	**8**	**1**	**–2**	....	....	....	....	....	....	....	....
	NHL Totals		**700**	**27**	**126**	**153**	**29**	**108**	**137**	**1025**	....	....	....	....	....	....	....	....	....	....	**66**	**1**	**12**	**13**	**131**	....	....	....

Played in NHL All-Star Game (1969, 1974, 1975)

Claimed by **Philadelphia** from **Chicago** in Expansion Draft, June 6, 1967. Traded to **Pittsburgh** by **Philadelphia** with Bobby Taylor for Gary Inness and cash, March 9, 1976.

• VARADA, Vaclav

RW – L. 6', 200 lbs. b: Vsetin, Czech., 4/26/1976. San Jose's 4th, 89th overall, in 1994.

Season	Club	League	GP	G	A	Pts	AG	AA	APts	PIM	PP	SH	GW	S	%	TGF	PGF	TGA	PGA	+/–	GP	G	A	Pts	PIM	PP	SH	GW
1992-93	TJ Vitkovice	Czech.	1	0	0	0	....	....	....	....	....	....	....	....	....	....	....	....	....	....	....	....	....	....	....	....	....	....
1993-94	HC Vitkovice	Czech-Rep	24	6	7	13	....	....	....	....	....	....	....	....	....	....	....	....	....	....	5	1	1	2	....	....	....	....
	Czech-Republic	EJC-A	5	3	3	6	....	....	....	6	....	....	....	....	....	....	....	....	....	....	....	....	....	....	....	....	....	....
1994-95	Tacoma Rockets	WHL	68	50	38	88	....	....	....	108	....	....	....	....	....	....	....	....	....	....	4	4	3	7	11	....	....	....
	Czech-Republic	WJC-A	7	6	4	10	....	....	....	25	....	....	....	....	....	....	....	....	....	....	....	....	....	....	....	....	....	....
1995-96	Kelowna Rockets	WHL	59	39	46	85	....	....	....	100	....	....	....	....	....	....	....	....	....	....	6	3	3	6	16	....	....	....
	Czech-Republic	WJC-A	6	5	1	6	....	....	....	8	....	....	....	....	....	....	....	....	....	....	....	....	....	....	....	....	....	....
	Buffalo Sabres	**NHL**	**1**	**0**	**0**	**0**	**0**	**0**	**0**	**0**	**0**	**0**	**0**	**2**	**0.0**	**0**	**0**	**0**	**0**	**0**	....	....	....	....	....	....	....	....
	Rochester Americans	AHL	5	3	0	3	....	....	....	4	....	....	....	....	....	....	....	....	....	....	....	....	....	....	....	....	....	....
1996-97	**Buffalo Sabres**	**NHL**	**5**	**0**	**0**	**0**	**0**	**0**	**0**	**2**	**0**	**0**	**0**	**2**	**0.0**	**0**	**0**	**0**	**0**	**0**	....	....	....	....	....	....	....	....
	Rochester Americans	AHL	53	23	25	48	....	....	....	81	....	....	....	....	....	....	....	....	....	....	10	1	6	7	27	....	....	....
1997-98	**Buffalo Sabres**	**NHL**	**27**	**5**	**6**	**11**	**6**	**6**	**12**	**15**	**0**	**0**	**1**	**27**	**18.5**	**13**	**0**	**13**	**0**	**0**	**15**	**3**	**4**	**7**	**18**	**0**	**0**	**0**
	Rochester Americans	AHL	45	30	26	56	....	....	....	74	....	....	....	....	....	....	....	....	....	....	....	....	....	....	....	....	....	....
1998-99	**Buffalo Sabres**	**NHL**	**72**	**7**	**24**	**31**	**8**	**23**	**31**	**61**	**1**	**0**	**1**	**123**	**5.7**	**52**	**8**	**36**	**3**	**11**	**21**	**5**	**4**	**9**	**14**	**1**	**0**	**0**
99-2000	HC Vitkovice	Czech-Rep	5	2	3	5	....	....	....	12	....	....	....	....	....	....	....	....	....	....	....	....	....	....	....	....	....	....
	Buffalo Sabres	**NHL**	**76**	**10**	**27**	**37**	**11**	**25**	**36**	**62**	**0**	**0**	**0**	**140**	**7.1**	**48**	**6**	**33**	**3**	**12**	**5**	**0**	**0**	**0**	**8**	**0**	**0**	**0**
	Czech-Republic	WC-A	9	2	4	6	....	....	....	6	....	....	....	....	....	....	....	....	....	....	....	....	....	....	....	....	....	....
	NHL Totals		**181**	**22**	**57**	**79**	**25**	**54**	**79**	**140**	**1**	**0**	**2**	**294**	**7.5**	**113**	**14**	**82**	**6**		**41**	**8**	**8**	**16**	**40**	**1**	**0**	**0**

Traded to **Buffalo** by **San Jose** with Martin Spahnel and Philadelphia's 1st (previously acquired by San Jose — later traded to Phoenix — Phoenix selected Daniel Briere) and 4th (previously acquired, Buffalo selected Mike Martone) round choices in 1996 Entry Draft for Doug Bodger, November 16, 1995.

• VARIS, Petri

Petri J. LW – L. 6'1", 200 lbs. b: Varkaus, Finland, 5/13/1969. San Jose's 7th, 132nd overall, in 1993.

Season	Club	League	GP	G	A	Pts	AG	AA	APts	PIM	PP	SH	GW	S	%	TGF	PGF	TGA	PGA	+/–	GP	G	A	Pts	PIM	PP	SH	GW
1986-87	Karhu-Kissat	Finland-Jr.	2	0	1	1	....	....	....	0	....	....	....	....	....	....	....	....	....	....	....	....	....	....	....	....	....	....
1987-88	Karhu-Kissat	Finland-2	42	9	15	24	....	....	....	21	....	....	....	....	....	....	....	....	....	....	....	....	....	....	....	....	....	....
1988-89	Karhu-Kissat	Finland-Jr.	7	4	5	9	....	....	....	10	....	....	....	....	....	....	....	....	....	....	....	....	....	....	....	....	....	....
	Karhu-Kissat	Finland-2	44	18	19	37	....	....	....	26	....	....	....	....	....	....	....	....	....	....	....	....	....	....	....	....	....	....
1989-90	Karhu-Kissat	Finland-2	42	30	24	54	....	....	....	44	....	....	....	....	....	....	....	....	....	....	....	....	....	....	....	....	....	....

			REGULAR SEASON																		PLAYOFFS							
Season	Club	League	GP	G	A	Pts	AG	AA	APts	PIM	PP	SH	GW	S	%	TGF	PGF	TGA	PGA	+/–	GP	G	A	Pts	PIM	PP	SH	GW
1990-91	KooKoo Kouvola	Finland-2	44	20	31	51	....	....	....	42	....	....	....	....	....	....	....	....	....	....	....	....	....	....	....	....	....	....
1991-92	Assat Pori	Finland	36	13	23	36	....	....	....	24	....	....	....	....	....	....	....	....	....	....	....	....	....	....	....	....	....	....
1992-93	Assat Pori	Finland	46	14	35	49	....	....	....	42	....	....	....	....	....	....	....	....	....	....	8	2	2	4	12	....	....	....
1993-94	Jokerit Helsinki	Finland	31	14	15	29	....	....	....	16	....	....	....	....	....	....	....	....	....	....	11	3	4	7	6	....	....	....
	Finland	Olympics	5	1	1	2	....	....	....	2	....	....	....	....	....	....	....	....	....	....	....	....	....	....	....	....	....	....
1994-95	Haukat Jarvenpaa	Finland-2	1	0	1	1	....	....	....	2	....	....	....	....	....	....	....	....	....	....	....	....	....	....	....	....	....	....
	Jokerit Helsinki	Finland	47	21	20	41	....	....	....	53	....	....	....	....	....	....	....	....	....	....	11	7	2	9	10	....	....	....
1995-96	Jokerit Helsinki	Finland	50	*28	28	56	....	....	....	22	....	....	....	....	....	....	....	....	....	....	11	*12	7	19	6	....	....	....
1996-97	Jokerit Helsinki	Finland	50	*36	23	*59	....	....	....	38	....	....	....	....	....	....	....	....	....	....	9	*7	4	11	14	....	....	....
	Jokerit Helsinki	EuroHL	6	2	8	10	....	....	....	2	....	....	....	....	....	....	....	....	....	....	....	....	....	....	....	....	....	....
	Finland	WC-A	8	2	3	5	....	....	....	2	....	....	....	....	....	....	....	....	....	....	....	....	....	....	....	....	....	....
1997-98	**Chicago Blackhawks**	**NHL**	**1**	**0**	**0**	**0**	**0**	**0**	**0**	**0**	**0**	**0**	**0**	**0**	**0.0**	**0**	**0**	**0**	**0**	**0**	....	....	....	....	....	....	....	....
	Indianapolis Ice	IHL	77	18	54	72	....	....	....	32	....	....	....	....	....	....	....	....	....	....	5	3	4	7	4	....	....	....
1998-99	Kolner Haie	Germany	52	10	25	35	....	....	....	22	....	....	....	....	....	....	....	....	....	....	5	3	0	5	4	....	....	....
99-2000	Jokerit Helsinki	Finland	53	21	25	46	....	....	....	42	....	....	....	....	....	....	....	....	....	....	10	0	6	6	14	....	....	....
	NHL Totals		**1**	**0**	**0**	**0**	**0**	**0**	**0**	**0**	**0**	**0**	**0**	**0**	**0.0**	**0**	**0**	**0**	**0**		....	....	....	....	....	....	....	....

Finnish Rookie of the Year (1992)

Rights traded to **Chicago** by **San Jose** with San Jose's 6th round choice (Jari Viuhkola) in 1998 Entry Draft for Murray Craven, July 25, 1997.

• VARLAMOV, Sergei

LW – L. 5'11", 195 lbs. b: Kiev, USSR, 7/21/1978.

Season	Club	League	GP	G	A	Pts	AG	AA	APts	PIM	PP	SH	GW	S	%	TGF	PGF	TGA	PGA	+/–	GP	G	A	Pts	PIM	PP	SH	GW
1995-96	Swift Current Broncos	WHL	55	23	21	44	....	....	....	65	....	....	....	....	....	....	....	....	....	....	....	....	....	....	....	....	....	....
1996-97	Swift Current Broncos	WHL	72	46	39	85	....	....	....	94	....	....	....	....	....	....	....	....	....	....	10	3	8	11	10	....	....	....
	Saint John Flames	AHL	1	0	0	0	....	....	....	0	....	....	....	....	....	....	....	....	....	....	....	....	....	....	....	....	....	....
1997-98	Swift Current Broncos	WHL	72	*66	53	*119	....	....	....	132	....	....	....	....	....	....	....	....	....	....	12	10	5	15	28	....	....	....
	Calgary Flames	**NHL**	**1**	**0**	**0**	**0**	**0**	**0**	**0**	**0**	**0**	**0**	**0**	**0**	**0.0**	....	....	....	....	**0**	....	....	....	....	....	....	....	....
	Saint John Flames	AHL	....	....	....	....	....	....	....	....	....	....	....	....	....	....	....	....	....	....	3	0	0	0	0	....	....	....
1998-99	Saint John Flames	AHL	76	24	33	57	....	....	....	66	....	....	....	....	....	....	....	....	....	....	7	0	4	4	8	....	....	....
99-2000	**Calgary Flames**	**NHL**	**7**	**3**	**0**	**3**	**3**	**0**	**3**	**0**	**0**	**0**	**1**	**11**	**27.3**	**5**	**0**	**5**	**0**	**0**	....	....	....	....	....	....	....	....
	Saint John Flames	AHL	68	20	21	41	....	....	....	88	....	....	....	....	....	....	....	....	....	....	3	0	0	0	24	....	....	....
	Ukraine	WC-A	6	0	5	5	....	....	....	42	....	....	....	....	....	....	....	....	....	....	....	....	....	....	....	....	....	....
	NHL Totals		**8**	**3**	**0**	**3**	**3**	**0**	**3**	**0**	**0**	**0**	**1**	**11**	**27.3**	**5**	**0**	**5**	**0**		....	....	....	....	....	....	....	....

WHL East First All-Star Team (1998) • Canadian Major Junior First All-Star Team (1998) • Canadian Major Junior Player of the Year (1998)

Signed as a free agent by **Calgary**, September 18, 1996.

• VARVIO, Jarkko

RW – R. 5'9", 175 lbs. b: Tampere, Finland, 4/28/1972. Minnesota's 1st, 34th overall, in 1992.

Season	Club	League	GP	G	A	Pts	AG	AA	APts	PIM	PP	SH	GW	S	%	TGF	PGF	TGA	PGA	+/–	GP	G	A	Pts	PIM	PP	SH	GW
1989-90	Ilves Tampere	Finland-Jr.	31	34	14	48	....	....	....	10	....	....	....	....	....	....	....	....	....	....	3	4	1	5	0	....	....	....
	Ilves Tampere	Finland	1	0	0	0	....	....	....	0	....	....	....	....	....	....	....	....	....	....	....	....	....	....	....	....	....	....
1990-91	Ilves Tampere	Finland-Jr.	7	10	7	17	....	....	....	12	....	....	....	....	....	....	....	....	....	....	7	6	6	12	2	....	....	....
	Finland	WJC-A	7	5	4	9	....	....	....	4	....	....	....	....	....	....	....	....	....	....	....	....	....	....	....	....	....	....
	Ilves Tampere	Finland	37	10	7	17	....	....	....	6	....	....	....	....	....	....	....	....	....	....	....	....	....	....	....	....	....	....
1991-92	HPK Hameenlinna	Finland-Jr.	1	2	4	6	....	....	....	0	....	....	....	....	....	....	....	....	....	....	....	....	....	....	....	....	....	....
	HPK Hameenlinna	Finland	41	25	9	34	....	....	....	6	....	....	....	....	....	....	....	....	....	....	....	....	....	....	....	....	....	....
	Finland	WJC-A	7	8	1	9	....	....	....	8	....	....	....	....	....	....	....	....	....	....	....	....	....	....	....	....	....	....
	Finland	WC-A	8	9	1	10	....	....	....	4	....	....	....	....	....	....	....	....	....	....	....	....	....	....	....	....	....	....
1992-93	HPK Hameenlinna	Finland-Jr.	2	3	2	5	....	....	....	4	....	....	....	....	....	....	....	....	....	....	....	....	....	....	....	....	....	....
	HPK Hameenlinna	Finland	40	29	19	48	....	....	....	16	....	....	....	....	....	....	....	....	....	....	12	3	2	5	8	....	....	....
	Finland	WC-A	6	2	0	2	....	....	....	6	....	....	....	....	....	....	....	....	....	....	....	....	....	....	....	....	....	....
1993-94	**Dallas Stars**	**NHL**	**8**	**2**	**3**	**5**	**2**	**2**	**4**	**4**	**0**	**0**	**1**	**17**	**11.8**	**6**	**2**	**3**	**0**	**1**	....	....	....	....	....	....	....	....
	Kalamazoo Wings	IHL	58	29	16	45	....	....	....	18	....	....	....	....	....	....	....	....	....	....	1	0	0	0	0	....	....	....
1994-95	HPK Hameenlinna	Finland	19	7	8	15	....	....	....	4	....	....	....	....	....	....	....	....	....	....	....	....	....	....	....	....	....	....
	Dallas Stars	**NHL**	**5**	**1**	**1**	**2**	**2**	**1**	**3**	**0**	**1**	**0**	**0**	**9**	**11.1**	**3**	**1**	**1**	**0**	**1**	....	....	....	....	....	....	....	....
	Kalamazoo Wings	IHL	7	0	0	0	....	....	....	2	....	....	....	....	....	....	....	....	....	....	....	....	....	....	....	....	....	....
1995-96	Lukko Rauma	Finland	47	14	13	27	....	....	....	32	....	....	....	....	....	....	....	....	....	....	8	5	0	5	4	....	....	....
1996-97	Lukko Rauma	Finland	40	9	11	20	....	....	....	40	....	....	....	....	....	....	....	....	....	....	....	....	....	....	....	....	....	....
	Lukko Rauma	EuroHL	5	3	2	5	....	....	....	2	....	....	....	....	....	....	....	....	....	....	....	....	....	....	....	....	....	....
	Finland	WC-A	8	0	0	0	....	....	....	4	....	....	....	....	....	....	....	....	....	....	....	....	....	....	....	....	....	....
1997-98	Tappara Tampere	Finland	47	19	13	32	....	....	....	22	....	....	....	....	....	....	....	....	....	....	4	0	2	2	4	....	....	....
1998-99	AIK Solna Stockholm	Sweden	27	17	10	27	....	....	....	8	....	....	....	....	....	....	....	....	....	....	....	....	....	....	....	....	....	....
	HV-71 Jonkoping	Sweden	13	1	1	2	....	....	....	4	....	....	....	....	....	....	....	....	....	....	....	....	....	....	....	....	....	....
99-2000	AIK Solna Stockholm	Sweden	26	4	9	13	....	....	....	12	....	....	....	....	....	....	....	....	....	....	....	....	....	....	....	....	....	....
	SC Rapperswil-Jona	Switz.	12	7	6	13	....	....	....	2	....	....	....	....	....	....	....	....	....	....	5	0	0	0	2	....	....	....
	NHL Totals		**13**	**3**	**4**	**7**	**4**	**3**	**7**	**4**	**1**	**0**	**1**	**26**	**11.5**	**9**	**3**	**4**	**0**		....	....	....	....	....	....	....	....

WC-A All-Star Team (1992) • Finnish First All-Star Team (1993)

Rights transferred to **Dallas** after **Minnesota** franchise relocated, June 9, 1993.

• VASILEVSKI, Alexander

RW – L. 5'11", 190 lbs. b: Kiev, USSR, 1/8/1975. St. Louis' 9th, 271st overall, in 1993.

Season	Club	League	GP	G	A	Pts	AG	AA	APts	PIM	PP	SH	GW	S	%	TGF	PGF	TGA	PGA	+/–	GP	G	A	Pts	PIM	PP	SH	GW
1992-93	Victoria Cougars	WHL	71	27	25	52	....	....	....	52	....	....	....	....	....	....	....	....	....	....	....	....	....	....	....	....	....	....
1993-94	Victoria Cougars	WHL	69	34	51	85	....	....	....	78	....	....	....	....	....	....	....	....	....	....	....	....	....	....	....	....	....	....
1994-95	Prince George Cougars	WHL	48	32	34	66	....	....	....	52	....	....	....	....	....	....	....	....	....	....	....	....	....	....	....	....	....	....
	Brandon Wheat Kings	WHL	23	6	11	17	....	....	....	39	....	....	....	....	....	....	....	....	....	....	18	3	6	9	34	....	....	....
	Brandon Wheat Kings	Mem-Cup	4	0	1	1	....	....	....	2	....	....	....	....	....	....	....	....	....	....	....	....	....	....	....	....	....	....
1995-96	**St. Louis Blues**	**NHL**	**1**	**0**	**0**	**0**	**0**	**0**	**0**	**0**	**0**	**0**	**0**	**0**	**0.0**	**0**	**0**	**1**	**0**	**–1**	....	....	....	....	....	....	....	....
	Worcester IceCats	AHL	69	18	21	39	....	....	....	112	....	....	....	....	....	....	....	....	....	....	4	2	1	3	10	....	....	....
1996-97	**St. Louis Blues**	**NHL**	**3**	**0**	**0**	**0**	**0**	**0**	**0**	**2**	**0**	**0**	**0**	**3**	**0.0**	**0**	**0**	**1**	**0**	**–1**	....	....	....	....	....	....	....	....
	Worcester IceCats	AHL	61	9	23	32	....	....	....	100	....	....	....	....	....	....	....	....	....	....	....	....	....	....	....	....	....	....
	Grand Rapids Griffins	IHL	10	1	5	6	....	....	....	43	....	....	....	....	....	....	....	....	....	....	5	0	1	1	19	....	....	....
1997-98	Hamilton Bulldogs	AHL	41	3	14	17	....	....	....	60	....	....	....	....	....	....	....	....	....	....	....	....	....	....	....	....	....	....
	Detroit Vipers	IHL	9	1	1	2	....	....	....	7	....	....	....	....	....	....	....	....	....	....	....	....	....	....	....	....	....	....
1998-99	Severstal Cherepovets	Russia	2	0	0	0	....	....	....	0	....	....	....	....	....	....	....	....	....	....	....	....	....	....	....	....	....	....
	Krylja Sovetov Moscow	Russia	7	2	1	3	....	....	....	4	....	....	....	....	....	....	....	....	....	....	....	....	....	....	....	....	....	....
99-2000	Muskegon Fury	UHL	19	10	8	18	....	....	....	22	....	....	....	....	....	....	....	....	....	....	....	....	....	....	....	....	....	....
	Long Beach Ice Dogs	IHL	51	8	25	33	....	....	....	109	....	....	....	....	....	....	....	....	....	....	5	0	3	3	4	....	....	....
	NHL Totals		**4**	**0**	**0**	**0**	**0**	**0**	**0**	**2**	**0**	**0**	**0**	**3**	**0.0**	**0**	**0**	**2**	**0**		....	....	....	....	....	....	....	....

• VASILIEV, Alexei

D – L. 6'1", 190 lbs. b: Yaroslavl, USSR, 9/1/1977. NY Rangers' 4th, 110th overall, in 1995.

Season	Club	League	GP	G	A	Pts	AG	AA	APts	PIM	PP	SH	GW	S	%	TGF	PGF	TGA	PGA	+/–	GP	G	A	Pts	PIM	PP	SH	GW
1993-94	Torpedo Yaroslavl	CIS	2	0	1	1	....	....	....	4	....	....	....	....	....	....	....	....	....	....	....	....	....	....	....	....	....	....
1994-95	Torpedo Yaroslavl-2	CIS-2	STATISTICS NOT AVAILABLE																									
1995-96	Torpedo Yaroslavl	CIS	40	4	7	11	....	....	....	4	....	....	....	....	....	....	....	....	....	....	....	....	....	....	....	....	....	....
1996-97	Torpedo Yaroslavl	Russia	44	2	8	10	....	....	....	10	....	....	....	....	....	....	....	....	....	....	9	1	1	2	8	....	....	....
1997-98	Hartford Wolf Pack	AHL	DID NOT PLAY – INJURED																									
1998-99	Hartford Wolf Pack	AHL	75	8	19	27	....	....	....	24	....	....	....	....	....	....	....	....	....	....	6	0	1	1	2	....	....	....
99-2000	**New York Rangers**	**NHL**	**1**	**0**	**0**	**0**	**0**	**0**	**0**	**2**	**0**	**0**	**0**	**0**	**0.0**						....	....	....	....	....	....	....	....
	Hartford Wolf Pack	AHL	75	10	28	38	....	....	....	20	....	....	....	....	....	....	....	....	....	....	15	3	1	4	2	....	....	....
	NHL Totals		**1**	**0**	**0**	**0**	**0**	**0**	**0**	**2**	**0**	**0**	**0**	**0**	**0.0**						....	....	....	....	....	....	....	....

• Missed entire 1997-98 season recovering from knee injury suffered in training camp, October, 1997.

• VASILJEVS, Herbert

C – R. 5'11", 180 lbs. b: Riga, USSR, 5/27/1976.

Season	Club	League	GP	G	A	Pts	AG	AA	APts	PIM	PP	SH	GW	S	%	TGF	PGF	TGA	PGA	+/–	GP	G	A	Pts	PIM	PP	SH	GW
			REGULAR SEASON																		PLAYOFFS							
1994-95	Krefeld Pinguine	Germany	42	4	5	9	....	....	....	24	....	....	....	....	....	....	....	....	....	....	15	1	4	5	10	....	....	....
1995-96	Guelph Storm	OHL	65	34	33	67	....	....	....	63	....	....	....	....	....	....	....	....	....	....	16	6	13	19	6	....	....	....
1996-97	Carolina Monarchs	AHL	54	13	18	31	....	....	....	30	....	....	....	....	....	....	....	....	....	....	....	....	....	....	....	....	....	....
	Port Huron Border Cats	ColHL	3	3	2	5	....	....	....	4	....	....	....	....	....	....	....	....	....	....	....	....	....	....	....	....	....	....
1997-98	Beast of New Haven	AHL	76	36	30	66	....	....	....	60	....	....	....	....	....	....	....	....	....	....	3	1	0	1	2	....	....	....
1998-99	**Florida Panthers**	**NHL**	**5**	**0**	**0**	**0**	**0**	**0**	**0**	**2**	**0**	**0**	**0**	**6**	**0.0**	**0**	**0**	**1**	**0**	**–1**	....	....	....	....	....	....	....	....
	Kentucky Thoroughblades	AHL	76	28	48	76	....	....	....	66	....	....	....	....	....	....	....	....	....	....	12	2	1	3	4	....	....	....
99-2000	**Atlanta Thrashers**	**NHL**	**7**	**1**	**0**	**1**	**1**	**0**	**1**	**4**	**0**	**0**	**0**	**2**	**50.0**	**2**	**1**	**5**	**1**	**–3**	....	....	....	....	....	....	....	....
	Orlando Solar Bears	IHL	73	25	35	60	....	....	....	60	....	....	....	....	....	....	....	....	....	....	6	2	2	4	6	....	....	....
	Latvia	WC-A	1	0	0	0	....	....	....	4	....	....	....	....	....	....	....	....	....	....	....	....	....	....	....	....	....	....
	NHL Totals		**12**	**1**	**0**	**1**	**1**	**0**	**1**	**6**	**0**	**0**	**0**	**8**	**12.5**	**2**	**1**	**6**	**1**		....	....	....	....	....	....	....	....

Signed as a free agent by **Florida**, October 3, 1996. Traded to **Atlanta** by **Florida** with Gord Murphy, Daniel Tjarnqvist and Ottawa's 6th round choice (previously acquired, later traded to Dallas - Dallas selected Justin Cox) in 1999 Entry Draft for Trevor Kidd, June 25, 1999.

• VASILYEV, Andrei

LW – R. 5'9", 180 lbs. b: Voskresensk, USSR, 3/30/1972. NY Islanders' 11th, 248th overall, in 1992.

Season	Club	League	GP	G	A	Pts	AG	AA	APts	PIM	PP	SH	GW	S	%	TGF	PGF	TGA	PGA	+/–	GP	G	A	Pts	PIM	PP	SH	GW
1991-92	CSKA Moscow	CIS	28	7	2	9	....	....	....	2	....	....	....	....	....	....	....	....	....	....	....	....	....	....	....	....	....	....
1992-93	Khimik Voskresensk	CIS	34	4	8	12	....	....	....	20	....	....	....	....	....	....	....	....	....	....	....	....	....	....	....	....	....	....
1993-94	CSKA Moscow	CIS	46	17	6	23	....	....	....	8	....	....	....	....	....	....	....	....	....	....	3	1	0	1	0	....	....	....
1994-95	**New York Islanders**	**NHL**	**2**	**0**	**0**	**0**	**0**	**0**	**0**	**2**	**0**	**0**	**0**	**2**	**0.0**	**0**	**0**	**0**	**0**	**0**	....	....	....	....	....	....	....	....
	Denver Grizzlies	IHL	74	28	37	65	....	....	....	48	....	....	....	....	....	....	....	....	....	....	13	9	4	13	22	....	....	....
1995-96	**New York Islanders**	**NHL**	**10**	**2**	**5**	**7**	**2**	**4**	**6**	**2**	**0**	**0**	**1**	**12**	**16.7**	**12**	**4**	**4**	**0**	**4**	....	....	....	....	....	....	....	....
	Utah Grizzlies	IHL	43	26	20	46	....	....	....	34	....	....	....	....	....	....	....	....	....	....	22	12	4	16	18	....	....	....
1996-97	**New York Islanders**	**NHL**	**3**	**0**	**0**	**0**	**0**	**0**	**0**	**2**	**0**	**0**	**0**	**1**	**0.0**	**0**	**0**	**3**	**0**	**–3**	....	....	....	....	....	....	....	....
	Utah Grizzlies	IHL	56	16	18	34	....	....	....	42	....	....	....	....	....	....	....	....	....	....	7	4	1	5	0	....	....	....
1997-98	Long Beach Ice Dogs	IHL	62	33	34	67	....	....	....	60	....	....	....	....	....	....	....	....	....	....	17	9	4	13	14	....	....	....
1998-99	**Phoenix Coyotes**	**NHL**	**1**	**0**	**0**	**0**	**0**	**0**	**0**	**0**	**0**	**0**	**0**	**0**	**0.0**	**0**	**0**	**2**	**0**	**–2**	....	....	....	....	....	....	....	....
	Las Vegas Thunder	IHL	15	3	6	9	....	....	....	6	....	....	....	....	....	....	....	....	....	....	....	....	....	....	....	....	....	....
	Grand Rapids Griffins	IHL	59	21	27	48	....	....	....	24	....	....	....	....	....	....	....	....	....	....	....	....	....	....	....	....	....	....
99-2000	Frankfurt Lions	Germany	54	26	21	47	....	....	....	18	....	....	....	....	....	....	....	....	....	....	5	2	1	3	30	....	....	....
	NHL Totals		**16**	**2**	**5**	**7**	**2**	**4**	**6**	**6**	**0**	**0**	**1**	**15**	**13.3**	**12**	**4**	**9**	**0**		....	....	....	....	....	....	....	....

Signed as a free agent by **Phoenix**, August 26, 1998.

• VASKE, Dennis

D – L. 6'2", 210 lbs. b: Rockford, IL, 10/11/1967. NY Islanders' 2nd, 38th overall, in 1986.

Season	Club	League	GP	G	A	Pts	AG	AA	APts	PIM	PP	SH	GW	S	%	TGF	PGF	TGA	PGA	+/–	GP	G	A	Pts	PIM	PP	SH	GW
1984-85	Armstrong High School	Hi-School	22	5	18	23	....	....	....	....	....	....	....	....	....	....	....	....	....	....	....	....	....	....	....	....	....	....
1985-86	Armstrong High School	Hi-School	20	9	13	22	....	....	....	....	....	....	....	....	....	....	....	....	....	....	....	....	....	....	....	....	....	....
1986-87	University of Minnesota-Duluth	WCHA	33	0	2	2	....	....	....	40	....	....	....	....	....	....	....	....	....	....	....	....	....	....	....	....	....	....
1987-88	University of Minnesota-Duluth	WCHA	39	1	6	7	....	....	....	90	....	....	....	....	....	....	....	....	....	....	....	....	....	....	....	....	....	....
1988-89	University of Minnesota-Duluth	WCHA	37	9	19	28	....	....	....	86	....	....	....	....	....	....	....	....	....	....	....	....	....	....	....	....	....	....
1989-90	University of Minnesota-Duluth	WCHA	37	5	24	29	....	....	....	72	....	....	....	....	....	....	....	....	....	....	....	....	....	....	....	....	....	....
1990-91	**New York Islanders**	**NHL**	**5**	**0**	**0**	**0**	**0**	**0**	**0**	**2**	**0**	**0**	**0**	**3**	**0.0**	**7**	**0**	**4**	**1**	**4**	....	....	....	....	....	....	....	....
	Capital District Islanders	AHL	67	10	10	20	....	....	....	65	....	....	....	....	....	....	....	....	....	....	....	....	....	....	....	....	....	....
1991-92	**New York Islanders**	**NHL**	**39**	**0**	**1**	**1**	**0**	**1**	**1**	**39**	**0**	**0**	**0**	**26**	**0.0**	**35**	**1**	**42**	**13**	**5**	....	....	....	....	....	....	....	....
	Capital District Islanders	AHL	31	1	11	12	....	....	....	59	....	....	....	....	....	....	....	....	....	....	....	....	....	....	....	....	....	....
	United States	WC-A	6	0	0	0	....	....	....	6	....	....	....	....	....	....	....	....	....	....	....	....	....	....	....	....	....	....
1992-93	**New York Islanders**	**NHL**	**27**	**1**	**5**	**6**	**1**	**3**	**4**	**32**	**0**	**0**	**0**	**15**	**6.7**	**34**	**0**	**28**	**3**	**9**	**18**	**0**	**6**	**6**	**14**	**0**	**0**	**0**
	Capital District Islanders	AHL	42	4	15	19	....	....	....	70	....	....	....	....	....	....	....	....	....	....	....	....	....	....	....	....	....	....
1993-94	**New York Islanders**	**NHL**	**65**	**2**	**11**	**13**	**2**	**9**	**11**	**76**	**0**	**0**	**0**	**71**	**2.8**	**71**	**5**	**67**	**22**	**21**	**4**	**0**	**1**	**1**	**2**	**0**	**0**	**0**
1994-95	**New York Islanders**	**NHL**	**41**	**1**	**11**	**12**	**2**	**16**	**18**	**53**	**0**	**0**	**0**	**48**	**2.1**	**44**	**7**	**53**	**19**	**3**	....	....	....	....	....	....	....	....
1995-96	**New York Islanders**	**NHL**	**19**	**1**	**6**	**7**	**1**	**5**	**6**	**21**	**1**	**0**	**1**	**19**	**5.3**	**18**	**8**	**36**	**13**	**–13**	....	....	....	....	....	....	....	....
1996-97	**New York Islanders**	**NHL**	**17**	**0**	**4**	**4**	**0**	**4**	**4**	**12**	**0**	**0**	**0**	**19**	**0.0**	**17**	**2**	**13**	**1**	**3**	....	....	....	....	....	....	....	....
1997-98	**New York Islanders**	**NHL**	**19**	**0**	**3**	**3**	**0**	**3**	**3**	**12**	**0**	**0**	**0**	**16**	**0.0**	**18**	**3**	**16**	**3**	**2**	....	....	....	....	....	....	....	....
1998-99	**Boston Bruins**	**NHL**	**3**	**0**	**0**	**0**	**0**	**0**	**0**	**6**	**0**	**0**	**0**	**0**	**0.0**	**0**	**0**	**3**	**0**	**–3**	....	....	....	....	....	....	....	....
	Providence Bruins	AHL	43	2	13	15	....	....	....	56	....	....	....	....	....	....	....	....	....	....	19	1	5	6	26	....	....	....
	NHL Totals		**235**	**5**	**41**	**46**	**6**	**41**	**47**	**253**	**1**	**0**	**1**	**217**	**2.3**	**244**	**26**	**262**	**75**		**22**	**0**	**7**	**7**	**16**	**0**	**0**	**0**

• Missed remainder of 1995-96 season recovering from head injury suffered in game vs. LA Kings, November 22, 1995. • Missed majority of 1996-97 season recovering from head injury suffered in game vs. Washington, November 29, 1996. • Missed remainder of 1997-98 season recovering from head injury suffered in game vs. Buffalo, November 22, 1997. Signed as a free agent by **Boston**, September 10, 1998.

• VASKO, Moose

Elmer "Moose" D – L. 6'2", 200 lbs. b: Duparquet, Que., 12/11/1935 d: 10/30/1998.

Season	Club	League	GP	G	A	Pts	AG	AA	APts	PIM	PP	SH	GW	S	%	TGF	PGF	TGA	PGA	+/–	GP	G	A	Pts	PIM	PP	SH	GW
1953-54	St. Catharines Teepees	OHA-Jr.	59	5	17	22	....	....	....	25	....	....	....	....	....	....	....	....	....	....	15	0	2	2	10	....	....	....
	St. Catharines Teepees	Mem-Cup	11	0	2	2	....	....	....	6	....	....	....	....	....	....	....	....	....	....	....	....	....	....	....	....	....	....
1954-55	St. Catharines Teepees	OHA-Jr.	49	16	20	36	....	....	....	75	....	....	....	....	....	....	....	....	....	....	11	2	3	5	17	....	....	....
1955-56	St. Catharines Teepees	OHA-Jr.	47	9	31	40	....	....	....	90	....	....	....	....	....	....	....	....	....	....	6	2	3	5	8	....	....	....
	Buffalo Bisons	AHL	4	0	3	3	....	....	....	4	....	....	....	....	....	....	....	....	....	....	3	1	0	1	2	....	....	....
1956-57	**Chicago Black Hawks**	**NHL**	**64**	**3**	**12**	**15**	**4**	**13**	**17**	**31**	....	....	....	....	....	....	....	....	....	....	....	....	....	....	....	....	....	....
1957-58	**Chicago Black Hawks**	**NHL**	**59**	**6**	**20**	**26**	**7**	**21**	**28**	**51**	....	....	....	....	....	....	....	....	....	....	....	....	....	....	....	....	....	....
1958-59	**Chicago Black Hawks**	**NHL**	**63**	**6**	**10**	**16**	**7**	**10**	**17**	**52**	....	....	....	....	....	....	....	....	....	....	**6**	**0**	**1**	**1**	**4**	**0**	**0**	**0**
1959-60	**Chicago Black Hawks**	**NHL**	**69**	**3**	**27**	**30**	**3**	**26**	**29**	**110**	....	....	....	....	....	....	....	....	....	....	**4**	**0**	**0**	**0**	**0**	**0**	**0**	**0**
1960-61 ♦	**Chicago Black Hawks**	**NHL**	**63**	**4**	**18**	**22**	**5**	**17**	**22**	**40**	....	....	....	....	....	....	....	....	....	....	**12**	**1**	**1**	**2**	**23**	**1**	**0**	**1**
1961-62	**Chicago Black Hawks**	**NHL**	**64**	**2**	**22**	**24**	**2**	**21**	**23**	**87**	....	....	....	....	....	....	....	....	....	....	**12**	**0**	**0**	**0**	**4**	**0**	**0**	**0**
1962-63	**Chicago Black Hawks**	**NHL**	**64**	**4**	**9**	**13**	**5**	**9**	**14**	**70**	....	....	....	....	....	....	....	....	....	....	**6**	**0**	**1**	**1**	**8**	**0**	**0**	**0**
1963-64	**Chicago Black Hawks**	**NHL**	**70**	**2**	**18**	**20**	**2**	**19**	**21**	**65**	....	....	....	....	....	....	....	....	....	....	**7**	**0**	**0**	**0**	**4**	**0**	**0**	**0**
1964-65	**Chicago Black Hawks**	**NHL**	**69**	**1**	**10**	**11**	**1**	**10**	**11**	**56**	....	....	....	....	....	....	....	....	....	....	**14**	**1**	**2**	**3**	**20**	**0**	**0**	**0**
1965-66	**Chicago Black Hawks**	**NHL**	**56**	**1**	**7**	**8**	**1**	**7**	**8**	**44**	....	....	....	....	....	....	....	....	....	....	**3**	**0**	**0**	**0**	**4**	**0**	**0**	**0**
1966-67			OUT OF HOCKEY – RETIRED																									
1967-68	**Minnesota North Stars**	**NHL**	**70**	**1**	**6**	**7**	**1**	**6**	**7**	**45**	**0**	**0**	**0**	**23**	**4.3**	**49**	**3**	**88**	**6**	**–36**	**14**	**0**	**2**	**2**	**6**	**0**	**0**	**0**
1968-69	**Minnesota North Stars**	**NHL**	**72**	**1**	**7**	**8**	**1**	**6**	**7**	**68**	**0**	**0**	**0**	**52**	**1.9**	**70**	**2**	**109**	**23**	**–18**	....	....	....	....	....	....	....	....
1969-70	**Minnesota North Stars**	**NHL**	**3**	**0**	**0**	**0**	**0**	**0**	**0**	**0**	**0**	**0**	**0**	**3**	**0.0**	**1**	**0**	**3**	**1**	**–1**	....	....	....	....	....	....	....	....
	Salt Lake Golden Eagles	WHL	54	4	6	10	....	....	....	34	....	....	....	....	....	....	....	....	....	....	....	....	....	....	....	....	....	....
	NHL Totals		**786**	**34**	**166**	**200**	**39**	**165**	**204**	**719**	....	....	....	....	....	....	....	....	....	....	**78**	**2**	**7**	**9**	**73**	....	....	....

NHL Second All-Star Team (1963, 1964) • Played in NHL All-Star Game (1961, 1963, 1964, 1969)

Claimed by **Minnesota** from **Chicago** in Expansion Draft, June 6, 1967.

• VASKO, Rick

Richard John "The Moose" D – L. 6', 185 lbs. b: St. Catharines, Ont., 1/12/1957. Detroit's 2nd, 37th overall, in 1977.

Season	Club	League	GP	G	A	Pts	AG	AA	APts	PIM	PP	SH	GW	S	%	TGF	PGF	TGA	PGA	+/–	GP	G	A	Pts	PIM	PP	SH	GW
1974-75	Markham Waxers	OHA-B	25	5	10	15	....	....	....	60	....	....	....	....	....	....	....	....	....	....	....	....	....	....	....	....	....	....
1975-76	Peterborough Petes	OMJHL	63	9	20	29	....	....	....	53	....	....	....	....	....	....	....	....	....	....	....	....	....	....	....	....	....	....
1976-77	Peterborough Petes	OMJHL	65	6	30	36	....	....	....	122	....	....	....	....	....	....	....	....	....	....	4	0	1	1	2	....	....	....
1977-78	**Detroit Red Wings**	**NHL**	**3**	**0**	**0**	**0**	**0**	**0**	**0**	**7**	**0**	**0**	**0**	**6**	**0.0**	**1**	**0**	**2**	**0**	**–1**	....	....	....	....	....	....	....	....
	Kansas City Red Wings	CHL	70	11	30	41	....	....	....	72	....	....	....	....	....	....	....	....	....	....	....	....	....	....	....	....	....	....
1978-79	Kansas City Red Wings	CHL	75	21	38	59	....	....	....	67	....	....	....	....	....	....	....	....	....	....	4	1	1	2	2	....	....	....
1979-80	**Detroit Red Wings**	**NHL**	**8**	**0**	**0**	**0**	**0**	**0**	**0**	**2**	**0**	**0**	**0**	**6**	**0.0**	**2**	**1**	**12**	**0**	**–11**	....	....	....	....	....	....	....	....
	Adirondack Red Wings	AHL	71	22	39	61	....	....	....	79	....	....	....	....	....	....	....	....	....	....	....	....	....	....	....	....	....	....
1980-81	**Detroit Red Wings**	**NHL**	**20**	**3**	**7**	**10**	**2**	**5**	**7**	**20**	**1**	**0**	**0**	**28**	**10.7**	**24**	**6**	**30**	**9**	**–3**	....	....	....	....	....	....	....	....
	Adirondack Red Wings	AHL	57	17	34	51	....	....	....	78	....	....	....	....	....	....	....	....	....	....	18	9	12	*21	31	....	....	....

			REGULAR SEASON																		PLAYOFFS							
Season	Club	League	GP	G	A	Pts	AG	AA	APts	PIM	PP	SH	GW	S	%	TGF	PGF	TGA	PGA	+/-	GP	G	A	Pts	PIM	PP	SH	GW
1981-82	Oklahoma City Stars	CHL	68	9	32	41				92											4	1	1	2	4			
1982-83	ZSC Zurich	Switz-2	STATISTICS NOT AVAILABLE																									
1983-84	ZSC Zurich	Switz.	36	12	10	22																						
	NHL Totals		**31**	**3**	**7**	**10**	**2**	**5**	**7**	**29**	**1**	**0**	**0**	**40**	**7.5**	**27**	**7**	**44**	**9**									

AHL First All-Star Team (1980) • Won Eddie Shore Award (Outstanding Defenseman - AHL) (1980)

Traded to **Calgary** by **Detroit** to complete transaction that sent Brad Smith to Detroit (February 24, 1981), May 28, 1981.

• VAUTOUR, Yvon

Yvon Jean RW – R. 6', 200 lbs. b: St. John, N.B., 9/10/1956. NY Islanders' 6th, 104th overall, in 1976.

Season	Club	League	GP	G	A	Pts	AG	AA	APts	PIM	PP	SH	GW	S	%	TGF	PGF	TGA	PGA	+/-	GP	G	A	Pts	PIM	PP	SH	GW
1971-72	Saint John Schooners	NBJHL	40	13	15	28				96																		
1972-73	Saint John Schooners	NBJHL	40	42	31	73				85																		
1973-74	Laval Nationale	QMJHL	61	38	39	77				118																		
1974-75	Laval Nationale	QMJHL	56	34	37	71				67											16	15	7	22	67			
1975-76	Laval Nationale	QMJHL	72	43	60	103				61																		
1976-77	Muskegon Mohawks	IHL	76	43	47	90				52											7	3	4	7	2			
	Fort Worth Texans	CHL																			2	0	0	0	0			
1977-78	Fort Worth Texans	CHL	64	14	21	35				84											14	2	6	8	16			
1978-79	Fort Worth Texans	CHL	69	20	20	40				130											5	2	1	3	15			
1979-80	**New York Islanders**	**NHL**	**17**	**3**	**1**	**4**	**3**	**1**	**4**	**24**	**0**	**0**	**1**	**16**	**18.8**	**5**	**0**	**12**	**1**	**–6**								
	Indianapolis Checkers	CHL	59	27	28	55				140											7	2	5	7	11			
1980-81	**Colorado Rockies**	**NHL**	**74**	**15**	**19**	**34**	**12**	**13**	**25**	**143**	**3**	**0**	**0**	**97**	**15.5**	**51**	**8**	**66**	**3**	**–20**								
1981-82	**Colorado Rockies**	**NHL**	**14**	**1**	**2**	**3**	**1**	**1**	**2**	**18**	**1**	**0**	**0**	**21**	**4.8**	**7**	**1**	**12**	**0**	**–6**								
1982-83	**New Jersey Devils**	**NHL**	**52**	**4**	**7**	**11**	**3**	**5**	**8**	**136**	**0**	**0**	**0**	**54**	**7.4**	**17**	**2**	**34**	**0**	**–19**								
	Moncton Alpines	AHL	14	7	5	12				25																		
	Wichita Wind	CHL	4	3	0	3				0																		
1983-84	**New Jersey Devils**	**NHL**	**42**	**3**	**4**	**7**	**2**	**3**	**5**	**78**	**0**	**0**	**1**	**44**	**6.8**	**11**	**2**	**28**	**1**	**–18**								
	Maine Mariners	AHL	24	8	12	20				117																		
1984-85	**Quebec Nordiques**	**NHL**	**5**	**0**	**0**	**0**	**0**	**0**	**0**	**2**	**0**	**0**	**0**	**1**	**0.0**	**0**	**0**	**0**	**0**	**0**								
	Fredericton Express	AHL	68	7	20	27				222											4	1	1	2	26			
1985-86			OUT OF HOCKEY – RETIRED																									
1986-87			OUT OF HOCKEY – RETIRED																									
1987-88	Saint John Schooners	NBSHL	28	17	11	28				98																		
1988-89	Saint John Vitos	NBSHL	27	17	25	42				118												4	11	15				
1989-90	Saint John Vitos	NBSHL	26	5	11	16				*182																		
	NHL Totals		**204**	**26**	**33**	**59**	**21**	**23**	**44**	**401**	**4**	**0**	**2**	**233**	**11.2**	**91**	**13**	**152**	**5**									

Claimed by **NY Islanders** as a fill-in during Expansion Draft, June 13, 1979. Claimed by **Colorado** from **NY Islanders** in Waiver Draft, October 8, 1980. Transferred to **New Jersey** after **Colorado** franchise relocated, June 30, 1982. Signed as a free agent by **Quebec**, October 18, 1984.

• VAYDIK, Greg

Gregory C – L. 6'1", 190 lbs. b: Yellowknife, N.W.T., 10/9/1955. Chicago's 1st, 7th overall, in 1975.

Season	Club	League	GP	G	A	Pts	AG	AA	APts	PIM	PP	SH	GW	S	%	TGF	PGF	TGA	PGA	+/-	GP	G	A	Pts	PIM	PP	SH	GW
1972-73	Drumheller Falcons	AJHL	STATISTICS NOT AVAILABLE																									
	Medicine Hat Tigers	WCJHL	38	5	3	8				6											17	0	0	0	0			
1973-74	Medicine Hat Tigers	WCJHL	68	33	41	74				24											6	4	4	8	7			
1974-75	Medicine Hat Tigers	WCJHL	61	55	51	106				37											5	4	7	11	4			
	Canada	WJC-A	3	0	1	1				0																		
1975-76	Dallas Black Hawks	CHL	17	5	5	10				2																		
1976-77	**Chicago Black Hawks**	**NHL**	**5**	**0**	**0**	**0**	**0**	**0**	**0**	**0**	**0**	**0**	**0**	**2**	**0.0**	**1**	**0**	**3**	**0**	**–2**								
	Dallas Black Hawks	CHL	68	29	32	61				10											5	0	3	3	0			
1977-78	Dallas Black Hawks	CHL	73	26	18	44				8											13	3	3	6	4			
1978-79	Rochester Americans	AHL	80	16	25	41				10																		
1979-80	New Brunswick Hawks	AHL	60	12	19	31				0																		
1980-81	Dallas Black Hawks	CHL	26	6	5	11				6																		
1981-82	Dallas Black Hawks	CHL	65	20	30	50				20											16	3	6	9	8			
	NHL Totals		**5**	**0**	**0**	**0**	**0**	**0**	**0**	**0**	**0**	**0**	**0**	**2**	**0.0**	**1**	**0**	**3**	**0**									

• Missed majority of 1975-76 season recovering from knee injury suffered in vs. Dallas (CHL), November 24, 1975.

• VEITCH, Darren

Darren William D – R. 5'11", 195 lbs. b: Saskatoon, Sask., 4/24/1960. Washington's 1st, 5th overall, in 1980.

Season	Club	League	GP	G	A	Pts	AG	AA	APts	PIM	PP	SH	GW	S	%	TGF	PGF	TGA	PGA	+/-	GP	G	A	Pts	PIM	PP	SH	GW
1976-77	Regina Blues	SJHL	60	15	21	36				121																		
	Regina Pats	WCJHL	1	0	0	0				0																		
1977-78	Regina Pats	WCJHL	71	13	32	45				135											9	0	2	2	4			
1978-79	Regina Pats	WHL	51	11	36	47				80																		
1979-80	Regina Pats	WHL	71	29	*93	122				118											18	13	18	31	13			
	Regina Pats	Mem-Cup	4	3	5	8				4																		
1980-81	**Washington Capitals**	**NHL**	**59**	**4**	**21**	**25**	**3**	**14**	**17**	**46**	**1**	**0**	**1**	**89**	**4.5**	**71**	**23**	**67**	**7**	**–12**								
	Hershey Bears	AHL	26	6	22	28				12											10	6	3	9	15			
1981-82	**Washington Capitals**	**NHL**	**67**	**9**	**44**	**53**	**7**	**29**	**36**	**54**	**5**	**0**	**1**	**203**	**4.4**	**128**	**60**	**101**	**16**	**–17**								
	Hershey Bears	AHL	10	5	10	15				16																		
1982-83	**Washington Capitals**	**NHL**	**10**	**0**	**8**	**8**	**0**	**6**	**6**	**0**	**0**	**0**	**0**	**23**	**0.0**	**15**	**6**	**11**	**1**	**–1**								
	Hershey Bears	AHL	5	0	1	1				2																		
1983-84	**Washington Capitals**	**NHL**	**46**	**6**	**18**	**24**	**5**	**12**	**17**	**17**	**4**	**0**	**0**	**120**	**5.0**	**65**	**28**	**43**	**6**	**0**	**5**	**0**	**1**	**1**	**15**	**0**	**0**	**0**
	Hershey Bears	AHL	11	1	6	7				4																		
1984-85	**Washington Capitals**	**NHL**	**75**	**3**	**18**	**21**	**2**	**12**	**14**	**37**	**2**	**0**	**0**	**126**	**2.4**	**101**	**22**	**81**	**33**	**31**	**5**	**0**	**1**	**1**	**4**	**0**	**0**	**0**
1985-86	**Washington Capitals**	**NHL**	**62**	**3**	**9**	**12**	**2**	**6**	**8**	**27**	**0**	**0**	**0**	**82**	**3.7**	**58**	**1**	**57**	**21**	**21**								
	Detroit Red Wings	**NHL**	**13**	**0**	**5**	**5**	**0**	**3**	**3**	**2**	**0**	**0**	**0**	**22**	**0.0**	**16**	**4**	**24**	**3**	**–9**								
1986-87	**Detroit Red Wings**	**NHL**	**77**	**13**	**45**	**58**	**11**	**33**	**44**	**52**	**7**	**1**	**2**	**164**	**7.9**	**120**	**46**	**85**	**25**	**14**	**12**	**3**	**4**	**7**	**8**	**2**	**0**	**1**
1987-88	**Detroit Red Wings**	**NHL**	**63**	**7**	**33**	**40**	**6**	**24**	**30**	**45**	**4**	**0**	**1**	**156**	**4.5**	**102**	**31**	**69**	**9**	**11**	**11**	**1**	**5**	**6**	**6**	**1**	**0**	**0**
1988-89	**Toronto Maple Leafs**	**NHL**	**37**	**3**	**7**	**10**	**3**	**5**	**8**	**16**	**1**	**0**	**0**	**69**	**4.3**	**31**	**10**	**48**	**10**	**–17**								
	Newmarket Saints	AHL	33	5	19	24				29											5	0	4	4	4			
1989-90	Newmarket Saints	AHL	78	13	54	67				30																		
1990-91	**Toronto Maple Leafs**	**NHL**	**2**	**0**	**1**	**1**	**0**	**1**	**1**	**0**	**0**	**0**	**0**	**2**	**0.0**	**3**	**1**	**6**	**0**	**–4**								
	Newmarket Saints	AHL	56	7	28	35				26																		
	Peoria Rivermen	IHL	18	2	14	16				10											19	4	12	16	10			
1991-92	Moncton Hawks	AHL	61	6	23	29				47											11	0	6	6	2			
	EV Landshut	Germany	14	2	4	6				4																		
1992-93	Peoria Rivermen	IHL	79	12	37	49				16											4	2	0	2	4			
1993-94	Peoria Rivermen	IHL	76	21	54	75				16											6	1	1	2	0			
1994-95	Peoria Rivermen	IHL	75	8	42	50				42											9	0	2	2	8			
1995-96	Peoria Rivermen	IHL	15	1	9	10				8																		
	Phoenix Roadrunners	IHL	43	1	15	16				12											1	0	0	0	0			
1996-97			OUT OF HOCKEY – RETIRED																									
1997-98	Phoenix Mustangs	WCHL	59	6	31	37				40											9	3	6	9	12			
1998-99	Phoenix Mustangs	WCHL	52	3	29	32				46											3	0	1	1	2			
	NHL Totals		**511**	**48**	**209**	**257**	**39**	**145**	**184**	**296**	**24**	**1**	**5**	**1056**	**4.5**	**710**	**232**	**592**	**131**		**33**	**4**	**11**	**15**	**33**	**3**	**0**	**1**

WHL All-Star Team (1980) • Memorial Cup All-Star Team (1980) • AHL Second All-Star Team (1990) • Won Governors' Trophy (Top Defenseman - IHL) (1994)

• Missed majority of 1982-83 season recovering from collarbone injury suffered in game vs. Vancouver, October 28, 1982. Traded to **Detroit** by **Washington** for John Barrett and Greg Smith, March 10, 1986. Traded to **Toronto** by **Detroit** for Miroslav Frycer, June 10, 1988. Traded to **St. Louis** by **Toronto** for Keith Osborne, March 5, 1991. Signed as a free agent by **Phoenix Mustangs**, October 6, 1997. • Retired in 1996-97 to work as colour analyst on Phoenix Roadrunners television broadcasts.

• VELISCHEK, Randy

Randy John D – L. 6', 200 lbs. b: Montreal, Que., 2/10/1962. Minnesota's 3rd, 53rd overall, in 1980.

			REGULAR SEASON																		PLAYOFFS							
Season	Club	League	GP	G	A	Pts	AG	AA	APts	PIM	PP	SH	GW	S	%	TGF	PGF	TGA	PGA	+/–	GP	G	A	Pts	PIM	PP	SH	GW
1977-78	Lac St-Louis Lions	QAAA	26	3	25	28																						
1978-79	Lac-St-Louis Lions	QAAA	39	13	31	44																						
1979-80	Providence College	ECAC	31	5	5	10				20																		
1980-81	Providence College	ECAC	33	3	12	15				26																		
1981-82	Providence College	ECAC	33	1	14	15				38																		
1982-83	Providence College	ECAC	41	18	34	52				50																		
	Minnesota North Stars	**NHL**	3	0	0	0	0	0	0	2	0	0	0	4	0.0	1	0	8	3	–4	9	0	0	0	0	0	0	0
1983-84	**Minnesota North Stars**	**NHL**	33	2	2	4	2	1	3	10	0	0	0	15	13.3	24	0	34	4	–6	1	0	0	0	0	0	0	0
	Salt Lake Golden Eagles	CHL	43	7	21	28				54											5	0	3	3	2			
1984-85	**Minnesota North Stars**	**NHL**	52	4	9	13	3	6	9	26	0	0	0	33	12.1	51	0	55	11	7	9	2	3	5	8	0	0	0
	Springfield Indians	AHL	26	2	7	9				22																		
1985-86	**New Jersey Devils**	**NHL**	47	2	7	9	2	5	7	39	0	0	0	24	8.3	45	1	95	31	–20								
	Maine Mariners	AHL	21	0	4	4				4																		
1986-87	**New Jersey Devils**	**NHL**	64	2	16	18	2	12	14	52	0	0	0	39	5.1	59	0	102	31	–12								
1987-88	**New Jersey Devils**	**NHL**	51	3	9	12	3	6	9	66	0	1	0	39	7.7	25	1	56	19	–13	19	0	2	2	20	0	0	0
1988-89	**New Jersey Devils**	**NHL**	80	4	14	18	3	10	13	70	0	1	0	77	5.2	61	1	136	74	–2								
1989-90	**New Jersey Devils**	**NHL**	62	0	6	6	0	4	4	72	0	0	0	34	0.0	44	0	56	16	4	6	0	0	0	4	0	0	0
1990-91	**Quebec Nordiques**	**NHL**	79	2	10	12	2	8	10	42	0	0	0	47	4.3	59	1	139	62	–19								
1991-92	**Quebec Nordiques**	**NHL**	38	2	3	5	2	2	4	22	0	0	0	23	8.7	23	1	42	17	–3								
	Halifax Citadels	AHL	16	3	6	9				0																		
1992-93	Halifax Citadels	AHL	49	6	16	22				18																		
1993-94	Cornwall Aces	AHL	18	1	6	7				17																		
	Milwaukee Admirals	IHL	53	7	11	18				28											4	0	0	0	2			
1994-95	Milwaukee Admirals	IHL	35	3	3	6				24											12	2	2	4	6			
1995-96	Durham Wasps	BH-Cup	3	3	6	9				2																		
	NHL Totals		**509**	**21**	**76**	**97**	**19**	**54**	**73**	**401**	**0**	**2**	**0**	**335**	**6.3**	**392**	**5**	**723**	**268**		**44**	**2**	**5**	**7**	**32**	**0**	**0**	**0**

ECAC Second All-Star Team (1982) • ECAC First All-Star Team (1983) • NCAA East First All-American Team (1983)

Claimed by **New Jersey** from **Minnesota** in Waiver Draft, October 7, 1985. Traded to **Quebec** by **New Jersey** to complete transaction that sent Peter Stastny to New Jersey (March 6, 1990), August 13, 1990. • Released from contract with Durham (Britain) to join New Jersey Devils' Media Department, September 28, 1995.

• VELLUCCI, Mike

D – L. 6'1", 180 lbs. b: Farmington, MI, 8/11/1966. Hartford's 3rd, 131st overall, in 1984.

Season	Club	League	GP	G	A	Pts	AG	AA	APts	PIM	PP	SH	GW	S	%	TGF	PGF	TGA	PGA	+/–	GP	G	A	Pts	PIM	PP	SH	GW
1982-83	Detroit Compuware	MNHL	70	23	20	43				98																		
1983-84	Belleville Bulls	OHL	67	2	20	22				83											3	1	0	1	6			
1984-85	Belleville Bulls	OHL	DID NOT PLAY – INJURED																									
1985-86	Belleville Bulls	OHL	64	11	32	43				154											24	2	5	7	45			
1986-87	Salt Lake Golden Eagles	IHL	60	5	30	35				94																		
1987-88	**Hartford Whalers**	**NHL**	2	0	0	0	0	0	0	11	0	0	0	2	0.0	0	0	1	0	–1								
	Binghamton Whalers	AHL	3	0	0	0				2																		
	Milwaukee Admirals	IHL	66	7	18	25				202																		
1988-89	Binghamton Whalers	AHL	37	9	9	18				59																		
	Indianapolis Ice	IHL	12	1	2	3				43																		
1989-90	Whitley Warriors	Britain	5	1	5	6				41																		
	Phoenix Roadrunners	IHL	4	0	0	0				5																		
	Winston-Salem Thunderbirds	ECHL	10	2	7	9				21																		
	Erie Panthers	ECHL	22	7	20	27				57											7	1	4	5	6			
1990-91			DID NOT PLAY																									
1991-92	Michigan Falcons	ColHL	56	17	33	50				103																		
	NHL Totals		**2**	**0**	**0**	**0**	**0**	**0**	**0**	**11**	**0**	**0**	**0**	**2**	**0.0**	**0**	**0**	**1**	**0**									

• Missed entire 1984-85 season recovering from injuries suffered in automobile accident, June, 1984.

• VENASKY, Vic

Victor William C – R. 5'11", 185 lbs. b: Thunder Bay, Ont., 6/3/1951. Los Angeles' 1st, 34th overall, in 1971.

Season	Club	League	GP	G	A	Pts	AG	AA	APts	PIM	PP	SH	GW	S	%	TGF	PGF	TGA	PGA	+/–	GP	G	A	Pts	PIM	PP	SH	GW
1966-67	Port Arthur Marrs	TBJHL																			5	1	0	1	0			
	Port Arthur Marrs	Mem-Cup	6	0	1	1				0																		
1967-68	Port Arthur Marrs	TBJHL	24	16	17	33				0																		
1968-69	Port Arthur Marrs	TBJHL	36	29	34	63				4																		
	Fort William Hurricanes	Mem-Cup	6	7	5	12				12																		
1969-70	Port Arthur Marrs	TBJHL	22	27	20	47				0																		
	Fort William Hurricanes	Mem-Cup	12	8	12	20				6																		
	Weyburn Red Wings	Mem-Cup	4	2	4	6				0																		
1970-71	University of Denver	WCHA	36	20	36	56				12																		
1971-72	University of Denver	WCHA	21	20	36	56				8																		
1972-73	**Los Angeles Kings**	**NHL**	77	15	19	34	14	15	29	10	1	0	1	176	8.5	41	5	57	5	–16								
1973-74	**Los Angeles Kings**	**NHL**	32	6	5	11	6	4	10	12	1	0	1	45	13.3	19	8	13	1	–1								
	Springfield Kings	AHL	21	8	15	23				8																		
	Portland Buckaroos	WHL	10	1	11	12				4											9	*7	2	9	8			
1974-75	**Los Angeles Kings**	**NHL**	17	1	2	3	1	1	2	0	1	0	0	17	5.9	6	2	2	1	3								
	Fort Worth Texans	CHL	14	5	11	16				6																		
	Springfield Indians	AHL	6	2	2	4				4																		
1975-76	**Los Angeles Kings**	**NHL**	80	18	26	44	16	19	35	12	4	0	5	103	17.5	57	11	57	5	–6	9	0	1	1	6	0	0	0
1976-77	**Los Angeles Kings**	**NHL**	80	14	26	40	13	20	33	18	1	1	2	120	11.7	56	7	56	9	2	9	1	4	5	6	1	0	0
1977-78	**Los Angeles Kings**	**NHL**	71	3	10	13	3	8	11	6	0	0	3	53	5.7	16	0	19	4	1	1	0	0	0	0	0	0	0
1978-79	**Los Angeles Kings**	**NHL**	73	4	13	17	3	9	12	8	0	0	1	47	8.5	23	1	28	6	0	2	0	0	0	0	0	0	0
1979-80	Binghamton Dusters	AHL	80	25	31	56				22																		
1980-81	HC Davos	Switz.	STATISTICS NOT AVAILABLE																									
	Thunder Bay Twins	CASH	STATISTICS NOT AVAILABLE																									
	NHL Totals		**430**	**61**	**101**	**162**	**56**	**76**	**132**	**66**	**8**	**1**	**13**	**561**	**10.9**	**218**	**34**	**232**	**31**		**21**	**1**	**5**	**6**	**12**	**1**	**0**	**0**

WCHA Second All-Star Team (1971) • NCAA West First All-American Team (1971)

• Regular season totals for Port Arthur (TBJHL) during 1966-67 season are unavailable. • Loaned to **Fort William** (TBJHL) and **Weyburn** (SJHL) by **Port Arthur** (TBJHL) for Memorial Cup playoffs, April, 1970.

• VENERUZZO, Gary

Gary Raymond W – L. 5'8", 165 lbs. b: Fort William, Ont., 6/28/1943.

Season	Club	League	GP	G	A	Pts	AG	AA	APts	PIM	PP	SH	GW	S	%	TGF	PGF	TGA	PGA	+/–	GP	G	A	Pts	PIM	PP	SH	GW
1959-60	Fort William Canadiens	TBJHL	STATISTICS NOT AVAILABLE																									
	Fort William Canadiens	Mem-Cup	2	0	0	0				0																		
1960-61	Fort William Canadiens	TBJHL	24	6	13	19				18											4	0	6	6	11			
	Fort William Canadiens	Mem-Cup	7	1	5	6				2																		
1961-62	Fort William Canadiens	TBJHL	30	30	31	*61				76																		
	Port Arthur North Stars	Mem-Cup	4	2	3	5				6																		
1962-63	Fort William Beavers	TBSHL	26	27	20	47				27											14	11	15	26	25			
	Fort William Canadiens	Mem-Cup	10	8	10	18				19																		
1963-64	Fort William Beavers	TBSHL	30	26	*35	*61				35											10	7	6	13	4			
1964-65	Tulsa Oilers	CPHL	60	11	17	28				29											10	1	4	5	8			
1965-66	Tulsa Oilers	CPHL	69	19	19	38				25											11	1	7	8	5			
1966-67	Victoria Maple Leafs	WHL	11	3	5	8				2																		
	Tulsa Oilers	CPHL	59	21	25	46				38																		
1967-68	**St. Louis Blues**	**NHL**	5	1	1	2	1	1	2	0	0	0	0	8	12.5	2	0	1	0	1	9	0	2	2	2	0	0	0
	Kansas City Blues	CPHL	63	24	51	75				36											7	4	2	6	10			
1968-69	Kansas City Blues	CHL	71	38	40	78				38											4	1	1	2	13			

			REGULAR SEASON																		PLAYOFFS							
Season	Club	League	GP	G	A	Pts	AG	AA	APts	PIM	PP	SH	GW	S	%	TGF	PGF	TGA	PGA	+/-	GP	G	A	Pts	PIM	PP	SH	GW
1969-70	Kansas City Blues	CHL	52	20	30	50	....	....	....	33	....	....	....	....	....	....	....	....	....	....	....	....	....	....	....	....	....	....
	Buffalo Bisons	AHL	21	8	11	19	....	....	....	2	....	....	....	....	....	....	....	....	....	....	14	6	5	11	9	....	....	....
1970-71	Kansas City Blues	CHL	2	2	0	2	....	....	....	2	....	....	....	....	....	....	....	....	....	....	....	....	....	....	....	....	....	....
	Seattle Totems	WHL	66	27	22	49	....	....	....	30	....	....	....	....	....	....	....	....	....	....	....	....	....	....	....	....	....	....
1971-72	**St. Louis Blues**	**NHL**	**2**	**0**	**0**	**0**	**0**	**0**	**0**	**0**	**0**	**0**	**0**	**1**	**0.0**	**1**	**0**	**2**	**0**	**-1**	....	....	....	....	....	....	....	....
	Denver Spurs	WHL	72	*41	45	86	....	....	....	41	....	....	....	....	....	....	....	....	....	....	9	2	6	8	10	....	....	....
1972-73	Los Angeles Sharks	WHA	78	43	30	73	....	....	....	34	....	....	....	....	....	....	....	....	....	....	6	3	0	3	4	....	....	....
1973-74	Los Angeles Sharks	WHA	78	39	29	68	....	....	....	68	....	....	....	....	....	....	....	....	....	....	....	....	....	....	....	....	....	....
1974-75	Michigan-Baltimore Stags	WHA	77	33	27	60	....	....	....	57	....	....	....	....	....	....	....	....	....	....	....	....	....	....	....	....	....	....
1975-76	Cincinnati Stingers	WHA	14	3	2	5	....	....	....	8	....	....	....	....	....	....	....	....	....	....	....	....	....	....	....	....	....	....
	Phoenix Roadrunners	WHA	61	19	24	43	....	....	....	27	....	....	....	....	....	....	....	....	....	....	5	2	0	2	7	....	....	....
1976-77	San Diego Mariners	WHA	40	14	11	25	....	....	....	18	....	....	....	....	....	....	....	....	....	....	7	0	0	0	0	....	....	....
1977-78	Thunder Bay Twins	OHA-Sr.	14	2	4	6	....	....	....	20	....	....	....	....	....	....	....	....	....	....	....	....	....	....	....	....	....	....
1978-79	Thunder Bay Twins	CASH	40	22	25	47	....	....	....	....	....	....	....	....	....	....	....	....	....	....	....	....	....	....	....	....	....	....
	NHL Totals		**7**	**1**	**1**	**2**	**1**	**1**	**2**	**0**	**0**	**0**	**0**	**9**	**11.1**	**3**	**0**	**3**	**0**		**9**	**0**	**2**	**2**	**2**	**0**	**0**	**0**
	Other Major League Totals		348	151	123	274	....	....	....	212	....	....	....	....	....	....	....	....	....	....	18	5	0	5	11	....	....	....

Won TBSHL Rookie-of-the Year Award (1963) • CPHL Second All-Star Team (1968) • CHL First All-Star Team (1969) • WHL First All-Star Team (1972)

Claimed by **St. Louis** from **Toronto** in Expansion Draft, June 6, 1967. Selected by **LA Sharks** (WHA) in 1972 WHA General Player Draft, February 12, 1972. Transferred to **Michigan** (WHA) when **LA Sharks** (WHA) franchise relocated, April 11, 1974. Selected by **Cincinnati** (WHA) from **Baltimore-Michigan** (WHA) in WHA Dispersal Draft, June 19, 1975. Traded to **Phoenix** (WHA) by **Cincinnati** (WHA) for Ron Serafini, November, 1975. Traded to **San Diego** (WHA) by **Phoenix** (WHA) for future considerations, August, 1976.

• VERBEEK, Pat

Patrick "Little Ball of Hate" W – R. 5'9", 192 lbs. b: Sarnia, Ont., 5/24/1964. New Jersey's 3rd, 43rd overall, in 1982.

Season	Club	League	GP	G	A	Pts	AG	AA	APts	PIM	PP	SH	GW	S	%	TGF	PGF	TGA	PGA	+/-	GP	G	A	Pts	PIM	PP	SH	GW
1979-80	Petrolia Jets	OHA-B	41	17	24	41	....	....	....	85	....	....	....	....	....	....	....	....	....	....	....	....	....	....	....	....	....	....
1980-81	Petrolia Jets	OHA-B	42	44	44	88	....	....	....	155	....	....	....	....	....	....	....	....	....	....	....	....	....	....	....	....	....	....
1981-82	Sudbury Wolves	OHL	66	37	51	88	....	....	....	180	....	....	....	....	....	....	....	....	....	....	....	....	....	....	....	....	....	....
1982-83	Sudbury Wolves	OHL	61	40	67	107	....	....	....	184	....	....	....	....	....	....	....	....	....	....	....	....	....	....	....	....	....	....
	Canada	WJC-A	7	2	2	4	....	....	....	6	....	....	....	....	....	....	....	....	....	....	....	....	....	....	....	....	....	....
	New Jersey Devils	**NHL**	**6**	**3**	**2**	**5**	**2**	**1**	**3**	**8**	**0**	**0**	**0**	**12**	**25.0**	**7**	**2**	**7**	**0**	**-2**	....	....	....	....	....	....	....	....
1983-84	**New Jersey Devils**	**NHL**	**79**	**20**	**27**	**47**	**16**	**18**	**34**	**158**	**5**	**1**	**2**	**167**	**12.0**	**76**	**26**	**92**	**23**	**-19**	....	....	....	....	....	....	....	....
1984-85	**New Jersey Devils**	**NHL**	**78**	**15**	**18**	**33**	**12**	**12**	**24**	**162**	**5**	**1**	**1**	**147**	**10.2**	**64**	**17**	**84**	**13**	**-24**	....	....	....	....	....	....	....	....
1985-86	**New Jersey Devils**	**NHL**	**76**	**25**	**28**	**53**	**20**	**19**	**39**	**79**	**4**	**1**	**0**	**159**	**15.7**	**80**	**21**	**92**	**9**	**-24**	....	....	....	....	....	....	....	....
1986-87	**New Jersey Devils**	**NHL**	**74**	**35**	**24**	**59**	**30**	**17**	**47**	**120**	**17**	**0**	**5**	**143**	**24.5**	**90**	**41**	**75**	**3**	**-23**	....	....	....	....	....	....	....	....
1987-88	**New Jersey Devils**	**NHL**	**73**	**46**	**31**	**77**	**39**	**22**	**61**	**227**	**13**	**0**	**8**	**179**	**25.7**	**118**	**46**	**49**	**6**	**29**	**20**	**4**	**8**	**12**	**51**	**2**	**0**	**1**
1988-89	**New Jersey Devils**	**NHL**	**77**	**26**	**21**	**47**	**22**	**15**	**37**	**189**	**9**	**0**	**1**	**175**	**14.9**	**69**	**24**	**63**	**0**	**-18**	....	....	....	....	....	....	....	....
	Canada	WEC-A	4	0	2	2	....	....	....	2	....	....	....	....	....	....	....	....	....	....	....	....	....	....	....	....	....	....
1989-90	**Hartford Whalers**	**NHL**	**80**	**44**	**45**	**89**	**38**	**32**	**70**	**228**	**14**	**0**	**5**	**219**	**20.1**	**137**	**62**	**85**	**11**	**1**	**7**	**2**	**2**	**4**	**26**	**1**	**0**	**1**
1990-91	**Hartford Whalers**	**NHL**	**80**	**43**	**39**	**82**	**40**	**30**	**70**	**246**	**15**	**0**	**5**	**247**	**17.4**	**121**	**54**	**76**	**9**	**0**	**6**	**3**	**2**	**5**	**40**	**2**	**0**	**0**
1991-92	**Hartford Whalers**	**NHL**	**76**	**22**	**35**	**57**	**20**	**26**	**46**	**243**	**10**	**0**	**3**	**163**	**13.5**	**90**	**44**	**67**	**5**	**-16**	**7**	**0**	**2**	**2**	**12**	**0**	**0**	**0**
1992-93	**Hartford Whalers**	**NHL**	**84**	**39**	**43**	**82**	**32**	**30**	**62**	**197**	**16**	**0**	**6**	**235**	**16.6**	**120**	**51**	**92**	**16**	**-7**	....	....	....	....	....	....	....	....
1993-94	**Hartford Whalers**	**NHL**	**84**	**37**	**38**	**75**	**34**	**30**	**64**	**177**	**15**	**1**	**3**	**226**	**16.4**	**104**	**44**	**87**	**12**	**-15**	....	....	....	....	....	....	....	....
	Canada	WC-A	8	1	1	2	....	....	....	4	....	....	....	....	....	....	....	....	....	....	....	....	....	....	....	....	....	....
1994-95	**Hartford Whalers**	**NHL**	**29**	**7**	**11**	**18**	**12**	**16**	**28**	**53**	**3**	**0**	**0**	**75**	**9.3**	**30**	**10**	**22**	**2**	**0**	....	....	....	....	....	....	....	....
	New York Rangers	**NHL**	**19**	**10**	**5**	**15**	**18**	**7**	**25**	**18**	**4**	**0**	**2**	**56**	**17.9**	**28**	**14**	**16**	**0**	**-2**	**10**	**4**	**6**	**10**	**20**	**3**	**0**	**0**
1995-96	**New York Rangers**	**NHL**	**69**	**41**	**41**	**82**	**40**	**34**	**74**	**129**	**17**	**0**	**6**	**252**	**16.3**	**120**	**51**	**41**	**1**	**29**	**11**	**3**	**6**	**9**	**12**	**1**	**0**	**0**
1996-97	Canada	W-Cup	1	0	0	0	....	....	....	0	....	....	....	....	....	....	....	....	....	....	....	....	....	....	....	....	....	....
	Dallas Stars	**NHL**	**81**	**17**	**36**	**53**	**18**	**32**	**50**	**128**	**5**	**0**	**4**	**172**	**9.9**	**77**	**20**	**54**	**0**	**3**	**7**	**1**	**3**	**4**	**16**	**1**	**0**	**0**
1997-98	**Dallas Stars**	**NHL**	**82**	**31**	**26**	**57**	**36**	**25**	**61**	**170**	**9**	**0**	**8**	**190**	**16.3**	**90**	**37**	**38**	**0**	**15**	**17**	**3**	**2**	**5**	**26**	**2**	**0**	**1**
1998-99♦	**Dallas Stars**	**NHL**	**78**	**17**	**17**	**34**	**20**	**16**	**36**	**133**	**8**	**0**	**2**	**134**	**12.7**	**62**	**24**	**27**	**0**	**11**	**18**	**3**	**4**	**7**	**14**	**0**	**0**	**1**
99-2000	**Detroit Red Wings**	**NHL**	**68**	**22**	**26**	**48**	**25**	**24**	**49**	**95**	**7**	**0**	**5**	**138**	**15.9**	**85**	**27**	**36**	**0**	**22**	**9**	**1**	**1**	**2**	**2**	**1**	**0**	**1**
	NHL Totals		**1293**	**500**	**513**	**1013**	**474**	**406**	**880**	**2760**	**176**	**4**	**66**	**3089**	**16.2**	**1568**	**615**	**1103**	**110**		**112**	**24**	**36**	**60**	**219**	**13**	**0**	**5**

Played in NHL All-Star Game (1991, 1996)

Traded to **Hartford** by **New Jersey** for Sylvain Turgeon, June 17, 1989. Traded to **NY Rangers** by **Hartford** for Glen Featherstone, Michael Stewart, NY Rangers' 1st round choice (Jean-Sebastien Giguere) in 1995 Entry Draft and 4th round choice (Steve Wasylko) in 1996 Entry Draft, March 23, 1995. Signed as a free agent by **Dallas**, August 21, 1996. Signed as a free agent by **Detroit**, November 11, 1999.

• VERMETTE, Mark

Mark A. RW – R. 6'1", 203 lbs. b: Cochenour, Ont., 10/3/1967. Quebec's 8th, 134th overall, in 1986.

Season	Club	League	GP	G	A	Pts	AG	AA	APts	PIM	PP	SH	GW	S	%	TGF	PGF	TGA	PGA	+/-	GP	G	A	Pts	PIM	PP	SH	GW
1983-84	Notre Dame Midget Hounds	SAHA	STATISTICS NOT AVAILABLE																									
1984-85	Notre Dame Hounds	Hi-School	43	24	28	52	....	....	....	....	....	....	....	....	....	....	....	....	....	....	....	....	....	....	....	....	....	....
1985-86	Lake Superior State	CCHA	32	1	4	5	....	....	....	7	....	....	....	....	....	....	....	....	....	....	....	....	....	....	....	....	....	....
1986-87	Lake Superior State	CCHA	38	19	17	36	....	....	....	59	....	....	....	....	....	....	....	....	....	....	....	....	....	....	....	....	....	....
1987-88	Lake Superior State	CCHA	46	*45	30	75	....	....	....	154	....	....	....	....	....	....	....	....	....	....	....	....	....	....	....	....	....	....
1988-89	**Quebec Nordiques**	**NHL**	**12**	**0**	**4**	**4**	**0**	**3**	**3**	**7**	**0**	**0**	**0**	**10**	**0.0**	**7**	**1**	**14**	**1**	**-7**	....	....	....	....	....	....	....	....
	Halifax Citadels	AHL	52	12	16	28	....	....	....	30	....	....	....	....	....	....	....	....	....	....	1	0	0	0	0	....	....	....
1989-90	**Quebec Nordiques**	**NHL**	**11**	**1**	**5**	**6**	**1**	**4**	**5**	**8**	**0**	**0**	**0**	**16**	**6.3**	**8**	**0**	**11**	**0**	**-3**	....	....	....	....	....	....	....	....
	Halifax Citadels	AHL	47	20	17	37	....	....	....	44	....	....	....	....	....	....	....	....	....	....	6	1	5	6	6	....	....	....
1990-91	**Quebec Nordiques**	**NHL**	**34**	**3**	**4**	**7**	**3**	**3**	**6**	**10**	**0**	**0**	**0**	**42**	**7.1**	**10**	**0**	**28**	**3**	**-15**	....	....	....	....	....	....	....	....
	Halifax Citadels	AHL	46	26	22	48	....	....	....	37	....	....	....	....	....	....	....	....	....	....	....	....	....	....	....	....	....	....
1991-92	**Quebec Nordiques**	**NHL**	**10**	**1**	**0**	**1**	**1**	**0**	**1**	**8**	**0**	**0**	**0**	**12**	**8.3**	**3**	**1**	**10**	**2**	**-6**	....	....	....	....	....	....	....	....
	Halifax Citadels	AHL	44	21	18	39	....	....	....	39	....	....	....	....	....	....	....	....	....	....	....	....	....	....	....	....	....	....
1992-93	Halifax Citadels	AHL	67	42	37	79	....	....	....	32	....	....	....	....	....	....	....	....	....	....	....	....	....	....	....	....	....	....
1993-94	Las Vegas Thunder	IHL	77	22	38	60	....	....	....	61	....	....	....	....	....	....	....	....	....	....	4	0	0	0	2	....	....	....
	NHL Totals		**67**	**5**	**13**	**18**	**5**	**10**	**15**	**33**	**0**	**0**	**0**	**80**	**6.3**	**28**	**2**	**63**	**6**		....	....	....	....	....	....	....	....

NCAA West All-American Team (1988) • CCHA First All-Star Team (1988)

• VERRET, Claude

C – L. 5'9", 165 lbs. b: Lachine, Que., 4/20/1963. Buffalo's 12th, 163rd overall, in 1982.

Season	Club	League	GP	G	A	Pts	AG	AA	APts	PIM	PP	SH	GW	S	%	TGF	PGF	TGA	PGA	+/-	GP	G	A	Pts	PIM	PP	SH	GW
1978-79	Ste-Foy Couillard	QAAA	38	13	11	24	....	....	....	....	....	....	....	....	....	....	....	....	....	....	....	....	....	....	....	....	....	....
1979-80	Ste-Foy Gouverneurs	QAAA	38	29	47	76	....	....	....	....	....	....	....	....	....	....	....	....	....	....	....	....	....	....	....	....	....	....
1980-81	Trois-Rivieres Draveurs	QMJHL	68	39	73	112	....	....	....	4	....	....	....	....	....	....	....	....	....	....	19	13	24	37	7	....	....	....
1981-82	Trois-Rivieres Draveurs	QMJHL	64	54	108	*162	....	....	....	14	....	....	....	....	....	....	....	....	....	....	23	13	*35	*48	4	....	....	....
1982-83	Trois-Rivieres Draveurs	QMJHL	68	73	115	188	....	....	....	21	....	....	....	....	....	....	....	....	....	....	4	3	6	9	4	....	....	....
1983-84	**Buffalo Sabres**	**NHL**	**11**	**2**	**5**	**7**	**2**	**3**	**5**	**2**	**1**	**0**	**0**	**14**	**14.3**	**12**	**7**	**8**	**0**	**-3**	....	....	....	....	....	....	....	....
	Rochester Americans	AHL	65	39	51	90	....	....	....	4	....	....	....	....	....	....	....	....	....	....	18	5	9	14	4	....	....	....
1984-85	**Buffalo Sabres**	**NHL**	**3**	**0**	**0**	**0**	**0**	**0**	**0**	**0**	**0**	**0**	**0**	**5**	**0.0**	**1**	**1**	**2**	**0**	**-2**	....	....	....	....	....	....	....	....
	Rochester Americans	AHL	76	40	53	93	....	....	....	12	....	....	....	....	....	....	....	....	....	....	5	2	5	7	0	....	....	....
1985-86	Rochester Americans	AHL	52	19	32	51	....	....	....	14	....	....	....	....	....	....	....	....	....	....	....	....	....	....	....	....	....	....
1986-87	EHC Kloten	Switz.	1	2	1	3	....	....	....	0	....	....	....	....	....	....	....	....	....	....	4	1	1	2	2	....	....	....
	Rochester Americans	AHL	36	13	12	25	....	....	....	2	....	....	....	....	....	....	....	....	....	....	8	3	3	6	0	....	....	....
1987-88	HC Rouen	France	18	13	22	35	....	....	....	20	....	....	....	....	....	....	....	....	....	....	10	16	14	30	....	....	....	....
1988-89	HC Rouen	France	38	48	58	106	....	....	....	6	....	....	....	....	....	....	....	....	....	....	5	7	9	16	4	....	....	....
1989-90	HC Rouen	France	31	31	35	66	....	....	....	4	....	....	....	....	....	....	....	....	....	....	4	2	2	4	0	....	....	....
1990-91	HC Rouen	France	28	19	37	56	....	....	....	4	....	....	....	....	....	....	....	....	....	....	9	7	14	21	0	....	....	....
1991-92	Paris Francais Volants	France-2	14	16	9	25	....	....	....	36	....	....	....	....	....	....	....	....	....	....	....	....	....	....	....	....	....	....
	HC Rouen	France	9	9	13	22	....	....	....	4	....	....	....	....	....	....	....	....	....	....	17	9	17	26	6	....	....	....
1992-93	HC Rouen	France	31	*40	43	*83	....	....	....	6	....	....	....	....	....	....	....	....	....	....	....	....	....	....	....	....	....	....
1993-94	HC Rouen	France	8	4	17	21	....	....	....	12	....	....	....	....	....	....	....	....	....	....	4	2	6	8	0	....	....	....
	HC Lausanne	Switz-2	19	18	20	38	....	....	....	6	....	....	....	....	....	....	....	....	....	....	13	11	10	21	4	....	....	....
1994-95	HC Lausanne	Switz-2	36	44	45	89	....	....	....	6	....	....	....	....	....	....	....	....	....	....	11	10	20	30	6	....	....	....
1995-96	HC Lausanne	Switz.	19	10	8	18	....	....	....	2	....	....	....	....	....	....	....	....	....	....	7	2	5	7	20	....	....	....
1996-97	HC Geneve-Servette	Switz-2	42	31	45	76	....	....	....	6	....	....	....	....	....	....	....	....	....	....	5	5	5	10	0	....	....	....

			REGULAR SEASON																		PLAYOFFS							
Season	**Club**	**League**	**GP**	**G**	**A**	**Pts**	**AG**	**AA**	**APts**	**PIM**	**PP**	**SH**	**GW**	**S**	**%**	**TGF**	**PGF**	**TGA**	**PGA**	**+/–**	**GP**	**G**	**A**	**Pts**	**PIM**	**PP**	**SH**	**GW**
1997-98	HC Geneve-Servette	Switz-2	42	31	45	76	....	....	....	6	....	....	....	....	....	....	....	....	....	....	5	5	5	10	0	....	....	....
1998-99	HC Lausanne	Switz-2	24	13	25	38	....	....	....	12	....	....	....	....	....	....	....	....	....	....	....	....	....	....	....	....	....	....
99-2000	HC Lausanne	Switz-2	32	17	29	46	....	....	....	8	....	....	....	....	....	....	....	....	....	....	3	0	2	2	0	....	....	....
	NHL Totals		**14**	**2**	**5**	**7**	**2**	**3**	**5**	**2**	**1**	**0**	**0**	**19**	**10.5**	**13**	**8**	**10**	**0**		....	....	....	....	....	....	....	....

Won Michel Bergeron Trophy (QMJHL Rookie-of-the-Year) (1981) • QMJHL First All-Star Team (1982) • Won Dudley "Red" Garrett Memorial Award (Top Rookie - AHL) (1984) • AHL Second All-Star Team (1985)

• VERSTRAETE, Leigh

RW – R. 5'11", 185 lbs. b: Pincher Creek, Alta., 1/6/1962. Toronto's 13th, 192nd overall, in 1982.

Season	Club	League	GP	G	A	Pts	AG	AA	APts	PIM	PP	SH	GW	S	%	TGF	PGF	TGA	PGA	+/–	GP	G	A	Pts	PIM	PP	SH	GW
1978-79	Billings Bighorns	WHL	32	4	4	8	....	....	....	58	....	....	....	....	....	....	....	....	....	....	2	0	0	0	5	....	....	....
1979-80	Billings Bighorns	WHL	10	1	0	1	....	....	....	47	....	....	....	....	....	....	....	....	....	....	....	....	....	....	....	....	....	....
	Calgary Wranglers	WHL	56	12	14	26	....	....	....	168	....	....	....	....	....	....	....	....	....	....	7	2	2	4	23	....	....	....
1980-81	Calgary Wranglers	WHL	71	22	18	40	....	....	....	372	....	....	....	....	....	....	....	....	....	....	21	6	5	11	155	....	....	....
1981-82	Calgary Wranglers	WHL	49	19	20	39	....	....	....	385	....	....	....	....	....	....	....	....	....	....	8	4	4	8	43	....	....	....
1982-83	**Toronto Maple Leafs**	**NHL**	**3**	**0**	**0**	**0**	**0**	**0**	**0**	**5**	**0**	**0**	**0**	**0**	**0.0**	**1**	**1**	**0**	**0**	**0**	....	....	....	....	....	....	....	....
	St. Catharines Saints	AHL	61	5	3	8	....	....	....	221	....	....	....	....	....	....	....	....	....	....	....	....	....	....	....	....	....	....
1983-84	St. Catharines Saints	AHL	51	0	7	7	....	....	....	183	....	....	....	....	....	....	....	....	....	....	....	....	....	....	....	....	....	....
	Muskegon Mohawks	IHL	19	5	5	10	....	....	....	123	....	....	....	....	....	....	....	....	....	....	....	....	....	....	....	....	....	....
1984-85	**Toronto Maple Leafs**	**NHL**	**2**	**0**	**0**	**0**	**0**	**0**	**0**	**0**	**0**	**0**	**0**	**2**	**0.0**	**0**	**0**	**0**	**0**	**0**	....	....	....	....	....	....	....	....
	St. Catharines Saints	AHL	43	5	8	13	....	....	....	164	....	....	....	....	....	....	....	....	....	....	....	....	....	....	....	....	....	....
1985-86	St. Catharines Saints	AHL	75	8	12	20	....	....	....	300	....	....	....	....	....	....	....	....	....	....	11	2	3	5	14	....	....	....
1986-87	Newmarket Saints	AHL	57	9	7	16	....	....	....	179	....	....	....	....	....	....	....	....	....	....	....	....	....	....	....	....	....	....
1987-88	**Toronto Maple Leafs**	**NHL**	**3**	**0**	**1**	**1**	**0**	**1**	**1**	**9**	**0**	**0**	**0**	**0**	**0.0**	**1**	**0**	**3**	**0**	**–2**	....	....	....	....	....	....	....	....
	Newmarket Saints	AHL	12	4	3	7	....	....	....	38	....	....	....	....	....	....	....	....	....	....	....	....	....	....	....	....	....	....
	NHL Totals		**8**	**0**	**1**	**1**	**0**	**1**	**1**	**14**	**0**	**0**	**0**	**2**	**0.0**	**2**	**1**	**3**	**0**		....	....	....	....	....	....	....	....

• VERVERGAERT, Dennis

Dennis Andrew RW – R. 6', 185 lbs. b: Hamilton, Ont., 3/30/1953. Vancouver's 1st, 3rd overall, in 1973.

Season	Club	League	GP	G	A	Pts	AG	AA	APts	PIM	PP	SH	GW	S	%	TGF	PGF	TGA	PGA	+/–	GP	G	A	Pts	PIM	PP	SH	GW
1970-71	St. Catharines Black Hawks	OMJHL	5	0	0	0	....	....	....	0	....	....	....	....	....	....	....	....	....	....	....	....	....	....	....	....	....	....
	London Knights	OMJHL	62	39	48	87	....	....	....	98	....	....	....	....	....	....	....	....	....	....	4	1	0	1	4	....	....	....
1971-72	London Knights	OMJHL	62	44	73	117	....	....	....	65	....	....	....	....	....	....	....	....	....	....	7	5	7	12	8	....	....	....
1972-73	London Knights	OMJHL	63	58	89	147	....	....	....	86	....	....	....	....	....	....	....	....	....	....	18	13	12	25	6	....	....	....
1973-74	**Vancouver Canucks**	**NHL**	**78**	**26**	**31**	**57**	**25**	**26**	**51**	**25**	**7**	**0**	**3**	**153**	**17.0**	**79**	**23**	**79**	**3**	**–20**	....	....	....	....	....	....	....	....
1974-75	**Vancouver Canucks**	**NHL**	**57**	**19**	**32**	**51**	**17**	**24**	**41**	**25**	**5**	**0**	**5**	**114**	**16.7**	**71**	**25**	**40**	**0**	**6**	**1**	**0**	**0**	**0**	**0**	**0**	**0**	**0**
1975-76	**Vancouver Canucks**	**NHL**	**80**	**37**	**34**	**71**	**33**	**25**	**58**	**53**	**11**	**0**	**4**	**207**	**17.9**	**103**	**29**	**79**	**4**	**–1**	**2**	**1**	**0**	**1**	**4**	**1**	**0**	**0**
1976-77	**Vancouver Canucks**	**NHL**	**79**	**27**	**18**	**45**	**24**	**14**	**38**	**38**	**7**	**0**	**1**	**178**	**15.2**	**66**	**24**	**78**	**1**	**–35**	....	....	....	....	....	....	....	....
1977-78	**Vancouver Canucks**	**NHL**	**80**	**21**	**33**	**54**	**19**	**26**	**45**	**23**	**6**	**0**	**1**	**136**	**15.4**	**81**	**25**	**80**	**0**	**–24**	....	....	....	....	....	....	....	....
1978-79	**Vancouver Canucks**	**NHL**	**35**	**9**	**17**	**26**	**8**	**12**	**20**	**13**	**2**	**1**	**3**	**57**	**15.8**	**32**	**6**	**23**	**0**	**3**	....	....	....	....	....	....	....	....
	Philadelphia Flyers	**NHL**	**37**	**9**	**7**	**16**	**8**	**5**	**13**	**6**	**2**	**0**	**1**	**54**	**16.7**	**28**	**5**	**28**	**1**	**–4**	**3**	**0**	**2**	**2**	**2**	**0**	**0**	**0**
1979-80	**Philadelphia Flyers**	**NHL**	**58**	**14**	**17**	**31**	**12**	**12**	**24**	**24**	**0**	**0**	**2**	**96**	**14.6**	**50**	**3**	**38**	**0**	**9**	**2**	**0**	**0**	**0**	**0**	**0**	**0**	**0**
1980-81	**Washington Capitals**	**NHL**	**79**	**14**	**27**	**41**	**11**	**18**	**29**	**40**	**2**	**0**	**2**	**111**	**12.6**	**56**	**11**	**56**	**6**	**–5**	....	....	....	....	....	....	....	....
	NHL Totals		**583**	**176**	**216**	**392**	**157**	**162**	**319**	**247**	**42**	**1**	**22**	**1106**	**15.9**	**566**	**151**	**501**	**15**		**8**	**1**	**2**	**3**	**6**	**1**	**0**	**0**

OMJHL Second All-Star Team (1972) • OMJHL First All-Star Team (1973) • Played in NHL All-Star Game (1976, 1978)

Traded to **Philadelphia** by **Vancouver** for Drew Callander and Kevin McCarthy, December 29, 1978. Signed as a free agent by **Washington**, October 6, 1980.

• VESEY, Jim

James Edward C/RW – R. 6'1", 202 lbs. b: Columbus, MA, 10/29/1965. St. Louis' 11th, 155th overall, in 1984.

Season	Club	League	GP	G	A	Pts	AG	AA	APts	PIM	PP	SH	GW	S	%	TGF	PGF	TGA	PGA	+/–	GP	G	A	Pts	PIM	PP	SH	GW
1983-84	Columbus Cardinals	Hi-School	21	39	48	87	....	....	....	....	....	....	....	....	....	....	....	....	....	....	....	....	....	....	....	....	....	....
1984-85	Merrimack College	ECAC-2	33	19	11	30	....	....	....	28	....	....	....	....	....	....	....	....	....	....	....	....	....	....	....	....	....	....
1985-86	Merrimack College	ECAC-2	32	29	32	61	....	....	....	67	....	....	....	....	....	....	....	....	....	....	....	....	....	....	....	....	....	....
1986-87	Merrimack College	ECAC-2	35	22	36	58	....	....	....	57	....	....	....	....	....	....	....	....	....	....	....	....	....	....	....	....	....	....
1987-88	Merrimack College	ECAC-2	33	33	50	83	....	....	....	95	....	....	....	....	....	....	....	....	....	....	7	7	5	12	....	....	....	....
1988-89	**St. Louis Blues**	**NHL**	**5**	**1**	**1**	**2**	**1**	**1**	**2**	**7**	**0**	**0**	**0**	**5**	**20.0**	**2**	**0**	**3**	**0**	**–1**	....	....	....	....	....	....	....	....
	Peoria Rivermen	IHL	76	47	46	93	....	....	....	137	....	....	....	....	....	....	....	....	....	....	4	1	2	3	6	....	....	....
1989-90	**St. Louis Blues**	**NHL**	**6**	**0**	**1**	**1**	**0**	**1**	**1**	**0**	**0**	**0**	**0**	**3**	**0.0**	**2**	**0**	**5**	**0**	**–3**	....	....	....	....	....	....	....	....
	Peoria Rivermen	IHL	60	47	44	91	....	....	....	75	....	....	....	....	....	....	....	....	....	....	5	1	3	4	21	....	....	....
1990-91	Peoria Rivermen	IHL	58	32	41	73	....	....	....	69	....	....	....	....	....	....	....	....	....	....	19	4	14	18	26	....	....	....
1991-92	**Boston Bruins**	**NHL**	**4**	**0**	**0**	**0**	**0**	**0**	**0**	**0**	**0**	**0**	**0**	**1**	**0.0**	**0**	**0**	**0**	**0**	**0**	....	....	....	....	....	....	....	....
	Maine Mariners	AHL	10	6	7	13	....	....	....	13	....	....	....	....	....	....	....	....	....	....	....	....	....	....	....	....	....	....
1992-93	Providence Bruins	AHL	71	38	39	77	....	....	....	42	....	....	....	....	....	....	....	....	....	....	6	2	5	7	4	....	....	....
1993-94	Phoenix Roadrunners	IHL	60	20	30	50	....	....	....	75	....	....	....	....	....	....	....	....	....	....	....	....	....	....	....	....	....	....
1994-95	Phoenix Roadrunners	IHL	41	10	10	20	....	....	....	62	....	....	....	....	....	....	....	....	....	....	....	....	....	....	....	....	....	....
	NHL Totals		**15**	**1**	**2**	**3**	**1**	**2**	**3**	**7**	**0**	**0**	**0**	**9**	**11.1**	**4**	**0**	**8**	**0**		....	....	....	....	....	....	....	....

NCAA (College Div.) East All-American Team (1986) • NCAA (College Div.) East Second All-American Team (1987) • IHL First All-Star Team (1989)

Traded to **Winnipeg** by **St. Louis** to complete transaction that sent Tom Draper to St. Louis (February 28, 1991), May 24, 1991. Traded to **Boston** by **Winnipeg** for future considerations, June 20, 1991. • Missed majority of 1991-92 season recovering from shoulder injury suffered in game vs. Hartford, November 14, 1991.

• VEYSEY, Sid

Sidney G. C – L. 5'11", 175 lbs. b: Woodstock, N.B., 7/30/1955. Vancouver's 10th, 182nd overall, in 1975.

Season	Club	League	GP	G	A	Pts	AG	AA	APts	PIM	PP	SH	GW	S	%	TGF	PGF	TGA	PGA	+/–	GP	G	A	Pts	PIM	PP	SH	GW
1971-72	Riverview Reds	NBJHL	26	22	23	45	....	....	....	62	....	....	....	....	....	....	....	....	....	....	....	....	....	....	....	....	....	....
	Moncton Beavers	NBJHL	15	15	13	28	....	....	....	52	....	....	....	....	....	....	....	....	....	....	....	....	....	....	....	....	....	....
1972-73	Moncton Beavers	NBJHL	37	31	*77	*108	....	....	....	69	....	....	....	....	....	....	....	....	....	....	8	7	4	11	*41	....	....	....
1973-74	Sherbrooke Castors	QMJHL	69	35	44	79	....	....	....	51	....	....	....	....	....	....	....	....	....	....	....	....	....	....	....	....	....	....
1974-75	Sherbrooke Castors	QMJHL	48	37	53	90	....	....	....	65	....	....	....	....	....	....	....	....	....	....	....	....	....	....	....	....	....	....
	Sherbrooke Castors	Mem-Cup	3	0	2	2	....	....	....	7	....	....	....	....	....	....	....	....	....	....	....	....	....	....	....	....	....	....
1975-76	Tulsa Oilers	CHL	1	0	0	0	....	....	....	0	....	....	....	....	....	....	....	....	....	....	....	....	....	....	....	....	....	....
	Fort Wayne Komets	IHL	73	36	51	87	....	....	....	97	....	....	....	....	....	....	....	....	....	....	9	7	6	13	14	....	....	....
1976-77	Tulsa Oilers	CHL	76	29	51	80	....	....	....	66	....	....	....	....	....	....	....	....	....	....	9	1	3	4	4	....	....	....
1977-78	**Vancouver Canucks**	**NHL**	**1**	**0**	**0**	**0**	**0**	**0**	**0**	**0**	**0**	**0**	**0**	**0**	**0.0**	**0**	**0**	**1**	**0**	**–1**	....	....	....	....	....	....	....	....
	Tulsa Oilers	CHL	54	16	17	33	....	....	....	64	....	....	....	....	....	....	....	....	....	....	....	....	....	....	....	....	....	....
1978-79	Newcastle Northmen	NNBHL	STATISTICS NOT AVAILABLE																									
1979-80	University of New Brunswick	AUAA	27	25	28	53	....	....	....	46	....	....	....	....	....	....	....	....	....	....	....	....	....	....	....	....	....	....
1980-81	University of New Brunswick	AUAA	20	17	20	37	....	....	....	46	....	....	....	....	....	....	....	....	....	....	2	0	5	5	2	....	....	....
1981-82	Fredericton Capitals	NBSHL	STATISTICS NOT AVAILABLE																									
	Fredericton Express	AHL	17	2	10	12	....	....	....	17	....	....	....	....	....	....	....	....	....	....	....	....	....	....	....	....	....	....
1982-83	Saint John Gulls	NBHA-I	24	17	19	36	....	....	....	39	....	....	....	....	....	....	....	....	....	....	11	4	11	15	18	....	....	....
	NHL Totals		**1**	**0**	**0**	**0**	**0**	**0**	**0**	**0**	**0**	**0**	**0**	**0**	**0.0**	**0**	**0**	**1**	**0**		....	....	....	....	....	....	....	....

QMJHL Second All-Star Team (1975) • Won Garry F. Longman Memorial Trophy (Top Rookie - IHL) (1976) • AUAA Second All-Star Team (1981)

• VIAL, Dennis

"Dancin' Bear" D/LW – L. 6'1", 220 lbs. b: Sault Ste. Marie, Ont., 4/10/1969. NY Rangers' 5th, 110th overall, in 1988.

Season	Club	League	GP	G	A	Pts	AG	AA	APts	PIM	PP	SH	GW	S	%	TGF	PGF	TGA	PGA	+/–	GP	G	A	Pts	PIM	PP	SH	GW
1984-85	Sault Ste. Marie Legionaires	OMHA	31	4	19	23	....	....	....	40	....	....	....	....	....	....	....	....	....	....	....	....	....	....	....	....	....	....
1985-86	Hamilton Kilty B's	OJHL-B	27	11	7	18	....	....	....	215	....	....	....	....	....	....	....	....	....	....	....	....	....	....	....	....	....	....
	Hamilton Steelhawks	OHL	31	1	1	2	....	....	....	66	....	....	....	....	....	....	....	....	....	....	....	....	....	....	....	....	....	....
1986-87	Hamilton Steelhawks	OHL	53	1	8	9	....	....	....	194	....	....	....	....	....	....	....	....	....	....	8	0	0	0	8	....	....	....
1987-88	Hamilton Steelhawks	OHL	52	3	17	20	....	....	....	229	....	....	....	....	....	....	....	....	....	....	13	2	2	4	49	....	....	....
1988-89	Niagara Falls Thunder	OHL	50	10	27	37	....	....	....	227	....	....	....	....	....	....	....	....	....	....	15	1	7	8	44	....	....	....
1989-90	Flint Spirits	IHL	79	6	29	35	....	....	....	351	....	....	....	....	....	....	....	....	....	....	4	0	0	0	10	....	....	....
1990-91	**New York Rangers**	**NHL**	**21**	**0**	**0**	**0**	**0**	**0**	**0**	**61**	**0**	**0**	**0**	**5**	**0.0**	**6**	**0**	**10**	**0**	**–4**	....	....	....	....	....	....	....	....
	Binghamton Rangers	AHL	40	2	7	9	....	....	....	250	....	....	....	....	....	....	....	....	....	....	....	....	....	....	....	....	....	....
	Detroit Red Wings	**NHL**	**9**	**0**	**0**	**0**	**0**	**0**	**0**	**16**	**0**	**0**	**0**	**3**	**0.0**	**0**	**0**	**3**	**0**	**–3**	....	....	....	....	....	....	....	....

			REGULAR SEASON																		PLAYOFFS							
Season	Club	League	GP	G	A	Pts	AG	AA	APts	PIM	PP	SH	GW	S	%	TGF	PGF	TGA	PGA	+/–	GP	G	A	Pts	PIM	PP	SH	GW
1991-92	**Detroit Red Wings**	**NHL**	**27**	**1**	**0**	**1**	**1**	**0**	**1**	**72**	**0**	**0**	**0**	**6**	**16.7**	**7**	**0**	**6**	**0**	**1**								
	Adirondack Red Wings	AHL	20	2	4	6				107											17	1	3	4	43			
1992-93	**Detroit Red Wings**	**NHL**	**9**	**0**	**1**	**1**	**0**	**1**	**1**	**20**	**0**	**0**	**0**	**5**	**0.0**	**4**	**0**	**3**	**0**	**1**								
	Adirondack Red Wings	AHL	30	2	11	13				177											11	1	1	2	14			
1993-94	**Ottawa Senators**	**NHL**	**55**	**2**	**5**	**7**	**2**	**4**	**6**	**214**	**0**	**0**	**0**	**37**	**5.4**	**25**	**1**	**46**	**13**	**–9**								
1994-95	**Ottawa Senators**	**NHL**	**27**	**0**	**4**	**4**	**0**	**6**	**6**	**65**	**0**	**0**	**0**	**9**	**0.0**	**12**	**0**	**15**	**3**	**0**								
1995-96	**Ottawa Senators**	**NHL**	**64**	**1**	**4**	**5**	**1**	**3**	**4**	**276**	**0**	**0**	**0**	**33**	**3.0**	**10**	**0**	**26**	**3**	**–13**								
1996-97	**Ottawa Senators**	**NHL**	**11**	**0**	**1**	**1**	**0**	**1**	**1**	**25**	**0**	**0**	**0**	**4**	**0.0**	**2**	**1**	**1**	**0**	**0**								
1997-98	**Ottawa Senators**	**NHL**	**19**	**0**	**0**	**0**	**0**	**0**	**0**	**45**	**0**	**0**	**0**	**9**	**0.0**	**1**	**0**	**1**	**0**	**0**								
	Chicago Wolves	IHL	24	1	3	4				86											1	0	0	0	2			
1998-99	Chicago Wolves	IHL	55	1	4	5				213																		
99-2000	Sheffield Steelers	Britain	24	2	3	5				78											7	0	1	1	10			
	NHL Totals		**242**	**4**	**15**	**19**	**4**	**15**	**19**	**794**	**0**	**0**	**0**	**111**	**3.6**	**67**	**2**	**111**	**19**									

Traded to **Detroit** by **NY Rangers** with Kevin Miller and Jim Cummins for Joey Kocur and Per Djoos, March 5, 1991. Traded to **Quebec** by **Detroit** with Doug Crossman for cash, June 15, 1992. Traded to **Detroit** by **Quebec** for cash, September 9, 1992. Traded to **Tampa Bay** by **Detroit** for Steve Maltais, June 8, 1993. Claimed by **Anaheim** from **Tampa Bay** in Expansion Draft, June 24, 1993. Claimed by **Ottawa** from **Anaheim** in Phase II of Expansion Draft, June 25, 1993.

• VICKERS, Steve

Stephen James "Sarge" LW – L. 6', 180 lbs. b: Toronto, Ont., 4/21/1951. NY Rangers' 1st, 10th overall, in 1971.

Season	Club	League	GP	G	A	Pts	AG	AA	APts	PIM	PP	SH	GW	S	%	TGF	PGF	TGA	PGA	+/–	GP	G	A	Pts	PIM	PP	SH	GW
1968-69	Markham Waxers	OHA-B	36	43	40	83																						
1969-70	Toronto Marlboros	OHA-Jr.	52	28	38	66				23											11	5	5	10	5			
1970-71	Toronto Marlboros	OHA-Jr.	62	43	64	107				51											13	8	12	20	5			
1971-72	Omaha Knights	CHL	70	36	23	59				45																		
1972-73	**New York Rangers**	**NHL**	**61**	**30**	**23**	**53**	**28**	**18**	**46**	**37**	**2**	**0**	**5**	**131**	**22.9**	**74**	**10**	**29**	**0**	**35**	**10**	**5**	**4**	**9**	**4**	**0**	**0**	**0**
1973-74	**New York Rangers**	**NHL**	**75**	**34**	**24**	**58**	**33**	**20**	**53**	**18**	**5**	**0**	**5**	**168**	**20.2**	**82**	**20**	**58**	**2**	**6**	**13**	**4**	**4**	**8**	**17**	**2**	**0**	**0**
1974-75	**New York Rangers**	**NHL**	**80**	**41**	**48**	**89**	**36**	**36**	**72**	**64**	**16**	**0**	**6**	**188**	**21.8**	**138**	**53**	**75**	**0**	**10**	**3**	**2**	**4**	**6**	**6**	**0**	**0**	**0**
1975-76	**New York Rangers**	**NHL**	**80**	**30**	**53**	**83**	**26**	**40**	**66**	**40**	**10**	**0**	**4**	**202**	**14.9**	**128**	**46**	**99**	**0**	**–17**								
1976-77	**New York Rangers**	**NHL**	**75**	**22**	**31**	**53**	**20**	**24**	**44**	**26**	**4**	**0**	**3**	**157**	**14.0**	**82**	**20**	**76**	**0**	**–14**								
1977-78	**New York Rangers**	**NHL**	**79**	**19**	**44**	**63**	**17**	**34**	**51**	**30**	**9**	**0**	**2**	**113**	**16.8**	**101**	**38**	**54**	**1**	**10**	**3**	**2**	**1**	**3**	**0**	**0**	**0**	**0**
1978-79	**New York Rangers**	**NHL**	**66**	**13**	**34**	**47**	**11**	**25**	**36**	**24**	**4**	**0**	**3**	**86**	**15.1**	**67**	**17**	**64**	**7**	**–7**	**18**	**5**	**3**	**8**	**13**	**1**	**0**	**1**
1979-80	**New York Rangers**	**NHL**	**75**	**29**	**33**	**62**	**25**	**24**	**49**	**38**	**12**	**0**	**2**	**98**	**29.6**	**95**	**32**	**44**	**1**	**20**	**9**	**2**	**2**	**4**	**4**	**0**	**0**	**1**
1980-81	**New York Rangers**	**NHL**	**73**	**19**	**39**	**58**	**15**	**26**	**41**	**40**	**5**	**1**	**3**	**85**	**22.4**	**76**	**15**	**56**	**2**	**7**	**12**	**4**	**7**	**11**	**14**	**1**	**0**	**0**
1981-82	**New York Rangers**	**NHL**	**34**	**9**	**11**	**20**	**7**	**7**	**14**	**13**	**2**	**0**	**2**	**48**	**18.8**	**35**	**10**	**21**	**0**	**4**								
	Springfield Indians	AHL	20	4	6	10				14																		
	NHL Totals		**698**	**246**	**340**	**586**	**218**	**254**	**472**	**330**	**69**	**1**	**35**	**1276**	**19.3**	**878**	**261**	**576**	**13**		**68**	**24**	**25**	**49**	**58**	**4**	**0**	**2**

OHA-Jr. First All-Star Team (1971) • Won Calder Memorial Trophy (1973) • NHL Second All-Star Team (1975) • Played in NHL All-Star Game (1975, 1976)

• VIGNEAULT, Alain

D – R. 5'11", 195 lbs. b: Quebec City, Que., 5/14/1961. St. Louis' 7th, 167th overall, in 1981.

Season	Club	League	GP	G	A	Pts	AG	AA	APts	PIM	PP	SH	GW	S	%	TGF	PGF	TGA	PGA	+/–	GP	G	A	Pts	PIM	PP	SH	GW
1979-80	Hull Olympiques	QMJHL	35	5	34	39				82																		
	Trois-Rivieres Draveurs	QMJHL	28	6	19	25				93											7	1	5	6	30			
1980-81	Trois-Rivieres Draveurs	QMJHL	67	7	55	62				181											19	4	6	10	53			
1981-82	**St. Louis Blues**	**NHL**	**14**	**1**	**2**	**3**	**1**	**1**	**2**	**43**	**0**	**0**	**0**	**9**	**11.1**	**8**	**0**	**14**	**5**	**–1**								
	Salt Lake Golden Eagles	CHL	64	2	10	12				266											7	1	1	2	37			
1982-83	**St. Louis Blues**	**NHL**	**28**	**1**	**3**	**4**	**1**	**2**	**3**	**39**	**0**	**0**	**0**	**13**	**7.7**	**12**	**1**	**16**	**1**	**–4**	**4**	**0**	**1**	**1**	**26**	**0**	**0**	**0**
	Salt Lake Golden Eagles	CHL	33	1	4	5				189																		
1983-84	Montana Magic	CHL	47	2	14	16				139																		
	Maine Mariners	AHL	11	0	1	1				46											1	0	0	0	4			
1984-1986			OUT OF HOCKEY – RETIRED																									
1986-1987	Trois Rivieres Draveurs	QMJHL	DID NOT PLAY – COACHING																									
1987-1992	Hull Olympiques	QMJHL	DID NOT PLAY – COACHING																									
1992-1995	**Ottawa Senators**	**NHL**	DID NOT PLAY – ASSISTANT COACH																									
1995-1997	Beaufort Harfangs	QMJHL	DID NOT PLAY – COACHING																									
1997-2000	**Montreal Canadiens**	**NHL**	DID NOT PLAY – COACHING																									
	NHL Totals		**42**	**2**	**5**	**7**	**2**	**3**	**5**	**82**	**0**	**0**	**0**	**22**	**9.1**	**20**	**1**	**30**	**6**		**4**	**0**	**1**	**1**	**26**	**0**	**0**	**0**

• VIITAKOSKI, Vesa

Vesa I. LW – L. 6'3", 215 lbs. b: Lappeenranta, Finland, 2/13/1971. Calgary's 3rd, 32nd overall, in 1990.

Season	Club	League	GP	G	A	Pts	AG	AA	APts	PIM	PP	SH	GW	S	%	TGF	PGF	TGA	PGA	+/–	GP	G	A	Pts	PIM	PP	SH	GW
1986-87	SaiPa Lappeenranta-B	Finland-Jr.	1	1	1	2				2																		
1987-88	SaiPa Lappeenranta-B	Finland-Jr.	20	21	11	32				16																		
1988-89	SaiPa Lappeenranta-B	Finland-Jr.	23	22	32	54				8																		
	SaiPa Lappeenranta	Finland	11	4	1	5				6																		
	Finland	EJC-A	6	8	8	16				6																		
1989-90	SaiPa Lappeenranta	Finland	44	24	10	34				8																		
	Finland	WJC-A	7	6	1	7				2																		
1990-91	Tappara Tampere	Finland	41	17	23	40				14											3	2	0	2	4			
	Finland	WJC-A	7	6	5	11				2																		
1991-92	Tappara Tampere	Finland	44	19	19	38				39																		
	Finland	WC-A	8	2	3	5				6																		
1992-93	Tappara Tampere	Finland	48	27	27	54				28																		
	Finland	WC-A	6	1	0	1				6																		
1993-94	**Calgary Flames**	**NHL**	**8**	**1**	**2**	**3**	**1**	**2**	**3**	**0**	**1**	**0**	**0**	**15**	**6.7**	**7**	**3**	**4**	**0**	**0**								
	Saint John Flames	AHL	67	28	39	67				24											5	1	2	3	2			
1994-95	Saint John Flames	AHL	56	17	26	43				8											4	0	1	1	2			
	Calgary Flames	**NHL**	**10**	**1**	**2**	**3**	**2**	**3**	**5**	**6**	**1**	**0**	**0**	**6**	**16.7**	**6**	**3**	**4**	**0**	**–1**								
1995-96	**Calgary Flames**	**NHL**	**5**	**0**	**0**	**0**	**0**	**0**	**0**	**2**	**0**	**0**	**0**	**7**	**0.0**	**0**	**0**	**1**	**0**	**–1**								
	Saint John Flames	AHL	48	18	29	47				48																		
	Cornwall Aces	AHL	10	7	6	13				4											8	1	3	4	2			
1996-97	HV-71 Jonkoping	Sweden	50	17	12	29				24											5	1	1	2	2			
1997-98	Ilves Tampere	Finland	47	11	19	30				12											9	2	4	6	4			
1998-99	Ilves Tampere	Finland	53	17	5	22				18											4	2	1	3	2			
	SaiPa Lappeenranta	EuroHL	6	3	1	4				0											6	0	2	2	0			
99-2000	Ilves Tampere	Finland	53	20	20	40				28											3	1	0	1	4			
	NHL Totals		**23**	**2**	**4**	**6**	**3**	**5**	**8**	**8**	**2**	**0**	**0**	**28**	**7.1**	**13**	**6**	**9**	**0**									

Finnish Rookie of the Year (1990)

Traded to **Colorado** by **Calgary** for Paxton Schulte, March 19, 1996.

• VILGRAIN, Claude

RW – R. 6'1", 205 lbs. b: Port-au-Prince, Haiti, 3/1/1963. Detroit's 6th, 107th overall, in 1982.

Season	Club	League	GP	G	A	Pts	AG	AA	APts	PIM	PP	SH	GW	S	%	TGF	PGF	TGA	PGA	+/–	GP	G	A	Pts	PIM	PP	SH	GW
1980-81	Laval Titan	QMJHL	72	20	31	51				65																		
1981-82	Laval Titan	QMJHL	58	26	29	55				64											17	14	10	24	4			
1982-83	Laval Titan	QMJHL	69	46	80	126				72											12	10	4	14	4			
1983-84	University of Moncton	AUAA	20	11	20	31				8																		
1984-85	University of Moncton	AUAA	24	*35	28	63				20																		
1985-86	University of Moncton	AUAA	19	17	20	37				25																		
	Canada	Nat-Team	1	0	1	1				0																		
1986-87	Canada	Nat-Team	78	28	42	70				38																		
1987-88	Canada	Nat-Team	61	21	20	41				41																		
	Canada	Olympics	6	0	0	0				0																		
	Vancouver Canucks	**NHL**	**6**	**1**	**1**	**2**	**1**	**1**	**2**	**0**	**0**	**0**	**0**	**7**	**14.3**	**4**	**1**	**6**	**0**	**–3**								
1988-89	Milwaukee Admirals	IHL	23	9	13	22				26																		
	Utica Devils	AHL	55	23	30	53				41											5	0	2	2	2			

Season	Club	League	GP	G	A	Pts	AG	AA	APts	PIM	PP	SH	GW	S	%	TGF	PGF	TGA	PGA	+/–	GP	G	A	Pts	PIM	PP	SH	GW
			REGULAR SEASON																		PLAYOFFS							
1989-90	**New Jersey Devils**	**NHL**	**6**	**1**	**2**	**3**	**1**	**1**	**2**	**4**	**0**	**0**	**0**	**13**	**7.7**	**2**	**0**	**4**	**1**	**–1**	**4**	**0**	**0**	**0**	**0**	**0**	**0**	**0**
	Utica Devils	AHL	73	37	52	89	....	....	....	32	....	....	....	....	....	....	....	....	....	....	....	....	....	....	....	....	....	....
1990-91	Utica Devils	AHL	59	32	46	78	....	....	....	26	....	....	....	....	....	....	....	....	....	....	....	....	....	....	....	....	....	....
1991-92	**New Jersey Devils**	**NHL**	**71**	**19**	**27**	**46**	**17**	**20**	**37**	**74**	**1**	**1**	**1**	**88**	**21.6**	**68**	**5**	**37**	**1**	**27**	**7**	**1**	**1**	**2**	**17**	**0**	**0**	**0**
1992-93	**New Jersey Devils**	**NHL**	**4**	**0**	**2**	**2**	**0**	**1**	**1**	**0**	**0**	**0**	**0**	**2**	**0.0**	**2**	**0**	**5**	**0**	**–3**	....	....	....	....	....	....	....	....
	Utica Devils	AHL	22	6	8	14	....	....	....	4	....	....	....	....	....	....	....	....	....	....	5	0	1	1	0	....	....	....
	Cincinnati Cyclones	IHL	57	19	26	45	....	....	....	22	....	....	....	....	....	....	....	....	....	....	....	....	....	....	....	....	....	....
1993-94	**Philadelphia Flyers**	**NHL**	**2**	**0**	**0**	**0**	**0**	**0**	**0**	**0**	**0**	**0**	**0**	**0**	**0.0**	**0**	**0**	**1**	**0**	**–1**	....	....	....	....	....	....	....	....
	Hershey Bears	AHL	76	30	53	83	....	....	....	45	....	....	....	....	....	....	....	....	....	....	11	1	6	7	2	....	....	....
1994-95	SC Herisau	Switz-2	40	30	35	65	....	....	....	54	....	....	....	....	....	....	....	....	....	....	....	....	....	....	....	....	....	....
	Canada	Nat-Team	10	5	11	16	....	....	....	6	....	....	....	....	....	....	....	....	....	....	....	....	....	....	....	....	....	....
1995-96	SC Herisau	Switz-2	36	27	41	68	....	....	....	44	....	....	....	....	....	....	....	....	....	....	5	5	5	10	12	....	....	....
1996-97	SC Herisau	Switz-2	42	30	46	76	....	....	....	64	....	....	....	....	....	....	....	....	....	....	....	....	....	....	....	....	....	....
1997-98	Frankfurt Lions	Germany	38	17	13	30	....	....	....	54	....	....	....	....	....	....	....	....	....	....	7	1	2	3	8	....	....	....
1998-99	Schwenningen Wild Wings	Germany	52	16	29	45	....	....	....	26	....	....	....	....	....	....	....	....	....	....	....	....	....	....	....	....	....	....
99-2000	EHC Biel-Bienne	Switz-2	36	26	44	70	....	....	....	16	....	....	....	....	....	....	....	....	....	....	9	2	10	12	....	....	....	....
	NHL Totals		**89**	**21**	**32**	**53**	**19**	**23**	**42**	**78**	**1**	**1**	**1**	**110**	**19.1**	**76**	**6**	**53**	**2**		**11**	**1**	**1**	**2**	**17**	**0**	**0**	**0**

QMJHL Second All-Star Team (1983)

Signed as a free agent by **Vancouver**, June 18, 1987. Traded to **New Jersey** by **Vancouver** for Tim Lenardon, March 7, 1989. Signed as a free agent by **Philadelphia**, August 3, 1993.

• VINCELETTE, Dan

Dan Daniel LW – L. 6'2", 202 lbs. b: Verdun, Que., 8/1/1967. Chicago's 3rd, 74th overall, in 1985.

Season	Club	League	GP	G	A	Pts	AG	AA	APts	PIM	PP	SH	GW	S	%	TGF	PGF	TGA	PGA	+/–	GP	G	A	Pts	PIM	PP	SH	GW
1982-83	Acton Vale CC	QAAA	STATISTICS NOT AVAILABLE																									
1983-84	Montreal West Cantonniers	QAAA	40	9	13	22	....	....	....	43	....	....	....	....	....	....	....	....	....	....	....	....	....	....	....	....	....	....
1984-85	Drummondville Voltigeurs	QMJHL	64	11	24	35	....	....	....	124	....	....	....	....	....	....	....	....	....	....	12	0	1	1	11	....	....	....
1985-86	Drummondville Voltigeurs	QMJHL	70	37	47	84	....	....	....	234	....	....	....	....	....	....	....	....	....	....	22	11	14	25	40	....	....	....
1986-87	Drummondville Voltigeurs	QMJHL	50	34	35	69	....	....	....	288	....	....	....	....	....	....	....	....	....	....	8	6	5	11	17	....	....	....
	Chicago Blackhawks	**NHL**	....	....	....	....	....	....	....	....	....	....	....	....	....	....	....	....	....	....	**3**	**0**	**0**	**0**	**0**	**0**	**0**	**0**
1987-88	**Chicago Blackhawks**	**NHL**	**69**	**6**	**11**	**17**	**5**	**8**	**13**	**109**	**2**	**0**	**0**	**67**	**9.0**	**37**	**10**	**46**	**4**	**–15**	**4**	**0**	**0**	**0**	**0**	**0**	**0**	**0**
1988-89	**Chicago Blackhawks**	**NHL**	**66**	**11**	**4**	**15**	**9**	**3**	**12**	**119**	**1**	**0**	**0**	**76**	**14.5**	**38**	**9**	**41**	**3**	**–9**	**5**	**0**	**0**	**0**	**4**	**0**	**0**	**0**
	Saginaw Hawks	IHL	2	0	0	0	....	....	....	14	....	....	....	....	....	....	....	....	....	....	....	....	....	....	....	....	....	....
1989-90	**Chicago Blackhawks**	**NHL**	**2**	**0**	**0**	**0**	**0**	**0**	**0**	**4**	**0**	**0**	**0**	**2**	**0.0**	**0**	**0**	**1**	**0**	**–1**	....	....	....	....	....	....	....	....
	Indianapolis Ice	IHL	49	16	13	29	....	....	....	262	....	....	....	....	....	....	....	....	....	....	....	....	....	....	....	....	....	....
	Quebec Nordiques	**NHL**	**11**	**0**	**1**	**1**	**0**	**1**	**1**	**25**	**0**	**0**	**0**	**15**	**0.0**	**3**	**0**	**9**	**0**	**–6**	....	....	....	....	....	....	....	....
	Halifax Citadels	AHL	....	....	....	....	....	....	....	....	....	....	....	....	....	....	....	....	....	....	2	0	0	0	4	....	....	....
1990-91	**Quebec Nordiques**	**NHL**	**16**	**0**	**1**	**1**	**0**	**1**	**1**	**38**	**0**	**0**	**0**	**16**	**0.0**	**2**	**0**	**12**	**0**	**–10**	....	....	....	....	....	....	....	....
	Halifax Citadels	AHL	24	4	9	13	....	....	....	85	....	....	....	....	....	....	....	....	....	....	....	....	....	....	....	....	....	....
	Indianapolis Ice	IHL	15	5	3	8	....	....	....	51	....	....	....	....	....	....	....	....	....	....	7	2	1	3	62	....	....	....
1991-92	**Chicago Blackhawks**	**NHL**	**29**	**3**	**5**	**8**	**3**	**4**	**7**	**56**	**0**	**0**	**0**	**28**	**10.7**	**18**	**2**	**24**	**2**	**–6**	....	....	....	....	....	....	....	....
	Indianapolis Ice	IHL	16	5	3	8	....	....	....	84	....	....	....	....	....	....	....	....	....	....	....	....	....	....	....	....	....	....
1992-93	Atlanta Knights	IHL	30	5	5	10	....	....	....	126	....	....	....	....	....	....	....	....	....	....	....	....	....	....	....	....	....	....
	San Diego Gulls	IHL	6	0	0	0	....	....	....	6	....	....	....	....	....	....	....	....	....	....	....	....	....	....	....	....	....	....
1993-94	Durham Wasps	Britain	10	3	2	5	....	....	....	36	....	....	....	....	....	....	....	....	....	....	6	0	0	0	52	....	....	....
1994-95			OUT OF HOCKEY – RETIRED																									
1995-96	San Francisco Spiders	IHL	35	3	7	10	....	....	....	96	....	....	....	....	....	....	....	....	....	....	4	0	0	0	15	....	....	....
1996-97	Acton Vale Nova	QSPHL	22	10	12	22	....	....	....	155	....	....	....	....	....	....	....	....	....	....	....	....	....	....	....	....	....	....
	NHL Totals		**193**	**20**	**22**	**42**	**17**	**17**	**34**	**351**	**3**	**0**	**0**	**204**	**9.8**	**98**	**21**	**133**	**9**		**12**	**0**	**0**	**0**	**4**	**0**	**0**	**0**

Traded to **Quebec** by **Chicago** with Mario Doyon and Everett Sanipass for Greg Millen, Michel Goulet and Quebec's 6th round choice (Kevin St. Jacques) in 1991 Entry Draft, March 5, 1990. Traded to **Chicago** by **Quebec** with Paul Gillis for Ryan McGill and Mike McNeill, March 5, 1991. Claimed by **Tampa Bay** from **Chicago** in Expansion Draft, June 18, 1992. Traded to **Philadelphia** by **Tampa Bay** for Steve Kasper, December 8, 1992.

• VIPOND, Pete

Peter John LW – L. 5'10", 175 lbs. b: Oshawa, Ont., 12/8/1949. Oakland's 7th, 76th overall, in 1969.

Season	Club	League	GP	G	A	Pts	AG	AA	APts	PIM	PP	SH	GW	S	%	TGF	PGF	TGA	PGA	+/–	GP	G	A	Pts	PIM	PP	SH	GW
1967-68	Whitby Warriors	OHA-B	STATISTICS NOT AVAILABLE																									
	Oshawa Generals	OHA-Jr.	32	6	10	16	....	....	....	6	....	....	....	....	....	....	....	....	....	....	....	....	....	....	....	....	....	....
1968-69	Oshawa Generals	OHA-Jr.	54	21	39	60	....	....	....	45	....	....	....	....	....	....	....	....	....	....	....	....	....	....	....	....	....	....
1969-70	Nelson Maple Leafs	WIHL	48	28	36	64	....	....	....	36	....	....	....	....	....	....	....	....	....	....	8	1	5	6	10	....	....	....
	Spokane Jets	Al-Cup	13	1	10	11	....	....	....	9	....	....	....	....	....	....	....	....	....	....	....	....	....	....	....	....	....	....
1970-71	Nelson Maple Leafs	WIHL	48	21	45	66	....	....	....	28	....	....	....	....	....	....	....	....	....	....	....	....	....	....	....	....	....	....
1971-72	Columbus Seals	IHL	66	23	39	62	....	....	....	24	....	....	....	....	....	....	....	....	....	....	....	....	....	....	....	....	....	....
1972-73	**California Golden Seals**	**NHL**	**3**	**0**	**0**	**0**	**0**	**0**	**0**	**0**	**0**	**0**	**0**	**2**	**0.0**	**0**	**0**	**0**	**0**	**0**	....	....	....	....	....	....	....	....
	Salt Lake Golden Eagles	WHL	66	33	24	57	....	....	....	17	....	....	....	....	....	....	....	....	....	....	9	1	3	4	2	....	....	....
1973-74	Tulsa Oilers	CHL	60	20	22	42	....	....	....	30	....	....	....	....	....	....	....	....	....	....	....	....	....	....	....	....	....	....
1974-75	Whitby Warriors	OHA-Sr.	37	19	18	37	....	....	....	9	....	....	....	....	....	....	....	....	....	....	....	....	....	....	....	....	....	....
1975-76	Whitby Warriors	OHA-Sr.	44	25	35	60	....	....	....	18	....	....	....	....	....	....	....	....	....	....	....	....	....	....	....	....	....	....
1976-77	Whitby Warriors	OHA-Sr.	34	22	26	48	....	....	....	21	....	....	....	....	....	....	....	....	....	....	....	....	....	....	....	....	....	....
1977-78	Whitby Warriors	OHA-Sr.	36	9	19	28	....	....	....	10	....	....	....	....	....	....	....	....	....	....	....	....	....	....	....	....	....	....
	NHL Totals		**3**	**0**	**0**	**0**	**0**	**0**	**0**	**0**	**0**	**0**	**0**	**2**	**0.0**	**0**	**0**	**0**	**0**		....	....	....	....	....	....	....	....

Loaned to **Spokane** (WIHL) by **Nelson** (WIHL) for Allan Cup playoffs, April, 1970.

• VIRTA, Hannu

D – L. 5'11", 183 lbs. b: Turku, Finland, 3/22/1963. Buffalo's 2nd, 38th overall, in 1981.

Season	Club	League	GP	G	A	Pts	AG	AA	APts	PIM	PP	SH	GW	S	%	TGF	PGF	TGA	PGA	+/–	GP	G	A	Pts	PIM	PP	SH	GW
1978-79	TPS Turku	Finland-Jr.	22	1	9	10	....	....	....	6	....	....	....	....	....	....	....	....	....	....	....	....	....	....	....	....	....	....
1979-80	TPS Turku	Finland-Jr.	STATISTICS NOT AVAILABLE																									
1980-81	TPS Turku	Finland-Jr.	29	22	22	44	....	....	....	55	....	....	....	....	....	....	....	....	....	....	....	....	....	....	....	....	....	....
	TPS Turku	Finland	1	0	1	1	....	....	....	0	....	....	....	....	....	....	....	....	....	....	4	0	1	1	4	....	....	....
1981-82	TPS Turku	Finland	36	5	12	17	....	....	....	6	....	....	....	....	....	....	....	....	....	....	7	1	1	2	2	....	....	....
	Finland	WJC-A	7	1	7	8	....	....	....	4	....	....	....	....	....	....	....	....	....	....	....	....	....	....	....	....	....	....
	Buffalo Sabres	**NHL**	**3**	**0**	**1**	**1**	**0**	**1**	**1**	**4**	....	....	....	....	....	....	....	....	....	....	**4**	**0**	**1**	**1**	**0**	**0**	**0**	**0**
1982-83	**Buffalo Sabres**	**NHL**	**74**	**13**	**24**	**37**	**11**	**17**	**28**	**18**	**2**	**2**	**1**	**169**	**7.7**	**112**	**33**	**76**	**4**	**7**	**10**	**1**	**2**	**3**	**4**	**0**	**0**	**0**
1983-84	**Buffalo Sabres**	**NHL**	**70**	**6**	**30**	**36**	**5**	**20**	**25**	**12**	**4**	**0**	**0**	**98**	**6.1**	**105**	**34**	**63**	**7**	**15**	**3**	**0**	**0**	**0**	**2**	**0**	**0**	**0**
1984-85	**Buffalo Sabres**	**NHL**	**51**	**1**	**23**	**24**	**1**	**16**	**17**	**16**	**0**	**0**	**0**	**57**	**1.8**	**58**	**15**	**46**	**1**	**–2**	....	....	....	....	....	....	....	....
1985-86	**Buffalo Sabres**	**NHL**	**47**	**5**	**23**	**28**	**4**	**15**	**19**	**16**	**1**	**0**	**0**	**81**	**6.2**	**64**	**20**	**45**	**3**	**2**	....	....	....	....	....	....	....	....
1986-87	TPS Turku	Finland	41	13	30	43	....	....	....	20	....	....	....	....	....	....	....	....	....	....	5	0	3	3	2	....	....	....
	Finland	WEC-A	8	0	4	4	....	....	....	4	....	....	....	....	....	....	....	....	....	....	....	....	....	....	....	....	....	....
1987-88	Finland	Can-Cup	5	0	1	1	....	....	....	0	....	....	....	....	....	....	....	....	....	....	....	....	....	....	....	....	....	....
	TPS Turku	Finland	44	10	28	38	....	....	....	20	....	....	....	....	....	....	....	....	....	....	....	....	....	....	....	....	....	....
1988-89	TPS Turku	Finland	43	7	25	32	....	....	....	30	....	....	....	....	....	....	....	....	....	....	10	1	7	8	0	....	....	....
	Finland	WEC-A	10	3	5	8	....	....	....	6	....	....	....	....	....	....	....	....	....	....	....	....	....	....	....	....	....	....
1989-90	TPS Turku	Finland	41	7	19	26	....	....	....	14	....	....	....	....	....	....	....	....	....	....	9	0	6	6	10	....	....	....
1990-91	TPS Turku	Finland	43	4	16	20	....	....	....	40	....	....	....	....	....	....	....	....	....	....	9	4	2	6	4	....	....	....
	Finland	WEC-A	7	0	2	2	....	....	....	4	....	....	....	....	....	....	....	....	....	....	....	....	....	....	....	....	....	....
1991-92	TPS Turku	Finland	43	6	22	28	....	....	....	32	....	....	....	....	....	....	....	....	....	....	3	1	4	5	0	....	....	....
1992-93	TPS Turku	Finland	39	1	18	19	....	....	....	18	....	....	....	....	....	....	....	....	....	....	12	2	2	4	14	....	....	....
1993-94	TPS Turku	Finland	47	3	17	20	....	....	....	18	....	....	....	....	....	....	....	....	....	....	....	....	....	....	....	....	....	....
	Finland	Olympics	8	2	1	3	....	....	....	2	....	....	....	....	....	....	....	....	....	....	....	....	....	....	....	....	....	....
	Finland	WC-A	8	1	4	5	....	....	....	6	....	....	....	....	....	....	....	....	....	....	....	....	....	....	....	....	....	....
1994-95	ZSC Zurich	Switz.	36	12	18	30	....	....	....	14	....	....	....	....	....	....	....	....	....	....	12	5	9	14	2	....	....	....
	Finland	WC-A	7	1	1	2	....	....	....	8	....	....	....	....	....	....	....	....	....	....	....	....	....	....	....	....	....	....
1995-96	ZSC Zurich	Switz-2	35	12	10	22	....	....	....	34	....	....	....	....	....	....	....	....	....	....	6	1	5	6	0	....	....	....
	Finland	WC-A	6	0	6	6	....	....	....	4	....	....	....	....	....	....	....	....	....	....	....	....	....	....	....	....	....	....

			REGULAR SEASON																		PLAYOFFS							
Season	Club	League	GP	G	A	Pts	AG	AA	APts	PIM	PP	SH	GW	S	%	TGF	PGF	TGA	PGA	+/–	GP	G	A	Pts	PIM	PP	SH	GW
1996-97	Finland	W-Cup	4	1	0	1	....	....	....	6	....	....	....	....	....	....	....	....	....	....	....	....	....	....	....	....	....	....
	TPS Turku	Finland	48	7	14	21	....	....	....	24	....	....	....	....	....	....	....	....	....	....	12	0	1	1	6	....	....	....
	TPS Turku	EuroHL	5	0	2	2	....	....	....	2	....	....	....	....	....	....	....	....	....	....	....	....	....	....	....	....	....	....
	Finland	WC-A	8	0	3	3	....	....	....	4	....	....	....	....	....	....	....	....	....	....	....	....	....	....	....	....	....	....
1997-98	ZSC Lions Zurich	Switz.	38	3	20	23	....	....	....	8	....	....	....	....	....	....	....	....	....	....	....	....	....	....	....	....	....	....
1998-2000	TPS Turku	Finland	DID NOT PLAY – ASSISTANT COACH																									
	NHL Totals		**245**	**25**	**101**	**126**	**21**	**69**	**90**	**66**	**7**	**2**	**1**	**405**	**6.2**	**339**	**102**	**230**	**15**		**17**	**1**	**3**	**4**	**6**	**0**	**0**	**0**

EJC-A All-Star Team (1981) • Finnish Rookie of the Year (1982) • Finnish First All-Star Team (1987, 1989, 1990, 1991, 1992)

• VIRTUE, Terry

Terry William　D – R. 6', 200 lbs.　b: Scarborough, Ont., 8/12/1970.

Season	Club	League	GP	G	A	Pts	AG	AA	APts	PIM	PP	SH	GW	S	%	TGF	PGF	TGA	PGA	+/–	GP	G	A	Pts	PIM	PP	SH	GW
1988-89	Hobbema Hawks	AJHL	STATISTICS NOT AVAILABLE																									
	Victoria Cougars	WHL	8	1	1	2	....	....	....	13	....	....	....	....	....	....	....	....	....	....	....	....	....	....	....	....	....	....
1989-90	Victoria Cougars	WHL	24	1	9	10	....	....	....	85	....	....	....	....	....	....	....	....	....	....	....	....	....	....	....	....	....	....
	Tri-City Americans	WHL	34	1	10	11	....	....	....	82	....	....	....	....	....	....	....	....	....	....	6	0	0	0	30	....	....	....
1990-91	Tri-City Americans	WHL	11	1	8	9	....	....	....	24	....	....	....	....	....	....	....	....	....	....	....	....	....	....	....	....	....	....
	Portland Winter Hawks	WHL	59	9	44	53	....	....	....	127	....	....	....	....	....	....	....	....	....	....	....	....	....	....	....	....	....	....
1991-92	Roanoke Valley Rebels	ECHL	38	4	22	26	....	....	....	165	....	....	....	....	....	....	....	....	....	....	....	....	....	....	....	....	....	....
	Louisville IceHawks	ECHL	23	1	15	16	....	....	....	58	....	....	....	....	....	....	....	....	....	....	13	0	8	8	49	....	....	....
1992-93	Louisville IceHawks	ECHL	28	0	17	17	....	....	....	84	....	....	....	....	....	....	....	....	....	....	....	....	....	....	....	....	....	....
	Wheeling Thunderbirds	ECHL	31	3	15	18	....	....	....	86	....	....	....	....	....	....	....	....	....	....	16	3	5	8	18	....	....	....
1993-94	Wheeling Thunderbirds	ECHL	34	5	28	33	....	....	....	61	....	....	....	....	....	....	....	....	....	....	6	2	2	4	4	....	....	....
	Cape Breton Oilers	AHL	26	4	6	10	....	....	....	10	....	....	....	....	....	....	....	....	....	....	5	0	0	0	17	....	....	....
1994-95	Worcester IceCats	AHL	73	14	25	39	....	....	....	183	....	....	....	....	....	....	....	....	....	....	....	....	....	....	....	....	....	....
	Atlanta Knights	IHL	1	0	0	0	....	....	....	2	....	....	....	....	....	....	....	....	....	....	....	....	....	....	....	....	....	....
1995-96	Worcester IceCats	AHL	76	7	31	38	....	....	....	234	....	....	....	....	....	....	....	....	....	....	4	0	0	0	4	....	....	....
1996-97	Worcester IceCats	AHL	80	16	26	42	....	....	....	220	....	....	....	....	....	....	....	....	....	....	5	0	4	4	8	....	....	....
1997-98	Worcester IceCats	AHL	74	8	26	34	....	....	....	233	....	....	....	....	....	....	....	....	....	....	11	1	4	5	41	....	....	....
1998-99	**Boston Bruins**	**NHL**	**4**	**0**	**0**	**0**	**0**	**0**	**0**	**0**	**0**	....	**0**	**2**	**0.0**	**3**	**0**	**1**	**0**	**2**	....	....	....	....	....	....	....	....
	Providence Bruins	AHL	76	8	48	56	....	....	....	117	....	....	....	....	....	....	....	....	....	....	17	2	12	14	29	....	....	....
99-2000	**New York Rangers**	**NHL**	**1**	**0**	**0**	**0**	**0**	**0**	**0**	**0**	**0**	**0**	**0**	**2**	**0.0**	**0**	**0**	**2**	**0**	**–2**	....	....	....	....	....	....	....	....
	Hartford Wolf Pack	AHL	67	5	22	27	....	....	....	166	....	....	....	....	....	....	....	....	....	....	23	3	7	10	51	....	....	....
	NHL Totals		**5**	**0**	**0**	**0**	**0**	**0**	**0**	**0**	**0**	**0**	**0**	**4**	**0.0**	**3**	**0**	**3**	**0**		....	....	....	....	....	....	....	....

AHL Second All-Star Team (1999)

Signed as a free agent by **St. Louis**, January 29, 1996. Signed as a free agent by **Boston**, August 28, 1998. Signed as a free agent by **NY Rangers**, July 29, 1999. • Played w/ RHI's Atlanta Fire Ants in 1994 (22-10-26-36-54).

• VISHEAU, Mark

Mark Andrew　D – R. 6'6", 222 lbs.　b: Burlington, Ont., 6/27/1973. Winnipeg's 4th, 84th overall, in 1992.

Season	Club	League	GP	G	A	Pts	AG	AA	APts	PIM	PP	SH	GW	S	%	TGF	PGF	TGA	PGA	+/–	GP	G	A	Pts	PIM	PP	SH	GW
1989-90	Burlington Cougars	OJHL-B	42	11	22	33	....	....	....	53	....	....	....	....	....	....	....	....	....	....	....	....	....	....	....	....	....	....
1990-91	London Knights	OHL	59	4	11	15	....	....	....	40	....	....	....	....	....	....	....	....	....	....	7	0	1	1	6	....	....	....
1991-92	London Knights	OHL	66	5	31	36	....	....	....	104	....	....	....	....	....	....	....	....	....	....	10	0	4	4	27	....	....	....
1992-93	London Knights	OHL	62	8	52	60	....	....	....	88	....	....	....	....	....	....	....	....	....	....	12	0	5	5	26	....	....	....
1993-94	**Winnipeg Jets**	**NHL**	**1**	**0**	**0**	**0**	**0**	**0**	**0**	**0**	**0**	**0**	**0**	**1**	**0.0**	**0**	**0**	**0**	**0**	**0**	....	....	....	....	....	....	....	....
	Moncton Hawks	AHL	48	4	5	9	....	....	....	58	....	....	....	....	....	....	....	....	....	....	....	....	....	....	....	....	....	....
1994-95	Springfield Falcons	AHL	35	0	4	4	....	....	....	94	....	....	....	....	....	....	....	....	....	....	....	....	....	....	....	....	....	....
1995-96	Cape Breton Oilers	AHL	8	0	0	0	....	....	....	30	....	....	....	....	....	....	....	....	....	....	....	....	....	....	....	....	....	....
	Minnesota Moose	IHL	10	0	0	0	....	....	....	25	....	....	....	....	....	....	....	....	....	....	....	....	....	....	....	....	....	....
	Wheeling Thunderbirds	ECHL	7	1	2	3	....	....	....	14	....	....	....	....	....	....	....	....	....	....	7	0	3	3	4	....	....	....
1996-97	Raleigh IceCaps	ECHL	15	1	5	6	....	....	....	61	....	....	....	....	....	....	....	....	....	....	....	....	....	....	....	....	....	....
	Quebec Rafales	IHL	64	3	10	13	....	....	....	173	....	....	....	....	....	....	....	....	....	....	9	1	1	2	11	....	....	....
1997-98	Milwaukee Admirals	IHL	72	4	12	16	....	....	....	227	....	....	....	....	....	....	....	....	....	....	....	....	....	....	....	....	....	....
1998-99	**Los Angeles Kings**	**NHL**	**28**	**1**	**3**	**4**	**1**	**3**	**4**	**107**	**0**	**0**	**0**	**10**	**10.0**	**6**	**0**	**15**	**2**	**–7**	....	....	....	....	....	....	....	....
	NHL Totals		**29**	**1**	**3**	**4**	**1**	**3**	**4**	**107**	**0**	**0**	**0**	**11**	**9.1**	**6**	**0**	**15**	**2**		....	....	....	....	....	....	....	....

Signed as a free agent by **LA Kings**, July 30, 1997.

• VISHNEVSKI, Vitaly

D – L. 6'1", 190 lbs.　b: Kharkov, USSR, 3/18/1980. Anaheim's 1st, 5th overall, in 1998.

Season	Club	League	GP	G	A	Pts	AG	AA	APts	PIM	PP	SH	GW	S	%	TGF	PGF	TGA	PGA	+/–	GP	G	A	Pts	PIM	PP	SH	GW
1995-96	Torpedo Yaroslavl-2	Russia-2	40	4	4	8	....	....	....	20	....	....	....	....	....	....	....	....	....	....	....	....	....	....	....	....	....	....
1996-97	Torpedo Yaroslavl-2	Russia-3	45	0	2	2	....	....	....	30	....	....	....	....	....	....	....	....	....	....	....	....	....	....	....	....	....	....
1997-98	Torpedo Yaroslavl-2	Russia-2	47	8	9	17	....	....	....	164	....	....	....	....	....	....	....	....	....	....	....	....	....	....	....	....	....	....
	Russia	EJC-A	6	2	6	8	....	....	....	24	....	....	....	....	....	....	....	....	....	....	....	....	....	....	....	....	....	....
1998-99	Torpedo Yaroslavl	Russia	34	3	4	7	....	....	....	38	....	....	....	....	....	....	....	....	....	....	10	0	0	0	4	....	....	....
	Russia	WJC-A	7	0	2	2	....	....	....	6	....	....	....	....	....	....	....	....	....	....	....	....	....	....	....	....	....	....
	Russia	WC-A	6	0	1	1	....	....	....	8	....	....	....	....	....	....	....	....	....	....	....	....	....	....	....	....	....	....
99-2000	**Mighty Ducks of Anaheim**	**NHL**	**31**	**1**	**1**	**2**	**1**	**1**	**2**	**26**	**1**	**0**	**0**	**17**	**5.9**	....	....	....	....	....	....	....	....	....	....	....	....	....
	Cincinnati Mighty Ducks	AHL	35	1	3	4	....	....	....	45	....	....	....	....	....	....	....	....	....	....	....	....	....	....	....	....	....	....
	NHL Totals		**31**	**1**	**1**	**2**	**1**	**1**	**2**	**26**	**1**	**0**	**0**	**17**	**5.9**	....	....	....	....	....	....	....	....	....	....	....	....	....

WJC-A All-Star Team (1999) • Named Best Defenseman at WJC-A (1999)

• VITOLINSH, Harijs

C – L. 6'3", 212 lbs.　b: Riga, Latvia, 4/30/1968. Winnipeg's 12th, 228th overall, in 1993.

Season	Club	League	GP	G	A	Pts	AG	AA	APts	PIM	PP	SH	GW	S	%	TGF	PGF	TGA	PGA	+/–	GP	G	A	Pts	PIM	PP	SH	GW
1986-87	Dynamo Riga	USSR	17	1	1	2	....	....	....	8	....	....	....	....	....	....	....	....	....	....	....	....	....	....	....	....	....	....
1987-88	Dynamo Riga	USSR	30	3	3	6	....	....	....	24	....	....	....	....	....	....	....	....	....	....	....	....	....	....	....	....	....	....
	Soviet Union	WJC-A	7	2	0	2	....	....	....	6	....	....	....	....	....	....	....	....	....	....	....	....	....	....	....	....	....	....
1988-89	Dynamo Riga	USSR	36	3	2	5	....	....	....	16	....	....	....	....	....	....	....	....	....	....	....	....	....	....	....	....	....	....
	Dynamo Riga	Super-S	7	1	0	1	....	....	....	2	....	....	....	....	....	....	....	....	....	....	....	....	....	....	....	....	....	....
1989-90	Dynamo Riga	Fr-Tour	1	0	0	0	....	....	....	0	....	....	....	....	....	....	....	....	....	....	....	....	....	....	....	....	....	....
	Dynamo Riga	USSR	45	7	6	13	....	....	....	18	....	....	....	....	....	....	....	....	....	....	....	....	....	....	....	....	....	....
1990-91	Dynamo Riga	Fr-Tour	1	0	0	0	....	....	....	0	....	....	....	....	....	....	....	....	....	....	....	....	....	....	....	....	....	....
	Dynamo Riga	USSR	46	12	19	31	....	....	....	22	....	....	....	....	....	....	....	....	....	....	....	....	....	....	....	....	....	....
1991-92	Dynamo Riga	CIS	30	12	5	17	....	....	....	10	....	....	....	....	....	....	....	....	....	....	....	....	....	....	....	....	....	....
1992-93	EHC Chur	Switz.	17	12	6	18	....	....	....	23	....	....	....	....	....	....	....	....	....	....	....	....	....	....	....	....	....	....
	Thunder Bay Thunder Hawks	ColHL	8	6	7	13	....	....	....	12	....	....	....	....	....	....	....	....	....	....	....	....	....	....	....	....	....	....
	New Haven Senators	AHL	7	6	3	9	....	....	....	4	....	....	....	....	....	....	....	....	....	....	....	....	....	....	....	....	....	....
	Latvia	WC-C	3	3	3	6	....	....	....	4	....	....	....	....	....	....	....	....	....	....	....	....	....	....	....	....	....	....
1993-94	**Winnipeg Jets**	**NHL**	**8**	**0**	**0**	**0**	**0**	**0**	**0**	**4**	**0**	**0**	**0**	**7**	**0.0**	**2**	**0**	**2**	**0**	**0**	....	....	....	....	....	....	....	....
	Moncton Hawks	AHL	70	28	34	62	....	....	....	41	....	....	....	....	....	....	....	....	....	....	20	1	3	4	4	....	....	....
1994-95	SC Rapperswil-Jona	Switz.	30	6	17	23	....	....	....	50	....	....	....	....	....	....	....	....	....	....	....	....	....	....	....	....	....	....
	Latvia	WC-B	7	3	4	7	....	....	....	16	....	....	....	....	....	....	....	....	....	....	....	....	....	....	....	....	....	....
1995-96	Rogle BK Angelholm	Sweden	19	3	2	5	....	....	....	24	....	....	....	....	....	....	....	....	....	....	....	....	....	....	....	....	....	....
	Latvia	WC-B	7	3	6	9	....	....	....	2	....	....	....	....	....	....	....	....	....	....	....	....	....	....	....	....	....	....
1996-97	EHC Chur	Switz-2	39	25	58	83	....	....	....	58	....	....	....	....	....	....	....	....	....	....	3	0	1	1	6	....	....	....
	Latvia	WC-A	8	4	5	9	....	....	....	4	....	....	....	....	....	....	....	....	....	....	....	....	....	....	....	....	....	....
1997-98	EHC Chur	Switz-2	STATISTICS NOT AVAILABLE																									

Season	Club	League	GP	G	A	Pts	AG	AA	APts	PIM	PP	SH	GW	S	%	TGF	PGF	TGA	PGA	+/–	GP	G	A	Pts	PIM	PP	SH	GW
			REGULAR SEASON																		PLAYOFFS							
1998-99	EHC Chur	Switz-2	40	32	49	81	....	....	....	93	....	....	....	....	....	....	....	....	....	....	4	2	3	5	....	....	....	....
	Latvia	WC-A	6	0	2	2	....	....	....	6	....	....	....	....	....	....	....	....	....	....	....	....	....	....	....	....	....	....
99-2000	EHC Chur	Switz-2	40	32	49	81	....	....	....	....	....	....	....	....	....	....	....	....	....	....	12	6	8	14	....	....	....	....
	Latvia	WC-A	7	1	1	2	....	....	....	14	....	....	....	....	....	....	....	....	....	....	....	....	....	....	....	....	....	....
	NHL Totals		**8**	**0**	**0**	**0**	**0**	**0**	**0**	**4**	**0**	**0**	**0**	**7**	**0.0**	**2**	**0**	**2**	**0**		....	....	....	....	....	....	....	....

WC-B All-Star Team (1996)

• Re-entered NHL draft. Originally Montreal's 10th choice, 188th overall, in 1988 Entry Draft.

• VIVEIROS, Emanuel

D – L. 6', 175 lbs. b: St. Albert, Alta., 1/8/1966. Edmonton's 6th, 106th overall, in 1984.

Season	Club	League	GP	G	A	Pts	AG	AA	APts	PIM	PP	SH	GW	S	%	TGF	PGF	TGA	PGA	+/–	GP	G	A	Pts	PIM	PP	SH	GW
1981-82	St. Albert Royals	AAHA	STATISTICS NOT AVAILABLE																									
	St. Albert Saints	AJHL	10	1	1	2	....	....	....	2	....	....	....	....	....	....	....	....	....	....	....	....	....	....	....	....	....	....
1982-83	Prince Albert Raiders	WHL	59	6	26	32	....	....	....	55	....	....	....	....	....	....	....	....	....	....	....	....	....	....	....	....	....	....
1983-84	Prince Albert Raiders	WHL	67	15	94	109	....	....	....	48	....	....	....	....	....	....	....	....	....	....	2	0	3	3	6	....	....	....
1984-85	Prince Albert Raiders	WHL	68	17	71	88	....	....	....	94	....	....	....	....	....	....	....	....	....	....	13	2	9	11	14	....	....	....
	Prince Albert Raiders	Mem-Cup	5	2	6	8	....	....	....	4	....	....	....	....	....	....	....	....	....	....	....	....	....	....	....	....	....	....
1985-86	Prince Albert Raiders	WHL	57	22	70	92	....	....	....	30	....	....	....	....	....	....	....	....	....	....	20	4	24	28	4	....	....	....
	Canada	WJC-A	7	1	1	2	....	....	....	2	....	....	....	....	....	....	....	....	....	....	....	....	....	....	....	....	....	....
	Minnesota North Stars	**NHL**	**4**	**0**	**1**	**1**	**0**	**1**	**1**	**0**	**0**	**0**	**0**	**4**	**0.0**	**7**	**0**	**5**	**0**	**2**	....	....	....	....	....	....	....	....
1986-87	**Minnesota North Stars**	**NHL**	**1**	**0**	**1**	**1**	**0**	**1**	**1**	**0**	**0**	**0**	**0**	**1**	**0.0**	**1**	**1**	**0**	**0**	**0**	....	....	....	....	....	....	....	....
	Springfield Indians	AHL	76	7	35	42	....	....	....	38	....	....	....	....	....	....	....	....	....	....	....	....	....	....	....	....	....	....
1987-88	**Minnesota North Stars**	**NHL**	**24**	**1**	**9**	**10**	**1**	**6**	**7**	**6**	**0**	**0**	**0**	**35**	**2.9**	**23**	**11**	**17**	**0**	**–5**	....	....	....	....	....	....	....	....
	Kalamazoo Wings	IHL	57	15	48	63	....	....	....	41	....	....	....	....	....	....	....	....	....	....	7	1	8	9	0	....	....	....
1988-89	Kalamazoo Wings	IHL	54	11	29	40	....	....	....	37	....	....	....	....	....	....	....	....	....	....	....	....	....	....	....	....	....	....
1989-90	ESC Kaufbeuren	Germany-2	8	2	7	9	....	....	....	8	....	....	....	....	....	....	....	....	....	....	....	....	....	....	....	....	....	....
1990-91	Albany Choppers	IHL	14	3	7	10	....	....	....	6	....	....	....	....	....	....	....	....	....	....	....	....	....	....	....	....	....	....
	Springfield Indians	AHL	48	2	22	24	....	....	....	29	....	....	....	....	....	....	....	....	....	....	7	0	2	2	4	....	....	....
1991-92	VSV Villach	Alpenliga	20	5	16	21	....	....	....	8	....	....	....	....	....	....	....	....	....	....	....	....	....	....	....	....	....	....
	VSV Villach	Austria	26	4	31	35	....	....	....	....	....	....	....	....	....	....	....	....	....	....	....	....	....	....	....	....	....	....
1992-93	VSV Villach	Alpenliga	29	8	20	28	....	....	....	12	....	....	....	....	....	....	....	....	....	....	....	....	....	....	....	....	....	....
	VSV Villach	Austria	25	5	17	22	....	....	....	....	....	....	....	....	....	....	....	....	....	....	....	....	....	....	....	....	....	....
1993-94	VSV Villach	Alpenliga	28	7	27	34	....	....	....	20	....	....	....	....	....	....	....	....	....	....	....	....	....	....	....	....	....	....
	VSV Villach	Austria	23	4	23	27	....	....	....	....	....	....	....	....	....	....	....	....	....	....	....	....	....	....	....	....	....	....
1994-95	VSV Villach	Alpenliga	10	2	5	7	....	....	....	0	....	....	....	....	....	....	....	....	....	....	....	....	....	....	....	....	....	....
	VSV Villach	Austria	13	2	11	13	....	....	....	18	....	....	....	....	....	....	....	....	....	....	12	5	11	16	51	....	....	....
1995-96	EHC Lustenau	Alpenliga	8	3	9	12	....	....	....	4	....	....	....	....	....	....	....	....	....	....	....	....	....	....	....	....	....	....
	EHC Lustenau	Austria	33	10	23	33	....	....	....	36	....	....	....	....	....	....	....	....	....	....	....	....	....	....	....	....	....	....
1996-97	Schwenningen Wild Wings	Germany	44	8	16	24	....	....	....	34	....	....	....	....	....	....	....	....	....	....	5	0	2	2	31	....	....	....
1997-98	Schwenningen Wild Wings	Germany	51	5	11	16	....	....	....	36	....	....	....	....	....	....	....	....	....	....	....	....	....	....	....	....	....	....
1998-99	EC Graz	Alpenliga	2	0	1	1	....	....	....	0	....	....	....	....	....	....	....	....	....	....	....	....	....	....	....	....	....	....
	VSV Sterzing	Alpenliga	2	1	0	1	....	....	....	0	....	....	....	....	....	....	....	....	....	....	3	0	0	0	2	....	....	....
	VSV Sterzing	Austria	22	3	12	15	....	....	....	26	....	....	....	....	....	....	....	....	....	....	3	1	0	1	12	....	....	....
99-2000	WEV Wein	IEL	27	7	6	13	....	....	....	16	....	....	....	....	....	....	....	....	....	....	....	....	....	....	....	....	....	....
	WEV Wein	Austria	11	4	4	8	....	....	....	12	....	....	....	....	....	....	....	....	....	....	....	....	....	....	....	....	....	....
	NHL Totals		**29**	**1**	**11**	**12**	**1**	**8**	**9**	**6**	**0**	**0**	**0**	**40**	**2.5**	**31**	**12**	**22**	**0**		....	....	....	....	....	....	....	....

WHL East Second All-Star Team (1985) • WHL East First All-Star Team (1986)

Traded to **Minnesota** by **Edmonton** with Marc Habscheid and Don Barber for Gord Sherven and Don Biggs, December 20, 1985. Signed as a free agent by **Hartford**, February 9, 1990.

• VOLCAN, Mickey

Michael Stephen D – R. 6', 190 lbs. b: Edmonton, Alta., 3/3/1962. Hartford's 3rd, 50th overall, in 1980.

Season	Club	League	GP	G	A	Pts	AG	AA	APts	PIM	PP	SH	GW	S	%	TGF	PGF	TGA	PGA	+/–	GP	G	A	Pts	PIM	PP	SH	GW
1977-78	St. Albert Saints	AJHL	60	28	40	68	....	....	....	106	....	....	....	....	....	....	....	....	....	....	....	....	....	....	....	....	....	....
1978-79	St. Albert Saints	AJHL	50	20	47	67	....	....	....	109	....	....	....	....	....	....	....	....	....	....	....	....	....	....	....	....	....	....
1979-80	University of North Dakota	WCHA	33	2	14	16	....	....	....	38	....	....	....	....	....	....	....	....	....	....	....	....	....	....	....	....	....	....
1980-81	**Hartford Whalers**	**NHL**	**49**	**2**	**11**	**13**	**2**	**7**	**9**	**26**	**0**	**0**	**0**	**49**	**4.1**	**47**	**2**	**63**	**6**	**–12**	....	....	....	....	....	....	....	....
	Binghamton Whalers	AHL	24	1	9	10	....	....	....	26	....	....	....	....	....	....	....	....	....	....	6	0	0	0	14	....	....	....
1981-82	**Hartford Whalers**	**NHL**	**26**	**1**	**5**	**6**	**1**	**3**	**4**	**29**	**1**	**0**	**0**	**45**	**2.2**	**19**	**2**	**41**	**7**	**–17**	....	....	....	....	....	....	....	....
	Binghamton Whalers	AHL	33	4	13	17	....	....	....	47	....	....	....	....	....	....	....	....	....	....	14	4	8	12	40	....	....	....
1982-83	**Hartford Whalers**	**NHL**	**68**	**4**	**13**	**17**	**3**	**9**	**12**	**73**	**0**	**0**	**0**	**72**	**5.6**	**56**	**6**	**96**	**16**	**–30**	....	....	....	....	....	....	....	....
1983-84	**Calgary Flames**	**NHL**	**19**	**1**	**4**	**5**	**1**	**3**	**4**	**18**	**0**	**0**	**1**	**13**	**7.7**	**19**	**0**	**24**	**3**	**–2**	....	....	....	....	....	....	....	....
	Colorado Flames	CHL	30	8	9	17	....	....	....	20	....	....	....	....	....	....	....	....	....	....	5	0	0	0	11	....	....	....
1984-85	Moncton Golden Flames	AHL	63	8	14	22	....	....	....	44	....	....	....	....	....	....	....	....	....	....	....	....	....	....	....	....	....	....
1985-86	Nova Scotia Oilers	AHL	66	12	36	48	....	....	....	114	....	....	....	....	....	....	....	....	....	....	....	....	....	....	....	....	....	....
1986-87	Baltimore Skipjacks	AHL	72	8	36	44	....	....	....	118	....	....	....	....	....	....	....	....	....	....	....	....	....	....	....	....	....	....
1987-88	JyP-HT Jyvaskyla	Finland	29	7	4	11	....	....	....	78	....	....	....	....	....	....	....	....	....	....	....	....	....	....	....	....	....	....
1988-89	EV Landshut	Germany-2	16	9	15	24	....	....	....	49	....	....	....	....	....	....	....	....	....	....	....	....	....	....	....	....	....	....
1989-90	Krefelder EV	Germany-2	25	8	27	35	....	....	....	60	....	....	....	....	....	....	....	....	....	....	....	....	....	....	....	....	....	....
	SC Riessersee	Germany-2	10	5	7	12	....	....	....	39	....	....	....	....	....	....	....	....	....	....	....	....	....	....	....	....	....	....
1990-91	Phoenix Roadrunners	IHL	59	13	29	42	....	....	....	103	....	....	....	....	....	....	....	....	....	....	11	0	6	6	11	....	....	....
	NHL Totals		**162**	**8**	**33**	**41**	**7**	**22**	**29**	**146**	**1**	**0**	**1**	**179**	**4.5**	**141**	**10**	**224**	**32**		....	....	....	....	....	....	....	....

Traded to **Calgary** by **Hartford** for Joel Quenneville and Richie Dunn, July 5, 1983.

• VOLCHKOV, Alexandre

C – L. 6'2", 204 lbs. b: Moscow, USSR, 9/25/1977. Washington's 1st, 4th overall, in 1996.

Season	Club	League	GP	G	A	Pts	AG	AA	APts	PIM	PP	SH	GW	S	%	TGF	PGF	TGA	PGA	+/–	GP	G	A	Pts	PIM	PP	SH	GW
1994-95	CSKA Moscow	CIS	1	0	0	0	....	....	....	0	....	....	....	....	....	....	....	....	....	....	....	....	....	....	....	....	....	....
1995-96	Barrie Colts	OHL	47	37	27	64	....	....	....	36	....	....	....	....	....	....	....	....	....	....	7	2	3	5	12	....	....	....
1996-97	Barrie Colts	OHL	56	29	53	82	....	....	....	76	....	....	....	....	....	....	....	....	....	....	9	6	9	15	12	....	....	....
	Russia	WJC-A	6	0	2	2	....	....	....	4	....	....	....	....	....	....	....	....	....	....	....	....	....	....	....	....	....	....
	Portland Pirates	AHL	....	....	....	....	....	....	....	....	....	....	....	....	....	....	....	....	....	....	4	0	0	0	0	....	....	....
1997-98	Portland Pirates	AHL	34	2	5	7	....	....	....	20	....	....	....	....	....	....	....	....	....	....	1	0	0	0	0	....	....	....
1998-99	Portland Pirates	AHL	27	3	8	11	....	....	....	24	....	....	....	....	....	....	....	....	....	....	....	....	....	....	....	....	....	....
	Cincinnati Cyclones	IHL	25	1	3	4	....	....	....	8	....	....	....	....	....	....	....	....	....	....	....	....	....	....	....	....	....	....
99-2000	**Washington Capitals**	**NHL**	**3**	**0**	**0**	**0**	**0**	**0**	**0**	**0**	**0**	**0**	**0**	**1**	**0.0**	**0**	**0**	**2**	**0**	**–2**	....	....	....	....	....	....	....	....
	Portland Pirates	AHL	35	11	15	26	....	....	....	47	....	....	....	....	....	....	....	....	....	....	....	....	....	....	....	....	....	....
	Hamilton Bulldogs	AHL	25	2	6	8	....	....	....	11	....	....	....	....	....	....	....	....	....	....	....	....	....	....	....	....	....	....
	NHL Totals		**3**	**0**	**0**	**0**	**0**	**0**	**0**	**0**	**0**	**0**	**0**	**1**	**0.0**	**0**	**0**	**2**	**0**		....	....	....	....	....	....	....	....

OHL Second All-Star Team (1997)

Traded to **Edmonton** by **Washington** for a conditional choice in 2001 Entry Draft, February 4, 2000.

• VOLEK, David

W – L. 6', 185 lbs. b: Prague, Czech., 6/18/1966. NY Islanders' 11th, 208th overall, in 1984.

Season	Club	League	GP	G	A	Pts	AG	AA	APts	PIM	PP	SH	GW	S	%	TGF	PGF	TGA	PGA	+/–	GP	G	A	Pts	PIM	PP	SH	GW
1982-83	Czechoslovakia	EJC-A	5	3	2	5	....	....	....	8	....	....	....	....	....	....	....	....	....	....	....	....	....	....	....	....	....	....
1983-84	Czechoslovakia	EJC-A	5	5	5	10	....	....	....	2	....	....	....	....	....	....	....	....	....	....	....	....	....	....	....	....	....	....
1984-85	HC Sparta Praha	Czech.	32	5	5	10	....	....	....	14	....	....	....	....	....	....	....	....	....	....	....	....	....	....	....	....	....	....
1985-86	HC Sparta Praha	Czech.	35	10	7	17	....	....	....	....	....	....	....	....	....	....	....	....	....	....	....	....	....	....	....	....	....	....
	Czechoslovakia	WJC-A	7	4	3	7	....	....	....	6	....	....	....	....	....	....	....	....	....	....	....	....	....	....	....	....	....	....
1986-87	HC Sparta Praha	Czech.	39	27	25	52	....	....	....	38	....	....	....	....	....	....	....	....	....	....	....	....	....	....	....	....	....	....
	Czechoslovakia	WEC-A	10	3	1	4	....	....	....	2	....	....	....	....	....	....	....	....	....	....	....	....	....	....	....	....	....	....
1987-88	Czechoslovakia	Can-Cup	6	2	2	4	....	....	....	2	....	....	....	....	....	....	....	....	....	....	....	....	....	....	....	....	....	....
	HC Sparta Praha	Czech.	42	29	18	47	....	....	....	58	....	....	....	....	....	....	....	....	....	....	....	....	....	....	....	....	....	....
	Czechoslovakia	Olympics	7	1	2	3	....	....	....	2	....	....	....	....	....	....	....	....	....	....	....	....	....	....	....	....	....	....
1988-89	**New York Islanders**	**NHL**	**77**	**25**	**34**	**59**	**21**	**24**	**45**	**24**	**9**	**0**	**7**	**229**	**10.9**	**90**	**42**	**63**	**4**	**–11**	....	....	....	....	....	....	....	....
1989-90	**New York Islanders**	**NHL**	**80**	**17**	**22**	**39**	**15**	**16**	**31**	**41**	**6**	**0**	**0**	**181**	**9.4**	**69**	**27**	**52**	**8**	**–2**	**5**	**1**	**4**	**5**	**0**	**0**	**0**	**0**

			REGULAR SEASON																		PLAYOFFS							
Season	Club	League	GP	G	A	Pts	AG	AA	APts	PIM	PP	SH	GW	S	%	TGF	PGF	TGA	PGA	+/-	GP	G	A	Pts	PIM	PP	SH	GW
1990-91	**New York Islanders**	**NHL**	**77**	**22**	**34**	**56**	**20**	**26**	**46**	**57**	**6**	**0**	**1**	**224**	**9.8**	**75**	**23**	**82**	**20**	**−10**	....	....	....	....	....	....	....	....
	Czechoslovakia	WEC-A	10	3	2	5	....	....	....	8	....	....	....	....	....	....	....	....	....	....	....	....	....	....	....	....	....	....
1991-92	**New York Islanders**	**NHL**	**74**	**18**	**42**	**60**	**16**	**32**	**48**	**35**	**4**	**1**	**2**	**167**	**10.8**	**87**	**26**	**86**	**25**	**0**	....	....	....	....	....	....	....	....
1992-93	**New York Islanders**	**NHL**	**56**	**8**	**13**	**21**	**7**	**9**	**16**	**34**	**2**	**0**	**1**	**118**	**6.8**	**38**	**5**	**41**	**7**	**−1**	**10**	**4**	**1**	**5**	**2**	**0**	**0**	**0**
1993-94	**New York Islanders**	**NHL**	**32**	**5**	**9**	**14**	**5**	**7**	**12**	**10**	**2**	**0**	**0**	**56**	**8.9**	**28**	**7**	**22**	**1**	**0**	....	....	....	....	....	....	....	....
1994-95	**New York Islanders**	**NHL**	DID NOT PLAY – INJURED																									
1995-96	HC Sparta Praha	Czech-Rep	5	3	2	5	....	....	....	....	....	....	....	....	....	....	....	....	....	....	....	....	....	....	....	....	....	....
	NHL Totals		**396**	**95**	**154**	**249**	**84**	**114**	**198**	**201**	**29**	**1**	**11**	**975**	**9.7**	**387**	**130**	**346**	**65**		**15**	**5**	**5**	**10**	**2**	**0**	**0**	**0**

NHL All-Rookie Team (1989)

• Missed entire 1994-95 season recovering from back surgery, September, 1994.

• VOLMAR, Doug

Douglas Steven RW – R. 6'1", 215 lbs. b: Cleveland, OH, 1/9/1945.

Season	Club	League	GP	G	A	Pts	AG	AA	APts	PIM	PP	SH	GW	S	%	TGF	PGF	TGA	PGA	+/-	GP	G	A	Pts	PIM	PP	SH	GW
1963-64	Cleveland Heights High	Hi-School	STATISTICS NOT AVAILABLE																									
1964-65	Michigan State Spartans	WCHA	25	27	9	36	....	....	....	21	....	....	....	....	....	....	....	....	....	....	....	....	....	....	....	....	....	....
1965-66	Michigan State Spartans	WCHA	25	24	27	*51	....	....	....	47	....	....	....	....	....	....	....	....	....	....	4	2	1	3	10	....	....	....
1966-67	Michigan State Spartans	WCHA	32	21	12	33	....	....	....	100	....	....	....	....	....	....	....	....	....	....	....	....	....	....	....	....	....	....
1967-68	United States	Nat-Team	45	53	13	66	....	....	....	....	....	....	....	....	....	....	....	....	....	....	....	....	....	....	....	....	....	....
	United States	Olympics	7	5	0	5	....	....	....	4	....	....	....	....	....	....	....	....	....	....	....	....	....	....	....	....	....	....
1968-69	Columbus Checkers	IHL	72	*63	28	91	....	....	....	74	....	....	....	....	....	....	....	....	....	....	3	2	1	3	0	....	....	....
1969-70	Fort Worth Wings	CHL	67	30	23	53	....	....	....	75	....	....	....	....	....	....	....	....	....	....	7	4	1	5	2	....	....	....
	Detroit Red Wings	**NHL**	....	....	....	....	....	....	....	....	....	....	....	....	....	....	....	....	....	....	**2**	**1**	**0**	**1**	**0**	**0**	**0**	**0**
	San Diego Gulls	WHL	....	....	....	....	....	....	....	....	....	....	....	....	....	....	....	....	....	....	2	0	3	3	0	....	....	....
1970-71	**Detroit Red Wings**	**NHL**	**2**	**0**	**1**	**1**	**0**	**1**	**1**	**2**	**0**	**0**	**0**	**0**	**0.0**	**1**	**1**	**0**	**0**	**0**	....	....	....	....	....	....	....	....
	Springfield Kings	AHL	69	*42	26	68	....	....	....	52	....	....	....	....	....	....	....	....	....	....	12	6	10	16	29	....	....	....
1971-72	**Detroit Red Wings**	**NHL**	**39**	**9**	**5**	**14**	**9**	**4**	**13**	**8**	**3**	**0**	**1**	**43**	**20.9**	**24**	**10**	**14**	**0**	**0**	....	....	....	....	....	....	....	....
	Tidewater Red Wings	AHL	20	8	8	16	....	....	....	8	....	....	....	....	....	....	....	....	....	....	....	....	....	....	....	....	....	....
1972-73	**Los Angeles Kings**	**NHL**	**21**	**4**	**2**	**6**	**4**	**2**	**6**	**16**	**0**	**0**	**1**	**33**	**12.1**	**12**	**0**	**14**	**0**	**−2**	....	....	....	....	....	....	....	....
1973-74	Portland Buckaroos	WHL	3	0	4	4	....	....	....	5	....	....	....	....	....	....	....	....	....	....	....	....	....	....	....	....	....	....
	Springfield Kings	AHL	25	11	5	16	....	....	....	20	....	....	....	....	....	....	....	....	....	....	....	....	....	....	....	....	....	....
	Richmond Robins	AHL	22	13	7	20	....	....	....	10	....	....	....	....	....	....	....	....	....	....	5	3	4	7	2	....	....	....
1974-75	San Diego Mariners	WHA	10	0	1	1	....	....	....	4	....	....	....	....	....	....	....	....	....	....	....	....	....	....	....	....	....	....
	Syracuse Blazers	NAHL	47	40	32	72	....	....	....	47	....	....	....	....	....	....	....	....	....	....	....	....	....	....	....	....	....	....
	NHL Totals		**62**	**13**	**8**	**21**	**13**	**7**	**20**	**26**	**3**	**0**	**2**	**76**	**17.1**	**37**	**11**	**28**	**0**		**2**	**1**	**0**	**1**	**0**	**0**	**0**	**0**
	Other Major League Totals		10	0	1	1	....	....	....	4	....	....	....	....	....	....	....	....	....	....	....	....	....	....	....	....	....	....

WCHA First All-Star Team (1966) • NCAA West First All-American Team (1966) • IHL Second All-Star Team (1969) • Won Garry F. Longman Memorial Trophy (Top Rookie - IHL) (1969)

Claimed by **San Diego** (WHL) from **Detroit** in Reverse Draft, June 12, 1969. Traded to **Detroit** by **San Diego** (WHL) for cash, July, 1969. Claimed by **LA Kings** from **Detroit** in Intra-League Draft, June 5, 1972. Traded to **Richmond** (AHL) by **Springfield** (AHL) for Roger Pelletier, February, 1974. Signed as a free agent by **San Diego** (WHA), June, 1974.

• VON STEFENELLI, Phil

D – L. 6'1", 200 lbs. b: Vancouver, B.C., 4/10/1969. Vancouver's 5th, 122nd overall, in 1988.

Season	Club	League	GP	G	A	Pts	AG	AA	APts	PIM	PP	SH	GW	S	%	TGF	PGF	TGA	PGA	+/-	GP	G	A	Pts	PIM	PP	SH	GW
1985-86	Richmond Sockeyes	BCJHL	41	6	11	17	....	....	....	28	....	....	....	....	....	....	....	....	....	....	....	....	....	....	....	....	....	....
1986-87	Richmond Sockeyes	BCJHL	35	5	19	24	....	....	....	39	....	....	....	....	....	....	....	....	....	....	....	....	....	....	....	....	....	....
	Langley Eagles	BCJHL	17	0	13	13	....	....	....	12	....	....	....	....	....	....	....	....	....	....	....	....	....	....	....	....	....	....
1987-88	Boston University	H-East	34	3	13	16	....	....	....	38	....	....	....	....	....	....	....	....	....	....	....	....	....	....	....	....	....	....
1988-89	Boston University	H-East	33	2	6	8	....	....	....	34	....	....	....	....	....	....	....	....	....	....	....	....	....	....	....	....	....	....
1989-90	Boston University	H-East	44	8	20	28	....	....	....	40	....	....	....	....	....	....	....	....	....	....	....	....	....	....	....	....	....	....
1990-91	Boston University	H-East	41	7	23	30	....	....	....	32	....	....	....	....	....	....	....	....	....	....	....	....	....	....	....	....	....	....
1991-92	Milwaukee Admirals	IHL	80	2	34	36	....	....	....	40	....	....	....	....	....	....	....	....	....	....	5	1	2	3	2	....	....	....
1992-93	Hamilton Canucks	AHL	78	11	20	31	....	....	....	75	....	....	....	....	....	....	....	....	....	....	....	....	....	....	....	....	....	....
1993-94	Hamilton Canucks	AHL	80	10	31	41	....	....	....	89	....	....	....	....	....	....	....	....	....	....	4	1	0	1	2	....	....	....
1994-95	Providence Bruins	AHL	75	6	13	19	....	....	....	93	....	....	....	....	....	....	....	....	....	....	13	2	4	6	6	....	....	....
1995-96	**Boston Bruins**	**NHL**	**27**	**0**	**4**	**4**	**0**	**3**	**3**	**16**	**0**	**0**	**0**	**20**	**0.0**	**15**	**5**	**11**	**3**	**2**	....	....	....	....	....	....	....	....
	Providence Bruins	AHL	42	9	21	30	....	....	....	52	....	....	....	....	....	....	....	....	....	....	....	....	....	....	....	....	....	....
1996-97	**Ottawa Senators**	**NHL**	**6**	**0**	**1**	**1**	**0**	**1**	**1**	**7**	**0**	**0**	**0**	**2**	**0.0**	**3**	**2**	**5**	**1**	**−3**	....	....	....	....	....	....	....	....
	Detroit Vipers	IHL	67	14	26	40	....	....	....	86	....	....	....	....	....	....	....	....	....	....	21	2	4	6	20	....	....	....
1997-98	EHC Chur	Switz-2	40	10	26	36	....	....	....	75	....	....	....	....	....	....	....	....	....	....	9	1	3	4	30	....	....	....
	HC Fassa	Italy	....	....	....	....	....	....	....	....	....	....	....	....	....	....	....	....	....	....	7	2	3	5	2	....	....	....
1998-99	Frankfurt Lions	Germany	51	4	12	16	....	....	....	75	....	....	....	....	....	....	....	....	....	....	8	0	0	0	6	....	....	....
	Frankfurt Lions	EuroHL	6	2	1	3	....	....	....	32	....	....	....	....	....	....	....	....	....	....	....	....	....	....	....	....	....	....
99-2000	Krefeld Pinguine	Germany	50	4	7	11	....	....	....	82	....	....	....	....	....	....	....	....	....	....	4	1	2	3	4	....	....	....
	NHL Totals		**33**	**0**	**5**	**5**	**0**	**4**	**4**	**23**	**0**	**0**	**0**	**22**	**0.0**	**18**	**7**	**16**	**4**		....	....	....	....	....	....	....	....

Signed as a free agent by **Boston**, September 10, 1994. Signed as a free agent by **Ottawa**, July 17, 1996. Signed as a free agent by **Tampa Bay**, July 22, 1999.

• VOPAT, Jan

D – L. 6', 205 lbs. b: Most, Czech., 3/22/1973. Hartford's 3rd, 57th overall, in 1992.

Season	Club	League	GP	G	A	Pts	AG	AA	APts	PIM	PP	SH	GW	S	%	TGF	PGF	TGA	PGA	+/-	GP	G	A	Pts	PIM	PP	SH	GW
1989-90	CHZ Litvinov	Czech-Jr.	STATISTICS NOT AVAILABLE																									
	Czechoslovakia	EJC-A	6	2	1	3	....	....	....	2	....	....	....	....	....	....	....	....	....	....	....	....	....	....	....	....	....	....
1990-91	CHZ Litvinov	Czech.	25	1	4	5	....	....	....	4	....	....	....	....	....	....	....	....	....	....	....	....	....	....	....	....	....	....
	Czechoslovakia	EJC-A	6	6	0	6	....	....	....	4	....	....	....	....	....	....	....	....	....	....	....	....	....	....	....	....	....	....
1991-92	CHZ Litvinov	Czech.	46	4	2	6	....	....	....	16	....	....	....	....	....	....	....	....	....	....	....	....	....	....	....	....	....	....
	Czechoslovakia	WJC-A	7	0	1	1	....	....	....	2	....	....	....	....	....	....	....	....	....	....	....	....	....	....	....	....	....	....
1992-93	CHZ Litvinov	Czech.	45	12	10	22	....	....	....	....	....	....	....	....	....	....	....	....	....	....	....	....	....	....	....	....	....	....
	Czech-Republic	WJC-A	7	6	4	10	....	....	....	6	....	....	....	....	....	....	....	....	....	....	....	....	....	....	....	....	....	....
1993-94	HC Chemopetrol Litvinov	Czech-Rep	41	9	19	28	....	....	....	0	....	....	....	....	....	....	....	....	....	....	4	1	1	2	....	....	....	....
	Czech-Republic	Olympics	8	0	1	1	....	....	....	8	....	....	....	....	....	....	....	....	....	....	....	....	....	....	....	....	....	....
1994-95	HC Chemopetrol Litvinov	Czech-Rep	42	7	18	25	....	....	....	49	....	....	....	....	....	....	....	....	....	....	4	0	2	2	2	....	....	....
	Czech-Republic	WC-A	8	0	1	1	....	....	....	6	....	....	....	....	....	....	....	....	....	....	....	....	....	....	....	....	....	....
1995-96	**Los Angeles Kings**	**NHL**	**11**	**1**	**4**	**5**	**1**	**3**	**4**	**4**	**0**	**0**	**0**	**13**	**7.7**	**15**	**6**	**7**	**1**	**3**	....	....	....	....	....	....	....	....
	Phoenix Roadrunners	IHL	47	0	9	9	....	....	....	34	....	....	....	....	....	....	....	....	....	....	4	0	2	2	4	....	....	....
1996-97	**Los Angeles Kings**	**NHL**	**33**	**4**	**5**	**9**	**4**	**4**	**8**	**22**	**0**	**0**	**1**	**44**	**9.1**	**26**	**2**	**25**	**4**	**3**	....	....	....	....	....	....	....	....
	Phoenix Roadrunners	IHL	4	0	6	6	....	....	....	6	....	....	....	....	....	....	....	....	....	....	....	....	....	....	....	....	....	....
1997-98	**Los Angeles Kings**	**NHL**	**21**	**1**	**5**	**6**	**1**	**5**	**6**	**10**	**0**	**0**	**1**	**13**	**7.7**	**18**	**1**	**13**	**4**	**8**	**2**	**0**	**1**	**1**	**2**	**0**	**0**	**0**
	Utah Grizzlies	IHL	38	8	13	21	....	....	....	24	....	....	....	....	....	....	....	....	....	....	....	....	....	....	....	....	....	....
1998-99	**Nashville Predators**	**NHL**	**55**	**5**	**6**	**11**	**6**	**6**	**12**	**28**	**0**	**0**	**0**	**46**	**10.9**	**40**	**4**	**48**	**12**	**0**	....	....	....	....	....	....	....	....
99-2000	**Nashville Predators**	**NHL**	**6**	**0**	**0**	**0**	**0**	**0**	**0**	**6**	**0**	**0**	**0**	**3**	**0.0**	**5**	**1**	**3**	**0**	**1**	....	....	....	....	....	....	....	....
	Milwaukee Admirals	IHL	2	1	0	1	....	....	....	2	....	....	....	....	....	....	....	....	....	....	....	....	....	....	....	....	....	....
	NHL Totals		**126**	**11**	**20**	**31**	**12**	**18**	**30**	**70**	**0**	**0**	**2**	**119**	**9.2**	**104**	**14**	**96**	**21**		**2**	**0**	**1**	**1**	**2**	**0**	**0**	**0**

• Brother of Roman

Rights traded to **LA Kings** by **Hartford** for LA Kings' 4th round choice (Ian MacNeil) in 1995 Entry Draft, May 31, 1995. Traded to **Nashville** by **LA Kings** with Kimmo Timonen for future considerations, June 26, 1998. • Missed remainder of 1999-2000 season recovering from rare skin allergy, December 10, 1999.

• VOPAT, Roman

C – L. 6'3", 223 lbs. b: Litvinov, Czech., 4/21/1976. St. Louis' 4th, 172nd overall, in 1994.

Season	Club	League	GP	G	A	Pts	AG	AA	APts	PIM	PP	SH	GW	S	%	TGF	PGF	TGA	PGA	+/-	GP	G	A	Pts	PIM	PP	SH	GW
1993-94	HC Chemopetrol Litvinov	Czech-Jr.	STATISTICS NOT AVAILABLE																									
	HC Chemopetrol Litvinov	Czech-Rep	7	0	0	0	....	....	....	0	....	....	....	....	....	....	....	....	....	....	....	....	....	....	....	....	....	....
	Czech-Republic	EJC-A	5	2	1	3	....	....	....	8	....	....	....	....	....	....	....	....	....	....	....	....	....	....	....	....	....	....
1994-95	Moose Jaw Warriors	WHL	72	23	20	43	....	....	....	141	....	....	....	....	....	....	....	....	....	....	10	4	1	5	28	....	....	....
	Peoria Rivermen	IHL	....	....	....	....	....	....	....	....	....	....	....	....	....	....	....	....	....	....	6	0	2	2	2	....	....	....

			REGULAR SEASON																		PLAYOFFS							
Season	Club	League	GP	G	A	Pts	AG	AA	APts	PIM	PP	SH	GW	S	%	TGF	PGF	TGA	PGA	+/–	GP	G	A	Pts	PIM	PP	SH	GW
1995-96	Moose Jaw Warriors	WHL	7	0	4	4	....	....	....	34	....	....	....	....	....	....	....	....	....	....	....	....	....	....	....	....	....	....
	Prince Albert Raiders	WHL	22	15	5	20	....	....	....	81	....	....	....	....	....	....	....	....	....	....	18	9	8	17	57	....	....	....
	St. Louis Blues	**NHL**	**25**	**2**	**3**	**5**	**2**	**2**	**4**	**48**	**1**	**0**	**1**	**33**	**6.1**	**6**	**1**	**14**	**1**	**–8**	....	....	....	....	....	....	....	....
	Worcester IceCats	AHL	5	2	0	2	....	....	....	14	....	....	....	....	....	....	....	....	....	....	....	....	....	....	....	....	....	....
1996-97	**Los Angeles Kings**	**NHL**	**29**	**4**	**5**	**9**	**4**	**4**	**8**	**60**	**1**	**0**	**2**	**54**	**7.4**	**16**	**1**	**23**	**1**	**–7**	....	....	....	....	....	....	....	....
	Phoenix Roadrunners	IHL	50	8	8	16	....	....	....	139	....	....	....	....	....	....	....	....	....	....	....	....	....	....	....	....	....	....
1997-98	**Los Angeles Kings**	**NHL**	**25**	**0**	**3**	**3**	**0**	**3**	**3**	**55**	**0**	**0**	**0**	**36**	**0.0**	**5**	**2**	**10**	**0**	**–7**	....	....	....	....	....	....	....	....
	Fredericton Canadiens	AHL	29	10	10	20	....	....	....	93	....	....	....	....	....	....	....	....	....	....	....	....	....	....	....	....	....	....
1998-99	**Los Angeles Kings**	**NHL**	**3**	**0**	**0**	**0**	**0**	**0**	**0**	**6**	**0**	**0**	**0**	**2**	**0.0**	**0**	**0**	**0**	**0**	**0**	....	....	....	....	....	....	....	....
	Chicago Blackhawks	**NHL**	**3**	**0**	**0**	**0**	**0**	**0**	**0**	**4**	**0**	**0**	**0**	**0**	**0.0**	**0**	**0**	**4**	**0**	**–4**	....	....	....	....	....	....	....	....
	Philadelphia Flyers	**NHL**	**48**	**0**	**3**	**3**	**0**	**3**	**3**	**80**	**0**	**0**	**0**	**25**	**0.0**	**6**	**0**	**9**	**0**	**–3**	....	....	....	....	....	....	....	....
99-2000	Philadelphia Phantoms	AHL	12	1	0	1	....	....	....	12	....	....	....	....	....	....	....	....	....	....	....	....	....	....	....	....	....	....
	Moskitos Essen	Germany	44	8	15	23	....	....	....	171	....	....	....	....	....	....	....	....	....	....	....	....	....	....	....	....	....	....
	NHL Totals		**133**	**6**	**14**	**20**	**6**	**12**	**18**	**253**	**2**	**0**	**3**	**150**	**4.0**	**33**	**4**	**60**	**2**		....	....	....	....	....	....	....	....

• Brother of Jan

Traded to **LA Kings** by **St. Louis** with Craig Johnson, Patrice Tardif, St. Louis 5th round choice (Peter Hogan) in 1996 Entry Draft and 1st round choice (Matt Zultek) in 1997 Entry Draft for Wayne Gretzky, February 27, 1996. Traded to **Colorado** by **Los Angeles** with Los Angeles' 6th round choice (later traded to Chicago, later traded to Ottawa, Ottawa selected Martin Brusek) in 1999 Entry Draft for Eric Lacroix, October 29, 1998. Traded to **Chicago** by **Colorado** with Los Angeles' 6th round choice (previously acquired, later traded to Ottawa, Ottawa selected Martin Brusek) in 1999 Entry Draft for Cam Russell, November 10, 1998. Traded to **Philadelphia** by **Chicago** for Mike Maneluk, November 17, 1998. Signed as a free agent by **Moskitos Essen** (Germany) following release by **Philadelphia**, December 19, 1999.

• VOROBIEV, Vladimir

LW – R. 6', 185 lbs. b: Cherepovets, USSR, 10/2/1972. NY Rangers' 10th, 240th overall, in 1992.

1992-93	Severstal Cherepovets	CIS	42	18	5	23	....	....	....	18	....	....	....	....	....	....	....	....	....	....	....	....	....	....	....	....	....	....
1993-94	Dynamo Moscow	CIS	11	3	1	4	....	....	....	2	....	....	....	....	....	....	....	....	....	....	....	....	....	....	....	....	....	....
1994-95	Dynamo Moscow	CIS	48	9	20	29	....	....	....	28	....	....	....	....	....	....	....	....	....	....	14	1	7	8	2	....	....	....
1995-96	Dynamo Moscow	CIS	42	19	9	28	....	....	....	49	....	....	....	....	....	....	....	....	....	....	9	2	8	10	2	....	....	....
1996-97	**New York Rangers**	**NHL**	**16**	**5**	**5**	**10**	**5**	**4**	**9**	**6**	**2**	**0**	**0**	**42**	**11.9**	**15**	**4**	**7**	**0**	**4**	....	....	....	....	....	....	....	....
	Binghamton Rangers	AHL	61	22	27	49	....	....	....	6	....	....	....	....	....	....	....	....	....	....	4	1	1	2	2	....	....	....
1997-98	**New York Rangers**	**NHL**	**15**	**2**	**2**	**4**	**2**	**2**	**4**	**6**	**0**	**0**	**1**	**27**	**7.4**	**8**	**5**	**13**	**0**	**–10**	....	....	....	....	....	....	....	....
	Hartford Wolf Pack	AHL	56	20	28	48	....	....	....	18	....	....	....	....	....	....	....	....	....	....	15	11	8	19	4	....	....	....
1998-99	Hartford Wolf Pack	AHL	65	24	41	65	....	....	....	22	....	....	....	....	....	....	....	....	....	....	....	....	....	....	....	....	....	....
	Edmonton Oilers	**NHL**	**2**	**2**	**0**	**2**	**2**	**0**	**2**	**2**	**0**	**0**	**0**	**5**	**40.0**	**2**	**0**	**1**	**0**	**1**	**1**	**0**	**0**	**0**	**0**	**0**	**0**	**0**
	Hamilton Bulldogs	AHL	8	3	6	9	....	....	....	2	....	....	....	....	....	....	....	....	....	....	6	0	1	1	2	....	....	....
99-2000	Hamilton Bulldogs	AHL	37	9	9	18	....	....	....	16	....	....	....	....	....	....	....	....	....	....	....	....	....	....	....	....	....	....
	Long Beach Ice Dogs	IHL	23	6	7	13	....	....	....	0	....	....	....	....	....	....	....	....	....	....	1	0	0	0	2	....	....	....
	NHL Totals		**33**	**9**	**7**	**16**	**9**	**6**	**15**	**14**	**2**	**0**	**1**	**74**	**12.2**	**25**	**9**	**21**	**0**		**1**	**0**	**0**	**0**	**0**	**0**	**0**	**0**

Traded to **Edmonton** by **NY Rangers** for Kevin Brown, March 23, 1999.

• VUJTEK, Vladimir

LW – L. 6'1", 190 lbs. b: Ostrava, Czech., 2/17/1972. Montreal's 5th, 73rd overall, in 1991.

1988-89	TJ Vitkovice	Czech.	3	0	1	1	....	....	....	0	....	....	....	....	....	....	....	....	....	....	....	....	....	....	....	....	....	....
1989-90	TJ Vitkovice	Czech.	22	3	4	7	....	....	....	....	....	....	....	....	....	....	....	....	....	....	7	4	3	7	....	....	....	....
1990-91	TJ Vitkovice	Czech.	26	7	4	11	....	....	....	....	....	....	....	....	....	....	....	....	....	....	....	....	....	....	....	....	....	....
	Tri-City Americans	WHL	37	26	18	44	....	....	....	74	....	....	....	....	....	....	....	....	....	....	7	2	3	5	4	....	....	....
1991-92	Tri-City Americans	WHL	53	41	61	102	....	....	....	114	....	....	....	....	....	....	....	....	....	....	....	....	....	....	....	....	....	....
	Montreal Canadiens	**NHL**	**2**	**0**	**0**	**0**	**0**	**0**	**0**	**0**	**0**	**0**	**0**	**1**	**0.0**	**0**	**0**	**1**	**0**	**–1**	....	....	....	....	....	....	....	....
1992-93	**Edmonton Oilers**	**NHL**	**30**	**1**	**10**	**11**	**1**	**7**	**8**	**8**	**0**	**0**	**0**	**49**	**2.0**	**16**	**4**	**13**	**0**	**–1**	....	....	....	....	....	....	....	....
	Cape Breton Oilers	AHL	20	10	9	19	....	....	....	14	....	....	....	....	....	....	....	....	....	....	1	0	0	0	0	....	....	....
1993-94	**Edmonton Oilers**	**NHL**	**40**	**4**	**15**	**19**	**4**	**12**	**16**	**14**	**1**	**0**	**0**	**66**	**6.1**	**25**	**4**	**28**	**0**	**–7**	....	....	....	....	....	....	....	....
1994-95	HC Vitkovice	Czech-Rep	18	5	7	12	....	....	....	51	....	....	....	....	....	....	....	....	....	....	....	....	....	....	....	....	....	....
	Cape Breton Oilers	AHL	30	10	11	21	....	....	....	30	....	....	....	....	....	....	....	....	....	....	....	....	....	....	....	....	....	....
	Las Vegas Thunder	IHL	1	0	0	0	....	....	....	0	....	....	....	....	....	....	....	....	....	....	....	....	....	....	....	....	....	....
1995-96	HC Vitkovice	Czech-Rep	26	6	7	13	....	....	....	....	....	....	....	....	....	....	....	....	....	....	4	1	1	2	....	....	....	....
1996-97	HC Assat-Pori	Finland	50	27	31	58	....	....	....	48	....	....	....	....	....	....	....	....	....	....	4	1	2	3	2	....	....	....
	Czech-Republic	WC-A	8	7	7	14	....	....	....	31	....	....	....	....	....	....	....	....	....	....	....	....	....	....	....	....	....	....
1997-98	**Tampa Bay Lightning**	**NHL**	**30**	**2**	**4**	**6**	**2**	**4**	**6**	**16**	**0**	**0**	**1**	**44**	**4.5**	**10**	**2**	**10**	**0**	**–2**	....	....	....	....	....	....	....	....
	Adirondack Red Wings	AHL	2	1	2	3	....	....	....	0	....	....	....	....	....	....	....	....	....	....	....	....	....	....	....	....	....	....
1998-99	HC Vitkovice	Czech-Rep	47	20	35	55	....	....	....	75	....	....	....	....	....	....	....	....	....	....	....	....	....	....	....	....	....	....
99-2000	**Atlanta Thrashers**	**NHL**	**3**	**0**	**0**	**0**	**0**	**0**	**0**	**0**	**0**	**0**	**0**	**2**	**0.0**	**0**	**0**	**0**	**0**	**0**	....	....	....	....	....	....	....	....
	HC Sparta Praha	Czech-Rep	21	12	19	31	....	....	....	10	....	....	....	....	....	....	....	....	....	....	8	2	3	5	10	....	....	....
	HC Sparta Praha	EuroHL	1	0	0	0	....	....	....	2	....	....	....	....	....	....	....	....	....	....	4	2	2	4	0	....	....	....
	NHL Totals		**105**	**7**	**29**	**36**	**7**	**23**	**30**	**38**	**1**	**0**	**1**	**162**	**4.3**	**51**	**10**	**52**	**0**		....	....	....	....	....	....	....	....

WHL West First All-Star Team (1992) • WC-A All-Star Team (1997)

Traded to **Edmonton** by **Montreal** with Shayne Corson and Brent Gilchrist for Vincent Damphousse and Edmonton's 4th round choice (Adam Wiesel) in 1993 Entry Draft, August 27, 1992. Traded to **Tampa Bay** by **Edmonton** with Edmonton's 3rd round choice (Dmitri Afanasenkov) in 1998 Entry Draft for Brantt Myhres and Toronto's 3rd round choice (previously acquired, Edmonton selected Alex Henry) in 1998 Entry Draft, July 16, 1997. • Missed majority of 1997-98 season recovering from Epstein-Barr Virus, December, 1997. Signed as a free agent by **Atlanta**, July 29, 1999. • Missed majority of 1999-2000 season recovering from facial injuries suffered in exhibition game vs. NY Rangers, September 18, 1999.

• VUKOTA, Mick

RW – R. 6'1", 225 lbs. b: Saskatoon, Sask., 9/14/1966.

1983-84	North Battleford North Stars	SJHL	STATISTICS NOT AVAILABLE																									
	Winnipeg Warriors	WHL	3	1	1	2	....	....	....	10	....	....	....	....	....	....	....	....	....	....	....	....	....	....	....	....	....	....
1984-85	Kelowna Wings	WHL	66	10	6	16	....	....	....	247	....	....	....	....	....	....	....	....	....	....	6	0	0	0	56	....	....	....
1985-86	Spokane Chiefs	WHL	64	19	14	33	....	....	....	369	....	....	....	....	....	....	....	....	....	....	9	6	4	10	68	....	....	....
1986-87	Spokane Chiefs	WHL	61	25	28	53	....	....	....	*337	....	....	....	....	....	....	....	....	....	....	4	0	0	0	40	....	....	....
1987-88	**New York Islanders**	**NHL**	**17**	**1**	**0**	**1**	**1**	**0**	**1**	**82**	**0**	**0**	**0**	**7**	**14.3**	**8**	**0**	**7**	**0**	**1**	**2**	**0**	**0**	**0**	**23**	**0**	**0**	**0**
	Springfield Indians	AHL	52	7	9	16	....	....	....	375	....	....	....	....	....	....	....	....	....	....	....	....	....	....	....	....	....	....
1988-89	**New York Islanders**	**NHL**	**48**	**2**	**2**	**4**	**2**	**1**	**3**	**237**	**0**	**0**	**0**	**19**	**10.5**	**4**	**0**	**21**	**0**	**–17**	....	....	....	....	....	....	....	....
	Springfield Indians	AHL	3	1	0	1	....	....	....	33	....	....	....	....	....	....	....	....	....	....	....	....	....	....	....	....	....	....
1989-90	**New York Islanders**	**NHL**	**76**	**4**	**8**	**12**	**3**	**6**	**9**	**290**	**0**	**0**	**0**	**55**	**7.3**	**24**	**0**	**15**	**1**	**10**	**1**	**0**	**0**	**0**	**17**	**0**	**0**	**0**
1990-91	**New York Islanders**	**NHL**	**60**	**2**	**4**	**6**	**2**	**3**	**5**	**238**	**0**	**0**	**0**	**39**	**5.1**	**12**	**1**	**24**	**0**	**–13**	....	....	....	....	....	....	....	....
	Capital District Islanders	AHL	2	0	0	0	....	....	....	9	....	....	....	....	....	....	....	....	....	....	....	....	....	....	....	....	....	....
1991-92	**New York Islanders**	**NHL**	**74**	**0**	**6**	**6**	**0**	**5**	**5**	**293**	**0**	**0**	**0**	**34**	**0.0**	**15**	**0**	**21**	**0**	**–6**	....	....	....	....	....	....	....	....
1992-93	**New York Islanders**	**NHL**	**74**	**2**	**5**	**7**	**2**	**3**	**5**	**216**	**0**	**0**	**0**	**37**	**5.4**	**16**	**1**	**12**	**0**	**3**	**15**	**0**	**0**	**0**	**16**	**0**	**0**	**0**
1993-94	**New York Islanders**	**NHL**	**72**	**3**	**1**	**4**	**3**	**1**	**4**	**237**	**0**	**0**	**0**	**26**	**11.5**	**8**	**1**	**12**	**0**	**–5**	**4**	**0**	**0**	**0**	**17**	**0**	**0**	**0**
1994-95	**New York Islanders**	**NHL**	**40**	**0**	**2**	**2**	**0**	**3**	**3**	**109**	**0**	**0**	**0**	**11**	**0.0**	**6**	**0**	**5**	**0**	**1**	....	....	....	....	....	....	....	....
1995-96	**New York Islanders**	**NHL**	**32**	**1**	**1**	**2**	**1**	**1**	**2**	**106**	**0**	**0**	**0**	**11**	**9.1**	**2**	**0**	**5**	**0**	**–3**	....	....	....	....	....	....	....	....
1996-97	**New York Islanders**	**NHL**	**17**	**1**	**0**	**1**	**1**	**0**	**1**	**71**	**0**	**0**	**0**	**7**	**14.3**	**1**	**0**	**3**	**0**	**–2**	....	....	....	....	....	....	....	....
	Utah Grizzlies	IHL	43	11	11	22	....	....	....	185	....	....	....	....	....	....	....	....	....	....	7	1	2	3	20	....	....	....
1997-98	**Tampa Bay Lightning**	**NHL**	**42**	**1**	**0**	**1**	**1**	**0**	**1**	**116**	**0**	**0**	**0**	**15**	**6.7**	**4**	**0**	**4**	**0**	**0**	....	....	....	....	....	....	....	....
	Montreal Canadiens	**NHL**	**22**	**0**	**0**	**0**	**0**	**0**	**0**	**76**	**0**	**0**	**0**	**8**	**0.0**	**0**	**0**	**4**	**0**	**–4**	**1**	**0**	**0**	**0**	**0**	**0**	**0**	**0**
1998-99	Utah Grizzlies	IHL	48	8	7	15	....	....	....	226	....	....	....	....	....	....	....	....	....	....	....	....	....	....	....	....	....	....
99-2000	Utah Grizzlies	IHL	71	6	15	21	....	....	....	249	....	....	....	....	....	....	....	....	....	....	4	0	0	0	2	....	....	....
	NHL Totals		**574**	**17**	**29**	**46**	**16**	**23**	**39**	**2071**	**0**	**0**	**0**	**269**	**6.3**	**100**	**3**	**133**	**1**		**23**	**0**	**0**	**0**	**73**	**0**	**0**	**0**

Signed as a free agent by **NY Islanders**, March 2, 1987. Claimed by **Tampa Bay** from **NY Islanders** in NHL Waiver Draft, September 28, 1997. Traded to **Montreal** by **Tampa Bay** with Patrick Poulin and Igor Ulanov for Stephane Richer, Darcy Tucker and David Wilkie, January 15, 1998.

• VYAZMIKIN, Igor W – L. 6'1", 194 lbs. b: Moscow, Soviet Union, 1/8/1966. Edmonton's 13th, 252nd overall, in 1987.

			REGULAR SEASON																		PLAYOFFS							
Season	Club	League	GP	G	A	Pts	AG	AA	APts	PIM	PP	SH	GW	S	%	TGF	PGF	TGA	PGA	+/-	GP	G	A	Pts	PIM	PP	SH	GW
1982-83	Soviet Union	EJC-A	5	9	3	12	....	....	....	8	....	....	....	....	....	....	....	....	....	....	....	....	....	....	....	....	....	....
1983-84	CSKA Moscow	USSR	38	8	12	20	....	....	....	4	....	....	....	....	....	....	....	....	....	....	....	....	....	....	....	....	....	....
	Soviet Union	WJC-A	7	6	5	11	....	....	....	6	....	....	....	....	....	....	....	....	....	....	....	....	....	....	....	....	....	....
	Soviet Union	EJC-A	5	12	4	16	....	....	....	8	....	....	....	....	....	....	....	....	....	....	....	....	....	....	....	....	....	....
1984-85	CSKA Moscow	USSR	26	6	5	11	....	....	....	6	....	....	....	....	....	....	....	....	....	....	....	....	....	....	....	....	....	....
1985-86	CSKA Moscow	USSR	19	7	6	13	....	....	....	6	....	....	....	....	....	....	....	....	....	....	....	....	....	....	....	....	....	....
	Soviet Union	WJC-A	7	5	5	10	....	....	....	6	....	....	....	....	....	....	....	....	....	....	....	....	....	....	....	....	....	....
1986-87	CSKA Moscow	USSR	4	0	0	0	....	....	....	0	....	....	....	....	....	....	....	....	....	....	....	....	....	....	....	....	....	....
1987-88	CSKA Moscow	USSR	8	1	0	1	....	....	....	16	....	....	....	....	....	....	....	....	....	....	....	....	....	....	....	....	....	....
1988-89	CSKA Moscow	USSR	30	10	7	17	....	....	....	20	....	....	....	....	....	....	....	....	....	....	....	....	....	....	....	....	....	....
1989-90	Khimik Voskresensk	USSR	34	11	13	24	....	....	....	26	....	....	....	....	....	....	....	....	....	....	....	....	....	....	....	....	....	....
	Khimik Voskresensk	Super-S	6	1	6	7	....	....	....	0	....	....	....	....	....	....	....	....	....	....	....	....	....	....	....	....	....	....
1990-91	Khimik Voskresensk	Fr-Tour	1	0	0	0	....	....	....	20	....	....	....	....	....	....	....	....	....	....	....	....	....	....	....	....	....	....
	Khimik Voskresensk	USSR	23	7	12	19	....	....	....	17	....	....	....	....	....	....	....	....	....	....	....	....	....	....	....	....	....	....
	Edmonton Oilers	**NHL**	**4**	**1**	**0**	**1**	**1**	**0**	**1**	**0**	**0**	**0**	**1**	**5**	**20.0**	**2**	**1**	**1**	**0**	**0**	....	....	....	....	....	....	....	....
	Cape Breton Oilers	AHL	33	12	19	31	....	....	....	21	....	....	....	....	....	....	....	....	....	....	4	3	2	5	10	....	....	....
1991-92	Milwaukee Admirals	IHL	8	3	5	8	....	....	....	2	....	....	....	....	....	....	....	....	....	....	....	....	....	....	....	....	....	....
	Phoenix Roadrunners	IHL	6	0	3	3	....	....	....	8	....	....	....	....	....	....	....	....	....	....	....	....	....	....	....	....	....	....
1992-93	Fargo-Moorhead Express	AmHA	24	17	39	56	....	....	....	57	....	....	....	....	....	....	....	....	....	....	....	....	....	....	....	....	....	....
1993-94	Rungsted IK	Denmark	28	28	31	59	....	....	....	60	....	....	....	....	....	....	....	....	....	....	....	....	....	....	....	....	....	....
1994-95	HC Fassa	Italy	12	8	17	25	....	....	....	6	....	....	....	....	....	....	....	....	....	....	....	....	....	....	....	....	....	....
1995-96	Hermes Kokkola	Finland-2	29	18	20	38	....	....	....	129	....	....	....	....	....	....	....	....	....	....	4	1	5	6	12	....	....	....
1996-97	Ilves Tampere	Finland	36	8	13	21	....	....	....	76	....	....	....	....	....	....	....	....	....	....	3	0	0	0	2	....	....	....
1997-98	CSKA Moscow	Russia	25	6	7	13	....	....	....	16	....	....	....	....	....	....	....	....	....	....	....	....	....	....	....	....	....	....
1998-99	Severstal Cherepovets	Russia	18	3	4	7	....	....	....	31	....	....	....	....	....	....	....	....	....	....	3	1	0	1	10	....	....	....
	NHL Totals		**4**	**1**	**0**	**1**	**1**	**0**	**1**	**0**	**0**	**0**	**1**	**5**	**20.0**	**2**	**1**	**1**	**0**		....	....	....	....	....	....	....	....

EJC-A All-Star Team (1983, 1984) • Named Best Forward at EJC-A (1983) • WJC-A All-Star Team (1986)

• VYSHEDKEVICH, Sergei D – L. 6', 195 lbs. b: Dedovsk, USSR, 1/3/1975. New Jersey's 3rd, 70th overall, in 1995.

			REGULAR SEASON																		PLAYOFFS							
Season	Club	League	GP	G	A	Pts	AG	AA	APts	PIM	PP	SH	GW	S	%	TGF	PGF	TGA	PGA	+/-	GP	G	A	Pts	PIM	PP	SH	GW
1994-95	Dynamo Moscow	CIS	49	6	7	13	....	....	....	67	....	....	....	....	....	....	....	....	....	....	14	2	0	2	12	....	....	....
1995-96	Dynamo Moscow	CIS	49	5	4	9	....	....	....	12	....	....	....	....	....	....	....	....	....	....	13	1	1	2	6	....	....	....
1996-97	Albany River Rats	AHL	65	8	27	35	....	....	....	16	....	....	....	....	....	....	....	....	....	....	12	0	6	6	0	....	....	....
1997-98	Albany River Rats	AHL	54	12	16	28	....	....	....	12	....	....	....	....	....	....	....	....	....	....	13	0	10	10	4	....	....	....
1998-99	Albany River Rats	AHL	79	11	38	49	....	....	....	28	....	....	....	....	....	....	....	....	....	....	5	0	3	3	0	....	....	....
99-2000	**Atlanta Thrashers**	**NHL**	**7**	**1**	**3**	**4**	**1**	**3**	**4**	**2**	**1**	**0**	**0**	**5**	**20.0**	**10**	**2**	**12**	**1**	**–3**	....	....	....	....	....	....	....	....
	Orlando Solar Bears	IHL	69	11	24	35	....	....	....	32	....	....	....	....	....	....	....	....	....	....	6	3	3	6	8	....	....	....
	NHL Totals		**7**	**1**	**3**	**4**	**1**	**3**	**4**	**2**	**1**	**0**	**0**	**5**	**20.0**	**10**	**2**	**12**	**1**		....	....	....	....	....	....	....	....

Traded to **Atlanta** by **New Jersey** for future considerations, June 25, 1999.

• WADDELL, Don D – L. 5'10", 180 lbs. b: Detroit, MI, 8/19/1958. Los Angeles' 3rd, 111th overall, in 1978.

			REGULAR SEASON																		PLAYOFFS							
Season	Club	League	GP	G	A	Pts	AG	AA	APts	PIM	PP	SH	GW	S	%	TGF	PGF	TGA	PGA	+/-	GP	G	A	Pts	PIM	PP	SH	GW
1975-76	Detroit Little Caesars	GLJHL	50	23	29	52	....	....	....	....	....	....	....	....	....	....	....	....	....	....	....	....	....	....	....	....	....	....
1976-77	Northern Michigan University	CCHA	28	11	34	45	....	....	....	40	....	....	....	....	....	....	....	....	....	....	....	....	....	....	....	....	....	....
1977-78	Northern Michigan University	CCHA	32	18	34	52	....	....	....	44	....	....	....	....	....	....	....	....	....	....	....	....	....	....	....	....	....	....
	United States	WJC-A	6	5	2	7	....	....	....	8	....	....	....	....	....	....	....	....	....	....	....	....	....	....	....	....	....	....
1978-79	Northern Michigan University	CCHA	23	5	20	25	....	....	....	24	....	....	....	....	....	....	....	....	....	....	....	....	....	....	....	....	....	....
1979-80	Northern Michigan University	CCHA	37	18	32	50	....	....	....	30	....	....	....	....	....	....	....	....	....	....	....	....	....	....	....	....	....	....
1980-81	**Los Angeles Kings**	**NHL**	**1**	**0**	**0**	**0**	**0**	**0**	**0**	**0**	**0**	**0**	**0**	**0**	**0.0**	**0**	**0**	**1**	**0**	**–1**	....	....	....	....	....	....	....	....
	Houston Apollos	CHL	31	4	5	9	....	....	....	23	....	....	....	....	....	....	....	....	....	....	....	....	....	....	....	....	....	....
	Saginaw Gears	IHL	40	4	18	22	....	....	....	33	....	....	....	....	....	....	....	....	....	....	13	2	4	6	6	....	....	....
1981-82	Saginaw Gears	IHL	77	26	69	95	....	....	....	61	....	....	....	....	....	....	....	....	....	....	14	1	*17	18	0	....	....	....
1982-83	Saginaw Gears	IHL	18	3	17	20	....	....	....	10	....	....	....	....	....	....	....	....	....	....	....	....	....	....	....	....	....	....
	New Haven Nighthawks	AHL	....	....	....	....	....	....	....	....	....	....	....	....	....	....	....	....	....	....	2	0	0	0	0	....	....	....
1983-84	Augsburger EV	Germany	8	6	5	11	....	....	....	10	....	....	....	....	....	....	....	....	....	....	....	....	....	....	....	....	....	....
1984-85	Flint Generals	IHL	35	3	14	17	....	....	....	10	....	....	....	....	....	....	....	....	....	....	....	....	....	....	....	....	....	....
	Toledo Goaldiggers	IHL	42	10	31	41	....	....	....	12	....	....	....	....	....	....	....	....	....	....	6	0	6	6	0	....	....	....
1985-86	Toledo Goaldiggers	IHL	63	19	50	69	....	....	....	113	....	....	....	....	....	....	....	....	....	....	....	....	....	....	....	....	....	....
	New Haven Nighthawks	AHL	6	1	4	5	....	....	....	9	....	....	....	....	....	....	....	....	....	....	5	1	2	3	4	....	....	....
1986-87	Flint Spirits	IHL	10	1	4	5	....	....	....	2	....	....	....	....	....	....	....	....	....	....	6	1	3	4	4	....	....	....
1987-88	New Haven Nighthawks	AHL	2	1	2	3	....	....	....	0	....	....	....	....	....	....	....	....	....	....	....	....	....	....	....	....	....	....
	Flint Spirits	IHL	71	17	58	75	....	....	....	61	....	....	....	....	....	....	....	....	....	....	15	5	10	15	6	....	....	....
1988-1989	Flint Spirits	IHL	DID NOT PLAY – COACHING																									
1989-1990	Flint Spirits	IHL	DID NOT PLAY – GENERAL MANAGER																									
1990-1995	San Diego Gulls	IHL	DID NOT PLAY – GENERAL MANAGER																									
1995-1997	Orlando Solar Bears	IHL	DID NOT PLAY – GENERAL MANAGER																									
1997-1998	**Detroit Red Wings**	**NHL**	DID NOT PLAY – ASSISTANT GENERAL MANAGER																									
1998-2000	**Atlanta Thrashers**	**NHL**	DID NOT PLAY – GENERAL MANAGER																									
	NHL Totals		**1**	**0**	**0**	**0**	**0**	**0**	**0**	**0**	**0**	**0**	**0**	**0**	**0.0**	**0**	**0**	**1**	**0**		....	....	....	....	....	....	....	....

CCHA First All-Star Team (1978, 1980) • IHL First All-Star Team (1982, 1986) • Won Governors' Trophy (Top Defenseman - IHL) (1982) • IHL Second All-Star Team (1988)

• WALKER, Gord RW – L. 6', 175 lbs. b: Castlegar, B.C., 8/12/1965. NY Rangers' 4th, 54th overall, in 1983.

			REGULAR SEASON																		PLAYOFFS							
Season	Club	League	GP	G	A	Pts	AG	AA	APts	PIM	PP	SH	GW	S	%	TGF	PGF	TGA	PGA	+/-	GP	G	A	Pts	PIM	PP	SH	GW
1981-82	Drumheller Miners	AJHL	60	35	44	79	....	....	....	90	....	....	....	....	....	....	....	....	....	....	....	....	....	....	....	....	....	....
1982-83	Portland Winter Hawks	WHL	66	24	30	54	....	....	....	95	....	....	....	....	....	....	....	....	....	....	14	5	8	13	12	....	....	....
	Portland Winter Hawks	Mem-Cup	4	0	2	2	....	....	....	2	....	....	....	....	....	....	....	....	....	....	....	....	....	....	....	....	....	....
1983-84	Portland Winter Hawks	WHL	58	28	41	69	....	....	....	65	....	....	....	....	....	....	....	....	....	....	14	8	11	19	18	....	....	....
1984-85	Kamloops Blazers	WHL	66	67	67	134	....	....	....	76	....	....	....	....	....	....	....	....	....	....	15	*13	14	27	34	....	....	....
1985-86	New Haven Nighthawks	AHL	46	11	28	39	....	....	....	66	....	....	....	....	....	....	....	....	....	....	....	....	....	....	....	....	....	....
1986-87	**New York Rangers**	**NHL**	**1**	**1**	**0**	**1**	**1**	**0**	**1**	**4**	**0**	**0**	**0**	**1**	**100.0**	**2**	**0**	**0**	**0**	**2**	....	....	....	....	....	....	....	....
	New Haven Nighthawks	AHL	59	24	20	44	....	....	....	58	....	....	....	....	....	....	....	....	....	....	7	3	2	5	0	....	....	....
1987-88	**New York Rangers**	**NHL**	**18**	**1**	**4**	**5**	**1**	**3**	**4**	**17**	**0**	**0**	**0**	**23**	**4.3**	**6**	**1**	**14**	**1**	**–8**	....	....	....	....	....	....	....	....
	New Haven Nighthawks	AHL	14	10	9	19	....	....	....	17	....	....	....	....	....	....	....	....	....	....	....	....	....	....	....	....	....	....
	Colorado Rangers	IHL	16	4	9	13	....	....	....	4	....	....	....	....	....	....	....	....	....	....	....	....	....	....	....	....	....	....
1988-89	**Los Angeles Kings**	**NHL**	**11**	**1**	**0**	**1**	**1**	**0**	**1**	**2**	**0**	**0**	**0**	**13**	**7.7**	**2**	**0**	**4**	**0**	**–2**	....	....	....	....	....	....	....	....
	New Haven Nighthawks	AHL	60	21	25	46	....	....	....	50	....	....	....	....	....	....	....	....	....	....	17	7	8	15	23	....	....	....
1989-90	**Los Angeles Kings**	**NHL**	**1**	**0**	**0**	**0**	**0**	**0**	**0**	**0**	**0**	**0**	**0**	**0**	**0.0**	**0**	**0**	**0**	**0**	**0**	....	....	....	....	....	....	....	....
	New Haven Nighthawks	AHL	24	14	7	21	....	....	....	8	....	....	....	....	....	....	....	....	....	....	....	....	....	....	....	....	....	....
1990-91	Canada	Nat-Team	13	1	3	4	....	....	....	8	....	....	....	....	....	....	....	....	....	....	....	....	....	....	....	....	....	....
	San Diego Gulls	IHL	22	3	7	10	....	....	....	24	....	....	....	....	....	....	....	....	....	....	....	....	....	....	....	....	....	....
	NHL Totals		**31**	**3**	**4**	**7**	**3**	**3**	**6**	**23**	**0**	**0**	**0**	**37**	**8.1**	**10**	**1**	**18**	**1**		....	....	....	....	....	....	....	....

WHL West First All-Star Team (1985)

Traded to **LA Kings** by **NY Rangers** with Mike Siltala for Joe Paterson, January 21, 1988.

• WALKER, Howard D – L. 6', 205 lbs. b: Grande Prairie, Alta., 8/5/1958.

			REGULAR SEASON																		PLAYOFFS							
Season	Club	League	GP	G	A	Pts	AG	AA	APts	PIM	PP	SH	GW	S	%	TGF	PGF	TGA	PGA	+/-	GP	G	A	Pts	PIM	PP	SH	GW
1974-75	The Pass Red Devils	AJHL	1	1	0	1	....	....	....	0	....	....	....	....	....	....	....	....	....	....	....	....	....	....	....	....	....	....
1975-76	The Pass Red Devils	AJHL	STATISTICS NOT AVAILABLE																									
1976-77	Penticton Vees	BCJHL	STATISTICS NOT AVAILABLE																									
1977-78	Penticton Vees	BCJHL	56	31	47	78	....	....	....	223	....	....	....	....	....	....	....	....	....	....	....	....	....	....	....	....	....	....
1978-79	University of North Dakota	WCHA	38	7	16	23	....	....	....	76	....	....	....	....	....	....	....	....	....	....	....	....	....	....	....	....	....	....

			REGULAR SEASON																		PLAYOFFS							
Season	**Club**	**League**	**GP**	**G**	**A**	**Pts**	**AG**	**AA**	**APts**	**PIM**	**PP**	**SH**	**GW**	**S**	**%**	**TGF**	**PGF**	**TGA**	**PGA**	**+/–**	**GP**	**G**	**A**	**Pts**	**PIM**	**PP**	**SH**	**GW**
1979-80	University of North Dakota	WCHA	39	7	18	25	....	....	....	57	....	....	....	....	....	....	....	....	....	....	....	....	....	....	....	....	....	....
1980-81	Washington Capitals	DN-Cup	2	0	0	0	....	....	....	0	....	....	....	....	....	....	....	....	....	....	....	....	....	....	....	....	....	....
	Washington Capitals	**NHL**	**64**	**2**	**11**	**13**	**2**	**7**	**9**	**100**	**2**	**0**	**0**	**68**	**2.9**	**64**	**8**	**61**	**14**	**9**	....	....	....	....	....	....	....	....
	Hershey Bears	AHL	7	1	0	1	....	....	....	24	....	....	....	....	....	....	....	....	....	....	....	....	....	....	....	....	....	....
1981-82	**Washington Capitals**	**NHL**	**16**	**0**	**2**	**2**	**0**	**1**	**1**	**26**	**0**	**0**	**0**	**18**	**0.0**	**9**	**1**	**18**	**1**	**–9**	....	....	....	....	....	....	....	....
	Hershey Bears	AHL	54	3	4	7	....	....	....	62	....	....	....	....	....	....	....	....	....	....	....	....	....	....	....	....	....	....
1982-83	**Calgary Flames**	**NHL**	**3**	**0**	**0**	**0**	**0**	**0**	**0**	**7**	**0**	**0**	**0**	**2**	**0.0**	**2**	**0**	**2**	**0**	**0**	....	....	....	....	....	....	....	....
	Colorado Flames	CHL	69	4	19	23	....	....	....	172	....	....	....	....	....	....	....	....	....	....	6	3	2	5	11	....	....	....
	NHL Totals		**83**	**2**	**13**	**15**	**2**	**8**	**10**	**133**	**2**	**0**	**0**	**88**	**2.3**	**75**	**9**	**81**	**15**		....	....	....	....	....	....	....	....

NCAA Championship All-Tournament Team (1979) • WCHA First All-Star Team (1980) • NCAA West First All-American Team (1980)

Signed as a free agent by **Washington**, June 5, 1980. Traded to **Calgary** by **Washington** with George White, Washington's 6th round choice (Mats Kihlstrom) in 1982 Entry Draft, 3rd round choice (Parry Berezan) in 1983 Entry Draft and 2nd round choice (Paul Ranheim) in 1984 Entry Draft for Pat Riggin and Ken Houston, June 9, 1982.

• WALKER, Kurt

Kurt Adrian D – R. 6'3", 200 lbs. b: Weymouth, MA, 6/10/1954.

Season	Club	League	GP	G	A	Pts	AG	AA	APts	PIM	PP	SH	GW	S	%	TGF	PGF	TGA	PGA	+/–	GP	G	A	Pts	PIM	PP	SH	GW
1971-72	Wingham Hawks	Hi-School	STATISTICS NOT AVAILABLE																									
1972-73	Northeastern University	ECAC	DID NOT PLAY – FRESHMAN																									
1973-74	Sherbrooke Castors	QMJHL	36	2	5	7	....	....	....	142	....	....	....	....	....	....	....	....	....	....	....	....	....	....	....	....	....	....
1974-75	Saginaw Gears	IHL	67	1	3	4	....	....	....	168	....	....	....	....	....	....	....	....	....	....	16	0	0	0	0	....	....	....
1975-76	**Toronto Maple Leafs**	**NHL**	**5**	**0**	**0**	**0**	**0**	**0**	**0**	**49**	**0**	**0**	**0**	**2**	**0.0**	**0**	**0**	**2**	**0**	**–2**	**6**	**0**	**0**	**0**	**24**	**0**	**0**	**0**
	Oklahoma City Blazers	CHL	59	4	5	9	....	....	....	184	....	....	....	....	....	....	....	....	....	....	....	....	....	....	....	....	....	....
1976-77	**Toronto Maple Leafs**	**NHL**	**26**	**2**	**3**	**5**	**2**	**2**	**4**	**24**	**0**	**0**	**0**	**6**	**33.3**	**10**	**0**	**5**	**0**	**5**	....	....	....	....	....	....	....	....
	Dallas Black Hawks	CHL	6	3	0	3	....	....	....	50	....	....	....	....	....	....	....	....	....	....	....	....	....	....	....	....	....	....
1977-78	**Toronto Maple Leafs**	**NHL**	**40**	**2**	**2**	**4**	**2**	**2**	**4**	**69**	**0**	**0**	**0**	**12**	**16.7**	**5**	**1**	**9**	**0**	**–5**	**10**	**0**	**0**	**0**	**10**	**0**	**0**	**0**
	Dallas Black Hawks	CHL	20	3	3	6	....	....	....	53	....	....	....	....	....	....	....	....	....	....	2	1	0	1	2	....	....	....
1978-79	Springfield Indians	AHL	11	0	1	1	....	....	....	22	....	....	....	....	....	....	....	....	....	....	....	....	....	....	....	....	....	....
	Tulsa Oilers	CHL	54	17	19	36	....	....	....	81	....	....	....	....	....	....	....	....	....	....	....	....	....	....	....	....	....	....
1979-80	Binghamton Dusters	AHL	6	0	0	0	....	....	....	4	....	....	....	....	....	....	....	....	....	....	....	....	....	....	....	....	....	....
	Syracuse Firebirds	AHL	11	1	4	5	....	....	....	18	....	....	....	....	....	....	....	....	....	....	....	....	....	....	....	....	....	....
	NHL Totals		**71**	**4**	**5**	**9**	**4**	**4**	**8**	**142**	**0**	**0**	**0**	**20**	**20.0**	**15**	**1**	**16**	**0**		**16**	**0**	**0**	**0**	**34**	**0**	**0**	**0**

Signed as a free agent by **Toronto**, September, 1975. Traded to **LA Kings** by **Toronto** with Scott Garland, Brian Glennie and Toronto's 2nd round choice (Mark Hardy) in 1979 Entry Draft for Dave Hutchison and Lorne Stamler, June 14, 1978.

• WALKER, Russ

RW – R. 6'2", 185 lbs. b: Red Deer, Alta., 5/24/1953. Los Angeles' 1st, 38th overall, in 1973.

Season	Club	League	GP	G	A	Pts	AG	AA	APts	PIM	PP	SH	GW	S	%	TGF	PGF	TGA	PGA	+/–	GP	G	A	Pts	PIM	PP	SH	GW
1969-70	Red Deer Royals	AAHA	STATISTICS NOT AVAILABLE																									
	Red Deer Rustlers	AJHL	1	0	0	0	....	....	....	0	....	....	....	....	....	....	....	....	....	....	....	....	....	....	....	....	....	....
	Lethbridge Silver Kings	AJHL	2	1	0	1	....	....	....	0	....	....	....	....	....	....	....	....	....	....	....	....	....	....	....	....	....	....
1970-71	Lethbridge Silver Kings	AJHL	STATISTICS NOT AVAILABLE																									
1971-72	Saskatoon Blades	WCJHL	68	24	28	52	....	....	....	218	....	....	....	....	....	....	....	....	....	....	8	1	7	8	27	....	....	....
1972-73	Saskatoon Blades	WCJHL	65	42	38	80	....	....	....	193	....	....	....	....	....	....	....	....	....	....	16	9	6	15	65	....	....	....
1973-74	Cleveland Crusaders	WHA	76	15	14	29	....	....	....	117	....	....	....	....	....	....	....	....	....	....	5	1	0	1	11	....	....	....
1974-75	Cleveland Crusaders	WHA	66	14	11	25	....	....	....	80	....	....	....	....	....	....	....	....	....	....	5	1	0	1	17	....	....	....
1975-76	Cleveland Crusaders	WHA	72	23	15	38	....	....	....	122	....	....	....	....	....	....	....	....	....	....	3	0	0	0	18	....	....	....
1976-77	**Los Angeles Kings**	**NHL**	**16**	**1**	**0**	**1**	**1**	**0**	**1**	**35**	**0**	**0**	**0**	**12**	**8.3**	**6**	**0**	**8**	**0**	**–2**	....	....	....	....	....	....	....	....
	Fort Worth Texans	CHL	53	23	17	40	....	....	....	106	....	....	....	....	....	....	....	....	....	....	5	1	2	3	9	....	....	....
1977-78	**Los Angeles Kings**	**NHL**	**1**	**0**	**0**	**0**	**0**	**0**	**0**	**6**	**0**	**0**	**0**	**0**	**0.0**	**0**	**0**	**0**	**0**	**0**	....	....	....	....	....	....	....	....
	Springfield Indians	AHL	77	30	36	66	....	....	....	79	....	....	....	....	....	....	....	....	....	....	4	2	0	2	0	....	....	....
1978-79	Springfield Indians	AHL	61	23	19	42	....	....	....	88	....	....	....	....	....	....	....	....	....	....	....	....	....	....	....	....	....	....
	NHL Totals		**17**	**1**	**0**	**1**	**1**	**0**	**1**	**41**	**0**	**0**	**0**	**12**	**8.3**	**6**	**0**	**8**	**0**		....	....	....	....	....	....	....	....
	Other Major League Totals		214	52	40	92	....	....	....	319	....	....	....	....	....	....	....	....	....	....	13	2	0	2	46	....	....	....

Selected by **Cleveland** (WHA) in 1973 WHA Amateur Draft, June, 1973. Traded to **Cincinnati** (WHA) by **Cleveland** (WHA) for Bernie MacNeil, May, 1976.

• WALKER, Scott

C – R. 5'10", 189 lbs. b: Cambridge, Ont., 7/19/1973. Vancouver's 4th, 124th overall, in 1993.

Season	Club	League	GP	G	A	Pts	AG	AA	APts	PIM	PP	SH	GW	S	%	TGF	PGF	TGA	PGA	+/–	GP	G	A	Pts	PIM	PP	SH	GW
1989-90	Kitchener Dutchmen	OJHL-B	6	0	5	5	....	....	....	4	....	....	....	....	....	....	....	....	....	....	....	....	....	....	....	....	....	....
	Cambridge Winterhawks	OJHL-B	27	7	22	29	....	....	....	87	....	....	....	....	....	....	....	....	....	....	....	....	....	....	....	....	....	....
1990-91	Cambridge Winterhawks	OJHL-B	45	10	27	37	....	....	....	241	....	....	....	....	....	....	....	....	....	....	....	....	....	....	....	....	....	....
1991-92	Owen Sound Platers	OHL	53	7	31	38	....	....	....	128	....	....	....	....	....	....	....	....	....	....	5	0	7	7	8	....	....	....
1992-93	Owen Sound Platers	OHL	57	23	68	91	....	....	....	110	....	....	....	....	....	....	....	....	....	....	8	1	5	6	16	....	....	....
	Canada	Nat-Team	2	3	0	3	....	....	....	0	....	....	....	....	....	....	....	....	....	....	....	....	....	....	....	....	....	....
1993-94	Hamilton Canucks	AHL	77	10	29	39	....	....	....	272	....	....	....	....	....	....	....	....	....	....	4	0	1	1	25	....	....	....
1994-95	Syracuse Crunch	AHL	74	14	38	52	....	....	....	334	....	....	....	....	....	....	....	....	....	....	....	....	....	....	....	....	....	....
	Vancouver Canucks	**NHL**	**11**	**0**	**1**	**1**	**0**	**1**	**1**	**33**	**0**	**0**	**0**	**8**	**0.0**	**4**	**0**	**4**	**0**	**0**	....	....	....	....	....	....	....	....
1995-96	**Vancouver Canucks**	**NHL**	**63**	**4**	**8**	**12**	**4**	**7**	**11**	**137**	**0**	**1**	**1**	**45**	**8.9**	**17**	**1**	**33**	**10**	**–7**	....	....	....	....	....	....	....	....
	Syracuse Crunch	AHL	15	3	12	15	....	....	....	52	....	....	....	....	....	....	....	....	....	....	16	9	8	17	39	....	....	....
1996-97	**Vancouver Canucks**	**NHL**	**64**	**3**	**15**	**18**	**3**	**13**	**16**	**132**	**0**	**0**	**0**	**55**	**5.5**	**27**	**0**	**29**	**4**	**2**	....	....	....	....	....	....	....	....
1997-98	**Vancouver Canucks**	**NHL**	**59**	**3**	**10**	**13**	**4**	**10**	**14**	**164**	**0**	**1**	**1**	**40**	**7.5**	**18**	**0**	**33**	**7**	**–8**	....	....	....	....	....	....	....	....
1998-99	**Nashville Predators**	**NHL**	**71**	**15**	**25**	**40**	**18**	**24**	**42**	**103**	**0**	**1**	**2**	**96**	**15.6**	**55**	**3**	**66**	**14**	**0**	....	....	....	....	....	....	....	....
	Canada	WC-A	10	2	3	5	....	....	....	16	....	....	....	....	....	....	....	....	....	....	....	....	....	....	....	....	....	....
99-2000	**Nashville Predators**	**NHL**	**69**	**7**	**21**	**28**	**8**	**19**	**27**	**90**	**0**	**1**	**0**	**98**	**7.1**	**42**	**1**	**67**	**10**	**–16**	....	....	....	....	....	....	....	....
	NHL Totals		**337**	**32**	**80**	**112**	**37**	**74**	**111**	**659**	**0**	**4**	**4**	**342**	**9.4**	**163**	**5**	**232**	**45**		....	....	....	....	....	....	....	....

OHL Second All-Star Team (1993)

Claimed by **Nashville** from **Vancouver** in Expansion Draft, June 26, 1998.

• WALL, Bob

Robert James Albert D – L. 5'10", 171 lbs. b: Richmond Hill, Ont., 12/1/1942.

Season	Club	League	GP	G	A	Pts	AG	AA	APts	PIM	PP	SH	GW	S	%	TGF	PGF	TGA	PGA	+/–	GP	G	A	Pts	PIM	PP	SH	GW
1958-59	Montreal Snowdon Ponsards	MMJHL	STATISTICS NOT AVAILABLE																									
1959-60	Hamilton Tiger Cubs	OHA-Jr.	48	3	11	14	....	....	....	44	....	....	....	....	....	....	....	....	....	....	....	....	....	....	....	....	....	....
1960-61	Hamilton Red Wings	OHA-Jr.	48	2	8	10	....	....	....	30	....	....	....	....	....	....	....	....	....	....	12	1	3	4	29	....	....	....
1961-62	Hamilton Red Wings	OHA-Jr.	44	7	22	29	....	....	....	28	....	....	....	....	....	....	....	....	....	....	10	3	3	6	26	....	....	....
	Hamilton Red Wings	Mem-Cup	14	2	*13	15	....	....	....	6	....	....	....	....	....	....	....	....	....	....	....	....	....	....	....	....	....	....
1962-63	Hamilton Red Wings	OHA-Jr.	36	5	30	35	....	....	....	27	....	....	....	....	....	....	....	....	....	....	5	0	6	6	2	....	....	....
	Pittsburgh Hornets	AHL	3	0	2	2	....	....	....	2	....	....	....	....	....	....	....	....	....	....	....	....	....	....	....	....	....	....
	Edmonton Flyers	WHL	7	0	0	0	....	....	....	0	....	....	....	....	....	....	....	....	....	....	....	....	....	....	....	....	....	....
1963-64	Cincinnati Wings	CPHL	59	10	20	30	....	....	....	16	....	....	....	....	....	....	....	....	....	....	....	....	....	....	....	....	....	....
	Quebec Aces	AHL	8	1	2	3	....	....	....	4	....	....	....	....	....	....	....	....	....	....	....	....	....	....	....	....	....	....
	Omaha Knights	CPHL	....	....	....	....	....	....	....	....	....	....	....	....	....	....	....	....	....	....	10	1	7	8	4	....	....	....
1964-65	**Detroit Red Wings**	**NHL**	**1**	**0**	**0**	**0**	**0**	**0**	**0**	**0**	....	....	....	....	....	....	....	....	....	....	**1**	**0**	**0**	**0**	**0**	**0**	**0**	**0**
	Memphis Wings	CPHL	70	8	38	46	....	....	....	83	....	....	....	....	....	....	....	....	....	....	....	....	....	....	....	....	....	....
1965-66	**Detroit Red Wings**	**NHL**	**8**	**1**	**1**	**2**	**1**	**1**	**2**	**8**	....	....	....	....	....	....	....	....	....	....	**6**	**0**	**0**	**0**	**2**	**0**	**0**	**0**
	Pittsburgh Hornets	AHL	63	10	35	45	....	....	....	26	....	....	....	....	....	....	....	....	....	....	3	0	1	1	8	....	....	....
1966-67	**Detroit Red Wings**	**NHL**	**31**	**2**	**2**	**4**	**2**	**2**	**4**	**26**	....	....	....	....	....	....	....	....	....	....	....	....	....	....	....	....	....	....
	Pittsburgh Hornets	AHL	41	7	25	32	....	....	....	29	....	....	....	....	....	....	....	....	....	....	9	2	2	4	4	....	....	....
1967-68	**Los Angeles Kings**	**NHL**	**71**	**5**	**18**	**23**	**6**	**18**	**24**	**66**	**1**	**0**	**2**	**148**	**3.4**	**77**	**14**	**94**	**22**	**–9**	**7**	**0**	**1**	**1**	**0**	**0**	**0**	**0**
1968-69	**Los Angeles Kings**	**NHL**	**71**	**13**	**13**	**26**	**14**	**12**	**26**	**16**	**1**	**1**	**1**	**147**	**8.8**	**38**	**6**	**51**	**13**	**–6**	**8**	**0**	**2**	**2**	**0**	**0**	**0**	**0**
1969-70	**Los Angeles Kings**	**NHL**	**70**	**5**	**13**	**18**	**5**	**12**	**17**	**26**	**5**	**0**	**1**	**116**	**4.3**	**54**	**25**	**65**	**10**	**–26**	....	....	....	....	....	....	....	....
1970-71	**St. Louis Blues**	**NHL**	**25**	**2**	**4**	**6**	**2**	**3**	**5**	**4**	**1**	**0**	**0**	**29**	**6.9**	**12**	**1**	**15**	**3**	**–1**	....	....	....	....	....	....	....	....
	Kansas City Blues	CHL	18	0	7	7	....	....	....	4	....	....	....	....	....	....	....	....	....	....	....	....	....	....	....	....	....	....
1971-72	**Detroit Red Wings**	**NHL**	**45**	**2**	**4**	**6**	**2**	**3**	**5**	**9**	**2**	**0**	**0**	**31**	**6.5**	**17**	**3**	**24**	**3**	**–7**	....	....	....	....	....	....	....	....
	Tidewater Red Wings	AHL	17	2	4	6	....	....	....	12	....	....	....	....	....	....	....	....	....	....	....	....	....	....	....	....	....	....
1972-73	Alberta Oilers	WHA	78	16	29	45	....	....	....	20	....	....	....	....	....	....	....	....	....	....	....	....	....	....	....	....	....	....

Season	Club	League	GP	G	A	Pts	AG	AA	APts	PIM	PP	SH	GW	S	%	TGF	PGF	TGA	PGA	+/–	GP	G	A	Pts	PIM	PP	SH	GW
			REGULAR SEASON																		PLAYOFFS							
1973-74	Edmonton Oilers	WHA	74	6	31	37	....	....	....	46	....	....	....	....	....	....	....	....	....	....	5	0	2	2	2	....	....	....
1974-75	San Diego Mariners	WHA	33	0	9	9	....	....	....	15	....	....	....	....	....	....	....	....	....	....	10	0	3	3	2	....	....	....
1975-76	San Diego Mariners	WHA	68	1	20	21	....	....	....	32	....	....	....	....	....	....	....	....	....	....	11	1	3	4	4	....	....	....
	NHL Totals		**322**	**30**	**55**	**85**	**32**	**51**	**83**	**155**	....	....	....	....	....	....	....	....	....	....	**22**	**0**	**3**	**3**	**2**	....	....	....
	Other Major League Totals		253	23	89	112	....	....	....	113	....	....	....	....	....	....	....	....	....	....	26	1	8	9	8	....	....	....

Claimed by **LA Kings** from **Detroit** in Expansion Draft, June 6, 1967. Traded to **St. Louis** by **LA Kings** for Ray Fortin, May 11, 1970. Traded to **Detroit** by **St. Louis** with Ab McDonald and Mike Lowe to complete transaction that sent Carl Brewer to Detroit (February 22, 1971), May 12, 1971. Selected by **Alberta** (WHA) in 1972 WHA General Player Draft, February 12, 1972. Traded to **San Diego** (WHA) by **Edmonton** (WHA) for Don Herriman, August, 1974.

• WALLIN, Jesse

D – L. 6'2", 190 lbs. b: Saskatoon, Sask., 3/10/1978. Detroit's 1st, 26th overall, in 1996.

Season	Club	League	GP	G	A	Pts	AG	AA	APts	PIM	PP	SH	GW	S	%	TGF	PGF	TGA	PGA	+/–	GP	G	A	Pts	PIM	PP	SH	GW
1993-94	North Battleford North Stars	SAHA	32	1	7	8	....	....	....	41	....	....	....	....	....	....	....	....	....	....	....	....	....	....	....	....	....	....
1994-95	Red Deer Rebels	WHL	72	4	20	24	....	....	....	72	....	....	....	....	....	....	....	....	....	....	....	....	....	....	....	....	....	....
1995-96	Red Deer Rebels	WHL	70	5	19	24	....	....	....	61	....	....	....	....	....	....	....	....	....	....	9	0	3	3	4	....	....	....
1996-97	Red Deer Rebels	WHL	59	6	33	39	....	....	....	70	....	....	....	....	....	....	....	....	....	....	16	1	4	5	10	....	....	....
	Canada	WJC-A	7	0	0	0	....	....	....	6	....	....	....	....	....	....	....	....	....	....	....	....	....	....	....	....	....	....
1997-98	Red Deer Rebels	WHL	14	1	6	7	....	....	....	17	....	....	....	....	....	....	....	....	....	....	5	0	1	1	2	....	....	....
	Canada	WJC-A	4	0	0	0	....	....	....	4	....	....	....	....	....	....	....	....	....	....	....	....	....	....	....	....	....	....
1998-99	Adirondack Red Wings	AHL	76	4	12	16	....	....	....	34	....	....	....	....	....	....	....	....	....	....	3	0	2	2	2	....	....	....
99-2000	**Detroit Red Wings**	**NHL**	**1**	**0**	**0**	**0**	**0**	**0**	**0**	**0**	**0**	**0**	**0**	**0**	**0.0**	**0**	**0**	**2**	**0**	**–2**	....	....	....	....	....	....	....	....
	Cincinnati Mighty Ducks	AHL	75	3	14	17	....	....	....	61	....	....	....	....	....	....	....	....	....	....	....	....	....	....	....	....	....	....
	NHL Totals		**1**	**0**	**0**	**0**	**0**	**0**	**0**	**0**	**0**	**0**	**0**	**0**	**0.0**	**0**	**0**	**2**	**0**		....	....	....	....	....	....	....	....

Canadian Major Junior Humanitarian Player of the Year (1997)

• WALLIN, Peter

RW – R. 5'9", 170 lbs. b: Stockholm, Sweden, 4/30/1957.

Season	Club	League	GP	G	A	Pts	AG	AA	APts	PIM	PP	SH	GW	S	%	TGF	PGF	TGA	PGA	+/–	GP	G	A	Pts	PIM	PP	SH	GW
1974-75	Djurgardens IF Stockholm	Sweden-Jr.	14	*18	11	29	....	....	....	....	....	....	....	....	....	....	....	....	....	....	....	....	....	....	....	....	....	....
	Djurgardens IF Stockholm	Sweden	1	0	0	0	....	....	....	2	....	....	....	....	....	....	....	....	....	....	....	....	....	....	....	....	....	....
1975-76	Djurgardens IF Stockholm	Sweden	12	3	4	7	....	....	....	0	....	....	....	....	....	....	....	....	....	....	....	....	....	....	....	....	....	....
1976-77	Djurgardens IF Stockholm	Sweden-2	40	24	34	58	....	....	....	....	....	....	....	....	....	....	....	....	....	....	....	....	....	....	....	....	....	....
1977-78	Djurgardens IF Stockholm	Sweden	36	12	16	28	....	....	....	22	....	....	....	....	....	....	....	....	....	....	....	....	....	....	....	....	....	....
1978-79	Djurgardens IF Stockholm	Sweden	36	14	19	33	....	....	....	34	....	....	....	....	....	....	....	....	....	....	6	2	2	4	6	....	....	....
	Sweden	WEC-A	8	1	3	4	....	....	....	2	....	....	....	....	....	....	....	....	....	....	....	....	....	....	....	....	....	....
1979-80	Djurgardens IF Stockholm	Sweden	30	11	15	26	....	....	....	66	....	....	....	....	....	....	....	....	....	....	....	....	....	....	....	....	....	....
	Djurgardens IF Stockholm	DN-Cup	3	0	0	0	....	....	....	2	....	....	....	....	....	....	....	....	....	....	....	....	....	....	....	....	....	....
	Sweden	Nat-Team	11	3	1	4	....	....	....	....	....	....	....	....	....	....	....	....	....	....	....	....	....	....	....	....	....	....
1980-81	Djurgardens IF Stockholm	Sweden	36	12	13	25	....	....	....	55	....	....	....	....	....	....	....	....	....	....	....	....	....	....	....	....	....	....
	Sweden	Nat-Team	6	1	1	2	....	....	....	0	....	....	....	....	....	....	....	....	....	....	....	....	....	....	....	....	....	....
	New York Rangers	**NHL**	**12**	**1**	**5**	**6**	**1**	**3**	**4**	**2**	**0**	**0**	**0**	**14**	**7.1**	**9**	**2**	**9**	**1**	**–1**	**14**	**2**	**6**	**8**	**6**	**0**	**0**	**0**
1981-82	**New York Rangers**	**NHL**	**40**	**2**	**9**	**11**	**2**	**6**	**8**	**12**	**0**	**0**	**1**	**50**	**4.0**	**21**	**3**	**17**	**0**	**1**	....	....	....	....	....	....	....	....
	Springfield Indians	AHL	16	4	10	14	....	....	....	8	....	....	....	....	....	....	....	....	....	....	....	....	....	....	....	....	....	....
1982-83	Tulsa Oilers	CHL	65	15	40	55	....	....	....	43	....	....	....	....	....	....	....	....	....	....	....	....	....	....	....	....	....	....
1983-84	Sodertalje SK	Sweden	28	12	13	25	....	....	....	38	....	....	....	....	....	....	....	....	....	....	....	....	....	....	....	....	....	....
1984-85	Sodertalje SK	Sweden	20	6	7	13	....	....	....	30	....	....	....	....	....	....	....	....	....	....	8	5	6	11	8	....	....	....
1985-86	Sodertalje SK	Sweden	31	12	18	30	....	....	....	37	....	....	....	....	....	....	....	....	....	....	7	3	3	6	4	....	....	....
	NHL Totals		**52**	**3**	**14**	**17**	**3**	**9**	**12**	**14**	**0**	**0**	**1**	**64**	**4.7**	**30**	**5**	**26**	**1**		**14**	**2**	**6**	**8**	**6**	**0**	**0**	**0**

Signed as a free agent by **NY Rangers**, March 8, 1981.

• WALSH, Jim

D – R. 6'1", 185 lbs. b: Norfolk, VA, 10/26/1956.

Season	Club	League	GP	G	A	Pts	AG	AA	APts	PIM	PP	SH	GW	S	%	TGF	PGF	TGA	PGA	+/–	GP	G	A	Pts	PIM	PP	SH	GW
1976-77	Northeastern University	ECAC	27	5	9	14	....	....	....	44	....	....	....	....	....	....	....	....	....	....	....	....	....	....	....	....	....	....
1977-78	Northeastern University	ECAC	27	3	26	29	....	....	....	69	....	....	....	....	....	....	....	....	....	....	....	....	....	....	....	....	....	....
1978-79	Northeastern University	ECAC	22	5	12	17	....	....	....	44	....	....	....	....	....	....	....	....	....	....	....	....	....	....	....	....	....	....
1979-80	Rochester Americans	AHL	33	2	4	6	....	....	....	64	....	....	....	....	....	....	....	....	....	....	....	....	....	....	....	....	....	....
1980-81	Rochester Americans	AHL	76	8	23	31	....	....	....	182	....	....	....	....	....	....	....	....	....	....	....	....	....	....	....	....	....	....
1981-82	**Buffalo Sabres**	**NHL**	**4**	**0**	**1**	**1**	**0**	**1**	**1**	**4**	....	....	....	....	....	....	....	....	....	....	....	....	....	....	....	....	....	....
	Rochester Americans	AHL	70	7	33	40	....	....	....	174	....	....	....	....	....	....	....	....	....	....	9	0	4	4	17	....	....	....
1982-83	Saginaw Gears	IHL	5	0	1	1	....	....	....	4	....	....	....	....	....	....	....	....	....	....	....	....	....	....	....	....	....	....
	Binghamton Whalers	AHL	49	1	13	14	....	....	....	93	....	....	....	....	....	....	....	....	....	....	....	....	....	....	....	....	....	....
1983-84	New Haven Nighthawks	AHL	13	0	5	5	....	....	....	14	....	....	....	....	....	....	....	....	....	....	....	....	....	....	....	....	....	....
	NHL Totals		**4**	**0**	**1**	**1**	**0**	**1**	**1**	**4**	....	....	....	....	....	....	....	....	....	....	....	....	....	....	....	....	....	....

Signed as a free agent by **Buffalo**, September 5, 1979.

• WALSH, Mike

Michael W – R. 6'2", 195 lbs. b: New York, NY, 4/3/1962.

Season	Club	League	GP	G	A	Pts	AG	AA	APts	PIM	PP	SH	GW	S	%	TGF	PGF	TGA	PGA	+/–	GP	G	A	Pts	PIM	PP	SH	GW
1980-81	Colgate University	ECAC	35	10	15	25	....	....	....	62	....	....	....	....	....	....	....	....	....	....	....	....	....	....	....	....	....	....
1981-82	Colgate University	ECAC	26	2	7	9	....	....	....	42	....	....	....	....	....	....	....	....	....	....	....	....	....	....	....	....	....	....
1982-83	Colgate University	ECAC	24	9	14	23	....	....	....	36	....	....	....	....	....	....	....	....	....	....	....	....	....	....	....	....	....	....
1983-84	Colgate University	ECAC	35	16	17	33	....	....	....	94	....	....	....	....	....	....	....	....	....	....	....	....	....	....	....	....	....	....
1984-85	Malmo IF	Sweden-3	33	*41	23	*64	....	....	....	....	....	....	....	....	....	....	....	....	....	....	....	....	....	....	....	....	....	....
1985-86	Malmo IF	Sweden-2	31	44	24	68	....	....	....	18	....	....	....	....	....	....	....	....	....	....	4	5	2	7	4	....	....	....
	Springfield Indians	AHL	2	1	0	1	....	....	....	0	....	....	....	....	....	....	....	....	....	....	....	....	....	....	....	....	....	....
1986-87	Springfield Indians	AHL	67	20	26	46	....	....	....	32	....	....	....	....	....	....	....	....	....	....	....	....	....	....	....	....	....	....
1987-88	**New York Islanders**	**NHL**	**1**	**0**	**0**	**0**	**0**	**0**	**0**	**0**	**0**	**0**	**0**	**2**	**0.0**	**0**	**0**	**0**	**0**	**0**	....	....	....	....	....	....	....	....
	Springfield Indians	AHL	77	27	23	50	....	....	....	48	....	....	....	....	....	....	....	....	....	....	....	....	....	....	....	....	....	....
1988-89	**New York Islanders**	**NHL**	**13**	**2**	**0**	**2**	**2**	**0**	**2**	**4**	**0**	**0**	**1**	**11**	**18.2**	**3**	**0**	**10**	**0**	**–7**	....	....	....	....	....	....	....	....
	Springfield Indians	AHL	68	31	34	65	....	....	....	73	....	....	....	....	....	....	....	....	....	....	....	....	....	....	....	....	....	....
1989-90	Springfield Indians	AHL	69	34	20	54	....	....	....	43	....	....	....	....	....	....	....	....	....	....	8	2	2	4	10	....	....	....
1990-91	SC Cortina	Italy	36	15	21	36	....	....	....	49	....	....	....	....	....	....	....	....	....	....	6	7	4	11	19	....	....	....
1991-92	Maine Mariners	AHL	76	27	24	51	....	....	....	42	....	....	....	....	....	....	....	....	....	....	....	....	....	....	....	....	....	....
1992-93	Providence Bruins	AHL	5	2	0	2	....	....	....	8	....	....	....	....	....	....	....	....	....	....	....	....	....	....	....	....	....	....
	NHL Totals		**14**	**2**	**0**	**2**	**2**	**0**	**2**	**4**	**0**	**0**	**1**	**13**	**15.4**	**3**	**0**	**10**	**0**		....	....	....	....	....	....	....	....

Signed as a free agent by **NY Islanders**, August, 1986.

• WALTER, Ryan

Ryan William C/LW – L. 6', 200 lbs. b: New Westminster, B.C., 4/23/1958. Washington's 1st, 2nd overall, in 1978.

Season	Club	League	GP	G	A	Pts	AG	AA	APts	PIM	PP	SH	GW	S	%	TGF	PGF	TGA	PGA	+/–	GP	G	A	Pts	PIM	PP	SH	GW
1973-74	Langley Lords	BCJHL	62	40	62	102	....	....	....	....	....	....	....	....	....	....	....	....	....	....	....	....	....	....	....	....	....	....
	Kamloops Chiefs	WCJHL	2	0	0	0	....	....	....	0	....	....	....	....	....	....	....	....	....	....	....	....	....	....	....	....	....	....
1974-75	Langley Lords	BCJHL	52	32	60	92	....	....	....	111	....	....	....	....	....	....	....	....	....	....	....	....	....	....	....	....	....	....
	Kamloops Chiefs	WCJHL	9	8	4	12	....	....	....	2	....	....	....	....	....	....	....	....	....	....	2	1	1	2	2	....	....	....
1975-76	Kamloops Chiefs	WHL	72	35	49	84	....	....	....	96	....	....	....	....	....	....	....	....	....	....	12	3	9	12	10	....	....	....
1976-77	Kamloops Chiefs	WCJHL	71	41	58	99	....	....	....	100	....	....	....	....	....	....	....	....	....	....	5	1	3	4	11	....	....	....
1977-78	Seattle Breakers	WCJHL	62	54	71	125	....	....	....	148	....	....	....	....	....	....	....	....	....	....	....	....	....	....	....	....	....	....
	Canada	WJC-A	6	5	3	8	....	....	....	4	....	....	....	....	....	....	....	....	....	....	....	....	....	....	....	....	....	....
1978-79	**Washington Capitals**	**NHL**	**69**	**28**	**28**	**56**	**24**	**20**	**44**	**70**	**6**	**0**	**1**	**156**	**17.9**	**87**	**25**	**83**	**20**	**–1**	....	....	....	....	....	....	....	....
	Canada	WEC-A	8	4	1	5	....	....	....	4	....	....	....	....	....	....	....	....	....	....	....	....	....	....	....	....	....	....
1979-80	**Washington Capitals**	**NHL**	**80**	**24**	**42**	**66**	**20**	**31**	**51**	**106**	**12**	**1**	**1**	**157**	**15.3**	**104**	**32**	**94**	**21**	**–1**	....	....	....	....	....	....	....	....
1980-81	**Washington Capitals**	**NHL**	**80**	**24**	**44**	**68**	**19**	**29**	**48**	**150**	**4**	**0**	**1**	**178**	**13.5**	**106**	**26**	**103**	**14**	**–9**	....	....	....	....	....	....	....	....
	Canada	WEC-A	8	0	1	1	....	....	....	2	....	....	....	....	....	....	....	....	....	....	....	....	....	....	....	....	....	....
1981-82	**Washington Capitals**	**NHL**	**78**	**38**	**49**	**87**	**30**	**33**	**63**	**142**	**19**	**1**	**3**	**183**	**20.8**	**141**	**58**	**103**	**17**	**–3**	....	....	....	....	....	....	....	....
	Canada	WEC-A	4	1	3	4	....	....	....	0	....	....	....	....	....	....	....	....	....	....	....	....	....	....	....	....	....	....
1982-83	**Montreal Canadiens**	**NHL**	**80**	**29**	**46**	**75**	**24**	**32**	**56**	**40**	**8**	**1**	**4**	**169**	**17.2**	**122**	**35**	**102**	**30**	**15**	**3**	**0**	**0**	**0**	**11**	**0**	**0**	**0**

			REGULAR SEASON																		PLAYOFFS							
Season	Club	League	GP	G	A	Pts	AG	AA	APts	PIM	PP	SH	GW	S	%	TGF	PGF	TGA	PGA	+/–	GP	G	A	Pts	PIM	PP	SH	GW
1983-84	**Montreal Canadiens**	**NHL**	73	20	29	49	16	20	36	83	7	1	4	117	17.1	82	28	84	19	–11	15	2	1	3	4	1	0	1
1984-85	**Montreal Canadiens**	**NHL**	72	19	19	38	15	13	28	59	11	0	0	120	15.8	61	23	61	5	–18	12	2	7	9	13	0	0	0
1985-86♦	**Montreal Canadiens**	**NHL**	69	15	34	49	12	23	35	45	9	0	1	115	13.0	87	45	52	1	–9	5	0	1	1	2	0	0	0
1986-87	**Montreal Canadiens**	**NHL**	76	23	23	46	20	17	37	34	11	0	4	117	19.7	79	34	58	7	–6	17	7	12	19	10	2	1	1
1987-88	**Montreal Canadiens**	**NHL**	61	13	23	36	11	16	27	39	6	0	3	93	14.0	71	21	40	2	12	11	2	4	6	6	2	0	1
1988-89	**Montreal Canadiens**	**NHL**	78	14	17	31	12	12	24	48	1	1	0	104	13.5	57	4	45	15	23	21	3	5	8	6	0	1	2
1989-90	**Montreal Canadiens**	**NHL**	70	8	16	24	7	11	18	59	1	0	1	109	7.3	45	7	52	18	4	11	0	2	2	0	0	0	0
1990-91	Montreal Canadiens	Fr-Tour	2	0	0	0	....	....	....	0	....	....	....	....	....	....	....	....	....	....	....	....	....	....	....	....	....	....
	Montreal Canadiens	**NHL**	25	0	1	1	0	1	1	12	0	0	0	14	0.0	7	0	11	1	–3	5	0	0	0	2	0	0	0
1991-92	**Vancouver Canucks**	**NHL**	67	6	11	17	5	8	13	49	1	1	0	73	8.2	32	5	45	24	6	13	0	3	3	8	0	0	0
1992-93	**Vancouver Canucks**	**NHL**	25	3	0	3	2	0	2	10	0	0	0	15	20.0	6	0	20	12	–2	....	....	....	....	....	....	....	....
	NHL Totals		**1003**	**264**	**382**	**646**	**217**	**266**	**483**	**946**	**96**	**6**	**23**	**1720**	**15.3**	**1087**	**343**	**953**	**206**		**113**	**16**	**35**	**51**	**62**	**5**	**2**	**5**

WCJHL All-Star Team (1978) • Won Bud Man of the Year Award (1992) • Played in NHL All-Star Game (1983)

Traded to **Montreal** by **Washington** with Rick Green for Rod Langway, Brian Engblom, Doug Jarvis and Craig Laughlin, September 9, 1982. • Missed majority of 1990-91 season recovering from wrist injury suffered in game vs. Hartford, October 13, 1990. Signed as a free agent by **Vancouver**, July 26, 1991.

• WALTON, Mike

Michael Robert "Shaky" C – L. 5'10", 175 lbs. b: Kirkland Lake, Ont., 1/3/1945.

Season	Club	League	GP	G	A	Pts	AG	AA	APts	PIM	PP	SH	GW	S	%	TGF	PGF	TGA	PGA	+/–	GP	G	A	Pts	PIM	PP	SH	GW
1961-62	St. Michael's Majors	MTJHL	26	13	11	24	....	....	....	12	....	....	....	....	....	....	....	....	....	....	12	7	7	14	10	....	....	....
	St. Michael's Majors	Mem-Cup	5	1	0	1	....	....	....	6	....	....	....	....	....	....	....	....	....	....	....	....	....	....	....	....	....	....
1962-63	Neil McNeil Maroons	MTJHL	38	22	22	44	....	....	....	32	....	....	....	....	....	....	....	....	....	....	8	4	3	7	10	....	....	....
	Neil McNeil Maroons	Mem-Cup	6	4	1	5	....	....	....	13	....	....	....	....	....	....	....	....	....	....	....	....	....	....	....	....	....	....
1963-64	Toronto Marlboros	OHA-Jr.	53	41	51	92	....	....	....	62	....	....	....	....	....	....	....	....	....	....	9	6	9	15	6	....	....	....
	Rochester Americans	AHL	2	0	0	0	....	....	....	0	....	....	....	....	....	....	....	....	....	....	....	....	....	....	....	....	....	....
	Toronto Marlboros	Mem-Cup	12	6	20	26	....	....	....	11	....	....	....	....	....	....	....	....	....	....	....	....	....	....	....	....	....	....
1964-65	Tulsa Oilers	CPHL	68	40	44	84	....	....	....	86	....	....	....	....	....	....	....	....	....	....	12	7	6	13	16	....	....	....
1965-66	**Toronto Maple Leafs**	**NHL**	6	1	3	4	1	3	4	0	....	....	....	....	....	....	....	....	....	....	....	....	....	....	....	....	....	....
	Rochester Americans	AHL	68	35	51	86	....	....	....	67	....	....	....	....	....	....	....	....	....	....	12	*8	4	*12	*43	....	....	....
1966-67♦	**Toronto Maple Leafs**	**NHL**	31	7	10	17	8	10	18	13	....	....	....	....	....	....	....	....	....	....	12	4	3	7	2	3	0	1
	Rochester Americans	AHL	36	19	33	52	....	....	....	28	....	....	....	....	....	....	....	....	....	....	....	....	....	....	....	....	....	....
1967-68	**Toronto Maple Leafs**	**NHL**	73	30	29	59	35	29	64	48	11	0	5	238	12.6	66	19	46	0	1	....	....	....	....	....	....	....	....
1968-69	**Toronto Maple Leafs**	**NHL**	66	22	21	43	23	19	42	34	8	0	5	205	10.7	64	28	45	0	–9	4	0	0	0	4	0	0	0
1969-70	**Toronto Maple Leafs**	**NHL**	58	21	34	55	23	32	55	68	7	0	6	242	8.7	74	36	49	0	–11	....	....	....	....	....	....	....	....
1970-71	**Toronto Maple Leafs**	**NHL**	23	3	10	13	3	8	11	21	2	0	0	68	4.4	21	12	23	0	–14	....	....	....	....	....	....	....	....
	Boston Bruins	**NHL**	22	3	5	8	3	4	7	10	0	0	0	44	6.8	17	1	5	0	11	5	2	0	2	19	1	0	0
1971-72♦	**Boston Bruins**	**NHL**	76	28	28	56	28	24	52	45	6	0	4	236	11.9	83	18	42	0	23	15	6	6	12	13	1	0	2
1972-73	**Boston Bruins**	**NHL**	56	25	22	47	23	17	40	37	0	0	2	128	19.5	60	8	42	0	10	5	1	1	2	2	0	0	0
1973-74	Minnesota Fighting Saints	WHA	78	57	60	*117	....	....	....	88	....	....	....	....	....	....	....	....	....	....	11	*10	8	18	16	....	....	....
1974-75	Minnesota Fighting Saints	WHA	75	48	45	93	....	....	....	33	....	....	....	....	....	....	....	....	....	....	12	*10	7	17	10	....	....	....
1975-76	Minnesota Fighting Saints	WHA	58	31	40	71	....	....	....	71	....	....	....	....	....	....	....	....	....	....	....	....	....	....	....	....	....	....
	Vancouver Canucks	**NHL**	10	8	8	16	7	6	13	9	2	0	2	27	29.6	17	8	4	0	5	2	0	0	0	5	0	0	0
1976-77	**Vancouver Canucks**	**NHL**	40	7	24	31	6	18	24	32	2	0	1	75	9.3	42	12	46	1	–15	....	....	....	....	....	....	....	....
1977-78	**Vancouver Canucks**	**NHL**	65	29	37	66	26	29	55	30	14	0	4	115	25.2	87	44	69	0	–26	....	....	....	....	....	....	....	....
1978-79	**St. Louis Blues**	**NHL**	22	7	11	18	6	8	14	6	3	0	0	41	17.1	25	12	27	1	–13	....	....	....	....	....	....	....	....
	Boston Bruins	**NHL**	14	4	2	6	3	1	4	0	0	0	1	15	26.7	7	0	9	1	–1	....	....	....	....	....	....	....	....
	Rochester Americans	AHL	1	1	2	3	....	....	....	2	....	....	....	....	....	....	....	....	....	....	....	....	....	....	....	....	....	....
	Chicago Black Hawks	**NHL**	26	6	3	9	5	2	7	4	3	0	1	37	16.2	15	8	11	0	–4	4	1	0	1	0	0	0	0
	New Brunswick Hawks	AHL	7	1	5	6	....	....	....	6	....	....	....	....	....	....	....	....	....	....	....	....	....	....	....	....	....	....
1979-80	Kolner EC	Germany	20	12	19	31	....	....	....	33	....	....	....	....	....	....	....	....	....	....	....	....	....	....	....	....	....	....
	NHL Totals		**588**	**201**	**247**	**448**	**200**	**210**	**410**	**357**	....	....	....	....	....	....	....	....	....	....	**47**	**14**	**10**	**24**	**45**	....	....	....
	Other Major League Totals		211	136	145	281	....	....	....	192	....	....	....	....	....	....	....	....	....	....	23	20	15	35	26	....	....	....

• Son of Bobby • CPHL First All-Star Team (1965) • Won Ken McKenzie Trophy (Rookie of the Year - CPHL) (1965) • Won Dudley "Red" Garrett Memorial Award (Top Rookie - AHL) (1966) • WHA Second All-Star Team (1974) • Won W. D. (Bill) Hunter Trophy (Scoring Leader - WHA) (1974) • Played in NHL All-Star Game (1968)

Traded to **Philadelphia** by **Toronto** with Bruce Gamble and Toronto's 1st round choice (Pierre Plante) in 1971 Amateur Draft for Bernie Parent and Philadelphia's 2nd round choice (Rick Kehoe) in 1971 Amateur Draft, February 1, 1971. Traded to **Boston** by **Philadelphia** for Danny Schock and Rick MacLeish, February 1, 1971. Selected by **LA Sharks** (WHA) in 1972 WHA General Player Draft, February 12, 1972. WHA rights traded to **Minnesota** (WHA) by **LA Sharks** (WHA) for cash, June, 1973. Traded to **Vancouver** by **Boston** with Chris Oddleifson and Fred O'Donnell for Bobby Schmautz, February 7, 1974. Traded to **St. Louis** by **Vancouver** for St. Louis' 4th round choice (Harold Luckner) in 1978 Amateur Draft and future considerations, June 12, 1978. Signed as a free agent by **Boston**, December 5, 1978. Signed as a free agent by **Chicago**, January 22, 1979.

• WALZ, Wes

C – R. 5'10", 185 lbs. b: Calgary, Alta., 5/15/1970. Boston's 3rd, 57th overall, in 1989.

Season	Club	League	GP	G	A	Pts	AG	AA	APts	PIM	PP	SH	GW	S	%	TGF	PGF	TGA	PGA	+/–	GP	G	A	Pts	PIM	PP	SH	GW
1986-87	Calgary North Stars	AAHA	STATISTICS NOT AVAILABLE																									
1987-88	Calgary North Stars	AAHA	35	47	52	99	....	....	....	72	....	....	....	....	....	....	....	....	....	....	....	....	....	....	....	....	....	....
	Prince Albert Raiders	WHL	1	1	1	2	....	....	....	0	....	....	....	....	....	....	....	....	....	....	....	....	....	....	....	....	....	....
1988-89	Lethbridge Hurricanes	WHL	63	29	75	104	....	....	....	32	....	....	....	....	....	....	....	....	....	....	8	1	5	6	6	....	....	....
1989-90	Lethbridge Hurricanes	WHL	56	54	86	140	....	....	....	69	....	....	....	....	....	....	....	....	....	....	19	13	*24	*37	33	....	....	....
	Canada	WJC-A	7	2	3	5	....	....	....	0	....	....	....	....	....	....	....	....	....	....	....	....	....	....	....	....	....	....
	Boston Bruins	**NHL**	2	1	1	2	1	1	2	0	1	0	0	1	100.0	3	2	2	0	–1	....	....	....	....	....	....	....	....
1990-91	**Boston Bruins**	**NHL**	56	8	8	16	7	6	13	32	1	0	1	57	14.0	26	2	41	3	–14	2	0	0	0	0	0	0	0
	Maine Mariners	AHL	20	8	12	20	....	....	....	19	....	....	....	....	....	....	....	....	....	....	2	0	0	0	21	....	....	....
1991-92	**Boston Bruins**	**NHL**	15	0	3	3	0	2	2	12	0	0	0	17	0.0	4	0	8	1	–3	....	....	....	....	....	....	....	....
	Maine Mariners	AHL	21	13	11	24	....	....	....	38	....	....	....	....	....	....	....	....	....	....	....	....	....	....	....	....	....	....
	Philadelphia Flyers	**NHL**	2	1	0	1	1	0	1	0	0	0	1	2	50.0	1	0	0	0	1	....	....	....	....	....	....	....	....
	Hershey Bears	AHL	41	13	28	41	....	....	....	37	....	....	....	....	....	....	....	....	....	....	6	1	2	3	0	....	....	....
1992-93	Hershey Bears	AHL	78	35	45	80	....	....	....	106	....	....	....	....	....	....	....	....	....	....	....	....	....	....	....	....	....	....
1993-94	**Calgary Flames**	**NHL**	53	11	27	38	10	21	31	16	1	0	0	79	13.9	55	15	21	1	20	6	3	0	3	2	0	0	0
	Saint John Flames	AHL	15	6	6	12	....	....	....	14	....	....	....	....	....	....	....	....	....	....	....	....	....	....	....	....	....	....
1994-95	**Calgary Flames**	**NHL**	39	6	12	18	11	18	29	11	4	0	1	73	8.2	31	9	15	0	7	1	0	0	0	0	0	0	0
1995-96	**Detroit Red Wings**	**NHL**	2	0	0	0	0	0	0	0	0	0	0	2	0.0	0	0	0	0	0	....	....	....	....	....	....	....	....
	Adirondack Red Wings	AHL	38	20	35	55	....	....	....	58	....	....	....	....	....	....	....	....	....	....	....	....	....	....	....	....	....	....
1996-97	EV Zug	Switz.	41	24	22	46	....	....	....	67	....	....	....	....	....	....	....	....	....	....	9	5	1	6	39	....	....	....
1997-98	EV Zug	Switz.	38	18	34	52	....	....	....	32	....	....	....	....	....	....	....	....	....	....	20	*16	*12	*28	18	....	....	....
	EV Zug	EuroHL	5	1	3	4	....	....	....	10	....	....	....	....	....	....	....	....	....	....	....	....	....	....	....	....	....	....
1998-99	EV Zug	Switz.	42	22	27	49	....	....	....	75	....	....	....	....	....	....	....	....	....	....	10	3	9	12	2	....	....	....
	EV Zug	EuroHL	6	7	5	12	....	....	....	4	....	....	....	....	....	....	....	....	....	....	2	0	0	0	12	....	....	....
99-2000	Long Beach Ice Dogs	IHL	6	4	3	7	....	....	....	8	....	....	....	....	....	....	....	....	....	....	....	....	....	....	....	....	....	....
	HC Lugano	Switz.	13	7	11	18	....	....	....	14	....	....	....	....	....	....	....	....	....	....	5	3	4	7	4	....	....	....
	HC Lugano	EuroHL	1	0	0	0	....	....	....	0	....	....	....	....	....	....	....	....	....	....	4	3	3	6	4	....	....	....
	NHL Totals		**169**	**27**	**51**	**78**	**30**	**48**	**78**	**71**	**7**	**0**	**3**	**231**	**11.7**	**120**	**28**	**87**	**5**		**9**	**3**	**0**	**3**	**2**	**0**	**0**	**0**

WHL East First All-Star Team (1990)

Traded to **Philadelphia** by **Boston** with Garry Galley and Boston's 3rd round choice (Milos Holan) in 1993 Entry Draft for Gord Murphy, Brian Dobbin, Philadelphia's 3rd round choice (Sergei Zholtok) in 1992 Entry Draft and 4th round choice (Charles Paquette) in 1993 Entry Draft, January 2, 1992. Signed as a free agent by **Calgary**, August 26, 1993. Signed as a free agent by **Detroit**, September 6, 1995. Signed as a free agent by **Long Beach** (IHL), October 12, 1999. Signed as a free agent by **Minnesota**, June 28, 2000.

• WAPPEL, Gord

Gordon Alexander D – L. 6'2", 205 lbs. b: Regina, Sask., 7/26/1958. Atlanta's 4th, 80th overall, in 1978.

Season	Club	League	GP	G	A	Pts	AG	AA	APts	PIM	PP	SH	GW	S	%	TGF	PGF	TGA	PGA	+/–	GP	G	A	Pts	PIM	PP	SH	GW
1973-74	Regina Blues	SJHL	50	2	4	6	....	....	....	55	....	....	....	....	....	....	....	....	....	....	....	....	....	....	....	....	....	....
1974-75	Regina Blues	SJHL	25	5	5	10	....	....	....	55	....	....	....	....	....	....	....	....	....	....	....	....	....	....	....	....	....	....
	Regina Pats	WCJHL	20	0	3	3	....	....	....	9	....	....	....	....	....	....	....	....	....	....	5	0	0	0	4	....	....	....
1975-76	Regina Pats	WCJHL	72	5	28	33	....	....	....	76	....	....	....	....	....	....	....	....	....	....	6	0	2	2	28	....	....	....
1976-77	Regina Pats	WCJHL	54	4	28	32	....	....	....	137	....	....	....	....	....	....	....	....	....	....	....	....	....	....	....	....	....	....
1977-78	Regina Pats	WCJHL	72	10	30	40	....	....	....	177	....	....	....	....	....	....	....	....	....	....	13	5	5	10	20	....	....	....

Season	Club	League	GP	G	A	Pts	AG	AA	APts	PIM	PP	SH	GW	S	%	TGF	PGF	TGA	PGA	+/–	GP	G	A	Pts	PIM	PP	SH	GW
			REGULAR SEASON																		PLAYOFFS							
1978-79	Tulsa Oilers	CHL	47	1	16	17	....	....	....	44	....	....	....	....	....	....	....	....	....	....	....	....	....	....	....	....	....	....
	Muskegon Mohawks	IHL	20	2	6	8	....	....	....	40	....	....	....	....	....	....	....	....	....	....	....	....	....	....	....	....	....	....
1979-80	**Atlanta Flames**	**NHL**	**2**	**0**	**0**	**0**	**0**	**0**	**0**	**0**	**0**	**0**	**0**	**2**	**0.0**	**2**	**0**	**1**	**0**	**1**	**2**	**0**	**0**	**0**	**4**	**0**	**0**	**0**
	Birmingham Bulls	CHL	76	4	20	24	....	....	....	122	....	....	....	....	....	....	....	....	....	....	....	....	....	....	....	....	....	....
1980-81	**Calgary Flames**	**NHL**	**7**	**0**	**1**	**1**	**0**	**1**	**1**	**4**	**0**	**0**	**0**	**3**	**0.0**	**7**	**0**	**7**	**1**	**1**	....	....	....	....	....	....	....	....
	Birmingham Bulls	CHL	44	6	19	25	....	....	....	89	....	....	....	....	....	....	....	....	....	....	....	....	....	....	....	....	....	....
	Nova Scotia Voyageurs	AHL	18	0	4	4	....	....	....	16	....	....	....	....	....	....	....	....	....	....	6	0	1	1	8	....	....	....
1981-82	**Calgary Flames**	**NHL**	**11**	**1**	**0**	**1**	**1**	**0**	**1**	**6**	**0**	**0**	**0**	**7**	**14.3**	**6**	**0**	**10**	**0**	**–4**	....	....	....	....	....	....	....	....
	Oklahoma City Stars	CHL	46	6	13	19	....	....	....	52	....	....	....	....	....	....	....	....	....	....	....	....	....	....	....	....	....	....
1982-83	Colorado Flames	CHL	70	10	34	44	....	....	....	110	....	....	....	....	....	....	....	....	....	....	6	0	8	8	2	....	....	....
	NHL Totals		**20**	**1**	**1**	**2**	**1**	**1**	**2**	**10**	**0**	**0**	**0**	**12**	**8.3**	**15**	**0**	**18**	**1**		**2**	**0**	**0**	**0**	**4**	**0**	**0**	**0**

Transferred to **Calgary** after **Atlanta** franchise relocated, June 24, 1980.

• WARD, Aaron

D – R. 6'2", 200 lbs. b: Windsor, Ont., 1/17/1973. Winnipeg's 1st, 5th overall, in 1991.

Season	Club	League	GP	G	A	Pts	AG	AA	APts	PIM	PP	SH	GW	S	%	TGF	PGF	TGA	PGA	+/–	GP	G	A	Pts	PIM	PP	SH	GW
1988-89	Nepean Raiders	OJHL	54	1	14	15	....	....	....	40	....	....	....	....	....	....	....	....	....	....	....	....	....	....	....	....	....	....
1989-90	Nepean Raiders	OJHL	52	6	33	39	....	....	....	85	....	....	....	....	....	....	....	....	....	....	....	....	....	....	....	....	....	....
1990-91	University of Michigan	CCHA	46	8	11	19	....	....	....	126	....	....	....	....	....	....	....	....	....	....	....	....	....	....	....	....	....	....
1991-92	University of Michigan	CCHA	42	7	12	19	....	....	....	64	....	....	....	....	....	....	....	....	....	....	....	....	....	....	....	....	....	....
1992-93	University of Michigan	CCHA	30	5	8	13	....	....	....	73	....	....	....	....	....	....	....	....	....	....	....	....	....	....	....	....	....	....
	Canada	Nat-Team	4	0	0	0	....	....	....	8	....	....	....	....	....	....	....	....	....	....	....	....	....	....	....	....	....	....
1993-94	**Detroit Red Wings**	**NHL**	**5**	**1**	**0**	**1**	**1**	**0**	**1**	**4**	**0**	**0**	**0**	**3**	**33.3**	**3**	**0**	**1**	**0**	**2**	....	....	....	....	....	....	....	....
	Adirondack Red Wings	AHL	58	4	12	16	....	....	....	87	....	....	....	....	....	....	....	....	....	....	9	2	6	8	6	....	....	....
1994-95	Adirondack Red Wings	AHL	76	11	24	35	....	....	....	87	....	....	....	....	....	....	....	....	....	....	4	0	1	1	0	....	....	....
	Detroit Red Wings	**NHL**	**1**	**0**	**1**	**1**	**0**	**1**	**1**	**2**	**0**	**0**	**0**	**0**	**0.0**	**1**	**0**	**0**	**0**	**1**	....	....	....	....	....	....	....	....
1995-96	Adirondack Red Wings	AHL	74	5	10	15	....	....	....	133	....	....	....	....	....	....	....	....	....	....	3	0	0	0	6	....	....	....
1996-97♦	**Detroit Red Wings**	**NHL**	**49**	**2**	**5**	**7**	**2**	**4**	**6**	**52**	**0**	**0**	**0**	**40**	**5.0**	**21**	**2**	**32**	**4**	**–9**	**19**	**0**	**0**	**0**	**17**	**0**	**0**	**0**
1997-98♦	**Detroit Red Wings**	**NHL**	**52**	**5**	**5**	**10**	**6**	**5**	**11**	**47**	**0**	**0**	**1**	**47**	**10.6**	**26**	**0**	**35**	**8**	**–1**	....	....	....	....	....	....	....	....
1998-99	**Detroit Red Wings**	**NHL**	**60**	**3**	**8**	**11**	**4**	**8**	**12**	**52**	**0**	**0**	**0**	**46**	**6.5**	**26**	**0**	**38**	**7**	**–5**	**8**	**0**	**1**	**1**	**8**	**0**	**0**	**0**
99-2000	**Detroit Red Wings**	**NHL**	**36**	**1**	**3**	**4**	**1**	**3**	**4**	**24**	**0**	**0**	**0**	**25**	**4.0**	**16**	**0**	**24**	**4**	**–4**	**3**	**0**	**0**	**0**	**0**	**0**	**0**	**0**
	NHL Totals		**203**	**12**	**22**	**34**	**14**	**21**	**35**	**181**	**0**	**0**	**1**	**161**	**7.5**	**93**	**2**	**130**	**23**		**30**	**0**	**1**	**1**	**25**	**0**	**0**	**0**

Traded to **Detroit** by **Winnipeg** with Toronto's 4th round choice (previously acquired by Winnipeg - later traded to Detroit - Detroit selected John Jakopin) in 1993 Entry Draft for Paul Ysebaert and future considerations (Alan Kerr, June 18, 1993), June 11, 1993. • Missed majority of 1999-2000 season recovering from shoulder injury suffered in game vs. Vancouver, January 19, 2000.

• WARD, Dixon

Dixon McRae RW – R. 6', 200 lbs. b: Leduc, Alta., 9/23/1968. Vancouver's 6th, 128th overall, in 1988.

Season	Club	League	GP	G	A	Pts	AG	AA	APts	PIM	PP	SH	GW	S	%	TGF	PGF	TGA	PGA	+/–	GP	G	A	Pts	PIM	PP	SH	GW
1986-87	Red Deer Rustlers	AJHL	59	46	40	86	....	....	....	153	....	....	....	....	....	....	....	....	....	....	....	....	....	....	....	....	....	....
1987-88	Red Deer Rebels	AJHL	51	60	71	131	....	....	....	167	....	....	....	....	....	....	....	....	....	....	....	....	....	....	....	....	....	....
1988-89	University of North Dakota	WCHA	37	8	9	17	....	....	....	26	....	....	....	....	....	....	....	....	....	....	....	....	....	....	....	....	....	....
1989-90	University of North Dakota	WCHA	45	35	34	69	....	....	....	44	....	....	....	....	....	....	....	....	....	....	....	....	....	....	....	....	....	....
1990-91	University of North Dakota	WCHA	43	34	35	69	....	....	....	84	....	....	....	....	....	....	....	....	....	....	....	....	....	....	....	....	....	....
1991-92	University of North Dakota	WCHA	38	33	31	64	....	....	....	90	....	....	....	....	....	....	....	....	....	....	....	....	....	....	....	....	....	....
1992-93	**Vancouver Canucks**	**NHL**	**70**	**22**	**30**	**52**	**18**	**21**	**39**	**82**	**4**	**1**	**0**	**111**	**19.8**	**78**	**15**	**40**	**11**	**34**	**9**	**2**	**3**	**5**	**0**	**2**	**0**	**0**
1993-94	**Vancouver Canucks**	**NHL**	**33**	**6**	**1**	**7**	**6**	**1**	**7**	**37**	**2**	**0**	**1**	**46**	**13.0**	**12**	**6**	**22**	**2**	**–14**	....	....	....	....	....	....	....	....
	Los Angeles Kings	**NHL**	**34**	**6**	**2**	**8**	**6**	**2**	**8**	**45**	**2**	**0**	**0**	**44**	**13.6**	**10**	**3**	**15**	**0**	**–8**	....	....	....	....	....	....	....	....
1994-95	**Toronto Maple Leafs**	**NHL**	**22**	**0**	**3**	**3**	**0**	**4**	**4**	**31**	**0**	**0**	**0**	**15**	**0.0**	**3**	**0**	**7**	**0**	**–4**	....	....	....	....	....	....	....	....
	St. John's Maple Leafs	AHL	6	3	3	6	....	....	....	19	....	....	....	....	....	....	....	....	....	....	....	....	....	....	....	....	....	....
	Detroit Vipers	IHL	7	3	6	9	....	....	....	7	....	....	....	....	....	....	....	....	....	....	5	3	0	3	7	....	....	....
1995-96	**Buffalo Sabres**	**NHL**	**8**	**2**	**2**	**4**	**2**	**2**	**4**	**6**	**0**	**0**	**1**	**12**	**16.7**	**5**	**1**	**3**	**0**	**1**	....	....	....	....	....	....	....	....
	Rochester Americans	AHL	71	38	56	94	....	....	....	74	....	....	....	....	....	....	....	....	....	....	19	11	*24	*35	8	....	....	....
1996-97	**Buffalo Sabres**	**NHL**	**79**	**13**	**32**	**45**	**14**	**28**	**42**	**36**	**1**	**2**	**4**	**93**	**14.0**	**59**	**6**	**54**	**18**	**17**	**12**	**2**	**3**	**5**	**6**	**0**	**0**	**1**
1997-98	**Buffalo Sabres**	**NHL**	**71**	**10**	**13**	**23**	**12**	**13**	**25**	**42**	**0**	**2**	**3**	**99**	**10.1**	**40**	**1**	**47**	**17**	**9**	**15**	**3**	**8**	**11**	**6**	**0**	**0**	**0**
1998-99	**Buffalo Sabres**	**NHL**	**78**	**20**	**24**	**44**	**23**	**23**	**46**	**44**	**2**	**1**	**4**	**101**	**19.8**	**55**	**10**	**59**	**24**	**10**	**21**	**7**	**5**	**12**	**32**	**0**	**2**	**3**
99-2000	**Buffalo Sabres**	**NHL**	**71**	**11**	**9**	**20**	**12**	**8**	**20**	**41**	**1**	**2**	**2**	**101**	**10.9**	**32**	**3**	**39**	**11**	**1**	**5**	**0**	**1**	**1**	**2**	**0**	**0**	**0**
	NHL Totals		**466**	**90**	**116**	**206**	**93**	**102**	**195**	**364**	**12**	**8**	**15**	**622**	**14.5**	**294**	**45**	**286**	**83**		**62**	**14**	**20**	**34**	**46**	**2**	**2**	**4**

WCHA Second All-Star Team (1991, 1992) • Won Jack A. Butterfield Trophy (Playoff MVP - AHL) (1996)

Traded to **LA Kings** by **Vancouver** for Jimmy Carson, January 8, 1994. Traded to **Toronto** by **LA Kings** with Guy Leveque, Kelly Fairchild and Shayne Toporowski for Eric Lacroix, Chris Snell and Toronto's 4th round choice (Eric Belanger) in 1996 Entry Draft, October 3, 1994. Signed as a free agent by **Buffalo**, September 20, 1995.

• WARD, Ed

Edward J. RW – R. 6'3", 220 lbs. b: Edmonton, Alta., 11/10/1969. Quebec's 7th, 108th overall, in 1988.

Season	Club	League	GP	G	A	Pts	AG	AA	APts	PIM	PP	SH	GW	S	%	TGF	PGF	TGA	PGA	+/–	GP	G	A	Pts	PIM	PP	SH	GW
1986-87	Sherwood Park Crusaders	AJHL	60	18	28	46	....	....	....	272	....	....	....	....	....	....	....	....	....	....	....	....	....	....	....	....	....	....
1987-88	Northern Michigan University	WCHA	25	0	2	2	....	....	....	40	....	....	....	....	....	....	....	....	....	....	....	....	....	....	....	....	....	....
1988-89	Northern Michigan University	WCHA	42	5	15	20	....	....	....	36	....	....	....	....	....	....	....	....	....	....	....	....	....	....	....	....	....	....
1989-90	Northern Michigan University	WCHA	39	5	11	16	....	....	....	77	....	....	....	....	....	....	....	....	....	....	....	....	....	....	....	....	....	....
1990-91	Northern Michigan University	WCHA	46	13	18	31	....	....	....	109	....	....	....	....	....	....	....	....	....	....	....	....	....	....	....	....	....	....
1991-92	Greensboro Monarchs	ECHL	12	4	8	12	....	....	....	21	....	....	....	....	....	....	....	....	....	....	....	....	....	....	....	....	....	....
	Halifax Citadels	AHL	51	7	11	18	....	....	....	65	....	....	....	....	....	....	....	....	....	....	....	....	....	....	....	....	....	....
1992-93	Halifax Citadels	AHL	70	13	19	32	....	....	....	56	....	....	....	....	....	....	....	....	....	....	....	....	....	....	....	....	....	....
1993-94	**Quebec Nordiques**	**NHL**	**7**	**1**	**0**	**1**	**1**	**0**	**1**	**5**	**0**	**0**	**0**	**3**	**33.3**	**2**	**0**	**2**	**0**	**0**	....	....	....	....	....	....	....	....
	Cornwall Aces	AHL	60	12	30	42	....	....	....	65	....	....	....	....	....	....	....	....	....	....	12	1	3	4	14	....	....	....
1994-95	Cornwall Aces	AHL	56	10	14	24	....	....	....	118	....	....	....	....	....	....	....	....	....	....	....	....	....	....	....	....	....	....
	Calgary Flames	**NHL**	**2**	**1**	**1**	**2**	**2**	**1**	**3**	**2**	**0**	**0**	**0**	**1**	**100.0**	**2**	**0**	**4**	**0**	**–2**	....	....	....	....	....	....	....	....
	Saint John Flames	AHL	11	4	5	9	....	....	....	20	....	....	....	....	....	....	....	....	....	....	5	1	0	1	10	....	....	....
1995-96	**Calgary Flames**	**NHL**	**41**	**3**	**5**	**8**	**3**	**4**	**7**	**44**	**0**	**0**	**0**	**33**	**9.1**	**12**	**1**	**13**	**0**	**–2**	....	....	....	....	....	....	....	....
	Saint John Flames	AHL	12	1	2	3	....	....	....	45	....	....	....	....	....	....	....	....	....	....	16	4	4	8	27	....	....	....
1996-97	**Calgary Flames**	**NHL**	**40**	**5**	**8**	**13**	**5**	**7**	**12**	**49**	**0**	**0**	**1**	**33**	**15.2**	**16**	**0**	**19**	**0**	**–3**	....	....	....	....	....	....	....	....
	Saint John Flames	AHL	1	0	0	0	....	....	....	0	....	....	....	....	....	....	....	....	....	....	....	....	....	....	....	....	....	....
	Detroit Vipers	IHL	31	7	6	13	....	....	....	45	....	....	....	....	....	....	....	....	....	....	....	....	....	....	....	....	....	....
1997-98	**Calgary Flames**	**NHL**	**64**	**4**	**5**	**9**	**5**	**5**	**10**	**122**	**0**	**0**	**0**	**52**	**7.7**	**21**	**1**	**22**	**1**	**–1**	....	....	....	....	....	....	....	....
1998-99	**Calgary Flames**	**NHL**	**68**	**3**	**5**	**8**	**4**	**5**	**9**	**67**	**0**	**0**	**0**	**56**	**5.4**	**14**	**1**	**17**	**0**	**–4**	....	....	....	....	....	....	....	....
99-2000	**Atlanta Thrashers**	**NHL**	**44**	**5**	**1**	**6**	**6**	**1**	**7**	**44**	**0**	**2**	**0**	**51**	**9.8**	**15**	**3**	**21**	**4**	**–5**	....	....	....	....	....	....	....	....
	Mighty Ducks of Anaheim	**NHL**	**8**	**1**	**0**	**1**	**1**	**0**	**1**	**15**	**0**	**0**	**0**	**5**	**20.0**	**1**	**0**	**3**	**0**	**–2**	....	....	....	....	....	....	....	....
	NHL Totals		**274**	**23**	**25**	**48**	**27**	**23**	**50**	**348**	**0**	**2**	**1**	**234**	**9.8**	**83**	**6**	**101**	**5**		....	....	....	....	....	....	....	....

Traded to **Calgary** by **Quebec** for Francois Groleau, March 23, 1995. Claimed by **Atlanta** from **Calgary** in Expansion Draft, June 25, 1999. Traded to **Anaheim** by **Atlanta** for a conditional choice in 2001 Entry Draft, March 14, 2000. Traded to **New Jersey** by **Anaheim** for New Jersey's 7th round choice in 2001 Entry Draft, June 12, 2000.

• WARD, Jason

Jason Robert RW – R. 6'2", 192 lbs. b: Chapleau, Ont., 1/16/1979. Montreal's 1st, 11th overall, in 1997.

Season	Club	League	GP	G	A	Pts	AG	AA	APts	PIM	PP	SH	GW	S	%	TGF	PGF	TGA	PGA	+/–	GP	G	A	Pts	PIM	PP	SH	GW
1994-95	Oshawa Legionaires	OJHL	47	30	31	61	....	....	....	75	....	....	....	....	....	....	....	....	....	....	....	....	....	....	....	....	....	....
1995-96	Niagara Falls Thunder	OHL	64	15	35	50	....	....	....	139	....	....	....	....	....	....	....	....	....	....	10	6	4	10	23	....	....	....
1996-97	Erie Otters	OHL	58	25	39	64	....	....	....	137	....	....	....	....	....	....	....	....	....	....	5	1	2	3	2	....	....	....
1997-98	Erie Otters	OHL	21	7	9	16	....	....	....	42	....	....	....	....	....	....	....	....	....	....	....	....	....	....	....	....	....	....
	Windsor Spitfires	OHL	26	19	27	46	....	....	....	34	....	....	....	....	....	....	....	....	....	....	....	....	....	....	....	....	....	....
	Fredericton Canadiens	AHL	7	1	0	1	....	....	....	2	....	....	....	....	....	....	....	....	....	....	1	0	0	0	2	....	....	....
	Canada	WJC-A	7	1	0	1	....	....	....	2	....	....	....	....	....	....	....	....	....	....	....	....	....	....	....	....	....	....

Season	Club	League	GP	G	A	Pts	AG	AA	APts	PIM	PP	SH	GW	S	%	TGF	PGF	TGA	PGA	+/–	GP	G	A	Pts	PIM	PP	SH	GW
			REGULAR SEASON																		PLAYOFFS							
1998-99	Windsor Spitfires	OHL	12	8	11	19	....	....	....	25	....	....	....	....	....	....	....	....	....	....	....	....	....	....	....	....	....	....
	Plymouth Whalers	OHL	23	14	13	27	....	....	....	28	....	....	....	....	....	....	....	....	....	....	11	6	8	14	12	....	....	....
	Canada	WJC-A	7	1	1	2	....	....	....	8	....	....	....	....	....	....	....	....	....	....	....	....	....	....	....	....	....	....
	Fredericton Canadiens	AHL	....	....	....	....	....	....	....	....	....	....	....	....	....	....	....	....	....	....	10	4	2	6	22	....	....	....
99-2000	**Montreal Canadiens**	**NHL**	**32**	**2**	**1**	**3**	**2**	**1**	**3**	**10**	**1**	**0**	**0**	**24**	**8.3**	**10**	**3**	**8**	**0**	**–1**	....	....	....	....	....	....	....	....
	Quebec Citadelles	AHL	40	14	12	26	....	....	....	30	....	....	....	....	....	....	....	....	....	....	3	2	1	3	4	....	....	....
	NHL Totals		**32**	**2**	**1**	**3**	**2**	**1**	**3**	**10**	**1**	**0**	**0**	**24**	**8.3**	**10**	**3**	**8**	**0**		....	....	....	....	....	....	....	....

• WARD, Joe

Joseph Michael C – L. 6', 180 lbs. b: Sarnia, Ont., 2/11/1961. Colorado's 2nd, 22nd overall, in 1980.

Season	Club	League	GP	G	A	Pts	AG	AA	APts	PIM	PP	SH	GW	S	%	TGF	PGF	TGA	PGA	+/–	GP	G	A	Pts	PIM	PP	SH	GW
1978-79	Seattle Breakers	WHL	61	18	30	48	....	....	....	66	....	....	....	....	....	....	....	....	....	....	....	....	....	....	....	....	....	....
1979-80	Seattle Breakers	WHL	59	32	37	69	....	....	....	90	....	....	....	....	....	....	....	....	....	....	....	....	....	....	....	....	....	....
1980-81	Seattle Breakers	WHL	40	28	23	51	....	....	....	48	....	....	....	....	....	....	....	....	....	....	....	....	....	....	....	....	....	....
	Colorado Rockies	**NHL**	**4**	**0**	**0**	**0**	**0**	**0**	**0**	**2**	**0**	**0**	**0**	**2**	**0.0**	**1**	**0**	**3**	**0**	**–2**	....	....	....	....	....	....	....	....
	Fort Worth Texans	CHL	....	....	....	....	....	....	....	....	....	....	....	....	....	....	....	....	....	....	5	2	2	4	2	....	....	....
1981-82	Fort Worth Texans	CHL	32	6	15	21	....	....	....	12	....	....	....	....	....	....	....	....	....	....	....	....	....	....	....	....	....	....
1982-83	Wichita Wind	CHL	7	0	2	2	....	....	....	2	....	....	....	....	....	....	....	....	....	....	....	....	....	....	....	....	....	....
	Muskegon Mohawks	IHL	53	34	25	59	....	....	....	4	....	....	....	....	....	....	....	....	....	....	4	1	2	3	4	....	....	....
1983-84	Muskegon Mohawks	IHL	9	3	2	5	....	....	....	2	....	....	....	....	....	....	....	....	....	....	....	....	....	....	....	....	....	....
	NHL Totals		**4**	**0**	**0**	**0**	**0**	**0**	**0**	**2**	**0**	**0**	**0**	**2**	**0.0**	**1**	**0**	**3**	**0**		....	....	....	....	....	....	....	....

• Son of Don

• WARD, Ron

Ronald Leon C – R. 5'11", 175 lbs. b: Cornwall, Ont., 9/12/1944.

Season	Club	League	GP	G	A	Pts	AG	AA	APts	PIM	PP	SH	GW	S	%	TGF	PGF	TGA	PGA	+/–	GP	G	A	Pts	PIM	PP	SH	GW
1963-64	Cornwall Colts	OHA-B	STATISTICS NOT AVAILABLE																									
	Lachine Maroons	Mem-Cup	4	0	0	0	....	....	....	6	....	....	....	....	....	....	....	....	....	....	....	....	....	....	....	....	....	....
	Smiths Falls Bears	Mem-Cup	5	0	2	2	....	....	....	6	....	....	....	....	....	....	....	....	....	....	....	....	....	....	....	....	....	....
1964-65	Cornwall Colts	OHA-B	36	29	31	60	....	....	....	....	....	....	....	....	....	....	....	....	....	....	....	....	....	....	....	....	....	....
1965-66	Tulsa Oilers	CPHL	69	6	22	28	....	....	....	37	....	....	....	....	....	....	....	....	....	....	7	1	2	3	9	....	....	....
1966-67	Tulsa Oilers	CPHL	42	12	15	27	....	....	....	46	....	....	....	....	....	....	....	....	....	....	....	....	....	....	....	....	....	....
1967-68	Phoenix Roadrunners	WHL	1	0	1	1	....	....	....	0	....	....	....	....	....	....	....	....	....	....	....	....	....	....	....	....	....	....
	Tulsa Oilers	CPHL	67	31	*54	*85	....	....	....	30	....	....	....	....	....	....	....	....	....	....	11	5	5	10	8	....	....	....
1968-69	Rochester Americans	AHL	73	35	43	78	....	....	....	18	....	....	....	....	....	....	....	....	....	....	....	....	....	....	....	....	....	....
1969-70	**Toronto Maple Leafs**	**NHL**	**18**	**0**	**1**	**1**	**0**	**1**	**1**	**2**	**0**	**0**	**0**	**11**	**0.0**	**0**	**0**	**0**	**0**	**0**	....	....	....	....	....	....	....	....
	Phoenix Roadrunners	WHL	22	7	9	16	....	....	....	12	....	....	....	....	....	....	....	....	....	....	....	....	....	....	....	....	....	....
	Tulsa Oilers	CHL	22	7	17	24	....	....	....	15	....	....	....	....	....	....	....	....	....	....	....	....	....	....	....	....	....	....
1970-71	Rochester Americans	AHL	69	23	16	39	....	....	....	33	....	....	....	....	....	....	....	....	....	....	....	....	....	....	....	....	....	....
1971-72	**Vancouver Canucks**	**NHL**	**71**	**2**	**4**	**6**	**2**	**3**	**5**	**4**	**0**	**1**	**0**	**45**	**4.4**	**9**	**0**	**54**	**43**	**–2**	....	....	....	....	....	....	....	....
1972-73	New York Raiders	WHA	77	51	67	118	....	....	....	28	....	....	....	....	....	....	....	....	....	....	....	....	....	....	....	....	....	....
1973-74	Vancouver Blazers	WHA	7	0	2	2	....	....	....	2	....	....	....	....	....	....	....	....	....	....	....	....	....	....	....	....	....	....
	Los Angeles Sharks	WHA	40	14	19	33	....	....	....	16	....	....	....	....	....	....	....	....	....	....	....	....	....	....	....	....	....	....
	Cleveland Crusaders	WHA	23	19	7	26	....	....	....	7	....	....	....	....	....	....	....	....	....	....	5	3	0	3	2	....	....	....
1974-75	Cleveland Crusaders	WHA	73	30	32	62	....	....	....	18	....	....	....	....	....	....	....	....	....	....	5	0	2	2	2	....	....	....
1975-76	Cleveland Crusaders	WHA	75	32	50	82	....	....	....	24	....	....	....	....	....	....	....	....	....	....	3	0	2	2	0	....	....	....
1976-77	Minnesota Fighting Saints	WHA	41	15	21	36	....	....	....	6	....	....	....	....	....	....	....	....	....	....	....	....	....	....	....	....	....	....
	Winnipeg Jets	WHA	14	4	7	11	....	....	....	2	....	....	....	....	....	....	....	....	....	....	....	....	....	....	....	....	....	....
	Calgary Cowboys	WHA	9	5	5	10	....	....	....	0	....	....	....	....	....	....	....	....	....	....	....	....	....	....	....	....	....	....
	NHL Totals		**89**	**2**	**5**	**7**	**2**	**4**	**6**	**6**	**0**	**1**	**0**	**56**	**3.6**	**9**	**0**	**54**	**43**		....	....	....	....	....	....	....	....
	Other Major League Totals		359	170	210	380				103											13	3	4	7	4			

CPHL Second All-Star Team (1968) • Won Dudley "Red" Garrett Memorial Award (Top Rookie - AHL) (1969) • WHA Second All-Star Team (1973)

Loaned to **Lachine** (MMJHL) and **Smiths Falls** (OHA-B) by **Cornwall**(MMJHL) for Memorial Cup playoffs, March, 1964. Traded to **Toronto** by **Vancouver** (WHL) for Brad Selwood and Rene Robert, May, 1969. Claimed by **Vancouver** from **Toronto** in Expansion Draft, June 10, 1970. Selected by **NY Raiders** (WHA) in 1972 WHA General Player Draft, February 12, 1972. Traded to **Vancouver** (WHA) by **NY Raiders** (WHA) with Pete Donnelly for Andre Lacroix, Don Herriman and WHA rights to Bernie Parent, June, 1973. Traded to **LA Sharks** (WHA) by **Vancouver** (WHA) for George Gardner and future considerations (Ralph MacSweyn, November 5, 1973), October, 1973. Traded to **Cleveland** (WHA) by **LA Sharks** (WHA) for Bill Young and Ted Hodgson, February, 1974. Transferred to **Minnesota** (WHA) after **LA Sharks** (WHA) franchise relocated, April 11, 1974. Signed as a free agent by **Winnipeg** (WHA) after **Minnesota** (WHA) franchise folded, January 17, 1977. Traded to **Calgary** (WHA) by **Winnipeg** (WHA) with Veli-Pekka Ketola and Heikki Riihiranta for Danny Lawson, Mike Ford and future considerations, March, 1977.

• WARE, Jeff

D – L. 6'4", 220 lbs. b: Toronto, Ont., 5/19/1977. Toronto's 1st, 15th overall, in 1995.

Season	Club	League	GP	G	A	Pts	AG	AA	APts	PIM	PP	SH	GW	S	%	TGF	PGF	TGA	PGA	+/–	GP	G	A	Pts	PIM	PP	SH	GW
1993-94	Wexford Raiders	OJHL	45	1	9	10	....	....	....	75	....	....	....	....	....	....	....	....	....	....	....	....	....	....	....	....	....	....
1994-95	Oshawa Generals	OHL	55	2	11	13	....	....	....	86	....	....	....	....	....	....	....	....	....	....	7	1	1	2	6	....	....	....
1995-96	Oshawa Generals	OHL	62	4	19	23	....	....	....	128	....	....	....	....	....	....	....	....	....	....	5	0	1	1	8	....	....	....
	St. John's Maple Leafs	AHL	4	0	0	0	....	....	....	4	....	....	....	....	....	....	....	....	....	....	4	0	0	0	2	....	....	....
1996-97	Oshawa Generals	OHL	24	1	10	11	....	....	....	38	....	....	....	....	....	....	....	....	....	....	13	0	3	3	34	....	....	....
	Canada	WJC-A	7	0	0	0	....	....	....	6	....	....	....	....	....	....	....	....	....	....	....	....	....	....	....	....	....	....
	Toronto Maple Leafs	**NHL**	**13**	**0**	**0**	**0**	**0**	**0**	**0**	**6**	**0**	**0**	**0**	**4**	**0.0**	**5**	**0**	**3**	**0**	**2**	....	....	....	....	....	....	....	....
	Oshawa Generals	Mem-Cup	4	0	0	0	....	....	....	39	....	....	....	....	....	....	....	....	....	....	....	....	....	....	....	....	....	....
1997-98	**Toronto Maple Leafs**	**NHL**	**2**	**0**	**0**	**0**	**0**	**0**	**0**	**0**	**0**	**0**	**0**	**0**	**0.0**	**1**	**0**	**0**	**0**	**1**	....	....	....	....	....	....	....	....
	St. John's Maple Leafs	AHL	67	0	3	3	....	....	....	182	....	....	....	....	....	....	....	....	....	....	4	0	0	0	4	....	....	....
1998-99	St. John's Maple Leafs	AHL	55	1	4	5	....	....	....	130	....	....	....	....	....	....	....	....	....	....	....	....	....	....	....	....	....	....
	Florida Panthers	**NHL**	**6**	**0**	**1**	**1**	**0**	**1**	**1**	**6**	**0**	**0**	**0**	**1**	**0.0**	**3**	**0**	**11**	**2**	**–6**	....	....	....	....	....	....	....	....
	Beast of New Haven	AHL	20	0	1	1	....	....	....	26	....	....	....	....	....	....	....	....	....	....	....	....	....	....	....	....	....	....
99-2000	Louisville Panthers	AHL	51	0	10	10	....	....	....	128	....	....	....	....	....	....	....	....	....	....	4	0	0	0	4	....	....	....
	NHL Totals		**21**	**0**	**1**	**1**	**0**	**1**	**1**	**12**	**0**	**0**	**0**	**5**	**0.0**	**9**	**0**	**14**	**2**		....	....	....	....	....	....	....	....

Traded to **Florida** by **Toronto** for David Nemirovsky, February 17, 1999.

• WARE, Michael

"Iron Mike" RW – R. 6'5", 216 lbs. b: York, Ont., 3/22/1967. Edmonton's 3rd, 62nd overall, in 1985.

Season	Club	League	GP	G	A	Pts	AG	AA	APts	PIM	PP	SH	GW	S	%	TGF	PGF	TGA	PGA	+/–	GP	G	A	Pts	PIM	PP	SH	GW
1983-84	Mississauga Reps	MTHL	30	14	20	34	....	....	....	50	....	....	....	....	....	....	....	....	....	....	....	....	....	....	....	....	....	....
1984-85	Hamilton Steelhawks	OHL	57	4	14	18	....	....	....	225	....	....	....	....	....	....	....	....	....	....	12	0	1	1	29	....	....	....
1985-86	Hamilton Steelhawks	OHL	44	8	11	19	....	....	....	155	....	....	....	....	....	....	....	....	....	....	....	....	....	....	....	....	....	....
1986-87	Cornwall Royals	OHL	50	5	19	24	....	....	....	173	....	....	....	....	....	....	....	....	....	....	5	0	1	1	10	....	....	....
1987-88	Nova Scotia Oilers	AHL	52	0	8	8	....	....	....	253	....	....	....	....	....	....	....	....	....	....	3	0	0	0	16	....	....	....
1988-89	**Edmonton Oilers**	**NHL**	**2**	**0**	**1**	**1**	**0**	**1**	**1**	**11**	**0**	**0**	**0**	**0**	**0.0**	**1**	**0**	**0**	**0**	**1**	....	....	....	....	....	....	....	....
	Cape Breton Oilers	AHL	48	1	11	12	....	....	....	317	....	....	....	....	....	....	....	....	....	....	....	....	....	....	....	....	....	....
1989-90	**Edmonton Oilers**	**NHL**	**3**	**0**	**0**	**0**	**0**	**0**	**0**	**4**	**0**	**0**	**0**	**1**	**0.0**	**0**	**0**	**1**	**0**	**–1**	....	....	....	....	....	....	....	....
	Cape Breton Oilers	AHL	54	6	13	19	....	....	....	191	....	....	....	....	....	....	....	....	....	....	6	0	3	3	29	....	....	....
1990-91	Cape Breton Oilers	AHL	43	4	8	12	....	....	....	176	....	....	....	....	....	....	....	....	....	....	3	0	0	0	4	....	....	....
1991-92			DID NOT PLAY																									
1992-93	Murrayfield Racers	Britain	33	26	34	60	....	....	....	218	....	....	....	....	....	....	....	....	....	....	7	10	7	17	24	....	....	....
1993-94	Murrayfield Racers	BH-Cup	11	7	4	11	....	....	....	50	....	....	....	....	....	....	....	....	....	....	....	....	....	....	....	....	....	....
	Murrayfield Racers	Britain	43	30	41	71	....	....	....	162	....	....	....	....	....	....	....	....	....	....	6	5	5	10	16	....	....	....
1994-95	Edinburgh Racers	BH-Cup	8	9	5	14	....	....	....	76	....	....	....	....	....	....	....	....	....	....	....	....	....	....	....	....	....	....
	Edinburgh Racers	Britain	40	38	41	79	....	....	....	218	....	....	....	....	....	....	....	....	....	....	6	8	6	14	6	....	....	....
1995-96	Cardiff Devils	BH-Cup	9	4	5	9	....	....	....	58	....	....	....	....	....	....	....	....	....	....	....	....	....	....	....	....	....	....
	Cardiff Devils	Britain	32	16	30	46	....	....	....	169	....	....	....	....	....	....	....	....	....	....	6	0	1	1	37	....	....	....
1996-97	Cardiff Devils	BH-Cup	8	1	3	4	....	....	....	49	....	....	....	....	....	....	....	....	....	....	....	....	....	....	....	....	....	....
	Cardiff Devils	Britain	38	6	12	18	....	....	....	79	....	....	....	....	....	....	....	....	....	....	5	0	1	1	29	....	....	....
1997-98	Sheffield Steelers	BH-Cup	11	0	3	3	....	....	....	10	....	....	....	....	....	....	....	....	....	....	....	....	....	....	....	....	....	....
	Sheffield Steelers	Britain	43	6	8	14	....	....	....	96	....	....	....	....	....	....	....	....	....	....	9	2	0	2	4	....	....	....

										REGULAR SEASON											PLAYOFFS							
Season	Club	League	GP	G	A	Pts	AG	AA	APts	PIM	PP	SH	GW	S	%	TGF	PGF	TGA	PGA	+/–	GP	G	A	Pts	PIM	PP	SH	GW
1998-99	Hannover Scorpions	Germany	44	4	2	6	....	....	....	103	....	....	....	....	....	....	....	....	....	....	....	....	....	....	....	....	....	....
99-2000	London Knights	BH-Cup	9	1	1	2	....	....	....	64	....	....	....	....	....	....	....	....	....	....	....	....	....	....	....	....	....	....
	London Knights	Britain	22	5	2	7	....	....	....	70	....	....	....	....	....	....	....	....	....	....	8	0	1	1	8	....	....	....
	NHL Totals		**5**	**0**	**1**	**1**	**0**	**1**	**1**	**15**	**0**	**0**	**0**	**1**	**0.0**	**1**	**0**	**1**	**0**		....	....	....	....	....	....	....	....

• Played w/ RHI's Florida Hammerheads in 1994 (5-1-3-4-10).

• WARNER, Bob

Robert Norman D – L. 5'11", 180 lbs. b: Grimsby, Ont., 12/13/1950.

Season	Club	League	GP	G	A	Pts	AG	AA	APts	PIM	PP	SH	GW	S	%	TGF	PGF	TGA	PGA	+/–	GP	G	A	Pts	PIM	PP	SH	GW
1969-70	Ottawa M&W Rangers	OJHL	STATISTICS NOT AVAILABLE																									
	Ottawa 67's	OHA-Jr.	7	0	0	0	....	....	....	2	....	....	....	....	....	....	....	....	....	....	....	....	....	....	....	....	....	....
	Ottawa M&W Rangers	Cen-Cup	5	0	2	2	....	....	....	12	....	....	....	....	....	....	....	....	....	....	....	....	....	....	....	....	....	....
1970-71	Johnstown Jets	IHL	71	20	24	44	....	....	....	139	....	....	....	....	....	....	....	....	....	....	10	5	5	10	18	....	....	....
1971-72	St. Mary's University	AUAA	18	5	10	15	....	....	....	33	....	....	....	....	....	....	....	....	....	....	....	....	....	....	....	....	....	....
1972-73	St. Mary's University	AUAA	21	6	15	21	....	....	....	66	....	....	....	....	....	....	....	....	....	....	....	....	....	....	....	....	....	....
1973-74	St. Mary's University	AUAA	17	4	11	15	....	....	....	15	....	....	....	....	....	....	....	....	....	....	....	....	....	....	....	....	....	....
1974-75	St. Mary's University	AUAA	18	4	19	23	....	....	....	48	....	....	....	....	....	....	....	....	....	....	....	....	....	....	....	....	....	....
1975-76	Oklahoma City Blazers	CHL	74	7	20	27	....	....	....	117	....	....	....	....	....	....	....	....	....	....	4	1	0	1	9	....	....	....
	Toronto Maple Leafs	**NHL**	....	....	....	....	....	....	....	....	....	....	....	....	....	....	....	....	....	....	**2**	**0**	**0**	**0**	**0**	**0**	**0**	**0**
1976-77	**Toronto Maple Leafs**	**NHL**	**10**	**1**	**1**	**2**	**1**	**1**	**2**	**4**	**0**	**0**	**0**	**9**	**11.1**	**5**	**0**	**1**	**0**	**4**	**2**	**0**	**0**	**0**	**0**	**0**	**0**	**0**
	Dallas Black Hawks	CHL	69	26	19	45	....	....	....	75	....	....	....	....	....	....	....	....	....	....	5	2	0	2	0	....	....	....
1977-78	Dallas Black Hawks	CHL	61	5	14	19	....	....	....	62	....	....	....	....	....	....	....	....	....	....	13	2	2	4	18	....	....	....
1978-79	New Brunswick Hawks	AHL	80	10	14	24	....	....	....	52	....	....	....	....	....	....	....	....	....	....	5	0	0	0	2	....	....	....
1979-80	New Brunswick Hawks	AHL	61	8	6	14	....	....	....	35	....	....	....	....	....	....	....	....	....	....	4	0	0	0	2	....	....	....
1980-81			OUT OF HOCKEY – RETIRED																									
1981-82	Cap Pele Capitals	NBSHL	....	....	....	....	....	....	....	....	....	....	....	....	....	....	....	....	....	....	17	6	16	22	....	....	....	....
	NHL Totals		**10**	**1**	**1**	**2**	**1**	**1**	**2**	**4**	**0**	**0**	**0**	**9**	**11.1**	**5**	**0**	**1**	**0**		**4**	**0**	**0**	**0**	**0**	**0**	**0**	**0**

AUAA First All-Star Team (1973, 1974)

Signed as a free agent by **Toronto**, September 3, 1975.

• WARNER, Jim

James Francis RW – R. 5'11", 180 lbs. b: Minneapolis, MN, 3/26/1954. NY Rangers' 23rd, 245th overall, in 1974.

Season	Club	League	GP	G	A	Pts	AG	AA	APts	PIM	PP	SH	GW	S	%	TGF	PGF	TGA	PGA	+/–	GP	G	A	Pts	PIM	PP	SH	GW
1972-73	Minnesota Jr. North Stars	MWJHL	56	21	17	38	....	....	....	22	....	....	....	....	....	....	....	....	....	....	....	....	....	....	....	....	....	....
1973-74	Minnesota Jr. North Stars	MWJHL	56	55	50	105	....	....	....	47	....	....	....	....	....	....	....	....	....	....	....	....	....	....	....	....	....	....
	United States	WJC-A	5	3	1	4	....	....	....	2	....	....	....	....	....	....	....	....	....	....	....	....	....	....	....	....	....	....
1974-75	Colorado College	WCHA	37	30	25	55	....	....	....	24	....	....	....	....	....	....	....	....	....	....	....	....	....	....	....	....	....	....
	United States	WEC-A	10	1	4	5	....	....	....	8	....	....	....	....	....	....	....	....	....	....	....	....	....	....	....	....	....	....
1975-76	Colorado College	WCHA	35	16	20	36	....	....	....	59	....	....	....	....	....	....	....	....	....	....	....	....	....	....	....	....	....	....
	United States	WEC-A	10	2	2	4	....	....	....	12	....	....	....	....	....	....	....	....	....	....	....	....	....	....	....	....	....	....
1976-77	Colorado College	WCHA	30	16	23	39	....	....	....	36	....	....	....	....	....	....	....	....	....	....	....	....	....	....	....	....	....	....
1977-78	Colorado College	WCHA	38	27	41	68	....	....	....	50	....	....	....	....	....	....	....	....	....	....	....	....	....	....	....	....	....	....
	United States	WEC-A	10	2	5	7	....	....	....	2	....	....	....	....	....	....	....	....	....	....	....	....	....	....	....	....	....	....
1978-79	New England Whalers	WHA	41	6	9	15	....	....	....	20	....	....	....	....	....	....	....	....	....	....	1	0	0	0	0	....	....	....
	Springfield Indians	AHL	40	17	7	24	....	....	....	15	....	....	....	....	....	....	....	....	....	....	....	....	....	....	....	....	....	....
1979-80	**Hartford Whalers**	**NHL**	**32**	**0**	**3**	**3**	**0**	**2**	**2**	**10**	**0**	**0**	**0**	**26**	**0.0**	**6**	**0**	**26**	**14**	**–6**	....	....	....	....	....	....	....	....
	Springfield Indians	AHL	45	14	19	33	....	....	....	22	....	....	....	....	....	....	....	....	....	....	....	....	....	....	....	....	....	....
	NHL Totals		**32**	**0**	**3**	**3**	**0**	**2**	**2**	**10**	**0**	**0**	**0**	**26**	**0.0**	**6**	**0**	**26**	**14**		....	....	....	....	....	....	....	....
	Other Major League Totals		41	6	9	15	....	....	....	20	....	....	....	....	....	....	....	....	....	....	1	0	0	0	0	....	....	....

WCHA Second All-Star Team (1975)

Signed as a free agent by **New England** (WHA), June, 1978. Rights retained by **Hartford** prior to Expansion Draft, June 9, 1979.

• WARRENER, Rhett

Rhett Adam D – R. 6'1", 209 lbs. b: Shaunavon, Sask., 1/27/1976. Florida's 2nd, 27th overall, in 1994.

Season	Club	League	GP	G	A	Pts	AG	AA	APts	PIM	PP	SH	GW	S	%	TGF	PGF	TGA	PGA	+/–	GP	G	A	Pts	PIM	PP	SH	GW
1991-92	Saskatoon Blazers	AAHA	33	6	5	11	....	....	....	71	....	....	....	....	....	....	....	....	....	....	....	....	....	....	....	....	....	....
	Saskatoon Blades	WHL	2	0	0	0	....	....	....	0	....	....	....	....	....	....	....	....	....	....	....	....	....	....	....	....	....	....
1992-93	Saskatoon Blades	WHL	68	2	17	19	....	....	....	100	....	....	....	....	....	....	....	....	....	....	9	0	0	0	14	....	....	....
1993-94	Saskatoon Blades	WHL	61	7	19	26	....	....	....	131	....	....	....	....	....	....	....	....	....	....	16	0	5	5	33	....	....	....
1994-95	Saskatoon Blades	WHL	66	13	26	39	....	....	....	137	....	....	....	....	....	....	....	....	....	....	10	0	3	3	6	....	....	....
1995-96	**Florida Panthers**	**NHL**	**28**	**0**	**3**	**3**	**0**	**2**	**2**	**46**	**0**	**0**	**0**	**19**	**0.0**	**16**	**0**	**16**	**4**	**4**	**21**	**0**	**1**	**1**	**0**	**0**	**0**	**0**
	Canada	WJC-A	6	0	0	0	....	....	....	4	....	....	....	....	....	....	....	....	....	....	....	....	....	....	....	....	....	....
	Carolina Monarchs	AHL	9	0	0	0	....	....	....	4	....	....	....	....	....	....	....	....	....	....	....	....	....	....	....	....	....	....
1996-97	**Florida Panthers**	**NHL**	**62**	**4**	**9**	**13**	**4**	**8**	**12**	**88**	**1**	**0**	**1**	**58**	**6.9**	**52**	**5**	**42**	**15**	**20**	**5**	**0**	**0**	**0**	**0**	**0**	**0**	**0**
1997-98	**Florida Panthers**	**NHL**	**79**	**0**	**4**	**4**	**0**	**4**	**4**	**99**	**0**	**0**	**0**	**66**	**0.0**	**33**	**1**	**77**	**29**	**–16**	....	....	....	....	....	....	....	....
1998-99	**Florida Panthers**	**NHL**	**48**	**0**	**7**	**7**	**0**	**7**	**7**	**64**	**0**	**0**	**0**	**33**	**0.0**	**32**	**4**	**44**	**15**	**–1**	....	....	....	....	....	....	....	....
	Buffalo Sabres	**NHL**	**13**	**1**	**0**	**1**	**1**	**0**	**1**	**20**	**0**	**0**	**0**	**11**	**9.1**	**8**	**0**	**7**	**2**	**3**	**20**	**1**	**3**	**4**	**32**	**0**	**0**	**0**
99-2000	**Buffalo Sabres**	**NHL**	**61**	**0**	**3**	**3**	**0**	**3**	**3**	**89**	**0**	**0**	**0**	**68**	**0.0**	**44**	**0**	**49**	**23**	**18**	**5**	**0**	**0**	**0**	**2**	**0**	**0**	**0**
	NHL Totals		**291**	**5**	**26**	**31**	**5**	**24**	**29**	**406**	**1**	**0**	**1**	**255**	**2.0**	**185**	**10**	**235**	**88**		**51**	**1**	**4**	**5**	**34**	**0**	**0**	**0**

Traded to **Buffalo** by **Florida** with Florida's 5th round choice (Ryan Miller) in 1999 Entry Draft for Mike Wilson, March 23, 1999.

• WARRINER, Todd

LW – L. 6'1", 200 lbs. b: Blenheim, Ont., 1/3/1974. Quebec's 1st, 4th overall, in 1992.

Season	Club	League	GP	G	A	Pts	AG	AA	APts	PIM	PP	SH	GW	S	%	TGF	PGF	TGA	PGA	+/–	GP	G	A	Pts	PIM	PP	SH	GW
1988-89	Blenheim Blades	OJHL-C	10	1	4	5	....	....	....	0	....	....	....	....	....	....	....	....	....	....	....	....	....	....	....	....	....	....
1989-90	Chatham Maroons	OJHL-B	40	24	21	45	....	....	....	12	....	....	....	....	....	....	....	....	....	....	....	....	....	....	....	....	....	....
1990-91	Windsor Spitfires	OHL	57	36	28	64	....	....	....	26	....	....	....	....	....	....	....	....	....	....	11	5	6	11	12	....	....	....
1991-92	Windsor Spitfires	OHL	50	41	41	82	....	....	....	64	....	....	....	....	....	....	....	....	....	....	7	5	4	9	6	....	....	....
1992-93	Windsor Spitfires	OHL	23	13	21	34	....	....	....	29	....	....	....	....	....	....	....	....	....	....	....	....	....	....	....	....	....	....
	Kitchener Rangers	OHL	32	19	24	43	....	....	....	35	....	....	....	....	....	....	....	....	....	....	7	5	14	19	14	....	....	....
1993-94	Canada	Nat-Team	50	11	20	31	....	....	....	33	....	....	....	....	....	....	....	....	....	....	....	....	....	....	....	....	....	....
	Canada	Olympics	4	1	1	2	....	....	....	0	....	....	....	....	....	....	....	....	....	....	....	....	....	....	....	....	....	....
	Kitchener Rangers	OHL	....	....	....	....	....	....	....	....	....	....	....	....	....	....	....	....	....	....	1	0	1	1	0	....	....	....
	Cornwall Aces	AHL	....	....	....	....	....	....	....	....	....	....	....	....	....	....	....	....	....	....	10	1	4	5	4	....	....	....
1994-95	St. John's Maple Leafs	AHL	46	8	10	18	....	....	....	22	....	....	....	....	....	....	....	....	....	....	4	1	0	1	2	....	....	....
	Toronto Maple Leafs	**NHL**	**5**	**0**	**0**	**0**	**0**	**0**	**0**	**0**	**0**	**0**	**0**	**1**	**0.0**	**0**	**0**	**3**	**0**	**–3**	....	....	....	....	....	....	....	....
1995-96	**Toronto Maple Leafs**	**NHL**	**57**	**7**	**8**	**15**	**7**	**7**	**14**	**26**	**1**	**0**	**0**	**79**	**8.9**	**27**	**7**	**31**	**0**	**–11**	**6**	**1**	**1**	**2**	**2**	**0**	**0**	**0**
	St. John's Maple Leafs	AHL	11	5	6	11	....	....	....	16	....	....	....	....	....	....	....	....	....	....	....	....	....	....	....	....	....	....
1996-97	**Toronto Maple Leafs**	**NHL**	**75**	**12**	**21**	**33**	**13**	**19**	**32**	**41**	**2**	**2**	**0**	**146**	**8.2**	**57**	**14**	**58**	**12**	**–3**	....	....	....	....	....	....	....	....
1997-98	**Toronto Maple Leafs**	**NHL**	**45**	**5**	**8**	**13**	**6**	**8**	**14**	**20**	**0**	**0**	**1**	**73**	**6.8**	**21**	**0**	**24**	**8**	**5**	....	....	....	....	....	....	....	....
1998-99	**Toronto Maple Leafs**	**NHL**	**53**	**9**	**10**	**19**	**11**	**10**	**21**	**28**	**1**	**0**	**1**	**96**	**9.4**	**24**	**4**	**37**	**11**	**–6**	**9**	**0**	**0**	**0**	**2**	**0**	**0**	**0**
99-2000	**Toronto Maple Leafs**	**NHL**	**18**	**3**	**1**	**4**	**3**	**1**	**4**	**2**	**0**	**0**	**0**	**33**	**9.1**	**8**	**0**	**4**	**2**	**6**	....	....	....	....	....	....	....	....
	Tampa Bay Lightning	**NHL**	**55**	**11**	**13**	**24**	**12**	**12**	**24**	**34**	**3**	**1**	**0**	**100**	**11.0**	**30**	**8**	**51**	**15**	**–14**	....	....	....	....	....	....	....	....
	NHL Totals		**308**	**47**	**61**	**108**	**52**	**57**	**109**	**151**	**7**	**3**	**2**	**528**	**8.9**	**167**	**33**	**208**	**48**		**15**	**1**	**1**	**2**	**4**	**0**	**0**	**0**

OHL First All-Star Team (1992)

Traded to **Toronto** by **Quebec** with Mats Sundin, Garth Butcher and Philadelphia's 1st round choice (previously acquired by Quebec — later traded to Washington — Washington selected Nolan Baumgartner) in 1994 Entry Draft for Wendel Clark, Sylvain Lefebvre, Landon Wilson and Toronto's 1st round choice (Jeffrey Kealty) in 1994 Entry Draft, June 28, 1994. Traded to **Tampa Bay** by **Toronto** for Tampa Bay's 3rd round choice (Mikael Tellqvist) in 2000 Entry Draft, November 29, 1999.

• WASHBURN, Steve

C – L. 6'2", 198 lbs. b: Ottawa, Ont., 4/10/1975. Florida's 5th, 78th overall, in 1993.

Season	Club	League	GP	G	A	Pts	AG	AA	APts	PIM	PP	SH	GW	S	%	TGF	PGF	TGA	PGA	+/–	GP	G	A	Pts	PIM	PP	SH	GW
1990-91	Gloucester Rangers	OJHL	56	21	30	51	....	....	....	47	....	....	....	....	....	....	....	....	....	....	....	....	....	....	....	....	....	....
1991-92	Ottawa 67's	OHL	59	5	17	22	....	....	....	10	....	....	....	....	....	....	....	....	....	....	11	2	3	5	4	....	....	....
1992-93	Ottawa 67's	OHL	66	20	38	58	....	....	....	54	....	....	....	....	....	....	....	....	....	....	....	....	....	....	....	....	....	....
1993-94	Ottawa 67's	OHL	65	30	50	80	....	....	....	88	....	....	....	....	....	....	....	....	....	....	17	7	16	23	10	....	....	....

Season	Club	League	GP	G	A	Pts	AG	AA	APts	PIM	PP	SH	GW	S	%	TGF	PGF	TGA	PGA	+/–	GP	G	A	Pts	PIM	PP	SH	GW
			REGULAR SEASON																		PLAYOFFS							
1994-95	Ottawa 67's	OHL	63	43	63	106				72																		
	Cincinnati Cyclones	IHL	6	3	1	4				0											9	1	3	4	4			
1995-96	**Florida Panthers**	**NHL**	1	0	1	1	0	1	1	0	0	0	0	1	0.0	1	0	0	0	1	1	0	1	1	0	0	0	0
	Carolina Monarchs	AHL	78	29	54	83				45																		
1996-97	**Florida Panthers**	**NHL**	18	3	6	9	3	5	8	4	1	0	0	21	14.3	14	2	10	0	2								
	Carolina Monarchs	AHL	60	23	40	63				66																		
1997-98	**Florida Panthers**	**NHL**	58	11	8	19	13	8	21	32	4	0	2	61	18.0	30	9	31	4	–6								
	Beast of New Haven	AHL	6	3	5	8				4											3	2	0	2	15			
1998-99	**Florida Panthers**	**NHL**	4	0	0	0	0	0	0	4	0	0	0	0	0.0	0	0	1	0	–1								
	Beast of New Haven	AHL	10	4	3	7				6																		
	Vancouver Canucks	**NHL**	8	0	0	0	0	0	0	2	0	0	0	6	0.0	0	0	0	0	0								
	Syracuse Crunch	AHL	13	1	6	7				6																		
99-2000	Milwaukee Admirals	IHL	12	0	4	4				16																		
	Philadelphia Flyers	**NHL**	1	0	0	0	0	0	0	0	0	0	0	1	0.0	0	0	0	0	0								
	Philadelphia Phantoms	AHL	61	19	52	71				93											5	0	2	2	8			
	NHL Totals		**90**	**14**	**15**	**29**	**16**	**14**	**30**	**42**	**5**	**0**	**2**	**90**	**15.6**	**45**	**11**	**42**	**4**		**1**	**0**	**1**	**1**	**0**	**0**	**0**	**0**

Claimed on waivers by **Vancouver** from **Florida**, February 18, 1999. Signed as a free agent by **Nashville**, August 11, 1999. Traded to **Philadelphia** by **Nashville** for a conditional choice in 2001 Entry Draft, November 16, 1999.

• WATSON, Bill

William Charles RW – R. 6′, 185 lbs. b: Pine Falls, Man., 3/30/1964. Chicago's 4th, 70th overall, in 1982.

Season	Club	League	GP	G	A	Pts	AG	AA	APts	PIM	PP	SH	GW	S	%	TGF	PGF	TGA	PGA	+/–	GP	G	A	Pts	PIM	PP	SH	GW
1980-81	Prince Albert Raiders	SJHL	54	30	39	69				27																		
	Prince Albert Raiders	Cen-Cup	STATISTICS NOT AVAILABLE																									
1981-82	Prince Albert Raiders	SJHL	47	43	41	84				37																		
	Prince Albert Raiders	Cen-Cup	STATISTICS NOT AVAILABLE																									
1982-83	University of Minnesota-Duluth	WCHA	22	5	10	15				10																		
1983-84	University of Minnesota-Duluth	WCHA	40	35	51	86				12																		
1984-85	University of Minnesota-Duluth	WCHA	42	46	54	100				46																		
1985-86	**Chicago Black Hawks**	**NHL**	52	8	16	24	6	11	17	2	2	0	0	67	11.9	36	9	31	0	–4	2	0	1	1	0	0	0	0
1986-87	**Chicago Blackhawks**	**NHL**	51	13	19	32	11	14	25	6	0	0	0	106	12.3	58	9	30	0	19	4	0	1	1	0	0	0	0
1987-88	**Chicago Blackhawks**	**NHL**	9	2	0	2	2	0	2	0	0	0	0	7	28.6	3	0	8	0	–5								
	Saginaw Hawks	IHL	35	15	20	35				10																		
1988-89	**Chicago Blackhawks**	**NHL**	3	0	1	1	0	1	1	4	0	0	0	2	0.0	1	1	0	0	0								
	Saginaw Hawks	IHL	42	26	24	50				18											3	1	0	1	2			
	NHL Totals		**115**	**23**	**36**	**59**	**19**	**26**	**45**	**12**	**2**	**0**	**0**	**182**	**12.6**	**98**	**19**	**69**	**0**		**6**	**0**	**2**	**2**	**0**	**0**	**0**	**0**

WCHA First All-Star Team (1984, 1985) • NCAA West First All-American Team (1984, 1985) • NCAA Championship All-Tournament Team (1985) • Won Hobey Baker Memorial Award (Top U.S. Collegiate Player) (1985)

• WATSON, Bryan

Bryan Joseph "Bugsy" D – R. 5′9″, 175 lbs. b: Bancroft, Ont., 11/14/1942.

Season	Club	League	GP	G	A	Pts	AG	AA	APts	PIM	PP	SH	GW	S	%	TGF	PGF	TGA	PGA	+/–	GP	G	A	Pts	PIM	PP	SH	GW
1960-61	Peterborough Petes	OHA-Jr.	18	0	1	1				4																		
1961-62	Peterborough Petes	OHA-Jr.	50	3	16	19				129																		
1962-63	Peterborough Petes	OHA-Jr.	49	9	22	31				80											6	0	3	3	10			
	Hull-Ottawa Canadiens	EPHL																			3	1	1	2	0			
1963-64	**Montreal Canadiens**	**NHL**	39	0	2	2	0	2	2	18											6	0	0	0	2	0	0	0
	Omaha Knights	CPHL	9	1	1	2				12																		
1964-65	**Montreal Canadiens**	**NHL**	5	0	1	1	0	1	1	7																		
	Quebec Aces	AHL	64	1	16	17				186											5	0	0	0	35			
1965-66	**Detroit Red Wings**	**NHL**	70	2	7	9	2	7	9	133											12	2	0	2	30	0	0	0
1966-67	**Detroit Red Wings**	**NHL**	48	0	1	1	0	1	1	66																		
	Memphis Wings	CPHL	16	1	3	4				76																		
1967-68	**Montreal Canadiens**	**NHL**	12	0	1	1	0	1	1	9	0	0	0	6	0.0	2	0	6	1	–3								
	Cleveland Barons	AHL	12	2	4	6				22																		
	Houston Apollos	CPHL	50	2	37	39				*293																		
1968-69	**Oakland Seals**	**NHL**	50	2	3	5	2	3	5	97	0	0	1	39	5.1	23	3	57	21	–16								
	Pittsburgh Penguins	**NHL**	18	0	4	4	0	4	4	35	0	0	0	34	0.0	11	2	25	5	–11								
1969-70	**Pittsburgh Penguins**	**NHL**	61	1	9	10	1	8	9	189	0	0	0	61	1.6	48	0	74	25	–1	10	0	0	0	17	0	0	0
	Baltimore Clippers	AHL	5	1	2	3				8																		
1970-71	**Pittsburgh Penguins**	**NHL**	43	2	6	8	2	5	7	119	0	0	0	48	4.2	27	0	47	15	–5								
1971-72	**Pittsburgh Penguins**	**NHL**	75	3	17	20	3	15	18	*212	0	0	1	106	2.8	77	3	95	26	5	4	0	0	0	21	0	0	0
1972-73	**Pittsburgh Penguins**	**NHL**	69	1	17	18	1	13	14	179	0	0	0	47	2.1	88	2	92	24	18								
1973-74	**Pittsburgh Penguins**	**NHL**	38	1	4	5	1	3	4	137	1	0	0	27	3.7	34	1	55	10	–12								
	St. Louis Blues	**NHL**	11	0	1	1	0	1	1	19	0	0	0	10	0.0	11	0	13	2	0								
	Detroit Red Wings	**NHL**	21	0	4	4	0	3	3	99	0	0	0	9	0.0	17	0	23	5	–1								
1974-75	**Detroit Red Wings**	**NHL**	70	1	13	14	1	10	11	238	0	1	0	68	1.5	65	2	122	30	–29								
1975-76	**Detroit Red Wings**	**NHL**	79	0	18	18	0	13	13	322	0	0	0	88	0.0	69	2	126	39	–20								
1976-77	**Detroit Red Wings**	**NHL**	14	0	1	1	0	1	1	39	0	0	0	4	0.0	12	0	17	7	2								
	Washington Capitals	**NHL**	56	1	14	15	1	11	12	91	0	0	0	54	1.9	49	1	76	23	–5								
1977-78	**Washington Capitals**	**NHL**	79	3	11	14	3	8	11	167	0	1	0	52	5.8	60	0	103	31	–12								
1978-79	**Washington Capitals**	**NHL**	20	0	1	1	0	1	1	36	0	0	0	16	0.0	10	0	21	4	–7								
	Cincinnati Stingers	WHA	21	0	2	2				56											3	0	1	1	2			
	NHL Totals		**878**	**17**	**135**	**152**	**17**	**111**	**128**	**2212**											**32**	**2**	**0**	**2**	**70**			
	Other Major League Totals		21	0	2	2				56											3	0	1	1	2			

CPHL First All-Star Team (1968) • Named Top Defenseman - CPHL (1968) • Won Tommy Ivan Trophy (MVP - CPHL) (1968)

Traded to **Chicago** by **Montreal** for Don Johns, June 8, 1965. Claimed by **Detroit** from **Chicago** in Intra-League Draft, June 9, 1965. Claimed by **Minnesota** from **Detroit** in Expansion Draft, June 6, 1967. Traded to **Montreal** by **Minnesota** for Bill Plager and the rights to Leo Thiffault and Barrie Meissner, June 6, 1967. Traded to **Oakland** by **Montreal** with cash for Oakland's 1st round choice (Michel Larocque) in 1972 Amateur Draft and future considerations (Tom Thurlby, September, 1968), June 28, 1968. Traded to **Pittsburgh** by **Oakland** with George Swarbrick and Tracy Pratt for Earl Ingarfield, Gene Ubriaco and Dick Mattiussi, January 30, 1969. Selected by **LA Sharks** (WHA) in 1972 WHA General Player Draft, February 12, 1972. Traded to **St. Louis** by **Pittsburgh** with Greg Polis and Pittsburgh's 2nd round choice (Bob Hess) in 1974 Amateur Draft for Steve Durbano, Ab DeMarco Jr. and Bob Kelly, January 17, 1974. Traded to **Detroit** by **St. Louis** with Chris Evans and Jean Hamel for Ted Harris, Bill Collins and Garnet Bailey, February 14, 1974. Traded to **Washington** by **Detroit** for Greg Joly, November 30, 1976. Signed as a free agent by **Cincinnati** (WHA) following release by **Washington**, March 2, 1979. Claimed by **Edmonton** from **Cincinnati** (WHA) in WHA Dispersal Draft, June 9, 1979.

• WATSON, Dave

David Gerald LW – L. 6′2″, 190 lbs. b: Kirkland Lake, Ont., 5/19/1958. Colorado's 4th, 58th overall, in 1978.

Season	Club	League	GP	G	A	Pts	AG	AA	APts	PIM	PP	SH	GW	S	%	TGF	PGF	TGA	PGA	+/–	GP	G	A	Pts	PIM	PP	SH	GW
1976-77	Sudbury Wolves	OMJHL	39	12	13	25				34																		
	Sault Ste. Marie Greyhounds	OMJHL	26	11	9	20				18											6	0	3	3	6			
1977-78	Sault Ste. Marie Greyhounds	OMJHL	65	21	30	51				112											13	5	3	8	8			
1978-79	**Colorado Rockies**	**NHL**	DID NOT PLAY – INJURED																									
1979-80	**Colorado Rockies**	**NHL**	5	0	0	0	0	0	0	2	0	0	0	1	0.0	1	0	2	0	–1								
	Fort Worth Texans	CHL	68	19	22	41				124											14	4	6	10	14			
1980-81	**Colorado Rockies**	**NHL**	13	0	1	1	0	1	1	8	0	0	0	6	0.0	2	1	3	0	–2								
	Fort Worth Texans	CHL	50	16	20	36				115																		
1981-82	Fort Worth Texans	CHL	68	15	14	29				107																		
1982-83	Carolina Thunderbirds	ACHL	66	53	49	*102				101											8	6	8	*14	28			
1983-84	Carolina Thunderbirds	ACHL	29	17	16	33				56											10	4	4	8	13			
1984-85	Carolina Thunderbirds	ACHL	64	31	54	85				138											10	3	*14	17	26			
1985-86	Carolina Thunderbirds	ACHL	9	3	3	6				21																		
	NHL Totals		**18**	**0**	**1**	**1**	**0**	**1**	**1**	**10**	**0**	**0**	**0**	**7**	**0.0**	**3**	**1**	**5**	**0**									

ACHL First All-Star Team (1983)

• Missed entire 1978-79 season recovering from knee injury suffered in training camp, September, 1978.

• WATSON, Jim

James Arthur "Watty" D – L. 6'2", 186 lbs. b: Malartic, Que., 6/28/1943.

Season	Club	League	REGULAR SEASON GP	G	A	Pts	AG	AA	APts	PIM	PP	SH	GW	S	%	TGF	PGF	TGA	PGA	+/-	PLAYOFFS GP	G	A	Pts	PIM	PP	SH	GW
1961-62	Hamilton Red Wings	OHA-Jr.	5	0	0	0				4																		
1962-63	Hamilton Red Wings	OHA-Jr.	15	0	0	0				25																		
1963-64	Detroit Red Wings	NHL	1	0	0	0	0	0	0	0																		
	Cincinnati Wings	CPHL	61	2	5	7				36																		
1964-65	Detroit Red Wings	NHL	1	0	0	0	0	0	0	2																		
	Pittsburgh Hornets	AHL	61	2	16	18				53																		
1965-66	Detroit Red Wings	NHL	2	0	0	0	0	0	0	4																		
	Memphis Wings	CPHL	69	4	11	15				126																		
1966-67	San Diego Gulls	WHL	72	4	19	23				*158																		
1967-68	Detroit Red Wings	NHL	61	0	3	3	0	3	3	87	0	0	0	55	0.0	34	0	57	3	–20								
1968-69	Detroit Red Wings	NHL	8	0	1	1	0	1	1	4	0	0	0	5	0.0	3	0	6	0	–3								
	Baltimore Clippers	AHL	25	2	8	10				58																		
	Fort Worth Wings	CHL	21	1	8	9				54																		
1969-70	Detroit Red Wings	NHL	4	0	0	0	0	0	0	0	0	0	0	6	0.0	0	0	0	0	0								
	Cleveland Barons	AHL	59	7	19	26				128																		
1970-71	Buffalo Sabres	NHL	78	2	9	11	2	7	9	147	0	0	0	114	1.8	75	3	122	22	–28								
1971-72	Buffalo Sabres	NHL	66	2	6	8	2	5	7	101	1	0	0	78	2.6	39	1	91	20	–33								
1972-73	Los Angeles Sharks	WHA	75	5	15	20				123											4	0	1	1	2			
1973-74	Los Angeles Sharks	WHA	48	0	6	6				28																		
	Greensboro Generals	SHL	2	0	1	1				0																		
	Chicago Cougars	WHA	23	0	5	5				22											18	2	3	5	18			
1974-75	Chicago Cougars	WHA	57	3	6	9				31																		
	Long Island Cougars	NAHL	4	0	1	1				6																		
1975-76	Quebec Nordiques	WHA	28	0	1	1				24																		
	NHL Totals		221	4	19	23	4	16	20	345																		
	Other Major League Totals		231	8	33	41				228											22	2	4	6	20			

Claimed by **Buffalo** from **Detroit** in Expansion Draft, June 10, 1970. Selected by **LA Sharks** (WHA) in 1972 WHA General Player Draft, February 12, 1972. Traded to **Chicago Cougars** (WHA) by **LA Sharks** (WHA) with Don Gordon for Bob Whitlock, February, 1974. Claimed by **Quebec** (WHA) from **Chicago** (WHA) in WHA Dispersal Draft, May 19, 1975.

• WATSON, Jimmy

James Charles D – L. 6', 195 lbs. b: Smithers, B.C., 8/19/1952. Philadelphia's 3rd, 39th overall, in 1972.

Season	Club	League	REGULAR SEASON GP	G	A	Pts	AG	AA	APts	PIM	PP	SH	GW	S	%	TGF	PGF	TGA	PGA	+/-	PLAYOFFS GP	G	A	Pts	PIM	PP	SH	GW
1968-69	Calgary Centennials	WCJHL	52	2	15	17				26											11	1	4	5	0			
1969-70	Calgary Centennials	WCJHL	35	3	15	18				18																		
1970-71	Calgary Centennials	WCJHL	64	9	35	44				118											11	3	7	10	8			
1971-72	Calgary Centennials	WCJHL	66	13	52	65				50											13	3	9	12	6			
1972-73	Philadelphia Flyers	NHL	4	0	1	1	0	1	1	5	0	0	0	4	0.0	3	3	1	0	–1	2	0	0	0	0	0	0	0
	Richmond Robins	AHL	73	5	33	38				83											4	1	2	3	6			
1973-74♦	Philadelphia Flyers	NHL	78	2	18	20	2	15	17	44	1	0	1	113	1.8	90	16	60	19	33	17	1	2	3	41	1	0	0
1974-75♦	Philadelphia Flyers	NHL	68	7	18	25	6	13	19	72	1	0	2	113	6.2	83	10	61	29	41	17	1	8	9	10	0	0	0
1975-76	Philadelphia Flyers	NHL	79	2	34	36	2	25	27	66	0	0	0	89	2.2	119	7	93	46	65	16	1	8	9	6	0	0	0
1976-77	Canada	Can-Cup	2	0	0	0				2																		
	Philadelphia Flyers	NHL	71	3	23	26	3	18	21	35	0	0	0	72	4.2	88	4	70	20	34	10	1	2	3	2	0	0	1
1977-78	Philadelphia Flyers	NHL	71	5	12	17	5	9	14	62	0	0	0	112	4.5	75	0	68	26	33	12	1	7	8	6	0	0	0
1978-79	Philadelphia Flyers	NHL	77	9	13	22	8	9	17	52	0	2	0	112	8.0	73	2	91	31	11	8	0	2	2	2	0	0	0
1979-80	Philadelphia Flyers	NHL	71	5	18	23	4	13	17	51	0	1	1	99	5.1	97	0	81	37	53	15	0	4	4	20	0	0	0
1980-81	Philadelphia Flyers	NHL	18	2	2	4	2	1	3	6	1	0	0	14	14.3	21	1	11	5	14								
1981-82	Philadelphia Flyers	NHL	76	3	9	12	2	6	8	99	0	0	1	67	4.5	74	4	87	29	12	4	0	1	1	2	0	0	0
	NHL Totals		613	38	148	186	34	110	144	492	3	3	5	795	4.8	723	47	623	242		101	5	34	39	89	1	0	1

• Brother of Joe • WCJHL All-Star Team (1972) • NHL Plus/Minus Leader (1980) • Played in NHL All-Star Game (1975, 1976, 1977, 1978, 1980)

• Missed majority of 1980-81 season recovering from back injury that required surgery, January, 1981.

• WATSON, Joe

Joseph John D – R. 5'10", 185 lbs. b: Smithers, B.C., 7/6/1943.

Season	Club	League	REGULAR SEASON GP	G	A	Pts	AG	AA	APts	PIM	PP	SH	GW	S	%	TGF	PGF	TGA	PGA	+/-	PLAYOFFS GP	G	A	Pts	PIM	PP	SH	GW
1961-62	Estevan Bruins	SJHL	49	6	10	16				22											10	1	3	4	4			
1962-63	Estevan Bruins	SJHL	53	5	24	29				74											11	2	10	12	14			
	Estevan Bruins	Mem-Cup	6	0	2	2				2																		
1963-64	Minneapolis Bruins	CPHL	71	0	20	20				55											5	0	0	0	2			
1964-65	Boston Bruins	NHL	4	0	1	1	0	1	1	0																		
	Minneapolis Bruins	CPHL	65	3	23	26				38											5	0	1	1	2			
1965-66	Oklahoma City Blazers	CPHL	69	8	24	32				58											9	1	3	4	6			
1966-67	Boston Bruins	NHL	69	2	13	15	2	13	15	38																		
1967-68	Philadelphia Flyers	NHL	73	5	14	19	6	14	20	56	1	0	1	91	5.5	80	6	95	33	12	7	1	1	2	28	0	0	0
1968-69	Philadelphia Flyers	NHL	60	2	8	10	2	7	9	14	0	0	0	82	2.4	49	1	86	17	–21	4	0	0	0	0	0	0	0
1969-70	Philadelphia Flyers	NHL	54	3	11	14	3	10	13	28	1	0	0	102	2.9	46	3	61	18	0								
1970-71	Philadelphia Flyers	NHL	57	3	7	10	3	6	9	50	0	0	0	61	4.9	43	1	39	6	9	1	0	0	0	0	0	0	0
1971-72	Philadelphia Flyers	NHL	65	3	7	10	3	6	9	38	0	0	1	110	2.7	39	0	76	20	–17								
1972-73	Philadelphia Flyers	NHL	63	2	24	26	2	19	21	46	0	0	1	72	2.8	87	8	77	28	30	11	0	2	2	12	0	0	0
1973-74♦	Philadelphia Flyers	NHL	74	1	17	18	1	14	15	34	0	0	0	75	1.3	73	2	54	11	28	17	1	4	5	24	0	0	0
1974-75♦	Philadelphia Flyers	NHL	80	6	17	23	5	13	18	42	0	0	0	115	5.2	92	6	84	40	42	17	0	4	4	6	0	0	0
1975-76	Philadelphia Flyers	NHL	78	2	22	24	2	16	18	28	0	0	2	88	2.3	96	2	73	35	56	16	1	1	2	10	0	0	0
1976-77	Philadelphia Flyers	NHL	77	4	26	30	4	20	24	39	0	0	1	101	4.0	87	1	82	25	29	10	0	0	0	2	0	0	0
1977-78	Philadelphia Flyers	NHL	65	5	9	14	5	7	12	22	0	0	1	68	7.4	57	0	47	13	23	1	0	0	0	0	0	0	0
1978-79	Colorado Rockies	NHL	16	0	2	2	0	1	1	12	0	0	0	20	0.0	13	1	30	5	–13								
	NHL Totals		835	38	178	216	38	147	185	447											84	3	12	15	82			

• Brother of Jimmy • CPHL First All-Star Team (1966) • Played in NHL All-Star Game (1974, 1977)

Claimed by **Philadelphia** from **Boston** in Expansion Draft, June 6, 1967. Traded to **Colorado** by **Philadelphia** for cash, August 31, 1978.

• WATT, Mike

LW – L. 6'2", 212 lbs. b: Seaforth, Ont., 3/31/1976. Edmonton's 3rd, 32nd overall, in 1994.

Season	Club	League	REGULAR SEASON GP	G	A	Pts	AG	AA	APts	PIM	PP	SH	GW	S	%	TGF	PGF	TGA	PGA	+/-	PLAYOFFS GP	G	A	Pts	PIM	PP	SH	GW
1990-91	Seaforth Centenaires	OJHL-D	39	15	23	38				43																		
1991-92	Stratford Cullitons	OJHL-B	40	5	21	26				103																		
1992-93	Stratford Cullitons	OJHL-B	45	20	35	55				100																		
1993-94	Stratford Cullitons	OJHL-B	48	34	34	68				165																		
1994-95	Michigan State Spartans	CCHA	39	12	6	18				64																		
1995-96	Michigan State Spartans	CCHA	37	17	22	39				60																		
	Canada	WJC-A	6	1	2	3				6																		
1996-97	Michigan State Spartans	CCHA	39	24	17	41				109																		
1997-98	Edmonton Oilers	NHL	14	1	2	3	1	2	3	4	0	0	1	14	7.1	6	3	7	0	–4								
	Hamilton Bulldogs	AHL	63	24	25	49				65											9	2	2	4	8			
1998-99	New York Islanders	NHL	75	8	17	25	9	16	25	12	0	0	4	75	10.7	31	2	39	8	–2								
99-2000	New York Islanders	NHL	45	5	6	11	6	6	12	17	0	1	0	49	10.2	15	0	33	10	–8								
	Lowell Lock Monsters	AHL	16	6	11	17				6											7	1	1	2	4			
	NHL Totals		134	14	25	39	16	24	40	33	0	1	5	138	10.1	52	5	79	18									

Traded to **NY Islanders** by **Edmonton** for Eric Fichaud, June 18, 1998. Claimed on waivers by **Nashville** from **NY Islanders**, May 23, 2000.

• WATTERS, Tim

Timothy John "Muddy" D – L. 5'11", 185 lbs. b: Kamloops, B.C., 7/25/1959. Winnipeg's 6th, 124th overall, in 1979.

Season	Club	League	REGULAR SEASON GP	G	A	Pts	AG	AA	APts	PIM	PP	SH	GW	S	%	TGF	PGF	TGA	PGA	+/-	PLAYOFFS GP	G	A	Pts	PIM	PP	SH	GW
1976-77	Kamloops Braves	BCJHL	60	10	38	48																						
	Kamloops Chiefs	WCJHL	15	3	0	3				29											2	0	0	0	0			
1977-78	Michigan Tech Huskies	WCHA	37	1	15	16				47																		

Season	Club	League	GP	G	A	Pts	AG	AA	APts	PIM	PP	SH	GW	S	%	TGF	PGF	TGA	PGA	+/-	GP	G	A	Pts	PIM	PP	SH	GW
			REGULAR SEASON																		PLAYOFFS							
1978-79	Michigan Tech Huskies	WCHA	38	6	21	27				48																		
1979-80	Canada	Nat-Team	56	8	21	29				43																		
	Canada	Olympics	6	1	1	2				0																		
1980-81	Michigan Tech Huskies	WCHA	43	12	38	50				36																		
1981-82	**Winnipeg Jets**	**NHL**	**69**	**2**	**22**	**24**	**2**	**15**	**17**	**97**	**0**	**0**	**0**	**66**	**3.0**	**94**	**3**	**102**	**25**	**14**	**4**	**0**	**1**	**1**	**8**	**0**	**0**	**0**
	Tulsa Oilers	CHL	5	1	2	3				0																		
1982-83	**Winnipeg Jets**	**NHL**	**77**	**5**	**18**	**23**	**4**	**12**	**16**	**98**	**2**	**0**	**1**	**57**	**8.8**	**85**	**5**	**125**	**35**	**–10**	**3**	**0**	**0**	**0**	**2**	**0**	**0**	**0**
	Canada	WEC-A	10	0	0	0				8																		
1983-84	**Winnipeg Jets**	**NHL**	**74**	**3**	**20**	**23**	**2**	**14**	**16**	**169**	**1**	**0**	**1**	**66**	**4.5**	**122**	**18**	**129**	**32**	**7**	**3**	**1**	**0**	**1**	**2**	**0**	**0**	**0**
1984-85	**Winnipeg Jets**	**NHL**	**63**	**2**	**20**	**22**	**2**	**14**	**16**	**74**	**0**	**0**	**1**	**54**	**3.7**	**80**	**1**	**78**	**19**	**20**	**8**	**0**	**1**	**1**	**16**	**0**	**0**	**0**
1985-86	**Winnipeg Jets**	**NHL**	**56**	**6**	**8**	**14**	**5**	**5**	**10**	**97**	**0**	**0**	**0**	**37**	**16.2**	**65**	**1**	**89**	**15**	**–10**								
1986-87	**Winnipeg Jets**	**NHL**	**63**	**3**	**13**	**16**	**3**	**9**	**12**	**119**	**0**	**0**	**0**	**44**	**6.8**	**52**	**0**	**56**	**9**	**5**	**10**	**0**	**0**	**0**	**21**	**0**	**0**	**0**
1987-88	Canada	Nat-Team	2	0	2	2				0																		
	Canada	Olympics	8	0	1	1				2																		
	Winnipeg Jets	**NHL**	**36**	**0**	**0**	**0**	**0**	**0**	**0**	**106**	**0**	**0**	**0**	**21**	**0.0**	**20**	**1**	**40**	**9**	**–12**	**4**	**0**	**0**	**0**	**4**	**0**	**0**	**0**
1988-89	**Los Angeles Kings**	**NHL**	**76**	**3**	**18**	**21**	**3**	**13**	**16**	**168**	**0**	**0**	**0**	**62**	**4.8**	**96**	**4**	**109**	**34**	**17**	**11**	**0**	**1**	**1**	**6**	**0**	**0**	**0**
1989-90	**Los Angeles Kings**	**NHL**	**62**	**1**	**10**	**11**	**1**	**7**	**8**	**92**	**0**	**0**	**0**	**50**	**2.0**	**70**	**3**	**75**	**31**	**23**	**4**	**0**	**0**	**0**	**6**	**0**	**0**	**0**
1990-91	**Los Angeles Kings**	**NHL**	**45**	**0**	**4**	**4**	**0**	**3**	**3**	**92**	**0**	**0**	**0**	**29**	**0.0**	**40**	**0**	**50**	**17**	**7**	**7**	**0**	**0**	**0**	**12**	**0**	**0**	**0**
1991-92	**Los Angeles Kings**	**NHL**	**37**	**0**	**7**	**7**	**0**	**5**	**5**	**92**	**0**	**0**	**0**	**29**	**0.0**	**24**	**0**	**45**	**19**	**–2**	**6**	**0**	**0**	**0**	**8**	**0**	**0**	**0**
	Phoenix Roadrunners	IHL	5	0	3	3				6																		
1992-93	**Los Angeles Kings**	**NHL**	**22**	**0**	**2**	**2**	**0**	**1**	**1**	**18**	**0**	**0**	**0**	**8**	**0.0**	**16**	**0**	**31**	**12**	**–3**	**22**	**0**	**2**	**2**	**30**	**0**	**0**	**0**
	Phoenix Roadrunners	IHL	31	3	3	6				43																		
1993-94	**Los Angeles Kings**	**NHL**	**60**	**1**	**9**	**10**	**1**	**7**	**8**	**67**	**0**	**1**	**0**	**38**	**2.6**	**38**	**0**	**70**	**21**	**–11**								
1994-95	**Los Angeles Kings**	**NHL**	**1**	**0**	**0**	**0**	**0**	**0**	**0**	**0**	**0**	**0**	**0**	**1**	**0.0**	**1**	**0**	**1**	**1**	**1**								
	Phoenix Roadrunners	IHL	36	1	8	9				58											7	0	1	1	10			
1995-1996	Phoenix Roadrunners	IHL	DID NOT PLAY – ASSISTANT COACH																									
1996-2000	Michigan Tech Huskies	WCHA	DID NOT PLAY – COACHING																									
	NHL Totals		**741**	**26**	**151**	**177**	**23**	**105**	**128**	**1289**	**3**	**1**	**3**	**562**	**4.6**	**803**	**36**	**1000**	**279**		**82**	**1**	**5**	**6**	**115**	**0**	**0**	**0**

WCHA First All-Star Team (1981) • NCAA West First All-American Team (1981) • NCAA Championship All-Tournament Team (1981)

Signed as a free agent by **LA Kings**, June 27, 1988.

• WATTS, Brian

Brian Alan LW – L. 6′, 180 lbs. b: Hagersville, Ont., 9/10/1947. Detroit's 2nd, 7th overall, in 1964.

Season	Club	League	GP	G	A	Pts	AG	AA	APts	PIM	PP	SH	GW	S	%	TGF	PGF	TGA	PGA	+/-	GP	G	A	Pts	PIM	PP	SH	GW
1964-65	Hamilton Red Wings	OHA-Jr.	49	5	8	13				31																		
1965-66	Hamilton Red Wings	OHA-Jr.	48	9	15	24				51											5	0	2	2	0			
1966-67	Michigan Tech Huskies	WCHA	DID NOT PLAY – FRESHMAN																									
1967-68	Michigan Tech Huskies	WCHA	32	14	17	31				39																		
1968-69	Michigan Tech Huskies	WCHA	31	7	15	22				38																		
1969-70	Michigan Tech Huskies	WCHA	31	16	20	36				60																		
1970-71	Port Huron Flags	IHL	44	9	14	23				25																		
1971-72	Fort Worth Wings	CHL	71	26	38	64				69											7	1	3	4	13			
1972-73	Virginia Wings	AHL	72	20	25	45				43											13	4	4	8	16			
1973-74	London Lions	Britain	70	34	30	64				30																		
1974-75	Virginia Wings	AHL	70	14	17	31				57											5	0	0	0	2			
1975-76	**Detroit Red Wings**	**NHL**	**4**	**0**	**0**	**0**	**0**	**0**	**0**	**0**	**0**	**0**	**0**	**0**	**0.0**	**0**	**0**	**0**	**0**	**0**								
	New Haven Nighthawks	CHL	57	8	9	17				14																		
1976-77	Bjorkloven IF	Sweden	25	7	1	8				6																		
	NHL Totals		**4**	**0**	**0**	**0**	**0**	**0**	**0**	**0**	**0**	**0**	**0**	**0**	**0.0**	**0**	**0**	**0**	**0**									

• WEBB, Steve

RW – R. 6′, 195 lbs. b: Peterborough, Ont., 4/20/1975. Buffalo's 8th, 176th overall, in 1994.

Season	Club	League	GP	G	A	Pts	AG	AA	APts	PIM	PP	SH	GW	S	%	TGF	PGF	TGA	PGA	+/-	GP	G	A	Pts	PIM	PP	SH	GW
1991-92	Peterborough Jr. Petes	OJHL-B	37	9	9	18				195																		
1992-93	Windsor Spitfires	OHL	63	14	25	39				184																		
1993-94	Windsor Spitfires	OHL	2	0	1	1				9																		
	Peterborough Petes	OHL	33	6	15	21				117											6	1	1	2	20			
1994-95	Peterborough Petes	OHL	42	8	16	24				109											11	3	3	6	22			
1995-96	Muskegon Fury	ColHL	58	18	24	42				263											5	1	2	3	22			
	Detroit Vipers	IHL	4	0	0	0				24																		
1996-97	**New York Islanders**	**NHL**	**41**	**1**	**4**	**5**	**1**	**4**	**5**	**144**	**1**	**0**	**0**	**21**	**4.8**	**10**	**2**	**18**	**0**	**–10**								
	Kentucky Thoroughblades	AHL	25	6	6	12				103											2	0	0	0	19			
1997-98	**New York Islanders**	**NHL**	**20**	**0**	**0**	**0**	**0**	**0**	**0**	**35**	**0**	**0**	**0**	**6**	**0.0**	**4**	**0**	**6**	**0**	**–2**								
	Kentucky Thoroughblades	AHL	37	5	13	18				139											3	0	1	1	10			
1998-99	**New York Islanders**	**NHL**	**45**	**0**	**0**	**0**	**0**	**0**	**0**	**32**	**0**	**0**	**0**	**18**	**0.0**	**2**	**0**	**12**	**0**	**–10**								
	Lowell Lock Monsters	AHL	23	2	4	6				80																		
99-2000	**New York Islanders**	**NHL**	**65**	**1**	**3**	**4**	**1**	**3**	**4**	**103**	**0**	**0**	**0**	**27**	**3.7**	**11**	**0**	**16**	**1**	**–4**								
	NHL Totals		**171**	**2**	**7**	**9**	**2**	**7**	**9**	**314**	**1**	**0**	**0**	**72**	**2.8**	**27**	**2**	**52**	**1**									

Signed as a free agent by **NY Islanders**, October 10, 1996.

• WEBSTER, Tom

Thomas Ronald RW – R. 5′10″, 170 lbs. b: Kirkland Lake, Ont., 10/4/1948. Boston's 4th, 19th overall, in 1966.

Season	Club	League	GP	G	A	Pts	AG	AA	APts	PIM	PP	SH	GW	S	%	TGF	PGF	TGA	PGA	+/-	GP	G	A	Pts	PIM	PP	SH	GW
1963-1965	Holy Name Irish	KLJHL	50	69	45	114																						
1965-66	Niagara Falls Canucks	OHA-B	3	15	9	24				6																		
	Niagara Falls Flyers	OHA-Jr.	43	16	27	43				16											6	2	3	5	0			
1966-67	Niagara Falls Flyers	OHA-Jr.	47	19	26	45				26											13	14	8	22	4			
1967-68	Niagara Falls Flyers	OHA-Jr.	54	50	64	*114				55											19	13	13	26	20			
	Niagara Falls Flyers	Mem-Cup	10	7	*11	*18				10																		
1968-69	**Boston Bruins**	**NHL**	**9**	**0**	**2**	**2**	**0**	**2**	**2**	**9**	**0**	**0**	**0**	**9**	**0.0**	**5**	**1**	**5**	**0**	**–1**	**1**	**0**	**0**	**0**	**0**	**0**	**0**	**0**
	Oklahoma City Blazers	CHL	44	29	42	71				31											12	*10	8	18	19			
1969-70	**Boston Bruins**	**NHL**	**2**	**0**	**1**	**1**	**0**	**1**	**1**	**2**	**0**	**0**	**0**	**4**	**0.0**	**3**	**2**	**2**	**0**	**–1**								
	Oklahoma City Blazers	CHL	49	29	35	64				49																		
1970-71	**Detroit Red Wings**	**NHL**	**78**	**30**	**37**	**67**	**30**	**31**	**61**	**40**	**7**	**0**	**5**	**183**	**16.4**	**85**	**29**	**104**	**1**	**–47**								
1971-72	**Detroit Red Wings**	**NHL**	**5**	**1**	**1**	**2**	**1**	**1**	**2**	**4**	**1**	**0**	**0**	**7**	**14.3**	**5**	**3**	**7**	**0**	**–5**								
	California Golden Seals	**NHL**	**7**	**2**	**1**	**3**	**2**	**1**	**3**	**6**	**0**	**0**	**0**	**6**	**33.3**	**6**	**3**	**3**	**1**	**1**								
1972-73	New England Whalers	WHA	77	53	50	103				89											15	12	14	26	6			
1973-74	New England Whalers	WHA	64	43	27	70				28											3	5	0	5	7			
1974-75	Canada	Summit	4	2	0	2				4																		
	New England Whalers	WHA	66	40	24	64				52											3	0	2	2	0			
1975-76	New England Whalers	WHA	55	33	50	83				24											17	10	9	19	6			
1976-77	New England Whalers	WHA	70	36	49	85				43											5	1	1	2	0			
1977-78	New England Whalers	WHA	20	15	5	20				5																		
1978-79			DID NOT PLAY – INJURED																									
1979-80	**Detroit Red Wings**	**NHL**	**1**	**0**	**0**	**0**	**0**	**0**	**0**	**0**	**0**	**0**	**0**	**1**	**0.0**	**0**	**0**	**0**	**0**	**0**								
	Adirondack Red Wings	AHL	12	4	5	9				2																		
	NHL Totals		**102**	**33**	**42**	**75**	**33**	**36**	**69**	**61**	**8**	**0**	**5**	**210**	**15.7**	**104**	**38**	**121**	**2**		**1**	**0**	**0**	**0**	**0**	**0**	**0**	**0**
	Other Major League Totals		352	220	205	425				241											43	28	26	54	19			

OHA-Jr. Second All-Star Team (1968) • WHA Second All-Star Team (1973)

Claimed by **Buffalo** from **Boston** in Expansion Draft, June 10, 1970. Traded to **Detroit** by **Buffalo** for Roger Crozier, June 10, 1970. Traded to **California** by **Detroit** for Ron Stackhouse, October 22, 1971. • Missed remainder of 1971-72 season recovering from back injury suffered in game vs. NY Rangers, November 5, 1971. • Selected by **New England** (WHA) in 1972 WHA General Player Draft, February 12, 1972. • Missed remainder of 1977-78 season and entire 1978-79 season recovering from spinal fusion surgery, February, 1978. Signed as a free agent by **Detroit**, September 15, 19790.

• WEIGHT, Doug

Douglas Daniel C – L. 5'11", 200 lbs. b: Warren, MI, 1/21/1971. NY Rangers' 2nd, 34th overall, in 1990.

			REGULAR SEASON																		PLAYOFFS							
Season	Club	League	GP	G	A	Pts	AG	AA	APts	PIM	PP	SH	GW	S	%	TGF	PGF	TGA	PGA	+/-	GP	G	A	Pts	PIM	PP	SH	GW
1988-89	Bloomfield Jets	NAJHL	34	26	53	79				105																		
1989-90	Lake Superior State	CCHA	46	21	48	69				44																		
1990-91	Lake Superior State	CCHA	42	29	46	75				86																		
	United States	WJC-A	7	5	*14	19				4																		
	New York Rangers	NHL																			1	0	0	0	0	0	0	0
1991-92	New York Rangers	NHL	53	8	22	30	7	17	24	23	0	0	2	72	11.1	45	17	34	3	–3	7	2	2	4	0	1	0	0
	Binghamton Rangers	AHL	9	3	14	17				2											4	1	4	5	6			
1992-93	New York Rangers	NHL	65	15	25	40	12	17	29	55	3	0	1	90	16.7	58	18	36	0	4								
	Edmonton Oilers	NHL	13	2	6	8	2	4	6	10	0	0	0	35	5.7	8	2	14	6	–2								
	United States	WC-A	6	0	6	6				12																		
1993-94	Edmonton Oilers	NHL	84	24	50	74	22	39	61	47	4	1	1	188	12.8	102	42	100	18	–22								
	United States	WC-A	8	0	4	4				16																		
1994-95	Star Bulls Rosenheim	Germany	8	2	3	5				18																		
	Edmonton Oilers	NHL	48	7	33	40	12	49	61	69	1	0	1	104	6.7	53	27	45	2	–17								
1995-96	Edmonton Oilers	NHL	82	25	79	104	25	65	90	95	9	0	2	204	12.3	129	59	94	5	–19								
1996-97	United States	W-Cup	7	3	4	7				12																		
	Edmonton Oilers	NHL	80	21	61	82	22	54	76	80	4	0	2	235	8.9	123	64	67	9	1	12	3	8	11	8	0	0	0
1997-98	Edmonton Oilers	NHL	79	26	44	70	30	43	73	69	9	0	4	205	12.7	103	50	61	9	1	12	2	7	9	14	2	0	1
	United States	Olympics	4	0	2	2				2																		
1998-99	Edmonton Oilers	NHL	43	6	31	37	7	30	37	12	1	0	0	79	7.6	55	26	39	2	–8	4	1	1	2	15	0	0	0
99-2000	Edmonton Oilers	NHL	77	21	51	72	24	47	71	54	3	1	4	167	12.6	96	36	68	14	6	5	3	2	5	4	2	0	1
	NHL Totals		624	155	402	557	163	365	528	514	34	2	17	1379	11.2	772	341	558	68		41	11	20	31	41	5	0	2

CCHA First All-Star Team (1991) • NCAA West Second All-American Team (1991) • Played in NHL All-Star Game (1996, 1998)

Traded to **Edmonton** by **NY Rangers** for Esa Tikkanen, March 17, 1993.

• WEINRICH, Eric

Eric John D – L. 6'1", 215 lbs. b: Roanoke, VA, 12/19/1966. New Jersey's 3rd, 32nd overall, in 1985.

Season	Club	League	GP	G	A	Pts	AG	AA	APts	PIM	PP	SH	GW	S	%	TGF	PGF	TGA	PGA	+/-	GP	G	A	Pts	PIM	PP	SH	GW
1983-84	North Yarmouth Academy	Hi-School	17	23	33	56																						
1984-85	North Yarmouth Academy	Hi-School	20	6	21	27																						
	United States	WJC-A	7	1	1	2				8																		
1985-86	University of Maine	H-East	34	0	14	14				26																		
	United States	WJC-A	7	1	0	1				4																		
1986-87	University of Maine	H-East	41	12	32	44				59																		
1987-88	University of Maine	H-East	8	4	7	11				22																		
	United States	Nat-Team	38	3	9	12				24																		
	United States	Olympics	3	0	0	0				0																		
1988-89	New Jersey Devils	NHL	2	0	0	0	0	0	0	0	0	0	0	3	0.0	1	0	3	1	–1								
	Utica Devils	AHL	80	17	27	44				70											5	0	1	1	4			
1989-90	New Jersey Devils	NHL	19	2	7	9	2	5	7	11	1	0	1	16	12.5	25	9	15	0	1	6	1	3	4	17	0	0	0
	Utica Devils	AHL	57	12	48	60				38																		
1990-91	New Jersey Devils	NHL	76	4	34	38	4	26	30	48	1	0	0	96	4.2	95	28	62	5	10	7	1	2	3	6	1	0	0
	United States	WEC-A	10	2	1	3				6																		
1991-92	United States	Can-Cup	8	0	0	0				2																		
	New Jersey Devils	NHL	76	7	25	32	6	19	25	55	5	0	0	97	7.2	95	25	66	6	10	7	0	2	2	4	0	0	0
1992-93	Hartford Whalers	NHL	79	7	29	36	6	20	26	76	0	2	2	104	6.7	114	27	129	31	–11								
	United States	WC-A	6	0	1	1				0																		
1993-94	Hartford Whalers	NHL	8	1	1	2	1	1	2	2	1	0	0	10	10.0	5	3	15	8	–5								
	Chicago Blackhawks	NHL	54	3	23	26	3	18	21	31	1	0	2	105	2.9	59	19	52	18	6	6	0	2	2	6	0	0	0
1994-95	Chicago Blackhawks	NHL	48	3	10	13	5	15	20	33	1	0	2	50	6.0	39	10	42	14	1	16	1	5	6	4	0	0	0
1995-96	Chicago Blackhawks	NHL	77	5	10	15	5	8	13	65	0	0	0	76	6.6	74	7	70	17	14	10	1	4	5	10	1	0	0
1996-97	United States	W-Cup	6	0	4	4				2																		
	Chicago Blackhawks	NHL	81	7	25	32	7	22	29	62	1	0	0	115	6.1	82	10	76	23	19	6	0	1	1	4	0	0	0
1997-98	United States	WC-A	6	0	2	2				16																		
	Chicago Blackhawks	NHL	82	2	21	23	2	21	23	106	0	0	0	85	2.4	71	14	79	32	10								
1998-99	Chicago Blackhawks	NHL	14	1	3	4	1	3	4	12	0	0	0	24	4.2	9	2	29	9	–13								
	Montreal Canadiens	NHL	66	6	12	18	7	12	19	77	4	0	1	95	6.3	55	22	57	12	–12								
	United States	WC-A	6	1	2	3				2																		
99-2000	Montreal Canadiens	NHL	77	4	25	29	4	23	27	39	2	0	0	120	3.3	86	35	68	21	4								
	United States	WC-A	7	0	2	2				4																		
	NHL Totals		759	52	225	277	53	193	246	617	17	2	8	996	5.2	810	211	763	197		58	4	19	23	51	2	0	0

Hockey East First All-Star Team (1987) • NCAA East Second All-American Team (1987) • AHL First All-Star Team (1990) • Won Eddie Shore Award (Outstanding Defenseman - AHL) (1990) • NHL All-Rookie Team (1991)

Traded to **Hartford** by **New Jersey** with Sean Burke for Bobby Holik and Hartford's 2nd round choice (Jay Pandolfo) in 1993 Entry Draft, August 28, 1992. Traded to **Chicago** by **Hartford** with Patrick Poulin for Steve Larmer and Bryan Marchment, November 2, 1993. Traded to **Montreal** by **Chicago** with Jeff Hackett, Alain Nasreddine and Tampa Bay's 4th round choice (previously acquired, Montreal selected Chris Dyment) in 1999 Entry Draft for Jocelyn Thibault, Dave Manson and Brad Brown, November 16, 1998.

• WEIR, Stan

Brian Stanley C – L. 6'1", 180 lbs. b: Ponoka, Alta., 3/17/1952. California's 2nd, 28th overall, in 1972.

Season	Club	League	GP	G	A	Pts	AG	AA	APts	PIM	PP	SH	GW	S	%	TGF	PGF	TGA	PGA	+/-	GP	G	A	Pts	PIM	PP	SH	GW
1969-70	Ponoka Stampeders	AJHL	42	35	26	*61				45																		
1970-71	Medicine Hat Tigers	WCJHL	66	52	59	111				88																		
1971-72	Medicine Hat Tigers	WCJHL	68	58	75	133				77											7	3	7	10	2			
1972-73	California Golden Seals	NHL	78	15	24	39	14	19	33	16	5	0	1	123	12.2	65	14	75	0	–24								
1973-74	California Golden Seals	NHL	58	9	7	16	9	6	15	10	1	0	0	65	13.8	23	3	58	5	–33								
1974-75	California Golden Seals	NHL	80	18	27	45	16	20	36	12	4	0	0	128	14.1	62	15	88	11	–30								
1975-76	Toronto Maple Leafs	NHL	64	19	32	51	17	24	41	22	5	0	3	90	21.1	77	24	50	7	10	9	1	3	4	0	1	0	1
1976-77	Toronto Maple Leafs	NHL	65	11	19	30	10	15	25	14	1	0	2	68	16.2	50	9	39	0	2	7	2	1	3	0	1	0	1
1977-78	Toronto Maple Leafs	NHL	30	12	5	17	11	4	15	4	0	0	0	39	30.8	23	1	22	0	0	13	3	1	4	0	1	0	1
	Tulsa Oilers	CHL	42	24	33	57				38																		
1978-79	Edmonton Oilers	WHA	68	31	30	61				20											13	2	5	7	2			
1979-80	Edmonton Oilers	NHL	79	33	33	66	28	24	52	40	3	2	2	129	25.6	92	16	113	39	2	3	0	0	0	2	0	0	0
1980-81	Edmonton Oilers	NHL	70	12	20	32	9	13	22	40	1	0	2	84	14.3	45	4	92	44	–7	5	0	0	0	2	0	0	0
1981-82	Edmonton Oilers	NHL	51	3	13	16	2	9	11	13	1	0	1	29	10.3	23	2	45	24	0								
	Colorado Rockies	NHL	10	2	3	5	2	2	4	10	0	0	1	12	16.7	6	0	17	4	–7								
1982-83	Detroit Red Wings	NHL	57	5	24	29	4	17	21	2	1	0	1	59	8.5	50	8	47	5	0								
1983-84	Montana Magic	CHL	73	21	44	65				20																		
1984-85	Milwaukee Admirals	IHL	26	7	14	21				5																		
1985-86			OUT OF HOCKEY – RETIRED																									
1986-87	Brantford Motts Clamatos	OHA-Sr.	17	2	0	2				4																		
1987-88	Dundas Real McCoys	OHA-Sr.	STATISTICS NOT AVAILABLE																									
	NHL Totals		642	139	207	346	122	153	275	183	22	2	13	826	16.8	516	96	646	139		37	6	5	11	4	3	0	3
	Other Major League Totals		68	31	30	61				20											13	2	5	7	2			

Won Ernie Love Trophy (AJHL Scoring Champion), 1970.

Selected by **Calgary-Cleveland** (WHA) in 1972 WHA General Player Draft, February 12, 1972. Traded to **Toronto** by **California** for Gary Sabourin, June 20, 1975. Signed as a free agent by **Edmonton** (WHA), June, 1978. Reclaimed by **Toronto** from **Edmonton** prior to Expansion Draft, June 9, 1979. Claimed on waivers by **Edmonton** from **Toronto**, July 4, 1979. Traded to **Colorado** by **Edmonton** for Ed Cooper, March 9, 1982. Traded to **Edmonton** by **Colorado** for Ed Cooper, July 2, 1982. Traded to **Detroit** by **Edmonton** for cash, September 14, 1982.

			REGULAR SEASON																			PLAYOFFS							
Season	Club	League	GP	G	A	Pts	AG	AA	APts	PIM	PP	SH	GW	S	%	TGF	PGF	TGA	PGA	+/–	GP	G	A	Pts	PIM	PP	SH	GW

● WEIR, Wally

Walter Edward D – R. 6'2", 200 lbs. b: Verdun, Que., 6/3/1954.

Season	Club	League	GP	G	A	Pts	AG	AA	APts	PIM	PP	SH	GW	S	%	TGF	PGF	TGA	PGA	+/–	GP	G	A	Pts	PIM	PP	SH	GW
1973-74	Lonqueil Rebels	QJHL-B	STATISTICS NOT AVAILABLE																									
1974-75			DID NOT PLAY																									
1975-76	Flint Generals	IHL	7	0	0	0	....	....	....	4	....	....	....	....	....	....	....	....	....	....	....	....	....	....	....	....	....	....
	Beauce Jaros	NAHL	56	6	20	26	....	....	....	180	....	....	....	....	....	....	....	....	....	....	....	....	....	....	....	....	....	....
1976-77	Quebec Nordiques	WHA	69	3	17	20	....	....	....	197	....	....	....	....	....	....	....	....	....	....	17	1	5	6	13	....	....	....
1977-78	Quebec Nordiques	WHA	13	0	0	0	....	....	....	47	....	....	....	....	....	....	....	....	....	....	11	1	2	3	50	....	....	....
1978-79	Quebec Nordiques	WHA	68	2	7	9	....	....	....	166	....	....	....	....	....	....	....	....	....	....	4	0	1	1	4	....	....	....
1979-80	**Quebec Nordiques**	**NHL**	73	3	12	15	3	9	12	133	0	0	0	91	3.3	56	1	86	13	–18	....	....	....	....	....	....	....	....
1980-81	**Quebec Nordiques**	**NHL**	54	6	8	14	5	5	10	77	0	0	0	50	12.0	30	3	32	5	0	3	0	0	0	15	0	0	0
	Rochester Americans	AHL	7	1	1	2	....	....	....	79	....	....	....	....	....	....	....	....	....	....	....	....	....	....	....	....	....	....
1981-82	**Quebec Nordiques**	**NHL**	62	3	5	8	2	3	5	173	0	0	0	44	6.8	25	1	53	13	–16	15	0	0	0	45	0	0	0
1982-83	**Quebec Nordiques**	**NHL**	58	5	11	16	4	8	12	135	1	0	0	50	10.0	37	2	28	4	11	4	0	1	1	19	0	0	0
1983-84	**Quebec Nordiques**	**NHL**	25	2	3	5	2	2	4	17	0	0	1	15	13.3	12	0	7	0	5	1	0	0	0	17	0	0	0
	Fredericton Express	AHL	44	6	17	23	....	....	....	45	....	....	....	....	....	....	....	....	....	....	7	2	2	4	14	....	....	....
1984-85	**Hartford Whalers**	**NHL**	34	2	3	5	2	2	4	56	0	0	0	24	8.3	15	0	26	4	–7	....	....	....	....	....	....	....	....
	Pittsburgh Penguins	**NHL**	14	0	3	3	0	2	2	34	0	0	0	8	0.0	8	0	8	1	1	....	....	....	....	....	....	....	....
1985-86	Baltimore Skipjacks	AHL	67	5	12	17	....	....	....	300	....	....	....	....	....	....	....	....	....	....	....	....	....	....	....	....	....	....
	NHL Totals		320	21	45	66	18	31	49	625	1	0	1	282	7.4	183	7	240	40		23	0	1	1	96	0	0	0
	Other Major League Totals		150	5	24	29	....	....	....	410	....	....	....	....	....	....	....	....	....	....	32	2	8	10	67	....	....	....

Signed as a free agent by **Quebec** (WHA), September, 1976. • Missed majority of 1977-78 season recovering from elbow injury suffered in training camp, October, 1977. Claimed by **Hartford** from **Quebec** in Waiver Draft, October 9, 1984. Claimed on waivers by **Pittsburgh** from **Hartford**, March 1, 1985.

● WELLS, Chris

C – L. 6'6", 223 lbs. b: Calgary, Alta., 11/12/1975. Pittsburgh's 1st, 24th overall, in 1994.

Season	Club	League	GP	G	A	Pts	AG	AA	APts	PIM	PP	SH	GW	S	%	TGF	PGF	TGA	PGA	+/–	GP	G	A	Pts	PIM	PP	SH	GW
1990-91	Calgary Royals	AAHA	35	13	14	27	....	....	....	33	....	....	....	....	....	....	....	....	....	....	....	....	....	....	....	....	....	....
1991-92	Seattle Thunderbirds	WHL	64	13	8	21	....	....	....	80	....	....	....	....	....	....	....	....	....	....	11	0	0	0	15	....	....	....
	Seattle Thunderbirds	Mem-Cup	4	0	1	1	....	....	....	2	....	....	....	....	....	....	....	....	....	....	....	....	....	....	....	....	....	....
1992-93	Seattle Thunderbirds	WHL	63	18	37	55	....	....	....	111	....	....	....	....	....	....	....	....	....	....	5	2	3	5	4	....	....	....
1993-94	Seattle Thunderbirds	WHL	69	30	44	74	....	....	....	150	....	....	....	....	....	....	....	....	....	....	9	6	5	11	23	....	....	....
1994-95	Seattle Thunderbirds	WHL	69	45	63	108	....	....	....	148	....	....	....	....	....	....	....	....	....	....	3	0	1	1	4	....	....	....
	Cleveland Lumberjacks	IHL	3	0	1	1	....	....	....	2	....	....	....	....	....	....	....	....	....	....	....	....	....	....	....	....	....	....
1995-96	**Pittsburgh Penguins**	**NHL**	54	2	2	4	2	2	4	59	0	1	0	25	8.0	9	0	18	3	–6	....	....	....	....	....	....	....	....
1996-97	Cleveland Lumberjacks	IHL	15	4	6	10	....	....	....	9	....	....	....	....	....	....	....	....	....	....	....	....	....	....	....	....	....	....
	Florida Panthers	**NHL**	47	2	6	8	2	5	7	42	0	0	0	29	6.9	17	0	12	0	5	3	0	0	0	0	0	0	0
1997-98	**Florida Panthers**	**NHL**	61	5	10	15	6	10	16	47	0	1	0	57	8.8	21	1	29	13	4	....	....	....	....	....	....	....	....
1998-99	**Florida Panthers**	**NHL**	20	0	2	2	0	2	2	31	0	0	0	28	0.0	5	0	21	12	–4	....	....	....	....	....	....	....	....
	Beast of New Haven	AHL	9	3	1	4	....	....	....	28	....	....	....	....	....	....	....	....	....	....	....	....	....	....	....	....	....	....
99-2000	**Florida Panthers**	**NHL**	13	0	0	0	0	0	0	14	0	0	0	5	0.0	0	0	6	1	–5	....	....	....	....	....	....	....	....
	Louisville Panthers	AHL	31	8	10	18	....	....	....	20	....	....	....	....	....	....	....	....	....	....	....	....	....	....	....	....	....	....
	Hartford Wolf Pack	AHL	14	2	2	4	....	....	....	6	....	....	....	....	....	....	....	....	....	....	20	3	4	7	38	....	....	....
	NHL Totals		195	9	20	29	10	19	29	193	0	2	0	144	6.3	52	1	86	29		3	0	0	0	0	0	0	0

WHL West First All-Star Team (1995)

Traded to **Florida** by **Pittsburgh** for Stu Barnes and Jason Woolley, November 19, 1996. Traded to **NY Rangers** by **Florida** for conditional choice in 2001 Entry Draft, March 13, 2000.

● WELLS, Jay

Gordon Jay D – L. 6'1", 210 lbs. b: Paris, Ont., 5/18/1959. Los Angeles' 1st, 16th overall, in 1979.

Season	Club	League	GP	G	A	Pts	AG	AA	APts	PIM	PP	SH	GW	S	%	TGF	PGF	TGA	PGA	+/–	GP	G	A	Pts	PIM	PP	SH	GW
1975-76	Preston Raiders	OJHL	20	2	10	12	....	....	....	....	....	....	....	....	....	....	....	....	....	....	....	....	....	....	....	....	....	....
1976-77	Kingston Canadians	OMJHL	59	4	7	11	....	....	....	90	....	....	....	....	....	....	....	....	....	....	14	1	1	2	20	....	....	....
1977-78	Kingston Canadians	OMJHL	68	9	13	22	....	....	....	195	....	....	....	....	....	....	....	....	....	....	5	1	2	3	6	....	....	....
1978-79	Kingston Canadians	OMJHL	48	6	21	27	....	....	....	100	....	....	....	....	....	....	....	....	....	....	11	2	7	9	29	....	....	....
1979-80	**Los Angeles Kings**	**NHL**	43	0	0	0	0	0	0	113	0	0	0	22	0.0	15	0	42	5	–22	4	0	0	0	11	0	0	0
	Binghamton Dusters	AHL	28	0	6	6	....	....	....	48	....	....	....	....	....	....	....	....	....	....	....	....	....	....	....	....	....	....
1980-81	**Los Angeles Kings**	**NHL**	72	5	13	18	4	9	13	155	0	0	1	75	6.7	72	6	72	15	9	4	0	0	0	27	0	0	0
1981-82	**Los Angeles Kings**	**NHL**	60	1	8	9	1	5	6	145	0	0	0	84	1.2	56	2	76	24	2	10	1	3	4	41	0	0	0
1982-83	**Los Angeles Kings**	**NHL**	69	3	12	15	2	8	10	167	0	0	1	105	2.9	79	4	96	32	11	....	....	....	....	....	....	....	....
1983-84	**Los Angeles Kings**	**NHL**	69	3	18	21	2	12	14	141	0	0	0	96	3.1	84	3	130	39	–10	....	....	....	....	....	....	....	....
1984-85	**Los Angeles Kings**	**NHL**	77	2	9	11	2	6	8	185	0	0	0	72	2.8	83	0	95	16	4	3	0	1	1	0	0	0	0
1985-86	**Los Angeles Kings**	**NHL**	79	11	31	42	9	21	30	226	4	0	2	113	9.7	113	24	124	42	7	....	....	....	....	....	....	....	....
	Canada	WEC-A	10	0	2	2	....	....	....	16	....	....	....	....	....	....	....	....	....	....	....	....	....	....	....	....	....	....
1986-87	**Los Angeles Kings**	**NHL**	77	7	29	36	6	21	27	155	6	0	2	115	6.1	107	39	129	42	–19	5	1	2	3	10	1	0	0
1987-88	**Los Angeles Kings**	**NHL**	58	2	23	25	2	16	18	159	1	0	0	76	2.6	75	17	89	28	–3	5	1	2	3	21	0	0	0
1988-89	**Philadelphia Flyers**	**NHL**	67	2	19	21	2	13	15	184	0	0	0	67	3.0	78	25	73	17	–3	18	0	2	2	51	0	0	0
1989-90	**Philadelphia Flyers**	**NHL**	59	3	16	19	3	11	14	129	0	0	1	76	3.9	66	12	70	20	4	....	....	....	....	....	....	....	....
	Buffalo Sabres	**NHL**	1	0	1	1	0	1	1	0	0	0	0	0	0.0	2	0	1	0	1	6	0	0	0	12	0	0	0
1990-91	**Buffalo Sabres**	**NHL**	43	1	2	3	1	2	3	86	0	0	0	36	2.8	24	2	42	2	–18	1	0	1	1	0	0	0	0
1991-92	**Buffalo Sabres**	**NHL**	41	2	9	11	2	7	9	157	0	0	0	26	7.7	29	0	43	11	–3	....	....	....	....	....	....	....	....
	New York Rangers	**NHL**	11	0	0	0	0	0	0	24	0	0	0	4	0.0	3	0	1	0	2	13	0	2	2	10	0	0	0
1992-93	**New York Rangers**	**NHL**	53	1	9	10	1	6	7	107	0	0	0	32	3.1	32	2	52	20	–2	....	....	....	....	....	....	....	....
1993-94♦	**New York Rangers**	**NHL**	79	2	7	9	2	5	7	110	0	0	0	64	3.1	35	2	37	8	4	23	0	0	0	20	0	0	0
1994-95	**New York Rangers**	**NHL**	43	2	7	9	4	10	14	36	0	0	0	38	5.3	20	1	24	5	0	10	0	0	0	8	0	0	0
1995-96	**St. Louis Blues**	**NHL**	76	0	3	3	0	2	2	67	0	0	0	24	0.0	20	1	37	10	–8	12	0	1	1	2	0	0	0
1996-97	**Tampa Bay Lightning**	**NHL**	21	0	0	0	0	0	0	13	0	0	0	16	0.0	6	0	10	1	–3	....	....	....	....	....	....	....	....
1997-1998	Portland Pirates	AHL	DID NOT PLAY – ASSISTANT COACH																									
1998-2000	Hershey Bears	AHL	DID NOT PLAY – ASSISTANT COACH																									
	NHL Totals		1098	47	216	263	43	155	198	2359	11	0	7	1141	4.1	999	140	1243	337		114	3	14	17	213	1	0	0

OMJHL First All-Star Team (1979)

Traded to **Philadelphia** by **LA Kings** for Doug Crossman, September 29, 1988. Traded to **Buffalo** by **Philadelphia** with Philadelphia's 4th round choice (Peter Ambroziak) in 1991 Entry Draft for Kevin Maguire and Buffalo's 2nd round choice (Mikael Renberg) in 1990 Entry Draft, March 5, 1990. Traded to **NY Rangers** by **Buffalo** for Randy Moller, March 9, 1992. Traded to **St. Louis** by **NY Rangers** for Doug Lidster, July 31, 1995. Signed as a free agent by **Tampa Bay**, August 3, 1996.

● WENSINK, John

LW – L. 6', 200 lbs. b: Pincher Creek, AB, 4/1/1953. St. Louis' 6th, 104th overall, in 1973.

Season	Club	League	GP	G	A	Pts	AG	AA	APts	PIM	PP	SH	GW	S	%	TGF	PGF	TGA	PGA	+/–	GP	G	A	Pts	PIM	PP	SH	GW
1970-71	Cornwall Royals	QMJHL	57	11	6	17	....	....	....	151	....	....	....	....	....	....	....	....	....	....	....	....	....	....	....	....	....	....
1971-72	Cornwall Royals	QMJHL	60	10	22	32	....	....	....	69	....	....	....	....	....	....	....	....	....	....	15	2	2	4	64	....	....	....
	Cornwall Royals	Mem-Cup	3	0	1	1	....	....	....	*39	....	....	....	....	....	....	....	....	....	....	....	....	....	....	....	....	....	....
1972-73	Cornwall Royals	QMJHL	52	9	26	35	....	....	....	242	....	....	....	....	....	....	....	....	....	....	16	1	6	7	55	....	....	....
1973-74	**St. Louis Blues**	**NHL**	3	0	0	0	0	0	0	0	0	0	0	0	0.0	0	0	0	0	0	....	....	....	....	....	....	....	....
	Rochester Americans	AHL	36	6	2	8	....	....	....	139	....	....	....	....	....	....	....	....	....	....	5	0	0	0	29	....	....	....
1974-75	Denver Spurs	CHL	21	3	8	11	....	....	....	75	....	....	....	....	....	....	....	....	....	....	....	....	....	....	....	....	....	....
1975-76	Denver Spurs	CHL	DID NOT PLAY – INJURED																									
1976-77	**Boston Bruins**	**NHL**	23	4	6	10	4	5	9	32	0	0	0	24	16.7	13	0	9	1	5	13	0	3	3	8	0	0	0
	Rochester Americans	AHL	49	11	15	26	....	....	....	145	....	....	....	....	....	....	....	....	....	....	....	....	....	....	....	....	....	....
1977-78	**Boston Bruins**	**NHL**	80	16	20	36	15	15	30	181	1	0	3	131	12.2	65	2	40	0	23	15	2	2	4	54	0	0	0
1978-79	**Boston Bruins**	**NHL**	76	28	18	46	24	13	37	106	0	0	4	131	21.4	77	6	51	0	20	8	0	1	1	19	0	0	0
1979-80	**Boston Bruins**	**NHL**	69	9	11	20	8	8	16	110	0	0	2	71	12.7	36	0	29	0	7	4	0	0	0	5	0	0	0
1980-81	**Quebec Nordiques**	**NHL**	53	6	3	9	5	2	7	124	0	0	1	55	10.9	16	1	29	0	–14	3	0	0	0	0	0	0	0
1981-82	**Colorado Rockies**	**NHL**	57	5	3	8	4	2	6	152	1	0	0	35	14.3	15	3	25	0	–13	....	....	....	....	....	....	....	....

Season	Club	League	REGULAR SEASON GP	G	A	Pts	AG	AA	APts	PIM	PP	SH	GW	S	%	TGF	PGF	TGA	PGA	+/-	PLAYOFFS GP	G	A	Pts	PIM	PP	SH	GW
1982-83	New Jersey Devils	NHL	42	2	7	9	2	5	7	135	1	0	0	30	6.7	15	4	19	0	–8	....	....	....	....	....	....	....	....
	Wichita Wind	CHL	7	1	0	1	....	....	....	36	....	....	....	....	....	....	....	....	....	....	....	....	....	....	....	....	....	....
1983-84	SIJ Nijmegen	Holland	PLAYER/COACH – STATISTICS UNAVAILABLE																									
1984-85	SIJ Nijmegen	Holland	14	15	12	27	....	....	....	39	....	....	....	....	....	....	....	....	....	....	....	....	....	....	....	....	....	....
	NHL Totals		403	70	68	138	62	50	112	840	3	0	10	477	14.7	237	16	202	1		43	2	6	8	86	0	0	0

• Missed remainder of 1974-75 and all of 1975-76 recovering from back surgery, January, 1975. Signed as a free agent by **Boston**, October 12, 1976. Claimed by **Quebec** from **Boston** in Waiver Draft, October 10, 1980. Signed as a free agent by **Colorado**, September 21, 1981. Transferred to **New Jersey** after **Colorado** franchise relocated, June 30, 1982.

• WERENKA, Brad

D – L. 6'1", 218 lbs. b: Two Hills, Alta., 2/12/1969. Edmonton's 2nd, 42nd overall, in 1987.

Season	Club	League	GP	G	A	Pts	AG	AA	APts	PIM	PP	SH	GW	S	%	TGF	PGF	TGA	PGA	+/-	GP	G	A	Pts	PIM	PP	SH	GW
1985-86	Fort Saskatchewan Traders	SJHL	29	12	23	35	....	....	....	24	....	....	....	....	....	....	....	....	....	....	....	....	....	....	....	....	....	....
1986-87	Northern Michigan University	WCHA	30	4	4	8	....	....	....	35	....	....	....	....	....	....	....	....	....	....	....	....	....	....	....	....	....	....
1987-88	Northern Michigan University	WCHA	34	7	23	30	....	....	....	26	....	....	....	....	....	....	....	....	....	....	....	....	....	....	....	....	....	....
1988-89	Northern Michigan University	WCHA	28	7	13	20	....	....	....	16	....	....	....	....	....	....	....	....	....	....	....	....	....	....	....	....	....	....
1989-90	Northern Michigan University	WCHA	8	2	5	7	....	....	....	8	....	....	....	....	....	....	....	....	....	....	....	....	....	....	....	....	....	....
1990-91	Northern Michigan University	WCHA	47	20	43	63	....	....	....	36	....	....	....	....	....	....	....	....	....	....	....	....	....	....	....	....	....	....
1991-92	Cape Breton Oilers	AHL	66	6	21	27	....	....	....	95	....	....	....	....	....	....	....	....	....	....	5	0	3	3	6	....	....	....
1992-93	Canada	Nat-Team	18	3	7	10	....	....	....	10	....	....	....	....	....	....	....	....	....	....	....	....	....	....	....	....	....	....
	Edmonton Oilers	NHL	27	5	4	9	4	3	7	24	0	1	1	38	13.2	32	9	25	3	1	....	....	....	....	....	....	....	....
	Cape Breton Oilers	AHL	4	1	1	2	....	....	....	4	....	....	....	....	....	....	....	....	....	....	16	4	17	21	12	....	....	....
1993-94	Edmonton Oilers	NHL	15	0	4	4	0	3	3	14	0	0	0	11	0.0	12	4	12	3	–1	....	....	....	....	....	....	....	....
	Cape Breton Oilers	AHL	25	6	17	23	....	....	....	19	....	....	....	....	....	....	....	....	....	....	....	....	....	....	....	....	....	....
	Canada	Olympics	8	2	2	4	....	....	....	8	....	....	....	....	....	....	....	....	....	....	....	....	....	....	....	....	....	....
	Quebec Nordiques	NHL	11	0	7	7	0	5	5	8	0	0	0	17	0.0	15	5	7	1	4	....	....	....	....	....	....	....	....
	Cornwall Aces	AHL	....	....	....	....	....	....	....	....	....	....	....	....	....	....	....	....	....	....	12	2	10	12	22	....	....	....
1994-95	Milwaukee Admirals	IHL	80	8	45	53	....	....	....	161	....	....	....	....	....	....	....	....	....	....	15	3	10	13	36	....	....	....
1995-96	Chicago Blackhawks	NHL	9	0	0	0	0	0	0	8	0	0	0	2	0.0	3	0	6	1	–2	....	....	....	....	....	....	....	....
	Indianapolis Ice	IHL	73	15	42	57	....	....	....	85	....	....	....	....	....	....	....	....	....	....	5	1	3	4	8	....	....	....
1996-97	Indianapolis Ice	IHL	82	20	56	76	....	....	....	83	....	....	....	....	....	....	....	....	....	....	4	1	4	5	6	....	....	....
1997-98	Pittsburgh Penguins	NHL	71	3	15	18	4	15	19	46	2	0	0	50	6.0	56	9	51	19	15	6	1	0	1	8	0	1	0
1998-99	Pittsburgh Penguins	NHL	81	6	18	24	7	17	24	93	1	0	4	77	7.8	71	6	78	30	17	13	1	1	2	6	0	0	0
99-2000	Pittsburgh Penguins	NHL	61	3	8	11	3	7	10	69	0	0	1	42	7.1	43	2	40	14	15	....	....	....	....	....	....	....	....
	Calgary Flames	NHL	12	1	1	2	1	1	2	21	0	0	0	20	5.0	10	0	17	5	–2	....	....	....	....	....	....	....	....
	NHL Totals		287	18	57	75	19	51	70	283	3	1	6	257	7.0	242	35	236	76		19	2	1	3	14	0	1	0

WCHA First All-Star Team (1991) • NCAA West First All-American Team (1991) • NCAA Championship All-Tournament Team (1991) • IHL First All-Star Team (1997) • Won Governors' Trophy (Top Defenseman - IHL) (1997)

Traded to **Quebec** by **Edmonton** for Steve Passmore, March 21, 1994. Signed as a free agent by **Chicago**, July 20, 1995. Signed as a free agent by **Pittsburgh**, July 31, 1997. Traded to **Calgary** by **Pittsburgh** for Tyler Moss and Rene Corbet, March 14, 2000.

• WESENBERG, Brian

RW – R. 6'3", 187 lbs. b: Peterborough, Ont., 5/9/1977. Anaheim's 2nd, 29th overall, in 1995.

Season	Club	League	GP	G	A	Pts	AG	AA	APts	PIM	PP	SH	GW	S	%	TGF	PGF	TGA	PGA	+/-	GP	G	A	Pts	PIM	PP	SH	GW
1993-94	Cobourg Cougars	OJHL	40	14	18	32	....	....	....	81	....	....	....	....	....	....	....	....	....	....	....	....	....	....	....	....	....	....
1994-95	Guelph Storm	OHL	66	17	27	44	....	....	....	81	....	....	....	....	....	....	....	....	....	....	14	2	3	5	18	....	....	....
1995-96	Guelph Storm	OHL	66	25	33	58	....	....	....	161	....	....	....	....	....	....	....	....	....	....	16	4	11	15	34	....	....	....
	Guelph Storm	Mem-Cup	3	0	0	0	....	....	....	8	....	....	....	....	....	....	....	....	....	....	....	....	....	....	....	....	....	....
1996-97	Guelph Storm	OHL	64	37	43	80	....	....	....	186	....	....	....	....	....	....	....	....	....	....	18	4	9	13	59	....	....	....
	Philadelphia Phantoms	AHL	....	....	....	....	....	....	....	....	....	....	....	....	....	....	....	....	....	....	3	0	0	0	7	....	....	....
1997-98	Philadelphia Phantoms	AHL	74	17	22	39	....	....	....	93	....	....	....	....	....	....	....	....	....	....	19	1	4	5	34	....	....	....
1998-99	Philadelphia Flyers	NHL	1	0	0	0	0	0	0	5	0	0	0	0	0.0	1	0	0	0	1	....	....	....	....	....	....	....	....
	Philadelphia Phantoms	AHL	71	23	20	43	....	....	....	169	....	....	....	....	....	....	....	....	....	....	16	5	3	8	28	....	....	....
99-2000	Philadelphia Phantoms	AHL	22	3	5	8	....	....	....	44	....	....	....	....	....	....	....	....	....	....	....	....	....	....	....	....	....	....
	Orlando Solar Bears	IHL	31	9	3	12	....	....	....	50	....	....	....	....	....	....	....	....	....	....	4	0	0	0	9	....	....	....
	NHL Totals		1	0	0	0	0	0	0	5	0	0	0	0	0.0	1	0	0	0		....	....	....	....	....	....	....	....

Traded to **Philadelphia** by **Anaheim** for Anatoli Semenov and Mike Crowley, March 19, 1996. Traded to **Atlanta** by **Philadelphia** for Eric Bertrand, December 9, 1999.

• WESLEY, Blake

Trevor Blake D – L. 6'1", 200 lbs. b: Red Deer, Alta., 7/10/1959. Philadelphia's 2nd, 22nd overall, in 1979.

Season	Club	League	GP	G	A	Pts	AG	AA	APts	PIM	PP	SH	GW	S	%	TGF	PGF	TGA	PGA	+/-	GP	G	A	Pts	PIM	PP	SH	GW
1974-75	Red Deer Rustlers	AJHL	3	1	0	1	....	....	....	4	....	....	....	....	....	....	....	....	....	....	....	....	....	....	....	....	....	....
1975-76	Red Deer Rustlers	AJHL	55	19	41	60	....	....	....	199	....	....	....	....	....	....	....	....	....	....	....	....	....	....	....	....	....	....
1976-77	Portland Winter Hawks	WCJHL	63	8	25	33	....	....	....	111	....	....	....	....	....	....	....	....	....	....	10	0	5	5	32	....	....	....
1977-78	Portland Winter Hawks	WCJHL	67	7	37	44	....	....	....	190	....	....	....	....	....	....	....	....	....	....	8	1	2	3	20	....	....	....
1978-79	Portland Winter Hawks	WHL	69	10	42	52	....	....	....	292	....	....	....	....	....	....	....	....	....	....	25	3	8	11	70	....	....	....
1979-80	Philadelphia Flyers	NHL	2	0	1	1	0	1	1	2	0	0	0	4	0.0	2	0	5	0	–3	....	....	....	....	....	....	....	....
	Maine Mariners	AHL	62	12	22	34	....	....	....	76	....	....	....	....	....	....	....	....	....	....	12	2	5	7	62	....	....	....
1980-81	Philadelphia Flyers	NHL	50	3	7	10	2	5	7	107	2	0	1	53	5.7	52	14	43	18	13	....	....	....	....	....	....	....	....
	Maine Mariners	AHL	24	6	10	16	....	....	....	20	....	....	....	....	....	....	....	....	....	....	9	1	8	9	53	....	....	....
1981-82	Hartford Whalers	NHL	78	9	18	27	7	12	19	123	3	0	1	115	7.8	87	19	135	33	–34	....	....	....	....	....	....	....	....
1982-83	Hartford Whalers	NHL	22	0	1	1	0	1	1	46	0	0	0	12	0.0	13	1	34	6	–16	....	....	....	....	....	....	....	....
	Quebec Nordiques	NHL	52	4	8	12	3	6	9	84	2	0	1	59	6.8	53	7	68	18	–4	4	0	0	0	2	0	0	0
1983-84	Quebec Nordiques	NHL	46	2	8	10	2	5	7	75	0	0	0	40	5.0	47	1	40	8	14	9	1	2	3	20	0	0	1
1984-85	Quebec Nordiques	NHL	21	0	2	2	0	1	1	28	0	0	0	11	0.0	7	0	11	2	–2	6	1	0	1	8	0	0	0
	Fredericton Express	AHL	25	3	4	7	....	....	....	80	....	....	....	....	....	....	....	....	....	....	2	1	0	1	2	....	....	....
1985-86	Toronto Maple Leafs	NHL	27	0	1	1	0	1	1	21	0	0	0	11	0.0	16	0	28	8	–4	....	....	....	....	....	....	....	....
	St. Catharines Saints	AHL	37	3	4	7	....	....	....	56	....	....	....	....	....	....	....	....	....	....	13	0	3	3	41	....	....	....
1986-87	Newmarket Saints	AHL	79	1	12	13	....	....	....	170	....	....	....	....	....	....	....	....	....	....	....	....	....	....	....	....	....	....
1987-88	Maine Mariners	AHL	34	0	3	3	....	....	....	124	....	....	....	....	....	....	....	....	....	....	1	0	0	0	2	....	....	....
	NHL Totals		298	18	46	64	14	32	46	486	7	0	3	305	5.9	277	42	364	93		19	2	2	4	30	0	0	1

• Brother of Glen • WHL Second Team All-Star (1979)

Traded to **Hartford** by **Philadelphia** with Rick MacLeish, Don Gillen and Philadelphia's 1st (Paul Lawless), 2nd (Mark Paterson) and 3rd (Kevin Dineen) round choices in 1982 Entry Draft for Ray Allison, Fred Arthur and Hartford's 1st (Ron Sutter), 2nd (later traded to Toronto - Toronto selected Peter Ihnacak) and 3rd (Miroslav Dvorak) round choices in 1982 Entry Draft, July 3, 1981. Traded to **Quebec** by **Hartford** for Pierre Lacroix, December 3, 1982. Signed as a free agent by **Toronto**, July 31, 1985. • Played w/ RHI's Portland Rage in 1993 (1-0-0-0-0).

• WESLEY, Glen

Glen Edwin D – L. 6'1", 205 lbs. b: Red Deer, Alta., 10/2/1968. Boston's 1st, 3rd overall, in 1987.

Season	Club	League	GP	G	A	Pts	AG	AA	APts	PIM	PP	SH	GW	S	%	TGF	PGF	TGA	PGA	+/-	GP	G	A	Pts	PIM	PP	SH	GW
1983-84	Red Deer Rustlers	AJHL	57	9	20	29	....	....	....	40	....	....	....	....	....	....	....	....	....	....	....	....	....	....	....	....	....	....
	Portland Winter Hawks	WHL	3	1	2	3	....	....	....	0	....	....	....	....	....	....	....	....	....	....	....	....	....	....	....	....	....	....
1984-85	Portland Winter Hawks	WHL	67	16	52	68	....	....	....	76	....	....	....	....	....	....	....	....	....	....	6	1	6	7	8	....	....	....
1985-86	Portland Winter Hawks	WHL	69	16	75	91	....	....	....	96	....	....	....	....	....	....	....	....	....	....	15	3	11	14	29	....	....	....
	Portland Winter Hawks	Mem-Cup	4	0	2	2	....	....	....	4	....	....	....	....	....	....	....	....	....	....	....	....	....	....	....	....	....	....
1986-87	Portland Winter Hawks	WHL	63	16	46	62	....	....	....	72	....	....	....	....	....	....	....	....	....	....	20	8	18	26	27	....	....	....
	Canada	WJC-A	6	2	1	3	....	....	....	4	....	....	....	....	....	....	....	....	....	....	....	....	....	....	....	....	....	....
1987-88	Boston Bruins	NHL	79	7	30	37	6	21	27	69	1	2	0	158	4.4	111	26	91	27	21	23	6	8	14	22	4	1	0
1988-89	Boston Bruins	NHL	77	19	35	54	16	25	41	61	8	1	1	181	10.5	136	48	92	27	23	10	0	2	2	4	0	0	0
1989-90	Boston Bruins	NHL	78	9	27	36	8	19	27	48	5	0	4	166	5.4	122	55	82	21	6	21	2	6	8	36	0	0	1
1990-91	Boston Bruins	NHL	80	11	32	43	10	24	34	78	5	1	1	199	5.5	135	53	109	27	0	19	2	9	11	19	2	0	0
1991-92	Boston Bruins	NHL	78	9	37	46	8	28	36	54	4	0	1	211	4.3	111	45	102	27	–9	15	2	4	6	16	0	0	0
1992-93	Boston Bruins	NHL	64	8	25	33	7	17	24	47	4	1	0	183	4.4	95	38	82	23	–2	4	0	0	0	0	0	0	0
1993-94	Boston Bruins	NHL	81	14	44	58	13	34	47	64	6	1	1	265	5.3	124	65	77	19	1	13	3	3	6	12	1	0	0
1994-95	Hartford Whalers	NHL	48	2	14	16	4	21	25	50	1	0	1	125	1.6	57	23	56	16	–6	....	....	....	....	....	....	....	....
1995-96	Hartford Whalers	NHL	68	8	16	24	8	13	21	88	6	0	1	129	6.2	73	30	91	39	–9	....	....	....	....	....	....	....	....
1996-97	Hartford Whalers	NHL	68	6	26	32	6	23	29	40	3	1	0	126	4.8	75	19	72	16	0	....	....	....	....	....	....	....	....

			REGULAR SEASON																		PLAYOFFS							
Season	Club	League	GP	G	A	Pts	AG	AA	APts	PIM	PP	SH	GW	S	%	TGF	PGF	TGA	PGA	+/–	GP	G	A	Pts	PIM	PP	SH	GW
1997-98	**Carolina Hurricanes**	**NHL**	**82**	**6**	**19**	**25**	**7**	**19**	**26**	**36**	**1**	**0**	**1**	**121**	**5.0**	**66**	**13**	**61**	**15**	**7**	....	....	....	....	....	....	....	....
1998-99	**Carolina Hurricanes**	**NHL**	**74**	**7**	**17**	**24**	**8**	**16**	**24**	**44**	**0**	**0**	**2**	**112**	**6.3**	**67**	**12**	**56**	**15**	**14**	**6**	**0**	**0**	**0**	**2**	**0**	**0**	**0**
99-2000	**Carolina Hurricanes**	**NHL**	**78**	**7**	**15**	**22**	**8**	**14**	**22**	**38**	**1**	**0**	**0**	**99**	**7.1**	**58**	**13**	**64**	**15**	**–4**	....	....	....	....	....	....	....	....
	NHL Totals		**955**	**113**	**337**	**450**	**109**	**274**	**383**	**717**	**45**	**7**	**13**	**2075**	**5.4**	**1230**	**440**	**1035**	**287**		**111**	**15**	**32**	**47**	**111**	**7**	**1**	**1**

• Brother of Blake • WHL West First All-Star Team (1986, 1987) • NHL All-Rookie Team (1988) • Played in NHL All-Star Game (1989)

Traded to **Hartford** by **Boston** for Hartford/Carolina's 1st round choices in 1995 (Kyle McLaren), 1996 (Jonathan Aitken) and 1997 (Sergei Samsonov) Entry Drafts, August 26, 1994. Transferred to **Carolina** after **Hartford** franchise relocated, June 25, 1997.

• WESTFALL, Ed

Edwin Vernon "Shadow" D/RW – R. 6'1", 197 lbs. b: Belleville, Ont., 9/19/1940.

Season	Club	League	GP	G	A	Pts	AG	AA	APts	PIM	PP	SH	GW	S	%	TGF	PGF	TGA	PGA	+/–	GP	G	A	Pts	PIM	PP	SH	GW
1957-58	Barrie Flyers	OHA-Jr.	51	3	10	13	....	....	....	60	....	....	....	....	....	....	....	....	....	....	4	0	0	0	4	....	....	....
1958-59	Barrie Flyers	OHA-Jr.	54	4	10	14	....	....	....	63	....	....	....	....	....	....	....	....	....	....	6	0	4	4	2	....	....	....
1959-60	Barrie Flyers	OHA-Jr.	48	7	28	35	....	....	....	63	....	....	....	....	....	....	....	....	....	....	6	0	4	4	28	....	....	....
	Kingston Frontenacs	EPHL	1	0	0	0	....	....	....	2	....	....	....	....	....	....	....	....	....	....	....	....	....	....	....	....	....	....
1960-61	Niagara Falls Flyers	OHA-Jr.	48	9	45	54	....	....	....	72	....	....	....	....	....	....	....	....	....	....	7	2	7	9	6	....	....	....
	Kingston Frontenacs	EPHL	2	0	0	0	....	....	....	0	....	....	....	....	....	....	....	....	....	....	....	....	....	....	....	....	....	....
1961-62	**Boston Bruins**	**NHL**	**63**	**2**	**9**	**11**	**2**	**9**	**11**	**53**	....	....	....	....	....	....	....	....	....	....	....	....	....	....	....	....	....	....
1962-63	**Boston Bruins**	**NHL**	**48**	**1**	**11**	**12**	**1**	**11**	**12**	**34**	....	....	....	....	....	....	....	....	....	....	....	....	....	....	....	....	....	....
	Kingston Frontenacs	EPHL	21	5	16	21	....	....	....	14	....	....	....	....	....	....	....	....	....	....	....	....	....	....	....	....	....	....
1963-64	**Boston Bruins**	**NHL**	**55**	**1**	**5**	**6**	**1**	**5**	**6**	**35**	....	....	....	....	....	....	....	....	....	....	....	....	....	....	....	....	....	....
	Providence Reds	AHL	13	1	3	4	....	....	....	8	....	....	....	....	....	....	....	....	....	....	3	0	0	0	4	....	....	....
1964-65	**Boston Bruins**	**NHL**	**68**	**12**	**15**	**27**	**14**	**15**	**29**	**65**	....	....	....	....	....	....	....	....	....	....	....	....	....	....	....	....	....	....
1965-66	**Boston Bruins**	**NHL**	**59**	**9**	**21**	**30**	**10**	**20**	**30**	**42**	....	....	....	....	....	....	....	....	....	....	....	....	....	....	....	....	....	....
1966-67	**Boston Bruins**	**NHL**	**70**	**12**	**24**	**36**	**14**	**23**	**37**	**26**	....	....	....	....	....	....	....	....	....	....	....	....	....	....	....	....	....	....
1967-68	**Boston Bruins**	**NHL**	**73**	**14**	**22**	**36**	**16**	**22**	**38**	**38**	**1**	**2**	**2**	**139**	**10.1**	**55**	**4**	**77**	**31**	**5**	**4**	**2**	**0**	**2**	**2**	**0**	**0**	**0**
1968-69	**Boston Bruins**	**NHL**	**70**	**18**	**24**	**42**	**19**	**21**	**40**	**22**	**1**	**4**	**4**	**139**	**12.9**	**66**	**5**	**74**	**33**	**20**	**10**	**3**	**7**	**10**	**11**	**0**	**2**	**2**
1969-70♦	**Boston Bruins**	**NHL**	**72**	**14**	**22**	**36**	**15**	**21**	**36**	**28**	**0**	**0**	**0**	**158**	**8.9**	**63**	**0**	**93**	**50**	**20**	**14**	**3**	**5**	**8**	**4**	**0**	**1**	**1**
1970-71	**Boston Bruins**	**NHL**	**78**	**25**	**34**	**59**	**25**	**28**	**53**	**48**	**0**	**7**	**5**	**149**	**16.8**	**99**	**0**	**75**	**34**	**58**	**7**	**1**	**2**	**3**	**2**	**0**	**1**	**0**
1971-72♦	**Boston Bruins**	**NHL**	**71**	**18**	**26**	**44**	**18**	**22**	**40**	**19**	**0**	**2**	**5**	**123**	**14.6**	**68**	**1**	**77**	**39**	**29**	**15**	**4**	**3**	**7**	**10**	**0**	**2**	**1**
1972-73	**New York Islanders**	**NHL**	**67**	**15**	**31**	**46**	**14**	**25**	**39**	**25**	**4**	**0**	**1**	**160**	**9.4**	**76**	**25**	**121**	**28**	**–42**	....	....	....	....	....	....	....	....
1973-74	**New York Islanders**	**NHL**	**68**	**19**	**23**	**42**	**18**	**19**	**37**	**28**	**6**	**0**	**0**	**177**	**10.7**	**65**	**17**	**90**	**37**	**–5**	....	....	....	....	....	....	....	....
1974-75	**New York Islanders**	**NHL**	**73**	**22**	**33**	**55**	**19**	**25**	**44**	**28**	**6**	**1**	**1**	**170**	**12.9**	**81**	**20**	**77**	**35**	**19**	**17**	**5**	**10**	**15**	**12**	**2**	**1**	**2**
1975-76	**New York Islanders**	**NHL**	**80**	**25**	**31**	**56**	**22**	**23**	**45**	**27**	**6**	**2**	**3**	**154**	**16.2**	**83**	**24**	**90**	**48**	**17**	**8**	**2**	**3**	**5**	**0**	**1**	**0**	**0**
1976-77	**New York Islanders**	**NHL**	**79**	**14**	**33**	**47**	**13**	**25**	**38**	**8**	**1**	**3**	**0**	**118**	**11.9**	**69**	**8**	**75**	**35**	**21**	**12**	**1**	**5**	**6**	**0**	**0**	**1**	**0**
1977-78	**New York Islanders**	**NHL**	**71**	**5**	**19**	**24**	**5**	**15**	**20**	**14**	**0**	**1**	**1**	**72**	**6.9**	**35**	**1**	**58**	**31**	**7**	**2**	**0**	**0**	**0**	**0**	**0**	**0**	**0**
1978-79	**New York Islanders**	**NHL**	**55**	**5**	**11**	**16**	**4**	**8**	**12**	**4**	**0**	**1**	**1**	**51**	**9.8**	**25**	**0**	**50**	**25**	**0**	**6**	**1**	**2**	**3**	**0**	**0**	**0**	**0**
	NHL Totals		**1220**	**231**	**394**	**625**	**230**	**337**	**567**	**544**	....	....	....	....	....	....	....	....	....	....	**95**	**22**	**37**	**59**	**41**	....	....	....

OHA-Jr. First All-Star Team (1961) • Won Bill Masterton Trophy (1977) • Played in NHL All-Star Game (1971, 1973, 1974, 1975)

Claimed by **NY Islanders** from **Boston** in Expansion Draft, June 6, 1972.

• WESTLUND, Tommy

RW – R. 6', 210 lbs. b: Fors, Sweden, 12/29/1974. Carolina's 5th, 93rd overall, in 1998.

Season	Club	League	GP	G	A	Pts	AG	AA	APts	PIM	PP	SH	GW	S	%	TGF	PGF	TGA	PGA	+/–	GP	G	A	Pts	PIM	PP	SH	GW
1991-92	Avesta BK	Sweden-3	27	11	9	20	....	....	....	8	....	....	....	....	....	....	....	....	....	....	....	....	....	....	....	....	....	....
1992-93	Avesta BK	Sweden-2	32	9	5	14	....	....	....	32	....	....	....	....	....	....	....	....	....	....	....	....	....	....	....	....	....	....
1993-94	Avesta BK	Sweden-2	31	20	11	31	....	....	....	34	....	....	....	....	....	....	....	....	....	....	....	....	....	....	....	....	....	....
1994-95	Avesta BK	Sweden-2	32	17	13	30	....	....	....	22	....	....	....	....	....	....	....	....	....	....	....	....	....	....	....	....	....	....
1995-96	Brynas IF Gavle	Sweden	18	2	1	3	....	....	....	2	....	....	....	....	....	....	....	....	....	....	....	....	....	....	....	....	....	....
	Brynas IF Gavle	Sweden-2	18	10	10	20	....	....	....	4	....	....	....	....	....	....	....	....	....	....	8	1	0	1	4	....	....	....
1996-97	Brynas IF Gavle	Sweden	50	21	13	34	....	....	....	16	....	....	....	....	....	....	....	....	....	....	....	....	....	....	....	....	....	....
1997-98	Brynas IF Gavle	Sweden	46	29	9	38	....	....	....	45	....	....	....	....	....	....	....	....	....	....	3	0	1	1	0	....	....	....
1998-99	Beast of New Haven	AHL	50	8	18	26	....	....	....	31	....	....	....	....	....	....	....	....	....	....	....	....	....	....	....	....	....	....
99-2000	**Carolina Hurricanes**	**NHL**	**81**	**4**	**8**	**12**	**4**	**7**	**11**	**19**	**0**	**1**	**0**	**67**	**6.0**	**21**	**1**	**39**	**9**	**–10**	....	....	....	....	....	....	....	....
	NHL Totals		**81**	**4**	**8**	**12**	**4**	**7**	**11**	**19**	**0**	**1**	**0**	**67**	**6.0**	**21**	**1**	**39**	**9**		....	....	....	....	....	....	....	....

• WHARRAM, Kenny

Kenneth Malcolm RW/C – R. 5'9", 160 lbs. b: North Bay, Ont., 7/2/1933.

Season	Club	League	GP	G	A	Pts	AG	AA	APts	PIM	PP	SH	GW	S	%	TGF	PGF	TGA	PGA	+/–	GP	G	A	Pts	PIM	PP	SH	GW
1949-50	North Bay Black Hawks	EOHL	2	0	1	1	....	....	....	0	....	....	....	....	....	....	....	....	....	....	....	....	....	....	....	....	....	....
1950-51	Galt Black Hawks	OHA-Jr.	53	35	38	73	....	....	....	28	....	....	....	....	....	....	....	....	....	....	3	2	3	5	2	....	....	....
1951-52	Galt Black Hawks	OHA-Jr.	45	35	79	114	....	....	....	37	....	....	....	....	....	....	....	....	....	....	....	....	....	....	....	....	....	....
	Chicago Black Hawks	**NHL**	**1**	**0**	**0**	**0**	**0**	**0**	**0**	**0**	....	....	....	....	....	....	....	....	....	....	....	....	....	....	....	....	....	....
1952-53	Galt Black Hawks	OHA-Jr.	54	34	40	74	....	....	....	42	....	....	....	....	....	....	....	....	....	....	11	9	*14	*23	2	....	....	....
1953-54	**Chicago Black Hawks**	**NHL**	**29**	**1**	**7**	**8**	**1**	**8**	**9**	**8**	....	....	....	....	....	....	....	....	....	....	....	....	....	....	....	....	....	....
	Quebec Aces	QHL	29	7	10	17	....	....	....	8	....	....	....	....	....	....	....	....	....	....	....	....	....	....	....	....	....	....
1954-55	Buffalo Bisons	AHL	63	33	49	82	....	....	....	15	....	....	....	....	....	....	....	....	....	....	10	*9	7	*16	4	....	....	....
1955-56	**Chicago Black Hawks**	**NHL**	**3**	**0**	**0**	**0**	**0**	**0**	**0**	**0**	....	....	....	....	....	....	....	....	....	....	....	....	....	....	....	....	....	....
	Buffalo Bisons	AHL	59	27	63	90	....	....	....	27	....	....	....	....	....	....	....	....	....	....	5	4	2	6	2	....	....	....
1956-57	Buffalo Bisons	AHL	64	28	49	77	....	....	....	18	....	....	....	....	....	....	....	....	....	....	....	....	....	....	....	....	....	....
1957-58	Buffalo Bisons	AHL	58	31	26	57	....	....	....	14	....	....	....	....	....	....	....	....	....	....	....	....	....	....	....	....	....	....
1958-59	**Chicago Black Hawks**	**NHL**	**66**	**10**	**9**	**19**	**12**	**9**	**21**	**14**	....	....	....	....	....	....	....	....	....	....	**6**	**0**	**2**	**2**	**2**	....	....	....
1959-60	**Chicago Black Hawks**	**NHL**	**59**	**14**	**11**	**25**	**16**	**11**	**27**	**16**	....	....	....	....	....	....	....	....	....	....	**4**	**1**	**1**	**2**	**0**	....	....	....
1960-61♦	**Chicago Black Hawks**	**NHL**	**64**	**16**	**29**	**45**	**18**	**28**	**46**	**12**	....	....	....	....	....	....	....	....	....	....	**12**	**3**	**5**	**8**	**12**	....	....	....
1961-62	**Chicago Black Hawks**	**NHL**	**62**	**14**	**23**	**37**	**16**	**22**	**38**	**24**	....	....	....	....	....	....	....	....	....	....	**12**	**3**	**4**	**7**	**8**	....	....	....
1962-63	**Chicago Black Hawks**	**NHL**	**55**	**20**	**18**	**38**	**23**	**18**	**41**	**17**	....	....	....	....	....	....	....	....	....	....	**6**	**1**	**5**	**6**	**0**	....	....	....
1963-64	**Chicago Black Hawks**	**NHL**	**70**	**39**	**32**	**71**	**49**	**34**	**83**	**18**	....	....	....	....	....	....	....	....	....	....	**7**	**2**	**2**	**4**	**6**	....	....	....
1964-65	**Chicago Black Hawks**	**NHL**	**68**	**24**	**20**	**44**	**29**	**20**	**49**	**27**	....	....	....	....	....	....	....	....	....	....	**12**	**2**	**3**	**5**	**4**	....	....	....
1965-66	**Chicago Black Hawks**	**NHL**	**69**	**26**	**17**	**43**	**30**	**16**	**46**	**28**	....	....	....	....	....	....	....	....	....	....	**6**	**1**	**0**	**1**	**4**	....	....	....
1966-67	**Chicago Black Hawks**	**NHL**	**70**	**31**	**34**	**65**	**36**	**33**	**69**	**21**	....	....	....	....	....	....	....	....	....	....	**6**	**2**	**2**	**4**	**2**	....	....	....
1967-68	**Chicago Black Hawks**	**NHL**	**74**	**27**	**42**	**69**	**32**	**42**	**74**	**18**	**9**	**1**	**3**	**177**	**15.3**	**99**	**30**	**76**	**5**	**–2**	**9**	**1**	**3**	**4**	**0**	**0**	**0**	**0**
1968-69	**Chicago Black Hawks**	**NHL**	**76**	**30**	**39**	**69**	**32**	**35**	**67**	**19**	**5**	**0**	**4**	**167**	**18.0**	**107**	**31**	**60**	**2**	**18**	....	....	....	....	....	....	....	....
	NHL Totals		**766**	**252**	**281**	**533**	**294**	**276**	**570**	**222**	....	....	....	....	....	....	....	....	....	....	**80**	**16**	**27**	**43**	**38**	....	....	....

AHL Second All-Star Team (1955) • NHL First All-Star Team (1964, 1967) • Won Lady Byng Trophy (1964) • Played in NHL All-Star Game (1961, 1968)

Traded to **Buffalo** (AHL) by **Chicago** for cash, August, 1956. Traded to **Chicago** by **Buffalo** (AHL) for Wally Hergesheimer and Frank Martin, May 5, 1958. • Suffered career-ending heart attack during training camp, September 18, 1969.

• WHEELDON, Simon

C – L. 5'11", 170 lbs. b: Vancouver, B.C., 8/30/1966. Edmonton's 11th, 229th overall, in 1984.

Season	Club	League	GP	G	A	Pts	AG	AA	APts	PIM	PP	SH	GW	S	%	TGF	PGF	TGA	PGA	+/–	GP	G	A	Pts	PIM	PP	SH	GW
1982-83	Kelowna Buckaroos	BCJHL	55	30	44	74	....	....	....	74	....	....	....	....	....	....	....	....	....	....	....	....	....	....	....	....	....	....
1983-84	Victoria Cougars	WHL	56	14	24	38	....	....	....	43	....	....	....	....	....	....	....	....	....	....	....	....	....	....	....	....	....	....
1984-85	Victoria Cougars	WHL	67	50	76	126	....	....	....	78	....	....	....	....	....	....	....	....	....	....	....	....	....	....	....	....	....	....
	Nova Scotia Voyageurs	AHL	4	0	1	1	....	....	....	0	....	....	....	....	....	....	....	....	....	....	1	0	0	0	0	....	....	....
1985-86	Victoria Cougars	WHL	70	61	96	157	....	....	....	85	....	....	....	....	....	....	....	....	....	....	....	....	....	....	....	....	....	....
1986-87	Flint Spirits	IHL	41	17	53	70	....	....	....	20	....	....	....	....	....	....	....	....	....	....	....	....	....	....	....	....	....	....
	New Haven Nighthawks	AHL	38	11	28	39	....	....	....	39	....	....	....	....	....	....	....	....	....	....	5	0	0	0	6	....	....	....
1987-88	**New York Rangers**	**NHL**	**5**	**0**	**1**	**1**	**0**	**1**	**1**	**4**	**0**	**0**	**0**	**2**	**0.0**	**1**	**0**	**3**	**0**	**–2**	....	....	....	....	....	....	....	....
	Colorado Rangers	IHL	69	45	54	99	....	....	....	80	....	....	....	....	....	....	....	....	....	....	13	8	11	19	12	....	....	....
1988-89	**New York Rangers**	**NHL**	**6**	**0**	**1**	**1**	**0**	**1**	**1**	**2**	**0**	**0**	**0**	**2**	**0.0**	**1**	**0**	**2**	**0**	**–1**	....	....	....	....	....	....	....	....
	Denver Rangers	IHL	74	50	56	106	....	....	....	77	....	....	....	....	....	....	....	....	....	....	4	0	2	2	6	....	....	....
1989-90	Flint Spirits	IHL	76	34	49	83	....	....	....	61	....	....	....	....	....	....	....	....	....	....	4	1	2	3	2	....	....	....
1990-91	**Winnipeg Jets**	**NHL**	**4**	**0**	**0**	**0**	**0**	**0**	**0**	**4**	**0**	**0**	**0**	**4**	**0.0**	**2**	**0**	**0**	**0**	**2**	....	....	....	....	....	....	....	....
	Moncton Hawks	AHL	66	30	38	68	....	....	....	38	....	....	....	....	....	....	....	....	....	....	8	4	3	7	2	....	....	....
1991-92	Baltimore Skipjacks	AHL	78	38	53	91	....	....	....	62	....	....	....	....	....	....	....	....	....	....	....	....	....	....	....	....	....	....

			REGULAR SEASON																		PLAYOFFS							
Season	Club	League	GP	G	A	Pts	AG	AA	APts	PIM	PP	SH	GW	S	%	TGF	PGF	TGA	PGA	+/–	GP	G	A	Pts	PIM	PP	SH	GW
1992-93	VEU Feldkirch	Alpenliga	30	19	32	51	....	....	....	38	....	....	....	....	....	....	....	....	....	....	....	....	....	....	....	....	....	....
	VEU Feldkirch	Austria	20	10	25	35	....	....	....	....	....	....	....	....	....	....	....	....	....	....	....	....	....	....	....	....	....	....
1993-94	VEU Feldkirch	Alpenliga	28	24	20	44	....	....	....	30	....	....	....	....	....	....	....	....	....	....	....	....	....	....	....	....	....	....
	VEU Feldkirch	Austria	27	19	26	45	....	....	....	24	....	....	....	....	....	....	....	....	....	....	....	....	....	....	....	....	....	....
1994-95	VEU Feldkirch	Alpenliga	17	24	15	39	....	....	....	24	....	....	....	....	....	....	....	....	....	....	....	....	....	....	....	....	....	....
	VEU Feldkirch	Austria	45	32	39	71	....	....	....	38	....	....	....	....	....	....	....	....	....	....	....	....	....	....	....	....	....	....
1995-96	VEU Feldkirch	Alpenliga	8	13	11	24	....	....	....	6	....	....	....	....	....	....	....	....	....	....	....	....	....	....	....	....	....	....
	VEU Feldkirch	Austria	37	*35	*50	*85	....	....	....	32	....	....	....	....	....	....	....	....	....	....	....	....	....	....	....	....	....	....
1996-97	VEU Feldkirch	Alpenliga	45	32	39	71	....	....	....	38	....	....	....	....	....	....	....	....	....	....	....	....	....	....	....	....	....	....
	VEU Feldkirch	Austria	11	9	5	14	....	....	....	14	....	....	....	....	....	....	....	....	....	....	6	5	2	7	6	....	....	....
	Austria	WC-B	7	4	0	4	....	....	....	2	....	....	....	....	....	....	....	....	....	....	....	....	....	....	....	....	....	....
1997-98	VEU Feldkirch	Alpenliga	16	8	9	17	....	....	....	30	....	....	....	....	....	....	....	....	....	....	5	4	10	14	....	....	....	....
	VEU Feldkirch	Austria	21	13	14	27	....	....	....	24	....	....	....	....	....	....	....	....	....	....	6	0	3	3	4	....	....	....
	VEU Feldkirch	EuroHL	10	6	6	12	....	....	....	8	....	....	....	....	....	....	....	....	....	....	....	....	....	....	....	....	....	....
	Austria	Olympics	4	0	1	1	....	....	....	8	....	....	....	....	....	....	....	....	....	....	....	....	....	....	....	....	....	....
	Austria	WC-A	3	1	0	1	....	....	....	2	....	....	....	....	....	....	....	....	....	....	....	....	....	....	....	....	....	....
1998-99	VEU Feldkirch	Alpenliga	35	19	30	49	....	....	....	46	....	....	....	....	....	....	....	....	....	....	....	....	....	....	....	....	....	....
	VEU Feldkirch	Austria	17	6	7	13	....	....	....	22	....	....	....	....	....	....	....	....	....	....	....	....	....	....	....	....	....	....
99-2000	Munich Barons	Germany	56	26	34	60	....	....	....	85	....	....	....	....	....	....	....	....	....	....	12	2	6	8	8	....	....	....
	Austria	WC-A	5	1	3	4	....	....	....	10	....	....	....	....	....	....	....	....	....	....	....	....	....	....	....	....	....	....
	NHL Totals		**15**	**0**	**2**	**2**	**0**	**2**	**2**	**10**	**0**	**0**	**0**	**8**	**0.0**	**4**	**0**	**5**	**0**		....	....	....	....	....	....	....	....

WHL West Second All-Star Team (1985, 1986) • IHL Second All-Star Team (1988, 1989)

Signed as a free agent by **NY Rangers**, September 8, 1986. Traded to **Winnipeg** by **NY Rangers** for Brian McReynolds, July 9, 1990. Traded to **Washington** by **Winnipeg** with Craig Duncanson and Brent Hughes for Bob Joyce, Tyler Larter and Kent Paynter, May 21, 1991.

• WHELDON, Donald

D – R. 6'2", 185 lbs. b: Falmouth, MA, 12/28/1954 d: 6/3/1985. St. Louis' 4th, 87th overall, in 1974.

Season	Club	League	GP	G	A	Pts	AG	AA	APts	PIM	PP	SH	GW	S	%	TGF	PGF	TGA	PGA	+/–	GP	G	A	Pts	PIM	PP	SH	GW
1971-72	Riverview Reds	NBJHL	24	6	11	17	....	....	....	59	....	....	....	....	....	....	....	....	....	....	....	....	....	....	....	....	....	....
	Moncton Beavers	NBJHL	15	3	12	15	....	....	....	10	....	....	....	....	....	....	....	....	....	....	....	....	....	....	....	....	....	....
1972-73	London Knights	OHA	65	2	7	9	....	....	....	70	....	....	....	....	....	....	....	....	....	....	....	....	....	....	....	....	....	....
1973-74	London Knights	OHA	70	5	27	32	....	....	....	88	....	....	....	....	....	....	....	....	....	....	....	....	....	....	....	....	....	....
1974-75	**St. Louis Blues**	**NHL**	**2**	**0**	**0**	**0**	**0**	**0**	**0**	**0**	**0**	**0**	**0**	**0**	**0.0**	**0**	**0**	**1**	**1**	**0**	....	....	....	....	....	....	....	....
	Denver Spurs	CHL	8	0	1	1	....	....	....	8	....	....	....	....	....	....	....	....	....	....	....	....	....	....	....	....	....	....
	Columbus Owls	IHL	43	6	12	18	....	....	....	28	....	....	....	....	....	....	....	....	....	....	5	2	1	3	2	....	....	....
1975-76	Winston-Salem Polar Bears	SHL	70	11	28	39	....	....	....	52	....	....	....	....	....	....	....	....	....	....	4	1	0	1	4	....	....	....
1976-77	Winston-Salem Polar Bears	SHL	37	9	13	22	....	....	....	14	....	....	....	....	....	....	....	....	....	....	....	....	....	....	....	....	....	....
	NHL Totals		**2**	**0**	**0**	**0**	**0**	**0**	**0**	**0**	**0**	**0**	**0**	**0**	**0.0**	**0**	**0**	**1**	**1**		....	....	....	....	....	....	....	....

• WHELTON, Bill

William M. D – L. 6'1", 180 lbs. b: Everett, MA, 8/28/1959. Winnipeg's 3rd, 61st overall, in 1979.

Season	Club	League	GP	G	A	Pts	AG	AA	APts	PIM	PP	SH	GW	S	%	TGF	PGF	TGA	PGA	+/–	GP	G	A	Pts	PIM	PP	SH	GW
1978-79	Boston University	ECAC	30	2	5	7	....	....	....	20	....	....	....	....	....	....	....	....	....	....	....	....	....	....	....	....	....	....
1979-80	Boston University	ECAC	30	4	14	18	....	....	....	39	....	....	....	....	....	....	....	....	....	....	....	....	....	....	....	....	....	....
1980-81	Boston University	ECAC	29	4	18	22	....	....	....	42	....	....	....	....	....	....	....	....	....	....	....	....	....	....	....	....	....	....
	Winnipeg Jets	**NHL**	**2**	**0**	**0**	**0**	**0**	**0**	**0**	**0**	**0**	**0**	**0**	**1**	**0.0**	**0**	**0**	**1**	**0**	**–1**	....	....	....	....	....	....	....	....
1981-82	Tulsa Oilers	CHL	66	2	18	20	....	....	....	51	....	....	....	....	....	....	....	....	....	....	3	0	0	0	2	....	....	....
1982-83	Sherbrooke Jets	AHL	72	4	16	20	....	....	....	73	....	....	....	....	....	....	....	....	....	....	....	....	....	....	....	....	....	....
1983-84	Sherbrooke Jets	AHL	67	2	14	16	....	....	....	32	....	....	....	....	....	....	....	....	....	....	....	....	....	....	....	....	....	....
1984-85	Kiekko-Reipas	Finland	34	2	3	5	....	....	....	54	....	....	....	....	....	....	....	....	....	....	....	....	....	....	....	....	....	....
1985-86	HC Brunico	Italy	35	12	21	33	....	....	....	61	....	....	....	....	....	....	....	....	....	....	5	1	4	5	4	....	....	....
	NHL Totals		**2**	**0**	**0**	**0**	**0**	**0**	**0**	**0**	**0**	**0**	**0**	**1**	**0.0**	**0**	**0**	**1**	**0**		....	....	....	....	....	....	....	....

• WHISTLE, Rob

Robert Douglas D – R. 6'2", 195 lbs. b: Thunder Bay, Ont., 4/4/1961.

Season	Club	League	GP	G	A	Pts	AG	AA	APts	PIM	PP	SH	GW	S	%	TGF	PGF	TGA	PGA	+/–	GP	G	A	Pts	PIM	PP	SH	GW
1976-77	Thunder Bay Flyers	TBJHL	28	10	21	31	....	....	....	....	....	....	....	....	....	....	....	....	....	....	....	....	....	....	....	....	....	....
1977-78	Thunder Bay Flyers	TBJHL	28	28	30	58	....	....	....	....	....	....	....	....	....	....	....	....	....	....	....	....	....	....	....	....	....	....
1978-79	Thunder Bay Flyers	TBJHL	18	10	12	22	....	....	....	22	....	....	....	....	....	....	....	....	....	....	....	....	....	....	....	....	....	....
1979-80	Kitchener Ranger B's	OHA-B	10	5	5	10	....	....	....	8	....	....	....	....	....	....	....	....	....	....	....	....	....	....	....	....	....	....
	Kitchener Rangers	OMJHL	55	2	5	7	....	....	....	68	....	....	....	....	....	....	....	....	....	....	....	....	....	....	....	....	....	....
1980-81	Kitchener Rangers	OMJHL	33	4	0	4	....	....	....	47	....	....	....	....	....	....	....	....	....	....	....	....	....	....	....	....	....	....
	Kitchener Rangers	Mem-Cup	5	0	1	1	....	....	....	0	....	....	....	....	....	....	....	....	....	....	....	....	....	....	....	....	....	....
1981-82	Sir Wilfred Laurier University	OUAA	STATISTICS NOT AVAILABLE																									
1982-83	Sir Wilfred Laurier University	OUAA	24	6	14	20	....	....	....	12	....	....	....	....	....	....	....	....	....	....	....	....	....	....	....	....	....	....
1983-84	Sir Wilfred Laurier University	OUAA	24	9	15	24	....	....	....	42	....	....	....	....	....	....	....	....	....	....	....	....	....	....	....	....	....	....
1984-85	Sir Wilfred Laurier University	OUAA	24	5	22	27	....	....	....	31	....	....	....	....	....	....	....	....	....	....	....	....	....	....	....	....	....	....
1985-86	**New York Rangers**	**NHL**	**32**	**4**	**2**	**6**	**3**	**1**	**4**	**10**	**1**	**0**	**1**	**30**	**13.3**	**22**	**3**	**21**	**1**	**–1**	**3**	**0**	**0**	**0**	**2**	**0**	**0**	**0**
	New Haven Nighthawks	AHL	20	1	4	5	....	....	....	5	....	....	....	....	....	....	....	....	....	....	....	....	....	....	....	....	....	....
1986-87	New Haven Nighthawks	AHL	55	4	12	16	....	....	....	30	....	....	....	....	....	....	....	....	....	....	7	1	1	2	7	....	....	....
1987-88	**St. Louis Blues**	**NHL**	**19**	**3**	**3**	**6**	**3**	**2**	**5**	**6**	**0**	**0**	**1**	**17**	**17.6**	**19**	**0**	**23**	**4**	**0**	**1**	**0**	**0**	**0**	**0**	**0**	**0**	**0**
	Peoria Rivermen	IHL	39	5	21	26	....	....	....	21	....	....	....	....	....	....	....	....	....	....	....	....	....	....	....	....	....	....
1988-89	Baltimore Skipjacks	AHL	61	2	24	26	....	....	....	30	....	....	....	....	....	....	....	....	....	....	....	....	....	....	....	....	....	....
	Peoria Rivermen	IHL	4	0	1	1	....	....	....	4	....	....	....	....	....	....	....	....	....	....	....	....	....	....	....	....	....	....
	NHL Totals		**51**	**7**	**5**	**12**	**6**	**3**	**9**	**16**	**1**	**0**	**2**	**47**	**14.9**	**41**	**3**	**44**	**5**		**4**	**0**	**0**	**0**	**2**	**0**	**0**	**0**

OUAA First All-Star Team (1985)

Signed as a free agent by **NY Rangers**, August 13, 1985. Traded to **St. Louis** by **NY Rangers** with Tony McKegney for Bruce Bell and future considerations, May 28, 1987. Traded to **Washington** by **St. Louis** for Washington's 6th round choice (Derek Frenette) in 1989 Entry Draft, October 19, 1988.

• WHITE, Bill

William Earl D – R. 6'2", 195 lbs. b: Toronto, Ont., 8/26/1939.

Season	Club	League	GP	G	A	Pts	AG	AA	APts	PIM	PP	SH	GW	S	%	TGF	PGF	TGA	PGA	+/–	GP	G	A	Pts	PIM	PP	SH	GW
1956-57	Weston Dukes	OHA-B	STATISTICS NOT AVAILABLE																									
	Toronto Marlboros	OHA-Jr.	2	0	0	0	....	....	....	4	....	....	....	....	....	....	....	....	....	....	....	....	....	....	....	....	....	....
1957-58	Toronto Marlboros	OHA-Jr.	52	2	7	9	....	....	....	34	....	....	....	....	....	....	....	....	....	....	13	1	2	3	18	....	....	....
	Toronto Marlboros	Mem-Cup	5	0	0	0	....	....	....	4	....	....	....	....	....	....	....	....	....	....	....	....	....	....	....	....	....	....
1958-59	Toronto Marlboros	OHA-Jr.	54	3	17	20	....	....	....	63	....	....	....	....	....	....	....	....	....	....	5	3	0	3	2	....	....	....
1959-60	Toronto Marlboros	OHA-Jr.	48	2	17	19	....	....	....	66	....	....	....	....	....	....	....	....	....	....	4	0	1	1	16	....	....	....
	Rochester Americans	AHL	1	0	0	0	....	....	....	0	....	....	....	....	....	....	....	....	....	....	....	....	....	....	....	....	....	....
1960-61	Sudbury Wolves	EPHL	21	1	2	3	....	....	....	20	....	....	....	....	....	....	....	....	....	....	....	....	....	....	....	....	....	....
	Rochester Americans	AHL	47	1	9	10	....	....	....	37	....	....	....	....	....	....	....	....	....	....	....	....	....	....	....	....	....	....
1961-62	Rochester Americans	AHL	67	5	21	26	....	....	....	58	....	....	....	....	....	....	....	....	....	....	2	0	1	1	2	....	....	....
1962-63	Springfield Indians	AHL	69	8	38	46	....	....	....	38	....	....	....	....	....	....	....	....	....	....	....	....	....	....	....	....	....	....
1963-64	Springfield Indians	AHL	72	7	31	38	....	....	....	76	....	....	....	....	....	....	....	....	....	....	....	....	....	....	....	....	....	....
1964-65	Springfield Indians	AHL	71	7	31	38	....	....	....	66	....	....	....	....	....	....	....	....	....	....	....	....	....	....	....	....	....	....
1965-66	Springfield Indians	AHL	68	5	14	19	....	....	....	42	....	....	....	....	....	....	....	....	....	....	6	0	2	2	6	....	....	....
1966-67	Springfield Indians	AHL	69	5	29	34	....	....	....	68	....	....	....	....	....	....	....	....	....	....	....	....	....	....	....	....	....	....
1967-68	**Los Angeles Kings**	**NHL**	**74**	**11**	**27**	**38**	**13**	**27**	**40**	**100**	**2**	**1**	**1**	**170**	**6.5**	**108**	**18**	**97**	**24**	**17**	**7**	**2**	**2**	**4**	**4**	**0**	**0**	**1**
1968-69	**Los Angeles Kings**	**NHL**	**75**	**5**	**28**	**33**	**5**	**25**	**30**	**38**	**0**	**0**	**0**	**163**	**3.1**	**106**	**22**	**133**	**29**	**–20**	**11**	**1**	**4**	**5**	**8**	**0**	**0**	**0**
1969-70	**Los Angeles Kings**	**NHL**	**40**	**4**	**11**	**15**	**4**	**10**	**14**	**21**	**2**	**0**	**0**	**62**	**6.5**	**39**	**8**	**73**	**27**	**–15**	....	....	....	....	....	....	....	....
	Chicago Black Hawks	**NHL**	**21**	**0**	**5**	**5**	**0**	**5**	**5**	**18**	**0**	**0**	**0**	**32**	**0.0**	**24**	**3**	**25**	**7**	**3**	**8**	**1**	**2**	**3**	**8**	**0**	**0**	**0**
1970-71	**Chicago Black Hawks**	**NHL**	**67**	**4**	**21**	**25**	**4**	**18**	**22**	**64**	**0**	**0**	**1**	**127**	**3.1**	**100**	**3**	**73**	**27**	**51**	**18**	**1**	**4**	**5**	**20**	**0**	**0**	**1**
1971-72	**Chicago Black Hawks**	**NHL**	**76**	**7**	**22**	**29**	**7**	**19**	**26**	**58**	**0**	**0**	**0**	**122**	**5.7**	**107**	**5**	**86**	**26**	**42**	**8**	**0**	**3**	**3**	**6**	**0**	**0**	**0**
1972-73	Team Canada	Summit-72	7	1	1	2	....	....	....	8	....	....	....	....	....	....	....	....	....	....	....	....	....	....	....	....	....	....
	Chicago Black Hawks	**NHL**	**72**	**9**	**38**	**47**	**8**	**30**	**38**	**80**	**1**	**0**	**2**	**176**	**5.1**	**151**	**40**	**115**	**34**	**30**	**16**	**1**	**6**	**7**	**10**	**0**	**1**	**0**
1973-74	**Chicago Black Hawks**	**NHL**	**69**	**5**	**31**	**36**	**5**	**26**	**31**	**52**	**0**	**0**	**1**	**85**	**5.9**	**136**	**29**	**73**	**17**	**51**	**11**	**1**	**7**	**8**	**14**	**1**	**0**	**0**
1974-75	**Chicago Black Hawks**	**NHL**	**51**	**4**	**23**	**27**	**3**	**17**	**20**	**20**	**2**	**0**	**0**	**83**	**4.8**	**93**	**26**	**77**	**19**	**9**	**8**	**0**	**3**	**3**	**4**	**0**	**0**	**0**

Season	Club	League	GP	G	A	Pts	AG	AA	APts	PIM	PP	SH	GW	S	%	TGF	PGF	TGA	PGA	+/–	GP	G	A	Pts	PIM	PP	SH	GW
			REGULAR SEASON																		PLAYOFFS							
1975-76	**Chicago Black Hawks**	**NHL**	**59**	**1**	**9**	**10**	**1**	**7**	**8**	**44**	**0**	**0**	**0**	**46**	**2.2**	**64**	**5**	**97**	**28**	**–10**	**4**	**0**	**1**	**1**	**2**	**0**	**0**	**0**
1976-77	**Chicago Black Hawks**	**NHL**	DID NOT PLAY – INJURED																									
1977-78	Oshawa Generals	OMJHL	DID NOT PLAY – COACHING																									
	NHL Totals		**604**	**50**	**215**	**265**	**50**	**184**	**234**	**495**	**7**	**1**	**5**	**1066**	**4.7**	**928**	**159**	**849**	**238**		**91**	**7**	**32**	**39**	**76**	**1**	**1**	**2**

NHL Second All-Star Team (1972, 1973, 1974) • Played in NHL All-Star Game (1969, 1970, 1971, 1972, 1973, 1974)

Traded to **Springfield** (AHL) by **Toronto** (Rochester-AHL) with Dick Mattiussi, Wally Boyer, Jim Wilcox and Roger Cote for Kent Douglas, June 7, 1962. NHL rights transferred to **LA Kings** after NHL club purchased **Springfield** (AHL) franchise, May, 1967. Traded to **Chicago** by **LA Kings** with Bryan Campbell and Gerry Desjardins for Gilles Marotte, Jim Stanfield and Denis Dejordy, February 20, 1970. • Suffered eventual career-ending neck injury in game vs. Montreal, April 16, 1976.

• WHITE, Brian D – R. 6'1", 180 lbs. b: Winchester, MA, 2/7/1976. Tampa Bay's 11th, 268th overall, in 1994.

Season	Club	League	GP	G	A	Pts	AG	AA	APts	PIM	PP	SH	GW	S	%	TGF	PGF	TGA	PGA	+/–	GP	G	A	Pts	PIM	PP	SH	GW
1993-94	Arlington Catholic High	Hi-School	40	14	18	32	....	....	....	81	....	....	....	....	....	....	....	....	....	....	....	....	....	....	....	....	....	....
1994-95	University of Maine	H-East	28	1	1	2	....	....	....	16	....	....	....	....	....	....	....	....	....	....	....	....	....	....	....	....	....	....
1995-96	University of Maine	H-East	39	0	4	4	....	....	....	18	....	....	....	....	....	....	....	....	....	....	....	....	....	....	....	....	....	....
1996-97	University of Maine	H-East	35	4	12	16	....	....	....	36	....	....	....	....	....	....	....	....	....	....	....	....	....	....	....	....	....	....
1997-98	University of Maine	H-East	33	0	12	12	....	....	....	45	....	....	....	....	....	....	....	....	....	....	....	....	....	....	....	....	....	....
	Long Beach Ice Dogs	IHL	1	0	0	0	....	....	....	0	....	....	....	....	....	....	....	....	....	....	....	....	....	....	....	....	....	....
1998-99	**Colorado Avalanche**	**NHL**	**2**	**0**	**0**	**0**	**0**	**0**	**0**	**0**	**0**	**0**	**0**	**0**	**0.0**	**0**	**0**	**0**	**0**	**0**	....	....	....	....	....	....	....	....
	Hershey Bears	AHL	71	4	8	12	....	....	....	41	....	....	....	....	....	....	....	....	....	....	4	0	1	1	2	....	....	....
99-2000	Hershey Bears	AHL	79	3	19	22	....	....	....	78	....	....	....	....	....	....	....	....	....	....	14	0	3	3	21	....	....	....
	NHL Totals		**2**	**0**	**0**	**0**	**0**	**0**	**0**	**0**	**0**	**0**	**0**	**0**	**0.0**	**0**	**0**	**0**	**0**		....	....	....	....	....	....	....	....

Signed as a free agent by **Colorado**, July 7, 1998.

• WHITE, Colin John Colin D – L. 6'4", 210 lbs. b: New Glasgow, N.S., 12/12/1977. New Jersey's 5th, 49th overall, in 1996.

Season	Club	League	GP	G	A	Pts	AG	AA	APts	PIM	PP	SH	GW	S	%	TGF	PGF	TGA	PGA	+/–	GP	G	A	Pts	PIM	PP	SH	GW
1994-95	Laval Titan	QMJHL	7	0	1	1	....	....	....	32	....	....	....	....	....	....	....	....	....	....	....	....	....	....	....	....	....	....
	Hull Olympiques	QMJHL	5	0	1	1	....	....	....	4	....	....	....	....	....	....	....	....	....	....	12	0	0	0	23	....	....	....
1995-96	Hull Olympiques	QMJHL	62	2	8	10	....	....	....	303	....	....	....	....	....	....	....	....	....	....	18	0	4	4	42	....	....	....
1996-97	Hull Olympiques	QMJHL	63	3	12	15	....	....	....	297	....	....	....	....	....	....	....	....	....	....	14	3	12	15	65	....	....	....
1997-98	Albany River Rats	AHL	76	3	13	16	....	....	....	235	....	....	....	....	....	....	....	....	....	....	13	0	0	0	55	....	....	....
1998-99	Albany River Rats	AHL	77	2	12	14	....	....	....	265	....	....	....	....	....	....	....	....	....	....	5	0	1	1	8	....	....	....
99-2000♦	**New Jersey Devils**	**NHL**	**21**	**2**	**1**	**3**	**2**	**1**	**3**	**40**	**0**	**0**	**1**	**29**	**6.9**	**11**	**0**	**10**	**2**	**3**	**23**	**1**	**5**	**6**	**18**	**0**	**0**	**1**
	Albany River Rats	AHL	52	5	21	26	....	....	....	176	....	....	....	....	....	....	....	....	....	....	....	....	....	....	....	....	....	....
	NHL Totals		**21**	**2**	**1**	**3**	**2**	**1**	**3**	**40**	**0**	**0**	**1**	**29**	**6.9**	**11**	**0**	**10**	**2**		**23**	**1**	**5**	**6**	**18**	**0**	**0**	**1**

• WHITE, Peter C – L. 5'11", 200 lbs. b: Montreal, Que., 3/15/1969. Edmonton's 4th, 92nd overall, in 1989.

Season	Club	League	GP	G	A	Pts	AG	AA	APts	PIM	PP	SH	GW	S	%	TGF	PGF	TGA	PGA	+/–	GP	G	A	Pts	PIM	PP	SH	GW
1984-85	Lac-St-Louis Lions	QAAA	42	16	32	48	....	....	....	....	....	....	....	....	....	....	....	....	....	....	....	....	....	....	....	....	....	....
1985-86	Lac St-Louis Lions	QAAA	42	38	62	100	....	....	....	....	....	....	....	....	....	....	....	....	....	....	....	....	....	....	....	....	....	....
1986-87	Pembroke Lumber Kings	OJHL	55	20	34	54	....	....	....	20	....	....	....	....	....	....	....	....	....	....	....	....	....	....	....	....	....	....
	Pembroke Lumber Kings	Cen-Cup	4	2	2	4	....	....	....	2	....	....	....	....	....	....	....	....	....	....	....	....	....	....	....	....	....	....
1987-88	Pembroke Lumber Kings	OJHL	56	*90	*136	*226	....	....	....	32	....	....	....	....	....	....	....	....	....	....	....	....	....	....	....	....	....	....
	Pembroke Lumber Kings	Cen-Cup	4	3	6	9	....	....	....	....	....	....	....	....	....	....	....	....	....	....	....	....	....	....	....	....	....	....
1988-89	Michigan State Spartans	CCHA	46	20	33	53	....	....	....	17	....	....	....	....	....	....	....	....	....	....	....	....	....	....	....	....	....	....
1989-90	Michigan State Spartans	CCHA	45	22	40	62	....	....	....	6	....	....	....	....	....	....	....	....	....	....	....	....	....	....	....	....	....	....
1990-91	Michigan State Spartans	CCHA	37	7	31	38	....	....	....	28	....	....	....	....	....	....	....	....	....	....	....	....	....	....	....	....	....	....
1991-92	Michigan State Spartans	CCHA	41	26	49	75	....	....	....	32	....	....	....	....	....	....	....	....	....	....	....	....	....	....	....	....	....	....
1992-93	Cape Breton Oilers	AHL	64	12	28	40	....	....	....	10	....	....	....	....	....	....	....	....	....	....	16	3	3	6	12	....	....	....
1993-94	**Edmonton Oilers**	**NHL**	**26**	**3**	**5**	**8**	**3**	**4**	**7**	**2**	**0**	**0**	**0**	**17**	**17.6**	**11**	**0**	**13**	**3**	**1**	....	....	....	....	....	....	....	....
	Cape Breton Oilers	AHL	45	21	49	70	....	....	....	12	....	....	....	....	....	....	....	....	....	....	5	2	3	5	2	....	....	....
1994-95	Cape Breton Oilers	AHL	65	36	*69	*105	....	....	....	30	....	....	....	....	....	....	....	....	....	....	....	....	....	....	....	....	....	....
	Edmonton Oilers	**NHL**	**9**	**2**	**4**	**6**	**4**	**6**	**10**	**0**	**2**	**0**	**0**	**13**	**15.4**	**6**	**2**	**3**	**0**	**1**	....	....	....	....	....	....	....	....
1995-96	**Edmonton Oilers**	**NHL**	**26**	**5**	**3**	**8**	**5**	**2**	**7**	**0**	**1**	**0**	**0**	**34**	**14.7**	**9**	**2**	**26**	**5**	**–14**	....	....	....	....	....	....	....	....
	Toronto Maple Leafs	**NHL**	**1**	**0**	**0**	**0**	**0**	**0**	**0**	**0**	**1**	**0**	**0**	**0**	**0.0**	**0**	**0**	**0**	**0**	**0**	....	....	....	....	....	....	....	....
	St. John's Maple Leafs	AHL	17	6	7	13	....	....	....	6	....	....	....	....	....	....	....	....	....	....	....	....	....	....	....	....	....	....
	Atlanta Knights	IHL	36	21	20	41	....	....	....	4	....	....	....	....	....	....	....	....	....	....	3	0	3	3	2	....	....	....
1996-97	Philadelphia Phantoms	AHL	80	*44	61	*105	....	....	....	28	....	....	....	....	....	....	....	....	....	....	10	6	8	14	6	....	....	....
1997-98	Philadelphia Phantoms	AHL	80	27	*78	*105	....	....	....	28	....	....	....	....	....	....	....	....	....	....	20	9	9	18	6	....	....	....
1998-99	**Philadelphia Flyers**	**NHL**	**3**	**0**	**0**	**0**	**0**	**0**	**0**	**0**	**0**	**0**	**0**	**0**	**0.0**	**0**	**0**	**0**	**0**	**0**	....	....	....	....	....	....	....	....
	Philadelphia Phantoms	AHL	77	31	59	90	....	....	....	20	....	....	....	....	....	....	....	....	....	....	16	4	13	17	12	....	....	....
99-2000	**Philadelphia Flyers**	**NHL**	**21**	**1**	**5**	**6**	**1**	**5**	**6**	**6**	**0**	**0**	**0**	**24**	**4.2**	**10**	**0**	**10**	**1**	**1**	**16**	**0**	**2**	**2**	**0**	**0**	**0**	**0**
	Philadelphia Phantoms	AHL	62	20	41	61	....	....	....	38	....	....	....	....	....	....	....	....	....	....	....	....	....	....	....	....	....	....
	NHL Totals		**86**	**11**	**17**	**28**	**13**	**17**	**30**	**8**	**4**	**0**	**0**	**88**	**12.5**	**36**	**4**	**52**	**9**		**16**	**0**	**2**	**2**	**0**	**0**	**0**	**0**

AHL Second All-Star Team (1995, 1997) • Won John B. Sollenberger Trophy (Top Scorer - AHL) (1995, 1997, 1998)

Traded to **Toronto** by **Edmonton** with Edmonton's 4th round choice (Jason Sessa) in 1996 Entry Draft for Kent Manderville, December 4, 1995. Signed as a free agent by **Philadelphia**, August 19, 1996.

• WHITE, Todd C – L. 5'10", 189 lbs. b: Kanata, Ont., 5/21/1975.

Season	Club	League	GP	G	A	Pts	AG	AA	APts	PIM	PP	SH	GW	S	%	TGF	PGF	TGA	PGA	+/–	GP	G	A	Pts	PIM	PP	SH	GW
1990-91	Powassan Passports	OJHL	38	34	38	72	....	....	....	118	....	....	....	....	....	....	....	....	....	....	....	....	....	....	....	....	....	....
1991-92	Kanata Valley Lasers	OJHL	55	39	49	88	....	....	....	30	....	....	....	....	....	....	....	....	....	....	....	....	....	....	....	....	....	....
1992-93	Kanata Valley Lasers	OJHL	49	51	87	138	....	....	....	46	....	....	....	....	....	....	....	....	....	....	....	....	....	....	....	....	....	....
1993-94	Clarkson University	ECAC	33	10	12	22	....	....	....	28	....	....	....	....	....	....	....	....	....	....	....	....	....	....	....	....	....	....
1994-95	Clarkson University	ECAC	34	13	16	29	....	....	....	44	....	....	....	....	....	....	....	....	....	....	....	....	....	....	....	....	....	....
1995-96	Clarkson University	ECAC	38	29	43	72	....	....	....	36	....	....	....	....	....	....	....	....	....	....	....	....	....	....	....	....	....	....
1996-97	Clarkson University	ECAC	37	*38	*36	*74	....	....	....	22	....	....	....	....	....	....	....	....	....	....	....	....	....	....	....	....	....	....
1997-98	**Chicago Blackhawks**	**NHL**	**7**	**1**	**0**	**1**	**1**	**0**	**1**	**2**	**0**	**0**	**0**	**3**	**33.3**	**4**	**0**	**4**	**0**	**0**	....	....	....	....	....	....	....	....
	Indianapolis Ice	IHL	65	46	36	82	....	....	....	28	....	....	....	....	....	....	....	....	....	....	5	2	3	5	4	....	....	....
1998-99	**Chicago Blackhawks**	**NHL**	**35**	**5**	**8**	**13**	**6**	**8**	**14**	**20**	**2**	**0**	**0**	**43**	**11.6**	**19**	**6**	**19**	**5**	**–1**	....	....	....	....	....	....	....	....
	Chicago Wolves	IHL	25	11	13	24	....	....	....	8	....	....	....	....	....	....	....	....	....	....	10	1	4	5	8	....	....	....
99-2000	**Chicago Blackhawks**	**NHL**	**1**	**0**	**0**	**0**	**0**	**0**	**0**	**0**	**0**	**0**	**0**	**0**	**0.0**	**0**	**0**	**0**	**0**	**0**	....	....	....	....	....	....	....	....
	Cleveland Lumberjacks	IHL	42	21	30	51	....	....	....	32	....	....	....	....	....	....	....	....	....	....	....	....	....	....	....	....	....	....
	Philadelphia Flyers	**NHL**	**3**	**1**	**0**	**1**	**1**	**0**	**1**	**0**	**0**	**0**	**0**	**4**	**25.0**	**1**	**0**	**2**	**0**	**–1**	....	....	....	....	....	....	....	....
	Philadelphia Phantoms	AHL	32	19	24	43	....	....	....	12	....	....	....	....	....	....	....	....	....	....	5	2	1	3	8	....	....	....
	NHL Totals		**46**	**7**	**8**	**15**	**8**	**8**	**16**	**22**	**2**	**0**	**0**	**50**	**14.0**	**24**	**6**	**25**	**5**		....	....	....	....	....	....	....	....

ECAC Second All-Star Team (1996) • NCAA East Second All-American Team (1996) • ECAC First All-Star Team (1997) • NCAA East First All-American Team (1997) • Won Garry F. Longman Memorial Trophy (Top Rookie - IHL) (1998)

Signed as a free agent by **Chicago**, August 27, 1997. Traded to **Philadelphia** by **Chicago** for a conditional choice in 2001 Entry Draft, January 26, 2000. Signed as a free agent by **Ottawa**, July 12, 2000.

• WHITE, Tony Anthony Raymond LW – L. 5'10", 175 lbs. b: Grand Falls, Nfld., 6/16/1954. Washington's 10th, 161st overall, in 1974.

Season	Club	League	GP	G	A	Pts	AG	AA	APts	PIM	PP	SH	GW	S	%	TGF	PGF	TGA	PGA	+/–	GP	G	A	Pts	PIM	PP	SH	GW
1970-71	Grand Falls Novas	Nfld-Jr.	STATISTICS NOT AVAILABLE																									
	Grand Falls Cataracts	Nfld-Sr.	....	....	....	....	....	....	....	....	....	....	....	....	....	....	....	....	....	....	1	0	0	0	0	....	....	....
1971-72	Grand Falls Cataracts	Nfld-Sr.	35	14	19	33	....	....	....	17	....	....	....	....	....	....	....	....	....	....	12	2	6	8	2	....	....	....
	Grand Falls Cataracts	Al-Cup	4	0	1	1	....	....	....	2	....	....	....	....	....	....	....	....	....	....	....	....	....	....	....	....	....	....
1972-73	Kitchener Rangers	OMJHL	60	20	33	53	....	....	....	65	....	....	....	....	....	....	....	....	....	....	....	....	....	....	....	....	....	....
1973-74	Kitchener Rangers	OMJHL	70	15	38	53	....	....	....	69	....	....	....	....	....	....	....	....	....	....	....	....	....	....	....	....	....	....
1974-75	**Washington Capitals**	**NHL**	**5**	**0**	**2**	**2**	**0**	**1**	**1**	**0**	**0**	**0**	**0**	**8**	**0.0**	**3**	**0**	**3**	**0**	**0**	....	....	....	....	....	....	....	....
	Dayton Gems	IHL	64	23	35	58	....	....	....	73	....	....	....	....	....	....	....	....	....	....	14	7	9	16	27	....	....	....
1975-76	**Washington Capitals**	**NHL**	**80**	**25**	**17**	**42**	**22**	**13**	**35**	**56**	**7**	**0**	**2**	**168**	**14.9**	**75**	**23**	**101**	**6**	**–43**	....	....	....	....	....	....	....	....
1976-77	**Washington Capitals**	**NHL**	**72**	**12**	**9**	**21**	**11**	**7**	**18**	**44**	**2**	**1**	**3**	**126**	**9.5**	**45**	**5**	**58**	**3**	**–15**	....	....	....	....	....	....	....	....

Season	Club	League	REGULAR SEASON GP	G	A	Pts	AG	AA	APts	PIM	PP	SH	GW	S	%	TGF	PGF	TGA	PGA	+/–	PLAYOFFS GP	G	A	Pts	PIM	PP	SH	GW
1977-78	**Washington Capitals**	**NHL**	**1**	**0**	**0**	**0**	**0**	**0**	**0**	**0**	**0**	**0**	**0**	**4**	**0.0**	**1**	**1**	**4**	**0**	**–4**	....	....	....	....	....	....	....	....
	Hershey Bears	AHL	68	24	29	53	....	....	....	28	....	....	....	....	....	....	....	....	....	....	....	....	....	....	....	....	....	....
1978-79	Springfield Indians	AHL	80	26	29	55	....	....	....	30	....	....	....	....	....	....	....	....	....	....	....	....	....	....	....	....	....	....
1979-80	**Minnesota North Stars**	**NHL**	**6**	**0**	**0**	**0**	**0**	**0**	**0**	**4**	**0**	**0**	**0**	**10**	**0.0**	**2**	**0**	**4**	**0**	**–2**	....	....	....	....	....	....	....	....
	Oklahoma City Stars	CHL	74	30	28	58	....	....	....	59	....	....	....	....	....	....	....	....	....	....	....	....	....	....	....	....	....	....
1980-81	Oklahoma City Stars	CHL	74	21	41	62	....	....	....	55	....	....	....	....	....	....	....	....	....	....	3	0	1	1	6	....	....	....
1981-82	EV Fussen	Germany	41	21	21	42	....	....	....	79	....	....	....	....	....	....	....	....	....	....	....	....	....	....	....	....	....	....
1982-83	EV Fussen	Germany	25	9	13	22	....	....	....	42	....	....	....	....	....	....	....	....	....	....	....	....	....	....	....	....	....	....
	NHL Totals		**164**	**37**	**28**	**65**	**33**	**21**	**54**	**104**	**9**	**1**	**5**	**316**	**11.7**	**126**	**29**	**170**	**9**		....	....	....	....	....	....	....	....

Signed as a free agent by **Minnesota**, September 17, 1979.

• WHITFIELD, Trent

C – L. 5'11", 200 lbs. b: Estevan, Sask., 6/17/1977. Boston's 5th, 100th overall, in 1996.

Season	Club	League	GP	G	A	Pts	AG	AA	APts	PIM	PP	SH	GW	S	%	TGF	PGF	TGA	PGA	+/–	GP	G	A	Pts	PIM	PP	SH	GW
1993-94	Saskatoon Blazers	SAHA	36	26	22	48	....	....	....	42	....	....	....	....	....	....	....	....	....	....	....	....	....	....	....	....	....	....
	Spokane Chiefs	WHL	5	1	1	2	....	....	....	0	....	....	....	....	....	....	....	....	....	....	....	....	....	....	....	....	....	....
	Spokane Chiefs	WHL	5	1	1	2	....	....	....	0	....	....	....	....	....	....	....	....	....	....	....	....	....	....	....	....	....	....
1994-95	Spokane Chiefs	WHL	48	8	17	25	....	....	....	26	....	....	....	....	....	....	....	....	....	....	11	7	6	13	5	....	....	....
1995-96	Spokane Chiefs	WHL	72	33	51	84	....	....	....	75	....	....	....	....	....	....	....	....	....	....	18	8	10	18	10	....	....	....
1996-97	Spokane Chiefs	WHL	58	34	42	76	....	....	....	74	....	....	....	....	....	....	....	....	....	....	9	5	7	12	10	....	....	....
1997-98	Spokane Chiefs	WHL	65	38	44	82	....	....	....	97	....	....	....	....	....	....	....	....	....	....	18	9	10	19	15	....	....	....
1998-99	Portland Pirates	AHL	50	10	8	18	....	....	....	20	....	....	....	....	....	....	....	....	....	....	....	....	....	....	....	....	....	....
	Hampton Roads Admirals	ECHL	19	13	12	25	....	....	....	12	....	....	....	....	....	....	....	....	....	....	4	2	0	2	14	....	....	....
99-2000	Portland Pirates	AHL	79	18	35	53	....	....	....	52	....	....	....	....	....	....	....	....	....	....	3	1	1	2	2	....	....	....
	Washington Capitals	**NHL**	....	....	....	....	....	....	....	....	....	....	....	....	....	....	....	....	....	....	**3**	**0**	**0**	**0**	**0**	**0**	**0**	**0**
	NHL Totals		....	....	....	....	....	....	....	....	....	....	....	....	....	....	....	....	....	....	**3**	**0**	**0**	**0**	**0**	**0**	**0**	**0**

WHL West First All-Star Team (1997) • WHL West Second All-Star Team (1998)

Signed as a free agent by **Washington**, September 1, 1998.

• WHITLOCK, Bob

Robert Angus C – R. 5'10", 175 lbs. b: Charlottetown, P.E.I., 7/16/1949.

Season	Club	League	GP	G	A	Pts	AG	AA	APts	PIM	PP	SH	GW	S	%	TGF	PGF	TGA	PGA	+/–	GP	G	A	Pts	PIM	PP	SH	GW
1966-67	Halifax Jr. Canadiens	X-Games	48	52	70	122	....	....	....	52	....	....	....	....	....	....	....	....	....	....	....	....	....	....	....	....	....	....
	Halifax Jr. Canadiens	Mem-Cup	18	14	18	32	....	....	....	18	....	....	....	....	....	....	....	....	....	....	....	....	....	....	....	....	....	....
1967-68	Fredericton Jr. Red Wings	SNBHL	5	2	3	5	....	....	....	28	....	....	....	....	....	....	....	....	....	....	....	....	....	....	....	....	....	....
	Halifax Jr. Canadiens	MJrHL	38	53	42	95	....	....	....	4	....	....	....	....	....	....	....	....	....	....	11	*9	*11	*20	0	....	....	....
1968-69	Kitchener Rangers	OHA-Jr.	22	9	15	24	....	....	....	51	....	....	....	....	....	....	....	....	....	....	....	....	....	....	....	....	....	....
	Edmonton Oil Kings	WCJHL	6	2	2	4	....	....	....	0	....	....	....	....	....	....	....	....	....	....	....	....	....	....	....	....	....	....
1969-70	**Minnesota North Stars**	**NHL**	**1**	**0**	**0**	**0**	**0**	**0**	**0**	**0**	**0**	**0**	**0**	**3**	**0.0**	**1**	**0**	**0**	**0**	**1**	....	....	....	....	....	....	....	....
	Iowa Stars	CHL	63	26	28	54	....	....	....	58	....	....	....	....	....	....	....	....	....	....	11	4	3	7	4	....	....	....
1970-71	Cleveland Barons	AHL	68	19	15	34	....	....	....	30	....	....	....	....	....	....	....	....	....	....	8	1	2	3	4	....	....	....
1971-72	Phoenix Roadrunners	WHL	64	33	46	79	....	....	....	69	....	....	....	....	....	....	....	....	....	....	4	2	2	4	4	....	....	....
1972-73	Chicago Cougars	WHA	75	23	28	51	....	....	....	53	....	....	....	....	....	....	....	....	....	....	....	....	....	....	....	....	....	....
1973-74	Chicago Cougars	WHA	52	16	19	35	....	....	....	44	....	....	....	....	....	....	....	....	....	....	....	....	....	....	....	....	....	....
	Los Angeles Sharks	WHA	14	4	10	14	....	....	....	4	....	....	....	....	....	....	....	....	....	....	....	....	....	....	....	....	....	....
1974-75	Indianapolis Racers	WHA	73	31	26	57	....	....	....	56	....	....	....	....	....	....	....	....	....	....	....	....	....	....	....	....	....	....
1975-76	Indianapolis Racers	WHA	30	7	15	22	....	....	....	16	....	....	....	....	....	....	....	....	....	....	....	....	....	....	....	....	....	....
	Mohawk Valley Comets	NAHL	32	15	20	35	....	....	....	42	....	....	....	....	....	....	....	....	....	....	....	....	....	....	....	....	....	....
1976-77	Erie Blades	NAHL	15	7	7	14	....	....	....	8	....	....	....	....	....	....	....	....	....	....	....	....	....	....	....	....	....	....
	Johnstown Jets	NAHL	20	8	8	16	....	....	....	26	....	....	....	....	....	....	....	....	....	....	....	....	....	....	....	....	....	....
1977-78	Trail Smoke Eaters	WIHL	....	31	27	58	....	....	....	59	....	....	....	....	....	....	....	....	....	....	....	....	....	....	....	....	....	....
	Charlottetown GJ's	NBSHL	STATISTICS NOT AVAILABLE																									
	NHL Totals		**1**	**0**	**0**	**0**	**0**	**0**	**0**	**0**	**0**	**0**	**0**	**3**	**0.0**	**1**	**0**	**0**	**0**		....	....	....	....	....	....	....	....
	Other Major League Totals		244	81	98	179	....	....	....	173	....	....	....	....	....	....	....	....	....	....	....	....	....	....	....	....	....	....

Won WHL Rookie of the Year Award (1972)

Signed as a free agent by **Minnesota**, October 2, 1969. Selected by **LA Sharks** (WHA) in 1972 WHA General Player Draft, February 12, 1972. Traded to **Chicago** (WHA) by **LA Sharks** (WHA) with Bob Liddington and the rights to Larry Cahan for Bill Young and future considerations, July, 1972. Traded to **LA Sharks** (WHA) by **Chicago** (WHA) for Don Gordon and Jim Watson, February 20, 1974. Transferred to **Michigan** (WHA) after **LA Sharks** relocated, April 11, 1974. Claimed by **Indianapolis** (WHA) from **Michigan** (WHA) in WHA Expansion Draft, May, 1974.

• WHITNEY, Ray

LW – R. 5'10", 175 lbs. b: Fort Saskatchewan, Alta., 5/8/1972. San Jose's 2nd, 23rd overall, in 1991.

Season	Club	League	GP	G	A	Pts	AG	AA	APts	PIM	PP	SH	GW	S	%	TGF	PGF	TGA	PGA	+/–	GP	G	A	Pts	PIM	PP	SH	GW
1987-88	Fort Saskatchewan Rangers	AAHA	71	80	155	235	....	....	....	119	....	....	....	....	....	....	....	....	....	....	....	....	....	....	....	....	....	....
1988-89	Spokane Chiefs	WHL	71	17	33	50	....	....	....	16	....	....	....	....	....	....	....	....	....	....	....	....	....	....	....	....	....	....
1989-90	Spokane Chiefs	WHL	71	57	56	113	....	....	....	50	....	....	....	....	....	....	....	....	....	....	6	3	4	7	6	....	....	....
1990-91	Spokane Chiefs	WHL	72	67	118	*185	....	....	....	36	....	....	....	....	....	....	....	....	....	....	15	13	18	*31	12	....	....	....
	Spokane Chiefs	Mem-Cup	4	5	*6	*11	....	....	....	4	....	....	....	....	....	....	....	....	....	....	....	....	....	....	....	....	....	....
1991-92	Kolner EC	Germany	10	3	6	9	....	....	....	4	....	....	....	....	....	....	....	....	....	....	....	....	....	....	....	....	....	....
	Canada	Nat-Team	5	1	0	1	....	....	....	6	....	....	....	....	....	....	....	....	....	....	....	....	....	....	....	....	....	....
	San Jose Sharks	**NHL**	**2**	**0**	**3**	**3**	**0**	**2**	**2**	**0**	**0**	**0**	**0**	**4**	**0.0**	**3**	**2**	**2**	**0**	**–1**	....	....	....	....	....	....	....	....
	San Diego Gulls	IHL	63	36	54	90	....	....	....	12	....	....	....	....	....	....	....	....	....	....	4	0	0	0	0	....	....	....
1992-93	**San Jose Sharks**	**NHL**	**26**	**4**	**6**	**10**	**3**	**4**	**7**	**4**	**1**	**0**	**0**	**24**	**16.7**	**12**	**4**	**22**	**0**	**–14**	....	....	....	....	....	....	....	....
	Kansas City Blades	IHL	46	20	33	53	....	....	....	14	....	....	....	....	....	....	....	....	....	....	12	5	7	12	2	....	....	....
1993-94	**San Jose Sharks**	**NHL**	**61**	**14**	**26**	**40**	**13**	**20**	**33**	**14**	**1**	**0**	**0**	**82**	**17.1**	**56**	**18**	**38**	**2**	**2**	**14**	**0**	**4**	**4**	**8**	**0**	**0**	**0**
1994-95	**San Jose Sharks**	**NHL**	**39**	**13**	**12**	**25**	**23**	**18**	**41**	**14**	**4**	**0**	**1**	**67**	**19.4**	**37**	**13**	**31**	**0**	**–7**	**11**	**4**	**4**	**8**	**2**	**0**	**0**	**1**
1995-96	**San Jose Sharks**	**NHL**	**60**	**17**	**24**	**41**	**17**	**20**	**37**	**16**	**4**	**2**	**2**	**106**	**16.0**	**58**	**17**	**74**	**10**	**–23**	....	....	....	....	....	....	....	....
1996-97	**San Jose Sharks**	**NHL**	**12**	**0**	**2**	**2**	**0**	**2**	**2**	**4**	**0**	**0**	**0**	**24**	**0.0**	**5**	**0**	**13**	**2**	**–6**	....	....	....	....	....	....	....	....
	Kentucky Thoroughblades	AHL	9	1	7	8	....	....	....	2	....	....	....	....	....	....	....	....	....	....	....	....	....	....	....	....	....	....
	Utah Grizzlies	IHL	43	13	35	48	....	....	....	34	....	....	....	....	....	....	....	....	....	....	7	3	1	4	6	....	....	....
1997-98	**Edmonton Oilers**	**NHL**	**9**	**1**	**3**	**4**	**1**	**3**	**4**	**0**	**0**	**0**	**0**	**19**	**5.3**	**6**	**4**	**3**	**0**	**–1**	....	....	....	....	....	....	....	....
	Florida Panthers	**NHL**	**68**	**32**	**29**	**61**	**38**	**28**	**66**	**28**	**12**	**0**	**2**	**156**	**20.5**	**77**	**34**	**33**	**0**	**10**	....	....	....	....	....	....	....	....
	Canada	WC-A	6	4	2	6	....	....	....	4	....	....	....	....	....	....	....	....	....	....	....	....	....	....	....	....	....	....
1998-99	**Florida Panthers**	**NHL**	**81**	**26**	**38**	**64**	**31**	**37**	**68**	**18**	**7**	**0**	**6**	**193**	**13.5**	**85**	**33**	**56**	**1**	**–3**	....	....	....	....	....	....	....	....
	Canada	WC-A	10	1	6	7	....	....	....	22	....	....	....	....	....	....	....	....	....	....	....	....	....	....	....	....	....	....
99-2000	**Florida Panthers**	**NHL**	**81**	**29**	**42**	**71**	**33**	**39**	**72**	**35**	**5**	**0**	**3**	**198**	**14.6**	**92**	**29**	**50**	**3**	**16**	**4**	**1**	**0**	**1**	**4**	**0**	**0**	**0**
	NHL Totals		**439**	**136**	**185**	**321**	**159**	**173**	**332**	**133**	**34**	**2**	**14**	**873**	**15.6**	**431**	**154**	**322**	**18**		**29**	**5**	**8**	**13**	**14**	**0**	**0**	**1**

WHL West First All-Star Team (1991) • Memorial Cup All-Star Team (1991) • Won George Parsons Trophy (Memorial Cup Tournament Most Sportsmanlike Player) (1991) • Played in NHL All-Star Game (2000)

Signed as a free agent by **Edmonton**, October 1, 1997. Claimed on waivers by **Florida** from **Edmonton**, November 6, 1997.

• WHYTE, Sean

Sean G. "Sheepdog" RW – R. 6', 198 lbs. b: Sudbury, Ont., 5/4/1970. Los Angeles' 7th, 165th overall, in 1989.

Season	Club	League	GP	G	A	Pts	AG	AA	APts	PIM	PP	SH	GW	S	%	TGF	PGF	TGA	PGA	+/–	GP	G	A	Pts	PIM	PP	SH	GW
1985-86	Gloucester Bantam Rangers	OMHA	34	23	15	38	....	....	....	45	....	....	....	....	....	....	....	....	....	....	....	....	....	....	....	....	....	....
1986-87	Guelph Jr. B's	OJHL-B	4	0	7	7	....	....	....	6	....	....	....	....	....	....	....	....	....	....	....	....	....	....	....	....	....	....
	Guelph Platers	OHL	41	1	3	4	....	....	....	13	....	....	....	....	....	....	....	....	....	....	....	....	....	....	....	....	....	....
1987-88	Guelph Platers	OHL	62	6	22	28	....	....	....	71	....	....	....	....	....	....	....	....	....	....	....	....	....	....	....	....	....	....
1988-89	Guelph Platers	OHL	53	20	44	64	....	....	....	57	....	....	....	....	....	....	....	....	....	....	....	....	....	....	....	....	....	....
1989-90	Owen Sound Platers	OHL	54	23	30	53	....	....	....	90	....	....	....	....	....	....	....	....	....	....	3	0	1	1	10	....	....	....
1990-91	Phoenix Roadrunners	IHL	60	18	17	35	....	....	....	61	....	....	....	....	....	....	....	....	....	....	4	1	0	1	2	....	....	....
1991-92	**Los Angeles Kings**	**NHL**	**3**	**0**	**0**	**0**	**0**	**0**	**0**	**0**	**0**	**0**	**0**	**0**	**0.0**	**0**	**0**	**1**	**0**	**–1**	....	....	....	....	....	....	....	....
	Phoenix Roadrunners	IHL	72	24	30	54	....	....	....	113	....	....	....	....	....	....	....	....	....	....	....	....	....	....	....	....	....	....
1992-93	**Los Angeles Kings**	**NHL**	**18**	**0**	**2**	**2**	**0**	**1**	**1**	**12**	**0**	**0**	**0**	**7**	**0.0**	**6**	**0**	**5**	**0**	**1**	....	....	....	....	....	....	....	....
	Phoenix Roadrunners	IHL	51	11	35	46	....	....	....	65	....	....	....	....	....	....	....	....	....	....	....	....	....	....	....	....	....	....
1993-94	Tulsa Oilers	CHL	50	42	29	71	....	....	....	93	....	....	....	....	....	....	....	....	....	....	....	....	....	....	....	....	....	....
	Cornwall Aces	AHL	18	6	9	15	....	....	....	16	....	....	....	....	....	....	....	....	....	....	9	1	2	3	2	....	....	....

			REGULAR SEASON																		PLAYOFFS							
Season	Club	League	GP	G	A	Pts	AG	AA	APts	PIM	PP	SH	GW	S	%	TGF	PGF	TGA	PGA	+/-	GP	G	A	Pts	PIM	PP	SH	GW
1994-95	Worcester IceCats	AHL	59	13	8	21	....	....	....	76	....	....	....	....	....	....	....	....	....	....	....	....	....	....	....	....	....	....
1995-96	Fort Worth Fire	CHL	51	15	37	52	....	....	....	94	....	....	....	....	....	....	....	....	....	....	....	....	....	....	....	....	....	....
	Phoenix Roadrunners	IHL	11	0	2	2	....	....	....	4	....	....	....	....	....	....	....	....	....	....	....	....	....	....	....	....	....	....
1996-97	El Paso Buzzards	WPHL	60	21	39	60	....	....	....	105	....	....	....	....	....	....	....	....	....	....	11	2	*14	16	36	....	....	....
1997-98	Phoenix Mustangs	WCHL	53	19	23	42	....	....	....	93	....	....	....	....	....	....	....	....	....	....	9	4	10	14	10	....	....	....
1998-99	Phoenix Mustangs	WCHL	65	16	34	50	....	....	....	80	....	....	....	....	....	....	....	....	....	....	3	2	0	2	4	....	....	....
99-2000	Phoenix Mustangs	WCHL	60	28	28	56	....	....	....	50	....	....	....	....	....	....	....	....	....	....	12	4	5	9	32	....	....	....
	NHL Totals		**21**	**0**	**2**	**2**	**0**	**1**	**1**	**12**	**0**	**0**	**0**	**7**	**0.0**	**6**	**0**	**6**	**0**		....	....	....	....	....	....	....	....

Signed as a free agent by **Phoenix Mustangs** (WCHL), September 4, 1997. • Served as Player/Assistant Coach with **Phoenix Mustangs** (WCHL) during 99-2000 season. Played w/ RHI's Phoenix Cobras in 1994 (20-11-15-26-51) and 1995 (24-18-29-47-64); Anaheim Bullfrogs in 1996 (4-1-1-2-6); 1997 (8-6-7-13-0); 1998 (13-3-14-17-12) and 1999 (25-13-23-36-52).

• WICKENHEISER, Doug

Douglas Peter C – L. 6'1", 200 lbs. b: Regina, Sask., 3/30/1961 d: 1/12/1999. Montreal's 1st, 1st overall, in 1980.

Season	Club	League	GP	G	A	Pts	AG	AA	APts	PIM	PP	SH	GW	S	%	TGF	PGF	TGA	PGA	+/-	GP	G	A	Pts	PIM	PP	SH	GW
1976-77	Regina Blues	SJHL	59	42	46	88	....	....	....	63	....	....	....	....	....	....	....	....	....	....	....	....	....	....	....	....	....	....
1977-78	Regina Pats	WCJHL	68	37	51	88	....	....	....	49	....	....	....	....	....	....	....	....	....	....	13	4	5	9	4	....	....	....
1978-79	Regina Pats	WHL	68	32	62	94	....	....	....	141	....	....	....	....	....	....	....	....	....	....	....	....	....	....	....	....	....	....
1979-80	Regina Pats	WHL	71	*89	81	*170	....	....	....	99	....	....	....	....	....	....	....	....	....	....	18	14	*26	*40	20	....	....	....
	Regina Pats	Mem-Cup	4	1	4	5	....	....	....	8	....	....	....	....	....	....	....	....	....	....	....	....	....	....	....	....	....	....
1980-81	**Montreal Canadiens**	**NHL**	**41**	**7**	**8**	**15**	**5**	**5**	**10**	**20**	**2**	**0**	**0**	**56**	**12.5**	**24**	**5**	**14**	**0**	**5**	....	....	....	....	....	....	....	....
1981-82	**Montreal Canadiens**	**NHL**	**56**	**12**	**23**	**35**	**9**	**15**	**24**	**43**	**1**	**0**	**3**	**94**	**12.8**	**56**	**11**	**27**	**0**	**18**	....	....	....	....	....	....	....	....
1982-83	**Montreal Canadiens**	**NHL**	**78**	**25**	**30**	**55**	**20**	**21**	**41**	**49**	**5**	**0**	**3**	**160**	**15.6**	**88**	**14**	**52**	**0**	**22**	....	....	....	....	....	....	....	....
1983-84	**Montreal Canadiens**	**NHL**	**27**	**5**	**5**	**10**	**4**	**3**	**7**	**6**	**0**	**0**	**1**	**26**	**19.2**	**14**	**0**	**14**	**1**	**1**	....	....	....	....	....	....	....	....
	St. Louis Blues	**NHL**	**46**	**7**	**21**	**28**	**6**	**14**	**20**	**19**	**2**	**0**	**1**	**118**	**5.9**	**43**	**10**	**45**	**22**	**10**	**11**	**2**	**2**	**4**	**2**	**0**	**1**	**1**
1984-85	**St. Louis Blues**	**NHL**	**68**	**23**	**20**	**43**	**19**	**14**	**33**	**36**	**1**	**2**	**3**	**155**	**14.8**	**60**	**5**	**76**	**30**	**9**	....	....	....	....	....	....	....	....
1985-86	**St. Louis Blues**	**NHL**	**36**	**8**	**11**	**19**	**6**	**7**	**13**	**16**	**0**	**0**	**2**	**53**	**15.1**	**30**	**1**	**30**	**12**	**11**	**19**	**2**	**5**	**7**	**12**	**1**	**0**	**1**
1986-87	**St. Louis Blues**	**NHL**	**80**	**13**	**15**	**28**	**11**	**11**	**22**	**37**	**5**	**2**	**1**	**131**	**9.9**	**48**	**15**	**66**	**11**	**–22**	**6**	**0**	**0**	**0**	**2**	**0**	**0**	**0**
1987-88	**Vancouver Canucks**	**NHL**	**80**	**7**	**19**	**26**	**6**	**14**	**20**	**36**	**0**	**2**	**2**	**123**	**5.7**	**43**	**2**	**89**	**33**	**–15**	....	....	....	....	....	....	....	....
1988-89	**New York Rangers**	**NHL**	**1**	**1**	**0**	**1**	**1**	**0**	**1**	**0**	**0**	**0**	**0**	**4**	**25.0**	**1**	**0**	**0**	**0**	**1**	....	....	....	....	....	....	....	....
	Flint Spirits	IHL	21	9	7	16	....	....	....	18	....	....	....	....	....	....	....	....	....	....	....	....	....	....	....	....	....	....
	Canada	Nat-Team	26	7	15	22	....	....	....	40	....	....	....	....	....	....	....	....	....	....	....	....	....	....	....	....	....	....
	Washington Capitals	**NHL**	**16**	**2**	**5**	**7**	**2**	**4**	**6**	**4**	**1**	**0**	**0**	**29**	**6.9**	**9**	**2**	**11**	**4**	**0**	**5**	**0**	**0**	**0**	**2**	**0**	**0**	**0**
	Baltimore Skipjacks	AHL	2	0	5	5	....	....	....	0	....	....	....	....	....	....	....	....	....	....	....	....	....	....	....	....	....	....
1989-90	Washington Capitals	Fr-Tour	4	1	0	1	....	....	....	10	....	....	....	....	....	....	....	....	....	....	....	....	....	....	....	....	....	....
	Washington Capitals	**NHL**	**27**	**1**	**8**	**9**	**1**	**6**	**7**	**20**	**0**	**0**	**0**	**44**	**2.3**	**14**	**0**	**21**	**8**	**1**	....	....	....	....	....	....	....	....
	Baltimore Skipjacks	AHL	35	9	19	28	....	....	....	22	....	....	....	....	....	....	....	....	....	....	12	2	5	7	22	....	....	....
1990-91	HC Asiago	Italy	35	25	32	57	....	....	....	9	....	....	....	....	....	....	....	....	....	....	....	....	....	....	....	....	....	....
1991-92	EHC Unna	Germany-3	8	14	6	20	....	....	....	36	....	....	....	....	....	....	....	....	....	....	....	....	....	....	....	....	....	....
	SV Bayreuth	Germany-2	4	4	3	7	....	....	....	6	....	....	....	....	....	....	....	....	....	....	....	....	....	....	....	....	....	....
	KAC Klagenfurt	Austria	22	7	12	19	....	....	....	....	....	....	....	....	....	....	....	....	....	....	....	....	....	....	....	....	....	....
1992-93	Peoria Rivermen	IHL	80	30	45	75	....	....	....	30	....	....	....	....	....	....	....	....	....	....	4	0	2	2	2	....	....	....
1993-94	Fort Wayne Komets	IHL	73	22	37	59	....	....	....	22	....	....	....	....	....	....	....	....	....	....	14	2	2	4	4	....	....	....
	NHL Totals		**556**	**111**	**165**	**276**	**90**	**114**	**204**	**286**	**17**	**6**	**16**	**993**	**11.2**	**430**	**65**	**445**	**121**		**41**	**4**	**7**	**11**	**18**	**1**	**1**	**2**

WHL All-Star Team (1980) • Canadian Major Junior Player of the Year (1980)

Traded to **St. Louis** by **Montreal** with Gilbert Delorme and Greg Paslawski for Perry Turnbull, December 21, 1983. Claimed by **Hartford** from **St. Louis** in Waiver Draft, October 5, 1987. Claimed by **Vancouver** from **Hartford** in Waiver Draft, October 5, 1987. Signed as a free agent by **NY Rangers**, August 12, 1988. Signed as a free agent by **Washington**, February 28, 1989.

• WIDING, Juha

Juha Markku "Whitey" C – . 6', 180 lbs. b: Oulu, Finland, 7/4/1947 d: 12/30/1984.

Season	Club	League	GP	G	A	Pts	AG	AA	APts	PIM	PP	SH	GW	S	%	TGF	PGF	TGA	PGA	+/-	GP	G	A	Pts	PIM	PP	SH	GW
1963-64	Goteborgs AIS	Sweden-2	18	12	....	12	....	....	....	....	....	....	....	....	....	....	....	....	....	....	....	....	....	....	....	....	....	....
1964-65	Brandon Wheat Kings	SJHL	45	23	15	38	....	....	....	26	....	....	....	....	....	....	....	....	....	....	9	3	5	8	6	....	....	....
1965-66	Brandon Wheat Kings	SJHL	50	*62	52	114	....	....	....	29	....	....	....	....	....	....	....	....	....	....	11	8	14	22	4	....	....	....
1966-67	Brandon Wheat Kings	CMJHL	43	70	74	144	....	....	....	64	....	....	....	....	....	....	....	....	....	....	9	5	10	15	6	....	....	....
	Port Arthur Marrs	Mem-Cup	5	2	2	4	....	....	....	4	....	....	....	....	....	....	....	....	....	....	....	....	....	....	....	....	....	....
1967-68	Omaha Knights	CPHL	62	27	33	60	....	....	....	19	....	....	....	....	....	....	....	....	....	....	....	....	....	....	....	....	....	....
1968-69	Omaha Knights	CHL	72	*41	39	80	....	....	....	58	....	....	....	....	....	....	....	....	....	....	7	2	4	6	0	....	....	....
1969-70	**New York Rangers**	**NHL**	**44**	**7**	**7**	**14**	**8**	**7**	**15**	**10**	**2**	**0**	**0**	**90**	**7.8**	**22**	**2**	**18**	**0**	**2**	....	....	....	....	....	....	....	....
	Los Angeles Kings	**NHL**	**4**	**0**	**2**	**2**	**0**	**2**	**2**	**2**	**0**	**0**	**0**	**12**	**0.0**	**3**	**1**	**5**	**2**	**–1**	....	....	....	....	....	....	....	....
1970-71	**Los Angeles Kings**	**NHL**	**78**	**25**	**40**	**65**	**25**	**34**	**59**	**24**	**5**	**0**	**4**	**202**	**12.4**	**87**	**16**	**83**	**1**	**–11**	....	....	....	....	....	....	....	....
1971-72	**Los Angeles Kings**	**NHL**	**78**	**27**	**28**	**55**	**27**	**24**	**51**	**26**	**3**	**0**	**3**	**192**	**14.1**	**64**	**16**	**86**	**2**	**–36**	....	....	....	....	....	....	....	....
1972-73	**Los Angeles Kings**	**NHL**	**77**	**16**	**54**	**70**	**15**	**43**	**58**	**30**	**0**	**0**	**3**	**189**	**8.5**	**97**	**32**	**79**	**0**	**–14**	....	....	....	....	....	....	....	....
1973-74	**Los Angeles Kings**	**NHL**	**71**	**27**	**30**	**57**	**26**	**25**	**51**	**26**	**5**	**0**	**4**	**175**	**15.4**	**74**	**17**	**62**	**1**	**–4**	**5**	**1**	**0**	**1**	**2**	**0**	**0**	**1**
1974-75	**Los Angeles Kings**	**NHL**	**80**	**26**	**34**	**60**	**23**	**25**	**48**	**46**	**7**	**0**	**3**	**186**	**14.0**	**83**	**29**	**36**	**0**	**18**	**3**	**0**	**2**	**2**	**0**	**0**	**0**	**0**
1975-76	**Los Angeles Kings**	**NHL**	**67**	**7**	**15**	**22**	**6**	**11**	**17**	**26**	**1**	**0**	**2**	**84**	**8.3**	**35**	**7**	**40**	**0**	**–12**	....	....	....	....	....	....	....	....
1976-77	**Los Angeles Kings**	**NHL**	**47**	**3**	**8**	**11**	**3**	**6**	**9**	**8**	**0**	**0**	**1**	**69**	**4.3**	**15**	**1**	**30**	**0**	**–16**	....	....	....	....	....	....	....	....
	Sweden	Can-Cup	5	1	1	2	....	....	....	0	....	....	....	....	....	....	....	....	....	....	....	....	....	....	....	....	....	....
	Cleveland Barons	**NHL**	**29**	**6**	**8**	**14**	**5**	**6**	**11**	**10**	**1**	**0**	**1**	**39**	**15.4**	**18**	**3**	**22**	**0**	**–7**	....	....	....	....	....	....	....	....
1977-78	Edmonton Oilers	WHA	71	18	24	42	....	....	....	8	....	....	....	....	....	....	....	....	....	....	5	0	1	1	0	....	....	....
	NHL Totals		**575**	**144**	**226**	**370**	**138**	**183**	**321**	**208**	**24**	**0**	**21**	**1238**	**11.6**	**498**	**124**	**461**	**6**		**8**	**1**	**2**	**3**	**2**	**0**	**0**	**1**
	Other Major League Totals		71	18	24	42	....	....	....	8	....	....	....	....	....	....	....	....	....	....	5	0	1	1	0	....	....	....

CHL Second All-Star Team (1969)

• Only games played and goals scored totals available for **Goteborgs AIS** in 1963-64 season. • Loaned to **Port Arthur** (TBJHL) by **Brandon** (MJHL) for Memorial Cup playoffs, March, 1964. Traded to **LA Kings** by **NY Rangers** with Real Lemieux for Ted Irvine, February 28, 1970. Selected by **Ontario-Ottawa** (WHA) in 1972 WHA General Player Draft, February 12, 1972. Traded to **Cleveland** by **LA Kings** with Gary Edwards for Jim Moxey and Gary Simmons, January 22, 1977. Signed as a free agent by **Edmonton** (WHA), June, 1978. Traded to **Indianapolis** (WHA) by **Edmonton** (WHA) for Bill Goldsworthy, June, 1978.

• WIDMER, Jason

D – L. 6', 200 lbs. b: Calgary, Alta., 8/1/1973. NY Islanders' 8th, 176th overall, in 1992.

Season	Club	League	GP	G	A	Pts	AG	AA	APts	PIM	PP	SH	GW	S	%	TGF	PGF	TGA	PGA	+/-	GP	G	A	Pts	PIM	PP	SH	GW
1988-89	Lethbridge Y's Men	AAHA	44	10	27	37	....	....	....	100	....	....	....	....	....	....	....	....	....	....	....	....	....	....	....	....	....	....
1989-90	Moose Jaw Warriors	WHL	58	1	8	9	....	....	....	33	....	....	....	....	....	....	....	....	....	....	....	....	....	....	....	....	....	....
1990-91	Lethbridge Hurricanes	WHL	58	2	12	14	....	....	....	55	....	....	....	....	....	....	....	....	....	....	16	0	1	1	12	....	....	....
1991-92	Lethbridge Hurricanes	WHL	40	2	19	21	....	....	....	181	....	....	....	....	....	....	....	....	....	....	5	0	4	4	9	....	....	....
1992-93	Lethbridge Hurricanes	WHL	55	3	15	18	....	....	....	140	....	....	....	....	....	....	....	....	....	....	4	0	3	3	2	....	....	....
	Capital District Islanders	AHL	4	0	0	0	....	....	....	2	....	....	....	....	....	....	....	....	....	....	....	....	....	....	....	....	....	....
1993-94	Lethbridge Hurricanes	WHL	64	11	31	42	....	....	....	191	....	....	....	....	....	....	....	....	....	....	9	3	5	8	34	....	....	....
1994-95	Canada	Nat-Team	6	1	4	5	....	....	....	4	....	....	....	....	....	....	....	....	....	....	....	....	....	....	....	....	....	....
	New York Islanders	**NHL**	**1**	**0**	**0**	**0**	**0**	**0**	**0**	**0**	**0**	**0**	**0**	**0**	**0.0**	**0**	**0**	**1**	**0**	**–1**	....	....	....	....	....	....	....	....
	Worcester IceCats	AHL	73	8	26	34	....	....	....	136	....	....	....	....	....	....	....	....	....	....	....	....	....	....	....	....	....	....
1995-96	**New York Islanders**	**NHL**	**4**	**0**	**0**	**0**	**0**	**0**	**0**	**7**	**0**	**0**	**0**	**1**	**0.0**	**2**	**0**	**2**	**0**	**0**	....	....	....	....	....	....	....	....
	Worcester IceCats	AHL	76	6	21	27	....	....	....	129	....	....	....	....	....	....	....	....	....	....	4	2	0	2	9	....	....	....
1996-97	**San Jose Sharks**	**NHL**	**2**	**0**	**1**	**1**	**0**	**1**	**1**	**0**	**0**	**0**	**0**	**0**	**0.0**	**2**	**0**	**1**	**0**	**1**	....	....	....	....	....	....	....	....
	Kentucky Thoroughblades	AHL	76	4	24	28	....	....	....	105	....	....	....	....	....	....	....	....	....	....	4	0	0	0	8	....	....	....
1997-98	Kentucky Thoroughblades	AHL	71	5	13	18	....	....	....	176	....	....	....	....	....	....	....	....	....	....	3	0	0	0	6	....	....	....
1998-99	Worcester IceCats	AHL	25	2	3	5	....	....	....	42	....	....	....	....	....	....	....	....	....	....	....	....	....	....	....	....	....	....
99-2000	Worcester IceCats	AHL	12	0	5	5	....	....	....	23	....	....	....	....	....	....	....	....	....	....	....	....	....	....	....	....	....	....
	NHL Totals		**7**	**0**	**1**	**1**	**0**	**1**	**1**	**7**	**0**	**0**	**0**	**1**	**0.0**	**4**	**0**	**4**	**0**		....	....	....	....	....	....	....	....

Signed as a free agent by **San Jose**, September 11, 1996. Signed as a free agent by **St. Louis**, July 28, 1998. • Suffered eventual career-ending knee injury in game vs. Springfield (AHL), January 3, 1999. • Officially announced retirement December 30, 1999.

• WIEMER, Jason

C – L. 6'1", 220 lbs. b: Kimberley, B.C., 4/14/1976. Tampa Bay's 1st, 8th overall, in 1994.

Season	Club	League	GP	G	A	Pts	AG	AA	APts	PIM	PP	SH	GW	S	%	TGF	PGF	TGA	PGA	+/–	Playoffs GP	G	A	Pts	PIM	PP	SH	GW
1991-92	Kimberley Dynamiters	RMJHL	45	33	33	66				211																		
	Portland Winter Hawks	WHL	2	0	1	1				0																		
1992-93	Portland Winter Hawks	WHL	68	18	34	52				159											16	7	3	10	27			
1993-94	Portland Winter Hawks	WHL	72	45	51	96				236											10	4	4	8	32			
1994-95	Portland Winter Hawks	WHL	16	10	14	24				63																		
	Tampa Bay Lightning	**NHL**	**36**	**1**	**4**	**5**	**2**	**6**	**8**	**44**	**0**	**0**	**0**	**10**	**10.0**	**9**	**0**	**11**	**0**	**–2**								
1995-96	**Tampa Bay Lightning**	**NHL**	**66**	**9**	**9**	**18**	**9**	**7**	**16**	**81**	**4**	**0**	**1**	**89**	**10.1**	**41**	**24**	**33**	**7**	**–9**	**6**	**1**	**0**	**1**	**28**	**1**	**0**	**0**
1996-97	**Tampa Bay Lightning**	**NHL**	**63**	**9**	**5**	**14**	**10**	**4**	**14**	**134**	**2**	**0**	**0**	**103**	**8.7**	**29**	**4**	**42**	**4**	**–13**								
	Adirondack Red Wings	AHL	4	1	0	1				7																		
1997-98	**Tampa Bay Lightning**	**NHL**	**67**	**8**	**9**	**17**	**9**	**9**	**18**	**132**	**2**	**0**	**0**	**106**	**7.5**	**30**	**4**	**42**	**7**	**–9**								
	Calgary Flames	**NHL**	**12**	**4**	**1**	**5**	**5**	**1**	**6**	**28**	**1**	**0**	**2**	**16**	**25.0**	**10**	**4**	**7**	**0**	**–1**								
1998-99	**Calgary Flames**	**NHL**	**78**	**8**	**13**	**21**	**9**	**13**	**22**	**177**	**1**	**0**	**1**	**128**	**6.3**	**43**	**14**	**44**	**3**	**–12**								
99-2000	**Calgary Flames**	**NHL**	**64**	**11**	**11**	**22**	**12**	**10**	**22**	**120**	**2**	**0**	**3**	**104**	**10.6**	**42**	**13**	**42**	**3**	**–10**								
	NHL Totals		**386**	**50**	**52**	**102**	**56**	**50**	**106**	**716**	**12**	**0**	**7**	**556**	**9.0**	**204**	**63**	**221**	**24**		**6**	**1**	**0**	**1**	**28**	**1**	**0**	**0**

Traded to **Calgary** by **Tampa Bay** for Sandy McCarthy and Calgary's 3rd (Brad Richards) and 5th (Curtis Rich) round choices in 1998 Entry Draft, March 24, 1998.

• WIEMER, Jim

James Duncan "Ripper" D – L. 6'4", 216 lbs. b: Sudbury, Ont., 1/9/1961. Buffalo's 5th, 83rd overall, in 1980.

Season	Club	League	GP	G	A	Pts	AG	AA	APts	PIM	PP	SH	GW	S	%	TGF	PGF	TGA	PGA	+/–	Playoffs GP	G	A	Pts	PIM	PP	SH	GW
1978-79	Peterborough Petes	OMJHL	61	15	12	27				50											18	4	4	8	15			
	Peterborough Petes	Mem-Cup	5	2	1	3				0																		
1979-80	Peterborough Petes	OMJHL	53	17	32	49				63											14	6	9	15	19			
	Canada	WJC-A	5	2	2	4				2																		
	Peterborough Petes	Mem-Cup	5	0	0	0				6																		
1980-81	Peterborough Petes	OMJHL	65	41	54	95				102											5	1	2	3	15			
1981-82	Rochester Americans	AHL	74	19	26	45				57											9	0	4	4	2			
1982-83	Rochester Americans	AHL	74	15	44	59				43											15	5	15	20	22			
	Buffalo Sabres	**NHL**																			**1**	**0**	**0**	**0**	**0**	**0**	**0**	**0**
1983-84	**Buffalo Sabres**	**NHL**	**64**	**5**	**15**	**20**	**4**	**10**	**14**	**48**	**0**	**1**	**0**	**91**	**5.5**	**63**	**7**	**61**	**6**	**1**								
	Rochester Americans	AHL	12	4	11	15				11											18	3	13	16	20			
1984-85	**Buffalo Sabres**	**NHL**	**10**	**3**	**2**	**5**	**2**	**1**	**3**	**4**	**2**	**0**	**0**	**22**	**13.6**	**10**	**6**	**9**	**0**	**–5**								
	Rochester Americans	AHL	13	1	9	10				24																		
	New York Rangers	**NHL**	**22**	**4**	**3**	**7**	**3**	**2**	**5**	**30**	**2**	**0**	**0**	**51**	**7.8**	**19**	**8**	**24**	**3**	**–10**	**1**	**0**	**0**	**0**	**0**	**0**	**0**	**0**
	New Haven Nighthawks	AHL	33	9	27	36				39																		
1985-86	**New York Rangers**	**NHL**	**7**	**3**	**0**	**3**	**2**	**0**	**2**	**2**	**0**	**0**	**1**	**22**	**13.6**	**11**	**4**	**7**	**0**	**0**	**8**	**1**	**0**	**1**	**6**	**1**	**0**	**1**
	New Haven Nighthawks	AHL	73	24	49	73				108																		
1986-87	New Haven Nighthawks	AHL	6	0	7	7				6																		
	Nova Scotia Oilers	AHL	59	9	25	34				72											5	0	4	4	2			
1987-88 ♦	**Edmonton Oilers**	**NHL**	**12**	**1**	**2**	**3**	**1**	**1**	**2**	**15**	**0**	**0**	**0**	**24**	**4.2**	**20**	**6**	**10**	**3**	**7**	**2**	**0**	**0**	**0**	**2**	**0**	**0**	**0**
	Nova Scotia Oilers	AHL	57	11	32	43				99											5	1	1	2	14			
1988-89	Cape Breton Oilers	AHL	51	12	29	41				80																		
	Los Angeles Kings	**NHL**	**9**	**2**	**3**	**5**	**2**	**2**	**4**	**20**	**0**	**1**	**1**	**17**	**11.8**	**5**	**1**	**2**	**0**	**2**	**10**	**2**	**1**	**3**	**19**	**0**	**0**	**1**
	New Haven Nighthawks	AHL	3	1	1	2				2											7	2	3	5	2			
1989-90	**Boston Bruins**	**NHL**	**61**	**5**	**14**	**19**	**4**	**10**	**14**	**63**	**0**	**0**	**1**	**90**	**5.6**	**50**	**8**	**33**	**2**	**11**	**8**	**0**	**1**	**1**	**4**	**0**	**0**	**0**
	Maine Mariners	AHL	6	3	4	7				27																		
1990-91	**Boston Bruins**	**NHL**	**61**	**4**	**19**	**23**	**4**	**14**	**18**	**62**	**0**	**0**	**1**	**86**	**4.7**	**52**	**6**	**47**	**4**	**3**	**16**	**1**	**3**	**4**	**14**	**1**	**0**	**0**
1991-92	**Boston Bruins**	**NHL**	**47**	**1**	**8**	**9**	**1**	**6**	**7**	**84**	**0**	**0**	**0**	**60**	**1.7**	**38**	**5**	**25**	**2**	**10**	**15**	**1**	**3**	**4**	**14**	**0**	**0**	**1**
	Maine Mariners	AHL	3	0	1	1				4																		
1992-93	**Boston Bruins**	**NHL**	**28**	**1**	**6**	**7**	**1**	**4**	**5**	**48**	**0**	**0**	**0**	**39**	**2.6**	**24**	**4**	**21**	**2**	**1**	**1**	**0**	**0**	**0**	**4**	**0**	**0**	**0**
	Providence Bruins	AHL	4	2	1	3				2																		
1993-94	**Boston Bruins**	**NHL**	**4**	**0**	**0**	**0**	**0**	**0**	**0**	**2**	**0**	**0**	**0**	**8**	**0.0**	**1**	**0**	**4**	**0**	**–3**								
	Providence Bruins	AHL	35	5	12	17				81																		
1994-95	Rochester Americans	AHL	45	9	29	38				74											5	0	2	2	6			
	NHL Totals		**325**	**29**	**72**	**101**	**24**	**50**	**74**	**378**	**4**	**2**	**4**	**510**	**5.7**	**293**	**55**	**243**	**22**		**62**	**5**	**8**	**13**	**63**	**2**	**0**	**3**

AHL First All-Star Team (1986) • Won Eddie Shore Award (Outstanding Defenseman - AHL) (1986)

Traded to **NY Rangers** by **Buffalo** with Steve Patrick for Dave Maloney and Chris Renaud, December 6, 1984. Traded to **Edmonton** by **NY Rangers** with Reijo Ruotsalainen, Clark Donatelli, Ville Kentala for Don Jackson, Mike Golden, Miloslav Horova and future considerations (Stu Kulak, March 10, 1987), October 23, 1986. Traded to **LA Kings** by **Edmonton** with Alan May for Brian Wilks and John English, March 7, 1989. Signed as a free agent by **Boston**, July 6, 1989.

• WILCOX, Barry

Barry Fredrick RW – L. 6'1", 190 lbs. b: New Westminster, B.C., 4/23/1948.

Season	Club	League	GP	G	A	Pts	AG	AA	APts	PIM	PP	SH	GW	S	%	TGF	PGF	TGA	PGA	+/–	Playoffs GP	G	A	Pts	PIM	PP	SH	GW
1967-68	New Westminster Royals	BCJHL	28	25	25	50																						
1968-1971	University of British Columbia	WCIAA	STATISTICS NOT AVAILABLE																									
1971-72	Rochester Americans	AHL	73	17	10	27				95																		
1972-73	**Vancouver Canucks**	**NHL**	**31**	**3**	**2**	**5**	**3**	**2**	**5**	**15**	**0**	**0**	**0**	**52**	**5.8**	**14**	**0**	**24**	**0**	**–10**								
	Seattle Totems	WHL	47	19	22	41				38																		
1973-74	Seattle Totems	WHL	6	0	1	1				10																		
1974-75	**Vancouver Canucks**	**NHL**	**2**	**0**	**0**	**0**	**0**	**0**	**0**	**0**	**0**	**0**	**0**	**0**	**0.0**	**0**	**0**	**0**	**0**	**0**								
	Seattle Totems	CHL	55	12	17	29				68																		
1975-76	Tulsa Oilers	CHL	44	8	8	16				36																		
1976-1980	Delta Kings	BCSHL	STATISTICS NOT AVAILABLE																									
1980-81	Jujyo-Seishi	Japan	PLAYER/COACH – STATISTICS UNAVAILABLE																									
	NHL Totals		**33**	**3**	**2**	**5**	**3**	**2**	**5**	**15**	**0**	**0**	**0**	**52**	**5.8**	**14**	**0**	**24**	**0**									

WCIAA First All-Star Team (1970, 1971)

Signed as a free agent by **Vancouver**, September, 1971. • Missed majority of 1973-74 season recovering from arm injury suffered in training camp, September, 1973.

• WILEY, Jim

James Thomas C – L. 6'2", 200 lbs. b: Sault Ste. Marie, Ont., 4/28/1950.

Season	Club	League	GP	G	A	Pts	AG	AA	APts	PIM	PP	SH	GW	S	%	TGF	PGF	TGA	PGA	+/–	Playoffs GP	G	A	Pts	PIM	PP	SH	GW
1966-67	Sault Ste. Marie Greyhounds	NOJHA	STATISTICS NOT AVAILABLE																									
1967-68	Sault Ste. Marie Greyhounds	NOJHA	STATISTICS NOT AVAILABLE																									
	Sault Ste. Marie Greyhounds	Mem-Cup	STATISTICS NOT AVAILABLE																									
1968-69	Lake Superior State	CCHA	26	9	15	24				4																		
1969-70	Lake Superior State	CCHA	25	21	17	38				11																		
1970-71	Lake Superior State	CCHA	25	18	19	37				13																		
1971-72	Lake Superior State	CCHA	28	22	34	56				24																		
1972-73	**Pittsburgh Penguins**	**NHL**	**4**	**0**	**1**	**1**	**0**	**1**	**1**	**0**	**0**	**0**	**0**	**7**	**0.0**	**1**	**0**	**0**	**0**	**1**								
	Hershey Bears	AHL	71	30	45	75				30											7	1	1	2	5			
1973-74	**Pittsburgh Penguins**	**NHL**	**22**	**0**	**3**	**3**	**0**	**2**	**2**	**2**	**0**	**0**	**0**	**12**	**0.0**	**6**	**0**	**10**	**0**	**–4**								
	Hershey Bears	AHL	47	21	33	54				26											14	5	11	*16	15			
1974-75	**Vancouver Canucks**	**NHL**	**1**	**0**	**0**	**0**	**0**	**0**	**0**	**0**	**0**	**0**	**0**	**0**	**0.0**	**0**	**0**	**0**	**0**	**0**								
	Seattle Totems	CHL	51	10	25	35				24																		
1975-76	**Vancouver Canucks**	**NHL**	**2**	**0**	**0**	**0**	**0**	**0**	**0**	**2**	**0**	**0**	**0**	**1**	**0.0**	**0**	**0**	**1**	**0**	**–1**								
	Tulsa Oilers	CHL	76	33	*63	*96				21											9	*5	4	9	38			
1976-77	**Vancouver Canucks**	**NHL**	**34**	**4**	**6**	**10**	**4**	**5**	**9**	**4**	**0**	**0**	**0**	**37**	**10.8**	**13**	**0**	**26**	**0**	**–13**								
	Tulsa Oilers	CHL	29	17	17	34				27											9	*4	4	8	4			

Season	Club	League	GP	G	A	Pts	AG	AA	APts	PIM	PP	SH	GW	S	%	TGF	PGF	TGA	PGA	+/–	GP	G	A	Pts	PIM	PP	SH	GW
			REGULAR SEASON																		PLAYOFFS							
1977-78	Tulsa Oilers	CHL	DID NOT PLAY – FRONT OFFICE STAFF																									
1978-79	Tulsa Oilers	CHL	73	23	45	68	....	....	....	29	....	....	....	....	....	....	....	....	....	....	....	....	....	....	....	....	....	....
1979-80	Tulsa Oilers	CHL	76	18	36	54	....	....	....	30	....	....	....	....	....	....	....	....	....	....	3	0	2	2	0	....	....	....
	NHL Totals		**63**	**4**	**10**	**14**	**4**	**8**	**12**	**8**	**0**	**0**	**0**	**57**	**7.0**	**20**	**0**	**37**	**0**		....	....	....	....	....	....	....	....

NCAA (College Div.) West All-American Team (1972) • CHL First All-Star Team (1975)

Signed as a free agent by **Pittsburgh**, June 25, 1972. Claimed by **Vancouver** from **Pittsburgh** in Intra-League Draft, June 10, 1974.

• WILKIE, Bob

D – R. 6'2", 215 lbs. b: Calgary, Alta., 2/11/1969. Detroit's 3rd, 41st overall, in 1987.

Season	Club	League	GP	G	A	Pts	AG	AA	APts	PIM	PP	SH	GW	S	%	TGF	PGF	TGA	PGA	+/–	GP	G	A	Pts	PIM	PP	SH	GW
1984-85	Calgary Buffaloes	AAHA	37	20	33	53	....	....	....	116	....	....	....	....	....	....	....	....	....	....	....	....	....	....	....	....	....	....
1985-86	Calgary Wranglers	WHL	63	8	19	27	....	....	....	56	....	....	....	....	....	....	....	....	....	....	....	....	....	....	....	....	....	....
1986-87	Calgary Wranglers	WHL	1	0	1	1	....	....	....	0	....	....	....	....	....	....	....	....	....	....	....	....	....	....	....	....	....	....
	Swift Current Broncos	WHL	64	12	37	49	....	....	....	50	....	....	....	....	....	....	....	....	....	....	4	1	3	4	2	....	....	....
1987-88	Swift Current Broncos	WHL	67	12	68	80	....	....	....	124	....	....	....	....	....	....	....	....	....	....	10	4	12	16	8	....	....	....
1988-89	Swift Current Broncos	WHL	62	18	67	85	....	....	....	89	....	....	....	....	....	....	....	....	....	....	12	1	11	12	47	....	....	....
	Swift Current Broncos	Mem-Cup	5	2	3	5	....	....	....	10	....	....	....	....	....	....	....	....	....	....	....	....	....	....	....	....	....	....
1989-90	Adirondack Red Wings	AHL	58	5	33	38	....	....	....	64	....	....	....	....	....	....	....	....	....	....	6	1	4	5	2	....	....	....
1990-91	**Detroit Red Wings**	**NHL**	**8**	**1**	**2**	**3**	**1**	**2**	**3**	**2**	**0**	**0**	**0**	**9**	**11.1**	**6**	**1**	**7**	**0**	**–2**	....	....	....	....	....	....	....	....
	Adirondack Red Wings	AHL	43	6	18	24	....	....	....	71	....	....	....	....	....	....	....	....	....	....	2	1	0	1	2	....	....	....
1991-92	Adirondack Red Wings	AHL	7	1	4	5	....	....	....	6	....	....	....	....	....	....	....	....	....	....	16	2	5	7	12	....	....	....
1992-93	Adirondack Red Wings	AHL	14	0	5	5	....	....	....	20	....	....	....	....	....	....	....	....	....	....	....	....	....	....	....	....	....	....
	Fort Wayne Komets	IHL	32	7	14	21	....	....	....	82	....	....	....	....	....	....	....	....	....	....	12	4	6	10	10	....	....	....
	Hershey Bears	AHL	28	7	25	32	....	....	....	18	....	....	....	....	....	....	....	....	....	....	....	....	....	....	....	....	....	....
1993-94	**Philadelphia Flyers**	**NHL**	**10**	**1**	**3**	**4**	**1**	**2**	**3**	**8**	**0**	**0**	**0**	**10**	**10.0**	**12**	**4**	**10**	**0**	**–2**	....	....	....	....	....	....	....	....
	Hershey Bears	AHL	69	8	53	61	....	....	....	100	....	....	....	....	....	....	....	....	....	....	9	1	4	5	8	....	....	....
1994-95	Hershey Bears	AHL	50	9	30	39	....	....	....	46	....	....	....	....	....	....	....	....	....	....	....	....	....	....	....	....	....	....
	Indianapolis Ice	IHL	29	5	22	27	....	....	....	30	....	....	....	....	....	....	....	....	....	....	....	....	....	....	....	....	....	....
1995-96	Augsburger Panther	Germany	6	0	1	1	....	....	....	43	....	....	....	....	....	....	....	....	....	....	....	....	....	....	....	....	....	....
	Cincinnati Cyclones	IHL	22	4	6	10	....	....	....	32	....	....	....	....	....	....	....	....	....	....	....	....	....	....	....	....	....	....
1996-97	Cincinnati Cyclones	IHL	DID NOT PLAY – INJURED																									
1997-98	Las Vegas Thunder	IHL	3	0	1	1	....	....	....	0	....	....	....	....	....	....	....	....	....	....	....	....	....	....	....	....	....	....
	Fresno Fighting Falcons	WCHL	54	13	50	63	....	....	....	60	....	....	....	....	....	....	....	....	....	....	5	1	7	8	38	....	....	....
1998-99	Pensacola Ice Pilots	ECHL	16	2	11	13	....	....	....	18	....	....	....	....	....	....	....	....	....	....	....	....	....	....	....	....	....	....
	Fresno Fighting Falcons	WCHL	10	3	4	7	....	....	....	12	....	....	....	....	....	....	....	....	....	....	7	1	2	3	18	....	....	....
99-2000	Anchorage Aces	WCHL	DID NOT PLAY – COACHING																									
	Anchorage Aces	WCHL	15	3	10	13	....	....	....	18	....	....	....	....	....	....	....	....	....	....	4	1	4	5	16	....	....	....
	NHL Totals		**18**	**2**	**5**	**7**	**2**	**4**	**6**	**10**	**0**	**0**	**0**	**19**	**10.5**	**18**	**5**	**17**	**0**		....	....	....	....	....	....	....	....

WCHL First All-Star Team (1998)

Traded to **Philadelphia** by **Detroit** for future considerations, February 2, 1993. Traded to **Chicago** by **Philadelphia** with Philadelphia's 5th round choice (Kyle Calder) in 1995 Entry Draft for Karl Dykhuis, February 16, 1995. • Missed majority of 1995-96 and entire 1996-97 seasons recovering from spinal disc surgery, January, 1996. Signed as a free agent by **Las Vegas** (IHL), August 14, 1997. • Relieved of duties as head coach of **Anchorage Aces**, November 10, 1999. Signed as a free agent by **Anchorage** (WCHL), January 3, 2000. • Played w/ RHI's Calgary Radz in 1993 (2-0-0-0-0).

• WILKIE, David

D – R. 6'2", 210 lbs. b: Ellensburgh, WA, 5/30/1974. Montreal's 1st, 20th overall, in 1992.

Season	Club	League	GP	G	A	Pts	AG	AA	APts	PIM	PP	SH	GW	S	%	TGF	PGF	TGA	PGA	+/–	GP	G	A	Pts	PIM	PP	SH	GW
1989-90	Seattle Northwest Americans	PIJHL	41	21	27	48	....	....	....	59	....	....	....	....	....	....	....	....	....	....	....	....	....	....	....	....	....	....
1990-91	Omaha Lancers	USHL	19	2	2	4	....	....	....	18	....	....	....	....	....	....	....	....	....	....	....	....	....	....	....	....	....	....
	Seattle Thunderbirds	WHL	25	1	1	2	....	....	....	22	....	....	....	....	....	....	....	....	....	....	....	....	....	....	....	....	....	....
1991-92	Kamloops Blazers	WHL	71	12	28	40	....	....	....	153	....	....	....	....	....	....	....	....	....	....	16	6	5	11	19	....	....	....
	Kamloops Blazers	Mem-Cup	5	1	1	2	....	....	....	4	....	....	....	....	....	....	....	....	....	....	....	....	....	....	....	....	....	....
1992-93	Kamloops Blazers	WHL	53	11	26	37	....	....	....	109	....	....	....	....	....	....	....	....	....	....	6	4	2	6	2	....	....	....
	United States	WJC-A	7	0	2	2	....	....	....	2	....	....	....	....	....	....	....	....	....	....	....	....	....	....	....	....	....	....
1993-94	Kamloops Blazers	WHL	27	11	18	29	....	....	....	18	....	....	....	....	....	....	....	....	....	....	....	....	....	....	....	....	....	....
	United States	WJC-A	6	2	1	3	....	....	....	0	....	....	....	....	....	....	....	....	....	....	....	....	....	....	....	....	....	....
	Regina Pats	WHL	29	27	21	48	....	....	....	16	....	....	....	....	....	....	....	....	....	....	4	1	4	5	4	....	....	....
1994-95	Fredericton Canadiens	AHL	70	10	43	53	....	....	....	34	....	....	....	....	....	....	....	....	....	....	1	0	0	0	0	....	....	....
	Montreal Canadiens	**NHL**	**1**	**0**	**0**	**0**	**0**	**0**	**0**	**0**	**0**	**0**	**0**	**0**	**0.0**	**0**	**0**	**0**	**0**	**0**	....	....	....	....	....	....	....	....
1995-96	**Montreal Canadiens**	**NHL**	**24**	**1**	**5**	**6**	**1**	**4**	**5**	**10**	**1**	**0**	**0**	**39**	**2.6**	**21**	**8**	**29**	**6**	**–10**	**6**	**1**	**2**	**3**	**12**	**0**	**0**	**0**
	Fredericton Canadiens	AHL	23	5	12	17	....	....	....	20	....	....	....	....	....	....	....	....	....	....	....	....	....	....	....	....	....	....
1996-97	**Montreal Canadiens**	**NHL**	**61**	**6**	**9**	**15**	**6**	**8**	**14**	**63**	**3**	**0**	**0**	**65**	**9.2**	**46**	**9**	**49**	**3**	**–9**	**2**	**0**	**0**	**0**	**2**	**0**	**0**	**0**
1997-98	**Montreal Canadiens**	**NHL**	**5**	**1**	**0**	**1**	**1**	**0**	**1**	**4**	**0**	**0**	**1**	**2**	**50.0**	**1**	**0**	**2**	**0**	**–1**	....	....	....	....	....	....	....	....
	Tampa Bay Lightning	**NHL**	**29**	**1**	**5**	**6**	**1**	**5**	**6**	**17**	**0**	**0**	**0**	**46**	**2.2**	**17**	**6**	**33**	**1**	**–21**	....	....	....	....	....	....	....	....
1998-99	**Tampa Bay Lightning**	**NHL**	**46**	**1**	**7**	**8**	**1**	**7**	**8**	**69**	**0**	**0**	**0**	**35**	**2.9**	**25**	**7**	**37**	**0**	**–19**	....	....	....	....	....	....	....	....
	Cleveland Lumberjacks	IHL	2	0	2	2	....	....	....	0	....	....	....	....	....	....	....	....	....	....	....	....	....	....	....	....	....	....
99-2000	Houston Aeros	IHL	57	4	24	28	....	....	....	71	....	....	....	....	....	....	....	....	....	....	11	1	8	9	10	....	....	....
	Hartford Wolf Pack	AHL	1	0	2	2	....	....	....	0	....	....	....	....	....	....	....	....	....	....	....	....	....	....	....	....	....	....
	Chicago Wolves	IHL	1	0	0	0	....	....	....	0	....	....	....	....	....	....	....	....	....	....	....	....	....	....	....	....	....	....
	NHL Totals		**166**	**10**	**26**	**36**	**10**	**24**	**34**	**163**	**4**	**0**	**1**	**187**	**5.3**	**110**	**30**	**150**	**10**		**8**	**1**	**2**	**3**	**14**	**0**	**0**	**0**

Traded to **Tampa Bay** by **Montreal** with Stephane Richer and Darcy Tucker for Patrick Poulin, Mick Vukota and Igor Ulanov, January 15, 1998.

• WILKINS, Barry

Barry James D – L. 6', 190 lbs. b: Toronto, Ont., 2/28/1947.

Season	Club	League	GP	G	A	Pts	AG	AA	APts	PIM	PP	SH	GW	S	%	TGF	PGF	TGA	PGA	+/–	GP	G	A	Pts	PIM	PP	SH	GW
1963-64	Woodbridge Dodgers	OHA-B	STATISTICS NOT AVAILABLE																									
1964-65	Niagara Falls Flyers	OHA-Jr.	51	2	12	14	....	....	....	45	....	....	....	....	....	....	....	....	....	....	9	0	0	0	2	....	....	....
	Niagara Falls Flyers	Mem-Cup	3	0	2	2	....	....	....	0	....	....	....	....	....	....	....	....	....	....	....	....	....	....	....	....	....	....
1965-66	Oshawa Generals	OHA-Jr.	47	8	11	19	....	....	....	128	....	....	....	....	....	....	....	....	....	....	17	3	7	10	36	....	....	....
	Oshawa Generals	Mem-Cup	14	2	6	8	....	....	....	37	....	....	....	....	....	....	....	....	....	....	....	....	....	....	....	....	....	....
1966-67	Oshawa Generals	OHA-Jr.	40	8	21	29	....	....	....	69	....	....	....	....	....	....	....	....	....	....	....	....	....	....	....	....	....	....
	Boston Bruins	**NHL**	**1**	**0**	**0**	**0**	**0**	**0**	**0**	**0**	....	....	....	....	....	....	....	....	....	....	....	....	....	....	....	....	....	....
1967-68	Oklahoma City Blazers	CPHL	69	6	27	33	....	....	....	146	....	....	....	....	....	....	....	....	....	....	7	1	0	1	12	....	....	....
1968-69	**Boston Bruins**	**NHL**	**1**	**1**	**0**	**1**	**1**	**0**	**1**	**0**	**0**	**0**	**0**	**1**	**100.0**	**1**	**0**	**0**	**0**	**1**	....	....	....	....	....	....	....	....
	Oklahoma City Blazers	CHL	69	14	32	46	....	....	....	164	....	....	....	....	....	....	....	....	....	....	12	3	7	10	26	....	....	....
1969-70	**Boston Bruins**	**NHL**	**6**	**0**	**0**	**0**	**0**	**0**	**0**	**2**	**0**	**0**	**0**	**2**	**0.0**	**1**	**0**	**2**	**0**	**–1**	....	....	....	....	....	....	....	....
	Oklahoma City Blazers	CHL	61	11	41	52	....	....	....	204	....	....	....	....	....	....	....	....	....	....	....	....	....	....	....	....	....	....
1970-71	**Vancouver Canucks**	**NHL**	**70**	**5**	**18**	**23**	**5**	**15**	**20**	**131**	**1**	**0**	**1**	**84**	**6.0**	**85**	**17**	**120**	**34**	**–18**	....	....	....	....	....	....	....	....
1971-72	**Vancouver Canucks**	**NHL**	**45**	**2**	**5**	**7**	**2**	**4**	**6**	**65**	**0**	**0**	**0**	**50**	**4.0**	**41**	**1**	**84**	**35**	**–9**	....	....	....	....	....	....	....	....
1972-73	**Vancouver Canucks**	**NHL**	**76**	**11**	**17**	**28**	**10**	**13**	**23**	**133**	**0**	**1**	**0**	**103**	**10.7**	**77**	**2**	**149**	**36**	**–38**	....	....	....	....	....	....	....	....
1973-74	**Vancouver Canucks**	**NHL**	**78**	**3**	**28**	**31**	**3**	**23**	**26**	**123**	**1**	**0**	**0**	**128**	**2.3**	**109**	**17**	**142**	**37**	**–13**	....	....	....	....	....	....	....	....
1974-75	**Vancouver Canucks**	**NHL**	**7**	**0**	**1**	**1**	**0**	**1**	**1**	**6**	**0**	**0**	**0**	**6**	**0.0**	**5**	**0**	**9**	**2**	**–2**	....	....	....	....	....	....	....	....
	Pittsburgh Penguins	**NHL**	**59**	**5**	**29**	**34**	**4**	**22**	**26**	**97**	**0**	**1**	**0**	**83**	**6.0**	**97**	**10**	**70**	**12**	**29**	**3**	**0**	**0**	**0**	**0**	**0**	**0**	**0**
1975-76	**Pittsburgh Penguins**	**NHL**	**75**	**0**	**27**	**27**	**0**	**20**	**20**	**106**	**0**	**0**	**0**	**68**	**0.0**	**92**	**7**	**107**	**21**	**–1**	**3**	**0**	**1**	**1**	**4**	**0**	**0**	**0**
1976-77	Edmonton Oilers	WHA	51	4	24	28	....	....	....	75	....	....	....	....	....	....	....	....	....	....	4	0	1	1	2	....	....	....
1977-78	Indianapolis Racers	WHA	79	2	21	23	....	....	....	79	....	....	....	....	....	....	....	....	....	....	....	....	....	....	....	....	....	....
1978-79	Philadelphia Firebirds	AHL	46	5	12	17	....	....	....	51	....	....	....	....	....	....	....	....	....	....	....	....	....	....	....	....	....	....
	NHL Totals		**418**	**27**	**125**	**152**	**25**	**98**	**123**	**663**	....	....	....	....	....	....	....	....	....	....	**6**	**0**	**1**	**1**	**4**	....	....	....
	Other Major League Totals		130	6	45	51	....	....	....	154	....	....	....	....	....	....	....	....	....	....	4	0	1	1	2	....	....	....

CHL First All-Star Team (1969) • CHL Second All-Star Team (1970)

Claimed by **Vancouver** from **Boston** in Expansion Draft, June 10, 1970. Selected by **Dayton-Houston** (WHA) in 1972 WHA General Player Draft, February 12, 1972. Traded to **Pittsburgh** by **Vancouver** for Ab Demarco Jr., November 4, 1974. WHA rights traded to **Edmonton** (WHA) by **Houston** (WHA) for future considerations, June, 1976. Traded to **Indianapolis** (WHA) by **Edmonton** (WHA) with Rusty Patenaude and Claude St. Sauveur for Blair MacDonald, Mike Zuke and Dave Inkpen, September, 1977.

• WILKINSON, Neil

D – R. 6'3", 194 lbs. b: Selkirk, Man., 8/15/1967. Minnesota's 2nd, 30th overall, in 1986.

			REGULAR SEASON																		PLAYOFFS							
Season	Club	League	GP	G	A	Pts	AG	AA	APts	PIM	PP	SH	GW	S	%	TGF	PGF	TGA	PGA	+/–	GP	G	A	Pts	PIM	PP	SH	GW
1985-86	Selkirk Steelers	MJHL	42	14	35	49				91																		
1986-87	Michigan State Spartans	CCHA	19	3	4	7				18																		
1987-88	Medicine Hat Tigers	WHL	55	11	21	32				157											5	1	0	1	2			
	Medicine Hat Tigers	Mem-Cup	1	0	0	0				0																		
1988-89	Kalamazoo Wings	IHL	39	5	15	20				96																		
1989-90	Minnesota North Stars	NHL	36	0	5	5	0	4	4	100	0	0	0	36	0.0	29	3	35	8	–1	7	0	2	2	11	0	0	0
	Kalamazoo Wings	IHL	20	6	7	13				62																		
1990-91	Minnesota North Stars	Fr-Tour	4	0	0	0				2																		
	Minnesota North Stars	NHL	50	2	9	11	2	7	9	117	0	0	0	55	3.6	37	7	49	14	–5	22	3	3	6	12	1	0	0
	Kalamazoo Wings	IHL	10	0	3	3				38																		
1991-92	San Jose Sharks	NHL	60	4	15	19	4	11	15	107	1	0	0	95	4.2	59	12	80	22	–11								
1992-93	San Jose Sharks	NHL	59	1	7	8	1	5	6	96	0	1	0	51	2.0	31	2	104	25	–50								
1993-94	Chicago Blackhawks	NHL	72	3	9	12	3	7	10	116	1	0	0	72	4.2	50	5	52	9	2	4	0	0	0	0	0	0	0
1994-95	Winnipeg Jets	NHL	40	1	4	5	2	6	8	75	0	0	0	25	4.0	16	1	48	7	–26								
1995-96	Winnipeg Jets	NHL	21	1	4	5	1	3	4	33	0	1	1	17	5.9	15	1	30	16	0								
	Pittsburgh Penguins	NHL	41	2	10	12	2	8	10	87	0	0	0	42	4.8	48	0	52	16	12	15	0	1	1	14	0	0	0
1996-97	Pittsburgh Penguins	NHL	23	0	0	0	0	0	0	36	0	0	0	16	0.0	8	0	24	4	–12	5	0	0	0	4	0	0	0
	Cleveland Lumberjacks	IHL	2	0	1	1				0																		
1997-98	Pittsburgh Penguins	NHL	34	2	4	6	2	4	6	24	1	0	0	19	10.5	17	3	19	5	0								
1998-99	Pittsburgh Penguins	NHL	24	0	0	0	0	0	0	22	0	0	0	11	0.0	7	0	9	0	–2								
	NHL Totals		460	16	67	83	17	55	72	813	3	2	1	439	3.6	317	34	502	126		53	3	6	9	41	1	0	0

Claimed by **San Jose** from **Minnesota** in Dispersal Draft, May 30, 1991. Traded to **Chicago** by **San Jose** to complete transaction that sent Jimmy Waite to San Jose (June 18, 1993), July 9, 1993. Traded to **Winnipeg** by **Chicago** for Chicago's 3rd round choice (previously acquired, Chicago selected Kevin McKay) in 1995 Entry Draft, June 3, 1994. Traded to **Pittsburgh** by **Winnipeg** for Norm Maciver, December 28, 1995.

• WILKS, Brian

C – R. 5'11", 175 lbs. b: North York, Ont., 2/27/1966. Los Angeles' 2nd, 24th overall, in 1984.

Season	Club	League	GP	G	A	Pts	AG	AA	APts	PIM	PP	SH	GW	S	%	TGF	PGF	TGA	PGA	+/–	GP	G	A	Pts	PIM	PP	SH	GW
1980-81	Toronto Midget Marlboros	MTHL	STATISTICS NOT AVAILABLE																									
	Markham Waxers	OJHL	2	0	1	1				0																		
1981-82	Toronto Midgêt Marlboros	MTHL	36	40	48	88				22																		
1982-83	Kitchener Rangers	OHL	69	6	17	23				25											1	0	0	0	0			
1983-84	Kitchener Rangers	OHL	64	21	54	75				36											16	6	14	20	9			
	Kitchener Rangers	Mem-Cup	4	6	2	8				0																		
1984-85	Kitchener Rangers	OHL	58	30	63	93				52											4	2	4	6	2			
	Los Angeles Kings	NHL	2	0	0	0	0	0	0	0	0	0	0	3	0.0	0	0	1	0	–1								
1985-86	Los Angeles Kings	NHL	43	4	8	12	3	5	8	25	0	0	0	31	12.9	20	3	24	0	–7								
1986-87	Los Angeles Kings	NHL	1	0	0	0	0	0	0	0	0	0	0	0	0.0	0	0	2	0	–2								
	New Haven Nighthawks	AHL	43	16	20	36				23											7	1	3	4	7			
1987-88	New Haven Nighthawks	AHL	18	4	8	12				26																		
1988-89	Los Angeles Kings	NHL	2	0	0	0	0	0	0	2	0	0	0	2	0.0	1	0	1	0	0								
	New Haven Nighthawks	AHL	44	15	19	34				48																		
	Cape Breton Oilers	AHL	12	4	11	15				27																		
1989-90	Cape Breton Oilers	AHL	53	13	20	33				85																		
	Muskegon Lumberjacks	IHL	15	6	11	17				10											15	7	10	17	41			
	NHL Totals		48	4	8	12	3	5	8	27	0	0	0	36	11.1	21	3	28	0									

Won George Parsons Trophy (Memorial Cup Tournament Most Sportsmanlike Player) (1984)

Traded to **Edmonton** by **LA Kings** with John English for Jim Wiemer and Alan May, March 7, 1989. Traded to **Pittsburgh** by **Edmonton** for future considerations, March 6, 1990.

• WILLARD, Rod

Rod Stephen LW – L. 6', 190 lbs. b: New Liskeard, Ont., 5/1/1960.

Season	Club	League	GP	G	A	Pts	AG	AA	APts	PIM	PP	SH	GW	S	%	TGF	PGF	TGA	PGA	+/–	GP	G	A	Pts	PIM	PP	SH	GW
1977-78	Cornwall Royals	QMJHL	66	12	29	41				27											9	1	6	7	21			
1978-79	Cornwall Royals	QMJHL	72	38	57	95				69											7	3	3	6	15			
1979-80	Cornwall Royals	QMJHL	55	29	50	79				84											18	6	8	14	18			
1980-81	Tulsa Oilers	CHL	4	0	0	0				0																		
	Fort Wayne Komets	IHL	79	32	29	61				92											12	4	5	9	14			
1981-82	New Brunswick Hawks	AHL	72	18	17	35				88											15	4	2	6	13			
1982-83	Toronto Maple Leafs	NHL	1	0	0	0	0	0	0	0	0	0	0	2	0.0	0	0	1	0	–1								
	St. Catharines Saints	AHL	46	6	11	17				22																		
	Springfield Indians	AHL	33	16	8	24				41																		
1983-84	Springfield Indians	AHL	76	17	19	36				76																		
1984-85	Fort Wayne Komets	IHL	18	2	8	10				19																		
	Kalamazoo Wings	IHL	10	2	1	3				0																		
	NHL Totals		1	0	0	0	0	0	0	0	0	0	0	2	0.0	0	0	1	0									

Signed as a free agent by **Toronto**, September 14, 1982. Traded to **Chicago** by **Toronto** for Dave Snopek, January 23, 1983.

• WILLIAMS, Butch

Butch Warren RW – R. 5'11", 195 lbs. b: Duluth, MN, 9/11/1952.

Season	Club	League	GP	G	A	Pts	AG	AA	APts	PIM	PP	SH	GW	S	%	TGF	PGF	TGA	PGA	+/–	GP	G	A	Pts	PIM	PP	SH	GW
1970-71	Oshawa Generals	OHA-Jr.	53	5	21	26				43																		
1971-72	Oshawa–Niagara Falls Flyers	OMJHL	47	13	18	31				101											6	0	1	1	41			
1972-73	New England-Clinton Comets	EHL	54	22	42	64				129																		
	Denver Spurs	WHL	13	2	5	7				15											5	1	2	3	2			
1973-74	St. Louis Blues	NHL	31	3	10	13	3	8	11	6	0	0	0	41	7.3	19	0	17	0	2								
	Denver Spurs	WHL	35	13	11	24				86																		
1974-75	California Golden Seals	NHL	63	11	21	32	10	16	26	118	2	0	0	109	10.1	53	14	56	1	–16								
	Denver Spurs	CHL	14	2	9	11				29																		
1975-76	California Golden Seals	NHL	14	0	4	4	0	3	3	7	0	0	0	10	0.0	7	2	12	0	–7								
	Salt Lake Golden Eagles	CHL	60	31	46	77				171											5	2	3	5	24			
1976-77	United States	Can-Cup	3	0	3	3				2																		
	Edmonton Oilers	WHA	29	3	10	13				16																		
	Rhode Island Reds	AHL	5	0	1	1				24																		
	United States	WEC-A	10	4	4	8				22																		
1977-78	Sun Valley Suns	X-Games	2	1	2	3				0																		
	NHL Totals		108	14	35	49	13	27	40	131	2	0	0	160	8.8	79	16	85	1									
	Other Major League Totals		29	3	10	13				16																		

• Brother of Tommy • CHL First All-Star Team (1975)

Claimed by **Clinton** (EHL) after **New England** (EHL) franchise folded, December, 1972. Traded to **New England** (EHL) by **Clinton** (EHL) for Dwight Winters, October, 1972. Signed as a free agent by **St. Louis**, August, 1972. Traded to **California** by **St. Louis** with Dave Gardner for Craig Patrick and Stan Gilbertson, November 11, 1974. Signed as a free agent by **Edmonton** (WHA), September, 1976.

• WILLIAMS, Darryl

Darryl C. LW – L. 5'11", 185 lbs. b: Mt. Pearl, Nfld., 2/9/1968.

Season	Club	League	GP	G	A	Pts	AG	AA	APts	PIM	PP	SH	GW	S	%	TGF	PGF	TGA	PGA	+/–	GP	G	A	Pts	PIM	PP	SH	GW
1984-85	Mount Pearl Blades	NFAHA	39	52	43	95																						
1985-86	Victoria Cougars	WHL	38	3	2	5				66																		
1986-87	Hamilton Steelhawks	OHL	24	2	4	6				36																		
	Belleville Bulls	OHL	34	7	6	13				72																		
1987-88	Belleville Bulls	OHL	63	29	39	68				169																		
1988-89	Belleville Bulls	OHL	46	24	21	45				137																		
	New Haven Nighthawks	AHL	15	5	5	10				24																		
1989-90	New Haven Nighthawks	AHL	51	9	13	22				124																		

			REGULAR SEASON																		PLAYOFFS							
Season	Club	League	GP	G	A	Pts	AG	AA	APts	PIM	PP	SH	GW	S	%	TGF	PGF	TGA	PGA	+/-	GP	G	A	Pts	PIM	PP	SH	GW
1990-91	New Haven Nighthawks	AHL	57	14	11	25	....	....	....	278	....	....	....	....	....	....	....	....	....	....	....	....	....	....	....	....	....	....
	Phoenix Roadrunners	IHL	12	1	2	3	....	....	....	53	....	....	....	....	....	....	....	....	....	....	7	1	0	1	12	....	....	....
1991-92	Phoenix Roadrunners	IHL	48	8	19	27	....	....	....	219	....	....	....	....	....	....	....	....	....	....	....	....	....	....	....	....	....	....
	New Haven Nighthawks	AHL	13	0	2	2	....	....	....	69	....	....	....	....	....	....	....	....	....	....	....	....	....	....	....	....	....	....
1992-93	**Los Angeles Kings**	**NHL**	**2**	**0**	**0**	**0**	**0**	**0**	**0**	**10**	**0**	**0**	**0**	**1**	**0.0**	**0**	**0**	**0**	**0**	**0**	....	....	....	....	....	....	....	....
	Phoenix Roadrunners	IHL	61	18	7	25	....	....	....	314	....	....	....	....	....	....	....	....	....	....	....	....	....	....	....	....	....	....
1993-94	Phoenix Roadrunners	IHL	52	11	18	29	....	....	....	237	....	....	....	....	....	....	....	....	....	....	....	....	....	....	....	....	....	....
1994-95	Detroit Vipers	IHL	66	10	12	22	....	....	....	268	....	....	....	....	....	....	....	....	....	....	4	0	0	0	14	....	....	....
1995-96	Detroit Vipers	IHL	72	8	19	27	....	....	....	294	....	....	....	....	....	....	....	....	....	....	12	0	3	3	30	....	....	....
1996-97	Long Beach Ice Dogs	IHL	82	13	17	30	....	....	....	215	....	....	....	....	....	....	....	....	....	....	14	2	2	4	26	....	....	....
1997-98	Long Beach Ice Dogs	IHL	82	16	17	33	....	....	....	184	....	....	....	....	....	....	....	....	....	....	17	6	6	12	52	....	....	....
1998-99	Long Beach Ice Dogs	IHL	65	13	15	28	....	....	....	122	....	....	....	....	....	....	....	....	....	....	....	....	....	....	....	....	....	....
99-2000	Long Beach Ice Dogs	IHL	DID NOT PLAY – ASSISTANT COACH																									
	NHL Totals		**2**	**0**	**0**	**0**	**0**	**0**	**0**	**10**	**0**	**0**	**0**	**1**	**0.0**	**0**	**0**	**0**	**0**		....	....	....	....	....	....	....	....

Signed as a free agent by **LA Kings**, May 19, 1989. • Officially announced retirement and named Assistant Coach of **Long Beach** (IHL), August 2, 1999.

• WILLIAMS, David

David A. D – R. 6'2", 195 lbs. b: Plainfield, NJ, 8/25/1967. New Jersey's 12th, 234th overall, in 1985.

Season	Club	League	GP	G	A	Pts	AG	AA	APts	PIM	PP	SH	GW	S	%	TGF	PGF	TGA	PGA	+/-	GP	G	A	Pts	PIM	PP	SH	GW
1984-85	Choate-Rosemary Hall	Hi-School	25	14	20	34	....	....	....	30	....	....	....	....	....	....	....	....	....	....	....	....	....	....	....	....	....	....
1985-86	Choate-Rosemary Hall	Hi-School	STATISTICS NOT AVAILABLE																									
1986-87	Dartmouth College	ECAC	23	2	19	21	....	....	....	20	....	....	....	....	....	....	....	....	....	....	....	....	....	....	....	....	....	....
1987-88	Dartmouth College	ECAC	25	8	14	22	....	....	....	30	....	....	....	....	....	....	....	....	....	....	....	....	....	....	....	....	....	....
1988-89	Dartmouth College	ECAC	25	4	11	15	....	....	....	28	....	....	....	....	....	....	....	....	....	....	....	....	....	....	....	....	....	....
1989-90	Dartmouth College	ECAC	26	3	12	15	....	....	....	32	....	....	....	....	....	....	....	....	....	....	....	....	....	....	....	....	....	....
1990-91	Muskegon Lumberjacks	IHL	14	1	2	3	....	....	....	4	....	....	....	....	....	....	....	....	....	....	....	....	....	....	....	....	....	....
	Knoxville Cherokees	ECHL	38	12	15	27	....	....	....	40	....	....	....	....	....	....	....	....	....	....	3	0	0	0	4	....	....	....
	United States	WEC-A	9	0	2	2	....	....	....	8	....	....	....	....	....	....	....	....	....	....	....	....	....	....	....	....	....	....
1991-92	**San Jose Sharks**	**NHL**	**56**	**3**	**25**	**28**	**3**	**19**	**22**	**40**	**2**	**0**	**1**	**91**	**3.3**	**68**	**24**	**71**	**14**	**−13**	....	....	....	....	....	....	....	....
	Kansas City Blades	IHL	18	2	3	5	....	....	....	22	....	....	....	....	....	....	....	....	....	....	....	....	....	....	....	....	....	....
	United States	WC-A	6	0	1	1	....	....	....	8	....	....	....	....	....	....	....	....	....	....	....	....	....	....	....	....	....	....
1992-93	**San Jose Sharks**	**NHL**	**40**	**1**	**11**	**12**	**1**	**8**	**9**	**49**	**1**	**0**	**0**	**60**	**1.7**	**26**	**9**	**54**	**10**	**−27**	....	....	....	....	....	....	....	....
	Kansas City Blades	IHL	31	1	11	12	....	....	....	28	....	....	....	....	....	....	....	....	....	....	....	....	....	....	....	....	....	....
1993-94	**Mighty Ducks of Anaheim**	**NHL**	**56**	**5**	**15**	**20**	**5**	**12**	**17**	**42**	**2**	**0**	**0**	**74**	**6.8**	**58**	**13**	**43**	**6**	**8**	....	....	....	....	....	....	....	....
	San Diego Gulls	IHL	16	1	6	7	....	....	....	17	....	....	....	....	....	....	....	....	....	....	....	....	....	....	....	....	....	....
1994-95	**Mighty Ducks of Anaheim**	**NHL**	**21**	**2**	**2**	**4**	**4**	**3**	**7**	**26**	**0**	**0**	**0**	**30**	**6.7**	**13**	**1**	**24**	**7**	**−5**	....	....	....	....	....	....	....	....
	San Diego Gulls	IHL	2	0	1	1	....	....	....	0	....	....	....	....	....	....	....	....	....	....	5	1	0	1	0	....	....	....
1995-96	Detroit Vipers	IHL	81	5	14	19	....	....	....	81	....	....	....	....	....	....	....	....	....	....	11	1	3	4	6	....	....	....
1996-97	Worcester IceCats	AHL	72	3	17	20	....	....	....	89	....	....	....	....	....	....	....	....	....	....	5	1	1	2	0	....	....	....
1997-98	Cincinnati Cyclones	IHL	80	3	15	18	....	....	....	78	....	....	....	....	....	....	....	....	....	....	8	0	2	2	8	....	....	....
	NHL Totals		**173**	**11**	**53**	**64**	**13**	**42**	**55**	**157**	**5**	**0**	**1**	**255**	**4.3**	**165**	**47**	**192**	**37**		....	....	....	....	....	....	....	....

ECAC First All-Star Team (1989)

Signed as a free agent by **San Jose**, August 9, 1991. Claimed by **Anaheim** from **San Jose** in Expansion Draft, June 24, 1993. Signed as a free agent by **Hartford**, August 25, 1995. Signed as a free agent by **St. Louis**, July 29, 1996.

• WILLIAMS, Fred

Frederick Richard "Fats" C – L. 5'11", 178 lbs. b: Saskatoon, Sask., 7/1/1956. Detroit's 1st, 4th overall, in 1976.

Season	Club	League	GP	G	A	Pts	AG	AA	APts	PIM	PP	SH	GW	S	%	TGF	PGF	TGA	PGA	+/-	GP	G	A	Pts	PIM	PP	SH	GW
1970-71	Saskatoon Blazers	SAHA	STATISTICS NOT AVAILABLE																									
1971-72	Saskatoon Blades	WCJHL	54	7	9	16	....	....	....	6	....	....	....	....	....	....	....	....	....	....	8	0	3	3	0	....	....	....
1972-73	Saskatoon Blades	WCJHL	67	7	18	25	....	....	....	24	....	....	....	....	....	....	....	....	....	....	16	1	1	2	6	....	....	....
1973-74	Saskatoon Blades	WCJHL	67	16	20	36	....	....	....	46	....	....	....	....	....	....	....	....	....	....	6	1	2	3	0	....	....	....
1974-75	Saskatoon Blades	WCJHL	59	21	49	70	....	....	....	61	....	....	....	....	....	....	....	....	....	....	17	8	16	24	43	....	....	....
1975-76	Saskatoon Blades	WHL	72	31	87	118	....	....	....	129	....	....	....	....	....	....	....	....	....	....	20	7	20	27	20	....	....	....
1976-77	**Detroit Red Wings**	**NHL**	**44**	**2**	**5**	**7**	**2**	**4**	**6**	**10**	**0**	**0**	**0**	**32**	**6.3**	**13**	**2**	**29**	**1**	**−17**	....	....	....	....	....	....	....	....
	Rhode Island Reds	AHL	34	7	19	26	....	....	....	24	....	....	....	....	....	....	....	....	....	....	....	....	....	....	....	....	....	....
1977-78	Kansas City Red Wings	CHL	32	0	6	6	....	....	....	12	....	....	....	....	....	....	....	....	....	....	....	....	....	....	....	....	....	....
	Philadelphia Firebirds	AHL	35	5	11	16	....	....	....	22	....	....	....	....	....	....	....	....	....	....	4	2	3	5	2	....	....	....
1978-79			OUT OF HOCKEY – RETIRED																									
1979-80	Maine Mariners	AHL	73	17	34	51	....	....	....	26	....	....	....	....	....	....	....	....	....	....	12	5	13	18	8	....	....	....
1980-81	Maine Mariners	AHL	79	21	34	55	....	....	....	78	....	....	....	....	....	....	....	....	....	....	20	8	8	16	20	....	....	....
1981-82	Maine Mariners	AHL	46	6	26	32	....	....	....	44	....	....	....	....	....	....	....	....	....	....	3	0	0	0	2	....	....	....
	NHL Totals		**44**	**2**	**5**	**7**	**2**	**4**	**6**	**10**	**0**	**0**	**0**	**32**	**6.3**	**13**	**2**	**29**	**1**		....	....	....	....	....	....	....	....

• Brother of Gord

Signed as a free agent by **Philadelphia**, September 15, 1979.

• WILLIAMS, Gord

Gordon James RW – R. 5'11", 190 lbs. b: Saskatoon, Sask., 4/10/1960. Philadelphia's 7th, 119th overall, in 1979.

Season	Club	League	GP	G	A	Pts	AG	AA	APts	PIM	PP	SH	GW	S	%	TGF	PGF	TGA	PGA	+/-	GP	G	A	Pts	PIM	PP	SH	GW
1976-77	Taber Golden Suns	AJHL	60	35	28	63	....	....	....	53	....	....	....	....	....	....	....	....	....	....	....	....	....	....	....	....	....	....
1977-78	Lethbridge Broncos	WCJHL	71	12	26	38	....	....	....	80	....	....	....	....	....	....	....	....	....	....	....	....	....	....	....	....	....	....
1978-79	Lethbridge Broncos	WHL	72	58	59	117	....	....	....	60	....	....	....	....	....	....	....	....	....	....	....	....	....	....	....	....	....	....
1979-80	Lethbridge Broncos	WHL	72	57	65	122	....	....	....	92	....	....	....	....	....	....	....	....	....	....	....	....	....	....	....	....	....	....
1980-81	Maine Mariners	AHL	65	14	12	26	....	....	....	62	....	....	....	....	....	....	....	....	....	....	12	3	5	8	4	....	....	....
1981-82	**Philadelphia Flyers**	**NHL**	**1**	**0**	**0**	**0**	**0**	**0**	**0**	**2**	**0**	**0**	**0**	**1**	**0.0**	**0**	**0**	**0**	**0**	**0**	....	....	....	....	....	....	....	....
	Maine Mariners	AHL	73	31	25	56	....	....	....	35	....	....	....	....	....	....	....	....	....	....	4	1	1	2	0	....	....	....
1982-83	**Philadelphia Flyers**	**NHL**	**1**	**0**	**0**	**0**	**0**	**0**	**0**	**0**	**0**	**0**	**0**	**1**	**0.0**	**0**	**0**	**0**	**0**	**0**	....	....	....	....	....	....	....	....
	Maine Mariners	AHL	56	26	37	63	....	....	....	34	....	....	....	....	....	....	....	....	....	....	8	2	4	6	4	....	....	....
	NHL Totals		**2**	**0**	**0**	**0**	**0**	**0**	**0**	**2**	**0**	**0**	**0**	**2**	**0.0**	**0**	**0**	**0**	**0**		....	....	....	....	....	....	....	....

• Brother of Fred

• WILLIAMS, Sean

Sean B. C – L. 6'1", 182 lbs. b: Oshawa, Ont., 1/28/1968. Chicago's 11th, 245th overall, in 1986.

Season	Club	League	GP	G	A	Pts	AG	AA	APts	PIM	PP	SH	GW	S	%	TGF	PGF	TGA	PGA	+/-	GP	G	A	Pts	PIM	PP	SH	GW
1983-84	Oshawa Legionaires	OMHA	42	15	28	43	....	....	....	34	....	....	....	....	....	....	....	....	....	....	....	....	....	....	....	....	....	....
1984-85	Oshawa Generals	OHL	40	6	7	13	....	....	....	28	....	....	....	....	....	....	....	....	....	....	5	1	0	1	0	....	....	....
1985-86	Oshawa Generals	OHL	55	15	23	38	....	....	....	23	....	....	....	....	....	....	....	....	....	....	6	2	3	5	4	....	....	....
1986-87	Oshawa Generals	OHL	62	21	23	44	....	....	....	32	....	....	....	....	....	....	....	....	....	....	25	7	5	12	19	....	....	....
	Oshawa Generals	Mem-Cup	4	1	1	2	....	....	....	5	....	....	....	....	....	....	....	....	....	....	....	....	....	....	....	....	....	....
1987-88	Oshawa Generals	OHL	65	*58	65	123	....	....	....	38	....	....	....	....	....	....	....	....	....	....	7	3	3	6	6	....	....	....
1988-89	Saginaw Hawks	IHL	77	32	27	59	....	....	....	75	....	....	....	....	....	....	....	....	....	....	6	0	3	3	0	....	....	....
1989-90	Indianapolis Ice	IHL	78	21	37	58	....	....	....	25	....	....	....	....	....	....	....	....	....	....	14	8	5	13	12	....	....	....
1990-91	Indianapolis Ice	IHL	82	46	52	98	....	....	....	59	....	....	....	....	....	....	....	....	....	....	7	1	2	3	12	....	....	....
1991-92	**Chicago Blackhawks**	**NHL**	**2**	**0**	**0**	**0**	**0**	**0**	**0**	**4**	**0**	**0**	**0**	**0**	**0.0**	**1**	**0**	**1**	**0**	**0**	....	....	....	....	....	....	....	....
	Indianapolis Ice	IHL	79	29	36	65	....	....	....	89	....	....	....	....	....	....	....	....	....	....	....	....	....	....	....	....	....	....
1992-93	Indianapolis Ice	IHL	81	28	37	65	....	....	....	66	....	....	....	....	....	....	....	....	....	....	5	0	1	1	4	....	....	....
1993-94	HC Gardena-Groden	Alpenliga	28	14	15	29	....	....	....	21	....	....	....	....	....	....	....	....	....	....	....	....	....	....	....	....	....	....
	HC Gardena-Groden	Italy	22	20	23	43	....	....	....	4	....	....	....	....	....	....	....	....	....	....	....	....	....	....	....	....	....	....
1994-95	Minnesota Moose	IHL	81	20	26	46	....	....	....	34	....	....	....	....	....	....	....	....	....	....	3	1	0	1	0	....	....	....
1995-96	Minnesota Moose	IHL	7	0	4	4	....	....	....	2	....	....	....	....	....	....	....	....	....	....	....	....	....	....	....	....	....	....
	NHL Totals		**2**	**0**	**0**	**0**	**0**	**0**	**0**	**4**	**0**	**0**	**0**	**0**	**0.0**	**1**	**0**	**1**	**0**		....	....	....	....	....	....	....	....

OHL First All-Star Team (1988)

• WILLIAMS, Tiger

David James LW – L. 5'11", 190 lbs. b: Weyburn, Sask., 2/3/1954. Toronto's 2nd, 31st overall, in 1974.

			REGULAR SEASON																		PLAYOFFS							
Season	Club	League	GP	G	A	Pts	AG	AA	APts	PIM	PP	SH	GW	S	%	TGF	PGF	TGA	PGA	+/–	GP	G	A	Pts	PIM	PP	SH	GW
1970-71	Vernon Lakers	BCJHL	STATISTICS NOT AVAILABLE																									
1971-72	Swift Current Broncos	WCJHL	68	12	22	34	....	....	....	278	....	....	....	....	....	....	....	....	....	....	....	....	....	....	....	....	....	....
1972-73	Swift Current Broncos	WCJHL	68	44	58	102	....	....	....	266	....	....	....	....	....	....	....	....	....	....	....	....	....	....	....	....	....	....
1973-74	Swift Current Broncos	WCJHL	68	52	56	108	....	....	....	310	....	....	....	....	....	....	....	....	....	....	12	14	10	24	23	....	....	....
1974-75	Oklahoma City Blazers	CHL	39	16	11	27	....	....	....	202	....	....	....	....	....	....	....	....	....	....	....	....	....	....	....	....	....	....
	Toronto Maple Leafs	**NHL**	42	10	19	29	9	14	23	187	2	0	0	83	12.0	50	12	36	2	4	7	1	3	4	25	1	0	0
1975-76	**Toronto Maple Leafs**	**NHL**	78	21	19	40	18	14	32	299	3	0	3	149	14.1	60	9	53	1	–1	10	0	0	0	75	0	0	0
1976-77	**Toronto Maple Leafs**	**NHL**	77	18	25	43	16	19	35	*338	1	0	0	157	11.5	67	3	54	1	11	9	3	6	9	29	0	0	1
1977-78	**Toronto Maple Leafs**	**NHL**	78	19	31	50	17	24	41	351	6	0	5	161	11.8	104	34	64	0	6	12	1	2	3	*63	0	0	0
1978-79	**Toronto Maple Leafs**	**NHL**	77	19	20	39	16	14	30	*298	6	0	4	157	12.1	76	27	58	2	–7	6	0	0	0	*48	0	0	0
1979-80	**Toronto Maple Leafs**	**NHL**	55	22	18	40	19	13	32	197	5	0	1	108	20.4	74	29	60	2	–13	....	....	....	....	....	....	....	....
	Vancouver Canucks	**NHL**	23	8	5	13	7	4	11	81	1	0	0	62	12.9	26	8	22	4	0	3	0	0	0	20	0	0	0
1980-81	**Vancouver Canucks**	**NHL**	77	35	27	62	27	18	45	*343	11	1	4	186	18.8	102	38	88	28	4	3	0	0	0	20	0	0	0
1981-82	**Vancouver Canucks**	**NHL**	77	17	21	38	13	14	27	341	5	1	1	138	12.3	69	18	65	8	–6	17	3	7	10	*116	0	0	2
1982-83	**Vancouver Canucks**	**NHL**	68	8	13	21	7	9	16	265	0	0	1	78	10.3	43	2	49	1	–7	4	0	3	3	12	0	0	0
1983-84	**Vancouver Canucks**	**NHL**	67	15	16	31	12	11	23	294	2	0	1	119	12.6	60	9	64	2	–11	4	1	0	1	13	0	0	0
1984-85	**Detroit Red Wings**	**NHL**	55	3	8	11	2	5	7	158	0	0	0	34	8.8	22	2	47	11	–16	....	....	....	....	....	....	....	....
	Adirondack Red Wings	AHL	8	5	2	7	....	....	....	4	....	....	....	....	....	....	....	....	....	....	....	....	....	....	....	....	....	....
	Los Angeles Kings	**NHL**	12	4	3	7	3	2	5	43	0	0	0	19	21.1	10	1	9	0	0	3	0	0	0	4	0	0	0
1985-86	**Los Angeles Kings**	**NHL**	72	20	29	49	16	19	35	320	5	0	1	138	14.5	82	20	69	1	–6	....	....	....	....	....	....	....	....
1986-87	**Los Angeles Kings**	**NHL**	76	16	18	34	14	13	27	358	1	0	3	118	13.6	64	8	57	0	–1	5	3	2	5	30	0	0	1
1987-88	**Los Angeles Kings**	**NHL**	2	0	0	0	0	0	0	6	0	0	0	2	0.0	1	0	0	0	1	....	....	....	....	....	....	....	....
	Hartford Whalers	**NHL**	26	6	0	6	5	0	5	87	1	0	1	31	19.4	12	2	8	0	2	....	....	....	....	....	....	....	....
	NHL Totals		962	241	272	513	201	193	394	3966	49	2	25	1740	13.9	922	222	803	63		83	12	23	35	455	1	0	4

Played in NHL All-Star Game (1981)

Traded to **Vancouver** by **Toronto** with Jerry Butler for Rick Vaive and Bill Derlago, February 18, 1980. Traded to **Detroit** by **Vancouver** for Rob McClanahan, August 8, 1984. Traded to **LA Kings** by **Detroit** for future considerations, March 12, 1985. Traded to **Hartford** by **LA Kings** for cash, October 15, 1987. • Played w/ RHI's Vancouver Voodoo in 1993 (1-1-1-2-2).

• WILLIAMS, Tom

Thomas Charles LW – R. 5'11", 187 lbs. b: Windsor, Ont., 2/7/1951. NY Rangers' 3rd, 27th overall, in 1971.

Season	Club	League	GP	G	A	Pts	AG	AA	APts	PIM	PP	SH	GW	S	%	TGF	PGF	TGA	PGA	+/–	GP	G	A	Pts	PIM	PP	SH	GW
1968-69	Hamilton Red Wings	OHA-Jr.	54	21	29	50	....	....	....	18	....	....	....	....	....	....	....	....	....	....	5	0	1	1	0	....	....	....
1969-70	Hamilton Red Wings	OHA-Jr.	54	23	27	50	....	....	....	17	....	....	....	....	....	....	....	....	....	....	....	....	....	....	....	....	....	....
1970-71	Hamilton Red Wings	OHA-Jr.	59	43	26	69	....	....	....	8	....	....	....	....	....	....	....	....	....	....	7	1	2	3	0	....	....	....
1971-72	**New York Rangers**	**NHL**	3	0	0	0	0	0	0	2	0	0	0	6	0.0	1	0	2	0	–1	....	....	....	....	....	....	....	....
	Omaha Knights	CHL	67	30	34	64	....	....	....	4	....	....	....	....	....	....	....	....	....	....	....	....	....	....	....	....	....	....
1972-73	**New York Rangers**	**NHL**	8	0	1	1	0	1	1	0	0	0	0	2	0.0	1	0	1	1	1	....	....	....	....	....	....	....	....
	Providence Reds	AHL	50	20	27	47	....	....	....	9	....	....	....	....	....	....	....	....	....	....	3	1	2	3	0	....	....	....
1973-74	**New York Rangers**	**NHL**	14	1	2	3	1	2	3	4	0	0	0	18	5.6	4	1	5	0	–2	....	....	....	....	....	....	....	....
	Los Angeles Kings	**NHL**	46	11	17	28	11	14	25	6	2	0	2	113	9.7	42	16	23	0	3	5	3	1	4	0	1	0	0
1974-75	**Los Angeles Kings**	**NHL**	74	24	22	46	21	16	37	16	6	0	3	188	12.8	66	23	29	0	14	3	0	0	0	0	0	0	0
1975-76	**Los Angeles Kings**	**NHL**	70	19	20	39	17	15	32	14	4	0	2	157	12.1	65	16	49	0	0	9	2	2	4	2	0	0	0
1976-77	**Los Angeles Kings**	**NHL**	80	35	39	74	32	30	62	14	15	0	3	233	15.0	111	49	48	0	14	9	3	4	7	2	1	0	0
1977-78	**Los Angeles Kings**	**NHL**	58	15	22	37	14	17	31	9	6	0	2	147	10.2	56	20	53	3	–14	2	0	0	0	0	0	0	0
	Springfield Indians	AHL	7	6	3	9	....	....	....	13	....	....	....	....	....	....	....	....	....	....	....	....	....	....	....	....	....	....
1978-79	**Los Angeles Kings**	**NHL**	44	10	15	25	9	11	20	8	3	0	2	84	11.9	37	13	31	0	–7	1	0	0	0	0	0	0	0
1979-80	Salt Lake Golden Eagles	CHL	11	1	3	4	....	....	....	0	....	....	....	....	....	....	....	....	....	....	....	....	....	....	....	....	....	....
	NHL Totals		397	115	138	253	105	106	211	73	36	0	14	948	12.1	383	138	241	4		29	8	7	15	4	2	0	0

CHL Second All-Star Team (1972) • Won Ken McKenzie Trophy (CHL's Rookie of the Year) (1972)

Traded to **LA Kings** by **NY Rangers** with Mike Murphy and Sheldon Kannegiesser for Gilles Marotte and Real Lemieux, November 30, 1973. Traded to **St. Louis** by **LA Kings** to complete three-team transaction that sent Barry Gibbs to LA Kings (June 9, 1979) and Terry Richardson to NY Islanders (June 9, 1979), August 16, 1979.

• WILLIAMS, Tommy

Thomas Mark RW – R. 5'11", 180 lbs. b: Duluth, MN, 4/17/1940 d: 2/8/1992. USHOF

Season	Club	League	GP	G	A	Pts	AG	AA	APts	PIM	PP	SH	GW	S	%	TGF	PGF	TGA	PGA	+/–	GP	G	A	Pts	PIM	PP	SH	GW
1958-59	United States	Nat-Team	50	21	12	33	....	....	....	22	....	....	....	....	....	....	....	....	....	....	5	1	1	2	0	....	....	....
	United States	WEC-A	8	7	2	9	....	....	....	....	....	....	....	....	....	....	....	....	....	....	....	....	....	....	....	....	....	....
1959-60	Fort William Hurricanes	NOHA	STATISTICS NOT AVAILABLE																									
	United States	Olympics	7	4	6	10	....	....	....	2	....	....	....	....	....	....	....	....	....	....	....	....	....	....	....	....	....	....
	Fort William Hurricanes	Mem-Cup	2	4	1	5	....	....	....	0	....	....	....	....	....	....	....	....	....	....	....	....	....	....	....	....	....	....
1960-61	Kingston Frontenacs	EPHL	51	16	26	42	....	....	....	18	....	....	....	....	....	....	....	....	....	....	5	0	2	2	0	....	....	....
1961-62	**Boston Bruins**	**NHL**	26	6	6	12	7	6	13	2	....	....	....	....	....	....	....	....	....	....	....	....	....	....	....	....	....	....
	Kingston Frontenacs	EPHL	36	10	18	28	....	....	....	35	....	....	....	....	....	....	....	....	....	....	....	....	....	....	....	....	....	....
1962-63	**Boston Bruins**	**NHL**	69	23	20	43	27	20	47	11	....	....	....	....	....	....	....	....	....	....	....	....	....	....	....	....	....	....
1963-64	**Boston Bruins**	**NHL**	37	8	15	23	10	16	26	8	....	....	....	....	....	....	....	....	....	....	....	....	....	....	....	....	....	....
1964-65	**Boston Bruins**	**NHL**	65	13	21	34	16	22	38	28	....	....	....	....	....	....	....	....	....	....	....	....	....	....	....	....	....	....
1965-66	**Boston Bruins**	**NHL**	70	16	22	38	18	21	39	31	....	....	....	....	....	....	....	....	....	....	....	....	....	....	....	....	....	....
1966-67	**Boston Bruins**	**NHL**	29	8	13	21	9	13	22	2	....	....	....	....	....	....	....	....	....	....	....	....	....	....	....	....	....	....
1967-68	**Boston Bruins**	**NHL**	68	18	32	50	21	32	53	14	0	0	4	136	13.2	65	5	36	0	24	4	1	0	1	2	0	0	0
1968-69	**Boston Bruins**	**NHL**	26	4	7	11	4	6	10	19	0	0	0	48	8.3	20	2	12	0	6	....	....	....	....	....	....	....	....
1969-70	**Minnesota North Stars**	**NHL**	75	15	52	67	16	49	65	18	2	0	0	165	9.1	90	33	77	1	–19	6	1	5	6	0	0	0	0
1970-71	**Minnesota North Stars**	**NHL**	41	10	13	23	10	11	21	16	3	0	2	61	16.4	26	4	27	0	–5	....	....	....	....	....	....	....	....
	California Golden Seals	**NHL**	18	7	10	17	7	8	15	8	2	0	0	44	15.9	20	6	37	11	–12	....	....	....	....	....	....	....	....
1971-72	**California Golden Seals**	**NHL**	32	3	9	12	3	8	11	2	0	0	0	41	7.3	15	5	29	2	–17	....	....	....	....	....	....	....	....
	Boston Braves	AHL	31	8	15	23	....	....	....	8	....	....	....	....	....	....	....	....	....	....	9	2	6	8	6	....	....	....
1972-73	New England Whalers	WHA	69	10	21	31	....	....	....	14	....	....	....	....	....	....	....	....	....	....	15	6	11	17	2	....	....	....
1973-74	New England Whalers	WHA	70	21	37	58	....	....	....	6	....	....	....	....	....	....	....	....	....	....	4	0	3	3	10	....	....	....
1974-75	**Washington Capitals**	**NHL**	73	22	36	58	19	27	46	12	7	2	1	135	16.3	60	22	128	42	–48	....	....	....	....	....	....	....	....
1975-76	**Washington Capitals**	**NHL**	34	8	13	21	7	10	17	6	2	0	0	39	20.5	31	15	50	1	–33	....	....	....	....	....	....	....	....
	New Haven Nighthawks	AHL	20	4	16	20	....	....	....	4	....	....	....	....	....	....	....	....	....	....	3	0	1	1	0	....	....	....
	NHL Totals		663	161	269	430	174	249	423	177	....	....	....	....	....	....	....	....	....		10	2	5	7	2	....	....	....
	Other Major League Totals		139	31	58	89	....	....	....	20	....	....	....	....	....	....	....	....	....	....	19	6	14	20	12	....	....	....

• Brother of Warren

• Missed majority of 1968-69 season recovering from knee injury suffered in game vs. Chicago, December 13, 1968. Traded to **Minnesota** by **Boston** with Barry Gibbs for Minnesota's 1st round choice (Don Tannahill) in 1969 Amateur Draft and future considerations (Fred O'Donnell, May 7, 1971), May 7, 1969. Traded to **California** by **Minnesota** with Dick Redmond for Ted Hampson and Wayne Muloin, March 7, 1971. Selected by **New England** (WHA) in 1972 WHA General Player Draft, February 12, 1972. Traded to **Boston** by **California** for cash, March 5, 1972. Traded to **Washington** by **Boston** for cash, July 22, 1974.

• WILLIS, Shane

RW – R. 6', 180 lbs. b: Edmonton, Alta., 6/13/1977. Carolina's 4th, 88th overall, in 1997.

Season	Club	League	GP	G	A	Pts	AG	AA	APts	PIM	PP	SH	GW	S	%	TGF	PGF	TGA	PGA	+/–	GP	G	A	Pts	PIM	PP	SH	GW
1992-93	Red Deer Bantam Raiders	AAHA	36	32	18	50	....	....	....	88	....	....	....	....	....	....	....	....	....	....	....	....	....	....	....	....	....	....
1993-94	Red Deer Midget Chiefs	AAHA	34	40	26	66	....	....	....	103	....	....	....	....	....	....	....	....	....	....	....	....	....	....	....	....	....	....
1994-95	Prince Albert Raiders	WHL	65	24	19	43	....	....	....	38	....	....	....	....	....	....	....	....	....	....	13	3	4	7	6	....	....	....
1995-96	Prince Albert Raiders	WHL	69	41	40	81	....	....	....	47	....	....	....	....	....	....	....	....	....	....	18	11	10	21	18	....	....	....
1996-97	Prince Albert Raiders	WHL	41	34	22	56	....	....	....	63	....	....	....	....	....	....	....	....	....	....	....	....	....	....	....	....	....	....
	Lethbridge Hurricanes	WHL	26	22	17	39	....	....	....	24	....	....	....	....	....	....	....	....	....	....	19	13	11	24	20	....	....	....
	Canada	WJC-A	7	0	0	0	....	....	....	0	....	....	....	....	....	....	....	....	....	....	....	....	....	....	....	....	....	....
	Lethbridge Hurricanes	Mem-Cup	5	2	2	4	....	....	....	4	....	....	....	....	....	....	....	....	....	....	....	....	....	....	....	....	....	....
1997-98	Lethbridge Hurricanes	WHL	64	58	54	112	....	....	....	73	....	....	....	....	....	....	....	....	....	....	4	2	3	5	6	....	....	....
	Beast of New Haven	AHL	1	0	1	1	....	....	....	2	....	....	....	....	....	....	....	....	....	....	....	....	....	....	....	....	....	....

			REGULAR SEASON																		PLAYOFFS							
Season	Club	League	GP	G	A	Pts	AG	AA	APts	PIM	PP	SH	GW	S	%	TGF	PGF	TGA	PGA	+/–	GP	G	A	Pts	PIM	PP	SH	GW
1998-99	**Carolina Hurricanes**	**NHL**	**7**	**0**	**0**	**0**	**0**	**0**	**0**	**0**	**0**	**0**	**0**	**1**	**0.0**	**0**	**0**	**2**	**0**	**–2**	....	....	....	....	....	....	....	....
	Beast of New Haven	AHL	73	31	50	81	....	....	....	49	....	....	....	....	....	....	....	....	....	....	....	....	....	....	....	....	....	....
99-2000	**Carolina Hurricanes**	**NHL**	**2**	**0**	**0**	**0**	**0**	**0**	**0**	**0**	**0**	**0**	**0**	**1**	**0.0**	**0**	**0**	**1**	**0**	**–1**	....	....	....	....	....	....	....	....
	Cincinnati Cyclones	IHL	80	35	25	60	....	....	....	64	....	....	....	....	....	....	....	....	....	....	11	5	3	8	8	....	....	....
	NHL Totals		**9**	**0**	**0**	**0**	**0**	**0**	**0**	**0**	**0**	**0**	**0**	**2**	**0.0**	**0**	**0**	**3**	**0**		....	....	....	....	....	....	....	....

WHL East First All-Star Team (1997, 1998) • AHL First All-Star Team (1999) • Won Dudley "Red" Garrett Memorial Trophy (Top Rookie - AHL) (1999)

• Re-entered NHL Entry Draft. Tampa Bay's 3rd choice, 56th overall, in 1995 Entry Draft.

• WILLSIE, Brian

RW – R. 6', 190 lbs. b: London, Ont., 3/16/1978. Colorado's 7th, 146th overall, in 1996.

Season	Club	League	GP	G	A	Pts	AG	AA	APts	PIM	PP	SH	GW	S	%	TGF	PGF	TGA	PGA	+/–	GP	G	A	Pts	PIM	PP	SH	GW
1993-94	Belmont Bombers	OJHL-D	13	9	5	14	....	....	....	14	....	....	....	....	....	....	....	....	....	....	....	....	....	....	....	....	....	....
1994-95	St. Thomas Stars	OJHL-B	45	35	47	82	....	....	....	47	....	....	....	....	....	....	....	....	....	....	....	....	....	....	....	....	....	....
1995-96	Guelph Storm	OHL	65	13	21	34	....	....	....	18	....	....	....	....	....	....	....	....	....	....	16	4	2	6	6	....	....	....
1996-97	Guelph Storm	OHL	64	37	31	68	....	....	....	37	....	....	....	....	....	....	....	....	....	....	18	15	4	19	10	....	....	....
1997-98	Guelph Storm	OHL	57	45	31	76	....	....	....	41	....	....	....	....	....	....	....	....	....	....	12	9	5	14	18	....	....	....
	Canada	WJC-A	7	0	2	2	....	....	....	4	....	....	....	....	....	....	....	....	....	....	....	....	....	....	....	....	....	....
1998-99	Hershey Bears	AHL	72	19	10	29	....	....	....	28	....	....	....	....	....	....	....	....	....	....	3	1	0	1	0	....	....	....
99-2000	**Colorado Avalanche**	**NHL**	**1**	**0**	**0**	**0**	**0**	**0**	**0**	**0**	**0**	**0**	**0**	**1**	**0.0**	**0**	**0**	**0**	**0**	**0**	....	....	....	....	....	....	....	....
	Hershey Bears	AHL	78	20	39	59	....	....	....	44	....	....	....	....	....	....	....	....	....	....	12	2	6	8	8	....	....	....
	NHL Totals		**1**	**0**	**0**	**0**	**0**	**0**	**0**	**0**	**0**	**0**	**0**	**1**	**0.0**	**0**	**0**	**0**	**0**		....	....	....	....	....	....	....	....

OHL First All-Star Team (1998)

• WILM, Clarke

C – L. 6', 202 lbs. b: Central Butte, Sask., 10/24/1976. Calgary's 5th, 150th overall, in 1995.

Season	Club	League	GP	G	A	Pts	AG	AA	APts	PIM	PP	SH	GW	S	%	TGF	PGF	TGA	PGA	+/–	GP	G	A	Pts	PIM	PP	SH	GW
1991-92	Saskatoon Blazers	SAHA	36	18	28	46	....	....	....	16	....	....	....	....	....	....	....	....	....	....	....	....	....	....	....	....	....	....
	Saskatoon Blades	WHL	....	....	....	....	....	....	....	....	....	....	....	....	....	....	....	....	....	....	1	0	0	0	0	....	....	....
1992-93	Saskatoon Blades	WHL	69	14	19	33	....	....	....	71	....	....	....	....	....	....	....	....	....	....	9	4	2	6	13	....	....	....
1993-94	Saskatoon Blades	WHL	70	18	32	50	....	....	....	181	....	....	....	....	....	....	....	....	....	....	16	0	9	9	19	....	....	....
1994-95	Saskatoon Blades	WHL	71	20	39	59	....	....	....	179	....	....	....	....	....	....	....	....	....	....	10	6	1	7	21	....	....	....
1995-96	Saskatoon Blades	WHL	72	49	61	110	....	....	....	83	....	....	....	....	....	....	....	....	....	....	4	1	1	2	4	....	....	....
1996-97	Saint John Flames	AHL	62	9	19	28	....	....	....	107	....	....	....	....	....	....	....	....	....	....	5	2	0	2	15	....	....	....
1997-98	Saint John Flames	AHL	68	13	26	39	....	....	....	112	....	....	....	....	....	....	....	....	....	....	21	5	9	14	8	....	....	....
1998-99	**Calgary Flames**	**NHL**	**78**	**10**	**8**	**18**	**12**	**8**	**20**	**53**	**2**	**2**	**0**	**94**	**10.6**	**36**	**3**	**36**	**14**	**11**	....	....	....	....	....	....	....	....
99-2000	**Calgary Flames**	**NHL**	**78**	**10**	**12**	**22**	**11**	**11**	**22**	**67**	**1**	**3**	**0**	**81**	**12.3**	**34**	**3**	**58**	**21**	**–6**	....	....	....	....	....	....	....	....
	NHL Totals		**156**	**20**	**20**	**40**	**23**	**19**	**42**	**120**	**3**	**5**	**0**	**175**	**11.4**	**70**	**6**	**94**	**35**		....	....	....	....	....	....	....	....

• WILSON, Behn

Behn Alexander D – L. 6'3", 210 lbs. b: Toronto, Ont., 12/19/1958. Philadelphia's 1st, 6th overall, in 1978.

Season	Club	League	GP	G	A	Pts	AG	AA	APts	PIM	PP	SH	GW	S	%	TGF	PGF	TGA	PGA	+/–	GP	G	A	Pts	PIM	PP	SH	GW
1974-75	Don Mills Flyers	OHA-B	44	24	45	69	....	....	....	....	....	....	....	....	....	....	....	....	....	....	....	....	....	....	....	....	....	....
1975-76	Ottawa 67's	OMJHL	63	5	16	21	....	....	....	131	....	....	....	....	....	....	....	....	....	....	12	3	2	5	46	....	....	....
1976-77	Ottawa 67's	OMJHL	31	8	29	37	....	....	....	115	....	....	....	....	....	....	....	....	....	....	....	....	....	....	....	....	....	....
	Windsor Spitfires	OMJHL	17	4	16	20	....	....	....	38	....	....	....	....	....	....	....	....	....	....	....	....	....	....	....	....	....	....
	Kalamazoo Wings	IHL	13	2	7	9	....	....	....	40	....	....	....	....	....	....	....	....	....	....	....	....	....	....	....	....	....	....
1977-78	Kingston Canadians	OMJHL	52	18	58	76	....	....	....	186	....	....	....	....	....	....	....	....	....	....	2	1	3	4	21	....	....	....
1978-79	**Philadelphia Flyers**	**NHL**	**80**	**13**	**36**	**49**	**11**	**26**	**37**	**197**	**6**	**0**	**2**	**174**	**7.5**	**128**	**34**	**110**	**29**	**13**	**5**	**1**	**0**	**1**	**8**	**0**	**0**	**0**
1979-80	**Philadelphia Flyers**	**NHL**	**61**	**9**	**25**	**34**	**8**	**18**	**26**	**212**	**4**	**0**	**1**	**119**	**7.6**	**92**	**20**	**69**	**18**	**21**	**19**	**4**	**9**	**13**	**66**	**0**	**0**	**2**
1980-81	**Philadelphia Flyers**	**NHL**	**77**	**16**	**47**	**63**	**12**	**31**	**43**	**237**	**2**	**2**	**2**	**216**	**7.4**	**144**	**37**	**99**	**31**	**39**	**12**	**2**	**10**	**12**	**36**	**1**	**0**	**0**
1981-82	**Philadelphia Flyers**	**NHL**	**59**	**13**	**23**	**36**	**10**	**15**	**25**	**135**	**5**	**0**	**3**	**130**	**10.0**	**102**	**37**	**84**	**25**	**6**	**4**	**1**	**4**	**5**	**10**	**1**	**0**	**0**
1982-83	**Philadelphia Flyers**	**NHL**	**62**	**8**	**24**	**32**	**7**	**17**	**24**	**92**	**3**	**0**	**2**	**117**	**6.8**	**53**	**14**	**38**	**2**	**3**	**3**	**0**	**1**	**1**	**2**	**0**	**0**	**0**
1983-84	**Chicago Black Hawks**	**NHL**	**59**	**10**	**22**	**32**	**8**	**15**	**23**	**143**	**3**	**0**	**1**	**141**	**7.1**	**76**	**15**	**89**	**23**	**–5**	**4**	**0**	**0**	**0**	**0**	**0**	**0**	**0**
1984-85	**Chicago Black Hawks**	**NHL**	**76**	**10**	**23**	**33**	**8**	**16**	**24**	**185**	**2**	**0**	**1**	**106**	**9.4**	**94**	**12**	**100**	**23**	**5**	**15**	**4**	**5**	**9**	**60**	**1**	**0**	**1**
1985-86	**Chicago Black Hawks**	**NHL**	**69**	**13**	**37**	**50**	**10**	**25**	**35**	**113**	**10**	**0**	**6**	**138**	**9.4**	**117**	**33**	**131**	**36**	**–11**	**2**	**0**	**0**	**0**	**2**	**0**	**0**	**0**
1986-87	**Chicago Blackhawks**	**NHL**	DID NOT PLAY – INJURED																									
1987-88	**Chicago Blackhawks**	**NHL**	**58**	**6**	**23**	**29**	**5**	**16**	**21**	**166**	**3**	**0**	**0**	**103**	**5.8**	**72**	**25**	**88**	**22**	**–19**	**3**	**0**	**0**	**0**	**6**	**0**	**0**	**0**
1988-89	**Vancouver Canucks**	**NHL**	DID NOT PLAY – INJURED																									
	NHL Totals		**601**	**98**	**260**	**358**	**79**	**179**	**258**	**1480**	**38**	**2**	**18**	**1244**	**7.9**	**878**	**227**	**808**	**209**		**67**	**12**	**29**	**41**	**190**	**3**	**0**	**3**

Played in NHL All-Star Game (1981)

Traded to **Chicago** by **Philadelphia** for Doug Crossman and Philadelphia's 2nd round choice (Scott Mellanby) in 1984 Entry Draft, June 8, 1983. • Missed entire 1986-87 season and entire 1988-89 season recovering from back injury originally suffered in game vs. Toronto, April 5, 1986. Claimed by **Vancouver** from **Chicago** in Waiver Draft, October 3, 1988.

• WILSON, Bert

Bertwin Hilliard LW – L. 6', 178 lbs. b: Orangeville, Ont., 10/17/1949 d: 1992. NY Rangers' 3rd, 23rd overall, in 1969.

Season	Club	League	GP	G	A	Pts	AG	AA	APts	PIM	PP	SH	GW	S	%	TGF	PGF	TGA	PGA	+/–	GP	G	A	Pts	PIM	PP	SH	GW
1967-68	London Nationals/Knights	OHA-Jr.	45	8	3	11	....	....	....	94	....	....	....	....	....	....	....	....	....	....	3	1	0	1	2	....	....	....
1968-69	London Nationals	OHA-Jr.	54	13	19	32	....	....	....	160	....	....	....	....	....	....	....	....	....	....	6	2	2	4	7	....	....	....
1969-70	Omaha Knights	CHL	32	7	6	13	....	....	....	103	....	....	....	....	....	....	....	....	....	....	12	3	2	5	15	....	....	....
	Buffalo Bisons	AHL	....	....	....	....	....	....	....	....	....	....	....	....	....	....	....	....	....	....	1	0	0	0	0	....	....	....
1970-71	Omaha Knights	CHL	69	13	15	28	....	....	....	164	....	....	....	....	....	....	....	....	....	....	11	0	4	4	29	....	....	....
1971-72	Providence Reds	AHL	59	11	12	23	....	....	....	105	....	....	....	....	....	....	....	....	....	....	5	0	2	2	16	....	....	....
1972-73	Providence Reds	AHL	72	15	24	39	....	....	....	131	....	....	....	....	....	....	....	....	....	....	4	2	0	2	15	....	....	....
1973-74	**New York Rangers**	**NHL**	**5**	**1**	**1**	**2**	**1**	**1**	**2**	**2**	**1**	**0**	**0**	**3**	**33.3**	**2**	**1**	**0**	**0**	**1**	....	....	....	....	....	....	....	....
	Providence Reds	AHL	72	24	31	55	....	....	....	200	....	....	....	....	....	....	....	....	....	....	15	5	6	11	22	....	....	....
1974-75	**New York Rangers**	**NHL**	**61**	**5**	**1**	**6**	**4**	**1**	**5**	**66**	**1**	**0**	**1**	**38**	**13.2**	**17**	**3**	**17**	**3**	**0**	....	....	....	....	....	....	....	....
1975-76	**St. Louis Blues**	**NHL**	**45**	**2**	**3**	**5**	**2**	**2**	**4**	**47**	**0**	**0**	**1**	**25**	**8.0**	**8**	**0**	**16**	**2**	**–6**	....	....	....	....	....	....	....	....
	Los Angeles Kings	**NHL**	**13**	**0**	**0**	**0**	**0**	**0**	**0**	**17**	**0**	**0**	**0**	**5**	**0.0**	**1**	**0**	**1**	**0**	**0**	**8**	**0**	**0**	**0**	**24**	**0**	**0**	**0**
1976-77	**Los Angeles Kings**	**NHL**	**77**	**4**	**3**	**7**	**4**	**2**	**6**	**64**	**0**	**0**	**1**	**54**	**7.4**	**20**	**0**	**39**	**10**	**–9**	**8**	**0**	**2**	**2**	**12**	**0**	**0**	**0**
1977-78	**Los Angeles Kings**	**NHL**	**79**	**7**	**16**	**23**	**6**	**12**	**18**	**127**	**0**	**0**	**0**	**78**	**9.0**	**38**	**0**	**44**	**6**	**0**	**2**	**0**	**0**	**0**	**2**	**0**	**0**	**0**
1978-79	**Los Angeles Kings**	**NHL**	**73**	**9**	**10**	**19**	**8**	**7**	**15**	**138**	**0**	**0**	**2**	**72**	**12.5**	**30**	**1**	**37**	**3**	**–5**	....	....	....	....	....	....	....	....
1979-80	**Los Angeles Kings**	**NHL**	**75**	**4**	**3**	**7**	**3**	**2**	**5**	**91**	**1**	**1**	**0**	**56**	**7.1**	**17**	**2**	**40**	**6**	**–19**	**2**	**0**	**0**	**0**	**4**	**0**	**0**	**0**
1980-81	**Calgary Flames**	**NHL**	**50**	**5**	**7**	**12**	**4**	**5**	**9**	**94**	**0**	**0**	**1**	**34**	**14.7**	**19**	**0**	**30**	**5**	**–6**	**1**	**0**	**0**	**0**	**0**	**0**	**0**	**0**
1981-82	Salt Lake Golden Eagles	CHL	52	6	23	29	....	....	....	124	....	....	....	....	....	....	....	....	....	....	10	3	2	5	30	....	....	....
1982-83	Salt Lake Golden Eagles	CHL	69	11	13	24	....	....	....	114	....	....	....	....	....	....	....	....	....	....	6	1	2	3	2	....	....	....
	NHL Totals		**478**	**37**	**44**	**81**	**32**	**32**	**64**	**646**	**3**	**1**	**6**	**365**	**10.1**	**152**	**7**	**224**	**35**		**21**	**0**	**2**	**2**	**42**	**0**	**0**	**0**

Traded to **St. Louis** by **NY Rangers** with Ted Irvine and Jerry Butler for Bill Collins and John Davidson, June 18, 1975. Traded to **LA Kings** by **St. Louis** with rights to Curt Brackenbury for cash, March 6, 1976. Traded to **Calgary** by **LA Kings** with Randy Holt for Garry Unger, June 6, 1980.

• WILSON, Carey

Carey John C – R. 6'2", 195 lbs. b: Winnipeg, Man., 5/19/1962. Chicago's 8th, 67th overall, in 1980.

Season	Club	League	GP	G	A	Pts	AG	AA	APts	PIM	PP	SH	GW	S	%	TGF	PGF	TGA	PGA	+/–	GP	G	A	Pts	PIM	PP	SH	GW
1978-79	Calgary Chinooks	AJHL	60	30	34	64	....	....	....	....	....	....	....	....	....	....	....	....	....	....	....	....	....	....	....	....	....	....
1979-80	Dartmouth College	ECAC	31	16	22	38	....	....	....	20	....	....	....	....	....	....	....	....	....	....	....	....	....	....	....	....	....	....
1980-81	Dartmouth College	ECAC	24	9	13	22	....	....	....	52	....	....	....	....	....	....	....	....	....	....	....	....	....	....	....	....	....	....
1981-82	HIFK Helsinki	Finland	29	15	17	32	....	....	....	58	....	....	....	....	....	....	....	....	....	....	7	1	4	5	6	....	....	....
	Canada	WJC-A	7	4	1	5	....	....	....	6	....	....	....	....	....	....	....	....	....	....	....	....	....	....	....	....	....	....
1982-83	HIFK Helsinki	Finland	36	16	24	40	....	....	....	62	....	....	....	....	....	....	....	....	....	....	4	2	0	2	12	....	....	....
1983-84	Canada	Nat-Team	56	19	24	43	....	....	....	34	....	....	....	....	....	....	....	....	....	....	....	....	....	....	....	....	....	....
	Canada	Olympics	7	3	3	6	....	....	....	6	....	....	....	....	....	....	....	....	....	....	....	....	....	....	....	....	....	....
	Calgary Flames	**NHL**	**15**	**2**	**5**	**7**	**2**	**3**	**5**	**2**	**0**	**0**	**0**	**11**	**18.2**	**10**	**1**	**10**	**0**	**–1**	**6**	**3**	**1**	**4**	**2**	**0**	**0**	**1**
1984-85	**Calgary Flames**	**NHL**	**74**	**24**	**48**	**72**	**20**	**33**	**53**	**27**	**4**	**0**	**3**	**128**	**18.8**	**97**	**17**	**56**	**0**	**24**	**4**	**0**	**0**	**0**	**0**	**0**	**0**	**0**
1985-86	**Calgary Flames**	**NHL**	**76**	**29**	**29**	**58**	**23**	**19**	**42**	**24**	**5**	**0**	**2**	**149**	**19.5**	**84**	**22**	**62**	**1**	**1**	**9**	**0**	**2**	**2**	**2**	**0**	**0**	**0**
1986-87	**Calgary Flames**	**NHL**	**80**	**20**	**36**	**56**	**17**	**26**	**43**	**42**	**3**	**1**	**2**	**140**	**14.3**	**78**	**16**	**75**	**11**	**–2**	**6**	**1**	**1**	**2**	**6**	**0**	**0**	**0**
1987-88	**Calgary Flames**	**NHL**	**34**	**9**	**21**	**30**	**8**	**15**	**23**	**18**	**3**	**0**	**3**	**61**	**14.8**	**43**	**12**	**39**	**10**	**2**	....	....	....	....	....	....	....	....
	Hartford Whalers	**NHL**	**36**	**18**	**20**	**38**	**15**	**14**	**29**	**22**	**7**	**1**	**6**	**77**	**23.4**	**45**	**16**	**40**	**6**	**–5**	**6**	**2**	**4**	**6**	**2**	**1**	**0**	**1**

			REGULAR SEASON																		PLAYOFFS							
Season	Club	League	GP	G	A	Pts	AG	AA	APts	PIM	PP	SH	GW	S	%	TGF	PGF	TGA	PGA	+/–	GP	G	A	Pts	PIM	PP	SH	GW
1988-89	Hartford Whalers	NHL	34	11	11	22	9	8	17	14	4	0	2	56	19.6	28	10	36	6	–12	....	....	....	....	....	....	....	....
	New York Rangers	NHL	41	21	34	55	18	24	42	45	10	0	3	108	19.4	71	33	37	0	1	4	1	2	3	2	0	0	0
1989-90	New York Rangers	NHL	41	9	17	26	8	12	20	57	4	0	1	64	14.1	48	26	19	1	4	10	2	1	3	0	1	0	0
1990-91	Hartford Whalers	NHL	45	8	15	23	7	11	18	16	4	0	1	59	13.6	33	13	34	0	–14	....	....	....	....	....	....	....	....
	Calgary Flames	NHL	12	3	3	6	3	2	5	2	0	0	1	20	15.0	10	5	7	3	1	7	2	2	4	0	1	0	0
1991-92	Calgary Flames	NHL	42	11	12	23	10	9	19	37	4	2	2	74	14.9	33	13	42	16	–6	....	....	....	....	....	....	....	....
1992-93	Calgary Flames	NHL	22	4	7	11	3	5	8	8	1	2	0	30	13.3	20	5	11	6	10	....	....	....	....	....	....	....	....
1993-1996			OUT OF HOCKEY – RETIRED																									
1996-97	Manitoba Moose	IHL	7	0	4	4	....	....	....	2	....	....	....	....	....	....	....	....	....	....	....	....	....	....	....	....	....	....
	NHL Totals		552	169	258	427	143	181	324	314	49	6	26	977	17.3	600	189	468	60		52	11	13	24	14	3	0	2

• Son of Jerry

Rights traded to **Calgary** by **Chicago** for Denis Cyr, November 8, 1982. Traded to **Hartford** by **Calgary** with Neil Sheehy and rights to Lane MacDonald for Dana Murzyn and Shane Churla, January 3, 1988. Traded to **NY Rangers** by **Hartford** with Hartford's 5th round choice (Lubos Rob) in 1990 Entry Draft for Brian Lawton, Norm MacIver and Don Maloney, December 26, 1988. Traded to **Hartford** by **NY Rangers** with NY Rangers' 3rd round choice (Michael Nylander) in 1991 Entry Draft for Jody Hull, July 9, 1990. Traded to **Calgary** by **Hartford** for Mark Hunter, March 5, 1991. • Suffered eventual career-ending knee injury in game vs. St. Louis, December 4, 1992.

• WILSON, Doug

Douglas Frederick   D – L. 6'1", 187 lbs.   b: Ottawa, Ont., 7/5/1957. Chicago's 1st, 6th overall, in 1977.

Season	Club	League	GP	G	A	Pts	AG	AA	APts	PIM	PP	SH	GW	S	%	TGF	PGF	TGA	PGA	+/–	GP	G	A	Pts	PIM	PP	SH	GW
1974-75	Ottawa 67's	OMJHL	55	29	58	87	....	....	....	75	....	....	....	....	....	....	....	....	....	....	7	2	3	5	6	....	....	....
1975-76	Ottawa 67's	OMJHL	58	26	62	88	....	....	....	142	....	....	....	....	....	....	....	....	....	....	12	5	10	*15	24	....	....	....
1976-77	Ottawa 67's	OMJHL	43	25	54	79	....	....	....	85	....	....	....	....	....	....	....	....	....	....	19	4	20	24	34	....	....	....
1977-78	Chicago Black Hawks	NHL	77	14	20	34	13	15	28	72	5	0	2	203	6.9	94	24	76	17	11	4	0	0	0	0	0	0	0
1978-79	Chicago Black Hawks	NHL	56	5	21	26	4	15	19	37	2	1	0	136	3.7	67	17	61	15	4	....	....	....	....	....	....	....	....
1979-80	Chicago Black Hawks	NHL	73	12	49	61	10	36	46	70	3	1	1	225	5.3	121	52	97	23	–5	7	2	8	10	6	0	0	0
1980-81	Chicago Black Hawks	NHL	76	12	39	51	9	26	35	80	3	0	1	245	4.9	130	49	99	24	6	3	0	3	3	2	0	0	0
1981-82	Chicago Black Hawks	NHL	76	39	46	85	31	31	62	54	14	1	3	325	12.0	163	54	141	33	1	15	3	10	13	32	0	1	1
1982-83	Chicago Black Hawks	NHL	74	18	51	69	15	35	50	58	3	0	3	260	6.9	153	59	105	33	22	13	4	11	15	12	0	1	0
1983-84	Chicago Black Hawks	NHL	66	13	45	58	10	31	41	64	4	1	1	199	6.5	117	45	113	30	–11	5	0	3	3	2	0	0	0
1984-85	Canada	Can-Cup	7	2	1	3	....	....	....	4	....	....	....	....	....	....	....	....	....	....	....	....	....	....	....	....	....	....
	Chicago Black Hawks	NHL	78	22	54	76	18	37	55	44	7	0	2	236	9.3	151	46	129	47	23	12	3	10	13	12	2	0	0
1985-86	Chicago Black Hawks	NHL	79	17	47	64	14	32	46	80	3	0	2	243	7.0	162	47	126	35	24	3	1	1	2	2	0	0	0
1986-87	Chicago Blackhawks	NHL	69	16	32	48	14	23	37	36	7	1	1	249	6.4	123	40	106	38	15	4	0	0	0	0	0	0	0
	NHL All-Stars	RV-87	2	1	1	2	....	....	....	0	....	....	....	....	....	....	....	....	....	....	....	....	....	....	....	....	....	....
1987-88	Chicago Blackhawks	NHL	27	8	24	32	7	17	24	28	6	1	1	87	9.2	53	34	47	11	–17	....	....	....	....	....	....	....	....
1988-89	Chicago Blackhawks	NHL	66	15	47	62	13	33	46	69	4	1	3	248	6.0	156	70	105	27	8	4	1	2	3	0	1	0	0
1989-90	Chicago Blackhawks	NHL	70	23	50	73	20	36	56	40	13	1	2	242	9.5	155	55	117	30	13	20	3	12	15	18	1	0	1
1990-91	Chicago Blackhawks	NHL	51	11	29	40	10	22	32	32	6	1	1	162	6.8	102	47	40	10	25	5	2	1	3	2	2	0	0
1991-92	San Jose Sharks	NHL	44	9	19	28	8	14	22	26	4	0	0	123	7.3	50	24	85	21	–38	....	....	....	....	....	....	....	....
1992-93	San Jose Sharks	NHL	42	3	17	20	2	12	14	40	1	0	0	110	2.7	51	23	68	12	–28	....	....	....	....	....	....	....	....
	NHL Totals		1024	237	590	827	198	415	613	830	85	9	23	3293	7.2	1848	686	1515	406		95	19	61	80	88	6	2	2

• Brother of Murray • OMJHL First All-Star Team (1977) • NHL First All-Star Team (1982) • Won James Norris Trophy (1982) • NHL Second All-Star Team (1985, 1990) • Played in NHL All-Star Game (1982, 1983, 1984, 1985, 1986, 1990, 1992)

• Missed majority of 1987-88 season recovering from shoulder surgery, December, 1987. Traded to **San Jose** by **Chicago** for Kerry Toporowski and San Jose's 2nd round choice (later traded to Winnipeg - Winnipeg selected Boris Mironov) in 1992 Entry Draft, September 6, 1991.

• WILSON, Landon

Landon Matthew "Moose"   RW – R. 6'2", 216 lbs.   b: St. Louis, MO, 3/13/1975. Toronto's 2nd, 19th overall, in 1993.

Season	Club	League	GP	G	A	Pts	AG	AA	APts	PIM	PP	SH	GW	S	%	TGF	PGF	TGA	PGA	+/–	GP	G	A	Pts	PIM	PP	SH	GW
1991-92	California Jr. Kings	WSJHL	38	50	42	92	....	....	....	135	....	....	....	....	....	....	....	....	....	....	....	....	....	....	....	....	....	....
1992-93	Dubuque Fighting Saints	USHL	43	29	36	65	....	....	....	284	....	....	....	....	....	....	....	....	....	....	....	....	....	....	....	....	....	....
1993-94	University of North Dakota	WCHA	35	18	15	33	....	....	....	*147	....	....	....	....	....	....	....	....	....	....	....	....	....	....	....	....	....	....
1994-95	University of North Dakota	WCHA	31	7	16	23	....	....	....	141	....	....	....	....	....	....	....	....	....	....	....	....	....	....	....	....	....	....
	United States	WJC-A	7	3	2	5	....	....	....	37	....	....	....	....	....	....	....	....	....	....	....	....	....	....	....	....	....	....
	Cornwall Aces	AHL	8	4	4	8	....	....	....	25	....	....	....	....	....	....	....	....	....	....	13	3	4	7	68	....	....	....
1995-96	Colorado Avalanche	NHL	7	1	0	1	1	0	1	6	0	0	0	6	16.7	3	0	0	0	3	....	....	....	....	....	....	....	....
	Cornwall Aces	AHL	53	21	13	34	....	....	....	154	....	....	....	....	....	....	....	....	....	....	8	1	3	4	22	....	....	....
1996-97	Colorado Avalanche	NHL	9	1	2	3	1	2	3	23	0	0	0	7	14.3	4	0	3	0	1	....	....	....	....	....	....	....	....
	Boston Bruins	NHL	40	7	10	17	7	9	16	49	0	0	0	76	9.2	28	5	29	0	–6	....	....	....	....	....	....	....	....
	Providence Bruins	AHL	2	2	1	3	....	....	....	2	....	....	....	....	....	....	....	....	....	....	10	3	4	7	16	....	....	....
1997-98	Boston Bruins	NHL	28	1	5	6	1	5	6	7	0	0	0	26	3.8	8	2	3	0	3	1	0	0	0	0	0	0	0
	Providence Bruins	AHL	42	18	10	28	....	....	....	146	....	....	....	....	....	....	....	....	....	....	....	....	....	....	....	....	....	....
1998-99	Boston Bruins	NHL	22	3	3	6	4	3	7	17	0	0	0	32	9.4	8	1	7	0	0	8	1	1	2	8	1	0	1
	Providence Bruins	AHL	48	31	22	53	....	....	....	89	....	....	....	....	....	....	....	....	....	....	11	7	1	8	19	....	....	....
99-2000	Boston Bruins	NHL	40	1	3	4	1	3	4	18	0	0	0	67	1.5	16	1	21	0	–6	....	....	....	....	....	....	....	....
	Providence Bruins	AHL	17	5	5	10	....	....	....	45	....	....	....	....	....	....	....	....	....	....	9	2	3	5	38	....	....	....
	NHL Totals		146	14	23	37	15	22	37	120	0	0	0	214	6.5	67	9	63	0		9	1	1	2	8	1	0	1

• Son of Rick • AHL First All-Star Team (1999)

Traded to **Quebec** by **Toronto** with Wendel Clark, Sylvain Lefebvre and Toronto's 1st round choice (Jeffrey Kealty) in 1994 Entry Draft for Mats Sundin, Garth Butcher, Todd Warriner and Philadelphia's 1st round choice (previously acquired by Quebec - later traded to Washington - Washington selected Nolan Baumgartner) in 1994 Entry Draft, June 28, 1994. Transferred to **Colorado** after **Quebec** franchise relocated, June 21, 1995. Traded to **Boston** by **Colorado** with Anders Myrvold for Boston's 1st round choice (Robyn Regehr) in 1998 Entry Draft, November 22, 1996. Signed as a free agent by **Phoenix**, July 7, 2000.

• WILSON, Mike

D – L. 6'6", 212 lbs.   b: Brampton, Ont., 2/26/1975. Vancouver's 1st, 20th overall, in 1993.

Season	Club	League	GP	G	A	Pts	AG	AA	APts	PIM	PP	SH	GW	S	%	TGF	PGF	TGA	PGA	+/–	GP	G	A	Pts	PIM	PP	SH	GW
1991-92	Georgetown Raiders	OJHL-B	41	9	13	22	....	....	....	65	....	....	....	....	....	....	....	....	....	....	....	....	....	....	....	....	....	....
1992-93	Sudbury Wolves	OHL	53	6	7	13	....	....	....	58	....	....	....	....	....	....	....	....	....	....	14	1	1	2	2	....	....	....
1993-94	Sudbury Wolves	OHL	60	4	22	26	....	....	....	62	....	....	....	....	....	....	....	....	....	....	9	1	3	4	8	....	....	....
1994-95	Sudbury Wolves	OHL	64	13	34	47	....	....	....	46	....	....	....	....	....	....	....	....	....	....	18	1	8	9	10	....	....	....
1995-96	Buffalo Sabres	NHL	58	4	8	12	4	7	11	41	1	0	1	52	7.7	54	2	59	20	13	....	....	....	....	....	....	....	....
	Rochester Americans	AHL	15	0	5	5	....	....	....	38	....	....	....	....	....	....	....	....	....	....	....	....	....	....	....	....	....	....
1996-97	Buffalo Sabres	NHL	77	2	9	11	2	8	10	51	0	0	1	57	3.5	54	0	68	27	13	10	0	1	1	2	0	0	0
1997-98	Buffalo Sabres	NHL	66	4	4	8	5	4	9	48	0	0	1	52	7.7	37	0	45	21	13	15	0	1	1	13	0	0	0
1998-99	Buffalo Sabres	NHL	30	1	2	3	1	2	3	47	0	0	1	40	2.5	21	1	22	12	10	....	....	....	....	....	....	....	....
	Florida Panthers	NHL	4	0	0	0	0	0	0	0	0	0	0	8	0.0	3	0	3	2	2	....	....	....	....	....	....	....	....
	Las Vegas Thunder	IHL	6	3	1	4	....	....	....	6	....	....	....	....	....	....	....	....	....	....	....	....	....	....	....	....	....	....
99-2000	Florida Panthers	NHL	60	4	16	20	4	15	19	35	0	0	2	65	6.2	61	12	49	10	10	4	0	0	0	0	0	0	0
	NHL Totals		295	15	39	54	16	36	52	222	1	0	6	274	5.5	230	15	246	92		29	0	2	2	15	0	0	0

Traded to **Buffalo** by **Vancouver** with Mike Peca and Vancouver's 1st round choice (Jay McKee) in 1995 Entry Draft for Alexander Mogilny and Buffalo's 5th round choice (Todd Norman) in 1995 Entry Draft, July 8, 1995. Traded to **Florida** by **Buffalo** for Rhett Warrener and Florida's 5th round choice (Ryan Miller) in 1999 Entry Draft, March 23, 1999.

• WILSON, Mitch

C – R. 5'8", 190 lbs.   b: Kelowna, B.C., 2/15/1962.

Season	Club	League	GP	G	A	Pts	AG	AA	APts	PIM	PP	SH	GW	S	%	TGF	PGF	TGA	PGA	+/–	GP	G	A	Pts	PIM	PP	SH	GW
1978-79	Kelowna Buckaroos	BCJHL	62	7	13	20	....	....	....	156	....	....	....	....	....	....	....	....	....	....	....	....	....	....	....	....	....	....
1979-80	Kelowna Buckaroos	BCJHL	55	17	22	39	....	....	....	223	....	....	....	....	....	....	....	....	....	....	....	....	....	....	....	....	....	....
1980-81	Seattle Breakers	WHL	64	8	23	31	....	....	....	253	....	....	....	....	....	....	....	....	....	....	5	3	0	3	31	....	....	....
1981-82	Seattle Breakers	WHL	60	18	17	35	....	....	....	436	....	....	....	....	....	....	....	....	....	....	10	3	7	10	55	....	....	....
1982-83	Wichita Wind	CHL	55	4	6	10	....	....	....	186	....	....	....	....	....	....	....	....	....	....	....	....	....	....	....	....	....	....
1983-84	Maine Mariners	AHL	71	6	8	14	....	....	....	349	....	....	....	....	....	....	....	....	....	....	17	3	6	9	98	....	....	....
1984-85	New Jersey Devils	NHL	9	0	2	2	0	1	1	21	0	0	0	7	0.0	4	0	3	0	1	....	....	....	....	....	....	....	....
	Maine Mariners	AHL	51	6	3	9	....	....	....	220	....	....	....	....	....	....	....	....	....	....	2	0	0	0	32	....	....	....
1985-86	Maine Mariners	AHL	64	4	3	7	....	....	....	217	....	....	....	....	....	....	....	....	....	....	3	0	0	0	2	....	....	....
1986-87	Pittsburgh Penguins	NHL	17	2	1	3	2	1	3	83	0	0	0	7	28.6	3	0	6	0	–3	....	....	....	....	....	....	....	....
	Baltimore Skipjacks	AHL	58	8	9	17	....	....	....	*353	....	....	....	....	....	....	....	....	....	....	....	....	....	....	....	....	....	....

Season	Club	League	REGULAR SEASON																		PLAYOFFS							
			GP	G	A	Pts	AG	AA	APts	PIM	PP	SH	GW	S	%	TGF	PGF	TGA	PGA	+/–	GP	G	A	Pts	PIM	PP	SH	GW
1987-88	Muskegon Lumberjacks	IHL	68	27	25	52	....	....	....	400	....	....	....	....	....	....	....	....	....	....	5	1	0	1	23	....	....	....
1988-89	Muskegon Lumberjacks	IHL	61	16	34	50	....	....	....	*382	....	....	....	....	....	....	....	....	....	....	11	4	5	9	83	....	....	....
1989-90	Muskegon Lumberjacks	IHL	63	13	24	37	....	....	....	283	....	....	....	....	....	....	....	....	....	....	15	1	4	5	97	....	....	....
1990-91	Muskegon Lumberjacks	IHL	78	14	19	33	....	....	....	387	....	....	....	....	....	....	....	....	....	....	4	1	2	3	34	....	....	....
1991-92	San Diego Gulls	IHL	12	0	0	0	....	....	....	55	....	....	....	....	....	....	....	....	....	....	....	....	....	....	....	....	....	....
	Louisville IceHawks	ECHL	25	9	11	20	....	....	....	144	....	....	....	....	....	....	....	....	....	....	....	....	....	....	....	....	....	....
	NHL Totals		**26**	**2**	**3**	**5**	**2**	**2**	**4**	**104**	**0**	**0**	**0**	**14**	**14.3**	**7**	**0**	**9**	**0**		....	....	....	....	....	....	....	....

Signed as a free agent by **New Jersey**, October 12, 1982. Signed as a free agent by **Pittsburgh**, July 24, 1986.

• WILSON, Murray

Murray Charles LW – L. 6'1", 185 lbs. b: Toronto, Ont., 11/7/1951. Montreal's 3rd, 11th overall, in 1971.

Season	Club	League	GP	G	A	Pts	AG	AA	APts	PIM	PP	SH	GW	S	%	TGF	PGF	TGA	PGA	+/–	GP	G	A	Pts	PIM	PP	SH	GW
1968-69	Ottawa 67's	OHA-Jr.	24	7	11	18	....	....	....	8	....	....	....	....	....	....	....	....	....	....	....	....	....	....	....	....	....	....
1969-70	Ottawa 67's	OHA-Jr.	46	24	26	50	....	....	....	48	....	....	....	....	....	....	....	....	....	....	7	2	2	4	10	....	....	....
1970-71	Ottawa 67's	OHA-Jr.	44	26	32	58	....	....	....	36	....	....	....	....	....	....	....	....	....	....	11	5	2	7	8	....	....	....
1971-72	Nova Scotia Voyageurs	AHL	65	11	21	32	....	....	....	30	....	....	....	....	....	....	....	....	....	....	15	2	7	9	11	....	....	....
1972-73♦	**Montreal Canadiens**	**NHL**	**52**	**18**	**9**	**27**	**17**	**7**	**24**	**16**	**0**	**0**	**3**	**68**	**26.5**	**33**	**1**	**18**	**0**	**14**	**16**	**2**	**4**	**6**	**6**	**0**	**0**	**1**
1973-74	**Montreal Canadiens**	**NHL**	**72**	**17**	**14**	**31**	**16**	**12**	**28**	**26**	**0**	**0**	**4**	**107**	**15.9**	**48**	**0**	**48**	**4**	**4**	**5**	**1**	**0**	**1**	**2**	**0**	**0**	**0**
1974-75	**Montreal Canadiens**	**NHL**	**73**	**24**	**18**	**42**	**21**	**13**	**34**	**44**	**4**	**0**	**6**	**135**	**17.8**	**64**	**10**	**45**	**4**	**13**	**5**	**0**	**3**	**3**	**4**	**0**	**0**	**0**
1975-76♦	**Montreal Canadiens**	**NHL**	**59**	**11**	**24**	**35**	**10**	**18**	**28**	**36**	**2**	**1**	**1**	**73**	**15.1**	**50**	**8**	**26**	**9**	**25**	**12**	**1**	**1**	**2**	**6**	**0**	**0**	**0**
1976-77♦	**Montreal Canadiens**	**NHL**	**60**	**13**	**14**	**27**	**12**	**11**	**23**	**26**	**1**	**0**	**1**	**83**	**15.7**	**46**	**2**	**20**	**1**	**25**	**14**	**1**	**6**	**7**	**14**	**0**	**0**	**0**
1977-78	**Montreal Canadiens**	**NHL**	**12**	**0**	**1**	**1**	**0**	**1**	**1**	**0**	**0**	**0**	**0**	**9**	**0.0**	**4**	**0**	**6**	**1**	**–1**	....	....	....	....	....	....	....	....
1978-79	**Los Angeles Kings**	**NHL**	**58**	**11**	**15**	**26**	**9**	**11**	**20**	**14**	**1**	**0**	**2**	**107**	**10.3**	**47**	**7**	**47**	**0**	**–7**	**1**	**0**	**0**	**0**	**0**	**0**	**0**	**0**
	NHL Totals		**386**	**94**	**95**	**189**	**85**	**73**	**158**	**162**	**8**	**1**	**17**	**582**	**16.2**	**292**	**28**	**210**	**19**		**53**	**5**	**14**	**19**	**32**	**0**	**0**	**1**

• Brother of Doug

• Missed majority of 1977-78 season recovering from spinal fusion surgery, October, 1977. Traded to **LA Kings** by **Montreal** with Montreal's 1st round choice (Jay Wells) in 1979 Entry Draft for LA King's 1st round choice (Gilbert Delorme) in 1981 Entry Draft, October 5, 1978.

• WILSON, Rick

Richard Gordon D – L. 6'1", 195 lbs. b: Prince Albert, Sask., 8/10/1950. Montreal's 6th, 66th overall, in 1970.

Season	Club	League	GP	G	A	Pts	AG	AA	APts	PIM	PP	SH	GW	S	%	TGF	PGF	TGA	PGA	+/–	GP	G	A	Pts	PIM	PP	SH	GW
1969-70	University of North Dakota	WCHA	30	2	9	11	....	....	....	32	....	....	....	....	....	....	....	....	....	....	....	....	....	....	....	....	....	....
1970-71	University of North Dakota	WCHA	33	6	9	15	....	....	....	113	....	....	....	....	....	....	....	....	....	....	....	....	....	....	....	....	....	....
1971-72	University of North Dakota	WCHA	25	7	19	26	....	....	....	38	....	....	....	....	....	....	....	....	....	....	....	....	....	....	....	....	....	....
1972-73	Nova Scotia Voyageurs	AHL	70	4	11	15	....	....	....	163	....	....	....	....	....	....	....	....	....	....	12	1	0	1	*56	....	....	....
1973-74	**Montreal Canadiens**	**NHL**	**21**	**0**	**2**	**2**	**0**	**2**	**2**	**6**	**0**	**0**	**0**	**9**	**0.0**	**16**	**0**	**9**	**1**	**8**	....	....	....	....	....	....	....	....
	Nova Scotia Voyageurs	AHL	47	4	19	23	....	....	....	65	....	....	....	....	....	....	....	....	....	....	....	....	....	....	....	....	....	....
1974-75	**St. Louis Blues**	**NHL**	**76**	**2**	**5**	**7**	**2**	**4**	**6**	**83**	**0**	**0**	**0**	**63**	**3.2**	**66**	**3**	**63**	**12**	**12**	**2**	**0**	**0**	**0**	**0**	**0**	**0**	**0**
1975-76	**St. Louis Blues**	**NHL**	**65**	**1**	**6**	**7**	**1**	**4**	**5**	**20**	**1**	**0**	**0**	**44**	**2.3**	**36**	**2**	**63**	**19**	**–10**	**1**	**0**	**0**	**0**	**0**	**0**	**0**	**0**
1976-77	**Detroit Red Wings**	**NHL**	**77**	**3**	**13**	**16**	**3**	**10**	**13**	**56**	**0**	**0**	**0**	**60**	**5.0**	**66**	**6**	**109**	**29**	**–20**	....	....	....	....	....	....	....	....
1977-78	Philadelphia Firebirds	AHL	75	4	28	32	....	....	....	101	....	....	....	....	....	....	....	....	....	....	4	0	1	1	2	....	....	....
1978-1980	University of North Dakota	WCHA	DID NOT PLAY – ASSISTANT COACH																									
1980-1986	Prince Albert Raiders	WHL	DID NOT PLAY – ASSISTANT COACH																									
1986-1988	Prince Albert Raiders	WHL	DID NOT PLAY – COACHING																									
1988-1989	**New York Islanders**	**NHL**	DID NOT PLAY – ASSISTANT COACH																									
1989-1992	**Los Angeles Kings**	**NHL**	DID NOT PLAY – ASSISTANT COACH																									
1992-1993	**Minnesota North Stars**	**NHL**	DID NOT PLAY – ASSISTANT COACH																									
1993-2000	**Dallas Stars**	**NHL**	DID NOT PLAY – ASSISTANT COACH																									
	NHL Totals		**239**	**6**	**26**	**32**	**6**	**20**	**26**	**165**	**1**	**0**	**0**	**176**	**3.4**	**184**	**11**	**244**	**61**		**3**	**0**	**0**	**0**	**0**	**0**	**0**	**0**

• Father of Landon • WCHA Second All-Star Team (1972) • AHL First All-Star Team (1978)

Traded to **St. Louis** by **Montreal** with Montreal's 5th round choice (Don Wheldon) in 1974 Amateur Draft for St. Louis' 4th round choice (Barry Legge) in 1974 Amateur Draft and future considerations (Glen Sather, June 14, 1974), May 27, 1974. Traded to **Detroit** by **St. Louis** to complete transaction that sent Doug Grant to St. Louis (March 9, 1976), June 16, 1976.

• WILSON, Rik

Rik William D – R. 6', 180 lbs. b: Long Beach, CA, 6/17/1962. St. Louis' 1st, 12th overall, in 1980.

Season	Club	League	GP	G	A	Pts	AG	AA	APts	PIM	PP	SH	GW	S	%	TGF	PGF	TGA	PGA	+/–	GP	G	A	Pts	PIM	PP	SH	GW
1978-79	Kingston Legionaires	OJHL	44	18	33	51	....	....	....	....	....	....	....	....	....	....	....	....	....	....	....	....	....	....	....	....	....	....
1979-80	Kingston Canadians	OMJHL	67	15	38	53	....	....	....	75	....	....	....	....	....	....	....	....	....	....	3	1	3	4	2	....	....	....
1980-81	Kingston Canadians	OMJHL	68	30	70	100	....	....	....	108	....	....	....	....	....	....	....	....	....	....	13	1	9	10	18	....	....	....
	Salt Lake Golden Eagles	IHL	....	....	....	....	....	....	....	....	....	....	....	....	....	....	....	....	....	....	4	1	1	2	2	....	....	....
1981-82	Kingston Canadians	OHL	16	9	10	19	....	....	....	38	....	....	....	....	....	....	....	....	....	....	....	....	....	....	....	....	....	....
	St. Louis Blues	**NHL**	**48**	**3**	**18**	**21**	**2**	**12**	**14**	**24**	**1**	**0**	**1**	**95**	**3.2**	**64**	**14**	**68**	**8**	**–10**	**9**	**0**	**3**	**3**	**14**	**0**	**0**	**0**
1982-83	**St. Louis Blues**	**NHL**	**56**	**3**	**11**	**14**	**2**	**8**	**10**	**50**	**1**	**0**	**1**	**77**	**3.9**	**44**	**8**	**51**	**5**	**–10**	....	....	....	....	....	....	....	....
	Salt Lake Golden Eagles	CHL	4	0	0	0	....	....	....	0	....	....	....	....	....	....	....	....	....	....	....	....	....	....	....	....	....	....
1983-84	**St. Louis Blues**	**NHL**	**48**	**7**	**11**	**18**	**6**	**7**	**13**	**53**	**2**	**0**	**1**	**72**	**9.7**	**57**	**10**	**48**	**5**	**4**	**11**	**0**	**0**	**0**	**9**	**0**	**0**	**0**
	Montana Magic	CHL	6	0	3	3	....	....	....	2	....	....	....	....	....	....	....	....	....	....	....	....	....	....	....	....	....	....
1984-85	**St. Louis Blues**	**NHL**	**51**	**8**	**16**	**24**	**6**	**11**	**17**	**39**	**3**	**0**	**0**	**85**	**9.4**	**62**	**15**	**36**	**3**	**14**	**2**	**0**	**1**	**1**	**0**	**0**	**0**	**0**
	Flint Generals	IHL	29	0	0	0	....	....	....	0	....	....	....	....	....	....	....	....	....	....	1	0	0	0	0	....	....	....
	Salt Lake Golden Eagles	IHL	2	0	0	0	....	....	....	0	....	....	....	....	....	....	....	....	....	....	....	....	....	....	....	....	....	....
1985-86	**St. Louis Blues**	**NHL**	**32**	**0**	**4**	**4**	**0**	**3**	**3**	**48**	**0**	**0**	**0**	**45**	**0.0**	**20**	**6**	**25**	**2**	**–9**	....	....	....	....	....	....	....	....
	Calgary Flames	**NHL**	**2**	**0**	**0**	**0**	**0**	**0**	**0**	**0**	**0**	**0**	**0**	**3**	**0.0**	**3**	**0**	**1**	**0**	**2**	....	....	....	....	....	....	....	....
	Nova Scotia Oilers	AHL	13	4	5	9	....	....	....	11	....	....	....	....	....	....	....	....	....	....	....	....	....	....	....	....	....	....
	Moncton Golden Flames	AHL	8	3	3	6	....	....	....	2	....	....	....	....	....	....	....	....	....	....	....	....	....	....	....	....	....	....
1986-87	Nova Scotia Oilers	AHL	45	8	13	21	....	....	....	109	....	....	....	....	....	....	....	....	....	....	5	1	3	4	20	....	....	....
1987-88	**Chicago Blackhawks**	**NHL**	**14**	**4**	**5**	**9**	**3**	**4**	**7**	**6**	**0**	**0**	**1**	**27**	**14.8**	**20**	**6**	**10**	**0**	**4**	....	....	....	....	....	....	....	....
	Saginaw Hawks	IHL	33	4	5	9	....	....	....	105	....	....	....	....	....	....	....	....	....	....	....	....	....	....	....	....	....	....
1988-89	VSV Villach	Austria	45	17	43	60	....	....	....	110	....	....	....	....	....	....	....	....	....	....	....	....	....	....	....	....	....	....
1989-90	ESV Kaufbeuren	Germany-2	9	2	7	9	....	....	....	44	....	....	....	....	....	....	....	....	....	....	....	....	....	....	....	....	....	....
	Peoria Rivermen	IHL	15	1	4	5	....	....	....	34	....	....	....	....	....	....	....	....	....	....	....	....	....	....	....	....	....	....
1990-91	VSV Villach	Austria	44	13	45	58	....	....	....	140	....	....	....	....	....	....	....	....	....	....	....	....	....	....	....	....	....	....
	New Haven Nighthawks	AHL	2	0	0	0	....	....	....	4	....	....	....	....	....	....	....	....	....	....	....	....	....	....	....	....	....	....
1991-92			DID NOT PLAY																									
1992-93	Fort Wayne Komets	IHL	2	0	0	0	....	....	....	4	....	....	....	....	....	....	....	....	....	....	....	....	....	....	....	....	....	....
	NHL Totals		**251**	**25**	**65**	**90**	**19**	**45**	**64**	**220**	**7**	**0**	**4**	**404**	**6.2**	**270**	**59**	**239**	**23**		**22**	**0**	**4**	**4**	**23**	**0**	**0**	**0**

OMJHL First All-Star Team (1981)

Traded to **Calgary** by **St. Louis** with Joe Mullen and Terry Johnson for Eddy Beers, Charlie Bourgeois and Gino Cavallini, February 1, 1986. Traded to **Chicago** by **Calgary** for Tom McMurchy, March 11, 1986. Signed as free agent by **St. Louis** July 19, 1989. • Played w/ RHI's St. Louis Vipers in 1993 (13-14-17-31-41); 1994 (10-9-14-23-43); 1994 (16-7-23-30-49) and 1996 (16-5-21-26-29).

• WILSON, Roger

Roger Sidney D – R. 5'11", 175 lbs. b: Sudbury, Ont., 9/18/1946.

Season	Club	League	GP	G	A	Pts	AG	AA	APts	PIM	PP	SH	GW	S	%	TGF	PGF	TGA	PGA	+/–	GP	G	A	Pts	PIM	PP	SH	GW
1965-66	Sudbury Wolves	NOJHA	40	10	33	43	....	....	....	....	....	....	....	....	....	....	....	....	....	....	....	....	....	....	....	....	....	....
1966-67	Sudbury Wolves	NOJHA	STATISTICS NOT AVAILABLE																									
	Columbus Checkers	IHL	3	0	0	0	....	....	....	9	....	....	....	....	....	....	....	....	....	....	....	....	....	....	....	....	....	....
1967-68	Greensboro Generals	EHL	71	9	31	40	....	....	....	182	....	....	....	....	....	....	....	....	....	....	11	3	4	7	21	....	....	....
1968-69	Dallas Black Hawks	CHL	4	0	0	0	....	....	....	13	....	....	....	....	....	....	....	....	....	....	....	....	....	....	....	....	....	....
	Greensboro Generals	EHL	70	9	28	37	....	....	....	128	....	....	....	....	....	....	....	....	....	....	8	1	2	3	10	....	....	....
1969-70	Dallas Black Hawks	CHL	3	0	0	0	....	....	....	0	....	....	....	....	....	....	....	....	....	....	....	....	....	....	....	....	....	....
	Greensboro Generals	EHL	69	13	26	39	....	....	....	205	....	....	....	....	....	....	....	....	....	....	16	2	2	4	8	....	....	....
1970-71	Greensboro Generals	EHL	71	21	49	70	....	....	....	285	....	....	....	....	....	....	....	....	....	....	9	4	5	9	12	....	....	....
1971-72	Dallas Black Hawks	CHL	72	4	20	24	....	....	....	173	....	....	....	....	....	....	....	....	....	....	12	1	4	5	20	....	....	....
1972-73	Dallas Black Hawks	CHL	65	7	27	34	....	....	....	120	....	....	....	....	....	....	....	....	....	....	7	0	1	1	12	....	....	....

Season	Club	League	GP	G	A	Pts	AG	AA	APts	PIM	PP	SH	GW	S	%	TGF	PGF	TGA	PGA	+/-	GP	G	A	Pts	PIM	PP	SH	GW
			REGULAR SEASON																		PLAYOFFS							
1973-74	Dallas Black Hawks	CHL	61	9	21	30				124											10	1	5	6	19			
1974-75	**Chicago Black Hawks**	**NHL**	**7**	**0**	**2**	**2**	**0**	**1**	**1**	**6**	**0**	**0**	**0**	**10**	**0.0**	**5**	**0**	**4**	**0**	**1**								
	Dallas Black Hawks	CHL	52	6	27	33				71											10	1	1	2	16			
	NHL Totals		**7**	**0**	**2**	**2**	**0**	**1**	**1**	**6**	**0**	**0**	**0**	**10**	**0.0**	**5**	**0**	**4**	**0**									

NOJHA First All-Star Team (1966) • EHL South First All-Star Team (1971)

• WILSON, Ron

Ronald Lee C – L. 5'9", 180 lbs. b: Toronto, Ont., 5/13/1956. Montreal's 15th, 133rd overall, in 1976.

Season	Club	League	GP	G	A	Pts	AG	AA	APts	PIM	PP	SH	GW	S	%	TGF	PGF	TGA	PGA	+/-	GP	G	A	Pts	PIM	PP	SH	GW
1972-73	Toronto Midet Marlboros	MTHL	STATISTICS NOT AVAILABLE																									
	Toronto Marlboros	OMJHL	21	1	11	12				2																		
1973-74	Markham Waxers	OHA-B	STATISTICS NOT AVAILABLE																									
	Hamilton Red Wings	OMJHL	6	1	0	1				2																		
1974-75	Markham Waxers	OHA-B	43	26	28	54				24																		
	Toronto Marlboros	OMJHL	16	6	12	18				6											23	9	17	26	6			
	Toronto Marlboros	Mem-Cup	4	0	3	3				2																		
1975-76	St. Catharines Black Hawks	OMJHL	64	37	62	99				44											4	1	6	7	7			
1976-77	Nova Scotia Voyageurs	AHL	67	15	21	36				18											6	0	0	0	0			
1977-78	Nova Scotia Voyageurs	AHL	59	15	25	40				17											11	4	4	8	9			
1978-79	Nova Scotia Voyageurs	AHL	77	33	42	75				91											10	5	6	11	14			
1979-80	**Winnipeg Jets**	**NHL**	**79**	**21**	**36**	**57**	**18**	**26**	**44**	**28**	**6**	**0**	**3**	**176**	**11.9**	**84**	**24**	**83**	**11**	**–12**								
1980-81	**Winnipeg Jets**	**NHL**	**77**	**18**	**33**	**51**	**14**	**22**	**36**	**55**	**4**	**1**	**0**	**192**	**9.4**	**79**	**23**	**106**	**16**	**–34**								
1981-82	**Winnipeg Jets**	**NHL**	**39**	**3**	**13**	**16**	**2**	**9**	**11**	**49**	**0**	**0**	**0**	**53**	**5.7**	**24**	**1**	**40**	**14**	**–3**								
	Tulsa Oilers	CHL	41	20	38	58				22											3	1	0	1	2			
1982-83	**Winnipeg Jets**	**NHL**	**12**	**6**	**3**	**9**	**5**	**2**	**7**	**4**	**2**	**0**	**0**	**20**	**30.0**	**12**	**1**	**6**	**2**	**7**	**3**	**2**	**2**	**4**	**2**	**0**	**0**	**0**
	Sherbrooke Jets	AHL	65	30	55	85				71																		
1983-84	**Winnipeg Jets**	**NHL**	**51**	**3**	**12**	**15**	**2**	**8**	**10**	**12**	**0**	**0**	**1**	**52**	**5.8**	**21**	**0**	**43**	**19**	**–3**								
	Sherbrooke Jets	AHL	22	10	30	40				16																		
1984-85	**Winnipeg Jets**	**NHL**	**75**	**10**	**9**	**19**	**8**	**6**	**14**	**31**	**1**	**1**	**1**	**65**	**15.4**	**23**	**1**	**54**	**24**	**–8**	**8**	**4**	**2**	**6**	**2**	**0**	**0**	**1**
1985-86	**Winnipeg Jets**	**NHL**	**54**	**6**	**7**	**13**	**5**	**5**	**10**	**16**	**0**	**2**	**0**	**64**	**9.4**	**20**	**1**	**42**	**21**	**–2**	**1**	**0**	**0**	**0**	**0**	**0**	**0**	**0**
	Sherbrooke Canadiens	AHL	10	9	8	17				9																		
1986-87	**Winnipeg Jets**	**NHL**	**80**	**3**	**13**	**16**	**3**	**9**	**12**	**13**	**0**	**0**	**0**	**76**	**3.9**	**24**	**0**	**46**	**32**	**10**	**10**	**1**	**2**	**3**	**0**	**0**	**0**	**0**
1987-88	**Winnipeg Jets**	**NHL**	**69**	**5**	**8**	**13**	**4**	**6**	**10**	**28**	**0**	**2**	**0**	**80**	**6.3**	**21**	**0**	**69**	**47**	**–1**	**1**	**0**	**0**	**0**	**2**	**0**	**0**	**0**
1988-89	Moncton Hawks	AHL	80	31	61	92				110											8	1	4	5	20			
1989-90	Moncton Hawks	AHL	47	16	37	53				39																		
	St. Louis Blues	**NHL**	**33**	**3**	**17**	**20**	**3**	**12**	**15**	**23**	**1**	**0**	**1**	**40**	**7.5**	**36**	**11**	**28**	**8**	**5**	**12**	**3**	**5**	**8**	**18**	**2**	**0**	**0**
1990-91	**St. Louis Blues**	**NHL**	**73**	**10**	**27**	**37**	**9**	**21**	**30**	**54**	**1**	**2**	**1**	**101**	**9.9**	**49**	**4**	**71**	**25**	**–1**	**7**	**0**	**0**	**0**	**28**	**0**	**0**	**0**
1991-92	**St. Louis Blues**	**NHL**	**64**	**12**	**17**	**29**	**11**	**13**	**24**	**46**	**5**	**2**	**2**	**100**	**12.0**	**47**	**14**	**51**	**28**	**10**	**6**	**0**	**1**	**1**	**0**	**0**	**0**	**0**
1992-93	**St. Louis Blues**	**NHL**	**78**	**8**	**11**	**19**	**7**	**8**	**15**	**44**	**0**	**3**	**1**	**75**	**10.7**	**29**	**1**	**67**	**31**	**–8**	**11**	**0**	**0**	**0**	**12**	**0**	**0**	**0**
1993-94	**Montreal Canadiens**	**NHL**	**48**	**2**	**10**	**12**	**2**	**8**	**10**	**12**	**0**	**0**	**0**	**39**	**5.1**	**15**	**0**	**34**	**17**	**–2**	**4**	**0**	**0**	**0**	**0**	**0**	**0**	**0**
1994-95	Detroit Vipers	IHL	12	6	9	15				10																		
	San Diego Gulls	IHL	58	8	25	33				60											5	2	0	2	8			
1995-96	Wheeling Thunderbirds	ECHL	46	12	30	42				72											2	0	3	3	6			
1996-2000	Springfield Falcons	AHL	DID NOT PLAY – ASSISTANT COACH																									
	NHL Totals		**832**	**110**	**216**	**326**	**93**	**155**	**248**	**415**	**20**	**13**	**10**	**1133**	**9.7**	**484**	**81**	**740**	**295**		**63**	**10**	**12**	**22**	**64**	**2**	**0**	**1**

AHL Second All-Star Team (1989)

Traded to **Winnipeg** by **Montreal** for cash, October 4, 1979. Traded to **St. Louis** by **Winnipeg** for Doug Evans, January 22, 1990. Signed as a free agent by **Montreal**, August 20, 1993.

• WILSON, Ron

Ronald Laurence D – R. 5'10", 170 lbs. b: Windsor, Ont., 5/28/1955. Toronto's 7th, 132nd overall, in 1975.

Season	Club	League	GP	G	A	Pts	AG	AA	APts	PIM	PP	SH	GW	S	%	TGF	PGF	TGA	PGA	+/-	GP	G	A	Pts	PIM	PP	SH	GW
1973-74	Providence College	ECAC	26	16	22	38																						
1974-75	Providence College	ECAC	27	26	*61	*87				12																		
	United States	WEC-A	10	1	2	3				4																		
1975-76	Providence College	ECAC	28	19	47	66				44																		
1976-77	Providence College	ECAC	30	17	42	59				62																		
	Dallas Black Hawks	CHL	4	1	0	1				2																		
1977-78	**Toronto Maple Leafs**	**NHL**	**13**	**2**	**1**	**3**	**2**	**1**	**3**	**0**	**1**	**0**	**0**	**11**	**18.2**	**3**	**2**	**6**	**0**	**–5**								
	Dallas Black Hawks	CHL	67	31	38	69				18																		
1978-79	**Toronto Maple Leafs**	**NHL**	**46**	**5**	**12**	**17**	**4**	**9**	**13**	**4**	**4**	**0**	**0**	**58**	**8.6**	**36**	**28**	**19**	**1**	**–10**	**3**	**0**	**1**	**1**	**0**	**0**	**0**	**0**
	New Brunswick Hawks	AHL	31	11	21	32				13																		
1979-80	**Toronto Maple Leafs**	**NHL**	**5**	**0**	**2**	**2**	**0**	**1**	**1**	**2**	**0**	**0**	**0**	**6**	**0.0**	**6**	**3**	**6**	**1**	**–2**	**3**	**1**	**2**	**3**	**2**	**1**	**0**	**0**
	New Brunswick Hawks	AHL	43	20	43	63				10											14	3	2	5	2			
1980-81	EHC Kloten	Switz.	38	22	23	45																						
	United States	WEC-A	8	3	4	7				2																		
1981-82	HC Davos	Switz.	38	24	23	47																						
1982-83	HC Davos	Switz.	36	32	32	64																						
1983-84	HC Davos	Switz.	36	33	39	72																						
1984-85	HC Davos	Switz.	38	39	62	101																						
	Minnesota North Stars	**NHL**	**13**	**4**	**8**	**12**	**3**	**5**	**8**	**2**	**0**	**0**	**0**	**27**	**14.8**	**21**	**7**	**15**	**0**	**–1**	**9**	**1**	**6**	**7**	**2**	**1**	**0**	**0**
1985-86	HC Davos	Switz.	27	28	41	69															5	6	2	8				
	Minnesota North Stars	**NHL**	**11**	**1**	**3**	**4**	**1**	**2**	**3**	**8**	**1**	**0**	**0**	**21**	**4.8**	**20**	**11**	**12**	**1**	**–2**	**5**	**2**	**4**	**6**	**4**	**1**	**0**	**0**
1986-87	**Minnesota North Stars**	**NHL**	**65**	**12**	**29**	**41**	**10**	**21**	**31**	**36**	**6**	**0**	**2**	**138**	**8.7**	**107**	**53**	**65**	**2**	**–9**								
	United States	WEC-A	10	1	3	4				12																		
1987-88	HC Davos	Switz.	36	8	24	32															6	2	5	7				
	Minnesota North Stars	**NHL**	**24**	**2**	**12**	**14**	**2**	**9**	**11**	**16**	**1**	**0**	**0**	**40**	**5.0**	**39**	**21**	**22**	**0**	**–4**								
1988-1989	ZSC Zurich	Switz-2	PLAYER/COACH – STATISTICS UNAVAILABLE																									
1989-1990	Milwaukee Admirals	IHL	DID NOT PLAY – ASSISTANT COACH																									
1990-1993	**Vancouver Canucks**	**NHL**	DID NOT PLAY – COACHING																									
1993-1997	**Mighty Ducks of Anaheim**	**NHL**	DID NOT PLAY – COACHING																									
1997-2000	**Washington Capitals**	**NHL**	DID NOT PLAY – COACHING																									
	NHL Totals		**177**	**26**	**67**	**93**	**22**	**48**	**70**	**68**	**13**	**0**	**2**	**301**	**8.6**	**232**	**125**	**145**	**5**		**20**	**4**	**13**	**17**	**8**	**3**	**0**	**0**

• Son of Larry • ECAC First All-Star Team (1975, 1976) • NCAA East First All-American Team (1975, 1976) • ECAC Second All-Star Team (1977) • CHL First All-Star Team (1978) • WEC-B All-Star Team (1983)

Signed as a free agent by **Minnesota**, March 7, 1985.

• WING, Murray

Murray Allan D – R. 5'11", 180 lbs. b: Thunder Bay, Ont., 10/14/1950. Boston's 9th, 83rd overall, in 1970.

Season	Club	League	GP	G	A	Pts	AG	AA	APts	PIM	PP	SH	GW	S	%	TGF	PGF	TGA	PGA	+/-	GP	G	A	Pts	PIM	PP	SH	GW
1967-68	Westfort Hurricanes	TBJHL	18	4	6	10				25																		
	Westfort Hurricanes	Mem-Cup	11	2	2	4				11																		
1968-69	Westfort Hurricanes	TBJHL	36	22	25	47				58																		
	Fort William Canadiens	Mem-Cup	6	1	3	4				9																		
1969-70	University of North Dakota	WCHA	DID NOT PLAY – FRESHMAN																									
1970-71	University of North Dakota	WCHA	29	3	10	13				18																		
1971-72	Oklahoma City Blazers	CHL	71	12	15	27				79											6	0	0	0	14			
1972-73	Boston Braves	AHL	57	2	10	12				37											10	2	6	8	2			
	San Diego Gulls	WHL	6	0	0	0				2																		
1973-74	**Detroit Red Wings**	**NHL**	**1**	**0**	**1**	**1**	**0**	**1**	**1**	**0**	**0**	**0**	**0**	**0**	**0.0**	**1**	**0**	**3**	**0**	**–2**								
	London Lions	Britain	71	21	21	42				24																		

Season	Club	League	REGULAR SEASON GP	G	A	Pts	AG	AA	APts	PIM	PP	SH	GW	S	%	TGF	PGF	TGA	PGA	+/–	PLAYOFFS GP	G	A	Pts	PIM	PP	SH	GW
1974-75	Thunder Bay Twins	USHL	44	16	35	51	....	....	....	23	....	....	....	....	....	....	....	....	....	....	....	....	....	....	....	....	....	....
1975-76	Thunder Bay Twins	OHA-Sr.	22	3	15	18	....	....	....	8	....	....	....	....	....	....	....	....	....	....	....	....	....	....	....	....	....	....
1976-77	Thunder Bay Twins	OHA-Sr.	12	2	11	13	....	....	....	2	....	....	....	....	....	....	....	....	....	....	....	....	....	....	....	....	....	....
	NHL Totals		**1**	**0**	**1**	**1**	**0**	**1**	**1**	**0**	**0**	**0**	**0**	**0**	**0.0**	**1**	**0**	**3**	**0**		....	....	....	....	....	....	....	....

USHL First All-Star Team (1975)

Traded to **Detroit** by **Boston** to complete transaction that sent Gary Doak to Boston (March 1, 1973), June 4, 1973.

• WINNES, Chris

Christopher R. RW – R. 6′, 201 lbs. b: Ridgefield, CT, 2/12/1968. Boston's 9th, 161st overall, in 1987.

Season	Club	League	GP	G	A	Pts	AG	AA	APts	PIM	PP	SH	GW	S	%	TGF	PGF	TGA	PGA	+/–	GP	G	A	Pts	PIM	PP	SH	GW
1985-86	Ridgewood High School	Hi-School	24	40	30	70	....	....	....	....	....	....	....	....	....	....	....	....	....	....	....	....	....	....	....	....	....	....
1986-87	Northwood Prep School	Hi-School	47	25	33	58	....	....	....	56	....	....	....	....	....	....	....	....	....	....	....	....	....	....	....	....	....	....
1987-88	University of New Hampshire	H-East	30	17	19	36	....	....	....	28	....	....	....	....	....	....	....	....	....	....	....	....	....	....	....	....	....	....
1988-89	University of New Hampshire	H-East	30	11	20	31	....	....	....	22	....	....	....	....	....	....	....	....	....	....	....	....	....	....	....	....	....	....
1989-90	University of New Hampshire	H-East	24	10	13	23	....	....	....	12	....	....	....	....	....	....	....	....	....	....	....	....	....	....	....	....	....	....
1990-91	University of New Hampshire	H-East	33	15	16	31	....	....	....	24	....	....	....	....	....	....	....	....	....	....	....	....	....	....	....	....	....	....
	Maine Mariners	AHL	7	3	1	4	....	....	....	0	....	....	....	....	....	....	....	....	....	....	1	0	2	2	0	....	....	....
	Boston Bruins	**NHL**	....	....	....	....	....	....	....	....	....	....	....	....	....	....	....	....	....	....	**1**	**0**	**0**	**0**	**0**	**0**	**0**	**0**
1991-92	**Boston Bruins**	**NHL**	**24**	**1**	**3**	**4**	**1**	**2**	**3**	**6**	**0**	**0**	**0**	**20**	**5.0**	**7**	**3**	**10**	**0**	**–6**	....	....	....	....	....	....	....	....
	Maine Mariners	AHL	45	12	35	47	....	....	....	30	....	....	....	....	....	....	....	....	....	....	....	....	....	....	....	....	....	....
	United States	WC-A	6	3	2	5	....	....	....	4	....	....	....	....	....	....	....	....	....	....	....	....	....	....	....	....	....	....
1992-93	**Boston Bruins**	**NHL**	**5**	**0**	**1**	**1**	**0**	**1**	**1**	**0**	**0**	**0**	**0**	**2**	**0.0**	**1**	**0**	**0**	**0**	**1**	....	....	....	....	....	....	....	....
	Providence Bruins	AHL	64	23	36	59	....	....	....	34	....	....	....	....	....	....	....	....	....	....	4	0	2	2	5	....	....	....
1993-94	**Philadelphia Flyers**	**NHL**	**4**	**0**	**2**	**2**	**0**	**2**	**2**	**0**	**0**	**0**	**0**	**4**	**0.0**	**3**	**0**	**2**	**0**	**1**	....	....	....	....	....	....	....	....
	Hershey Bears	AHL	70	29	21	50	....	....	....	20	....	....	....	....	....	....	....	....	....	....	7	1	3	4	0	....	....	....
1994-95	Hershey Bears	AHL	78	26	40	66	....	....	....	39	....	....	....	....	....	....	....	....	....	....	6	2	2	4	17	....	....	....
1995-96	Michigan K-Wings	IHL	27	6	13	19	....	....	....	14	....	....	....	....	....	....	....	....	....	....	....	....	....	....	....	....	....	....
	Fort Wayne Komets	IHL	39	6	7	13	....	....	....	12	....	....	....	....	....	....	....	....	....	....	2	0	0	0	0	....	....	....
1996-97	HC Merano	Italy	10	10	2	12	....	....	....	6	....	....	....	....	....	....	....	....	....	....	2	1	3	4	4	....	....	....
	Utah Grizzlies	IHL	5	0	0	0	....	....	....	0	....	....	....	....	....	....	....	....	....	....	....	....	....	....	....	....	....	....
1997-98	San Antonio Dragons	IHL	3	0	0	0	....	....	....	0	....	....	....	....	....	....	....	....	....	....	....	....	....	....	....	....	....	....
	Hartford Wolf Pack	AHL	64	17	23	40	....	....	....	16	....	....	....	....	....	....	....	....	....	....	13	1	4	5	2	....	....	....
1998-99	Manitoba Moose	IHL	11	2	0	2	....	....	....	0	....	....	....	....	....	....	....	....	....	....	....	....	....	....	....	....	....	....
	Hartford Wolf Pack	AHL	33	7	6	13	....	....	....	25	....	....	....	....	....	....	....	....	....	....	1	0	0	0	0	....	....	....
99-2000	Binghamton Icemen	UHL	14	7	7	14	....	....	....	0	....	....	....	....	....	....	....	....	....	....	3	0	4	4	0	....	....	....
	Louisville Panthers	AHL	12	1	3	4	....	....	....	6	....	....	....	....	....	....	....	....	....	....	....	....	....	....	....	....	....	....
	Providence Bruins	AHL	2	1	1	2	....	....	....	0	....	....	....	....	....	....	....	....	....	....	....	....	....	....	....	....	....	....
	Springfield Falcons	AHL	38	6	17	23	....	....	....	4	....	....	....	....	....	....	....	....	....	....	5	2	2	4	0	....	....	....
	NHL Totals		**33**	**1**	**6**	**7**	**1**	**5**	**6**	**6**	**0**	**0**	**0**	**26**	**3.8**	**11**	**3**	**12**	**0**		**1**	**0**	**0**	**0**	**0**	**0**	**0**	**0**

Signed as a free agent by **Philadelphia**, August 4, 1993. Signed as a free agent by **NY Rangers**, July 21, 1998. Signed as a free agent by **Binghamton** (UHL), September 27, 1999.

• WISEMAN, Brian

C – L. 5′8″, 175 lbs. b: Chatham, Ont., 7/13/1971. NY Rangers' 11th, 257th overall, in 1991.

Season	Club	League	GP	G	A	Pts	AG	AA	APts	PIM	PP	SH	GW	S	%	TGF	PGF	TGA	PGA	+/–	GP	G	A	Pts	PIM	PP	SH	GW
1986-87	Dresden Kings	OJHL-C	33	12	29	41	....	....	....	53	....	....	....	....	....	....	....	....	....	....	....	....	....	....	....	....	....	....
1987-88	Chatham Maroons	OJHL-B	41	26	33	59	....	....	....	35	....	....	....	....	....	....	....	....	....	....	....	....	....	....	....	....	....	....
1988-89	Chatham Maroons	OJHL-B	42	36	*71	*107	....	....	....	34	....	....	....	....	....	....	....	....	....	....	....	....	....	....	....	....	....	....
1989-90	Chatham Maroons	OJHL-B	40	*70	*77	*147	....	....	....	32	....	....	....	....	....	....	....	....	....	....	....	....	....	....	....	....	....	....
1990-91	University of Michigan	CCHA	47	25	33	58	....	....	....	58	....	....	....	....	....	....	....	....	....	....	....	....	....	....	....	....	....	....
1991-92	University of Michigan	CCHA	44	27	44	71	....	....	....	38	....	....	....	....	....	....	....	....	....	....	....	....	....	....	....	....	....	....
1992-93	University of Michigan	CCHA	35	13	37	50	....	....	....	40	....	....	....	....	....	....	....	....	....	....	....	....	....	....	....	....	....	....
1993-94	University of Michigan	CCHA	40	19	50	69	....	....	....	44	....	....	....	....	....	....	....	....	....	....	....	....	....	....	....	....	....	....
1994-95	Chicago Wolves	IHL	75	17	55	72	....	....	....	52	....	....	....	....	....	....	....	....	....	....	3	1	1	2	4	....	....	....
1995-96	Chicago Wolves	IHL	73	33	55	88	....	....	....	117	....	....	....	....	....	....	....	....	....	....	....	....	....	....	....	....	....	....
1996-97	**Toronto Maple Leafs**	**NHL**	**3**	**0**	**0**	**0**	**0**	**0**	**0**	**0**	**0**	**0**	**0**	**1**	**0.0**	**0**	**0**	**0**	**0**	**0**	....	....	....	....	....	....	....	....
	St. John's Maple Leafs	AHL	71	33	62	95	....	....	....	83	....	....	....	....	....	....	....	....	....	....	7	5	4	9	8	....	....	....
1997-98	Houston Aeros	IHL	78	26	72	98	....	....	....	86	....	....	....	....	....	....	....	....	....	....	4	0	3	3	8	....	....	....
1998-99	Houston Aeros	IHL	77	21	*88	*109	....	....	....	106	....	....	....	....	....	....	....	....	....	....	19	3	13	16	26	....	....	....
99-2000	Houston Aeros	IHL	72	15	38	53	....	....	....	52	....	....	....	....	....	....	....	....	....	....	3	0	1	1	6	....	....	....
	NHL Totals		**3**	**0**	**0**	**0**	**0**	**0**	**0**	**0**	**0**	**0**	**0**	**1**	**0.0**	**0**	**0**	**0**	**0**		....	....	....	....	....	....	....	....

CCHA First All-Star Team (1994) • NCAA West First All-American Team (1994) • IHL First All-Star Team (1998, 1999) • Won Leo P. Lamoureux Memorial Trophy (Top Scorer - IHL) (1999) • Won James Gatschene Memorial Trophy (MVP - IHL) (1999)

Signed as a free agent by **Toronto**, August 14, 1996. Signed as a free agent by **Houston** (IHL), August 4, 1997. Signed as a free agent by **Toronto**, July 13, 1999.

• WISTE, Jim

James Andrew C – L. 5′10″, 185 lbs. b: Moose Jaw, Sask., 2/18/1946.

Season	Club	League	GP	G	A	Pts	AG	AA	APts	PIM	PP	SH	GW	S	%	TGF	PGF	TGA	PGA	+/–	GP	G	A	Pts	PIM	PP	SH	GW
1962-63	Moose Jaw Canucks	SJHL	47	22	20	42	....	....	....	47	....	....	....	....	....	....	....	....	....	....	5	2	7	9	6	....	....	....
1963-64	Moose Jaw Canucks	SJHL	61	37	60	97	....	....	....	124	....	....	....	....	....	....	....	....	....	....	5	1	5	6	15	....	....	....
1964-65	University of Denver	WCHA	DID NOT PLAY – FRESHMAN																									
1965-66	University of Denver	WCHA	32	16	14	30	....	....	....	36	....	....	....	....	....	....	....	....	....	....	....	....	....	....	....	....	....	....
1966-67	University of Denver	WCHA	30	24	28	52	....	....	....	35	....	....	....	....	....	....	....	....	....	....	....	....	....	....	....	....	....	....
1967-68	University of Denver	WCHA	34	21	36	57	....	....	....	25	....	....	....	....	....	....	....	....	....	....	....	....	....	....	....	....	....	....
1968-69	**Chicago Black Hawks**	**NHL**	**3**	**0**	**0**	**0**	**0**	**0**	**0**	**0**	**0**	**0**	**0**	**3**	**0.0**	**1**	**0**	**0**	**0**	**1**	....	....	....	....	....	....	....	....
	Dallas Black Hawks	CHL	68	32	44	76	....	....	....	77	....	....	....	....	....	....	....	....	....	....	10	7	6	13	6	....	....	....
1969-70	**Chicago Black Hawks**	**NHL**	**26**	**0**	**8**	**8**	**0**	**7**	**7**	**8**	**0**	**0**	**0**	**11**	**0.0**	**12**	**2**	**12**	**2**	**0**	....	....	....	....	....	....	....	....
	Dallas Black Hawks	CHL	11	6	9	15	....	....	....	27	....	....	....	....	....	....	....	....	....	....	....	....	....	....	....	....	....	....
1970-71	**Vancouver Canucks**	**NHL**	**23**	**1**	**2**	**3**	**1**	**2**	**3**	**0**	**0**	**0**	**0**	**9**	**11.1**	**5**	**2**	**11**	**0**	**–8**	....	....	....	....	....	....	....	....
	Seattle Totems	WHL	29	11	13	24	....	....	....	32	....	....	....	....	....	....	....	....	....	....	....	....	....	....	....	....	....	....
	Rochester Americans	AHL	....	....	....	....	....	....	....	....	....	....	....	....	....	....	....	....	....	....	10	2	8	10	35	....	....	....
1971-72	Seattle Totems	WHL	4	0	0	0	....	....	....	0	....	....	....	....	....	....	....	....	....	....	....	....	....	....	....	....	....	....
	Rochester Americans	AHL	13	4	8	12	....	....	....	2	....	....	....	....	....	....	....	....	....	....	....	....	....	....	....	....	....	....
	Providence Reds	AHL	53	12	26	38	....	....	....	35	....	....	....	....	....	....	....	....	....	....	3	0	1	1	0	....	....	....
1972-73	Cleveland Crusaders	WHA	70	28	43	71	....	....	....	24	....	....	....	....	....	....	....	....	....	....	9	3	8	11	13	....	....	....
1973-74	Cleveland Crusaders	WHA	76	23	35	58	....	....	....	26	....	....	....	....	....	....	....	....	....	....	5	0	1	1	0	....	....	....
1974-75	Indianapolis Racers	WHA	75	13	28	41	....	....	....	30	....	....	....	....	....	....	....	....	....	....	....	....	....	....	....	....	....	....
1975-76	Indianapolis Racers	WHA	7	0	2	2	....	....	....	0	....	....	....	....	....	....	....	....	....	....	....	....	....	....	....	....	....	....
	Mohawk Valley Comets	NAHL	5	0	1	1	....	....	....	0	....	....	....	....	....	....	....	....	....	....	....	....	....	....	....	....	....	....
	NHL Totals		**52**	**1**	**10**	**11**	**1**	**9**	**10**	**8**	**0**	**0**	**0**	**23**	**4.3**	**18**	**4**	**23**	**2**		....	....	....	....	....	....	....	....
	Other Major League Totals		228	64	108	172				80											14	3	9	12	13			

WCHA First All-Star Team (1967, 1968) • NCAA West First All-American Team (1967, 1968)

Signed as a free agent by **Chicago**, September 27, 1968. Claimed by **Vancouver** from **Chicago** in Expansion Draft, June 10, 1970. Loaned to **Seattle** (WHL) by **Vancouver** with Ed Hatoum for the remainder of the 1970-71 season for Bobby Schmautz, February 9, 1971. Traded to **NY Rangers** by **Vancouver** with Gary Doak for Dave Balon, Wayne Connelly and Ron Stewart, November 16, 1971. Selected by **NY Raiders** (WHA) in 1972 WHA General Player Draft, February 12, 1972. Signed as a free agent by **Cleveland** (WHA) after securing release from **NY Raiders**, August, 1972. Claimed by **Indianapolis** (WHA) from **Cleveland** (WHA) in WHA Expansion Draft, May, 1974.

• WITEHALL, Johan

LW – L. 6′1″, 198 lbs. b: Kungsbacka, Sweden, 1/7/1972. NY Rangers' 8th, 207th overall, in 1998.

Season	Club	League	GP	G	A	Pts	AG	AA	APts	PIM	PP	SH	GW	S	%	TGF	PGF	TGA	PGA	+/–	GP	G	A	Pts	PIM	PP	SH	GW
1991-92	Hanhals Kungsbacka IF	Sweden-2	32	23	14	37	....	....	....	52	....	....	....	....	....	....	....	....	....	....	....	....	....	....	....	....	....	....
1992-93	Hanhals Kungsbacka IF	Sweden 2	29	12	7	19	....	....	....	34	....	....	....	....	....	....	....	....	....	....	....	....	....	....	....	....	....	....
1993-94	Hanhals Kungsbacka IF	Sweden 2	30	13	12	25	....	....	....	66	....	....	....	....	....	....	....	....	....	....	....	....	....	....	....	....	....	....
1994-95	Hanhals Kungsbacka IF	Sweden-3	32	*38	13	*51	....	....	....	44	....	....	....	....	....	....	....	....	....	....	....	....	....	....	....	....	....	....
1995-96	Hanhals Kungsbacka IF	Sweden-3	36	*43	17	60	....	....	....	48	....	....	....	....	....	....	....	....	....	....	....	....	....	....	....	....	....	....
1996-97	IK Oskarshamn	Sweden 2	32	19	16	35	....	....	....	38	....	....	....	....	....	....	....	....	....	....	....	....	....	....	....	....	....	....

			REGULAR SEASON																		PLAYOFFS							
Season	Club	League	GP	G	A	Pts	AG	AA	APts	PIM	PP	SH	GW	S	%	TGF	PGF	TGA	PGA	+/–	GP	G	A	Pts	PIM	PP	SH	GW
1997-98	Leksands IF	Sweden	42	12	4	16	....	....	....	34	....	....	....	....	....	....	....	....	....	....	2	0	0	0	2	....	....	....
	Leksands IF	EuroHL	5	3	0	3	....	....	....	2	....	....	....	....	....	....	....	....	....	....	....	....	....	....	....	....	....	....
1998-99	**New York Rangers**	**NHL**	**4**	**0**	**0**	**0**	**0**	**0**	**0**	**0**	**0**	**0**	**0**	**1**	**0.0**	**0**	**0**	**0**	**0**	**0**	....	....	....	....	....	....	....	....
	Hartford Wolf Pack	AHL	62	14	15	29	....	....	....	56	....	....	....	....	....	....	....	....	....	....	7	1	2	3	6	....	....	....
99-2000	**New York Rangers**	**NHL**	**9**	**1**	**1**	**2**	**1**	**1**	**2**	**2**	**0**	**0**	**0**	**6**	**16.7**	**2**	**0**	**2**	**0**	**0**	....	....	....	....	....	....	....	....
	Hartford Wolf Pack	AHL	73	17	24	41	....	....	....	65	....	....	....	....	....	....	....	....	....	....	17	6	7	13	10	....	....	....
	NHL Totals		**13**	**1**	**1**	**2**	**1**	**1**	**2**	**2**	**0**	**0**	**0**	**7**	**14.3**	**2**	**0**	**2**	**0**		....	....	....	....	....	....	....	....

• WITHERSPOON, Jim

James D – R. 6'3", 205 lbs. b: Toronto, Ont., 10/3/1951.

Season	Club	League	GP	G	A	Pts	AG	AA	APts	PIM	PP	SH	GW	S	%	TGF	PGF	TGA	PGA	+/–	GP	G	A	Pts	PIM	PP	SH	GW
1967-68	Newmarket Orioles	OHA-B	STATISTICS NOT AVAILABLE																									
1968-69	Markham Waxers	OHA-B	STATISTICS NOT AVAILABLE																									
1969-70	Newmarket Redmen	OHA-C	STATISTICS NOT AVAILABLE																									
1970-71	Ohio State University	CCHA	29	4	10	14	....	....	....	107	....	....	....	....	....	....	....	....	....	....	....	....	....	....	....	....	....	....
1971-72	Ohio State University	CCHA	29	3	22	25	....	....	....	64	....	....	....	....	....	....	....	....	....	....	....	....	....	....	....	....	....	....
1972-73	Ohio State University	CCHA	25	6	23	29	....	....	....	80	....	....	....	....	....	....	....	....	....	....	....	....	....	....	....	....	....	....
1973-74	Ohio State University	CCHA	31	7	26	33	....	....	....	52	....	....	....	....	....	....	....	....	....	....	....	....	....	....	....	....	....	....
1974-75	Springfield Indians	AHL	61	3	9	12	....	....	....	33	....	....	....	....	....	....	....	....	....	....	16	0	1	1	4	....	....	....
1975-76	**Los Angeles Kings**	**NHL**	**2**	**0**	**0**	**0**	**0**	**0**	**0**	**2**	**0**	**0**	**0**	**0**	**0.0**	**0**	**0**	**1**	**0**	**–1**	....	....	....	....	....	....	....	....
	Fort Worth Texans	CHL	61	0	13	13	....	....	....	102	....	....	....	....	....	....	....	....	....	....	....	....	....	....	....	....	....	....
1976-77	Fort Worth Texans	CHL	30	1	4	5	....	....	....	69	....	....	....	....	....	....	....	....	....	....	....	....	....	....	....	....	....	....
1977-78	Springfield Indians	AHL	STATISTICS NOT AVAILABLE																									
	NHL Totals		**2**	**0**	**0**	**0**	**0**	**0**	**0**	**2**	**0**	**0**	**0**	**0**	**0.0**	**0**	**0**	**1**	**0**		....	....	....	....	....	....	....	....

CCHA Second All-Star Team (1973)

Signed as a free agent by **LA Kings**, August, 1974.

• WITT, Brendan

D – L. 6'2", 226 lbs. b: Humbolt, Sask., 2/20/1975. Washington's 1st, 11th overall, in 1993.

Season	Club	League	GP	G	A	Pts	AG	AA	APts	PIM	PP	SH	GW	S	%	TGF	PGF	TGA	PGA	+/–	GP	G	A	Pts	PIM	PP	SH	GW
1990-91	Saskatoon Blazers	SAHA	31	5	13	18	....	....	....	42	....	....	....	....	....	....	....	....	....	....	....	....	....	....	....	....	....	....
	Seattle Thunderbirds	WHL	....	....	....	....	....	....	....	....	....	....	....	....	....	....	....	....	....	....	1	0	0	0	0	....	....	....
1991-92	Seattle Thunderbirds	WHL	67	3	9	12	....	....	....	212	....	....	....	....	....	....	....	....	....	....	15	1	1	2	84	....	....	....
	Seattle Thunderbirds	Mem-Cup	4	0	1	1	....	....	....	11	....	....	....	....	....	....	....	....	....	....	....	....	....	....	....	....	....	....
1992-93	Seattle Thunderbirds	WHL	70	2	26	28	....	....	....	239	....	....	....	....	....	....	....	....	....	....	5	1	2	3	30	....	....	....
1993-94	Seattle Thunderbirds	WHL	56	8	31	39	....	....	....	235	....	....	....	....	....	....	....	....	....	....	9	3	8	11	23	....	....	....
	Canada	WJC-A	7	0	0	0	....	....	....	6	....	....	....	....	....	....	....	....	....	....	....	....	....	....	....	....	....	....
1994-95			DID NOT PLAY																									
1995-96	**Washington Capitals**	**NHL**	**48**	**2**	**3**	**5**	**2**	**2**	**4**	**85**	**0**	**0**	**1**	**44**	**4.5**	**20**	**0**	**27**	**3**	**–4**	....	....	....	....	....	....	....	....
1996-97	**Washington Capitals**	**NHL**	**44**	**3**	**2**	**5**	**3**	**2**	**5**	**88**	**0**	**0**	**0**	**41**	**7.3**	**17**	**0**	**39**	**2**	**–20**	....	....	....	....	....	....	....	....
	Portland Pirates	AHL	30	2	4	6	....	....	....	56	....	....	....	....	....	....	....	....	....	....	5	1	0	1	30	....	....	....
1997-98	**Washington Capitals**	**NHL**	**64**	**1**	**7**	**8**	**1**	**7**	**8**	**112**	**0**	**0**	**0**	**68**	**1.5**	**37**	**1**	**57**	**10**	**–11**	**16**	**1**	**0**	**1**	**14**	**0**	**0**	**0**
1998-99	**Washington Capitals**	**NHL**	**54**	**2**	**5**	**7**	**2**	**5**	**7**	**87**	**0**	**0**	**0**	**51**	**3.9**	**20**	**0**	**32**	**6**	**–6**	....	....	....	....	....	....	....	....
99-2000	**Washington Capitals**	**NHL**	**77**	**1**	**7**	**8**	**1**	**6**	**7**	**114**	**0**	**0**	**0**	**64**	**1.6**	**55**	**1**	**72**	**23**	**5**	**3**	**0**	**0**	**0**	**0**	**0**	**0**	**0**
	NHL Totals		**287**	**9**	**24**	**33**	**9**	**22**	**31**	**486**	**0**	**0**	**1**	**268**	**3.4**	**149**	**2**	**227**	**44**		**19**	**1**	**0**	**1**	**14**	**0**	**0**	**0**

WHL West First All-Star Team (1993, 1994) • Canadian Major Junior First All-Star Team (1994)

• Sat out entire 1994-95 season after failing to come to contract terms with Washington.

• WOLANIN, Craig

Craig W. D – L. 6'4", 215 lbs. b: Grosse Pointe, MI, 7/27/1967. New Jersey's 1st, 3rd overall, in 1985.

Season	Club	League	GP	G	A	Pts	AG	AA	APts	PIM	PP	SH	GW	S	%	TGF	PGF	TGA	PGA	+/–	GP	G	A	Pts	PIM	PP	SH	GW
1983-84	Detroit Compuware	MNHL	69	8	42	50	....	....	....	86	....	....	....	....	....	....	....	....	....	....	....	....	....	....	....	....	....	....
1984-85	Kitchener Rangers	OHL	60	5	16	21	....	....	....	95	....	....	....	....	....	....	....	....	....	....	4	1	1	2	2	....	....	....
1985-86	**New Jersey Devils**	**NHL**	**44**	**2**	**16**	**18**	**2**	**11**	**13**	**74**	**0**	**0**	**1**	**45**	**4.4**	**48**	**6**	**63**	**14**	**–7**	....	....	....	....	....	....	....	....
1986-87	**New Jersey Devils**	**NHL**	**68**	**4**	**6**	**10**	**3**	**4**	**7**	**109**	**0**	**0**	**0**	**68**	**5.9**	**46**	**2**	**95**	**20**	**–31**	....	....	....	....	....	....	....	....
	United States	WEC-A	9	0	0	0	....	....	....	32	....	....	....	....	....	....	....	....	....	....	....	....	....	....	....	....	....	....
1987-88	**New Jersey Devils**	**NHL**	**78**	**6**	**25**	**31**	**5**	**18**	**23**	**170**	**1**	**1**	**3**	**113**	**5.3**	**79**	**18**	**89**	**28**	**0**	**18**	**2**	**5**	**7**	**51**	**1**	**0**	**0**
1988-89	**New Jersey Devils**	**NHL**	**56**	**3**	**8**	**11**	**3**	**6**	**9**	**69**	**0**	**0**	**0**	**70**	**4.3**	**40**	**3**	**59**	**13**	**–9**	....	....	....	....	....	....	....	....
1989-90	**New Jersey Devils**	**NHL**	**37**	**1**	**7**	**8**	**1**	**5**	**6**	**47**	**0**	**0**	**0**	**35**	**2.9**	**28**	**1**	**41**	**1**	**–13**	....	....	....	....	....	....	....	....
	Utica Devils	AHL	6	2	4	6	....	....	....	2	....	....	....	....	....	....	....	....	....	....	....	....	....	....	....	....	....	....
	Quebec Nordiques	**NHL**	**13**	**0**	**3**	**3**	**0**	**2**	**2**	**10**	**0**	**0**	**0**	**25**	**0.0**	**15**	**0**	**30**	**17**	**2**	....	....	....	....	....	....	....	....
1990-91	**Quebec Nordiques**	**NHL**	**80**	**5**	**13**	**18**	**5**	**10**	**15**	**89**	**0**	**1**	**0**	**109**	**4.6**	**74**	**1**	**133**	**47**	**–13**	....	....	....	....	....	....	....	....
	United States	WEC-A	10	2	2	4	....	....	....	22	....	....	....	....	....	....	....	....	....	....	....	....	....	....	....	....	....	....
1991-92	United States	Can-Cup	8	0	2	2	....	....	....	2	....	....	....	....	....	....	....	....	....	....	....	....	....	....	....	....	....	....
	Quebec Nordiques	**NHL**	**69**	**2**	**11**	**13**	**2**	**8**	**10**	**80**	**0**	**0**	**0**	**71**	**2.8**	**57**	**0**	**98**	**29**	**–12**	....	....	....	....	....	....	....	....
1992-93	**Quebec Nordiques**	**NHL**	**24**	**1**	**4**	**5**	**1**	**3**	**4**	**49**	**0**	**0**	**0**	**17**	**5.9**	**26**	**0**	**24**	**7**	**9**	**4**	**0**	**0**	**0**	**4**	**0**	**0**	**0**
1993-94	**Quebec Nordiques**	**NHL**	**63**	**6**	**10**	**16**	**6**	**8**	**14**	**80**	**0**	**0**	**0**	**78**	**7.7**	**63**	**4**	**70**	**27**	**16**	....	....	....	....	....	....	....	....
	United States	WC-A	8	2	1	3	....	....	....	4	....	....	....	....	....	....	....	....	....	....	....	....	....	....	....	....	....	....
1994-95	**Quebec Nordiques**	**NHL**	**40**	**3**	**6**	**9**	**5**	**9**	**14**	**40**	**0**	**0**	**0**	**36**	**8.3**	**37**	**2**	**36**	**13**	**12**	**6**	**1**	**1**	**2**	**4**	**0**	**0**	**0**
1995-96♦	**Colorado Avalanche**	**NHL**	**75**	**7**	**20**	**27**	**7**	**16**	**23**	**50**	**0**	**3**	**0**	**73**	**9.6**	**80**	**2**	**81**	**28**	**25**	**7**	**1**	**0**	**1**	**8**	**0**	**0**	**1**
1996-97	**Tampa Bay Lightning**	**NHL**	**15**	**0**	**0**	**0**	**0**	**0**	**0**	**8**	**0**	**0**	**0**	**12**	**0.0**	**5**	**0**	**15**	**1**	**–9**	....	....	....	....	....	....	....	....
	Toronto Maple Leafs	**NHL**	**23**	**0**	**4**	**4**	**0**	**4**	**4**	**13**	**0**	**0**	**0**	**31**	**0.0**	**15**	**0**	**15**	**3**	**3**	....	....	....	....	....	....	....	....
1997-98	**Toronto Maple Leafs**	**NHL**	**10**	**0**	**0**	**0**	**0**	**0**	**0**	**6**	**0**	**0**	**0**	**5**	**0.0**	**1**	**0**	**10**	**0**	**–9**	....	....	....	....	....	....	....	....
1998-99	Detroit Vipers	IHL	16	0	5	5	....	....	....	21	....	....	....	....	....	....	....	....	....	....	11	0	0	0	12	....	....	....
	NHL Totals		**695**	**40**	**133**	**173**	**40**	**104**	**144**	**894**	**1**	**5**	**4**	**788**	**5.1**	**614**	**39**	**859**	**248**		**35**	**4**	**6**	**10**	**67**	**1**	**0**	**1**

Traded to **Quebec** by **New Jersey** with future considerations (Randy Velischek, August 13, 1990) for Peter Stastny, March 6, 1990. Transferred to **Colorado** after **Quebec** franchise relocated, June 21, 1995. Traded to **Tampa Bay** by **Colorado** for Tampa Bay's 2nd round choice (Ramzi Abid) in 1998 Entry Draft, July 29, 1996. Traded to **Toronto** by **Tampa Bay** for Toronto's 3rd round choice (later traded to Edmonton - Edmonton Selected Alex Henry) in 1998 Entry Draft, January 31, 1997. • Missed majority of 1997-98 and 1998-99 seasons recovering from knee injury suffered in game vs. Montreal, November 1, 1997. Signed as a free agent by **Detroit** (IHL), January 31, 1999.

• WOLF, Bennett

Bennett Martin D – R. 6'3", 205 lbs. b: Kitchener, Ont., 10/23/1959. Pittsburgh's 2nd, 52nd overall, in 1979.

Season	Club	League	GP	G	A	Pts	AG	AA	APts	PIM	PP	SH	GW	S	%	TGF	PGF	TGA	PGA	+/–	GP	G	A	Pts	PIM	PP	SH	GW
1976-77	Kitchener Greenshirts	OHA-B	38	3	16	19	....	....	....	200	....	....	....	....	....	....	....	....	....	....	....	....	....	....	....	....	....	....
	Kitchener Rangers	OMJHL	7	0	1	1	....	....	....	16	....	....	....	....	....	....	....	....	....	....	1	0	0	0	0	....	....	....
1977-78	Toronto Marlboros	OMJHL	66	3	13	16	....	....	....	334	....	....	....	....	....	....	....	....	....	....	5	0	1	1	37	....	....	....
1978-79	Toronto Marlboros	OMJHL	18	0	3	3	....	....	....	48	....	....	....	....	....	....	....	....	....	....	....	....	....	....	....	....	....	....
	Kitchener Rangers	OMJHL	47	3	18	21	....	....	....	279	....	....	....	....	....	....	....	....	....	....	10	0	4	4	73	....	....	....
1979-80	Grand Rapids Owls	IHL	51	3	14	17	....	....	....	408	....	....	....	....	....	....	....	....	....	....	....	....	....	....	....	....	....	....
	Syracuse Firebirds	AHL	....	....	....	....	....	....	....	....	....	....	....	....	....	....	....	....	....	....	4	0	0	0	39	....	....	....
1980-81	**Pittsburgh Penguins**	**NHL**	**24**	**0**	**1**	**1**	**0**	**1**	**1**	**94**	**0**	**0**	**0**	**14**	**0.0**	**7**	**0**	**11**	**3**	**–1**	....	....	....	....	....	....	....	....
	Binghamton Whalers	AHL	14	2	2	4	....	....	....	106	....	....	....	....	....	....	....	....	....	....	....	....	....	....	....	....	....	....
1981-82	**Pittsburgh Penguins**	**NHL**	**1**	**0**	**0**	**0**	**0**	**0**	**0**	**2**	....	....	....	....	....	....	....	....	....	....	....	....	....	....	....	....	....	....
	Erie Blades	AHL	45	0	4	4	....	....	....	153	....	....	....	....	....	....	....	....	....	....	....	....	....	....	....	....	....	....
1982-83	**Pittsburgh Penguins**	**NHL**	**5**	**0**	**0**	**0**	**0**	**0**	**0**	**37**	**0**	**0**	**0**	**1**	**0.0**	**1**	**0**	**5**	**2**	**–2**	....	....	....	....	....	....	....	....
	Baltimore Skipjacks	AHL	61	1	10	11	....	....	....	223	....	....	....	....	....	....	....	....	....	....	....	....	....	....	....	....	....	....
1983-84	Baltimore Skipjacks	AHL	63	3	13	16	....	....	....	349	....	....	....	....	....	....	....	....	....	....	10	0	2	2	24	....	....	....
1984-85	Baltimore Skipjacks	AHL	55	0	8	8	....	....	....	285	....	....	....	....	....	....	....	....	....	....	13	0	2	2	89	....	....	....
	NHL Totals		**30**	**0**	**1**	**1**	**0**	**1**	**1**	**133**	**0**	**0**	**0**	**15**	**0.0**	**8**	**0**	**16**	**5**		....	....	....	....	....	....	....	....

• WONG, Mike

Michael Anthony C – L. 6'3", 204 lbs. b: Minneapolis, MN, 1/14/1955. Detroit's 7th, 77th overall, in 1975.

Season	Club	League	GP	G	A	Pts	AG	AA	APts	PIM	PP	SH	GW	S	%	TGF	PGF	TGA	PGA	+/–	GP	G	A	Pts	PIM	PP	SH	GW
1973-74	Minnesota Jr. North Stars	MWJHL	57	24	32	56	....	....	....	128	....	....	....	....	....	....	....	....	....	....	....	....	....	....	....	....	....	....
	United States	WJC-A	5	0	0	0	....	....	....	4	....	....	....	....	....	....	....	....	....	....	....	....	....	....	....	....	....	....
1974-75	Montreal Jr. Canadiens	QMJHL	67	27	41	68	....	....	....	130	....	....	....	....	....	....	....	....	....	....	....	....	....	....	....	....	....	....

			REGULAR SEASON																		PLAYOFFS							
Season	Club	League	GP	G	A	Pts	AG	AA	APts	PIM	PP	SH	GW	S	%	TGF	PGF	TGA	PGA	+/–	GP	G	A	Pts	PIM	PP	SH	GW
1975-76	**Detroit Red Wings**	**NHL**	22	1	1	2	1	1	2	12	0	0	0	9	11.1	3	2	12	0	–11	....	....	....	....	....	....	....	....
	Kalamazoo Wings	IHL	39	20	22	42	....	....	....	81	....	....	....	....	....	....	....	....	....	....	....	....	....	....	....	....	....	....
1976-77	Kalamazoo Wings	IHL	24	12	10	22	....	....	....	22	....	....	....	....	....	....	....	....	....	....	....	....	....	....	....	....	....	....
	Rhode Island Reds	AHL	18	3	5	8	....	....	....	6	....	....	....	....	....	....	....	....	....	....	....	....	....	....	....	....	....	....
1977-78	Kalamazoo Wings	IHL	8	0	1	1	....	....	....	0	....	....	....	....	....	....	....	....	....	....	....	....	....	....	....	....	....	....
	Muskegon Mohawks	IHL	58	23	18	41	....	....	....	63	....	....	....	....	....	....	....	....	....	....	4	1	0	1	18	....	....	....
1978-79	Kalamazoo Wings	IHL	6	2	2	4	....	....	....	21	....	....	....	....	....	....	....	....	....	....	....	....	....	....	....	....	....	....
	Johnstown Wings	NEHL	53	18	26	44	....	....	....	81	....	....	....	....	....	....	....	....	....	....	....	....	....	....	....	....	....	....
	NHL Totals		22	1	1	2	1	1	2	12	0	0	0	9	11.1	3	2	12	0		....	....	....	....	....	....	....	....

• WOOD, Dody

Darin Michael C – L. 6′, 200 lbs. b: Chetwynd, B.C., 3/18/1972. San Jose's 4th, 45th overall, in 1991.

Season	Club	League	GP	G	A	Pts	AG	AA	APts	PIM	PP	SH	GW	S	%	TGF	PGF	TGA	PGA	+/–	GP	G	A	Pts	PIM	PP	SH	GW
1989-90	Fort St. John Huskies	PCJHL	44	51	73	124	....	....	....	270	....	....	....	....	....	....	....	....	....	....	....	....	....	....	....	....	....	....
	Seattle Thunderbirds	WHL	....	....	....	....	....	....	....	....	....	....	....	....	....	....	....	....	....	....	5	0	0	0	2	....	....	....
1990-91	Seattle Thunderbirds	WHL	69	28	37	65	....	....	....	272	....	....	....	....	....	....	....	....	....	....	6	0	1	1	2	....	....	....
1991-92	Seattle Thunderbirds	WHL	37	13	19	32	....	....	....	232	....	....	....	....	....	....	....	....	....	....	....	....	....	....	....	....	....	....
	Swift Current Broncos	WHL	3	0	2	2	....	....	....	14	....	....	....	....	....	....	....	....	....	....	7	2	1	3	37	....	....	....
1992-93	**San Jose Sharks**	**NHL**	13	1	1	2	1	1	2	71	0	0	0	10	10.0	3	0	9	1	–5	....	....	....	....	....	....	....	....
	Kansas City Blades	IHL	36	3	2	5	....	....	....	216	....	....	....	....	....	....	....	....	....	....	6	0	1	1	15	....	....	....
1993-94	Kansas City Blades	IHL	48	5	15	20	....	....	....	320	....	....	....	....	....	....	....	....	....	....	....	....	....	....	....	....	....	....
1994-95	Kansas City Blades	IHL	44	5	13	18	....	....	....	255	....	....	....	....	....	....	....	....	....	....	21	7	10	17	87	....	....	....
	San Jose Sharks	**NHL**	9	1	1	2	2	1	3	29	0	0	0	5	20.0	2	0	2	0	0	....	....	....	....	....	....	....	....
1995-96	**San Jose Sharks**	**NHL**	32	3	6	9	3	5	8	138	0	1	0	33	9.1	13	0	19	6	0	....	....	....	....	....	....	....	....
1996-97	**San Jose Sharks**	**NHL**	44	3	2	5	3	2	5	193	0	0	0	43	7.0	8	0	11	0	–3	....	....	....	....	....	....	....	....
	Kansas City Blades	IHL	6	3	6	9	....	....	....	35	....	....	....	....	....	....	....	....	....	....	....	....	....	....	....	....	....	....
1997-98	**San Jose Sharks**	**NHL**	8	0	0	0	0	0	0	40	0	0	0	4	0.0	1	0	4	0	–3	....	....	....	....	....	....	....	....
	Kansas City Blades	IHL	2	0	1	1	....	....	....	31	....	....	....	....	....	....	....	....	....	....	....	....	....	....	....	....	....	....
	Albany River Rats	AHL	34	4	13	17	....	....	....	185	....	....	....	....	....	....	....	....	....	....	13	2	0	2	55	....	....	....
1998-99	Kansas City Blades	IHL	60	11	16	27	....	....	....	286	....	....	....	....	....	....	....	....	....	....	3	0	1	1	25	....	....	....
99-2000	Kansas City Blades	IHL	77	13	28	41	....	....	....	*341	....	....	....	....	....	....	....	....	....	....	....	....	....	....	....	....	....	....
	NHL Totals		106	8	10	18	9	9	18	471	0	1	0	95	8.4	27	0	45	7		....	....	....	....	....	....	....	....

Traded to **New Jersey** by **San Jose** with Doug Bodger for John MacLean and Ken Sutton, December 7, 1997.

• WOOD, Randy

Randolph B. LW/C – L. 6′, 195 lbs. b: Princeton, NJ, 10/12/1963.

Season	Club	League	GP	G	A	Pts	AG	AA	APts	PIM	PP	SH	GW	S	%	TGF	PGF	TGA	PGA	+/–	GP	G	A	Pts	PIM	PP	SH	GW
1982-83	Yale University	ECAC	26	5	14	19	....	....	....	10	....	....	....	....	....	....	....	....	....	....	....	....	....	....	....	....	....	....
1983-84	Yale University	ECAC	18	7	7	14	....	....	....	10	....	....	....	....	....	....	....	....	....	....	....	....	....	....	....	....	....	....
1984-85	Yale University	ECAC	32	25	28	53	....	....	....	23	....	....	....	....	....	....	....	....	....	....	....	....	....	....	....	....	....	....
1985-86	Yale University	ECAC	31	25	30	55	....	....	....	26	....	....	....	....	....	....	....	....	....	....	....	....	....	....	....	....	....	....
	United States	WEC-A	4	0	0	0	....	....	....	4	....	....	....	....	....	....	....	....	....	....	....	....	....	....	....	....	....	....
1986-87	**New York Islanders**	**NHL**	6	1	0	1	1	0	1	4	0	0	0	4	25.0	1	0	2	0	–1	13	1	3	4	14	0	0	1
	Springfield Indians	AHL	75	23	24	47	....	....	....	57	....	....	....	....	....	....	....	....	....	....	....	....	....	....	....	....	....	....
1987-88	**New York Islanders**	**NHL**	75	22	16	38	19	11	30	80	0	1	2	106	20.8	46	1	57	10	–2	5	1	0	1	6	0	0	0
	Springfield Indians	AHL	1	0	1	1	....	....	....	0	....	....	....	....	....	....	....	....	....	....	....	....	....	....	....	....	....	....
1988-89	**New York Islanders**	**NHL**	77	15	13	28	13	9	22	44	0	0	0	115	13.0	38	0	88	32	–18	....	....	....	....	....	....	....	....
	Springfield Indians	AHL	1	1	1	2	....	....	....	0	....	....	....	....	....	....	....	....	....	....	....	....	....	....	....	....	....	....
	United States	WEC-A	10	1	1	2	....	....	....	6	....	....	....	....	....	....	....	....	....	....	....	....	....	....	....	....	....	....
1989-90	**New York Islanders**	**NHL**	74	24	24	48	21	17	38	39	6	1	3	185	13.0	76	22	84	20	–10	5	1	1	2	4	0	0	0
1990-91	**New York Islanders**	**NHL**	76	24	18	42	22	14	36	45	6	1	3	186	12.9	62	10	78	14	–12	....	....	....	....	....	....	....	....
1991-92	United States	Can-Cup	3	0	2	2	....	....	....	0	....	....	....	....	....	....	....	....	....	....	....	....	....	....	....	....	....	....
	New York Islanders	**NHL**	8	2	2	4	2	2	4	21	0	0	0	30	6.7	6	1	8	0	–3	....	....	....	....	....	....	....	....
	Buffalo Sabres	**NHL**	70	20	16	36	18	12	30	65	7	1	3	185	10.8	63	16	83	27	–9	7	2	1	3	6	0	0	0
1992-93	**Buffalo Sabres**	**NHL**	82	18	25	43	15	17	32	77	3	2	2	176	10.2	67	14	55	8	6	8	1	4	5	4	1	0	0
1993-94	**Buffalo Sabres**	**NHL**	84	22	16	38	20	12	32	71	2	2	5	161	13.7	53	4	54	16	11	6	0	0	0	0	0	0	0
1994-95	**Toronto Maple Leafs**	**NHL**	48	13	11	24	23	16	39	34	1	1	2	125	10.4	43	7	39	10	7	7	2	0	2	6	1	0	1
1995-96	**Toronto Maple Leafs**	**NHL**	46	7	9	16	7	7	14	36	1	0	0	101	6.9	24	1	40	13	–4	....	....	....	....	....	....	....	....
	Dallas Stars	**NHL**	30	1	4	5	1	3	4	26	0	0	0	58	1.7	9	0	30	10	–11	....	....	....	....	....	....	....	....
1996-97	**New York Islanders**	**NHL**	65	6	5	11	6	4	10	61	0	1	2	96	6.3	17	0	40	16	–7	....	....	....	....	....	....	....	....
	NHL Totals		741	175	159	334	168	124	292	603	26	10	22	1528	11.5	505	76	658	176		51	8	9	17	40	2	0	2

ECAC Second All-Star Team (1985) • ECAC First All-Star Team (1986) • NCAA East Second All-Star Team (1986)

Signed as a free agent by **NY Islanders**, September 17, 1986. Traded to **Buffalo** by **NY Islanders** with Pat LaFontaine, Randy Hillier and NY Islanders' 4th round choice (Dean Melanson) in 1992 Entry Draft for Pierre Turgeon, Uwe Krupp, Benoit Hogue and Dave McLlwain, October 25, 1991. Claimed by **Toronto** from **Buffalo** in NHL Waiver Draft, January 18, 1995. Traded to **Dallas** by **Toronto** with Benoit Hogue for Dave Gagner and Dallas' 6th round choice (Dmitriy Yakushin) in 1996 Entry Draft, January 29, 1996. Signed as a free agent by **NY Islanders**, October 2, 1996.

• WOODLEY, Dan

RW – R. 5′11″, 185 lbs. b: Oklahoma City, OK, 12/29/1967. Vancouver's 1st, 7th overall, in 1986.

Season	Club	League	GP	G	A	Pts	AG	AA	APts	PIM	PP	SH	GW	S	%	TGF	PGF	TGA	PGA	+/–	GP	G	A	Pts	PIM	PP	SH	GW
1983-84	Summerland Buckaroos	BCJHL	54	17	34	51	....	....	....	111	....	....	....	....	....	....	....	....	....	....	....	....	....	....	....	....	....	....
	Portland Winter Hawks	WHL	6	1	2	3	....	....	....	2	....	....	....	....	....	....	....	....	....	....	8	1	3	4	4	....	....	....
1984-85	Portland Winter Hawks	WHL	63	21	36	57	....	....	....	108	....	....	....	....	....	....	....	....	....	....	1	0	0	0	0	....	....	....
1985-86	Portland Winter Hawks	WHL	62	45	47	92	....	....	....	100	....	....	....	....	....	....	....	....	....	....	12	0	8	8	31	....	....	....
	Portland Winter Hawks	Mem-Cup	3	0	2	2	....	....	....	15	....	....	....	....	....	....	....	....	....	....	....	....	....	....	....	....	....	....
1986-87	Portland Winter Hawks	WHL	47	30	50	80	....	....	....	81	....	....	....	....	....	....	....	....	....	....	19	*19	17	*36	52	....	....	....
1987-88	**Vancouver Canucks**	**NHL**	5	2	0	2	2	0	2	17	0	0	0	3	66.7	3	1	1	0	1	....	....	....	....	....	....	....	....
	Flint Spirits	IHL	69	29	37	66	....	....	....	104	....	....	....	....	....	....	....	....	....	....	9	1	3	4	26	....	....	....
1988-89	Milwaukee Admirals	IHL	30	9	12	21	....	....	....	48	....	....	....	....	....	....	....	....	....	....	....	....	....	....	....	....	....	....
	Sherbrooke Canadiens	AHL	30	9	16	25	....	....	....	69	....	....	....	....	....	....	....	....	....	....	4	1	6	7	5	....	....	....
1989-90	Sherbrooke Canadiens	AHL	65	18	40	58	....	....	....	144	....	....	....	....	....	....	....	....	....	....	10	1	6	7	58	....	....	....
1990-91	Fredericton Canadiens	AHL	4	0	0	0	....	....	....	4	....	....	....	....	....	....	....	....	....	....	....	....	....	....	....	....	....	....
	Kansas City Blades	IHL	20	6	4	10	....	....	....	30	....	....	....	....	....	....	....	....	....	....	....	....	....	....	....	....	....	....
	Albany Choppers	IHL	31	8	17	25	....	....	....	36	....	....	....	....	....	....	....	....	....	....	....	....	....	....	....	....	....	....
1991-92	Winston-Salem Thunderbirds	ECHL	57	24	42	66	....	....	....	102	....	....	....	....	....	....	....	....	....	....	5	3	3	6	2	....	....	....
1992-93	Flint Bulldogs	ColHL	39	20	36	56	....	....	....	112	....	....	....	....	....	....	....	....	....	....	6	4	7	11	21	....	....	....
1993-94	Muskegon Fury	ColHL	58	43	58	101	....	....	....	217	....	....	....	....	....	....	....	....	....	....	1	0	0	0	0	....	....	....
1994-95	Muskegon Mohawks	ColHL	43	25	26	51	....	....	....	87	....	....	....	....	....	....	....	....	....	....	....	....	....	....	....	....	....	....
	Saginaw Wheels	ColHL	11	11	4	15	....	....	....	18	....	....	....	....	....	....	....	....	....	....	2	1	1	2	24	....	....	....
	NHL Totals		5	2	0	2	2	0	2	17	0	0	0	3	66.7	3	1	1	0		....	....	....	....	....	....	....	....

Traded to **Montreal** by **Vancouver** for Jose Charbonneau, January 25, 1989.

• WOODS, Paul

Paul William "Woodsy" LW – L. 5′10″, 175 lbs. b: Hespeler, Ont., 4/12/1955. Montreal's 5th, 51st overall, in 1975.

Season	Club	League	GP	G	A	Pts	AG	AA	APts	PIM	PP	SH	GW	S	%	TGF	PGF	TGA	PGA	+/–	GP	G	A	Pts	PIM	PP	SH	GW
1972-73	Sault Ste. Marie Greyhounds	OMJHL	60	30	34	64	....	....	....	65	....	....	....	....	....	....	....	....	....	....	....	....	....	....	....	....	....	....
1973-74	Sault Ste. Marie Greyhounds	OMJHL	48	17	32	49	....	....	....	91	....	....	....	....	....	....	....	....	....	....	....	....	....	....	....	....	....	....
1974-75	Sault Ste. Marie Greyhounds	OMJHL	62	38	81	119	....	....	....	116	....	....	....	....	....	....	....	....	....	....	....	....	....	....	....	....	....	....
1975-76	Nova Scotia Voyageurs	AHL	67	17	21	38	....	....	....	38	....	....	....	....	....	....	....	....	....	....	9	2	1	3	0	....	....	....
1976-77	Nova Scotia Voyageurs	AHL	45	20	18	38	....	....	....	51	....	....	....	....	....	....	....	....	....	....	12	1	3	4	6	....	....	....
1977-78	**Detroit Red Wings**	**NHL**	80	19	23	42	17	18	35	52	3	2	3	107	17.8	83	13	83	31	18	7	0	5	5	4	0	0	0
1978-79	**Detroit Red Wings**	**NHL**	80	14	23	37	12	17	29	59	1	3	1	127	11.0	60	12	110	36	–26	....	....	....	....	....	....	....	....
	Canada	WEC-A	8	0	0	0	....	....	....	2	....	....	....	....	....	....	....	....	....	....	....	....	....	....	....	....	....	....
1979-80	**Detroit Red Wings**	**NHL**	79	6	20	26	5	15	20	24	0	0	0	114	5.3	46	6	89	30	–19	....	....	....	....	....	....	....	....
1980-81	**Detroit Red Wings**	**NHL**	67	8	16	24	6	11	17	45	1	1	1	74	10.8	42	4	79	31	–10	....	....	....	....	....	....	....	....
1981-82	**Detroit Red Wings**	**NHL**	75	10	17	27	8	11	19	48	0	1	1	68	14.7	48	1	83	31	–5	....	....	....	....	....	....	....	....

			REGULAR SEASON																		PLAYOFFS							
Season	Club	League	GP	G	A	Pts	AG	AA	APts	PIM	PP	SH	GW	S	%	TGF	PGF	TGA	PGA	+/–	GP	G	A	Pts	PIM	PP	SH	GW
1982-83	**Detroit Red Wings**	**NHL**	63	13	20	33	11	14	25	30	0	1	3	82	15.9	44	0	67	21	–2	....	....	....	....	....	....	....	....
1983-84	**Detroit Red Wings**	**NHL**	57	2	5	7	2	3	5	18	0	0	0	33	6.1	19	1	50	16	–16	....	....	....	....	....	....	....	....
1984-85	Adirondack Red Wings	AHL	26	2	11	13	....	....	....	8	....	....	....	....	....	....	....	....	....	....	....	....	....	....	....	....	....	....
	NHL Totals		**501**	**72**	**124**	**196**	**61**	**89**	**150**	**276**	**5**	**8**	**9**	**605**	**11.9**	**342**	**37**	**561**	**196**		**7**	**0**	**5**	**5**	**4**	**0**	**0**	**0**

Claimed by **Detroit** from **Montreal** in Waiver Draft, October 10, 1977.

• WOOLLEY, Jason

Jason Douglas D – L. 6'1", 188 lbs. b: Toronto, Ont., 7/27/1969. Washington's 4th, 61st overall, in 1989.

Season	Club	League	GP	G	A	Pts	AG	AA	APts	PIM	PP	SH	GW	S	%	TGF	PGF	TGA	PGA	+/–	GP	G	A	Pts	PIM	PP	SH	GW
1986-87	St. Michael's Buzzers	OJHL-B	35	13	22	35	....	....	....	40	....	....	....	....	....	....	....	....	....	....	....	....	....	....	....	....	....	....
1987-88	St. Michael's Buzzers	OJHL-B	31	19	37	56	....	....	....	22	....	....	....	....	....	....	....	....	....	....	....	....	....	....	....	....	....	....
1988-89	Michigan State Spartans	CCHA	47	12	25	37	....	....	....	26	....	....	....	....	....	....	....	....	....	....	....	....	....	....	....	....	....	....
1989-90	Michigan State Spartans	CCHA	45	10	38	48	....	....	....	26	....	....	....	....	....	....	....	....	....	....	....	....	....	....	....	....	....	....
1990-91	Michigan State Spartans	CCHA	40	15	44	59	....	....	....	24	....	....	....	....	....	....	....	....	....	....	....	....	....	....	....	....	....	....
1991-92	Canada	Nat-Team	60	14	30	44	....	....	....	36	....	....	....	....	....	....	....	....	....	....	....	....	....	....	....	....	....	....
	Canada	Olympics	8	0	5	5	....	....	....	4	....	....	....	....	....	....	....	....	....	....	....	....	....	....	....	....	....	....
	Washington Capitals	**NHL**	1	0	0	0	0	0	0	0	0	0	0	2	0.0	1	0	0	0	1	....	....	....	....	....	....	....	....
	Baltimore Skipjacks	AHL	15	1	10	11	....	....	....	6	....	....	....	....	....	....	....	....	....	....	....	....	....	....	....	....	....	....
	Canada	WC-A	6	1	2	3	....	....	....	2	....	....	....	....	....	....	....	....	....	....	....	....	....	....	....	....	....	....
1992-93	**Washington Capitals**	**NHL**	26	0	2	2	0	1	1	10	0	0	0	11	0.0	18	3	13	1	3	....	....	....	....	....	....	....	....
	Baltimore Skipjacks	AHL	29	14	27	41	....	....	....	22	....	....	....	....	....	....	....	....	....	....	1	0	2	2	0	....	....	....
1993-94	**Washington Capitals**	**NHL**	10	1	2	3	1	2	3	4	0	0	0	15	6.7	9	3	4	0	2	4	1	0	1	4	0	0	1
	Portland Pirates	AHL	41	12	29	41	....	....	....	14	....	....	....	....	....	....	....	....	....	....	9	2	2	4	4	....	....	....
1994-95	Detroit Vipers	IHL	48	8	28	36	....	....	....	38	....	....	....	....	....	....	....	....	....	....	....	....	....	....	....	....	....	....
	Florida Panthers	**NHL**	34	4	9	13	7	13	20	18	1	0	0	76	5.3	31	11	21	0	–1	....	....	....	....	....	....	....	....
1995-96	**Florida Panthers**	**NHL**	52	6	28	34	6	23	29	32	3	0	0	98	6.1	72	44	40	3	–9	13	2	6	8	14	1	0	1
1996-97	**Florida Panthers**	**NHL**	3	0	0	0	0	0	0	2	0	0	0	7	0.0	3	1	1	0	1	....	....	....	....	....	....	....	....
	Pittsburgh Penguins	**NHL**	57	6	30	36	6	27	33	28	2	0	1	79	7.6	82	29	51	1	3	5	0	3	3	0	0	0	0
1997-98	**Buffalo Sabres**	**NHL**	71	9	26	35	11	25	36	35	3	0	2	129	7.0	72	34	30	0	8	15	2	9	11	12	1	0	1
1998-99	**Buffalo Sabres**	**NHL**	80	10	33	43	12	32	44	62	4	0	2	154	6.5	91	37	38	0	16	21	4	11	15	10	2	0	1
99-2000	**Buffalo Sabres**	**NHL**	74	8	25	33	9	23	32	52	2	0	2	113	7.1	81	30	39	2	14	5	0	2	2	2	0	0	0
	NHL Totals		**408**	**44**	**155**	**199**	**52**	**146**	**198**	**243**	**15**	**0**	**7**	**684**	**6.4**	**460**	**192**	**237**	**7**		**63**	**9**	**31**	**40**	**42**	**4**	**0**	**4**

CCHA First All-Star Team (1991) • NCAA West First All-American Team (1991)

Signed as a free agent by **Florida**, February 15, 1995. Traded to **Pittsburgh** by **Florida** with Stu Barnes for Chris Wells, November 19, 1996. Traded to **Buffalo** by **Pittsburgh** for Buffalo's 5th round choice (Robert Scuderi) in 1998 Entry Draft, September 24, 1997.

• WORRELL, Peter

LW – L. 6'6", 235 lbs. b: Pierrefonds, Que., 8/18/1977. Florida's 7th, 166th overall, in 1995.

Season	Club	League	GP	G	A	Pts	AG	AA	APts	PIM	PP	SH	GW	S	%	TGF	PGF	TGA	PGA	+/–	GP	G	A	Pts	PIM	PP	SH	GW
1994-95	Hull Olympiques	QMJHL	56	1	8	9	....	....	....	243	....	....	....	....	....	....	....	....	....	....	21	0	1	1	91	....	....	....
	Hull Olympiques	Mem-Cup	3	0	0	0	....	....	....	9	....	....	....	....	....	....	....	....	....	....	....	....	....	....	....	....	....	....
1995-96	Hull Olympiques	QMJHL	63	23	36	59	....	....	....	464	....	....	....	....	....	....	....	....	....	....	18	11	8	19	81	....	....	....
1996-97	Hull Olympiques	QMJHL	62	17	46	63	....	....	....	437	....	....	....	....	....	....	....	....	....	....	14	3	13	16	83	....	....	....
	Hull Olympiques	Mem-Cup	4	1	3	4	....	....	....	17	....	....	....	....	....	....	....	....	....	....	....	....	....	....	....	....	....	....
1997-98	**Florida Panthers**	**NHL**	19	0	0	0	0	0	0	153	0	0	0	15	0.0	0	0	4	0	–4	....	....	....	....	....	....	....	....
	Beast of New Haven	AHL	50	15	12	27	....	....	....	309	....	....	....	....	....	....	....	....	....	....	1	0	1	1	6	....	....	....
1998-99	**Florida Panthers**	**NHL**	62	4	5	9	5	5	10	258	0	0	2	50	8.0	13	1	12	0	0	....	....	....	....	....	....	....	....
	Beast of New Haven	AHL	10	3	1	4	....	....	....	65	....	....	....	....	....	....	....	....	....	....	....	....	....	....	....	....	....	....
99-2000	**Florida Panthers**	**NHL**	48	3	6	9	3	6	9	169	2	0	1	45	6.7	19	8	18	0	–7	4	1	0	1	8	0	0	0
	NHL Totals		**129**	**7**	**11**	**18**	**8**	**11**	**19**	**580**	**2**	**0**	**3**	**110**	**6.4**	**32**	**9**	**34**	**0**		**4**	**1**	**0**	**1**	**8**	**0**	**0**	**0**

• WORTMAN, Kevin

D – R. 6', 200 lbs. b: Saugus, MA, 2/22/1969. Calgary's 9th, 168th overall, in 1989.

Season	Club	League	GP	G	A	Pts	AG	AA	APts	PIM	PP	SH	GW	S	%	TGF	PGF	TGA	PGA	+/–	GP	G	A	Pts	PIM	PP	SH	GW
1987-88	Mass Bay Chiefs	MBAHL	STATISTICS NOT AVAILABLE																									
1988-89	USA International University	ECAC-2	STATISTICS NOT AVAILABLE																									
1989-90	USA International University	ECAC-2	STATISTICS NOT AVAILABLE																									
1990-91	USA International University	ECAC-2	28	21	25	46	....	....	....	6	....	....	....	....	....	....	....	....	....	....	....	....	....	....	....	....	....	....
1991-92	Salt Lake Golden Eagles	IHL	82	12	34	46	....	....	....	34	....	....	....	....	....	....	....	....	....	....	5	1	0	1	0	....	....	....
1992-93	Salt Lake Golden Eagles	IHL	82	13	50	63	....	....	....	24	....	....	....	....	....	....	....	....	....	....	....	....	....	....	....	....	....	....
1993-94	**Calgary Flames**	**NHL**	5	0	0	0	0	0	0	2	0	0	0	2	0.0	5	1	3	0	1	....	....	....	....	....	....	....	....
	Saint John Flames	AHL	72	17	32	49	....	....	....	32	....	....	....	....	....	....	....	....	....	....	7	1	5	6	16	....	....	....
1994-95	Kansas City Blades	IHL	80	6	28	34	....	....	....	22	....	....	....	....	....	....	....	....	....	....	21	1	1	2	4	....	....	....
1995-96	Fort Wayne Komets	IHL	82	12	21	33	....	....	....	26	....	....	....	....	....	....	....	....	....	....	5	2	4	6	4	....	....	....
1996-97	JyP-HT Jyvaskyla	Finland	49	8	15	23	....	....	....	26	....	....	....	....	....	....	....	....	....	....	4	1	2	3	0	....	....	....
1997-98	JyP Jyvaskyla	Finland	48	10	16	26	....	....	....	28	....	....	....	....	....	....	....	....	....	....	....	....	....	....	....	....	....	....
1998-99	JyP Jyvaskyla	Finland	53	13	13	26	....	....	....	65	....	....	....	....	....	....	....	....	....	....	3	1	0	1	4	....	....	....
99-2000	Schwenningen Wild Wings	Germany	67	4	14	18	....	....	....	45	....	....	....	....	....	....	....	....	....	....	....	....	....	....	....	....	....	....
	NHL Totals		**5**	**0**	**0**	**0**	**0**	**0**	**0**	**2**	**0**	**0**	**0**	**2**	**0.0**	**5**	**1**	**3**	**0**		....	....	....	....	....	....	....	....

IHL Second All-Star Team (1993)

Signed as a free agent by **San Jose**, August 25, 1994.

• WOTTON, Mark

Mark A. D – L. 6'1", 195 lbs. b: Foxwarren, Man., 11/16/1973. Vancouver's 11th, 237th overall, in 1992.

Season	Club	League	GP	G	A	Pts	AG	AA	APts	PIM	PP	SH	GW	S	%	TGF	PGF	TGA	PGA	+/–	GP	G	A	Pts	PIM	PP	SH	GW
1988-89	Foxwarren Blades	MAHA	60	10	30	40	....	....	....	70	....	....	....	....	....	....	....	....	....	....	....	....	....	....	....	....	....	....
1989-90	Saskatoon Blades	WHL	51	2	3	5	....	....	....	31	....	....	....	....	....	....	....	....	....	....	7	1	1	2	15	....	....	....
1990-91	Saskatoon Blades	WHL	45	4	11	15	....	....	....	37	....	....	....	....	....	....	....	....	....	....	....	....	....	....	....	....	....	....
1991-92	Saskatoon Blades	WHL	64	11	25	36	....	....	....	62	....	....	....	....	....	....	....	....	....	....	21	2	6	8	22	....	....	....
1992-93	Saskatoon Blades	WHL	71	15	51	66	....	....	....	90	....	....	....	....	....	....	....	....	....	....	9	6	5	11	18	....	....	....
1993-94	Saskatoon Blades	WHL	65	12	34	46	....	....	....	108	....	....	....	....	....	....	....	....	....	....	16	3	12	15	32	....	....	....
1994-95	Syracuse Crunch	AHL	75	12	29	41	....	....	....	50	....	....	....	....	....	....	....	....	....	....	....	....	....	....	....	....	....	....
	Vancouver Canucks	**NHL**	1	0	0	0	0	0	0	0	0	0	0	2	0.0	1	0	0	0	1	5	0	0	0	4	0	0	0
1995-96	Syracuse Crunch	AHL	80	10	35	45	....	....	....	96	....	....	....	....	....	....	....	....	....	....	15	1	12	13	20	....	....	....
1996-97	**Vancouver Canucks**	**NHL**	36	3	6	9	3	5	8	19	0	1	0	41	7.3	32	0	34	10	8	....	....	....	....	....	....	....	....
	Syracuse Crunch	AHL	27	2	8	10	....	....	....	25	....	....	....	....	....	....	....	....	....	....	2	0	0	0	4	....	....	....
1997-98	**Vancouver Canucks**	**NHL**	5	0	0	0	0	0	0	6	0	0	0	3	0.0	2	0	4	0	–2	....	....	....	....	....	....	....	....
	Syracuse Crunch	AHL	56	12	21	33	....	....	....	80	....	....	....	....	....	....	....	....	....	....	5	0	0	0	12	....	....	....
1998-99	Syracuse Crunch	AHL	72	4	31	35	....	....	....	74	....	....	....	....	....	....	....	....	....	....	....	....	....	....	....	....	....	....
99-2000	Michigan K-Wings	IHL	70	3	7	10	....	....	....	72	....	....	....	....	....	....	....	....	....	....	....	....	....	....	....	....	....	....
	NHL Totals		**42**	**3**	**6**	**9**	**3**	**5**	**8**	**25**	**0**	**1**	**0**	**46**	**6.5**	**35**	**0**	**38**	**10**		**5**	**0**	**0**	**0**	**4**	**0**	**0**	**0**

WHL East Second All-Star Team (1994)

Signed as a free agent by **Dallas**, July 19, 1999.

• WOYTOWICH, Bob

Robert Ivan "Augie" D – R. 6', 185 lbs. b: Winnipeg, Man., 8/18/1941 d: 7/30/1988.

Season	Club	League	GP	G	A	Pts	AG	AA	APts	PIM	PP	SH	GW	S	%	TGF	PGF	TGA	PGA	+/–	GP	G	A	Pts	PIM	PP	SH	GW
1958-59	Transcona Rangers	MJHL	28	7	3	10	....	....	....	34	....	....	....	....	....	....	....	....	....	....	4	0	1	1	4	....	....	....
1959-60	Winnipeg Rangers	MJHL	27	7	16	23	....	....	....	68	....	....	....	....	....	....	....	....	....	....	12	6	2	8	*34	....	....	....
1960-61	Winnipeg Rangers	MJHL	30	8	21	29	....	....	....	82	....	....	....	....	....	....	....	....	....	....	9	3	7	10	6	....	....	....
	Seattle Totems	WHL	2	0	0	0	....	....	....	0	....	....	....	....	....	....	....	....	....	....	....	....	....	....	....	....	....	....
1961-62	Winnipeg Rangers	MJHL	40	9	18	27	....	....	....	65	....	....	....	....	....	....	....	....	....	....	....	....	....	....	....	....	....	....
	Brandon Wheat Kings	Mem-Cup	7	1	3	4	....	....	....	12	....	....	....	....	....	....	....	....	....	....	....	....	....	....	....	....	....	....
1962-63	Sudbury Wolves	EPHL	71	17	27	44	....	....	....	69	....	....	....	....	....	....	....	....	....	....	8	0	3	3	8	....	....	....
1963-64	St. Paul Rangers	CPHL	68	9	31	40	....	....	....	101	....	....	....	....	....	....	....	....	....	....	11	2	4	6	8	....	....	....
1964-65	**Boston Bruins**	**NHL**	21	2	10	12	2	10	12	16	....	....	....	....	....	....	....	....	....	....	....	....	....	....	....	....	....	....
	Hershey Bears	AHL	48	5	21	26	....	....	....	56	....	....	....	....	....	....	....	....	....	....	....	....	....	....	....	....	....	....

Season	Club	League	GP	G	A	Pts	AG	AA	APts	PIM	PP	SH	GW	S	%	TGF	PGF	TGA	PGA	+/–	GP	G	A	Pts	PIM	PP	SH	GW
			REGULAR SEASON																		PLAYOFFS							
1965-66	**Boston Bruins**	**NHL**	**68**	**2**	**17**	**19**	**2**	**16**	**18**	**75**	....	....	....	....	....	....	....	....	....	....	....	....	....	....	....	....	....	....
1966-67	**Boston Bruins**	**NHL**	**64**	**2**	**7**	**9**	**2**	**7**	**9**	**43**	....	....	....	....	....	....	....	....	....	....	....	....	....	....	....	....	....	....
1967-68	**Minnesota North Stars**	**NHL**	**66**	**4**	**17**	**21**	**5**	**17**	**22**	**63**	**2**	**0**	**0**	**86**	**4.7**	**72**	**18**	**81**	**4**	**–23**	**14**	**0**	**1**	**1**	**18**	**0**	**0**	**0**
1968-69	**Pittsburgh Penguins**	**NHL**	**71**	**9**	**20**	**29**	**9**	**18**	**27**	**62**	**1**	**2**	**0**	**127**	**7.1**	**88**	**28**	**101**	**15**	**–26**	....	....	....	....	....	....	....	....
1969-70	**Pittsburgh Penguins**	**NHL**	**68**	**8**	**25**	**33**	**9**	**23**	**32**	**49**	**5**	**0**	**0**	**155**	**5.2**	**85**	**31**	**89**	**23**	**–12**	**10**	**1**	**2**	**3**	**2**	**0**	**0**	**0**
1970-71	**Pittsburgh Penguins**	**NHL**	**78**	**4**	**22**	**26**	**4**	**18**	**22**	**30**	**2**	**0**	**0**	**149**	**2.7**	**90**	**24**	**77**	**19**	**8**	....	....	....	....	....	....	....	....
1971-72	**Pittsburgh Penguins**	**NHL**	**31**	**1**	**4**	**5**	**1**	**3**	**4**	**8**	**1**	**0**	**0**	**36**	**2.8**	**19**	**7**	**38**	**7**	**–19**	....	....	....	....	....	....	....	....
	Los Angeles Kings	**NHL**	**36**	**0**	**4**	**4**	**0**	**3**	**3**	**6**	**0**	**0**	**0**	**19**	**0.0**	**31**	**9**	**40**	**10**	**–8**	....	....	....	....	....	....	....	....
1972-73	Winnipeg Jets	WHA	62	2	4	6	....	....	....	47	....	....	....	....	....	....	....	....	....	....	14	1	1	2	4	....	....	....
1973-74	Winnipeg Jets	WHA	72	6	28	34	....	....	....	43	....	....	....	....	....	....	....	....	....	....	4	0	0	0	0	....	....	....
1974-75	Winnipeg Jets	WHA	24	0	4	4	....	....	....	8	....	....	....	....	....	....	....	....	....	....	....	....	....	....	....	....	....	....
	Indianapolis Racers	WHA	42	0	8	8	....	....	....	28	....	....	....	....	....	....	....	....	....	....	....	....	....	....	....	....	....	....
1975-76	Indianapolis Racers	WHA	42	1	7	8	....	....	....	14	....	....	....	....	....	....	....	....	....	....	....	....	....	....	....	....	....	....
1976-77	Mohawk Valley Comets	NAHL	37	0	10	10	....	....	....	4	....	....	....	....	....	....	....	....	....	....	....	....	....	....	....	....	....	....
1977-78	Steinbach Stallions	CCSHL	4	0	1	1	....	....	....	7	....	....	....	....	....	....	....	....	....	....	....	....	....	....	....	....	....	....
	NHL Totals		**503**	**32**	**126**	**158**	**34**	**115**	**149**	**352**	....	....	....	....	....	....	....	....	....	....	**24**	**1**	**3**	**4**	**20**	....	....	....
	Other Major League Totals		242	9	51	60	....	....	....	140	....	....	....	....	....	....	....	....	....	....	18	1	1	2	4	....	....	....

CPHL First All-Star Team (1964) • Played in NHL All-Star Game (1970)

Claimed by **Boston** from **NY Rangers** in Intra-League Draft, June 10, 1964. Claimed by **Minnesota** from **Boston** in Expansion Draft, June 6, 1967. Traded to **Pittsburgh** by **Minnesota** for Pittsburgh's 1st round choice (later traded to Montreal - Montreal selected Dave Gardner) in 1972 Amateur Draft, October 1, 1968. Traded to **LA Kings** by **Pittsburgh** for Al McDonough, January 11, 1972. Selected by **Winnipeg** (WHA) in 1972 WHA General Player Draft, February 12, 1972. Traded to **Indianapolis** (WHA) by **Winnipeg** (WHA) for cash, December, 1974.

• WREN, Bob

C – L. 5'10", 185 lbs. b: Preston, Ont., 9/16/1974. Los Angeles' 3rd, 94th overall, in 1993.

Season	Club	League	GP	G	A	Pts	AG	AA	APts	PIM	PP	SH	GW	S	%	TGF	PGF	TGA	PGA	+/–	GP	G	A	Pts	PIM	PP	SH	GW
1989-90	Guelph Jr. B's	OJHL-B	48	24	36	60	....	....	....	82	....	....	....	....	....	....	....	....	....	....	....	....	....	....	....	....	....	....
1990-91	Guelph Jr. B's	OJHL-B	18	17	13	30	....	....	....	51	....	....	....	....	....	....	....	....	....	....	....	....	....	....	....	....	....	....
	Kingston Voyageurs	OJHL	14	10	15	25	....	....	....	34	....	....	....	....	....	....	....	....	....	....	....	....	....	....	....	....	....	....
1991-92	Detroit Ambassadors	OHL	62	13	36	49	....	....	....	58	....	....	....	....	....	....	....	....	....	....	7	3	4	7	19	....	....	....
1992-93	Detroit Jr. Red Wings	OHL	63	57	88	145	....	....	....	91	....	....	....	....	....	....	....	....	....	....	15	4	11	15	20	....	....	....
1993-94	Detroit Jr. Red Wings	OHL	57	45	64	109	....	....	....	81	....	....	....	....	....	....	....	....	....	....	17	12	18	30	20	....	....	....
1994-95	Springfield Falcons	AHL	61	16	15	31	....	....	....	118	....	....	....	....	....	....	....	....	....	....	....	....	....	....	....	....	....	....
	Richmond Renegades	ECHL	2	0	1	1	....	....	....	0	....	....	....	....	....	....	....	....	....	....	....	....	....	....	....	....	....	....
1995-96	Detroit Vipers	IHL	1	0	0	0	....	....	....	0	....	....	....	....	....	....	....	....	....	....	....	....	....	....	....	....	....	....
	Knoxville Cherokees	ECHL	50	21	35	56	....	....	....	257	....	....	....	....	....	....	....	....	....	....	8	4	11	15	32	....	....	....
1996-97	Baltimore Bandits	AHL	72	23	36	59	....	....	....	97	....	....	....	....	....	....	....	....	....	....	3	1	1	2	0	....	....	....
1997-98	**Mighty Ducks of Anaheim**	**NHL**	**3**	**0**	**0**	**0**	**0**	**0**	**0**	**0**	**0**	**0**	**0**	**4**	**0.0**	**1**	**0**	**1**	**0**	**0**	....	....	....	....	....	....	....	....
	Cincinnati Mighty Ducks	AHL	77	*42	58	100	....	....	....	151	....	....	....	....	....	....	....	....	....	....	....	....	....	....	....	....	....	....
1998-99	Cincinnati Mighty Ducks	AHL	73	27	43	70	....	....	....	102	....	....	....	....	....	....	....	....	....	....	3	1	2	3	8	....	....	....
99-2000	Cincinnati Mighty Ducks	AHL	57	24	38	62	....	....	....	61	....	....	....	....	....	....	....	....	....	....	....	....	....	....	....	....	....	....
	NHL Totals		**3**	**0**	**0**	**0**	**0**	**0**	**0**	**0**	**0**	**0**	**0**	**4**	**0.0**	**1**	**0**	**1**	**0**		....	....	....	....	....	....	....	....

OHL Second All-Star Team (1993, 1994)

Signed as a free agent by **Hartford**, September 6, 1994. Signed as a free agent by **Anaheim**, August 1, 1997.

• WRIGHT, Jamie

LW – L. 6', 195 lbs. b: Kitchener, Ont., 5/13/1976. Dallas' 3rd, 98th overall, in 1994.

Season	Club	League	GP	G	A	Pts	AG	AA	APts	PIM	PP	SH	GW	S	%	TGF	PGF	TGA	PGA	+/–	GP	G	A	Pts	PIM	PP	SH	GW
1991-92	Elmira Sugar Kings	OJHL-B	44	17	11	28	....	....	....	46	....	....	....	....	....	....	....	....	....	....	....	....	....	....	....	....	....	....
1992-93	Elmira Sugar Kings	OJHL-B	47	22	32	54	....	....	....	52	....	....	....	....	....	....	....	....	....	....	....	....	....	....	....	....	....	....
1993-94	Guelph Storm	OHL	65	17	15	32	....	....	....	34	....	....	....	....	....	....	....	....	....	....	8	2	1	3	10	....	....	....
1994-95	Guelph Storm	OHL	65	43	39	82	....	....	....	36	....	....	....	....	....	....	....	....	....	....	14	6	8	14	6	....	....	....
1995-96	Guelph Storm	OHL	55	30	36	66	....	....	....	45	....	....	....	....	....	....	....	....	....	....	16	10	12	22	35	....	....	....
	Canada	WJC-A	6	1	2	3	....	....	....	2	....	....	....	....	....	....	....	....	....	....	....	....	....	....	....	....	....	....
1996-97	Michigan K-Wings	IHL	60	6	8	14	....	....	....	34	....	....	....	....	....	....	....	....	....	....	1	0	0	0	0	....	....	....
1997-98	**Dallas Stars**	**NHL**	**21**	**4**	**2**	**6**	**5**	**2**	**7**	**2**	**0**	**0**	**2**	**15**	**26.7**	**11**	**0**	**3**	**0**	**8**	**5**	**0**	**0**	**0**	**0**	**0**	**0**	**0**
	Michigan K-Wings	IHL	53	15	11	26	....	....	....	31	....	....	....	....	....	....	....	....	....	....	....	....	....	....	....	....	....	....
1998-99	**Dallas Stars**	**NHL**	**11**	**0**	**0**	**0**	**0**	**0**	**0**	**0**	**0**	**0**	**0**	**10**	**0.0**	**2**	**0**	**5**	**0**	**–3**	....	....	....	....	....	....	....	....
	Michigan K-Wings	IHL	64	16	15	31	....	....	....	92	....	....	....	....	....	....	....	....	....	....	2	0	0	0	2	....	....	....
99-2000	**Dallas Stars**	**NHL**	**23**	**1**	**4**	**5**	**1**	**4**	**5**	**16**	**0**	**0**	**0**	**15**	**6.7**	**7**	**0**	**3**	**0**	**4**	....	....	....	....	....	....	....	....
	Michigan K-Wings	IHL	49	12	4	16	....	....	....	64	....	....	....	....	....	....	....	....	....	....	....	....	....	....	....	....	....	....
	NHL Totals		**55**	**5**	**6**	**11**	**6**	**6**	**12**	**18**	**0**	**0**	**2**	**40**	**12.5**	**20**	**0**	**11**	**0**		**5**	**0**	**0**	**0**	**0**	**0**	**0**	**0**

• WRIGHT, John

John Gilbert Brereton C – R. 5'11", 175 lbs. b: Toronto, Ont., 11/9/1948. Toronto's 1st, 4th overall, in 1966.

Season	Club	League	GP	G	A	Pts	AG	AA	APts	PIM	PP	SH	GW	S	%	TGF	PGF	TGA	PGA	+/–	GP	G	A	Pts	PIM	PP	SH	GW
1965-66	York Steel	OHA-B	36	26	18	44	....	....	....	....	....	....	....	....	....	....	....	....	....	....	....	....	....	....	....	....	....	....
	Toronto Marlboros	OHA-Jr.	1	1	0	1	....	....	....	2	....	....	....	....	....	....	....	....	....	....	....	....	....	....	....	....	....	....
1966-67	Toronto Marlboros	OHA-Jr.	48	9	27	36	....	....	....	18	....	....	....	....	....	....	....	....	....	....	17	0	4	4	6	....	....	....
	Toronto Marlboros	Mem-Cup	9	2	3	5	....	....	....	2	....	....	....	....	....	....	....	....	....	....	....	....	....	....	....	....	....	....
1967-68	Toronto Marlboros	OHA-Jr.	54	22	42	64	....	....	....	31	....	....	....	....	....	....	....	....	....	....	5	1	3	4	2	....	....	....
1968-69	University of Toronto	OUAA	15	18	19	37	....	....	....	....	....	....	....	....	....	....	....	....	....	....	....	....	....	....	....	....	....	....
1969-70	University of Toronto	OUAA	15	21	19	40	....	....	....	....	....	....	....	....	....	....	....	....	....	....	....	....	....	....	....	....	....	....
1970-71	University of Toronto	OUAA	15	11	13	24	....	....	....	18	....	....	....	....	....	....	....	....	....	....	16	21	10	31	....	....	....	....
1971-72	University of Toronto	OUAA	38	26	41	67	....	....	....	....	....	....	....	....	....	....	....	....	....	....	....	....	....	....	....	....	....	....
1972-73	**Vancouver Canucks**	**NHL**	**71**	**10**	**27**	**37**	**9**	**21**	**30**	**32**	**0**	**0**	**1**	**121**	**8.3**	**47**	**2**	**90**	**29**	**–16**	....	....	....	....	....	....	....	....
1973-74	**Vancouver Canucks**	**NHL**	**20**	**3**	**3**	**6**	**3**	**2**	**5**	**11**	**1**	**0**	**0**	**24**	**12.5**	**8**	**2**	**10**	**2**	**–2**	....	....	....	....	....	....	....	....
	St. Louis Blues	**NHL**	**32**	**3**	**6**	**9**	**3**	**5**	**8**	**22**	**0**	**0**	**0**	**43**	**7.0**	**11**	**0**	**14**	**2**	**–1**	....	....	....	....	....	....	....	....
1974-75	**Kansas City Scouts**	**NHL**	**4**	**0**	**0**	**0**	**0**	**0**	**0**	**2**	**0**	**0**	**0**	**5**	**0.0**	**0**	**0**	**3**	**0**	**–3**	....	....	....	....	....	....	....	....
	Providence Reds	AHL	68	30	40	70	....	....	....	47	....	....	....	....	....	....	....	....	....	....	6	0	0	0	4	....	....	....
	NHL Totals		**127**	**16**	**36**	**52**	**15**	**28**	**43**	**67**	**1**	**0**	**1**	**193**	**8.3**	**66**	**4**	**117**	**33**		....	....	....	....	....	....	....	....

OQAA First All-Star Team (1969) • OUAA First All-Star Team (1972)

Claimed by **Vancouver** (WHL) from **Toronto** in Reverse Draft, June, 1970. NHL rights transferred to **Vancouver** when owners of **Vancouver** (WHL) club awarded NHL expansion team, May 20, 1970. Traded to **St. Louis** by **Vancouver** for Mike Lampman, December 10, 1973. Claimed by **Kansas City** from **St. Louis** in Expansion Draft, June, 1974.

• WRIGHT, Keith

Keith Edward LW – L. 6', 180 lbs. b: Aurora, Ont., 4/13/1944.

Season	Club	League	GP	G	A	Pts	AG	AA	APts	PIM	PP	SH	GW	S	%	TGF	PGF	TGA	PGA	+/–	GP	G	A	Pts	PIM	PP	SH	GW
1960-61	Peterborough Petes	OHA-Jr.	48	5	10	15	....	....	....	50	....	....	....	....	....	....	....	....	....	....	5	0	1	1	2	....	....	....
1961-62	Peterborough Petes	OHA-Jr.	50	13	22	35	....	....	....	67	....	....	....	....	....	....	....	....	....	....	....	....	....	....	....	....	....	....
1962-63	Peterborough Petes	OHA-Jr.	50	21	23	44	....	....	....	59	....	....	....	....	....	....	....	....	....	....	6	0	2	2	0	....	....	....
1963-64	Peterborough Petes	OHA-Jr.	5	2	3	5	....	....	....	6	....	....	....	....	....	....	....	....	....	....	3	1	0	1	4	....	....	....
1964-65	Omaha Knights	CPHL	55	21	14	35	....	....	....	49	....	....	....	....	....	....	....	....	....	....	....	....	....	....	....	....	....	....
1965-66	Oklahoma City Blazers	CPHL	68	16	22	38	....	....	....	66	....	....	....	....	....	....	....	....	....	....	9	2	3	5	7	....	....	....
1966-67	Oklahoma City Blazers	CPHL	10	0	3	3	....	....	....	2	....	....	....	....	....	....	....	....	....	....	....	....	....	....	....	....	....	....
	California Seals	WHL	36	2	17	19	....	....	....	19	....	....	....	....	....	....	....	....	....	....	5	0	1	1	0	....	....	....
1967-68	**Philadelphia Flyers**	**NHL**	**1**	**0**	**0**	**0**	**0**	**0**	**0**	**0**	**0**	**0**	**0**	**1**	**0.0**	**1**	**0**	**0**	**0**	**1**	....	....	....	....	....	....	....	....
	Quebec Aces	AHL	72	20	23	43	....	....	....	42	....	....	....	....	....	....	....	....	....	....	15	6	6	12	4	....	....	....
1968-69			OUT OF HOCKEY – RETIRED																									
1969-70			OUT OF HOCKEY – RETIRED																									

			REGULAR SEASON																		PLAYOFFS							
Season	Club	League	GP	G	A	Pts	AG	AA	APts	PIM	PP	SH	GW	S	%	TGF	PGF	TGA	PGA	+/-	GP	G	A	Pts	PIM	PP	SH	GW
1970-71	Quebec Aces	AHL	39	0	14	14	....	....	....	22	....	....	....	....	....	....	....	....	....	....	....	....	....	....	....	....	....	....
	Oklahoma City Blazers	CHL	14	1	2	3	....	....	....	2	....	....	....	....	....	....	....	....	....	....	5	0	0	0	0	....	....	....
1971-72			OUT OF HOCKEY – RETIRED																									
1972-73	Orillia Terriers	OHA-Sr.	37	13	20	33				52	....	....	....	....	....	....	....	....	....	....	....	....	....	....	....	....	....	....
	NHL Totals		**1**	**0**	**0**	**0**	**0**	**0**	**0**	**0**	**0**	**0**	**0**	**1**	**0.0**	**1**	**0**	**0**	**0**		....	....	....	....	....	....	....	....

Claimed by **Omaha** (CPHL) from **Montreal** in Reverse Draft, June 10, 1964. Claimed by **NY Rangers** from **Omaha** (CPHL) in Intra-League Draft, June 8, 1965. Claimed on waivers by **Boston** from **NY Rangers** June 9, 1965. Claimed by **Philadelphia** from **Boston** in Expansion Draft, June 6, 1967. Traded to **Quebec** (AHL) by **Philadelphia** for cash, December, 1968.

• WRIGHT, Larry

Larry Dale C – L. 6'2", 180 lbs. b: Regina, Sask., 10/8/1951. Philadelphia's 1st, 8th overall, in 1971.

Season	Club	League	GP	G	A	Pts	AG	AA	APts	PIM	PP	SH	GW	S	%	TGF	PGF	TGA	PGA	+/-	GP	G	A	Pts	PIM	PP	SH	GW
1966-67	Regina Pat Canadians	SAHA	STATISTICS NOT AVAILABLE																									
1967-68	Regina Pats	WCJHL	60	20	47	67	....	....	....	10	....	....	....	....	....	....	....	....	....	....	4	1	0	1	0	....	....	....
1968-69	Regina Blues	SJHL	STATISTICS NOT AVAILABLE																									
	Regina Pats	Mem-Cup	11	7	10	17	....	....	....	5	....	....	....	....	....	....	....	....	....	....	....	....	....	....	....	....	....	....
1969-70	U. of Minnesota-Duluth	WCHA	24	11	11	22	....	....	....	8	....	....	....	....	....	....	....	....	....	....	....	....	....	....	....	....	....	....
1970-71	Regina Pats	WCJHL	59	24	60	84	....	....	....	43	....	....	....	....	....	....	....	....	....	....	6	1	3	4	7	....	....	....
1971-72	**Philadelphia Flyers**	**NHL**	**27**	**0**	**1**	**1**	**0**	**1**	**1**	**2**	**0**	**0**	**0**	**21**	**0.0**	**3**	**1**	**9**	**1**	**–6**	....	....	....	....	....	....	....	....
	Richmond Robins	AHL	44	10	12	22	....	....	....	10	....	....	....	....	....	....	....	....	....	....	....	....	....	....	....	....	....	....
1972-73	**Philadelphia Flyers**	**NHL**	**9**	**0**	**1**	**1**	**0**	**1**	**1**	**4**	**0**	**0**	**0**	**6**	**0.0**	**2**	**1**	**4**	**0**	**–3**	....	....	....	....	....	....	....	....
	Richmond Robins	AHL	61	26	25	51	....	....	....	29	....	....	....	....	....	....	....	....	....	....	4	1	3	4	2	....	....	....
1973-74	Richmond Robins	AHL	52	18	25	43	....	....	....	23	....	....	....	....	....	....	....	....	....	....	....	....	....	....	....	....	....	....
1974-75	**California Golden Seals**	**NHL**	**2**	**0**	**0**	**0**	**0**	**0**	**0**	**0**	**0**	**0**	**0**	**1**	**0.0**	**0**	**0**	**2**	**0**	**–2**	....	....	....	....	....	....	....	....
	Salt Lake Golden Eagles	CHL	14	0	3	3	....	....	....	9	....	....	....	....	....	....	....	....	....	....	11	1	4	5	2	....	....	....
1975-76	**Philadelphia Flyers**	**NHL**	**2**	**1**	**0**	**1**	**1**	**0**	**1**	**0**	**0**	**0**	**0**	**3**	**33.3**	**1**	**0**	**0**	**0**	**1**	....	....	....	....	....	....	....	....
	Richmond Robins	AHL	72	28	35	63	....	....	....	38	....	....	....	....	....	....	....	....	....	....	6	2	3	5	0	....	....	....
1976-77	Dusseldorfer EG	Germany	43	30	36	66	....	....	....	....	....	....	....	....	....	....	....	....	....	....	....	....	....	....	....	....	....	....
1977-78	**Detroit Red Wings**	**NHL**	**66**	**3**	**6**	**9**	**3**	**5**	**8**	**13**	**0**	**0**	**0**	**46**	**6.5**	**27**	**8**	**31**	**0**	**–12**	....	....	....	....	....	....	....	....
1978-79	Kansas City Red Wings	CHL	51	6	24	30	....	....	....	17	....	....	....	....	....	....	....	....	....	....	1	0	1	1	7	....	....	....
	NHL Totals		**106**	**4**	**8**	**12**	**4**	**7**	**11**	**19**	**0**	**0**	**0**	**77**	**5.2**	**33**	**10**	**46**	**1**		....	....	....	....	....	....	....	....

Traded to **California** by **Philadelphia** with Al MacAdam and Philadelphia's 1st round choice (Ron Chipperfield) in 1974 Amateur Draft for Reggie Leach, May 24, 1974. Signed as a free agent by **Philadelphia**, September, 1975. Signed as a free agent by **Detroit**, October 22, 1977.

• WRIGHT, Tyler

C – R. 5'11", 185 lbs. b: Canora, Sask., 4/6/1973. Edmonton's 1st, 12th overall, in 1991.

Season	Club	League	GP	G	A	Pts	AG	AA	APts	PIM	PP	SH	GW	S	%	TGF	PGF	TGA	PGA	+/-	GP	G	A	Pts	PIM	PP	SH	GW
1988-89	Swift Current Blazers	SAHA	36	20	13	33	....	....	....	102	....	....	....	....	....	....	....	....	....	....	....	....	....	....	....	....	....	....
1989-90	Swift Current Broncos	WHL	67	14	18	32	....	....	....	119	....	....	....	....	....	....	....	....	....	....	4	0	0	0	12	....	....	....
1990-91	Swift Current Broncos	WHL	66	41	51	92	....	....	....	157	....	....	....	....	....	....	....	....	....	....	3	0	0	0	6	....	....	....
1991-92	Swift Current Broncos	WHL	63	36	46	82	....	....	....	185	....	....	....	....	....	....	....	....	....	....	8	2	5	7	16	....	....	....
	Canada	WJC-A	7	1	0	1	....	....	....	16	....	....	....	....	....	....	....	....	....	....	....	....	....	....	....	....	....	....
1992-93	Swift Current Broncos	WHL	37	24	41	65	....	....	....	76	....	....	....	....	....	....	....	....	....	....	17	9	17	26	*49	....	....	....
	Canada	WJC-A	7	3	3	6	....	....	....	6	....	....	....	....	....	....	....	....	....	....	....	....	....	....	....	....	....	....
	Edmonton Oilers	**NHL**	**7**	**1**	**1**	**2**	**1**	**1**	**2**	**19**	**0**	**0**	**0**	**7**	**14.3**	**3**	**0**	**8**	**1**	**–4**	....	....	....	....	....	....	....	....
	Swift Current Broncos	Mem-Cup	4	1	3	4	....	....	....	6	....	....	....	....	....	....	....	....	....	....	....	....	....	....	....	....	....	....
1993-94	**Edmonton Oilers**	**NHL**	**5**	**0**	**0**	**0**	**0**	**0**	**0**	**4**	**0**	**0**	**0**	**2**	**0.0**	**0**	**0**	**3**	**0**	**–3**	....	....	....	....	....	....	....	....
	Cape Breton Oilers	AHL	65	14	27	41	....	....	....	160	....	....	....	....	....	....	....	....	....	....	5	2	0	2	11	....	....	....
1994-95	Cape Breton Oilers	AHL	70	16	15	31	....	....	....	184	....	....	....	....	....	....	....	....	....	....	....	....	....	....	....	....	....	....
	Edmonton Oilers	**NHL**	**6**	**1**	**0**	**1**	**2**	**0**	**2**	**14**	**0**	**0**	**0**	**6**	**16.7**	**3**	**0**	**2**	**0**	**1**	....	....	....	....	....	....	....	....
1995-96	**Edmonton Oilers**	**NHL**	**23**	**1**	**0**	**1**	**1**	**0**	**1**	**33**	**0**	**0**	**0**	**18**	**5.6**	**4**	**0**	**11**	**0**	**–7**	....	....	....	....	....	....	....	....
	Cape Breton Oilers	AHL	31	6	12	18	....	....	....	158	....	....	....	....	....	....	....	....	....	....	....	....	....	....	....	....	....	....
1996-97	**Pittsburgh Penguins**	**NHL**	**45**	**2**	**2**	**4**	**2**	**2**	**4**	**70**	**0**	**0**	**2**	**30**	**6.7**	**4**	**0**	**17**	**6**	**–7**	....	....	....	....	....	....	....	....
	Cleveland Lumberjacks	IHL	10	4	3	7	....	....	....	34	....	....	....	....	....	....	....	....	....	....	14	4	2	6	44	....	....	....
1997-98	**Pittsburgh Penguins**	**NHL**	**82**	**3**	**4**	**7**	**4**	**4**	**8**	**112**	**1**	**0**	**0**	**46**	**6.5**	**15**	**2**	**26**	**10**	**–3**	**6**	**0**	**1**	**1**	**4**	**0**	**0**	**0**
1998-99	**Pittsburgh Penguins**	**NHL**	**61**	**0**	**0**	**0**	**0**	**0**	**0**	**90**	**0**	**0**	**0**	**16**	**0.0**	**3**	**0**	**10**	**5**	**–2**	**13**	**0**	**0**	**0**	**19**	**0**	**0**	**0**
99-2000	**Pittsburgh Penguins**	**NHL**	**50**	**12**	**10**	**22**	**13**	**9**	**22**	**45**	**0**	**0**	**1**	**68**	**17.6**	**27**	**0**	**34**	**11**	**4**	**11**	**3**	**1**	**4**	**17**	**0**	**0**	**0**
	Wilkes-Barre Penguins	AHL	25	5	15	20	....	....	....	86	....	....	....	....	....	....	....	....	....	....	....	....	....	....	....	....	....	....
	NHL Totals		**279**	**20**	**17**	**37**	**23**	**16**	**39**	**387**	**1**	**0**	**3**	**193**	**10.4**	**59**	**2**	**111**	**33**		**30**	**3**	**2**	**5**	**40**	**0**	**0**	**0**

Traded to **Pittsburgh** by **Edmonton** for Pittsburgh's 7th round choice (Brandon Lafrance) in 1996 Entry Draft, June 22, 1996. Selected by **Columbus** from **Pittsburgh** in Expansion Draft, June 23, 2000.

• WYLIE, Duane

Duane Steven C – L. 5'8", 170 lbs. b: Spokane, WA, 11/10/1950. NY Rangers' 6th, 81st overall, in 1970.

Season	Club	League	GP	G	A	Pts	AG	AA	APts	PIM	PP	SH	GW	S	%	TGF	PGF	TGA	PGA	+/-	GP	G	A	Pts	PIM	PP	SH	GW
1967-68	Moose Jaw Canucks	WCJHL	29	4	7	11	....	....	....	24	....	....	....	....	....	....	....	....	....	....	....	....	....	....	....	....	....	....
1968-69	Moose Jaw Canucks	SJHL	STATISTICS NOT AVAILABLE																									
1969-70	St. Catharines Black Hawks	OHA-Jr.	53	18	23	41	....	....	....	54	....	....	....	....	....	....	....	....	....	....	10	6	9	15	4	....	....	....
1970-71	Flint Generals	IHL	64	15	26	41	....	....	....	31	....	....	....	....	....	....	....	....	....	....	7	2	1	3	2	....	....	....
1971-72	Flint Generals	IHL	72	26	39	65	....	....	....	43	....	....	....	....	....	....	....	....	....	....	4	0	1	1	2	....	....	....
1972-73	Dallas Black Hawks	CHL	61	11	19	30	....	....	....	46	....	....	....	....	....	....	....	....	....	....	7	1	2	3	8	....	....	....
1973-74	Dallas Black Hawks	CHL	72	30	27	57	....	....	....	39	....	....	....	....	....	....	....	....	....	....	10	*6	2	8	4	....	....	....
1974-75	**Chicago Black Hawks**	**NHL**	**6**	**1**	**3**	**4**	**1**	**2**	**3**	**2**	**0**	**0**	**0**	**7**	**14.3**	**4**	**0**	**7**	**2**	**–1**	....	....	....	....	....	....	....	....
	Dallas Black Hawks	CHL	73	24	37	61	....	....	....	62	....	....	....	....	....	....	....	....	....	....	10	3	1	4	6	....	....	....
1975-76	Dallas Black Hawks	CHL	74	30	40	70	....	....	....	28	....	....	....	....	....	....	....	....	....	....	10	2	6	8	2	....	....	....
1976-77	**Chicago Black Hawks**	**NHL**	**8**	**2**	**0**	**2**	**2**	**0**	**2**	**0**	**1**	**0**	**0**	**12**	**16.7**	**2**	**1**	**6**	**1**	**–4**	....	....	....	....	....	....	....	....
	Dallas Black Hawks	CHL	71	23	32	55	....	....	....	20	....	....	....	....	....	....	....	....	....	....	5	2	0	2	0	....	....	....
1977-78	Dallas Black Hawks	CHL	77	17	29	46	....	....	....	24	....	....	....	....	....	....	....	....	....	....	13	4	5	9	2	....	....	....
	NHL Totals		**14**	**3**	**3**	**6**	**3**	**2**	**5**	**2**	**1**	**0**	**0**	**19**	**15.8**	**6**	**1**	**13**	**3**		....	....	....	....	....	....	....	....

Signed as a free agent by **Chicago**, October 12, 1972.

• WYROZUB, Randy

William Randall C – L. 5'11", 180 lbs. b: Lacombe, Alta., 4/8/1950. Buffalo's 4th, 43rd overall, in 1970.

Season	Club	League	GP	G	A	Pts	AG	AA	APts	PIM	PP	SH	GW	S	%	TGF	PGF	TGA	PGA	+/-	GP	G	A	Pts	PIM	PP	SH	GW
1968-69	Ponoka Stampeders	AJHL	STATISTICS NOT AVAILABLE																									
1969-70	Edmonton Oil Kings	WCJHL	58	24	34	58	....	....	....	23	....	....	....	....	....	....	....	....	....	....	18	11	7	18	6	....	....	....
1970-71	**Buffalo Sabres**	**NHL**	**16**	**2**	**2**	**4**	**2**	**2**	**4**	**6**	**1**	**0**	**0**	**22**	**9.1**	**4**	**1**	**12**	**0**	**–9**	....	....	....	....	....	....	....	....
	Salt Lake Golden Eagles	WHL	23	7	4	11	....	....	....	2	....	....	....	....	....	....	....	....	....	....	....	....	....	....	....	....	....	....
1971-72	**Buffalo Sabres**	**NHL**	**34**	**3**	**4**	**7**	**3**	**3**	**6**	**0**	**0**	**0**	**0**	**36**	**8.3**	**12**	**1**	**13**	**0**	**–2**	....	....	....	....	....	....	....	....
	Cincinnati Swords	AHL	35	14	14	28	....	....	....	10	....	....	....	....	....	....	....	....	....	....	....	....	....	....	....	....	....	....
1972-73	**Buffalo Sabres**	**NHL**	**45**	**3**	**3**	**6**	**3**	**2**	**5**	**4**	**0**	**0**	**2**	**23**	**13.0**	**8**	**0**	**9**	**0**	**–1**	....	....	....	....	....	....	....	....
1973-74	**Buffalo Sabres**	**NHL**	**5**	**0**	**1**	**1**	**0**	**1**	**1**	**0**	**0**	**0**	**0**	**4**	**0.0**	**1**	**0**	**3**	**1**	**–1**	....	....	....	....	....	....	....	....
	Cincinnati Swords	AHL	69	22	35	57	....	....	....	17	....	....	....	....	....	....	....	....	....	....	5	0	3	3	0	....	....	....
1974-75	Richmond Robins	AHL	71	21	32	53	....	....	....	31	....	....	....	....	....	....	....	....	....	....	7	2	3	5	6	....	....	....
1975-76	Indianapolis Racers	WHA	55	11	14	25	....	....	....	8	....	....	....	....	....	....	....	....	....	....	....	....	....	....	....	....	....	....
	Mohawk Valley Comets	NAHL	11	6	7	13	....	....	....	0	....	....	....	....	....	....	....	....	....	....	4	1	2	3	2	....	....	....
1976-77	Mohawk Valley Comets	NAHL	73	26	57	83	....	....	....	18	....	....	....	....	....	....	....	....	....	....	5	4	2	6	2	....	....	....
1977-78	San Francisco Shamrocks	PHL	42	27	33	60	....	....	....	12	....	....	....	....	....	....	....	....	....	....	....	....	....	....	....	....	....	....
1978-79	Tucson Rustlers	PHL	29	15	20	35	....	....	....	0	....	....	....	....	....	....	....	....	....	....	....	....	....	....	....	....	....	....
	Erie Blades	NEHL	19	6	10	16	....	....	....	6	....	....	....	....	....	....	....	....	....	....	....	....	....	....	....	....	....	....
	NHL Totals		**100**	**8**	**10**	**18**	**8**	**8**	**16**	**10**	**1**	**0**	**2**	**85**	**9.4**	**25**	**2**	**37**	**1**		....	....	....	....	....	....	....	....
	Other Major League Totals		55	11	14	25	....	....	....	8	....	....	....	....	....	....	....	....	....	....	....	....	....	....	....	....	....	....

PHL First All-Star Team (1978)

• Selected by **Alberta** (WHA) in 1972 WHA General Player Draft, February 12, 1972. Claimed by **Washington** from **Buffalo** in Expansion Draft, June 12, 1974. WHA rights traded to **Edmonton** (WHA) by **Indianapolis** (WHA) for cash, September, 1975.

Season	Club	League	GP	G	A	Pts	AG	AA	APts	PIM	PP	SH	GW	S	%	TGF	PGF	TGA	PGA	+/–	GP	G	A	Pts	PIM	PP	SH	GW
			REGULAR SEASON																		PLAYOFFS							

• YACHMENEV, Vitali

RW – L. 5'9", 191 lbs. b: Chelyabinsk, USSR, 1/8/1975. Los Angeles' 3rd, 59th overall, in 1994.

Season	Club	League	GP	G	A	Pts	AG	AA	APts	PIM	PP	SH	GW	S	%	TGF	PGF	TGA	PGA	+/–	GP	G	A	Pts	PIM	PP	SH	GW
1990-91	Tractor Chelyabinsk	CIS-Jr.	80	88	60	148				72																		
1991-92	Tractor Chelyabinsk	CIS-Jr.	80	82	70	152				20																		
1992-93	Traktor Chelyabinsk	CIS-2	51	23	20	43				12																		
	Russia	EJC-A	6	2	5	7				2																		
1993-94	North Bay Centennials	OHL	66	*61	52	113				18											18	13	19	32	12			
	North Bay Centennials	Mem-Cup	3	1	3	4				2																		
1994-95	North Bay Centennials	OHL	59	53	52	105				8											6	1	8	9	2			
	Russia	WJC-A	7	3	4	7				2																		
	Phoenix Roadrunners	IHL																			4	1	0	1	0			
1995-96	**Los Angeles Kings**	**NHL**	**80**	**19**	**34**	**53**	**19**	**28**	**47**	**16**	**6**	**1**	**2**	**133**	**14.3**	**91**	**41**	**58**	**5**	**–3**								
1996-97	**Los Angeles Kings**	**NHL**	**65**	**10**	**22**	**32**	**11**	**20**	**31**	**10**	**2**	**0**	**2**	**97**	**10.3**	**46**	**10**	**55**	**10**	**–9**								
1997-98	**Los Angeles Kings**	**NHL**	**4**	**0**	**1**	**1**	**0**	**1**	**1**	**4**	**0**	**0**	**0**	**4**	**0.0**	**2**	**0**	**1**	**0**	**1**								
	Long Beach Ice Dogs	IHL	59	23	28	51				14											17	8	9	17	4			
1998-99	**Nashville Predators**	**NHL**	**55**	**7**	**10**	**17**	**8**	**10**	**18**	**10**	**0**	**1**	**2**	**83**	**8.4**	**28**	**1**	**42**	**5**	**–10**								
	Milwaukee Admirals	IHL	16	7	6	13				0																		
99-2000	**Nashville Predators**	**NHL**	**68**	**16**	**16**	**32**	**18**	**15**	**33**	**12**	**1**	**1**	**3**	**120**	**13.3**	**49**	**6**	**46**	**8**	**5**								
	NHL Totals		**272**	**52**	**83**	**135**	**56**	**74**	**130**	**52**	**9**	**3**	**9**	**437**	**11.9**	**216**	**58**	**202**	**28**									

Canadian Major Junior Rookie of the Year (1994)

Traded to **Nashville** by **LA Kings** for cash, July 7, 1998.

• YAKE, Terry

Terry Donald C – R. 5'11", 190 lbs. b: New Westminster, B.C., 10/22/1968. Hartford's 3rd, 81st overall, in 1987.

Season	Club	League	GP	G	A	Pts	AG	AA	APts	PIM	PP	SH	GW	S	%	TGF	PGF	TGA	PGA	+/–	GP	G	A	Pts	PIM	PP	SH	GW
1984-85	Pembina Valley Hawks	RMJHL	STATISTICS NOT AVAILABLE																									
	Brandon Wheat Kings	WHL	11	1	1	2				0																		
1985-86	Brandon Wheat Kings	WHL	72	26	26	52				49																		
1986-87	Brandon Wheat Kings	WHL	71	44	58	102				64																		
1987-88	Brandon Wheat Kings	WHL	72	55	85	140				59											4	5	6	11	12			
1988-89	**Hartford Whalers**	**NHL**	**2**	**0**	**0**	**0**	**0**	**0**	**0**	**0**	**0**	**0**	**0**	**0**	**0.0**	**2**	**1**	**0**	**0**	**1**								
	Binghamton Whalers	AHL	75	39	56	95				57																		
1989-90	**Hartford Whalers**	**NHL**	**2**	**0**	**1**	**1**	**0**	**1**	**1**	**0**	**0**	**0**	**0**	**2**	**0.0**	**1**	**0**	**2**	**0**	**–1**								
	Binghamton Whalers	AHL	77	13	42	55				37																		
1990-91	**Hartford Whalers**	**NHL**	**19**	**1**	**4**	**5**	**1**	**3**	**4**	**10**	**0**	**0**	**1**	**19**	**5.3**	**8**	**1**	**16**	**6**	**–3**	**6**	**1**	**1**	**2**	**16**	**0**	**1**	**0**
	Springfield Indians	AHL	60	35	42	77				56											15	9	9	18	10			
1991-92	**Hartford Whalers**	**NHL**	**15**	**1**	**1**	**2**	**1**	**1**	**2**	**4**	**0**	**0**	**0**	**12**	**8.3**	**3**	**0**	**8**	**3**	**–2**								
	Springfield Indians	AHL	53	21	34	55				63											8	3	4	7	2			
1992-93	**Hartford Whalers**	**NHL**	**66**	**22**	**31**	**53**	**18**	**21**	**39**	**46**	**4**	**1**	**2**	**98**	**22.4**	**74**	**17**	**71**	**17**	**3**								
	Springfield Indians	AHL	16	8	14	22				27																		
1993-94	**Mighty Ducks of Anaheim**	**NHL**	**82**	**21**	**31**	**52**	**20**	**24**	**44**	**44**	**5**	**0**	**2**	**188**	**11.2**	**80**	**27**	**60**	**9**	**2**								
1994-95	**Toronto Maple Leafs**	**NHL**	**19**	**3**	**2**	**5**	**5**	**3**	**8**	**2**	**1**	**0**	**2**	**26**	**11.5**	**9**	**3**	**5**	**0**	**1**								
	Denver Grizzlies	IHL	2	0	3	3				2											17	4	11	15	16			
1995-96	Milwaukee Admirals	IHL	70	32	56	88				70											5	3	6	9	4			
1996-97	Rochester Americans	AHL	78	34	*67	101				77											10	8	8	16	2			
1997-98	**St. Louis Blues**	**NHL**	**65**	**10**	**15**	**25**	**12**	**15**	**27**	**38**	**3**	**1**	**4**	**60**	**16.7**	**42**	**11**	**35**	**5**	**1**	**10**	**2**	**1**	**3**	**6**	**2**	**0**	**1**
1998-99	**St. Louis Blues**	**NHL**	**60**	**9**	**18**	**27**	**11**	**17**	**28**	**34**	**3**	**0**	**4**	**59**	**15.3**	**44**	**24**	**31**	**2**	**–9**	**13**	**1**	**2**	**3**	**14**	**1**	**0**	**0**
	Worcester IceCats	AHL	24	8	11	19				26																		
99-2000	**St. Louis Blues**	**NHL**	**26**	**4**	**9**	**13**	**4**	**8**	**12**	**22**	**2**	**0**	**2**	**26**	**15.4**	**19**	**7**	**10**	**0**	**2**								
	Washington Capitals	**NHL**	**35**	**6**	**5**	**11**	**7**	**5**	**12**	**12**	**1**	**0**	**1**	**29**	**20.7**	**15**	**1**	**15**	**3**	**2**	**3**	**0**	**0**	**0**	**0**	**0**	**0**	**0**
	NHL Totals		**391**	**77**	**117**	**194**	**79**	**98**	**177**	**212**	**19**	**2**	**18**	**519**	**14.8**	**297**	**92**	**253**	**45**		**32**	**4**	**4**	**8**	**36**	**3**	**1**	**1**

Claimed by **Anaheim** from **Hartford** in Expansion Draft, June 24, 1993. Traded to **Toronto** by **Anaheim** for David Sacco, September 28, 1994. Signed as a free agent by **Buffalo**, September 17, 1996. Signed as a free agent by **St. Louis**, July 24, 1997. Claimed by **Atlanta** from **St. Louis** in Expansion Draft, June 25, 1999. Claimed on waivers by **Washington** from **St. Louis**, January 18, 2000.

• YAKUSHIN, Dmitri

D – L. 6', 200 lbs. b: Kharkov, USSR, 1/21/1978. Toronto's 9th, 140th overall, in 1996.

Season	Club	League	GP	G	A	Pts	AG	AA	APts	PIM	PP	SH	GW	S	%	TGF	PGF	TGA	PGA	+/–	GP	G	A	Pts	PIM	PP	SH	GW
1995-96	Pembroke Lumber Kings	OJHL	31	8	5	13				62																		
1996-97	Edmonton Ice	WHL	63	3	14	17				103																		
1997-98	Edmonton Ice	WHL	29	1	10	11				41																		
	Regina Pats	WHL	13	0	14	14				16											9	2	8	10	12			
1998-99	St. John's Maple Leafs	AHL	71	2	6	8				65											4	0	0	0	0			
99-2000	**Toronto Maple Leafs**	**NHL**	**2**	**0**	**0**	**0**	**0**	**0**	**0**	**2**	**0**	**0**	**0**	**1**	**0.0**	**0**	**0**	**0**	**0**	**0**								
	St. John's Maple Leafs	AHL	64	1	13	14				106																		
	Ukraine	WC-A	6	1	1	2				6																		
	NHL Totals		**2**	**0**	**0**	**0**	**0**	**0**	**0**	**2**	**0**	**0**	**0**	**1**	**0.0**	**0**	**0**	**0**	**0**									

• YAREMCHUK, Gary

"The General" C – L. 6', 185 lbs. b: Edmonton, Alta., 8/15/1961. Toronto's 2nd, 24th overall, in 1981.

Season	Club	League	GP	G	A	Pts	AG	AA	APts	PIM	PP	SH	GW	S	%	TGF	PGF	TGA	PGA	+/–	GP	G	A	Pts	PIM	PP	SH	GW
1978-79	Fort Saskatchewan Traders	AJHL	STATISTICS NOT AVAILABLE																									
1979-80	Fort Saskatchewan Traders	AJHL	27	27	44	71				61																		
	Portland Winter Hawks	WHL	41	21	34	55				23											6	1	4	5	2			
1980-81	Portland Winter Hawks	WHL	72	56	79	135				121																		
1981-82	**Toronto Maple Leafs**	**NHL**	**18**	**0**	**3**	**3**	**0**	**2**	**2**	**10**	**0**	**0**	**0**	**6**	**0.0**	**6**	**0**	**14**	**1**	**–7**								
	Cincinnati Tigers	CHL	53	21	35	56				101											4	0	2	2	4			
1982-83	**Toronto Maple Leafs**	**NHL**	**3**	**0**	**0**	**0**	**0**	**0**	**0**	**2**	**0**	**0**	**0**	**3**	**0.0**	**0**	**0**	**1**	**0**	**–1**								
	St. Catharines Saints	AHL	61	17	28	45				72																		
1983-84	**Toronto Maple Leafs**	**NHL**	**1**	**0**	**0**	**0**	**0**	**0**	**0**	**0**	**0**	**0**	**0**	**1**	**0.0**	**1**	**1**	**1**	**0**	**–1**								
	St. Catharines Saints	AHL	73	24	37	61				84											7	5	1	6	2			
1984-85	**Toronto Maple Leafs**	**NHL**	**12**	**1**	**1**	**2**	**1**	**1**	**2**	**16**	**0**	**0**	**0**	**7**	**14.3**	**3**	**0**	**10**	**0**	**–7**								
	St. Catharines Saints	AHL	66	17	47	64				75																		
1985-86	Adirondack Red Wings	AHL	60	12	32	44				90											1	1	0	1	0			
1986-87	Jokerit Helsinki	Finland	20	7	21	28				116																		
1987-88	Karpat Oulu	Finland	36	16	27	43				92																		
1988-89	Kiekko-Kouvola	Finland	44	12	27	39				50																		
1989-90	Kiekko-Kouvola	Finland	42	16	19	35				81																		
1990-91	EHC Dubendorf	Switz-2	STATISTICS NOT AVAILABLE																									
1991-92	HC Amiens	France	30	25	39	64				82																		
1992-93	HC Gardena-Groden	Alpenliga	21	9	21	30				69																		
	HC Gardena-Groden	Italy	16	9	19	28				8											2	0	2	2	6			
1993-94	Durham Wasps	BH-Cup	5	2	5	7				6																		
	Durham Wasps	Britain	40	53	93	146				57																		
	NHL Totals		**34**	**1**	**4**	**5**	**1**	**3**	**4**	**28**	**0**	**0**	**0**	**17**	**5.9**	**10**	**1**	**26**	**1**									

• Brother of Ken

Signed as a free agent by **Detroit**, August 13, 1985.

• YAREMCHUK, Ken

C – R. 5'11", 185 lbs. b: Edmonton, Alta., 1/1/1964. Chicago's 1st, 7th overall, in 1982.

Season	Club	League	GP	G	A	Pts	AG	AA	APts	PIM	PP	SH	GW	S	%	TGF	PGF	TGA	PGA	+/–	GP	G	A	Pts	PIM	PP	SH	GW
1978-79	Edmonton Bay Drugs	AAHA	STATISTICS NOT AVAILABLE																									
1979-80	Fort Saskatchewan Traders	AJHL	59	40	72	112				39																		
	Portland Winter Hawks	WHL																			2	1	0	1	0			
1980-81	Portland Winter Hawks	WHL	72	35	72	107				105											9	2	8	10	24			

			REGULAR SEASON																		PLAYOFFS							
Season	Club	League	GP	G	A	Pts	AG	AA	APts	PIM	PP	SH	GW	S	%	TGF	PGF	TGA	PGA	+/–	GP	G	A	Pts	PIM	PP	SH	GW
1981-82	Portland Winter Hawks	WHL	72	58	99	157	....	....	....	181	....	....	....	....	....	....	....	....	....	....	15	10	21	31	12	....	....	....
	Portland Winter Hawks	Mem-Cup	4	1	4	5	....	....	....	2	....	....	....	....	....	....	....	....	....	....	....	....	....	....	....	....	....	....
1982-83	Portland Winter Hawks	WHL	66	51	*109	160	....	....	....	76	....	....	....	....	....	....	....	....	....	....	14	11	15	26	12	....	....	....
	Portland Winter Hawks	Mem-Cup	3	4	7	*11	....	....	....	0	....	....	....	....	....	....	....	....	....	....	....	....	....	....	....	....	....	....
1983-84	**Chicago Black Hawks**	**NHL**	**47**	**6**	**7**	**13**	**5**	**5**	**10**	**19**	**0**	**0**	**0**	**49**	**12.2**	**19**	**1**	**25**	**0**	**–7**	**1**	**0**	**0**	**0**	**0**	**0**	**0**	**0**
1984-85	**Chicago Black Hawks**	**NHL**	**63**	**10**	**16**	**26**	**8**	**11**	**19**	**16**	**2**	**0**	**0**	**72**	**13.9**	**39**	**8**	**37**	**0**	**–6**	**15**	**5**	**5**	**10**	**37**	**0**	**0**	**1**
	Milwaukee Admirals	IHL	7	4	6	10	....	....	....	9	....	....	....	....	....	....	....	....	....	....	....	....	....	....	....	....	....	....
1985-86	**Chicago Black Hawks**	**NHL**	**78**	**14**	**20**	**34**	**11**	**13**	**24**	**43**	**0**	**0**	**2**	**82**	**17.1**	**53**	**2**	**68**	**0**	**–17**	**3**	**1**	**1**	**2**	**2**	**0**	**0**	**0**
1986-87	**Toronto Maple Leafs**	**NHL**	**20**	**3**	**8**	**11**	**3**	**6**	**9**	**16**	**0**	**0**	**0**	**33**	**9.1**	**13**	**2**	**11**	**0**	**0**	**6**	**0**	**0**	**0**	**0**	**0**	**0**	**0**
	Newmarket Saints	AHL	14	2	4	6	....	....	....	21	....	....	....	....	....	....	....	....	....	....	....	....	....	....	....	....	....	....
1987-88	Canada	Nat-Team	38	15	18	33	....	....	....	63	....	....	....	....	....	....	....	....	....	....	....	....	....	....	....	....	....	....
	Canada	Olympics	8	3	3	6	....	....	....	2	....	....	....	....	....	....	....	....	....	....	....	....	....	....	....	....	....	....
	Toronto Maple Leafs	**NHL**	**16**	**2**	**5**	**7**	**2**	**4**	**6**	**10**	**0**	**0**	**0**	**14**	**14.3**	**7**	**2**	**14**	**2**	**–7**	**6**	**0**	**2**	**2**	**10**	**0**	**0**	**0**
1988-89	**Toronto Maple Leafs**	**NHL**	**11**	**1**	**0**	**1**	**1**	**0**	**1**	**2**	**0**	**0**	**0**	**13**	**7.7**	**1**	**0**	**6**	**0**	**–5**	....	....	....	....	....	....	....	....
	Newmarket Saints	AHL	55	25	33	58	....	....	....	145	....	....	....	....	....	....	....	....	....	....	5	7	7	14	12	....	....	....
1989-90	HC Asiago	Italy	34	37	76	113	....	....	....	32	....	....	....	....	....	....	....	....	....	....	6	5	6	11	8	....	....	....
1990-91	EV Zug	Switz.	26	17	14	31	....	....	....	....	....	....	....	....	....	....	....	....	....	....	....	....	....	....	....	....	....	....
1991-92	EV Zug	Switz.	36	29	25	54	....	....	....	65	....	....	....	....	....	....	....	....	....	....	....	....	....	....	....	....	....	....
	Canada	Nat-Team	3	0	0	0	....	....	....	0	....	....	....	....	....	....	....	....	....	....	....	....	....	....	....	....	....	....
1992-93	EV Zug	Switz.	36	27	33	60	....	....	....	57	....	....	....	....	....	....	....	....	....	....	5	0	1	1	18	....	....	....
	Canada	Nat-Team	2	0	5	5	....	....	....	0	....	....	....	....	....	....	....	....	....	....	....	....	....	....	....	....	....	....
1993-94	EV Zug	Switz.	36	17	39	56	....	....	....	19	....	....	....	....	....	....	....	....	....	....	2	1	0	1	0	....	....	....
1994-95	EV Zug	Switz.	36	26	45	71	....	....	....	55	....	....	....	....	....	....	....	....	....	....	12	5	12	17	24	....	....	....
1995-96	EV Zug	Switz.	26	16	30	46	....	....	....	69	....	....	....	....	....	....	....	....	....	....	6	1	4	5	6	....	....	....
1996-97	HC Davos	Switz.	46	31	38	69	....	....	....	60	....	....	....	....	....	....	....	....	....	....	5	2	2	4	16	....	....	....
1997-98	HC Davos	Switz.	39	20	22	42	....	....	....	76	....	....	....	....	....	....	....	....	....	....	18	11	14	25	34	....	....	....
1998-99	SC Rapperswil-Jona	Switz.	45	14	20	34	....	....	....	103	....	....	....	....	....	....	....	....	....	....	4	0	1	1	10	....	....	....
	NHL Totals		**235**	**36**	**56**	**92**	**30**	**39**	**69**	**106**	**2**	**0**	**2**	**263**	**13.7**	**132**	**15**	**161**	**2**		**31**	**6**	**8**	**14**	**49**	**0**	**0**	**1**

• Brother of Gary • WHL First All-Star Team (1982) • WHL Second All-Star Team (1983) • Memorial Cup All-Star Team (1983)

Transferred to **Toronto** by **Chicago** with Jerome Dupont and Chicago's 4th round choice (Joe Sacco) in 1987 Entry Draft as compensation for Chicago's signing of free agent Gary Nylund, September 6, 1986.

• YASHIN, Alexei

C – R. 6′3″, 225 lbs. b: Sverdlovsk, USSR, 11/5/1973. Ottawa's 1st, 2nd overall, in 1992.

Season	Club	League	GP	G	A	Pts	AG	AA	APts	PIM	PP	SH	GW	S	%	TGF	PGF	TGA	PGA	+/–	GP	G	A	Pts	PIM	PP	SH	GW
1990-91	Automobilist Sverdlovsk	USSR	26	2	1	3	....	....	....	10	....	....	....	....	....	....	....	....	....	....	....	....	....	....	....	....	....	....
	Soviet Union	EJC-A	5	1	3	4	....	....	....	2	....	....	....	....	....	....	....	....	....	....	....	....	....	....	....	....	....	....
1991-92	Dynamo Moscow	CIS	35	7	5	12	....	....	....	19	....	....	....	....	....	....	....	....	....	....	....	....	....	....	....	....	....	....
	Russia	WJC-A	7	4	2	6	....	....	....	2	....	....	....	....	....	....	....	....	....	....	....	....	....	....	....	....	....	....
1992-93	Dynamo Moscow	CIS	27	10	12	22	....	....	....	18	....	....	....	....	....	....	....	....	....	....	10	7	3	10	18	....	....	....
	Russia	WJC-A	3	1	0	1	....	....	....	4	....	....	....	....	....	....	....	....	....	....	....	....	....	....	....	....	....	....
	Russia	WC-A	8	2	1	3	....	....	....	5	....	....	....	....	....	....	....	....	....	....	....	....	....	....	....	....	....	....
1993-94	**Ottawa Senators**	**NHL**	**83**	**30**	**49**	**79**	**28**	**38**	**66**	**22**	**11**	**2**	**3**	**232**	**12.9**	**94**	**39**	**126**	**22**	**–49**	....	....	....	....	....	....	....	....
	Russia	WC-A	5	1	2	3	....	....	....	8	....	....	....	....	....	....	....	....	....	....	....	....	....	....	....	....	....	....
1994-95	Las Vegas Thunder	IHL	24	15	20	35	....	....	....	32	....	....	....	....	....	....	....	....	....	....	....	....	....	....	....	....	....	....
	Ottawa Senators	**NHL**	**47**	**21**	**23**	**44**	**37**	**34**	**71**	**20**	**11**	**0**	**1**	**154**	**13.6**	**59**	**25**	**55**	**1**	**–20**	....	....	....	....	....	....	....	....
1995-96	CSKA Moscow	CIS	4	2	2	4	....	....	....	4	....	....	....	....	....	....	....	....	....	....	....	....	....	....	....	....	....	....
	Ottawa Senators	**NHL**	**46**	**15**	**24**	**39**	**15**	**20**	**35**	**28**	**8**	**0**	**1**	**143**	**10.5**	**51**	**22**	**44**	**0**	**–15**	....	....	....	....	....	....	....	....
	Russia	WC-A	8	4	5	9	....	....	....	4	....	....	....	....	....	....	....	....	....	....	....	....	....	....	....	....	....	....
1996-97	Russia	W-Cup	5	0	2	2	....	....	....	6	....	....	....	....	....	....	....	....	....	....	....	....	....	....	....	....	....	....
	Ottawa Senators	**NHL**	**82**	**35**	**40**	**75**	**37**	**36**	**73**	**44**	**10**	**0**	**5**	**291**	**12.0**	**100**	**35**	**82**	**10**	**–7**	**7**	**1**	**5**	**6**	**2**	**1**	**0**	**0**
	Russia	WC-A	5	3	0	3	....	....	....	12	....	....	....	....	....	....	....	....	....	....	....	....	....	....	....	....	....	....
1997-98	**Ottawa Senators**	**NHL**	**82**	**33**	**39**	**72**	**39**	**38**	**77**	**24**	**5**	**0**	**6**	**291**	**11.3**	**97**	**32**	**63**	**4**	**6**	**11**	**5**	**3**	**8**	**8**	**3**	**0**	**2**
	Russia	Olympics	6	3	3	6	....	....	....	0	....	....	....	....	....	....	....	....	....	....	....	....	....	....	....	....	....	....
1998-99	**Ottawa Senators**	**NHL**	**82**	**44**	**50**	**94**	**52**	**48**	**100**	**54**	**19**	**0**	**5**	**337**	**13.1**	**119**	**47**	**64**	**8**	**16**	**4**	**0**	**0**	**0**	**10**	**0**	**0**	**0**
	Russia	WC-A	6	8	1	9	....	....	....	6	....	....	....	....	....	....	....	....	....	....	....	....	....	....	....	....	....	....
99-2000	**Ottawa Senators**	**NHL**	DID NOT PLAY – SUSPENDED																									
	Russia	WC-A	5	1	1	2	....	....	....	8	....	....	....	....	....	....	....	....	....	....	....	....	....	....	....	....	....	....
	NHL Totals		**422**	**178**	**225**	**403**	**208**	**214**	**422**	**192**	**64**	**2**	**21**	**1448**	**12.3**	**520**	**200**	**434**	**45**		**22**	**6**	**8**	**14**	**20**	**4**	**0**	**2**

CIS First All-Star Team (1993) • NHL Second All-Star Team (1999) • Played in NHL All-Star Game (1994, 1999)

• Suspended for entire 1999-2000 season by **Ottawa** for refusing to report to team, November 9, 1999. • Independent arbitrator ruled that Yashin was eligible to play for Team Russia at 2000 World Hockey Championships.

• YATES, Ross

Ross Richard C – R. 5′11″, 170 lbs. b: Montreal, Que., 6/18/1959.

Season	Club	League	GP	G	A	Pts	AG	AA	APts	PIM	PP	SH	GW	S	%	TGF	PGF	TGA	PGA	+/–	GP	G	A	Pts	PIM	PP	SH	GW
1975-76	Montreal-Bourassa Canadiens	QAAA	STATISTICS NOT AVAILABLE																									
1976-77	Mount Allison University	AUAA	20	7	7	14	....	....	....	18	....	....	....	....	....	....	....	....	....	....	....	....	....	....	....	....	....	....
1977-78	Mount Allison University	AUAA	20	8	21	29	....	....	....	38	....	....	....	....	....	....	....	....	....	....	....	....	....	....	....	....	....	....
1978-79	Mount Allison University	AUAA	20	*21	26	*47	....	....	....	34	....	....	....	....	....	....	....	....	....	....	....	....	....	....	....	....	....	....
1979-80	Mount Allison University	AUAA	27	23	*54	77	....	....	....	14	....	....	....	....	....	....	....	....	....	....	....	....	....	....	....	....	....	....
1980-81	Mount Allison University	AUAA	21	16	*56	*72	....	....	....	12	....	....	....	....	....	....	....	....	....	....	....	....	....	....	....	....	....	....
	Binghamton Whalers	AHL	14	4	1	5	....	....	....	2	....	....	....	....	....	....	....	....	....	....	5	0	0	0	0	....	....	....
1981-82	Binghamton Whalers	AHL	80	22	23	45	....	....	....	53	....	....	....	....	....	....	....	....	....	....	15	6	5	11	10	....	....	....
1982-83	Binghamton Whalers	AHL	77	41	*84	*125	....	....	....	28	....	....	....	....	....	....	....	....	....	....	5	0	6	6	2	....	....	....
1983-84	**Hartford Whalers**	**NHL**	**7**	**1**	**1**	**2**	**1**	**1**	**2**	**4**	**0**	**0**	**0**	**6**	**16.7**	**3**	**1**	**2**	**0**	**0**	....	....	....	....	....	....	....	....
	Binghamton Whalers	AHL	69	35	*73	108	....	....	....	82	....	....	....	....	....	....	....	....	....	....	....	....	....	....	....	....	....	....
1984-85	Mannheimer ERC	Germany	35	31	39	70	....	....	....	45	....	....	....	....	....	....	....	....	....	....	9	9	8	*17	6	....	....	....
	Fredericton Express	AHL	....	....	....	....	....	....	....	....	....	....	....	....	....	....	....	....	....	....	5	0	2	2	4	....	....	....
1985-86	Mannheimer ERC	Germany	36	20	41	61	....	....	....	38	....	....	....	....	....	....	....	....	....	....	3	1	3	4	....	....	....	....
	Rochester Americans	AHL	22	4	8	12	....	....	....	4	....	....	....	....	....	....	....	....	....	....	....	....	....	....	....	....	....	....
1986-87	EHC Kloten	Switz.	36	35	30	65	....	....	....	....	....	....	....	....	....	....	....	....	....	....	4	0	0	0	....	....	....	....
1987-88	EHC Kloten	Switz.	36	31	36	67	....	....	....	....	....	....	....	....	....	....	....	....	....	....	7	0	*8	8	....	....	....	....
1988-89	EHC Kloten	Switz.	36	34	*37	71	....	....	....	....	....	....	....	....	....	....	....	....	....	....	6	2	5	7	....	....	....	....
1989-90	EHC Kloten	Switz.	36	16	23	39	....	....	....	....	....	....	....	....	....	....	....	....	....	....	....	....	....	....	....	....	....	....
1990-91	SC Rapperswil-Jona	Switz-2	36	26	40	66	....	....	....	....	....	....	....	....	....	....	....	....	....	....	....	....	....	....	....	....	....	....
1991-92	EHC Kloten	Switz.	2	0	0	0	....	....	....	0	....	....	....	....	....	....	....	....	....	....	....	....	....	....	....	....	....	....
	HC Auronzo	Italy-2	24	29	40	69	....	....	....	26	....	....	....	....	....	....	....	....	....	....	....	....	....	....	....	....	....	....
1992-1993	Schwenninger ERC	Germany	DID NOT PLAY – COACHING																									
1993-1996	Kassel Huskies	Germany	DID NOT PLAY – COACHING																									
1996-2000	Hamburg Crocodiles	Germany	DID NOT PLAY – COACHING																									
	NHL Totals		**7**	**1**	**1**	**2**	**1**	**1**	**2**	**4**	**0**	**0**	**0**	**6**	**16.7**	**3**	**1**	**2**	**0**		....	....	....	....	....	....	....	....

AUAA First All-Star Team (1981) • AHL First All-Star Team (1983) • Won Fred T. Hunt Memorial Trophy (Sportsmanship - AHL) (1983) • Won John B. Sollenberger Trophy (Top Scorer - AHL) (1983) • Won Les Cunningham Award (MVP - AHL) (1983)

Signed as a free agent by **Hartford**, August 6, 1981.

• YAWNEY, Trent

Trent G. D – L. 6′3″, 195 lbs. b: Hudson Bay, Sask., 9/29/1965. Chicago's 2nd, 45th overall, in 1984.

Season	Club	League	GP	G	A	Pts	AG	AA	APts	PIM	PP	SH	GW	S	%	TGF	PGF	TGA	PGA	+/–	GP	G	A	Pts	PIM	PP	SH	GW
1981-82	Saskatoon Blues	SAHA	STATISTICS NOT AVAILABLE																									
	Saskatoon Blades	WHL	6	1	0	1	....	....	....	0	....	....	....	....	....	....	....	....	....	....	....	....	....	....	....	....	....	....
1982-83	Saskatoon Blades	WHL	59	6	31	37	....	....	....	44	....	....	....	....	....	....	....	....	....	....	6	0	2	2	0	....	....	....
1983-84	Saskatoon Blades	WHL	72	13	46	59	....	....	....	81	....	....	....	....	....	....	....	....	....	....	....	....	....	....	....	....	....	....
1984-85	Saskatoon Blades	WHL	72	16	51	67	....	....	....	158	....	....	....	....	....	....	....	....	....	....	3	1	6	7	7	....	....	....
1985-86	Canada	Nat-Team	73	6	15	21	....	....	....	60	....	....	....	....	....	....	....	....	....	....	....	....	....	....	....	....	....	....

			REGULAR SEASON																		PLAYOFFS							
Season	Club	League	GP	G	A	Pts	AG	AA	APts	PIM	PP	SH	GW	S	%	TGF	PGF	TGA	PGA	+/–	GP	G	A	Pts	PIM	PP	SH	GW
1986-87	Canada	Nat-Team	51	4	15	19	....	....	....	37	....	....	....	....	....	....	....	....	....	....	....	....	....	....	....	....	....	....
1987-88	Canada	Nat-Team	60	4	12	16	....	....	....	81	....	....	....	....	....	....	....	....	....	....	....	....	....	....	....	....	....	....
	Canada	Olympics	8	1	1	2	....	....	....	6	....	....	....	....	....	....	....	....	....	....	....	....	....	....	....	....	....	....
	Chicago Blackhawks	**NHL**	15	2	8	10	2	6	8	15	2	0	0	26	7.7	25	11	22	9	1	5	0	4	4	8	0	0	0
1988-89	**Chicago Blackhawks**	**NHL**	69	5	19	24	4	13	17	116	3	1	0	75	6.7	82	20	110	43	–5	15	3	6	9	20	0	1	0
1989-90	**Chicago Blackhawks**	**NHL**	70	5	15	20	4	11	15	82	1	0	1	58	8.6	76	21	79	18	–6	20	3	5	8	27	3	0	1
1990-91	**Chicago Blackhawks**	**NHL**	61	3	13	16	3	10	13	77	3	0	0	52	5.8	55	18	49	18	6	1	0	0	0	0	0	0	0
	Canada	WEC-A	10	2	4	6	....	....	....	4	....	....	....	....	....	....	....	....	....	....	....	....	....	....	....	....	....	....
1991-92	**Calgary Flames**	**NHL**	47	4	9	13	4	7	11	45	1	0	0	33	12.1	51	14	61	19	–5	....	....	....	....	....	....	....	....
	Indianapolis Ice	IHL	9	2	3	5	....	....	....	12	....	....	....	....	....	....	....	....	....	....	....	....	....	....	....	....	....	....
	Canada	WC-A	6	0	1	1	....	....	....	4	....	....	....	....	....	....	....	....	....	....	....	....	....	....	....	....	....	....
1992-93	**Calgary Flames**	**NHL**	63	1	16	17	1	11	12	67	0	0	0	61	1.6	63	9	68	23	9	6	3	2	5	6	1	0	0
1993-94	**Calgary Flames**	**NHL**	58	6	15	21	6	12	18	60	1	1	1	62	9.7	64	13	46	16	21	7	0	0	0	16	0	0	0
1994-95	**Calgary Flames**	**NHL**	37	0	2	2	0	3	3	108	0	0	0	20	0.0	16	0	29	9	–4	2	0	0	0	2	0	0	0
1995-96	**Calgary Flames**	**NHL**	69	0	3	3	0	2	2	88	0	0	0	51	0.0	37	2	60	24	–1	4	0	0	0	2	0	0	0
1996-97	**St. Louis Blues**	**NHL**	39	0	2	2	0	2	2	17	0	0	0	8	0.0	15	0	15	2	2	....	....	....	....	....	....	....	....
1997-98	**Chicago Blackhawks**	**NHL**	45	1	0	1	1	0	1	76	0	0	0	19	5.3	13	0	21	3	–5	....	....	....	....	....	....	....	....
1998-99	**Chicago Blackhawks**	**NHL**	20	0	0	0	0	0	0	32	0	0	0	11	0.0	3	0	13	4	–6	....	....	....	....	....	....	....	....
99-2000	**Chicago Blackhawks**	**NHL**	DID NOT PLAY – ASSISTANT COACH																									
	NHL Totals		593	27	102	129	25	77	102	783	11	2	2	476	5.7	500	108	573	188		60	9	17	26	81	4	1	1

Traded to **Calgary** by **Chicago** for Stephane Matteau, December 16, 1991. Signed as a free agent by **St. Louis**, July 31, 1996. Signed as a free agent by **Chicago**, September 25, 1997. • Missed remainder of 1998-99 season recovering from arm injury suffered in game vs. Colorado, January 9, 1999. • Officially announced retirement and named Assistant Coach of **Chicago**, February 24, 1999. • Named Head Coach of expansion **Norfolk Admirals** (AHL) franchise, June 23, 2000.

• YEGOROV, Alexei

RW – L. 5'11", 185 lbs. b: St. Petersburg, USSR, 5/21/1975. San Jose's 3rd, 66th overall, in 1994.

Season	Club	League	GP	G	A	Pts	AG	AA	APts	PIM	PP	SH	GW	S	%	TGF	PGF	TGA	PGA	+/–	GP	G	A	Pts	PIM	PP	SH	GW
1992-93	SKA St. Peterburg	CIS	17	1	2	3	....	....	....	10	....	....	....	....	....	....	....	....	....	....	6	3	1	4	6	....	....	....
1993-94	SKA St. Peterburg	CIS	23	5	3	8	....	....	....	18	....	....	....	....	....	....	....	....	....	....	6	0	0	0	4	....	....	....
1994-95	SKA St. Peterburg	CIS	10	2	1	3	....	....	....	10	....	....	....	....	....	....	....	....	....	....	....	....	....	....	....	....	....	....
	Fort Worth Fire	CHL	18	4	10	14	....	....	....	15	....	....	....	....	....	....	....	....	....	....	....	....	....	....	....	....	....	....
1995-96	**San Jose Sharks**	**NHL**	9	3	2	5	3	2	5	2	2	0	0	10	30.0	6	3	8	0	–5	....	....	....	....	....	....	....	....
	Kansas City Blades	IHL	65	31	25	56	....	....	....	84	....	....	....	....	....	....	....	....	....	....	5	2	0	2	8	....	....	....
1996-97	**San Jose Sharks**	**NHL**	2	0	1	1	0	1	1	0	0	0	0	0	0.0	1	0	0	0	1	....	....	....	....	....	....	....	....
	Kentucky Thoroughblades	AHL	75	26	32	58	....	....	....	59	....	....	....	....	....	....	....	....	....	....	4	0	1	1	2	....	....	....
1997-98	Kentucky Thoroughblades	AHL	79	32	52	84	....	....	....	56	....	....	....	....	....	....	....	....	....	....	3	2	0	2	0	....	....	....
1998-99	Torpedo Yaroslavl	Russia	13	3	1	4	....	....	....	8	....	....	....	....	....	....	....	....	....	....	....	....	....	....	....	....	....	....
	SKA St. Petersburg	Russia	25	8	8	16	....	....	....	30	....	....	....	....	....	....	....	....	....	....	....	....	....	....	....	....	....	....
99-2000	Adirondack IceHawks	UHL	41	16	26	42	....	....	....	35	....	....	....	....	....	....	....	....	....	....	....	....	....	....	....	....	....	....
	Long Beach Ice Dogs	IHL	20	4	9	13	....	....	....	8	....	....	....	....	....	....	....	....	....	....	6	1	0	1	2	....	....	....
	NHL Totals		11	3	3	6	3	3	6	2	2	0	0	10	30.0	7	3	8	0		....	....	....	....	....	....	....	....

Claimed by **Atlanta** from **San Jose** in Expansion Draft, June 25, 1999.

• YELLE, Stephane

C – L. 6'1", 190 lbs. b: Ottawa, Ont., 5/9/1974. New Jersey's 9th, 186th overall, in 1992.

Season	Club	League	GP	G	A	Pts	AG	AA	APts	PIM	PP	SH	GW	S	%	TGF	PGF	TGA	PGA	+/–	GP	G	A	Pts	PIM	PP	SH	GW
1990-91	Cumberland Barons	OJHL-B	33	20	30	50	....	....	....	16	....	....	....	....	....	....	....	....	....	....	....	....	....	....	....	....	....	....
1991-92	Oshawa Generals	OHL	55	12	14	26	....	....	....	20	....	....	....	....	....	....	....	....	....	....	7	2	0	2	1	....	....	....
1992-93	Oshawa Generals	OHL	66	24	50	74	....	....	....	20	....	....	....	....	....	....	....	....	....	....	10	2	4	6	4	....	....	....
1993-94	Oshawa Generals	OHL	66	35	69	104	....	....	....	22	....	....	....	....	....	....	....	....	....	....	5	1	7	8	2	....	....	....
1994-95	Cornwall Aces	AHL	40	18	15	33	....	....	....	22	....	....	....	....	....	....	....	....	....	....	13	7	7	14	8	....	....	....
1995-96♦	**Colorado Avalanche**	**NHL**	71	13	14	27	13	11	24	30	0	2	1	93	14.0	42	4	38	15	15	22	1	4	5	8	0	1	0
1996-97	**Colorado Avalanche**	**NHL**	79	9	17	26	10	15	25	38	0	1	1	89	10.1	37	0	55	19	1	12	1	6	7	2	0	0	0
1997-98	**Colorado Avalanche**	**NHL**	81	7	15	22	8	15	23	48	0	1	0	93	7.5	29	0	65	26	–10	7	1	0	1	12	0	0	0
1998-99	**Colorado Avalanche**	**NHL**	72	8	7	15	9	7	16	40	1	0	0	99	8.1	22	1	49	20	–8	10	0	1	1	6	0	0	0
99-2000	**Colorado Avalanche**	**NHL**	79	8	14	22	9	13	22	28	0	1	1	90	8.9	42	2	60	29	9	17	1	2	3	4	0	0	0
	NHL Totals		382	45	67	112	49	61	110	184	1	5	3	464	9.7	172	7	267	109		68	4	13	17	32	0	1	0

Traded to **Quebec** by **New Jersey** with New Jersey's 11th round choice (Steven Low) in 1994 Entry Draft for Quebec's 11th round choice (Mike Hansen) in 1994 Entry Draft, June 1, 1994. Transferred to **Colorado** after **Quebec** franchise relocated, June 21, 1995.

• YLONEN, Juha

Juha Petteri C – L. 6'1", 185 lbs. b: Helsinki, Finland, 2/13/1972. Winnipeg's 3rd, 91st overall, in 1991.

Season	Club	League	GP	G	A	Pts	AG	AA	APts	PIM	PP	SH	GW	S	%	TGF	PGF	TGA	PGA	+/–	GP	G	A	Pts	PIM	PP	SH	GW
1988-89	Kiekko Espoo	Finland-Jr.	31	9	14	23	....	....	....	8	....	....	....	....	....	....	....	....	....	....	....	....	....	....	....	....	....	....
1989-90	Kiekko Espoo	Finland-Jr.	4	1	5	6	....	....	....	0	....	....	....	....	....	....	....	....	....	....	5	1	5	6	0	....	....	....
	Kiekko Espoo	Finland-2	38	10	17	27	....	....	....	12	....	....	....	....	....	....	....	....	....	....	....	....	....	....	....	....	....	....
1990-91	Kiekko Espoo	Finland-Jr.	5	3	1	4	....	....	....	2	....	....	....	....	....	....	....	....	....	....	....	....	....	....	....	....	....	....
	Kiekko Espoo	Finland-2	40	12	21	33	....	....	....	4	....	....	....	....	....	....	....	....	....	....	....	....	....	....	....	....	....	....
	Finland	WJC-A	6	1	1	2	....	....	....	2	....	....	....	....	....	....	....	....	....	....	....	....	....	....	....	....	....	....
1991-92	HPK Hameenlinna	Finland-Jr.	2	1	2	3	....	....	....	0	....	....	....	....	....	....	....	....	....	....	....	....	....	....	....	....	....	....
	HPK Hameenlinna	Finland-2	9	8	14	22	....	....	....	0	....	....	....	....	....	....	....	....	....	....	....	....	....	....	....	....	....	....
	Finland	WJC-A	7	1	5	6	....	....	....	0	....	....	....	....	....	....	....	....	....	....	....	....	....	....	....	....	....	....
	HPK Hameenlinna	Finland	43	7	11	18	....	....	....	8	....	....	....	....	....	....	....	....	....	....	....	....	....	....	....	....	....	....
1992-93	HPK Hameenlinna	Finland	48	8	18	26	....	....	....	22	....	....	....	....	....	....	....	....	....	....	12	3	5	8	2	....	....	....
	HPK Hameenlinna	Finland-Jr.	2	2	1	3	....	....	....	0	....	....	....	....	....	....	....	....	....	....	1	0	0	0	0	....	....	....
	Finland	WC-A	1	0	0	0	....	....	....	0	....	....	....	....	....	....	....	....	....	....	....	....	....	....	....	....	....	....
1993-94	Jokerit Helsinki	Finland	37	5	11	16	....	....	....	2	....	....	....	....	....	....	....	....	....	....	12	1	3	4	8	....	....	....
1994-95	Jokerit Helsinki	Finland	50	13	15	28	....	....	....	10	....	....	....	....	....	....	....	....	....	....	11	3	2	5	0	....	....	....
	Finland	WC-A	8	1	3	4	....	....	....	2	....	....	....	....	....	....	....	....	....	....	....	....	....	....	....	....	....	....
1995-96	Jokerit Helsinki	Finland	24	3	13	16	....	....	....	20	....	....	....	....	....	....	....	....	....	....	11	4	5	9	4	....	....	....
	Finland	WC-A	6	0	2	2	....	....	....	4	....	....	....	....	....	....	....	....	....	....	....	....	....	....	....	....	....	....
1996-97	Finland	W-Cup	4	1	3	4	....	....	....	0	....	....	....	....	....	....	....	....	....	....	....	....	....	....	....	....	....	....
	Phoenix Coyotes	**NHL**	2	0	0	0	0	0	0	0	0	0	0	2	0.0	0	0	0	0	0	....	....	....	....	....	....	....	....
	Springfield Falcons	AHL	70	20	41	61	....	....	....	6	....	....	....	....	....	....	....	....	....	....	17	5	*16	21	4	....	....	....
1997-98	**Phoenix Coyotes**	**NHL**	55	1	11	12	1	11	12	10	0	1	0	60	1.7	18	0	36	15	–3	....	....	....	....	....	....	....	....
	Finland	Olympics	6	0	0	0	....	....	....	8	....	....	....	....	....	....	....	....	....	....	....	....	....	....	....	....	....	....
1998-99	**Phoenix Coyotes**	**NHL**	59	6	17	23	7	16	23	20	2	0	1	66	9.1	37	2	30	13	18	2	0	2	2	2	0	0	0
99-2000	**Phoenix Coyotes**	**NHL**	76	6	23	29	7	21	28	12	0	1	1	82	7.3	39	2	59	16	–6	1	0	0	0	0	0	0	0
	NHL Totals		192	13	51	64	15	48	63	42	2	2	2	210	6.2	94	4	125	44		3	0	2	2	2	0	0	0

Rights transferred to **Phoenix** after **Winnipeg** franchise relocated, July 1, 1996.

• YORK, Harry

C – L. 6'2", 215 lbs. b: Ponoka, Alta., 4/16/1974.

Season	Club	League	GP	G	A	Pts	AG	AA	APts	PIM	PP	SH	GW	S	%	TGF	PGF	TGA	PGA	+/–	GP	G	A	Pts	PIM	PP	SH	GW
1993-94	Bonnyville Pontiacs	AJHL	STATISTICS NOT AVAILABLE																									
1994-95	Fort McMurray Oil Barons	AJHL	54	36	73	*109	....	....	....	....	....	....	....	....	....	....	....	....	....	....	....	....	....	....	....	....	....	....
1995-96	Nashville Knights	ECHL	64	33	50	83	....	....	....	122	....	....	....	....	....	....	....	....	....	....	....	....	....	....	....	....	....	....
	Atlanta Knights	IHL	2	0	0	0	....	....	....	15	....	....	....	....	....	....	....	....	....	....	....	....	....	....	....	....	....	....
	Worcester IceCats	AHL	13	8	5	13	....	....	....	2	....	....	....	....	....	....	....	....	....	....	4	0	4	4	4	....	....	....
1996-97	**St. Louis Blues**	**NHL**	74	14	18	32	15	16	31	24	3	1	3	86	16.3	55	12	46	4	1	5	0	0	0	2	0	0	0
1997-98	**St. Louis Blues**	**NHL**	58	4	6	10	5	6	11	31	0	0	0	42	9.5	25	3	22	0	0	....	....	....	....	....	....	....	....
	New York Rangers	**NHL**	2	0	0	0	0	0	0	0	0	0	0	2	0.0	0	0	1	0	–1	....	....	....	....	....	....	....	....

			REGULAR SEASON																		PLAYOFFS							
Season	Club	League	GP	G	A	Pts	AG	AA	APts	PIM	PP	SH	GW	S	%	TGF	PGF	TGA	PGA	+/-	GP	G	A	Pts	PIM	PP	SH	GW
1998-99	**New York Rangers**	**NHL**	**5**	**0**	**0**	**0**	**0**	**0**	**0**	**4**	**0**	**0**	**0**	**5**	**0.0**	**0**	**0**	**1**	**0**	**–1**	....	....	....	....	....	....	....	....
	Pittsburgh Penguins	**NHL**	**2**	**0**	**0**	**0**	**0**	**0**	**0**	**0**	**0**	**0**	**0**	**0**	**0.0**	**0**	**0**	**0**	**0**	**0**	....	....	....	....	....	....	....	....
	Vancouver Canucks	**NHL**	**49**	**7**	**9**	**16**	**8**	**9**	**17**	**20**	**1**	**0**	**0**	**55**	**12.7**	**25**	**5**	**28**	**6**	**–2**	....	....	....	....	....	....	....	....
99-2000	**Vancouver Canucks**	**NHL**	**54**	**4**	**13**	**17**	**4**	**12**	**16**	**20**	**1**	**1**	**0**	**50**	**8.0**	**22**	**1**	**38**	**13**	**–4**	....	....	....	....	....	....	....	....
	Syracuse Crunch	AHL	1	0	0	0	....	....	....	15	....	....	....	....	....	....	....	....	....	....	....	....	....	....	....	....	....	....
	NHL Totals		**244**	**29**	**46**	**75**	**32**	**43**	**75**	**99**	**5**	**2**	**3**	**240**	**12.1**	**127**	**21**	**136**	**23**		**5**	**0**	**0**	**0**	**2**	**0**	**0**	**0**

Named AJHL MVP (1995) • Won AJHL Scoring Title (1995).

Signed as a free agent by **St. Louis**, May 1, 1996. Traded to **NY Rangers** by **St. Louis** for Mike Eastwood, March 24, 1998. Traded to **Pittsburgh** by **NY Rangers** with Alexei Kovalev for Petr Nedved, Chris Tamer and Sean Pronger, November 25, 1998. Claimed on waivers by **Vancouver** from **Pittsburgh**, December 7, 1998. • Played w/ RHI's Chicago Cheetahs in 1995 (24-24-47-71-25).

• YORK, Jason

D – R. 6'1", 200 lbs. b: Nepean, Ont., 5/20/1970. Detroit's 6th, 129th overall, in 1990.

Season	Club	League	GP	G	A	Pts	AG	AA	APts	PIM	PP	SH	GW	S	%	TGF	PGF	TGA	PGA	+/-	GP	G	A	Pts	PIM	PP	SH	GW
1986-87	Smiths Falls Bears	OJHL	46	6	13	19	....	....	....	86	....	....	....	....	....	....	....	....	....	....	....	....	....	....	....	....	....	....
1987-88	Hamilton Steelhawks	OHL	58	4	9	13	....	....	....	110	....	....	....	....	....	....	....	....	....	....	....	....	....	....	....	....	....	....
1988-89	Windsor Spitfires	OHL	65	19	44	63	....	....	....	105	....	....	....	....	....	....	....	....	....	....	....	....	....	....	....	....	....	....
1989-90	Windsor Spitfires	OHL	39	9	30	39	....	....	....	38	....	....	....	....	....	....	....	....	....	....	....	....	....	....	....	....	....	....
	Kitchener Rangers	OHL	25	11	25	36	....	....	....	17	....	....	....	....	....	....	....	....	....	....	17	3	19	22	10	....	....	....
	Kitchener Rangers	Mem-Cup	5	1	4	5	....	....	....	0	....	....	....	....	....	....	....	....	....	....	....	....	....	....	....	....	....	....
1990-91	Windsor Spitfires	OHL	66	13	80	93	....	....	....	40	....	....	....	....	....	....	....	....	....	....	11	3	10	13	12	....	....	....
1991-92	Adirondack Red Wings	AHL	49	4	20	24	....	....	....	32	....	....	....	....	....	....	....	....	....	....	5	0	1	1	0	....	....	....
1992-93	**Detroit Red Wings**	**NHL**	**2**	**0**	**0**	**0**	**0**	**0**	**0**	**0**	**0**	**0**	**0**	**1**	**0.0**	**1**	**0**	**1**	**0**	**0**	....	....	....	....	....	....	....	....
	Adirondack Red Wings	AHL	77	15	40	55	....	....	....	86	....	....	....	....	....	....	....	....	....	....	11	0	3	3	18	....	....	....
1993-94	**Detroit Red Wings**	**NHL**	**7**	**1**	**2**	**3**	**1**	**2**	**3**	**2**	**0**	**0**	**0**	**9**	**11.1**	**5**	**3**	**2**	**0**	**0**	....	....	....	....	....	....	....	....
	Adirondack Red Wings	AHL	74	10	56	66	....	....	....	98	....	....	....	....	....	....	....	....	....	....	12	3	11	14	22	....	....	....
1994-95	**Detroit Red Wings**	**NHL**	**10**	**1**	**2**	**3**	**2**	**3**	**5**	**2**	**0**	**0**	**0**	**6**	**16.7**	**3**	**1**	**2**	**0**	**0**	....	....	....	....	....	....	....	....
	Adirondack Red Wings	AHL	5	1	3	4	....	....	....	4	....	....	....	....	....	....	....	....	....	....	....	....	....	....	....	....	....	....
	Mighty Ducks of Anaheim	**NHL**	**15**	**0**	**8**	**8**	**0**	**12**	**12**	**12**	**0**	**0**	**0**	**22**	**0.0**	**18**	**5**	**12**	**3**	**4**	....	....	....	....	....	....	....	....
1995-96	**Mighty Ducks of Anaheim**	**NHL**	**79**	**3**	**21**	**24**	**3**	**17**	**20**	**88**	**0**	**0**	**0**	**106**	**2.8**	**68**	**16**	**90**	**31**	**–7**	....	....	....	....	....	....	....	....
1996-97	**Ottawa Senators**	**NHL**	**75**	**4**	**17**	**21**	**4**	**15**	**19**	**67**	**1**	**0**	**0**	**121**	**3.3**	**78**	**20**	**77**	**11**	**–8**	**7**	**0**	**0**	**0**	**4**	**0**	**0**	**0**
1997-98	**Ottawa Senators**	**NHL**	**73**	**3**	**13**	**16**	**4**	**13**	**17**	**62**	**0**	**0**	**0**	**109**	**2.8**	**66**	**14**	**61**	**17**	**8**	**7**	**1**	**1**	**2**	**7**	**1**	**0**	**0**
1998-99	**Ottawa Senators**	**NHL**	**79**	**4**	**31**	**35**	**5**	**30**	**35**	**48**	**2**	**0**	**0**	**177**	**2.3**	**93**	**27**	**69**	**20**	**17**	**4**	**1**	**1**	**2**	**4**	**0**	**0**	**0**
99-2000	**Ottawa Senators**	**NHL**	**79**	**8**	**22**	**30**	**9**	**20**	**29**	**60**	**1**	**0**	**1**	**159**	**5.0**	**93**	**20**	**90**	**14**	**–3**	**6**	**0**	**2**	**2**	**2**	**0**	**0**	**0**
	NHL Totals		**419**	**24**	**116**	**140**	**28**	**112**	**140**	**341**	**4**	**0**	**1**	**710**	**3.4**	**425**	**106**	**404**	**96**		**24**	**2**	**4**	**6**	**17**	**1**	**0**	**0**

AHL First All-Star Team (1994)

Traded to **Anaheim** by **Detroit** with Mike Sillinger for Stu Grimson, Mark Ferner and Anaheim's 6th round choice (Magnus Nilsson) in 1996 Entry Draft, April 4, 1995. Traded to **Ottawa** by **Anaheim** with Shaun Van Allen for Ted Drury and the rights to Marc Moro, October 1, 1996.

• YORK, Mike

Michael C – R. 5'9", 179 lbs. b: Pontiac, MI, 1/3/1978. NY Rangers' 7th, 136th overall, in 1997.

Season	Club	League	GP	G	A	Pts	AG	AA	APts	PIM	PP	SH	GW	S	%	TGF	PGF	TGA	PGA	+/-	GP	G	A	Pts	PIM	PP	SH	GW
1992-93	Michigan Nationals	MNHL	50	45	50	95	....	....	....	....	....	....	....	....	....	....	....	....	....	....	....	....	....	....	....	....	....	....
1993-94	Detroit Compuware	MNHL	85	136	140	276	....	....	....	....	....	....	....	....	....	....	....	....	....	....	....	....	....	....	....	....	....	....
1994-95	Thornhill Islanders	OJHL	49	39	54	93	....	....	....	44	....	....	....	....	....	....	....	....	....	....	11	7	6	13	0	....	....	....
1995-96	Michigan State Spartans	CCHA	39	12	27	39	....	....	....	20	....	....	....	....	....	....	....	....	....	....	....	....	....	....	....	....	....	....
1996-97	Michigan State Spartans	CCHA	37	18	29	47	....	....	....	42	....	....	....	....	....	....	....	....	....	....	....	....	....	....	....	....	....	....
	United States	WJC-A	6	5	5	10	....	....	....	4	....	....	....	....	....	....	....	....	....	....	....	....	....	....	....	....	....	....
1997-98	Michigan State Spartans	CCHA	40	27	34	61	....	....	....	38	....	....	....	....	....	....	....	....	....	....	....	....	....	....	....	....	....	....
1998-99	Michigan State Spartans	CCHA	42	22	32	*54	....	....	....	41	....	....	....	....	....	....	....	....	....	....	....	....	....	....	....	....	....	....
	Hartford Wolf Pack	AHL	3	2	2	4	....	....	....	0	....	....	....	....	....	....	....	....	....	....	6	3	1	4	0	....	....	....
99-2000	**New York Rangers**	**NHL**	**82**	**26**	**24**	**50**	**29**	**22**	**51**	**18**	**8**	**0**	**4**	**177**	**14.7**	....	....	....	....	....	....	....	....	....	....	....	....	....
	NHL Totals		**82**	**26**	**24**	**50**	**29**	**22**	**51**	**18**	**8**	**0**	**4**	**177**	**14.7**	....	....	....	....		....	....	....	....	....	....	....	....

OJHL Bauer Divison Rookie-of-the-Year (1995) • OJHL Bauer Divison All-Star Team (1995) • CCHA Second All-Star Team (1998) • NCAA West First All-American Team (1998, 1999) • CCHA First All-Star Team (1999) • NHL All-Rookie Team (2000)

• YOUNG, B.J.

RW – R. 5'10", 178 lbs. b: Anchorage, AK, 7/23/1977. Detroit's 5th, 157th overall, in 1997.

Season	Club	League	GP	G	A	Pts	AG	AA	APts	PIM	PP	SH	GW	S	%	TGF	PGF	TGA	PGA	+/-	GP	G	A	Pts	PIM	PP	SH	GW
1992-93	Anchorage North Stars	AAHL	50	48	60	108	....	....	....	94	....	....	....	....	....	....	....	....	....	....	....	....	....	....	....	....	....	....
1993-94	Tri-City Americans	WHL	54	19	24	43	....	....	....	66	....	....	....	....	....	....	....	....	....	....	2	1	1	2	2	....	....	....
1994-95	Tri-City Americans	WHL	30	6	3	9	....	....	....	39	....	....	....	....	....	....	....	....	....	....	....	....	....	....	....	....	....	....
	Red Deer Rebels	WHL	21	5	9	14	....	....	....	33	....	....	....	....	....	....	....	....	....	....	....	....	....	....	....	....	....	....
1995-96	Red Deer Rebels	WHL	67	49	45	94	....	....	....	144	....	....	....	....	....	....	....	....	....	....	8	4	9	13	12	....	....	....
1996-97	Red Deer Rebels	WHL	63	*58	56	114	....	....	....	97	....	....	....	....	....	....	....	....	....	....	16	8	14	22	26	....	....	....
1997-98	Adirondack Red Wings	AHL	65	15	22	37	....	....	....	191	....	....	....	....	....	....	....	....	....	....	3	0	2	2	6	....	....	....
1998-99	Adirondack Red Wings	AHL	58	13	17	30	....	....	....	150	....	....	....	....	....	....	....	....	....	....	3	1	0	1	6	....	....	....
99-2000	**Detroit Red Wings**	**NHL**	**1**	**0**	**0**	**0**	**0**	**0**	**0**	**0**	**0**	**0**	**0**	**1**	**0.0**	**0**	**0**	**0**	**0**	**0**	....	....	....	....	....	....	....	....
	Cincinnati Mighty Ducks	AHL	71	25	26	51	....	....	....	147	....	....	....	....	....	....	....	....	....	....	....	....	....	....	....	....	....	....
	NHL Totals		**1**	**0**	**0**	**0**	**0**	**0**	**0**	**0**	**0**	**0**	**0**	**1**	**0.0**	**0**	**0**	**0**	**0**		....	....	....	....	....	....	....	....

WHL East First All-Star Team (1997)

• YOUNG, Brian

Brian Donald D – R. 6'1", 183 lbs. b: Jasper, Alta., 10/2/1958. Chicago's 4th, 63rd overall, in 1978.

Season	Club	League	GP	G	A	Pts	AG	AA	APts	PIM	PP	SH	GW	S	%	TGF	PGF	TGA	PGA	+/-	GP	G	A	Pts	PIM	PP	SH	GW
1974-75	Estevan Bruins	SJHL	STATISTICS NOT AVAILABLE																									
1975-76	New Westminster Bruins	WCJHL	72	4	32	36	....	....	....	77	....	....	....	....	....	....	....	....	....	....	17	0	13	13	36	....	....	....
	New Westminster Bruins	Mem-Cup	4	0	3	3	....	....	....	5	....	....	....	....	....	....	....	....	....	....	....	....	....	....	....	....	....	....
1976-77	New Westminster Bruins	WCJHL	69	7	34	41	....	....	....	75	....	....	....	....	....	....	....	....	....	....	12	0	5	5	26	....	....	....
	New Westminster Bruins	Mem-Cup	....	....	....	....	....	....	....	....	....	....	....	....	....	....	....	....	....	....	....	....	....	....	....	....	....	....
1977-78	New Westminster Bruins	WCJHL	63	14	43	57	....	....	....	70	....	....	....	....	....	....	....	....	....	....	21	7	18	25	10	....	....	....
	Canada	WJC-A	6	0	2	2	....	....	....	2	....	....	....	....	....	....	....	....	....	....	....	....	....	....	....	....	....	....
	New Westminster Bruins	Mem-Cup	5	1	1	2	....	....	....	6	....	....	....	....	....	....	....	....	....	....	....	....	....	....	....	....	....	....
1978-79	New Brunswick Hawks	AHL	79	10	16	26	....	....	....	35	....	....	....	....	....	....	....	....	....	....	5	0	2	2	2	....	....	....
1979-80	New Brunswick Hawks	AHL	73	18	30	48	....	....	....	82	....	....	....	....	....	....	....	....	....	....	17	2	11	13	20	....	....	....
1980-81	**Chicago Black Hawks**	**NHL**	**8**	**0**	**2**	**2**	**0**	**1**	**1**	**6**	**0**	**0**	**0**	**5**	**0.0**	**3**	**1**	**9**	**3**	**–4**	....	....	....	....	....	....	....	....
	Dallas Black Hawks	CHL	53	7	16	23	....	....	....	43	....	....	....	....	....	....	....	....	....	....	6	1	2	3	11	....	....	....
1981-82	New Brunswick Hawks	AHL	3	0	0	0	....	....	....	0	....	....	....	....	....	....	....	....	....	....	14	0	1	1	7	....	....	....
	Schwenninger ERC	Germany	44	11	17	28	....	....	....	102	....	....	....	....	....	....	....	....	....	....	....	....	....	....	....	....	....	....
1982-83	Schwenninger ERC	Germany	35	6	16	22	....	....	....	86	....	....	....	....	....	....	....	....	....	....	....	....	....	....	....	....	....	....
1983-84	Schwenninger ERC	Germany	35	5	9	14	....	....	....	52	....	....	....	....	....	....	....	....	....	....	....	....	....	....	....	....	....	....
1984-85	Schwenninger ERC	Germany	36	7	21	28	....	....	....	62	....	....	....	....	....	....	....	....	....	....	3	1	1	2	....	....	....	....
1985-86	Kolner EC	Germany	25	10	11	21	....	....	....	63	....	....	....	....	....	....	....	....	....	....	10	2	10	12	....	....	....	....
1986-87	Kolner EC	Germany	16	1	12	13	....	....	....	32	....	....	....	....	....	....	....	....	....	....	....	....	....	....	....	....	....	....
1987-88	EHC Chur	Switz-2	36	19	12	31	....	....	....	....	....	....	....	....	....	....	....	....	....	....	....	....	....	....	....	....	....	....
1988-89	EHC Chur	Switz-2	10	3	7	10	....	....	....	....	....	....	....	....	....	....	....	....	....	....	....	....	....	....	....	....	....	....
1989-90	EHC Chur	Switz-2	36	18	9	27	....	....	....	....	....	....	....	....	....	....	....	....	....	....	....	....	....	....	....	....	....	....
	NHL Totals		**8**	**0**	**2**	**2**	**0**	**1**	**1**	**6**	**0**	**0**	**0**	**5**	**0.0**	**3**	**1**	**9**	**3**		....	....	....	....	....	....	....	....

WCJHL Second All-Star Team (1978) • Memorial Cup All-Star Team (1978) • AHL Second All-Star Team (1980)

• YOUNG, C.J.

Carl Joshua RW – R. 5'10", 180 lbs. b: Waban, MA, 1/1/1968. New Jersey's 1st, 5th overall, in 1989 Supplemental Draft.

Season	Club	League	GP	G	A	Pts	AG	AA	APts	PIM	PP	SH	GW	S	%	TGF	PGF	TGA	PGA	+/-	GP	G	A	Pts	PIM	PP	SH	GW
1983-1985	Belmont Hill Hillies	Hi-School	STATISTICS NOT AVAILABLE																									
1985-86	Belmont Hill Hillies	Hi-School	21	19	19	38	....	....	....	4	....	....	....	....	....	....	....	....	....	....	....	....	....	....	....	....	....	....
1986-87	Harvard University	ECAC	34	17	12	29	....	....	....	30	....	....	....	....	....	....	....	....	....	....	....	....	....	....	....	....	....	....

Season	Club	League	GP	G	A	Pts	AG	AA	APts	PIM	PP	SH	GW	S	%	TGF	PGF	TGA	PGA	+/–	GP	G	A	Pts	PIM	PP	SH	GW
			REGULAR SEASON																		PLAYOFFS							
1987-88	Harvard University	ECAC	28	13	16	29	....	....	....	40	....	....	....	....	....	....	....	....	....	....	....	....	....	....	....	....	....	....
	United States	WJC-A	7	2	1	3	....	....	....	8	....	....	....	....	....	....	....	....	....	....	....	....	....	....	....	....	....	....
1988-89	Harvard University	ECAC	36	20	31	51	....	....	....	36	....	....	....	....	....	....	....	....	....	....	....	....	....	....	....	....	....	....
1989-90	Harvard University	ECAC	28	21	28	49	....	....	....	32	....	....	....	....	....	....	....	....	....	....	....	....	....	....	....	....	....	....
1990-91	Salt Lake Golden Eagles	IHL	80	31	36	67	....	....	....	43	....	....	....	....	....	....	....	....	....	....	4	1	2	3	2	....	....	....
1991-92	United States	Nat-Team	49	17	17	34	....	....	....	38	....	....	....	....	....	....	....	....	....	....	....	....	....	....	....	....	....	....
	Salt Lake Golden Eagles	IHL	9	2	2	4	....	....	....	2	....	....	....	....	....	....	....	....	....	....	5	0	1	1	4	....	....	....
1992-93	**Calgary Flames**	**NHL**	**28**	**3**	**2**	**5**	**2**	**1**	**3**	**20**	**1**	**0**	**0**	**21**	**14.3**	**9**	**3**	**20**	**7**	**–7**	....	....	....	....	....	....	....	....
	Boston Bruins	**NHL**	**15**	**4**	**5**	**9**	**3**	**3**	**6**	**12**	**0**	**0**	**1**	**22**	**18.2**	**11**	**0**	**10**	**0**	**1**	....	....	....	....	....	....	....	....
	Providence Bruins	AHL	7	4	3	7	....	....	....	26	....	....	....	....	....	....	....	....	....	....	6	1	0	1	16	....	....	....
	NHL Totals		**43**	**7**	**7**	**14**	**5**	**4**	**9**	**32**	**1**	**0**	**1**	**43**	**16.3**	**20**	**3**	**30**	**7**		....	....	....	....	....	....	....	....

ECAC Second All-Star Team (1989) • ECAC First All-Star Team (1990)

Signed as a free agent by **Calgary**, October 5, 1990. Traded to **Boston** by **Calgary** for Brent Ashton, February 1, 1993.

• YOUNG, Howie Howard John "Wild Thing" D/RW – R. 5'11", 175 lbs. b: Toronto, Ont., 8/2/1937 d: 11/24/1999.

Season	Club	League	GP	G	A	Pts	AG	AA	APts	PIM	PP	SH	GW	S	%	TGF	PGF	TGA	PGA	+/–	GP	G	A	Pts	PIM	PP	SH	GW
1953-54	St. Michael's Midget Majors	MTHL	STATISTICS NOT AVAILABLE																									
	Scarbourough Scouts	OHA-B	STATISTICS NOT AVAILABLE																									
1954-55	Kitchener Canucks	OHA-Jr.	49	6	7	13	....	....	....	155	....	....	....	....	....	....	....	....	....	....	....	....	....	....	....	....	....	....
1955-56	Kitchener Canucks	OHA-Jr.	28	2	5	7	....	....	....	40	....	....	....	....	....	....	....	....	....	....	....	....	....	....	....	....	....	....
1956-57	Hamilton Tiger Cubs	OHA-Jr.	52	5	15	20	....	....	....	*228	....	....	....	....	....	....	....	....	....	....	4	0	1	1	28	....	....	....
1957-58	Hamilton Tiger Cubs	OHA-Jr.	40	3	7	10	....	....	....	163	....	....	....	....	....	....	....	....	....	....	....	....	....	....	....	....	....	....
1958-59	New Westminster Royals	WHL	4	0	1	1	....	....	....	26	....	....	....	....	....	....	....	....	....	....	....	....	....	....	....	....	....	....
	Chicoutimi Sagueneens	QHL	50	4	16	20	....	....	....	*180	....	....	....	....	....	....	....	....	....	....	....	....	....	....	....	....	....	....
1959-60	Rochester Americans	AHL	68	7	7	14	....	....	....	170	....	....	....	....	....	....	....	....	....	....	....	....	....	....	....	....	....	....
1960-61	Hershey Bears	AHL	33	1	5	6	....	....	....	160	....	....	....	....	....	....	....	....	....	....	....	....	....	....	....	....	....	....
	Detroit Red Wings	**NHL**	**29**	**0**	**8**	**8**	**0**	**8**	**8**	**108**	....	....	....	....	....	....	....	....	....	....	**11**	**2**	**2**	**4**	***30**	**0**	**0**	**0**
1961-62	**Detroit Red Wings**	**NHL**	**30**	**0**	**2**	**2**	**0**	**2**	**2**	**67**	....	....	....	....	....	....	....	....	....	....	....	....	....	....	....	....	....	....
	Edmonton Flyers	WHL	24	3	15	18	....	....	....	97	....	....	....	....	....	....	....	....	....	....	12	3	10	13	*49	....	....	....
1962-63	**Detroit Red Wings**	**NHL**	**64**	**4**	**5**	**9**	**5**	**5**	**10**	***273**	....	....	....	....	....	....	....	....	....	....	**8**	**0**	**2**	**2**	**16**	**0**	**0**	**0**
1963-64	**Chicago Black Hawks**	**NHL**	**39**	**0**	**7**	**7**	**0**	**7**	**7**	**99**	....	....	....	....	....	....	....	....	....	....	....	....	....	....	....	....	....	....
	Los Angeles Blades	WHL	13	2	4	6	....	....	....	40	....	....	....	....	....	....	....	....	....	....	4	0	2	2	21	....	....	....
1964-65	Los Angeles Blades	WHL	65	10	20	30	....	....	....	*227	....	....	....	....	....	....	....	....	....	....	....	....	....	....	....	....	....	....
1965-66	Los Angeles Blades	WHL	44	5	11	16	....	....	....	*170	....	....	....	....	....	....	....	....	....	....	....	....	....	....	....	....	....	....
1966-67	Los Angeles Blades	WHL	29	5	17	22	....	....	....	43	....	....	....	....	....	....	....	....	....	....	....	....	....	....	....	....	....	....
	Detroit Red Wings	**NHL**	**44**	**3**	**14**	**17**	**3**	**14**	**17**	**100**	....	....	....	....	....	....	....	....	....	....	....	....	....	....	....	....	....	....
1967-68	**Detroit Red Wings**	**NHL**	**62**	**2**	**17**	**19**	**2**	**17**	**19**	**112**	**0**	**0**	**0**	**87**	**2.3**	**71**	**3**	**68**	**16**	**16**	....	....	....	....	....	....	....	....
	Fort Worth Wings	CPHL	5	1	2	3	....	....	....	12	....	....	....	....	....	....	....	....	....	....	....	....	....	....	....	....	....	....
1968-69	**Chicago Black Hawks**	**NHL**	**57**	**3**	**7**	**10**	**3**	**6**	**9**	**67**	**0**	**0**	**0**	**64**	**4.7**	**23**	**1**	**37**	**2**	**–13**	....	....	....	....	....	....	....	....
1969-70	Rochester Americans	AHL	56	17	20	37	....	....	....	75	....	....	....	....	....	....	....	....	....	....	....	....	....	....	....	....	....	....
	Vancouver Canucks	WHL	16	0	3	3	....	....	....	44	....	....	....	....	....	....	....	....	....	....	....	....	....	....	....	....	....	....
1970-71	**Vancouver Canucks**	**NHL**	**11**	**0**	**2**	**2**	**0**	**2**	**2**	**25**	**0**	**0**	**0**	**18**	**0.0**	**6**	**2**	**13**	**2**	**–7**	....	....	....	....	....	....	....	....
	Phoenix Roadrunners	WHL	57	11	32	43	....	....	....	136	....	....	....	....	....	....	....	....	....	....	10	0	3	3	21	....	....	....
1971-72	San Diego Gulls	WHL	DID NOT PLAY – SUSPENDED																									
1972-73	Phoenix Roadrunners	WHL	71	20	38	58	....	....	....	223	....	....	....	....	....	....	....	....	....	....	10	1	5	6	31	....	....	....
1973-74	Phoenix Roadrunners	WHL	71	37	32	69	....	....	....	124	....	....	....	....	....	....	....	....	....	....	9	3	3	6	6	....	....	....
1974-75	Phoenix Roadrunners	WHA	30	3	12	15	....	....	....	44	....	....	....	....	....	....	....	....	....	....	....	....	....	....	....	....	....	....
	Winnipeg Jets	WHA	42	13	10	23	....	....	....	42	....	....	....	....	....	....	....	....	....	....	....	....	....	....	....	....	....	....
1975-76			DID NOT PLAY																									
1976-77	Phoenix Roadrunners	WHA	26	1	3	4	....	....	....	23	....	....	....	....	....	....	....	....	....	....	....	....	....	....	....	....	....	....
	Oklahoma City Blazers	CHL	4	0	0	0	....	....	....	8	....	....	....	....	....	....	....	....	....	....	....	....	....	....	....	....	....	....
1977-78	Phoenix Roadrunners	PHL	39	4	11	15	....	....	....	63	....	....	....	....	....	....	....	....	....	....	....	....	....	....	....	....	....	....
1978-79	Los Angeles Blades	PHL	14	0	2	2	....	....	....	22	....	....	....	....	....	....	....	....	....	....	....	....	....	....	....	....	....	....
1979-1985			OUT OF HOCKEY – RETIRED																									
1985-86	Flint Generals	IHL	4	0	1	1	....	....	....	2	....	....	....	....	....	....	....	....	....	....	....	....	....	....	....	....	....	....
	New York Slapshots	NAHL	7	0	1	1	....	....	....	18	....	....	....	....	....	....	....	....	....	....	....	....	....	....	....	....	....	....
	NHL Totals		**336**	**12**	**62**	**74**	**13**	**61**	**74**	**851**	....	....	....	....	....	....	....	....	....	....	**19**	**2**	**4**	**6**	**46**	....	....	....
	Other Major League Totals		98	17	25	42	....	....	....	109																		

WHL First All-Star Team (1974)

Loaned to **New Westminster** (WHL) by **Toronto** for cash, October, 1958. Loaned transferred to **Chicoutimi** by **Toronto** for cash, October 26, 1958. Traded to **Hershey** (AHL) by **Toronto** (Rochester-AHL) for cash, August, 1960. Traded to **Detroit** by **Hershey** (AHL) for Jack McIntyre, Marc Reaume and Pete Conacher, January, 1961. Traded to **Chicago** by **Detroit** for Ron Ingram and Roger Crozier, June 5, 1963. Traded to **LA Blades** (WHL) by **Chicago** for cash and future considerations (rights to Wayne Smith, July, 1964) with Chicago retaining NHL rights, February 11, 1964. Traded to **Detroit** by **Chicago** (LA Blades-WHL) for loan of Murray Hall and Al Lebrun for remainder of 1966-67 season and future considerations (Murray Hall, Al Lebrun and Rick Morris, June, 1967), December 20, 1966. Traded to **Oakland** by **Detroit** with Gary Jarrett, Doug Roberts and Chris Worthy for Bob Baun and Ron Harris, May 27, 1968. Claimed on waivers by **Chicago** from **Oakland**, October 2, 1968. • Rights transferred to **Vancouver** after NHL club purchased Vancouver (WHL) franchise, December 19, 1969. Loaned to **Phoenix** (WHL) by **Vancouver** for remainder of 1970-71 season, November 7, 1970. Claimed by **San Diego** (WHL) from **Vancouver** in Reverse Draft, June, 1971. • Suspended by **San Diego** (WHL) for refusing to report to team, September, 1971. Traded to **Phoenix** (WHL) by **San Diego** (WHL) for cash, August, 1972. WHA rights transferred to **Phoenix** (WHA) after owners of **Phoenix** (WHL) franchise granted WHA expansion team, September 14, 1973. Traded to **Winnipeg** (WHA) by **Phoenix** (WHA) for cash, January, 1975. Signed as a free agent by **Phoenix** (WHA), February 12, 1977.

• YOUNG, Scott Scott Allen "Duck" RW – R. 6'1", 200 lbs. b: Clinton, MA, 10/1/1967. Hartford's 1st, 11th overall, in 1986.

Season	Club	League	GP	G	A	Pts	AG	AA	APts	PIM	PP	SH	GW	S	%	TGF	PGF	TGA	PGA	+/–	GP	G	A	Pts	PIM	PP	SH	GW
1984-85	St. Marks High School	Hi-School	23	28	41	69	....	....	....		....	....	....	....	....	....	....	....	....	....	....	....	....	....	....	....	....	....
	United States	WJC-A	7	1	2	3	....	....	....	4	....	....	....	....	....	....	....	....	....	....	....	....	....	....	....	....	....	....
1985-86	Boston University	H-East	38	16	13	29	....	....	....	31	....	....	....	....	....	....	....	....	....	....	....	....	....	....	....	....	....	....
	United States	WJC-A	7	1	3	4	....	....	....	8	....	....	....	....	....	....	....	....	....	....	....	....	....	....	....	....	....	....
1986-87	Boston University	H-East	33	15	21	36	....	....	....	24	....	....	....	....	....	....	....	....	....	....	....	....	....	....	....	....	....	....
	United States	WJC-A	7	7	2	9	....	....	....	2	....	....	....	....	....	....	....	....	....	....	....	....	....	....	....	....	....	....
	United States	WEC-A	4	0	1	1	....	....	....	2	....	....	....	....	....	....	....	....	....	....	....	....	....	....	....	....	....	....
1987-88	United States	Nat-Team	56	11	47	58	....	....	....	31	....	....	....	....	....	....	....	....	....	....	....	....	....	....	....	....	....	....
	United States	Olympics	6	2	6	8	....	....	....	4	....	....	....	....	....	....	....	....	....	....	....	....	....	....	....	....	....	....
	Hartford Whalers	**NHL**	**7**	**0**	**0**	**0**	**0**	**0**	**0**	**2**	**0**	**0**	**0**	**6**	**0.0**	**1**	**0**	**7**	**0**	**–6**	**4**	**1**	**0**	**1**	**0**	**0**	**0**	**0**
1988-89	**Hartford Whalers**	**NHL**	**76**	**19**	**40**	**59**	**16**	**28**	**44**	**27**	**6**	**0**	**2**	**203**	**9.4**	**106**	**60**	**67**	**0**	**–21**	**4**	**2**	**0**	**2**	**4**	**0**	**0**	**0**
	United States	WEC-A	10	0	7	7	....	....	....	6	....	....	....	....	....	....	....	....	....	....	....	....	....	....	....	....	....	....
1989-90	**Hartford Whalers**	**NHL**	**80**	**24**	**40**	**64**	**21**	**29**	**50**	**47**	**10**	**2**	**5**	**239**	**10.0**	**111**	**62**	**84**	**11**	**–24**	**7**	**2**	**0**	**2**	**2**	**0**	**0**	**0**
1990-91	**Hartford Whalers**	**NHL**	**34**	**6**	**9**	**15**	**5**	**7**	**12**	**8**	**3**	**1**	**2**	**94**	**6.4**	**38**	**18**	**33**	**4**	**–9**	....	....	....	....	....	....	....	....
♦	**Pittsburgh Penguins**	**NHL**	**43**	**11**	**16**	**27**	**10**	**12**	**22**	**33**	**3**	**1**	**3**	**116**	**9.5**	**43**	**14**	**37**	**11**	**3**	**17**	**1**	**6**	**7**	**2**	**1**	**0**	**0**
1991-92	HC Bolzano	Alpenliga	15	19	11	30	....	....	....	14	....	....	....	....	....	....	....	....	....	....	....	....	....	....	....	....	....	....
	HC Bolzano	Italy	18	22	17	39	....	....	....	6	....	....	....	....	....	....	....	....	....	....	5	4	3	7	7	....	....	....
	United States	Nat-Team	10	2	4	6	....	....	....	21	....	....	....	....	....	....	....	....	....	....	....	....	....	....	....	....	....	....
	United States	Olympics	8	2	1	3	....	....	....	2	....	....	....	....	....	....	....	....	....	....	....	....	....	....	....	....	....	....
1992-93	**Quebec Nordiques**	**NHL**	**82**	**30**	**30**	**60**	**25**	**21**	**46**	**20**	**9**	**6**	**5**	**225**	**13.3**	**115**	**49**	**82**	**21**	**5**	**6**	**4**	**1**	**5**	**0**	**0**	**0**	**2**
1993-94	**Quebec Nordiques**	**NHL**	**76**	**26**	**25**	**51**	**24**	**19**	**43**	**14**	**6**	**1**	**1**	**236**	**11.0**	**73**	**26**	**75**	**24**	**–4**	....	....	....	....	....	....	....	....
	United States	WC-A	8	3	1	4	....	....	....	4	....	....	....	....	....	....	....	....	....	....	....	....	....	....	....	....	....	....
1994-95	EV Landshut	Germany	4	6	1	7	....	....	....	6	....	....	....	....	....	....	....	....	....	....	....	....	....	....	....	....	....	....
	Frankfurt Lions	Germany	1	1	0	1	....	....	....	0	....	....	....	....	....	....	....	....	....	....	....	....	....	....	....	....	....	....
	Quebec Nordiques	**NHL**	**48**	**18**	**21**	**39**	**32**	**31**	**63**	**14**	**3**	**3**	**0**	**167**	**10.8**	**57**	**24**	**31**	**7**	**9**	**6**	**3**	**3**	**6**	**2**	**0**	**1**	**0**
1995-96 ♦	**Colorado Avalanche**	**NHL**	**81**	**21**	**39**	**60**	**21**	**32**	**53**	**50**	**7**	**0**	**5**	**229**	**9.2**	**86**	**31**	**62**	**9**	**2**	**22**	**3**	**12**	**15**	**10**	**0**	**0**	**0**
1996-97	United States	W-Cup	7	2	2	4	....	....	....	4	....	....	....	....	....	....	....	....	....	....	....	....	....	....	....	....	....	....
	Colorado Avalanche	**NHL**	**72**	**18**	**19**	**37**	**19**	**17**	**36**	**14**	**7**	**0**	**0**	**164**	**11.0**	**58**	**32**	**35**	**4**	**–5**	**17**	**4**	**2**	**6**	**14**	**2**	**0**	**0**

										REGULAR SEASON											PLAYOFFS							
Season	**Club**	**League**	**GP**	**G**	**A**	**Pts**	**AG**	**AA**	**APts**	**PIM**	**PP**	**SH**	**GW**	**S**	**%**	**TGF**	**PGF**	**TGA**	**PGA**	**+/–**	**GP**	**G**	**A**	**Pts**	**PIM**	**PP**	**SH**	**GW**
1997-98	**Mighty Ducks of Anaheim**	**NHL**	**73**	**13**	**20**	**33**	**15**	**20**	**35**	**22**	**4**	**2**	**1**	**187**	**7.0**	**50**	**21**	**71**	**29**	**–13**	....	....	....	....	....	....	....	....
1998-99	**St. Louis Blues**	**NHL**	**75**	**24**	**28**	**52**	**28**	**27**	**55**	**27**	**8**	**0**	**4**	**205**	**11.7**	**74**	**27**	**40**	**1**	**8**	**13**	**4**	**7**	**11**	**10**	**1**	**0**	**1**
99-2000	**St. Louis Blues**	**NHL**	**75**	**24**	**15**	**39**	**27**	**14**	**41**	**18**	**6**	**1**	**7**	**244**	**9.8**	**71**	**30**	**32**	**3**	**12**	**6**	**6**	**2**	**8**	**8**	**3**	**0**	**0**
	NHL Totals		**822**	**234**	**302**	**536**	**243**	**257**	**500**	**296**	**72**	**17**	**35**	**2315**	**10.1**	**883**	**394**	**656**	**124**		**102**	**30**	**33**	**63**	**52**	**7**	**1**	**3**

WJC-A All-Star Team (1987) • ECAC First All-Star Team (1989)

Traded to **Pittsburgh** by **Hartford** for Rob Brown, December 21, 1990. Traded to **Quebec** by **Pittsburgh** for Bryan Fogarty, March 10, 1992. Transferred to **Colorado** after **Quebec** franchise relocated, June 21, 1995. Traded to **Anaheim** by **Colorado** for Anaheim's 3rd round choice (later traded to Florida - Florida selected Lance Ward) in 1998 Entry Draft, September 17, 1997. Signed as a free agent by **St. Louis**, July 28, 1998.

• YOUNG, Tim

Timothy Michael "Blade" C – R. 6'1", 190 lbs. b: Scarborough, Ont., 2/22/1955. Los Angeles' 1st, 16th overall, in 1975.

Season	Club	League	GP	G	A	Pts	AG	AA	APts	PIM	PP	SH	GW	S	%	TGF	PGF	TGA	PGA	+/–	GP	G	A	Pts	PIM	PP	SH	GW
1972-73	Pembroke Lumber Kings	OJHL	55	41	40	81	....	....	....	148	....	....	....	....	....	....	....	....	....	....	....	....	....	....	....	....	....	....
1973-74	Ottawa 67's	OMJHL	69	45	61	106	....	....	....	161	....	....	....	....	....	....	....	....	....	....	7	4	1	5	6	....	....	....
1974-75	Ottawa 67's	OMJHL	70	56	*107	163	....	....	....	127	....	....	....	....	....	....	....	....	....	....	5	3	4	7	8	....	....	....
1975-76	**Minnesota North Stars**	**NHL**	**63**	**18**	**33**	**51**	**16**	**25**	**41**	**71**	**5**	**0**	**2**	**127**	**14.2**	**60**	**17**	**54**	**1**	**–10**	....	....	....	....	....	....	....	....
	New Haven Nighthawks	AHL	13	7	13	20	....	....	....	6	....	....	....	....	....	....	....	....	....	....	....	....	....	....	....	....	....	....
1976-77	**Minnesota North Stars**	**NHL**	**80**	**29**	**66**	**95**	**26**	**51**	**77**	**58**	**10**	**0**	**2**	**223**	**13.0**	**115**	**49**	**98**	**0**	**–32**	**2**	**1**	**1**	**2**	**2**	**0**	**0**	**0**
1977-78	**Minnesota North Stars**	**NHL**	**78**	**23**	**35**	**58**	**21**	**27**	**48**	**64**	**5**	**0**	**2**	**217**	**10.6**	**78**	**23**	**92**	**0**	**–37**	....	....	....	....	....	....	....	....
1978-79	**Minnesota North Stars**	**NHL**	**73**	**24**	**32**	**56**	**21**	**23**	**44**	**46**	**8**	**0**	**5**	**147**	**16.3**	**78**	**31**	**61**	**2**	**–12**	....	....	....	....	....	....	....	....
1979-80	**Minnesota North Stars**	**NHL**	**77**	**31**	**43**	**74**	**26**	**31**	**57**	**24**	**5**	**2**	**5**	**220**	**14.1**	**101**	**25**	**73**	**11**	**14**	**15**	**2**	**5**	**7**	**4**	**1**	**1**	**0**
1980-81	Minnesota North Stars	DN-Cup	3	1	2	3	....	....	....	6	....	....	....	....	....	....	....	....	....	....	....	....	....	....	....	....	....	....
	Minnesota North Stars	**NHL**	**74**	**25**	**41**	**66**	**19**	**27**	**46**	**40**	**10**	**0**	**4**	**214**	**11.7**	**107**	**53**	**63**	**15**	**6**	**12**	**3**	**14**	**17**	**9**	**0**	**0**	**1**
1981-82	**Minnesota North Stars**	**NHL**	**49**	**10**	**31**	**41**	**8**	**21**	**29**	**67**	**1**	**0**	**1**	**125**	**8.0**	**62**	**19**	**50**	**7**	**0**	**4**	**1**	**1**	**2**	**10**	**0**	**0**	**0**
1982-83	**Minnesota North Stars**	**NHL**	**70**	**18**	**35**	**53**	**15**	**24**	**39**	**31**	**6**	**2**	**2**	**152**	**11.8**	**76**	**33**	**71**	**27**	**–1**	**2**	**0**	**2**	**2**	**2**	**0**	**0**	**0**
1983-84	**Winnipeg Jets**	**NHL**	**44**	**15**	**19**	**34**	**12**	**13**	**25**	**25**	**3**	**0**	**0**	**77**	**19.5**	**50**	**17**	**56**	**12**	**–11**	**1**	**0**	**1**	**1**	**0**	**0**	**0**	**0**
1984-85	**Philadelphia Flyers**	**NHL**	**20**	**2**	**6**	**8**	**2**	**4**	**6**	**12**	**0**	**0**	**1**	**25**	**8.0**	**16**	**2**	**13**	**1**	**2**	....	....	....	....	....	....	....	....
	Hershey Bears	AHL	49	19	29	48	....	....	....	56	....	....	....	....	....	....	....	....	....	....	....	....	....	....	....	....	....	....
	NHL Totals		**628**	**195**	**341**	**536**	**166**	**246**	**412**	**438**	**53**	**4**	**24**	**1527**	**12.8**	**743**	**269**	**631**	**76**		**36**	**7**	**24**	**31**	**27**	**1**	**1**	**1**

Played in NHL All-Star Game (1977)

Traded to **Minnesota** by **LA Kings** for Minnesota's 2nd round choice (Steve Clippingdale) in 1976 Amateur Draft, August 15, 1975. Traded to **Winnipeg** by **Minnesota** for Craig Levie and Tom Ward, August 3, 1983. Traded to **Philadelphia** by **Winnipeg** for future considerations, October 16, 1984.

• YOUNG, Warren

Warren Howard C – L. 6'3", 195 lbs. b: Toronto, Ont., 1/11/1956. California's 4th, 59th overall, in 1976.

Season	Club	League	GP	G	A	Pts	AG	AA	APts	PIM	PP	SH	GW	S	%	TGF	PGF	TGA	PGA	+/–	GP	G	A	Pts	PIM	PP	SH	GW
1974-75	Dixie Beehives	OHA-B	44	32	25	57	....	....	....	50	....	....	....	....	....	....	....	....	....	....	....	....	....	....	....	....	....	....
1975-76	Michigan Tech Huskies	WCHA	42	16	15	31	....	....	....	48	....	....	....	....	....	....	....	....	....	....	....	....	....	....	....	....	....	....
1976-77	Michigan Tech Huskies	WCHA	37	19	26	45	....	....	....	86	....	....	....	....	....	....	....	....	....	....	....	....	....	....	....	....	....	....
1977-78	Michigan Tech Huskies	WCHA	32	14	16	30	....	....	....	54	....	....	....	....	....	....	....	....	....	....	....	....	....	....	....	....	....	....
1978-79	Michigan Tech Huskies	WCHA	26	11	7	18	....	....	....	45	....	....	....	....	....	....	....	....	....	....	....	....	....	....	....	....	....	....
	Oklahoma City Stars	CHL	4	0	1	1	....	....	....	2	....	....	....	....	....	....	....	....	....	....	....	....	....	....	....	....	....	....
1979-80	Baltimore Clippers	EHL	65	*53	53	106	....	....	....	75	....	....	....	....	....	....	....	....	....	....	....	....	....	....	....	....	....	....
	Oklahoma City Stars	CHL	13	4	8	12	....	....	....	9	....	....	....	....	....	....	....	....	....	....	....	....	....	....	....	....	....	....
1980-81	Oklahoma City Stars	CHL	77	26	33	59	....	....	....	42	....	....	....	....	....	....	....	....	....	....	3	1	1	2	7	....	....	....
1981-82	**Minnesota North Stars**	**NHL**	**1**	**0**	**0**	**0**	**0**	**0**	**0**	**0**	**0**	**0**	**0**	**0**	**0.0**	**0**	**0**	**3**	**0**	**–3**	....	....	....	....	....	....	....	....
	Nashville South Stars	CHL	60	31	28	59	....	....	....	154	....	....	....	....	....	....	....	....	....	....	....	....	....	....	....	....	....	....
1982-83	**Minnesota North Stars**	**NHL**	**4**	**1**	**1**	**2**	**1**	**1**	**2**	**0**	**0**	**0**	**0**	**2**	**50.0**	**2**	**0**	**2**	**0**	**0**	....	....	....	....	....	....	....	....
	Birmingham South Stars	CHL	75	26	58	84	....	....	....	144	....	....	....	....	....	....	....	....	....	....	13	3	3	6	57	....	....	....
1983-84	**Pittsburgh Penguins**	**NHL**	**15**	**1**	**7**	**8**	**1**	**5**	**6**	**19**	**0**	**0**	**0**	**12**	**8.3**	**13**	**1**	**14**	**0**	**–2**	....	....	....	....	....	....	....	....
	Baltimore Skipjacks	AHL	59	25	38	63	....	....	....	142	....	....	....	....	....	....	....	....	....	....	10	2	6	8	18	....	....	....
1984-85	**Pittsburgh Penguins**	**NHL**	**80**	**40**	**32**	**72**	**33**	**22**	**55**	**174**	**9**	**0**	**3**	**130**	**30.8**	**113**	**39**	**94**	**0**	**–20**	....	....	....	....	....	....	....	....
1985-86	**Detroit Red Wings**	**NHL**	**79**	**22**	**24**	**46**	**18**	**16**	**34**	**161**	**9**	**0**	**1**	**95**	**23.2**	**75**	**32**	**77**	**0**	**–34**	....	....	....	....	....	....	....	....
1986-87	**Pittsburgh Penguins**	**NHL**	**50**	**8**	**13**	**21**	**7**	**9**	**16**	**103**	**3**	**0**	**1**	**52**	**15.4**	**34**	**9**	**31**	**1**	**–5**	....	....	....	....	....	....	....	....
	Baltimore Skipjacks	AHL	22	8	7	15	....	....	....	95	....	....	....	....	....	....	....	....	....	....	....	....	....	....	....	....	....	....
1987-88	**Pittsburgh Penguins**	**NHL**	**7**	**0**	**0**	**0**	**0**	**0**	**0**	**15**	**0**	**0**	**0**	**3**	**0.0**	**1**	**0**	**5**	**0**	**–4**	....	....	....	....	....	....	....	....
	Muskegon Lumberjacks	IHL	60	25	26	51	....	....	....	325	....	....	....	....	....	....	....	....	....	....	4	0	0	0	42	....	....	....
	NHL Totals		**236**	**72**	**77**	**149**	**60**	**53**	**113**	**472**	**21**	**0**	**5**	**294**	**24.5**	**238**	**81**	**226**	**1**		....	....	....	....	....	....	....	....

EHL Second All-Star Team (1980) • CHL Second All-Star Team (1983) • NHL All-Rookie Team (1985)

Signed as a free agent by **Minnesota**, October 22, 1981. Signed as a free agent by **Pittsburgh**, August 12, 1983. Signed as a free agent by **Detroit**, July 10, 1985. Traded to **Pittsburgh** by **Detroit** for cash, October 8, 1986. • Played w/ RHI's Pittsburgh Phantoms 1993-94 (4-1-3-4-20).

• YOUNGHANS, Tom

Thomas A. RW – R. 5'11", 175 lbs. b: St. Paul, MN, 1/22/1953.

Season	Club	League	GP	G	A	Pts	AG	AA	APts	PIM	PP	SH	GW	S	%	TGF	PGF	TGA	PGA	+/–	GP	G	A	Pts	PIM	PP	SH	GW
1974-75	University of Minnesota	WCHA	22	13	15	28	....	....	....	22	....	....	....	....	....	....	....	....	....	....	....	....	....	....	....	....	....	....
1975-76	University of Minnesota	WCHA	44	19	24	43	....	....	....	94	....	....	....	....	....	....	....	....	....	....	....	....	....	....	....	....	....	....
	United States	WEC-A	10	2	2	4	....	....	....	8	....	....	....	....	....	....	....	....	....	....	....	....	....	....	....	....	....	....
1976-77	**Minnesota North Stars**	**NHL**	**78**	**8**	**6**	**14**	**7**	**5**	**12**	**35**	**1**	**3**	**0**	**54**	**14.8**	**21**	**1**	**70**	**39**	**–11**	**2**	**0**	**0**	**0**	**0**	**0**	**0**	**0**
	United States	WEC-A	10	0	4	4	....	....	....	8	....	....	....	....	....	....	....	....	....	....	....	....	....	....	....	....	....	....
1977-78	**Minnesota North Stars**	**NHL**	**72**	**10**	**8**	**18**	**9**	**6**	**15**	**100**	**1**	**0**	**0**	**71**	**14.1**	**29**	**2**	**57**	**20**	**–10**	....	....	....	....	....	....	....	....
	Fort Worth Texans	CHL	6	3	2	5	....	....	....	2	....	....	....	....	....	....	....	....	....	....	....	....	....	....	....	....	....	....
	United States	WEC-A	10	2	1	3	....	....	....	6	....	....	....	....	....	....	....	....	....	....	....	....	....	....	....	....	....	....
1978-79	**Minnesota North Stars**	**NHL**	**76**	**8**	**10**	**18**	**7**	**7**	**14**	**50**	**0**	**0**	**1**	**70**	**11.4**	**25**	**0**	**69**	**21**	**–23**	....	....	....	....	....	....	....	....
1979-80	**Minnesota North Stars**	**NHL**	**79**	**10**	**6**	**16**	**8**	**4**	**12**	**92**	**0**	**1**	**0**	**79**	**12.7**	**30**	**0**	**57**	**24**	**–3**	**15**	**2**	**1**	**3**	**17**	**0**	**2**	**0**
1980-81	Minnesota North Stars	DN-Cup	2	0	0	0	....	....	....	2	....	....	....	....	....	....	....	....	....	....	....	....	....	....	....	....	....	....
	Minnesota North Stars	**NHL**	**74**	**4**	**6**	**10**	**3**	**4**	**7**	**79**	**1**	**1**	**2**	**55**	**7.3**	**18**	**1**	**60**	**35**	**–8**	**5**	**0**	**0**	**0**	**4**	**0**	**0**	**0**
1981-82	United States	Can-Cup	4	0	0	0	....	....	....	0	....	....	....	....	....	....	....	....	....	....	....	....	....	....	....	....	....	....
	Minnesota North Stars	**NHL**	**3**	**1**	**0**	**1**	**1**	**0**	**1**	**0**	**0**	**1**	**0**	**2**	**50.0**	**1**	**0**	**1**	**1**	**1**	....	....	....	....	....	....	....	....
	Nashville South Stars	CHL	5	5	3	8	....	....	....	2	....	....	....	....	....	....	....	....	....	....	....	....	....	....	....	....	....	....
	New York Rangers	**NHL**	**47**	**3**	**5**	**8**	**2**	**3**	**5**	**17**	**0**	**0**	**0**	**37**	**8.1**	**14**	**0**	**32**	**18**	**0**	**2**	**0**	**0**	**0**	**0**	**0**	**0**	**0**
	Springfield Indians	AHL	7	4	0	4	....	....	....	16	....	....	....	....	....	....	....	....	....	....	....	....	....	....	....	....	....	....
	NHL Totals		**429**	**44**	**41**	**85**	**37**	**29**	**66**	**373**	**3**	**6**	**3**	**368**	**12.0**	**138**	**4**	**346**	**158**		**24**	**2**	**1**	**3**	**21**	**0**	**2**	**0**

Signed as a free agent by **Minnesota**, September 14, 1976. Traded to **NY Rangers** by **Minnesota** for cash, October 30, 1981.

• YSEBAERT, Paul

Paul Robert C – L. 6'1", 194 lbs. b: Sarnia, Ont., 5/15/1966. New Jersey's 4th, 74th overall, in 1984.

Season	Club	League	GP	G	A	Pts	AG	AA	APts	PIM	PP	SH	GW	S	%	TGF	PGF	TGA	PGA	+/–	GP	G	A	Pts	PIM	PP	SH	GW
1982-83	Petrolia Jets	OJHL-B	40	23	30	53	....	....	....	24	....	....	....	....	....	....	....	....	....	....	....	....	....	....	....	....	....	....
	Newmarket Flyers	OJHL	2	0	0	0	....	....	....	19	....	....	....	....	....	....	....	....	....	....	....	....	....	....	....	....	....	....
1983-84	Petrolia Jets	OJHL-B	33	35	42	77	....	....	....	18	....	....	....	....	....	....	....	....	....	....	....	....	....	....	....	....	....	....
1984-85	Bowling Green University	CCHA	42	23	32	55	....	....	....	54	....	....	....	....	....	....	....	....	....	....	....	....	....	....	....	....	....	....
1985-86	Bowling Green University	CCHA	42	23	45	68	....	....	....	50	....	....	....	....	....	....	....	....	....	....	....	....	....	....	....	....	....	....
1986-87	Bowling Green University	CCHA	45	27	58	85	....	....	....	44	....	....	....	....	....	....	....	....	....	....	....	....	....	....	....	....	....	....
	Canada	Nat-Team	5	1	0	1	....	....	....	4	....	....	....	....	....	....	....	....	....	....	....	....	....	....	....	....	....	....
1987-88	Utica Devils	AHL	78	30	49	79	....	....	....	60	....	....	....	....	....	....	....	....	....	....	....	....	....	....	....	....	....	....
1988-89	**New Jersey Devils**	**NHL**	**5**	**0**	**4**	**4**	**0**	**3**	**3**	**0**	**0**	**0**	**0**	**4**	**0.0**	**6**	**2**	**2**	**0**	**2**	....	....	....	....	....	....	....	....
	Utica Devils	AHL	56	36	44	80	....	....	....	22	....	....	....	....	....	....	....	....	....	....	5	0	1	1	4	....	....	....
1989-90	**New Jersey Devils**	**NHL**	**5**	**1**	**2**	**3**	**1**	**1**	**2**	**0**	**0**	**0**	**0**	**6**	**16.7**	**4**	**1**	**3**	**0**	**0**	....	....	....	....	....	....	....	....
	Utica Devils	AHL	74	53	52	*105	....	....	....	61	....	....	....	....	....	....	....	....	....	....	5	2	4	6	0	....	....	....
1990-91	**New Jersey Devils**	**NHL**	**11**	**4**	**3**	**7**	**4**	**2**	**6**	**6**	**1**	**0**	**0**	**14**	**28.6**	**8**	**2**	**5**	**0**	**1**	....	....	....	....	....	....	....	....
	Detroit Red Wings	**NHL**	**51**	**15**	**18**	**33**	**14**	**14**	**28**	**16**	**5**	**0**	**1**	**114**	**13.2**	**49**	**16**	**46**	**5**	**–8**	**2**	**0**	**2**	**2**	**0**	**0**	**0**	**0**
1991-92	**Detroit Red Wings**	**NHL**	**79**	**35**	**40**	**75**	**32**	**30**	**62**	**55**	**3**	**4**	**3**	**211**	**16.6**	**114**	**29**	**56**	**15**	**44**	**10**	**1**	**0**	**1**	**10**	**0**	**0**	**0**
1992-93	**Detroit Red Wings**	**NHL**	**80**	**34**	**28**	**62**	**28**	**19**	**47**	**42**	**3**	**3**	**8**	**186**	**18.3**	**91**	**20**	**64**	**12**	**19**	**7**	**3**	**1**	**4**	**2**	**0**	**1**	**1**
1993-94	**Winnipeg Jets**	**NHL**	**60**	**9**	**18**	**27**	**8**	**14**	**22**	**18**	**1**	**0**	**0**	**120**	**7.5**	**39**	**13**	**39**	**5**	**–8**	....	....	....	....	....	....	....	....
	Chicago Blackhawks	**NHL**	**11**	**5**	**3**	**8**	**5**	**2**	**7**	**8**	**2**	**0**	**1**	**31**	**16.1**	**14**	**7**	**6**	**0**	**1**	**6**	**0**	**0**	**0**	**8**	**0**	**0**	**0**

			REGULAR SEASON																		PLAYOFFS							
Season	**Club**	**League**	**GP**	**G**	**A**	**Pts**	**AG**	**AA**	**APts**	**PIM**	**PP**	**SH**	**GW**	**S**	**%**	**TGF**	**PGF**	**TGA**	**PGA**	**+/–**	**GP**	**G**	**A**	**Pts**	**PIM**	**PP**	**SH**	**GW**
1994-95	**Chicago Blackhawks**	**NHL**	**15**	**4**	**5**	**9**	**7**	**7**	**14**	**6**	**0**	**0**	**1**	**23**	**17.4**	**14**	**2**	**8**	**0**	**4**	....	....	....	....	....	....	....	....
	Tampa Bay Lightning	**NHL**	**29**	**8**	**11**	**19**	**14**	**16**	**30**	**12**	**0**	**0**	**0**	**70**	**11.4**	**33**	**7**	**29**	**2**	**–1**	....	....	....	....	....	....	....	....
1995-96	**Tampa Bay Lightning**	**NHL**	**55**	**16**	**15**	**31**	**16**	**12**	**28**	**16**	**4**	**1**	**1**	**135**	**11.9**	**57**	**27**	**53**	**4**	**–19**	**5**	**0**	**0**	**0**	**0**	**0**	**0**	**0**
1996-97	**Tampa Bay Lightning**	**NHL**	**39**	**5**	**12**	**17**	**5**	**11**	**16**	**4**	**2**	**0**	**0**	**91**	**5.5**	**26**	**6**	**23**	**4**	**1**	....	....	....	....	....	....	....	....
1997-98	**Tampa Bay Lightning**	**NHL**	**82**	**13**	**27**	**40**	**15**	**26**	**41**	**32**	**2**	**1**	**0**	**145**	**9.0**	**56**	**23**	**89**	**13**	**–43**	....	....	....	....	....	....	....	....
1998-99	**Tampa Bay Lightning**	**NHL**	**10**	**0**	**1**	**1**	**0**	**1**	**1**	**2**	**0**	**0**	**0**	**10**	**0.0**	**2**	**0**	**10**	**3**	**–5**	....	....	....	....	....	....	....	....
	Cleveland Lumberjacks	IHL	27	6	11	17	....	....	....	14	....	....	....	....	....	....	....	....	....	....	....	....	....	....	....	....	....	....
99-2000	SC Rapperswil-Jona	Switz.	32	14	11	25	....	....	....	49	....	....	....	....	....	....	....	....	....	....	....	....	....	....	....	....	....	....
	NHL Totals		**532**	**149**	**187**	**336**	**149**	**158**	**307**	**217**	**23**	**9**	**15**	**1160**	**12.8**	**513**	**155**	**433**	**63**		**30**	**4**	**3**	**7**	**20**	**0**	**1**	**1**

CCHA Second All-Star Team (1986, 1987) • AHL First All-Star Team (1990) • Won John B. Sollenberger Trophy (Top Scorer - AHL) (1990) • Won Les Cunningham Award (MVP - AHL) (1990) • Won Alka-Seltzer Plus Award (1992)

Traded to **Detroit** by **New Jersey** for Lee Norwood and Detroit's 4th round choice (Scott McCabe) in 1992 Entry Draft, November 27, 1990. Traded to **Winnipeg** by **Detroit** with future considerations (Alan Kerr, June 18, 1993) for Aaron Ward and Toronto's 4th round choice (previously acquired by Winnipeg - later traded to Detroit - Detroit selected John Jakopin) in 1993 Entry Draft, June 11, 1993. Traded to **Chicago** by **Winnipeg** for Chicago's 3rd round choice (later traded back to Chicago — Chicago selected Kevin McKay) in 1995 Entry Draft, March 21, 1994. Traded to **Tampa Bay** by **Chicago** with Rich Sutter for Jim Cummins, Tom Tilley and Jeff Buchanan, February 22, 1995.

• YUSHKEVICH, Dimitri

D – R. 6′, 208 lbs. b: Yaroslavl, USSR, 11/19/1971. Philadelphia's 6th, 122nd overall, in 1991.

Season	Club	League	GP	G	A	Pts	AG	AA	APts	PIM	PP	SH	GW	S	%	TGF	PGF	TGA	PGA	+/–	GP	G	A	Pts	PIM	PP	SH	GW
1988-89	Torpedo Yaroslavl	USSR	23	2	1	3	....	....	....	8	....	....	....	....	....	....	....	....	....	....	....	....	....	....	....	....	....	....
	Soviet Union	WJC-A	7	0	3	3	....	....	....	2	....	....	....	....	....	....	....	....	....	....	....	....	....	....	....	....	....	....
	Soviet Union	EJC-A	6	3	2	5	....	....	....	16	....	....	....	....	....	....	....	....	....	....	....	....	....	....	....	....	....	....
1989-90	Torpedo Yaroslavl	USSR	41	2	3	5	....	....	....	39	....	....	....	....	....	....	....	....	....	....	....	....	....	....	....	....	....	....
	Soviet Union	WJC-A	7	0	4	4	....	....	....	8	....	....	....	....	....	....	....	....	....	....	....	....	....	....	....	....	....	....
1990-91	Torpedo Yaroslavl	USSR	41	10	4	14	....	....	....	22	....	....	....	....	....	....	....	....	....	....	....	....	....	....	....	....	....	....
	Soviet Union	WJC-A	7	2	4	6	....	....	....	2	....	....	....	....	....	....	....	....	....	....	....	....	....	....	....	....	....	....
1991-92	Dynamo Moscow	CIS	35	5	7	12	....	....	....	14	....	....	....	....	....	....	....	....	....	....	....	....	....	....	....	....	....	....
	Russia	Olympics	8	1	2	3	....	....	....	4	....	....	....	....	....	....	....	....	....	....	....	....	....	....	....	....	....	....
	Russia	WC-A	6	1	1	2	....	....	....	4	....	....	....	....	....	....	....	....	....	....	....	....	....	....	....	....	....	....
1992-93	**Philadelphia Flyers**	**NHL**	**82**	**5**	**27**	**32**	**4**	**19**	**23**	**71**	**1**	**0**	**1**	**155**	**3.2**	**109**	**13**	**122**	**38**	**12**	....	....	....	....	....	....	....	....
	Russia	WC-A	7	1	4	5	....	....	....	10	....	....	....	....	....	....	....	....	....	....	....	....	....	....	....	....	....	....
1993-94	**Philadelphia Flyers**	**NHL**	**75**	**5**	**25**	**30**	**5**	**19**	**24**	**86**	**1**	**0**	**2**	**136**	**3.7**	**86**	**9**	**113**	**28**	**–8**	....	....	....	....	....	....	....	....
	Russia	WC-A	6	1	2	3	....	....	....	12	....	....	....	....	....	....	....	....	....	....	....	....	....	....	....	....	....	....
1994-95	Torpedo Yaroslavl	CIS	10	3	4	7	....	....	....	8	....	....	....	....	....	....	....	....	....	....	....	....	....	....	....	....	....	....
	Philadelphia Flyers	**NHL**	**40**	**5**	**9**	**14**	**9**	**13**	**22**	**47**	**3**	**1**	**1**	**80**	**6.3**	**45**	**15**	**44**	**10**	**–4**	**15**	**1**	**5**	**6**	**12**	**0**	**0**	**0**
1995-96	**Toronto Maple Leafs**	**NHL**	**69**	**1**	**10**	**11**	**1**	**8**	**9**	**54**	**1**	**0**	**0**	**96**	**1.0**	**48**	**10**	**81**	**29**	**–14**	**4**	**0**	**0**	**0**	**0**	**0**	**0**	**0**
1996-97	Russia	W-Cup	5	1	1	2	....	....	....	2	....	....	....	....	....	....	....	....	....	....	....	....	....	....	....	....	....	....
	Toronto Maple Leafs	**NHL**	**74**	**4**	**10**	**14**	**4**	**9**	**13**	**56**	**1**	**1**	**1**	**99**	**4.0**	**58**	**5**	**105**	**28**	**–24**	....	....	....	....	....	....	....	....
1997-98	**Toronto Maple Leafs**	**NHL**	**72**	**0**	**12**	**12**	**0**	**12**	**12**	**78**	**0**	**0**	**0**	**92**	**0.0**	**58**	**6**	**82**	**17**	**–13**	....	....	....	....	....	....	....	....
	Russia	Olympics	6	0	0	0	....	....	....	2	....	....	....	....	....	....	....	....	....	....	....	....	....	....	....	....	....	....
1998-99	**Toronto Maple Leafs**	**NHL**	**78**	**6**	**22**	**28**	**7**	**21**	**28**	**88**	**2**	**1**	**0**	**95**	**6.3**	**96**	**17**	**75**	**21**	**25**	**17**	**1**	**5**	**6**	**22**	**1**	**0**	**0**
99-2000	**Toronto Maple Leafs**	**NHL**	**77**	**3**	**24**	**27**	**3**	**22**	**25**	**55**	**2**	**1**	**1**	**103**	**2.9**	**86**	**22**	**92**	**30**	**2**	**12**	**1**	**1**	**2**	**4**	**0**	**0**	**0**
	NHL Totals		**567**	**29**	**139**	**168**	**33**	**123**	**156**	**535**	**11**	**4**	**6**	**856**	**3.4**	**586**	**97**	**714**	**201**		**48**	**3**	**11**	**14**	**38**	**1**	**0**	**0**

Named Best Defenseman at WC-A (1993) • Played in NHL All-Star Game (2000)

Traded to **Toronto** by **Philadelphia** with Philadelphia's 2nd round choice (Francis Larivee) in 1996 Entry Draft for Toronto's 1st round choice (Dainius Zubrus) in 1996 Entry Draft, 2nd round choice (Jean-Marc Pelletier) in 1997 Entry Draft and LA Kings' 4th round choice (previously acquired by Toronto - later traded to LA Kings - LA Kings selected Mikael Simons) in 1996 Entry Draft, August 30, 1995.

• YZERMAN, Steve

Stephen Gregory "Stevie Wonder" C – R. 5′11″, 185 lbs. b: Cranbrook, B.C., 5/9/1965. Detroit's 1st, 4th overall, in 1983.

Season	Club	League	GP	G	A	Pts	AG	AA	APts	PIM	PP	SH	GW	S	%	TGF	PGF	TGA	PGA	+/–	GP	G	A	Pts	PIM	PP	SH	GW
1980-81	Nepean Raiders	OJHL	50	38	*54	92	....	....	....	44	....	....	....	....	....	....	....	....	....	....	....	....	....	....	....	....	....	....
1981-82	Peterborough Petes	OHL	58	21	43	64	....	....	....	65	....	....	....	....	....	....	....	....	....	....	6	0	1	1	16	....	....	....
1982-83	Peterborough Petes	OHL	56	42	49	91	....	....	....	33	....	....	....	....	....	....	....	....	....	....	4	1	4	5	0	....	....	....
	Canada	WJC-A	7	2	3	5	....	....	....	2	....	....	....	....	....	....	....	....	....	....	....	....	....	....	....	....	....	....
1983-84	**Detroit Red Wings**	**NHL**	**80**	**39**	**48**	**87**	**31**	**33**	**64**	**33**	**13**	**0**	**2**	**177**	**22.0**	**133**	**62**	**91**	**3**	**–17**	**4**	**3**	**3**	**6**	**0**	**1**	**0**	**1**
1984-85	Canada	Can-Cup	4	0	0	0	....	....	....	0	....	....	....	....	....	....	....	....	....	....	....	....	....	....	....	....	....	....
	Detroit Red Wings	**NHL**	**80**	**30**	**59**	**89**	**24**	**40**	**64**	**58**	**9**	**0**	**3**	**231**	**13.0**	**138**	**53**	**104**	**2**	**–17**	**3**	**2**	**1**	**3**	**2**	**0**	**0**	**0**
	Canada	WEC-A	10	3	4	7	....	....	....	6	....	....	....	....	....	....	....	....	....	....	....	....	....	....	....	....	....	....
1985-86	**Detroit Red Wings**	**NHL**	**51**	**14**	**28**	**42**	**11**	**19**	**30**	**16**	**3**	**0**	**3**	**132**	**10.6**	**72**	**31**	**74**	**9**	**–24**	....	....	....	....	....	....	....	....
1986-87	**Detroit Red Wings**	**NHL**	**80**	**31**	**59**	**90**	**27**	**43**	**70**	**43**	**9**	**1**	**2**	**217**	**14.3**	**125**	**53**	**87**	**14**	**–1**	**16**	**5**	**13**	**18**	**8**	**1**	**0**	**0**
1987-88	**Detroit Red Wings**	**NHL**	**64**	**50**	**52**	**102**	**43**	**37**	**80**	**44**	**10**	**6**	**6**	**242**	**20.7**	**132**	**42**	**75**	**15**	**30**	**3**	**1**	**3**	**4**	**6**	**0**	**0**	**0**
1988-89	**Detroit Red Wings**	**NHL**	**80**	**65**	**90**	**155**	**55**	**64**	**119**	**61**	**17**	**3**	**7**	**388**	**16.8**	**189**	**65**	**152**	**45**	**17**	**6**	**5**	**5**	**10**	**2**	**2**	**0**	**0**
	Canada	WEC-A	8	5	7	12	....	....	....	2	....	....	....	....	....	....	....	....	....	....	....	....	....	....	....	....	....	....
1989-90	**Detroit Red Wings**	**NHL**	**79**	**62**	**65**	**127**	**54**	**47**	**101**	**79**	**16**	**7**	**8**	**332**	**18.7**	**162**	**52**	**166**	**50**	**–6**	....	....	....	....	....	....	....	....
	Canada	WEC-A	10	10	10	*20	....	....	....	8	....	....	....	....	....	....	....	....	....	....	....	....	....	....	....	....	....	....
1990-91	**Detroit Red Wings**	**NHL**	**80**	**51**	**57**	**108**	**47**	**43**	**90**	**34**	**12**	**6**	**4**	**326**	**15.6**	**141**	**51**	**141**	**49**	**–2**	**7**	**3**	**3**	**6**	**4**	**1**	**0**	**0**
1991-92	**Detroit Red Wings**	**NHL**	**79**	**45**	**58**	**103**	**41**	**44**	**85**	**64**	**9**	**8**	**9**	**295**	**15.3**	**143**	**51**	**102**	**36**	**26**	**11**	**3**	**5**	**8**	**12**	**0**	**1**	**1**
1992-93	**Detroit Red Wings**	**NHL**	**84**	**58**	**79**	**137**	**48**	**55**	**103**	**44**	**13**	**7**	**6**	**307**	**18.9**	**174**	**61**	**114**	**34**	**33**	**7**	**4**	**3**	**7**	**4**	**1**	**1**	**1**
1993-94	**Detroit Red Wings**	**NHL**	**58**	**24**	**58**	**82**	**22**	**45**	**67**	**36**	**7**	**3**	**3**	**217**	**11.1**	**103**	**30**	**81**	**19**	**11**	**3**	**1**	**3**	**4**	**0**	**0**	**0**	**0**
1994-95	**Detroit Red Wings**	**NHL**	**47**	**12**	**26**	**38**	**21**	**38**	**59**	**40**	**4**	**0**	**1**	**134**	**9.0**	**67**	**34**	**36**	**9**	**6**	**15**	**4**	**8**	**12**	**0**	**2**	**0**	**1**
1995-96	**Detroit Red Wings**	**NHL**	**80**	**36**	**59**	**95**	**35**	**49**	**84**	**64**	**16**	**2**	**8**	**220**	**16.4**	**130**	**61**	**63**	**23**	**29**	**18**	**8**	**12**	**20**	**4**	**4**	**0**	**1**
1996-97	Canada	W-Cup	6	2	1	3	....	....	....	0	....	....	....	....	....	....	....	....	....	....	....	....	....	....	....	....	....	....
♦	**Detroit Red Wings**	**NHL**	**81**	**22**	**63**	**85**	**23**	**56**	**79**	**78**	**8**	**0**	**3**	**232**	**9.5**	**123**	**49**	**72**	**20**	**22**	**20**	**7**	**6**	**13**	**4**	**3**	**0**	**2**
1997-98 ♦	**Detroit Red Wings**	**NHL**	**75**	**24**	**45**	**69**	**28**	**44**	**72**	**46**	**6**	**2**	**0**	**188**	**12.8**	**96**	**41**	**67**	**15**	**3**	**22**	**6**	***18**	***24**	**22**	**3**	**1**	**0**
	Canada	Olympics	6	1	1	2	....	....	....	10	....	....	....	....	....	....	....	....	....	....	....	....	....	....	....	....	....	....
1998-99	**Detroit Red Wings**	**NHL**	**80**	**29**	**45**	**74**	**34**	**43**	**77**	**42**	**13**	**2**	**4**	**231**	**12.6**	**105**	**39**	**78**	**20**	**8**	**10**	**9**	**4**	**13**	**0**	**4**	**0**	**2**
99-2000	**Detroit Red Wings**	**NHL**	**78**	**35**	**44**	**79**	**39**	**41**	**80**	**34**	**15**	**2**	**6**	**234**	**15.0**	**128**	**51**	**66**	**17**	**28**	**8**	**0**	**4**	**4**	**0**	**0**	**0**	**0**
	NHL Totals		**1256**	**627**	**935**	**1562**	**583**	**741**	**1324**	**816**	**180**	**49**	**75**	**4103**	**15.3**	**2161**	**826**	**1569**	**380**		**153**	**61**	**91**	**152**	**68**	**22**	**3**	**9**

NHL All-Rookie Team (1984) • Won Lester B. Pearson Award (1989) • WEC-A All-Star Team (1989, 1990) • Named Best Forward at WEC-A (1990) • Won Conn Smythe Trophy (1998) • NHL First All-Star Team (2000) • Won Frank J. Selke Trophy (2000) • Played in NHL All-Star Game (1984, 1988, 1989, 1990, 1991, 1992, 1993, 1997, 2000)

• ZABRANSKY, Libor

D – L. 6′3″, 196 lbs. b: Brno, Czech., 11/25/1973. St. Louis' 8th, 209th overall, in 1995.

Season	Club	League	GP	G	A	Pts	AG	AA	APts	PIM	PP	SH	GW	S	%	TGF	PGF	TGA	PGA	+/–	GP	G	A	Pts	PIM	PP	SH	GW
1994-95	HC Ceske Budejovice	Czech-Rep	44	2	6	8	....	....	....	54	....	....	....	....	....	....	....	....	....	....	9	0	4	4	6	....	....	....
1995-96	HC Ceske Budejovice	Czech-Rep	40	4	7	11	....	....	....		....	....	....	....	....	....	....	....	....	....	10	0	1	1		....	....	....
1996-97	**St. Louis Blues**	**NHL**	**34**	**1**	**5**	**6**	**1**	**4**	**5**	**44**	**0**	**0**	**1**	**26**	**3.8**	**23**	**3**	**31**	**10**	**–1**	....	....	....	....	....	....	....	....
	Worcester IceCats	AHL	23	3	6	9	....	....	....	24	....	....	....	....	....	....	....	....	....	....	5	2	5	7	6	....	....	....
1997-98	**St. Louis Blues**	**NHL**	**6**	**0**	**1**	**1**	**0**	**1**	**1**	**6**	**0**	**0**	**0**	**2**	**0.0**	**1**	**1**	**3**	**0**	**–3**	....	....	....	....	....	....	....	....
	Worcester IceCats	AHL	54	2	17	19	....	....	....	61	....	....	....	....	....	....	....	....	....	....	6	1	1	2	8	....	....	....
1998-99	Worcester IceCats	AHL	6	0	0	0	....	....	....	18	....	....	....	....	....	....	....	....	....	....	....	....	....	....	....	....	....	....
	HC Slovnaft Vsetin	Czech-Rep	31	3	9	12	....	....	....	57	....	....	....	....	....	....	....	....	....	....	12	1	2	3		....	....	....
99-2000	HC Slovnaft Vsetin	Czech-Rep	47	6	17	23	....	....	....	69	....	....	....	....	....	....	....	....	....	....	9	0	2	2	10	....	....	....
	NHL Totals		**40**	**1**	**6**	**7**	**1**	**5**	**6**	**50**	**0**	**0**	**1**	**28**	**3.6**	**24**	**4**	**34**	**10**									

• ZAHARKO, Miles

D – L. 6′, 197 lbs. b: Mannville, Alta., 4/30/1957. Atlanta's 1st, 20th overall, in 1977.

Season	Club	League	GP	G	A	Pts	AG	AA	APts	PIM	PP	SH	GW	S	%	TGF	PGF	TGA	PGA	+/–	GP	G	A	Pts	PIM	PP	SH	GW
1973-74	Bellingham Blazers	BCJHL	64	4	21	25	....	....	....	79	....	....	....	....	....	....	....	....	....	....	....	....	....	....	....	....	....	....
1974-75	Vermilion Bruins	AJHL	60	40	44	84	....	....	....	110	....	....	....	....	....	....	....	....	....	....	....	....	....	....	....	....	....	....
1975-76	New Westminster Bruins	WCJHL	70	10	44	54	....	....	....	45	....	....	....	....	....	....	....	....	....	....	17	2	5	7	20	....	....	....
	New Westminster Bruins	Mem-Cup	4	0	3	3	....	....	....	8	....	....	....	....	....	....	....	....	....	....	....	....	....	....	....	....	....	....
1976-77	New Westminster Bruins	WCJHL	72	14	48	62	....	....	....	68	....	....	....	....	....	....	....	....	....	....	14	1	10	11	20	....	....	....
	New Westminster Bruins	Mem-Cup	5	1	4	5	....	....	....	0	....	....	....	....	....	....	....	....	....	....	....	....	....	....	....	....	....	....

			REGULAR SEASON																		PLAYOFFS							
Season	Club	League	GP	G	A	Pts	AG	AA	APts	PIM	PP	SH	GW	S	%	TGF	PGF	TGA	PGA	+/–	GP	G	A	Pts	PIM	PP	SH	GW
1977-78	**Atlanta Flames**	**NHL**	**71**	**1**	**19**	**20**	**1**	**15**	**16**	**26**	**0**	**0**	**0**	**54**	**1.9**	**57**	**2**	**77**	**9**	**–13**	**1**	**0**	**0**	**0**	**0**	**0**	**0**	**0**
	Nova Scotia Voyageurs	AHL	8	0	3	3	....	....	....	6	....	....	....	....	....	....	....	....	....	....	....	....	....	....	....	....	....	....
1978-79	**Chicago Black Hawks**	**NHL**	**1**	**0**	**0**	**0**	**0**	**0**	**0**	**0**	**0**	**0**	**0**	**0**	**0.0**	**0**	**0**	**0**	**0**	**0**	....	....	....	....	....	....	....	....
	Tulsa Oilers	CHL	54	2	20	22	....	....	....	28	....	....	....	....	....	....	....	....	....	....	....	....	....	....	....	....	....	....
	New Brunswick Hawks	AHL	13	1	6	7	....	....	....	2	....	....	....	....	....	....	....	....	....	....	5	1	4	5	2	....	....	....
1979-80	New Brunswick Hawks	AHL	77	2	20	22	....	....	....	34	....	....	....	....	....	....	....	....	....	....	17	2	14	16	16	....	....	....
1980-81	**Chicago Black Hawks**	**NHL**	**42**	**3**	**11**	**14**	**2**	**7**	**9**	**40**	**0**	**0**	**1**	**58**	**5.2**	**58**	**4**	**52**	**20**	**22**	**2**	**0**	**0**	**0**	**0**	**0**	**0**	**0**
	New Brunswick Hawks	AHL	33	7	18	25	....	....	....	27	....	....	....	....	....	....	....	....	....	....	....	....	....	....	....	....	....	....
1981-82	**Chicago Black Hawks**	**NHL**	**15**	**1**	**2**	**3**	**1**	**1**	**2**	**18**	**0**	**0**	**0**	**20**	**5.0**	**11**	**0**	**17**	**5**	**–1**	....	....	....	....	....	....	....	....
	New Brunswick Hawks	AHL	52	6	12	18	....	....	....	50	....	....	....	....	....	....	....	....	....	....	15	0	9	9	4	....	....	....
1982-83	Springfield Indians	AHL	54	6	18	24	....	....	....	20	....	....	....	....	....	....	....	....	....	....	....	....	....	....	....	....	....	....
1983-84	SC Duisberg	Germany	12	4	3	7	....	....	....	22	....	....	....	....	....	....	....	....	....	....	....	....	....	....	....	....	....	....
	NHL Totals		**129**	**5**	**32**	**37**	**4**	**23**	**27**	**84**	**0**	**0**	**1**	**132**	**3.8**	**126**	**6**	**146**	**34**		**3**	**0**	**0**	**0**	**0**	**0**	**0**	**0**

AHL Second All-Star Team (1982)

Traded to **Chicago** by **Atlanta** with Tom Lysiak, Pat Ribble, Greg Fox and Harold Phillipoff for Ivan Boldirev, Phil Russell and Darcy Rota, March 13, 1979. Claimed by Chicago as fill in Expansion Draft, June 13, 1979.

• ZAINE, Rod

Rodney Carl "Zainer" C – L. 5'10", 180 lbs. b: Ottawa, Ont., 5/18/1946.

Season	Club	League	GP	G	A	Pts	AG	AA	APts	PIM	PP	SH	GW	S	%	TGF	PGF	TGA	PGA	+/–	GP	G	A	Pts	PIM	PP	SH	GW
1962-63	Smiths Falls Bears	OJHL	STATISTICS NOT AVAILABLE																									
1963-64	Oshawa Generals	OHA-Jr.	55	6	11	17	....	....	....	32	....	....	....	....	....	....	....	....	....	....	2	0	0	0	0	....	....	....
1964-65	Ottawa Jr. Montagnards	OJHL	24	18	31	49	....	....	....	56	....	....	....	....	....	....	....	....	....	....	....	....	....	....	....	....	....	....
1965-66	Smiths Falls Bears	OJHL	34	35	56	91	....	....	....	46	....	....	....	....	....	....	....	....	....	....	....	....	....	....	....	....	....	....
1966-67	Clinton Comets	EHL	72	13	23	36	....	....	....	16	....	....	....	....	....	....	....	....	....	....	9	1	3	4	0	....	....	....
1967-68	Clinton Comets	EHL	72	24	53	77	....	....	....	68	....	....	....	....	....	....	....	....	....	....	14	5	7	12	5	....	....	....
1968-69	Ottawa Nationals	OHA-Sr.	6	3	1	4	....	....	....	4	....	....	....	....	....	....	....	....	....	....	....	....	....	....	....	....	....	....
1969-70	Baltimore Clippers	AHL	53	19	23	42	....	....	....	36	....	....	....	....	....	....	....	....	....	....	5	1	2	3	4	....	....	....
1970-71	**Pittsburgh Penguins**	**NHL**	**37**	**8**	**5**	**13**	**8**	**4**	**12**	**21**	**2**	**0**	**0**	**34**	**23.5**	**20**	**3**	**25**	**0**	**–8**	....	....	....	....	....	....	....	....
	Baltimore Clippers	AHL	8	1	2	3	....	....	....	4	....	....	....	....	....	....	....	....	....	....	....	....	....	....	....	....	....	....
	Amarillo Wranglers	CHL	27	4	11	15	....	....	....	20	....	....	....	....	....	....	....	....	....	....	....	....	....	....	....	....	....	....
1971-72	**Buffalo Sabres**	**NHL**	**24**	**2**	**1**	**3**	**2**	**1**	**3**	**4**	**0**	**0**	**1**	**23**	**8.7**	**8**	**0**	**23**	**1**	**–14**	....	....	....	....	....	....	....	....
	Cincinnati Swords	AHL	32	8	15	23	....	....	....	6	....	....	....	....	....	....	....	....	....	....	10	5	5	10	10	....	....	....
1972-73	Chicago Cougars	WHA	74	3	14	17	....	....	....	25	....	....	....	....	....	....	....	....	....	....	....	....	....	....	....	....	....	....
1973-74	Chicago Cougars	WHA	78	5	13	18	....	....	....	17	....	....	....	....	....	....	....	....	....	....	18	2	1	3	2	....	....	....
1974-75	Chicago Cougars	WHA	68	3	6	9	....	....	....	16	....	....	....	....	....	....	....	....	....	....	....	....	....	....	....	....	....	....
	NHL Totals		**61**	**10**	**6**	**16**	**10**	**5**	**15**	**25**	**2**	**0**	**1**	**57**	**17.5**	**28**	**3**	**48**	**1**		....	....	....	....	....	....	....	....
	Other Major League Totals		220	11	33	44	....	....	....	58	....	....	....	....	....	....	....	....	....	....	18	2	1	3	2	....	....	....

Signed as a free agent by **Baltimore** (AHL), October, 1969. Traded to **Pittsburgh** by **Baltimore** (AHL) for cash, July, 1970. Claimed by **Buffalo** from **Pittsburgh** in Intra-League Draft, June 8, 1971. Claimed by **Atlanta** from **Buffalo** in Expansion Draft, June 6, 1972. Selected by **Chicago** (WHA) in 1972 WHA General Player Draft, February 12, 1972. Selected by **Toronto** (WHA) from **Chicago** (WHA) in WHA Dispersal Draft, June 19, 1975.

• ZALAPSKI, Zarley

Zarley Bennett D – L. 6'1", 215 lbs. b: Edmonton, Alta., 4/22/1968. Pittsburgh's 1st, 4th overall, in 1986.

Season	Club	League	GP	G	A	Pts	AG	AA	APts	PIM	PP	SH	GW	S	%	TGF	PGF	TGA	PGA	+/–	GP	G	A	Pts	PIM	PP	SH	GW
1984-85	Fort Saskatchewan Traders	AJHL	23	17	30	47	....	....	....	14	....	....	....	....	....	....	....	....	....	....	....	....	....	....	....	....	....	....
1985-86	Fort Saskatchewan Traders	AJHL	27	20	33	53	....	....	....	46	....	....	....	....	....	....	....	....	....	....	....	....	....	....	....	....	....	....
	Canada	Nat-Team	32	2	4	6	....	....	....	10	....	....	....	....	....	....	....	....	....	....	....	....	....	....	....	....	....	....
1986-87	Canada	Nat-Team	74	11	29	40	....	....	....	28	....	....	....	....	....	....	....	....	....	....	....	....	....	....	....	....	....	....
	Canada	WEC-A	10	0	3	3	....	....	....	2	....	....	....	....	....	....	....	....	....	....	....	....	....	....	....	....	....	....
1987-88	Canada	Nat-Team	47	3	13	16	....	....	....	32	....	....	....	....	....	....	....	....	....	....	....	....	....	....	....	....	....	....
	Canada	Olympics	8	1	3	4	....	....	....	2	....	....	....	....	....	....	....	....	....	....	....	....	....	....	....	....	....	....
	Pittsburgh Penguins	**NHL**	**15**	**3**	**8**	**11**	**3**	**6**	**9**	**7**	**0**	**0**	**0**	**31**	**9.7**	**29**	**6**	**21**	**8**	**10**	....	....	....	....	....	....	....	....
1988-89	**Pittsburgh Penguins**	**NHL**	**58**	**12**	**33**	**45**	**10**	**23**	**33**	**57**	**5**	**1**	**2**	**95**	**12.6**	**120**	**61**	**72**	**22**	**9**	**11**	**1**	**8**	**9**	**13**	**1**	**0**	**0**
1989-90	**Pittsburgh Penguins**	**NHL**	**51**	**6**	**25**	**31**	**5**	**18**	**23**	**37**	**5**	**0**	**2**	**85**	**7.1**	**74**	**36**	**74**	**22**	**–14**	....	....	....	....	....	....	....	....
1990-91	**Pittsburgh Penguins**	**NHL**	**66**	**12**	**36**	**48**	**11**	**27**	**38**	**59**	**5**	**1**	**1**	**135**	**8.9**	**103**	**35**	**84**	**31**	**15**	....	....	....	....	....	....	....	....
	Hartford Whalers	**NHL**	**11**	**3**	**3**	**6**	**3**	**2**	**5**	**6**	**3**	**0**	**0**	**21**	**14.3**	**14**	**8**	**13**	**0**	**–7**	**6**	**1**	**3**	**4**	**8**	**0**	**0**	**1**
1991-92	**Hartford Whalers**	**NHL**	**79**	**20**	**37**	**57**	**18**	**28**	**46**	**120**	**4**	**0**	**3**	**230**	**8.7**	**132**	**52**	**112**	**25**	**–7**	**7**	**2**	**3**	**5**	**6**	**0**	**0**	**0**
1992-93	**Hartford Whalers**	**NHL**	**83**	**14**	**51**	**65**	**12**	**35**	**47**	**94**	**8**	**1**	**0**	**192**	**7.3**	**134**	**66**	**157**	**55**	**–34**	....	....	....	....	....	....	....	....
1993-94	**Hartford Whalers**	**NHL**	**56**	**7**	**30**	**37**	**6**	**23**	**29**	**56**	**0**	**0**	**0**	**121**	**5.8**	**76**	**31**	**68**	**17**	**–6**	....	....	....	....	....	....	....	....
	Calgary Flames	**NHL**	**13**	**3**	**7**	**10**	**3**	**5**	**8**	**18**	**1**	**0**	**1**	**35**	**8.6**	**22**	**14**	**12**	**4**	**0**	**7**	**0**	**3**	**3**	**2**	**0**	**0**	**0**
1994-95	**Calgary Flames**	**NHL**	**48**	**4**	**24**	**28**	**7**	**35**	**42**	**46**	**1**	**0**	**1**	**76**	**5.3**	**61**	**12**	**51**	**11**	**9**	**7**	**0**	**4**	**4**	**4**	**0**	**0**	**0**
1995-96	**Calgary Flames**	**NHL**	**80**	**12**	**17**	**29**	**12**	**14**	**26**	**115**	**5**	**0**	**1**	**145**	**8.3**	**107**	**30**	**105**	**39**	**11**	**4**	**0**	**1**	**1**	**10**	**0**	**0**	**0**
1996-97	**Calgary Flames**	**NHL**	**2**	**0**	**0**	**0**	**0**	**0**	**0**	**0**	**0**	**0**	**0**	**7**	**0.0**	**1**	**0**	**3**	**1**	**–1**	....	....	....	....	....	....	....	....
1997-98	**Calgary Flames**	**NHL**	**35**	**2**	**7**	**9**	**2**	**7**	**9**	**41**	**2**	**0**	**1**	**46**	**4.3**	**31**	**11**	**37**	**5**	**–12**	....	....	....	....	....	....	....	....
	Montreal Canadiens	**NHL**	**28**	**1**	**5**	**6**	**1**	**5**	**6**	**22**	**0**	**1**	**0**	**27**	**3.7**	**15**	**2**	**21**	**7**	**–1**	**6**	**0**	**1**	**1**	**4**	**0**	**0**	**0**
1998-99	ZSC Lions Zurich	Switz.	11	1	5	6	....	....	....	37	....	....	....	....	....	....	....	....	....	....	3	1	0	1	4	....	....	....
99-2000	Long Beach Ice Dogs	IHL	7	0	5	5	....	....	....	6	....	....	....	....	....	....	....	....	....	....	....	....	....	....	....	....	....	....
	Utah Grizzlies	IHL	56	4	24	28	....	....	....	69	....	....	....	....	....	....	....	....	....	....	5	1	1	2	4	....	....	....
	Philadelphia Flyers	**NHL**	**12**	**0**	**2**	**2**	**0**	**2**	**2**	**6**	**0**	**0**	**0**	**6**	**0.0**	**9**	**1**	**12**	**4**	**0**	....	....	....	....	....	....	....	....
	NHL Totals		**637**	**99**	**285**	**384**	**93**	**230**	**323**	**684**	**39**	**4**	**12**	**1252**	**7.9**	**928**	**365**	**842**	**251**		**48**	**4**	**23**	**27**	**47**	**1**	**0**	**1**

NHL All-Rookie Team (1989) • Played in NHL All-Star Game (1993)

Traded to **Hartford** by **Pittsburgh** with John Cullen and Jeff Parker for Ron Francis, Grant Jennings and Ulf Samuelsson, March 4, 1991. Traded to **Calgary** by **Hartford** with James Patrick and Michael Nylander for Gary Suter, Paul Ranheim and Ted Drury, March 10, 1994. Traded to **Montreal** by **Calgary** with Jonas Hoglund for Valeri Bure and Montreal's 4th round choice (Shaun Sutter) in 1998 Entry Draft, February 1, 1998. Signed as a free agent by **NY Rangers**, August 31, 1998. Signed as a free agent to try-out contract by **Long Beach** (IHL), September 14, 1999. Signed as a free agent by **Utah** (IHL), November 5, 1999. Signed as a free agent by **Philadelphia**, February 15, 2000.

• ZAMUNER, Rob

Robert F. LW – L. 6'3", 208 lbs. b: Oakville, Ont., 9/17/1969. NY Rangers' 3rd, 45th overall, in 1989.

Season	Club	League	GP	G	A	Pts	AG	AA	APts	PIM	PP	SH	GW	S	%	TGF	PGF	TGA	PGA	+/–	GP	G	A	Pts	PIM	PP	SH	GW
1985-86	Oakville Oaks	OMHA	48	43	50	93	....	....	....	66	....	....	....	....	....	....	....	....	....	....	....	....	....	....	....	....	....	....
1986-87	Guelph Jr. Bees	OJHL-B	3	6	7	13	....	....	....	15	....	....	....	....	....	....	....	....	....	....	....	....	....	....	....	....	....	....
	Guelph Platers	OHL	62	6	15	21	....	....	....	8	....	....	....	....	....	....	....	....	....	....	....	....	....	....	....	....	....	....
1987-88	Guelph Platers	OHL	58	20	41	61	....	....	....	18	....	....	....	....	....	....	....	....	....	....	....	....	....	....	....	....	....	....
1988-89	Guelph Platers	OHL	66	46	65	111	....	....	....	38	....	....	....	....	....	....	....	....	....	....	7	5	5	10	9	....	....	....
1989-90	Flint Spirits	IHL	77	44	35	79	....	....	....	32	....	....	....	....	....	....	....	....	....	....	4	1	0	1	6	....	....	....
1990-91	Binghamton Rangers	AHL	80	25	58	83	....	....	....	50	....	....	....	....	....	....	....	....	....	....	9	7	6	13	35	....	....	....
1991-92	**New York Rangers**	**NHL**	**9**	**1**	**2**	**3**	**1**	**2**	**3**	**2**	**0**	**0**	**0**	**11**	**9.1**	**3**	**0**	**3**	**0**	**0**	....	....	....	....	....	....	....	....
	Binghamton Rangers	AHL	61	19	53	72	....	....	....	42	....	....	....	....	....	....	....	....	....	....	11	8	9	17	8	....	....	....
1992-93	**Tampa Bay Lightning**	**NHL**	**84**	**15**	**28**	**43**	**12**	**19**	**31**	**74**	**1**	**0**	**0**	**183**	**8.2**	**64**	**21**	**79**	**11**	**–25**	....	....	....	....	....	....	....	....
1993-94	**Tampa Bay Lightning**	**NHL**	**59**	**6**	**6**	**12**	**6**	**5**	**11**	**42**	**0**	**0**	**1**	**109**	**5.5**	**18**	**1**	**34**	**8**	**–9**	....	....	....	....	....	....	....	....
1994-95	**Tampa Bay Lightning**	**NHL**	**43**	**9**	**6**	**15**	**16**	**9**	**25**	**24**	**0**	**3**	**1**	**74**	**12.2**	**23**	**2**	**33**	**9**	**–3**	....	....	....	....	....	....	....	....
1995-96	**Tampa Bay Lightning**	**NHL**	**72**	**15**	**20**	**35**	**15**	**16**	**31**	**62**	**0**	**3**	**4**	**152**	**9.9**	**50**	**4**	**63**	**28**	**11**	**6**	**2**	**3**	**5**	**10**	**0**	**1**	**0**
1996-97	**Tampa Bay Lightning**	**NHL**	**82**	**17**	**33**	**50**	**18**	**29**	**47**	**56**	**0**	**4**	**3**	**216**	**7.9**	**62**	**0**	**91**	**32**	**3**	....	....	....	....	....	....	....	....
	Canada	WC-A	11	4	2	6	....	....	....	16	....	....	....	....	....	....	....	....	....	....	....	....	....	....	....	....	....	....
1997-98	**Tampa Bay Lightning**	**NHL**	**77**	**14**	**12**	**26**	**16**	**12**	**28**	**41**	**0**	**3**	**4**	**126**	**11.1**	**42**	**10**	**88**	**25**	**–31**	....	....	....	....	....	....	....	....
	Canada	Olympics	6	1	0	1	....	....	....	8	....	....	....	....	....	....	....	....	....	....	....	....	....	....	....	....	....	....
	Canada	WC-A	5	0	2	2	....	....	....	4	....	....	....	....	....	....	....	....	....	....	....	....	....	....	....	....	....	....
1998-99	**Tampa Bay Lighning**	**NHL**	**58**	**8**	**11**	**19**	**9**	**11**	**20**	**24**	**1**	**1**	**2**	**89**	**9.0**	**26**	**3**	**60**	**22**	**–15**	....	....	....	....	....	....	....	....
99-2000	**Ottawa Senators**	**NHL**	**57**	**9**	**12**	**21**	**10**	**11**	**21**	**32**	**0**	**1**	**0**	**103**	**8.7**	**30**	**2**	**37**	**3**	**–6**	**6**	**2**	**0**	**2**	**2**	**0**	**0**	**1**
	NHL Totals		**541**	**94**	**130**	**224**	**103**	**114**	**217**	**357**	**2**	**15**	**15**	**1063**	**8.8**	**318**	**43**	**488**	**138**		**12**	**4**	**3**	**7**	**12**	**0**	**1**	**1**

Signed as a free agent by **Tampa Bay**, July 13, 1992. Traded to **Ottawa** by **Tampa Bay** with a conditional 2nd round choice in 2000, 2001 or 2002 Entry Draft for Andreas Johansson, June 29, 1999.

• ZANUSSI, Joe
Joseph Lawrence D – R. 5'10", 180 lbs. b: Rossland, B.C., 9/25/1947.

			REGULAR SEASON																		PLAYOFFS							
Season	Club	League	GP	G	A	Pts	AG	AA	APts	PIM	PP	SH	GW	S	%	TGF	PGF	TGA	PGA	+/–	GP	G	A	Pts	PIM	PP	SH	GW
1966-67	Edmonton Oil Kings	CMJHL	42	11	17	28				33											9	2	2	4	6			
1967-68	Swift Current Broncos	WCJHL	57	17	48	65				46																		
	Estevan Bruins	Mem-Cup	4	0	0	0				2																		
1968-69	Johnstown Jets	EHL	72	20	36	56				107											3	2	1	3	12			
1969-70	Fort Worth Wings	CHL	56	4	9	13				65											7	1	0	1	16			
1970-71	Fort Worth Wings	CHL	72	13	19	32				172											3	0	1	1	4			
1971-72	Fort Worth Wings	CHL	48	4	24	28				69											7	0	1	1	18			
1972-73	Winnipeg Jets	WHA	73	4	21	25				53											14	2	5	7	6			
1973-74	Winnipeg Jets	WHA	76	3	22	25				53											4	0	0	0	0			
1974-75	**New York Rangers**	**NHL**	**8**	**0**	**2**	**2**	**0**	**1**	**1**	**4**	**0**	**0**	**0**	**8**	**0.0**	**7**	**1**	**2**	**1**	**5**								
	Providence Reds	AHL	64	22	36	58				76											3	1	0	1	4			
1975-76	Providence Reds	AHL	11	8	11	19				29																		
	Boston Bruins	**NHL**	**60**	**1**	**7**	**8**	**1**	**5**	**6**	**30**	**0**	**0**	**0**	**77**	**1.3**	**32**	**2**	**38**	**10**	**2**	**4**	**0**	**1**	**1**	**2**	**0**	**0**	**0**
	Rochester Americans	AHL	2	0	1	1				2																		
1976-77	**Boston Bruins**	**NHL**	**8**	**0**	**1**	**1**	**0**	**1**	**1**	**8**	**0**	**0**	**0**	**12**	**0.0**	**8**	**0**	**8**	**1**	**1**								
	Rochester Americans	AHL	17	1	9	10				18																		
	St. Louis Blues	**NHL**	**11**	**0**	**3**	**3**	**0**	**2**	**2**	**4**	**0**	**0**	**0**	**11**	**0.0**	**5**	**2**	**10**	**1**	**–6**								
	Kansas City Blues	CHL	30	4	14	18				26											10	2	2	4	14			
1977-78	Salt Lake Golden Eagles	CHL	71	10	24	34				74											6	1	4	5	2			
	NHL Totals		**87**	**1**	**13**	**14**	**1**	**9**	**10**	**46**	**0**	**0**	**0**	**108**	**0.9**	**52**	**5**	**58**	**13**		**4**	**0**	**1**	**1**	**2**	**0**	**0**	**0**
	Other Major League Totals		149	7	43	50				106											18	2	5	7	6			

• Brother of Ron • CHL Second All-Star Team (1971) • Shared Tommy Ivan Trophy (MVP - CHL) with Andre Dupont, Gerry Ouellette & Peter McDuffe (1971) • AHL First All-Star Team (1975) • Won Eddie Shore Award (Outstanding Defenseman - AHL) (1975) • CHL First All-Star Team (1978)

Traded to **NY Rangers** by **Detroit** with Detroit's 1st round choice (Al Blanchard) in 1972 Amateur Draft for Gary Doak and Rick Newell, May 24, 1972. Selected by **Winnipeg** (WHA) in 1972 WHA General Player Draft, February 12, 1972. Traded to **Boston** by **NY Rangers** with Brad Park and Jean Ratelle for Phil Esposito and Carol Vadnais, November 7, 1975. Traded to **St. Louis** by **Boston** for Rick Smith, December 20, 1976.

• ZANUSSI, Ron
Ronald Kenneth RW – R. 5'11", 180 lbs. b: Toronto, Ont., 8/31/1956. Minnesota's 4th, 51st overall, in 1976.

Season	Club	League	GP	G	A	Pts	AG	AA	APts	PIM	PP	SH	GW	S	%	TGF	PGF	TGA	PGA	+/–	GP	G	A	Pts	PIM	PP	SH	GW
1973-74	London Squires	OHA-B	65	21	20	41				110																		
1974-75	London Knights	OMJHL	69	34	52	86				123																		
1975-76	London Knights	OMJHL	40	17	19	36				55											5	2	1	3	8			
1976-77	Fort Wayne Komets	IHL	77	53	33	86				138											9	9	6	15	20			
1977-78	**Minnesota North Stars**	**NHL**	**68**	**15**	**17**	**32**	**14**	**13**	**27**	**89**	**4**	**0**	**2**	**97**	**15.5**	**51**	**13**	**60**	**2**	**–20**								
	Fort Worth Texans	CHL	6	2	1	3				5																		
1978-79	**Minnesota North Stars**	**NHL**	**63**	**14**	**16**	**30**	**12**	**12**	**24**	**82**	**3**	**0**	**0**	**98**	**14.3**	**56**	**12**	**43**	**4**	**5**								
	Oklahoma City Stars	CHL	4	3	1	4				6																		
1979-80	**Minnesota North Stars**	**NHL**	**72**	**14**	**31**	**45**	**12**	**23**	**35**	**93**	**2**	**0**	**3**	**129**	**10.9**	**76**	**15**	**57**	**0**	**4**	**14**	**0**	**4**	**4**	**17**	**0**	**0**	**0**
1980-81	Minnesota North Stars	DN-Cup	2	0	1	1				6																		
	Minnesota North Stars	**NHL**	**41**	**6**	**11**	**17**	**5**	**7**	**12**	**89**	**0**	**0**	**0**	**43**	**14.0**	**31**	**3**	**25**	**0**	**3**								
	Oklahoma City Stars	CHL	3	3	2	5				5																		
	Toronto Maple Leafs	**NHL**	**12**	**3**	**0**	**3**	**2**	**0**	**2**	**6**	**0**	**0**	**0**	**15**	**20.0**	**4**	**0**	**15**	**4**	**–7**	**3**	**0**	**0**	**0**	**0**	**0**	**0**	**0**
1981-82	**Toronto Maple Leafs**	**NHL**	**43**	**0**	**8**	**8**	**0**	**5**	**5**	**14**	**0**	**0**	**0**	**25**	**0.0**	**16**	**1**	**40**	**21**	**–4**								
	Cincinnati Tigers	CHL	21	12	9	21				32											4	0	2	2	4			
1982-83	Sherbrooke Jets	AHL	72	9	21	30				53																		
1983-84	St. Catharines Saints	AHL	54	4	15	19				59																		
	NHL Totals		**299**	**52**	**83**	**135**	**45**	**60**	**105**	**373**	**9**	**0**	**5**	**407**	**12.8**	**234**	**44**	**240**	**31**		**17**	**0**	**4**	**4**	**17**	**0**	**0**	**0**

• Brother of Joe • Shared (with Garth MacGuigan) Garry F. Longman Memorial Trophy (Top Rookie - IHL) (1977)

Claimed by **Minnesota** as a fill-in during **Cleveland-Minnesota** Dispersal Draft, June 15, 1978. Traded to **Toronto** by **Minnesota** with Minnesota's 3rd round choice (Ernie Godden) in 1981 Entry Draft for Toronto's 2nd round choice (Dave Donnelly) in 1981 Entry Draft, March 10, 1981.

• ZAVISHA, Brad
Bradley J. LW – L. 6'2", 205 lbs. b: Hines Creek, Alta., 1/4/1972. Quebec's 3rd, 43rd overall, in 1990.

Season	Club	League	GP	G	A	Pts	AG	AA	APts	PIM	PP	SH	GW	S	%	TGF	PGF	TGA	PGA	+/–	GP	G	A	Pts	PIM	PP	SH	GW
1987-88	St. Albert Saints	AJHL	35	10	20	30				84																		
1988-89	Seattle Thunderbirds	WHL	52	8	13	21				43																		
1989-90	Seattle Thunderbirds	WHL	69	22	38	60				124											13	1	6	7	16			
1990-91	Seattle Thunderbirds	WHL	24	15	12	27				40																		
	Portland Winter Hawks	WHL	48	25	22	47				41																		
1991-92	Portland Winter Hawks	WHL	11	7	4	11				18																		
	Lethbridge Broncos	WHL	59	44	40	84				160											5	3	1	4	18			
1992-93	**Edmonton Oilers**	**NHL**	DID NOT PLAY – INJURED																									
1993-94	**Edmonton Oilers**	**NHL**	**2**	**0**	**0**	**0**	**0**	**0**	**0**	**0**	**0**	**0**	**0**	**1**	**0.0**	**0**	**0**	**2**	**0**	**–2**								
	Cape Breton Oilers	AHL	58	19	15	34				114											2	0	0	0	2			
1994-95	Cape Breton Oilers	AHL	62	13	20	33				55																		
	Hershey Bears	AHL	9	3	0	3				12																		
1995-96	Hershey Bears	AHL	5	1	0	1				2																		
	Michigan K-Wings	IHL	5	1	0	1				2																		
	ESV Kaufbeuren	Germany-2	1	0	0	0				2																		
1996-97	Manchester Storm	BH-Cup	8	2	4	6				10																		
	Manchester Storm	Britain	40	10	13	23				18											6	1	0	1	0			
	Manchester Storm	EuroHL	6	0	1	1				6																		
1997-98	Birmingham Bulls	ECHL	70	19	36	55				90											4	0	0	0	4			
	NHL Totals		**2**	**0**	**0**	**0**	**0**	**0**	**0**	**0**	**0**	**0**	**0**	**1**	**0.0**	**0**	**0**	**2**	**0**									

WHL East First All-Star Team (1992)

Traded to **Edmonton** by **Quebec** with Ron Tugnutt for Martin Rucinsky, March 10, 1992. • Missed entire 1992-93 season recovering from knee injury suffered in training camp, September 23, 1992. Traded to **Philadelphia** by **Edmonton** with Edmonton's 6th round choice (Jamie Sokolosky) in 1995 Entry Draft for Ryan McGill, March 13, 1995.

• ZEDNIK, Richard
LW – L. 6', 199 lbs. b: Bystrica, Czech., 1/6/1976. Washington's 10th, 249th overall, in 1994.

Season	Club	League	GP	G	A	Pts	AG	AA	APts	PIM	PP	SH	GW	S	%	TGF	PGF	TGA	PGA	+/–	GP	G	A	Pts	PIM	PP	SH	GW
1992-93	SK Banska	Slovakia-2	STATISTICS NOT AVAILABLE																									
	Slovakia	EJC-A	4	8	2	10				6																		
1993-94	SK Banska	Slovakia-2	25	3	6	9																						
	Slovakia	EJC-A	6	8	12	20				10																		
1994-95	Portland Winter Hawks	WHL	65	35	51	86				89											9	5	5	10	20			
1995-96	Portland Winter Hawks	WHL	61	44	37	81				154											7	8	4	12	23			
	Slovakia	WJC-A	6	5	2	7				10																		
	Washington Capitals	**NHL**	**1**	**0**	**0**	**0**	**0**	**0**	**0**	**0**	**0**	**0**	**0**	**0**	**0.0**	**0**	**0**	**0**	**0**	**0**								
	Portland Pirates	AHL	1	1	1	2				0											21	4	5	9	26			
1996-97	Slovakia	W-Cup	3	0	0	0				0																		
	Washington Capitals	**NHL**	**11**	**2**	**1**	**3**	**2**	**1**	**3**	**4**	**1**	**0**	**0**	**21**	**9.5**	**5**	**2**	**8**	**0**	**–5**								
	Portland Pirates	AHL	56	15	20	35				70											5	1	0	1	6			
1997-98	**Washington Capitals**	**NHL**	**65**	**17**	**9**	**26**	**20**	**9**	**29**	**28**	**2**	**0**	**2**	**148**	**11.5**	**37**	**5**	**34**	**0**	**–2**	**17**	**7**	**3**	**10**	**16**	**2**	**0**	**0**
1998-99	**Washington Capitals**	**NHL**	**49**	**9**	**8**	**17**	**11**	**8**	**19**	**50**	**1**	**0**	**2**	**115**	**7.8**	**24**	**5**	**25**	**0**	**–6**								
99-2000	**Washington Capitals**	**NHL**	**69**	**19**	**16**	**35**	**21**	**15**	**36**	**54**	**1**	**0**	**2**	**179**	**10.6**	**53**	**6**	**41**	**0**	**6**	**5**	**0**	**0**	**0**	**5**	**0**	**0**	**0**
	NHL Totals		**195**	**47**	**34**	**81**	**54**	**33**	**87**	**136**	**5**	**0**	**6**	**463**	**10.2**	**119**	**18**	**108**	**0**		**22**	**7**	**3**	**10**	**21**	**2**	**0**	**0**

WHL West Second All-Star Team (1996)

			REGULAR SEASON																		PLAYOFFS							
Season	**Club**	**League**	**GP**	**G**	**A**	**Pts**	**AG**	**AA**	**APts**	**PIM**	**PP**	**SH**	**GW**	**S**	**%**	**TGF**	**PGF**	**TGA**	**PGA**	**+/–**	**GP**	**G**	**A**	**Pts**	**PIM**	**PP**	**SH**	**GW**

• ZEHR, Jeff

LW – L. 6'3", 195 lbs. b: Woodstock, Ont., 12/10/1978. NY Islanders' 3rd, 31st overall, in 1997.

Season	Club	League	GP	G	A	Pts	AG	AA	APts	PIM	PP	SH	GW	S	%	TGF	PGF	TGA	PGA	+/–	GP	G	A	Pts	PIM	PP	SH	GW
1993-94	Tavistock Braves	OJHL-D	6	2	1	3	....	....	....	6	....	....	....	....	....	....	....	....	....	....	....	....	....	....	....	....	....	....
1994-95	Stratford Cullitons	OJHL-B	44	26	32	58	....	....	....	143	....	....	....	....	....	....	....	....	....	....	....	....	....	....	....	....	....	....
1995-96	Windsor Spitfires	OHL	56	4	21	25	....	....	....	103	....	....	....	....	....	....	....	....	....	....	7	0	1	1	2	....	....	....
1996-97	Windsor Spitfires	OHL	57	27	32	59	....	....	....	196	....	....	....	....	....	....	....	....	....	....	5	2	1	3	4	....	....	....
1997-98	Windsor Spitfires	OHL	20	12	18	30	....	....	....	67	....	....	....	....	....	....	....	....	....	....	....	....	....	....	....	....	....	....
	Erie Otters	OHL	32	15	24	39	....	....	....	91	....	....	....	....	....	....	....	....	....	....	5	0	3	3	24	....	....	....
1998-99	Erie Otters	OHL	28	20	23	43	....	....	....	78	....	....	....	....	....	....	....	....	....	....	....	....	....	....	....	....	....	....
	Sarnia Sting	OHL	14	4	10	14	....	....	....	43	....	....	....	....	....	....	....	....	....	....	6	3	4	7	27	....	....	....
99-2000	**Boston Bruins**	**NHL**	**4**	**0**	**0**	**0**	**0**	**0**	**0**	**2**	**0**	**0**	**0**	**3**	**0.0**	**0**	**0**	**1**	**0**	**–1**	....	....	....	....	....	....	....	....
	Providence Bruins	AHL	12	3	3	6	....	....	....	37	....	....	....	....	....	....	....	....	....	....	....	....	....	....	....	....	....	....
	NHL Totals		**4**	**0**	**0**	**0**	**0**	**0**	**0**	**2**	**0**	**0**	**0**	**3**	**0.0**	**0**	**0**	**1**	**0**		....	....	....	....	....	....	....	....

Signed as a free agent by **Boston**, June 21, 1999. • Missed majority of 1999-2000 season recovering from knee injury suffered in practice, December 22, 1999.

• ZEIDEL, Larry

Lawrence "The Rock" D – L. 5'11", 185 lbs. b: Montreal, Que., 6/1/1928.

Season	Club	League	GP	G	A	Pts	AG	AA	APts	PIM	PP	SH	GW	S	%	TGF	PGF	TGA	PGA	+/–	GP	G	A	Pts	PIM	PP	SH	GW
1944-45	Porcupine Combines	NOJHA	....	2	1	3	....	....	....	2	....	....	....	....	....	....	....	....	....	....	....	....	....	....	....	....	....	....
	Porcupine Combines	Mem-Cup	2	0	0	0	....	....	....	0	....	....	....	....	....	....	....	....	....	....	....	....	....	....	....	....	....	....
1945-46	Verdun Maple Leafs	QJHL	17	2	7	9	....	....	....	34	....	....	....	....	....	....	....	....	....	....	3	1	1	2	2	....	....	....
1946-47	Barrie Flyers	OHA	28	7	13	20	....	....	....	48	....	....	....	....	....	....	....	....	....	....	5	2	0	2	0	....	....	....
1947-48	Quebec Aces	QSHL	48	7	20	27	....	....	....	82	....	....	....	....	....	....	....	....	....	....	10	1	3	4	13	....	....	....
1948-49	Quebec Aces	QSHL	52	4	18	22	....	....	....	92	....	....	....	....	....	....	....	....	....	....	....	....	....	....	....	....	....	....
1949-50	Quebec Aces	QSHL	55	7	19	26	....	....	....	*176	....	....	....	....	....	....	....	....	....	....	13	1	4	5	*49	....	....	....
1950-51	Saskatoon Quakers	WCMHL	58	5	27	32	....	....	....	*169	....	....	....	....	....	....	....	....	....	....	8	2	2	4	*18	....	....	....
	Saskatoon Quakers	Alx-Cup	4	1	0	1	....	....	....	*20	....	....	....	....	....	....	....	....	....	....	....	....	....	....	....	....	....	....
1951-52♦	**Detroit Red Wings**	**NHL**	**19**	**1**	**0**	**1**	**1**	**0**	**1**	**14**	....	....	....	....	....	....	....	....	....	....	**5**	**0**	**0**	**0**	**0**	**0**	**0**	**0**
	Indianapolis Capitols	AHL	43	6	17	23	....	....	....	99	....	....	....	....	....	....	....	....	....	....	....	....	....	....	....	....	....	....
1952-53	**Detroit Red Wings**	**NHL**	**9**	**0**	**0**	**0**	**0**	**0**	**0**	**8**	....	....	....	....	....	....	....	....	....	....	....	....	....	....	....	....	....	....
	Edmonton Flyers	WHL	59	4	22	26	....	....	....	114	....	....	....	....	....	....	....	....	....	....	15	2	6	8	*26	....	....	....
1953-54	**Chicago Black Hawks**	**NHL**	**64**	**1**	**6**	**7**	**1**	**7**	**8**	**102**	....	....	....	....	....	....	....	....	....	....	....	....	....	....	....	....	....	....
1954-55	Edmonton Flyers	WHL	70	10	40	50	....	....	....	142	....	....	....	....	....	....	....	....	....	....	9	2	5	7	2	....	....	....
	Edmonton Flyers	Ed-Cup	2	0	0	0	....	....	....	*46	....	....	....	....	....	....	....	....	....	....	....	....	....	....	....	....	....	....
1955-56	Hershey Bears	AHL	56	5	27	32	....	....	....	128	....	....	....	....	....	....	....	....	....	....	....	....	....	....	....	....	....	....
1956-57	Hershey Bears	AHL	64	9	19	28	....	....	....	*211	....	....	....	....	....	....	....	....	....	....	7	0	5	5	21	....	....	....
1957-58	Hershey Bears	AHL	58	2	16	18	....	....	....	152	....	....	....	....	....	....	....	....	....	....	11	0	6	6	20	....	....	....
1958-59	Hershey Bears	AHL	67	8	24	32	....	....	....	129	....	....	....	....	....	....	....	....	....	....	13	4	6	10	*59	....	....	....
1959-60	Hershey Bears	AHL	66	5	19	24	....	....	....	*293	....	....	....	....	....	....	....	....	....	....	....	....	....	....	....	....	....	....
1960-61	Hershey Bears	AHL	70	4	25	29	....	....	....	149	....	....	....	....	....	....	....	....	....	....	8	0	2	2	8	....	....	....
1961-62	Hershey Bears	AHL	70	3	19	22	....	....	....	146	....	....	....	....	....	....	....	....	....	....	7	0	1	1	20	....	....	....
1962-63	Hershey Bears	AHL	66	4	29	33	....	....	....	127	....	....	....	....	....	....	....	....	....	....	14	1	6	7	*51	....	....	....
1963-64	Seattle Totems	WHL	66	5	19	24	....	....	....	163	....	....	....	....	....	....	....	....	....	....	....	....	....	....	....	....	....	....
	Cleveland Barons	AHL	2	0	1	1	....	....	....	2	....	....	....	....	....	....	....	....	....	....	9	0	4	4	12	....	....	....
1964-65	Seattle Totems	WHL	64	2	12	14	....	....	....	202	....	....	....	....	....	....	....	....	....	....	7	1	2	3	2	....	....	....
1965-66	Cleveland Barons	AHL	72	3	12	15	....	....	....	*162	....	....	....	....	....	....	....	....	....	....	12	1	3	4	14	....	....	....
1966-67	Cleveland Barons	AHL	72	5	24	29	....	....	....	124	....	....	....	....	....	....	....	....	....	....	....	....	....	....	....	....	....	....
1967-68	**Philadelphia Flyers**	**NHL**	**57**	**1**	**10**	**11**	**1**	**10**	**11**	**68**	**0**	**0**	**1**	**33**	**3.0**	**50**	**4**	**54**	**20**	**12**	**7**	**0**	**1**	**1**	**12**	**0**	**0**	**0**
1968-69	**Philadelphia Flyers**	**NHL**	**9**	**0**	**0**	**0**	**0**	**0**	**0**	**6**	**0**	**0**	**0**	**4**	**0.0**	**0**	**0**	**3**	**0**	**–3**	....	....	....	....	....	....	....	....
	NHL Totals		**158**	**3**	**16**	**19**	**3**	**17**	**20**	**198**	....	....	....	....	....	....	....	....	....	....	**12**	**0**	**1**	**1**	**12**	....	....	....

QSHL First All-Star Team (1950) • WCMHL Second All-Star Team (1951) • WHL First All-Star Team (1955) • AHL Second All-Star Team (1959)

Signed as a free agent by **Saskatoon** (WCMHL), September 8, 1950. Traded to **Chicago** by **Detroit** with Larry Wilson and Lou Jankowski for cash, September 12, 1953. Traded to **Detroit** by **Chicago** for cash, June, 1954. Traded to **Hershey** (AHL) by **Detroit** (Edmonton-WHL) with Jimmy Uniac for Hugh Coflin, August, 1955. Traded to **Montreal** by **Seattle** (WHL) for cash, June, 1965. Traded to **Cleveland** (AHL) by **Montreal** for cash, June, 1965. Traded to **Philadelphia** by **Cleveland** (AHL) for cash, October 23, 1967.

• ZELEPUKIN, Valeri

LW – L. 6'1", 200 lbs. b: Voskresensk, USSR, 9/17/1968. New Jersey's 13th, 221st overall, in 1990.

Season	Club	League	GP	G	A	Pts	AG	AA	APts	PIM	PP	SH	GW	S	%	TGF	PGF	TGA	PGA	+/–	GP	G	A	Pts	PIM	PP	SH	GW
1984-85	Khimik Voskresensk	USSR	5	0	0	0	....	....	....	2	....	....	....	....	....	....	....	....	....	....	....	....	....	....	....	....	....	....
1985-86	Khimik Voskresensk	USSR	33	2	2	4	....	....	....	10	....	....	....	....	....	....	....	....	....	....	....	....	....	....	....	....	....	....
1986-87	Khimik Voskresensk	USSR	19	1	0	1	....	....	....	4	....	....	....	....	....	....	....	....	....	....	....	....	....	....	....	....	....	....
1987-88	CSKA Moscow	USSR	19	3	1	4	....	....	....	8	....	....	....	....	....	....	....	....	....	....	....	....	....	....	....	....	....	....
	Soviet Union	WJC-A	7	6	1	7	....	....	....	4	....	....	....	....	....	....	....	....	....	....	....	....	....	....	....	....	....	....
1988-89	CSKA Moscow	USSR	17	2	3	5	....	....	....	2	....	....	....	....	....	....	....	....	....	....	....	....	....	....	....	....	....	....
	CSKA Moscow	Super-S	7	2	1	3	....	....	....	0	....	....	....	....	....	....	....	....	....	....	....	....	....	....	....	....	....	....
1989-90	Khimik Voskresensk	Fr-Tour	1	0	1	1	....	....	....	0	....	....	....	....	....	....	....	....	....	....	....	....	....	....	....	....	....	....
	Khimik Voskresensk	USSR	46	17	14	31	....	....	....	26	....	....	....	....	....	....	....	....	....	....	....	....	....	....	....	....	....	....
	Khimik Voskresensk	Super-S	6	3	1	4	....	....	....	0	....	....	....	....	....	....	....	....	....	....	....	....	....	....	....	....	....	....
1990-91	Khimik Voskresensk	USSR	34	11	6	17	....	....	....	38	....	....	....	....	....	....	....	....	....	....	....	....	....	....	....	....	....	....
	Khimik Voskresensk	Super-S	7	4	4	8	....	....	....	2	....	....	....	....	....	....	....	....	....	....	....	....	....	....	....	....	....	....
	Soviet Union	WEC-A	9	0	4	4	....	....	....	5	....	....	....	....	....	....	....	....	....	....	....	....	....	....	....	....	....	....
1991-92	**New Jersey Devils**	**NHL**	**44**	**13**	**18**	**31**	**12**	**14**	**26**	**28**	**3**	**0**	**3**	**94**	**13.8**	**49**	**10**	**28**	**0**	**11**	**4**	**1**	**1**	**2**	**2**	**0**	**0**	**0**
	Utica Devils	AHL	22	20	9	29	....	....	....	8	....	....	....	....	....	....	....	....	....	....	....	....	....	....	....	....	....	....
1992-93	**New Jersey Devils**	**NHL**	**78**	**23**	**41**	**64**	**19**	**28**	**47**	**70**	**5**	**1**	**2**	**174**	**13.2**	**93**	**20**	**55**	**1**	**19**	**5**	**0**	**2**	**2**	**0**	**0**	**0**	**0**
1993-94	**New Jersey Devils**	**NHL**	**82**	**26**	**31**	**57**	**24**	**24**	**48**	**70**	**8**	**0**	**0**	**155**	**16.8**	**101**	**29**	**36**	**0**	**36**	**20**	**5**	**2**	**7**	**14**	**1**	**0**	**0**
1994-95♦	**New Jersey Devils**	**NHL**	**4**	**1**	**2**	**3**	**2**	**3**	**5**	**6**	**0**	**0**	**0**	**6**	**16.7**	**4**	**1**	**0**	**0**	**3**	**18**	**1**	**2**	**3**	**12**	**0**	**0**	**1**
1995-96	**New Jersey Devils**	**NHL**	**61**	**6**	**9**	**15**	**6**	**7**	**13**	**107**	**3**	**0**	**1**	**86**	**7.0**	**22**	**6**	**29**	**3**	**–10**	....	....	....	....	....	....	....	....
1996-97	Russia	W-Cup	3	0	0	0	....	....	....	20	....	....	....	....	....	....	....	....	....	....	....	....	....	....	....	....	....	....
	New Jersey Devils	**NHL**	**71**	**14**	**24**	**38**	**15**	**21**	**36**	**36**	**3**	**0**	**2**	**111**	**12.6**	**47**	**7**	**51**	**1**	**–10**	**8**	**3**	**2**	**5**	**2**	**1**	**0**	**1**
1997-98	**New Jersey Devils**	**NHL**	**35**	**2**	**8**	**10**	**2**	**8**	**10**	**32**	**0**	**0**	**0**	**54**	**3.7**	**17**	**4**	**13**	**0**	**0**	....	....	....	....	....	....	....	....
	Edmonton Oilers	**NHL**	**33**	**2**	**10**	**12**	**2**	**10**	**12**	**57**	**0**	**0**	**0**	**47**	**4.3**	**19**	**8**	**14**	**1**	**–2**	**8**	**1**	**2**	**3**	**2**	**0**	**0**	**0**
	Russia	Olympics	6	1	2	3	....	....	....	0	....	....	....	....	....	....	....	....	....	....	....	....	....	....	....	....	....	....
1998-99	**Philadelphia Flyers**	**NHL**	**74**	**16**	**9**	**25**	**19**	**9**	**28**	**48**	**0**	**0**	**5**	**129**	**12.4**	**42**	**8**	**35**	**1**	**0**	**4**	**1**	**0**	**1**	**4**	**0**	**0**	**1**
99-2000	**Philadelphia Flyers**	**NHL**	**77**	**11**	**21**	**32**	**12**	**19**	**31**	**55**	**2**	**0**	**3**	**125**	**8.8**	**49**	**16**	**48**	**12**	**–3**	**18**	**1**	**2**	**3**	**12**	**1**	**0**	**0**
	NHL Totals		**559**	**114**	**173**	**287**	**113**	**143**	**256**	**509**	**24**	**1**	**16**	**981**	**11.6**	**443**	**109**	**309**	**19**		**85**	**13**	**13**	**26**	**48**	**3**	**0**	**3**

• Missed majority of 1994-95 season recovering from eye injury suffered in practice, January 24, 1995. Traded to **Edmonton** by **New Jersey** with Bill Guerin for Jason Arnott and Bryan Muir, January 4, 1998. Traded to **Philadelphia** by **Edmonton** for Daniel Lacroix, October 5, 1998.

• ZEMLAK, Richard

RW – R. 6'2", 190 lbs. b: Wynard, Sask., 3/3/1963. St. Louis' 9th, 209th overall, in 1981.

Season	Club	League	GP	G	A	Pts	AG	AA	APts	PIM	PP	SH	GW	S	%	TGF	PGF	TGA	PGA	+/–	GP	G	A	Pts	PIM	PP	SH	GW
1979-80	Melville Millionaires	SJHL	STATISTICS NOT AVAILABLE																									
	Regina Blues	SJHL	30	4	7	11	....	....	....	80	....	....	....	....	....	....	....	....	....	....	....	....	....	....	....	....	....	....
1980-81	Spokane Flyers	WHL	72	19	19	38	....	....	....	132	....	....	....	....	....	....	....	....	....	....	4	1	1	2	6	....	....	....
1981-82	Spokane Flyers	WHL	26	9	20	29	....	....	....	113	....	....	....	....	....	....	....	....	....	....	....	....	....	....	....	....	....	....
	Winnipeg Warriors	WHL	2	1	2	3	....	....	....	0	....	....	....	....	....	....	....	....	....	....	....	....	....	....	....	....	....	....
	Medicine Hat Tigers	WHL	41	11	20	31	....	....	....	70	....	....	....	....	....	....	....	....	....	....	....	....	....	....	....	....	....	....
	Salt Lake Golden Eagles	CHL	6	0	0	0	....	....	....	2	....	....	....	....	....	....	....	....	....	....	1	0	0	0	0	....	....	....
1982-83	Medicine Hat Tigers	WHL	51	20	17	37	....	....	....	119	....	....	....	....	....	....	....	....	....	....	....	....	....	....	....	....	....	....
	Nanaimo Islanders	WHL	18	2	8	10	....	....	....	50	....	....	....	....	....	....	....	....	....	....	....	....	....	....	....	....	....	....
1983-84	Montana Magic	CHL	14	2	2	4	....	....	....	17	....	....	....	....	....	....	....	....	....	....	....	....	....	....	....	....	....	....
	Toledo Goaldiggers	IHL	45	8	19	27	....	....	....	101	....	....	....	....	....	....	....	....	....	....	....	....	....	....	....	....	....	....
1984-85	Muskegon Mohawks	IHL	64	19	18	37	....	....	....	223	....	....	....	....	....	....	....	....	....	....	17	5	4	9	68	....	....	....
	Fredericton Express	AHL	16	3	4	7	....	....	....	59	....	....	....	....	....	....	....	....	....	....	....	....	....	....	....	....	....	....
1985-86	Fredericton Express	AHL	58	6	5	11	....	....	....	305	....	....	....	....	....	....	....	....	....	....	3	0	0	0	49	....	....	....
	Muskegon Lumberjacks	IHL	3	1	2	3	....	....	....	36	....	....	....	....	....	....	....	....	....	....	....	....	....	....	....	....	....	....

Season	Club	League	REGULAR SEASON																		PLAYOFFS							
			GP	G	A	Pts	AG	AA	APts	PIM	PP	SH	GW	S	%	TGF	PGF	TGA	PGA	+/–	GP	G	A	Pts	PIM	PP	SH	GW
1986-87	**Quebec Nordiques**	**NHL**	**20**	**0**	**2**	**2**	**0**	**1**	**1**	**47**	**0**	**0**	**0**	**2**	**0.0**	**2**	**0**	**2**	**0**	**0**	....	....	....	....	....	....	....	....
	Fredericton Express	AHL	29	9	6	15	....	....	....	201	....	....	....	....	....	....	....	....	....	....	....	....	....	....	....	....	....	....
1987-88	**Minnesota North Stars**	**NHL**	**54**	**1**	**4**	**5**	**1**	**3**	**4**	**307**	**0**	**0**	**0**	**19**	**5.3**	**7**	**0**	**22**	**0**	**–15**	....	....	....	....	....	....	....	....
1988-89	**Minnesota North Stars**	**NHL**	**3**	**0**	**0**	**0**	**0**	**0**	**0**	**13**	**0**	**0**	**0**	**1**	**0.0**	**1**	**0**	**0**	**0**	**1**	....	....	....	....	....	....	....	....
	Kalamazoo Wings	IHL	2	1	3	4	....	....	....	22	....	....	....	....	....	....	....	....	....	....	....	....	....	....	....	....	....	....
	Pittsburgh Penguins	**NHL**	**31**	**0**	**0**	**0**	**0**	**0**	**0**	**135**	**0**	**0**	**0**	**2**	**0.0**	**0**	**0**	**4**	**0**	**–4**	**1**	**0**	**0**	**0**	**10**	**0**	**0**	**0**
	Muskegon Lumberjacks	IHL	18	5	4	9	....	....	....	55	....	....	....	....	....	....	....	....	....	....	8	1	1	2	35	....	....	....
1989-90	**Pittsburgh Penguins**	**NHL**	**19**	**1**	**5**	**6**	**1**	**4**	**5**	**43**	**1**	**0**	**0**	**11**	**9.1**	**7**	**1**	**13**	**1**	**–6**	....	....	....	....	....	....	....	....
	Muskegon Lumberjacks	IHL	61	17	39	56	....	....	....	263	....	....	....	....	....	....	....	....	....	....	14	3	4	7	*105	....	....	....
1990-91	Salt Lake Golden Eagles	IHL	59	14	20	34	....	....	....	194	....	....	....	....	....	....	....	....	....	....	3	0	1	1	14	....	....	....
1991-92	**Calgary Flames**	**NHL**	**5**	**0**	**1**	**1**	**0**	**1**	**1**	**42**	**0**	**0**	**0**	**4**	**0.0**	**1**	**0**	**3**	**0**	**–2**	....	....	....	....	....	....	....	....
	Salt Lake Golden Eagles	IHL	60	5	14	19	....	....	....	204	....	....	....	....	....	....	....	....	....	....	3	0	0	0	0	....	....	....
1992-93	Milwaukee Admirals	IHL	62	3	9	12	....	....	....	301	....	....	....	....	....	....	....	....	....	....	2	1	1	2	6	....	....	....
1993-94	Milwaukee Admirals	IHL	61	3	8	11	....	....	....	243	....	....	....	....	....	....	....	....	....	....	2	0	0	0	16	....	....	....
	NHL Totals		**132**	**2**	**12**	**14**	**2**	**9**	**11**	**587**	**1**	**0**	**0**	**39**	**5.1**	**18**	**1**	**44**	**1**		**1**	**0**	**0**	**0**	**10**	**0**	**0**	**0**

Rights traded to **Quebec** by **St. Louis** with rights to Dan Wood and Roger Hagglund for cash, June 22, 1984. Claimed by **Minnesota** from **Quebec** in Waiver Draft, October 5, 1987. Traded to **Pittsburgh** by **Minnesota** for the rights to Rob Gaudreau, November 1, 1988. Signed as a free agent by **Calgary**, November 8, 1990.

• ZENT, Jason

LW – L. 5'11", 204 lbs. b: Buffalo, NY, 4/15/1971. NY Islanders' 3rd, 44th overall, in 1989.

Season	Club	League	GP	G	A	Pts	AG	AA	APts	PIM	PP	SH	GW	S	%	TGF	PGF	TGA	PGA	+/–	GP	G	A	Pts	PIM	PP	SH	GW
1984-85	Depew Saints	NYAHL	48	40	30	70	....	....	....	26	....	....	....	....	....	....	....	....	....	....	....	....	....	....	....	....	....	....
1985-86	Depew Saints	NYAHL	55	50	23	73	....	....	....	24	....	....	....	....	....	....	....	....	....	....	....	....	....	....	....	....	....	....
1986-87	Depew Saints	NYAHL	40	44	38	82	....	....	....	56	....	....	....	....	....	....	....	....	....	....	....	....	....	....	....	....	....	....
1987-88	The Nichols School	Hi-School	21	20	16	36	....	....	....	28	....	....	....	....	....	....	....	....	....	....	....	....	....	....	....	....	....	....
1988-89	The Nichols School	Hi-School	29	49	32	81	....	....	....	26	....	....	....	....	....	....	....	....	....	....	....	....	....	....	....	....	....	....
1989-90	The Nichols School	Hi-School	27	36	38	74	....	....	....		....	....	....	....	....	....	....	....	....	....	....	....	....	....	....	....	....	....
	United States	WJC-A	7	1	0	1	....	....	....	4	....	....	....	....	....	....	....	....	....	....	....	....	....	....	....	....	....	....
1990-91	University of Wisconsin	WCHA	39	19	18	37	....	....	....	51	....	....	....	....	....	....	....	....	....	....	....	....	....	....	....	....	....	....
1991-92	University of Wisconsin	WCHA	39	22	17	39	....	....	....	128	....	....	....	....	....	....	....	....	....	....	....	....	....	....	....	....	....	....
1992-93	University of Wisconsin	WCHA	40	26	12	38	....	....	....	92	....	....	....	....	....	....	....	....	....	....	....	....	....	....	....	....	....	....
1993-94	University of Wisconsin	WCHA	42	20	21	41	....	....	....	120	....	....	....	....	....	....	....	....	....	....	....	....	....	....	....	....	....	....
1994-95	P.E.I. Senators	AHL	55	15	11	26	....	....	....	46	....	....	....	....	....	....	....	....	....	....	9	6	1	7	6	....	....	....
1995-96	P.E.I. Senators	AHL	68	14	5	19	....	....	....	61	....	....	....	....	....	....	....	....	....	....	5	2	1	3	4	....	....	....
1996-97	**Ottawa Senators**	**NHL**	**22**	**3**	**3**	**6**	**3**	**3**	**6**	**9**	**0**	**0**	**0**	**20**	**15.0**	**7**	**0**	**2**	**0**	**5**	....	....	....	....	....	....	....	....
	Worcester IceCats	AHL	45	14	10	24	....	....	....	45	....	....	....	....	....	....	....	....	....	....	5	3	3	6	4	....	....	....
1997-98	**Ottawa Senators**	**NHL**	**3**	**0**	**0**	**0**	**0**	**0**	**0**	**4**	**0**	**0**	**0**	**1**	**0.0**	**0**	**0**	**0**	**0**	**0**	....	....	....	....	....	....	....	....
	Detroit Vipers	IHL	4	1	0	1	....	....	....	0	....	....	....	....	....	....	....	....	....	....	....	....	....	....	....	....	....	....
	Worcester IceCats	AHL	66	25	17	42	....	....	....	67	....	....	....	....	....	....	....	....	....	....	11	2	0	2	6	....	....	....
1998-99	**Philadelphia Flyers**	**NHL**	**2**	**0**	**0**	**0**	**0**	**0**	**0**	**0**	**0**	**0**	**0**	**1**	**0.0**	**0**	**0**	**0**	**0**	**0**	....	....	....	....	....	....	....	....
	Philadelphia Phantoms	AHL	64	13	13	26	....	....	....	82	....	....	....	....	....	....	....	....	....	....	16	2	4	6	22	....	....	....
99-2000	Philadelphia Phantoms	AHL	11	0	0	0	....	....	....	22	....	....	....	....	....	....	....	....	....	....	....	....	....	....	....	....	....	....
	NHL Totals		**27**	**3**	**3**	**6**	**3**	**3**	**6**	**13**	**0**	**0**	**0**	**22**	**13.6**	**7**	**0**	**2**	**0**		....	....	....	....	....	....	....	....

NCAA Championship All-Tournament Team (1992)

Traded to **Ottawa** by **NY Islanders** for Ottawa's 5th round choice (Andy Berenzweig) in 1996 Entry Draft, October 15, 1994. Signed as a free agent by **Philadelphia**, July 28, 1998.

• ZETTERSTROM, Lars

D – L. 6'1", 198 lbs. b: Stockholm, Sweden, 11/6/1953.

Season	Club	League	GP	G	A	Pts	AG	AA	APts	PIM	PP	SH	GW	S	%	TGF	PGF	TGA	PGA	+/–	GP	G	A	Pts	PIM	PP	SH	GW
1971-72	Farjestads BK Karlstad	Sweden-Jr.	STATISTICS NOT AVAILABLE																									
	Sweden	EJC-A	5	0	1	1	....	....	....	6	....	....	....	....	....	....	....	....	....	....	....	....	....	....	....	....	....	....
1972-73	Farjestads BK Karlstad	Sweden	14	2	4	6	....	....	....	2	....	....	....	....	....	....	....	....	....	....	13	1	4	5	0	....	....	....
1973-74	Farjestads BK Karlstad	Sweden	11	4	2	6	....	....	....	6	....	....	....	....	....	....	....	....	....	....	20	1	0	1	8	....	....	....
1974-75	Farjestads BK Karlstad	Sweden	28	10	9	19	....	....	....	24	....	....	....	....	....	....	....	....	....	....	....	....	....	....	....	....	....	....
1975-76	Farjestads BK Karlstad	Sweden	35	9	6	15	....	....	....	25	....	....	....	....	....	....	....	....	....	....	....	1	0	1	2	....	....	....
1976-77	Farjestads BK Karlstad	Sweden	33	5	3	8	....	....	....	14	....	....	....	....	....	....	....	....	....	....	5	1	1	2	4	....	....	....
	Sweden	WEC-A	10	1	1	2	....	....	....	16	....	....	....	....	....	....	....	....	....	....	....	....	....	....	....	....	....	....
1977-78	Farjestads BK Karlstad	Sweden	36	6	6	12	....	....	....	42	....	....	....	....	....	....	....	....	....	....	....	....	....	....	....	....	....	....
	Sweden	WEC-A	9	0	5	5	....	....	....	4	....	....	....	....	....	....	....	....	....	....	....	....	....	....	....	....	....	....
1978-79	**Vancouver Canucks**	**NHL**	**14**	**0**	**1**	**1**	**0**	**1**	**1**	**2**	**0**	**0**	**0**	**12**	**0.0**	**3**	**1**	**13**	**1**	**–10**	....	....	....	....	....	....	....	....
	Dallas Black Hawks	CHL	56	1	33	34	....	....	....	33	....	....	....	....	....	....	....	....	....	....	9	2	4	6	6	....	....	....
1979-80	Cincinnati Stingers	CHL	27	3	14	17	....	....	....	14	....	....	....	....	....	....	....	....	....	....	....	....	....	....	....	....	....	....
1980-81	Farjestads BK Karlstad	Sweden	35	4	6	10	....	....	....	40	....	....	....	....	....	....	....	....	....	....	7	0	3	3	6	....	....	....
1981-82	Farjestads BK Karlstad	Sweden	31	5	4	9	....	....	....	45	....	....	....	....	....	....	....	....	....	....	2	0	0	0	2	....	....	....
1982-83	Farjestads BK Karlstad	Sweden	32	2	3	5	....	....	....	28	....	....	....	....	....	....	....	....	....	....	8	1	0	1	8	....	....	....
1983-84	Hammaro HC	Sweden-3	STATISTICS NOT AVAILABLE																									
1984-85	Hammaro HC	Sweden-3	26	9	12	21	....	....	....		....	....	....	....	....	....	....	....	....	....	....	....	....	....	....	....	....	....
1985-86	Hammaro HC	Sweden-3	35	6	13	19	....	....	....		....	....	....	....	....	....	....	....	....	....	....	....	....	....	....	....	....	....
1986-87	Hammaro HC	Sweden-3	24	5	4	9	....	....	....	8	....	....	....	....	....	....	....	....	....	....	....	....	....	....	....	....	....	....
	NHL Totals		**14**	**0**	**1**	**1**	**0**	**1**	**1**	**2**	**0**	**0**	**0**	**12**	**0.0**	**3**	**1**	**13**	**1**		....	....	....	....	....	....	....	....

Signed as a free agent by **Vancouver**, June 5, 1978. Claimed by **Quebec** from **Vancouver** in Expansion Draft, June 13, 1979.

• ZETTLER, Rob

D – L. 6'3", 200 lbs. b: Sept Iles, Que., 3/8/1968. Minnesota's 5th, 55th overall, in 1986.

Season	Club	League	GP	G	A	Pts	AG	AA	APts	PIM	PP	SH	GW	S	%	TGF	PGF	TGA	PGA	+/–	GP	G	A	Pts	PIM	PP	SH	GW
1983-84	Sault Ste. Marie Legionaires	NOHA	40	9	24	33	....	....	....	28	....	....	....	....	....	....	....	....	....	....	....	....	....	....	....	....	....	....
1984-85	Sault Ste. Marie Greyhounds	OHL	60	2	14	16	....	....	....	37	....	....	....	....	....	....	....	....	....	....	....	....	....	....	....	....	....	....
	Sault Ste. Marie Greyhounds	Mem-Cup	4	0	1	1	....	....	....	2	....	....	....	....	....	....	....	....	....	....	....	....	....	....	....	....	....	....
1985-86	Sault Ste. Marie Greyhounds	OHL	57	5	23	28	....	....	....	92	....	....	....	....	....	....	....	....	....	....	....	....	....	....	....	....	....	....
1986-87	Sault Ste. Marie Greyhounds	OHL	64	13	22	35	....	....	....	89	....	....	....	....	....	....	....	....	....	....	4	0	0	0	0	....	....	....
1987-88	Sault Ste. Marie Greyhounds	OHL	64	7	41	48	....	....	....	77	....	....	....	....	....	....	....	....	....	....	6	2	2	4	9	....	....	....
	Kalamazoo Wings	IHL	2	0	1	1	....	....	....	0	....	....	....	....	....	....	....	....	....	....	7	0	2	2	2	....	....	....
1988-89	**Minnesota North Stars**	**NHL**	**2**	**0**	**0**	**0**	**0**	**0**	**0**	**0**	**0**	**0**	**0**	**0**	**0.0**	**0**	**0**	**1**	**0**	**–1**	....	....	....	....	....	....	....	....
	Kalamazoo Wings	IHL	80	5	21	26	....	....	....	79	....	....	....	....	....	....	....	....	....	....	6	0	1	1	26	....	....	....
1989-90	**Minnesota North Stars**	**NHL**	**31**	**0**	**8**	**8**	**0**	**6**	**6**	**45**	**0**	**0**	**0**	**21**	**0.0**	**26**	**2**	**42**	**11**	**–7**	....	....	....	....	....	....	....	....
	Kalamazoo Wings	IHL	41	6	10	16	....	....	....	64	....	....	....	....	....	....	....	....	....	....	7	0	0	0	6	....	....	....
1990-91	**Minnesota North Stars**	**NHL**	**47**	**1**	**4**	**5**	**1**	**3**	**4**	**119**	**0**	**0**	**0**	**30**	**3.3**	**30**	**1**	**64**	**25**	**–10**	....	....	....	....	....	....	....	....
	Kalamazoo Wings	IHL	1	0	0	0	....	....	....	2	....	....	....	....	....	....	....	....	....	....	....	....	....	....	....	....	....	....
1991-92	**San Jose Sharks**	**NHL**	**74**	**1**	**8**	**9**	**1**	**6**	**7**	**99**	**0**	**0**	**0**	**72**	**1.4**	**59**	**2**	**112**	**32**	**–23**	....	....	....	....	....	....	....	....
1992-93	**San Jose Sharks**	**NHL**	**80**	**0**	**7**	**7**	**0**	**5**	**5**	**150**	**0**	**0**	**0**	**60**	**0.0**	**43**	**1**	**130**	**38**	**–50**	....	....	....	....	....	....	....	....
1993-94	**San Jose Sharks**	**NHL**	**42**	**0**	**3**	**3**	**0**	**2**	**2**	**65**	**0**	**0**	**0**	**28**	**0.0**	**21**	**2**	**43**	**17**	**–7**	....	....	....	....	....	....	....	....
	Philadelphia Flyers	**NHL**	**33**	**0**	**4**	**4**	**0**	**3**	**3**	**69**	**0**	**0**	**0**	**27**	**0.0**	**24**	**1**	**51**	**9**	**–19**	....	....	....	....	....	....	....	....
1994-95	**Philadelphia Flyers**	**NHL**	**32**	**0**	**1**	**1**	**0**	**1**	**1**	**34**	**0**	**0**	**0**	**17**	**0.0**	**14**	**0**	**28**	**11**	**–3**	**1**	**0**	**0**	**0**	**2**	**0**	**0**	**0**
1995-96	**Toronto Maple Leafs**	**NHL**	**29**	**0**	**1**	**1**	**0**	**1**	**1**	**48**	**0**	**0**	**0**	**11**	**0.0**	**8**	**0**	**14**	**5**	**–1**	**2**	**0**	**0**	**0**	**0**	**0**	**0**	**0**
1996-97	**Toronto Maple Leafs**	**NHL**	**48**	**2**	**12**	**14**	**2**	**11**	**13**	**51**	**0**	**0**	**0**	**31**	**6.5**	**37**	**0**	**39**	**10**	**8**	....	....	....	....	....	....	....	....
	Utah Grizzlies	IHL	30	0	10	10	....	....	....	60	....	....	....	....	....	....	....	....	....	....	....	....	....	....	....	....	....	....
1997-98	**Toronto Maple Leafs**	**NHL**	**59**	**0**	**7**	**7**	**0**	**7**	**7**	**108**	**0**	**0**	**0**	**28**	**0.0**	**30**	**2**	**44**	**8**	**–8**	....	....	....	....	....	....	....	....

			REGULAR SEASON																		PLAYOFFS							
Season	Club	League	GP	G	A	Pts	AG	AA	APts	PIM	PP	SH	GW	S	%	TGF	PGF	TGA	PGA	+/–	GP	G	A	Pts	PIM	PP	SH	GW
1998-99	**Nashville Predators**	**NHL**	**2**	**0**	**0**	**0**	**0**	**0**	**0**	**2**	**0**	**0**	**0**	**0**	**0.0**	**0**	**0**	**2**	**0**	**–2**	....	....	....	....	....	....	....	....
	Utah Grizzlies	IHL	77	2	16	18	....	....	....	136	....	....	....	....	....	....	....	....	....	....	....	....	....	....	....	....	....	....
99-2000	**Washington Capitals**	**NHL**	**12**	**0**	**2**	**2**	**0**	**2**	**2**	**19**	**0**	**0**	**0**	**15**	**0.0**	**6**	**0**	**7**	**0**	**–1**	**5**	**0**	**0**	**0**	**2**	**0**	**0**	**0**
	Portland Pirates	AHL	23	2	2	4	....	....	....	27	....	....	....	....	....	....	....	....	....	....	....	....	....	....	....	....	....	....
	NHL Totals		**491**	**4**	**57**	**61**	**4**	**47**	**51**	**809**	**0**	**0**	**0**	**340**	**1.2**	**298**	**11**	**577**	**166**		**8**	**0**	**0**	**0**	**4**	**0**	**0**	**0**

Claimed by **San Jose** from **Minnesota** in Dispersal Draft, May 30, 1991. Traded to **Philadelphia** by **San Jose** for Viacheslav Butsayev, February 1, 1994. Traded to **Toronto** by **Philadelphia** for Toronto's 5th round choice (Per-Ragna Bergqvist) in 1996 Entry Draft, July 8, 1995. Claimed by **Nashville** from **Toronto** in Expansion Draft, June 26, 1998. Signed as a free agent by **Washington**, September 7, 1999. • Missed majority of 1999-2000 season recovering from head injury suffered in game vs. Albany (AHL), October 21, 1999.

• ZEZEL, Peter

C – L. 5'11", 220 lbs. b: Toronto, Ont., 4/22/1965. Philadelphia's 1st, 41st overall, in 1983.

Season	Club	League	GP	G	A	Pts	AG	AA	APts	PIM	PP	SH	GW	S	%	TGF	PGF	TGA	PGA	+/–	GP	G	A	Pts	PIM	PP	SH	GW
1981-82	Don Mills Flyers	MTHL	40	43	51	94	....	....	....	36	....	....	....	....	....	....	....	....	....	....	....	....	....	....	....	....	....	....
1982-83	Toronto Marlboros	OHL	66	35	39	74	....	....	....	28	....	....	....	....	....	....	....	....	....	....	4	2	4	6	0	....	....	....
1983-84	Toronto Marlboros	OHL	68	47	86	133	....	....	....	31	....	....	....	....	....	....	....	....	....	....	9	7	5	12	4	....	....	....
1984-85	**Philadelphia Flyers**	**NHL**	**65**	**15**	**46**	**61**	**12**	**31**	**43**	**26**	**8**	**0**	**2**	**91**	**16.5**	**90**	**36**	**33**	**1**	**22**	**19**	**1**	**8**	**9**	**28**	**1**	**0**	**0**
1985-86	**Philadelphia Flyers**	**NHL**	**79**	**17**	**37**	**54**	**14**	**25**	**39**	**76**	**4**	**0**	**4**	**144**	**11.8**	**78**	**18**	**42**	**9**	**27**	**5**	**3**	**1**	**4**	**4**	**1**	**0**	**1**
1986-87	**Philadelphia Flyers**	**NHL**	**71**	**33**	**39**	**72**	**29**	**28**	**57**	**71**	**6**	**2**	**7**	**181**	**18.2**	**92**	**28**	**58**	**15**	**21**	**25**	**3**	**10**	**13**	**10**	**1**	**1**	**1**
1987-88	**Philadelphia Flyers**	**NHL**	**69**	**22**	**35**	**57**	**19**	**25**	**44**	**42**	**14**	**0**	**1**	**133**	**16.5**	**80**	**37**	**49**	**13**	**7**	**7**	**3**	**2**	**5**	**7**	**0**	**0**	**0**
1988-89	**Philadelphia Flyers**	**NHL**	**26**	**4**	**13**	**17**	**3**	**9**	**12**	**15**	**0**	**0**	**0**	**34**	**11.8**	**21**	**6**	**30**	**2**	**–13**	....	....	....	....	....	....	....	....
	St. Louis Blues	**NHL**	**52**	**17**	**36**	**53**	**14**	**25**	**39**	**27**	**5**	**1**	**4**	**115**	**14.8**	**75**	**28**	**68**	**20**	**–1**	**10**	**6**	**6**	**12**	**4**	**1**	**1**	**1**
1989-90	**St. Louis Blues**	**NHL**	**73**	**25**	**47**	**72**	**21**	**34**	**55**	**30**	**7**	**0**	**3**	**158**	**15.8**	**101**	**47**	**72**	**9**	**–9**	**12**	**1**	**7**	**8**	**4**	**1**	**0**	**0**
1990-91	**Washington Capitals**	**NHL**	**20**	**7**	**5**	**12**	**6**	**4**	**10**	**10**	**6**	**0**	**0**	**21**	**33.3**	**14**	**8**	**20**	**1**	**–13**	....	....	....	....	....	....	....	....
	Toronto Maple Leafs	**NHL**	**32**	**14**	**14**	**28**	**13**	**11**	**24**	**4**	**6**	**0**	**5**	**69**	**20.3**	**37**	**16**	**33**	**5**	**–7**	....	....	....	....	....	....	....	....
1991-92	**Toronto Maple Leafs**	**NHL**	**64**	**16**	**33**	**49**	**15**	**25**	**40**	**26**	**4**	**0**	**1**	**125**	**12.8**	**65**	**20**	**79**	**12**	**–22**	....	....	....	....	....	....	....	....
1992-93	**Toronto Maple Leafs**	**NHL**	**70**	**12**	**23**	**35**	**10**	**16**	**26**	**24**	**0**	**0**	**4**	**102**	**11.8**	**44**	**5**	**48**	**9**	**0**	**20**	**2**	**1**	**3**	**6**	**0**	**0**	**0**
1993-94	**Toronto Maple Leafs**	**NHL**	**41**	**8**	**8**	**16**	**7**	**6**	**13**	**19**	**0**	**0**	**0**	**47**	**17.0**	**21**	**0**	**34**	**18**	**5**	**18**	**2**	**4**	**6**	**8**	**0**	**0**	**1**
1994-95	**Dallas Stars**	**NHL**	**30**	**6**	**5**	**11**	**11**	**7**	**18**	**19**	**0**	**0**	**1**	**47**	**12.8**	**13**	**1**	**28**	**10**	**–6**	**3**	**1**	**0**	**1**	**0**	**0**	**0**	**0**
	Kalamazoo Wings	IHL	2	0	0	0	....	....	....	0	....	....	....	....	....	....	....	....	....	....	....	....	....	....	....	....	....	....
1995-96	**St. Louis Blues**	**NHL**	**57**	**8**	**13**	**21**	**8**	**11**	**19**	**12**	**2**	**0**	**1**	**87**	**9.2**	**32**	**12**	**32**	**10**	**–2**	**10**	**3**	**0**	**3**	**2**	**0**	**1**	**0**
1996-97	**St. Louis Blues**	**NHL**	**35**	**4**	**9**	**13**	**4**	**8**	**12**	**12**	**0**	**0**	**1**	**49**	**8.2**	**21**	**2**	**21**	**8**	**6**	....	....	....	....	....	....	....	....
	New Jersey Devils	**NHL**	**18**	**0**	**3**	**3**	**0**	**3**	**3**	**4**	**0**	**0**	**0**	**13**	**0.0**	**8**	**0**	**4**	**0**	**4**	**2**	**0**	**0**	**0**	**10**	**0**	**0**	**0**
1997-98	**New Jersey Devils**	**NHL**	**5**	**0**	**3**	**3**	**0**	**3**	**3**	**0**	**0**	**0**	**0**	**3**	**0.0**	**3**	**0**	**2**	**1**	**2**	....	....	....	....	....	....	....	....
	Albany River Rats	AHL	35	13	37	50	....	....	....	18	....	....	....	....	....	....	....	....	....	....	....	....	....	....	....	....	....	....
	Vancouver Canucks	**NHL**	**25**	**5**	**12**	**17**	**6**	**12**	**18**	**2**	**2**	**0**	**1**	**37**	**13.5**	**29**	**5**	**16**	**5**	**13**	....	....	....	....	....	....	....	....
1998-99	**Vancouver Canucks**	**NHL**	**41**	**6**	**8**	**14**	**7**	**8**	**15**	**16**	**1**	**0**	**2**	**45**	**13.3**	**19**	**2**	**20**	**8**	**5**	....	....	....	....	....	....	....	....
	NHL Totals		**873**	**219**	**389**	**608**	**199**	**291**	**490**	**435**	**65**	**3**	**37**	**1501**	**14.6**	**843**	**271**	**689**	**156**		**131**	**25**	**39**	**64**	**83**	**5**	**3**	**4**

Traded to **St. Louis** by **Philadelphia** for Mike Bullard, November 29, 1988. Traded to **Washington** by **St. Louis** with Mike Lalor for Geoff Courtnall, July 13, 1990. Traded to **Toronto** by **Washington** with Bob Rouse for Al Iafrate, January 16, 1991. Transferred to **Dallas** by **Toronto** with Grant Marshall as compensation for Toronto's signing of free agent Mike Craig, August 10, 1994. Signed as a free agent by **St. Louis**, October 19, 1995. Traded to **New Jersey** by **St. Louis** for Chris McAlpine and New Jersey's 9th round choice (James Desmarais) in 1999 Entry Draft, February 11, 1997. Traded to **Vancouver** by **New Jersey** for Vancouver's 5th round choice (Anton But) in 1998 Entry Draft, February 5, 1998.

• ZHAMNOV, Alexei

C – L. 6'1", 200 lbs. b: Moscow, USSR, 10/1/1970. Winnipeg's 5th, 77th overall, in 1990.

Season	Club	League	GP	G	A	Pts	AG	AA	APts	PIM	PP	SH	GW	S	%	TGF	PGF	TGA	PGA	+/–	GP	G	A	Pts	PIM	PP	SH	GW
1988-89	Dynamo Moscow	USSR	4	0	0	0	....	....	....	0	....	....	....	....	....	....	....	....	....	....	....	....	....	....	....	....	....	....
1989-90	Dynamo Moscow	Fr-Tour	1	0	1	1	....	....	....	2	....	....	....	....	....	....	....	....	....	....	....	....	....	....	....	....	....	....
	Dynamo Moscow	USSR	43	11	6	17	....	....	....	21	....	....	....	....	....	....	....	....	....	....	....	....	....	....	....	....	....	....
	Soviet Union	WJC-A	7	6	1	7	....	....	....	6	....	....	....	....	....	....	....	....	....	....	....	....	....	....	....	....	....	....
1990-91	Dynamo Moscow	Fr-Tour	1	0	0	0	....	....	....	0	....	....	....	....	....	....	....	....	....	....	....	....	....	....	....	....	....	....
	Dynamo Moscow	USSR	46	16	12	28	....	....	....	24	....	....	....	....	....	....	....	....	....	....	....	....	....	....	....	....	....	....
	Dynamo Moscow	Super-S	7	1	1	2	....	....	....	0	....	....	....	....	....	....	....	....	....	....	....	....	....	....	....	....	....	....
	Soviet Union	WEC-A	10	4	5	9	....	....	....	12	....	....	....	....	....	....	....	....	....	....	....	....	....	....	....	....	....	....
1991-92	Soviet Union	Can-Cup	5	3	0	3	....	....	....	2	....	....	....	....	....	....	....	....	....	....	....	....	....	....	....	....	....	....
	Dynamo Moscow	CIS	39	15	21	36	....	....	....	28	....	....	....	....	....	....	....	....	....	....	....	....	....	....	....	....	....	....
	Russia	Olympics	8	0	3	3	....	....	....	8	....	....	....	....	....	....	....	....	....	....	....	....	....	....	....	....	....	....
	Russia	WC-A	6	0	0	0	....	....	....	29	....	....	....	....	....	....	....	....	....	....	....	....	....	....	....	....	....	....
1992-93	**Winnipeg Jets**	**NHL**	**68**	**25**	**47**	**72**	**21**	**32**	**53**	**58**	**6**	**1**	**4**	**163**	**15.3**	**121**	**42**	**79**	**7**	**7**	**6**	**0**	**2**	**2**	**2**	**0**	**0**	**0**
1993-94	**Winnipeg Jets**	**NHL**	**61**	**26**	**45**	**71**	**24**	**35**	**59**	**62**	**7**	**0**	**1**	**196**	**13.3**	**102**	**44**	**80**	**2**	**–20**	....	....	....	....	....	....	....	....
1994-95	**Winnipeg Jets**	**NHL**	**48**	**30**	**35**	**65**	**53**	**52**	**105**	**20**	**9**	**0**	**4**	**155**	**19.4**	**82**	**32**	**48**	**3**	**5**	....	....	....	....	....	....	....	....
1995-96	**Winnipeg Jets**	**NHL**	**58**	**22**	**37**	**59**	**22**	**30**	**52**	**65**	**5**	**0**	**2**	**199**	**11.1**	**97**	**49**	**57**	**5**	**–4**	**6**	**2**	**1**	**3**	**8**	**0**	**0**	**0**
1996-97	Russia	W-Cup	4	0	2	2	....	....	....	6	....	....	....	....	....	....	....	....	....	....	....	....	....	....	....	....	....	....
	Chicago Blackhawks	**NHL**	**74**	**20**	**42**	**62**	**21**	**37**	**58**	**56**	**6**	**1**	**2**	**208**	**9.6**	**85**	**28**	**56**	**17**	**18**	....	....	....	....	....	....	....	....
1997-98	**Chicago Blackhawks**	**NHL**	**70**	**21**	**28**	**49**	**25**	**27**	**52**	**61**	**6**	**2**	**3**	**193**	**10.9**	**76**	**26**	**50**	**16**	**16**	....	....	....	....	....	....	....	....
	Russia	Olympics	6	2	1	3	....	....	....	2	....	....	....	....	....	....	....	....	....	....	....	....	....	....	....	....	....	....
1998-99	**Chicago Blackhawks**	**NHL**	**76**	**20**	**41**	**61**	**23**	**40**	**63**	**50**	**8**	**1**	**2**	**200**	**10.0**	**85**	**38**	**79**	**22**	**–10**	....	....	....	....	....	....	....	....
99-2000	**Chicago Blackhawks**	**NHL**	**71**	**23**	**37**	**60**	**26**	**34**	**60**	**61**	**5**	**0**	**7**	**175**	**13.1**	**100**	**31**	**81**	**19**	**7**	....	....	....	....	....	....	....	....
	Russia	WC-A	5	0	1	1	....	....	....	0	....	....	....	....	....	....	....	....	....	....	....	....	....	....	....	....	....	....
	NHL Totals		**526**	**187**	**312**	**499**	**215**	**287**	**502**	**433**	**52**	**5**	**25**	**1489**	**12.6**	**748**	**290**	**530**	**91**		**12**	**2**	**3**	**5**	**10**	**0**	**0**	**0**

NHL Second All-Star Team (1995)

Traded to **Chicago** by **Phoenix** with Craig Mills and Phoenix's 1st round choice (Ty Jones) in 1997 Entry Draft for Jeremy Roenick, August 16, 1996.

• ZHITNIK, Alexei

Alexei N. D – L. 5'11", 204 lbs. b: Kiev, USSR, 10/10/1972. Los Angeles' 3rd, 81st overall, in 1991.

Season	Club	League	GP	G	A	Pts	AG	AA	APts	PIM	PP	SH	GW	S	%	TGF	PGF	TGA	PGA	+/–	GP	G	A	Pts	PIM	PP	SH	GW
1989-90	Sokol Kiev	USSR	31	3	4	7	....	....	....	16	....	....	....	....	....	....	....	....	....	....	....	....	....	....	....	....	....	....
	Soviet Union	EJC-A	6	2	2	4	....	....	....	2	....	....	....	....	....	....	....	....	....	....	....	....	....	....	....	....	....	....
1990-91	Sokol Kiev	Fr-Tour	1	0	0	0	....	....	....	0	....	....	....	....	....	....	....	....	....	....	....	....	....	....	....	....	....	....
	Sokol Kiev	USSR	46	1	4	5	....	....	....	46	....	....	....	....	....	....	....	....	....	....	....	....	....	....	....	....	....	....
	Soviet Union	WJC-A	7	1	1	2	....	....	....	2	....	....	....	....	....	....	....	....	....	....	....	....	....	....	....	....	....	....
1991-92	Soviet Union	Can-Cup	5	0	0	0	....	....	....	4	....	....	....	....	....	....	....	....	....	....	....	....	....	....	....	....	....	....
	CSKA Moscow	CIS	44	2	7	9	....	....	....	52	....	....	....	....	....	....	....	....	....	....	....	....	....	....	....	....	....	....
	Russia	WJC-A	7	1	1	2	....	....	....	2	....	....	....	....	....	....	....	....	....	....	....	....	....	....	....	....	....	....
	Russia	Olympics	8	1	0	1	....	....	....	0	....	....	....	....	....	....	....	....	....	....	....	....	....	....	....	....	....	....
	Russia	WC-A	6	0	2	2	....	....	....	6	....	....	....	....	....	....	....	....	....	....	....	....	....	....	....	....	....	....
1992-93	**Los Angeles Kings**	**NHL**	**78**	**12**	**36**	**48**	**10**	**25**	**35**	**80**	**5**	**0**	**2**	**136**	**8.8**	**104**	**42**	**77**	**12**	**–3**	**24**	**3**	**9**	**12**	**26**	**2**	**0**	**1**
1993-94	**Los Angeles Kings**	**NHL**	**81**	**12**	**40**	**52**	**11**	**31**	**42**	**101**	**11**	**0**	**1**	**227**	**5.3**	**128**	**59**	**99**	**19**	**–11**	....	....	....	....	....	....	....	....
	Russia	WC-A	6	1	0	1	....	....	....	8	....	....	....	....	....	....	....	....	....	....	....	....	....	....	....	....	....	....
1994-95	**Los Angeles Kings**	**NHL**	**11**	**2**	**5**	**7**	**4**	**7**	**11**	**27**	**2**	**0**	**0**	**33**	**6.1**	**19**	**8**	**14**	**0**	**–3**	....	....	....	....	....	....	....	....
	Buffalo Sabres	**NHL**	**21**	**2**	**5**	**7**	**4**	**7**	**11**	**34**	**1**	**0**	**0**	**33**	**6.1**	**23**	**11**	**15**	**0**	**–3**	**5**	**0**	**1**	**1**	**14**	**0**	**0**	**0**
1995-96	**Buffalo Sabres**	**NHL**	**80**	**6**	**30**	**36**	**6**	**25**	**31**	**58**	**5**	**0**	**0**	**193**	**3.1**	**109**	**50**	**112**	**28**	**–25**	....	....	....	....	....	....	....	....
	Russia	WC-A	8	1	1	2	....	....	....	6	....	....	....	....	....	....	....	....	....	....	....	....	....	....	....	....	....	....
1996-97	Russia	W-Cup	3	0	1	1	....	....	....	2	....	....	....	....	....	....	....	....	....	....	....	....	....	....	....	....	....	....
	Buffalo Sabres	**NHL**	**80**	**7**	**28**	**35**	**7**	**25**	**32**	**95**	**3**	**1**	**0**	**170**	**4.1**	**92**	**22**	**86**	**26**	**10**	**12**	**1**	**0**	**1**	**16**	**0**	**0**	**0**
1997-98	**Buffalo Sabres**	**NHL**	**78**	**15**	**30**	**45**	**18**	**29**	**47**	**102**	**2**	**3**	**3**	**191**	**7.9**	**103**	**31**	**80**	**27**	**19**	**15**	**0**	**3**	**3**	**36**	**0**	**0**	**0**
	Russia	Olympics	6	0	2	2	....	....	....	2	....	....	....	....	....	....	....	....	....	....	....	....	....	....	....	....	....	....
1998-99	**Buffalo Sabres**	**NHL**	**81**	**7**	**26**	**33**	**8**	**25**	**33**	**96**	**3**	**1**	**2**	**185**	**3.8**	**76**	**28**	**79**	**25**	**–6**	**21**	**4**	**11**	**15**	***52**	**4**	**0**	**2**
99-2000	**Buffalo Sabres**	**NHL**	**74**	**2**	**11**	**13**	**2**	**10**	**12**	**95**	**1**	**0**	**0**	**139**	**1.4**	**67**	**14**	**75**	**16**	**–6**	**4**	**0**	**0**	**0**	**8**	**0**	**0**	**0**
	Russia	WC-A	6	0	1	1	....	....	....	2	....	....	....	....	....	....	....	....	....	....	....	....	....	....	....	....	....	....
	NHL Totals		**584**	**65**	**211**	**276**	**70**	**184**	**254**	**688**	**33**	**5**	**8**	**1307**	**5.0**	**721**	**265**	**637**	**153**		**81**	**8**	**24**	**32**	**152**	**6**	**0**	**3**

WC-A All-Star Team (1996) • Named Best Defenseman at WC-A (1996) • Played in NHL All-Star Game (1999)

Traded to **Buffalo** by **LA Kings** with Robb Stauber, Charlie Huddy and LA Kings' 5th round choice (Marian Menhart) in 1995 Entry Draft for Philippe Boucher, Denis Tsygurov and Grant Fuhr, February 14, 1995.

• ZHOLTOK, Sergei

C – R. 6', 187 lbs. b: Riga, Latvia, 2/12/1972. Boston's 2nd, 55th overall, in 1992.

			REGULAR SEASON																		PLAYOFFS							
Season	Club	League	GP	G	A	Pts	AG	AA	APts	PIM	PP	SH	GW	S	%	TGF	PGF	TGA	PGA	+/–	GP	G	A	Pts	PIM	PP	SH	GW
1989-90	Dynamo Riga	USSR-Jr.	STATISTICS NOT AVAILABLE																									
	Soviet Union	EJC-A	6	6	4	10	....	....	....	6	....	....	....	....	....	....	....	....	....	....	....	....	....	....	....	....	....	....
1990-91	Dynamo Riga	Fr-Tour	1	0	0	0	....	....	....	0	....	....	....	....	....	....	....	....	....	....	....	....	....	....	....	....	....	....
	Dynamo Riga	USSR	39	4	0	4	....	....	....	16	....	....	....	....	....	....	....	....	....	....	....	....	....	....	....	....	....	....
	Soviet Union	WJC-A	7	2	2	4	....	....	....	2	....	....	....	....	....	....	....	....	....	....	....	....	....	....	....	....	....	....
1991-92	Dynamo Riga	CIS	27	6	3	9	....	....	....	6	....	....	....	....	....	....	....	....	....	....	....	....	....	....	....	....	....	....
	Russia	WJC-A	7	2	4	6	....	....	....	6	....	....	....	....	....	....	....	....	....	....	....	....	....	....	....	....	....	....
1992-93	**Boston Bruins**	**NHL**	**1**	**0**	**1**	**1**	**0**	**1**	**1**	**0**	**0**	**0**	**0**	**2**	**0.0**	**1**	**0**	**0**	**0**	**1**	....	....	....	....	....	....	....	....
	Providence Bruins	AHL	64	31	35	66	....	....	....	57	....	....	....	....	....	....	....	....	....	....	6	3	5	8	4	....	....	....
1993-94	**Boston Bruins**	**NHL**	**24**	**2**	**1**	**3**	**2**	**1**	**3**	**2**	**1**	**0**	**0**	**25**	**8.0**	**3**	**1**	**10**	**1**	**–7**	....	....	....	....	....	....	....	....
	Providence Bruins	AHL	54	29	33	62	....	....	....	16	....	....	....	....	....	....	....	....	....	....	....	....	....	....	....	....	....	....
	Latvia	WC-B	4	6	1	7	....	....	....	4	....	....	....	....	....	....	....	....	....	....	....	....	....	....	....	....	....	....
1994-95	Providence Bruins	AHL	78	23	35	58	....	....	....	42	....	....	....	....	....	....	....	....	....	....	13	8	5	13	6	....	....	....
1995-96	Las Vegas Thunder	IHL	82	51	50	101	....	....	....	30	....	....	....	....	....	....	....	....	....	....	15	7	13	20	6	....	....	....
1996-97	**Ottawa Senators**	**NHL**	**57**	**12**	**16**	**28**	**13**	**14**	**27**	**19**	**5**	**0**	**0**	**96**	**12.5**	**42**	**15**	**25**	**0**	**2**	**7**	**1**	**1**	**2**	**0**	**1**	**0**	**0**
	Las Vegas Thunder	IHL	19	13	14	27	....	....	....	20	....	....	....	....	....	....	....	....	....	....	....	....	....	....	....	....	....	....
	Latvia	WC-A	5	3	3	6	....	....	....	2	....	....	....	....	....	....	....	....	....	....	....	....	....	....	....	....	....	....
1997-98	**Ottawa Senators**	**NHL**	**78**	**10**	**13**	**23**	**12**	**13**	**25**	**16**	**7**	**0**	**1**	**127**	**7.9**	**34**	**17**	**24**	**0**	**–7**	**11**	**0**	**2**	**2**	**0**	**0**	**0**	**0**
1998-99	**Montreal Canadiens**	**NHL**	**70**	**7**	**15**	**22**	**8**	**14**	**22**	**6**	**2**	**0**	**3**	**102**	**6.9**	**31**	**13**	**30**	**0**	**–12**	....	....	....	....	....	....	....	....
	Fredericton Canadiens	AHL	7	3	4	7	....	....	....	0	....	....	....	....	....	....	....	....	....	....	....	....	....	....	....	....	....	....
	Latvia	WC-A	6	4	0	4	....	....	....	0	....	....	....	....	....	....	....	....	....	....	....	....	....	....	....	....	....	....
99-2000	**Montreal Canadiens**	**NHL**	**68**	**26**	**12**	**38**	**29**	**11**	**40**	**28**	**9**	**0**	**7**	**163**	**16.0**	**57**	**23**	**33**	**1**	**2**	....	....	....	....	....	....	....	....
	Quebec Citadelles	AHL	1	0	1	1	....	....	....	2	....	....	....	....	....	....	....	....	....	....	....	....	....	....	....	....	....	....
	NHL Totals		**298**	**57**	**58**	**115**	**64**	**54**	**118**	**71**	**24**	**0**	**11**	**515**	**11.1**	**168**	**69**	**122**	**2**		**18**	**1**	**3**	**4**	**0**	**1**	**0**	**0**

Signed as a free agent by **Ottawa**, July 10, 1996. Signed as a free agent by **Montreal**, September 9, 1998.

• ZMOLEK, Doug

D – L. 6'2", 222 lbs. b: Rochester, MN, 11/3/1970. Minnesota's 1st, 7th overall, in 1989.

Season	Club	League	GP	G	A	Pts	AG	AA	APts	PIM	PP	SH	GW	S	%	TGF	PGF	TGA	PGA	+/–	GP	G	A	Pts	PIM	PP	SH	GW
1987-88	John Marshall Rockets	Hi-School	27	4	32	36	....	....	....	....	....	....	....	....	....	....	....	....	....	....	....	....	....	....	....	....	....	....
1988-89	John Marshall Rockets	Hi-School	29	17	41	58	....	....	....	....	....	....	....	....	....	....	....	....	....	....	....	....	....	....	....	....	....	....
1989-90	University of Minnesota	WCHA	40	1	10	11	....	....	....	52	....	....	....	....	....	....	....	....	....	....	....	....	....	....	....	....	....	....
	United States	WJC-A	7	0	1	1	....	....	....	2	....	....	....	....	....	....	....	....	....	....	....	....	....	....	....	....	....	....
1990-91	University of Minnesota	WCHA	34	11	6	17	....	....	....	38	....	....	....	....	....	....	....	....	....	....	....	....	....	....	....	....	....	....
1991-92	University of Minnesota	WCHA	41	6	20	26	....	....	....	84	....	....	....	....	....	....	....	....	....	....	....	....	....	....	....	....	....	....
1992-93	**San Jose Sharks**	**NHL**	**84**	**5**	**10**	**15**	**4**	**7**	**11**	**229**	**2**	**0**	**0**	**94**	**5.3**	**64**	**12**	**142**	**40**	**–50**	....	....	....	....	....	....	....	....
1993-94	**San Jose Sharks**	**NHL**	**68**	**0**	**4**	**4**	**0**	**3**	**3**	**122**	**0**	**0**	**0**	**29**	**0.0**	**35**	**0**	**69**	**25**	**–9**	....	....	....	....	....	....	....	....
	Dallas Stars	**NHL**	**7**	**1**	**0**	**1**	**1**	**0**	**1**	**11**	**0**	**0**	**0**	**3**	**33.3**	**6**	**0**	**5**	**0**	**1**	**7**	**0**	**1**	**1**	**4**	**0**	**0**	**0**
1994-95	**Dallas Stars**	**NHL**	**42**	**0**	**5**	**5**	**0**	**7**	**7**	**67**	**0**	**0**	**0**	**28**	**0.0**	**22**	**2**	**39**	**13**	**–6**	**5**	**0**	**0**	**0**	**10**	**0**	**0**	**0**
1995-96	**Dallas Stars**	**NHL**	**42**	**1**	**5**	**6**	**1**	**4**	**5**	**65**	**0**	**0**	**0**	**26**	**3.8**	**36**	**6**	**45**	**16**	**1**	....	....	....	....	....	....	....	....
	Los Angeles Kings	**NHL**	**16**	**1**	**0**	**1**	**1**	**0**	**1**	**22**	**0**	**0**	**0**	**10**	**10.0**	**8**	**0**	**21**	**7**	**–6**	....	....	....	....	....	....	....	....
1996-97	**Los Angeles Kings**	**NHL**	**57**	**1**	**0**	**1**	**1**	**0**	**1**	**116**	**0**	**0**	**0**	**28**	**3.6**	**21**	**0**	**56**	**13**	**–22**	....	....	....	....	....	....	....	....
1997-98	**Los Angeles Kings**	**NHL**	**46**	**0**	**8**	**8**	**0**	**8**	**8**	**111**	**0**	**0**	**0**	**23**	**0.0**	**22**	**0**	**31**	**9**	**0**	**2**	**0**	**0**	**0**	**2**	**0**	**0**	**0**
1998-99	**Chicago Blackhawks**	**NHL**	**62**	**0**	**14**	**14**	**0**	**13**	**13**	**102**	**0**	**0**	**0**	**33**	**0.0**	**40**	**1**	**60**	**22**	**1**	....	....	....	....	....	....	....	....
99-2000	**Chicago Blackhawks**	**NHL**	**43**	**2**	**7**	**9**	**2**	**6**	**8**	**60**	**0**	**0**	**0**	**24**	**8.3**	**31**	**3**	**30**	**8**	**6**	....	....	....	....	....	....	....	....
	NHL Totals		**467**	**11**	**53**	**64**	**10**	**48**	**58**	**905**	**2**	**0**	**0**	**298**	**3.7**	**285**	**24**	**498**	**153**		**14**	**0**	**1**	**1**	**16**	**0**	**0**	**0**

WCHA Second All-Star Team (1992) • NCAA West Second All-American Team (1992)

Claimed by **San Jose** from **Minnesota** in Dispersal Draft, May 30, 1991. Traded to **Dallas** by **San Jose** with Mike Lalor for Ulf Dahlen and Dallas' 7th round choice (Brad Mehalko) in 1995 Entry Draft, March 19, 1994. Traded to **LA Kings** by **Dallas** with Shane Churla for Darryl Sydor and LA Kings' 5th round choice (Ryan Christie) in 1996 Entry Draft, February 17, 1996. Traded to **Chicago** by **LA Kings** for Chicago's 3rd round choice (Frantisek Kaberle) in 1999 Entry Draft, September 3, 1998.

• ZOMBO, Rick

Richard J. D – R. 6'1", 202 lbs. b: Des Plaines, IL, 5/8/1963. Detroit's 6th, 149th overall, in 1981.

Season	Club	League	GP	G	A	Pts	AG	AA	APts	PIM	PP	SH	GW	S	%	TGF	PGF	TGA	PGA	+/–	GP	G	A	Pts	PIM	PP	SH	GW
1979-80	Royal York Major Midgets	OMHA	STATISTICS NOT AVAILABLE																									
1980-81	Austin Mavericks	USHL	43	10	26	36	....	....	....	73	....	....	....	....	....	....	....	....	....	....	....	....	....	....	....	....	....	....
1981-82	University of North Dakota	WCHA	45	1	15	16	....	....	....	31	....	....	....	....	....	....	....	....	....	....	....	....	....	....	....	....	....	....
1982-83	University of North Dakota	WCHA	35	5	11	16	....	....	....	41	....	....	....	....	....	....	....	....	....	....	....	....	....	....	....	....	....	....
	United States	WJC-A	7	0	0	0	....	....	....	0	....	....	....	....	....	....	....	....	....	....	....	....	....	....	....	....	....	....
1983-84	University of North Dakota	WCHA	34	7	24	31	....	....	....	40	....	....	....	....	....	....	....	....	....	....	....	....	....	....	....	....	....	....
1984-85	**Detroit Red Wings**	**NHL**	**1**	**0**	**0**	**0**	**0**	**0**	**0**	**0**	**0**	**0**	**0**	**0**	**0.0**	**0**	**0**	**3**	**0**	**–3**	....	....	....	....	....	....	....	....
	Adirondack Red Wings	AHL	56	3	32	35	....	....	....	70	....	....	....	....	....	....	....	....	....	....	....	....	....	....	....	....	....	....
1985-86	**Detroit Red Wings**	**NHL**	**14**	**0**	**1**	**1**	**0**	**1**	**1**	**16**	**0**	**0**	**0**	**8**	**0.0**	**3**	**0**	**16**	**3**	**–10**	....	....	....	....	....	....	....	....
	Adirondack Red Wings	AHL	69	7	34	41	....	....	....	94	....	....	....	....	....	....	....	....	....	....	17	0	4	4	40	....	....	....
1986-87	**Detroit Red Wings**	**NHL**	**44**	**1**	**4**	**5**	**1**	**3**	**4**	**59**	**0**	**0**	**0**	**28**	**3.6**	**33**	**6**	**44**	**11**	**–6**	**7**	**0**	**1**	**1**	**9**	**0**	**0**	**0**
	Adirondack Red Wings	AHL	25	0	6	6	....	....	....	22	....	....	....	....	....	....	....	....	....	....	....	....	....	....	....	....	....	....
1987-88	**Detroit Red Wings**	**NHL**	**62**	**3**	**14**	**17**	**3**	**10**	**13**	**96**	**0**	**0**	**2**	**48**	**6.3**	**74**	**3**	**69**	**22**	**24**	**16**	**0**	**6**	**6**	**55**	**0**	**0**	**0**
1988-89	**Detroit Red Wings**	**NHL**	**75**	**1**	**20**	**21**	**1**	**14**	**15**	**106**	**1**	**0**	**0**	**64**	**1.6**	**94**	**3**	**105**	**36**	**22**	**6**	**0**	**1**	**1**	**16**	**0**	**0**	**0**
1989-90	**Detroit Red Wings**	**NHL**	**77**	**5**	**20**	**25**	**4**	**14**	**18**	**95**	**0**	**0**	**0**	**62**	**8.1**	**98**	**9**	**125**	**49**	**13**	....	....	....	....	....	....	....	....
1990-91	**Detroit Red Wings**	**NHL**	**77**	**4**	**19**	**23**	**4**	**14**	**18**	**55**	**0**	**0**	**0**	**68**	**5.9**	**69**	**1**	**119**	**49**	**–2**	**7**	**1**	**0**	**1**	**10**	**0**	**0**	**0**
1991-92	**Detroit Red Wings**	**NHL**	**3**	**0**	**0**	**0**	**0**	**0**	**0**	**15**	**0**	**0**	**0**	**1**	**0.0**	**1**	**0**	**5**	**1**	**–3**	....	....	....	....	....	....	....	....
	St. Louis Blues	**NHL**	**64**	**3**	**15**	**18**	**3**	**11**	**14**	**46**	**0**	**0**	**0**	**47**	**6.4**	**55**	**2**	**74**	**25**	**4**	**6**	**0**	**2**	**2**	**12**	**0**	**0**	**0**
1992-93	**St. Louis Blues**	**NHL**	**71**	**0**	**15**	**15**	**0**	**10**	**10**	**78**	**0**	**0**	**0**	**43**	**0.0**	**49**	**2**	**73**	**24**	**–2**	**11**	**0**	**1**	**1**	**12**	**0**	**0**	**0**
1993-94	**St. Louis Blues**	**NHL**	**74**	**2**	**8**	**10**	**2**	**6**	**8**	**85**	**0**	**0**	**0**	**53**	**3.8**	**59**	**6**	**93**	**25**	**–15**	**4**	**0**	**0**	**0**	**11**	**0**	**0**	**0**
1994-95	**St. Louis Blues**	**NHL**	**23**	**1**	**4**	**5**	**2**	**6**	**8**	**24**	**0**	**0**	**1**	**18**	**5.6**	**19**	**0**	**20**	**8**	**7**	**3**	**0**	**0**	**0**	**2**	**0**	**0**	**0**
1995-96	**Boston Bruins**	**NHL**	**67**	**4**	**10**	**14**	**4**	**8**	**12**	**53**	**0**	**0**	**1**	**68**	**5.9**	**60**	**4**	**80**	**17**	**–7**	....	....	....	....	....	....	....	....
1996-97	Phoenix Roadrunners	IHL	23	0	6	6	....	....	....	22	....	....	....	....	....	....	....	....	....	....	....	....	....	....	....	....	....	....
	NHL Totals		**652**	**24**	**130**	**154**	**24**	**97**	**121**	**728**	**1**	**0**	**4**	**508**	**4.7**	**614**	**36**	**826**	**270**		**60**	**1**	**11**	**12**	**127**	**0**	**0**	**0**

WCHA Second All-Star Team (1984)

Traded to **St. Louis** by **Detroit** for Vincent Riendeau, October 18, 1991. Traded to **Boston** by **St. Louis** for Fred Knipscheer, October 2, 1995. Signed as a free agent by **LA Kings**, December 13, 1996.

• ZUBOV, Sergei

D – R. 6'1", 200 lbs. b: Moscow, USSR, 7/22/1970. NY Rangers' 6th, 85th overall, in 1990.

Season	Club	League	GP	G	A	Pts	AG	AA	APts	PIM	PP	SH	GW	S	%	TGF	PGF	TGA	PGA	+/–	GP	G	A	Pts	PIM	PP	SH	GW
1987-88	Soviet Union	EJC-A	6	0	2	2	....	....	....	2	....	....	....	....	....	....	....	....	....	....	....	....	....	....	....	....	....	....
1988-89	CSKA Moscow	USSR	29	1	4	5	....	....	....	10	....	....	....	....	....	....	....	....	....	....	....	....	....	....	....	....	....	....
	CSKA Moscow	USSR-Jr.	STATISTICS NOT AVAILABLE																									
	Soviet Union	WJC-A	7	0	5	5	....	....	....	4	....	....	....	....	....	....	....	....	....	....	....	....	....	....	....	....	....	....
1989-90	CSKA Moscow	Fr-Tour	1	0	0	0	....	....	....	0	....	....	....	....	....	....	....	....	....	....	....	....	....	....	....	....	....	....
	CSKA Moscow	USSR	48	6	2	8	....	....	....	16	....	....	....	....	....	....	....	....	....	....	....	....	....	....	....	....	....	....
	Soviet Union	WJC-A	7	1	3	4	....	....	....	14	....	....	....	....	....	....	....	....	....	....	....	....	....	....	....	....	....	....
1990-91	CSKA Moscow	Fr-Tour	1	1	0	1	....	....	....	25	....	....	....	....	....	....	....	....	....	....	....	....	....	....	....	....	....	....
	CSKA Moscow	USSR	41	6	5	11	....	....	....	12	....	....	....	....	....	....	....	....	....	....	....	....	....	....	....	....	....	....
	CSKA Moscow	Super-S	7	0	1	1	....	....	....	0	....	....	....	....	....	....	....	....	....	....	....	....	....	....	....	....	....	....
1991-92	CSKA Moscow	CIS	44	4	7	11	....	....	....	8	....	....	....	....	....	....	....	....	....	....	....	....	....	....	....	....	....	....
	Russia	Olympics	8	0	1	1	....	....	....	0	....	....	....	....	....	....	....	....	....	....	....	....	....	....	....	....	....	....
	Russia	WC-A	6	2	2	4	....	....	....	10	....	....	....	....	....	....	....	....	....	....	....	....	....	....	....	....	....	....
1992-93	CSKA Moscow	CIS	1	0	1	1	....	....	....	0	....	....	....	....	....	....	....	....	....	....	....	....	....	....	....	....	....	....
	New York Rangers	**NHL**	**49**	**8**	**23**	**31**	**7**	**16**	**23**	**4**	**3**	**0**	**0**	**93**	**8.6**	**78**	**22**	**67**	**10**	**–1**	....	....	....	....	....	....	....	....
	Binghamton Rangers	AHL	30	7	29	36	....	....	....	14	....	....	....	....	....	....	....	....	....	....	11	5	5	10	2	....	....	....
1993-94♦	**New York Rangers**	**NHL**	**78**	**12**	**77**	**89**	**11**	**60**	**71**	**39**	**9**	**0**	**1**	**222**	**5.4**	**163**	**78**	**73**	**8**	**20**	**22**	**5**	**14**	**19**	**0**	**2**	**0**	**0**
	Binghamton Rangers	AHL	2	1	2	3	....	....	....	0	....	....	....	....	....	....	....	....	....	....	....	....	....	....	....	....	....	....
1994-95	**New York Rangers**	**NHL**	**38**	**10**	**26**	**36**	**18**	**38**	**56**	**18**	**6**	**0**	**0**	**116**	**8.6**	**67**	**33**	**42**	**6**	**–2**	**10**	**3**	**8**	**11**	**2**	**1**	**0**	**0**

			REGULAR SEASON																		PLAYOFFS							
Season	Club	League	GP	G	A	Pts	AG	AA	APts	PIM	PP	SH	GW	S	%	TGF	PGF	TGA	PGA	+/–	GP	G	A	Pts	PIM	PP	SH	GW
1995-96	**Pittsburgh Penguins**	**NHL**	**64**	**11**	**55**	**66**	**11**	**45**	**56**	**22**	**3**	**2**	**1**	**141**	**7.8**	**151**	**60**	**79**	**16**	**28**	**18**	**1**	**14**	**15**	**26**	**1**	**0**	**0**
1996-97	Russia	W-Cup	4	1	1	2	....	....	....	0	....	....	....	....	....	....	....	....	....	....	....	....	....	....	....	....	....	....
	Dallas Stars	**NHL**	**78**	**13**	**30**	**43**	**14**	**27**	**41**	**24**	**1**	**0**	**3**	**133**	**9.8**	**111**	**32**	**69**	**9**	**19**	**7**	**0**	**3**	**3**	**2**	**0**	**0**	**0**
1997-98	**Dallas Stars**	**NHL**	**73**	**10**	**47**	**57**	**12**	**46**	**58**	**16**	**5**	**1**	**2**	**148**	**6.8**	**122**	**61**	**58**	**13**	**16**	**17**	**4**	**5**	**9**	**2**	**3**	**0**	**1**
1998-99♦	**Dallas Stars**	**NHL**	**81**	**10**	**41**	**51**	**12**	**40**	**52**	**20**	**5**	**0**	**3**	**155**	**6.5**	**121**	**64**	**61**	**13**	**9**	**23**	**1**	**12**	**13**	**4**	**0**	**0**	**0**
99-2000	**Dallas Stars**	**NHL**	**77**	**9**	**33**	**42**	**10**	**31**	**41**	**18**	**3**	**1**	**3**	**179**	**5.0**	**112**	**39**	**88**	**13**	**–2**	**18**	**2**	**7**	**9**	**6**	**1**	**1**	**0**
	NHL Totals		**538**	**83**	**332**	**415**	**95**	**303**	**398**	**161**	**35**	**4**	**13**	**1187**	**7.0**	**925**	**389**	**537**	**88**		**115**	**16**	**63**	**79**	**42**	**8**	**1**	**1**

EJC-A All-Star Team (1988) • Named Best Defenseman at EJC-A (1988) • Played in NHL All-Star Game (1998, 1999, 2000)

Traded to **Pittsburgh** by **NY Rangers** with Petr Nedved for Luc Robitaille and Ulf Samuelsson, August 31, 1995. Traded to **Dallas** by **Pittsburgh** for Kevin Hatcher, June 22, 1996.

• ZUBRUS, Dainius

RW – L. 6'3", 220 lbs. b: Elektrenai, USSR, 6/16/1978. Philadelphia's 1st, 15th overall, in 1996.

Season	Club	League	GP	G	A	Pts	AG	AA	APts	PIM	PP	SH	GW	S	%	TGF	PGF	TGA	PGA	+/–	GP	G	A	Pts	PIM	PP	SH	GW
1995-96	Pembroke Lumber Kings	OJHL	28	19	13	32	....	....	....	73	....	....	....	....	....	....	....	....	....	....	....	....	....	....	....	....	....	....
	Caledon Canadians	OJHL	7	3	7	10	....	....	....	2	....	....	....	....	....	....	....	....	....	....	17	11	12	23	4	....	....	....
1996-97	**Philadelphia Flyers**	**NHL**	**68**	**8**	**13**	**21**	**8**	**12**	**20**	**22**	**1**	**0**	**2**	**71**	**11.3**	**31**	**4**	**24**	**0**	**3**	**19**	**5**	**4**	**9**	**12**	**1**	**0**	**1**
1997-98	**Philadelphia Flyers**	**NHL**	**69**	**8**	**25**	**33**	**9**	**24**	**33**	**42**	**1**	**0**	**5**	**101**	**7.9**	**64**	**10**	**25**	**0**	**29**	**5**	**0**	**1**	**1**	**2**	**0**	**0**	**0**
1998-99	**Philadelphia Flyers**	**NHL**	**63**	**3**	**5**	**8**	**4**	**5**	**9**	**25**	**0**	**1**	**0**	**49**	**6.1**	**14**	**0**	**22**	**3**	**–5**	....	....	....	....	....	....	....	....
	Montreal Canadiens	**NHL**	**17**	**3**	**5**	**8**	**4**	**5**	**9**	**4**	**0**	**0**	**1**	**31**	**9.7**	**9**	**1**	**12**	**1**	**–3**	....	....	....	....	....	....	....	....
99-2000	**Montreal Canadiens**	**NHL**	**73**	**14**	**28**	**42**	**16**	**26**	**42**	**54**	**3**	**0**	**1**	**139**	**10.1**	**59**	**15**	**49**	**4**	**–1**	....	....	....	....	....	....	....	....
	NHL Totals		**290**	**36**	**76**	**112**	**41**	**72**	**113**	**147**	**5**	**1**	**9**	**391**	**9.2**	**177**	**30**	**132**	**8**		**24**	**5**	**5**	**10**	**14**	**1**	**0**	**1**

Traded to **Montreal** by **Philadelphia** with Philadelphia's 2nd round choice (Matt Carkner) in 1999 Entry Draft and NY Islanders' 6th round choice (previously acquired, Montreal selected Scott Selig) in 2000 Entry Draft for Mark Recchi, March 10, 1999.

• ZUKE, Mike

C – R. 6', 180 lbs. b: Sault Ste. Marie, Ont., 4/16/1954. St. Louis' 3rd, 79th overall, in 1974.

Season	Club	League	GP	G	A	Pts	AG	AA	APts	PIM	PP	SH	GW	S	%	TGF	PGF	TGA	PGA	+/–	GP	G	A	Pts	PIM	PP	SH	GW
1971-72	Sault Ste. Marie Greyhounds	NOJHA	48	34	*62	*96	....	....	....	23	....	....	....	....	....	....	....	....	....	....	....	....	....	....	....	....	....	....
1972-73	Michigan Tech Huskies	CCHA	38	23	30	53	....	....	....	20	....	....	....	....	....	....	....	....	....	....	....	....	....	....	....	....	....	....
1973-74	Michigan Tech Huskies	CCHA	40	28	47	75	....	....	....	38	....	....	....	....	....	....	....	....	....	....	....	....	....	....	....	....	....	....
1974-75	Michigan Tech Huskies	WCHA	42	35	43	78	....	....	....	20	....	....	....	....	....	....	....	....	....	....	....	....	....	....	....	....	....	....
1975-76	Michigan Tech Huskies	WCHA	43	47	*57	104	....	....	....	42	....	....	....	....	....	....	....	....	....	....	....	....	....	....	....	....	....	....
1976-77	Mohawk Valley Comets	NAHL	48	42	29	71	....	....	....	33	....	....	....	....	....	....	....	....	....	....	....	....	....	....	....	....	....	....
	Indianapolis Racers	WHA	15	3	4	7	....	....	....	2	....	....	....	....	....	....	....	....	....	....	....	....	....	....	....	....	....	....
1977-78	Edmonton Oilers	WHA	71	23	34	57	....	....	....	47	....	....	....	....	....	....	....	....	....	....	5	2	3	5	0	....	....	....
1978-79	**St. Louis Blues**	**NHL**	**34**	**9**	**17**	**26**	**8**	**12**	**20**	**18**	**3**	**0**	**0**	**80**	**11.3**	**41**	**18**	**39**	**8**	**–8**	....	....	....	....	....	....	....	....
	Salt Lake Golden Eagles	CHL	29	9	13	22	....	....	....	4	....	....	....	....	....	....	....	....	....	....	....	....	....	....	....	....	....	....
1979-80	**St. Louis Blues**	**NHL**	**69**	**22**	**42**	**64**	**19**	**31**	**50**	**30**	**6**	**1**	**1**	**172**	**12.8**	**86**	**37**	**57**	**6**	**–2**	**3**	**0**	**0**	**0**	**2**	**0**	**0**	**0**
1980-81	**St. Louis Blues**	**NHL**	**74**	**24**	**44**	**68**	**19**	**29**	**48**	**57**	**10**	**1**	**1**	**145**	**16.6**	**100**	**46**	**59**	**20**	**15**	**11**	**4**	**5**	**9**	**4**	**3**	**0**	**0**
1981-82	**St. Louis Blues**	**NHL**	**76**	**13**	**40**	**53**	**10**	**27**	**37**	**41**	**1**	**1**	**2**	**159**	**8.2**	**86**	**38**	**91**	**25**	**–18**	**8**	**1**	**1**	**2**	**2**	**0**	**0**	**0**
1982-83	**St. Louis Blues**	**NHL**	**43**	**8**	**16**	**24**	**7**	**11**	**18**	**14**	**0**	**0**	**1**	**58**	**13.8**	**30**	**3**	**35**	**5**	**–3**	**4**	**1**	**0**	**1**	**4**	**0**	**0**	**1**
	Salt Lake Golden Eagles	CHL	13	7	8	15	....	....	....	0	....	....	....	....	....	....	....	....	....	....	....	....	....	....	....	....	....	....
1983-84	**Hartford Whalers**	**NHL**	**75**	**6**	**23**	**29**	**5**	**16**	**21**	**36**	**1**	**0**	**0**	**84**	**7.1**	**43**	**22**	**78**	**39**	**–18**	....	....	....	....	....	....	....	....
1984-85	**Hartford Whalers**	**NHL**	**67**	**4**	**12**	**16**	**3**	**8**	**11**	**12**	**0**	**0**	**1**	**54**	**7.4**	**27**	**0**	**56**	**25**	**–4**	....	....	....	....	....	....	....	....
1985-86	**Hartford Whalers**	**NHL**	**17**	**0**	**2**	**2**	**0**	**1**	**1**	**12**	**0**	**0**	**0**	**2**	**0.0**	**4**	**0**	**15**	**9**	**–2**	....	....	....	....	....	....	....	....
	NHL Totals		**455**	**86**	**196**	**282**	**71**	**135**	**206**	**220**	**21**	**3**	**6**	**754**	**11.4**	**417**	**164**	**430**	**137**		**26**	**6**	**6**	**12**	**12**	**3**	**0**	**1**
	Other Major League Totals		86	26	38	64	....	....	....	49	....	....	....	....	....	....	....	....	....	....	5	2	3	5	0	....	....	....

NOJHA First All-Star Team (1972) • WCHA First All-Star Team (1974, 1976) • NCAA West First All-American Team (1974) • WCHA Second All-Star Team (1975) • NCAA West First All-American Team (1976)

Selected by **Indianapolis** (WHA) in 1974 WHA Amateur Draft, May, 1974. Traded to **Edmonton** (WHA) by **Indianapolis** (WHA) with Blair MacDonald and Dave Inkpen for Barry Wilkins, Rusty Patenaude and Claude St. Sauveur, September, 1977. Signed as a free agent by **St. Louis**, September 29, 1978. Claimed by **Hartford** from **St. Louis** in Waiver Draft, October 3, 1983.

• ZYUZIN, Andrei

D – R. 6'1", 195 lbs. b: Ufa, USSR, 1/21/1978. San Jose's 1st, 2nd overall, in 1996.

Season	Club	League	GP	G	A	Pts	AG	AA	APts	PIM	PP	SH	GW	S	%	TGF	PGF	TGA	PGA	+/–	GP	G	A	Pts	PIM	PP	SH	GW
1994-95	Ufa Salavat	CIS	30	3	0	3	....	....	....	16	....	....	....	....	....	....	....	....	....	....	....	....	....	....	....	....	....	....
1995-96	Ufa Salavat	CIS	41	6	3	9	....	....	....	24	....	....	....	....	....	....	....	....	....	....	....	....	....	....	....	....	....	....
	Russia	WJC-A	7	1	4	5	....	....	....	2	....	....	....	....	....	....	....	....	....	....	....	....	....	....	....	....	....	....
	Russia	EJC-A	5	5	2	7	....	....	....	8	....	....	....	....	....	....	....	....	....	....	....	....	....	....	....	....	....	....
1996-97	Ufa Salavat	Russia	32	7	10	17	....	....	....	28	....	....	....	....	....	....	....	....	....	....	7	1	1	2	4	....	....	....
	Russia	WJC-A	6	1	1	2	....	....	....	6	....	....	....	....	....	....	....	....	....	....	....	....	....	....	....	....	....	....
1997-98	**San Jose Sharks**	**NHL**	**56**	**6**	**7**	**13**	**7**	**7**	**14**	**66**	**2**	**0**	**2**	**72**	**8.3**	**47**	**16**	**25**	**2**	**8**	**6**	**1**	**0**	**1**	**14**	**0**	**0**	**1**
	Kentucky Thoroughblades	AHL	17	4	5	9	....	....	....	28	....	....	....	....	....	....	....	....	....	....	....	....	....	....	....	....	....	....
1998-99	**San Jose Sharks**	**NHL**	**25**	**3**	**1**	**4**	**4**	**1**	**5**	**38**	**2**	**0**	**0**	**44**	**6.8**	**17**	**4**	**9**	**1**	**5**	....	....	....	....	....	....	....	....
	Kentucky Thoroughblades	AHL	23	2	12	14	....	....	....	42	....	....	....	....	....	....	....	....	....	....	....	....	....	....	....	....	....	....
99-2000	**Tampa Bay Lightning**	**NHL**	**34**	**2**	**9**	**11**	**2**	**8**	**10**	**33**	**0**	**0**	**0**	**47**	**4.3**	**31**	**6**	**41**	**5**	**–11**	....	....	....	....	....	....	....	....
	NHL Totals		**115**	**11**	**17**	**28**	**13**	**16**	**29**	**137**	**4**	**0**	**2**	**163**	**6.7**	**95**	**26**	**75**	**8**		**6**	**1**	**0**	**1**	**14**	**0**	**0**	**1**

EJC-A All-Star Team (1996) • Named Best Defenseman at EJC-A (1996)

• Suspended for remainder of 1998-99 season by **San Jose** for being leaving team without permission, April 1, 1999. Traded to **Tampa Bay** by **San Jose** with Bill Houlder, Shawn Burr and Steve Guolla for Niklas Sundstrom and NY Rangers' 3rd round choice (previously acquired, later traded to Chicago - Chicago selected Igor Radulov) in 2000 Entry Draft, August 4, 1999. • Missed remainder of 1999-2000 season recovering from shoulder injury suffered in game vs. NY Islanders, January 13, 2000.

CHAPTER 79

Using the Goaltender Register

Ralph Dinger

THE GOALTENDER REGISTER begins on page 1783. It contains the complete statistical history of every goaltender who has played in the National Hockey League.

Here are notes on various statistical categories:

Biographical – This field contains the goaltender's name, and given names (if these names are different than the name by which he is commonly known. For example, Gump Worsley's given names are Lorne John, while the given names of Al Rollins were Elwin Ira), nicknames, position (**G** – goaltender) and catching glove side (**R** – right, **L** – left). Additional items in a goaltender's biographical data are identical to those used for players. *See page 646.*

Season – From 1917–18 to the present day, the hockey season started in the fall and ended the following spring and is represented in the Goaltender Register as, for example, 1997–98. For players who retired or did not play for three or more seasons but later returned to the game, those years are represented as two four-digit dates, for example, 1964–1967.

Club – *See page 646.*

League – *See page 646.* A full list of the leagues found in *Total Hockey* and their abbreviations can be found on pages 1973 and 1974.

GP – Games Played – *See page 646.*

W – Wins – The goaltender in net when his team scores the game-winning goal is credited with the win. If a goaltender (Jones) enters a game with his team leading 4–0 and his team eventually wins the game 5–4, Jones receives credit for the victory. One win has been deducted from Terry Sawchuk's win total in 1962–63. In a game played December 9, 1962 at Detroit, the Red Wings defeated Toronto 4–3. The starting goaltender for Detroit in that game was Dennis Riggin. Following an injury to Riggin at the 12:51 mark of the second period, Sawchuk came in to finish the game. The score at the time of the change was 4–3 and, though Sawchuk shutout the Maple Leafs the rest of the way, the win has now been credited to Riggin who was in net when Detroit scored the winning goal. Previously, Sawchuk had been credited with a win for this game.

L – Losses – The goaltender who allows the game-winning goal is charged with the loss. If a goaltender enters a game with his team losing 4–0 and his team eventually loses the game 5–4, that goaltender is still charged with the loss. A goaltender removed for an extra attacker in a tie game is charged with the loss if his team surrenders an empty-net game-winning goal. For example, on April 1, 1989, the Toronto Maple Leafs needed a win over the St. Louis Blues to stay in contention for a playoff spot. With the game tied 3–3 in overtime, the Leafs pulled goaltender Allan Bester for an extra attacker. The Blues scored the winning goal into the empty net, but Bester was still charged with the loss. Until 1941–42, goaltenders were required to serve their own penalties. If the goalie's replacement allowed the winning goal, the penalized goaltender was still charged with the loss.

T – Ties – The goaltender in net when a tying goal is scored is credited with a tie. If a goaltender enters a game with his team winning 4–0 and the game ends 4–4, that goaltender is still credited with a tie. The NHL has not had a playoff game end in a tie since March 23, 1935, when the Black Hawks and Maroons played to a 0–0 tie in the first game of a two-game, total-goals series. Since 1935, two playoff games were suspended with tie scores: Game two of the 1951 semifinals between Toronto and Boston was suspended at 11:45 p.m. with the score tied 1–1 due to Toronto's Sunday curfew laws. A game in the 1988 Stanley Cup finals was suspended with the score tied 3–3 when a power failure at the old Boston Garden stopped play late in the second period. These games would have been replayed if a seventh game was required to determine a series winner. Individual statistics recorded in these suspended games (including minutes played for goaltenders) are accepted as official.

Mins – Minutes played – Playing time for each goaltender, rounded off to the nearest minute. Goaltenders must play at least 30 seconds of each minute to receive credit for playing the full minute. For instance, a goaltender who leaves the game at the 4:29 mark of the second period is credited with playing 24 minutes of that game. His replacement would be credited with playing 36 minutes if he finished the game. Those goalies who play less than 30 seconds in an entire game are credited with one minute of playing time. The goaltender (or goaltenders) who played the rest of the game is still credited with playing the full 60 minutes. A note of explanation is included to explain this discrepancy. Although goaltenders have been removed from the net for an extra attacker since the 1930s, that time was not removed from a goaltender's minutes played until the 1980s. Note: Terry Sawchuk and Jacques Plante have had their minutes reduced by 40 in 1954–55 because a game between the two clubs was forfeited to the Red Wings after the first period. (See page 157.)

GA – goals against – Goals scored against the goaltender. Prior to 1963–64, empty-net goals were charged against the goaltender who had been removed. Since 1963–64, goals scored into an empty net are counted against the team, but not against the goaltender who had been removed. Due to new research, goals scored into an empty net between 1955–56 and 1962–63 have now been subtracted from goaltender totals.

SO – Shutouts – Games played without allowing a goal. To register a shutout, the goaltender must play the entire game without allowing a goal. If two or more goaltenders play in a game in which their team does not allow a goal, they are considered to have shared the shutout, but no credit is given in the two goalies' statistical data panels.

Avg – Goals-against average — Goals allowed per 60 minutes of play. The goals-against average (**Avg**) is calculated by dividing goals against (**GA**) by minutes played (**Mins**) and multiplying the results by 60. Note that some modern minor leagues and college conferences calculate goaltender Mins down to the second. These fractional totals are reflected in their goaltender averages. In addition, some U.S. high school leagues play 40 or 45-minute games. The USAHA (1918 to 1926) also played 45-minute games. Goaltender averages for these leagues reflect these shorter game lengths.

AAvg – Adjusted average – A statistic similar to *Total Hockey*'s Adjusted Goals, Adjusted Assists and Adjusted Points. (*See page 613*). Adjusted Average (**AAvg**) factors the league-wide goals-against average for the season in question against 3.06, the average of the NHL's goals-against average each season since 1917–18. This factor is multiplied by an individual goaltender's Avg. to determine his Adjusted Average. For example, let us consider goaltenders Smith and Jones with identical averages of 3.00. Smith played in 1952–53 when the league-wide average was a stingy 2.40 goals-against. Dividing the all-time NHL average of 3.06 by the 1952–53 mark of 2.40, yields a factor of 1.28. Smith's 3.00, multiplied by the factor of 1.28, adjusts to 3.84. Jones played in the 1981–82 season when the league-wide average had grown to 4.01. Dividing the all-time average of 3.06 by the 1981–82 mark of 4.01, yields a factor of 0.76. Smith's 3.00 adjusts to 2.28. (In this example, all figures have been rounded off to two decimal places.)

To further remove bias from our formula, we harness the power of the computer to remove each goaltender's individual goals against (**GA**) from the calculation of the league-wide **Avg** in the season being adjusted.

Eff – Goaltender's Efficiency – Combines shots against (**SA**) with Avg, rewarding goaltenders who face a higher number of shots. To calculate **Eff**: (**Avg** x **GA**) divided by (**SA** divided by 10). Like conventional Avg, a lower **Eff** is better.

SA – Shots against – The number of shots-on-goal faced by each goaltender. Although shots-on-goal have been tabulated for many years, shots faced by goaltenders has only been an official statistic since 1982–83.

S% – Save percentage – Percentage of saves per 100 shots. The Save percentage (**S%**) is calculated by subtracting goals against (**GA**) from shots against (SA) and dividing that total by shots against (SA). Calculated since 1982–83.

SAPG – Shots against per game – The average shots faced per 60 minutes of play. The shots against per game (**SAPG**) average is calculated by dividing 60 by minutes played (**Mins**) and multiplying by shots against (**SA**). For example, a goaltender facing 177 shots in 305 minutes of playing time faces an average of 34.8 shots-per-game.

NHL Totals – Total of all primary NHL statistics found in the data panel.

Other Major League Totals – This field includes the total of all the other major leagues an NHL goaltender performed in from 1893 to date. *(See page 611.)* To be categorized as major a league must fall into one of the following three categories: it must have been professional, challenged for the Stanley Cup and/or competed with other major leagues to sign the top hockey talent of the day.

Award and All-Star Notes – *See page 646.*

Trade Notes – This field contains details on NHL trades, drafts (Waiver, Reverse, Intra-League, Inter-League, Expansion and Dispersal) and free agent signings. WHA trade notes, draft information and free agent signings are included for every goaltender who played in both the WHA and the NHL. Trade notes and free agent signings for every goaltender who played in the NHL and the PCHA, WCHL and the WHL from 1917–18 to 1925–26 have also been included. Trades between minor league teams are also included if available.

Special notes concerning injuries and other oddities and curiosities are indicated by a bullet (•). An asterisk (*) is used to indicate league- or tournament-leading statistics.

CHAPTER 80

Goaltender Register

Career Records for All NHL Goaltenders

• ABBOTT, George George Henry "Preacher" G – L. 5'7", 153 lbs. b: Sydenham, Ont., 8/3/1911.

			REGULAR SEASON													PLAYOFFS											
Season	**Club**	**League**	**GP**	**W**	**L**	**T**	**Mins**	**GA**	**SO**	**Avg**	**AAvg**	**Eff**	**SA**	**S%**	**SAPG**	**GP**	**W**	**L**	**T**	**Mins**	**GA**	**SO**	**Avg**	**Eff**	**SA**	**S%**	**SAPG**
1943-44	**Boston Bruins**	**NHL**	**1**	**0**	**1**	**0**	**60**	**7**	**0**	**7.00**	**5.24**	....	....	....	....	....	....	....	....	....	....	....	....	....	....	....	....
	NHL Totals		**1**	**0**	**1**	**0**	**60**	**7**	**0**	**7.00**	....	....	....	....	....	....	....	....	....	....	....	....	....	....	....	....	....

• **Toronto's** practice goaltender loaned to **Boston** to replace injured Bert Gardiner, November 27, 1943. (Toronto 7, Boston 4)

• ADAMS, John John Matthew G – L. 6', 200 lbs. b: Port Arthur, Ont., 7/27/1946.

Season	Club	League	GP	W	L	T	Mins	GA	SO	Avg	AAvg	Eff	SA	S%	SAPG	GP	W	L	T	Mins	GA	SO	Avg	Eff	SA	S%	SAPG
1963-64	Port Arthur North Stars	TBJHL	STATISTICS NOT AVAILABLE																								
	Port Arthur North Stars	Mem-Cup	6	3	3	0	360	25	0	4.17	....	....	....	....	....	....	....	....	....	....	....	....	....	....	....	....	....
1964-65	Port Arthur North Stars	TBJHL	22	13	8	1	1320	88	0	4.00	....	....	....	....	....	....	....	....	....	....	....	....	....	....	....	....	....
	Port Arthur North Stars	Mem-Cup	5	1	3	0	250	25	0	6.00	....	....	....	....	....	....	....	....	....	....	....	....	....	....	....	....	....
1965-66	Port Arthur North Stars	TBJHL	26	18	6	2	1530	93	0	3.65	....	....	....	....	....	....	....	....	....	....	....	....	....	....	....	....	....
	Fort William Canadians	Mem-Cup	11	6	4	0	630	33	0	3.14	....	....	....	....	....	....	....	....	....	....	....	....	....	....	....	....	....
1966-67	Port Arthur Marrs	TBJHL	30	20	8	2	1800	114	*3	3.80	....	....	....	....	....	5	4	1	0	320	17	0	*3.19	....	....	....	....
	Port Arthur Marrs	Mem-Cup	19	11	8	0	1160	71	1	3.67	....	....	....	....	....	....	....	....	....	....	....	....	....	....	....	....	....
1967-68	Dayton Gems	IHL	45	....	....	....	2570	148	2	3.46	....	....	....	....	....	4	....	....	....	240	21	0	5.25	....	....	....	....
1968-69	Dayton Gems	IHL	32	....	....	....	1900	91	2	2.87	....	....	....	....	....	6	....	....	....	365	15	1	*2.47	....	....	....	....
1969-70	Oklahoma City Blazers	CHL	51	18	26	7	3027	176	*5	3.49	....	....	....	....	....	....	....	....	....	....	....	....	....	....	....	....	....
1970-71	Oklahoma City Blazers	CHL	*57	25	22	10	3417	195	3	3.42	....	....	....	....	....	5	1	4	0	280	21	0	4.50	....	....	....	....
1971-72	Oklahoma City Blazers	CHL	43	15	15	3	2168	129	2	3.57	....	....	....	....	....	....	....	....	....	....	....	....	....	....	....	....	....
1972-73	**Boston Bruins**	**NHL**	**14**	**9**	**3**	**1**	**780**	**39**	**1**	**3.00**	**2.83**	....	....	....	....	....	....	....	....	....	....	....	....	....	....	....	....
	Boston Braves	AHL	23	....	....	....	1179	65	1	3.31	....	....	....	....	....	8	4	4	0	420	34	0	4.86	....	....	....	....
1973-74	San Diego Gulls	WHL	*69	*38	26	4	*4094	223	1	3.27	....	....	....	....	....	4	0	4	0	261	19	0	4.37	....	....	....	....
1974-75	**Washington Capitals**	**NHL**	**8**	**0**	**7**	**0**	**400**	**46**	**0**	**6.90**	**6.26**	....	....	....	....	....	....	....	....	....	....	....	....	....	....	....	....
	Richmond Robins	AHL	28	7	13	3	1424	105	1	4.42	....	....	....	....	....	....	....	....	....	....	....	....	....	....	....	....	....
1975-76	Thunder Bay Twins	OHA-Sr.	12	....	....	....	720	33	*3	2.75	....	....	....	....	....	....	....	....	....	....	....	....	....	....	....	....	....
1976-77	Thunder Bay Twins	TBSHL	STATISTICS NOT AVAILABLE																								
1977-78	Thunder Bay Twins	TBSHL	STATISTICS NOT AVAILABLE																								
1978-79	Thunder Bay Twins	CIHL	19	....	....	....	1181	66	0	3.35	....	....	....	....	....	....	....	....	....	....	....	....	....	....	....	....	....
1979-80	Thunder Bay Twins	CASH	STATISTICS NOT AVAILABLE																								
	NHL Totals		**22**	**9**	**10**	**1**	**1180**	**85**	**1**	**4.32**	....	....	....	....	....	....	....	....	....	....	....	....	....	....	....	....	....

Shared James Norris Memorial Trophy (fewest goals against - IHL) with Pat Rupp (1969) • CHL First All-Star Team (1972) • WHL Second All-Star Team (1974) • OHA-Sr. Second All-Star Team (1976)

Traded to **San Diego** (WHL) by **Boston** to complete transaction that sent Ken Broderick to Boston (March 10, 1973), June 12, 1973. Traded to **Washington** by **San Diego** (WHL) for cash, July 11, 1974.

• AIKEN, Don Donald John Judson G – L. 5'11", 165 lbs. b: Arlington, MA, 1/1/1932.

Season	Club	League	GP	W	L	T	Mins	GA	SO	Avg	AAvg	Eff	SA	S%	SAPG	GP	W	L	T	Mins	GA	SO	Avg	Eff	SA	S%	SAPG
1949-50	Arlington High	Hi-School	STATISTICS NOT AVAILABLE																								
1950-51	Boston Calculators	MBAHL	STATISTICS NOT AVAILABLE																								
1951-52	Boston Calculators	MBAHL	STATISTICS NOT AVAILABLE																								
1952-53	USA Military Academy	NCAA	STATISTICS NOT AVAILABLE																								
1953-54	Boston University	ECAC	DID NOT PLAY – TRANSFERRED COLLEGES																								
1954-55	Boston University	ECAC	23	4	19	0	1380	163	0	7.09	....	....	....	....	....	....	....	....	....	....	....	....	....	....	....	....	....
1955-56	Boston Calculators	MBAHL	STATISTICS NOT AVAILABLE																								
1956-57	Boston Calculators	MBAHL	STATISTICS NOT AVAILABLE																								
1957-58	**Montreal Canadiens**	**NHL**	**1**	**0**	**1**	**0**	**34**	**6**	**0**	**10.59**	**11.66**	....	....	....	....	....	....	....	....	....	....	....	....	....	....	....	....
	NHL Totals		**1**	**0**	**1**	**0**	**34**	**6**	**0**	**10.59**	....	....	....	....	....	....	....	....	....	....	....	....	....	....	....	....	....

• **Boston's** practice goaltender loaned to **Montreal** to replace injured Jacques Plante in 2nd period, March 13, 1958. (Boston 7, Montreal 3) • At the time of his appearance with Montreal, he was employed as a mathematician with the U.S. Air Force. • Served as Boston's practice goaltender for 13 seasons.

• AITKENHEAD, Andy G – L. 5'9", 145 lbs. b: Glasgow, Scotland, 3/6/1904 d: 1968.

Season	Club	League	GP	W	L	T	Mins	GA	SO	Avg	AAvg	Eff	SA	S%	SAPG	GP	W	L	T	Mins	GA	SO	Avg	Eff	SA	S%	SAPG
1921-22	Yorkton Terriers	N-SSHL	6	3	3	0	480	19	0	2.38	....	....	....	....	....	....	....	....	....	....	....	....	....	....	....	....	....
1922-23	Saskatoon St. George	N-SJHL	STATISTICS NOT AVAILABLE																								
	Saskatoon Quakers	Mem-Cup	2	1	0	1	120	3	0	1.50	....	....	....	....	....	....	....	....	....	....	....	....	....	....	....	....	....
1923-24	Saskatoon Nationals	SCSHL	5	*4	0	1	350	5	*1	*0.86	....	....	....	....	....	2	1	1	0	120	5	0	*2.50	....	....	....	....
	Saskatoon Nationals	Al-Cup	2	1	1	0	120	7	0	3.50	....	....	....	....	....	....	....	....	....	....	....	....	....	....	....	....	....
1924-25	Yorkton Terriers	SIHA	STATISTICS NOT AVAILABLE																								
1925-26	Saskatoon Empires	N-SSHL	4	*4	0	0	240	12	*1	*3.00	....	....	....	....	....	....	....	....	....	....	....	....	....	....	....	....	....
	Saskatoon Empires	Al-Cup	2	0	1	1	140	9	0	3.86	....	....	....	....	....	....	....	....	....	....	....	....	....	....	....	....	....
1926-27	Saskatoon Sheiks	PrHL	32	14	15	3	1902	94	*7	2.97	....	....	....	....	....	4	1	3	0	240	7	0	1.75	....	....	....	....
1927-28	Saskatoon Sheiks	PrHL	28	*18	5	5	1733	41	*7	*1.42	....	....	....	....	....	....	....	....	....	....	....	....	....	....	....	....	....
1928-29	Springfield Indians	Can-Am	40	13	14	13	2550	58	6	1.36	....	....	....	....	....	....	....	....	....	....	....	....	....	....	....	....	....
1929-30	Portland Buckaroos	PCHL	36	*20	10	6	2160	34	*16	*0.94	....	....	....	....	....	4	1	3	0	240	8	0	2.00	....	....	....	....
1930-31	Portland Buckaroos	PCHL	35	12	15	8	2100	61	6	1.74	....	....	....	....	....	....	....	....	....	....	....	....	....	....	....	....	....
1931-32	Bronx Tigers	Can-Am	33	16	13	4	2040	74	4	2.18	....	....	....	....	....	4	0	1	1	130	5	0	2.31	....	....	....	....
1932-33♦	**New York Rangers**	**NHL**	***48**	**23**	**17**	**8**	**2970**	**107**	**3**	**2.16**	**2.87**	....	....	....	....	**8**	***6**	**1**	**1**	**488**	**13**	***2**	**1.60**	....	....	....	....
1933-34	**New York Rangers**	**NHL**	***48**	**21**	**19**	**8**	**2990**	**113**	**7**	**2.27**	**2.85**	....	....	....	....	**2**	**0**	**1**	**1**	**120**	**2**	**1**	**1.00**	....	....	....	....
1934-35	**New York Rangers**	**NHL**	**10**	**3**	**7**	**0**	**610**	**37**	**1**	**3.64**	**4.46**	....	....	....	....	....	....	....	....	....	....	....	....	....	....	....	....
	Philadelphia Arrows	Can-Am	1	1	0	0	60	2	0	2.00	....	....	....	....	....	....	....	....	....	....	....	....	....	....	....	....	....
	Portland Buckaroos	NWHL	21	11	4	6	1260	40	5	*1.90	....	....	....	....	....	3	1	2	0	180	4	1	*1.33	....	....	....	....
1935-36	Portland Buckaroos	NWHL	40	18	14	8	2520	68	5	*1.62	....	....	....	....	....	3	1	2	0	190	5	0	*1.58	....	....	....	....
1936-37	Portland Buckaroos	PCHL	40	22	13	5	2400	72	*7	*1.80	....	....	....	....	....	3	3	0	0	180	3	0	*1.00	....	....	....	....
	Spokane Clippers	PCHL	1	1	0	0	60	0	1	0.00	....	....	....	....	....	....	....	....	....	....	....	....	....	....	....	....	....
1937-38	Portland Buckaroos	PCHL	42	16	18	8	2620	85	5	*1.95	....	....	....	....	....	2	1	1	0	120	4	0	2.00	....	....	....	....
1938-39	Portland Buckaroos	PCHL	48	*31	9	8	2880	114	*9	*2.38	....	....	....	....	....	5	*4	1	0	300	10	*1	*2.00	....	....	....	....
	Seattle Seahawks	PCHL	1	....	....	....	60	3	0	3.00	....	....	....	....	....	....	....	....	....	....	....	....	....	....	....	....	....
1939-40	Portland Buckaroos	PCHL	40	17	18	5	2400	98	4	*2.45	....	....	....	....	....	5	1	4	0	300	17	0	3.40	....	....	....	....
1940-41	Portland Buckaroos	PCHL	1	1	0	0	60	2	0	2.00	....	....	....	....	....	....	....	....	....	....	....	....	....	....	....	....	....
	NHL Totals		**106**	**47**	**43**	**16**	**6570**	**257**	**11**	**2.35**	....	....	....	....	....	**10**	**6**	**2**	**2**	**608**	**15**	**3**	**1.48**	....	....	....	....

Signed as a free agent by **Saskatoon** (PrHL), November 10, 1926. Claimed by **NY Rangers** from **Saskatoon** (PrHL) in Inter-League Draft, May 12, 1928. Traded to **Portland** (PCHL) by **NY Rangers** for cash, October, 1929. Traded to **NY Rangers** by **Portland** (PCHL) for cash, April 19, 1931. Loaned to **Portland** (NWHL) by **NY Rangers** for cash, December 30, 1934.

Season	Club	League	GP	W	L	T	Mins	GA	SO	Avg	AAvg	Eff	SA	S%	SAPG	GP	W	L	T	Mins	GA	SO	Avg	Eff	SA	S%	SAPG
			REGULAR SEASON													PLAYOFFS											

• ALMAS, Red Ralph Clayton G – R. 5'9", 160 lbs. b: Saskatoon, Sask., 4/26/1924.

Season	Club	League	GP	W	L	T	Mins	GA	SO	Avg	AAvg	Eff	SA	S%	SAPG	GP	W	L	T	Mins	GA	SO	Avg	Eff	SA	S%	SAPG
1941-42	Saskatoon Quakers	N-SJHL	8	6	2	0	490	22	0	*2.69	....	....	....	....	....	6	*4	1	1	360	22	0	*3.67	....	....	....	....
	Saskatoon Quakers	Mem-Cup	3	0	2	1	190	12	0	3.79	....	....	....	....	....	....	....	....	....	....	....	....	....	....	....	....	....
1942-43	Windsor Chrysler	MOHL	2	....	....	....	120	8	0	4.00	....	....	....	....	....	....	....	....	....	....	....	....	....	....	....	....	....
1943-44	Saskatoon Navy	N-SSHL	17	*16	1	0	1030	71	0	4.14	....	....	....	....	....	4	1	3	0	240	21	0	5.25	....	....	....	....
1944-45	Cornwallis Navy	X-Games	STATISTICS NOT AVAILABLE																								
1945-46	Saskatoon Elks	WCSHL	35	14	19	2	2160	147	1	4.08	....	....	....	....	....	3	0	3	0	180	14	0	4.67	....	....	....	....
1946-47	**Detroit Red Wings**	**NHL**	**1**	**0**	**1**	**0**	**60**	**5**	**0**	**5.00**	**4.83**	....	....	....	....	**5**	**1**	**3**	....	**263**	**13**	**0**	**2.97**	....	....	....	....
	Indianapolis Capitols	AHL	64	33	18	13	3840	215	3	3.36	....	....	....	....	....	....	....	....	....	....	....	....	....	....	....	....	....
1947-48	Indianapolis Capitols	AHL	65	31	28	6	3890	246	0	3.79	....	....	....	....	....	....	....	....	....	....	....	....	....	....	....	....	....
1948-49	St. Louis Flyers	AHL	66	39	18	9	3920	189	5	2.89	....	....	....	....	....	7	3	4	0	465	22	0	2.84	....	....	....	....
1949-50	St. Louis Flyers	AHL	55	29	21	5	3300	182	4	3.31	....	....	....	....	....	2	0	2	0	120	10	0	5.00	....	....	....	....
1950-51	**Chicago Black Hawks**	**NHL**	**1**	**0**	**1**	**0**	**60**	**5**	**0**	**5.00**	**5.63**	....	....	....	....	....	....	....	....	....	....	....	....	....	....	....	....
	St. Louis Flyers	AHL	70	32	34	4	4280	251	3	3.52	....	....	....	....	....	....	....	....	....	....	....	....	....	....	....	....	....
1951-52	St. Louis Flyers	AHL	68	28	39	1	4100	262	2	3.83	....	....	....	....	....	....	....	....	....	....	....	....	....	....	....	....	....
1952-53	**Detroit Red Wings**	**NHL**	**1**	**0**	**0**	**1**	**60**	**3**	**0**	**3.00**	**3.82**	....	....	....	....	....	....	....	....	....	....	....	....	....	....	....	....
	St. Louis Flyers	AHL	53	23	29	1	3200	200	1	3.75	....	....	....	....	....	....	....	....	....	....	....	....	....	....	....	....	....
1953-54	Buffalo Bisons	AHL	9	4	5	0	540	45	0	5.00	....	....	....	....	....	....	....	....	....	....	....	....	....	....	....	....	....
	Victoria Cougars	WHL	56	20	26	10	3360	174	2	3.10	....	....	....	....	....	....	....	....	....	....	....	....	....	....	....	....	....
1954-55	Calgary Stampeders	WHL	2	1	0	1	120	9	0	4.50	....	....	....	....	....	....	....	....	....	....	....	....	....	....	....	....	....
	NHL Totals		**3**	**0**	**2**	**1**	**180**	**13**	**0**	**4.33**	....	....	....	....	....	**5**	**1**	**3**	....	**263**	**13**	**0**	**2.97**	....	....	....	....

AHL Second All-Star Team (1949)

Traded to **Chicago** (St. Louis-AHL) by **Detroit** with Barry Sullivan, Lloyd Doran, Tony Licari and Thain Simon for Hec Highton and Joe Lund, September 9, 1948. Traded to **Detroit** by **Chicago** with Guyle Fielder and Steve Hrymnak for cash, September 23, 1952.

• ANDERSON, Lorne Lorne Robert G – R. 5'11", 166 lbs. b: Renfrew, Ont., 7/26/1931 d: 3/20/1984.

Season	Club	League	GP	W	L	T	Mins	GA	SO	Avg	AAvg	Eff	SA	S%	SAPG	GP	W	L	T	Mins	GA	SO	Avg	Eff	SA	S%	SAPG
1947-48	Renfrew Lions	NOJHA	STATISTICS NOT AVAILABLE																								
	Atlantic City Sea Gulls	EAHL	2	....	....	....	120	15	0	7.50	....	....	....	....	....	....	....	....	....	....	....	....	....	....	....	....	....
1948-49	Renfrew Lions	NOJHA	10	8	2	0	610	38	1	3.74	....	....	....	....	....	19	15	4	0	1160	72	1	3.72	....	....	....	....
1949-50	Renfrew Lions	NOJHA	12	....	....	....	720	46	0	3.83	....	....	....	....	....	6	....	....	....	360	23	0	3.83	....	....	....	....
	Pembroke Lumber Kings	LSLHL	....	....	....	....	....	....	....	....	....	....	....	....	....	2	1	1	0	120	11	0	5.50	....	....	....	....
1950-51	Atlantic City Sea Gulls	EAHL	52	....	....	....	3120	213	0	4.10	....	....	....	....	....	....	....	....	....	....	....	....	....	....	....	....	....
1951-52	New York Rovers	EAHL	61	25	34	2	3685	231	1	3.76	....	....	....	....	....	....	....	....	....	....	....	....	....	....	....	....	....
	Boston Olympics	EAHL	2	0	2	0	120	6	0	3.00	....	....	....	....	....	....	....	....	....	....	....	....	....	....	....	....	....
	New York Rangers	**NHL**	**3**	**1**	**2**	**0**	**180**	**18**	**0**	**6.00**	**7.11**	....	....	....	....	....	....	....	....	....	....	....	....	....	....	....	....
	New Haven Ramblers	EAHL	....	....	....	....	....	....	....	....	....	....	....	....	....	2	....	....	....	120	7	0	3.50	....	....	....	....
1952-53	Sudbury Wolves	NOHA	48	31	15	2	2880	165	0	*3.44	....	....	....	....	....	7	3	4	0	430	28	0	3.91	....	....	....	....
	Sudbury Wolves	Al-Cup	2	0	2	0	94	8	0	5.11	....	....	....	....	....	....	....	....	....	....	....	....	....	....	....	....	....
1953-54	Sudbury Wolves	NOHA	31	....	....	....	1860	92	1	*2.97	....	....	....	....	....	7	3	4	0	420	19	*1	2.71	....	....	....	....
1954-55	Sudbury Wolves	NOHA	57	....	....	....	3420	215	2	3.77	....	....	....	....	....	....	....	....	....	....	....	....	....	....	....	....	....
1955-56	North Bay Trappers	NOHA	52	....	....	....	3120	169	3	3.25	....	....	....	....	....	7	....	....	....	420	25	0	3.57	....	....	....	....
1956-57	Pembroke Lumber Kings	EOHL	32	....	....	....	1920	140	1	4.38	....	....	....	....	....	....	....	....	....	....	....	....	....	....	....	....	....
1957-58	Renfrew Royals	UOVHL	STATISTICS NOT AVAILABLE																								
1958-59	Renfrew Royals	UOVHL	17	4	13	0	1020	112	0	6.59	....	....	....	....	....	....	....	....	....	....	....	....	....	....	....	....	....
	Pembroke Lumber Kings	UOVHL	....	....	....	....	....	....	....	....	....	....	....	....	....	9	6	3	0	540	36	0	4.00	....	....	....	....
1959-60	Pembroke Lumber Kings	UOVHL	9	7	2	0	540	24	2	2.67	....	....	....	....	....	6	2	4	0	360	25	0	4.17	....	....	....	....
1960-61	Pembroke Lumber Kings	UOVHL	28	8	15	5	1680	145	0	5.18	....	....	....	....	....	7	3	4	0	440	39	0	5.32	....	....	....	....
	NHL Totals		**3**	**1**	**2**	**0**	**180**	**18**	**0**	**6.00**	....	....	....	....	....	....	....	....	....	....	....	....	....	....	....	....	....

• ASKEY, Tom G – L. 6'2", 185 lbs. b: Kenmore, NY, 10/4/1974. Anaheim's 8th, 186th overall in 1993.

Season	Club	League	GP	W	L	T	Mins	GA	SO	Avg	AAvg	Eff	SA	S%	SAPG	GP	W	L	T	Mins	GA	SO	Avg	Eff	SA	S%	SAPG
1991-92	Wheatfield Blades	EmJHL	STATISTICS NOT AVAILABLE																								
1992-93	Ohio State University	CCHA	25	2	19	0	1235	125	0	6.07	....	....	....	....	....	....	....	....	....	....	....	....	....	....	....	....	....
1993-94	Ohio State University	CCHA	27	3	19	4	1488	103	0	4.15	....	....	....	....	....	....	....	....	....	....	....	....	....	....	....	....	....
1994-95	Ohio State University	CCHA	26	4	19	2	1387	121	0	5.23	....	....	....	....	....	....	....	....	....	....	....	....	....	....	....	....	....
1995-96	Ohio State University	CCHA	26	8	11	4	1340	68	0	3.05	....	....	....	....	....	....	....	....	....	....	....	....	....	....	....	....	....
1996-97	Baltimore Bandits	AHL	40	17	18	2	2238	140	1	3.75	....	....	....	....	....	3	0	3	....	137	11	0	4.79	....	....	....	....
	United States	WC-A	1	1	0	0	60	4	0	4.00	....	....	....	....	....	....	....	....	....	....	....	....	....	....	....	....	....
1997-98	**Mighty Ducks of Anaheim**	**NHL**	**7**	**0**	**1**	**2**	**273**	**12**	**0**	**2.64**	**3.15**	**2.80**	**113**	**.894**	**24.8**	....	....	....	....	....	....	....	....	....	....	....	....
	Cincinnati Mighty Ducks	AHL	32	10	16	4	1753	104	3	3.56	....	....	....	....	....	....	....	....	....	....	....	....	....	....	....	....	....
1998-99	Cincinnati Mighty Ducks	AHL	53	21	22	3	2893	131	3	2.72	....	....	....	....	....	3	0	3	....	178	13	0	4.38	....	....	....	....
	Mighty Ducks of Anaheim	**NHL**	....	....	....	....	....	....	....	....	....	....	....	....	....	**1**	**0**	**1**	....	**30**	**2**	**0**	**4.00**	**7.27**	**11**	**.818**	**22.0**
99-2000	Kansas City Blades	IHL	13	3	5	3	658	43	0	3.92	....	....	....	....	....	....	....	....	....	....	....	....	....	....	....	....	....
	Houston Aeros	IHL	13	4	7	1	727	33	0	2.72	....	....	....	....	....	....	....	....	....	....	....	....	....	....	....	....	....
	NHL Totals		**7**	**0**	**1**	**2**	**273**	**12**	**0**	**2.64**	....	....	**113**	**.894**	**24.8**	**1**	**0**	**1**	....	**30**	**2**	**0**	**4.00**	....	**11**	**.818**	**22.0**

CCHA Second All-Star Team (1996)

• ASTROM, Hardy G – L. 6', 170 lbs. b: Skelleftea, Sweden, 3/29/1951.

Season	Club	League	GP	W	L	T	Mins	GA	SO	Avg	AAvg	Eff	SA	S%	SAPG	GP	W	L	T	Mins	GA	SO	Avg	Eff	SA	S%	SAPG
1968-1974	IFK Lulea	Sweden-2	STATISTICS NOT AVAILABLE																								
1974-75	Skelleftea AIK	Sweden	30	....	....	....	1800	96	0	3.20	....	....	....	....	....	5	....	....	....	307	19	....	3.71	....	....	....	....
1975-76	Skelleftea AIK	Sweden	36	....	....	....	2160	149	1	4.14	....	....	....	....	....	....	....	....	....	....	....	....	....	....	....	....	....
1976-77	Sweden	Can-Cup	4	1	2	1	240	17	....	4.00	....	....	....	....	....	....	....	....	....	....	....	....	....	....	....	....	....
	Skelleftea AIK	Sweden	35	....	....	....	2092	142	0	4.07	....	....	....	....	....	....	....	....	....	....	....	....	....	....	....	....	....
	Sweden	WEC-A	4	1	2	0	188	10	1	3.19	....	....	....	....	....	....	....	....	....	....	....	....	....	....	....	....	....
1977-78	**New York Rangers**	**NHL**	**4**	**2**	**2**	**0**	**240**	**14**	**0**	**3.50**	**3.28**	....	....	....	....	....	....	....	....	....	....	....	....	....	....	....	....
	New Haven Nighthawks	AHL	27	17	5	3	1572	69	*5	*2.63	....	....	....	....	....	....	....	....	....	....	....	....	....	....	....	....	....
	Sweden	WEC-A	4	....	....	....	208	15	....	4.33	....	....	....	....	....	....	....	....	....	....	....	....	....	....	....	....	....
1978-79	Skelleftea AIK	Sweden	26	....	....	....	1515	101	0	4.00	....	....	....	....	....	....	....	....	....	....	....	....	....	....	....	....	....
1979-80	**Colorado Rockies**	**NHL**	**49**	**9**	**27**	**6**	**2574**	**161**	**0**	**3.75**	**3.32**	....	....	....	....	....	....	....	....	....	....	....	....	....	....	....	....
1980-81	**Colorado Rockies**	**NHL**	**30**	**6**	**15**	**6**	**1642**	**103**	**0**	**3.76**	**3.04**	....	....	....	....	....	....	....	....	....	....	....	....	....	....	....	....
	Fort Worth Texans	CHL	7	1	5	0	345	21	0	3.65	....	....	....	....	....	1	0	0	0	20	3	0	9.00	....	....	....	....
1981-82	Oklahoma City Stars	CHL	35	12	18	1	1911	154	0	4.84	....	....	....	....	....	2	0	1	0	61	8	0	7.87	....	....	....	....
1982-83	MoDo AIK	Sweden-2	STATISTICS NOT AVAILABLE																								
1983-84	MoDo AIK	Sweden	36	....	....	....	1083	39	....	2.16	....	....	....	....	....	....	....	....	....	....	....	....	....	....	....	....	....
1984-85	Sodertalje SK	Sweden	27	....	....	....	1508	85	*3	3.38	....	....	....	....	....	8	*5	3	0	495	26	*1	*3.15	....	....	....	....
1985-86	Sodertalje SK	Sweden	28	....	....	....	1650	87	0	3.16	....	....	....	....	....	7	4	3	0	420	23	0	3.29	....	....	....	....
	NHL Totals		**83**	**17**	**44**	**12**	**4456**	**278**	**0**	**3.74**	....	....	....	....	....	....	....	....	....	....	....	....	....	....	....	....	....

Signed as a free agent by **NY Rangers**, March 15, 1977. Rights traded to **Colorado** by **NY Rangers** for Bill Lochead, July 2, 1979.

• AUBIN, Jean-Sebastien G – R. 5'11", 183 lbs. b: Montreal, Que., 7/19/1977. Pittsburgh's 2nd, 76th overall in 1995.

Season	Club	League	GP	W	L	T	Mins	GA	SO	Avg	AAvg	Eff	SA	S%	SAPG	GP	W	L	T	Mins	GA	SO	Avg	Eff	SA	S%	SAPG
1993-94	Montreal-Bourassa Canadiens	QAAA	27	14	13	0	1524	96	1	3.74	....	....	....	....	....	....	....	....	....	....	....	....	....	....	....	....	....
1994-95	Sherbrooke Faucons	QMJHL	27	13	10	1	1287	73	1	3.40	....	....	....	....	....	3	1	2	....	185	11	0	3.57	....	....	....	....
1995-96	Sherbrooke Faucons	QMJHL	40	18	14	2	2140	127	0	3.57	....	....	....	....	....	4	1	3	....	238	23	0	5.55	....	....	....	....
1996-97	Laval Titan	QMJHL	11	2	6	1	532	41	0	4.62	....	....	....	....	....	....	....	....	....	....	....	....	....	....	....	....	....
	Moncton Wildcats	QMJHL	22	9	12	0	1252	67	1	3.21	....	....	....	....	....	....	....	....	....	....	....	....	....	....	....	....	....
	Sherbrooke Faucons	QMJHL	4	3	1	0	249	8	0	1.93	....	....	....	....	....	1	0	1	....	60	4	0	4.00	....	....	....	....
1997-98	Syracuse Crunch	AHL	8	2	4	1	380	26	0	4.10	....	....	....	....	....	....	....	....	....	....	....	....	....	....	....	....	....
	Dayton Bombers	ECHL	21	15	2	2	1177	59	1	3.01	....	....	....	....	....	3	1	1	....	142	4	0	1.69	....	....	....	....

Season	Club	League	GP	W	L	T	Mins	GA	SO	Avg	AAvg	Eff	SA	S%	SAPG	GP	W	L	T	Mins	GA	SO	Avg	Eff	SA	S%	SAPG
			REGULAR SEASON													PLAYOFFS											
1998-99	**Pittsburgh Penguins**	**NHL**	**17**	**4**	**3**	**6**	**756**	**28**	**2**	**2.22**	**2.64**	**2.04**	**304**	**.908**	**24.1**	....	....	....	....	....	....	....	....	....	....	....	....
	Kansas City Blades	IHL	13	5	7	1	751	41	0	3.28	....	....	....	....	....	....	....	....	....	....	....	....	....	....	....	....	....
99-2000	**Pittsburgh Penguins**	**NHL**	**51**	**23**	**21**	**3**	**2789**	**120**	**2**	**2.58**	**2.95**	**2.22**	**1392**	**.914**	**29.9**	....	....	....	....	....	....	....	....	....	....	....	....
	Wilkes-Barre Penguins	AHL	11	2	8	0	538	39	0	4.35	....	....	....	....	....	....	....	....	....	....	....	....	....	....	....	....	....
	NHL Totals		**68**	**27**	**24**	**9**	**3545**	**148**	**4**	**2.50**	....	....	**1696**	**.913**	**28.7**	....	....	....	....	....	....	....	....	....	....	....	....

• BACH, Ryan

G – L. 6′1″, 185 lbs. b: Sherwood Park, Alta., 10/21/1973. Detroit's 11th, 262nd overall in 1992.

Season	Club	League	GP	W	L	T	Mins	GA	SO	Avg	AAvg	Eff	SA	S%	SAPG	GP	W	L	T	Mins	GA	SO	Avg	Eff	SA	S%	SAPG
1991-92	Notre Dame Hounds	SJHL	33	16	11	6	1062	124	0	4.00	....	....	....	....	....	....	....	....	....	....	....	....	....	....	....	....	....
1992-93	Colorado College	WCHA	4	1	3	0	239	11	0	2.76	....	....	....	....	....	....	....	....	....	....	....	....	....	....	....	....	....
1993-94	Colorado College	WCHA	30	17	7	5	1733	105	0	3.64	....	....	....	....	....	....	....	....	....	....	....	....	....	....	....	....	....
1994-95	Colorado College	WCHA	27	18	5	1	1522	83	0	3.27	....	....	....	....	....	....	....	....	....	....	....	....	....	....	....	....	....
1995-96	Colorado College	WCHA	23	*17	4	2	1390	62	2	2.68	....	....	....	....	....	....	....	....	....	....	....	....	....	....	....	....	....
1996-97	Utica Blizzard	ColHL	2	0	1	1	119	8	0	4.03	....	....	....	....	....	....	....	....	....	....	....	....	....	....	....	....	....
	Toledo Storm	ECHL	20	5	11	3	1168	74	0	3.80	....	....	....	....	....	....	....	....	....	....	....	....	....	....	....	....	....
	Adirondack Red Wings	AHL	13	2	3	1	451	29	0	3.86	....	....	....	....	....	1	0	0	....	46	3	0	3.92	....	....	....	....
1997-98	Houston Aeros	IHL	43	26	9	6	2452	95	5	2.32	....	....	....	....	....	....	....	....	....	....	....	....	....	....	....	....	....
1998-99	Utah Grizzlies	IHL	4	2	1	0	197	9	0	2.74	....	....	....	....	....	....	....	....	....	....	....	....	....	....	....	....	....
	Los Angeles Kings	**NHL**	**3**	**0**	**3**	**0**	**108**	**8**	**0**	**4.44**	**5.28**	**5.38**	**66**	**.879**	**36.7**	....	....	....	....	....	....	....	....	....	....	....	....
	Long Beach Ice Dogs	IHL	27	10	9	5	1491	74	1	2.98	....	....	....	....	....	3	0	2	....	152	7	0	2.76	....	....	....	....
99-2000	Louisville Panthers	AHL	11	4	4	1	603	33	0	3.28	....	....	....	....	....	....	....	....	....	....	....	....	....	....	....	....	....
	Wilkes-Barre Penguins	AHL	28	8	18	2	1590	100	0	3.77	....	....	....	....	....	....	....	....	....	....	....	....	....	....	....	....	....
	Kansas City Blades	IHL	6	3	3	0	358	19	0	3.18	....	....	....	....	....	....	....	....	....	....	....	....	....	....	....	....	....
	NHL Totals		**3**	**0**	**3**	**0**	**108**	**8**	**0**	**4.44**	....	....	**66**	**.879**	**36.7**	....	....	....	....	....	....	....	....	....	....	....	....

WCHA First All-Star Team (1995, 1996) • NCAA West Second All-American Team (1995) • NCAA West First All-American Team (1996)

Traded to **Los Angeles** by **Detroit** for Los Angeles' 6th round choice (Per Backer) in 2000 Entry Draft, October 22, 1998. Signed as a free agent by **Florida**, July 27, 1999.

• BAILEY, Scott

G – L. 6′, 195 lbs. b: Calgary, Alta., 5/2/1972. Boston's 3rd, 112th overall in 1992.

Season	Club	League	GP	W	L	T	Mins	GA	SO	Avg	AAvg	Eff	SA	S%	SAPG	GP	W	L	T	Mins	GA	SO	Avg	Eff	SA	S%	SAPG
1988-89	Calgary Midget Flames	AAHA	STATISTICS NOT AVAILABLE																								
	Moose Jaw Warriors	WHL	2	0	1	0	34	7	0	12.35	....	....	....	....	....	....	....	....	....	....	....	....	....	....	....	....	....
1989-90	Calgary Midget Flames	AAHA	17	....	....	....	991	55	1	3.33	....	....	....	....	....	....	....	....	....	....	....	....	....	....	....	....	....
1990-91	Spokane Chiefs	WHL	46	33	11	0	2537	157	*4	3.71	....	....	....	....	....	....	....	....	....	....	....	....	....	....	....	....	....
	Spokane Chiefs	Mem-Cup	1	1	0	0	60	4	0	4.00	....	....	....	....	....	....	....	....	....	....	....	....	....	....	....	....	....
1991-92	Spokane Chiefs	WHL	65	34	23	5	3798	206	1	3.30	....	....	....	....	....	10	5	5	....	605	43	0	4.26	....	....	....	....
1992-93	Johnstown Chiefs	ECHL	36	13	15	3	1750	112	1	3.84	....	....	....	....	....	....	....	....	....	....	....	....	....	....	....	....	....
1993-94	Providence Bruins	AHL	7	2	2	2	377	24	0	3.82	....	....	....	....	....	....	....	....	....	....	....	....	....	....	....	....	....
	Charlotte Checkers	ECHL	36	22	11	3	2180	130	1	3.58	....	....	....	....	....	3	1	2	....	187	12	0	3.83	....	....	....	....
1994-95	Providence Bruins	AHL	52	25	16	9	2936	147	2	3.00	....	....	....	....	....	9	4	4	....	504	31	*2	3.69	....	....	....	....
1995-96	**Boston Bruins**	**NHL**	**11**	**5**	**1**	**2**	**571**	**31**	**0**	**3.26**	**3.24**	**3.83**	**264**	**.883**	**27.7**	....	....	....	....	....	....	....	....	....	....	....	....
	Providence Bruins	AHL	37	15	19	3	2210	120	1	3.26	....	....	....	....	....	2	1	1	....	119	6	0	3.03	....	....	....	....
1996-97	**Boston Bruins**	**NHL**	**8**	**1**	**5**	**0**	**394**	**24**	**0**	**3.65**	**3.93**	**4.84**	**181**	**.867**	**27.6**	....	....	....	....	....	....	....	....	....	....	....	....
	Providence Bruins	AHL	31	11	17	2	1735	112	0	3.87	....	....	....	....	....	7	3	4	....	453	23	0	3.05	....	....	....	....
1997-98	San Antonio Dragons	IHL	37	11	17	3	1898	118	1	3.73	....	....	....	....	....	....	....	....	....	....	....	....	....	....	....	....	....
1998-99	Orlando Solar Bears	IHL	17	5	7	0	749	36	0	2.88	....	....	....	....	....	....	....	....	....	....	....	....	....	....	....	....	....
	Birmingham Bulls	ECHL	27	16	8	2	1557	90	1	3.47	....	....	....	....	....	5	2	3	....	299	21	0	4.21	....	....	....	....
99-2000	Tappara Tampere	Finland	6	0	4	2	347	29	0	5.01	....	....	....	....	....	....	....	....	....	....	....	....	....	....	....	....	....
	Charlotte Checkers	ECHL	31	10	16	4	1735	93	2	3.22	....	....	....	....	....	....	....	....	....	....	....	....	....	....	....	....	....
	Saint John Flames	AHL	4	0	1	0	135	11	0	4.90	....	....	....	....	....	....	....	....	....	....	....	....	....	....	....	....	....
	NHL Totals		**19**	**6**	**6**	**2**	**965**	**55**	**0**	**3.42**	....	....	**445**	**.876**	**27.7**	....	....	....	....	....	....	....	....	....	....	....	....

WHL West Second All-Star Team (1991, 1992)

Signed as a free agent by **Charlotte** (ECHL), December 10, 1999. Loaned to **Saint John** (AHL) by **Charlotte** (ECHL), February 6, 2000.

• BAKER, Steve

G – L. 6′3″, 200 lbs. b: Boston, MA, 5/6/1957. NY Rangers' 4th, 44th overall in 1977.

Season	Club	League	GP	W	L	T	Mins	GA	SO	Avg	AAvg	Eff	SA	S%	SAPG	GP	W	L	T	Mins	GA	SO	Avg	Eff	SA	S%	SAPG
1974-75	Owen Sound Grays	OHA-B	22	....	....	....	1320	38	5	1.73	....	....	....	....	....	....	....	....	....	....	....	....	....	....	....	....	....
1975-76	Union College Dutchmen	ECAC	9	8	1	0	480	21	0	2.62	....	....	....	....	....	....	....	....	....	....	....	....	....	....	....	....	....
1976-77	Union College Dutchmen	ECAC	19	16	3	0	1117	67	0	3.60	....	....	....	....	....	2	1	1	0	120	10	0	5.00	....	....	....	....
1977-78	Union College Dutchmen	ECAC	5	3	1	1	300	16	0	3.20	....	....	....	....	....	....	....	....	....	....	....	....	....	....	....	....	....
	Toledo Goaldiggers	IHL	10	....	....	....	544	46	0	5.07	....	....	....	....	....	....	....	....	....	....	....	....	....	....	....	....	....
1978-79	New Haven Nighthawks	AHL	24	15	5	4	1435	82	1	3.43	....	....	....	....	....	5	2	3	0	297	17	0	3.43	....	....	....	....
1979-80	**New York Rangers**	**NHL**	**27**	**9**	**8**	**6**	**1391**	**79**	**1**	**3.41**	**3.01**					....	....	....	....	....	....	....	....	....	....	....	....
	New Haven Nighthawks	AHL	9	6	1	1	492	29	0	3.54	....	....	....	....	....	....	....	....	....	....	....	....	....	....	....	....	....
1980-81	New Haven Nighthawks	AHL	25	10	11	4	1497	90	1	3.57	....	....	....	....	....	....	....	....	....	....	....	....	....	....	....	....	....
	New York Rangers	**NHL**	**21**	**10**	**6**	**5**	**1260**	**73**	**2**	**3.48**	**2.81**					**14**	**7**	**7**	....	**826**	**55**	**0**	**4.00**	....	....	....	....
1981-82	United States	Can-Cup	1	0	0	1	60	4	0	4.00	....	....	....	....	....	....	....	....	....	....	....	....	....	....	....	....	....
	Springfield Indians	AHL	11	2	7	1	503	42	0	5.01	....	....	....	....	....	....	....	....	....	....	....	....	....	....	....	....	....
	New York Rangers	**NHL**	**6**	**1**	**5**	**0**	**328**	**33**	**0**	**6.04**	**4.67**					....	....	....	....	....	....	....	....	....	....	....	....
1982-83	**New York Rangers**	**NHL**	**3**	**0**	**1**	**0**	**102**	**5**	**0**	**2.94**	**2.36**	**3.34**	**44**	**.886**	**25.9**	....	....	....	....	....	....	....	....	....	....	....	....
	Tulsa Oilers	CHL	*49	22	27	0	*2901	186	0	3.85	....	....	....	....	....	....	....	....	....	....	....	....	....	....	....	....	....
1983-84	Binghamton Whalers	AHL	6	0	4	1	345	35	0	6.09	....	....	....	....	....	....	....	....	....	....	....	....	....	....	....	....	....
	Maine Mariners	AHL	13	5	5	2	744	41	0	3.31	....	....	....	....	....	6	3	3	0	353	23	0	3.91	....	....	....	....
	NHL Totals		**57**	**20**	**20**	**11**	**3081**	**190**	**3**	**3.70**	....	....	....	....	....	**14**	**7**	**7**	....	**826**	**55**	**0**	**4.00**	....	....	....	....

• BALES, Mike

Michael R. G – L. 6′1″, 200 lbs. b: Prince Albert, Sask., 8/6/1971. Boston's 4th, 105th overall in 1990.

Season	Club	League	GP	W	L	T	Mins	GA	SO	Avg	AAvg	Eff	SA	S%	SAPG	GP	W	L	T	Mins	GA	SO	Avg	Eff	SA	S%	SAPG
1988-89	Estevan Bruins	SJHL	44	....	....	....	2412	197	1	4.90	....	....	....	....	....	....	....	....	....	....	....	....	....	....	....	....	....
1989-90	Ohio State University	CCHA	21	6	13	2	1117	95	0	5.11	....	....	....	....	....	....	....	....	....	....	....	....	....	....	....	....	....
1990-91	Ohio State University	CCHA	*39	11	24	3	*2180	184	0	5.06	....	....	....	....	....	....	....	....	....	....	....	....	....	....	....	....	....
1991-92	Ohio State University	CCHA	36	11	20	5	2060	180	0	5.24	....	....	....	....	....	....	....	....	....	....	....	....	....	....	....	....	....
1992-93	**Boston Bruins**	**NHL**	**1**	**0**	**0**	**0**	**25**	**1**	**0**	**2.40**	**2.06**	**2.40**	**10**	**.900**	**24.0**	....	....	....	....	....	....	....	....	....	....	....	....
	Providence Bruins	AHL	44	22	17	0	2363	166	1	4.21	....	....	....	....	....	2	0	2	....	118	8	0	4.07	....	....	....	....
1993-94	Providence Bruins	AHL	33	9	15	4	1757	130	0	4.44	....	....	....	....	....	....	....	....	....	....	....	....	....	....	....	....	....
1994-95	P.E.I. Senators	AHL	45	25	16	3	2649	160	2	3.62	....	....	....	....	....	9	6	3	....	530	24	*2	2.72	....	....	....	....
	Ottawa Senators	**NHL**	**1**	**0**	**0**	**0**	**3**	**0**	**0**	**0.00**	**0.00**	**0.00**	**1**	**1.000**	**20.0**	....	....	....	....	....	....	....	....	....	....	....	....
1995-96	**Ottawa Senators**	**NHL**	**20**	**2**	**14**	**1**	**1040**	**72**	**0**	**4.15**	**4.14**	**5.34**	**560**	**.871**	**32.3**	....	....	....	....	....	....	....	....	....	....	....	....
	P.E.I. Senators	AHL	2	0	2	0	118	11	0	5.58	....	....	....	....	....	....	....	....	....	....	....	....	....	....	....	....	....
1996-97	**Ottawa Senators**	**NHL**	**1**	**0**	**1**	**0**	**52**	**4**	**0**	**4.62**	**4.97**	**10.27**	**18**	**.778**	**20.8**	....	....	....	....	....	....	....	....	....	....	....	....
	Baltimore Bandits	AHL	46	13	21	8	2544	130	3	3.07	....	....	....	....	....	....	....	....	....	....	....	....	....	....	....	....	....
1997-98	Rochester Americans	AHL	39	13	19	5	2229	127	0	3.42	....	....	....	....	....	....	....	....	....	....	....	....	....	....	....	....	....
1998-99	Michigan K-Wings	IHL	32	11	17	3	1773	96	1	3.25	....	....	....	....	....	....	....	....	....	....	....	....	....	....	....	....	....
99-2000	Michigan K-Wings	IHL	25	9	9	5	1341	56	0	2.50	....	....	....	....	....	....	....	....	....	....	....	....	....	....	....	....	....
	NHL Totals		**23**	**2**	**15**	**1**	**1120**	**77**	**0**	**4.13**	....	....	**589**	**.869**	**31.6**	....	....	....	....	....	....	....	....	....	....	....	....

Signed as a free agent by **Ottawa**, July 4, 1994. Signed as a free agent by **Buffalo**, September 9, 1997. Signed as a free agent by **Dallas**, July 8, 1998.

• BANNERMAN, Murray

G – L. 5′11″, 185 lbs. b: Fort Frances, Ont., 4/27/1957. Vancouver's 5th, 58th overall in 1977.

Season	Club	League	GP	W	L	T	Mins	GA	SO	Avg	AAvg	Eff	SA	S%	SAPG	GP	W	L	T	Mins	GA	SO	Avg	Eff	SA	S%	SAPG
1972-73	St. James Canadians	MJHL	31	....	....	....	1778	104	*1	*3.51	....	....	....	....	....	....	....	....	....	....	....	....	....	....	....	....	....
1973-74	St. James Canadians	MJHL	17	....	....	....	930	69	0	4.45	....	....	....	....	....	....	....	....	....	....	....	....	....	....	....	....	....
	Winnipeg Clubs	WCJHL	6	....	....	....	258	29	0	6.74	....	....	....	....	....	....	....	....	....	....	....	....	....	....	....	....	....
1974-75	Winnipeg Clubs	WCJHL	28	3	12	5	1351	113	0	5.02	....	....	....	....	....	....	....	....	....	....	....	....	....	....	....	....	....

			REGULAR SEASON													PLAYOFFS											
Season	Club	League	GP	W	L	T	Mins	GA	SO	Avg	AAvg	Eff	SA	S%	SAPG	GP	W	L	T	Mins	GA	SO	Avg	Eff	SA	S%	SAPG
1975-76	Assiniboine Park Monarchs	MJHL	8	....	....	....	480	22	1	2.75	....	....	....	....	....	....	....	....	....	....	....	....	....	....	....	....	....
	Victoria Cougars	WCJHL	44	23	15	3	2450	178	1	4.36	....	....	....	....	....	15	7	5	3	*878	50	0	3.42	....	....	....	....
1976-77	Victoria Cougars	WCJHL	67	....	....	....	3893	262	2	4.04	....	....	....	....	....	4	....	....	....	234	20	0	5.13	....	....	....	....
1977-78	Fort Wayne Komets	IHL	44	....	....	....	2435	133	1	3.28	....	....	....	....	....	6	....	....	....	335	26	0	4.66	....	....	....	....
	Vancouver Canucks	**NHL**	**1**	**0**	**0**	**0**	**20**	**0**	**0**	**0.00**	**0.00**	....	....	....	....	....	....	....	....	....	....	....	....	....	....	....	....
1978-79	New Brunswick Hawks	AHL	47	22	14	5	2557	152	0	3.57	....	....	....	....	....	3	1	1	0	122	10	0	4.92	....	....	....	....
1979-80	New Brunswick Hawks	AHL	*61	32	20	5	3361	186	*3	3.32	....	....	....	....	....	*17	*10	6	0	*1049	51	0	2.92	....	....	....	....
1980-81	**Chicago Black Hawks**	**NHL**	**15**	**2**	**10**	**2**	**865**	**62**	**0**	**4.30**	**3.48**	....	....	....	....	....	....	....	....	....	....	....	....	....	....	....	....
1981-82	**Chicago Black Hawks**	**NHL**	**29**	**11**	**12**	**4**	**1671**	**116**	**1**	**4.17**	**3.22**	....	....	....	....	**10**	**5**	**4**	....	**555**	**35**	**0**	**3.78**	....	....	....	....
1982-83	**Chicago Black Hawks**	**NHL**	**41**	**24**	**12**	**5**	**2460**	**127**	**4**	**3.10**	**2.48**	**3.07**	**1283**	**.901**	**31.3**	**8**	**4**	**4**	....	**480**	**32**	**0**	**4.00**	....	....	....	....
1983-84	**Chicago Black Hawks**	**NHL**	**56**	**23**	**29**	**4**	**3335**	**188**	**2**	**3.38**	**2.65**	**3.81**	**1667**	**.887**	**30.0**	**5**	**2**	**3**	....	**300**	**17**	**0**	**3.40**	**3.38**	**171**	**.901**	**34.2**
1984-85	**Chicago Black Hawks**	**NHL**	**60**	**27**	**25**	**4**	**3371**	**215**	**0**	**3.83**	**3.05**	**4.46**	**1847**	**.884**	**32.9**	**15**	**9**	**6**	....	**906**	**72**	**0**	**4.77**	**6.28**	**547**	**.868**	**36.2**
1985-86	**Chicago Black Hawks**	**NHL**	**48**	**20**	**19**	**6**	**2689**	**201**	**1**	**4.48**	**3.51**	**5.85**	**1538**	**.869**	**34.3**	**2**	**0**	**1**	....	**81**	**9**	**0**	**6.67**	**15.01**	**40**	**.775**	**29.6**
1986-87	**Chicago Blackhawks**	**NHL**	**39**	**9**	**18**	**8**	**2059**	**142**	**0**	**4.14**	**3.52**	**5.24**	**1122**	**.873**	**32.7**	....	....	....	....	....	....	....	....	....	....	....	....
1987-88	Baltimore Skipjacks	AHL	41	6	21	5	2014	154	0	4.59	....	....	....	....	....	....	....	....	....	....	....	....	....	....	....	....	....
	Saginaw Hawks	IHL	3	0	2	0	140	15	0	6.43	....	....	....	....	....	....	....	....	....	....	....	....	....	....	....	....	....
	NHL Totals		**289**	**116**	**125**	**33**	**16470**	**1051**	**8**	**3.83**	....	....	....	....	....	**40**	**20**	**18**	....	**2322**	**165**	**0**	**4.26**	....	....	....	....

MJHL Second All-Star Team (1973) • IHL First All-Star Team (1978) • AHL Second All-Star Team (1980) • Played in NHL All-Star Game (1983, 1984)

Traded to **Chicago** by **Vancouver** to complete transaction that sent Pit Martin to Vancouver (November 4, 1977), May 27, 1978.

• BARON, Marco

Marco Joseph G – L. 5'11", 180 lbs. b: Montreal, Que., 4/8/1959. Boston's 6th, 99th overall in 1979.

Season	Club	League	GP	W	L	T	Mins	GA	SO	Avg	AAvg	Eff	SA	S%	SAPG	GP	W	L	T	Mins	GA	SO	Avg	Eff	SA	S%	SAPG
1975-76	Montreal Juniors	QMJHL	23	....	....	....	1376	81	2	3.53	....	....	....	....	....	....	....	....	....	....	....	....	....	....	....	....	....
1976-77	Montreal Juniors	QMJHL	41	....	....	....	2006	182	1	5.44	....	....	....	....	....	....	....	....	....	....	....	....	....	....	....	....	....
1977-78	Verdun Eperviers	QMJHL	61	....	....	....	3395	251	0	4.44	....	....	....	....	....	13	....	....	....	780	51	0	3.92	....	....	....	....
1978-79	Verdun Eperviers	QMJHL	67	....	....	....	3630	230	4	3.80	....	....	....	....	....	11	....	....	....	610	46	0	4.52	....	....	....	....
1979-80	**Boston Bruins**	**NHL**	**1**	**0**	**0**	**0**	**40**	**2**	**0**	**3.00**	**2.65**	....	....	....	....	....	....	....	....	....	....	....	....	....	....	....	....
	Binghamton Dusters	AHL	6	0	5	0	265	26	0	5.89	....	....	....	....	....	....	....	....	....	....	....	....	....	....	....	....	....
	Grand Rapids Owls	IHL	35	....	....	....	1995	135	0	4.06	....	....	....	....	....	....	....	....	....	....	....	....	....	....	....	....	....
1980-81	Springfield Indians	AHL	23	12	11	0	1300	79	1	3.45	....	....	....	....	....	....	....	....	....	....	....	....	....	....	....	....	....
	Boston Bruins	**NHL**	**10**	**3**	**4**	**1**	**507**	**24**	**0**	**2.84**	**2.29**	....	....	....	....	**1**	**0**	**1**	....	**20**	**3**	**0**	**9.00**	....	....	....	....
1981-82	Erie Blades	AHL	2	1	1	0	119	8	0	4.04	....	....	....	....	....	....	....	....	....	....	....	....	....	....	....	....	....
	Boston Bruins	**NHL**	**44**	**22**	**16**	**4**	**2515**	**144**	**1**	**3.44**	**2.65**	....	....	....	....	....	....	....	....	....	....	....	....	....	....	....	....
1982-83	**Boston Bruins**	**NHL**	**9**	**6**	**3**	**0**	**516**	**33**	**0**	**3.84**	**3.08**	**5.44**	**233**	**.858**	**27.1**	....	....	....	....	....	....	....	....	....	....	....	....
	Baltimore Skipjacks	AHL	22	8	11	1	1260	97	0	4.62	....	....	....	....	....	....	....	....	....	....	....	....	....	....	....	....	....
1983-84	Moncton Alpines	AHL	16	6	7	3	858	45	0	3.15	....	....	....	....	....	....	....	....	....	....	....	....	....	....	....	....	....
	Los Angeles Kings	**NHL**	**21**	**3**	**14**	**4**	**1211**	**87**	**0**	**4.31**	**3.40**	**5.92**	**633**	**.863**	**31.4**	....	....	....	....	....	....	....	....	....	....	....	....
1984-85	Sherbrooke Canadiens	AHL	1	0	0	0	32	5	0	9.37	....	....	....	....	....	....	....	....	....	....	....	....	....	....	....	....	....
	Edmonton Oilers	**NHL**	**1**	**0**	**1**	**0**	**33**	**2**	**0**	**3.64**	**2.90**	**8.09**	**9**	**.778**	**16.4**	....	....	....	....	....	....	....	....	....	....	....	....
	Nova Scotia Oilers	AHL	17	8	7	1	1010	45	0	2.67	....	....	....	....	....	6	2	4	0	406	25	0	3.69	....	....	....	....
	NHL Totals		**86**	**34**	**38**	**9**	**4822**	**292**	**1**	**3.63**	....	....	....	....	....	**1**	**0**	**1**	....	**20**	**3**	**0**	**9.00**	....	....	....	....

QMJHL Second All-Star Team (1978)

Traded to **LA Kings** by **Boston** for Bob LaForest, January 3, 1984. Signed as a free agent by **Edmonton**, February 21, 1985.

• BARRASSO, Tom

Thomas Patrick G – R. 6'3", 211 lbs. b: Boston, MA, 3/31/1965. Buffalo's 1st, 5th overall in 1983.

Season	Club	League	GP	W	L	T	Mins	GA	SO	Avg	AAvg	Eff	SA	S%	SAPG	GP	W	L	T	Mins	GA	SO	Avg	Eff	SA	S%	SAPG
1981-82	Acton-Boxboro Colonials	Hi-School	23	....	....	....	1035	32	7	1.86	....	....	....	....	....	....	....	....	....	....	....	....	....	....	....	....	....
1982-83	Acton-Boxboro Colonials	Hi-School.	23	22	1	0	1035	17	10	0.99	....	....	....	....	....	....	....	....	....	....	....	....	....	....	....	....	....
	United States	WJC-A	3	....	....	....	140	12	....	5.14	....	....	....	....	....	....	....	....	....	....	....	....	....	....	....	....	....
1983-84	**Buffalo Sabres**	**NHL**	**42**	**26**	**12**	**3**	**2475**	**117**	**2**	**2.84**	**2.22**	**3.03**	**1098**	**.893**	**26.6**	**3**	**0**	**2**	....	**139**	**8**	**0**	**3.45**	**4.68**	**59**	**.864**	**25.5**
1984-85	United States	Can-Cup	5	2	2	1	252	13	0	3.00	....	....	....	....	....	....	....	....	....	....	....	....	....	....	....	....	....
	Buffalo Sabres	**NHL**	**54**	**25**	**18**	**10**	**3248**	**144**	***5**	***2.66**	**2.10**	**3.01**	**1274**	**.887**	**23.5**	**5**	**2**	**3**	....	**300**	**22**	**0**	**4.40**	**6.41**	**151**	**.854**	**30.2**
	Rochester Americans	AHL	5	3	1	1	267	6	1	1.35	....	....	....	....	....	....	....	....	....	....	....	....	....	....	....	....	....
1985-86	**Buffalo Sabres**	**NHL**	**60**	**29**	**24**	**5**	**3561**	**214**	**2**	**3.61**	**2.81**	**4.34**	**1778**	**.880**	**30.0**	....	....	....	....	....	....	....	....	....	....	....	....
	United States	WEC-A	5	....	....	....	260	18	....	4.15	....	....	....	....	....	....	....	....	....	....	....	....	....	....	....	....	....
1986-87	**Buffalo Sabres**	**NHL**	**46**	**17**	**23**	**2**	**2501**	**152**	**2**	**3.65**	**3.09**	**4.62**	**1202**	**.874**	**28.8**	....	....	....	....	....	....	....	....	....	....	....	....
1987-88	United States	Can-Cup	1	0	1	0	60	5	0	5.00	....	....	....	....	....	....	....	....	....	....	....	....	....	....	....	....	....
	Buffalo Sabres	**NHL**	**54**	**25**	**18**	**8**	**3133**	**173**	**2**	**3.31**	**2.75**	**3.45**	**1658**	**.896**	**31.8**	**4**	**1**	**3**	....	**224**	**16**	**0**	**4.29**	**5.72**	**120**	**.867**	**32.1**
1988-89	**Buffalo Sabres**	**NHL**	**10**	**2**	**7**	**0**	**545**	**45**	**0**	**4.95**	**4.13**	**7.82**	**285**	**.842**	**31.4**	....	....	....	....	....	....	....	....	....	....	....	....
	Pittsburgh Penguins	**NHL**	**44**	**18**	**15**	**7**	**2406**	**162**	**0**	**4.04**	**3.37**	**4.53**	**1445**	**.888**	**36.0**	**11**	**7**	**4**	....	**631**	**40**	**0**	**3.80**	**3.91**	**389**	**.897**	**37.0**
1989-90	**Pittsburgh Penguins**	**NHL**	**24**	**7**	**12**	**3**	**1294**	**101**	**0**	**4.68**	**3.98**	**6.32**	**748**	**.865**	**34.7**	....	....	....	....	....	....	....	....	....	....	....	....
1990-91 ♦	**Pittsburgh Penguins**	**NHL**	**48**	**27**	**16**	**3**	**2754**	**165**	**1**	**3.59**	**3.23**	**3.75**	**1579**	**.896**	**34.4**	**20**	**12**	**7**	....	**1175**	**51**	***1**	***2.60**	**2.11**	**629**	**.919**	**32.1**
1991-92 ♦	**Pittsburgh Penguins**	**NHL**	**57**	**25**	**22**	**9**	**3329**	**196**	**1**	**3.53**	**3.16**	**4.07**	**1702**	**.885**	**30.7**	***21**	***16**	**5**	....	***1233**	**58**	**1**	**2.82**	**2.63**	**622**	**.907**	**30.3**
1992-93	**Pittsburgh Penguins**	**NHL**	**63**	***43**	**14**	**5**	**3702**	**186**	**4**	**3.01**	**2.57**	**2.97**	**1885**	**.901**	**30.6**	**12**	**7**	**5**	....	**722**	**35**	***2**	**2.91**	**2.75**	**370**	**.905**	**30.7**
1993-94	**Pittsburgh Penguins**	**NHL**	**44**	**22**	**15**	**5**	**2482**	**139**	**2**	**3.36**	**3.23**	**3.58**	**1304**	**.893**	**31.5**	**6**	**2**	**4**	....	**356**	**17**	**0**	**2.87**	**3.01**	**162**	**.895**	**27.3**
1994-95	**Pittsburgh Penguins**	**NHL**	**2**	**0**	**1**	**1**	**125**	**8**	**0**	**3.84**	**4.02**	**4.10**	**75**	**.893**	**36.0**	**2**	**0**	**1**	....	**80**	**8**	**0**	**6.00**	**11.71**	**41**	**.805**	**30.8**
1995-96	**Pittsburgh Penguins**	**NHL**	**49**	**29**	**16**	**2**	**2799**	**160**	**2**	**3.43**	**3.42**	**3.38**	**1626**	**.902**	**34.9**	**10**	**4**	**5**	....	**558**	**26**	**1**	**2.80**	**2.16**	**337**	**.923**	**36.2**
1996-97	**Pittsburgh Penguins**	**NHL**	**5**	**0**	**5**	**0**	**270**	**26**	**0**	**5.78**	**6.23**	**8.08**	**186**	**.860**	**41.3**	....	....	....	....	....	....	....	....	....	....	....	....
1997-98	**Pittsburgh Penguins**	**NHL**	**63**	**31**	**14**	**13**	**3542**	**122**	**7**	**2.07**	**2.45**	**1.62**	**1556**	**.922**	**26.4**	**6**	**2**	**4**	....	**376**	**17**	**0**	**2.71**	**2.69**	**171**	**.901**	**27.3**
1998-99	**Pittsburgh Penguins**	**NHL**	**43**	**19**	**16**	**3**	**2306**	**98**	**4**	**2.55**	**3.03**	**2.52**	**993**	**.901**	**25.8**	**13**	**6**	**7**	....	**787**	**35**	**1**	**2.67**	**2.67**	**350**	**.900**	**26.7**
99-2000	**Pittsburgh Penguins**	**NHL**	**18**	**5**	**7**	**2**	**870**	**46**	**1**	**3.17**	**3.63**	**3.78**	**386**	**.881**	**26.6**	....	....	....	....	....	....	....	....	....	....	....	....
	Ottawa Senators	**NHL**	**7**	**3**	**4**	**0**	**418**	**22**	**0**	**3.16**	**3.61**	**3.82**	**182**	**.879**	**26.1**	**6**	**2**	**4**	....	**372**	**16**	**0**	**2.58**	**2.46**	**168**	**.905**	**27.1**
	NHL Totals		**733**	**353**	**259**	**81**	**41760**	**2276**	**35**	**3.27**	....	....	**20962**	**.891**	**30.1**	**119**	**61**	**54**	....	**6953**	**349**	**6**	**3.01**	....	**3569**	**.902**	**30.8**

NHL All-Rookie Team (1984) • NHL First All-Star Team (1984) • Won Calder Memorial Trophy (1984) • Won Vezina Trophy (1984) • NHL Second All-Star Team (1985, 1993) • Shared William Jennings Trophy with Bob Sauve (1985) • Played in NHL All-Star Game (1985)

Traded to **Pittsburgh** by **Buffalo** with Buffalo's 3rd round choice (Joe Dziedzic) in 1990 Entry Draft for Doug Bodger and Darrin Shannon, November 12, 1988. • Missed majority of 1994-95 season recovering from wrist surgery, January 20, 1995. • Missed majority of 1996-97 season recovering from shoulder injury originally suffered in game vs. Montreal, February 5, 1996. Traded to **Ottawa** by **Pittsburgh** for Ron Tugnutt and Janne Laukkanen, March 14, 2000.

• BASSEN, Hank

Henry "Red" G – L. 5'10", 180 lbs. b: Calgary, Alta., 12/6/1932.

Season	Club	League	GP	W	L	T	Mins	GA	SO	Avg	AAvg	Eff	SA	S%	SAPG	GP	W	L	T	Mins	GA	SO	Avg	Eff	SA	S%	SAPG
1949-50	Calgary Buffaloes	WCJHL	30	11	18	1	1800	111	0	3.70	....	....	....	....	....	....	....	....	....	....	....	....	....	....	....	....	....
1950-51	Calgary Buffaloes	WCJHL	37	8	27	2	2280	176	*2	4.63	....	....	....	....	....	....	....	....	....	....	....	....	....	....	....	....	....
	Medicine Hat Tigers	WCJHL	1	0	1	0	60	10	0	10.00	....	....	....	....	....	....	....	....	....	....	....	....	....	....	....	....	....
1951-52	Calgary Buffaloes	WCJHL	42	21	17	4	2580	132	1	3.07	....	....	....	....	....	3	0	3	0	180	13	0	4.33	....	....	....	....
1952-53	Calgary Buffaloes	WCJHL	30	14	13	3	1860	145	0	4.68	....	....	....	....	....	3	0	3	0	180	11	0	3.67	....	....	....	....
1953-54	Chatham Maroons	OHA-Sr.	55	22	30	3	3300	205	2	3.73	....	....	....	....	....	6	2	4	0	360	25	*1	4.17	....	....	....	....
1954-55	Buffalo Bisons	AHL	37	13	19	5	2220	121	3	3.27	....	....	....	....	....	....	....	....	....	....	....	....	....	....	....	....	....
	Chicago Black Hawks	**NHL**	**21**	**4**	**9**	**8**	**1260**	**63**	**0**	**3.00**	**3.66**	....	....	....	....	....	....	....	....	....	....	....	....	....	....	....	....
1955-56	Buffalo Bisons	AHL	55	26	23	4	3300	201	0	3.80	....	....	....	....	....	5	2	3	0	299	20	0	4.01	....	....	....	....
	Chicago Black Hawks	**NHL**	**12**	**2**	**9**	**1**	**720**	**40**	**1**	**3.33**	**4.12**	....	....	....	....	....	....	....	....	....	....	....	....	....	....	....	....
1956-57	Calgary Stampeders	WHL	68	29	35	4	4125	223	5	3.24	....	....	....	....	....	3	1	2	0	180	12	0	4.00	....	....	....	....
1957-58	Seattle Totems	WHL	60	27	27	6	3600	184	3	3.06	....	....	....	....	....	9	5	4	0	557	21	0	*2.26	....	....	....	....
1958-59	Springfield Indians	AHL	29	13	14	2	1740	102	1	3.52	....	....	....	....	....	....	....	....	....	....	....	....*	....	....	....	....	....
1959-60	Vancouver Canucks	WHL	*70	*44	19	6	4220	172	*5	*2.45	....	....	....	....	....	*11	*9	2	0	*696	22	0	*1.90	....	....	....	....
1960-61	**Detroit Red Wings**	**NHL**	**34**	**13**	**12**	**9**	**1990**	**98**	**0**	**2.95**	**3.04**	....	....	....	....	**4**	**1**	**2**	....	**220**	**9**	**0**	**2.45**	....	....	....	....
1961-62	**Detroit Red Wings**	**NHL**	**27**	**9**	**12**	**6**	**1620**	**75**	**3**	**2.78**	**2.83**	....	....	....	....	....	....	....	....	....	....	....	....	....	....	....	....
	Edmonton Flyers	WHL	9	4	4	1	557	30	0	3.23	....	....	....	....	....	....	....	....	....	....	....	....	....	....	....	....	....
	Sudbury Wolves	EPHL	3	1	2	0	180	14	0	4.67	....	....	....	....	....	....	....	....	....	....	....	....	....	....	....	....	....
1962-63	**Detroit Red Wings**	**NHL**	**16**	**6**	**5**	**5**	**960**	**51**	**0**	**3.19**	**3.33**	....	....	....	....	....	....	....	....	....	....	....	....	....	....	....	....
	Pittsburgh Hornets	AHL	40	15	23	2	2400	134	2	3.35	....	....	....	....	....	....	....	....	....	....	....	....	....	....	....	....	....

			REGULAR SEASON													PLAYOFFS											
Season	Club	League	GP	W	L	T	Mins	GA	SO	Avg	AAvg	Eff	SA	S%	SAPG	GP	W	L	T	Mins	GA	SO	Avg	Eff	SA	S%	SAPG
1963-64	Cincinnati Wings	CPHL	7	0	6	1	420	39	0	5.57	....	....	....	....	....	....	....	....	....	....	....	....	....	....	....	....	....
	Detroit Red Wings	NHL	1	0	1	0	60	4	0	4.00	4.45	....	....	....	....	....	....	....	....	....	....	....	....	....	....	....	....
	Pittsburgh Hornets	AHL	26	9	15	2	1560	82	1	3.15	....	....	....	....	....	1	0	1	0	60	4	0	4.00	....	....	....	....
1964-65	Pittsburgh Hornets	AHL	57	24	25	7	3430	182	2	3.18	....	....	....	....	....	4	1	3	0	240	15	0	3.75	....	....	....	....
1965-66	Detroit Red Wings	NHL	11	3	3	0	406	17	0	2.51	2.53	....	....	....	....	1	0	1	....	54	2	0	2.22	....	....	....	....
1966-67	Detroit Red Wings	NHL	8	2	4	0	384	22	0	3.44	3.55	....	....	....	....	....	....	....	....	....	....	....	....	....	....	....	....
	Pittsburgh Hornets	AHL	10	6	3	1	570	18	3	1.89	....	....	....	....	....	9	*8	1	0	541	15	1	*1.66	....	....	....	....
1967-68	Pittsburgh Penguins	NHL	25	7	10	3	1299	62	1	2.86	3.18	....	....	....	....	....	....	....	....	....	....	....	....	....	....	....	....
	NHL Totals		155	46	65	32	8699	432	5	2.98	....	....	....	....	....	5	1	3	....	274	11	0	2.41	....	....	....	....

• Father of Bob • WCJHL Second All-Star Team (1950) • WCJHL First All-Star Team (1952) • OHA-Sr. First All-Star Team (1954) • WHL First All-Star Team (1960) • Won WHL Leading Goaltender Award (1960) • Won Leader Cup (WHL - MVP) (tied with Guyle Fielder) (1960)

Traded to **Detroit** by **Chicago** with Johnny Wilson, Forbes Kennedy and Bill Preston for Ted Lindsay and Glenn Hall, July 23, 1957. Traded to **Springfield** (AHL) by **Detroit** with Dennis Olson and Bill McCreary for Gerry Ehman, May 1, 1958. Traded to **Vancouver** (WHL) by **Springfield** (AHL) for Colin Kilburn and $7,500, July, 1959. Claimed by **Detroit** from **Vancouver** (WHL) in Inter-League Draft, June, 1960. Traded to **Pittsburgh** by **Detroit** for Roy Edwards, September 7, 1967.

• BASTIEN, Baz

Aldege G – L. 5'7", 160 lbs. b: Timmins, Ont., 8/29/1919 d: 3/15/1983.

Season	Club	League	GP	W	L	T	Mins	GA	SO	Avg	AAvg	Eff	SA	S%	SAPG	GP	W	L	T	Mins	GA	SO	Avg	Eff	SA	S%	SAPG
1938-39	North Bay Trappers	NOJHA	STATISTICS NOT AVAILABLE																								
	North Bay Trappers	Mem-Cup	2	0	2	0	140	12	0	5.14	....	....	....	....	....	....	....	....	....	....	....	....	....	....	....	....	....
1939-40	Port Colburne Sailors	OHA-Sr.	17	12	5	0	1030	47	*2	2.74	....	....	....	....	....	4	1	3	0	240	23	0	5.75	....	....	....	....
	Atlantic City Seagulls	EAHL	2	....	....	....	90	4	0	2.67	....	....	....	....	....	2	1	1	0	120	9	0	4.50	....	....	....	....
1940-41	Toronto Marlboros	OHA-Sr.	15	10	4	0	890	35	1	2.36	....	....	....	....	....	11	*8	3	0	675	19	*1	*1.69	....	....	....	....
	Toronto Marlboros	Al-Cup	9	3	4	0	370	17	1	2.76	....	....	....	....	....	....	....	....	....	....	....	....	....	....	....	....	....
1941-42	Toronto Marlboros	OHA-Sr.	28	13	11	4	1740	81	1	2.79	....	....	....	....	....	6	2	4	0	391	18	0	*2.76	....	....	....	....
1942-43	Cornwall Flyers	QSHL	30	....	....	....	1760	97	*4	*3.31	....	....	....	....	....	6	2	4	0	366	22	0	3.61	....	....	....	....
1943-44			MILITARY SERVICE																								
1944-45			MILITARY SERVICE																								
1945-46	Toronto Maple Leafs	NHL	5	0	4	1	300	20	0	4.00	3.66	....	....	....	....	....	....	....	....	....	....	....	....	....	....	....	....
	Pittsburgh Hornets	AHL	38	16	15	7	2280	144	1	3.79	....	....	....	....	....	6	3	3	0	385	20	0	3.12	....	....	....	....
1946-47	Pittsburgh Hornets	AHL	40	23	12	5	2400	104	*7	*2.60	....	....	....	....	....	12	7	5	0	720	29	1	2.42	....	....	....	....
	Hollywood Wolves	PCHL	22	....	....	....	1320	33	5	*1.50	....	....	....	....	....	....	....	....	....	....	....	....	....	....	....	....	....
1947-48	Pittsburgh Hornets	AHL	68	38	18	12	4080	170	*5	*2.50	....	....	....	....	....	2	0	2	0	130	6	0	2.77	....	....	....	....
1948-49	Pittsburgh Hornets	AHL	68	39	19	10	4080	175	6	*2.57	....	....	....	....	....	....	....	....	....	....	....	....	....	....	....	....	....
	NHL Totals		5	0	4	1	300	20	0	4.00	....	....	....	....	....	....	....	....	....	....	....	....	....	....	....	....	....

AHL First All-Star Team (1947, 1948, 1949) • Won Harry "Hap" Holmes Memorial Award (fewest goals against - AHL) (1948, 1949) • Suffered career-ending eye injury in training camp, September 19, 1949.

• BAUMAN, Gary

Gary Glenwood G – L. 5'11", 175 lbs. b: Innisfail, Alta., 7/21/1940.

Season	Club	League	GP	W	L	T	Mins	GA	SO	Avg	AAvg	Eff	SA	S%	SAPG	GP	W	L	T	Mins	GA	SO	Avg	Eff	SA	S%	SAPG
1958-59	Prince Albert Mintos	SJHL	25	....	....	....	1500	104	0	4.16	....	....	....	....	....	4	....	....	....	240	10	0	*2.50	....	....	....	....
1959-60	Prince Albert Mintos	SJHL	55	....	....	....	3320	212	4	3.83	....	....	....	....	....	7	....	....	....	420	28	0	4.00	....	....	....	....
1960-61	Michigan Tech Huskies	WCHA	DID NOT PLAY – FRESHMAN																								
1961-62	Michigan Tech Huskies	WCHA	25	24	1	0	1500	61	0	2.44	....	....	....	....	....	....	....	....	....	....	....	....	....	....	....	....	....
1962-63	Michigan Tech Huskies	WCHA	26	16	9	1	1560	70	3	2.69	....	....	....	....	....	....	....	....	....	....	....	....	....	....	....	....	....
1963-64	Michigan Tech Huskies	NCAA	24	12	12	0	1440	67	3	2.79	....	....	....	....	....	....	....	....	....	....	....	....	....	....	....	....	....
1964-65	Omaha Knights	CPHL	43	22	16	5	2580	159	1	3.70	....	....	....	....	....	6	2	4	0	360	19	*1	3.17	....	....	....	....
1965-66	Quebec Aces	AHL	52	*36	11	4	3142	154	4	2.94	....	....	....	....	....	6	2	4	0	360	25	0	4.17	....	....	....	....
1966-67	Montreal Canadiens	NHL	2	1	1	0	120	5	0	2.50	2.57	....	....	....	....	....	....	....	....	....	....	....	....	....	....	....	....
	Quebec Aces	AHL	40	21	15	4	2330	128	2	3.30	....	....	....	....	....	5	2	3	0	300	18	0	3.60	....	....	....	....
1967-68	Minnesota North Stars	NHL	26	5	13	5	1294	75	0	3.48	3.89	....	....	....	....	....	....	....	....	....	....	....	....	....	....	....	....
	Rochester Americans	AHL	3	0	2	0	140	10	0	4.29	....	....	....	....	....	....	....	....	....	....	....	....	....	....	....	....	....
1968-69	Minnesota North Stars	NHL	7	0	4	1	304	22	0	4.34	4.50	....	....	....	....	....	....	....	....	....	....	....	....	....	....	....	....
	Memphis South Stars	CHL	6	....	....	....	360	30	0	5.00	....	....	....	....	....	....	....	....	....	....	....	....	....	....	....	....	....
1969-70			STATISTICS NOT AVAILABLE																								
1970-71	Calgary Stampeders	ASHL	STATISTICS NOT AVAILABLE																								
1971-72	Calgary Stampeders	PrSHL	3	3	0	0	180	6	0	2.00	....	....	....	....	....	....	....	....	....	....	....	....	....	....	....	....	....
	NHL Totals		35	6	18	6	1718	102	0	3.56	....	....	....	....	....	....	....	....	....	....	....	....	....	....	....	....	....

WCHA First All-Star Team (1962, 1963, 1964) • NCAA West First All-American Team (1963, 1964) • Played in NHL All-Star Game (1967)

Signed as a free agent by **Montreal**, September 20, 1964. Claimed by **Minnesota** from **Montreal** in Expansion Draft, June 6, 1967. Claimed by **Vancouver** (WHL) from **Minnesota** in Reverse Draft, June 12, 1969.

• BEAUPRE, Don

Donald William G – L. 5'10", 172 lbs. b: Waterloo, Ont., 9/19/1961. Minnesota's 2nd, 37th overall in 1980.

Season	Club	League	GP	W	L	T	Mins	GA	SO	Avg	AAvg	Eff	SA	S%	SAPG	GP	W	L	T	Mins	GA	SO	Avg	Eff	SA	S%	SAPG
1978-79	Sudbury Wolves	OMJHL	54	....	....	....	3248	260	2	4.78	....	....	....	....	....	10	....	....	....	600	44	0	4.40	....	....	....	....
1979-80	Sudbury Wolves	OMJHL	59	28	29	2	3447	248	0	4.32	....	....	....	....	....	9	5	4	....	552	38	0	4.13	....	....	....	....
1980-81	Minnesota North Stars	DN-Cup	1	0	1	0	60	3	0	3.00	....	....	....	....	....	....	....	....	....	....	....	....	....	....	....	....	....
	Minnesota North Stars	NHL	44	18	14	11	2585	138	0	3.20	2.58	3.36	1313	.895	30.5	6	4	2	....	360	26	0	4.33	....	....	....	....
1981-82	Minnesota North Stars	NHL	29	11	8	9	1634	101	0	3.71	2.86	4.12	909	.889	33.4	2	0	1	....	60	4	0	4.00	....	....	....	....
	Nashville South Stars	CHL	5	2	3	0	299	25	0	5.02	....	....	....	....	....	....	....	....	....	....	....	....	....	....	....	....	....
1982-83	Minnesota North Stars	NHL	36	19	10	5	2011	120	0	3.58	2.87	4.10	1048	.885	31.3	4	2	2	....	245	20	0	4.90	....	....	....	....
	Birmingham South Stars	CHL	10	8	2	0	599	31	0	3.11	....	....	....	....	....	....	....	....	....	....	....	....	....	....	....	....	....
1983-84	Minnesota North Stars	NHL	33	16	13	2	1791	123	0	4.12	3.25	5.22	971	.873	32.5	13	6	7	....	782	40	1	3.07	3.23	380	.895	29.2
	Salt Lake Golden Eagles	CHL	7	2	5	0	419	30	0	4.30	....	....	....	....	....	....	....	....	....	....	....	....	....	....	....	....	....
1984-85	Minnesota North Stars	NHL	31	10	17	3	1770	109	1	3.69	2.94	4.31	934	.883	31.7	4	1	1	....	184	12	0	3.91	5.87	80	.850	26.1
1985-86	Minnesota North Stars	NHL	52	25	20	6	3073	182	1	3.55	2.76	3.82	1690	.892	33.0	5	2	3	....	300	17	0	3.40	3.66	158	.892	31.6
1986-87	Minnesota North Stars	NHL	47	17	20	6	2622	174	1	3.98	3.38	4.81	1439	.879	32.9	....	....	....	....	....	....	....	....	....	....	....	....
1987-88	Minnesota North Stars	NHL	43	10	22	3	2288	161	0	4.22	3.53	5.41	1257	.872	33.0	....	....	....	....	....	....	....	....	....	....	....	....
1988-89	Minnesota North Stars	NHL	1	0	1	0	59	3	0	3.05	2.54	3.52	26	.885	26.4	....	....	....	....	....	....	....	....	....	....	....	....
	Kalamazoo Wings	IHL	3	1	2	0	179	9	1	3.02	....	....	....	....	....	....	....	....	....	....	....	....	....	....	....	....	....
	Washington Capitals	NHL	11	5	4	0	578	28	1	2.91	2.42	3.03	269	.896	27.9	....	....	....	....	....	....	....	....	....	....	....	....
	Baltimore Skipjacks	AHL	30	14	12	2	1715	102	0	3.57	....	....	....	....	....	....	....	....	....	....	....	....	....	....	....	....	....
1989-90	Washington Capitals	Fr-Tour	2	....	....	....	91	8	....	5.27	....	....	....	....	....	....	....	....	....	....	....	....	....	....	....	....	....
	Washington Capitals	NHL	48	23	18	5	2793	150	2	3.22	2.72	3.55	1362	.890	29.3	8	4	3	....	401	18	0	2.69	2.59	187	.904	28.0
1990-91	Washington Capitals	NHL	45	20	18	3	2572	113	*5	2.64	2.36	2.72	1095	.897	25.5	11	5	5	....	624	29	*1	2.79	2.75	294	.901	28.3
	Baltimore Skipjacks	AHL	2	2	0	0	120	3	0	1.50	....	....	....	....	....	....	....	....	....	....	....	....	....	....	....	....	....
1991-92	Washington Capitals	NHL	54	29	17	6	3108	166	1	3.20	2.86	3.70	1435	.884	27.7	7	3	4	....	419	22	0	3.15	3.27	212	.896	30.4
	Baltimore Skipjacks	AHL	3	1	1	1	184	10	0	3.26	....	....	....	....	....	....	....	....	....	....	....	....	....	....	....	....	....
1992-93	Washington Capitals	NHL	58	27	23	5	3282	181	1	3.31	2.83	3.92	1530	.882	28.0	2	1	1	....	119	9	0	4.54	6.29	65	.862	32.8
1993-94	Washington Capitals	NHL	53	24	16	8	2853	135	2	2.84	2.72	3.42	1122	.880	23.6	8	5	2	....	429	21	1	2.94	3.23	191	.890	26.7
1994-95	Ottawa Senators	NHL	38	8	25	3	2161	121	1	3.36	3.54	3.48	1167	.896	32.4	....	....	....	....	....	....	....	....	....	....	....	....
1995-96	Ottawa Senators	NHL	33	6	23	0	1770	110	1	3.73	3.72	4.60	892	.877	30.2	....	....	....	....	....	....	....	....	....	....	....	....
	Toronto Maple Leafs	NHL	8	0	5	0	336	26	0	4.64	4.62	7.10	170	.847	30.4	2	0	0	....	20	2	0	6.00	9.23	13	.846	39.0
1996-97	Toronto Maple Leafs	NHL	3	0	3	0	110	10	0	5.45	5.87	9.08	60	.833	32.7	....	....	....	....	....	....	....	....	....	....	....	....
	St. John's Maple Leafs	AHL	47	24	16	4	2623	128	3	2.93	....	....	....	....	....	....	....	....	....	....	....	....	....	....	....	....	....
	Utah Grizzlies	IHL	4	2	2	0	238	13	0	3.27	....	....	....	....	....	7	3	4	....	438	17	1	2.32	....	....	....	....
	NHL Totals		667	268	277	75	37396	2151	17	3.45	....	....	18689	.885	30.0	72	33	31	....	3943	220	3	3.35	....	....	....	....

OMJHL First All-Star Team (1980) • Played in NHL All-Star Game (1981, 1992)

Traded to **Washington** by **Minnesota** for rights to Claudio Scremin, November 1, 1988. Traded to **Ottawa** by **Washington** for Ottawa's 5th round choice (Benoit Gratton) in 1995 Entry Draft, January 18, 1995. Traded to **NY Islanders** by **Ottawa** with Martin Straka and Bryan Berard for Damian Rhodes and Wade Redden, January 23, 1996. Traded to **Toronto** by **NY Islanders** with Kirk Muller to complete transaction that sent Damian Rhodes and Ken Belanger to NY Islanders (January 23, 1996), January 23, 1996.

Season	Club	League	GP	W	L	T	Mins	GA	SO	Avg	AAvg	Eff	SA	S%	SAPG	GP	W	L	T	Mins	GA	SO	Avg	Eff	SA	S%	SAPG
			REGULAR SEASON													PLAYOFFS											

• BEAUREGARD, Stephane

G – R. 5'11", 190 lbs. b: Cowansville, Que., 1/10/1968. Winnipeg's 3rd, 52nd overall in 1988.

Season	Club	League	GP	W	L	T	Mins	GA	SO	Avg	AAvg	Eff	SA	S%	SAPG	GP	W	L	T	Mins	GA	SO	Avg	Eff	SA	S%	SAPG
1986-87	St-Jean Castors	QMJHL	13	6	7	0	785	58	0	4.43	....	....	....	....	....	5	1	3	....	260	26	0	6.00	....	....	....	....
1987-88	St-Jean Castors	QMJHL	66	38	20	3	3766	229	2	3.65	....	....	....	....	....	7	3	4	....	423	34	0	4.82	....	....	....	....
1988-89	Moncton Hawks	AHL	15	4	8	2	824	62	0	4.51	....	....	....	....	....	....	....	....	....	....	....	....	....	....	....	....	....
	Fort Wayne Komets	IHL	16	9	5	0	830	43	0	3.10	....	....	....	....	....	9	4	4	....	484	21	*1	*2.60	....	....	....	....
1989-90	**Winnipeg Jets**	**NHL**	**19**	**7**	**8**	**3**	**1079**	**59**	**0**	**3.28**	**2.78**	**3.40**	**570**	**.896**	**31.7**	**4**	**1**	**3**	....	**238**	**12**	**0**	**3.03**	**3.46**	**105**	**.886**	**26.5**
	Fort Wayne Komets	IHL	33	20	8	3	1949	115	0	3.54	....	....	....	....	....	....	....	....	....	....	....	....	....	....	....	....	....
1990-91	**Winnipeg Jets**	**NHL**	**16**	**3**	**10**	**1**	**836**	**55**	**0**	**3.95**	**3.56**	**5.14**	**423**	**.870**	**30.4**	....	....	....	....	....	....	....	....	....	....	....	....
	Moncton Hawks	AHL	9	3	4	1	504	20	1	2.38	....	....	....	....	....	1	1	0	....	60	1	0	1.00	....	....	....	....
	Fort Wayne Komets	IHL	32	14	13	2	1761	109	0	3.71	....	....	....	....	....	*19	*10	9	....	*1158	57	0	2.95	....	....	....	....
1991-92	**Winnipeg Jets**	**NHL**	**26**	**6**	**8**	**6**	**1267**	**61**	**2**	**2.89**	**2.58**	**2.89**	**611**	**.900**	**28.9**	....	....	....	....	....	....	....	....	....	....	....	....
1992-93	**Philadelphia Flyers**	**NHL**	**16**	**3**	**9**	**0**	**802**	**59**	**0**	**4.41**	**3.78**	**6.42**	**405**	**.854**	**30.3**	....	....	....	....	....	....	....	....	....	....	....	....
	Hershey Bears	AHL	13	5	5	3	794	48	0	3.63	....	....	....	....	....	....	....	....	....	....	....	....	....	....	....	....	....
1993-94	**Winnipeg Jets**	**NHL**	**13**	**0**	**4**	**1**	**418**	**34**	**0**	**4.88**	**4.70**	**7.86**	**211**	**.839**	**30.3**	....	....	....	....	....	....	....	....	....	....	....	....
	Moncton Hawks	AHL	37	18	11	6	2082	121	1	3.49	....	....	....	....	....	*21	*12	9	....	*1305	57	*2	2.62	....	....	....	....
1994-95	Springfield Falcons	AHL	24	10	11	3	1381	73	2	3.17	....	....	....	....	....	....	....	....	....	....	....	....	....	....	....	....	....
1995-96	San Francisco Spiders	IHL	*69	*36	24	8	*4022	207	1	3.09	....	....	....	....	....	4	1	3	....	241	10	0	2.49	....	....	....	....
1996-97	Quebec Rafales	IHL	67	35	20	11	3945	174	4	2.65	....	....	....	....	....	9	5	3	....	498	19	0	2.29	....	....	....	....
1997-98	Chicago Wolves	IHL	18	10	6	0	917	49	1	3.20	....	....	....	....	....	14	10	4	....	820	36	1	2.63	....	....	....	....
1998-99	HC Davos	Switz.	*45	....	....	....	2638	151	....	3.44	....	....	....	....	....	6	2	4	....	370	23	0	3.73	....	....	....	....
99-2000	Schwenningen Wild Wings	Germany	*58	....	....	....	*3301	178	4	3.24	....	....	....	....	....	....	....	....	....	....	....	....	....	....	....	....	....
	NHL Totals		**90**	**19**	**39**	**11**	**4402**	**268**	**2**	**3.65**	....	....	**2220**	**.879**	**30.3**	**4**	**1**	**3**	....	**238**	**12**	**0**	**3.03**	....	**105**	**.886**	**26.5**

QMJHL First All-Star Team (1988) • Canadian Major Junior Goaltender of the year (1988) • IHL First All-Star Team (1996) • Won James Gatschene Memorial Trophy (MVP- IHL) (1996)

Traded to **Buffalo** by **Winnipeg** for Christian Ruuttu and future considerations, June 15, 1992. Traded to **Chicago** by **Buffalo** with Buffalo's 4th round choice (Eric Daze) in 1993 Entry Draft for Dominik Hasek, August 7, 1992. Traded to **Winnipeg** by **Chicago** for Christian Ruuttu, August 10, 1992. Traded to **Philadelphia** by **Winnipeg** for future considerations, October 1, 1992. Traded to **Winnipeg** by **Philadelphia** for future considerations, June 11, 1993. Signed as a free agent by **Washington**, August 20, 1997.

• BEDARD, Jim

James Arthur G – L. 5'10", 181 lbs. b: Niagara Falls, Ont., 11/14/1956. Washington's 6th, 91st overall in 1976.

Season	Club	League	GP	W	L	T	Mins	GA	SO	Avg	AAvg	Eff	SA	S%	SAPG	GP	W	L	T	Mins	GA	SO	Avg	Eff	SA	S%	SAPG
1972-73	Welland Cougars	OHA-B	42	....	....	....	2485	178	0	4.30	....	....	....	....	....	....	....	....	....	....	....	....	....	....	....	....	....
1973-74	Sudbury Wolves	OMJHL	28	....	....	....	1635	117	0	4.29	....	....	....	....	....	....	....	....	....	....	....	....	....	....	....	....	....
1974-75	Sudbury Wolves	OMJHL	51	....	....	....	3060	187	0	3.67	....	....	....	....	....	13	....	....	....	750	43	0	3.44	....	....	....	....
1975-76	Sudbury Wolves	OMJHL	58	....	....	....	3328	177	1	3.15	....	....	....	....	....	17	9	7	1	1000	62	1	3.60	....	....	....	....
1976-77	Dayton Gems	IHL	48	....	....	....	2693	168	0	3.74	....	....	....	....	....	2	....	....	....	120	9	0	4.50	....	....	....	....
1977-78	**Washington Capitals**	**NHL**	**43**	**11**	**23**	**7**	**2492**	**152**	**1**	**3.66**	**3.44**	....	....	....	....	....	....	....	....	....	....	....	....	....	....	....	....
	Hershey Bears	AHL	14	6	7	1	766	39	0	3.05	....	....	....	....	....	....	....	....	....	....	....	....	....	....	....	....	....
1978-79	**Washington Capitals**	**NHL**	**30**	**6**	**17**	**6**	**1740**	**126**	**0**	**4.34**	**3.86**	....	....	....	....	....	....	....	....	....	....	....	....	....	....	....	....
	Hershey Bears	AHL	26	9	11	2	1404	88	0	3.76	....	....	....	....	....	....	....	....	....	....	....	....	....	....	....	....	....
1979-80	Hershey Bears	AHL	2	....	....	....	60	9	0	9.00	....	....	....	....	....	....	....	....	....	....	....	....	....	....	....	....	....
	Cincinnati Stingers	CHL	8	3	4	0	385	32	0	4.99	....	....	....	....	....	....	....	....	....	....	....	....	....	....	....	....	....
	Rochester Americans	AHL	6	....	....	....	339	20	0	3.54	....	....	....	....	....	....	....	....	....	....	....	....	....	....	....	....	....
	Tulsa Oilers	CHL	3	0	3	0	177	10	0	3.39	....	....	....	....	....	....	....	....	....	....	....	....	....	....	....	....	....
	Dayton Gems	IHL	16	....	....	....	858	55	0	3.85	....	....	....	....	....	....	....	....	....	....	....	....	....	....	....	....	....
1980-81	TPS Turku	Finland	29	....	....	....	....	112	0	3.90	....	....	....	....	....	....	....	....	....	....	....	....	....	....	....	....	....
1981-82	TPS Turku	Finland	27	....	....	....	1620	95	1	3.52	....	....	....	....	....	....	....	....	....	....	....	....	....	....	....	....	....
1982-83	Kettera Imatra	Finland-2	11	....	....	....	380	44	0	6.95	....	....	....	....	....	....	....	....	....	....	....	....	....	....	....	....	....
1983-84	TuTo Turku	Finland-2	35	....	....	....	1172	130	....	6.66	....	....	....	....	....	....	....	....	....	....	....	....	....	....	....	....	....
1984-85	TuTo Turku	Finland-2	44	....	....	....	2640	139	0	3.28	....	....	....	....	....	....	....	....	....	....	....	....	....	....	....	....	....
1985-86	TuTo Turku	Finland-2	44	....	....	....	1413	127	0	5.39	....	....	....	....	....	....	....	....	....	....	....	....	....	....	....	....	....
1986-87	TuTo Turku	Finland-2	34	....	....	....	2040	80	....	2.36	....	....	....	....	....	....	....	....	....	....	....	....	....	....	....	....	....
1987-88	TuTo Turku	Finland-2	36	....	....	....	2160	86	....	2.39	....	....	....	....	....	....	....	....	....	....	....	....	....	....	....	....	....
1988-89	HPK Hameenlinna	Finland	31	....	....	....	1737	123	0	4.25	....	....	....	....	....	....	....	....	....	....	....	....	....	....	....	....	....
1989-90	Kiekko-67 Turku	Finland-2	31	....	....	....	1577	122	1	4.64	....	....	....	....	....	....	....	....	....	....	....	....	....	....	....	....	....
1990-91	Kiekko-67 Turku	Finland-2	37	19	12	3	2177	108	0	2.98	....	....	....	....	....	....	....	....	....	....	....	....	....	....	....	....	....
1991-92	Kiekko-67 Turku	Finland-2	40	19	18	3	2310	161	0	4.18	....	....	....	....	....	....	....	....	....	....	....	....	....	....	....	....	....
1992-93	Turku HT	Finland-3	STATISTICS NOT AVAILABLE																								
1993-94	TuTo Turku	Finland-2	37	....	....	....	2220	132	0	3.57	....	....	....	....	....	5	4	1	....	300	12	0	2.40	....	....	....	....
	NHL Totals		**73**	**17**	**40**	**13**	**4232**	**278**	**1**	**3.94**	....	....	....	....	....	....	....	....	....	....	....	....	....	....	....	....	....

OMJHL First All-Star Team (1976)

• BEHREND, Marc

G – L. 6'1", 180 lbs. b: Madison, WI, 1/11/1961. Winnipeg's 5th, 85th overall in 1981.

Season	Club	League	GP	W	L	T	Mins	GA	SO	Avg	AAvg	Eff	SA	S%	SAPG	GP	W	L	T	Mins	GA	SO	Avg	Eff	SA	S%	SAPG
1980-81	University of Wisconsin	WCHA	16	11	4	1	913	50	0	3.29	....	....	....	....	....	....	....	....	....	....	....	....	....	....	....	....	....
1981-82	University of Wisconsin	WCHA	25	21	3	1	1502	65	2	2.60	....	....	....	....	....	....	....	....	....	....	....	....	....	....	....	....	....
1982-83	University of Wisconsin	WCHA	19	17	1	1	1315	49	2	*2.24	....	....	....	....	....	....	....	....	....	....	....	....	....	....	....	....	....
1983-84	United States	Nat-Team	33	....	....	....	1898	100	....	3.16	....	....	....	....	....	....	....	....	....	....	....	....	....	....	....	....	....
	United States	Olympics	4	1	2	1	200	11	0	3.30	....	....	....	....	....	....	....	....	....	....	....	....	....	....	....	....	....
	Winnipeg Jets	**NHL**	**6**	**2**	**4**	**0**	**351**	**32**	**0**	**5.47**	**4.31**	**9.51**	**184**	**.826**	**31.5**	**2**	**0**	**2**	**0**	**121**	**9**	**0**	**4.46**	**4.41**	**91**	**.901**	**45.1**
1984-85	**Winnipeg Jets**	**NHL**	**24**	**8**	**10**	**3**	**1218**	**87**	**1**	**4.45**	**3.55**	**6.20**	**624**	**.861**	**30.7**	**4**	**1**	**1**	**0**	**179**	**10**	**0**	**3.35**	**3.42**	**98**	**.898**	**32.8**
	Sherbrooke Canadiens	AHL	7	2	3	2	427	25	0	3.51	....	....	....	....	....	....	....	....	....	....	....	....	....	....	....	....	....
1985-86	**Winnipeg Jets**	**NHL**	**9**	**2**	**5**	**0**	**422**	**41**	**0**	**5.83**	**4.56**	**10.87**	**220**	**.814**	**31.3**	**1**	**0**	**0**	**0**	**12**	**0**	**0**	**0.00**	**0.00**	**7**	**1.000**	**35.0**
	Sherbrooke Canadiens	AHL	35	16	5	2	2028	132	1	3.91	....	....	....	....	....	....	....	....	....	....	....	....	....	....	....	....	....
1986-87	Sherbrooke Canadiens	AHL	19	8	5	0	1124	62	0	3.31	....	....	....	....	....	1	0	1	0	59	3	0	3.05	....	....	....	....
	NHL Totals		**39**	**12**	**19**	**3**	**1991**	**160**	**1**	**4.82**	....	....	**1028**	**.844**	**31.0**	**7**	**1**	**3**	**0**	**312**	**19**	**0**	**3.65**	....	**196**	**.903**	**37.7**

NCAA Championship All-Tournament Team (1981, 1983) • NCAA Championship Tournament MVP (1981, 1983) • WCHA Second All-Star Team (1982)

• BELANGER, Yves

G – L. 5'11", 170 lbs. b: Baie Comeau, Que., 9/30/1952.

Season	Club	League	GP	W	L	T	Mins	GA	SO	Avg	AAvg	Eff	SA	S%	SAPG	GP	W	L	T	Mins	GA	SO	Avg	Eff	SA	S%	SAPG
1969-70	Sherbrooke Castors	QJHL	47	....	....	....	2780	225	0	4.86	....	....	....	....	....	....	....	....	....	....	....	....	....	....	....	....	....
1970-71	Sherbrooke Castors	QJHL	39	....	....	....	2340	182	0	4.67	....	....	....	....	....	8	....	....	....	460	50	0	6.52	....	....	....	....
1971-72	Sherbrooke Castors	QMJHL	38	....	....	....	2280	188	2	4.95	....	....	....	....	....	1	....	....	....	39	4	0	6.15	....	....	....	....
1972-73	Syracuse Blazers	EHL	38	....	....	....	2255	90	*5	2.39	....	....	....	....	....	7	7	0	0	436	11	1	1.51	....	....	....	....
1973-74	Jacksonville Barons	AHL	54	17	27	4	2878	199	0	4.15	....	....	....	....	....	....	....	....	....	....	....	....	....	....	....	....	....
1974-75	**St. Louis Blues**	**NHL**	**11**	**6**	**3**	**2**	**640**	**29**	**1**	**2.72**	**2.45**	....	....	....	....	....	....	....	....	....	....	....	....	....	....	....	....
	Denver Spurs	CHL	36	19	13	3	2060	105	0	3.06	....	....	....	....	....	....	....	....	....	....	....	....	....	....	....	....	....
1975-76	**St. Louis Blues**	**NHL**	**31**	**11**	**17**	**1**	**1763**	**113**	**0**	**3.85**	**3.50**	....	....	....	....	....	....	....	....	....	....	....	....	....	....	....	....
	Providence Reds	AHL	10	3	4	3	620	37	0	3.58	....	....	....	....	....	2	0	2	0	120	8	0	4.00	....	....	....	....
1976-77	**St. Louis Blues**	**NHL**	**3**	**2**	**0**	**0**	**140**	**7**	**0**	**3.00**	**2.79**	....	....	....	....	....	....	....	....	....	....	....	....	....	....	....	....
	Kansas City Blues	CHL	31	21	4	4	1826	83	1	2.73	....	....	....	....	....	....	....	....	....	....	....	....	....	....	....	....	....
1977-78	**St. Louis Blues**	**NHL**	**3**	**0**	**3**	**0**	**144**	**15**	**0**	**6.25**	**5.87**	....	....	....	....	....	....	....	....	....	....	....	....	....	....	....	....
	Atlanta Flames	**NHL**	**17**	**7**	**8**	**0**	**937**	**55**	**1**	**3.52**	**3.30**	....	....	....	....	....	....	....	....	....	....	....	....	....	....	....	....
	Salt Lake Golden Eagles	CHL	9	5	3	0	492	20	1	2.44	....	....	....	....	....	....	....	....	....	....	....	....	....	....	....	....	....
1978-79	**Atlanta Flames**	**NHL**	**5**	**1**	**2**	**0**	**182**	**21**	**0**	**6.92**	**6.13**	....	....	....	....	....	....	....	....	....	....	....	....	....	....	....	....
	Philadelphia Firebirds	AHL	22	4	14	1	1235	108	0	5.25	....	....	....	....	....	....	....	....	....	....	....	....	....	....	....	....	....
1979-80	**Boston Bruins**	**NHL**	**8**	**2**	**0**	**3**	**328**	**19**	**0**	**3.48**	**3.08**	....	....	....	....	....	....	....	....	....	....	....	....	....	....	....	....
	Binghamton Dusters	AHL	25	7	13	1	1334	95	0	4.27	....	....	....	....	....	....	....	....	....	....	....	....	....	....	....	....	....
1980-81	Charlottetown Islanders	PEI-Sr.	STATISTICS NOT AVAILABLE																								
1981-82	Cap Pele Caps	NBHA-I	22	....	....	....	1296	69	*1	*3.19	....	....	....	....	....	....	....	....	....	....	....	....	....	....	....	....	....
1982-83	Cap Pele Caps	NBHA-I	21	....	....	....	1226	81	0	*3.96	....	....	....	....	....	7	3	4	0	420	19	0	2.72	....	....	....	....

Season	Club	League	REGULAR SEASON GP	W	L	T	Mins	GA	SO	Avg	AAvg	Eff	SA	S%	SAPG	PLAYOFFS GP	W	L	T	Mins	GA	SO	Avg	Eff	SA	S%	SAPG
1983-84	Charlottetown GJ's	PEI-Sr.	STATISTICS NOT AVAILABLE																								
1984-1986			OUT OF HOCKEY – RETIRED																								
1986-87	Charlottetown Islanders	NBSHL	2	2	0	0	120	6	0	3.00	....	....	....	....	....	....	....	....	....	....	....	....	....	....	....	....	....
	NHL Totals		**78**	**29**	**33**	**6**	**4134**	**259**	**2**	**3.76**	....	....	....	....	....	....	....	....	....	....	....	....	....	....	....	....	....

EHL South First All-Star Team (1973) • Won George L. Davis Jr. Trophy (fewest goals against - EHL) (1973) • CHL First All-Star Team (1977) • Shared Terry Sawchuk Trophy (fewest goals against - CHL) with Gord McRae (1977)

Signed as a free agent by **Cleveland** (WHA), August, 1972. Traded to **St. Louis** by **Cleveland** (WHA) for cash, August, 1974. Traded to **Atlanta** by **St. Louis** with Bob MacMillan, Dick Redmond and St. Louis' 2nd round choice (Mike Perovich) in 1979 Entry Draft for Phil Myre, Curt Bennett and Barry Gibbs, December 12, 1977. Signed as a free agent by **Boston**, October 8, 1979.

• BELFOUR, Ed

Edward J. "The Eagle" G – L. 5'11", 192 lbs. b: Carman, Man., 4/21/1965.

Season	Club	League	GP	W	L	T	Mins	GA	SO	Avg	AAvg	Eff	SA	S%	SAPG	GP	W	L	T	Mins	GA	SO	Avg	Eff	SA	S%	SAPG
1982-83	Carman Collegiate	Hi-School	STATISTICS NOT AVAILABLE																								
1983-84	Winkler Flyers	MJHL	14	....	....	....	818	68	0	5.06	....	....	....	....	....	....	....	....	....	....	....	....	....	....	....	....	....
1984-85	Winkler Flyers	MJHL	34	....	....	....	1973	145	1	4.41	....	....	....	....	....	7	....	....	....	528	41	0	4.66	....	....	....	....
1985-86	Winkler Flyers	MJHL	33	....	....	....	1943	124	1	3.83	....	....	....	....	....	....	....	....	....	....	....	....	....	....	....	....	....
1986-87	University of North Dakota	WCHA	34	29	4	0	2049	81	3	2.43	....	....	....	....	....	....	....	....	....	....	....	....	....	....	....	....	....
1987-88	Saginaw Hawks	IHL	61	32	25	0	*3446	183	3	3.19	....	....	....	....	....	9	4	5	....	561	33	0	3.53	....	....	....	....
1988-89	**Chicago Blackhawks**	**NHL**	**23**	**4**	**12**	**3**	**1148**	**74**	**0**	**3.87**	**3.22**	**4.73**	**605**	**.878**	**31.6**	....	....	....	....	....	....	....	....	....	....	....	....
	Saginaw Hawks	IHL	29	12	10	0	1760	92	0	3.10	....	....	....	....	....	5	2	3	....	298	14	0	2.82	....	....	....	....
1989-90	Canada	Nat-Team	33	13	12	6	1808	93	0	3.08	....	....	....	....	....	....	....	....	....	....	....	....	....	....	....	....	....
	Chicago Blackhawks	**NHL**	....	....	....	....	....	....	....	....	....	....	....	....	....	**9**	**4**	**2**	....	**409**	**17**	**0**	**2.49**	**2.12**	**200**	**.915**	**29.3**
1990-91	**Chicago Blackhawks**	**NHL**	***74**	***43**	**19**	**7**	***4127**	**170**	**4**	***2.47**	**2.19**	**2.23**	**1883**	**.910**	**27.4**	**6**	**2**	**4**	....	**295**	**20**	**0**	**4.07**	**4.45**	**183**	**.891**	**37.2**
1991-92	Canada	Can-Cup	DID NOT PLAY – SPARE GOALTENDER																								
	Chicago Blackhawks	**NHL**	**52**	**21**	**18**	**10**	**2928**	**132**	***5**	**2.70**	**2.40**	**2.87**	**1241**	**.894**	**25.4**	**18**	**12**	**4**	....	**949**	**39**	**1**	***2.47**	**2.42**	**398**	**.902**	**25.2**
1992-93	**Chicago Blackhawks**	**NHL**	***71**	**41**	**18**	**11**	***4106**	**177**	***7**	**2.59**	**2.20**	**2.44**	**1880**	**.906**	**27.5**	**4**	**0**	**4**	....	**249**	**13**	**0**	**3.13**	**4.19**	**97**	**.866**	**23.4**
1993-94	**Chicago Blackhawks**	**NHL**	**70**	**37**	**24**	**6**	**3998**	**178**	***7**	**2.67**	**2.55**	**2.51**	**1892**	**.906**	**28.4**	**6**	**2**	**4**	....	**360**	**15**	**0**	**2.50**	**1.96**	**191**	**.921**	**31.8**
1994-95	**Chicago Blackhawks**	**NHL**	**42**	**22**	**15**	**3**	**2450**	**93**	***5**	**2.28**	**2.37**	**2.14**	**990**	**.906**	**24.2**	**16**	**9**	**7**	....	**1014**	**37**	**1**	**2.19**	**1.69**	**479**	**.923**	**28.3**
1995-96	**Chicago Blackhawks**	**NHL**	**50**	**22**	**17**	**10**	**2956**	**135**	**1**	**2.74**	**2.72**	**2.69**	**1373**	**.902**	**27.9**	**9**	**6**	**3**	....	**666**	**23**	**1**	**2.07**	**1.47**	**323**	**.929**	**29.1**
1996-97	**Chicago Blackhawks**	**NHL**	**33**	**11**	**15**	**6**	**1966**	**88**	**1**	**2.69**	**2.89**	**2.50**	**946**	**.907**	**28.9**	....	....	....	....	....	....	....	....	....	....	....	....
	San Jose Sharks	**NHL**	**13**	**3**	**9**	**0**	**757**	**43**	**1**	**3.41**	**3.67**	**3.95**	**371**	**.884**	**29.4**	....	....	....	....	....	....	....	....	....	....	....	....
1997-98	**Dallas Stars**	**NHL**	**61**	**37**	**12**	**10**	**3581**	**112**	**9**	***1.88**	**2.22**	**1.58**	**1335**	**.916**	**22.4**	**17**	**10**	**7**	....	**1039**	**31**	**1**	***1.79**	**1.39**	**399**	**.922**	**23.0**
1998-99♦	**Dallas Stars**	**NHL**	**61**	**35**	**15**	**9**	**3536**	**117**	**5**	**1.99**	**2.35**	**1.70**	**1373**	**.915**	**23.3**	***23**	***16**	**7**	....	***1544**	**43**	***3**	***1.67**	**1.16**	**617**	**.930**	**24.0**
99-2000	**Dallas Stars**	**NHL**	**62**	**32**	**21**	**7**	**3620**	**127**	**4**	**2.10**	**2.39**	**1.70**	**1571**	**.919**	**26.0**	***23**	**14**	**9**	....	**1443**	**45**	***4**	**1.87**	**1.29**	**651**	**.931**	**27.1**
	NHL Totals		**612**	**308**	**195**	**82**	**35173**	**1446**	**49**	**2.47**	....	....	**15460**	**.906**	**26.4**	**131**	**75**	**51**	....	**7968**	**283**	**11**	**2.13**	....	**3538**	**.920**	**26.6**

WCHA First All-Star Team (1987) • NCAA Championship All-Tournament Team (1987) • IHL First All-Star Team (1988) • Shared Garry F. Longman Memorial Trophy (Top Rookie - IHL) with John Cullen (1988) • NHL All-Rookie Team (1991) • NHL First All-Star Team (1991, 1993) • Won Trico Goaltender Award (1991) • Won Calder Memorial Trophy (1991) • Won William M. Jennings Trophy (1991, 1993, 1995) • Won Vezina Trophy (1991, 1993) • NHL Second All-Star Team (1995) • Shared William M. Jennings Trophy with Roman Turek (1999) • Played in NHL All-Star Game (1992, 1993, 1996, 1998, 1999)

Signed as a free agent by **Chicago**, September 25, 1987. Traded to **San Jose** by **Chicago** for Chris Terreri, Ulf Dahlen and Michal Sykora, January 25, 1997. Signed as a free agent by **Dallas**, July 2, 1997.

• BELHUMEUR, Michel

G – L. 5'10", 160 lbs. b: Sorel, Que., 9/2/1949. Philadelphia's 4th, 40th overall in 1969.

Season	Club	League	GP	W	L	T	Mins	GA	SO	Avg	AAvg	Eff	SA	S%	SAPG	GP	W	L	T	Mins	GA	SO	Avg	Eff	SA	S%	SAPG
1964-65	Sorel Eperviers	QJHL	5	1	4	0	300	22	0	6.40	....	....	....	....	....	....	....	....	....	....	....	....	....	....	....	....	....
1965-66	Sorel Eperviers	QJHL	4	1	3	0	220	27	0	7.36	....	....	....	....	....	....	....	....	....	....	....	....	....	....	....	....	....
1966-67	Sorel Eperviers	QJHL	2	1	1	0	120	5	0	2.50	....	....	....	....	....	....	....	....	....	....	....	....	....	....	....	....	....
1967-68	Sorel Eperviers	QJHL	STATISTICS NOT AVAILABLE																								
1968-69	Drummondville Rangers	QJHL	34	....	....	....	2105	135	3	3.85	....	....	....	....	....	....	....	....	....	....	....	....	....	....	....	....	....
1969-70	Quebec Aces	AHL	2	....	....	....	100	10	0	6.00	....	....	....	....	....	....	....	....	....	....	....	....	....	....	....	....	....
	Charlotte Checkers	EHL	14	....	....	....	840	42	1	3.00	....	....	....	....	....	....	....	....	....	....	....	....	....	....	....	....	....
1970-71	Quebec Aces	AHL	37	12	15	8	2083	110	2	3.17	....	....	....	....	....	1	0	1	0	60	4	0	4.00	....	....	....	....
1971-72	Richmond Robins	AHL	45	20	17	8	2645	122	1	2.77	....	....	....	....	....	....	....	....	....	....	....	....	....	....	....	....	....
1972-73	**Philadelphia Flyers**	**NHL**	**23**	**9**	**7**	**3**	**1117**	**60**	**0**	**3.22**	**3.04**	....	....	....	....	**1**	**0**	**0**	....	**10**	**1**	**0**	**6.00**	....	....	....	....
	Richmond Robins	AHL	12	....	....	....	671	49	0	4.38	....	....	....	....	....	....	....	....	....	....	....	....	....	....	....	....	....
1973-74	Richmond Robins	AHL	45	13	23	7	2567	179	0	4.18	....	....	....	....	....	3	1	2	0	191	13	*1	4.08	....	....	....	....
1974-75	**Washington Capitals**	**NHL**	**35**	**0**	**24**	**3**	**1812**	**162**	**0**	**5.36**	**4.90**	....	....	....	....	....	....	....	....	....	....	....	....	....	....	....	....
1975-76	**Washington Capitals**	**NHL**	**7**	**0**	**5**	**1**	**377**	**32**	**0**	**5.09**	**4.62**	....	....	....	....	....	....	....	....	....	....	....	....	....	....	....	....
	Richmond Robins	AHL	45	19	24	2	2679	159	3	3.56	....	....	....	....	....	4	2	1	0	194	7	0	2.16	....	....	....	....
1976-77	Tulsa Oilers	CHL	34	17	12	3	1966	131	1	4.00	....	....	....	....	....	1	0	1	0	70	4	0	3.43	....	....	....	....
1977-78	Tulsa Oilers	CHL	24	8	14	0	1319	96	0	4.37	....	....	....	....	....	5	2	3	0	305	15	0	2.95	....	....	....	....
1978-79	Utica Mohawks	NEHL	24	....	....	....	1308	89	2	4.08	....	....	....	....	....	....	....	....	....	....	....	....	....	....	....	....	....
	New Jersey-Hampton Aces	NEHL	11	....	....	....	665	37	1	3.34	....	....	....	....	....	....	....	....	....	....	....	....	....	....	....	....	....
	NHL Totals		**65**	**9**	**36**	**7**	**3306**	**254**	**0**	**4.61**	....	....	....	....	....	**1**	**0**	**0**	....	**10**	**1**	**0**	**6.00**	....	....	....	....

AHL Second All-Star Team (1972)

Claimed by **Washington** from **Philadelphia** in Expansion Draft, June 12, 1974. Signed as a free agent by **Atlanta**, October 7, 1976.

• BELL, Gordie

G – L. 5'10", 164 lbs. b: Portage la Prairie, Man., 3/13/1925 d: 11/3/1980.

Season	Club	League	GP	W	L	T	Mins	GA	SO	Avg	AAvg	Eff	SA	S%	SAPG	GP	W	L	T	Mins	GA	SO	Avg	Eff	SA	S%	SAPG
1941-42	Portage Terriers	MJHL	17	*14	2	0	1000	77	0	*4.62	....	....	....	....	....	5	*5	0	0	300	22	0	*4.40	....	....	....	....
	Portage Terriers	Mem-Cup	10	9	1	0	600	52	0	5.20	....	....	....	....	....	....	....	....	....	....	....	....	....	....	....	....	....
1942-43	Buffalo Bisons	AHL	52	28	17	7	3220	125	*9	*2.33	....	....	....	....	....	9	*7	2	0	550	16	*1	*1.75	....	....	....	....
1943-44	Winnipeg Navy	WNDHL	10	....	....	....	600	35	0	3.50	....	....	....	....	....	....	....	....	....	....	....	....	....	....	....	....	....
	Cornwallis Navy	X-Games	2	2	0	0	120	6	0	3.00	....	....	....	....	....	....	....	....	....	....	....	....	....	....	....	....	....
	Cornwallis Navy	Al-Cup	5	4	1	0	300	15	0	3.00	....	....	....	....	....	....	....	....	....	....	....	....	....	....	....	....	....
1944-45	Cornwallis Navy	X-Games	5	....	....	....	250	24	0	5.76	....	....	....	....	....	....	....	....	....	....	....	....	....	....	....	....	....
1945-46	**Toronto Maple Leafs**	**NHL**	**8**	**3**	**5**	**0**	**480**	**31**	**0**	**3.88**	**3.55**	....	....	....	....	....	....	....	....	....	....	....	....	....	....	....	....
	Providence Reds	AHL	37	14	19	4	2220	152	1	4.10	....	....	....	....	....	2	0	2	0	120	7	0	3.50	....	....	....	....
1946-47	Pittsburgh Hornets	AHL	23	11	7	5	1380	80	1	3.48	....	....	....	....	....	....	....	....	....	....	....	....	....	....	....	....	....
	Hollywood Wolves	PCHL	26	....	....	....	1560	67	1	2.58	....	....	....	....	....	7	4	3	0	420	17	1	2.43	....	....	....	....
1947-48	Washington Lions	AHL	64	14	42	6	3840	332	1	5.19	....	....	....	....	....	....	....	....	....	....	....	....	....	....	....	....	....
1948-49	Fort Worth Rangers	USHL	13	5	5	3	780	57	0	4.38	....	....	....	....	....	....	....	....	....	....	....	....	....	....	....	....	....
	Springfield Indians	AHL	4	1	3	0	240	16	0	4.00	....	....	....	....	....	....	....	....	....	....	....	....	....	....	....	....	....
	Omaha Knights	USHL	36	21	7	7	2160	84	0	2.33	....	....	....	....	....	4	2	2	0	254	18	0	4.25	....	....	....	....
1949-50	Louisville Blades	USHL	29	13	13	3	1740	121	0	4.17	....	....	....	....	....	....	....	....	....	....	....	....	....	....	....	....	....
	Buffalo Bisons	AHL	36	17	14	5	2160	114	2	3.17	....	....	....	....	....	3	1	2	0	188	14	0	4.47	....	....	....	....
1950-51	Buffalo Bisons	AHL	7	5	2	0	420	23	0	3.29	....	....	....	....	....	....	....	....	....	....	....	....	....	....	....	....	....
	Springfield Indians	AHL	51	20	29	2	3120	186	2	3.58	....	....	....	....	....	2	0	2	0	120	15	0	7.50	....	....	....	....
1951-52	Syracuse Warriors	AHL	63	24	38	1	3820	244	0	3.83	....	....	....	....	....	....	....	....	....	....	....	....	....	....	....	....	....
1952-53	Syracuse Warriors	AHL	64	31	31	2	3870	200	*6	3.10	....	....	....	....	....	4	1	3	0	239	8	0	2.01	....	....	....	....
1953-54	Syracuse Warriors	AHL	49	21	25	3	2940	176	0	3.59	....	....	....	....	....	....	....	....	....	....	....	....	....	....	....	....	....
1954-55	Springfield Indians	AHL	10	2	8	0	600	47	0	4.70	....	....	....	....	....	....	....	....	....	....	....	....	....	....	....	....	....
1955-56	Springfield Indians	AHL	11	4	7	0	660	57	0	5.18	....	....	....	....	....	....	....	....	....	....	....	....	....	....	....	....	....
	Trois-Rivieres Lions	QHL	14	6	8	0	852	48	1	3.38	....	....	....	....	....	....	....	....	....	....	....	....	....	....	....	....	....
	New York Rangers	**NHL**	....	....	....	....	....	....	....	....	....	....	....	....	....	**2**	**1**	**1**	....	**120**	**9**	**0**	**4.50**	....	....	....	....
1956-57	Trois-Rivieres Lions	QHL	4	2	1	1	250	10	0	2.40	....	....	....	....	....	....	....	....	....	....	....	....	....	....	....	....	....
	Belleville McFarlands	EOHL	41	19	17	5	2460	154	0	3.75	....	....	....	....	....	9	4	5	0	540	30	*2	3.33	....	....	....	....
1957-58	Belleville McFarlands	EOHL	49	*29	17	3	2940	176	*4	3.59	....	....	....	....	....	30	21	8	1	1817	81	3	2.67	....	....	....	....
	Belleville McFarlands	Al-Cup	14	10	4	0	850	43	1	3.04	....	....	....	....	....	....	....	....	....	....	....	....	....	....	....	....	....

			REGULAR SEASON													PLAYOFFS											
Season	Club	League	GP	W	L	T	Mins	GA	SO	Avg	AAvg	Eff	SA	S%	SAPG	GP	W	L	T	Mins	GA	SO	Avg	Eff	SA	S%	SAPG
1958-59	Belleville McFarlands	EOHL	46	....	....	....	2760	156	*2	3.39	....	....	....	....	....	....	....	....	....	....	....	....	....	....	....	....	....
	Canada	WEC-A	6	5	1	0	360	9	2	1.50	....	....	....	....	....	....	....	....	....	....	....	....	....	....	....	....	....
1959-60	Belleville McFarlands	OHA-Sr.	9	....	....	....	500	39	0	4.68	....	....	....	....	....	....	....	....	....	....	....	....	....	....	....	....	....
	NHL Totals		**8**	**3**	**5**	**0**	**480**	**31**	**0**	**3.88**	....	....	....	....	....	**2**	**1**	**1**	....	**120**	**9**	**0**	**4.50**	....	....	....	....

• Brother of Joe • AHL First All-Star Team (1943) • USHL Second All-Star Team (1949)

Claimed by **NY Rangers** from **Buffalo** (AHL) in Inter-League Draft, May 8, 1943. • Rights returned to **Buffalo** (AHL) by **NY Rangers** after failing to come to contract terms. Traded to **Toronto** by **Buffalo** (AHL) for cash, September 22, 1945. Traded to **Washington** (AHL) by **Toronto** for cash with Toronto retaining right of recall, October 5, 1947. Traded to **Springfield** (AHL) by **Toronto** with Armand Lemieux, Leo Curick and Rod Roy for Eldie Kobussen, April 20, 1948. Traded to **Montreal** (Buffalo-AHL) by **Springfield** (AHL) with the rights to Sid McNabney for Hub Macey, December 21, 1948. Signed as a free agent by **NY Rangers**, March 22, 1956.

• BENEDICT, Clint

Clinton Stephen G – L. b: Ottawa, Ont., 9/26/1892 d: 11/12/1976. **HHOF**

Season	Club	League	GP	W	L	T	Mins	GA	SO	Avg	AAvg	Eff	SA	S%	SAPG	GP	W	L	T	Mins	GA	SO	Avg	Eff	SA	S%	SAPG
1909-10	Ottawa Stewartons	OCHL	7	5	2	0	420	21	0	*3.00	....	....	....	....	....	1	0	1	0	60	2	0	2.00	....	....	....	....
1910-11	Ottawa New Edinburghs	IPAHU	5	*5	0	0	300	18	0	*3.60	....	....	....	....	....	3	3	0	0	180	13	0	4.25	....	....	....	....
	Ottawa New Edinburghs	OCHL	6	2	3	1	360	24	0	4.00	....	....	....	....	....	....	....	....	....	....	....	....	....	....	....	....	....
1911-12	Ottawa New Edinburghs	IPAHU	11	*11	0	0	657	34	0	*3.11	....	....	....	....	....	4	*3	1	0	237	18	0	4.56	....	....	....	....
1912-13	Ottawa Senators	NHA	10	7	2	1	275	16	1	3.49	....	....	....	....	....	....	....	....	....	....	....	....	....	....	....	....	....
1913-14	Ottawa Senators	NHA	9	5	3	0	474	29	0	3.67	....	....	....	....	....	....	....	....	....	....	....	....	....	....	....	....	....
1914-15	Ottawa Senators	NHA	20	*14	6	0	1243	65	0	3.14	....	....	....	....	....	2	1	1	0	120	2	1	0.50	....	....	....	....
1915-16	Ottawa Senators	NHA	24	13	11	0	1447	72	*1	*2.99	....	....	....	....	....	....	....	....	....	....	....	....	....	....	....	....	....
1916-17	Ottawa Senators	NHA	18	*14	4	0	1103	50	*1	*2.72	....	....	....	....	....	2	1	1	0	120	7	0	3.50	....	....	....	....
1917-18	**Ottawa Senators**	**NHL**	***22**	**9**	**13**	**0**	***1337**	**114**	***1**	**5.12**	**3.40**	....	....	....	....	....	....	....	....	....	....	....	....	....	....	....	....
1918-19	**Ottawa Senators**	**NHL**	***18**	***12**	**6**	**0**	***1152**	**53**	***2**	***2.76**	**1.72**	....	....	....	....	**5**	**1**	**4**	**0**	**300**	**26**	**0**	**5.20**	....	....	....	....
1919-20	**Ottawa Senators**	**NHL**	***24**	***19**	**5**	**0**	**1443**	**64**	***5**	***2.66**	**1.47**	....	....	....	....	....	....	....	....	....	....	....	....	....	....	....	....
♦	Ottawa Senators	St-Cup	5	3	2	....	300	11	1	2.20	....	....	....	....	....	....	....	....	....	....	....	....	....	....	....	....	....
1920-21	**Ottawa Senators**	**NHL**	***24**	***14**	**10**	**0**	***1462**	**75**	***2**	***3.08**	**2.03**	....	....	....	....	**2**	**2**	**0**	**0**	**120**	**0**	**2**	**0.00**	....	....	....	....
♦	Ottawa Senators	St-Cup	5	3	2	0	300	12	0	2.40	....	....	....	....	....	....	....	....	....	....	....	....	....	....	....	....	....
1921-22	**Ottawa Senators**	**NHL**	***24**	***14**	**8**	**2**	***1510**	**84**	***2**	***3.34**	**2.44**	....	....	....	....	**2**	**0**	**1**	**1**	**120**	**5**	**1**	**2.50**	....	....	....	....
1922-23	**Ottawa Senators**	**NHL**	***24**	***14**	**9**	**1**	**1486**	**54**	***4**	***2.18**	**1.83**	....	....	....	....	**2**	**2**	**0**	**0**	**120**	**2**	**1**	**1.00**	....	....	....	....
♦	Ottawa Senators	St-Cup	6	5	1	0	361	8	1	1.33	....	....	....	....	....	....	....	....	....	....	....	....	....	....	....	....	....
1923-24	**Ottawa Senators**	**NHL**	**22**	***15**	**7**	**0**	**1356**	**45**	***3**	***1.99**	**2.12**	....	....	....	....	**2**	**0**	**2**	**0**	**120**	**5**	**0**	**2.50**	....	....	....	....
1924-25	**Montreal Maroons**	**NHL**	**30**	**9**	**19**	**2**	**1843**	**65**	**2**	**2.12**	**2.51**	....	....	....	....	....	....	....	....	....	....	....	....	....	....	....	....
1925-26	**Montreal Maroons**	**NHL**	***36**	**20**	**11**	**5**	***2288**	**73**	**6**	**1.91**	**2.45**	....	....	....	....	**4**	**2**	**0**	**0**	**240**	**5**	**1**	**1.25**	....	....	....	....
♦	Montreal Maroons	St-Cup	4	3	1	0	240	3	3	0.75	....	....	....	....	....	....	....	....	....	....	....	....	....	....	....	....	....
1926-27	**Montreal Maroons**	**NHL**	**43**	**20**	**19**	**4**	**2748**	**65**	**13**	***1.42**	**2.10**	....	....	....	....	**2**	**0**	**1**	**1**	**132**	**2**	**0**	**0.91**	....	....	....	....
1927-28	**Montreal Maroons**	**NHL**	***44**	**24**	**14**	**6**	**2690**	**76**	**7**	**1.70**	**2.69**	....	....	....	....	***9**	***5**	**3**	**1**	***555**	**8**	***4**	***0.86**	....	....	....	....
1928-29	**Montreal Maroons**	**NHL**	**37**	**14**	**16**	**7**	**2300**	**57**	**11**	**1.49**	**3.12**	....	....	....	....	....	....	....	....	....	....	....	....	....	....	....	....
1929-30	**Montreal Maroons**	**NHL**	**14**	**6**	**6**	**1**	**752**	**38**	**0**	**3.03**	**3.13**	....	....	....	....	....	....	....	....	....	....	....	....	....	....	....	....
1930-31	Windsor Bulldogs	IHL	40	20	15	5	2478	92	1	2.23	....	....	....	....	....	....	....	....	....	....	....	....	....	....	....	....	....
	NHL Totals		**362**	**190**	**143**	**28**	**22367**	**863**	**58**	**2.32**	....	....	....	....	....	**28**	**12**	**11**	**3**	**1707**	**53**	**9**	**1.86**	....	....	....	....
	Other Major League Totals		81	53	26	1	4542	232	3	3.06	....	....	....	....	....	4	2	2	....	240	9	1	2.25	....	....	....	....

Rights retained by **Ottawa** after NHA folded, November 26, 1917. • 1922-23 Stanley Cup totals includes series with Regina (WCHL) and Edmonton (PCHA). Traded to **Montreal Maroons** by **Ottawa** with Punch Broadbent for cash, October 20, 1924. • First goaltender to wear a mask in a NHL game, February 20, 1930. (Montreal Maroons 3, NY Americans 3)

• BENNETT, Harvey

Harvey A. G – L. 6', 175 lbs. b: Edington, Sask., 7/23/1925.

Season	Club	League	GP	W	L	T	Mins	GA	SO	Avg	AAvg	Eff	SA	S%	SAPG	GP	W	L	T	Mins	GA	SO	Avg	Eff	SA	S%	SAPG
1941-42	Regina Abbotts	S-SJHL	13	*8	3	1	730	28	0	*2.30	....	....	....	....	....	5	3	2	0	300	16	0	3.20	....	....	....	....
	Regina Abbotts	M-Cup	9	4	2	3	580	27	1	2.79	....	....	....	....	....	....	....	....	....	....	....	....	....	....	....	....	....
1942-43	Oshawa Generals	OHA-Jr.	14	12	2	0	840	42	*3	*3.00	....	....	....	....	....	7	*6	1	0	420	20	*1	*2.86	....	....	....	....
	Oshawa Generals	M-Cup	9	5	4	0	540	35	0	3.89	....	....	....	....	....	....	....	....	....	....	....	....	....	....	....	....	....
1943-44	Oshawa Generals	OHA-Jr.	26	*23	3	0	1540	69	*3	*2.69	....	....	....	....	....	11	*8	3	0	660	31	*1	*2.82	....	....	....	....
	Oshawa Generals	M-Cup	10	*9	1	0	600	29	0	2.90	....	....	....	....	....	....	....	....	....	....	....	....	....	....	....	....	....
1944-45	**Boston Bruins**	**NHL**	**25**	**10**	**12**	**2**	**1470**	**103**	**0**	**4.20**	**3.53**	....	....	....	....	....	....	....	....	....	....	....	....	....	....	....	....
	Boston Olympics	EAHL	13	10	2	1	780	35	1	2.69	....	....	....	....	....	4	4	0	0	240	5	0	*1.25	....	....	....	....
1945-46	Boston Olympics	EAHL	45	*27	11	7	2700	145	2	*3.22	....	....	....	....	....	12	....	....	....	720	30	0	*2.50	....	....	....	....
1946-47	Hershey Bears	AHL	60	*34	15	11	3600	161	5	2.68	....	....	....	....	....	....	....	....	....	....	....	....	....	....	....	....	....
1947-48	Providence Reds	AHL	63	*40	19	4	3780	242	0	3.84	....	....	....	....	....	5	1	4	0	300	23	0	4.60	....	....	....	....
1948-49	Providence Reds	AHL	67	*43	18	6	4020	212	3	3.16	....	....	....	....	....	14	*8	6	0	900	41	1	2.73	....	....	....	....
1949-50	Providence Reds	AHL	60	31	26	3	3600	219	0	3.65	....	....	....	....	....	4	2	2	0	240	16	0	4.00	....	....	....	....
1950-51	Providence Reds	AHL	57	19	33	5	4270	218	2	3.40	....	....	....	....	....	....	....	....	....	....	....	....	....	....	....	....	....
1951-52	Providence Reds	AHL	47	24	19	3	2780	160	1	3.45	....	....	....	....	....	14	*8	6	0	885	31	1	2.10	....	....	....	....
1952-53	Providence Reds	AHL	58	27	31	1	3520	224	1	3.82	....	....	....	....	....	....	....	....	....	....	....	....	....	....	....	....	....
1953-54	Providence Reds	AHL	59	23	33	3	3540	230	2	3.90	....	....	....	....	....	....	....	....	....	....	....	....	....	....	....	....	....
1954-55	Providence Reds	AHL	48	14	29	5	2880	192	0	4.00	....	....	....	....	....	....	....	....	....	....	....	....	....	....	....	....	....
1955-56	Providence Reds	AHL	3	0	3	0	180	17	0	5.67	....	....	....	....	....	....	....	....	....	....	....	....	....	....	....	....	....
	Chatham Maroons	OHA-Sr.	9	....	....	....	540	44	0	4.88	....	....	....	....	....	....	....	....	....	....	....	....	....	....	....	....	....
1956-57	Providence Reds	AHL	7	4	3	0	420	29	0	4.14	....	....	....	....	....	....	....	....	....	....	....	....	....	....	....	....	....
1957-58	Providence Reds	AHL	1	0	1	0	70	2	0	1.71	....	....	....	....	....	....	....	....	....	....	....	....	....	....	....	....	....
	Trois-Rivieres Lions	QHL	1	0	1	0	60	6	0	6.00	....	....	....	....	....	....	....	....	....	....	....	....	....	....	....	....	....
1958-59	Washington Presidents	EHL	3	1	2	0	180	18	0	6.00	....	....	....	....	....	....	....	....	....	....	....	....	....	....	....	....	....
	Providence Reds	AHL	10	1	9	0	600	39	1	3.90	....	....	....	....	....	....	....	....	....	....	....	....	....	....	....	....	....
	NHL Totals		**25**	**10**	**12**	**2**	**1470**	**103**	**0**	**4.20**	....	....	....	....	....	....	....	....	....	....	....	....	....	....	....	....	....

• Father of Harvey Jr., Curt and Bill • EAHL First All-Star Team (1946) • Won George L. Davis Jr. Trophy (fewest goals against - EAHL) (1946) • AHL Second All-Star Team (1947)

• BERGERON, Jean-Claude

G – L. 6'2", 192 lbs. b: Hauterive, Que., 10/14/1968. Montreal's 6th, 104th overall in 1988.

Season	Club	League	GP	W	L	T	Mins	GA	SO	Avg	AAvg	Eff	SA	S%	SAPG	GP	W	L	T	Mins	GA	SO	Avg	Eff	SA	S%	SAPG
1985-86	Shawinigan Catartactes	QMJHL	33	13	16	1	1796	156	0	5.21	....	....	....	....	....	....	....	....	....	....	....	....	....	....	....	....	....
1986-87	Verdun Jr. Canadiens	QMJHL	52	16	32	2	2991	306	0	6.14	....	....	....	....	....	....	....	....	....	....	....	....	....	....	....	....	....
1987-88	Verdun Jr. Canadiens	QMJHL	49	13	31	3	2715	265	0	5.86	....	....	....	....	....	....	....	....	....	....	....	....	....	....	....	....	....
1988-89	Verdun Jr. Canadiens	QMJHL	44	8	34	1	2417	199	0	4.94	....	....	....	....	....	....	....	....	....	....	....	....	....	....	....	....	....
	Sherbrooke Canadiens	AHL	5	4	1	0	302	18	0	3.58	....	....	....	....	....	....	....	....	....	....	....	....	....	....	....	....	....
1989-90	Sherbrooke Canadiens	AHL	40	21	8	7	2254	103	2	*2.74	....	....	....	....	....	9	6	2	....	497	28	0	3.38	....	....	....	....
1990-91	Montreal Canadiens	Fr-Tour	2	1	0	0	59	2	0	2.03	....	....	....	....	....	....	....	....	....	....	....	....	....	....	....	....	....
	Montreal Canadiens	**NHL**	**18**	**7**	**6**	**2**	**941**	**59**	**0**	**3.76**	**3.38**	**5.21**	**426**	**.862**	**27.2**	....	....	....	....	....	....	....	....	....	....	....	....
	Fredericton Canadiens	AHL	18	12	6	0	1083	59	1	3.27	....	....	....	....	....	10	5	5	....	546	32	0	3.52	....	....	....	....
1991-92	Fredericton Canadiens	AHL	13	5	7	1	791	57	0	4.32	....	....	....	....	....	....	....	....	....	....	....	....	....	....	....	....	....
	Peoria Rivermen	IHL	27	14	9	3	1632	96	1	3.53	....	....	....	....	....	6	3	3	....	352	24	0	4.09	....	....	....	....
1992-93	**Tampa Bay Lightning**	**NHL**	**21**	**8**	**10**	**1**	**1163**	**71**	**0**	**3.66**	**3.14**	**4.53**	**574**	**.876**	**29.6**	....	....	....	....	....	....	....	....	....	....	....	....
	Atlanta Knights	IHL	31	21	7	1	1722	92	1	3.21	....	....	....	....	....	6	3	3	....	368	19	0	3.10	....	....	....	....
1993-94	**Tampa Bay Lightning**	**NHL**	**3**	**1**	**1**	**1**	**134**	**7**	**0**	**3.13**	**3.01**	**3.18**	**69**	**.899**	**30.9**	....	....	....	....	....	....	....	....	....	....	....	....
	Atlanta Knights	IHL	48	27	11	7	2755	141	0	3.07	....	....	....	....	....	2	1	1	....	153	6	0	2.34	....	....	....	....
1994-95	Atlanta Knights	IHL	6	3	3	0	324	24	0	4.44	....	....	....	....	....	....	....	....	....	....	....	....	....	....	....	....	....
	Tampa Bay Lightning	**NHL**	**17**	**3**	**9**	**1**	**883**	**49**	**1**	**3.33**	**3.49**	**4.36**	**374**	**.869**	**25.4**	....	....	....	....	....	....	....	....	....	....	....	....
1995-96	**Tampa Bay Lightning**	**NHL**	**12**	**2**	**6**	**2**	**595**	**42**	**0**	**4.24**	**4.22**	**7.12**	**250**	**.832**	**25.2**	....	....	....	....	....	....	....	....	....	....	....	....
	Atlanta Knights	IHL	25	9	10	3	1326	92	0	4.16	....	....	....	....	....	....	....	....	....	....	....	....	....	....	....	....	....
1996-97	**Los Angeles Kings**	**NHL**	**1**	**0**	**1**	**0**	**56**	**4**	**0**	**4.29**	**4.62**	**4.90**	**35**	**.886**	**37.5**	....	....	....	....	....	....	....	....	....	....	....	....
	Phoenix Roadrunners	IHL	42	11	19	7	2296	127	0	3.32	....	....	....	....	....	....	....	....	....	....	....	....	....	....	....	....	....

Season	Club	League	REGULAR SEASON													PLAYOFFS											
			GP	W	L	T	Mins	GA	SO	Avg	AAvg	Eff	SA	S%	SAPG	GP	W	L	T	Mins	GA	SO	Avg	Eff	SA	S%	SAPG
1997-98			DID NOT PLAY																								
1998-99	Joliette Blizzard	QSPHL	15	12	1	1	850	45	0	3.18	....	....	....	....	....	11	9	2	0	199	27	1	2.38	....	....	....	....
99-2000	Joliette Blizzard	QSPHL	13	8	5	0	732	50	0	4.10	....	....	....	....	....	....	....	....	....	....	....	....	....	....	....	....	....
	NHL Totals		**72**	**21**	**33**	**7**	**3772**	**232**	**1**	**3.69**	....	....	**1728**	**.866**	**27.5**	....	....	....	....	....	....	....	....	....	....	....	....

AHL First All-Star Team (1990) • Shared Harry "Hap" Holmes Trophy (fewest goals-against - AHL) with Andre Racicot (1990) • Won Baz Bastien Memorial Trophy (Top Goaltender - AHL) (1990) • Shared James Norris Memorial Trophy (fewest goals-against - IHL) with Mike Greenlay (1994)

Traded to **Tampa Bay** by **Montreal** for Frederic Chabot, June 19, 1992. Signed as a free agent by **Los Angeles**, August 28, 1996.

• BERNHARDT, Tim

Timothy John G – L. 5'9", 160 lbs. b: Sarnia, Ont., 1/17/1958. Atlanta's 2nd, 47th overall in 1978.

Season	Club	League	GP	W	L	T	Mins	GA	SO	Avg	AAvg	Eff	SA	S%	SAPG	GP	W	L	T	Mins	GA	SO	Avg	Eff	SA	S%	SAPG
1974-75	Sarnia Black Hawks	OMHA	STATISTICS NOT AVAILABLE																								
1975-76	Cornwall Royals	QMJHL	51	....	....	....	2985	195	2	3.92	....	....	....	....	....	8	4	4	0	488	30	0	3.69	....	....	....	....
1976-77	Cornwall Royals	QMJHL	44	....	....	....	2497	151	0	*3.63	....	....	....	....	....	12	4	5	3	720	47	0	3.92	....	....	....	....
1977-78	Cornwall Royals	QMJHL	54	....	....	....	3165	179	2	*3.39	....	....	....	....	....	9	5	4	0	540	27	2	3.00	....	....	....	....
	Canada	WJC-A	3	2	1	0	180	6	0	2.00	....	....	....	....	....	....	....	....	....	....	....	....	....	....	....	....	....
1978-79	Tulsa Oilers	CHL	46	15	26	3	2705	191	0	4.24	....	....	....	....	....	....	....	....	....	....	....	....	....	....	....	....	....
1979-80	Birmingham Bulls	CHL	34	15	16	1	1933	122	1	3.79	....	....	....	....	....	3	1	2	0	160	17	0	6.38	....	....	....	....
1980-81	Birmingham Bulls	CHL	29	11	13	2	1598	106	1	3.98	....	....	....	....	....	....	....	....	....	....	....	....	....	....	....	....	....
1981-82	Oklahoma City Stars	CHL	10	1	8	0	526	45	0	5.13	....	....	....	....	....	....	....	....	....	....	....	....	....	....	....	....	....
	Rochester Americans	AHL	29	15	10	2	1586	95	0	3.59	....	....	....	....	....	9	4	3	0	527	29	0	3.30	....	....	....	....
1982-83	**Calgary Flames**	**NHL**	**6**	**0**	**5**	**0**	**280**	**21**	**0**	**4.50**	**3.61**	**6.43**	**147**	**.857**	**31.5**	....	....	....	....	....	....	....	....	....	....	....	....
	Colorado Flames	CHL	34	19	11	1	1896	122	0	3.86	....	....	....	....	....	5	2	3	0	304	19	0	3.75	....	....	....	....
1983-84	St. Catharines Saints	AHL	42	25	13	4	2501	154	0	3.69	....	....	....	....	....	5	2	3	0	288	17	0	3.54	....	....	....	....
1984-85	St. Catharines Saints	AHL	14	5	7	2	801	55	0	4.12	....	....	....	....	....	....	....	....	....	....	....	....	....	....	....	....	....
	Toronto Maple Leafs	**NHL**	**37**	**13**	**19**	**4**	**2182**	**136**	**0**	**3.74**	**2.98**	**4.60**	**1106**	**.877**	**30.4**	....	....	....	....	....	....	....	....	....	....	....	....
1985-86	**Toronto Maple Leafs**	**NHL**	**23**	**4**	**12**	**3**	**1266**	**107**	**0**	**5.07**	**3.97**	**7.46**	**727**	**.853**	**34.5**	....	....	....	....	....	....	....	....	....	....	....	....
	St. Catharines Saints	AHL	14	6	4	2	776	38	1	2.94	....	....	....	....	....	3	0	3	0	140	12	0	5.14	....	....	....	....
1986-87	**Toronto Maple Leafs**	**NHL**	**1**	**0**	**0**	**0**	**20**	**3**	**0**	**9.00**	**7.62**	**38.57**	**7**	**.571**	**21.0**	....	....	....	....	....	....	....	....	....	....	....	....
	Newmarket Saints	AHL	31	6	17	0	1705	117	1	4.12	....	....	....	....	....	....	....	....	....	....	....	....	....	....	....	....	....
1987-88	Newmarket Saints	AHL	49	22	19	4	2704	166	0	3.68	....	....	....	....	....	....	....	....	....	....	....	....	....	....	....	....	....
1988-89	Newmarket Saints	AHL	37	17	16	2	2004	145	1	4.34	....	....	....	....	....	....	....	....	....	....	....	....	....	....	....	....	....
1989-90	Newmarket Saints	AHL	14	4	7	1	755	51	0	4.71	....	....	....	....	....	....	....	....	....	....	....	....	....	....	....	....	....
	NHL Totals		**67**	**17**	**36**	**7**	**3748**	**267**	**0**	**4.27**	....	....	**1987**	**.866**	**31.8**	....	....	....	....	....	....	....	....	....	....	....	....

QMJHL West Second All-Star Team (1976) • QMJHL First All-Star Team (1977, 1978) • AHL Second All-Star Team (1984)

Transferred to **Calgary** after **Atlanta** franchise relocated, June 24, 1980. Signed as a free agent by **Toronto**, December 5, 1984.

• BERTHIAUME, Daniel

Daniel J. "The Bandit" G – L. 5'9", 155 lbs. b: Longueuil, Que., 1/26/1966. Winnipeg's 3rd, 60th overall in 1985.

Season	Club	League	GP	W	L	T	Mins	GA	SO	Avg	AAvg	Eff	SA	S%	SAPG	GP	W	L	T	Mins	GA	SO	Avg	Eff	SA	S%	SAPG
1981-82	Richileau Selectes	QAAA	30	20	8	2	1797	125	0	4.17	....	....	....	....	....	....	....	....	....	....	....	....	....	....	....	....	....
1982-83	Richileau Selectes	QAAA	44	23	13	8	2607	171	0	3.94	....	....	....	....	....	....	....	....	....	....	....	....	....	....	....	....	....
1983-84	Drummondville Voltigeurs	QMJHL	28	....	....	....	1562	131	0	5.03	....	....	....	....	....	3	....	....	....	154	16	0	6.23	....	....	....	....
1984-85	Drummondville Voltigeurs	QMJHL	3	....	....	....	179	17	0	5.70	....	....	....	....	....	....	....	....	....	....	....	....	....	....	....	....	....
	Chicoutimi Sagueneens	QMJHL	56	....	....	....	3168	198	2	3.75	....	....	....	....	....	14	8	6	0	770	51	0	3.97	....	....	....	....
1985-86	Chicoutimi Sagueneens	QMJHL	66	34	29	3	3718	286	1	4.62	....	....	....	....	....	9	4	5	0	580	37	0	3.83	....	....	....	....
	Winnipeg Jets	**NHL**	....	....	....	....	....	....	....	....	....	....	....	....	....	**1**	**0**	**1**	....	**68**	**4**	**0**	**3.53**	**3.28**	**43**	**.907**	**37.9**
1986-87	**Winnipeg Jets**	**NHL**	**31**	**18**	**7**	**3**	**1758**	**93**	**1**	**3.17**	**2.68**	**3.64**	**810**	**.885**	**27.6**	**8**	**4**	**4**	....	**439**	**21**	**0**	**2.87**	**2.87**	**210**	**.900**	**28.7**
	Sherbrooke Canadiens	AHL	7	4	3	0	420	23	0	3.29	....	....	....	....	....	....	....	....	....	....	....	....	....	....	....	....	....
1987-88	**Winnipeg Jets**	**NHL**	**56**	**22**	**19**	**7**	**3010**	**176**	**2**	**3.51**	**2.92**	**4.15**	**1489**	**.882**	**29.7**	**5**	**1**	**4**	....	**300**	**25**	**0**	**5.00**	**8.12**	**154**	**.838**	**30.8**
1988-89	**Winnipeg Jets**	**NHL**	**9**	**0**	**8**	**0**	**443**	**44**	**0**	**5.96**	**4.97**	**10.28**	**255**	**.827**	**34.5**	....	....	....	....	....	....	....	....	....	....	....	....
	Moncton Hawks	AHL	21	6	9	2	1083	76	0	4.21	....	....	....	....	....	3	1	2	0	180	11	0	3.67	....	....	....	....
1989-90	**Winnipeg Jets**	**NHL**	**24**	**10**	**11**	**3**	**1387**	**86**	**1**	**3.72**	**3.15**	**4.80**	**667**	**.871**	**28.9**	....	....	....	....	....	....	....	....	....	....	....	....
	Minnesota North Stars	**NHL**	**5**	**1**	**3**	**0**	**240**	**14**	**0**	**3.50**	**2.96**	**4.71**	**104**	**.865**	**26.0**	....	....	....	....	....	....	....	....	....	....	....	....
1990-91	**Los Angeles Kings**	**NHL**	**37**	**20**	**11**	**4**	**2119**	**117**	**1**	**3.31**	**2.97**	**3.57**	**1086**	**.892**	**30.8**	....	....	....	....	....	....	....	....	....	....	....	....
1991-92	**Los Angeles Kings**	**NHL**	**19**	**7**	**10**	**1**	**979**	**66**	**0**	**4.04**	**3.62**	**4.93**	**541**	**.878**	**33.2**	....	....	....	....	....	....	....	....	....	....	....	....
	Boston Bruins	**NHL**	**8**	**1**	**4**	**2**	**399**	**21**	**0**	**3.16**	**2.83**	**4.25**	**156**	**.865**	**23.5**	....	....	....	....	....	....	....	....	....	....	....	....
1992-93	EC Graz	Alpenliga	28	....	....	....	....	110	0	4.07	....	....	....	....	....	....	....	....	....	....	....	....	....	....	....	....	....
	Ottawa Senators	**NHL**	**25**	**2**	**17**	**1**	**1326**	**95**	**0**	**4.30**	**3.69**	**5.53**	**739**	**.871**	**33.4**	....	....	....	....	....	....	....	....	....	....	....	....
1993-94	**Ottawa Senators**	**NHL**	**1**	**0**	**0**	**0**	**1**	**2**	**0**	**120.00**	**115.33**	**1200.0**	**2**	**.000**	**120.0**	....	....	....	....	....	....	....	....	....	....	....	....
	P.E.I. Senators	AHL	30	8	16	3	1640	130	0	4.76	....	....	....	....	....	....	....	....	....	....	....	....	....	....	....	....	....
	Adirondack Red Wings	AHL	11	7	2	0	552	35	0	3.80	....	....	....	....	....	11	6	4	0	632	30	0	2.85	....	....	....	....
1994-95	Providence Bruins	AHL	2	0	1	1	126	7	0	3.32	....	....	....	....	....	....	....	....	....	....	....	....	....	....	....	....	....
	Wheeling Thunderbirds	ECHL	10	6	1	1	600	41	0	4.10	....	....	....	....	....	....	....	....	....	....	....	....	....	....	....	....	....
	Roanoke Express	ECHL	21	15	4	2	1196	47	0	2.36	....	....	....	....	....	8	4	4	0	464	23	1	2.97	....	....	....	....
	Detroit Vipers	IHL	....	....	....	....	....	....	....	....	....	....	....	....	....	5	2	3	0	331	14	0	2.53	....	....	....	....
1995-96	Detroit Vipers	IHL	7	4	3	0	401	19	2	2.84	....	....	....	....	....	....	....	....	....	....	....	....	....	....	....	....	....
	Roanoke Express	ECHL	39	22	13	3	2109	112	*2	3.19	....	....	....	....	....	2	0	2	0	116	6	0	3.09	....	....	....	....
1996-97	Central Texas Stampede	WPHL	*54	30	20	0	*3034	171	*2	*3.38	....	....	....	....	....	*11	5	6	0	*678	43	*1	3.80	....	....	....	....
1997-98	Roanoke Express	ECHL	30	17	8	3	1711	74	2	*2.59	....	....	....	....	....	2	2	0	....	120	4	0	2.00	....	....	....	....
1998-99	Roanoke Express	ECHL	35	18	12	5	2105	97	2	2.76	....	....	....	....	....	10	6	4	....	608	19	1	1.88	....	....	....	....
99-2000	Roanoke Express	ECHL	37	21	12	4	2103	87	2	2.48	....	....	....	....	....	2	0	2	....	118	6	0	3.04	....	....	....	....
	NHL Totals		**215**	**81**	**90**	**21**	**11662**	**714**	**5**	**3.67**	....	....	**5849**	**.878**	**30.1**	**14**	**5**	**9**	....	**807**	**50**	**0**	**3.72**	....	**407**	**.877**	**30.3**

QMJHL First All-Star Team (1985) • WPHL First All-Star Team (1997) • Named WPHL's Top Goaltender (1997) • ECHL Second All-Star Team (2000)

Traded to **Minnesota** by **Winnipeg** for future considerations, January 22, 1990. Traded to **LA Kings** by **Minnesota** for Craig Duncanson, September 6, 1990. Traded to **Boston** by **LA Kings** for future considerations, January 18, 1992. Traded to **Winnipeg** by **Boston** for Doug Evans, June 10, 1992. Signed as a free agent by **Ottawa**, December 15, 1992. Traded to **Detroit** by **Ottawa** for Steve Konroyd, March 21, 1994. • Played w/ RHI's New Jersey R&R in 1994 (19-9-9-(1)-894-66-0-7.05); Detroit Mustangs in 1995 (20-10-7-(2)-916-139-0-7.28) and Philadelphia Bulldogs in 1996 (13-5-3-(3)-525-89-0-8.13).

• BESTER, Allan

"Ernie" G – L. 5'7", 155 lbs. b: Hamilton, Ont., 3/26/1964. Toronto's 3rd, 49th overall in 1983.

Season	Club	League	GP	W	L	T	Mins	GA	SO	Avg	AAvg	Eff	SA	S%	SAPG	GP	W	L	T	Mins	GA	SO	Avg	Eff	SA	S%	SAPG
1981-82	Hamilton Kilty A's	OJHL	STATISTICS NOT AVAILABLE																								
	Brantford Alexanders	OHL	19	4	11	0	970	68	0	4.21	....	....	....	....	....	....	....	....	....	....	....	....	....	....	....	....	....
1982-83	Brantford Alexanders	OHL	56	29	21	3	3210	188	0	3.51	....	....	....	....	....	8	3	3	....	480	20	*1	*2.50	....	....	....	....
1983-84	**Toronto Maple Leafs**	**NHL**	**32**	**11**	**16**	**4**	**1848**	**134**	**0**	**4.35**	**3.43**	**5.10**	**1144**	**.883**	**37.1**	....	....	....	....	....	....	....	....	....	....	....	....
	Brantford Alexanders	OHL	23	12	9	1	1271	71	1	3.35	....	....	....	....	....	1	0	1	....	60	5	0	5.00	....	....	....	....
1984-85	**Toronto Maple Leafs**	**NHL**	**15**	**3**	**9**	**1**	**767**	**54**	**1**	**4.22**	**3.37**	**5.30**	**430**	**.874**	**33.6**	....	....	....	....	....	....	....	....	....	....	....	....
	St. Catharines Saints	AHL	30	9	18	1	1669	133	0	4.78	....	....	....	....	....	....	....	....	....	....	....	....	....	....	....	....	....
1985-86	**Toronto Maple Leafs**	**NHL**	**1**	**0**	**0**	**0**	**20**	**2**	**0**	**6.00**	**4.69**	**24.00**	**5**	**.600**	**15.0**	....	....	....	....	....	....	....	....	....	....	....	....
	St. Catharines Saints	AHL	50	23	23	3	2855	173	1	3.64	....	....	....	....	....	11	7	3	....	637	27	0	2.54	....	....	....	....
1986-87	**Toronto Maple Leafs**	**NHL**	**36**	**10**	**14**	**3**	**1808**	**110**	**2**	**3.65**	**3.09**	**4.05**	**991**	**.889**	**32.9**	**1**	**0**	**0**	....	**39**	**1**	**0**	**1.54**	**0.91**	**17**	**.941**	**26.2**
	Newmarket Saints	AHL	3	1	0	0	190	6	0	1.89	....	....	....	....	....	....	....	....	....	....	....	....	....	....	....	....	....
1987-88	**Toronto Maple Leafs**	**NHL**	**30**	**8**	**12**	**5**	**1607**	**102**	**2**	**3.81**	**3.18**	**4.42**	**879**	**.884**	**32.8**	**5**	**2**	**3**	....	**253**	**21**	**0**	**4.98**	**7.75**	**135**	**.844**	**32.0**
1988-89	**Toronto Maple Leafs**	**NHL**	**43**	**17**	**20**	**3**	**2460**	**156**	**2**	**3.80**	**3.16**	**4.17**	**1420**	**.890**	**34.6**	....	....	....	....	....	....	....	....	....	....	....	....
1989-90	**Toronto Maple Leafs**	**NHL**	**42**	**20**	**16**	**0**	**2206**	**165**	**0**	**4.49**	**3.82**	**5.72**	**1296**	**.873**	**35.2**	**4**	**0**	**3**	....	**196**	**14**	**0**	**4.29**	**5.01**	**120**	**.883**	**36.7**
	Newmarket Saints	AHL	5	2	1	1	264	18	0	4.09	....	....	....	....	....	....	....	....	....	....	....	....	....	....	....	....	....
1990-91	**Toronto Maple Leafs**	**NHL**	**6**	**0**	**4**	**0**	**247**	**18**	**0**	**4.37**	**3.93**	**6.10**	**129**	**.860**	**31.3**	....	....	....	....	....	....	....	....	....	....	....	....
	Newmarket Saints	AHL	19	7	8	4	1157	58	1	3.01	....	....	....	....	....	....	....	....	....	....	....	....	....	....	....	....	....
	Detroit Red Wings	**NHL**	**3**	**0**	**3**	**0**	**178**	**13**	**0**	**4.38**	**3.94**	**5.75**	**99**	**.869**	**33.4**	**1**	**0**	**0**	....	**20**	**1**	**0**	**3.00**	**2.50**	**12**	**.917**	**36.0**
1991-92	**Detroit Red Wings**	**NHL**	**1**	**0**	**0**	**0**	**31**	**2**	**0**	**3.87**	**3.47**	**8.60**	**9**	**.778**	**17.4**	....	....	....	....	....	....	....	....	....	....	....	....
	Adirondack Red Wings	AHL	22	13	8	0	1268	78	0	3.69	....	....	....	....	....	*19	*14	5	....	1174	50	*1	*2.56	....	....	....	....
1992-93	Adirondack Red Wings	AHL	41	16	15	5	2268	133	1	3.52	....	....	....	....	....	10	7	3	....	633	26	*1	2.46	....	....	....	....
1993-94	San Diego Gulls	IHL	46	22	14	6	2543	150	1	3.54	....	....	....	....	....	8	4	4	....	419	28	0	4.00	....	....	....	....

			REGULAR SEASON													PLAYOFFS											
Season	**Club**	**League**	**GP**	**W**	**L**	**T**	**Mins**	**GA**	**SO**	**Avg**	**AAvg**	**Eff**	**SA**	**S%**	**SAPG**	**GP**	**W**	**L**	**T**	**Mins**	**GA**	**SO**	**Avg**	**Eff**	**SA**	**S%**	**SAPG**
1994-95	San Diego Gulls	IHL	58	28	23	5	3250	183	1	3.38	....	....	....	....	....	4	2	2	....	272	13	0	2.86	....	....	....	....
1995-96	Orlando Solar Bears	IHL	51	32	16	2	2947	176	1	3.58	....	....	....	....	....	*23	11	12	....	*1343	65	2	2.90	....	....	....	....
	Dallas Stars	**NHL**	**10**	**4**	**5**	**1**	**601**	**30**	**0**	**3.00**	**2.98**	**3.03**	**297**	**.899**	**29.7**	....	....	....	....	....	....	....	....	....	....	....	....
1996-97	Orlando Solar Bears	IHL	61	37	13	3	3115	132	2	2.54	....	....	....	....	....	10	4	4	....	512	27	0	3.16	....	....	....	....
1997-98	Orlando Solar Bears	IHL	26	13	8	1	1330	66	1	2.98	....	....	....	....	....	2	1	0	....	76	6	0	4.68	....	....	....	....
	NHL Totals		**219**	**73**	**99**	**17**	**11773**	**786**	**7**	**4.01**	....	....	**6699**	**.883**	**34.1**	**11**	**2**	**6**	....	**508**	**37**	**0**	**4.37**	....	**284**	**.870**	**33.5**

OHL First All-Star Team (1983) • Won Jack Butterfield Trophy (Playoff MVP - AHL) (1992)

Traded to **Detroit** by **Toronto** for Detroit's 6th round choice (Alexander Kuzminsky) in 1991 Entry Draft, March 5, 1991. Signed as a free agent by **Anaheim**, September 9, 1993. Signed as a free agent by **Dallas**, January 21, 1996.

• BEVERIDGE, Bill
William Stephen G – L. 5'8", 170 lbs. b: Ottawa, Ont., 7/1/1909 d: 2/13/1995.

Season	**Club**	**League**	**GP**	**W**	**L**	**T**	**Mins**	**GA**	**SO**	**Avg**	**AAvg**	**Eff**	**SA**	**S%**	**SAPG**	**GP**	**W**	**L**	**T**	**Mins**	**GA**	**SO**	**Avg**	**Eff**	**SA**	**S%**	**SAPG**
1924-25	Ottawa Jr. Shamrocks	OCJHL	5	2	3	0	300	12	0	2.40	....	....	....	....	....	....	....	....	....	....	....	....	....	....	....	....	....
	Ottawa Shamrocks	OCHL	6	3	3	0	400	23	0	3.45	....	....	....	....	....	....	....	....	....	....	....	....	....	....	....	....	....
1925-26	Ottawa Shamrocks	OCHL	15	5	10	0	900	41	2	2.73	....	....	....	....	....	....	....	....	....	....	....	....	....	....	....	....	....
1926-27	Ottawa New Edinburghs	OCHL	....	....	....	....	....	....	....	....	....	....	....	....	....	5	*3	2	0	300	4	*2	*0.80	....	....	....	....
1927-28	Ottawa New Edinburghs	OCHL	15	10	4	1	900	27	....	1.80	....	....	....	....	....	6	3	3	0	360	9	2	1.50	....	....	....	....
1928-29	Ottawa New Edinburghs	OCHL	15	9	6	0	900	17	*7	*1.13	....	....	....	....	....	2	2	0	0	120	6	0	3.00	....	....	....	....
1929-30	Ottawa New Edinburghs	OCHL	1	0	1	0	60	3	0	3.00	....	....	....	....	....	....	....	....	....	....	....	....	....	....	....	....	....
	Detroit Cougars	**NHL**	**39**	**14**	**20**	**5**	**2410**	**109**	**2**	**2.71**	**2.77**	....	....	....	....	....	....	....	....	....	....	....	....	....	....	....	....
1930-31	**Ottawa Senators**	**NHL**	**9**	**0**	**8**	**0**	**520**	**32**	**0**	**3.69**	**4.75**	....	....	....	....	....	....	....	....	....	....	....	....	....	....	....	....
1931-32	Providence Reds	Can-Am	40	*23	11	6	2510	108	5	2.58	....	....	....	....	....	5	*5	0	0	310	6	1	*1.16	....	....	....	....
1932-33	**Ottawa Senators**	**NHL**	**35**	**7**	**19**	**8**	**2195**	**95**	**5**	**2.60**	**3.53**	....	....	....	....	....	....	....	....	....	....	....	....	....	....	....	....
	Providence Reds	Can-Am	5	2	3	0	300	10	1	2.00	....	....	....	....	....	....	....	....	....	....	....	....	....	....	....	....	....
1933-34	**Ottawa Senators**	**NHL**	***48**	**13**	**29**	**6**	**3000**	**143**	**3**	**2.86**	**3.71**	....	....	....	....	....	....	....	....	....	....	....	....	....	....	....	....
1934-35	**St. Louis Eagles**	**NHL**	***48**	**11**	**31**	**6**	**2990**	**144**	**3**	**2.89**	**3.57**	....	....	....	....	....	....	....	....	....	....	....	....	....	....	....	....
1935-36	**Montreal Maroons**	**NHL**	**32**	**14**	**13**	**5**	**1970**	**71**	**1**	**2.16**	**3.04**	....	....	....	....	....	....	....	....	....	....	....	....	....	....	....	....
1936-37	**Montreal Maroons**	**NHL**	**21**	**12**	**6**	**3**	**1290**	**47**	**1**	**2.19**	**2.69**	....	....	....	....	**5**	**2**	**3**	....	**300**	**11**	**0**	**2.20**	....	....	....	....
1937-38	**Montreal Maroons**	**NHL**	***48**	**12**	**30**	**6**	**2980**	**149**	**2**	**3.00**	**3.71**	....	....	....	....	....	....	....	....	....	....	....	....	....	....	....	....
1938-39	Syracuse Stars	IAHL	4	3	1	0	240	11	1	2.75	....	....	....	....	....	....	....	....	....	....	....	....	....	....	....	....	....
	New Haven Eagles	IAHL	50	13	25	10	3000	144	5	2.88	....	....	....	....	....	....	....	....	....	....	....	....	....	....	....	....	....
	Providence Reds	IAHL	2	0	2	0	120	9	0	4.50	....	....	....	....	....	5	2	3	0	360	15	1	2.50	....	....	....	....
1939-40	Syracuse Stars	IAHL	*56	20	27	9	3450	169	3	2.94	....	....	....	....	....	....	....	....	....	....	....	....	....	....	....	....	....
1940-41	Buffalo Bisons	AHL	55	19	27	9	3470	172	3	2.97	....	....	....	....	....	....	....	....	....	....	....	....	....	....	....	....	....
1941-42	Cleveland Barons	AHL	31	16	12	2	1870	73	7	2.34	....	....	....	....	....	5	3	2	0	310	12	0	2.32	....	....	....	....
1942-43	Cleveland Barons	AHL	33	13	15	5	2050	109	1	3.19	....	....	....	....	....	....	....	....	....	....	....	....	....	....	....	....	....
	New York Rangers	**NHL**	**17**	**4**	**10**	**3**	**1020**	**89**	**1**	**5.24**	**4.55**	....	....	....	....	....	....	....	....	....	....	....	....	....	....	....	....
1943-44	Ottawa Commandos	QSHL	1	0	1	0	60	12	0	12.00	....	....	....	....	....	....	....	....	....	....	....	....	....	....	....	....	....
1944-45	Ottawa Commandos	QSHL	3	....	....	....	180	16	0	5.33	....	....	....	....	....	....	....	....	....	....	....	....	....	....	....	....	....
	NHL Totals		**297**	**87**	**166**	**42**	**18375**	**879**	**18**	**2.87**	....	....	....	....	....	**5**	**2**	**3**	....	**300**	**11**	**0**	**2.20**	....	....	....	....

Loaned to **Detroit** by **Ottawa** for the 1929-30 season for cash, November 27, 1929. Transferred to **St. Louis** after **Ottawa** franchise relocated, September 22, 1934. Claimed by **Montreal Canadiens** from **St. Louis** in Dispersal Draft, October 15, 1935. Traded to **Montreal Maroons** by **Montreal Canadiens** for cash, October, 1935. Loaned to **NY Rangers** by **Cleveland** (AHL) to replace injured Jim Franks, January 26, 1943.

• BIBEAULT, Paul
G – L. 5'9", 160 lbs. b: Montreal, Que., 4/13/1919 d: 8/2/1970.

Season	**Club**	**League**	**GP**	**W**	**L**	**T**	**Mins**	**GA**	**SO**	**Avg**	**AAvg**	**Eff**	**SA**	**S%**	**SAPG**	**GP**	**W**	**L**	**T**	**Mins**	**GA**	**SO**	**Avg**	**Eff**	**SA**	**S%**	**SAPG**
1938-39	Verdun Jr. Maple Leafs	QJHL	11	*9	0	2	660	23	1	*2.09	....	....	....	....	....	3	2	1	0	180	10	0	3.33	....	....	....	....
	Verdun Maple Leafs	QSHL	....	....	....	....	....	....	....	....	....	....	....	....	....	1	0	1	0	60	4	0	4.00	....	....	....	....
	Verdun Jr. Maple Leafs	Mem-Cup	7	4	3	0	420	19	0	2.71	....	....	....	....	....	....	....	....	....	....	....	....	....	....	....	....	....
1939-40	Verdun Maple Leafs	QSHL	30	11	11	8	1800	112	0	3.73	....	....	....	....	....	8	3	5	0	480	26	*1	*3.25	....	....	....	....
1940-41	Montreal Canadiens	QSHL	34	....	....	....	2040	121	0	3.56	....	....	....	....	....	....	....	....	....	....	....	....	....	....	....	....	....
	Montreal Canadiens	**NHL**	**4**	**1**	**2**	**0**	**210**	**15**	**0**	**4.29**	**4.91**	....	....	....	....	....	....	....	....	....	....	....	....	....	....	....	....
1941-42	**Montreal Canadiens**	**NHL**	**38**	**17**	**19**	**2**	**2380**	**131**	**1**	**3.30**	**3.25**	....	....	....	....	**3**	**1**	**2**	....	**180**	**8**	***1**	**2.67**	....	....	....	....
	Washington Lions	AHL	13	3	7	3	820	39	0	2.85	....	....	....	....	....	....	....	....	....	....	....	....	....	....	....	....	....
1942-43	**Montreal Canadiens**	**NHL**	***50**	**19**	**19**	**12**	**3010**	**191**	**1**	**3.81**	**3.25**	....	....	....	....	**5**	**1**	**4**	....	**320**	**18**	**1**	**3.38**	....	....	....	....
1943-44	**Toronto Maple Leafs**	**NHL**	**29**	**13**	**14**	**2**	**1740**	**87**	***5**	**3.00**	**2.18**	....	....	....	....	**5**	**1**	**4**	....	**300**	**23**	**0**	**4.60**	....	....	....	....
1944-45	**Boston Bruins**	**NHL**	**26**	**6**	**18**	**2**	**1530**	**116**	**0**	**4.55**	**3.86**	....	....	....	....	**7**	**3**	**4**	....	**437**	**22**	**0**	**3.02**	....	....	....	....
1945-46	**Boston Bruins**	**NHL**	**16**	**8**	**4**	**4**	**960**	**45**	**2**	**2.81**	**2.54**	....	....	....	....	....	....	....	....	....	....	....	....	....	....	....	....
	Montreal Canadiens	**NHL**	**10**	**4**	**6**	**0**	**600**	**30**	**0**	**3.00**	**2.72**	....	....	....	....	....	....	....	....	....	....	....	....	....	....	....	....
1946-47	**Chicago Black Hawks**	**NHL**	**41**	**13**	**25**	**3**	**2460**	**170**	**1**	**4.15**	**4.17**	....	....	....	....	....	....	....	....	....	....	....	....	....	....	....	....
	Fort Worth Rangers	USHL	11	....	....	....	660	30	1	2.73	....	....	....	....	....	9	4	*5	0	540	30	*1	3.33	....	....	....	....
1947-48	Buffalo Bisons	AHL	25	15	8	2	1500	83	0	3.32	....	....	....	....	....	....	....	....	....	....	....	....	....	....	....	....	....
1948-49	Dallas Texans	USHL	65	24	26	15	3900	246	2	3.78	....	....	....	....	....	4	2	2	0	240	11	*1	*2.75	....	....	....	....
1949-50	Cincinnati Mohawks	AHL	15	7	7	1	900	51	0	3.40	....	....	....	....	....	....	....	....	....	....	....	....	....	....	....	....	....
1950-51	Cincinnati Mohawks	AHL	18	8	8	1	1099	58	0	3.17	....	....	....	....	....	....	....	....	....	....	....	....	....	....	....	....	....
1951-52	Cincinnati Mohawks	AHL	16	5	10	1	980	60	0	3.67	....	....	....	....	....	1	1	0	0	94	1	0	0.64	....	....	....	....
1952-53			DID NOT PLAY																								
1953-54	Cincinnati Mohawks	IHL	3	....	....	....	180	8	0	2.67	....	....	....	....	....	....	....	....	....	....	....	....	....	....	....	....	....
1954-55	Cincinnati Mohawks	IHL	2	....	....	....	120	5	0	2.50	....	....	....	....	....	....	....	....	....	....	....	....	....	....	....	....	....
	NHL Totals		**214**	**81**	**107**	**25**	**12890**	**785**	**10**	**3.65**	....	....	....	....	....	**20**	**6**	**14**	....	**1237**	**71**	**2**	**3.44**	....	....	....	....

QSHL Second All-Star Team (1940) • NHL Second All-Star Team (1944) • USHL First All-Star Team (1949) • Won Charles Gardiner Memorial Trophy (USHL - Top Goaltender) (1949) • Won Herman W. Paterson Cup (USHL - MVP) (1949)

Signed as a free agent by **Montreal**, March 6, 1941. Loaned to **Toronto** by **Montreal** for remainder of 1943-44 season, December 22, 1943. Loaned to **Boston** by **Montreal** as a war-time replacement for Frank Brimsek, December 27, 1944. Returned to **Montreal** by **Boston** as an injury replacement for Bill Durnan, January 6, 1946. Mike McMahon was loaned to **Boston** on January 8, 1946 as compensation for recalling Bibeault. Traded to **Chicago** by **Montreal** for George Allen with both teams holding right of recall, September 23, 1946. • Players returned to original teams, June 2, 1947.

• BIERK, Zac
G – L. 6'4", 186 lbs. b: Peterborough, Ont., 9/17/1976. Tampa Bay's 8th, 212th overall in 1995.

Season	**Club**	**League**	**GP**	**W**	**L**	**T**	**Mins**	**GA**	**SO**	**Avg**	**AAvg**	**Eff**	**SA**	**S%**	**SAPG**	**GP**	**W**	**L**	**T**	**Mins**	**GA**	**SO**	**Avg**	**Eff**	**SA**	**S%**	**SAPG**
1992-93	Trinity College	Hi-School	STATISTICS NOT AVAILABLE																								
1993-94	Peterborough Jr. Petes	OJHL	4	....	....	....	205	17	0	4.98	....	....	....	....	....	....	....	....	....	....	....	....	....	....	....	....	....
	Peterborough Petes	OHL	9	0	4	2	423	37	0	5.22	....	....	....	....	....	1	0	0	....	33	7	0	12.70	....	....	....	....
1994-95	Peterborough Petes	OHL	35	11	15	5	1779	117	0	3.95	....	....	....	....	....	6	2	3	....	301	24	0	4.78	....	....	....	....
1995-96	Peterborough Petes	OHL	58	31	16	6	3292	174	2	3.17	....	....	....	....	....	*22	*14	7	....	*1383	83	0	3.60	....	....	....	....
	Peterborough Petes	Mem-Cup	5	*3	2	0	303	14	0	2.77	....	....	....	....	....	....	....	....	....	....	....	....	....	....	....	....	....
1996-97	Peterborough Petes	OHL	49	*28	16	0	2744	151	2	3.30	....	....	....	....	....	11	6	5	....	666	35	0	3.15	....	....	....	....
1997-98	**Tampa Bay Lightning**	**NHL**	**13**	**1**	**4**	**1**	**433**	**30**	**0**	**4.16**	**4.97**	**5.94**	**210**	**.857**	**29.1**	....	....	....	....	....	....	....	....	....	....	....	....
	Adirondack Red Wings	AHL	12	1	6	1	557	36	0	3.87	....	....	....	....	....	....	....	....	....	....	....	....	....	....	....	....	....
1998-99	**Tampa Bay Lightning**	**NHL**	**1**	**0**	**1**	**0**	**59**	**2**	**0**	**2.03**	**2.41**	**1.93**	**21**	**.905**	**21.4**	....	....	....	....	....	....	....	....	....	....	....	....
	Cleveland Lumberjacks	IHL	27	11	12	4	1556	79	0	3.05	....	....	....	....	....	....	....	....	....	....	....	....	....	....	....	....	....
99-2000	**Tampa Bay Lightning**	**NHL**	**12**	**4**	**4**	**1**	**509**	**31**	**0**	**3.65**	**4.18**	**3.67**	**308**	**.899**	**36.3**	....	....	....	....	....	....	....	....	....	....	....	....
	Detroit Vipers	IHL	15	4	8	2	846	46	1	3.26	....	....	....	....	....	....	....	....	....	....	....	....	....	....	....	....	....
	NHL Totals		**26**	**5**	**9**	**2**	**1001**	**63**	**0**	**3.78**	....	....	**539**	**.883**	**32.3**	....	....	....	....	....	....	....	....	....	....	....	....

OHL First All-Star Team (1997)

• Missed remainder of 1998-99 season recovering from Meniere's Disease which was diagnosed on March 25, 1999. Selected by **Minnesota** from **Tampa Bay** in Expansion Draft, June 23, 2000.

Season	Club	League	REGULAR SEASON GP	W	L	T	Mins	GA	SO	Avg	AAvg	Eff	SA	S%	SAPG	PLAYOFFS GP	W	L	T	Mins	GA	SO	Avg	Eff	SA	S%	SAPG

• BILLINGTON, Craig

Craig R. G – L. 5'10", 170 lbs. b: London, Ont., 9/11/1966. New Jersey's 2nd, 23rd overall in 1984.

Season	Club	League	GP	W	L	T	Mins	GA	SO	Avg	AAvg	Eff	SA	S%	SAPG	GP	W	L	T	Mins	GA	SO	Avg	Eff	SA	S%	SAPG
1982-83	London Diamonds	OJHL-B	23	....	....	....	1338	76	0	3.41	....	....	....	....	....	....	....	....	....	....	....	....	....	....	....	....	....
1983-84	Belleville Bulls	OHL	44	20	19	0	2335	162	1	4.16	....	....	....	....	....	1	0	0	....	30	3	0	6.00	....	....	....	....
1984-85	Belleville Bulls	OHL	47	26	19	0	2544	180	1	4.25	....	....	....	....	....	14	7	5	....	761	47	1	3.71	....	....	....	....
	Canada	WJC-A	5	3	0	2	300	13	1	2.60	....	....	....	....	....	....	....	....	....	....	....	....	....	....	....	....	....
1985-86	Belleville Bulls	OHL	3	2	1	0	180	11	0	3.67	....	....	....	....	....	20	9	6	....	1133	68	0	3.60	....	....	....	....
	Canada	WJC-A	5	4	1	0	300	14	0	2.80	....	....	....	....	....	....	....	....	....	....	....	....	....	....	....	....	....
	New Jersey Devils	**NHL**	**18**	**4**	**9**	**1**	**901**	**77**	**0**	**5.13**	**4.02**	**8.20**	**482**	**.840**	**32.1**	....	....	....	....	....	....	....	....	....	....	....	....
1986-87	**New Jersey Devils**	**NHL**	**22**	**4**	**13**	**2**	**1114**	**89**	**0**	**4.79**	**4.07**	**7.49**	**569**	**.844**	**30.6**	....	....	....	....	....	....	....	....	....	....	....	....
	Maine Mariners	AHL	20	9	8	2	1151	70	0	3.65	....	....	....	....	....	....	....	....	....	....	....	....	....	....	....	....	....
1987-88	Utica Devils	AHL	*59	22	27	8	*3404	208	1	3.67	....	....	....	....	....	....	....	....	....	....	....	....	....	....	....	....	....
1988-89	**New Jersey Devils**	**NHL**	**3**	**1**	**1**	**0**	**140**	**11**	**0**	**4.71**	**3.92**	**7.97**	**65**	**.831**	**27.9**	....	....	....	....	....	....	....	....	....	....	....	....
	Utica Devils	AHL	41	17	18	6	2432	150	2	3.70	....	....	....	....	....	4	1	3	....	220	18	0	4.91	....	....	....	....
1989-90	Utica Devils	AHL	38	20	13	1	2087	138	0	3.97	....	....	....	....	....	....	....	....	....	....	....	....	....	....	....	....	....
1990-91	Canada	Nat-Team	34	17	14	2	1879	110	2	3.51	....	....	....	....	....	....	....	....	....	....	....	....	....	....	....	....	....
	Canada	WEC-A	3	0	0	1	46	3	0	3.91	....	....	....	....	....	....	....	....	....	....	....	....	....	....	....	....	....
1991-92	**New Jersey Devils**	**NHL**	**26**	**13**	**7**	**1**	**1363**	**69**	**2**	**3.04**	**2.72**	**3.29**	**637**	**.892**	**28.0**	....	....	....	....	....	....	....	....	....	....	....	....
1992-93	**New Jersey Devils**	**NHL**	**42**	**21**	**16**	**4**	**2389**	**146**	**2**	**3.67**	**3.15**	**4.55**	**1178**	**.876**	**29.6**	**2**	**0**	**1**	....	**78**	**5**	**0**	**3.85**	**4.94**	**39**	**.872**	**30.0**
1993-94	**Ottawa Senators**	**NHL**	**63**	**11**	**41**	**4**	**3319**	**254**	**0**	**4.59**	**4.46**	**6.47**	**1801**	**.859**	**32.6**	....	....	....	....	....	....	....	....	....	....	....	....
1994-95	**Ottawa Senators**	**NHL**	**9**	**0**	**6**	**2**	**472**	**32**	**0**	**4.07**	**4.27**	**5.43**	**240**	**.867**	**30.5**	....	....	....	....	....	....	....	....	....	....	....	....
	Boston Bruins	**NHL**	**8**	**5**	**1**	**0**	**373**	**19**	**0**	**3.06**	**3.21**	**4.15**	**140**	**.864**	**22.5**	**1**	**0**	**0**	....	**25**	**1**	**0**	**2.40**	**2.40**	**10**	**.900**	**24.0**
1995-96	**Boston Bruins**	**NHL**	**27**	**10**	**13**	**3**	**1380**	**79**	**1**	**3.43**	**3.41**	**4.56**	**594**	**.867**	**25.8**	**1**	**0**	**1**	....	**60**	**6**	**0**	**6.00**	**12.86**	**28**	**.786**	**28.0**
1996-97	**Colorado Avalanche**	**NHL**	**23**	**11**	**8**	**2**	**1200**	**53**	**1**	**2.65**	**2.85**	**2.40**	**584**	**.909**	**29.2**	**1**	**0**	**0**	....	**20**	**1**	**0**	**3.00**	**2.31**	**13**	**.923**	**39.0**
1997-98	**Colorado Avalanche**	**NHL**	**23**	**8**	**7**	**4**	**1162**	**45**	**1**	**2.32**	**2.76**	**1.78**	**588**	**.923**	**30.4**	**1**	**0**	**0**	....	**1**	**0**	**0**	**0.00**	**0.00**	**0**	**.000**	**0.0**
1998-99	**Colorado Avalanche**	**NHL**	**21**	**11**	**8**	**1**	**1086**	**52**	**0**	**2.87**	**3.42**	**3.03**	**492**	**.894**	**27.2**	**1**	**0**	**0**	....	**9**	**1**	**0**	**6.67**	**11.12**	**6**	**.833**	**40.0**
99-2000	**Washington Capitals**	**NHL**	**13**	**3**	**6**	**1**	**611**	**28**	**2**	**2.75**	**3.14**	**2.48**	**310**	**.910**	**30.4**	**1**	**0**	**0**	....	**20**	**1**	**0**	**3.00**	**5.00**	**6**	**.833**	**18.0**
	NHL Totals		**298**	**102**	**136**	**25**	**15510**	**954**	**9**	**3.69**	....	....	**7680**	**.876**	**29.7**	**8**	**0**	**2**	....	**213**	**15**	**0**	**4.23**	....	**102**	**.853**	**28.7**

Named Best Goaltender at WJC-A (1985) • OHL First All-Star Team (1985) • Played in NHL All-Star Game (1993)

Traded to **Ottawa** by **New Jersey** with Troy Mallette and New Jersey's 4th round choice (Cosmo Dupaul) in 1993 Entry Draft for Peter Sidorkiewicz and future considerations (Mike Peluso, June 26, 1993), June 20, 1993. Traded to **Boston** by **Ottawa** for NY Islanders' 8th round choice (previously acquired, Ottawa selected Ray Schultz) in 1995 Entry Draft, April 7, 1995. Signed as a free agent by **Florida**, September 5, 1996. Claimed by **Colorado** from **Florida** in NHL Waiver Draft, September 30, 1996. Traded to **Washington** by **Colorado** for future considerations, July 16, 1999.

• BINETTE, Andre

G – L. 5'8", 140 lbs. b: Montreal, Que., 12/2/1933.

Season	Club	League	GP	W	L	T	Mins	GA	SO	Avg	AAvg	Eff	SA	S%	SAPG	GP	W	L	T	Mins	GA	SO	Avg	Eff	SA	S%	SAPG
1953-54	Trois-Rivieres Flambeaux	QJHL	48	24	22	2	2850	180	1	3.79	....	....	....	....	....	3	....	....	....	180	22	0	7.33	....	....	....	....
1954-55	**Montreal Canadiens**	**NHL**	**1**	**1**	**0**	**0**	**60**	**4**	**0**	**4.00**	**4.84**	....	....	....	....	....	....	....	....	....	....	....	....	....	....	....	....
	Shawinigan Cataracts	QHL	4	2	2	0	240	16	0	4.00	....	....	....	....	....	1	0	1	0	60	4	0	4.00	....	....	....	....
1955-56	Cornwall Colts	EOHL	2	0	2	0	120	16	0	8.00	....	....	....	....	....	....	....	....	....	....	....	....	....	....	....	....	....
1956-57	Troy Bruins	IHL	20	....	....	....	1200	75	1	3.75	....	....	....	....	....	....	....	....	....	....	....	....	....	....	....	....	....
	Clinton Comets	EHL	38	....	....	....	2280	181	0	4.76	....	....	....	....	....	....	....	....	....	....	....	....	....	....	....	....	....
1957-58	Chatham Maroons	NOHA	1	1	0	0	60	2	0	2.00	....	....	....	....	....	....	....	....	....	....	....	....	....	....	....	....	....
	Toledo Mercurys	IHL	46	....	....	....	2740	174	3	3.81	....	....	....	....	....	....	....	....	....	....	....	....	....	....	....	....	....
1958-1961			OUT OF HOCKEY – RETIRED																								
1961-62	Montreal Olympics	QSHL	3	2	1	0	180	12	0	4.00	....	....	....	....	....	13	*8	5	0	780	33	*2	*2.54	....	....	....	....
	Montreal Olympics	Al-Cup	16	11	5	0	971	42	4	2.60	....	....	....	....	....	....	....	....	....	....	....	....	....	....	....	....	....
	NHL Totals		**1**	**1**	**0**	**0**	**60**	**4**	**0**	**4.00**	....	....	....	....	....	....	....	....	....	....	....	....	....	....	....	....	....

Promoted to **Montreal** from **Montreal Royals** (QHL) to replace injured Jacques Plante, November 11, 1954. (Montreal 7, Chicago 4)

• BINKLEY, Les

Leslie John G – R. 6', 175 lbs. b: Owen Sound, Ont., 6/6/1934.

Season	Club	League	GP	W	L	T	Mins	GA	SO	Avg	AAvg	Eff	SA	S%	SAPG	GP	W	L	T	Mins	GA	SO	Avg	Eff	SA	S%	SAPG
1949-1951	Owen Sound Mintos	OHA-B	STATISTICS NOT AVAILABLE																								
1951-52	Galt Black Hawks	OHA-Jr.	47	31	13	2	2780	178	*4	3.84	....	....	....	....	....	3	0	3	0	190	16	0	5.05	....	....	....	....
1952-53	Galt Black Hawks	OHA-Jr.	55	....	....	....	3300	213	1	3.87	....	....	....	....	....	11	....	....	....	660	51	0	4.64	....	....	....	....
1953-54	Galt Black Hawks	OHA-Jr.	54	20	33	1	3240	250	0	4.63	....	....	....	....	....	....	....	....	....	....	....	....	....	....	....	....	....
	Kitchener Greenshirts	OHA-Jr.	4	2	2	0	240	17	0	4.25	....	....	....	....	....	4	1	3	0	240	16	0	4.00	....	....	....	....
1954-55	Walkerton Capitols	OSBHL	STATISTICS NOT AVAILABLE																								
	Kitchener-Waterloo Dutchmen	OHA-Sr.	3	....	....	....	180	12	0	4.00	....	....	....	....	....	....	....	....	....	....	....	....	....	....	....	....	....
1955-56	Fort Wayne Komets	IHL	3	1	2	0	180	13	0	4.33	....	....	....	....	....	....	....	....	....	....	....	....	....	....	....	....	....
	Baltimore-Charlotte Clippers	EHL	59	21	37	1	3540	302	0	5.11	....	....	....	....	....	....	....	....	....	....	....	....	....	....	....	....	....
1956-57	Charlotte Clippers	EHL	64	*50	13	1	3840	239	0	3.79	....	....	....	....	....	13	*8	5	0	780	35	*2	*2.69	....	....	....	....
1957-58	Charlotte Clippers	EHL	64	*38	25	1	3840	237	0	3.70	....	....	....	....	....	12	5	7	0	720	46	*1	3.83	....	....	....	....
1958-59	Toledo Mercurys	IHL	52	....	....	....	3100	205	1	3.97	....	....	....	....	....	....	....	....	....	....	....	....	....	....	....	....	....
	Cleveland Barons	AHL	1	0	1	0	60	3	0	3.00	....	....	....	....	....	....	....	....	....	....	....	....	....	....	....	....	....
1959-60	Toledo-St. Louis Mercurys	IHL	67	28	35	4	4020	294	2	4.39	....	....	....	....	....	....	....	....	....	....	....	....	....	....	....	....	....
1960-61	Toledo Mercurys	IHL	1	1	0	0	60	0	1	0.00	....	....	....	....	....	....	....	....	....	....	....	....	....	....	....	....	....
	Cleveland Barons	AHL	8	4	1	1	450	11	0	1.47	....	....	....	....	....	4	0	4	0	240	18	0	4.50	....	....	....	....
1961-62	Cleveland Barons	AHL	60	31	26	3	3600	181	5	3.02	....	....	....	....	....	3	1	2	0	201	10	0	2.99	....	....	....	....
1962-63	Cleveland Barons	AHL	63	28	27	7	3780	203	4	3.22	....	....	....	....	....	7	*4	3	0	420	22	1	3.14	....	....	....	....
1963-64	Cleveland Barons	AHL	65	34	27	3	3885	180	3	2.77	....	....	....	....	....	....	....	....	....	....	....	....	....	....	....	....	....
1964-65	Cleveland Barons	AHL	40	14	23	2	2330	152	0	3.91	....	....	....	....	....	....	....	....	....	....	....	....	....	....	....	....	....
1965-66	Cleveland Barons	AHL	*66	34	30	2	*3932	192	2	2.93	....	....	....	....	....	*12	*8	4	0	*696	27	1	2.33	....	....	....	....
1966-67	San Diego Gulls	WHL	55	15	36	2	3200	190	1	3.56	....	....	....	....	....	....	....	....	....	....	....	....	....	....	....	....	....
1967-68	**Pittsburgh Penguins**	**NHL**	**54**	**20**	**24**	**10**	**3141**	**151**	**6**	**2.88**	**3.20**	....	....	....	....	....	....	....	....	....	....	....	....	....	....	....	....
1968-69	**Pittsburgh Penguins**	**NHL**	**50**	**10**	**31**	**8**	**2885**	**158**	**0**	**3.29**	**3.42**	....	....	....	....	....	....	....	....	....	....	....	....	....	....	....	....
1969-70	**Pittsburgh Penguins**	**NHL**	**27**	**10**	**13**	**1**	**1477**	**79**	**3**	**3.21**	**3.42**	....	....	....	....	**7**	**5**	**2**	....	**428**	**15**	**0**	**2.10**	....	....	....	....
1970-71	**Pittsburgh Penguins**	**NHL**	**34**	**11**	**11**	**10**	**1870**	**89**	**2**	**2.86**	**2.82**	....	....	....	....	....	....	....	....	....	....	....	....	....	....	....	....
1971-72	**Pittsburgh Penguins**	**NHL**	**31**	**7**	**15**	**5**	**1673**	**98**	**0**	**3.51**	**3.56**	....	....	....	....	....	....	....	....	....	....	....	....	....	....	....	....
1972-73	Ottawa Nationals	WHA	30	10	17	1	1709	106	0	3.72	....	....	....	....	....	4	1	3	0	223	17	0	4.57	....	....	....	....
1973-74	Toronto Toros	WHA	27	14	9	1	1412	77	1	3.27	....	....	....	....	....	5	2	2	0	182	17	0	5.60	....	....	....	....
1974-75	Toronto Toros	WHA	17	6	4	0	772	47	0	3.65	....	....	....	....	....	1	0	1	0	59	5	0	5.08	....	....	....	....
1975-76	Toronto Toros	WHA	7	0	6	0	335	32	0	5.73	....	....	....	....	....	....	....	....	....	....	....	....	....	....	....	....	....
	Buffalo Norsemen	NAHL	24	....	....	....	1194	85	0	4.27	....	....	....	....	....	....	....	....	....	....	....	....	....	....	....	....	....
	NHL Totals		**196**	**58**	**94**	**34**	**11046**	**575**	**11**	**3.12**	....	....	....	....	....	**7**	**5**	**2**	....	**428**	**15**	**0**	**2.10**	....	....	....	....
	Other Major League Totals		81	30	36	2	4228	262	1	3.72	....	....	....	....	....	10	3	6	....	464	39	0	5.04	....	....	....	....

EHL Second All-Star Team (1957) • Won Dudley "Red" Garrett Memorial Award (Top Rookie - AHL) (1962) • AHL Second All-Star Team (1964, 1966) • Won Harry "Hap" Holmes Memorial Award (fewest goals against - AHL) (1966) • WHL Second All-Star Team (1967)

Signed by **Cleveland** (AHL) as assistant trainer and practice goaltender, September, 1957. Traded to **San Diego** (WHL) by **Cleveland** (AHL) for cash, September, 1966. Traded to **Pittsburgh** by **San Diego** (WHL) for cash, October, 1967. Selected by **Ontario-Ottawa** (WHA) in 1972 WHA General Player Draft, February 12, 1972. Transferred to **Toronto** (WHA) after **Ottawa** (WHA) franchise relocated, May, 1973.

• BIRON, Martin

G – L. 6'1", 154 lbs. b: Lac St. Charles, Que., 8/15/1977. Buffalo's 2nd, 16th overall in 1995.

Season	Club	League	GP	W	L	T	Mins	GA	SO	Avg	AAvg	Eff	SA	S%	SAPG	GP	W	L	T	Mins	GA	SO	Avg	Eff	SA	S%	SAPG
1993-94	Trois-Rivieres Estacades	QAAA	23	14	8	1	1412	80	1	3.40	....	....	....	....	....	....	....	....	....	....	....	....	....	....	....	....	....
1994-95	Beauport Harfangs	QMJHL	56	29	16	9	3193	132	3	*2.48	....	....	....	....	....	16	8	7	....	900	37	*4	2.47	....	....	....	....
1995-96	Beauport Harfangs	QMJHL	55	29	17	7	3201	152	1	2.85	....	....	....	....	....	*19	*12	7	....	1134	64	0	3.39	....	....	....	....
	Buffalo Sabres	**NHL**	**3**	**0**	**2**	**0**	**119**	**10**	**0**	**5.04**	**5.01**	**7.88**	**64**	**.844**	**32.3**	....	....	....	....	....	....	....	....	....	....	....	....
1996-97	Beauport Harfangs	QMJHL	18	6	9	1	928	61	1	3.94	....	....	....	....	....	....	....	....	....	....	....	....	....	....	....	....	....
	Canada	WJC-A	1	0	0	0	1	0	0	0.00	....	....	....	....	....	....	....	....	....	....	....	....	....	....	....	....	....
	Hull Olympiques	QMJHL	16	11	4	1	974	43	2	2.65	....	....	....	....	....	6	3	1	....	325	19	0	3.51	....	....	....	....

			REGULAR SEASON														PLAYOFFS											
Season	Club	League	GP	W	L	T	Mins	GA	SO	Avg	AAvg	Eff	SA	S%	SAPG	GP	W	L	T	Mins	GA	SO	Avg	Eff	SA	S%	SAPG
1997-98	South Carolina Stingrays	ECHL	2	0	1	1	86	3	0	2.09	....	....	....	....	....	....	....	....	....	....	....	....	....	....	....	....	....
	Rochester Americans	AHL	41	14	18	6	2312	113	*5	2.93	....	....	....	....	....	4	1	3	....	239	16	0	4.01	....	....	....	....
1998-99	**Buffalo Sabres**	**NHL**	**6**	**1**	**2**	**1**	**281**	**10**	**0**	**2.14**	**2.54**	**1.78**	**120**	**.917**	**25.6**	....	....	....	....	....	....	....	....	....	....	....	....
	Rochester Americans	AHL	52	36	13	3	3129	108	*6	*2.07	....	....	....	....	....	*20	12	8	....	1167	42	1	*2.16	....	....	....	....
99-2000	**Buffalo Sabres**	**NHL**	**41**	**19**	**18**	**2**	**2229**	**90**	**5**	**2.42**	**2.76**	**2.20**	**988**	**.909**	**26.6**	....	....	....	....	....	....	....	....	....	....	....	....
	Rochester Americans	AHL	6	6	0	0	344	12	1	2.09	....	....	....	....	....	....	....	....	....	....	....	....	....	....	....	....	....
	NHL Totals		**50**	**20**	**22**	**3**	**2629**	**110**	**5**	**2.51**	....	....	**1172**	**.906**	**26.7**	....	....	....	....	....	....	....	....	....	....	....	....

• Brother of Mathieu • Canadian Major Junior First All-Star Team (1995) • Canadian Major Junior Goaltender of the Year (1995) • AHL First All-Star Team (1999) • Shared Harry "Hap" Holmes Memorial Trophy (fewest goals against - AHL) with Tom Draper (1999) • Won Baz Bastien Memorial Trophy (Top Goaltender - AHL) (1999)

• BITTNER, Richard

Richard John G – L. 6', 170 lbs. b: New Haven, CT, 1/12/1922.

Season	Club	League	GP	W	L	T	Mins	GA	SO	Avg	AAvg	Eff	SA	S%	SAPG	GP	W	L	T	Mins	GA	SO	Avg	Eff	SA	S%	SAPG
1943-44	New Haven Eagles	EAHL	12	1	11	0	700	68	0	5.83	....	....	....	....	....	....	....	....	....	....	....	....	....	....	....	....	....
	Brooklyn Crescents	EAHL	4	0	4	0	240	28	0	7.25	....	....	....	....	....	11	1	*10	0	660	87	0	7.91	....	....	....	....
1944-45	Washington Lions	EAHL	12	3	8	1	720	53	0	4.42	....	....	....	....	....	4	0	4	0	240	29	0	7.11	....	....	....	....
1945-46	Washington Lions	EAHL	9	1	6	2	540	46	0	5.11	....	....	....	....	....	6	2	4	0	360	26	0	4.33	....	....	....	....
1946-47	New Haven All-Stars	X-Games	STATISTICS NOT AVAILABLE																								
	San Francisco Shamrocks	PCHL	1	0	1	0	60	7	0	7.00	....	....	....	....	....	....	....	....	....	....	....	....	....	....	....	....	....
1947-48	Washington Lions	AHL	6	....	....	....	360	37	0	6.17	....	....	....	....	....	....	....	....	....	....	....	....	....	....	....	....	....
	Atlantic City Sea Gulls	EAHL	3	1	2	0	180	16	0	5.33	....	....	....	....	....	....	....	....	....	....	....	....	....	....	....	....	....
1948-49	New Haven All-Stars	X-Games	STATISTICS NOT AVAILABLE																								
	United States	WEC	STATISTICS NOT AVAILABLE																								
1949-50	Boston Olympics	EAHL	36	14	17	5	2160	145	1	4.03	....	....	....	....	....	5	1	2	2	300	14	0	2.80	....	....	....	....
	Boston Bruins	**NHL**	**1**	**0**	**0**	**1**	**60**	**3**	**0**	**3.00**	**3.35**	....	....	....	....	....	....	....	....	....	....	....	....	....	....	....	....
1950-51	New Haven All-Stars	X-Games	STATISTICS NOT AVAILABLE																								
1951-52	Boston Olympics	EAHL	2	1	1	0	120	9	0	4.50	....	....	....	....	....	....	....	....	....	....	....	....	....	....	....	....	....
	Atlantic City Sea Gulls	EAHL	2	0	2	0	120	9	0	4.50	....	....	....	....	....	1	1	0	0	60	1	0	1.00	....	....	....	....
1952-53	Springfield Indians	EAHL	2	0	2	0	120	10	0	5.00	....	....	....	....	....	....	....	....	....	....	....	....	....	....	....	....	....
	Troy Uncle Sam Trojans	EAHL	1	1	0	0	60	4	0	4.00	....	....	....	....	....	....	....	....	....	....	....	....	....	....	....	....	....
1953-54	Clinton Comets	NYOHL	STATISTICS NOT AVAILABLE																								
1954-55	New Haven Blades	EHL	45	22	21	2	2700	196	1	4.36	....	....	....	....	....	4	0	4	0	240	27	0	6.75	....	....	....	....
1955-1961			DID NOT PLAY – REFEREE																								
1961-62	Minneapolis Millers	IHL	1	1	0	0	60	0	1	0.00	....	....	....	....	....	....	....	....	....	....	....	....	....	....	....	....	....
1962-63	St. Paul Saints	IHL	1	0	1	0	60	12	0	12.00	....	....	....	....	....	....	....	....	....	....	....	....	....	....	....	....	....
	NHL Totals		**1**	**0**	**0**	**1**	**60**	**3**	**0**	**3.00**	....	....	....	....	....	....	....	....	....	....	....	....	....	....	....	....	....

Promoted to **Boston** from **Boston Olympics** (EAHL) to replace injured Jack Gelineau, February 12, 1950. (Montreal 3, Boston 3)

• BLAKE, Mike

Michael W. G – L. 6', 185 lbs. b: Kitchener, Ont., 4/6/1956.

Season	Club	League	GP	W	L	T	Mins	GA	SO	Avg	AAvg	Eff	SA	S%	SAPG	GP	W	L	T	Mins	GA	SO	Avg	Eff	SA	S%	SAPG
1977-78	Ohio State University	CCHA	18	....	....	....	980	71	0	4.35	....	....	....	....	....	....	....	....	....	....	....	....	....	....	....	....	....
1978-79	Ohio State University	CCHA	21	....	....	....	1080	78	0	4.33	....	....	....	....	....	....	....	....	....	....	....	....	....	....	....	....	....
1979-80	Ohio State University	CCHA	15	8	4	1	775	48	0	3.72	....	....	....	....	....	....	....	....	....	....	....	....	....	....	....	....	....
1980-81	Ohio State University	CCHA	37	22	9	3	2098	125	2	3.57	....	....	....	....	....	....	....	....	....	....	....	....	....	....	....	....	....
1981-82	**Los Angeles Kings**	**NHL**	**2**	**0**	**0**	**0**	**51**	**2**	**0**	**2.35**	**1.81**	....	....	....	....	....	....	....	....	....	....	....	....	....	....	....	....
	Saginaw Gears	IHL	36	....	....	....	1984	151	0	4.57	....	....	....	....	....	10	....	....	....	621	37	0	3.57	....	....	....	....
1982-83	**Los Angeles Kings**	**NHL**	**9**	**4**	**4**	**0**	**432**	**30**	**0**	**4.17**	**3.35**	**5.93**	**211**	**.858**	**29.3**	....	....	....	....	....	....	....	....	....	....	....	....
	New Haven Nighthawks	AHL	20	8	7	4	1178	72	1	3.67	....	....	....	....	....	7	5	2	0	428	16	0	*2.24	....	....	....	....
1983-84	**Los Angeles Kings**	**NHL**	**29**	**9**	**11**	**5**	**1634**	**118**	**0**	**4.33**	**3.42**	**5.73**	**891**	**.868**	**32.7**	....	....	....	....	....	....	....	....	....	....	....	....
	New Haven Nighthawks	AHL	16	7	8	0	864	64	0	4.44	....	....	....	....	....	....	....	....	....	....	....	....	....	....	....	....	....
1984-85	New Haven Nighthawks	AHL	42	17	19	4	2425	168	1	4.16	....	....	....	....	....	....	....	....	....	....	....	....	....	....	....	....	....
	NHL Totals		**40**	**13**	**15**	**5**	**2117**	**150**	**0**	**4.25**	....	....	....	....	....	....	....	....	....	....	....	....	....	....	....	....	....

CCHA First All-Star Team (1981)

Signed as a free agent by **LA Kings**, January 5, 1982.

• BLUE, John

G – L. 5'10", 185 lbs. b: Huntington Beach, CA, 2/19/1966. Winnipeg's 9th, 197th overall in 1986.

Season	Club	League	GP	W	L	T	Mins	GA	SO	Avg	AAvg	Eff	SA	S%	SAPG	GP	W	L	T	Mins	GA	SO	Avg	Eff	SA	S%	SAPG
1983-84	Des Moines Buccaneers	USHL	15	....	....	....	753	63	0	5.02	....	....	....	....	....	....	....	....	....	....	....	....	....	....	....	....	....
1984-85	University of Minnesota	WCHA	34	23	10	0	1964	111	2	3.39	....	....	....	....	....	....	....	....	....	....	....	....	....	....	....	....	....
1985-86	University of Minnesota	WCHA	29	20	6	0	1588	80	2	3.02	....	....	....	....	....	....	....	....	....	....	....	....	....	....	....	....	....
1986-87	University of Minnesota	WCHA	33	21	9	1	1889	99	3	3.14	....	....	....	....	....	....	....	....	....	....	....	....	....	....	....	....	....
1987-88	United States	Nat-Team	13	3	4	1	588	33	0	3.37	....	....	....	....	....	....	....	....	....	....	....	....	....	....	....	....	....
	United States	Olympics	DID NOT PLAY – SPARE GOALTENDER																								
	Kalamazoo Wings	IHL	15	3	8	4	847	65	0	4.60	....	....	....	....	....	1	0	1	0	40	6	0	9.00	....	....	....	....
1988-89	Kalamazoo Wings	IHL	17	8	6	0	970	69	0	4.27	....	....	....	....	....	....	....	....	....	....	....	....	....	....	....	....	....
	Virginia Lancers	ECHL	10	....	....	....	570	38	0	4.00	....	....	....	....	....	....	....	....	....	....	....	....	....	....	....	....	....
1989-90	Phoenix Roadrunners	IHL	19	5	10	3	986	92	0	5.65	....	....	....	....	....	....	....	....	....	....	....	....	....	....	....	....	....
	Knoxville Cherokees	ECHL	19	6	10	1	1000	85	0	5.15	....	....	....	....	....	....	....	....	....	....	....	....	....	....	....	....	....
	Kalamazoo Wings	IHL	4	2	1	1	232	18	0	4.65	....	....	....	....	....	....	....	....	....	....	....	....	....	....	....	....	....
	United States	WEC-A	5	2	2	0	204	17	0	4.99	....	....	....	....	....	....	....	....	....	....	....	....	....	....	....	....	....
1990-91	Maine Mariners	AHL	10	3	4	2	545	22	0	2.42	....	....	....	....	....	1	0	1	0	40	7	0	10.50	....	....	....	....
	Albany Choppers	IHL	19	11	6	0	1077	71	0	3.96	....	....	....	....	....	....	....	....	....	....	....	....	....	....	....	....	....
	Kalamazoo Wings	IHL	1	1	0	0	64	2	0	1.88	....	....	....	....	....	....	....	....	....	....	....	....	....	....	....	....	....
	Peoria Rivermen	IHL	4	4	0	0	240	12	0	3.00	....	....	....	....	....	....	....	....	....	....	....	....	....	....	....	....	....
	Knoxville Cherokees	ECHL	3	1	1	0	149	13	0	5.23	....	....	....	....	....	....	....	....	....	....	....	....	....	....	....	....	....
1991-92	Maine Mariners	AHL	43	11	23	6	2168	165	1	4.57	....	....	....	....	....	....	....	....	....	....	....	....	....	....	....	....	....
	United States	WC-A	DID NOT PLAY – SPARE GOALTENDER																								
1992-93	**Boston Bruins**	**NHL**	**23**	**9**	**8**	**4**	**1322**	**64**	**1**	**2.90**	**2.48**	**3.11**	**597**	**.893**	**27.1**	**2**	**0**	**1**	....	**96**	**5**	**0**	**3.13**	**3.19**	**49**	**.898**	**30.6**
	Providence Bruins	AHL	19	14	4	1	1159	67	0	3.47	....	....	....	....	....	....	....	....	....	....	....	....	....	....	....	....	....
1993-94	**Boston Bruins**	**NHL**	**18**	**5**	**8**	**3**	**944**	**47**	**0**	**2.99**	**2.87**	**3.45**	**407**	**.885**	**25.9**	....	....	....	....	....	....	....	....	....	....	....	....
	Providence Bruins	AHL	24	7	11	4	1298	76	1	3.51	....	....	....	....	....	....	....	....	....	....	....	....	....	....	....	....	....
1994-95	Providence Bruins	AHL	10	6	3	0	577	30	0	3.11	....	....	....	....	....	4	1	3	0	219	19	0	5.19	....	....	....	....
1995-96	Phoenix Roadrunners	IHL	8	1	5	0	309	21	0	4.07	....	....	....	....	....	....	....	....	....	....	....	....	....	....	....	....	....
	Fort Wayne Komets	IHL	5	1	2	2	249	19	0	4.58	....	....	....	....	....	....	....	....	....	....	....	....	....	....	....	....	....
	Buffalo Sabres	**NHL**	**5**	**2**	**2**	**0**	**255**	**15**	**0**	**3.53**	**3.51**	**3.86**	**137**	**.891**	**32.2**	....	....	....	....	....	....	....	....	....	....	....	....
	Rochester Americans	AHL	14	4	6	1	672	41	0	3.66	....	....	....	....	....	1	0	1	0	27	1	0	2.24	....	....	....	....
1996-97	Austin Ice Bats	WPHL	33	17	11	5	1955	113	1	3.47	....	....	....	....	....	2	0	2	0	97	11	0	6.82	....	....	....	....
	United States	WC-A	1	1	0	0	60	1	0	1.00	....	....	....	....	....	....	....	....	....	....	....	....	....	....	....	....	....
	NHL Totals		**46**	**16**	**18**	**7**	**2521**	**126**	**1**	**3.00**	....	....	**1141**	**.890**	**27.2**	**2**	**0**	**1**	....	**96**	**5**	**0**	**3.13**	....	**49**	**.898**	**30.6**

WCHA Second All-Star Team (1985) • WCHA First All-Star Team (1986)

Traded to **Minnesota** by **Winnipeg** for Winnipeg's 7th round choice (Markus Akerblom) in 1988 Entry Draft, March 7, 1988. Signed as a free agent by **Boston**, August 1, 1991. Signed as a free agent by **Buffalo**, December 28, 1995.

• BOISVERT, Gilles

G – L. 5'8", 152 lbs. b: Trois Rivieres, Que., 2/15/1933.

Season	Club	League	GP	W	L	T	Mins	GA	SO	Avg	AAvg	Eff	SA	S%	SAPG	GP	W	L	T	Mins	GA	SO	Avg	Eff	SA	S%	SAPG
1949-50	Trois-Rivieres Reds	QJHL-B	20	*14	5	1	1220	64	*3	*3.15	....	....	....	....	....	4	1	3	0	240	17	0	4.25	....	....	....	....
1950-51	Cap-de-la-Madelaine Caps	QJHL-B	STATISTICS NOT AVAILABLE																								
	Trois-Rivieres Reds	QJHL	5	2	3	0	300	19	1	3.80	....	....	....	....	....	....	....	....	....	....	....	....	....	....	....	....	....
1951-52	Cap-de-la-Madelaine Caps	QJHL-B	STATISTICS NOT AVAILABLE																								
	Trois-Rivieres Reds	QJHL	....	....	....	....	....	....	....	....	....	....	....	....	....	5	0	5	0	309	19	0	3.69	....	....	....	....
1952-53	Barrie-Kitchener Canucks	OHA-Jr.	51	....	....	....	3060	217	0	4.25	....	....	....	....	....	....	....	....	....	....	....	....	....	....	....	....	....

			REGULAR SEASON													PLAYOFFS											
Season	Club	League	GP	W	L	T	Mins	GA	SO	Avg	AAvg	Eff	SA	S%	SAPG	GP	W	L	T	Mins	GA	SO	Avg	Eff	SA	S%	SAPG
1953-54	Amherst Meteors	NBSHL	40	18	19	2	2410	152	0	3.78	....	....	....	....	....	7	2	5	0	436	27	1	3.72	....	....	....	....
	Sydney Millionaires	MMHL	9	5	4	0	543	21	3	2.32	....	....	....	....	....	3	2	1	0	180	4	1	1.33	....	....	....	....
1954-55	Montreal Royals	QHL	7	3	3	0	393	21	0	3.21	....	....	....	....	....	14	7	7	0	*840	41	*2	2.93	....	....	....	....
	Hershey Bears	AHL	5	4	1	0	300	11	1	2.20	....	....	....	....	....	....	....	....	....	....	....	....	....	....	....	....	....
1955-56	Edmonton Flyers	WHL	60	30	28	2	3669	214	2	3.50	....	....	....	....	....	....	....	....	....	....	....	....	....	....	....	....	....
1956-57	Hull-Ottawa Canadiens	QHL	10	5	3	1	574	23	0	2.40	....	....	....	....	....	....	....	....	....	....	....	....	....	....	....	....	....
	Rochester Americans	AHL	1	1	0	0	60	1	0	1.00	....	....	....	....	....	....	....	....	....	....	....	....	....	....	....	....	....
	Hull-Ottawa Canadiens	EOHL	17	....	....	....	1000	54	1	3.24	....	....	....	....	....	....	....	....	....	....	....	....	....	....	....	....	....
1957-58	Chicoutimi Sagueneens	QHL	51	*31	16	4	3060	150	*5	*2.94	....	....	....	....	....	6	2	4	0	373	13	1	*2.09	....	....	....	....
1958-59	Chicoutimi Sagueneens	QHL	51	23	27	1	3060	190	1	3.73	....	....	....	....	....	....	....	....	....	....	....	....	....	....	....	....	....
1959-60	Sudbury Wolves	EPHL	12	5	5	1	690	47	0	4.09	....	....	....	....	....	....	....	....	....	....	....	....	....	....	....	....	....
	Cleveland Barons	AHL	24	13	6	5	1440	67	2	2.79	....	....	....	....	....	....	....	....	....	....	....	....	....	....	....	....	....
	Detroit Red Wings	**NHL**	**3**	**0**	**3**	**0**	**180**	**9**	**0**	**3.00**	**3.14**	....	....	....	....	....	....	....	....	....	....	....	....	....	....	....	....
	Edmonton Flyers	WHL	11	7	4	0	660	39	0	3.55	....	....	....	....	....	....	....	....	....	....	....	....	....	....	....	....	....
1960-61	Ottawa Senators	OCHL	17	....	....	....	1020	54	2	3.17	....	....	....	....	....	....	....	....	....	....	....	....	....	....	....	....	....
	Spokane Comets	WHL	36	16	19	0	2113	137	2	3.89	....	....	....	....	....	....	....	....	....	....	....	....	....	....	....	....	....
	Calgary Stampeders	WHL	3	1	2	0	180	12	0	4.00	....	....	....	....	....	....	....	....	....	....	....	....	....	....	....	....	....
1961-62	Hershey Bears	AHL	4	1	2	0	200	12	0	3.60	....	....	....	....	....	....	....	....	....	....	....	....	....	....	....	....	....
	Sudbury Wolves	EPHL	5	1	2	2	300	23	0	4.60	....	....	....	....	....	....	....	....	....	....	....	....	....	....	....	....	....
	Edmonton Flyers	WHL	44	23	18	3	2659	157	2	3.54	....	....	....	....	....	12	8	4	0	722	43	0	3.57	....	....	....	....
1962-63	Pittsburgh Hornets	AHL	12	3	8	1	720	58	1	4.83	....	....	....	....	....	....	....	....	....	....	....	....	....	....	....	....	....
	Edmonton Flyers	WHL	47	21	26	0	2820	174	0	3.70	....	....	....	....	....	3	1	2	0	182	9	0	*2.97	....	....	....	....
1963-64	St. Paul Rangers	CPHL	3	0	3	0	180	15	0	5.00	....	....	....	....	....	....	....	....	....	....	....	....	....	....	....	....	....
	Baltimore Clippers	AHL	7	1	4	1	420	27	0	3.86	....	....	....	....	....	....	....	....	....	....	....	....	....	....	....	....	....
1964-65	Vancouver Canucks	WHL	10	5	5	0	600	28	1	2.80	....	....	....	....	....	....	....	....	....	....	....	....	....	....	....	....	....
	Baltimore Clippers	AHL	26	15	8	3	1570	89	0	3.40	....	....	....	....	....	....	....	....	....	....	....	....	....	....	....	....	....
1965-66	Baltimore Clippers	AHL	28	9	17	0	1601	100	0	3.75	....	....	....	....	....	....	....	....	....	....	....	....	....	....	....	....	....
1966-67	Baltimore Clippers	AHL	3	1	0	1	140	6	1	2.57	....	....	....	....	....	1	0	0	0	15	2	0	8.00	....	....	....	....
1967-68	Baltimore Clippers	AHL	18	5	9	2	1030	59	2	3.44	....	....	....	....	....	....	....	....	....	....	....	....	....	....	....	....	....
1968-69	Baltimore Clippers	AHL	16	9	5	2	956	49	2	3.08	....	....	....	....	....	1	0	0	0	40	2	0	3.00	....	....	....	....
1969-70	Baltimore Clippers	AHL	3	1	0	0	90	4	0	2.67	....	....	....	....	....	....	....	....	....	....	....	....	....	....	....	....	....
	NHL Totals		**3**	**0**	**3**	**0**	**180**	**9**	**0**	**3.00**	....	....	....	....	....	....	....	....	....	....	....	....	....	....	....	....	....

NBSHL First All-Star Team (1954) • NBSHL MVP (1954) • QHL Second All-Star Team (1958) • Won Vezina Memorial Trophy (Top Goaltender - QHL) (1958)

Claimed by **Boston** (Hershey-AHL) from **Montreal Royals** (QHL) in Inter-League Draft, June 1, 1955. Traded to **Detroit** by **Boston** with Real Chevrefils, Norm Corcoran, Warren Godfrey and Ed Sandford for Terry Sawchuk, Marcel Bonin, Lorne Davis and Vic Stasiuk, June 3, 1955. Loaned to **Cleveland** (AHL) by **Detroit** (Sudbury-EPHL) for cash, November, 1959. Promoted to **Detroit** from **Cleveland** (AHL) to replace Terry Sawchuk in games on November 26, 28, 29, 1959. Traded to **Baltimore** (AHL) by **Detroit** for cash, June, 1963.

• BOUCHARD, Dan

Daniel Hector G – L. 6′, 190 lbs. b: Val d'Or, Que., 12/12/1950. Boston's 5th, 27th overall in 1970.

Season	Club	League	GP	W	L	T	Mins	GA	SO	Avg	AAvg	Eff	SA	S%	SAPG	GP	W	L	T	Mins	GA	SO	Avg	Eff	SA	S%	SAPG
1968-69	Sorel Eperviers	MMJHL	STATISTICS NOT AVAILABLE																								
	Sorel Eperviers	Mem-Cup	19	14	5	0	1140	65	1	3.42	....	....	....	....	....	....	....	....	....	....	....	....	....	....	....	....	....
1969-70	London Knights	OHA-Jr.	41	....	....	....	2452	159	2	3.89	....	....	....	....	....	12	4	5	3	711	48	0	4.05	....	....	....	....
1970-71	Hershey Bears	AHL	36	12	16	2	2029	106	1	3.13	....	....	....	....	....	....	....	....	....	....	....	....	....	....	....	....	....
1971-72	Boston Braves	AHL	50	*27	13	7	*2915	122	*4	2.51	....	....	....	....	....	6	2	3	0	311	14	0	2.70	....	....	....	....
	Oklahoma City Blazers	CHL	1	1	0	0	60	3	0	3.00	....	....	....	....	....	....	....	....	....	....	....	....	....	....	....	....	....
1972-73	**Atlanta Flames**	**NHL**	**34**	**9**	**15**	**10**	**1944**	**100**	**2**	**3.09**	**2.91**	....	....	....	....	....	....	....	....	....	....	....	....	....	....	....	....
1973-74	**Atlanta Flames**	**NHL**	**46**	**19**	**18**	**8**	**2660**	**123**	**5**	**2.77**	**2.66**	....	....	....	....	**1**	**0**	**1**	....	**60**	**4**	**0**	**4.00**	....	....	....	....
1974-75	**Atlanta Flames**	**NHL**	**40**	**20**	**15**	**5**	**2400**	**111**	**3**	**2.78**	**2.50**	....	....	....	....	....	....	....	....	....	....	....	....	....	....	....	....
1975-76	**Atlanta Flames**	**NHL**	**47**	**19**	**17**	**8**	**2671**	**113**	**2**	**2.54**	**2.28**	....	....	....	....	**2**	**0**	**2**	....	**120**	**3**	**0**	**1.50**	....	....	....	....
1976-77	**Atlanta Flames**	**NHL**	**42**	**17**	**17**	**5**	**2378**	**139**	**1**	**3.51**	**3.27**	....	....	....	....	**1**	**0**	**1**	....	**60**	**5**	**0**	**5.00**	....	....	....	....
1977-78	**Atlanta Flames**	**NHL**	**58**	**25**	**12**	**19**	**3340**	**153**	**2**	**2.75**	**2.56**	....	....	....	....	**2**	**0**	**2**	....	**120**	**7**	**0**	**3.50**	....	....	....	....
	Canada	WEC-A	6	2	4	0	344	24	0	4.19	....	....	....	....	....	....	....	....	....	....	....	....	....	....	....	....	....
1978-79	**Atlanta Flames**	**NHL**	***64**	***32**	**21**	**7**	**3624**	**201**	**3**	**3.33**	**2.94**	....	....	....	....	**2**	**0**	**2**	....	**100**	**9**	**0**	**5.40**	....	....	....	....
1979-80	**Atlanta Flames**	**NHL**	**53**	**23**	**19**	**10**	**3076**	**163**	**2**	**3.18**	**2.80**	....	....	....	....	**4**	**1**	**3**	....	**241**	**14**	**0**	**3.49**	....	....	....	....
1980-81	**Calgary Flames**	**NHL**	**14**	**4**	**5**	**3**	**760**	**51**	**0**	**4.03**	**3.26**	....	....	....	....	....	....	....	....	....	....	....	....	....	....	....	....
	Quebec Nordiques	**NHL**	**29**	**19**	**5**	**5**	**1740**	**92**	**2**	**3.17**	**2.56**	....	....	....	....	**5**	**2**	**3**	....	**286**	**19**	***1**	**3.99**	....	....	....	....
1981-82	**Quebec Nordiques**	**NHL**	**60**	**27**	**22**	**11**	**3572**	**230**	**1**	**3.86**	**2.98**	....	....	....	....	**11**	**4**	**7**	....	**677**	**38**	**0**	**3.37**	....	....	....	....
1982-83	**Quebec Nordiques**	**NHL**	**50**	**20**	**21**	**8**	**2947**	**197**	**1**	**4.01**	**3.22**	**5.00**	**1579**	**.875**	**32.1**	**4**	**1**	**3**	....	**242**	**11**	**0**	**2.73**	....	....	....	....
1983-84	**Quebec Nordiques**	**NHL**	**57**	**29**	**18**	**8**	**3373**	**180**	**1**	**3.20**	**2.50**	**3.78**	**1523**	**.882**	**27.1**	**9**	**5**	**4**	....	**543**	**25**	**0**	**2.76**	**3.08**	**224**	**.888**	**24.8**
1984-85	**Quebec Nordiques**	**NHL**	**29**	**12**	**13**	**4**	**1738**	**101**	**0**	**3.49**	**2.78**	**4.28**	**824**	**.877**	**28.4**	**1**	**0**	**1**	....	**60**	**7**	**0**	**7.00**	**20.42**	**24**	**.708**	**24.0**
1985-86	**Winnipeg Jets**	**NHL**	**32**	**11**	**14**	**2**	**1696**	**107**	**2**	**3.79**	**2.96**	**5.13**	**790**	**.865**	**27.9**	**1**	**0**	**1**	....	**40**	**5**	**0**	**7.50**	**17.05**	**22**	**.773**	**33.0**
1986-87	EHC Fribourg-Gotteron	Switz.	7	....	....	....	151	7	0	2.78	....	....	....	....	....	....	....	....	....	....	....	....	....	....	....	....	....
	NHL Totals		**655**	**286**	**232**	**113**	**37919**	**2061**	**27**	**3.26**	....	....	....	....	....	**43**	**13**	**30**	....	**2549**	**147**	**1**	**3.46**	....	....	....	....

AHL First All-Star Team (1972) • Shared Harry "Hap" Holmes Memorial Award (fewest goals against - AHL) with Ross Brooks (1972)

Claimed by **Atlanta** from **Boston** in Expansion Draft, June 6, 1972. Transferred to **Calgary** after **Atlanta** franchise relocated, June 24, 1980. Traded to **Quebec** by **Calgary** for Jamie Hislop, January 30, 1981. Traded to **Winnipeg** by **Quebec** for Winnipeg's 7th round choice (Mark Vermette) in 1986 Entry Draft, October 14, 1985.

• BOUCHER, Brian

G – L. 6′1″, 190 lbs. b: Woonsocket, RI, 1/2/1977. Philadelphia's 1st, 22nd overall in 1995.

Season	Club	League	GP	W	L	T	Mins	GA	SO	Avg	AAvg	Eff	SA	S%	SAPG	GP	W	L	T	Mins	GA	SO	Avg	Eff	SA	S%	SAPG
1993-94	Mount St. Charles Mounties	Hi-School	15	*14	0	1	*504	*8	*9	*0.57	....	....	....	....	....	4	*4	0	0	*180	*6	*1	*1.20	....	....	....	....
1994-95	Wexford Raiders	OJHL	8	....	....	....	425	23	0	3.25	....	....	....	....	....	....	....	....	....	....	....	....	....	....	....	....	....
	Tri-City Americans	WHL	35	17	11	2	1969	108	1	3.29	....	....	....	....	....	13	6	5	....	795	50	0	3.77	....	....	....	....
1995-96	Tri-City Americans	WHL	55	33	19	2	3183	181	1	3.41	....	....	....	....	....	11	6	5	....	653	37	*2	3.40	....	....	....	....
	United States	WJC-A	4	3	1	0	220	13	0	3.55	....	....	....	....	....	....	....	....	....	....	....	....	....	....	....	....	....
1996-97	Tri-City Americans	WHL	41	10	24	6	2458	149	1	3.64	....	....	....	....	....	....	....	....	....	....	....	....	....	....	....	....	....
	United States	WJC-A	6	4	1	1	357	9	*2	1.51	....	....	....	....	....	....	....	....	....	....	....	....	....	....	....	....	....
1997-98	Philadelphia Phantoms	AHL	34	16	12	3	1901	101	0	3.19	....	....	....	....	....	2	0	0	....	30	1	0	1.95	....	....	....	....
1998-99	Philadelphia Phantoms	AHL	36	20	8	5	2061	89	2	2.59	....	....	....	....	....	16	9	7	....	947	45	0	2.85	....	....	....	....
99-2000	**Philadelphia Flyers**	**NHL**	**35**	**20**	**10**	**3**	**2038**	**65**	**4**	***1.91**	**2.17**	**1.57**	**790**	**.918**	**23.3**	**18**	**11**	**7**	....	**1183**	**40**	**1**	**2.03**	**1.68**	**484**	**.917**	**24.5**
	Philadelphia Phantoms	AHL	1	0	0	1	65	3	0	2.77	....	....	....	....	....	....	....	....	....	....	....	....	....	....	....	....	....
	NHL Totals		**35**	**20**	**10**	**3**	**2038**	**65**	**4**	**1.91**	....	....	**790**	**.918**	**23.3**	**18**	**11**	**7**	....	**1183**	**40**	**1**	**2.03**	....	**484**	**.917**	**24.5**

WHL West Second All-Star Team (1996) • WJC-A All-Star Team (1997) • WHL West First All-Star Team (1997) • NHL All-Rookie Team (2000)

• BOURQUE, Claude

Claude Hennessey G – L. 5′6″, 140 lbs. b: Oxford, N.S., 3/31/1915 d: 5/13/1982.

Season	Club	League	GP	W	L	T	Mins	GA	SO	Avg	AAvg	Eff	SA	S%	SAPG	GP	W	L	T	Mins	GA	SO	Avg	Eff	SA	S%	SAPG
1928-29	Moncton St. Mary's	NBAHA	6	3	2	1	360	8	*2	1.33	....	....	....	....	....	....	....	....	....	....	....	....	....	....	....	....	....
1929-30	Moncton St. Mary's	NBAHA	6	3	2	1	280	11	0	2.36	....	....	....	....	....	....	....	....	....	....	....	....	....	....	....	....	....
1930-31	Moncton CCJA	MCJHL	4	3	1	0	240	2	*3	*0.50	....	....	....	....	....	....	....	....	....	....	....	....	....	....	....	....	....
	Moncton CNR	MCIHL	2	1	1	0	120	4	0	2.00	....	....	....	....	....	....	....	....	....	....	....	....	....	....	....	....	....
	Moncton Aberdeen	Hi-School	4	*4	0	0	240	5	*2	*1.25	....	....	....	....	....	1	0	1	0	60	3	0	3.00	....	....	....	....
1931-32	Moncton CCJA	MCJHL	6	*6	0	0	360	13	2	*2.11	....	....	....	....	....	3	*2	1	0	180	10	0	*3.33	....	....	....	....
1932-33	Moncton Red Indians	MCJHL	5	*4	0	1	330	8	*2	*1.46	....	....	....	....	....	2	*2	0	0	120	5	0	*2.50	....	....	....	....
	Moncton Red Indians	Mem-Cup	8	6	1	1	480	18	0	2.25	....	....	....	....	....	....	....	....	....	....	....	....	....	....	....	....	....
1933-34	Montreal Jr. Canadiens	QJHL	8	....	....	....	480	14	1	*1.75	....	....	....	....	....	2	....	....	....	120	5	0	*2.50	....	....	....	....
1934-35	Montreal Jr. Canadiens	QJHL	10	....	....	....	600	46	0	4.60	....	....	....	....	....	1	....	....	....	60	5	0	5.00	....	....	....	....
1935-36	Montreal Sr. Canadiens	QSHL	21	....	....	....	1260	73	1	3.56	....	....	....	....	....	....	....	....	....	....	....	....	....	....	....	....	....
1936-37	Montreal Royals	QSHL	19	....	....	....	1140	44	2	2.32	....	....	....	....	....	5	....	....	....	300	13	0	2.60	....	....	....	....
1937-38	Verdun Maple Leafs	MCHL	18	....	....	....	1080	52	1	2.89	....	....	....	....	....	8	....	....	....	480	26	0	3.25	....	....	....	....
1938-39	**Montreal Canadiens**	**NHL**	**25**	**7**	**13**	**5**	**1560**	**69**	**2**	**2.65**	**3.20**	....	....	....	....	**3**	**1**	**2**	....	**188**	**8**	**1**	**2.55**	....	....	....	....
	Verdun Maple Leafs	QSHL	2	....	....	....	120	4	0	2.00	....	....	....	....	....	....	....	....	....	....	....	....	....	....	....	....	....
	Kansas City Greyhounds	AHA	3	0	3	0	214	15	0	4.21	....	....	....	....	....	....	....	....	....	....	....	....	....	....	....	....	....

Season	Club	League	GP	W	L	T	Mins	GA	SO	Avg	AAvg	Eff	SA	S%	SAPG	GP	W	L	T	Mins	GA	SO	Avg	Eff	SA	S%	SAPG
			REGULAR SEASON													PLAYOFFS											
1939-40	**Montreal Canadiens**	**NHL**	36	9	24	3	2210	121	2	3.29	4.18	....	....	....	....	....	....	....	....	....	....	....	....	....	....	....	....
	Detroit Red Wings	**NHL**	1	0	1	0	60	3	0	3.00	3.66	....	....	....	....	....	....	....	....	....	....	....	....	....	....	....	....
	New Haven Eagles	IAHL	6	1	5	0	360	26	0	4.33	....	....	....	....	....	....	....	....	....	....	....	....	....	....	....	....	....
1940-41	Philadelphia Rockets	AHL	*56	25	25	6	*3470	167	1	2.89	....	....	....	....	....	....	....	....	....	....	....	....	....	....	....	....	....
1941-42	Buffalo Bisons	AHL	54	24	24	5	3350	150	4	2.69	....	....	....	....	....	....	....	....	....	....	....	....	....	....	....	....	....
1942-43	Lachine RCAF	MCHL	34	....	....	....	2040	142	1	4.18	....	....	....	....	....	12	....	....	....	720	24	0	2.83	....	....	....	....
	NHL Totals		62	16	38	8	3830	193	4	3.02	....	....	....	....	....	3	1	2	....	188	8	1	2.55	....	....	....	....

MCHL First All-Star Team (1938) • AHL Second All-Star Team (1942)

Rights traded to **Montreal Canadiens** by **Montreal Maroons** for cash, September 14, 1938. Loaned to **Detroit** by **Montreal** to replace injured Tiny Thompson, February 15, 1940. (NY Rangers 3, Detroit 1). Traded to **NY Rangers** by **Montreal** for Bert Gardiner and cash, April 26, 1940.

• BOUTIN, Rollie

Roland David G – L. 5'9", 179 lbs. b: Westlock, Alta., 11/6/1957. Washington's 7th, 111th overall in 1977.

Season	Club	League	GP	W	L	T	Mins	GA	SO	Avg	AAvg	Eff	SA	S%	SAPG	GP	W	L	T	Mins	GA	SO	Avg	Eff	SA	S%	SAPG
1973-74	Prince Albert Raiders	SJHL	32	....	....	....	1920	119	1	3.89	....	....	....	....	....	....	....	....	....	....	....	....	....	....	....	....	....
	Swift Current Broncos	WCJHL	1	....	....	....	60	3	0	3.00	....	....	....	....	....	....	....	....	....	....	....	....	....	....	....	....	....
1974-75	Lethbridge Broncos	WCJHL	39	....	....	....	2196	162	1	4.43	....	....	....	....	....	3	0	3	0	180	11	0	3.49	....	....	....	....
1975-76	Lethbridge Broncos	WCJHL	61	....	....	....	3430	259	0	4.53	....	....	....	....	....	7	....	....	....	420	37	0	5.29	....	....	....	....
1976-77	Lethbridge Broncos	WCJHL	59	....	....	....	3296	246	1	4.45	....	....	....	....	....	15	....	....	....	855	63	0	4.42	....	....	....	....
1977-78	Port Huron Flags	IHL	58	....	....	....	3192	205	1	3.85	....	....	....	....	....	17	11	6	0	1002	68	0	4.07	....	....	....	....
1978-79	**Washington Capitals**	**NHL**	2	0	1	0	90	10	0	6.67	5.91	....	....	....	....	....	....	....	....	....	....	....	....	....	....	....	....
	Hershey Bears	AHL	30	13	8	5	1624	105	0	3.88	....	....	....	....	....	4	1	3	0	240	16	0	4.00	....	....	....	....
	Port Huron Flags	IHL	9	....	....	....	464	24	0	3.10	....	....	....	....	....	3	1	1	0	138	9	0	3.91	....	....	....	....
1979-80	**Washington Capitals**	**NHL**	18	7	7	1	927	54	0	3.50	3.09	....	....	....	....	....	....	....	....	....	....	....	....	....	....	....	....
	Hershey Bears	AHL	15	11	2	0	821	34	0	2.48	....	....	....	....	....	....	....	....	....	....	....	....	....	....	....	....	....
1980-81	**Washington Capitals**	**NHL**	2	0	2	0	120	11	0	5.50	4.45	....	....	....	....	....	....	....	....	....	....	....	....	....	....	....	....
	Hershey Bears	AHL	53	32	15	5	3056	182	*3	3.57	....	....	....	....	....	7	5	2	0	420	20	*1	2.88	....	....	....	....
1981-82	Hershey Bears	AHL	*62	27	27	4	*3459	238	1	4.13	....	....	....	....	....	3	0	2	0	107	13	0	7.30	....	....	....	....
1982-83	Birmingham South Stars	CHL	11	1	8	1	619	48	0	4.65	....	....	....	....	....	....	....	....	....	....	....	....	....	....	....	....	....
	Salt Lake Golden Eagles	CHL	14	8	4	1	807	43	1	3.20	....	....	....	....	....	5	2	2	0	251	21	0	5.02	....	....	....	....
1983-84	Binghamton Whalers	AHL	45	23	20	1	2623	188	3	4.30	....	....	....	....	....	....	....	....	....	....	....	....	....	....	....	....	....
	NHL Totals		22	7	10	1	1137	75	0	3.96	....	....	....	....	....	....	....	....	....	....	....	....	....	....	....	....	....

AHL Second All-Star Team (1981)

Traded to **Minnesota** by **Washington** with Wes Jarvis for Robbie Moore and Minnesota's 11th round choice (Anders Huss) in 1983 Entry Draft, August 4, 1982. Signed as a free agent by **Hartford**, December 8, 1983.

• BOUVRETTE, Lionel

G – L. 5'9", 165 lbs. b: Hawkesbury, Ont., 6/10/1914.

Season	Club	League	GP	W	L	T	Mins	GA	SO	Avg	AAvg	Eff	SA	S%	SAPG	GP	W	L	T	Mins	GA	SO	Avg	Eff	SA	S%	SAPG
1931-32	Montreal St-Francis Xavier	MCJHL	10	....	....	....	600	16	3	1.60	....	....	....	....	....	2	2	0	0	120	3	0	*1.50	....	....	....	....
1932-33	Montreal St-Francis Xavier	MCJHL	11	....	....	....	660	29	*1	2.64	....	....	....	....	....	2	2	0	0	120	3	0	1.50	....	....	....	....
1933-34	Montreal St-Francis Xavier	MCJHL	8	....	....	....	480	23	*1	2.87	....	....	....	....	....	....	....	....	....	....	....	....	....	....	....	....	....
	Montreal St-Francis Xavier	MCJHL	1	0	1	0	60	5	0	5.00	....	....	....	....	....	....	....	....	....	....	....	....	....	....	....	....	....
1934-35	Montreal Lafontaine	MCHL	STATISTICS NOT AVAILABLE																								
1935-36	Montreal Lafontaine	MCHL	4	....	....	....	240	26	0	6.50	....	....	....	....	....	....	....	....	....	....	....	....	....	....	....	....	....
1936-37	Montreal Lafontaine	MCHL	STATISTICS NOT AVAILABLE																								
1937-38	Montreal Lafontaine	MCHL	STATISTICS NOT AVAILABLE																								
1938-39	Montreal Concordia	MCHL	5	....	....	....	300	12	1	2.40	....	....	....	....	....	3	....	....	....	180	9	0	3.00	....	....	....	....
1939-40	Montreal Concordia	MCHL	30	....	....	....	1800	106	1	3.53	....	....	....	....	....	5	....	....	....	300	17	*1	3.40	....	....	....	....
1940-41	Montreal Concordia	MCHL	35	....	....	....	2100	174	0	4.97	....	....	....	....	....	....	....	....	....	....	....	....	....	....	....	....	....
1941-42	Quebec Aces	QSHL	33	....	....	....	1980	92	*5	2.79	....	....	....	....	....	6	....	....	....	360	16	0	2.67	....	....	....	....
	Quebec Aces	Al-Cup	8	4	4	0	480	27	1	3.38	....	....	....	....	....	....	....	....	....	....	....	....	....	....	....	....	....
1942-43	Quebec Aces	QSHL	33	....	....	....	1980	123	1	3.73	....	....	....	....	....	4	....	....	....	240	12	0	3.00	....	....	....	....
	New York Rangers	**NHL**	1	0	1	0	60	6	0	6.00	5.08	....	....	....	....	....	....	....	....	....	....	....	....	....	....	....	....
1943-44	Quebec Aces	QSHL	24	15	7	2	1440	65	*3	*2.71	....	....	....	....	....	6	....	....	....	360	21	0	3.50	....	....	....	....
	Quebec Aces	Al-Cup	9	*9	0	0	540	27	0	3.00	....	....	....	....	....	....	....	....	....	....	....	....	....	....	....	....	....
1944-45	Quebec Aces	QSHL	24	....	....	....	1440	89	*2	*3.71	....	....	....	....	....	7	....	....	....	420	17	0	*2.43	....	....	....	....
1945-46	Quebec Aces	QSHL	31	....	....	....	1860	115	1	3.71	....	....	....	....	....	....	....	....	....	....	....	....	....	....	....	....	....
1946-47	Quebec Aces	QSHL	8	....	....	....	480	39	0	4.88	....	....	....	....	....	4	1	3	0	240	19	0	4.75	....	....	....	....
	NHL Totals		1	0	1	0	60	6	0	6.00	....	....	....	....	....	....	....	....	....	....	....	....	....	....	....	....	....

MCHL First All-Star Team (1940, 1941) • Won Vimy Trophy (MVP - QSHL) (1944)

Rights awarded to **Quebec** (QSHL) by Quebec League officials, October 28, 1941. Loaned to **NY Rangers** by **Montreal** (Quebec-QSHL) to replace injured Jim Franks, March 18, 1943. (Montreal 6, NY Rangers 3)

• BOWER, Johnny

John William "The China Wall" G – L. 5'11", 189 lbs. b: Prince Albert, Sask., 11/8/1924. **HHOF**

Season	Club	League	GP	W	L	T	Mins	GA	SO	Avg	AAvg	Eff	SA	S%	SAPG	GP	W	L	T	Mins	GA	SO	Avg	Eff	SA	S%	SAPG
1944-45	Prince Albert Black Hawks	SJHL	10	5	4	1	630	27	0	*2.57	....	....	....	....	....	....	....	....	....	....	....	....	....	....	....	....	....
	Laura Beavers	AAHA-I	....	....	....	....	....	....	....	....	....	....	....	....	....	1	1	0	0	60	3	0	3.00	....	....	....	....
	Prince Albert Black Hawks	M-Cup	3	0	3	0	180	23	0	7.67	....	....	....	....	....	....	....	....	....	....	....	....	....	....	....	....	....
1945-46	Cleveland Barons	AHL	41	18	17	6	2460	160	4	3.90	....	....	....	....	....	....	....	....	....	....	....	....	....	....	....	....	....
	Providence Reds	AHL	1	0	1	0	48	4	0	5.00	....	....	....	....	....	....	....	....	....	....	....	....	....	....	....	....	....
1946-47	Cleveland Barons	AHL	40	22	11	7	2400	124	3	3.10	....	....	....	....	....	....	....	....	....	....	....	....	....	....	....	....	....
1947-48	Cleveland Barons	AHL	31	18	6	6	1880	83	1	2.65	....	....	....	....	....	....	....	....	....	....	....	....	....	....	....	....	....
1948-49	Cleveland Barons	AHL	37	23	9	5	2200	127	3	3.43	....	....	....	....	....	5	2	3	0	329	23	0	4.19	....	....	....	....
1949-50	Cleveland Barons	AHL	61	*38	15	8	3660	201	*5	3.30	....	....	....	....	....	9	4	5	0	548	27	0	2.96	....	....	....	....
1950-51	Cleveland Barons	AHL	70	*44	21	5	4280	213	5	2.99	....	....	....	....	....	11	8	3	0	703	32	0	2.73	....	....	....	....
1951-52	Cleveland Barons	AHL	68	44	19	5	4110	165	3	2.41	....	....	....	....	....	5	2	3	0	300	17	0	3.40	....	....	....	....
1952-53	Cleveland Barons	AHL	61	*40	19	2	3680	155	*6	2.53	....	....	....	....	....	*11	*7	4	0	*745	21	*4	*1.69	....	....	....	....
1953-54	**New York Rangers**	**NHL**	*70	29	31	10	*4200	182	5	2.60	3.35	....	....	....	....	....	....	....	....	....	....	....	....	....	....	....	....
1954-55	**New York Rangers**	**NHL**	5	2	2	1	300	13	0	2.60	3.14	....	....	....	....	....	....	....	....	....	....	....	....	....	....	....	....
	Vancouver Canucks	WHL	63	30	25	8	3780	171	*7	*2.71	....	....	....	....	....	5	1	4	0	300	16	0	3.20	....	....	....	....
1955-56	Providence Reds	AHL	61	*45	14	2	3710	174	3	2.81	....	....	....	....	....	*9	*7	2	0	540	23	0	*2.56	....	....	....	....
1956-57	**New York Rangers**	**NHL**	2	0	2	0	120	6	0	3.00	3.45	....	....	....	....	....	....	....	....	....	....	....	....	....	....	....	....
	Providence Reds	AHL	57	30	19	8	3501	138	4	*2.37	....	....	....	....	....	5	1	4	0	300	15	0	3.00	....	....	....	....
1957-58	Cleveland Barons	AHL	64	37	23	3	3870	140	*8	*2.17	....	....	....	....	....	....	....	....	....	....	....	....	....	....	....	....	....
1958-59	**Toronto Maple Leafs**	**NHL**	39	15	17	7	2340	106	3	2.72	2.88	....	....	....	....	*12	5	7	....	*746	38	0	3.06	....	....	....	....
1959-60	**Toronto Maple Leafs**	**NHL**	66	34	24	8	3960	177	5	2.68	2.76	....	....	....	....	*10	4	6	....	*645	31	0	2.88	....	....	....	....
1960-61	**Toronto Maple Leafs**	**NHL**	58	*33	15	10	3480	145	2	*2.50	2.51	....	....	....	....	3	0	3	....	180	8	0	2.67	....	....	....	....
1961-62♦	**Toronto Maple Leafs**	**NHL**	59	31	18	10	3540	151	2	2.56	2.56	....	....	....	....	10	*6	3	....	579	20	0	*2.07	....	....	....	....
1962-63♦	**Toronto Maple Leafs**	**NHL**	42	20	15	7	2520	109	1	2.60	2.67	....	....	....	....	10	*8	2	....	600	16	*2	*1.60	....	....	....	....
1963-64♦	**Toronto Maple Leafs**	**NHL**	51	24	16	11	3009	106	5	*2.11	2.27	....	....	....	....	*14	*8	6	....	*850	30	*2	*2.12	....	....	....	....
1964-65	**Toronto Maple Leafs**	**NHL**	34	13	13	8	2040	81	3	*2.38	2.51	....	....	....	....	5	2	3	....	321	13	0	2.43	....	....	....	....
1965-66	**Toronto Maple Leafs**	**NHL**	35	18	10	5	1998	75	3	*2.25	2.23	....	....	....	....	2	0	2	....	120	8	0	4.00	....	....	....	....
1966-67♦	**Toronto Maple Leafs**	**NHL**	27	12	9	3	1431	63	2	2.64	2.70	....	....	....	....	4	2	0	....	183	5	*1	1.64	....	....	....	....

			REGULAR SEASON													PLAYOFFS											
Season	Club	League	GP	W	L	T	Mins	GA	SO	Avg	AAvg	Eff	SA	S%	SAPG	GP	W	L	T	Mins	GA	SO	Avg	Eff	SA	S%	SAPG
1967-68	Toronto Maple Leafs	NHL	43	14	18	7	2239	84	4	2.25	2.48																
1968-69	Toronto Maple Leafs	NHL	20	5	4	3	779	37	2	2.85	2.95					4	0	2	....	154	11	0	4.29				
1969-70	Toronto Maple Leafs	NHL	1	0	1	0	60	5	0	5.00	5.31																
	NHL Totals		552	250	195	90	32016	1340	37	2.51						74	35	34	....	4378	180	5	2.47				

AHL Second All-Star Team (1951) • AHL First All-Star Team (1952, 1953, 1956, 1957 1958) • Won Harry "Hap" Holmes Memorial Award (fewest goals against - AHL) (1952, 1957, 1958) • Won WHL Leading Goaltender Award (1955) • Won Les Cunningham Award (MVP - AHL) (1956, 1957, 1958) • NHL First All-Star Team (1961) • Won Vezina Trophy (1961) • Shared Vezina Trophy with Terry Sawchuk (1965) • Played in NHL All-Star Game (1961, 1962, 1963, 1964)

• Also known as John Kizkan. Traded to **NY Rangers** by **Cleveland** (AHL) with Eldred Kobussen for Emile Francis, Neil Strain and cash, July 20, 1953. Traded to **Cleveland** (AHL) by **NY Rangers** for Ed MacQueen and cash, July 31, 1957. Claimed by **Toronto** from **Cleveland** (AHL) in Inter-League Draft, June 3, 1958.

• BRANIGAN, Andy

Andrew John G. 5'11", 190 lbs. b: Winnipeg, Man., 4/11/1922 d: 4/13/1995.

Season	Club	League	GP	W	L	T	Mins	GA	SO	Avg	AAvg	Eff	SA	S%	SAPG	GP	W	L	T	Mins	GA	SO	Avg	Eff	SA	S%	SAPG
1940-41	New York Americans	NHL	1	0	0	0	7	0	0	0.00	0.00																
	NHL Totals		1	0	0	0	7	0	0	0.00																	

• NY Americans defenseman replaced injured Chuck Rayner in 3rd period, February 28, 1941. (Detroit 5, NY Americans 4)

• BRATHWAITE, Fred

G – L. 5'7", 175 lbs. b: Ottawa, Ont., 11/24/1972.

Season	Club	League	GP	W	L	T	Mins	GA	SO	Avg	AAvg	Eff	SA	S%	SAPG	GP	W	L	T	Mins	GA	SO	Avg	Eff	SA	S%	SAPG
1988-89	Smiths Falls Bears	OJHL	38	16	18	1	2130	187	0	5.27																	
1989-90	OrilliaTerriers	OJHL-B	15	....	....	....	782	47	0	3.61																	
	Oshawa Generals	OHL	20	11	2	1	886	43	1	2.91						10	4	2	....	451	22	0	*2.93				
	Oshawa Generals	Mem-Cup	1	1	0	0	52	1	0	1.15																	
1990-91	Oshawa Generals	OHL	39	25	6	3	1986	112	1	3.38						13	*9	2	....	677	43	0	3.81				
1991-92	Oshawa Generals	OHL	24	12	7	2	1248	81	0	3.89																	
	London Knights	OHL	23	15	6	2	1325	61	*4	2.76						10	5	5	....	615	36	0	3.51				
1992-93	Detroit Jr. Red Wings	OHL	37	23	10	4	2192	134	0	3.67						15	9	6	....	858	48	1	3.36				
1993-94	Edmonton Oilers	NHL	19	3	10	3	982	58	0	3.54	3.40	3.93	523	.889	32.0												
	Cape Breton Oilers	AHL	2	1	1	0	119	6	0	3.04																	
1994-95	Edmonton Oilers	NHL	14	2	5	1	601	40	0	3.99	4.19	5.47	292	.863	29.2												
1995-96	Edmonton Oilers	NHL	7	0	2	0	293	12	0	2.46	2.44	2.11	140	.914	28.7												
	Cape Breton Oilers	AHL	31	12	16	0	1699	110	1	3.88																	
1996-97	Manitoba Moose	IHL	58	22	22	5	2945	167	1	3.40																	
1997-98	Manitoba Moose	IHL	51	23	18	4	2736	138	1	3.03						2	0	1	0	72	4	0	3.30				
1998-99	Canada	Nat-Team	24	6	8	3	989	47	2	2.85																	
	Calgary Flames	NHL	28	11	9	7	1663	68	1	2.45	2.91	2.09	796	.915	28.7												
	Canada	WC-A	DID NOT PLAY – SPARE GOALTENDER																								
99-2000	Calgary Flames	NHL	61	25	25	7	3448	158	5	2.75	3.14	2.61	1664	.905	29.0												
	Saint John Flames	AHL	2	2	0	0	120	4	0	2.00																	
	Canada	WC-A	1	0	1	0	59	4	0	4.07																	
	NHL Totals		129	41	51	18	6987	336	6	2.89			3415	.902	29.3												

• Scored a goal while with Detroit (OHL), April 20, 1993. • Scored a goal while with Manitoba (IHL), November 9, 1996.

Signed as a free agent by **Edmonton**, October 6, 1993. Signed as a free agent by **Calgary**, January 6, 1999.

• BRIMSEK, Frank

Francis Charles "Mr. Zero" G – L. 5'9", 170 lbs. b: Eveleth, MN, 9/26/1915 d: 11/11/1998. USHOF HHOF

Season	Club	League	GP	W	L	T	Mins	GA	SO	Avg	AAvg	Eff	SA	S%	SAPG	GP	W	L	T	Mins	GA	SO	Avg	Eff	SA	S%	SAPG
1934-35	Eveleth Rangers	USJHA	STATISTICS NOT AVAILABLE																								
	Pittsburgh Yellowjackets	X-Games	16	14	2	0	960	39	1	2.44																	
1935-36	Pittsburgh Yellowjackets	EAHL	38	*20	16	2	2280	74	*8	1.95						8	4	3	1	480	19	2	2.36				
1936-37	Pittsburgh Yellowjackets	EAHL	47	19	23	5	2820	142	3	3.02																	
1937-38	Providence Reds	IAHL	*48	25	16	7	2950	86	5	*1.75						7	*5	2	0	515	16	0	1.86				
	New Haven Eagles	IAHL	....	....	....	....	....	....	....	....						1	0	1	0	93	3	0	1.94				
1938-39	Providence Reds	IAHL	9	5	2	2	570	18	0	1.89																	
♦	Boston Bruins	NHL	43	*33	9	1	2610	68	*10	*1.56	1.78					*12	*8	4	....	*863	18	1	*1.25				
1939-40	Boston Bruins	NHL	*48	*31	12	5	2950	98	6	1.99	2.35					6	2	4	....	360	15	0	2.50				
1940-41 ♦	Boston Bruins	NHL	*48	27	8	13	*3040	102	*6	2.01	2.19					*11	*8	3	....	*678	23	*1	*2.04				
1941-42	Boston Bruins	NHL	47	24	17	6	2930	115	3	*2.35	2.21					5	2	3	....	307	16	0	3.13				
1942-43	Boston Bruins	NHL	*50	24	17	9	3000	176	1	3.52	2.96					9	4	5	....	560	33	0	3.54				
1943-44	Coast Guard Cutters	X-Games	27	19	6	2	1620	83	1	3.07						5	4	0	0	300	4	1	0.80				
1944-45			MILITARY SERVICE																								
1945-46	Boston Bruins	NHL	34	16	14	4	2040	111	2	3.26	2.96					*10	5	5	....	*651	29	0	2.67				
1946-47	Boston Bruins	NHL	*60	26	23	11	*3600	175	3	2.92	2.77					5	1	4	....	343	16	0	2.80				
1947-48	Boston Bruins	NHL	*60	23	24	13	*3600	168	3	2.80	2.89					5	1	4	....	317	20	0	3.79				
1948-49	Boston Bruins	NHL	54	26	20	8	3240	147	1	2.72	3.05					5	1	4	....	316	16	0	3.04				
1949-50	Chicago Black Hawks	NHL	*70	22	38	10	*4200	244	5	3.49	4.12																
	NHL Totals		514	252	182	80	31210	1404	40	2.70						68	32	36	....	4395	186	2	2.54				

EAHL Second All-Star Team (1936) • Won George L. Davis Jr. Trophy (fewest goals against - EAHL) (1936) • IAHL First All-Star Team (1938) • NHL First All-Star Team (1939, 1942) • Won Calder Trophy (1939) • Won Vezina Trophy (1939, 1942) • NHL Second All-Star Team (1940, 1941, 1943, 1946, 1947, 1948) • Played in NHL All-Star Game (1939, 1947, 1948)

Signed as a free agent by **Boston**, October 27, 1938. Traded to **Chicago** by **Boston** for cash, September 8, 1949.

• BROCHU, Martin

G – L. 5'11", 204 lbs. b: Anjou, Que., 3/10/1973.

Season	Club	League	GP	W	L	T	Mins	GA	SO	Avg	AAvg	Eff	SA	S%	SAPG	GP	W	L	T	Mins	GA	SO	Avg	Eff	SA	S%	SAPG
1989-90	Montreal-Bourassa Canadiens.	QAAA	27	11	14	1	1471	103	3	4.20						3	1	2	0	193	10	1	3.10				
1990-91	Granby Bisons	QMJHL	16	6	5	0	622	39	....	3.76																	
1991-92	Granby Bisons	QMJHL	52	15	29	2	2772	278	0	4.72																	
1992-93	Hull Olympiques	QMJHL	29	9	15	1	1453	137	0	5.66						2	0	1	....	69	7	0	6.07				
1993-94	Fredericton Canadiens	AHL	32	10	11	3	1505	76	2	3.03																	
1994-95	Fredericton Canadiens	AHL	44	18	18	4	2475	145	0	3.51																	
1995-96	Fredericton Canadiens	AHL	17	6	8	2	986	70	0	4.26																	
	Wheeling Thunderbirds	ECHL	19	10	6	2	1060	51	1	2.89																	
	Portland Pirates	AHL	5	2	2	1	287	15	0	3.14						12	7	4	....	700	28	*2	*2.40				
1996-97	Portland Pirates	AHL	55	23	17	7	2962	150	2	3.04						5	2	3	....	324	13	0	2.41				
1997-98	Portland Pirates	AHL	37	16	14	1	1926	96	2	2.99						6	3	2	....	296	16	0	3.24				
1998-99	Washington Capitals	NHL	2	0	2	0	120	6	0	3.00	3.57	3.27	55	.891	27.5												
	Portland Pirates	AHL	20	6	10	3	1164	57	2	2.94																	
	Utah Grizzlies	IHL	5	1	3	1	298	13	0	2.62																	
99-2000	Portland Pirates	AHL	54	32	15	6	3192	116	4	2.18						2	0	2	....	80	7	0	5.27				
	NHL Totals		2	0	2	0	120	6	0	3.00			55	.891	27.5												

AHL First All-Star Team (2000) • Won Baz Bastien Memorial Trophy (Top Goaltender - AHL) (2000) • Won Les Cunningham Award (MVP - AHL) (2000)

Signed as a free agent by **Montreal**, September 22, 1992. Traded to **Washington** by **Montreal** for future considerations, March 15, 1996.

• BRODA, Turk

Walter Edward G – L. 5'9", 180 lbs. b: Brandon, Man., 5/15/1914 d: 10/17/1972. HHOF

Season	Club	League	GP	W	L	T	Mins	GA	SO	Avg	AAvg	Eff	SA	S%	SAPG	GP	W	L	T	Mins	GA	SO	Avg	Eff	SA	S%	SAPG
1931-32	Brandon Athletics	MAHA	STATISTICS NOT AVAILABLE																								
1932-33	Brandon Native Sons	MJHL	STATISTICS NOT AVAILABLE																								
	Brandon Native Sons	Mem-Cup	7	2	2	3	460	9	0	1.17																	
1933-34	Winnipeg Jr. Monarchs	MJHL	12	1	11	0	720	51	0	4.25						3	1	2	0	180	12	0	4.00				
	Winnipeg Monarchs	MHL-Sr.	1	0	1	0	60	6	0	6.00																	
	St. Michael's Majors	Mem-Cup	DID NOT PLAY – SPARE GOALTENDER																								
1934-35	Detroit Farm Crest	MOHL	2	1	1	0	120	4	0	2.00																	

			REGULAR SEASON													PLAYOFFS											
Season	Club	League	GP	W	L	T	Mins	GA	SO	Avg	AAvg	Eff	SA	S%	SAPG	GP	W	L	T	Mins	GA	SO	Avg	Eff	SA	S%	SAPG
1935-36	Detroit Olympics	IHL	47	*26	18	3	2890	101	6	*2.10	....	....	....	....	....	6	*6	0	0	365	8	*1	*1.32	....	....	....	....
1936-37	**Toronto Maple Leafs**	**NHL**	**45**	**22**	**19**	**4**	**2770**	**106**	**3**	**2.30**	**2.82**	....	....	....	....	**2**	**0**	**2**	....	**133**	**5**	**0**	**2.26**	....	....	....	....
1937-38	**Toronto Maple Leafs**	**NHL**	***48**	**24**	**15**	**9**	**2980**	**127**	**6**	**2.56**	**3.09**	....	....	....	....	**7**	**4**	**3**	....	**452**	**13**	**1**	**1.73**	....	....	....	....
1938-39	**Toronto Maple Leafs**	**NHL**	***48**	**19**	**20**	**9**	***2990**	**107**	**8**	**2.15**	**2.52**	....	....	....	....	**10**	**5**	**5**	....	**617**	**20**	***2**	**1.94**	....	....	....	....
1939-40	**Toronto Maple Leafs**	**NHL**	**47**	**25**	**17**	**5**	**2900**	**108**	**4**	**2.23**	**2.67**	....	....	....	....	**10**	**6**	**4**	....	**657**	**19**	**1**	**1.74**	....	....	....	....
1940-41	**Toronto Maple Leafs**	**NHL**	***48**	***28**	**14**	**6**	**2970**	**99**	**5**	***2.00**	**2.18**	....	....	....	....	**7**	**3**	**4**	....	**438**	**15**	**0**	**2.05**	....	....	....	....
1941-42♦	**Toronto Maple Leafs**	**NHL**	***48**	**27**	**18**	**3**	***2960**	**136**	***6**	**2.76**	**2.65**	....	....	....	....	***13**	***8**	**5**	....	***780**	**31**	***1**	**2.38**	....	....	....	....
1942-43	**Toronto Maple Leafs**	**NHL**	***50**	**22**	**19**	**9**	**3000**	**159**	**1**	**3.18**	**2.62**	....	....	....	....	**6**	**2**	**4**	....	**439**	**20**	**0**	**2.73**	....	....	....	....
	Victoria Navy	NNDHL	STATISTICS NOT AVAILABLE																								
	San Diego Skyhawks	X-Games	STATISTICS NOT AVAILABLE																								
1943-44			MILITARY SERVICE																								
1944-45			MILITARY SERVICE																								
1945-46	**Toronto Maple Leafs**	**NHL**	**15**	**6**	**6**	**3**	**900**	**53**	**0**	**3.53**	**3.23**	....	....	....	....	....	....	....	....	....	....	....	....	....	....	....	....
1946-47♦	**Toronto Maple Leafs**	**NHL**	***60**	**31**	**19**	**10**	***3600**	**172**	**4**	**2.87**	**2.72**	....	....	....	....	***11**	***8**	**3**	....	**680**	**27**	***1**	**2.38**	....	....	....	....
1947-48♦	**Toronto Maple Leafs**	**NHL**	***60**	***32**	**15**	**13**	***3600**	**143**	**5**	***2.38**	**2.39**	....	....	....	....	**9**	***8**	**1**	....	**557**	**20**	***1**	***2.15**	....	....	....	....
1948-49♦	**Toronto Maple Leafs**	**NHL**	***60**	**22**	**25**	**13**	***3600**	**161**	**5**	**2.68**	**3.00**	....	....	....	....	**9**	***8**	**1**	....	**574**	**15**	***1**	***1.57**	....	....	....	....
1949-50	**Toronto Maple Leafs**	**NHL**	**68**	**30**	**25**	**12**	**4040**	**167**	***9**	**2.48**	**2.72**	....	....	....	....	**7**	**3**	**4**	....	**450**	**10**	***3**	***1.33**	....	....	....	....
1950-51♦	**Toronto Maple Leafs**	**NHL**	**31**	**14**	**11**	**5**	**1827**	**68**	**6**	**2.23**	**2.47**	....	....	....	....	**8**	***5**	**1**	....	**492**	**9**	***2**	**1.10**	....	....	....	....
1951-52	**Toronto Maple Leafs**	**NHL**	**1**	**0**	**1**	**0**	**30**	**3**	**0**	**6.00**	**7.06**	....	....	....	....	**2**	**0**	**2**	....	**120**	**7**	**0**	**3.50**	....	....	....	....
	NHL Totals		**629**	**302**	**224**	**101**	**38167**	**1609**	**62**	**2.53**	....	....	....	....	....	**101**	**60**	**39**	....	**6389**	**211**	**13**	**1.98**	....	....	....	....

NHL First All-Star Team (1941, 1948) • Won Vezina Trophy (1941, 1948) • NHL Second All-Star Team (1942) • Played in NHL All-Star Game (1947, 1948, 1949, 1950)

Traded to **Toronto** by **Detroit** (Detroit-IHL) for $8,000, May 6, 1936.

• BRODERICK, Ken   Kenneth Lorne   G – R. 5'10", 178 lbs.   b: Toronto, Ont., 2/16/1942.

Season	Club	League	GP	W	L	T	Mins	GA	SO	Avg	AAvg	Eff	SA	S%	SAPG	GP	W	L	T	Mins	GA	SO	Avg	Eff	SA	S%	SAPG
1958-59	Toronto Midget Marlboros	MTHL	STATISTICS NOT AVAILABLE																								
	Toronto Marlboros	OHA-Jr.	1	0	1	0	40	5	0	7.50	....	....	....	....	....	....	....	....	....	....	....	....	....	....	....	....	....
1959-60	Toronto Marlboros	OHA-Jr.	48	*28	17	3	2880	180	4	3.75	....	....	....	....	....	4	0	4	0	240	17	0	4.25	....	....	....	....
1960-61	Toronto Marlboros	OHA-Jr.	45	9	27	9	2700	187	0	4.15	....	....	....	....	....	....	....	....	....	....	....	....	....	....	....	....	....
1961-62	Brampton 7-Ups	MTJHL	31	....	....	....	1860	155	1	5.00	....	....	....	....	....	5	1	4	0	300	37	0	7.40	....	....	....	....
1962-63	University of British Columbia	WCIAA	STATISTICS NOT AVAILABLE																								
1963-64	Canada	Nat-Team	STATISTICS NOT AVAILABLE																								
	Canada	Olympics	6	1	1	0	173	12	....	4.16	....	....	....	....	....	....	....	....	....	....	....	....	....	....	....	....	....
1964-65	Canada	Nat-Team	STATISTICS NOT AVAILABLE																								
	Canada	WEC-A	5	4	1	0	300	11	2	2.20	....	....	....	....	....	....	....	....	....	....	....	....	....	....	....	....	....
1965-66	Vancouver Canucks	WHL	3	1	1	1	190	8	0	2.53	....	....	....	....	....	....	....	....	....	....	....	....	....	....	....	....	....
	Canada	WEC-A	3	3	0	0	180	2	2	0.67	....	....	....	....	....	....	....	....	....	....	....	....	....	....	....	....	....
1966-67	Canada	Nat-Team	STATISTICS NOT AVAILABLE																								
1967-68	Winnipeg Nationals	WCSHL	9	....	....	....	540	23	1	2.77	....	....	....	....	....	....	....	....	....	....	....	....	....	....	....	....	....
	Hull Nationals	QSHL	1	1	0	0	60	3	0	3.00	....	....	....	....	....	....	....	....	....	....	....	....	....	....	....	....	....
	Canada	Olympics	5	3	2	0	280	12	1	2.57	....	....	....	....	....	....	....	....	....	....	....	....	....	....	....	....	....
1968-69	Phoenix Roadrunners	WHL	34	9	17	5	1904	115	2	3.62	....	....	....	....	....	....	....	....	....	....	....	....	....	....	....	....	....
1969-70	Iowa Stars	CHL	16	9	5	2	930	44	2	2.84	....	....	....	....	....	....	....	....	....	....	....	....	....	....	....	....	....
	Minnesota North Stars	**NHL**	**7**	**2**	**4**	**0**	**360**	**26**	**0**	**4.33**	**4.61**	....	....	....	....	....	....	....	....	....	....	....	....	....	....	....	....
	Phoenix Roadrunners	WHL	8	3	2	1	440	23	1	3.14	....	....	....	....	....	....	....	....	....	....	....	....	....	....	....	....	....
1970-71	Oakville Oaks	OHA-Sr.	40	....	....	....	2400	202	0	5.05	....	....	....	....	....	....	....	....	....	....	....	....	....	....	....	....	....
	Galt Hornets	Al-Cup	STATISTICS NOT AVAILABLE																								
1971-72	San Diego Gulls	WHL	42	18	15	7	2359	128	*3	3.26	....	....	....	....	....	2	0	2	0	119	6	0	3.03	....	....	....	....
1972-73	San Diego Gulls	WHL	51	*24	20	6	*2977	146	*3	*2.94	....	....	....	....	....	3	0	3	0	145	17	0	7.02	....	....	....	....
1973-74	**Boston Bruins**	**NHL**	**5**	**2**	**2**	**1**	**300**	**16**	**0**	**3.20**	**3.09**	....	....	....	....	....	....	....	....	....	....	....	....	....	....	....	....
	Boston Braves	AHL	6	1	4	0	318	18	0	3.39	....	....	....	....	....	....	....	....	....	....	....	....	....	....	....	....	....
	San Diego Gulls	WHL	4	1	3	0	220	19	0	5.18	....	....	....	....	....	....	....	....	....	....	....	....	....	....	....	....	....
1974-75	**Boston Bruins**	**NHL**	**15**	**7**	**6**	**0**	**804**	**32**	**1**	**2.39**	**2.15**	....	....	....	....	....	....	....	....	....	....	....	....	....	....	....	....
	Rochester Americans	AHL	3	1	2	0	180	15	0	5.00	....	....	....	....	....	....	....	....	....	....	....	....	....	....	....	....	....
	Binghamton Dusters	NAHL	2	0	2	0	120	10	0	5.00	....	....	....	....	....	....	....	....	....	....	....	....	....	....	....	....	....
1975-76	Rochester Americans	AHL	42	22	13	7	2541	36	2	3.21	....	....	....	....	....	3	1	2	0	180	12	0	4.00	....	....	....	....
1976-77	Edmonton Oilers	WHA	40	18	18	1	2301	134	*4	3.49	....	....	....	....	....	3	1	2	0	179	10	0	3.35	....	....	....	....
1977-78	Edmonton Oilers	WHA	9	2	5	0	497	42	0	5.07	....	....	....	....	....	....	....	....	....	....	....	....	....	....	....	....	....
	Quebec Nordiques	WHA	24	9	8	1	1140	83	0	4.37	....	....	....	....	....	2	0	1	0	48	2	0	2.50	....	....	....	....
	NHL Totals		**27**	**11**	**12**	**1**	**1464**	**74**	**1**	**3.03**	....	....	....	....	....	....	....	....	....	....	....	....	....	....	....	....	....
	Other Major League Totals		73	29	31	2	3938	259	4	3.95	....	....	....	....	....	5	1	3	....	227	12	0	3.17	....	....	....	....

• Brother of Len • Olympic Games All-Star Team (1968) • Named Best Goaltender at Olympic Games (1968) • WHL First All-Star Team (1973) • Won WHL Leading Goaltender Award (1973)
• Won Leader Cup (WHL - MVP) (1973)

• Shared shutout with Seth Martin in 1964 Olympics (Canada 8, Switzerland 0), January 8, 1964. Rights traded to **Minnesota** by **Toronto** for cash, June 6, 1967. Signed as a free agent by **San Diego** (WHL), June 12, 1971. Traded to **Boston** by **San Diego** (WHL) for cash and future considerations (John Adams, June 12, 1973), March 10, 1973. Signed as a free agent by **Edmonton** (WHA), September 28, 1976. Traded to **Quebec** (WHA) by **Edmonton** (WHA) with Dave Inkpen, Warren Miller and Rick Morris for Pierre Guite and Don McLeod, November, 1977.

• BRODERICK, Len   Leonard Francis   G – L. 5'11", 175 lbs.   b: Toronto, Ont., 10/11/1938.

Season	Club	League	GP	W	L	T	Mins	GA	SO	Avg	AAvg	Eff	SA	S%	SAPG	GP	W	L	T	Mins	GA	SO	Avg	Eff	SA	S%	SAPG
1955-56	Toronto Marlboros	OHA-Jr.	5	4	1	0	300	8	1	1.60	....	....	....	....	....	11	8	2	1	660	26	1	*2.36	....	....	....	....
1956-57	Toronto Marlboros	OHA-Jr.	42	28	11	3	2520	104	*8	*2.48	....	....	....	....	....	9	5	4	0	540	27	1	3.00	....	....	....	....
	Toronto Marlboros	Mem-Cup	11	*8	1	2	670	20	*4	*1.79	....	....	....	....	....	....	....	....	....	....	....	....	....	....	....	....	....
1957-58	Toronto Marlboros	OHA-Jr.	40	16	15	9	2400	131	1	*3.28	....	....	....	....	....	18	9	7	2	1062	62	0	3.50	....	....	....	....
	Montreal Canadiens	**NHL**	**1**	**1**	**0**	**0**	**60**	**2**	**0**	**2.00**	**2.19**	....	....	....	....	....	....	....	....	....	....	....	....	....	....	....	....
	Toronto Marlboros	Mem-Cup	5	1	4	0	282	23	0	4.89	....	....	....	....	....	....	....	....	....	....	....	....	....	....	....	....	....
1958-59	Toronto Marlboros	OHA-Jr.	23	....	....	....	1380	72	1	3.13	....	....	....	....	....	5	1	4	0	300	24	0	4.80	....	....	....	....
1959-60	Oakville Oaks	OHA-Sr.	STATISTICS NOT AVAILABLE																								
	St. Paul Saints	IHL	3	....	....	....	180	16	0	5.33	....	....	....	....	....	....	....	....	....	....	....	....	....	....	....	....	....
	NHL Totals		**1**	**1**	**0**	**0**	**60**	**2**	**0**	**2.00**	....	....	....	....	....	....	....	....	....	....	....	....	....	....	....	....	....

• Brother of Ken

Loaned to **Montreal** by **Toronto** (Toronto/OHA-Jr.) to replace Jacques Plante, October 30, 1957. (Montreal 6, Toronto 2)

• BRODEUR, Martin   Martin Pierre   G – L. 6'2", 205 lbs.   b: Montreal, Que., 5/6/1972. New Jersey's 1st, 20th overall in 1990.

Season	Club	League	GP	W	L	T	Mins	GA	SO	Avg	AAvg	Eff	SA	S%	SAPG	GP	W	L	T	Mins	GA	SO	Avg	Eff	SA	S%	SAPG
1988-89	Montreal-Bourassa Canadiens	QAAA	27	13	12	1	1580	98	0	3.72	....	....	....	....	....	....	....	....	....	....	....	....	....	....	....	....	....
1989-90	St-Hyacinthe Laser	QMJHL	42	23	13	2	2333	156	0	4.01	....	....	....	....	....	12	5	7	....	678	46	0	4.07	....	....	....	....
1990-91	St-Hyacinthe Laser	QMJHL	52	22	24	4	2946	162	2	3.30	....	....	....	....	....	4	0	4	....	232	16	0	4.14	....	....	....	....
1991-92	St-Hyacinthe Laser	QMJHL	48	27	16	4	2846	161	2	3.39	....	....	....	....	....	5	2	3	....	317	14	0	2.65	....	....	....	....
	New Jersey Devils	**NHL**	**4**	**2**	**1**	**0**	**179**	**10**	**0**	**3.35**	**3.00**	**3.94**	**85**	**.882**	**28.5**	**1**	**0**	**1**	....	**32**	**3**	**0**	**5.63**	**11.26**	**15**	**.800**	**28.1**
1992-93	Utica Devils	AHL	32	14	13	5	1952	131	0	4.03	....	....	....	....	....	4	1	3	....	258	18	0	4.19	....	....	....	....
1993-94	**New Jersey Devils**	**NHL**	**47**	**27**	**11**	**8**	**2625**	**105**	**3**	**2.40**	**2.29**	**2.04**	**1238**	**.915**	**28.3**	**17**	**8**	**9**	....	**1171**	**38**	**1**	**1.95**	**1.40**	**531**	**.928**	**27.2**
1994-95♦	**New Jersey Devils**	**NHL**	**40**	**19**	**11**	**6**	**2184**	**89**	**3**	**2.45**	**2.55**	**2.40**	**908**	**.902**	**24.9**	***20**	***16**	**4**	....	***1222**	**34**	***3**	***1.67**	**1.23**	**463**	**.927**	**22.7**
1995-96	**New Jersey Devils**	**NHL**	**77**	**34**	**30**	**12**	***4433**	**173**	**6**	**2.34**	**2.31**	**2.07**	**1954**	**.911**	**26.4**	....	....	....	....	....	....	....	....	....	....	....	....
	Canada	WC-A	3	....	....	....	180	9	0	3.00	....	....	....	....	....	....	....	....	....	....	....	....	....	....	....	....	....
1996-97	Canada	W-Cup	2	0	1	0	60	4	0	4.00	....	....	....	....	....	....	....	....	....	....	....	....	....	....	....	....	....
	New Jersey Devils	**NHL**	**67**	**37**	**14**	**13**	**3838**	**120**	***10**	***1.88**	**2.00**	**1.38**	**1633**	**.927**	**25.5**	**10**	**5**	**5**	....	**659**	**19**	**2**	***1.73**	**1.23**	**268**	**.929**	**24.4**

			REGULAR SEASON													PLAYOFFS											
Season	**Club**	**League**	**GP**	**W**	**L**	**T**	**Mins**	**GA**	**SO**	**Avg**	**AAvg**	**Eff**	**SA**	**S%**	**SAPG**	**GP**	**W**	**L**	**T**	**Mins**	**GA**	**SO**	**Avg**	**Eff**	**SA**	**S%**	**SAPG**
1997-98	**New Jersey Devils**	**NHL**	**70**	***43**	**17**	**8**	**4128**	**130**	**10**	**1.89**	**2.23**	**1.57**	**1569**	**.917**	**22.8**	**6**	**2**	**4**	....	**366**	**12**	**0**	**1.97**	**1.44**	**164**	**.927**	**26.9**
	Canada	Olympics	DID NOT PLAY – SPARE GOALTENDER																								
1998-99	**New Jersey Devils**	**NHL**	***70**	***39**	**21**	**10**	***4239**	**162**	**4**	**2.29**	**2.71**	**2.15**	**1728**	**.906**	**24.5**	**7**	**3**	**4**	....	**425**	**20**	**0**	**2.82**	**4.06**	**139**	**.856**	**19.6**
99-2000♦	**New Jersey Devils**	**NHL**	**72**	***43**	**20**	**8**	**4312**	**161**	**6**	**2.24**	**2.55**	**2.01**	**1797**	**.910**	**25.0**	***23**	***16**	**7**	....	***1450**	**39**	**2**	***1.61**	**1.17**	**537**	**.927**	**22.2**
	NHL Totals		**447**	**244**	**125**	**65**	**25938**	**950**	**42**	**2.20**	....	....	**10912**	**.913**	**25.2**	**84**	**50**	**34**	....	**5325**	**165**	**8**	**1.86**	....	**2117**	**.922**	**23.9**

QMJHL Second All-Star Team (1992) • NHL All-Rookie Team (1994) • Won Calder Memorial Trophy (1994) • NHL Second All-Star Team (1997, 1998) • Shared William M. Jennings Trophy with Mike Dunham (1997) • Won William M. Jennings Trophy (1998) • Played in NHL All-Star Game (1996, 1997, 1998, 1999, 2000)

• Scored a goal in playoffs vs. Montreal, April 17, 1997.

• BRODEUR, Richard

"King Richard" G – L. 5'7", 160 lbs. b: Longueuil, Que., 9/15/1952. NY Islanders' 7th, 97th overall in 1972.

Season	Club	League	GP	W	L	T	Mins	GA	SO	Avg	AAvg	Eff	SA	S%	SAPG	GP	W	L	T	Mins	GA	SO	Avg	Eff	SA	S%	SAPG
1970-71	Verdun Maple Leafs	QJHL	6	1	4	1	360	47	0	7.83	....	....	....	....	....	....	....	....	....	....	....	....	....	....	....	....	....
	Cornwall Royals	QJHL	35	....	....	....	2100	144	0	4.11	....	....	....	....	....	....	....	....	....	....	....	....	....	....	....	....	....
1971-72	Cornwall Royals	QMJHL	58	*40	17	1	3481	170	*5	*2.93	....	....	....	....	....	*16	*12	3	1	960	44	0	2.75	....	....	....	....
	Cornwall Royals	Mem-Cup	3	*2	1	0	179	4	*1	*1.34	....	....	....	....	....	....	....	....	....	....	....	....	....	....	....	....	....
1972-73	Quebec Nordiques	WHA	24	5	14	2	1288	102	0	4.75	....	....	....	....	....	....	....	....	....	....	....	....	....	....	....	....	....
1973-74	Quebec Nordiques	WHA	30	15	12	1	1607	89	1	3.32	....	....	....	....	....	....	....	....	....	....	....	....	....	....	....	....	....
	Maine Nordiques	NAHL	16	10	5	1	927	47	0	3.04	....	....	....	....	....	....	....	....	....	....	....	....	....	....	....	....	....
1974-75	Quebec Nordiques	WHA	51	29	21	0	2938	188	0	3.84	....	....	....	....	....	*15	8	7	0	*906	48	1	3.18	....	....	....	....
1975-76	Quebec Nordiques	WHA	*69	*44	21	2	*3967	244	2	3.69	....	....	....	....	....	5	1	4	0	299	22	0	4.41	....	....	....	....
1976-77	Quebec Nordiques	WHA	53	29	18	2	2906	167	2	3.45	....	....	....	....	....	17	*12	5	0	1007	55	*1	3.28	....	....	....	....
1977-78	Quebec Nordiques	WHA	36	18	15	2	1962	121	0	3.70	....	....	....	....	....	11	5	5	0	622	38	*1	3.67	....	....	....	....
1978-79	Quebec Nordiques	WHA	42	25	13	3	2433	126	*3	3.11	....	....	....	....	....	3	0	2	0	114	14	0	7.37	....	....	....	....
1979-80	**New York Islanders**	**NHL**	**2**	**1**	**0**	**0**	**80**	**6**	**0**	**4.50**	**3.98**	....	....	....	....	....	....	....	....	....	....	....	....	....	....	....	....
	Indianapolis Checkers	CHL	46	22	19	5	2722	131	*4	*2.88	....	....	....	....	....	6	3	3	0	357	12	*1	*2.02	....	....	....	....
1980-81	**Vancouver Canucks**	**NHL**	**52**	**17**	**18**	**16**	**3024**	**177**	**0**	**3.51**	**2.83**	....	....	....	....	**3**	**0**	**3**	....	**185**	**13**	**0**	**4.22**	....	....	....	....
1981-82	**Vancouver Canucks**	**NHL**	**52**	**20**	**18**	**12**	**3010**	**168**	**2**	**3.35**	**2.58**	....	....	....	....	**17**	**11**	**6**	....	**1089**	**49**	**0**	**2.70**	....	....	....	....
1982-83	**Vancouver Canucks**	**NHL**	**58**	**21**	**26**	**8**	**3291**	**208**	**0**	**3.79**	**3.04**	**4.80**	**1641**	**.873**	**29.9**	**3**	**0**	**3**	....	**193**	**13**	**0**	**4.04**	....	....	....	....
1983-84	**Vancouver Canucks**	**NHL**	**36**	**10**	**21**	**5**	**2110**	**141**	**1**	**4.01**	**3.16**	**5.30**	**1067**	**.868**	**30.3**	**4**	**1**	**3**	....	**222**	**12**	**1**	**3.24**	**3.38**	**115**	**.896**	**31.1**
1984-85	**Vancouver Canucks**	**NHL**	**51**	**16**	**27**	**6**	**2930**	**228**	**0**	**4.67**	**3.75**	**6.76**	**1574**	**.855**	**32.2**	....	....	....	....	....	....	....	....	....	....	....	....
	Fredericton Express	AHL	4	3	0	1	249	13	0	3.13	....	....	....	....	....	....	....	....	....	....	....	....	....	....	....	....	....
1985-86	**Vancouver Canucks**	**NHL**	***64**	**19**	**32**	**8**	***3541**	**240**	**2**	**4.07**	**3.18**	**5.67**	**1724**	**.861**	**29.2**	**2**	**0**	**2**	....	**120**	**12**	**0**	**6.00**	**9.11**	**79**	**.848**	**39.5**
1986-87	**Vancouver Canucks**	**NHL**	**53**	**20**	**25**	**5**	**2972**	**178**	**1**	**3.59**	**3.04**	**4.59**	**1391**	**.872**	**28.1**	....	....	....	....	....	....	....	....	....	....	....	....
1987-88	**Vancouver Canucks**	**NHL**	**11**	**3**	**6**	**2**	**670**	**49**	**0**	**4.39**	**3.66**	**6.20**	**347**	**.859**	**31.1**	....	....	....	....	....	....	....	....	....	....	....	....
	Fredericton Express	AHL	2	0	1	0	99	8	0	4.85	....	....	....	....	....	....	....	....	....	....	....	....	....	....	....	....	....
	Hartford Whalers	**NHL**	**6**	**4**	**2**	**0**	**340**	**15**	**0**	**2.65**	**2.21**	**2.80**	**142**	**.894**	**25.1**	**4**	**1**	**3**	....	**200**	**12**	**0**	**3.60**	**4.97**	**87**	**.862**	**26.1**
1988-89	Binghamton Whalers	AHL	6	1	2	0	222	21	0	5.68	....	....	....	....	....	....	....	....	....	....	....	....	....	....	....	....	....
	NHL Totals		**385**	**131**	**175**	**62**	**21968**	**1410**	**6**	**3.85**	....	....	....	....	....	**33**	**13**	**20**	....	**2009**	**111**	**1**	**3.32**	....	....	....	....
	Other Major League Totals		305	165	114	12	17101	1037	8	3.64	....	....	....	....	....	51	26	23	....	2948	177	3	3.60	....	....	....	....

Won Jacques Plante Trophy (Best Goaltender - QMJHL) (1972) • QMJHL First All-Star Team (1972) • Won Stafford Smythe Memorial Trophy (Memorial Cup Tournament MVP) (1972) • WHA Second All-Star Team (1979) • CHL First All-Star Team (1980) • Shared Terry Sawchuk Trophy (fewest goals against - CHL) with Jim Park (1980)

Selected by **Quebec** (WHA) in 1972 WHA General Player Draft, February 12, 1972. Reclaimed by **NY Islanders** from **Quebec** prior to Expansion Draft, June 9, 1979. Claimed as a priority selection by **Quebec**, June 9, 1979. Traded to **NY Islanders** by **Quebec** for Goran Hogasta, August, 1979. Traded to **Vancouver** by **NY Islanders** with NY Islanders' 5th round choice (Moe Lemay) in 1981 Entry Draft for Vancouver's 5th round choice (Jacques Sylvestre) in 1981 Entry Draft, October 6, 1980. Traded to **Hartford** by **Vancouver** for Steve Weeks, March 8, 1988.

• BROMLEY, Gary

Gary Bert "Bones" G – L. 5'10", 160 lbs. b: Edmonton, Alta., 1/19/1950.

Season	Club	League	GP	W	L	T	Mins	GA	SO	Avg	AAvg	Eff	SA	S%	SAPG	GP	W	L	T	Mins	GA	SO	Avg	Eff	SA	S%	SAPG
1968-69	Regina Pats	SJHL	STATISTICS NOT AVAILABLE																								
	Regina Pats	Mem-Cup	11	4	7	0	680	48	0	4.24	....	....	....	....	....	....	....	....	....	....	....	....	....	....	....	....	....
1969-70	Regina Pats	SJHL	34	....	....	....	2002	119	0	3.57	....	....	....	....	....	....	....	....	....	....	....	....	....	....	....	....	....
	Weyburn Red Wings	Mem-Cup	2	0	1	0	9	2	0	13.33	....	....	....	....	....	....	....	....	....	....	....	....	....	....	....	....	....
1970-71	Regina Pats	WCJHL	42	....	....	....	2457	152	2	3.71	....	....	....	....	....	6	....	....	....	340	24	0	4.24	....	....	....	....
1971-72	Charlotte Checkers	EHL	27	....	....	....	1620	73	4	2.70	....	....	....	....	....	1	0	1	0	60	7	0	7.00	....	....	....	....
	Cincinnati Swords	AHL	3	1	1	1	180	6	1	2.00	....	....	....	....	....	....	....	....	....	....	....	....	....	....	....	....	....
1972-73	Cincinnati Swords	AHL	31	....	....	....	1711	76	0	2.66	....	....	....	....	....	3	3	0	0	180	5	*1	1.67	....	....	....	....
1973-74	**Buffalo Sabres**	**NHL**	**12**	**3**	**5**	**3**	**598**	**33**	**0**	**3.31**	**3.20**	....	....	....	....	....	....	....	....	....	....	....	....	....	....	....	....
	Cincinnati Swords	AHL	34	19	11	3	1906	89	1	2.80	....	....	....	....	....	5	1	4	0	302	17	0	3.37	....	....	....	....
1974-75	**Buffalo Sabres**	**NHL**	**50**	**26**	**11**	**11**	**2787**	**144**	**4**	**3.10**	**2.79**	....	....	....	....	....	....	....	....	....	....	....	....	....	....	....	....
1975-76	**Buffalo Sabres**	**NHL**	**1**	**0**	**1**	**0**	**60**	**7**	**0**	**7.00**	**6.34**	....	....	....	....	....	....	....	....	....	....	....	....	....	....	....	....
	Providence Reds	AHL	7	4	1	1	405	30	0	4.44	....	....	....	....	....	....	....	....	....	....	....	....	....	....	....	....	....
1976-77	Calgary Cowboys	WHA	28	6	9	2	1237	79	0	3.83	....	....	....	....	....	....	....	....	....	....	....	....	....	....	....	....	....
1977-78	Winnipeg Jets	WHA	39	25	12	1	2250	124	1	3.31	....	....	....	....	....	5	4	0	0	268	7	0	*1.57	....	....	....	....
1978-79	**Vancouver Canucks**	**NHL**	**38**	**11**	**19**	**6**	**2144**	**136**	**2**	**3.81**	**3.38**	....	....	....	....	**3**	**1**	**2**	....	**180**	**14**	**0**	**4.67**	....	....	....	....
	Dallas Black Hawks	CHL	4	2	1	1	250	6	1	1.44	....	....	....	....	....	....	....	....	....	....	....	....	....	....	....	....	....
1979-80	**Vancouver Canucks**	**NHL**	**15**	**8**	**2**	**4**	**860**	**43**	**1**	**3.00**	**2.65**	....	....	....	....	**4**	**1**	**3**	....	**180**	**11**	**0**	**3.67**	....	....	....	....
	Dallas Black Hawks	CHL	21	8	9	3	1289	88	0	4.10	....	....	....	....	....	....	....	....	....	....	....	....	....	....	....	....	....
1980-81	**Vancouver Canucks**	**NHL**	**20**	**6**	**6**	**4**	**978**	**62**	**0**	**3.80**	**3.07**	....	....	....	....	....	....	....	....	....	....	....	....	....	....	....	....
	Dallas Black Hawks	CHL	2	1	1	0	127	8	0	3.78	....	....	....	....	....	....	....	....	....	....	....	....	....	....	....	....	....
1981-82	New Haven Nighthawks	AHL	44	22	17	3	2538	148	3	3.50	....	....	....	....	....	3	1	1	0	208	10	0	2.88	....	....	....	....
	NHL Totals		**136**	**54**	**44**	**28**	**7427**	**425**	**7**	**3.43**	....	....	....	....	....	**7**	**2**	**5**	....	**360**	**25**	**0**	**4.17**	....	....	....	....
	Other Major League Totals		67	31	21	3	3487	203	1	3.49	....	....	....	....	....	5	4	0	....	268	7	0	1.57	....	....	....	....

Loaned to **Weyburn** (SJHL) by **Regina** (SJHL) as emergency injury replacement during Memorial Cup playoffs, May, 1970. Signed as a free agent by **Buffalo**, September 29, 1971. Selected by **NY Raiders** (WHA) in 1972 WHA General Player Draft, February 12, 1972. WHA rights traded to **Calgary** (WHA) by **San Diego** (WHA), August, 1976. Signed as a free agent by **Winnipeg** (WHA) after **Calgary** (WHA) franchise folded, May 31, 1977. Signed as a free agent by **Vancouver**, May 23, 1978. Traded to **LA Kings** by **Vancouver** to complete transaction that sent Doug Halward to Vancouver (March 8, 1981), May 12, 1981.

• BROOKS, Art

G. b: Guelph, Ont., 1892 Deceased.

Season	Club	League	GP	W	L	T	Mins	GA	SO	Avg	AAvg	Eff	SA	S%	SAPG	GP	W	L	T	Mins	GA	SO	Avg	Eff	SA	S%	SAPG
1906-07	Guelph Lyons	OHA-Jr.	3	3	0	0	180	8	0	2.67	....	....	....	....	....	....	....	....	....	....	....	....	....	....	....	....	....
1907-08			DID NOT PLAY																								
1908-09	Pittsburgh Duquesne	WPHL	4	0	3	1	250	19	0	4.56	....	....	....	....	....	....	....	....	....	....	....	....	....	....	....	....	....
1909-10	Owen Sound Seniors	OHA-Sr.	STATISTICS NOT AVAILABLE																								
1910-11	Owen Sound Seniors	OHA-Sr.	STATISTICS NOT AVAILABLE																								
1911-12	Guelph Maple Leafs	OHA-Sr.	STATISTICS NOT AVAILABLE																								
1912-13	Owen Sound Seniors	OHA-Sr.	STATISTICS NOT AVAILABLE																								
1913-14			STATISTICS NOT AVAILABLE																								
1914-15			MILITARY SERVICE																								
1915-16			MILITARY SERVICE																								
1916-17	NY Irish-Americans	AAHL	DID NOT PLAY – SUSPENDED																								
	Toronto Arenas	NHA	4	2	2	0	238	16	0	4.03	....	....	....	....	....	....	....	....	....	....	....	....	....	....	....	....	....
1917-18	**Toronto Arenas**	**NHL**	**4**	**2**	**2**	**0**	**220**	**23**	**0**	**6.27**	**4.09**	....	....	....	....	....	....	....	....	....	....	....	....	....	....	....	....
	NHL Totals		**4**	**2**	**2**	**0**	**220**	**23**	**0**	**6.27**	....	....	....	....	....	....	....	....	....	....	....	....	....	....	....	....	....
	Other Major League Totals		4	2	2	0	238	16	0	4.03	....	....	....	....	....	....	....	....	....	....	....	....	....	....	....	....	....

Signed as a free agent by **Pittsburgh** (WPHL), November 1, 1908. • Suspended by USAHA for signing amateur contract with NY Irish Americans (AAHL), January 8, 1917. Signed as a free agent by **Toronto Arenas** (NHA), January 30, 1917. Claimed by **Montreal Canadiens** (NHA) from **Toronto Arenas** (NHA) in Dispersal Draft, February 11, 1917. Signed as a free agent by **Toronto**, December 15, 1917.

• BROOKS, Ross
Donald Ross G – L. 5'8", 173 lbs. b: Toronto, Ont., 10/17/1937.

			REGULAR SEASON													PLAYOFFS											
Season	Club	League	GP	W	L	T	Mins	GA	SO	Avg	AAvg	Eff	SA	S%	SAPG	GP	W	L	T	Mins	GA	SO	Avg	Eff	SA	S%	SAPG
1954-55	Barrie Flyers	OHA-Jr.	11	....	....	....	660	69	0	6.27	....	....	....	....	....	....	....	....	....	....	....	....	....	....	....	....	....
1955-56	Lakeshore Bruins	OHA-B	STATISTICS NOT AVAILABLE																								
1956-57	Barrie Flyers	OHA-Jr.	43	11	31	1	2580	182	4	4.23	....	....	....	....	....	2	0	2	0	120	9	0	4.50	....	....	....	....
1957-58	Barrie Flyers	OHA-Jr.	23	....	....	....	1380	110	1	4.78	....	....	....	....	....	3	1	2	0	180	16	0	5.33	....	....	....	....
1958-59	North Bay-Windsor-Kitchener	NOHA	12	....	....	....	720	63	0	5.25	....	....	....	....	....	....	....	....	....	....	....	....	....	....	....	....	....
	Washington Presidents	EHL	26	....	....	....	1560	118	1	4.54	....	....	....	....	....	....	....	....	....	....	....	....	....	....	....	....	....
1959-60	Philadelphia Ramblers	EHL	....	....	....	....	....	....	....	....	....	....	....	....	....	2	1	1	0	120	5	0	2.50	....	....	....	....
1960-61	Philadelphia Ramblers	EHL	64	32	28	4	3840	278	0	4.34	....	....	....	....	....	3	0	3	0	180	13	0	4.33	....	....	....	....
	Jersey Devils	EHL	1	1	0	0	60	3	0	3.00	....	....	....	....	....	....	....	....	....	....	....	....	....	....	....	....	....
	Providence Reds	AHL	2	....	....	....	20	3	0	9.00	....	....	....	....	....	....	....	....	....	....	....	....	....	....	....	....	....
1961-62	Philadelphia Ramblers	EHL	68	28	38	2	4080	337	0	4.96	....	....	....	....	....	3	....	....	....	180	12	0	4.00	....	....	....	....
	Long Island Ducks	EHL	1	0	1	0	60	7	0	7.00	....	....	....	....	....	....	....	....	....	....	....	....	....	....	....	....	....
	Johnstown Jets	EHL	2	0	2	0	120	16	0	8.00	....	....	....	....	....	3	0	3	0	180	12	0	4.00	....	....	....	....
1962-63	Philadelphia Ramblers	EHL	63	27	33	3	3780	272	3	4.32	....	....	....	....	....	3	0	3	0	180	13	0	4.33	....	....	....	....
1963-64	EHL Roving Goaltender	EHL	16	....	....	....	960	68	1	4.25	....	....	....	....	....	....	....	....	....	....	....	....	....	....	....	....	....
	Providence Reds	AHL	3	2	1	0	180	6	0	2.00	....	....	....	....	....	....	....	....	....	....	....	....	....	....	....	....	....
1964-65	Providence Reds	AHL	12	1	10	0	725	70	1	5.79	....	....	....	....	....	....	....	....	....	....	....	....	....	....	....	....	....
1965-66	Providence Reds	AHL	13	3	9	1	770	66	0	5.14	....	....	....	....	....	....	....	....	....	....	....	....	....	....	....	....	....
1966-67	Providence Reds	AHL	32	9	16	6	1849	137	0	4.45	....	....	....	....	....	....	....	....	....	....	....	....	....	....	....	....	....
1967-68	Providence Reds	AHL	19	7	10	1	1120	82	0	4.39	....	....	....	....	....	1	0	0	0	20	1	0	3.00	....	....	....	....
1968-69	Providence Reds	AHL	22	7	10	0	1097	80	0	4.38	....	....	....	....	....	....	....	....	....	....	....	....	....	....	....	....	....
1969-70	Providence Reds	AHL	13	....	....	....	612	43	0	4.22	....	....	....	....	....	....	....	....	....	....	....	....	....	....	....	....	....
1970-71	Providence Reds	AHL	12	1	7	3	657	40	1	3.65	....	....	....	....	....	....	....	....	....	....	....	....	....	....	....	....	....
	Phoenix Roadrunners	WHL	1	0	1	0	60	5	0	5.00	....	....	....	....	....	....	....	....	....	....	....	....	....	....	....	....	....
	Oklahoma City Blazers	CHL	9	....	....	....	530	44	0	4.99	....	....	....	....	....	1	0	1	0	20	5	0	15.00	....	....	....	....
1971-72	Boston Braves	AHL	30	14	8	7	1639	65	1	*2.38	....	....	....	....	....	5	2	2	0	248	12	0	2.90	....	....	....	....
1972-73	Boston Braves	AHL	7	....	....	....	379	16	0	2.52	....	....	....	....	....	....	....	....	....	....	....	....	....	....	....	....	....
	Boston Bruins	**NHL**	**16**	**11**	**1**	**3**	**910**	**40**	**1**	**2.64**	**2.48**	....	....	....	....	**1**	**0**	**0**	....	**20**	**3**	**0**	**9.00**	....	....	....	....
1973-74	**Boston Bruins**	**NHL**	**21**	**16**	**3**	**0**	**1170**	**46**	**3**	**2.36**	**2.27**	....	....	....	....	....	....	....	....	....	....	....	....	....	....	....	....
	Boston Braves	AHL	5	3	0	1	280	15	0	3.21	....	....	....	....	....	....	....	....	....	....	....	....	....	....	....	....	....
1974-75	**Boston Bruins**	**NHL**	**17**	**10**	**3**	**3**	**967**	**48**	**0**	**2.98**	**2.69**	....	....	....	....	....	....	....	....	....	....	....	....	....	....	....	....
1975-76	Rochester Americans	AHL	34	20	12	2	2056	103	2	3.00	....	....	....	....	....	4	2	2	0	239	17	0	4.27	....	....	....	....
	NHL Totals		**54**	**37**	**7**	**6**	**3047**	**134**	**4**	**2.64**	....	....	....	....	....	**1**	**0**	**0**	....	**20**	**3**	**0**	**9.00**	....	....	....	....

Shared Harry "Hap" Holmes Memorial Award (fewest goals against - AHL) with Dan Bouchard (1972)

• Signed as an emergency injury replacement goaltender by **EHL** for 1963-64 season. Signed as a free agent by **Boston**, October 2, 1971.

• BROPHY, Frank
G – L. 5'6", 150 lbs. b: Quebec City, Que., 1900 Deceased.

Season	Club	League	GP	W	L	T	Mins	GA	SO	Avg	AAvg	Eff	SA	S%	SAPG	GP	W	L	T	Mins	GA	SO	Avg	Eff	SA	S%	SAPG
1914-15	Quebec Crescents	QCHL	STATISTICS NOT AVAILABLE																								
1915-16	Quebec Crescents	QCHL	STATISTICS NOT AVAILABLE																								
1916-17	Quebec St. Pats	QCHL	5	2	3	0	300	19	0	3.80	....	....	....	....	....	....	....	....	....	....	....	....	....	....	....	....	....
1917-18	Montreal St. Anns	MCHL	9	6	2	1	537	19	2	2.12	....	....	....	....	....	2	1	1	0	120	5	0	2.50	....	....	....	....
	Montreal Westmount	MCHL	STATISTICS NOT AVAILABLE																								
1918-19	Montreal Vickers	MCHL	10	*9	0	1	600	24	*1	2.40	....	....	....	....	....	....	....	....	....	....	....	....	....	....	....	....	....
1919-20	**Quebec Bulldogs**	**NHL**	**21**	**3**	**18**	**0**	**1249**	**148**	**0**	**7.11**	**5.22**	....	....	....	....	....	....	....	....	....	....	....	....	....	....	....	....
	Quebec Crescents	QCHL	1	1	0	0	60	2	0	2.00	....	....	....	....	....	....	....	....	....	....	....	....	....	....	....	....	....
1920-21	Quebec Telegraph	QCHL	STATISTICS NOT AVAILABLE																								
	NHL Totals		**21**	**3**	**18**	**0**	**1249**	**148**	**0**	**7.11**	....	....	....	....	....	....	....	....	....	....	....	....	....	....	....	....	....

MCHL First All-Star Team (1918, 1919)

Signed as a free agent by **Quebec**, November 25, 1919.

• BROWN, Andy
Andrew Conrad G – L. 6', 185 lbs. b: Hamilton, Ont., 2/15/1944.

Season	Club	League	GP	W	L	T	Mins	GA	SO	Avg	AAvg	Eff	SA	S%	SAPG	GP	W	L	T	Mins	GA	SO	Avg	Eff	SA	S%	SAPG
1962-63	Guelph Royals	OHA-Jr.	20	....	....	....	1200	100	1	5.00	....	....	....	....	....	....	....	....	....	....	....	....	....	....	....	....	....
	Brampton 7-Ups	MTJHL	20	....	....	....	1175	109	0	5.54	....	....	....	....	....	....	....	....	....	....	....	....	....	....	....	....	....
1963-64			STATISTICS NOT AVAILABLE																								
1964-65	Gander Flyers	Nfld-Sr.	18	5	13	0	1079	105	1	5.84	....	....	....	....	....	....	....	....	....	....	....	....	....	....	....	....	....
1965-66	Baltimore Clippers	AHL	1	0	0	0	14	3	0	12.86	....	....	....	....	....	....	....	....	....	....	....	....	....	....	....	....	....
	Johnstown Jets	EHL	70	39	29	2	4200	253	0	3.61	....	....	....	....	....	3	0	3	0	180	14	0	4.67	....	....	....	....
1966-67	Long Island Ducks	EHL	45	23	19	3	2676	137	3	3.07	....	....	....	....	....	3	0	3	0	180	15	0	5.00	....	....	....	....
	Johnstown Jets	EHL	1	0	1	0	60	6	0	6.00	....	....	....	....	....	....	....	....	....	....	....	....	....	....	....	....	....
1967-68	Johnstown Jets	EHL	72	38	25	9	4320	273	4	3.79	....	....	....	....	....	2	0	2	0	....	13	0	8.33	....	....	....	....
1968-69	Baltimore Clippers	AHL	41	16	19	3	2211	134	2	3.64	....	....	....	....	....	....	....	....	....	....	....	....	....	....	....	....	....
1969-70	Baltimore Clippers	AHL	40	....	....	....	2082	125	1	3.60	....	....	....	....	....	....	....	....	....	....	....	....	....	....	....	....	....
1970-71	Baltimore Clippers	AHL	50	*28	13	8	*2954	141	4	2.86	....	....	....	....	....	6	2	4	0	360	18	*1	3.00	....	....	....	....
1971-72	**Detroit Red Wings**	**NHL**	**10**	**4**	**5**	**1**	**560**	**37**	**0**	**3.96**	**4.01**	....	....	....	....	....	....	....	....	....	....	....	....	....	....	....	....
	Fort Worth Wings	CHL	16	9	4	3	960	52	0	3.25	....	....	....	....	....	....	....	....	....	....	....	....	....	....	....	....	....
	Tidewater Wings	AHL	23	4	16	1	1278	86	0	4.04	....	....	....	....	....	....	....	....	....	....	....	....	....	....	....	....	....
1972-73	**Detroit Red Wings**	**NHL**	**7**	**2**	**1**	**2**	**337**	**20**	**0**	**3.56**	**3.36**	....	....	....	....	....	....	....	....	....	....	....	....	....	....	....	....
	Fort Worth Wings	CHL	22	....	....	....	1300	86	2	3.97	....	....	....	....	....	....	....	....	....	....	....	....	....	....	....	....	....
	Pittsburgh Penguins	**NHL**	**9**	**3**	**4**	**2**	**520**	**41**	**0**	**4.73**	**4.47**	....	....	....	....	....	....	....	....	....	....	....	....	....	....	....	....
1973-74	**Pittsburgh Penguins**	**NHL**	**36**	**13**	**16**	**4**	**1956**	**115**	**1**	**3.53**	**3.42**	....	....	....	....	....	....	....	....	....	....	....	....	....	....	....	....
1974-75	Indianapolis Racers	WHA	52	15	35	0	2979	206	2	4.15	....	....	....	....	....	....	....	....	....	....	....	....	....	....	....	....	....
1975-76	Indianapolis Racers	WHA	24	9	11	2	1368	82	1	3.60	....	....	....	....	....	....	....	....	....	....	....	....	....	....	....	....	....
1976-77	Indianapolis Racers	WHA	10	1	4	1	430	26	0	3.63	....	....	....	....	....	....	....	....	....	....	....	....	....	....	....	....	....
	NHL Totals		**62**	**22**	**26**	**9**	**3373**	**213**	**1**	**3.79**	....	....	....	....	....	....	....	....	....	....	....	....	....	....	....	....	....
	Other Major League Totals		86	25	50	3	4777	314	3	3.94	....	....	....	....	....	....	....	....	....	....	....	....	....	....	....	....	....

• Son of Adam • EHL North Second All-Star Team (1966) • AHL First All-Star Team (1971)

Loaned to **Johnstown** (EHL) by **Long Island** (EHL) as emergency injury replacement, January 25, 1967. Claimed by **Detroit** from **Baltimore** (AHL) in Inter-League Draft, June 7, 1971. Selected by **Minnesota** (WHA) in 1972 WHA General Player Draft, February 12, 1972. Traded to **Pittsburgh** by **Detroit** for Pittsburgh's 3rd round choice (Nelson Pyatt) in 1973 Amateur Draft and cash, February 25, 1973. WHA rights traded to **Indianapolis** (WHA) by **Minnesota** (WHA) for future considerations, July, 1974. • Last NHL goaltender to play without a facemask.

• BROWN, Ken
Kenneth Murray G – L. 5'11", 175 lbs. b: Port Arthur, Ont., 12/19/1948.

Season	Club	League	GP	W	L	T	Mins	GA	SO	Avg	AAvg	Eff	SA	S%	SAPG	GP	W	L	T	Mins	GA	SO	Avg	Eff	SA	S%	SAPG
1964-65	Moose Jaw Canucks	SJHL	13	....	....	....	780	60	1	4.61	....	....	....	....	....	....	....	....	....	....	....	....	....	....	....	....	....
1965-66	Moose Jaw Canucks	SJHL	14	....	....	....	830	60	0	4.34	....	....	....	....	....	....	....	....	....	....	....	....	....	....	....	....	....
	Estevan Bruins	SJHL	20	....	....	....	1190	46	1	2.32	....	....	....	....	....	3	....	....	....	180	13	0	4.33	....	....	....	....
	Estevan Bruins	Mem-Cup	2	1	0	0	100	3	0	1.80	....	....	....	....	....	....	....	....	....	....	....	....	....	....	....	....	....
1966-67	Moose Jaw Canucks	CMJHL	54	24	18	12	3240	174	*3	*3.22	....	....	....	....	....	14	7	3	4	840	55	0	3.93	....	....	....	....
1967-68	Moose Jaw Canucks	WCJHL	58	30	23	5	3480	236	0	4.07	....	....	....	....	....	10	4	5	1	600	56	1	5.60	....	....	....	....
	Estevan Bruins	Mem-Cup	7	3	4	0	426	26	0	3.66	....	....	....	....	....	....	....	....	....	....	....	....	....	....	....	....	....
1968-69	Dallas Black Hawks	CHL	23	....	....	....	1320	79	0	3.59	....	....	....	....	....	....	....	....	....	....	....	....	....	....	....	....	....
1969-70	Dallas Black Hawks	CHL	46	22	19	4	2720	142	4	3.13	....	....	....	....	....	....	....	....	....	....	....	....	....	....	....	....	....
1970-71	**Chicago Black Hawks**	**NHL**	**1**	**0**	**0**	**0**	**18**	**1**	**0**	**3.33**	**3.29**	....	....	....	....	....	....	....	....	....	....	....	....	....	....	....	....
	Dallas Black Hawks	CHL	26	....	....	....	1528	92	0	3.61	....	....	....	....	....	1	1	0	0	60	2	0	2.00	....	....	....	....
1971-72	Dallas Black Hawks	CHL	31	13	10	2	1683	90	2	3.20	....	....	....	....	....	*11	*7	3	0	*650	29	0	2.67	....	....	....	....

Season	Club	League	GP	W	L	T	Mins	GA	SO	Avg	AAvg	Eff	SA	S%	SAPG	GP	W	L	T	Mins	GA	SO	Avg	Eff	SA	S%	SAPG
			REGULAR SEASON													PLAYOFFS											
1972-73	Alberta Oilers	WHA	20	10	8	0	1034	63	1	3.66	....	....	....	....	....	....	....	....	....	....	....	....	....	....	....	....	....
1973-74	Winston-Salem Polar Bears	SHL	29	10	17	0	1575	145	0	5.53	....	....	....	....	....	5	3	2	0	285	12	0	*2.53	....	....	....	....
1974-75	Edmonton Oilers	WHA	32	11	11	0	1466	86	2	3.52	....	....	....	....	....	....	....	....	....	....	....	....	....	....	....	....	....
	NHL Totals		**1**	**0**	**0**	**0**	**18**	**1**	**0**	**3.33**	....	....	....	....	....	....	....	....	....	....	....	....	....	....	....	....	....
	Other Major League Totals		52	21	19	0	2500	149	3	3.58	....	....	....	....	....	....	....	....	....	....	....	....	....	....	....	....	....

CMJHL First All-Star Team (1967)

Selected by **Calgary-Cleveland** (WHA) in 1972 WHA General Player Draft, February 12, 1972. WHA rights traded to **Alberta** (WHA) by **Cleveland** (WHA) for cash, July, 1972.

• BRUNETTA, Mario

G – L. 6'3", 180 lbs. b: Quebec City, Que., 1/25/1967. Quebec's 9th, 162nd overall in 1985.

Season	Club	League	GP	W	L	T	Mins	GA	SO	Avg	AAvg	Eff	SA	S%	SAPG	GP	W	L	T	Mins	GA	SO	Avg	Eff	SA	S%	SAPG
1982-83	Ste-Foy Gouverneurs	QAAA	22	17	4	1	1316	64	0	2.91	....	....	....	....	....	....	....	....	....	....	....	....	....	....	....	....	....
1983-84	Ste-Foy Gouverneurs	QAAA	39	11	23	4	2169	162	0	4.48	....	....	....	....	....	....	....	....	....	....	....	....	....	....	....	....	....
1984-85	Quebec Remparts	QMJHL	45	20	21	1	2255	192	0	5.11	....	....	....	....	....	2	0	2	0	120	13	0	6.50	....	....	....	....
1985-86	Laval Titans	QMJHL	63	30	25	1	3383	279	0	4.95	....	....	....	....	....	14	9	5	0	834	60	0	4.32	....	....	....	....
1986-87	Laval Titans	QMJHL	59	27	25	4	3469	261	1	4.51	....	....	....	....	....	14	8	6	0	820	63	0	4.61	....	....	....	....
1987-88	**Quebec Nordiques**	**NHL**	**29**	**10**	**12**	**1**	**1550**	**96**	**0**	**3.72**	**3.10**	**4.59**	**778**	**.877**	**30.1**	....	....	....	....	....	....	....	....	....	....	....	....
	Fredericton Express	AHL	5	4	1	0	300	24	0	4.80	....	....	....	....	....	....	....	....	....	....	....	....	....	....	....	....	....
1988-89	**Quebec Nordiques**	**NHL**	**5**	**1**	**3**	**0**	**226**	**19**	**0**	**5.04**	**4.20**	**8.18**	**117**	**.838**	**31.1**	....	....	....	....	....	....	....	....	....	....	....	....
	Halifax Citadels	AHL	36	14	14	5	1898	124	0	3.92	....	....	....	....	....	3	0	2	0	142	12	0	5.07	....	....	....	....
1989-90	**Quebec Nordiques**	**NHL**	**6**	**1**	**2**	**0**	**191**	**13**	**0**	**4.08**	**3.46**	**5.36**	**99**	**.869**	**31.1**	....	....	....	....	....	....	....	....	....	....	....	....
	Halifax Citadels	AHL	24	8	14	2	1444	99	0	4.11	....	....	....	....	....	....	....	....	....	....	....	....	....	....	....	....	....
1990-91	HC Asiago	Italy	42	....	....	....	2446	160	3	3.92	....	....	....	....	....	....	....	....	....	....	....	....	....	....	....	....	....
1991-92	HC Asiago	Italy	29	....	....	....	1746	116	1	3.98	....	....	....	....	....	11	....	....	....	668	43	1	3.86	....	....	....	....
1992-93	HC Asiago	Italy	22	....	....	....	1320	94	....	4.27	....	....	....	....	....	....	....	....	....	....	....	....	....	....	....	....	....
1993-94	HC Milano	Italy	29	....	....	....	1551	81	....	3.13	....	....	....	....	....	....	....	....	....	....	....	....	....	....	....	....	....
1994-95	HC Milano	Italy	STATISTICS NOT AVAILABLE																								
	Italy	WC-A	4	1	2	1	167	13	0	4.67	....	....	....	....	....	....	....	....	....	....	....	....	....	....	....	....	....
1995-96	HC Varese	Italy	40	....	....	....	1555	69	....	2.66	....	....	....	....	....	....	....	....	....	....	....	....	....	....	....	....	....
1996-97	Eisbaren Berlin	Germany	46	....	....	....	2729	144	0	3.17	....	....	....	....	....	8	....	....	....	493	24	*1	2.92	....	....	....	....
1997-98	Eisbaren Berlin	Germany	40	....	....	....	2277	101	2	2.66	....	....	....	....	....	*10	*7	3	....	*607	29	*1	3.00	....	....	....	....
	Italy	Olympics	1	0	1	0	23	4	0	10.17	....	....	....	....	....	....	....	....	....	....	....	....	....	....	....	....	....
	Italy	WC-A	1	0	1	0	60	5	0	5.00	....	....	....	....	....	....	....	....	....	....	....	....	....	....	....	....	....
1998-99	Eisbaren Berlin	Germany	25	....	....	....	1296	77	0	3.56	....	....	....	....	....	....	....	....	....	....	....	....	....	....	....	....	....
99-2000	Vastra Frolunda	Sweden	28	....	....	....	1620	71	3	2.63	....	....	....	....	....	....	....	....	....	....	....	....	....	....	....	....	....
	NHL Totals		**40**	**12**	**17**	**1**	**1967**	**128**	**0**	**3.90**	....	....	**994**	**.871**	**30.3**	....	....	....	....	....	....	....	....	....	....	....	....

• BULLOCK, Bruce

Bruce John G – R. 5'7", 160 lbs. b: Toronto, Ont., 5/9/1949.

Season	Club	League	GP	W	L	T	Mins	GA	SO	Avg	AAvg	Eff	SA	S%	SAPG	GP	W	L	T	Mins	GA	SO	Avg	Eff	SA	S%	SAPG
1968-69	Clarkson College	ECAC	28	19	7	2	1676	96	3	3.44	....	....	....	....	....	....	....	....	....	....	....	....	....	....	....	....	....
1969-70	Clarkson College	ECAC	27	25	2	0	1550	79	4	3.06	....	....	....	....	....	....	....	....	....	....	....	....	....	....	....	....	....
1970-71	Clarkson College	ECAC	30	28	1	1	1800	71	1	2.37	....	....	....	....	....	....	....	....	....	....	....	....	....	....	....	....	....
1971-72	Dallas Black Hawks	CHL	5	0	2	1	220	15	0	3.75	....	....	....	....	....	....	....	....	....	....	....	....	....	....	....	....	....
	Seattle Totems	WHL	10	3	7	0	564	43	0	4.57	....	....	....	....	....	....	....	....	....	....	....	....	....	....	....	....	....
1972-73	**Vancouver Canucks**	**NHL**	**14**	**3**	**8**	**3**	**840**	**67**	**0**	**4.79**	**4.54**	....	....	....	....	....	....	....	....	....	....	....	....	....	....	....	....
	Seattle Totems	WHL	13	7	6	0	750	45	0	3.60	....	....	....	....	....	....	....	....	....	....	....	....	....	....	....	....	....
1973-74	Seattle Totems	WHL	46	22	20	3	2703	165	2	3.66	....	....	....	....	....	....	....	....	....	....	....	....	....	....	....	....	....
1974-75	**Vancouver Canucks**	**NHL**	**1**	**0**	**1**	**0**	**60**	**4**	**0**	**4.00**	**3.61**	....	....	....	....	....	....	....	....	....	....	....	....	....	....	....	....
	Seattle Totems	CHL	48	14	20	7	2580	168	1	3.91	....	....	....	....	....	....	....	....	....	....	....	....	....	....	....	....	....
1975-76	Beauce Jaros	NAHL	19	....	....	....	1067	60	2	3.37	....	....	....	....	....	....	....	....	....	....	....	....	....	....	....	....	....
	Tulsa Oilers	CHL	17	13	3	0	958	39	1	2.44	....	....	....	....	....	6	*6	0	0	360	10	*1	*1.67	....	....	....	....
1976-77	**Vancouver Canucks**	**NHL**	**1**	**0**	**0**	**0**	**27**	**3**	**0**	**6.67**	**6.20**	....	....	....	....	....	....	....	....	....	....	....	....	....	....	....	....
	Tulsa Oilers	CHL	40	20	14	6	2347	135	1	3.45	....	....	....	....	....	8	4	4	0	480	21	0	2.63	....	....	....	....
1977-78	Phoenix Roadrunners	PHL	31	....	....	....	1747	104	*1	3.57	....	....	....	....	....	....	....	....	....	....	....	....	....	....	....	....	....
1978-79	Phoenix Roadrunners	PHL	31	....	....	....	1872	100	*1	3.21	....	....	....	....	....	....	....	....	....	....	....	....	....	....	....	....	....
	NHL Totals		**16**	**3**	**9**	**3**	**927**	**74**	**0**	**4.79**	....	....	....	....	....	....	....	....	....	....	....	....	....	....	....	....	....

NCAA East First All-American Team (1970, 1971) • NCAA Championship All-Tournament Team (1970) • ECAC First All-Star Team (1971) • PHL Second All-Star Team (1978)

Traded to **Vancouver** (Seattle-WHL) by **Chicago** (Dallas-CHL) for cash, February 26, 1972.

• BURKE, Sean

Sean M. G – L. 6'4", 210 lbs. b: Windsor, Ont., 1/29/1967. New Jersey's 2nd, 24th overall in 1985.

Season	Club	League	GP	W	L	T	Mins	GA	SO	Avg	AAvg	Eff	SA	S%	SAPG	GP	W	L	T	Mins	GA	SO	Avg	Eff	SA	S%	SAPG
1983-84	St. Michael's Buzzers	OJHL-B	25	....	....	....	1482	120	0	4.86	....	....	....	....	....	....	....	....	....	....	....	....	....	....	....	....	....
1984-85	Toronto Marlboros	OHL	49	25	21	3	2987	211	0	4.24	....	....	....	....	....	5	1	3	....	266	25	0	5.64	....	....	....	....
1985-86	Toronto Marlboros	OHL	47	16	27	3	2840	233	0	4.92	....	....	....	....	....	4	0	4	....	238	24	0	6.05	....	....	....	....
	Canada	WJC-A	2	1	1	0	120	7	0	3.50	....	....	....	....	....	....	....	....	....	....	....	....	....	....	....	....	....
1986-87	Canada	Nat-Team	42	27	13	2	2550	130	0	3.05	....	....	....	....	....	....	....	....	....	....	....	....	....	....	....	....	....
	Canada	WEC-A	5	2	2	1	300	12	0	2.40	....	....	....	....	....	....	....	....	....	....	....	....	....	....	....	....	....
1987-88	Canada	Nat-Team	37	19	9	2	1962	92	1	2.81	....	....	....	....	....	....	....	....	....	....	....	....	....	....	....	....	....
	Canada	Olympics	4	1	2	1	238	12	....	3.02	....	....	....	....	....	....	....	....	....	....	....	....	....	....	....	....	....
	New Jersey Devils	**NHL**	**13**	**10**	**1**	**0**	**689**	**35**	**1**	**3.05**	**2.54**	**3.56**	**300**	**.883**	**26.1**	**17**	**9**	**8**	....	**1001**	**57**	***1**	**3.42**	**3.79**	**515**	**.889**	**30.9**
1988-89	**New Jersey Devils**	**NHL**	**62**	**22**	**31**	**9**	**3590**	**230**	**3**	**3.84**	**3.20**	**4.84**	**1823**	**.874**	**30.5**	....	....	....	....	....	....	....	....	....	....	....	....
	Canada	WEC-A	5	....	....	....	275	10	....	2.18	....	....	....	....	....	....	....	....	....	....	....	....	....	....	....	....	....
1989-90	**New Jersey Devils**	**NHL**	**52**	**22**	**22**	**6**	**2914**	**175**	**0**	**3.60**	**3.05**	**4.34**	**1453**	**.880**	**29.9**	**2**	**0**	**2**	....	**125**	**8**	**0**	**3.84**	**5.39**	**57**	**.860**	**27.4**
1990-91	**New Jersey Devils**	**NHL**	**35**	**8**	**12**	**8**	**1870**	**112**	**0**	**3.59**	**3.23**	**4.60**	**875**	**.872**	**28.1**	....	....	....	....	....	....	....	....	....	....	....	....
	Canada	WEC-A	8	5	1	2	479	21	0	2.63	....	....	....	....	....	....	....	....	....	....	....	....	....	....	....	....	....
1991-92	Canada	Can-Cup	DID NOT PLAY – SPARE GOALTENDER																								
	Canada	Nat-Team	31	18	6	4	1721	75	1	2.61	....	....	....	....	....	....	....	....	....	....	....	....	....	....	....	....	....
	Canada	Olympics	7	5	2	0	429	17	0	2.37	....	....	....	....	....	....	....	....	....	....	....	....	....	....	....	....	....
	San Diego Gulls	IHL	7	4	2	1	424	17	0	2.41	....	....	....	....	....	3	0	3	....	160	13	0	4.88	....	....	....	....
1992-93	**Hartford Whalers**	**NHL**	**50**	**16**	**27**	**3**	**2656**	**184**	**0**	**4.16**	**3.58**	**5.15**	**1485**	**.876**	**33.5**	....	....	....	....	....	....	....	....	....	....	....	....
1993-94	**Hartford Whalers**	**NHL**	**47**	**17**	**24**	**5**	**2750**	**137**	**2**	**2.99**	**2.87**	**2.81**	**1458**	**.906**	**31.8**	....	....	....	....	....	....	....	....	....	....	....	....
1994-95	**Hartford Whalers**	**NHL**	**42**	**17**	**19**	**4**	**2418**	**108**	**0**	**2.68**	**2.80**	**2.35**	**1233**	**.912**	**30.6**	....	....	....	....	....	....	....	....	....	....	....	....
1995-96	**Hartford Whalers**	**NHL**	**66**	**28**	**28**	**6**	**3669**	**190**	**4**	**3.11**	**3.09**	**2.91**	**2034**	**.907**	**33.3**	....	....	....	....	....	....	....	....	....	....	....	....
1996-97	**Hartford Whalers**	**NHL**	**51**	**22**	**22**	**6**	**2985**	**134**	**4**	**2.69**	**2.89**	**2.31**	**1560**	**.914**	**31.4**	....	....	....	....	....	....	....	....	....	....	....	....
	Canada	WC-A	11	7	1	3	608	22	3	2.17	....	....	....	....	....	....	....	....	....	....	....	....	....	....	....	....	....
1997-98	**Carolina Hurricanes**	**NHL**	**25**	**7**	**11**	**5**	**1415**	**66**	**1**	**2.80**	**3.34**	**2.82**	**655**	**.899**	**27.8**	....	....	....	....	....	....	....	....	....	....	....	....
	Vancouver Canucks	**NHL**	**16**	**2**	**9**	**4**	**838**	**49**	**0**	**3.51**	**4.20**	**4.34**	**396**	**.876**	**28.4**	....	....	....	....	....	....	....	....	....	....	....	....
	Philadelphia Flyers	**NHL**	**11**	**7**	**3**	**0**	**632**	**27**	**1**	**2.56**	**3.05**	**2.22**	**311**	**.913**	**29.5**	**5**	**1**	**4**	....	**283**	**17**	**0**	**3.60**	**5.06**	**121**	**.860**	**25.7**
1998-99	**Florida Panthers**	**NHL**	**59**	**21**	**24**	**14**	**3402**	**151**	**3**	**2.66**	**3.17**	**2.47**	**1624**	**.907**	**28.6**	....	....	....	....	....	....	....	....	....	....	....	....
99-2000	**Florida Panthers**	**NHL**	**7**	**2**	**5**	**0**	**418**	**18**	**0**	**2.58**	**2.95**	**2.23**	**208**	**.913**	**29.9**	....	....	....	....	....	....	....	....	....	....	....	....
	Phoenix Coyotes	**NHL**	**35**	**17**	**14**	**3**	**2074**	**88**	**3**	**2.55**	**2.91**	**2.20**	**1022**	**.914**	**29.6**	**5**	**1**	**4**	....	**296**	**16**	**0**	**3.24**	**3.10**	**167**	**.904**	**33.9**
	NHL Totals		**571**	**218**	**252**	**73**	**32320**	**1704**	**22**	**3.16**	....	....	**16437**	**.896**	**30.5**	**29**	**11**	**18**	....	**1705**	**98**	**1**	**3.45**	....	**860**	**.886**	**30.3**

WEC-A All-Star Team (1991) • Played in NHL All-Star Game (1989)

Traded to **Hartford** by **New Jersey** with Eric Weinrich for Bobby Holik and Hartford's 2nd round choice (Jay Pandolfo) in 1993 Entry Draft, August 28, 1992. Transferred to **Carolina** after **Hartford** franchise relocated, June 25, 1997. Traded to **Vancouver** by **Carolina** with Geoff Sanderson and Enrico Ciccone for Kirk McLean and Martin Gelinas, January 3, 1998. Traded to **Philadelphia** by **Vancouver** for Garth Snow, March 4, 1998. Signed as a free agent by **Florida**, September 12, 1998. Traded to **Phoenix** by **Florida** with Florida's 5th round choice (Nate Kiser) in 2000 Entry Draft for Mikhail Shtalenkov and Phoenix's 4th round choice (Chris Eade) in 2000 Entry Draft, November 18, 1999.

			REGULAR SEASON													PLAYOFFS											
Season	Club	League	GP	W	L	T	Mins	GA	SO	Avg	AAvg	Eff	SA	S%	SAPG	GP	W	L	T	Mins	GA	SO	Avg	Eff	SA	S%	SAPG

• BUZINSKI, Steve

Steven Rudolph "Puck Goes Inski" G – L. 5'8", 140 lbs. b: Dunblane, Sask., 10/15/1917.

Season	Club	League	GP	W	L	T	Mins	GA	SO	Avg	AAvg	Eff	SA	S%	SAPG	GP	W	L	T	Mins	GA	SO	Avg	Eff	SA	S%	SAPG
1934-35	Saskatoon Nutana	SCJHL	6	*5	0	1	420	8	*1	*1.37	....	....	....	....	....	2	0	2	0	120	8	0	4.00	....	....	....	....
1935-36	Prince Albert St. Marks	SAHA	....	....	....	....	....	....	....	....	....	....	....	....	....	2	0	2	0	120	17	0	8.50	....	....	....	....
1936-37	Prince Albert Mintos	N-SSHL	2	....	....	....	120	13	0	6.50	....	....	....	....	....	....	....	....	....	....	....	....	....	....	....	....	....
1937-1941	Swift Current Indians	SAHA-I	STATISTICS NOT AVAILABLE																								
1941-42	Swift Current Indians	SAHA-I	....	....	....	....	....	....	....	....	....	....	....	....	....	8	6	1	1	480	16	0	2.00	....	....	....	....
1942-43	**New York Rangers**	**NHL**	**9**	**2**	**6**	**1**	**560**	**55**	**0**	**5.89**	**5.08**	....	....	....	....	....	....	....	....	....	....	....	....	....	....	....	....
	Swift Current Indians	SAHA-I	STATISTICS NOT AVAILABLE																								
1943-44			MILITARY SERVICE																								
1944-45			MILITARY SERVICE																								
1945-1950	Swift Curent Indians	SAHA-I	STATISTICS NOT AVAILABLE																								
1950-51	Swift Curent Indians	SAHA-I	24	10	11	3	1470	80	0	3.37	....	....	....	....	....	5	1	3	1	310	21	0	4.06	....	....	....	....
	NHL Totals		**9**	**2**	**6**	**1**	**560**	**55**	**0**	**5.89**	....	....	....	....	....	....	....	....	....	....	....	....	....	....	....	....	....

Signed as free agent by **NY Rangers** as a war-time replacement for Jim Henry, October, 1942.

• CALEY, Don

Donald Thomas G – L. 5'10", 160 lbs. b: Dauphin, Man., 10/9/1945.

Season	Club	League	GP	W	L	T	Mins	GA	SO	Avg	AAvg	Eff	SA	S%	SAPG	GP	W	L	T	Mins	GA	SO	Avg	Eff	SA	S%	SAPG
1963-64	Weyburn Red Wings	SJHL	18	....	....	....	1080	75	0	4.16	....	....	....	....	....	5	1	4	0	300	29	0	5.80	....	....	....	....
1964-65	Weyburn Red Wings	SJHL	54	36	15	3	3240	188	*2	3.49	....	....	....	....	....	15	....	....	....	900	45	*1	*3.00	....	....	....	....
	Peterborough Petes	OHA-Jr.	1	1	0	0	60	1	0	1.00	....	....	....	....	....	....	....	....	....	....	....	....	....	....	....	....	....
1965-66	Weyburn Red Wings	SJHL	56	36	14	6	3360	165	*4	2.95	....	....	....	....	....	12	....	....	....	720	29	1	2.42	....	....	....	....
	Estevan Bruins	Mem-Cup	11	5	6	0	680	39	0	3.44	....	....	....	....	....	....	....	....	....	....	....	....	....	....	....	....	....
1966-67	Pittsburgh Hornets	AHL	20	6	11	2	1122	71	2	3.80	....	....	....	....	....	....	....	....	....	....	....	....	....	....	....	....	....
1967-68	**St. Louis Blues**	**NHL**	**1**	**0**	**0**	**0**	**30**	**3**	**0**	**6.00**	**6.66**	....	....	....	....	....	....	....	....	....	....	....	....	....	....	....	....
	Kansas City Blues	CPHL	55	*26	23	5	3203	176	1	3.30	....	....	....	....	....	7	4	3	0	420	22	*1	3.14	....	....	....	....
1968-69	Buffalo Bisons	AHL	1	0	1	0	60	5	0	5.00	....	....	....	....	....	....	....	....	....	....	....	....	....	....	....	....	....
	Omaha Knights	CHL	34	....	....	....	1899	102	1	3.23	....	....	....	....	....	6	3	3	0	316	14	*1	2.66	....	....	....	....
1969-70	Phoenix Roadrunners	WHL	28	8	11	7	1578	83	0	3.16	....	....	....	....	....	....	....	....	....	....	....	....	....	....	....	....	....
1970-71	Phoenix Roadrunners	WHL	24	9	9	3	1306	67	2	3.08	....	....	....	....	....	4	2	2	0	207	10	0	2.90	....	....	....	....
1971-72	Phoenix Roadrunners	WHL	44	21	16	2	2425	129	2	3.19	....	....	....	....	....	3	1	2	0	199	13	0	3.91	....	....	....	....
1972-73	Phoenix Roadrunners	WHL	39	19	11	7	2236	128	2	3.43	....	....	....	....	....	*8	*7	1	0	*435	23	*1	3.17	....	....	....	....
1973-74	Phoenix Roadrunners	WHL	7	4	3	0	427	26	0	3.68	....	....	....	....	....	....	....	....	....	....	....	....	....	....	....	....	....
	NHL Totals		**1**	**0**	**0**	**0**	**30**	**3**	**0**	**6.00**	....	....	....	....	....	....	....	....	....	....	....	....	....	....	....	....	....

SJHL First All-Star Team (1966) • WHL First All-Star Team (1972) • WHL Second All-Star Team (1973)

Claimed by **St. Louis** from **Detroit** in Expansion Draft, June 6, 1967. Traded to **NY Rangers** by **St. Louis** with Wayne Rivers for Camille Henry, Bill Plager and Robbie Irons, June 13, 1968. Traded to **Phoenix** (WHL) by **NY Rangers** with Sandy Snow for Peter McDuffe, July 3, 1969.

• CAPRICE, Frank

Francis J. G – L. 5'9", 150 lbs. b: Hamilton, Ont., 5/2/1962. Vancouver's 8th, 178th overall in 1981.

Season	Club	League	GP	W	L	T	Mins	GA	SO	Avg	AAvg	Eff	SA	S%	SAPG	GP	W	L	T	Mins	GA	SO	Avg	Eff	SA	S%	SAPG
1978-79	Hamilton Kilty B's	OHA-B	STATISTICS NOT AVAILABLE																								
1979-80	London Knights	OMJHL	18	3	7	3	919	74	1	4.84	....	....	....	....	....	3	1	1	0	94	10	0	6.38	....	....	....	....
1980-81	London Knights	OMJHL	42	11	26	0	2171	190	0	5.25	....	....	....	....	....	....	....	....	....	....	....	....	....	....	....	....	....
1981-82	London Knights	OHL	45	24	17	2	2614	196	0	4.50	....	....	....	....	....	4	1	3	0	240	18	0	4.50	....	....	....	....
	Canada	WJC-A	3	3	0	0	180	7	0	2.33	....	....	....	....	....	....	....	....	....	....	....	....	....	....	....	....	....
	Dallas Black Hawks	CHL	3	0	3	0	178	19	0	6.40	....	....	....	....	....	....	....	....	....	....	....	....	....	....	....	....	....
1982-83	**Vancouver Canucks**	**NHL**	**1**	**0**	**0**	**0**	**20**	**3**	**0**	**9.00**	**7.22**	**33.75**	**8**	**.625**	**24.0**	....	....	....	....	....	....	....	....	....	....	....	....
	Fredericton Express	AHL	14	5	8	1	819	50	0	3.67	....	....	....	....	....	....	....	....	....	....	....	....	....	....	....	....	....
1983-84	**Vancouver Canucks**	**NHL**	**19**	**8**	**8**	**2**	**1098**	**62**	**1**	**3.39**	**2.67**	**4.00**	**525**	**.882**	**28.7**	....	....	....	....	....	....	....	....	....	....	....	....
	Fredericton Express	AHL	18	11	5	2	1089	49	2	2.70	....	....	....	....	....	....	....	....	....	....	....	....	....	....	....	....	....
1984-85	**Vancouver Canucks**	**NHL**	**28**	**8**	**14**	**3**	**1523**	**122**	**0**	**4.81**	**3.85**	**7.17**	**818**	**.851**	**32.2**	....	....	....	....	....	....	....	....	....	....	....	....
1985-86	**Vancouver Canucks**	**NHL**	**7**	**0**	**3**	**2**	**308**	**28**	**0**	**5.45**	**4.26**	**9.85**	**155**	**.819**	**30.2**	....	....	....	....	....	....	....	....	....	....	....	....
	Fredericton Express	AHL	26	12	11	2	1526	109	0	4.29	....	....	....	....	....	6	2	4	0	333	22	0	3.96	....	....	....	....
1986-87	**Vancouver Canucks**	**NHL**	**25**	**8**	**11**	**2**	**1390**	**89**	**0**	**3.84**	**3.25**	**5.32**	**643**	**.862**	**27.8**	....	....	....	....	....	....	....	....	....	....	....	....
	Fredericton Express	AHL	12	5	5	0	686	47	0	4.11	....	....	....	....	....	....	....	....	....	....	....	....	....	....	....	....	....
1987-88	**Vancouver Canucks**	**NHL**	**22**	**7**	**10**	**2**	**1250**	**87**	**0**	**4.18**	**3.49**	**5.81**	**626**	**.861**	**30.0**	....	....	....	....	....	....	....	....	....	....	....	....
1988-89	Milwaukee Admirals	IHL	39	24	12	0	2204	143	2	3.89	....	....	....	....	....	2	0	1	0	91	5	0	3.30	....	....	....	....
1989-90	Maine Mariners	AHL	10	2	6	1	550	46	0	5.02	....	....	....	....	....	....	....	....	....	....	....	....	....	....	....	....	....
	Milwaukee Admirals	IHL	20	8	6	3	1098	78	0	4.26	....	....	....	....	....	3	0	2	0	142	10	0	4.23	....	....	....	....
1990-91			STATISTICS NOT AVAILABLE																								
1991-92			STATISTICS NOT AVAILABLE																								
1992-93	HC Gardena-Groden	Italy	19	....	....	....	1140	93	....	4.89	....	....	....	....	....	....	....	....	....	....	....	....	....	....	....	....	....
1993-94	HC Gardena-Groden	Italy	22	....	....	....	1204	100	....	4.98	....	....	....	....	....	....	....	....	....	....	....	....	....	....	....	....	....
1994-95	HC Gardena-Groden	Italy	STATISTICS NOT AVAILABLE																								
1995-96	HC Gardena-Groden	Italy	36	....	....	....	1678	100	....	3.58	....	....	....	....	....	....	....	....	....	....	....	....	....	....	....	....	....
1996-97	Cardiff Devils	BH-Cup	7	7	0	0	430	14	1	1.95	....	....	....	....	....	....	....	....	....	....	....	....	....	....	....	....	....
	Cardiff Devils	Britain	12	....	....	....	705	38	....	3.23	....	....	....	....	....	1	....	....	....	60	3	0	3.00	....	....	....	....
1997-98	Cardiff Devils	BH-Cup	8	....	....	....	480	16	1	2.00	....	....	....	....	....	....	....	....	....	....	....	....	....	....	....	....	....
	Cardiff Devils	Britain	21	....	....	....	1242	61	....	2.95	....	....	....	....	....	2	....	....	....	120	4	....	2.00	....	....	....	....
1998-99	Corpus Christi Icerays	WPHL	15	9	5	1	847	48	0	3.40	....	....	....	....	....	....	....	....	....	....	....	....	....	....	....	....	....
	Ayr Scottish Eagles	Britain	7	2	5	0	391	24	0	3.49	....	....	....	....	....	4	0	3	1	210	11	0	3.14	....	....	....	....
	NHL Totals		**102**	**31**	**46**	**11**	**5589**	**391**	**1**	**4.20**	....	....	**2775**	**.859**	**29.8**	....	....	....	....	....	....	....	....	....	....	....	....

• Played w/ RHI's Vancouver Voodoo in 1994 (2-0-0-1-(0)-77-7-0-4.34)

• CAREY, Jim

G – L. 6'2", 205 lbs. b: Dorchester, MA, 5/31/1974. Washington's 2nd, 32nd overall in 1992.

Season	Club	League	GP	W	L	T	Mins	GA	SO	Avg	AAvg	Eff	SA	S%	SAPG	GP	W	L	T	Mins	GA	SO	Avg	Eff	SA	S%	SAPG
1989-90	Boston College Prep School	Hi-School	20	12	0	0	1200	20	0	1.00	....	....	....	....	....	....	....	....	....	....	....	....	....	....	....	....	....
1990-91	Catholic Memorial Knights	Hi-School	14	14	0	0	840	20	6	1.66	....	....	....	....	....	....	....	....	....	....	....	....	....	....	....	....	....
1991-92	Catholic Memorial Knights	Hi-School	21	19	2	*0	940	34	8	1.63	....	....	....	....	....	....	....	....	....	....	....	....	....	....	....	....	....
1992-93	University of Wisconsin	WCHA	26	15	8	1	1525	78	1	3.07	....	....	....	....	....	....	....	....	....	....	....	....	....	....	....	....	....
	United States	WJC-A	4	2	2	0	240	14	0	3.50	....	....	....	....	....	....	....	....	....	....	....	....	....	....	....	....	....
1993-94	University of Wisconsin	WCHA	*40	*24	13	1	*2247	114	*1	*3.04	....	....	....	....	....	....	....	....	....	....	....	....	....	....	....	....	....
1994-95	Portland Pirates	AHL	55	30	14	11	3281	151	*6	2.76	....	....	....	....	....	....	....	....	....	....	....	....	....	....	....	....	....
	Washington Capitals	**NHL**	**28**	**18**	**6**	**3**	**1604**	**57**	**4**	**2.13**	**2.22**	**1.86**	**654**	**.913**	**24.5**	**7**	**2**	**4**	....	**358**	**25**	**0**	**4.19**	**6.94**	**151**	**.834**	**25.3**
1995-96	**Washington Capitals**	**NHL**	**71**	**35**	**24**	**9**	**4069**	**153**	***9**	**2.26**	**2.23**	**2.12**	**1631**	**.906**	**24.1**	**3**	**0**	**1**	....	**97**	**10**	**0**	**6.19**	**15.87**	**39**	**.744**	**24.1**
1996-97	United States	W-Cup	DID NOT PLAY – SPARE GOALTENDER																								
	Washington Capitals	**NHL**	**40**	**17**	**18**	**3**	**2293**	**105**	**1**	**2.75**	**2.96**	**2.93**	**984**	**.893**	**25.7**	....	....	....	....	....	....	....	....	....	....	....	....
	Boston Bruins	**NHL**	**19**	**5**	**13**	**0**	**1004**	**64**	**0**	**3.82**	**4.12**	**4.93**	**496**	**.871**	**29.6**	....	....	....	....	....	....	....	....	....	....	....	....
1997-98	**Boston Bruins**	**NHL**	**10**	**3**	**2**	**1**	**496**	**24**	**2**	**2.90**	**3.46**	**3.09**	**225**	**.893**	**27.2**	....	....	....	....	....	....	....	....	....	....	....	....
	Providence Bruins	AHL	10	2	7	1	604	40	0	3.97	....	....	....	....	....	....	....	....	....	....	....	....	....	....	....	....	....
1998-99	Providence Bruins	AHL	30	17	8	3	1750	68	3	2.33	....	....	....	....	....	....	....	....	....	....	....	....	....	....	....	....	....
	Cincinnati Cyclones	IHL	2	1	0	1	120	2	0	1.00	....	....	....	....	....	....	....	....	....	....	....	....	....	....	....	....	....
	St. Louis Blues	**NHL**	**4**	**1**	**2**	**0**	**202**	**13**	**0**	**3.86**	**4.59**	**6.60**	**76**	**.829**	**22.6**	....	....	....	....	....	....	....	....	....	....	....	....
	NHL Totals		**172**	**79**	**65**	**16**	**9668**	**416**	**16**	**2.58**	....	....	**4066**	**.898**	**25.2**	**10**	**2**	**5**	....	**455**	**35**	**0**	**4.62**	....	**190**	**.816**	**25.1**

WCHA Second All-Star Team (1993) • AHL First All-Star Team (1995) • Won Dudley "Red" Garrett Memorial Trophy (Top Rookie - AHL) (1995) • Won Baz Bastien Memorial Trophy (Top Goaltender - AHL) (1995) • NHL All-Rookie Team (1995) • NHL First All-Star Team (1996) • Won Vezina Trophy (1996)

Traded to **Boston** by **Washington** with Anson Carter, Jason Allison and Washington's 3rd round choice (Lee Goren) in 1997 Entry Draft for Bill Ranford, Adam Oates and Rick Tocchet, March 1, 1997. Signed as a free agent by **St. Louis**, March 1, 1999.

• CARON, Jacques

Jacques Joseph G – L. 6'2", 185 lbs. b: Noranda, Que., 4/21/1940.

Season	Club	League	GP	W	L	T	Mins	GA	SO	Avg	AAvg	Eff	SA	S%	SAPG	GP	W	L	T	Mins	GA	SO	Avg	Eff	SA	S%	SAPG
			REGULAR SEASON													PLAYOFFS											
1956-57	Toronto Marlboros	OHA-Jr.	10	....	....	....	600	29	2	2.90	....	....	....	....	....	....	....	....	....	....	....	....	....	....	....	....	....
1957-58	Peterborough Petes	OHA-Jr.	31	....	....	....	1840	113	1	3.68	....	....	....	....	....	4	....	....	....	240	14	0	3.50	....	....	....	....
1958-59	Peterborough Petes	OHA-Jr.	43	24	14	4	2580	129	2	*3.00	....	....	....	....	....	13	9	3	1	780	35	2	2.69	....	....	....	....
	Peterborough Petes	Mem-Cup	2	0	2	0	120	9	0	4.50	....	....	....	....	....	....	....	....	....	....	....	....	....	....	....	....	....
1959-60	Washington Presidents	EHL	55	....	....	....	3300	218	3	3.97	....	....	....	....	....	....	....	....	....	....	....	....	....	....	....	....	....
1960-61	Rouyn-Noranda Alouettes	NOHA	STATISTICS NOT AVAILABLE																								
	Rouyn-Noranda Alouettes	Al-Cup	3	0	3	0	180	13	0	4.33	....	....	....	....	....	....	....	....	....	....	....	....	....	....	....	....	....
1961-62	Springfield Indians	AHL	5	4	1	0	310	17	1	3.29	....	....	....	....	....	....	....	....	....	....	....	....	....	....	....	....	....
	Charlotte Clippers	EHL	5	....	....	....	300	26	0	5.20	....	....	....	....	....	....	....	....	....	....	....	....	....	....	....	....	....
1962-63	Springfield Indians	AHL	38	12	14	7	2180	112	2	3.08	....	....	....	....	....	....	....	....	....	....	....	....	....	....	....	....	....
1963-64	Springfield Indians	AHL	31	12	14	1	1780	110	0	3.71	....	....	....	....	....	....	....	....	....	....	....	....	....	....	....	....	....
1964-65	Springfield Indians	AHL	55	21	29	4	3321	195	2	3.52	....	....	....	....	....	....	....	....	....	....	....	....	....	....	....	....	....
1965-66	Springfield Indians	AHL	33	15	15	1	1832	80	2	2.62	....	....	....	....	....	6	3	3	0	360	14	0	2.33	....	....	....	....
1966-67	Springfield Indians	AHL	35	11	17	5	1866	136	1	4.37	....	....	....	....	....	....	....	....	....	....	....	....	....	....	....	....	....
1967-68	Los Angeles Kings	NHL	1	0	1	0	60	4	0	4.00	4.44	....	....	....	....	....	....	....	....	....	....	....	....	....	....	....	....
	Springfield Kings	AHL	42	19	18	4	2393	151	0	3.79	....	....	....	....	....	....	....	....	....	....	....	....	....	....	....	....	....
1968-69	Los Angeles Kings	NHL	3	0	1	0	140	9	0	3.86	3.99	....	....	....	....	....	....	....	....	....	....	....	....	....	....	....	....
	Denver Spurs	WHL	31	7	21	3	1764	122	2	4.15	....	....	....	....	....	....	....	....	....	....	....	....	....	....	....	....	....
1969-70	Denver Spurs	WHL	31	8	16	4	1548	120	0	4.65	....	....	....	....	....	....	....	....	....	....	....	....	....	....	....	....	....
1970-71	Denver Spurs	WHL	30	10	13	4	1668	109	2	3.92	....	....	....	....	....	2	0	2	0	120	9	0	4.50	....	....	....	....
1971-72	St. Louis Blues	NHL	28	14	8	5	1619	68	1	2.52	2.54	....	....	....	....	9	4	5	....	499	26	0	3.13	....	....	....	....
	Denver Spurs	WHL	20	15	3	0	1160	45	0	2.32	....	....	....	....	....	....	....	....	....	....	....	....	....	....	....	....	....
1972-73	St. Louis Blues	NHL	30	8	14	5	1562	92	1	3.53	3.34	....	....	....	....	3	0	2	....	140	8	0	3.43	....	....	....	....
1973-74	Vancouver Canucks	NHL	10	2	5	1	465	38	0	4.90	4.75	....	....	....	....	....	....	....	....	....	....	....	....	....	....	....	....
1974-75	Syracuse Eagles	AHL	50	16	21	9	2755	170	0	3.70	....	....	....	....	....	1	0	1	0	60	8	0	8.00	....	....	....	....
1975-76	Syracuse Blazers	NAHL	32	....	....	....	1725	90	3	3.10	....	....	....	....	....	....	....	....	....	....	....	....	....	....	....	....	....
	Cleveland Crusaders	WHA	2	1	0	1	130	8	0	3.69	....	....	....	....	....	....	....	....	....	....	....	....	....	....	....	....	....
1976-77	Syracuse Blazers	NAHL	22	....	....	....	1307	83	1	3.63	....	....	....	....	....	....	....	....	....	....	....	....	....	....	....	....	....
	Cincinnati Stingers	WHA	24	13	6	2	1292	61	3	2.83	....	....	....	....	....	1	0	1	0	14	3	0	12.86	....	....	....	....
1977-78	Binghamton Dusters	AHL	1	0	0	0	1	0	0	0.00	....	....	....	....	....	....	....	....	....	....	....	....	....	....	....	....	....
1978-79			DID NOT PLAY																								
1979-80			DID NOT PLAY																								
1980-81	Binghamton Whalers	AHL	1	0	0	0	19	1	0	3.16	....	....	....	....	....	....	....	....	....	....	....	....	....	....	....	....	....
	NHL Totals		72	24	29	11	3846	211	2	3.29	....	....	....	....	....	12	4	7	....	639	34	0	3.19	....	....	....	....
	Other Major League Totals		26	14	6	3	1422	69	3	2.91	....	....	....	....	....	1	0	1	....	14	3	0	12.86	....	....	....	....

NAHL First All-Star Team (1976)

Rights transferred to **LA Kings** when NHL club purchased **Springfield** (AHL) franchise, May, 1967. Claimed by **St. Louis** (Denver-WHL) from **LA Kings** in Reverse Draft, June 12, 1969. Selected by **Dayton-Houston** (WHA) in 1972 WHA General Player Draft, February 12, 1972. Claimed by **Vancouver** (Seattle-WHL) from **St. Louis** in Reverse Draft, June 15, 1973. Traded to **Buffalo** by **Vancouver** for future considerations, September 15, 1974. WHA rights traded to **Cleveland** (WHA) by **Houston** (WHA) for future considerations, February, 1976. Signed as a free agent by **Cincinnati** (WHA) after **Cleveland** (WHA) franchise folded, July, 1976.

• CARTER, Lyle

Lyle Dwight G – L. 6'1", 185 lbs. b: Truro, N.S., 4/29/1945.

Season	Club	League	GP	W	L	T	Mins	GA	SO	Avg	AAvg	Eff	SA	S%	SAPG	GP	W	L	T	Mins	GA	SO	Avg	Eff	SA	S%	SAPG
1962-63	Brampton 7-Ups	MTJHL	11	....	....	....	640	52	0	4.88	....	....	....	....	....	....	....	....	....	....	....	....	....	....	....	....	....
	Windsor Maple Leafs	NSSHL	12	....	....	....	720	77	0	6.24	....	....	....	....	....	....	....	....	....	....	....	....	....	....	....	....	....
1963-64	Buchans Miners	Nfld-Sr.	20	*15	5	0	1200	69	0	3.45	....	....	....	....	....	11	6	5	0	660	59	0	5.36	....	....	....	....
1964-65	New Glasgow Rangers	NSSHL	45	....	....	....	2700	172	0	*3.76	....	....	....	....	....	....	....	....	....	....	....	....	....	....	....	....	....
1965-66	Orillia Pepsi-Colas	OHA-Sr.	STATISTICS NOT AVAILABLE																								
1966-67	Gander Flyers	Nfld-Sr.	40	*26	12	1	2350	152	0	*3.88	....	....	....	....	....	10	5	5	0	620	43	0	4.16	....	....	....	....
	Conception Bay Ceebees	Nfld-Sr.	....	....	....	....	....	....	....	....	....	....	....	....	....	2	0	1	0	79	3	0	2.28	....	....	....	....
1967-68	Cleveland Barons	AHL	2	....	....	....	120	12	0	6.00	....	....	....	....	....	....	....	....	....	....	....	....	....	....	....	....	....
	Toledo Blades	IHL	1	1	0	0	60	4	0	4.00	....	....	....	....	....	....	....	....	....	....	....	....	....	....	....	....	....
1968-69	Clinton Comets	EHL	72	*44	18	10	4320	169	*13	*2.35	....	....	....	....	....	15	8	7	0	900	40	0	*2.67	....	....	....	....
1969-70	Montreal Voyageurs	AHL	5	....	....	....	154	8	0	3.12	....	....	....	....	....	....	....	....	....	....	....	....	....	....	....	....	....
	Clinton Comets	EHL	5	....	....	....	300	11	3	2.20	....	....	....	....	....	....	....	....	....	....	....	....	....	....	....	....	....
1970-71	Montreal Voyageurs	AHL	1	0	1	0	40	5	0	7.50	....	....	....	....	....	....	....	....	....	....	....	....	....	....	....	....	....
	Muskegon Mohawks	IHL	50	30	15	4	2958	120	*6	*2.44	....	....	....	....	....	6	2	4	0	360	20	0	3.33	....	....	....	....
1971-72	Baltimore Clippers	AHL	6	1	2	1	237	15	0	3.79	....	....	....	....	....	....	....	....	....	....	....	....	....	....	....	....	....
	Salt Lake Golden Eagles	WHL	9	4	3	2	538	26	0	2.89	....	....	....	....	....	....	....	....	....	....	....	....	....	....	....	....	....
	California Golden Seals	NHL	15	4	7	0	721	50	0	4.16	4.22	....	....	....	....	....	....	....	....	....	....	....	....	....	....	....	....
	Oklahoma City Blazers	CHL	....	....	....	....	....	....	....	....	....	....	....	....	....	5	2	3	0	279	18	0	3.87	....	....	....	....
1972-73	Salt Lake Golden Eagles	WHL	35	17	14	4	2009	120	1	3.58	....	....	....	....	....	2	2	0	0	120	7	0	3.50	....	....	....	....
1973-74	New Haven Nighthawks	AHL	37	17	11	6	2034	101	1	2.97	....	....	....	....	....	10	4	6	0	636	33	0	3.11	....	....	....	....
1974-75	Syracuse Eagles	AHL	32	5	20	1	1561	133	0	5.11	....	....	....	....	....	....	....	....	....	....	....	....	....	....	....	....	....
	Greensboro Generals	SHL	4	....	....	....	216	17	0	4.72	....	....	....	....	....	....	....	....	....	....	....	....	....	....	....	....	....
	NHL Totals		15	4	7	0	721	50	0	4.16	....	....	....	....	....	....	....	....	....	....	....	....	....	....	....	....	....

EHL North First All-Star Team (1969) • Won George L. Davis Jr. Trophy (fewest goals against - EHL) (1969) • IHL First All-Star Team (1971) • Won James Norris Memorial Trophy (fewest goals against - IHL) (1971) • Won James Gatschene Memorial Trophy (MVP - IHL) (1971)

Signed as a free agent by **Montreal** (Cleveland-AHL), March 30, 1968. Traded to **California** by **Montreal** with John French for Randy Rota, October, 1971. Claimed by **Minnesota** (Jacksonville-AHL) from **California** in Reverse Draft, June 10, 1973. Traded to **Syracuse** (AHL) by **Minnesota** for cash, August, 1974.

• CASEY, Jon

Jonathan J. G – L. 5'10", 155 lbs. b: Grand Rapids, MN, 3/29/1962.

Season	Club	League	GP	W	L	T	Mins	GA	SO	Avg	AAvg	Eff	SA	S%	SAPG	GP	W	L	T	Mins	GA	SO	Avg	Eff	SA	S%	SAPG
1980-81	University of North Dakota	WCHA	5	3	1	0	300	19	0	3.80	....	....	....	....	....	....	....	....	....	....	....	....	....	....	....	....	....
1981-82	University of North Dakota	WCHA	18	15	3	0	1038	48	1	2.77	....	....	....	....	....	....	....	....	....	....	....	....	....	....	....	....	....
	United States	WJC-A	5	1	2	0	219	15	0	4.11	....	....	....	....	....	....	....	....	....	....	....	....	....	....	....	....	....
1982-83	University of North Dakota	WCHA	17	9	6	2	1020	42	0	2.51	....	....	....	....	....	....	....	....	....	....	....	....	....	....	....	....	....
1983-84	University of North Dakota	WCHA	37	25	10	2	2180	115	2	3.13	....	....	....	....	....	....	....	....	....	....	....	....	....	....	....	....	....
	Minnesota North Stars	NHL	2	1	0	0	84	6	0	4.29	3.38	4.36	59	.898	42.1	....	....	....	....	....	....	....	....	....	....	....	....
1984-85	Baltimore Skipjacks	AHL	46	30	11	4	2646	116	*4	*2.63	....	....	....	....	....	*13	8	3	....	689	38	0	3.31	....	....	....	....
1985-86	Minnesota North Stars	NHL	26	11	11	1	1402	91	0	3.89	3.04	4.49	789	.885	33.8	....	....	....	....	....	....	....	....	....	....	....	....
	Springfield Indians	AHL	9	4	3	1	464	30	0	3.88	....	....	....	....	....	....	....	....	....	....	....	....	....	....	....	....	....
1986-87	Springfield Indians	AHL	13	1	8	0	770	56	0	4.36	....	....	....	....	....	....	....	....	....	....	....	....	....	....	....	....	....
	Indianapolis Checkers	IHL	31	14	15	0	1794	133	0	4.45	....	....	....	....	....	....	....	....	....	....	....	....	....	....	....	....	....
1987-88	Minnesota North Stars	NHL	14	1	7	4	663	41	0	3.71	3.09	4.37	348	.882	31.5	....	....	....	....	....	....	....	....	....	....	....	....
	Kalamazoo Wings	IHL	42	24	13	5	2541	154	2	3.64	....	....	....	....	....	7	3	3	....	382	26	0	4.08	....	....	....	....
1988-89	Minnesota North Stars	NHL	55	18	17	12	2961	151	1	3.06	2.53	3.06	1509	.900	30.6	4	1	3	....	211	16	0	4.55	6.02	121	.868	34.4
1989-90	Minnesota North Stars	NHL	61	*31	22	4	3407	183	3	3.22	2.72	3.35	1757	.896	30.9	7	3	4	....	415	21	1	3.04	2.92	219	.904	31.7
	United States	WEC-A	6	4	2	0	334	15	0	2.69	....	....	....	....	....	....	....	....	....	....	....	....	....	....	....	....	....
1990-91	Minnesota North Stars	Fr-Tour	3	....	....	....	111	9	....	4.86	....	....	....	....	....	....	....	....	....	....	....	....	....	....	....	....	....
	Minnesota North Stars	NHL	55	21	20	11	3185	158	3	2.98	2.67	3.25	1450	.891	27.3	*23	*14	7	....	*1205	61	*1	3.04	3.25	571	.893	28.4
1991-92	Minnesota North Stars	NHL	52	19	23	5	2911	165	2	3.40	3.04	4.00	1401	.882	28.9	7	3	4	....	437	22	0	3.02	2.95	225	.902	30.9
	Kalamazoo Wings	IHL	4	2	1	1	250	11	0	2.64	....	....	....	....	....	....	....	....	....	....	....	....	....	....	....	....	....
1992-93	Minnesota North Stars	NHL	60	26	26	5	3476	193	3	3.33	2.85	3.82	1683	.885	29.1	....	....	....	....	....	....	....	....	....	....	....	....
1993-94	Boston Bruins	NHL	57	30	15	9	3192	153	4	2.88	2.76	3.42	1289	.881	24.2	11	5	6	....	698	34	0	2.92	3.22	308	.890	26.5
1994-95	St. Louis Blues	NHL	19	7	5	4	872	40	0	2.75	2.88	2.75	400	.900	27.5	2	0	1	....	30	2	0	4.00	8.00	10	.800	20.0
1995-96	St. Louis Blues	NHL	9	2	3	0	395	25	0	3.80	3.78	5.28	180	.861	27.3	12	6	6	....	747	36	1	2.89	2.75	378	.905	30.4
	Peoria Rivermen	IHL	43	21	19	2	2514	128	3	3.05	....	....	....	....	....	....	....	....	....	....	....	....	....	....	....	....	....

			REGULAR SEASON													PLAYOFFS											
Season	Club	League	GP	W	L	T	Mins	GA	SO	Avg	AAvg	Eff	SA	S%	SAPG	GP	W	L	T	Mins	GA	SO	Avg	Eff	SA	S%	SAPG
1996-97	**St. Louis Blues**	**NHL**	**15**	**3**	**8**	**0**	**707**	**40**	**0**	**3.39**	**3.65**	**4.54**	**299**	**.866**	**25.4**	....	....	....	....	....	....	....	....	....	....	....	....
	Worcester IceCats	AHL	4	2	1	1	245	10	0	2.45	....	....	....	....	....	....	....	....	....	....	....	....	....	....	....	....	....
1997-98	Kansas City Blades	IHL	24	9	13	2	1340	62	2	2.78	....	....	....	....	....	....	....	....	....	....	....	....	....	....	....	....	....
	NHL Totals		**425**	**170**	**157**	**55**	**23255**	**1246**	**16**	**3.21**	....	....	**11164**	**.888**	**28.8**	**66**	**32**	**31**	....	**3743**	**192**	**3**	**3.08**	....	**1832**	**.895**	**29.4**

WCHA First All-Star Team (1982, 1984) • WCHA Second All-Star Team (1983) • NCAA West First All-American Team (1984) • AHL First All-Star Team (1985) • Won Harry "Hap" Holmes Memorial Trophy (fewest goals against - AHL) (1985) • Won Baz Bastien Memorial Trophy (Top Goaltender - AHL) (1985) • Played in NHL All-Star Game (1993)

Signed as a free agent by **Minnesota**, April 1, 1984. Transferred to **Dallas** after **Minnesota** franchise relocated, June 9, 1993. Traded to **Boston** by **Dallas** for Andy Moog to complete transaction that sent Gord Murphy to Dallas (June 20, 1993), June 25, 1993. Signed as a free agent by **St. Louis**, June 29, 1994.

• CHABOT, Frederic

G – L. 5′11″, 187 lbs. b: Hebertville-Station, Que., 2/12/1968. New Jersey's 10th, 192nd overall in 1986.

Season	Club	League	GP	W	L	T	Mins	GA	SO	Avg	AAvg	Eff	SA	S%	SAPG	GP	W	L	T	Mins	GA	SO	Avg	Eff	SA	S%	SAPG
1985-86	Trois-Rivieres Selects	QAAA	34	25	9	0	2038	139	0	3.90	....	....	....	....	....	....	....	....	....	....	....	....	....	....	....	....	....
1986-87	Drummondville Voltigeurs	QMJHL	62	31	29	0	3508	293	1	5.01	....	....	....	....	....	8	2	6	....	481	40	0	4.99	....	....	....	....
1987-88	Drummondville Voltigeurs	QMJHL	58	27	24	4	3276	237	1	4.34	....	....	....	....	....	16	10	6	....	1019	56	*1	*3.30	....	....	....	....
	Drummondville Voltigeurs	Mem-Cup	3	0	*3	0	158	18	0	6.86	....	....	....	....	....	....	....	....	....	....	....	....	....	....	....	....	....
1988-89	Moose Jaw Warriors	WHL	26	....	....	....	1385	114	....	4.94	....	....	....	....	....	....	....	....	....	....	....	....	....	....	....	....	....
	Prince Albert Raiders	WHL	28	....	....	....	1572	88	....	3.36	....	....	....	....	....	4	1	1	....	199	16	0	4.82	....	....	....	....
1989-90	Sherbrooke Canadiens	AHL	2	1	1	0	119	8	0	4.03	....	....	....	....	....	....	....	....	....	....	....	....	....	....	....	....	....
	Fort Wayne Komets	IHL	23	6	13	3	1208	87	1	4.32	....	....	....	....	....	....	....	....	....	....	....	....	....	....	....	....	....
1990-91	**Montreal Canadiens**	**NHL**	**3**	**0**	**0**	**1**	**108**	**6**	**0**	**3.33**	**2.99**	**4.44**	**45**	**.867**	**25.0**	....	....	....	....	....	....	....	....	....	....	....	....
	Fredericton Canadiens	AHL	35	9	15	5	1800	122	0	4.07	....	....	....	....	....	....	....	....	....	....	....	....	....	....	....	....	....
1991-92	Fredericton Canadiens	AHL	30	17	9	4	1761	79	2	*2.69	....	....	....	....	....	7	3	4	....	457	20	0	2.63	....	....	....	....
	Winston-Salem Thunderbirds	ECHL	24	15	7	2	1449	71	0	*2.94	....	....	....	....	....	....	....	....	....	....	....	....	....	....	....	....	....
1992-93	**Montreal Canadiens**	**NHL**	**1**	**0**	**0**	**0**	**40**	**1**	**0**	**1.50**	**1.28**	**0.79**	**19**	**.947**	**28.5**	....	....	....	....	....	....	....	....	....	....	....	....
	Fredericton Canadiens	AHL	45	22	17	4	2544	141	0	3.33	....	....	....	....	....	4	1	3	....	261	16	0	3.68	....	....	....	....
1993-94	**Montreal Canadiens**	**NHL**	**1**	**0**	**1**	**0**	**60**	**5**	**0**	**5.00**	**4.81**	**10.42**	**24**	**.792**	**24.0**	....	....	....	....	....	....	....	....	....	....	....	....
	Fredericton Canadiens	AHL	3	0	1	1	143	12	0	5.03	....	....	....	....	....	....	....	....	....	....	....	....	....	....	....	....	....
	Las Vegas Thunder	IHL	2	1	1	0	110	5	0	2.72	....	....	....	....	....	....	....	....	....	....	....	....	....	....	....	....	....
	Philadelphia Flyers	**NHL**	**4**	**0**	**1**	**1**	**70**	**5**	**0**	**4.29**	**4.12**	**5.36**	**40**	**.875**	**34.3**	....	....	....	....	....	....	....	....	....	....	....	....
	Hershey Bears	AHL	28	13	5	6	1464	63	2	*2.58	....	....	....	....	....	11	7	4	....	665	32	0	2.89	....	....	....	....
1994-95	Cincinnati Cyclones	IHL	48	25	12	7	2622	128	1	2.93	....	....	....	....	....	5	3	2	....	326	16	0	2.94	....	....	....	....
1995-96	Cincinnati Cyclones	IHL	38	23	9	4	2147	88	3	*2.46	....	....	....	....	....	14	9	5	....	854	37	1	2.60	....	....	....	....
1996-97	Houston Aeros	IHL	*72	*39	26	7	*4265	180	*7	2.53	....	....	....	....	....	13	8	5	....	777	34	*2	2.63	....	....	....	....
1997-98	**Los Angeles Kings**	**NHL**	**12**	**3**	**3**	**2**	**554**	**29**	**0**	**3.14**	**3.75**	**3.41**	**267**	**.891**	**28.9**	....	....	....	....	....	....	....	....	....	....	....	....
	Houston Aeros	IHL	22	12	7	2	1237	46	1	2.23	....	....	....	....	....	4	1	3	....	238	11	0	2.77	....	....	....	....
1998-99	**Montreal Canadiens**	**NHL**	**11**	**1**	**3**	**0**	**430**	**16**	**0**	**2.23**	**2.65**	**1.90**	**188**	**.915**	**26.2**	....	....	....	....	....	....	....	....	....	....	....	....
	Houston Aeros	IHL	21	16	4	1	1259	49	3	2.34	....	....	....	....	....	....	....	....	....	....	....	....	....	....	....	....	....
99-2000	Houston Aeros	IHL	*62	*36	19	7	*3695	131	4	2.13	....	....	....	....	....	11	6	5	....	658	20	*3	1.82	....	....	....	....
	NHL Totals		**32**	**4**	**8**	**4**	**1262**	**62**	**0**	**2.95**	....	....	**583**	**.894**	**27.7**	....	....	....	....	....	....	....	....	....	....	....	....

WHL East All-Star Team (1989) • Won Baz Bastien Award (Top Goaltender - AHL) (1994) • IHL Second All-Star Team (1996) • IHL First All-Star Team (1997, 2000) • Won James Gatschene Memorial Trophy (MVP - IHL) (1997) • Won James Norris Memorial Trophy (fewest goals against - IHL) (2000) • Won James Gatschene Memorial Trophy (MVP - IHL) (tied with Nikolai Khabibulin) (2000)

Signed as a free agent by **Montreal**, January 16, 1990. Claimed by **Tampa Bay** from **Montreal** in Expansion Draft, June 18, 1992. Traded to **Montreal** by **Tampa Bay** for Jean-Claude Bergeron, June 19, 1992. Traded to **Philadelphia** by **Montreal** for cash, February 21, 1994. Signed as a free agent by **Florida**, August 11, 1994. Signed as a free agent by **LA Kings**, September 3, 1997. Claimed by **Nashville** from **LA Kings** in Expansion Draft, June 26, 1998. Claimed on waivers by **LA Kings** from **Nashville**, July 18, 1998. Claimed by **Montreal** from **LA Kings** in NHL Waiver Draft, October 5, 1998. Selected by **Columbus** from **Montreal** in Expansion Draft, June 23, 2000.

• CHABOT, Lorne

"Chabotsky" G – L. 6′1″, 185 lbs. b: Montreal, Que., 10/5/1900 d: 10/10/1946.

Season	Club	League	GP	W	L	T	Mins	GA	SO	Avg	AAvg	Eff	SA	S%	SAPG	GP	W	L	T	Mins	GA	SO	Avg	Eff	SA	S%	SAPG
1919-20	Laval University	MCHL	STATISTICS NOT AVAILABLE																								
	Brandon Wheat Kings	MHL-Sr.	STATISTICS NOT AVAILABLE																								
1920-21	Brandon Wheat Kings	MHL-Sr.	1	1	0	0	60	3	0	3.00	....	....	....	....	....	....	....	....	....	....	....	....	....	....	....	....	....
1921-22	Brandon Wheat Kings	MHL-Sr.	STATISTICS NOT AVAILABLE																								
1922-23	Port Arthur Ports	MHL-Sr.	16	11	5	0	960	57	0	3.56	....	....	....	....	....	2	1	1	0	120	3	*1	1.50	....	....	....	....
1923-24	Port Arthur Ports	MHL-Sr.	15	11	4	0	900	37	1	2.46	....	....	....	....	....	2	0	1	1	120	6	0	3.00	....	....	....	....
1924-25	Port Arthur Ports	MHL-Sr.	20	12	8	0	1200	51	*3	2.55	....	....	....	....	....	2	2	0	0	120	4	0	2.00	....	....	....	....
	Port Arthur Ports	Al-Cup	8	6	1	1	480	16	1	2.00	....	....	....	....	....	....	....	....	....	....	....	....	....	....	....	....	....
1925-26	Port Arthur Ports	TBSHL	20	*14	6	0	1200	42	2	2.10	....	....	....	....	....	3	2	0	1	180	4	1	1.33	....	....	....	....
	Port Arthur Ports	Al-Cup	6	5	1	0	360	13	1	2.17	....	....	....	....	....	....	....	....	....	....	....	....	....	....	....	....	....
1926-27	**New York Rangers**	**NHL**	**36**	**22**	**9**	**5**	**2307**	**56**	**10**	**1.46**	**2.17**	....	....	....	....	**2**	**0**	**1**	**1**	**120**	**3**	**1**	**1.50**	....	....	....	....
	Springfield Indians	Can-Am	1	1	0	0	60	2	0	2.00	....	....	....	....	....	....	....	....	....	....	....	....	....	....	....	....	....
1927-28♦	**New York Rangers**	**NHL**	***44**	**19**	**16**	**9**	**2730**	**79**	**11**	**1.74**	**2.76**	....	....	....	....	**6**	**2**	**2**	**1**	**321**	**8**	**1**	**1.50**	....	....	....	....
1928-29	**Toronto Maple Leafs**	**NHL**	**43**	**20**	**18**	**5**	**2458**	**66**	**12**	**1.61**	**3.40**	....	....	....	....	**4**	**2**	**2**	**0**	**242**	**5**	**0**	**1.24**	....	....	....	....
1929-30	**Toronto Maple Leafs**	**NHL**	**42**	**16**	**20**	**6**	**2620**	**113**	**6**	**2.59**	**2.63**	....	....	....	....	....	....	....	....	....	....	....	....	....	....	....	....
1930-31	**Toronto Maple Leafs**	**NHL**	**37**	**21**	**8**	**8**	**2300**	**80**	**6**	**2.09**	**2.63**	....	....	....	....	**2**	**0**	**1**	**1**	**139**	**4**	**0**	**1.73**	....	....	....	....
1931-32♦	**Toronto Maple Leafs**	**NHL**	**44**	**22**	**16**	**6**	**2698**	**106**	**4**	**2.36**	**2.87**	....	....	....	....	***7**	***5**	**1**	**1**	**438**	**15**	**0**	**2.05**	....	....	....	....
1932-33	**Toronto Maple Leafs**	**NHL**	***48**	**24**	**18**	**6**	**2946**	**111**	**5**	**2.26**	**3.02**	....	....	....	....	***9**	**4**	**5**	**0**	***686**	**18**	***2**	**1.57**	....	....	....	....
1933-34	**Montreal Canadiens**	**NHL**	**47**	**21**	**20**	**6**	**2928**	**101**	**8**	**2.07**	**2.57**	....	....	....	....	**2**	**0**	**1**	**1**	**131**	**4**	**0**	**1.83**	....	....	....	....
1934-35	**Chicago Black Hawks**	**NHL**	***48**	**26**	**17**	**5**	**2940**	**88**	**8**	***1.80**	**2.10**	....	....	....	....	**2**	**0**	**1**	**1**	**124**	**1**	**1**	**0.48**	....	....	....	....
1935-36	**Montreal Maroons**	**NHL**	**16**	**8**	**3**	**5**	**1010**	**35**	**2**	**2.08**	**2.92**	....	....	....	....	**3**	**0**	**3**	**0**	**297**	**6**	**0**	***1.21**	....	....	....	....
1936-37	**New York Americans**	**NHL**	**6**	**2**	**3**	**1**	**370**	**25**	**1**	**4.05**	**5.06**	....	....	....	....	....	....	....	....	....	....	....	....	....	....	....	....
	NHL Totals		**411**	**201**	**148**	**62**	**25307**	**860**	**73**	**2.04**	....	....	....	....	....	**37**	**13**	**17**	**6**	**2498**	**64**	**5**	**1.54**	....	....	....	....

NHL First All-Star Team (1935) • Won Vezina Trophy (1935)

Signed as a free agent by **NY Rangers**, September 2, 1926. • Recorded shutout (2-0) in NHL debut vs. Montreal Canadiens, November 27, 1926. Traded to **Toronto** by **NY Rangers** with $10,000 for John Ross Roach, October 18, 1928. Traded to **Montreal Canadiens** by **Toronto** for George Hainsworth, October 1, 1933. Traded to **Chicago** by **Montreal Canadiens** with Howie Morenz and Marty Burke for Lionel Conacher, Roger Jenkins and Leroy Goldsworthy, October 3, 1934. • Missed majority of 1935-36 season recovering from knee injury suffered in training camp, October 23, 1935. Traded to **Montreal Canadiens** by **Chicago** for cash, February 8, 1936. Traded to **Montreal Maroons** by **Montreal Canadiens** for Bill Miller, Toe Blake and the rights to Ken Grivel, February, 1936. Traded to **NY Americans** by **Montreal Maroons** for cash, October 22, 1936.

• CHADWICK, Ed

Edwin Walter "Chad" G – L. 5′11″, 184 lbs. b: Fergus, Ont., 5/8/1933.

Season	Club	League	GP	W	L	T	Mins	GA	SO	Avg	AAvg	Eff	SA	S%	SAPG	GP	W	L	T	Mins	GA	SO	Avg	Eff	SA	S%	SAPG
1950-51	St. Michael's Majors	OHA-Jr.	40	....	....	....	2350	148	2	3.78	....	....	....	....	....	....	....	....	....	....	....	....	....	....	....	....	....
1951-52	St. Michael's Majors	OHA-Jr.	49	28	17	3	2900	168	0	3.48	....	....	....	....	....	8	5	3	0	490	31	*1	3.80	....	....	....	....
1952-53	St. Michael's Majors	OHA-Jr.	46	....	....	....	2760	151	3	3.28	....	....	....	....	....	16	8	8	0	960	59	0	3.69	....	....	....	....
	Pittsburgh Hornets	AHL	1	1	0	0	60	1	0	1.00	....	....	....	....	....	....	....	....	....	....	....	....	....	....	....	....	....
1953-54	Stratford Indians	OHA-Sr.	4	....	....	....	210	17	0	4.86	....	....	....	....	....	....	....	....	....	....	....	....	....	....	....	....	....
	Pittsburgh Hornets	AHL	2	1	1	0	120	9	0	4.50	....	....	....	....	....	....	....	....	....	....	....	....	....	....	....	....	....
1954-55	Sault Ste. Marie Greyhounds	NOHA	38	....	....	....	2240	96	3	*2.57	....	....	....	....	....	14	....	....	....	840	34	*2	*2.43	....	....	....	....
	Buffalo Bisons	AHL	2	1	1	0	120	10	0	5.00	....	....	....	....	....	....	....	....	....	....	....	....	....	....	....	....	....
1955-56	Winnipeg Warriors	WHL	68	*39	27	2	4129	204	2	2.96	....	....	....	....	....	20	*16	4	0	1232	52	*1	2.53	....	....	....	....
	Toronto Maple Leafs	**NHL**	**5**	**2**	**0**	**3**	**300**	**3**	**2**	**0.60**	**0.73**	....	....	....	....	....	....	....	....	....	....	....	....	....	....	....	....
1956-57	**Toronto Maple Leafs**	**NHL**	***70**	**21**	**34**	**15**	***4200**	**186**	**5**	**2.66**	**3.06**	....	....	....	....	....	....	....	....	....	....	....	....	....	....	....	....
1957-58	**Toronto Maple Leafs**	**NHL**	***70**	**21**	**38**	**11**	***4200**	**223**	**4**	**3.19**	**3.60**	....	....	....	....	....	....	....	....	....	....	....	....	....	....	....	....
1958-59	**Toronto Maple Leafs**	**NHL**	**31**	**12**	**15**	**4**	**1860**	**92**	**3**	**2.97**	**3.17**	....	....	....	....	....	....	....	....	....	....	....	....	....	....	....	....
1959-60	**Toronto Maple Leafs**	**NHL**	**4**	**1**	**2**	**1**	**240**	**15**	**0**	**3.75**	**3.93**	....	....	....	....	....	....	....	....	....	....	....	....	....	....	....	....
	Rochester Americans	AHL	67	*39	24	4	4020	184	4	*2.75	....	....	....	....	....	*12	5	7	0	*720	35	0	*2.92	....	....	....	....
1960-61	Rochester Americans	AHL	*71	32	35	4	*4300	236	2	3.29	....	....	....	....	....	....	....	....	....	....	....	....	....	....	....	....	....
1961-62	**Boston Bruins**	**NHL**	**4**	**0**	**3**	**1**	**240**	**22**	**0**	**5.50**	**5.68**	....	....	....	....	....	....	....	....	....	....	....	....	....	....	....	....
	Kingston Frontenacs	EPHL	67	36	23	8	4020	214	2	3.19	....	....	....	....	....	11	6	5	0	671	36	*1	3.22	....	....	....	....
1962-63	Hershey Bears	AHL	*68	34	26	7	*4080	219	*6	3.22	....	....	....	....	....	*15	*8	7	0	*922	42	*1	2.73	....	....	....	....
1963-64	Hershey Bears	AHL	57	31	22	3	3340	189	2	3.40	....	....	....	....	....	6	3	3	0	360	29	0	4.84	....	....	....	....

Season	Club	League	REGULAR SEASON													PLAYOFFS											
			GP	W	L	T	Mins	GA	SO	Avg	AAvg	Eff	SA	S%	SAPG	GP	W	L	T	Mins	GA	SO	Avg	Eff	SA	S%	SAPG
1964-65	Buffalo Bisons	AHL	61	33	21	6	3696	186	*5	3.02	....	....	....	....	....	9	5	4	0	542	18	*2	*1.99	....	....	....	....
1965-66	Buffalo Bisons	AHL	34	14	18	1	1983	102	3	3.09	....	....	....	....	....	....	....	....	....	....	....	....	....	....	....	....	....
1966-67	Buffalo Bisons	AHL	36	5	23	2	1829	158	0	5.18	....	....	....	....	....	....	....	....	....	....	....	....	....	....	....	....	....
1967-68	Buffalo Bisons	AHL	18	5	8	1	881	55	1	3.75	....	....	....	....	....	1	0	0	0	53	5	0	5.66	....	....	....	....
	NHL Totals		**184**	**57**	**92**	**35**	**11040**	**541**	**14**	**2.94**	....	....	....	....	....	....	....	....	....	....	....	....	....	....	....	....	....

AHL First All-Star Team (1960) • Won Harry "Hap" Holmes Memorial Award (fewest goals against - AHL) (1960) • AHL Second All-Star Team (1961, 1965)

Recalled by **Toronto** from **Winnipeg** (WHL) to replace injured Harry Lumley in games from February 8 - 15, 1956. Traded to **Boston** by **Toronto** for Don Simmons, January 31, 1961. Traded to **Detroit** (Hershey-AHL) by **Boston** with Barry Ashbee for Bob Perreault, June, 1962. Traded to **Chicago** by **Hershey** (AHL) for cash, August, 1964.

• CHAMPOUX, Bob

Robert Joseph G – L. 5'10", 175 lbs. b: Ste-Hilaire, Que., 12/2/1942.

Season	Club	League	GP	W	L	T	Mins	GA	SO	Avg	AAvg	Eff	SA	S%	SAPG	GP	W	L	T	Mins	GA	SO	Avg	Eff	SA	S%	SAPG
1960-61	Palestre Nationale	MMJHL	39	....	....	....	2340	120	3	3.08	....	....	....	....	....	....	....	....	....	....	....	....	....	....	....	....	....
1961-62	Montreal Jr. Canadiens	OHA-Jr.	8	....	....	....	480	25	0	3.13	....	....	....	....	....	....	....	....	....	....	....	....	....	....	....	....	....
1962-63	St-Jerome Alouettes	MMJHL	STATISTICS NOT AVAILABLE																								
1963-64	Cincinnati Wings	CPHL	60	10	44	5	3610	337	1	5.60	....	....	....	....	....	....	....	....	....	....	....	....	....	....	....	....	....
	Detroit Red Wings	**NHL**	....	....	....	....	....	....	....	....	....	....	....	....	....	**1**	**1**	**0**	....	**55**	**4**	**0**	**4.36**	....	....	....	....
1964-65	Memphis Wings	CPHL	4	1	3	0	240	16	0	4.00	....	....	....	....	....	....	....	....	....	....	....	....	....	....	....	....	....
	Minneapolis Bruins	CPHL	1	1	0	0	60	0	1	0.00	....	....	....	....	....	....	....	....	....	....	....	....	....	....	....	....	....
	Pittsburgh Hornets	AHL	13	4	8	0	740	50	1	4.05	....	....	....	....	....	....	....	....	....	....	....	....	....	....	....	....	....
1965-66	Pittsburgh Hornets	AHL	8	4	3	0	412	21	1	3.06	....	....	....	....	....	....	....	....	....	....	....	....	....	....	....	....	....
	Memphis Wings	CPHL	1	0	1	0	60	6	0	6.00	....	....	....	....	....	....	....	....	....	....	....	....	....	....	....	....	....
1966-67	San Diego Gulls	WHL	20	7	11	1	1140	72	0	3.86	....	....	....	....	....	....	....	....	....	....	....	....	....	....	....	....	....
1967-68	San Diego Gulls	WHL	33	15	16	2	1957	111	0	3.40	....	....	....	....	....	5	3	2	0	306	12	0	2.35	....	....	....	....
1968-69	San Diego Gulls	WHL	37	13	15	6	2048	123	*3	3.60	....	....	....	....	....	7	3	4	0	399	21	0	3.16	....	....	....	....
1969-70	San Diego Gulls	WHL	1	0	1	0	60	4	0	4.00	....	....	....	....	....	....	....	....	....	....	....	....	....	....	....	....	....
	Kansas City Blues	CHL	2	2	0	0	120	10	0	5.00	....	....	....	....	....	....	....	....	....	....	....	....	....	....	....	....	....
	Dallas Black Hawks	CHL	25	8	16	1	1460	89	2	3.66	....	....	....	....	....	....	....	....	....	....	....	....	....	....	....	....	....
1970-71	San Diego Gulls	WHL	2	0	1	1	120	6	0	3.00	....	....	....	....	....	....	....	....	....	....	....	....	....	....	....	....	....
	Jacksonville Rockets	EHL	21	....	....	....	1260	112	0	5.33	....	....	....	....	....	....	....	....	....	....	....	....	....	....	....	....	....
1971-72			OUT OF HOCKEY – RETIRED																								
1972-73	San Diego Gulls	WHL	24	8	9	5	1339	74	1	3.31	....	....	....	....	....	4	2	1	0	214	10	*1	2.80	....	....	....	....
1973-74	San Diego Gulls	WHL	2	0	2	0	120	8	0	4.00	....	....	....	....	....	....	....	....	....	....	....	....	....	....	....	....	....
	California Golden Seals	**NHL**	**17**	**2**	**11**	**3**	**923**	**80**	**0**	**5.20**	**5.07**	....	....	....	....	....	....	....	....	....	....	....	....	....	....	....	....
	Salt Lake Golden Eagles	WHL	44	23	16	3	2586	139	2	3.23	....	....	....	....	....	3	1	1	0	140	10	0	4.29	....	....	....	....
1974-75	Winston-Salem Polar Bears	SHL	22	....	....	....	1287	91	0	4.24	....	....	....	....	....	7	3	4	0	422	30	0	4.27	....	....	....	....
	Syracuse Blazers	NAHL	3	2	1	0	171	8	1	2.80	....	....	....	....	....	....	....	....	....	....	....	....	....	....	....	....	....
1975-76	Winston-Salem Polar Bears	SHL	47	18	20	9	2770	161	0	3.49	....	....	....	....	....	4	0	4	0	214	18	0	5.05	....	....	....	....
1976-77	Winston-Salem Polar Bears	SHL	23	....	....	....	1269	78	1	3.69	....	....	....	....	....	....	....	....	....	....	....	....	....	....	....	....	....
	NHL Totals		**17**	**2**	**11**	**3**	**923**	**80**	**0**	**5.20**	....	....	....	....	....	**1**	**1**	**0**	....	**55**	**4**	**0**	**4.36**	....	....	....	....

Loaned to **San Diego** (WHL) by **Detroit**, September, 1966. Traded to **San Diego** (WHL) by **Detroit** for cash, October, 1967. Loaned to **Kansas City** (CHL) by **San Diego** (WHL) for loan of Gary Edwards, November, 1969. Signed as a free agent by **California** (Salt Lake-CHL) after securing release from **San Diego** (WHL), November, 1973.

• CHEEVERS, Gerry

Gerald Michael "Cheesy" G – L. 5'11", 185 lbs. b: St. Catharines, Ont., 12/7/1940. **HHOF**

Season	Club	League	GP	W	L	T	Mins	GA	SO	Avg	AAvg	Eff	SA	S%	SAPG	GP	W	L	T	Mins	GA	SO	Avg	Eff	SA	S%	SAPG
1956-57	St. Michael's Midget Majors	MTHL	STATISTICS NOT AVAILABLE																								
	St. Michael's Majors	OHA-Jr.	1	....	....	....	60	4	0	4.00	....	....	....	....	....	....	....	....	....	....	....	....	....	....	....	....	....
1957-58	St. Michael's Majors	OHA-Jr.	1	1	0	0	60	3	0	3.00	....	....	....	....	....	....	....	....	....	....	....	....	....	....	....	....	....
1958-59	St. Michael's Buzzers	OHA-B	STATISTICS NOT AVAILABLE																								
	St. Michael's Majors	OHA-Jr.	6	....	....	....	360	28	0	4.67	....	....	....	....	....	....	....	....	....	....	....	....	....	....	....	....	....
1959-60	St. Michael's Majors	OHA-Jr.	36	18	13	5	2160	111	*5	*3.08	....	....	....	....	....	10	....	....	....	600	33	0	3.30	....	....	....	....
1960-61	St. Michael's Majors	OHA-Jr.	30	12	20	5	1775	94	2	3.18	....	....	....	....	....	20	....	....	....	1200	52	*1	*2.60	....	....	....	....
	St. Michael's Majors	Mem-Cup	9	7	2	0	540	21	1	2.33	....	....	....	....	....	....	....	....	....	....	....	....	....	....	....	....	....
1961-62	Pittsburgh Hornets	AHL	5	2	2	1	300	21	0	4.20	....	....	....	....	....	....	....	....	....	....	....	....	....	....	....	....	....
	Sault Ste. Marie Thunderbirds	EPHL	29	13	13	3	1740	103	1	3.55	....	....	....	....	....	....	....	....	....	....	....	....	....	....	....	....	....
	Toronto Maple Leafs	**NHL**	**2**	**1**	**1**	**0**	**120**	**6**	**0**	**3.00**	**3.07**	....	....	....	....	....	....	....	....	....	....	....	....	....	....	....	....
	Rochester Americans	AHL	19	9	9	1	1140	69	1	3.63	....	....	....	....	....	2	2	0	0	120	8	0	4.00	....	....	....	....
1962-63	Rochester Americans	AHL	19	7	9	3	1140	75	1	3.95	....	....	....	....	....	....	....	....	....	....	....	....	....	....	....	....	....
	Sudbury Wolves	EPHL	51	17	24	10	3060	212	4	4.15	....	....	....	....	....	*8	*4	4	0	485	29	*1	3.59	....	....	....	....
1963-64	Rochester Americans	AHL	66	*38	25	2	3960	187	3	2.84	....	....	....	....	....	2	0	2	0	120	8	0	4.00	....	....	....	....
1964-65	Rochester Americans	AHL	*72	*48	21	3	*4359	195	*5	*2.68	....	....	....	....	....	10	*8	2	0	615	24	0	2.34	....	....	....	....
1965-66	**Boston Bruins**	**NHL**	**7**	**0**	**4**	**1**	**340**	**34**	**0**	**6.00**	**6.15**	....	....	....	....	....	....	....	....	....	....	....	....	....	....	....	....
	Oklahoma City Blazers	CPHL	30	16	9	5	1760	73	3	*2.49	....	....	....	....	....	9	*8	1	0	540	19	0	*2.11	....	....	....	....
1966-67	**Boston Bruins**	**NHL**	**22**	**5**	**10**	**6**	**1298**	**72**	**1**	**3.33**	**3.46**	....	....	....	....	....	....	....	....	....	....	....	....	....	....	....	....
	Oklahoma City Blazers	CPHL	26	14	6	5	1520	71	1	*2.80	....	....	....	....	....	11	*8	3	0	677	29	*1	*2.57	....	....	....	....
1967-68	**Boston Bruins**	**NHL**	**47**	**23**	**17**	**5**	**2646**	**125**	**3**	**2.83**	**3.14**	....	....	....	....	**4**	**0**	**4**	....	**240**	**15**	**0**	**3.75**	....	....	....	....
1968-69	**Boston Bruins**	**NHL**	**52**	**28**	**12**	**12**	**3112**	**145**	**3**	**2.80**	**2.89**	....	....	....	....	**9**	**6**	**3**	....	**572**	**16**	***3**	**1.68**	....	....	....	....
1969-70♦	**Boston Bruins**	**NHL**	**41**	**24**	**8**	**8**	**2384**	**108**	**4**	**2.72**	**2.88**	....	....	....	....	***13**	***12**	**1**	....	***781**	**29**	**0**	**2.23**	....	....	....	....
1970-71	**Boston Bruins**	**NHL**	**40**	**27**	**8**	**5**	**2400**	**109**	**3**	**2.73**	**2.69**	....	....	....	....	**6**	**3**	**3**	....	**360**	**21**	**0**	**3.50**	....	....	....	....
1971-72♦	**Boston Bruins**	**NHL**	**41**	**27**	**5**	**8**	**2420**	**101**	**2**	**2.50**	**2.51**	....	....	....	....	**8**	***6**	**2**	....	**483**	**21**	***2**	**2.61**	....	....	....	....
1972-73	Cleveland Crusaders	WHA	52	32	20	0	3144	149	*5	*2.84	....	....	....	....	....	9	5	4	0	548	22	0	*2.41	....	....	....	....
1973-74	Cleveland Crusaders	WHA	*59	30	20	6	*3562	180	*4	3.03	....	....	....	....	....	5	1	4	0	303	18	0	3.56	....	....	....	....
1974-75	Team Canada	Summit-74	7	1	3	3	420	24	0	3.43	....	....	....	....	....	....	....	....	....	....	....	....	....	....	....	....	....
	Cleveland Crusaders	WHA	52	26	24	2	3076	167	*4	3.26	....	....	....	....	....	5	1	4	0	300	23	0	4.60	....	....	....	....
1975-76	Cleveland Crusaders	WHA	28	11	14	1	1570	95	1	*3.63	....	....	....	....	....	....	....	....	....	....	....	....	....	....	....	....	....
	Boston Bruins	**NHL**	**15**	**8**	**2**	**5**	**900**	**41**	**1**	**2.73**	**2.47**	....	....	....	....	**6**	**2**	**4**	....	**392**	**14**	**1**	**2.14**	....	....	....	....
1976-77	Canada	Can-Cup	DID NOT PLAY – SPARE GOALTENDER																								
	Boston Bruins	**NHL**	**45**	**30**	**10**	**5**	**2700**	**137**	**3**	**3.04**	**2.82**	....	....	....	....	***14**	**8**	**5**	....	***858**	**44**	**1**	**3.08**	....	....	....	....
1977-78	**Boston Bruins**	**NHL**	**21**	**10**	**5**	**2**	**1086**	**48**	**1**	**2.65**	**2.48**	....	....	....	....	**12**	**8**	**4**	....	**731**	**35**	**1**	**2.87**	....	....	....	....
1978-79	**Boston Bruins**	**NHL**	**43**	**23**	**9**	**10**	**2509**	**132**	**1**	**3.16**	**2.79**	....	....	....	....	**6**	**4**	**2**	....	**360**	**15**	**0**	**2.50**	....	....	....	....
	NHL All-Stars	Chal-Cup	1	0	1	0	60	6	0	6.00	....	....	....	....	....	....	....	....	....	....	....	....	....	....	....	....	....
1979-80	**Boston Bruins**	**NHL**	**42**	**24**	**11**	**7**	**2479**	**116**	**4**	**2.81**	**2.47**	....	....	....	....	**10**	**4**	**6**	....	**619**	**32**	**0**	**3.10**	....	....	....	....
1980-1984	**Boston Bruins**	**NHL**	DID NOT PLAY – COACHING																								
	NHL Totals		**418**	**230**	**102**	**74**	**24394**	**1174**	**26**	**2.89**	....	....	....	....	....	**88**	**53**	**34**	....	**5396**	**242**	**8**	**2.69**	....	....	....	....
	Other Major League Totals		191	99	78	9	11352	591	14	3.12	....	....	....	....	....	19	7	12	....	1151	63	0	3.28	....	....	....	....

AHL First All-Star Team (1965) • Won Harry "Hap" Holmes Memorial Award (fewest goals against - AHL) (1965) • Won Terry Sawchuk Trophy (fewest goals against - CPHL) (1967) • WHA First All-Star Team (1973) • Won Ben Hatskin Trophy (WHA Top Goaltender) (1973) • WHA Second All-Star Team (1974, 1975) • Played in NHL All-Star Game (1969)

Promoted to **Toronto** from **Sault Ste. Marie** (EPHL) to replace injured Johnny Bower in games on December 2 (Toronto 6, Chicago 4) and December 3 (Detroit 3, Toronto 1), 1961. Claimed by **Boston** from **Toronto** in Intra-League Draft, June 9, 1965. Selected by **New England** (WHA) in WHA General Player Draft, February 12, 1972. WHA rights traded to **Cleveland** (WHA) by **New England** (WHA) for cash, June, 1972. • Suspended by **Cleveland** (WHA) for leaving team and refusing to play, January 25, 1976. Signed as a free agent by **Boston** after securing his release from **Cleveland** (WHA), January 27, 1976.

• CHEVELDAE, Tim

Timothy M. G – L. 5'10", 195 lbs. b: Melville, Sask., 2/15/1968. Detroit's 4th, 64th overall in 1986.

Season	Club	League	GP	W	L	T	Mins	GA	SO	Avg	AAvg	Eff	SA	S%	SAPG	GP	W	L	T	Mins	GA	SO	Avg	Eff	SA	S%	SAPG
1983-84	Yorkton Mallers	SAHA	STATISTICS NOT AVAILABLE																								
1984-85	Melville Millionaires	SJHL	23	....	....	....	1167	98	0	5.04	....	....	....	....	....	....	....	....	....	....	....	....	....	....	....	....	....
1985-86	Saskatoon Blades	WHL	36	21	10	3	2030	165	0	4.88	....	....	....	....	....	8	6	2	....	480	29	0	3.63	....	....	....	....
1986-87	Saskatoon Blades	WHL	33	20	11	0	1909	133	2	4.18	....	....	....	....	....	5	4	1	....	308	20	0	3.90	....	....	....	....
1987-88	Saskatoon Blades	WHL	66	44	19	3	3798	235	1	3.71	....	....	....	....	....	6	4	2	....	364	27	0	4.45	....	....	....	....
1988-89	**Detroit Red Wings**	**NHL**	**2**	**0**	**2**	**0**	**122**	**9**	**0**	**4.43**	**3.69**	**5.39**	**74**	**.878**	**36.4**	....	....	....	....	....	....	....	....	....	....	....	....
	Adirondack Red Wings	AHL	30	20	8	0	1694	98	1	3.47	....	....	....	....	....	2	1	0	....	99	9	0	5.45	....	....	....	....
1989-90	**Detroit Red Wings**	**NHL**	**28**	**10**	**9**	**8**	**1600**	**101**	**0**	**3.79**	**3.21**	**4.48**	**854**	**.882**	**32.0**	....	....	....	....	....	....	....	....	....	....	....	....
	Adirondack Red Wings	AHL	31	17	8	6	1848	116	0	3.77	....	....	....	....	....	....	....	....	....	....	....	....	....	....	....	....	....

Season	Club	League	REGULAR SEASON GP	W	L	T	Mins	GA	SO	Avg	AAvg	Eff	SA	S%	SAPG	PLAYOFFS GP	W	L	T	Mins	GA	SO	Avg	Eff	SA	S%	SAPG
1990-91	Detroit Red Wings	NHL	65	30	26	5	3615	214	2	3.55	3.20	4.43	1716	.875	28.5	7	3	4	....	398	22	0	3.32	3.51	208	.894	31.4
1991-92	Detroit Red Wings	NHL	*72	*38	23	9	*4236	226	2	3.20	2.86	3.66	1978	.886	28.0	11	3	7	....	597	25	*2	2.51	2.27	277	.910	27.8
1992-93	Detroit Red Wings	NHL	67	34	24	7	3880	210	4	3.25	2.78	3.60	1897	.889	29.3	7	3	4	....	423	24	0	3.40	4.08	200	.880	28.4
1993-94	Detroit Red Wings	NHL	30	16	9	1	1572	91	1	3.47	3.34	4.34	727	.875	27.7	....	....	....	....	....	....	....	....	....	....	....	....
	Adirondack Red Wings	AHL	2	1	0	1	125	7	0	3.36	....	....	....	....	....	....	....	....	....	....	....	....	....	....	....	....	....
	Winnipeg Jets	NHL	14	5	8	1	788	52	1	3.96	3.81	4.25	485	.893	36.9	....	....	....	....	....	....	....	....	....	....	....	....
1994-95	Winnipeg Jets	NHL	30	8	16	3	1571	97	0	3.70	3.90	4.39	818	.881	31.2	....	....	....	....	....	....	....	....	....	....	....	....
1995-96	Winnipeg Jets	NHL	30	8	18	3	1695	111	0	3.93	3.92	4.60	948	.883	33.6	....	....	....	....	....	....	....	....	....	....	....	....
	Hershey Bears	AHL	8	4	3	0	457	31	0	4.07	....	....	....	....	....	4	2	2	....	250	14	0	3.36	....	....	....	....
1996-97	Boston Bruins	NHL	2	0	1	0	93	5	0	3.23	3.48	4.89	33	.848	21.3	....	....	....	....	....	....	....	....	....	....	....	....
	Fort Wayne Komets	IHL	21	6	9	4	1137	75	0	3.96	....	....	....	....	....	....	....	....	....	....	....	....	....	....	....	....	....
1997-98	Las Vegas Thunder	IHL	38	9	17	5	1942	128	0	3.95	....	....	....	....	....	....	....	....	....	....	....	....	....	....	....	....	....
1998-2000	Saskatoon Blades	WHL	DID NOT PLAY – ASSISTANT COACH																								
	NHL Totals		340	149	136	37	19172	1116	10	3.49	....	....	9530	.883	29.8	25	9	15	....	1418	71	2	3.00	....	685	.896	29.0

WHL East All-Star Team (1988) • Played in NHL All-Star Game (1992)

Traded to **Winnipeg** by **Detroit** with Dallas Drake for Bob Essensa and Sergei Bautin, March 8, 1994. Traded to **Philadelphia** by **Winnipeg** with Winnipeg's 3rd round choice (Chester Gallant) in 1996 Entry Draft for Dominic Roussel, February 27, 1996. Signed as a free agent by **Boston**, August 27, 1996.

• CHEVRIER, Alain

Alain Gerald G – L. 5'8", 180 lbs. b: Cornwall, Ont., 4/23/1961.

Season	Club	League	GP	W	L	T	Mins	GA	SO	Avg	AAvg	Eff	SA	S%	SAPG	GP	W	L	T	Mins	GA	SO	Avg	Eff	SA	S%	SAPG
1978-79	Ottawa Jr. Senators	OJHL	STATISTICS NOT AVAILABLE																								
	Cornwall Royals	QMJHL	7	....	....	....	332	37	0	6.69	....	....	....	....	....	....	....	....	....	....	....	....	....	....	....	....	....
1979-80	Ottawa Jr. Senators	OJHL	34	....	....	....	1818	119	0	3.93	....	....	....	....	....	....	....	....	....	....	....	....	....	....	....	....	....
1980-81	University of Miami-Ohio	NCAA	16	....	....	....	778	44	0	3.39	....	....	....	....	....	....	....	....	....	....	....	....	....	....	....	....	....
1981-82	University of Miami-Ohio	CCHA	19	8	10	1	1053	73	0	4.16	....	....	....	....	....	....	....	....	....	....	....	....	....	....	....	....	....
1982-83	University of Miami-Ohio	CCHA	33	15	16	1	1894	125	....	3.96	....	....	....	....	....	....	....	....	....	....	....	....	....	....	....	....	....
1983-84	University of Miami-Ohio	CCHA	32	9	19	1	1509	123	....	4.89	....	....	....	....	....	....	....	....	....	....	....	....	....	....	....	....	....
1984-85	Fort Wayne Komets	IHL	56	26	21	7	3219	194	0	3.62	....	....	....	....	....	9	5	4	0	556	28	0	3.02	....	....	....	....
1985-86	New Jersey Devils	NHL	37	11	18	2	1862	143	0	4.61	3.61	6.93	951	.850	30.6	....	....	....	....	....	....	....	....	....	....	....	....
1986-87	New Jersey Devils	NHL	58	24	26	2	3153	227	0	4.32	3.68	5.47	1793	.873	34.1	....	....	....	....	....	....	....	....	....	....	....	....
1987-88	New Jersey Devils	NHL	45	18	19	3	2354	148	1	3.77	3.14	5.00	1117	.868	28.5	....	....	....	....	....	....	....	....	....	....	....	....
1988-89	Winnipeg Jets	NHL	22	8	8	2	1092	78	1	4.29	3.58	6.04	554	.859	30.4	....	....	....	....	....	....	....	....	....	....	....	....
	Chicago Blackhawks	NHL	27	13	11	2	1573	92	0	3.51	2.92	4.36	740	.876	28.2	16	9	7	....	1013	44	0	2.61	2.37	484	.909	28.7
1989-90	Chicago Blackhawks	NHL	39	16	14	3	1894	132	0	4.18	3.55	6.14	898	.853	28.4	....	....	....	....	....	....	....	....	....	....	....	....
	Pittsburgh Penguins	NHL	3	1	2	0	166	14	0	5.06	4.29	7.96	89	.843	32.2	....	....	....	....	....	....	....	....	....	....	....	....
1990-91	Detroit Red Wings	NHL	3	0	2	0	108	11	0	6.11	5.50	12.22	55	.800	30.6	....	....	....	....	....	....	....	....	....	....	....	....
	San Diego Gulls	IHL	32	10	16	1	1689	124	0	4.40	....	....	....	....	....	....	....	....	....	....	....	....	....	....	....	....	....
	NHL Totals		234	91	100	14	12202	845	2	4.16	....	....	6197	.864	30.5	16	9	7	....	1013	44	0	2.61	....	484	.909	28.7

Signed as a free agent by **New Jersey**, May 31, 1985. Traded to **Winnipeg** by **New Jersey** with New Jersey's 7th round choice (Doug Evans) in 1989 Entry Draft for Steve Rooney and Winnipeg's 3rd round choice (Brad Bombardir) in 1990 Entry Draft, July 19, 1988. Traded to **Chicago** by **Winnipeg** for Chicago's 4th round choice (Allain Roy) in 1989 Entry Draft, January 19, 1989. Traded to **Pittsburgh** by **Chicago** for future considerations, March 6, 1990. Signed as a free agent by **Detroit**, July 5, 1990.

• CLANCY, King

Francis Michael G. 5'7", 155 lbs. b: Ottawa, Ont., 2/25/1903 d: 11/8/1986. **HHOF**

Season	Club	League	GP	W	L	T	Mins	GA	SO	Avg	AAvg	Eff	SA	S%	SAPG	GP	W	L	T	Mins	GA	SO	Avg	Eff	SA	S%	SAPG
1922-23♦	Ottawa Senators	St-Cup	....	....	....	....	....	....	....	....	....	....	....	....	....	1	0	0	0	2	0	0	0.00	....	....	....	....
1924-25	Ottawa Senators	NHL	1	0	0	0	2	0	0	0.00	0.00	....	....	....	....	....	....	....	....	....	....	....	....	....	....	....	....
1931-32	Toronto Maple Leafs	NHL	1	0	0	0	1	1	0	60.00	73.44	....	....	....	....	....	....	....	....	....	....	....	....	....	....	....	....
	NHL Totals		2	0	0	0	3	1	0	20.00	....	....	....	....	....	....	....	....	....	....	....	....	....	....	....	....	....

• **Ottawa** defenseman replaced penalized Alex Connell, December 27, 1924. (Ottawa 4, Toronto 3) • **Toronto** defenseman replaced penalized Lorne Chabot, March 15, 1932. (Detroit 6, Toronto 2).

• CLEGHORN, Odie

James Ogilvie G. 5'9", 195 lbs. b: Montreal, Que., 9/19/1891 d: 7/13/1956.

Season	Club	League	GP	W	L	T	Mins	GA	SO	Avg	AAvg	Eff	SA	S%	SAPG	GP	W	L	T	Mins	GA	SO	Avg	Eff	SA	S%	SAPG
1925-26	Pittsburgh Pirates	NHL	1	1	0	0	60	2	0	2.00	2.64	....	....	....	....	....	....	....	....	....	....	....	....	....	....	....	....
	NHL Totals		1	1	0	0	60	2	0	2.00	....	....	....	....	....	....	....	....	....	....	....	....	....	....	....	....	....

• **Pittsburgh** playing coach replaced Roy Worters, February 23, 1926. (Pittsburgh 3, Montreal Canadiens 2)

• CLEGHORN, Sprague

Sprague Horace "Peg" G. 5'10", 190 lbs. b: Montreal, Que., 3/11/1890 d: 7/11/1956. **HHOF**

Season	Club	League	GP	W	L	T	Mins	GA	SO	Avg	AAvg	Eff	SA	S%	SAPG	GP	W	L	T	Mins	GA	SO	Avg	Eff	SA	S%	SAPG
1918-19	Ottawa Senators	NHL	1	0	0	0	3	0	0	0.00	0.00	....	....	....	....	....	....	....	....	....	....	....	....	....	....	....	....
1921-22	Montreal Canadiens	NHL	1	0	0	0	2	0	0	0.00	0.00	....	....	....	....	....	....	....	....	....	....	....	....	....	....	....	....
	NHL Totals		2	0	0	0	5	0	0	0.00	....	....	....	....	....	....	....	....	....	....	....	....	....	....	....	....	....

• **Ottawa** defenseman replaced penalized Clint Benedict, February 18, 1919. (Ottawa 4, Toronto 3) • **Montreal** defenseman replaced penalized Georges Vezina, February 1, 1922. (Ottawa 4, Montreal 2)

• CLIFFORD, Chris

G – L. 5'9", 167 lbs. b: Kingston, Ont., 5/26/1966. Chicago's 6th, 111th overall in 1984.

Season	Club	League	GP	W	L	T	Mins	GA	SO	Avg	AAvg	Eff	SA	S%	SAPG	GP	W	L	T	Mins	GA	SO	Avg	Eff	SA	S%	SAPG
1982-83	Brockville Braves	OJHL	32	....	....	....	1746	126	1	4.33	....	....	....	....	....	....	....	....	....	....	....	....	....	....	....	....	....
1983-84	Kingston Canadians	OHL	50	16	28	0	2808	229	2	4.89	....	....	....	....	....	....	....	....	....	....	....	....	....	....	....	....	....
1984-85	Kingston Canadians	OHL	52	15	34	0	2768	241	0	5.22	....	....	....	....	....	....	....	....	....	....	....	....	....	....	....	....	....
	Chicago Black Hawks	NHL	1	0	0	0	20	0	0	0.00	0.00	0.00	8	1.000	24.0	....	....	....	....	....	....	....	....	....	....	....	....
1985-86	Kingston Canadians	OHL	50	26	21	3	2988	178	1	3.57	....	....	....	....	....	10	5	5	0	564	31	1	3.30	....	....	....	....
1986-87	Kingston Frontenacs	OHL	44	18	25	0	2576	188	1	4.38	....	....	....	....	....	12	6	6	0	730	42	0	3.45	....	....	....	....
1987-88	Saginaw Hawks	IHL	22	9	7	2	1146	80	0	4.19	....	....	....	....	....	....	....	....	....	....	....	....	....	....	....	....	....
1988-89	Chicago Blackhawks	NHL	1	0	0	0	4	0	0	0.00	0.00	0.00	0	.000	0.0	....	....	....	....	....	....	....	....	....	....	....	....
	Saginaw Hawks	IHL	7	4	2	0	321	23	0	4.30	....	....	....	....	....	....	....	....	....	....	....	....	....	....	....	....	....
1989-90	Muskegon Lumberjacks	IHL	23	17	4	1	1352	77	0	3.42	....	....	....	....	....	6	3	3	0	360	24	0	4.01	....	....	....	....
	Virginia Lancers	ECHL	10	7	1	0	547	16	0	1.75	....	....	....	....	....	....	....	....	....	....	....	....	....	....	....	....	....
1990-91	Muskegon Lumberjacks	IHL	*56	24	26	4	*3247	215	1	3.97	....	....	....	....	....	5	1	4	0	299	20	0	4.01	....	....	....	....
1991-92	Fort Wayne Komets	IHL	2	2	0	0	120	4	0	2.00	....	....	....	....	....	....	....	....	....	....	....	....	....	....	....	....	....
	Louisville IceHawks	ECHL	*56	29	19	6	*3151	223	0	4.25	....	....	....	....	....	13	7	6	0	780	53	0	4.08	....	....	....	....
1992-93	Muskegon Fury	ColHL	19	8	8	2	1038	82	1	4.74	....	....	....	....	....	2	....	....	....	117	11	0	5.64	....	....	....	....
1993-94	Louisville Icehawks	ECHL	35	11	18	4	1894	152	0	4.82	....	....	....	....	....	1	0	0	0	8	1	0	7.17	....	....	....	....
	NHL Totals		2	0	0	0	24	0	0	0.00	....	....	8	1.000	20.0	....	....	....	....	....	....	....	....	....	....	....	....

• Scored a goal with Kingston (OHL), January 7, 1987.

Signed as a free agent by **Pittsburgh**, September 6, 1989.

• CLOUTIER, Dan

G – L. 6'1", 182 lbs. b: Mont-Laurier, Que., 4/22/1976. NY Rangers' 1st, 26th overall in 1994.

Season	Club	League	GP	W	L	T	Mins	GA	SO	Avg	AAvg	Eff	SA	S%	SAPG	GP	W	L	T	Mins	GA	SO	Avg	Eff	SA	S%	SAPG
1990-91	Kapuskasing Flyers	NOHA	STATISTICS NOT AVAILABLE																								
1991-92	St. Thomas Stars	OJHL-B	14	....	....	....	823	80	0	5.83	....	....	....	....	....	....	....	....	....	....	....	....	....	....	....	....	....
1992-93	Timmons Golden Bears	NOJHA	5	4	0	0	255	10	0	2.35	....	....	....	....	....	....	....	....	....	....	....	....	....	....	....	....	....
	Sault Ste. Marie Greyhounds	OHL	12	4	6	0	572	44	0	4.62	....	....	....	....	....	4	1	2	....	231	12	0	3.12	....	....	....	....
1993-94	Sault Ste. Marie Greyhounds	OHL	55	28	14	6	2934	174	*2	3.56	....	....	....	....	....	14	*10	4	....	833	52	0	3.75	....	....	....	....
1994-95	Sault Ste. Marie Greyhounds	OHL	45	15	26	2	2518	185	1	4.41	....	....	....	....	....	....	....	....	....	....	....	....	....	....	....	....	....
	Canada	WJC-A	3	3	0	0	180	8	0	2.67	....	....	....	....	....	....	....	....	....	....	....	....	....	....	....	....	....

Season	Club	League	REGULAR SEASON													PLAYOFFS											
			GP	W	L	T	Mins	GA	SO	Avg	AAvg	Eff	SA	S%	SAPG	GP	W	L	T	Mins	GA	SO	Avg	Eff	SA	S%	SAPG
1995-96	Sault Ste. Marie Greyhounds	OHL	13	9	3	0	641	43	0	4.02	....	....	....	....	....	....	....	....	....	....	....	....	....	....	....	....	....
	Guelph Storm	OHL	17	12	2	2	1004	35	2	2.09	....	....	....	....	....	16	11	5	....	993	52	*2	3.14	....	....	....	....
	Guelph Storm	Mem-Cup	3	0	*3	0	180	12	0	4.00	....	....	....	....	....	....	....	....	....	....	....	....	....	....	....	....	....
1996-97	Binghamton Rangers	AHL	60	23	28	8	3367	199	3	3.55	....	....	....	....	....	4	1	3	....	236	13	0	3.31	....	....	....	....
1997-98	**New York Rangers**	**NHL**	**12**	**4**	**5**	**1**	**551**	**23**	**0**	**2.50**	**2.98**	**2.32**	**248**	**.907**	**27.0**	....	....	....	....	....	....	....	....	....	....	....	....
	Hartford Wolf Pack	AHL	24	12	8	3	1417	62	0	2.63	....	....	....	....	....	8	5	3	....	478	24	0	3.01	....	....	....	....
1998-99	**New York Rangers**	**NHL**	**22**	**6**	**8**	**3**	**1097**	**49**	**0**	**2.68**	**3.19**	**2.30**	**570**	**.914**	**31.2**	....	....	....	....	....	....	....	....	....	....	....	....
99-2000	**Tampa Bay Lightning**	**NHL**	**52**	**9**	**30**	**3**	**2492**	**145**	**0**	**3.49**	**4.01**	**4.02**	**1258**	**.885**	**30.3**	....	....	....	....	....	....	....	....	....	....	....	....
	NHL Totals		**86**	**19**	**43**	**7**	**4140**	**217**	**0**	**3.14**	....	....	**2076**	**.895**	**30.1**	....	....	....	....	....	....	....	....	....	....	....	....

OHL Second All-Star Team (1996)

Traded to **Tampa Bay** by **NY Rangers** with Niklas Sundstrom and NY Rangers' 1st (Nikita Alexeev) and 3rd (later traded to San Jose - later traded to Chicago - Chicago selected Igor Radulov) round choices in 2000 Entry Draft for Chicago's 1st round choice (previously acquired, NY Rangers selected Pavel Brendl) in 1999 Entry Draft, June 26, 1999.

• CLOUTIER, Jacques

G – L. 5'7", 168 lbs. b: Noranda, Que., 1/3/1960. Buffalo's 4th, 55th overall in 1979.

Season	Club	League	GP	W	L	T	Mins	GA	SO	Avg	AAvg	Eff	SA	S%	SAPG	GP	W	L	T	Mins	GA	SO	Avg	Eff	SA	S%	SAPG
1976-77	Trois Rivieres Draveurs	QMJHL	24	....	....	....	1109	93	0	5.03	....	....	....	....	....	....	....	....	....	....	....	....	....	....	....	....	....
1977-78	Trois Rivieres Draveurs	QMJHL	71	*46	17	7	4134	240	*4	3.48	....	....	....	....	....	13	....	....	....	779	40	1	3.08	....	....	....	....
	Trois Rivieres Draveurs	Mem-Cup	4	1	*3	0	240	18	0	4.50	....	....	....	....	....	....	....	....	....	....	....	....	....	....	....	....	....
1978-79	Trois Rivieres Draveurs	QMJHL	72	*58	8	6	4168	218	*4	*3.14	....	....	....	....	....	13	....	....	....	780	36	0	*2.77	....	....	....	....
	Trois Rivieres Draveurs	Mem-Cup	4	2	2	0	240	13	0	3.25	....	....	....	....	....	....	....	....	....	....	....	....	....	....	....	....	....
1979-80	Trois Rivieres Draveurs	QMJHL	55	27	20	7	3222	231	*2	4.30	....	....	....	....	....	7	3	4	0	420	33	0	4.71	....	....	....	....
1980-81	Rochester Americans	AHL	*61	27	27	6	*3478	209	1	3.61	....	....	....	....	....	....	....	....	....	....	....	....	....	....	....	....	....
1981-82	**Buffalo Sabres**	**NHL**	**7**	**5**	**1**	**0**	**311**	**13**	**0**	**2.51**	**1.94**	**2.09**	**156**	**.917**	**30.1**	....	....	....	....	....	....	....	....	....	....	....	....
	Rochester Americans	AHL	23	14	7	2	1366	64	0	2.81	....	....	....	....	....	....	....	....	....	....	....	....	....	....	....	....	....
1982-83	**Buffalo Sabres**	**NHL**	**25**	**10**	**7**	**6**	**1390**	**81**	**0**	**3.50**	**2.81**	**4.96**	**572**	**.858**	**24.7**	....	....	....	....	....	....	....	....	....	....	....	....
	Rochester Americans	AHL	13	7	3	1	634	42	0	3.97	....	....	....	....	....	16	*12	4	0	992	47	0	2.84	....	....	....	....
1983-84	Rochester Americans	AHL	*51	26	22	1	*2841	172	1	3.63	....	....	....	....	....	*18	9	9	0	*1145	68	0	3.56	....	....	....	....
1984-85	**Buffalo Sabres**	**NHL**	**1**	**0**	**0**	**1**	**65**	**4**	**0**	**3.69**	**2.94**	**3.99**	**37**	**.892**	**34.2**	....	....	....	....	....	....	....	....	....	....	....	....
	Rochester Americans	AHL	14	10	2	1	803	36	0	2.69	....	....	....	....	....	....	....	....	....	....	....	....	....	....	....	....	....
1985-86	**Buffalo Sabres**	**NHL**	**15**	**5**	**9**	**1**	**872**	**49**	**1**	**3.37**	**2.63**	**3.86**	**428**	**.886**	**29.4**	....	....	....	....	....	....	....	....	....	....	....	....
	Rochester Americans	AHL	14	10	2	2	835	38	1	2.73	....	....	....	....	....	....	....	....	....	....	....	....	....	....	....	....	....
	Canada	WEC-A	5	....	....	....	298	15	....	3.02	....	....	....	....	....	....	....	....	....	....	....	....	....	....	....	....	....
1986-87	**Buffalo Sabres**	**NHL**	**40**	**11**	**19**	**5**	**2167**	**137**	**0**	**3.79**	**3.21**	**5.02**	**1035**	**.868**	**28.7**	....	....	....	....	....	....	....	....	....	....	....	....
1987-88	**Buffalo Sabres**	**NHL**	**20**	**4**	**8**	**2**	**851**	**67**	**0**	**4.72**	**3.94**	**7.03**	**450**	**.851**	**31.7**	....	....	....	....	....	....	....	....	....	....	....	....
1988-89	**Buffalo Sabres**	**NHL**	**36**	**15**	**14**	**0**	**1786**	**108**	**0**	**3.63**	**3.02**	**4.57**	**857**	**.874**	**28.8**	**4**	**1**	**3**	....	**238**	**10**	**1**	**2.52**	**2.33**	**108**	**.907**	**27.2**
	Rochester Americans	AHL	11	2	7	0	527	41	0	4.67	....	....	....	....	....	....	....	....	....	....	....	....	....	....	....	....	....
1989-90	**Chicago Blackhawks**	**NHL**	**43**	**18**	**15**	**2**	**2178**	**112**	**2**	**3.09**	**2.61**	**3.72**	**931**	**.880**	**25.6**	**4**	**0**	**2**	....	**175**	**8**	**0**	**2.74**	**2.92**	**75**	**.893**	**25.7**
1990-91	**Chicago Blackhawks**	**NHL**	**10**	**2**	**3**	**0**	**403**	**24**	**0**	**3.57**	**3.21**	**4.90**	**175**	**.863**	**26.1**	....	....	....	....	....	....	....	....	....	....	....	....
	Quebec Nordiques	**NHL**	**15**	**3**	**8**	**2**	**829**	**61**	**0**	**4.41**	**3.97**	**5.11**	**526**	**.884**	**38.1**	....	....	....	....	....	....	....	....	....	....	....	....
1991-92	**Quebec Nordiques**	**NHL**	**26**	**6**	**14**	**3**	**1345**	**88**	**0**	**3.93**	**3.53**	**4.86**	**712**	**.876**	**31.8**	....	....	....	....	....	....	....	....	....	....	....	....
1992-93	**Quebec Nordiques**	**NHL**	**3**	**0**	**2**	**1**	**154**	**10**	**0**	**3.90**	**3.34**	**6.00**	**65**	**.846**	**25.3**	....	....	....	....	....	....	....	....	....	....	....	....
1993-94	**Quebec Nordiques**	**NHL**	**14**	**3**	**2**	**1**	**475**	**24**	**0**	**3.03**	**2.91**	**3.13**	**232**	**.897**	**29.3**	....	....	....	....	....	....	....	....	....	....	....	....
1994-1995	Cornwall Aces	AHL	DID NOT PLAY – ASSISTANT COACH																								
1995-1996	Cornwall Aces	AHL	DID NOT PLAY – ASSISTANT COACH																								
	Colorado Avalanche	**NHL**	DID NOT PLAY – ASSISTANT COACH																								
1996-2000	**Colorado Avalanche**	**NHL**	DID NOT PLAY – ASSISTANT COACH																								
	NHL Totals		**255**	**82**	**102**	**24**	**12826**	**778**	**3**	**3.64**	....	....	....	....	....	**8**	**1**	**5**	....	**413**	**18**	**1**	**2.62**	....	**183**	**.902**	**26.6**

QMJHL First All-Star Team (1978, 1979)

Traded to **Chicago** by **Buffalo** for future considerations, September 28, 1989. Traded to **Quebec** by **Chicago** for Tony McKegney, January 29, 1991.

• COLVIN, Les

G – L. 5'6", 150 lbs. b: Oshawa, Ont., 2/8/1921.

Season	Club	League	GP	W	L	T	Mins	GA	SO	Avg	AAvg	Eff	SA	S%	SAPG	GP	W	L	T	Mins	GA	SO	Avg	Eff	SA	S%	SAPG
1936-37	Oshawa Generals	OHA-Jr.	1	....	....	....	60	4	0	4.00	....	....	....	....	....	....	....	....	....	....	....	....	....	....	....	....	....
1937-38	Oshawa Generals	OHA-Jr.	4	....	....	....	240	20	1	5.00	....	....	....	....	....	....	....	....	....	....	....	....	....	....	....	....	....
1938-39	Oshawa Generals	OHA-Jr.	7	....	....	....	420	8	1	*1.14	....	....	....	....	....	4	4	0	0	240	7	*1	*1.75	....	....	....	....
1939-40	Washington Eagles	EAHL	23	....	....	....	1380	79	0	3.43	....	....	....	....	....	3	1	2	0	180	11	0	3.67	....	....	....	....
1940-41	Washington Eagles	EAHL	27	....	....	....	1620	74	0	2.74	....	....	....	....	....	1	....	....	....	60	3	0	3.00	....	....	....	....
	New York Rovers	EAHL	3	....	....	....	180	11	0	3.67	....	....	....	....	....	....	....	....	....	....	....	....	....	....	....	....	....
1941-42			MILITARY SERVICE																								
1942-43	Toronto Army Daggers	TIHL	1	0	1	0	60	8	0	8.00	....	....	....	....	....	....	....	....	....	....	....	....	....	....	....	....	....
1943-44			MILITARY SERVICE																								
1944-45			MILITARY SERVICE																								
1945-46			DID NOT PLAY																								
1946-47	Shawinigan Cataracts	QSHL	10	....	....	....	600	51	0	5.10	....	....	....	....	....	4	....	....	....	240	22	0	5.40	....	....	....	....
1947-48	Vancouver Canucks	PCHL	50	25	23	2	3000	197	1	3.94	....	....	....	....	....	....	....	....	....	....	....	....	....	....	....	....	....
	Los Angeles Monarchs	PCHL	4	1	3	0	240	21	0	4.20	....	....	....	....	....	....	....	....	....	....	....	....	....	....	....	....	....
	Portland Penguins	PCHL	1	1	0	0	60	3	0	3.00	....	....	....	....	....	....	....	....	....	....	....	....	....	....	....	....	....
1948-49	Shawinigan Cataracts	QSHL	36	....	....	....	2307	56	10	1.46	....	....	....	....	....	....	....	....	....	....	....	....	....	....	....	....	....
	Boston Bruins	**NHL**	**1**	**0**	**1**	**0**	**60**	**4**	**0**	**4.00**	**4.49**	....	....	....	....	....	....	....	....	....	....	....	....	....	....	....	....
1949-50	Moncton Hawks	NBSHL	70	31	32	7	4200	270	3	3.87	....	....	....	....	....	4	0	4	0	250	22	0	5.28	....	....	....	....
1950-51	Moncton Hawks	MMHL	69	16	*45	5	4060	312	0	4.61	....	....	....	....	....	6	1	5	0	360	22	0	3.67	....	....	....	....
1951-52	North Bay Trappers	NOHA	18	....	....	....	1080	81	1	4.50	....	....	....	....	....	11	....	....	....	660	42	0	3.82	....	....	....	....
1952-53	North Bay Trappers	NOHA	47	21	23	2	2820	203	1	4.32	....	....	....	....	....	7	....	....	....	420	28	0	4.00	....	....	....	....
	NHL Totals		**1**	**0**	**1**	**0**	**60**	**4**	**0**	**4.00**	....	....	....	....	....	....	....	....	....	....	....	....	....	....	....	....	....

EAHL Second All-Star Team (1941)

Loaned to **Boston** by **Shawinigan** (QSHL) to replace Frank Brimsek, January 22, 1949. (Montreal 4, Boston 2)

• CONACHER, Charlie

Charles William "The Big Bomber" G. 6'1", 195 lbs. b: Toronto, Ont., 12/20/1909 d: 12/30/1967. **HHOF**

Season	Club	League	GP	W	L	T	Mins	GA	SO	Avg	AAvg	Eff	SA	S%	SAPG	GP	W	L	T	Mins	GA	SO	Avg	Eff	SA	S%	SAPG
1932-33	**Toronto Maple Leafs**	**NHL**	**2**	**0**	**0**	**0**	**4**	**0**	**0**	**0.00**	**0.00**	....	....	....	....	....	....	....	....	....	....	....	....	....	....	....	....
1934-35	**Toronto Maple Leafs**	**NHL**	**1**	**0**	**0**	**0**	**3**	**0**	**0**	**0.00**	**0.00**	....	....	....	....	....	....	....	....	....	....	....	....	....	....	....	....
1938-39	**Detroit Red Wings**	**NHL**	**1**	**0**	**0**	**0**	**3**	**0**	**0**	**0.00**	**0.00**	....	....	....	....	....	....	....	....	....	....	....	....	....	....	....	....
	NHL Totals		**4**	**0**	**0**	**0**	**10**	**0**	**0**	**0.00**	....	....	....	....	....	....	....	....	....	....	....	....	....	....	....	....	....

• **Toronto** right winger replaced penalized Lorne Chabot, November 20, 1932, (NY Rangers 7, Toronto 0) and March 16, 1933. (Detroit 1, Toronto 0) • **Toronto** right winger replaced injured George Hainsworth in 3rd period, March 16, 1935. (Toronto 5, Montreal Canadiens 3) • **Detroit** right winger replaced injured Tiny Thompson, February 21, 1939. (NY Rangers 7, Detroit 3)

• CONNELL, Alex

"The Ottawa Fireman" G – R. 5'9", 150 lbs. b: Ottawa, Ont., 2/8/1902 d: 5/10/1958. **HHOF**

Season	Club	League	GP	W	L	T	Mins	GA	SO	Avg	AAvg	Eff	SA	S%	SAPG	GP	W	L	T	Mins	GA	SO	Avg	Eff	SA	S%	SAPG
1917-18	Kingston Frontenacs	OHA-Jr.	4	*4	0	0	240	11	0	*2.75	....	....	....	....	....	4	3	1	0	240	18	0	4.50	....	....	....	....
1918-19	Kingston Frontenacs	OHA-Jr.	5	3	2	0	305	24	0	4.72	....	....	....	....	....	4	0	1	3	240	20	0	5.00	....	....	....	....
1919-20	Ottawa Cliffsides	OCHL	7	4	3	0	430	8	2	1.12	....	....	....	....	....	....	....	....	....	....	....	....	....	....	....	....	....
1920-21	Ottawa St. Brigids	OCHL	11	*8	2	1	660	12	*2	*1.09	....	....	....	....	....	8	*6	1	1	520	14	1	1.62	....	....	....	....
1921-22	Ottawa Gunners	OCHL	14	*10	3	1	860	18	*5	*1.26	....	....	....	....	....	6	5	1	0	360	17	0	2.83	....	....	....	....
1922-23	Ottawa St. Brigids	OCHL	17	8	8	1	1090	26	*4	1.43	....	....	....	....	....	....	....	....	....	....	....	....	....	....	....	....	....
1923-24	Ottawa St. Brigids	OCHL	12	8	4	0	740	14	5	1.14	....	....	....	....	....	....	....	....	....	....	....	....	....	....	....	....	....
1924-25	**Ottawa Senators**	**NHL**	***30**	**17**	**12**	**1**	**1852**	**66**	***7**	**2.14**	**2.53**	....	....	....	....	....	....	....	....	....	....	....	....	....	....	....	....
1925-26	**Ottawa Senators**	**NHL**	***36**	***24**	**8**	**4**	**2251**	**42**	***15**	***1.12**	**1.36**	....	....	....	....	**2**	**0**	**1**	**1**	**120**	**2**	**0**	***1.00**	....	....	....	....
1926-27♦	**Ottawa Senators**	**NHL**	***44**	***30**	**10**	**4**	**2782**	**69**	**13**	**1.49**	**2.21**	....	....	....	....	**6**	***3**	**0**	**3**	**400**	**4**	***2**	***0.60**	....	....	....	....
1927-28	**Ottawa Senators**	**NHL**	***44**	**20**	**14**	**10**	**2760**	**57**	***15**	**1.24**	**1.91**	....	....	....	....	**2**	**0**	**2**	**0**	**120**	**3**	**0**	**1.50**	....	....	....	....
1928-29	**Ottawa Senators**	**NHL**	***44**	**14**	**17**	**13**	***2820**	**67**	**7**	**1.43**	**2.98**	....	....	....	....	....	....	....	....	....	....	....	....	....	....	....	....
1929-30	**Ottawa Senators**	**NHL**	***44**	**21**	**15**	**8**	**2780**	**118**	**3**	**2.55**	**2.59**	....	....	....	....	**2**	**0**	**1**	**1**	**120**	**6**	**0**	**3.00**	....	....	....	....

			REGULAR SEASON													PLAYOFFS											
Season	Club	League	GP	W	L	T	Mins	GA	SO	Avg	AAvg	Eff	SA	S%	SAPG	GP	W	L	T	Mins	GA	SO	Avg	Eff	SA	S%	SAPG
1930-31	**Ottawa Senators**	**NHL**	**36**	**10**	**22**	**4**	**2190**	**110**	**3**	**3.01**	**3.92**	....	....	....	....	....	....	....	....	....	....	....	....	....	....	....	....
1931-32	**Detroit Falcons**	**NHL**	***48**	**18**	**20**	**10**	***3050**	**108**	**6**	**2.12**	**2.54**	....	....	....	....	**2**	**0**	**1**	**1**	**120**	**3**	**0**	**1.50**	....	....	....	....
1932-33	**Ottawa Senators**	**NHL**	**15**	**4**	**8**	**2**	**845**	**36**	**1**	**2.56**	**3.44**	....	....	....	....	....	....	....	....	....	....	....	....	....	....	....	....
1933-34	**New York Americans**	**NHL**	**1**	**1**	**0**	**0**	**40**	**2**	**0**	**3.00**	**3.80**	....	....	....	....	....	....	....	....	....	....	....	....	....	....	....	....
1934-35♦	**Montreal Maroons**	**NHL**	***48**	**24**	**19**	**5**	**2970**	**92**	***9**	**1.86**	**2.18**	....	....	....	....	***7**	***5**	**0**	**2**	**429**	**8**	***2**	***1.12**	....	....	....	....
1935-36			OUT OF HOCKEY – RETIRED																								
1936-37	**Montreal Maroons**	**NHL**	**27**	**10**	**11**	**6**	**1710**	**63**	**2**	**2.21**	**2.71**	....	....	....	....	....	....	....	....	....	....	....	....	....	....	....	....
	NHL Totals		**417**	**193**	**156**	**67**	**26050**	**830**	**81**	**1.91**	....	....	....	....	....	**21**	**8**	**5**	**8**	**1309**	**26**	**4**	**1.19**	....	....	....	....

Signed as a free agent by **Ottawa**, November 18, 1924. • Established NHL record for consecutive shutouts (6), January 31 – February 18, 1928. Claimed by **Detroit** from **Ottawa** in Dispersal Draft for 1931-32 season, September 26, 1931. Loaned to **NY Americans** by **Ottawa** to replace injured Roy Worters, March 15, 1934. (NY Americans 3, Ottawa 2). Traded to **Montreal Maroons** by **Ottawa** for future considerations (Glenn Brydson, October 22, 1934), October 2, 1934.

• CORSI, Jim

James G – L. 5'10", 180 lbs. b: Montreal, Que., 6/19/1954.

Season	Club	League	GP	W	L	T	Mins	GA	SO	Avg	AAvg	Eff	SA	S%	SAPG	GP	W	L	T	Mins	GA	SO	Avg	Eff	SA	S%	SAPG
1973-74	Loyola University	QUAA	11	....	....	....	660	30	1	2.73	....	....	....	....	....	....	....	....	....	....	....	....	....	....	....	....	....
1974-75	Loyola University	QUAA	40	....	....	....	2359	109	2	2.72	....	....	....	....	....	....	....	....	....	....	....	....	....	....	....	....	....
1975-76	Concordia University	QUAA	20	19	0	1	1200	36	2	1.80	....	....	....	....	....	....	....	....	....	....	....	....	....	....	....	....	....
1976-77	Maine Nordiques	NAHL	54	....	....	....	2988	181	1	3.57	....	....	....	....	....	12	7	5	0	714	46	*1	3.87	....	....	....	....
1977-78	Quebec Nordiques	WHA	23	10	7	0	1089	82	0	4.52	....	....	....	....	....	....	....	....	....	....	....	....	....	....	....	....	....
1978-79	Binghamton Dusters	AHL	4	1	2	0	211	7	0	1.99	....	....	....	....	....	....	....	....	....	....	....	....	....	....	....	....	....
	Quebec Nordiques	WHA	40	16	20	1	2291	126	*3	3.30	....	....	....	....	....	2	0	1	0	66	7	0	6.36	....	....	....	....
1979-80	**Edmonton Oilers**	**NHL**	**26**	**8**	**14**	**3**	**1366**	**83**	**0**	**3.65**	**3.23**	....	....	....	....	....	....	....	....	....	....	....	....	....	....	....	....
	Houston Apollos	CHL	17	8	5	2	959	57	0	3.57	....	....	....	....	....	....	....	....	....	....	....	....	....	....	....	....	....
	Oklahoma City Stars	CHL	11	5	6	0	645	28	1	2.60	....	....	....	....	....	....	....	....	....	....	....	....	....	....	....	....	....
1980-81	HC Gardena-Groden	Italy	STATISTICS NOT AVAILABLE																								
	Italy	WEC-B	7	*6	0	1	420	18	0	2.57	....	....	....	....	....	....	....	....	....	....	....	....	....	....	....	....	....
1981-82	HC Gardena-Groden	Italy	STATISTICS NOT AVAILABLE																								
	Italy	WEC-A	7	1	5	1	390	38	0	5.84	....	....	....	....	....	....	....	....	....	....	....	....	....	....	....	....	....
1982-83	HC Gardena-Groden	Italy	STATISTICS NOT AVAILABLE																								
	Italy	WEC-A	10	1	8	1	568	50	0	5.28	....	....	....	....	....	....	....	....	....	....	....	....	....	....	....	....	....
1983-84	HC Bolzano-Bozen	Italy	18	16	1	1	1080	60	....	3.33	....	....	....	....	....	6	4	2	0	360	28	0	4.67	....	....	....	....
1984-85	HC Varese	Italy	STATISTICS NOT AVAILABLE																								
	Italy	WEC-B	7	5	0	2	420	22	0	3.14	....	....	....	....	....	....	....	....	....	....	....	....	....	....	....	....	....
1985-86	HC Varese	Italy	STATISTICS NOT AVAILABLE																								
	Italy	WEC-B	7	4	3	0	420	16	*1	2.29	....	....	....	....	....	....	....	....	....	....	....	....	....	....	....	....	....
1986-87	HC Varese	Italy	36	....	....	....	2134	103	1	2.90	....	....	....	....	....	....	....	....	....	....	....	....	....	....	....	....	....
	Italy	WEC-B	7	2	4	1	420	29	0	4.14	....	....	....	....	....	....	....	....	....	....	....	....	....	....	....	....	....
1987-88	HC Varese	Italy	STATISTICS NOT AVAILABLE																								
1988-89	HC Varese	Italy	42	....	....	....	2520	116	0	*2.76	....	....	....	....	....	5	....	....	....	300	8	*1	*1.60	....	....	....	....
	Italy	WEC-B	7	*5	1	1	420	16	*2	2.29	....	....	....	....	....	....	....	....	....	....	....	....	....	....	....	....	....
1989-90	HC Varese	Italy	STATISTICS NOT AVAILABLE																								
	Italy	WEC-B	5	2	2	1	299	14	0	2.81	....	....	....	....	....	....	....	....	....	....	....	....	....	....	....	....	....
1990-91	HC Varese	Italy	44	....	....	....	2610	165	0	3.79	....	....	....	....	....	....	....	....	....	....	....	....	....	....	....	....	....
1991-92	HC Varese	Italy	STATISTICS NOT AVAILABLE																								
	NHL Totals		**26**	**8**	**14**	**3**	**1366**	**83**	**0**	**3.65**	....	....	....	....	....	....	....	....	....	....	....	....	....	....	....	....	....
	Other Major League Totals		63	26	27	1	3380	208	3	3.69	....	....	....	....	....	2	0	1	....	66	7	0	6.36	....	....	....	....

QUAA Second All-Star Team (1975) • QUAA First All-Star Team (1976) • CIAU MVP (1976) • WEC-B All-Star Team (1981, 1987) • Named Best Goaltender at WEC-B (1986)

• Played professional soccer with Montreal Olympics of the NASL, 1971-72. Signed as a free agent by **Quebec** (WHA), September, 1976. Signed as a free agent by **Edmonton**, October 4, 1979. Traded to **Minnesota** by **Edmonton** for future considerations, March 11, 1980.

• COURTEAU, Maurice

Maurice Laurent G – L. 5'8", 162 lbs. b: Quebec City, Que., 2/18/1920.

Season	Club	League	GP	W	L	T	Mins	GA	SO	Avg	AAvg	Eff	SA	S%	SAPG	GP	W	L	T	Mins	GA	SO	Avg	Eff	SA	S%	SAPG
1935-36	Noranda Copper Kings	NOJHA	2	1	1	0	120	9	0	4.50	....	....	....	....	....	....	....	....	....	....	....	....	....	....	....	....	....
1936-37	Noranda Copper Kings	NOJHA	STATISTICS NOT AVAILABLE																								
1937-38	Noranda Copper Kings	NOJHA	16	1	13	2	960	86	0	5.37	....	....	....	....	....	....	....	....	....	....	....	....	....	....	....	....	....
1938-39	Atlantic City Seagulls	EAHL	53	22	*25	6	3180	184	2	3.47	....	....	....	....	....	....	....	....	....	....	....	....	....	....	....	....	....
1939-40	Shawinigan Cataracts	QPHL	40	....	....	....	2400	155	1	3.88	....	....	....	....	....	....	....	....	....	....	....	....	....	....	....	....	....
1940-41	Quebec Royal Rifles	QCHL	33	17	11	5	1980	117	0	3.54	....	....	....	....	....	4	....	....	....	240	14	*1	3.50	....	....	....	....
1941-42	Quebec Aces	QSHL	7	....	....	....	420	15	1	2.14	....	....	....	....	....	1	0	1	0	60	5	0	5.00	....	....	....	....
1942-43	Philadelphia Falcons	EAHL	26	....	....	....	1560	88	2	*3.39	....	....	....	....	....	....	....	....	....	....	....	....	....	....	....	....	....
1943-44	**Boston Bruins**	**NHL**	**6**	**2**	**4**	**0**	**360**	**33**	**0**	**5.50**	**4.13**	....	....	....	....	....	....	....	....	....	....	....	....	....	....	....	....
	Boston Olympics	EAHL	36	*34	1	1	2160	79	4	*2.19	....	....	....	....	....	10	4	6	0	600	42	0	4.20	....	....	....	....
	Providence Reds	AHL	1	0	0	1	60	2	0	2.00	....	....	....	....	....	....	....	....	....	....	....	....	....	....	....	....	....
1944-45	Boston Olympics	EAHL	33	22	9	2	1980	129	1	3.91	....	....	....	....	....	8	*7	0	1	480	26	0	3.25	....	....	....	....
1945-46	Sherbrooke Randies	QPHL	11	....	....	....	660	38	0	3.45	....	....	....	....	....	....	....	....	....	....	....	....	....	....	....	....	....
1946-47	Philadelphia Rockets	AHL	7	0	6	0	380	49	0	7.74	....	....	....	....	....	....	....	....	....	....	....	....	....	....	....	....	....
	San Francisco Shamrocks	PCHL	24	....	....	....	1440	145	0	6.04	....	....	....	....	....	....	....	....	....	....	....	....	....	....	....	....	....
1947-48	New York Rovers	QSHL	12	....	....	....	720	57	0	4.75	....	....	....	....	....	....	....	....	....	....	....	....	....	....	....	....	....
	Philadelphia Rockets	AHL	30	8	21	1	1800	144	1	4.80	....	....	....	....	....	....	....	....	....	....	....	....	....	....	....	....	....
1948-49			DID NOT PLAY																								
1949-50	Magog Volants	ETSHL	19	....	....	....	1140	82	*2	4.32	....	....	....	....	....	....	....	....	....	....	....	....	....	....	....	....	....
	NHL Totals		**6**	**2**	**4**	**0**	**360**	**33**	**0**	**5.50**	....	....	....	....	....	....	....	....	....	....	....	....	....	....	....	....	....

EAHL Second All-Star Team (1943, 1945) • EAHL First All-Star Team (1944) • Won George L. Davis Jr. Trophy (fewest goals against - EAHL) (1944)

• COUSINEAU, Marcel

G – L. 5'9", 183 lbs. b: Delson, Que., 4/30/1973. Boston's 3rd, 62nd overall in 1991.

Season	Club	League	GP	W	L	T	Mins	GA	SO	Avg	AAvg	Eff	SA	S%	SAPG	GP	W	L	T	Mins	GA	SO	Avg	Eff	SA	S%	SAPG
1989-90	Richelieu Riverains	QAAA	27	22	5	0	1618	104	0	3.83	....	....	....	....	....	....	....	....	....	....	....	....	....	....	....	....	....
1990-91	Beauport Harfangs	QMJHL	49	13	29	3	2739	196	1	4.29	....	....	....	....	....	....	....	....	....	....	....	....	....	....	....	....	....
1991-92	Beauport Harfangs	QMJHL	*67	26	32	5	*3673	241	0	3.94	....	....	....	....	....	....	....	....	....	....	....	....	....	....	....	....	....
1992-93	Drummondville Voltigeurs	QMJHL	60	20	32	2	3298	225	0	4.09	....	....	....	....	....	9	3	6	....	498	37	*1	4.45	....	....	....	....
1993-94	St. John's Maple Leafs	AHL	37	13	11	9	2015	118	0	3.51	....	....	....	....	....	....	....	....	....	....	....	....	....	....	....	....	....
1994-95	St. John's Maple Leafs	AHL	58	22	27	6	3342	171	4	3.07	....	....	....	....	....	3	0	3	....	179	9	0	3.01	....	....	....	....
1995-96	St. John's Maple Leafs	AHL	62	21	26	13	3629	192	1	3.17	....	....	....	....	....	4	1	3	....	258	11	0	2.56	....	....	....	....
1996-97	**Toronto Maple Leafs**	**NHL**	**13**	**3**	**5**	**1**	**566**	**31**	**1**	**3.29**	**3.54**	**3.22**	**317**	**.902**	**33.6**	....	....	....	....	....	....	....	....	....	....	....	....
	St. John's Maple Leafs	AHL	19	7	8	3	1053	58	0	3.30	....	....	....	....	....	11	6	5	....	658	28	0	2.55	....	....	....	....
1997-98	**Toronto Maple Leafs**	**NHL**	**2**	**0**	**0**	**0**	**17**	**0**	**0**	**0.00**	**0.00**	**0.00**	**9**	**1.000**	**31.8**	....	....	....	....	....	....	....	....	....	....	....	....
	St. John's Maple Leafs	AHL	57	17	25	13	3306	167	1	3.03	....	....	....	....	....	4	1	3	....	254	10	0	2.36	....	....	....	....
1998-99	**New York Islanders**	**NHL**	**6**	**0**	**4**	**0**	**293**	**14**	**0**	**2.87**	**3.41**	**3.38**	**119**	**.882**	**24.4**	....	....	....	....	....	....	....	....	....	....	....	....
	Lowell Lock Monsters	AHL	53	26	17	7	3034	139	3	2.75	....	....	....	....	....	3	0	3	....	186	13	0	4.20	....	....	....	....
99-2000	**Los Angeles Kings**	**NHL**	**5**	**1**	**1**	**0**	**171**	**6**	**0**	**2.11**	**2.41**	**1.98**	**64**	**.906**	**22.5**	....	....	....	....	....	....	....	....	....	....	....	....
	Long Beach Ice Dogs	IHL	23	15	6	1	1328	62	0	2.80	....	....	....	....	....	....	....	....	....	....	....	....	....	....	....	....	....
	NHL Totals		**26**	**4**	**10**	**1**	**1047**	**51**	**1**	**2.92**	....	....	**509**	**.900**	**29.2**	....	....	....	....	....	....	....	....	....	....	....	....

Signed as a free agent by **Toronto**, November 13, 1993. Signed as a free agent by **NY Islanders**, July 29, 1998. Traded to **LA Kings** by **NY Islanders** with Zigmund Palffy, Brian Smolinski and New Jersey's 4th round choice (previously acquired, LA Kings selected Daniel Johanssen) in 1999 Entry Draft for Olli Jokinen, Josh Green, Mathieu Biron and LA Kings' 1st round choice (Taylor Pyatt) in 1999 Entry Draft, June 20, 1999.

• COWLEY, Wayne

Wayne R. G – L. 6', 185 lbs. b: Scarborough, Ont., 12/4/1964.

Season	Club	League	GP	W	L	T	Mins	GA	SO	Avg	AAvg	Eff	SA	S%	SAPG	GP	W	L	T	Mins	GA	SO	Avg	Eff	SA	S%	SAPG
1980-81	Mississauga Reps	MTHL	STATISTICS NOT AVAILABLE																								
1981-82	Georgetown Geminis	OJHL-B	STATISTICS NOT AVAILABLE																								
1982-83	Georgetown Geminis	OJHL-B	14	....	....	....	836	74	0	5.31	....	....	....	....	....	....	....	....	....	....	....	....	....	....	....	....	....
1983-84	Georgetown Geminis	OJHL-B	37	....	....	....	2170	157	0	4.34	....	....	....	....	....	....	....	....	....	....	....	....	....	....	....	....	....

Season	Club	League	GP	W	L	T	Mins	GA	SO	Avg	AAvg	Eff	SA	S%	SAPG	GP	W	L	T	Mins	GA	SO	Avg	Eff	SA	S%	SAPG
			REGULAR SEASON													PLAYOFFS											
1984-85	Oakville Blades	OJHL-B	35	....	....	....	2086	132	*3	*3.80	....	....	....	....	....	....	....	....	....	....	....	....	....	....	....	....	....
1985-86	Colgate University	ECAC	7	2	2	0	313	23	1	4.42	....	....	....	....	....	....	....	....	....	....	....	....	....	....	....	....	....
1986-87	Colgate University	ECAC	31	21	8	1	1805	106	0	3.52	....	....	....	....	....	....	....	....	....	....	....	....	....	....	....	....	....
1987-88	Colgate University	ECAC	20	11	7	1	1162	58	1	2.99	....	....	....	....	....	....	....	....	....	....	....	....	....	....	....	....	....
1988-89	Salt Lake Golden Eagles	IHL	29	17	7	1	1423	94	0	3.96	....	....	....	....	....	2	1	0	0	69	6	0	5.22	....	....	....	....
1989-90	Salt Lake Golden Eagles	IHL	36	15	12	5	2009	124	1	3.70	....	....	....	....	....	3	0	0	0	118	6	0	3.05	....	....	....	....
1990-91	Salt Lake Golden Eagles	IHL	7	3	4	0	377	23	1	3.66	....	....	....	....	....	....	....	....	....	....	....	....	....	....	....	....	....
	Cincinnati Cyclones	ECHL	30	19	9	2	1680	108	1	3.85	....	....	....	....	....	4	1	3	0	249	13	*1	3.13	....	....	....	....
1991-92	Solihull Barons	Aut-Cup	8	3	5	0	463	48	0	6.22	....	....	....	....	....	....	....	....	....	....	....	....	....	....	....	....	....
	Blackburn Blackhawks	Britain-2	2	....	....	....	115	7	....	3.65	....	....	....	....	....	....	....	....	....	....	....	....	....	....	....	....	....
	Raleigh IceCaps	ECHL	38	16	18	2	2213	137	0	3.71	....	....	....	....	....	....	....	....	....	....	....	....	....	....	....	....	....
	Cape Breton Oilers	AHL	11	6	5	0	644	42	0	3.91	....	....	....	....	....	1	0	1	0	61	3	0	2.95	....	....	....	....
1992-93	Cape Breton Oilers	AHL	42	14	17	6	2334	152	1	3.91	....	....	....	....	....	16	*14	2	0	1014	47	*1	2.78	....	....	....	....
	Wheeling Thunderbirds	ECHL	1	1	0	0	60	3	0	3.00	....	....	....	....	....	....	....	....	....	....	....	....	....	....	....	....	....
1993-94	**Edmonton Oilers**	**NHL**	**1**	**0**	**1**	**0**	**57**	**3**	**0**	**3.16**	**3.04**	**2.71**	**35**	**.914**	**36.8**	....	....	....	....	....	....	....	....	....	....	....	....
	Cape Breton Oilers	AHL	44	20	17	5	2486	150	0	3.62	....	....	....	....	....	5	1	4	0	0	20	0	4.66	....	....	....	....
1994-95	Worcester IceCats	AHL	45	11	25	6	2597	153	1	3.53	....	....	....	....	....	....	....	....	....	....	....	....	....	....	....	....	....
	Milwaukee Admirals	IHL	2	0	0	1	79	4	0	3.04	....	....	....	....	....	....	....	....	....	....	....	....	....	....	....	....	....
1995-96	Sheffield Steelers	BH-Cup	2	2	0	0	125	5	0	2.40	....	....	....	....	....	....	....	....	....	....	....	....	....	....	....	....	....
	Sheffield Steelers	Britain	20	....	....	....	1160	62	....	*3.21	....	....	....	....	....	7	....	....	....	420	17	*2	*2.43	....	....	....	....
1996-97	Wedemark Scorpions	Germany	43	....	....	....	2324	175	1	4.51	....	....	....	....	....	7	....	....	....	410	30	0	4.39	....	....	....	....
1997-98	Newcastle Cobras	BH-Cup	9	....	....	....	503	26	0	3.10	....	....	....	....	....	....	....	....	....	....	....	....	....	....	....	....	....
	Newcastle Cobras	Britain	28	....	....	....	1612	94	....	3.50	....	....	....	....	....	6	....	....	....	367	20	....	3.27	....	....	....	....
1998-99	Newcastle Riverkings	BH-Cup	5	....	....	....	300	15	0	3.00	....	....	....	....	....	....	....	....	....	....	....	....	....	....	....	....	....
	Newcastle Riverkings	Britain	29	....	....	....	1673	87	0	3.12	....	....	....	....	....	....	....	....	....	....	....	....	....	....	....	....	....
99-2000	Great Britain	WC-Q	DID NOT PLAY – SPARE GOALTENDER																								
	Flint Generals	UHL	7	6	1	0	419	21	0	3.01	....	....	....	....	....	....	....	....	....	....	....	....	....	....	....	....	....
	NHL Totals		**1**	**0**	**1**	**0**	**57**	**3**	**0**	**3.16**	....	....	**35**	**.914**	**36.8**	....	....	....	....	....	....	....	....	....	....	....	....

ECHL Second All-Star Team (1991)

Signed as a free agent by **Calgary**, May 1, 1988. Signed as a free agent by **Edmonton**, September 13, 1993. Signed as an emergency back-up goaltender by **Dayton** (ECHL), February 18, 2000. Loaned to **Flint** (UHL) by **Dayton** (ECHL), February 26, 2000. • Played w/ RHI's Las Vegas Flash in 1994 (13-3-6-1-503-76-0-7.24)

• COX, Abbie

Albert Edward G – L. 5'6", 140 lbs. b: London, Ont., 7/19/1904.

Season	Club	League	GP	W	L	T	Mins	GA	SO	Avg	AAvg	Eff	SA	S%	SAPG	GP	W	L	T	Mins	GA	SO	Avg	Eff	SA	S%	SAPG
1921-22	Ottawa Munitions	OCHL	12	4	7	2	720	42	1	3.50	....	....	....	....	....	2	0	2	0	120	11	0	5.50	....	....	....	....
1922-23	Iroquois Falls Papermakers	NOJHA	STATISTICS NOT AVAILABLE																								
1923-24	New Haven Bears	USAHA	12	*6	6	0	730	21	2	1.73	....	....	....	....	....	....	....	....	....	....	....	....	....	....	....	....	....
1924-25	Boston Maples	USAHA	21	6	15	0	995	58	0	2.21	....	....	....	....	....	....	....	....	....	....	....	....	....	....	....	....	....
1925-26	NY Knickerbockers	USAHA	DID NOT PLAY – SUSPENDED																								
1926-27	Springfield Indians	Can-Am	31	14	12	5	1950	51	6	1.57	....	....	....	....	....	6	*3	1	2	360	6	*2	*1.00	....	....	....	....
1927-28	Springfield Indians	Can-Am	40	*24	13	3	2450	71	12	1.74	....	....	....	....	....	4	2	2	0	240	7	*1	*1.75	....	....	....	....
1928-29	Windsor Bulldogs	Can-Pro	34	22	9	3	2100	64	7	1.83	....	....	....	....	....	8	*5	3	0	530	7	*3	*0.79	....	....	....	....
1929-30	Windsor Bulldogs	IHL	41	20	13	8	2440	89	3	2.19	....	....	....	....	....	....	....	....	....	....	....	....	....	....	....	....	....
	Montreal Maroons	**NHL**	**1**	**1**	**0**	**0**	**60**	**2**	**0**	**2.00**	**2.06**	....	....	....	....	....	....	....	....	....	....	....	....	....	....	....	....
1930-31	Windsor Bulldogs	IHL	1	0	0	1	70	4	0	3.43	....	....	....	....	....	....	....	....	....	....	....	....	....	....	....	....	....
	Detroit Olympics	IHL	39	19	11	9	2470	78	8	1.89	....	....	....	....	....	6	0	6	0	370	19	0	3.08	....	....	....	....
1931-32	Pittsburgh Yellowjackets	IHL	31	12	13	5	1930	84	5	2.61	....	....	....	....	....	....	....	....	....	....	....	....	....	....	....	....	....
1932-33	Detroit Olympics	IHL	13	....	....	....	780	51	2	3.92	....	....	....	....	....	....	....	....	....	....	....	....	....	....	....	....	....
	Windsor Bulldogs	IHL	2	2	0	0	120	2	0	1.00	....	....	....	....	....	....	....	....	....	....	....	....	....	....	....	....	....
1933-34	Detroit Olympics	IHL	38	....	....	....	2280	80	5	2.11	....	....	....	....	....	6	3	3	0	360	17	0	2.83	....	....	....	....
	New York Americans	**NHL**	**1**	**0**	**1**	**0**	**24**	**3**	**0**	**7.50**	**9.50**	....	....	....	....	....	....	....	....	....	....	....	....	....	....	....	....
	Detroit Red Wings	**NHL**	**2**	**0**	**0**	**1**	**109**	**5**	**0**	**2.75**	**3.48**	....	....	....	....	....	....	....	....	....	....	....	....	....	....	....	....
	Cleveland Indians	IHL	1	0	1	0	60	4	0	4.00	....	....	....	....	....	....	....	....	....	....	....	....	....	....	....	....	....
1934-35	Quebec Castors	Can-Am	43	19	18	6	2660	114	*5	2.57	....	....	....	....	....	3	1	2	0	180	6	*1	2.00	....	....	....	....
1935-36	Springfield Indians	Can-Am	38	15	20	3	2320	129	*6	3.34	....	....	....	....	....	....	....	....	....	....	....	....	....	....	....	....	....
	Montreal Canadiens	**NHL**	**1**	**0**	**0**	**1**	**70**	**1**	**0**	**0.86**	**1.21**	....	....	....	....	....	....	....	....	....	....	....	....	....	....	....	....
	Philadelphia Ramblers	Can-Am	1	....	....	....	60	4	0	4.00	....	....	....	....	....	....	....	....	....	....	....	....	....	....	....	....	....
1936-37	Kansas City Greyhounds	AHA	10	0	8	2	646	31	0	2.88	....	....	....	....	....	....	....	....	....	....	....	....	....	....	....	....	....
	NHL Totals		**5**	**1**	**1**	**2**	**263**	**11**	**0**	**2.51**	....	....	....	....	....	....	....	....	....	....	....	....	....	....	....	....	....

Signed as a free agent by **NY Rangers**, November 9, 1926. Traded to **Windsor** (Can-Pro) by **NY Rangers** for cash, September, 1928. Loaned to **Montreal Maroons** by **Windsor** (IHL) to replace injured Clint Benedict and Flat Walsh, February 1, 1930. (Montreal Maroons 7, NY Americans 2). Loaned to **Detroit** (IHL) by **Windsor** (IHL) for cash, November 21, 1930. Loaned to **NY Americans** by **Windsor** (IHL) to replace injured Roy Worters, November 12, 1933. (Detroit 5, NY Americans 2). Loaned to **Detroit** by **Windsor** (IHL) to replace injured John Ross Roach, December 10, 1933 (Detroit 4, Montreal Maroons 1) and December 17, 1933. (NY Americans 4, Detroit 4). Loaned to **Montreal Canadiens** by **Springfield** (Can-Am) to replace injured Wilf Cude, February 16, 1936. (Montreal Canadiens 1, NY Rangers 1)

• CRAIG, Jim

James D. G – L. 6'1", 190 lbs. b: North Easton, MA, 5/31/1957. Atlanta's 4th, 72nd overall in 1977.

Season	Club	League	GP	W	L	T	Mins	GA	SO	Avg	AAvg	Eff	SA	S%	SAPG	GP	W	L	T	Mins	GA	SO	Avg	Eff	SA	S%	SAPG
1974-75	Oliver Ames High School	Hi-School	57	54	2	1	3420	118	....	2.11	....	....	....	....	....	....	....	....	....	....	....	....	....	....	....	....	....
1975-76	Massasoit Jr. College	NCAA-2	STATISTICS NOT AVAILABLE																								
1976-77	Boston University	ECAC	DID NOT PLAY – FRESHMAN																								
1977-78	Boston University	ECAC	16	16	0	0	967	60	0	3.72	....	....	....	....	....	5	5	0	0	305	17	0	3.34	....	....	....	....
1978-79	Boston University	ECAC	19	13	4	2	1009	60	1	3.57	....	....	....	....	....	2	1	1	0	120	8	0	4.00	....	....	....	....
	United States	WEC-A	5	2	1	2	280	10	0	2.14	....	....	....	....	....	....	....	....	....	....	....	....	....	....	....	....	....
1979-80	United States	Nat-Team	48	....	....	....	2790	110	0	2.37	....	....	....	....	....	....	....	....	....	....	....	....	....	....	....	....	....
	United States	Olympics	7	6	0	1	420	15	0	2.14	....	....	....	....	....	....	....	....	....	....	....	....	....	....	....	....	....
	Atlanta Flames	**NHL**	**4**	**1**	**2**	**1**	**206**	**13**	**0**	**3.79**	**3.35**	....	....	....	....	....	....	....	....	....	....	....	....	....	....	....	....
1980-81	**Boston Bruins**	**NHL**	**23**	**9**	**7**	**6**	**1272**	**78**	**0**	**3.68**	**2.97**	....	....	....	....	....	....	....	....	....	....	....	....	....	....	....	....
1981-82	Erie Blades	AHL	13	3	9	1	742	57	0	4.61	....	....	....	....	....	....	....	....	....	....	....	....	....	....	....	....	....
1982-83	United States	Nat-Team	26	....	....	....	1385	61	2	2.64	....	....	....	....	....	....	....	....	....	....	....	....	....	....	....	....	....
1983-84	**Minnesota North Stars**	**NHL**	**3**	**1**	**1**	**0**	**110**	**9**	**0**	**4.91**	**3.87**	**7.89**	**56**	**.839**	**30.5**	....	....	....	....	....	....	....	....	....	....	....	....
	Salt Lake Golden Eagles	CHL	27	....	....	....	1532	108	1	4.23	....	....	....	....	....	3	....	....	....	177	12	0	4.07	....	....	....	....
	NHL Totals		**30**	**11**	**10**	**7**	**1588**	**100**	**0**	**3.78**	....	....	....	....	....	....	....	....	....	....	....	....	....	....	....	....	....

ECAC First All-Star Team (1979) • NCAA East First All-American Team (1979) • WEC-B All-Star Team (1983)

Traded to **Boston** by **Atlanta** for Boston's 2nd round choice (Steve Konroyd) in 1980 Entry Draft and 3rd round choice (Mike Vernon) in 1981 Entry Draft, June 2, 1980. Signed as a free agent by **Minnesota**, March 2, 1983.

• CRHA, Jiri

"George" G – L. 5'11", 170 lbs. b: Pardubice, Czech., 4/13/1950.

Season	Club	League	GP	W	L	T	Mins	GA	SO	Avg	AAvg	Eff	SA	S%	SAPG	GP	W	L	T	Mins	GA	SO	Avg	Eff	SA	S%	SAPG
1969-70	Dukla Jihlava	Czech.	19	....	....	....	1140	45	1	2.37	....	....	....	....	....	....	....	....	....	....	....	....	....	....	....	....	....
1970-71	Dukla Jihlava	Czech.	32	....	....	....	1825	75	2	2.46	....	....	....	....	....	....	....	....	....	....	....	....	....	....	....	....	....
1971-72	Tesla Pardubice	Czech.	STATISTICS NOT AVAILABLE																								
1972-73	Tesla Pardubice	Czech.	STATISTICS NOT AVAILABLE																								
	Czechoslovakia	WEC-A	2	2	0	0	120	3	0	1.50	....	....	....	....	....	....	....	....	....	....	....	....	....	....	....	....	....
1973-74	Tesla Pardubice	Czech.	STATISTICS NOT AVAILABLE																								
	Czechoslovakia	WEC-A	5	3	1	0	260	10	1	2.31	....	....	....	....	....	....	....	....	....	....	....	....	....	....	....	....	....
1974-75	Tesla Pardubice	Czech.	STATISTICS NOT AVAILABLE																								
	Czechoslovakia	WEC-A	2	0	1	0	75	5	0	4.00	....	....	....	....	....	....	....	....	....	....	....	....	....	....	....	....	....
1975-76	Tesla Pardubice	Czech.	STATISTICS NOT AVAILABLE																								
	Czechoslovakia	Olympics	2	....	....	....	37	1	0	1.62	....	....	....	....	....	....	....	....	....	....	....	....	....	....	....	....	....
1976-77	Tesla Pardubice	Czech.	44	....	....	....	2640	145	....	3.30	....	....	....	....	....	....	....	....	....	....	....	....	....	....	....	....	....
1977-78	Pojistovna Pardubice	Czech.	44	....	....	....	2595	128	....	2.96	....	....	....	....	....	....	....	....	....	....	....	....	....	....	....	....	....
	Czechoslovakia	WEC-A	1	1	0	0	60	2	0	2.00	....	....	....	....	....	....	....	....	....	....	....	....	....	....	....	....	....

Season	Club	League	GP	W	L	T	Mins	GA	SO	Avg	AAvg	Eff	SA	S%	SAPG	GP	W	L	T	Mins	GA	SO	Avg	Eff	SA	S%	SAPG
			REGULAR SEASON													PLAYOFFS											
1978-79	Pojistovna Pardubice	Czech.	37	....	....	....	2220	117	....	3.16	....	....	....	....	....	....	....	....	....	....	....	....	....	....	....	....	....
1979-80	New Brunswick Hawks	AHL	7	4	1	2	404	15	1	2.23	....	....	....	....	....	....	....	....	....	....	....	....	....	....	....	....	....
	Toronto Maple Leafs	**NHL**	**15**	**8**	**7**	**0**	**830**	**50**	**0**	**3.61**	**3.19**	....	....	....	....	**2**	**0**	**2**	....	**121**	**10**	**0**	**4.96**	....	....	....	....
1980-81	**Toronto Maple Leafs**	**NHL**	**54**	**20**	**20**	**11**	**3112**	**211**	**0**	**4.07**	**3.30**	....	....	....	....	**3**	**0**	**2**	....	**65**	**11**	**0**	**10.15**	....	....	....	....
1981-82	Cincinnati Tigers	CHL	2	1	0	0	81	11	0	8.15	....	....	....	....	....	....	....	....	....	....	....	....	....	....	....	....	....
1982-83	St. Catharines Saints	AHL	1	....	....	....	60	6	0	6.00	....	....	....	....	....	....	....	....	....	....	....	....	....	....	....	....	....
1983-84	SV Bayreuth	Germany-2	STATISTICS NOT AVAILABLE																								
1984-85			OUT OF HOCKEY – RETIRED																								
1985-1991	EHC Freiburg	Germany-2	STATISTICS NOT AVAILABLE																								
1991-92	EHC Freiburg	Germany	40	....	....	....	2376	161	0	4.07	....	....	....	....	....	....	....	....	....	....	....	....	....	....	....	....	....
1992-93	EHC Freiburg	Germany	41	12	23	2	2427	149	0	3.68	....	....	....	....	....	....	....	....	....	....	....	....	....	....	....	....	....
	NHL Totals		**69**	**28**	**27**	**11**	**3942**	**261**	**0**	**3.97**	....	....	....	....	....	**5**	**0**	**4**	....	**186**	**21**	**0**	**6.77**	....	....	....	....

Signed as a free agent by **Toronto**, February 4, 1980.

• CROZIER, Roger

Roger Allan G – R. 5'8", 165 lbs. b: Bracebridge, Ont., 3/16/1942 d: 1/11/1996.

Season	Club	League	GP	W	L	T	Mins	GA	SO	Avg	AAvg	Eff	SA	S%	SAPG	GP	W	L	T	Mins	GA	SO	Avg	Eff	SA	S%	SAPG
1959-60	St. Catharines Teepees	OHA-Jr.	48	25	19	4	2880	191	1	3.98	....	....	....	....	....	17	....	....	....	1020	52	0	*3.06	....	....	....	....
	St. Catharines Teepees	Mem-Cup	14	8	5	1	850	58	0	4.09	....	....	....	....	....	....	....	....	....	....	....	....	....	....	....	....	....
1960-61	St. Catharines Teepees	OHA-Jr.	48	18	24	6	2880	204	0	4.25	....	....	....	....	....	6	....	....	....	360	21	0	3.50	....	....	....	....
	Buffalo Bisons	AHL	3	2	0	0	130	5	0	2.31	....	....	....	....	....	....	....	....	....	....	....	....	....	....	....	....	....
1961-62	St. Catharines Teepees	OHA-Jr.	45	....	....	....	2670	174	1	3.91	....	....	....	....	....	6	....	....	....	360	19	0	3.17	....	....	....	....
	Sault Ste. Marie Thunderbirds	EPHL	3	0	1	2	180	12	0	4.00	....	....	....	....	....	....	....	....	....	....	....	....	....	....	....	....	....
	Buffalo Bisons	AHL	1	0	1	0	60	4	0	4.00	....	....	....	....	....	....	....	....	....	....	....	....	....	....	....	....	....
1962-63	Buffalo Bisons	AHL	4	3	1	0	240	10	0	2.50	....	....	....	....	....	....	....	....	....	....	....	....	....	....	....	....	....
	St. Louis Braves	EPHL	*70	26	35	9	*4200	299	1	4.27	....	....	....	....	....	....	....	....	....	....	....	....	....	....	....	....	....
1963-64	**Detroit Red Wings**	**NHL**	**15**	**5**	**6**	**4**	**900**	**51**	**2**	**3.40**	**3.81**	....	....	....	....	**3**	**0**	**2**	....	**126**	**5**	**0**	**2.38**	....	....	....	....
	Pittsburgh Hornets	AHL	44	30	13	1	2640	103	4	*2.34	....	....	....	....	....	3	1	2	0	184	9	0	2.93	....	....	....	....
1964-65	**Detroit Red Wings**	**NHL**	***70**	***40**	**22**	**7**	***4168**	**168**	***6**	**2.42**	**2.52**	....	....	....	....	**7**	**3**	**4**	....	**420**	**23**	**0**	**3.29**	....	....	....	....
1965-66	**Detroit Red Wings**	**NHL**	***64**	**27**	**24**	**12**	**3734**	**173**	***7**	**2.78**	**2.77**	....	....	....	....	***12**	**6**	**5**	....	***668**	**26**	***1**	**2.34**	....	....	....	....
1966-67	**Detroit Red Wings**	**NHL**	**58**	**22**	**29**	**4**	**3256**	**182**	**4**	**3.35**	**3.52**	....	....	....	....	....	....	....	....	....	....	....	....	....	....	....	....
1967-68	Fort Worth Wings	CPHL	5	3	2	0	265	12	0	2.49	....	....	....	....	....	....	....	....	....	....	....	....	....	....	....	....	....
	Detroit Red Wings	**NHL**	**34**	**9**	**18**	**2**	**1729**	**95**	**1**	**3.30**	**3.68**	....	....	....	....	....	....	....	....	....	....	....	....	....	....	....	....
1968-69	**Detroit Red Wings**	**NHL**	**38**	**12**	**16**	**3**	**1820**	**101**	**0**	**3.33**	**3.46**	....	....	....	....	....	....	....	....	....	....	....	....	....	....	....	....
1969-70	**Detroit Red Wings**	**NHL**	**34**	**16**	**6**	**9**	**1877**	**83**	**0**	**2.65**	**2.80**	....	....	....	....	**1**	**0**	**1**	....	**34**	**3**	**0**	**5.29**	....	....	....	....
1970-71	**Buffalo Sabres**	**NHL**	**44**	**9**	**20**	**7**	**2198**	**135**	**1**	**3.69**	**3.68**	....	....	....	....	....	....	....	....	....	....	....	....	....	....	....	....
1971-72	**Buffalo Sabres**	**NHL**	**63**	**13**	**34**	**14**	**3654**	**214**	**2**	**3.51**	**3.58**	....	....	....	....	....	....	....	....	....	....	....	....	....	....	....	....
1972-73	**Buffalo Sabres**	**NHL**	**49**	**23**	**13**	**7**	**2633**	**121**	**3**	**2.76**	**2.59**	....	....	....	....	**4**	**2**	**2**	....	**249**	**11**	**0**	**2.65**	....	....	....	....
1973-74	**Buffalo Sabres**	**NHL**	**12**	**4**	**5**	**0**	**615**	**39**	**0**	**3.80**	**3.68**	....	....	....	....	....	....	....	....	....	....	....	....	....	....	....	....
1974-75	**Buffalo Sabres**	**NHL**	**23**	**17**	**2**	**1**	**1260**	**55**	**3**	**2.62**	**2.36**	....	....	....	....	**5**	**3**	**2**	....	**292**	**14**	**0**	**2.88**	....	....	....	....
1975-76	**Buffalo Sabres**	**NHL**	**11**	**8**	**2**	**0**	**620**	**27**	**1**	**2.61**	**2.36**	....	....	....	....	....	....	....	....	....	....	....	....	....	....	....	....
1976-77	**Washington Capitals**	**NHL**	**3**	**1**	**0**	**0**	**103**	**2**	**0**	**1.17**	**1.09**	....	....	....	....	....	....	....	....	....	....	....	....	....	....	....	....
	NHL Totals		**518**	**206**	**197**	**70**	**28567**	**1446**	**30**	**3.04**	....	....	....	....	....	**32**	**14**	**16**	....	**1789**	**82**	**1**	**2.75**	....	....	....	....

OHA-Jr. First All-Star Team (1960, 1961, 1962) • AHL Second All-Star Team (1964) • Won Harry "Hap" Holmes Memorial Award (fewest goals against - AHL) (1964) • Won Dudley "Red" Garrett Memorial Award (Top Rookie - AHL) (1964) • NHL First All-Star Team (1965) • Won Calder Memorial Trophy (1965) • Won Conn Smythe Trophy (1966)

Traded to **Detroit** by **Chicago** with Ron Ingram for Howie Young, June 5, 1963. Traded to **Buffalo** by **Detroit** for Tom Webster, June 10, 1970. Traded to **Washington** by **Buffalo** for cash, March 3, 1977.

• CUDE, Wilf

Wilfred Reginald G – L. 5'9", 146 lbs. b: Barry, Wales, 7/4/1910 d: 5/5/1968.

Season	Club	League	GP	W	L	T	Mins	GA	SO	Avg	AAvg	Eff	SA	S%	SAPG	GP	W	L	T	Mins	GA	SO	Avg	Eff	SA	S%	SAPG
1925-1928	St. Vital ACC	MAHA	STATISTICS NOT AVAILABLE																								
1928-29	Winnipeg Wellingtons	WSrHL	STATISTICS NOT AVAILABLE																								
1929-30	Melville Millionaires	S-SSHL	20	13	6	1	1290	40	3	1.86	....	....	....	....	....	2	1	1	0	120	3	*1	1.50	....	....	....	....
1930-31	**Philadelphia Quakers**	**NHL**	**30**	**2**	**25**	**3**	**1850**	**130**	**1**	**4.22**	**5.69**	....	....	....	....	....	....	....	....	....	....	....	....	....	....	....	....
1931-32	**Boston Bruins**	**NHL**	**2**	**1**	**1**	**0**	**120**	**6**	**1**	**3.00**	**3.67**	....	....	....	....	....	....	....	....	....	....	....	....	....	....	....	....
	Chicago Black Hawks	**NHL**	**1**	**0**	**0**	**0**	**41**	**9**	**0**	**13.17**	**16.23**	....	....	....	....	....	....	....	....	....	....	....	....	....	....	....	....
	Syracuse Stars	IHL	1	0	0	1	70	1	0	0.86	....	....	....	....	....	....	....	....	....	....	....	....	....	....	....	....	....
	Boston Cubs	Can-Am	15	7	7	1	900	46	1	3.00	....	....	....	....	....	....	....	....	....	....	....	....	....	....	....	....	....
1932-33	Philadelphia Arrows	Can-Am	32	21	9	2	1950	64	*4	*1.97	....	....	....	....	....	5	2	*3	0	300	15	*1	3.00	....	....	....	....
1933-34	**Montreal Canadiens**	**NHL**	**1**	**1**	**0**	**0**	**60**	**0**	**1**	***0.00**	**0.00**	....	....	....	....	....	....	....	....	....	....	....	....	....	....	....	....
	Syracuse Stars	IHL	19	....	....	....	1140	39	3	2.05	....	....	....	....	....	....	....	....	....	....	....	....	....	....	....	....	....
	Detroit Red Wings	**NHL**	**29**	**15**	**6**	**8**	**1860**	**47**	**4**	***1.52**	**1.87**	....	....	....	....	***9**	**4**	**5**	**0**	***593**	**21**	**1**	**2.12**	....	....	....	....
1934-35	**Montreal Canadiens**	**NHL**	***48**	**19**	**23**	**6**	**2960**	**145**	**1**	**2.94**	**3.64**	....	....	....	....	**2**	**0**	**1**	**1**	**120**	**6**	**0**	**3.00**	....	....	....	....
1935-36	**Montreal Canadiens**	**NHL**	**47**	**11**	**26**	**10**	**2940**	**122**	**6**	**2.49**	**3.59**	....	....	....	....	....	....	....	....	....	....	....	....	....	....	....	....
1936-37	**Montreal Canadiens**	**NHL**	**44**	**22**	**17**	**5**	**2730**	**99**	**5**	**2.18**	**2.65**	....	....	....	....	**5**	**2**	**3**	....	**352**	**13**	**0**	**2.22**	....	....	....	....
1937-38	**Montreal Canadiens**	**NHL**	**47**	**18**	**17**	**12**	**2990**	**126**	**3**	**2.53**	**3.05**	....	....	....	....	**3**	**1**	**2**	....	**192**	**11**	**0**	**3.44**	....	....	....	....
1938-39	**Montreal Canadiens**	**NHL**	**23**	**8**	**11**	**4**	**1440**	**77**	**2**	**3.21**	**3.94**	....	....	....	....	....	....	....	....	....	....	....	....	....	....	....	....
1939-40	**Montreal Canadiens**	**NHL**	**7**	**1**	**5**	**1**	**415**	**24**	**0**	**3.47**	**4.27**	....	....	....	....	....	....	....	....	....	....	....	....	....	....	....	....
	New Haven Eagles	IAHL	44	23	18	1	2690	146	3	3.26	....	....	....	....	....	3	1	2	0	180	11	0	3.44	....	....	....	....
1940-41	**Montreal Canadiens**	**NHL**	**3**	**2**	**1**	**0**	**180**	**13**	**0**	**4.33**	**4.95**	....	....	....	....	....	....	....	....	....	....	....	....	....	....	....	....
	NHL Totals		**282**	**100**	**132**	**49**	**17586**	**798**	**24**	**2.72**	....	....	....	....	....	**19**	**7**	**11**	**1**	**1257**	**51**	**1**	**2.43**	....	....	....	....

NHL Second All-Star Team (1936, 1937) • Played in NHL All-Star Game (1937, 1939)

Signed as a free agent by **Pittsburgh**, February 18, 1930. Transferred to **Philadelphia** after **Pittsburgh** franchise relocated, October 18, 1930. • Signed as a utility back-up goaltender by **NHL** for 1931-32 season after **Philadelphia** franchise suspended operations, September 27, 1931. Traded to **Montreal Canadiens** by **Philadelphia** for cash, October 19, 1933. Loaned to **Detroit** by **Montreal Canadiens** for balance of 1933-34 season for cash, January 2, 1934.

• CUTTS, Don

Donald Edward G – L. 6'3", 190 lbs. b: Edmonton, Alta., 2/24/1953. NY Islanders' 6th, 97th overall in 1973.

Season	Club	League	GP	W	L	T	Mins	GA	SO	Avg	AAvg	Eff	SA	S%	SAPG	GP	W	L	T	Mins	GA	SO	Avg	Eff	SA	S%	SAPG
1970-71	RPI Engineers	ECAC	8	....	....	....	480	20	....	2.73	....	....	....	....	....	....	....	....	....	....	....	....	....	....	....	....	....
1971-72	RPI Engineers	ECAC	21	....	....	....	1260	72	1	3.43	....	....	....	....	....	....	....	....	....	....	....	....	....	....	....	....	....
1972-73	RPI Engineers	ECAC	30	....	....	....	1800	109	1	3.54	....	....	....	....	....	....	....	....	....	....	....	....	....	....	....	....	....
1973-74	RPI Engineers	ECAC	30	14	15	1	1800	137	0	4.57	....	....	....	....	....	....	....	....	....	....	....	....	....	....	....	....	....
1974-75	Fort Worth Texans	CHL	15	2	10	0	773	58	0	4.50	....	....	....	....	....	....	....	....	....	....	....	....	....	....	....	....	....
	Muskegon Mohawks	IHL	9	....	....	....	550	24	2	2.62	....	....	....	....	....	1	0	1	0	54	5	0	5.55	....	....	....	....
1975-76	Muskegon Mohawks	IHL	58	....	....	....	3356	158	5	2.82	....	....	....	....	....	4	1	3	0	240	19	0	4.75	....	....	....	....
1976-77	Fort Worth Texans	CHL	34	12	14	7	1957	111	2	3.40	....	....	....	....	....	....	....	....	....	....	....	....	....	....	....	....	....
	Kalamazoo Wings	IHL	1	....	....	....	60	3	0	3.00	....	....	....	....	....	....	....	....	....	....	....	....	....	....	....	....	....
1977-78	Fort Worth Texans	CHL	44	23	13	2	2358	113	2	*2.88	....	....	....	....	....	6	3	2	0	350	15	0	*2.57	....	....	....	....
1978-79	Fort Wayne Komets	IHL	27	....	....	....	1368	100	0	4.37	....	....	....	....	....	....	....	....	....	....	....	....	....	....	....	....	....
	Fort Worth Texans	CHL	7	1	3	0	283	17	0	3.60	....	....	....	....	....	3	0	2	0	151	7	0	2.78	....	....	....	....
1979-80	Muskegon Mohawks	IHL	25	....	....	....	1379	72	4	3.13	....	....	....	....	....	....	....	....	....	....	....	....	....	....	....	....	....
	Edmonton Oilers	**NHL**	**6**	**1**	**2**	**1**	**269**	**16**	**0**	**3.57**	**3.16**	....	....	....	....	....	....	....	....	....	....	....	....	....	....	....	....
	Houston Apollos	CHL	28	11	13	3	1636	83	2	3.04	....	....	....	....	....	5	1	3	0	274	20	0	4.38	....	....	....	....
1980-81	Oklahoma City Stars	CHL	2	1	1	0	120	12	0	6.00	....	....	....	....	....	3	0	2	0	134	8	0	3.58	....	....	....	....
	H-Reipas Lahti	Finland	26	....	....	....	1560	97	1	3.72	....	....	....	....	....	....	....	....	....	....	....	....	....	....	....	....	....
1981-82	Muskegon Mohawks	IHL	24	....	....	....	1315	117	0	5.34	....	....	....	....	....	....	....	....	....	....	....	....	....	....	....	....	....
	NHL Totals		**6**	**1**	**2**	**1**	**269**	**16**	**0**	**3.57**	....	....	....	....	....	....	....	....	....	....	....	....	....	....	....	....	....

ECAC Second All-Star Team (1972, 1973) • IHL First All-Star Team (1976) • Won James Norris Memorial Trophy (fewest goals against - IHL) (1976)

Signed as a free agent by **Edmonton**, January 12, 1980.

• CYR, Claude

G – L. 5'10", 180 lbs. b: Montreal, Que., 3/27/1939 Deceased.

			REGULAR SEASON													PLAYOFFS											
Season	Club	League	GP	W	L	T	Mins	GA	SO	Avg	AAvg	Eff	SA	S%	SAPG	GP	W	L	T	Mins	GA	SO	Avg	Eff	SA	S%	SAPG
1956-57	L'Abord-a-Plouffe	MMJHL	36	15	18	3	2160	113	3	3.14	....	....	....	....	....	....	....	....	....	....	....	....	....	....	....	....	....
1957-58	Hull-Ottawa Canadiens	X-Games	13	....	....	....	780	57	0	4.38	....	....	....	....	....	....	....	....	....	....	....	....	....	....	....	....	....
	Hull-Ottawa Canadiens	EOHL	11	....	....	....	660	59	1	5.36	....	....	....	....	....	....	....	....	....	....	....	....	....	....	....	....	....
1958-59	Hull-Ottawa Canadiens	X-Games	STATISTICS NOT AVAILABLE																								
	Hull-Ottawa Canadiens	EOHL	26	....	....	....	1560	114	0	4.38	....	....	....	....	....	1	....	....	....	60	4	0	4.00	....	....	....	....
	Montreal Canadiens	**NHL**	**1**	**0**	**0**	**0**	**20**	**1**	**0**	**3.00**	**3.19**	....	....	....	....	....	....	....	....	....	....	....	....	....	....	....	....
	Hull-Ottawa Canadiens	Mem-Cup	9	4	4	1	550	21	1	2.29	....	....	....	....	....	....	....	....	....	....	....	....	....	....	....	....	....
1959-60	Hull-Ottawa Canadiens	EPHL	6	2	4	0	360	22	0	3.67	....	....	....	....	....	....	....	....	....	....	....	....	....	....	....	....	....
	Montreal Royals	EPHL	7	2	4	1	420	27	0	3.86	....	....	....	....	....	....	....	....	....	....	....	....	....	....	....	....	....
	Cleveland Barons	AHL	2	0	2	0	120	7	0	3.50	....	....	....	....	....	....	....	....	....	....	....	....	....	....	....	....	....
	Calgary Stampeders	WHL	4	1	3	0	240	15	0	3.75	....	....	....	....	....	....	....	....	....	....	....	....	....	....	....	....	....
1960-61	Montreal Royals	EPHL	13	3	6	4	780	41	0	3.15	....	....	....	....	....	....	....	....	....	....	....	....	....	....	....	....	....
	Trail Smoke Eaters	WIHL	7	6	1	0	420	19	0	2.71	....	....	....	....	....	2	1	0	0	74	4	0	3.24	....	....	....	....
	Canada	WEC-A	2	1	0	0	74	0	0	0.00	....	....	....	....	....	....	....	....	....	....	....	....	....	....	....	....	....
1961-62	Knoxville Knights	EHL	61	....	....	....	3660	211	3	3.46	....	....	....	....	....	8	4	4	0	480	17	1	*2.12	....	....	....	....
1962-63	Philadelphia-Knoxville	EHL	36	....	....	....	2160	118	5	3.28	....	....	....	....	....	....	....	....	....	....	....	....	....	....	....	....	....
1963-64	Verdun Pirates	QSHL	STATISTICS NOT AVAILABLE																								
1964-65	Sherbrooke Beavers	QSHL	STATISTICS NOT AVAILABLE																								
1965-66	Victoriaville Tigers	QSHL	16	....	....	....	960	82	*1	5.13	....	....	....	....	....	....	....	....	....	....	....	....	....	....	....	....	....
1966-67	Drummondville Eagles	QSHL	27	....	....	....	1620	102	2	3.78	....	....	....	....	....	9	*8	1	0	540	19	*1	*2.11	....	....	....	....
	Drummondville Eagles	Al-Cup	11	*10	1	0	677	23	*2	*2.04	....	....	....	....	....	....	....	....	....	....	....	....	....	....	....	....	....
1967-68	Drummondville Eagles	QSHL	23	13	9	1	1380	93	0	4.04	....	....	....	....	....	9	5	4	0	546	40	0	4.60	....	....	....	....
	NHL Totals		**1**	**0**	**0**	**0**	**20**	**1**	**0**	**3.00**	....	....	....	....	....	....	....	....	....	....	....	....	....	....	....	....	....

QSHL First All-Star Team (1968)

Promoted to **Montreal** from **Hull-Ottawa** (EOHL) and replaced Claude Pronovost at start of 3rd period, March 19, 1959. (Toronto 6, Montreal 3)

• DADSWELL, Doug

G – L. 5'10", 180 lbs. b: Scarborough, Ont., 2/7/1964.

Season	Club	League	GP	W	L	T	Mins	GA	SO	Avg	AAvg	Eff	SA	S%	SAPG	GP	W	L	T	Mins	GA	SO	Avg	Eff	SA	S%	SAPG
1979-80	St. Michael's Midget Buzzers	MTHL	STATISTICS NOT AVAILABLE																								
1980-81	St. Michael's Buzzers	OHA-B	STATISTICS NOT AVAILABLE																								
1981-82	Richmond Hill Dynes	OJHL-B	STATISTICS NOT AVAILABLE																								
1982-83	Richmond Hill Dynes	OJHL-B	27	13	12	1	1575	149	0	5.67	....	....	....	....	....	....	....	....	....	....	....	....	....	....	....	....	....
1983-84	Pickering Panthers	OJHL-B	26	....	....	....	1520	98	0	3.86	....	....	....	....	....	....	....	....	....	....	....	....	....	....	....	....	....
1984-85	Cornell University	ECAC	28	17	10	1	1654	97	0	3.52	....	....	....	....	....	....	....	....	....	....	....	....	....	....	....	....	....
1985-86	Cornell University	ECAC	30	20	7	3	1815	92	1	3.04	....	....	....	....	....	....	....	....	....	....	....	....	....	....	....	....	....
1986-87	**Calgary Flames**	**NHL**	**2**	**0**	**1**	**1**	**125**	**10**	**0**	**4.80**	**4.07**	**6.58**	**73**	**.863**	**35.0**	....	....	....	....	....	....	....	....	....	....	....	....
	Moncton Golden Flames	AHL	42	23	12	0	2276	138	1	3.64	....	....	....	....	....	6	2	4	0	326	23	0	4.20	....	....	....	....
1987-88	**Calgary Flames**	**NHL**	**25**	**8**	**7**	**2**	**1221**	**89**	**0**	**4.37**	**3.65**	**6.19**	**628**	**.858**	**30.9**	....	....	....	....	....	....	....	....	....	....	....	....
1988-89	Salt Lake Golden Eagles	IHL	32	15	10	0	1723	110	0	3.83	....	....	....	....	....	....	....	....	....	....	....	....	....	....	....	....	....
	Indianapolis Ice	IHL	24	4	15	0	1207	122	0	6.06	....	....	....	....	....	....	....	....	....	....	....	....	....	....	....	....	....
1989-90			DID NOT PLAY																								
1990-91	Canada	Nat-Team	28	16	6	1	1599	78	0	2.92	....	....	....	....	....	....	....	....	....	....	....	....	....	....	....	....	....
1991-92	Cincinnati Cyclones	ECHL	24	14	9	1	1361	89	0	3.92	....	....	....	....	....	....	....	....	....	....	....	....	....	....	....	....	....
	Utica Devils	AHL	22	7	9	2	1168	67	0	3.44	....	....	....	....	....	2	0	2	0	119	8	0	4.03	....	....	....	....
1992-93	Cincinnati Cyclones	IHL	17	5	11	1	1006	63	1	3.76	....	....	....	....	....	....	....	....	....	....	....	....	....	....	....	....	....
	Birmingham Bulls	ECHL	8	3	3	0	401	36	0	5.39	....	....	....	....	....	....	....	....	....	....	....	....	....	....	....	....	....
	NHL Totals		**27**	**8**	**8**	**3**	**1346**	**99**	**0**	**4.41**	....	....	**701**	**.859**	**31.2**	....	....	....	....	....	....	....	....	....	....	....	....

ECAC Second All-Star Team (1986) • NCAA East First All-American Team (1986)

Signed as a free agent by **Calgary**, August 6, 1986. • Played w/ RHI's Calgary Rads in 1993 season (10-5-4-0-377-68-0-8.66)

• DAFOE, Byron

Byron Jaromir "Lord" G – L. 5'11", 190 lbs. b: Sussex, England, 2/25/1971. Washington's 2nd, 35th overall in 1989.

Season	Club	League	GP	W	L	T	Mins	GA	SO	Avg	AAvg	Eff	SA	S%	SAPG	GP	W	L	T	Mins	GA	SO	Avg	Eff	SA	S%	SAPG
1987-88	Juan de Fuca Whalers	BCJHL	32	....	....	....	1716	129	0	4.51	....	....	....	....	....	....	....	....	....	....	....	....	....	....	....	....	....
1988-89	Portland Winter Hawks	WHL	59	29	24	3	3279	291	1	5.32	....	....	....	....	....	*18	10	8	....	*1091	81	*1	4.45	....	....	....	....
1989-90	Washington Capitals	Fr-Tour	2	....	....	....	60	3	0	3.00	....	....	....	....	....	....	....	....	....	....	....	....	....	....	....	....	....
	Portland Winter Hawks	WHL	40	14	21	3	2265	193	0	5.11	....	....	....	....	....	....	....	....	....	....	....	....	....	....	....	....	....
1990-91	Portland Winter Hawks	WHL	8	1	5	1	414	41	0	5.94	....	....	....	....	....	....	....	....	....	....	....	....	....	....	....	....	....
	Prince Albert Raiders	WHL	32	13	12	4	1839	124	0	4.05	....	....	....	....	....	....	....	....	....	....	....	....	....	....	....	....	....
1991-92	Baltimore Skipjacks	AHL	33	12	16	4	1847	119	0	3.87	....	....	....	....	....	....	....	....	....	....	....	....	....	....	....	....	....
	New Haven Nighthawks	AHL	7	3	2	1	364	22	0	3.63	....	....	....	....	....	....	....	....	....	....	....	....	....	....	....	....	....
	Hampton Roads Admirals	ECHL	10	6	4	0	562	26	0	2.78	....	....	....	....	....	....	....	....	....	....	....	....	....	....	....	....	....
1992-93	**Washington Capitals**	**NHL**	**1**	**0**	**0**	**0**	**1**	**0**	**0**	**0.00**	**0.00**	**0.00**	**0**	**.000**	**0.0**	....	....	....	....	....	....	....	....	....	....	....	....
	Baltimore Skipjacks	AHL	48	16	20	7	2617	191	1	4.38	....	....	....	....	....	5	2	3	....	241	22	0	5.48	....	....	....	....
1993-94	**Washington Capitals**	**NHL**	**5**	**2**	**2**	**0**	**230**	**13**	**0**	**3.39**	**3.26**	**4.36**	**101**	**.871**	**26.3**	**2**	**0**	**2**	....	**118**	**5**	**0**	**2.54**	**3.26**	**39**	**.872**	**19.8**
	Portland Pirates	AHL	47	24	16	4	2661	148	1	3.34	....	....	....	....	....	1	0	0	....	9	1	0	6.79	....	....	....	....
1994-95	**Washington Capitals**	**NHL**	**4**	**1**	**1**	**1**	**187**	**11**	**0**	**3.53**	**3.70**	**4.85**	**80**	**.863**	**25.7**	**1**	**0**	**0**	....	**20**	**1**	**0**	**3.00**	**10.00**	**3**	**.667**	**9.0**
	Phoenix Roadrunners	IHL	49	25	16	6	2743	169	2	3.70	....	....	....	....	....	....	....	....	....	....	....	....	....	....	....	....	....
	Portland Pirates	AHL	6	5	0	0	330	16	0	2.91	....	....	....	....	....	7	3	4	....	416	29	0	4.18	....	....	....	....
1995-96	**Los Angeles Kings**	**NHL**	**47**	**14**	**24**	**8**	**2666**	**172**	**1**	**3.87**	**3.87**	**4.33**	**1539**	**.888**	**34.6**	....	....	....	....	....	....	....	....	....	....	....	....
1996-97	**Los Angeles Kings**	**NHL**	**40**	**13**	**17**	**5**	**2162**	**112**	**0**	**3.11**	**3.35**	**2.96**	**1178**	**.905**	**32.7**	....	....	....	....	....	....	....	....	....	....	....	....
1997-98	**Boston Bruins**	**NHL**	**65**	**30**	**25**	**9**	**3693**	**138**	**6**	**2.24**	**2.66**	**1.93**	**1602**	**.914**	**26.0**	**6**	**2**	**4**	....	**422**	**14**	**1**	**1.99**	**1.75**	**159**	**.912**	**22.6**
1998-99	**Boston Bruins**	**NHL**	**68**	**32**	**23**	**11**	**4001**	**133**	***10**	**1.99**	**2.35**	**1.47**	**1800**	**.926**	**27.0**	**12**	**6**	**6**	....	**768**	**26**	**2**	**2.03**	**1.60**	**330**	**.921**	**25.8**
99-2000	**Boston Bruins**	**NHL**	**41**	**13**	**16**	**10**	**2307**	**114**	**3**	**2.96**	**3.39**	**3.28**	**1030**	**.889**	**26.8**	....	....	....	....	....	....	....	....	....	....	....	....
	NHL Totals		**271**	**105**	**108**	**44**	**15247**	**693**	**20**	**2.73**	....	....	**7330**	**.905**	**28.8**	**21**	**8**	**12**	....	**1328**	**46**	**3**	**2.08**	....	**531**	**.913**	**24.0**

• Also known as Byron Kubick. AHL First All-Star Team (1994) • Shared Harry "Hap" Holmes Trophy (fewest goals-against - AHL) with Olaf Kolzig (1994) • NHL Second All-Star Team (1999)

Traded to **Los Angeles** by **Washington** with Dimitri Khristich for Los Angeles' 1st round choice (Alexander Volchkov) and Dallas' 4th round choice (previously acquired, Washington selected Justin Davis) in 1996 Entry Draft, July 8, 1995. Traded to **Boston** by **Los Angeles** with Dimitri Khristich for Jozef Stumpel, Sandy Moger and Boston's 4th round choice (later traded to New Jersey - New Jersey selected Pierre Dagenais) in 1998 Entry Draft, August 29, 1997.

• D'ALESSIO, Corrie

Corrie Vince G – L. 5'11", 155 lbs. b: Cornwall, Ont., 9/9/1969. Vancouver's 4th, 107th overall in 1988.

Season	Club	League	GP	W	L	T	Mins	GA	SO	Avg	AAvg	Eff	SA	S%	SAPG	GP	W	L	T	Mins	GA	SO	Avg	Eff	SA	S%	SAPG
1985-86	Pembroke Lumber Kings	OJHL	20	14	3	0	982	59	0	3.60	....	....	....	....	....	....	....	....	....	....	....	....	....	....	....	....	....
1986-87	Pembroke Lumber Kings	OJHL	25	15	6	0	1327	95	0	4.30	....	....	....	....	....	....	....	....	....	....	....	....	....	....	....	....	....
1987-88	Cornell University	ECAC	25	17	8	0	1457	67	0	2.76	....	....	....	....	....	....	....	....	....	....	....	....	....	....	....	....	....
1988-89	Cornell University	ECAC	29	15	13	1	1684	96	1	3.42	....	....	....	....	....	....	....	....	....	....	....	....	....	....	....	....	....
1989-90	Cornell University	ECAC	16	6	7	2	887	50	0	3.38	....	....	....	....	....	....	....	....	....	....	....	....	....	....	....	....	....
1990-91	Cornell University	ECAC	24	10	8	3	1160	67	0	3.47	....	....	....	....	....	....	....	....	....	....	....	....	....	....	....	....	....
1991-92	Milwaukee Admirals	IHL	27	9	14	2	1435	96	0	4.01	....	....	....	....	....	2	0	2	0	119	12	0	6.05	....	....	....	....
1992-93	**Hartford Whalers**	**NHL**	**1**	**0**	**0**	**0**	**11**	**0**	**0**	**0.00**	**0.00**	**0.00**	**3**	**1.000**	**16.4**	....	....	....	....	....	....	....	....	....	....	....	....
	Springfield Indians	AHL	23	3	13	2	1120	77	0	4.13	....	....	....	....	....	4	1	0	0	75	3	0	2.40	....	....	....	....
1993-94	Las Vegas Thunder	IHL	1	1	0	0	35	1	0	1.70	....	....	....	....	....	....	....	....	....	....	....	....	....	....	....	....	....
	NHL Totals		**1**	**0**	**0**	**0**	**11**	**0**	**0**	**0.00**	....	....	**3**	**1.000**	**16.4**	....	....	....	....	....	....	....	....	....	....	....	....

Traded to **Hartford** by **Vancouver** with cash for Kay Whitmore, October 1, 1992.

• DALEY, Joe

Thomas Joseph "The Holy Goalie" G – L. 5'10", 170 lbs. b: Winnipeg, Man., 2/20/1943.

Season	Club	League	GP	W	L	T	Mins	GA	SO	Avg	AAvg	Eff	SA	S%	SAPG	GP	W	L	T	Mins	GA	SO	Avg	Eff	SA	S%	SAPG
1961-62	Weyburn Red Wings	SJHL	53	17	29	7	3180	177	2	3.34	....	....	....	....	....	....	....	....	....	....	....	....	....	....	....	....	....
	Sudbury Wolves	EPHL	1	0	1	0	60	6	0	6.00	....	....	....	....	....	....	....	....	....	....	....	....	....	....	....	....	....
1962-63	Weyburn Red Wings	SJHL	51	28	17	6	3060	152	3	2.98	....	....	....	....	....	8	....	....	....	480	23	1	3.19	....	....	....	....

			REGULAR SEASON													PLAYOFFS											
Season	Club	League	GP	W	L	T	Mins	GA	SO	Avg	AAvg	Eff	SA	S%	SAPG	GP	W	L	T	Mins	GA	SO	Avg	Eff	SA	S%	SAPG
1963-64	Johnstown Jets	EHL	66	40	22	4	3960	221	4	3.35	....	....	....	....	....	10	5	5	0	600	27	1	2.70	....	....	....	....
	Cincinnati Wings	CPHL	1	0	1	0	60	3	0	3.00	....	....	....	....	....	....	....	....	....	....	....	....	....	....	....	....	....
	Pittsburgh Hornets	AHL	2	1	1	0	120	7	0	3.50	....	....	....	....	....	2	0	1	0	60	6	0	6.00	....	....	....	....
1964-65	Johnstown Jets	EHL	*72	41	31	0	*4320	292	2	4.06	....	....	....	....	....	5	2	3	0	300	19	1	3.80	....	....	....	....
1965-66	Memphis Wings	CPHL	68	25	31	12	4040	212	2	3.15	....	....	....	....	....	....	....	....	....	....	....	....	....	....	....	....	....
	San Francisco Seals	WHL	8	5	2	1	426	17	2	2.39	....	....	....	....	....	....	....	....	....	....	....	....	....	....	....	....	....
1966-67	Pittsburgh Hornets	AHL	16	11	1	3	948	43	0	2.72	....	....	....	....	....	....	....	....	....	....	....	....	....	....	....	....	....
	Memphis Wings	CPHL	50	23	21	5	2960	169	0	3.42	....	....	....	....	....	7	3	4	0	433	27	0	3.74	....	....	....	....
1967-68	Baltimore Clippers	AHL	56	23	25	8	3300	192	2	3.49	....	....	....	....	....	....	....	....	....	....	....	....	....	....	....	....	....
1968-69	**Pittsburgh Penguins**	**NHL**	**29**	**10**	**13**	**3**	**1615**	**87**	**2**	**3.23**	**3.35**	....	....	....	....	....	....	....	....	....	....	....	....	....	....	....	....
1969-70	**Pittsburgh Penguins**	**NHL**	**9**	**1**	**5**	**3**	**528**	**26**	**0**	**2.95**	**3.13**	....	....	....	....	....	....	....	....	....	....	....	....	....	....	....	....
	Baltimore Clippers	AHL	34	....	....	....	1867	107	0	3.44	....	....	....	....	....	5	1	4	0	315	25	0	4.76	....	....	....	....
1970-71	**Buffalo Sabres**	**NHL**	**38**	**12**	**16**	**8**	**2073**	**128**	**1**	**3.70**	**3.68**	....	....	....	....	....	....	....	....	....	....	....	....	....	....	....	....
1971-72	**Detroit Red Wings**	**NHL**	**29**	**11**	**10**	**5**	**1620**	**85**	**0**	**3.15**	**3.19**	....	....	....	....	....	....	....	....	....	....	....	....	....	....	....	....
1972-73	Winnipeg Jets	WHA	29	17	10	1	1718	83	2	2.90	....	....	....	....	....	7	5	2	0	422	25	0	3.55	....	....	....	....
1973-74	Winnipeg Jets	WHA	41	19	20	1	2454	163	0	3.99	....	....	....	....	....	2	0	2	0	119	8	0	4.03	....	....	....	....
1974-75	Winnipeg Jets	WHA	51	23	21	4	2902	175	1	3.62	....	....	....	....	....	....	....	....	....	....	....	....	....	....	....	....	....
1975-76	Winnipeg Jets	WHA	62	41	17	1	3612	171	*5	2.84	....	....	....	....	....	12	*10	1	0	671	29	1	2.59	....	....	....	....
1976-77	Winnipeg Jets	WHA	65	*39	23	2	*3818	206	3	3.24	....	....	....	....	....	*20	11	9	0	*1186	71	*1	3.59	....	....	....	....
1977-78	Winnipeg Jets	WHA	37	21	11	1	2075	114	1	3.30	....	....	....	....	....	5	4	1	0	271	13	0	2.88	....	....	....	....
1978-79	Winnipeg Jets	WHA	23	7	11	3	1256	90	0	4.30	....	....	....	....	....	3	0	0	0	37	3	0	4.86	....	....	....	....
	NHL Totals		**105**	**34**	**44**	**19**	**5836**	**326**	**3**	**3.35**	....	....	....	....	....	....	....	....	....	....	....	....	....	....	....	....	....
	Other Major League Totals		308	167	113	13	17835	1002	12	3.37	....	....	....	....	....	49	30	15	....	2706	149	2	3.30	....	....	....	....

SJHL Second All-Star Team (1962) • EHL Rookie of the Year (1964) • WHA First All-Star Team (1976) • WHA Second All-Star Team (1977)

Claimed by **Pittsburgh** from **Detroit** in Expansion Draft, June 6, 1967. Claimed on waivers by **Buffalo** from **Pittsburgh**, June 9, 1970. Traded to **Detroit** by **Buffalo** for Don Luce and Mike Robitaille, May 25, 1971. Selected by **Winnipeg** (WHA) in 1972 WHA General Player Draft, February 12, 1972. Claimed by **Cleveland** (AHL) from **Detroit** in Reverse Draft, June, 1972.

• DAMORE, Nick

G – L. 5'6", 160 lbs. b: Niagara Falls, Ont., 7/10/1916.

Season	Club	League	GP	W	L	T	Mins	GA	SO	Avg	AAvg	Eff	SA	S%	SAPG	GP	W	L	T	Mins	GA	SO	Avg	Eff	SA	S%	SAPG
1932-33	Niagara Falls Cataracts	OHA-Jr.	1	1	0	0	60	1	0	1.00	....	....	....	....	....	....	....	....	....	....	....	....	....	....	....	....	....
1933-34			STATISTICS NOT AVAILABLE																								
1934-35	Hershey B'ars	EAHL	21	10	9	2	1260	56	3	2.67	....	....	....	....	....	6	3	3	0	360	22	0	3.67	....	....	....	....
1935-36	Hershey B'ars	EAHL	22	16	5	1	1320	42	*5	*1.91	....	....	....	....	....	5	....	....	....	300	15	0	3.00	....	....	....	....
	Baltimore Orioles	EAHL	1	0	1	0	60	5	0	5.00	....	....	....	....	....	....	....	....	....	....	....	....	....	....	....	....	....
1936-37	Hershey B'ars	EAHL	34	18	9	7	2040	61	1	*1.79	....	....	....	....	....	4	*3	1	0	250	9	*1	2.16	....	....	....	....
1937-38	Hershey B'ars	EAHL	57	*31	15	11	3420	135	*7	*2.36	....	....	....	....	....	....	....	....	....	....	....	....	....	....	....	....	....
1938-39	Providence Reds	IAHL	43	16	18	9	2700	126	6	2.80	....	....	....	....	....	....	....	....	....	....	....	....	....	....	....	....	....
	Hershey Bears	IAHL	....	....	....	....	....	....	....	....	....	....	....	....	....	2	1	1	0	120	8	0	4.00	....	....	....	....
1939-40	Hershey Bears	IAHL	42	21	18	3	2580	109	4	2.53	....	....	....	....	....	6	3	3	0	360	15	1	2.50	....	....	....	....
1940-41	Hershey Bears	AHL	*56	24	23	9	*3470	189	4	3.27	....	....	....	....	....	*10	*6	4	0	640	20	*2	*1.88	....	....	....	....
1941-42	Hershey Bears	AHL	56	33	17	6	3450	169	4	2.94	....	....	....	....	....	10	6	4	0	620	27	1	2.61	....	....	....	....
	Boston Bruins	**NHL**	**1**	**1**	**0**	**0**	**60**	**3**	**0**	**3.00**	**2.93**	....	....	....	....	....	....	....	....	....	....	....	....	....	....	....	....
1942-43	Hershey Bears	AHL	54	*34	13	7	3330	162	2	2.92	....	....	....	....	....	6	2	4	0	370	23	1	3.73	....	....	....	....
1943-44	Hershey Bears	AHL	54	*30	16	8	3240	133	6	*2.46	....	....	....	....	....	7	3	4	0	425	18	0	2.54	....	....	....	....
1944-45	Hershey Bears	AHL	57	27	23	7	3420	176	7	3.09	....	....	....	....	....	11	6	5	0	660	29	0	2.63	....	....	....	....
1945-46	Hershey Bears	AHL	46	20	21	5	2760	160	3	3.48	....	....	....	....	....	....	....	....	....	....	....	....	....	....	....	....	....
1946-47	Philadelphia Rockets	AHL	56	5	44	7	3360	342	1	6.11	....	....	....	....	....	....	....	....	....	....	....	....	....	....	....	....	....
1947-1950			DID NOT PLAY																								
1950-51	Johnstown Jets	EAHL	23	....	....	....	1380	91	*2	3.95	....	....	....	....	....	6	2	4	0	360	27	0	4.50	....	....	....	....
1951-52	Washington Lions	EAHL	12	2	9	1	720	57	0	4.75	....	....	....	....	....	....	....	....	....	....	....	....	....	....	....	....	....
	NHL Totals		**1**	**1**	**0**	**0**	**60**	**3**	**0**	**3.00**	....	....	....	....	....	....	....	....	....	....	....	....	....	....	....	....	....

• Brother of Hank • EAHL Second All-Star Team (1935) • EAHL First All-Star Team (1936, 1937, 1938) • Won George L. Davis Jr. Trophy (fewest goals against - EAHL) (1937, 1938) • AHL First All-Star Team (1944, 1945, 1946)

Promoted to **Boston** from **Hershey** (AHL) to replace injured Frank Brimsek, January 25, 1942. (Boston 7, Montreal 3).

• D'AMOUR, Marc

Marc G. G – L. 5'9", 190 lbs. b: Sudbury, Ont., 5/29/1961.

Season	Club	League	GP	W	L	T	Mins	GA	SO	Avg	AAvg	Eff	SA	S%	SAPG	GP	W	L	T	Mins	GA	SO	Avg	Eff	SA	S%	SAPG
1978-79	Sault Ste. Marie Greyhounds	OMJHL	30	....	....	....	1501	149	0	5.96	....	....	....	....	....	....	....	....	....	....	....	....	....	....	....	....	....
1979-80	Sault Ste. Marie Greyhounds	OMJHL	33	6	15	0	1429	117	0	4.91	....	....	....	....	....	....	....	....	....	....	....	....	....	....	....	....	....
1980-81	Sault Ste. Marie Greyhounds	OMJHL	16	7	1	1	653	38	0	3.49	....	....	....	....	....	14	5	4	0	683	41	0	3.60	....	....	....	....
1981-82	Sault Ste. Marie Greyhounds	OHL	46	28	12	1	2384	130	1	*3.27	....	....	....	....	....	10	3	2	0	504	30	0	3.57	....	....	....	....
1982-83	Colorado Flames	CHL	42	16	21	2	2373	153	1	3.87	....	....	....	....	....	1	0	1	0	59	4	0	4.08	....	....	....	....
1983-84	Colorado Flames	CHL	36	18	12	1	1917	131	0	4.10	....	....	....	....	....	1	0	0	0	20	0	0	0.00	....	....	....	....
1984-85	Moncton Golden Flames	AHL	37	18	14	2	2051	115	0	3.36	....	....	....	....	....	....	....	....	....	....	....	....	....	....	....	....	....
	Salt Lake Golden Eagles	IHL	12	7	2	2	694	33	0	2.85	....	....	....	....	....	....	....	....	....	....	....	....	....	....	....	....	....
1985-86	**Calgary Flames**	**NHL**	**15**	**2**	**4**	**2**	**560**	**32**	**0**	**3.43**	**2.68**	**3.54**	**310**	**.897**	**33.2**	....	....	....	....	....	....	....	....	....	....	....	....
	Moncton Golden Flames	AHL	21	6	9	3	1129	72	0	3.83	....	....	....	....	....	5	1	4	0	296	20	0	4.05	....	....	....	....
1986-87	Binghamton Whalers	AHL	8	5	3	0	461	30	0	3.90	....	....	....	....	....	....	....	....	....	....	....	....	....	....	....	....	....
	Salt Lake Golden Eagles	IHL	10	3	6	0	523	37	0	4.24	....	....	....	....	....	....	....	....	....	....	....	....	....	....	....	....	....
	Canada	Nat-Team	1	0	0	0	30	4	0	8.00	....	....	....	....	....	....	....	....	....	....	....	....	....	....	....	....	....
1987-88	Salt Lake Golden Eagles	IHL	*62	26	19	5	3245	177	0	3.27	....	....	....	....	....	*19	*12	7	0	*1123	67	0	3.58	....	....	....	....
1988-89	**Philadelphia Flyers**	**NHL**	**1**	**0**	**0**	**0**	**19**	**0**	**0**	**0.00**	**0.00**	**0.00**	**14**	**1.000**	**44.2**	....	....	....	....	....	....	....	....	....	....	....	....
	Hershey Bears	AHL	39	19	13	3	2174	127	0	3.51	....	....	....	....	....	....	....	....	....	....	....	....	....	....	....	....	....
	Indianapolis Ice	IHL	6	2	3	0	324	20	0	3.70	....	....	....	....	....	....	....	....	....	....	....	....	....	....	....	....	....
1989-90	Hershey Bears	AHL	43	15	20	6	2505	148	2	3.54	....	....	....	....	....	....	....	....	....	....	....	....	....	....	....	....	....
1990-91	Hershey Bears	AHL	28	10	8	4	1331	80	0	3.61	....	....	....	....	....	2	0	1	0	80	5	0	3.75	....	....	....	....
	Fort Wayne Komets	IHL	3	1	0	0	136	9	0	3.97	....	....	....	....	....	....	....	....	....	....	....	....	....	....	....	....	....
1991-92	Hershey Bears	AHL	21	9	8	2	1073	79	0	4.42	....	....	....	....	....	....	....	....	....	....	....	....	....	....	....	....	....
	NHL Totals		**16**	**2**	**4**	**2**	**579**	**32**	**0**	**3.32**			**324**	**.901**	**33.6**	....	....	....	....	....	....	....	....	....	....	....	....

Signed as a free agent by **Calgary**, June 7, 1982. Signed as a free agent by **Philadelphia**, September 30, 1988.

• DARRAGH, Jack

G – L. 5'10", 168 lbs. b: Ottawa, Ont.,, 12/4/1890 d: 6/25/1924.

Season	Club	League	GP	W	L	T	Mins	GA	SO	Avg	AAvg	Eff	SA	S%	SAPG	GP	W	L	T	Mins	GA	SO	Avg	Eff	SA	S%	SAPG
1919-20	**Ottawa Senators**	**NHL**	**1**	**0**	**0**	**0**	**2**	**0**	**0**	**0.00**	**0.00**	....	....	....	....	....	....	....	....	....	....	....	....	....	....	....	....
	NHL Totals		**1**	**0**	**0**	**0**	**2**	**0**	**0**	**0.00**	....	....	....	....	....	....	....	....	....	....	....	....	....	....	....	....	....

Ottawa right winger replaced penalized Clint Benedict, January 24, 1920. (Toronto 5, Ottawa 3)

• DASKALAKIS, Cleon

G – L. 5'9", 175 lbs. b: Boston, MA, 9/29/1962.

Season	Club	League	GP	W	L	T	Mins	GA	SO	Avg	AAvg	Eff	SA	S%	SAPG	GP	W	L	T	Mins	GA	SO	Avg	Eff	SA	S%	SAPG
1979-80	South Shore Bruins	NEJHL	24	....	....	....	1165	63	0	3.24	....	....	....	....	....	....	....	....	....	....	....	....	....	....	....	....	....
1980-81	Boston University	ECAC	8	4	2	0	399	24	0	3.61	....	....	....	....	....	....	....	....	....	....	....	....	....	....	....	....	....
	United States	WJC-A	3	....	....	....	141	14	0	5.95	....	....	....	....	....	....	....	....	....	....	....	....	....	....	....	....	....
1981-82	Boston University	ECAC	20	9	6	3	1101	59	3	3.22	....	....	....	....	....	....	....	....	....	....	....	....	....	....	....	....	....
1982-83	Boston University	ECAC	24	15	7	1	1398	78	1	3.35	....	....	....	....	....	....	....	....	....	....	....	....	....	....	....	....	....
1983-84	Boston University	ECAC	35	25	10	0	1972	96	1	2.92	....	....	....	....	....	....	....	....	....	....	....	....	....	....	....	....	....
1984-85	**Boston Bruins**	**NHL**	**8**	**1**	**2**	**1**	**289**	**24**	**0**	**4.98**	**3.97**	**8.48**	**141**	**.830**	**29.3**	....	....	....	....	....	....	....	....	....	....	....	....
	Hershey Bears	AHL	30	9	13	4	1614	119	0	4.42	....	....	....	....	....	....	....	....	....	....	....	....	....	....	....	....	....
1985-86	**Boston Bruins**	**NHL**	**2**	**0**	**2**	**0**	**120**	**10**	**0**	**5.00**	**3.91**	**7.94**	**63**	**.841**	**31.5**	....	....	....	....	....	....	....	....	....	....	....	....
	Moncton Golden Flames	AHL	41	19	14	6	2343	141	0	3.61	....	....	....	....	....	6	4	1	0	372	13	0	*2.10	....	....	....	....
1986-87	**Boston Bruins**	**NHL**	**2**	**2**	**0**	**0**	**97**	**7**	**0**	**4.33**	**3.67**	**5.94**	**51**	**.863**	**31.5**	....	....	....	....	....	....	....	....	....	....	....	....
	Moncton Golden Flames	AHL	27	8	14	0	1452	118	0	4.88	....	....	....	....	....	1	0	0	0	36	2	0	3.33	....	....	....	....

Season	Club	League	GP	W	L	T	Mins	GA	SO	Avg	AAvg	Eff	SA	S%	SAPG	GP	W	L	T	Mins	GA	SO	Avg	Eff	SA	S%	SAPG
			REGULAR SEASON													PLAYOFFS											
1987-88	Hershey Bears	AHL	3	1	1	0	122	9	0	4.43	....	....	....	....	....	....	....	....	....	....	....	....	....	....	....	....	....
	Binghamton Whalers	AHL	6	2	2	1	344	27	0	4.71	....	....	....	....	....	....	....	....	....	....	....	....	....	....	....	....	....
	Rochester Americans	AHL	8	4	3	0	382	22	0	3.46	....	....	....	....	....	....	....	....	....	....	....	....	....	....	....	....	....
	Milwaukee Admirals	IHL	9	1	5	3	483	47	0	5.84	....	....	....	....	....	....	....	....	....	....	....	....	....	....	....	....	....
1988-89	United States	Nat-Team	1	0	0	0	20	1	0	3.00	....	....	....	....	....	....	....	....	....	....	....	....	....	....	....	....	....
	United States	WEC-A	DID NOT PLAY – SPARE GOALTENDER																								
	NHL Totals		**12**	**3**	**4**	**1**	**506**	**41**	**0**	**4.86**	....	....	**255**	**.839**	**30.2**	....	....	....	....	....	....	....	....	....	....	....	....

ECAC Second All-Star Team (1983) • ECAC First All-Star Team (1984) • NCAA East First All-American Team (1984)

Signed as a free agent by **Boston**, June 1, 1984.

• DAVIDSON, John

John Arthur "J.D." G – L. 6'3", 205 lbs. b: Ottawa, Ont., 2/27/1953. St. Louis' 1st, 5th overall in 1973.

Season	Club	League	GP	W	L	T	Mins	GA	SO	Avg	AAvg	Eff	SA	S%	SAPG	GP	W	L	T	Mins	GA	SO	Avg	Eff	SA	S%	SAPG
1969-70	Lethbridge Sugar Kings	AJHL	STATISTICS NOT AVAILABLE																								
	Calgary Centennials	WCJHL	1	0	0	0	3	0	0	0.00	....	....	....	....	....	....	....	....	....	....	....	....	....	....	....	....	....
1970-71	Lethbridge Native Sons	AJHL	46	....	....	....	2760	142	*3	*3.09	....	....	....	....	....	....	....	....	....	....	....	....	....	....	....	....	....
	Calgary Centennials	WCJHL	....	....	....	....	....	....	....	....	....	....	....	....	....	1	0	0	0	19	1	0	3.16	....	....	....	....
1971-72	Calgary Centennials	WCJHL	66	....	....	....	3970	157	*8	*2.37	....	....	....	....	....	13	6	6	1	780	39	0	3.00	....	....	....	....
	Edmonton Oil Kings	Mem-Cup	2	0	2	0	118	9	0	4.58	....	....	....	....	....	....	....	....	....	....	....	....	....	....	....	....	....
1972-73	Calgary Centennials	WCJHL	63	....	....	....	3735	201	2	3.30	....	....	....	....	....	....	....	....	....	....	....	....	....	....	....	....	....
1973-74	**St. Louis Blues**	**NHL**	**39**	**13**	**19**	**7**	**2300**	**118**	**0**	**3.08**	**2.97**	....	....	....	....	....	....	....	....	....	....	....	....	....	....	....	....
1974-75	**St. Louis Blues**	**NHL**	**40**	**17**	**15**	**7**	**2360**	**144**	**0**	**3.66**	**3.31**	....	....	....	....	**1**	**0**	**1**	....	**60**	**4**	**0**	**4.00**	....	....	....	....
	Denver Spurs	CHL	7	4	2	1	420	27	0	3.86	....	....	....	....	....	....	....	....	....	....	....	....	....	....	....	....	....
1975-76	**New York Rangers**	**NHL**	**56**	**22**	**28**	**5**	**3207**	**212**	**3**	**3.97**	**3.62**	....	....	....	....	....	....	....	....	....	....	....	....	....	....	....	....
1976-77	**New York Rangers**	**NHL**	**39**	**14**	**14**	**6**	**2116**	**125**	**1**	**3.54**	**3.30**	....	....	....	....	....	....	....	....	....	....	....	....	....	....	....	....
	New Haven Nighthawks	AHL	2	....	....	....	119	5	0	2.52	....	....	....	....	....	....	....	....	....	....	....	....	....	....	....	....	....
1977-78	**New York Rangers**	**NHL**	**34**	**14**	**13**	**4**	**1848**	**98**	**1**	**3.18**	**2.98**	....	....	....	....	**2**	**1**	**1**	....	**122**	**7**	**0**	**3.44**	....	....	....	....
1978-79	**New York Rangers**	**NHL**	**39**	**20**	**12**	**5**	**2232**	**131**	**0**	**3.52**	**3.12**	....	....	....	....	***18**	**11**	**7**	....	***1106**	**42**	***1**	**2.28**	....	....	....	....
1979-80	**New York Rangers**	**NHL**	**41**	**20**	**15**	**4**	**2306**	**122**	**2**	**3.17**	**2.80**	....	....	....	....	**9**	**4**	**5**	....	**541**	**21**	**0**	**2.33**	....	....	....	....
	New Haven Nighthawks	AHL	4	1	3	0	238	16	0	4.02	....	....	....	....	....	....	....	....	....	....	....	....	....	....	....	....	....
1980-81	**New York Rangers**	**NHL**	**10**	**1**	**7**	**1**	**560**	**48**	**0**	**5.14**	**4.16**	....	....	....	....	....	....	....	....	....	....	....	....	....	....	....	....
1981-82	**New York Rangers**	**NHL**	**1**	**1**	**0**	**0**	**60**	**1**	**0**	**1.00**	**0.77**	....	....	....	....	**1**	**0**	**0**	....	**33**	**3**	**0**	**5.45**	....	....	....	....
	Springfield Indians	AHL	8	3	4	0	437	24	0	3.30	....	....	....	....	....	....	....	....	....	....	....	....	....	....	....	....	....
1982-83	**New York Rangers**	**NHL**	**2**	**1**	**1**	**0**	**120**	**5**	**0**	**2.50**	**2.01**	**2.27**	**55**	**.909**	**27.5**	....	....	....	....	....	....	....	....	....	....	....	....
	NHL Totals		**301**	**123**	**124**	**39**	**17109**	**1004**	**7**	**3.52**	....	....	....	....	....	**31**	**16**	**14**	....	**1862**	**77**	**1**	**2.48**	....	....	....	....

AJHL Second All-Star Team (1971) • WCJHL All-Star Team (1972, 1973) • First goaltender to spend full season in NHL directly from junior without minor league experience.

Loaned to **Edmonton** (WCJHL) by **Calgary** (WCJHL) for Memorial Cup Tournament, May 8, 1972. Traded to **NY Rangers** by **St. Louis** with Bill Collins for Jerry Butler, Ted Irvine and Bert Wilson, June 18, 1975.

• DECOURCY, Bob

Robert Philip G – R. 5'11", 160 lbs. b: Toronto, Ont., 6/12/1927.

Season	Club	League	GP	W	L	T	Mins	GA	SO	Avg	AAvg	Eff	SA	S%	SAPG	GP	W	L	T	Mins	GA	SO	Avg	Eff	SA	S%	SAPG
1943-44	St. Michael's Midget Majors	OHA	10	*10	0	0	600	3	*8	*0.30	....	....	....	....	....	....	....	....	....	....	....	....	....	....	....	....	....
1944-45	St. Michael's Buzzers	OHA-B	6	6	0	0	360	16	0	2.67	....	....	....	....	....	9	*8	1	0	540	22	2	2.44	....	....	....	....
1945-46	St. Michael's Majors	OHA-Jr.	1	0	0	0	20	0	0	0.00	....	....	....	....	....	....	....	....	....	....	....	....	....	....	....	....	....
1946-47	Hamilton Szabos	OHA-Jr.	20	....	....	....	1200	176	0	8.80	....	....	....	....	....	....	....	....	....	....	....	....	....	....	....	....	....
	New York Rovers	EAHL	2	0	2	0	120	9	0	4.50	....	....	....	....	....	6	3	2	1	360	22	0	3.67	....	....	....	....
1947-48	New York Rovers	EAHL	14	....	....	....	840	92	0	6.57	....	....	....	....	....	....	....	....	....	....	....	....	....	....	....	....	....
	New York Rangers	**NHL**	**1**	**0**	**1**	**0**	**29**	**6**	**0**	**12.41**	**12.97**	....	....	....	....	....	....	....	....	....	....	....	....	....	....	....	....
	New York Rovers	QSHL	10	....	....	....	600	55	0	5.50	....	....	....	....	....	....	....	....	....	....	....	....	....	....	....	....	....
	St. Paul Saints	USHL	8	....	....	....	480	21	2	2.62	....	....	....	....	....	....	....	....	....	....	....	....	....	....	....	....	....
1948-49	Kansas City Pla-Mors	USHL	2	0	1	1	120	6	0	3.00	....	....	....	....	....	....	....	....	....	....	....	....	....	....	....	....	....
	Omaha Knights	USHL	9	3	5	1	540	32	0	3.56	....	....	....	....	....	....	....	....	....	....	....	....	....	....	....	....	....
1949-50	St. Paul Saints	USHL	13	3	10	0	780	69	0	5.30	....	....	....	....	....	....	....	....	....	....	....	....	....	....	....	....	....
1950-51	St. Michael's Monarchs	OHA-Sr.	1	....	....	....	60	5	0	5.00	....	....	....	....	....	....	....	....	....	....	....	....	....	....	....	....	....
	NHL Totals		**1**	**0**	**1**	**0**	**29**	**6**	**0**	**12.41**	....	....	....	....	....	....	....	....	....	....	....	....	....	....	....	....	....

• **NY Rangers'** spare goaltender replaced injured Chuck Rayner in 2nd period, November 12, 1947. (Boston 8, NY Rangers 2).

• DEFELICE, Norm

G – L. 5'10", 150 lbs. b: Schumacher, Ont., 1/19/1933.

Season	Club	League	GP	W	L	T	Mins	GA	SO	Avg	AAvg	Eff	SA	S%	SAPG	GP	W	L	T	Mins	GA	SO	Avg	Eff	SA	S%	SAPG
1951-52	Waterloo Hurricanes	OHA-Jr.	18	....	....	....	1050	138	0	7.89	....	....	....	....	....	....	....	....	....	....	....	....	....	....	....	....	....
1952-53	St. Catharines Teepees	OHA-Jr.	20	....	....	....	1200	55	2	2.75	....	....	....	....	....	2	....	....	....	120	8	0	4.00	....	....	....	....
1953-54	Sydney Millionaires	MMHL	69	35	30	3	4182	236	*7	*3.39	....	....	....	....	....	12	5	7	0	730	35	1	2.88	....	....	....	....
	Hershey Bears	AHL	1	0	1	0	60	4	0	4.00	....	....	....	....	....	....	....	....	....	....	....	....	....	....	....	....	....
1954-55	Johnstown Jets	IHL	37	....	....	....	2220	122	0	3.30	....	....	....	....	....	....	....	....	....	....	....	....	....	....	....	....	....
	Hershey Bears	AHL	21	9	11	1	1260	82	1	3.90	....	....	....	....	....	....	....	....	....	....	....	....	....	....	....	....	....
	Toledo Mercurys	IHL	4	....	....	....	240	21	0	5.25	....	....	....	....	....	....	....	....	....	....	....	....	....	....	....	....	....
	Washington Lions	EHL	1	1	0	0	60	5	0	5.00	....	....	....	....	....	....	....	....	....	....	....	....	....	....	....	....	....
1955-56	Hershey Bears	AHL	22	7	13	2	1320	91	0	4.14	....	....	....	....	....	....	....	....	....	....	....	....	....	....	....	....	....
	Washington Lions	EHL	4	....	....	....	240	12	0	3.00	....	....	....	....	....	....	....	....	....	....	....	....	....	....	....	....	....
1956-57	Hershey Bears	AHL	8	6	1	1	490	21	2	2.57	....	....	....	....	....	....	....	....	....	....	....	....	....	....	....	....	....
	Boston Bruins	**NHL**	**10**	**3**	**5**	**2**	**600**	**30**	**0**	**3.00**	**3.46**	....	....	....	....	....	....	....	....	....	....	....	....	....	....	....	....
	Springfield Indians	AHL	8	1	6	1	500	38	0	4.56	....	....	....	....	....	....	....	....	....	....	....	....	....	....	....	....	....
1957-58	Clinton Comets	EHL	45	....	....	....	2700	162	1	3.60	....	....	....	....	....	....	....	....	....	....	....	....	....	....	....	....	....
	Trois-Rivieres Lions	QHL	2	0	2	0	120	10	0	5.00	....	....	....	....	....	....	....	....	....	....	....	....	....	....	....	....	....
	Charlotte Clippers	EHL	1	0	1	0	60	8	0	8.00	....	....	....	....	....	....	....	....	....	....	....	....	....	....	....	....	....
	Washington Presidents	EHL	....	....	....	....	....	....	....	....	....	....	....	....	....	12	*8	4	0	720	32	*1	*2.67	....	....	....	....
1958-59	Clinton Comets	EHL	63	*41	20	2	3780	177	3	*2.82	....	....	....	....	....	8	*8	0	0	480	18	*1	*2.25	....	....	....	....
1959-60	Clinton Comets	EHL	37	....	....	....	2220	97	4	*2.62	....	....	....	....	....	8	3	5	0	480	23	0	2.88	....	....	....	....
	Greensboro Generals	EHL	1	1	0	0	60	4	0	4.00	....	....	....	....	....	....	....	....	....	....	....	....	....	....	....	....	....
1960-61	Clinton Comets	EHL	60	29	29	2	3600	220	*6	3.49	....	....	....	....	....	4	1	3	0	240	15	0	3.75	....	....	....	....
1961-62	Clinton Comets	EHL	68	*45	22	1	4080	193	*5	*2.99	....	....	....	....	....	6	1	5	0	360	22	0	3.65	....	....	....	....
1962-63	Clinton Comets	EHL	63	36	21	6	3780	163	*8	*2.59	....	....	....	....	....	13	8	5	0	780	45	0	3.23	....	....	....	....
1963-64	Clinton Comets	EHL	66	35	24	7	3960	193	*8	*2.92	....	....	....	....	....	12	7	5	0	730	45	1	3.70	....	....	....	....
1964-65	Clinton Comets	EHL	69	....	....	....	4140	*164	*15	*2.38	....	....	....	....	....	11	5	6	0	670	32	0	2.86	....	....	....	....
1965-66	Jersey Devils	EHL	62	....	....	....	3720	239	1	3.85	....	....	....	....	....	....	....	....	....	....	....	....	....	....	....	....	....
	Long Island Ducks	EHL	3	2	1	0	180	6	0	2.00	....	....	....	....	....	....	....	....	....	....	....	....	....	....	....	....	....
1966-67	Jersey Devils	EHL	52	....	....	....	3120	146	0	2.81	....	....	....	....	....	9	5	4	0	540	29	0	3.22	....	....	....	....
1967-68	Galt Hornets	OHA-Sr.	29	....	....	....	1740	62	*5	*2.14	....	....	....	....	....	....	....	....	....	....	....	....	....	....	....	....	....
1968-69	Long Island Ducks	EHL	23	....	....	....	1380	75	1	3.26	....	....	....	....	....	....	....	....	....	....	....	....	....	....	....	....	....
1969-70	Galt Hornets	OHA-Sr.	13	....	....	....	780	32	1	2.46	....	....	....	....	....	....	....	....	....	....	....	....	....	....	....	....	....
	NHL Totals		**10**	**3**	**5**	**2**	**600**	**30**	**0**	**3.00**	....	....	....	....	....	....	....	....	....	....	....	....	....	....	....	....	....

EHL First All-Star Team (1959, 1962, 1963) • Won George L. Davis Jr. Trophy (fewest goals against - EHL) (1959, 1960, 1962, 1963, 1964, 1965) • EHL Second All-Star Team (1961, 1964) • EHL North First All-Star Team (1965) • EHL North Second All-Star Team (1967)

Loaned to **Sydney** (MMHL) by **Boston** for cash, October 5, 1953. Promoted to **Boston** from **Hershey** (AHL) to replace Terry Sawchuk who was hospitalized for nervous exhaustion, December 13, 1956. Traded to **Springfield** (AHL) by **Boston** with future considerations (Floyd Smith, June, 1957) and the loan of Jack Bionda for Don Simmons, January 22, 1957. Traded to **Jersey** (EHL) by **Clinton** (EHL) with Hec Lalande, Ted Sydlowski and Benny Woit for Ed Babiuk, Pat Kelly and Borden Smith, August, 1965. Traded to **Long Island** (EHL) by **Jersey** (EHL) for Bob Brown, September, 1968.

• DEJORDY, Denis
Denis Emile G – L. 5'9", 185 lbs. b: St. Hyacinthe, Que., 11/12/1938.

Season	Club	League	GP	W	L	T	Mins	GA	SO	Avg	AAvg	Eff	SA	S%	SAPG	GP	W	L	T	Mins	GA	SO	Avg	Eff	SA	S%	SAPG
			REGULAR SEASON													PLAYOFFS											
1956-57	Dixie Beehives	OHA-B	STATISTICS NOT AVAILABLE																								
1957-58	St. Catharines Teepees	OHA-Jr.	52	*32	14	6	3120	174	1	3.35	....	....	....	....	....	8	3	4	1	480	36	0	4.50	....	....	....	....
	Buffalo Bisons	AHL	1	0	1	0	60	5	0	5.00	....	....	....	....	....	....	....	....	....	....	....	....	....	....	....	....	....
1958-59	St. Catharines Teepees	OHA-Jr.	53	*40	10	3	3180	169	1	3.19	....	....	....	....	....	7	2	4	1	420	18	0	2.57	....	....	....	....
	Peterborough Petes	Mem-Cup	5	1	4	0	300	23	0	4.60	....	....	....	....	....	....	....	....	....	....	....	....	....	....	....	....	....
1959-60	Sault Ste. Marie Thunderbirds	EPHL	69	27	31	11	4140	258	1	3.74	....	....	....	....	....	....	....	....	....	....	....	....	....	....	....	....	....
1960-61	Sault Ste. Marie Thunderbirds	EPHL	33	16	14	3	1980	115	2	3.48	....	....	....	....	....	....	....	....	....	....	....	....	....	....	....	....	....
	Buffalo Bisons	AHL	40	20	18	2	2400	127	3	3.18	....	....	....	....	....	4	0	4	0	264	18	0	4.09	....	....	....	....
1961-62	Buffalo Bisons	AHL	*69	*36	30	3	*4170	210	*8	3.02	....	....	....	....	....	*11	6	5	0	706	20	*2	1.70	....	....	....	....
1962-63	**Chicago Black Hawks**	**NHL**	**5**	**2**	**1**	**2**	**290**	**12**	**0**	**2.48**	**2.58**	....	....	....	....	....	....	....	....	....	....	....	....	....	....	....	....
	Buffalo Bisons	AHL	67	*37	23	7	4020	187	*6	2.79	....	....	....	....	....	13	*8	5	0	802	28	1	*2.09	....	....	....	....
1963-64	**Chicago Black Hawks**	**NHL**	**6**	**2**	**3**	**1**	**340**	**19**	**0**	**3.35**	**3.73**	....	....	....	....	**1**	**0**	**0**	....	**20**	**2**	**0**	**6.00**	....	....	....	....
	St. Louis Braves	CPHL	1	0	1	0	60	5	0	5.00	....	....	....	....	....	....	....	....	....	....	....	....	....	....	....	....	....
1964-65	**Chicago Black Hawks**	**NHL**	**30**	**16**	**11**	**3**	**1760**	**74**	**3**	**2.52**	**2.68**	....	....	....	....	**2**	**0**	**1**	....	**80**	**9**	**0**	**6.75**	....	....	....	....
	Buffalo Bisons	AHL	7	3	4	0	450	20	1	2.67	....	....	....	....	....	....	....	....	....	....	....	....	....	....	....	....	....
1965-66	St. Louis Braves	CPHL	*70	30	31	9	*4200	217	6	3.10	....	....	....	....	....	5	1	4	0	300	18	0	3.60	....	....	....	....
1966-67	**Chicago Black Hawks**	**NHL**	**44**	**22**	**12**	**7**	**2536**	**104**	**4**	**2.46**	**2.49**	....	....	....	....	**4**	**1**	**2**	....	**184**	**10**	**0**	**3.26**	....	....	....	....
1967-68	**Chicago Black Hawks**	**NHL**	**50**	**23**	**15**	**11**	**2838**	**128**	**4**	**2.71**	**3.00**	....	....	....	....	**11**	**5**	**6**	....	**662**	**34**	**0**	**3.08**	....	....	....	....
1968-69	**Chicago Black Hawks**	**NHL**	**53**	**22**	**22**	**7**	**2981**	**156**	**2**	**3.14**	**3.26**	....	....	....	....	....	....	....	....	....	....	....	....	....	....	....	....
	Dallas Black Hawks	CHL	15	8	4	3	899	41	1	2.74	....	....	....	....	....	....	....	....	....	....	....	....	....	....	....	....	....
1969-70	**Chicago Black Hawks**	**NHL**	**10**	**3**	**5**	**1**	**557**	**25**	**0**	**2.69**	**2.85**	....	....	....	....	....	....	....	....	....	....	....	....	....	....	....	....
	Los Angeles Kings	**NHL**	**21**	**5**	**11**	**4**	**1147**	**62**	**0**	**3.24**	**3.45**	....	....	....	....	....	....	....	....	....	....	....	....	....	....	....	....
1970-71	**Los Angeles Kings**	**NHL**	**60**	**18**	**29**	**11**	**3375**	**214**	**1**	**3.80**	**3.81**	....	....	....	....	....	....	....	....	....	....	....	....	....	....	....	....
1971-72	**Los Angeles Kings**	**NHL**	**5**	**0**	**5**	**0**	**291**	**23**	**0**	**4.74**	**4.80**	....	....	....	....	....	....	....	....	....	....	....	....	....	....	....	....
	Montreal Canadiens	**NHL**	**7**	**3**	**2**	**1**	**332**	**25**	**0**	**4.52**	**4.58**	....	....	....	....	....	....	....	....	....	....	....	....	....	....	....	....
1972-73	**Detroit Red Wings**	**NHL**	**24**	**8**	**11**	**3**	**1331**	**83**	**1**	**3.74**	**3.54**	....	....	....	....	....	....	....	....	....	....	....	....	....	....	....	....
	Fort Worth Wings	CHL	10	....	....	....	560	41	0	4.39	....	....	....	....	....	....	....	....	....	....	....	....	....	....	....	....	....
1973-74	**Detroit Red Wings**	**NHL**	**1**	**0**	**1**	**0**	**20**	**4**	**0**	**12.00**	**11.60**	....	....	....	....	....	....	....	....	....	....	....	....	....	....	....	....
	Baltimore Clippers	AHL	42	21	13	6	2428	131	1	3.23	....	....	....	....	....	4	1	3	0	252	22	0	5.23	....	....	....	....
	NHL Totals		**316**	**124**	**128**	**51**	**17798**	**929**	**15**	**3.13**	....	....	....	....	....	**18**	**6**	**9**	....	**946**	**55**	**0**	**3.49**	....	....	....	....

OHA-Jr. First All-Star Team (1959) • AHL First All-Star Team (1963) • Won Harry "Hap" Holmes Memorial Award (fewest goals against - AHL) (1963) • Won Les Cunningham Award (MVP - AHL) (1963) • CPHL First All-Star Team (1966) • Shared Vezina Trophy with Glenn Hall (1967) • AHL Second All-Star Team (1974)

Traded to **LA Kings** by **Chicago** with Gilles Marotte and Jim Stanfield for Bill White, Bryan Campbell and Gerry Desjardins, February 20, 1970. Traded to **Montreal** by **LA Kings** with Dale Hoganson, Noel Price and Doug Robinson for Rogie Vachon, November 4, 1971. Traded to **NY Islanders** by **Montreal** with Glenn Resch, Germain Gagnon, Tony Featherstone, Murray Anderson and Alex Campbell for cash, June 26, 1972. Traded to **Detroit** by **NY Islanders** with Don McLaughlin for Arnie Brown and Gerry Gray, October 4, 1972.

• DELGUIDICE, Matt
G – R. 5'9", 170 lbs. b: West Haven, CT, 3/5/1967. Boston's 5th, 77th overall in 1987.

Season	Club	League	GP	W	L	T	Mins	GA	SO	Avg	AAvg	Eff	SA	S%	SAPG	GP	W	L	T	Mins	GA	SO	Avg	Eff	SA	S%	SAPG
1981-1986	East Haven Comets	Hi-School	STATISTICS NOT AVAILABLE																								
1986-87	St. Anselm College Hawks	ECAC-2	24	5	11	3	1437	76	0	3.17	....	....	....	....	....	....	....	....	....	....	....	....	....	....	....	....	....
1987-88	University of Maine	H-East	DID NOT PLAY – ACADEMICALLY INELIGIBLE																								
1988-89	University of Maine	H-East	20	16	4	0	1090	57	1	*3.14	....	....	....	....	....	4	3	1	0	254	16	0	3.78	....	....	....	....
1989-90	University of Maine	H-East	23	16	4	0	1257	68	0	3.25	....	....	....	....	....	5	3	1	0	244	15	0	3.69	....	....	....	....
1990-91	**Boston Bruins**	**NHL**	**1**	**0**	**0**	**0**	**10**	**0**	**0**	**0.00**	**0.00**	**0.00**	**7**	**1.000**	**42.0**	....	....	....	....	....	....	....	....	....	....	....	....
	Maine Mariners	AHL	52	23	18	9	2893	160	2	3.32	....	....	....	....	....	2	1	1	0	82	5	0	3.66	....	....	....	....
1991-92	**Boston Bruins**	**NHL**	**10**	**2**	**5**	**1**	**424**	**28**	**0**	**3.96**	**3.55**	**4.64**	**239**	**.883**	**33.8**	....	....	....	....	....	....	....	....	....	....	....	....
	Maine Mariners	AHL	25	5	15	0	1369	101	0	4.43	....	....	....	....	....	....	....	....	....	....	....	....	....	....	....	....	....
1992-93	Providence Bruins	AHL	9	0	7	1	478	58	0	7.28	....	....	....	....	....	....	....	....	....	....	....	....	....	....	....	....	....
	San Diego Gulls	IHL	1	0	0	0	20	2	0	6.00	....	....	....	....	....	....	....	....	....	....	....	....	....	....	....	....	....
1993-94	Albany River Rats	AHL	5	1	2	2	309	19	0	3.68	....	....	....	....	....	....	....	....	....	....	....	....	....	....	....	....	....
	Springfield Indians	AHL	1	0	0	1	65	3	0	2.77	....	....	....	....	....	....	....	....	....	....	....	....	....	....	....	....	....
	Raleigh IceCaps	ECHL	31	18	9	4	1877	92	1	*2.94	....	....	....	....	....	12	6	6	0	706	37	0	3.14	....	....	....	....
1994-95	Charlotte Checkers	ECHL	5	2	2	1	303	15	0	2.97	....	....	....	....	....	....	....	....	....	....	....	....	....	....	....	....	....
	Nashville Knights	ECHL	18	7	8	2	1009	81	0	4.82	....	....	....	....	....	2	0	1	0	74	6	0	4.84	....	....	....	....
	Atlanta Knights	IHL	1	0	0	0	52	5	0	5.70	....	....	....	....	....	....	....	....	....	....	....	....	....	....	....	....	....
1995-96	Roanoke Express	ECHL	35	13	10	3	1738	103	3	3.56	....	....	....	....	....	2	0	1	0	60	3	0	2.98	....	....	....	....
1996-97	Amarillo Rattlers	WPHL	49	13	26	7	2620	193	0	4.42	....	....	....	....	....	....	....	....	....	....	....	....	....	....	....	....	....
1997-98	Amarillo Rattlers	WPHL	31	7	17	4	1598	124	0	4.65	....	....	....	....	....	....	....	....	....	....	....	....	....	....	....	....	....
	Monroe Moccasins	WPHL	16	9	7	0	922	48	2	3.12	....	....	....	....	....	....	....	....	....	....	....	....	....	....	....	....	....
1998-99	Monroe Moccasins	WPHL	8	5	3	0	478	36	0	4.52	....	....	....	....	....	....	....	....	....	....	....	....	....	....	....	....	....
	Corpus Christi Icerays	WPHL	4	1	2	1	199	11	0	3.32	....	....	....	....	....	....	....	....	....	....	....	....	....	....	....	....	....
	NHL Totals		**11**	**2**	**5**	**1**	**434**	**28**	**0**	**3.87**	....	....	**246**	**.886**	**34.0**	....	....	....	....	....	....	....	....	....	....	....	....

NCAA (College Div.) East Second All-American Team (1987) • Played w/ RHI's San Diego Barracudas in 1994 (9-1-1-2-245-44-0-8.61); New Jersey R&R (3-2-1-0-116-15-0-6.20) and Ottawa Loggers (8-3-3-0-355-48-0-6.48) in 1995 and New Jersey R&R in 1996 (17-5-9-2-758-115-1-7.28)

• DENIS, Marc
G – L. 6', 190 lbs. b: Montreal, Que., 8/1/1977. Colorado's 1st, 25th overall in 1995.

Season	Club	League	GP	W	L	T	Mins	GA	SO	Avg	AAvg	Eff	SA	S%	SAPG	GP	W	L	T	Mins	GA	SO	Avg	Eff	SA	S%	SAPG
1992-93	Montreal-Bourassa Canadiens	QAAA	26	....	....	....	1559	74	5	2.87	....	....	....	....	....	....	....	....	....	....	....	....	....	....	....	....	....
1993-94	Trois-Rivieres Canadiens	QAAA	36	....	....	....	2093	158	3	4.53	....	....	....	....	....	....	....	....	....	....	....	....	....	....	....	....	....
1994-95	Chicoutimi Sagueneens	QMJHL	32	17	9	1	1688	98	0	3.48	....	....	....	....	....	6	4	2	....	372	19	1	3.06	....	....	....	....
1995-96	Chicoutimi Sagueneens	QMJHL	51	23	21	4	2951	157	2	3.19	....	....	....	....	....	16	8	8	....	957	69	0	4.33	....	....	....	....
	Canada	WJC-A	2	2	0	0	120	2	0	1.00	....	....	....	....	....	....	....	....	....	....	....	....	....	....	....	....	....
1996-97	Chicoutimi Sagueneens	QMJHL	41	22	15	2	2323	104	4	*2.69	....	....	....	....	....	*21	*11	10	....	*1229	70	*1	3.42	....	....	....	....
	Canada	WJC-A	7	5	0	2	419	13	1	1.86	....	....	....	....	....	....	....	....	....	....	....	....	....	....	....	....	....
	Colorado Avalanche	**NHL**	**1**	**0**	**1**	**0**	**60**	**3**	**0**	**3.00**	**3.23**	**3.46**	**26**	**.885**	**26.0**	....	....	....	....	....	....	....	....	....	....	....	....
	Hershey Bears	AHL	....	....	....	....	....	....	....	....	....	....	....	....	....	4	1	0	....	56	1	0	1.08	....	....	....	....
	Chicoutimi Sagueneens	Mem-Cup	3	0	*3	0	179	15	0	5.02	....	....	....	....	....	....	....	....	....	....	....	....	....	....	....	....	....
1997-98	Hershey Bears	AHL	47	17	23	4	2588	125	1	2.90	....	....	....	....	....	6	3	3	....	346	15	0	2.59	....	....	....	....
1998-99	**Colorado Avalanche**	**NHL**	**4**	**1**	**1**	**1**	**217**	**9**	**0**	**2.49**	**2.96**	**2.04**	**110**	**.918**	**30.4**	....	....	....	....	....	....	....	....	....	....	....	....
	Hershey Bears	AHL	52	20	23	5	2908	137	4	2.83	....	....	....	....	....	3	1	1	....	143	7	0	2.93	....	....	....	....
99-2000	**Colorado Avalanche**	**NHL**	**23**	**9**	**8**	**3**	**1203**	**51**	**3**	**2.54**	**2.90**	**2.10**	**618**	**.917**	**30.8**	....	....	....	....	....	....	....	....	....	....	....	....
	NHL Totals		**28**	**10**	**10**	**4**	**1480**	**63**	**3**	**2.55**	....	....	**754**	**.916**	**30.6**	....	....	....	....	....	....	....	....	....	....	....	....

Named Best Goaltender at WJC-A (1997) • QMJHL First All-Star Team (1997) • Canadian Major Junior First All-Star Team (1997) • Canadian Major Junior Goaltender of the Year (1997)

Traded to **Columbus** by **Colorado** for Columbus' 2nd round choice (later traded to Carolina - Carolina selected Tomas Kurka) in 2000 Entry Draft, June 7, 2000.

• DeROUVILLE, Philippe
G – L. 6'1", 185 lbs. b: Victoriaville, Que., 8/7/1974. Pittsburgh's 5th, 115th overall in 1992.

Season	Club	League	GP	W	L	T	Mins	GA	SO	Avg	AAvg	Eff	SA	S%	SAPG	GP	W	L	T	Mins	GA	SO	Avg	Eff	SA	S%	SAPG
1989-90	Magog Cantonniers	QAAA	21	15	6	0	1213	90	0	4.45	....	....	....	....	....	....	....	....	....	....	....	....	....	....	....	....	....
1990-91	Longueuil College-Francais	QMJHL	20	13	6	0	1030	50	0	2.91	....	....	....	....	....	....	....	....	....	....	....	....	....	....	....	....	....
1991-92	Verdun College-Francais	QMJHL	34	20	6	3	1854	99	2	3.20	....	....	....	....	....	11	7	3	....	593	28	1	2.83	....	....	....	....
1992-93	Verdun College-Francais	QMJHL	61	30	27	2	3491	210	1	3.61	....	....	....	....	....	4	0	4	....	256	18	0	3.61	....	....	....	....
	Canada	WJC-A	1	0	1	0	60	7	0	7.00	....	....	....	....	....	....	....	....	....	....	....	....	....	....	....	....	....
1993-94	Verdun College-Francais	QMJHL	51	28	22	0	2845	145	1	*3.06	....	....	....	....	....	4	0	4	....	210	14	0	4.00	....	....	....	....
1994-95	Cleveland Lumberjacks	IHL	41	24	10	5	2369	131	1	3.32	....	....	....	....	....	4	1	3	....	263	18	0	4.09	....	....	....	....
	Pittsburgh Penguins	**NHL**	**1**	**1**	**0**	**0**	**60**	**3**	**0**	**3.00**	**3.14**	**3.33**	**27**	**.889**	**27.0**	....	....	....	....	....	....	....	....	....	....	....	....
1995-96	Cleveland Lumberjacks	IHL	38	19	11	3	2008	129	1	3.86	....	....	....	....	....	....	....	....	....	....	....	....	....	....	....	....	....
1996-97	**Pittsburgh Penguins**	**NHL**	**2**	**0**	**2**	**0**	**111**	**6**	**0**	**3.24**	**3.49**	**2.95**	**66**	**.909**	**35.7**	....	....	....	....	....	....	....	....	....	....	....	....
	Kansas City Blades	IHL	26	11	11	4	1470	69	2	2.82	....	....	....	....	....	2	0	1	....	32	4	0	7.35	....	....	....	....

Season	Club	League	GP	W	L	T	Mins	GA	SO	Avg	AAvg	Eff	SA	S%	SAPG	GP	W	L	T	Mins	GA	SO	Avg	Eff	SA	S%	SAPG
			REGULAR SEASON													PLAYOFFS											
1997-98	Louisville RiverFrogs	ECHL	8	5	2	1	480	27	0	3.38	....	....	....	....	....	....	....	....	....	....	....	....	....	....	....	....	....
	Hartford Wolf Pack	AHL	3	0	2	1	184	10	0	3.26	....	....	....	....	....	....	....	....	....	....	....	....	....	....	....	....	....
	Utah Grizzlies	IHL	30	18	9	1	1524	65	3	2.56	....	....	....	....	....	2	1	1	....	129	7	0	3.25	....	....	....	....
1998-99	Utah Grizzlies	IHL	5	0	2	0	142	12	0	5.07	....	....	....	....	....	....	....	....	....	....	....	....	....	....	....	....	....
	San Antonio Iguanas	CHL	5	3	2	0	181	13	0	4.31	....	....	....	....	....	....	....	....	....	....	....	....	....	....	....	....	....
	Fredericton Canadiens	AHL	19	6	6	2	921	46	0	3.00	....	....	....	....	....	....	....	....	....	....	....	....	....	....	....	....	....
99-2000	ERC Inglostadt	Germany-2	45	....	....	....	2515	111	2	2.65	....	....	....	....	....	....	....	....	....	....	....	....	....	....	....	....	....
	NHL Totals		**3**	**1**	**2**	**0**	**171**	**9**	**0**	**3.16**	....	....	**93**	**.903**	**32.6**	....	....	....	....	....	....	....	....	....	....	....	....

QMJHL Second All-Star Team (1993, 1994)

• DESJARDINS, Gerry

Gerard Ferdinand G – L. 5'11", 190 lbs. b: Sudbury, Ont., 7/22/1944.

Season	Club	League	GP	W	L	T	Mins	GA	SO	Avg	AAvg	Eff	SA	S%	SAPG	GP	W	L	T	Mins	GA	SO	Avg	Eff	SA	S%	SAPG
1960-1962	Sudbury Bell Telephone	NBHL	STATISTICS NOT AVAILABLE																								
1962-63	Toronto Marlboros	OHA-Jr.	30	....	....	....	1780	97	2	3.27	....	....	....	....	....	....	....	....	....	....	....	....	....	....	....	....	....
1963-64	Garson Native Sons	NOJHA	STATISTICS NOT AVAILABLE																								
	London Nationals	OHA-B	STATISTICS NOT AVAILABLE																								
1964-65	Toronto Marlboros	OHA-Jr.	53	32	14	7	3180	202	1	3.81	....	....	....	....	....	19	....	....	....	1140	57	0	3.00	....	....	....	....
1965-66	Houston Apollos	CPHL	20	6	8	5	1160	73	0	3.78	....	....	....	....	....	....	....	....	....	....	....	....	....	....	....	....	....
1966-67	Houston Apollos	CPHL	36	15	16	5	2160	130	1	3.61	....	....	....	....	....	6	2	4	0	328	18	0	3.29	....	....	....	....
1967-68	Cleveland Barons	AHL	*66	26	26	14	*3934	226	3	3.45	....	....	....	....	....	....	....	....	....	....	....	....	....	....	....	....	....
1968-69	**Los Angeles Kings**	**NHL**	**60**	**18**	**34**	**6**	**3499**	**190**	**4**	**3.26**	**3.40**	....	....	....	....	**9**	**3**	**4**	....	**431**	**28**	**0**	**3.90**	....	....	....	....
1969-70	**Los Angeles Kings**	**NHL**	**43**	**7**	**29**	**5**	**2453**	**159**	**3**	**3.89**	**4.20**	....	....	....	....	....	....	....	....	....	....	....	....	....	....	....	....
	Chicago Black Hawks	**NHL**	**4**	**4**	**0**	**0**	**240**	**8**	**0**	**2.00**	**2.12**	....	....	....	....	....	....	....	....	....	....	....	....	....	....	....	....
1970-71	**Chicago Black Hawks**	**NHL**	**22**	**12**	**6**	**3**	**1217**	**49**	**0**	**2.42**	**2.38**	....	....	....	....	....	....	....	....	....	....	....	....	....	....	....	....
1971-72	**Chicago Black Hawks**	**NHL**	**6**	**1**	**2**	**3**	**360**	**21**	**0**	**3.50**	**3.54**	....	....	....	....	**1**	**1**	**0**	....	**60**	**5**	**0**	**5.00**	....	....	....	....
1972-73	**New York Islanders**	**NHL**	**44**	**5**	**35**	**3**	**2498**	**195**	**0**	**4.68**	**4.48**	....	....	....	....	....	....	....	....	....	....	....	....	....	....	....	....
1973-74	**New York Islanders**	**NHL**	**36**	**9**	**17**	**6**	**1945**	**101**	**0**	**3.12**	**3.01**	....	....	....	....	....	....	....	....	....	....	....	....	....	....	....	....
1974-75	Michigan-Baltimore Stags	WHA	41	9	28	1	2282	162	0	4.26	....	....	....	....	....	....	....	....	....	....	....	....	....	....	....	....	....
	Buffalo Sabres	**NHL**	**9**	**6**	**2**	**1**	**540**	**25**	**0**	**2.78**	**2.51**	....	....	....	....	***15**	**7**	**5**	....	**760**	**43**	**0**	**3.39**	....	....	....	....
1975-76	**Buffalo Sabres**	**NHL**	**55**	**29**	**15**	**11**	**3280**	**161**	**2**	**2.95**	**2.66**	....	....	....	....	**9**	**4**	**5**	....	**563**	**28**	**0**	**2.98**	....	....	....	....
1976-77	**Buffalo Sabres**	**NHL**	**49**	**31**	**12**	**6**	**2871**	**126**	**3**	**2.63**	**2.43**	....	....	....	....	**1**	**0**	**1**	....	**60**	**4**	**0**	**4.00**	....	....	....	....
1977-78	**Buffalo Sabres**	**NHL**	**3**	**0**	**1**	**0**	**111**	**7**	**0**	**3.78**	**3.54**	....	....	....	....	....	....	....	....	....	....	....	....	....	....	....	....
	NHL Totals		**331**	**122**	**153**	**44**	**19014**	**1042**	**12**	**3.29**	....	....	....	....	....	**35**	**15**	**15**	....	**1874**	**108**	**0**	**3.46**	....	....	....	....
	Other Major League Totals		41	9	28	1	2282	162	0	4.26	....	....	....	....	....	....	....	....	....	....	....	....	....	....	....	....	....

AHL First All-Star Team (1968) • Won Dudley "Red" Garrett Memorial Award (Top Rookie - AHL) (1968) • Played in NHL All-Star Game (1977)

Traded to **LA Kings** by **Montreal** for LA Kings' 1st round choices in 1969 (later traded to Minnesota - Minnesota selected Dick Redmond) and 1972 (Steve Shutt) Amateur Drafts, June 11, 1968. Traded to **Chicago** by **LA Kings** with Bill White and Bryan Campbell for Denis Dejordy, Gilles Marotte and Jim Stanfield, February 20, 1970. Traded to **California** by **Chicago** with Kerry Bond and Gerry Pinder for Gary Smith, September 9, 1971. Traded to **Chicago** by **California** for Paul Shmyr and Gilles Meloche, October 18, 1971. Selected by **NY Raiders** (WHA) in 1972 WHA General Player Draft, February 12, 1972. Claimed by **NY Islanders** from **Chicago** in Expansion Draft, June 6, 1972. WHA rights traded to **Michigan** (WHA) by **New York-Jersey** (WHA) for cash, May, 1974. Rights traded to **Buffalo** by **NY Islanders** for the rights to Garry Lariviere, February 19, 1975.

• DICKIE, Bill

William Rufus G – R. 5'8", 185 lbs. b: Campbellton, N.B., 2/20/1916 d: 12/23/1997.

Season	Club	League	GP	W	L	T	Mins	GA	SO	Avg	AAvg	Eff	SA	S%	SAPG	GP	W	L	T	Mins	GA	SO	Avg	Eff	SA	S%	SAPG
1932-33	Campbellton Collegiate	Hi-School	STATISTICS NOT AVAILABLE																								
1933-34	Mount Allison University	MIHC	4	*3	1	0	240	3	*2	*0.75	....	....	....	....	....	....	....	....	....	....	....	....	....	....	....	....	....
	Mount Allison University	NBCHL	7	*7	0	0	430	11	1	*1.53	....	....	....	....	....	2	*2	0	0	120	3	0	*1.50	....	....	....	....
	Mount Allison University	Al-Cup	6	3	2	1	360	20	0	3.33	....	....	....	....	....	....	....	....	....	....	....	....	....	....	....	....	....
1934-35	Mount Allison University	MIHC	4	*3	0	1	250	10	0	*2.40	....	....	....	....	....	....	....	....	....	....	....	....	....	....	....	....	....
	Mount Allison University	NBCHL	6	4	2	0	370	15	0	2.43	....	....	....	....	....	2	1	1	0	120	6	0	3.00	....	....	....	....
1935-36	Mount Allison University	X-Games	1	0	1	0	60	2	0	2.00	....	....	....	....	....	....	....	....	....	....	....	....	....	....	....	....	....
1936-37	Mount Allison University	MIHC	4	3	0	1	240	3	2	*0.75	....	....	....	....	....	1	0	1	0	60	6	0	6.00	....	....	....	....
1937-38	Saint John Beavers	SNBHL	29	16	11	1	1780	69	4	*2.33	....	....	....	....	....	4	1	3	0	195	11	0	3.39	....	....	....	....
1938-39	Saint John Beavers	X-Games	34	20	9	5	2050	85	4	2.49	....	....	....	....	....	....	....	....	....	....	....	....	....	....	....	....	....
	Saint John Beavers	Al-Cup	13	8	4	1	809	38	1	2.82	....	....	....	....	....	....	....	....	....	....	....	....	....	....	....	....	....
1939-40	Sydney Millionaires	CBSHL	35	*26	8	1	2100	85	*5	*2.43	....	....	....	....	....	4	3	1	0	240	13	0	*3.25	....	....	....	....
1940-41	Sydney Millionaires	CBSHL	40	*24	15	1	2400	125	3	*3.12	....	....	....	....	....	4	1	3	0	120	11	0	5.50	....	....	....	....
	Sydney Millionaires	Al-Cup	17	10	5	2	1040	53	1	3.06	....	....	....	....	....	....	....	....	....	....	....	....	....	....	....	....	....
1941-42	Montreal Pats	MCSHL	40	10	21	9	2400	139	2	3.48	....	....	....	....	....	....	....	....	....	....	....	....	....	....	....	....	....
	Chicago Black Hawks	**NHL**	**1**	**1**	**0**	**0**	**60**	**3**	**0**	**3.00**	**2.93**	....	....	....	....	....	....	....	....	....	....	....	....	....	....	....	....
1942-1945			MILITARY SERVICE																								
	NHL Totals		**1**	**1**	**0**	**0**	**60**	**3**	**0**	**3.00**	....	....	....	....	....	....	....	....	....	....	....	....	....	....	....	....	....

Loaned to **Chicago** by **Montreal** (Montreal Pats-MCSHL) to replace injured Sam LoPresti, February 5, 1942. (Chicago 4, Montreal 3).

• DION, Connie

G – R. 5'4", 140 lbs. b: St. Remi de Rinqwick, Que., 8/11/1918.

Season	Club	League	GP	W	L	T	Mins	GA	SO	Avg	AAvg	Eff	SA	S%	SAPG	GP	W	L	T	Mins	GA	SO	Avg	Eff	SA	S%	SAPG
1937-38	Verdun Jr. Maple Leafs	QJHL	12	....	....	....	720	22	*2	1.83	....	....	....	....	....	4	....	....	....	240	11	0	*2.75	....	....	....	....
	Verdun Maple Leafs	QSHL	1	1	0	0	60	2	0	2.00	....	....	....	....	....	....	....	....	....	....	....	....	....	....	....	....	....
	Verdun Jr. Maple Leafs	Mem-Cup	5	2	2	0	300	14	2	2.80	....	....	....	....	....	....	....	....	....	....	....	....	....	....	....	....	....
1938-39	Lachine Rapides	QPHL	38	....	....	....	2280	126	2	3.32	....	....	....	....	....	6	....	....	....	360	20	0	3.33	....	....	....	....
1939-40	Sherbrooke Red Raiders	QPHL	41	....	....	....	2460	130	*4	3.17	....	....	....	....	....	8	6	2	0	480	22	*1	*2.75	....	....	....	....
	Sherbrooke Red Raiders	Al-Cup	2	0	2	0	120	16	0	8.00	....	....	....	....	....	....	....	....	....	....	....	....	....	....	....	....	....
1940-41	Cornwall Flyers	QSHL	34	....	....	....	2040	122	1	3.68	....	....	....	....	....	4	....	....	....	240	14	0	3.50	....	....	....	....
1941-42	Cornwall Flyers	QSHL	37	20	14	3	2220	122	1	3.30	....	....	....	....	....	5	2	3	0	310	19	0	3.68	....	....	....	....
1942-43	Cornwall Flyers	QSHL	5	....	....	....	280	14	0	3.00	....	....	....	....	....	....	....	....	....	....	....	....	....	....	....	....	....
1943-44	**Detroit Red Wings**	**NHL**	**26**	**17**	**7**	**2**	**1560**	**80**	**1**	**3.08**	**2.25**	....	....	....	....	**5**	**1**	**4**	....	**300**	**17**	**0**	**3.40**	....	....	....	....
1944-45	**Detroit Red Wings**	**NHL**	**12**	**6**	**4**	**2**	**720**	**39**	**0**	**3.25**	**2.68**	....	....	....	....	....	....	....	....	....	....	....	....	....	....	....	....
	Indianapolis Capitols	AHL	39	14	19	6	2340	121	3	3.10	....	....	....	....	....	5	1	4	0	300	18	0	3.60	....	....	....	....
1945-46	St. Louis Flyers	AHL	8	1	6	1	480	40	0	5.00	....	....	....	....	....	....	....	....	....	....	....	....	....	....	....	....	....
	Buffalo Bisons	AHL	34	24	6	4	2040	84	1	2.47	....	....	....	....	....	12	*8	4	0	730	35	*1	*2.88	....	....	....	....
1946-47	Buffalo Bisons	AHL	61	33	17	11	3660	166	6	2.72	....	....	....	....	....	4	2	2	0	240	13	0	3.25	....	....	....	....
1947-48	Buffalo Bisons	AHL	43	26	15	2	2580	155	2	3.60	....	....	....	....	....	8	4	4	0	480	28	0	3.50	....	....	....	....
	Houston Huskies	USHL	7	4	3	0	420	30	0	4.28	....	....	....	....	....	....	....	....	....	....	....	....	....	....	....	....	....
1948-49	Buffalo Bisons	AHL	*68	33	27	8	*4080	213	4	3.13	....	....	....	....	....	....	....	....	....	....	....	....	....	....	....	....	....
	New York Rovers	QSHL	1	1	0	0	60	2	0	2.00	....	....	....	....	....	....	....	....	....	....	....	....	....	....	....	....	....
1949-50	Buffalo Bisons	AHL	34	15	15	4	2040	92	3	*2.71	....	....	....	....	....	2	0	2	0	120	11	0	5.50	....	....	....	....
	Louisville Blades	USHL	4	0	4	0	240	27	0	6.75	....	....	....	....	....	....	....	....	....	....	....	....	....	....	....	....	....
1950-51	Buffalo Bisons	AHL	63	35	24	4	3840	259	1	4.05	....	....	....	....	....	4	0	4	0	273	19	0	4.18	....	....	....	....
1951-52			DID NOT PLAY																								
1952-53	Sherbrooke Saints	QMHL	13	3	7	3	820	38	1	2.78	....	....	....	....	....	7	3	4	0	430	21	0	2.93	....	....	....	....
1953-54	Glace Bay Miners	MMHL	18	7	9	1	1079	85	0	4.73	....	....	....	....	....	....	....	....	....	....	....	....	....	....	....	....	....
	NHL Totals		**38**	**23**	**11**	**4**	**2280**	**119**	**1**	**3.13**	....	....	....	....	....	**5**	**1**	**4**	....	**300**	**17**	**0**	**3.40**	....	....	....	....

AHL Second All-Star Team (1945, 1946, 1950) • Won Harry "Hap" Holmes Memorial Award (fewest goals against - AHL) (1950)

Traded to **Washington** (AHL) by **Montreal** for cash, October 9, 1941. • Did not report to Washington (AHL), October, 1941. Signed as a free agent by **Detroit**, January 25, 1944. Traded to **St. Louis** (AHL) by **Detroit** for cash, August 24, 1945. Traded to **Buffalo** (AHL) by **St. Louis** (AHL) with John Horeck and John Baby Sr. for Hec Pozzo and cash, November 5, 1945.

• DION, Michel

Michel J. G – L. 5'10", 185 lbs. b: Granby, Que., 2/11/1954.

Season	Club	League	GP	W	L	T	Mins	GA	SO	Avg	AAvg	Eff	SA	S%	SAPG	GP	W	L	T	Mins	GA	SO	Avg	Eff	SA	S%	SAPG
1969-70	Montreal Jr. Canadiens	OHA-Jr.	8	....	....	....	430	39	0	5.44	....	....	....	....	....	....	....	....	....	....	....	....	....	....	....	....	....
1970-71			PLAYED PROFESSIONAL BASEBALL																								
1971-72			PLAYED PROFESSIONAL BASEBALL																								

			REGULAR SEASON													PLAYOFFS											
Season	Club	League	GP	W	L	T	Mins	GA	SO	Avg	AAvg	Eff	SA	S%	SAPG	GP	W	L	T	Mins	GA	SO	Avg	Eff	SA	S%	SAPG
1972-73	Granby Vics	QJHL	STATISTICS NOT AVAILABLE																								
	Montreal Red-White-Blue	QMJHL	8	....	....	....	479	39	0	4.88	....	....	....	....	....	....	....	....	....	....	....	....	....	....	....	....	....
1973-74	Montreal Red-White-Blue	QMJHL	31	....	....	....	1840	135	0	4.40	....	....	....	....	....	1	....	....	....	60	4	0	4.00	....	....	....	....
1974-75	Indianapolis Racers	WHA	1	0	1	0	59	4	0	4.07	....	....	....	....	....	....	....	....	....	....	....	....	....	....	....	....	....
	Mohawk Valley Comets	NAHL	28	10	12	2	1476	96	0	3.90	....	....	....	....	....	3	....	....	....	189	9	0	3.00	....	....	....	....
1975-76	Mohawk Valley Comets	NAHL	22	....	....	....	1295	83	0	3.84	....	....	....	....	....	....	....	....	....	....	....	....	....	....	....	....	....
	Indianapolis Racers	WHA	31	14	15	1	1860	85	0	*2.74	....	....	....	....	....	3	0	2	0	126	5	0	2.38	....	....	....	....
1976-77	Indianapolis Racers	WHA	42	17	19	3	2286	128	1	3.36	....	....	....	....	....	4	2	2	0	245	17	0	4.16	....	....	....	....
1977-78	Cincinnati Stingers	WHA	45	21	17	1	2356	140	*4	3.57	....	....	....	....	....	....	....	....	....	....	....	....	....	....	....	....	....
1978-79	Cincinnati Stingers	WHA	30	10	14	2	1681	93	0	3.32	....	....	....	....	....	....	....	....	....	....	....	....	....	....	....	....	....
1979-80	**Quebec Nordiques**	**NHL**	**50**	**15**	**25**	**6**	**2773**	**171**	**2**	**3.70**	**3.28**	....	....	....	....	....	....	....	....	....	....	....	....	....	....	....	....
1980-81	**Quebec Nordiques**	**NHL**	**12**	**0**	**8**	**3**	**688**	**61**	**0**	**5.32**	**4.31**	....	....	....	....	....	....	....	....	....	....	....	....	....	....	....	....
	Indianapolis Checkers	CHL	6	2	3	0	364	19	0	3.13	....	....	....	....	....	....	....	....	....	....	....	....	....	....	....	....	....
	Winnipeg Jets	**NHL**	**14**	**3**	**6**	**3**	**757**	**61**	**0**	**4.83**	**3.91**	....	....	....	....	....	....	....	....	....	....	....	....	....	....	....	....
1981-82	**Pittsburgh Penguins**	**NHL**	**62**	**25**	**24**	**12**	**3580**	**226**	**0**	**3.79**	**2.92**	....	....	....	....	**5**	**2**	**3**	....	**304**	**22**	**0**	**4.34**	....	....	....	....
1982-83	**Pittsburgh Penguins**	**NHL**	**49**	**12**	**30**	**4**	**2791**	**198**	**0**	**4.26**	**3.43**	**5.58**	**1511**	**.869**	**32.5**	....	....	....	....	....	....	....	....	....	....	....	....
1983-84	**Pittsburgh Penguins**	**NHL**	**30**	**2**	**19**	**4**	**1553**	**138**	**0**	**5.33**	**4.22**	**7.85**	**937**	**.853**	**36.2**	....	....	....	....	....	....	....	....	....	....	....	....
1984-85	**Pittsburgh Penguins**	**NHL**	**10**	**3**	**6**	**0**	**553**	**43**	**0**	**4.67**	**3.73**	**6.35**	**316**	**.864**	**34.3**	....	....	....	....	....	....	....	....	....	....	....	....
	Baltimore Skipjacks	AHL	21	10	6	2	1118	65	0	3.49	....	....	....	....	....	5	2	2	0	229	9	0	2.36	....	....	....	....
	NHL Totals		**227**	**60**	**118**	**32**	**12695**	**898**	**2**	**4.24**	....	....	....	....	....	**5**	**2**	**3**	....	**304**	**22**	**0**	**4.34**	....	....	....	....
	Other Major League Totals		149	62	66	7	8242	450	5	3.28	....	....	....	....	....	7	2	4	....	371	22	0	3.56	....	....	....	....

Won Ben Hatskin Trophy (WHA Top Goaltender) (1976) • Played in NHL All-Star Game (1982)

• Played professional baseball w/ Montreal Expos organization in 1971 and 1972. Selected by **Indianapolis** (WHA) in 1974 WHA Amateur Draft, May, 1974. Signed as a free agent by **Cincinnati** (WHA), October 12, 1977. Claimed by **Quebec** from **Cincinnati** (WHA) in WHA Dispersal Draft, June 9, 1979. Traded to **Winnipeg** by **Quebec** for cash, February 10, 1981. Signed as a free agent by **Pittsburgh**, June 30, 1981.

• DOLSON, Dolly

Clarence Edward G – L. 5'7", 160 lbs. b: Hespeler, Ont., 5/23/1897.

Season	Club	League	GP	W	L	T	Mins	GA	SO	Avg	AAvg	Eff	SA	S%	SAPG	GP	W	L	T	Mins	GA	SO	Avg	Eff	SA	S%	SAPG
1914-15	Galt Garrison	OHA-Jr.	6	3	3	0	360	18	0	3.00	....	....	....	....	....	....	....	....	....	....	....	....	....	....	....	....	....
1915-1918			MILITARY SERVICE																								
1918-19			DID NOT PLAY																								
1919-1923	Galt Intermediates	OHA-I	STATISTICS NOT AVAILABLE																								
1923-24	Stratford Indians	OHA-Sr.	12	*9	2	1	730	28	*2	*2.30	....	....	....	....	....	2	*2	0	0	120	3	*1	*1.50	....	....	....	....
	Stratford Indians	Al-Cup	2	1	1	0	120	4	0	2.00	....	....	....	....	....	....	....	....	....	....	....	....	....	....	....	....	....
1924-25	Stratford Indians	OHA-Sr.	20	12	8	0	1230	63	*2	3.07	....	....	....	....	....	2	1	1	0	120	6	1	3.00	....	....	....	....
1925-26	Stratford Indians	OHA-Sr.	20	6	13	1	1280	66	0	3.09	....	....	....	....	....	....	....	....	....	....	....	....	....	....	....	....	....
	Montreal CNR	MRTHL	1	1	0	0	60	1	0	1.00	....	....	....	....	....	1	*1	0	0	60	1	0	*1.00	....	....	....	....
1926-27	Stratford Nationals	Can-Pro	30	19	11	0	1835	76	2	2.49	....	....	....	....	....	2	0	2	0	120	4	0	2.00	....	....	....	....
1927-28	Stratford Nationals	Can-Pro	41	24	12	5	2520	51	*11	*1.21	....	....	....	....	....	5	*4	0	1	300	3	*2	*0.60	....	....	....	....
1928-29	**Detroit Cougars**	**NHL**	***44**	**19**	**16**	**9**	**2750**	**63**	**10**	**1.37**	**2.84**	....	....	....	....	**2**	**0**	**2**	**0**	**120**	**7**	**0**	**3.50**	....	....	....	....
1929-30	**Detroit Cougars**	**NHL**	**5**	**0**	**4**	**1**	**320**	**24**	**0**	**4.50**	**4.67**	....	....	....	....	....	....	....	....	....	....	....	....	....	....	....	....
	London Panthers	IHL	31	....	....	....	1860	60	5	1.94	....	....	....	....	....	2	0	2	0	120	4	0	2.00	....	....	....	....
1930-31	**Detroit Falcons**	**NHL**	***44**	**16**	**21**	**7**	**2750**	**105**	**6**	**2.29**	**2.90**	....	....	....	....	....	....	....	....	....	....	....	....	....	....	....	....
1931-32	Cleveland Indians	IHL	14	2	9	3	880	54	0	3.68	....	....	....	....	....	....	....	....	....	....	....	....	....	....	....	....	....
1932-33	Cleveland Indians	IHL	10	....	....	....	600	36	0	3.60	....	....	....	....	....	....	....	....	....	....	....	....	....	....	....	....	....
	NHL Totals		**93**	**35**	**41**	**17**	**5820**	**192**	**16**	**1.98**	....	....	....	....	....	**2**	**0**	**2**	**0**	**120**	**7**	**0**	**3.50**	....	....	....	....

Signed as a free agent by **Stratford** (Can-Pro), September 12, 1926. Claimed by **Detroit** from **Stratford** (Can-Pro) in Inter-League Draft, May 12, 1928.

• DOPSON, Rob

Robert James G – L. 6', 200 lbs. b: Smiths Falls, Ont., 8/21/1967.

Season	Club	League	GP	W	L	T	Mins	GA	SO	Avg	AAvg	Eff	SA	S%	SAPG	GP	W	L	T	Mins	GA	SO	Avg	Eff	SA	S%	SAPG
1982-83	Smiths Falls Settlers	OJHL-B	2	0	1	0	80	14	0	10.50	....	....	....	....	....	....	....	....	....	....	....	....	....	....	....	....	....
1983-84	Smiths Falls Settlers	OJHL-B	27	10	14	1	1590	157	0	5.92	....	....	....	....	....	....	....	....	....	....	....	....	....	....	....	....	....
1984-85	Newmarket Flyers	OJHL	32	17	12	5	1910	163	0	5.12	....	....	....	....	....	....	....	....	....	....	....	....	....	....	....	....	....
	Kitchener Rangers	OHL	2	1	1	0	100	8	0	4.80	....	....	....	....	....	....	....	....	....	....	....	....	....	....	....	....	....
1985-86	Nepean Raiders	OJHL	20	11	3	0	872	47	1	3.23	....	....	....	....	....	....	....	....	....	....	....	....	....	....	....	....	....
	Kitchener Rangers	OHL	8	5	2	0	403	32	0	4.76	....	....	....	....	....	....	....	....	....	....	....	....	....	....	....	....	....
1986-87	Smiths Falls Bears	OJHL	30	12	11	5	1640	98	1	3.59	....	....	....	....	....	....	....	....	....	....	....	....	....	....	....	....	....
1987-88	Sir Wilfred Laurier University	OUAA	6	....	....	....	336	23	0	4.12	....	....	....	....	....	....	....	....	....	....	....	....	....	....	....	....	....
1988-89	Sir Wilfred Laurier University	OUAA	23	....	....	....	1323	64	0	2.90	....	....	....	....	....	....	....	....	....	....	....	....	....	....	....	....	....
1989-90	Sir Wilfred Laurier University	OUAA	22	....	....	....	1319	57	0	2.59	....	....	....	....	....	....	....	....	....	....	....	....	....	....	....	....	....
1990-91	Muskegon Lumberjacks	IHL	24	10	10	0	1243	90	0	4.34	....	....	....	....	....	....	....	....	....	....	....	....	....	....	....	....	....
	Louisville IceHawks	ECHL	3	3	0	0	180	12	0	4.00	....	....	....	....	....	5	3	1	0	270	16	0	3.55	....	....	....	....
1991-92	Muskegon Lumberjacks	IHL	29	13	12	2	1655	90	*4	3.26	....	....	....	....	....	12	8	4	0	697	40	0	3.44	....	....	....	....
1992-93	Cleveland Lumberjacks	IHL	50	26	15	3	2825	167	1	3.55	....	....	....	....	....	4	0	4	0	203	20	0	5.91	....	....	....	....
1993-94	**Pittsburgh Penguins**	**NHL**	**2**	**0**	**0**	**0**	**45**	**3**	**0**	**4.00**	**3.84**	**5.22**	**23**	**.870**	**30.7**	....	....	....	....	....	....	....	....	....	....	....	....
	Cleveland Lumberjacks	IHL	32	9	10	8	1681	109	0	3.89	....	....	....	....	....	....	....	....	....	....	....	....	....	....	....	....	....
1994-95	Houston Aeros	IHL	41	17	16	2	2102	119	0	3.40	....	....	....	....	....	1	0	0	0	40	6	0	9.00	....	....	....	....
1995-96	Louisiana IceGators	ECHL	2	1	0	1	120	4	0	2.00	....	....	....	....	....	....	....	....	....	....	....	....	....	....	....	....	....
	Kansas City Blades	IHL	5	1	0	1	183	10	0	3.28	....	....	....	....	....	....	....	....	....	....	....	....	....	....	....	....	....
	Houston Aeros	IHL	33	9	13	2	1518	96	0	3.79	....	....	....	....	....	....	....	....	....	....	....	....	....	....	....	....	....
1996-97	Houston Aeros	IHL	12	5	4	1	637	36	0	3.39	....	....	....	....	....	....	....	....	....	....	....	....	....	....	....	....	....
1997-98	Ayr Scottish Eagles	BH-Cup	11	....	....	....	660	29	0	2.64	....	....	....	....	....	....	....	....	....	....	....	....	....	....	....	....	....
	Ayr Scottish Eagles	Britain	29	....	....	....	1742	70	0	2.42	....	....	....	....	....	9	....	....	....	567	19	0	2.01	....	....	....	....
1998-99	Nippon Paper Kushiro	Japan	33	....	....	....	1681	93	0	3.22	....	....	....	....	....	5	2	3	0	298	18	0	3.62	....	....	....	....
	Canada	Nat-Team	3	2	0	0	147	7	0	2.86	....	....	....	....	....	....	....	....	....	....	....	....	....	....	....	....	....
	Lake Charles Ice Pirates	WPHL	....	....	....	....	....	....	....	....	....	....	....	....	....	9	4	5	0	541	29	*1	3.22	....	....	....	....
99-2000	Nippon Paper Kushiro	Japan	25	....	....	....	1459	66	0	2.71	....	....	....	....	....	2	1	1	0	159	4	0	1.51	....	....	....	....
	NHL Totals		**2**	**0**	**0**	**0**	**45**	**3**	**0**	**4.00**	....	....	**23**	**.870**	**30.7**	....	....	....	....	....	....	....	....	....	....	....	....

Won Jack Kennedy Trophy (Outstanding Player in OUAA Championship Series) (1990) • OUAA Second All-Star Team (1990)

Signed as a free agent by **Pittsburgh**, July 6, 1991.

• DOWIE, Bruce

G – L. 5'10", 170 lbs. b: Oakville, Ont., 12/9/1962.

Season	Club	League	GP	W	L	T	Mins	GA	SO	Avg	AAvg	Eff	SA	S%	SAPG	GP	W	L	T	Mins	GA	SO	Avg	Eff	SA	S%	SAPG
1978-79	Oakville Midget Blades	OMHA	14	....	....	....	840	26	0	1.85	....	....	....	....	....	....	....	....	....	....	....	....	....	....	....	....	....
1979-80	Toronto Marlboros	OMJHL	60	31	24	3	3513	247	0	4.22	....	....	....	....	....	4	0	4	0	253	19	0	4.51	....	....	....	....
1980-81	Toronto Marlboros	OMJHL	57	28	26	0	3215	253	0	4.73	....	....	....	....	....	5	2	2	0	272	23	0	5.07	....	....	....	....
1981-82	Toronto Marlboros	OHL	37	16	17	0	2022	150	1	4.45	....	....	....	....	....	2	0	2	0	120	10	0	5.00	....	....	....	....
1982-83	Toronto Marlboros	OHL	30	19	8	3	1830	123	0	4.03	....	....	....	....	....	2	....	....	....	120	10	0	5.00	....	....	....	....
	St. Catharines Saints	AHL	8	2	3	1	424	35	0	4.95	....	....	....	....	....	....	....	....	....	....	....	....	....	....	....	....	....
1983-84	**Toronto Maple Leafs**	**NHL**	**2**	**0**	**1**	**0**	**72**	**4**	**0**	**3.33**	**2.62**	**3.10**	**43**	**.907**	**35.8**	....	....	....	....	....	....	....	....	....	....	....	....
	Muskegon Mohawks	IHL	25	....	....	....	1306	100	2	4.59	....	....	....	....	....	....	....	....	....	....	....	....	....	....	....	....	....
	St. Catharines Saints	AHL	9	2	2	1	410	41	0	6.00	....	....	....	....	....	....	....	....	....	....	....	....	....	....	....	....	....
1984-85	St. Catharines Saints	AHL	10	2	7	1	596	55	0	5.54	....	....	....	....	....	....	....	....	....	....	....	....	....	....	....	....	....
	Toledo Goaldiggers	IHL	5	2	1	2	310	20	0	3.87	....	....	....	....	....	....	....	....	....	....	....	....	....	....	....	....	....
1985-86	St. Catharines Saints	AHL	5	1	1	0	139	14	0	6.04	....	....	....	....	....	....	....	....	....	....	....	....	....	....	....	....	....
1986-87	Newmarket Saints	AHL	4	0	2	0	155	13	0	5.03	....	....	....	....	....	....	....	....	....	....	....	....	....	....	....	....	....
	Dundas Real McCoys	OHA-Sr.	15	9	5	0	853	55	0	3.87	....	....	....	....	....	....	....	....	....	....	....	....	....	....	....	....	....
	NHL Totals		**2**	**0**	**1**	**0**	**72**	**4**	**0**	**3.33**	....	....	**43**	**.907**	**35.8**	....	....	....	....	....	....	....	....	....	....	....	....

Signed as a free agent by **Toronto**, May 6, 1983.

• DRAPER, Tom Thomas Edward G – L. 5'11", 185 lbs. b: Outremont, Que., 11/20/1966. Winnipeg's 8th, 165th overall in 1985.

			REGULAR SEASON													PLAYOFFS											
Season	Club	League	GP	W	L	T	Mins	GA	SO	Avg	AAvg	Eff	SA	S%	SAPG	GP	W	L	T	Mins	GA	SO	Avg	Eff	SA	S%	SAPG
1981-82	Lac St-Louis Lions	QAAA	25	17	4	4	1498	85	0	3.40	....	....	....	....	....	....	....	....	....	....	....	....	....	....	....	....	....
1982-83	Lac St-Louis Lions	QAAA	28	15	8	5	1677	149	0	5.34	....	....	....	....	....	....	....	....	....	....	....	....	....	....	....	....	....
1983-84	University of Vermont	ECAC	20	8	12	0	1205	82	0	4.08	....	....	....	....	....	....	....	....	....	....	....	....	....	....	....	....	....
1984-85	University of Vermont	ECAC	24	5	17	0	1316	90	0	4.11	....	....	....	....	....	....	....	....	....	....	....	....	....	....	....	....	....
1985-86	University of Vermont	ECAC	29	15	12	1	1697	87	1	3.08	....	....	....	....	....	....	....	....	....	....	....	....	....	....	....	....	....
1986-87	University of Vermont	ECAC	29	16	13	0	1662	96	2	3.47	....	....	....	....	....	....	....	....	....	....	....	....	....	....	....	....	....
1987-88	Tappara Tampere	Finland	28	16	3	9	1619	87	0	3.22	....	....	....	....	....	10	....	....	....	600	25	2	2.50	....	....	....	....
1988-89	**Winnipeg Jets**	**NHL**	**2**	**1**	**1**	**0**	**120**	**12**	**0**	**6.00**	**5.00**	**10.91**	**66**	**.818**	**33.0**	....	....	....	....	....	....	....	....	....	....	....	....
	Moncton Hawks	AHL	*54	27	17	5	*2962	171	2	3.46	....	....	....	....	....	7	5	2	....	419	24	0	3.44	....	....	....	....
1989-90	**Winnipeg Jets**	**NHL**	**6**	**2**	**4**	**0**	**359**	**26**	**0**	**4.35**	**3.69**	**7.39**	**153**	**.830**	**25.6**	....	....	....	....	....	....	....	....	....	....	....	....
	Moncton Hawks	AHL	51	20	24	3	2844	167	1	3.52	....	....	....	....	....	....	....	....	....	....	....	....	....	....	....	....	....
1990-91	Moncton Hawks	AHL	30	15	13	2	1779	95	1	3.20	....	....	....	....	....	....	....	....	....	....	....	....	....	....	....	....	....
	Fort Wayne Komets	IHL	10	5	3	1	564	32	0	3.40	....	....	....	....	....	....	....	....	....	....	....	....	....	....	....	....	....
	Peoria Rivermen	IHL	10	6	3	1	584	36	0	3.70	....	....	....	....	....	4	2	1	....	214	10	0	2.80	....	....	....	....
1991-92	**Buffalo Sabres**	**NHL**	**26**	**10**	**9**	**5**	**1403**	**75**	**1**	**3.21**	**2.87**	**3.38**	**712**	**.895**	**30.4**	**7**	**3**	**4**	....	**433**	**19**	**1**	**2.63**	**2.49**	**201**	**.905**	**27.9**
	Rochester Americans	AHL	9	4	3	2	531	28	0	3.16	....	....	....	....	....	....	....	....	....	....	....	....	....	....	....	....	....
1992-93	**Buffalo Sabres**	**NHL**	**11**	**5**	**6**	**0**	**664**	**41**	**0**	**3.70**	**3.17**	**4.41**	**344**	**.881**	**31.1**	....	....	....	....	....	....	....	....	....	....	....	....
	Rochester Americans	AHL	5	3	2	0	303	22	0	4.36	....	....	....	....	....	....	....	....	....	....	....	....	....	....	....	....	....
1993-94	**New York Islanders**	**NHL**	**7**	**1**	**3**	**0**	**227**	**16**	**0**	**4.23**	**4.07**	**5.74**	**118**	**.864**	**31.2**	....	....	....	....	....	....	....	....	....	....	....	....
	Salt Lake Golden Eagles	IHL	35	7	23	3	1933	140	0	4.34	....	....	....	....	....	....	....	....	....	....	....	....	....	....	....	....	....
1994-95	Minnesota Moose	IHL	59	25	20	6	3063	187	1	3.66	....	....	....	....	....	2	0	2	....	118	10	0	5.07	....	....	....	....
1995-96	**Winnipeg Jets**	**NHL**	**1**	**0**	**0**	**0**	**34**	**3**	**0**	**5.29**	**5.26**	**11.34**	**14**	**.786**	**24.7**	....	....	....	....	....	....	....	....	....	....	....	....
	Milwaukee Admirals	IHL	31	14	12	3	1793	101	1	3.38	....	....	....	....	....	....	....	....	....	....	....	....	....	....	....	....	....
1996-97	Long Beach Ice Dogs	IHL	39	28	7	3	2267	87	2	2.30	....	....	....	....	....	*18	*13	5	....	*1096	41	*2	2.24	....	....	....	....
1997-98	Quebec Rafales	IHL	43	15	22	4	2418	131	2	3.25	....	....	....	....	....	....	....	....	....	....	....	....	....	....	....	....	....
	Cleveland Lumberjacks	IHL	9	4	2	2	497	20	0	2.41	....	....	....	....	....	10	5	5	....	582	32	0	3.30	....	....	....	....
1998-99	Rochester Americans	AHL	26	14	9	3	1568	60	0	2.30	....	....	....	....	....	2	0	0	....	86	4	0	2.79	....	....	....	....
99-2000	Lukko Rauma	Finland	*52	*27	17	7	*3143	116	6	2.21	....	....	....	....	....	4	1	3	....	273	7	1	*1.54	....	....	....	....
	NHL Totals		**53**	**19**	**23**	**5**	**2807**	**173**	**1**	**3.70**	....	....	**1407**	**.877**	**30.1**	**7**	**3**	**4**	....	**433**	**19**	**1**	**2.63**	....	**201**	**.905**	**27.9**

ECAC First All-Star Team (1986, 1987) • AHL Second All-Star Team (1989) • Shared Harry "Hap" Holmes Memorial Trophy (fewest goals against - AHL) with Martin Biron (1999)

Traded to **St. Louis** by **Winnipeg** for future considerations (Jim Vesey, May 24, 1991), February 28, 1991. Traded to **Winnipeg** by **St. Louis** for future considerations, May 24, 1991. Traded to **Buffalo** by **Winnipeg** for Buffalo's 7th round choice (Artur Oktyabrev) in 1992 Entry Draft, June 22, 1991. Traded to **NY Islanders** by **Buffalo** for NY Islanders' 7th round choice (Steve Plouffe) in 1994 Entry Draft, September 30, 1993. Signed as a free agent by **Winnipeg**, December 14, 1995.

• DRYDEN, Dave David Murray G – L. 6'1", 186 lbs. b: Hamilton, Ont., 9/5/1941.

			REGULAR SEASON													PLAYOFFS											
Season	Club	League	GP	W	L	T	Mins	GA	SO	Avg	AAvg	Eff	SA	S%	SAPG	GP	W	L	T	Mins	GA	SO	Avg	Eff	SA	S%	SAPG
1958-59	Aurora Bears	OHA-B	48	....	....	....	2880	170	*3	3.52	....	....	....	....	....	....	....	....	....	....	....	....	....	....	....	....	....
1959-60	St. Michael's Majors	OHA-Jr.	12	5	6	1	720	39	1	3.25	....	....	....	....	....	1	0	0	0	20	2	0	6.00	....	....	....	....
1960-61	St. Michael's Majors	OHA-Jr.	18	....	....	....	1080	66	1	3.67	....	....	....	....	....	....	....	....	....	....	....	....	....	....	....	....	....
1961-62	Toronto Marlboros	MTJHL	32	17	8	6	1880	99	*3	3.16	....	....	....	....	....	12	7	5	0	720	49	0	4.08	....	....	....	....
	New York Rangers	**NHL**	**1**	**0**	**1**	**0**	**40**	**3**	**0**	**4.50**	**4.61**	....	....	....	....	....	....	....	....	....	....	....	....	....	....	....	....
	Rochester Americans	AHL	1	0	0	0	20	2	0	6.00	....	....	....	....	....	....	....	....	....	....	....	....	....	....	....	....	....
1962-63	Galt Terriers	OHA-Sr.	40	....	....	....	2400	174	2	4.35	....	....	....	....	....	4	....	....	....	240	27	0	6.75	....	....	....	....
1963-64	Galt Terriers	OHA-Sr.	39	....	....	....	2340	141	0	*3.62	....	....	....	....	....	11	6	5	0	660	36	*1	3.27	....	....	....	....
1964-65	Galt Hornets	OHA-Sr.	35	....	....	....	2040	106	1	3.10	....	....	....	....	....	1	0	1	0	60	6	0	6.00	....	....	....	....
	Buffalo Bisons	AHL	4	4	0	0	240	6	1	1.50	....	....	....	....	....	....	....	....	....	....	....	....	....	....	....	....	....
1965-66	**Chicago Black Hawks**	**NHL**	**11**	**3**	**4**	**1**	**453**	**23**	**0**	**3.05**	**3.08**	....	....	....	....	**1**	**0**	**0**	....	**13**	**0**	**0**	**0.00**	....	....	....	....
1966-67	St. Louis Braves	CPHL	48	17	17	14	2880	158	2	3.29	....	....	....	....	....	....	....	....	....	....	....	....	....	....	....	....	....
1967-68	**Chicago Black Hawks**	**NHL**	**27**	**7**	**8**	**5**	**1268**	**69**	**1**	**3.26**	**3.63**	....	....	....	....	....	....	....	....	....	....	....	....	....	....	....	....
1968-69	**Chicago Black Hawks**	**NHL**	**30**	**11**	**11**	**2**	**1479**	**79**	**3**	**3.20**	**3.32**	....	....	....	....	....	....	....	....	....	....	....	....	....	....	....	....
1969-70	Dallas Black Hawks	CHL	2	0	2	0	120	6	0	3.00	....	....	....	....	....	....	....	....	....	....	....	....	....	....	....	....	....
1970-71	Salt Lake Golden Eagles	WHL	8	1	6	0	364	34	0	5.60	....	....	....	....	....	....	....	....	....	....	....	....	....	....	....	....	....
	Buffalo Sabres	**NHL**	**10**	**3**	**3**	**0**	**409**	**23**	**1**	**3.37**	**3.34**	....	....	....	....	....	....	....	....	....	....	....	....	....	....	....	....
1971-72	**Buffalo Sabres**	**NHL**	**20**	**3**	**9**	**5**	**1026**	**68**	**0**	**3.98**	**4.04**	....	....	....	....	....	....	....	....	....	....	....	....	....	....	....	....
1972-73	**Buffalo Sabres**	**NHL**	**37**	**14**	**13**	**7**	**2018**	**89**	**3**	**2.65**	**2.49**	....	....	....	....	**2**	**0**	**2**	....	**120**	**9**	**0**	**4.50**	....	....	....	....
1973-74	**Buffalo Sabres**	**NHL**	**53**	**23**	**20**	**8**	**2987**	**148**	**1**	**2.97**	**2.86**	....	....	....	....	....	....	....	....	....	....	....	....	....	....	....	....
1974-75	Chicago Cougars	WHA	45	18	26	1	2728	176	1	3.87	....	....	....	....	....	....	....	....	....	....	....	....	....	....	....	....	....
1975-76	Edmonton Oilers	WHA	62	22	34	5	3567	235	1	3.95	....	....	....	....	....	3	0	3	0	180	15	0	5.00	....	....	....	....
1976-77	Edmonton Oilers	WHA	24	10	13	0	1416	77	1	3.26	....	....	....	....	....	....	....	....	....	....	....	....	....	....	....	....	....
1977-78	Edmonton Oilers	WHA	48	21	23	2	2578	150	2	3.49	....	....	....	....	....	2	0	1	0	91	6	0	3.96	....	....	....	....
1978-79	Edmonton Oilers	WHA	*63	*41	17	2	*3531	170	*3	*2.89	....	....	....	....	....	*13	6	7	0	*687	42	0	3.67	....	....	....	....
1979-80	**Edmonton Oilers**	**NHL**	**14**	**2**	**7**	**3**	**744**	**53**	**0**	**4.27**	**3.78**	....	....	....	....	....	....	....	....	....	....	....	....	....	....	....	....
	Edmonton Oilers	**NHL**	DID NOT PLAY – ASSISTANT COACH																								
1980-1982	Peterborough Petes	OMJHL	DID NOT PLAY – COACHING																								
	NHL Totals		**203**	**66**	**76**	**31**	**10424**	**555**	**9**	**3.19**	....	....	....	....	....	**3**	**0**	**2**	....	**133**	**9**	**0**	**4.06**	....	....	....	....
	Other Major League Totals		242	112	113	10	13820	808	8	3.51	....	....	....	....	....	18	6	11	....	958	63	0	3.95	....	....	....	....

• Brother of Ken • OHA-B First All-Star Team (1959) • OHA-Sr. Second All-Star Team (1963) • OHA-Sr. First All-Star Team (1964, 1965) • CPHL Second All-Star Team (1967) • WHA First All-Star Team (1979) • Won Ben Hatskin Trophy (WHA Top Goaltender) (1979) • Won Gary Davidson Trophy (WHA MVP) (1979) • Played in NHL All-Star Game (1974)

Loaned to **NY Rangers** by **Toronto** (Toronto-MTJHL) to replace injured Gump Worsley in 2nd period, February 3, 1962. (Toronto 4, NY Rangers 1). Signed as a free agent by **Chicago** (Buffalo-AHL), March 12, 1965. • Suspended by **Chicago** (Dallas-CHL) after refusing assignment to minors, October, 1969. Traded to **Pittsburgh** by **Chicago** for cash, June 10, 1970. Traded to **Buffalo** by **Pittsburgh** for cash, October 9, 1970. Selected by **New England** (WHA) in 1972 WHA General Player Draft, February 12, 1972. WHA rights traded to **Chicago** (WHA) by **New England** (WHA) for future considerations, June, 1974. Claimed by **Edmonton** (WHA) from **Chicago** (WHA) in WHA Dispersal Draft, May 19, 1975. Traded to **New England** (WHA) by **Edmonton** (WHA) with Jack Carlson, Steve Carlson, Dave Keon and John McKenzie for future considerations (Dave Debol, June, 1977), Dan Arndt and cash, January, 1977. • Suspended by **New England** (WHA) for refusing to report to WHA club, January, 1977. Traded to **Edmonton** (WHA) by **New England** (WHA) with Brett Callighen and future considerations for Jean-Louis Levasseur, September, 1977. Reclaimed by **Buffalo** from **Edmonton** prior to Expansion Draft, June 9, 1979. Claimed as a priority selection by **Edmonton**, June 9, 1979.

• DRYDEN, Ken Kenneth Wayne G – L. 6'4", 205 lbs. b: Hamilton, Ont., 8/8/1947. Boston's 3rd, 14th overall in 1964. **HHOF**

			REGULAR SEASON													PLAYOFFS											
Season	Club	League	GP	W	L	T	Mins	GA	SO	Avg	AAvg	Eff	SA	S%	SAPG	GP	W	L	T	Mins	GA	SO	Avg	Eff	SA	S%	SAPG
1963-64	Humber Valley	MTHL	STATISTICS NOT AVAILABLE																								
1964-65	Etobicoke Indians	OHA-B	STATISTICS NOT AVAILABLE																								
1965-66	Cornell University	ECAC	DID NOT PLAY – FRESHMAN																								
1966-67	Cornell University	ECAC	27	26	0	1	1646	40	4	1.46	....	....	....	....	....	....	....	....	....	....	....	....	....	....	....	....	....
1967-68	Cornell University	ECAC	29	25	2	0	1620	41	6	1.52	....	....	....	....	....	....	....	....	....	....	....	....	....	....	....	....	....
1968-69	Cornell University	ECAC	27	25	2	0	1578	47	3	1.79	....	....	....	....	....	....	....	....	....	....	....	....	....	....	....	....	....
	Canada	WEC-A	2	1	1	0	120	4	1	2.00	....	....	....	....	....	....	....	....	....	....	....	....	....	....	....	....	....
1969-70	Canada	Nat-Team	STATISTICS NOT AVAILABLE																								
1970-71	Montreal Voyageurs	AHL	33	16	7	8	1899	84	3	2.68	....	....	....	....	....	....	....	....	....	....	....	....	....	....	....	....	....
♦	**Montreal Canadiens**	**NHL**	**6**	**6**	**0**	**0**	**327**	**9**	**0**	**1.65**	**1.63**	....	....	....	....	***20**	***12**	**8**	....	***1221**	**61**	**0**	**3.00**	....	....	....	....
1971-72	**Montreal Canadiens**	**NHL**	***64**	***39**	**8**	**15**	***3800**	**142**	**8**	**2.24**	**2.23**	....	....	....	....	**6**	**2**	**4**	....	**360**	**17**	**0**	**2.83**	....	....	....	....
1972-73	Team Canada	Summit-72	4	2	2	0	240	19	0	4.75	....	....	....	....	....	....	....	....	....	....	....	....	....	....	....	....	....
♦	**Montreal Canadiens**	**NHL**	**54**	***33**	**7**	**13**	**3165**	**119**	***6**	***2.26**	**2.10**	....	....	....	....	***17**	***12**	**5**	....	***1039**	**50**	**1**	**2.89**	....	....	....	....
1973-74			DID NOT PLAY																								
1974-75	**Montreal Canadiens**	**NHL**	**56**	**30**	**9**	**16**	**3320**	**149**	**4**	**2.69**	**2.41**	....	....	....	....	**11**	**6**	**5**	....	**688**	**29**	**2**	**2.53**	....	....	....	....
1975-76♦	**Montreal Canadiens**	**NHL**	**62**	***42**	**10**	**8**	**3580**	**121**	***8**	***2.03**	**1.81**	....	....	....	....	***13**	***12**	**1**	....	***780**	**25**	**1**	***1.92**	....	....	....	....

			REGULAR SEASON													PLAYOFFS											
Season	Club	League	GP	W	L	T	Mins	GA	SO	Avg	AAvg	Eff	SA	S%	SAPG	GP	W	L	T	Mins	GA	SO	Avg	Eff	SA	S%	SAPG
1976-77♦	**Montreal Canadiens**	**NHL**	**56**	***41**	**6**	**8**	**3275**	**117**	***10**	**2.14**	**1.96**	....	....	....	....	***14**	***12**	**2**	....	**849**	**22**	***4**	***1.55**	....	....	....	....
1977-78♦	**Montreal Canadiens**	**NHL**	**52**	**37**	**7**	**7**	**3071**	**105**	**5**	***2.05**	**1.90**	....	....	....	....	***15**	***12**	**3**	....	***919**	**29**	***2**	***1.89**	....	....	....	....
1978-79♦	**Montreal Canadiens**	**NHL**	**47**	**30**	**10**	**7**	**2814**	**108**	***5**	***2.30**	**2.01**	....	....	....	....	**16**	***12**	**4**	....	**990**	**41**	**0**	**2.48**	....	....	....	....
	NHL All-Stars	Chal-Cup	2	1	1	0	120	7	0	3.50	....	....	....	....	....	....	....	....	....	....	....	....	....	....	....	....	....
	NHL Totals		**397**	**258**	**57**	**74**	**23352**	**870**	**46**	**2.24**	....	....	....	....	....	**112**	**80**	**32**	....	**6846**	**274**	**10**	**2.40**	....	....	....	....

• Brother of Dave • ECAC First All-Star Team (1967, 1968, 1969) • NCAA East First All-American Team (1967, 1968, 1969) • NCAA Championship All-Tournament Team (1967) • Won Conn Smythe Trophy (1971) • NHL Second All-Star Team (1972) • Won Calder Memorial Trophy (1972) • NHL First All-Star Team (1973, 1976, 1977, 1978, 1979) • Won Vezina Trophy (1973, 1976) • Shared Vezina Trophy with Michel Larocque (1977, 1978, 1979) • Played in NHL All-Star Game (1972, 1975, 1976, 1977, 1978)

Rights traded to **Montreal** by **Boston** with Alex Campbell for Guy Allen and Paul Reid, June, 1964. Promoted to **Montreal** from **Montreal Voyageurs** (AHL), March, 1971. • Sat out entire 1973-74 season after failing to come to contract terms with Montreal.

• DUFFUS, Parris

G – L. 6'2", 192 lbs. b: Denver, CO, 1/27/1970. St. Louis' 6th, 180th overall in 1990.

Season	Club	League	GP	W	L	T	Mins	GA	SO	Avg	AAvg	Eff	SA	S%	SAPG	GP	W	L	T	Mins	GA	SO	Avg	Eff	SA	S%	SAPG
1989-90	Melfort Mustangs	SJHL	51	....	....	....	2828	226	....	4.79	....	....	....	....	....	....	....	....	....	....	....	....	....	....	....	....	....
1990-91	Cornell University	ECAC	4	0	0	0	37	3	0	4.86	....	....	....	....	....	....	....	....	....	....	....	....	....	....	....	....	....
1991-92	Cornell University	ECAC	28	14	11	3	1677	74	1	2.65	....	....	....	....	....	....	....	....	....	....	....	....	....	....	....	....	....
1992-93	Hampton Roads Admirals	ECHL	4	3	1	0	245	13	0	3.18	....	....	....	....	....	....	....	....	....	....	....	....	....	....	....	....	....
	Peoria Rivermen	IHL	37	16	15	4	2149	142	0	3.96	....	....	....	....	....	1	0	1	....	59	5	0	5.08	....	....	....	....
1993-94	Peoria Rivermen	IHL	36	19	10	3	1845	141	0	4.58	....	....	....	....	....	2	0	1	....	92	6	0	3.88	....	....	....	....
1994-95	Peoria Rivermen	IHL	29	17	7	3	1581	71	*3	2.69	....	....	....	....	....	7	4	2	....	409	17	0	2.49	....	....	....	....
1995-96	Minnesota Moose	IHL	35	10	17	2	1812	100	1	3.31	....	....	....	....	....	....	....	....	....	....	....	....	....	....	....	....	....
	United States	WC-A	7	4	3	0	425	18	1	2.54	....	....	....	....	....	....	....	....	....	....	....	....	....	....	....	....	....
1996-97	**Phoenix Coyotes**	**NHL**	**1**	**0**	**0**	**0**	**29**	**1**	**0**	**2.07**	**2.23**	**2.59**	**8**	**.875**	**16.6**	....	....	....	....	....	....	....	....	....	....	....	....
	Las Vegas Thunder	IHL	58	28	19	6	3266	176	3	3.23	....	....	....	....	....	3	0	3	....	175	8	0	2.73	....	....	....	....
1997-98	HPK Hameenlinna	Finland	31	11	13	0	1436	79	0	3.30	....	....	....	....	....	....	....	....	....	....	....	....	....	....	....	....	....
	Cincinnati Cyclones	IHL	17	10	5	0	916	47	0	3.08	....	....	....	....	....	5	1	3	....	252	12	0	2.85	....	....	....	....
1998-99	Berlin Capitals	Germany	38	....	....	....	2256	126	1	3.35	....	....	....	....	....	....	....	....	....	....	....	....	....	....	....	....	....
	United States	WC-Q	3	3	0	0	130	1	1	0.46	....	....	....	....	....	....	....	....	....	....	....	....	....	....	....	....	....
	Jokerit Helsinki	Finland	15	7	8	0	894	34	*5	2.28	....	....	....	....	....	3	0	3	....	167	13	0	4.67	....	....	....	....
	United States	WC-A	5	....	....	....	258	7	....	1.63	....	....	....	....	....	....	....	....	....	....	....	....	....	....	....	....	....
99-2000	HIFK Helsinki	Finland	29	11	10	7	1767	72	1	2.44	....	....	....	....	....	7	4	3	....	433	24	0	3.33	....	....	....	....
	HIFK Helsinki	EuroHL	3	....	....	....	130	7	0	3.24	....	....	....	....	....	....	....	....	....	....	....	....	....	....	....	....	....
	Fort Wayne Komets	UHL	3	3	0	0	180	10	0	3.33	....	....	....	....	....	....	....	....	....	....	....	....	....	....	....	....	....
	NHL Totals		**1**	**0**	**0**	**0**	**29**	**1**	**0**	**2.07**	....	....	**8**	**.875**	**16.6**	....	....	....	....	....	....	....	....	....	....	....	....

ECAC Second All-Star Team (1992) • NCAA East First All-American Team (1992)

Signed as a free agent by **Winnipeg**, August 4, 1995. Transferred to **Phoenix** after **Winnipeg** franchise relocated, July 1, 1996.

• DUMAS, Michel

Michel Joseph G – L. 5'9", 180 lbs. b: St. Antoine-de-Pontbriand, Que, 7/8/1949.

Season	Club	League	GP	W	L	T	Mins	GA	SO	Avg	AAvg	Eff	SA	S%	SAPG	GP	W	L	T	Mins	GA	SO	Avg	Eff	SA	S%	SAPG
1966-67	Thetford Mines Canadiens	QJHL	10	....	....	....	600	25	0	2.50	....	....	....	....	....	....	....	....	....	....	....	....	....	....	....	....	....
	Thetford Mines Canadiens	Mem-Cup	6	4	1	0	336	20	0	3.57	....	....	....	....	....	....	....	....	....	....	....	....	....	....	....	....	....
1967-68	Thetford Mines Canadiens	QJHL	....	....	....	....	....	....	....	....	....	....	....	....	....	7	3	4	0	440	44	0	6.00	....	....	....	....
1968-69	Thetford Mines Canadiens	QJHL	STATISTICS NOT AVAILABLE																								
1969-70	Oklahoma City Blazers	CHL	2	0	1	0	80	9	0	6.75	....	....	....	....	....	....	....	....	....	....	....	....	....	....	....	....	....
	Dayton Gems	IHL	54	....	....	....	3000	180	3	3.60	....	....	....	....	....	13	8	5	0	746	36	0	2.90	....	....	....	....
1970-71	Dayton Gems	IHL	49	....	....	....	2811	167	1	3.56	....	....	....	....	....	5	....	....	....	300	19	0	3.80	....	....	....	....
1971-72	Dallas Black Hawks	CHL	*44	*30	10	4	2415	124	*3	*3.08	....	....	....	....	....	2	1	1	0	111	9	0	4.86	....	....	....	....
1972-73	Dallas Black Hawks	CHL	37	....	....	....	2160	108	1	3.00	....	....	....	....	....	4	....	....	....	200	16	0	4.80	....	....	....	....
1973-74	Dallas Black Hawks	CHL	*67	*26	23	16	*3896	194	*3	2.98	....	....	....	....	....	*10	*8	2	0	*580	15	*1	*1.55	....	....	....	....
1974-75	**Chicago Black Hawks**	**NHL**	**3**	**2**	**0**	**0**	**121**	**7**	**0**	**3.47**	**3.14**	....	....	....	....	**1**	**0**	**0**	....	**19**	**1**	**0**	**3.16**	....	....	....	....
	Dallas Black Hawks	CHL	52	26	20	6	3093	160	*4	3.10	....	....	....	....	....	....	....	....	....	....	....	....	....	....	....	....	....
1975-76	**Chicago Black Hawks**	**NHL**	DID NOT PLAY – SPARE GOALTENDER																								
1976-77	**Chicago Black Hawks**	**NHL**	**5**	**0**	**1**	**2**	**241**	**17**	**0**	**4.23**	**3.94**	....	....	....	....	....	....	....	....	....	....	....	....	....	....	....	....
	NHL Totals		**8**	**2**	**1**	**2**	**362**	**24**	**0**	**3.98**	....	....	....	....	....	**1**	**0**	**0**	....	**19**	**1**	**0**	**3.16**	....	....	....	....

CHL Second All-Star Team (1972, 1974) • Won Terry Sawchuk Trophy (fewest goals against - CHL) (1972)

• Regular season totals for **Thetford Mines** (QJHL) during 1967-68 season are unavailable. Signed as a free agent by **Chicago**, October 7, 1971. • On active roster for entire 1975-76 season but did not play. • Suffered career-ending eye injury in game vs. Colorado, December 26, 1976.

• DUNHAM, Mike

Michael G – L. 6'3", 200 lbs. b: Johnson City, NY, 6/1/1972. New Jersey's 4th, 53rd overall in 1990.

Season	Club	League	GP	W	L	T	Mins	GA	SO	Avg	AAvg	Eff	SA	S%	SAPG	GP	W	L	T	Mins	GA	SO	Avg	Eff	SA	S%	SAPG
1987-88	The Canterbury School	Hi-School	29	....	....	....	1740	69	4	2.37	....	....	....	....	....	....	....	....	....	....	....	....	....	....	....	....	....
1988-89	The Canterbury School	Hi-School	25	....	....	....	1500	63	2	2.52	....	....	....	....	....	....	....	....	....	....	....	....	....	....	....	....	....
1989-90	The Canterbury School	Hi-School	32	....	....	....	1558	68	3	1.96	....	....	....	....	....	....	....	....	....	....	....	....	....	....	....	....	....
1990-91	University of Maine	H-East	23	14	5	2	1275	63	0	*2.96	....	....	....	....	....	....	....	....	....	....	....	....	....	....	....	....	....
	United States	WJC-A	3	2	1	0	180	11	0	3.67	....	....	....	....	....	....	....	....	....	....	....	....	....	....	....	....	....
1991-92	University of Maine	H-East	7	6	0	0	382	14	1	2.20	....	....	....	....	....	....	....	....	....	....	....	....	....	....	....	....	....
	United States	WJC-A	6	5	0	1	360	14	....	2.33	....	....	....	....	....	....	....	....	....	....	....	....	....	....	....	....	....
	United States	Nat-Team	3	0	1	1	157	10	0	3.82	....	....	....	....	....	....	....	....	....	....	....	....	....	....	....	....	....
	United States	Olympics	DID NOT PLAY – SPARE GOALTENDER																								
	United States	WC-A	3	0	1	0	107	7	....	3.92	....	....	....	....	....	....	....	....	....	....	....	....	....	....	....	....	....
1992-93	University of Maine	H-East	25	*21	1	1	1429	63	0	2.65	....	....	....	....	....	....	....	....	....	....	....	....	....	....	....	....	....
	United States	WC-A	1	1	0	0	60	1	0	1.00	....	....	....	....	....	....	....	....	....	....	....	....	....	....	....	....	....
1993-94	United States	Nat-Team	33	22	9	2	1983	125	2	3.78	....	....	....	....	....	....	....	....	....	....	....	....	....	....	....	....	....
	United States	Olympics	3	0	1	2	180	15	0	5.00	....	....	....	....	....	....	....	....	....	....	....	....	....	....	....	....	....
	Albany River Rats	AHL	5	2	2	1	304	26	0	5.12	....	....	....	....	....	....	....	....	....	....	....	....	....	....	....	....	....
1994-95	Albany River Rats	AHL	35	20	7	8	2120	99	1	2.80	....	....	....	....	....	7	6	1	....	419	20	1	2.86	....	....	....	....
1995-96	Albany River Rats	AHL	44	30	10	2	2592	109	1	2.52	....	....	....	....	....	3	1	2	....	182	5	1	1.65	....	....	....	....
1996-97	**New Jersey Devils**	**NHL**	**26**	**8**	**7**	**1**	**1013**	**43**	**2**	**2.55**	**2.74**	**2.40**	**456**	**.906**	**27.0**	....	....	....	....	....	....	....	....	....	....	....	....
	Albany River Rats	AHL	3	1	1	1	184	12	0	3.91	....	....	....	....	....	....	....	....	....	....	....	....	....	....	....	....	....
1997-98	**New Jersey Devils**	**NHL**	**15**	**5**	**5**	**3**	**773**	**29**	**1**	**2.25**	**2.68**	**1.97**	**332**	**.913**	**25.8**	....	....	....	....	....	....	....	....	....	....	....	....
	United States	WC-A	2	0	1	0	40	4	0	6.00	....	....	....	....	....	....	....	....	....	....	....	....	....	....	....	....	....
1998-99	**Nashville Predators**	**NHL**	**44**	**16**	**23**	**3**	**2472**	**127**	**1**	**3.08**	**3.68**	**2.82**	**1387**	**.908**	**33.7**	....	....	....	....	....	....	....	....	....	....	....	....
99-2000	**Nashville Predators**	**NHL**	**52**	**19**	**27**	**6**	**3077**	**146**	**0**	**2.85**	**3.26**	**2.63**	**1584**	**.908**	**30.9**	....	....	....	....	....	....	....	....	....	....	....	....
	Milwaukee Admirals	IHL	1	1	0	0	60	1	0	1.00	....	....	....	....	....	....	....	....	....	....	....	....	....	....	....	....	....
	NHL Totals		**137**	**48**	**62**	**13**	**7335**	**345**	**4**	**2.82**	....	....	**3759**	**.908**	**30.7**	....	....	....	....	....	....	....	....	....	....	....	....

WJC-A All-Star Team (1992) • Named Best Goaltender at WJC-A (1992) • Hockey East First All-Star Team (1993) • NCAA East First All-American Team (1993) • Shared Harry "Hap" Holmes Memorial Trophy (fewest goals against - AHL) with Corey Schwab (1995) • Shared Jack A. Butterfield Trophy (Playoff MVP - AHL) with Corey Schwab (1995) • AHL Second All-Star Team (1996) • Shared William M. Jennings Trophy with Martin Brodeur (1997)

Claimed by **Nashville** from **New Jersey** in Expansion Draft, June 26, 1998.

• DUPUIS, Bob

Robert A. G – L. 5'11", 167 lbs. b: North Bay, Ont., 8/26/1952.

Season	Club	League	GP	W	L	T	Mins	GA	SO	Avg	AAvg	Eff	SA	S%	SAPG	GP	W	L	T	Mins	GA	SO	Avg	Eff	SA	S%	SAPG
1969-70	North Bay Trappers	NOJHA	30	....	....	....	1786	134	0	5.16	....	....	....	....	....	....	....	....	....	....	....	....	....	....	....	....	....
1970-71	North Bay Trappers	NOJHA	STATISTICS NOT AVAILABLE																								
1971-72	North Bay Trappers	NOJHA	46	....	....	....	2745	227	1	4.96	....	....	....	....	....	....	....	....	....	....	....	....	....	....	....	....	....
1972-73	Cape Cod Cubs	EHL	14	....	....	....	840	102	0	4.79	....	....	....	....	....	....	....	....	....	....	....	....	....	....	....	....	....
1973-74	Macon Whoopees	SHL	19	....	....	....	842	79	1	5.63	....	....	....	....	....	....	....	....	....	....	....	....	....	....	....	....	....
1974-75	Cambridge Hornets	OHA-Sr.	27	....	....	....	1620	114	1	4.22	....	....	....	....	....	....	....	....	....	....	....	....	....	....	....	....	....
1975-76	Cambridge Hornets	OHA-Sr.	21	....	....	....	1260	81	1	3.83	....	....	....	....	....	....	....	....	....	....	....	....	....	....	....	....	....
1976-77	Cambridge Hornets	OHA-Sr.	21	....	....	....	1260	81	*3	3.62	....	....	....	....	....	....	....	....	....	....	....	....	....	....	....	....	....
1977-78	Cambridge Hornets	OHA-Sr.	20	....	....	....	1200	77	*1	3.91	....	....	....	....	....	....	....	....	....	....	....	....	....	....	....	....	....

			REGULAR SEASON													PLAYOFFS											
Season	Club	League	GP	W	L	T	Mins	GA	SO	Avg	AAvg	Eff	SA	S%	SAPG	GP	W	L	T	Mins	GA	SO	Avg	Eff	SA	S%	SAPG
1978-79	Barrie Flyers	OlHA	16	....	....	....	960	82	0	5.13	....	....	....	....	....	....	....	....	....	....	....	....	....	....	....	....	....
1979-80	Canada	Nat-Team	STATISTICS NOT AVAILABLE																								
	Canada	Olympics	3	1	2	0	122	7	0	3.44	....	....	....	....	....	....	....	....	....	....	....	....	....	....	....	....	....
	Edmonton Oilers	**NHL**	**1**	**0**	**1**	**0**	**60**	**4**	**0**	**4.00**	**3.54**	....	....	....	....	....	....	....	....	....	....	....	....	....	....	....	....
	Houston Apollos	CHL	4	1	1	0	123	13	0	6.34	....	....	....	....	....	....	....	....	....	....	....	....	....	....	....	....	....
1980-81	Milwaukee Admirals	IHL	17	....	....	....	959	78	0	4.88	....	....	....	....	....	....	....	....	....	....	....	....	....	....	....	....	....
	Hampton Aces	EHL	15	....	....	....	716	72	0	6.03	....	....	....	....	....	....	....	....	....	....	....	....	....	....	....	....	....
	NHL Totals		**1**	**0**	**1**	**0**	**60**	**4**	**0**	**4.00**	....	....	....	....	....	....	....	....	....	....	....	....	....	....	....	....	....

Signed as a free agent by **Edmonton**, March, 1980.

• DURNAN, Bill

William Ronald G – R. 6', 190 lbs. b: Toronto, Ont., 1/22/1916 d: 10/31/1972. **HHOF**

Season	Club	League	GP	W	L	T	Mins	GA	SO	Avg	AAvg	Eff	SA	S%	SAPG	GP	W	L	T	Mins	GA	SO	Avg	Eff	SA	S%	SAPG
1931-32	North Toronto Juniors	TJrHL	8	....	....	....	480	17	1	2.12	....	....	....	....	....	4	....	....	....	240	10	1	2.50	....	....	....	....
1932-33	Sudbury Wolves	NOJHA	6	....	....	....	360	6	2	1.00	....	....	....	....	....	2	....	....	....	120	4	0	2.00	....	....	....	....
1933-34	Toronto Torontos	TIHL	11	....	....	....	660	21	4	1.91	....	....	....	....	....	1	0	1	0	60	5	0	5.00	....	....	....	....
	Toronto British Consols	TMHL	15	*12	2	1	910	31	*1	*2.04	....	....	....	....	....	5	0	2	3	350	21	0	3.60	....	....	....	....
1934-35	Toronto All-Stars	TIHL	2	....	....	....	120	9	0	4.50	....	....	....	....	....	....	....	....	....	....	....	....	....	....	....	....	....
	Toronto McColl	TMHL	15	....	....	....	900	62	0	4.13	....	....	....	....	....	....	....	....	....	....	....	....	....	....	....	....	....
1935-36	Toronto Dominions	TMHL	1	0	1	0	60	6	0	6.00	....	....	....	....	....	....	....	....	....	....	....	....	....	....	....	....	....
1936-37	Kirkland Lake Blue Devils	NOHA	4	4	0	0	240	5	0	1.25	....	....	....	....	....	4	1	0	3	240	8	1	2.00	....	....	....	....
1937-38	Kirkland Lake Blue Devils	NOHA	11	*8	1	1	610	27	1	2.66	....	....	....	....	....	2	*2	0	0	120	2	*1	*1.00	....	....	....	....
	Kirkland Lake Blue Devils	Al-Cup	2	0	2	0	120	11	0	5.50	....	....	....	....	....	....	....	....	....	....	....	....	....	....	....	....	....
1938-39	Kirkland Lake Blue Devils	NOHA	7	*7	0	0	420	7	*3	*1.00	....	....	....	....	....	2	*2	0	0	120	3	*1	*1.50	....	....	....	....
	Kirkland Lake Blue Devils	Al-Cup	5	3	2	0	299	12	2	2.41	....	....	....	....	....	....	....	....	....	....	....	....	....	....	....	....	....
1939-40	Kirkland Lake Blue Devils	X-Games	6	....	....	....	360	12	1	2.00	....	....	....	....	....	....	....	....	....	....	....	1	....	....	....	....	....
	Kirkland Lake Blue Devils	Al-Cup	17	14	1	2	1040	35	1	2.02	....	....	....	....	....	....	....	....	....	....	....	....	....	....	....	....	....
1940-41	Montreal Royals	QSHL	34	....	....	....	2000	100	1	3.00	....	....	....	....	....	8	8	0	0	480	24	*1	3.00	....	....	....	....
	Montreal Royals	Al-Cup	14	8	5	1	850	49	1	3.46	....	....	....	....	....	....	....	....	....	....	....	....	....	....	....	....	....
1941-42	Montreal Royals	QSHL	39	....	....	....	2340	143	0	3.67	....	....	....	....	....	....	....	....	....	....	....	....	....	....	....	....	....
1942-43	Montreal Royals	QSHL	31	....	....	....	1860	130	0	4.19	....	....	....	....	....	4	....	....	....	240	11	0	2.75	....	....	....	....
1943-44♦	**Montreal Canadiens**	**NHL**	***50**	***38**	**5**	**7**	***3000**	**109**	**2**	***2.18**	**1.49**	....	....	....	....	***9**	***8**	**1**	....	***549**	**14**	***1**	***1.53**	....	....	....	....
1944-45	**Montreal Canadiens**	**NHL**	***50**	***38**	**8**	**4**	***3000**	**121**	**1**	***2.42**	**1.88**	....	....	....	....	**6**	**2**	**4**	....	**373**	**15**	**0**	**2.41**	....	....	....	....
1945-46♦	**Montreal Canadiens**	**NHL**	**40**	***24**	**11**	**5**	**2400**	**104**	***4**	***2.60**	**2.29**	....	....	....	....	**9**	***8**	**1**	....	**581**	**20**	**0**	***2.07**	....	....	....	....
1946-47	**Montreal Canadiens**	**NHL**	***60**	***34**	**16**	**10**	***3600**	**138**	**4**	***2.30**	**2.10**	....	....	....	....	***11**	**6**	**5**	....	***720**	**23**	***1**	***1.92**	....	....	....	....
1947-48	**Montreal Canadiens**	**NHL**	**59**	**20**	**28**	**10**	**3505**	**162**	**5**	**2.77**	**2.85**	....	....	....	....	....	....	....	....	....	....	....	....	....	....	....	....
1948-49	**Montreal Canadiens**	**NHL**	***60**	**28**	**23**	**9**	***3600**	**126**	***10**	***2.10**	**2.25**	....	....	....	....	**7**	**3**	**4**	....	**468**	**17**	**0**	**2.18**	....	....	....	....
1949-50	**Montreal Canadiens**	**NHL**	**64**	**26**	**21**	**17**	**3840**	**141**	**8**	***2.20**	**2.37**	....	....	....	....	**3**	**0**	**3**	....	**180**	**10**	**0**	**3.33**	....	....	....	....
1950-51	Ottawa Senators	QMHL	DID NOT PLAY – COACHING																								
	NHL Totals		**383**	**208**	**112**	**62**	**22945**	**901**	**34**	**2.36**	....	....	....	....	....	**45**	**27**	**18**	....	**2871**	**99**	**2**	**2.07**	....	....	....	....

NHL First All-Star Team (1944, 1945, 1946, 1947, 1949, 1950) • Won Vezina Trophy (1944, 1945, 1946, 1947, 1949, 1950) • Played in NHL All-Star Game (1947, 1948, 1949)

Signed as a free agent by **Montreal**, October 30, 1943. • Named Head Coach of **Ottawa** (QMHL), September 13, 1950.

• DYCK, Ed

Edwin Paul G – L. 5'11", 160 lbs. b: Warman, Sask., 10/29/1950. Vancouver's 3rd, 30th overall in 1970.

Season	Club	League	GP	W	L	T	Mins	GA	SO	Avg	AAvg	Eff	SA	S%	SAPG	GP	W	L	T	Mins	GA	SO	Avg	Eff	SA	S%	SAPG
1966-67	Swift Current Broncos	X-Games	1	0	0	0	40	7	0	10.50	....	....	....	....	....	....	....	....	....	....	....	....	....	....	....	....	....
1967-68	Estevan Bruins	WCJHL	4	....	....	....	240	12	0	3.00	....	....	....	....	....	2	2	0	0	120	5	0	2.50	....	....	....	....
1968-69	Estevan-Calgary Centennials	WCJHL	36	....	....	....	2111	120	1	3.41	....	....	....	....	....	....	....	....	....	....	....	....	....	....	....	....	....
1969-70	Calgary Centennials	WCJHL	*60	....	....	....	3599	193	3	3.22	....	....	....	....	....	16	7	7	2	960	45	*1	*2.81	....	....	....	....
1970-71	Calgary Centennials	WCJHL	66	....	....	....	4069	172	4	*2.53	....	....	....	....	....	11	5	4	2	641	29	0	2.71	....	....	....	....
1971-72	**Vancouver Canucks**	**NHL**	**12**	**1**	**6**	**2**	**573**	**35**	**0**	**3.66**	**3.71**	....	....	....	....	....	....	....	....	....	....	....	....	....	....	....	....
	Rochester Americans	AHL	10	4	3	2	554	43	1	4.66	....	....	....	....	....	....	....	....	....	....	....	....	....	....	....	....	....
	Seattle Totems	WHL	6	1	5	0	360	31	0	5.17	....	....	....	....	....	....	....	....	....	....	....	....	....	....	....	....	....
1972-73	**Vancouver Canucks**	**NHL**	**25**	**5**	**17**	**1**	**1297**	**98**	**1**	**4.53**	**4.30**	....	....	....	....	....	....	....	....	....	....	....	....	....	....	....	....
	Seattle Totems	WHL	13	3	6	3	617	50	0	4.86	....	....	....	....	....	....	....	....	....	....	....	....	....	....	....	....	....
1973-74	**Vancouver Canucks**	**NHL**	**12**	**2**	**5**	**2**	**583**	**45**	**0**	**4.63**	**4.49**	....	....	....	....	....	....	....	....	....	....	....	....	....	....	....	....
	Seattle Totems	WHL	4	2	1	1	173	10	1	3.47	....	....	....	....	....	....	....	....	....	....	....	....	....	....	....	....	....
1974-75	Indianapolis Racers	WHA	32	3	21	3	1692	123	0	4.36	....	....	....	....	....	....	....	....	....	....	....	....	....	....	....	....	....
1975-76	HC Boden	Sweden-2	STATISTICS NOT AVAILABLE																								
	NHL Totals		**49**	**8**	**28**	**5**	**2453**	**178**	**1**	**4.35**	....	....	....	....	....	....	....	....	....	....	....	....	....	....	....	....	....
	Other Major League Totals		32	3	21	3	1692	123	0	4.36	....	....	....	....	....	....	....	....	....	....	....	....	....	....	....	....	....

WCJHL Second All-Star Team (1970) • WCJHL First All-Star Team (1971)

Selected by **Calgary-Cleveland** (WHA) in 1972 WHA General Player Draft, February 12, 1972. WHA rights traded to **Indianapolis** (WHA) by **Cleveland** (WHA) for future considerations, April, 1974. Loaned to **Boden** (Sweden) by **Indianapolis** (WHA) for 1975-76 season as compensation for Indianapolis' signing of free agent Leif Holmqvist, June, 1974.

• EDWARDS, Don

Donald Laurie "Dart" G – L. 5'9", 160 lbs. b: Hamilton, Ont., 9/28/1955. Buffalo's 6th, 89th overall in 1975.

Season	Club	League	GP	W	L	T	Mins	GA	SO	Avg	AAvg	Eff	SA	S%	SAPG	GP	W	L	T	Mins	GA	SO	Avg	Eff	SA	S%	SAPG
1973-74	Kitchener Rangers	OMJHL	35	....	....	....	2089	95	*3	*2.73	....	....	....	....	....	....	....	....	....	....	....	....	....	....	....	....	....
1974-75	Kitchener Rangers	OMJHL	55	....	....	....	3294	258	1	4.70	....	....	....	....	....	....	....	....	....	....	....	....	....	....	....	....	....
1975-76	Hershey Bears	AHL	39	23	12	2	2253	128	3	3.41	....	....	....	....	....	5	1	3	0	293	18	0	3.68	....	....	....	....
1976-77	Hershey Bears	AHL	47	26	15	6	2797	136	*5	2.91	....	....	....	....	....	....	....	....	....	....	....	....	....	....	....	....	....
	Buffalo Sabres	**NHL**	**25**	**16**	**7**	**2**	**1480**	**62**	**2**	**2.51**	**2.32**	....	....	....	....	**5**	**2**	**3**	....	**300**	**15**	**0**	**3.00**	....	....	....	....
1977-78	**Buffalo Sabres**	**NHL**	***72**	***38**	**16**	**17**	***4209**	**185**	**5**	**2.64**	**2.45**	....	....	....	....	**8**	**3**	**5**	....	**482**	**22**	**0**	**2.74**	....	....	....	....
1978-79	**Buffalo Sabres**	**NHL**	**54**	**26**	**18**	**9**	**3160**	**159**	**2**	**3.02**	**2.66**	....	....	....	....	....	....	....	....	....	....	....	....	....	....	....	....
1979-80	**Buffalo Sabres**	**NHL**	**49**	**27**	**9**	**12**	**2920**	**125**	**2**	**2.57**	**2.25**	....	....	....	....	**6**	**3**	**3**	....	**360**	**17**	**1**	**2.83**	....	....	....	....
1980-81	**Buffalo Sabres**	**NHL**	**45**	**23**	**10**	**12**	**2700**	**133**	***3**	**2.96**	**2.38**	....	....	....	....	**8**	**4**	**4**	....	**503**	**28**	**0**	**3.34**	....	....	....	....
1981-82	Canada	Can-Cup	1	1	0	0	60	3	0	3.00	....	....	....	....	....	....	....	....	....	....	....	....	....	....	....	....	....
	Buffalo Sabres	**NHL**	**62**	**26**	**23**	**9**	**3500**	**205**	**0**	**3.51**	**2.70**	....	....	....	....	**4**	**1**	**3**	....	**214**	**16**	**0**	**4.49**	....	....	....	....
1982-83	**Calgary Flames**	**NHL**	**39**	**16**	**15**	**6**	**2209**	**148**	**1**	**4.02**	**3.23**	**4.74**	**1255**	**.882**	**34.1**	**5**	**1**	**2**	....	**226**	**22**	**0**	**5.84**	....	....	....	....
1983-84	**Calgary Flames**	**NHL**	**41**	**13**	**19**	**5**	**2303**	**157**	**0**	**4.09**	**3.22**	**5.28**	**1217**	**.871**	**31.7**	**6**	**2**	**1**	....	**217**	**12**	**0**	**3.32**	**3.00**	**133**	**.910**	**36.8**
1984-85	**Calgary Flames**	**NHL**	**34**	**11**	**15**	**2**	**1691**	**115**	**1**	**4.08**	**3.26**	**5.47**	**858**	**.866**	**30.4**	....	....	....	....	....	....	....	....	....	....	....	....
1985-86	**Toronto Maple Leafs**	**NHL**	**38**	**12**	**23**	**0**	**2009**	**160**	**0**	**4.78**	**3.75**	**6.71**	**1140**	**.860**	**34.0**	....	....	....	....	....	....	....	....	....	....	....	....
1986-87	Brantford Mott's Clamatos	OHA-Sr.	17	14	1	0	966	52	0	3.42	....	....	....	....	....	....	....	....	....	....	....	....	....	....	....	....	....
1987-88	Nova Scotia Oilers	AHL	3	....	....	....	180	18	0	6.00	....	....	....	....	....	....	....	....	....	....	....	....	....	....	....	....	....
	NHL Totals		**459**	**208**	**155**	**74**	**26181**	**1449**	**16**	**3.32**	....	....	....	....	....	**42**	**16**	**21**	....	**2302**	**132**	**1**	**3.44**	....	....	....	....

OMJHL First All-Star Team (1974, 1975) • AHL Second All-Star Team (1976) • NHL Second All-Star Team (1978, 1980) • Shared Vezina Trophy with Bob Sauve (1980) • Played in NHL All-Star Game (1980, 1982)

Traded to **Calgary** by **Buffalo** with Richie Dunn, Buffalo's 2nd round choice (Rich Kromm) in 1982 Entry Draft and 1st round choice (Dan Quinn) in 1983 Entry Draft for Calgary's 1st (Paul Cyr) and 2nd (Jens Johansson) round choices in 1982 Entry Draft and 1st (Normand Lacombe) and 2nd (John Tucker) round choices in 1987 Entry Draft, May 29, 1982. Traded to **Toronto** by **Calgary** for Toronto's 4th round choice (Tim Harris) in 1987 Entry Draft, May 29, 1985.

• EDWARDS, Gary

Gary William "Suitcase" G – L. 5'9", 165 lbs. b: Toronto, Ont., 10/5/1947. St. Louis' 1st, 6th overall in 1968.

Season	Club	League	GP	W	L	T	Mins	GA	SO	Avg	AAvg	Eff	SA	S%	SAPG	GP	W	L	T	Mins	GA	SO	Avg	Eff	SA	S%	SAPG
1965-66	Toronto Westvairs	OHA-B	STATISTICS NOT AVAILABLE																								
1966-67	Toronto Westvairs	OHA-B	STATISTICS NOT AVAILABLE																								
	Toronto Marlboros	OHA-Jr.	8	....	....	....	480	37	0	4.62	....	....	....	....	....	....	....	....	....	....	....	....	....	....	....	....	....
1967-68	Toronto Marlboros	OHA-Jr.	38	....	....	....	2250	120	2	3.20	....	....	....	....	....	5	....	....	....	290	18	0	3.72	....	....	....	....
1968-69	**St. Louis Blues**	**NHL**	**1**	**0**	**0**	**0**	**4**	**0**	**0**	**0.00**	**0.00**	....	....	....	....	....	....	....	....	....	....	....	....	....	....	....	....
	Kansas City Blues	CHL	32	....	....	....	1760	92	*4	3.00	....	....	....	....	....	4	1	3	0	240	18	0	4.50	....	....	....	....
1969-70	**St. Louis Blues**	**NHL**	**1**	**0**	**1**	**0**	**60**	**4**	**0**	**4.00**	**4.24**	....	....	....	....	....	....	....	....	....	....	....	....	....	....	....	....
	Kansas City Blues	CHL	34	11	17	6	2040	115	2	3.38	....	....	....	....	....	....	....	....	....	....	....	....	....	....	....	....	....
	San Diego Gulls	WHL	3	2	0	1	180	3	1	1.00	....	....	....	....	....	....	....	....	....	....	....	....	....	....	....	....	....

			REGULAR SEASON													PLAYOFFS											
Season	**Club**	**League**	**GP**	**W**	**L**	**T**	**Mins**	**GA**	**SO**	**Avg**	**AAvg**	**Eff**	**SA**	**S%**	**SAPG**	**GP**	**W**	**L**	**T**	**Mins**	**GA**	**SO**	**Avg**	**Eff**	**SA**	**S%**	**SAPG**
1970-71	San Diego Gulls	WHL	4	4	0	0	240	12	0	3.00	....	....	....	....	....	....	....	....	....	....	....	....	....	....	....	....	....
	Kansas City Blues	CHL	35	....	....	....	1980	85	2	2.58	....	....	....	....	....	....	....	....	....	....	....	....	....	....	....	....	....
1971-72	**Los Angeles Kings**	**NHL**	**44**	**13**	**23**	**5**	**2503**	**150**	**2**	**3.60**	**3.67**	....	....	....	....	....	....	....	....	....	....	....	....	....	....	....	....
1972-73	**Los Angeles Kings**	**NHL**	**27**	**9**	**16**	**1**	**1560**	**94**	**1**	**3.62**	**3.42**	....	....	....	....	....	....	....	....	....	....	....	....	....	....	....	....
1973-74	**Los Angeles Kings**	**NHL**	**18**	**5**	**7**	**2**	**929**	**50**	**1**	**3.23**	**3.12**	....	....	....	....	**1**	**1**	**0**	....	**60**	**1**	**0**	**1.00**	....	....	....	....
1974-75	**Los Angeles Kings**	**NHL**	**27**	**15**	**3**	**8**	**1561**	**61**	**3**	**2.34**	**2.10**	....	....	....	....	....	....	....	....	....	....	....	....	....	....	....	....
1975-76	**Los Angeles Kings**	**NHL**	**29**	**12**	**13**	**4**	**1740**	**103**	**0**	**3.55**	**3.22**	....	....	....	....	**2**	**1**	**1**	....	**120**	**9**	**0**	**4.50**	....	....	....	....
1976-77	**Los Angeles Kings**	**NHL**	**10**	**0**	**6**	**2**	**501**	**39**	**0**	**4.67**	**4.35**	....	....	....	....	....	....	....	....	....	....	....	....	....	....	....	....
	Cleveland Barons	**NHL**	**17**	**4**	**10**	**3**	**999**	**68**	**2**	**4.08**	**3.80**	....	....	....	....	....	....	....	....	....	....	....	....	....	....	....	....
1977-78	**Cleveland Barons**	**NHL**	**30**	**6**	**18**	**5**	**1700**	**128**	**0**	**4.52**	**4.27**	....	....	....	....	....	....	....	....	....	....	....	....	....	....	....	....
1978-79	**Minnesota North Stars**	**NHL**	**25**	**6**	**11**	**5**	**1337**	**83**	**0**	**3.72**	**3.29**	....	....	....	....	....	....	....	....	....	....	....	....	....	....	....	....
1979-80	**Minnesota North Stars**	**NHL**	**26**	**9**	**7**	**10**	**1539**	**82**	**0**	**3.20**	**2.83**	....	....	....	....	**7**	**3**	**3**	....	**337**	**22**	**0**	**3.92**	....	....	....	....
1980-81	Minnesota North Stars	DN-Cup	2	2	0	0	115	4	1	2.07	....	....	....	....	....	....	....	....	....	....	....	....	....	....	....	....	....
	Edmonton Oilers	**NHL**	**15**	**5**	**3**	**4**	**729**	**44**	**0**	**3.62**	**2.93**	....	....	....	....	**1**	**0**	**0**	....	**20**	**2**	**0**	**6.00**	....	....	....	....
1981-82	**St. Louis Blues**	**NHL**	**10**	**1**	**5**	**1**	**480**	**45**	**1**	**5.63**	**4.36**	....	....	....	....	....	....	....	....	....	....	....	....	....	....	....	....
	Pittsburgh Penguins	**NHL**	**6**	**3**	**2**	**1**	**360**	**22**	**1**	**3.67**	**2.83**	....	....	....	....	....	....	....	....	....	....	....	....	....	....	....	....
	NHL Totals		**286**	**88**	**125**	**51**	**16002**	**973**	**11**	**3.65**	....	....	....	....	....	**11**	**5**	**4**	....	**537**	**34**	**0**	**3.80**	....	....	....	....

Loaned to **San Diego** (WHL) by **St. Louis** (Kansas City-CHL) for the loan of Bob Champoux, November, 1969. Claimed by **Buffalo** from **St. Louis** in Expansion Draft, June 10, 1970. Loaned to **St. Louis** (Kansas City-CHL) by **Buffalo** for cash, October, 1970. Claimed by **LA Kings** from **Buffalo** in Intra-League Draft, June 8, 1971. Traded to **Cleveland** by **LA Kings** with Juha Widing for Gary Simmons and Jim Moxey, January 22, 1977. Placed on **Minnesota** reserve list after Cleveland-Minnesota Dispersal Draft, June 15, 1978. Traded to **Edmonton** by **Minnesota** for future considerations, February 2, 1981. Claimed by **St. Louis** from **Edmonton** in Waiver Draft, October 8, 1981. Claimed on waivers by **Pittsburgh** from **St. Louis**, February 14, 1982.

• EDWARDS, Marv

Marvin Wayne G – L. 5'8", 155 lbs. b: St. Catharines, Ont., 8/15/1935.

Season	Club	League	GP	W	L	T	Mins	GA	SO	Avg	AAvg	Eff	SA	S%	SAPG	GP	W	L	T	Mins	GA	SO	Avg	Eff	SA	S%	SAPG
1950-51	St. Catharines Teepees	OHA-Jr.	1	0	1	0	60	11	0	11.00	....	....	....	....	....	....	....	....	....	....	....	....	....	....	....	....	....
1951-52	St. Catharines Teepees	OHA-Jr.	48	....	....	....	2880	198	2	4.13	....	....	....	....	....	13	7	6	0	780	47	0	3.62	....	....	....	....
1952-53	St. Catharines Teepees	OHA-Jr.	36	....	....	....	2160	149	2	4.14	....	....	....	....	....	1	....	....	....	60	5	0	5.00	....	....	....	....
	Barrie Flyers	Mem-Cup	10	*8	2	0	600	37	0	3.70	....	....	....	....	....	....	....	....	....	....	....	....	....	....	....	....	....
1953-54	St. Catharines Teepees	OHA-Jr.	49	....	....	....	2940	182	*4	3.71	....	....	....	....	....	15	....	....	....	900	55	*1	3.67	....	....	....	....
	St. Catharines Teepees	Mem-Cup	11	*8	2	1	670	28	0	2.51	....	....	....	....	....	....	....	....	....	....	....	....	....	....	....	....	....
1954-55	St. Catharines Teepees	OHA-Jr.	47	*32	13	2	2820	162	1	3.45	....	....	....	....	....	6	....	....	....	360	20	0	3.33	....	....	....	....
	Buffalo Bisons	AHL	2	1	1	0	120	6	0	3.00	....	....	....	....	....	....	....	....	....	....	....	....	....	....	....	....	....
1955-56	Windsor-Chatham Maroons	OHA-Sr.	34	....	....	....	2040	158	0	4.72	....	....	....	....	....	11	8	3	0	660	38	0	3.45	....	....	....	....
	Chatham Maroons	Al-Cup	17	8	7	2	1040	55	0	3.17	....	....	....	....	....	....	....	....	....	....	....	....	....	....	....	....	....
1956-57	Chatham Maroons	OHA-Sr.	52	28	22	2	3120	183	5	3.52	....	....	....	....	....	6	2	4	0	360	14	0	*2.33	....	....	....	....
	Calgary Stampeders	WHL	2	0	2	0	119	5	0	2.52	....	....	....	....	....	....	....	....	....	....	....	....	....	....	....	....	....
	Buffalo Bisons	AHL	1	0	1	0	60	4	0	4.00	....	....	....	....	....	....	....	....	....	....	....	....	....	....	....	....	....
1957-58	Windsor Bulldogs	NOHA	57	25	30	2	3420	213	1	3.73	....	....	....	....	....	13	7	4	2	780	42	1	3.23	....	....	....	....
	Buffalo Bisons	AHL	2	0	2	0	120	10	0	5.00	....	....	....	....	....	....	....	....	....	....	....	....	....	....	....	....	....
1958-59	North Bay Trappers	NOHA	35	....	....	....	2100	180	0	5.14	....	....	....	....	....	....	....	....	....	....	....	....	....	....	....	....	....
	Canada	WEC-A	2	2	0	0	120	0	2	0.00	....	....	....	....	....	....	....	....	....	....	....	....	....	....	....	....	....
1959-60	Milwaukee Falcons	IHL	64	24	39	1	3840	296	3	4.62	....	....	....	....	....	....	....	....	....	....	....	....	....	....	....	....	....
	Minneapolis Millers	IHL	....	....	....	....	....	....	....	....	....	....	....	....	....	6	2	4	0	360	17	1	2.83	....	....	....	....
1960-61	Johnstown Jets	EHL	64	40	22	2	3840	215	4	3.36	....	....	....	....	....	12	*10	2	0	720	18	*4	*1.50	....	....	....	....
	New Haven Blades	EHL	1	....	....	....	60	3	0	3.00	....	....	....	....	....	....	....	....	....	....	....	....	....	....	....	....	....
1961-62	Johnstown Jets	EHL	55	....	....	....	3300	193	3	3.51	....	....	....	....	....	....	....	....	....	....	....	....	....	....	....	....	....
1962-63	Knoxville Knights	EHL	1	1	0	0	60	1	0	1.00	....	....	....	....	....	....	....	....	....	....	....	....	....	....	....	....	....
	Nashville Dixie Flyers	EHL	68	16	48	4	4080	262	1	3.85	....	....	....	....	....	3	0	3	0	184	13	0	4.24	....	....	....	....
1963-64	Nashville Dixie Flyers	EHL	70	37	29	4	4200	230	5	3.29	....	....	....	....	....	3	0	3	0	180	14	0	4.67	....	....	....	....
	Clinton Comets	EHL	....	....	....	....	....	....	....	....	....	....	....	....	....	3	2	1	0	180	9	0	3.00	....	....	....	....
1964-65	Nashville Dixie Flyers	EHL	71	*54	17	0	4260	193	7	2.72	....	....	....	....	....	13	8	5	0	780	34	1	2.62	....	....	....	....
1965-66	Nashville Dixie Flyers	EHL	71	42	22	7	4260	174	*7	*2.45	....	....	....	....	....	11	*11	0	0	660	13	*2	*1.18	....	....	....	....
1966-67	Nashville Dixie Flyers	EHL	72	*51	19	2	4320	168	*6	*2.33	....	....	....	....	....	14	*11	3	0	840	29	*1	2.07	....	....	....	....
1967-68	Portland Buckaroos	WHL	40	21	16	2	2366	93	4	*2.36	....	....	....	....	....	5	1	4	0	328	16	1	2.93	....	....	....	....
1968-69	**Pittsburgh Penguins**	**NHL**	**1**	**0**	**1**	**0**	**60**	**3**	**0**	**3.00**	**3.10**	....	....	....	....	....	....	....	....	....	....	....	....	....	....	....	....
	Amarillo Wranglers	CHL	39	....	....	....	2190	116	1	3.18	....	....	....	....	....	....	....	....	....	....	....	....	....	....	....	....	....
	Baltimore Clippers	AHL	14	6	7	1	839	42	2	3.00	....	....	....	....	....	4	1	3	0	200	13	0	3.90	....	....	....	....
1969-70	**Toronto Maple Leafs**	**NHL**	**25**	**10**	**9**	**4**	**1420**	**77**	**1**	**3.25**	**3.46**	....	....	....	....	....	....	....	....	....	....	....	....	....	....	....	....
1970-71	Phoenix Roadrunners	WHL	53	27	17	6	2949	157	2	3.19	....	....	....	....	....	7	3	4	0	410	24	0	3.51	....	....	....	....
1971-72	Phoenix Roadrunners	WHL	35	19	11	3	1891	103	1	3.26	....	....	....	....	....	3	1	2	0	186	11	0	3.55	....	....	....	....
1972-73	**California Golden Seals**	**NHL**	**21**	**4**	**14**	**2**	**1207**	**87**	**1**	**4.32**	**4.10**	....	....	....	....	....	....	....	....	....	....	....	....	....	....	....	....
1973-74	**California Golden Seals**	**NHL**	**14**	**1**	**10**	**1**	**780**	**51**	**0**	**3.92**	**3.80**	....	....	....	....	....	....	....	....	....	....	....	....	....	....	....	....
	NHL Totals		**61**	**15**	**34**	**7**	**3467**	**218**	**2**	**3.77**	....	....	....	....	....	....	....	....	....	....	....	....	....	....	....	....	....

Won George L. Davis Jr. Trophy (fewest goals against - EHL) (1961, 1966, 1967) • EHL First All-Star Team (1964) • EHL South First All-Star Team (1965, 1966, 1967) • Shared WHL Leading Goaltender Award with Jim McLeod (1968) • CHL First All-Star Team (1969)

Traded to **Windsor** (NOHA) by **Chatham** (NOHA) for Don Head, October, 1957. Traded to **North Bay** (NOHA) by **Windsor** (NOHA) for John Utendale, December, 1958. Signed as a free agent by **Pittsburgh**, September, 1967. Claimed by **Toronto** from **Pittsburgh** in Intra-League Draft, June 11, 1969. Claimed by **California** (Salt Lake-WHL) from **Toronto** in Reverse Draft, June 8, 1972.

• EDWARDS, Roy

Allen Roy G – R. 5'8", 165 lbs. b: Seneca Township, Ont., 3/12/1937 d: 8/16/1999.

Season	Club	League	GP	W	L	T	Mins	GA	SO	Avg	AAvg	Eff	SA	S%	SAPG	GP	W	L	T	Mins	GA	SO	Avg	Eff	SA	S%	SAPG
1955-56	St. Catharines Teepees	OHA-Jr.	41	26	12	3	2460	160	1	3.90	....	....	....	....	....	6	....	....	....	360	26	0	4.33	....	....	....	....
1956-57	St. Catharines Teepees	OHA-Jr.	49	24	23	2	2940	179	3	3.65	....	....	....	....	....	14	....	....	....	840	55	1	3.93	....	....	....	....
1957-58	Whitby Dunlops	EOHL	7	....	....	....	420	21	0	3.00	....	....	....	....	....	....	....	....	....	....	....	....	....	....	....	....	....
	Fort Wayne Komets	IHL	25	....	....	....	1500	84	0	3.36	....	....	....	....	....	....	....	....	....	....	....	....	....	....	....	....	....
	Canada	WEC-A	7	*7	0	0	420	6	*3	0.86	....	....	....	....	....	....	....	....	....	....	....	....	....	....	....	....	....
1958-59	Calgary Stampeders	WHL	63	*42	20	1	3780	192	2	3.05	....	....	....	....	....	8	4	4	0	480	27	0	3.37	....	....	....	....
1959-60	Buffalo Bisons	AHL	*72	33	35	4	*4360	267	4	3.67	....	....	....	....	....	....	....	....	....	....	....	....	....	....	....	....	....
1960-61	Buffalo Bisons	AHL	30	12	16	1	1800	128	1	4.27	....	....	....	....	....	....	....	....	....	....	....	....	....	....	....	....	....
	Sault Ste. Marie Thunderbirds	EPHL	37	16	15	6	2220	119	3	3.22	....	....	....	....	....	12	7	5	0	739	34	0	2.76	....	....	....	....
1961-62	Sault Ste. Marie Thunderbirds	EPHL	36	4	26	6	2160	157	1	4.36	....	....	....	....	....	....	....	....	....	....	....	....	....	....	....	....	....
	Pittsburgh Hornets	AHL	10	1	8	1	600	52	0	5.20	....	....	....	....	....	....	....	....	....	....	....	....	....	....	....	....	....
	Portland Buckeroos	WHL	8	3	5	0	480	32	0	4.00	....	....	....	....	....	....	....	....	....	....	....	....	....	....	....	....	....
1962-63	Calgary Stampeders	WHL	*70	23	44	2	4140	274	0	3.97	....	....	....	....	....	....	....	....	....	....	....	....	....	....	....	....	....
	Spokane Comets	WHL	1	0	1	0	60	3	0	3.00	....	....	....	....	....	....	....	....	....	....	....	....	....	....	....	....	....
1963-64	Buffalo Bisons	AHL	47	14	27	6	2820	155	2	3.30	....	....	....	....	....	....	....	....	....	....	....	....	....	....	....	....	....
	St. Louis Braves	CPHL	3	1	1	1	180	8	0	2.66	....	....	....	....	....	....	....	....	....	....	....	....	....	....	....	....	....
1964-65	St. Louis Braves	CPHL	65	12	47	6	3900	302	1	4.65	....	....	....	....	....	....	....	....	....	....	....	....	....	....	....	....	....
1965-66	Buffalo Bisons	AHL	40	15	22	2	2389	140	3	3.52	....	....	....	....	....	....	....	....	....	....	....	....	....	....	....	....	....
1966-67	Buffalo Bisons	AHL	39	9	24	5	2235	189	0	5.07	....	....	....	....	....	....	....	....	....	....	....	....	....	....	....	....	....
1967-68	**Detroit Red Wings**	**NHL**	**41**	**15**	**15**	**8**	**2177**	**127**	**0**	**3.50**	**3.93**	....	....	....	....	....	....	....	....	....	....	....	....	....	....	....	....
	Fort Worth Wings	CPHL	9	8	0	1	540	12	4	1.33	....	....	....	....	....	....	....	....	....	....	....	....	....	....	....	....	....
1968-69	**Detroit Red Wings**	**NHL**	**40**	**18**	**11**	**6**	**2099**	**89**	**4**	**2.54**	**2.61**	....	....	....	....	....	....	....	....	....	....	....	....	....	....	....	....
	Fort Worth Wings	CHL	10	4	2	3	560	28	0	3.00	....	....	....	....	....	....	....	....	....	....	....	....	....	....	....	....	....
1969-70	**Detroit Red Wings**	**NHL**	**47**	**24**	**15**	**6**	**2683**	**116**	**2**	**2.59**	**2.73**	....	....	....	....	**4**	**0**	**3**	....	**206**	**11**	**0**	**3.20**	....	....	....	....
1970-71	**Detroit Red Wings**	**NHL**	**37**	**11**	**19**	**7**	**2104**	**119**	**0**	**3.39**	**3.36**	....	....	....	....	....	....	....	....	....	....	....	....	....	....	....	....

Season	Club	League	REGULAR SEASON GP	W	L	T	Mins	GA	SO	Avg	AAvg	Eff	SA	S%	SAPG	PLAYOFFS GP	W	L	T	Mins	GA	SO	Avg	Eff	SA	S%	SAPG
1971-72	**Pittsburgh Penguins**	**NHL**	**15**	**2**	**8**	**4**	**847**	**36**	**0**	**2.55**	**2.57**	....	....	....	....	....	....	....	....	....	....	....	....	....	....	....	....
1972-73	**Detroit Red Wings**	**NHL**	**52**	**27**	**17**	**7**	**3012**	**132**	***6**	**2.63**	**2.46**	....	....	....	....	....	....	....	....	....	....	....	....	....	....	....	....
1973-74	**Detroit Red Wings**	**NHL**	**4**	**0**	**3**	**0**	**187**	**18**	**0**	**5.78**	**5.60**	....	....	....	....	....	....	....	....	....	....	....	....	....	....	....	....
	NHL Totals		**236**	**97**	**88**	**38**	**13109**	**637**	**12**	**2.92**	....	....	....	....	....	**4**	**0**	**3**	....	**206**	**11**	**0**	**3.20**	....	....	....	....

WHL Prairie Division First All-Star Team (1959) • Won WHL Prairie Division Rookie of the Year Award (1959)

Claimed by **Pittsburgh** from **Chicago** in Expansion Draft, June 6, 1967. Traded to **Detroit** by **Pittsburgh** for Hank Bassen, September 7, 1967. Claimed on waivers by **Pittsburgh** from **Detroit**, June 7, 1971. • Retired to recover from stress and nervous exhaustion, December 30, 1971. Traded to **Detroit** by **Pittsburgh** for cash, October 6, 1972 . Claimed on waivers by **Buffalo** from **Detroit**, May 20, 1974.

• ELIOT, Darren

Darren Joseph G – R. 6'1", 175 lbs. b: Hamilton, Ont., 11/26/1961. Los Angeles' 8th, 115th overall in 1980.

Season	Club	League	GP	W	L	T	Mins	GA	SO	Avg	AAvg	Eff	SA	S%	SAPG	GP	W	L	T	Mins	GA	SO	Avg	Eff	SA	S%	SAPG
1977-78	Oshawa Parkway TV	OMHA	18	....	....	....	1080	55	0	3.06	....	....	....	....	....	....	....	....	....	....	....	....	....	....	....	....	....
1978-79	Oshawa Legionnaires	OHA-B	26	....	....	....	1580	93	0	3.53	....	....	....	....	....	....	....	....	....	....	....	....	....	....	....	....	....
1979-80	Cornell University	ECAC	26	14	8	0	1362	94	0	4.14	....	....	....	....	....	5	3	2	0	300	20	0	4.00	....	....	....	....
1980-81	Cornell University	ECAC	18	8	7	0	912	52	1	3.42	....	....	....	....	....	3	1	1	0	119	7	0	2.33	....	....	....	....
1981-82	Cornell University	ECAC	7	1	3	0	338	25	0	4.44	....	....	....	....	....	....	....	....	....	....	....	....	....	....	....	....	....
1982-83	Cornell University	ECAC	26	13	10	3	1606	100	1	3.74	....	....	....	....	....	....	....	....	....	....	....	....	....	....	....	....	....
1983-84	Canada	Nat-Team	31	....	....	....	1676	111	0	3.97	....	....	....	....	....	....	....	....	....	....	....	....	....	....	....	....	....
	Canada	Olympics	2	0	0	0	40	2	0	3.00	....	....	....	....	....	....	....	....	....	....	....	....	....	....	....	....	....
	New Haven Nighthawks	AHL	7	4	1	0	365	30	0	4.93	....	....	....	....	....	....	....	....	....	....	....	....	....	....	....	....	....
1984-85	**Los Angeles Kings**	**NHL**	**33**	**12**	**11**	**6**	**1882**	**137**	**0**	**4.37**	**3.49**	**6.34**	**944**	**.855**	**30.1**	....	....	....	....	....	....	....	....	....	....	....	....
1985-86	**Los Angeles Kings**	**NHL**	**27**	**5**	**17**	**3**	**1481**	**121**	**0**	**4.90**	**3.84**	**7.40**	**801**	**.849**	**32.5**	....	....	....	....	....	....	....	....	....	....	....	....
	New Haven Nighthawks	AHL	3	1	2	1	180	19	0	6.33	....	....	....	....	....	1	0	1	0	60	4	0	4.00	....	....	....	....
1986-87	**Los Angeles Kings**	**NHL**	**24**	**8**	**13**	**2**	**1404**	**103**	**1**	**4.40**	**3.74**	**6.55**	**692**	**.851**	**29.6**	**1**	**0**	**0**	....	**40**	**7**	**0**	**10.50**	**25.34**	**29**	**.759**	**43.5**
	New Haven Nighthawks	AHL	4	2	2	0	239	15	0	3.77	....	....	....	....	....	....	....	....	....	....	....	....	....	....	....	....	....
1987-88	**Detroit Red Wings**	**NHL**	**3**	**0**	**0**	**1**	**97**	**9**	**0**	**5.57**	**4.64**	**8.95**	**56**	**.839**	**34.6**	....	....	....	....	....	....	....	....	....	....	....	....
	Adirondack Red Wings	AHL	43	23	11	7	2445	136	0	3.34	....	....	....	....	....	10	4	6	0	614	45	0	4.40	....	....	....	....
1988-89	Rochester Americans	AHL	23	8	6	2	969	59	0	3.65	....	....	....	....	....	....	....	....	....	....	....	....	....	....	....	....	....
	Buffalo Sabres	**NHL**	**2**	**0**	**0**	**0**	**67**	**7**	**0**	**6.27**	**5.22**	**10.21**	**43**	**.837**	**38.5**	....	....	....	....	....	....	....	....	....	....	....	....
	NHL Totals		**89**	**25**	**41**	**12**	**4931**	**377**	**1**	**4.59**	....	....	**2536**	**.851**	**30.9**	**1**	**0**	**0**	....	**40**	**7**	**0**	**10.50**	....	**29**	**.759**	**43.5**

ECAC First All-Star Team (1983) • NCAA East First All-American Team (1983)

Signed as a free agent by **Detroit**, June 30, 1987. Signed as a free agent by **Buffalo**, February 27, 1989.

• ELLACOTT, Ken

Kenneth George G – L. 5'8", 160 lbs. b: Paris, Ont., 3/3/1959. Vancouver's 3rd, 47th overall in 1979.

Season	Club	League	GP	W	L	T	Mins	GA	SO	Avg	AAvg	Eff	SA	S%	SAPG	GP	W	L	T	Mins	GA	SO	Avg	Eff	SA	S%	SAPG
1976-77	Hespeler Hawks	OHA-B	41	....	....	....	2460	216	0	5.27	....	....	....	....	....	....	....	....	....	....	....	....	....	....	....	....	....
1977-78	Peterborough Petes	OMJHL	55	....	....	....	3270	200	0	3.65	....	....	....	....	....	21	*11	6	4	1260	74	1	3.42	....	....	....	....
	Peterborough Petes	Mem-Cup	5	*3	2	0	301	17	*1	*3.39	....	....	....	....	....	....	....	....	....	....	....	....	....	....	....	....	....
1978-79	Peterborough Petes	OMJHL	48	....	....	....	2856	169	3	3.53	....	....	....	....	....	19	....	....	....	1140	61	1	3.21	....	....	....	....
	Peterborough Petes	Mem-Cup	5	*3	2	0	303	16	0	3.17	....	....	....	....	....	....	....	....	....	....	....	....	....	....	....	....	....
1979-80	Dallas Black Hawks	CHL	*54	19	28	5	*3155	198	*4	3.77	....	....	....	....	....	....	....	....	....	....	....	....	....	....	....	....	....
1980-81	Dallas Black Hawks	CHL	40	27	7	5	2336	119	1	3.06	....	....	....	....	....	4	....	....	....	180	13	0	4.33	....	....	....	....
1981-82	Dallas Black Hawks	CHL	*68	31	25	5	*3742	282	1	4.52	....	....	....	....	....	*16	9	7	0	*1015	62	0	3.66	....	....	....	....
1982-83	**Vancouver Canucks**	**NHL**	**12**	**2**	**3**	**4**	**555**	**41**	**0**	**4.43**	**3.56**	**5.88**	**309**	**.867**	**33.4**	....	....	....	....	....	....	....	....	....	....	....	....
	Fredericton Express	AHL	17	11	6	0	998	63	0	3.79	....	....	....	....	....	12	6	6	0	743	41	0	3.31	....	....	....	....
1983-84	Montana Magic	CHL	41	....	....	....	2441	208	1	5.11	....	....	....	....	....	....	....	....	....	....	....	....	....	....	....	....	....
1984-85	Flamboro Motts Clamatos	OHA-Sr.	STATISTICS NOT AVAILABLE																								
1985-86	Flamboro Flames	OHA-Sr.	STATISTICS NOT AVAILABLE																								
	NHL Totals		**12**	**2**	**3**	**4**	**555**	**41**	**0**	**4.43**	....	....	**309**	**.867**	**33.4**	....	....	....	....	....	....	....	....	....	....	....	....

Memorial Cup All-Star Team (1978) • Won Hap Emms Memorial Trophy (Memorial Cup Tournament Top Goaltender) (1978) • OMJHL First All-Star Team (1979) • Shared Terry Sawchuk Trophy (fewest goals against - CHL) with Paul Harrison (1981)

• ERICKSON, Chad

G – R. 5'10", 175 lbs. b: Minneapolis, MN, 8/21/1970. New Jersey's 8th, 138th overall in 1988.

Season	Club	League	GP	W	L	T	Mins	GA	SO	Avg	AAvg	Eff	SA	S%	SAPG	GP	W	L	T	Mins	GA	SO	Avg	Eff	SA	S%	SAPG
1986-87	Warroad Warriors	Hi-School	21	....	....	....	945	36	1	2.29	....	....	....	....	....	....	....	....	....	....	....	....	....	....	....	....	....
1987-88	Warroad Warriors	Hi-School	24	....	....	....	1080	33	7	1.83	....	....	....	....	....	....	....	....	....	....	....	....	....	....	....	....	....
1988-89	University of Minnesota-Duluth	WCHA	15	5	7	1	821	49	0	3.58	....	....	....	....	....	....	....	....	....	....	....	....	....	....	....	....	....
1989-90	University of Minnesota-Duluth	WCHA	39	19	19	1	2301	141	0	3.68	....	....	....	....	....	....	....	....	....	....	....	....	....	....	....	....	....
1990-91	University of Minnesota-Duluth	WCHA	40	14	19	7	2393	159	0	3.99	....	....	....	....	....	....	....	....	....	....	....	....	....	....	....	....	....
1991-92	**New Jersey Devils**	**NHL**	**2**	**1**	**1**	**0**	**120**	**9**	**0**	**4.50**	**4.03**	**7.36**	**55**	**.836**	**27.5**	....	....	....	....	....	....	....	....	....	....	....	....
	Utica Devils	AHL	43	18	19	3	2341	147	2	3.77	....	....	....	....	....	2	0	2	0	127	11	0	5.20	....	....	....	....
1992-93	Utica Devils	AHL	9	1	7	1	505	47	0	5.58	....	....	....	....	....	....	....	....	....	....	....	....	....	....	....	....	....
	Cincinnati Cyclones	IHL	10	2	6	1	516	42	0	4.88	....	....	....	....	....	....	....	....	....	....	....	....	....	....	....	....	....
	Birmingham Bulls	ECHL	14	6	6	2	856	54	0	3.79	....	....	....	....	....	....	....	....	....	....	....	....	....	....	....	....	....
1993-94	Albany River Rats	AHL	4	2	1	0	183	13	0	4.25	....	....	....	....	....	....	....	....	....	....	....	....	....	....	....	....	....
	Raleigh IceCaps	ECHL	32	19	9	3	1883	101	0	3.22	....	....	....	....	....	6	3	1	0	286	21	0	4.40	....	....	....	....
1994-95	Albany River Rats	AHL	1	1	0	0	60	2	0	2.00	....	....	....	....	....	....	....	....	....	....	....	....	....	....	....	....	....
	Providence Bruins	AHL	7	1	6	0	351	33	0	5.64	....	....	....	....	....	....	....	....	....	....	....	....	....	....	....	....	....
	Springfield Falcons	AHL	1	0	0	0	23	3	0	7.78	....	....	....	....	....	....	....	....	....	....	....	....	....	....	....	....	....
	Raleigh IceCaps	ECHL	11	1	8	1	587	45	0	4.60	....	....	....	....	....	....	....	....	....	....	....	....	....	....	....	....	....
1995-96	Birmingham Bulls	ECHL	44	16	20	4	2410	201	0	5.00	....	....	....	....	....	....	....	....	....	....	....	....	....	....	....	....	....
1996-97	Austin Ice-Bats	WPHL	32	18	11	2	1875	122	0	3.90	....	....	....	....	....	5	2	2	0	281	19	0	4.06	....	....	....	....
1997-98	Austin Ice-Bats	WPHL	51	26	13	10	2987	172	0	3.45	....	....	....	....	....	....	....	....	....	....	....	....	....	....	....	....	....
1998-99	San Angelo Outlaws	WPHL	49	31	14	3	2841	156	0	3.29	....	....	....	....	....	*17	*9	7	....	*1033	58	0	3.37	....	....	....	....
99-2000	Tulsa Oilers	CHL	45	25	16	2	2541	145	1	3.42	....	....	....	....	....	3	0	2	....	164	10	0	3.67	....	....	....	....
	NHL Totals		**2**	**1**	**1**	**0**	**120**	**9**	**0**	**4.50**	....	....	**55**	**.836**	**27.5**	....	....	....	....	....	....	....	....	....	....	....	....

WCHA Second All-Star Team (1990) • NCAA West First All-American Team (1990)

• ESCHE, Robert

Robert L. G – L. 6'1", 204 lbs. b: Utica, NY, 1/22/1978. Phoenix's 5th, 139th overall in 1996.

Season	Club	League	GP	W	L	T	Mins	GA	SO	Avg	AAvg	Eff	SA	S%	SAPG	GP	W	L	T	Mins	GA	SO	Avg	Eff	SA	S%	SAPG
1994-95	Gloucester Rangers	OJHL	20	10	6	0	1034	70	0	4.06	....	....	....	....	....	....	....	....	....	....	....	....	....	....	....	....	....
1995-96	Detroit Jr. Whalers	OHL	23	13	6	0	1219	76	1	3.74	....	....	....	....	....	3	0	2	....	105	4	0	2.29	....	....	....	....
1996-97	Detroit Jr. Whalers	OHL	58	24	28	2	3241	206	2	3.81	....	....	....	....	....	5	1	4	....	317	19	0	3.60	....	....	....	....
	United States	WJC-A	DID NOT PLAY – SPARE GOALTENDER																								
1997-98	Plymouth Whalers	OHL	48	29	13	4	2810	135	3	2.88	....	....	....	....	....	15	8	7	....	869	45	0	3.11	....	....	....	....
	United States	WJC-A	4	1	3	0	238	13	0	3.28	....	....	....	....	....	....	....	....	....	....	....	....	....	....	....	....	....
1998-99	**Phoenix Coyotes**	**NHL**	**3**	**0**	**1**	**0**	**130**	**7**	**0**	**3.23**	**3.84**	**4.52**	**50**	**.860**	**23.1**	....	....	....	....	....	....	....	....	....	....	....	....
	Springfield Falcons	AHL	55	24	20	6	2957	138	1	2.80	....	....	....	....	....	1	0	1	....	60	4	0	4.02	....	....	....	....
99-2000	**Phoenix Coyotes**	**NHL**	**8**	**2**	**5**	**0**	**408**	**23**	**0**	**3.38**	**3.86**	**3.62**	**215**	**.893**	**31.6**	....	....	....	....	....	....	....	....	....	....	....	....
	Houston Aeros	IHL	7	4	2	1	419	16	2	2.29	....	....	....	....	....	....	....	....	....	....	....	....	....	....	....	....	....
	Springfield Falcons	AHL	21	9	9	2	1207	61	2	3.03	....	....	....	....	....	3	1	2	....	180	12	0	4.01	....	....	....	....
	United States	WC-A	2	1	0	1	120	1	1	0.50	....	....	....	....	....	....	....	....	....	....	....	....	....	....	....	....	....
	NHL Totals		**11**	**2**	**6**	**0**	**538**	**30**	**0**	**3.35**	....	....	**265**	**.887**	**29.6**	....	....	....	....	....	....	....	....	....	....	....	....

OHL Second All-Star Team (1998)

• ESPOSITO, Tony

Anthony James "Tony 0" G – R. 5'11", 185 lbs. b: Sault Ste. Marie, Ont., 4/23/1943. **HHOF**

Season	Club	League	GP	W	L	T	Mins	GA	SO	Avg	AAvg	Eff	SA	S%	SAPG	GP	W	L	T	Mins	GA	SO	Avg	Eff	SA	S%	SAPG
1962-63	Sault Ste. Marie Greyhounds	NOJHA	STATISTICS NOT AVAILABLE																								
1963-64	Michigan Tech Huskies	WCHA	DID NOT PLAY – FRESHMAN																								
1964-65	Michigan Tech Huskies	WCHA	17	....	....	....	1020	40	1	2.35	....	....	....	....	....	....	....	....	....	....	....	....	....	....	....	....	....
1965-66	Michigan Tech Huskies	WCHA	19	....	....	....	1140	51	1	2.68	....	....	....	....	....	....	....	....	....	....	....	....	....	....	....	....	....

			REGULAR SEASON													PLAYOFFS											
Season	**Club**	**League**	**GP**	**W**	**L**	**T**	**Mins**	**GA**	**SO**	**Avg**	**AAvg**	**Eff**	**SA**	**S%**	**SAPG**	**GP**	**W**	**L**	**T**	**Mins**	**GA**	**SO**	**Avg**	**Eff**	**SA**	**S%**	**SAPG**
1966-67	Michigan Tech Huskies	WCHA	15				900	39	0	2.60																	
1967-68	Vancouver Canucks	WHL	*63	*25	*33	4	*3734	199	*4	3.20																	
1968-69♦	**Montreal Canadiens**	**NHL**	**13**	**5**	**4**	**4**	**746**	**34**	**2**	**2.73**	**2.82**																
	Houston Apollos	CHL	19	10	7	2	1139	46	1	2.42						1	0	1	0	59	3	0	3.05				
1969-70	**Chicago Black Hawks**	**NHL**	**63**	***38**	**17**	**8**	**3763**	**136**	***15**	**2.17**	**2.26**					**8**	**4**	**4**		**480**	**27**	**0**	**3.38**				
1970-71	**Chicago Black Hawks**	**NHL**	**57**	***35**	**14**	**6**	**3325**	**126**	**6**	**2.27**	**2.21**					**18**	**11**	**7**		**1151**	**42**	***2**	***2.19**				
1971-72	**Chicago Black Hawks**	**NHL**	**48**	**31**	**10**	**6**	**2780**	**82**	***9**	***1.77**	**1.76**					**5**	**2**	**3**		**300**	**16**	**0**	**3.20**				
1972-73	Team Canada	Summit-72	4	2	1	1	240	13	0	3.25																	
	Chicago Black Hawks	**NHL**	**56**	**32**	**17**	**7**	**3340**	**140**	**4**	**2.51**	**2.34**					**15**	**10**	**5**		**895**	**46**	**1**	**3.08**				
1973-74	**Chicago Black Hawks**	**NHL**	**70**	**34**	**14**	**21**	**4143**	**141**	**10**	**2.04**	**1.93**					**10**	**6**	**4**		**584**	**28**	***2**	**2.88**				
1974-75	**Chicago Black Hawks**	**NHL**	**71**	**34**	**30**	**7**	***4219**	**193**	**6**	**2.74**	**2.45**					**8**	**3**	**5**		**472**	**34**	**0**	**4.32**				
1975-76	**Chicago Black Hawks**	**NHL**	***68**	**30**	**23**	**13**	***4003**	**198**	**4**	**2.97**	**2.67**					**4**	**0**	**4**		**240**	**13**	**0**	**3.25**				
1976-77	**Chicago Black Hawks**	**NHL**	***69**	**25**	**36**	**8**	***4067**	**234**	**2**	**3.45**	**3.22**					**2**	**0**	**2**		**120**	**6**	**0**	**3.00**				
	Canada	WEC-A	9	6	2	1	510	27	1	3.17																	
1977-78	**Chicago Black Hawks**	**NHL**	**64**	**28**	**22**	**14**	**3840**	**168**	**5**	**2.63**	**2.44**					**4**	**0**	**4**		**252**	**19**	**0**	**4.52**				
1978-79	**Chicago Black Hawks**	**NHL**	**63**	**24**	**28**	**11**	***3780**	**206**	**4**	**3.27**	**2.88**					**4**	**0**	**4**		**243**	**14**	**0**	**3.46**				
	NHL All-Stars	Chal-Cup	DID NOT PLAY – SPARE GOALTENDER																								
1979-80	**Chicago Black Hawks**	**NHL**	***69**	**31**	**22**	**16**	***4140**	**205**	***6**	**2.97**	**2.61**					**6**	**3**	**3**		**373**	**14**	**0**	**2.25**				
1980-81	**Chicago Black Hawks**	**NHL**	***66**	**29**	**23**	**14**	***3935**	**246**	**0**	**3.75**	**3.03**					**3**	**0**	**3**		**215**	**15**	**0**	**4.19**				
1981-82	United States	Can-Cup	5	2	3	0	300	20	0	4.00																	
	Chicago Black Hawks	**NHL**	**52**	**19**	**25**	**8**	**3069**	**231**	**1**	**4.52**	**3.51**					**7**	**3**	**3**		**381**	**16**	***1**	**2.52**				
1982-83	**Chicago Black Hawks**	**NHL**	**39**	**23**	**11**	**5**	**2340**	**135**	**1**	**3.46**	**2.77**	**3.88**	**1203**	**.888**	**30.8**	**5**	**3**	**2**		**311**	**18**	**0**	**3.47**				
1983-84	**Chicago Black Hawks**	**NHL**	**18**	**5**	**10**	**3**	**1095**	**88**	**1**	**4.82**	**3.80**	**6.82**	**622**	**.859**	**34.1**												
	NHL Totals		**886**	**423**	**306**	**151**	**52585**	**2563**	**76**	**2.92**						**99**	**45**	**53**		**6017**	**308**	**6**	**3.07**				

• Brother of Phil • WCHA First All-Star Team (1965, 1966, 1967) • NCAA West First All-American Team (1965, 1966, 1967) • NCAA Championship All-Tournament Team (1965) • NHL First All-Star Team (1970, 1972, 1980) • Won Calder Memorial Trophy (1970) • Won Vezina Trophy (1970) • Shared Vezina Trophy with Gary Smith (1972) • NHL Second All-Star Team (1973, 1974) • Won Vezina Trophy (tied with Bernie Parent) (1974) • Played in NHL All-Star Game (1970, 1971, 1972, 1973, 1974, 1980)

Signed as a free agent by **Montreal** (Cleveland-AHL), September 29, 1967. Loaned to **Vancouver** (WHL) by **Montreal** for cash, October, 1967. Claimed by **Chicago** from **Montreal** in Intra-League Draft, June 11, 1969.

• ESSENSA, Bob

Robert Earle G – L. 6′, 188 lbs. b: Toronto, Ont., 1/14/1965. Winnipeg's 5th, 71st overall in 1983.

Season	Club	League	GP	W	L	T	Mins	GA	SO	Avg	AAvg	Eff	SA	S%	SAPG	GP	W	L	T	Mins	GA	SO	Avg	Eff	SA	S%	SAPG
1981-82	Henry Carr Crusaders	OJHL	17				948	79	0	4.99																	
1982-83	Henry Carr Crusaders	OJHL	31				1840	98	2	3.20																	
	Markham Waxers	OJHL	1	1	0	0	60	1	0	1.00																	
1983-84	Michigan State Spartans	CCHA	17	11	4	0	946	44	2	2.79																	
1984-85	Michigan State Spartans	CCHA	18	15	2	0	1059	29	2	1.64																	
1985-86	Michigan State Spartans	CCHA	23	17	4	1	1333	74	1	3.33																	
1986-87	Michigan State Spartans	CCHA	25	19	3	1	1383	64	2	2.78																	
1987-88	Moncton Hawks	AHL	27	7	11	1	1287	100	1	4.66																	
1988-89	**Winnipeg Jets**	**NHL**	**20**	**6**	**8**	**3**	**1102**	**68**	**1**	**3.70**	**3.08**	**4.38**	**574**	**.882**	**31.3**												
	Fort Wayne Komets	IHL	22	14	7	0	1287	70	0	3.26																	
1989-90	**Winnipeg Jets**	**NHL**	**36**	**18**	**9**	**5**	**2035**	**107**	**1**	**3.15**	**2.66**	**3.41**	**988**	**.892**	**29.1**	**4**	**2**	**1**		**206**	**12**	**0**	**3.50**	**4.20**	**100**	**.880**	**29.1**
	Moncton Hawks	AHL	6	3	3	0	358	15	0	2.51																	
	Canada	WEC-A	4				101	5	0	2.97																	
1990-91	**Winnipeg Jets**	**NHL**	**55**	**19**	**24**	**6**	**2916**	**153**	**4**	**3.15**	**2.83**	**3.22**	**1496**	**.898**	**30.8**												
	Moncton Hawks	AHL	2	1	0	1	125	6	0	2.88																	
1991-92	**Winnipeg Jets**	**NHL**	**47**	**21**	**17**	**6**	**2627**	**126**	***5**	**2.88**	**2.57**	**2.58**	**1407**	**.910**	**32.1**	**1**	**0**	**0**		**33**	**3**	**0**	**5.45**	**9.62**	**17**	**.824**	**30.9**
1992-93	**Winnipeg Jets**	**NHL**	**67**	**33**	**26**	**6**	**3855**	**227**	**2**	**3.53**	**3.02**	**3.78**	**2119**	**.893**	**33.0**	**6**	**2**	**4**		**367**	**20**	**0**	**3.27**	**3.57**	**183**	**.891**	**29.9**
1993-94	**Winnipeg Jets**	**NHL**	**56**	**19**	**30**	**6**	**3136**	**201**	**1**	**3.85**	**3.72**	**4.51**	**1714**	**.883**	**32.8**												
	Detroit Red Wings	**NHL**	**13**	**4**	**7**	**2**	**778**	**34**	**1**	**2.62**	**2.51**	**2.64**	**337**	**.899**	**26.0**	**2**	**0**	**2**		**109**	**9**	**0**	**4.95**	**10.36**	**43**	**.791**	**23.7**
1994-95	San Diego Gulls	IHL	16	6	8	1	919	52	0	3.39						1	0	1		59	3	0	3.05				
1995-96	Adirondack Red Wings	AHL	3	1	2	0	179	11	0	3.69																	
	Fort Wayne Komets	IHL	45	24	14	5	2529	122	1	2.89						5	2	3		299	12	0	2.41				
1996-97	**Edmonton Oilers**	**NHL**	**19**	**4**	**8**	**0**	**868**	**41**	**1**	**2.83**	**3.05**	**2.86**	**406**	**.899**	**28.1**												
1997-98	**Edmonton Oilers**	**NHL**	**16**	**6**	**6**	**1**	**825**	**35**	**0**	**2.55**	**3.04**	**2.21**	**404**	**.913**	**29.4**	**1**	**0**	**0**		**27**	**1**	**0**	**2.22**	**2.02**	**11**	**.909**	**24.4**
1998-99	**Edmonton Oilers**	**NHL**	**39**	**12**	**14**	**6**	**2091**	**96**	**0**	**2.75**	**3.27**	**2.71**	**974**	**.901**	**27.9**												
99-2000	**Phoenix Coyotes**	**NHL**	**30**	**13**	**10**	**3**	**1573**	**73**	**1**	**2.78**	**3.18**	**2.82**	**719**	**.898**	**27.4**												
	NHL Totals		**398**	**155**	**159**	**44**	**21806**	**1161**	**17**	**3.19**			**11138**	**.896**	**30.6**	**14**	**4**	**7**		**742**	**45**	**0**	**3.64**		**354**	**.873**	**28.6**

CCHA First All-Star Team (1985) • CCHA Second All-Star Team (1986) • NHL All-Rookie Team (1990)

Traded to **Detroit** by **Winnipeg** with Sergei Bautin for Tim Cheveldae and Dallas Drake, March 8, 1994. Traded to **Edmonton** by **Detroit** for future considerations, June 14, 1996. Signed as a free agent by **Phoenix**, September 5, 1999. Signed as a free agent by **Vancouver**, July 26, 2000.

• EVANS, Claude

G – L. 5′8″, 165 lbs. b: Longueuil, Que., 4/28/1933 Deceased.

Season	Club	League	GP	W	L	T	Mins	GA	SO	Avg	AAvg	Eff	SA	S%	SAPG	GP	W	L	T	Mins	GA	SO	Avg	Eff	SA	S%	SAPG
1949-50	Montreal Nationale	QJHL	1	1	0	0	60	1	0	1.00																	
1950-51	Montreal Nationale	QJHL	44	25	19	0	2670	186	0	4.18						3	1	2	0	180	14	0	4.67				
1951-52	Montreal Nationale	QJHL	50	28	21	1	3000	198	1	3.96						9	4	5	0	544	33	0	3.64				
1952-53	Cincinnati Mohawks	IHL	*60	*43	13	4	*3600	152	*5	*2.53						9	*8	1	0	540	19	*1	*2.11				
1953-54	Montreal Royals	QHL	14	6	5	3	870	43	2	2.97						2	1	1	0	120	5	0	2.50				
	Valleyfield Braves	QHL	8	3	5	0	480	31	0	3.88																	
	Providence Reds	AHL	3	0	3	0	180	14	0	4.67																	
	Victoria Cougars	WHL	14	7	6	1	840	46	0	3.28						5	1	4	0	300	28	0	5.60				
1954-55	Montreal Royals	QHL	21	10	8	3	1270	73	0	3.45																	
	Montreal Canadiens	**NHL**	**4**	**1**	**2**	**0**	**200**	**12**	**0**	**3.60**	**4.37**																
	Quebec Aces	QHL	13	9	3	1	750	40	2	3.20						4	2	2	0	240	11	1	2.75				
	Chicoutimi Sagueneens	QHL	4	2	2	0	240	15	0	3.75																	
1955-56	Quebec Aces	QHL	57	21	33	8	3410	199	2	3.50																	
1956-57	Springfield Indians	AHL	32	8	23	0	1960	143	1	4.47																	
1957-58	Springfield Indians	AHL	53	27	21	5	3252	173	1	3.19						*13	6	7	0	*783	40	*3	3.07				
	Boston Bruins	**NHL**	**1**	**0**	**0**	**1**	**60**	**4**	**0**	**4.00**	**4.39**																
1958-59	Springfield Indians	AHL	21	9	11	0	1220	84	2	4.13																	
	Trois-Rivieres Lions	QHL	38	*21	16	1	2280	116	*3	3.05						*8	*3	5	0	*484	26	0	3.22				
1959-60	Trois-Rivieres Lions	EPHL	62	28	25	9	3720	207	4	3.34						7	3	4	0	422	15	0	*2.13				
1960-61	Kitchener-Waterloo Beavers	EPHL	17	6	7	4	1020	69	0	4.06																	
	Vancouver Canucks	WHL	53	27	23	3	3180	147	6	2.77						9	4	5	0	575	24	0	2.50				
1961-62	Vancouver Canucks	WHL	40	11	26	3	2427	165	2	4.08																	
	Pittsburgh Hornets	AHL	19	2	17	0	1140	132	0	6.95																	
1962-1965	Drummondville Eagles	QSHL	STATISTICS NOT AVAILABLE																								
1965-66	Victoriaville Tigers	QSHL	3				180	20	0	6.67																	
	Trois-Rivieres Leafs	QIHA	24	10	12	2	1440	128	0	5.33																	
	NHL Totals		**5**	**1**	**2**	**1**	**260**	**16**	**0**	**3.69**																	

QJHL Second All-Star Team (1952) • IHL Second All-Star Team (1953) • QHL Second All-Star Team (1959)

Promoted to **Montreal** from **Montreal Royals** (QHL) to replace injured Jacques Plante in games from November 13 through 18, 1955. Promoted to **Boston** from **Springfield** (AHL) to replace injured Harry Lumley, March 6, 1958. (Chicago 4, Boston 4)

• EXELBY, Randy

G – L. 5′9″, 170 lbs. b: Toronto, Ont., 8/13/1965. Montreal's 1st, 20th overall in 1986 Supplemental Draft.

Season	Club	League	GP	W	L	T	Mins	GA	SO	Avg	AAvg	Eff	SA	S%	SAPG	GP	W	L	T	Mins	GA	SO	Avg	Eff	SA	S%	SAPG
1982-83	Streetsville Derbys	OJHL-B	17				971	64	0	3.96																	
	Richmond Hill Dynes	OJHL	3	0	3	0	160	22	0	8.07																	
1983-84	Lake Superior State	CCHA	21	6	10	0	905	75	0	4.97																	

Season	Club	League	REGULAR SEASON													PLAYOFFS											
			GP	W	L	T	Mins	GA	SO	Avg	AAvg	Eff	SA	S%	SAPG	GP	W	L	T	Mins	GA	SO	Avg	Eff	SA	S%	SAPG
1984-85	Lake Superior State	CCHA	36	22	11	1	1999	112	0	3.36	....	....	....	....	....	....	....	....	....	....	....	....	....	....	....	....	....
1985-86	Lake Superior State	CCHA	28	14	11	1	1625	98	0	3.62	....	....	....	....	....	....	....	....	....	....	....	....	....	....	....	....	....
1986-87	Lake Superior State	CCHA	28	12	9	1	1357	91	0	4.02	....	....	....	....	....	....	....	....	....	....	....	....	....	....	....	....	....
1987-88	Sherbrooke Canadiens	AHL	19	7	10	0	1050	49	0	2.80	....	....	....	....	....	4	2	2	0	212	13	0	3.68	....	....	....	....
1988-89	**Montreal Canadiens**	**NHL**	**1**	**0**	**0**	**0**	**3**	**0**	**0**	**0.00**	**0.00**	**0.00**	**1**	**1.000**	**20.0**	....	....	....	....	....	....	....	....	....	....	....	....
	Sherbrooke Canadiens	AHL	52	31	13	6	2935	146	6	2.98	....	....	....	....	....	6	1	4	0	329	24	0	4.38	....	....	....	....
1989-90	**Edmonton Oilers**	**NHL**	**1**	**0**	**1**	**0**	**60**	**5**	**0**	**5.00**	**4.24**	**8.33**	**30**	**.833**	**30.0**	....	....	....	....	....	....	....	....	....	....	....	....
	Phoenix Roadrunners	IHL	41	11	18	5	2146	163	0	4.56	....	....	....	....	....	....	....	....	....	....	....	....	....	....	....	....	....
1990-91	Springfield Indians	AHL	4	1	2	1	245	20	0	4.90	....	....	....	....	....	....	....	....	....	....	....	....	....	....	....	....	....
	Kansas City Blades	IHL	16	0	13	0	785	65	0	4.97	....	....	....	....	....	....	....	....	....	....	....	....	....	....	....	....	....
	Louisville IceHawks	ECHL	13	6	5	1	743	60	0	4.84	....	....	....	....	....	....	....	....	....	....	....	....	....	....	....	....	....
	NHL Totals		**2**	**0**	**1**	**0**	**63**	**5**	**0**	**4.76**	....	....	**31**	**.839**	**29.5**	....	....	....	....	....	....	....	....	....	....	....	....

AHL First All-Star Team (1989) • Shared Harry "Hap" Holmes Memorial Award (fewest goals against - AHL) with Francois Gravel (1989) • Won Aldege "Baz" Bastien Memorial Award (Top Goaltender - AHL) (1989)

Traded to **Edmonton** by **Montreal** for cash, October 2, 1989.

• FANKHOUSER, Scott

G – L. 6′2″, 195 lbs. b: Bismark, ND, 7/1/1975. St. Louis' 8th, 276th overall in 1994.

Season	Club	League	GP	W	L	T	Mins	GA	SO	Avg	AAvg	Eff	SA	S%	SAPG	GP	W	L	T	Mins	GA	SO	Avg	Eff	SA	S%	SAPG
1993-94	Loomis-Chaffe Prep School	Hi-School	STATISTICS NOT AVAILABLE																								
1994-95	U. of Massachusetts-Lowell	H-East	11	4	4	1	499	37	0	4.44	....	....	....	....	....	....	....	....	....	....	....	....	....	....	....	....	....
1995-96	Melfort Mustangs	SJHL	45	31	9	4	2544	109	3	2.57	....	....	....	....	....	....	....	....	....	....	....	....	....	....	....	....	....
1996-97	U. of Massachusetts-Lowell	H-East	11	2	4	1	517	38	0	4.41	....	....	....	....	....	....	....	....	....	....	....	....	....	....	....	....	....
1997-98	U. of Massachusetts-Lowell	H-East	16	4	7	2	798	48	0	3.61	....	....	....	....	....	....	....	....	....	....	....	....	....	....	....	....	....
1998-99	U. of Massachusetts-Lowell	H-East	32	16	14	0	1729	80	1	2.78	....	....	....	....	....	....	....	....	....	....	....	....	....	....	....	....	....
99-2000	**Atlanta Thrashers**	**NHL**	**16**	**2**	**11**	**2**	**920**	**49**	**0**	**3.20**	**3.66**	**3.48**	**451**	**.891**	**29.4**	....	....	....	....	....	....	....	....	....	....	....	....
	Greenville Growl	ECHL	7	6	1	0	419	18	0	2.58	....	....	....	....	....	....	....	....	....	....	....	....	....	....	....	....	....
	Orlando Solar Bears	IHL	6	2	2	1	320	14	0	2.63	....	....	....	....	....	....	....	....	....	....	....	....	....	....	....	....	....
	Louisville Panthers	AHL	1	0	1	0	59	3	0	3.05	....	....	....	....	....	....	....	....	....	....	....	....	....	....	....	....	....
	NHL Totals		**16**	**2**	**11**	**2**	**920**	**49**	**0**	**3.20**	....	....	**451**	**.891**	**29.4**	....	....	....	....	....	....	....	....	....	....	....	....

Signed as a free agent by **Atlanta**, August 24, 1999.

• FARR, Rocky

Norman Richard G – R. 5′10″, 175 lbs. b: Toronto, Ont., 4/7/1947.

Season	Club	League	GP	W	L	T	Mins	GA	SO	Avg	AAvg	Eff	SA	S%	SAPG	GP	W	L	T	Mins	GA	SO	Avg	Eff	SA	S%	SAPG
1963-64	Notre Dame Monarchs	MMJHL	2	....	....	....	120	7	0	3.50	....	....	....	....	....	....	....	....	....	....	....	....	....	....	....	....	....
	Montreal Jr. Canadiens	OHA-Jr.	11	....	....	....	660	33	2	3.00	....	....	....	....	....	2	....	....	....	100	9	0	5.40	....	....	....	....
1964-65	Montreal Jr. Canadiens	OHA-Jr.	10	....	....	....	600	40	0	4.00	....	....	....	....	....	....	....	....	....	....	....	....	....	....	....	....	....
1965-66	London Nationals	OHA-Jr.	47	11	29	7	2820	232	0	4.94	....	....	....	....	....	....	....	....	....	....	....	....	....	....	....	....	....
1966-67	London-Oshawa	OHA-Jr.	24	....	....	....	1440	112	0	4.63	....	....	....	....	....	4	....	....	....	240	17	0	4.86	....	....	....	....
1967-68	Houston Apollos	CPHL	18	4	10	1	888	53	1	3.58	....	....	....	....	....	....	....	....	....	....	....	....	....	....	....	....	....
	Cleveland Barons	AHL	5	2	2	0	270	17	0	3.78	....	....	....	....	....	....	....	....	....	....	....	....	....	....	....	....	....
1968-69	Denver Spurs	WHL	46	16	23	4	2667	180	2	4.05	....	....	....	....	....	....	....	....	....	....	....	....	....	....	....	....	....
	Cleveland Barons	AHL	3	2	0	1	180	3	1	1.00	....	....	....	....	....	....	....	....	....	....	....	....	....	....	....	....	....
1969-70	Denver Spurs	WHL	47	16	21	7	2769	188	1	4.07	....	....	....	....	....	....	....	....	....	....	....	....	....	....	....	....	....
1970-71	Springfield Kings	AHL	4	0	3	1	166	18	0	6.50	....	....	....	....	....	....	....	....	....	....	....	....	....	....	....	....	....
	Salt Lake Golden Eagles	WHL	25	6	15	0	1276	83	3	3.91	....	....	....	....	....	....	....	....	....	....	....	....	....	....	....	....	....
	Fort Worth Wings	CHL	1	0	0	0	15	0	0	0.00	....	....	....	....	....	1	0	1	0	60	4	0	4.00	....	....	....	....
1971-72	Cincinnati Swords	AHL	*52	20	16	10	2843	145	2	3.06	....	....	....	....	....	9	4	3	0	472	21	0	2.66	....	....	....	....
1972-73	**Buffalo Sabres**	**NHL**	**1**	**0**	**1**	**0**	**29**	**3**	**0**	**6.21**	**5.86**	....	....	....	....	....	....	....	....	....	....	....	....	....	....	....	....
	Cincinnati Swords	AHL	48	....	....	....	2746	121	3	2.64	....	....	....	....	....	12	....	....	....	720	35	0	2.91	....	....	....	....
1973-74	**Buffalo Sabres**	**NHL**	**11**	**2**	**4**	**1**	**480**	**25**	**0**	**3.13**	**3.02**	....	....	....	....	....	....	....	....	....	....	....	....	....	....	....	....
	Cincinnati Swords	AHL	16	7	3	2	812	47	1	3.47	....	....	....	....	....	....	....	....	....	....	....	....	....	....	....	....	....
1974-75	**Buffalo Sabres**	**NHL**	**7**	**0**	**1**	**2**	**213**	**14**	**0**	**3.94**	**3.56**	....	....	....	....	....	....	....	....	....	....	....	....	....	....	....	....
1975-76	Springfield Indians	AHL	6	0	3	1	222	30	0	8.11	....	....	....	....	....	....	....	....	....	....	....	....	....	....	....	....	....
	Johnstown Jets	NAHL	1	0	1	0	60	8	0	8.00	....	....	....	....	....	....	....	....	....	....	....	....	....	....	....	....	....
	NHL Totals		**19**	**2**	**6**	**3**	**722**	**42**	**0**	**3.49**	....	....	....	....	....	....	....	....	....	....	....	....	....	....	....	....	....

Claimed by **Cleveland** (AHL) (Montreal) from **Montreal** in Reverse Draft, June 13, 1968. Claimed by **Buffalo** from **Montreal** in Expansion Draft, June 10, 1970. Traded to **Kansas City** by **Buffalo** for cash, October 1, 1975.

• FAVELL, Doug

Douglas Robert G – L. 5′10″, 172 lbs. b: St. Catharines, Ont., 4/5/1945.

Season	Club	League	GP	W	L	T	Mins	GA	SO	Avg	AAvg	Eff	SA	S%	SAPG	GP	W	L	T	Mins	GA	SO	Avg	Eff	SA	S%	SAPG
1962-63	St. Catharines Black Hawks	OHA-Jr.	1	....	....	....	60	2	0	2.00	....	....	....	....	....	....	....	....	....	....	....	....	....	....	....	....	....
1963-64	Niagara Falls Flyers	OHA-Jr.	28	....	....	....	1748	98	3	3.36	....	....	....	....	....	....	....	....	....	....	....	....	....	....	....	....	....
1964-65	Niagara Falls Flyers	OHA-Jr.	22	....	....	....	1320	79	0	3.59	....	....	....	....	....	3	2	1	0	180	9	0	3.00	....	....	....	....
	Minneapolis Bruins	CPHL	1	1	0	0	60	3	0	3.00	....	....	....	....	....	....	....	....	....	....	....	....	....	....	....	....	....
	Niagara Falls Flyers	Mem-Cup	2	1	0	0	80	3	0	2.25	....	....	....	....	....	....	....	....	....	....	....	....	....	....	....	....	....
1965-66	Oklahoma City Blazers	CPHL	18	4	8	5	1060	59	0	3.34	....	....	....	....	....	....	....	....	....	....	....	....	....	....	....	....	....
	San Francisco Seals	WHL	2	1	1	0	120	6	0	3.00	....	....	....	....	....	2	0	2	0	113	10	0	5.31	....	....	....	....
1966-67	Oklahoma City Blazers	CPHL	33	14	13	4	1860	88	1	2.83	....	....	....	....	....	....	....	....	....	....	....	....	....	....	....	....	....
1967-68	**Philadelphia Flyers**	**NHL**	**37**	**15**	**15**	**6**	**2192**	**83**	**4**	**2.27**	**2.50**	....	....	....	....	**2**	**1**	**1**	....	**120**	**8**	**0**	**4.00**	....	....	....	....
1968-69	**Philadelphia Flyers**	**NHL**	**21**	**3**	**12**	**5**	**1195**	**71**	**1**	**3.56**	**3.70**	....	....	....	....	**1**	**0**	**1**	....	**60**	**5**	**0**	**5.00**	....	....	....	....
	Quebec Aces	AHL	4	0	4	0	199	16	0	4.82	....	....	....	....	....	....	....	....	....	....	....	....	....	....	....	....	....
1969-70	**Philadelphia Flyers**	**NHL**	**15**	**4**	**5**	**4**	**820**	**43**	**1**	**3.15**	**3.35**	....	....	....	....	....	....	....	....	....	....	....	....	....	....	....	....
1970-71	**Philadelphia Flyers**	**NHL**	**44**	**16**	**15**	**9**	**2434**	**108**	**2**	**2.66**	**2.62**	....	....	....	....	**2**	**0**	**2**	....	**120**	**8**	**0**	**4.00**	....	....	....	....
1971-72	**Philadelphia Flyers**	**NHL**	**54**	**18**	**25**	**9**	**2993**	**140**	**5**	**2.81**	**2.83**	....	....	....	....	....	....	....	....	....	....	....	....	....	....	....	....
1972-73	**Philadelphia Flyers**	**NHL**	**44**	**20**	**15**	**4**	**2419**	**114**	**3**	**2.83**	**2.66**	....	....	....	....	**11**	**5**	**6**	....	**669**	**29**	**1**	**2.60**	....	....	....	....
1973-74	**Toronto Maple Leafs**	**NHL**	**32**	**14**	**7**	**9**	**1752**	**79**	**0**	**2.71**	**2.61**	....	....	....	....	**3**	**0**	**3**	....	**181**	**10**	**0**	**3.31**	....	....	....	....
1974-75	**Toronto Maple Leafs**	**NHL**	**39**	**12**	**17**	**6**	**2149**	**145**	**1**	**4.05**	**3.68**	....	....	....	....	....	....	....	....	....	....	....	....	....	....	....	....
1975-76	**Toronto Maple Leafs**	**NHL**	**3**	**0**	**2**	**1**	**160**	**15**	**0**	**5.63**	**5.10**	....	....	....	....	....	....	....	....	....	....	....	....	....	....	....	....
	Oklahoma City Blazers	CHL	4	3	1	0	240	12	0	3.00	....	....	....	....	....	....	....	....	....	....	....	....	....	....	....	....	....
1976-77	**Colorado Rockies**	**NHL**	**30**	**8**	**15**	**3**	**1614**	**105**	**0**	**3.90**	**3.64**	....	....	....	....	....	....	....	....	....	....	....	....	....	....	....	....
1977-78	**Colorado Rockies**	**NHL**	**47**	**13**	**20**	**11**	**2663**	**159**	**1**	**3.58**	**3.37**	....	....	....	....	**2**	**0**	**2**	....	**120**	**6**	**0**	**3.00**	....	....	....	....
1978-79	**Colorado Rockies**	**NHL**	**7**	**0**	**5**	**2**	**380**	**34**	**0**	**5.37**	**4.76**	....	....	....	....	....	....	....	....	....	....	....	....	....	....	....	....
	Philadelphia Firebirds	AHL	32	12	15	4	1834	137	1	4.48	....	....	....	....	....	....	....	....	....	....	....	....	....	....	....	....	....
	NHL Totals		**373**	**123**	**153**	**69**	**20771**	**1096**	**18**	**3.17**	....	....	....	....	....	**21**	**6**	**15**	....	**1270**	**66**	**1**	**3.12**	....	....	....	....

Claimed by **Philadelphia** from **Boston** in Expansion Draft, June 6, 1967. • Missed remainder of 1969-70 season recovering from heel injury suffered in dressing room accident, February 11, 1970. Traded to **Toronto** by **Philadelphia** to complete transaction that sent Bernie Parent and Toronto's 2nd round choice (Larry Goodenough) in 1973 Amateur Draft to Philadelphia for Philadelphia's 1st round choice (Bob Neely) in 1973 Amateur Draft (May 15, 1973), July 27, 1973. Traded to **Colorado** by **Toronto** for cash, September 15, 1976. Claimed by **Edmonton** from **Colorado** in Expansion Draft, June 13, 1979. • Only player to be claimed in both the 1967 and 1979 Expansion Drafts.

• FERNANDEZ, Manny

Emmanuel G – L. 6′, 185 lbs. b: Etobicoke, Ont., 8/27/1974. Quebec's 4th, 52nd overall in 1992.

Season	Club	League	GP	W	L	T	Mins	GA	SO	Avg	AAvg	Eff	SA	S%	SAPG	GP	W	L	T	Mins	GA	SO	Avg	Eff	SA	S%	SAPG
1990-91	Lac St-Louis Lions	QAAA	20	13	5	0	1176	69	3	3.52	....	....	....	....	....	....	....	....	....	....	....	....	....	....	....	....	....
1991-92	Laval Titan	QMJHL	31	14	13	2	1593	99	1	3.73	....	....	....	....	....	9	3	5	....	468	39	0	5.00	....	....	....	....
1992-93	Laval Titan	QMJHL	43	26	14	2	2347	141	1	3.60	....	....	....	....	....	13	*12	1	....	818	42	0	3.08	....	....	....	....
	Laval Titan	Mem-Cup	5	2	*3	0	300	17	0	3.40	....	....	....	....	....	....	....	....	....	....	....	....	....	....	....	....	....
1993-94	Laval Titan	QMJHL	51	29	14	1	2776	143	*5	3.09	....	....	....	....	....	19	14	5	....	1116	49	*1	*2.63	....	....	....	....
	Laval Titan	Mem-Cup	5	2	*3	0	304	17	0	3.36	....	....	....	....	....	....	....	....	....	....	....	....	....	....	....	....	....
1994-95	Kalamazoo Wings	IHL	46	21	10	9	2470	115	2	2.79	....	....	....	....	....	14	10	2	....	753	34	1	2.71	....	....	....	....
	Dallas Stars	**NHL**	**1**	**0**	**1**	**0**	**59**	**3**	**0**	**3.05**	**3.19**	**3.39**	**27**	**.889**	**27.5**	....	....	....	....	....	....	....	....	....	....	....	....
1995-96	**Dallas Stars**	**NHL**	**5**	**0**	**1**	**1**	**249**	**19**	**0**	**4.58**	**4.56**	**7.19**	**121**	**.843**	**29.2**	....	....	....	....	....	....	....	....	....	....	....	....
	Michigan K-Wings	IHL	47	22	15	9	2664	133	*4	3.00	....	....	....	....	....	6	5	1	....	372	14	0	*2.26	....	....	....	....
1996-97	Michigan K-Wings	IHL	48	20	24	2	2720	142	2	3.13	....	....	....	....	....	4	1	3	....	277	15	0	3.25	....	....	....	....

Season	Club	League	REGULAR SEASON													PLAYOFFS											
			GP	W	L	T	Mins	GA	SO	Avg	AAvg	Eff	SA	S%	SAPG	GP	W	L	T	Mins	GA	SO	Avg	Eff	SA	S%	SAPG
1997-98	**Dallas Stars**	**NHL**	**2**	**1**	**0**	**0**	**69**	**2**	**0**	**1.74**	**2.07**	**0.99**	**35**	**.943**	**30.4**	**1**	**0**	**0**	....	**2**	**0**	**0**	**0.00**	**0.00**	**0**	**.000**	**0.0**
	Michigan K-Wings	IHL	55	27	17	5	3022	139	5	2.76	....	....	....	....	....	2	0	2	....	88	7	0	4.73	....	....	....	....
1998-99	**Dallas Stars**	**NHL**	**1**	**0**	**1**	**0**	**60**	**2**	**0**	**2.00**	**2.38**	**1.38**	**29**	**.931**	**29.0**	....	....	....	....	....	....	....	....	....	....	....	....
	Houston Aeros	IHL	50	34	6	9	2949	116	2	2.36	....	....	....	....	....	*19	*11	8	....	*1126	49	1	2.61	....	....	....	....
99-2000	**Dallas Stars**	**NHL**	**24**	**11**	**8**	**3**	**1353**	**48**	**1**	**2.13**	**2.43**	**1.70**	**603**	**.920**	**26.7**	**1**	**0**	**0**	....	**17**	**1**	**0**	**3.53**	**4.41**	**8**	**.875**	**28.2**
	NHL Totals		**33**	**12**	**11**	**4**	**1790**	**74**	**1**	**2.48**	....	....	**815**	**.909**	**27.3**	**2**	**0**	**0**	....	**19**	**1**	**0**	**3.16**	....	**8**	**.875**	**25.3**

QMJHL First All-Star Team (1994) • IHL Second All-Star Team (1995)

Rights traded to **Dallas** by **Quebec** for Tommy Sjodin and Dallas' 3rd round choice (Chris Drury) in 1994 Entry Draft, February 13, 1994. Traded to **Minnesota** by **Dallas** with Brad Lukowich for Minnesota's 3rd round choice (Joel Lundqvist) in 2000 Entry Draft and 4th round choice in 2002 Entry Draft, June 12, 2000.

• FICHAUD, Eric

G – L. 5'11", 171 lbs. b: Anjou, Que., 11/4/1975. Toronto's 1st, 16th overall in 1994.

Season	Club	League	GP	W	L	T	Mins	GA	SO	Avg	AAvg	Eff	SA	S%	SAPG	GP	W	L	T	Mins	GA	SO	Avg	Eff	SA	S%	SAPG
1991-92	Montreal-Bourassa Canadiens	QAAA	28	12	15	1	1678	110	0	3.95	....	....	....	....	....	....	....	....	....	....	....	....	....	....	....	....	....
1992-93	Chicoutimi Sagueneens	QMJHL	43	18	13	1	2039	149	0	4.38	....	....	....	....	....	....	....	....	....	....	....	....	....	....	....	....	....
1993-94	Chicoutimi Sagueneens	QMJHL	*63	*37	21	3	*3493	192	4	3.30	....	....	....	....	....	*26	*16	10	....	*1560	86	*1	3.31	....	....	....	....
	Chicoutimi Sagueneens	Mem-Cup	4	2	2	0	240	10	*1	2.50	....	....	....	....	....	....	....	....	....	....	....	....	....	....	....	....	....
1994-95	Chicoutimi Sagueneens	QMJHL	46	21	19	4	2637	151	4	3.44	....	....	....	....	....	7	2	5	....	428	20	0	2.80	....	....	....	....
1995-96	**New York Islanders**	**NHL**	**24**	**7**	**12**	**2**	**1234**	**68**	**1**	**3.31**	**3.29**	**3.42**	**659**	**.897**	**32.0**	....	....	....	....	....	....	....	....	....	....	....	....
	Worcester IceCats	AHL	34	13	15	6	1989	97	1	2.93	....	....	....	....	....	2	1	1	....	127	7	0	3.30	....	....	....	....
1996-97	**New York Islanders**	**NHL**	**34**	**9**	**14**	**4**	**1759**	**91**	**0**	**3.10**	**3.34**	**3.14**	**897**	**.899**	**30.6**	....	....	....	....	....	....	....	....	....	....	....	....
	Canada	WC-A	DID NOT PLAY – SPARE GOALTENDER																								
1997-98	**New York Islanders**	**NHL**	**17**	**3**	**8**	**3**	**807**	**40**	**0**	**2.97**	**3.54**	**2.82**	**422**	**.905**	**31.4**	....	....	....	....	....	....	....	....	....	....	....	....
	Utah Grizzlies	IHL	1	0	0	0	40	3	0	4.45	....	....	....	....	....	....	....	....	....	....	....	....	....	....	....	....	....
1998-99	**Nashville Predators**	**NHL**	**9**	**0**	**6**	**0**	**447**	**24**	**0**	**3.22**	**3.83**	**3.37**	**229**	**.895**	**30.7**	....	....	....	....	....	....	....	....	....	....	....	....
	Milwaukee Admirals	IHL	8	5	2	1	480	25	0	3.13	....	....	....	....	....	....	....	....	....	....	....	....	....	....	....	....	....
99-2000	**Carolina Hurricanes**	**NHL**	**9**	**3**	**5**	**1**	**490**	**24**	**1**	**2.94**	**3.36**	**3.43**	**206**	**.883**	**25.2**	....	....	....	....	....	....	....	....	....	....	....	....
	Quebec Citadelles	AHL	6	4	1	1	368	17	0	2.77	....	....	....	....	....	3	0	3	....	177	10	0	3.39	....	....	....	....
	NHL Totals		**93**	**22**	**45**	**10**	**4737**	**247**	**2**	**3.13**	....	....	**2413**	**.898**	**30.6**	....	....	....	....	....	....	....	....	....	....	....	....

Canadian Major Junior Second All-Star Team (1994) • Memorial Cup All-Star Team (1994) • Won Hap Emms Memorial Trophy (Memorial Cup Tournament Top Goaltender) (1994) • QMJHL First All-Star Team (1995)

Traded to **NY Islanders** by **Toronto** for Benoit Hogue, NY Islanders' 3rd round choice (Ryan Pepperall) in 1995 Entry Draft and 5th round choice (Brandon Sugden) in 1996 Entry Draft, April 6, 1995. Traded to **Edmonton** by **NY Islanders** for Mike Watt, June 18, 1998. Traded to **Nashville** by **Edmonton** with Drake Berehowsky and Greg de Vries for Mikhail Shtalenkov and Jim Dowd, October 1, 1998. Traded to **Carolina** by **Nashville** for Toronto's 4th round choice (previously acquired, Nashville selected Yevgeny Pavlov) in 1999 Entry Draft and future considerations, June 26, 1999. Claimed on waivers by **Montreal** from **Carolina**, February 11, 2000.

• FISET, Stephane

G – L. 6'1", 215 lbs. b: Montreal, Que., 6/17/1970. Quebec's 3rd, 24th overall in 1988.

Season	Club	League	GP	W	L	T	Mins	GA	SO	Avg	AAvg	Eff	SA	S%	SAPG	GP	W	L	T	Mins	GA	SO	Avg	Eff	SA	S%	SAPG
1986-87	Montreal-Bourassa Canadiens	QAAA	29	7	20	1	1445	142	0	5.89	....	....	....	....	....	....	....	....	....	....	....	....	....	....	....	....	....
1987-88	Victoriaville Tigres	QMJHL	40	15	17	4	2221	146	1	3.94	....	....	....	....	....	2	0	2	....	163	10	0	3.68	....	....	....	....
1988-89	Victoriaville Tigres	QMJHL	43	25	14	0	2401	138	1	*3.45	....	....	....	....	....	12	*9	2	....	711	33	0	*2.78	....	....	....	....
	Canada	WJC-A	6	3	2	1	329	18	0	3.28	....	....	....	....	....	....	....	....	....	....	....	....	....	....	....	....	....
1989-90	**Quebec Nordiques**	**NHL**	**6**	**0**	**5**	**1**	**342**	**34**	**0**	**5.96**	**5.06**	**10.18**	**199**	**.829**	**34.9**	....	....	....	....	....	....	....	....	....	....	....	....
	Victoriaville Tigres	QMJHL	24	14	6	3	1383	63	1	*2.73	....	....	....	....	....	*14	7	6	....	*790	49	0	3.72	....	....	....	....
	Canada	WJC-A	7	*5	1	1	420	18	*1	2.57	....	....	....	....	....	....	....	....	....	....	....	....	....	....	....	....	....
1990-91	**Quebec Nordiques**	**NHL**	**3**	**0**	**2**	**1**	**186**	**12**	**0**	**3.87**	**3.48**	**3.78**	**123**	**.902**	**39.7**	....	....	....	....	....	....	....	....	....	....	....	....
	Halifax Citadels	AHL	36	10	15	8	1902	131	0	4.13	....	....	....	....	....	....	....	....	....	....	....	....	....	....	....	....	....
1991-92	**Quebec Nordiques**	**NHL**	**23**	**7**	**10**	**2**	**1133**	**71**	**1**	**3.76**	**3.37**	**4.13**	**646**	**.890**	**34.2**	....	....	....	....	....	....	....	....	....	....	....	....
	Halifax Citadels	AHL	29	8	14	6	1675	110	*3	3.94	....	....	....	....	....	....	....	....	....	....	....	....	....	....	....	....	....
1992-93	**Quebec Nordiques**	**NHL**	**37**	**18**	**9**	**4**	**1939**	**110**	**0**	**3.40**	**2.91**	**3.96**	**945**	**.884**	**29.2**	**1**	**0**	**0**	....	**21**	**1**	**0**	**2.86**	**2.38**	**12**	**.917**	**34.3**
	Halifax Citadels	AHL	3	2	1	0	180	11	0	3.67	....	....	....	....	....	....	....	....	....	....	....	....	....	....	....	....	....
1993-94	**Quebec Nordiques**	**NHL**	**50**	**20**	**25**	**4**	**2798**	**158**	**2**	**3.39**	**3.26**	**3.74**	**1434**	**.890**	**30.8**	....	....	....	....	....	....	....	....	....	....	....	....
	Cornwall Aces	AHL	1	0	1	0	60	4	0	4.00	....	....	....	....	....	....	....	....	....	....	....	....	....	....	....	....	....
	Canada	WC-A	2	2	0	0	120	3	0	1.50	....	....	....	....	....	....	....	....	....	....	....	....	....	....	....	....	....
1994-95	**Quebec Nordiques**	**NHL**	**32**	**17**	**10**	**3**	**1879**	**87**	**2**	**2.78**	**2.91**	**2.50**	**968**	**.910**	**30.9**	**4**	**1**	**2**	....	**209**	**16**	**0**	**4.59**	**6.39**	**115**	**.861**	**33.0**
1995-96♦	**Colorado Avalanche**	**NHL**	**37**	**22**	**6**	**7**	**2107**	**103**	**1**	**2.93**	**2.91**	**2.98**	**1012**	**.898**	**28.8**	**1**	**0**	**0**	....	**1**	**0**	**0**	**0.00**	**0.00**	**0**	**.000**	**0.0**
1996-97	**Los Angeles Kings**	**NHL**	**44**	**13**	**24**	**5**	**2482**	**132**	**4**	**3.19**	**3.44**	**2.99**	**1410**	**.906**	**34.1**	....	....	....	....	....	....	....	....	....	....	....	....
1997-98	**Los Angeles Kings**	**NHL**	**60**	**26**	**25**	**8**	**3497**	**158**	**2**	**2.71**	**3.24**	**2.48**	**1728**	**.909**	**29.6**	**2**	**0**	**2**	....	**93**	**7**	**0**	**4.52**	**5.19**	**61**	**.885**	**39.4**
1998-99	**Los Angeles Kings**	**NHL**	**42**	**18**	**21**	**1**	**2403**	**104**	**3**	**2.60**	**3.09**	**2.22**	**1217**	**.915**	**30.4**	....	....	....	....	....	....	....	....	....	....	....	....
99-2000	**Los Angeles Kings**	**NHL**	**47**	**20**	**15**	**7**	**2592**	**119**	**1**	**2.75**	**3.14**	**2.71**	**1208**	**.901**	**28.0**	**4**	**0**	**3**	....	**200**	**10**	**0**	**3.00**	**3.06**	**98**	**.898**	**29.4**
	NHL Totals		**381**	**161**	**152**	**43**	**21358**	**1088**	**16**	**3.06**	....	....	**10890**	**.900**	**30.6**	**12**	**1**	**7**	....	**524**	**34**	**0**	**3.89**	....	**286**	**.881**	**32.7**

QMJHL First All-Star Team (1989) • Canadian Major Junior Goaltender of the Year (1989) • WJC-A All-Star Team (1990) • Named Best Goaltender at WJC-A (1990)

Transferred to **Colorado** after **Quebec** franchise relocated, June 21, 1995. Traded to **Los Angeles** by **Colorado** with Colorado's 1st round choice (Mathieu Biron) in 1998 Entry Draft for Eric Lacroix and Los Angeles' 1st round choice (Martin Skoula) in 1998 Entry Draft, June 20, 1996.

• FITZPATRICK, Mark

G – L. 6'2", 195 lbs. b: Toronto, Ont., 11/13/1968. Los Angeles' 2nd, 27th overall in 1987.

Season	Club	League	GP	W	L	T	Mins	GA	SO	Avg	AAvg	Eff	SA	S%	SAPG	GP	W	L	T	Mins	GA	SO	Avg	Eff	SA	S%	SAPG
1983-84	Revelstoke Rangers	BCJHL	21	....	....	....	1019	90	0	5.30	....	....	....	....	....	....	....	....	....	....	....	....	....	....	....	....	....
1984-85	Medicine Hat Tigers	WHL	3	1	2	0	180	9	0	3.00	....	....	....	....	....	1	0	0	0	20	2	0	6.00	....	....	....	....
	Calgary Canucks	AJHL	29	....	....	....	1631	102	2	3.75	....	....	....	....	....	....	....	....	....	....	....	....	....	....	....	....	....
1985-86	Medicine Hat Tigers	WHL	41	26	6	1	2074	99	1	*2.86	....	....	....	....	....	*19	*11	5	....	*986	58	0	3.53	....	....	....	....
1986-87	Medicine Hat Tigers	WHL	50	31	11	4	2844	159	4	3.35	....	....	....	....	....	20	12	8	....	1224	71	1	3.48	....	....	....	....
	Medicine Hat Tigers	Mem-Cup	5	*4	1	0	300	10	*1	*2.00	....	....	....	....	....	....	....	....	....	....	....	....	....	....	....	....	....
1987-88	Medicine Hat Tigers	WHL	63	36	15	6	3600	194	2	3.23	....	....	....	....	....	16	12	4	....	959	52	*1	*3.25	....	....	....	....
	Medicine Hat Tigers	Mem-Cup	5	*4	1	0	280	17	0	*3.64	....	....	....	....	....	....	....	....	....	....	....	....	....	....	....	....	....
1988-89	**Los Angeles Kings**	**NHL**	**17**	**6**	**7**	**3**	**957**	**64**	**0**	**4.01**	**3.34**	**4.53**	**566**	**.887**	**35.5**	....	....	....	....	....	....	....	....	....	....	....	....
	New Haven Nighthawks	AHL	18	10	5	1	980	54	1	3.31	....	....	....	....	....	....	....	....	....	....	....	....	....	....	....	....	....
	New York Islanders	**NHL**	**11**	**3**	**5**	**2**	**627**	**41**	**0**	**3.92**	**3.26**	**5.13**	**313**	**.869**	**30.0**	....	....	....	....	....	....	....	....	....	....	....	....
1989-90	**New York Islanders**	**NHL**	**47**	**19**	**19**	**5**	**2653**	**150**	**3**	**3.39**	**2.87**	**3.45**	**1472**	**.898**	**33.3**	**4**	**0**	**2**	....	**152**	**13**	**0**	**5.13**	**9.39**	**71**	**.817**	**28.0**
1990-91	**New York Islanders**	**NHL**	**2**	**1**	**1**	**0**	**120**	**6**	**0**	**3.00**	**2.70**	**3.00**	**60**	**.900**	**30.0**	....	....	....	....	....	....	....	....	....	....	....	....
	Capital District Islanders	AHL	12	3	7	2	734	47	0	3.84	....	....	....	....	....	....	....	....	....	....	....	....	....	....	....	....	....
1991-92	**New York Islanders**	**NHL**	**30**	**11**	**13**	**5**	**1743**	**93**	**0**	**3.20**	**2.86**	**3.14**	**949**	**.902**	**32.7**	....	....	....	....	....	....	....	....	....	....	....	....
	Capital District Islanders	AHL	14	6	5	1	782	39	0	2.99	....	....	....	....	....	....	....	....	....	....	....	....	....	....	....	....	....
1992-93	**New York Islanders**	**NHL**	**39**	**17**	**15**	**5**	**2253**	**130**	**0**	**3.46**	**2.96**	**4.22**	**1066**	**.878**	**28.4**	**3**	**0**	**1**	....	**77**	**4**	**0**	**3.12**	**5.43**	**23**	**.826**	**17.9**
	Capital District Islanders	AHL	5	1	3	1	284	18	0	3.80	....	....	....	....	....	....	....	....	....	....	....	....	....	....	....	....	....
1993-94	**Florida Panthers**	**NHL**	**28**	**12**	**8**	**6**	**1603**	**73**	**1**	**2.73**	**2.62**	**2.36**	**844**	**.914**	**31.6**	....	....	....	....	....	....	....	....	....	....	....	....
1994-95	**Florida Panthers**	**NHL**	**15**	**6**	**7**	**2**	**819**	**36**	**2**	**2.64**	**2.76**	**2.63**	**361**	**.900**	**26.4**	....	....	....	....	....	....	....	....	....	....	....	....
1995-96	**Florida Panthers**	**NHL**	**34**	**15**	**11**	**3**	**1786**	**88**	**0**	**2.96**	**2.94**	**3.22**	**810**	**.891**	**27.2**	**2**	**0**	**0**	....	**60**	**6**	**0**	**6.00**	**12.00**	**30**	**.800**	**30.0**
1996-97	**Florida Panthers**	**NHL**	**30**	**8**	**9**	**9**	**1680**	**66**	**0**	**2.36**	**2.53**	**2.02**	**771**	**.914**	**27.5**	....	....	....	....	....	....	....	....	....	....	....	....
1997-98	**Florida Panthers**	**NHL**	**12**	**2**	**7**	**2**	**640**	**32**	**1**	**3.00**	**3.58**	**3.62**	**265**	**.879**	**24.8**	....	....	....	....	....	....	....	....	....	....	....	....
	Fort Wayne Komets	IHL	2	1	1	0	119	8	0	4.03	....	....	....	....	....	....	....	....	....	....	....	....	....	....	....	....	....
	Tampa Bay Lightning	**NHL**	**34**	**7**	**24**	**1**	**1938**	**102**	**1**	**3.16**	**3.78**	**3.31**	**975**	**.895**	**30.2**	....	....	....	....	....	....	....	....	....	....	....	....

Season	Club	League	REGULAR SEASON													PLAYOFFS											
			GP	W	L	T	Mins	GA	SO	Avg	AAvg	Eff	SA	S%	SAPG	GP	W	L	T	Mins	GA	SO	Avg	Eff	SA	S%	SAPG
1998-99	Chicago Blackhawks	NHL	27	6	8	6	1403	64	0	2.74	3.26	2.57	682	.906	29.2	....	....	....	....	....	....	....	....	....	....	....	....
99-2000	Carolina Hurricanes	NHL	3	0	2	0	107	8	0	4.49	5.13	5.28	68	.882	38.1	....	....	....	....	....	....	....	....	....	....	....	....
	Cincinnati Cyclones	IHL	24	11	11	1	1379	59	4	2.57	....	....	....	....	....	....	....	....	....	....	....	....	....	....	....	....	....
	NHL Totals		329	113	136	49	18329	953	8	3.12	....	....	9202	.896	30.1	9	0	3	....	289	23	0	4.78	....	124	.815	25.7

WHL East Second All-Star Team (1986, 1988) • Won Hap Emms Memorial Trophy (Memorial Cup Tournament Top Goaltender) (1987, 1988) • Won Bill Masterton Memorial Trophy (1992)

Traded to **NY Islanders** by **Los Angeles** with Wayne McBean and future considerations (Doug Crossman, May 23, 1989) for Kelly Hrudey, February 22, 1989. Traded to **Quebec** by **NY Islanders** with NY Islanders' 1st round choice (Adam Deadmarsh) in 1993 Entry Draft for Ron Hextall and Quebec's 1st round choice (Todd Bertuzzi) in 1993 Entry Draft, June 20, 1993. Claimed by **Florida** from **Quebec** in Expansion Draft, June 24, 1993. Traded to **Tampa Bay** by **Florida** with Jody Hull for Dino Ciccarelli and Jeff Norton, January 15, 1998. Traded to **Chicago** by **Tampa Bay** with Tampa Bay's 4th round choice (later traded to Montreal - Montreal selected Chris Dyment) in 1999 Entry Draft for Michal Sykora, July 17, 1998. Signed as a free agent by **Carolina**, August 19, 1999

• FLAHERTY, Wade

G – L. 6', 170 lbs. b: Terrace, B.C., 1/11/1968. Buffalo's 10th, 181st overall in 1988.

Season	Club	League	GP	W	L	T	Mins	GA	SO	Avg	AAvg	Eff	SA	S%	SAPG	GP	W	L	T	Mins	GA	SO	Avg	Eff	SA	S%	SAPG
1984-85	Terrace Titans	BCAHA	STATISTICS NOT AVAILABLE																								
	Kelowna Wings	WHL	1	0	0	0	55	5	0	5.45	....	....	....	....	....	....	....	....	....	....	....	....	....	....	....	....	....
1985-86	Williams Lake Mustangs	PCJHL	STATISTICS NOT AVAILABLE																								
	Seattle Thunderbirds	WHL	9	1	3	0	271	36	0	7.97	....	....	....	....	....	....	....	....	....	....	....	....	....	....	....	....	....
	Spokane Chiefs	WHL	5	0	3	0	161	21	0	7.83	....	....	....	....	....	....	....	....	....	....	....	....	....	....	....	....	....
1986-87	Nanaimo Clippers	BCJHL	15	....	....	....	830	53	0	3.83	....	....	....	....	....	....	....	....	....	....	....	....	....	....	....	....	....
	Victoria Cougars	WHL	3	0	2	0	127	16	0	7.56	....	....	....	....	....	....	....	....	....	....	....	....	....	....	....	....	....
1987-88	Victoria Cougars	WHL	36	20	15	0	2052	135	0	3.95	....	....	....	....	....	5	2	3	0	300	18	0	3.60	....	....	....	....
1988-89	Victoria Cougars	WHL	42	21	19	0	2408	180	4	4.49	....	....	....	....	....	....	....	....	....	....	....	....	....	....	....	....	....
1989-90	Greensboro Monarchs	ECHL	27	12	10	0	1308	96	0	4.40	....	....	....	....	....	....	....	....	....	....	....	....	....	....	....	....	....
1990-91	Kansas City Blades	IHL	*56	16	31	4	2990	224	0	4.49	....	....	....	....	....	....	....	....	....	....	....	....	....	....	....	....	....
1991-92	San Jose Sharks	NHL	3	0	3	0	178	13	0	4.38	3.92	4.75	120	.892	40.4	....	....	....	....	....	....	....	....	....	....	....	....
	Kansas City Blades	IHL	43	26	14	3	2603	140	1	3.23	....	....	....	....	....	1	0	0	....	1	0	0	0.00	....	....	....	....
1992-93	San Jose Sharks	NHL	1	0	1	0	60	5	0	5.00	4.28	5.43	46	.891	46.0	....	....	....	....	....	....	....	....	....	....	....	....
	Kansas City Blades	IHL	*61	*34	19	7	*3642	195	2	3.21	....	....	....	....	....	*12	6	6	....	733	34	*1	2.78	....	....	....	....
1993-94	Kansas City Blades	IHL	*60	32	19	9	*3564	202	0	3.40	....	....	....	....	....	....	....	....	....	....	....	....	....	....	....	....	....
1994-95	San Jose Sharks	NHL	18	5	6	1	852	44	1	3.10	3.25	3.00	455	.903	32.0	7	2	3	....	377	31	0	4.93	6.92	221	.860	35.2
1995-96	San Jose Sharks	NHL	24	3	12	1	1137	92	0	4.85	4.85	6.48	689	.866	36.4	....	....	....	....	....	....	....	....	....	....	....	....
1996-97	San Jose Sharks	NHL	7	2	4	0	359	31	0	5.18	5.59	7.95	202	.847	33.8	....	....	....	....	....	....	....	....	....	....	....	....
	Kentucky Thoroughblades	AHL	19	8	6	2	1032	54	1	3.14	....	....	....	....	....	3	1	2	....	200	11	0	3.30	....	....	....	....
1997-98	New York Islanders	NHL	16	4	4	3	694	23	3	1.99	2.37	1.48	309	.926	26.7	....	....	....	....	....	....	....	....	....	....	....	....
	Utah Grizzlies	IHL	24	16	5	3	1341	40	3	1.79	....	....	....	....	....	....	....	....	....	....	....	....	....	....	....	....	....
1998-99	New York Islanders	NHL	20	5	11	2	1048	53	0	3.03	3.61	3.27	491	.892	28.1	....	....	....	....	....	....	....	....	....	....	....	....
	Lowell Lock Monsters	AHL	5	1	3	1	305	16	0	3.15	....	....	....	....	....	....	....	....	....	....	....	....	....	....	....	....	....
99-2000	New York Islanders	NHL	4	0	1	1	182	7	0	2.31	2.64	2.00	81	.914	26.7	....	....	....	....	....	....	....	....	....	....	....	....
	NHL Totals		93	19	42	8	4510	268	4	3.57	....	....	2393	.888	31.8	7	2	3	....	377	31	0	4.93	....	221	.860	35.2

WHL West Second All-Star Team (1988) • Playoff MVP - ECHL (1990) • Shared James Norris Memorial Trophy (fewest goals against - IHL) with Arturs Irbe (1992) • IHL Second All-Star Team (1993, 1994)

Signed as a free agent by **San Jose**, September 3, 1991. Signed as a free agent by **NY Islanders**, July 22, 1997.

• FORBES, Jake

Vernon Vivian "Jumpin' Jackie" G – L. 5'6", 140 lbs. b: Toronto, Ont., 7/4/1897 Deceased.

Season	Club	League	GP	W	L	T	Mins	GA	SO	Avg	AAvg	Eff	SA	S%	SAPG	GP	W	L	T	Mins	GA	SO	Avg	Eff	SA	S%	SAPG
1916-17	Toronto Aura Lee	OHA-Jr.	6	*6	0	0	360	14	0	2.33	....	....	....	....	....	6	4	2	0	360	18	0	3.00	....	....	....	....
1917-18	Toronto Aura Lee	OHA-Jr.	4	3	1	0	240	13	0	3.25	....	....	....	....	....	....	....	....	....	....	....	....	....	....	....	....	....
1918-19	Toronto Goodyears	TIHL	STATISTICS NOT AVAILABLE																								
1919-20	Toronto Aura Lee	OHA-Jr.	6	2	4	0	360	27	0	4.50	....	....	....	....	....	....	....	....	....	....	....	....	....	....	....	....	....
	Toronto Goodyears	TIHL	STATISTICS NOT AVAILABLE																								
	Toronto St. Pats	NHL	5	2	3	0	300	21	0	4.20	2.65	....	....	....	....	....	....	....	....	....	....	....	....	....	....	....	....
1920-21	Toronto St. Pats	NHL	20	13	7	0	1221	78	0	3.83	2.69	....	....	....	....	2	0	2	0	120	7	0	3.50	....	....	....	....
1921-22	Toronto St. Pats	NHL	DID NOT PLAY – SUSPENDED																								
1922-23	Hamilton Tigers	NHL	*24	6	18	0	1470	110	0	4.49	4.82	....	....	....	....	....	....	....	....	....	....	....	....	....	....	....	....
1923-24	Hamilton Tigers	NHL	*24	9	15	0	1483	68	1	2.75	3.19	....	....	....	....	....	....	....	....	....	....	....	....	....	....	....	....
1924-25	Hamilton Tigers	NHL	*30	*19	10	1	1833	60	6	1.96	2.29	....	....	....	....	....	....	....	....	....	....	....	....	....	....	....	....
1925-26	New York Americans	NHL	*36	12	20	4	2240	86	2	2.30	3.04	....	....	....	....	....	....	....	....	....	....	....	....	....	....	....	....
1926-27	New York Americans	NHL	*44	17	25	2	2715	91	8	2.01	3.07	....	....	....	....	....	....	....	....	....	....	....	....	....	....	....	....
1927-28	New York Americans	NHL	16	3	11	2	980	51	2	3.12	5.13	....	....	....	....	....	....	....	....	....	....	....	....	....	....	....	....
	Providence Reds	Can-Am	13	....	....	....	780	20	2	1.46	....	....	....	....	....	....	....	....	....	....	....	....	....	....	....	....	....
	Niagara Falls Cataracts	Can-Pro	8	....	....	....	480	16	1	2.00	....	....	....	....	....	....	....	....	....	....	....	....	....	....	....	....	....
1928-29	New York Americans	NHL	1	1	0	0	60	3	0	3.00	6.28	....	....	....	....	....	....	....	....	....	....	....	....	....	....	....	....
	New Haven Eagles	Can-Am	26	....	....	....	1560	29	9	*1.06	....	....	....	....	....	2	1	1	0	123	4	0	1.95	....	....	....	....
1929-30	New York Americans	NHL	1	0	0	1	70	1	0	0.86	0.88	....	....	....	....	....	....	....	....	....	....	....	....	....	....	....	....
	New Haven Eagles	Can-Am	40	....	....	....	2400	101	3	2.44	....	....	....	....	....	....	....	....	....	....	....	....	....	....	....	....	....
1930-31	New Haven Eagles	Can-Am	40	....	....	....	2400	140	3	3.37	....	....	....	....	....	....	....	....	....	....	....	....	....	....	....	....	....
	Philadelphia Quakers	NHL	2	0	2	0	120	7	0	3.50	4.46	....	....	....	....	....	....	....	....	....	....	....	....	....	....	....	....
1931-32	New York Americans	NHL	6	3	3	0	360	16	0	2.67	3.27	....	....	....	....	....	....	....	....	....	....	....	....	....	....	....	....
	Springfield Indians	Can-Am	3	....	....	....	180	16	0	5.05	....	....	....	....	....	....	....	....	....	....	....	....	....	....	....	....	....
	Bronx Tigers	Can-Am	7	....	....	....	420	16	0	2.09	....	....	....	....	....	....	....	....	....	....	....	....	....	....	....	....	....
1932-33	New York Americans	NHL	1	0	0	1	70	2	0	1.71	2.29	....	....	....	....	....	....	....	....	....	....	....	....	....	....	....	....
	New Haven Eagles	Can-Am	5	....	....	....	300	15	0	3.11	....	....	....	....	....	....	....	....	....	....	....	....	....	....	....	....	....
1933-34	Windsor Bulldogs	IHL	36	....	....	....	2160	89	6	2.41	....	....	....	....	....	....	....	....	....	....	....	....	....	....	....	....	....
1934-35	Syracuse Stars	IHL	8	5	3	0	510	21	0	2.47	....	....	....	....	....	....	....	....	....	....	....	....	....	....	....	....	....
	London Tecumsehs	IHL	8	4	3	1	500	20	0	2.40	....	....	....	....	....	5	2	*3	0	320	12	*1	2.25	....	....	....	....
1935-36	Rochester Cardinals	IHL	5	2	3	0	300	20	0	4.00	....	....	....	....	....	....	....	....	....	....	....	....	....	....	....	....	....
	Syracuse Stars	IHL	5	2	3	0	330	15	0	2.73	....	....	....	....	....	....	....	....	....	....	....	....	....	....	....	....	....
	NHL Totals		210	85	114	11	12922	594	19	2.76	....	....	....	....	....	2	0	2	0	120	7	0	3.50	....	....	....	....

Can-Am First All-Star Team (1930)

Signed as a free agent by **Toronto**, February 28, 1920. • Suspended for entire 1921-22 season by **Toronto** for refusing to accept contract terms, December 12, 1921. Traded to **Hamilton** by **Toronto** for cash, May 27, 1922. Rights transferred to **NY Americans** after NHL club purchased **Hamilton** franchise, November 7, 1925. Loaned to **Providence** (Can-Am) by **NY Americans** for cash, December 7, 1927. Loan transferred to **Niagara Falls** (Can-Pro) from **Providence** (Can-Am) by **NY Americans**, January 12, 1928. Loaned to **Philadelphia** by **NY Americans** (New Haven-AHL) to replace injured Wilf Cude, January 13 (Montreal Canadiens 2, Philadelphia 1) and January 17, 1931. (Detroit 5, Philadelphia 2)

• FORD, Brian

G – L. 5'10", 170 lbs. b: Edmonton, Alta., 9/22/1961.

Season	Club	League	GP	W	L	T	Mins	GA	SO	Avg	AAvg	Eff	SA	S%	SAPG	GP	W	L	T	Mins	GA	SO	Avg	Eff	SA	S%	SAPG
1977-78	Edmonton Little Brickmen	AAHA	STATISTICS NOT AVAILABLE																								
	St. Albert Saints	AJHL	1	1	0	0	60	3	0	3.00	....	....	....	....	....	....	....	....	....	....	....	....	....	....	....	....	....
1978-79	Edmonton Little Brickmen	AAHA	STATISTICS NOT AVAILABLE																								
1979-80	St. Albert Saints	AJHL	....	....	....	....	....	....	....	....	....	....	....	....	....	6	4	1	1	360	14	0	2.33	....	....	....	....
	Red Deer Rustlers	Cen-Cup	STATISTICS NOT AVAILABLE																								
1980-81	Billings Bighorns	WHL	44	14	26	0	2435	204	0	5.03	....	....	....	....	....	3	....	....	....	193	15	0	4.66	....	....	....	....
1981-82	Billings Bighorns	WHL	53	19	26	1	2791	256	0	5.50	....	....	....	....	....	5	1	4	0	226	26	0	6.90	....	....	....	....
1982-83	Fredericton Express	AHL	27	14	7	2	1443	84	0	3.49	....	....	....	....	....	1	0	0	0	11	1	0	5.56	....	....	....	....
	Carolina Thunderbirds	ACHL	4	....	....	....	203	7	0	2.07	....	....	....	....	....	....	....	....	....	....	....	....	....	....	....	....	....
1983-84	Quebec Nordiques	NHL	3	1	1	0	123	13	0	6.34	5.00	11.77	70	.814	34.1	....	....	....	....	....	....	....	....	....	....	....	....
	Fredericton Express	AHL	36	17	17	1	2132	105	2	*2.96	....	....	....	....	....	4	1	3	0	223	18	0	4.84	....	....	....	....
1984-85	Muskegon Mohawks	IHL	22	17	5	0	1321	59	1	2.68	....	....	....	....	....	....	....	....	....	....	....	....	....	....	....	....	....
	Pittsburgh Penguins	NHL	8	2	6	0	457	48	0	6.30	5.04	10.36	292	.836	38.3	....	....	....	....	....	....	....	....	....	....	....	....
	Baltimore Skipjacks	AHL	6	3	3	0	363	21	0	3.47	....	....	....	....	....	....	....	....	....	....	....	....	....	....	....	....	....

Season	Club	League	REGULAR SEASON													PLAYOFFS											
			GP	W	L	T	Mins	GA	SO	Avg	AAvg	Eff	SA	S%	SAPG	GP	W	L	T	Mins	GA	SO	Avg	Eff	SA	S%	SAPG
1985-86	Baltimore Skipjacks	AHL	39	12	20	4	2230	136	1	3.66	....	....	....	....	....	....	....	....	....	....	....	....	....	....	....	....	....
	Muskegon Lumberjacks	IHL	9	4	4	0	513	33	0	3.06	....	....	....	....	....	13	*12	1	0	793	41	0	*3.10	....	....	....	....
1986-87	Baltimore Skipjacks	AHL	32	10	11	0	1541	99	0	3.85	....	....	....	....	....	....	....	....	....	....	....	....	....	....	....	....	....
1987-88	Springfield Indians	AHL	35	12	15	4	1898	118	0	3.73	....	....	....	....	....	....	....	....	....	....	....	....	....	....	....	....	....
1988-89	Fredericton Capitals	NBSHL	30	....	....	....	1378	100	0	4.35	....	....	....	....	....	....	....	....	....	....	....	....	....	....	....	....	....
	Rochester Americans	AHL	19	12	4	1	1075	60	2	3.35	....	....	....	....	....	....	....	....	....	....	....	....	....	....	....	....	....
1989-90	Rochester Americans	AHL	19	7	6	4	1076	69	0	3.85	....	....	....	....	....	....	....	....	....	....	....	....	....	....	....	....	....
1990-91	Saint John Vitos	NBSHL	22	....	....	....	1320	101	*1	4.59	....	....	....	....	....	....	....	....	....	....	....	....	....	....	....	....	....
	Moncton Hawks	AHL	1	0	1	0	60	5	0	5.00	....	....	....	....	....	1	0	0	0	1	1	0	60.00	....	....	....	....
1991-92	Saint John Vitos	NBSHL	DID NOT PLAY – ASSISTANT COACH																								
	NHL Totals		**11**	**3**	**7**	**0**	**580**	**61**	**0**	**6.31**	....	....	**362**	**.831**	**37.4**	....	....	....	....	....	....	....	....	....	....	....	....

Shared Harry "Hap" Holmes Memorial Award (fewest goals against - AHL) with Clint Malarchuk (1983) • AHL First All-Star Team (1984) • Won Harry "Hap" Holmes Memorial Award (fewest goals against - AHL) (1984) • Won Aldege "Baz" Bastien Memorial Award (Top Goaltender - AHL) (1984)

Signed as a free agent by **Quebec**, August 1, 1982. Traded to **Pittsburgh** by **Quebec** for Tom Thornbury, December 6, 1984.

• FOSTER, Norm

Norman Richard G – L. 5'9", 175 lbs. b: Vancouver, B.C., 2/10/1965. Boston's 11th, 231st overall in 1983.

Season	Club	League	GP	W	L	T	Mins	GA	SO	Avg	AAvg	Eff	SA	S%	SAPG	GP	W	L	T	Mins	GA	SO	Avg	Eff	SA	S%	SAPG
1981-82	Penticton Knights	BCJHL	21	....	....	....	1187	58	0	2.93	....	....	....	....	....	....	....	....	....	....	....	....	....	....	....	....	....
1982-83	Penticton Knights	BCJHL	33	....	....	....	1999	156	0	4.68	....	....	....	....	....	....	....	....	....	....	....	....	....	....	....	....	....
1983-84	Michigan State Spartans	CCHA	32	23	8	0	1815	83	1	2.74	....	....	....	....	....	....	....	....	....	....	....	....	....	....	....	....	....
1984-85	Michigan State Spartans	CCHA	26	22	4	0	1531	67	0	2.63	....	....	....	....	....	....	....	....	....	....	....	....	....	....	....	....	....
	Canada	WJC-A	2	2	0	0	120	1	1	0.50	....	....	....	....	....	....	....	....	....	....	....	....	....	....	....	....	....
1985-86	Michigan State Spartans	CCHA	24	17	5	1	1414	87	0	3.69	....	....	....	....	....	....	....	....	....	....	....	....	....	....	....	....	....
1986-87	Michigan State Spartans	CCHA	24	14	7	1	1383	90	1	3.90	....	....	....	....	....	....	....	....	....	....	....	....	....	....	....	....	....
1987-88	Milwaukee Admirals	IHL	38	10	22	1	2001	170	0	5.10	....	....	....	....	....	....	....	....	....	....	....	....	....	....	....	....	....
1988-89	Maine Mariners	AHL	47	16	17	6	2411	156	1	3.88	....	....	....	....	....	....	....	....	....	....	....	....	....	....	....	....	....
1989-90	Maine Mariners	AHL	*64	23	28	10	*3664	217	3	3.55	....	....	....	....	....	....	....	....	....	....	....	....	....	....	....	....	....
1990-91	**Boston Bruins**	**NHL**	**3**	**2**	**1**	**0**	**184**	**14**	**0**	**4.57**	**4.11**	**7.80**	**82**	**.829**	**26.7**	....	....	....	....	....	....	....	....	....	....	....	....
	Maine Mariners	AHL	2	1	1	0	122	7	0	3.44	....	....	....	....	....	....	....	....	....	....	....	....	....	....	....	....	....
	Cape Breton Oilers	AHL	40	15	14	7	2207	135	1	3.67	....	....	....	....	....	2	0	2	0	128	8	0	3.75	....	....	....	....
1991-92	**Edmonton Oilers**	**NHL**	**10**	**5**	**3**	**0**	**439**	**20**	**0**	**2.73**	**2.44**	**2.98**	**183**	**.891**	**25.0**	....	....	....	....	....	....	....	....	....	....	....	....
	Cape Breton Oilers	AHL	29	15	13	1	1699	119	0	4.20	....	....	....	....	....	3	1	2	0	193	14	0	4.35	....	....	....	....
1992-93	Cape Breton Oilers	AHL	10	5	5	0	560	53	0	5.68	....	....	....	....	....	....	....	....	....	....	....	....	....	....	....	....	....
	Kansas City Blades	IHL	8	6	1	1	489	28	0	3.44	....	....	....	....	....	1	0	0	0	16	0	0	0.00	....	....	....	....
1993-94	Hershey Bears	AHL	17	5	9	1	775	58	0	4.49	....	....	....	....	....	....	....	....	....	....	....	....	....	....	....	....	....
1994-95	Detroit Vipers	IHL	18	9	5	1	797	59	0	4.44	....	....	....	....	....	....	....	....	....	....	....	....	....	....	....	....	....
	Las Vegas Thunder	IHL	14	8	3	1	677	35	0	3.10	....	....	....	....	....	....	....	....	....	....	....	....	....	....	....	....	....
	Detroit Falcons	ColHL	3	2	1	0	179	7	1	2.35	....	....	....	....	....	....	....	....	....	....	....	....	....	....	....	....	....
	NHL Totals		**13**	**7**	**4**	**0**	**623**	**34**	**0**	**3.27**	....	....	**265**	**.872**	**25.5**	....	....	....	....	....	....	....	....	....	....	....	....

CCHA Second All-Star Team (1984) • NCAA Championship All-Tournament Team (1985)

Traded to **Edmonton** by **Boston** for Edmonton's 6th round choice (Jiri Dopita) in 1992 Entry Draft, September 11, 1991. Signed as a free agent by **Philadelphia**, August 4, 1993.

• FOUNTAIN, Mike

G – L. 6'1", 180 lbs. b: North York, Ont., 1/26/1972. Vancouver's 3rd, 45th overall in 1992.

Season	Club	League	GP	W	L	T	Mins	GA	SO	Avg	AAvg	Eff	SA	S%	SAPG	GP	W	L	T	Mins	GA	SO	Avg	Eff	SA	S%	SAPG
1988-89	Huntsville Blair McCanns	OJHL-C	22	*18	3	2	1306	82	0	3.77	....	....	....	....	....	....	....	....	....	....	....	....	....	....	....	....	....
1989-90	Chatham Maroons	OJHL-B	21	....	....	....	1249	76	0	3.65	....	....	....	....	....	....	....	....	....	....	....	....	....	....	....	....	....
1990-91	Sault Ste. Marie Greyhounds	OHL	7	5	2	0	380	19	0	3.00	....	....	....	....	....	....	....	....	....	....	....	....	....	....	....	....	....
	Oshawa Generals	OHL	30	17	5	1	1483	84	0	3.40	....	....	....	....	....	8	1	4	....	292	26	0	5.34	....	....	....	....
1991-92	Oshawa Generals	OHL	40	18	13	6	2260	149	1	3.96	....	....	....	....	....	7	3	4	....	429	26	0	3.64	....	....	....	....
	Canada	WJC-A	DID NOT PLAY – SPARE GOALTENDER																								
1992-93	Canada	Nat-Team	13	7	5	1	745	37	1	2.98	....	....	....	....	....	....	....	....	....	....	....	....	....	....	....	....	....
	Hamilton Canucks	AHL	12	2	8	0	618	46	0	4.47	....	....	....	....	....	....	....	....	....	....	....	....	....	....	....	....	....
1993-94	Hamilton Canucks	AHL	*70	*34	28	6	*4005	241	*4	3.61	....	....	....	....	....	3	0	2	....	146	12	0	4.92	....	....	....	....
1994-95	Syracuse Crunch	AHL	61	25	29	7	3618	225	2	3.73	....	....	....	....	....	....	....	....	....	....	....	....	....	....	....	....	....
1995-96	Syracuse Crunch	AHL	54	21	27	3	3060	184	1	3.61	....	....	....	....	....	15	8	7	....	915	57	*2	3.74	....	....	....	....
1996-97	**Vancouver Canucks**	**NHL**	**6**	**2**	**2**	**0**	**245**	**14**	**1**	**3.43**	**3.69**	**3.56**	**135**	**.896**	**33.1**	....	....	....	....	....	....	....	....	....	....	....	....
	Syracuse Crunch	AHL	25	8	14	2	1462	78	1	3.20	....	....	....	....	....	2	0	2	....	120	12	0	6.02	....	....	....	....
1997-98	**Carolina Hurricanes**	**NHL**	**3**	**0**	**3**	**0**	**163**	**10**	**0**	**3.68**	**4.39**	**5.41**	**68**	**.853**	**25.0**	....	....	....	....	....	....	....	....	....	....	....	....
	Beast of New Haven	AHL	50	25	19	5	2922	139	3	2.85	....	....	....	....	....	....	....	....	....	....	....	....	....	....	....	....	....
1998-99	Beast of New Haven	AHL	51	23	24	3	2989	150	2	3.01	....	....	....	....	....	....	....	....	....	....	....	....	....	....	....	....	....
99-2000	**Ottawa Senators**	**NHL**	**1**	**0**	**0**	**0**	**16**	**1**	**0**	**3.75**	**4.28**	**6.25**	**6**	**.833**	**22.5**	....	....	....	....	....	....	....	....	....	....	....	....
	Grand Rapids Griffins	IHL	36	21	7	4	1851	77	3	2.50	....	....	....	....	....	1	0	0	....	20	4	0	12.00	....	....	....	....
	NHL Totals		**10**	**2**	**5**	**0**	**424**	**25**	**1**	**3.54**	....	....	**209**	**.880**	**29.6**	....	....	....	....	....	....	....	....	....	....	....	....

OHL First All-Star Team (1992) • AHL Second All-Star Team (1994)

• Recorded a shutout (3-0) in NHL debut vs. New Jersey, November 14, 1996. Signed as a free agent by **Carolina**, August 19, 1997. Signed as a free agent by **Ottawa**, July 30, 1999.

• FOWLER, Hec

Hector Norman Bostock G – L. 5'11", 190 lbs. b: Saskatoon, Sask., 10/14/1892.

Season	Club	League	GP	W	L	T	Mins	GA	SO	Avg	AAvg	Eff	SA	S%	SAPG	GP	W	L	T	Mins	GA	SO	Avg	Eff	SA	S%	SAPG
1909-10	Saskatoon Rovers	SCJHL	STATISTICS NOT AVAILABLE																								
	Saskatoon Bankers	SCSHL	1	1	0	0	60	2	0	2.00	....	....	....	....	....	....	....	....	....	....	....	....	....	....	....	....	....
1910-11	Saskatoon Westerns	SCSHL	STATISTICS NOT AVAILABLE																								
1911-12	Saskatoon Wholesalers	SPHL	....	....	....	....	....	....	....	....	....	....	....	....	....	1	1	0	0	60	1	0	1.00	....	....	....	....
1912-1915			DID NOT PLAY																								
1915-16	Saskatoon Pilgrims	N-SSHL	STATISTICS NOT AVAILABLE																								
	Saskatoon Pilgrims	Al-Cup	2	0	2	0	120	10	0	5.00	....	....	....	....	....	....	....	....	....	....	....	....	....	....	....	....	....
1916-17	Spokane Canaries	PCHA	23	8	15	0	1383	143	0	6.20	....	....	....	....	....	....	....	....	....	....	....	....	....	....	....	....	....
1917-18	Seattle Metropolitans	PCHA	18	*11	7	0	1168	65	*1	3.34	....	....	....	....	....	2	1	1	0	120	3	0	1.50	....	....	....	....
1918-19			MILITARY SERVICE																								
1919-20	Victoria Aristocrats	PCHA	22	10	12	0	1327	71	1	3.21	....	....	....	....	....	....	....	....	....	....	....	....	....	....	....	....	....
1920-21	Victoria Aristocrats	PCHA	24	10	13	1	1541	88	*3	3.43	....	....	....	....	....	....	....	....	....	....	....	....	....	....	....	....	....
1921-22	Victoria Aristocrats	PCHA	24	11	12	1	1468	70	1	2.86	....	....	....	....	....	....	....	....	....	....	....	....	....	....	....	....	....
1922-23	Victoria Cougars	PCHA	*30	*16	14	0	*1846	85	4	2.76	....	....	....	....	....	2	1	1	0	120	5	0	2.50	....	....	....	....
1923-24	Victoria Cougars	PCHA	*30	11	18	1	1843	103	0	3.35	....	....	....	....	....	....	....	....	....	....	....	....	....	....	....	....	....
1924-25	**Boston Bruins**	**NHL**	**7**	**1**	**6**	**0**	**409**	**42**	**0**	**6.16**	**7.97**	....	....	....	....	....	....	....	....	....	....	....	....	....	....	....	....
	Edmonton Eskimos	WCHL	8	5	3	0	480	29	1	3.63	....	....	....	....	....	....	....	....	....	....	....	....	....	....	....	....	....
1925-26			DID NOT PLAY																								
1926-27	Edmonton Eskimos	PrHL	32	12	18	2	1879	127	0	4.06	....	....	....	....	....	....	....	....	....	....	....	....	....	....	....	....	....
1927-28			DID NOT PLAY																								
1928-29	Oakland Sheiks	Cal-Pro	STATISTICS NOT AVAILABLE																								
1929-30	Oakland Sheiks	Cal-Pro	42	*24	12	6	2520	72	....	*1.71	....	....	....	....	....	4	*3	0	1	250	5	1	*1.20	....	....	....	....
1930-31	Oakland Sheiks	Cal-Pro	....	....	....	....	....	....	....	....	....	....	....	....	....	4	*2	1	1	254	11	0	*2.60	....	....	....	....
	NHL Totals		**7**	**1**	**6**	**0**	**409**	**42**	**0**	**6.16**	....	....	....	....	....	....	....	....	....	....	....	....	....	....	....	....	....
	Other Major League Totals		179	82	94	3	11056	654	11	3.55	....	....	....	....	....	4	2	2	....	240	8	0	2.00	....	....	....	....

PCHA First All-Star Team (1917) • PCHA Second All-Star Team (1918)

Signed as a free agent by **Seattle** (PCHA), December 25, 1917. Signed as a free agent by **Victoria** (PCHA), December 14, 1919. Traded to **Boston** by **Victoria** (PCHA) for cash, October 29, 1924. Signed as a free agent by **Edmonton** (WCHL), January 28, 1925.

Season	Club	League	GP	W	L	T	Mins	GA	SO	Avg	AAvg	Eff	SA	S%	SAPG	GP	W	L	T	Mins	GA	SO	Avg	Eff	SA	S%	SAPG
			REGULAR SEASON													PLAYOFFS											

• FRANCIS, Emile

Emile Percy "The Cat" G – L. 5'6", 145 lbs. b: North Battleford, Sask., 9/13/1926. **HHOF**

Season	Club	League	GP	W	L	T	Mins	GA	SO	Avg	AAvg	Eff	SA	S%	SAPG	GP	W	L	T	Mins	GA	SO	Avg	Eff	SA	S%	SAPG
1941-42	North Battleford Beavers	N-SJHL	4	0	4	0	240	34	0	8.50																	
1942-43	North Battleford Beavers	N-SJHL	8				480	59	0	7.37																	
1943-44	Philadelphia Falcons	EAHL	14				840	78	0	5.57																	
1944-45	Washington Lions	EAHL	36				2160	243	0	6.75						8	1	6	1	479	57	0	7.12				
1945-46	Moose Jaw Canucks	S-SJHL	18	*18	0	0	1080	55	0	*3.06						4	*4	0	0	240	8	*1	*2.00				
	Regina Capitals	WCSHL	1				60	5	0	5.00																	
	Moose Jaw Canucks	Mem-Cup	8	4	4	0	480	38	0	4.75																	
1946-47	**Chicago Black Hawks**	**NHL**	**19**	**6**	**12**	**1**	**1140**	**104**	**0**	**5.47**	**5.50**																
	Regina Capitals	WCSHL	32				1920	148	0	4.63																	
1947-48	**Chicago Black Hawks**	**NHL**	**54**	**18**	**31**	**5**	**3240**	**183**	**1**	**3.39**	**3.63**																
	Kansas City Pla-Mors	USHL	7	3	2	2	420	24	1	3.42																	
1948-49	**New York Rangers**	**NHL**	**2**	**2**	**0**	**0**	**120**	**4**	**0**	**2.00**	**2.24**																
	New Haven Ramblers	AHL	49	15	27	7	2940	203	4	4.14																	
1949-50	**New York Rangers**	**NHL**	**1**	**0**	**1**	**0**	**60**	**8**	**0**	**8.00**	**8.96**																
	New Haven Ramblers	AHL	68	22	36	10	4080	246	1	3.62																	
1950-51	**New York Rangers**	**NHL**	**5**	**1**	**1**	**2**	**260**	**14**	**0**	**3.23**	**3.64**																
	Cincinnati Mohawks	AHL	53	20	26	7	3280	167	2	3.05																	
1951-52	**New York Rangers**	**NHL**	**14**	**4**	**7**	**3**	**840**	**42**	**0**	**3.00**	**3.54**																
	Cincinnati Mohawks	AHL	51	24	22	5	3160	162	4	3.08						6	3	3	0	360	18	0	3.00				
1952-53	Vancouver Canucks	WHL	70	*32	28	10	4200	216	5	*3.08						9	4	5	0	550	30	0	3.27				
1953-54	Cleveland Barons	AHL	65	*37	28	0	3900	204	*5	3.14						9	*7	2	0	540	28	0	3.11				
1954-55	Cleveland Barons	AHL	57	28	26	3	3420	204	2	3.58						3	1	2	0	158	12	0	4.56				
1955-56	Saskatoon Quakers	WHL	68	27	33	8	4185	239	5	3.43						3	0	3	0	180	17	0	5.67				
1956-57	Seattle Americans	WHL	68	35	27	6	4167	214	4	3.08						6	2	4	0	358	20	0	3.35				
1957-58	Victoria Cougars	WHL	67	18	47	2	4040	294	2	4.37																	
1958-59	Spokane Spokes	WHL	68	25	37	6	4150	269	1	3.89						4	1	3	0	240	16	0	4.00				
1959-60	Spokane Spokes	WHL	68	19	46	3	4080	300	0	4.41																	
	Seattle Totems	WHL	1	1	0	0	60	2	0	2.00																	
	NHL Totals		**95**	**31**	**52**	**11**	**5660**	**355**	**1**	**3.76**																	

• Father of Bobby • WHL First All-Star Team (1953) • Won WHL Leading Goaltender Award (1953) • Won Leader Cup (MVP - WHL) (1953) • AHL Second All-Star Team (1954) • WHL Coast Division Second All-Star Team (1957) • Won Lester Patrick Trophy (1982)

Traded to **NY Rangers** by **Chicago** with Alex Kaleta for Jim Henry, October 7, 1948. Traded to **Cleveland** (AHL) by **NY Rangers** with Neil Strain and cash for Johnny Bower and Eldred Kobussen, July 20, 1953.

• FRANKS, Jim

James Reginald G – L. 5'11", 156 lbs. b: Melville, Sask., 11/8/1914 Deceased.

Season	Club	League	GP	W	L	T	Mins	GA	SO	Avg	AAvg	Eff	SA	S%	SAPG	GP	W	L	T	Mins	GA	SO	Avg	Eff	SA	S%	SAPG
1932-33	Regina Pats	S-SJHL	2				120	3	0	1.50						2	*2	0	0	120	0	*2	*0.00				
	Regina Pats	Mem-Cup	13	7	3	3	840	10	0	0.77																	
1933-34	Melville Millionaires	S-SJHL	STATISTICS NOT AVAILABLE																								
1934-35	Kerrobert Tigers	SIHA	STATISTICS NOT AVAILABLE																								
1935-36	Prince Albert Mintos	N-SSHL	18	11	6	1	1110	70	1	3.78						3	2	1	0	180	7	0	2.33				
	Prince Albert Mintos	Al-Cup	7	5	2	0	430	17	0	2.37																	
1936-37	Pittsburgh Hornets	AHL	20	8	9	3	1230	57	1	2.78						1	1	0	0	60	1	0	1.00				
♦	**Detroit Red Wings**	**NHL**														**1**	**0**	**1**		**30**	**2**	**0**	**4.00**				
1937-38	**Detroit Red Wings**	**NHL**	**1**	**1**	**0**	**0**	**60**	**3**	**0**	**3.00**	**3.61**																
	Pittsburgh Hornets	AHL	9	3	4	2	560	24	1	2.57																	
1938-39	Pittsburgh Hornets	AHL	33	16	14	3	2030	103	1	3.04																	
	Syracuse Stars	AHL	1	0	0	1	70	3	0	2.57																	
	Kansas City Greyhounds	AHA	4	3	1	0	240	10	1	2.50																	
1939-40	Indianapolis Capitols	AHL	29	16	7	6	1830	68	2	2.23																	
1940-41	Indianapolis Capitols	AHL	*56	17	28	11	*3500	168	1	2.88																	
1941-42	Omaha Knights	AHA	39	19	14	6	2397	116	1	2.90						8	*8	0	0	497	16	0	*1.93				
1942-43	**New York Rangers**	**NHL**	**23**	**5**	**14**	**4**	**1380**	**103**	**0**	**4.48**	**3.86**																
	Pittsburgh Hornets	AHL	4	1	3	0	240	19	0	4.45																	
1943-44	**Detroit Red Wings**	**NHL**	**17**	**6**	**8**	**3**	**1020**	**69**	**1**	**4.06**	**3.03**																
	Boston Bruins	**NHL**	**1**	**0**	**1**	**0**	**60**	**6**	**0**	**6.00**	**4.48**																
	Buffalo Bisons	AHL	1	1	0	0	60	1	0	1.00																	
1944-45	Buffalo Bisons	AHL	1	0	0	1	60	2	0	2.00																	
	St. Louis Flyers	AHL	29	5	21	3	1740	115	1	3.97																	
	NHL Totals		**42**	**12**	**23**	**7**	**2520**	**181**	**1**	**4.31**						**1**	**0**	**1**		**30**	**2**	**0**	**4.00**				

Signed as a free agent by **Detroit**, May 7, 1936. Loaned to **NY Rangers** by **Detroit** for 1942-43 season as a war-time replacement for Jim Henry, October, 1942. • Suspended by **Detroit** for refusing assignment to **Indianapolis** (AHL), October, 1943. Suspension lifted after Franks agreed to play "road games only" for club, December, 1943. Loaned to **Boston** by **Detroit** to replace injured Bert Gardiner, January 29, 1944. (Detroit 6, Boston 1).

• FREDERICK, Ray

G – L. 6', 154 lbs. b: Fort Frances, Ont., 7/31/1929.

Season	Club	League	GP	W	L	T	Mins	GA	SO	Avg	AAvg	Eff	SA	S%	SAPG	GP	W	L	T	Mins	GA	SO	Avg	Eff	SA	S%	SAPG
1943-44	Fort Frances Maple Leafs	TBSHL	STATISTICS NOT AVAILABLE																								
	Fort Frances Maple Leafs	Al-Cup	2	0	2	0	120	23	0	11.50																	
1944-45	Port Arthur Bruins	TBJHL	STATISTICS NOT AVAILABLE																								
	Fort Francis West Enders	TBSHL	5				270	41	0	9.11																	
1945-46	Hamilton Lloyds	OHA-Jr.	12				720	94	0	7.83																	
1946-47	Fort Frances Canadians	TBSHL	STATISTICS NOT AVAILABLE																								
	Fort Frances Canadians	Al-Cup	4	1	3	0	240	18	0	4.50																	
1947-48	Brandon Wheat Kings	MJHL	24	*15	9	0	1460	99	*2	4.07						5	1	3	1	310	29	0	5.00				
1948-49	Brandon Wheat Kings	MJHL	30	*27	3	0	1800	78	*2	*2.60						7	4	2	1	440	23	*1	*3.14				
	Brandon Wheat Kings	Mem-Cup	18	*11	6	1	1090	49	1	2.70																	
1949-50	Edmonton Flyers	WCSHL	47				2820	159	0	3.38						6	2	4	0	360	23	0	3.83				
1950-51	Edmonton Flyers	WCSHL	60				3600	198	2	3.30						8				480	27	*1	3.37				
1951-52	Chicoutimi Sagueneens	QMHL	14	5	6	3	870	40	0	2.76																	
	Charlottetown Islanders	MMHL	54	26	22	6	3216	193	2	3.60						4	0	4	0	264	15	0	3.41				
1952-53	Ottawa Senators	QMHL	*60	27	26	7	*3720	191	5	3.08						11	5	6	0	726	33	1	2.73				
1953-54	Ottawa Senators	QHL	60	28	27	5	3656	172	*9	2.82						22	*12	10	0	1364	48	0	2.11				
1954-55	Ottawa Senators	QHL	27	10	17	0	1626	90	1	3.32																	
	Chicago Black Hawks	**NHL**	**5**	**0**	**4**	**1**	**300**	**22**	**0**	**4.40**	**5.37**																
	Buffalo Bisons	AHL	22	15	7	0	1320	83	0	3.77						10	5	5	0	639	32	*1	3.00				
1955-56	Calgary Stampeders	WHL	60	34	26	0	3627	203	6	3.36						8	4	4	0	505	35	0	4.16				
1956-57	Chicoutimi Sagueneens	QHL	64	32	28	4	3886	190	4	2.93						*10	6	4	0	605	26	*1	*2.59				
1957-58	Cornwall Chevies	EOHL	38				2280	180	1	4.74						7				420	23	1	3.28				
1958-59	Sudbury Wolves	NOHA	53				3180	207	1	3.91						5				300	19	0	3.80				
	NHL Totals		**5**	**0**	**4**	**1**	**300**	**22**	**0**	**4.40**																	

MJHL Second All-Star Team (1948) • MJHL First All-Star Team (1949) • QMHL Second All-Star Team (1953) • QHL Second All-Star Team (1954)

Traded to **Charlottetown** (MMHL) by **Chicoutimi** (QMHL) for cash, December 9, 1951. Signed as a free agent by **Ottawa** (QMHL), September 15, 1952. Traded to **Chicago** by **Ottawa** (QHL) for cash, February 10, 1955.

• FRIESEN, Karl

G – L. 6', 185 lbs. b: Winnipeg, Man., 6/30/1958.

Season	Club	League	GP	W	L	T	Mins	GA	SO	Avg	AAvg	Eff	SA	S%	SAPG	GP	W	L	T	Mins	GA	SO	Avg	Eff	SA	S%	SAPG
1975-76	West Kildonan Northstars	MJHL	11				658	44	0	4.01																	
1976-77	West Kildonan Northstars	MJHL	STATISTICS NOT AVAILABLE																								
1977-78	West Kildonan Northstars	MJHL	38				2091	164	0	4.71						18	12	6	0	1042	71	1	4.08				
1978-79	West Kildonan Northstars	MJHL	37				2194	144	1	3.94																	

Season	Club	League	GP	W	L	T	Mins	GA	SO	Avg	AAvg	Eff	SA	S%	SAPG	GP	W	L	T	Mins	GA	SO	Avg	Eff	SA	S%	SAPG
			REGULAR SEASON													PLAYOFFS											
1979-80	St. Boniface Mohawks	CASH	STATISTICS NOT AVAILABLE																								
1980-81	SB Rosenheim	Germany	44	....	....	....	2592	140	....	3.24	....	....	....	....	....	3	....	....	....	180	8	....	2.67	....	....	....	....
	West Germany	WEC-A	4	1	2	1	240	20	0	5.00	....	....	....	....	....	....	....	....	....	....	....	....	....	....	....	....	....
1981-82	SB Rosenheim	Germany	42	....	....	....	2469	147	....	3.57	....	....	....	....	....	7	....	....	....	420	15	....	2.14	....	....	....	....
	West Germany	WEC-A	7	2	4	1	420	30	0	4.28	....	....	....	....	....	....	....	....	....	....	....	....	....	....	....	....	....
1982-83	SB Rosenheim	Germany	36	....	....	....	2160	103	....	2.86	....	....	....	....	....	9	....	....	....	480	36	....	4.50	....	....	....	....
	West Germany	WEC-A	5	....	....	....	300	21	....	4.20	....	....	....	....	....	....	....	....	....	....	....	....	....	....	....	....	....
1983-84	SB Rosenheim	Germany	42	....	....	....	2490	136	....	3.28	....	....	....	....	....	4	....	....	....	240	10	....	2.50	....	....	....	....
	West Germany	Olympics	5	3	1	1	300	16	0	3.20	....	....	....	....	....	....	....	....	....	....	....	....	....	....	....	....	....
1984-85	West Germany	Can-Cup	4	0	3	1	240	21	0	5.25	....	....	....	....	....	....	....	....	....	....	....	....	....	....	....	....	....
	SB Rosenheim	Germany	35	*23	5	6	2100	99	2	2.83	....	....	....	....	....	9	*9	0	....	547	22	0	2.41	....	....	....	....
	West Germany	WEC-A	9	3	5	1	580	34	*1	3.51	....	....	....	....	....	....	....	....	....	....	....	....	....	....	....	....	....
1985-86	Maine Mariners	AHL	35	16	11	5	1983	115	2	3.48	....	....	....	....	....	5	1	4	0	340	14	0	2.47	....	....	....	....
1986-87	**New Jersey Devils**	**NHL**	**4**	**0**	**2**	**1**	**130**	**16**	**0**	**7.38**	**6.26**	**14.76**	**80**	**.800**	**36.9**	....	....	....	....	....	....	....	....	....	....	....	....
	SB Rosenheim	Germany	14	10	2	2	840	39	1	2.79	....	....	....	....	....	7	3	4	....	424	18	0	2.55	....	....	....	....
	West Germany	WEC-A	5	2	2	1	300	19	0	3.80	....	....	....	....	....	....	....	....	....	....	....	....	....	....	....	....	....
1987-88	SB Rosenheim	Germany	33	*22	7	4	1980	85	*3	2.58	....	....	....	....	....	14	8	6	....	840	33	*3	2.36	....	....	....	....
	West Germany	Olympics	6	3	2	0	328	17	0	3.11	....	....	....	....	....	....	....	....	....	....	....	....	....	....	....	....	....
1988-89	SB Rosenheim	Germany	36	19	8	9	2160	98	....	2.72	....	....	....	....	....	11	*9	2	....	655	27	0	2.47	....	....	....	....
	West Germany	WEC-A	8	1	5	2	480	31	1	3.87	....	....	....	....	....	....	....	....	....	....	....	....	....	....	....	....	....
1989-90	SB Rosenheim	Germany	18	14	4	0	1060	43	0	2.43	....	....	....	....	....	11	8	3	....	526	37	0	4.22	....	....	....	....
1990-91	SB Rosenheim	Germany	40	....	....	....	2340	105	....	2.69	....	....	....	....	....	11	....	....	....	612	36	....	3.53	....	....	....	....
1991-92	SB Rosenheim	Germany	44	....	....	....	2447	133	....	3.26	....	....	....	....	....	9	....	....	....	547	27	....	2.96	....	....	....	....
	Germany	Olympics	1	0	1	0	60	5	0	5.00	....	....	....	....	....	....	....	....	....	....	....	....	....	....	....	....	....
1992-93	EC Hedos Munich	Germany	44	21	15	8	2640	111	....	2.52	....	....	....	....	....	4	....	....	....	240	14	....	3.50	....	....	....	....
1993-94	EC Hedos Munich	Germany	44	....	....	....	2172	81	....	2.24	....	....	....	....	....	10	....	....	....	600	25	....	2.50	....	....	....	....
1994-95	Munich Mad Dogs	Germany	26	....	....	....	1409	71	....	3.02	....	....	....	....	....	....	....	....	....	....	....	....	....	....	....	....	....
1995-96	Star Bulls Rosenheim	Germany	28	....	....	....	1571	81	....	3.09	....	....	....	....	....	4	....	....	....	240	18	....	4.50	....	....	....	....
	NHL Totals		**4**	**0**	**2**	**1**	**130**	**16**	**0**	**7.38**	....	....	**80**	**.800**	**36.9**	....	....	....	....	....	....	....	....	....	....	....	....

German Player of the Year (1982, 1988, 1989, 1990) • Shared Harry "Hap" Holmes Memorial Award (fewest goals against - AHL) with Sam St. Laurent (1986)

Signed as a free agent by **New Jersey**, April 24, 1985. • Munich Mad Dogs (Germany) folded after 27 games during 1994-95 season.

• FROESE, Bob

Robert Glenn G – L. 5′11″, 176 lbs. b: St. Catharines, Ont., 6/30/1958. St. Louis' 11th, 160th overall in 1978.

Season	Club	League	GP	W	L	T	Mins	GA	SO	Avg	AAvg	Eff	SA	S%	SAPG	GP	W	L	T	Mins	GA	SO	Avg	Eff	SA	S%	SAPG
1974-75	St. Catharines Black Hawks	OMJHL	15	....	....	....	871	71	0	4.89	....	....	....	....	....	....	....	....	....	....	....	....	....	....	....	....	....
1975-76	St. Catharines Black Hawks	OMJHL	39	....	....	....	1976	193	0	5.86	....	....	....	....	....	4	1	3	0	240	20	0	5.00	....	....	....	....
1976-77	Oshawa Generals	OMJHL	39	....	....	....	2063	161	*2	4.68	....	....	....	....	....	....	....	....	....	....	....	....	....	....	....	....	....
1977-78	Niagara Falls Flyers	OMJHL	53	....	....	....	3128	246	0	4.72	....	....	....	....	....	4	2	2	0	236	17	0	4.36	....	....	....	....
1978-79	Saginaw Gears	IHL	21	....	....	....	1050	58	0	3.31	....	....	....	....	....	....	....	....	....	....	....	....	....	....	....	....	....
	Milwaukee Admirals	IHL	14	....	....	....	715	42	1	3.52	....	....	....	....	....	7	....	....	....	334	23	0	4.14	....	....	....	....
1979-80	Maine Mariners	AHL	1	0	1	0	60	5	0	5.00	....	....	....	....	....	....	....	....	....	....	....	....	....	....	....	....	....
	Saginaw Gears	IHL	52	....	....	....	2827	178	0	3.78	....	....	....	....	....	4	....	....	....	213	13	0	3.66	....	....	....	....
1980-81	Saginaw Gears	IHL	43	....	....	....	2298	114	3	2.98	....	....	....	....	....	*13	*12	1	0	*806	29	*2	*2.16	....	....	....	....
1981-82	Maine Mariners	AHL	33	16	11	4	1900	104	2	3.28	....	....	....	....	....	....	....	....	....	....	....	....	....	....	....	....	....
1982-83	**Philadelphia Flyers**	**NHL**	**25**	**17**	**4**	**2**	**1407**	**59**	**4**	**2.52**	**2.01**	**2.61**	**569**	**.896**	**24.3**	....	....	....	....	....	....	....	....	....	....	....	....
	Maine Mariners	AHL	33	18	11	3	1966	110	2	3.36	....	....	....	....	....	....	....	....	....	....	....	....	....	....	....	....	....
1983-84	**Philadelphia Flyers**	**NHL**	**48**	**28**	**13**	**7**	**2863**	**150**	**2**	**3.14**	**2.46**	**3.55**	**1326**	**.887**	**27.8**	**3**	**0**	**2**	....	**154**	**11**	**0**	**4.29**	**6.13**	**77**	**.857**	**30.0**
1984-85	**Philadelphia Flyers**	**NHL**	**17**	**13**	**2**	**0**	**923**	**37**	**1**	**2.41**	**1.91**	**2.09**	**427**	**.913**	**27.8**	**4**	**0**	**1**	....	**146**	**11**	**0**	**4.52**	**7.00**	**71**	**.845**	**29.2**
	Hershey Bears	AHL	4	1	2	1	245	15	0	3.67	....	....	....	....	....	....	....	....	....	....	....	....	....	....	....	....	....
1985-86	**Philadelphia Flyers**	**NHL**	**51**	***31**	**10**	**3**	**2728**	**116**	***5**	***2.55**	**1.97**	**2.33**	**1270**	**.909**	**27.9**	**5**	**2**	**3**	....	**293**	**15**	**0**	**3.07**	**3.68**	**125**	**.880**	**25.6**
1986-87	**Philadelphia Flyers**	**NHL**	**3**	**3**	**0**	**0**	**180**	**8**	**0**	**2.67**	**2.26**	**2.43**	**88**	**.909**	**29.3**	....	....	....	....	....	....	....	....	....	....	....	....
	New York Rangers	**NHL**	**28**	**14**	**11**	**0**	**1474**	**92**	**0**	**3.74**	**3.17**	**4.39**	**784**	**.883**	**31.9**	**4**	**1**	**1**	....	**165**	**10**	**0**	**3.64**	**3.79**	**96**	**.896**	**34.9**
	Canada	WEC-A	5	1	3	1	300	18	1	3.60	....	....	....	....	....	....	....	....	....	....	....	....	....	....	....	....	....
1987-88	**New York Rangers**	**NHL**	**25**	**8**	**11**	**3**	**1443**	**85**	**0**	**3.53**	**2.94**	**4.30**	**697**	**.878**	**29.0**	....	....	....	....	....	....	....	....	....	....	....	....
1988-89	**New York Rangers**	**NHL**	**30**	**9**	**14**	**4**	**1621**	**102**	**1**	**3.78**	**3.15**	**4.87**	**791**	**.871**	**29.3**	**2**	**0**	**2**	....	**72**	**8**	**0**	**6.67**	**10.46**	**51**	**.843**	**42.5**
1989-90	**New York Rangers**	**NHL**	**15**	**5**	**7**	**1**	**812**	**45**	**0**	**3.33**	**2.82**	**4.22**	**355**	**.873**	**26.2**	....	....	....	....	....	....	....	....	....	....	....	....
	NHL Totals		**242**	**128**	**72**	**20**	**13451**	**694**	**13**	**3.10**	....	....	**6307**	**.890**	**28.1**	**18**	**3**	**9**	....	**830**	**55**	**0**	**3.98**	....	**420**	**.869**	**30.4**

NHL Second All-Star Team (1986) • Shared William M. Jennings Trophy with Darren Jensen (1986) • Played in NHL All-Star Game (1986)

Signed as a free agent by **Philadelphia**, June 18, 1981. Traded to **NY Rangers** by **Philadelphia** for Kjell Samuelsson and NY Rangers' 2nd round choice (Patrik Juhlin) in 1989 Entry Draft, December 18, 1986.

• FUHR, Grant

Grant S. "CoCo" G – R. 5′10″, 201 lbs. b: Spruce Grove, Alta., 9/28/1962. Edmonton's 1st, 8th overall in 1981.

Season	Club	League	GP	W	L	T	Mins	GA	SO	Avg	AAvg	Eff	SA	S%	SAPG	GP	W	L	T	Mins	GA	SO	Avg	Eff	SA	S%	SAPG
1979-80	Victoria Cougars	WHL	43	30	12	0	2488	130	2	3.14	....	....	....	....	....	8	5	3	....	465	22	0	2.84	....	....	....	....
1980-81	Victoria Cougars	WHL	59	48	9	1	3448	160	*4	*2.78	....	....	....	....	....	15	12	3	....	899	45	*1	*3.00	....	....	....	....
	Victoria Cougars	Mem-Cup	4	1	*3	0	239	18	0	4.52	....	....	....	....	....	....	....	....	....	....	....	....	....	....	....	....	....
1981-82	**Edmonton Oilers**	**NHL**	**48**	**28**	**5**	**14**	**2847**	**157**	**0**	**3.31**	**2.54**	**3.39**	**1532**	**.898**	**32.3**	**5**	**2**	**3**	....	**309**	**26**	**0**	**5.05**	....	....	....	....
1982-83	**Edmonton Oilers**	**NHL**	**32**	**13**	**12**	**5**	**1803**	**129**	**0**	**4.29**	**3.45**	**5.68**	**974**	**.868**	**32.4**	**1**	**0**	**0**	....	**11**	**0**	**0**	**0.00**	....	....	....	....
	Moncton Alpines	AHL	10	4	5	1	604	40	0	3.98	....	....	....	....	....	....	....	....	....	....	....	....	....	....	....	....	....
1983-84♦	**Edmonton Oilers**	**NHL**	**45**	**30**	**10**	**4**	**2625**	**171**	**1**	**3.91**	**3.08**	**4.57**	**1463**	**.883**	**33.4**	**16**	**11**	**4**	....	**883**	**44**	**1**	**2.99**	**2.68**	**491**	**.910**	**33.4**
1984-85	Canada	Can-Cup	2	1	0	1	120	6	0	3.00	....	....	....	....	....	....	....	....	....	....	....	....	....	....	....	....	....
♦	**Edmonton Oilers**	**NHL**	**46**	**26**	**8**	**7**	**2559**	**165**	**1**	**3.87**	**3.09**	**4.48**	**1426**	**.884**	**33.4**	***18**	***15**	**3**	....	**1064**	**55**	**0**	**3.10**	**3.27**	**522**	**.895**	**29.4**
1985-86	**Edmonton Oilers**	**NHL**	**40**	**29**	**8**	**0**	**2184**	**143**	**0**	**3.93**	**3.07**	**4.34**	**1296**	**.890**	**35.6**	**9**	**5**	**4**	....	**541**	**28**	**0**	**3.11**	**3.19**	**273**	**.897**	**30.3**
1986-87♦	**Edmonton Oilers**	**NHL**	**44**	**22**	**13**	**3**	**2388**	**137**	**0**	**3.44**	**2.91**	**4.10**	**1149**	**.881**	**28.9**	**19**	**14**	**5**	....	**1148**	**47**	**0**	**2.46**	**2.26**	**511**	**.908**	**26.7**
	NHL All-Stars	RV-87	2	1	1	0	120	8	0	4.00	....	....	....	....	....	....	....	....	....	....	....	....	....	....	....	....	....
1987-88	Canada	Can-Cup	9	6	1	2	575	32	0	3.00	....	....	....	....	....	....	....	....	....	....	....	....	....	....	....	....	....
♦	**Edmonton Oilers**	**NHL**	***75**	***40**	**24**	**9**	***4304**	**246**	***4**	**3.43**	**2.85**	**4.08**	**2066**	**.881**	**28.8**	***19**	***16**	**2**	....	***1136**	**55**	**0**	**2.90**	**3.39**	**471**	**.883**	**24.9**
1988-89	**Edmonton Oilers**	**NHL**	**59**	**23**	**26**	**6**	**3341**	**213**	**1**	**3.83**	**3.19**	**4.76**	**1714**	**.876**	**30.8**	**7**	**3**	**4**	....	**417**	**24**	**1**	**3.45**	**3.65**	**227**	**.894**	**32.7**
	Canada	WEC-A	5	1	3	1	298	18	1	3.62	....	....	....	....	....	....	....	....	....	....	....	....	....	....	....	....	....
1989-90♦	**Edmonton Oilers**	**NHL**	**21**	**9**	**7**	**3**	**1081**	**70**	**1**	**3.89**	**3.30**	**5.12**	**532**	**.868**	**29.5**	....	....	....	....	....	....	....	....	....	....	....	....
	Cape Breton Oilers	AHL	2	2	0	0	120	6	0	3.01	....	....	....	....	....	....	....	....	....	....	....	....	....	....	....	....	....
1990-91	**Edmonton Oilers**	**NHL**	**13**	**6**	**4**	**3**	**778**	**39**	**1**	**3.01**	**2.70**	**3.09**	**380**	**.897**	**29.3**	**17**	**8**	**7**	....	**1019**	**51**	**0**	**3.00**	**3.14**	**488**	**.895**	**28.7**
	Cape Breton Oilers	AHL	4	2	2	0	240	17	0	4.25	....	....	....	....	....	....	....	....	....	....	....	....	....	....	....	....	....
1991-92	**Toronto Maple Leafs**	**NHL**	**66**	**25**	**33**	**5**	**3774**	**230**	**2**	**3.66**	**3.29**	**4.35**	**1933**	**.881**	**30.7**	....	....	....	....	....	....	....	....	....	....	....	....
1992-93	**Toronto Maple Leafs**	**NHL**	**29**	**13**	**9**	**4**	**1665**	**87**	**1**	**3.14**	**2.68**	**3.31**	**826**	**.895**	**29.8**	....	....	....	....	....	....	....	....	....	....	....	....
	Buffalo Sabres	**NHL**	**29**	**11**	**15**	**2**	**1694**	**98**	**0**	**3.47**	**2.97**	**3.77**	**903**	**.891**	**32.0**	**8**	**3**	**4**	....	**474**	**27**	**1**	**3.42**	**4.28**	**216**	**.875**	**27.3**
1993-94	**Buffalo Sabres**	**NHL**	**32**	**13**	**12**	**3**	**1726**	**106**	**2**	**3.68**	**3.54**	**4.30**	**907**	**.883**	**31.5**	....	....	....	....	....	....	....	....	....	....	....	....
	Rochester Americans	AHL	5	3	0	2	310	10	0	1.94	....	....	....	....	....	....	....	....	....	....	....	....	....	....	....	....	....
1994-95	**Buffalo Sabres**	**NHL**	**3**	**1**	**2**	**0**	**180**	**12**	**0**	**4.00**	**4.19**	**5.65**	**85**	**.859**	**28.3**	....	....	....	....	....	....	....	....	....	....	....	....
	Los Angeles Kings	**NHL**	**14**	**1**	**7**	**3**	**698**	**47**	**0**	**4.04**	**4.25**	**5.01**	**379**	**.876**	**32.6**	....	....	....	....	....	....	....	....	....	....	....	....
1995-96	**St. Louis Blues**	**NHL**	***79**	**30**	**28**	**16**	**4365**	**209**	**3**	**2.87**	**2.85**	**2.78**	**2157**	**.903**	**29.6**	**2**	**1**	**0**	....	**69**	**1**	**0**	**0.87**	**0.19**	**45**	**.978**	**39.1**
1996-97	**St. Louis Blues**	**NHL**	**73**	**33**	**27**	**11**	**4261**	**193**	**3**	**2.72**	**2.92**	**2.71**	**1940**	**.901**	**27.3**	**6**	**2**	**4**	....	**357**	**13**	**2**	**2.18**	**1.55**	**183**	**.929**	**30.8**
1997-98	**St. Louis Blues**	**NHL**	**58**	**29**	**21**	**6**	**3274**	**138**	**3**	**2.53**	**3.02**	**2.58**	**1354**	**.898**	**24.8**	**10**	**6**	**4**	....	**616**	**28**	**0**	**2.73**	**2.57**	**297**	**.906**	**28.9**

Season	Club	League	GP	W	L	T	Mins	GA	SO	Avg	AAvg	Eff	SA	S%	SAPG	GP	W	L	T	Mins	GA	SO	Avg	Eff	SA	S%	SAPG
			REGULAR SEASON													PLAYOFFS											
1998-99	**St. Louis Blues**	**NHL**	**39**	**16**	**11**	**8**	**2193**	**89**	**2**	**2.44**	**2.90**	**2.63**	**827**	**.892**	**22.6**	**13**	**6**	**6**	....	**790**	**31**	**1**	**2.35**	**2.39**	**305**	**.898**	**23.2**
99-2000	**Calgary Flames**	**NHL**	**23**	**5**	**13**	**2**	**1205**	**77**	**0**	**3.83**	**4.39**	**5.50**	**536**	**.856**	**26.7**	....	....	....	....	....	....	....	....	....	....	....	....
	Saint John Flames	AHL	2	0	2	0	99	10	0	6.05	....	....	....	....	....	....	....	....	....	....	....	....	....	....	....	....	....
	NHL Totals		**868**	**403**	**295**	**114**	**48945**	**2756**	**25**	**3.38**	....	....	**24379**	**.887**	**29.9**	**150**	**92**	**50**	....	**8834**	**430**	**6**	**2.92**	....	....	....	....

WHL First All-Star Team (1980, 1981) • NHL Second All-Star Team (1982) • Canada Cup All-Star Team (1987) • NHL First All-Star Team (1988) • Won Vezina Trophy (1988) • Shared William M. Jennings Trophy with Dominik Hasek (1994) • Played in NHL All-Star Game (1982, 1984, 1985, 1986, 1988, 1989)

Traded to **Toronto** by **Edmonton** with Glenn Anderson and Craig Berube for Vincent Damphousse, Peter Ing, Scott Thornton, Luke Richardson, future considerations and cash, September 19, 1991. Traded to **Buffalo** by **Toronto** with Toronto's 5th round choice (Kevin Popp) in 1995 Entry Draft for Dave Andreychuk, Daren Puppa and Buffalo's 1st round choice (Kenny Jonsson) in 1993 Entry Draft, February 2, 1993. Traded to **Los Angeles** by **Buffalo** with Philippe Boucher and Denis Tsygurov for Alexei Zhitnik, Robb Stauber, Charlie Huddy and Los Angeles' 5th round choice (Marian Menhart) in 1995 Entry Draft, February 14, 1995. Signed as a free agent by **St. Louis**, July 14, 1995. Traded to **Calgary** by **St. Louis** for Calgary's 3rd round choice (Justin Papineau) in 2000 Entry Draft, September 4, 1999. • Statistics for suspended game vs. Boston on May 24, 1988 are included in playoff record.

• GAGE, Joaquin

Joaquin Jesse G – L. 6', 200 lbs. b: Vancouver, B.C., 10/19/1973. Edmonton's 6th, 109th overall in 1992.

Season	Club	League	GP	W	L	T	Mins	GA	SO	Avg	AAvg	Eff	SA	S%	SAPG	GP	W	L	T	Mins	GA	SO	Avg	Eff	SA	S%	SAPG
1990-91	Bellingham Ice Hawks	BCJHL	16	....	....	....	751	64	0	5.11	....	....	....	....	....	....	....	....	....	....	....	....	....	....	....	....	....
	Chilliwack Chiefs	BCJHL	2	1	0	0	85	11	0	7.76	....	....	....	....	....	....	....	....	....	....	....	....	....	....	....	....	....
	Portland Winter Hawks	WHL	3	0	3	0	180	17	0	5.70	....	....	....	....	....	....	....	....	....	....	....	....	....	....	....	....	....
1991-92	Portland Winter Hawks	WHL	63	27	30	4	3635	269	2	4.44	....	....	....	....	....	6	2	4	....	366	28	0	4.59	....	....	....	....
1992-93	Portland Winter Hawks	WHL	38	21	16	1	2302	153	2	3.99	....	....	....	....	....	8	5	2	....	427	30	0	4.22	....	....	....	....
1993-94	Prince Albert Raiders	WHL	53	24	25	3	3041	212	1	4.18	....	....	....	....	....	....	....	....	....	....	....	....	....	....	....	....	....
1994-95	Cape Breton Oilers	AHL	54	17	28	5	3010	207	0	4.13	....	....	....	....	....	....	....	....	....	....	....	....	....	....	....	....	....
	Edmonton Oilers	**NHL**	**2**	**0**	**2**	**0**	**99**	**7**	**0**	**4.24**	**4.44**	**7.42**	**40**	**.825**	**24.2**	....	....	....	....	....	....	....	....	....	....	....	....
1995-96	**Edmonton Oilers**	**NHL**	**16**	**2**	**8**	**1**	**717**	**45**	**0**	**3.77**	**3.75**	**4.85**	**350**	**.871**	**29.3**	....	....	....	....	....	....	....	....	....	....	....	....
	Cape Breton Oilers	AHL	21	8	11	0	1162	80	0	4.13	....	....	....	....	....	....	....	....	....	....	....	....	....	....	....	....	....
1996-97	Hamilton Bulldogs	AHL	29	7	14	4	1558	91	0	3.50	....	....	....	....	....	....	....	....	....	....	....	....	....	....	....	....	....
	Wheeling Nailers	ECHL	3	1	0	0	120	8	0	4.00	....	....	....	....	....	....	....	....	....	....	....	....	....	....	....	....	....
1997-98	Raleigh IceCaps	ECHL	39	19	14	3	2173	116	1	3.20	....	....	....	....	....	....	....	....	....	....	....	....	....	....	....	....	....
	Syracuse Crunch	AHL	2	1	1	0	120	7	0	3.50	....	....	....	....	....	....	....	....	....	....	....	....	....	....	....	....	....
1998-99	Augusta Lynx	ECHL	5	5	0	0	300	16	0	3.20	....	....	....	....	....	....	....	....	....	....	....	....	....	....	....	....	....
	Portland Pirates	AHL	26	8	11	3	1429	69	2	2.90	....	....	....	....	....	....	....	....	....	....	....	....	....	....	....	....	....
	Providence Bruins	AHL	3	0	2	0	130	9	0	4.16	....	....	....	....	....	....	....	....	....	....	....	....	....	....	....	....	....
	Syracuse Crunch	AHL	12	2	8	2	706	46	0	3.91	....	....	....	....	....	....	....	....	....	....	....	....	....	....	....	....	....
99-2000	Canada	Nat-Team	29	13	10	2	1530	83	0	3.25	....	....	....	....	....	....	....	....	....	....	....	....	....	....	....	....	....
	Hamilton Bulldogs	AHL	1	0	1	0	59	3	0	3.03	....	....	....	....	....	10	5	5	....	580	28	0	2.89	....	....	....	....
	NHL Totals		**18**	**2**	**10**	**1**	**816**	**52**	**0**	**3.82**	....	....	**390**	**.867**	**28.7**	....	....	....	....	....	....	....	....	....	....	....	....

• GAGNON, David

David Anthony G – L. 6', 185 lbs. b: Windsor, Ont., 10/31/1967.

Season	Club	League	GP	W	L	T	Mins	GA	SO	Avg	AAvg	Eff	SA	S%	SAPG	GP	W	L	T	Mins	GA	SO	Avg	Eff	SA	S%	SAPG
1986-87	Windsor Royals	OJHL-B	30	....	....	....	1779	190	0	6.41	....	....	....	....	....	....	....	....	....	....	....	....	....	....	....	....	....
1987-88	Colgate University	ECAC	13	6	4	2	743	43	1	3.47	....	....	....	....	....	....	....	....	....	....	....	....	....	....	....	....	....
1988-89	Colgate University	ECAC	28	17	9	2	1622	102	0	3.77	....	....	....	....	....	....	....	....	....	....	....	....	....	....	....	....	....
1989-90	Colgate University	ECAC	33	28	3	1	1986	93	0	2.81	....	....	....	....	....	....	....	....	....	....	....	....	....	....	....	....	....
1990-91	**Detroit Red Wings**	**NHL**	**2**	**0**	**1**	**0**	**35**	**6**	**0**	**10.29**	**9.26**	**22.05**	**28**	**.786**	**48.0**	....	....	....	....	....	....	....	....	....	....	....	....
	Adirondack Red Wings	AHL	24	8	8	5	1356	94	0	4.16	....	....	....	....	....	....	....	....	....	....	....	....	....	....	....	....	....
	Hampton Roads Admirals	ECHL	10	7	1	2	606	26	2	2.57	....	....	....	....	....	11	*10	1	0	696	27	0	*2.32	....	....	....	....
1991-92	Fort Wayne Komets	IHL	2	2	0	0	125	7	0	3.36	....	....	....	....	....	....	....	....	....	....	....	....	....	....	....	....	....
	Toledo Storm	ECHL	7	4	2	0	354	18	0	3.05	....	....	....	....	....	....	....	....	....	....	....	....	....	....	....	....	....
1992-93	Adirondack Red Wings	AHL	1	0	1	0	60	5	0	5.00	....	....	....	....	....	....	....	....	....	....	....	....	....	....	....	....	....
	Fort Wayne Komets	IHL	31	15	11	2	1771	116	0	3.93	....	....	....	....	....	1	0	0	0	6	0	0	0.00	....	....	....	....
1993-94	Fort Wayne Komets	IHL	19	7	6	3	1026	58	0	3.39	....	....	....	....	....	....	....	....	....	....	....	....	....	....	....	....	....
	Toledo Storm	ECHL	20	13	5	0	1122	65	1	3.48	....	....	....	....	....	*14	*12	2	0	*909	41	0	*2.70	....	....	....	....
1994-95	Roanoke Express	ECHL	29	17	7	5	1738	82	1	2.83	....	....	....	....	....	....	....	....	....	....	....	....	....	....	....	....	....
	Minnesota Moose	IHL	16	5	4	2	767	55	0	4.30	....	....	....	....	....	1	0	1	0	60	9	0	9.00	....	....	....	....
1995-96	Minnesota Moose	IHL	52	18	25	4	2721	188	0	4.14	....	....	....	....	....	....	....	....	....	....	....	....	....	....	....	....	....
1996-97	Roanoke Express	ECHL	60	34	18	6	3386	181	3	3.21	....	....	....	....	....	3	1	2	0	219	10	0	2.73	....	....	....	....
1997-98	Roanoke Express	ECHL	43	25	13	4	2466	119	2	2.89	....	....	....	....	....	7	3	4	....	441	15	1	2.04	....	....	....	....
1998-99	Roanoke Express	ECHL	34	20	9	5	2033	87	2	2.57	....	....	....	....	....	3	0	2	....	139	6	0	2.59	....	....	....	....
99-2000	Roanoke Express	ECHL	37	23	8	2	2085	87	0	2.50	....	....	....	....	....	2	1	1	....	120	7	0	3.50	....	....	....	....
	NHL Totals		**2**	**0**	**1**	**0**	**35**	**6**	**0**	**10.29**	....	....	**28**	**.786**	**48.0**	....	....	....	....	....	....	....	....	....	....	....	....

OJHL-B First All-Star Team (1987) • ECAC First All-Star Team (1990) • Shared Playoff MVP Award - ECHL (1991) with Dave Flanagan • Playoff MVP - ECHL (1994) • ECHL Second All-Star Team (1995)

Signed as a free agent by **Detroit**, June 11, 1990.

• GAMBLE, Bruce

Bruce George "Paladin" G – L. 5'9", 200 lbs. b: Port Arthur, Ont., 5/24/1938 d: 12/29/1982.

Season	Club	League	GP	W	L	T	Mins	GA	SO	Avg	AAvg	Eff	SA	S%	SAPG	GP	W	L	T	Mins	GA	SO	Avg	Eff	SA	S%	SAPG
1952-53	Port Arthur Bruins	TBJHL	11	....	....	....	660	82	0	7.45	....	....	....	....	....	....	....	....	....	....	....	....	....	....	....	....	....
1953-54	Port Arthur Bruins	TBJHL	36	20	15	1	2160	150	0	4.17	....	....	....	....	....	9	....	....	....	540	42	0	4.67	....	....	....	....
1954-55	Port Arthur Bruins	TBJHL	STATISTICS NOT AVAILABLE																								
1955-56	Port Arthur North Stars	TBJHL	31	19	10	2	1860	97	0	*3.13	....	....	....	....	....	9	*8	1	....	540	27	0	*3.00	....	....	....	....
	Port Arthur North Stars	Mem-Cup	13	7	6	0	800	53	0	4.74	....	....	....	....	....	....	....	....	....	....	....	....	....	....	....	....	....
1956-57	Guelph Biltmores	OHA-Jr.	40	....	....	....	2360	102	6	2.59	....	....	....	....	....	10	....	....	....	600	34	0	3.40	....	....	....	....
	Guelph Biltmores	Mem-Cup	6	1	4	1	370	28	0	4.54	....	....	....	....	....	....	....	....	....	....	....	....	....	....	....	....	....
1957-58	Guelph Biltmores	OHA-Jr.	50	13	32	5	3000	205	1	4.10	....	....	....	....	....	....	....	....	....	....	....	....	....	....	....	....	....
	Providence Reds	AHL	1	1	0	0	60	1	0	1.00	....	....	....	....	....	....	....	....	....	....	....	....	....	....	....	....	....
	Hull-Ottawa Canadiens	Mem-Cup	13	*10	3	0	610	30	2	2.95	....	....	....	....	....	....	....	....	....	....	....	....	....	....	....	....	....
1958-59	Vancouver Canucks	WHL	65	29	26	10	3900	199	*7	3.06	....	....	....	....	....	5	2	3	0	300	11	*2	2.20	....	....	....	....
	New York Rangers	**NHL**	**2**	**0**	**2**	**0**	**120**	**6**	**0**	**3.00**	**3.19**	....	....	....	....	....	....	....	....	....	....	....	....	....	....	....	....
1959-60	Providence Reds	AHL	71	37	32	2	4280	231	4	3.24	....	....	....	....	....	5	1	4	0	328	19	0	3.48	....	....	....	....
1960-61	Providence Reds	AHL	19	6	13	0	1140	85	0	4.47	....	....	....	....	....	....	....	....	....	....	....	....	....	....	....	....	....
	Boston Bruins	**NHL**	**52**	**12**	**33**	**7**	**3120**	**193**	**0**	**3.71**	**3.96**	....	....	....	....	....	....	....	....	....	....	....	....	....	....	....	....
1961-62	Portland Buckaroos	WHL	41	28	11	2	2476	108	2	*2.62	....	....	....	....	....	....	....	....	....	....	....	....	....	....	....	....	....
	Boston Bruins	**NHL**	**28**	**6**	**18**	**4**	**1680**	**121**	**1**	**4.32**	**4.57**	....	....	....	....	....	....	....	....	....	....	....	....	....	....	....	....
1962-63	Kingston Frontenacs	EPHL	68	*39	18	11	4080	220	1	3.23	....	....	....	....	....	5	*4	1	0	300	13	*1	*2.60	....	....	....	....
1963-64	Springfield Indians	AHL	21	5	12	3	1230	80	0	3.90	....	....	....	....	....	....	....	....	....	....	....	....	....	....	....	....	....
1964-65	Springfield Indians	AHL	DID NOT PLAY – SUSPENDED																								
1965-66	**Toronto Maple Leafs**	**NHL**	**10**	**5**	**2**	**3**	**501**	**21**	**4**	**2.51**	**2.53**	....	....	....	....	....	....	....	....	....	....	....	....	....	....	....	....
	Tulsa Oilers	CPHL	54	21	24	9	3240	155	4	2.87	....	....	....	....	....	....	....	....	....	....	....	....	....	....	....	....	....
1966-67♦	**Toronto Maple Leafs**	**NHL**	**23**	**5**	**10**	**4**	**1185**	**67**	**0**	**3.39**	**3.52**	....	....	....	....	....	....	....	....	....	....	....	....	....	....	....	....
	Tulsa Oilers	CPHL	7	2	4	1	420	24	0	3.43	....	....	....	....	....	....	....	....	....	....	....	....	....	....	....	....	....
	Rochester Americans	AHL	5	2	3	0	300	25	0	5.00	....	....	....	....	....	1	0	0	0	40	4	0	6.00	....	....	....	....
1967-68	**Toronto Maple Leafs**	**NHL**	**41**	**19**	**13**	**3**	**2201**	**85**	**5**	**2.32**	**2.56**	....	....	....	....	....	....	....	....	....	....	....	....	....	....	....	....
1968-69	**Toronto Maple Leafs**	**NHL**	**61**	**28**	**20**	**11**	**3446**	**161**	**3**	**2.80**	**2.89**	....	....	....	....	**3**	**0**	**2**	....	**86**	**13**	**0**	**9.07**	....	....	....	....
1969-70	**Toronto Maple Leafs**	**NHL**	**52**	**19**	**24**	**9**	**3057**	**156**	**5**	**3.06**	**3.26**	....	....	....	....	....	....	....	....	....	....	....	....	....	....	....	....

Season	Club	League	GP	W	L	T	Mins	GA	SO	Avg	AAvg	Eff	SA	S%	SAPG	GP	W	L	T	Mins	GA	SO	Avg	Eff	SA	S%	SAPG
			REGULAR SEASON													PLAYOFFS											
1970-71	Toronto Maple Leafs	NHL	23	6	14	1	1286	83	2	3.87	3.85	....	....	....	....	....	....	....	....	....	....	....	....	....	....	....	....
	Philadelphia Flyers	NHL	11	3	6	2	660	37	0	3.36	3.33	....	....	....	....	2	0	2	....	120	12	0	6.00	....	....	....	....
1971-72	Philadelphia Flyers	NHL	24	7	8	2	1186	58	2	2.93	2.96	....	....	....	....	....	....	....	....	....	....	....	....	....	....	....	....
	NHL Totals		327	110	150	46	18442	988	22	3.21	....	....	....	....	....	5	0	4	....	206	25	0	7.28	....	....	....	....

OHA-Jr. First All-Star Team (1957) • WHL Coast Division Second All-Star Team (1959) • Won WHL Coast Division Rookie of the Year Award (1959) • EPHL First All-Star Team (1963) • Played in NHL All-Star Game (1968)

Promoted to **NY Rangers** from **Vancouver** (WHL) to replace injured Gump Worsley in games on February 11, 12, 1959. Claimed by **Boston** from **NY Rangers** in Intra-League Draft, June 10, 1959. Loaned to **Portland** (WHL) by **Boston** to complete transaction that sent Don Head to Boston (May, 1961), September, 1961. Traded to **Springfield** (AHL) by **Boston** with Terry Gray, Randy Miller and Dale Rolfe for Bob McCord, June, 1963. • Suspended for entire 1964-65 season by **Springfield** (AHL) for refusing to report to team, September, 1964. Traded to **Toronto** by **Springfield** (AHL) for Larry Johnston and Bill Smith, September, 1965. Traded to **Philadelphia** by **Toronto** with Mike Walton and Toronto's 1st round choice (Pierre Plante) in 1971 Amateur Draft for Bernie Parent and Philadelphia's 2nd round choice (Rick Kehoe) in 1971 Amateur Draft, February 1, 1971. • Suffered career-ending heart attack during game vs. Vancouver, February 9, 1972.

• GAMBLE, Troy

Troy C. G – L. 5'11", 195 lbs. b: New Glasgow, N.S., 4/7/1967. Vancouver's 2nd, 25th overall in 1985.

Season	Club	League	GP	W	L	T	Mins	GA	SO	Avg	AAvg	Eff	SA	S%	SAPG	GP	W	L	T	Mins	GA	SO	Avg	Eff	SA	S%	SAPG
1983-84	Hobbena Hawks	AJHL	22	....	....	....	1102	43	0	3.47	....	....	....	....	....	....	....	....	....	....	....	....	....	....	....	....	....
1984-85	Medicine Hat Tigers	WHL	37	27	6	2	2095	100	*3	*2.86	....	....	....	....	....	2	1	1	0	120	9	0	4.50	....	....	....	....
1985-86	Medicine Hat Tigers	WHL	45	28	11	0	2264	142	0	3.76	....	....	....	....	....	11	5	4	0	530	31	0	3.51	....	....	....	....
1986-87	**Vancouver Canucks**	**NHL**	1	0	1	0	60	4	0	4.00	3.39	6.96	23	.826	23.0	....	....	....	....	....	....	....	....	....	....	....	....
	Medicine Hat Tigers	WHL	11	7	3	0	646	46	0	4.27	....	....	....	....	....	....	....	....	....	....	....	....	....	....	....	....	....
	Spokane Chiefs	WHL	38	17	17	1	2155	163	0	4.54	....	....	....	....	....	5	0	5	0	298	35	0	7.05	....	....	....	....
1987-88	Spokane Chiefs	WHL	67	36	26	1	3824	235	0	3.69	....	....	....	....	....	15	7	8	0	875	56	1	3.84	....	....	....	....
1988-89	**Vancouver Canucks**	**NHL**	5	2	3	0	302	12	0	2.38	1.98	2.04	140	.914	27.8	....	....	....	....	....	....	....	....	....	....	....	....
	Milwaukee Admirals	IHL	42	23	9	0	2198	138	0	3.77	....	....	....	....	....	11	5	5	0	640	35	0	3.28	....	....	....	....
1989-90	Milwaukee Admirals	IHL	*56	22	21	4	2779	160	2	4.21	....	....	....	....	....	5	2	2	0	216	19	0	5.28	....	....	....	....
1990-91	**Vancouver Canucks**	**NHL**	47	16	16	6	2433	140	1	3.45	3.10	4.18	1156	.879	28.5	4	1	3	....	249	16	0	3.86	4.64	133	.880	32.0
1991-92	**Vancouver Canucks**	**NHL**	19	4	9	3	1009	73	0	4.34	3.90	6.12	518	.859	30.8	....	....	....	....	....	....	....	....	....	....	....	....
	Milwaukee Admirals	IHL	9	2	4	2	521	31	0	3.57	....	....	....	....	....	....	....	....	....	....	....	....	....	....	....	....	....
1992-93	Hamilton Canucks	AHL	14	1	10	2	769	62	0	4.84	....	....	....	....	....	....	....	....	....	....	....	....	....	....	....	....	....
	Cincinnati Cyclones	IHL	33	11	18	2	1762	134	0	4.56	....	....	....	....	....	....	....	....	....	....	....	....	....	....	....	....	....
1993-94	Kalamazoo Wings	IHL	48	25	13	5	2607	146	*2	3.36	....	....	....	....	....	2	0	1	0	80	7	0	5.25	....	....	....	....
1994-95	Houston Aeros	IHL	43	18	17	5	2421	132	1	3.27	....	....	....	....	....	4	1	3	0	203	16	0	4.72	....	....	....	....
1995-96	Houston Aeros	IHL	52	16	25	5	2722	174	0	3.83	....	....	....	....	....	....	....	....	....	....	....	....	....	....	....	....	....
	NHL Totals		72	22	29	9	3804	229	1	3.61	....	....	1837	.875	29.0	4	1	3	....	249	16	0	3.86	....	133	.880	32.0

WHL East First All-Star Team (1985) • WHL West First All-Star Team (1988)

Signed as a free agent by **Dallas**, August 28, 1993.

• GARDINER, Bert

G – L. 5'11", 160 lbs. b: Saskatoon, Sask., 3/25/1913.

Season	Club	League	GP	W	L	T	Mins	GA	SO	Avg	AAvg	Eff	SA	S%	SAPG	GP	W	L	T	Mins	GA	SO	Avg	Eff	SA	S%	SAPG
1931-32	Saskatoon Mercuries	SCJHL	3	1	2	0	210	18	0	5.14	....	....	....	....	....	....	....	....	....	....	....	....	....	....	....	....	....
	Calgary Jimmies	CCJHL	2	2	0	0	120	2	0	1.00	....	....	....	....	....	....	....	....	....	....	....	....	....	....	....	....	....
	Calgary Jimmies	Mem-Cup	5	2	3	0	300	11	0	2.20	....	....	....	....	....	....	....	....	....	....	....	....	....	....	....	....	....
1932-33	Calgary Jimmies	CCJHL	2	2	0	0	120	2	0	1.00	....	....	....	....	....	....	....	....	....	....	....	....	....	....	....	....	....
	Calgary Jimmies	Mem-Cup	7	5	2	0	420	16	1	2.29	....	....	....	....	....	....	....	....	....	....	....	....	....	....	....	....	....
1933-34	Saskatoon Quakers	N-SSHL	14	6	7	1	910	53	0	3.49	....	....	....	....	....	4	3	1	0	240	8	1	2.00	....	....	....	....
1934-35	Brooklyn Crescents	EAHL	21	*15	5	1	1260	35	*6	*1.67	....	....	....	....	....	8	*7	1	0	560	13	*1	*1.39	....	....	....	....
1935-36	**New York Rangers**	**NHL**	1	1	0	0	60	1	0	1.00	1.41	....	....	....	....	....	....	....	....	....	....	....	....	....	....	....	....
	Philadelphia Arrows	Can-Am	45	26	16	3	2760	94	5	*2.04	....	....	....	....	....	4	3	1	0	265	4	*1	0.91	....	....	....	....
1936-37	Philadelphia Ramblers	IAHL	49	*28	13	8	3020	104	4	*2.07	....	....	....	....	....	6	3	3	0	360	15	*2	2.50	....	....	....	....
1937-38	Philadelphia Ramblers	IAHL	*48	*26	18	4	*2950	108	*8	2.20	....	....	....	....	....	5	3	2	0	369	10	*2	*1.63	....	....	....	....
1938-39	Philadelphia Ramblers	IAHL	52	*32	16	4	3230	150	2	2.79	....	....	....	....	....	5	3	2	0	335	11	0	1.97	....	....	....	....
	New York Rangers	**NHL**	....	....	....	....	....	....	....	....	....	....	....	....	....	6	3	3	....	433	12	0	1.66	....	....	....	....
1939-40	Philadelphia Rockets	IAHL	54	15	31	8	3350	170	4	3.04	....	....	....	....	....	....	....	....	....	....	....	....	....	....	....	....	....
	New Haven Eagles	IAHL	3	3	0	0	180	4	1	1.67	....	....	....	....	....	....	....	....	....	....	....	....	....	....	....	....	....
1940-41	**Montreal Canadiens**	**NHL**	42	13	23	6	2600	119	2	2.75	3.14	....	....	....	....	3	1	2	....	214	8	0	2.24	....	....	....	....
1941-42	**Montreal Canadiens**	**NHL**	10	1	8	1	620	42	0	4.06	4.01	....	....	....	....	....	....	....	....	....	....	....	....	....	....	....	....
	Washington Lions	AHL	34	12	19	3	2080	99	4	2.86	....	....	....	....	....	2	0	2	0	120	7	0	3.50	....	....	....	....
1942-43	**Chicago Black Hawks**	**NHL**	*50	17	18	15	*3020	180	1	3.58	3.02	....	....	....	....	....	....	....	....	....	....	....	....	....	....	....	....
1943-44	**Boston Bruins**	**NHL**	41	17	19	5	2460	212	1	5.17	4.03	....	....	....	....	....	....	....	....	....	....	....	....	....	....	....	....
	NHL Totals		144	49	68	27	8760	554	4	3.79	....	....	....	....	....	9	4	5	....	647	20	0	1.85	....	....	....	....

EAHL First All-Star Team (1935) • Won George L. Davis Jr. Trophy (fewest goals against - EAHL) (1935) • Can-Am First All-Star Team (1936) • IAHL First All-Star Team (1939) • IAHL Second All-Star Team (1940)

Signed as a free agent by **NY Rangers**, October 18, 1935. Traded to **Montreal** by **NY Rangers** with cash for Claude Bourque, April 26, 1940. Loaned to **Chicago** by **Montreal** for cash, October 12, 1942. Traded to **Boston** by **Montreal** for cash with Montreal holding right of repurchase, October 30, 1943.

• GARDINER, Charlie

Charles Robert "Chuck" G – R. 176 lbs. b: Edinburgh, Scotland, 12/31/1904 d: 6/13/1934. **HHOF**

Season	Club	League	GP	W	L	T	Mins	GA	SO	Avg	AAvg	Eff	SA	S%	SAPG	GP	W	L	T	Mins	GA	SO	Avg	Eff	SA	S%	SAPG
1921-22	Winnipeg Tigers	MJHL	1	0	1	0	60	6	0	6.00	....	....	....	....	....	....	....	....	....	....	....	....	....	....	....	....	....
1922-23	Winnipeg Tigers	MJHL	6	....	....	....	370	19	0	3.08	....	....	....	....	....	....	....	....	....	....	....	....	....	....	....	....	....
1923-24	Winnipeg Tigers	MJHL	....	....	....	....	....	....	....	....	....	....	....	....	....	1	1	0	0	60	0	1	*0.00	....	....	....	....
1924-25	Selkirk Fishermen	MHL-Sr.	18	....	....	....	1080	33	2	1.83	....	....	....	....	....	2	0	2	0	120	6	0	3.00	....	....	....	....
1925-26	Winnipeg Maroons	CHL	38	....	....	....	2280	82	6	2.16	....	....	....	....	....	5	....	....	....	300	10	1	2.00	....	....	....	....
1926-27	Winnipeg Maroons	AHA	36	17	14	5	2203	77	6	2.14	....	....	....	....	....	3	0	3	0	180	8	0	2.67	....	....	....	....
1927-28	**Chicago Black Hawks**	**NHL**	40	6	32	2	2420	114	3	2.83	4.77	....	....	....	....	....	....	....	....	....	....	....	....	....	....	....	....
1928-29	**Chicago Black Hawks**	**NHL**	*44	7	29	8	2758	85	5	1.85	3.99	....	....	....	....	....	....	....	....	....	....	....	....	....	....	....	....
1929-30	**Chicago Black Hawks**	**NHL**	*44	21	18	5	2750	111	3	2.42	2.44	....	....	....	....	2	0	1	1	172	3	0	1.05	....	....	....	....
1930-31	**Chicago Black Hawks**	**NHL**	*44	24	17	3	2710	78	*12	1.73	2.13	....	....	....	....	9	5	3	1	638	14	*2	1.32	....	....	....	....
1931-32	**Chicago Black Hawks**	**NHL**	*48	18	19	11	2989	92	4	*1.85	2.18	....	....	....	....	2	1	1	0	120	6	*1	3.00	....	....	....	....
1932-33	**Chicago Black Hawks**	**NHL**	*48	16	20	12	*3010	101	5	2.01	2.65	....	....	....	....	....	....	....	....	....	....	....	....	....	....	....	....
1933-34♦	**Chicago Black Hawks**	**NHL**	*48	20	17	11	3050	83	*10	1.63	1.98	....	....	....	....	8	*6	1	1	542	12	*2	*1.33	....	....	....	....
	NHL Totals		316	112	152	52	19687	664	42	2.02	....	....	....	....	....	21	12	6	3	1472	35	5	1.43	....	....	....	....

NHL First All-Star Team (1931, 1932, 1934) • Won Vezina Trophy (1932, 1934) • NHL Second All-Star Team (1933) • Played in NHL All-Star Game (1934)

Signed as a free agent by **Winnipeg** (AHA), November 3, 1926. Traded to **Chicago** by **Winnipeg** (AHA) with Cecil Browne for cash, April 8, 1927.

• GARDNER, George

George Edward "Bud" G – L. 5'8", 165 lbs. b: Lachine, Que., 10/8/1942.

Season	Club	League	GP	W	L	T	Mins	GA	SO	Avg	AAvg	Eff	SA	S%	SAPG	GP	W	L	T	Mins	GA	SO	Avg	Eff	SA	S%	SAPG
1961-62	Victoriaville Bruins	QJHL	49	28	19	2	2940	172	3	3.51	....	....	....	....	....	10	7	3	0	600	21	*2	*2.10	....	....	....	....
1962-63	Niagara Falls Flyers	OHA-Jr.	50	....	....	....	3000	146	3	2.92	....	....	....	....	....	9	....	....	....	540	21	0	*2.33	....	....	....	....
	Niagara Falls Flyers	Mem-Cup	15	9	6	0	910	50	1	3.30	....	....	....	....	....	....	....	....	....	....	....	....	....	....	....	....	....
1963-64	Minneapolis Bruins	CPHL	63	30	27	6	3780	235	1	3.63	....	....	....	....	....	5	1	4	0	300	21	0	4.20	....	....	....	....
1964-65	Memphis Wings	CPHL	66	25	32	9	3960	229	1	3.47	....	....	....	....	....	....	....	....	....	....	....	....	....	....	....	....	....
1965-66	Pittsburgh Hornets	AHL	*66	34	30	1	*3932	196	*7	2.99	....	....	....	....	....	3	0	3	0	180	14	0	4.67	....	....	....	....
	Detroit Red Wings	**NHL**	1	1	0	0	60	1	0	1.00	1.01	....	....	....	....	....	....	....	....	....	....	....	....	....	....	....	....
1966-67	**Detroit Red Wings**	**NHL**	11	3	6	0	560	36	0	3.86	4.01	....	....	....	....	....	....	....	....	....	....	....	....	....	....	....	....
	Pittsburgh Hornets	AHL	28	18	6	4	1680	76	2	*2.71	....	....	....	....	....	....	....	....	....	....	....	....	....	....	....	....	....
	Memphis Wings	CPHL	16	4	9	3	960	72	0	4.50	....	....	....	....	....	....	....	....	....	....	....	....	....	....	....	....	....
1967-68	**Detroit Red Wings**	**NHL**	12	3	2	2	534	32	0	3.60	4.01	....	....	....	....	....	....	....	....	....	....	....	....	....	....	....	....
	Fort Worth Wings	CPHL	12	4	7	0	680	39	0	3.44	....	....	....	....	....	....	....	....	....	....	....	....	....	....	....	....	....
1968-69	Vancouver Canucks	WHL	*53	*25	18	9	*3073	154	2	3.01	....	....	....	....	....	....	....	....	....	....	....	....	....	....	....	....	....
1969-70	Vancouver Canucks	WHL	*62	*41	14	6	*3556	171	3	*2.89	....	....	....	....	....	*11	*8	3	0	*664	35	0	3.16	....	....	....	....

			REGULAR SEASON													PLAYOFFS											
Season	Club	League	GP	W	L	T	Mins	GA	SO	Avg	AAvg	Eff	SA	S%	SAPG	GP	W	L	T	Mins	GA	SO	Avg	Eff	SA	S%	SAPG
1970-71	**Vancouver Canucks**	**NHL**	**18**	**6**	**8**	**1**	**922**	**52**	**0**	**3.38**	**3.35**	....	....	....	....	....	....	....	....	....	....	....	....	....	....	....	....
	Rochester Americans	AHL	4	0	1	3	240	13	0	3.25	....	....	....	....	....	....	....	....	....	....	....	....	....	....	....	....	....
1971-72	**Vancouver Canucks**	**NHL**	**24**	**3**	**14**	**3**	**1237**	**86**	**0**	**4.17**	**4.25**	....	....	....	....	....	....	....	....	....	....	....	....	....	....	....	....
1972-73	Los Angeles Sharks	WHA	49	19	22	4	2713	149	1	3.30	....	....	....	....	....	3	1	2	0	116	11	0	5.69	....	....	....	....
1973-74	Los Angeles Sharks	WHA	2	0	2	0	120	13	0	6.50	....	....	....	....	....	....	....	....	....	....	....	....	....	....	....	....	....
	Vancouver Blazers	WHA	28	4	21	1	1590	125	0	4.72	....	....	....	....	....	....	....	....	....	....	....	....	....	....	....	....	....
	Roanoke Valley Rebels	SHL	4	....	....	....	245	18	0	4.41	....	....	....	....	....	....	....	....	....	....	....	....	....	....	....	....	....
	NHL Totals		**66**	**16**	**30**	**6**	**3313**	**207**	**0**	**3.75**	....	....	....	....	....	....	....	....	....	....	....	....	....	....	....	....	....
	Other Major League Totals		79	23	45	5	4423	287	1	3.89	....	....	....	....	....	3	1	2	....	116	11	0	5.69	....	....	....	....

AHL Second All-Star Team (1966) • WHL Second All-Star Team (1970) • Won WHL Leading Goaltender Award (1970)

Claimed by **Boston** from **Kingston** (EPHL) in Inter-League Draft, June 4, 1963. Claimed by **Detroit** from **Boston** in Intra-League Draft, June 10, 1964. Promoted to **Detroit** from **Pittsburgh** (AHL) to replace Roger Crozier, March 20, 1966. (Detroit 6, Toronto 1). Claimed by **Rochester** (AHL) from **Detroit** in Reverse Draft, June 13, 1968. Rights transferred to **Vancouver** (WHL) after WHL club purchased **Rochester** (AHL) franchise, August 13, 1968. NHL rights transferred to **Vancouver** after NHL club purchased **Vancouver** (WHL) franchise, December 19, 1969. Selected by **LA Sharks** (WHA) in 1972 WHA General Player Draft, February 12, 1972. Traded to **Vancouver** (WHA) by **LA Sharks** (WHA) with future considerations (Ralph MacSweyn, November 5, 1973) for Ron Ward, October, 1973.

• GARNER, Tyrone

G – L. 6'1", 200 lbs. b: Stoney Creek, Ont., 7/27/1978. NY Islanders' 4th, 83rd overall in 1996.

Season	Club	League	GP	W	L	T	Mins	GA	SO	Avg	AAvg	Eff	SA	S%	SAPG	GP	W	L	T	Mins	GA	SO	Avg	Eff	SA	S%	SAPG
1994-95	Stoney Creek Spirit	OJHL-B	10	....	....	....	589	62	0	6.32	....	....	....	....	....	....	....	....	....	....	....	....	....	....	....	....	....
1995-96	Oshawa Generals	OHL	32	11	15	4	1697	112	0	3.96	....	....	....	....	....	....	....	....	....	....	....	....	....	....	....	....	....
	Hamilton Kilty B's	OJHL	8	....	....	....	419	28	0	4.01	....	....	....	....	....	....	....	....	....	....	....	....	....	....	....	....	....
1996-97	Oshawa Generals	OHL	9	6	1	0	434	20	0	2.76	....	....	....	....	....	3	1	0	....	88	6	0	4.09	....	....	....	....
1997-98	Oshawa Generals	OHL	54	23	17	8	2946	162	1	3.30	....	....	....	....	....	7	3	4	....	450	25	0	3.33	....	....	....	....
1998-99	Oshawa Generals	OHL	44	24	15	3	2496	124	4	2.98	....	....	....	....	....	15	9	6	0	901	57	0	3.80	....	....	....	....
	Calgary Flames	**NHL**	**3**	**0**	**2**	**0**	**139**	**12**	**0**	**5.18**	**6.16**	**8.40**	**74**	**.838**	**31.9**	....	....	....	....	....	....	....	....	....	....	....	....
99-2000	Saint John Flames	AHL	19	4	8	4	940	70	0	4.47	....	....	....	....	....	....	....	....	....	....	....	....	....	....	....	....	....
	Dayton Bombers	ECHL	3	0	2	0	113	11	0	5.86	....	....	....	....	....	....	....	....	....	....	....	....	....	....	....	....	....
	Johnstown Chiefs	ECHL	17	8	6	3	971	48	0	2.97	....	....	....	....	....	1	0	1	....	59	2	0	2.03	....	....	....	....
	NHL Totals		**3**	**0**	**2**	**0**	**139**	**12**	**0**	**5.18**	....	....	**74**	**.838**	**31.9**	....	....	....	....	....	....	....	....	....	....	....	....

OHL Second All-Star Team (1999)

Traded to **Calgary** by **NY Islanders** with Marty McInnis and Calgary's sixth round choice (previously acquired, Calgary selected Ilja Demidov) in 1997 Entry Draft for Robert Reichel, March 18, 1997.

• GARRETT, John

John Murdoch "Chi Chi" G – L. 5'8", 175 lbs. b: Trenton, Ont., 6/17/1951. St. Louis' 2nd, 38th overall in 1971.

Season	Club	League	GP	W	L	T	Mins	GA	SO	Avg	AAvg	Eff	SA	S%	SAPG	GP	W	L	T	Mins	GA	SO	Avg	Eff	SA	S%	SAPG
1969-70	Peterborough Petes	OHA-Jr.	48	....	....	....	2850	142	*3	*2.99	....	....	....	....	....	6	2	4	0	360	21	0	3.50	....	....	....	....
	Montreal Jr. Canadiens	Mem-Cup	9	7	1	0	371	19	0	3.07	....	....	....	....	....	....	....	....	....	....	....	....	....	....	....	....	....
1970-71	Peterborough Petes	OHA-Jr.	51	....	....	....	3062	151	5	*2.96	....	....	....	....	....	5	0	3	2	298	22	0	4.43	....	....	....	....
1971-72	Kansas City Blues	CHL	35	13	14	7	2041	121	*3	3.55	....	....	....	....	....	....	....	....	....	....	....	....	....	....	....	....	....
1972-73	Portland Buckaroos	WHL	17	6	8	2	951	52	2	3.28	....	....	....	....	....	....	....	....	....	....	....	....	....	....	....	....	....
	Richmond Robins	AHL	37	....	....	....	2138	117	0	3.26	....	....	....	....	....	3	0	3	0	123	17	0	8.29	....	....	....	....
1973-74	Minnesota Fighting Saints	WHA	40	21	18	0	2290	137	1	3.59	....	....	....	....	....	7	4	2	0	372	25	0	4.03	....	....	....	....
1974-75	Minnesota Fighting Saints	WHA	58	30	23	2	3294	180	2	3.28	....	....	....	....	....	12	6	6	0	726	41	1	3.39	....	....	....	....
1975-76	Minnesota Fighting Saints	WHA	52	26	22	4	3179	177	2	3.34	....	....	....	....	....	....	....	....	....	....	....	....	....	....	....	....	....
	Toronto Toros	WHA	9	3	6	0	551	33	1	3.59	....	....	....	....	....	....	....	....	....	....	....	....	....	....	....	....	....
1976-77	Birmingham Bulls	WHA	65	24	34	4	3803	224	*4	3.53	....	....	....	....	....	....	....	....	....	....	....	....	....	....	....	....	....
1977-78	Birmingham Bulls	WHA	*58	24	31	1	3306	210	2	3.81	....	....	....	....	....	5	1	4	0	271	26	0	5.76	....	....	....	....
1978-79	New England Whalers	WHA	41	20	17	4	2496	149	2	3.58	....	....	....	....	....	8	4	3	0	447	32	0	4.30	....	....	....	....
1979-80	**Hartford Whalers**	**NHL**	**52**	**16**	**24**	**11**	**3046**	**202**	**0**	**3.98**	**3.53**	....	....	....	....	**1**	**0**	**1**	....	**60**	**8**	**0**	**8.00**	....	....	....	....
1980-81	**Hartford Whalers**	**NHL**	**54**	**15**	**27**	**12**	**3152**	**241**	**0**	**4.59**	**3.74**	....	....	....	....	....	....	....	....	....	....	....	....	....	....	....	....
	Canada	WEC-A	3	....	....	....	120	8	....	4.00	....	....	....	....	....	....	....	....	....	....	....	....	....	....	....	....	....
1981-82	**Hartford Whalers**	**NHL**	**16**	**5**	**6**	**4**	**898**	**63**	**0**	**4.21**	**3.25**	....	....	....	....	....	....	....	....	....	....	....	....	....	....	....	....
	Quebec Nordiques	**NHL**	**12**	**4**	**5**	**3**	**720**	**62**	**0**	**5.17**	**4.00**	....	....	....	....	**5**	**3**	**2**	....	**323**	**21**	**0**	**3.90**	....	....	....	....
1982-83	**Quebec Nordiques**	**NHL**	**17**	**6**	**8**	**2**	**953**	**64**	**0**	**4.03**	**3.24**	**5.09**	**507**	**.874**	**31.9**	....	....	....	....	....	....	....	....	....	....	....	....
	Vancouver Canucks	**NHL**	**17**	**7**	**6**	**3**	**934**	**48**	**1**	**3.08**	**2.47**	**2.92**	**506**	**.905**	**32.5**	**1**	**1**	**0**	....	**60**	**4**	**0**	**4.00**	....	....	....	....
1983-84	**Vancouver Canucks**	**NHL**	**29**	**14**	**10**	**2**	**1653**	**113**	**0**	**4.10**	**3.23**	**6.11**	**758**	**.851**	**27.5**	**2**	**0**	**0**	....	**18**	**0**	**0**	**0.00**	**0.00**	**5**	**1.000**	**16.7**
1984-85	**Vancouver Canucks**	**NHL**	**10**	**1**	**5**	**0**	**407**	**44**	**0**	**6.49**	**5.19**	**11.75**	**243**	**.819**	**35.8**	....	....	....	....	....	....	....	....	....	....	....	....
1985-86	Fredericton Express	AHL	3	2	1	0	179	9	0	3.02	....	....	....	....	....	....	....	....	....	....	....	....	....	....	....	....	....
	NHL Totals		**207**	**68**	**91**	**37**	**11763**	**837**	**1**	**4.27**	....	....	....	....	....	**9**	**4**	**3**	....	**461**	**33**	**0**	**4.30**	....	....	....	....
	Other Major League Totals		323	148	151	15	18919	1110	14	3.52	....	....	....	....	....	32	15	15	....	1816	124	1	4.10	....	....	....	....

OHA-Jr. Second All-Star Team (1970) • OHA-Jr. First All-Star Team (1971) • WHA First All-Star Team (1977) • Played in NHL All-Star Game (1983)

Rights traded to **Chicago** by **St. Louis** to complete transaction that sent Danny O'Shea to St. Louis (February 8, 1972), September 19, 1972. Selected by **Minnesota** (WHA) in 1973 WHA Professional Player Draft, June, 1973. Signed as a free agent by **Toronto** (WHA) after **Minnesota** (WHA) franchise folded, March 10, 1976. Transferred to **Birmingham** (WHA) after **Toronto** (WHA) franchise relocated, June 30, 1976. Traded to **New England** (WHA) by **Birmingham** (WHA) for future considerations, September, 1978. Reclaimed by **Chicago** from **Hartford** prior to Expansion Draft, June 9, 1979. Claimed by **Hartford** as a priority selection, June 9, 1979. Traded to **Quebec** by **Hartford** for Michel Plasse and Quebec's 4th round choice (Ron Chyzowski) in 1983 Entry Draft, January 12, 1982. Traded to **Vancouver** by **Quebec** for Anders Eldebrink, February 4, 1983.

• GATHERUM, Dave

G – L. 5'8", 170 lbs. b: Fort William, Ont., 3/28/1932.

Season	Club	League	GP	W	L	T	Mins	GA	SO	Avg	AAvg	Eff	SA	S%	SAPG	GP	W	L	T	Mins	GA	SO	Avg	Eff	SA	S%	SAPG
1948-49	Fort William Hurricanes	TBJHL	12	3	8	1	720	67	*1	5.58	....	....	....	....	....	1	0	1	0	60	8	0	8.00	....	....	....	....
1949-50	Fort William Hurricanes	TBJHL	17	10	6	1	1020	82	0	4.24	....	....	....	....	....	5	....	....	....	300	17	*1	3.40	....	....	....	....
1950-51	Fort William Hurricanes	TBJHL	21	11	10	0	1260	84	0	4.00	....	....	....	....	....	12	....	....	....	720	52	0	4.33	....	....	....	....
1951-52	Fort William Hurricanes	TBJHL	30	15	14	1	1800	128	0	4.27	....	....	....	....	....	9	*7	2	0	540	30	0	3.33	....	....	....	....
	Fort William Hurricanes	Mem-Cup	12	5	5	2	760	36	0	2.80	....	....	....	....	....	....	....	....	....	....	....	....	....	....	....	....	....
1952-53	Shawinigan Cataracts	QMHL	30	6	21	3	1830	112	0	3.67	....	....	....	....	....	....	....	....	....	....	....	....	....	....	....	....	....
	Edmonton Flyers	WHL	6	3	1	2	360	14	0	2.30	....	....	....	....	....	....	....	....	....	....	....	....	....	....	....	....	....
	St. Louis Flyers	AHL	11	3	8	0	660	55	0	5.00	....	....	....	....	....	....	....	....	....	....	....	....	....	....	....	....	....
1953-54	Sherbrooke Saints	QHL	53	24	24	5	3240	176	4	3.26	....	....	....	....	....	4	1	3	0	240	13	0	3.25	....	....	....	....
	Detroit Red Wings	**NHL**	**3**	**2**	**0**	**1**	**180**	**3**	**1**	**1.00**	**1.26**	....	....	....	....	....	....	....	....	....	....	....	....	....	....	....	....
1954-55	Quebec Aces	QHL	20	9	10	0	1174	74	1	3.78	....	....	....	....	....	....	....	....	....	....	....	....	....	....	....	....	....
	Edmonton Flyers	WHL	4	1	2	1	240	15	0	3.75	....	....	....	....	....	....	....	....	....	....	....	....	....	....	....	....	....
	New Westminster Royals	WHL	4	1	1	2	240	10	0	2.50	....	....	....	....	....	....	....	....	....	....	....	....	....	....	....	....	....
1955-56	Kelowna Packers	OSHL	52	22	28	2	3120	221	1	4.25	....	....	....	....	....	10	4	6	0	600	37	0	3.70	....	....	....	....
	New Westminster Royals	WHL	7	1	6	0	422	32	0	4.55	....	....	....	....	....	....	....	....	....	....	....	....	....	....	....	....	....
	Vernon Canadians	Al-Cup	10	4	6	0	600	37	0	3.70	....	....	....	....	....	....	....	....	....	....	....	....	....	....	....	....	....
1956-57	Kelowna Packers	OSHL	49	....	....	....	2940	213	1	4.34	....	....	....	....	....	7	2	5	0	420	30	0	4.29	....	....	....	....
1957-58	Kelowna Packers	OSHL	51	....	....	....	3060	183	0	*3.61	....	....	....	....	....	12	*8	3	1	720	32	1	*2.67	....	....	....	....
	Kelowna Packers	Al-Cup	17	11	6	0	1020	41	*4	*2.41	....	....	....	....	....	....	....	....	....	....	....	....	....	....	....	....	....
1958-59	Kelowna Packers	OSHL	53	....	....	....	3180	189	*2	*3.57	....	....	....	....	....	....	....	....	....	....	....	....	....	....	....	....	....
	Nelson Maple Leafs	WIHL	....	....	....	....	....	....	....	....	....	....	....	....	....	1	1	0	0	60	4	0	4.00	....	....	....	....
	NHL Totals		**3**	**2**	**0**	**1**	**180**	**3**	**1**	**1.00**	....	....	....	....	....	....	....	....	....	....	....	....	....	....	....	....	....

OSHL First All-Star Team (1956, 1958)

Promoted to **Detroit** from **Sherbrooke** (QHL) to replace injured Terry Sawchuk in games on October 11, 16, 17, 1953. • Recorded a shutout (4-0) in NHL debut vs. Toronto, October 11, 1953. • NHL record for longest shutout sequence by a goaltender from start of career (100:21), October 11, 16, 1953.

• GAUTHIER, Paul

Paul Joseph Alphonse G – R. 5'5", 125 lbs. b: Winnipeg, Man., 3/6/1915.

Season	Club	League	GP	W	L	T	Mins	GA	SO	Avg	AAvg	Eff	SA	S%	SAPG	GP	W	L	T	Mins	GA	SO	Avg	Eff	SA	S%	SAPG
1932-33	Winnipeg Monarchs	MJHL	1	1	0	0	60	1	0	1.00	....	....	....	....	....	....	....	....	....	....	....	....	....	....	....	....	....
1933-34	Winnipeg Monarchs	MJHL	STATISTICS NOT AVAILABLE																								
1934-35	Winnipeg Monarchs	MJHL	7	....	....	....	420	15	0	*2.14	....	....	....	....	....	4	4	0	0	240	12	0	3.00	....	....	....	....
	Winnipeg Monarchs	Mem-Cup	8	*6	2	0	480	25	1	3.13	....	....	....	....	....	....	....	....	....	....	....	....	....	....	....	....	....

			REGULAR SEASON													PLAYOFFS											
Season	Club	League	GP	W	L	T	Mins	GA	SO	Avg	AAvg	Eff	SA	S%	SAPG	GP	W	L	T	Mins	GA	SO	Avg	Eff	SA	S%	SAPG
1935-36	Montreal Canadiens	MCHL	1	0	1	0	30	3	0	6.00	....	....	....	....	....	....	....	....	....	....	....	....	....	....	....	....	....
	Pittsburgh Shamrocks	IHL	16	7	9	0	990	56	0	3.39	....	....	....	....	....	....	....	....	....	....	....	....	....	....	....	....	....
1936-37	Minneapolis Millers	AHA	48	23	21	4	2880	105	6	2.19	....	....	....	....	....	6	*6	0	0	408	8	*1	*1.18	....	....	....	....
1937-38	New Haven Eagles	AHL	47	13	27	7	2910	126	5	2.60	....	....	....	....	....	1	0	1	0	60	2	0	2.00	....	....	....	....
	Montreal Canadiens	**NHL**	**1**	**0**	**0**	**1**	**70**	**2**	**0**	**1.71**	**2.06**	....	....	....	....	....	....	....	....	....	....	....	....	....	....	....	....
1938-39	Spokane Clippers	PCHL	34	....	....	....	2040	105	3	3.09	....	....	....	....	....	....	....	....	....	....	....	....	....	....	....	....	....
	New Haven Eagles	AHL	6	1	5	0	370	30	0	4.86	....	....	....	....	....	....	....	....	....	....	....	....	....	....	....	....	....
1939-40	Kansas City Greyhounds	AHA	47	20	27	0	2871	163	6	3.41	....	....	....	....	....	....	....	....	....	....	....	....	....	....	....	....	....
1940-41	Seattle Olympics	PCHL	41	....	....	....	2460	131	1	3.20	....	....	....	....	....	2	1	1	0	120	5	0	2.50	....	....	....	....
1941-42	Washington Lions	AHL	9	5	4	0	540	34	0	3.78	....	....	....	....	....	....	....	....	....	....	....	....	....	....	....	....	....
	New Haven Eagles	AHL	1	0	1	0	60	8	0	8.00	....	....	....	....	....	....	....	....	....	....	....	....	....	....	....	....	....
1942-43	Washington Lions	AHL	41	10	26	5	2530	203	0	4.81	....	....	....	....	....	....	....	....	....	....	....	....	....	....	....	....	....
1943-44	Buffalo Bisons	AHL	1	1	0	0	60	3	0	3.00	....	....	....	....	....	....	....	....	....	....	....	....	....	....	....	....	....
	Cleveland Barons	AHL	46	29	10	7	2760	139	4	3.02	....	....	....	....	....	4	1	3	0	240	25	0	6.25	....	....	....	....
1944-45	Cleveland Barons	AHL	4	3	0	1	240	15	0	3.75	....	....	....	....	....	....	....	....	....	....	....	....	....	....	....	....	....
1945-46			MILITARY SERVICE																								
1946-47	Houston Huskies	USHL	16	4	10	2	960	69	1	4.31	....	....	....	....	....	....	....	....	....	....	....	....	....	....	....	....	....
	Philadelphia Rockets	AHL	1	0	1	0	60	9	0	9.00	....	....	....	....	....	....	....	....	....	....	....	....	....	....	....	....	....
	Buffalo Bisons	AHL	3	3	0	0	180	7	0	2.33	....	....	....	....	....	....	....	....	....	....	....	....	....	....	....	....	....
	San Francisco Shamrocks	PCHL	5	....	....	....	300	19	0	3.80	....	....	....	....	....	....	....	....	....	....	....	....	....	....	....	....	....
1947-48	Houston Huskies	USHL	27	16	9	1	1640	112	1	4.10	....	....	....	....	....	7	5	2	0	423	19	0	2.70	....	....	....	....
	Omaha Knights	USHL	5	1	3	1	310	29	0	5.61	....	....	....	....	....	....	....	....	....	....	....	....	....	....	....	....	....
1948-49	Washington Lions	AHL	13	1	9	0	716	72	0	6.03	....	....	....	....	....	....	....	....	....	....	....	....	....	....	....	....	....
	NHL Totals		**1**	**0**	**0**	**1**	**70**	**2**	**0**	**1.71**	....	....	....	....	....	....	....	....	....	....	....	....	....	....	....	....	....

Signed as a free agent by **Montreal** (MCHL), January 26, 1936. Loaned to **Pittsburgh** (IHL) by **Montreal** (MCHL) for cash, February 6, 1936. Signed as a free agent by **Montreal Canadiens**, October, 1937. Loaned to **New Haven** (AHL) by **Montreal Canadiens** for cash, October, 1937. Promoted to **Montreal Canadiens** from **New Haven** (AHL) to replace injured Wilf Cude, January 13, 1938. (Montreal Canadiens 2, Chicago 2). Loaned to **Kansas City** (AHA) by **Montreal** for cash, October, 1939. Loaned to **Seattle** (PCHL) by **Montreal** for cash, October, 1940. NHL rights loaned to **Boston** by **Montreal** for remainder of 1941-42 season for loan of Terry Reardon, November 5, 1941.

• GAUTHIER, Sean

Sean D. G – L. 5'11", 200 lbs. b: Sudbury, Ont., 3/28/1971. Winnipeg's 7th, 181st overall in 1991.

Season	Club	League	GP	W	L	T	Mins	GA	SO	Avg	AAvg	Eff	SA	S%	SAPG	GP	W	L	T	Mins	GA	SO	Avg	Eff	SA	S%	SAPG
1987-88	Oakville Blades	OJHL-B	28	....	....	....	1491	110	2	4.43	....	....	....	....	....	....	....	....	....	....	....	....	....	....	....	....	....
1988-89	Kingston Raiders	OHL	37	7	18	1	1528	141	0	5.54	....	....	....	....	....	....	....	....	....	....	....	....	....	....	....	....	....
1989-90	Kingston Frontenacs	OHL	32	17	9	0	1602	101	0	3.78	....	....	....	....	....	2	0	1	....	76	6	0	4.74	....	....	....	....
1990-91	Kingston Frontenacs	OHL	59	16	36	3	3200	282	0	5.29	....	....	....	....	....	....	....	....	....	....	....	....	....	....	....	....	....
1991-92	Moncton Hawks	AHL	25	8	10	5	1415	88	1	3.73	....	....	....	....	....	2	0	0	....	26	2	0	4.62	....	....	....	....
	Fort Wayne Komets	IHL	18	10	4	2	978	59	1	3.62	....	....	....	....	....	2	0	0	....	48	7	0	8.74	....	....	....	....
1992-93	Moncton Hawks	AHL	38	10	16	9	2196	145	0	3.96	....	....	....	....	....	2	0	1	....	75	6	0	4.80	....	....	....	....
1993-94	Moncton Hawks	AHL	13	3	5	1	616	41	0	3.99	....	....	....	....	....	....	....	....	....	....	....	....	....	....	....	....	....
	Fort Wayne Komets	IHL	22	9	9	3	1139	66	0	3.48	....	....	....	....	....	....	....	....	....	....	....	....	....	....	....	....	....
1994-95	Fort Wayne Komets	IHL	5	0	2	1	217	15	0	4.13	....	....	....	....	....	....	....	....	....	....	....	....	....	....	....	....	....
	Canada	Nat-Team	STATISTICS NOT AVAILABLE																								
1995-96	South Carolina Stingrays	ECHL	49	31	11	7	2891	149	0	3.09	....	....	....	....	....	8	5	3	....	478	24	0	3.01	....	....	....	....
	St. John's Maple Leafs	AHL	5	1	1	0	173	9	0	3.12	....	....	....	....	....	....	....	....	....	....	....	....	....	....	....	....	....
1996-97	Pensacola Ice Pilots	ECHL	46	23	21	1	2692	168	1	3.74	....	....	....	....	....	12	8	4	....	749	44	*1	3.52	....	....	....	....
1997-98	Pensacola Ice Pilots	ECHL	54	29	17	7	3213	194	0	3.62	....	....	....	....	....	*19	12	7	....	1180	58	1	2.95	....	....	....	....
1998-99	**San Jose Sharks**	**NHL**	**1**	**0**	**0**	**0**	**3**	**0**	**0**	**0.00**	**0.00**	**0.00**	**2**	**1.000**	**40.0**	....	....	....	....	....	....	....	....	....	....	....	....
	Kentucky Thoroughblades	AHL	40	18	15	6	2376	99	1	2.50	....	....	....	....	....	4	0	1	....	130	8	0	3.68	....	....	....	....
99-2000	Louisiana Ice Gators	ECHL	22	12	6	3	1230	62	0	3.02	....	....	....	....	....	....	....	....	....	....	....	....	....	....	....	....	....
	Louisville Panthers	AHL	39	24	12	2	2259	102	3	2.71	....	....	....	....	....	4	1	3	....	239	14	0	3.52	....	....	....	....
	NHL Totals		**1**	**0**	**0**	**0**	**3**	**0**	**0**	**0.00**	....	....	**2**	**1.000**	**40.0**	....	....	....	....	....	....	....	....	....	....	....	....

ECHL Second All-Star Team (1996, 1998)

Signed as a free agent by **San Jose**, July 23, 1998. Signed as a free agent by **Florida**, January 13, 2000. • Played w/ RHI's LA Blades in 1995 (22-8-9-5-(3)-1023-133-0-6.24) and 1996 (19-6-8-1-(1)-733-92-0-6.02) and w/ Sacramento River Rats in 1997 (5-2-2-0-(0)-233-35-0-7.22)

• GELINEAU, Jack

John Edward G – L. 6', 180 lbs. b: Toronto, Ont., 11/11/1924 d: 11/12/1998.

Season	Club	League	GP	W	L	T	Mins	GA	SO	Avg	AAvg	Eff	SA	S%	SAPG	GP	W	L	T	Mins	GA	SO	Avg	Eff	SA	S%	SAPG
1942-43	Montreal Catholic High	Hi-School	STATISTICS NOT AVAILABLE																								
1943-44	Toronto Young Rangers	OHA-Jr.	11	1	9	1	680	58	1	5.12	....	....	....	....	....	....	....	....	....	....	....	....	....	....	....	....	....
	Toronto CIL	TMHL	4	0	4	0	240	22	0	5.50	....	....	....	....	....	....	....	....	....	....	....	....	....	....	....	....	....
	Toronto RCAF	TNDHL	7	5	2	0	420	21	1	3.00	....	....	....	....	....	1	0	1	0	60	3	0	3.00	....	....	....	....
1944-45	Montreal RCAF	MCHL	8	....	....	....	480	24	0	3.00	....	....	....	....	....	5	....	....	....	300	28	0	5.60	....	....	....	....
	Montreal Royals	QJHL	5	2	3	0	300	19	3	3.80	....	....	....	....	....	9	2	7	0	528	43	0	4.96	....	....	....	....
1945-46	McGill University	MCHL	15	13	2	0	900	52	1	3.47	....	....	....	....	....	....	....	....	....	....	....	....	....	....	....	....	....
1946-47	McGill University	MCHL	16	10	5	1	960	45	1	2.81	....	....	....	....	....	....	....	....	....	....	....	....	....	....	....	....	....
1947-48	McGill University	MCHL	20	14	6	0	1200	62	1	3.10	....	....	....	....	....	....	....	....	....	....	....	....	....	....	....	....	....
1948-49	McGill University	MCHL	6	3	3	0	360	20	0	3.33	....	....	....	....	....	....	....	....	....	....	....	....	....	....	....	....	....
	Boston Bruins	**NHL**	**4**	**2**	**2**	**0**	**240**	**12**	**0**	**3.00**	**3.37**	....	....	....	....	....	....	....	....	....	....	....	....	....	....	....	....
1949-50	**Boston Bruins**	**NHL**	**67**	**22**	**30**	**15**	**4020**	**220**	**3**	**3.28**	**3.80**	....	....	....	....	....	....	....	....	....	....	....	....	....	....	....	....
1950-51	**Boston Bruins**	**NHL**	***70**	**22**	**30**	**18**	***4200**	**197**	**4**	**2.81**	**3.18**	....	....	....	....	**4**	**1**	**2**	....	**260**	**7**	**1**	**1.62**	....	....	....	....
1951-52	Quebec Aces	QMHL	12	6	4	2	740	42	0	3.41	....	....	....	....	....	12	8	4	0	739	28	1	2.27	....	....	....	....
1952-53	Quebec Aces	QMHL	21	8	9	4	1300	59	1	2.72	....	....	....	....	....	21	*13	8	0	1303	51	1	*2.35	....	....	....	....
1953-54	Quebec Aces	QHL	57	24	27	6	3466	158	5	2.74	....	....	....	....	....	14	....	....	....	840	26	*4	*1.86	....	....	....	....
	Chicago Black Hawks	**NHL**	**2**	**0**	**2**	**0**	**120**	**18**	**0**	**9.00**	**11.57**	....	....	....	....	....	....	....	....	....	....	....	....	....	....	....	....
	Quebec Aces	Ed-Cup	3	1	2	0	179	14	0	4.69	....	....	....	....	....	....	....	....	....	....	....	....	....	....	....	....	....
1954-55	Quebec Aces	QHL	11	4	7	0	640	38	1	3.56	....	....	....	....	....	4	1	3	0	240	14	0	3.50	....	....	....	....
	NHL Totals		**143**	**46**	**64**	**33**	**8580**	**447**	**7**	**3.13**	....	....	....	....	....	**4**	**1**	**2**	....	**260**	**7**	**1**	**1.62**	....	....	....	....

Won Calder Memorial Trophy (1950)

Signed as a free agent by **Quebec** (QMHL) with Boston retaining his NHL rights, November 1, 1951. NHL rights traded to **Chicago** by **Boston** for cash, November 28, 1953.

• GIACOMIN, Ed

Edward G – L. 5'11", 180 lbs. b: Sudbury, Ont., 6/6/1939. **HHOF**

Season	Club	League	GP	W	L	T	Mins	GA	SO	Avg	AAvg	Eff	SA	S%	SAPG	GP	W	L	T	Mins	GA	SO	Avg	Eff	SA	S%	SAPG
1957-58	Commack Comets	NBHL	STATISTICS NOT AVAILABLE																								
1958-59	Sudbury Bell Telephone	NBHL	STATISTICS NOT AVAILABLE																								
	Washington Eagles	EAHL	4	4	0	0	240	13	0	3.25	....	....	....	....	....	....	....	....	....	....	....	....	....	....	....	....	....
1959-60	Clinton-NY Rovers	EAHL	51	....	....	....	3060	206	3	4.04	....	....	....	....	....	....	....	....	....	....	....	....	....	....	....	....	....
	Providence Reds	AHL	1	1	0	0	60	4	0	4.00	....	....	....	....	....	....	....	....	....	....	....	....	....	....	....	....	....
1960-61	Providence Reds	AHL	43	17	24	0	2510	183	0	4.37	....	....	....	....	....	....	....	....	....	....	....	....	....	....	....	....	....
	New York Rovers	EHL	12	2	10	0	720	54	0	4.50	....	....	....	....	....	....	....	....	....	....	....	....	....	....	....	....	....
1961-62	Providence Reds	AHL	40	20	19	1	2400	144	2	3.60	....	....	....	....	....	....	....	....	....	....	....	....	....	....	....	....	....
1962-63	Providence Reds	AHL	39	22	14	2	2340	102	4	*2.62	....	....	....	....	....	6	2	4	0	359	31	0	5.18	....	....	....	....
1963-64	Providence Reds	AHL	*69	30	34	5	*4140	232	*6	3.37	....	....	....	....	....	3	1	2	0	120	12	0	4.00	....	....	....	....
1964-65	Providence Reds	AHL	59	19	38	2	3527	226	0	3.84	....	....	....	....	....	....	....	....	....	....	....	....	....	....	....	....	....
1965-66	**New York Rangers**	**NHL**	**36**	**8**	**19**	**7**	**2096**	**128**	**0**	**3.66**	**3.77**	....	....	....	....	....	....	....	....	....	....	....	....	....	....	....	....
	Baltimore Clippers	AHL	7	3	4	0	420	21	0	3.00	....	....	....	....	....	....	....	....	....	....	....	....	....	....	....	....	....
1966-67	**New York Rangers**	**NHL**	***68**	***30**	**27**	**11**	***3981**	**173**	***9**	**2.61**	**2.63**	....	....	....	....	**4**	**0**	**4**	....	**246**	**14**	**0**	**3.41**	....	....	....	....
1967-68	**New York Rangers**	**NHL**	***66**	***36**	**20**	**10**	***3940**	**160**	***8**	**2.44**	**2.68**	....	....	....	....	**6**	**2**	**4**	....	**360**	**18**	**0**	**3.00**	....	....	....	....
1968-69	**New York Rangers**	**NHL**	***70**	***37**	**23**	**7**	***4114**	**175**	**7**	**2.55**	**2.61**	....	....	....	....	**3**	**0**	**3**	....	**180**	**10**	**0**	**3.33**	....	....	....	....
1969-70	**New York Rangers**	**NHL**	***70**	**35**	**21**	**14**	***4148**	**163**	**6**	**2.36**	**2.47**	....	....	....	....	**5**	**2**	**3**	....	**280**	**19**	**0**	**4.07**	....	....	....	....
1970-71	**New York Rangers**	**NHL**	**45**	**27**	**10**	**7**	**2641**	**95**	***8**	**2.16**	**2.11**	....	....	....	....	**12**	**7**	**5**	....	**759**	**28**	**0**	**2.21**	....	....	....	....
1971-72	**New York Rangers**	**NHL**	**44**	**24**	**10**	**9**	**2551**	**115**	**1**	**2.70**	**2.72**	....	....	....	....	***10**	***6**	**4**	....	***600**	**27**	**0**	**2.70**	....	....	....	....
1972-73	**New York Rangers**	**NHL**	**43**	**26**	**11**	**6**	**2580**	**125**	**4**	**2.91**	**2.73**	....	....	....	....	**10**	**5**	**4**	....	**539**	**23**	**1**	**2.56**	....	....	....	....

Season	Club	League	GP	W	L	T	Mins	GA	SO	Avg	AAvg	Eff	SA	S%	SAPG	GP	W	L	T	Mins	GA	SO	Avg	Eff	SA	S%	SAPG
			REGULAR SEASON													PLAYOFFS											
1973-74	**New York Rangers**	**NHL**	**56**	**30**	**15**	**10**	**3286**	**168**	**5**	**3.07**	**2.96**	....	....	....	....	**13**	**7**	**6**	....	**788**	**37**	**0**	**2.82**	....	....	....	....
1974-75	**New York Rangers**	**NHL**	**37**	**13**	**12**	**8**	**2069**	**120**	**1**	**3.48**	**3.15**	....	....	....	....	**2**	**0**	**2**	....	**86**	**4**	**0**	**2.79**	....	....	....	....
1975-76	**New York Rangers**	**NHL**	**4**	**0**	**3**	**1**	**240**	**19**	**0**	**4.75**	**4.31**	....	....	....	....	....	....	....	....	....	....	....	....	....	....	....	....
	Detroit Red Wings	**NHL**	**29**	**12**	**14**	**3**	**1740**	**100**	**2**	**3.45**	**3.13**	....	....	....	....	....	....	....	....	....	....	....	....	....	....	....	....
1976-77	**Detroit Red Wings**	**NHL**	**33**	**8**	**18**	**3**	**1791**	**107**	**3**	**3.58**	**3.33**	....	....	....	....	....	....	....	....	....	....	....	....	....	....	....	....
1977-78	**Detroit Red Wings**	**NHL**	**9**	**3**	**5**	**1**	**516**	**27**	**0**	**3.14**	**2.94**	....	....	....	....	....	....	....	....	....	....	....	....	....	....	....	....
	NHL Totals		**610**	**289**	**208**	**97**	**35693**	**1675**	**54**	**2.82**	....	....	....	....	....	**65**	**29**	**35**	....	**3838**	**180**	**1**	**2.81**	....	....	....	....

NHL First All-Star Team (1967, 1971) • NHL Second All-Star Team (1968, 1969, 1970) • Shared Vezina Trophy with Gilles Villemure (1971) • Played in NHL All-Star Game (1967, 1968, 1969, 1970, 1971, 1973)

• Hired as assistant trainer and practice goaltender by **Clinton** (EHL), September, 1959. Traded to **NY Rangers** by **Providence** (AHL) for Marcel Paille, Aldo Guidolin, Sandy McGregor and Jim Mikol, May 18, 1965. • McGregor refused to report to Providence and was replaced with Buzz Deschamps. Claimed on waivers by **Detroit** from **NY Rangers**, October 31, 1975.

• GIGUERE, Jean-Sebastien

G – L. 6', 185 lbs. b: Montreal, Que., 5/16/1977. Hartford's 1st, 13th overall in 1995.

Season	Club	League	GP	W	L	T	Mins	GA	SO	Avg	AAvg	Eff	SA	S%	SAPG	GP	W	L	T	Mins	GA	SO	Avg	Eff	SA	S%	SAPG
1992-93	Laval Regents	QAAA	25	12	11	2	1498	76	0	3.02	....	....	....	....	....	....	....	....	....	....	....	....	....	....	....	....	....
1993-94	Verdun College-Francais	QMJHL	25	13	5	2	1234	66	1	3.21	....	....	....	....	....	....	....	....	....	....	....	....	....	....	....	....	....
1994-95	Halifax Mooseheads	QMJHL	47	14	27	5	2755	181	2	3.94	....	....	....	....	....	7	3	4	....	417	17	1	*2.45	....	....	....	....
1995-96	Halifax Mooseheads	QMJHL	55	26	23	2	3230	185	1	3.44	....	....	....	....	....	6	1	5	....	354	24	0	4.07	....	....	....	....
1996-97	**Hartford Whalers**	**NHL**	**8**	**1**	**4**	**0**	**394**	**24**	**0**	**3.65**	**3.93**	**4.36**	**201**	**.881**	**30.6**	....	....	....	....	....	....	....	....	....	....	....	....
	Halifax Mooseheads	QMJHL	50	28	19	3	3014	170	2	3.38	....	....	....	....	....	16	9	7	....	954	58	0	3.65	....	....	....	....
1997-98	Saint John Flames	AHL	31	16	10	3	1758	72	2	2.46	....	....	....	....	....	10	5	3	....	536	27	0	3.02	....	....	....	....
1998-99	**Calgary Flames**	**NHL**	**15**	**6**	**7**	**1**	**860**	**46**	**0**	**3.21**	**3.82**	**3.30**	**447**	**.897**	**31.2**	....	....	....	....	....	....	....	....	....	....	....	....
	Saint John Flames	AHL	39	18	16	3	2145	123	3	3.44	....	....	....	....	....	7	3	2	....	304	21	0	4.14	....	....	....	....
99-2000	**Calgary Flames**	**NHL**	**7**	**1**	**3**	**1**	**330**	**15**	**0**	**2.73**	**3.12**	**2.34**	**175**	**.914**	**31.8**	....	....	....	....	....	....	....	....	....	....	....	....
	Saint John Flames	AHL	41	17	17	3	2243	114	0	3.05	....	....	....	....	....	3	0	3	....	178	9	0	3.03	....	....	....	....
	NHL Totals		**30**	**8**	**14**	**2**	**1584**	**85**	**0**	**3.22**	....	....	**823**	**.897**	**31.2**	....	....	....	....	....	....	....	....	....	....	....	....

QMJHL Second All-Star Team (1997) • Shared Harry "Hap" Holmes Memorial Trophy (fewest goals against - AHL) with Tyler Moss (1998)

Transferred to **Carolina** after **Hartford** franchise relocated, June 25, 1997. Traded to **Calgary** by **Carolina** with Andrew Cassels for Gary Roberts and Trevor Kidd, August 25, 1997. Traded to **Anaheim** by **Calgary** for Anaheim's 2nd round choice (later traded to Washington - Washington selected Matt Pettinger) in 2000 Entry Draft, June 10, 2000.

• GILBERT, Gilles

Gilles Joseph Gerard G – L. 6'1", 175 lbs. b: St. Esprit, Que., 3/31/1949. Minnesota's 3rd, 25th overall in 1969.

Season	Club	League	GP	W	L	T	Mins	GA	SO	Avg	AAvg	Eff	SA	S%	SAPG	GP	W	L	T	Mins	GA	SO	Avg	Eff	SA	S%	SAPG
1966-67	Trois-Rivieres Reds	QJHL	43	23	18	2	2540	188	1	4.44	....	....	....	....	....	14	9	5	0	850	65	0	4.59	....	....	....	....
	Thetford Mines Canadiens	M-Cup	5	3	1	0	276	18	0	3.91	....	....	....	....	....	....	....	....	....	....	....	....	....	....	....	....	....
1967-68	Trois-Rivieres Reds	QJHL	STATISTICS NOT AVAILABLE																								
1968-69	London Knights	OHA-Jr.	37	....	....	....	2200	167	1	4.55	....	....	....	....	....	....	....	....	....	....	....	....	....	....	....	....	....
1969-70	Iowa Stars	CHL	39	17	16	5	2340	127	2	3.26	....	....	....	....	....	4	2	2	0	245	14	0	3.43	....	....	....	....
	Minnesota North Stars	**NHL**	**1**	**0**	**1**	**0**	**60**	**6**	**0**	**6.00**	**6.37**	....	....	....	....	....	....	....	....	....	....	....	....	....	....	....	....
1970-71	**Minnesota North Stars**	**NHL**	**17**	**5**	**9**	**2**	**931**	**59**	**0**	**3.80**	**3.77**	....	....	....	....	....	....	....	....	....	....	....	....	....	....	....	....
1971-72	**Minnesota North Stars**	**NHL**	**4**	**1**	**2**	**1**	**218**	**11**	**0**	**3.03**	**3.06**	....	....	....	....	....	....	....	....	....	....	....	....	....	....	....	....
	Cleveland Barons	AHL	41	20	15	5	2319	140	2	3.62	....	....	....	....	....	4	1	2	0	187	18	0	5.78	....	....	....	....
1972-73	**Minnesota North Stars**	**NHL**	**22**	**10**	**10**	**2**	**1320**	**67**	**2**	**3.05**	**2.87**	....	....	....	....	**1**	**0**	**1**	....	**60**	**4**	**0**	**4.00**	....	....	....	....
1973-74	**Boston Bruins**	**NHL**	**54**	**34**	**12**	**8**	**3210**	**158**	**6**	**2.95**	**2.84**	....	....	....	....	**16**	**10**	**6**	....	**977**	**43**	**1**	**2.64**	....	....	....	....
1974-75	**Boston Bruins**	**NHL**	**53**	**23**	**17**	**11**	**3029**	**158**	**3**	**3.13**	**2.82**	....	....	....	....	**3**	**1**	**2**	....	**188**	**12**	**0**	**3.83**	....	....	....	....
1975-76	**Boston Bruins**	**NHL**	**55**	**33**	**8**	**10**	**3123**	**151**	**3**	**2.90**	**2.61**	....	....	....	....	**6**	**3**	**3**	....	**360**	**19**	***2**	**3.17**	....	....	....	....
1976-77	**Boston Bruins**	**NHL**	**34**	**18**	**13**	**3**	**2040**	**97**	**1**	**2.85**	**2.64**	....	....	....	....	**1**	**0**	**1**	....	**20**	**3**	**0**	**9.00**	....	....	....	....
1977-78	**Boston Bruins**	**NHL**	**25**	**15**	**6**	**2**	**1326**	**56**	**2**	**2.53**	**2.36**	....	....	....	....	....	....	....	....	....	....	....	....	....	....	....	....
1978-79	**Boston Bruins**	**NHL**	**23**	**12**	**8**	**2**	**1254**	**74**	**0**	**3.54**	**3.13**	....	....	....	....	**5**	**3**	**2**	....	**314**	**16**	**0**	**3.06**	....	....	....	....
1979-80	**Boston Bruins**	**NHL**	**33**	**20**	**9**	**3**	**1933**	**88**	**1**	**2.73**	**2.40**	....	....	....	....	....	....	....	....	....	....	....	....	....	....	....	....
1980-81	**Detroit Red Wings**	**NHL**	**48**	**11**	**24**	**9**	**2618**	**175**	**0**	**4.01**	**3.25**	....	....	....	....	....	....	....	....	....	....	....	....	....	....	....	....
1981-82	**Detroit Red Wings**	**NHL**	**27**	**6**	**10**	**6**	**1478**	**105**	**0**	**4.26**	**3.29**	....	....	....	....	....	....	....	....	....	....	....	....	....	....	....	....
1982-83	**Detroit Red Wings**	**NHL**	**20**	**4**	**14**	**1**	**1137**	**85**	**0**	**4.49**	**3.61**	**6.75**	**565**	**.850**	**29.8**	....	....	....	....	....	....	....	....	....	....	....	....
	NHL Totals		**416**	**192**	**143**	**60**	**23677**	**1290**	**18**	**3.27**	....	....	....	....	....	**32**	**17**	**15**	....	**1919**	**97**	**3**	**3.03**	....	....	....	....

Played in NHL All-Star Game (1974)

Loaned to **Thetford Mines** (QJHL) by **Trois-Rivieres** (QJHL) for Memorial Cup playoffs, April, 1967. Traded to **Boston** by **Minnesota** for Fred Stanfield, May 22, 1973. Traded to **Detroit** by **Boston** for Rogie Vachon, July 15, 1980.

• GILL, Andre

Andre Marcel G – L. 5'7", 145 lbs. b: Sorel, Que., 9/19/1941.

Season	Club	League	GP	W	L	T	Mins	GA	SO	Avg	AAvg	Eff	SA	S%	SAPG	GP	W	L	T	Mins	GA	SO	Avg	Eff	SA	S%	SAPG
1960-61	Sorel Royals	MMJHL	41	....	....	....	2460	197	1	4.80	....	....	....	....	....	....	....	....	....	....	....	....	....	....	....	....	....
1961-62	Sorel Royals	MMJHL	STATISTICS NOT AVAILABLE																								
1962-63	Hershey Bears	AHL	4	2	2	0	240	12	0	3.00	....	....	....	....	....	....	....	....	....	....	....	....	....	....	....	....	....
1963-64	Minneapolis Bruins	CPHL	5	4	1	0	300	16	0	3.20	....	....	....	....	....	....	....	....	....	....	....	....	....	....	....	....	....
	Hershey Bears	AHL	19	5	9	2	1000	60	0	3.60	....	....	....	....	....	....	....	....	....	....	....	....	....	....	....	....	....
1964-65	Hershey Bears	AHL	7	2	4	0	369	25	0	4.07	....	....	....	....	....	....	....	....	....	....	....	....	....	....	....	....	....
1965-66	Hershey Bears	AHL	18	6	9	0	966	55	1	3.42	....	....	....	....	....	....	....	....	....	....	....	....	....	....	....	....	....
1966-67	Hershey Bears	AHL	56	28	18	10	3334	161	*4	2.90	....	....	....	....	....	....	....	....	....	....	....	....	....	....	....	....	....
1967-68	Hershey Bears	AHL	46	23	17	5	2564	134	0	3.14	....	....	....	....	....	5	1	4	0	307	15	0	2.93	....	....	....	....
	Boston Bruins	**NHL**	**5**	**3**	**2**	**0**	**270**	**13**	**1**	**2.89**	**3.21**	....	....	....	....	....	....	....	....	....	....	....	....	....	....	....	....
1968-69	Hershey Bears	AHL	27	15	10	2	1548	83	0	3.22	....	....	....	....	....	....	....	....	....	....	....	....	....	....	....	....	....
1969-70	Hershey Bears	AHL	52	....	....	....	3043	161	1	3.17	....	....	....	....	....	7	3	4	0	441	20	0	2.72	....	....	....	....
1970-71	Hershey Bears	AHL	40	18	14	8	2284	102	4	*2.67	....	....	....	....	....	4	1	3	0	240	16	0	4.00	....	....	....	....
1971-72	Hershey Bears	AHL	40	17	13	9	2310	114	2	2.96	....	....	....	....	....	3	0	3	0	194	13	0	4.02	....	....	....	....
1972-73	Chicago Cougars	WHA	33	4	24	0	1709	118	0	4.14	....	....	....	....	....	....	....	....	....	....	....	....	....	....	....	....	....
1973-74	Chicago Cougars	WHA	13	4	7	2	803	46	0	3.44	....	....	....	....	....	11	6	5	0	614	38	0	3.71	....	....	....	....
	Long Island Cougars	NAHL	18	....	....	....	1137	50	0	2.63	....	....	....	....	....	5	....	....	....	286	13	0	2.73	....	....	....	....
1974-75	Hampton Gulls	SHL	24	....	....	....	1406	70	1	*2.99	....	....	....	....	....	11	....	....	....	660	39	1	3.55	....	....	....	....
1975-76			DID NOT PLAY																								
1976-77	Richmond Wildcats	SHL	17	....	....	....	884	53	0	3.60	....	....	....	....	....	....	....	....	....	....	....	....	....	....	....	....	....
	NHL Totals		**5**	**3**	**2**	**0**	**270**	**13**	**1**	**2.89**	....	....	....	....	....	....	....	....	....	....	....	....	....	....	....	....	....
	Other Major League Totals		46	8	31	2	2512	164	0	3.92	....	....	....	....	....	11	6	5	....	614	38	0	3.71	....	....	....	....

AHL First All-Star Team (1967) • Won Harry "Hap" Holmes Memorial Award (fewest goals against - AHL) (1967) • SHL Second All-Star Team (1975)

Promoted to **Boston** by **Hershey** (AHL) to replace injured Gerry Cheevers, December 23, 1967. • Recorded a shutout (4-0) in NHL debut vs. NY Rangers, December 23, 1967. Selected by **Dayton-Houston** (WHA) in 1972 WHA General Player Draft, February 12, 1972. WHA rights traded to **Chicago** (WHA) by **Houston** (WHA) for cash, September, 1972.

• GOODMAN, Paul

G – L. 5'10", 165 lbs. b: Selkirk, Man., 2/25/1905 d: 10/1/1959.

Season	Club	League	GP	W	L	T	Mins	GA	SO	Avg	AAvg	Eff	SA	S%	SAPG	GP	W	L	T	Mins	GA	SO	Avg	Eff	SA	S%	SAPG
1931-32	Selkirk Fishermen	MHL-Sr.	12	....	....	....	720	17	4	1.92	....	....	....	....	....	2	....	....	....	120	3	0	1.50	....	....	....	....
	Selkirk Fishermen	Al-Cup	2	0	2	0	120	4	0	2.00	....	....	....	....	....	....	....	....	....	....	....	....	....	....	....	....	....
1932-33	Selkirk Fishermen	MHL-Sr.	16	....	....	....	960	26	1	1.63	....	....	....	....	....	4	....	....	....	240	4	*1	*1.00	....	....	....	....
1933-34	Selkirk Fishermen	MHL-Sr.	16	....	....	....	960	30	*2	1.88	....	....	....	....	....	4	....	....	....	240	12	0	3.00	....	....	....	....
1934-35	Selkirk Fishermen	MHL-Sr.	10	....	....	....	600	29	0	2.90	....	....	....	....	....	2	....	....	....	120	12	0	3.00	....	....	....	....
1935-36	Wichita Skyhawks	AHA	48	16	32	0	2880	114	7	2.90	....	....	....	....	....	....	....	....	....	....	....	....	....	....	....	....	....
1936-37	Wichita Skyhawks	AHA	48	18	*27	3	2880	87	9	1.77	....	....	....	....	....	....	....	....	....	....	....	....	....	....	....	....	....
1937-38	Wichita Skyhawks	AHA	47	23	20	4	2820	130	1	2.69	....	....	....	....	....	4	1	3	0	240	15	1	3.75	....	....	....	....
♦	**Chicago Black Hawks**	**NHL**	....	....	....	....	....	....	....	....	....	....	....	....	....	**1**	**0**	**1**	....	**60**	**5**	**0**	**5.00**	....	....	....	....
1938-39	Wichita Skyhawks	AHA	45	13	*32	0	2737	156	0	3.42	....	....	....	....	....	3	0	3	0	182	19	0	6.26	....	....	....	....

Season	Club	League	GP	W	L	T	Mins	GA	SO	Avg	AAvg	Eff	SA	S%	SAPG	GP	W	L	T	Mins	GA	SO	Avg	Eff	SA	S%	SAPG
			REGULAR SEASON													PLAYOFFS											
1939-40	**Chicago Black Hawks**	**NHL**	**31**	**16**	**10**	**5**	**1920**	**62**	**4**	**1.94**	**2.31**	....	....	....	....	**2**	**0**	**2**	....	**127**	**5**	**0**	**2.36**	....	....	....	....
	Providence Reds	IAHL	21	10	9	2	1300	58	2	2.68	....	....	....	....	....	....	....	....	....	....	....	....	....	....	....	....	....
1940-41	**Chicago Black Hawks**	**NHL**	**21**	**7**	**10**	**4**	**1320**	**55**	**2**	**2.50**	**2.83**	....	....	....	....	....	....	....	....	....	....	....	....	....	....	....	....
	NHL Totals		**52**	**23**	**20**	**9**	**3240**	**117**	**6**	**2.17**	....	....	....	....	....	**3**	**0**	**3**	....	**187**	**10**	**0**	**3.21**	....	....	....	....

• GORDON, Scott

Scott M. G – L. 5'10", 175 lbs. b: Brockton, MA, 2/6/1963.

Season	Club	League	GP	W	L	T	Mins	GA	SO	Avg	AAvg	Eff	SA	S%	SAPG	GP	W	L	T	Mins	GA	SO	Avg	Eff	SA	S%	SAPG
1980-81	Oliver Ames Tigers	Hi-School	STATISTICS NOT AVAILABLE																								
1981-82	Kimball Union Wildcats	Hi-School	STATISTICS NOT AVAILABLE																								
1982-83	Boston College	ECAC	9	3	3	0	371	15	0	2.43	....	....	....	....	....	....	....	....	....	....	....	....	....	....	....	....	....
1983-84	Boston College	ECAC	35	21	13	0	2034	127	1	3.75	....	....	....	....	....	....	....	....	....	....	....	....	....	....	....	....	....
1984-85	Boston College	H-East	36	23	11	2	2179	131	1	3.61	....	....	....	....	....	....	....	....	....	....	....	....	....	....	....	....	....
1985-86	Boston College	H-East	32	17	8	1	1852	112	2	3.63	....	....	....	....	....	....	....	....	....	....	....	....	....	....	....	....	....
1986-87	Fredericton Express	AHL	32	9	12	2	1616	120	0	4.46	....	....	....	....	....	....	....	....	....	....	....	....	....	....	....	....	....
1987-88	Baltimore Skipjacks	AHL	34	7	17	3	1638	145	0	5.31	....	....	....	....	....	....	....	....	....	....	....	....	....	....	....	....	....
1988-89	Halifax Citadels	AHL	2	0	2	0	116	10	0	5.17	....	....	....	....	....	....	....	....	....	....	....	....	....	....	....	....	....
	Johnstown Chiefs	ECHL	31	18	9	3	1839	117	*2	*3.82	....	....	....	....	....	11	7	4	0	647	36	0	3.34	....	....	....	....
1989-90	**Quebec Nordiques**	**NHL**	**10**	**2**	**8**	**0**	**597**	**53**	**0**	**5.33**	**4.53**	**7.68**	**368**	**.856**	**37.0**	....	....	....	....	....	....	....	....	....	....	....	....
	Halifax Citadels	AHL	48	28	16	3	2851	158	0	3.33	....	....	....	....	....	6	2	4	0	340	28	0	4.94	....	....	....	....
1990-91	**Quebec Nordiques**	**NHL**	**13**	**0**	**8**	**0**	**485**	**48**	**0**	**5.94**	**5.36**	**12.67**	**225**	**.787**	**27.8**	....	....	....	....	....	....	....	....	....	....	....	....
	Halifax Citadels	AHL	24	12	10	2	1410	87	2	3.70	....	....	....	....	....	....	....	....	....	....	....	....	....	....	....	....	....
	United States	WEC-A	2	0	1	0	72	9	0	7.50	....	....	....	....	....	....	....	....	....	....	....	....	....	....	....	....	....
1991-92	United States	Nat-Team	29	13	12	3	1666	112	0	4.03	....	....	....	....	....	....	....	....	....	....	....	....	....	....	....	....	....
	United States	Olympics	1	0	0	0	17	2	0	3.53	....	....	....	....	....	....	....	....	....	....	....	....	....	....	....	....	....
	Halifax Citadels	AHL	7	3	3	1	424	27	0	3.82	....	....	....	....	....	....	....	....	....	....	....	....	....	....	....	....	....
	New Haven Nighthawks	AHL	4	3	1	0	239	11	0	2.76	....	....	....	....	....	2	0	2	0	119	9	0	4.54	....	....	....	....
1992-93	Nashville Knights	ECHL	23	13	9	1	1380	99	0	4.30	....	....	....	....	....	9	5	4	0	548	40	0	4.38	....	....	....	....
1993-94	Knoxville Cherokees	ECHL	26	15	10	1	1517	98	0	3.87	....	....	....	....	....	....	....	....	....	....	....	....	....	....	....	....	....
	Atlanta Knights	IHL	5	0	1	3	233	13	0	3.34	....	....	....	....	....	....	....	....	....	....	....	....	....	....	....	....	....
	NHL Totals		**23**	**2**	**16**	**0**	**1082**	**101**	**0**	**5.60**	....	....	**593**	**.830**	**32.9**	....	....	....	....	....	....	....	....	....	....	....	....

Hockey East First All-Star Team (1986) • ECHL First All-Star Team (1989)

Signed as a free agent by **Quebec**, October 2, 1986.

• GOSSELIN, Mario

"Goose" G – L. 5'8", 160 lbs. b: Thetford Mines, Que., 6/15/1963. Quebec's 3rd, 55th overall in 1982.

Season	Club	League	GP	W	L	T	Mins	GA	SO	Avg	AAvg	Eff	SA	S%	SAPG	GP	W	L	T	Mins	GA	SO	Avg	Eff	SA	S%	SAPG
1979-80	Montreal L'est Cantonniers	QAAA	19	8	6	0	1140	78	0	4.09	....	....	....	....	....	....	....	....	....	....	....	....	....	....	....	....	....
1980-81	Shawinigan Cataracts	QMJHL	21	4	9	0	907	75	0	4.96	....	....	....	....	....	1	0	0	0	20	2	0	6.00	....	....	....	....
1981-82	Shawinigan Cataracts	QMJHL	*60	33	25	2	*3404	230	0	4.05	....	....	....	....	....	14	7	7	0	788	58	0	4.42	....	....	....	....
1982-83	Shawinigan Cataracts	QMJHL	46	32	9	1	2556	133	*3	*3.12	....	....	....	....	....	8	5	3	0	457	29	0	3.81	....	....	....	....
	Canada	WJC-A	DID NOT PLAY – SPARE GOALTENDER																								
1983-84	Canada	Nat-Team	36	....	....	....	2007	126	0	3.77	....	....	....	....	....	....	....	....	....	....	....	....	....	....	....	....	....
	Canada	Olympics	7	4	3	0	380	14	0	2.21	....	....	....	....	....	....	....	....	....	....	....	....	....	....	....	....	....
	Quebec Nordiques	**NHL**	**3**	**2**	**0**	**0**	**148**	**3**	**1**	**1.22**	**0.96**	**0.55**	**67**	**.955**	**27.2**	....	....	....	....	....	....	....	....	....	....	....	....
1984-85	**Quebec Nordiques**	**NHL**	**35**	**19**	**11**	**3**	**1960**	**109**	**1**	**3.34**	**2.66**	**4.10**	**887**	**.877**	**27.2**	**17**	**9**	**8**	....	**1059**	**54**	**0**	**3.06**	**3.49**	**473**	**.886**	**26.8**
1985-86	**Quebec Nordiques**	**NHL**	**31**	**14**	**14**	**1**	**1726**	**111**	**2**	**3.86**	**3.01**	**5.38**	**796**	**.861**	**27.7**	**1**	**0**	**1**	....	**40**	**5**	**0**	**7.50**	**17.05**	**22**	**.773**	**33.0**
	Fredericton Express	AHL	5	2	2	1	304	15	0	2.96	....	....	....	....	....	....	....	....	....	....	....	....	....	....	....	....	....
1986-87	**Quebec Nordiques**	**NHL**	**30**	**13**	**11**	**1**	**1625**	**86**	**0**	**3.18**	**2.69**	**3.61**	**758**	**.887**	**28.0**	**11**	**7**	**4**	....	**654**	**37**	**0**	**3.39**	**3.85**	**326**	**.887**	**29.9**
1987-88	**Quebec Nordiques**	**NHL**	**54**	**20**	**28**	**4**	**3002**	**189**	**2**	**3.78**	**3.15**	**5.02**	**1422**	**.867**	**28.4**	....	....	....	....	....	....	....	....	....	....	....	....
1988-89	**Quebec Nordiques**	**NHL**	**39**	**11**	**19**	**3**	**2064**	**146**	**0**	**4.24**	**3.54**	**5.60**	**1105**	**.868**	**32.1**	....	....	....	....	....	....	....	....	....	....	....	....
	Halifax Citadels	AHL	3	3	0	0	183	9	0	2.95	....	....	....	....	....	....	....	....	....	....	....	....	....	....	....	....	....
1989-90	**Los Angeles Kings**	**NHL**	**26**	**7**	**11**	**1**	**1226**	**79**	**0**	**3.87**	**3.28**	**5.21**	**587**	**.865**	**28.7**	**3**	**0**	**2**	....	**63**	**3**	**0**	**2.90**	**3.78**	**23**	**.870**	**21.9**
1990-91	Phoenix Roadrunners	IHL	46	24	15	4	2673	172	1	3.86	....	....	....	....	....	11	7	4	0	670	43	0	3.85	....	....	....	....
1991-92	Springfield Indians	AHL	47	28	11	5	2606	142	0	3.27	....	....	....	....	....	6	1	4	0	319	18	0	3.39	....	....	....	....
1992-93	**Hartford Whalers**	**NHL**	**16**	**5**	**9**	**1**	**867**	**57**	**0**	**3.94**	**3.38**	**4.50**	**499**	**.886**	**34.5**	....	....	....	....	....	....	....	....	....	....	....	....
	Springfield Indians	AHL	23	8	7	7	1345	75	0	3.35	....	....	....	....	....	....	....	....	....	....	....	....	....	....	....	....	....
1993-94	**Hartford Whalers**	**NHL**	**7**	**0**	**4**	**0**	**239**	**21**	**0**	**5.27**	**5.07**	**10.34**	**107**	**.804**	**26.9**	....	....	....	....	....	....	....	....	....	....	....	....
	Springfield Indians	AHL	2	2	0	0	120	5	0	2.50	....	....	....	....	....	....	....	....	....	....	....	....	....	....	....	....	....
	NHL Totals		**241**	**91**	**107**	**14**	**12857**	**801**	**6**	**3.74**	....	....	**6228**	**.871**	**29.1**	**32**	**16**	**15**	....	**1816**	**99**	**0**	**3.27**	....	**844**	**.883**	**27.9**

QMJHL Second All-Star Team (1982) • QMJHL First All-Star Team (1983) • Played in NHL All-Star Game (1986)

• Recorded a shutout (5-0) in NHL debut vs. St. Louis, February 26, 1984. Signed as a free agent by **LA Kings**, June 14, 1989. Signed as a free agent by **Hartford**, September 4, 1991.
• Suffered eventual career-ending knee injury in game vs. Florida, November 27, 1993.

• GOVERDE, David

David W. G – R. 6', 210 lbs. b: Toronto, Ont., 4/9/1970. Los Angeles' 4th, 91st overall in 1990.

Season	Club	League	GP	W	L	T	Mins	GA	SO	Avg	AAvg	Eff	SA	S%	SAPG	GP	W	L	T	Mins	GA	SO	Avg	Eff	SA	S%	SAPG
1986-87	North York Rangers	MTHL	21	....	....	....	672	47	3	2.24	....	....	....	....	....	....	....	....	....	....	....	....	....	....	....	....	....
1987-88	Windsor Spitfires	OHL	10	5	3	1	471	28	0	3.57	....	....	....	....	....	....	....	....	....	....	....	....	....	....	....	....	....
1988-89	Windsor Spitfires	OHL	5	0	3	0	221	24	0	6.52	....	....	....	....	....	....	....	....	....	....	....	....	....	....	....	....	....
	Sudbury Wolves	OHL	39	16	15	4	2189	156	0	4.28	....	....	....	....	....	....	....	....	....	....	....	....	....	....	....	....	....
1989-90	Sudbury Wolves	OHL	52	28	12	7	2941	182	0	3.71	....	....	....	....	....	7	3	3	....	394	25	0	3.81	....	....	....	....
1990-91	Phoenix Roadrunners	IHL	40	11	19	5	2007	137	0	4.10	....	....	....	....	....	....	....	....	....	....	....	....	....	....	....	....	....
1991-92	**Los Angeles Kings**	**NHL**	**2**	**1**	**1**	**0**	**120**	**9**	**0**	**4.50**	**4.03**	**6.43**	**63**	**.857**	**31.5**	....	....	....	....	....	....	....	....	....	....	....	....
	Phoenix Roadrunners	IHL	36	11	19	3	1951	129	1	3.97	....	....	....	....	....	....	....	....	....	....	....	....	....	....	....	....	....
	New Haven Nighthawks	AHL	5	1	3	0	248	17	0	4.11	....	....	....	....	....	....	....	....	....	....	....	....	....	....	....	....	....
1992-93	**Los Angeles Kings**	**NHL**	**2**	**0**	**2**	**0**	**98**	**13**	**0**	**7.96**	**6.82**	**20.29**	**51**	**.745**	**31.2**	....	....	....	....	....	....	....	....	....	....	....	....
	Phoenix Roadrunners	IHL	45	18	21	3	2569	173	1	4.04	....	....	....	....	....	....	....	....	....	....	....	....	....	....	....	....	....
1993-94	**Los Angeles Kings**	**NHL**	**1**	**0**	**1**	**0**	**60**	**7**	**0**	**7.00**	**6.73**	**13.24**	**37**	**.811**	**37.0**	....	....	....	....	....	....	....	....	....	....	....	....
	Phoenix Roadrunners	IHL	30	15	13	1	1716	93	0	3.25	....	....	....	....	....	....	....	....	....	....	....	....	....	....	....	....	....
	Portland Pirates	AHL	1	0	1	0	59	4	0	4.01	....	....	....	....	....	....	....	....	....	....	....	....	....	....	....	....	....
	Peoria Rivermen	IHL	5	4	1	0	299	13	0	2.61	....	....	....	....	....	1	0	1	....	59	7	0	7.05	....	....	....	....
1994-95	Detroit Falcons	ColHL	4	4	0	0	240	10	0	2.50	....	....	....	....	....	....	....	....	....	....	....	....	....	....	....	....	....
	Phoenix Roadrunners	IHL	2	0	2	0	76	5	0	3.95	....	....	....	....	....	....	....	....	....	....	....	....	....	....	....	....	....
	Detroit Vipers	IHL	15	8	5	0	814	49	0	3.61	....	....	....	....	....	....	....	....	....	....	....	....	....	....	....	....	....
1995-96	Saint John Flames	AHL	1	0	0	0	47	9	0	11.40	....	....	....	....	....	....	....	....	....	....	....	....	....	....	....	....	....
	Louisville IceHawks	ECHL	12	5	5	1	697	46	*1	3.96	....	....	....	....	....	....	....	....	....	....	....	....	....	....	....	....	....
	Toledo Storm	ECHL	31	23	3	4	1817	79	*1	2.61	....	....	....	....	....	11	8	3	....	666	32	0	2.88	....	....	....	....
1996-97	Fort Wayne Komets	IHL	1	0	1	0	60	7	0	7.00	....	....	....	....	....	....	....	....	....	....	....	....	....	....	....	....	....
	Toledo Storm	ECHL	44	23	14	6	2554	126	*5	2.96	....	....	....	....	....	5	2	3	....	346	15	0	*2.59	....	....	....	....
1997-98	Phoenix Mustangs	WCHL	53	30	21	2	3149	178	2	3.39	....	....	....	....	....	9	3	5	....	492	38	0	4.63	....	....	....	....
1998-99	Phoenix Mustangs	WCHL	58	26	25	6	*3378	211	2	3.75	....	....	....	....	....	3	1	2	....	179	11	0	3.69	....	....	....	....
99-2000	Phoenix Mustangs	WCHL	*55	24	27	3	*3175	186	2	3.52	....	....	....	....	....	*12	*10	2	....	*750	29	*2	2.32	....	....	....	....
	NHL Totals		**5**	**1**	**4**	**0**	**278**	**29**	**0**	**6.26**	....	....	**151**	**.808**	**32.6**	....	....	....	....	....	....	....	....	....	....	....	....

ECHL Second All-Star Team (1997) • WCHL Second All-Star Team (1998)

Signed a s free agent by **Phoenix** (WCHL), August 12, 1997. • Played w/ RHI's Orlando Rollerblades in 1995 (18-4-12-0-(2)-773-121-0-7.51); Empire State Cobras in 1996 (13-6-5-2-(3)-622-74-0-5.71) and Anaheim Bullfrogs in 1997 (13-6-4-0-(2)-505-66-0-6.26)

• GRAHAME, John

John Gillies Mark G – L. 6'2", 210 lbs. b: Denver, CO, 8/31/1975. Boston's 7th, 229th overall in 1994.

Season	Club	League	GP	W	L	T	Mins	GA	SO	Avg	AAvg	Eff	SA	S%	SAPG	GP	W	L	T	Mins	GA	SO	Avg	Eff	SA	S%	SAPG
1993-94	Sioux City Musketeers	USHL	20	....	....	....	1200	73	0	3.70	....	....	....	....	....	....	....	....	....	....	....	....	....	....	....	....	....
1994-95	Lake Superior State	CCHA	28	16	7	3	1616	75	2	2.79	....	....	....	....	....	....	....	....	....	....	....	....	....	....	....	....	....
1995-96	Lake Superior State	CCHA	29	21	4	2	1558	66	2	2.54	....	....	....	....	....	....	....	....	....	....	....	....	....	....	....	....	....
	United States	WC-A	1	0	0	0	39	4	0	6.15	....	....	....	....	....	....	....	....	....	....	....	....	....	....	....	....	....

			REGULAR SEASON													PLAYOFFS											
Season	Club	League	GP	W	L	T	Mins	GA	SO	Avg	AAvg	Eff	SA	S%	SAPG	GP	W	L	T	Mins	GA	SO	Avg	Eff	SA	S%	SAPG
1996-97	Lake Superior State	CCHA	37	19	13	4	2197	134	3	3.66	....	....	....	....	....	....	....	....	....	....	....	....	....	....	....	....	....
1997-98	Providence Bruins	AHL	55	15	31	4	3053	164	3	3.22	....	....	....	....	....	....	....	....	....	....	....	....	....	....	....	....	....
1998-99	Providence Bruins	AHL	48	*37	9	1	2771	134	3	2.90	....	....	....	....	....	19	*15	4	....	*1209	48	1	2.38	....	....	....	....
99-2000	**Boston Bruins**	**NHL**	**24**	**7**	**10**	**5**	**1344**	**55**	**2**	**2.46**	**2.81**	**2.22**	**609**	**.910**	**27.2**	....	....	....	....	....	....	....	....	....	....	....	....
	Providence Bruins	AHL	27	11	13	2	1528	86	1	3.38	....	....	....	....	....	13	10	3	....	839	35	0	2.50	....	....	....	....
	NHL Totals		**24**	**7**	**10**	**5**	**1344**	**55**	**2**	**2.46**	....	....	**609**	**.910**	**27.2**	....	....	....	....	....	....	....	....	....	....	....	....

• Son of Ron

• GRAHAME, Ron

Ronald Ian G – L. 5'11", 175 lbs. b: Victoria, B.C., 6/7/1950.

Season	Club	League	GP	W	L	T	Mins	GA	SO	Avg	AAvg	Eff	SA	S%	SAPG	GP	W	L	T	Mins	GA	SO	Avg	Eff	SA	S%	SAPG
1968-69	Victoria Cougars	BCJHL	23	....	....	....	2380	73	0	3.17	....	....	....	....	....	....	....	....	....	....	....	....	....	....	....	....	....
1969-70	University of Denver	WCHA	30	19	10	1	1800	103	1	3.43	....	....	....	....	....	....	....	....	....	....	....	....	....	....	....	....	....
1970-71	University of Denver	WCHA	17	9	7	1	1020	70	1	4.12	....	....	....	....	....	....	....	....	....	....	....	....	....	....	....	....	....
1971-72	University of Denver	WCHA	37	26	11	0	2200	132	0	3.60	....	....	....	....	....	....	....	....	....	....	....	....	....	....	....	....	....
1972-73	University of Denver	WCHA	35	27	7	1	2094	102	2	*2.92	....	....	....	....	....	....	....	....	....	....	....	....	....	....	....	....	....
1973-74	Macon Whoopees	SHL	46	....	....	....	2588	178	0	4.13	....	....	....	....	....	....	....	....	....	....	....	....	....	....	....	....	....
	Houston Aeros	WHA	4	3	0	1	250	5	1	1.20	....	....	....	....	....	....	....	....	....	....	....	....	....	....	....	....	....
1974-75	Houston Aeros	WHA	43	*33	10	0	2590	131	*4	*3.03	....	....	....	....	....	13	*12	1	0	780	26	*3	*2.00	....	....	....	....
1975-76	Houston Aeros	WHA	57	39	17	0	3343	182	3	3.27	....	....	....	....	....	*14	6	8	0	817	54	1	3.97	....	....	....	....
1976-77	Houston Aeros	WHA	39	27	10	2	2345	107	*4	*2.74	....	....	....	....	....	9	4	5	0	561	36	0	3.85	....	....	....	....
1977-78	**Boston Bruins**	**NHL**	**40**	**26**	**6**	**7**	**2328**	**107**	**3**	**2.76**	**2.58**	....	....	....	....	**4**	**2**	**1**	....	**202**	**7**	**0**	**2.08**	....	....	....	....
1978-79	**Los Angeles Kings**	**NHL**	**34**	**11**	**19**	**2**	**1940**	**136**	**0**	**4.21**	**3.74**	....	....	....	....	....	....	....	....	....	....	....	....	....	....	....	....
1979-80	**Los Angeles Kings**	**NHL**	**26**	**9**	**11**	**4**	**1405**	**98**	**2**	**4.19**	**3.71**	....	....	....	....	....	....	....	....	....	....	....	....	....	....	....	....
1980-81	**Los Angeles Kings**	**NHL**	**6**	**3**	**2**	**1**	**360**	**28**	**0**	**4.67**	**3.78**	....	....	....	....	....	....	....	....	....	....	....	....	....	....	....	....
	Quebec Nordiques	**NHL**	**8**	**1**	**5**	**1**	**439**	**40**	**0**	**5.47**	**4.43**	....	....	....	....	....	....	....	....	....	....	....	....	....	....	....	....
	Binghamton Whalers	AHL	22	....	....	....	1240	72	0	3.48	....	....	....	....	....	5	....	....	....	289	22	0	4.57	....	....	....	....
	NHL Totals		**114**	**50**	**43**	**15**	**6472**	**409**	**5**	**3.79**	....	....	....	....	....	**4**	**2**	**1**	....	**202**	**7**	**0**	**2.08**	....	....	....	....
	Other Major League Totals		143	102	37	3	8528	425	12	2.99						36	22	14	....	2158	116	4	3.23				

• Father of John • WCHA First All-Star Team (1973) • NCAA West First All-American Team (1973) • WHA First All-Star Team (1975) • Won Ben Hatskin Trophy (WHA Top Goaltender) (1975, 1977) • Won WHA Playoff MVP Trophy (1975) • WHA Second All-Star Team (1976)

Selected by **NY Raiders** (WHA) in 1972 WHA General Player Draft, February 12, 1972. WHA rights traded to **Houston** (WHA) by **NY Raiders** (WHA) for Ray Larose, June, 1973. Signed as a free agent by **Boston**, October 13, 1977. Traded to **LA Kings** by **Boston** for LA Kings' 1st round choice (Ray Bourque) in 1979 Entry Draft, October 9, 1978. Sold to **Quebec** by **LA Kings** for cash, December 12, 1980.

• GRANT, Benny

Benjamin Cameron G – L. 5'11", 160 lbs. b: Owen Sound, Ont., 7/14/1908 d: 7/30/1991.

Season	Club	League	GP	W	L	T	Mins	GA	SO	Avg	AAvg	Eff	SA	S%	SAPG	GP	W	L	T	Mins	GA	SO	Avg	Eff	SA	S%	SAPG
1924-25	Owen Sound Greys	X-Games	1	0	0	0	20	0	0	0.00	....	....	....	....	....	....	....	....	....	....	....	....	....	....	....	....	....
1925-26	Owen Sound Greys	X-Games	3	2	1	0	150	4	1	1.60	....	....	....	....	....	....	....	....	....	....	....	....	....	....	....	....	....
1926-27	Owen Sound Greys	X-Games	16	12	3	1	960	35	2	2.19	....	....	....	....	....	....	....	....	....	....	....	....	....	....	....	....	....
1927-28	London Panthers	Can-Pro	6	1	4	1	249	24	0	5.78	....	....	....	....	....	....	....	....	....	....	....	....	....	....	....	....	....
1928-29	**Toronto Maple Leafs**	**NHL**	**3**	**1**	**0**	**0**	**110**	**3**	**0**	**1.64**	**3.43**	....	....	....	....	....	....	....	....	....	....	....	....	....	....	....	....
1929-30	**Toronto Maple Leafs**	**NHL**	**2**	**1**	**1**	**0**	**130**	**11**	**0**	**5.08**	**5.25**	....	....	....	....	....	....	....	....	....	....	....	....	....	....	....	....
	New York Americans	**NHL**	**7**	**3**	**4**	**0**	**420**	**25**	**0**	**3.57**	**3.69**	....	....	....	....	....	....	....	....	....	....	....	....	....	....	....	....
	Minneapolis Millers	AHA	21	....	....	....	1260	36	3	1.71	....	....	....	....	....	....	....	....	....	....	....	....	....	....	....	....	....
1930-31	**Toronto Maple Leafs**	**NHL**	**7**	**1**	**5**	**1**	**430**	**19**	**2**	**2.65**	**3.38**	....	....	....	....	....	....	....	....	....	....	....	....	....	....	....	....
	Boston Tigers/Cubs	Can-Am	26	10	12	4	1609	69	1	2.57	....	....	....	....	....	9	*3	4	2	712	23	0	*1.94	....	....	....	....
1931-32	**Toronto Maple Leafs**	**NHL**	**5**	**1**	**2**	**1**	**320**	**18**	**1**	**3.38**	**4.15**	....	....	....	....	....	....	....	....	....	....	....	....	....	....	....	....
	Syracuse Stars	IHL	27	11	12	4	1700	66	4	2.33	....	....	....	....	....	....	....	....	....	....	....	....	....	....	....	....	....
1932-33	Syracuse Stars	IHL	44	23	15	6	2640	119	2	2.70	....	....	....	....	....	6	2	3	1	360	10	0	*1.60	....	....	....	....
1933-34	Syracuse-Windsor	IHL	9	....	....	....	500	26	0	3.12	....	....	....	....	....	....	....	....	....	....	....	....	....	....	....	....	....
	New York Americans	**NHL**	**5**	**1**	**4**	**0**	**320**	**18**	**1**	**3.38**	**4.30**	....	....	....	....	....	....	....	....	....	....	....	....	....	....	....	....
1934-35	Boston Cubs	Can-Am	10	5	3	1	590	20	1	2.03	....	....	....	....	....	....	....	....	....	....	....	....	....	....	....	....	....
	Philadelphia Arrows	Can-Am	32	10	21	1	1930	114	1	3.54	....	....	....	....	....	....	....	....	....	....	....	....	....	....	....	....	....
1935-36	New Haven Eagles	Can-Am	28	11	15	2	1740	93	2	3.21	....	....	....	....	....	....	....	....	....	....	....	....	....	....	....	....	....
	Springfield Indians	Can-Am	8	6	1	1	490	14	3	1.71	....	....	....	....	....	3	0	2	1	180	9	0	3.00	....	....	....	....
1936-37	Springfield Indians	IAHL	50	23	18	9	3090	125	*7	2.43	....	....	....	....	....	5	2	3	0	300	14	1	2.60	....	....	....	....
1937-38	Springfield Indians	IAHL	45	9	28	7	2790	174	3	3.20	....	....	....	....	....	....	....	....	....	....	....	....	....	....	....	....	....
1938-39	Springfield Indians	IAHL	52	15	28	9	3240	174	5	3.22	....	....	....	....	....	3	1	2	0	180	7	1	2.33	....	....	....	....
1939-40	Springfield Indians	IAHL	54	24	24	6	*3330	149	3	2.68	....	....	....	....	....	3	1	2	0	180	10	0	3.33	....	....	....	....
1940-41	St. Paul Saints	AHA	48	25	23	0	2991	116	*7	2.33	....	....	....	....	....	4	1	3	0	262	10	0	2.29	....	....	....	....
1941-42	St. Paul Saints	AHA	50	28	17	5	3060	99	10	*1.94	....	....	....	....	....	2	0	2	0	120	7	0	3.50	....	....	....	....
1942-43			DID NOT PLAY																								
1943-44	**Toronto Maple Leafs**	**NHL**	**20**	**9**	**9**	**2**	**1200**	**83**	**0**	**4.15**	**3.10**	....	....	....	....	....	....	....	....	....	....	....	....	....	....	....	....
	Boston Bruins	**NHL**	**1**	**0**	**1**	**0**	**60**	**10**	**0**	**10.00**	**7.50**	....	....	....	....	....	....	....	....	....	....	....	....	....	....	....	....
	NHL Totals		**50**	**17**	**26**	**4**	**2990**	**187**	**4**	**3.75**	....	....	....	....	....	....	....	....	....	....	....	....	....	....	....	....	....

AHA First All-Star Team (1942)

Traded to **Toronto** by **London** (Can-Pro) for cash, January, 1928. Loaned to **NY Americans** by **Toronto** for cash, December 18, 1929. Loaned to **Minneapolis** (AHA) by **Toronto** for cash, January 24, 1930. Loaned to **Boston** (Can-Am) by **Toronto** for cash, December 26, 1930. Loaned to **NY Americans** by **Toronto** to replace injured Moe Roberts, December 9, 1933. Signed as a free agent by **Toronto** as a war-time replacement for Turk Broda, October, 1942. Loaned to **Boston** by **Toronto** to replace Maurice Courteau, March 18, 1944. (Toronto 10, Boston 2)

• GRANT, Doug

Douglas Munro G – L. 6'1", 200 lbs. b: Corner Brook, Nfld., 7/27/1948.

Season	Club	League	GP	W	L	T	Mins	GA	SO	Avg	AAvg	Eff	SA	S%	SAPG	GP	W	L	T	Mins	GA	SO	Avg	Eff	SA	S%	SAPG
1964-65	Corner Brook Pats	Nfld-Jr.	STATISTICS NOT AVAILABLE																								
1965-66			STATISTICS NOT AVAILABLE																								
1966-67	Corner Brook Royals	Nfld-Sr.	23	12	8	2	1360	113	1	4.99	....	....	....	....	....	3	1	2	0	190	16	0	5.05	....	....	....	....
1967-68	Corner Brook Royals	Nfld-Sr.	40	19	16	5	2400	174	0	4.35	....	....	....	....	....	12	*8	4	0	730	51	*1	*4.19	....	....	....	....
	Corner Brook Royals	Al-Cup	8	3	5	0	464	40	1	5.17	....	....	....	....	....	....	....	....	....	....	....	....	....	....	....	....	....
1968-69	Corner Brook Royals	Nfld-Sr.	39	17	18	4	2340	169	*3	4.33	....	....	....	....	....	....	....	....	....	....	....	....	....	....	....	....	....
	Corner Brook Royals	Al-Cup	4	1	2	0	120	20	0	6.00	....	....	....	....	....	....	....	....	....	....	....	....	....	....	....	....	....
1969-70	Corner Brook Royals	Nfld-Sr.	40	18	17	5	2400	177	2	4.43	....	....	....	....	....	7	3	4	0	429	26	0	3.64	....	....	....	....
1970-71	Corner Brook Royals	Nfld-Sr.	35	*16	13	6	2100	150	*2	4.29	....	....	....	....	....	11	3	8	0	659	55	0	5.01	....	....	....	....
1971-72	Memorial University	AUAA	14	....	....	....	850	29	*2	*2.05	....	....	....	....	....	....	....	....	....	....	....	....	....	....	....	....	....
	Fort Worth Wings	CHL	3	2	1	0	180	9	0	3.00	....	....	....	....	....	....	....	....	....	....	....	....	....	....	....	....	....
	Grand Falls Cataracts	Al-Cup	1	0	1	0	60	6	0	6.00	....	....	....	....	....	....	....	....	....	....	....	....	....	....	....	....	....
1972-73	Virginia Wings	AHL	51	....	....	....	3037	129	*6	2.54	....	....	....	....	....	12	6	6	0	717	42	*1	3.51	....	....	....	....
1973-74	**Detroit Red Wings**	**NHL**	**37**	**15**	**16**	**2**	**2018**	**140**	**1**	**4.16**	**4.06**	....	....	....	....	....	....	....	....	....	....	....	....	....	....	....	....
	Virginia Wings	AHL	6	1	3	2	359	20	1	3.34	....	....	....	....	....	....	....	....	....	....	....	....	....	....	....	....	....
1974-75	**Detroit Red Wings**	**NHL**	**7**	**1**	**5**	**0**	**380**	**34**	**0**	**5.37**	**4.86**	....	....	....	....	....	....	....	....	....	....	....	....	....	....	....	....
	Virginia Wings	AHL	35	14	11	8	1978	106	1	3.21	....	....	....	....	....	3	2	1	0	180	16	0	5.33	....	....	....	....
1975-76	**Detroit Red Wings**	**NHL**	**2**	**1**	**1**	**0**	**120**	**8**	**0**	**4.00**	**3.62**	....	....	....	....	....	....	....	....	....	....	....	....	....	....	....	....
	New Haven Nighthawks	AHL	23	8	13	2	1392	95	0	4.10	....	....	....	....	....	....	....	....	....	....	....	....	....	....	....	....	....
1976-77	**St. Louis Blues**	**NHL**	**17**	**7**	**7**	**3**	**960**	**50**	**1**	**3.13**	**2.91**	....	....	....	....	....	....	....	....	....	....	....	....	....	....	....	....
	Kansas City Blues	CHL	20	10	6	4	1199	57	*3	2.85	....	....	....	....	....	....	....	....	....	....	....	....	....	....	....	....	....
1977-78	**St. Louis Blues**	**NHL**	**9**	**3**	**3**	**2**	**500**	**24**	**0**	**2.88**	**2.70**	....	....	....	....	....	....	....	....	....	....	....	....	....	....	....	....
	Salt Lake Golden Eagles	CHL	35	17	13	3	2068	107	1	3.10	....	....	....	....	....	....	....	....	....	....	....	....	....	....	....	....	....
1978-79	**St. Louis Blues**	**NHL**	**4**	**0**	**2**	**1**	**190**	**23**	**0**	**7.26**	**6.44**	....	....	....	....	....	....	....	....	....	....	....	....	....	....	....	....
	Salt Lake Golden Eagles	CHL	31	15	12	3	1871	91	3	2.92	....	....	....	....	....	4	1	2	0	198	15	0	4.54	....	....	....	....

Season	Club	League	REGULAR SEASON GP	W	L	T	Mins	GA	SO	Avg	AAvg	Eff	SA	S%	SAPG	PLAYOFFS GP	W	L	T	Mins	GA	SO	Avg	Eff	SA	S%	SAPG
1979-80	**St. Louis Blues**	**NHL**	**1**	**0**	**0**	**0**	**31**	**1**	**0**	**1.94**	**1.71**	....	....	....	....	....	....	....	....	....	....	....	....	....	....	....	....
	Salt Lake Golden Eagles	CHL	38	24	12	2	2283	130	1	3.42	....	....	....	....	....	9	7	2	0	483	27	0	3.35	....	....	....	....
1980-81	Salt Lake Golden Eagles	CHL	5	3	1	0	260	14	1	3.23	....	....	....	....	....	....	....	....	....	....	....	....	....	....	....	....	....
1981-82	Salt Lake Golden Eagles	CHL	7	2	3	0	354	34	0	5.76	....	....	....	....	....	....	....	....	....	....	....	....	....	....	....	....	....
	NHL Totals		**77**	**27**	**34**	**8**	**4199**	**280**	**2**	**4.00**	....	....	....	....	....	....	....	....	....	....	....	....	....	....	....	....	....

Nfld.-Sr. First All-Star Team (1971) • AUAA First All-Star Team (1972) • AHL First All-Star Team (1973) • CHL Second All-Star Team (1978) • Shared Terry Sawchuk Trophy (fewest goals against - CHL) with Ed Staniowski (1978) • Shared Terry Sawchuk Trophy (fewest goals against - CHL) with Terry Richardson (1979)

Signed as a free agent by **Detroit**, March 1, 1972. Traded to **St. Louis** by **Detroit** for future considerations (Rick Wilson, June 16, 1976), March 9, 1976.

• GRATTON, Gilles

Gilles Andre "Grattony the Loony" G – L. 5'11", 160 lbs. b: LaSalle, Que., 7/28/1952. Buffalo's 5th, 69th overall in 1972.

Season	Club	League	GP	W	L	T	Mins	GA	SO	Avg	AAvg	Eff	SA	S%	SAPG	GP	W	L	T	Mins	GA	SO	Avg	Eff	SA	S%	SAPG
1969-70	Oshawa Generals	OHA-Jr.	26	....	....	....	1550	129	0	4.99	....	....	....	....	....	....	....	....	....	....	....	....	....	....	....	....	....
1970-71	Oshawa Generals	OHA-Jr.	47	....	....	....	2808	234	0	5.00	....	....	....	....	....	....	....	....	....	....	....	....	....	....	....	....	....
1971-72	Oshawa Generals	OMJHL	50	....	....	....	3000	178	3	3.55	....	....	....	....	....	10	5	4	1	600	31	0	3.10	....	....	....	....
1972-73	Ottawa Nationals	WHA	51	25	22	3	3021	187	0	3.71	....	....	....	....	....	2	0	1	0	87	7	0	4.83	....	....	....	....
1973-74	Toronto Toros	WHA	57	26	24	3	3200	188	2	3.53	....	....	....	....	....	10	5	3	0	539	25	*1	2.78	....	....	....	....
1974-75	Team Canada	Summit-74	1	0	0	0	2	0	0	0.00	....	....	....	....	....	....	....	....	....	....	....	....	....	....	....	....	....
	Toronto Toros	WHA	53	30	20	1	2881	185	2	3.85	....	....	....	....	....	1	0	1	0	36	5	0	8.33	....	....	....	....
1975-76	**St. Louis Blues**	**NHL**	**6**	**2**	**0**	**2**	**265**	**11**	**0**	**2.49**	**2.25**	....	....	....	....	....	....	....	....	....	....	....	....	....	....	....	....
1976-77	**New York Rangers**	**NHL**	**41**	**11**	**18**	**7**	**2034**	**143**	**0**	**4.22**	**3.95**	....	....	....	....	....	....	....	....	....	....	....	....	....	....	....	....
1977-78	New Haven Nighthawks	AHL	1	0	1	0	60	6	0	6.00	....	....	....	....	....	....	....	....	....	....	....	....	....	....	....	....	....
	NHL Totals		**47**	**13**	**18**	**9**	**2299**	**154**	**0**	**4.02**	....	....	....	....	....	....	....	....	....	....	....	....	....	....	....	....	....
	Other Major League Totals		161	81	66	7	9102	560	4	3.69	....	....	....	....	....	13	5	5	....	662	37	1	3.35	....	....	....	....

• Brother of Norm • OMJHL Second All-Star Team (1972)

Selected by **Edmonton** (WHA) in 1972 WHA General Player Draft, February 12, 1972. WHA rights traded to **Ottawa** (WHA) by **Edmonton** (WHA) for cash, September, 1972. Transferred to **Toronto** (WHA) after **Ottawa** (WHA) franchise relocated, May, 1973. Rights traded to **St. Louis** by **Buffalo** for cash, July 3, 1975. • Placed on "voluntary retired" list after walking out on the team following game vs. NY Islanders, November 28, 1975. St. Louis refused to place Gratton on waivers, blocking his attempt to sign with Toronto (WHA). Signed as a free agent by **NY Rangers** after securing release from **St. Louis**, March 24, 1976.

• GRAY, Gerry

Gerald Robert G – L. 6', 165 lbs. b: Brantford, Ont., 1/28/1948.

Season	Club	League	GP	W	L	T	Mins	GA	SO	Avg	AAvg	Eff	SA	S%	SAPG	GP	W	L	T	Mins	GA	SO	Avg	Eff	SA	S%	SAPG
1965-66	Hamilton Red Wings	OHA-Jr.	32	....	....	....	1920	151	0	4.72	....	....	....	....	....	1	0	0	0	20	0	0	0.00	....	....	....	....
1966-67	Hamilton Red Wings	OHA-Jr.	44	....	....	....	2600	142	1	3.28	....	....	....	....	....	17	....	....	....	1020	59	0	3.47	....	....	....	....
1967-68	Hamilton Red Wings	OHA-Jr.	45	....	....	....	2680	138	0	3.09	....	....	....	....	....	11	....	....	....	641	45	0	4.21	....	....	....	....
1968-69	Fort Worth Wings	CHL	40	....	....	....	2125	127	2	3.59	....	....	....	....	....	....	....	....	....	....	....	....	....	....	....	....	....
1969-70	Cleveland Barons	AHL	35	....	....	....	1997	131	1	3.94	....	....	....	....	....	....	....	....	....	....	....	....	....	....	....	....	....
1970-71	**Detroit Red Wings**	**NHL**	**7**	**1**	**4**	**1**	**380**	**30**	**0**	**4.74**	**4.70**	....	....	....	....	....	....	....	....	....	....	....	....	....	....	....	....
	Fort Worth Wings	CHL	33	....	....	....	1940	90	2	2.78	....	....	....	....	....	....	....	....	....	....	....	....	....	....	....	....	....
1971-72	Tidewater Wings	AHL	18	7	7	2	1009	45	2	2.68	....	....	....	....	....	....	....	....	....	....	....	....	....	....	....	....	....
	Fort Worth Wings	CHL	32	14	11	6	1633	95	0	3.49	....	....	....	....	....	7	....	....	....	444	30	0	4.05	....	....	....	....
1972-73	**New York Islanders**	**NHL**	**1**	**0**	**1**	**0**	**60**	**5**	**0**	**5.00**	**4.72**	....	....	....	....	....	....	....	....	....	....	....	....	....	....	....	....
	New Haven Nighthawks	AHL	36	....	....	....	2071	156	0	4.51	....	....	....	....	....	....	....	....	....	....	....	....	....	....	....	....	....
1973-74	Jacksonville Barons	AHL	30	5	16	4	1464	113	0	4.63	....	....	....	....	....	....	....	....	....	....	....	....	....	....	....	....	....
1974-75	Brantford Foresters	OHA-Sr.	6	....	....	....	360	27	0	4.56	....	....	....	....	....	....	....	....	....	....	....	....	....	....	....	....	....
1975-76	Cambridge Hornets	OHA-Sr.	22	....	....	....	1320	82	0	3.76	....	....	....	....	....	....	....	....	....	....	....	....	....	....	....	....	....
1976-77	Brantford Alexanders	OHA-Sr.	19	....	....	....	1140	89	1	4.60	....	....	....	....	....	....	....	....	....	....	....	....	....	....	....	....	....
1977-78	Brantford Alexanders	OHA-Sr.	15	....	....	....	900	84	0	5.57	....	....	....	....	....	....	....	....	....	....	....	....	....	....	....	....	....
	NHL Totals		**8**	**1**	**5**	**1**	**440**	**35**	**0**	**4.77**	....	....	....	....	....	....	....	....	....	....	....	....	....	....	....	....	....

OHA-Jr. First All-Star Team (1968) • Shared Terry Sawchuk Trophy (fewest goals against - CHL) with Don McLeod (1971)

Traded to **NY Islanders** by **Detroit** with Arnie Brown for Denis Dejordy and Don McLaughlin, October 4, 1972.

• GRAY, Harrison

Harrison Leroy G. 5'11", 165 lbs. b: Calgary, Alta., 9/5/1941.

Season	Club	League	GP	W	L	T	Mins	GA	SO	Avg	AAvg	Eff	SA	S%	SAPG	GP	W	L	T	Mins	GA	SO	Avg	Eff	SA	S%	SAPG
1959-60	Edmonton Oil Kings	CAHL	STATISTICS NOT AVAILABLE																								
	Lethbridge Native Sons	Mem-Cup	3	0	3	0	180	25	0	8.33	....	....	....	....	....	....	....	....	....	....	....	....	....	....	....	....	....
1960-1962	Edmonton Oil Kings	CAHL	STATISTICS NOT AVAILABLE																								
1961-62	Edmonton Flyers	WHL	1	0	0	0	20	0	0	0.00	....	....	....	....	....	....	....	....	....	....	....	....	....	....	....	....	....
	Edmonton Oil Kings	Mem-Cup	21	14	7	0	1271	56	3	2.64	....	....	....	....	....	....	....	....	....	....	....	....	....	....	....	....	....
1962-63	Edmonton Flyers	WHL	14	0	13	1	840	87	0	6.21	....	....	....	....	....	....	....	....	....	....	....	....	....	....	....	....	....
1963-64	**Detroit Red Wings**	**NHL**	**1**	**0**	**1**	**0**	**40**	**5**	**0**	**7.50**	**8.35**	....	....	....	....	....	....	....	....	....	....	....	....	....	....	....	....
	Cincinnati Wings	CPHL	3	1	1	1	180	10	0	3.33	....	....	....	....	....	....	....	....	....	....	....	....	....	....	....	....	....
1964-65	Knoxville Knights	EHL	55	....	....	....	3300	208	2	3.78	....	....	....	....	....	10	5	5	0	600	37	0	3.70	....	....	....	....
1965-66	Knoxville Knights	EHL	28	14	14	0	1680	118	0	4.21	....	....	....	....	....	....	....	....	....	....	....	....	....	....	....	....	....
	New Haven Blades	EHL	37	....	....	....	2220	170	1	4.59	....	....	....	....	....	3	0	3	0	180	15	0	5.00	....	....	....	....
1966-67	Florida Rockets	EHL	72	27	43	2	4320	314	2	4.36	....	....	....	....	....	....	....	....	....	....	....	....	....	....	....	....	....
1967-68	Florida Rockets	EHL	72	30	34	8	4320	286	3	3.97	....	....	....	....	....	5	2	3	0	300	20	0	4.00	....	....	....	....
1968-69	Jacksonville Rockets	EHL	54	....	....	....	3240	226	1	4.18	....	....	....	....	....	1	1	0	0	60	2	0	2.00	....	....	....	....
1969-70	Drumheller Miners	ASHL	17	....	....	....	1020	72	1	4.24	....	....	....	....	....	....	....	....	....	....	....	....	....	....	....	....	....
	NHL Totals		**1**	**0**	**1**	**0**	**40**	**5**	**0**	**7.50**	....	....	....	....	....	....	....	....	....	....	....	....	....	....	....	....	....

• **Detroit's** spare goaltender replaced injured Terry Sawchuk at start of 2nd period, November 28, 1963. (Montreal 7, Detroit 3).

• GREENLAY, Mike

G – L. 6'3", 200 lbs. b: Vitoria, Brazil, 9/15/1968. Edmonton's 9th, 189th overall in 1986.

Season	Club	League	GP	W	L	T	Mins	GA	SO	Avg	AAvg	Eff	SA	S%	SAPG	GP	W	L	T	Mins	GA	SO	Avg	Eff	SA	S%	SAPG
1985-86	Calgary Royals	AAHA	STATISTICS NOT AVAILABLE																								
1986-87	Lake Superior State	CCHA	17	7	5	0	744	44	0	3.54	....	....	....	....	....	....	....	....	....	....	....	....	....	....	....	....	....
1987-88	Lake Superior State	CCHA	19	10	3	3	1023	57	0	3.34	....	....	....	....	....	....	....	....	....	....	....	....	....	....	....	....	....
1988-89	Lake Superior State	CCHA	2	1	1	0	85	6	0	4.23	....	....	....	....	....	....	....	....	....	....	....	....	....	....	....	....	....
	Saskatoon Blades	WHL	20	10	8	1	1128	86	0	4.57	....	....	....	....	....	6	2	0	0	174	16	0	5.52	....	....	....	....
	Saskatoon Blades	Mem-Cup	4	2	2	0	243	14	0	3.46	....	....	....	....	....	....	....	....	....	....	....	....	....	....	....	....	....
1989-90	**Edmonton Oilers**	**NHL**	**2**	**0**	**0**	**0**	**20**	**4**	**0**	**12.00**	**10.17**	**28.24**	**17**	**.765**	**51.0**	....	....	....	....	....	....	....	....	....	....	....	....
	Cape Breton Oilers	AHL	46	19	18	5	2595	146	2	3.38	....	....	....	....	....	5	1	3	0	306	26	0	5.09	....	....	....	....
1990-91	Cape Breton Oilers	AHL	11	5	2	0	493	33	0	4.02	....	....	....	....	....	....	....	....	....	....	....	....	....	....	....	....	....
	Knoxville Cherokees	ECHL	29	17	9	2	1725	108	2	3.75	....	....	....	....	....	....	....	....	....	....	....	....	....	....	....	....	....
1991-92	Cape Breton Oilers	AHL	3	1	1	1	144	12	0	5.00	....	....	....	....	....	....	....	....	....	....	....	....	....	....	....	....	....
	Knoxville Cherokees	ECHL	27	8	12	2	1415	113	0	4.79	....	....	....	....	....	....	....	....	....	....	....	....	....	....	....	....	....
1992-93	Louisville IceHawks	ECHL	27	12	11	2	1437	96	1	4.01	....	....	....	....	....	....	....	....	....	....	....	....	....	....	....	....	....
	Atlanta Knights	IHL	12	5	3	2	637	40	0	3.77	....	....	....	....	....	....	....	....	....	....	....	....	....	....	....	....	....
1993-94	Atlanta Knights	IHL	34	16	10	4	1741	104	0	3.58	....	....	....	....	....	13	*11	1	0	749	29	*1	*2.32	....	....	....	....
1994-95	Atlanta Knights	IHL	20	7	10	0	1059	72	0	4.08	....	....	....	....	....	....	....	....	....	....	....	....	....	....	....	....	....
	Hershey Bears	AHL	16	5	5	2	704	46	0	3.92	....	....	....	....	....	5	2	3	0	270	12	0	2.66	....	....	....	....
1995-96	Houston Aeros	IHL	1	0	1	0	17	2	0	6.86	....	....	....	....	....	....	....	....	....	....	....	....	....	....	....	....	....
	NHL Totals		**2**	**0**	**0**	**0**	**20**	**4**	**0**	**12.00**	....	....	**17**	**.765**	**51.0**	....	....	....	....	....	....	....	....	....	....	....	....

Memorial Cup All-Star Team (1989) • Won Hap Emms Memorial Trophy (Memorial Cup Tournament Top Goaltender) (1989) • Shared James Norris Memorial Trophy (fewest goals against - IHL) with J.C. Bergeron (1994)

Signed as a free agent by **Tampa Bay**, July 29, 1992. Traded to **Philadelphia** by **Tampa Bay** for Scott LaGrand, February 2, 1995.

• GUENETTE, Steve

Steven P. G – L. 5'10", 175 lbs. b: Gloucester, Ont., 11/13/1965.

			REGULAR SEASON													PLAYOFFS											
Season	Club	League	GP	W	L	T	Mins	GA	SO	Avg	AAvg	Eff	SA	S%	SAPG	GP	W	L	T	Mins	GA	SO	Avg	Eff	SA	S%	SAPG
1982-83	Gloucester Rangers	OJHL	30				1546	124	0	4.81																	
1983-84	Guelph Platers	OHL	38	9	20	1	1808	155	0	5.14																	
1984-85	Guelph Platers	OHL	47	16	22	4	2593	200	1	4.63																	
1985-86	Guelph Platers	OHL	50	26	20	1	2910	165	*3	3.40						20	15	3	0	1167	54	1	2.77				
	Guelph Platers	Mem-Cup	4	*3	1	0	240	12	0	*3.00																	
1986-87	**Pittsburgh Penguins**	**NHL**	**2**	**0**	**2**	**0**	**113**	**8**	**0**	**4.25**	**3.60**	**6.30**	**54**	**.852**	**28.7**												
	Baltimore Skipjacks	AHL	54	21	23	0	3035	157	5	3.10																	
1987-88	**Pittsburgh Penguins**	**NHL**	**19**	**12**	**7**	**0**	**1092**	**61**	**1**	**3.35**	**2.79**	**3.51**	**582**	**.895**	**32.0**												
	Muskegon Lumberjacks	IHL	33	23	4	5	1943	91	*4	*2.81																	
1988-89	**Pittsburgh Penguins**	**NHL**	**11**	**5**	**6**	**0**	**574**	**41**	**0**	**4.29**	**3.57**	**5.71**	**308**	**.867**	**32.2**												
	Muskegon Lumberjacks	IHL	10	6	4	0	597	39	0	*3.92																	
	Salt Lake Golden Eagles	IHL	30	24	5	0	1810	82	2	*2.72						*13	*8	5	0	*782	44	0	3.38				
1989-90	Calgary Flames	Fr-Tour	1	0	0	0	27	0	0	0.00																	
	Calgary Flames	**NHL**	**2**	**1**	**1**	**0**	**119**	**8**	**0**	**4.03**	**3.41**	**6.45**	**50**	**.840**	**25.2**												
	Salt Lake Golden Eagles	IHL	47	22	21	4	2779	160	0	3.45						*10	4	4	0	545	35	*1	3.85				
1990-91	**Calgary Flames**	**NHL**	**1**	**1**	**0**	**0**	**60**	**4**	**0**	**4.00**	**3.60**	**5.33**	**30**	**.867**	**30.0**												
	Salt Lake Golden Eagles	IHL	43	*26	13	4	2521	137	2	3.26						2	0	1	0	59	9	0	9.15				
1991-92	Kalamazoo Wings	IHL	21	7	9	3	1094	70	1	3.84																	
	NHL Totals		**35**	**19**	**16**	**0**	**1958**	**122**	**1**	**3.74**			**1024**	**.881**	**31.4**												

OHL Second All-Star Team (1986) • Memorial Cup All-Star Team (1986) • Won Hap Emms Memorial Trophy (Memorial Cup Tournament Top Goaltender) (1986) • IHL Second All-Star Team (1988, 1989) • Won James Norris Memorial Trophy (fewest goals against - IHL) (1988)

Signed as a free agent by **Pittsburgh**, April 6, 1985. Traded to **Calgary** by **Pittsburgh** for Calgary's 6th round choice (Mike Needham) in 1989 Entry Draft, January 9, 1989. Traded to **Minnesota** by **Calgary** for Minnesota's 7th round choice (Matt Hoffman) in 1991 Entry Draft, May 30, 1991.

• HACKETT, Jeff

G – L. 6'1", 195 lbs. b: London, Ont., 6/1/1968. NY Islanders' 2nd, 34th overall in 1987.

			REGULAR SEASON													PLAYOFFS											
Season	Club	League	GP	W	L	T	Mins	GA	SO	Avg	AAvg	Eff	SA	S%	SAPG	GP	W	L	T	Mins	GA	SO	Avg	Eff	SA	S%	SAPG
1984-85	London Diamonds	OJHL-B	18				1078	73	1	4.06																	
1985-86	London Diamonds	OJHL-B	19				1150	66	0	3.43																	
1986-87	Oshawa Generals	OHL	31	18	9	2	1672	85	2	3.05						15	8	7		895	40	0	2.68				
	Oshawa Generals	Mem-Cup	3	2	1	0	180	12	0	4.00																	
1987-88	Oshawa Generals	OHL	53	30	21	2	3165	205	0	3.89						7	3	4		438	31	0	4.25				
	Canada	WJC-A	DID NOT PLAY – SPARE GOALTENDER																								
1988-89	**New York Islanders**	**NHL**	**13**	**4**	**7**	**0**	**662**	**39**	**0**	**3.53**	**2.94**	**4.18**	**329**	**.881**	**29.8**												
	Springfield Indians	AHL	29	12	14	2	1677	116	0	4.15																	
1989-90	Springfield Indians	AHL	54	24	25	3	3045	187	1	3.68						*17	*10	5		934	60	0	3.85				
1990-91	**New York Islanders**	**NHL**	**30**	**5**	**18**	**1**	**1508**	**91**	**0**	**3.62**	**3.26**	**4.45**	**741**	**.877**	**29.5**												
1991-92	**San Jose Sharks**	**NHL**	**42**	**11**	**27**	**1**	**2314**	**148**	**0**	**3.84**	**3.45**	**4.16**	**1366**	**.892**	**35.4**												
1992-93	**San Jose Sharks**	**NHL**	**36**	**2**	**30**	**1**	**2000**	**176**	**0**	**5.28**	**4.56**	**7.62**	**1220**	**.856**	**36.6**												
1993-94	**Chicago Blackhawks**	**NHL**	**22**	**2**	**12**	**3**	**1084**	**62**	**0**	**3.43**	**3.30**	**3.76**	**566**	**.890**	**31.3**												
1994-95	**Chicago Blackhawks**	**NHL**	**7**	**1**	**3**	**2**	**328**	**13**	**0**	**2.38**	**2.49**	**2.06**	**150**	**.913**	**27.4**	**2**	**0**	**0**		**26**	**1**	**0**	**2.31**	**2.10**	**11**	**.909**	**25.4**
1995-96	**Chicago Blackhawks**	**NHL**	**35**	**18**	**11**	**4**	**2000**	**80**	**4**	**2.40**	**2.38**	**2.03**	**948**	**.916**	**28.4**	**1**	**0**	**1**		**60**	**5**	**0**	**5.00**	**7.81**	**32**	**.844**	**32.0**
1996-97	**Chicago Blackhawks**	**NHL**	**41**	**19**	**18**	**4**	**2473**	**89**	**2**	**2.16**	**2.31**	**1.59**	**1212**	**.927**	**29.4**	**6**	**2**	**4**		**345**	**25**	**0**	**4.35**	**5.72**	**190**	**.868**	**33.0**
1997-98	**Chicago Blackhawks**	**NHL**	**58**	**21**	**25**	**11**	**3441**	**126**	**8**	**2.20**	**2.61**	**1.82**	**1520**	**.917**	**26.5**												
	Canada	WC-A	2	0	1	1	120	9	0	4.50																	
1998-99	**Chicago Blackhawks**	**NHL**	**10**	**2**	**6**	**1**	**524**	**33**	**0**	**3.78**	**4.50**	**4.87**	**256**	**.871**	**29.3**												
	Montreal Canadiens	**NHL**	**53**	**24**	**20**	**9**	**3091**	**117**	**5**	**2.27**	**2.69**	**1.95**	**1360**	**.914**	**26.4**												
99-2000	**Montreal Canadiens**	**NHL**	**56**	**23**	**25**	**7**	**3301**	**132**	**3**	**2.40**	**2.74**	**2.05**	**1543**	**.914**	**28.0**												
	NHL Totals		**403**	**132**	**202**	**44**	**22726**	**1106**	**22**	**2.92**			**11211**	**.901**	**29.6**	**9**	**2**	**5**		**431**	**31**	**0**	**4.32**		**233**	**.867**	**32.4**

Won Jack A. Butterfield Trophy (Playoff MVP - AHL) (1990)

Claimed by **San Jose** from **NY Islanders** in Expansion Draft, May 30, 1991. Traded to **Chicago** by **San Jose** for Chicago's 3rd round choice (Alexei Yegorov) in 1994 Entry Draft, July 13, 1993. Traded to **Montreal** by **Chicago** with Eric Weinrich, Alain Nasreddine and Tampa Bay's 4th round choice (previously acquired, Montreal selected Chris Dyment) in 1999 Entry Draft for Jocelyn Thibault, Dave Manson and Brad Brown, November 16, 1998.

• HAINSWORTH, George

G – L. 5'6", 150 lbs. b: Toronto, Ont., 6/26/1895 d: 10/9/1950. **HHOF**

			REGULAR SEASON													PLAYOFFS											
Season	Club	League	GP	W	L	T	Mins	GA	SO	Avg	AAvg	Eff	SA	S%	SAPG	GP	W	L	T	Mins	GA	SO	Avg	Eff	SA	S%	SAPG
1910-11	Berlin Mavericks	OMHA	STATISTICS NOT AVAILABLE																								
1911-12	Berlin Union Jacks	OHA-Jr.	4	*3	1	0	240	13	0	3.25						6	2	3	1	360	30	0	5.00				
1912-13	Berlin City Seniors	OHA-Sr.	4	*3	1	0	240	12	1	3.00						8	4	3	1	480	35	1	4.38				
1913-14	Berlin City Seniors	OHA-Sr.	7	*7	0	0	420	11	0	*1.57						9	7	1	1	590	31	1	3.15				
1914-15	Berlin City Seniors	OHA-Sr.	5	*5	0	0	300	9	1	*1.80						4	2	1	1	240	19	1	4.75				
1915-16	Berlin City Seniors	OHA-Sr.	8	*8	0	0	480	18	*1	2.85						4	2	2	0	280	18	0	3.86				
1916-17	Toronto Kew Beach	TIHL	STATISTICS NOT AVAILABLE																								
1917-18	Kitchener Greenshirts	OHA-Sr.	9	*9	0	0	540	31	0	*3.44						5	3	1	1	298	10	1	2.01				
1918-19	Kitchener Greenshirts	OHA-Sr.	9	5	3	1	570	28	0	2.95																	
1919-20	Kitchener Greenshirts	OHA-Sr.	8	*6	2	0	480	16	*1	*2.00						2	0	1	1	150	6	0	2.40				
1920-21	Kitchener Greenshirts	OHA-Sr.	10	7	3	0	600	22	*3	2.20						1	0	1	0	60	6	0	6.00				
1921-22	Kitchener Greenshirts	OHA-Sr.	10	3	7	0	600	38	*1	3.80																	
1922-23	Kitchener Greenshirts	OHA-Sr.	12	8	4	0	720	32	1	2.67																	
1923-24	Saskatoon Crescents	WCHL	*30	15	12	3	*1871	73	*4	2.34																	
1924-25	Saskatoon Crescents	WCHL	*28	16	11	1	*1698	75	2	2.65						2	0	1	1	120	6	0	3.00				
1925-26	Saskatoon Crescents	WHL	*30	17	12	1	1821	64	4	2.11						2	0	1	1	129	4	0	1.86				
1926-27	**Montreal Canadiens**	**NHL**	***44**	**28**	**14**	**2**	**2732**	**67**	***14**	**1.47**	**2.18**					**4**	**1**	**1**	**2**	**252**	**6**	**1**	**1.43**				
1927-28	**Montreal Canadiens**	**NHL**	***44**	***26**	**11**	**7**	**2730**	**48**	**13**	***1.05**	**1.60**					**2**	**0**	**1**	**1**	**128**	**3**	**0**	**1.41**				
1928-29	**Montreal Canadiens**	**NHL**	***44**	**22**	**7**	**15**	**2800**	**43**	***22**	***0.92**	**1.84**					**3**	**0**	**3**	**0**	**180**	**5**	**0**	**1.67**				
1929-30♦	**Montreal Canadiens**	**NHL**	**42**	**20**	**13**	**9**	**2680**	**108**	***4**	**2.42**	**2.44**					***6**	***5**	**0**	**1**	***481**	**6**	***3**	***0.75**				
1930-31♦	**Montreal Canadiens**	**NHL**	***44**	**26**	**10**	**8**	**2740**	**89**	**8**	**1.95**	**2.43**					***10**	***6**	**4**	**0**	***722**	**21**	***2**	**1.75**				
1931-32	**Montreal Canadiens**	**NHL**	***48**	***25**	**16**	**7**	**2998**	**110**	**6**	**2.20**	**2.64**					**4**	**1**	**3**	**0**	**300**	**13**	**0**	**2.60**				
1932-33	**Montreal Canadiens**	**NHL**	***48**	**18**	**25**	**5**	**2980**	**115**	**8**	**2.32**	**3.11**					**2**	**0**	**1**	**1**	**120**	**8**	**0**	**4.00**				
1933-34	**Toronto Maple Leafs**	**NHL**	***48**	***26**	**13**	**9**	***3010**	**119**	**3**	**2.37**	**2.99**					**5**	**2**	**3**	**0**	**302**	**11**	**0**	**2.19**				
1934-35	**Toronto Maple Leafs**	**NHL**	***48**	***30**	**14**	**4**	**2957**	**111**	**8**	**2.25**	**2.69**					***7**	**3**	**4**	**0**	***460**	**12**	***2**	**1.57**				
1935-36	**Toronto Maple Leafs**	**NHL**	***48**	**23**	**19**	**6**	**3000**	**106**	**8**	**2.12**	**2.98**					***9**	**4**	**5**	**0**	***541**	**27**	**0**	**2.99**				
1936-37	**Toronto Maple Leafs**	**NHL**	**3**	**0**	**2**	**1**	**190**	**9**	**0**	**2.84**	**3.52**																
	Montreal Canadiens	**NHL**	**4**	**2**	**1**	**1**	**270**	**12**	**0**	**2.67**	**3.31**																
	NHL Totals		**465**	**246**	**145**	**74**	**29087**	**937**	**94**	**1.93**						**52**	**22**	**25**	**5**	**3486**	**112**	**8**	**1.93**				
	Other Major League Totals		88	48	35	5	5390	212	10	2.36						4	0	2		249	10	0	2.41				

WHL All-Star Team (1926) • Won Vezina Trophy (1927, 1928, 1929) • Played in NHL All-Star Game (1934)

• Suspended from playing in OHA-Sr. in 1916-17 after transfer to Toronto Aura Lee was denied, October, 1916. Signed as a free agent by **Saskatoon** (WCHL), October 11, 1923. Traded to **Montreal Canadiens** by **Saskatoon** (WHL) for cash, August 23, 1926. Traded to **Toronto** by **Montreal Canadiens** for Lorne Chabot, October 1, 1933. Signed as a free agent by **Montreal Canadiens**, November 24, 1936.

• HALL, Glenn

Glenn Henry "Mr. Goalie" G – L. 5'11", 180 lbs. b: Humboldt, Sask., 10/3/1931. **HHOF**

			REGULAR SEASON													PLAYOFFS											
Season	Club	League	GP	W	L	T	Mins	GA	SO	Avg	AAvg	Eff	SA	S%	SAPG	GP	W	L	T	Mins	GA	SO	Avg	Eff	SA	S%	SAPG
1947-48	Humboldt Indians	N-SJHL	5				300	17	0	3.40						2	0	2	0	120	15	0	7.50				
1948-49	Humboldt Indians	N-SJHL	24	13	9	2	1420	86	1	3.63						7	3	4	0	420	36	0	5.14				
1949-50	Windsor Spitfires	OHA-Jr.	43	31	11	1	2580	152	0	3.53						11	6	5	0	660	37	0	3.36				
1950-51	Windsor Spitfires	OHA-Jr.	54	32	18	4	3240	167	*6	3.09						8				480	30	0	3.75				
1951-52	Indianapolis Capitols	AHL	*68	22	40	6	*4190	272	0	3.89																	
1952-53	Edmonton Flyers	WHL	63	27	27	9	3780	207	2	3.29						15	*10	5	0	905	53	0	3.51				
	Detroit Red Wings	**NHL**	**6**	**4**	**1**	**1**	**360**	**10**	**1**	**1.67**	**2.12**																
1953-54	Edmonton Flyers	WHL	*70	29	30	11	*4200	259	0	3.70						13	7	6	0	783	44	*2	3.37				

			REGULAR SEASON													PLAYOFFS											
Season	Club	League	GP	W	L	T	Mins	GA	SO	Avg	AAvg	Eff	SA	S%	SAPG	GP	W	L	T	Mins	GA	SO	Avg	Eff	SA	S%	SAPG
1954-55	Edmonton Flyers	WHL	66	*38	18	10	3960	187	5	2.83	....	....	....	....	....	16	11	5	0	1000	43	1	2.58	....	....	....	....
	Detroit Red Wings	**NHL**	2	2	0	0	120	2	0	1.00	1.21	....	....	....	....	....	....	....	....	....	....	....	....	....	....	....	....
1955-56	**Detroit Red Wings**	**NHL**	*70	30	24	16	*4200	147	*12	2.10	2.49	....	....	....	....	*10	5	5	....	*604	28	0	2.78	....	....	....	....
1956-57	**Detroit Red Wings**	**NHL**	*70	*38	20	12	*4200	155	4	2.21	2.46	....	....	....	....	5	1	4	....	300	15	0	3.00	....	....	....	....
1957-58	**Chicago Black Hawks**	**NHL**	*70	24	39	7	*4200	200	7	2.86	3.15	....	....	....	....	....	....	....	....	....	....	....	....	....	....	....	....
1958-59	**Chicago Black Hawks**	**NHL**	*70	28	29	13	*4200	208	1	2.97	3.18	....	....	....	....	6	2	4	....	360	21	0	3.50	....	....	....	....
1959-60	**Chicago Black Hawks**	**NHL**	*70	28	29	13	*4200	179	*6	2.56	2.61	....	....	....	....	4	0	4	....	249	14	0	3.37	....	....	....	....
1960-61♦	**Chicago Black Hawks**	**NHL**	*70	29	24	17	*4200	176	*6	2.51	2.51	....	....	....	....	*12	*8	4	....	*772	26	*2	*2.02	....	....	....	....
1961-62	**Chicago Black Hawks**	**NHL**	*70	31	26	13	*4200	184	*9	2.63	2.63	....	....	....	....	*12	*6	6	....	*720	31	*2	2.58	....	....	....	....
1962-63	**Chicago Black Hawks**	**NHL**	66	30	20	15	3910	161	*5	2.47	2.50	....	....	....	....	6	2	4	....	360	25	0	4.17	....	....	....	....
1963-64	**Chicago Black Hawks**	**NHL**	65	*34	19	11	3860	148	7	2.30	2.48	....	....	....	....	7	3	4	....	408	22	0	3.24	....	....	....	....
1964-65	**Chicago Black Hawks**	**NHL**	41	18	17	5	2440	99	4	2.43	2.56	....	....	....	....	*13	*7	6	....	*760	28	1	2.21	....	....	....	....
1965-66	**Chicago Black Hawks**	**NHL**	*64	*34	21	7	*3747	164	4	2.63	2.60	....	....	....	....	6	2	4	....	347	22	0	3.80	....	....	....	....
1966-67	**Chicago Black Hawks**	**NHL**	32	19	5	5	1664	66	2	*2.38	2.42	....	....	....	....	3	1	2	....	176	8	0	2.73	....	....	....	....
1967-68	**St. Louis Blues**	**NHL**	49	19	21	9	2858	118	5	2.48	2.74	....	....	....	....	*18	8	10	....	*1111	45	*1	2.43	....	....	....	....
1968-69	**St. Louis Blues**	**NHL**	41	19	12	8	2354	85	*8	2.17	2.22	....	....	....	....	3	0	2	....	131	5	0	2.29	....	....	....	....
1969-70	**St. Louis Blues**	**NHL**	18	7	8	3	1010	49	1	2.91	3.09	....	....	....	....	7	4	3	....	421	21	0	2.99	....	....	....	....
1970-71	**St. Louis Blues**	**NHL**	32	13	11	8	1761	71	2	2.42	2.38	....	....	....	....	3	0	3	....	180	9	0	3.00	....	....	....	....
	NHL Totals		906	407	326	163	53484	2222	84	2.49	....	....	....	....	....	115	49	65	....	6899	320	6	2.78	....	....	....	....

WHL First All-Star Team (1955) • NHL Second All-Star Team (1956, 1961, 1962, 1967) • Won Calder Memorial Trophy (1956) • NHL First All-Star Team (1957, 1958, 1960, 1963, 1964, 1966, 1969) • Won Vezina Trophy (1963) • Shared Vezina Trophy with Denis Dejordy (1967) • Won Conn Smythe Trophy (1968) • Shared Vezina Trophy with Jacques Plante (1969) • Played in NHL All-Star Game (1955, 1956, 1957, 1958, 1960, 1961, 1962, 1963, 1964, 1965, 1967, 1968, 1969)

Promoted to **Detroit** from **Edmonton** (WHL) to replace injured Terry Sawchuk in games from December 27, 1952 through January 11, 1953 and February 12, 13, 1955. Traded to **Chicago** by **Detroit** with Ted Lindsay for Johnny Wilson, Forbes Kennedy, Bill Preston and Hank Bassen, July 23, 1957. Claimed by **St. Louis** from **Chicago** in Expansion Draft, June 6, 1967.

• HAMEL, Pierre

G – L. 5'9", 170 lbs. b: Montreal, Que., 9/16/1952.

Season	Club	League	GP	W	L	T	Mins	GA	SO	Avg	AAvg	Eff	SA	S%	SAPG	GP	W	L	T	Mins	GA	SO	Avg	Eff	SA	S%	SAPG
1969-70	St-Victor Voisons	QJHA-B	STATISTICS NOT AVAILABLE																								
	Verdun Maple Leafs	QJHL	12	....	....	....	680	79	0	6.97	....	....	....	....	....	1	0	0	0	6	1	0	10.00	....	....	....	....
1970-71	Verdun Maple Leafs	QJHL	43	....	....	....	2580	200	0	4.65	....	....	....	....	....	1	0	1	0	30	7	0	14.00	....	....	....	....
1971-72	Laval Titans	QMJHL	15	....	....	....	870	86	0	5.93	....	....	....	....	....	....	....	....	....	....	....	....	....	....	....	....	....
	Drummondville Rangers	QMJHL	34	....	....	....	2000	120	1	3.60	....	....	....	....	....	8	....	....	....	450	28	0	3.73	....	....	....	....
1972-73	Trail Smoke Eaters	WIHL	STATISTICS NOT AVAILABLE																								
1973-74	Trail Smoke Eaters	WIHL	30	....	....	....	1800	105	1	3.50	....	....	....	....	....	....	....	....	....	....	....	....	....	....	....	....	....
	Salt Lake Golden Eagles	WHL	1	0	1	0	60	4	0	4.00	....	....	....	....	....	....	....	....	....	....	....	....	....	....	....	....	....
1974-75	**Toronto Maple Leafs**	**NHL**	4	1	2	0	195	18	0	5.54	5.01	....	....	....	....	....	....	....	....	....	....	....	....	....	....	....	....
	Oklahoma City Blazers	CHL	44	22	12	6	2349	125	3	3.19	....	....	....	....	....	1	0	0	0	22	2	0	5.45	....	....	....	....
1975-76	Oklahoma City Blazers	CHL	39	14	12	6	2038	107	2	3.15	....	....	....	....	....	2	0	2	0	82	8	0	5.85	....	....	....	....
1976-77	Oklahoma City Blazers	CHL	33	5	19	4	1696	162	0	5.73	....	....	....	....	....	....	....	....	....	....	....	....	....	....	....	....	....
1977-78	Dallas Black Hawks	CHL	36	15	16	1	1982	126	0	3.81	....	....	....	....	....	1	0	0	0	20	2	0	6.00	....	....	....	....
1978-79	**Toronto Maple Leafs**	**NHL**	1	0	0	0	1	0	0	0.00	0.00	....	....	....	....	....	....	....	....	....	....	....	....	....	....	....	....
	New Brunswick Hawks	AHL	37	18	12	5	2068	119	0	2.45	....	....	....	....	....	3	1	2	0	187	13	0	4.17	....	....	....	....
1979-80	**Winnipeg Jets**	**NHL**	35	9	19	3	1947	130	0	4.01	3.56	....	....	....	....	....	....	....	....	....	....	....	....	....	....	....	....
1980-81	**Winnipeg Jets**	**NHL**	29	3	20	4	1623	128	0	4.73	3.84	....	....	....	....	....	....	....	....	....	....	....	....	....	....	....	....
	Tulsa Oilers	CHL	9	2	5	1	478	3	0	4.14	....	....	....	....	....	....	....	....	....	....	....	....	....	....	....	....	....
1981-82	Tulsa Oilers	CHL	5	3	1	0	247	14	0	3.40	....	....	....	....	....	....	....	....	....	....	....	....	....	....	....	....	....
	Fredericton Express	AHL	29	5	15	3	1571	114	1	4.35	....	....	....	....	....	....	....	....	....	....	....	....	....	....	....	....	....
1982-83	Sherbrooke Jets	AHL	2	1	1	0	119	6	0	3.02	....	....	....	....	....	....	....	....	....	....	....	....	....	....	....	....	....
	Dusseldorfer EG	Germany-2	STATISTICS NOT AVAILABLE																								
1983-84	Carolina Thunderbirds	ACHL	38	....	....	....	2192	151	*2	4.13	....	....	....	....	....	8	....	....	....	500	26	0	3.12	....	....	....	....
1984-85	Carolina Thunderbirds	ACHL	36	....	....	....	1909	109	*1	3.42	....	....	....	....	....	8	....	....	....	452	27	0	3.58	....	....	....	....
	NHL Totals		69	13	41	7	3766	276	0	4.40	....	....	....	....	....	....	....	....	....	....	....	....	....	....	....	....	....

CHL Second All-Star Team (1976) • ACHL First All-Star Team (1984)

Signed as a free agent by **Toronto**, September 27, 1974. Claimed by **Winnipeg** from **Toronto** in Expansion Draft, June 13, 1979.

• HANLON, Glen

Glen A. "Red" G – R. 6', 185 lbs. b: Brandon, Man., 2/20/1957. Vancouver's 3rd, 40th overall in 1977.

Season	Club	League	GP	W	L	T	Mins	GA	SO	Avg	AAvg	Eff	SA	S%	SAPG	GP	W	L	T	Mins	GA	SO	Avg	Eff	SA	S%	SAPG
1973-74	Brandon Travellers	MJHL	20	....	....	....	1059	64	*1	3.63	....	....	....	....	....	....	....	....	....	....	....	....	....	....	....	....	....
1974-75	Brandon Wheat Kings	WCJHL	43	....	....	....	2498	176	0	4.22	....	....	....	....	....	5	....	....	....	284	29	0	6.13	....	....	....	....
1975-76	Brandon Wheat Kings	WCJHL	*64	....	....	....	*3523	234	*4	3.99	....	....	....	....	....	5	....	....	....	300	33	0	6.60	....	....	....	....
	New Westminster Bruins	Mem-Cup	4	*2	1	0	179	10	0	3.35	....	....	....	....	....	....	....	....	....	....	....	....	....	....	....	....	....
1976-77	Brandon Wheat Kings	WCJHL	65	....	....	....	3784	195	*4	*3.09	....	....	....	....	....	*16	....	....	....	*913	53	0	3.48	....	....	....	....
1977-78	**Vancouver Canucks**	**NHL**	4	1	2	1	200	9	0	2.70	2.53	....	....	....	....	....	....	....	....	....	....	....	....	....	....	....	....
	Tulsa Oilers	CHL	53	25	23	3	3123	160	*3	3.07	....	....	....	....	....	2	1	1	0	120	5	0	2.50	....	....	....	....
1978-79	**Vancouver Canucks**	**NHL**	31	12	13	5	1821	94	3	3.10	2.74	....	....	....	....	....	....	....	....	....	....	....	....	....	....	....	....
1979-80	**Vancouver Canucks**	**NHL**	57	17	29	10	3341	193	0	3.47	3.07	....	....	....	....	2	0	0	....	60	3	0	3.00	....	....	....	....
1980-81	**Vancouver Canucks**	**NHL**	17	5	8	0	798	59	1	4.44	3.59	....	....	....	....	....	....	....	....	....	....	....	....	....	....	....	....
	Dallas Black Hawks	CHL	4	3	1	0	239	8	1	2.01	....	....	....	....	....	....	....	....	....	....	....	....	....	....	....	....	....
1981-82	**Vancouver Canucks**	**NHL**	28	8	14	5	1610	106	1	3.95	3.05	....	....	....	....	....	....	....	....	....	....	....	....	....	....	....	....
	St. Louis Blues	**NHL**	2	0	1	0	76	8	0	6.32	4.88	....	....	....	....	3	0	2	....	109	9	0	4.95	....	....	....	....
1982-83	**St. Louis Blues**	**NHL**	14	3	8	1	671	50	0	4.47	3.59	5.40	414	.879	37.0	....	....	....	....	....	....	....	....	....	....	....	....
	New York Rangers	**NHL**	21	9	10	1	1173	67	0	3.43	2.75	3.62	635	.894	32.5	1	0	1	....	60	5	0	5.00	....	....	....	....
1983-84	**New York Rangers**	**NHL**	50	28	14	4	2837	166	1	3.51	2.76	3.86	1508	.890	31.9	5	2	3	....	308	13	1	2.53	1.98	166	.922	32.3
1984-85	**New York Rangers**	**NHL**	44	14	20	7	2510	175	0	4.18	3.34	5.08	1439	.878	34.4	3	0	3	....	168	14	0	5.00	7.07	99	.859	35.4
1985-86	**New York Rangers**	**NHL**	23	5	12	1	1170	65	0	3.33	2.60	3.56	608	.893	31.2	3	0	0	....	75	6	0	4.80	9.00	32	.813	25.6
	Adirondack Red Wings	AHL	10	5	4	1	605	33	0	3.27	....	....	....	....	....	....	....	....	....	....	....	....	....	....	....	....	....
	New Haven Nighthawks	AHL	5	3	2	0	279	22	0	4.73	....	....	....	....	....	....	....	....	....	....	....	....	....	....	....	....	....
1986-87	**Detroit Red Wings**	**NHL**	36	11	16	5	1963	104	1	3.18	2.69	3.39	975	.893	29.8	8	5	2	....	467	13	*2	*1.67	0.96	227	.943	29.2
1987-88	**Detroit Red Wings**	**NHL**	47	22	17	5	2623	141	*4	3.23	2.68	3.53	1292	.891	29.6	8	4	3	....	431	22	*1	3.06	3.94	171	.871	23.8
1988-89	**Detroit Red Wings**	**NHL**	39	13	14	8	2092	124	1	3.56	2.96	4.18	1055	.882	30.3	2	0	1	....	78	7	0	5.38	8.01	47	.851	36.2
1989-90	**Detroit Red Wings**	**NHL**	45	15	18	5	2290	154	1	4.03	3.42	5.35	1159	.867	30.4	....	....	....	....	....	....	....	....	....	....	....	....
1990-91	**Detroit Red Wings**	**NHL**	19	4	6	3	862	46	0	3.20	2.87	3.36	438	.895	30.5	....	....	....	....	....	....	....	....	....	....	....	....
	San Diego Gulls	IHL	11	6	4	0	603	39	0	3.88	....	....	....	....	....	....	....	....	....	....	....	....	....	....	....	....	....
1991-92			OUT OF HOCKEY – RETIRED																								
1992-1999	**Vancouver Canucks**	**NHL**	DID NOT PLAY – ASSISTANT COACH																								
1999-2000	Portland Pirates	AHL	DID NOT PLAY – COACHING																								
	NHL Totals		477	167	202	61	26037	1561	13	3.60	....	....	....	....	....	35	11	15	....	1756	92	4	3.14	....	....	....	....

WCJHL All-Star Team (1976, 1977) • CHL First All-Star Team (1978) • Won Ken McKenzie Trophy (CHL's Rookie of the Year) (1978)

Traded to **St. Louis** by **Vancouver** for Rick Heinz, Tony Currie, Jim Nill and St. Louis' 4th round choice (Shawn Kilroy) in 1982 Entry Draft, March 9, 1982. Traded to **NY Rangers** by **St. Louis** with Vaclav Nedomansky for Andre Dore, January 4, 1983. Traded to **Detroit** by **NY Rangers** with NY Rangers' 3rd round choices in 1987 (Dennis Holland) and 1988 (Guy Dupuis) Entry Drafts for Kelly Kisio, Lane Lambert, Jim Leavins and Detroit's 5th round choice (later traded to Winnipeg–Winnipeg selected Benoit LeBeau) in 1988 Entry Draft, July 29, 1986. • Served as Vancouver's Goaltending Coach, 1992-1999.

• HARRISON, Paul

Paul Douglas G – L. 6'1", 196 lbs. b: Timmins, Ont., 2/11/1955. Minnesota's 2nd, 40th overall in 1975.

Season	Club	League	GP	W	L	T	Mins	GA	SO	Avg	AAvg	Eff	SA	S%	SAPG	GP	W	L	T	Mins	GA	SO	Avg	Eff	SA	S%	SAPG
1973-74	Oshawa Generals	OMJHL	33	....	....	....	1968	131	1	3.99	....	....	....	....	....	....	....	....	....	....	....	....	....	....	....	....	....
1974-75	Oshawa Generals	OMJHL	34	....	....	....	2040	153	2	4.50	....	....	....	....	....	4	....	....	....	240	17	0	4.25	....	....	....	....
1975-76	**Minnesota North Stars**	**NHL**	6	0	4	1	307	28	0	5.47	4.96	....	....	....	....	....	....	....	....	....	....	....	....	....	....	....	....
	Providence Reds	AHL	3	1	1	1	145	13	0	5.38	....	....	....	....	....	....	....	....	....	....	....	....	....	....	....	....	....
1976-77	**Minnesota North Stars**	**NHL**	2	0	2	0	120	11	0	5.50	5.12	....	....	....	....	....	....	....	....	....	....	....	....	....	....	....	....
	New Haven Nighthawks	AHL	*55	*32	17	6	*3265	172	2	3.16	....	....	....	....	....	6	2	4	0	363	25	0	4.13	....	....	....	....

Season	Club	League	REGULAR SEASON													PLAYOFFS											
			GP	W	L	T	Mins	GA	SO	Avg	AAvg	Eff	SA	S%	SAPG	GP	W	L	T	Mins	GA	SO	Avg	Eff	SA	S%	SAPG
1977-78	**Minnesota North Stars**	**NHL**	**27**	**6**	**16**	**2**	**1555**	**99**	**1**	**3.82**	**3.59**	....	....	....	....	....	....	....	....	....	....	....	....	....	....	....	....
1978-79	**Toronto Maple Leafs**	**NHL**	**25**	**8**	**12**	**3**	**1403**	**82**	**1**	**3.51**	**3.11**	....	....	....	....	**2**	**0**	**1**	....	**91**	**7**	**0**	**4.62**	....	....	....	....
1979-80	**Toronto Maple Leafs**	**NHL**	**30**	**9**	**17**	**2**	**1492**	**110**	**0**	**4.42**	**3.92**	....	....	....	....	....	....	....	....	....	....	....	....	....	....	....	....
	New Brunswick Hawks	AHL	9	4	3	1	485	30	0	3.71	....	....	....	....	....	....	....	....	....	....	....	....	....	....	....	....	....
1980-81	Dallas Black Hawks	CHL	37	24	7	2	2047	92	*4	2.70	....	....	....	....	....	4	....	....	....	179	16	0	5.33	....	....	....	....
	Toronto Maple Leafs	**NHL**	....	....	....	....	....	....	....	....	....	....	....	....	....	**1**	**0**	**0**	....	**40**	**1**	**0**	**1.50**	....	....	....	....
1981-82	**Pittsburgh Penguins**	**NHL**	**13**	**3**	**7**	**0**	**700**	**64**	**0**	**5.49**	**4.25**	....	....	....	....	....	....	....	....	....	....	....	....	....	....	....	....
	Buffalo Sabres	**NHL**	**6**	**2**	**1**	**1**	**229**	**14**	**0**	**3.67**	**2.83**	....	....	....	....	**1**	**0**	**0**	....	**26**	**1**	**0**	**2.31**	....	....	....	....
	NHL Totals		**109**	**28**	**59**	**9**	**5806**	**408**	**2**	**4.22**	....	....	....	....	....	**4**	**0**	**1**	....	**157**	**9**	**0**	**3.44**	....	....	....	....

AHL Second All-Star Team (1977) • CHL Second All-Star Team (1981) • Shared Terry Sawchuk Trophy (fewest goals against - CHL) with Ken Ellacott (1981)

Traded to **Toronto** by **Minnesota** for Toronto's 4th round choice (Terry Tait) in 1981 Entry Draft, June 14, 1978. Traded to **Pittsburgh** by **Toronto** for future considerations, September 11, 1981. Claimed on waivers by **Buffalo** from **Pittsburgh**, February 8, 1982.

• HASEK, Dominik

"The Dominator" G – L. 5'11", 168 lbs. b: Pardubice, Czech., 1/29/1965. Chicago's 11th, 207th overall in 1983.

Season	Club	League	GP	W	L	T	Mins	GA	SO	Avg	AAvg	Eff	SA	S%	SAPG	GP	W	L	T	Mins	GA	SO	Avg	Eff	SA	S%	SAPG
1981-82	HC Pardubice	Czech.	12	....	....	....	661	34	....	3.09	....	....	....	....	....	....	....	....	....	....	....	....	....	....	....	....	....
	Czechoslovakia	EJC-A	5	....	....	....	20	1	....	3.00	....	....	....	....	....	....	....	....	....	....	....	....	....	....	....	....	....
1982-83	HC Pardubice	Czech.	42	....	....	....	2358	105	....	2.67	....	....	....	....	....	....	....	....	....	....	....	....	....	....	....	....	....
	Czechoslovakia	WEC-A	2	1	1	0	120	5	1	2.50	....	....	....	....	....	....	....	....	....	....	....	....	....	....	....	....	....
1983-84	HC Pardubice	Czech.	40	....	....	....	2304	108	....	2.81	....	....	....	....	....	....	....	....	....	....	....	....	....	....	....	....	....
1984-85	Czechoslovakia	Can-Cup	4	0	3	1	188	12	0	4.00	....	....	....	....	....	....	....	....	....	....	....	....	....	....	....	....	....
	HC Pardubice	Czech.	42	....	....	....	2419	131	....	3.25	....	....	....	....	....	....	....	....	....	....	....	....	....	....	....	....	....
	Czechoslovakia	WJC-A	7	4	0	2	380	10	0	1.89	....	....	....	....	....	....	....	....	....	....	....	....	....	....	....	....	....
1985-86	HC Pardubice	Czech.	45	....	....	....	2689	138	....	3.08	....	....	....	....	....	....	....	....	....	....	....	....	....	....	....	....	....
	Czechoslovakia	WEC-A	9	5	3	1	538	19	0	2.12	....	....	....	....	....	....	....	....	....	....	....	....	....	....	....	....	....
1986-87	HC Pardubice	Czech.	43	....	....	....	2515	103	....	2.46	....	....	....	....	....	....	....	....	....	....	....	....	....	....	....	....	....
	Czechoslovakia	WEC-A	9	5	2	2	520	19	1	2.19	....	....	....	....	....	....	....	....	....	....	....	....	....	....	....	....	....
1987-88	Czechoslovakia	Can-Cup	6	2	3	1	360	20	0	3.00	....	....	....	....	....	....	....	....	....	....	....	....	....	....	....	....	....
	HC Pardubice	Czech.	31	....	....	....	1862	93	....	3.00	....	....	....	....	....	....	....	....	....	....	....	....	....	....	....	....	....
	Czechoslovakia	Olympics	5	3	2	0	217	18	1	4.98	....	....	....	....	....	....	....	....	....	....	....	....	....	....	....	....	....
1988-89	HC Pardubice	Czech.	42	....	....	....	2507	114	....	2.73	....	....	....	....	....	....	....	....	....	....	....	....	....	....	....	....	....
	Czechoslovakia	WEC-A	10	4	4	2	600	21	*2	2.10	....	....	....	....	....	....	....	....	....	....	....	....	....	....	....	....	....
1989-90	Dukla Jihlava	Czech.	40	....	....	....	2251	80	....	2.13	....	....	....	....	....	....	....	....	....	....	....	....	....	....	....	....	....
	Czechoslovakia	WEC-A	8	5	3	0	480	20	1	2.50	....	....	....	....	....	....	....	....	....	....	....	....	....	....	....	....	....
1990-91	**Chicago Blackhawks**	**NHL**	**5**	**3**	**0**	**1**	**195**	**8**	**0**	**2.46**	**2.21**	**2.12**	**93**	**.914**	**28.6**	**3**	**0**	**0**	....	**69**	**3**	**0**	**2.61**	**2.01**	**39**	**.923**	**33.9**
	Indianapolis Ice	IHL	33	20	11	1	1903	80	*5	*2.52	....	....	....	....	....	1	1	0	....	60	3	0	3.00	....	....	....	....
1991-92	Czechoslovakia	Can-Cup	5	1	4	0	300	18	0	4.00	....	....	....	....	....	....	....	....	....	....	....	....	....	....	....	....	....
	Chicago Blackhawks	**NHL**	**20**	**10**	**4**	**1**	**1014**	**44**	**1**	**2.60**	**2.32**	**2.77**	**413**	**.893**	**24.4**	**3**	**0**	**2**	....	**158**	**8**	**0**	**3.04**	**3.47**	**70**	**.886**	**26.6**
	Indianapolis Ice	IHL	20	7	10	3	1162	69	1	3.56	....	....	....	....	....	....	....	....	....	....	....	....	....	....	....	....	....
1992-93	**Buffalo Sabres**	**NHL**	**28**	**11**	**10**	**4**	**1429**	**75**	**0**	**3.15**	**2.69**	**3.28**	**720**	**.896**	**30.2**	**1**	**1**	**0**	....	**45**	**1**	**0**	**1.33**	**0.55**	**24**	**.958**	**32.0**
1993-94	**Buffalo Sabres**	**NHL**	**58**	**30**	**20**	**6**	**3358**	**109**	***7**	***1.95**	**1.85**	**1.37**	**1552**	**.930**	**27.7**	**7**	**3**	**4**	....	**484**	**13**	**2**	***1.61**	**0.80**	**261**	**.950**	**32.4**
1994-95	HC Pardubice	Czech-Rep	2	1	0	1	124	6	0	2.90	....	....	....	....	....	....	....	....	....	....	....	....	....	....	....	....	....
	Buffalo Sabres	**NHL**	**41**	**19**	**14**	**7**	**2416**	**85**	***5**	***2.11**	**2.19**	**1.47**	**1221**	**.930**	**30.3**	**5**	**1**	**4**	....	**309**	**18**	**0**	**3.50**	**4.81**	**131**	**.863**	**25.4**
1995-96	**Buffalo Sabres**	**NHL**	**59**	**22**	**30**	**6**	**3417**	**161**	**2**	**2.83**	**2.81**	**2.27**	**2011**	**.920**	**35.3**	....	....	....	....	....	....	....	....	....	....	....	....
1996-97	**Buffalo Sabres**	**NHL**	**67**	**37**	**20**	**10**	**4037**	**153**	**5**	**2.27**	**2.43**	**1.60**	**2177**	**.930**	**32.4**	**3**	**1**	**1**	....	**153**	**5**	**0**	**1.96**	**1.44**	**68**	**.926**	**26.7**
1997-98	**Buffalo Sabres**	**NHL**	***72**	**33**	**23**	**13**	***4220**	**147**	***13**	**2.09**	**2.48**	**1.43**	**2149**	**.932**	**30.6**	**15**	**10**	**5**	....	**948**	**32**	**1**	**2.03**	**1.26**	**514**	**.938**	**32.5**
	Czech-Republic	Olympics	6	*5	1	0	*369	6	*2	*0.97	....	....	....	....	....	....	....	....	....	....	....	....	....	....	....	....	....
1998-99	**Buffalo Sabres**	**NHL**	**64**	**30**	**18**	**14**	**3817**	**119**	**9**	**1.87**	**2.21**	**1.19**	**1877**	**.937**	**29.5**	**19**	**13**	**6**	....	**1217**	**36**	**2**	**1.77**	**1.09**	**587**	**.939**	**28.9**
99-2000	**Buffalo Sabres**	**NHL**	**35**	**15**	**11**	**6**	**2066**	**76**	**3**	**2.21**	**2.52**	**1.79**	**937**	**.919**	**27.2**	**5**	**1**	**4**	....	**301**	**12**	**0**	**2.39**	**1.95**	**147**	**.918**	**29.3**
	NHL Totals		**449**	**210**	**150**	**68**	**25969**	**977**	**45**	**2.26**	....	....	**13150**	**.926**	**30.4**	**61**	**30**	**26**	....	**3684**	**128**	**5**	**2.08**	....	**1841**	**.930**	**30.0**

WJC-A All-Star Team (1983) • Czechoslovakian Goaltender-of-the-Year (1986, 1987, 1988, 1989, 1990) • Czechoslovakian Player-of-the-Year (1987, 1989, 1990) • WEC-A All-Star Team (1987, 1989, 1990) • Named Best Goaltender at WEC-A (1987, 1989) • Czechoslovakian First All-Star Team (1988, 1989, 1990) • IHL First All-Star Team (1991) • NHL All-Rookie Team (1992) • NHL First All-Star Team (1994, 1995, 1997, 1998, 1999) • Shared William M. Jennings Trophy with Grant Fuhr (1994) • Won Vezina Trophy (1994, 1995, 1997, 1998, 1999) • Won Lester B. Pearson Award (1997, 1998) • Won Hart Trophy (1997, 1998) • Named Best Goaltender at Olympic Games (1998) • Played in NHL All-Star Game (1996, 1997, 1998, 1999)

Traded to **Buffalo** by **Chicago** for Stephane Beauregard and Buffalo's 4th round choice (Eric Daze) in 1993 Entry Draft, August 7, 1992.

• HAYWARD, Brian

Brian George G – L. 5'10", 180 lbs. b: Toronto, Ont., 6/25/1960.

Season	Club	League	GP	W	L	T	Mins	GA	SO	Avg	AAvg	Eff	SA	S%	SAPG	GP	W	L	T	Mins	GA	SO	Avg	Eff	SA	S%	SAPG
1976-77	Markham Waxers	OHA-B	26	....	....	....	1558	107	0	4.11	....	....	....	....	....	....	....	....	....	....	....	....	....	....	....	....	....
1977-78	Guelph Platers	OJHL	STATISTICS NOT AVAILABLE													....	....	....	....	....	....	....	....	....	....	....	....
	Guelph Platers	Cen-Cup	STATISTICS NOT AVAILABLE																								
1978-79	Cornell University	ECAC	25	18	6	0	1469	95	0	3.88	....	....	....	....	....	3	2	1	0	179	14	0	4.66	....	....	....	....
1979-80	Cornell University	ECAC	12	2	7	0	508	52	0	6.02	....	....	....	....	....	....	....	....	....	....	....	....	....	....	....	....	....
1980-81	Cornell University	ECAC	19	11	4	1	967	58	1	3.54	....	....	....	....	....	4	2	1	0	181	18	0	4.50	....	....	....	....
1981-82	Cornell University	ECAC	22	11	10	1	1249	66	0	3.17	....	....	....	....	....	....	....	....	....	....	....	....	....	....	....	....	....
1982-83	**Winnipeg Jets**	**NHL**	**24**	**10**	**12**	**2**	**1440**	**89**	**1**	**3.71**	**2.98**	**4.20**	**786**	**.887**	**32.8**	**3**	**0**	**3**	....	**160**	**14**	**0**	**5.25**	....	....	....	....
	Sherbrooke Jets	AHL	22	6	11	3	1208	89	1	4.42	....	....	....	....	....	....	....	....	....	....	....	....	....	....	....	....	....
1983-84	**Winnipeg Jets**	**NHL**	**28**	**7**	**18**	**2**	**1530**	**124**	**0**	**4.86**	**3.84**	**7.01**	**860**	**.856**	**33.7**	....	....	....	....	....	....	....	....	....	....	....	....
	Sherbrooke Jets	AHL	15	4	8	0	781	69	0	5.30	....	....	....	....	....	....	....	....	....	....	....	....	....	....	....	....	....
1984-85	**Winnipeg Jets**	**NHL**	**61**	**33**	**17**	**7**	**3436**	**220**	**0**	**3.84**	**3.06**	**4.66**	**1814**	**.879**	**31.7**	**6**	**2**	**4**	....	**309**	**23**	**0**	**4.47**	**6.59**	**156**	**.853**	**30.3**
1985-86	**Winnipeg Jets**	**NHL**	**52**	**13**	**28**	**5**	**2721**	**217**	**0**	**4.79**	**3.76**	**7.57**	**1373**	**.842**	**30.3**	**2**	**0**	**1**	....	**68**	**6**	**0**	**5.29**	**10.24**	**31**	**.806**	**27.4**
	Sherbrooke Canadiens	AHL	3	2	0	1	185	5	0	1.62	....	....	....	....	....	....	....	....	....	....	....	....	....	....	....	....	....
1986-87	**Montreal Canadiens**	**NHL**	**37**	**19**	**13**	**4**	**2178**	**102**	**1**	***2.81**	**2.37**	**2.99**	**959**	**.894**	**26.4**	**13**	**6**	**5**	....	**708**	**32**	**0**	**2.71**	**2.82**	**308**	**.896**	**26.1**
1987-88	**Montreal Canadiens**	**NHL**	**39**	**22**	**10**	**4**	**2247**	**107**	**2**	**2.86**	**2.37**	**2.97**	**1032**	**.896**	**27.6**	**4**	**2**	**2**	....	**230**	**9**	**0**	**2.35**	**2.49**	**85**	**.894**	**22.2**
1988-89	**Montreal Canadiens**	**NHL**	**36**	**20**	**13**	**3**	**2091**	**101**	**1**	**2.90**	**2.40**	**3.28**	**894**	**.887**	**25.7**	**2**	**1**	**1**	....	**124**	**7**	**0**	**3.39**	**4.39**	**54**	**.870**	**26.1**
1989-90	**Montreal Canadiens**	**NHL**	**29**	**10**	**12**	**6**	**1674**	**94**	**1**	**3.37**	**2.85**	**4.11**	**770**	**.878**	**27.6**	**1**	**0**	**0**	....	**33**	**2**	**0**	**3.64**	**4.04**	**18**	**.889**	**32.7**
1990-91	Montreal Canadiens	Fr-Tour	2	1	1	0	64	2	0	1.87	....	....	....	....	....	....	....	....	....	....	....	....	....	....	....	....	....
	Minnesota North Stars	**NHL**	**26**	**6**	**15**	**3**	**1473**	**77**	**2**	**3.14**	**2.82**	**3.59**	**674**	**.886**	**27.5**	**6**	**0**	**2**	....	**171**	**11**	**0**	**3.86**	**5.66**	**75**	**.853**	**26.3**
	Kalamazoo Wings	IHL	2	2	0	0	120	5	0	2.50	....	....	....	....	....	....	....	....	....	....	....	....	....	....	....	....	....
1991-92	**San Jose Sharks**	**NHL**	**7**	**1**	**4**	**0**	**305**	**25**	**0**	**4.92**	**4.41**	**6.95**	**177**	**.859**	**34.8**	....	....	....	....	....	....	....	....	....	....	....	....
	Kansas City Blades	IHL	2	1	1	0	119	3	1	1.51	....	....	....	....	....	....	....	....	....	....	....	....	....	....	....	....	....
1992-93	**San Jose Sharks**	**NHL**	**18**	**2**	**14**	**1**	**930**	**86**	**0**	**5.55**	**4.77**	**8.54**	**559**	**.846**	**36.1**	....	....	....	....	....	....	....	....	....	....	....	....
	NHL Totals		**357**	**143**	**156**	**37**	**20025**	**1242**	**8**	**3.72**	....	....	**9898**	**.875**	**29.7**	**37**	**11**	**18**	....	**1803**	**104**	**0**	**3.46**	....	....	....	....

Centennial Cup All-Star Team (1978) • ECAC First All-Star Team (1982) • NCAA East First All-American Team (1982) • Shared William M. Jennings Trophy with Patrick Roy (1987, 1988, 1989)

Signed as a free agent by **Winnipeg**, May 5, 1982. Traded to **Montreal** by **Winnipeg** for Steve Penney and the rights to Jan Ingman, August 19, 1986. Traded to **Minnesota** by **Montreal** for Jayson More, November 7, 1990. Claimed by **San Jose** from **Minnesota** in Dispersal Draft, May 30, 1991. • Missed majority of 1991-92 season recovering from back injury suffered in game vs. Buffalo, October 19, 1991. • Suffered eventual career-ending back injury in game vs. Detroit, January 15, 1993.

• HEAD, Don

Donald Charles G – L. 5'10", 200 lbs. b: Mt. Dennis, Ont., 6/30/1933.

Season	Club	League	GP	W	L	T	Mins	GA	SO	Avg	AAvg	Eff	SA	S%	SAPG	GP	W	L	T	Mins	GA	SO	Avg	Eff	SA	S%	SAPG
1950-51	Weston Dukes	OHA-B	STATISTICS NOT AVAILABLE																								
1951-52	Toronto Marlboros	OHA-Jr.	37	....	....	....	2220	107	*4	*2.87	....	....	....	....	....	....	....	....	....	....	....	....	....	....	....	....	....
1952-53	Weston Dukes	OHA-B	STATISTICS NOT AVAILABLE																								
1953-54	Stratford Indians	OHA-Sr.	14	....	....	....	840	53	1	3.79	....	....	....	....	....	....	....	....	....	....	....	....	....	....	....	....	....
1954-55	Stratford Indians	OHA-Sr.	13	....	....	....	780	49	0	3.77	....	....	....	....	....	....	....	....	....	....	....	....	....	....	....	....	....
1955-56	Stratford Indians	OHA-Sr.	47	....	....	....	2820	186	*3	3.96	....	....	....	....	....	6	....	....	....	360	25	0	4.17	....	....	....	....
1956-57	Windsor Bulldogs	OHA-Sr.	50	30	17	3	3000	144	*6	*2.88	....	....	....	....	....	12	....	....	....	720	50	0	4.17	....	....	....	....
1957-58	Chatham Maroons	NOHA	49	....	....	....	2940	168	3	3.43	....	....	....	....	....	....	....	....	....	....	....	....	....	....	....	....	....
1958-59	Chatham Maroons	NOHA	47	....	....	....	2820	152	*6	3.23	....	....	....	....	....	10	....	....	....	600	27	*1	2.70	....	....	....	....
1959-60	Windsor Bulldogs	OHA-Sr.	48	....	....	....	2860	138	*3	*2.90	....	....	....	....	....	17	....	....	....	1020	47	*3	*2.76	....	....	....	....
	Canada	Olympics	7	5	1	0	385	12	*2	1.87	....	....	....	....	....	....	....	....	....	....	....	....	....	....	....	....	....

Season	Club	League	REGULAR SEASON GP	W	L	T	Mins	GA	SO	Avg	AAvg	Eff	SA	S%	SAPG	PLAYOFFS GP	W	L	T	Mins	GA	SO	Avg	Eff	SA	S%	SAPG
1960-61	Portland Buckaroos	WHL	*70	*38	23	9	*4290	192	*7	*2.69	....	....	....	....	....	*14	*10	4	0	*846	30	*2	*2.13	....	....	....	....
1961-62	**Boston Bruins**	**NHL**	**38**	**9**	**26**	**3**	**2280**	**158**	**2**	**4.16**	**4.43**	....	....	....	....	....	....	....	....	....	....	....	....	....	....	....	....
	Portland Buckaroos	WHL	5	3	1	1	300	16	0	3.20	....	....	....	....	....	....	....	....	....	....	....	....	....	....	....	....	....
1962-63	Portland Buckaroos	WHL	*70	*43	21	6	*4200	178	4	*2.54	....	....	....	....	....	7	3	4	0	423	22	0	3.12	....	....	....	....
1963-64	Portland Buckaroos	WHL	16	6	9	1	940	57	0	3.64	....	....	....	....	....	....	....	....	....	....	....	....	....	....	....	....	....
1964-65	Portland Buckaroos	WHL	51	26	20	4	3055	153	3	3.00	....	....	....	....	....	9	*8	1	0	554	13	*3	*1.41	....	....	....	....
1965-66	Portland Buckaroos	WHL	36	20	12	3	2154	100	4	*2.79	....	....	....	....	....	....	....	....	....	....	....	....	....	....	....	....	....
1966-67	Portland Buckaroos	WHL	44	26	13	5	2714	120	3	2.65	....	....	....	....	....	4	0	3	0	225	10	0	2.67	....	....	....	....
1967-68	Seattle Totems	WHL	46	23	19	4	2717	114	3	2.52	....	....	....	....	....	*9	*8	1	0	*556	20	*2	*2.17	....	....	....	....
1968-69	Seattle Totems	WHL	44	22	13	4	2377	120	1	3.03	....	....	....	....	....	4	0	4	0	245	19	0	4.65	....	....	....	....
1969-70	Seattle Totems	WHL	20	8	10	2	1200	71	0	3.55	....	....	....	....	....	....	....	....	....	....	....	....	....	....	....	....	....
1970-71	Seattle Totems	WHL	16	4	7	3	769	45	0	3.51	....	....	....	....	....	....	....	....	....	....	....	....	....	....	....	....	....
	NHL Totals		**38**	**9**	**26**	**3**	**2280**	**158**	**2**	**4.16**	....	....	....	....	....	....	....	....	....	....	....	....	....	....	....	....	....

NOHA First All-Star Team (1959) • WHL First All-Star Team (1961, 1963, 1968) • Won WHL Rookie of the Year Award (1961) • Won WHL Leading Goaltender Award (1961, 1963) • WHL Second All-Star Team (1965, 1966) • Shared WHL Leading Goaltender Award with Dave Kelly (1966)

Traded to **Chatham** (NOHA) by **Windsor** (OHA-Sr.) for Marv Edwards, October, 1957. Traded to **Boston** by **Portland** (WHL) for Jack Bionda and future considerations (Gene Achtymichuk and Don Ward (August, 1961) and the loan of Bruce Gamble (September, 1961), May, 1961. Traded to **Portland** (WHL) by **Boston** for cash, June 10, 1962. Traded to **Seattle** (WHL) by **Portland** (WHL) for Jim McLeod and cash, September, 1967.

• HEALY, Glenn

G – L. 5′9″, 192 lbs. b: Pickering, Ont., 8/23/1962.

Season	Club	League	GP	W	L	T	Mins	GA	SO	Avg	AAvg	Eff	SA	S%	SAPG	GP	W	L	T	Mins	GA	SO	Avg	Eff	SA	S%	SAPG
1979-80	Pickering Panthers	OHA-B	31	....	....	....	1850	123	0	3.99	....	....	....	....	....	....	....	....	....	....	....	....	....	....	....	....	....
1980-81	Pickering Panthers	OHA-B	35	....	....	....	2080	120	1	3.46	....	....	....	....	....	....	....	....	....	....	....	....	....	....	....	....	....
1981-82	Western Michigan University	CCHA	27	7	19	1	1569	116	0	4.44	....	....	....	....	....	....	....	....	....	....	....	....	....	....	....	....	....
1982-83	Western Michigan University	CCHA	30	8	19	2	1732	116	0	4.01	....	....	....	....	....	....	....	....	....	....	....	....	....	....	....	....	....
1983-84	Western Michigan University	CCHA	38	19	16	3	2241	146	0	3.90	....	....	....	....	....	....	....	....	....	....	....	....	....	....	....	....	....
1984-85	Western Michigan University	CCHA	37	21	14	2	2171	118	0	3.26	....	....	....	....	....	....	....	....	....	....	....	....	....	....	....	....	....
1985-86	**Los Angeles Kings**	**NHL**	**1**	**0**	**0**	**0**	**51**	**6**	**0**	**7.06**	**5.52**	**12.10**	**35**	**.829**	**41.2**	....	....	....	....	....	....	....	....	....	....	....	....
	Toledo	IHL	7	....	....	....	402	28	0	4.18	....	....	....	....	....	....	....	....	....	....	....	....	....	....	....	....	....
	New Haven Nighthawks	AHL	43	21	15	4	2410	160	0	3.98	....	....	....	....	....	2	0	2	....	49	11	0	5.55	....	....	....	....
1986-87	New Haven Nighthawks	AHL	47	21	15	0	2828	173	1	3.67	....	....	....	....	....	7	3	4	....	427	19	0	2.67	....	....	....	....
1987-88	**Los Angeles Kings**	**NHL**	**34**	**12**	**18**	**1**	**1869**	**135**	**1**	**4.33**	**3.62**	**5.82**	**1005**	**.866**	**32.3**	**4**	**1**	**3**	....	**240**	**20**	**0**	**5.00**	**7.81**	**128**	**.844**	**32.0**
1988-89	**Los Angeles Kings**	**NHL**	**48**	**25**	**19**	**2**	**2699**	**192**	**0**	**4.27**	**3.57**	**5.43**	**1509**	**.873**	**33.5**	**3**	**0**	**1**	....	**97**	**6**	**0**	**3.71**	**3.77**	**59**	**.898**	**36.5**
1989-90	**New York Islanders**	**NHL**	**39**	**12**	**19**	**6**	**2197**	**128**	**2**	**3.50**	**2.96**	**3.70**	**1210**	**.894**	**33.0**	**4**	**1**	**2**	....	**166**	**9**	**0**	**3.25**	**3.70**	**79**	**.886**	**28.6**
1990-91	**New York Islanders**	**NHL**	**53**	**18**	**24**	**9**	**2999**	**166**	**0**	**3.32**	**2.98**	**3.54**	**1557**	**.893**	**31.2**	....	....	....	....	....	....	....	....	....	....	....	....
1991-92	**New York Islanders**	**NHL**	**37**	**14**	**16**	**4**	**1960**	**124**	**1**	**3.80**	**3.41**	**4.51**	**1045**	**.881**	**32.0**	....	....	....	....	....	....	....	....	....	....	....	....
1992-93	**New York Islanders**	**NHL**	**47**	**22**	**20**	**2**	**2655**	**146**	**1**	**3.30**	**2.82**	**3.66**	**1316**	**.889**	**29.7**	**18**	**9**	**8**	....	**1109**	**59**	**0**	**3.19**	**3.59**	**524**	**.887**	**28.3**
1993-94♦	**New York Rangers**	**NHL**	**29**	**10**	**12**	**2**	**1368**	**69**	**2**	**3.03**	**2.91**	**3.69**	**567**	**.878**	**24.9**	**2**	**0**	**0**	....	**68**	**1**	**0**	**0.88**	**0.52**	**17**	**.941**	**15.0**
1994-95	**New York Rangers**	**NHL**	**17**	**8**	**6**	**1**	**888**	**35**	**1**	**2.36**	**2.47**	**2.19**	**377**	**.907**	**25.5**	**5**	**2**	**1**	....	**230**	**13**	**0**	**3.39**	**4.74**	**93**	**.860**	**24.3**
1995-96	**New York Rangers**	**NHL**	**44**	**17**	**14**	**11**	**2564**	**124**	**2**	**2.90**	**2.88**	**2.91**	**1237**	**.900**	**28.9**	....	....	....	....	....	....	....	....	....	....	....	....
1996-97	**New York Rangers**	**NHL**	**23**	**5**	**12**	**4**	**1357**	**59**	**1**	**2.61**	**2.81**	**2.44**	**632**	**.907**	**27.9**	....	....	....	....	....	....	....	....	....	....	....	....
1997-98	**Toronto Maple Leafs**	**NHL**	**21**	**4**	**10**	**2**	**1068**	**53**	**0**	**2.98**	**3.56**	**3.49**	**453**	**.883**	**25.4**	....	....	....	....	....	....	....	....	....	....	....	....
1998-99	Chicago Wolves	IHL	10	6	3	1	597	33	0	3.32	....	....	....	....	....	....	....	....	....	....	....	....	....	....	....	....	....
	Toronto Maple Leafs	**NHL**	**9**	**6**	**3**	**0**	**546**	**27**	**0**	**2.97**	**3.53**	**3.12**	**257**	**.895**	**28.2**	**1**	**0**	**0**	....	**20**	**0**	**0**	**0.00**	**0.00**	**5**	**1.000**	**15.0**
99-2000	**Toronto Maple Leafs**	**NHL**	**20**	**9**	**10**	**0**	**1164**	**59**	**2**	**3.04**	**3.48**	**3.40**	**527**	**.888**	**27.2**	....	....	....	....	....	....	....	....	....	....	....	....
	NHL Totals		**422**	**162**	**183**	**44**	**23385**	**1323**	**13**	**3.39**	....	....	**11727**	**.887**	**30.1**	**37**	**13**	**15**	....	**1930**	**108**	**0**	**3.36**	....	**905**	**.881**	**28.1**

CCHA Second All-Star Team (1985) • NCAA West Second All-American Team (1985)

Signed as a free agent by **Los Angeles**, June 13, 1985. Signed as a free agent by **NY Islanders**, August 16, 1989. Claimed by **Anaheim** from **NY Islanders** in Expansion Draft, June 24, 1993. Claimed by **Tampa Bay** from **Anaheim** in Phase II of Expansion Draft, June 25, 1993. Traded to **NY Rangers** by **Tampa Bay** for Tampa Bay's 3rd round choice (previously acquired, Tampa Bay selected Allan Egeland) in 1993 Entry Draft, June 25, 1993. Signed as a free agent by **Toronto**, August 8, 1997.

• HEBERT, Guy

Guy Andre G – L. 5′11″, 185 lbs. b: Troy, NY, 1/7/1967. St. Louis' 8th, 159th overall in 1987.

Season	Club	League	GP	W	L	T	Mins	GA	SO	Avg	AAvg	Eff	SA	S%	SAPG	GP	W	L	T	Mins	GA	SO	Avg	Eff	SA	S%	SAPG
1985-86	Hamilton College	NCAA-2	18	4	12	2	1011	69	2	4.09	....	....	....	....	....	....	....	....	....	....	....	....	....	....	....	....	....
1986-87	Hamilton College	NCAA-2	18	12	5	0	1070	40	3	2.19	....	....	....	....	....	2	1	1	....	134	6	0	2.69	....	....	....	....
1987-88	Hamilton College	NCAA-2	9	5	3	0	510	22	1	2.58	....	....	....	....	....	1	0	1	....	60	3	0	3.00	....	....	....	....
1988-89	Hamilton College	NCAA-2	25	18	7	0	1454	62	2	2.56	....	....	....	....	....	2	1	1	....	126	4	0	1.90	....	....	....	....
1989-90	Peoria Rivermen	IHL	30	7	13	7	1706	124	1	4.36	....	....	....	....	....	2	0	1	....	76	5	0	3.95	....	....	....	....
1990-91	Peoria Rivermen	IHL	36	24	10	1	2093	100	2	2.87	....	....	....	....	....	8	3	4	....	458	32	0	4.19	....	....	....	....
1991-92	**St. Louis Blues**	**NHL**	**13**	**5**	**5**	**1**	**738**	**36**	**0**	**2.93**	**2.62**	**2.68**	**393**	**.908**	**32.0**	....	....	....	....	....	....	....	....	....	....	....	....
	Peoria Rivermen	IHL	29	20	9	0	1731	98	0	3.40	....	....	....	....	....	4	3	1	....	239	9	0	2.26	....	....	....	....
1992-93	**St. Louis Blues**	**NHL**	**24**	**8**	**8**	**2**	**1210**	**74**	**1**	**3.67**	**3.14**	**4.31**	**630**	**.883**	**31.2**	**1**	**0**	**0**	....	**2**	**0**	**0**	**0.00**	**0.00**	**1**	**1.000**	**30.0**
1993-94	**Anaheim Mighty Ducks**	**NHL**	**52**	**20**	**27**	**3**	**2991**	**141**	**2**	**2.83**	**2.71**	**2.64**	**1513**	**.907**	**30.4**	....	....	....	....	....	....	....	....	....	....	....	....
	United States	WC-A	6	4	2	0	300	18	0	3.60	....	....	....	....	....	....	....	....	....	....	....	....	....	....	....	....	....
1994-95	**Mighty Ducks of Anaheim**	**NHL**	**39**	**12**	**20**	**4**	**2092**	**109**	**2**	**3.13**	**3.29**	**3.01**	**1132**	**.904**	**32.5**	....	....	....	....	....	....	....	....	....	....	....	....
1995-96	**Mighty Ducks of Anaheim**	**NHL**	**59**	**28**	**23**	**5**	**3326**	**157**	**4**	**2.83**	**2.81**	**2.44**	**1820**	**.914**	**32.8**	....	....	....	....	....	....	....	....	....	....	....	....
1996-97	United States	W-Cup	1	1	0	0	60	3	0	3.00	....	....	....	....	....	....	....	....	....	....	....	....	....	....	....	....	....
	Mighty Ducks of Anaheim	**NHL**	**67**	**29**	**25**	**12**	**3863**	**172**	**4**	**2.67**	**2.87**	**2.15**	**2133**	**.919**	**33.1**	**9**	**4**	**4**	....	**534**	**18**	**1**	**2.02**	**1.43**	**255**	**.929**	**28.7**
1997-98	**Mighty Ducks of Anaheim**	**NHL**	**46**	**13**	**24**	**6**	**2660**	**130**	**3**	**2.93**	**3.50**	**2.84**	**1339**	**.903**	**30.2**	....	....	....	....	....	....	....	....	....	....	....	....
1998-99	**Mighty Ducks of Anaheim**	**NHL**	**69**	**31**	**29**	**9**	**4083**	**165**	**6**	**2.42**	**2.87**	**1.89**	**2114**	**.922**	**31.1**	**4**	**0**	**3**	....	**208**	**15**	**0**	**4.33**	**5.24**	**124**	**.879**	**35.8**
99-2000	**Mighty Ducks of Anaheim**	**NHL**	**68**	**28**	**31**	**9**	**3976**	**166**	**4**	**2.51**	**2.86**	**2.31**	**1805**	**.908**	**27.2**	....	....	....	....	....	....	....	....	....	....	....	....
	NHL Totals		**437**	**174**	**192**	**51**	**24939**	**1150**	**26**	**2.77**	....	....	**12879**	**.911**	**31.0**	**14**	**4**	**7**	....	**744**	**33**	**1**	**2.66**	....	**380**	**.913**	**30.6**

IHL Second All-Star Team (1991) • Shared James Norris Memorial Trophy (fewest goals against - IHL) with Pat Jablonski (1991) • Played in NHL All-Star Game (1997)

Claimed by **Anaheim** from **St. Louis** in Expansion Draft, June 24, 1993.

• HEBERT, Sammy

G – R. 5′10″, 145 lbs. b: Ottawa, Ont., 3/31/1894 d: 7/23/1965.

Season	Club	League	GP	W	L	T	Mins	GA	SO	Avg	AAvg	Eff	SA	S%	SAPG	GP	W	L	T	Mins	GA	SO	Avg	Eff	SA	S%	SAPG
1910-11	Ottawa Cedar	OHA-I	STATISTICS NOT AVAILABLE																								
1911-12	Ottawa Stewartons	IPAHU	6	2	3	0	375	35	0	5.60	....	....	....	....	....	....	....	....	....	....	....	....	....	....	....	....	....
1912-13	Ottawa Stewartons	OCHL	STATISTICS NOT AVAILABLE																								
1913-14	Ottawa New Edinburghs	X-Games	1	1	0	0	60	3	0	3.00	....	....	....	....	....	....	....	....	....	....	....	....	....	....	....	....	....
	Toronto Ontarios	NHA	19	4	15	0	1160	108	0	5.59	....	....	....	....	....	....	....	....	....	....	....	....	....	....	....	....	....
1914-15	Ottawa Senators	NHA	2	0	0	0	23	1	0	2.61	....	....	....	....	....	....	....	....	....	....	....	....	....	....	....	....	....
	Ottawa New Edinburghs	OCHL	STATISTICS NOT AVAILABLE																								
1915-16			MILITARY SERVICE																								
1916-17	Quebec Bulldogs	NHA	15	7	6	0	874	95	0	6.52	....	....	....	....	....	....	....	....	....	....	....	....	....	....	....	....	....
	Ottawa Senators	NHA	1	0	1	0	60	8	0	8.00	....	....	....	....	....	....	....	....	....	....	....	....	....	....	....	....	....
1917-18♦	**Toronto Arenas**	**NHL**	**2**	**1**	**0**	**0**	**80**	**10**	**0**	**7.50**	**4.86**	....	....	....	....	....	....	....	....	....	....	....	....	....	....	....	....
	Ottawa Ordinance Corps	ONDHL	STATISTICS NOT AVAILABLE																								
1918-19			MILITARY SERVICE																								
1919-20	Ottawa City Cedar	OCHL	STATISTICS NOT AVAILABLE																								
1920-21	Ottawa City Cedar	OCHL	STATISTICS NOT AVAILABLE																								

			REGULAR SEASON													PLAYOFFS											
Season	**Club**	**League**	**GP**	**W**	**L**	**T**	**Mins**	**GA**	**SO**	**Avg**	**AAvg**	**Eff**	**SA**	**S%**	**SAPG**	**GP**	**W**	**L**	**T**	**Mins**	**GA**	**SO**	**Avg**	**Eff**	**SA**	**S%**	**SAPG**
1921-22	Saskatoon Sheiks	WCHL	23	5	18	0	1380	131	0	5.70	....	....	....	....	....	....	....	....	....	....	....	....	....	....	....	....	....
1922-23	Saskatoon Sheiks	WCHL	19	4	13	2	1219	79	0	3.89	....	....	....	....	....	....	....	....	....	....	....	....	....	....	....	....	....
1923-24	**Ottawa Senators**	**NHL**	**2**	**1**	**1**	**0**	**120**	**9**	**0**	**4.50**	**5.24**	....	....	....	....	....	....	....	....	....	....	....	....	....	....	....	....
	NHL Totals		**4**	**2**	**1**	**0**	**200**	**19**	**0**	**5.70**	....	....	....	....	....	....	....	....	....	....	....	....	....	....	....	....	....
	Other Major League Totals		79	20	53	2	4716	422	0	5.37	....	....	....	....	....	....	....	....	....	....	....	....	....	....	....	....	....

Signed as a free agent by **Toronto Ontarios** (NHA), December 29, 1913. Traded to **Ottawa** (NHA) by **Toronto Ontarios/Shamrocks** (NHA) with cash for Skene Ronan, December 25, 1914. Traded to **Montreal Canadiens** (NHA) by **Ottawa** (NHA) for Jack Fournier, January 16, 1917. Traded to **Quebec** (NHA) by **Montreal Canadiens** (NHA) for Tommy Smith, January 16, 1917. Loaned to **Ottawa** (NHA) by **Quebec** (NHA) as emergency replacement for Clint Benedict, January 24, 1917. (Toronto 8, Ottawa 5). Signed as a free agent by **Toronto**, December 5, 1917. Traded to **Ottawa** by **Toronto** for cash, February 11, 1918. NHL rights awarded to **Quebec** when team returned to NHL, November 25, 1919. Signed as a free agent by **Saskatoon** (WCHL), December 2, 1921. Signed as a free agent by **Ottawa**, February 29, 1924.

• HEINZ, Rick
Richard D. G – L. 5'10", 165 lbs. b: Essex, Ont., 5/30/1955.

Season	Club	League	GP	W	L	T	Mins	GA	SO	Avg	AAvg	Eff	SA	S%	SAPG	GP	W	L	T	Mins	GA	SO	Avg	Eff	SA	S%	SAPG
1972-73	Windsor Royals	OHA-B	STATISTICS NOT AVAILABLE																								
1973-74	Chatham Maroons	OHA-B	STATISTICS NOT AVAILABLE																								
1974-75	University of Minnesota-Duluth	WCHA	20	6	11	2	1187	94	0	4.75	....	....	....	....	....	....	....	....	....	....	....	....	....	....	....	....	....
1975-76	University of Minnesota-Duluth	WCHA	34	14	20	0	2029	162	0	4.79	....	....	....	....	....	....	....	....	....	....	....	....	....	....	....	....	....
1976-77	University of Minnesota-Duluth	WCHA	23	6	15	2	1332	123	0	5.54	....	....	....	....	....	....	....	....	....	....	....	....	....	....	....	....	....
1977-78	University of Minnesota-Duluth	WCHA	33	13	18	1	1961	157	0	4.80	....	....	....	....	....	....	....	....	....	....	....	....	....	....	....	....	....
1978-79	Port Huron Flags	IHL	54	....	....	....	2800	157	5	3.36	....	....	....	....	....	6	....	....	....	281	18	1	3.84	....	....	....	....
	Salt Lake Golden Eagles	CHL	1	0	1	0	59	3	0	3.05	....	....	....	....	....	....	....	....	....	....	....	....	....	....	....	....	....
1979-80	Salt Lake Golden Eagles	CHL	39	22	11	5	2353	119	0	3.03	....	....	....	....	....	5	1	3	0	324	16	0	2.96	....	....	....	....
1980-81	**St. Louis Blues**	**NHL**	**4**	**2**	**1**	**1**	**220**	**8**	**0**	**2.18**	**1.76**	....	....	....	....	....	....	....	....	....	....	....	....	....	....	....	....
	Salt Lake Golden Eagles	CHL	36	19	14	3	2210	128	3	3.48	....	....	....	....	....	*14	*10	4	0	*859	39	0	*2.72	....	....	....	....
1981-82	**St. Louis Blues**	**NHL**	**9**	**2**	**5**	**0**	**433**	**35**	**0**	**4.85**	**3.75**	....	....	....	....	....	....	....	....	....	....	....	....	....	....	....	....
	Salt Lake Golden Eagles	CHL	19	14	3	2	433	35	0	3.65	....	....	....	....	....	....	....	....	....	....	....	....	....	....	....	....	....
	Vancouver Canucks	**NHL**	**3**	**2**	**1**	**0**	**180**	**9**	**1**	**3.00**	**2.32**	....	....	....	....	....	....	....	....	....	....	....	....	....	....	....	....
1982-83	**St. Louis Blues**	**NHL**	**9**	**1**	**5**	**1**	**335**	**24**	**1**	**4.30**	**3.45**	**6.41**	**161**	**.851**	**28.8**	....	....	....	....	....	....	....	....	....	....	....	....
	Salt Lake Golden Eagles	CHL	17	9	8	0	1031	58	1	3.38	....	....	....	....	....	....	....	....	....	....	....	....	....	....	....	....	....
1983-84	**St. Louis Blues**	**NHL**	**22**	**7**	**7**	**3**	**1118**	**80**	**0**	**4.29**	**3.38**	**6.37**	**539**	**.852**	**28.9**	**1**	**0**	**0**	....	**8**	**1**	**0**	**7.50**	....	....	....	....
1984-85	**St. Louis Blues**	**NHL**	**2**	**0**	**0**	**0**	**70**	**3**	**0**	**2.57**	**2.05**	**2.97**	**26**	**.885**	**22.3**	....	....	....	....	....	....	....	....	....	....	....	....
	Peoria Rivermen	IHL	43	24	12	4	2443	129	2	3.17	....	....	....	....	....	10	6	4	0	607	31	1	3.06	....	....	....	....
1985-86	Binghamton Whalers	AHL	1	0	1	0	60	9	0	9.00	....	....	....	....	....	....	....	....	....	....	....	....	....	....	....	....	....
	Salt Lake Golden Eagles	IHL	52	22	20	0	3000	185	1	3.70	....	....	....	....	....	5	1	4	0	299	26	0	5.22	....	....	....	....
1986-87	Salt Lake Golden Eagles	IHL	51	29	20	0	3026	201	1	3.99	....	....	....	....	....	16	12	4	0	912	57	0	3.75	....	....	....	....
	NHL Totals		**49**	**14**	**19**	**5**	**2356**	**159**	**2**	**4.05**	....	....	....	....	....	**1**	**0**	**0**	....	**8**	**1**	**0**	**7.50**	....	....	....	....

IHL Second All-Star Team (1979) • CHL Second All-Star Team (1980) • IHL First All-Star Team (1985) • Won James Norris Memorial Trophy (fewest goals against - IHL) (1985)

Signed as a free agent by **St. Louis**, April 16, 1979. Traded to **Vancouver** by **St. Louis** with Tony Currie, Jim Nill and St. Louis' 4th round choice (Shawn Kilroy) in 1982 Entry Draft for Glen Hanlon, March 9, 1982. Traded to **St. Louis** by **Vancouver** for cash, June 3, 1982.

• HENDERSON, John
John Duncan "Long John" G – L. 6'1", 174 lbs. b: Toronto, Ont., 3/25/1933.

Season	Club	League	GP	W	L	T	Mins	GA	SO	Avg	AAvg	Eff	SA	S%	SAPG	GP	W	L	T	Mins	GA	SO	Avg	Eff	SA	S%	SAPG
1950-51	Toronto Marlboros	OHA-Jr.	12	....	....	....	720	39	1	3.25	....	....	....	....	....	....	....	....	....	....	....	....	....	....	....	....	....
1951-52	Toronto Marlboros	OHA-Jr.	16	....	....	....	960	39	1	2.44	....	....	....	....	....	6	2	4	0	360	26	0	4.33	....	....	....	....
1952-53	Toronto Marlboros	OHA-Jr.	50	....	....	....	3000	128	3	*2.56	....	....	....	....	....	7	....	....	....	420	23	0	3.29	....	....	....	....
	Pittsburgh Hornets	AHL	1	0	1	0	60	1	0	1.00	....	....	....	....	....	....	....	....	....	....	....	....	....	....	....	....	....
1953-54	Springfield Indians	QHL	22	8	11	3	1357	93	0	4.11	....	....	....	....	....	....	....	....	....	....	....	....	....	....	....	....	....
	Syracuse Warriors	AHL	21	3	17	1	1260	141	0	6.71	....	....	....	....	....	....	....	....	....	....	....	....	....	....	....	....	....
1954-55	**Boston Bruins**	**NHL**	**45**	**15**	**14**	**15**	**2628**	**109**	**5**	**2.49**	**3.00**	....	....	....	....	**2**	**0**	**2**	....	**120**	**8**	**0**	**4.00**	....	....	....	....
	Hershey Bears	AHL	15	7	5	3	900	46	0	3.07	....	....	....	....	....	....	....	....	....	....	....	....	....	....	....	....	....
1955-56	Hershey Bears	AHL	42	12	26	4	2400	175	0	4.17	....	....	....	....	....	....	....	....	....	....	....	....	....	....	....	....	....
	Boston Bruins	**NHL**	**1**	**0**	**1**	**0**	**60**	**4**	**0**	**4.00**	**4.90**	....	....	....	....	....	....	....	....	....	....	....	....	....	....	....	....
	Whitby Dunlops	EOHL	23	....	....	....	1380	76	1	*3.30	....	....	....	....	....	....	....	....	....	....	....	....	....	....	....	....	....
1956-57	Whitby Dunlops	EOHL	16	....	....	....	960	38	*2	2.37	....	....	....	....	....	8	....	....	....	480	17	1	*2.12	....	....	....	....
	Whitby Dunlops	Al-Cup	18	12	6	0	1090	64	0	3.52	....	....	....	....	....	....	....	....	....	....	....	....	....	....	....	....	....
1957-58	Whitby Dunlops	EOHL	22	....	....	....	1320	70	1	*3.18	....	....	....	....	....	....	....	....	....	....	....	....	....	....	....	....	....
	Hull-Ottawa Canadiens	EOHL	1	0	1	0	60	6	0	6.00	....	....	....	....	....	....	....	....	....	....	....	....	....	....	....	....	....
	Canada	WEC-A	DID NOT PLAY – SPARE GOALTENDER																								
1958-59	Whitby Dunlops	EOHL	50	....	....	....	3000	145	2	*2.90	....	....	....	....	....	10	....	....	....	600	24	*2	*2.40	....	....	....	....
1959-60	Whitby Dunlops	OHA-Sr.	53	....	....	....	3180	191	*3	3.67	....	....	....	....	....	11	....	....	....	660	47	0	4.27	....	....	....	....
	Cleveland Barons	AHL	1	1	0	0	60	3	0	3.00	....	....	....	....	....	....	....	....	....	....	....	....	....	....	....	....	....
1960-61	Kingston Frontenacs	EPHL	39	15	17	7	2340	145	1	3.72	....	....	....	....	....	5	1	4	0	303	14	0	2.77	....	....	....	....
1961-1965			OUT OF HOCKEY – RETIRED																								
1965-66	Oklahoma City Blazers	CPHL	2	1	1	0	120	7	0	3.50	....	....	....	....	....	....	....	....	....	....	....	....	....	....	....	....	....
	San Francisco Seals	WHL	10	3	6	1	613	40	0	3.92	....	....	....	....	....	....	....	....	....	....	....	....	....	....	....	....	....
	Victoria Cougars	WHL	14	8	6	0	844	51	1	3.63	....	....	....	....	....	*14	*8	6	0	*890	42	0	2.83	....	....	....	....
1966-67	California Seals	WHL	3	2	1	0	180	9	0	3.00	....	....	....	....	....	....	....	....	....	....	....	....	....	....	....	....	....
	Hershey Bears	AHL	16	9	5	0	866	46	3	3.19	....	....	....	....	....	5	1	4	0	300	15	0	3.00	....	....	....	....
1967-68	Hershey Bears	AHL	32	11	13	3	1756	112	0	3.83	....	....	....	....	....	....	....	....	....	....	....	....	....	....	....	....	....
1968-69	Hershey Bears	AHL	41	23	14	3	2252	109	2	2.90	....	....	....	....	....	11	*8	3	0	660	32	*2	2.91	....	....	....	....
1969-70	Hershey Bears	AHL	6	....	....	....	306	24	0	4.71	....	....	....	....	....	....	....	....	....	....	....	....	....	....	....	....	....
	NHL Totals		**46**	**15**	**15**	**15**	**2688**	**113**	**5**	**2.52**	....	....	....	....	....	**2**	**0**	**2**	....	**120**	**8**	**0**	**4.00**	....	....	....	....

Traded to **Boston** by **Toronto** for Ray Gariepy, September 23, 1954. Promoted to **Boston** from **Hershey** (AHL) to replace injured Terry Sawchuk, January 15, 1956. (Toronto 4, Boston 1). • Suspended by **Boston** for refusing to report to training camp, September, 1956. Signed as a free agent by **Whitby** (EOHL) following release by Boston, January 22, 1957.

• HENRY, Gord
Gordon David G – L. 6', 185 lbs. b: Owen Sound, Ont., 8/17/1926 d: 10/3/1972.

Season	Club	League	GP	W	L	T	Mins	GA	SO	Avg	AAvg	Eff	SA	S%	SAPG	GP	W	L	T	Mins	GA	SO	Avg	Eff	SA	S%	SAPG
1940-1943	Owen Sound Orphans	OHA-Jr.	STATISTICS NOT AVAILABLE																								
1943-44	Philadelphia Falcons	EAHL	28	....	....	....	1680	129	1	4.61	....	....	....	....	....	12	6	6	0	720	52	0	4.33	....	....	....	....
1944-45	Hershey Bears	AHL	3	1	1	1	180	10	0	3.33	....	....	....	....	....	....	....	....	....	....	....	....	....	....	....	....	....
	Philadelphia Falcons	EAHL	35	....	....	....	2100	160	*3	4.57	....	....	....	....	....	12	....	....	....	720	47	*1	3.92	....	....	....	....
1945-46	Hershey Bears	AHL	16	6	5	5	960	61	0	3.81	....	....	....	....	....	3	1	2	0	180	10	1	3.33	....	....	....	....
	Baltimore Clippers	EAHL	4	....	....	....	240	27	0	5.50	....	....	....	....	....	....	....	....	....	....	....	....	....	....	....	....	....
	Philadelphia Falcons	EAHL	1	....	....	....	60	3	0	3.00	....	....	....	....	....	....	....	....	....	....	....	....	....	....	....	....	....
	New York Rovers	EAHL	1	1	0	0	60	0	1	0.00	....	....	....	....	....	....	....	....	....	....	....	....	....	....	....	....	....
1946-47	Boston Olympics	EAHL	43	21	17	5	2580	201	1	4.67	....	....	....	....	....	....	....	....	....	....	....	....	....	....	....	....	....
	Hershey Bears	AHL	5	2	1	1	260	13	0	3.00	....	....	....	....	....	11	*8	3	0	660	16	*5	*1.45	....	....	....	....
1947-48	Hershey Bears	AHL	*68	25	30	13	*4080	273	1	4.01	....	....	....	....	....	1	0	0	0	20	2	0	6.00	....	....	....	....
1948-49	**Boston Bruins**	**NHL**	**1**	**1**	**0**	**0**	**60**	**0**	**1**	**0.00**	**0.00**	....	....	....	....	....	....	....	....	....	....	....	....	....	....	....	....
	Hershey Bears	AHL	66	28	33	5	3960	249	3	3.71	....	....	....	....	....	11	7	4	0	694	26	*1	*2.25	....	....	....	....
1949-50	**Boston Bruins**	**NHL**	**2**	**0**	**2**	**0**	**120**	**5**	**0**	**2.50**	**2.79**	....	....	....	....	....	....	....	....	....	....	....	....	....	....	....	....
	Hershey Bears	AHL	64	19	35	10	3840	270	1	4.22	....	....	....	....	....	....	....	....	....	....	....	....	....	....	....	....	....
1950-51	Hershey Bears	AHL	*70	38	28	4	*4270	242	3	3.40	....	....	....	....	....	6	3	3	0	415	17	0	2.46	....	....	....	....
	Boston Bruins	**NHL**	....	....	....	....	....	....	....	....	....	....	....	....	....	**2**	**0**	**2**	....	**120**	**10**	**0**	**5.00**	....	....	....	....
1951-52	Hershey Bears	AHL	*68	35	28	5	*4120	211	4	3.07	....	....	....	....	....	5	1	4	0	348	14	0	2.42	....	....	....	....
1952-53	Hershey Bears	AHL	*64	31	*32	1	3870	214	5	3.32	....	....	....	....	....	3	0	3	0	189	12	0	3.81	....	....	....	....
	Boston Bruins	**NHL**	....	....	....	....	....	....	....	....	....	....	....	....	....	**3**	**0**	**2**	....	**163**	**11**	**0**	**4.05**	....	....	....	....
1953-54	Hershey Bears	AHL	63	33	26	4	3780	211	1	3.35	....	....	....	....	....	9	4	*5	0	570	24	*1	2.53	....	....	....	....

			REGULAR SEASON													PLAYOFFS											
Season	Club	League	GP	W	L	T	Mins	GA	SO	Avg	AAvg	Eff	SA	S%	SAPG	GP	W	L	T	Mins	GA	SO	Avg	Eff	SA	S%	SAPG
1954-55	Hershey Bears	AHL	23	9	11	3	1380	85	0	3.70	....	....	....	....	....	....	....	....	....	....	....	....	....	....	....	....	....
1955-56	Owen Sound Mercurys	OHA-Sr.	22	....	....	....	1280	77	1	3.61	....	....	....	....	....	3	....	....	....	180	11	0	3.67	....	....	....	....
1956-57	Philadelphia Ramblers	EHL	1	0	1	0	60	6	0	6.00	....	....	....	....	....	....	....	....	....	....	....	....	....	....	....	....	....
	NHL Totals		**3**	**1**	**2**	**0**	**180**	**5**	**1**	**1.67**	....	....	....	....	....	**5**	**0**	**4**	....	**283**	**21**	**0**	**4.45**	....	....	....	....

EAHL Second All-Star Team (1944) • AHL Second All-Star Team (1952)

• Recorded shutout (3-0) in NHL debut vs. Montreal, January 23, 1949. • Missed remainder of 1954-55 season recovering from injuries suffered in automobile accident, January 18, 1955.

• HENRY, Jim

Samuel James "Sugar Jim" G – L. 5'9", 165 lbs. b: Winnipeg, Man., 10/23/1920.

Season	Club	League	GP	W	L	T	Mins	GA	SO	Avg	AAvg	Eff	SA	S%	SAPG	GP	W	L	T	Mins	GA	SO	Avg	Eff	SA	S%	SAPG
1937-38	Winnipeg Lombards	WJrHL	STATISTICS NOT AVAILABLE																								
1938-39	Brandon Elks	MJHL	15	....	....	....	900	44	*1	2.96	....	....	....	....	....	7	....	....	....	420	30	0	4.29	....	....	....	....
	Brandon Elks	M-Cup	6	3	3	0	360	26	1	4.33	....	....	....	....	....	....	....	....	....	....	....	....	....	....	....	....	....
1939-40	Brandon Elks	MJHL	23	....	....	....	1380	82	0	3.57	....	....	....	....	....	3	3	0	0	180	6	*1	*2.00	....	....	....	....
1940-41	Regina Rangers	S-SJHL	29	....	....	....	1740	87	*2	*3.00	....	....	....	....	....	8	....	....	....	480	22	1	2.75	....	....	....	....
	Regina Rangers	Al-Cup	14	*9	4	1	840	38	2	2.71	....	....	....	....	....	....	....	....	....	....	....	....	....	....	....	....	....
1941-42	**New York Rangers**	**NHL**	***48**	***29**	**17**	**2**	***2960**	**143**	**1**	**2.90**	**2.80**	....	....	....	....	**6**	**2**	**4**	....	**360**	**13**	***1**	***2.17**	....	....	....	....
1942-43	Ottawa Staff Clerks	ONDHL	8	....	....	....	480	53	0	6.63	....	....	....	....	....	....	....	....	....	....	....	....	....	....	....	....	....
	Ottawa Commandos	QSHL	23	....	....	....	1380	84	1	3.65	....	....	....	....	....	....	....	....	....	....	....	....	....	....	....	....	....
	Ottawa Commandos	Al-Cup	12	9	2	1	740	35	2	2.84	....	....	....	....	....	....	....	....	....	....	....	....	....	....	....	....	....
1943-44	Red Deer Army	CNDHL	16	....	....	....	960	52	0	3.25	....	....	....	....	....	5	....	....	....	300	19	0	3.80	....	....	....	....
1944-45	Calgary Navy	CNDHL	15	....	....	....	900	92	0	6.13	....	....	....	....	....	....	....	....	....	....	....	....	....	....	....	....	....
1945-46	**New York Rangers**	**NHL**	**11**	**1**	**7**	**2**	**623**	**42**	**1**	**4.04**	**3.71**	....	....	....	....	....	....	....	....	....	....	....	....	....	....	....	....
	New Haven Eagles	AHL	25	8	15	2	1500	96	1	3.84	....	....	....	....	....	....	....	....	....	....	....	....	....	....	....	....	....
1946-47	**New York Rangers**	**NHL**	**2**	**0**	**2**	**0**	**120**	**9**	**0**	**4.50**	**4.35**	....	....	....	....	....	....	....	....	....	....	....	....	....	....	....	....
	New Haven Ramblers	AHL	58	20	28	10	3480	197	5	3.40	....	....	....	....	....	3	1	2	0	180	11	0	3.67	....	....	....	....
1947-48	**New York Rangers**	**NHL**	**48**	**17**	**18**	**13**	**2880**	**153**	**2**	**3.19**	**3.37**	....	....	....	....	....	....	....	....	....	....	....	....	....	....	....	....
	New Haven Ramblers	AHL	13	6	6	1	780	40	1	3.08	....	....	....	....	....	....	....	....	....	....	....	....	....	....	....	....	....
1948-49	**Chicago Black Hawks**	**NHL**	***60**	**21**	**31**	**8**	***3600**	**211**	**0**	**3.52**	**4.20**	....	....	....	....	....	....	....	....	....	....	....	....	....	....	....	....
1949-50	Kansas City Pla-Mors	USHL	68	29	27	12	4080	255	*3	3.75	....	....	....	....	....	3	0	3	0	180	20	0	6.67	....	....	....	....
1950-51	Omaha Knights	USHL	7	5	2	0	420	18	1	2.57	....	....	....	....	....	....	....	....	....	....	....	....	....	....	....	....	....
	Indianapolis Capitols	AHL	58	37	19	2	3520	202	0	3.44	....	....	....	....	....	3	0	3	0	190	11	0	3.47	....	....	....	....
1951-52	**Boston Bruins**	**NHL**	***70**	**25**	**29**	**16**	***4200**	**176**	**7**	**2.51**	**2.93**	....	....	....	....	**7**	**3**	**4**	....	**448**	**18**	**1**	**2.41**	....	....	....	....
1952-53	**Boston Bruins**	**NHL**	***70**	**28**	**29**	**13**	***4200**	**172**	**7**	**2.46**	**3.15**	....	....	....	....	***9**	**5**	**4**	....	***510**	**26**	**0**	**3.06**	....	....	....	....
1953-54	**Boston Bruins**	**NHL**	***70**	**32**	**28**	**10**	***4200**	**181**	**8**	**2.59**	**3.34**	....	....	....	....	**4**	**0**	**4**	....	**240**	**16**	**0**	**4.00**	....	....	....	....
1954-55	**Boston Bruins**	**NHL**	**27**	**8**	**12**	**6**	**1572**	**79**	**1**	**3.02**	**3.70**	....	....	....	....	**3**	**1**	**2**	....	**183**	**8**	**0**	**2.62**	....	....	....	....
1955-56	Sault Ste. Marie Greyhounds	NOHA	STATISTICS NOT AVAILABLE																								
1956-57	Winnipeg Maroons	X-Games	STATISTICS NOT AVAILABLE																								
1957-58	Winnipeg Maroons	X-Games	STATISTICS NOT AVAILABLE																								
	Winnipeg Maroons	Al-Cup	12	10	2	0	720	31	1	2.58	....	....	....	....	....	....	....	....	....	....	....	....	....	....	....	....	....
1958-59	Warroad Lakers	MHL-Sr.	14	....	....	....	840	41	0	*2.92	....	....	....	....	....	....	....	....	....	....	....	....	....	....	....	....	....
1959-60	St. Paul Saints	IHL	9	....	....	....	540	35	0	3.89	....	....	....	....	....	....	....	....	....	....	....	....	....	....	....	....	....
	Winnipeg Maroons	Al-Cup	3	1	2	0	179	6	0	2.01	....	....	....	....	....	....	....	....	....	....	....	....	....	....	....	....	....
	NHL Totals		**406**	**161**	**173**	**70**	**24355**	**1166**	**27**	**2.87**	....	....	....	....	....	**29**	**11**	**18**	....	**1741**	**81**	**2**	**2.79**	....	....	....	....

CNDHL First All-Star Team (1944) • USHL First All-Star Team (1950) • Won Charles Gardiner Memorial Trophy (USHL - Top Goaltender) (1950) • NHL Second All-Star Team (1952) • Played in NHL All-Star Game (1952)

Signed as a free agent by **NY Rangers**, October 28, 1941. Traded to **Chicago** by **NY Rangers** for Emile Francis and Alex Kaleta, October 7, 1948. Traded to **Detroit** by **Chicago** with Metro Prystai, Gaye Stewart and Bob Goldham for Harry Lumley, Jack Stewart, Al Dewsbury, Pete Babando and Don Morrison, July 13, 1950. Traded to **Boston** by **Detroit** for cash, September 28, 1951. Signed as a free agent by **St. Paul** (IHL), February 8, 1960.

• HERRON, Denis

Denis Bernard G – L. 5'11", 165 lbs. b: Chambly, Que., 6/18/1952. Pittsburgh's 3rd, 40th overall in 1972.

Season	Club	League	GP	W	L	T	Mins	GA	SO	Avg	AAvg	Eff	SA	S%	SAPG	GP	W	L	T	Mins	GA	SO	Avg	Eff	SA	S%	SAPG
1969-70	Trois Rivieres Draveurs	QJHL	2	0	1	0	96	10	0	6.25	....	....	....	....	....	....	....	....	....	....	....	....	....	....	....	....	....
1970-71	Trois Rivieres Draveurs	QJHL	33	....	....	....	1980	136	0	4.12	....	....	....	....	....	7	....	....	....	420	23	1	3.29	....	....	....	....
1971-72	Trois Rivieres Draveurs	QMJHL	40	....	....	....	2400	160	2	4.00	....	....	....	....	....	4	....	....	....	200	19	0	5.70	....	....	....	....
1972-73	**Pittsburgh Penguins**	**NHL**	**18**	**6**	**7**	**2**	**967**	**55**	**2**	**3.41**	**3.22**	....	....	....	....	....	....	....	....	....	....	....	....	....	....	....	....
	Hershey Bears	AHL	21	....	....	....	1185	63	0	3.19	....	....	....	....	....	4	....	....	....	240	16	0	4.00	....	....	....	....
1973-74	**Pittsburgh Penguins**	**NHL**	**5**	**1**	**3**	**0**	**260**	**18**	**0**	**4.15**	**4.01**	....	....	....	....	....	....	....	....	....	....	....	....	....	....	....	....
	Salt Lake Golden Eagles	WHL	9	6	2	1	530	32	0	3.62	....	....	....	....	....	....	....	....	....	....	....	....	....	....	....	....	....
	Hershey Bears	AHL	17	10	4	1	967	52	0	3.22	....	....	....	....	....	4	4	0	0	242	7	0	*1.73	....	....	....	....
1974-75	Hershey Bears	AHL	12	2	7	2	615	45	0	4.39	....	....	....	....	....	....	....	....	....	....	....	....	....	....	....	....	....
	Pittsburgh Penguins	**NHL**	**3**	**1**	**1**	**0**	**108**	**11**	**0**	**6.11**	**5.53**	....	....	....	....	....	....	....	....	....	....	....	....	....	....	....	....
	Kansas City Scouts	**NHL**	**22**	**4**	**13**	**4**	**1280**	**80**	**0**	**3.75**	**3.39**	....	....	....	....	....	....	....	....	....	....	....	....	....	....	....	....
1975-76	**Kansas City Scouts**	**NHL**	**64**	**11**	**39**	**11**	**3620**	**243**	**0**	**4.03**	**3.68**	....	....	....	....	....	....	....	....	....	....	....	....	....	....	....	....
1976-77	**Pittsburgh Penguins**	**NHL**	**34**	**15**	**11**	**5**	**1920**	**94**	**1**	**2.94**	**2.73**	....	....	....	....	**3**	**1**	**2**	....	**180**	**11**	**0**	**3.67**	....	....	....	....
1977-78	**Pittsburgh Penguins**	**NHL**	**60**	**20**	**25**	**15**	**3534**	**210**	**0**	**3.57**	**3.36**	....	....	....	....	....	....	....	....	....	....	....	....	....	....	....	....
	Canada	WEC-A	5	3	1	0	255	12	0	2.82	....	....	....	....	....	....	....	....	....	....	....	....	....	....	....	....	....
1978-79	**Pittsburgh Penguins**	**NHL**	**56**	**22**	**19**	**12**	**3208**	**180**	**0**	**3.37**	**2.98**	....	....	....	....	**7**	**2**	**5**	....	**421**	**24**	**0**	**3.42**	....	....	....	....
1979-80	**Montreal Canadiens**	**NHL**	**34**	**25**	**3**	**3**	**1909**	**80**	**0**	**2.51**	**2.21**	....	....	....	....	**5**	**2**	**3**	....	**300**	**15**	**0**	**3.00**	....	....	....	....
1980-81	**Montreal Canadiens**	**NHL**	**25**	**6**	**9**	**6**	**1147**	**67**	**1**	**3.50**	**2.83**	....	....	....	....	....	....	....	....	....	....	....	....	....	....	....	....
1981-82	**Montreal Canadiens**	**NHL**	**27**	**12**	**6**	**8**	**1547**	**68**	***3**	***2.64**	**2.03**	....	....	....	....	....	....	....	....	....	....	....	....	....	....	....	....
1982-83	**Pittsburgh Penguins**	**NHL**	**31**	**5**	**18**	**5**	**1707**	**151**	**1**	**5.31**	**4.29**	**8.61**	**931**	**.838**	**32.7**	....	....	....	....	....	....	....	....	....	....	....	....
1983-84	**Pittsburgh Penguins**	**NHL**	**38**	**8**	**24**	**2**	**2028**	**138**	**1**	**4.08**	**3.22**	**4.69**	**1200**	**.885**	**35.5**	....	....	....	....	....	....	....	....	....	....	....	....
1984-85	**Pittsburgh Penguins**	**NHL**	**42**	**10**	**22**	**3**	**2193**	**170**	**1**	**4.65**	**3.72**	**5.80**	**1362**	**.875**	**37.3**	....	....	....	....	....	....	....	....	....	....	....	....
1985-86	**Pittsburgh Penguins**	**NHL**	**3**	**0**	**3**	**0**	**180**	**14**	**0**	**4.67**	**3.65**	**7.11**	**92**	**.848**	**30.7**	....	....	....	....	....	....	....	....	....	....	....	....
	Baltimore Clippers	AHL	27	10	11	4	1510	86	0	3.42	....	....	....	....	....	....	....	....	....	....	....	....	....	....	....	....	....
	NHL Totals		**462**	**146**	**203**	**76**	**25608**	**1579**	**10**	**3.70**	....	....	....	....	....	**15**	**5**	**10**	....	**901**	**50**	**0**	**3.33**	....	....	....	....

QMJHL Second All-Star Team (1972) • Shared Vezina Trophy with Richard Sevigny and Michel Larocque (1981) • Shared William M. Jennings Trophy with Rick Wamsley (1982)

Traded to **Kansas City** by **Pittsburgh** with Jean-Guy Lagace for Michel Plasse, January 10, 1975. Signed as a free agent by **Pittsburgh**, August 7, 1976. Traded to **Montreal** by **Pittsburgh** with Pittsburgh's 2nd round choice (Jocelyn Gauvreau) in 1982 Entry Draft for Pat Hughes and Robbie Holland, August 30, 1979. Traded to **Pittsburgh** by **Montreal** for Pittsburgh's 3rd round choice (later traded to St. Louis - St. Louis selected Nelson Emerson) in 1985 Entry Draft, September 15, 1982.

• HEXTALL, Ron

Ronald Jeffrey G – L. 6'3", 192 lbs. b: Brandon, Man., 5/3/1964. Philadelphia's 6th, 119th overall in 1982.

Season	Club	League	GP	W	L	T	Mins	GA	SO	Avg	AAvg	Eff	SA	S%	SAPG	GP	W	L	T	Mins	GA	SO	Avg	Eff	SA	S%	SAPG
1980-81	Melville Millionaires	SJHL	37	7	24	0	2001	219	0	6.57	....	....	....	....	....	....	....	....	....	....	....	....	....	....	....	....	....
1981-82	Brandon Wheat Kings	WHL	30	12	11	0	1398	133	0	5.71	....	....	....	....	....	3	0	2	....	103	16	0	9.32	....	....	....	....
1982-83	Brandon Wheat Kings	WHL	44	13	30	0	2589	249	0	5.77	....	....	....	....	....	....	....	....	....	....	....	....	....	....	....	....	....
1983-84	Brandon Wheat Kings	WHL	46	29	13	2	2670	190	0	4.27	....	....	....	....	....	10	5	5	....	592	37	0	3.75	....	....	....	....
1984-85	Hershey Bears	AHL	11	4	6	0	555	34	0	3.68	....	....	....	....	....	....	....	....	....	....	....	....	....	....	....	....	....
	Kalamazoo Wings	IHL	19	6	11	1	1103	80	0	4.35	....	....	....	....	....	....	....	....	....	....	....	....	....	....	....	....	....
1985-86	Hershey Bears	AHL	*53	30	19	2	*3061	174	*5	3.41	....	....	....	....	....	13	5	7	....	780	42	*1	3.23	....	....	....	....
1986-87	**Philadelphia Flyers**	**NHL**	***66**	***37**	**21**	**6**	***3799**	**190**	**1**	**3.00**	**2.52**	**2.95**	**1933**	**.902**	**30.5**	***26**	**15**	**11**	....	***1540**	**71**	***2**	**2.77**	**2.56**	**769**	**.908**	**30.0**
	NHL All-Stars	RV-87	DID NOT PLAY – SPARE GOALTENDER																								
1987-88	Canada	Can-Cup	DID NOT PLAY – SPARE GOALTENDER																								
	Philadelphia Flyers	**NHL**	**62**	**30**	**22**	**7**	**3561**	**208**	**0**	**3.50**	**2.91**	**4.01**	**1817**	**.886**	**30.6**	**7**	**2**	**4**	....	**379**	**30**	**0**	**4.75**	**7.27**	**196**	**.847**	**31.0**
1988-89	**Philadelphia Flyers**	**NHL**	**64**	**30**	**28**	**6**	**3756**	**202**	**0**	**3.23**	**2.67**	**3.51**	**1860**	**.891**	**29.7**	**15**	**8**	**7**	....	**886**	**49**	**0**	**3.32**	**3.66**	**445**	**.890**	**30.1**
1989-90	**Philadelphia Flyers**	**NHL**	**8**	**4**	**2**	**1**	**419**	**29**	**0**	**4.15**	**3.52**	**5.50**	**219**	**.868**	**31.4**	....	....	....	....	....	....	....	....	....	....	....	....
	Hershey Bears	AHL	1	1	0	0	49	3	0	3.67	....	....	....	....	....	....	....	....	....	....	....	....	....	....	....	....	....
1990-91	**Philadelphia Flyers**	**NHL**	**36**	**13**	**16**	**5**	**2035**	**106**	**0**	**3.13**	**2.81**	**3.38**	**982**	**.892**	**29.0**	....	....	....	....	....	....	....	....	....	....	....	....
1991-92	**Philadelphia Flyers**	**NHL**	**45**	**16**	**21**	**6**	**2668**	**151**	**3**	**3.40**	**3.04**	**3.97**	**1294**	**.883**	**29.1**	....	....	....	....	....	....	....	....	....	....	....	....
	Canada	WC-A	5	1	2	1	273	13	0	2.86	....	....	....	....	....	....	....	....	....	....	....	....	....	....	....	....	....
1992-93	**Quebec Nordiques**	**NHL**	**54**	**29**	**16**	**5**	**2988**	**172**	**0**	**3.45**	**2.95**	**3.88**	**1529**	**.888**	**30.7**	**6**	**2**	**4**	....	**372**	**18**	**0**	**2.90**	**2.47**	**211**	**.915**	**34.0**

			REGULAR SEASON													PLAYOFFS											
Season	Club	League	GP	W	L	T	Mins	GA	SO	Avg	AAvg	Eff	SA	S%	SAPG	GP	W	L	T	Mins	GA	SO	Avg	Eff	SA	S%	SAPG
1993-94	**New York Islanders**	NHL	65	27	26	6	3581	184	5	3.08	2.96	3.15	1801	.898	30.2	3	0	3	....	158	16	0	6.08	12.16	80	.800	30.4
1994-95	**Philadelphia Flyers**	NHL	31	17	9	4	1824	88	1	2.89	3.03	3.18	801	.890	26.3	15	10	5	....	897	42	0	2.81	2.70	437	.904	29.2
1995-96	**Philadelphia Flyers**	NHL	53	31	13	7	3102	112	4	*2.17	2.14	1.88	1292	.913	25.0	12	6	6	....	760	27	0	2.13	1.80	319	.915	25.2
1996-97	**Philadelphia Flyers**	NHL	55	31	16	5	3094	132	5	2.56	2.75	2.63	1285	.897	24.9	8	4	3	....	444	22	0	2.97	3.22	203	.892	27.4
1997-98	**Philadelphia Flyers**	NHL	46	21	17	7	2688	97	4	2.17	2.58	1.93	1089	.911	24.3	1	0	0	....	20	1	0	3.00	3.75	8	.875	24.0
1998-99	**Philadelphia Flyers**	NHL	23	10	7	4	1235	52	0	2.53	3.01	2.84	464	.888	22.5	....	....	....	....	....	....	....	....	....	....	....	....
	NHL Totals		608	296	214	69	34750	1723	23	2.97	....	....	16366	.895	28.3	93	47	43	....	5456	276	2	3.04	....	2668	.897	29.3

• Son of Bryan Jr. • AHL First All-Star Team (1986) • Won Dudley "Red" Garrett Memorial Trophy (Top Rookie - AHL) (1986) • NHL All-Rookie Team (1987) • NHL First All-Star Team (1987) • Won Vezina Trophy (1987) • Won Conn Smythe Trophy (1987) • Scored a goal vs. Boston, December 8, 1987 • Scored a goal in playoffs vs. Washington, April 11, 1989. • Played in NHL All-Star Game (1988)

Traded to **Quebec** by **Philadelphia** with Steve Duchesne, Peter Forsberg, Kerry Huffman, Mike Ricci, Philadelphia's 1st round choice (Jocelyn Thibault) in 1993 Entry Draft, $15,000,000 and future considerations (Chris Simon and Philadelphia's 1st round choice (later traded to Toronto — later traded to Washington — Washington selected Nolan Baumgartner) in 1994 Entry Draft, July 21, 1992) for Eric Lindros, June 30, 1992. Traded to **NY Islanders** by **Quebec** with Quebec's 1st round choice (Todd Bertuzzi) in 1993 Entry Draft for Mark Fitzpatrick and NY Islanders' 1st round choice (Adam Deadmarsh) in 1993 Entry Draft, June 20, 1993. Traded to **Philadelphia** by **NY Islanders** with NY Islanders' 6th round choice (Dimitri Tertyshny) in 1995 Entry Draft for Tommy Soderstrom, September 22, 1994.

• HIGHTON, Hec

Hector Salisbury G – R. 6', 175 lbs. b: Medicine Hat, Alta., 12/10/1923.

Season	Club	League	GP	W	L	T	Mins	GA	SO	Avg	AAvg	Eff	SA	S%	SAPG	GP	W	L	T	Mins	GA	SO	Avg	Eff	SA	S%	SAPG
1940-41	Spokane Bombers	PCHL	....	....	....	....	....	....	....	....	....	....	....	....	....	1	0	1	0	60	5	0	5.00	....	....	....	....
1941-42			MILITARY SERVICE																								
1942-43	New Westminster Spitfires	PCHL	10	....	....	....	600	33	*1	3.30	....	....	....	....	....	3	1	2	0	190	18	0	5.68	....	....	....	....
1943-44	**Chicago Black Hawks**	NHL	24	10	14	0	1440	108	0	4.50	3.39	....	....	....	....	....	....	....	....	....	....	....	....	....	....	....	....
	Providence Reds	AHL	27	5	21	1	1620	125	0	4.62	....	....	....	....	....	....	....	....	....	....	....	....	....	....	....	....	....
1944-45	Providence Reds	AHL	4	0	4	0	240	29	0	7.25	....	....	....	....	....	....	....	....	....	....	....	....	....	....	....	....	....
	St. Louis Flyers	AHL	26	7	15	4	1560	118	0	4.54	....	....	....	....	....	....	....	....	....	....	....	....	....	....	....	....	....
1945-46	St. Louis Flyers	AHL	52	20	24	8	3120	215	1	4.13	....	....	....	....	....	....	....	....	....	....	....	....	....	....	....	....	....
1946-47	St. Louis Flyers	AHL	59	16	32	11	3540	257	0	4.36	....	....	....	....	....	....	....	....	....	....	....	....	....	....	....	....	....
1947-48	St. Louis Flyers	AHL	65	21	34	10	3900	278	0	4.28	....	....	....	....	....	....	....	....	....	....	....	....	....	....	....	....	....
1948-49	Los Angeles Monarchs	PCHL	70	28	33	9	4200	271	1	3.87	....	....	....	....	....	7	4	3	0	434	25	0	3.46	....	....	....	....
1949-50	Los Angeles Monarchs	PCHL	62	26	28	8	3720	209	3	3.37	....	....	....	....	....	17	10	7	0	1032	50	3	2.91	....	....	....	....
1950-51	Victoria Cougars	PCHL	19	7	8	4	1140	68	0	3.58	....	....	....	....	....	....	....	....	....	....	....	....	....	....	....	....	....
	Vancouver Canucks	PCHL	48	13	21	13	2860	173	3	3.63	....	....	....	....	....	....	....	....	....	....	....	....	....	....	....	....	....
	Portland Eagles	PCHL	....	....	....	....	....	....	....	....	....	....	....	....	....	7	3	4	0	480	20	1	2.50	....	....	....	....
	NHL Totals		24	10	14	0	1440	108	0	4.50	....	....	....	....	....	....	....	....	....	....	....	....	....	....	....	....	....

Traded to **Providence** (AHL) by **Chicago** with Gord Buttrey and cash for Mike Karakas, January 7, 1944. Traded to **Chicago** (St. Louis-AHL) by **Providence** (AHL) for cash, February 4, 1945. Traded to **Detroit** by **Chicago** (St. Louis-AHL) with Joe Lund for Red Almas, Lloyd Doran, Tony Licari, Barry Sullivan and Thain Simon, September 9, 1948. Loaned to **Los Angeles** (PCHL) by **Detroit** for cash, October 11, 1948. Traded to **Victoria** (PCHL) by **Los Angeles** (PCHL) for cash, September 16, 1950.

• HIMES, Normie

Norman Lawrence G. 5'9", 145 lbs. b: Galt, Ont., 4/13/1903 d: 9/14/1958.

Season	Club	League	GP	W	L	T	Mins	GA	SO	Avg	AAvg	Eff	SA	S%	SAPG	GP	W	L	T	Mins	GA	SO	Avg	Eff	SA	S%	SAPG
1927-28	**New York Americans**	NHL	1	0	0	0	19	0	0	0.00	0.00	....	....	....	....	....	....	....	....	....	....	....	....	....	....	....	....
1928-29	**New York Americans**	NHL	1	0	1	0	60	3	0	3.00	6.28	....	....	....	....	....	....	....	....	....	....	....	....	....	....	....	....
	NHL Totals		2	0	1	0	79	3	0	2.28	....	....	....	....	....	....	....	....	....	....	....	....	....	....	....	....	....

• NY Americans' center replaced injured Joe Miller in 3rd period, December 5, 1927. (NY Americans 0, Pittsburgh 0) • NY Americans' center replaced Jake Forbes, December 1, 1928. (Toronto 3, NY Americans 0)

• HIRSCH, Corey

G – L. 5'10", 175 lbs. b: Medicine Hat, Alta., 8/10/1972. NY Rangers' 7th, 169th overall in 1991.

Season	Club	League	GP	W	L	T	Mins	GA	SO	Avg	AAvg	Eff	SA	S%	SAPG	GP	W	L	T	Mins	GA	SO	Avg	Eff	SA	S%	SAPG
1987-88	Calgary Canucks	AJHL	32	....	....	....	1538	91	1	3.55	....	....	....	....	....	....	....	....	....	....	....	....	....	....	....	....	....
1988-89	Kamloops Blazers	WHL	32	11	12	2	1516	106	2	4.20	....	....	....	....	....	5	3	2	....	245	19	0	4.65	....	....	....	....
1989-90	Kamloops Blazers	WHL	*63	*48	13	0	3608	230	*3	3.82	....	....	....	....	....	*17	*14	3	....	*1043	60	0	*3.45	....	....	....	....
	Kamloops Blazers	Mem-Cup	3	0	*3	0	191	18	0	5.65	....	....	....	....	....	....	....	....	....	....	....	....	....	....	....	....	....
1990-91	Kamloops Blazers	WHL	38	26	7	1	1970	100	3	*3.05	....	....	....	....	....	11	5	6	....	623	42	0	4.04	....	....	....	....
1991-92	Kamloops Blazers	WHL	48	35	10	2	2732	124	*5	*2.72	....	....	....	....	....	*16	*11	5	....	954	35	*2	*2.20	....	....	....	....
	Kamloops Blazers	Mem-Cup	5	*4	1	0	300	13	*1	*2.60	....	....	....	....	....	....	....	....	....	....	....	....	....	....	....	....	....
1992-93	**New York Rangers**	NHL	4	1	2	1	224	14	0	3.75	3.21	4.53	116	.879	31.1	....	....	....	....	....	....	....	....	....	....	....	....
	Binghamton Rangers	AHL	46	*35	4	5	2692	125	1	*2.79	....	....	....	....	....	14	7	7	....	831	46	0	3.32	....	....	....	....
1993-94	Canada	Nat-Team	45	24	17	3	2653	124	0	2.80	....	....	....	....	....	....	....	....	....	....	....	....	....	....	....	....	....
	Canada	Olympics	8	5	2	1	495	18	0	2.18	....	....	....	....	....	....	....	....	....	....	....	....	....	....	....	....	....
	Binghamton Rangers	AHL	10	5	4	1	610	38	0	3.73	....	....	....	....	....	....	....	....	....	....	....	....	....	....	....	....	....
1994-95	Binghamton Rangers	AHL	57	31	20	5	3371	175	0	3.11	....	....	....	....	....	....	....	....	....	....	....	....	....	....	....	....	....
	Canada	WC-A	8	4	3	1	488	21	0	2.58	....	....	....	....	....	....	....	....	....	....	....	....	....	....	....	....	....
1995-96	**Vancouver Canucks**	NHL	41	17	14	6	2338	114	1	2.93	2.91	2.85	1173	.903	30.1	6	2	3	....	338	21	0	3.73	4.72	166	.873	29.5
1996-97	**Vancouver Canucks**	NHL	39	12	20	4	2127	116	2	3.27	3.53	3.48	1090	.894	30.7	....	....	....	....	....	....	....	....	....	....	....	....
1997-98	**Vancouver Canucks**	NHL	1	0	0	0	50	5	0	6.00	7.16	8.82	34	.853	40.8	....	....	....	....	....	....	....	....	....	....	....	....
	Syracuse Crunch	AHL	60	30	22	6	3512	187	1	3.19	....	....	....	....	....	5	2	3	....	297	10	1	*2.02	....	....	....	....
1998-99	**Vancouver Canucks**	NHL	20	3	8	3	919	48	1	3.13	3.73	3.45	435	.890	28.4	....	....	....	....	....	....	....	....	....	....	....	....
	Syracuse Crunch	AHL	5	2	3	0	300	14	0	2.80	....	....	....	....	....	....	....	....	....	....	....	....	....	....	....	....	....
99-2000	Milwaukee Admirals	IHL	19	9	8	1	1098	49	0	2.68	....	....	....	....	....	....	....	....	....	....	....	....	....	....	....	....	....
	Utah Grizzlies	IHL	17	9	5	1	937	42	3	2.69	....	....	....	....	....	2	0	2	....	121	4	0	1.99	....	....	....	....
	NHL Totals		105	33	44	14	5658	297	4	3.15	....	....	2848	.896	30.2	6	2	3	....	338	21	0	3.73	....	166	.873	29.5

WHL West Second All-Star Team (1990) • WHL West First All-Star Team (1991, 1992) • Canadian Major Junior Goaltender of the Year (1992) • Memorial Cup All-Star Team (1992) • Won Hap Emms Memorial Trophy (Memorial Cup Tournament Top Goaltender) (1992) • AHL First All-Star Team (1993) • Won Dudley "Red" Garrett Memorial Trophy (AHL Rookie of the Year) (1993) • Shared Harry "Hap" Holmes Memorial Trophy (fewest goals-against - AHL) with Boris Rousson (1993) • NHL All-Rookie Team (1996)

Traded to **Vancouver** by **NY Rangers** for Nathan Lafayette, April 7, 1995. Signed as a free agent by **Nashville**, August 10, 1999. Traded to **Anaheim** by **Nashville** for future considerations, March 14, 2000.

• HNILICKA, Milan

G – L. 6', 180 lbs. b: Litomerice, Czech., 6/25/1973. NY Islanders' 4th, 70th overall in 1991.

Season	Club	League	GP	W	L	T	Mins	GA	SO	Avg	AAvg	Eff	SA	S%	SAPG	GP	W	L	T	Mins	GA	SO	Avg	Eff	SA	S%	SAPG
1989-90	Poldi Kladno	Czech.	24	....	....	....	1113	70	....	3.77	....	....	....	....	....	....	....	....	....	....	....	....	....	....	....	....	....
1990-91	Poldi Kladno	Czech.	40	....	....	....	2122	98	0	2.80	....	....	....	....	....	....	....	....	....	....	....	....	....	....	....	....	....
	Czechoslovakia	WJC-A	5	4	1	0	269	14	1	3.12	....	....	....	....	....	....	....	....	....	....	....	....	....	....	....	....	....
1991-92	Poldi Kladno	Czech.	38	....	....	....	2066	128	0	3.73	....	....	....	....	....	....	....	....	....	....	....	....	....	....	....	....	....
1992-93	Swift Current Broncos	WHL	*65	*46	12	2	3679	206	2	3.36	....	....	....	....	....	*17	*12	5	....	*1017	54	*2	3.19	....	....	....	....
1993-94	Richmond Renegades	ECHL	43	18	16	5	2299	155	4	4.05	....	....	....	....	....	....	....	....	....	....	....	....	....	....	....	....	....
	Salt Lake City Golden Eagles	IHL	8	5	1	0	378	25	0	3.97	....	....	....	....	....	....	....	....	....	....	....	....	....	....	....	....	....
1994-95	Denver Grizzlies	IHL	15	9	4	1	798	47	1	3.53	....	....	....	....	....	....	....	....	....	....	....	....	....	....	....	....	....
1995-96	Poldi Kladno	Czech-Rep	33	....	....	....	1959	93	1	2.84	....	....	....	....	....	8	....	....	....	493	24	....	2.92	....	....	....	....
1996-97	Poldi Kladno	Czech-Rep	48	....	....	....	2736	120	4	2.63	....	....	....	....	....	3	....	....	....	151	14	0	5.56	....	....	....	....
	Czech-Republic	WC-A	1	1	0	0	60	3	0	3.00	....	....	....	....	....	....	....	....	....	....	....	....	....	....	....	....	....
1997-98	HC Sparta Praha	Czech-Rep	49	....	....	....	2847	99	....	2.09	....	....	....	....	....	11	....	....	....	632	31	....	3.00	....	....	....	....
	Czech-Republic	Olympics	DID NOT PLAY – SPARE GOALTENDER																								
	Czech-Republic	WC-A	8	4	1	2	430	10	2	1.39	....	....	....	....	....	....	....	....	....	....	....	....	....	....	....	....	....

Season	Club	League	REGULAR SEASON GP	W	L	T	Mins	GA	SO	Avg	AAvg	Eff	SA	S%	SAPG	PLAYOFFS GP	W	L	T	Mins	GA	SO	Avg	Eff	SA	S%	SAPG
1998-99	HC Sparta Praha	Czech-Rep	*50	....	....	....	*2877	109	....	2.27	....	....	....	....	....	8	....	....	....	507	13	....	*1.54	....	....	....	....
	Czech-Republic	WC-A	7	4	2	0	440	16	1	2.18	....	....	....	....	....	....	....	....	....	....	....	....	....	....	....	....	....
99-2000	**New York Rangers**	**NHL**	**2**	**0**	**1**	**0**	**86**	**5**	**0**	**3.49**	**3.99**	**3.97**	**44**	**.886**	**30.7**	....	....	....	....	....	....	....	....	....	....	....	....
	Hartford Wolf Pack	AHL	36	22	11	0	1979	71	5	2.15	....	....	....	....	....	3	0	1	....	99	6	0	3.64	....	....	....	....
	NHL Totals		**2**	**0**	**1**	**0**	**86**	**5**	**0**	**3.49**	....	....	**44**	**.886**	**30.7**	....	....	....	....	....	....	....	....	....	....	....	....

• Shared Harry "Hap" Holmes Memorial Trophy (fewest goals against - AHL) with Jean-Francois Labbe (2000)

Signed as a free agent by **NY Rangers**, July 15, 1999.

• HODGE, Charlie

Charles Edward G – L. 5'6", 150 lbs. b: Lachine, Que., 7/28/1933.

Season	Club	League	GP	W	L	T	Mins	GA	SO	Avg	AAvg	Eff	SA	S%	SAPG	GP	W	L	T	Mins	GA	SO	Avg	Eff	SA	S%	SAPG
1949-50	Montreal Jr. Canadiens	QJHL	STATISTICS NOT AVAILABLE																								
	Montreal Jr. Canadiens	Mem-Cup	2	0	2	0	122	11	0	5.41	....	....	....	....	....	....	....	....	....	....	....	....	....	....	....	....	....
1950-51	Montreal Jr. Canadiens	QJHL	23	14	8	0	1320	57	1	*2.59	....	....	....	....	....	9	4	5	0	564	31	0	3.30	....	....	....	....
1951-52	Montreal Jr. Canadiens	QJHL	45	32	10	3	2700	100	3	*2.22	....	....	....	....	....	11	*9	2	0	669	19	0	*1.70	....	....	....	....
	Montreal Royals	QMHL	1	0	0	0	40	3	0	4.50	....	....	....	....	....	....	....	....	....	....	....	....	....	....	....	....	....
	Montreal Jr. Canadiens	Mem-Cup	8	4	4	0	480	32	1	4.00	....	....	....	....	....	....	....	....	....	....	....	....	....	....	....	....	....
1952-53	Montreal Jr. Canadiens	QJHL	44	*35	9	0	2640	100	*5	*2.27	....	....	....	....	....	7	....	....	....	560	18	0	2.57	....	....	....	....
	Montreal Royals	QMHL	1	0	1	0	60	4	0	4.00	....	....	....	....	....	....	....	....	....	....	....	....	....	....	....	....	....
1953-54	Cincinnati Mohawks	IHL	62	....	....	....	3720	145	*10	*2.34	....	....	....	....	....	11	*8	3	0	660	19	*2	*1.73	....	....	....	....
	Buffalo Bisons	AHL	3	2	1	0	180	10	0	3.33	....	....	....	....	....	....	....	....	....	....	....	....	....	....	....	....	....
1954-55	**Montreal Canadiens**	**NHL**	**14**	**7**	**3**	**4**	**840**	**31**	**1**	**2.21**	**2.66**	....	....	....	....	**4**	**1**	**2**	....	**84**	**6**	**0**	**4.29**	....	....	....	....
	Providence Reds	AHL	5	3	2	0	300	18	1	3.60	....	....	....	....	....	....	....	....	....	....	....	....	....	....	....	....	....
	Montreal Royals	QHL	35	17	17	1	2100	113	2	3.23	....	....	....	....	....	....	....	....	....	....	....	....	....	....	....	....	....
1955-56	Seattle Americans	WHL	70	31	37	2	4245	239	6	3.38	....	....	....	....	....	....	....	....	....	....	....	....	....	....	....	....	....
1956-57	Rochester Americans	AHL	41	18	18	4	2460	132	2	3.22	....	....	....	....	....	....	....	....	....	....	....	....	....	....	....	....	....
	Shawinigan Cataracts	QHL	14	7	5	2	859	39	2	2.72	....	....	....	....	....	....	....	....	....	....	....	....	....	....	....	....	....
1957-58	**Montreal Canadiens**	**NHL**	**12**	**8**	**2**	**2**	**720**	**31**	**1**	**2.58**	**2.82**	....	....	....	....	....	....	....	....	....	....	....	....	....	....	....	....
	Montreal Royals	QHL	48	23	21	4	2880	153	4	3.19	....	....	....	....	....	7	2	4	0	380	25	1	3.95	....	....	....	....
1958-59	Montreal Royals	QHL	24	15	8	1	1440	67	1	2.79	....	....	....	....	....	2	2	0	0	120	4	0	*2.00	....	....	....	....
	Rochester Americans	AHL	4	0	4	0	240	12	0	3.00	....	....	....	....	....	....	....	....	....	....	....	....	....	....	....	....	....
♦	**Montreal Canadiens**	**NHL**	**2**	**1**	**1**	**0**	**120**	**6**	**0**	**3.00**	**3.19**	....	....	....	....	....	....	....	....	....	....	....	....	....	....	....	....
1959-60	Montreal Royals	EPHL	33	15	12	6	1980	96	*5	2.91	....	....	....	....	....	....	....	....	....	....	....	....	....	....	....	....	....
	Hull-Ottawa Canadiens	EPHL	26	15	6	5	1560	74	*2	2.85	....	....	....	....	....	7	3	4	0	430	24	0	3.35	....	....	....	....
♦	**Montreal Canadiens**	**NHL**	**1**	**0**	**1**	**0**	**60**	**3**	**0**	**3.00**	**3.13**	....	....	....	....	....	....	....	....	....	....	....	....	....	....	....	....
1960-61	**Montreal Canadiens**	**NHL**	**30**	**18**	**8**	**4**	**1800**	**74**	**4**	**2.47**	**2.51**	....	....	....	....	....	....	....	....	....	....	....	....	....	....	....	....
	Montreal Royals	EPHL	22	5	13	4	1320	74	0	3.36	....	....	....	....	....	....	....	....	....	....	....	....	....	....	....	....	....
1961-62	Quebec Aces	AHL	65	28	33	4	3900	185	5	2.85	....	....	....	....	....	....	....	....	....	....	....	....	....	....	....	....	....
1962-63	Quebec Aces	AHL	67	31	25	11	4020	190	4	2.84	....	....	....	....	....	....	....	....	....	....	....	....	....	....	....	....	....
1963-64	**Montreal Canadiens**	**NHL**	**62**	**33**	**18**	**11**	**3720**	**140**	***8**	**2.26**	**2.43**	....	....	....	....	**7**	**3**	**4**	....	**420**	**16**	**1**	**2.29**	....	....	....	....
	Quebec Aces	AHL	10	4	6	0	600	32	1	3.20	....	....	....	....	....	....	....	....	....	....	....	....	....	....	....	....	....
1964-65♦	**Montreal Canadiens**	**NHL**	**53**	**26**	**16**	**10**	**3180**	**135**	**3**	**2.55**	**2.69**	....	....	....	....	**5**	**3**	**2**	....	**300**	**10**	**1**	**2.00**	....	....	....	....
1965-66♦	**Montreal Canadiens**	**NHL**	**26**	**12**	**7**	**2**	**1301**	**56**	**1**	**2.58**	**2.59**	....	....	....	....	....	....	....	....	....	....	....	....	....	....	....	....
1966-67	**Montreal Canadiens**	**NHL**	**37**	**11**	**15**	**7**	**2055**	**88**	**3**	**2.57**	**2.62**	....	....	....	....	....	....	....	....	....	....	....	....	....	....	....	....
1967-68	**Oakland Seals**	**NHL**	**58**	**13**	**29**	**13**	**3311**	**158**	**3**	**2.86**	**3.18**	....	....	....	....	....	....	....	....	....	....	....	....	....	....	....	....
1968-69	**Oakland Seals**	**NHL**	**14**	**4**	**6**	**1**	**781**	**48**	**0**	**3.69**	**3.83**	....	....	....	....	....	....	....	....	....	....	....	....	....	....	....	....
	Vancouver Canucks	WHL	13	7	2	4	779	32	0	2.54	....	....	....	....	....	8	*8	0	0	*497	12	*1	*1.45	....	....	....	....
1969-70	**Oakland Seals**	**NHL**	**14**	**3**	**5**	**2**	**738**	**43**	**0**	**3.50**	**3.72**	....	....	....	....	....	....	....	....	....	....	....	....	....	....	....	....
1970-71	**Vancouver Canucks**	**NHL**	**35**	**15**	**13**	**5**	**1967**	**112**	**0**	**3.42**	**3.39**	....	....	....	....	....	....	....	....	....	....	....	....	....	....	....	....
	NHL Totals		**358**	**151**	**124**	**61**	**20593**	**925**	**24**	**2.70**	....	....	....	....	....	**16**	**7**	**8**	....	**804**	**32**	**2**	**2.39**	....	....	....	....

QJHL First All-Star Team (1952, 1953) • IHL Second All-Star Team (1954) • QHL Second All-Star Team (1955) • QHL First All-Star Team (1958) • AHL Second All-Star Team (1963) • NHL Second All-Star Team (1964, 1965) • Won Vezina Trophy (1964) • Shared Vezina Trophy with Gump Worsley (1966) • Played in NHL All-Star Game (1964, 1965, 1967)

Promoted to **Montreal** from **Montreal** (QHL) to replace Jacques Plante, March 21, 22, 1959 and March 13, 1960. Claimed by **California** from **Montreal** in Expansion Draft, June 6, 1967. Claimed by **Vancouver** from **Oakland** in Expansion Draft, June 10, 1970.

• HODSON, Kevin

Kevin T. G – L. 6', 182 lbs. b: Winnipeg, Man., 3/27/1972.

Season	Club	League	GP	W	L	T	Mins	GA	SO	Avg	AAvg	Eff	SA	S%	SAPG	GP	W	L	T	Mins	GA	SO	Avg	Eff	SA	S%	SAPG
1989-90	Winnipeg South Blues	MJHL	35	....	....	....	1900	115	2	3.40	....	....	....	....	....	....	....	....	....	....	....	....	....	....	....	....	....
1990-91	Sault Ste. Marie Greyhounds	OHL	30	18	11	0	1638	88	*2	*3.22	....	....	....	....	....	10	*9	1	....	581	28	0	*2.89	....	....	....	....
1991-92	Sault Ste. Marie Greyhounds	OHL	50	28	12	4	2722	151	0	3.33	....	....	....	....	....	18	12	6	....	1116	54	1	2.90	....	....	....	....
	Sault Ste. Marie Greyhounds	Mem-Cup	4	3	1	0	210	12	0	3.43	....	....	....	....	....	....	....	....	....	....	....	....	....	....	....	....	....
1992-93	Sault Ste. Marie Greyhounds	OHL	26	18	5	2	1470	76	1	*3.10	....	....	....	....	....	14	11	2	....	755	34	0	2.70	....	....	....	....
	Indianapolis Ice	IHL	14	5	9	0	777	53	0	4.09	....	....	....	....	....	....	....	....	....	....	....	....	....	....	....	....	....
	Sault Ste. Marie Greyhounds	Mem-Cup	4	*3	0	1	240	12	0	*3.00	....	....	....	....	....	....	....	....	....	....	....	....	....	....	....	....	....
1993-94	Adirondack Red Wings	AHL	37	20	10	5	2082	102	2	2.94	....	....	....	....	....	3	0	2	....	89	10	0	6.77	....	....	....	....
1994-95	Adirondack Red Wings	AHL	51	19	22	8	2731	161	1	3.54	....	....	....	....	....	4	0	4	....	237	14	0	3.53	....	....	....	....
1995-96	**Detroit Red Wings**	**NHL**	**4**	**2**	**0**	**0**	**163**	**3**	**1**	**1.10**	**1.09**	**0.49**	**67**	**.955**	**24.7**	....	....	....	....	....	....	....	....	....	....	....	....
	Adirondack Red Wings	AHL	32	13	13	2	1654	87	0	3.16	....	....	....	....	....	3	0	2	....	150	8	0	3.21	....	....	....	....
1996-97	**Detroit Red Wings**	**NHL**	**6**	**2**	**2**	**1**	**294**	**8**	**1**	**1.63**	**1.75**	**1.14**	**114**	**.930**	**23.3**	....	....	....	....	....	....	....	....	....	....	....	....
	Quebec Rafales	IHL	2	1	1	0	118	7	0	3.54	....	....	....	....	....	....	....	....	....	....	....	....	....	....	....	....	....
1997-98♦	**Detroit Red Wings**	**NHL**	**21**	**9**	**3**	**3**	**988**	**44**	**2**	**2.67**	**3.18**	**2.65**	**444**	**.901**	**27.0**	**1**	**0**	**0**	....	**1**	**0**	**0**	**0.00**	**0.00**	**0**	**.000**	**0.0**
1998-99	**Detroit Red Wings**	**NHL**	**4**	**0**	**2**	**0**	**175**	**9**	**0**	**3.09**	**3.67**	**3.52**	**79**	**.886**	**27.1**	....	....	....	....	....	....	....	....	....	....	....	....
	Adirondack Red Wings	AHL	6	1	3	2	349	19	0	3.27	....	....	....	....	....	....	....	....	....	....	....	....	....	....	....	....	....
	Tampa Bay Lightning	**NHL**	**5**	**2**	**1**	**1**	**238**	**11**	**0**	**2.77**	**3.29**	**2.58**	**118**	**.907**	**29.7**	....	....	....	....	....	....	....	....	....	....	....	....
99-2000	**Tampa Bay Lightning**	**NHL**	**24**	**2**	**7**	**4**	**769**	**47**	**0**	**3.67**	**4.20**	**5.27**	**327**	**.856**	**25.5**	....	....	....	....	....	....	....	....	....	....	....	....
	Detroit Vipers	IHL	9	2	6	0	505	22	0	2.61	....	....	....	....	....	....	....	....	....	....	....	....	....	....	....	....	....
	NHL Totals		**64**	**17**	**15**	**9**	**2627**	**122**	**4**	**2.79**	....	....	**1149**	**.894**	**26.2**	**1**	**0**	**0**	....	**1**	**0**	**0**	**0.00**	....	**0**	**.000**	**0.0**

Memorial Cup All-Star Team (1993) • Won Hap Emms Memorial Trophy (Memorial Cup Tournament Top Goaltender) (1993)

Signed as a free agent by **Chicago**, August 17, 1992. Signed as a free agent by **Detroit**, June 16, 1993. • Played 16 seconds in playoff game vs. Chicago, May 17, 1998. Traded to **Tampa Bay** by **Detroit** with San Jose's 2nd round choice (previously acquired, Tampa Bay selected Sheldon Keefe) in 1999 Entry Draft for Wendel Clark and Detroit's 6th round choice (previously acquired, Detroit selected Kent McDonnell) in 1999 Entry Draft, March 23, 1999. Traded to **Montreal** by **Tampa Bay** for Montreal's 7th round choice (later traded to Philadelphia - Philadelphia selected John Eichelberger) in 2000 Entry Draft, June 2, 2000.

• HOFFORT, Bruce

Bruce W. G – L. 5'10", 185 lbs. b: North Battleford, Sask., 7/30/1966.

Season	Club	League	GP	W	L	T	Mins	GA	SO	Avg	AAvg	Eff	SA	S%	SAPG	GP	W	L	T	Mins	GA	SO	Avg	Eff	SA	S%	SAPG
1985-86	Melville Millionaires	SJHL	40	15	18	2	2198	167	2	4.56	....	....	....	....	....	4	0	3	0	196	23	0	7.04	....	....	....	....
1986-87	Humboldt Broncos	SJHL	STATISTICS NOT AVAILABLE																								
	Humboldt Broncos	Cen-Cup	STATISTICS NOT AVAILABLE																								
1987-88	Lake Superior State	CCHA	31	23	4	3	1787	79	2	2.65	....	....	....	....	....	....	....	....	....	....	....	....	....	....	....	....	....
1988-89	Lake Superior State	CCHA	44	27	10	5	2595	117	0	2.71	....	....	....	....	....	....	....	....	....	....	....	....	....	....	....	....	....
1989-90	**Philadelphia Flyers**	**NHL**	**7**	**3**	**0**	**2**	**329**	**19**	**0**	**3.47**	**2.94**	**4.15**	**159**	**.881**	**29.0**	....	....	....	....	....	....	....	....	....	....	....	....
	Hershey Bears	AHL	40	16	18	4	2284	139	1	3.65	....	....	....	....	....	....	....	....	....	....	....	....	....	....	....	....	....
1990-91	**Philadelphia Flyers**	**NHL**	**2**	**1**	**0**	**1**	**39**	**3**	**0**	**4.62**	**4.15**	**6.93**	**20**	**.850**	**30.8**	....	....	....	....	....	....	....	....	....	....	....	....
	Hershey Bears	AHL	18	3	12	1	913	74	0	4.86	....	....	....	....	....	....	....	....	....	....	....	....	....	....	....	....	....
	Kansas City Blades	IHL	18	6	7	0	883	68	0	4.62	....	....	....	....	....	....	....	....	....	....	....	....	....	....	....	....	....
1991-92	San Diego Gulls	IHL	26	11	9	4	1474	89	0	3.62	....	....	....	....	....	....	....	....	....	....	....	....	....	....	....	....	....
	NHL Totals		**9**	**4**	**0**	**3**	**368**	**22**	**0**	**3.59**	....	....	**179**	**.877**	**29.2**	....	....	....	....	....	....	....	....	....	....	....	....

CCHA First All-Star Team (1988, 1989) • NCAA Championship All-Tournament Team (1988) • NCAA Championship Tournament MVP (1988) • NCAA West First All-American Team (1989)

Signed as a free agent by **Philadelphia**, June 30, 1989.

• HOGANSON, Paul Paul Edward G – R. 5'11", 175 lbs. b: Toronto, Ont., 11/12/1949. Pittsburgh's 5th, 62nd overall in 1969.

			REGULAR SEASON													PLAYOFFS											
Season	Club	League	GP	W	L	T	Mins	GA	SO	Avg	AAvg	Eff	SA	S%	SAPG	GP	W	L	T	Mins	GA	SO	Avg	Eff	SA	S%	SAPG
1965-66	Humber Valley Packers	MTHL	STATISTICS NOT AVAILABLE																								
1966-67	Hamilton Red Wings	OHA-Jr.	5	....	....	....	290	19	0	3.93	....	....	....	....	....	....	....	....	....	....	....	....	....	....	....	....	....
1967-68	Quebec Remparts	QJHL	STATISTICS NOT AVAILABLE																								
	Hamilton Red Wings	OHA-Jr.	1	....	....	....	60	5	0	5.00	....	....	....	....	....	....	....	....	....	....	....	....	....	....	....	....	....
1968-69	Hamilton Red Wings	OHA-Jr.	1	....	....	....	60	3	0	3.00	....	....	....	....	....	....	....	....	....	....	....	....	....	....	....	....	....
	Kitchener Rangers	OHA-Jr.	22	....	....	....	1320	125	0	5.68	....	....	....	....	....	....	....	....	....	....	....	....	....	....	....	....	....
	Toronto Marlboros	OHA-Jr.	22	....	....	....	1310	84	0	3.84	....	....	....	....	....	6	....	....	....	360	28	0	4.67	....	....	....	....
1969-70	Fort Wayne Komets	IHL	37	....	....	....	2101	121	3	3.46	....	....	....	....	....	3	0	3	0	180	14	0	4.67	....	....	....	....
	Baltimore Clippers	AHL	3	....	....	....	100	5	0	3.00	....	....	....	....	....	....	....	....	....	....	....	....	....	....	....	....	....
1970-71	**Pittsburgh Penguins**	**NHL**	**2**	**0**	**1**	**0**	**57**	**7**	**0**	**7.37**	**7.30**	....	....	....	....	....	....	....	....	....	....	....	....	....	....	....	....
	Amarillo Wranglers	CHL	48	....	....	....	2828	203	0	4.37	....	....	....	....	....	....	....	....	....	....	....	....	....	....	....	....	....
1971-72	Fort Wayne Komets	IHL	52	....	....	....	3074	161	2	3.14	....	....	....	....	....	8	4	4	0	480	25	0	3.12	....	....	....	....
1972-73	Hershey Bears	AHL	41	....	....	....	2251	110	3	2.98	....	....	....	....	....	3	....	....	....	179	14	0	4.69	....	....	....	....
1973-74	Los Angeles Sharks	WHA	27	6	16	0	1308	102	0	4.68	....	....	....	....	....	....	....	....	....	....	....	....	....	....	....	....	....
	Greensboro Generals	SHL	3	....	....	....	180	12	0	4.00	....	....	....	....	....	....	....	....	....	....	....	....	....	....	....	....	....
1974-75	Baltimore-Michigan Stags	WHA	32	9	19	2	1776	121	2	4.09	....	....	....	....	....	....	....	....	....	....	....	....	....	....	....	....	....
	Tulsa Oilers	CHL	6	3	3	0	320	19	0	3.56	....	....	....	....	....	....	....	....	....	....	....	....	....	....	....	....	....
1975-76	New England Whalers	WHA	4	1	2	0	224	16	0	4.29	....	....	....	....	....	....	....	....	....	....	....	....	....	....	....	....	....
	Cincinnati Stingers	WHA	45	19	24	0	2392	145	2	3.64	....	....	....	....	....	....	....	....	....	....	....	....	....	....	....	....	....
1976-77	Binghamton Dusters	NAHL	8	....	....	....	480	440	0	5.05	....	....	....	....	....	....	....	....	....	....	....	....	....	....	....	....	....
	Cincinnati Stingers	WHA	17	5	6	1	823	64	1	4.67	....	....	....	....	....	....	....	....	....	....	....	....	....	....	....	....	....
	Indianapolis Racers	WHA	11	3	2	0	395	24	0	3.65	....	....	....	....	....	5	3	2	0	348	17	*1	*2.93	....	....	....	....
1977-78	Cincinnati Stingers	WHA	7	1	2	1	326	24	0	4.42	....	....	....	....	....	....	....	....	....	....	....	....	....	....	....	....	....
	Hampton Gulls	AHL	3	1	1	1	155	11	0	4.26	....	....	....	....	....	....	....	....	....	....	....	....	....	....	....	....	....
	San Francisco Shamrocks	PHL	11	....	....	....	660	614	0	3.90	....	....	....	....	....	....	....	....	....	....	....	....	....	....	....	....	....
1978-79	Tucson Rustlers	PHL	37	....	....	....	2058	170	1	4.96	....	....	....	....	....	....	....	....	....	....	....	....	....	....	....	....	....
	NHL Totals		**2**	**0**	**1**	**0**	**57**	**7**	**0**	**7.37**	....	....	....	....	....	....	....	....	....	....	....	....	....	....	....	....	....
	Other Major League Totals		143	44	71	4	7244	496	5	4.11	....	....	....	....	....	5	3	2	....	348	17	1	2.93	....	....	....	....

OHA-Jr. Second All-Star Team (1969) • IHL Second All-Star Team (1972)

Selected by **LA Sharks** (WHA) in 1972 WHA General Player Draft, February 12, 1972. Transferred to **Michigan** (WHA) after **LA Sharks** (WHA) franchise relocated, April 11, 1974. Selected by **New England** (WHA) from **Michigan-Baltimore** (WHA) in WHA Dispersal Draft, May 19, 1975. Signed as a free agent by **Cincinnati** (WHA) after securing release from **New England** (WHA), November, 1975. Traded to **Indianapolis** (WHA) by **Cincinnati** (WHA) for cash, February, 1976. Signed as a free agent by **Cincinnati** (WHA) after **Indianapolis** (WHA) franchise folded, February, 1978.

• HOGOSTA, Goran G – L. 6'1", 179 lbs. b: Appelbo, Sweden, 4/15/1954.

Season	Club	League	GP	W	L	T	Mins	GA	SO	Avg	AAvg	Eff	SA	S%	SAPG	GP	W	L	T	Mins	GA	SO	Avg	Eff	SA	S%	SAPG
1971-72	Tunabro IK	Sweden	11	....	....	....	660	64	0	5.82	....	....	....	....	....	....	....	....	....	....	....	....	....	....	....	....	....
	Sweden	EJC-A	2	....	....	....	70	2	....	1.71	....	....	....	....	....	....	....	....	....	....	....	....	....	....	....	....	....
1972-73	Tunabro IK	Sweden	10	....	....	....	600	59	0	5.90	....	....	....	....	....	6	3	0	3	360	21	0	3.50	....	....	....	....
	Sweden	EJC-A	4	....	....	....	210	11	....	3.14	....	....	....	....	....	....	....	....	....	....	....	....	....	....	....	....	....
1973-74	Tunabro IK	Sweden	10	....	....	....	600	62	0	6.20	....	....	....	....	....	....	....	....	....	....	....	....	....	....	....	....	....
1974-75	Leksands IF	Sweden	30	....	....	....	1800	80	0	2.67	....	....	....	....	....	5	....	....	....	304	15	0	2.96	....	....	....	....
	Sweden	WEC-A	4	2	2	0	220	12	2	3.27	....	....	....	....	....	....	....	....	....	....	....	....	....	....	....	....	....
1975-76	Leksands IF	Sweden	27	....	....	....	1620	118	0	4.37	....	....	....	....	....	....	....	....	....	....	....	....	....	....	....	....	....
	Sweden	WEC-A	6	4	2	0	360	20	0	3.33	....	....	....	....	....	....	....	....	....	....	....	....	....	....	....	....	....
1976-77	Sweden	Can-Cup	1	1	0	0	60	1	0	1.00	....	....	....	....	....	....	....	....	....	....	....	....	....	....	....	....	....
	Leksands IF	Sweden	33	....	....	....	1921	126	0	3.94	....	....	....	....	....	4	....	....	....	245	16	0	3.92	....	....	....	....
	Sweden	WEC-A	7	6	1	0	412	9	0	1.31	....	....	....	....	....	....	....	....	....	....	....	....	....	....	....	....	....
1977-78	**New York Islanders**	**NHL**	**1**	**0**	**0**	**0**	**9**	**0**	**0**	**0.00**	**0.00**	....	....	....	....	....	....	....	....	....	....	....	....	....	....	....	....
	Fort Worth Texans	CHL	5	3	2	0	297	19	0	3.84	....	....	....	....	....	....	....	....	....	....	....	....	....	....	....	....	....
	Hershey Bears	AHL	23	6	13	2	1254	82	1	3.92	....	....	....	....	....	....	....	....	....	....	....	....	....	....	....	....	....
	Sweden	WEC-A	7	2	4	0	392	22	0	3.37	....	....	....	....	....	....	....	....	....	....	....	....	....	....	....	....	....
1978-79	Fort Worth Texans	CHL	61	25	29	4	3332	195	2	3.51	....	....	....	....	....	3	1	2	0	167	9	0	3.23	....	....	....	....
1979-80	**Quebec Nordiques**	**NHL**	**21**	**5**	**12**	**3**	**1199**	**83**	**1**	**4.15**	**3.68**	....	....	....	....	....	....	....	....	....	....	....	....	....	....	....	....
	Syracuse Firebirds	AHL	17	4	9	4	1037	69	0	3.99	....	....	....	....	....	....	....	....	....	....	....	....	....	....	....	....	....
1980-81	Vastra Frolunda	Sweden	18	....	....	....	1078	76	0	4.23	....	....	....	....	....	1	0	1	0	60	6	0	6.00	....	....	....	....
1981-82	Vastra Frolunda	Sweden	28	....	....	....	1582	89	0	3.38	....	....	....	....	....	....	....	....	....	....	....	....	....	....	....	....	....
1982-83	Vastra Frolunda	Sweden	34	....	....	....	1980	140	1	4.24	....	....	....	....	....	....	....	....	....	....	....	....	....	....	....	....	....
1983-84	Vastra Frolunda	Sweden	36	....	....	....	1093	151	1	8.29	....	....	....	....	....	....	....	....	....	....	....	....	....	....	....	....	....
1984-85			OUT OF HOCKEY – RETIRED																								
1985-86			OUT OF HOCKEY – RETIRED																								
1986-87	Leksands IF	Sweden	4	2	1	0	200	16	0	4.80	....	....	....	....	....	....	....	....	....	....	....	....	....	....	....	....	....
	NHL Totals		**22**	**5**	**12**	**3**	**1208**	**83**	**1**	**4.12**	....	....	....	....	....	....	....	....	....	....	....	....	....	....	....	....	....

Named Best Goaltender at EJC-A (1973) • WEC-A All-Star Team (1977) • Named Best Goaltender at WEC-A (1977)

Signed as a free agent by **NY Islanders**, June 17, 1977. • Shared shutout (9-0) w/ Billy Smith in NHL debut vs. Atlanta, November 1, 1977. Traded to **Quebec** by **NY Islanders** for Richard Brodeur, August, 1979.

• HOLDEN, Mark G – L. 5'10", 165 lbs. b: Weymouth, MA, 6/12/1957. Montreal's 16th, 160th overall in 1977.

Season	Club	League	GP	W	L	T	Mins	GA	SO	Avg	AAvg	Eff	SA	S%	SAPG	GP	W	L	T	Mins	GA	SO	Avg	Eff	SA	S%	SAPG
1976-77	Brown University	ECAC	5	0	0	0	82	5	0	3.68	....	....	....	....	....	....	....	....	....	....	....	....	....	....	....	....	....
1977-78	Brown University	ECAC	10	4	6	0	590	33	1	3.36	....	....	....	....	....	....	....	....	....	....	....	....	....	....	....	....	....
1978-79	Brown University	ECAC	13	7	6	0	755	49	0	3.90	....	....	....	....	....	....	....	....	....	....	....	....	....	....	....	....	....
1979-80	Brown University	ECAC	26	10	14	2	1508	93	0	3.70	....	....	....	....	....	....	....	....	....	....	....	....	....	....	....	....	....
1980-81	Nova Scotia Voyageurs	AHL	42	20	17	1	2223	127	2	3.43	....	....	....	....	....	3	0	3	0	159	12	0	4.53	....	....	....	....
1981-82	**Montreal Canadiens**	**NHL**	**1**	**0**	**0**	**0**	**20**	**0**	**0**	**0.00**	**0.00**	....	....	....	....	....	....	....	....	....	....	....	....	....	....	....	....
	Nova Scotia Voyageurs	AHL	44	19	19	5	2534	142	0	3.36	....	....	....	....	....	7	2	5	0	435	21	0	2.90	....	....	....	....
1982-83	**Montreal Canadiens**	**NHL**	**2**	**0**	**1**	**1**	**87**	**6**	**0**	**4.14**	**3.32**	**5.91**	**42**	**.857**	**29.0**	....	....	....	....	....	....	....	....	....	....	....	....
	Nova Scotia Voyageurs	AHL	41	21	16	1	2369	160	0	4.05	....	....	....	....	....	6	3	2	0	319	13	0	2.44	....	....	....	....
1983-84	**Montreal Canadiens**	**NHL**	**1**	**0**	**1**	**0**	**52**	**4**	**0**	**4.62**	**3.64**	**10.87**	**17**	**.765**	**19.6**	....	....	....	....	....	....	....	....	....	....	....	....
	Nova Scotia Voyageurs	AHL	47	19	8	7	2739	153	0	3.35	....	....	....	....	....	10	4	6	0	534	40	0	4.49	....	....	....	....
1984-85	**Winnipeg Jets**	**NHL**	**4**	**2**	**0**	**0**	**213**	**15**	**0**	**4.23**	**3.37**	**6.10**	**104**	**.856**	**29.3**	....	....	....	....	....	....	....	....	....	....	....	....
	Nova Scotia Oilers	AHL	22	8	12	1	1261	87	1	4.14	....	....	....	....	....	....	....	....	....	....	....	....	....	....	....	....	....
1985-86	Sherbrooke Canadiens	AHL	12	5	7	0	696	52	0	4.48	....	....	....	....	....	....	....	....	....	....	....	....	....	....	....	....	....
	Fort Wayne Komets	IHL	9	3	3	0	496	26	1	3.14	....	....	....	....	....	....	....	....	....	....	....	....	....	....	....	....	....
1986-87	Dartmouth Mounties	NSSHL	STATISTICS NOT AVAILABLE																								
1987-88	Dartmouth Mounties	NSSHL	STATISTICS NOT AVAILABLE																								
	NHL Totals		**8**	**2**	**2**	**1**	**372**	**25**	**0**	**4.03**	....	....	....	....	....	....	....	....	....	....	....	....	....	....	....	....	....

NCAA East First All-American Team (1980)

Traded to **Winnipeg** by **Montreal** for Doug Soetaert, October 9, 1984.

• HOLLAND, Ken Kenneth Mark G – L. 5'8", 160 lbs. b: Vernon, B.C., 11/10/1955. Toronto's 13th, 188th overall in 1975.

Season	Club	League	GP	W	L	T	Mins	GA	SO	Avg	AAvg	Eff	SA	S%	SAPG	GP	W	L	T	Mins	GA	SO	Avg	Eff	SA	S%	SAPG
1973-74	Vernon Lakers	BCJHL	16	....	....	....	960	59	0	3.69	....	....	....	....	....	....	....	....	....	....	....	....	....	....	....	....	....
1974-75	Medicine Hat Tigers	WCJHL	37	23	10	4	2114	138	1	3.91	....	....	....	....	....	4	1	3	0	230	16	0	4.17	....	....	....	....
1975-76	Medicine Hat Tigers	WCJHL	41	22	11	1	2152	150	2	4.18	....	....	....	....	....	9	4	4	0	528	30	0	3.41	....	....	....	....
1976-77	Binghamton Dusters	NAHL	48	....	....	....	2620	165	0	3.78	....	....	....	....	....	6	....	....	....	320	22	0	4.13	....	....	....	....
1977-78	Binghamton Dusters	AHL	39	12	19	3	2057	147	0	4.28	....	....	....	....	....	....	....	....	....	....	....	....	....	....	....	....	....
1978-79	Binghamton Dusters	AHL	41	19	17	3	2315	151	0	3.91	....	....	....	....	....	*10	5	5	0	*572	39	*1	4.09	....	....	....	....
1979-80	Springfield Indians	AHL	37	15	14	5	2092	129	2	3.70	....	....	....	....	....	....	....	....	....	....	....	....	....	....	....	....	....

			REGULAR SEASON													PLAYOFFS											
Season	Club	League	GP	W	L	T	Mins	GA	SO	Avg	AAvg	Eff	SA	S%	SAPG	GP	W	L	T	Mins	GA	SO	Avg	Eff	SA	S%	SAPG
1980-81	**Hartford Whalers**	**NHL**	**1**	**0**	**1**	**0**	**60**	**7**	**0**	**7.00**	**5.66**	....	....	....	....	....	....	....	....	....	....	....	....	....	....	....	....
	Binghamton Whalers	AHL	47	15	25	4	2543	168	2	3.96	....	....	....	....	....	2	0	2	0	79	3	0	2.28	....	....	....	....
1981-82	Binghamton Whalers	AHL	46	27	13	4	2733	133	2	2.92	....	....	....	....	....	*15	8	7	0	*888	57	0	3.85	....	....	....	....
1982-83	Binghamton Whalers	AHL	*48	23	18	5	2700	196	0	4.36	....	....	....	....	....	3	1	2	0	180	16	0	5.33	....	....	....	....
1983-84	**Detroit Red Wings**	**NHL**	**3**	**0**	**1**	**1**	**146**	**10**	**0**	**4.11**	**3.24**	**7.75**	**53**	**.811**	**21.8**	....	....	....	....	....	....	....	....	....	....	....	....
	Adirondack Red Wings	AHL	42	19	15	6	2495	154	0	3.70	....	....	....	....	....	7	3	4	0	416	25	0	3.61	....	....	....	....
1984-85	Adirondack Red Wings	AHL	43	13	22	6	2478	176	0	4.26	....	....	....	....	....	....	....	....	....	....	....	....	....	....	....	....	....
1985-1994	**Detroit Red Wings**	**NHL**	DID NOT PLAY – SCOUTING																								
1994-1997	**Detroit Red Wings**	**NHL**	DID NOT PLAY – ASSISTANT GENERAL MANAGER																								
1997-2000	**Detroit Red Wings**	**NHL**	DID NOT PLAY – GENERAL MANAGER																								
	NHL Totals		**4**	**0**	**2**	**1**	**206**	**17**	**0**	**4.95**	....	....	....	....	....	....	....	....	....	....	....	....	....	....	....	....	....

NAHL Second All-Star Team (1977) • AHL Second All-Star Team (1982)

Signed as a free agent by **Hartford**, July 17, 1980. Signed as a free agent by **Detroit**, July 6, 1983.

• HOLLAND, Robbie

G – L. 6'1", 180 lbs. b: Montreal, Que., 9/10/1957. Montreal's 8th, 64th overall in 1977.

Season	Club	League	GP	W	L	T	Mins	GA	SO	Avg	AAvg	Eff	SA	S%	SAPG	GP	W	L	T	Mins	GA	SO	Avg	Eff	SA	S%	SAPG
1974-75	Longueuil Lions	QJHL	36	....	....	....	2139	187	0	5.25	....	....	....	....	....	....	....	....	....	....	....	....	....	....	....	....	....
1975-76	Montreal Jr. Canadiens	QMJHL	37	....	....	....	1995	147	0	4.42	....	....	....	....	....	6	....	....	....	360	21	0	3.50	....	....	....	....
1976-77	Montreal Jr. Canadiens	QMJHL	45	....	....	....	2314	184	0	4.77	....	....	....	....	....	13	....	....	....	780	64	0	4.92	....	....	....	....
1977-78	Nova Scotia Voyageurs	AHL	38	13	14	11	2270	120	1	3.17	....	....	....	....	....	5	3	2	0	299	14	0	2.81	....	....	....	....
1978-79	Nova Scotia Voyageurs	AHL	43	18	19	2	2377	154	*2	3.89	....	....	....	....	....	1	0	1	0	60	7	0	7.00	....	....	....	....
1979-80	**Pittsburgh Penguins**	**NHL**	**34**	**10**	**17**	**6**	**1974**	**126**	**1**	**3.83**	**3.39**	....	....	....	....	....	....	....	....	....	....	....	....	....	....	....	....
1980-81	**Pittsburgh Penguins**	**NHL**	**10**	**1**	**5**	**3**	**539**	**45**	**0**	**5.01**	**4.06**	....	....	....	....	....	....	....	....	....	....	....	....	....	....	....	....
	Binghamton Whalers	AHL	7	1	4	0	354	28	0	4.75	....	....	....	....	....	....	....	....	....	....	....	....	....	....	....	....	....
	Indianapolis Checkers	CHL	15	6	6	2	845	41	1	2.91	....	....	....	....	....	3	....	....	....	179	13	0	4.36	....	....	....	....
1981-82	Indianapolis Checkers	CHL	30	15	11	1	1672	95	0	3.41	....	....	....	....	....	....	....	....	....	....	....	....	....	....	....	....	....
	Toledo Goaldiggers	IHL	7	....	....	....	423	25	0	3.55	....	....	....	....	....	....	....	....	....	....	....	....	....	....	....	....	....
1982-83	Indianapolis Checkers	CHL	37	24	11	1	2111	101	*4	*2.87	....	....	....	....	....	3	2	1	0	200	13	0	3.90	....	....	....	....
1983-84	Indianapolis Checkers	CHL	39	....	....	....	2149	131	0	3.66	....	....	....	....	....	7	....	....	....	379	22	0	3.48	....	....	....	....
1984-85	Indianapolis Checkers	IHL	57	....	....	....	3344	184	*4	3.28	....	....	....	....	....	6	....	....	....	359	21	*1	3.51	....	....	....	....
1985-86	Springfield Indians	AHL	8	6	2	0	478	23	0	2.88	....	....	....	....	....	....	....	....	....	....	....	....	....	....	....	....	....
	Indianapolis Checkers	IHL	44	....	....	....	2246	146	0	3.90	....	....	....	....	....	4	....	....	....	182	15	0	4.94	....	....	....	....
1986-87	Milwaukee Admirals	IHL	66	....	....	....	3915	268	1	4.11	....	....	....	....	....	6	....	....	....	360	30	0	5.00	....	....	....	....
	NHL Totals		**44**	**11**	**22**	**9**	**2513**	**171**	**1**	**4.08**	....	....	....	....	....	....	....	....	....	....	....	....	....	....	....	....	....

Shared Harry "Hap" Holmes Memorial Award (fewest goals against - AHL) with Maurice Barrett (1978) • Shared Terry Sawchuk Trophy (fewest goals against - CHL) with Kelly Hrudey (1982, 1983) • CHL Second All-Star Team (1983)

Traded to **Pittsburgh** by **Montreal** with Pat Hughes for Denis Herron and Pittsburgh's 2nd round choice (Jocelyn Gauvreau) in 1982 Entry Draft, August 30, 1979. Rights traded to **NY Islanders** by **Pittsburgh** for future considerations, September 28, 1981.

• HOLMES, Hap

Harry G – L. 5'10", 170 lbs. b: Aurora, Ont., 2/21/1892 d: 6/27/1941. **HHOF**

Season	Club	League	GP	W	L	T	Mins	GA	SO	Avg	AAvg	Eff	SA	S%	SAPG	GP	W	L	T	Mins	GA	SO	Avg	Eff	SA	S%	SAPG
1907-08	Toronto Young Toronto	OMHA	STATISTICS NOT AVAILABLE																								
1908-09	Parkdale Canoe Club	OHA-Sr.	3	0	3	0	180	22	0	7.33	....	....	....	....	....	....	....	....	....	....	....	....	....	....	....	....	....
1909-10	Parkdale Canoe Club	OHA-Sr.	4	2	2	0	240	26	0	6.50	....	....	....	....	....	....	....	....	....	....	....	....	....	....	....	....	....
1910-11	Parkdale Canoe Club	OHA-Sr.	4	*3	1	0	240	12	0	3.00	....	....	....	....	....	2	0	1	1	120	9	0	4.50	....	....	....	....
1911-12	Toronto Tecumsehs	X-Games	1	1	0	0	60	3	0	3.00	....	....	....	....	....	....	....	....	....	....	....	....	....	....	....	....	....
1912-13	Toronto Blueshirts	NHA	15	6	7	0	779	58	*1	4.47	....	....	....	....	....	....	....	....	....	....	....	....	....	....	....	....	....
1913-14♦	Toronto Blueshirts	NHA	20	*13	7	0	1204	65	*1	3.24	....	....	....	....	....	5	4	1	0	315	10	2	1.90	....	....	....	....
1914-15	Toronto Blueshirts	NHA	20	8	12	0	1218	84	0	4.18	....	....	....	....	....	....	....	....	....	....	....	....	....	....	....	....	....
1915-16	Seattle Metropolitans	PCHA	18	9	9	0	1080	66	0	3.67	....	....	....	....	....	....	....	....	....	....	....	....	....	....	....	....	....
	PCHA All-Stars	X-Games	1	0	1	0	60	6	0	6.00	....	....	....	....	....	....	....	....	....	....	....	....	....	....	....	....	....
1916-17♦	Seattle Metropolitans	PCHA	24	*16	8	0	1465	80	*2	*3.28	....	....	....	....	....	4	*3	1	0	140	11	0	2.75	....	....	....	....
1917-18	**Toronto Arenas**	**NHL**	**16**	**9**	**7**	**0**	**965**	**76**	**0**	**4.73**	**3.03**	....	....	....	....	***2**	***1**	**1**	**0**	***120**	**7**	**0**	***3.50**	....	....	....	....
♦	Toronto Arenas	St-Cup	5	3	2	....	300	21	0	4.20	....	....	....	....	....	....	....	....	....	....	....	....	....	....	....	....	....
1918-19	**Toronto Arenas**	**NHL**	**2**	**0**	**2**	**0**	**120**	**9**	**0**	**4.50**	**3.33**	....	....	....	....	....	....	....	....	....	....	....	....	....	....	....	....
	Seattle Metropolitans	PCHA	20	11	9	0	1225	46	0	*2.25	....	....	....	....	....	2	1	1	1	120	5	0	2.50	....	....	....	....
	Seattle Metropolitans	St-Cup	5	2	2	1	336	10	2	1.79	....	....	....	....	....	....	....	....	....	....	....	....	....	....	....	....	....
1919-20	Seattle Metropolitans	PCHA	22	12	10	0	1340	55	*4	*2.46	....	....	....	....	....	2	1	1	0	120	3	1	1.50	....	....	....	....
	Seattle Metropolitans	St-Cup	5	2	3	0	300	15	0	3.00	....	....	....	....	....	....	....	....	....	....	....	....	....	....	....	....	....
1920-21	Seattle Metropolitans	PCHA	24	12	11	1	1551	68	0	*2.63	....	....	....	....	....	2	0	2	0	120	13	0	6.50	....	....	....	....
1921-22	Seattle Metropolitans	PCHA	24	*12	11	1	1479	64	*4	*2.60	....	....	....	....	....	2	0	2	0	120	2	0	1.00	....	....	....	....
1922-23	Seattle Metropolitans	PCHA	*30	*15	15	0	1844	106	2	3.45	....	....	....	....	....	....	....	....	....	....	....	....	....	....	....	....	....
1923-24	Seattle Metropolitans	PCHA	*30	*14	16	0	1824	99	*2	3.26	....	....	....	....	....	2	0	1	1	134	4	0	1.79	....	....	....	....
1924-25	Victoria Cougars	WCHL	*28	16	12	0	1683	63	*3	*2.25	....	....	....	....	....	4	2	0	2	240	5	1	1.25	....	....	....	....
♦	Victoria Cougars	St-Cup	4	3	1	0	240	8	0	2.00	....	....	....	....	....	....	....	....	....	....	....	....	....	....	....	....	....
1925-26	Victoria Cougars	WHL	*30	15	11	4	*1894	53	4	*1.68	....	....	....	....	....	4	*2	0	2	249	6	1	*1.45	....	....	....	....
	Victoria Cougars	St-Cup	4	1	3	0	240	10	0	2.50	....	....	....	....	....	....	....	....	....	....	....	....	....	....	....	....	....
1926-27	**Detroit Cougars**	**NHL**	**41**	**11**	**26**	**4**	**2685**	**100**	**6**	**2.23**	**3.45**	....	....	....	....	....	....	....	....	....	....	....	....	....	....	....	....
1927-28	**Detroit Cougars**	**NHL**	***44**	**19**	**19**	**6**	**2740**	**79**	**11**	**1.73**	**2.75**	....	....	....	....	....	....	....	....	....	....	....	....	....	....	....	....
	NHL Totals		**103**	**39**	**54**	**10**	**6510**	**264**	**17**	**2.43**	....	....	....	....	....	**2**	**1**	**1**	**0**	**120**	**7**	**0**	**3.50**	....	....	....	....
	Other Major League Totals		306	159	139	6	18646	913	23	2.94	....	....	....	....	....	27	13	9	....	1558	59	5	2.27	....	....	....	....

PCHA Second All-Star Team (1916, 1917, 1919, 1920, 1921, 1922, 1923) • WCHL All-Star Team (1925)

Signed as a free agent by **Toronto Tecumsehs** (NHA), December, 1911. • Team unable to play 1911-12 season due to slow completion of artifical ice arena. Jumped NHA contract to sign with **Seattle** (PCHA), November 12, 1915. Signed as a free agent by **Montreal Wanderers**, November, 1917. Loaned to **Seattle** (PCHA) by **Montreal Wanderers**, December 12, 1917. Loaned to **Toronto** by **Seattle** (PCHA), January 4, 1918 and recalled December 27, 1918. Signed as a free agent by **Victoria** (WCHL), November 7, 1924. • 1924-25 playoff totals includes WCHL series against Calgary and Saskatoon. Rights transferred to **Detroit** after NHL club purchased **Victoria** (WHL) franchise, May 26, 1926.

• HORNER, Red

George Reginald G. 6', 190 lbs. b: Lynden, Ont., 5/28/1909. **HHOF**

Season	Club	League	GP	W	L	T	Mins	GA	SO	Avg	AAvg	Eff	SA	S%	SAPG	GP	W	L	T	Mins	GA	SO	Avg	Eff	SA	S%	SAPG
1931-32	**Toronto Maple Leafs**	**NHL**	**1**	**0**	**0**	**0**	**1**	**1**	**0**	**60.00**	**73.44**	....	....	....	....	....	....	....	....	....	....	....	....	....	....	....	....
	NHL Totals		**1**	**0**	**0**	**0**	**1**	**1**	**0**	**60.00**	....	....	....	....	....	....	....	....	....	....	....	....	....	....	....	....	....

• **Toronto** defenseman replaced penalized Lorne Chabot, March 15, 1932. (Detroit 6, Toronto 2)

• HRIVNAK, Jim

G – L. 6'2", 195 lbs. b: Montreal, Que., 5/28/1968. Washington's 4th, 61st overall in 1986.

Season	Club	League	GP	W	L	T	Mins	GA	SO	Avg	AAvg	Eff	SA	S%	SAPG	GP	W	L	T	Mins	GA	SO	Avg	Eff	SA	S%	SAPG
1983-84	Montreal Concordia	QAAA	15	6	8	1	897	68	0	4.54	....	....	....	....	....	....	....	....	....	....	....	....	....	....	....	....	....
1984-85	Montreal Concordia	QAAA	34	8	22	1	1822	182	0	5.99	....	....	....	....	....	....	....	....	....	....	....	....	....	....	....	....	....
1985-86	Merrimack College	NCAA-2	21	12	6	2	1230	75	0	3.66	....	....	....	....	....	....	....	....	....	....	....	....	....	....	....	....	....
1986-87	Merrimack College	NCAA-2	34	27	7	0	1950	80	3	2.46	....	....	....	....	....	....	....	....	....	....	....	....	....	....	....	....	....
1987-88	Merrimack College	NCAA-2	37	31	6	0	2119	84	4	2.38	....	....	....	....	....	....	....	....	....	....	....	....	....	....	....	....	....
1988-89	Merrimack College	NCAA-2	22	18	4	0	1295	52	4	2.41	....	....	....	....	....	....	....	....	....	....	....	....	....	....	....	....	....
	Baltimore Skipjacks	AHL	10	1	8	0	502	55	0	6.57	....	....	....	....	....	....	....	....	....	....	....	....	....	....	....	....	....
1989-90	**Washington Capitals**	**NHL**	**11**	**5**	**5**	**0**	**609**	**36**	**0**	**3.55**	**3.01**	**4.36**	**293**	**.877**	**28.9**	....	....	....	....	....	....	....	....	....	....	....	....
	Baltimore Skipjacks	AHL	47	24	19	2	2722	139	*4	3.06	....	....	....	....	....	6	4	2	0	360	19	0	3.17	....	....	....	....
1990-91	**Washington Capitals**	**NHL**	**9**	**4**	**2**	**1**	**432**	**26**	**0**	**3.61**	**3.25**	**4.15**	**226**	**.885**	**31.4**	....	....	....	....	....	....	....	....	....	....	....	....
	Baltimore Skipjacks	AHL	42	20	16	6	2481	134	1	3.24	....	....	....	....	....	6	2	3	0	324	21	0	3.89	....	....	....	....
1991-92	**Washington Capitals**	**NHL**	**12**	**6**	**3**	**0**	**605**	**35**	**0**	**3.47**	**3.11**	**4.43**	**274**	**.872**	**27.2**	....	....	....	....	....	....	....	....	....	....	....	....
	Baltimore Skipjacks	AHL	22	10	8	3	1303	73	0	3.36	....	....	....	....	....	....	....	....	....	....	....	....	....	....	....	....	....
1992-93	**Washington Capitals**	**NHL**	**27**	**13**	**9**	**2**	**1421**	**83**	**0**	**3.50**	**3.00**	**4.29**	**677**	**.877**	**28.6**	....	....	....	....	....	....	....	....	....	....	....	....
	Winnipeg Jets	**NHL**	**3**	**2**	**1**	**0**	**180**	**13**	**0**	**4.33**	**3.71**	**5.86**	**96**	**.865**	**32.0**	....	....	....	....	....	....	....	....	....	....	....	....

			REGULAR SEASON													PLAYOFFS											
Season	Club	League	GP	W	L	T	Mins	GA	SO	Avg	AAvg	Eff	SA	S%	SAPG	GP	W	L	T	Mins	GA	SO	Avg	Eff	SA	S%	SAPG
1993-94	**St. Louis Blues**	**NHL**	**23**	**4**	**10**	**0**	**970**	**69**	**0**	**4.27**	**4.11**	**5.23**	**563**	**.877**	**34.8**	....	....	....	....	....	....	....	....	....	....	....	....
1994-95	Milwaukee Admirals	IHL	28	17	10	1	1634	106	0	3.89	....	....	....	....	....	....	....	....	....	....	....	....	....	....	....	....	....
	Kansas City Blades	IHL	10	3	5	2	550	35	0	3.81	....	....	....	....	....	2	0	2	0	118	7	0	3.55	....	....	....	....
1995-96	Carolina Monarchs	AHL	11	1	4	1	458	27	0	3.54	....	....	....	....	....	....	....	....	....	....	....	....	....	....	....	....	....
	Las Vegas Thunder	IHL	13	10	1	1	713	34	0	2.86	....	....	....	....	....	....	....	....	....	....	....	....	....	....	....	....	....
	Kansas City Blades	IHL	4	1	1	0	154	11	0	4.29	....	....	....	....	....	....	....	....	....	....	....	....	....	....	....	....	....
1996-97	Kolner Haie	Germany	21	....	....	....	1144	53	1	2.78	....	....	....	....	....	2	....	....	....	121	7	0	3.47	....	....	....	....
	Kolner Haie	EuroHL	2	0	0	2	120	3	0	1.50	....	....	....	....	....	....	....	....	....	....	....	....	....	....	....	....	....
1997-98	Manchester Storm	BH-Cup	8	....	....	....	480	19	0	2.38	....	....	....	....	....	....	....	....	....	....	....	....	....	....	....	....	....
	Manchester Storm	Britain	24	....	....	....	1487	62	....	2.50	....	....	....	....	....	....	....	....	....	....	....	....	....	....	....	....	....
	Manchester Storm	EuroHL	4	1	2	0	207	14	0	4.06	....	....	....	....	....	....	....	....	....	....	....	....	....	....	....	....	....
1998-99	Hamburg Scorpions	Germany-2	32	11	14	1	1785	114	4	3.83	....	....	....	....	....	3	0	0	1	133	5	0	2.26	....	....	....	....
99-2000	HC Ambri-Piotta	Finland	24	6	12	5	1410	74	1	3.15	....	....	....	....	....	....	....	....	....	....	....	....	....	....	....	....	....
	NHL Totals		**85**	**34**	**30**	**3**	**4217**	**262**	**0**	**3.73**	....	....	**2129**	**.877**	**30.3**	....	....	....	....	....	....	....	....	....	....	....	....

NCAA (College Div.) East First All-American Team (1987)

Traded to **Winnipeg** by **Washington** with Washington's 2nd round choice (Alexei Budayev) in 1993 Entry Draft for Rick Tabaracci, March 22, 1993. Traded to **St. Louis** by **Winnipeg** for St. Louis' 6th round choice (later traded to Florida - later traded to Edmonton - later traded to Winnipeg - Winnipeg selected Chris Kibermanis) in 1994 Entry Draft and future considerations, July 29, 1993.

• HRUDEY, Kelly

Kelly Stephen G – L. 5'10", 189 lbs. b: Edmonton, Alta., 1/13/1961. NY Islanders' 2nd, 38th overall in 1980.

Season	Club	League	GP	W	L	T	Mins	GA	SO	Avg	AAvg	Eff	SA	S%	SAPG	GP	W	L	T	Mins	GA	SO	Avg	Eff	SA	S%	SAPG
1978-79	Medicine Hat Tigers	WHL	57	12	34	7	3093	318	0	6.17	....	....	....	....	....	....	....	....	....	....	....	....	....	....	....	....	....
1979-80	Medicine Hat Tigers	WHL	57	25	23	4	3049	212	1	4.17	....	....	....	....	....	13	6	6	....	638	48	0	4.51	....	....	....	....
1980-81	Medicine Hat Tigers	WHL	55	32	19	1	3023	200	4	3.97	....	....	....	....	....	4	1	3	....	244	17	0	4.18	....	....	....	....
	Indianapolis Checkers	CHL	....	....	....	....	....	....	....	....	....	....	....	....	....	2	....	....	....	135	8	0	3.56	....	....	....	....
1981-82	Indianapolis Checkers	CHL	51	27	19	4	3033	149	1	*2.95	....	....	....	....	....	13	11	2	....	842	34	*1	*2.42	....	....	....	....
1982-83	Indianapolis Checkers	CHL	47	*26	17	1	2744	139	2	3.04	....	....	....	....	....	10	*7	3	....	*637	28	0	*2.64	....	....	....	....
1983-84	**New York Islanders**	**NHL**	**12**	**7**	**2**	**0**	**535**	**28**	**0**	**3.14**	**2.47**	**3.04**	**289**	**.903**	**32.4**	....	....	....	....	....	....	....	....	....	....	....	....
	Indianapolis Checkers	CHL	6	3	2	1	370	21	0	3.40	....	....	....	....	....	....	....	....	....	....	....	....	....	....	....	....	....
1984-85	**New York Islanders**	**NHL**	**41**	**19**	**17**	**3**	**2335**	**141**	**2**	**3.62**	**2.88**	**4.14**	**1234**	**.886**	**31.7**	**5**	**1**	**3**	....	**281**	**8**	**0**	**1.71**	**0.92**	**149**	**.946**	**31.8**
1985-86	**New York Islanders**	**NHL**	**45**	**19**	**15**	**8**	**2563**	**137**	**1**	**3.21**	**2.50**	**3.02**	**1455**	**.906**	**34.1**	**2**	**0**	**2**	....	**120**	**6**	**0**	**3.00**	**3.05**	**59**	**.898**	**29.5**
	Canada	WEC-A	5	....	....	....	299	22	....	4.41	....	....	....	....	....	....	....	....	....	....	....	....	....	....	....	....	....
1986-87	**New York Islanders**	**NHL**	**46**	**21**	**15**	**7**	**2634**	**145**	**0**	**3.30**	**2.79**	**3.93**	**1219**	**.881**	**27.8**	**14**	**7**	**7**	....	**842**	**38**	**0**	**2.71**	**2.22**	**464**	**.918**	**33.1**
1987-88	Canada	Can-Cup	DID NOT PLAY – SPARE GOALTENDER																								
	New York Islanders	**NHL**	**47**	**22**	**17**	**5**	**2751**	**153**	**3**	**3.34**	**2.78**	**3.48**	**1467**	**.896**	**32.0**	**6**	**2**	**4**	....	**381**	**23**	**0**	**3.62**	**5.41**	**154**	**.851**	**24.3**
1988-89	**New York Islanders**	**NHL**	***50**	**18**	**24**	**3**	***2800**	**183**	**0**	**3.92**	**3.27**	**4.92**	**1457**	**.874**	**31.2**	....	....	....	....	....	....	....	....	....	....	....	....
	Los Angeles Kings	**NHL**	***16**	**10**	**4**	**2**	***974**	**47**	**1**	**2.90**	**2.41**	**2.78**	**491**	**.904**	**30.2**	**10**	**4**	**6**	....	**566**	**35**	**0**	**3.71**	**4.43**	**293**	**.881**	**31.1**
1989-90	**Los Angeles Kings**	**NHL**	**52**	**22**	**21**	**6**	**2860**	**194**	**2**	**4.07**	**3.46**	**5.15**	**1532**	**.873**	**32.1**	**9**	**4**	**4**	....	**539**	**39**	**0**	**4.34**	**6.39**	**265**	**.853**	**29.5**
1990-91	**Los Angeles Kings**	**NHL**	**47**	**26**	**13**	**6**	**2730**	**132**	**3**	**2.90**	**2.60**	**2.90**	**1321**	**.900**	**29.0**	**12**	**6**	**6**	....	**798**	**37**	**0**	**2.78**	**2.69**	**382**	**.903**	**28.7**
1991-92	**Los Angeles Kings**	**NHL**	**60**	**26**	**17**	**13**	**3509**	**197**	**1**	**3.37**	**3.02**	**3.46**	**1916**	**.897**	**32.8**	**6**	**2**	**4**	....	**355**	**22**	**0**	**3.72**	**4.57**	**179**	**.877**	**30.3**
1992-93	**Los Angeles Kings**	**NHL**	**50**	**18**	**21**	**6**	**2718**	**175**	**2**	**3.86**	**3.31**	**4.35**	**1552**	**.887**	**34.3**	**20**	**10**	**10**	....	**1261**	**74**	**0**	**3.52**	**3.97**	**656**	**.887**	**31.2**
1993-94	**Los Angeles Kings**	**NHL**	**64**	**22**	**31**	**7**	**3713**	**228**	**1**	**3.68**	**3.55**	**3.78**	**2219**	**.897**	**35.9**	....	....	....	....	....	....	....	....	....	....	....	....
1994-95	**Los Angeles Kings**	**NHL**	**35**	**14**	**13**	**5**	**1894**	**99**	**0**	**3.14**	**3.30**	**2.83**	**1099**	**.910**	**34.8**	....	....	....	....	....	....	....	....	....	....	....	....
1995-96	**Los Angeles Kings**	**NHL**	**36**	**7**	**15**	**10**	**2077**	**113**	**0**	**3.26**	**3.24**	**3.03**	**1214**	**.907**	**35.1**	....	....	....	....	....	....	....	....	....	....	....	....
	Phoenix Roadrunners	IHL	1	0	1	0	50	5	0	5.95	....	....	....	....	....	....	....	....	....	....	....	....	....	....	....	....	....
1996-97	**San Jose Sharks**	**NHL**	**48**	**16**	**24**	**5**	**2631**	**140**	**0**	**3.19**	**3.44**	**3.54**	**1263**	**.889**	**28.8**	....	....	....	....	....	....	....	....	....	....	....	....
1997-98	**San Jose Sharks**	**NHL**	**28**	**4**	**16**	**2**	**1360**	**62**	**1**	**2.74**	**3.27**	**2.83**	**600**	**.897**	**26.5**	**1**	**0**	**0**	....	**20**	**1**	**0**	**3.00**	**5.00**	**6**	**.833**	**18.0**
	NHL Totals		**677**	**271**	**265**	**88**	**38084**	**2174**	**17**	**3.43**	....	....	**20328**	**.893**	**32.0**	**85**	**36**	**46**	....	**5163**	**283**	**0**	**3.29**	....	**2607**	**.891**	**30.3**

WHL Second All-Star Team (1981) • CHL First All-Star Team (1982, 1983) • Shared Terry Sawchuk Trophy (fewest goals against - CHL) with Rob Holland (1982, 1983) • Won Tommy Ivan Trophy (MVP - CHL) (1983)

Traded to **LA Kings** by **NY Islanders** for Mark Fitzpatrick, Wayne McBean and future considerations (Doug Crossman, May 23, 1989) February 22, 1989. Signed as a free agent by **San Jose**, August 18, 1996.

• HURME, Jani

G – L. 6', 186 lbs. b: Turku, Finland, 1/7/1975. Ottawa's 2nd, 58th overall in 1997.

Season	Club	League	GP	W	L	T	Mins	GA	SO	Avg	AAvg	Eff	SA	S%	SAPG	GP	W	L	T	Mins	GA	SO	Avg	Eff	SA	S%	SAPG
1992-93	TPS Turku	Finland-Jr.	12	....	....	....	669	47	0	4.22	....	....	....	....	....	1	....	....	....	60	0	1	0.00	....	....	....	....
1993-94	TPS Turku	Finland	1	....	....	....	2	0	0	0.00	....	....	....	....	....	....	....	....	....	....	....	....	....	....	....	....	....
	Kiekko-67 Turku	Finland-2	3	....	....	....	190	7	0	2.21	....	....	....	....	....	....	....	....	....	....	....	....	....	....	....	....	....
	Kiekko-67 Turku	Finland-Jr.	18	....	....	....	....	....	....	3.16	....	....	....	....	....	....	....	....	....	....	....	....	....	....	....	....	....
1994-95	Kiekko-67 Turku	Finland-2	19	....	....	....	1049	53	....	3.03	....	....	....	....	....	3	....	....	....	180	6	....	2.00	....	....	....	....
	TPS Turku	Finland-Jr.	2	....	....	....	125	5	0	2.40	....	....	....	....	....	....	....	....	....	....	....	....	....	....	....	....	....
	Kiekko-67 Turku	Finland-Jr.	9	....	....	....	540	47	....	5.22	....	....	....	....	....	....	....	....	....	....	....	....	....	....	....	....	....
1995-96	TPS Turku	Finland	16	....	....	....	946	34	2	2.16	....	....	....	....	....	10	....	....	....	545	22	2	2.42	....	....	....	....
	Kiekko-67 Turku	Finland 2	16	....	....	....	968	39	1	2.42	....	....	....	....	....	....	....	....	....	....	....	....	....	....	....	....	....
	TPS Turku	Finland-Jr.	13	....	....	....	777	34	1	2.63	....	....	....	....	....	....	....	....	....	....	....	....	....	....	....	....	....
1996-97	TPS Turku	Finland	48	31	11	6	2917	101	6	2.08	....	....	....	....	....	12	6	6	....	722	39	0	3.24	....	....	....	....
	Finland	WC-A	DID NOT PLAY – SPARE GOALTENDER																								
1997-98	Detroit Vipers	IHL	6	2	2	2	290	20	0	4.13	....	....	....	....	....	....	....	....	....	....	....	....	....	....	....	....	....
	Indianapolis Ice	IHL	29	11	11	3	1506	83	1	3.30	....	....	....	....	....	3	1	0	....	129	10	0	4.62	....	....	....	....
1998-99	Detroit Vipers	IHL	12	7	3	1	643	26	1	2.43	....	....	....	....	....	....	....	....	....	....	....	....	....	....	....	....	....
	Cincinnati Cyclones	IHL	26	14	9	2	1428	81	0	3.40	....	....	....	....	....	....	....	....	....	....	....	....	....	....	....	....	....
99-2000	**Ottawa Senators**	**NHL**	**1**	**1**	**0**	**0**	**60**	**2**	**0**	**2.00**	**2.28**	**2.11**	**19**	**.895**	**19.0**	....	....	....	....	....	....	....	....	....	....	....	....
	Grand Rapids Griffins	IHL	52	29	15	4	2948	107	4	2.18	....	....	....	....	....	*17	*10	7	....	*1028	37	1	2.16	....	....	....	....
	NHL Totals		**1**	**1**	**0**	**0**	**60**	**2**	**0**	**2.00**	....	....	**19**	**.895**	**19.0**	....	....	....	....	....	....	....	....	....	....	....	....

IHL Second All-Star Team (2000)

• ING, Peter

Peter A. G – L. 6'2", 170 lbs. b: Toronto, Ont., 4/28/1969. Toronto's 3rd, 48th overall in 1988.

Season	Club	League	GP	W	L	T	Mins	GA	SO	Avg	AAvg	Eff	SA	S%	SAPG	GP	W	L	T	Mins	GA	SO	Avg	Eff	SA	S%	SAPG
1985-86	Toronto Midget Marlboros	MTHL	35	....	....	....	1800	91	4	3.03	....	....	....	....	....	....	....	....	....	....	....	....	....	....	....	....	....
	Markham Waxers	OJHL	DID NOT PLAY – SPARE GOALTENDER													....	....	....	....	....	....	....	....	....	....	....	....
1986-87	Windsor Spitfires	OHL	28	13	11	3	1615	105	0	3.90	....	....	....	....	....	5	4	0	0	161	9	0	3.35	....	....	....	....
1987-88	Windsor Spitfires	OHL	43	30	7	1	2422	125	2	3.10	....	....	....	....	....	3	2	0	0	225	7	0	1.87	....	....	....	....
1988-89	Windsor Spitfires	OHL	19	7	7	3	1043	76	*1	4.37	....	....	....	....	....	....	....	....	....	....	....	....	....	....	....	....	....
	London Knights	OHL	32	18	11	2	1848	104	*2	3.38	....	....	....	....	....	21	11	9	0	1093	82	0	4.50	....	....	....	....
1989-90	**Toronto Maple Leafs**	**NHL**	**3**	**0**	**2**	**1**	**182**	**18**	**0**	**5.93**	**5.03**	**9.98**	**107**	**.832**	**35.3**	....	....	....	....	....	....	....	....	....	....	....	....
	Newmarket Saints	AHL	48	16	19	12	2829	184	0	3.90	....	....	....	....	....	....	....	....	....	....	....	....	....	....	....	....	....
	Canada	Nat-Team	10	2	2	4	460	29	....	3.78	....	....	....	....	....	....	....	....	....	....	....	....	....	....	....	....	....
	London Knights	OHL	8	6	2	0	480	27	0	3.38	....	....	....	....	....	....	....	....	....	....	....	....	....	....	....	....	....
1990-91	**Toronto Maple Leafs**	**NHL**	**56**	**16**	**29**	**8**	**3126**	**200**	**1**	**3.84**	**3.47**	**4.48**	**1716**	**.883**	**32.9**	....	....	....	....	....	....	....	....	....	....	....	....
1991-92	**Edmonton Oilers**	**NHL**	**12**	**3**	**4**	**0**	**463**	**33**	**0**	**4.28**	**3.84**	**5.60**	**252**	**.869**	**32.7**	....	....	....	....	....	....	....	....	....	....	....	....
	Cape Breton Oilers	AHL	24	9	10	4	1411	92	0	3.91	....	....	....	....	....	1	0	1	0	60	9	0	9.00	....	....	....	....
1992-93	Detroit Falcons	ColHL	3	2	1	0	136	6	0	2.65	....	....	....	....	....	....	....	....	....	....	....	....	....	....	....	....	....
	San Diego Gulls	IHL	17	11	4	1	882	53	0	3.61	....	....	....	....	....	4	2	2	0	183	13	0	4.26	....	....	....	....
1993-94	**Detroit Red Wings**	**NHL**	**3**	**1**	**2**	**0**	**170**	**15**	**0**	**5.29**	**5.09**	**7.78**	**102**	**.853**	**36.0**	....	....	....	....	....	....	....	....	....	....	....	....
	Adirondack Red Wings	AHL	7	3	3	1	425	26	1	3.67	....	....	....	....	....	....	....	....	....	....	....	....	....	....	....	....	....
	Las Vegas Thunder	IHL	30	16	7	4	1627	91	0	3.36	....	....	....	....	....	2	0	1	0	40	4	0	5.87	....	....	....	....

Season	Club	League	GP	W	L	T	Mins	GA	SO	Avg	AAvg	Eff	SA	S%	SAPG	GP	W	L	T	Mins	GA	SO	Avg	Eff	SA	S%	SAPG
			REGULAR SEASON													PLAYOFFS											
1994-95	Fort Wayne Komets	IHL	36	15	18	2	2018	119	2	3.54	....	....	....	....	....	2	0	1	0	94	5	0	3.19	....	....	....	....
1995-96	Fort Wayne Komets	IHL	31	12	16	0	1674	109	2	3.91	....	....	....	....	....	....	....	....	....	....	....	....	....	....	....	....	....
	Cincinnati Cyclones	IHL	1	0	1	0	60	8	0	8.00	....	....	....	....	....	....	....	....	....	....	....	....	....	....	....	....	....
	NHL Totals		**74**	**20**	**37**	**9**	**3941**	**266**	**1**	**4.05**	....	....	**2177**	**.878**	**33.1**	....	....	....	....	....	....	....	....	....	....	....	....

Traded to **Edmonton** by **Toronto** with Vincent Damphousse, Scott Thornton, Luke Richardson, future considerations and cash for Grant Fuhr, Glenn Anderson and Craig Berube, September 19, 1991. Traded to **Detroit** by **Edmonton** for Detroit's 7th round choice (Chris Wickenheiser) in 1994 Entry Draft and future considerations, August 30, 1993.

• INNESS, Gary

Gary George G – L. 6', 195 lbs. b: Toronto, Ont., 5/28/1949.

Season	Club	League	GP	W	L	T	Mins	GA	SO	Avg	AAvg	Eff	SA	S%	SAPG	GP	W	L	T	Mins	GA	SO	Avg	Eff	SA	S%	SAPG
1968-69	McMaster University	OQUA	STATISTICS NOT AVAILABLE																								
1969-70	McMaster University	OQUA	STATISTICS NOT AVAILABLE																								
1970-71	McMaster University	OUAA	16	....	....	....	888	70	0	4.73	....	....	....	....	....	....	....	....	....	....	....	....	....	....	....	....	....
1971-72	McMaster University	OUAA	18	....	....	....	1060	59	0	3.44	....	....	....	....	....	....	....	....	....	....	....	....	....	....	....	....	....
1972-73	University of Toronto	OUAA	9	....	....	....	540	24	0	2.67	....	....	....	....	....	....	....	....	....	....	....	....	....	....	....	....	....
1973-74	**Pittsburgh Penguins**	**NHL**	**20**	**7**	**10**	**1**	**1032**	**56**	**0**	**3.26**	**3.15**	....	....	....	....	....	....	....	....	....	....	....	....	....	....	....	....
	Hershey Bears	AHL	20	11	4	4	1160	56	1	2.89	....	....	....	....	....	....	....	....	....	....	....	....	....	....	....	....	....
1974-75	**Pittsburgh Penguins**	**NHL**	**57**	**24**	**18**	**10**	**3122**	**161**	**2**	**3.09**	**2.78**	....	....	....	....	**9**	**5**	**4**	....	**540**	**24**	**0**	**2.67**	....	....	....	....
1975-76	Hershey Bears	AHL	2	0	2	0	119	9	0	4.54	....	....	....	....	....	....	....	....	....	....	....	....	....	....	....	....	....
	Pittsburgh Penguins	**NHL**	**23**	**8**	**9**	**2**	**1212**	**82**	**0**	**4.06**	**3.69**	....	....	....	....	....	....	....	....	....	....	....	....	....	....	....	....
	Philadelphia Flyers	**NHL**	**2**	**2**	**0**	**0**	**120**	**3**	**0**	**1.50**	**1.36**	....	....	....	....	....	....	....	....	....	....	....	....	....	....	....	....
1976-77	**Philadelphia Flyers**	**NHL**	**6**	**1**	**0**	**2**	**210**	**9**	**0**	**2.57**	**2.39**	....	....	....	....	....	....	....	....	....	....	....	....	....	....	....	....
1977-78	Indianapolis Racers	WHA	52	14	30	4	2850	200	0	4.21	....	....	....	....	....	....	....	....	....	....	....	....	....	....	....	....	....
1978-79	Indianapolis Racers	WHA	11	3	6	0	609	51	0	5.02	....	....	....	....	....	....	....	....	....	....	....	....	....	....	....	....	....
	Washington Capitals	**NHL**	**37**	**14**	**14**	**8**	**2107**	**130**	**0**	**3.70**	**3.28**	....	....	....	....	....	....	....	....	....	....	....	....	....	....	....	....
1979-80	**Washington Capitals**	**NHL**	**14**	**2**	**9**	**2**	**727**	**44**	**0**	**3.63**	**3.21**	....	....	....	....	....	....	....	....	....	....	....	....	....	....	....	....
	Hershey Bears	AHL	11	4	4	3	673	44	0	3.92	....	....	....	....	....	8	7	1	0	531	25	0	2.82	....	....	....	....
1980-81	**Washington Capitals**	**NHL**	**3**	**0**	**1**	**2**	**180**	**9**	**0**	**3.00**	**2.42**	....	....	....	....	....	....	....	....	....	....	....	....	....	....	....	....
	Hershey Bears	AHL	10	4	2	2	529	31	1	3.52	....	....	....	....	....	4	0	3	0	198	12	0	3.64	....	....	....	....
	NHL Totals		**162**	**58**	**61**	**27**	**8710**	**494**	**2**	**3.40**	....	....	....	....	....	**9**	**5**	**4**	....	**540**	**24**	**0**	**2.67**	....	....	....	....
	Other Major League Totals		63	17	36	4	3459	251	0	4.35	....	....	....	....	....	....	....	....	....	....	....	....	....	....	....	....	....

Signed as a free agent by **Pittsburgh**, June, 1973. Traded to **Philadelphia** by **Pittsburgh** with future considerations for Bobby Taylor and Ed Van Impe, March 9, 1976. Signed as a free agent by **Indianapolis** (WHA), September, 1977. Signed as a free agent by **Washington**, December 19, 1978.

• IRBE, Arturs

G – L. 5'8", 190 lbs. b: Riga, Latvia, 2/2/1967. Minnesota's 11th, 196th overall in 1989.

Season	Club	League	GP	W	L	T	Mins	GA	SO	Avg	AAvg	Eff	SA	S%	SAPG	GP	W	L	T	Mins	GA	SO	Avg	Eff	SA	S%	SAPG
1984-85	Dynamo Riga	USSR-Jr.	STATISTICS NOT AVAILABLE																								
	Soviet Union	EJC-A	5	....	....	....	300	5	....	1.00	....	....	....	....	....	....	....	....	....	....	....	....	....	....	....	....	....
1985-86	Dynamo Riga	USSR-Jr.	STATISTICS NOT AVAILABLE																								
1986-87	Dynamo Riga	USSR-Jr.	STATISTICS NOT AVAILABLE																								
	Dynamo Riga	USSR	2	....	....	....	27	1	0	2.22	....	....	....	....	....	....	....	....	....	....	....	....	....	....	....	....	....
1987-88	Dynamo Riga	USSR	34	....	....	....	1870	86	4	2.69	....	....	....	....	....	....	....	....	....	....	....	....	....	....	....	....	....
1988-89	Dynamo Riga	USSR	40	....	....	....	2460	116	4	2.85	....	....	....	....	....	....	....	....	....	....	....	....	....	....	....	....	....
	Dynamo Riga	Super-S	7	....	....	....	425	23	....	3.25	....	....	....	....	....	....	....	....	....	....	....	....	....	....	....	....	....
1989-90	Dynamo Riga	Fr-Tour	1	....	....	....	63	2	0	1.90	....	....	....	....	....	....	....	....	....	....	....	....	....	....	....	....	....
	Dynamo Riga	USSR	48	....	....	....	2880	115	2	2.42	....	....	....	....	....	....	....	....	....	....	....	....	....	....	....	....	....
	CSKA Moscow	Super-S	4	....	....	....	240	10	....	2.50	....	....	....	....	....	....	....	....	....	....	....	....	....	....	....	....	....
	Soviet Union	WEC-A	6	4	0	1	315	5	*1	0.95	....	....	....	....	....	....	....	....	....	....	....	....	....	....	....	....	....
1990-91	Dynamo Riga	Fr-Tour	1	1	0	0	60	4	0	4.00	....	....	....	....	....	....	....	....	....	....	....	....	....	....	....	....	....
	Dynamo Riga	USSR	46	....	....	....	2713	133	5	2.94	....	....	....	....	....	....	....	....	....	....	....	....	....	....	....	....	....
1991-92	**San Jose Sharks**	**NHL**	**13**	**2**	**6**	**3**	**645**	**48**	**0**	**4.47**	**4.01**	**5.88**	**365**	**.868**	**34.0**	....	....	....	....	....	....	....	....	....	....	....	....
	Kansas City Blades	IHL	32	24	7	1	1955	80	0	*2.46	....	....	....	....	....	*15	*12	3	....	914	44	0	*2.89	....	....	....	....
1992-93	**San Jose Sharks**	**NHL**	**36**	**7**	**26**	**0**	**2074**	**142**	**1**	**4.11**	**3.53**	**4.67**	**1250**	**.886**	**36.2**	....	....	....	....	....	....	....	....	....	....	....	....
	Kansas City Blades	IHL	6	3	3	0	364	20	0	3.30	....	....	....	....	....	....	....	....	....	....	....	....	....	....	....	....	....
1993-94	**San Jose Sharks**	**NHL**	***74**	**30**	**28**	**16**	***4412**	**209**	**3**	**2.84**	**2.72**	**2.88**	**2064**	**.899**	**28.1**	**14**	**7**	**7**	....	**806**	**50**	**0**	**3.72**	**4.66**	**399**	**.875**	**29.7**
1994-95	**San Jose Sharks**	**NHL**	**38**	**14**	**19**	**3**	**2043**	**111**	**4**	**3.26**	**3.43**	**3.43**	**1056**	**.895**	**31.0**	**6**	**2**	**4**	....	**316**	**27**	**0**	**5.13**	**7.53**	**184**	**.853**	**34.9**
1995-96	**San Jose Sharks**	**NHL**	**22**	**4**	**12**	**4**	**1112**	**85**	**0**	**4.59**	**4.58**	**6.43**	**607**	**.860**	**32.8**	....	....	....	....	....	....	....	....	....	....	....	....
	Kansas City Blades	IHL	4	1	2	1	226	16	0	4.24	....	....	....	....	....	....	....	....	....	....	....	....	....	....	....	....	....
	Latvia	WC-B	4	3	0	1	240	7	0	1.75	....	....	....	....	....	....	....	....	....	....	....	....	....	....	....	....	....
1996-97	**Dallas Stars**	**NHL**	**35**	**17**	**12**	**3**	**1965**	**88**	**3**	**2.69**	**2.89**	**2.87**	**825**	**.893**	**25.2**	**1**	**0**	**0**	....	**13**	**0**	**0**	**0.00**	**0.00**	**4**	**1.000**	**18.5**
	Latvia	WC-A	5	4	0	1	300	10	1	2.00	....	....	....	....	....	....	....	....	....	....	....	....	....	....	....	....	....
1997-98	**Vancouver Canucks**	**NHL**	**41**	**14**	**11**	**6**	**1999**	**91**	**2**	**2.73**	**3.26**	**2.53**	**982**	**.907**	**29.5**	....	....	....	....	....	....	....	....	....	....	....	....
	Latvia	WC-A	6	3	2	1	358	17	1	2.85	....	....	....	....	....	....	....	....	....	....	....	....	....	....	....	....	....
1998-99	**Carolina Hurricanes**	**NHL**	**62**	**27**	**20**	**12**	**3643**	**135**	**6**	**2.22**	**2.63**	**1.71**	**1753**	**.923**	**28.9**	**6**	**2**	**4**	....	**408**	**15**	**0**	**2.21**	**1.83**	**181**	**.917**	**26.6**
	Latvia	WC-A	4	....	....	....	238	12	....	3.03	....	....	....	....	....	....	....	....	....	....	....	....	....	....	....	....	....
99-2000	**Carolina Hurricanes**	**NHL**	***75**	**34**	**28**	**9**	**4345**	**175**	**5**	**2.42**	**2.76**	**2.28**	**1858**	**.906**	**25.7**	....	....	....	....	....	....	....	....	....	....	....	....
	Latvia	WC-A	5	3	1	1	420	17	0	2.43	....	....	....	....	....	....	....	....	....	....	....	....	....	....	....	....	....
	NHL Totals		**396**	**149**	**162**	**56**	**22238**	**1084**	**24**	**2.92**	....	....	**10760**	**.899**	**29.0**	**27**	**11**	**15**	....	**1543**	**92**	**0**	**3.58**	....	**768**	**.880**	**29.9**

Named Best Goaltender at EJC-A (1985) • USSR Rookie-of-the-Year (1988) • Named Best Goaltender at WEC-A (1990) • IHL First All-Star Team (1992) • Shared James Norris Memorial Trophy (fewest goals against - IHL) with Wade Flaherty (1992) • Played in NHL All-Star Game (1994, 1999)

Claimed by **San Jose** from **Minnesota** in Dispersal Draft, May 30, 1991. Signed as a free agent by **Dallas**, August 19, 1996. Signed as a free agent by **Vancouver**, August 25, 1997. Signed as a free agent by **Carolina**, September 14, 1998.

• IRELAND, Randy

G – L. 6', 165 lbs. b: Rosetown, Sask., 4/5/1957. Buffalo's 5th, 82nd overall in 1978.

Season	Club	League	GP	W	L	T	Mins	GA	SO	Avg	AAvg	Eff	SA	S%	SAPG	GP	W	L	T	Mins	GA	SO	Avg	Eff	SA	S%	SAPG
1972-73	Estevan Bruins	SJHL	STATISTICS NOT AVAILABLE																								
1973-74	Saskatoon Blades	WCJHL	35	16	14	2	1883	124	0	3.95	....	....	....	....	....	1	0	1	0	20	3	0	9.00	....	....	....	....
1974-75	Saskatoon Blades	WCJHL	28	12	10	5	1654	114	1	4.14	....	....	....	....	....	7	4	1	0	420	16	1	2.78	....	....	....	....
1975-76	Saskatoon Blades	WCJHL	40	15	13	8	2218	148	0	4.00	....	....	....	....	....	15	....	....	....	785	50	0	3.82	....	....	....	....
1976-77	Saskatoon Blades	WCJHL	1	0	1	0	60	7	0	7.00	....	....	....	....	....	....	....	....	....	....	....	....	....	....	....	....	....
	Portland Winter Hawks	WCJHL	46	....	....	....	2589	162	3	3.76	....	....	....	....	....	10	....	....	....	611	27	*1	*2.65	....	....	....	....
1977-78	Flint Generals	IHL	45	....	....	....	2617	205	0	4.70	....	....	....	....	....	3	....	....	....	119	8	0	4.03	....	....	....	....
1978-79	**Buffalo Sabres**	**NHL**	**2**	**0**	**0**	**0**	**30**	**3**	**0**	**6.00**	**5.31**	....	....	....	....	....	....	....	....	....	....	....	....	....	....	....	....
	Hershey Bears	AHL	29	9	16	1	1477	113	0	4.59	....	....	....	....	....	....	....	....	....	....	....	....	....	....	....	....	....
1979-80	Rochester Americans	AHL	29	9	10	5	1559	94	0	3.62	....	....	....	....	....	1	0	1	0	60	6	0	6.00	....	....	....	....
1980-81	Oklahoma City Stars	CHL	2	2	0	0	120	8	0	4.00	....	....	....	....	....	....	....	....	....	....	....	....	....	....	....	....	....
	Baltimore Clippers	EHL	33	....	....	....	1776	105	2	3.55	....	....	....	....	....	....	....	....	....	....	....	....	....	....	....	....	....
	Richmond Rifles	EHL	13	....	....	....	770	48	0	3.74	....	....	....	....	....	4	....	....	....	240	23	0	5.75	....	....	....	....
1981-82	Mohawk Valley Stars	ACHL	25	....	....	....	1234	89	0	4.33	....	....	....	....	....	8	....	....	....	467	29	0	3.73	....	....	....	....
1982-83	Mohawk Valley Stars	ACHL	38	....	....	....	2044	148	1	4.39	....	....	....	....	....	9	....	....	....	*544	33	0	3.63	....	....	....	....
	NHL Totals		**2**	**0**	**0**	**0**	**30**	**3**	**0**	**6.00**	....	....	....	....	....	....	....	....	....	....	....	....	....	....	....	....	....

• Re-entered NHL draft. Originally Chicago's 3rd choice, 60th overall, in 1977 Amateur Draft.

Traded to **Richmond** (EHL) by **Baltimore** (EHL) with Paul Pacific for Dale Yakiwchuk, Jim Lockhurst and Gord Gejdos, February, 1981.

• IRONS, Robbie

Robert Richard G – L. 5'8", 150 lbs. b: Toronto, Ont., 11/19/1946.

Season	Club	League	GP	W	L	T	Mins	GA	SO	Avg	AAvg	Eff	SA	S%	SAPG	GP	W	L	T	Mins	GA	SO	Avg	Eff	SA	S%	SAPG
1964-65	Etobicoke Indians	OHA-B	STATISTICS NOT AVAILABLE																								
1965-66	Etobicoke Indians	OHA-B	STATISTICS NOT AVAILABLE																								
1966-67	Kitchener Rangers	OHA-Jr.	33	....	....	....	1940	95	*3	2.94	....	....	....	....	....	13	....	....	....	780	49	0	3.77	....	....	....	....
1967-68	Fort Wayne Komets	IHL	43	....	....	....	2398	134	1	3.35	....	....	....	....	....	5	1	3	0	262	19	0	4.35	....	....	....	....
1968-69	Kansas City Blues	CHL	24	....	....	....	1309	83	0	3.80	....	....	....	....	....	....	....	....	....	....	....	....	....	....	....	....	....
	St. Louis Blues	**NHL**	**1**	**0**	**0**	**0**	**3**	**0**	**0**	**0.00**	**0.00**	....	....	....	....	....	....	....	....	....	....	....	....	....	....	....	....

			REGULAR SEASON													PLAYOFFS											
Season	Club	League	GP	W	L	T	Mins	GA	SO	Avg	AAvg	Eff	SA	S%	SAPG	GP	W	L	T	Mins	GA	SO	Avg	Eff	SA	S%	SAPG
1969-70	Kansas City Blues	CHL	30	10	16	4	1800	104	2	3.47	....	....	....	....	....	....	....	....	....	....	....	....	....	....	....	....	....
1970-71	Kansas City Blues	CHL	6	....	....	....	360	23	0	3.83	....	....	....	....	....	....	....	....	....	....	....	....	....	....	....	....	....
	Fort Wayne Komets	IHL	31	....	....	....	1811	80	1	2.25	....	....	....	....	....	4	0	4	0	240	22	0	5.50	....	....	....	....
1971-72	Fort Wayne Komets	IHL	21	....	....	....	1251	83	1	4.00	....	....	....	....	....	....	....	....	....	....	....	....	....	....	....	....	....
1972-73	Fort Wayne Komets	IHL	46	....	....	....	2737	132	2	2.89	....	....	....	....	....	1	1	0	0	60	0	1	0.00	....	....	....	....
1973-74	Fort Wayne Komets	IHL	47	....	....	....	2701	148	2	3.29	....	....	....	....	....	....	....	....	....	....	....	....	....	....	....	....	....
1974-75	Fort Wayne Komets	IHL	46	....	....	....	2713	146	2	3.27	....	....	....	....	....	....	....	....	....	....	....	....	....	....	....	....	....
1975-76	Fort Wayne Komets	IHL	63	....	....	....	3321	199	1	3.60	....	....	....	....	....	9	5	4	0	530	39	0	5.44	....	....	....	....
1976-77	Fort Wayne Komets	IHL	41	....	....	....	2248	141	1	3.70	....	....	....	....	....	....	....	....	....	....	....	....	....	....	....	....	....
1977-78	Fort Wayne Komets	IHL	39	....	....	....	2152	129	0	3.60	....	....	....	....	....	7	....	....	....	319	20	0	3.76	....	....	....	....
1978-79	Fort Wayne Komets	IHL	54	....	....	....	2490	193	1	3.90	....	....	....	....	....	13	7	6	0	780	56	0	4.29	....	....	....	....
1979-80	Fort Wayne Komets	IHL	41	....	....	....	2188	147	1	4.03	....	....	....	....	....	14	....	....	....	806	44	1	3.28	....	....	....	....
1980-81	Fort Wayne Komets	IHL	51	....	....	....	2719	168	0	3.71	....	....	....	....	....	11	....	....	....	633	47	0	4.45	....	....	....	....
	NHL Totals		**1**	**0**	**0**	**0**	**3**	**0**	**0**	**0.00**	....	....	....	....	....	....	....	....	....	....	....	....	....	....	....	....	....

Shared James Norris Memorial Trophy (fewest goals against - IHL) with Don Atchison (1973) • IHL Second All-Star Team (1981)

Traded to **St. Louis** by **NY Rangers** with Camille Henry and Bill Plager for Don Caley and Wayne Rivers, June 13, 1968. • Replaced Glenn Hall in 1st period vs. NY Rangers after Hall was given a game misconduct, November 13, 1968. Shares NHL record (w/ Christian Soucy) for having shortest career (three minutes) in league history.

• IRONSTONE, Joe

Joseph "Kelly" G – R. 5'6", 180 lbs. b: Sudbury, Ont., 6/28/1898 d: 1972.

Season	Club	League	GP	W	L	T	Mins	GA	SO	Avg	AAvg	Eff	SA	S%	SAPG	GP	W	L	T	Mins	GA	SO	Avg	Eff	SA	S%	SAPG
1921-22	Sudbury Wolves	NOHA	6	3	2	0	350	12	0	2.06	....	....	....	....	....	....	....	....	....	....	....	....	....	....	....	....	....
	Sudbury Legion	NOHA	3	*3	0	0	180	4	0	1.33	....	....	....	....	....	2	0	1	1	120	5	0	2.50	....	....	....	....
1922-23	Sudbury Wolves	NOHA	8	4	4	0	478	23	*2	2.89	....	....	....	....	....	....	....	....	....	....	....	....	....	....	....	....	....
1923-24	Sudbury Wolves	NOHA	STATISTICS NOT AVAILABLE																								
1924-25	**Ottawa Senators**	**NHL**	DID NOT PLAY – SPARE GOALTENDER																								
1925-26	**New York Americans**	**NHL**	**1**	**0**	**0**	**0**	**40**	**3**	**0**	**4.50**	**5.96**	....	....	....	....	....	....	....	....	....	....	....	....	....	....	....	....
1926-27	Niagara Falls Cataracts	Can-Pro	23	6	15	1	1429	64	1	2.69	....	....	....	....	....	....	....	....	....	....	....	....	....	....	....	....	....
1927-28	Niagara Falls Cataracts	Can-Pro	14	3	6	5	890	33	1	2.22	....	....	....	....	....	....	....	....	....	....	....	....	....	....	....	....	....
	Toronto Ravinas	Can-Pro	26	13	10	3	1610	46	7	1.77	....	....	....	....	....	2	0	2	0	120	11	0	5.50	....	....	....	....
	Toronto Maple Leafs	**NHL**	**1**	**0**	**0**	**1**	**70**	**0**	**1**	**0.00**	**0.00**	....	....	....	....	....	....	....	....	....	....	....	....	....	....	....	....
1928-29	London Panthers	Can-Pro	42	16	22	4	2580	109	3	2.53	....	....	....	....	....	....	....	....	....	....	....	....	....	....	....	....	....
1929-30	London Panthers	IHL	10	....	....	....	350	35	0	3.76	....	....	....	....	....	....	....	....	....	....	....	....	....	....	....	....	....
	Kitchener Flying Dutchmen	Can-Pro	15	7	8	0	910	39	*2	*2.57	....	....	....	....	....	....	....	....	....	....	....	....	....	....	....	....	....
1930-31	Marquette Iron Rangers	NMHL	STATISTICS NOT AVAILABLE																								
	Guelph Maple Leafs	OPHL	19	8	10	1	1180	53	1	2.69	....	....	....	....	....	....	....	....	....	....	....	....	....	....	....	....	....
	Syracuse Stars	IHL	13	1	10	2	830	51	1	3.69	....	....	....	....	....	....	....	....	....	....	....	....	....	....	....	....	....
1931-32			STATISTICS NOT AVAILABLE																								
1932-33			STATISTICS NOT AVAILABLE																								
1933-34	Sudbury Legion	NOHA	STATISTICS NOT AVAILABLE																								
1934-35	Sudbury Legion	NOHA	10	....	....	....	600	42	0	4.20	....	....	....	....	....	....	....	....	....	....	....	....	....	....	....	....	....
1935-36	Falconbridge Falcons	NOHA	6	....	....	....	360	12	*1	*2.00	....	....	....	....	....	3	....	....	....	180	9	0	*3.00	....	....	....	....
	Sudbury Wolves	NOHA	1	0	1	0	60	6	0	6.00	....	....	....	....	....	....	....	....	....	....	....	....	....	....	....	....	....
	NHL Totals		**2**	**0**	**0**	**1**	**110**	**3**	**1**	**1.64**	....	....	....	....	....	....	....	....	....	....	....	....	....	....	....	....	....

Signed as a free agent by **Ottawa**, October 30, 1924. Signed as a free agent by **NY Americans**, October 30, 1925. Traded to **Toronto** (Can-Pro) by **NY Americans** for cash, January 6, 1928. Loaned to **Toronto** by **Toronto** (Can-Pro) to replace injured John Ross Roach, March 3, 1928. (Toronto 0, NY Americans 0). Claimed by **NY Americans** from **Toronto** (Can-Pro) in Inter-League Draft, May 12, 1928. Traded to **London** (Can-Pro) by **NY Americans** for cash, October 30, 1928. Loaned to **Marquette** (NMHL) by **London** (IHL), January 3, 1930. Loan transferred to **Kitchener** (Can-Pro) from **Marquette** (NMHL) by **London** (IHL), January 27, 1930. Traded to **Syracuse** (IHL) by **Guelph** (OPHL) for cash, February 12, 1931.

• JABLONSKI, Pat

Patrick D. G – R. 6', 180 lbs. b: Toledo, OH, 6/20/1967. St. Louis' 6th, 138th overall in 1985.

Season	Club	League	GP	W	L	T	Mins	GA	SO	Avg	AAvg	Eff	SA	S%	SAPG	GP	W	L	T	Mins	GA	SO	Avg	Eff	SA	S%	SAPG
1984-85	Detroit Compuware	NAJHL	29	....	....	....	1483	95	0	3.84	....	....	....	....	....	....	....	....	....	....	....	....	....	....	....	....	....
1985-86	Windsor Spitfires	OHL	29	6	16	4	1600	119	1	4.46	....	....	....	....	....	6	0	3	....	263	20	0	4.56	....	....	....	....
1986-87	Windsor Spitfires	OHL	41	22	14	2	2328	128	*3	3.30	....	....	....	....	....	12	8	4	....	710	38	0	3.21	....	....	....	....
	United States	WJC-A	4	....	....	....	200	13	....	3.90	....	....	....	....	....	....	....	....	....	....	....	....	....	....	....	....	....
1987-88	Peoria Rivermen	IHL	5	2	2	1	285	17	0	3.58	....	....	....	....	....	....	....	....	....	....	....	....	....	....	....	....	....
	Windsor Spitfires	OHL	18	14	3	0	994	48	2	2.90	....	....	....	....	....	9	*8	0	....	537	28	0	3.13	....	....	....	....
	Windsor Spitfires	Mem-Cup	4	3	1	0	240	16	0	4.00	....	....	....	....	....	....	....	....	....	....	....	....	....	....	....	....	....
1988-89	Peoria Rivermen	IHL	35	11	20	0	2051	163	1	4.77	....	....	....	....	....	3	0	2	....	130	13	0	6.00	....	....	....	....
1989-90	**St. Louis Blues**	**NHL**	**4**	**0**	**3**	**0**	**208**	**17**	**0**	**4.90**	**4.15**	**8.50**	**98**	**.827**	**28.3**	....	....	....	....	....	....	....	....	....	....	....	....
	Peoria Rivermen	IHL	36	14	17	4	2023	165	0	4.89	....	....	....	....	....	4	1	3	....	223	19	0	5.11	....	....	....	....
1990-91	**St. Louis Blues**	**NHL**	**8**	**2**	**3**	**3**	**492**	**25**	**0**	**3.05**	**2.74**	**3.34**	**228**	**.890**	**27.8**	**3**	**0**	**0**	....	**90**	**5**	**0**	**3.33**	**4.76**	**35**	**.857**	**23.3**
	Peoria Rivermen	IHL	29	23	3	2	1738	87	0	3.00	....	....	....	....	....	10	7	2	....	532	23	0	2.59	....	....	....	....
1991-92	United States	Can-Cup	DID NOT PLAY – SPARE GOALTENDER																								
	St. Louis Blues	**NHL**	**10**	**3**	**6**	**0**	**468**	**38**	**0**	**4.87**	**4.37**	**7.15**	**259**	**.853**	**33.2**	....	....	....	....	....	....	....	....	....	....	....	....
	Peoria Rivermen	IHL	8	6	1	1	493	29	1	3.53	....	....	....	....	....	....	....	....	....	....	....	....	....	....	....	....	....
1992-93	**Tampa Bay Lightning**	**NHL**	**43**	**8**	**24**	**4**	**2268**	**150**	**1**	**3.97**	**3.41**	**4.99**	**1194**	**.874**	**31.6**	....	....	....	....	....	....	....	....	....	....	....	....
	United States	WC-A	2	....	....	....	62	1	....	0.96	....	....	....	....	....	....	....	....	....	....	....	....	....	....	....	....	....
1993-94	**Tampa Bay Lightning**	**NHL**	**15**	**5**	**6**	**3**	**834**	**54**	**0**	**3.88**	**3.73**	**5.60**	**374**	**.856**	**26.9**	....	....	....	....	....	....	....	....	....	....	....	....
	St. John's Maple Leafs	AHL	16	12	3	1	962	49	1	3.05	....	....	....	....	....	11	6	5	....	676	36	0	3.19	....	....	....	....
1994-95	Chicago Wolves	IHL	4	0	4	0	216	17	0	4.71	....	....	....	....	....	....	....	....	....	....	....	....	....	....	....	....	....
	Houston Aeros	IHL	3	1	1	1	179	9	0	3.01	....	....	....	....	....	....	....	....	....	....	....	....	....	....	....	....	....
	United States	WC-A	6	....	....	....	360	15	....	2.50	....	....	....	....	....	....	....	....	....	....	....	....	....	....	....	....	....
1995-96	**St. Louis Blues**	**NHL**	**1**	**0**	**0**	**0**	**8**	**1**	**0**	**7.50**	**7.46**	**15.00**	**5**	**.800**	**37.5**	....	....	....	....	....	....	....	....	....	....	....	....
	Montreal Canadiens	**NHL**	**23**	**5**	**9**	**6**	**1264**	**62**	**0**	**2.94**	**2.92**	**2.70**	**676**	**.908**	**32.1**	**1**	**0**	**0**	....	**49**	**1**	**0**	**1.22**	**0.72**	**17**	**.941**	**20.8**
1996-97	**Montreal Canadiens**	**NHL**	**17**	**4**	**6**	**2**	**754**	**50**	**0**	**3.98**	**4.29**	**4.54**	**438**	**.886**	**34.9**	....	....	....	....	....	....	....	....	....	....	....	....
	Phoenix Coyotes	**NHL**	**2**	**0**	**1**	**0**	**59**	**2**	**0**	**2.03**	**2.18**	**1.69**	**24**	**.917**	**24.4**	....	....	....	....	....	....	....	....	....	....	....	....
1997-98	**Carolina Hurricanes**	**NHL**	**5**	**1**	**4**	**0**	**279**	**14**	**0**	**3.01**	**3.59**	**3.66**	**115**	**.878**	**24.7**	....	....	....	....	....	....	....	....	....	....	....	....
	Cleveland Lumberjacks	IHL	34	13	13	6	1950	98	0	3.01	....	....	....	....	....	....	....	....	....	....	....	....	....	....	....	....	....
	Quebec Rafales	IHL	7	3	3	0	368	21	0	3.42	....	....	....	....	....	....	....	....	....	....	....	....	....	....	....	....	....
1998-99	Chicago Wolves	IHL	36	22	7	7	2119	106	1	3.00	....	....	....	....	....	3	2	1	....	185	11	0	3.57	....	....	....	....
99-2000	Vastra Frolunda	Sweden	27	....	....	....	1624	65	4	2.40	....	....	....	....	....	5	....	....	....	298	18	0	3.62	....	....	....	....
	NHL Totals		**128**	**28**	**62**	**18**	**6634**	**413**	**1**	**3.74**	....	....	**3411**	**.879**	**30.9**	**4**	**0**	**0**	....	**139**	**6**	**0**	**2.59**	....	**52**	**.885**	**22.4**

Shared James Norris Memorial Trophy (fewest goals against - IHL) with Guy Hebert (1991)

Traded to **Tampa Bay** by **St. Louis** with Steve Tuttle, Darin Kimble and Rob Robinson for future considerations, June 19, 1992. Traded to **Toronto** by **Tampa Bay** for cash, February 21, 1994. Claimed by **St. Louis** from **Toronto** in NHL Waiver Draft, October 2, 1995. Traded to **Montreal** by **St. Louis** for J.J. Daigneault, November 7, 1995. Traded to **Phoenix** by **Montreal** for Steve Cheredaryk, March 18, 1997. Signed as a free agent by **Carolina**, August 12, 1997.

• JACKSON, Doug

G – L. 5'10", 150 lbs. b: Winnipeg, Man., 12/12/1924.

Season	Club	League	GP	W	L	T	Mins	GA	SO	Avg	AAvg	Eff	SA	S%	SAPG	GP	W	L	T	Mins	GA	SO	Avg	Eff	SA	S%	SAPG
1938-39	Winnipeg Excelsiors	MAHA	17	....	....	....	1020	51	*6	3.00	....	....	....	....	....	....	....	....	....	....	....	....	....	....	....	....	....
1939-40	Winnipeg Excelsiors	MAHA	STATISTICS NOT AVAILABLE																								
1940-41	Winnipeg JV Rangers	MAHA	STATISTICS NOT AVAILABLE																								
1941-42	Winnipeg JV Rangers	MAHA	STATISTICS NOT AVAILABLE																								
	Winnipeg Rangers	MJHL	2	....	....	....	120	13	0	6.50	....	....	....	....	....	....	....	....	....	....	....	....	....	....	....	....	....
	Winnipeg Rangers	Mem-Cup	13	10	3	0	780	62	0	4.77	....	....	....	....	....	....	....	....	....	....	....	....	....	....	....	....	....
1942-43	Winnipeg Rangers	MJHL	13	....	....	....	780	51	0	*3.92	....	....	....	....	....	6	....	....	....	360	23	0	3.83	....	....	....	....
1943-44	Montreal Royals	QJHL	2	2	0	0	120	5	0	2.50	....	....	....	....	....	4	*4	0	0	240	11	0	2.75	....	....	....	....
1944-45			MILITARY SERVICE																								
1945-46	Kansas City Pla-Mors	USHL	52	....	....	....	3120	169	2	3.25	....	....	....	....	....	12	8	4	0	720	33	....	2.75	....	....	....	....
1946-47	Kansas City Pla-Mors	USHL	54	26	17	11	3240	177	3	3.27	....	....	....	....	....	12	10	2	0	720	21	*1	*1.75	....	....	....	....
1947-48	**Chicago Black Hawks**	**NHL**	**6**	**2**	**3**	**1**	**360**	**42**	**0**	**7.00**	**7.46**	....	....	....	....	....	....	....	....	....	....	....	....	....	....	....	....
	Kansas City Pla-Mors	USHL	59	32	25	2	3540	220	*4	3.72	....	....	....	....	....	7	3	4	0	434	23	0	3.18	....	....	....	....

Season	Club	League	REGULAR SEASON													PLAYOFFS											
			GP	W	L	T	Mins	GA	SO	Avg	AAvg	Eff	SA	S%	SAPG	GP	W	L	T	Mins	GA	SO	Avg	Eff	SA	S%	SAPG
1948-49	Vancouver Canucks	PCHL	66	31	29	6	3960	241	1	3.65	....	....	....	....	....	3	0	3	0	203	14	0	4.14	....	....	....	....
1949-50	Los Angeles Monarchs	PCHL	8	4	2	2	480	38	0	4.75	....	....	....	....	....	....	....	....	....	....	....	....	....	....	....	....	....
	San Francisco Shamrocks	PCHL	5	1	2	2	300	20	0	4.00	....	....	....	....	....	....	....	....	....	....	....	....	....	....	....	....	....
	Victoria Cougars	PCHL	1	0	1	0	60	11	0	11.00	....	....	....	....	....	....	....	....	....	....	....	....	....	....	....	....	....
1950-51			REINSTATED AS AN AMATEUR																								
1951-52	Nanaimo Clippers	PCSHL	41	....	....	....	2460	147	1	3.65	....	....	....	....	....	6	4	2	0	360	19	0	3.17	....	....	....	....
	NHL Totals		**6**	**2**	**3**	**1**	**360**	**42**	**0**	**7.00**	....	....	....	....	....	....	....	....	....	....	....	....	....	....	....	....	....

USHL Second All-Star Team (1946)

Traded to **Vancouver** (PCHL) by **Chicago** for cash, May 31, 1948.

• JACKSON, Percy

G – L. 5'9", 165 lbs. b: Canmore, Alta., 9/21/1907.

Season	Club	League	GP	W	L	T	Mins	GA	SO	Avg	AAvg	Eff	SA	S%	SAPG	GP	W	L	T	Mins	GA	SO	Avg	Eff	SA	S%	SAPG
1926-27	Trail Smoke Eaters	WRHL	STATISTICS NOT AVAILABLE																								
1927-28	Trail Smoke Eaters	WRHL	STATISTICS NOT AVAILABLE																								
1928-29	Vancouver Lions	PCHL	35	*25	7	3	2160	51	*11	*1.42	....	....	....	....	....	3	*3	0	0	180	3	1	*1.00	....	....	....	....
1929-30	Vancouver Lions	PCHL	36	*20	8	8	2160	46	10	1.28	....	....	....	....	....	4	*3	1	0	240	6	0	*1.50	....	....	....	....
1930-31	Vancouver Lions	PCHL	34	14	12	8	2040	56	7	1.65	....	....	....	....	....	4	*3	1	0	240	7	*2	1.75	....	....	....	....
1931-32	**Boston Bruins**	**NHL**	**4**	**1**	**1**	**1**	**232**	**8**	**0**	**2.07**	**2.53**	....	....	....	....	....	....	....	....	....	....	....	....	....	....	....	....
	Boston Cubs	Can-Am	25	14	9	2	1540	62	2	2.42	....	....	....	....	....	5	1	4	0	300	15	0	3.00	....	....	....	....
1932-33	Boston Cubs	Can-Am	45	21	16	8	2800	105	2	2.25	....	....	....	....	....	7	*5	2	0	420	14	0	*2.00	....	....	....	....
1933-34	Boston Cubs	Can-Am	41	18	16	7	2560	104	4	2.44	....	....	....	....	....	5	2	3	0	300	13	0	2.60	....	....	....	....
	New York Americans	**NHL**	**1**	**0**	**1**	**0**	**60**	**9**	**0**	**9.00**	**11.45**	....	....	....	....	....	....	....	....	....	....	....	....	....	....	....	....
1934-35	**New York Rangers**	**NHL**	**1**	**0**	**1**	**0**	**60**	**8**	**0**	**8.00**	**9.74**	....	....	....	....	....	....	....	....	....	....	....	....	....	....	....	....
	Providence Reds	Can-Am	1	1	0	0	60	2	0	2.00	....	....	....	....	....	....	....	....	....	....	....	....	....	....	....	....	....
	Boston Cubs	Can-Am	39	*24	10	5	2340	105	1	2.69	....	....	....	....	....	3	*3	0	0	180	2	*1	*0.67	....	....	....	....
1935-36	**Boston Bruins**	**NHL**	**1**	**0**	**0**	**0**	**40**	**1**	**0**	**1.50**	**2.11**	....	....	....	....	....	....	....	....	....	....	....	....	....	....	....	....
	Boston Cubs	Can-Am	46	20	22	4	2840	129	0	2.73	....	....	....	....	....	....	....	....	....	....	....	....	....	....	....	....	....
	Philadelphia Ramblers	Can-Am	1	0	1	0	60	6	0	6.00	....	....	....	....	....	....	....	....	....	....	....	....	....	....	....	....	....
1936-37	Vancouver Lions	PCHL	40	....	....	....	2400	105	3	2.62	....	....	....	....	....	3	1	2	0	180	6	0	2.00	....	....	....	....
1937-38	Vancouver Lions	PCHL	42	19	18	5	2580	91	5	2.12	....	....	....	....	....	6	*4	2	0	374	8	*2	*1.28	....	....	....	....
1938-39	Vancouver Lions	PCHL	48	15	24	9	2880	195	0	4.06	....	....	....	....	....	2	0	2	0	120	10	0	5.00	....	....	....	....
1939-40	Vancouver Lions	PCHL	40	*22	16	2	2400	125	1	3.12	....	....	....	....	....	5	*4	1	0	300	12	0	*2.40	....	....	....	....
1940-41	Portland Buckaroos	PCHL	1	1	0	0	60	1	0	1.00	....	....	....	....	....	....	....	....	....	....	....	....	....	....	....	....	....
	Vancouver Lions	PCHL	48	22	21	5	2880	145	3	3.02	....	....	....	....	....	6	*5	1	0	360	11	*1	1.83	....	....	....	....
1941-42	Tulsa Oilers	AHA	50	13	34	3	3010	188	1	3.75	....	....	....	....	....	2	0	2	0	120	9	0	4.50	....	....	....	....
1942-43	Vancouver St. Regis	PCHL	3	....	....	....	180	14	0	4.67	....	....	....	....	....	5	....	....	....	300	18	0	*3.60	....	....	....	....
1943-44	Vancouver St. Regis	NWIHL	24	....	....	....	1440	142	0	5.92	....	....	....	....	....	3	0	3	0	180	24	0	8.00	....	....	....	....
	Vancouver RCAF Seahawks	NNDHL	3	*2	1	0	180	19	0	6.33	....	....	....	....	....	....	....	....	....	....	....	....	....	....	....	....	....
	Vancouver Maple Leafs	NNDHL	2	1	1	0	120	12	0	6.00	....	....	....	....	....	4	*3	1	0	240	22	0	5.50	....	....	....	....
	NHL Totals		**7**	**1**	**3**	**1**	**392**	**26**	**0**	**3.98**	....	....	....	....	....	....	....	....	....	....	....	....	....	....	....	....	....

Loaned to **NY Americans** by **Boston** to replace injured Roy Worters, March 18, 1934. (NY Americans 9, Boston 5). Traded to **NY Rangers** by **Boston** for Jean Pusie, November 1, 1934. Traded to **Boston** by **NY Rangers** for cash, November 18, 1934.

• JAKS, Pauli

G – L. 6', 194 lbs. b: Schaffhausen, Switz., 1/25/1972. Los Angeles' 4th, 108th overall in 1991.

Season	Club	League	GP	W	L	T	Mins	GA	SO	Avg	AAvg	Eff	SA	S%	SAPG	GP	W	L	T	Mins	GA	SO	Avg	Eff	SA	S%	SAPG
1990-91	HC Ambri-Piotta	Switz.	22	....	....	....	1247	100	0	4.81	....	....	....	....	....	....	....	....	....	....	....	....	....	....	....	....	....
	Switzerland	WJC-A	5	1	4	0	300	30	0	6.00	....	....	....	....	....	....	....	....	....	....	....	....	....	....	....	....	....
1991-92	HC Ambri-Piotta	Switz.	33	25	7	1	1890	97	2	2.93	....	....	....	....	....	....	....	....	....	....	....	....	....	....	....	....	....
	Switzerland	WJC-A	5	1	4	0	300	31	0	6.20	....	....	....	....	....	....	....	....	....	....	....	....	....	....	....	....	....
1992-93	HC Ambri-Piotta	Switz.	29	....	....	....	1740	92	....	3.17	....	....	....	....	....	....	....	....	....	....	....	....	....	....	....	....	....
1993-94	Phoenix Roadrunners	IHL	33	16	13	1	1712	101	0	3.54	....	....	....	....	....	....	....	....	....	....	....	....	....	....	....	....	....
1994-95	Phoenix Roadrunners	IHL	15	2	4	4	635	44	0	4.15	....	....	....	....	....	....	....	....	....	....	....	....	....	....	....	....	....
	Los Angeles Kings	**NHL**	**1**	**0**	**0**	**0**	**40**	**2**	**0**	**3.00**	**3.14**	**2.40**	**25**	**.920**	**37.5**	....	....	....	....	....	....	....	....	....	....	....	....
1995-96	HC Ambri-Piotta	Switz.	30	....	....	....	1799	106	....	3.53	....	....	....	....	....	....	....	....	....	....	....	....	....	....	....	....	....
	Switzerland	WC-B	1	1	0	0	60	1	0	1.00	....	....	....	....	....	....	....	....	....	....	....	....	....	....	....	....	....
1996-97	HC Ambri-Piotta	Switz.	42	....	....	....	2486	143	....	3.45	....	....	....	....	....	....	....	....	....	....	....	....	....	....	....	....	....
1997-98	HC Ambri-Piotta	Switz.	28	....	....	....	1645	81	....	2.95	....	....	....	....	....	3	....	....	....	169	12	....	4.26	....	....	....	....
1998-99	HC Ambri-Piotta	Switz.	41	....	....	....	2440	90	....	*2.21	....	....	....	....	....	*15	....	....	....	*915	30	....	1.97	....	....	....	....
	Switzerland	WC-A	....	....	....	....	....	....	....	....	....	....	....	....	....	....	....	....	....	....	....	....	....	....	....	....	....
99-2000	HC Ambri-Piotta	Switz.	39	....	....	....	2211	92	3	2.50	....	....	....	....	....	9	....	....	....	485	24	1	2.97	....	....	....	....
	Switzerland	WC-A	DID NOT PLAY – SPARE GOALTENDER																								
	NHL Totals		**1**	**0**	**0**	**0**	**40**	**2**	**0**	**3.00**	....	....	**25**	**.920**	**37.5**	....	....	....	....	....	....	....	....	....	....	....	....

WJC-A All-Star Team (1991) • Named Best Goaltender at WJC-A (1991)

• JANASZAK, Steve

Steven James G – R. 6'1", 210 lbs. b: St. Paul, MN, 1/7/1957.

Season	Club	League	GP	W	L	T	Mins	GA	SO	Avg	AAvg	Eff	SA	S%	SAPG	GP	W	L	T	Mins	GA	SO	Avg	Eff	SA	S%	SAPG
1974-75	Hill-Murray Pioneers	Hi-School	STATISTICS NOT AVAILABLE																								
1975-76	University of Minnesota	WCHA	4	1	2	0	240	21	0	5.25	....	....	....	....	....	....	....	....	....	....	....	....	....	....	....	....	....
1976-77	University of Minnesota	WCHA	17	6	9	2	1100	86	0	4.69	....	....	....	....	....	....	....	....	....	....	....	....	....	....	....	....	....
1977-78	University of Minnesota	WCHA	28	14	10	2	1653	106	3	3.85	....	....	....	....	....	....	....	....	....	....	....	....	....	....	....	....	....
1978-79	University of Minnesota	WCHA	41	29	11	1	2428	131	1	3.23	....	....	....	....	....	....	....	....	....	....	....	....	....	....	....	....	....
1979-80	United States	Nat-Team	17	....	....	....	894	47	2	3.15	....	....	....	....	....	....	....	....	....	....	....	....	....	....	....	....	....
	United States	Olympics	DID NOT PLAY – SPARE GOALTENDER																								
	Minnesota North Stars	**NHL**	**1**	**0**	**0**	**1**	**60**	**2**	**0**	**2.00**	**1.77**	....	....	....	....	....	....	....	....	....	....	....	....	....	....	....	....
	Oklahoma City Stars	CHL	1	1	0	0	60	2	0	2.00	....	....	....	....	....	....	....	....	....	....	....	....	....	....	....	....	....
	Tulsa Oilers	CHL	1	0	1	0	59	6	0	6.10	....	....	....	....	....	....	....	....	....	....	....	....	....	....	....	....	....
	Baltimore Clippers	EHL	4	....	....	....	219	19	0	5.21	....	....	....	....	....	....	....	....	....	....	....	....	....	....	....	....	....
1980-81	Fort Worth Texans	CHL	6	0	6	0	357	26	0	4.37	....	....	....	....	....	....	....	....	....	....	....	....	....	....	....	....	....
	Fort Wayne Komets	IHL	42	....	....	....	2196	130	0	3.55	....	....	....	....	....	3	....	....	....	104	7	0	4.04	....	....	....	....
1981-82	Fort Worth Texans	CHL	37	8	24	0	1962	152	2	4.65	....	....	....	....	....	....	....	....	....	....	....	....	....	....	....	....	....
	Colorado Rockies	**NHL**	**2**	**0**	**1**	**0**	**100**	**13**	**0**	**7.80**	**6.03**	....	....	....	....	....	....	....	....	....	....	....	....	....	....	....	....
	United States	WEC-A	3	....	....	....	180	17	....	5.66	....	....	....	....	....	....	....	....	....	....	....	....	....	....	....	....	....
1982-83	Wichita Wind	CHL	35	13	18	1	1996	147	0	4.42	....	....	....	....	....	....	....	....	....	....	....	....	....	....	....	....	....
	NHL Totals		**3**	**0**	**1**	**1**	**160**	**15**	**0**	**5.63**	....	....	....	....	....	....	....	....	....	....	....	....	....	....	....	....	....

NCAA Championship All-Tournament Team (1979) • NCAA Championship Tournament MVP (1979)

Signed as a free agent by **Minnesota**, March, 1980. Signed as a free agent by **Colorado**, April 14, 1980. Traded to **Calgary** by **Colorado** for future considerations, September 18, 1982.

• JANECYK, Bob

Robert T. G – L. 6'1", 180 lbs. b: Chicago, IL, 5/18/1957.

Season	Club	League	GP	W	L	T	Mins	GA	SO	Avg	AAvg	Eff	SA	S%	SAPG	GP	W	L	T	Mins	GA	SO	Avg	Eff	SA	S%	SAPG
1975-1979	Chicago State University	NCAA-2	STATISTICS NOT AVAILABLE																								
1979-80	Flint Generals	IHL	2	....	....	....	119	5	0	2.53	....	....	....	....	....	....	....	....	....	....	....	....	....	....	....	....	....
	Chicago Cardinals	ConHL	1	0	1	0	60	6	0	6.00	....	....	....	....	....	....	....	....	....	....	....	....	....	....	....	....	....
	Fort Wayne Komets	IHL	40	....	....	....	2208	128	1	3.48	....	....	....	....	....	3	....	....	....	89	4	0	2.70	....	....	....	....
1980-81	New Brunswick Hawks	AHL	34	11	18	1	1915	131	0	4.10	....	....	....	....	....	....	....	....	....	....	....	....	....	....	....	....	....
1981-82	New Brunswick Hawks	AHL	53	32	13	7	3224	153	2	2.85	....	....	....	....	....	14	*11	2	0	818	32	*1	*2.35	....	....	....	....
1982-83	Springfield Indians	AHL	47	19	24	4	*2754	167	*3	3.64	....	....	....	....	....	....	....	....	....	....	....	....	....	....	....	....	....
1983-84	**Chicago Black Hawks**	**NHL**	**8**	**2**	**3**	**1**	**412**	**28**	**0**	**4.08**	**3.21**	**4.82**	**237**	**.882**	**34.5**	....	....	....	....	....	....	....	....	....	....	....	....
	Springfield Indians	AHL	30	14	11	4	1664	94	0	3.39	....	....	....	....	....	....	....	....	....	....	....	....	....	....	....	....	....
1984-85	**Los Angeles Kings**	**NHL**	**51**	**22**	**21**	**8**	**3002**	**183**	**2**	**3.66**	**2.91**	**4.52**	**1483**	**.877**	**29.6**	**3**	**0**	**3**	....	**184**	**10**	**0**	**3.26**	**3.26**	**100**	**.900**	**32.6**
1985-86	**Los Angeles Kings**	**NHL**	**38**	**14**	**16**	**4**	**2083**	**162**	**0**	**4.67**	**3.66**	**6.70**	**1130**	**.857**	**32.5**	....	....	....	....	....	....	....	....	....	....	....	....
1986-87	**Los Angeles Kings**	**NHL**	**7**	**4**	**3**	**0**	**420**	**34**	**0**	**4.86**	**4.12**	**7.44**	**222**	**.847**	**31.7**	....	....	....	....	....	....	....	....	....	....	....	....

Season	Club	League	REGULAR SEASON													PLAYOFFS											
			GP	W	L	T	Mins	GA	SO	Avg	AAvg	Eff	SA	S%	SAPG	GP	W	L	T	Mins	GA	SO	Avg	Eff	SA	S%	SAPG
1987-88	**Los Angeles Kings**	**NHL**	**5**	**1**	**4**	**0**	**303**	**23**	**0**	**4.55**	**3.79**	**6.34**	**165**	**.861**	**32.7**	....	....	....	....	....	....	....	....	....	....	....	....
	New Haven Nighthawks	AHL	37	19	13	3	2162	125	1	3.47	....	....	....	....	....	....	....	....	....	....	....	....	....	....	....	....	....
1988-89	**Los Angeles Kings**	**NHL**	**1**	**0**	**0**	**0**	**30**	**2**	**0**	**4.00**	**3.33**	**3.64**	**22**	**.909**	**44.0**	....	....	....	....	....	....	....	....	....	....	....	....
	New Haven Nighthawks	AHL	34	14	13	6	1992	131	1	3.95	....	....	....	....	....	....	....	....	....	....	....	....	....	....	....	....	....
	NHL Totals		**110**	**43**	**47**	**13**	**6250**	**432**	**2**	**4.15**	....	....	**3259**	**.867**	**31.3**	**3**	**0**	**3**	....	**184**	**10**	**0**	**3.26**	....	**100**	**.900**	**32.6**

NCAA (College Div.) West All-American Team (1976, 1977, 1978) • IHL Second All-Star Team (1980) • AHL First All-Star Team (1982, 1983) • Shared Harry "Hap" Holmes Memorial Award (fewest goals against - AHL) with Warren Skorodenski (1982)

Signed as a free agent by **Chicago**, June 3, 1980. Traded to **LA Kings** by **Chicago** with Chicago's 1st (Craig Redmond), 3rd (John English) and 4th (Tom Glavine) round choices in 1984 Entry Draft for LA Kings' 1st (Ed Olczyk) and 4th (Tommy Eriksson) round choices in 1984 Entry Draft, June 9, 1984.

• JENKINS, Roger

Joseph Roger "Broadway" G. 5'11", 173 lbs. b: Appleton, WI, 11/18/1911.

Season	Club	League	GP	W	L	T	Mins	GA	SO	Avg	AAvg	Eff	SA	S%	SAPG	GP	W	L	T	Mins	GA	SO	Avg	Eff	SA	S%	SAPG
1938-39	**New York Americans**	**NHL**	**1**	**0**	**1**	**0**	**30**	**7**	**0**	**14.00**	**16.96**	....	....	....	....	....	....	....	....	....	....	....	....	....	....	....	....
	NHL Totals		**1**	**0**	**1**	**0**	**30**	**7**	**0**	**14.00**	....	....	....	....	....	....	....	....	....	....	....	....	....	....	....	....	....

• **NY Americans'** defenseman replaced injured Earl Robertson in 2nd period, March 18, 1939. (NY Rangers 11, NY Americans 5)

• JENSEN, Al

Allan Raymond G – L. 5'10", 180 lbs. b: Hamilton, Ont., 11/27/1958. Detroit's 4th, 31st overall in 1978.

Season	Club	League	GP	W	L	T	Mins	GA	SO	Avg	AAvg	Eff	SA	S%	SAPG	GP	W	L	T	Mins	GA	SO	Avg	Eff	SA	S%	SAPG
1975-76	Hamilton Fincups	OMJHL	28	....	....	....	1451	97	0	3.97	....	....	....	....	....	3	2	0	0	140	6	1	2.58	....	....	....	....
	Hamilton Fincups	Mem-Cup	DID NOT PLAY – SPARE GOALTENDER																								
1976-77	St. Catharines Fincups	OMJHL	48	....	....	....	2727	168	*2	3.70	....	....	....	....	....	13	7	5	1	707	36	1	2.97	....	....	....	....
	Canada	WJC-A	7	5	1	1	400	19	....	2.85	....	....	....	....	....	....	....	....	....	....	....	....	....	....	....	....	....
1977-78	Hamilton Fincups	OMJHL	43	....	....	....	2582	146	*3	*3.35	....	....	....	....	....	17	8	5	4	967	43	*1	*2.54	....	....	....	....
	Canada	WJC-A	3	....	....	....	180	12	....	4.00	....	....	....	....	....	....	....	....	....	....	....	....	....	....	....	....	....
1978-79	Kalamazoo Wings	IHL	47	....	....	....	2596	156	2	3.61	....	....	....	....	....	12	....	....	....	718	34	0	2.84	....	....	....	....
1979-80	Adirondack Red Wings	AHL	57	27	24	5	*3406	199	2	3.51	....	....	....	....	....	4	0	4	0	212	15	0	4.25	....	....	....	....
1980-81	**Detroit Red Wings**	**NHL**	**1**	**0**	**1**	**0**	**60**	**7**	**0**	**7.00**	**5.66**	....	....	....	....	....	....	....	....	....	....	....	....	....	....	....	....
	Adirondack Red Wings	AHL	60	27	21	3	3169	203	*3	3.84	....	....	....	....	....	11	7	4	0	626	46	0	4.41	....	....	....	....
1981-82	**Washington Capitals**	**NHL**	**26**	**8**	**8**	**4**	**1274**	**81**	**0**	**3.81**	**2.94**	....	....	....	....	....	....	....	....	....	....	....	....	....	....	....	....
	Hershey Bears	AHL	8	4	1	1	407	24	0	3.54	....	....	....	....	....	3	2	1	0	162	9	0	3.33	....	....	....	....
1982-83	**Washington Capitals**	**NHL**	**40**	**22**	**12**	**6**	**2358**	**135**	**1**	**3.44**	**2.75**	**4.07**	**1140**	**.882**	**29.0**	**3**	**1**	**2**	....	**139**	**10**	**0**	**4.32**	....	....	....	....
	Hershey Bears	AHL	6	....	....	....	316	14	1	2.66	....	....	....	....	....	....	....	....	....	....	....	....	....	....	....	....	....
1983-84	**Washington Capitals**	**NHL**	**43**	**25**	**13**	**3**	**2414**	**117**	**4**	**2.91**	**2.28**	**3.42**	**995**	**.882**	**24.7**	**6**	**3**	**1**	....	**258**	**14**	**0**	**3.26**	**3.80**	**120**	**.883**	**27.9**
	Hershey Bears	AHL	3	1	2	0	180	16	0	5.33	....	....	....	....	....	....	....	....	....	....	....	....	....	....	....	....	....
1984-85	**Washington Capitals**	**NHL**	**14**	**10**	**3**	**1**	**803**	**34**	**1**	**2.54**	**2.02**	**2.93**	**295**	**.885**	**22.0**	**3**	**1**	**2**	....	**201**	**8**	**0**	**2.39**	**2.22**	**86**	**.907**	**25.7**
	Binghamton Whalers	AHL	3	2	1	0	180	9	0	3.00	....	....	....	....	....	....	....	....	....	....	....	....	....	....	....	....	....
1985-86	**Washington Capitals**	**NHL**	**44**	**28**	**9**	**3**	**2437**	**129**	**2**	**3.18**	**2.47**	**3.51**	**1168**	**.890**	**28.8**	....	....	....	....	....	....	....	....	....	....	....	....
1986-87	**Washington Capitals**	**NHL**	**6**	**1**	**3**	**1**	**328**	**27**	**0**	**4.94**	**4.19**	**7.25**	**184**	**.853**	**33.7**	....	....	....	....	....	....	....	....	....	....	....	....
	Binghamton Whalers	AHL	13	5	6	0	684	42	0	3.68	....	....	....	....	....	....	....	....	....	....	....	....	....	....	....	....	....
	Los Angeles Kings	**NHL**	**5**	**1**	**4**	**0**	**300**	**27**	**0**	**5.40**	**4.58**	**9.47**	**154**	**.825**	**30.8**	....	....	....	....	....	....	....	....	....	....	....	....
1987-88	New Haven Nighthawks	AHL	20	5	12	3	1129	84	0	4.46	....	....	....	....	....	....	....	....	....	....	....	....	....	....	....	....	....
	NHL Totals		**179**	**95**	**53**	**18**	**9974**	**557**	**8**	**3.35**	....	....	....	....	....	**12**	**5**	**5**	....	**598**	**32**	**0**	**3.21**	....	....	....	....

OMJHL Second All-Star Team (1977) • OMJHL First All-Star Team (1978) • Shared William M. Jennings Trophy with Pat Riggin (1984)

Traded to **Washington** by **Detroit** for Mark Lofthouse, July 23, 1981. Traded to **LA Kings** by **Washington** for Garry Galley, February 14, 1987.

• JENSEN, Darren

Darren Aksel G – L. 5'9", 165 lbs. b: Creston, B.C., 5/27/1960. Hartford's 5th, 92nd overall in 1980.

Season	Club	League	GP	W	L	T	Mins	GA	SO	Avg	AAvg	Eff	SA	S%	SAPG	GP	W	L	T	Mins	GA	SO	Avg	Eff	SA	S%	SAPG
1977-78	Penticton Vees	BCJHL	29	22	7	0	1732	133	0	4.60	....	....	....	....	....	....	....	....	....	....	....	....	....	....	....	....	....
1978-79	Penticton Vees	BCJHL	42	16	21	1	2475	187	0	5.33	....	....	....	....	....	....	....	....	....	....	....	....	....	....	....	....	....
1979-80	University of North Dakota	WCHA	15	....	....	....	890	33	1	2.22	....	....	....	....	....	....	....	....	....	....	....	....	....	....	....	....	....
1980-81	University of North Dakota	WCHA	25	....	....	....	1510	110	0	4.37	....	....	....	....	....	....	....	....	....	....	....	....	....	....	....	....	....
1981-82	University of North Dakota	WCHA	16	....	....	....	910	45	1	2.97	....	....	....	....	....	....	....	....	....	....	....	....	....	....	....	....	....
1982-83	University of North Dakota	WCHA	16	....	....	....	905	45	0	2.98	....	....	....	....	....	....	....	....	....	....	....	....	....	....	....	....	....
1983-84	Fort Wayne Komets	IHL	56	40	12	3	3325	162	*4	*2.92	....	....	....	....	....	6	2	4	0	358	21	0	3.52	....	....	....	....
1984-85	**Philadelphia Flyers**	**NHL**	**1**	**0**	**1**	**0**	**60**	**7**	**0**	**7.00**	**5.58**	**16.33**	**30**	**.767**	**30.0**	....	....	....	....	....	....	....	....	....	....	....	....
	Hershey Bears	AHL	39	12	20	6	2263	150	1	3.98	....	....	....	....	....	....	....	....	....	....	....	....	....	....	....	....	....
1985-86	**Philadelphia Flyers**	**NHL**	**29**	**15**	**9**	**1**	**1436**	**88**	**2**	**3.68**	**2.87**	**4.28**	**756**	**.884**	**31.6**	....	....	....	....	....	....	....	....	....	....	....	....
	Hershey Bears	AHL	14	11	1	1	795	38	1	2.87	....	....	....	....	....	7	5	1	0	365	19	0	3.12	....	....	....	....
1986-87	Hershey Bears	AHL	60	26	26	0	3429	215	0	3.76	....	....	....	....	....	4	1	2	0	203	15	0	4.43	....	....	....	....
1987-88	Fredericton Express	AHL	42	18	19	4	2459	158	0	3.86	....	....	....	....	....	12	7	5	0	715	40	0	3.36	....	....	....	....
1988-89	Milwaukee Admirals	IHL	11	7	2	0	555	36	0	3.89	....	....	....	....	....	....	....	....	....	....	....	....	....	....	....	....	....
	NHL Totals		**30**	**15**	**10**	**1**	**1496**	**95**	**2**	**3.81**	....	....	**786**	**.879**	**31.5**	....	....	....	....	....	....	....	....	....	....	....	....

NCAA Championship All-Tournament Team (1982) • IHL First All-Star Team (1984) • Won James Norris Memorial Trophy (fewest goals against - IHL) (1984) • Won Garry F. Longman Memorial Trophy (Top Rookie - IHL) (1984) • Won James Gatschene Memorial Trophy (MVP - IHL) (1984) • Shared William M. Jennings Trophy with Bob Froese (1986)

Signed as a free agent by **Philadelphia**, May 1, 1984. Traded to **Vancouver** by **Philadelphia** with Daryl Stanley for Wendell Young and Vancouver's 3rd round choice (Kimbi Daniels) in 1990 Entry Draft, August 31, 1987.

• JOHNSON, Bob

Robert Martin G – L. 6'1", 185 lbs. b: Farmington, MI, 11/12/1948.

Season	Club	League	GP	W	L	T	Mins	GA	SO	Avg	AAvg	Eff	SA	S%	SAPG	GP	W	L	T	Mins	GA	SO	Avg	Eff	SA	S%	SAPG
1967-68	Michigan State Spartans	WCHA	17	....	....	....	1020	69	0	4.06	....	....	....	....	....	....	....	....	....	....	....	....	....	....	....	....	....
1968-69	Michigan State Spartans	WCHA	13	....	....	....	760	49	0	3.87	....	....	....	....	....	....	....	....	....	....	....	....	....	....	....	....	....
1969-70	Michigan State Spartans	WCHA	5	....	....	....	280	23	0	4.93	....	....	....	....	....	....	....	....	....	....	....	....	....	....	....	....	....
1970-71	Toledo Hornets	IHL	44	....	....	....	2478	176	0	4.26	....	....	....	....	....	....	....	....	....	....	....	....	....	....	....	....	....
	Fort Worth Wings	CHL	1	....	....	....	60	3	0	3.00	....	....	....	....	....	....	....	....	....	....	....	....	....	....	....	....	....
1971-72	Denver Spurs	WHL	37	19	10	6	2030	96	1	*2.83	....	....	....	....	....	5	4	1	0	299	5	*2	*1.00	....	....	....	....
1972-73	**St. Louis Blues**	**NHL**	**12**	**6**	**5**	**0**	**583**	**26**	**0**	**2.68**	**2.52**	....	....	....	....	....	....	....	....	....	....	....	....	....	....	....	....
	Denver Spurs	WHL	30	11	10	6	1589	91	2	3.44	....	....	....	....	....	4	1	3	0	245	16	0	3.92	....	....	....	....
1973-74	Hershey Bears	AHL	43	18	15	9	2426	131	0	3.23	....	....	....	....	....	10	8	2	0	608	31	*1	3.05	....	....	....	....
1974-75	**Pittsburgh Penguins**	**NHL**	**12**	**3**	**4**	**1**	**476**	**40**	**0**	**5.04**	**4.57**	....	....	....	....	....	....	....	....	....	....	....	....	....	....	....	....
	Hershey Bears	AHL	31	11	13	5	1750	106	1	3.63	....	....	....	....	....	....	....	....	....	....	....	....	....	....	....	....	....
1975-76	Denver-Ottawa	WHA	24	8	14	1	1334	88	0	3.96	....	....	....	....	....	....	....	....	....	....	....	....	....	....	....	....	....
	Cleveland Crusaders	WHA	18	9	8	0	1043	56	1	3.22	....	....	....	....	....	2	0	2	0	120	8	0	4.00	....	....	....	....
1976-77	Rhode Island Reds	AHL	10	2	8	0	568	43	0	4.54	....	....	....	....	....	....	....	....	....	....	....	....	....	....	....	....	....
	Hampton Gulls	SHL	3	....	....	....	180	8	0	2.67	....	....	....	....	....	....	....	....	....	....	....	....	....	....	....	....	....
	Binghamton Dusters	NAHL	5	....	....	....	275	22	0	4.78	....	....	....	....	....	....	....	....	....	....	....	....	....	....	....	....	....
	NHL Totals		**24**	**9**	**9**	**1**	**1059**	**66**	**0**	**3.74**	....	....	....	....	....	....	....	....	....	....	....	....	....	....	....	....	....
	Other Major League Totals		42	17	22	1	2377	144	1	3.63	....	....	....	....	....	2	0	2	....	120	8	0	4.00	....	....	....	....

• Father of Brent • WHL Second All-Star Team (1972) • Shared WHL Leading Goaltender Award with Peter McDuffe (1972)

Signed as a free agent by **Detroit**, September 29, 1970. Traded to **St. Louis** (Denver-WHL) by **Detroit** for cash, October 1, 1971. Traded to **Pittsburgh** by **St. Louis** for Nick Harbaruk, October 4, 1973. Signed as a free agent by **Denver** (WHA), September, 1975. Signed as a free agent by **Cleveland** (WHA) after **Denver/Ottawa** (WHA) franchise folded, January 17, 1976.

• JOHNSON, Brent

G – L. 6'2", 200 lbs. b: Farmington, MI, 3/12/1977. Colorado's 5th, 129th overall in 1995.

			REGULAR SEASON													PLAYOFFS											
Season	Club	League	GP	W	L	T	Mins	GA	SO	Avg	AAvg	Eff	SA	S%	SAPG	GP	W	L	T	Mins	GA	SO	Avg	Eff	SA	S%	SAPG
1993-94	Detroit Compuware	OJHL	18	....	....	....	1024	49	1	3.52	....	....	....	....	....	....	....	....	....	....	....	....	....	....	....	....	....
1994-95	Owen Sound Platers	OHL	18	3	9	1	904	75	0	4.98	....	....	....	....	....	....	....	....	....	....	....	....	....	....	....	....	....
1995-96	Owen Sound Platers	OHL	58	24	28	1	3211	243	1	4.54	....	....	....	....	....	6	2	4	....	371	29	0	4.69	....	....	....	....
1996-97	Owen Sound Platers	OHL	50	20	28	1	2798	201	1	4.31	....	....	....	....	....	4	0	4	....	253	24	0	5.69	....	....	....	....
1997-98	Worcester IceCats	AHL	42	14	15	7	2240	119	0	3.19	....	....	....	....	....	6	3	2	....	332	19	0	3.43	....	....	....	....
1998-99	**St. Louis Blues**	**NHL**	**6**	**3**	**2**	**0**	**286**	**10**	**0**	**2.10**	**2.50**	**1.65**	**127**	**.921**	**26.6**	....	....	....	....	....	....	....	....	....	....	....	....
	Worcester IceCats	AHL	49	22	22	4	2925	146	2	2.99	....	....	....	....	....	4	1	3	....	238	12	0	3.02	....	....	....	....
99-2000	Worcester IceCats	AHL	58	24	27	5	3319	161	3	2.91	....	....	....	....	....	9	4	5	....	561	23	1	2.46	....	....	....	....
	NHL Totals		**6**	**3**	**2**	**0**	**286**	**10**	**0**	**2.10**	....	....	**127**	**.921**	**26.6**	....	....	....	....	....	....	....	....	....	....	....	....

• Son of Bob

Traded to **St. Louis** by **Colorado** for San Jose's third round choice (previously acquired, Colorado selected Rick Berry) in 1997 Entry Draft, May 30, 1997.

• JOHNSTON, Eddie

Edward Joseph G – L. 6', 190 lbs. b: Montreal, Que., 11/24/1935.

Season	Club	League	GP	W	L	T	Mins	GA	SO	Avg	AAvg	Eff	SA	S%	SAPG	GP	W	L	T	Mins	GA	SO	Avg	Eff	SA	S%	SAPG
1953-54	Montreal Jr. Royals	QJHL	35	....	....	....	....	226	0	6.46	....	....	....	....	....	4	0	4	0	240	32	0	8.00	....	....	....	....
1954-55	Trois-Rivieres Flambeaux	QJHL	46	20	24	2	2760	169	1	3.67	....	....	....	....	....	10	3	7	0	613	29	*1	2.84	....	....	....	....
1955-56	Montreal Jr. Canadiens	QJHL	STATISTICS NOT AVAILABLE																								
	Chatham Maroons	OHA-Sr.	7	....	....	....	420	31	0	4.29	....	....	....	....	....	....	....	....	....	....	....	....	....	....	....	....	....
	Moncton Hawks	ACSHL	1	1	0	0	60	2	0	2.00	....	....	....	....	....	....	....	....	....	....	....	....	....	....	....	....	....
	Chicoutimi Sagueneens	QHL	1	0	0	0	20	1	0	3.00	....	....	....	....	....	....	....	....	....	....	....	....	....	....	....	....	....
	Montreal Jr. Canadiens	Mem-Cup	10	5	4	1	598	27	2	2.71	....	....	....	....	....	....	....	....	....	....	....	....	....	....	....	....	....
1956-57	Winnipeg Warriors	WHL	50	17	32	1	3040	192	2	3.79	....	....	....	....	....	....	....	....	....	....	....	....	....	....	....	....	....
1957-58	Shawinigan Cataracts	QHL	*63	*31	27	5	*3760	230	*5	3.65	....	....	....	....	....	*14	*8	6	0	*880	49	1	3.34	....	....	....	....
1958-59	Edmonton Flyers	WHL	49	26	21	2	2960	163	1	3.30	....	....	....	....	....	3	0	3	0	180	12	0	4.00	....	....	....	....
1959-60	Johnstown Jets	EHL	63	....	....	....	3780	169	4	2.69	....	....	....	....	....	13	9	4	0	780	25	*2	*1.92	....	....	....	....
1960-61	Hull-Ottawa Canadiens	EPHL	*70	*41	20	9	*4200	187	*11	*2.67	....	....	....	....	....	*14	*8	6	0	*857	27	0	*1.89	....	....	....	....
1961-62	Spokane Comets	WHL	*70	*37	28	5	*4310	237	3	3.30	....	....	....	....	....	*16	*9	7	0	*972	58	*1	3.58	....	....	....	....
1962-63	**Boston Bruins**	**NHL**	**50**	**11**	**27**	**10**	**2913**	**193**	**1**	**3.98**	**4.34**	....	....	....	....	....	....	....	....	....	....	....	....	....	....	....	....
1963-64	**Boston Bruins**	**NHL**	***70**	**18**	**40**	**12**	***4200**	**211**	**6**	**3.01**	**3.41**	....	....	....	....	....	....	....	....	....	....	....	....	....	....	....	....
1964-65	**Boston Bruins**	**NHL**	**47**	**11**	**32**	**4**	**2820**	**163**	**3**	**3.47**	**3.82**	....	....	....	....	....	....	....	....	....	....	....	....	....	....	....	....
1965-66	**Boston Bruins**	**NHL**	**33**	**10**	**19**	**2**	**1744**	**108**	**1**	**3.72**	**3.83**	....	....	....	....	....	....	....	....	....	....	....	....	....	....	....	....
	Los Angeles Blades	WHL	5	2	2	0	260	10	1	2.31	....	....	....	....	....	....	....	....	....	....	....	....	....	....	....	....	....
1966-67	**Boston Bruins**	**NHL**	**34**	**8**	**21**	**2**	**1880**	**116**	**0**	**3.70**	**3.89**	....	....	....	....	....	....	....	....	....	....	....	....	....	....	....	....
1967-68	**Boston Bruins**	**NHL**	**28**	**11**	**8**	**5**	**1524**	**73**	**0**	**2.87**	**3.19**	....	....	....	....	....	....	....	....	....	....	....	....	....	....	....	....
1968-69	**Boston Bruins**	**NHL**	**24**	**14**	**6**	**4**	**1440**	**74**	**2**	**3.08**	**3.19**	....	....	....	....	**1**	**0**	**1**	....	**65**	**4**	**0**	**3.69**	....	....	....	....
1969-70♦	**Boston Bruins**	**NHL**	**37**	**16**	**9**	**11**	**2176**	**108**	**3**	**2.98**	**3.17**	....	....	....	....	**1**	**0**	**1**	....	**60**	**4**	**0**	**4.00**	....	....	....	....
1970-71	**Boston Bruins**	**NHL**	**38**	**30**	**6**	**2**	**2280**	**96**	**4**	**2.53**	**2.49**	....	....	....	....	**1**	**0**	**1**	....	**60**	**7**	**0**	**7.00**	....	....	....	....
1971-72♦	**Boston Bruins**	**NHL**	**38**	**27**	**8**	**3**	**2260**	**102**	**2**	**2.71**	**2.73**	....	....	....	....	**7**	***6**	**1**	....	**420**	**13**	**1**	***1.86**	....	....	....	....
1972-73	Team Canada	Summit-72	DID NOT PLAY – SPARE GOALTENDER																								
	Boston Bruins	**NHL**	**45**	**24**	**17**	**1**	**2510**	**137**	**5**	**3.27**	**3.09**	....	....	....	....	**3**	**1**	**2**	....	**160**	**9**	**0**	**3.38**	....	....	....	....
1973-74	**Toronto Maple Leafs**	**NHL**	**26**	**12**	**9**	**4**	**1516**	**78**	**1**	**3.09**	**2.98**	....	....	....	....	**1**	**0**	**1**	....	**60**	**6**	**0**	**6.00**	....	....	....	....
1974-75	**St. Louis Blues**	**NHL**	**30**	**12**	**13**	**5**	**1800**	**93**	**2**	**3.10**	**2.80**	....	....	....	....	**1**	**0**	**1**	....	**60**	**5**	**0**	**5.00**	....	....	....	....
1975-76	**St. Louis Blues**	**NHL**	**38**	**11**	**17**	**9**	**2152**	**130**	**1**	**3.62**	**3.28**	....	....	....	....	....	....	....	....	....	....	....	....	....	....	....	....
1976-77	**St. Louis Blues**	**NHL**	**38**	**13**	**16**	**5**	**2111**	**108**	**1**	**3.07**	**2.85**	....	....	....	....	**3**	**0**	**2**	....	**138**	**9**	**0**	**3.91**	....	....	....	....
1977-78	**St. Louis Blues**	**NHL**	**12**	**5**	**6**	**1**	**650**	**45**	**0**	**4.15**	**3.90**	....	....	....	....	....	....	....	....	....	....	....	....	....	....	....	....
	Chicago Black Hawks	**NHL**	**4**	**1**	**3**	**0**	**240**	**17**	**0**	**4.25**	**3.99**	....	....	....	....	....	....	....	....	....	....	....	....	....	....	....	....
1978-1979	New Brunswick Hawks	AHL	DID NOT PLAY – COACHING																								
1979-1980	**Chicago Black Hawks**	**NHL**	DID NOT PLAY – COACHING																								
1980-1983	**Pittsburgh Penguins**	**NHL**	DID NOT PLAY – COACHING																								
1983-1988	**Pittsburgh Penguins**	**NHL**	DID NOT PLAY – GENERAL MANAGER																								
1988-1989	**Pittsburgh Penguins**	**NHL**	DID NOT PLAY – ASSISTANT GENERAL MANAGER																								
1989-1992	**Hartford Whalers**	**NHL**	DID NOT PLAY – GENERAL MANAGER																								
1992-1993			OUT OF HOCKEY – RETIRED																								
1993-1997	**Pittsburgh Penguins**	**NHL**	DID NOT PLAY – COACHING																								
1997-2000	**Pittsburgh Penguins**	**NHL**	DID NOT PLAY – ASSISTANT GENERAL MANAGER																								
1999-2000	**Pittsburgh Penguins**	**NHL**	DID NOT PLAY – ASSISTANT COACH																								
	NHL Totals		**592**	**234**	**257**	**80**	**34216**	**1852**	**32**	**3.25**	....	....	....	....	....	**18**	**7**	**10**	....	**1023**	**57**	**1**	**3.34**	....	....	....	....

EHL First All-Star Team (1960) • EPHL First All-Star Team (1961) • WHL Second All-Star Team (1962)

Traded to **Chicago** by **Montreal** for cash, September 10, 1959. Claimed by **Boston** from **Spokane** (WHL) in Inter-League Draft, June 4, 1962. Traded to **Toronto** by **Boston** to complete transaction that sent Jacques Plante to Boston (March 3, 1973), May 22, 1973. Traded to **St. Louis** by **Toronto** for Gary Sabourin, May 27, 1974. Traded to **Chicago** by **St. Louis** for cash, January 27, 1978.

• JOSEPH, Curtis

"Cujo" G – L. 5'11", 190 lbs. b: Keswick, Ont., 4/29/1967.

Season	Club	League	GP	W	L	T	Mins	GA	SO	Avg	AAvg	Eff	SA	S%	SAPG	GP	W	L	T	Mins	GA	SO	Avg	Eff	SA	S%	SAPG
1984-85	Newmarket Flyers	OJHL	2	1	1	0	120	16	0	8.00	....	....	....	....	....	....	....	....	....	....	....	....	....	....	....	....	....
	King City Dukes	OJHL-B	18	....	....	....	947	76	0	4.82	....	....	....	....	....	....	....	....	....	....	....	....	....	....	....	....	....
1985-86	Richmond Hill Dynes	OJHL	33	12	18	0	1716	156	1	5.45	....	....	....	....	....	....	....	....	....	....	....	....	....	....	....	....	....
1986-87	Richmond Hill Dynes	OJHL	30	14	7	6	1764	128	1	4.35	....	....	....	....	....	....	....	....	....	....	....	....	....	....	....	....	....
1987-88	Notre Dame Hounds	SJHL	36	25	4	7	2174	94	1	2.59	....	....	....	....	....	....	....	....	....	....	....	....	....	....	....	....	....
	Notre Dame Hounds	Cen-Cup	5	*4	1	0	321	17	0	*3.17	....	....	....	....	....	....	....	....	....	....	....	....	....	....	....	....	....
1988-89	University of Wisconsin	WCHA	38	21	11	5	2267	94	1	2.49	....	....	....	....	....	....	....	....	....	....	....	....	....	....	....	....	....
1989-90	Peoria Rivermen	IHL	23	10	8	2	1241	80	0	3.87	....	....	....	....	....	....	....	....	....	....	....	....	....	....	....	....	....
	St. Louis Blues	**NHL**	**15**	**9**	**5**	**1**	**852**	**48**	**0**	**3.38**	**2.86**	**3.73**	**435**	**.890**	**30.6**	**6**	**4**	**1**	....	**327**	**18**	**0**	**3.30**	**3.56**	**167**	**.892**	**30.6**
1990-91	**St. Louis Blues**	**NHL**	**30**	**16**	**10**	**2**	**1710**	**89**	**0**	**3.12**	**2.80**	**3.18**	**874**	**.898**	**30.7**	....	....	....	....	....	....	....	....	....	....	....	....
1991-92	**St. Louis Blues**	**NHL**	**60**	**27**	**20**	**10**	**3494**	**175**	**2**	**3.01**	**2.68**	**2.70**	**1953**	**.910**	**33.5**	**6**	**2**	**4**	....	**379**	**23**	**0**	**3.64**	**3.86**	**217**	**.894**	**34.4**
1992-93	**St. Louis Blues**	**NHL**	**68**	**29**	**28**	**9**	**3890**	**196**	**1**	**3.02**	**2.57**	**2.69**	**2202**	**.911**	**34.0**	**11**	**7**	**4**	....	**715**	**27**	***2**	**2.27**	**1.40**	**438**	**.938**	**36.8**
1993-94	**St. Louis Blues**	**NHL**	**71**	**36**	**23**	**11**	**4127**	**213**	**1**	**3.10**	**2.98**	**2.77**	**2382**	**.911**	**34.6**	**4**	**0**	**4**	....	**246**	**15**	**0**	**3.66**	**3.47**	**158**	**.905**	**38.5**
1994-95	**St. Louis Blues**	**NHL**	**36**	**20**	**10**	**1**	**1914**	**89**	**1**	**2.79**	**2.92**	**2.75**	**904**	**.902**	**28.3**	**7**	**3**	**3**	....	**392**	**24**	**0**	**3.67**	**4.95**	**178**	**.865**	**27.2**
1995-96	Las Vegas Thunder	IHL	15	12	2	1	874	29	1	1.99	....	....	....	....	....	....	....	....	....	....	....	....	....	....	....	....	....
	Edmonton Oilers	**NHL**	**34**	**15**	**16**	**2**	**1936**	**111**	**0**	**3.44**	**3.43**	**3.93**	**971**	**.886**	**30.1**	....	....	....	....	....	....	....	....	....	....	....	....
	Canada	WC-A	8	....	....	....	409	12	*2	1.94	....	....	....	....	....	....	....	....	....	....	....	....	....	....	....	....	....
1996-97	Canada	W-Cup	7	5	2	0	468	18	1	2.00	....	....	....	....	....	....	....	....	....	....	....	....	....	....	....	....	....
	Edmonton Oilers	**NHL**	**72**	**32**	**29**	**9**	**4100**	**200**	**6**	**2.93**	**3.16**	**2.73**	**2144**	**.907**	**31.4**	**12**	**5**	**7**	....	**767**	**36**	**2**	**2.82**	**2.51**	**405**	**.911**	**31.7**
1997-98	**Edmonton Oilers**	**NHL**	**71**	**29**	**31**	**9**	**4132**	**181**	**8**	**2.63**	**3.14**	**2.50**	**1901**	**.905**	**27.6**	**12**	**5**	**7**	....	**716**	**23**	**3**	**1.93**	**1.39**	**319**	....	**26.7**
	Canada	Olympics	DID NOT PLAY – SPARE GOALTENDER																								
1998-99	**Toronto Maple Leafs**	**NHL**	**67**	**35**	**24**	**7**	**4001**	**171**	**3**	**2.56**	**3.04**	**2.30**	**1903**	**.910**	**28.5**	**17**	**9**	**8**	....	**1011**	**41**	**1**	**2.43**	**2.26**	**440**	**.907**	**26.1**
99-2000	**Toronto Maple Leafs**	**NHL**	**63**	**36**	**20**	**7**	**3801**	**158**	**4**	**2.49**	**2.84**	**2.12**	**1854**	**.915**	**29.3**	**12**	**6**	**6**	....	**729**	**25**	**1**	**2.06**	**1.40**	**369**	**.932**	**30.4**
	NHL Totals		**587**	**284**	**216**	**68**	**33957**	**1631**	**26**	**2.88**	....	....	**17523**	**.907**	**31.0**	**87**	**41**	**44**	....	**5282**	**232**	**9**	**2.64**	....	**2691**	**.914**	**30.6**

WCHA First All-Star Team (1989) • NCAA West Second All-American Team (1989) • Played in NHL All-Star Game (1994, 2000)

Signed as a free agent by **St. Louis**, June 16, 1989. Traded to **Edmonton** by **St. Louis** with the rights to Michael Grier for St. Louis' 1st round choices (previously acquired) in 1996 (Marty Reasoner) and 1997 (later traded to LA Kings - LA Kings selected Matt Zultek) Entry Drafts, August 4, 1995. Signed as a free agent by **Toronto**, July 15, 1998.

• JUNKIN, Joe

Joseph Brian G – L. 5'11", 180 lbs. b: Lindsay, Ont., 9/8/1946.

Season	Club	League	GP	W	L	T	Mins	GA	SO	Avg	AAvg	Eff	SA	S%	SAPG	GP	W	L	T	Mins	GA	SO	Avg	Eff	SA	S%	SAPG
1966-67	Bobcaygeon Bobcats	OHA-B	STATISTICS NOT AVAILABLE																								
1967-68	Belleville Mohawks	OHA-Sr.	24	....	....	....	1410	100	0	4.26	....	....	....	....	....	....	....	....	....	....	....	....	....	....	....	....	....
1968-69	Oklahoma City Blazers	CHL	27	....	....	....	1420	78	0	3.30	....	....	....	....	....	5	0	4	0	230	19	0	4.96	....	....	....	....
	Boston Bruins	**NHL**	**1**	**0**	**0**	**0**	**8**	**0**	**0**	**0.00**	**0.00**	....	....	....	....	....	....	....	....	....	....	....	....	....	....	....	....
1969-70	Oklahoma City Blazers	CHL	9	4	4	0	500	38	1	4.56	....	....	....	....	....	....	....	....	....	....	....	....	....	....	....	....	....
	Hershey Bears	AHL	17	....	....	....	969	63	0	3.90	....	....	....	....	....	....	....	....	....	....	....	....	....	....	....	....	....

			REGULAR SEASON													PLAYOFFS											
Season	**Club**	**League**	**GP**	**W**	**L**	**T**	**Mins**	**GA**	**SO**	**Avg**	**AAvg**	**Eff**	**SA**	**S%**	**SAPG**	**GP**	**W**	**L**	**T**	**Mins**	**GA**	**SO**	**Avg**	**Eff**	**SA**	**S%**	**SAPG**
1970-71	Hershey Bears	AHL	DID NOT PLAY – INJURED																								
1971-72	Fenelon Falls Flyers	UOVHL	STATISTICS NOT AVAILABLE																								
1972-73	Long Island Ducks	EHL	2	....	....	....	80	12	0	9.23	....	....	....	....	....	....	....	....	....	....	....	....	....	....	....	....	....
	Syracuse Blazers	EHL	34	....	....	....	2071	90	*5	2.61	....	....	....	....	....	7	3	3	0	399	17	*1	2.57	....	....	....	....
1973-74	New York-Jersey Knights	WHA	53	21	25	4	3122	197	1	3.79	....	....	....	....	....	....	....	....	....	....	....	....	....	....	....	....	....
1974-75	San Diego Mariners	WHA	16	6	7	0	839	46	1	3.29	....	....	....	....	....	....	....	....	....	....	....	....	....	....	....	....	....
	Syracuse Blazers	NAHL	20	11	8	0	1183	72	0	3.65	....	....	....	....	....	6	3	3	0	360	21	*1	3.50	....	....	....	....
1975-76	Tidewater Sharks	SHL	7	1	5	1	390	30	0	4.62	....	....	....	....	....	....	....	....	....	....	....	....	....	....	....	....	....
	Roanoke Valley Rebels	SHL	29	12	13	3	1686	97	1	3.45	....	....	....	....	....	....	....	....	....	....	....	....	....	....	....	....	....
	NHL Totals		**1**	**0**	**0**	**0**	**8**	**0**	**0**	**0.00**	....	....	....	....	....	....	....	....	....	....	....	....	....	....	....	....	....
	Other Major League Totals		69	27	32	4	3961	243	2	3.68	....	....	....	....	....	....	....	....	....	....	....	....	....	....	....	....	....

EHL North First All-Star Team (1973)

Signed as a free agent by **Boston**, September 12, 1968. • Missed entire 1970-71 season recovering from retina-reattachment surgery, July, 1970. Signed as a free agent by **NY Raiders** (WHA), September, 1972. Transferred to **San Diego** (WHA) after **New York-Jersey** (WHA) franchise relocated, April 30, 1974. Traded to **Cincinnati** (WHA) by **San Diego** (WHA) for Cincinnati's 3rd round choice (Mark Suzor) in 1976 WHA Amateur Draft, June, 1975.

• KAARELA, Jari

Jari Pekka G – L. 5'10", 165 lbs. b: Tampere, Finland, 8/8/1958.

Season	Club	League	GP	W	L	T	Mins	GA	SO	Avg	AAvg	Eff	SA	S%	SAPG	GP	W	L	T	Mins	GA	SO	Avg	Eff	SA	S%	SAPG
1977-78	Ilves Tampere	Finland	STATISTICS NOT AVAILABLE																								
1978-79	SaiPa Lappeenranta	Finland-2	STATISTICS NOT AVAILABLE																								
1979-80	SaiPa Lappeenranta	Finland-2	STATISTICS NOT AVAILABLE																								
1980-81	Fort Worth Texans	CHL	36	13	20	2	2093	133	1	3.81	....	....	....	....	....	....	....	....	....	....	....	....	....	....	....	....	....
	Colorado Rockies	**NHL**	**5**	**2**	**2**	**0**	**220**	**22**	**0**	**6.00**	**4.86**	....	....	....	....	....	....	....	....	....	....	....	....	....	....	....	....
	Indianapolis Checkers	CHL	2	2	0	0	120	4	1	2.00	....	....	....	....	....	....	....	....	....	....	....	....	....	....	....	....	....
1981-82	Muskegon Mohawks	IHL	49	....	....	....	2682	219	1	4.90	....	....	....	....	....	....	....	....	....	....	....	....	....	....	....	....	....
	Fort Worth Texans	CHL	2	0	2	0	120	13	0	6.50	....	....	....	....	....	....	....	....	....	....	....	....	....	....	....	....	....
1982-83	K-Reipas	Finland-2	STATISTICS NOT AVAILABLE																								
1983-84	Karpat Oulu	Finland	8	....	....	....	480	24	0	3.00	....	....	....	....	....	....	....	....	....	....	....	....	....	....	....	....	....
1984-85	HIFK Helsinki	Finland	15	....	....	....	899	55	0	3.67	....	....	....	....	....	....	....	....	....	....	....	....	....	....	....	....	....
1985-86	HIFK Helsinki	Finland	14	....	....	....	690	48	0	4.18	....	....	....	....	....	2	0	1	0	89	14	0	9.44	....	....	....	....
	NHL Totals		**5**	**2**	**2**	**0**	**220**	**22**	**0**	**6.00**	....	....	....	....	....	....	....	....	....	....	....	....	....	....	....	....	....

Signed as a free agent by **Colorado**, February 9, 1981. Traded to **NY Islanders** by **Colorado** with Mike McEwen for Glenn Resch and Steve Tambellini, March 10, 1981.

• KAMPPURI, Hannu

Hannu Juhani G – R. 6', 175 lbs. b: Helsinki, Finland, 6/1/1957.

Season	Club	League	GP	W	L	T	Mins	GA	SO	Avg	AAvg	Eff	SA	S%	SAPG	GP	W	L	T	Mins	GA	SO	Avg	Eff	SA	S%	SAPG
1973-74	Karhu Karpat	Finland	STATISTICS NOT AVAILABLE																								
1974-75	Jokerit Helsinki	Finland	STATISTICS NOT AVAILABLE																								
1975-76	Jokerit Helsinki	Finland	STATISTICS NOT AVAILABLE																								
	Finland	WJC-A	3	0	2	0	65	10	0	9.23	....	....	....	....	....	....	....	....	....	....	....	....	....	....	....	....	....
1976-77	Jokerit Helsinki	Finland	STATISTICS NOT AVAILABLE																								
	Finland	WJC-A	DID NOT PLAY – SPARE GOALTENDER																								
1977-78	Jokerit Helsinki	Finland	36	....	....	....	1456	177	....	7.29	....	....	....	....	....	....	....	....	....	....	....	....	....	....	....	....	....
1978-79	Jokerit Helsinki	Finland	36	....	....	....	2160	161	0	4.47	....	....	....	....	....	....	....	....	....	....	....	....	....	....	....	....	....
	Edmonton Oilers	WHA	2	0	1	0	90	10	0	6.67	....	....	....	....	....	....	....	....	....	....	....	....	....	....	....	....	....
1979-80	Houston Apollos	CHL	19	6	11	2	1119	88	0	4.72	....	....	....	....	....	2	....	....	....	103	9	0	5.24	....	....	....	....
	Baltimore Clippers	EHL	3	....	....	....	....	4	1	1.33	....	....	....	....	....	....	....	....	....	....	....	....	....	....	....	....	....
1980-81	Tappara Tampere	Finland	36	....	....	....	2160	118	0	3.27	....	....	....	....	....	....	....	....	....	....	....	....	....	....	....	....	....
1981-82	Tappara Tampere	Finland	36	....	....	....	2160	118	0	3.67	....	....	....	....	....	....	....	....	....	....	....	....	....	....	....	....	....
	Finland	WEC-A	6	3	2	1	355	20	0	3.38	....	....	....	....	....	....	....	....	....	....	....	....	....	....	....	....	....
1982-83	Tappara Tampere	Finland	36	....	....	....	2160	121	0	3.36	....	....	....	....	....	....	....	....	....	....	....	....	....	....	....	....	....
1983-84	Tappara Tampere	Finland	37	....	....	....	2220	102	0	2.77	....	....	....	....	....	....	....	....	....	....	....	....	....	....	....	....	....
1984-85	**New Jersey Devils**	**NHL**	**13**	**1**	**10**	**1**	**645**	**54**	**0**	**5.02**	**4.01**	**7.72**	**351**	**.846**	**32.7**	....	....	....	....	....	....	....	....	....	....	....	....
	Maine Mariners	AHL	7	4	2	0	340	19	0	3.35	....	....	....	....	....	....	....	....	....	....	....	....	....	....	....	....	....
	Fort Wayne Komets	IHL	1	0	1	0	60	4	0	4.00	....	....	....	....	....	....	....	....	....	....	....	....	....	....	....	....	....
1985-86	SaiPa Lappeenranta	Finland	34	....	....	....	2109	147	....	4.18	....	....	....	....	....	....	....	....	....	....	....	....	....	....	....	....	....
	Finland	WEC-A	5	....	....	....	299	16	0	3.21	....	....	....	....	....	....	....	....	....	....	....	....	....	....	....	....	....
1986-87	Karpat Oulu	Finland	44	....	....	....	2666	159	0	*3.58	....	....	....	....	....	9	4	5	0	540	27	0	3.00	....	....	....	....
	Finland	WEC-A	3	....	....	....	136	7	0	3.09	....	....	....	....	....	....	....	....	....	....	....	....	....	....	....	....	....
1987-88	Karpat Oulu	Finland	STATISTICS NOT AVAILABLE																								
1988-89	KooKoo Kouvola	Finland	41	....	....	....	2403	171	0	4.27	....	....	....	....	....	....	....	....	....	....	....	....	....	....	....	....	....
1989-90	KooKoo Kouvola	Finland	42	10	28	4	2403	193	0	4.82	....	....	....	....	....	....	....	....	....	....	....	....	....	....	....	....	....
	NHL Totals		**13**	**1**	**10**	**1**	**645**	**54**	**0**	**5.02**	....	....	**351**	**.846**	**32.7**	....	....	....	....	....	....	....	....	....	....	....	....
	Other Major League Totals		2	0	1	0	90	10	0	6.67	....	....	....	....	....	....	....	....	....	....	....	....	....	....	....	....	....

Signed as a free agent by **Edmonton** (WHA), March, 1978. Signed as a free agent by **New Jersey**, August 1, 1984.

• KARAKAS, Mike

G – L. 5'11", 147 lbs. b: Aurora, MN, 12/12/1911 Deceased. **USHOF**

Season	Club	League	GP	W	L	T	Mins	GA	SO	Avg	AAvg	Eff	SA	S%	SAPG	GP	W	L	T	Mins	GA	SO	Avg	Eff	SA	S%	SAPG
1929-30	Eveleth Rangers	CHL	STATISTICS NOT AVAILABLE																								
1930-31	Chicago Shamrocks	AHA	8	5	2	0	435	16	0	2.21	....	....	....	....	....	....	....	....	....	....	....	....	....	....	....	....	....
1931-32	Chicago Shamrocks	AHA	45	*29	11	5	2624	65	9	1.59	....	....	....	....	....	4	*3	1	0	242	10	0	2.48	....	....	....	....
1932-33	St. Louis Flyers	AHA	43	23	19	1	2702	85	*5	1.89	....	....	....	....	....	4	2	2	0	284	6	*1	1.27	....	....	....	....
1933-34	Tulsa Oilers	AHA	48	23	25	0	2918	110	7	2.26	....	....	....	....	....	4	2	2	0	260	7	*1	1.62	....	....	....	....
1934-35	Tulsa Oilers	AHA	41	20	17	4	2640	77	4	*1.52	....	....	....	....	....	2	0	2	0	130	8	0	3.69	....	....	....	....
1935-36	**Chicago Black Hawks**	**NHL**	***48**	**21**	**19**	**8**	**2990**	**92**	**9**	**1.85**	**2.55**	....	....	....	....	**2**	**1**	**1**	**0**	**120**	**7**	**0**	**3.50**	....	....	....	....
1936-37	**Chicago Black Hawks**	**NHL**	***48**	**14**	***27**	**7**	**2978**	**131**	**5**	**2.64**	**3.30**	....	....	....	....	....	....	....	....	....	....	....	....	....	....	....	....
1937-38♦	**Chicago Black Hawks**	**NHL**	***48**	**14**	**25**	**9**	**2980**	**139**	**1**	**2.80**	**3.42**	....	....	....	....	***8**	***6**	**2**	....	***525**	**15**	***2**	**1.71**	....	....	....	....
1938-39	**Chicago Black Hawks**	**NHL**	***48**	**12**	***28**	**8**	**2988**	**132**	**5**	**2.65**	**3.21**	....	....	....	....	....	....	....	....	....	....	....	....	....	....	....	....
1939-40	**Chicago Black Hawks**	**NHL**	**17**	**7**	**9**	**1**	**1050**	**58**	**0**	**3.31**	**4.11**	....	....	....	....	....	....	....	....	....	....	....	....	....	....	....	....
	Providence Reds	AHL	14	7	5	2	860	43	1	3.00	....	....	....	....	....	8	*6	2	0	545	21	*2	2.31	....	....	....	....
	Montreal Canadiens	**NHL**	**5**	**0**	**4**	**1**	**310**	**18**	**0**	**3.48**	**4.27**	....	....	....	....	....	....	....	....	....	....	....	....	....	....	....	....
1940-41	Providence Reds	AHL	*56	*31	21	4	*3450	171	0	2.97	....	....	....	....	....	4	1	3	0	279	13	0	2.60	....	....	....	....
1941-42	Providence Reds	AHL	*56	17	*32	7	*3470	237	1	4.10	....	....	....	....	....	....	....	....	....	....	....	....	....	....	....	....	....
	New Haven Eagles	AHL	1	0	1	0	60	7	0	7.00	....	....	....	....	....	....	....	....	....	....	....	....	....	....	....	....	....
	Springfield Indians	AHL	....	....	....	....	....	....	....	....	....	....	....	....	....	3	0	2	0	160	7	0	2.63	....	....	....	....
1942-43	Providence Reds	AHL	*56	27	*27	2	3430	216	2	3.78	....	....	....	....	....	2	0	2	0	130	7	0	3.23	....	....	....	....
1943-44	Providence Reds	AHL	24	6	15	3	1440	67	0	3.63	....	....	....	....	....	....	....	....	....	....	....	....	....	....	....	....	....
	Chicago Black Hawks	**NHL**	**26**	**12**	**9**	**5**	**1560**	**79**	**3**	**3.04**	**2.21**	....	....	....	....	***9**	**4**	**5**	....	***549**	**24**	***1**	**2.62**	....	....	....	....
1944-45	**Chicago Black Hawks**	**NHL**	**48**	**12**	***29**	**7**	**2880**	**187**	***4**	**3.90**	**3.27**	....	....	....	....	....	....	....	....	....	....	....	....	....	....	....	....
1945-46	**Chicago Black Hawks**	**NHL**	**48**	**22**	**19**	**7**	**2880**	**166**	**1**	**3.46**	**3.17**	....	....	....	....	**4**	**0**	**4**	....	**240**	**26**	**0**	**6.50**	....	....	....	....
1946-47	Providence Reds	AHL	62	21	31	10	3720	266	0	4.29	....	....	....	....	....	....	....	....	....	....	....	....	....	....	....	....	....
1947-48	Providence Reds	AHL	2	1	1	0	120	7	0	3.50	....	....	....	....	....	....	....	....	....	....	....	....	....	....	....	....	....
	NHL Totals		**336**	**114**	**169**	**53**	**20616**	**1002**	**28**	**2.92**	....	....	....	....	....	**23**	**11**	**12**	**0**	**1434**	**72**	**3**	**3.01**	....	....	....	....

AHA First All-Star Team (1935) • NHL Rookie of the Year (1936) • AHL First All-Star Team (1941) • AHL Second All-Star Team (1943) • NHL Second All-Star Team (1945)

Signed as a free agent by **Chicago**, October 28, 1935. • Suspended by **Chicago** for remainder of 1939-40 season after refusing assignment to **Providence** (AHL), December 30, 1939. • Suspension lifted by NHL President Frank Calder and rights loaned to **Montreal** for remainder of 1939-40 season after Montreal goaltender Wilf Cude suffered season-ending shoulder injury, February 23, 1940. Traded to **Providence** (AHL) by **Chicago** for cash, May 14, 1940. Traded to **Chicago** by **Providence** (AHL) for Hec Highton, Gord Buttrey and $10,000, January 7, 1944.

• KEANS, Doug

Douglas Frederick G – L. 5'7", 185 lbs. b: Pembroke, Ont., 1/7/1958. Los Angeles' 2nd, 94th overall in 1978.

			REGULAR SEASON													PLAYOFFS											
Season	Club	League	GP	W	L	T	Mins	GA	SO	Avg	AAvg	Eff	SA	S%	SAPG	GP	W	L	T	Mins	GA	SO	Avg	Eff	SA	S%	SAPG
1975-76	Oshawa Legionaires	OMHA	STATISTICS NOT AVAILABLE																								
	Oshawa Generals	OMJHL	1	0	0	0	29	4	0	8.28	....	....	....	....	....	....	....	....	....	....	....	....	....	....	....	....	....
1976-77	Oshawa Generals	OMJHL	48	....	....	....	2632	291	0	6.63	....	....	....	....	....	....	....	....	....	....	....	....	....	....	....	....	....
1977-78	Oshawa Generals	OMJHL	42	....	....	....	2500	172	1	4.13	....	....	....	....	....	5	1	3	1	299	23	0	4.63	....	....	....	....
1978-79	Saginaw Gears	IHL	59	....	....	....	3207	217	0	4.06	....	....	....	....	....	2	....	....	....	120	10	0	5.05	....	....	....	....
1979-80	Saginaw Gears	IHL	22	....	....	....	1070	67	1	3.76	....	....	....	....	....	....	....	....	....	....	....	....	....	....	....	....	....
	Binghamton Dusters	AHL	7	3	3	2	429	25	0	3.50	....	....	....	....	....	....	....	....	....	....	....	....	....	....	....	....	....
	Los Angeles Kings	**NHL**	**10**	**3**	**3**	**3**	**559**	**23**	**0**	**2.47**	**2.18**	....	....	....	....	**1**	**0**	**1**	....	**40**	**7**	**0**	**10.50**	....	....	....	....
1980-81	**Los Angeles Kings**	**NHL**	**9**	**2**	**3**	**1**	**454**	**37**	**0**	**4.89**	**3.96**	....	....	....	....	....	....	....	....	....	....	....	....	....	....	....	....
	Houston Apollos	CHL	11	3	4	4	699	27	0	2.32	....	....	....	....	....	....	....	....	....	....	....	....	....	....	....	....	....
	Oklahoma City Stars	CHL	9	3	5	0	492	32	1	3.90	....	....	....	....	....	....	....	....	....	....	....	....	....	....	....	....	....
1981-82	**Los Angeles Kings**	**NHL**	**31**	**8**	**10**	**7**	**1436**	**103**	**0**	**4.30**	**3.33**	....	....	....	....	**2**	**0**	**1**	....	**32**	**1**	**0**	**1.88**	....	....	....	....
	New Haven Nighthawks	AHL	13	5	5	1	686	33	2	2.89	....	....	....	....	....	....	....	....	....	....	....	....	....	....	....	....	....
1982-83	**Los Angeles Kings**	**NHL**	**6**	**0**	**2**	**2**	**304**	**24**	**0**	**4.74**	**3.81**	**8.24**	**138**	**.826**	**27.2**	....	....	....	....	....	....	....	....	....	....	....	....
	New Haven Nighthawks	AHL	30	13	13	2	1724	125	0	4.35	....	....	....	....	....	....	....	....	....	....	....	....	....	....	....	....	....
1983-84	**Boston Bruins**	**NHL**	**33**	**19**	**8**	**3**	**1779**	**92**	**2**	**3.10**	**2.43**	**3.61**	**791**	**.884**	**26.7**	....	....	....	....	....	....	....	....	....	....	....	....
1984-85	**Boston Bruins**	**NHL**	**25**	**16**	**6**	**3**	**1497**	**82**	**1**	**3.29**	**2.62**	**4.03**	**669**	**.877**	**26.8**	**4**	**2**	**2**	....	**240**	**15**	**0**	**3.75**	**5.11**	**110**	**.864**	**27.5**
1985-86	**Boston Bruins**	**NHL**	**30**	**14**	**13**	**3**	**1757**	**107**	**0**	**3.65**	**2.85**	**4.99**	**782**	**.863**	**26.7**	....	....	....	....	....	....	....	....	....	....	....	....
1986-87	**Boston Bruins**	**NHL**	**36**	**18**	**8**	**4**	**1942**	**108**	**0**	**3.34**	**2.82**	**3.97**	**909**	**.881**	**28.1**	**2**	**0**	**2**	....	**120**	**11**	**0**	**5.50**	**10.43**	**58**	**.810**	**29.0**
1987-88	**Boston Bruins**	**NHL**	**30**	**16**	**11**	**0**	**1660**	**90**	**1**	**3.25**	**2.70**	**3.89**	**751**	**.880**	**27.1**	....	....	....	....	....	....	....	....	....	....	....	....
	Maine Mariners	AHL	10	8	2	0	600	34	0	3.40	....	....	....	....	....	10	5	5	0	617	42	0	4.08	....	....	....	....
1988-89	Baltimore Skipjacks	AHL	4	1	3	0	239	17	0	4.27	....	....	....	....	....	....	....	....	....	....	....	....	....	....	....	....	....
	Springfield Indians	AHL	32	11	16	2	1737	124	0	4.28	....	....	....	....	....	....	....	....	....	....	....	....	....	....	....	....	....
1989-90			DID NOT PLAY																								
1990-91			DID NOT PLAY																								
1991-92			DID NOT PLAY																								
1992-93	Minnesota Iron Rangers	AmHA	8	2	6	0	481	39	0	4.86	....	....	....	....	....	....	....	....	....	....	....	....	....	....	....	....	....
	Jacksonville Bullets	SunHL	15	8	5	0	801	53	*1	3.97	....	....	....	....	....	5	2	2	1	301	17	0	3.39	....	....	....	....
1993-94			DID NOT PLAY																								
1994-95			DID NOT PLAY																								
1995-96	Jacksonville Bullets	SunHL	9	5	3	0	430	53	0	5.15	....	....	....	....	....	....	....	....	....	....	....	....	....	....	....	....	....
	NHL Totals		**210**	**96**	**64**	**26**	**11388**	**666**	**4**	**3.51**	....	....	....	....	....	**9**	**2**	**6**	....	**432**	**34**	**0**	**4.72**	....	....	....	....

Claimed on waivers by **Boston** from **LA Kings**, May 24, 1983.

• KEENAN, Don

Donald Robert James G – L. 6', 170 lbs. b: Toronto, Ontario, 8/8/1938.

Season	Club	League	GP	W	L	T	Mins	GA	SO	Avg	AAvg	Eff	SA	S%	SAPG	GP	W	L	T	Mins	GA	SO	Avg	Eff	SA	S%	SAPG
1955-56	St. Michael's Majors	OHA-Jr.	2	....	....	....	120	10	0	5.00	....	....	....	....	....	....	....	....	....	....	....	....	....	....	....	....	....
	St. Francis Xavier X-Men	MIHC	DID NOT PLAY – SPARE GOALTENDER																								
1956-57	St. Francis Xavier X-Men	MIHC	7	5	0	2	420	22	0	3.14	....	....	....	....	....	6	*5	0	1	360	10	*2	*1.67	....	....	....	....
1957-58	St. Francis Xavier X-Men	MIHC	7	*7	0	0	420	18	*1	*2.57	....	....	....	....	....	5	*4	0	1	300	11	0	*2.20	....	....	....	....
1958-59	**Boston Bruins**	**NHL**	**1**	**0**	**1**	**0**	**60**	**4**	**0**	**4.00**	**4.26**	....	....	....	....	....	....	....	....	....	....	....	....	....	....	....	....
1959-60	University of Toronto	OQAA	STATISTICS NOT AVAILABLE																								
	NHL Totals		**1**	**0**	**1**	**0**	**60**	**4**	**0**	**4.00**	....	....	....	....	....	....	....	....	....	....	....	....	....	....	....	....	....

Loaned to **Boston** by **Toronto** (St. Michael's/OHA-Jr.) to replace Harry Lumley, March 7, 1959. (Toronto 4, Boston 1).

• KERR, Davey

David Alexander G – R. 5'10", 160 lbs. b: Toronto, Ont., 1/11/1910 d: 5/11/1978.

Season	Club	League	GP	W	L	T	Mins	GA	SO	Avg	AAvg	Eff	SA	S%	SAPG	GP	W	L	T	Mins	GA	SO	Avg	Eff	SA	S%	SAPG
1924-25	Toronto Canoe Club	OHA-Jr.	3	2	0	0	140	5	0	2.14	....	....	....	....	....	2	0	2	0	120	7	0	3.50	....	....	....	....
1925-26	Toronto Canoe Club	OHA-Jr.	7	3	3	0	380	22	0	3.47	....	....	....	....	....	....	....	....	....	....	....	....	....	....	....	....	....
1926-27	Iroquois Papermakers	NOJHA	STATISTICS NOT AVAILABLE																								
1927-28	Iroquois Papermakers	NOHA	STATISTICS NOT AVAILABLE																								
1928-29	Iroquois Papermakers	NOHA	STATISTICS NOT AVAILABLE																								
1929-30	Montreal AAA	MCHL	9	*8	0	1	540	6	4	*0.67	....	....	....	....	....	2	1	1	0	150	2	*1	*0.80	....	....	....	....
	Montreal CPR	MCHL	9	3	2	4	540	10	3	1.11	....	....	....	....	....	2	0	1	0	120	4	0	2.00	....	....	....	....
	Montreal AAA	Al-Cup	9	*7	0	2	610	5	*5	*0.49	....	....	....	....	....	....	....	....	....	....	....	....	....	....	....	....	....
1930-31	**Montreal Maroons**	**NHL**	**29**	**13**	**11**	**4**	**1769**	**70**	**1**	**2.37**	**3.01**	....	....	....	....	**2**	**0**	**2**	**0**	**120**	**8**	**0**	**4.00**	....	....	....	....
1931-32	Windsor Bulldogs	IHL	34	14	13	7	2140	68	6	1.91	....	....	....	....	....	....	....	....	....	....	....	....	....	....	....	....	....
	New York Americans	**NHL**	**1**	**0**	**1**	**0**	**60**	**6**	**0**	**6.00**	**7.36**	....	....	....	....	....	....	....	....	....	....	....	....	....	....	....	....
1932-33	**Montreal Maroons**	**NHL**	**25**	**14**	**8**	**3**	**1520**	**58**	**4**	**2.29**	**3.07**	....	....	....	....	**2**	**0**	**2**	**0**	**120**	**5**	**0**	**2.50**	....	....	....	....
	Philadelphia Arrows	Can-Am	16	8	3	5	1020	31	2	1.82	....	....	....	....	....	....	....	....	....	....	....	....	....	....	....	....	....
1933-34	**Montreal Maroons**	**NHL**	***48**	**19**	**18**	**11**	**3060**	**122**	**6**	**2.39**	**3.02**	....	....	....	....	**4**	**1**	**2**	**1**	**240**	**7**	**1**	**1.75**	....	....	....	....
1934-35	**New York Rangers**	**NHL**	**37**	**19**	**12**	**6**	**2290**	**94**	**4**	**2.46**	**2.97**	....	....	....	....	**4**	**1**	**1**	**2**	**240**	**10**	**0**	**2.50**	....	....	....	....
1935-36	**New York Rangers**	**NHL**	**47**	**18**	**17**	**12**	**2980**	**95**	**8**	**1.91**	**2.64**	....	....	....	....	....	....	....	....	....	....	....	....	....	....	....	....
1936-37	**New York Rangers**	**NHL**	***48**	**19**	**20**	**9**	**3020**	**106**	**4**	**2.11**	**2.55**	....	....	....	....	***9**	***6**	**3**	....	***553**	**10**	***4**	***1.08**	....	....	....	....
1937-38	**New York Rangers**	**NHL**	***48**	**27**	**15**	**6**	**2960**	**96**	***8**	**1.95**	**2.27**	....	....	....	....	**3**	**1**	**2**	....	**262**	**8**	**0**	**1.83**	....	....	....	....
1938-39	**New York Rangers**	**NHL**	***48**	**26**	**16**	**6**	**2970**	**105**	**6**	**2.12**	**2.48**	....	....	....	....	**1**	**0**	**1**	....	**119**	**2**	**0**	**1.01**	....	....	....	....
1939-40♦	**New York Rangers**	**NHL**	***48**	**27**	**11**	**10**	**3000**	**77**	***8**	***1.54**	**1.76**	....	....	....	....	***12**	***8**	**4**	....	***770**	**20**	***3**	***1.56**	....	....	....	....
1940-41	**New York Rangers**	**NHL**	***48**	**21**	**19**	**8**	**3010**	**125**	**2**	**2.49**	**2.80**	....	....	....	....	**3**	**1**	**2**	....	**192**	**6**	**0**	**1.88**	....	....	....	....
	NHL Totals		**427**	**203**	**148**	**75**	**26639**	**954**	**51**	**2.15**	....	....	....	....	....	**40**	**18**	**19**	**3**	**2616**	**76**	**8**	**1.74**	....	....	....	....

NHL Second All-Star Team (1938) • NHL First All-Star Team (1940) • Won Vezina Trophy (1940)

Signed as a free agent by **Montreal Maroons**, September 2, 1930. Loaned to **NY Americans** by **Montreal Maroons** to replace injured Roy Worters, March 8, 1932. (Montreal Canadiens 6, NY Americans 1). Traded to **NY Rangers** by **Montreal Maroons** for cash, December 14, 1934.

• KHABIBULIN, Nikolai

"Bulin Wall" G – L. 6'1", 196 lbs. b: Sverdlovsk, USSR, 1/13/1973. Winnipeg's 8th, 204th overall in 1992.

Season	Club	League	GP	W	L	T	Mins	GA	SO	Avg	AAvg	Eff	SA	S%	SAPG	GP	W	L	T	Mins	GA	SO	Avg	Eff	SA	S%	SAPG
1988-89	Avtomo Sverdlovsk	USSR-Jr.	STATISTICS NOT AVAILABLE																								
	Avtomo Sverdlovsk	USSR-2	1	0	0	0	3	0	0	0.00	....	....	....	....	....	....	....	....	....	....	....	....	....	....	....	....	....
1989-90	Avtomo Sverdlovsk	USSR-Jr.	STATISTICS NOT AVAILABLE																								
1990-91	Sputnick Nizhy	USSR-Jr.	STATISTICS NOT AVAILABLE																								
	Soviet Union	EJC-A	5	....	....	....	242	11	....	2.73	....	....	....	....	....	....	....	....	....	....	....	....	....	....	....	....	....
1991-92	CSKA Moscow	CIS	2	....	....	....	34	2	0	3.52	....	....	....	....	....	....	....	....	....	....	....	....	....	....	....	....	....
	Russia	WJC-A	6	*6	0	0	289	7	*2	*1.45	....	....	....	....	....	....	....	....	....	....	....	....	....	....	....	....	....
	Russia	Olympics	DID NOT PLAY – SPARE GOALTENDER																								
1992-93	CSKA Moscow	CIS	13	....	....	....	491	27	....	3.29	....	....	....	....	....	....	....	....	....	....	....	....	....	....	....	....	....
	Soviet Union	WJC-A	6	2	3	1	340	15	1	2.65	....	....	....	....	....	....	....	....	....	....	....	....	....	....	....	....	....
1993-94	CSKA Moscow	CIS	46	....	....	....	2625	116	....	2.65	....	....	....	....	....	3	....	....	....	193	11	....	3.42	....	....	....	....
	Russian Penguins	IHL	12	2	7	2	639	47	0	4.41	....	....	....	....	....	....	....	....	....	....	....	....	....	....	....	....	....
1994-95	Springfield Falcons	AHL	23	9	9	3	1240	80	0	3.87	....	....	....	....	....	....	....	....	....	....	....	....	....	....	....	....	....
	Winnipeg Jets	**NHL**	**26**	**8**	**9**	**4**	**1339**	**76**	**0**	**3.41**	**3.58**	**3.58**	**723**	**.895**	**32.4**	....	....	....	....	....	....	....	....	....	....	....	....
1995-96	**Winnipeg Jets**	**NHL**	**53**	**26**	**20**	**3**	**2914**	**152**	**2**	**3.13**	**3.11**	**2.87**	**1656**	**.908**	**34.1**	**6**	**2**	**4**	....	**359**	**19**	**0**	**3.18**	**2.82**	**214**	**.911**	**35.8**
1996-97	Russia	W-Cup	2	0	2	0	100	10	0	6.00	....	....	....	....	....	....	....	....	....	....	....	....	....	....	....	....	....
	Phoenix Coyotes	**NHL**	**72**	**30**	**33**	**6**	**4091**	**193**	**7**	**2.83**	**3.05**	**2.61**	**2094**	**.908**	**30.7**	**7**	**3**	**4**	....	**426**	**15**	**1**	**2.11**	**1.43**	**222**	**.932**	**31.3**

			REGULAR SEASON													PLAYOFFS											
Season	Club	League	GP	W	L	T	Mins	GA	SO	Avg	AAvg	Eff	SA	S%	SAPG	GP	W	L	T	Mins	GA	SO	Avg	Eff	SA	S%	SAPG
1997-98	**Phoenix Coyotes**	**NHL**	**70**	**30**	**28**	**10**	**4026**	**184**	**4**	**2.74**	**3.27**	**2.75**	**1835**	**.900**	**27.3**	**4**	**2**	**1**	....	**185**	**13**	**0**	**4.22**	**5.18**	**106**	**.877**	**34.4**
1998-99	**Phoenix Coyotes**	**NHL**	**63**	**32**	**23**	**7**	**3657**	**130**	**8**	**2.13**	**2.52**	**1.65**	**1681**	**.923**	**27.6**	**7**	**3**	**4**	....	**449**	**18**	**0**	**2.41**	**1.84**	**236**	**.924**	**31.5**
99-2000	Long Beach Ice Dogs	IHL	33	21	11	1	1936	59	5	*1.83	....	....	....	....	....	5	2	3	....	321	15	0	2.81	....	....	....	....
	NHL Totals		**284**	**126**	**113**	**30**	**16027**	**735**	**21**	**2.75**	....	....	**7989**	**.908**	**29.9**	**24**	**10**	**13**	....	**1419**	**65**	**1**	**2.75**	....	**778**	**.916**	**32.9**

• Won James Gatschene Memorial Trophy (MVP - IHL) (tied with Frederic Chabot) (2000) • Played in NHL All-Star Game (1998, 1999)

Transferred to **Phoenix** after **Winnipeg** franchise relocated, July 1, 1996. • Sat out entire 1999-2000 NHL season after failing to come to contract terms with **Phoenix**. Signed as a free agent by **Long Beach** (IHL) with **Phoenix** retaining NHL rights, January 14, 2000.

• KIDD, Trevor

G – L. 6'2", 190 lbs. b: Dugald, Man., 3/29/1972. Calgary's 1st, 11th overall in 1990.

Season	Club	League	GP	W	L	T	Mins	GA	SO	Avg	AAvg	Eff	SA	S%	SAPG	GP	W	L	T	Mins	GA	SO	Avg	Eff	SA	S%	SAPG
1987-88	Eastman Selects	MAHA	14	....	....	....	840	66	0	4.72	....	....	....	....	....	....	....	....	....	....	....	....	....	....	....	....	....
1988-89	Brandon Wheat Kings	WHL	32	11	13	1	1509	102	0	4.06	....	....	....	....	....	....	....	....	....	....	....	....	....	....	....	....	....
1989-90	Brandon Wheat Kings	WHL	*63	24	32	2	*3676	254	2	4.15	....	....	....	....	....	....	....	....	....	....	....	....	....	....	....	....	....
	Canada	WJC-A	DID NOT PLAY – SPARE GOALTENDER																								
1990-91	Brandon Wheat Kings	WHL	30	10	19	1	1730	117	0	4.06	....	....	....	....	....	....	....	....	....	....	....	....	....	....	....	....	....
	Canada	WJC-A	6	....	....	....	340	15	....	2.65	....	....	....	....	....	....	....	....	....	....	....	....	....	....	....	....	....
	Spokane Chiefs	WHL	14	8	3	0	749	44	0	3.52	....	....	....	....	....	15	*14	1	....	926	32	2	*2.07	....	....	....	....
	Spokane Chiefs	Mem-Cup	3	*3	0	0	180	5	0	*1.67	....	....	....	....	....	....	....	....	....	....	....	....	....	....	....	....	....
1991-92	Canada	Nat-Team	28	18	4	4	1349	79	2	3.51	....	....	....	....	....	....	....	....	....	....	....	....	....	....	....	....	....
	Canada	WJC-A	7	2	3	2	420	29	1	4.14	....	....	....	....	....	....	....	....	....	....	....	....	....	....	....	....	....
	Canada	Olympics	1	1	0	0	60	0	1	0.00	....	....	....	....	....	....	....	....	....	....	....	....	....	....	....	....	....
	Calgary Flames	**NHL**	**2**	**1**	**1**	**0**	**120**	**8**	**0**	**4.00**	**3.58**	**5.71**	**56**	**.857**	**28.0**	....	....	....	....	....	....	....	....	....	....	....	....
	Canada	WC-A	1	1	0	0	60	3	0	3.00	....	....	....	....	....	....	....	....	....	....	....	....	....	....	....	....	....
1992-93	Salt Lake Golden Eagles	IHL	29	10	16	1	1696	111	1	3.93	....	....	....	....	....	....	....	....	....	....	....	....	....	....	....	....	....
1993-94	**Calgary Flames**	**NHL**	**31**	**13**	**7**	**6**	**1614**	**85**	**0**	**3.16**	**3.04**	**3.57**	**752**	**.887**	**28.0**	....	....	....	....	....	....	....	....	....	....	....	....
1994-95	**Calgary Flames**	**NHL**	***43**	**22**	**14**	**6**	***2463**	**107**	**3**	**2.61**	**2.72**	**2.39**	**1170**	**.909**	**28.5**	**7**	**3**	**4**	....	**434**	**26**	**1**	**3.59**	**5.16**	**181**	**.856**	**25.0**
1995-96	**Calgary Flames**	**NHL**	**47**	**15**	**21**	**8**	**2570**	**119**	**3**	**2.78**	**2.76**	**2.93**	**1130**	**.895**	**26.4**	**2**	**0**	**1**	....	**83**	**9**	**0**	**6.51**	**14.65**	**40**	**.775**	**28.9**
1996-97	**Calgary Flames**	**NHL**	**55**	**21**	**23**	**6**	**2979**	**141**	**4**	**2.84**	**3.06**	**2.83**	**1416**	**.900**	**28.5**	....	....	....	....	....	....	....	....	....	....	....	....
1997-98	**Carolina Hurricanes**	**NHL**	**47**	**21**	**21**	**3**	**2685**	**97**	**3**	**2.17**	**2.58**	**1.70**	**1237**	**.922**	**27.6**	....	....	....	....	....	....	....	....	....	....	....	....
1998-99	**Carolina Hurricanes**	**NHL**	**25**	**7**	**10**	**6**	**1358**	**61**	**2**	**2.70**	**3.21**	**2.57**	**640**	**.905**	**28.3**	....	....	....	....	....	....	....	....	....	....	....	....
99-2000	**Florida Panthers**	**NHL**	**28**	**14**	**11**	**2**	**1574**	**69**	**1**	**2.63**	**3.00**	**2.24**	**809**	**.915**	**30.8**	....	....	....	....	....	....	....	....	....	....	....	....
	Louisville Panthers	AHL	1	0	1	0	60	5	0	5.04	....	....	....	....	....	....	....	....	....	....	....	....	....	....	....	....	....
	NHL Totals		**278**	**114**	**108**	**37**	**15363**	**687**	**16**	**2.68**	....	....	**7210**	**.905**	**28.2**	**9**	**3**	**5**	....	**517**	**35**	**1**	**4.06**	....	**221**	**.842**	**25.6**

WHL East First All-Star Team (1990) • Canadian Major Junior Goaltender of the Year (1990)

Traded to **Carolina** by **Calgary** with Gary Roberts for Andrew Cassels and Jean-Sebastien Giguere, August 25, 1997. Claimed by **Atlanta** from **Carolina** in Expansion Draft, June 25, 1999. Traded to **Florida** by **Atlanta** for Gord Murphy, Herbert Vasiljevs, Daniel Tjarnqvist and Ottawa's 6th round choice (previously acquired and later traded to Dallas - Dallas selected Justin Cox) in 1999 Entry Draft, June 25, 1999.

• KING, Scott

Scott Glenndale Martin G – L. 6'1", 185 lbs. b: Thunder Bay, Ont., 6/25/1967. Detroit's 10th, 190th overall in 1986.

Season	Club	League	GP	W	L	T	Mins	GA	SO	Avg	AAvg	Eff	SA	S%	SAPG	GP	W	L	T	Mins	GA	SO	Avg	Eff	SA	S%	SAPG
1984-85	Richmond Sockeyes	BCJHL	40	23	9	0	2067	174	0	5.05	....	....	....	....	....	....	....	....	....	....	....	....	....	....	....	....	....
1985-86	Vernon Lakers	BCJHL	29	17	9	0	1718	133	0	4.64	....	....	....	....	....	....	....	....	....	....	....	....	....	....	....	....	....
1986-87	University of Maine	H-East	21	11	6	1	1111	58	0	3.13	....	....	....	....	....	2	1	1	0	115	7	0	3.65	....	....	....	....
	Abbotsford Falcons	BCJHL	11	....	....	....	582	52	0	5.43	....	....	....	....	....	....	....	....	....	....	....	....	....	....	....	....	....
1987-88	University of Maine	H-East	33	25	5	1	1762	91	0	3.10	....	....	....	....	....	6	4	2	0	340	20	0	3.53	....	....	....	....
1988-89	University of Maine	H-East	27	13	8	0	1394	83	0	3.57	....	....	....	....	....	3	1	2	0	189	17	0	5.40	....	....	....	....
1989-90	University of Maine	H-East	29	17	7	2	1526	67	1	2.63	....	....	....	....	....	4	2	2	0	240	9	1	2.25	....	....	....	....
1990-91	**Detroit Red Wings**	**NHL**	**1**	**0**	**0**	**0**	**45**	**2**	**0**	**2.67**	**2.40**	**4.85**	**11**	**.818**	**14.7**	....	....	....	....	....	....	....	....	....	....	....	....
	Adirondack Red Wings	AHL	24	8	10	2	1287	91	0	4.24	....	....	....	....	....	1	0	0	0	32	4	0	7.50	....	....	....	....
	Hampton Roads Admirals	ECHL	15	8	4	1	819	57	0	4.17	....	....	....	....	....	....	....	....	....	....	....	....	....	....	....	....	....
1991-92	**Detroit Red Wings**	**NHL**	**1**	**0**	**0**	**0**	**16**	**1**	**0**	**3.75**	**3.36**	**7.50**	**5**	**.800**	**18.8**	....	....	....	....	....	....	....	....	....	....	....	....
	Adirondack Red Wings	AHL	33	14	14	3	1904	112	0	3.53	....	....	....	....	....	....	....	....	....	....	....	....	....	....	....	....	....
	Toledo Storm	ECHL	7	4	2	1	424	25	0	3.54	....	....	....	....	....	....	....	....	....	....	....	....	....	....	....	....	....
1992-93	Adirondack Red Wings	AHL	1	1	0	0	60	1	0	1.00	....	....	....	....	....	....	....	....	....	....	....	....	....	....	....	....	....
	Toledo Storm	ECHL	*45	*26	11	7	*2602	153	2	3.53	....	....	....	....	....	*14	*10	3	0	*823	52	0	3.79	....	....	....	....
	NHL Totals		**2**	**0**	**0**	**0**	**61**	**3**	**0**	**2.95**	....	....	**16**	**.813**	**15.7**	....	....	....	....	....	....	....	....	....	....	....	....

Hockey East First All-Star Team (1988, 1990) • Hockey East Second All-Star Team (1989) • ECHL Second All-Star Team (1993)

• KLEISINGER, Terry

G – R. 6', 190 lbs. b: Regina, Sask., 10/10/1960.

Season	Club	League	GP	W	L	T	Mins	GA	SO	Avg	AAvg	Eff	SA	S%	SAPG	GP	W	L	T	Mins	GA	SO	Avg	Eff	SA	S%	SAPG
1979-80	Nanaimo Clippers	BCJHL	49	....	....	....	2588	200	0	4.63	....	....	....	....	....	....	....	....	....	....	....	....	....	....	....	....	....
1980-81	University of Wisconsin	WCHA	16	11	5	0	1011	61	2	3.62	....	....	....	....	....	1	0	1	0	34	7	0	12.36	....	....	....	....
1981-82	University of Wisconsin	WCHA	22	14	8	0	1337	59	4	2.65	....	....	....	....	....	5	3	2	0	300	10	2	2.00	....	....	....	....
1982-83	University of Wisconsin	WCHA	18	11	6	1	1021	48	3	2.82	....	....	....	....	....	1	1	0	0	60	1	0	1.00	....	....	....	....
1983-84	University of Wisconsin	WCHA	24	11	11	1	1406	96	0	4.10	....	....	....	....	....	2	0	2	0	109	12	0	6.63	....	....	....	....
1984-85			DID NOT PLAY																								
1985-86	**New York Rangers**	**NHL**	**4**	**0**	**2**	**0**	**191**	**14**	**0**	**4.40**	**3.44**	**5.65**	**109**	**.872**	**34.2**	....	....	....	....	....	....	....	....	....	....	....	....
	Flint Spirits	IHL	4	0	3	0	200	25	0	7.50	....	....	....	....	....	....	....	....	....	....	....	....	....	....	....	....	....
	Toledo Goaldiggers	IHL	14	1	10	0	786	76	0	5.80	....	....	....	....	....	....	....	....	....	....	....	....	....	....	....	....	....
	New Haven Nighthawks	AHL	10	2	5	2	497	34	0	4.10	....	....	....	....	....	....	....	....	....	....	....	....	....	....	....	....	....
1986-87	New Haven Nighthawks	AHL	1	0	1	0	40	4	0	6.00	....	....	....	....	....	....	....	....	....	....	....	....	....	....	....	....	....
	Flint Spirits	IHL	2	0	0	0	53	5	0	5.66	....	....	....	....	....	....	....	....	....	....	....	....	....	....	....	....	....
	Indianapolis Checkers	IHL	4	0	4	0	240	25	0	6.25	....	....	....	....	....	....	....	....	....	....	....	....	....	....	....	....	....
	NHL Totals		**4**	**0**	**2**	**0**	**191**	**14**	**0**	**4.40**	....	....	**109**	**.872**	**34.2**	....	....	....	....	....	....	....	....	....	....	....	....

• Missed entire 1984-85 season recovering from mononucleosis. Signed as a free agent by **NY Rangers**, October 8, 1985.

• KLYMKIW, Julian

G – R. 5'11", 180 lbs. b: Winnipeg, Man., 7/16/1933.

Season	Club	League	GP	W	L	T	Mins	GA	SO	Avg	AAvg	Eff	SA	S%	SAPG	GP	W	L	T	Mins	GA	SO	Avg	Eff	SA	S%	SAPG
1951-52	Brandon Wheat Kings	MJHL	16	8	8	0	960	66	0	4.13	....	....	....	....	....	....	....	....	....	....	....	....	....	....	....	....	....
1952-53	Brandon Wheat Kings	MJHL	36	*23	11	1	2160	123	*1	3.36	....	....	....	....	....	4	....	....	....	240	18	0	4.50	....	....	....	....
1953-54	EHL Roving Goaltender	EHL	57	....	....	....	3420	239	1	4.19	....	....	....	....	....	....	....	....	....	....	....	....	....	....	....	....	....
1954-55	Brandon Wheat Kings	MHL-Sr.	24	....	....	....	1440	95	*2	*3.96	....	....	....	....	....	....	....	....	....	....	....	....	....	....	....	....	....
1955-56			STATISTICS NOT AVAILABLE																								
1956-57	Winnipeg Warriors	WHL	4	2	2	0	240	20	0	5.00	....	....	....	....	....	....	....	....	....	....	....	....	....	....	....	....	....
	Sault Ste. Marie Greyhounds	NOHA	33	....	....	....	1980	133	1	4.03	....	....	....	....	....	....	....	....	....	....	....	....	....	....	....	....	....
1957-58	Winnipeg Warriors	WHL	3	0	2	1	180	8	0	2.67	....	....	....	....	....	....	....	....	....	....	....	....	....	....	....	....	....
	Winnipeg Maroons	Al-Cup	1	1	0	0	60	2	0	2.00	....	....	....	....	....	....	....	....	....	....	....	....	....	....	....	....	....
1958-59	**New York Rangers**	**NHL**	**1**	**0**	**0**	**0**	**19**	**2**	**0**	**6.32**	**6.72**	....	....	....	....	....	....	....	....	....	....	....	....	....	....	....	....
1959-60			DID NOT PLAY																								
1960-61			DID NOT PLAY																								
1961-62	Warroad Lakers	OMHL	1	....	....	....	60	3	0	3.00	....	....	....	....	....	....	....	....	....	....	....	....	....	....	....	....	....
	Winnipeg Maroons	Al-Cup	2	....	....	....	110	7	0	3.82	....	....	....	....	....	....	....	....	....	....	....	....	....	....	....	....	....
1962-63	Winnipeg Maroons	SSHL	6	....	....	....	360	25	0	4.17	....	....	....	....	....	....	....	....	....	....	....	....	....	....	....	....	....
	Winnipeg Maroons	Al-Cup	10	....	....	....	610	35	0	3.44	....	....	....	....	....	....	....	....	....	....	....	....	....	....	....	....	....
1963-64	Winnipeg Maroons	X-Games	STATISTICS NOT AVAILABLE																								
1964-65	Winnipeg Maroons	SSHL	2	....	....	....	120	8	0	4.00	....	....	....	....	....	....	....	....	....	....	....	....	....	....	....	....	....
	NHL Totals		**1**	**0**	**0**	**0**	**19**	**2**	**0**	**6.32**	....	....	....	....	....	....	....	....	....	....	....	....	....	....	....	....	....

• Served as a roving goaltender for **EHL** (Troy-Louisville-Grand Rapids) for 1953-54 season. **Detroit's** assistant trainer/practice goaltender loaned to **NY Rangers** to replace injured Gump Worsley in 3rd period, October 12, 1958. (Detroit 3, NY Rangers 0).

• KNICKLE, Rick

G – L. 5'10", 175 lbs. b: Chatham, N.B., 2/26/1960. Buffalo's 7th, 116th overall in 1979.

			REGULAR SEASON													PLAYOFFS											
Season	Club	League	GP	W	L	T	Mins	GA	SO	Avg	AAvg	Eff	SA	S%	SAPG	GP	W	L	T	Mins	GA	SO	Avg	Eff	SA	S%	SAPG
1976-77	Coles Harbour Colts	MJrHL	13	....	....	....	780	40	1	3.08	....	....	....	....	....	....	....	....	....	....	....	....	....	....	....	....	....
1977-78	Brandon Travellers	MJHL	7	....	....	....	427	26	0	3.65	....	....	....	....	....	....	....	....	....	....	....	....	....	....	....	....	....
	Brandon Wheat Kings	WCJHL	49	34	5	7	2806	182	0	3.89	....	....	....	....	....	8	4	4	....	450	36	0	4.82	....	....	....	....
1978-79	Brandon Wheat Kings	WHL	38	26	3	8	2240	118	1	*3.16	....	....	....	....	....	16	12	3	....	886	41	*1	*2.78	....	....	....	....
	Brandon Wheat Kings	Mem-Cup	2	0	2	0	123	11	0	3.57	....	....	....	....	....	....	....	....	....	....	....	....	....	....	....	....	....
1979-80	Brandon Wheat Kings	WHL	33	11	14	1	1604	125	0	4.68	....	....	....	....	....	....	....	....	....	....	....	....	....	....	....	....	....
	Muskegon Mohawks	IHL	16	....	....	....	829	52	0	3.76	....	....	....	....	....	3	....	....	....	156	17	0	6.54	....	....	....	....
1980-81	Erie Blades	EHL	43	....	....	....	2347	125	1	*3.20	....	....	....	....	....	8	....	....	....	446	14	0	*1.88	....	....	....	....
1981-82	Rochester Americans	AHL	31	10	12	5	1753	108	1	3.70	....	....	....	....	....	3	0	2	....	125	7	0	3.37	....	....	....	....
1982-83	Flint Generals	IHL	27	....	....	....	1638	92	2	3.37	....	....	....	....	....	3	....	....	....	193	10	0	3.11	....	....	....	....
	Rochester Americans	AHL	4	0	3	0	143	11	0	4.64	....	....	....	....	....	....	....	....	....	....	....	....	....	....	....	....	....
1983-84	Flint Generals	IHL	60	32	21	5	3518	203	3	3.46	....	....	....	....	....	8	8	0	....	480	24	0	3.00	....	....	....	....
1984-85	Flint Generals	IHL	36	18	11	3	2018	115	2	3.42	....	....	....	....	....	7	3	4	....	401	27	0	4.04	....	....	....	....
	Sherbrooke Canadiens	AHL	14	7	6	0	780	53	0	4.08	....	....	....	....	....	....	....	....	....	....	....	....	....	....	....	....	....
1985-86	Saginaw Generals	IHL	39	16	15	2	2235	135	2	3.62	....	....	....	....	....	3	2	1	....	193	12	0	3.73	....	....	....	....
1986-87	Saginaw Generals	IHL	26	9	13	0	1413	113	0	4.80	....	....	....	....	....	5	1	4	....	329	21	0	3.83	....	....	....	....
1987-88	Flint Spirits	IHL	1	0	1	0	60	4	0	4.00	....	....	....	....	....	....	....	....	....	....	....	....	....	....	....	....	....
	Peoria Rivermen	IHL	13	2	8	1	705	58	0	4.94	....	....	....	....	....	6	3	3	....	294	20		4.08	....	....	....	....
1988-89	Fort Wayne Komets	IHL	47	22	16	0	2716	141	1	*3.11	....	....	....	....	....	4	1	2	....	173	15	0	5.20	....	....	....	....
1989-90	Flint Spirits	IHL	55	25	24	1	2998	210	1	4.20	....	....	....	....	....	2	0	2	....	101	13	0	7.72	....	....	....	....
1990-91	Albany Choppers	IHL	14	4	6	2	679	52	0	4.59	....	....	....	....	....	....	....	....	....	....	....	....	....	....	....	....	....
	Springfield Indians	AHL	9	6	0	2	509	28	0	3.30	....	....	....	....	....	....	....	....	....	....	....	....	....	....	....	....	....
1991-92	San Diego Gulls	IHL	46	*28	13	4	2686	155	0	3.46	....	....	....	....	....	2	0	1	....	78	3	0	2.31	....	....	....	....
1992-93	San Diego Gulls	IHL	41	33	4	4	2437	88	*4	*2.17	....	....	....	....	....	....	....	....	....	....	....	....	....	....	....	....	....
	Los Angeles Kings	**NHL**	**10**	**6**	**4**	**0**	**532**	**35**	**0**	**3.95**	**3.38**	**4.73**	**292**	**.880**	**32.9**	....	....	....	....	....	....	....	....	....	....	....	....
1993-94	**Los Angeles Kings**	**NHL**	**4**	**1**	**2**	**0**	**174**	**9**	**0**	**3.10**	**2.98**	**3.93**	**71**	**.873**	**24.5**	....	....	....	....	....	....	....	....	....	....	....	....
	Phoenix Roadrunners	IHL	25	8	9	3	1292	89	1	4.13	....	....	....	....	....	....	....	....	....	....	....	....	....	....	....	....	....
1994-95	Detroit Vipers	IHL	49	24	15	5	2725	134	*3	2.95	....	....	....	....	....	....	....	....	....	....	....	....	....	....	....	....	....
1995-96	Detroit Vipers	IHL	18	9	5	1	872	50	0	3.44	....	....	....	....	....	....	....	....	....	....	....	....	....	....	....	....	....
	Las Vegas Thunder	IHL	7	6	1	0	420	27	0	3.86	....	....	....	....	....	4	1	0	....	126	7	0	3.33	....	....	....	....
1996-97	Milwaukee Admirals	IHL	19	5	9	1	940	60	0	3.83	....	....	....	....	....	....	....	....	....	....	....	....	....	....	....	....	....
	NHL Totals		**14**	**7**	**6**	**0**	**706**	**44**	**0**	**3.74**	....	....	**363**	**.879**	**30.8**	....	....	....	....	....	....	....	....	....	....	....	....

WHL First All-Star Team (1979) • EHL First All-Star Team (1981) • IHL Second All-Star Team (1984, 1992) • IHL First All-Star Team (1989, 1993) • Won James Norris Memorial Trophy (fewest goals against - IHL) (1989) • Shared James Norris Memorial Trophy (fewest goals against - IHL) with Clint Malarchuk (1993)

Signed as a free agent by **Montreal**, February 8, 1985. Signed as a free agent by **LA Kings**, February 16, 1993.

• KOCHAN, Dieter

G – L. 6'1", 180 lbs. b: Saskatoon, SK, 5/11/1974. Vancouver's 3rd, 98th overall in 1993.

Season	Club	League	GP	W	L	T	Mins	GA	SO	Avg	AAvg	Eff	SA	S%	SAPG	GP	W	L	T	Mins	GA	SO	Avg	Eff	SA	S%	SAPG
1990-91	Edgewood Eagles	Hi-School	STATISTICS NOT AVAILABLE																								
1991-92	Sioux City Musketeers	USHL	23	7	10	0	1131	100	0	5.31	....	....	....	....	....	....	....	....	....	....	....	....	....	....	....	....	....
1992-93	Kelowna Spartans	BCJHL	44	34	8	0	2582	137	1	3.18	....	....	....	....	....	15	12	3	0	927	48	1	3.10	....	....	....	....
1993-94	Northern Michigan University	WCHA	20	9	7	0	985	57	2	3.47	....	....	....	....	....	....	....	....	....	....	....	....	....	....	....	....	....
1994-95	Northern Michigan University	WCHA	29	8	17	3	1512	107	0	4.25	....	....	....	....	....	....	....	....	....	....	....	....	....	....	....	....	....
1995-96	Northern Michigan University	WCHA	31	7	21	2	1627	123	0	4.54	....	....	....	....	....	....	....	....	....	....	....	....	....	....	....	....	....
1996-97	Northern Michigan University	WCHA	26	8	15	2	1528	99	0	3.89	....	....	....	....	....	....	....	....	....	....	....	....	....	....	....	....	....
1997-98	Louisville Riverfrogs	ECHL	18	7	9	2	980	61	1	3.73	....	....	....	....	....	....	....	....	....	....	....	....	....	....	....	....	....
1998-99	Binghamton Icemen	UHL	40	18	16	5	2322	115	2	2.97	....	....	....	....	....	4	1	2	....	208	9	0	2.60	....	....	....	....
99-2000	Binghamton Icemen	UHL	43	29	11	3	2544	110	4	2.59	....	....	....	....	....	....	....	....	....	....	....	....	....	....	....	....	....
	Orlando Solar Bears	IHL	4	4	0	0	240	4	1	1.00	....	....	....	....	....	....	....	....	....	....	....	....	....	....	....	....	....
	Springfield Falcons	AHL	2	1	1	0	120	5	1	2.50	....	....	....	....	....	....	....	....	....	....	....	....	....	....	....	....	....
	Tampa Bay Lightning	**NHL**	**5**	**1**	**4**	**0**	**238**	**17**	**0**	**4.29**	**4.91**	**6.57**	**111**	**.847**	**28.0**	....	....	....	....	....	....	....	....	....	....	....	....
	Grand Rapids Griffins	IHL	2	1	0	1	93	1	0	0.64	....	....	....	....	....	....	....	....	....	....	....	....	....	....	....	....	....
	NHL Totals		**5**	**1**	**4**	**0**	**238**	**17**	**0**	**4.29**	....	....	**111**	**.847**	**28.0**	....	....	....	....	....	....	....	....	....	....	....	....

UHL Second All-Star Team (2000) • Scored goal vs. Winston-Salem (ECHL), January 5, 1999.

Signed as a free agent by **Tampa Bay**, March 27, 2000.

• KOLZIG, Olaf

"Godzilla" G – L. 6'3", 225 lbs. b: Johannesburg, South Africa, 4/9/1970. Washington's 1st, 19th overall in 1989.

Season	Club	League	GP	W	L	T	Mins	GA	SO	Avg	AAvg	Eff	SA	S%	SAPG	GP	W	L	T	Mins	GA	SO	Avg	Eff	SA	S%	SAPG
1985-86	Dartmouth Oland Exports	NSAHA	STATISTICS NOT AVAILABLE																								
1986-87	Abbottsford Pilots	BCAHA	17	5	9	0	857	81	0	3.65	....	....	....	....	....	....	....	....	....	....	....	....	....	....	....	....	....
1987-88	Abbottsford Flyers	BCJHL	STATISTICS NOT AVAILABLE																								
	New Westminster Bruins	WHL	15	6	5	0	650	48	1	4.43	....	....	....	....	....	3	0	3	....	149	11	0	4.43	....	....	....	....
1988-89	Tri-City Americans	WHL	30	16	10	2	1671	97	1	*3.48	....	....	....	....	....	....	....	....	....	....	....	....	....	....	....	....	....
1989-90	Washington Capitals	Fr-Tour	2	....	....	....	65	4	....	3.69	....	....	....	....	....	....	....	....	....	....	....	....	....	....	....	....	....
	Washington Capitals	**NHL**	**2**	**0**	**2**	**0**	**120**	**12**	**0**	**6.00**	**5.09**	**11.43**	**63**	**.810**	**31.5**	....	....	....	....	....	....	....	....	....	....	....	....
	Tri-City Americans	WHL	48	27	27	3	2504	250	1	4.38	....	....	....	....	....	6	4	0	....	318	27	0	5.09	....	....	....	....
1990-91	Baltimore Skipjacks	AHL	26	10	12	1	1367	72	0	3.16	....	....	....	....	....	....	....	....	....	....	....	....	....	....	....	....	....
	Hampton Roads Admirals	ECHL	21	11	9	1	1248	71	2	3.41	....	....	....	....	....	3	1	2	....	180	14	0	4.66	....	....	....	....
1991-92	Baltimore Skipjacks	AHL	28	5	17	2	1503	105	1	4.19	....	....	....	....	....	....	....	....	....	....	....	....	....	....	....	....	....
	Hampton Roads Admirals	ECHL	14	11	3	0	847	41	0	2.90	....	....	....	....	....	....	....	....	....	....	....	....	....	....	....	....	....
1992-93	**Washington Capitals**	**NHL**	**1**	**0**	**0**	**0**	**20**	**2**	**0**	**6.00**	**5.14**	**17.14**	**7**	**.714**	**21.0**	....	....	....	....	....	....	....	....	....	....	....	....
	Rochester Americans	AHL	49	25	16	4	2737	168	0	3.68	....	....	....	....	....	*17	9	8	....	*1040	61	0	3.52	....	....	....	....
1993-94	**Washington Capitals**	**NHL**	**7**	**0**	**3**	**0**	**224**	**20**	**0**	**5.36**	**5.16**	**8.38**	**128**	**.844**	**34.3**	....	....	....	....	....	....	....	....	....	....	....	....
	Portland Pirates	AHL	29	16	8	5	1725	88	3	3.06	....	....	....	....	....	17	*12	5	....	1035	44	0	*2.55	....	....	....	....
1994-95	**Washington Capitals**	**NHL**	**14**	**2**	**8**	**2**	**724**	**30**	**0**	**2.49**	**2.60**	**2.45**	**305**	**.902**	**25.3**	**2**	**1**	**0**	....	**44**	**1**	**0**	**1.36**	**0.65**	**21**	**.952**	**28.6**
	Portland Pirates	AHL	2	1	0	1	125	3	0	1.44	....	....	....	....	....	....	....	....	....	....	....	....	....	....	....	....	....
1995-96	**Washington Capitals**	**NHL**	**18**	**4**	**8**	**2**	**897**	**46**	**0**	**3.08**	**3.06**	**3.49**	**406**	**.887**	**27.2**	**5**	**2**	**3**	....	**341**	**11**	**0**	***1.94**	**1.28**	**167**	**.934**	**29.4**
	Portland Pirates	AHL	5	5	0	0	300	7	1	1.40	....	....	....	....	....	....	....	....	....	....	....	....	....	....	....	....	....
1996-97	Germany	W-Cup	1	0	1	0	45	5	0	6.67	....	....	....	....	....	....	....	....	....	....	....	....	....	....	....	....	....
	Washington Capitals	**NHL**	**29**	**8**	**15**	**4**	**1645**	**71**	**2**	**2.59**	**2.78**	**2.43**	**758**	**.906**	**27.6**	....	....	....	....	....	....	....	....	....	....	....	....
	Germany	WC-A	4	0	3	0	199	13	0	3.92	....	....	....	....	....	....	....	....	....	....	....	....	....	....	....	....	....
1997-98	**Washington Capitals**	**NHL**	**64**	**33**	**18**	**10**	**3788**	**139**	**5**	**2.20**	**2.61**	**1.77**	**1729**	**.920**	**27.4**	**21**	**12**	**9**	....	**1351**	**44**	***4**	**1.95**	**1.16**	**740**	**.941**	**32.9**
	Germany	Olympics	2	2	0	0	120	2	1	1.00	....	....	....	....	....	....	....	....	....	....	....	....	....	....	....	....	....
1998-99	**Washington Capitals**	**NHL**	**64**	**26**	**31**	**3**	**3586**	**154**	**4**	**2.58**	**3.07**	**2.58**	**1538**	**.900**	**25.7**	....	....	....	....	....	....	....	....	....	....	....	....
99-2000	**Washington Capitals**	**NHL**	**73**	**41**	**20**	**11**	***4371**	**163**	**5**	**2.24**	**2.55**	**1.87**	**1957**	**.917**	**26.9**	**5**	**1**	**4**	....	**284**	**16**	**0**	**3.38**	**5.25**	**103**	**.845**	**21.8**
	NHL Totals		**272**	**114**	**105**	**32**	**15375**	**637**	**16**	**2.49**	....	....	**6891**	**.908**	**26.9**	**33**	**16**	**16**	....	**2020**	**72**	**4**	**2.14**	....	**1031**	**.930**	**30.6**

WHL West Second All-Star Team (1989) • Shared Harry "Hap" Holmes Trophy (fewest goals against - AHL) with Byron Dafoe (1994) • Won Jack Butterfield Trophy (Playoff MVP - AHL) (1994) • NHL First All-Star Team (2000) • Won Vezina Trophy (2000) • Played in NHL All-Star Game (1998, 2000)

• Scored a goal with Tri-City (WHL), November 29, 1989.

• KUNTAR, Les

G – L. 6'2", 195 lbs. b: Elma, NY, 7/28/1969. Montreal's 8th, 122nd overall in 1987.

Season	Club	League	GP	W	L	T	Mins	GA	SO	Avg	AAvg	Eff	SA	S%	SAPG	GP	W	L	T	Mins	GA	SO	Avg	Eff	SA	S%	SAPG
1986-87	Nicholls High School	Hi-School	22	....	....	....	1585	56	*3	....	....	....	....	....	....	....	....	....	....	....	....	....	....	....	....	....	....
1987-88	St. Lawrence University	ECAC	10	6	1	0	488	27	0	3.32	....	....	....	....	....	....	....	....	....	....	....	....	....	....	....	....	....
1988-89	St. Lawrence University	ECAC	14	11	2	0	786	31	0	2.37	....	....	....	....	....	....	....	....	....	....	....	....	....	....	....	....	....
1989-90	St. Lawrence University	ECAC	20	7	11	1	1136	80	0	4.23	....	....	....	....	....	....	....	....	....	....	....	....	....	....	....	....	....
1990-91	St. Lawrence University	ECAC	*33	*19	11	1	*1797	97	*1	*3.24	....	....	....	....	....	....	....	....	....	....	....	....	....	....	....	....	....
1991-92	Fredericton Canadiens	AHL	11	7	3	0	638	26	0	2.45	....	....	....	....	....	....	....	....	....	....	....	....	....	....	....	....	....
	United States	Nat-Team	13	3	5	3	725	57	0	4.72	....	....	....	....	....	....	....	....	....	....	....	....	....	....	....	....	....
1992-93	Fredericton Canadiens	AHL	42	16	14	7	2315	130	0	3.37	....	....	....	....	....	1	0	1	0	64	6	0	5.63	....	....	....	....

Season	Club	League	REGULAR SEASON													PLAYOFFS											
			GP	W	L	T	Mins	GA	SO	Avg	AAvg	Eff	SA	S%	SAPG	GP	W	L	T	Mins	GA	SO	Avg	Eff	SA	S%	SAPG
1993-94	**Montreal Canadiens**	**NHL**	**6**	**2**	**2**	**0**	**302**	**16**	**0**	**3.18**	**3.06**	**3.91**	**130**	**.877**	**25.8**	....	....	....	....	....	....	....	....	....	....	....	....
	Fredericton Canadiens	AHL	34	10	17	3	1804	109	1	3.62	....	....	....	....	....	....	....	....	....	....	....	....	....	....	....	....	....
	United States	WC-A	4	0	2	0	135	11	0	4.89	....	....	....	....	....	....	....	....	....	....	....	....	....	....	....	....	....
1994-95	Worcester IceCats	AHL	24	6	10	5	1241	77	2	3.72	....	....	....	....	....	....	....	....	....	....	....	....	....	....	....	....	....
	Hershey Bears	AHL	32	15	13	2	1802	89	0	2.96	....	....	....	....	....	2	0	1	0	70	5	0	4.28	....	....	....	....
1995-96	Hershey Bears	AHL	20	7	8	2	1020	71	0	4.18	....	....	....	....	....	....	....	....	....	....	....	....	....	....	....	....	....
	Fort Wayne Komets	IHL	8	2	3	1	387	26	1	4.03	....	....	....	....	....	....	....	....	....	....	....	....	....	....	....	....	....
1996-97	Rochester Americans	AHL	21	6	9	3	1052	60	0	3.42	....	....	....	....	....	....	....	....	....	....	....	....	....	....	....	....	....
	Pensacola Ice Pilots	ECHL	4	2	2	0	220	13	0	3.55	....	....	....	....	....	....	....	....	....	....	....	....	....	....	....	....	....
	Cleveland Lumberjacks	IHL	1	1	0	0	60	4	0	4.00	....	....	....	....	....	....	....	....	....	....	....	....	....	....	....	....	....
	Utah Grizzlies	IHL	3	1	0	0	87	1	0	0.69	....	....	....	....	....	....	....	....	....	....	....	....	....	....	....	....	....
	NHL Totals		**6**	**2**	**2**	**0**	**302**	**16**	**0**	**3.18**	....	....	**130**	**.877**	**25.8**	....	....	....	....	....	....	....	....	....	....	....	....

ECAC First All-Star Team (1991)

Signed as a free agent by **Philadelphia**, June 30, 1995.

• KURT, Gary

Gary David G – L. 6'3", 205 lbs. b: Kitchener, Ont., 3/9/1947.

Season	Club	League	GP	W	L	T	Mins	GA	SO	Avg	AAvg	Eff	SA	S%	SAPG	GP	W	L	T	Mins	GA	SO	Avg	Eff	SA	S%	SAPG
1963-64	Kitchener Rangers	OHA-Jr.	11	....	....	....	620	49	0	4.74	....	....	....	....	....	....	....	....	....	....	....	....	....	....	....	....	....
1964-65	Kitchener Greenshirts	OHA-B		STATISTICS NOT AVAILABLE																							
	Kitchener Rangers	OHA-Jr.	21	....	....	....	1240	103	0	4.98	....	....	....	....	....	....	....	....	....	....	....	....	....	....	....	....	....
1965-66	Kitchener Rangers	OHA-Jr.	9	....	....	....	540	33	1	3.67	....	....	....	....	....	17	....	....	....	1020	67	1	3.94	....	....	....	....
1966-67	Kitchener Rangers	OHA-Jr.	16	....	....	....	940	69	0	4.40	....	....	....	....	....	....	....	....	....	....	....	....	....	....	....	....	....
1967-68	Omaha Knights	CPHL	34	5	21	3	1842	124	0	4.04	....	....	....	....	....	....	....	....	....	....	....	....	....	....	....	....	....
1968-69	Omaha Knights	CPHL	35	....	....	....	1940	108	1	3.34	....	....	....	....	....	3	1	0	0	104	5	0	2.88	....	....	....	....
1969-70	Cleveland Barons	AHL	40	....	....	....	2320	121	2	3.13	....	....	....	....	....	....	....	....	....	....	....	....	....	....	....	....	....
1970-71	Cleveland Barons	AHL	42	24	12	3	2263	101	3	*2.67	....	....	....	....	....	7	4	3	0	420	20	0	2.85	....	....	....	....
1971-72	**California Golden Seals**	**NHL**	**16**	**1**	**7**	**5**	**838**	**60**	**0**	**4.30**	**4.37**	....	....	....	....	....	....	....	....	....	....	....	....	....	....	....	....
	Baltimore Clippers	AHL	17	12	4	1	1020	47	1	2.76	....	....	....	....	....	....	....	....	....	....	....	....	....	....	....	....	....
1972-73	New York Raiders	WHA	36	10	21	0	1881	150	0	4.78	....	....	....	....	....	....	....	....	....	....	....	....	....	....	....	....	....
1973-74	New York-Jersey Knights	WHA	20	8	10	0	1089	75	0	4.13	....	....	....	....	....	....	....	....	....	....	....	....	....	....	....	....	....
	Syracuse Blazers	NAHL	24	....	....	....	1357	66	0	2.92	....	....	....	....	....	....	....	....	....	....	....	....	....	....	....	....	....
1974-75	Phoenix Roadrunners	WHA	47	25	16	4	2841	156	2	3.29	....	....	....	....	....	4	1	2	0	207	12	0	3.48	....	....	....	....
1975-76	Phoenix Roadrunners	WHA	40	18	20	2	2369	147	1	3.72	....	....	....	....	....	....	....	....	....	....	....	....	....	....	....	....	....
1976-77	Phoenix Roadrunners	WHA	33	11	19	1	1752	162	0	5.55	....	....	....	....	....	....	....	....	....	....	....	....	....	....	....	....	....
	Oklahoma City Blazers	CHL	3	....	....	....	180	15	0	5.00	....	....	....	....	....	....	....	....	....	....	....	....	....	....	....	....	....
1977-78				DID NOT PLAY																							
1978-79	Cambridge Hornets	OHA-Sr.	19	....	....	....	1140	86	0	4.53	....	....	....	....	....	....	....	....	....	....	....	....	....	....	....	....	....
	NHL Totals		**16**	**1**	**7**	**5**	**838**	**60**	**0**	**4.30**	....	....	....	....	....	....	....	....	....	....	....	....	....	....	....	....	....
	Other Major League Totals		176	72	86	7	9932	690	3	4.17	....	....	....	....	....	4	1	2	....	207	12	0	3.48	....	....	....	....

AHL Second All-Star Team (1971) • Won Harry "Hap" Holmes Memorial Award (fewest goals against - AHL) (1971) • NAHL First All-Star Team (1974)

Claimed by **Cleveland** (AHL) from **NY Rangers** in Reverse Draft, June 12, 1969. Claimed by **California** from **Cleveland** (AHL) in Inter-League Draft, June 7, 1971. Selected by **NY Raiders** (WHA) in 1972 WHA General Player Draft, February 12, 1972. Transferred to **San Diego** (WHA) after **New York-Jersey** (WHA) franchise relocated, April 30, 1974. Claimed by **Phoenix** (WHA) from **San Diego** (WHA) in 1974 WHA Expansion Draft, May 30, 1974.

• LABBE, Jean-Francois

G – L. 5'9", 170 lbs. b: Sherbrooke, Que., 6/15/1972.

Season	Club	League	GP	W	L	T	Mins	GA	SO	Avg	AAvg	Eff	SA	S%	SAPG	GP	W	L	T	Mins	GA	SO	Avg	Eff	SA	S%	SAPG
1988-89	Montreal L'est Cantonniers	QAAA	42	27	14	1	2522	151	0	3.59	....	....	....	....	....	....	....	....	....	....	....	....	....	....	....	....	....
1989-90	Trois Rivieres Draveurs	QMJHL	28	13	10	0	1499	106	1	4.24	....	....	....	....	....	3	1	1	....	132	8	0	3.64	....	....	....	....
1990-91	Trois Rivieres Draveurs	QMJHL	54	*35	14	0	2870	158	5	3.30	....	....	....	....	....	5	1	4	....	230	19	0	4.96	....	....	....	....
1991-92	Trois Rivieres Draveurs	QMJHL	48	*31	13	3	2749	142	1	3.10	....	....	....	....	....	*15	*10	3	....	791	33	*1	*2.50	....	....	....	....
1992-93	Hull Olympiques	QMJHL	46	26	18	2	2701	156	2	3.46	....	....	....	....	....	10	6	3	....	518	24	*1	*2.78	....	....	....	....
1993-94	Thunder Bay Senators	ColHL	52	*35	11	4	*2900	150	*2	*3.10	....	....	....	....	....	8	7	1	....	493	18	*2	*2.19	....	....	....	....
	P.E.I. Senators	AHL	7	4	3	0	389	22	0	3.39	....	....	....	....	....	....	....	....	....	....	....	....	....	....	....	....	....
1994-95	P.E.I. Senators	AHL	32	13	14	3	1817	94	2	3.10	....	....	....	....	....	....	....	....	....	....	....	....	....	....	....	....	....
1995-96	Cornwall Aces	AHL	55	25	21	5	2972	144	3	2.91	....	....	....	....	....	8	3	5	....	471	21	1	2.68	....	....	....	....
1996-97	Hershey Bears	AHL	66	*34	22	9	3811	160	*6	*2.52	....	....	....	....	....	*23	*14	8	....	*1364	59	1	2.60	....	....	....	....
1997-98	Hamilton Bulldogs	AHL	52	24	17	11	3138	149	2	2.85	....	....	....	....	....	7	3	4	....	413	20	0	2.90	....	....	....	....
1998-99	Hartford Wolf Pack	AHL	*59	28	26	3	*3392	182	2	3.22	....	....	....	....	....	7	3	4	....	447	22	0	2.95	....	....	....	....
99-2000	**New York Rangers**	**NHL**	**1**	**0**	**1**	**0**	**60**	**3**	**0**	**3.00**	**3.43**	**4.09**	**22**	**.864**	**22.0**	....	....	....	....	....	....	....	....	....	....	....	....
	Hartford Wolf Pack	AHL	49	27	13	7	2853	120	1	2.52	....	....	....	....	....	*22	*15	7	....	*1320	48	3	2.18	....	....	....	....
	NHL Totals		**1**	**0**	**1**	**0**	**60**	**3**	**0**	**3.00**	....	....	**22**	**.864**	**22.0**	....	....	....	....	....	....	....	....	....	....	....	....

QMJHL First All-Star Team (1992) • ColHL First All-Star Team (1994) • Named ColHL's Rookie of the Year (1994) • Named ColHL's Outstanding Goaltender (1994) • Named ColHL's Playoff MVP (1994) • AHL First All-Star Team (1997) • Won Harry "Hap" Holmes Memorial Trophy (fewest goals against - AHL) (1997) • Won Baz Bastien Memorial Trophy (Top Goaltender - AHL) (1997) • Won Les Cunningham Award (MVP - AHL) (1997) • Shared Harry "Hap" Holmes Memorial Trophy (fewest goals against - AHL) with Milan Hnilicka (2000)

Signed as a free agent by **Ottawa**, May 12, 1994. Traded to **Colorado** by **Ottawa** for future considerations, September 20, 1995. Signed as a free agent by **Edmonton**, September 2, 1997. Signed as a free agent by **NY Rangers**, July 30, 1998. • Scored goal with Hartford (AHL) vs. Quebec (AHL), February 5, 2000.

• LABRECQUE, Patrick

G – L. 6', 190 lbs. b: Laval, Que., 3/6/1971. Quebec's 5th, 90th overall in 1991.

Season	Club	League	GP	W	L	T	Mins	GA	SO	Avg	AAvg	Eff	SA	S%	SAPG	GP	W	L	T	Mins	GA	SO	Avg	Eff	SA	S%	SAPG
1987-88	Laval-Laurentides	QAAA	21	17	3	1	1274	81	0	3.82	....	....	....	....	....	....	....	....	....	....	....	....	....	....	....	....	....
1988-89	St-Jean Beavers	QMJHL	30	....	....	....	1417	140	0	5.93	....	....	....	....	....	....	....	....	....	....	....	....	....	....	....	....	....
1989-90	St-Jean Lynx	QMJHL	48	21	24	0	2630	196	1	4.47	....	....	....	....	....	....	....	....	....	....	....	....	....	....	....	....	....
1990-91	St-Jean Lynx	QMJHL	59	17	34	6	3375	216	1	3.84	....	....	....	....	....	....	....	....	....	....	....	....	....	....	....	....	....
1991-92	Halifax Citadels	AHL	29	5	12	8	1570	114	0	4.36	....	....	....	....	....	....	....	....	....	....	....	....	....	....	....	....	....
1992-93	Greensboro Monarchs	ECHL	11	6	3	2	650	31	0	2.86	....	....	....	....	....	1	0	1	....	59	5	0	5.08	....	....	....	....
	Halifax Citadels	AHL	20	3	12	2	914	76	0	4.99	....	....	....	....	....	....	....	....	....	....	....	....	....	....	....	....	....
1993-94	Cornwall Aces	AHL	4	1	2	0	198	8	1	2.42	....	....	....	....	....	....	....	....	....	....	....	....	....	....	....	....	....
	Greensboro Monarchs	ECHL	29	17	8	2	1609	89	0	3.32	....	....	....	....	....	1	0	0	....	22	4	0	10.80	....	....	....	....
1994-95	Fredericton Canadiens	AHL	35	15	17	1	1913	104	1	3.26	....	....	....	....	....	*16	*10	6	....	*967	40	1	2.48	....	....	....	....
	Wheeling Thunderbirds	ECHL	5	2	3	0	281	22	0	4.69	....	....	....	....	....	....	....	....	....	....	....	....	....	....	....	....	....
1995-96	**Montreal Canadiens**	**NHL**	**2**	**0**	**1**	**0**	**98**	**7**	**0**	**4.29**	**4.27**	**6.39**	**47**	**.851**	**28.8**	....	....	....	....	....	....	....	....	....	....	....	....
	Fredericton Canadiens	AHL	48	23	18	6	2686	153	3	3.42	....	....	....	....	....	7	3	3	....	405	31	0	4.59	....	....	....	....
1996-97	Fredericton Canadiens	AHL	12	1	7	1	602	31	0	3.09	....	....	....	....	....	....	....	....	....	....	....	....	....	....	....	....	....
	Quebec Rafales	IHL	9	2	6	0	482	29	0	3.61	....	....	....	....	....	....	....	....	....	....	....	....	....	....	....	....	....
1997-98	Baton Rouge Kingfish	ECHL	34	17	13	4	1935	107	0	3.32	....	....	....	....	....	....	....	....	....	....	....	....	....	....	....	....	....
	Hershey Bears	AHL	....	....	....	....	....	....	....	....	....	....	....	....	....	1	0	0	....	10	0	0	0.00	....	....	....	....
1998-99	SC Bietigheim-Bissingen	Germany-3	40	....	....	....	2404	124	2	3.09	....	....	....	....	....	13	....	....	....	783	47	0	3.60	....	....	....	....
99-2000	EHC Harz	Germany-2	11	7	4	0	657	43	0	3.93	....	....	....	....	....	....	....	....	....	....	....	....	....	....	....	....	....
	San Angelo Outlaws	WPHL	8	2	6	0	428	34	0	4.76	....	....	....	....	....	....	....	....	....	....	....	....	....	....	....	....	....
	Fort Wayne Komets	UHL	7	4	1	0	337	11	1	1.96	....	....	....	....	....	1	0	1	....	59	3	0	3.07	....	....	....	....
	Bakersfield Condors	WCHL	5	2	2	1	297	17	0	3.43	....	....	....	....	....	4	1	3	....	200	14	0	4.20	....	....	....	....
	NHL Totals		**2**	**0**	**1**	**0**	**98**	**7**	**0**	**4.29**	....	....	**47**	**.851**	**28.8**	....	....	....	....	....	....	....	....	....	....	....	....

Signed as a free agent by **Montreal**, June 21, 1994.

• LACHER, Blaine

G – L. 6'1", 205 lbs. b: Medicine Hat, Alta., 9/5/1970.

Season	Club	League	GP	W	L	T	Mins	GA	SO	Avg	AAvg	Eff	SA	S%	SAPG	GP	W	L	T	Mins	GA	SO	Avg	Eff	SA	S%	SAPG
1989-90	Melville Millionaires	SJHL	39	....	....	....	2250	134	1	3.57	....	....	....	....	....	....	....	....	....	....	....	....	....	....	....	....	....
1990-91	Lake Superior State	CCHA		DID NOT PLAY – ACADEMICALLY INELIGIBLE																							
1991-92	Lake Superior State	CCHA	9	5	3	0	410	22	0	3.22	....	....	....	....	....	....	....	....	....	....	....	....	....	....	....	....	....
1992-93	Lake Superior State	CCHA	34	24	5	3	1915	86	2	2.70	....	....	....	....	....	....	....	....	....	....	....	....	....	....	....	....	....
1993-94	Lake Superior State	CCHA	30	20	5	4	1785	59	6	*1.98	....	....	....	....	....	....	....	....	....	....	....	....	....	....	....	....	....

			REGULAR SEASON													PLAYOFFS											
Season	**Club**	**League**	**GP**	**W**	**L**	**T**	**Mins**	**GA**	**SO**	**Avg**	**AAvg**	**Eff**	**SA**	**S%**	**SAPG**	**GP**	**W**	**L**	**T**	**Mins**	**GA**	**SO**	**Avg**	**Eff**	**SA**	**S%**	**SAPG**
1994-95	**Boston Bruins**	**NHL**	**35**	**19**	**11**	**2**	**1965**	**79**	**4**	**2.41**	**2.51**	**2.37**	**805**	**.902**	**24.6**	**5**	**1**	**4**	....	**283**	**12**	**0**	**2.54**	**2.44**	**125**	**.904**	**26.5**
	Providence Bruins	AHL	1	0	1	0	59	3	0	3.03	....	....	....	....	....	....	....	....	....	....	....	....	....	....	....	....	....
1995-96	**Boston Bruins**	**NHL**	**12**	**3**	**5**	**2**	**671**	**44**	**0**	**3.93**	**3.91**	**6.09**	**284**	**.845**	**25.4**	....	....	....	....	....	....	....	....	....	....	....	....
	Providence Bruins	AHL	9	3	5	0	462	30	0	3.90	....	....	....	....	....	....	....	....	....	....	....	....	....	....	....	....	....
	Cleveland Lumberjacks	IHL	8	3	4	1	478	28	0	3.51	....	....	....	....	....	3	0	3	....	191	10	0	3.14	....	....	....	....
1996-97	Grand Rapids Griffins	IHL	11	1	8	1	510	32	0	3.76	....	....	....	....	....	....	....	....	....	....	....	....	....	....	....	....	....
	NHL Totals		**47**	**22**	**16**	**4**	**2636**	**123**	**4**	**2.80**	....	....	**1089**	**.887**	**24.8**	**5**	**1**	**4**	....	**283**	**12**	**0**	**2.54**	....	**125**	**.904**	**26.5**

NCAA Championship All-Tournament Team (1994)

Signed as a free agent by **Boston**, June 2, 1994.

• LACROIX, Frenchy

Alphonse Albert G – L. 5'7", 136 lbs. b: Newton, MA, 10/21/1897 Deceased.

Season	Club	League	GP	W	L	T	Mins	GA	SO	Avg	AAvg	Eff	SA	S%	SAPG	GP	W	L	T	Mins	GA	SO	Avg	Eff	SA	S%	SAPG
1914-15	Newton High School	Hi-School	7	5	1	1	294	15	0	2.04	....	....	....	....	....	1	1	0	0	40	1	0	1.00	....	....	....	....
1915-16	Newton High School	Hi-School	7	5	2	0	280	9	2	1.29	....	....	....	....	....	....	....	....	....	....	....	....	....	....	....	....	....
1916-17	Newton High School	Hi-School	8	7	0	1	320	10	4	1.25	....	....	....	....	....	....	....	....	....	....	....	....	....	....	....	....	....
1917-18	Boston Navy Yard	USNHL	11	7	4	0	455	22	*3	*1.93	....	....	....	....	....	....	....	....	....	....	....	....	....	....	....	....	....
1918-19	Boston Navy Yard	X-Games	STATISTICS NOT AVAILABLE																								
1919-20	Boston AA Unicorn	X-Games	3	2	1	0	135	8	0	2.67	....	....	....	....	....	....	....	....	....	....	....	....	....	....	....	....	....
1920-21	Boston AA Unicorn	X-Games	DID NOT PLAY – SPARE GOALTENDER																								
1921-22	Boston AA Unicorn	BCSHL	1	1	0	0	45	2	0	2.00	....	....	....	....	....	....	....	....	....	....	....	....	....	....	....	....	....
1922-23	Boston AA Unicorn	USAHA	9	*9	0	0	405	10	*4	*1.11	....	....	....	....	....	4	*3	1	0	180	4	*1	*1.00	....	....	....	....
1923-24	Boston AA Unicorn	USAHA	6	3	3	0	270	10	1	1.67	....	....	....	....	....	3	1	2	0	180	8	0	2.67	....	....	....	....
	United States	Olympics	5	4	1	0	225	6	4	1.20	....	....	....	....	....	....	....	....	....	....	....	....	....	....	....	....	....
1924-25	Boston AA Unicorn	USAHA	21	15	6	0	955	40	*4	1.88	....	....	....	....	....	4	1	3	0	150	10	*1	3.00	....	....	....	....
1925-26	**Montreal Canadiens**	**NHL**	**5**	**1**	**4**	**0**	**280**	**16**	**0**	**3.43**	**4.58**	....	....	....	....	....	....	....	....	....	....	....	....	....	....	....	....
1926-27	**Montreal Canadiens**	**NHL**	DID NOT PLAY – SPARE GOALTENDER																								
1927-28	Providence Reds	Can-Am	4	1	3	0	250	12	0	2.88	....	....	....	....	....	....	....	....	....	....	....	....	....	....	....	....	....
	Lewiston St. Doms	NEHL	22	8	12	2	1350	42	5	1.87	....	....	....	....	....	5	....	....	....	305	16	0	3.15	....	....	....	....
1928-29	Lewiston St. Doms	NEHL	4	3	1	0	240	9	0	2.25	....	....	....	....	....	3	2	1	0	240	8	*1	*2.67	....	....	....	....
1929-30	Providence Reds	Can-Am	1	1	0	0	60	2	0	2.00	....	....	....	....	....	....	....	....	....	....	....	....	....	....	....	....	....
1930-31	Boston Tigers	Can-Am	4	1	3	0	240	13	0	3.25	....	....	....	....	....	....	....	....	....	....	....	....	....	....	....	....	....
	NHL Totals		**5**	**1**	**4**	**0**	**280**	**16**	**0**	**3.43**	....	....	....	....	....	....	....	....	....	....	....	....	....	....	....	....	....

USNHL First All-Star Team (1918)

Signed as a free agent by **Montreal Canadiens**, November 10, 1925.

• LAFERRIERE, Rick

Richard Jacques G – L. 5'8", 165 lbs. b: Hawkesbury, Ont., 1/3/1961. Colorado's 3rd, 64th overall in 1980.

Season	Club	League	GP	W	L	T	Mins	GA	SO	Avg	AAvg	Eff	SA	S%	SAPG	GP	W	L	T	Mins	GA	SO	Avg	Eff	SA	S%	SAPG
1978-79	Peterborough Petes	OMJHL	21	....	....	....	1279	76	1	3.56	....	....	....	....	....	....	....	....	....	....	....	....	....	....	....	....	....
1979-80	Peterborough Petes	OMJHL	55	....	....	....	3118	170	2	*3.27	....	....	....	....	....	14	12	....	....	863	38	0	2.64	....	....	....	....
	Canada	WJC-A	4	2	2	0	240	13	0	3.25	....	....	....	....	....	....	....	....	....	....	....	....	....	....	....	....	....
	Peterborough Petes	Mem-Cup	5	*3	2	0	305	21	0	4.13	....	....	....	....	....	....	....	....	....	....	....	....	....	....	....	....	....
1980-81	Peterborough Petes	OMJHL	34	15	15	2	1959	144	0	4.41	....	....	....	....	....	....	....	....	....	....	....	....	....	....	....	....	....
	Brantford Alexanders	OMJHL	20	11	8	0	1155	93	0	4.83	....	....	....	....	....	....	....	....	....	....	....	....	....	....	....	....	....
1981-82	Brantford Alexanders	OHL	20	....	....	....	1155	92	0	4.83	....	....	....	....	....	4	....	....	....	194	19	0	5.90	....	....	....	....
	Fort Worth Texans	CHL	37	8	26	2	2155	189	1	5.26	....	....	....	....	....	....	....	....	....	....	....	....	....	....	....	....	....
	Colorado Rockies	**NHL**	**1**	**0**	**0**	**0**	**20**	**1**	**0**	**3.00**	**2.32**	....	....	....	....	....	....	....	....	....	....	....	....	....	....	....	....
1982-83	Muskegon Mohawks	IHL	44	....	....	....	2578	186	0	4.33	....	....	....	....	....	2	....	....	....	120	8	0	4.00	....	....	....	....
1983-84	Muskegon Mohawks	IHL	16	....	....	....	817	83	0	6.09	....	....	....	....	....	....	....	....	....	....	....	....	....	....	....	....	....
	Tulsa Oilers	CHL	2	....	....	....	79	4	0	3.03	....	....	....	....	....	1	0	0	0	20	2	0	6.00	....	....	....	....
	NHL Totals		**1**	**0**	**0**	**0**	**20**	**1**	**0**	**3.00**	....	....	....	....	....	....	....	....	....	....	....	....	....	....	....	....	....

OMJHL Second All-Star Team (1980) • Memorial Cup All-Star Team (1980) • Won Hap Emms Memorial Trophy (Memorial Cup Tournament Top Goaltender) (1980)

• **NY Islanders'** spare goaltender replaced Chico Resch at start of 3rd period, February 23, 1982. (Detroit 6, Colorado 3).

• LaFOREST, Mark

Mark Andrew "Trees" G – L. 5'11", 190 lbs. b: Welland, Ont., 7/10/1962.

Season	Club	League	GP	W	L	T	Mins	GA	SO	Avg	AAvg	Eff	SA	S%	SAPG	GP	W	L	T	Mins	GA	SO	Avg	Eff	SA	S%	SAPG
1980-81	Welland Cougars	OHA-B	22	....	....	....	1262	117	0	5.56	....	....	....	....	....	....	....	....	....	....	....	....	....	....	....	....	....
1981-82	Niagara Falls Flyers	OHL	24	10	13	1	1365	105	1	4.62	....	....	....	....	....	5	1	2	....	300	19	0	3.80	....	....	....	....
1982-83	North Bay Centennials	OHL	54	34	17	1	3140	195	0	3.73	....	....	....	....	....	8	4	4	....	474	31	0	3.92	....	....	....	....
1983-84	Adirondack Red Wings	AHL	7	3	3	1	351	29	0	4.96	....	....	....	....	....	....	....	....	....	....	....	....	....	....	....	....	....
	Kalamazoo Wings	IHL	13	4	5	2	718	48	1	4.01	....	....	....	....	....	....	....	....	....	....	....	....	....	....	....	....	....
1984-85	Adirondack Red Wings	AHL	11	2	3	1	430	35	0	4.88	....	....	....	....	....	....	....	....	....	....	....	....	....	....	....	....	....
	Mohawk Valley Comets	ACHL	8	....	....	....	420	60	0	8.57	....	....	....	....	....	....	....	....	....	....	....	....	....	....	....	....	....
1985-86	**Detroit Red Wings**	**NHL**	**28**	**4**	**21**	**0**	**1383**	**114**	**1**	**4.95**	**3.88**	**7.61**	**742**	**.846**	**32.2**	....	....	....	....	....	....	....	....	....	....	....	....
	Adirondack Red Wings	AHL	19	13	5	1	1142	57	0	2.99	....	....	....	....	....	*17	*12	5	....	*1075	58	0	3.24	....	....	....	....
1986-87	**Detroit Red Wings**	**NHL**	**5**	**2**	**1**	**0**	**219**	**12**	**0**	**3.29**	**2.79**	**3.56**	**111**	**.892**	**30.4**	....	....	....	....	....	....	....	....	....	....	....	....
	Adirondack Red Wings	AHL	37	23	8	0	2229	105	*3	2.83	....	....	....	....	....	....	....	....	....	....	....	....	....	....	....	....	....
1987-88	**Philadelphia Flyers**	**NHL**	**21**	**5**	**9**	**2**	**972**	**60**	**1**	**3.70**	**3.08**	**4.64**	**478**	**.874**	**29.5**	**2**	**1**	**0**	....	**48**	**1**	**0**	**1.25**	**1.04**	**12**	**.917**	**15.0**
	Hershey Bears	AHL	5	2	1	2	309	13	0	2.52	....	....	....	....	....	....	....	....	....	....	....	....	....	....	....	....	....
1988-89	**Philadelphia Flyers**	**NHL**	**17**	**5**	**7**	**2**	**933**	**64**	**0**	**4.12**	**3.43**	**5.31**	**497**	**.871**	**32.0**	....	....	....	....	....	....	....	....	....	....	....	....
	Hershey Bears	AHL	3	2	0	0	185	9	0	2.92	....	....	....	....	....	12	7	5	....	744	27	1	2.18	....	....	....	....
1989-90	**Toronto Maple Leafs**	**NHL**	**27**	**9**	**14**	**0**	**1343**	**87**	**0**	**3.89**	**3.30**	**4.42**	**765**	**.886**	**34.2**	....	....	....	....	....	....	....	....	....	....	....	....
	Newmarket Saints	AHL	10	6	4	0	604	33	1	3.28	....	....	....	....	....	....	....	....	....	....	....	....	....	....	....	....	....
1990-91	Binghamton Rangers	AHL	45	25	14	2	2452	129	0	3.16	....	....	....	....	....	9	3	4	....	442	28	1	3.80	....	....	....	....
1991-92	Binghamton Rangers	AHL	43	25	15	3	2559	146	1	3.42	....	....	....	....	....	11	7	4	....	662	34	0	3.08	....	....	....	....
1992-93	New Haven Senators	AHL	30	10	18	1	1688	121	1	4.30	....	....	....	....	....	....	....	....	....	....	....	....	....	....	....	....	....
	Brantford Smoke	ColHL	10	5	3	1	565	35	1	3.72	....	....	....	....	....	....	....	....	....	....	....	....	....	....	....	....	....
1993-94	**Ottawa Senators**	**NHL**	**5**	**0**	**2**	**0**	**182**	**17**	**0**	**5.60**	**5.39**	**9.92**	**96**	**.823**	**31.6**	....	....	....	....	....	....	....	....	....	....	....	....
	P.E.I. Senators	AHL	43	9	25	5	2359	161	0	4.09	....	....	....	....	....	....	....	....	....	....	....	....	....	....	....	....	....
1994-95	Milwaukee Admirals	IHL	42	19	13	7	2325	123	2	3.17	....	....	....	....	....	15	8	7	....	937	40	*2	2.56	....	....	....	....
1995-96	Milwaukee Admirals	IHL	53	26	20	7	3079	191	0	3.72	....	....	....	....	....	5	2	3	....	315	18	0	3.42	....	....	....	....
1996-97	Binghamton Rangers	AHL	9	0	4	1	393	26	0	3.97	....	....	....	....	....	....	....	....	....	....	....	....	....	....	....	....	....
	Utica Blizzard	ColHL	6	1	2	2	312	31	0	5.95	....	....	....	....	....	....	....	....	....	....	....	....	....	....	....	....	....
	NHL Totals		**103**	**25**	**54**	**4**	**5032**	**354**	**2**	**4.22**	....	....	**2689**	**.868**	**32.1**	**2**	**1**	**0**	....	**48**	**1**	**0**	**1.25**	....	**12**	**.917**	**15.0**

• Brother of Bob • Won Baz Bastien Memorial Trophy (Top Goaltender - AHL) (1987, 1991) • AHL Second All-Star Team (1991)

Signed as a free agent by **Detroit**, April 29, 1983. Traded to **Philadelphia** by **Detroit** for Philadelphia's 2nd round choice (Bob Wilkie) in 1987 Entry Draft, June 13, 1987. Traded to **Toronto** by **Philadelphia** for Toronto's 5th round choice (later traded to Winnipeg - Winnipeg selected Juha Ylonen) in 1991 Entry Draft and Philadelphia's 7th round choice (previously acquired, Philadelphia selected Andrei Lomakin) in 1991 Entry Draft, September 8, 1989. Traded to **NY Rangers** by **Toronto** with Tie Domi for Greg Johnston, June 28, 1990. Claimed by **Ottawa** from **NY Rangers** in Expansion Draft, June 18, 1992.

• LALIME, Patrick

G – L. 6'3", 185 lbs. b: St. Bonaventure, Que., 7/7/1974. Pittsburgh's 6th, 156th overall in 1993.

Season	Club	League	GP	W	L	T	Mins	GA	SO	Avg	AAvg	Eff	SA	S%	SAPG	GP	W	L	T	Mins	GA	SO	Avg	Eff	SA	S%	SAPG
1990-91	D'abitibi Forestiers	QAAA	26	9	17	0	1595	151	0	5.81	....	....	....	....	....	....	....	....	....	....	....	....	....	....	....	....	....
1991-92	Valleyfield Braves	QJHL	STATISTICS NOT AVAILABLE																								
	Shawinigan Cataractes	QMJHL	6	....	....	....	272	25	0	5.50	....	....	....	....	....	....	....	....	....	....	....	....	....	....	....	....	....
1992-93	Shawinigan Cataracts	QMJHL	44	10	24	4	2467	192	0	4.67	....	....	....	....	....	....	....	....	....	....	....	....	....	....	....	....	....
1993-94	Shawinigan Cataracts	QMJHL	48	22	20	0	2733	192	1	4.22	....	....	....	....	....	5	1	3	....	223	25	0	6.73	....	....	....	....
1994-95	Hampton Roads Admirals	ECHL	26	15	7	3	1470	82	2	3.35	....	....	....	....	....	....	....	....	....	....	....	....	....	....	....	....	....
	Cleveland Lumberjacks	IHL	23	7	10	4	1230	91	0	4.44	....	....	....	....	....	....	....	....	....	....	....	....	....	....	....	....	....
1995-96	Cleveland Lumberjacks	IHL	41	20	12	7	2314	149	0	3.86	....	....	....	....	....	....	....	....	....	....	....	....	....	....	....	....	....
1996-97	**Pittsburgh Penguins**	**NHL**	**39**	**21**	**12**	**2**	**2058**	**101**	**3**	**2.94**	**3.17**	**2.55**	**1166**	**.913**	**34.0**	....	....	....	....	....	....	....	....	....	....	....	....
	Cleveland Lumberjacks	IHL	14	6	6	2	834	45	1	3.24	....	....	....	....	....	....	....	....	....	....	....	....	....	....	....	....	....

			REGULAR SEASON													PLAYOFFS											
Season	Club	League	GP	W	L	T	Mins	GA	SO	Avg	AAvg	Eff	SA	S%	SAPG	GP	W	L	T	Mins	GA	SO	Avg	Eff	SA	S%	SAPG
1997-98	Grand Rapids Griffins	IHL	31	10	10	9	1749	76	2	2.61	....	....	....	....	....	1	0	1	....	77	4	0	3.11	....	....	....	....
1998-99	Kansas City Blades	IHL	*66	*39	20	4	*3789	190	2	3.01	....	....	....	....	....	3	1	2	....	179	6	1	2.01	....	....	....	....
99-2000	**Ottawa Senators**	**NHL**	**38**	**19**	**14**	**3**	**2038**	**79**	**3**	**2.33**	**2.66**	**2.21**	**834**	**.905**	**24.6**	....	....	....	....	....	....	....	....	....	....	....	....
	NHL Totals		**77**	**40**	**26**	**5**	**4096**	**180**	**6**	**2.64**	....	....	**2000**	**.910**	**29.3**	....	....	....	....	....	....	....	....	....	....	....	....

NHL All-Rookie Team (1997) • IHL First All-Star Team (1999)

Rights traded to **Anaheim** by **Pittsburgh** for Sean Pronger, March 24, 1998. Traded to **Ottawa** by **Anaheim** for Ted Donato and the rights to Antti-Jussi Niemi, June 18, 1999.

• LAMOTHE, Marc

G – L. 6'2", 210 lbs. b: New Liskeard, Ont., 2/27/1974. Montreal's 6th, 92nd overall in 1992.

Season	Club	League	GP	W	L	T	Mins	GA	SO	Avg	AAvg	Eff	SA	S%	SAPG	GP	W	L	T	Mins	GA	SO	Avg	Eff	SA	S%	SAPG
1990-91	Ottawa Jr. Senators	OJHL	25	13	7	0	1220	82	1	4.03	....	....	....	....	....	....	....	....	....	....	....	....	....	....	....	....	....
1991-92	Kingston Frontenacs	OHL	42	10	25	2	2378	189	1	4.77	....	....	....	....	....	....	....	....	....	....	....	....	....	....	....	....	....
1992-93	Kingston Frontenacs	OHL	45	23	12	6	2489	162	1	3.91	....	....	....	....	....	15	8	5	....	753	48	1	3.82	....	....	....	....
1993-94	Kingston Frontenacs	OHL	48	23	20	5	2828	177	*2	3.76	....	....	....	....	....	6	2	2	....	224	12	0	3.21	....	....	....	....
1994-95	Fredericton Canadiens	AHL	9	2	5	0	428	32	0	4.48	....	....	....	....	....	....	....	....	....	....	....	....	....	....	....	....	....
	Wheeling Thunderbirds	ECHL	13	9	2	1	737	38	0	3.10	....	....	....	....	....	....	....	....	....	....	....	....	....	....	....	....	....
1995-96	Fredericton Canadiens	AHL	23	5	9	3	1166	73	1	3.76	....	....	....	....	....	3	1	2	....	161	9	0	3.36	....	....	....	....
1996-97	Indianapolis Ice	IHL	38	20	14	4	2271	100	1	2.64	....	....	....	....	....	1	0	0	....	20	1	0	3.00	....	....	....	....
1997-98	Indianapolis Ice	IHL	31	18	10	2	1772	72	3	2.44	....	....	....	....	....	4	1	3	....	177	10	0	3.38	....	....	....	....
1998-99	Indianapolis Ice	IHL	32	9	16	6	1823	115	1	3.78	....	....	....	....	....	6	3	3	....	338	10	*2	1.78	....	....	....	....
	Detroit Vipers	IHL	DID NOT PLAY – SPARE GOALTENDER																								
99-2000	**Chicago Blackhawks**	**NHL**	**2**	**1**	**1**	**0**	**116**	**10**	**0**	**5.17**	**5.91**	**10.34**	**50**	**.800**	**25.9**	....	....	....	....	....	....	....	....	....	....	....	....
	Cleveland Lumberjacks	IHL	44	19	18	4	2455	112	2	2.74	....	....	....	....	....	4	2	2	....	325	12	0	2.21	....	....	....	....
	NHL Totals		**2**	**1**	**1**	**0**	**116**	**10**	**0**	**5.17**	....	....	**50**	**.800**	**25.9**	....	....	....	....	....	....	....	....	....	....	....	....

Signed as a free agent by **Chicago**, September 26, 1996.

• LANGKOW, Scott

G – L. 5'11", 190 lbs. b: Sherwood Park, Alta., 4/21/1975. Winnipeg's 2nd, 31st overall in 1993.

Season	Club	League	GP	W	L	T	Mins	GA	SO	Avg	AAvg	Eff	SA	S%	SAPG	GP	W	L	T	Mins	GA	SO	Avg	Eff	SA	S%	SAPG
1990-91	Sherwood Park Flyers	AAHA	32	....	....	....	1920	128	0	4.00	....	....	....	....	....	....	....	....	....	....	....	....	....	....	....	....	....
1991-92	Abbotsford Pilots	PIJHL	STATISTICS NOT AVAILABLE																								
	Portland Winter Hawks	WHL	1	0	0	0	33	2	0	3.46	....	....	....	....	....	....	....	....	....	....	....	....	....	....	....	....	....
1992-93	Portland Winter Hawks	WHL	34	24	8	2	2064	119	2	3.46	....	....	....	....	....	9	6	3	....	535	31	0	3.48	....	....	....	....
1993-94	Portland Winter Hawks	WHL	39	27	9	1	2302	121	2	3.15	....	....	....	....	....	10	6	4	....	600	34	0	3.40	....	....	....	....
1994-95	Portland Winter Hawks	WHL	63	20	36	5	*3638	240	1	3.96	....	....	....	....	....	8	3	5	....	510	30	0	3.53	....	....	....	....
1995-96	**Winnipeg Jets**	**NHL**	**1**	**0**	**0**	**0**	**6**	**0**	**0**	**0.00**	**0.00**	**0.00**	**2**	**1.000**	**20.0**	....	....	....	....	....	....	....	....	....	....	....	....
	Springfield Falcons	AHL	39	18	15	6	2329	116	3	2.99	....	....	....	....	....	7	4	2	....	393	23	0	3.51	....	....	....	....
1996-97	Springfield Falcons	AHL	33	15	9	7	1929	85	0	2.64	....	....	....	....	....	....	....	....	....	....	....	....	....	....	....	....	....
1997-98	**Phoenix Coyotes**	**NHL**	**3**	**0**	**1**	**1**	**137**	**10**	**0**	**4.38**	**5.23**	**7.30**	**60**	**.833**	**26.3**	....	....	....	....	....	....	....	....	....	....	....	....
	Springfield Falcons	AHL	51	30	13	5	2874	128	3	2.67	....	....	....	....	....	4	1	3	....	216	14	0	3.88	....	....	....	....
1998-99	**Phoenix Coyotes**	**NHL**	**1**	**0**	**0**	**0**	**35**	**3**	**0**	**5.14**	**6.11**	**9.07**	**17**	**.824**	**29.1**	....	....	....	....	....	....	....	....	....	....	....	....
	Las Vegas Thunder	IHL	27	7	14	2	1402	97	1	4.15	....	....	....	....	....	....	....	....	....	....	....	....	....	....	....	....	....
	Utah Grizzlies	IHL	21	10	9	2	1227	59	1	2.89	....	....	....	....	....	....	....	....	....	....	....	....	....	....	....	....	....
99-2000	**Atlanta Thrashers**	**NHL**	**15**	**3**	**11**	**0**	**765**	**55**	**0**	**4.31**	**4.94**	**6.00**	**395**	**.861**	**31.0**	....	....	....	....	....	....	....	....	....	....	....	....
	Orlando Solar Bears	IHL	27	14	8	2	1487	57	4	2.30	....	....	....	....	....	6	2	3	....	381	16	0	2.52	....	....	....	....
	NHL Totals		**20**	**3**	**12**	**1**	**943**	**68**	**0**	**4.33**	....	....	**474**	**.857**	**30.2**	....	....	....	....	....	....	....	....	....	....	....	....

• Brother of Daymond • WHL West Second All-Star Team (1994, 1995) • Shared Harry "Hap" Holmes Memorial Trophy (fewest goals against - AHL) with Manny Legace (1996) • AHL First All-Star Team (1998) • Won Baz Bastien Memorial Trophy (Top Goaltender - AHL) (1998)

Transferred to **Phoenix** after **Winnipeg** franchise relocated, July 1, 1996. Traded to **Atlanta** by **Phoenix** for future considerations, June 25, 1999.

• LAROCQUE, Michel

Michel Raymond "Bunny" G – L. 5'10", 200 lbs. b: Hull, Que., 4/6/1952 d: 7/29/1992. Montreal's 2nd, 6th overall in 1972.

Season	Club	League	GP	W	L	T	Mins	GA	SO	Avg	AAvg	Eff	SA	S%	SAPG	GP	W	L	T	Mins	GA	SO	Avg	Eff	SA	S%	SAPG
1967-68	Ottawa 67's	OHA-Jr.	4	....	....	....	210	32	0	9.14	....	....	....	....	....	....	....	....	....	....	....	....	....	....	....	....	....
1968-69	Ottawa 67's	OHA-Jr.	4	....	....	....	190	24	0	7.58	....	....	....	....	....	....	....	....	....	....	....	....	....	....	....	....	....
1969-70	Ottawa 67's	OHA-Jr.	*51	....	....	....	*3060	185	*3	*3.63	....	....	....	....	....	11	4	6	1	625	36	3	3.46	....	....	....	....
1970-71	Ottawa 67's	OHA-Jr.	56	....	....	....	3345	189	*5	3.39	....	....	....	....	....	....	....	....	....	....	....	....	....	....	....	....	....
1971-72	Ottawa 67's	OMJHL	55	....	....	....	3287	189	*4	*3.45	....	....	....	....	....	18	8	7	3	1029	55	1	3.21	....	....	....	....
1972-73	Nova Scotia Voyageurs	AHL	47	....	....	....	2705	113	1	*2.50	....	....	....	....	....	*13	....	....	....	*760	36	0	2.84	....	....	....	....
1973-74	**Montreal Canadiens**	**NHL**	**27**	**15**	**8**	**2**	**1431**	**69**	**0**	**2.89**	**2.79**	....	....	....	....	**6**	**2**	**4**	....	**364**	**18**	**0**	**2.97**	....	....	....	....
1974-75	**Montreal Canadiens**	**NHL**	**25**	**17**	**5**	**3**	**1480**	**74**	**3**	**3.00**	**2.71**	....	....	....	....	....	....	....	....	....	....	....	....	....	....	....	....
1975-76♦	**Montreal Canadiens**	**NHL**	**22**	**16**	**1**	**3**	**1220**	**50**	**2**	**2.46**	**2.22**	....	....	....	....	....	....	....	....	....	....	....	....	....	....	....	....
1976-77♦	**Montreal Canadiens**	**NHL**	**26**	**19**	**2**	**4**	**1525**	**53**	**4**	***2.09**	**1.93**	....	....	....	....	....	....	....	....	....	....	....	....	....	....	....	....
1977-78♦	**Montreal Canadiens**	**NHL**	**30**	**22**	**3**	**4**	**1729**	**77**	**1**	**2.67**	**2.49**	....	....	....	....	....	....	....	....	....	....	....	....	....	....	....	....
1978-79♦	**Montreal Canadiens**	**NHL**	**34**	**22**	**7**	**4**	**1986**	**94**	**3**	**2.84**	**2.50**	....	....	....	....	**1**	**0**	**0**	....	**20**	**0**	**0**	**0.00**	....	....	....	....
1979-80	**Montreal Canadiens**	**NHL**	**39**	**17**	**13**	**8**	**2259**	**125**	**3**	**3.32**	**2.93**	....	....	....	....	**5**	**4**	**1**	....	**300**	**11**	**1**	**2.20**	....	....	....	....
1980-81	**Montreal Canadiens**	**NHL**	**28**	**16**	**9**	**3**	**1623**	**82**	**1**	**3.03**	**2.44**	....	....	....	....	....	....	....	....	....	....	....	....	....	....	....	....
	Toronto Maple Leafs	**NHL**	**8**	**3**	**3**	**2**	**460**	**40**	**0**	**5.22**	**4.23**	....	....	....	....	**2**	**0**	**1**	....	**75**	**8**	**0**	**6.40**	....	....	....	....
1981-82	**Toronto Maple Leafs**	**NHL**	**50**	**10**	**24**	**8**	**2647**	**207**	**0**	**4.69**	**3.64**	....	....	....	....	....	....	....	....	....	....	....	....	....	....	....	....
1982-83	**Toronto Maple Leafs**	**NHL**	**16**	**3**	**8**	**3**	**835**	**68**	**0**	**4.89**	**3.93**	**7.32**	**454**	**.850**	**32.6**	....	....	....	....	....	....	....	....	....	....	....	....
	Philadelphia Flyers	**NHL**	**2**	**0**	**1**	**1**	**120**	**8**	**0**	**4.00**	**3.21**	**5.71**	**56**	**.857**	**28.0**	....	....	....	....	....	....	....	....	....	....	....	....
1983-84	Springfield Indians	AHL	5	3	2	0	301	21	0	4.18	....	....	....	....	....	....	....	....	....	....	....	....	....	....	....	....	....
	St. Louis Blues	**NHL**	**5**	**0**	**5**	**0**	**300**	**31**	**0**	**6.20**	**4.89**	**11.72**	**164**	**.811**	**32.8**	....	....	....	....	....	....	....	....	....	....	....	....
1984-85	Peoria Rivermen	IHL	13	7	3	3	786	41	0	3.13	....	....	....	....	....	....	....	....	....	....	....	....	....	....	....	....	....
	NHL Totals		**312**	**160**	**89**	**45**	**17615**	**978**	**17**	**3.33**	....	....	....	....	....	**14**	**6**	**6**	....	**759**	**37**	**1**	**2.92**	....	....	....	....

OHA-Jr. Second All-Star Team (1971) • OMJHL First All-Star Team (1972) • AHL Second All-Star Team (1973) • Shared Harry "Hap" Holmes Memorial Award (fewest goals against - AHL) with Michel Deguise (1973) • Shared Vezina Trophy with Ken Dryden (1977, 1978, 1979) • Shared Vezina Trophy with Denis Herron and Richard Sevigny (1981)

Traded to **Toronto** by **Montreal** for Robert Picard, March 10, 1981. Traded to **Philadelphia** by **Toronto** for Rick St. Croix, January 11, 1983. Traded to **St. Louis** by **Philadelphia** for cash, January 5, 1984.

• LASKOWSKI, Gary

G – L. 6'1", 175 lbs. b: Ottawa, Ont., 6/6/1959.

Season	Club	League	GP	W	L	T	Mins	GA	SO	Avg	AAvg	Eff	SA	S%	SAPG	GP	W	L	T	Mins	GA	SO	Avg	Eff	SA	S%	SAPG
1977-78	Gloucester Rangers	OJHL	STATISTICS NOT AVAILABLE																								
1978-79	St. Lawrence University	ECAC	21	5	15	0	1130	93	0	4.94	....	....	....	....	....	....	....	....	....	....	....	....	....	....	....	....	....
1979-80	St. Lawrence University	ECAC	17	3	13	0	904	72	0	4.78	....	....	....	....	....	....	....	....	....	....	....	....	....	....	....	....	....
1980-81	St. Lawrence University	ECAC	21	10	10	1	1196	64	0	3.21	....	....	....	....	....	....	....	....	....	....	....	....	....	....	....	....	....
1981-82	St. Lawrence University	ECAC	15	7	7	0	851	50	0	3.53	....	....	....	....	....	....	....	....	....	....	....	....	....	....	....	....	....
1982-83	**Los Angeles Kings**	**NHL**	**46**	**15**	**20**	**4**	**2277**	**173**	**0**	**4.56**	**3.68**	**6.51**	**1212**	**.857**	**31.9**	....	....	....	....	....	....	....	....	....	....	....	....
1983-84	**Los Angeles Kings**	**NHL**	**13**	**4**	**7**	**1**	**665**	**55**	**0**	**4.96**	**3.91**	**8.50**	**321**	**.829**	**29.0**	....	....	....	....	....	....	....	....	....	....	....	....
	New Haven Nighthawks	AHL	22	....	....	....	1179	97	0	4.94	....	....	....	....	....	....	....	....	....	....	....	....	....	....	....	....	....
	NHL Totals		**59**	**19**	**27**	**5**	**2942**	**228**	**0**	**4.65**	....	....	**1533**	**.851**	**31.3**	....	....	....	....	....	....	....	....	....	....	....	....

Signed as a free agent by **LA Kings**, October 22, 1982.

• LAXTON, Gord

G – L. 5'10", 195 lbs. b: Montreal, Que., 3/16/1955. Pittsburgh's 1st, 13th overall in 1975.

Season	Club	League	GP	W	L	T	Mins	GA	SO	Avg	AAvg	Eff	SA	S%	SAPG	GP	W	L	T	Mins	GA	SO	Avg	Eff	SA	S%	SAPG
1972-73	Chilliwack Bruins	BCJHL	25	....	....	....	1350	75	0	3.33	....	....	....	....	....	4	0	3	0	126	14	0	6.67	....	....	....	....
1973-74	New Westminster Bruins	WCJHL	25	....	....	....	1350	75	0	3.33	....	....	....	....	....	4				126	14	0	6.67	....	....	....	....
1974-75	New Westminster Bruins	WCJHL	70	....	....	....	3980	239	3	3.60	....	....	....	....	....	18	....	....	....	1081	67	0	3.71	....	....	....	....
	New Westminster Bruins	Mem-Cup	3	*2	1	0	180	14	0	4.67	....	....	....	....	....	....	....	....	....	....	....	....	....	....	....	....	....
1975-76	**Pittsburgh Penguins**	**NHL**	**8**	**3**	**4**	**0**	**414**	**31**	**0**	**4.49**	**4.07**	....	....	....	....	....	....	....	....	....	....	....	....	....	....	....	....
	Hershey Bears	AHL	31	16	11	4	1857	104	0	3.36	....	....	....	....	....	*6	4	2	0	*309	19	0	3.69	....	....	....	....
1976-77	**Pittsburgh Penguins**	**NHL**	**6**	**1**	**3**	**0**	**253**	**26**	**0**	**6.17**	**5.75**	....	....	....	....	....	....	....	....	....	....	....	....	....	....	....	....
	Hershey Bears	AHL	18	4	11	0	958	80	0	5.01	....	....	....	....	....	....	....	....	....	....	....	....	....	....	....	....	....

			REGULAR SEASON													PLAYOFFS											
Season	Club	League	GP	W	L	T	Mins	GA	SO	Avg	AAvg	Eff	SA	S%	SAPG	GP	W	L	T	Mins	GA	SO	Avg	Eff	SA	S%	SAPG
1977-78	**Pittsburgh Penguins**	**NHL**	**2**	**0**	**1**	**0**	**73**	**9**	**0**	**7.40**	**6.94**	....	....	....	....	....	....	....	....	....	....	....	....	....	....	....	....
	Grand Rapids Owls	IHL	45	....	....	....	2651	183	0	4.14	....	....	....	....	....	....	....	....	....	....	....	....	....	....	....	....	....
1978-79	**Pittsburgh Penguins**	**NHL**	**1**	**0**	**1**	**0**	**60**	**8**	**0**	**8.00**	**7.08**	....	....	....	....	....	....	....	....	....	....	....	....	....	....	....	....
	Grand Rapids Owls	IHL	63	....	....	....	3742	192	3	3.08	....	....	....	....	....	19	10	9	0	1178	81	1	4.13	....	....	....	....
1979-80	Syracuse Firebirds	AHL	2	0	1	0	69	11	0	9.56	....	....	....	....	....	....	....	....	....	....	....	....	....	....	....	....	....
	Grand Rapids Owls	IHL	20	....	....	....	1197	90	0	4.51	....	....	....	....	....	....	....	....	....	....	....	....	....	....	....	....	....
1980-81	Binghamton Whalers	AHL	2	0	2	0	118	12	0	6.10	....	....	....	....	....	....	....	....	....	....	....	....	....	....	....	....	....
	Port Huron Flags	IHL	52	....	....	....	2923	207	0	4.25	....	....	....	....	....	3	0	3	0	191	12	0	3.77	....	....	....	....
1981-82	Erie Blades	AHL	31	2	23	1	1672	172	0	6.17	....	....	....	....	....	....	....	....	....	....	....	....	....	....	....	....	....
	Muskegon Mohawks	IHL	3	....	....	....	175	11	0	3.71	....	....	....	....	....	....	....	....	....	....	....	....	....	....	....	....	....
1982-83	Muskegon Mohawks	IHL	40	....	....	....	2326	158	1	4.08	....	....	....	....	....	2	1	1	0	120	8	0	4.00	....	....	....	....
	NHL Totals		**17**	**4**	**9**	**0**	**800**	**74**	**0**	**5.55**	....	....	....	....	....	....	....	....	....	....	....	....	....	....	....	....	....

IHL First All-Star Team (1979) • Won James Norris Memorial Trophy (fewest goals against - IHL) (1979)

• LeBLANC, Ray

Raymond J. G – L. 5'10", 170 lbs. b: Fitchburg, MA, 10/24/1964.

Season	Club	League	GP	W	L	T	Mins	GA	SO	Avg	AAvg	Eff	SA	S%	SAPG	GP	W	L	T	Mins	GA	SO	Avg	Eff	SA	S%	SAPG
1982-83	Markham Waxers	OJHL	6	2	2	1	305	28	0	5.55	....	....	....	....	....	....	....	....	....	....	....	....	....	....	....	....	....
	Dixie Beehives	OJHL	29	16	8	3	1722	111	0	3.90	....	....	....	....	....	....	....	....	....	....	....	....	....	....	....	....	....
1983-84	Kitchener Rangers	OHL	*54	*39	7	1	2965	185	1	3.74	....	....	....	....	....	....	....	....	....	....	....	....	....	....	....	....	....
	Kitchener Rangers	Mem-Cup	4	*3	1	0	240	18	0	4.50	....	....	....	....	....	....	....	....	....	....	....	....	....	....	....	....	....
1984-85	Pinebridge Bucks	ACHL	40	....	....	....	2178	150	0	4.13	....	....	....	....	....	....	....	....	....	....	....	....	....	....	....	....	....
1985-86	Carolina Thunderbirds	ACHL	42	....	....	....	2505	133	3	3.19	....	....	....	....	....	....	....	....	....	....	....	....	....	....	....	....	....
1986-87	Flint Spirits	IHL	64	33	23	1	3417	222	0	3.90	....	....	....	....	....	4	1	3	....	233	17	0	4.38	....	....	....	....
1987-88	Flint Spirits	IHL	62	27	19	8	3269	239	1	4.39	....	....	....	....	....	16	10	6	....	925	55	1	3.57	....	....	....	....
1988-89	Flint Spirits	IHL	15	5	9	0	852	67	0	4.72	....	....	....	....	....	....	....	....	....	....	....	....	....	....	....	....	....
	New Haven Nighthawks	AHL	1	0	0	0	20	3	0	9.00	....	....	....	....	....	....	....	....	....	....	....	....	....	....	....	....	....
	Saginaw Hawks	IHL	29	19	7	2	1655	99	0	3.59	....	....	....	....	....	1	0	1	....	5	9	0	3.05	....	....	....	....
1989-90	Indianapolis Ice	IHL	23	15	6	2	1334	71	2	3.19	....	....	....	....	....	....	....	....	....	....	....	....	....	....	....	....	....
	Fort Wayne Komets	IHL	15	3	3	3	680	44	0	3.88	....	....	....	....	....	3	0	2	....	139	11	0	4.75	....	....	....	....
1990-91	Fort Wayne Komets	IHL	21	10	8	0	1072	69	0	3.86	....	....	....	....	....	....	....	....	....	....	....	....	....	....	....	....	....
	Indianapolis Ice	IHL	3	2	0	0	145	7	0	2.90	....	....	....	....	....	1	0	0	....	19	1	0	3.20	....	....	....	....
1991-92	United States	Nat-Team	17	5	10	1	891	54	0	3.63	....	....	....	....	....	....	....	....	....	....	....	....	....	....	....	....	....
	United States	Olympics	8	5	2	1	463	17	*2	2.20	....	....	....	....	....	....	....	....	....	....	....	....	....	....	....	....	....
	Chicago Blackhawks	**NHL**	**1**	**1**	**0**	**0**	**60**	**1**	**0**	**1.00**	**0.90**	**0.45**	**22**	**.955**	**22.0**	....	....	....	....	....	....	....	....	....	....	....	....
	Indianapolis Ice	IHL	25	14	9	2	1468	84	2	3.43	....	....	....	....	....	....	....	....	....	....	....	....	....	....	....	....	....
1992-93	Indianapolis Ice	IHL	56	23	22	7	3201	206	0	3.86	....	....	....	....	....	5	1	4	....	276	23	0	5.00	....	....	....	....
1993-94	Indianapolis Ice	IHL	2	0	1	0	112	8	0	4.25	....	....	....	....	....	....	....	....	....	....	....	....	....	....	....	....	....
	Cincinnati Cyclones	IHL	34	17	9	3	1779	104	1	3.51	....	....	....	....	....	5	0	3	....	159	9	0	3.39	....	....	....	....
1994-95	Chicago Wolves	IHL	44	19	14	6	2375	129	1	3.26	....	....	....	....	....	3	0	3	....	177	14	0	4.73	....	....	....	....
1995-96	Chicago Wolves	IHL	31	10	14	2	1614	97	0	3.61	....	....	....	....	....	....	....	....	....	....	....	....	....	....	....	....	....
1996-97	Chicago Wolves	IHL	38	15	14	2	1911	103	2	3.23	....	....	....	....	....	....	....	....	....	....	....	....	....	....	....	....	....
1997-98	Chicago Wolves	IHL	14	9	3	0	728	34	0	2.80	....	....	....	....	....	....	....	....	....	....	....	....	....	....	....	....	....
	Flint Generals	UHL	29	12	4	5	1303	79	2	3.64	....	....	....	....	....	....	....	....	....	....	....	....	....	....	....	....	....
1998-99	Jacksonville Lizard Kings	ECHL	53	29	19	1	2982	163	1	3.28	....	....	....	....	....	2	0	2	0	118	8	0	4.07	....	....	....	....
99-2000	Jacksonville Lizard Kings	ECHL	56	22	25	8	3030	183	0	3.62	....	....	....	....	....	....	....	....	....	....	....	....	....	....	....	....	....
	NHL Totals		**1**	**1**	**0**	**0**	**60**	**1**	**0**	**1.00**	....	....	**22**	**.955**	**22.0**	....	....	....	....	....	....	....	....	....	....	....	....

ACHL Second All-Star Team (1985) • ACHL First All-Star Team (1986) • IHL Second All-Star Team (1987)

Signed as a free agent by **Chicago**, July 5, 1989.

• LEDUC, Albert

"Battleship" G. 5'9", 180 lbs. b: Valleyfield, Que., 11/22/1902 d: 7/31/1990.

Season	Club	League	GP	W	L	T	Mins	GA	SO	Avg	AAvg	Eff	SA	S%	SAPG	GP	W	L	T	Mins	GA	SO	Avg	Eff	SA	S%	SAPG
1931-32	**Montreal Canadiens**	**NHL**	**1**	**0**	**0**	**0**	**2**	**1**	**0**	**30.00**	**36.72**	....	....	....	....	....	....	....	....	....	....	....	....	....	....	....	....
	NHL Totals		**1**	**0**	**0**	**0**	**2**	**1**	**0**	**30.00**	....	....	....	....	....	....	....	....	....	....	....	....	....	....	....	....	....

• **Montreal Canadiens'** defenseman replaced penalized George Hainsworth, December 2, 1931. (Chicago 2, Montreal Canadiens 1)

• LEGACE, Manny

Emmanuel Fernandez G – L. 5'9", 162 lbs. b: Toronto, Ont., 2/4/1973. Hartford's 5th, 188th overall in 1993.

Season	Club	League	GP	W	L	T	Mins	GA	SO	Avg	AAvg	Eff	SA	S%	SAPG	GP	W	L	T	Mins	GA	SO	Avg	Eff	SA	S%	SAPG
1987-88	Alliston Hornets	OJHL-C	16	7	9	0	960	83	0	5.17	....	....	....	....	....	....	....	....	....	....	....	....	....	....	....	....	....
1988-89	Vaughan Raiders	OJHL-B	23	....	....	....	1303	92	1	4.24	....	....	....	....	....	....	....	....	....	....	....	....	....	....	....	....	....
1989-90	Vaughan Raiders	OJHL-B	21	8	11	1	1180	89	1	4.53	....	....	....	....	....	....	....	....	....	....	....	....	....	....	....	....	....
	Thornhill Thunderbirds	OJHL-B	8	3	3	2	480	30	0	3.75	....	....	....	....	....	....	....	....	....	....	....	....	....	....	....	....	....
1990-91	Niagara Falls Thunder	OHL	30	13	11	2	1515	107	0	4.24	....	....	....	....	....	4	1	1	....	119	10	0	5.04	....	....	....	....
1991-92	Niagara Falls Thunder	OHL	43	21	16	3	2384	143	0	3.60	....	....	....	....	....	14	8	5	....	791	56	0	4.25	....	....	....	....
1992-93	Niagara Falls Thunder	OHL	48	22	19	3	2630	171	0	3.90	....	....	....	....	....	4	0	4	....	240	18	0	4.50	....	....	....	....
	Canada	WJC-A	6	*6	0	0	360	10	1	1.67	....	....	....	....	....	....	....	....	....	....	....	....	....	....	....	....	....
1993-94	Canada	Nat-Team	16	8	6	0	859	36	2	2.51	....	....	....	....	....	....	....	....	....	....	....	....	....	....	....	....	....
	Canada	Olympics	DID NOT PLAY – SPARE GOALTENDER																								
1994-95	Springfield Falcons	AHL	39	12	17	6	2169	128	2	3.54	....	....	....	....	....	....	....	....	....	....	....	....	....	....	....	....	....
1995-96	Springfield Falcons	AHL	37	20	12	4	2196	83	*5	*2.27	....	....	....	....	....	4	1	3	....	220	18	0	4.91	....	....	....	....
1996-97	Springfield Falcons	AHL	36	17	14	5	2119	107	1	3.03	....	....	....	....	....	12	9	3	....	745	25	*2	2.01	....	....	....	....
	Richmond Renegades	ECHL	3	2	1	0	157	8	0	3.05	....	....	....	....	....	....	....	....	....	....	....	....	....	....	....	....	....
1997-98	Springfield Falcons	AHL	6	4	2	0	345	16	0	2.78	....	....	....	....	....	....	....	....	....	....	....	....	....	....	....	....	....
	Las Vegas Thunder	IHL	41	18	16	4	2106	111	1	3.16	....	....	....	....	....	4	1	3	....	237	16	0	4.05	....	....	....	....
1998-99	**Los Angeles Kings**	**NHL**	**17**	**2**	**9**	**2**	**899**	**39**	**0**	**2.60**	**3.09**	**2.31**	**439**	**.911**	**29.3**	....	....	....	....	....	....	....	....	....	....	....	....
	Long Beach Ice Dogs	IHL	33	22	8	1	1796	67	2	2.24	....	....	....	....	....	6	4	2	....	338	9	0	*1.60	....	....	....	....
99-2000	**Detroit Red Wings**	**NHL**	**4**	**4**	**0**	**0**	**240**	**11**	**0**	**2.75**	**3.14**	**2.59**	**117**	**.906**	**29.3**	....	....	....	....	....	....	....	....	....	....	....	....
	Manitoba Moose	IHL	42	17	18	5	2409	104	2	2.59	....	....	....	....	....	2	0	2	....	141	7	0	2.97	....	....	....	....
	NHL Totals		**21**	**6**	**9**	**2**	**1139**	**50**	**0**	**2.63**	....	....	**556**	**.910**	**29.3**	....	....	....	....	....	....	....	....	....	....	....	....

OHL First All-Star Team (1993) • AHL First All-Star Team (1996) • Shared Harry "Hap" Holmes Memorial Trophy (fewest goals against - AHL) with Scott Langkow (1996) • Won Baz Bastien Memorial Trophy (Top Goaltender - AHL) (1996)

Rights transferred to **Carolina** after **Hartford** franchise relocated, June 25, 1997. Traded to **LA Kings** by **Carolina** for future considerations, July 31, 1998. Signed as a free agent by **Detroit**, August 9, 1999. • Played w/ RHI's Toronto Planets in 1993 (13-10-3-(0)-611-67-0-5.26)

• LEGRIS, Claude

G – L. 5'9", 160 lbs. b: Verdun, Que., 11/6/1956. Detroit's 8th, 120th overall in 1976.

Season	Club	League	GP	W	L	T	Mins	GA	SO	Avg	AAvg	Eff	SA	S%	SAPG	GP	W	L	T	Mins	GA	SO	Avg	Eff	SA	S%	SAPG
1972-73	Sorel Eperviers	QMJHL	26	....	....	....	1530	156	0	6.12	....	....	....	....	....	5	....	....	....	300	36	0	7.20	....	....	....	....
1973-74	Sorel Eperviers	QMJHL	48	....	....	....	2880	216	*2	4.50	....	....	....	....	....	12	....	....	....	680	53	0	4.68	....	....	....	....
1974-75	Sorel Eperviers	QMJHL	47	....	....	....	2513	231	0	5.52	....	....	....	....	....	....	....	....	....	....	....	....	....	....	....	....	....
1975-76	Sorel Eperviers	QMJHL	67	....	....	....	3862	301	0	4.68	....	....	....	....	....	5	....	....	....	300	23	0	4.60	....	....	....	....
1976-77	Campbellton Tigers	NNBHL	STATISTICS NOT AVAILABLE																								
1977-78	Campbellton Tigers	NNBHL	1	1	0	0	60	1	0	1.00	....	....	....	....	....	4	....	....	....	232	13	0	3.36	....	....	....	....
	Bathurst Alpines	NNBHL	....	....	....	....	....	....	....	....	....	....	....	....	....	1	1	0	0	60	1	0	1.00	....	....	....	....
1978-79	Kalamazoo Wings	IHL	16	....	....	....	730	55	0	4.52	....	....	....	....	....	....	....	....	....	....	....	....	....	....	....	....	....
1979-80	Adirondack Red Wings	AHL	17	3	6	5	898	64	0	4.27	....	....	....	....	....	....	....	....	....	....	....	....	....	....	....	....	....
	Johnstown Red Wings	EHL	1	....	....	....	33	4	0	7.27	....	....	....	....	....	....	....	....	....	....	....	....	....	....	....	....	....
1980-81	**Detroit Red Wings**	**NHL**	**3**	**0**	**1**	**0**	**63**	**4**	**0**	**3.81**	**3.08**	....	....	....	....	....	....	....	....	....	....	....	....	....	....	....	....
	Adirondack Red Wings	AHL	2	1	1	0	120	7	0	3.50	....	....	....	....	....	....	....	....	....	....	....	....	....	....	....	....	....
	Kalamazoo Wings	IHL	52	....	....	....	3010	154	5	3.07	....	....	....	....	....	6	2	2	0	251	17	1	4.06	....	....	....	....

			REGULAR SEASON													PLAYOFFS											
Season	Club	League	GP	W	L	T	Mins	GA	SO	Avg	AAvg	Eff	SA	S%	SAPG	GP	W	L	T	Mins	GA	SO	Avg	Eff	SA	S%	SAPG
1981-82	**Detroit Red Wings**	**NHL**	**1**	**0**	**0**	**1**	**28**	**0**	**0**	**0.00**	**0.00**	....	....	....	....	....	....	....	....	....	....	....	....	....	....	....	....
	Springfield Indians	AHL	18	7	9	1	1002	71	0	4.25	....	....	....	....	....	....	....	....	....	....	....	....	....	....	....	....	....
	Kalamazoo Wings	IHL	7	....	....	....	396	28	0	4.24	....	....	....	....	....	....	....	....	....	....	....	....	....	....	....	....	....
1982-83	Adirondack Red Wings	AHL	32	11	12	2	1680	118	0	4.21	....	....	....	....	....	....	....	....	....	....	....	....	....	....	....	....	....
	NHL Totals		**4**	**0**	**1**	**1**	**91**	**4**	**0**	**2.64**	....	....	....	....	....	....	....	....	....	....	....	....	....	....	....	....	....

QMJHL East Division Second All-Star Team (1976) • IHL First All-Star Team (1981) • Shared James Norris Memorial Trophy (fewest goals against - IHL) with Georges Gagnon (1981)

• LEHMAN, Hugh

Frederick Hugh "Old Eagle Eyes" G – L. 5'8", 168 lbs. b: Pembroke, Ont., 10/27/1885 d: 4/8/1961. **HHOF**

Season	Club	League	GP	W	L	T	Mins	GA	SO	Avg	AAvg	Eff	SA	S%	SAPG	GP	W	L	T	Mins	GA	SO	Avg	Eff	SA	S%	SAPG
1903-04	Pembroke Lumber Kings	OVHL	5	1	4	0	300	22	0	....	....	....	....	....	....	....	....	....	....	....	....	....	....	....	....	....	....
1904-05	Pembroke Lumber Kings	OVHL	STATISTICS NOT AVAILABLE																								
1905-06	Pembroke Lumber Kings	OVHL	8	*8	0	0	480	13	*1	*1.67	....	....	....	....	....	1	1	0	0	60	0	1	0.00	....	....	....	....
1906-07	Canadian Soo Pros	IHL	24	13	11	0	1440	123	0	5.13	....	....	....	....	....	....	....	....	....	....	....	....	....	....	....	....	....
1907-08	Michigan Soo Pros	MOHL	DID NOT PLAY																								
	Pembroke Lumber Kings	OVHL	STATISTICS NOT AVAILABLE																								
1908-09	Berlin Professionals	OPHL	15	9	6	0	890	72	0	4.85	....	....	....	....	....	....	....	....	....	....	....	....	....	....	....	....	....
1909-10	Berlin Professionals	OPHL	6	*6	0	0	360	18	0	*3.00	....	....	....	....	....	....	....	....	....	....	....	....	....	....	....	....	....
	Galt Professionals	OPHL	....	....	....	....	....	....	....	....	....	....	....	....	....	2	0	2	0	120	15	0	7.50	....	....	....	....
1910-11	Berlin Professionals	OPHL	15	7	8	0	900	87	0	5.80	....	....	....	....	....	....	....	....	....	....	....	....	....	....	....	....	....
1911-12	New Westminster Royals	PCHA	15	*9	6	0	911	77	0	*5.07	....	....	....	....	....	....	....	....	....	....	....	....	....	....	....	....	....
	PCHA All-Stars	X-Games	3	*2	1	0	180	12	0	*4.00	....	....	....	....	....	....	....	....	....	....	....	....	....	....	....	....	....
1912-13	New Westminster Royals	PCHA	12	4	8	0	739	51	0	4.14	....	....	....	....	....	....	....	....	....	....	....	....	....	....	....	....	....
1913-14	New Westminster Royals	PCHA	16	7	9	0	997	81	0	4.87	....	....	....	....	....	....	....	....	....	....	....	....	....	....	....	....	....
1914-15♦	Vancouver Millionaires	PCHA	17	*14	3	0	1043	71	*1	*4.08	....	....	....	....	....	3	*3	0	0	180	8	0	2.67	....	....	....	....
	PCHA All-Stars	X-Games	2	*2	0	0	120	9	0	*4.50	....	....	....	....	....	....	....	....	....	....	....	....	....	....	....	....	....
1915-16	Vancouver Millionaires	PCHA	18	9	9	0	1091	69	0	3.79	....	....	....	....	....	....	....	....	....	....	....	....	....	....	....	....	....
	PCHA All-Stars	X-Games	2	1	1	0	120	9	0	*4.50	....	....	....	....	....	....	....	....	....	....	....	....	....	....	....	....	....
1916-17	Vancouver Millionaires	PCHA	23	14	9	0	1404	124	0	5.30	....	....	....	....	....	....	....	....	....	....	....	....	....	....	....	....	....
1917-18	Vancouver Millionaires	PCHA	18	9	9	0	1179	60	*1	*3.05	....	....	....	....	....	2	1	0	1	120	2	1	1.00	....	....	....	....
	Vancouver Millionaires	St-Cup	5	2	3	....	300	18	0	3.60	....	....	....	....	....	....	....	....	....	....	....	....	....	....	....	....	....
1918-19	Vancouver Millionaires	PCHA	20	*12	8	0	1277	55	1	2.58	....	....	....	....	....	2	1	1	0	120	7	0	3.50	....	....	....	....
1919-20	Vancouver Millionaires	PCHA	22	11	11	0	1334	65	1	2.92	....	....	....	....	....	2	1	1	0	120	7	0	3.50	....	....	....	....
1920-21	Vancouver Millionaires	PCHA	24	13	11	0	1449	78	*3	3.23	....	....	....	....	....	2	2	0	0	120	2	1	1.00	....	....	....	....
	Vancouver Millionaires	St-Cup	5	2	3	0	300	12	0	2.40	....	....	....	....	....	....	....	....	....	....	....	....	....	....	....	....	....
1921-22	Vancouver Millionaires	PCHA	22	*12	10	0	1318	62	*4	2.82	....	....	....	....	....	2	0	2	0	120	0	2	0.00	....	....	....	....
	Vancouver Millionaires	St-Cup	7	3	4	0	425	18	2	2.54	....	....	....	....	....	....	....	....	....	....	....	....	....	....	....	....	....
1922-23	Vancouver Maroons	PCHA	25	*16	8	1	1571	61	*5	*2.33	....	....	....	....	....	2	1	1	0	120	3	1	1.50	....	....	....	....
	Vancouver Maroons	St-Cup	4	1	3	0	240	10	0	2.50	....	....	....	....	....	....	....	....	....	....	....	....	....	....	....	....	....
1923-24	Vancouver Maroons	PCHA	*30	13	16	1	*1846	80	1	*2.60	....	....	....	....	....	2	1	1	0	134	3	0	1.34	....	....	....	....
	Vancouver Maroons	St-Cup	5	1	4	....	300	15	0	3.00	....	....	....	....	....	....	....	....	....	....	....	....	....	....	....	....	....
1924-25	Vancouver Maroons	WCHL	11	7	4	0	663	29	0	2.62	....	....	....	....	....	....	....	....	....	....	....	....	....	....	....	....	....
1925-26	Vancouver Maroons	WHL	*30	10	18	2	1839	90	3	2.94	....	....	....	....	....	....	....	....	....	....	....	....	....	....	....	....	....
1926-27	**Chicago Black Hawks**	**NHL**	***44**	**19**	**22**	**3**	***2797**	**116**	**5**	**2.49**	**3.91**	....	....	....	....	**2**	**0**	**1**	**1**	**120**	**10**	**0**	**5.00**	....	....	....	....
1927-28	**Chicago Black Hawks**	**NHL**	**4**	**1**	**2**	**1**	**250**	**20**	**1**	**4.80**	**7.81**	....	....	....	....	....	....	....	....	....	....	....	....	....	....	....	....
	NHL Totals		**48**	**20**	**24**	**4**	**3047**	**136**	**6**	**2.68**	....	....	....	....	....	**2**	**0**	**1**	**1**	**120**	**10**	**0**	**5.00**	....	....	....	....
	Other Major League Totals		363	195	164	4	22251	1353	20	3.65	....	....	....	....	....	19	10	8	....	1154	47	5	2.44	....	....	....	....

PCHA All-Star Team (1912 , 1914, 1915, 1924) • PCHA First All-Star Team (1916, 1918, 1919, 1920, 1921, 1922, 1923)

Signed as a free agent by **Canadian Soo** (IHL), November 30, 1906. Signed as a free agent by **Michigan Soo** (IHL), November 3, 1907. Signed as a free agent by **Brantford** (OPHL) after **Michigan Soo** (IHL) franchise folded, December 10, 1907. Signed with **Pembroke** (OVHL) after leaving **Brantford** (OPHL), December, 1907. Traded to **Chicago** by **Vancouver** (WHL) for cash, October 9, 1926. • 1922 St-Cup totals include series vs. Regina.

• LEMELIN, Reggie

Rejean M. G – L. 5'11", 170 lbs. b: Quebec City, Que., 11/19/1954. Philadelphia's 6th, 125th overall in 1974.

Season	Club	League	GP	W	L	T	Mins	GA	SO	Avg	AAvg	Eff	SA	S%	SAPG	GP	W	L	T	Mins	GA	SO	Avg	Eff	SA	S%	SAPG
1972-73	Sherbrooke Castors	QMJHL	28	....	....	....	1660	146	0	5.28	....	....	....	....	....	2	....	....	....	120	12	0	6.00	....	....	....	....
1973-74	Sherbrooke Castors	QMJHL	35	....	....	....	2060	158	0	4.60	....	....	....	....	....	1	....	....	....	60	3	0	3.00	....	....	....	....
1974-75	Philadelphia Firebirds	NAHL	43	21	16	2	2277	131	3	3.45	....	....	....	....	....	....	....	....	....	....	....	....	....	....	....	....	....
1975-76	Richmond Robins	AHL	7	....	....	....	402	30	0	4.48	....	....	....	....	....	....	....	....	....	....	....	....	....	....	....	....	....
	Philadelphia Firebirds	NAHL	29	....	....	....	1601	97	1	3.63	....	....	....	....	....	3	....	....	....	171	15	0	5.26	....	....	....	....
1976-77	Springfield Indians	AHL	3	2	1	0	180	10	0	3.33	....	....	....	....	....	....	....	....	....	....	....	....	....	....	....	....	....
	Philadelphia Firebirds	NAHL	51	26	19	1	2763	170	1	3.61	....	....	....	....	....	3	....	....	....	191	14	0	4.40	....	....	....	....
1977-78	Philadelphia Firebirds	AHL	*60	31	21	7	*3585	177	4	2.96	....	....	....	....	....	2	0	2	0	119	12	0	6.05	....	....	....	....
1978-79	**Atlanta Flames**	**NHL**	**18**	**8**	**8**	**1**	**994**	**55**	**0**	**3.32**	**2.93**	....	....	....	....	**1**	**0**	**0**	....	**20**	**0**	**0**	**0.00**	....	....	....	....
	Philadelphia Firebirds	AHL	13	3	9	1	780	36	0	2.77	....	....	....	....	....	....	....	....	....	....	....	....	....	....	....	....	....
1979-80	**Atlanta Flames**	**NHL**	**3**	**0**	**2**	**0**	**150**	**15**	**0**	**6.00**	**5.31**	....	....	....	....	....	....	....	....	....	....	....	....	....	....	....	....
	Birmingham Bulls	CHL	38	13	21	2	2188	137	0	3.76	....	....	....	....	....	2	0	1	0	79	5	0	3.80	....	....	....	....
1980-81	**Calgary Flames**	**NHL**	**29**	**14**	**6**	**7**	**1629**	**88**	**2**	**3.24**	**2.61**	....	....	....	....	**6**	**3**	**3**	....	**366**	**22**	**0**	**3.61**	....	....	....	....
	Birmingham Bulls	CHL	13	3	8	2	757	56	0	4.44	....	....	....	....	....	....	....	....	....	....	....	....	....	....	....	....	....
1981-82	**Calgary Flames**	**NHL**	**34**	**10**	**15**	**6**	**1866**	**135**	**0**	**4.34**	**3.36**	....	....	....	....	....	....	....	....	....	....	....	....	....	....	....	....
1982-83	**Calgary Flames**	**NHL**	**39**	**16**	**12**	**8**	**2211**	**133**	**0**	**3.61**	**2.89**	**4.03**	**1192**	**.888**	**32.3**	**7**	**3**	**3**	....	**327**	**27**	**0**	**4.95**	....	....	....	....
1983-84	**Calgary Flames**	**NHL**	**51**	**21**	**12**	**9**	**2568**	**150**	**0**	**3.50**	**2.75**	**3.74**	**1405**	**.893**	**32.8**	**8**	**4**	**4**	....	**448**	**32**	**0**	**4.29**	**4.73**	**290**	**.890**	**38.8**
1984-85	**Calgary Flames**	**NHL**	**56**	**30**	**12**	**10**	**3176**	**183**	**1**	**3.46**	**2.75**	**3.87**	**1638**	**.888**	**30.9**	**4**	**1**	**3**	....	**248**	**15**	**1**	**3.63**	**4.25**	**128**	**.883**	**31.0**
1985-86	**Calgary Flames**	**NHL**	**60**	**29**	**24**	**4**	**3369**	**229**	**1**	**4.08**	**3.19**	**5.23**	**1787**	**.872**	**31.8**	**3**	**0**	**1**	....	**109**	**7**	**0**	**3.85**	**5.61**	**48**	**.854**	**26.4**
1986-87	**Calgary Flames**	**NHL**	**34**	**16**	**9**	**1**	**1735**	**94**	**2**	**3.25**	**2.75**	**3.70**	**825**	**.886**	**28.5**	**2**	**0**	**1**	....	**101**	**6**	**0**	**3.56**	**4.54**	**47**	**.872**	**27.9**
1987-88	**Boston Bruins**	**NHL**	**49**	**24**	**17**	**6**	**2828**	**138**	**3**	**2.93**	**2.43**	**3.25**	**1244**	**.889**	**26.4**	**17**	**11**	**6**	....	**1027**	**45**	***1**	***2.63**	**2.75**	**430**	**.895**	**25.1**
1988-89	**Boston Bruins**	**NHL**	**40**	**19**	**15**	**6**	**2392**	**120**	**0**	**3.01**	**2.49**	**3.40**	**1061**	**.887**	**26.6**	**4**	**1**	**3**	....	**252**	**16**	**0**	**3.81**	**5.44**	**112**	**.857**	**26.7**
1989-90	**Boston Bruins**	**NHL**	**43**	**22**	**15**	**2**	**2310**	**108**	**2**	**2.81**	**2.37**	**3.03**	**1002**	**.892**	**26.0**	**3**	**0**	**1**	....	**135**	**13**	**0**	**5.78**	**13.18**	**57**	**.772**	**25.3**
1990-91	**Boston Bruins**	**NHL**	**33**	**17**	**10**	**3**	**1829**	**111**	**1**	**3.64**	**3.28**	**4.80**	**841**	**.868**	**27.6**	**2**	**0**	**0**	....	**32**	**0**	**0**	**0.00**	**0.00**	**18**	**1.000**	**33.8**
1991-92	**Boston Bruins**	**NHL**	**8**	**5**	**1**	**0**	**407**	**23**	**0**	**3.39**	**3.04**	**3.71**	**210**	**.890**	**31.0**	**2**	**0**	**0**	....	**54**	**3**	**0**	**3.33**	**4.34**	**23**	**.870**	**25.6**
1992-93	**Boston Bruins**	**NHL**	**10**	**5**	**4**	**0**	**542**	**31**	**0**	**3.43**	**2.94**	**4.73**	**225**	**.862**	**24.9**	....	....	....	....	....	....	....	....	....	....	....	....
	NHL Totals		**507**	**236**	**162**	**63**	**28006**	**1613**	**12**	**3.46**	....	....	....	....	....	**59**	**23**	**25**	....	**3119**	**186**	**2**	**3.58**	....	....	....	....

AHL First All-Star Team (1978) • Shared William M. Jennings Trophy with Andy Moog (1990) • Played in NHL All-Star Game (1989)

Signed as a free agent by **Atlanta**, August 17, 1978. Transferred to **Calgary** after **Atlanta** franchise relocated, June 24, 1980. Signed as a free agent by **Boston**, August 13, 1987.

• LENARDUZZI, Mike

Michael P. G – L. 6'1", 165 lbs. b: London, Ont., 9/14/1972. Hartford's 3rd, 57th overall in 1990.

Season	Club	League	GP	W	L	T	Mins	GA	SO	Avg	AAvg	Eff	SA	S%	SAPG	GP	W	L	T	Mins	GA	SO	Avg	Eff	SA	S%	SAPG
1987-88	London Legionaires	OMHA	STATISTICS NOT AVAILABLE																								
1988-89	Markham Waxers	OJHL	23	....	....	....	1149	111	0	5.80	....	....	....	....	....	....	....	....	....	....	....	....	....	....	....	....	....
	Oshawa Generals	OHL	6	0	0	2	166	9	0	3.25	....	....	....	....	....	....	....	....	....	....	....	....	....	....	....	....	....
1989-90	Oshawa Generals	OHL	12	6	3	1	444	32	0	4.32	....	....	....	....	....	....	....	....	....	....	....	....	....	....	....	....	....
	Sault Ste. Marie Greyhounds	OHL	20	8	8	2	1117	66	0	3.55	....	....	....	....	....	....	....	....	....	....	....	....	....	....	....	....	....
1990-91	Sault Ste. Marie Greyhounds	OHL	35	19	8	3	1966	107	0	3.27	....	....	....	....	....	5	3	1	....	268	13	*1	2.91	....	....	....	....
	Sault Ste. Marie Greyhounds	Mem-Cup	2	0	2	0	114	8	0	4.21	....	....	....	....	....	....	....	....	....	....	....	....	....	....	....	....	....
1991-92	Sault Ste. Marie Greyhounds	OHL	9	5	3	0	486	33	0	4.07	....	....	....	....	....	....	....	....	....	....	....	....	....	....	....	....	....
	Ottawa 67's	OHL	18	5	12	1	986	60	1	3.65	....	....	....	....	....	....	....	....	....	....	....	....	....	....	....	....	....
	Sudbury Wolves	OHL	22	11	5	4	1201	84	2	4.20	....	....	....	....	....	11	4	7	....	651	38	0	3.50	....	....	....	....
	Springfield Indians	AHL	....	....	....	....	....	....	....	....	....	....	....	....	....	1	0	0	....	39	2	0	3.08	....	....	....	....
1992-93	**Hartford Whalers**	**NHL**	**3**	**1**	**1**	**1**	**168**	**9**	**0**	**3.21**	**2.75**	**3.32**	**87**	**.897**	**31.1**	....	....	....	....	....	....	....	....	....	....	....	....
	Springfield Indians	AHL	36	10	17	5	1945	142	0	4.38	....	....	....	....	....	2	1	0	....	100	5	0	3.00	....	....	....	....
1993-94	**Hartford Whalers**	**NHL**	**1**	**0**	**0**	**0**	**21**	**1**	**0**	**2.86**	**2.75**	**2.38**	**12**	**.917**	**34.3**	....	....	....	....	....	....	....	....	....	....	....	....
	Springfield Indians	AHL	22	5	7	2	984	73	0	4.45	....	....	....	....	....	....	....	....	....	....	....	....	....	....	....	....	....
	Salt Lake Golden Eagles	IHL	4	0	4	0	211	22	0	6.25	....	....	....	....	....	....	....	....	....	....	....	....	....	....	....	....	....
1994-95	London Blues	ColHL	43	19	16	0	2198	172	0	4.69	....	....	....	....	....	5	1	2	....	274	20	0	4.37	....	....	....	....

			REGULAR SEASON													PLAYOFFS											
Season	**Club**	**League**	**GP**	**W**	**L**	**T**	**Mins**	**GA**	**SO**	**Avg**	**AAvg**	**Eff**	**SA**	**S%**	**SAPG**	**GP**	**W**	**L**	**T**	**Mins**	**GA**	**SO**	**Avg**	**Eff**	**SA**	**S%**	**SAPG**
1995-96	Saginaw Wheels	ColHL	43	14	15	3	2153	155	0	4.32	....	....	....	....	....	5	1	4	....	299	19	0	3.82	....	....	....	....
1996-97	Hershey Bears	AHL	2	0	0	0	13	0	0	0.00	....	....	....	....	....	....	....	....	....	....	....	....	....	....	....	....	....
	Mobile Mystics	ECHL	37	15	10	8	1932	118	1	3.66	....	....	....	....	....	1	0	1	....	60	4	0	4.00	....	....	....	....
1997-98	Mobile Mystics	ECHL	44	21	13	2	2201	122	2	3.32	....	....	....	....	....	3	0	2	....	133	11	0	4.96	....	....	....	....
1998-99	HC Milano Saima	Alpenliga	STATISTICS NOT AVAILABLE																								
	Amarillo Rattlers	WPHL	9	2	3	2	344	24	0	4.19	....	....	....	....	....	....	....	....	....	....	....	....	....	....	....	....	....
99-2000	Baton Rouge Kingfish	ECHL	54	25	20	2	2749	167	0	3.64	....	....	....	....	....	2	0	2	....	133	11	0	4.96	....	....	....	....
	NHL Totals		**4**	**1**	**1**	**1**	**189**	**10**	**0**	**3.17**	....	....	**99**	**.899**	**31.4**	....	....	....	....	....	....	....	....	....	....	....	....

• LESSARD, Mario

G – L. 5'9", 190 lbs. b: East Broughton, Que., 6/25/1954. Los Angeles' 7th, 154th overall in 1974.

Season	Club	League	GP	W	L	T	Mins	GA	SO	Avg	AAvg	Eff	SA	S%	SAPG	GP	W	L	T	Mins	GA	SO	Avg	Eff	SA	S%	SAPG
1969-1971	Sherbrooke Castors	QJHL	STATISTICS NOT AVAILABLE																								
1971-72	Sherbrooke Castors	QMJHL	17	....	....	....	1020	72	2	4.24	....	....	....	....	....	3	0	2	0	133	24	0	10.83	....	....	....	....
1972-73	Sherbrooke Castors	QMJHL	37	....	....	....	2180	161	0	4.43	....	....	....	....	....	6	....	....	....	360	24	0	4.00	....	....	....	....
1973-74	Sherbrooke Castors	QMJHL	36	....	....	....	2140	180	0	5.05	....	....	....	....	....	4	....	....	....	240	24	0	6.00	....	....	....	....
1974-75	Saginaw Gears	IHL	59	....	....	....	3186	171	4	3.22	....	....	....	....	....	17	10	7	0	1016	64	2	3.78	....	....	....	....
1975-76	Saginaw Gears	IHL	62	....	....	....	3323	187	3	3.38	....	....	....	....	....	12	7	5	0	722	31	1	2.58	....	....	....	....
1976-77	Fort Worth Texans	CHL	4	1	3	0	192	11	0	3.44	....	....	....	....	....	....	....	....	....	....	....	....	....	....	....	....	....
	Saginaw Gears	IHL	44	....	....	....	2489	144	0	3.47	....	....	....	....	....	18	12	6	0	1059	52	1	2.95	....	....	....	....
1977-78	Springfield Indians	AHL	57	30	19	6	3295	204	1	3.71	....	....	....	....	....	4	1	3	0	239	10	*1	2.51	....	....	....	....
1978-79	**Los Angeles Kings**	**NHL**	**49**	**23**	**15**	**10**	**2860**	**148**	**4**	**3.10**	**2.73**	....	....	....	....	**2**	**0**	**2**	....	**126**	**8**	**0**	**3.81**	....	....	....	....
1979-80	**Los Angeles Kings**	**NHL**	**50**	**18**	**22**	**7**	**2836**	**185**	**0**	**3.91**	**3.47**	....	....	....	....	**4**	**1**	**2**	....	**207**	**14**	**0**	**4.06**	....	....	....	....
1980-81	**Los Angeles Kings**	**NHL**	**64**	***35**	**18**	**11**	**3746**	**203**	**2**	**3.25**	**2.61**	....	....	....	....	**4**	**1**	**3**	....	**220**	**20**	**0**	**5.45**	....	....	....	....
1981-82	**Los Angeles Kings**	**NHL**	**52**	**13**	**28**	**8**	**2933**	**213**	**2**	**4.36**	**3.38**	....	....	....	....	**10**	**4**	**5**	....	**583**	**41**	**0**	**4.22**	....	....	....	....
1982-83	**Los Angeles Kings**	**NHL**	**19**	**3**	**10**	**2**	**888**	**68**	**1**	**4.59**	**3.69**	**7.23**	**432**	**.843**	**29.2**	....	....	....	....	....	....	....	....	....	....	....	....
	Birmingham South Stars	CHL	8	4	2	0	405	28	0	4.15	....	....	....	....	....	*11	6	3	0	*637	35	0	3.30	....	....	....	....
1983-84	**Los Angeles Kings**	**NHL**	**6**	**0**	**4**	**1**	**266**	**26**	**0**	**5.86**	**4.62**	**9.52**	**160**	**.838**	**36.1**	....	....	....	....	....	....	....	....	....	....	....	....
	New Haven Nighthawks	AHL	5	1	3	1	281	27	0	5.77	....	....	....	....	....	....	....	....	....	....	....	....	....	....	....	....	....
	NHL Totals		**240**	**92**	**97**	**39**	**13529**	**843**	**9**	**3.74**	....	....	**592**	**-.424**	**2.6**	**20**	**6**	**12**	....	**1136**	**83**	**0**	**4.38**	....	....	....	....

IHL First All-Star Team (1977) • AHL Second All-Star Team (1978) • NHL Second All-Star Team (1981) • Played in NHL All-Star Game (1981)

• Recorded shutout (6-0) in NHL debut vs. Buffalo, October 26, 1978.

• LEVASSEUR, Jean-Louis

G – L. 5'10", 160 lbs. b: Noranda, Que., 6/16/1949.

Season	Club	League	GP	W	L	T	Mins	GA	SO	Avg	AAvg	Eff	SA	S%	SAPG	GP	W	L	T	Mins	GA	SO	Avg	Eff	SA	S%	SAPG
1972-73	Orillia Terriers	OHA-Sr.	35	....	....	....	2100	114	1	3.26	....	....	....	....	....	....	....	....	....	....	....	....	....	....	....	....	....
	Tulsa Oilers	CHL	4	....	....	....	169	13	1	4.62	....	....	....	....	....	....	....	....	....	....	....	....	....	....	....	....	....
1973-74	Orillia Terriers	OHA-Sr.	14	....	....	....	840	48	1	3.43	....	....	....	....	....	....	....	....	....	....	....	....	....	....	....	....	....
1974-75	Johnstown Jets	NAHL	28	....	....	....	1504	79	1	3.15	....	....	....	....	....	12	8	4	0	654	29	0	2.66	....	....	....	....
1975-76	Johnstown Jets	NAHL	30	....	....	....	1757	89	1	3.04	....	....	....	....	....	5	....	....	....	264	19	0	4.32	....	....	....	....
	Minnesota Fighting Saints	WHA	4	2	1	0	193	10	0	3.11	....	....	....	....	....	....	....	....	....	....	....	....	....	....	....	....	....
1976-77	Minnesota Fighting Saints	WHA	30	15	11	2	1715	78	2	2.73	....	....	....	....	....	....	....	....	....	....	....	....	....	....	....	....	....
	Edmonton Oilers	WHA	21	6	12	3	1213	88	0	4.35	....	....	....	....	....	2	0	2	0	133	10	0	4.51	....	....	....	....
1977-78	New England Whalers	WHA	27	14	11	2	1655	91	3	3.30	....	....	....	....	....	*12	*8	4	0	*719	31	0	2.59	....	....	....	....
1978-79	Binghamton Dusters	AHL	25	10	12	2	1463	92	0	3.77	....	....	....	....	....	....	....	....	....	....	....	....	....	....	....	....	....
	Springfield Indians	AHL	9	4	3	0	480	30	0	3.75	....	....	....	....	....	....	....	....	....	....	....	....	....	....	....	....	....
	Quebec Nordiques	WHA	3	0	1	0	140	14	0	6.00	....	....	....	....	....	1	0	1	0	59	8	0	8.14	....	....	....	....
1979-80	**Minnesota North Stars**	**NHL**	**1**	**0**	**1**	**0**	**60**	**7**	**0**	**7.00**	**6.19**	....	....	....	....	....	....	....	....	....	....	....	....	....	....	....	....
	Oklahoma City Stars	CHL	37	19	14	3	2225	107	*4	2.89	....	....	....	....	....	....	....	....	....	....	....	....	....	....	....	....	....
1980-81	Oklahoma City Stars	CHL	21	9	8	1	1120	72	0	3.86	....	....	....	....	....	....	....	....	....	....	....	....	....	....	....	....	....
	NHL Totals		**1**	**0**	**1**	**0**	**60**	**7**	**0**	**7.00**	....	....	....	....	....	....	....	....	....	....	....	....	....	....	....	....	....
	Other Major League Totals		85	37	36	7	4916	281	5	3.43	....	....	....	....	....	15	8	7	....	911	49	0	3.23	....	....	....	....

OHA-Sr. First All-Star Team (1973)

Signed as a free agent by **Minnesota** (WHA), September, 1974. Traded to **Edmonton** (WHA) by **Minnesota** (WHA) with Mike Antonovich, Bill Butters, Dave Keon, Jack Carlson, Steve Carlson and John McKenzie fror cash, January, 1977. Traded to **New England** (WHA) by **Edmonton** (WHA) for Brett Callighen, Dave Dryden and future considerations, September, 1977. Traded to **Quebec** (WHA) by **New England** (WHA) for Warren Miller, September, 1978. Signed as a free agent by **Minnesota**, October 2, 1979.

• LEVINSKY, Alex

"Mine Boy" G. 5'10", 184 lbs. b: Syracuse, NY, 2/2/1910 d: 1990.

Season	Club	League	GP	W	L	T	Mins	GA	SO	Avg	AAvg	Eff	SA	S%	SAPG	GP	W	L	T	Mins	GA	SO	Avg	Eff	SA	S%	SAPG
1931-32	**Toronto Maple Leafs**	**NHL**	**1**	**0**	**0**	**0**	**1**	**1**	**0**	**60.00**	**73.44**	....	....	....	....	....	....	....	....	....	....	....	....	....	....	....	....
	NHL Totals		**1**	**0**	**0**	**0**	**1**	**1**	**0**	**60.00**	....	....	....	....	....	....	....	....	....	....	....	....	....	....	....	....	....

• **Toronto** defenseman replaced penalized Lorne Chabot, March 15, 1932. (Detroit 6, Toronto 2)

• LINDBERGH, Pelle

Per-Eric G – L. 5'9", 165 lbs. b: Stockholm, Sweden, 5/24/1959 d: 11/10/1985. Philadelphia's 3rd, 35th overall in 1979.

Season	Club	League	GP	W	L	T	Mins	GA	SO	Avg	AAvg	Eff	SA	S%	SAPG	GP	W	L	T	Mins	GA	SO	Avg	Eff	SA	S%	SAPG
1975-76	AIK Solna Stockholm	Sweden-Jr.	STATISTICS NOT AVAILABLE																								
	Sweden	EJC-A	3	....	....	....	180	4	....	1.33	....	....	....	....	....	....	....	....	....	....	....	....	....	....	....	....	....
1976-77	AIK Solna Stockholm	Sweden-Jr.	STATISTICS NOT AVAILABLE																								
	Sweden	EJC-A	3	....	....	....	180	3	....	1.00	....	....	....	....	....	....	....	....	....	....	....	....	....	....	....	....	....
1977-78	AIK Solna Stockholm	Sweden-Jr.	STATISTICS NOT AVAILABLE																								
	Sweden	WJC-A	4	....	....	....	240	10	0	2.50	....	....	....	....	....	....	....	....	....	....	....	....	....	....	....	....	....
1978-79	AIK Solna Stockholm	Sweden	6	....	....	....	360	38	0	6.33	....	....	....	....	....	....	....	....	....	....	....	....	....	....	....	....	....
	Sweden	WEC-A	6	1	4	1	360	38	0	6.33	....	....	....	....	....	....	....	....	....	....	....	....	....	....	....	....	....
1979-80	AIK Solna Stockholm	Sweden	32	....	....	....	1866	106	1	3.41	....	....	....	....	....	....	....	....	....	....	....	....	....	....	....	....	....
	Sweden	Olympics	5	2	1	2	300	18	0	3.60	....	....	....	....	....	....	....	....	....	....	....	....	....	....	....	....	....
1980-81	Maine Mariners	AHL	51	31	14	5	3035	165	1	3.26	....	....	....	....	....	*20	*10	7	0	*1120	66	0	3.54	....	....	....	....
1981-82	Sweden	Can-Cup	2	0	0	0	92	9	0	6.00	....	....	....	....	....	....	....	....	....	....	....	....	....	....	....	....	....
	Philadelphia Flyers	**NHL**	**8**	**2**	**4**	**2**	**480**	**35**	**0**	**4.38**	**3.38**	....	....	....	....	....	....	....	....	....	....	....	....	....	....	....	....
	Maine Mariners	AHL	25	17	7	2	1505	83	0	3.31	....	....	....	....	....	....	....	....	....	....	....	....	....	....	....	....	....
1982-83	**Philadelphia Flyers**	**NHL**	**40**	**23**	**13**	**3**	**2333**	**116**	**3**	**2.98**	**2.38**	**3.26**	**1060**	**.891**	**27.3**	**3**	**0**	**3**	....	**180**	**18**	**0**	**6.00**	....	....	....	....
	Sweden	WEC-A	9	4	4	1	540	27	0	3.00	....	....	....	....	....	....	....	....	....	....	....	....	....	....	....	....	....
1983-84	**Philadelphia Flyers**	**NHL**	**36**	**16**	**13**	**3**	**1999**	**135**	**1**	**4.05**	**3.19**	**5.66**	**966**	**.860**	**29.0**	**2**	**0**	**1**	....	**26**	**3**	**0**	**6.92**	**15.97**	**13**	**.769**	**30.0**
	Springfield Indians	AHL	4	4	0	0	240	12	0	3.00	....	....	....	....	....	....	....	....	....	....	....	....	....	....	....	....	....
1984-85	**Philadelphia Flyers**	**NHL**	***65**	***40**	**17**	**7**	***3858**	**194**	**2**	**3.02**	**2.39**	**3.04**	**1929**	**.899**	**30.0**	***18**	**12**	**6**	....	**1008**	**42**	***3**	**2.50**	**2.14**	**490**	**.914**	**29.2**
1985-86	**Philadelphia Flyers**	**NHL**	**8**	**6**	**2**	**0**	**480**	**23**	**1**	**2.88**	**2.25**	**3.33**	**199**	**.884**	**24.9**	....	....	....	....	....	....	....	....	....	....	....	....
	NHL Totals		**157**	**87**	**49**	**15**	**9150**	**503**	**7**	**3.30**	....	....	....	....	....	**23**	**12**	**10**	....	**1214**	**63**	**3**	**3.11**	....	....	....	....

Named Best Goaltender at EJC-A (1976, 1977) • WJC-A All-Star Team (1979) • Named Best Goaltender at WJC-A (1979) • Swedish World All-Star Team (1979, 1980, 1983) • AHL First All-Star Team (1981) • Shared Harry "Hap" Holmes Memorial Award (fewest goals against - AHL) with Robbie Moore (1981) • Won Dudley "Red" Garrett Memorial Award (Top Rookie - AHL) (1981) • Won Les Cunningham Award (MVP - AHL) (1981) • NHL All-Rookie Team (1983) • NHL First All-Star Team (1985) • Won Vezina Trophy (1985) • Played in NHL All-Star Game (1983, 1985) • Died of injuries suffered in automobile accident, November 10, 1985.

• LINDSAY, Bert

Leslie Bertrand G – R. 5'7", 160 lbs. b: Garafraxa County, Ont., 7/23/1881 d: 11/11/1960.

Season	Club	League	GP	W	L	T	Mins	GA	SO	Avg	AAvg	Eff	SA	S%	SAPG	GP	W	L	T	Mins	GA	SO	Avg	Eff	SA	S%	SAPG
1903-04	McGill University	MCHL	4	1	3	0	240	18	0	4.50	....	....	....	....	....	....	....	....	....	....	....	....	....	....	....	....	....
1904-05	McGill University	MCHL	4	*3	1	0	240	13	0	*3.25	....	....	....	....	....	....	....	....	....	....	....	....	....	....	....	....	....
1905-06	McGill University	MCHL	4	1	3	0	240	35	0	8.75	....	....	....	....	....	....	....	....	....	....	....	....	....	....	....	....	....
1906-07	Renfrew Riversides	UOVHL	STATISTICS NOT AVAILABLE																								
	Latchford Athletics	TPHL	STATISTICS NOT AVAILABLE																								
1907-08	Renfrew Riversides	UOVHL	4	*4	0	0	240	16	0	4.00	....	....	....	....	....	....	....	....	....	....	....	....	....	....	....	....	....
	Brockville Invincibles	FAHL	1	1	0	0	60	0	1	0.00	....	....	....	....	....	....	....	....	....	....	....	....	....	....	....	....	....

			REGULAR SEASON													PLAYOFFS											
Season	Club	League	GP	W	L	T	Mins	GA	SO	Avg	AAvg	Eff	SA	S%	SAPG	GP	W	L	T	Mins	GA	SO	Avg	Eff	SA	S%	SAPG
1908-09	Edmonton Pros	X-Games	3	3	0	0	180	10	0	3.33																	
	Edmonton Pros	St-Cup	2	1	1	0	120	13	0	6.50																	
	Strathcona Pros	X-Games	1	0	1	0	60	11	0	11.00																	
	Renfrew Creamery Kings	FAHL	6	*6	0	0	360	25	0	4.17																	
1909-10	Renfrew Creamery Kings	FAHL	1	0	1	0	60	11	0	11.00																	
	Renfrew Creamery Kings	NHA	12	8	3	1	730	54	0	4.44																	
1910-11	Renfrew Millionaires	NHA	16	8	8	0	960	101	0	6.31																	
1911-12	Victoria Aristocrats	PCHA	16	7	9	0	*975	90	0	5.54																	
1912-13	Victoria Aristocrats	PCHA	*15	*10	5	0	*927	56	*1	*3.62						3	2	1	0	180	12	0	4.00				
1913-14	Victoria Aristocrats	PCHA	16	*10	6	0	1005	80	0	4.78						3	0	3	0	195	13	0	4.00				
1914-15	Victoria Aristocrats	PCHA	17	4	13	0	1054	116	0	6.60																	
	PCHA All-Stars	X-Games	2	0	2	0	120	12	0	6.00																	
1915-16	Montreal Wanderers	NHA	23	10	13	0	1380	110	*1	4.78																	
1916-17	Montreal Wanderers	NHA	15	3	12	0	879	95	0	6.48																	
1917-18	**Montreal Wanderers**	**NHL**	**4**	**1**	**3**	**0**	**240**	**35**	**0**	**8.75**	**5.91**																
1918-19	**Toronto Arenas**	**NHL**	**16**	**5**	**11**	**0**	**998**	**83**	**0**	**4.99**	**4.06**																
	NHL Totals		**20**	**6**	**14**	**0**	**1238**	**118**	**0**	**5.72**																	
	Other Major League Totals		130	60	69	1	7910	702	2	5.32						6	2	4		375	25	0	4.00				

• Father of Ted • PCHA All-Star Team (1913)

Claimed by **Toronto Tecumsehs** (NHA) in NHA Dispersal Draft, November 12, 1911. Jumped contract with **Toronto Tecumsehs** (NHA) to sign with **Victoria** (PCHA), November 28, 1911. Signed as a free agent by **Montreal Wanderers** (NHA), December 2, 1915. Signed as a free agent by **Toronto**, December 28, 1918.

• LITTMAN, David

David K. G – L. 6', 183 lbs. b: Cranston, RI, 6/13/1967. Buffalo's 12th, 211th overall in 1987.

Season	Club	League	GP	W	L	T	Mins	GA	SO	Avg	AAvg	Eff	SA	S%	SAPG	GP	W	L	T	Mins	GA	SO	Avg	Eff	SA	S%	SAPG
1984-85	Oyster Bay Gulls	NYJHL	STATISTICS NOT AVAILABLE																								
1985-86	Boston College	H.East	7	4	0	1	312	18	0	3.46																	
1986-87	Boston College	H-East	21	15	5	0	1182	68	0	3.45																	
1987-88	Boston College	H-East	30	11	16	2	1726	116	0	4.03																	
1988-89	Boston College	H-East	*32	19	9	4	*1945	107	0	3.30																	
1989-90	Rochester Americans	AHL	14	5	6	1	681	37	0	3.26																	
	Phoenix Roadrunners	IHL	18	8	7	2	1047	64	0	3.67																	
1990-91	**Buffalo Sabres**	**NHL**	**1**	**0**	**0**	**0**	**36**	**3**	**0**	**5.00**	**4.49**	**8.33**	**18**	**.833**	**30.0**												
	Rochester Americans	AHL	*56	*33	13	5	*3155	160	3	3.04						8	4	2		378	16	0	2.54				
1991-92	**Buffalo Sabres**	**NHL**	**1**	**0**	**1**	**0**	**60**	**4**	**0**	**4.00**	**3.58**	**5.52**	**29**	**.862**	**29.0**												
	Rochester Americans	AHL	*60	*28	20	9	*3498	172	*3	2.95						15	8	7		879	43	*1	2.94				
1992-93	**Tampa Bay Lightning**	**NHL**	**1**	**0**	**1**	**0**	**45**	**7**	**0**	**9.33**	**8.00**	**31.10**	**21**	**.667**	**28.0**												
	Atlanta Knights	IHL	44	23	12	4	2390	134	0	3.36						3	1	2		178	8	0	2.70				
1993-94	Providence Bruins	AHL	25	10	11	3	1385	83	0	3.60																	
	Fredericton Canadiens	AHL	16	8	7	0	872	63	0	4.33																	
	United States	WC-A	1	0	1	0	45	6	0	8.00																	
1994-95	Richmond Renegades	ECHL	8	4	2	0	346	13	1	2.25						*17	*12	4		*953	37	*3	*2.33				
1995-96	Los Angeles Ice Dogs	IHL	43	17	16	5	2245	145	1	3.88																	
1996-97	San Antonio Dragons	IHL	45	20	16	5	2437	138	2	3.40						4	1	3		230	11	0	2.87				
1997-98	Orlando Solar Bears	IHL	44	21	13	6	2303	102	0	2.66						16	8	8		966	48	1	2.98				
1998-99	Orlando Solar Bears	IHL	55	32	17	1	2981	144	2	2.90						2	0	0		46	4	0	5.22				
99-2000	Orlando Solar Bears	IHL	2	1	1	0	119	7	0	3.52																	
	NHL Totals		**3**	**0**	**2**	**0**	**141**	**14**	**0**	**5.96**			**68**	**.794**	**28.9**												

Hockey East Second All-Star Team (1988) • Hockey East First All-Star Team (1989) • NCAA East Second All-American Team (1989) • AHL First All-Star Team (1991) • Shared Harry "Hap" Holmes Memorial Trophy (fewest goals against - AHL) with Darcy Wakaluk (1991) • AHL Second All-Star Team (1992) • Won Harry "Hap" Holmes Memorial Trophy (fewest goals against - AHL) (1992)

Signed as a free agent by **Tampa Bay**, August 27, 1992. Signed as a free agent by **Boston**, August 6, 1993. • Played w/ RHI's LA Blades in 1995 (3-1-1-0-(0)-122-23-0-9.04)

• LIUT, Mike

Michael Dennis G – L. 6'2", 195 lbs. b: Weston, Ont., 1/7/1956. St. Louis' 5th, 56th overall in 1976.

Season	Club	League	GP	W	L	T	Mins	GA	SO	Avg	AAvg	Eff	SA	S%	SAPG	GP	W	L	T	Mins	GA	SO	Avg	Eff	SA	S%	SAPG
1971-72	Markham Waxers	OHA-B	STATISTICS NOT AVAILABLE																								
1972-73	Bowling Green University	CCHA	DID NOT PLAY – FRESHMAN																								
1973-74	Bowling Green University	CCHA	24	10	12	0	1272	88	1	4.15																	
1974-75	Bowling Green University	CCHA	20	12	6	1	1174	78	0	3.99																	
1975-76	Bowling Green University	CCHA	21	13	5	0	1171	50	2	2.56																	
1976-77	Bowling Green University	CCHA	24	18	4	0	1346	61	2	2.72																	
1977-78	Cincinnati Stingers	WHA	27	8	12	0	1215	86	0	4.25																	
1978-79	Cincinnati Stingers	WHA	54	23	27	4	3181	184	*3	3.47						3	1	2	0	179	10	0	3.35				
1979-80	**St. Louis Blues**	**NHL**	**64**	***32**	**23**	**9**	**3661**	**194**	**2**	**3.18**	**2.80**					**3**	**0**	**3**		**193**	**12**	**0**	**3.73**				
1980-81	**St. Louis Blues**	**NHL**	**61**	**33**	**14**	**13**	**3570**	**199**	**1**	**3.34**	**2.69**					**11**	**5**	**6**		**685**	**50**	**0**	**4.38**				
1981-82	Canada	Can-Cup	6	4	1	1	360	19	1	3.17																	
	St. Louis Blues	**NHL**	***64**	**28**	**28**	**7**	***3691**	**250**	**2**	**4.06**	**3.14**					**10**	**5**	**3**		**494**	**27**	**0**	**3.28**				
1982-83	**St. Louis Blues**	**NHL**	***68**	**21**	**27**	**13**	***3794**	**235**	**1**	**3.72**	**2.98**	**4.56**	**1919**	**.878**	**30.3**	**4**	**1**	**3**		**240**	**15**	**0**	**3.75**				
1983-84	**St. Louis Blues**	**NHL**	**58**	**25**	**29**	**4**	**3425**	**197**	**3**	**3.45**	**2.71**	**4.01**	**1697**	**.884**	**29.7**	**11**	**6**	**5**		**714**	**29**	**1**	**2.44**	**1.95**	**362**	**.920**	**30.4**
1984-85	**St. Louis Blues**	**NHL**	**32**	**12**	**12**	**6**	**1869**	**119**	**1**	**3.82**	**3.04**	**4.58**	**992**	**.880**	**31.8**												
	Hartford Whalers	**NHL**	**12**	**4**	**7**	**1**	**731**	**36**	**1**	**2.95**	**2.35**	**2.53**	**419**	**.914**	**34.4**												
1985-86	**Hartford Whalers**	**NHL**	**57**	**27**	**23**	**4**	**3282**	**198**	**2**	**3.62**	**2.82**	**4.55**	**1574**	**.874**	**28.8**	**8**	**5**	**2**		**441**	**14**	***1**	***1.90**	**1.18**	**226**	**.938**	**30.7**
1986-87	**Hartford Whalers**	**NHL**	**59**	**31**	**22**	**5**	**3476**	**187**	***4**	**3.23**	**2.73**	**3.72**	**1625**	**.885**	**28.0**	**6**	**2**	**4**		**332**	**25**	**0**	**4.52**	**7.11**	**159**	**.843**	**28.7**
1987-88	**Hartford Whalers**	**NHL**	**60**	**25**	**28**	**5**	**3532**	**187**	**2**	**3.18**	**2.64**	**3.67**	**1620**	**.885**	**27.5**	**3**	**1**	**1**		**160**	**11**	**0**	**4.13**	**5.54**	**82**	**.866**	**30.8**
1988-89	**Hartford Whalers**	**NHL**	**35**	**13**	**19**	**1**	**2006**	**142**	**1**	**4.25**	**3.55**	**5.88**	**1027**	**.862**	**30.7**												
1989-90	**Hartford Whalers**	**NHL**	**29**	**15**	**12**	**1**	**1683**	**74**	***3**	***2.64**	**2.23**	**2.62**	**745**	**.901**	**26.6**												
	Washington Capitals	**NHL**	**8**	**4**	**4**	**0**	**478**	**17**	***1**	***2.13**	**1.80**	**1.67**	**217**	**.922**	**27.2**	**9**	**4**	**4**		**507**	**28**	**0**	**3.31**	**4.16**	**223**	**.874**	**26.4**
1990-91	**Washington Capitals**	**NHL**	**35**	**13**	**16**	**3**	**1834**	**114**	**0**	**3.73**	**3.36**	**5.41**	**786**	**.855**	**25.7**	**2**	**0**	**1**		**48**	**4**	**0**	**5.00**	**6.67**	**30**	**.867**	**37.5**
1991-92	**Washington Capitals**	**NHL**	**21**	**10**	**7**	**2**	**1123**	**70**	**1**	**3.74**	**3.35**	**4.69**	**558**	**.875**	**29.8**												
	NHL Totals		**663**	**293**	**271**	**74**	**38155**	**2219**	**25**	**3.49**			**13179**	**.832**	**20.7**	**67**	**29**	**32**		**3814**	**215**	**2**	**3.38**				
	Other Major League Totals		81	31	39	4	4396	270	3	3.69						3	1	2		179	10	0	3.35				

CCHA First All-Star Team (1975, 1977) • CCHA Second All-Star Team (1976) • NHL First All-Star Team (1981) • Won Lester B. Pearson Award (1981) • NHL Second All-Star Team (1987) • Played in NHL All-Star Game (1981)

Selected by **New England** (WHA) in 1976 WHA Amateur Draft, May, 1976. WHA rights traded to **Cincinnati** (WHA) by **New England** (WHA) for Greg Carroll and Bryan Maxwell, May, 1977. Reclaimed by **St. Louis** from **Cincinnati** (WHA) prior to Expansion Draft, June 9, 1979. Traded to **Hartford** by **St. Louis** with Jorgen Pettersson for Mark Johnson and Greg Millen, February 21, 1985. Traded to **Washington** by **Hartford** for Yvon Corriveau, March 6, 1990.

• LOCKETT, Ken

Kenneth Richard G – L. 6', 160 lbs. b: Toronto, Ont., 8/30/1947.

Season	Club	League	GP	W	L	T	Mins	GA	SO	Avg	AAvg	Eff	SA	S%	SAPG	GP	W	L	T	Mins	GA	SO	Avg	Eff	SA	S%	SAPG
1967-68	North York Rangers	OHA-B	STATISTICS NOT AVAILABLE																								
1968-69	Fort Wayne Komets	IHL	6				300	28	0	5.60																	
1969-70	Fort Wayne Komets	IHL	2				120	10	0	5.00																	
	Owen Sound Mercurys	OHA-Sr.	9				520	45	0	5.19																	
1970-71	University of Guelph	OQAA	15				900	54	0	3.60																	
1971-72	University of Guelph	OUAA	17				1020	64	0	3.76																	
1972-73	Baltimore Clippers	AHL	32				1809	139	0	4.57																	
1973-74	Baltimore Clippers	AHL	37	21	11	4	2128	99	2	2.79						5	3	2	0	300	18	0	3.60				

Season	Club	League	REGULAR SEASON													PLAYOFFS											
			GP	W	L	T	Mins	GA	SO	Avg	AAvg	Eff	SA	S%	SAPG	GP	W	L	T	Mins	GA	SO	Avg	Eff	SA	S%	SAPG
1974-75	**Vancouver Canucks**	**NHL**	**25**	**6**	**7**	**1**	**912**	**48**	**2**	**3.16**	**2.85**	....	....	....	....	**1**	**0**	**1**	....	**60**	**6**	**0**	**6.00**	....	....	....	....
1975-76	**Vancouver Canucks**	**NHL**	**30**	**7**	**8**	**7**	**1436**	**83**	**0**	**3.47**	**3.14**	....	....	....	....	....	....	....	....	....	....	....	....	....	....	....	....
1976-77	San Diego Mariners	WHA	45	18	19	1	2397	148	1	3.70	....	....	....	....	....	5	1	3	0	260	19	0	4.38	....	....	....	....
	NHL Totals		**55**	**13**	**15**	**8**	**2348**	**131**	**2**	**3.35**	....	....	....	....	....	**1**	**0**	**1**	....	**60**	**6**	**0**	**6.00**	....	....	....	....
	Other Major League Totals		45	18	19	1	2397	148	1	3.70	....	....	....	....	....	5	1	3	....	260	19	0	4.38	....	....	....	....

OUAA First All-Star Team (1972)

Traded to **Vancouver** by **Baltimore** (AHL), August, 1974. WHA rights claimed by **Phoenix** (WHA) in WHA Dispersal Draft, June 19, 1975. Signed as a free agent by **San Diego** (WHA), September, 1976.

• LOCKHART, Howard

"Holes" G – L. 5'8", 180 lbs. b: North Bay, Ontario, 1895 Deceased.

Season	Club	League	GP	W	L	T	Mins	GA	SO	Avg	AAvg	Eff	SA	S%	SAPG	GP	W	L	T	Mins	GA	SO	Avg	Eff	SA	S%	SAPG
1911-12	North Bay Juniors	NOJHA	STATISTICS NOT AVAILABLE																								
1912-13	North Bay Seniors	NOHA	8	5	3	0	480	36	0	4.50	....	....	....	....	....	2	1	1	0	120	16	0	8.00	....	....	....	....
1913-1916	North Bay Intermediates	NOIHA	STATISTICS NOT AVAILABLE																								
1916-17	Toronto 228th Battalion	NHA	12	7	5	0	720	69	*1	5.75	....	....	....	....	....	....	....	....	....	....	....	....	....	....	....	....	....
1917-18			MILITARY SERVICE																								
1918-19			MILITARY SERVICE																								
1919-20	**Toronto St. Pats**	**NHL**	**7**	**4**	**2**	**0**	**310**	**25**	**0**	**4.84**	**3.08**	....	....	....	....	....	....	....	....	....	....	....	....	....	....	....	....
	Quebec Bulldogs	**NHL**	**1**	**0**	**1**	**0**	**60**	**11**	**0**	**11.00**	**7.09**	....	....	....	....	....	....	....	....	....	....	....	....	....	....	....	....
1920-21	**Hamilton Tigers**	**NHL**	***24**	**6**	**18**	**0**	**1454**	**132**	**1**	**5.45**	**4.35**	....	....	....	....	....	....	....	....	....	....	....	....	....	....	....	....
1921-22	**Hamilton Tigers**	**NHL**	***24**	**6**	**17**	**0**	**1409**	**103**	**0**	**4.39**	**3.50**	....	....	....	....	....	....	....	....	....	....	....	....	....	....	....	....
1922-23			DID NOT PLAY																								
1923-24	**Toronto St. Pats**	**NHL**	**1**	**0**	**1**	**0**	**60**	**5**	**0**	**5.00**	**5.79**	....	....	....	....	....	....	....	....	....	....	....	....	....	....	....	....
1924-25	**Boston Bruins**	**NHL**	**2**	**0**	**2**	**0**	**120**	**11**	**0**	**5.50**	**6.80**	....	....	....	....	....	....	....	....	....	....	....	....	....	....	....	....
1925-26			DID NOT PLAY																								
1926-27	Hamilton Tigers	Can-Pro	19	9	9	1	1165	50	0	2.58	....	....	....	....	....	....	....	....	....	....	....	....	....	....	....	....	....
	NHL Totals		**59**	**16**	**41**	**0**	**3413**	**287**	**1**	**5.05**	....	....	....	....	....	....	....	....	....	....	....	....	....	....	....	....	....
	Other Major League Totals		12	7	5	0	720	69	1	5.75	....	....	....	....	....	....	....	....	....	....	....	....	....	....	....	....	....

Signed as a free agent by **Toronto**, December 15, 1919. Loaned to **Quebec** by **Toronto**, March 6, 1920. (Toronto 11, Quebec 2). Traded to **Hamilton** by **Toronto** for cash, December 16, 1920. Signed as a free agent by **Toronto**, December 18, 1923. Traded to **Boston** by **Toronto** for cash, December 24, 1924. Signed as a free agent by **Hamilton** (Can-Pro), November 12, 1926.

• LOPRESTI, Pete

Peter Jon G – L. 6'1", 195 lbs. b: Virginia, MN, 5/23/1954. Minnesota's 3rd, 42nd overall in 1974.

Season	Club	League	GP	W	L	T	Mins	GA	SO	Avg	AAvg	Eff	SA	S%	SAPG	GP	W	L	T	Mins	GA	SO	Avg	Eff	SA	S%	SAPG
1972-73	University of Denver	WCHA	4	2	2	0	240	13	0	3.25	....	....	....	....	....	....	....	....	....	....	....	....	....	....	....	....	....
1973-74	University of Denver	WCHA	38	22	13	3	2280	155	1	4.10	....	....	....	....	....	4	2	1	1	240	9	0	2.25	....	....	....	....
1974-75	New Haven Nighthawks	AHL	11	4	4	3	658	36	0	3.28	....	....	....	....	....	....	....	....	....	....	....	....	....	....	....	....	....
	Minnesota North Stars	**NHL**	**35**	**9**	**20**	**3**	**1964**	**137**	**1**	**4.19**	**3.81**	....	....	....	....	....	....	....	....	....	....	....	....	....	....	....	....
1975-76	**Minnesota North Stars**	**NHL**	**34**	**7**	**22**	**1**	**1789**	**123**	**1**	**4.13**	**3.76**	....	....	....	....	....	....	....	....	....	....	....	....	....	....	....	....
	United States	WEC-A	5	....	....	....	300	27	....	5.40	....	....	....	....	....	....	....	....	....	....	....	....	....	....	....	....	....
1976-77	United States	Can-Cup	2	1	1	0	120	6	0	3.00	....	....	....	....	....	....	....	....	....	....	....	....	....	....	....	....	....
	Minnesota North Stars	**NHL**	**44**	**13**	**20**	**10**	**2590**	**156**	**1**	**3.61**	**3.37**	....	....	....	....	**2**	**0**	**2**	....	**77**	**6**	**0**	**4.68**	....	....	....	....
1977-78	**Minnesota North Stars**	**NHL**	**53**	**12**	**35**	**6**	**3065**	**216**	**2**	**4.23**	**4.01**	....	....	....	....	....	....	....	....	....	....	....	....	....	....	....	....
	United States	WEC-A	9	2	5	2	540	50	0	5.56	....	....	....	....	....	....	....	....	....	....	....	....	....	....	....	....	....
1978-79	**Minnesota North Stars**	**NHL**	**7**	**2**	**4**	**0**	**345**	**28**	**0**	**4.87**	**4.31**	....	....	....	....	....	....	....	....	....	....	....	....	....	....	....	....
	Oklahoma City Stars	CHL	33	16	15	0	1928	129	0	4.01	....	....	....	....	....	....	....	....	....	....	....	....	....	....	....	....	....
1979-80			DID NOT PLAY																								
1980-81	Wichita Wind	CHL	36	9	25	0	2029	161	1	4.76	....	....	....	....	....	....	....	....	....	....	....	....	....	....	....	....	....
	Edmonton Oilers	**NHL**	**2**	**0**	**1**	**0**	**105**	**8**	**0**	**4.57**	**3.69**	....	....	....	....	....	....	....	....	....	....	....	....	....	....	....	....
	NHL Totals		**175**	**43**	**102**	**20**	**9858**	**668**	**5**	**4.07**	....	....	....	....	....	**2**	**0**	**2**	....	**77**	**6**	**0**	**4.68**	....	....	....	....

• Son of Sam

Claimed by **Edmonton** from **Minnesota** in Expansion Draft, June 13, 1979.

• LOPRESTI, Sam

G – L. 5'11", 200 lbs. b: Eveleth, MN, 1/30/1917 d: 12/11/1984. **USHOF**

Season	Club	League	GP	W	L	T	Mins	GA	SO	Avg	AAvg	Eff	SA	S%	SAPG	GP	W	L	T	Mins	GA	SO	Avg	Eff	SA	S%	SAPG
1935-36	Eveleth Jr. College	Hi-School	STATISTICS NOT AVAILABLE																								
1936-37	Eveleth Rangers	TBSHL	2	....	....	....	120	9	0	4.50	....	....	....	....	....	....	....	....	....	....	....	....	....	....	....	....	....
1937-38	St. Paul Saints	AHA	48	10	36	2	2952	178	2	3.62	....	....	....	....	....	....	....	....	....	....	....	....	....	....	....	....	....
1938-39	St. Paul Saints	AHA	44	23	21	0	2684	122	1	2.73	....	....	....	....	....	3	0	3	0	180	11	0	3.67	....	....	....	....
1939-40	St. Paul Saints	AHA	47	29	18	0	2848	121	4	2.55	....	....	....	....	....	7	*6	1	0	420	9	*2	*1.29	....	....	....	....
1940-41	Kansas City Americans	AHA	18	9	9	0	1142	61	0	3.21	....	....	....	....	....	....	....	....	....	....	....	....	....	....	....	....	....
	Chicago Black Hawks	**NHL**	**27**	**9**	**15**	**3**	**1670**	**84**	**1**	**3.02**	**3.48**	....	....	....	....	**5**	**2**	**3**	....	**343**	**12**	**0**	**2.10**	....	....	....	....
1941-42	**Chicago Black Hawks**	**NHL**	**47**	**21**	**23**	**3**	**2860**	**152**	**3**	**3.19**	**3.13**	....	....	....	....	**3**	**1**	**2**	....	**187**	**5**	***1**	**1.60**	....	....	....	....
1942-43			MILITARY SERVICE																								
1943-44	San Diego Skyhawks	SCHL	STATISTICS NOT AVAILABLE																								
1944-45	San Diego Skyhawks	PCHL	STATISTICS NOT AVAILABLE																								
1945-46			DID NOT PLAY																								
1946-47	Duluth Coolerators	TBSHL	4	....	....	....	240	30	0	7.50	....	....	....	....	....	....	....	....	....	....	....	....	....	....	....	....	....
1947-48			DID NOT PLAY																								
1948-49	Duluth Steelers	NAHL	STATISTICS NOT AVAILABLE																								
1949-50	Eveleth Rangers	NAHL	30	17	13	0	1800	114	0	3.79	....	....	....	....	....	....	....	....	....	....	....	....	....	....	....	....	....
1950-51	Eveleth Rangers	NAHL	20	....	....	....	1200	99	0	4.98	....	....	....	....	....	....	....	....	....	....	....	....	....	....	....	....	....
	NHL Totals		**74**	**30**	**38**	**6**	**4530**	**236**	**4**	**3.13**	....	....	....	....	....	**8**	**3**	**5**	....	**530**	**17**	**1**	**1.92**	....	....	....	....

• Father of Pete

AHA Second All-Star Team (1940) • NAHL MVP (1950)

• LORENZ, Danny

G – L. 5'10", 187 lbs. b: Murrayville, B.C., 12/12/1969. NY Islanders' 4th, 58th overall in 1988.

Season	Club	League	GP	W	L	T	Mins	GA	SO	Avg	AAvg	Eff	SA	S%	SAPG	GP	W	L	T	Mins	GA	SO	Avg	Eff	SA	S%	SAPG
1985-86	Burnaby Hawks	BCJHL	25	....	....	....	1305	62	0	5.81	....	....	....	....	....	....	....	....	....	....	....	....	....	....	....	....	....
1986-87	Seattle Thunderbirds	WHL	38	12	21	2	2103	199	0	5.68	....	....	....	....	....	....	....	....	....	....	....	....	....	....	....	....	....
1987-88	Seattle Thunderbirds	WHL	62	20	37	2	3302	314	0	5.71	....	....	....	....	....	....	....	....	....	....	....	....	....	....	....	....	....
1988-89	Springfield Indians	AHL	4	2	1	0	210	12	0	3.43	....	....	....	....	....	....	....	....	....	....	....	....	....	....	....	....	....
	Seattle Thunderbirds	WHL	*68	31	33	4	*4003	240	*3	3.60	....	....	....	....	....	....	....	....	....	....	....	....	....	....	....	....	....
1989-90	Seattle Thunderbirds	WHL	56	37	15	2	3226	221	0	4.11	....	....	....	....	....	13	6	7	....	751	40	0	3.21	....	....	....	....
1990-91	**New York Islanders**	**NHL**	**2**	**0**	**1**	**0**	**80**	**5**	**0**	**3.75**	**3.37**	**5.21**	**36**	**.861**	**27.0**	....	....	....	....	....	....	....	....	....	....	....	....
	Capital District Islanders	AHL	17	5	9	2	940	70	0	4.47	....	....	....	....	....	....	....	....	....	....	....	....	....	....	....	....	....
	Richmond Renegades	ECHL	20	6	9	2	1020	75	0	4.41	....	....	....	....	....	....	....	....	....	....	....	....	....	....	....	....	....
1991-92	**New York Islanders**	**NHL**	**2**	**0**	**2**	**0**	**120**	**10**	**0**	**5.00**	**4.48**	**8.33**	**60**	**.833**	**30.0**	....	....	....	....	....	....	....	....	....	....	....	....
	Capital District Islanders	AHL	53	22	22	7	3050	181	2	3.56	....	....	....	....	....	7	3	4	....	442	25	0	3.39	....	....	....	....
1992-93	**New York Islanders**	**NHL**	**4**	**1**	**2**	**0**	**157**	**10**	**0**	**3.82**	**3.27**	**4.90**	**78**	**.872**	**29.8**	....	....	....	....	....	....	....	....	....	....	....	....
	Capital District Islanders	AHL	44	16	17	5	2412	146	1	3.63	....	....	....	....	....	4	0	3	....	219	12	0	3.29	....	....	....	....
1993-94	Salt Lake Golden Eagles	IHL	20	4	12	0	982	91	0	5.56	....	....	....	....	....	....	....	....	....	....	....	....	....	....	....	....	....
	Springfield Indians	AHL	14	5	7	1	801	59	0	4.42	....	....	....	....	....	2	0	0	....	35	0	0	0.00	....	....	....	....
1994-95	Cincinnati Cyclones	IHL	41	24	10	3	2222	126	0	3.40	....	....	....	....	....	5	2	3	....	308	16	0	3.12	....	....	....	....
1995-96	Cincinnati Cyclones	IHL	46	28	12	5	2694	139	1	3.10	....	....	....	....	....	5	1	2	....	199	11	0	3.31	....	....	....	....
1996-97	Milwaukee Admirals	IHL	67	33	27	6	3903	221	0	3.40	....	....	....	....	....	3	0	3	....	187	11	0	3.53	....	....	....	....
1997-98	Milwaukee Admirals	IHL	54	28	18	4	2718	140	0	3.09	....	....	....	....	....	10	5	5	....	622	31	1	2.99	....	....	....	....
1998-99	Adler Mannheim	Germany	22	....	....	....	1051	54	2	3.08	....	....	....	....	....	....	....	....	....	....	....	....	....	....	....	....	....
	Houston Aeros	IHL	7	3	2	2	418	13	0	1.87	....	....	....	....	....	1	0	0	....	38	2	0	3.16	....	....	....	....

Season	Club	League	REGULAR SEASON GP	W	L	T	Mins	GA	SO	Avg	AAvg	Eff	SA	S%	SAPG	PLAYOFFS GP	W	L	T	Mins	GA	SO	Avg	Eff	SA	S%	SAPG
99-2000	Tallahassee Tiger Sharks	ECHL	33	15	12	2	1749	105	0	3.60	....	....	....	....	....	....	....	....	....	....	....	....	....	....	....	....	....
	Tacoma Sabercats	WCHL	2	2	0	0	120	2	1	1.00	....	....	....	....	....	....	....	....	....	....	....	....	....	....	....	....	....
	Rochester Americans	AHL	4	0	2	1	168	15	0	5.36	....	....	....	....	....	....	....	....	....	....	....	....	....	....	....	....	....
	NHL Totals		**8**	**1**	**5**	**0**	**357**	**25**	**0**	**4.20**	....	....	**174**	**.856**	**29.2**	....	....	....	....	....	....	....	....	....	....	....	....

WHL West First All-Star Team (1989, 1990)

Signed as a free agent by **Florida**, June 14, 1994.

• LOUSTEL, Ron

Ronald David G – L. 5'11", 185 lbs. b: Winnipeg, Man., 3/7/1962. Winnipeg's 6th, 107th overall in 1980.

Season	Club	League	GP	W	L	T	Mins	GA	SO	Avg	AAvg	Eff	SA	S%	SAPG	GP	W	L	T	Mins	GA	SO	Avg	Eff	SA	S%	SAPG
1978-79	Kelowna Buckaroos	BCJHL	44	....	....	....	2493	203	0	4.88	....	....	....	....	....	....	....	....	....	....	....	....	....	....	....	....	....
1979-80	Saskatoon Blades	WHL	41	....	....	....	2203	181	0	4.92	....	....	....	....	....	....	....	....	....	....	....	....	....	....	....	....	....
1980-81	Saskatoon Blades	WHL	55	....	....	....	2932	278	0	5.60	....	....	....	....	....	....	....	....	....	....	....	....	....	....	....	....	....
	Winnipeg Jets	**NHL**	**1**	**0**	**1**	**0**	**60**	**10**	**0**	**10.00**	**8.09**	....	....	....	....	....	....	....	....	....	....	....	....	....	....	....	....
	Tulsa Oilers	CHL	1	0	0	0	29	5	0	10.34	....	....	....	....	....	....	....	....	....	....	....	....	....	....	....	....	....
1981-82	Saskatoon Blades	WHL	42	....	....	....	2280	172	0	4.53	....	....	....	....	....	....	....	....	....	....	....	....	....	....	....	....	....
1982-83	Brandon Wheat Kings	WHL	28	7	20	0	1627	192	0	7.08	....	....	....	....	....	....	....	....	....	....	....	....	....	....	....	....	....
	Fort Wayne Komets	IHL	1	....	....	....	33	3	0	5.45	....	....	....	....	....	....	....	....	....	....	....	....	....	....	....	....	....
	NHL Totals		**1**	**0**	**1**	**0**	**60**	**10**	**0**	**10.00**	....	....	....	....	....	....	....	....	....	....	....	....	....	....	....	....	....

• LOW, Ron

Ronald Albert G – L. 6'1", 205 lbs. b: Birtle, Man., 6/21/1950. Toronto's 8th, 103rd overall in 1970.

Season	Club	League	GP	W	L	T	Mins	GA	SO	Avg	AAvg	Eff	SA	S%	SAPG	GP	W	L	T	Mins	GA	SO	Avg	Eff	SA	S%	SAPG
1967-68	Dauphin Kings	MJHL	STATISTICS NOT AVAILABLE																								
	Winnipeg Jets	WCJHL	16	....	....	....	960	92	0	5.75	....	....	....	....	....	....	....	....	....	....	....	....	....	....	....	....	....
1968-69	Dauphin Kings	MJHL	STATISTICS NOT AVAILABLE																								
	Dauphin Kings	Mem-Cup	12	7	5	0	730	55	0	4.52	....	....	....	....	....	....	....	....	....	....	....	....	....	....	....	....	....
1969-70	Dauphin Kings	MJHL	*33	....	....	....	2001	119	0	3.57	....	....	....	....	....	....	....	....	....	....	....	....	....	....	....	....	....
	Dauphin Kings	Mem-Cup	6	2	4	0	293	26	1	5.32	....	....	....	....	....	....	....	....	....	....	....	....	....	....	....	....	....
1970-71	Jacksonville Rockets	EHL	49	....	....	....	2940	293	1	5.98	....	....	....	....	....	....	....	....	....	....	....	....	....	....	....	....	....
	Tulsa Oilers	CHL	4	....	....	....	192	11	0	5.11	....	....	....	....	....	....	....	....	....	....	....	....	....	....	....	....	....
1971-72	Richmond Robins	AHL	1	1	0	0	60	2	0	2.00	....	....	....	....	....	....	....	....	....	....	....	....	....	....	....	....	....
	Tulsa Oilers	CHL	43	21	18	2	*2428	135	1	3.33	....	....	....	....	....	8	....	....	....	474	15	*1	*1.89	....	....	....	....
1972-73	**Toronto Maple Leafs**	**NHL**	**42**	**12**	**24**	**4**	**2343**	**152**	**1**	**3.89**	**3.69**	....	....	....	....	....	....	....	....	....	....	....	....	....	....	....	....
1973-74	Tulsa Oilers	CHL	56	23	23	8	3213	169	1	3.16	....	....	....	....	....	....	....	....	....	....	....	....	....	....	....	....	....
1974-75	**Washington Capitals**	**NHL**	**48**	**8**	**36**	**2**	**2588**	**235**	**1**	**5.45**	**5.02**	....	....	....	....	....	....	....	....	....	....	....	....	....	....	....	....
1975-76	**Washington Capitals**	**NHL**	**43**	**6**	**31**	**2**	**2289**	**208**	**0**	**5.45**	**5.02**	....	....	....	....	....	....	....	....	....	....	....	....	....	....	....	....
1976-77	**Washington Capitals**	**NHL**	**54**	**16**	**27**	**5**	**2918**	**188**	**0**	**3.87**	**3.62**	....	....	....	....	....	....	....	....	....	....	....	....	....	....	....	....
1977-78	**Detroit Red Wings**	**NHL**	**32**	**9**	**12**	**9**	**1816**	**102**	**1**	**3.37**	**3.16**	....	....	....	....	**4**	**1**	**3**	....	**240**	**17**	**0**	**4.25**	....	....	....	....
1978-79	Kansas City Red Wings	CHL	*63	*33	28	2	*3795	244	0	3.86	....	....	....	....	....	5	1	4	0	237	15	0	3.80	....	....	....	....
1979-80	**Quebec Nordiques**	**NHL**	**15**	**5**	**7**	**2**	**828**	**51**	**0**	**3.70**	**3.27**	....	....	....	....	....	....	....	....	....	....	....	....	....	....	....	....
	Syracuse Firebirds	AHL	15	5	9	1	905	70	0	4.64	....	....	....	....	....	....	....	....	....	....	....	....	....	....	....	....	....
	Edmonton Oilers	**NHL**	**11**	**8**	**2**	**1**	**650**	**37**	**0**	**3.42**	**3.02**	....	....	....	....	**3**	**0**	**3**	....	**212**	**12**	**0**	**3.40**	....	....	....	....
1980-81	**Edmonton Oilers**	**NHL**	**24**	**5**	**13**	**3**	**1260**	**93**	**0**	**4.43**	**3.59**	....	....	....	....	....	....	....	....	....	....	....	....	....	....	....	....
	Wichita Wind	CHL	2	0	2	0	120	10	0	5.00	....	....	....	....	....	....	....	....	....	....	....	....	....	....	....	....	....
1981-82	**Edmonton Oilers**	**NHL**	**29**	**17**	**7**	**1**	**1554**	**100**	**0**	**3.86**	**2.98**	....	....	....	....	....	....	....	....	....	....	....	....	....	....	....	....
1982-83	**Edmonton Oilers**	**NHL**	**3**	**0**	**1**	**0**	**104**	**10**	**0**	**5.77**	**4.63**	**10.49**	**55**	**.818**	**31.7**	....	....	....	....	....	....	....	....	....	....	....	....
	Moncton Alpines	AHL	6	....	....	....	365	22	1	3.62	....	....	....	....	....	....	....	....	....	....	....	....	....	....	....	....	....
	New Jersey Devils	**NHL**	**11**	**2**	**7**	**1**	**608**	**41**	**0**	**4.05**	**3.25**	**4.83**	**344**	**.881**	**33.9**	....	....	....	....	....	....	....	....	....	....	....	....
1983-84	**New Jersey Devils**	**NHL**	**44**	**8**	**25**	**4**	**2218**	**161**	**0**	**4.36**	**3.44**	**6.20**	**1133**	**.858**	**30.6**	....	....	....	....	....	....	....	....	....	....	....	....
1984-85	**New Jersey Devils**	**NHL**	**26**	**6**	**11**	**4**	**1326**	**85**	**1**	**3.85**	**3.07**	**5.21**	**628**	**.865**	**28.4**	....	....	....	....	....	....	....	....	....	....	....	....
1985-86	Nova Scotia Oilers	AHL	6	1	5	0	299	24	0	4.82	....	....	....	....	....	....	....	....	....	....	....	....	....	....	....	....	....
1986-1987	Nova Scotia Oilers	AHL	DID NOT PLAY – ASSISTANT COACH																								
1987-1988	Nova Scotia Oilers	AHL	DID NOT PLAY – COACHING																								
1988-1989	Cape Breton Oilers	AHL	DID NOT PLAY – COACHING																								
1989-1994	**Edmonton Oilers**	**NHL**	DID NOT PLAY – ASSISTANT COACH																								
1994-1999	**Edmonton Oilers**	**NHL**	DID NOT PLAY – COACHING																								
1999-2000	Houston Aeros	AHL	DID NOT PLAY – COACHING																								
	NHL Totals		**382**	**102**	**203**	**38**	**20502**	**1463**	**4**	**4.28**	....	....	....	....	....	**7**	**1**	**6**	....	**452**	**29**	**0**	**3.85**	....	....	....	....

EHL South Rookie of the Year (1971) • CHL Second All-Star Team (1974) • CHL First All-Star Team (1979) • Won Tommy Ivan Trophy (MVP - CHL) (1979)

Claimed by **Washington** from **Toronto** in Expansion Draft, June 12, 1974. Signed as a free agent by **Detroit**, August 17, 1977. Claimed by **Quebec** from **Detroit** in Expansion Draft, June 13, 1979. Traded to **Edmonton** by **Quebec** for Ron Chipperfield, March 11, 1980. Traded to **New Jersey** by **Edmonton** with Jim McTaggart for Lindsay Middlebrook and Paul Miller, February 19, 1983. • Named Head Coach of **NY Rangers**, July 12, 2000.

• LOZINSKI, Larry

Lawrence Peter G – R. 5'11", 175 lbs. b: Hudson Bay, Sask., 3/11/1958. Detroit's 16th, 219th overall in 1978.

Season	Club	League	GP	W	L	T	Mins	GA	SO	Avg	AAvg	Eff	SA	S%	SAPG	GP	W	L	T	Mins	GA	SO	Avg	Eff	SA	S%	SAPG
1975-76	Maple Ridge Blazers	BCJHL	34	....	....	....	2122	116	1	3.28	....	....	....	....	....	....	....	....	....	....	....	....	....	....	....	....	....
1976-77	Abbotsford Flyers	BCJHL	65	28	34	3	3897	294	4	4.53	....	....	....	....	....	....	....	....	....	....	....	....	....	....	....	....	....
1977-78	Flin Flon Bombers	WCJHL	37	14	17	5	1939	178	0	5.51	....	....	....	....	....	16	....	....	....	941	86	0	5.48	....	....	....	....
	New Westminster Bruins	Mem-Cup	1	0	0	0	34	1	0	1.76	....	....	....	....	....	....	....	....	....	....	....	....	....	....	....	....	....
1978-79	Kansas City Red Wings	CHL	13	4	6	1	688	45	0	3.92	....	....	....	....	....	....	....	....	....	....	....	....	....	....	....	....	....
1979-80	Kalamazoo Wings	IHL	69	....	....	....	4000	232	5	3.48	....	....	....	....	....	10	....	....	....	597	24	1	2.41	....	....	....	....
1980-81	**Detroit Red Wings**	**NHL**	**30**	**6**	**11**	**7**	**1459**	**105**	**0**	**4.32**	**3.50**	....	....	....	....	....	....	....	....	....	....	....	....	....	....	....	....
	Adirondack Red Wings	AHL	16	4	9	1	789	53	0	4.03	....	....	....	....	....	....	....	....	....	....	....	....	....	....	....	....	....
1981-82	Adirondack Red Wings	AHL	55	25	23	4	3207	175	1	3.27	....	....	....	....	....	5	....	....	....	280	22	0	4.71	....	....	....	....
1982-83	Adirondack Red Wings	AHL	32	....	....	....	1709	128	*3	4.49	....	....	....	....	....	6	2	4	0	390	22	0	3.38	....	....	....	....
	Kalamazoo K-Wings	IHL	12	....	....	....	674	51	0	4.54	....	....	....	....	....	....	....	....	....	....	....	....	....	....	....	....	....
	NHL Totals		**30**	**6**	**11**	**7**	**1459**	**105**	**0**	**4.32**	....	....	....	....	....	....	....	....	....	....	....	....	....	....	....	....	....

IHL First All-Star Team (1980) • Won James Norris Memorial Trophy (fewest goals against - IHL) (1980)

• LUMLEY, Harry

"Apple Cheeks" G – L. 6', 195 lbs. b: Owen Sound, Ont., 11/11/1926 d: 9/13/1998. **HHOF**

Season	Club	League	GP	W	L	T	Mins	GA	SO	Avg	AAvg	Eff	SA	S%	SAPG	GP	W	L	T	Mins	GA	SO	Avg	Eff	SA	S%	SAPG
1942-43	Barrie Colts	OHA-Jr.	STATISTICS NOT AVAILABLE																								
1943-44	**Detroit Red Wings**	**NHL**	**2**	**0**	**2**	**0**	**120**	**13**	**0**	**6.50**	**4.87**	....	....	....	....	....	....	....	....	....	....	....	....	....	....	....	....
	Indianapolis Capitols	AHL	52	19	18	15	3120	147	0	2.84	....	....	....	....	....	5	1	4	0	300	18	0	3.60	....	....	....	....
	New York Rangers	**NHL**	**1**	**0**	**0**	**0**	**20**	**0**	**0**	**0.00**	**0.00**	....	....	....	....	....	....	....	....	....	....	....	....	....	....	....	....
1944-45	**Detroit Red Wings**	**NHL**	**37**	**24**	**10**	**3**	**2220**	**119**	**1**	**3.22**	**2.62**	....	....	....	....	***14**	**7**	**7**	....	***871**	**31**	**2**	***2.14**	....	....	....	....
	Indianapolis Capitols	AHL	21	11	5	5	1260	46	2	2.14	....	....	....	....	....	....	....	....	....	....	....	....	....	....	....	....	....
1945-46	**Detroit Red Wings**	**NHL**	***50**	**20**	**20**	**10**	***3000**	**159**	**2**	**3.18**	**2.87**	....	....	....	....	**5**	**1**	**4**	....	**310**	**16**	***1**	**3.10**	....	....	....	....
1946-47	**Detroit Red Wings**	**NHL**	**52**	**22**	**20**	**10**	**3120**	**159**	**3**	**3.06**	**2.93**	....	....	....	....	....	....	....	....	....	....	....	....	....	....	....	....
1947-48	**Detroit Red Wings**	**NHL**	***60**	**30**	**18**	**12**	**3592**	**147**	***7**	**2.46**	**2.48**	....	....	....	....	***10**	**4**	**6**	....	***600**	**30**	**0**	**3.00**	....	....	....	....
1948-49	**Detroit Red Wings**	**NHL**	***60**	***34**	**19**	**7**	***3600**	**145**	**6**	**2.42**	**2.66**	....	....	....	....	***11**	**4**	**7**	....	***726**	**26**	**0**	**2.15**	....	....	....	....
1949-50♦	**Detroit Red Wings**	**NHL**	**63**	***33**	**16**	**14**	**3780**	**148**	**7**	**2.35**	**2.56**	....	....	....	....	***14**	***8**	**6**	....	**910**	**28**	***3**	**1.85**	....	....	....	....
1950-51	**Chicago Black Hawks**	**NHL**	**64**	**12**	**41**	**10**	**3785**	**246**	**3**	**3.90**	**4.75**	....	....	....	....	....	....	....	....	....	....	....	....	....	....	....	....
1951-52	**Chicago Black Hawks**	**NHL**	***70**	**17**	**44**	**9**	**4180**	**241**	**2**	**3.46**	**4.35**	....	....	....	....	....	....	....	....	....	....	....	....	....	....	....	....
1952-53	**Toronto Maple Leafs**	**NHL**	***70**	**27**	**30**	**13**	***4200**	**167**	***10**	**2.39**	**3.04**	....	....	....	....	....	....	....	....	....	....	....	....	....	....	....	....
1953-54	**Toronto Maple Leafs**	**NHL**	**69**	**32**	**24**	**13**	**4140**	**128**	***13**	***1.86**	**2.26**	....	....	....	....	**5**	**1**	**4**	....	**321**	**15**	**0**	**2.80**	....	....	....	....
1954-55	**Toronto Maple Leafs**	**NHL**	***69**	**23**	**24**	**22**	***4140**	**134**	**8**	***1.94**	**2.24**	....	....	....	....	**4**	**0**	**4**	....	**240**	**14**	**0**	**3.50**	....	....	....	....
1955-56	**Toronto Maple Leafs**	**NHL**	**59**	**21**	**28**	**10**	**3527**	**157**	**3**	**2.67**	**3.31**	....	....	....	....	**5**	**1**	**4**	....	**304**	**13**	**1**	**2.57**	....	....	....	....
1956-57	Buffalo Bisons	AHL	*63	25	36	2	*3780	264	0	4.19	....	....	....	....	....	....	....	....	....	....	....	....	....	....	....	....	....
1957-58	Buffalo Bisons	AHL	17	7	9	1	1029	63	1	3.67	....	....	....	....	....	....	....	....	....	....	....	....	....	....	....	....	....
	Boston Bruins	**NHL**	**24**	**11**	**10**	**3**	**1440**	**70**	**3**	**2.92**	**3.21**	....	....	....	....	**1**	**0**	**1**	....	**60**	**5**	**0**	**5.00**	....	....	....	....
1958-59	**Boston Bruins**	**NHL**	**11**	**8**	**2**	**1**	**660**	**27**	**1**	**2.45**	**2.59**	....	....	....	....	**7**	**3**	**4**	....	**436**	**20**	**0**	**2.75**	....	....	....	....
	Providence Reds	AHL	58	27	29	2	3480	208	4	3.59	....	....	....	....	....	....	....	....	....	....	....	....	....	....	....	....	....

			REGULAR SEASON													PLAYOFFS											
Season	**Club**	**League**	**GP**	**W**	**L**	**T**	**Mins**	**GA**	**SO**	**Avg**	**AAvg**	**Eff**	**SA**	**S%**	**SAPG**	**GP**	**W**	**L**	**T**	**Mins**	**GA**	**SO**	**Avg**	**Eff**	**SA**	**S%**	**SAPG**
1959-60	**Boston Bruins**	**NHL**	**42**	**16**	**21**	**5**	**2520**	**146**	**2**	**3.48**	**3.72**	....	....	....	....	....	....	....	....	....	....	....	....	....	....	....	....
1960-61	Kingston Frontenacs	EPHL	2	1	1	0	120	7	0	3.50	....	....	....	....	....	....	....	....	....	....	....	....	....	....	....	....	....
	Winnipeg Warriors	WHL	61	17	40	4	3660	213	0	3.49	....	....	....	....	....	....	....	....	....	....	....	....	....	....	....	....	....
	NHL Totals		**803**	**330**	**329**	**142**	**48044**	**2206**	**71**	**2.75**	....	....	....	....	....	**76**	**29**	**47**	....	**4778**	**198**	**7**	**2.49**	....	....	....	....

NHL First All-Star Team (1954, 1955) • Won Vezina Trophy (1954) • AHL Second All-Star Team (1957) • Played in NHL All-Star Game (1951, 1954, 1955)

Loaned to **NY Rangers** by **Detroit** to replace injured Ken McAuley, December 23, 1943. (Detroit 5, NY Rangers 3). Traded to **Chicago** by **Detroit** with Jack Stewart, Al Dewsbury, Pete Babando and Don Morrison for Metro Prystai, Gaye Stewart, Bob Goldham and Jim Henry, July 13, 1950. Traded to **Toronto** by **Chicago** for Al Rollins, Gus Mortson, Cal Gardner and Ray Hannigan, September 11, 1952. Traded to **Chicago** by **Toronto** with Eric Nesterenko for $40,000, May 21, 1956. Traded to **Boston** by **Chicago** for cash, January, 1958.

• LUONGO, Roberto

G – L. 6'3", 175 lbs. b: Montreal, Que., 4/4/1979. NY Islanders' 1st, 4th overall in 1997.

Season	Club	League	GP	W	L	T	Mins	GA	SO	Avg	AAvg	Eff	SA	S%	SAPG	GP	W	L	T	Mins	GA	SO	Avg	Eff	SA	S%	SAPG
1994-95	Montreal-Bourassa College	QAAA	25	10	14	0	94	1465	0	3.85	....	....	....	....	....	....	....	....	....	....	....	....	....	....	....	....	....
1995-96	Val d'Or Foreurs	QMJHL	23	6	11	4	1201	74	0	3.70	....	....	....	....	....	3	0	1	....	68	5	0	4.41	....	....	....	....
1996-97	Val d'Or Foreurs	QMJHL	60	32	22	2	3305	171	2	3.10	....	....	....	....	....	13	8	5	....	777	44	0	3.40	....	....	....	....
1997-98	Val d'Or Foreurs	QMJHL	54	27	20	5	3046	157	*7	3.09	....	....	....	....	....	*17	*14	3	....	*1019	37	*2	*2.18	....	....	....	....
	Canada	WJC-A	3	....	....	....	145	7	....	2.89	....	....	....	....	....	....	....	....	....	....	....	....	....	....	....	....	....
	Val d'Or Foreurs	Mem-Cup	3	0	*3	0	180	19	0	6.33	....	....	....	....	....	....	....	....	....	....	....	....	....	....	....	....	....
1998-99	Val d'Or Foreurs	QMJHL	21	6	10	2	1176	77	1	3.93	....	....	....	....	....	....	....	....	....	....	....	....	....	....	....	....	....
	Acadie Bathurst Titan	QMJHL	22	14	7	1	1340	74	0	3.31	....	....	....	....	....	*23	*16	6	....	*1400	64	0	2.74	....	....	....	....
	Canada	WJC-A	7	....	....	....	405	13	....	1.93	....	....	....	....	....	....	....	....	....	....	....	....	....	....	....	....	....
	Acadie Bathurst Titan	Mem-Cup	3	0	*3	0	180	11	0	3.67	....	....	....	....	....	....	....	....	....	....	....	....	....	....	....	....	....
99-2000	**New York Islanders**	**NHL**	**24**	**7**	**14**	**1**	**1292**	**70**	**1**	**3.25**	**3.72**	**3.12**	**730**	**.904**	**33.9**	....	....	....	....	....	....	....	....	....	....	....	....
	Lowell Lock Monsters	AHL	26	10	12	4	1517	74	1	2.93	....	....	....	....	....	6	3	3	....	359	18	0	3.01	....	....	....	....
	NHL Totals		**24**	**7**	**14**	**1**	**1292**	**70**	**1**	**3.25**	....	....	**730**	**.904**	**33.9**	....	....	....	....	....	....	....	....	....	....	....	....

WJC-A All-Star Team (1999) • Named Best Goaltender at WJC-A (1999)

Traded to **Florida** by **NY Islanders** with Olli Jokinen for Mark Parrish and Oleg Kvasha, June 24, 2000.

• MacKENZIE, Shawn

Shawn Kenneth G – L. 5'10", 175 lbs. b: Bedford, N.S., 8/22/1962. Colorado's 8th, 169th overall in 1980.

Season	Club	League	GP	W	L	T	Mins	GA	SO	Avg	AAvg	Eff	SA	S%	SAPG	GP	W	L	T	Mins	GA	SO	Avg	Eff	SA	S%	SAPG
1979-80	Windsor Spitfires	OMJHL	41	17	14	1	1964	158	0	4.83	....	....	....	....	....	13	6	6	0	680	45	0	3.97	....	....	....	....
1980-81	Windsor Spitfires	OMJHL	*60	30	27	2	*3540	282	1	4.78	....	....	....	....	....	11	3	4	0	622	47	0	4.53	....	....	....	....
1981-82	Windsor Spitfires	OHL	17	6	11	0	1001	77	0	4.62	....	....	....	....	....	....	....	....	....	....	....	....	....	....	....	....	....
	Oshawa Generals	OHL	32	20	12	0	1934	124	1	3.85	....	....	....	....	....	12	7	5	0	707	53	0	4.50	....	....	....	....
1982-83	**New Jersey Devils**	**NHL**	**4**	**0**	**1**	**0**	**130**	**15**	**0**	**6.92**	**5.56**	**15.26**	**68**	**.779**	**31.4**	....	....	....	....	....	....	....	....	....	....	....	....
	Wichita Wind	CHL	36	10	23	2	2083	148	1	4.26	....	....	....	....	....	....	....	....	....	....	....	....	....	....	....	....	....
1983-84	Maine Mariners	AHL	34	14	13	5	1946	113	0	3.48	....	....	....	....	....	1	0	0	0	0	0	0	0.00	....	....	....	....
1984-85	Maine Mariners	AHL	24	8	8	3	1254	70	3	3.35	....	....	....	....	....	2	0	1	0	69	9	0	7.83	....	....	....	....
1985-86	Hershey Bears	AHL	10	5	3	0	521	36	0	4.15	....	....	....	....	....	....	....	....	....	....	....	....	....	....	....	....	....
	Kalamazoo Wings	IHL	6	4	2	0	362	27	0	4.40	....	....	....	....	....	....	....	....	....	....	....	....	....	....	....	....	....
1986-87	Maine Mariners	AHL	6	3	2	0	321	19	1	3.55	....	....	....	....	....	....	....	....	....	....	....	....	....	....	....	....	....
	NHL Totals		**4**	**0**	**1**	**0**	**130**	**15**	**0**	**6.92**	....	....	**68**	**.779**	**31.4**	....	....	....	....	....	....	....	....	....	....	....	....

Transferred to **New Jersey** after **Colorado** franchise relocated, June 30, 1982.

• MADELEY, Darrin

Darrin R. G – L. 5'11", 170 lbs. b: Holland Landing, Ont., 2/25/1968.

Season	Club	League	GP	W	L	T	Mins	GA	SO	Avg	AAvg	Eff	SA	S%	SAPG	GP	W	L	T	Mins	GA	SO	Avg	Eff	SA	S%	SAPG
1984-85	Bradford Blues	OJHL-C	10	7	2	0	549	30	0	3.28	....	....	....	....	....	....	....	....	....	....	....	....	....	....	....	....	....
1985-86	Bradford Blues	OJHL-C	4	2	1	0	200	15	0	4.50	....	....	....	....	....	....	....	....	....	....	....	....	....	....	....	....	....
	Newmarket Flyers	OJHL	3	0	1	0	84	6	0	4.29	....	....	....	....	....	....	....	....	....	....	....	....	....	....	....	....	....
	Orillia Travelways	OJHL	DID NOT PLAY – SPARE GOALTENDER																								
1986-87	Richmond Hill Dynes	OJHL	14	6	9	1	816	67	*2	4.92	....	....	....	....	....	....	....	....	....	....	....	....	....	....	....	....	....
1987-88	Richmond Hill Dynes	OJHL-B	32	....	....	....	1660	129	0	4.66	....	....	....	....	....	....	....	....	....	....	....	....	....	....	....	....	....
1988-89	Richmond Hill Dynes	OJHL-B	27	....	....	....	1404	124	0	5.30	....	....	....	....	....	....	....	....	....	....	....	....	....	....	....	....	....
1989-90	Lake Superior State	CCHA	30	21	7	1	1683	68	1	2.42	....	....	....	....	....	....	....	....	....	....	....	....	....	....	....	....	....
1990-91	Lake Superior State	CCHA	36	*29	3	3	2137	93	1	*2.61	....	....	....	....	....	....	....	....	....	....	....	....	....	....	....	....	....
1991-92	Lake Superior State	CCHA	36	23	6	4	2144	69	2	*2.05	....	....	....	....	....	....	....	....	....	....	....	....	....	....	....	....	....
1992-93	**Ottawa Senators**	**NHL**	**2**	**0**	**2**	**0**	**90**	**10**	**0**	**6.67**	**5.72**	**15.16**	**44**	**.773**	**29.3**	....	....	....	....	....	....	....	....	....	....	....	....
	New Haven Senators	AHL	41	10	16	9	2295	127	0	3.32	....	....	....	....	....	....	....	....	....	....	....	....	....	....	....	....	....
1993-94	**Ottawa Senators**	**NHL**	**32**	**3**	**18**	**5**	**1583**	**115**	**0**	**4.36**	**4.21**	**5.78**	**868**	**.868**	**32.9**	....	....	....	....	....	....	....	....	....	....	....	....
	P.E.I. Senators	AHL	6	0	4	0	270	26	0	5.77	....	....	....	....	....	....	....	....	....	....	....	....	....	....	....	....	....
1994-95	**Ottawa Senators**	**NHL**	**5**	**1**	**3**	**0**	**255**	**15**	**0**	**3.53**	**3.70**	**3.60**	**147**	**.898**	**34.6**	....	....	....	....	....	....	....	....	....	....	....	....
	P.E.I. Senators	AHL	3	1	1	1	185	8	0	2.59	....	....	....	....	....	....	....	....	....	....	....	....	....	....	....	....	....
	Detroit Vipers	IHL	9	7	2	0	498	20	1	2.41	....	....	....	....	....	....	....	....	....	....	....	....	....	....	....	....	....
1995-96	P.E.I. Senators	AHL	1	1	0	0	60	4	0	4.00	....	....	....	....	....	....	....	....	....	....	....	....	....	....	....	....	....
	Detroit Vipers	IHL	40	16	14	4	2047	108	0	3.17	....	....	....	....	....	7	3	3	....	355	23	0	3.89	....	....	....	....
1996-97	Detroit Vipers	IHL	4	2	0	0	177	11	0	3.72	....	....	....	....	....	....	....	....	....	....	....	....	....	....	....	....	....
	Saint John Flames	AHL	46	11	18	11	2316	124	0	3.21	....	....	....	....	....	2	0	0	....	58	0	0	0.00	....	....	....	....
1997-98	TPS Turku	Finland	2	1	0	0	85	2	0	1.41	....	....	....	....	....	....	....	....	....	....	....	....	....	....	....	....	....
	Richmond Renegades	ECHL	5	1	1	0	137	8	0	3.49	....	....	....	....	....	....	....	....	....	....	....	....	....	....	....	....	....
1998-99	Star Bulls Rosenheim	Germany	3	....	....	....	127	8	0	3.78	....	....	....	....	....	....	....	....	....	....	....	....	....	....	....	....	....
	Pensacola Ice Pilots	ECHL	32	12	16	3	1792	92	3	3.08	....	....	....	....	....	....	....	....	....	....	....	....	....	....	....	....	....
	NHL Totals		**39**	**4**	**23**	**5**	**1928**	**140**	**0**	**4.36**	....	....	**1059**	**.868**	**33.0**	....	....	....	....	....	....	....	....	....	....	....	....

CCHA Second All-Star Team (1990) • CCHA First All-Star Team (1991, 1992) • NCAA West First All-American Team (1991, 1992) • NCAA Championship All-Tournament Team (1991, 1992) • AHL Second All-Star Team (1993)

Signed as a free agent by **Ottawa**, June 20, 1992. Signed as a free agent by **San Jose**, October 22, 1996.

• MALARCHUK, Clint

Clint Regan G – L. 6', 185 lbs. b: Grande Prairie, Alta., 5/1/1961. Quebec's 3rd, 74th overall in 1981.

Season	Club	League	GP	W	L	T	Mins	GA	SO	Avg	AAvg	Eff	SA	S%	SAPG	GP	W	L	T	Mins	GA	SO	Avg	Eff	SA	S%	SAPG
1978-79	Fort Saskatchewan Traders	AJHL	STATISTICS NOT AVAILABLE																								
	Portland Winter Hawks	WHL	2	2	0	0	120	4	0	2.00	....	....	....	....	....	....	....	....	....	....	....	....	....	....	....	....	....
1979-80	Portland Winter Hawks	WHL	37	21	10	0	1948	147	0	4.53	....	....	....	....	....	1	0	0	0	40	3	0	4.50	....	....	....	....
1980-81	Portland Winter Hawks	WHL	38	28	8	0	2235	142	3	3.81	....	....	....	....	....	5	3	2	0	307	21	0	4.10	....	....	....	....
1981-82	**Quebec Nordiques**	**NHL**	**2**	**0**	**1**	**1**	**120**	**14**	**0**	**7.00**	**5.41**	**14.85**	**66**	**.788**	**33.0**	....	....	....	....	....	....	....	....	....	....	....	....
	Fredericton Express	AHL	51	15	34	2	2906	247	0	5.10	....	....	....	....	....	....	....	....	....	....	....	....	....	....	....	....	....
1982-83	**Quebec Nordiques**	**NHL**	**15**	**8**	**5**	**2**	**900**	**71**	**0**	**4.73**	**3.80**	**6.50**	**517**	**.863**	**34.5**	....	....	....	....	....	....	....	....	....	....	....	....
	Fredericton Express	AHL	25	14	6	5	1506	78	0	*3.11	....	....	....	....	....	....	....	....	....	....	....	....	....	....	....	....	....
1983-84	**Quebec Nordiques**	**NHL**	**23**	**10**	**9**	**2**	**1215**	**80**	**0**	**3.95**	**3.11**	**5.35**	**591**	**.865**	**29.2**	....	....	....	....	....	....	....	....	....	....	....	....
	Fredericton Express	AHL	11	5	5	1	663	40	0	3.62	....	....	....	....	....	....	....	....	....	....	....	....	....	....	....	....	....
1984-85	Fredericton Express	AHL	*56	26	25	4	*3347	198	2	3.55	....	....	....	....	....	6	2	4	0	379	20	0	3.17	....	....	....	....
1985-86	**Quebec Nordiques**	**NHL**	**46**	**26**	**12**	**4**	**2657**	**142**	**4**	**3.21**	**2.49**	**3.36**	**1358**	**.895**	**30.7**	**3**	**0**	**2**	....	**143**	**11**	**0**	**4.62**	**6.27**	**81**	**.864**	**34.0**
1986-87	**Quebec Nordiques**	**NHL**	**54**	**18**	**26**	**9**	**3092**	**175**	**1**	**3.40**	**2.87**	**3.94**	**1512**	**.884**	**29.3**	**3**	**0**	**2**	....	**140**	**8**	**0**	**3.43**	**4.90**	**56**	**.857**	**24.0**
	NHL All-Stars	RV-87	DID NOT PLAY – SPARE GOALTENDER																								
1987-88	**Washington Capitals**	**NHL**	**54**	**24**	**20**	**4**	**2926**	**154**	***4**	**3.16**	**2.62**	**3.63**	**1340**	**.885**	**27.5**	**4**	**0**	**2**	....	**193**	**15**	**0**	**4.66**	**7.36**	**95**	**.842**	**29.5**
1988-89	**Washington Capitals**	**NHL**	**42**	**16**	**18**	**7**	**2428**	**141**	**1**	**3.48**	**2.89**	**4.29**	**1145**	**.877**	**28.3**	....	....	....	....	....	....	....	....	....	....	....	....
	Buffalo Sabres	**NHL**	**7**	**3**	**1**	**1**	**326**	**13**	**1**	**2.39**	**1.99**	**2.19**	**142**	**.908**	**26.1**	**1**	**0**	**1**	**0**	**59**	**5**	**0**	**5.08**	**7.94**	**32**	**.844**	**32.5**
1989-90	**Buffalo Sabres**	**NHL**	**29**	**14**	**11**	**2**	**1596**	**89**	**0**	**3.35**	**2.83**	**3.26**	**914**	**.903**	**34.4**	....	....	....	....	....	....	....	....	....	....	....	....
1990-91	**Buffalo Sabres**	**NHL**	**37**	**12**	**14**	**10**	**2131**	**119**	**1**	**3.35**	**3.01**	**3.66**	**1090**	**.891**	**30.7**	**4**	**2**	**2**	....	**246**	**17**	**0**	**4.15**	**6.08**	**116**	**.853**	**28.3**
1991-92	**Buffalo Sabres**	**NHL**	**29**	**10**	**13**	**3**	**1639**	**102**	**0**	**3.73**	**3.34**	**4.21**	**903**	**.887**	**33.1**	....	....	....	....	....	....	....	....	....	....	....	....
	Rochester Americans	AHL	2	2	0	0	120	3	1	1.50	....	....	....	....	....	....	....	....	....	....	....	....	....	....	....	....	....
1992-93	San Diego Gulls	IHL	27	17	3	3	1516	72	3	2.85	....	....	....	....	....	*12	6	4	0	668	34	0	3.05	....	....	....	....
1993-94	Las Vegas Thunder	IHL	55	*34	10	7	3076	172	1	3.35	....	....	....	....	....	5	1	3	0	257	16	0	3.74	....	....	....	....
1994-95	Las Vegas Thunder	IHL	38	15	13	3	2039	127	0	3.74	....	....	....	....	....	2	0	0	0	32	2	0	3.70	....	....	....	....

Season	Club	League	REGULAR SEASON													PLAYOFFS											
			GP	W	L	T	Mins	GA	SO	Avg	AAvg	Eff	SA	S%	SAPG	GP	W	L	T	Mins	GA	SO	Avg	Eff	SA	S%	SAPG
1995-1996	Las Vegas Thunder	IHL	DID NOT PLAY – ASSISTANT GENERAL MANAGER																								
	Las Vegas Thunder	IHL	1	0	0	0	4	0	0	0.00																	
1996-1997	Las Vegas Thunder	IHL	DID NOT PLAY – ASSISTANT GENERAL MANAGER																								
	Las Vegas Thunder	IHL	3	1	1	0	63	6	0	5.63																	
1997-1998	Las Vegas Thunder	IHL	DID NOT PLAY – ASSISTANT GENERAL MANAGER																								
	Las Vegas Thunder	IHL	DID NOT PLAY – COACHING																								
1998-2000	Idaho Steelheads	WPHL	DID NOT PLAY – COACHING																								
	NHL Totals		**338**	**141**	**130**	**45**	**19030**	**1100**	**12**	**3.47**	....	....	**9578**	**.885**	**30.2**	**15**	**2**	**9**	**0**	**781**	**56**	**0**	**4.30**	....	**380**	**.853**	**29.2**

Shared Harry "Hap" Holmes Memorial Award (fewest goals against - AHL) with Brian Ford (1983) • Shared James Norris Memorial Trophy (fewest goals against - IHL) with Rick Knickle (1993)

Traded to **Washington** by **Quebec** with Dale Hunter for Gaetan Duchesne, Alan Haworth and Washington's 1st round choice (Joe Sakic) in 1987 Entry Draft, June 13, 1987. Traded to **Buffalo** by **Washington** with Grant Ledyard and Washington's 6th round choice (Brian Holzinger) in 1991 Entry Draft for Calle Johansson and Buffalo's 2nd round choice (Byron Dafoe) in 1989 Entry Draft, March 7, 1989. • Came out of retirement with **Las Vegas** (IHL) to play first 4 minutes of game vs. **Kansas City** (IHL) before becoming first player in team history to have number retired, March 5, 1996. • Named Head Coach of **Las Vegas** (IHL), March 14, 1998.

• MANELUK, George

G – L. 5′11″, 185 lbs. b: Winnipeg, Man., 7/25/1967. NY Islanders' 4th, 76th overall in 1987.

Season	Club	League	GP	W	L	T	Mins	GA	SO	Avg	AAvg	Eff	SA	S%	SAPG	GP	W	L	T	Mins	GA	SO	Avg	Eff	SA	S%	SAPG
1985-86	University of Manitoba	CWUAA	2	1	1	0	120	14	0	7.00																	
1986-87	Brandon Wheat Kings	WHL	58	16	35	4	3258	315	0	5.80																	
1987-88	Brandon Wheat Kings	WHL	64	24	33	3	3651	297	0	4.88						4	1	3	0	271	22	0	4.87				
	Springfield Indians	AHL	2	0	1	1	125	9	0	4.32																	
	Peoria Rivermen	IHL	3	1	2	0	148	14	0	5.68						1	0	1	0	60	5	0	5.00				
1988-89	Springfield Indians	AHL	24	7	13	0	1202	84	0	4.19																	
1989-90	Springfield Indians	AHL	27	11	9	1	1382	94	1	4.08						4	2	1	0	174	9	0	3.10				
	Winston-Salem Thunderbirds	ECHL	3	2	0	0	140	11	0	4.71																	
1990-91	**New York Islanders**	**NHL**	**4**	**1**	**1**	**0**	**140**	**15**	**0**	**6.43**	**5.79**	**10.26**	**94**	**.840**	**40.3**												
	Capital District Islanders	AHL	29	10	14	1	1524	103	1	4.06																	
1991-92	New Haven Nighthawks	AHL	54	25	22	0	2863	175	1	3.67						3	1	2	0	216	13	0	3.61				
1992-93	Springfield Indians	AHL	7	4	3	0	343	23	0	4.02						14	6	7	0	778	53	0	4.09				
	Phoenix Roadrunners	IHL	2	1	1	0	120	10	0	5.00																	
	Muskegon Fury	ColHL	27	....	....	....	1494	113	*1	4.54						1	0	1	0	59	6	0	6.10				
1993-94	Springfield Indians	AHL	31	8	14	6	1515	107	0	4.24																	
1994-95	Wichita Thunder	CHL	44	27	10	2	2439	153	2	3.76						9	6	3	0	476	37	0	4.65				
1995-96	Louisiana IceGators	ECHL	36	18	13	2	1969	129	0	3.93						3	0	2	0	160	14	0	5.25				
	Los Angeles Ice Dogs	IHL	1	0	0	0	9	0	0	0.00																	
	NHL Totals		**4**	**1**	**1**	**0**	**140**	**15**	**0**	**6.43**	....	....	**94**	**.840**	**40.3**												

CHL Second All-Star Team (1995)

• MANIAGO, Cesare

"Hail Cesare" G – L. 6′3″, 195 lbs. b: Trail, B.C., 1/13/1939.

Season	Club	League	GP	W	L	T	Mins	GA	SO	Avg	AAvg	Eff	SA	S%	SAPG	GP	W	L	T	Mins	GA	SO	Avg	Eff	SA	S%	SAPG
1957-58	St. Michael's Majors	OHA-Jr.	48	21	19	7	2880	173	*2	3.60																	
1958-59	St. Michael's Majors	OHA-Jr.	42	....	....	....	2520	131	*4	3.12																	
1959-60	Kitchener-Waterloo Dutchmen	OHA-Sr.	38	....	....	....	2240	149	0	3.99																	
	Chatham Maroons	Al-Cup	14	10	3	1	850	40	*3	*2.82																	
1960-61	**Toronto Maple Leafs**	**NHL**	**7**	**4**	**2**	**1**	**420**	**17**	**0**	**2.43**	**2.49**					**2**	**1**	**1**	....	**145**	**6**	**0**	**2.48**				
	Vancouver Canucks	WHL	2	2	0	0	120	5	0	2.50																	
	Sudbury Wolves	EPHL	11	7	3	1	660	19	3	1.73																	
	Spokane Comets	WHL	30	17	10	3	1800	90	1	3.00						4	1	3	0	240	19	0	4.75				
1961-62	Hull-Ottawa Canadiens	EPHL	68	*37	21	10	4080	168	3	*2.47						*13	*8	5	0	*823	32	0	*2.33				
1962-63	**Montreal Canadiens**	**NHL**	**14**	**5**	**5**	**4**	**820**	**42**	**0**	**3.07**	**3.20**																
	Quebec Aces	AHL	5	2	3	0	300	19	0	3.80																	
	Spokane Comets	WHL	1	0	1	0	60	4	0	4.00																	
	Hull-Ottawa Canadiens	EPHL	28	13	11	4	1680	86	1	3.07						3	0	3	0	185	9	0	2.92				
1963-64	Buffalo Bisons	AHL	27	11	13	1	1630	103	0	3.82																	
	Omaha Knights	CPHL	6	2	2	2	360	23	0	3.83																	
1964-65	Minneapolis Bruins	CPHL	67	34	26	7	4020	184	*6	*2.75						5	1	4	0	300	19	*1	3.80				
1965-66	**New York Rangers**	**NHL**	**28**	**9**	**16**	**3**	**1613**	**94**	**2**	**3.50**	**3.58**																
	Baltimore Clippers	AHL	27	11	16	0	1572	83	1	3.17																	
1966-67	**New York Rangers**	**NHL**	**6**	**0**	**1**	**1**	**219**	**14**	**0**	**3.84**	**3.97**																
1967-68	**Minnesota North Stars**	**NHL**	**52**	**21**	**17**	**9**	**2877**	**133**	**6**	**2.77**	**3.07**					**14**	**7**	**7**	....	**893**	**39**	**0**	**2.62**				
1968-69	**Minnesota North Stars**	**NHL**	**64**	**18**	**33**	**10**	**3599**	**198**	**1**	**3.30**	**3.44**																
1969-70	**Minnesota North Stars**	**NHL**	**50**	**9**	**24**	**16**	**2887**	**163**	**2**	**3.39**	**3.63**					**3**	**1**	**2**	....	**180**	**6**	***1**	**2.00**				
1970-71	**Minnesota North Stars**	**NHL**	**40**	**19**	**15**	**6**	**2380**	**107**	**5**	**2.70**	**2.66**					**8**	**3**	**5**	....	**480**	**28**	**0**	**3.50**				
1971-72	**Minnesota North Stars**	**NHL**	**43**	**20**	**17**	**4**	**2539**	**112**	**3**	**2.65**	**2.67**					**4**	**1**	**3**	....	**238**	**12**	**0**	**3.03**				
1972-73	**Minnesota North Stars**	**NHL**	**47**	**21**	**18**	**6**	**2736**	**132**	**5**	**2.89**	**2.71**					**5**	**2**	**3**	....	**309**	**9**	***2**	***1.75**				
1973-74	**Minnesota North Stars**	**NHL**	**40**	**12**	**18**	**10**	**2378**	**138**	**1**	**3.48**	**3.37**																
1974-75	**Minnesota North Stars**	**NHL**	**37**	**11**	**21**	**4**	**2129**	**149**	**1**	**4.20**	**3.82**																
1975-76	**Minnesota North Stars**	**NHL**	**47**	**13**	**27**	**5**	**2704**	**151**	**2**	**3.35**	**3.03**																
1976-77	**Vancouver Canucks**	**NHL**	**47**	**17**	**21**	**9**	**2699**	**151**	**1**	**3.36**	**3.13**																
1977-78	**Vancouver Canucks**	**NHL**	**46**	**10**	**24**	**8**	**2570**	**172**	**1**	**4.02**	**3.80**																
	NHL Totals		**568**	**189**	**259**	**96**	**32570**	**1773**	**30**	**3.27**	....	....	....	....	....	**36**	**15**	**21**	....	**2245**	**100**	**3**	**2.67**	....	....	....	....

EPHL First All-Star Team (1962) • CPHL First All-Star Team (1965) • Won Terry Sawchuk Trophy (fewest goals against - CPHL) (1965) • Won Tommy Ivan Trophy (MVP - CPHL) (1965)

Claimed by **Montreal** from **Toronto** (Rochester-AHL) in Inter-League Draft, June 12, 1961. Traded to **NY Rangers** by **Montreal** with Garry Peters for Noel Price, Earl Ingarfield, Gord Labossiere, Dave McComb and cash, June 8, 1965. Claimed by **Minnesota** from **NY Rangers** in Expansion Draft, June 6, 1967. Traded to **Vancouver** by **Minnesota** for Gary Smith, August 23, 1976.

• MARACLE, Norm

G – L. 5′8″, 195 lbs. b: Belleville, Ont., 10/2/1974. Detroit's 6th, 126th overall in 1993.

Season	Club	League	GP	W	L	T	Mins	GA	SO	Avg	AAvg	Eff	SA	S%	SAPG	GP	W	L	T	Mins	GA	SO	Avg	Eff	SA	S%	SAPG
1990-91	Calgary North Stars	AMHL	29	....	....	....	1740	99	0	3.43																	
1991-92	Saskatoon Blades	WHL	29	13	6	3	1529	87	1	3.41						15	9	5	....	860	37	0	3.38				
1992-93	Saskatoon Blades	WHL	53	27	18	3	1939	160	1	3.27						9	4	5	....	569	33	0	3.48				
1993-94	Saskatoon Blades	WHL	56	*41	13	1	3219	148	2	2.76						16	*11	5	....	940	48	*1	3.06				
1994-95	Adirondack Red Wings	AHL	39	12	15	2	1997	119	0	3.57																	
1995-96	Adirondack Red Wings	AHL	54	24	18	6	2949	135	2	2.75						1	0	1	....	30	4	0	8.11				
1996-97	Adirondack Red Wings	AHL	*68	*34	22	9	*3843	173	5	2.70						4	1	3	....	192	10	1	3.13				
1997-98	**Detroit Red Wings**	**NHL**	**4**	**2**	**0**	**1**	**178**	**6**	**0**	**2.02**	**2.41**	**1.92**	**63**	**.905**	**21.2**												
	Adirondack Red Wings	AHL	*66	27	29	8	*3709	190	1	3.07						3	0	3	....	180	10	0	3.33				
1998-99	**Detroit Red Wings**	**NHL**	**16**	**6**	**5**	**2**	**821**	**31**	**0**	**2.27**	**2.70**	**1.86**	**379**	**.918**	**27.7**	**2**	**0**	**0**	....	**58**	**3**	**0**	**3.10**	**4.23**	**22**	**.864**	**22.8**
	Adirondack Red Wings	AHL	6	3	3	0	359	18	0	3.01																	
99-2000	**Atlanta Thrashers**	**NHL**	**32**	**4**	**19**	**2**	**1618**	**94**	**1**	**3.49**	**4.00**	**3.85**	**852**	**.890**	**31.6**												
	NHL Totals		**52**	**12**	**24**	**5**	**2617**	**131**	**1**	**3.00**	....	....	**1294**	**.899**	**29.7**	**2**	**0**	**0**	....	**58**	**3**	**0**	**3.10**	....	**22**	**.864**	**22.8**

WHL East Second All-Star Team (1993) • WHL East First All-Star Team (1994) • Canadian Major Junior First All-Star Team (1994) • Canadian Major Junior Goaltender of the Year (1994) • AHL Second All-Star Team (1997, 1998)

Claimed by **Atlanta** from **Detroit** in Expansion Draft, June 25, 1999.

• MAROIS, Jean

G – L. 5′8″, 155 lbs. b: Quebec City, Que., 5/11/1924.

Season	Club	League	GP	W	L	T	Mins	GA	SO	Avg	AAvg	Eff	SA	S%	SAPG	GP	W	L	T	Mins	GA	SO	Avg	Eff	SA	S%	SAPG
1939-40	St. Michael's Buzzers	OHA-B	1	1	0	0	60	3	0	3.00																	
1940-41	St. Michael's Buzzers	OHA-B	5	2	2	1	370	16	0	2.59																	
1941-42	St. Michael's Buzzers	OHA-B	2	0	2	0	120	9	0	4.50																	
	St. Michael's Majors	OHA-Jr.	4	1	3	0	240	22	0	5.50						2	0	1	0	100	10	0	6.00				

			REGULAR SEASON													PLAYOFFS											
Season	**Club**	**League**	**GP**	**W**	**L**	**T**	**Mins**	**GA**	**SO**	**Avg**	**AAvg**	**Eff**	**SA**	**S%**	**SAPG**	**GP**	**W**	**L**	**T**	**Mins**	**GA**	**SO**	**Avg**	**Eff**	**SA**	**S%**	**SAPG**
1942-43	St. Michael's Majors	OHA-Jr.	20	8	11	1	1230	99	0	4.83	....	....	....	....	....	6	3	3	0	360	35	*1	5.95	....	....	....	....
	Toronto Tip Tops	TIHL	1	0	0	1	70	4	0	3.43	....	....	....	....	....	....	....	....	....	....	....	....	....	....	....	....	....
	St. Michael's Majors	Mem-Cup	2	2	0	0	120	7	0	3.50	....	....	....	....	....	....	....	....	....	....	....	....	....	....	....	....	....
1943-44	St. Michael's Majors	OHA-Jr.	14	11	3	0	840	44	1	3.14	....	....	....	....	....	6	....	....	....	360	20	0	3.38	....	....	....	....
	Toronto Maple Leafs	**NHL**	**1**	**1**	**0**	**0**	**60**	**4**	**0**	**4.00**	**2.98**	....	....	....	....	....	....	....	....	....	....	....	....	....	....	....	....
1944-45			MILITARY SERVICE																								
1945-46	Quebec Aces	QSHL	7	....	....	....	420	38	0	5.43	....	....	....	....	....	6	1	3	2	360	28	0	4.67	....	....	....	....
1946-47	Quebec Aces	QSHL	32	....	....	....	1920	119	0	3.72	....	....	....	....	....	....	....	....	....	....	....	....	....	....	....	....	....
1947-48	Quebec Aces	QSHL	35	....	....	....	2080	120	0	3.46	....	....	....	....	....	10	6	4	0	600	30	1	3.00	....	....	....	....
1948-49	Quebec Aces	QSHL	59	22	31	6	3540	205	4	3.47	....	....	....	....	....	3	0	3	0	180	18	0	6.00	....	....	....	....
1949-50	Shawinigan Cataracts	QSHL	46	13	31	6	2820	204	3	4.34	....	....	....	....	....	....	....	....	....	....	....	....	....	....	....	....	....
1950-51	Quebec Aces	QMHL	60	31	22	7	3600	192	*3	3.20	....	....	....	....	....	19	*12	7	0	1140	55	1	2.89	....	....	....	....
1951-52	Quebec Aces	QMHL	48	*31	12	5	2950	126	*6	*2.56	....	....	....	....	....	8	6	2	0	519	18	1	2.08	....	....	....	....
1952-53	Quebec Aces	QMHL	36	13	14	8	2220	118	1	3.19	....	....	....	....	....	1	0	1	0	60	6	0	6.00	....	....	....	....
1953-54	Quebec Aces	QHL	15	6	7	2	927	54	0	3.50	....	....	....	....	....	1	1	1	0	120	6	0	3.00	....	....	....	....
	Hershey Bears	AHL	6	4	2	0	360	16	0	2.67	....	....	....	....	....	....	....	....	....	....	....	....	....	....	....	....	....
	Providence Reds	AHL	3	2	1	0	180	11	0	3.67	....	....	....	....	....	....	....	....	....	....	....	....	....	....	....	....	....
	Chicago Black Hawks	**NHL**	**2**	**0**	**2**	**0**	**120**	**11**	**0**	**5.50**	**7.02**	....	....	....	....	....	....	....	....	....	....	....	....	....	....	....	....
	Quebec Aces	Ed-Cup	3	0	3	0	180	14	0	4.67	....	....	....	....	....	....	....	....	....	....	....	....	....	....	....	....	....
1954-55	Providence Reds	AHL	11	4	6	1	660	47	0	4.27	....	....	....	....	....	....	....	....	....	....	....	....	....	....	....	....	....
	Quebec Aces	QHL	17	9	7	1	1013	56	1	3.32	....	....	....	....	....	....	....	....	....	....	....	....	....	....	....	....	....
	NHL Totals		**3**	**1**	**2**	**0**	**180**	**15**	**0**	**5.00**	....	....	....	....	....	....	....	....	....	....	....	....	....	....	....	....	....

QSHL Second All-Star Team (1949) • QMHL Second All-Star Team (1951) • QMHL First All-Star Team (1952)

Promoted to **Toronto** from **St. Michael's** (OHA-Jr.) to replace injured Benny Grant, November 18, 1943. (Montreal 5, Toronto 2). Loaned to **Chicago** by **Quebec** (QHL), November 21, 1953.

• MARTIN, Seth

G – L. 5'11", 180 lbs. b: Rossland, B.C., 5/4/1933.

Season	Club	League	GP	W	L	T	Mins	GA	SO	Avg	AAvg	Eff	SA	S%	SAPG	GP	W	L	T	Mins	GA	SO	Avg	Eff	SA	S%	SAPG
1950-51	Lethbridge Native Sons	WCJHL	30	....	....	....	1800	98	0	3.27	....	....	....	....	....	2	....	....	....	80	3	0	*2.25	....	....	....	....
1951-52	Lethbridge Native Sons	WCJHL	36	23	12	1	2160	138	1	3.84	....	....	....	....	....	4	0	4	0	240	30	0	7.50	....	....	....	....
1952-53	Lethbridge Native Sons	WCJHL	27	17	6	4	1620	115	0	4.26	....	....	....	....	....	25	16	7	2	1540	96	2	3.74	....	....	....	....
1953-54	Trail Smoke Eaters	WIHL	28	....	....	....	1680	139	0	4.96	....	....	....	....	....	4	1	3	0	240	21	0	5.20	....	....	....	....
	Kelowna Packers	OSHL	3	....	....	....	180	7	0	2.33	....	....	....	....	....	....	....	....	....	....	....	....	....	....	....	....	....
1954-55	Trail Smoke Eaters	WIHL	28	....	....	....	1680	134	*1	4.78	....	....	....	....	....	4	....	....	....	240	13	0	*3.25	....	....	....	....
1955-56	Trail Smoke Eaters	WIHL	39	....	....	....	2340	183	0	4.69	....	....	....	....	....	10	5	5	0	600	35	1	3.50	....	....	....	....
1956-57	Trail Smoke Eaters	WIHL	26	....	....	....	1560	89	0	*3.42	....	....	....	....	....	9	....	....	....	540	42	0	4.67	....	....	....	....
1957-58	Trail Smoke Eaters	WIHL	47	....	....	....	2820	211	1	4.49	....	....	....	....	....	7	3	4	0	420	29	0	4.14	....	....	....	....
1958-59	Trail Smoke Eaters	WIHL	39	17	20	2	2340	165	*4	4.23	....	....	....	....	....	7	3	4	0	379	29	0	4.60	....	....	....	....
1959-60	Trail Smoke Eaters	WIHL	37	....	....	....	2220	185	0	5.00	....	....	....	....	....	11	*9	2	0	660	45	1	4.09	....	....	....	....
	Spokane Spokes	WHL	2	0	2	0	120	8	0	4.00	....	....	....	....	....	....	....	....	....	....	....	....	....	....	....	....	....
	Vancouver Canucks	WHL	1	0	1	0	40	4	0	6.00	....	....	....	....	....	....	....	....	....	....	....	....	....	....	....	....	....
	Trail Smoke Eaters	Al-Cup	15	8	6	1	915	56	1	3.67	....	....	....	....	....	....	....	....	....	....	....	....	....	....	....	....	....
1960-61	Trail Smoke Eaters	WIHL	37	*34	3	0	2220	111	0	3.00	....	....	....	....	....	13	11	1	0	780	30	0	2.31	....	....	....	....
	Canada	WEC-A	5	4	0	1	280	6	0	1.28	....	....	....	....	....	....	....	....	....	....	....	....	....	....	....	....	....
1961-62	Portland Buckaroos	WHL	1	....	....	....	60	1	0	1.00	....	....	....	....	....	....	....	....	....	....	....	....	....	....	....	....	....
	Trail Smoke Eaters	WIHL	31	....	....	....	1860	112	*2	*3.70	....	....	....	....	....	....	....	....	....	....	....	....	....	....	....	....	....
1962-63	Canada	Nat-Team	STATISTICS NOT AVAILABLE																								
	Canada	WEC-A	7	4	2	1	420	23	1	3.29	....	....	....	....	....	....	....	....	....	....	....	....	....	....	....	....	....
1963-64	Rossland Miners	WIHL	23	12	9	0	1380	90	*1	3.91	....	....	....	....	....	5	2	3	0	300	22	0	4.40	....	....	....	....
	Canada	Olympics	6	4	1	0	247	5	1	1.21	....	....	....	....	....	....	....	....	....	....	....	....	....	....	....	....	....
1964-65	Rossland Warriors	WIHL	41	15	24	2	2460	192	0	4.68	....	....	....	....	....	....	....	....	....	....	....	....	....	....	....	....	....
	Nelson Maple Leafs	Al-Cup	12	7	5	0	700	40	2	3.43	....	....	....	....	....	....	....	....	....	....	....	....	....	....	....	....	....
1965-66	Rossland Warriors	WIHL	24	13	9	0	1380	104	0	4.52	....	....	....	....	....	1	0	1	0	60	5	0	5.00	....	....	....	....
	Nelson Maple Leafs	WIHL	1	0	0	0	20	1	0	3.00	....	....	....	....	....	....	....	....	....	....	....	....	....	....	....	....	....
	Canada	WEC-A	4	2	2	0	240	8	0	2.00	....	....	....	....	....	....	....	....	....	....	....	....	....	....	....	....	....
	Kimberley Dynamiters	WIHL	....	....	....	....	....	....	....	....	....	....	....	....	....	1	0	1	0	60	3	0	3.00	....	....	....	....
1966-67	Rossland Warriors	WIHL	33	....	....	....	1980	158	0	4.79	....	....	....	....	....	....	....	....	....	....	....	....	....	....	....	....	....
	Canada	WEC-A	6	3	2	1	360	14	0	2.33	....	....	....	....	....	....	....	....	....	....	....	....	....	....	....	....	....
1967-68	**St. Louis Blues**	**NHL**	**30**	**8**	**10**	**7**	**1552**	**67**	**1**	**2.59**	**2.87**	....	....	....	....	**2**	**0**	**0**	....	**73**	**5**	**0**	**4.11**	....	....	....	....
1968-69	Trail Smoke Eaters	WIHL	17	....	....	....	1020	67	1	3.94	....	....	....	....	....	....	....	....	....	....	....	....	....	....	....	....	....
1969-70	Spokane Jets	WIHL	24	....	....	....	1440	56	*3	*2.33	....	....	....	....	....	7	*7	0	0	420	9	*1	*1.29	....	....	....	....
	Spokane Jets	Al-Cup	11	*9	2	0	660	24	*2	*2.18	....	....	....	....	....	....	....	....	....	....	....	....	....	....	....	....	....
1970-71			DID NOT PLAY																								
1971-72			DID NOT PLAY																								
1972-73	Spokane Jets	WIHL	3	....	....	....	180	14	0	4.66	....	....	....	....	....	....	....	....	....	....	....	....	....	....	....	....	....
	Portland Buckaroos	WHL	2	0	2	0	100	11	0	6.59	....	....	....	....	....	....	....	....	....	....	....	....	....	....	....	....	....
	NHL Totals		**30**	**8**	**10**	**7**	**1552**	**67**	**1**	**2.59**	....	....	....	....	....	**2**	**0**	**0**	....	**73**	**5**	**0**	**4.11**	....	....	....	....

WEC-A All-Star Team (1961, 1966) • Named Best Goaltender at WEC-A (1961, 1963, 1966) • Olympic Games All-Star Team (1964) • Named Best Goaltender at Olympic Games (1964)

• Shared shutout with Ken Broderick in 1964 Olympics. Canada 8, Switzerland 0, January 8, 1964. Signed as a free agent by **St. Louis**, June 6, 1967. Claimed by **Buffalo** (AHL) from **St. Louis** in Reverse Draft, June 13, 1968. Traded to **St. Louis** by **Buffalo** (AHL) for cash, June 27, 1968.

• MASON, Bob

Robert T. G – R. 6'1", 180 lbs. b: International Falls, MN, 4/22/1961.

Season	Club	League	GP	W	L	T	Mins	GA	SO	Avg	AAvg	Eff	SA	S%	SAPG	GP	W	L	T	Mins	GA	SO	Avg	Eff	SA	S%	SAPG
1981-82	University of Minnesota-Duluth.	WCHA	27	9	15	3	1401	115	0	4.45	....	....	....	....	....	....	....	....	....	....	....	....	....	....	....	....	....
1982-83	University of Minnesota-Duluth.	WCHA	43	26	16	1	2594	151	1	3.49	....	....	....	....	....	....	....	....	....	....	....	....	....	....	....	....	....
1983-84	United States	Nat-Team	33	17	10	5	1895	89	0	2.82	....	....	....	....	....	....	....	....	....	....	....	....	....	....	....	....	....
	United States	Olympics	3	1	0	1	160	10	0	3.75	....	....	....	....	....	....	....	....	....	....	....	....	....	....	....	....	....
	Washington Capitals	**NHL**	**2**	**2**	**0**	**0**	**120**	**3**	**0**	**1.50**	**1.18**	**0.98**	**46**	**.935**	**23.0**	....	....	....	....	....	....	....	....	....	....	....	....
	Hershey Bears	AHL	5	1	4	0	282	26	0	5.53	....	....	....	....	....	....	....	....	....	....	....	....	....	....	....	....	....
1984-85	**Washington Capitals**	**NHL**	**12**	**8**	**2**	**1**	**661**	**31**	**1**	**2.81**	**2.24**	**2.99**	**291**	**.893**	**26.4**	....	....	....	....	....	....	....	....	....	....	....	....
	Binghamton Whalers	AHL	20	10	6	1	1052	58	1	3.31	....	....	....	....	....	....	....	....	....	....	....	....	....	....	....	....	....
1985-86	**Washington Capitals**	**NHL**	**1**	**1**	**0**	**0**	**16**	**0**	**0**	**0.00**	**0.00**	**0.00**	**5**	**1.000**	**18.8**	....	....	....	....	....	....	....	....	....	....	....	....
	Binghamton Whalers	AHL	34	20	11	2	1940	126	0	3.90	....	....	....	....	....	3	1	1	0	124	9	0	4.35	....	....	....	....
1986-87	**Washington Capitals**	**NHL**	**45**	**20**	**18**	**5**	**2536**	**137**	**0**	**3.24**	**2.74**	**3.56**	**1247**	**.890**	**29.5**	**4**	**2**	**2**	....	**309**	**9**	**1**	**1.75**	**1.10**	**143**	**.937**	**27.8**
	Binghamton Whalers	AHL	2	1	1	0	119	4	0	2.02	....	....	....	....	....	....	....	....	....	....	....	....	....	....	....	....	....
1987-88	United States	Can-Cup	DID NOT PLAY – SPARE GOALTENDER																								
	Chicago Blackhawks	**NHL**	**41**	**13**	**18**	**8**	**2312**	**160**	**0**	**4.15**	**3.47**	**4.91**	**1353**	**.882**	**35.1**	**1**	**0**	**1**	....	**60**	**3**	**0**	**3.00**	**2.90**	**31**	**.903**	**31.0**
1988-89	**Quebec Nordiques**	**NHL**	**22**	**5**	**14**	**1**	**1168**	**92**	**0**	**4.73**	**3.95**	**6.94**	**627**	**.853**	**32.2**	....	....	....	....	....	....	....	....	....	....	....	....
	Halifax Citadels	AHL	23	11	7	1	1278	73	1	3.43	....	....	....	....	....	2	0	2	0	97	9	0	5.57	....	....	....	....
1989-90	Washington Capitals	Fr-Tour	1	0	1	0	30	4	0	8.00	....	....	....	....	....	....	....	....	....	....	....	....	....	....	....	....	....
	Washington Capitals	**NHL**	**16**	**4**	**9**	**1**	**822**	**48**	**0**	**3.50**	**2.96**	**4.32**	**389**	**.877**	**28.4**	....	....	....	....	....	....	....	....	....	....	....	....
	Baltimore Skipjacks	AHL	13	9	2	2	770	44	0	3.43	....	....	....	....	....	6	2	4	0	373	20	0	3.22	....	....	....	....
1990-91	**Vancouver Canucks**	**NHL**	**6**	**2**	**4**	**0**	**353**	**29**	**0**	**4.93**	**4.44**	**7.60**	**188**	**.846**	**32.0**	....	....	....	....	....	....	....	....	....	....	....	....
	Milwaukee Admirals	IHL	22	8	12	1	1199	82	0	4.10	....	....	....	....	....	....	....	....	....	....	....	....	....	....	....	....	....
1991-92	Milwaukee Admirals	IHL	51	27	18	4	3024	171	1	3.39	....	....	....	....	....	3	1	2	0	179	15	0	5.03	....	....	....	....
1992-93	Hamilton Canucks	AHL	44	20	19	3	2601	159	0	3.67	....	....	....	....	....	....	....	....	....	....	....	....	....	....	....	....	....

Season	Club	League	REGULAR SEASON													PLAYOFFS											
			GP	W	L	T	Mins	GA	SO	Avg	AAvg	Eff	SA	S%	SAPG	GP	W	L	T	Mins	GA	SO	Avg	Eff	SA	S%	SAPG
1993-94	Milwaukee Admirals	IHL	40	21	9	8	2206	132	0	3.59	....	....	....	....	....	3	0	1	0	141	9	0	3.83	....	....	....	....
1994-95	Fort Wayne Komets	IHL	1	0	1	0	60	5	0	5.00	....	....	....	....	....	....	....	....	....	....	....	....	....	....	....	....	....
	Milwaukee Admirals	IHL	13	7	4	1	745	50	0	4.03	....	....	....	....	....	....	....	....	....	....	....	....	....	....	....	....	....
	NHL Totals		**145**	**55**	**65**	**16**	**7988**	**500**	**1**	**3.76**	....	....	**4146**	**.879**	**31.1**	**5**	**2**	**3**	....	**369**	**12**	**1**	**1.95**	....	**174**	**.931**	**28.3**

WCHA First All-Star Team (1983)

Signed as a free agent by **Washington**, February 21, 1984. Signed as a free agent by **Chicago**, June 12, 1987. Traded to **Quebec** by **Chicago** for Mike Eagles, July 5, 1988. Traded to **Washington** by **Quebec** for future considerations, June 17, 1989. Signed as a free agent by **Vancouver**, December 1, 1990.

• MASON, Chris

G – L. 6', 200 lbs. b: Red Deer, Alta., 4/20/1976. New Jersey's 7th, 122nd overall in 1995.

Season	Club	League	GP	W	L	T	Mins	GA	SO	Avg	AAvg	Eff	SA	S%	SAPG	GP	W	L	T	Mins	GA	SO	Avg	Eff	SA	S%	SAPG
1992-93	Red Deer Chiefs	AAHA	20	....	....	....	1280	76	0	3.35	....	....	....	....	....	....	....	....	....	....	....	....	....	....	....	....	....
1993-94	Victoria Cougars	WHL	5	1	4	0	237	27	0	6.84	....	....	....	....	....	....	....	....	....	....	....	....	....	....	....	....	....
1994-95	Prince George Cougars	WHL	44	8	30	1	2288	192	1	5.03	....	....	....	....	....	....	....	....	....	....	....	....	....	....	....	....	....
1995-96	Prince George Cougars	WHL	59	16	37	1	3289	236	1	4.31	....	....	....	....	....	....	....	....	....	....	....	....	....	....	....	....	....
1996-97	Prince George Cougars	WHL	50	19	24	4	2851	172	2	3.62	....	....	....	....	....	15	9	6	....	938	44	*1	2.81	....	....	....	....
1997-98	Cincinnati Mighty Ducks	AHL	47	13	19	7	2368	136	0	3.45	....	....	....	....	....	....	....	....	....	....	....	....	....	....	....	....	....
1998-99	**Nashville Predators**	**NHL**	**3**	**0**	**0**	**0**	**69**	**6**	**0**	**5.22**	**6.21**	**7.12**	**44**	**.864**	**38.3**	....	....	....	....	....	....	....	....	....	....	....	....
	Milwaukee Admirals	IHL	34	15	12	6	1901	92	1	2.90	....	....	....	....	....	....	....	....	....	....	....	....	....	....	....	....	....
99-2000	Milwaukee Admirals	IHL	53	20	21	8	2952	137	2	2.78	....	....	....	....	....	3	1	2	....	252	11	0	2.62	....	....	....	....
	NHL Totals		**3**	**0**	**0**	**0**	**69**	**6**	**0**	**5.22**	....	....	**44**	**.864**	**38.3**	....	....	....	....	....	....	....	....	....	....	....	....

Signed as a free agent by **Anaheim**, June 27, 1997. Traded to **Nashville** by **Anaheim** with Marc Moro for Dominic Roussel, October 5, 1998.

• MATTSSON, Markus

Markus Rainer G – R. 6', 180 lbs. b: Suoneiemi, Finland, 7/30/1957. NY Islanders' 6th, 87th overall in 1977.

Season	Club	League	GP	W	L	T	Mins	GA	SO	Avg	AAvg	Eff	SA	S%	SAPG	GP	W	L	T	Mins	GA	SO	Avg	Eff	SA	S%	SAPG
1973-74	Ilves Tampere	Finland	STATISTICS NOT AVAILABLE																								
1974-75	Ilves Tampere	Finland	STATISTICS NOT AVAILABLE																								
	Finland	EJC-A	3	....	....	....	180	9	....	3.00	....	....	....	....	....	....	....	....	....	....	....	....	....	....	....	....	....
	Finland	WJC-A	5	1	3	1	300	14	0	2.80	....	....	....	....	....	....	....	....	....	....	....	....	....	....	....	....	....
1975-76	Ilves Tampere	Finland	STATISTICS NOT AVAILABLE																								
	Finland	EJC-A	4	....	....	....	240	16	....	4.00	....	....	....	....	....	....	....	....	....	....	....	....	....	....	....	....	....
1976-77	Finland	Can-Cup	2	1	1	0	80	14	0	11.00	....	....	....	....	....	....	....	....	....	....	....	....	....	....	....	....	....
	Ilves Tampere	Finland	STATISTICS NOT AVAILABLE																								
1977-78	Tulsa Oilers	CHL	2	1	1	0	92	6	0	3.91	....	....	....	....	....	....	....	....	....	....	....	....	....	....	....	....	....
	Quebec Nordiques	WHA	6	1	3	0	266	30	0	6.77	....	....	....	....	....	....	....	....	....	....	....	....	....	....	....	....	....
	Winnipeg Jets	WHA	10	4	5	0	511	30	0	3.52	....	....	....	....	....	....	....	....	....	....	....	....	....	....	....	....	....
1978-79	Winnipeg Jets	WHA	52	25	21	3	2990	181	0	3.63	....	....	....	....	....	....	....	....	....	....	....	....	....	....	....	....	....
1979-80	**Winnipeg Jets**	**NHL**	**21**	**5**	**11**	**4**	**1200**	**65**	**2**	**3.25**	**2.87**	....	....	....	....	....	....	....	....	....	....	....	....	....	....	....	....
	Tulsa Oilers	CHL	20	10	7	2	1196	56	2	2.81	....	....	....	....	....	....	....	....	....	....	....	....	....	....	....	....	....
1980-81	**Winnipeg Jets**	**NHL**	**31**	**3**	**21**	**4**	**1707**	**128**	**1**	**4.50**	**3.65**	....	....	....	....	....	....	....	....	....	....	....	....	....	....	....	....
	Tulsa Oilers	CHL	5	3	2	0	298	10	1	2.01	....	....	....	....	....	....	....	....	....	....	....	....	....	....	....	....	....
1981-82	Finland	Can-Cup	2	0	2	0	120	15	0	7.50	....	....	....	....	....	....	....	....	....	....	....	....	....	....	....	....	....
	Tulsa Oilers	CHL	50	26	23	0	2963	195	0	3.95	....	....	....	....	....	1	0	1	0	60	7	0	7.00	....	....	....	....
1982-83	**Minnesota North Stars**	**NHL**	**2**	**1**	**1**	**0**	**100**	**6**	**1**	**3.60**	**2.89**	**3.09**	**70**	**.914**	**42.0**	....	....	....	....	....	....	....	....	....	....	....	....
	Birmingham South Stars	CHL	28	17	10	0	1614	89	1	3.31	....	....	....	....	....	....	....	....	....	....	....	....	....	....	....	....	....
	Los Angeles Kings	**NHL**	**19**	**5**	**5**	**4**	**899**	**65**	**1**	**4.34**	**3.49**	**6.21**	**454**	**.857**	**30.3**	....	....	....	....	....	....	....	....	....	....	....	....
1983-84	**Los Angeles Kings**	**NHL**	**19**	**7**	**8**	**2**	**1101**	**79**	**1**	**4.31**	**3.40**	**6.42**	**530**	**.851**	**28.9**	....	....	....	....	....	....	....	....	....	....	....	....
	New Haven Nighthawks	AHL	31	16	10	1	1701	110	0	3.88	....	....	....	....	....	....	....	....	....	....	....	....	....	....	....	....	....
1984-85	Tappara Tampere	Finland	26	....	....	....	1560	101	0	3.88	....	....	....	....	....	....	....	....	....	....	....	....	....	....	....	....	....
1985-86	Tappara Tampere	Finland	34	....	....	....	2041	109	*4	3.20	....	....	....	....	....	8	*6	2	0	479	11	*1	*1.38	....	....	....	....
1986-87	Tappara Tampere	Finland	33	....	....	....	1905	98	0	3.09	....	....	....	....	....	9	5	4	0	540	27	*1	*3.00	....	....	....	....
	NHL Totals		**92**	**21**	**46**	**14**	**5007**	**343**	**6**	**4.11**	....	....	....	....	....	....	....	....	....	....	....	....	....	....	....	....	....
	Other Major League Totals		68	30	29	3	3767	241	0	3.84	....	....	....	....	....	....	....	....	....	....	....	....	....	....	....	....	....

Finnish Rookie of the Year (1975) • Finnish First All-Star Team (1986)

Selected by **Houston** (WHA) in 1977 WHA Amateur Draft, May, 1977. WHA rights traded to **Winnipeg** (WHA) by **Houston** (WHA) for future considerations, June, 1977. Traded to **Quebec** (WHA) by **Winnipeg** (WHA) for future considerations, February, 1978. Traded to **Winnipeg** (WHA) by **Quebec** (WHA) for future considerations, March, 1978. Reclaimed by **NY Islanders** from **Winnipeg** prior to Expansion Draft, June 9, 1979. Claimed as a priority selection by **Winnipeg**, June 9, 1979. Signed as a free agent by **Minnesota**, September 24, 1982. Traded to **LA Kings** by **Minnesota** for LA Kings' 3rd round choice (Stephane Roy) in 1985 Entry Draft, February 1, 1983.

• MAY, Darrell

Darrell Gerald G – L. 6', 175 lbs. b: Edmonton, Alta., 3/6/1962. Vancouver's 4th, 91st overall in 1980.

Season	Club	League	GP	W	L	T	Mins	GA	SO	Avg	AAvg	Eff	SA	S%	SAPG	GP	W	L	T	Mins	GA	SO	Avg	Eff	SA	S%	SAPG
1978-79	Portland Winter Hawks	WHL	21	12	2	2	1113	64	0	3.45	....	....	....	....	....	2	1	0	0	80	7	0	5.25	....	....	....	....
1979-80	Portland Winter Hawks	WHL	43	32	8	1	2416	143	1	3.55	....	....	....	....	....	8	3	5	0	439	27	0	3.69	....	....	....	....
1980-81	Portland Winter Hawks	WHL	36	28	7	1	2128	122	3	3.44	....	....	....	....	....	4	....	....	....	243	21	0	5.19	....	....	....	....
1981-82	Portland Winter Hawks	WHL	53	31	20	2	3097	226	0	4.38	....	....	....	....	....	15	....	....	....	851	59	0	4.16	....	....	....	....
	Portland Winter Hawks	Mem-Cup	2	1	0	0	77	7	0	5.45	....	....	....	....	....	....	....	....	....	....	....	....	....	....	....	....	....
1982-83	Fort Wayne Komets	IHL	46	....	....	....	2584	177	0	4.11	....	....	....	....	....	2	....	....	....	120	13	0	6.50	....	....	....	....
1983-84	Erie Golden Blades	ACHL	43	21	16	2	2404	163	1	4.07	....	....	....	....	....	7	....	....	....	461	16	*1	*2.08	....	....	....	....
1984-85	Peoria Rivermen	IHL	19	13	4	2	1133	56	1	2.97	....	....	....	....	....	10	6	4	0	609	33	0	3.25	....	....	....	....
	Erie Golden Blades	ACHL	43	....	....	....	2580	170	*1	3.95	....	....	....	....	....	....	....	....	....	....	....	....	....	....	....	....	....
1985-86	**St. Louis Blues**	**NHL**	**3**	**1**	**2**	**0**	**184**	**13**	**0**	**4.24**	**3.31**	**6.41**	**86**	**.849**	**28.0**	....	....	....	....	....	....	....	....	....	....	....	....
	Peoria Rivermen	IHL	56	33	21	0	3321	179	1	3.23	....	....	....	....	....	11	6	5	0	634	38	1	3.60	....	....	....	....
1986-87	Peoria Rivermen	IHL	58	26	31	1	3420	214	2	3.75	....	....	....	....	....	....	....	....	....	....	....	....	....	....	....	....	....
1987-88	**St. Louis Blues**	**NHL**	**3**	**0**	**3**	**0**	**180**	**18**	**0**	**6.00**	**5.00**	**10.09**	**107**	**.832**	**35.7**	....	....	....	....	....	....	....	....	....	....	....	....
	Peoria Rivermen	IHL	48	22	19	5	2754	162	1	3.53	....	....	....	....	....	....	....	....	....	....	....	....	....	....	....	....	....
1988-89	Peoria Rivermen	IHL	52	20	22	0	2908	202	0	4.17	....	....	....	....	....	2	0	2	0	137	13	0	5.69	....	....	....	....
	NHL Totals		**6**	**1**	**5**	**0**	**364**	**31**	**0**	**5.11**	....	....	**193**	**.839**	**31.8**	....	....	....	....	....	....	....	....	....	....	....	....

IHL First All-Star Team (1986, 1987) • Won James Gatschene Memorial Trophy (MVP - IHL) (1986)

Signed as a free agent by **St. Louis**, October 9, 1985. Traded to **Montreal** by **St. Louis** with Jocelyn Lemieux and St. Louis' 2nd round choice (Patrice Brisebois) in 1989 Entry Draft for Sergio Momesso and Vincent Riendeau, August 9, 1988.

• MAYER, Gilles

"The Needle" G – L. 5'6", 135 lbs. b: Ottawa, Ont., 8/24/1930.

Season	Club	League	GP	W	L	T	Mins	GA	SO	Avg	AAvg	Eff	SA	S%	SAPG	GP	W	L	T	Mins	GA	SO	Avg	Eff	SA	S%	SAPG
1944-45	Hull Volants	OCHL	7	*6	1	0	420	15	*1	*2.14	....	....	....	....	....	4	2	2	0	240	18	0	4.50	....	....	....	....
1945-46	Hull Volants	OCHL	5	....	....	....	300	35	0	6.99	....	....	....	....	....	....	....	....	....	....	....	....	....	....	....	....	....
1946-47	Lake Placid Roamers	X-Games	STATISTICS NOT AVAILABLE																								
1947-48	Barrie Flyers	OHA-Jr.	19	....	....	....	1140	59	3	3.11	....	....	....	....	....	10	8	2	0	600	36	0	3.60	....	....	....	....
	Barrie Flyers	Mem-Cup	5	4	1	0	300	20	0	4.00	....	....	....	....	....	....	....	....	....	....	....	....	....	....	....	....	....
1948-49	Barrie Flyers	OHA-Jr.	46	*26	16	4	2760	134	*5	*2.91	....	....	....	....	....	8	8	0	0	480	21	*1	*2.63	....	....	....	....
	Barrie Flyers	Mem-Cup	8	4	4	0	490	22	1	2.69	....	....	....	....	....	....	....	....	....	....	....	....	....	....	....	....	....
1949-50	Pittsburgh Hornets	AHL	50	20	19	11	3000	142	4	2.84	....	....	....	....	....	....	....	....	....	....	....	....	....	....	....	....	....
	Toronto Maple Leafs	**NHL**	**1**	**0**	**1**	**0**	**60**	**2**	**0**	**2.00**	**2.23**	....	....	....	....	....	....	....	....	....	....	....	....	....	....	....	....
1950-51	Pittsburgh Hornets	AHL	71	31	33	7	*4350	174	*6	*2.40	....	....	....	....	....	*13	*9	4	0	835	26	*2	*1.87	....	....	....	....
1951-52	Pittsburgh Hornets	AHL	*68	*46	19	3	*4120	175	*5	2.55	....	....	....	....	....	11	*8	3	0	753	24	*1	*1.91	....	....	....	....
1952-53	Pittsburgh Hornets	AHL	62	36	20	6	3760	146	*6	*2.33	....	....	....	....	....	10	6	4	0	695	20	0	1.73	....	....	....	....
1953-54	Pittsburgh Hornets	AHL	68	33	30	5	4080	212	3	3.12	....	....	....	....	....	5	2	3	0	330	13	*1	*2.36	....	....	....	....
	Toronto Maple Leafs	**NHL**	**1**	**0**	**0**	**1**	**60**	**3**	**0**	**3.00**	**3.81**	....	....	....	....	....	....	....	....	....	....	....	....	....	....	....	....
1954-55	Pittsburgh Hornets	AHL	*64	31	25	8	*3840	179	*3	*2.80	....	....	....	....	....	*10	*7	3	0	639	28	*1	*2.63	....	....	....	....
	Toronto Maple Leafs	**NHL**	**1**	**1**	**0**	**0**	**60**	**1**	**0**	**1.00**	**1.21**	....	....	....	....	....	....	....	....	....	....	....	....	....	....	....	....
1955-56	Pittsburgh Hornets	AHL	56	40	12	4	3360	151	*5	*2.70	....	....	....	....	....	4	1	3	0	312	14	0	2.69	....	....	....	....
	Toronto Maple Leafs	**NHL**	**6**	**1**	**5**	**0**	**360**	**18**	**0**	**3.00**	**3.68**	....	....	....	....	....	....	....	....	....	....	....	....	....	....	....	....
1956-57	Hershey Bears	AHL	29	14	12	3	1740	103	1	3.55	....	....	....	....	....	....	....	....	....	....	....	....	....	....	....	....	....

			REGULAR SEASON													PLAYOFFS											
Season	**Club**	**League**	**GP**	**W**	**L**	**T**	**Mins**	**GA**	**SO**	**Avg**	**AAvg**	**Eff**	**SA**	**S%**	**SAPG**	**GP**	**W**	**L**	**T**	**Mins**	**GA**	**SO**	**Avg**	**Eff**	**SA**	**S%**	**SAPG**
1957-58	Hershey Bears	AHL	22	12	7	3	1358	62	0	2.74	....	....	....	....	....	....	....	....	....	....	....	....	....	....	....	....	....
1958-59	Hershey Bears	AHL	19	....	....	....	1140	61	0	3.21	....	....	....	....	....	....	....	....	....	....	....	....	....	....	....	....	....
1959-60	Cleveland Barons	AHL	41	19	19	3	2460	126	3	3.07	....	....	....	....	....	7	3	4	0	420	22	*1	3.14	....	....	....	....
1960-61	Cleveland Barons	AHL	66	32	34	0	3960	222	3	3.36	....	....	....	....	....	....	....	....	....	....	....	....	....	....	....	....	....
1961-62	Providence Reds	AHL	30	16	13	1	1800	122	1	4.07	....	....	....	....	....	3	1	2	0	185	11	0	3.57	....	....	....	....
1962-63	Providence Reds	AHL	34	16	15	3	2040	99	1	2.91	....	....	....	....	....	....	....	....	....	....	....	....	....	....	....	....	....
	NHL Totals		**9**	**2**	**6**	**1**	**540**	**24**	**0**	**2.67**	....	....	....	....	....	....	....	....	....	....	....	....	....	....	....	....	....

AHL First All-Star Team (1951, 1954, 1955) • Won Harry "Hap" Holmes Memorial Award (fewest goals against - AHL) (1951, 1953, 1954, 1955, 1956) • AHL Second All-Star Team (1953, 1956)

Promoted to **Toronto** from **Pittsburgh** (AHL) to replace Turk Broda, December 1, 1949. (Detroit 2, Toronto 1). Promoted to **Toronto** from **Pittsburgh** (AHL) to replace Harry Lumley, March 4, 1954 (Toronto 3, Detroit 3) and October 21, 1954 (Toronto 3, Montreal 1). Traded to **Detroit** (Hershey-AHL) by **Toronto** (Pittsburgh-AHL) with Jack Price, Willie Marshall, Bob Hassard, Bob Solinger and Ray Gariepy for cash, July 7, 1956. Traded to **Cleveland** (AHL) by **Hershey** (AHL) for Gord Hollingworth and Claude Dufour, June, 1959.

• McAULEY, Ken

Kenneth Leslie "Tubby" G – R. 5'10", 190 lbs. b: Edmonton, Alta., 1/9/1921.

Season	Club	League	GP	W	L	T	Mins	GA	SO	Avg	AAvg	Eff	SA	S%	SAPG	GP	W	L	T	Mins	GA	SO	Avg	Eff	SA	S%	SAPG
1938-39	Edmonton Maple Leafs	EJrHL	11	....	....	....	660	38	0	3.45	....	....	....	....	....	....	....	....	....	....	....	....	....	....	....	....	....
1939-40	Edmonton Maple Leafs	EJrHL		STATISTICS NOT AVAILABLE																							
1940-41	Edmonton Maple Leafs	EJrHL		STATISTICS NOT AVAILABLE																							
1941-42	Regina Rangers	S-SSHL	32	11	16	5	1970	136	2	4.14	....	....	....	....	....	3	0	3	0	180	15	0	5.00	....	....	....	....
1942-43				MILITARY SERVICE																							
1943-44	**New York Rangers**	**NHL**	***50**	**6**	**39**	**5**	**2980**	**310**	**0**	**6.24**	**5.20**	....	....	....	....	....	....	....	....	....	....	....	....	....	....	....	....
1944-45	**New York Rangers**	**NHL**	**46**	**11**	**25**	**10**	**2760**	**227**	**1**	**4.93**	**4.36**	....	....	....	....	....	....	....	....	....	....	....	....	....	....	....	....
1945-46	Edmonton Flyers	WCSHL	36	24	10	2	2200	130	0	3.55	....	....	....	....	....	8	4	4	0	490	31	0	3.80	....	....	....	....
1946-47	Edmonton Flyers	WCSHL	40	22	16	2	2460	139	1	3.39	....	....	....	....	....	1	0	1	0	60	5	0	5.00	....	....	....	....
1947-48	Saskatoon Quakers	WCSHL	48	10	36	2	2900	234	0	4.84	....	....	....	....	....	....	....	....	....	....	....	....	....	....	....	....	....
1948-49	Saskatoon Quakers	WCSHL	6	....	....	....	353	42	0	7.14	....	....	....	....	....	....	....	....	....	....	....	....	....	....	....	....	....
1949-50	Kimberley Dynamiters	WIHL	1	1	0	0	60	2	0	2.00	....	....	....	....	....	....	....	....	....	....	....	....	....	....	....	....	....
	NHL Totals		**96**	**17**	**64**	**15**	**5740**	**537**	**1**	**5.61**	....	....	....	....	....	....	....	....	....	....	....	....	....	....	....	....	....

Signed as a free agent by **NY Rangers**, October 16, 1943.

• McCARTAN, Jack

John William G. 6'1", 195 lbs. b: St. Paul, MN, 8/5/1935. **USHOF**

Season	Club	League	GP	W	L	T	Mins	GA	SO	Avg	AAvg	Eff	SA	S%	SAPG	GP	W	L	T	Mins	GA	SO	Avg	Eff	SA	S%	SAPG
1955-56	University of Minnesota	WCHA	24	....	....	....	1440	67	0	2.79	....	....	....	....	....	....	....	....	....	....	....	....	....	....	....	....	....
1956-57	University of Minnesota	WCHA	15	....	....	....	900	43	0	2.87	....	....	....	....	....	....	....	....	....	....	....	....	....	....	....	....	....
1957-58	University of Minnesota	WCHA	28	....	....	....	1680	89	1	3.18	....	....	....	....	....	....	....	....	....	....	....	....	....	....	....	....	....
1958-59	United States	Nat-Team	29	....	....	....	1740	104	0	3.65	....	....	....	....	....	3	....	....	....	180	12	0	4.00	....	....	....	....
1959-60	Minneapolis Rangers	CHL	5	....	....	....	300	17	1	3.40	....	....	....	....	....	....	....	....	....	....	....	....	....	....	....	....	....
	United States	Olympics	5	*5	0	0	300	11	0	*2.20	....	....	....	....	....	....	....	....	....	....	....	....	....	....	....	....	....
	New York Rangers	**NHL**	**4**	**1**	**1**	**2**	**240**	**7**	**0**	**1.75**	**1.82**	....	....	....	....	....	....	....	....	....	....	....	....	....	....	....	....
1960-61	**New York Rangers**	**NHL**	**8**	**1**	**6**	**1**	**440**	**35**	**1**	**4.77**	**4.97**	....	....	....	....	....	....	....	....	....	....	....	....	....	....	....	....
	Kitchener-Waterloo Beavers	EPHL	52	25	21	6	3120	145	2	2.79	....	....	....	....	....	7	3	4	0	421	20	*2	2.85	....	....	....	....
1961-62	Kitchener-Waterloo Beavers	EPHL	*70	36	24	10	*4200	217	*5	3.10	....	....	....	....	....	7	3	4	0	451	20	0	2.66	....	....	....	....
1962-63	Los Angeles Blades	WHL	60	31	27	2	3600	187	4	3.12	....	....	....	....	....	3	1	2	0	181	9	0	2.98	....	....	....	....
1963-64	St. Louis Braves	CPHL	*67	31	30	6	*4020	262	3	3.91	....	....	....	....	....	6	2	4	0	361	27	0	4.49	....	....	....	....
1964-65	St. Louis Braves	CPHL	5	1	4	0	300	27	0	5.40	....	....	....	....	....	....	....	....	....	....	....	....	....	....	....	....	....
	Los Angeles Blades	WHL	32	8	22	2	1948	122	1	3.76	....	....	....	....	....	....	....	....	....	....	....	....	....	....	....	....	....
1965-66	San Francisco Seals	WHL	53	23	27	3	3229	183	2	3.40	....	....	....	....	....	....	....	....	....	....	....	....	....	....	....	....	....
1966-67	California Seals	WHL	61	25	26	10	3784	200	1	3.17	....	....	....	....	....	5	2	3	0	300	13	0	2.60	....	....	....	....
1967-68	Omaha Knights	CPHL	43	9	25	7	2380	148	1	3.77	....	....	....	....	....	....	....	....	....	....	....	....	....	....	....	....	....
1968-69	San Diego Gulls	WHL	43	20	14	6	2380	134	0	3.38	....	....	....	....	....	1	0	0	0	20	2	0	6.00	....	....	....	....
1969-70	San Diego Gulls	WHL	52	21	20	9	3025	162	3	3.21	....	....	....	....	....	4	0	3	0	199	19	0	5.73	....	....	....	....
1970-71	San Diego Gulls	WHL	*55	24	20	11	*3239	161	3	2.98	....	....	....	....	....	6	2	4	0	379	24	0	3.80	....	....	....	....
1971-72	San Diego Gulls	WHL	36	14	16	2	1955	112	0	3.44	....	....	....	....	....	2	0	2	0	118	6	0	3.05	....	....	....	....
1972-73	Minnesota Fighting Saints	WHA	38	15	19	1	2160	129	1	3.58	....	....	....	....	....	4	1	2	0	213	14	0	3.94	....	....	....	....
1973-74	Minnesota Fighting Saints	WHA	2	0	0	0	42	5	0	7.14	....	....	....	....	....	....	....	....	....	....	....	....	....	....	....	....	....
	Suncoast Suns	SHL	6	....	....	....	323	26	0	4.83	....	....	....	....	....	....	....	....	....	....	....	....	....	....	....	....	....
1974-75	Minnesota Fighting Saints	WHA	2	1	0	0	61	5	0	4.92	....	....	....	....	....	....	....	....	....	....	....	....	....	....	....	....	....
	NHL Totals		**12**	**2**	**7**	**3**	**680**	**42**	**1**	**3.71**	....	....	....	....	....	....	....	....	....	....	....	....	....	....	....	....	....
	Other Major League Totals		42	16	19	1	2263	139	1	3.69	....	....	....	....	....	4	1	2	....	213	14	0	3.94	....	....	....	....

WCHA First All-Star Team (1957, 1958) • NCAA West First All-American Team (1958) • Named Best Goaltender at Olympic Games (1960) • WHL Second All-Star Team (1969) • WHL First All-Star Team (1970, 1971)

Signed to five-game amateur tryout contract by **NY Rangers** following 1960 Winter Olympic Games, March 2, 1960. Traded to **LA Blades** (WHL) by **NY Rangers** for cash, October 2, 1962. Claimed by **Chicago** from **LA Blades** (WHL) in Inter-League Draft, June 4, 1963. Traded to **LA Blades** (WHL) by **Chicago** for cash, January, 1965. Traded to **San Francisco** (WHL) by **LA Blades** (WHL) for Paul Jackson, June, 1965. NHL rights transferred to **California** after owners of **San Francisco** (WHL) franchise granted expansion team, April 6, 1966. Claimed by **San Diego** (WHL) from **Oakland** in Reverse Draft, June 13, 1968. Selected by **Minnesota** (WHA) in 1972 WHA General Player Draft, February 12, 1972.

• McCOOL, Frank

"Ulcers" G – L. 6', 170 lbs. b: Calgary, Alta., 10/27/1918 d: 5/20/1973.

Season	Club	League	GP	W	L	T	Mins	GA	SO	Avg	AAvg	Eff	SA	S%	SAPG	GP	W	L	T	Mins	GA	SO	Avg	Eff	SA	S%	SAPG
1936-37	Calgary Bronks	ASHL	2	....	....	....	120	9	0	4.50	....	....	....	....	....	....	....	....	....	....	....	....	....	....	....	....	....
	Calgary Canadians	CCJHL	1	....	....	....	60	3	0	3.00	....	....	....	....	....	....	....	....	....	....	....	....	....	....	....	....	....
1937-38	Calgary Columbus Club	CCSHL	12	....	....	....	720	47	*1	3.92	....	....	....	....	....	3	....	....	....	180	8	0	2.67	....	....	....	....
	Calgary Canadians	Mem-Cup	4	1	3	0	240	19	0	4.75	....	....	....	....	....	....	....	....	....	....	....	....	....	....	....	....	....
1938-39	Calgary Columbus Club	CCSHL		STATISTICS NOT AVAILABLE																							
1939-40	Gonzaga University	WKHL	8	....	....	....	480	46	0	5.75	....	....	....	....	....	....	....	....	....	....	....	....	....	....	....	....	....
1940-41	Gonzaga University	SCSHL		STATISTICS NOT AVAILABLE																							
1941-42	Gonzaga University	SCSHL		STATISTICS NOT AVAILABLE																							
1942-43	Calgary Currie Army	ASHL	24	....	....	....	1440	81	*1	*3.37	....	....	....	....	....	5	3	2	0	300	20	0	4.00	....	....	....	....
	Calgary Currie Army	Al-Cup	5	2	3	0	300	20	0	4.00	....	....	....	....	....	....	....	....	....	....	....	....	....	....	....	....	....
1943-44				MILITARY SERVICE																							
1944-45♦	**Toronto Maple Leafs**	**NHL**	***50**	**24**	**22**	**4**	***3000**	**161**	***4**	**3.22**	**2.60**	....	....	....	....	**13**	***8**	**5**	....	**807**	**30**	***4**	**2.23**	....	....	....	....
1945-46	**Toronto Maple Leafs**	**NHL**	**22**	**10**	**9**	**3**	**1320**	**81**	**0**	**3.68**	**3.38**	....	....	....	....	....	....	....	....	....	....	....	....	....	....	....	....
	NHL Totals		**72**	**34**	**31**	**7**	**4320**	**242**	**4**	**3.36**	....	....	....	....	....	**13**	**8**	**5**	....	**807**	**30**	**4**	**2.23**	....	....	....	....

Won Calder Memorial Trophy (1945)

Signed as a free agent by **Toronto**, October 25, 1944.

• McDUFFE, Peter

Peter Arnold G – L. 5'9", 180 lbs. b: Milton, Ont., 2/16/1948.

Season	Club	League	GP	W	L	T	Mins	GA	SO	Avg	AAvg	Eff	SA	S%	SAPG	GP	W	L	T	Mins	GA	SO	Avg	Eff	SA	S%	SAPG
1964-65	St. Catharines Black Hawks	OHA-Jr.	2	0	1	0	80	9	0	6.92	....	....	....	....	....	....	....	....	....	....	....	....	....	....	....	....	....
1965-66	St. Catharines Black Hawks	OHA-Jr.	21	....	....	....	1260	112	0	5.33	....	....	....	....	....	....	....	....	....	....	....	....	....	....	....	....	....
1966-67	St. Catharines Black Hawks	OHA-Jr.	30	....	....	....	1840	90	2	*2.93	....	....	....	....	....	6	....	....	....	360	26	0	4.33	....	....	....	....
	Buffalo Bisons	AHL	2	0	2	0	120	13	0	6.50	....	....	....	....	....	....	....	....	....	....	....	....	....	....	....	....	....
1967-68	St. Catharines Black Hawks	OHA-Jr.	50	....	....	....	3036	192	0	3.79	....	....	....	....	....	5	....	....	....	300	34	0	6.80	....	....	....	....
1968-69	Greensboro Generals	EHL	65	....	....	....	3900	246	4	3.78	....	....	....	....	....	8	....	....	....	480	28	0	3.50	....	....	....	....
1969-70	Omaha Rangers	CHL	*59	*26	24	9	*3500	174	2	2.98	....	....	....	....	....	*12	*8	4	0	*720	31	*1	*2.58	....	....	....	....
1970-71	Omaha Rangers	CHL	*57	....	....	....	*3420	57	3	2.77	....	....	....	....	....	*11	*8	3	0	*692	26	*2	*2.36	....	....	....	....
1971-72	**St. Louis Blues**	**NHL**	**10**	**0**	**6**	**0**	**467**	**29**	**0**	**3.73**	**3.78**	....	....	....	....	**1**	**0**	**1**	....	**60**	**7**	**0**	**7.00**	....	....	....	....
	Denver Spurs	WHL	21	10	7	2	1126	65	1	3.46	....	....	....	....	....	4	4	0	0	240	6	1	1.50	....	....	....	....
1972-73	**New York Rangers**	**NHL**	**1**	**1**	**0**	**0**	**60**	**1**	**0**	**1.00**	**0.94**	....	....	....	....	....	....	....	....	....	....	....	....	....	....	....	....
1973-74	**New York Rangers**	**NHL**	**6**	**3**	**2**	**1**	**340**	**18**	**0**	**3.18**	**3.07**	....	....	....	....	....	....	....	....	....	....	....	....	....	....	....	....
	Providence Reds	AHL	36	17	12	6	2098	123	0	3.51	....	....	....	....	....	*14	8	6	0	*883	45	*1	3.05	....	....	....	....
1974-75	**Kansas City Scouts**	**NHL**	**36**	**7**	**25**	**4**	**2100**	**148**	**0**	**4.23**	**3.85**	....	....	....	....	....	....	....	....	....	....	....	....	....	....	....	....

			REGULAR SEASON													PLAYOFFS											
Season	Club	League	GP	W	L	T	Mins	GA	SO	Avg	AAvg	Eff	SA	S%	SAPG	GP	W	L	T	Mins	GA	SO	Avg	Eff	SA	S%	SAPG
1975-76	**Detroit Red Wings**	**NHL**	**4**	**0**	**3**	**1**	**240**	**22**	**0**	**5.50**	**4.99**	....	....	....	....	....	....	....	....	....	....	....	....	....	....	....	....
	New Haven Nighthawks	AHL	21	8	9	3	1245	85	0	4.10	....	....	....	....	....	1	0	1	0	60	4	0	4.00	....	....	....	....
1976-77	Rhode Island Reds	AHL	11	....	....	....	621	46	0	4.44	....	....	....	....	....	....	....	....	....	....	....	....	....	....	....	....	....
	New Haven Nighthawks	AHL	6	....	....	....	323	32	0	5.94	....	....	....	....	....	....	....	....	....	....	....	....	....	....	....	....	....
1977-78	Indianapolis Racers	WHA	12	1	6	1	539	39	0	4.34	....	....	....	....	....	....	....	....	....	....	....	....	....	....	....	....	....
1978-79			OUT OF HOCKEY – RETIRED																								
1979-80	Georgetown Gyros	GBSHL	32	....	....	....	1920	141	0	4.41	....	....	....	....	....	....	....	....	....	....	....	....	....	....	....	....	....
1980-81	Georgetown Gyros	OHA-I	34	....	....	....	2060	111	0	3.23	....	....	....	....	....	....	....	....	....	....	....	....	....	....	....	....	....
	NHL Totals		**57**	**11**	**36**	**6**	**3207**	**218**	**0**	**4.08**	....	....	....	....	....	**1**	**0**	**1**	....	**60**	**7**	**0**	**7.00**	....	....	....	....
	Other Major League Totals		12	1	6	1	539	39	0	4.34	....	....	....	....	....	....	....	....	....	....	....	....	....	....	....	....	....

OHA-Jr. First All-Star Team (1967) • EHL South First All-Star Team (1969) • EHL South Rookie of the Year (1969) • CHL Second All-Star Team (1970) • CHL First All-Star Team (1971) • Shared Tommy Ivan Trophy (MVP - CHL) with Andre Dupont, Gerry Ouellette & Joe Zanussi (1971) • Shared WHL Leading Goaltender Award with Bob Johnson (1972)

Claimed by **Phoenix** (WHL) from **Chicago** in Reverse Draft, June 12, 1969. Traded to **NY Rangers** by **Phoenix** (WHL) for Don Caley and Sandy Snow, July 3, 1969. Traded to **St. Louis** by **NY Rangers** for St. Louis' 1st round choice (Steve Vickers) in 1971 Amateur Draft, May 25, 1971. Selected by **NY Raiders** (WHA) in 1972 WHA General Player Draft, February 12, 1972. Traded to **NY Rangers** by **St. Louis** with Curt Bennett to complete transaction that sent Steve Durbano to St. Louis (May 24, 1972), June 7, 1972. Claimed by **Kansas City** from **NY Rangers** in Expansion Draft, June 12, 1974. Traded to **Detroit** by **Kansas City** with Glen Burdon for Gary Bergman and Bill McKenzie, August 22, 1975. Signed as a free agent by **Indianapolis** (WHA), September, 1977.

• McGRATTAN, Tom

G – L. 6'2", 170 lbs. b: Brantford, Ont., 10/19/1927.

Season	Club	League	GP	W	L	T	Mins	GA	SO	Avg	AAvg	Eff	SA	S%	SAPG	GP	W	L	T	Mins	GA	SO	Avg	Eff	SA	S%	SAPG
1944-45	Brantford Lions	OHA-B	12	*10	2	0	720	37	0	3.17	....	....	....	....	....	4	1	3	0	240	20	0	5.00	....	....	....	....
1945-46	Galt Red Wings	OHA-Jr.	21	....	....	....	1260	66	2	3.14	....	....	....	....	....	3	....	....	....	180	14	0	4.67	....	....	....	....
1946-47	Windsor Spitfires	OHA-Jr.	16	....	....	....	960	62	0	3.87	....	....	....	....	....	....	....	....	....	....	....	....	....	....	....	....	....
	Windsor Spitfires	IHL	3	2	1	0	180	17	0	5.67	....	....	....	....	....	....	....	....	....	....	....	....	....	....	....	....	....
	Stratford Kroehlers	OHA-Jr.	....	....	....	....	....	....	....	....	....	....	....	....	....	2	0	2	0	120	10	0	5.00	....	....	....	....
1947-48	Detroit Bright's Goodyears	IHL	15	....	....	....	900	75	1	5.00	....	....	....	....	....	2	0	2	0	120	11	0	5.50	....	....	....	....
	Detroit Red Wings	**NHL**	**1**	**0**	**0**	**0**	**8**	**1**	**0**	**7.50**	**7.81**	....	....	....	....	....	....	....	....	....	....	....	....	....	....	....	....
1948-49	Owen Sound Mercurys	OHA-Sr.	25	....	....	....	1500	125	0	5.00	....	....	....	....	....	4	....	....	....	240	26	0	6.50	....	....	....	....
1949-50	Brantford Nationals	OSrBL	STATISTICS NOT AVAILABLE																								
	NHL Totals		**1**	**0**	**0**	**0**	**8**	**1**	**0**	**7.50**	....	....	....	....	....	....	....	....	....	....	....	....	....	....	....	....	....

Signed as a free agent by **Detroit**, March 20, 1945. • **Detroit's** spare goaltender replaced injured Harry Lumley in 3rd period, November 9, 1947. (Toronto 6, Detroit 0)

• McKAY, Ross

Ross Lee G – R. 5'11", 175 lbs. b: Edmonton, Alta., 3/3/1964.

Season	Club	League	GP	W	L	T	Mins	GA	SO	Avg	AAvg	Eff	SA	S%	SAPG	GP	W	L	T	Mins	GA	SO	Avg	Eff	SA	S%	SAPG
1981-82	Calgary Northmen	AAHA	STATISTICS NOT AVAILABLE																								
	Calgary Wranglers	WHL	1	....	....	....	53	1	0	1.13	....	....	....	....	....	....	....	....	....	....	....	....	....	....	....	....	....
1982-83	Calgary Wranglers	WHL	29	14	6	0	1404	91	0	3.89	....	....	....	....	....	2	....	....	....	35	5	0	8.57	....	....	....	....
1983-84	Calgary Wranglers	WHL	42	....	....	....	2342	175	0	4.48	....	....	....	....	....	1	0	1	0	60	9	0	9.00	....	....	....	....
1984-85	University of Saskatchewan	CWUAA	18	....	....	....	1099	59	*2	3.22	....	....	....	....	....	....	....	....	....	....	....	....	....	....	....	....	....
1985-86	University of Saskatchewan	CWUAA	15	....	....	....	887	59	*2	3.99	....	....	....	....	....	....	....	....	....	....	....	....	....	....	....	....	....
1986-87	University of Saskatchewan	CWUAA	18	....	....	....	996	58	0	3.49	....	....	....	....	....	....	....	....	....	....	....	....	....	....	....	....	....
1987-88	University of Saskatchewan	CWUAA	16	*12	3	0	920	42	1	*2.74	....	....	....	....	....	2	1	1	0	148	11	0	4.46	....	....	....	....
1988-89	Binghamton Whalers	AHL	19	5	9	2	938	81	1	5.18	....	....	....	....	....	....	....	....	....	....	....	....	....	....	....	....	....
	Indianapolis Ice	IHL	5	1	3	0	187	18	0	5.78	....	....	....	....	....	....	....	....	....	....	....	....	....	....	....	....	....
1989-90	Binghamton Whalers	AHL	18	0	10	1	713	58	0	4.88	....	....	....	....	....	....	....	....	....	....	....	....	....	....	....	....	....
	Knoxville Cherokees	ECHL	8	4	2	1	426	20	0	2.81	....	....	....	....	....	....	....	....	....	....	....	....	....	....	....	....	....
1990-91	**Hartford Whalers**	**NHL**	**1**	**0**	**0**	**0**	**35**	**3**	**0**	**5.14**	**4.62**	**10.28**	**15**	**.800**	**25.7**	....	....	....	....	....	....	....	....	....	....	....	....
	Springfield Indians	AHL	23	7	10	3	1275	75	0	3.53	....	....	....	....	....	3	1	2	0	191	11	0	3.46	....	....	....	....
	NHL Totals		**1**	**0**	**0**	**0**	**35**	**3**	**0**	**5.14**	....	....	**15**	**.800**	**25.7**	....	....	....	....	....	....	....	....	....	....	....	....

CWUAA Second All-Star Team (1985, 1987) • CWUAA First All-Star Team (1988)

Signed as a free agent by **Hartford**, May 2, 1988.

• McKENZIE, Bill

William Ian G – R. 5'11", 180 lbs. b: St. Thomas, Ont., 3/12/1949.

Season	Club	League	GP	W	L	T	Mins	GA	SO	Avg	AAvg	Eff	SA	S%	SAPG	GP	W	L	T	Mins	GA	SO	Avg	Eff	SA	S%	SAPG
1969-70	Ohio State University	CCHA	25	....	....	....	1500	79	4	3.16	....	....	....	....	....	....	....	....	....	....	....	....	....	....	....	....	....
1970-71	Ohio State University	CCHA	24	....	....	....	1420	65	2	2.74	....	....	....	....	....	....	....	....	....	....	....	....	....	....	....	....	....
1971-72	Ohio State University	CCHA	22	....	....	....	1280	48	2	2.25	....	....	....	....	....	....	....	....	....	....	....	....	....	....	....	....	....
1972-73	Port Huron Wings	IHL	45	....	....	....	2532	120	2	2.84	....	....	....	....	....	5	3	2	0	280	6	*2	*1.29	....	....	....	....
1973-74	**Detroit Red Wings**	**NHL**	**13**	**4**	**4**	**4**	**720**	**43**	**1**	**3.58**	**3.46**	....	....	....	....	....	....	....	....	....	....	....	....	....	....	....	....
	Virginia Wings	AHL	29	8	13	2	1470	99	1	4.04	....	....	....	....	....	....	....	....	....	....	....	....	....	....	....	....	....
	London Lions	Britain	2	....	....	....	120	6	0	3.00	....	....	....	....	....	....	....	....	....	....	....	....	....	....	....	....	....
1974-75	**Detroit Red Wings**	**NHL**	**13**	**1**	**9**	**2**	**740**	**58**	**0**	**4.70**	**4.26**	....	....	....	....	....	....	....	....	....	....	....	....	....	....	....	....
	Virginia Wings	AHL	14	8	6	0	700	33	1	2.82	....	....	....	....	....	....	....	....	....	....	....	....	....	....	....	....	....
1975-76	**Kansas City Scouts**	**NHL**	**22**	**1**	**16**	**1**	**1120**	**97**	**0**	**5.20**	**4.74**	....	....	....	....	....	....	....	....	....	....	....	....	....	....	....	....
1976-77	Rhode Island Reds	AHL	2	0	1	1	125	10	0	4.80	....	....	....	....	....	....	....	....	....	....	....	....	....	....	....	....	....
	Colorado Rockies	**NHL**	**5**	**0**	**2**	**1**	**200**	**8**	**0**	**2.40**	**2.23**	....	....	....	....	....	....	....	....	....	....	....	....	....	....	....	....
	Oklahoma City Blazers	CHL	6	2	3	1	358	24	0	4.02	....	....	....	....	....	....	....	....	....	....	....	....	....	....	....	....	....
	Kansas City Blues	CHL	10	7	2	1	513	25	0	2.92	....	....	....	....	....	*10	*8	2	0	*634	23	*2	*2.18	....	....	....	....
1977-78	**Colorado Rockies**	**NHL**	**12**	**3**	**6**	**2**	**654**	**42**	**0**	**3.85**	**3.61**	....	....	....	....	....	....	....	....	....	....	....	....	....	....	....	....
	Hampton Gulls	AHL	12	7	4	0	645	38	1	3.53	....	....	....	....	....	....	....	....	....	....	....	....	....	....	....	....	....
	Philadelphia Firebirds	AHL	5	1	4	0	305	22	1	4.33	....	....	....	....	....	....	....	....	....	....	....	....	....	....	....	....	....
1978-79	Tulsa Oilers	CHL	35	6	25	1	1935	164	0	5.09	....	....	....	....	....	....	....	....	....	....	....	....	....	....	....	....	....
1979-80	**Colorado Rockies**	**NHL**	**26**	**9**	**12**	**3**	**1342**	**78**	**1**	**3.49**	**3.09**	....	....	....	....	....	....	....	....	....	....	....	....	....	....	....	....
	Fort Worth Texans	CHL	9	2	5	1	521	29	1	3.34	....	....	....	....	....	....	....	....	....	....	....	....	....	....	....	....	....
	NHL Totals		**91**	**18**	**49**	**13**	**4776**	**326**	**2**	**4.10**	....	....	....	....	....	....	....	....	....	....	....	....	....	....	....	....	....

IHL First All-Star Team (1973)

Signed as a free agent by **Detroit**, October 4, 1972. Traded to **Kansas City** by **Detroit** with Gary Bergman for Peter McDuffe and Glen Burdon, August 22, 1975. Transferred to **Colorado** after **Kansas City** franchise relocated, July 15, 1976.

• McKICHAN, Steve

G – L. 5'11", 180 lbs. b: Strathroy, Ont., 5/29/1967. Vancouver's 2nd, 7th overall in 1988 Supplemental Draft.

Season	Club	League	GP	W	L	T	Mins	GA	SO	Avg	AAvg	Eff	SA	S%	SAPG	GP	W	L	T	Mins	GA	SO	Avg	Eff	SA	S%	SAPG
1983-84	Strathroy Blades	OJHL-B	1	0	1	0	45	9	0	12.00	....	....	....	....	....	....	....	....	....	....	....	....	....	....	....	....	....
1984-85	Strathroy Blades	OJHL-B	23	....	....	....	1372	165	0	7.26	....	....	....	....	....	....	....	....	....	....	....	....	....	....	....	....	....
1985-86	Strathroy Blades	OJHL-B	17	....	....	....	1020	99	0	5.82	....	....	....	....	....	....	....	....	....	....	....	....	....	....	....	....	....
1986-87	University of Miami-Ohio	CCHA	28	3	19	0	1351	130	0	5.77	....	....	....	....	....	....	....	....	....	....	....	....	....	....	....	....	....
1987-88	University of Miami-Ohio	CCHA	34	12	17	1	1767	140	1	4.75	....	....	....	....	....	....	....	....	....	....	....	....	....	....	....	....	....
1988-89	University of Miami-Ohio	CCHA	21	4	15	0	1014	85	0	5.03	....	....	....	....	....	....	....	....	....	....	....	....	....	....	....	....	....
1989-90	Virginia Lancers	ECHL	28	16	11	2	1445	97	0	4.02	....	....	....	....	....	3	1	2	0	209	11	0	3.16	....	....	....	....
	Milwaukee Admirals	IHL	1	1	0	0	40	2	0	3.00	....	....	....	....	....	....	....	....	....	....	....	....	....	....	....	....	....
1990-91	**Vancouver Canucks**	**NHL**	**1**	**0**	**0**	**0**	**20**	**2**	**0**	**6.00**	**5.39**	**15.00**	**8**	**.750**	**24.0**	....	....	....	....	....	....	....	....	....	....	....	....
	Milwaukee Admirals	IHL	30	12	10	2	1571	87	2	3.32	....	....	....	....	....	4	1	2	0	212	13	0	3.68	....	....	....	....
	NHL Totals		**1**	**0**	**0**	**0**	**20**	**2**	**0**	**6.00**	....	....	**8**	**.750**	**24.0**	....	....	....	....	....	....	....	....	....	....	....	....

• Suffered eventual career-ending neck injury in game vs. Peoria (IHL), December 15, 1990.

• McLACHLAN, Murray

G – L. 6', 195 lbs. b: London, Ont., 10/20/1948.

Season	Club	League	GP	W	L	T	Mins	GA	SO	Avg	AAvg	Eff	SA	S%	SAPG	GP	W	L	T	Mins	GA	SO	Avg	Eff	SA	S%	SAPG
1965-66	Toronto Westclairs	OHA-B	STATISTICS NOT AVAILABLE																								
1966-67	Toronto Westclairs	OHA-B	STATISTICS NOT AVAILABLE																								
1967-68	University of Minnesota	WCHA	22	13	9	0	1320	71	2	3.23	....	....	....	....	....	....	....	....	....	....	....	....	....	....	....	....	....
1968-69	University of Minnesota	WCHA	24	12	7	2	1178	53	1	2.70	....	....	....	....	....	....	....	....	....	....	....	....	....	....	....	....	....
1969-70	University of Minnesota	WCHA	25	*18	7	0	1500	81	*2	*3.24	....	....	....	....	....	....	....	....	....	....	....	....	....	....	....	....	....

			REGULAR SEASON													PLAYOFFS											
Season	**Club**	**League**	**GP**	**W**	**L**	**T**	**Mins**	**GA**	**SO**	**Avg**	**AAvg**	**Eff**	**SA**	**S%**	**SAPG**	**GP**	**W**	**L**	**T**	**Mins**	**GA**	**SO**	**Avg**	**Eff**	**SA**	**S%**	**SAPG**
1970-71	**Toronto Maple Leafs**	**NHL**	**2**	**0**	**1**	**0**	**25**	**4**	**0**	**9.60**	**9.50**	....	....	....	....	....	....	....	....	....	....	....	....	....	....	....	....
	Tulsa Oilers	CHL	38	17	17	4	2271	144	0	3.84	....	....	....	....	....	....	....	....	....	....	....	....	....	....	....	....	....
1971-72	Tulsa Oilers	CHL	15	8	7	0	892	49	1	3.29	....	....	....	....	....	....	....	....	....	....	....	....	....	....	....	....	....
	NHL Totals		**2**	**0**	**1**	**0**	**25**	**4**	**0**	**9.60**	....	....	....	....	....	....	....	....	....	....	....	....	....	....	....	....	....

WCHA First All-Star Team (1969, 1970) • NCAA West First All-American Team (1970)

Signed as a free agent by **Toronto**, October 1, 1970.

• McLEAN, Kirk

Kirk Alan G – L. 6′, 180 lbs. b: Willowdale, Ont., 6/26/1966. New Jersey's 6th, 107th overall in 1984.

Season	Club	League	GP	W	L	T	Mins	GA	SO	Avg	AAvg	Eff	SA	S%	SAPG	GP	W	L	T	Mins	GA	SO	Avg	Eff	SA	S%	SAPG
1982-83	Don Mills Flyers	MTHL	26	....	....	....	1575	52	0	2.01	....	....	....	....	....	....	....	....	....	....	....	....	....	....	....	....	....
1983-84	Oshawa Generals	OHL	17	5	9	0	940	67	0	4.28	....	....	....	....	....	....	....	....	....	....	....	....	....	....	....	....	....
1984-85	Oshawa Generals	OHL	47	23	17	2	2581	143	1	*3.32	....	....	....	....	....	5	1	3	....	271	21	0	4.65	....	....	....	....
1985-86	Oshawa Generals	OHL	51	24	21	2	2830	169	1	3.58	....	....	....	....	....	4	1	2	....	201	18	0	5.37	....	....	....	....
	New Jersey Devils	**NHL**	**2**	**1**	**1**	**0**	**111**	**11**	**0**	**5.95**	**4.65**	**11.09**	**59**	**.814**	**31.9**	....	....	....	....	....	....	....	....	....	....	....	....
1986-87	**New Jersey Devils**	**NHL**	**4**	**1**	**1**	**0**	**160**	**10**	**0**	**3.75**	**3.18**	**5.14**	**73**	**.863**	**27.4**	....	....	....	....	....	....	....	....	....	....	....	....
	Maine Mariners	AHL	45	15	23	4	2606	140	1	3.22	....	....	....	....	....	....	....	....	....	....	....	....	....	....	....	....	....
1987-88	**Vancouver Canucks**	**NHL**	**41**	**11**	**27**	**3**	**2380**	**147**	**1**	**3.71**	**3.09**	**4.63**	**1178**	**.875**	**29.7**	....	....	....	....	....	....	....	....	....	....	....	....
1988-89	**Vancouver Canucks**	**NHL**	**42**	**20**	**17**	**3**	**2477**	**127**	**4**	**3.08**	**2.55**	**3.35**	**1169**	**.891**	**28.3**	**5**	**2**	**3**	....	**302**	**18**	**0**	**3.58**	**3.86**	**167**	**.892**	**33.2**
1989-90	**Vancouver Canucks**	**NHL**	***63**	**21**	**30**	**10**	***3739**	**216**	**0**	**3.47**	**2.94**	**4.15**	**1804**	**.880**	**28.9**	....	....	....	....	....	....	....	....	....	....	....	....
	Canada	WEC-A	10	4	3	1	457	27	0	3.54	....	....	....	....	....	....	....	....	....	....	....	....	....	....	....	....	....
1990-91	**Vancouver Canucks**	**NHL**	**41**	**10**	**22**	**3**	**1969**	**131**	**0**	**3.99**	**3.60**	**5.32**	**983**	**.867**	**30.0**	**2**	**1**	**1**	....	**123**	**7**	**0**	**3.41**	**3.62**	**66**	**.894**	**32.2**
1991-92	**Vancouver Canucks**	**NHL**	**65**	***38**	**17**	**9**	**3852**	**176**	***5**	**2.74**	**2.44**	**2.71**	**1780**	**.901**	**27.7**	**13**	**6**	**7**	....	**785**	**33**	***2**	**2.52**	**2.28**	**364**	**.909**	**27.8**
1992-93	**Vancouver Canucks**	**NHL**	**54**	**28**	**21**	**5**	**3261**	**184**	**3**	**3.39**	**2.90**	**3.86**	**1615**	**.886**	**29.7**	**12**	**6**	**6**	....	**754**	**42**	**0**	**3.34**	**3.80**	**369**	**.886**	**29.4**
1993-94	**Vancouver Canucks**	**NHL**	**52**	**23**	**26**	**3**	**3128**	**156**	**3**	**2.99**	**2.87**	**3.26**	**1430**	**.891**	**27.4**	***24**	**15**	**9**	....	***1544**	**59**	***4**	**2.29**	**1.65**	**820**	**.928**	**31.9**
1994-95	**Vancouver Canucks**	**NHL**	**40**	**18**	**12**	**10**	**2374**	**109**	**1**	**2.75**	**2.88**	**2.63**	**1140**	**.904**	**28.8**	**11**	**4**	**7**	....	**660**	**36**	**0**	**3.27**	**3.50**	**336**	**.893**	**30.5**
1995-96	**Vancouver Canucks**	**NHL**	**45**	**15**	**21**	**9**	**2645**	**156**	**2**	**3.54**	**3.53**	**4.27**	**1292**	**.879**	**29.3**	**1**	**0**	**1**	....	**21**	**3**	**0**	**8.57**	**21.43**	**12**	**.750**	**34.3**
1996-97	**Vancouver Canucks**	**NHL**	**44**	**21**	**18**	**3**	**2581**	**138**	**0**	**3.21**	**3.46**	**3.55**	**1247**	**.889**	**29.0**	....	....	....	....	....	....	....	....	....	....	....	....
1997-98	**Vancouver Canucks**	**NHL**	**29**	**6**	**17**	**4**	**1583**	**97**	**1**	**3.68**	**4.41**	**4.46**	**800**	**.879**	**30.3**	....	....	....	....	....	....	....	....	....	....	....	....
	Carolina Hurricanes	**NHL**	**8**	**4**	**2**	**0**	**401**	**22**	**0**	**3.29**	**3.93**	**4.00**	**181**	**.878**	**27.1**	....	....	....	....	....	....	....	....	....	....	....	....
	Florida Panthers	**NHL**	**7**	**4**	**2**	**1**	**406**	**22**	**0**	**3.25**	**3.88**	**3.45**	**207**	**.894**	**30.6**	....	....	....	....	....	....	....	....	....	....	....	....
1998-99	**Florida Panthers**	**NHL**	**30**	**9**	**10**	**4**	**1597**	**73**	**2**	**2.74**	**3.26**	**2.75**	**727**	**.900**	**27.3**	....	....	....	....	....	....	....	....	....	....	....	....
99-2000	**New York Rangers**	**NHL**	**22**	**7**	**8**	**4**	**1206**	**58**	**0**	**2.89**	**3.30**	**3.00**	**558**	**.896**	**27.8**	....	....	....	....	....	....	....	....	....	....	....	....
	NHL Totals		**589**	**237**	**252**	**71**	**33870**	**1833**	**22**	**3.25**	....	....	**16243**	**.887**	**28.8**	**68**	**34**	**34**	....	**4189**	**198**	**6**	**2.84**	....	**2134**	**.907**	**30.6**

NHL Second All-Star Team (1992) • Played in NHL All-Star Game (1990, 1992)

Traded to **Vancouver** by **New Jersey** with Greg Adams and New Jersey's 2nd round choice (Leif Rohlin) in 1988 Entry Draft for Patrik Sundstrom and Vancouver's 2nd (Jeff Christian) and 4th (Matt Ruchty) round choices in 1988 Entry Draft, September 15, 1987. Traded to **Carolina** by **Vancouver** with Martin Gelinas for Sean Burke, Geoff Sanderson and Enrico Ciccone, January 3, 1998. Traded to **Florida** by **Carolina** for Ray Sheppard, March 24, 1998. Signed as a free agent by **NY Rangers**, July 20, 1999.

• McLELLAND, Dave

David Ivan G – L. 5′9″, 165 lbs. b: Penticton, B.C., 11/20/1952. Vancouver's 6th, 83rd overall in 1972.

Season	Club	League	GP	W	L	T	Mins	GA	SO	Avg	AAvg	Eff	SA	S%	SAPG	GP	W	L	T	Mins	GA	SO	Avg	Eff	SA	S%	SAPG
1968-69	Penticton Broncos	BCJHL	32	....	....	....	1920	125	3.9	....	....	....	....	....	....	....	....	....	....	....	....	....	....	....	....	....	....
1969-70	New Westminster Royals	BCJHL	STATISTICS NOT AVAILABLE																								
1970-71	Penticton Broncos	BCJHL	58	36	17	4	3460	142	*2	*2.46	....	....	....	....	....	....	....	....	....	....	....	....	....	....	....	....	....
1971-72	Brandon Wheat Kings	WCJHL	65	....	....	....	3778	285	1	4.53	....	....	....	....	....	11	....	....	....	662	54	0	4.89	....	....	....	....
1972-73	**Vancouver Canucks**	**NHL**	**2**	**1**	**1**	**0**	**120**	**10**	**0**	**5.00**	**4.72**	....	....	....	....	....	....	....	....	....	....	....	....	....	....	....	....
	Des Moines Capitols	IHL	2	0	1	0	84	13	0	9.28	....	....	....	....	....	....	....	....	....	....	....	....	....	....	....	....	....
	Seattle Totems	WHL	6	0	1	0	141	11	0	4.68	....	....	....	....	....	....	....	....	....	....	....	....	....	....	....	....	....
1973-74	Des Moines Capitols	IHL	55	....	....	....	3071	146	1	2.85	....	....	....	....	....	9	8	1	0	540	14	*2	*1.55	....	....	....	....
1974-75	Des Moines Capitols	IHL	32	....	....	....	1705	94	1	3.31	....	....	....	....	....	2	0	2	0	120	9	0	4.50	....	....	....	....
	NHL Totals		**2**	**1**	**1**	**0**	**120**	**10**	**0**	**5.00**	....	....	....	....	....	....	....	....	....	....	....	....	....	....	....	....	....

BCJHL First All-Star Team (1971)

• McLENNAN, Jamie

James Joseph "Noodles" G – L. 6′, 190 lbs. b: Edmonton, Alta., 6/30/1971. NY Islanders' 3rd, 48th overall in 1991.

Season	Club	League	GP	W	L	T	Mins	GA	SO	Avg	AAvg	Eff	SA	S%	SAPG	GP	W	L	T	Mins	GA	SO	Avg	Eff	SA	S%	SAPG
1987-88	St. Albert Royals	AAHA	21	....	....	....	1224	80	0	3.92	....	....	....	....	....	....	....	....	....	....	....	....	....	....	....	....	....
1988-89	Spokane Chiefs	WHL	11	....	....	....	578	63	0	6.54	....	....	....	....	....	....	....	....	....	....	....	....	....	....	....	....	....
	Lethbridge Hurricanes	WHL	7	....	....	....	368	22	0	3.59	....	....	....	....	....	....	....	....	....	....	....	....	....	....	....	....	....
1989-90	Lethbridge Hurricanes	WHL	34	20	4	2	1690	110	1	3.91	....	....	....	....	....	13	6	5	....	677	44	0	3.90	....	....	....	....
1990-91	Lethbridge Hurricanes	WHL	56	32	18	4	3230	205	0	3.81	....	....	....	....	....	*16	8	8	....	*970	56	0	3.46	....	....	....	....
1991-92	Capital District Islanders	AHL	18	4	10	2	952	60	1	3.78	....	....	....	....	....	....	....	....	....	....	....	....	....	....	....	....	....
	Richmond Renegades	ECHL	32	16	12	2	1837	114	0	3.72	....	....	....	....	....	....	....	....	....	....	....	....	....	....	....	....	....
1992-93	Capital District Islanders	AHL	38	17	14	6	2171	117	1	3.23	....	....	....	....	....	1	0	1	....	20	5	0	15.00	....	....	....	....
1993-94	**New York Islanders**	**NHL**	**22**	**8**	**7**	**6**	**1287**	**61**	**0**	**2.84**	**2.73**	**2.71**	**639**	**.905**	**29.8**	**2**	**0**	**1**	....	**82**	**6**	**0**	**4.39**	**5.60**	**47**	**.872**	**34.4**
	Salt Lake Golden Eagles	IHL	24	8	12	2	1320	80	0	3.64	....	....	....	....	....	....	....	....	....	....	....	....	....	....	....	....	....
1994-95	**New York Islanders**	**NHL**	**21**	**6**	**11**	**2**	**1185**	**67**	**0**	**3.39**	**3.56**	**4.21**	**539**	**.876**	**27.3**	....	....	....	....	....	....	....	....	....	....	....	....
	Denver Grizzlies	IHL	4	3	0	1	239	12	0	3.00	....	....	....	....	....	11	8	2	....	640	23	1	*2.15	....	....	....	....
1995-96	**New York Islanders**	**NHL**	**13**	**3**	**9**	**1**	**636**	**39**	**0**	**3.68**	**3.66**	**4.20**	**342**	**.886**	**32.3**	....	....	....	....	....	....	....	....	....	....	....	....
	Utah Grizzlies	IHL	14	9	2	2	728	29	0	2.39	....	....	....	....	....	....	....	....	....	....	....	....	....	....	....	....	....
	Worcester IceCats	AHL	22	14	7	1	1216	57	0	2.81	....	....	....	....	....	2	0	2	....	119	8	0	4.04	....	....	....	....
1996-97	Worcester IceCats	AHL	39	18	13	4	2152	100	2	2.79	....	....	....	....	....	4	2	2	....	262	16	0	3.67	....	....	....	....
1997-98	**St. Louis Blues**	**NHL**	**30**	**16**	**8**	**2**	**1658**	**60**	**2**	**2.17**	**2.58**	**2.11**	**618**	**.903**	**22.4**	**1**	**0**	**0**	....	**14**	**1**	**0**	**4.29**	**10.73**	**4**	**.750**	**17.1**
1998-99	**St. Louis Blues**	**NHL**	**33**	**13**	**14**	**4**	**1763**	**70**	**3**	**2.38**	**2.83**	**2.60**	**640**	**.891**	**21.8**	**1**	**0**	**1**	....	**37**	**0**	**0**	**0.00**	**0.00**	**7**	**1.000**	**11.4**
99-2000	**St. Louis Blues**	**NHL**	**19**	**9**	**5**	**2**	**1009**	**33**	**2**	**1.96**	**2.23**	**1.90**	**341**	**.903**	**20.3**	....	....	....	....	....	....	....	....	....	....	....	....
	NHL Totals		**138**	**55**	**54**	**17**	**7538**	**330**	**7**	**2.63**	....	....	**3119**	**.894**	**24.8**	**4**	**0**	**2**	....	**133**	**7**	**0**	**3.16**	....	**58**	**.879**	**26.2**

WHL East First All-Star Team (1991) • Won Bill Masterton Memorial Trophy (1998)

Signed as a free agent by **St. Louis**, July 15, 1996. Selected by **Minnesota** from **St. Louis** in Expansion Draft, June 23, 2000.

• McLEOD, Don

Donald Martin "Smokey" G – L. 6′, 190 lbs. b: Trail, B.C., 8/24/1946. Pittsburgh's 11th, 164th overall in 1973.

Season	Club	League	GP	W	L	T	Mins	GA	SO	Avg	AAvg	Eff	SA	S%	SAPG	GP	W	L	T	Mins	GA	SO	Avg	Eff	SA	S%	SAPG
1963-64	Trail Smoke Eaters	WIHL	8	0	7	0	502	55	0	6.57	....	....	....	....	....	....	....	....	....	....	....	....	....	....	....	....	....
1964-65	Edmonton Oil Kings	CAHL	STATISTICS NOT AVAILABLE																								
1965-66	Edmonton Oil Kings	ASHL	29	....	....	....	1740	115	0	3.97	....	....	....	....	....	9	6	3	0	520	27	0	3.12	....	....	....	....
	Edmonton Oil Kings	Mem-Cup	19	*15	4	0	1100	49	*3	*2.67	....	....	....	....	....	....	....	....	....	....	....	....	....	....	....	....	....
1966-67	Edmonton Oil Kings	CMJHL	38	....	....	....	2280	126	1	3.32	....	....	....	....	....	9	2	3	4	522	34	*2	3.91	....	....	....	....
1967-68	Quebec Aces	AHL	2	0	1	0	80	10	0	7.50	....	....	....	....	....	....	....	....	....	....	....	....	....	....	....	....	....
	Springfield Kings	AHL	9	6	2	1	540	27	0	3.00	....	....	....	....	....	4	1	3	0	240	13	0	3.25	....	....	....	....
	Fort Worth Wings	CPHL	17	5	6	5	1020	51	0	3.00	....	....	....	....	....	....	....	....	....	....	....	....	....	....	....	....	....
1968-69	Baltimore Clippers	AHL	7	2	3	1	379	28	0	4.43	....	....	....	....	....	....	....	....	....	....	....	....	....	....	....	....	....
	Springfield Kings	AHL	34	15	13	2	1833	105	0	3.44	....	....	....	....	....	....	....	....	....	....	....	....	....	....	....	....	....
1969-70	Fort Worth Wings	CHL	37	18	11	8	2200	109	1	2.97	....	....	....	....	....	3	0	3	0	176	11	0	3.75	....	....	....	....
1970-71	**Detroit Red Wings**	**NHL**	**14**	**3**	**7**	**0**	**698**	**60**	**0**	**5.16**	**5.14**	....	....	....	....	....	....	....	....	....	....	....	....	....	....	....	....
	Fort Worth Wings	CHL	36	....	....	....	2124	90	2	*2.57	....	....	....	....	....	3	....	....	....	207	15	0	4.35	....	....	....	....
1971-72	**Philadelphia Flyers**	**NHL**	**4**	**0**	**3**	**1**	**181**	**14**	**0**	**4.64**	**4.70**	....	....	....	....	....	....	....	....	....	....	....	....	....	....	....	....
	Richmond Robins	AHL	5	1	3	1	300	14	0	2.80	....	....	....	....	....	....	....	....	....	....	....	....	....	....	....	....	....
	Providence Reds	AHL	19	6	8	4	1083	66	0	2.73	....	....	....	....	....	....	....	....	....	....	....	....	....	....	....	....	....
1972-73	Houston Aeros	WHA	41	19	20	1	2410	145	1	3.61	....	....	....	....	....	3	0	3	0	178	8	0	2.70	....	....	....	....
1973-74	Houston Aeros	WHA	49	*33	13	3	2971	127	3	*2.56	....	....	....	....	....	*14	*12	2	0	*842	35	0	*2.49	....	....	....	....
1974-75	Team Canada	Summit-74	1	0	1	0	58	8	0	8.28	....	....	....	....	....	....	....	....	....	....	....	....	....	....	....	....	....
	Vancouver Blazers	WHA	*72	*33	35	2	*4184	233	1	3.34	....	....	....	....	....	....	....	....	....	....	....	....	....	....	....	....	....
1975-76	Calgary Cowboys	WHA	63	30	27	3	3534	206	1	3.50	....	....	....	....	....	10	5	5	0	559	37	0	3.97	....	....	....	....

			REGULAR SEASON													PLAYOFFS											
Season	Club	League	GP	W	L	T	Mins	GA	SO	Avg	AAvg	Eff	SA	S%	SAPG	GP	W	L	T	Mins	GA	SO	Avg	Eff	SA	S%	SAPG
1976-77	Calgary Cowboys	WHA	*67	25	34	5	3701	210	3	3.40																	
1977-78	Quebec Nordiques	WHA	7	2	4	0	403	28	0	4.17																	
	Edmonton Oilers	WHA	33	15	10	1	1723	102	2	3.55						4	1	3	0	207	16	1	4.64				
	NHL Totals		**18**	**3**	**10**	**1**	**879**	**74**	**0**	**5.05**																	
	Other Major League Totals		332	157	143	15	18926	1051	11	3.33						31	18	13		1786	96	1	3.23				

Shared Terry Sawchuk Trophy (fewest goals against - CHL) with Gerry Gray (1971) • WHA First All-Star Team (1974) • Won Ben Hatskin Trophy (WHA Top Goaltender) (1974)

Claimed by **Philadelphia** (Quebec-AHL) from **Detroit** in Reverse Draft, June, 1971. Selected by **Houston** (WHA) in 1972 WHA General Player Draft, February 12, 1972. Signed as a free agent by **Vancouver** (WHA) after securing release from **Houston** (WHA), August 15, 1974. Transferred to **Calgary** (WHA) after **Vancouver** (WHA) franchise relocated, May 7, 1975. Claimed by **Quebec** (WHA) from **Calgary** (WHA) in WHA Dispersal Auction, August, 1977. Traded to **Edmonton** (WHA) by **Quebec** (WHA) with Pierre Guite for Dave Inkpen, Ken Broderick, Warren Miller and Rick Morris, November, 1977.

• McLEOD, Jim
James Bradley G – L. 5'8", 170 lbs. b: Port Arthur, Ont., 4/7/1937.

Season	Club	League	GP	W	L	T	Mins	GA	SO	Avg	AAvg	Eff	SA	S%	SAPG	GP	W	L	T	Mins	GA	SO	Avg	Eff	SA	S%	SAPG
1955-56	Port Arthur Bearcats	TBSHL	STATISTICS NOT AVAILABLE																								
1956-57	Vernon Canadians	OSHL	4				240	15	0	3.75																	
1957-58	Vernon Canadians	OSHL	2				120	12	0	6.00																	
1958-59	Vernon Canadians	OSHL	6				360	30	1	5.00																	
1959-60	Vernon Canadians	OSHL	44				2640	148	2	*3.36						13	7	5	1	780	44	1	3.38				
	Kelowna Packers	Al-Cup	3	0	3	0	180	20	0	6.67																	
1960-61	Muskegon Zephyrs	IHL	62				3720	269	1	4.34						13	5	8	0	780	48	0	3.38				
	Seattle Totems	WHL	7	5	2	0	428	24	0	3.36																	
1961-62	Muskegon Zephyrs	IHL	47				2820	157	1	3.34						9	8	1	0	540	28	0	3.11				
	Seattle Totems	WHL	12	6	6	0	720	37	0	3.08																	
1962-63	San Francisco Seals	WHL	67	*43	23	1	4090	202	4	3.01						*17	*10	7	0	1054	56	*3	3.19				
1963-64	Los Angeles Blades	WHL	39	18	15	6	2340	127	*4	3.26						5	2	2	0	260	14	0	*3.23				
1964-65	Seattle Totems	WHL	65	*35	27	3	3970	181	*5	2.74						7	3	4	0	420	19	1	2.71				
1965-66	Seattle Totems	WHL	46	20	23	2	2751	167	2	3.64																	
1966-67	Seattle Totems	WHL	42	26	11	4	2528	101	4	*2.40						*8	*6	2	0	*480	15	*1	1.88				
1967-68	Portland Buckaroos	WHL	33	18	10	4	1961	73	4	2.23						7	4	3	0	407	17	1	2.51				
1968-69	Portland Buckaroos	WHL	42	23	9	8	2363	90	*3	*2.29						8	4	3	0	433	27	0	3.74				
1969-70	Portland Buckaroos	WHL	33	21	9	0	1794	103	0	3.44						9	5	4	0	539	25	*2	*2.78				
1970-71	Portland Buckaroos	WHL	47	*32	10	3	2710	122	*5	*2.70						*11	*8	3	0	*678	23	*1	*2.03				
1971-72	**St. Louis Blues**	**NHL**	**16**	**6**	**6**	**4**	**880**	**44**	**0**	**3.00**	**3.03**																
	Portland Buckaroos	WHL	13	9	3	0	735	34	0	2.78						*11	*5	6	0	*658	39	0	3.55				
1972-73	Chicago Cougars	WHA	54	22	25	2	2996	166	1	3.32																	
1973-74	New York-Jersey Knights	WHA	10	3	7	0	517	36	0	4.18																	
	Los Angeles Sharks	WHA	17	4	13	0	969	69	1	4.27																	
1974-75	Michigan-Baltimore	WHA	16	3	6	1	694	53	0	4.58																	
	Syracuse Blazers	NAHL	3	3	0	0	180	5	0	1.67																	
	Greensboro Generals	SHL	2				120	8	0	4.00																	
	NHL Totals		**16**	**6**	**6**	**4**	**880**	**44**	**0**	**3.00**																	
	Other Major League Totals		97	32	51	3	5176	324	2	3.76																	

OSHL First All-Star Team (1960) • WHL First All-Star Team (1965, 1969) • Won WHL Leading Goaltender Award (1965, 1967, 1971) • WHL Second All-Star Team (1968, 1971) • Shared WHL Leading Goaltender Award with Marv Edwards (1968) • Shared WHL Leading Goaltender Award with Dave Kelly (1969)

Traded to **Portland** (WHL) by **Seattle** (WHL) with cash for Don Head, September, 1967. Claimed by **St. Louis** from **Portland** (WHL) in Inter-League Draft, June 7, 1971. Selected by **Chicago** (WHA) in 1972 WHA General Player Draft, February 12, 1972. Traded to **NY Raiders** (WHA) by **Chicago** (WHA) for cash, July, 1973. Traded to **LA Sharks** (WHA) by **New York-Jersey** (WHA) for Earl Heiskala and Russ Gillow, January, 1974. Transferred to **Michigan** (WHA) after **LA Sharks** (WHA) franchise relocated, April 1974.

• McNAMARA, Gerry
Gerald Lionel G – L. 6'2", 190 lbs. b: Sturgeon Falls, Ont., 9/22/1934.

Season	Club	League	GP	W	L	T	Mins	GA	SO	Avg	AAvg	Eff	SA	S%	SAPG	GP	W	L	T	Mins	GA	SO	Avg	Eff	SA	S%	SAPG
1951-52	St. Michael's Majors	OHA-Jr.	5	2	3	0	280	20	0	4.29																	
1952-53	St. Michael's Majors	OHA-Jr.	10				600	30	0	3.00						1				60	4	0	4.00				
1953-54	St. Michael's Majors	OHA-Jr.	57				3420	205	2	3.59						8				480	41	0	5.12				
1954-55	St. Michael's Majors	OHA-Jr.	46	25	18	3	2750	149	2	3.24						2				120	8	0	4.00				
1955-56	Pittsburgh Hornets	AHL	5	1	4	0	300	19	0	3.80																	
1956-57	Winnipeg Warriors	WHL	16	4	11	1	965	60	0	3.73																	
	Hershey Bears	AHL	22	10	12	0	1320	92	0	4.18						7	3	4	0	430	16	*2	*2.23				
1957-58	Buffalo Bisons	AHL	37	14	21	2	2245	149	0	3.98																	
1958-59	Cleveland Barons	AHL	49	29	18	2	2940	155	3	3.16						7	3	4	0	420	18	*1	2.57				
1959-60	Sudbury Wolves	EPHL	59	31	21	7	3520	236	2	4.02						*14	7	7	0	850	41	*1	2.89				
	Rochester Americans	AHL	2	0	2	0	120	13	0	6.50																	
1960-61	Sudbury Wolves	EPHL	52	18	27	7	3120	210	3	4.04																	
	Rochester Americans	AHL	1	0	1	0	60	5	0	5.00																	
	Toronto Maple Leafs	**NHL**	**5**	**2**	**2**	**1**	**300**	**12**	**0**	**2.40**	**2.47**																
1961-62	Pittsburgh Hornets	AHL	35	5	30	0	2100	148	0	4.23																	
	Portland Buckeroos	WHL	6	1	3	2	380	25	0	3.95																	
1962-63	Rochester Americans	AHL	32	10	18	3	1920	123	1	3.84																	
1963-64	Charlotte Checkers	EHL	29				1740	109	1	3.76																	
1964-65			DID NOT PLAY																								
1965-66			DID NOT PLAY																								
1966-67	Toronto Grads	OHA-Sr.	31				1830	112	2	3.67																	
1967-68	Toronto Marlboros	OHA-Sr.	37				2210	111	0	3.01																	
1968-69	Orillia Terriers	OHA-Sr.	29				1697	105	1	3.71																	
1969-70	**Toronto Maple Leafs**	**NHL**	**2**	**0**	**0**	**0**	**23**	**2**	**0**	**5.22**	**5.54**																
	Orillia Terriers	OHA-Sr.	25				1500	61	*3	*2.44																	
1970-71	Orillia Terriers	OHA-Sr.	STATISTICS NOT AVAILABLE																								
1971-72	Orillia Terriers	OHA-Sr.	31				1817	112	*3	3.70																	
1972-73	Barrie Flyers	Al-Cup	1	1	0	0	60	3	0	3.00																	
	NHL Totals		**7**	**2**	**2**	**1**	**323**	**14**	**0**	**2.60**																	

OHA-Sr. First All-Star Team (1970) • OHA-Sr. Second All-Star Team (1972)

• McNEIL, Gerry
Gerard George G – L. 5'7", 155 lbs. b: Quebec City, Que., 4/17/1926.

Season	Club	League	GP	W	L	T	Mins	GA	SO	Avg	AAvg	Eff	SA	S%	SAPG	GP	W	L	T	Mins	GA	SO	Avg	Eff	SA	S%	SAPG
1943-44	Montreal Royals	QJHL	3				180	10	0	3.33																	
	Montreal Royals	QSHL	21				1260	110	1	5.24						7	3	4	0	420	30	0	4.29				
1944-45	Montreal Royals	QSHL	23	*18	4	1	1350	90	0	4.00						7	4	3	0	420	30	*1	4.29				
1945-46	Montreal Royals	QSHL	26	21	3	2	1560	87	1	*3.35						11	*7	2	2	660	31	0	*2.82				
1946-47	Montreal Royals	QSHL	40	25	13	2	2400	124	*2	*3.10						11	*7	4	0	660	22	0	*2.00				
1947-48	**Montreal Canadiens**	**NHL**	**2**	**0**	**1**	**1**	**95**	**7**	**0**	**4.42**	**4.61**																
	Montreal Royals	QSHL	47	33	14	0	2820	156	*3	3.32						3	0	3	0	180	9	0	3.00				
1948-49	Montreal Royals	QSHL	59	35	19	5	3540	178	*5	3.02						9	3	4	0	540	25	1	2.78				
1949-50	**Montreal Canadiens**	**NHL**	**6**	**3**	**1**	**2**	**360**	**9**	**1**	**1.50**	**1.66**					**2**	**1**	**1**		**135**	**5**	**0**	**2.22**				
	Cincinnati Mohawks	AHL	55	12	30	13	3300	201	3	3.65																	
1950-51	**Montreal Canadiens**	**NHL**	***70**	**25**	**30**	**15**	***4200**	**184**	**6**	**2.63**	**2.94**					***11**	***5**	**6**		***785**	**25**	**1**	**1.91**				
1951-52	**Montreal Canadiens**	**NHL**	***70**	**34**	**26**	**10**	***4200**	**164**	**5**	**2.34**	**2.70**					***11**	**4**	**7**		***688**	**23**	**1**	**2.01**				
1952-53♦	**Montreal Canadiens**	**NHL**	**66**	**25**	**23**	**18**	**3960**	**140**	***10**	**2.12**	**2.64**					**8**	***5**	**3**		**486**	**16**	***2**	**1.98**				
1953-54	**Montreal Canadiens**	**NHL**	**53**	**28**	**19**	**6**	**3180**	**114**	**6**	**2.15**	**2.69**					**3**	**2**	**1**		**190**	**3**	**1**	**0.95**				
1954-55	Jonquiere Marquis	QJHL	DID NOT PLAY – COACHING																								
1955-56	Montreal Royals	QHL	54	30	17	7	3330	128	*5	*2.31						19	9	10	0	1161	63	1	3.26				
1956-57♦	**Montreal Canadiens**	**NHL**	**9**	**4**	**5**	**0**	**540**	**31**	**0**	**3.44**	**3.98**																
	Montreal Royals	QHL	59	26	28	4	3610	175	3	2.91						4	0	4	0	245	11	0	2.69				
1957-58	Rochester Americans	AHL	*68	28	34	6	*4158	229	5	3.30																	

Season	Club	League	REGULAR SEASON GP	W	L	T	Mins	GA	SO	Avg	AAvg	Eff	SA	S%	SAPG	PLAYOFFS GP	W	L	T	Mins	GA	SO	Avg	Eff	SA	S%	SAPG
1958-59	Rochester Americans	AHL	66	31	30	5	4010	199	2	2.98	....	....	....	....	....	5	1	4	0	304	12	0	*2.37	....	....	....	....
1959-60	Montreal Royals	EPHL	28	13	9	6	1680	67	5	*2.39	....	....	....	....	....	*14	*8	6	0	842	34	*1	2.42	....	....	....	....
1960-61	Quebec Aces	AHL	50	21	27	1	2933	176	3	3.60	....	....	....	....	....	....	....	....	....	....	....	....	....	....	....	....	....
	NHL Totals		**276**	**119**	**105**	**52**	**16535**	**649**	**28**	**2.36**	....	....	....	....	....	**35**	**17**	**18**	....	**2284**	**72**	**5**	**1.89**	....	....	....	....

QSHL 1st All-Star Team (1947, 1948, 1949) • Won Byng of Vimy Trophy (MVP - QSHL) (1947, 1948, 1949) • NHL Second All-Star Team (1953) • QHL First All-Star Team (1956) • Won Vezina Memorial Trophy (Top Goaltender - QHL) (1956) • AHL Second All-Star Team (1958) • Played in NHL All-Star Game (1951, 1952, 1953)

• McRAE, Gord

Gordon Alexander "The Bird" G – L. 6', 180 lbs. b: Sherbrooke, Que., 4/12/1948.

Season	Club	League	GP	W	L	T	Mins	GA	SO	Avg	AAvg	Eff	SA	S%	SAPG	GP	W	L	T	Mins	GA	SO	Avg	Eff	SA	S%	SAPG
1967-68	Michigan Tech Huskies	WCHA	12	....	....	....	720	25	2	2.08	....	....	....	....	....	....	....	....	....	....	....	....	....	....	....	....	....
1968-69	Michigan Tech Huskies	WCHA	28	....	....	....	1680	84	1	3.00	....	....	....	....	....	....	....	....	....	....	....	....	....	....	....	....	....
1969-70	Michigan Tech Huskies	WCHA	31	....	....	....	1860	112	1	3.61	....	....	....	....	....	....	....	....	....	....	....	....	....	....	....	....	....
1970-71	Charlotte-Jersey Devils	EHL	24	....	....	....	1440	69	3	2.88	....	....	....	....	....	7	7	0	0	420	8	*3	*1.14	....	....	....	....
1971-72	Orillia Terriers	OHA-Sr.	2	....	....	....	120	11	0	5.50	....	....	....	....	....	....	....	....	....	....	....	....	....	....	....	....	....
	Providence Reds	AHL	3	2	1	0	140	8	0	3.42	....	....	....	....	....	....	....	....	....	....	....	....	....	....	....	....	....
	Tulsa Oilers	CHL	17	5	5	6	879	54	0	3.68	....	....	....	....	....	7	3	4	0	372	28	0	4.51	....	....	....	....
1972-73	**Toronto Maple Leafs**	**NHL**	**11**	**7**	**3**	**0**	**620**	**39**	**0**	**3.77**	**3.56**	....	....	....	....	....	....	....	....	....	....	....	....	....	....	....	....
	Tulsa Oilers	CHL	*43	18	19	6	*2459	154	3	3.75	....	....	....	....	....	....	....	....	....	....	....	....	....	....	....	....	....
1973-74	Oklahoma City Blazers	CHL	39	20	14	4	2222	119	2	3.21	....	....	....	....	....	8	....	....	....	460	17	*1	2.21	....	....	....	....
1974-75	**Toronto Maple Leafs**	**NHL**	**20**	**10**	**3**	**6**	**1063**	**57**	**0**	**3.22**	**2.91**	....	....	....	....	**7**	**2**	**5**	....	**441**	**21**	**0**	**2.86**	....	....	....	....
	Oklahoma City Blazers	CHL	29	4	16	4	1483	99	0	4.01	....	....	....	....	....	....	....	....	....	....	....	....	....	....	....	....	....
1975-76	**Toronto Maple Leafs**	**NHL**	**20**	**6**	**5**	**2**	**956**	**59**	**0**	**3.70**	**3.35**	....	....	....	....	**1**	**0**	**0**	....	**13**	**1**	**0**	**4.62**	....	....	....	....
1976-77	**Toronto Maple Leafs**	**NHL**	**2**	**0**	**1**	**1**	**120**	**9**	**0**	**4.50**	**4.18**	....	....	....	....	....	....	....	....	....	....	....	....	....	....	....	....
	Dallas Black Hawks	CHL	30	17	6	7	1796	81	1	*2.71	....	....	....	....	....	3	1	2	0	179	10	0	3.35	....	....	....	....
1977-78	**Toronto Maple Leafs**	**NHL**	**18**	**7**	**10**	**1**	**1040**	**57**	**1**	**3.29**	**3.08**	....	....	....	....	....	....	....	....	....	....	....	....	....	....	....	....
	NHL Totals		**71**	**30**	**22**	**10**	**3799**	**221**	**1**	**3.49**	....	....	....	....	....	**8**	**2**	**5**	....	**454**	**22**	**0**	**2.91**	....	....	....	....

CHL First All-Star Team (1977) • Shared Terry Sawchuk Trophy (fewest goals against - CHL) with Yves Belanger (1977)

Signed as a free agent by **Toronto** (Tulsa - CHL), December 18, 1971.

• MELANSON, Rollie

Roland Joseph G – L. 5'10", 185 lbs. b: Moncton, N.B., 6/28/1960. NY Islanders' 4th, 59th overall in 1979.

Season	Club	League	GP	W	L	T	Mins	GA	SO	Avg	AAvg	Eff	SA	S%	SAPG	GP	W	L	T	Mins	GA	SO	Avg	Eff	SA	S%	SAPG
1976-77	Moncton Century Flyers	NBAHA	70	....	....	....	4198	147	*14	2.09	....	....	....	....	....	6	*4	1	1	360	14	0	2.33	....	....	....	....
1977-78	Windsor Spitfires	OMJHL	44	....	....	....	2592	195	1	4.51	....	....	....	....	....	5	1	2	1	258	13	0	3.02	....	....	....	....
1978-79	Windsor Spitfires	OMJHL	*62	....	....	....	*3461	254	1	4.40	....	....	....	....	....	7	....	....	....	392	31	0	4.74	....	....	....	....
1979-80	Windsor Spitfires	OMJHL	22	11	8	0	1099	90	0	4.91	....	....	....	....	....	....	....	....	....	....	....	....	....	....	....	....	....
	Oshawa Generals	OMJHL	38	26	12	0	2240	136	*3	3.64	....	....	....	....	....	7	3	4	0	420	32	0	4.57	....	....	....	....
1980-81 ♦	**New York Islanders**	**NHL**	**11**	**8**	**1**	**1**	**620**	**32**	**0**	**3.10**	**2.50**	....	....	....	....	**3**	**1**	**0**	....	**92**	**6**	**0**	**3.91**	....	....	....	....
	Indianapolis Checkers	CHL	*52	31	16	3	*3056	131	2	*2.57	....	....	....	....	....	....	....	....	....	....	....	....	....	....	....	....	....
1981-82 ♦	**New York Islanders**	**NHL**	**36**	**22**	**7**	**6**	**2115**	**114**	**0**	**3.23**	**2.48**	....	....	....	....	**3**	**0**	**1**	....	**64**	**5**	**0**	**4.69**	....	....	....	....
1982-83 ♦	**New York Islanders**	**NHL**	**44**	**24**	**12**	**5**	**2460**	**109**	**1**	**2.66**	**2.12**	**2.40**	**1206**	**.910**	**29.4**	**5**	**2**	**2**	....	**238**	**10**	**0**	**2.52**	....	....	....	....
1983-84	**New York Islanders**	**NHL**	**37**	**20**	**11**	**2**	**2019**	**110**	**0**	**3.27**	**2.57**	**3.19**	**1129**	**.903**	**33.6**	**6**	**0**	**1**	....	**87**	**5**	**0**	**3.45**	**5.39**	**32**	**.844**	**22.1**
1984-85	**New York Islanders**	**NHL**	**8**	**3**	**3**	**0**	**425**	**35**	**0**	**4.94**	**3.94**	**6.73**	**257**	**.864**	**36.3**	....	....	....	....	....	....	....	....	....	....	....	....
	Minnesota North Stars	**NHL**	**20**	**5**	**10**	**3**	**1142**	**78**	**0**	**4.10**	**3.27**	**5.45**	**587**	**.867**	**30.8**	....	....	....	....	....	....	....	....	....	....	....	....
1985-86	**Minnesota North Stars**	**NHL**	**6**	**2**	**1**	**2**	**325**	**24**	**0**	**4.43**	**3.46**	**6.08**	**175**	**.863**	**32.3**	....	....	....	....	....	....	....	....	....	....	....	....
	Los Angeles Kings	**NHL**	**22**	**4**	**16**	**1**	**1246**	**87**	**0**	**4.19**	**3.27**	**5.57**	**654**	**.867**	**31.5**	....	....	....	....	....	....	....	....	....	....	....	....
	New Haven Nighthawks	AHL	3	1	2	0	179	13	0	4.36	....	....	....	....	....	....	....	....	....	....	....	....	....	....	....	....	....
1986-87	**Los Angeles Kings**	**NHL**	**46**	**18**	**21**	**6**	**2734**	**168**	**1**	**3.69**	**3.13**	**4.37**	**1420**	**.882**	**31.2**	**5**	**1**	**4**	....	**260**	**24**	**0**	**5.54**	**8.63**	**154**	**.844**	**35.5**
1987-88	**Los Angeles Kings**	**NHL**	**47**	**17**	**20**	**7**	**2676**	**195**	**2**	**4.37**	**3.66**	**6.09**	**1399**	**.861**	**31.4**	**1**	**0**	**1**	....	**60**	**9**	**0**	**9.00**	**16.20**	**50**	**.820**	**50.0**
1988-89	**Los Angeles Kings**	**NHL**	**4**	**1**	**1**	**0**	**178**	**19**	**0**	**6.40**	**5.33**	**11.16**	**109**	**.826**	**36.7**	....	....	....	....	....	....	....	....	....	....	....	....
	New Haven Nighthawks	AHL	29	11	15	3	1734	106	1	3.67	....	....	....	....	....	*17	9	8	0	*1019	74	1	4.36	....	....	....	....
1989-90	Utica Devils	AHL	48	24	19	3	2737	167	1	3.66	....	....	....	....	....	5	1	4	0	298	20	0	4.03	....	....	....	....
1990-91	**New Jersey Devils**	**NHL**	**1**	**0**	**0**	**0**	**20**	**2**	**0**	**6.00**	**5.39**	**17.14**	**7**	**.714**	**21.0**	....	....	....	....	....	....	....	....	....	....	....	....
	Utica Devils	AHL	54	23	28	1	3058	208	0	4.08	....	....	....	....	....	....	....	....	....	....	....	....	....	....	....	....	....
1991-92	**Montreal Canadiens**	**NHL**	**9**	**5**	**3**	**0**	**492**	**22**	**2**	**2.68**	**2.40**	**3.02**	**195**	**.887**	**23.8**	....	....	....	....	....	....	....	....	....	....	....	....
1992-93	Brantford Smoke	ColHL	14	10	4	0	811	54	*1	4.00	....	....	....	....	....	15	*11	3	0	844	50	0	3.55	....	....	....	....
1993-94	Saint John Flames	AHL	7	1	2	0	270	20	0	4.44	....	....	....	....	....	....	....	....	....	....	....	....	....	....	....	....	....
1994-1995	Saint John Flames	AHL	DID NOT PLAY – ASSISTANT COACH																								
1995-1997	Moncton Wildcats	QMJHL	DID NOT PLAY – ASSISTANT COACH																								
1997-2000	**Montreal Canadiens**	**NHL**	DID NOT PLAY – ASSISTANT COACH																								
	NHL Totals		**291**	**129**	**106**	**33**	**16452**	**995**	**6**	**3.63**	....	....	....	....	....	**23**	**4**	**9**	....	**801**	**59**	**0**	**4.42**	....	....	....	....

OMJHL Second All-Star Team (1979) • CHL First All-Star Team (1981) • Won Ken McKenzie Trophy (Rookie of the Year - CHL) (1981) • NHL Second All-Star Team (1983) • Shared William M. Jennings Trophy with Billy Smith (1983) • ColHL Playoff MVP (1993)

Traded to **Minnesota** by **NY Islanders** for Minnesota's 1st round choice (Brad Dalgarno) in 1985 Entry Draft, November 19, 1984. Traded to **NY Rangers** by **Minnesota** for NY Rangers' 2nd round choice (Neil Wilkinson) in 1986 Entry Draft and 4th round choice (John Weisbrod) in 1987 Entry Draft, December 9, 1985. Traded to **LA Kings** by **NY Rangers** with Grant Ledyard for Brian MacLellan and LA Kings' 4th round choice (Mike Sullivan) in 1987 Entry Draft, December 9, 1985. Signed as a free agent by **New Jersey**, August 10, 1989. Traded to **Montreal** by **New Jersey** with Kirk Muller for Stephane Richer and Tom Chorske, September 20, 1991. • Missed majority of 1991-92 season recovering from groin injury suffered in game vs. Hartford, January 11, 1992.

• MELOCHE, Gilles

G – L. 5'9", 185 lbs. b: Montreal, Que., 7/12/1950. Chicago's 5th, 70th overall in 1970.

Season	Club	League	GP	W	L	T	Mins	GA	SO	Avg	AAvg	Eff	SA	S%	SAPG	GP	W	L	T	Mins	GA	SO	Avg	Eff	SA	S%	SAPG
1969-70	Verdun Jr. Maple Leafs	QJHL	45	....	....	....	2679	221	*1	4.95	....	....	....	....	....	11	5	6	0	654	34	0	3.12	....	....	....	....
	Verdun Jr. Maple Leafs	Mem-Cup	8	4	4	0	474	35	0	4.43	....	....	....	....	....	....	....	....	....	....	....	....	....	....	....	....	....
1970-71	**Chicago Black Hawks**	**NHL**	**2**	**2**	**0**	**0**	**120**	**6**	**0**	**3.00**	**2.97**	....	....	....	....	....	....	....	....	....	....	....	....	....	....	....	....
	Flint Generals	IHL	33	....	....	....	1866	104	2	3.34	....	....	....	....	....	3	....	....	....	183	11	0	3.61	....	....	....	....
1971-72	**California Golden Seals**	**NHL**	**56**	**16**	**25**	**13**	**3121**	**173**	**4**	**3.33**	**3.38**	....	....	....	....	....	....	....	....	....	....	....	....	....	....	....	....
1972-73	**California Golden Seals**	**NHL**	***59**	**12**	**32**	**14**	***3473**	**235**	**1**	**4.06**	**3.88**	....	....	....	....	....	....	....	....	....	....	....	....	....	....	....	....
1973-74	**California Golden Seals**	**NHL**	**47**	**9**	**33**	**5**	**2800**	**198**	**1**	**4.24**	**4.15**	....	....	....	....	....	....	....	....	....	....	....	....	....	....	....	....
1974-75	**California Golden Seals**	**NHL**	**47**	**9**	**27**	**10**	**2771**	**186**	**1**	**4.03**	**3.66**	....	....	....	....	....	....	....	....	....	....	....	....	....	....	....	....
1975-76	**California Golden Seals**	**NHL**	**41**	**12**	**23**	**6**	**2440**	**140**	**1**	**3.44**	**3.12**	....	....	....	....	....	....	....	....	....	....	....	....	....	....	....	....
1976-77	**Cleveland Barons**	**NHL**	**51**	**19**	**24**	**6**	**2961**	**171**	**2**	**3.47**	**3.23**	....	....	....	....	....	....	....	....	....	....	....	....	....	....	....	....
1977-78	**Cleveland Barons**	**NHL**	**54**	**16**	**27**	**8**	**3100**	**195**	**1**	**3.77**	**3.56**	....	....	....	....	....	....	....	....	....	....	....	....	....	....	....	....
1978-79	**Minnesota North Stars**	**NHL**	**53**	**20**	**25**	**7**	**3118**	**173**	**2**	**3.33**	**2.94**	....	....	....	....	....	....	....	....	....	....	....	....	....	....	....	....
1979-80	**Minnesota North Stars**	**NHL**	**54**	**27**	**20**	**5**	**3141**	**160**	**1**	**3.06**	**2.69**	....	....	....	....	**11**	**5**	**4**	....	**564**	**34**	**1**	**3.62**	....	....	....	....
1980-81	Minnesota North Stars	DN-Cup	1	....	....	....	29	0	0	0.00	....	....	....	....	....	....	....	....	....	....	....	....	....	....	....	....	....
	Minnesota North Stars	**NHL**	**38**	**17**	**14**	**6**	**2215**	**120**	**2**	**3.25**	**2.62**	....	....	....	....	**13**	**8**	**5**	....	**802**	**47**	**0**	**3.52**	....	....	....	....
1981-82	**Minnesota North Stars**	**NHL**	**51**	**26**	**15**	**9**	**3026**	**175**	**1**	**3.47**	**2.67**	....	....	....	....	**4**	**1**	**2**	....	**184**	**8**	**0**	**2.61**	....	....	....	....
	Canada	WEC-A	5	3	2	0	299	16	1	3.21	....	....	....	....	....	....	....	....	....	....	....	....	....	....	....	....	....
1982-83	**Minnesota North Stars**	**NHL**	**47**	**20**	**13**	**11**	**2689**	**160**	**1**	**3.57**	**2.86**	**4.05**	**1411**	**.887**	**31.5**	**5**	**2**	**3**	....	**319**	**18**	**0**	**3.39**	....	....	....	....
1983-84	**Minnesota North Stars**	**NHL**	**52**	**21**	**17**	**8**	**2883**	**201**	**2**	**4.18**	**3.30**	**5.51**	**1524**	**.868**	**31.7**	**4**	**1**	**2**	....	**200**	**11**	**0**	**3.30**	**4.13**	**88**	**.875**	**26.4**
1984-85	**Minnesota North Stars**	**NHL**	**32**	**10**	**13**	**6**	**1817**	**115**	**0**	**3.80**	**3.03**	**4.60**	**949**	**.879**	**31.3**	**8**	**4**	**3**	....	**395**	**25**	**1**	**3.80**	**3.71**	**256**	**.902**	**38.9**
1985-86	**Pittsburgh Penguins**	**NHL**	**34**	**13**	**15**	**5**	**1989**	**119**	**0**	**3.59**	**2.80**	**4.26**	**1003**	**.881**	**30.3**	....	....	....	....	....	....	....	....	....	....	....	....
1986-87	**Pittsburgh Penguins**	**NHL**	**43**	**13**	**19**	**7**	**2343**	**134**	**0**	**3.43**	**2.90**	**4.09**	**1123**	**.881**	**28.8**	....	....	....	....	....	....	....	....	....	....	....	....
1987-88	**Pittsburgh Penguins**	**NHL**	**27**	**8**	**9**	**5**	**1394**	**95**	**0**	**4.09**	**3.41**	**5.38**	**722**	**.868**	**31.1**	....	....	....	....	....	....	....	....	....	....	....	....
	NHL Totals		**788**	**270**	**351**	**131**	**45401**	**2756**	**20**	**3.64**	....	....	....	....	....	**45**	**21**	**19**	....	**2464**	**143**	**2**	**3.48**	....	....	....	....

QJHL First All-Star Team (1970) • Played in NHL All-Star Game (1980, 1982)

Traded to **California** by **Chicago** with Paul Shmyr for Gerry Desjardins, October 18, 1971. Transferred to **Cleveland** after **California** franchise relocated, August 26, 1976. Protected by **Minnesota** prior to Cleveland - Minnesota Dispersal Draft, June 15, 1978. Traded to **Edmonton** by **Minnesota** for Paul Houck, May 31, 1985. Traded to **Pittsburgh** by **Edmonton** for Marty McSorley, Tim Hrynewich and future considerations (Craig Muni, October 6, 1986), September 11, 1985.

• MICALEF, Corrado

G – R. 5'8", 172 lbs. b: Montreal, Que., 4/20/1961. Detroit's 2nd, 44th overall in 1981.

			REGULAR SEASON													PLAYOFFS											
Season	Club	League	GP	W	L	T	Mins	GA	SO	Avg	AAvg	Eff	SA	S%	SAPG	GP	W	L	T	Mins	GA	SO	Avg	Eff	SA	S%	SAPG
1978-79	Sherbrooke Castors	QMJHL	42	....	....	....	2045	142	1	4.17	....	....	....	....	....	4	....	....	....	38	2	0	3.16	....	....	....	....
1979-80	Sherbrooke Castors	QMJHL	64	37	17	7	3598	252	1	*4.20	....	....	....	....	....	15	10	5	0	842	52	0	3.71	....	....	....	....
1980-81	Sherbrooke Castors	QMJHL	64	35	26	3	3764	280	*2	4.46	....	....	....	....	....	14	7	7	0	842	46	*1	*3.28	....	....	....	....
	Canada	WJC-A	5	1	2	1	207	20	0	5.79	....	....	....	....	....	....	....	....	....	....	....	....	....	....	....	....	....
	Cornwall Royals	Mem-Cup	3	3	0	0	140	6	0	*2.57	....	....	....	....	....	....	....	....	....	....	....	....	....	....	....	....	....
1981-82	**Detroit Red Wings**	**NHL**	**18**	**4**	**10**	**1**	**809**	**63**	**0**	**4.67**	**3.61**	....	....	....	....	....	....	....	....	....	....	....	....	....	....	....	....
	Adirondack Red Wings	AHL	1	0	0	0	10	0	0	0.00	....	....	....	....	....	....	....	....	....	....	....	....	....	....	....	....	....
	Kalamazoo Wings	IHL	20	....	....	....	1146	91	1	4.76	....	....	....	....	....	1	....	....	....	25	5	0	11.90	....	....	....	....
1982-83	**Detroit Red Wings**	**NHL**	**34**	**11**	**13**	**5**	**1756**	**106**	**2**	**3.62**	**2.90**	**5.01**	**766**	**.862**	**26.2**	....	....	....	....	....	....	....	....	....	....	....	....
	Adirondack Red Wings	AHL	11	6	5	0	660	37	0	3.36	....	....	....	....	....	....	....	....	....	....	....	....	....	....	....	....	....
1983-84	**Detroit Red Wings**	**NHL**	**14**	**5**	**8**	**1**	**808**	**52**	**0**	**3.86**	**3.04**	**5.56**	**361**	**.856**	**26.8**	**1**	**0**	**0**	....	**7**	**2**	**0**	**17.14**	**68.56**	**5**	**.600**	**42.9**
	Adirondack Red Wings	AHL	29	14	10	5	1767	132	0	4.48	....	....	....	....	....	1	0	0	0	1	0	0	0.00	....	....	....	....
1984-85	**Detroit Red Wings**	**NHL**	**36**	**5**	**19**	**7**	**1856**	**136**	**0**	**4.40**	**3.52**	**6.07**	**986**	**.862**	**31.9**	**2**	**0**	**0**	....	**42**	**6**	**0**	**8.57**	**28.57**	**18**	**.667**	**25.7**
	Adirondack Red Wings	AHL	1	1	0	0	60	2	0	2.00	....	....	....	....	....	....	....	....	....	....	....	....	....	....	....	....	....
1985-86	**Detroit Red Wings**	**NHL**	**11**	**1**	**9**	**1**	**565**	**52**	**0**	**5.52**	**4.32**	**8.39**	**342**	**.848**	**36.3**	....	....	....	....	....	....	....	....	....	....	....	....
	Kalamazoo Wings	IHL	7	....	....	....	398	29	0	4.37	....	....	....	....	....	....	....	....	....	....	....	....	....	....	....	....	....
	Adirondack Red Wings	AHL	25	12	9	2	1436	93	0	3.89	....	....	....	....	....	....	....	....	....	....	....	....	....	....	....	....	....
	Canada	WEC-A	DID NOT PLAY – SPARE GOALTENDER																								
1986-87	Adirondack Red Wings	AHL	1	0	1	0	59	5	0	5.08	....	....	....	....	....	....	....	....	....	....	....	....	....	....	....	....	....
	HC Fribourg-Gotteron	Switz.	13	....	....	....	710	66	0	5.57	....	....	....	....	....	....	....	....	....	....	....	....	....	....	....	....	....
1987-88			STATISTICS NOT AVAILABLE																								
1988-89	CS Villard-de-Lans	France	17	....	....	....	1013	78	0	4.62	....	....	....	....	....	....	....	....	....	....	....	....	....	....	....	....	....
1989-90	CS Villard-de-Lans	France-2	30	....	....	....	1670	168	0	6.04	....	....	....	....	....	....	....	....	....	....	....	....	....	....	....	....	....
1990-91	HC Briacon	France	28	....	....	....	1643	85	0	3.11	....	....	....	....	....	....	....	....	....	....	....	....	....	....	....	....	....
1991-92	HC Briacon	France	19	....	....	....	1093	54	1	2.96	....	....	....	....	....	....	....	....	....	....	....	....	....	....	....	....	....
1992-93	HC Varese	Italy	19	....	....	....	1077	84	0	4.68	....	....	....	....	....	....	....	....	....	....	....	....	....	....	....	....	....
1993-94	HC Courmaosta	Italy	26	....	....	....	1433	95	0	3.98	....	....	....	....	....	....	....	....	....	....	....	....	....	....	....	....	....
1994-95	HC Courmaosta	Italy	STATISTICS NOT AVAILABLE																								
1995-96	San Francisco Spiders	IHL	18	4	8	2	851	56	0	3.95	....	....	....	....	....	....	....	....	....	....	....	....	....	....	....	....	....
1996-97	EHC Trier	Germany-2	39	....	....	....	2249	139	4	3.63	....	....	....	....	....	....	....	....	....	....	....	....	....	....	....	....	....
1997-98	EHC Trier	Germany-2	STATISTICS NOT AVAILABLE																								
1998-99	EHC Harz	Germany-2	42	....	....	....	2479	115	*5	2.78	....	....	....	....	....	4	....	....	....	235	5	1	1.28	....	....	....	....
99-2000	ESC Erfurt	Germany-2	48	....	....	....	2714	120	*6	2.65	....	....	....	....	....	....	....	....	....	....	....	....	....	....	....	....	....
	NHL Totals		**113**	**26**	**59**	**15**	**5794**	**409**	**2**	**4.24**	....	....	....	....	....	**3**	**0**	**0**	....	**49**	**8**	**0**	**9.80**	....	**23**	**.652**	**28.2**

QMJHL Second All-Star Team (1980) • QMJHL First All-Star Team (1981) • Memorial Cup All-Star Team (1981) • Won Hap Emms Memorial Trophy (Memorial Cup Tournament Top Goaltender) (1981)

• Loaned to **Cornwall** (QMJHL) by **Sherbrooke** (QMJHL) for Memorial Cup Tournament, May, 1981. • Played w/ RHI's Montreal Roadrunners in 1994 (18-4-4-0-527-79-0-7.19) and 1995 (13-7-3-1-566-61-0-5.17); Orlando Rollergators in 1996 (5-2-1-0-161-31-0-9.24) and San Jose Rhinos in 1997 (16-8-4-1-592-72-0-5.84)

• MICHAUD, Alfie

G. 5'10", 177 lbs. b: Selkirk, Man., 11/6/1976.

Season	Club	League	GP	W	L	T	Mins	GA	SO	Avg	AAvg	Eff	SA	S%	SAPG	GP	W	L	T	Mins	GA	SO	Avg	Eff	SA	S%	SAPG
1995-96	Lebret Eagles	SJHL	44	....	....	....	2547	121	2	2.85	....	....	....	....	....	....	....	....	....	....	....	....	....	....	....	....	....
1996-97	University of Maine	H-East	29	*17	8	1	1515	78	1	3.09	....	....	....	....	....	....	....	....	....	....	....	....	....	....	....	....	....
1997-98	University of Maine	H-East	32	15	12	4	1794	94	2	3.14	....	....	....	....	....	....	....	....	....	....	....	....	....	....	....	....	....
1998-99	University of Maine	H-East	37	*28	6	3	2147	83	3	2.32	....	....	....	....	....	....	....	....	....	....	....	....	....	....	....	....	....
99-2000	**Vancouver Canucks**	**NHL**	**2**	**0**	**1**	**0**	**69**	**5**	**0**	**4.35**	**4.97**	**8.06**	**27**	**.815**	**23.5**	....	....	....	....	....	....	....	....	....	....	....	....
	Syracuse Crunch	AHL	38	10	17	5	2052	132	0	3.86	....	....	....	....	....	....	....	....	....	....	....	....	....	....	....	....	....
	NHL Totals		**2**	**0**	**1**	**0**	**69**	**5**	**0**	**4.35**	....	....	**27**	**.815**	**23.5**	....	....	....	....	....	....	....	....	....	....	....	....

NCAA Championship All-Tournament Team (1999) • NCAA Championship Tournament MVP (1999)

Signed as a free agent by **Vancouver**, July 12, 1999.

• MIDDLEBROOK, Lindsay

G – R. 5'7", 160 lbs. b: Collingwood, Ont., 9/7/1955.

Season	Club	League	GP	W	L	T	Mins	GA	SO	Avg	AAvg	Eff	SA	S%	SAPG	GP	W	L	T	Mins	GA	SO	Avg	Eff	SA	S%	SAPG
1972-73	Wexford Raiders	OHA-B	STATISTICS NOT AVAILABLE																								
1973-74	St. Louis University	CCHA	2	0	1	0	41	6	0	8.82	....	....	....	....	....	....	....	....	....	....	....	....	....	....	....	....	....
1974-75	St. Louis University	CCHA	24	....	....	....	1459	71	1	2.98	....	....	....	....	....	....	....	....	....	....	....	....	....	....	....	....	....
1975-76	St. Louis University	CCHA	30	....	....	....	1767	88	0	2.99	....	....	....	....	....	....	....	....	....	....	....	....	....	....	....	....	....
1976-77	St. Louis University	CCHA	18	....	....	....	1058	54	1	3.07	....	....	....	....	....	....	....	....	....	....	....	....	....	....	....	....	....
1977-78	New Haven Nighthawks	AHL	17	5	9	3	968	71	0	4.40	....	....	....	....	....	....	....	....	....	....	....	....	....	....	....	....	....
	Toledo Goaldiggers	IHL	16	....	....	....	949	45	*2	2.85	....	....	....	....	....	13	....	....	....	739	32	0	2.60	....	....	....	....
1978-79	New Haven Nighthawks	AHL	*54	*29	19	5	*3221	173	1	3.22	....	....	....	....	....	5	2	3	0	301	16	0	3.19	....	....	....	....
1979-80	**Winnipeg Jets**	**NHL**	**10**	**2**	**8**	**0**	**580**	**40**	**0**	**4.14**	**3.66**	....	....	....	....	....	....	....	....	....	....	....	....	....	....	....	....
	Tulsa Oilers	CHL	37	16	15	3	2073	102	0	2.95	....	....	....	....	....	2	0	2	0	119	8	0	4.03	....	....	....	....
1980-81	**Winnipeg Jets**	**NHL**	**14**	**0**	**9**	**3**	**653**	**65**	**0**	**5.97**	**4.84**	....	....	....	....	....	....	....	....	....	....	....	....	....	....	....	....
	Tulsa Oilers	CHL	36	17	16	2	2115	120	2	3.63	....	....	....	....	....	8	4	4	0	479	33	0	4.13	....	....	....	....
1981-82	**Minnesota North Stars**	**NHL**	**3**	**0**	**0**	**2**	**140**	**7**	**0**	**3.00**	**2.32**	....	....	....	....	....	....	....	....	....	....	....	....	....	....	....	....
	Nashville South Stars	CHL	31	17	11	2	1868	93	*3	2.99	....	....	....	....	....	3	0	3	0	179	11	0	3.69	....	....	....	....
1982-83	**New Jersey Devils**	**NHL**	**9**	**0**	**6**	**1**	**412**	**37**	**0**	**5.39**	**4.33**	**9.07**	**220**	**.832**	**32.0**	....	....	....	....	....	....	....	....	....	....	....	....
	Wichita Wind	CHL	13	6	7	0	779	46	0	3.54	....	....	....	....	....	....	....	....	....	....	....	....	....	....	....	....	....
	Edmonton Oilers	**NHL**	**1**	**1**	**0**	**0**	**60**	**3**	**0**	**3.00**	**2.41**	**2.73**	**33**	**.909**	**33.0**	....	....	....	....	....	....	....	....	....	....	....	....
	Moncton Alpines	AHL	11	6	4	1	669	42	0	3.77	....	....	....	....	....	....	....	....	....	....	....	....	....	....	....	....	....
1983-84	Montana Magic	CHL	36	10	22	3	2104	162	0	4.62	....	....	....	....	....	....	....	....	....	....	....	....	....	....	....	....	....
1984-85	Toledo Goaldiggers	IHL	50	18	25	3	2791	183	0	3.93	....	....	....	....	....	6	2	4	0	339	24	0	4.25	....	....	....	....
1985-86	Milwaukee Admirals	IHL	56	33	10	0	3318	191	*3	3.45	....	....	....	....	....	5	1	4	0	298	18	1	3.62	....	....	....	....
1986-87	Danville Fighting Saints	AAHL	STATISTICS NOT AVAILABLE																								
	NHL Totals		**37**	**3**	**23**	**6**	**1845**	**152**	**0**	**4.94**	....	....	....	....	....	....	....	....	....	....	....	....	....	....	....	....	....

CCHA First All-Star Team (1975) • AHL First All-Star Team (1979) • CHL Second All-Star Team (1981)

Signed as a free agent by **NY Rangers**, October 12, 1977. Claimed by **Winnipeg** from **NY Rangers** in Expansion Draft, June 13, 1979. Traded to **Minnesota** by **Winnipeg** for cash, July 31, 1981. Signed as a free agent by **New Jersey**, September 25, 1982. Traded to **Edmonton** by **New Jersey** with Paul Miller for Ron Low and Jim McTaggart, February 19, 1983.

• MILLAR, Al

Franklin Allan G – L. 5'11", 175 lbs. b: Winnipeg, Man., 9/18/1929 Deceased.

Season	Club	League	GP	W	L	T	Mins	GA	SO	Avg	AAvg	Eff	SA	S%	SAPG	GP	W	L	T	Mins	GA	SO	Avg	Eff	SA	S%	SAPG
1947-48	Winnipeg Canadiens	MJHL	17	10	4	2	1010	65	0	*3.80	....	....	....	....	....	6	2	4	0	310	29	0	5.61	....	....	....	....
1948-49	St-Hyacinthe Flyers	QJHL	28	14	12	1	1680	85	1	3.04	....	....	....	....	....	....	....	....	....	....	....	....	....	....	....	....	....
	Montreal Nationale	QJHL	2	1	1	0	120	11	1	5.50	....	....	....	....	....	....	....	....	....	....	....	....	....	....	....	....	....
	Montreal Jr. Canadiens	QJHL	....	....	....	....	....	....	....	....	....	....	....	....	....	1	0	1	0	60	4	0	4.00	....	....	....	....
1949-50	Quebec Aces	QSHL	37	21	14	2	2250	109	2	2.91	....	....	....	....	....	13	7	*6	0	780	35	*2	2.69	....	....	....	....
1950-51	New Haven Ramblers	AHL	19	3	16	0	1160	105	1	5.43	....	....	....	....	....	....	....	....	....	....	....	....	....	....	....	....	....
	Kansas City Royals	USHL	4	2	2	0	240	15	1	3.75	....	....	....	....	....	....	....	....	....	....	....	....	....	....	....	....	....
	Portland Eagles	PCHL	28	15	10	3	1680	95	0	3.39	....	....	....	....	....	....	....	....	....	....	....	....	....	....	....	....	....
1951-52	Shawinigan Cataracts	QMHL	60	19	34	7	3680	200	5	3.26	....	....	....	....	....	....	....	....	....	....	....	....	....	....	....	....	....
1952-53	Quebec Aces	QMHL	4	1	3	0	240	22	0	5.50	....	....	....	....	....	....	....	....	....	....	....	....	....	....	....	....	....
	Charlottetown Islanders	MMHL	67	37	26	4	4038	200	6	*3.01	....	....	....	....	....	18	9	9	0	1142	61	1	3.20	....	....	....	....
1953-54	Sudbury Wolves	NOHA	32	18	13	1	1920	120	2	3.75	....	....	....	....	....	4	3	1	0	250	8	0	1.92	....	....	....	....
1954-55	Sault Ste. Marie Indians	NOHA	60	27	27	6	3600	190	*5	3.17	....	....	....	....	....	7	3	4	0	400	18	1	2.70	....	....	....	....
1955-56	Sault Ste. Marie Indians	NOHA	60	26	29	5	3600	207	3	3.45	....	....	....	....	....	7	3	4	0	420	22	0	3.14	....	....	....	....
	Quebec Aces	QHL	3	2	1	0	180	8	1	2.67	....	....	....	....	....	7	3	4	0	426	20	0	2.82	....	....	....	....
1956-57	Quebec Aces	QHL	*65	38	20	7	*3988	165	*5	*2.48	....	....	....	....	....	16	*13	3	0	960	48	*1	3.00	....	....	....	....

			REGULAR SEASON													PLAYOFFS											
Season	Club	League	GP	W	L	T	Mins	GA	SO	Avg	AAvg	Eff	SA	S%	SAPG	GP	W	L	T	Mins	GA	SO	Avg	Eff	SA	S%	SAPG
1957-58	Springfield Indians	AHL	14	2	9	3	873	56	1	3.85						5	3	2	0								
	Quebec Aces	QHL	25	9	15	1	1500	97	0	3.88						13	7	6	0	827	28	*2	*2.03				
	Boston Bruins	**NHL**	**6**	**1**	**4**	**1**	**360**	**25**	**0**	**4.17**	**4.61**																
	Buffalo Bisons	AHL	5	2	3	0	300	19	0	3.80																	
	Chicoutimi Sagueneens	QHL	1	0	1	0	60	7	0	7.00																	
1958-59	Quebec Aces	QHL	*62	21	33	8	3809	232	1	3.65																	
1959-60	Quebec Aces	AHL	61	16	42	2	3660	273	2	4.48																	
1960-61	Hershey Bears	AHL	32	14	16	1	1894	90	2	2.85																	
	Sudbury Wolves	EPHL	2	2	0	0	120	7	0	3.50																	
1961-62	Seattle Totems	WHL	58	30	23	5	3540	182	3	3.08						2	0	2	0	119	6	0	3.03				
1962-63	Seattle Totems	WHL	*70	35	33	2	4200	232	0	3.31						*17	9	8	0	*1061	56	0	3.17				
1963-64	Denver Invaders	WHL	*70	*44	23	3	4230	198	*4	*2.81						3	1	2	0	179	13	0	4.36				
1964-65	Victoria Maple Leafs	WHL	64	31	31	2	3835	208	4	3.25						*10	5	5	0	*600	25	0	2.50				
1965-66	Victoria Maple Leafs	WHL	51	29	18	4	3100	160	0	3.10																	
	Tulsa Oilers	CPHL	16	8	5	3	960	43	1	2.69						*11	4	7	0	*694	47	*1	4.06				
1966-67	Tulsa Oilers	CPHL	62	12	36	14	3732	241	1	3.87																	
1967-68	Quebec Aces	AHL	33	15	12	4	1771	100	1	3.39						5	3	2	0	298	18	0	3.62				
1968-69	Vancouver Canucks	WHL	12	4	4	1	580	34	0	3.52																	
1969-70	Rochester Americans	AHL	11	3	8	0	577	52	0	5.41																	
	NHL Totals		**6**	**1**	**4**	**1**	**360**	**25**	**0**	**4.17**																	

QSHL Second All-Star Team (1950) • QMHL Second All-Star Team (1952) • MMHL First All-Star Team (1953) • NOHA Second All-Star Team (1956) • QHL First All-Star Team (1957) • Won Vezina Memorial Trophy (Top Goaltender - QHL) (1957) • WHL First All-Star Team (1962, 1964) • Won WHL Leading Goaltender Award (1962, 1964)

Signed as a free agent by **New Haven** (AHL), September 17, 1950. Signed as a free agent by **Kansas City** (USHL) (after New Haven folded), December 10, 1950. Traded to **Portland** (PCHL) by **Kansas City** (USHL) for Wally Bak, January, 1951. Traded to **Quebec** (QMHL) by **Detroit** for cash, September 16, 1951. Promoted to **Boston** from **Quebec** (AHL) to replace injured Don Simmons in games from January 1 through 12, 1958. Traded to **Detroit** (Hershey-AHL) by **Boston** (Quebec-AHL) with Myron Stankiewicz for Claude Dufour, June, 1960. Transferred to **Seattle** (WHL) by **Detroit** as compensation for the loss of Les Hunt and Marc Boileau, November 5, 1961. Traded to **Toronto** (Denver-WHL) by **Seattle** (WHL) for cash, September, 1963. Traded to **Philadelphia** by **Toronto** for cash, September, 1967. Traded to **Vancouver** (WHL) by **Philadelphia** for cash, October, 1968. Rights transferred to **Vancouver** after NHL club purchased **Vancouver** (WHL) franchise, December 19, 1969.

• MILLEN, Greg

Gregory H. G – R. 5'9", 175 lbs. b: Toronto, Ont., 6/25/1957. Pittsburgh's 4th, 102nd overall in 1977.

Season	Club	League	GP	W	L	T	Mins	GA	SO	Avg	AAvg	Eff	SA	S%	SAPG	GP	W	L	T	Mins	GA	SO	Avg	Eff	SA	S%	SAPG
1973-74	Markham Waxers	OHA-B	STATISTICS NOT AVAILABLE																								
1974-75	Peterborough Petes	OMJHL	27				1584	90	2	*3.41						5				300	14	0	2.80				
1975-76	Peterborough Petes	OMJHL	58				3282	233	0	4.26																	
1976-77	Peterborough Petes	OMJHL	59				3457	244	0	4.23						4	1	3	0	240	23	0	5.75				
1977-78	Sault Ste. Marie Greyhounds	OMJHL	25				1469	105	1	4.29						13	6	6	1	774	61	0	4.73				
	Kalamazoo Wings	IHL	3				180	14	0	4.67																	
1978-79	**Pittsburgh Penguins**	**NHL**	**28**	**14**	**11**	**1**	**1532**	**86**	**2**	**3.37**	**2.98**																
1979-80	**Pittsburgh Penguins**	**NHL**	**44**	**18**	**18**	**7**	**2586**	**157**	**2**	**3.64**	**3.22**					**5**	**2**	**3**		**300**	**21**	**0**	**4.20**				
1980-81	**Pittsburgh Penguins**	**NHL**	**63**	**25**	**27**	**10**	**3721**	**258**	**0**	**4.16**	**3.38**					**5**	**2**	**3**		**325**	**19**	**0**	**3.51**				
1981-82	**Hartford Whalers**	**NHL**	**55**	**11**	**30**	**12**	**3201**	**229**	**0**	**4.29**	**3.32**																
	Canada	WEC-A	5	2	1	2	300	14	1	2.80																	
1982-83	**Hartford Whalers**	**NHL**	**60**	**14**	**38**	**6**	**3520**	**282**	**1**	**4.81**	**3.90**	**6.60**	**2056**	**.863**	**35.0**												
1983-84	**Hartford Whalers**	**NHL**	***60**	**21**	**30**	**9**	***3583**	**221**	**2**	**3.70**	**2.91**	**4.50**	**1817**	**.878**	**30.4**												
1984-85	**Hartford Whalers**	**NHL**	**44**	**16**	**22**	**6**	**2659**	**187**	**1**	**4.22**	**3.37**	**6.13**	**1288**	**.855**	**29.1**												
	St. Louis Blues	**NHL**	**10**	**2**	**7**	**1**	**607**	**35**	**0**	**3.46**	**2.76**	**4.47**	**271**	**.871**	**26.8**	**1**	**0**	**1**		**60**	**2**	**0**	**2.00**	**1.14**	**35**	**.943**	**35.0**
1985-86	**St. Louis Blues**	**NHL**	**36**	**14**	**16**	**6**	**2168**	**129**	**1**	**3.57**	**2.78**	**4.04**	**1140**	**.887**	**31.5**	**10**	**6**	**3**		**586**	**29**	**0**	**2.97**	**2.61**	**330**	**.912**	**33.8**
1986-87	**St. Louis Blues**	**NHL**	**42**	**15**	**18**	**9**	**2482**	**146**	**0**	**3.53**	**2.99**	**4.47**	**1152**	**.873**	**27.8**	**4**	**1**	**3**		**250**	**10**	**0**	**2.40**	**1.97**	**122**	**.918**	**29.3**
1987-88	**St. Louis Blues**	**NHL**	**48**	**21**	**19**	**7**	**2854**	**167**	**1**	**3.51**	**2.92**	**4.20**	**1396**	**.880**	**29.3**	**10**	**5**	**5**		**600**	**38**	**0**	**3.80**	**5.73**	**252**	**.849**	**25.2**
1988-89	**St. Louis Blues**	**NHL**	**52**	**22**	**20**	**7**	**3019**	**170**	***6**	**3.38**	**2.81**	**4.07**	**1411**	**.880**	**28.0**	**10**	**5**	**5**		**649**	**34**	**0**	**3.14**	**3.47**	**308**	**.890**	**28.5**
1989-90	**St. Louis Blues**	**NHL**	**21**	**11**	**7**	**3**	**1245**	**61**	**1**	**2.94**	**2.48**	**3.23**	**556**	**.890**	**26.8**												
	Quebec Nordiques	**NHL**	**18**	**3**	**14**	**1**	**1080**	**95**	**0**	**5.28**	**4.50**	**7.74**	**648**	**.853**	**36.0**												
	Chicago Blackhawks	**NHL**	**10**	**5**	**4**	**1**	**575**	**32**	**0**	**3.34**	**2.83**	**4.00**	**267**	**.880**	**27.9**	**14**	**6**	**6**		**613**	**40**	**0**	**3.92**	**5.23**	**300**	**.867**	**29.4**
1990-91	**Chicago Blackhawks**	**NHL**	**3**	**0**	**1**	**0**	**58**	**4**	**0**	**4.14**	**3.72**	**5.18**	**32**	**.875**	**33.1**												
1991-92	Maine Mariners	AHL	11	2	5	2	599	37	0	3.71																	
	Detroit Red Wings	**NHL**	**10**	**3**	**2**	**3**	**487**	**22**	**0**	**2.71**	**2.42**	**2.81**	**212**	**.896**	**26.1**												
	San Diego Gulls	IHL	5	2	3	0	296	20	0	4.05																	
	NHL Totals		**604**	**215**	**284**	**89**	**35377**	**2281**	**17**	**3.87**						**59**	**27**	**29**		**3383**	**193**	**0**	**3.42**				

Signed as a free agent by **Hartford**, June 15, 1981. Traded to **St. Louis** by **Hartford** with Mark Johnson for Mike Liut and Jorgen Pettersson, February 21, 1985. Traded to **Quebec** by **St. Louis** with Tony Hrkac for Jeff Brown, December 13, 1989. Traded to **Chicago** by **Quebec** with Michel Goulet and Quebec's 6th round choice (Kevin St. Jacques) in 1991 Entry Draft for Mario Doyon, Everett Sanipass and Dan Vincelette, March 5, 1990. Traded to **NY Rangers** by **Chicago** for future considerations, September 24, 1991. Traded to **Detroit** by **NY Rangers** for future considerations, December 26, 1991.

• MILLER, Joe

Joseph Anthony G. 5'9", 170 lbs. b: Morrisburg, Ont., 10/6/1900 d: 8/12/1963.

Season	Club	League	GP	W	L	T	Mins	GA	SO	Avg	AAvg	Eff	SA	S%	SAPG	GP	W	L	T	Mins	GA	SO	Avg	Eff	SA	S%	SAPG
1916-17	Pittsburgh AA	X-Games	40	37	3	0	2447	63	5	1.54																	
1917-18	Renfrew Creamery Kings	X-Games	7	4	3	0	432	16	0	2.22																	
1918-19	Ottawa New Edinburghs	OCHL	4	3	1	0	240	5	2	1.25																	
1919-20	Ottawa New Edinburghs	OCHL	7	4	2	0	400	10	1	1.50																	
1920-21	Ottawa New Edinburghs	OCHL	11	4	6	1	675	25	0	2.22																	
1921-22	Ottawa New Edinburghs	OCHL	13	4	7	2	780	30	2	2.31																	
1922-23	Ottawa New Edinburghs	OCHL	18	10	6	2	1200	43	2	2.15						5	1	3	1	340	8	1	1.41				
1923-24	Ottawa New Edinburghs	OCHL	12	*9	3	0	720	18	1	1.50						2	0	2	0	120	5	0	2.50				
1924-25	Fort Pitt Hornets	USAHA	22	*17	5	0	1020	39	*1	*1.72						4	1	3	0	220	9	0	2.45				
1925-26	St. Paul Saints	CHL	38				2280	70	6	1.84																	
1926-27	St. Paul Saints	AHA	30	13	12	5	1850	54	*10	1.75																	
1927-28	**New York Americans**	**NHL**	**28**	**8**	**16**	**4**	**1721**	**77**	**5**	**2.68**	**4.43**																
	Niagara Falls Cataracts	Can-Pro	13				780	30	2	2.31																	
♦	**New York Rangers**	**NHL**														**3**	**2**	**1**	**0**	**180**	**3**	**1**	**1.00**				
1928-29	**Pittsburgh Pirates**	**NHL**	***44**	**9**	**27**	**8**	**2780**	**80**	**11**	**1.73**	**3.69**																
1929-30	**Pittsburgh Pirates**	**NHL**	**43**	**5**	**35**	**3**	**2630**	**179**	**0**	**4.08**	**4.39**																
1930-31	**Philadelphia Quakers**	**NHL**	**12**	**2**	**9**	**1**	**740**	**47**	**0**	**3.81**	**4.93**																
1931-32	Syracuse Stars	IHL	20	5	11	4	1260	51	3	2.43																	
	NHL Totals		**127**	**24**	**87**	**16**	**7871**	**383**	**16**	**2.92**						**3**	**2**	**1**	**0**	**180**	**3**	**1**	**1.00**				

NHL rights traded to **NY Americans** by **Pittsburgh** for the rights to Odie Cleghorn and the loan of Jesse Spring, January 23, 1926. Signed as a free agent by **St. Paul** (AHA), October 21, 1926. Loaned to **Niagara Falls** (Can-Pro) by **NY Americans** for cash, February 7, 1928. Loaned to **NY Rangers** by **NY Americans** to replace injured Lorne Chabot for remainder of Stanley Cup Finals, April 10, 1928. Traded to **Pittsburgh** by **NY Americans** with $20,000 for Roy Worters, November 1, 1928. Transferred to **Philadelphia** after **Pittsburgh** franchise relocated, October 26, 1930.

• MINARD, Mike

Michael Edward Roger G – L. 6'3", 205 lbs. b: Owen Sound, Ont., 11/1/1976. Edmonton's 4th, 83rd overall in 1995.

Season	Club	League	GP	W	L	T	Mins	GA	SO	Avg	AAvg	Eff	SA	S%	SAPG	GP	W	L	T	Mins	GA	SO	Avg	Eff	SA	S%	SAPG
1992-93	St. Mary's Lincolns	OJHL-B	23				1374	162	0	3.10																	
1993-94	St. Mary's Lincolns	OJHL-B	31	*25	5	0	1710	78	1	*2.74																	
1994-95	Chilliwack Chiefs	BCJHL	40				2330	136	0	3.50																	
1995-96	Barrie Colts	OHL	1	0	1	0	52	8	0	9.23																	
	Detroit Jr. Whalers	OHL	42	25	10	4	2314	128	2	3.32						17	9	6		922	55	1	3.58				
1996-97	Hamilton Bulldogs	AHL	3	1	1	0	100	7	0	4.20																	
	Wheeling Nailers	ECHL	23	3	7	1	899	69	0	4.60						3	0	2		148	16	0	6.47				
1997-98	Hamilton Bulldogs	AHL	2	1	0	0	80	2	0	1.50																	
	Brantford Smoke	UHL	2	1	1	0	74	7	0	5.63																	
	New Orleans Brass	ECHL	11	6	2	0	429	30	0	4.19																	
	Milwaukee Admirals	IHL	8	2	2	0	362	19	0	3.15																	

			REGULAR SEASON													PLAYOFFS											
Season	**Club**	**League**	**GP**	**W**	**L**	**T**	**Mins**	**GA**	**SO**	**Avg**	**AAvg**	**Eff**	**SA**	**S%**	**SAPG**	**GP**	**W**	**L**	**T**	**Mins**	**GA**	**SO**	**Avg**	**Eff**	**SA**	**S%**	**SAPG**
1998-99	Dayton Bombers	ECHL	15	8	5	2	788	42	1	3.20	....	....	....	....	....	....	....	....	....	....	....	....	....	....	....	....	....
	Milwaukee Admirals	IHL	10	3	5	0	531	27	0	3.05	....	....	....	....	....	....	....	....	....	....	....	....	....	....	....	....	....
	Hamilton Bulldogs	AHL	11	8	3	0	645	30	1	2.79	....	....	....	....	....	1	0	0	....	20	0	0	0.00	....	....	....	....
99-2000	**Edmonton Oilers**	**NHL**	**1**	**1**	**0**	**0**	**60**	**3**	**0**	**3.00**	**3.43**	**2.50**	**36**	**.917**	**36.0**	....	....	....	....	....	....	....	....	....	....	....	....
	Hamilton Bulldogs	AHL	38	16	12	5	1987	102	0	3.08	....	....	....	....	....	1	0	0	....	23	0	0	0.00	....	....	....	....
	NHL Totals		**1**	**1**	**0**	**0**	**60**	**3**	**0**	**3.00**	....	....	**36**	**.917**	**36.0**	....	....	....	....	....	....	....	....	....	....	....	....

• MIO, Eddie

Edward Dario G – L. 5'10", 180 lbs. b: Windsor, Ont., 1/31/1954. Chicago's 7th, 124th overall in 1974.

Season	Club	League	GP	W	L	T	Mins	GA	SO	Avg	AAvg	Eff	SA	S%	SAPG	GP	W	L	T	Mins	GA	SO	Avg	Eff	SA	S%	SAPG
1971-72	Windsor Spitfires	OJHL	STATISTICS NOT AVAILABLE																								
1972-73	Colorado College	WCHA	23	6	17	0	1322	119	0	5.40	....	....	....	....	....	....	....	....	....	....	....	....	....	....	....	....	....
1973-74	Colorado College	WCHA	13	4	7	2	698	57	0	4.90	....	....	....	....	....	....	....	....	....	....	....	....	....	....	....	....	....
1974-75	Colorado College	WCHA	21	....	....	....	1260	83	0	3.95	....	....	....	....	....	....	....	....	....	....	....	....	....	....	....	....	....
1975-76	Colorado College	WCHA	34	15	18	1	2038	144	0	4.24	....	....	....	....	....	....	....	....	....	....	....	....	....	....	....	....	....
1976-77	Tidewater Sharks	SHL	19	....	....	....	1123	66	1	3.53	....	....	....	....	....	....	....	....	....	....	....	....	....	....	....	....	....
	Erie Blades	NAHL	17	....	....	....	771	42	0	3.27	....	....	....	....	....	2	0	1	0	80	8	0	6.00	....	....	....	....
1977-78	Hampton Gulls	AHL	19	5	9	0	949	53	2	3.35	....	....	....	....	....	....	....	....	....	....	....	....	....	....	....	....	....
	Indianapolis Racers	WHA	17	6	8	0	900	64	0	4.27	....	....	....	....	....	....	....	....	....	....	....	....	....	....	....	....	....
1978-79	Dallas Black Hawks	CHL	7	4	3	0	424	25	0	3.54	....	....	....	....	....	....	....	....	....	....	....	....	....	....	....	....	....
	Indianapolis Racers	WHA	5	2	2	1	242	13	1	3.22	....	....	....	....	....	....	....	....	....	....	....	....	....	....	....	....	....
	Edmonton Oilers	WHA	22	7	10	0	1068	71	1	3.99	....	....	....	....	....	3	0	0	0	90	6	0	4.00	....	....	....	....
1979-80	**Edmonton Oilers**	**NHL**	**34**	**9**	**13**	**5**	**1711**	**120**	**1**	**4.21**	**3.74**	....	....	....	....	....	....	....	....	....	....	....	....	....	....	....	....
1980-81	**Edmonton Oilers**	**NHL**	**43**	**16**	**15**	**9**	**2393**	**155**	**0**	**3.89**	**3.15**	....	....	....	....	....	....	....	....	....	....	....	....	....	....	....	....
1981-82	Wichita Wind	CHL	11	3	8	0	657	46	0	4.20	....	....	....	....	....	....	....	....	....	....	....	....	....	....	....	....	....
	New York Rangers	**NHL**	**25**	**13**	**6**	**5**	**1500**	**89**	**0**	**3.56**	**2.75**	....	....	....	....	**8**	**4**	**3**	....	**443**	**28**	**0**	**3.79**	....	....	....	....
1982-83	**New York Rangers**	**NHL**	**41**	**16**	**18**	**6**	**2365**	**136**	**2**	**3.45**	**2.76**	**4.05**	**1159**	**.883**	**29.4**	**8**	**5**	**3**	....	**480**	**32**	**0**	**4.00**	....	....	....	....
1983-84	**Detroit Red Wings**	**NHL**	**24**	**7**	**11**	**3**	**1295**	**95**	**1**	**4.40**	**3.47**	**6.17**	**677**	**.860**	**31.4**	**1**	**0**	**1**	....	**63**	**3**	**0**	**2.86**	**3.58**	**24**	**.875**	**22.9**
	Adirondack Red Wings	AHL	4	1	1	2	250	11	0	2.64	....	....	....	....	....	....	....	....	....	....	....	....	....	....	....	....	....
1984-85	**Detroit Red Wings**	**NHL**	**7**	**1**	**3**	**2**	**376**	**27**	**0**	**4.31**	**3.44**	**6.69**	**174**	**.845**	**27.8**	....	....	....	....	....	....	....	....	....	....	....	....
	Adirondack Red Wings	AHL	33	19	12	1	1871	871	2	3.75	....	....	....	....	....	....	....	....	....	....	....	....	....	....	....	....	....
1985-86	**Detroit Red Wings**	**NHL**	**18**	**2**	**7**	**0**	**788**	**83**	**0**	**6.32**	**4.96**	**11.58**	**453**	**.817**	**34.5**	....	....	....	....	....	....	....	....	....	....	....	....
	Adirondack Red Wings	AHL	8	4	1	3	487	32	0	3.94	....	....	....	....	....	....	....	....	....	....	....	....	....	....	....	....	....
	NHL Totals		**192**	**64**	**73**	**30**	**10428**	**705**	**4**	**4.06**	....	....	....	....	....	**17**	**9**	**7**	....	**986**	**63**	**0**	**3.83**	....	....	....	....
	Other Major League Totals		44	15	20	1	2210	148	2	4.02	....	....	....	....	....	3	0	0	....	90	6	0	4.00	....	....	....	....

WCHA Second All-Star Team (1975) • NCAA West First All-American Team (1975, 1976) • WCHA First All-Star Team (1976)

Selected by **Vancouver** (WHA) in 1974 WHA Amateur Draft, May, 1974. Signed as a free agent by **Birmingham** (WHA) after **Calgary** (WHA) franchise folded, May 31, 1977. Traded to **Indianapolis** (WHA) by **Birmingham** (WHA) for cash, February, 1978. NHL rights traded to **Minnesota** by **Chicago** with future considerations (Pierre Plante, May 4, 1978) for Doug Hicks and Minnesota's 3rd round choice (Marcel Frere) in 1980 Entry Draft, March 14, 1978. Traded to **Edmonton** (WHA) by **Indianapolis** (WHA) with Wayne Gretzky and Peter Driscoll for $700,000 and future considerations, November 2, 1978. Reclaimed by **Minnesota** from **Edmonton** prior to Expansion Draft, June 9, 1979. Claimed as priority selection by **Edmonton**, June 9, 1979. Traded to **NY Rangers** by **Edmonton** for Lance Nethery, December 11, 1981. Traded to **Detroit** by **NY Rangers** with Ron Duguay and Eddie Johnstone for Willie Huber, Mike Blaisdell and Mark Osborne, June 13, 1983.

• MITCHELL, Ivan

Ivan Joseph Gordon "Mike" G. b: , , 1896 Deceased.

Season	Club	League	GP	W	L	T	Mins	GA	SO	Avg	AAvg	Eff	SA	S%	SAPG	GP	W	L	T	Mins	GA	SO	Avg	Eff	SA	S%	SAPG
1913-14	Toronto Canoe Club	OHA-Jr.	4	1	3	0	240	21	0	5.25	....	....	....	....	....	....	....	....	....	....	....	....	....	....	....	....	....
1914-15	Toronto R & AA	OHA-Jr.	6	5	1	0	370	23	0	3.73	....	....	....	....	....	1	0	1	0	60	14	0	14.00	....	....	....	....
1915-16	Toronto R & AA	OHA-Sr.	4	0	4	0	240	32	0	8.00	....	....	....	....	....	....	....	....	....	....	....	....	....	....	....	....	....
1916-17			MILITARY SERVICE																								
1917-18	New York Wanderers	USAHA	STATISTICS NOT AVAILABLE																								
1918-19	Toronto Veterans	OHA-Sr.	2	0	2	0	120	22	0	11.00	....	....	....	....	....	....	....	....	....	....	....	....	....	....	....	....	....
1919-20	Toronto Granites	OHA-Sr.	1	1	0	0	60	3	0	3.00	....	....	....	....	....	....	....	....	....	....	....	....	....	....	....	....	....
	Toronto St. Pats	**NHL**	**16**	**6**	**7**	**0**	**830**	**60**	**0**	**4.34**	**2.72**	....	....	....	....	....	....	....	....	....	....	....	....	....	....	....	....
1920-21	**Toronto St. Pats**	**NHL**	**4**	**2**	**2**	**0**	**240**	**22**	**0**	**5.50**	**4.02**	....	....	....	....	....	....	....	....	....	....	....	....	....	....	....	....
1921-22	**Toronto St. Pats**	**NHL**	**2**	**2**	**0**	**0**	**120**	**6**	**0**	**3.00**	**2.30**	....	....	....	....	....	....	....	....	....	....	....	....	....	....	....	....
	NHL Totals		**22**	**10**	**9**	**0**	**1190**	**88**	**0**	**4.44**	....	....	....	....	....	....	....	....	....	....	....	....	....	....	....	....	....
	Other Major League Totals		6	5	1	0	370	23	0	3.73	....	....	....	....	....	1	0	1	....	60	14	0	14.00	....	....	....	....

Signed as a free agent by **Toronto**, December 15, 1919. Signed as a free agent by **Hamilton**, December 5, 1921. Loaned to **Toronto** by **Hamilton** to replace injured John Ross Roach, December 13, 1921. • Missed remainder of 1921-22 season recovering from eventual career-ending illness that required treatment at Mayo Clinic in Baltimore, MD.

• MOFFAT, Mike

Michael Anthony G – L. 5'10", 165 lbs. b: Galt, Ont., 2/4/1962. Boston's 7th, 165th overall in 1980.

Season	Club	League	GP	W	L	T	Mins	GA	SO	Avg	AAvg	Eff	SA	S%	SAPG	GP	W	L	T	Mins	GA	SO	Avg	Eff	SA	S%	SAPG
1979-80	Kingston Canadians	OMJHL	21	7	7	1	968	71	0	4.40	....	....	....	....	....	2	0	1	0	104	8	0	4.62	....	....	....	....
1980-81	Kingston Canadians	OMJHL	57	33	21	3	3442	211	0	3.68	....	....	....	....	....	14	6	6	0	814	56	0	4.13	....	....	....	....
1981-82	Kingston Canadians	OHL	46	19	21	4	2666	184	1	4.15	....	....	....	....	....	4	0	1	0	199	17	0	5.13	....	....	....	....
	Canada	WJC-A	4	3	0	1	240	7	1	1.75	....	....	....	....	....	....	....	....	....	....	....	....	....	....	....	....	....
	Boston Bruins	**NHL**	**2**	**2**	**0**	**0**	**120**	**6**	**0**	**3.00**	**2.32**	....	....	....	....	**11**	**6**	**5**	....	**663**	**38**	**0**	**3.44**	....	....	....	....
1982-83	**Boston Bruins**	**NHL**	**13**	**4**	**6**	**1**	**673**	**49**	**0**	**4.37**	**3.51**	**7.90**	**271**	**.819**	**24.2**	....	....	....	....	....	....	....	....	....	....	....	....
	Baltimore Skipjacks	AHL	17	5	8	3	937	78	0	4.99	....	....	....	....	....	....	....	....	....	....	....	....	....	....	....	....	....
1983-84	**Boston Bruins**	**NHL**	**4**	**1**	**1**	**1**	**186**	**15**	**0**	**4.84**	**3.81**	**8.96**	**81**	**.815**	**26.1**	....	....	....	....	....	....	....	....	....	....	....	....
	Hershey Bears	AHL	30	8	13	4	1592	124	0	4.67	....	....	....	....	....	....	....	....	....	....	....	....	....	....	....	....	....
1984-85	Nova Scotia Oilers	AHL	1	0	1	0	60	9	0	9.00	....	....	....	....	....	....	....	....	....	....	....	....	....	....	....	....	....
1985-86	Sir Wilfred Laurier University	OUAA	6	5	1	0	360	19	0	3.20	....	....	....	....	....	....	....	....	....	....	....	....	....	....	....	....	....
1986-87	Sir Wilfred Laurier University	OUAA	STATISTICS NOT AVAILABLE																								
	Canada	Nat-Team	6	2	3	1	333	18	0	3.24	....	....	....	....	....	....	....	....	....	....	....	....	....	....	....	....	....
	NHL Totals		**19**	**7**	**7**	**2**	**979**	**70**	**0**	**4.29**	....	....	**352**	**.801**	**21.6**	**11**	**6**	**5**	....	**663**	**38**	**0**	**3.44**	....	....	....	....

OMJHL Second All-Star Team (1981) • WJC-A All-Star Team (1982) • Named Best Goaltender at WJC-A (1982)

• MOOG, Andy

Donald Andrew G – L. 5'8", 175 lbs. b: Penticton, B.C., 2/18/1960. Edmonton's 6th, 132nd overall in 1980.

Season	Club	League	GP	W	L	T	Mins	GA	SO	Avg	AAvg	Eff	SA	S%	SAPG	GP	W	L	T	Mins	GA	SO	Avg	Eff	SA	S%	SAPG
1976-77	Kamloops Braves	BCJHL	44	18	26	0	2735	173	1	3.81	....	....	....	....	....	....	....	....	....	....	....	....	....	....	....	....	....
1977-78	Penticton Vees	BCJHL	38	19	19	0	2280	194	0	5.11	....	....	....	....	....	....	....	....	....	....	....	....	....	....	....	....	....
1978-79	Billings Bighorns	WHL	26	13	5	4	1306	90	4	4.13	....	....	....	....	....	5	1	3	....	229	21	0	5.50	....	....	....	....
1979-80	Billings Bighorns	WHL	46	23	14	1	2435	149	1	3.67	....	....	....	....	....	3	2	1	....	190	10	0	3.16	....	....	....	....
1980-81	**Edmonton Oilers**	**NHL**	**7**	**3**	**3**	**0**	**313**	**20**	**0**	**3.83**	**3.10**	**4.51**	**170**	**.882**	**32.6**	**9**	**5**	**4**	....	**526**	**32**	**0**	**3.65**	....	....	....	....
	Wichita Wind	CHL	29	14	13	1	1602	89	0	3.33	....	....	....	....	....	5	3	2	....	300	16	0	3.20	....	....	....	....
1981-82	**Edmonton Oilers**	**NHL**	**8**	**3**	**5**	**0**	**399**	**32**	**0**	**4.81**	**3.72**	**7.58**	**203**	**.842**	**30.5**	....	....	....	....	....	....	....	....	....	....	....	....
	Wichita Wind	CHL	40	23	13	3	2391	119	1	2.99	....	....	....	....	....	7	3	4	....	434	23	0	3.18	....	....	....	....
1982-83	**Edmonton Oilers**	**NHL**	**50**	**33**	**8**	**7**	**2833**	**167**	**1**	**3.54**	**2.84**	**3.86**	**1531**	**.891**	**32.4**	**16**	**11**	**5**	....	**949**	**48**	**0**	**3.03**	....	....	....	....
1983-84♦	**Edmonton Oilers**	**NHL**	**38**	**27**	**8**	**1**	**2212**	**139**	**1**	**3.77**	**2.97**	**4.44**	**1179**	**.882**	**32.0**	**7**	**4**	**0**	....	**263**	**12**	**0**	**2.74**	**2.99**	**110**	**.891**	**25.1**
1984-85♦	**Edmonton Oilers**	**NHL**	**39**	**22**	**9**	**3**	**2019**	**111**	**1**	**3.30**	**2.62**	**3.49**	**1050**	**.894**	**31.2**	**2**	**0**	**0**	....	**20**	**0**	**0**	**0.00**	**0.00**	**3**	**1.000**	**9.0**
1985-86	**Edmonton Oilers**	**NHL**	**47**	**27**	**9**	**7**	**2664**	**164**	**1**	**3.69**	**2.88**	**4.09**	**1480**	**.889**	**33.3**	**1**	**1**	**0**	....	**60**	**1**	**0**	**1.00**	**0.37**	**27**	**.963**	**27.0**
1986-87♦	**Edmonton Oilers**	**NHL**	**46**	**28**	**11**	**3**	**2461**	**144**	**0**	**3.51**	**2.97**	**4.15**	**1218**	**.882**	**29.7**	**2**	**2**	**0**	....	**120**	**8**	**0**	**4.00**	**8.65**	**37**	**.784**	**18.5**
1987-88	Canada	Nat-Team	27	10	7	5	1438	86	0	3.58	....	....	....	....	....	....	....	....	....	....	....	....	....	....	....	....	....
	Canada	Olympics	4	4	0	0	240	9	1	2.25	....	....	....	....	....	....	....	....	....	....	....	....	....	....	....	....	....
	Boston Bruins	**NHL**	**6**	**4**	**2**	**0**	**360**	**17**	**1**	**2.83**	**2.36**	**2.66**	**181**	**.906**	**30.2**	**7**	**1**	**4**	....	**354**	**25**	**0**	**4.24**	**6.39**	**166**	**.849**	**28.1**
1988-89	**Boston Bruins**	**NHL**	**41**	**18**	**14**	**8**	**2482**	**133**	**1**	**3.22**	**2.67**	**3.97**	**1079**	**.877**	**26.1**	**6**	**4**	**2**	....	**359**	**14**	**0**	**2.34**	**2.41**	**136**	**.897**	**22.7**
1989-90	**Boston Bruins**	**NHL**	**46**	**24**	**10**	**7**	**2536**	**122**	**3**	**2.89**	**2.44**	**3.08**	**1145**	**.893**	**27.1**	**20**	**13**	**7**	....	**1195**	**44**	***2**	***2.21**	**2.00**	**486**	**.909**	**24.4**
1990-91	**Boston Bruins**	**NHL**	**51**	**25**	**13**	**9**	**2844**	**136**	**4**	**2.87**	**2.57**	**2.99**	**1307**	**.896**	**27.6**	**19**	**10**	**9**	....	**1133**	**60**	**0**	**3.18**	**3.35**	**569**	**.895**	**30.1**
1991-92	**Boston Bruins**	**NHL**	**62**	**28**	**22**	**9**	**3640**	**196**	**1**	**3.23**	**2.89**	**3.67**	**1727**	**.887**	**28.5**	**15**	**8**	**7**	....	**866**	**46**	**1**	**3.19**	**3.81**	**385**	**.881**	**26.7**
1992-93	**Boston Bruins**	**NHL**	**55**	**37**	**14**	**3**	**3194**	**168**	**3**	**3.16**	**2.70**	**3.91**	**1357**	**.876**	**25.5**	**3**	**0**	**3**	....	**161**	**14**	**0**	**5.22**	**10.91**	**67**	**.791**	**25.0**
1993-94	**Dallas Stars**	**NHL**	**55**	**24**	**20**	**7**	**3121**	**170**	**2**	**3.27**	**3.14**	**3.47**	**1604**	**.894**	**30.8**	**4**	**1**	**3**	....	**246**	**12**	**0**	**2.93**	**2.91**	**121**	**.901**	**29.5**
1994-95	**Dallas Stars**	**NHL**	**31**	**10**	**12**	**7**	**1770**	**72**	**2**	**2.44**	**2.55**	**2.08**	**846**	**.915**	**28.7**	**5**	**1**	**4**	....	**277**	**16**	**0**	**3.47**	**3.29**	**169**	**.905**	**36.6**

Season	Club	League	REGULAR SEASON GP	W	L	T	Mins	GA	SO	Avg	AAvg	Eff	SA	S%	SAPG	PLAYOFFS GP	W	L	T	Mins	GA	SO	Avg	Eff	SA	S%	SAPG
1995-96	**Dallas Stars**	**NHL**	**41**	**13**	**19**	**7**	**2228**	**111**	**1**	**2.99**	**2.97**	**3.00**	**1106**	**.900**	**29.8**	....	....	....	....	....	....	....	....	....	....	....	....
1996-97	**Dallas Stars**	**NHL**	**48**	**28**	**13**	**5**	**2738**	**98**	**3**	**2.15**	**2.30**	**1.88**	**1121**	**.913**	**24.6**	**7**	**3**	**4**	....	**449**	**21**	**0**	**2.81**	**2.76**	**214**	**.902**	**28.6**
1997-98	**Montreal Canadiens**	**NHL**	**42**	**18**	**17**	**5**	**2337**	**97**	**3**	**2.49**	**2.97**	**2.36**	**1024**	**.905**	**26.3**	**9**	**4**	**5**	....	**474**	**24**	**1**	**3.04**	**3.58**	**204**	**.882**	**25.8**
	NHL Totals		**713**	**372**	**209**	**88**	**40151**	**2097**	**28**	**3.13**	....	....	**19328**	**.892**	**28.9**	**132**	**68**	**57**	....	**7452**	**377**	**4**	**3.04**	....	....	....	....

WHL Second All-Star Team (1980) • CHL Second All-Star Team (1982) • Shared William Jennings Trophy with Rejean Lemelin (1990) • Played in NHL All-Star Game (1985, 1986, 1991, 1997)

• Statistics (Mins., GA) for suspended game vs. Edmonton on May 24, 1988 are included in playoff record.

Traded to **Boston** by **Edmonton** for Geoff Courtnall, Bill Ranford and Boston's 2nd round choice (Petro Koivunen) in 1988 Entry Draft, March 8, 1988. Traded to **Dallas** by **Boston**for Jon Casey to complete transaction that sent Gord Murphy to Dallas (June 20, 1993), June 25, 1993. Signed as a free agent by **Montreal**, July 17, 1997.

• MOORE, Alfie

Alfred Ernest G – R. 5'11", 155 lbs. b: Toronto, Ont., 12/1/1905.

Season	Club	League	GP	W	L	T	Mins	GA	SO	Avg	AAvg	Eff	SA	S%	SAPG	GP	W	L	T	Mins	GA	SO	Avg	Eff	SA	S%	SAPG
1920-21	Toronto Canoe Club	OHA-Jr.	3	3	0	0	180	2	*1	*0.67	....	....	....	....	....	....	....	....	....	....	....	....	....	....	....	....	....
1921-22	Toronto Aura Lee	OHA-Jr.	3	*3	0	0	180	4	0	*1.33	....	....	....	....	....	....	....	....	....	....	....	....	....	....	....	....	....
1922-23	Toronto Aura Lee	OHA-Jr.	1	0	1	0	60	3	0	3.00	....	....	....	....	....	....	....	....	....	....	....	....	....	....	....	....	....
1923-24	Toronto Aura Lee	OHA-Jr.	4	2	1	1	290	7	1	*1.45	....	....	....	....	....	....	....	....	....	....	....	....	....	....	....	....	....
	Toronto Aura Lee	OHA-Jr.	3	0	2	0	160	11	0	4.13	....	....	....	....	....	....	....	....	....	....	....	....	....	....	....	....	....
1924-25	Toronto Aura Lee	OHA-Sr.	8	2	6	0	520	31	0	3.58	....	....	....	....	....	....	....	....	....	....	....	....	....	....	....	....	....
1925-26	London Ravens	OHA-Sr.	20	*14	5	1	1300	51	0	2.35	....	....	....	....	....	2	1	0	1	120	6	0	3.00	....	....	....	....
	London Ravens	Al-Cup	2	0	1	1	120	7	0	3.50	....	....	....	....	....	....	....	....	....	....	....	....	....	....	....	....	....
1926-27	London Ravens	OHA-Sr.	STATISTICS NOT AVAILABLE																								
	Chicago Cardinals	AHA	12	4	7	1	720	22	3	1.83	....	....	....	....	....	....	....	....	....	....	....	....	....	....	....	....	....
1927-28	Kitchener Millionaires	Can-Pro	1	0	1	0	70	3	0	2.57	....	....	....	....	....	....	....	....	....	....	....	....	....	....	....	....	....
	Chicago Cardinals	AHA	STATISTICS NOT AVAILABLE																								
1928-29	Kitchener Flying Dutchmen	Can-Pro	42	19	19	4	2600	112	7	2.59	....	....	....	....	....	3	1	2	0	230	6	1	1.57	....	....	....	....
1929-30	Cleveland Indians	IHL	42	*24	9	9	2610	78	*8	1.79	....	....	....	....	....	6	*5	1	0	390	9	*2	*1.38	....	....	....	....
1930-31	Springfield Indians	Can-Am	40	*29	2	2	2459	99	2	2.42	....	....	....	....	....	7	*3	2	0	570	19	0	2.00	....	....	....	....
1931-32	Springfield Indians	Can-Am	22	5	13	4	1350	64	0	2.84	....	....	....	....	....	....	....	....	....	....	....	....	....	....	....	....	....
1932-33	Springfield Indians	Can-Am	13	6	5	2	810	30	1	2.22	....	....	....	....	....	....	....	....	....	....	....	....	....	....	....	....	....
	Cleveland Indians	IHL	24	....	....	....	1440	77	3	3.21	....	....	....	....	....	....	....	....	....	....	....	....	....	....	....	....	....
1933-34	New Haven Eagles	Can-Am	41	12	*25	4	2530	107	4	2.54	....	....	....	....	....	....	....	....	....	....	....	....	....	....	....	....	....
1934-35	New Haven Eagles	Can-Am	48	16	*23	9	3000	145	2	2.90	....	....	....	....	....	....	....	....	....	....	....	....	....	....	....	....	....
	Philadelphia Arrows	Can-Am	1	0	1	0	60	1	0	1.00	....	....	....	....	....	....	....	....	....	....	....	....	....	....	....	....	....
1935-36	New Haven Eagles	Can-Am	20	8	10	2	1240	56	3	2.71	....	....	....	....	....	....	....	....	....	....	....	....	....	....	....	....	....
	Springfield Indians	Can-Am	1	0	0	1	70	2	0	1.71	....	....	....	....	....	....	....	....	....	....	....	....	....	....	....	....	....
	Providence Reds	Can-Am	6	4	2	0	360	16	1	2.67	....	....	....	....	....	....	....	....	....	....	....	....	....	....	....	....	....
	Boston Cubs	Can-Am	1	0	1	0	60	3	0	3.00	....	....	....	....	....	....	....	....	....	....	....	....	....	....	....	....	....
1936-37	New Haven Eagles	IAHL	28	9	14	5	1750	73	3	2.50	....	....	....	....	....	....	....	....	....	....	....	....	....	....	....	....	....
	New York Americans	**NHL**	**18**	**7**	**11**	**0**	**1110**	**64**	**1**	**3.46**	**4.37**	....	....	....	....	....	....	....	....	....	....	....	....	....	....	....	....
1937-38	Pittsburgh Hornets	IAHL	39	19	14	6	2430	80	7	1.98	....	....	....	....	....	2	0	2	0	130	8	0	3.69	....	....	....	....
♦	**Chicago Black Hawks**	**NHL**	....	....	....	....	....	....	....	....	....	....	....	....	....	**1**	**1**	**0**	....	**60**	**1**	**0**	**1.00**	....	....	....	....
1938-39	**New York Americans**	**NHL**	**2**	**0**	**2**	**0**	**120**	**14**	**0**	**7.00**	**8.51**	....	....	....	....	**2**	**0**	**2**	....	**120**	**6**	**0**	**3.00**	....	....	....	....
	Hershey Bears	IAHL	53	*31	18	4	3260	105	7	*1.93	....	....	....	....	....	3	1	2	0	180	8	0	2.66	....	....	....	....
1939-40	Hershey Bears	IAHL	13	6	5	2	810	45	1	3.33	....	....	....	....	....	....	....	....	....	....	....	....	....	....	....	....	....
	Indianapolis Capitols	IAHL	27	10	13	4	1670	76	4	2.73	....	....	....	....	....	5	2	3	0	342	12	0	*2.11	....	....	....	....
	Detroit Red Wings	**NHL**	**1**	**0**	**1**	**0**	**60**	**3**	**0**	**3.00**	**3.66**	....	....	....	....	....	....	....	....	....	....	....	....	....	....	....	....
1940-41	Springfield Indians	AHL	8	4	3	1	500	24	1	2.88	....	....	....	....	....	....	....	....	....	....	....	....	....	....	....	....	....
	New Haven Eagles	AHL	3	1	0	2	200	11	0	3.30	....	....	....	....	....	....	....	....	....	....	....	....	....	....	....	....	....
	Cleveland Barons	AHL	8	3	4	1	490	27	0	3.31	....	....	....	....	....	6	4	2	0	360	16	0	2.67	....	....	....	....
1941-42	Philadelphia Rockets	AHL	19	6	11	2	1160	79	1	4.09	....	....	....	....	....	....	....	....	....	....	....	....	....	....	....	....	....
	Buffalo Bisons	AHL	2	0	1	1	130	7	0	3.23	....	....	....	....	....	....	....	....	....	....	....	....	....	....	....	....	....
	NHL Totals		**21**	**7**	**14**	**0**	**1290**	**81**	**1**	**3.77**	....	....	....	....	....	**3**	**1**	**2**	....	**180**	**7**	**0**	**2.33**	....	....	....	....

IAHL Second All-Star Team (1939)

Signed as a free agent by **Chicago Cardinals** (AHA), January 30, 1927. Signed as a free agent by **Kitchener** (Can-Pro), October 27, 1927. Transferred to **Toronto** (IHL) after **Kitchener** (Can-Pro) franchise relocated, September, 1929. Traded to **Cleveland** (IHL) by **Toronto** (IHL) for Winton Fisher, October 18, 1929. Claimed by **NY Rangers** from **Cleveland** (IHL) in Inter-League Draft, April 15, 1930. Loaned to **Springfield** (Can-Am) by **NY Rangers** for cash, October, 1930. Traded to **Cleveland** (IHL) by **NY Rangers** after Springfield (Can-Am) folded, December 18, 1932. Signed as a free agent by **New Haven** (Can-Am), October, 1933. Traded to **NY Americans** by **New Haven** (IAHL) for Lloyd Jackson and cash, November, 1936. • Recorded a shutout (4-0) in NHL debut vs. Montreal Canadiens, January 30, 1937. Loaned to **Chicago** by **NY Americans** (Pittsburgh-IAHL) to replace injured Mike Karakas for game one of Stanley Cup Finals, April 5, 1938. Traded to **Detroit** by **NY Americans** for cash, November 7, 1939. Promoted to **Detroit** by **Indianapolis** (IAHL) to replace injured Tiny Thompson, January 9, 1940. (Boston 3, Detroit 1). Traded to **Buffalo** (AHL) by **Philadelphia** (AHL) for cash, February 23, 1942. Traded to **Pittsburgh** (AHL) by **Buffalo** (AHL) for cash, October 13, 1942.

• MOORE, Robbie

Robert David G – R. 5'5", 155 lbs. b: Sarnia, Ont., 5/3/1954.

Season	Club	League	GP	W	L	T	Mins	GA	SO	Avg	AAvg	Eff	SA	S%	SAPG	GP	W	L	T	Mins	GA	SO	Avg	Eff	SA	S%	SAPG
1971-72	Sarnia Steeplejacks	OHA-B	18	....	....	....	1069	64	1	3.59	....	....	....	....	....	....	....	....	....	....	....	....	....	....	....	....	....
1972-73	University of Michigan	WCHA	31	....	....	....	1840	176	0	5.74	....	....	....	....	....	....	....	....	....	....	....	....	....	....	....	....	....
1973-74	University of Michigan	WCHA	36	....	....	....	2000	144	0	4.32	....	....	....	....	....	....	....	....	....	....	....	....	....	....	....	....	....
1974-75	University of Michigan	WCHA	24	....	....	....	1420	94	0	3.97	....	....	....	....	....	....	....	....	....	....	....	....	....	....	....	....	....
1975-76	University of Michigan	WCHA	37	....	....	....	2137	157	1	4.41	....	....	....	....	....	....	....	....	....	....	....	....	....	....	....	....	....
1976-77	University of Western Ontario	OUAA	30	....	....	....	770	52	0	4.05	....	....	....	....	....	....	....	....	....	....	....	....	....	....	....	....	....
1978-79	Maine Mariners	AHL	26	12	6	6	1489	84	1	3.38	....	....	....	....	....	4	1	2	0	163	9	0	3.31	....	....	....	....
	Philadelphia Flyers	**NHL**	**5**	**3**	**0**	**1**	**237**	**7**	**2**	**1.77**	**1.56**	....	....	....	....	**5**	**3**	**2**	....	**268**	**18**	**0**	**4.03**	....	....	....	....
1979-80	Maine Mariners	AHL	32	14	11	4	1830	106	1	3.48	....	....	....	....	....	7	5	2	0	448	21	*1	*2.81	....	....	....	....
1980-81	Maine Mariners	AHL	25	11	11	2	1431	92	1	3.86	....	....	....	....	....	4	0	3	0	139	14	0	6.04	....	....	....	....
1981-82	Nashville South Stars	CHL	39	18	17	1	2204	159	0	4.33	....	....	....	....	....	....	....	....	....	....	....	....	....	....	....	....	....
1982-83	**Washington Capitals**	**NHL**	**1**	**0**	**1**	**0**	**20**	**1**	**0**	**3.00**	**2.41**	**3.75**	**8**	**.875**	**24.0**	....	....	....	....	....	....	....	....	....	....	....	....
	Hershey Bears	AHL	35	15	14	1	1798	115	0	3.84	....	....	....	....	....	1	0	1	0	87	3	0	2.07	....	....	....	....
1983-84	Milwaukee Admirals	IHL	49	....	....	....	2788	195	0	4.20	....	....	....	....	....	4	....	....	....	206	13	0	3.79	....	....	....	....
	NHL Totals		**6**	**3**	**1**	**1**	**257**	**8**	**2**	**1.87**	....	....	**8**	**.000**	**1.9**	**5**	**3**	**2**	....	**268**	**18**	**0**	**4.03**	....	....	....	....

NCAA West First All-American Team (1974) • WCHA Second All-Star Team (1976) • Shared Harry "Hap" Holmes Memorial Award (fewest goals against - AHL) with Pete Peters (1979) • Shared Harry "Hap" Holmes Memorial Award (fewest goals against - AHL) with Rick St. Croix (1980) • Shared Harry "Hap" Holmes Memorial Award (fewest goals against - AHL) with Pelle Lindbergh (1981)

Signed as a free agent by **Philadelphia**, November 7, 1978. • Recorded a shutout (5-0) in NHL debut vs. Colorado, March 6, 1979. Signed as a free agent by **Minnesota**, July 27, 1981. Traded to **Washington** by **Minnesota** with Minnesota's 11th round choice (Anders Huss) in 1983 Entry Draft for Wes Jarvis and Rollie Boutin, August 4, 1982.

• MORISSETTE, Jean-Guy

G – L. 5'8", 140 lbs. b: Causapscal, N.B., 12/16/1937.

Season	Club	League	GP	W	L	T	Mins	GA	SO	Avg	AAvg	Eff	SA	S%	SAPG	GP	W	L	T	Mins	GA	SO	Avg	Eff	SA	S%	SAPG
1955-56	Jonquiere Aces	QJHL	STATISTICS NOT AVAILABLE																								
	Chicoutimi Sagueneens	QHL	1	....	....	....	60	3	0	3.00	....	....	....	....	....	....	....	....	....	....	....	....	....	....	....	....	....
1956-1961	Jonquiere Aces	QPHL	STATISTICS NOT AVAILABLE																								
1961-62	Causapscal Pioneers	LSLHL	STATISTICS NOT AVAILABLE																								
	Amherst Ramblers	NSSHL	7	5	2	0	420	20	1	2.86	....	....	....	....	....	9	*8	1	0	540	26	*2	*2.89	....	....	....	....
	Amherst Ramblers	Al-Cup	8	5	3	0	491	29	0	3.54	....	....	....	....	....	....	....	....	....	....	....	....	....	....	....	....	....
1962-63	Amherst-Moncton Hawks	NSSHL	55	....	....	....	3300	228	*1	*4.15	....	....	....	....	....	11	*8	3	0	660	31	0	2.82	....	....	....	....
	Moncton Hawks	Al-Cup	15	10	5	0	910	51	0	3.36	....	....	....	....	....	....	....	....	....	....	....	....	....	....	....	....	....
1963-64	**Montreal Canadiens**	**NHL**	**1**	**0**	**1**	**0**	**36**	**4**	**0**	**6.67**	**7.42**	....	....	....	....	....	....	....	....	....	....	....	....	....	....	....	....
	Omaha Knights	CPHL	7	4	1	2	420	22	0	3.14	....	....	....	....	....	....	....	....	....	....	....	....	....	....	....	....	....
	Quebec Aces	AHL	1	1	0	0	60	2	0	2.00	....	....	....	....	....	....	....	....	....	....	....	....	....	....	....	....	....
	Cleveland Barons	AHL	5	2	2	1	310	14	1	2.71	....	....	....	....	....	*9	*9	0	0	540	17	0	*1.89	....	....	....	....
1964-65	Cleveland Barons	AHL	11	4	6	1	670	38	0	3.40	....	....	....	....	....	....	....	....	....	....	....	....	....	....	....	....	....
	Baltimore Clippers	AHL	20	9	10	0	1173	70	1	3.58	....	....	....	....	....	....	....	....	....	....	....	....	....	....	....	....	....
	Omaha Knights	CPHL	12	4	6	2	720	39	3	3.25	....	....	....	....	....	....	....	....	....	....	....	....	....	....	....	....	....
	Victoria Maple Leafs	WHL	....	....	....	....	....	....	....	....	....	....	....	....	....	2	1	1	0	125	6	0	2.88	....	....	....	....

			REGULAR SEASON													PLAYOFFS											
Season	Club	League	GP	W	L	T	Mins	GA	SO	Avg	AAvg	Eff	SA	S%	SAPG	GP	W	L	T	Mins	GA	SO	Avg	Eff	SA	S%	SAPG
1965-66	Cleveland Barons	AHL	8	4	2	0	398	24	0	3.62	....	....	....	....	....	1	0	0	0	24	1	0	2.50	....	....	....	....
1966-67	California Seals	WHL	8	5	2	0	440	21	1	2.86	....	....	....	....	....	....	....	....	....	....	....	....	....	....	....	....	....
	Quebec Aces	AHL	9	3	2	1	409	19	0	2.79	....	....	....	....	....	....	....	....	....	....	....	....	....	....	....	....	....
1967-68	Vancouver Canucks	WHL	11	1	8	1	638	58	0	5.45	....	....	....	....	....	....	....	....	....	....	....	....	....	....	....	....	....
1968-69			DID NOT PLAY																								
1969-70	Victoriaville Tigers	QSHL	STATISTICS NOT AVAILABLE																								
1970-71	Grand Falls Cataracts	Nfld-Sr.	35	14	16	5	2100	144	1	4.11	....	....	....	....	....	19	*13	6	0	1140	47	2	*2.47	....	....	....	....
	Grand Falls Cataracts	Al-Cup	5	2	3	0	380	19	0	3.00	....	....	....	....	....	....	....	....	....	....	....	....	....	....	....	....	....
1971-72	Grand Falls Cataracts	Nfld-Sr.	33	*25	5	3	1980	77	*5	*2.33	....	....	....	....	....	11	*11	0	0	660	22	*2	2.00	....	....	....	....
	Grand Falls Cataracts	Al-Cup	3	0	3	0	164	15	0	5.49	....	....	....	....	....	....	....	....	....	....	....	....	....	....	....	....	....
	NHL Totals		**1**	**0**	**1**	**0**	**36**	**4**	**0**	**6.67**	....	....	....	....	....	....	....	....	....	....	....	....	....	....	....	....	....

• **Montreal's** spare goaltender replaced injured Gump Worsley in 2nd period, October 30, 1963. (Toronto 6, Montreal 3). • Missed majority of 1963-64 season recovering from broken cheekbone suffered in practice, October 31, 1963. Loaned to **NY Rangers** by **Montreal** for remainder of 1964-65 season with the trade of Bill Hicke for Dick Duff and Dave McComb, December 22, 1964. Claimed by **Hershey** (AHL) from **Montreal** in Reverse Draft, June 15, 1966. Loaned to **Quebec** (AHL) by **California** (WHL) for the loan of Ed Hoekstra, January, 1967.

• MOSS, Tyler

G – R. 6′, 184 lbs. b: Ottawa, Ont., 6/29/1975. Tampa Bay's 2nd, 29th overall in 1993.

Season	Club	League	GP	W	L	T	Mins	GA	SO	Avg	AAvg	Eff	SA	S%	SAPG	GP	W	L	T	Mins	GA	SO	Avg	Eff	SA	S%	SAPG
1991-92	Nepean Raiders	OJHL	26	7	12	1	1335	109	0	4.90	....	....	....	....	....	....	....	....	....	....	....	....	....	....	....	....	....
1992-93	Kingston Frontenacs	OHL	31	13	7	5	1537	97	0	3.79	....	....	....	....	....	6	1	2	....	228	19	0	5.00	....	....	....	....
1993-94	Kingston Frontenacs	OHL	13	6	4	3	795	42	1	3.17	....	....	....	....	....	3	0	2	....	136	8	0	3.53	....	....	....	....
1994-95	Kingston Frontenacs	OHL	*57	33	17	5	*3249	164	1	3.03	....	....	....	....	....	6	2	4	....	333	27	0	4.86	....	....	....	....
1995-96	Atlanta Knights	IHL	40	11	19	4	2030	138	1	4.08	....	....	....	....	....	3	0	3	....	213	11	0	3.10	....	....	....	....
1996-97	Adirondack Red Wings	AHL	11	1	5	2	507	42	1	4.97	....	....	....	....	....	....	....	....	....	....	....	....	....	....	....	....	....
	Grand Rapids Griffins	IHL	15	5	6	1	715	35	0	2.94	....	....	....	....	....	....	....	....	....	....	....	....	....	....	....	....	....
	Muskegon Fury	ColHL	2	1	1	0	119	5	0	2.51	....	....	....	....	....	....	....	....	....	....	....	....	....	....	....	....	....
	Saint John Flames	AHL	9	6	1	1	534	17	0	1.91	....	....	....	....	....	5	2	3	....	242	15	0	3.72	....	....	....	....
1997-98	**Calgary Flames**	**NHL**	**6**	**2**	**3**	**1**	**367**	**20**	**0**	**3.27**	**3.90**	**3.52**	**186**	**.892**	**30.4**	....	....	....	....	....	....	....	....	....	....	....	....
	Saint John Flames	AHL	39	19	10	7	2194	91	0	2.49	....	....	....	....	....	15	8	5	....	761	37	0	2.91	....	....	....	....
1998-99	**Calgary Flames**	**NHL**	**11**	**3**	**7**	**0**	**550**	**23**	**0**	**2.51**	**2.98**	**1.96**	**295**	**.922**	**32.2**	....	....	....	....	....	....	....	....	....	....	....	....
	Saint John Flames	AHL	9	2	5	1	475	25	0	3.16	....	....	....	....	....	....	....	....	....	....	....	....	....	....	....	....	....
	Orlando Solar Bears	IHL	9	6	2	1	515	21	1	2.45	....	....	....	....	....	17	10	7	....	1017	53	0	3.13	....	....	....	....
99-2000	Wilkes-Barre Penguins	AHL	4	1	1	1	188	11	0	3.52	....	....	....	....	....	....	....	....	....	....	....	....	....	....	....	....	....
	Kansas City Blades	IHL	36	18	12	5	2116	105	3	2.98	....	....	....	....	....	....	....	....	....	....	....	....	....	....	....	....	....
	NHL Totals		**17**	**5**	**10**	**1**	**917**	**43**	**0**	**2.81**	....	....	**481**	**.911**	**31.5**	....	....	....	....	....	....	....	....	....	....	....	....

OHL First All-Star Team (1995) • Shared Harry "Hap" Holmes Memorial Trophy (fewest goals against - AHL) with Jean-Sebastien Giguere (1998)

Traded to **Calgary** by **Tampa Bay** for Jamie Huscroft, March 18, 1997. Traded to **Pittsburgh** by **Calgary** with Rene Corbet for Brad Werenka, March 14, 2000. • Played w/ RHI's Florida Hammerheads in 1993 (1-0-0-0-8-4-0-24.00)

• MOWERS, Johnny

John Thomas "Mum" G – L. 5′11″, 185 lbs. b: Niagara Falls, Ont., 10/29/1916 d: 1995.

Season	Club	League	GP	W	L	T	Mins	GA	SO	Avg	AAvg	Eff	SA	S%	SAPG	GP	W	L	T	Mins	GA	SO	Avg	Eff	SA	S%	SAPG
1935-36	Niagara Falls Cataracts	OHA-Sr.	STATISTICS NOT AVAILABLE																								
	Niagara Falls Cataracts	Al-Cup	2	0	2	0	120	12	0	6.00	....	....	....	....	....	....	....	....	....	....	....	....	....	....	....	....	....
1936-37	Niagara Falls Cataracts	OHA-Sr.	18	....	....	....	1080	54	0	*3.00	....	....	....	....	....	9	....	....	....	540	30	0	3.33	....	....	....	....
1937-38	Niagara Falls Cataracts	OHA-Sr.	16	....	....	....	960	50	0	3.12	....	....	....	....	....	7	*7	0	0	420	16	0	*2.29	....	....	....	....
1938-39	Niagara Falls Cataracts	OHA-Sr.	20	....	....	....	1200	63	4	3.15	....	....	....	....	....	....	....	....	....	....	....	....	....	....	....	....	....
1939-40	Detroit Pontiacs	MOHL	20	....	....	....	1200	84	0	4.20	....	....	....	....	....	....	....	....	....	....	....	....	....	....	....	....	....
	Omaha Knights	AHA	21	16	5	0	1272	41	3	1.93	....	....	....	....	....	9	4	*5	0	610	21	1	2.07	....	....	....	....
1940-41	**Detroit Red Wings**	**NHL**	***48**	**21**	**16**	**11**	***3040**	**102**	**4**	**2.01**	**2.19**	....	....	....	....	**9**	**4**	**5**	....	**561**	**20**	**0**	**2.14**	....	....	....	....
1941-42	**Detroit Red Wings**	**NHL**	**47**	**19**	**25**	**3**	**2880**	**144**	**5**	**3.00**	**2.92**	....	....	....	....	**12**	**7**	**5**	....	**720**	**38**	**0**	**3.17**	....	....	....	....
1942-43♦	**Detroit Red Wings**	**NHL**	***50**	***25**	**14**	**11**	**3010**	**124**	***6**	***2.47**	**1.96**	....	....	....	....	***10**	***8**	**2**	....	***679**	**22**	***2**	***1.94**	....	....	....	....
1943-44	Toronto RCAF	TNDHL	9	3	6	0	540	53	0	5.89	....	....	....	....	....	....	....	....	....	....	....	....	....	....	....	....	....
1944-45			MILITARY SERVICE																								
1945-46	Wembley Lions	Britain	STATISTICS NOT AVAILABLE																								
1946-47	**Detroit Red Wings**	**NHL**	**7**	**0**	**6**	**1**	**420**	**29**	**0**	**4.14**	**4.02**	....	....	....	....	**1**	**0**	**1**	....	**40**	**5**	**0**	**7.50**	....	....	....	....
1947-48	Indianapolis Capitols	AHL	2	1	1	0	120	7	0	3.50	....	....	....	....	....	....	....	....	....	....	....	....	....	....	....	....	....
	NHL Totals		**152**	**65**	**61**	**26**	**9350**	**399**	**15**	**2.56**	....	....	....	....	....	**32**	**19**	**13**	....	**2000**	**85**	**2**	**2.55**	....	....	....	....

NHL First All-Star Team (1943) • Won Vezina Trophy (1943)

Signed as a free agent by **Detroit**, October 2, 1939.

• MRAZEK, Jerome

Jerome John G – L. 5′9″, 160 lbs. b: Prince Albert, Sask., 10/15/1951. Philadelphia's 8th, 106th overall in 1971.

Season	Club	League	GP	W	L	T	Mins	GA	SO	Avg	AAvg	Eff	SA	S%	SAPG	GP	W	L	T	Mins	GA	SO	Avg	Eff	SA	S%	SAPG
1967-68	Moose Jaw Canucks	WCJHL	4	....	....	....	130	7	0	3.23	....	....	....	....	....	....	....	....	....	....	....	....	....	....	....	....	....
1968-69	Moose Jaw Canucks	SJHL	STATISTICS NOT AVAILABLE																								
1969-70	Moose Jaw Canucks	SJHL	31	....	....	....	1829	125	0	4.10	....	....	....	....	....	....	....	....	....	....	....	....	....	....	....	....	....
	Weyburn Red Wings	Mem-Cup	21	12	9	0	1217	76	1	3.75	....	....	....	....	....	....	....	....	....	....	....	....	....	....	....	....	....
1970-71	University of Minnesota-Duluth	WCHA	4	2	1	0	200	17	0	5.10	....	....	....	....	....	....	....	....	....	....	....	....	....	....	....	....	....
1971-72	University of Minnesota-Duluth	WCHA	27	12	13	1	1590	114	0	4.30	....	....	....	....	....	....	....	....	....	....	....	....	....	....	....	....	....
1972-73	University of Minnesota-Duluth	WCHA	27	14	13	0	1608	119	0	4.44	....	....	....	....	....	....	....	....	....	....	....	....	....	....	....	....	....
1973-74	University of Minnesota-Duluth	WCHA	29	17	12	0	1729	115	1	3.99	....	....	....	....	....	....	....	....	....	....	....	....	....	....	....	....	....
1974-75	Des Moines Capitols	IHL	50	....	....	....	2787	154	2	3.32	....	....	....	....	....	5	2	3	0	311	13	0	*2.51	....	....	....	....
1975-76	**Philadelphia Flyers**	**NHL**	**1**	**0**	**0**	**0**	**6**	**1**	**0**	**10.00**	**9.06**	....	....	....	....	....	....	....	....	....	....	....	....	....	....	....	....
	Richmond Robins	AHL	20	5	9	4	1135	72	2	3.81	....	....	....	....	....	5	3	2	0	289	14	0	2.91	....	....	....	....
1976-77	Springfield Indians	AHL	33	....	....	....	1685	151	0	5.38	....	....	....	....	....	....	....	....	....	....	....	....	....	....	....	....	....
	Hershey Bears	AHL	10	....	....	....	537	38	0	4.24	....	....	....	....	....	6	2	4	0	358	21	0	3.52	....	....	....	....
1977-78	Maine Mariners	AHL	27	12	10	4	1488	80	3	3.33	....	....	....	....	....	....	....	....	....	....	....	....	....	....	....	....	....
	Hershey Bears	AHL	14	2	10	1	831	67	0	4.84	....	....	....	....	....	....	....	....	....	....	....	....	....	....	....	....	....
	NHL Totals		**1**	**0**	**0**	**0**	**6**	**1**	**0**	**10.00**	....	....	....	....	....	....	....	....	....	....	....	....	....	....	....	....	....

Loaned to **Weyburn** (SJHL) by **Moose Jaw** (SJHL) for Memorial Cup playoffs, March, 1970.

• MUMMERY, Harry

Harold "Mum" G. 5′11″, 220 lbs. b: Chicago, IL, 8/25/1889 d: 12/9/1945.

Season	Club	League	GP	W	L	T	Mins	GA	SO	Avg	AAvg	Eff	SA	S%	SAPG	GP	W	L	T	Mins	GA	SO	Avg	Eff	SA	S%	SAPG
1919-20	**Quebec Bulldogs**	**NHL**	**3**	**1**	**1**	**0**	**142**	**18**	**0**	**7.61**	**4.91**	....	....	....	....	....	....	....	....	....	....	....	....	....	....	....	....
1921-22	**Hamilton Tigers**	**NHL**	**1**	**1**	**0**	**0**	**50**	**2**	**0**	**2.40**	**1.84**	....	....	....	....	....	....	....	....	....	....	....	....	....	....	....	....
	NHL Totals		**4**	**2**	**1**	**0**	**192**	**20**	**0**	**6.25**	....	....	....	....	....	....	....	....	....	....	....	....	....	....	....	....	....

• **Quebec** defenseman replaced injured Frank Brophy, February 4, March 8 and 10, 1920. • **Hamilton** defenseman replaced injured Howard Lockhart in 1st period, January 21, 1922. (Hamilton 7, Ottawa 6)

• MUNRO, Dunc

Duncan Brown G. 5′8″, 190 lbs. b: Moray, Scotland, 1/19/1901 d: 1/3/1958.

Season	Club	League	GP	W	L	T	Mins	GA	SO	Avg	AAvg	Eff	SA	S%	SAPG	GP	W	L	T	Mins	GA	SO	Avg	Eff	SA	S%	SAPG
1924-25	**Montreal Maroons**	**NHL**	**1**	**0**	**0**	**0**	**2**	**0**	**0**	**0.00**	**0.00**	....	....	....	....	....	....	....	....	....	....	....	....	....	....	....	....
	NHL Totals		**1**	**0**	**0**	**0**	**2**	**0**	**0**	**0.00**	....	....	....	....	....	....	....	....	....	....	....	....	....	....	....	....	....

• **Montreal Maroons'** defenseman replaced penalized Clint Benedict, December 20, 1924. (Hamilton 3, Montreal Maroons 1)

			REGULAR SEASON													PLAYOFFS											
Season	Club	League	GP	W	L	T	Mins	GA	SO	Avg	AAvg	Eff	SA	S%	SAPG	GP	W	L	T	Mins	GA	SO	Avg	Eff	SA	S%	SAPG

• MURPHY, Hal

G – R. 5'9", 140 lbs. b: Montreal, Que., 7/6/1927 Deceased.

Season	Club	League	GP	W	L	T	Mins	GA	SO	Avg	AAvg	Eff	SA	S%	SAPG	GP	W	L	T	Mins	GA	SO	Avg	Eff	SA	S%	SAPG
1952-53	Montreal Royals	QMHL	3	2	1	0	180	6	0	2.00	....	....	....	....	....	....	....	....	....	....	....	....	....	....	....	....	....
	Montreal Canadiens	**NHL**	**1**	**1**	**0**	**0**	**60**	**4**	**0**	**4.00**	**5.10**	....	....	....	....	....	....	....	....	....	....	....	....	....	....	....	....
1953-54	George Williams University	QUAA	STATISTICS NOT AVAILABLE																								
	Ottawa Senators	QHL	3	2	1	0	180	11	0	3.67	....	....	....	....	....	....	....	....	....	....	....	....	....	....	....	....	....
	NHL Totals		**1**	**1**	**0**	**0**	**60**	**4**	**0**	**4.00**	....	....	....	....	....	....	....	....	....	....	....	....	....	....	....	....	....

Promoted to **Montreal** from **Montreal Royals** (QMHL) to replace injured Gerry McNeil, November 8, 1952. (Montreal 6, Chicago 4)

• MURRAY, Mickey

Mickey Edward Kevin G – R. 5'10", 168 lbs. b: Peterbourgh, Ont., 10/14/1898 Deceased.

Season	Club	League	GP	W	L	T	Mins	GA	SO	Avg	AAvg	Eff	SA	S%	SAPG	GP	W	L	T	Mins	GA	SO	Avg	Eff	SA	S%	SAPG
1916-17	Peterborough Juniors	OHA-Jr.	3	2	1	0	180	15	0	5.00	....	....	....	....	....	2	0	2	0	120	21	0	10.50	....	....	....	....
1917-18	Peterborough Juniors	OHA-Jr.	3	*3	0	0	180	7	0	2.33	....	....	....	....	....	4	1	3	0	240	37	0	9.25	....	....	....	....
1918-19			STATISTICS NOT AVAILABLE																								
1919-20	Peterborough Seniors	OHA-Sr.	....	....	....	....	....	....	....	....	....	....	....	....	....	5	3	2	0	300	24	0	4.80	....	....	....	....
1920-21	Peterborough Seniors	OHA-Sr.	4	1	3	0	240	22	0	5.50	....	....	....	....	....	....	....	....	....	....	....	....	....	....	....	....	....
1921-22			STATISTICS NOT AVAILABLE																								
1922-23	North Toronto Rangers	OHA-Sr.	STATISTICS NOT AVAILABLE																								
1923-24	North Toronto Rangers	OHA-Sr.	STATISTICS NOT AVAILABLE																								
1924-25	Galt Terriers	OHA-Sr.	20	7	12	1	1200	48	1	*2.48	....	....	....	....	....	....	....	....	....	....	....	....	....	....	....	....	....
1925-26	Galt Terriers	OHA-Sr.	20	*14	4	2	1200	33	3	*1.65	....	....	....	....	....	2	0	1	1	120	8	0	4.00	....	....	....	....
1926-27	Galt Terriers	OHA-Sr.	10	4	6	0	600	30	0	3.00	....	....	....	....	....	....	....	....	....	....	....	....	....	....	....	....	....
1927-28	Providence Reds	Can-Am	21	6	10	5	1310	42	1	1.92	....	....	....	....	....	....	....	....	....	....	....	....	....	....	....	....	....
	Philadelphia Arrows	Can-Am	3	1	2	0	200	4	1	1.20	....	....	....	....	....	....	....	....	....	....	....	....	....	....	....	....	....
1928-29	Providence Reds	Can-Am	40	18	12	0	2540	58	*12	1.37	....	....	....	....	....	6	1	3	2	363	14	1	2.31	....	....	....	....
1929-30	Providence Reds	Can-Am	39	*23	11	5	2394	96	*6	*2.41	....	....	....	....	....	3	*3	0	0	180	4	0	*1.33	....	....	....	....
	Montreal Canadiens	**NHL**	**1**	**0**	**1**	**0**	**60**	**4**	**0**	**4.00**	**4.13**	....	....	....	....	....	....	....	....	....	....	....	....	....	....	....	....
1930-31	Providence Reds	Can-Am	40	23	11	6	2470	96	*4	*2.33	....	....	....	....	....	2	1	1	0	142	7	0	2.96	....	....	....	....
1931-32	Philadelphia Arrows	Can-Am	38	13	*20	5	2352	97	3	2.48	....	....	....	....	....	....	....	....	....	....	....	....	....	....	....	....	....
1932-33			DID NOT PLAY																								
1933-34	St. Louis Flyers	AHA	48	*26	18	4	3050	84	7	*1.65	....	....	....	....	....	7	2	4	1	460	12	1	1.57	....	....	....	....
1934-35	St. Louis Flyers	AHA	46	*29	14	3	2920	97	6	1.99	....	....	....	....	....	6	3	3	0	370	18	0	2.92	....	....	....	....
1935-36	St. Louis Flyers	AHA	47	27	16	4	2941	87	*9	1.78	....	....	....	....	....	1	0	0	1	80	1	0	0.75	....	....	....	....
1936-37	Kansas City Greyhounds	AHA	36	21	13	2	2189	54	*11	*1.48	....	....	....	....	....	3	0	3	0	180	10	3	3.33	....	....	....	....
1937-38	Kansas City Greyhounds	AHA	48	21	22	5	3005	120	0	2.40	....	....	....	....	....	....	....	....	....	....	....	....	....	....	....	....	....
1938-39	St. Paul Saints	AHA	4	1	3	0	240	20	1	5.00	....	....	....	....	....	....	....	....	....	....	....	....	....	....	....	....	....
	NHL Totals		**1**	**0**	**1**	**0**	**60**	**4**	**0**	**4.00**	....	....	....	....	....	....	....	....	....	....	....	....	....	....	....	....	....

Can-Am Second All-Star Team (1930) • AHA Second All-Star Team (1935, 1936, 1938)

Signed as a free agent by **Providence** (Can-Am), December 6, 1927. Promoted to **Montreal Canadiens** from **Providence** (Can-Am) to replace injured George Hainsworth, February 25, 1930. (NY Americans 4, Montreal Canadiens 2)

• MUZZATTI, Jason

Jason M. G – L. 6'2", 210 lbs. b: Toronto, Ont., 2/3/1970. Calgary's 1st, 21st overall in 1988.

Season	Club	League	GP	W	L	T	Mins	GA	SO	Avg	AAvg	Eff	SA	S%	SAPG	GP	W	L	T	Mins	GA	SO	Avg	Eff	SA	S%	SAPG
1985-86	St. Michael's Buzzers	OJHL-B	11	6	3	0	517	48	0	5.57	....	....	....	....	....	....	....	....	....	....	....	....	....	....	....	....	....
1986-87	St. Michael's Buzzers	OJHL-B	20	10	5	2	1054	69	1	3.93	....	....	....	....	....	....	....	....	....	....	....	....	....	....	....	....	....
1987-88	Michigan State Spartans	CCHA	33	19	9	3	1915	109	0	3.41	....	....	....	....	....	....	....	....	....	....	....	....	....	....	....	....	....
1988-89	Michigan State Spartans	CCHA	42	32	9	1	2515	127	3	*3.03	....	....	....	....	....	....	....	....	....	....	....	....	....	....	....	....	....
1989-90	Michigan State Spartans	CCHA	33	*24	6	0	1976	99	0	3.01	....	....	....	....	....	....	....	....	....	....	....	....	....	....	....	....	....
1990-91	Michigan State Spartans	CCHA	22	8	10	2	1204	75	1	3.74	....	....	....	....	....	....	....	....	....	....	....	....	....	....	....	....	....
1991-92	Salt Lake Golden Eagles	IHL	52	24	22	5	3033	167	2	3.30	....	....	....	....	....	4	1	3	....	247	18	0	4.37	....	....	....	....
1992-93	Canada	Nat-Team	16	6	9	0	880	53	0	3.84	....	....	....	....	....	....	....	....	....	....	....	....	....	....	....	....	....
	Indianapolis Ice	IHL	12	5	6	1	707	48	0	4.07	....	....	....	....	....	....	....	....	....	....	....	....	....	....	....	....	....
	Salt Lake Golden Eagles	IHL	13	5	6	1	747	52	0	4.18	....	....	....	....	....	....	....	....	....	....	....	....	....	....	....	....	....
1993-94	**Calgary Flames**	**NHL**	**1**	**0**	**1**	**0**	**60**	**8**	**0**	**8.00**	**7.69**	**18.29**	**35**	**.771**	**35.0**	....	....	....	....	....	....	....	....	....	....	....	....
	Saint John Flames	AHL	51	26	21	3	2939	183	2	3.74	....	....	....	....	....	7	3	4	....	415	19	0	2.75	....	....	....	....
1994-95	**Calgary Flames**	**NHL**	**1**	**0**	**0**	**0**	**10**	**0**	**0**	**0.00**	**0.00**	**0.00**	**8**	**1.000**	**48.0**	....	....	....	....	....	....	....	....	....	....	....	....
	Saint John Flames	AHL	31	10	14	4	1741	101	2	3.48	....	....	....	....	....	....	....	....	....	....	....	....	....	....	....	....	....
1995-96	**Hartford Whalers**	**NHL**	**22**	**4**	**8**	**3**	**1013**	**49**	**1**	**2.90**	**2.88**	**2.58**	**551**	**.911**	**32.6**	....	....	....	....	....	....	....	....	....	....	....	....
	Springfield Falcons	AHL	5	4	0	1	300	12	1	2.40	....	....	....	....	....	....	....	....	....	....	....	....	....	....	....	....	....
1996-97	**Hartford Whalers**	**NHL**	**31**	**9**	**13**	**5**	**1591**	**91**	**0**	**3.43**	**3.70**	**3.83**	**815**	**.888**	**30.7**	....	....	....	....	....	....	....	....	....	....	....	....
1997-98	**New York Rangers**	**NHL**	**6**	**0**	**3**	**2**	**313**	**17**	**0**	**3.26**	**3.89**	**3.55**	**156**	**.891**	**29.9**	....	....	....	....	....	....	....	....	....	....	....	....
	Hartford Wolf Pack	AHL	17	11	5	1	999	57	0	3.42	....	....	....	....	....	....	....	....	....	....	....	....	....	....	....	....	....
	San Jose Sharks	**NHL**	**1**	**0**	**0**	**0**	**27**	**2**	**0**	**4.44**	**5.29**	**6.83**	**13**	**.846**	**28.9**	....	....	....	....	....	....	....	....	....	....	....	....
	Kentucky Thoroughblades	AHL	7	2	3	2	430	25	0	3.49	....	....	....	....	....	3	0	3	....	153	13	0	5.07	....	....	....	....
1998-99	Eisbaren Berlin	Germany	4	....	....	....	240	12	0	3.00	....	....	....	....	....	3	0	3	....	166	14	0	5.06	....	....	....	....
99-2000	Tappara Tampere	Finland	41	26	9	5	2479	94	5	2.28	....	....	....	....	....	4	1	3	....	252	14	0	3.33	....	....	....	....
	NHL Totals		**62**	**13**	**25**	**10**	**3014**	**167**	**1**	**3.32**	....	....	**1578**	**.894**	**31.4**	....	....	....	....	....	....	....	....	....	....	....	....

CCHA Second All-Star Team (1988) • CCHA First All-Star Team (1990) • NCAA West Second All-American Team (1990)

Claimed on waivers by **Hartford** from **Calgary**, October 6, 1995. Transferred to **Carolina** after **Hartford** franchise relocated, June 25, 1997. Traded to **NY Rangers** by **Carolina** for NY Rangers' 4th round choice (Tommy Westlund) in 1998 Entry Draft, August 8, 1997. Traded to **San Jose** by **NY Rangers** for Rich Brennan, March 24, 1998. • Missed majority of 1998-99 season recovering from minor heart surgery, September 1998.

• MYLLYS, Jarmo

G – L. 5'8", 160 lbs. b: Savonlinna, Finland, 5/29/1965. Minnesota's 9th, 172nd overall in 1987.

Season	Club	League	GP	W	L	T	Mins	GA	SO	Avg	AAvg	Eff	SA	S%	SAPG	GP	W	L	T	Mins	GA	SO	Avg	Eff	SA	S%	SAPG
1981-82	SaiPa Lappeenranta	Finland-Jr.	STATISTICS NOT AVAILABLE																								
1982-83	SaiPa Lappeenranta	Finland-2	STATISTICS NOT AVAILABLE																								
	Finland	EJC-A	STATISTICS NOT AVAILABLE																								
1983-84	Lukko Rauma	Finland-Jr.	STATISTICS NOT AVAILABLE																								
	Ilves Tampere	Finland	9	....	....	....	540	27	....	3.00	....	....	....	....	....	....	....	....	....	....	....	....	....	....	....	....	....
	Finland	WJC-A	4	3	1	0	240	13	0	3.25	....	....	....	....	....	....	....	....	....	....	....	....	....	....	....	....	....
1984-85	Lukko Rauma	Finland-Jr.	STATISTICS NOT AVAILABLE																								
	Ilves Tampere	Finland	9	....	....	....	540	23	....	2.55	....	....	....	....	....	....	....	....	....	....	....	....	....	....	....	....	....
	Finland	WJC-A	1	1	0	0	60	2	0	2.00	....	....	....	....	....	....	....	....	....	....	....	....	....	....	....	....	....
1985-86	Ilves Tampere	Finland-Jr.	16	....	....	....	1032	71	....	4.13	....	....	....	....	....	....	....	....	....	....	....	....	....	....	....	....	....
1986-87	Lukko Rauma	Finland	43	....	....	....	2542	160	0	3.78	....	....	....	....	....	....	....	....	....	....	....	....	....	....	....	....	....
	Finland	WEC-A	8	4	3	1	464	27	0	3.49	....	....	....	....	....	....	....	....	....	....	....	....	....	....	....	....	....
1987-88	Finland	Can-Cup	1	....	....	....	20	1	0	3.00	....	....	....	....	....	....	....	....	....	....	....	....	....	....	....	....	....
	Lukko Rauma	Finland	43	....	....	....	2468	160	....	3.72	....	....	....	....	....	8	....	....	....	480	....	....	....	....	....	....	....
	Finland	Olympics	6	4	1	1	360	11	1	1.83	....	....	....	....	....	....	....	....	....	....	....	....	....	....	....	....	....
1988-89	**Minnesota North Stars**	**NHL**	**6**	**1**	**4**	**0**	**238**	**22**	**0**	**5.55**	**4.62**	**8.85**	**138**	**.841**	**34.8**	....	....	....	....	....	....	....	....	....	....	....	....
	Kalamazoo Wings	IHL	28	13	8	4	1523	93	0	3.66	....	....	....	....	....	6	2	4	0	419	22	0	3.15	....	....	....	....
1989-90	**Minnesota North Stars**	**NHL**	**4**	**0**	**3**	**0**	**156**	**16**	**0**	**6.15**	**5.22**	**11.86**	**83**	**.807**	**31.9**	....	....	....	....	....	....	....	....	....	....	....	....
	Kalamazoo Wings	IHL	49	31	9	3	2715	159	1	3.51	....	....	....	....	....	7	2	4	0	356	22	0	3.71	....	....	....	....
1990-91	Minnesota North Stars	Fr-Tour	3	....	....	....	85	4	0	2.82	....	....	....	....	....	....	....	....	....	....	....	....	....	....	....	....	....
	Minnesota North Stars	**NHL**	**2**	**0**	**2**	**0**	**78**	**8**	**0**	**6.15**	**5.53**	**8.63**	**57**	**.860**	**43.8**	....	....	....	....	....	....	....	....	....	....	....	....
	Kalamazoo Wings	IHL	38	24	13	1	2278	144	1	3.79	....	....	....	....	....	10	6	4	0	600	26	0	*2.60	....	....	....	....
1991-92	**San Jose Sharks**	**NHL**	**27**	**3**	**18**	**1**	**1374**	**115**	**0**	**5.02**	**4.52**	**6.70**	**862**	**.867**	**37.6**	....	....	....	....	....	....	....	....	....	....	....	....
	Kansas City Blades	IHL	5	5	0	0	307	15	0	2.93	....	....	....	....	....	....	....	....	....	....	....	....	....	....	....	....	....
1992-93	KooKoo Kouvola	Finland-2	39	....	....	....	2310	120	....	3.11	....	....	....	....	....	6	....	....	....	359	24	....	4.01	....	....	....	....
1993-94	Lukko Rauma	Finland	46	....	....	....	2762	131	2	*2.05	....	....	....	....	....	....	....	....	....	....	....	....	....	....	....	....	....
	Finland	Olympics	5	5	0	0	300	3	*2	0.60	....	....	....	....	....	....	....	....	....	....	....	....	....	....	....	....	....
	Finland	WC-A	7	....	....	....	400	10	....	1.35	....	....	....	....	....	....	....	....	....	....	....	....	....	....	....	....	....

Season	Club	League	REGULAR SEASON													PLAYOFFS											
			GP	W	L	T	Mins	GA	SO	Avg	AAvg	Eff	SA	S%	SAPG	GP	W	L	T	Mins	GA	SO	Avg	Eff	SA	S%	SAPG
1994-95	Lulea HF	Sweden	37	....	....	....	2220	106	*4	2.86	....	....	....	....	....	9	....	....	....	540	28	0	3.11	....	....	....	....
	Finland	WC-A	7	5	1	1	420	12	2	1.71	....	....	....	....	....	....	....	....	....	....	....	....	....	....	....	....	....
1995-96	Lulea HF	Sweden	39	....	....	....	2340	104	1	2.67	....	....	....	....	....	7	....	....	....	780	29	0	*2.23	....	....	....	....
	Finland	WC-A	4	0	2	2	238	12	0	3.02	....	....	....	....	....	....	....	....	....	....	....	....	....	....	....	....	....
1996-97	Finland	W-Cup	2	1	1	0	120	8	0	4.00	....	....	....	....	....	....	....	....	....	....	....	....	....	....	....	....	....
	Lulea HF	Sweden	37	....	....	....	2158	80	*5	*2.22	....	....	....	....	....	10	....	....	....	612	25	*1	2.45	....	....	....	....
	Lulea HF	EuroHL	4	....	....	....	240	9	....	2.25	....	....	....	....	....	....	....	....	....	....	....	....	....	....	....	....	....
	Finland	WC-A	6	4	2	0	357	10	1	1.68	....	....	....	....	....	....	....	....	....	....	....	....	....	....	....	....	....
1997-98	Lulea HF	Sweden	43	....	....	....	2534	111	....	2.63	....	....	....	....	....	3	....	....	....	180	10	....	3.33	....	....	....	....
	Finland	Olympics	4	1	3	0	237	14	0	3.54	....	....	....	....	....	....	....	....	....	....	....	....	....	....	....	....	....
	Finland	WC-A	2	1	1	0	119	4	1	2.02	....	....	....	....	....	....	....	....	....	....	....	....	....	....	....	....	....
1998-99	Lulea HF	Sweden	47	....	....	....	2839	129	2	2.73	....	....	....	....	....	9	....	....	....	570	22	0	2.32	....	....	....	....
99-2000	Lulea HF	Sweden	40	....	....	....	2422	105	*6	2.60	....	....	....	....	....	9	....	....	....	535	23	1	2.58	....	....	....	....
	NHL Totals		**39**	**4**	**27**	**1**	**1846**	**161**	**0**	**5.23**	....	....	**1140**	**.859**	**37.1**	....	....	....	....	....	....	....	....	....	....	....	....

EJC-A All-Star Team (1983) • Named Best Goaltender at EJC-A (1983) • Finnish First All-Star Team (1988, 1994) • Finnish Player of the Year (1988) • IHL Second All-Star Team (1990, 1991) • Named Best Goaltender at WC-A (1995)

Claimed by **San Jose** from **Minnesota** in Dispersal Draft, May 30, 1991. Traded to **Toronto** by **San Jose** for cash, June 15, 1992.

• MYLNIKOV, Sergei

G – L. 5'10", 176 lbs. b: Chelyabinsk, Soviet Union, 10/6/1958. Quebec's 8th, 127th overall in 1989.

Season	Club	League	GP	W	L	T	Mins	GA	SO	Avg	AAvg	Eff	SA	S%	SAPG	GP	W	L	T	Mins	GA	SO	Avg	Eff	SA	S%	SAPG
1976-77	Traktor Chelyabinsk	USSR	2	....	....	....	120	2	....	1.00	....	....	....	....	....	....	....	....	....	....	....	....	....	....	....	....	....
	Soviet Union	WJC-A	2	....	....	....	80	4	....	3.00	....	....	....	....	....	....	....	....	....	....	....	....	....	....	....	....	....
1977-78	Traktor Chelyabinsk	USSR	22	....	....	....	1320	71	....	3.22	....	....	....	....	....	....	....	....	....	....	....	....	....	....	....	....	....
	Soviet Union	WJC-A	3	1	0	0	110	3	0	1.63	....	....	....	....	....	....	....	....	....	....	....	....	....	....	....	....	....
1978-79	Traktor Chelyabinsk	USSR	32	....	....	....	1862	90	....	2.90	....	....	....	....	....	....	....	....	....	....	....	....	....	....	....	....	....
1979-80	Traktor Chelyabinsk	USSR	17	....	....	....	1023	58	....	3.40	....	....	....	....	....	....	....	....	....	....	....	....	....	....	....	....	....
1980-81	SKA Leningrad	USSR	40	....	....	....	2415	157	....	3.90	....	....	....	....	....	....	....	....	....	....	....	....	....	....	....	....	....
1981-82	SKA Leningrad	USSR	42	....	....	....	2310	132	....	3.42	....	....	....	....	....	....	....	....	....	....	....	....	....	....	....	....	....
1982-83	Traktor Chelyabinsk	USSR	37	....	....	....	1954	124	....	3.80	....	....	....	....	....	....	....	....	....	....	....	....	....	....	....	....	....
1983-84	Traktor Chelyabinsk	USSR	37	....	....	....	2173	91	....	2.51	....	....	....	....	....	....	....	....	....	....	....	....	....	....	....	....	....
1984-85	Traktor Chelyabinsk	USSR	28	....	....	....	1360	74	....	3.26	....	....	....	....	....	....	....	....	....	....	....	....	....	....	....	....	....
	Soviet Union	WEC-A	1	0	0	0	20	3	0	9.00	....	....	....	....	....	....	....	....	....	....	....	....	....	....	....	....	....
1985-86	Traktor Chelyabinsk	USSR	37	....	....	....	2126	96	....	2.70	....	....	....	....	....	....	....	....	....	....	....	....	....	....	....	....	....
	CSKA Moscow	Super-S	6	....	....	....	364	16	....	2.64	....	....	....	....	....	....	....	....	....	....	....	....	....	....	....	....	....
	Soviet Union	WEC-A	3	3	0	0	180	4	0	1.33	....	....	....	....	....	....	....	....	....	....	....	....	....	....	....	....	....
1986-87	Traktor Chelyabinsk	USSR	36	....	....	....	2059	103	....	3.00	....	....	....	....	....	....	....	....	....	....	....	....	....	....	....	....	....
	Soviet Union	RV-87	DID NOT PLAY – SPARE GOALTENDER																								
	Soviet Union	WEC-A	DID NOT PLAY – SPARE GOALTENDER																								
1987-88	Soviet Union	Can-Cup	6	5	1	0	365	18	1	3.00	....	....	....	....	....	....	....	....	....	....	....	....	....	....	....	....	....
	Traktor Chelyabinsk	USSR	28	....	....	....	1559	69	....	2.65	....	....	....	....	....	....	....	....	....	....	....	....	....	....	....	....	....
	Soviet Union	Olympics	8	*7	1	0	480	13	*2	1.62	....	....	....	....	....	....	....	....	....	....	....	....	....	....	....	....	....
1988-89	Traktor Chelyabinsk	USSR	33	....	....	....	1980	85	....	2.58	....	....	....	....	....	....	....	....	....	....	....	....	....	....	....	....	....
	CSKA Moscow	Super-S	6	....	....	....	327	16	....	2.93	....	....	....	....	....	....	....	....	....	....	....	....	....	....	....	....	....
	Soviet Union	WEC-A	7	*7	0	0	420	11	1	1.57	....	....	....	....	....	....	....	....	....	....	....	....	....	....	....	....	....
1989-90	**Quebec Nordiques**	**NHL**	**10**	**1**	**7**	**2**	**568**	**47**	**0**	**4.96**	**4.21**	**7.06**	**330**	**.858**	**34.9**	....	....	....	....	....	....	....	....	....	....	....	....
	Soviet Union	WEC-A	5	4	1	0	280	8	1	1.71	....	....	....	....	....	....	....	....	....	....	....	....	....	....	....	....	....
	NHL Totals		**10**	**1**	**7**	**2**	**568**	**47**	**0**	**4.96**	....	....	**330**	**.858**	**34.9**	....	....	....	....	....	....	....	....	....	....	....	....

USSR First All-Star Team (1988)

• MYRE, Phil

Phillipe Louis G – L. 6'1", 185 lbs. b: Ste-Anne-de-Bellevue, Que., 11/1/1948. Montreal's 1st, 5th overall in 1966.

Season	Club	League	GP	W	L	T	Mins	GA	SO	Avg	AAvg	Eff	SA	S%	SAPG	GP	W	L	T	Mins	GA	SO	Avg	Eff	SA	S%	SAPG
1963-64	Victoriaville Bruins	OJHL	....	....	....	....	....	....	....	....	....	....	....	....	....	2	1	1	0	120	12	0	6.00	....	....	....	....
	Victoriaville Bruins	Mem-Cup	1	0	1	0	60	8	0	8.00	....	....	....	....	....	....	....	....	....	....	....	....	....	....	....	....	....
1964-65	Victoriaville Bruins	QJHL	21	14	7	0	1260	82	*3	3.91	....	....	....	....	....	9	7	2	0	540	36	0	4.00	....	....	....	....
	Victoriaville Bruins	Mem-Cup	3	0	3	0	180	24	0	8.00	....	....	....	....	....	....	....	....	....	....	....	....	....	....	....	....	....
1965-66	Shawinigan Bruins	QJHL	44	*38	6	0	2620	136	1	3.11	....	....	....	....	....	12	*8	4	0	730	34	*3	*2.79	....	....	....	....
	Shawinigan Bruins	Mem-Cup	15	11	4	0	900	41	0	2.73	....	....	....	....	....	....	....	....	....	....	....	....	....	....	....	....	....
1966-67	Niagara Falls Flyers	OHA-Jr.	34	....	....	....	2010	135	1	4.03	....	....	....	....	....	9	....	....	....	540	44	0	4.89	....	....	....	....
1967-68	Niagara Falls Flyers	OHA-Jr.	50	....	....	....	2970	153	4	3.09	....	....	....	....	....	19	....	....	....	1140	72	0	3.79	....	....	....	....
	Niagara Falls Flyers	Mem-Cup	10	7	3	0	621	34	1	3.29	....	....	....	....	....	....	....	....	....	....	....	....	....	....	....	....	....
1968-69	Houston Apollos	CHL	*53	24	19	10	*3150	150	2	2.83	....	....	....	....	....	2	0	2	0	119	7	0	3.53	....	....	....	....
1969-70	**Montreal Canadiens**	**NHL**	**10**	**4**	**3**	**2**	**503**	**19**	**0**	**2.27**	**2.40**	....	....	....	....	....	....	....	....	....	....	....	....	....	....	....	....
	Montreal Voyageurs	AHL	15	....	....	....	900	37	0	2.47	....	....	....	....	....	....	....	....	....	....	....	....	....	....	....	....	....
1970-71 ♦	**Montreal Canadiens**	**NHL**	**30**	**13**	**11**	**4**	**1677**	**87**	**1**	**3.11**	**3.08**	....	....	....	....	....	....	....	....	....	....	....	....	....	....	....	....
1971-72	**Montreal Canadiens**	**NHL**	**9**	**4**	**5**	**0**	**528**	**32**	**0**	**3.64**	**3.69**	....	....	....	....	....	....	....	....	....	....	....	....	....	....	....	....
1972-73	**Atlanta Flames**	**NHL**	**46**	**16**	**23**	**5**	**2736**	**138**	**2**	**3.03**	**2.85**	....	....	....	....	....	....	....	....	....	....	....	....	....	....	....	....
1973-74	**Atlanta Flames**	**NHL**	**36**	**11**	**16**	**6**	**2020**	**112**	**0**	**3.33**	**3.22**	....	....	....	....	**3**	**0**	**3**	....	**186**	**13**	**0**	**4.19**	....	....	....	....
1974-75	**Atlanta Flames**	**NHL**	**40**	**14**	**16**	**10**	**2400**	**114**	**5**	**2.85**	**2.56**	....	....	....	....	....	....	....	....	....	....	....	....	....	....	....	....
1975-76	**Atlanta Flames**	**NHL**	**37**	**16**	**16**	**4**	**2129**	**123**	**1**	**3.47**	**3.14**	....	....	....	....	....	....	....	....	....	....	....	....	....	....	....	....
1976-77	**Atlanta Flames**	**NHL**	**43**	**17**	**17**	**7**	**2422**	**124**	**3**	**3.07**	**2.85**	....	....	....	....	**2**	**1**	**1**	....	**120**	**5**	**0**	**2.50**	....	....	....	....
1977-78	**Atlanta Flames**	**NHL**	**9**	**2**	**7**	**0**	**523**	**43**	**0**	**4.93**	**4.64**	....	....	....	....	....	....	....	....	....	....	....	....	....	....	....	....
	St. Louis Blues	**NHL**	**44**	**11**	**25**	**8**	**2620**	**159**	**1**	**3.64**	**3.43**	....	....	....	....	....	....	....	....	....	....	....	....	....	....	....	....
1978-79	**St. Louis Blues**	**NHL**	**39**	**9**	**22**	**8**	**2259**	**163**	**1**	**4.33**	**3.86**	....	....	....	....	....	....	....	....	....	....	....	....	....	....	....	....
1979-80	**Philadelphia Flyers**	**NHL**	**41**	**18**	**7**	**15**	**2367**	**141**	**0**	**3.57**	**3.16**	....	....	....	....	**6**	**5**	**1**	....	**384**	**16**	**1**	**2.50**	....	....	....	....
1980-81	**Philadelphia Flyers**	**NHL**	**16**	**6**	**5**	**4**	**900**	**61**	**0**	**4.07**	**3.29**	....	....	....	....	....	....	....	....	....	....	....	....	....	....	....	....
	Colorado Rockies	**NHL**	**10**	**3**	**6**	**1**	**580**	**33**	**0**	**3.41**	**2.75**	....	....	....	....	....	....	....	....	....	....	....	....	....	....	....	....
	Canada	WEC-A	7	2	5	0	359	26	0	4.34	....	....	....	....	....	....	....	....	....	....	....	....	....	....	....	....	....
1981-82	**Colorado Rockies**	**NHL**	**24**	**2**	**17**	**2**	**1256**	**112**	**0**	**5.35**	**4.15**	....	....	....	....	....	....	....	....	....	....	....	....	....	....	....	....
	Fort Worth Texans	CHL	10	4	5	1	615	40	0	3.90	....	....	....	....	....	....	....	....	....	....	....	....	....	....	....	....	....
1982-83	**Buffalo Sabres**	**NHL**	**5**	**3**	**2**	**0**	**300**	**21**	**0**	**4.20**	**3.37**	**5.80**	**152**	**.862**	**30.4**	**1**	**0**	**0**	....	**57**	**7**	**0**	**7.37**	....	....	....	....
	Rochester Americans	AHL	43	28	8	5	2541	156	0	3.68	....	....	....	....	....	....	....	....	....	....	....	....	....	....	....	....	....
1983-84	Rochester Americans	AHL	33	19	9	1	1803	104	4	3.46	....	....	....	....	....	....	....	....	....	....	....	....	....	....	....	....	....
	NHL Totals		**439**	**149**	**198**	**76**	**25220**	**1482**	**14**	**3.53**	....	....	....	....	....	**12**	**6**	**5**	....	**747**	**41**	**1**	**3.29**	....	....	....	....

QJHL Second All-Star Team (1965, 1966) • OHA-Jr. Second All-Star Team (1968) • CHL Second All-Star Team (1969) • Won Terry Sawchuk Trophy (fewest goals against - CHL) (1969)

• Regular season totals for **Victoriaville** (QJHL) in 1963-64 are unavailable. Claimed by **Atlanta** from **Montreal** in Expansion Draft, June 6, 1972. Traded to **St. Louis** by **Atlanta** with Curt Bennett and Barry Gibbs for Yves Belanger, Dick Redmond, Bob MacMillan and St. Louis' 2nd round choice (Mike Perovich) in 1979 Entry Draft, December 12, 1977. Traded to **Philadelphia** by **St. Louis** for Blake Dunlop and Rick Lapointe, June 7, 1979. Traded to **Colorado** by **Philadelphia** for cash, February 26, 1981. Signed as a free agent by **Buffalo**, September 11, 1982.

• NABOKOV, Evgeni

Evgeni Vitorovich G – L. 6', 195 lbs. b: Ust-Kamenogorsk, USSR, 7/25/1975. San Jose's 9th, 219th overall in 1994.

Season	Club	League	GP	W	L	T	Mins	GA	SO	Avg	AAvg	Eff	SA	S%	SAPG	GP	W	L	T	Mins	GA	SO	Avg	Eff	SA	S%	SAPG
1992-93	Torpedo Ust Kamenogorsk	CIS	4	....	....	....	109	5	0	2.75	....	....	....	....	....	....	....	....	....	....	....	....	....	....	....	....	....
1993-94	Torpedo Ust Kamenogorsk	CIS	11	....	....	....	539	29	0	3.22	....	....	....	....	....	....	....	....	....	....	....	....	....	....	....	....	....
1994-95	Dynamo Moscow	CIS	24	....	....	....	1265	40	....	1.89	....	....	....	....	....	....	....	....	....	....	....	....	....	....	....	....	....
1995-96	Dynamo Moscow	CIS	39	....	....	....	2008	67	5	2.00	....	....	....	....	....	6	....	....	....	298	7	....	1.41	....	....	....	....
1996-97	Dynamo Moscow	Russia	27	....	....	....	1588	56	2	2.11	....	....	....	....	....	4	....	....	....	255	12	0	2.82	....	....	....	....
1997-98	Kentucky Thoroughblades	AHL	33	10	21	2	1866	122	0	3.92	....	....	....	....	....	1	0	0	....	23	1	0	2.59	....	....	....	....
1998-99	Kentucky Thoroughblades	AHL	43	26	14	1	2429	106	5	2.62	....	....	....	....	....	11	6	5	....	599	30	*2	3.00	....	....	....	....

			REGULAR SEASON													PLAYOFFS											
Season	Club	League	GP	W	L	T	Mins	GA	SO	Avg	AAvg	Eff	SA	S%	SAPG	GP	W	L	T	Mins	GA	SO	Avg	Eff	SA	S%	SAPG
99-2000	**San Jose Sharks**	**NHL**	**11**	**2**	**2**	**1**	**414**	**15**	**1**	**2.17**	**2.48**	**1.96**	**166**	**.910**	**24.1**	**1**	**0**	**0**	....	**20**	**0**	**0**	**0.00**	**0.00**	**10**	**1.000**	**30.0**
	Kentucky Thoroughblades	AHL	2	1	1	0	120	3	1	1.50	....	....	....	....	....	....	....	....	....	....	....	....	....	....	....	....	....
	Cleveland Lumberjacks	IHL	20	12	4	3	1164	52	0	2.68	....	....	....	....	....	....	....	....	....	....	....	....	....	....	....	....	....
	NHL Totals		**11**	**2**	**2**	**1**	**414**	**15**	**1**	**2.17**	....	....	**166**	**.910**	**24.1**	**1**	**0**	**0**	....	**20**	**0**	**0**	**0.00**	....	**10**	**1.000**	**30.0**

• NEWTON, Cam

Cameron Charles G – L. 5'11", 170 lbs. b: Peterborough, Ont., 2/25/1950. Pittsburgh's 8th, 102nd overall in 1970.

Season	Club	League	GP	W	L	T	Mins	GA	SO	Avg	AAvg	Eff	SA	S%	SAPG	GP	W	L	T	Mins	GA	SO	Avg	Eff	SA	S%	SAPG
1966-67	Toronto Marlboros	OHA-Jr.	18	....	....	....	1044	59	0	3.39	....	....	....	....	....	10	....	....	....	600	32	0	3.20	....	....	....	....
1967-68	Toronto Marlboros	OHA-Jr.	18	....	....	....	1030	60	0	3.50	....	....	....	....	....	1	0	0	0	10	0	0	0.00	....	....	....	....
1968-69	Toronto Marlboros	OHA-Jr.	27	....	....	....	1600	129	0	4.84	....	....	....	....	....	....	....	....	....	....	....	....	....	....	....	....	....
	Kitchener Rangers	OHA-Jr.	24	....	....	....	1440	135	0	5.63	....	....	....	....	....	....	....	....	....	....	....	....	....	....	....	....	....
1969-70	Kitchener Rangers	OHA-Jr.	42	....	....	....	2520	179	1	4.26	....	....	....	....	....	4	0	3	0	206	23	0	7.82	....	....	....	....
1970-71	**Pittsburgh Penguins**	**NHL**	**5**	**1**	**3**	**1**	**281**	**16**	**0**	**3.42**	**3.38**	....	....	....	....	....	....	....	....	....	....	....	....	....	....	....	....
	Amarillo Wranglers	CHL	15	....	....	....	873	68	0	4.74	....	....	....	....	....	....	....	....	....	....	....	....	....	....	....	....	....
1971-72	Hershey Bears	AHL	35	13	17	4	2065	131	0	3.80	....	....	....	....	....	1	0	1	0	60	7	0	7.00	....	....	....	....
1972-73	**Pittsburgh Penguins**	**NHL**	**11**	**3**	**4**	**0**	**533**	**35**	**0**	**3.94**	**3.72**	....	....	....	....	....	....	....	....	....	....	....	....	....	....	....	....
	Hershey Bears	AHL	19	....	....	....	1121	53	2	2.83	....	....	....	....	....	....	....	....	....	....	....	....	....	....	....	....	....
1973-74	Chicago Cougars	WHA	45	25	18	2	2732	143	1	3.14	....	....	....	....	....	10	2	5	0	486	34	0	4.20	....	....	....	....
1974-75	Chicago Cougars	WHA	32	12	20	0	1905	126	0	3.97	....	....	....	....	....	....	....	....	....	....	....	....	....	....	....	....	....
1975-76	Denver-Ottawa Civics	WHA	10	4	6	0	573	35	1	3.66	....	....	....	....	....	....	....	....	....	....	....	....	....	....	....	....	....
	Cleveland Crusaders	WHA	15	7	7	1	896	48	0	3.21	....	....	....	....	....	1	0	1	0	60	6	0	6.00	....	....	....	....
1976-77	Erie Blades	NAHL	4	....	....	....	122	5	1	1.96	....	....	....	....	....	....	....	....	....	....	....	....	....	....	....	....	....
	NHL Totals		**16**	**4**	**7**	**1**	**814**	**51**	**0**	**3.76**	....	....	....	....	....	....	....	....	....	....	....	....	....	....	....	....	....
	Other Major League Totals		102	48	51	3	6106	352	2	3.46	....	....	....	....	....	11	2	6	....	546	40	0	4.40	....	....	....	....

Signed as a free agent by **Chicago** (WHA), May, 1973. Claimed by **Denver** (WHA) from **Chicago** (WHA) in 1975 WHA Expansion Draft, May, 1975. Signed as a free agent by **Cleveland** (WHA) after **Denver-Ottawa** (WHA) franchise folded, January 17, 1976.

• NORRIS, Jack

John Wayne G – L. 5'10", 185 lbs. b: Saskatoon, Sask., 8/5/1942.

Season	Club	League	GP	W	L	T	Mins	GA	SO	Avg	AAvg	Eff	SA	S%	SAPG	GP	W	L	T	Mins	GA	SO	Avg	Eff	SA	S%	SAPG
1959-60	Estevan Bruins	SJHL	19	....	....	....	1160	82	1	4.24	....	....	....	....	....	....	....	....	....	....	....	....	....	....	....	....	....
1960-61	Estevan Bruins	SJHL	49	....	....	....	2940	148	3	3.02	....	....	....	....	....	7	....	....	....	380	20	0	3.16	....	....	....	....
1961-62	Estevan Bruins	SJHL	42	....	....	....	2420	87	*7	*2.16	....	....	....	....	....	10	6	3	1	620	25	0	*2.42	....	....	....	....
1962-63	Estevan Bruins	SJHL	54	....	....	....	3240	139	5	*2.57	....	....	....	....	....	12	7	4	1	740	37	0	3.00	....	....	....	....
	Estevan Bruins	Mem-Cup	6	2	4	0	370	23	0	3.73	....	....	....	....	....	....	....	....	....	....	....	....	....	....	....	....	....
1963-64	Los Angeles Blades	WHL	31	13	16	2	1836	115	2	3.71	....	....	....	....	....	8	4	4	0	491	31	0	3.79	....	....	....	....
	Minneapolis Bruins	CPHL	4	2	1	1	240	19	0	4.75	....	....	....	....	....	....	....	....	....	....	....	....	....	....	....	....	....
1964-65	Los Angeles Blades	WHL	38	18	19	1	2307	146	1	3.80	....	....	....	....	....	....	....	....	....	....	....	....	....	....	....	....	....
	Boston Bruins	**NHL**	**23**	**10**	**11**	**2**	**1380**	**85**	**1**	**3.70**	**4.03**	....	....	....	....	....	....	....	....	....	....	....	....	....	....	....	....
1965-66	Los Angeles Blades	WHL	20	5	15	0	1200	117	0	5.85	....	....	....	....	....	....	....	....	....	....	....	....	....	....	....	....	....
	Oklahoma City Blazers	CPHL	18	9	7	2	1040	51	1	2.94	....	....	....	....	....	....	....	....	....	....	....	....	....	....	....	....	....
1966-67	Los Angeles Blades	WHL	35	14	17	3	2102	133	2	3.80	....	....	....	....	....	....	....	....	....	....	....	....	....	....	....	....	....
1967-68	**Chicago Black Hawks**	**NHL**	**7**	**2**	**3**	**0**	**334**	**22**	**1**	**3.95**	**4.39**	....	....	....	....	....	....	....	....	....	....	....	....	....	....	....	....
	Dallas Black Hawks	CPHL	39	13	15	10	2423	132	0	3.27	....	....	....	....	....	....	....	....	....	....	....	....	....	....	....	....	....
1968-69	**Chicago Black Hawks**	**NHL**	**3**	**1**	**0**	**0**	**100**	**10**	**0**	**6.00**	**6.22**	....	....	....	....	....	....	....	....	....	....	....	....	....	....	....	....
	Dallas Black Hawks	CHL	36	....	....	....	2099	98	*4	*2.80	....	....	....	....	....	*11	*10	1	0	*660	26	0	*2.36	....	....	....	....
1969-70	Montreal Voyageurs	AHL	55	....	....	....	3265	149	4	2.74	....	....	....	....	....	8	4	4	0	495	24	*1	2.91	....	....	....	....
1970-71	**Los Angeles Kings**	**NHL**	**25**	**7**	**11**	**2**	**1305**	**85**	**0**	**3.91**	**3.89**	....	....	....	....	....	....	....	....	....	....	....	....	....	....	....	....
1971-72	Seattle Totems	WHL	38	5	28	5	2219	152	2	4.14	....	....	....	....	....	....	....	....	....	....	....	....	....	....	....	....	....
	Springfield Kings	AHL	10	5	4	1	569	36	0	3.80	....	....	....	....	....	2	0	2	0	108	14	0	7.78	....	....	....	....
1972-73	Alberta Oilers	WHA	*64	28	29	3	*3702	189	1	3.06	....	....	....	....	....	....	....	....	....	....	....	....	....	....	....	....	....
1973-74	Edmonton Oilers	WHA	53	23	24	1	2954	158	2	3.21	....	....	....	....	....	3	0	2	0	111	9	0	4.86	....	....	....	....
1974-75	Phoenix Roadrunners	WHA	33	14	15	4	1962	107	1	3.27	....	....	....	....	....	2	0	2	0	100	10	0	6.00	....	....	....	....
1975-76	Phoenix Roadrunners	WHA	41	21	14	4	2412	128	1	3.18	....	....	....	....	....	5	2	3	0	298	17	0	3.42	....	....	....	....
	NHL Totals		**58**	**20**	**25**	**4**	**3119**	**202**	**2**	**3.89**	....	....	....	....	....	....	....	....	....	....	....	....	....	....	....	....	....
	Other Major League Totals		191	86	82	12	11030	582	5	3.17	....	....	....	....	....	10	2	7	....	509	36	0	4.24	....	....	....	....

SJHL First All-Star Team (1962, 1963) • AHL Second All-Star Team (1970)

Promoted to **Boston** from **LA Blades** (WHL) after Ed Johnston suffered hand injury in game vs. Toronto, January 30, 1965. Traded to **Chicago** by **Boston** with Gilles Marotte and Pit Martin for Phil Esposito, Ken Hodge and Fred Stanfield, May 15, 1967. Claimed by **Montreal** from **Chicago** in Intra-League Draft, June 11, 1969. Traded to **LA Kings** by **Montreal** with Larry Mickey and Lucien Grenier for Leon Rochefort, Gregg Boddy and Wayne Thomas, May 22, 1970. Claimed by **Seattle** (WHL) from **LA Kings** in Reverse Draft, June, 1971. Selected by **Calgary-Cleveland** (WHA) in 1972 WHA General Player Draft, February 12, 1972. WHA rights traded to **Alberta** (WHA) by **Cleveland** (WHA) for cash, June, 1972. Traded to **Indianapolis** (WHA) by **Edmonton** (WHA) for future considerations, June, 1974. Traded to **Phoenix** (WHA) by **Indianapolis** (WHA) for Ray Reeson, September, 1974.

• OLESCHUK, Bill

William Stephen G – L. 6'3", 194 lbs. b: Edmonton, Alta., 7/20/1955. Kansas City's 7th, 110th overall in 1975.

Season	Club	League	GP	W	L	T	Mins	GA	SO	Avg	AAvg	Eff	SA	S%	SAPG	GP	W	L	T	Mins	GA	SO	Avg	Eff	SA	S%	SAPG
1971-72	Edmonton Maple Leafs	AJHL	22	....	....	....	1320	99	0	4.58	....	....	....	....	....	....	....	....	....	....	....	....	....	....	....	....	....
1972-73	Edmonton Mets	AJHL	STATISTICS NOT AVAILABLE																								
	Winnipeg Jets	WCJHL	1	....	....	....	20	2	0	6.00	....	....	....	....	....	....	....	....	....	....	....	....	....	....	....	....	....
1973-74	Prince Albert Raiders	SJHL	10	....	....	....	2280	38	0	3.85	....	....	....	....	....	....	....	....	....	....	....	....	....	....	....	....	....
	Swift Current Broncos	WCJHL	11	....	....	....	518	36	0	4.17	....	....	....	....	....	....	....	....	....	....	....	....	....	....	....	....	....
1974-75	Lethbridge Broncos	WCJHL	2	....	....	....	80	8	0	6.00	....	....	....	....	....	....	....	....	....	....	....	....	....	....	....	....	....
	Saskatoon Blades	WCJHL	41	24	12	5	2419	121	*4	3.00	....	....	....	....	....	12	7	5	0	672	37	0	3.30	....	....	....	....
1975-76	**Kansas City Scouts**	**NHL**	**1**	**0**	**1**	**0**	**60**	**4**	**0**	**4.00**	**3.62**	....	....	....	....	....	....	....	....	....	....	....	....	....	....	....	....
	Port Huron Flags	IHL	44	....	....	....	2417	145	0	3.60	....	....	....	....	....	9	....	....	....	443	24	0	3.25	....	....	....	....
1976-77	Baltimore Clippers	SHL	30	....	....	....	1780	97	1	3.27	....	....	....	....	....	....	....	....	....	....	....	....	....	....	....	....	....
	Oklahoma City Blazers	CHL	3	0	3	0	159	15	0	5.66	....	....	....	....	....	....	....	....	....	....	....	....	....	....	....	....	....
1977-78	**Colorado Rockies**	**NHL**	**2**	**0**	**2**	**0**	**100**	**9**	**0**	**5.40**	**5.07**	....	....	....	....	....	....	....	....	....	....	....	....	....	....	....	....
	Phoenix Roadrunners	CHL	9	2	6	1	549	45	0	4.92	....	....	....	....	....	....	....	....	....	....	....	....	....	....	....	....	....
	Hampton Gulls	AHL	11	1	9	1	616	40	0	3.90	....	....	....	....	....	....	....	....	....	....	....	....	....	....	....	....	....
	Philadelphia Firebirds	AHL	2	0	1	0	65	9	0	8.30	....	....	....	....	....	....	....	....	....	....	....	....	....	....	....	....	....
	Flint Generals	IHL	13	....	....	....	702	57	0	4.87	....	....	....	....	....	4	....	....	....	204	10	0	2.94	....	....	....	....
1978-79	**Colorado Rockies**	**NHL**	**40**	**6**	**19**	**8**	**2118**	**136**	**1**	**3.85**	**3.42**	....	....	....	....	....	....	....	....	....	....	....	....	....	....	....	....
1979-80	**Colorado Rockies**	**NHL**	**12**	**1**	**6**	**2**	**557**	**39**	**0**	**4.20**	**3.72**	....	....	....	....	....	....	....	....	....	....	....	....	....	....	....	....
	Fort Worth Texans	CHL	43	24	14	5	2478	134	1	3.24	....	....	....	....	....	2	1	1	0	72	8	0	6.67	....	....	....	....
1980-81	Fort Worth Texans	CHL	36	10	22	1	2054	122	0	3.56	....	....	....	....	....	5	....	....	....	300	14	0	2.80	....	....	....	....
1981-82	Dallas Black Hawks	CHL	7	2	4	0	322	26	0	4.84	....	....	....	....	....	....	....	....	....	....	....	....	....	....	....	....	....
1982-83	Peoria Prancers	IHL	29	....	....	....	1448	147	1	6.09	....	....	....	....	....	....	....	....	....	....	....	....	....	....	....	....	....
1983-84	Fort Wayne Komets	IHL	1	....	....	....	60	7	0	7.00	....	....	....	....	....	....	....	....	....	....	....	....	....	....	....	....	....
	NHL Totals		**55**	**7**	**28**	**10**	**2835**	**188**	**1**	**3.98**	....	....	....	....	....	....	....	....	....	....	....	....	....	....	....	....	....

Won WCJHL Top Goaltender Award (1975)

Transferred to **Colorado** after **Kansas City** franchise relocated, July 15, 1976.

• OLESEVICH, Dan

Daniel John G – R. 6', 170 lbs. b: Port Colborne, Ont., 9/16/1937 d: 7/15/1983.

Season	Club	League	GP	W	L	T	Mins	GA	SO	Avg	AAvg	Eff	SA	S%	SAPG	GP	W	L	T	Mins	GA	SO	Avg	Eff	SA	S%	SAPG
1953-54	Hamilton Tiger Cubs	OHA-Jr.	5	....	....	....	300	23	0	4.60	....	....	....	....	....	....	....	....	....	....	....	....	....	....	....	....	....
1954-55	Hamilton Tiger Cubs	OHA-Jr.	DID NOT PLAY – SPARE GOALTENDER																								
1955-56	Hamilton Tiger Cubs	OHA-Jr.	1	0	1	0	60	6	0	6.00	....	....	....	....	....	....	....	....	....	....	....	....	....	....	....	....	....
1956-57	Hamilton Tiger Cubs	OHA-Jr.	2	0	2	0	120	12	0	6.00	....	....	....	....	....	....	....	....	....	....	....	....	....	....	....	....	....
1957-58	Edmonton Oil Kings	X-Games	STATISTICS NOT AVAILABLE																								
	Edmonton Flyers	WHL	1	1	0	0	60	1	0	1.00	....	....	....	....	....	....	....	....	....	....	....	....	....	....	....	....	....
	Edmonton Oil Kings	Mem-Cup	4	0	4	0	240	20	0	5.00	....	....	....	....	....	....	....	....	....	....	....	....	....	....	....	....	....
1958-59	Charlotte-Johnstown	EHL	30	....	....	....	1800	121	2	4.03	....	....	....	....	....	....	....	....	....	....	....	....	....	....	....	....	....
	Windsor Bulldogs	NOHA	26	....	....	....	1560	90	1	3.46	....	....	....	....	....	....	....	....	....	....	....	....	....	....	....	....	....

Season	Club	League	GP	W	L	T	Mins	GA	SO	Avg	AAvg	Eff	SA	S%	SAPG	GP	W	L	T	Mins	GA	SO	Avg	Eff	SA	S%	SAPG
			REGULAR SEASON													PLAYOFFS											
1959-60			DID NOT PLAY																								
1960-61			DID NOT PLAY																								
1961-62	**New York Rangers**	**NHL**	**1**	**0**	**0**	**1**	**29**	**2**	**0**	**4.14**	**4.24**	....	....	....	....	....	....	....	....	....	....	....	....	....	....	....	....
	NHL Totals		**1**	**0**	**0**	**1**	**29**	**2**	**0**	**4.14**	....	....	....	....	....	....	....	....	....	....	....	....	....	....	....	....	....

• Retired after 1958-59 season and was hired as Detroit's assistant trainer/practice goaltender. Loaned to **NY Rangers** by **Detroit** to replace injured Gump Worsley in 2nd period, October 21, 1961. (NY Rangers 4, Detroit 4)

• O'NEILL, Mike

Michael A. G – L. 5'7", 155 lbs. b: LaSalle, Que., 11/3/1967. Winnipeg's 1st, 15th overall in 1988 Supplemental Draft.

Season	Club	League	GP	W	L	T	Mins	GA	SO	Avg	AAvg	Eff	SA	S%	SAPG	GP	W	L	T	Mins	GA	SO	Avg	Eff	SA	S%	SAPG
1982-83	Lac St-Louis Lions	QAAA	20	7	8	5	1198	107	0	5.34	....	....	....	....	....	....	....	....	....	....	....	....	....	....	....	....	....
	Lac St-Louis Lions	QAAA	22	13	7	2	1318	81	0	3.67	....	....	....	....	....	....	....	....	....	....	....	....	....	....	....	....	....
1983-84	Lower Canada College	CEGEP	STATISTICS NOT AVAILABLE																								
1984-85	Lower Canada College	CEGEP	STATISTICS NOT AVAILABLE																								
1985-86	Yale University	ECAC	6	3	1	0	389	17	0	3.53	....	....	....	....	....	....	....	....	....	....	....	....	....	....	....	....	....
1986-87	Yale University	ECAC	16	9	6	1	964	55	2	3.42	....	....	....	....	....	....	....	....	....	....	....	....	....	....	....	....	....
1987-88	Yale University	ECAC	24	6	17	0	1385	101	0	4.37	....	....	....	....	....	....	....	....	....	....	....	....	....	....	....	....	....
1988-89	Yale University	ECAC	25	10	14	1	1490	93	0	3.74	....	....	....	....	....	....	....	....	....	....	....	....	....	....	....	....	....
1989-90	Tappara Tampere	Finland	41	23	13	5	2369	127	2	3.22	....	....	....	....	....	7	....	....	....	420	31	0	4.43	....	....	....	....
1990-91	Fort Wayne Komets	IHL	8	5	2	1	490	31	0	3.80	....	....	....	....	....	....	....	....	....	....	....	....	....	....	....	....	....
	Moncton Hawks	AHL	30	13	7	6	1613	84	0	3.12	....	....	....	....	....	8	3	4	....	435	29	0	4.00	....	....	....	....
1991-92	**Winnipeg Jets**	**NHL**	**1**	**0**	**0**	**0**	**13**	**1**	**0**	**4.62**	**4.14**	**6.60**	**7**	**.857**	**32.3**	....	....	....	....	....	....	....	....	....	....	....	....
	Moncton Hawks	AHL	32	14	16	2	1902	108	1	3.41	....	....	....	....	....	11	4	7	....	670	43	*1	3.85	....	....	....	....
	Fort Wayne Komets	IHL	33	22	6	3	1858	97	*4	3.13	....	....	....	....	....	....	....	....	....	....	....	....	....	....	....	....	....
1992-93	**Winnipeg Jets**	**NHL**	**2**	**0**	**0**	**1**	**73**	**6**	**0**	**4.93**	**4.22**	**8.70**	**34**	**.824**	**27.9**	....	....	....	....	....	....	....	....	....	....	....	....
	Moncton Hawks	AHL	30	13	10	4	1649	88	1	3.20	....	....	....	....	....	....	....	....	....	....	....	....	....	....	....	....	....
1993-94	**Winnipeg Jets**	**NHL**	**17**	**0**	**9**	**1**	**738**	**51**	**0**	**4.15**	**3.99**	**5.54**	**382**	**.866**	**31.1**	....	....	....	....	....	....	....	....	....	....	....	....
	Moncton Hawks	AHL	12	8	4	0	716	33	1	2.76	....	....	....	....	....	....	....	....	....	....	....	....	....	....	....	....	....
	Fort Wayne Komets	IHL	11	4	4	3	642	38	0	3.55	....	....	....	....	....	....	....	....	....	....	....	....	....	....	....	....	....
1994-95	Fort Wayne Komets	IHL	28	11	12	4	1603	109	0	4.08	....	....	....	....	....	....	....	....	....	....	....	....	....	....	....	....	....
	Phoenix Roadrunners	IHL	21	13	4	4	1256	64	1	3.06	....	....	....	....	....	9	4	5	....	535	33	0	3.70	....	....	....	....
1995-96	Baltimore Bandits	AHL	*74	31	31	7	*4250	250	2	3.53	....	....	....	....	....	12	6	6	....	689	43	0	3.75	....	....	....	....
1996-97	**Mighty Ducks of Anaheim**	**NHL**	**1**	**0**	**0**	**0**	**31**	**3**	**0**	**5.81**	**6.25**	**17.43**	**10**	**.700**	**19.4**	....	....	....	....	....	....	....	....	....	....	....	....
	Long Beach Ice Dogs	IHL	45	26	12	6	2644	145	1	3.29	....	....	....	....	....	1	0	0	....	7	0	0	0.00	....	....	....	....
1997-98	Portland Pirates	AHL	47	16	18	10	2640	135	1	3.07	....	....	....	....	....	6	2	3	....	305	16	0	3.15	....	....	....	....
1998-99	VSV Villach	Austria	42	35	5	1	2540	104	0	2.49	....	....	....	....	....	....	....	....	....	....	....	....	....	....	....	....	....
99-2000	Michigan K-Wings	IHL	4	1	1	0	155	6	1	2.33	....	....	....	....	....	....	....	....	....	....	....	....	....	....	....	....	....
	Long Beach Ice Dogs	IHL	25	7	12	5	1423	71	0	2.99	....	....	....	....	....	1	0	1	....	60	3	0	3.01	....	....	....	....
	NHL Totals		**21**	**0**	**9**	**2**	**855**	**61**	**0**	**4.28**	....	....	**433**	**.859**	**30.4**	....	....	....	....	....	....	....	....	....	....	....	....

ECAC First All-Star Team (1987, 1989) • NCAA East First All-American Team (1989)

Signed as a free agent by **Anaheim**, July 14, 1995. Signed as a free agent by **Washington**, August 20, 1997. Signed as a free agent by **LA Kings**, July 21, 1999.

• OSGOOD, Chris

G – L. 5'10", 160 lbs. b: Peace River, Alta., 11/26/1972. Detroit's 3rd, 54th overall in 1991.

Season	Club	League	GP	W	L	T	Mins	GA	SO	Avg	AAvg	Eff	SA	S%	SAPG	GP	W	L	T	Mins	GA	SO	Avg	Eff	SA	S%	SAPG
1987-88	Medicine Hat Elks	AAHA	STATISTICS NOT AVAILABLE																								
1988-89	Medicine Hat Midget Tigers	AAHA	26	....	....	....	1441	88	0	3.66	....	....	....	....	....	....	....	....	....	....	....	....	....	....	....	....	....
1989-90	Medicine Hat Tigers	WHL	57	24	28	2	3094	228	0	4.42	....	....	....	....	....	3	0	3	....	173	17	0	5.91	....	....	....	....
1990-91	Medicine Hat Tigers	WHL	46	23	18	3	2630	173	2	3.95	....	....	....	....	....	12	7	5	....	712	42	0	3.54	....	....	....	....
1991-92	Medicine Hat Tigers	WHL	15	10	3	0	819	44	0	3.22	....	....	....	....	....	....	....	....	....	....	....	....	....	....	....	....	....
	Brandon Wheat Kings	WHL	16	3	10	1	890	60	1	4.04	....	....	....	....	....	....	....	....	....	....	....	....	....	....	....	....	....
	Seattle Thunderbirds	WHL	21	12	7	1	1217	65	1	3.20	....	....	....	....	....	15	9	6	....	904	51	0	3.38	....	....	....	....
	Seattle Thunderbirds	Mem-Cup	4	1	*3	0	240	18	0	4.50	....	....	....	....	....	....	....	....	....	....	....	....	....	....	....	....	....
1992-93	Adirondack Red Wings	AHL	45	19	19	4	2438	159	0	3.91	....	....	....	....	....	1	0	1	....	59	2	0	2.03	....	....	....	....
1993-94	**Detroit Red Wings**	**NHL**	**41**	**23**	**8**	**5**	**2206**	**105**	**2**	**2.86**	**2.74**	**3.01**	**999**	**.895**	**27.2**	**6**	**3**	**2**	....	**307**	**12**	**1**	**2.35**	**2.56**	**110**	**.891**	**21.5**
	Adirondack Red Wings	AHL	4	3	1	0	239	13	0	3.26	....	....	....	....	....	....	....	....	....	....	....	....	....	....	....	....	....
1994-95	**Detroit Red Wings**	**NHL**	**19**	**14**	**5**	**0**	**1087**	**41**	**1**	**2.26**	**2.36**	**1.87**	**496**	**.917**	**27.4**	**2**	**0**	**0**	....	**68**	**2**	**0**	**1.76**	**1.41**	**25**	**.920**	**22.1**
	Adirondack Red Wings	AHL	2	1	1	0	120	6	0	3.00	....	....	....	....	....	....	....	....	....	....	....	....	....	....	....	....	....
1995-96	**Detroit Red Wings**	**NHL**	**50**	***39**	**6**	**5**	**2933**	**106**	**5**	**2.17**	**2.14**	**1.93**	**1190**	**.911**	**24.3**	**15**	**8**	**7**	....	**936**	**33**	**2**	**2.12**	**2.17**	**322**	**.898**	**20.6**
1996-97♦	**Detroit Red Wings**	**NHL**	**47**	**23**	**13**	**9**	**2769**	**106**	**6**	**2.30**	**2.46**	**2.07**	**1175**	**.910**	**25.5**	**2**	**0**	**0**	....	**47**	**2**	**0**	**2.55**	**2.43**	**21**	**.905**	**26.8**
1997-98♦	**Detroit Red Wings**	**NHL**	**64**	**33**	**20**	**11**	**3807**	**140**	**6**	**2.21**	**2.62**	**1.93**	**1605**	**.913**	**25.3**	***22**	***16**	**6**	....	***1361**	**48**	**2**	**2.12**	**1.73**	**588**	**.918**	**25.9**
1998-99	**Detroit Red Wings**	**NHL**	**63**	**34**	**25**	**4**	**3691**	**149**	**3**	**2.42**	**2.87**	**2.18**	**1654**	**.910**	**26.9**	**6**	**4**	**2**	....	**358**	**14**	**1**	**2.35**	**1.91**	**172**	**.919**	**28.8**
99-2000	**Detroit Red Wings**	**NHL**	**53**	**30**	**14**	**8**	**3148**	**126**	**6**	**2.40**	**2.74**	**2.24**	**1349**	**.907**	**25.7**	**9**	**5**	**4**	....	**547**	**18**	**2**	**1.97**	**1.50**	**237**	**.924**	**26.0**
	NHL Totals		**337**	**196**	**91**	**42**	**19641**	**773**	**29**	**2.36**	....	....	**8468**	**.909**	**25.9**	**62**	**36**	**21**	....	**3624**	**129**	**8**	**2.14**	....	**1475**	**.913**	**24.4**

WHL East Second All-Star Team (1991) • NHL Second All-Star Team (1996) • Shared William M. Jennings Trophy with Mike Vernon (1996) • Played in NHL All-Star Game (1996, 1997, 1998)

• Scored a goal while with Medicine Hat (WHL), January 3, 1991. • Scored a goal vs. Hartford, March 6, 1996.

• OUIMET, Ted

Edward John G. 5'9", 165 lbs. b: Noranda, Que., 7/6/1947.

Season	Club	League	GP	W	L	T	Mins	GA	SO	Avg	AAvg	Eff	SA	S%	SAPG	GP	W	L	T	Mins	GA	SO	Avg	Eff	SA	S%	SAPG
1964-65	Montreal Jr. Canadiens	OHA-Jr.	5	....	....	....	300	20	0	4.00	....	....	....	....	....	1	....	....	....	20	0	0	0.00	....	....	....	....
1965-66	Montreal Jr. Canadiens	OHA-Jr.	32	....	....	....	1920	88	*3	*2.75	....	....	....	....	....	10	....	....	....	600	28	1	2.80	....	....	....	....
1966-67	Montreal Jr. Canadiens	OHA-Jr.	41	....	....	....	2450	177	2	4.33	....	....	....	....	....	6	....	....	....	320	27	0	5.09	....	....	....	....
1967-68	London Nationals/Knights	OHA-Jr.	35	....	....	....	2093	166	0	4.76	....	....	....	....	....	2	....	....	....	120	7	0	3.50	....	....	....	....
1968-69	Kansas City Blues	CHL	22	....	....	....	....	64	2	3.07	....	....	....	....	....	....	....	....	....	....	....	....	....	....	....	....	....
	St. Louis Blues	**NHL**	**1**	**0**	**1**	**0**	**60**	**2**	**0**	**2.00**	**2.07**	....	....	....	....	....	....	....	....	....	....	....	....	....	....	....	....
1969-70	Kansas City Blues	CHL	6	1	4	1	360	29	0	4.83	....	....	....	....	....	....	....	....	....	....	....	....	....	....	....	....	....
	San Diego Gulls	WHL	18	10	8	0	1050	71	0	4.06	....	....	....	....	....	3	2	1	0	165	12	0	4.37	....	....	....	....
1970-71	Kansas City Blues	CHL	8	....	....	....	....	32	0	4.00	....	....	....	....	....	....	....	....	....	....	....	....	....	....	....	....	....
	Port Huron Flags	IHL	27	....	....	....	1588	104	1	3.93	....	....	....	....	....	3	....	....	....	140	14	0	6.00	....	....	....	....
1971-72	Port Huron Wings	IHL	1	1	0	0	60	5	0	5.00	....	....	....	....	....	....	....	....	....	....	....	....	....	....	....	....	....
	Jacksonville Rockets	EHL	17	....	....	....	870	72	0	4.97	....	....	....	....	....	14	....	....	....	840	45	1	3.21	....	....	....	....
	Syracuse Blazers	EHL	18	8	10	0	1130	77	0	4.19	....	....	....	....	....	14	....	....	....	840	45	1	3.21	....	....	....	....
1972-73	Cleveland-Jacksonville	AHL	19	....	....	....	909	74	0	4.88	....	....	....	....	....	....	....	....	....	....	....	....	....	....	....	....	....
1973-74	Syracuse Blazers	NAHL	35	....	....	....	2119	105	0	2.97	....	....	....	....	....	6	....	....	....	341	12	0	*2.11	....	....	....	....
1974-75	New England Whalers	WHA	1	0	0	0	20	3	0	9.00	....	....	....	....	....	....	....	....	....	....	....	....	....	....	....	....	....
	Cape Cod Codders	NAHL	45	21	16	4	2551	161	2	3.79	....	....	....	....	....	4	....	....	....	240	14	0	3.50	....	....	....	....
	NHL Totals		**1**	**0**	**1**	**0**	**60**	**2**	**0**	**2.00**	....	....	....	....	....	....	....	....	....	....	....	....	....	....	....	....	....
	Other Major League Totals		1	0	0	0	20	3	0	9.00	....	....	....	....	....	....	....	....	....	....	....	....	....	....	....	....	....

NAHL First All-Star Team (1974)

Traded to **St. Louis** by **Montreal** for cash, June 11, 1968. Signed as a free agent by **Jacksonville** (EHL), October, 1971. Traded to **Syracuse** (EHL) by **Jacksonville** (EHL) for cash, December, 1971. Traded to **Cleveland** (WHA) by **Syracuse** (NAHL) for John Raynak and cash, October, 1974. Traded to **New England** (WHA) by **Cleveland** (WHA) for cash, December, 1974. Traded to **Cleveland** (WHA) by **New England** (WHA) for cash, January, 1976.

• PAGEAU, Paul

G – R. 5'9", 160 lbs. b: Montreal, Que., 10/1/1959.

Season	Club	League	GP	W	L	T	Mins	GA	SO	Avg	AAvg	Eff	SA	S%	SAPG	GP	W	L	T	Mins	GA	SO	Avg	Eff	SA	S%	SAPG
1976-77	Quebec Remparts	QMJHL	19	....	....	....	955	56	0	3.52	....	....	....	....	....	....	....	....	....	....	....	....	....	....	....	....	....
1977-78	Quebec Remparts	QMJHL	33	....	....	....	1656	138	0	5.00	....	....	....	....	....	3	....	....	....	83	8	0	5.78	....	....	....	....
1978-79	Quebec Remparts	QMJHL	7	....	....	....	345	28	0	4.87	....	....	....	....	....	....	....	....	....	....	....	....	....	....	....	....	....
	Shawinigan Cataracts	QMJHL	43	....	....	....	2352	199	0	5.08	....	....	....	....	....	4	....	....	....	236	27	0	6.86	....	....	....	....
1979-80	Shawinigan Cataracts	QMJHL	43	19	18	4	2438	175	*2	4.31	....	....	....	....	....	7	3	4	0	421	34	0	4.85	....	....	....	....
	Canada	Nat-Team	10	....	....	....	506	16	1	1.89	....	....	....	....	....	....	....	....	....	....	....	....	....	....	....	....	....
	Canada	Olympics	4	2	1	0	238	11	1	2.77	....	....	....	....	....	....	....	....	....	....	....	....	....	....	....	....	....

			REGULAR SEASON													PLAYOFFS											
Season	Club	League	GP	W	L	T	Mins	GA	SO	Avg	AAvg	Eff	SA	S%	SAPG	GP	W	L	T	Mins	GA	SO	Avg	Eff	SA	S%	SAPG
1980-81	**Los Angeles Kings**	**NHL**	**1**	**0**	**1**	**0**	**60**	**8**	**0**	**8.00**	**6.47**	....	....	....	....	....	....	....	....	....	....	....	....	....	....	....	....
	Houston Apollos	CHL	21	9	9	3	1282	64	0	3.00	....	....	....	....	....	....	....	....	....	....	....	....	....	....	....	....	....
	Oklahoma City Stars	CHL	11	4	4	0	590	32	0	3.25	....	....	....	....	....	....	....	....	....	....	....	....	....	....	....	....	....
	Saginaw Gears	IHL	1	....	....	....	60	4	0	4.00	....	....	....	....	....	....	....	....	....	....	....	....	....	....	....	....	....
1981-82	Saginaw Gears	IHL	29	....	....	....	1621	140	0	5.18	....	....	....	....	....	4	....	....	....	249	18	0	4.34	....	....	....	....
1982-83	Saginaw Gears	IHL	11	....	....	....	614	47	0	4.59	....	....	....	....	....	....	....	....	....	....	....	....	....	....	....	....	....
	New Haven Nighthawks	AHL	37	17	14	2	1939	123	2	3.81	....	....	....	....	....	6	2	3	0	374	21	0	3.37	....	....	....	....
1983-84	Sherbrooke Jets	AHL	45	12	26	3	2432	205	0	5.06	....	....	....	....	....	....	....	....	....	....	....	....	....	....	....	....	....
1984-85	Sherbrooke Canadiens	AHL	20	8	11	0	1074	66	0	3.69	....	....	....	....	....	3	0	1	0	80	5	0	3.75	....	....	....	....
	Flint Generals	IHL	6	0	5	0	3331	37	0	6.71	....	....	....	....	....	....	....	....	....	....	....	....	....	....	....	....	....
	NHL Totals		**1**	**0**	**1**	**0**	**60**	**8**	**0**	**8.00**	....	....	....	....	....	....	....	....	....	....	....	....	....	....	....	....	....

QMJHL First All-Star Team (1980)

Signed as a free agent by **LA Kings**, May 6, 1980.

• PAILLE, Marcel

G – L. 5'8", 175 lbs. b: Shawinigan Falls, Que., 12/8/1932.

Season	Club	League	GP	W	L	T	Mins	GA	SO	Avg	AAvg	Eff	SA	S%	SAPG	GP	W	L	T	Mins	GA	SO	Avg	Eff	SA	S%	SAPG
1948-49	Shawinigan Technique	QAHA	STATISTICS NOT AVAILABLE																								
1949-50	Quebec Citadelle	QJHL	18	13	5	0	1080	60	3	3.33	....	....	....	....	....	15	9	6	0	926	50	0	*3.24	....	....	....	....
1950-51	Quebec Citadelle	QJHL	46	*33	13	0	2764	135	0	2.93	....	....	....	....	....	13	*9	4	0	804	40	0	*2.99	....	....	....	....
	Quebec Citadelle	Mem-Cup	10	6	4	0	600	40	2	4.00	....	....	....	....	....	....	....	....	....	....	....	....	....	....	....	....	....
1951-52	Quebec Citadelle	QJHL	....	....	....	....	....	....	....	....	....	....	....	....	....	14	7	7	0	844	38	1	2.70	....	....	....	....
1952-53	Quebec Citadelle	QJHL	48	30	15	3	286	149	1	3.12	....	....	....	....	....	9	....	....	....	540	20	0	*2.22	....	....	....	....
	Quebec Citadelle	Mem-Cup	8	4	4	0	480	39	0	4.88	....	....	....	....	....	....	....	....	....	....	....	....	....	....	....	....	....
1953-54	Matane Red Rockets	LSLHL	65	....	....	....	3900	182	*5	*2.80	....	....	....	....	....	....	....	....	....	....	....	....	....	....	....	....	....
1954-55	North Bay Trappers	NOHA	59	24	25	10	3540	228	1	3.86	....	....	....	....	....	13	....	....	....	780	40	1	3.08	....	....	....	....
1955-56	Chicoutimi Sagueneens	QHL	*61	30	26	4	*3632	176	2	2.91	....	....	....	....	....	5	1	4	0	300	19	0	3.80	....	....	....	....
1956-57	Cleveland Barons	AHL	62	*34	25	3	3750	200	*7	3.20	....	....	....	....	....	*12	*8	4	0	*767	31	0	2.43	....	....	....	....
1957-58	**New York Rangers**	**NHL**	**33**	**11**	**15**	**7**	**1980**	**102**	**1**	**3.09**	**3.42**	....	....	....	....	....	....	....	....	....	....	....	....	....	....	....	....
	Providence Reds	AHL	41	19	20	2	2491	124	4	2.99	....	....	....	....	....	5	1	4	0	300	17	1	3.40	....	....	....	....
1958-59	**New York Rangers**	**NHL**	**1**	**0**	**0**	**1**	**60**	**4**	**0**	**4.00**	**4.26**	....	....	....	....	....	....	....	....	....	....	....	....	....	....	....	....
	Buffalo Bisons	AHL	*70	*38	27	4	*4200	195	3	2.79	....	....	....	....	....	11	*6	5	0	664	27	*1	2.44	....	....	....	....
1959-60	**New York Rangers**	**NHL**	**17**	**6**	**9**	**2**	**1020**	**67**	**1**	**3.94**	**4.18**	....	....	....	....	....	....	....	....	....	....	....	....	....	....	....	....
	Springfield Indians	AHL	57	32	20	5	3420	183	2	3.21	....	....	....	....	....	10	*8	2	0	628	31	0	2.96	....	....	....	....
1960-61	**New York Rangers**	**NHL**	**4**	**1**	**2**	**1**	**240**	**16**	**0**	**4.00**	**4.13**	....	....	....	....	....	....	....	....	....	....	....	....	....	....	....	....
	Springfield Indians	AHL	67	*46	20	1	4020	188	*8	*2.81	....	....	....	....	....	4	*4	0	....	226	5	0	*1.33	....	....	....	....
1961-62	**New York Rangers**	**NHL**	**10**	**4**	**4**	**2**	**600**	**28**	**0**	**2.80**	**2.86**	....	....	....	....	....	....	....	....	....	....	....	....	....	....	....	....
	Springfield Indians	AHL	45	29	14	2	2770	115	2	*2.49	....	....	....	....	....	*11	*8	3	0	*758	21	*2	*1.66	....	....	....	....
1962-63	**New York Rangers**	**NHL**	**3**	**0**	**1**	**2**	**180**	**10**	**0**	**3.33**	**3.47**	....	....	....	....	....	....	....	....	....	....	....	....	....	....	....	....
	Baltimore Clippers	AHL	41	18	20	3	2460	146	0	3.56	....	....	....	....	....	....	....	....	....	....	....	....	....	....	....	....	....
1963-64	Vancouver Canucks	WHL	*70	26	41	3	4230	254	2	3.60	....	....	....	....	....	....	....	....	....	....	....	....	....	....	....	....	....
	Denver Invaders	WHL	....	....	....	....	....	....	....	....	....	....	....	....	....	3	1	2	0	194	12	0	3.71	....	....	....	....
1964-65	**New York Rangers**	**NHL**	**39**	**10**	**21**	**7**	**2262**	**135**	**0**	**3.58**	**3.93**	....	....	....	....	....	....	....	....	....	....	....	....	....	....	....	....
1965-66	Providence Reds	AHL	60	17	40	2	3650	243	1	3.99	....	....	....	....	....	....	....	....	....	....	....	....	....	....	....	....	....
1966-67	Providence Reds	AHL	42	4	30	7	2471	188	0	4.56	....	....	....	....	....	....	....	....	....	....	....	....	....	....	....	....	....
1967-68	Providence Reds	AHL	54	23	23	8	3200	188	1	3.53	....	....	....	....	....	8	4	4	0	460	19	0	*2.48	....	....	....	....
1968-69	Providence Reds	AHL	58	25	26	6	3321	202	2	3.65	....	....	....	....	....	9	5	4	0	544	28	0	3.09	....	....	....	....
1969-70	Providence Reds	AHL	62	....	....	....	3565	211	2	3.55	....	....	....	....	....	....	....	....	....	....	....	....	....	....	....	....	....
1970-71	Providence Reds	AHL	51	24	17	9	2789	167	1	3.59	....	....	....	....	....	10	4	*6	0	599	32	*1	3.21	....	....	....	....
1971-72	Providence Reds	AHL	34	15	16	2	1981	110	3	3.33	....	....	....	....	....	5	1	4	0	303	18	0	3.56	....	....	....	....
1972-73	Philadelphia Blazers	WHA	15	2	8	0	611	49	0	4.81	....	....	....	....	....	....	....	....	....	....	....	....	....	....	....	....	....
1973-74	Richmond Robins	AHL	21	5	11	4	1201	85	0	4.24	....	....	....	....	....	2	0	2	0	119	9	0	4.54	....	....	....	....
	NHL Totals		**107**	**32**	**52**	**22**	**6342**	**362**	**2**	**3.42**	....	....	....	....	....	....	....	....	....	....	....	....	....	....	....	....	....
	Other Major League Totals		15	2	8	0	611	49	0	4.81	....	....	....	....	....	....	....	....	....	....	....	....	....	....	....	....	....

QJHL Second All-Star Team (1951, 1952, 1953) • Won William Northey Trophy (Top Rookie - QHL) (1956) • AHL Second All-Star Team (1957, 1960) • AHL First All-Star Team (1959, 1961, 1962) • Won Harry "Hap" Holmes Memorial Award (fewest goals against - AHL) (1961, 1962) • WHL Second All-Star Team (1964)

Signed as a free agent by **North Bay** (NOHA), September 28, 1954. Claimed by **NY Rangers** from **Chicoutimi** (QHL) in Inter-League Draft, June 5, 1956. • Recorded a shutout (5-0) in NHL debut vs. Boston, November 2, 1957. Traded to **Providence** (AHL) by **NY Rangers** with Aldo Guidolin, Sandy McGregor and Jim Mikol for Ed Giacomin, May 18, 1965. Selected by **Chicago** (WHA) in 1972 WHA General Player Draft, February 12, 1972. WHA rights traded to **Philadelphia** (WHA) by **Chicago** (WHA) for future considerations, June, 1972.

• PALMATEER, Mike

Michael Scott "The Popcorn Kid" G – R. 5'9", 170 lbs. b: Toronto, Ont., 1/13/1954. Toronto's 5th, 85th overall in 1974.

Season	Club	League	GP	W	L	T	Mins	GA	SO	Avg	AAvg	Eff	SA	S%	SAPG	GP	W	L	T	Mins	GA	SO	Avg	Eff	SA	S%	SAPG
1971-72	Markham Waxers	OHA-B	STATISTICS NOT AVAILABLE																								
1972-73	Toronto Marlboros	OMJHL	31	....	....	....	1860	87	5	2.81	....	....	....	....	....	....	....	....	....	....	....	....	....	....	....	....	....
	Toronto Marlboros	Mem-Cup	3	*2	1	0	180	6	0	2.00	....	....	....	....	....	....	....	....	....	....	....	....	....	....	....	....	....
1973-74	Toronto Marlboros	OMJHL	32	....	....	....	1895	120	0	3.80	....	....	....	....	....	....	....	....	....	....	....	....	....	....	....	....	....
1974-75	Saginaw Gears	IHL	20	....	....	....	1095	70	2	3.84	....	....	....	....	....	....	....	....	....	....	....	....	....	....	....	....	....
	Oklahoma City Blazers	CHL	16	7	5	2	841	39	1	2.78	....	....	....	....	....	5	2	3	0	278	18	0	3.88	....	....	....	....
1975-76	Oklahoma City Blazers	CHL	42	15	21	4	2272	137	1	3.61	....	....	....	....	....	3	0	2	0	158	8	0	3.04	....	....	....	....
1976-77	**Toronto Maple Leafs**	**NHL**	**50**	**23**	**18**	**8**	**2877**	**154**	**4**	**3.21**	**2.98**	....	....	....	....	**6**	**3**	**3**	....	**360**	**16**	**0**	**2.67**	....	....	....	....
	Dallas Black Hawks	CHL	3	0	2	1	171	5	0	1.75	....	....	....	....	....	....	....	....	....	....	....	....	....	....	....	....	....
1977-78	**Toronto Maple Leafs**	**NHL**	**63**	**34**	**19**	**9**	**3760**	**172**	**5**	**2.74**	**2.55**	....	....	....	....	**13**	**6**	**7**	....	**795**	**32**	***2**	**2.42**	....	....	....	....
1978-79	**Toronto Maple Leafs**	**NHL**	**58**	**26**	**21**	**10**	**3396**	**167**	**4**	**2.95**	**2.59**	....	....	....	....	**5**	**2**	**3**	....	**298**	**17**	**0**	**3.42**	....	....	....	....
1979-80	**Toronto Maple Leafs**	**NHL**	**38**	**16**	**14**	**3**	**2039**	**125**	**2**	**3.68**	**3.26**	....	....	....	....	**1**	**0**	**1**	....	**60**	**7**	**0**	**7.00**	....	....	....	....
1980-81	Washington Capitals	DN-Cup	2	2	0	0	115	4	0	2.07	....	....	....	....	....	....	....	....	....	....	....	....	....	....	....	....	....
	Washington Capitals	**NHL**	**49**	**18**	**19**	**9**	**2679**	**172**	**2**	**3.85**	**3.11**	....	....	....	....	....	....	....	....	....	....	....	....	....	....	....	....
1981-82	**Washington Capitals**	**NHL**	**11**	**2**	**7**	**2**	**584**	**47**	**0**	**4.83**	**3.74**	....	....	....	....	....	....	....	....	....	....	....	....	....	....	....	....
1982-83	St. Catharines Saints	AHL	2	1	0	1	125	4	1	1.92	....	....	....	....	....	....	....	....	....	....	....	....	....	....	....	....	....
	Toronto Maple Leafs	**NHL**	**53**	**21**	**23**	**7**	**2965**	**197**	**0**	**3.99**	**3.21**	**5.12**	**1534**	**.872**	**31.0**	**4**	**1**	**3**	....	**252**	**17**	**0**	**4.05**	....	....	....	....
1983-84	**Toronto Maple Leafs**	**NHL**	**34**	**9**	**17**	**4**	**1831**	**149**	**0**	**4.88**	**3.86**	**7.37**	**986**	**.849**	**32.3**	....	....	....	....	....	....	....	....	....	....	....	....
	NHL Totals		**356**	**149**	**138**	**52**	**20131**	**1183**	**17**	**3.53**	....	....	....	....	....	**29**	**12**	**17**	....	**1765**	**89**	**2**	**3.03**	....	....	....	....

OMJHL First All-Star Team (1973)

Traded to **Washington** by **Toronto** with Toronto's 3rd round choice (Torrie Robertson) in 1980 Entry Draft for Robert Picard, Tim Coulis and Washington's 2nd round choice (Bob McGill) in 1980 Entry Draft, June 11, 1980. • Missed majority of 1981-82 season recovering from knee surgery, September, 1981. Traded to **Toronto** by **Washington** for cash, September 9, 1982.

• PANG, Darren

Darren R. G – L. 5'5", 155 lbs. b: Meaford, Ont., 2/17/1964.

Season	Club	League	GP	W	L	T	Mins	GA	SO	Avg	AAvg	Eff	SA	S%	SAPG	GP	W	L	T	Mins	GA	SO	Avg	Eff	SA	S%	SAPG
1980-81	Nepean Raiders	OJHL	41	....	....	....	2316	154	0	3.99	....	....	....	....	....	....	....	....	....	....	....	....	....	....	....	....	....
1981-82	Belleville Bulls	OHL	47	15	21	1	2234	173	0	4.65	....	....	....	....	....	....	....	....	....	....	....	....	....	....	....	....	....
1982-83	Belleville Bulls	OHL	12	3	8	0	570	44	0	4.63	....	....	....	....	....	....	....	....	....	....	....	....	....	....	....	....	....
	Ottawa 67's	OHL	47	28	14	3	2729	166	1	3.65	....	....	....	....	....	9	5	4	0	510	33	0	3.88	....	....	....	....
1983-84	Ottawa 67's	OHL	43	29	10	1	2318	117	2	3.03	....	....	....	....	....	13	....	....	....	726	41	*1	*3.31	....	....	....	....
	Ottawa 67's	Mem-Cup	5	*3	1	0	226	13	0	*3.45	....	....	....	....	....	....	....	....	....	....	....	....	....	....	....	....	....
1984-85	**Chicago Black Hawks**	**NHL**	**1**	**0**	**1**	**0**	**60**	**4**	**0**	**4.00**	**3.19**	**7.27**	**22**	**.818**	**22.0**	....	....	....	....	....	....	....	....	....	....	....	....
	Milwaukee Admirals	IHL	53	19	29	3	3129	226	0	4.33	....	....	....	....	....	....	....	....	....	....	....	....	....	....	....	....	....
1985-86	Saginaw Generals	IHL	44	21	21	0	2638	148	2	3.37	....	....	....	....	....	8	3	5	0	492	32	0	3.90	....	....	....	....
1986-87	Nova Scotia Oilers	AHL	7	4	2	0	389	21	0	3.24	....	....	....	....	....	3	1	2	0	200	11	0	3.30	....	....	....	....
	Saginaw Generals	IHL	44	25	16	0	2500	151	0	3.62	....	....	....	....	....	....	....	....	....	....	....	....	....	....	....	....	....
1987-88	**Chicago Blackhawks**	**NHL**	**45**	**17**	**23**	**1**	**2548**	**163**	**0**	**3.84**	**3.20**	**4.17**	**1501**	**.891**	**35.3**	**4**	**1**	**3**	....	**240**	**18**	**0**	**4.50**	**6.23**	**130**	**.862**	**32.5**

			REGULAR SEASON														PLAYOFFS											
Season	Club	League	GP	W	L	T	Mins	GA	SO	Avg	AAvg	Eff	SA	S%	SAPG	GP	W	L	T	Mins	GA	SO	Avg	Eff	SA	S%	SAPG
1988-89	**Chicago Blackhawks**	**NHL**	35	10	11	6	1644	120	0	4.38	3.66	5.74	915	.869	33.4	2	0	0	....	10	0	0	0.00	0.00	4	1.000	24.0
	Saginaw Hawks	IHL	2	1	0	0	89	6	0	4.04	....	....	....	....	....	....	....	....	....	....	....	....	....	....	....	....	....
1989-90	Indianapolis Ice	IHL	7	4	1	2	401	17	1	2.54	....	....	....	....	....	4	3	1	0	253	12	0	2.85	....	....	....	....
	NHL Totals		81	27	35	7	4252	287	0	4.05	....	....	2438	.882	34.4	6	1	3	....	250	18	0	4.32	....	134	.866	32.2

OHL First All-Star Team (1984) • Memorial Cup All-Star Team (1984) • Won Hap Emms Memorial Trophy (Memorial Cup Tournament Top Goaltender) (1984) • IHL Second All-Star Team (1987) • NHL All-Rookie Team (1988)

Signed as a free agent by **Chicago**, August 15, 1984. • Suffered career-ending knee injury in training camp, September 21, 1990.

• PARENT, Bernie
Bernard Marcel G – L. 5'10", 180 lbs. b: Montreal, Que., 4/3/1945. **HHOF**

Season	Club	League	GP	W	L	T	Mins	GA	SO	Avg	AAvg	Eff	SA	S%	SAPG	GP	W	L	T	Mins	GA	SO	Avg	Eff	SA	S%	SAPG
1962-63	Rosemount Raiders	QJHL	STATISTICS NOT AVAILABLE																								
1963-64	Niagara Falls Flyers	OHA-Jr.	28	....	....	....	1680	80	4	*2.86	....	....	....	....	....	4	0	4	0	240	26	0	6.50	....	....	....	....
1964-65	Niagara Falls Flyers	OHA-Jr.	34	....	....	....	2004	86	2	*2.58	....	....	....	....	....	8	*6	2	0	480	15	1	*1.86	....	....	....	....
	Niagara Falls Flyers	Mem-Cup	13	*10	2	0	700	19	2	*1.63	....	....	....	....	....	....	....	....	....	....	....	....	....	....	....	....	....
1965-66	**Boston Bruins**	**NHL**	39	11	20	3	2083	128	1	3.69	3.81	....	....	....	....	....	....	....	....	....	....	....	....	....	....	....	....
	Oklahoma City Blazers	CPHL	3	1	1	1	180	11	0	3.67	....	....	....	....	....	....	....	....	....	....	....	....	....	....	....	....	....
1966-67	**Boston Bruins**	**NHL**	18	4	12	2	1022	62	0	3.64	3.79	....	....	....	....	....	....	....	....	....	....	....	....	....	....	....	....
	Oklahoma City Blazers	CPHL	14	10	4	0	820	37	*4	2.70	....	....	....	....	....	....	....	....	....	....	....	....	....	....	....	....	....
1967-68	**Philadelphia Flyers**	**NHL**	38	16	17	5	2248	93	4	2.48	2.74	....	....	....	....	5	2	3	....	355	8	0	*1.35	....	....	....	....
1968-69	**Philadelphia Flyers**	**NHL**	58	17	23	16	3365	151	1	2.69	2.77	....	....	....	....	3	0	3	....	180	12	0	4.00	....	....	....	....
1969-70	**Philadelphia Flyers**	**NHL**	62	13	29	20	3680	171	3	2.79	2.95	....	....	....	....	....	....	....	....	....	....	....	....	....	....	....	....
1970-71	**Philadelphia Flyers**	**NHL**	30	9	12	6	1586	73	2	2.76	2.72	....	....	....	....	....	....	....	....	....	....	....	....	....	....	....	....
	Toronto Maple Leafs	**NHL**	18	7	7	3	1040	46	0	2.65	2.62	....	....	....	....	4	2	2	....	235	9	0	2.30	....	....	....	....
1971-72	**Toronto Maple Leafs**	**NHL**	47	17	18	9	2715	116	3	2.56	2.57	....	....	....	....	4	1	3	....	243	13	0	3.21	....	....	....	....
1972-73	Philadelphia Blazers	WHA	63	*33	28	0	3653	220	2	3.61	....	....	....	....	....	1	0	1	0	70	3	0	2.57	....	....	....	....
1973-74♦	**Philadelphia Flyers**	**NHL**	*73	*47	13	12	*4314	136	*12	*1.89	1.78	....	....	....	....	*17	*12	5	....	*1042	35	*2	2.02	....	....	....	....
1974-75♦	**Philadelphia Flyers**	**NHL**	68	*44	14	10	4041	137	*12	*2.03	1.80	....	....	....	....	*15	*10	5	....	*922	29	*4	*1.89	....	....	....	....
1975-76	**Philadelphia Flyers**	**NHL**	11	6	2	3	615	24	0	2.34	2.11	....	....	....	....	8	4	4	....	480	27	0	3.38	....	....	....	....
1976-77	**Philadelphia Flyers**	**NHL**	61	35	13	12	3525	159	5	2.71	2.50	....	....	....	....	3	0	3	....	123	8	0	3.90	....	....	....	....
1977-78	**Philadelphia Flyers**	**NHL**	49	29	6	13	2923	108	*7	2.22	2.06	....	....	....	....	12	7	5	....	722	33	0	2.74	....	....	....	....
1978-79	**Philadelphia Flyers**	**NHL**	36	16	12	7	1979	89	4	2.70	2.38	....	....	....	....	....	....	....	....	....	....	....	....	....	....	....	....
	NHL Totals		608	271	198	121	35136	1493	54	2.55	....	....	....	....	....	71	38	33	....	4302	174	6	2.43	....	....	....	....
	Other Major League Totals		63	33	28	0	3653	220	2	3.61	....	....	....	....	....	1	0	1	....	70	3	0	2.57	....	....	....	....

OHA-Jr. Second All-Star Team (1964) • OHA-Jr. First All-Star Team (1965) • WHA Second All-Star Team (1973) • NHL First All-Star Team (1974, 1975) • Won Vezina Trophy (tied with Tony Esposito) (1974) • Won Conn Smythe Trophy (1974, 1975) • Won Vezina Trophy (1975) • Played in NHL All-Star Game (1969, 1970, 1974, 1975, 1977)

Claimed by **Philadelphia** from **Boston** in Expansion Draft, June 6, 1967. Traded to **Toronto** by **Philadelphia** with Philadelphia's 2nd round choice (Rick Kehoe) in 1971 Amateur Draft for Bruce Gamble, Mike Walton and Toronto's 1st round choice (Pierre Plante) in 1971 Amateur Draft, February 1, 1971. Selected by **Miami-Philadelphia** (WHA) in WHA General Player Draft, February 12, 1972. • Suspended by **Philadelphia** (WHA) for leaving team following game vs. Cleveland (WHA), April 4, 1973. WHA rights traded to **NY Raiders** (WHA) by **Philadelphia-Vancouver** (WHA) with Dan Herriman and Andre Lacroix for Ron Ward and Pete Donnelly, June, 1973. Traded to **Philadelphia** by **Toronto** with Toronto's 2nd round choice (Larry Goodenough) in 1973 Amateur Draft for Philadelphia's 1st round choice (Bob Neely) in 1973 Amateur Draft and future considerations (Doug Favell, July 27, 1973), May 15, 1973. • Suffered career-ending eye injury in game vs. NY Rangers, February 17, 1979.

• PARENT, Bob
Robert John G – R. 5'9", 175 lbs. b: Windsor, Ont., 2/19/1958. Toronto's 3rd, 65th overall in 1978.

Season	Club	League	GP	W	L	T	Mins	GA	SO	Avg	AAvg	Eff	SA	S%	SAPG	GP	W	L	T	Mins	GA	SO	Avg	Eff	SA	S%	SAPG
1975-76	Windsor Spitfires	OMJHL	9	5	4	0	377	53	0	8.44	....	....	....	....	....	....	....	....	....	....	....	....	....	....	....	....	....
1976-77	Windsor Spitfires	OMJHL	39	....	....	....	1689	161	0	5.73	....	....	....	....	....	7	5	2	0	332	19	0	3.43	....	....	....	....
1977-78	Windsor Spitfires	OMJHL	11	....	....	....	604	37	0	3.66	....	....	....	....	....	....	....	....	....	....	....	....	....	....	....	....	....
	Kitchener Rangers	OMJHL	48	....	....	....	2848	182	1	3.81	....	....	....	....	....	9	3	6	0	532	45	0	4.95	....	....	....	....
1978-79	Saginaw Gears	IHL	2	....	....	....	49	10	0	12.24	....	....	....	....	....	....	....	....	....	....	....	....	....	....	....	....	....
	Port Huron Flags	IHL	24	....	....	....	1177	73	0	3.72	....	....	....	....	....	....	....	....	....	....	....	....	....	....	....	....	....
1979-80	Port Huron Flags	IHL	37	....	....	....	2212	137	0	3.72	....	....	....	....	....	11	6	5	0	671	36	0	3.22	....	....	....	....
1980-81	Hampton Aces	EHL	46	....	....	....	2536	200	1	4.73	....	....	....	....	....	....	....	....	....	....	....	....	....	....	....	....	....
	New Brunswick Hawks	AHL	2	0	2	0	80	5	0	3.75	....	....	....	....	....	13	7	6	0	845	39	0	2.77	....	....	....	....
1981-82	**Toronto Maple Leafs**	**NHL**	2	0	2	0	120	13	0	6.50	5.02	....	....	....	....	....	....	....	....	....	....	....	....	....	....	....	....
	Cincinnati Tigers	CHL	65	*34	24	3	3680	252	2	4.11	....	....	....	....	....	3	1	2	0	180	13	0	4.33	....	....	....	....
1982-83	**Toronto Maple Leafs**	**NHL**	1	0	0	0	40	2	0	3.00	2.41	2.73	22	.909	33.0	....	....	....	....	....	....	....	....	....	....	....	....
	St. Catharines Saints	AHL	46	18	20	3	2485	180	1	4.35	....	....	....	....	....	....	....	....	....	....	....	....	....	....	....	....	....
1983-84	St. Catharines Saints	AHL	18	6	11	0	900	73	0	4.87	....	....	....	....	....	....	....	....	....	....	....	....	....	....	....	....	....
	Muskegon Mohawks	IHL	35	....	....	....	2063	185	0	5.38	....	....	....	....	....	....	....	....	....	....	....	....	....	....	....	....	....
	NHL Totals		3	0	2	0	160	15	0	5.63	....	....	....	....	....												

• PARENT, Rich
G – L. 6'3", 195 lbs. b: Montreal, Que., 1/12/1973.

Season	Club	League	GP	W	L	T	Mins	GA	SO	Avg	AAvg	Eff	SA	S%	SAPG	GP	W	L	T	Mins	GA	SO	Avg	Eff	SA	S%	SAPG
1991-92	Fort McMurray Oil Barons	AJHL	23	....	....	....	1363	90	0	3.96	....	....	....	....	....	....	....	....	....	....	....	....	....	....	....	....	....
	Vernon Lakers	BCJHL	2	0	1	0	52	5	0	5.77	....	....	....	....	....	....	....	....	....	....	....	....	....	....	....	....	....
1992-93	Spokane Chiefs	WHL	36	12	14	2	1767	129	2	4.38	....	....	....	....	....	1	0	0	....	5	0	0	0.00	....	....	....	....
1993-94	Fort McMurray Oil Barons	AJHL	29	....	....	....	1712	91	1	3.19	....	....	....	....	....	....	....	....	....	....	....	....	....	....	....	....	....
1994-95	Muskegon Fury	ColHL	35	17	11	3	1867	112	1	3.60	....	....	....	....	....	13	7	3	....	725	47	1	3.89	....	....	....	....
1995-96	Muskegon Fury	ColHL	36	23	7	4	2087	85	2	2.44	....	....	....	....	....	....	....	....	....	....	....	....	....	....	....	....	....
	Rochester Americans	AHL	2	0	1	0	90	6	0	4.02	....	....	....	....	....	....	....	....	....	....	....	....	....	....	....	....	....
	Detroit Vipers	IHL	19	16	0	1	1040	48	2	2.77	....	....	....	....	....	7	3	3	....	363	22	0	3.64	....	....	....	....
1996-97	Detroit Vipers	IHL	53	31	13	4	2815	104	4	2.22	....	....	....	....	....	15	8	3	....	786	21	1	*1.60	....	....	....	....
1997-98	**St. Louis Blues**	**NHL**	1	0	0	0	12	0	0	0.00	0.00	0.00	1	1.000	5.0	....	....	....	....	....	....	....	....	....	....	....	....
	Manitoba Moose	IHL	26	8	12	2	1334	69	3	3.10	....	....	....	....	....	....	....	....	....	....	....	....	....	....	....	....	....
	Detroit Vipers	IHL	7	4	0	3	417	15	0	2.15	....	....	....	....	....	5	1	0	....	157	6	0	2.29	....	....	....	....
1998-99	**St. Louis Blues**	**NHL**	10	4	3	1	519	22	1	2.54	3.02	2.90	193	.886	22.3	....	....	....	....	....	....	....	....	....	....	....	....
	Worcester IceCats	AHL	20	8	8	2	1100	56	1	3.05	....	....	....	....	....	....	....	....	....	....	....	....	....	....	....	....	....
99-2000	Utah Grizzlies	IHL	27	17	7	3	1571	58	1	2.21	....	....	....	....	....	....	....	....	....	....	....	....	....	....	....	....	....
	Tampa Bay Lightning	**NHL**	14	2	7	1	698	43	0	3.70	4.24	4.51	353	.878	30.3	....	....	....	....	....	....	....	....	....	....	....	....
	Detroit Vipers	IHL	10	3	5	1	539	23	1	2.56	....	....	....	....	....	....	....	....	....	....	....	....	....	....	....	....	....
	NHL Totals		25	6	10	2	1229	65	1	3.17	....	....	547	.881	26.7												

ColHL First All-Star Team (1996) • Named ColHL's Outstanding Goaltender (1996) • Shared James Norris Memorial Trophy (fewest goals against - IHL) with Jeff Reese (1997)

Signed as a free agent by **St. Louis**, July 31, 1997. Traded to **Tampa Bay** by **St. Louis** with Chris McAlpine for Stephane Richer, January 13, 2000. Traded to **Ottawa** by **Tampa Bay** for Ottawa's 7th round choice (later traded to NY Islanders - later traded to Buffalo - Buffalo selected Paul Gaustad) in 2000 Entry Draft, June 4, 2000.

• PARRO, Dave
David E. G – L. 5'11", 165 lbs. b: Saskatoon, Sask., 4/30/1957. Boston's 2nd, 34th overall in 1977.

Season	Club	League	GP	W	L	T	Mins	GA	SO	Avg	AAvg	Eff	SA	S%	SAPG	GP	W	L	T	Mins	GA	SO	Avg	Eff	SA	S%	SAPG
1973-74	Saskatoon Olympics	SJHL	29	....	....	....	1740	137	0	4.21	....	....	....	....	....	....	....	....	....	....	....	....	....	....	....	....	....
1974-75	Saskatoon Olympics	SJHL	35	....	....	....	2100	136	0	4.34	....	....	....	....	....	....	....	....	....	....	....	....	....	....	....	....	....
	Saskatoon Blades	WCJHL	1	1	0	0	60	2	0	2.00	....	....	....	....	....	....	....	....	....	....	....	....	....	....	....	....	....
1975-76	Saskatoon Blades	WCJHL	36	28	6	2	2100	119	1	3.40	....	....	....	....	....	9	1	3	1	414	31	0	4.49	....	....	....	....
1976-77	Saskatoon Blades	WCJHL	69	28	26	12	3956	246	1	3.73	....	....	....	....	....	6	2	4	0	360	23	0	3.83	....	....	....	....
1977-78	Rochester Americans	AHL	46	25	16	3	2694	164	0	3.65	....	....	....	....	....	3	2	1	0	180	9	0	3.00	....	....	....	....
1978-79	Grand Rapids Owls	IHL	7	....	....	....	419	25	0	3.58	....	....	....	....	....	....	....	....	....	....	....	....	....	....	....	....	....
	Rochester Americans	AHL	36	12	15	5	2065	130	*2	3.78	....	....	....	....	....	....	....	....	....	....	....	....	....	....	....	....	....
1979-80	Hershey Bears	AHL	54	20	30	3	3159	172	0	3.27	....	....	....	....	....	8	5	3	0	479	34	0	4.26	....	....	....	....
1980-81	**Washington Capitals**	**NHL**	18	4	7	2	811	49	1	3.63	2.93	....	....	....	....	....	....	....	....	....	....	....	....	....	....	....	....
	Hershey Bears	AHL	14	7	6	1	834	60	0	4.32	....	....	....	....	....	....	....	....	....	....	....	....	....	....	....	....	....
1981-82	**Washington Capitals**	**NHL**	52	16	26	7	2942	206	1	4.20	3.25	....	....	....	....	....	....	....	....	....	....	....	....	....	....	....	....
1982-83	**Washington Capitals**	**NHL**	6	1	3	1	261	19	0	4.37	3.51	6.54	127	.850	29.2	....	....	....	....	....	....	....	....	....	....	....	....
	Hershey Bears	AHL	47	21	20	4	2714	175	1	3.87	....	....	....	....	....	4	1	3	0	240	15	0	3.75	....	....	....	....

Season	Club	League	REGULAR SEASON GP	W	L	T	Mins	GA	SO	Avg	AAvg	Eff	SA	S%	SAPG	PLAYOFFS GP	W	L	T	Mins	GA	SO	Avg	Eff	SA	S%	SAPG
1983-84	**Washington Capitals**	**NHL**	**1**	**0**	**0**	**0**	**1**	**0**	**0**	**0.00**	**0.00**	**0.00**	**0**	**.000**	**0.0**	....	....	....	....	....	....	....	....	....	....	....	....
	Hershey Bears	AHL	42	12	21	5	2277	190	1	5.01	....	....	....	....	....	....	....	....	....	....	....	....	....	....	....	....	....
1984-85	Salt Lake Golden Eagles	IHL	28	11	14	3	1672	102	0	3.66	....	....	....	....	....	....	....	....	....	....	....	....	....	....	....	....	....
1985-86	Flint Generals	IHL	46	10	34	0	2527	235	0	5.30	....	....	....	....	....	....	....	....	....	....	....	....	....	....	....	....	....
	Fort Wayne Komets	IHL	5	1	3	1	305	18	0	3.54	....	....	....	....	....	....	....	....	....	....	....	....	....	....	....	....	....
1986-87	Indianapolis Checkers	IHL	32	16	14	0	1780	124	*3	4.18	....	....	....	....	....	....	....	....	....	....	....	....	....	....	....	....	....
	NHL Totals		**77**	**21**	**36**	**10**	**4015**	**274**	**2**	**4.09**	....	....	....	....	....	....	....	....	....	....	....	....	....	....	....	....	....

WCJHL Second All-Star Team (1977) • AHL Second All-Star Team (1983)

Claimed by **Quebec** from **Boston** in Expansion Draft, June 13, 1979. Traded to **Washington** by **Quebec** for Nelson Burton, June 15, 1979.

• PASSMORE, Steve

G – L. 5'9", 165 lbs. b: Thunder Bay, Ont., 1/29/1973. Quebec's 10th, 196th overall in 1992.

Season	Club	League	GP	W	L	T	Mins	GA	SO	Avg	AAvg	Eff	SA	S%	SAPG	GP	W	L	T	Mins	GA	SO	Avg	Eff	SA	S%	SAPG
1988-89	West Island Deltas	BCAHA	STATISTICS NOT AVAILABLE																								
	Tri-City Americans	WHL	1	0	1	0	60	6	0	6.00	....	....	....	....	....	....	....	....	....	....	....	....	....	....	....	....	....
1989-90	West Island Deltas	BCAHA	STATISTICS NOT AVAILABLE																								
	Tri-City Americans	WHL	4	....	....	....	215	17	0	4.74	....	....	....	....	....	....	....	....	....	....	....	....	....	....	....	....	....
1990-91	Victoria Cougars	WHL	35	3	25	1	1838	190	0	6.20	....	....	....	....	....	....	....	....	....	....	....	....	....	....	....	....	....
1991-92	Victoria Cougars	WHL	*71	15	50	5	*4228	347	0	4.92	....	....	....	....	....	....	....	....	....	....	....	....	....	....	....	....	....
1992-93	Victoria Cougars	WHL	43	14	24	2	2402	150	1	3.75	....	....	....	....	....	....	....	....	....	....	....	....	....	....	....	....	....
	Kamloops Blazers	WHL	25	19	6	0	1479	69	1	2.80	....	....	....	....	....	7	4	2	....	401	22	1	3.29	....	....	....	....
1993-94	Kamloops Blazers	WHL	36	22	9	2	1927	88	1	*2.74	....	....	....	....	....	*18	*11	7	....	*1099	60	0	3.28	....	....	....	....
	Kamloops Blazers	Mem-Cup	4	*4	0	0	240	8	*1	*2.00	....	....	....	....	....	....	....	....	....	....	....	....	....	....	....	....	....
1994-95	Cape Breton Oilers	AHL	25	8	13	3	1455	93	0	3.83	....	....	....	....	....	....	....	....	....	....	....	....	....	....	....	....	....
1995-96	Cape Breton Oilers	AHL	2	1	0	0	90	2	0	1.33	....	....	....	....	....	....	....	....	....	....	....	....	....	....	....	....	....
1996-97	Hamilton Bulldogs	AHL	27	12	12	3	1568	70	1	2.68	....	....	....	....	....	22	12	10	....	1325	61	*2	2.76	....	....	....	....
	Raleigh IceCaps	ECHL	2	1	1	0	118	13	0	6.56	....	....	....	....	....	....	....	....	....	....	....	....	....	....	....	....	....
1997-98	San Antonio Dragons	IHL	14	3	8	2	736	56	0	4.56	....	....	....	....	....	....	....	....	....	....	....	....	....	....	....	....	....
	Hamilton Bulldogs	AHL	27	11	10	6	1655	87	2	3.15	....	....	....	....	....	3	0	2	....	132	14	0	6.33	....	....	....	....
1998-99	**Edmonton Oilers**	**NHL**	**6**	**1**	**4**	**1**	**362**	**17**	**0**	**2.82**	**3.35**	**2.62**	**183**	**.907**	**30.3**	....	....	....	....	....	....	....	....	....	....	....	....
	Hamilton Bulldogs	AHL	54	24	21	7	3148	117	4	2.23	....	....	....	....	....	11	5	6	....	680	31	0	2.74	....	....	....	....
99-2000	**Chicago Blackhawks**	**NHL**	**24**	**7**	**12**	**3**	**1388**	**63**	**1**	**2.72**	**3.11**	**2.62**	**654**	**.904**	**28.3**	....	....	....	....	....	....	....	....	....	....	....	....
	Cleveland Lumberjacks	IHL	2	1	0	1	120	3	1	1.50	....	....	....	....	....	....	....	....	....	....	....	....	....	....	....	....	....
	NHL Totals		**30**	**8**	**16**	**4**	**1750**	**80**	**1**	**2.74**	....	....	**837**	**.904**	**28.7**	....	....	....	....	....	....	....	....	....	....	....	....

WHL West First All-Star Team (1993, 1994) • Won Fred Hunt Memorial Trophy (Sportsmanship - AHL) (1997) • AHL Second All-Star Team (1999)

Traded to **Edmonton** by **Quebec** for Brad Werenka, March 21, 1994. • Missed the majority of the 1995-96 season while being treated for a rare blood disorder, October, 1995. Signed as a free agent by **Chicago**, July 8, 1999. Traded to **LA Kings** by **Chicago** for LA Kings' 4th round choice (Olli Malmivaara) in 2000 Entry Draft, May 1, 2000.

• PATRICK, Lester

Curtis Lester "The Silver Fox" G. 6'1", 180 lbs. b: Drummondville, Que., 12/30/1883 d: 6/1/1960. **HHOF**

Season	Club	League	GP	W	L	T	Mins	GA	SO	Avg	AAvg	Eff	SA	S%	SAPG	GP	W	L	T	Mins	GA	SO	Avg	Eff	SA	S%	SAPG
1921-22	Victoria Aristocrats	PCHA	1	0	0	0	10	1	0	6.00	....	....	....	....	....	....	....	....	....	....	....	....	....	....	....	....	....
1927-28♦	**New York Rangers**	**NHL**	....	....	....	....	....	....	....	....	....	....	....	....	....	**1**	**1**	**0**	**0**	**46**	**1**	**0**	**1.30**	....	....	....	....
	NHL Totals		....	....	....	....	....	....	....	....	....	....	....	....	....	**1**	**1**	**0**	**0**	**46**	**1**	**0**	**1.30**	....	....	....	....

• **NY Rangers'** coach/general manager replaced injured Lorne Chabot in 2nd period, April 7, 1928. (NY Rangers 2, Montreal Maroons 1)

• PEETERS, Pete

Peter H. G – L. 6'1", 195 lbs. b: Edmonton, Alta., 8/17/1957. Philadelphia's 9th, 135th overall in 1977.

Season	Club	League	GP	W	L	T	Mins	GA	SO	Avg	AAvg	Eff	SA	S%	SAPG	GP	W	L	T	Mins	GA	SO	Avg	Eff	SA	S%	SAPG
1974-75	Edmonton Crusaders	AJHL	35	....	....	....	2012	114	0	3.25	....	....	....	....	....	....	....	....	....	....	....	....	....	....	....	....	....
1975-76	Medicine Hat Tigers	WCJHL	37	....	....	....	2074	147	0	4.25	....	....	....	....	....	....	....	....	....	....	....	....	....	....	....	....	....
1976-77	Medicine Hat Tigers	WCJHL	62	....	....	....	3423	232	1	4.07	....	....	....	....	....	4	....	....	....	204	17	0	5.00	....	....	....	....
1977-78	Milwaukee Admirals	IHL	32	....	....	....	1698	93	1	3.29	....	....	....	....	....	....	....	....	....	....	....	....	....	....	....	....	....
	Maine Mariners	AHL	17	8	2	2	855	40	1	2.80	....	....	....	....	....	11	*8	3	0	562	25	*1	*2.67	....	....	....	....
1978-79	**Philadelphia Flyers**	**NHL**	**5**	**1**	**2**	**1**	**280**	**16**	**0**	**3.43**	**3.03**	....	....	....	....	....	....	....	....	....	....	....	....	....	....	....	....
	Maine Mariners	AHL	35	25	6	3	2067	100	*2	*2.90	....	....	....	....	....	6	5	0	0	329	15	0	*2.74	....	....	....	....
1979-80	**Philadelphia Flyers**	**NHL**	**40**	**29**	**5**	**5**	**2373**	**108**	**1**	**2.73**	**2.40**	....	....	....	....	**13**	**8**	**5**	....	**799**	**37**	**1**	**2.78**	....	....	....	....
1980-81	**Philadelphia Flyers**	**NHL**	**40**	**22**	**12**	**5**	**2333**	**115**	**2**	**2.96**	**2.38**	....	....	....	....	**3**	**2**	**1**	....	**180**	**12**	**0**	**4.00**	....	....	....	....
1981-82	**Philadelphia Flyers**	**NHL**	**44**	**23**	**18**	**3**	**2591**	**160**	**0**	**3.71**	**2.86**	....	....	....	....	**4**	**1**	**2**	....	**220**	**17**	**0**	**4.64**	....	....	....	....
1982-83	**Boston Bruins**	**NHL**	**62**	***40**	**11**	**9**	**3611**	**142**	***8**	***2.36**	**1.87**	**2.26**	**1482**	**.904**	**24.6**	***17**	**9**	**8**	....	***1024**	**61**	**1**	**3.57**	....	....	....	....
1983-84	**Boston Bruins**	**NHL**	**50**	**29**	**16**	**2**	**2868**	**151**	**0**	**3.16**	**2.47**	**3.90**	**1222**	**.876**	**25.6**	**3**	**0**	**3**	....	**180**	**10**	**0**	**3.33**	**4.90**	**68**	**.853**	**22.7**
1984-85	Canada	Can-Cup	4	3	1	0	234	13	0	3.00	....	....	....	....	....	....	....	....	....	....	....	....	....	....	....	....	....
	Boston Bruins	**NHL**	**51**	**19**	**26**	**4**	**2975**	**172**	**1**	**3.47**	**2.76**	**4.57**	**1307**	**.868**	**26.4**	**1**	**0**	**1**	....	**60**	**4**	**0**	**4.00**	**6.15**	**26**	**.846**	**26.0**
1985-86	**Boston Bruins**	**NHL**	**8**	**3**	**4**	**1**	**485**	**31**	**0**	**3.84**	**3.00**	**4.86**	**245**	**.873**	**30.3**	....	....	....	....	....	....	....	....	....	....	....	....
	Washington Capitals	**NHL**	**34**	**19**	**11**	**3**	**2021**	**113**	**1**	**3.35**	**2.61**	**4.16**	**910**	**.876**	**27.0**	**9**	**5**	**4**	....	**544**	**24**	**0**	**2.65**	**2.51**	**253**	**.905**	**27.9**
1986-87	**Washington Capitals**	**NHL**	**37**	**17**	**11**	**4**	**2002**	**107**	**0**	**3.21**	**2.71**	**3.69**	**930**	**.885**	**27.9**	**3**	**1**	**2**	....	**180**	**9**	**0**	**3.00**	**3.55**	**76**	**.882**	**25.3**
	Binghamton Whalers	AHL	4	3	0	0	245	4	1	0.98	....	....	....	....	....	....	....	....	....	....	....	....	....	....	....	....	....
1987-88	**Washington Capitals**	**NHL**	**35**	**14**	**12**	**5**	**1896**	**88**	**2**	***2.78**	**2.31**	**2.82**	**866**	**.898**	**27.4**	**12**	**7**	**5**	....	**654**	**34**	**0**	**3.12**	**3.25**	**326**	**.896**	**29.9**
1988-89	**Washington Capitals**	**NHL**	**33**	**20**	**7**	**3**	**1854**	**88**	**4**	**2.85**	**2.36**	**3.17**	**790**	**.889**	**25.6**	**6**	**2**	**4**	....	**359**	**24**	**0**	**4.01**	**5.87**	**164**	**.854**	**27.4**
1989-90	**Philadelphia Flyers**	**NHL**	**24**	**1**	**13**	**5**	**1140**	**72**	**1**	**3.79**	**3.21**	**4.50**	**606**	**.881**	**31.9**	....	....	....	....	....	....	....	....	....	....	....	....
1990-91	**Philadelphia Flyers**	**NHL**	**26**	**9**	**7**	**1**	**1270**	**61**	**1**	**2.88**	**2.58**	**2.82**	**623**	**.902**	**29.4**	....	....	....	....	....	....	....	....	....	....	....	....
	Hershey Bears	AHL	2	0	1	0	105	11	0	6.29	....	....	....	....	....	....	....	....	....	....	....	....	....	....	....	....	....
	NHL Totals		**489**	**246**	**155**	**51**	**27699**	**1424**	**21**	**3.08**	....	....	....	....	....	**71**	**35**	**35**	....	**4200**	**232**	**2**	**3.31**	....	....	....	....

AHL Second All-Star Team (1979) • Shared Harry "Hap" Holmes Memorial Award (fewest goals against - AHL) with Robbie Moore (1979) • NHL First All-Star Team (1983) • Won Vezina Trophy (1983) • Played in NHL All-Star Game (1980, 1981, 1983, 1984)

Traded to **Boston** by **Philadelphia** for Brad McCrimmon, June 9, 1982. Traded to **Washington** by **Boston** for Pat Riggin, November 14, 1985. Signed as a free agent by **Philadelphia**, June 17, 1989. Traded to **Winnipeg** by **Philadelphia** with Keith Acton for future considerations, September 28, 1989. Traded to **Philadelphia** by **Winnipeg** with Keith Acton for Toronto's 5th round choice (previously acquired, Winnipeg selected Juha Ylonen) in 1991 Entry Draft and the cancellation of future considerations owed Philadelphia from the trade for Shawn Cronin (July 21, 1989), October 3, 1989.

• PELLETIER, Jean-Marc

G – L. 6'3", 200 lbs. b: Atlanta, GA, 3/4/1978. Philadelphia's 1st, 30th overall in 1997.

Season	Club	League	GP	W	L	T	Mins	GA	SO	Avg	AAvg	Eff	SA	S%	SAPG	GP	W	L	T	Mins	GA	SO	Avg	Eff	SA	S%	SAPG
1993-94	Richelieu Riverains	QAAA	24	14	8	2	1440	91	0	3.79	....	....	....	....	....	....	....	....	....	....	....	....	....	....	....	....	....
1994-95	Richelieu Riverains	QAAA	21	15	6	0	1260	71	0	3.36	....	....	....	....	....	....	....	....	....	....	....	....	....	....	....	....	....
1995-96	Cornell University	ECAC	5	1	2	0	179	15	0	5.03	....	....	....	....	....	....	....	....	....	....	....	....	....	....	....	....	....
1996-97	Cornell University	ECAC	11	5	2	3	679	28	1	2.47	....	....	....	....	....	....	....	....	....	....	....	....	....	....	....	....	....
1997-98	Rimouski Oceanic	QMJHL	34	17	11	3	1913	118	0	3.70	....	....	....	....	....	16	11	3	....	895	51	1	3.42	....	....	....	....
	United States	WJC-A	4	2	1	0	180	5	1	1.66	....	....	....	....	....	....	....	....	....	....	....	....	....	....	....	....	....
1998-99	**Philadelphia Flyers**	**NHL**	**1**	**0**	**1**	**0**	**60**	**5**	**0**	**5.00**	**5.95**	**8.62**	**29**	**.828**	**29.0**	....	....	....	....	....	....	....	....	....	....	....	....
	Philadelphia Phantoms	AHL	47	25	16	4	2636	122	2	2.78	....	....	....	....	....	1	0	0	....	27	0	0	0.00	....	....	....	....
99-2000	Philadelphia Phantoms	AHL	24	14	10	0	1405	58	3	2.48	....	....	....	....	....	....	....	....	....	....	....	....	....	....	....	....	....
	Cincinnati Cyclones	IHL	22	14	4	2	1278	52	2	2.44	....	....	....	....	....	3	1	1	....	160	8	1	3.00	....	....	....	....
	NHL Totals		**1**	**0**	**1**	**0**	**60**	**5**	**0**	**5.00**	....	....	**29**	**.828**	**29.0**	....	....	....	....	....	....	....	....	....	....	....	....

Traded to **Carolina** by **Philadelphia** with Rod Brind'Amour and Philadelphia's 2nd round choice (later traded to Colorado - Colorado selected Argis Saviels) in 2000 Entry Draft for Keith Primeau and Carolina's 5th round choice (later traded to NY Islanders - NY Islanders selected Kristofer Ottoson) in 2000 Entry Draft, January 23, 2000.

• PELLETIER, Marcel

Marcel Gerard G – R. 5'11", 180 lbs. b: Drummondville, Que., 12/6/1927.

Season	Club	League	GP	W	L	T	Mins	GA	SO	Avg	AAvg	Eff	SA	S%	SAPG	GP	W	L	T	Mins	GA	SO	Avg	Eff	SA	S%	SAPG
1946-47	Verdun Jr. Maple Leafs	QJHL	24	11	9	4	1410	79	3	3.36	....	....	....	....	....	5	2	3	0	360	23	0	4.60	....	....	....	....
1947-48	Verdun Jr. Maple Leafs	QJHL	15	5	9	1	900	49	1	3.27	....	....	....	....	....	3	0	2	1	180	7	0	2.33	....	....	....	....
1948-49	Kitchener-Waterloo Dutchmen	OHA-Sr.	40	27	11	2	2380	105	4	*2.65	....	....	....	....	....	12	6	6	0	720	31	*1	*2.58	....	....	....	....
1949-50	Quebec Aces	QSHL	23	14	8	1	1410	66	2	2.81	....	....	....	....	....	....	....	....	....	....	....	....	....	....	....	....	....
	Kansas City Mohawks	USHL	2	1	1	0	120	12	0	6.00	....	....	....	....	....	....	....	....	....	....	....	....	....	....	....	....	....

			REGULAR SEASON													PLAYOFFS											
Season	Club	League	GP	W	L	T	Mins	GA	SO	Avg	AAvg	Eff	SA	S%	SAPG	GP	W	L	T	Mins	GA	SO	Avg	Eff	SA	S%	SAPG
1950-51	Milwaukee Sea Gulls	USHL	41	13	23	5	2506	177	1	4.24	....	....	....	....	....	....	....	....	....	....	....	....	....	....	....	....	....
	Chicago Black Hawks	**NHL**	**6**	**1**	**5**	**0**	**355**	**29**	**0**	**4.90**	**5.57**	....	....	....	....	....	....	....	....	....	....	....	....	....	....	....	....
	Omaha Knights	USHL	1	0	0	1	70	5	0	4.29	....	....	....	....	....	....	....	....	....	....	....	....	....	....	....	....	....
1951-52	Chicoutimi Sagueneens	QMHL	46	21	19	6	2840	139	2	2.94	....	....	....	....	....	18	*11	7	0	1123	43	*3	2.30	....	....	....	....
1952-53	Chicoutimi Sagueneens	QMHL	59	*33	15	11	3680	149	*6	*2.43	....	....	....	....	....	20	11	9	0	1280	53	*3	2.46	....	....	....	....
1953-54	Seattle Bombers	WHL	68	22	39	7	4080	236	2	3.47	....	....	....	....	....	....	....	....	....	....	....	....	....	....	....	....	....
1954-55	Victoria Cougars	WHL	70	33	29	8	*4080	197	6	2.81	....	....	....	....	....	4	1	3	0	245	14	0	3.43	....	....	....	....
1955-56	Victoria Cougars	WHL	69	35	29	5	4216	191	*8	2.72	....	....	....	....	....	9	5	4	0	547	28	*1	3.07	....	....	....	....
1956-57	Victoria Cougars	WHL	69	29	33	7	4240	198	4	2.80	....	....	....	....	....	3	1	2	0	199	6	0	1.81	....	....	....	....
	Seattle Americans	WHL	1	1	0	0	60	2	0	2.00	....	....	....	....	....	....	....	....	....	....	....	....	....	....	....	....	....
	New Westminster Royals	WHL	....	....	....	....	....	....	....	....	....	....	....	....	....	2	0	2	0	119	7	0	3.53	....	....	....	....
1957-58	Vancouver Canucks	WHL	*70	*44	21	5	*4250	173	*8	*2.44	....	....	....	....	....	11	*8	3	0	738	31	0	2.52	....	....	....	....
1958-59	Victoria Cougars	WHL	69	30	35	4	4180	247	5	3.55	....	....	....	....	....	3	0	3	0	180	12	0	4.00	....	....	....	....
1959-60	Victoria Cougars	WHL	*70	37	29	4	4240	190	2	2.69	....	....	....	....	....	11	6	5	0	671	27	*2	2.41	....	....	....	....
1960-61	Victoria Cougars	WHL	*70	27	41	2	4220	263	1	3.74	....	....	....	....	....	5	2	3	0	335	12	0	2.15	....	....	....	....
1961-62	Los Angeles Blades	WHL	67	24	37	6	4080	281	0	4.13	....	....	....	....	....	....	....	....	....	....	....	....	....	....	....	....	....
1962-63	**New York Rangers**	**NHL**	**2**	**0**	**1**	**0**	**40**	**3**	**0**	**4.50**	**4.69**	....	....	....	....	....	....	....	....	....	....	....	....	....	....	....	....
	Baltimore Clippers	AHL	30	16	10	4	1800	91	1	3.03	....	....	....	....	....	3	1	2	0	180	12	0	4.00	....	....	....	....
1963-64	St. Paul Rangers	CPHL	61	34	23	3	3660	181	*9	2.97	....	....	....	....	....	*11	5	6	0	661	48	0	4.36	....	....	....	....
1964-65	Baltimore Clippers	AHL	11	5	5	1	639	37	1	3.47	....	....	....	....	....	....	....	....	....	....	....	....	....	....	....	....	....
	St. Paul Rangers	CPHL	32	19	7	5	1863	89	0	2.87	....	....	....	....	....	11	*8	3	0	660	27	0	*2.45	....	....	....	....
1965-66	Los Angeles Blades	WHL	48	15	31	2	2900	199	0	4.12	....	....	....	....	....	....	....	....	....	....	....	....	....	....	....	....	....
	San Francisco Seals	WHL	....	....	....	....	....	....	....	....	....	....	....	....	....	3	2	1	0	182	7	0	2.31	....	....	....	....
1966-67	New Jersey Devils	EHL	23	....	....	....	1380	63	1	2.74	....	....	....	....	....	7	....	....	....	420	14	*1	*2.00	....	....	....	....
1967-68	Rimouski Kades	QSHL	43	....	....	....	2580	143	*6	3.37	....	....	....	....	....	....	....	....	....	....	....	....	....	....	....	....	....
1968-69	New Jersey Devils	EHL	1	1	0	0	60	1	0	1.00	....	....	....	....	....	....	....	....	....	....	....	....	....	....	....	....	....
	NHL Totals		**8**	**1**	**6**	**0**	**395**	**32**	**0**	**4.86**	....	....	....	....	....	....	....	....	....	....	....	....	....	....	....	....	....

QMHL First All-Star Team (1953) • WHL First All-Star Team (1956) • WHL Coast Division First All-Star Team (1957) • WHL Coast Division Second All-Star Team (1958) • Won WHL Leading Goaltender Award (1958) • WHL Second All-Star Team (1961) • CPHL First All-Star Team (1964)

Loaned to **Chicago** by **Milwaukee** (USHL) to replace injured Harry Lumley, January, 1951. Claimed by **Seattle** (WHL) from **Chicoutimi** (QMHL) in Inter-League Draft, June 10, 1953. Traded to **Vancouver** (WHL) by **Victoria** (WHL) for Carl Kaiser and Fred Brown, August, 1957. Signed as a free agent by **NY Rangers**, June, 1962.

• PENNEY, Steve

G – L. 6'1", 190 lbs. b: Ste-Foy, Que., 2/2/1961. Montreal's 10th, 166th overall in 1980.

Season	Club	League	GP	W	L	T	Mins	GA	SO	Avg	AAvg	Eff	SA	S%	SAPG	GP	W	L	T	Mins	GA	SO	Avg	Eff	SA	S%	SAPG
1978-79	Shawinigan Cataracts	QMJHL	36	....	....	....	1631	180	0	6.62	....	....	....	....	....	1	0	0	0	4	0	0	0.00	....	....	....	....
1979-80	Shawinigan Cataracts	QMJHL	31	9	14	5	1682	143	0	5.10	....	....	....	....	....	....	....	....	....	....	....	....	....	....	....	....	....
1980-81	Shawinigan Cataracts	QMJHL	62	30	25	4	3456	244	0	4.24	....	....	....	....	....	5	1	4	0	279	21	0	4.52	....	....	....	....
1981-82	Nova Scotia Voyageurs	AHL	6	2	1	1	308	22	0	4.29	....	....	....	....	....	....	....	....	....	....	....	....	....	....	....	....	....
	Flint Generals	IHL	36	....	....	....	2040	147	1	4.32	....	....	....	....	....	4	0	4	0	222	17	0	4.59	....	....	....	....
1982-83	Flint Generals	IHL	48	....	....	....	2552	179	0	4.21	....	....	....	....	....	3	0	2	0	111	10	0	5.40	....	....	....	....
1983-84	Nova Scotia Voyageurs	AHL	27	11	12	4	1571	92	0	3.51	....	....	....	....	....	....	....	....	....	....	....	....	....	....	....	....	....
	Montreal Canadiens	**NHL**	**4**	**0**	**4**	**0**	**240**	**19**	**0**	**4.75**	**3.74**	**7.85**	**115**	**.835**	**28.8**	**15**	**9**	**6**	....	**871**	**32**	***3**	***2.20**	**1.99**	**354**	**.910**	**24.4**
1984-85	**Montreal Canadiens**	**NHL**	**54**	**26**	**18**	**8**	**3252**	**167**	**1**	**3.08**	**2.44**	**3.83**	**1344**	**.876**	**24.8**	**12**	**6**	**6**	....	**733**	**40**	**1**	**3.27**	**4.36**	**300**	**.867**	**24.6**
1985-86	**Montreal Canadiens**	**NHL**	**18**	**6**	**8**	**2**	**990**	**72**	**0**	**4.36**	**3.41**	**7.02**	**447**	**.839**	**27.1**	....	....	....	....	....	....	....	....	....	....	....	....
1986-87	**Winnipeg Jets**	**NHL**	**7**	**1**	**4**	**1**	**327**	**25**	**0**	**4.59**	**3.89**	**8.56**	**134**	**.813**	**24.6**	....	....	....	....	....	....	....	....	....	....	....	....
	Sherbrooke Canadiens	AHL	4	1	2	0	199	12	0	3.62	....	....	....	....	....	....	....	....	....	....	....	....	....	....	....	....	....
1987-88	**Winnipeg Jets**	**NHL**	**8**	**2**	**4**	**1**	**385**	**30**	**0**	**4.68**	**3.90**	**7.55**	**186**	**.839**	**29.0**	....	....	....	....	....	....	....	....	....	....	....	....
	Moncton Hawks	AHL	28	9	14	4	1541	107	0	4.17	....	....	....	....	....	....	....	....	....	....	....	....	....	....	....	....	....
	NHL Totals		**91**	**35**	**38**	**12**	**5194**	**313**	**1**	**3.62**	....	....	**2226**	**.859**	**25.7**	**27**	**15**	**12**	....	**1604**	**72**	**4**	**2.69**	....	**654**	**.890**	**24.5**

NHL All-Rookie Team (1985)

Traded to **Winnipeg** by **Montreal** with the rights to Jan Ingman for Brian Hayward, August 19, 1986.

• PERREAULT, Bob

Robert M. "Miche" G – L. 5'8", 170 lbs. b: Trois Rivieres, Que., 1/28/1931 Deceased.

Season	Club	League	GP	W	L	T	Mins	GA	SO	Avg	AAvg	Eff	SA	S%	SAPG	GP	W	L	T	Mins	GA	SO	Avg	Eff	SA	S%	SAPG
1948-49	Trois-Rivieres Reds	QJHL	46	26	16	4	2830	142	6	3.01	....	....	....	....	....	8	4	4	0	490	29	0	3.55	....	....	....	....
1949-50	Trois-Rivieres Reds	QJHL	36	22	12	2	2190	91	*4	2.49	....	....	....	....	....	9	4	5	0	549	30	0	3.28	....	....	....	....
1950-51	Trois-Rivieres Reds	QJHL	35	25	10	0	2108	96	2	2.73	....	....	....	....	....	8	4	4	0	517	30	0	3.48	....	....	....	....
1951-52	Providence Reds	AHL	22	8	13	0	1250	95	0	4.56	....	....	....	....	....	1	0	1	0	60	7	0	7.00	....	....	....	....
1952-53	Providence Reds	AHL	6	1	5	0	360	26	0	4.33	....	....	....	....	....	....	....	....	....	....	....	....	....	....	....	....	....
	Sherbrooke Saints	QMHL	29	15	11	3	1780	84	1	2.83	....	....	....	....	....	....	....	....	....	....	....	....	....	....	....	....	....
1953-54	Montreal Royals	QHL	58	34	20	4	3528	160	4	2.72	....	....	....	....	....	9	5	4	0	544	22	2	2.43	....	....	....	....
1954-55	Shawinigan Cataracts	QHL	58	*37	18	3	3490	129	*10	*2.22	....	....	....	....	....	12	*9	3	0	720	31	1	*2.58	....	....	....	....
1955-56	Shawinigan Cataracts	QHL	57	*40	14	3	3450	146	4	2.54	....	....	....	....	....	11	6	5	0	665	24	*2	*2.17	....	....	....	....
	Montreal Canadiens	**NHL**	**6**	**3**	**3**	**0**	**360**	**12**	**1**	**2.00**	**2.44**	....	....	....	....	....	....	....	....	....	....	....	....	....	....	....	....
1956-57	Shawinigan Cataracts	QHL	41	12	22	7	2556	132	0	3.10	....	....	....	....	....	....	....	....	....	....	....	....	....	....	....	....	....
	Rochester Americans	AHL	24	15	7	1	1440	66	3	2.75	....	....	....	....	....	10	5	5	0	637	27	*2	2.54	....	....	....	....
1957-58	Hershey Bears	AHL	47	26	17	4	2820	128	3	2.72	....	....	....	....	....	11	*8	3	0	660	31	0	2.82	....	....	....	....
1958-59	Hershey Bears	AHL	52	....	....	....	3000	134	*6	*2.68	....	....	....	....	....	*13	*8	5	0	*780	35	*1	2.69	....	....	....	....
	Detroit Red Wings	**NHL**	**3**	**2**	**1**	**0**	**180**	**9**	**1**	**3.00**	**3.19**	....	....	....	....	....	....	....	....	....	....	....	....	....	....	....	....
1959-60	Hershey Bears	AHL	66	26	33	7	3960	205	*5	3.11	....	....	....	....	....	....	....	....	....	....	....	....	....	....	....	....	....
1960-61	Hershey Bears	AHL	41	22	16	3	2460	116	3	2.83	....	....	....	....	....	*8	*4	4	0	*504	24	0	2.86	....	....	....	....
1961-62	Hershey Bears	AHL	66	*36	25	5	3960	189	4	2.86	....	....	....	....	....	7	3	4	0	451	17	0	2.26	....	....	....	....
1962-63	**Boston Bruins**	**NHL**	**22**	**3**	**12**	**7**	**1287**	**82**	**1**	**3.82**	**4.04**	....	....	....	....	....	....	....	....	....	....	....	....	....	....	....	....
	Rochester Americans	AHL	10	3	4	2	600	27	0	2.70	....	....	....	....	....	2	0	2	0	120	11	0	5.50	....	....	....	....
1963-64	San Francisco Seals	WHL	*70	32	35	3	4230	257	0	3.65	....	....	....	....	....	*11•	*8	3	0	*677	41	0	3.63	....	....	....	....
1964-65	San Francisco Seals	WHL	*69	30	37	2	*4164	268	0	3.86	....	....	....	....	....	....	....	....	....	....	....	....	....	....	....	....	....
1965-66	Rochester Americans	AHL	41	26	10	1	2361	121	3	3.07	....	....	....	....	....	9	7	2	0	532	17	*2	*1.92	....	....	....	....
1966-67	Rochester Americans	AHL	54	30	17	5	3149	158	*4	3.01	....	....	....	....	....	*13	6	7	0	*785	38	*2	2.90	....	....	....	....
1967-68	Rochester Americans	AHL	57	*31	15	7	3101	149	*6	2.88	....	....	....	....	....	9	5	3	0	515	28	1	3.26	....	....	....	....
1968-69	Rochester Americans	AHL	19	5	10	1	913	63	0	4.14	....	....	....	....	....	....	....	....	....	....	....	....	....	....	....	....	....
1969-70	Des Moines Oak Leafs	IHL	27	....	....	....	1467	66	1	*2.70	....	....	....	....	....	....	....	....	....	....	....	....	....	....	....	....	....
1970-71	Des Moines Oak Leafs	IHL	19	....	....	....	1062	57	1	3.22	....	....	....	....	....	8	....	....	....	478	21	0	2.63	....	....	....	....
1971-72	Des Moines Oak Leafs	IHL	51	....	....	....	3139	176	1	3.36	....	....	....	....	....	3	0	3	0	180	15	0	5.00	....	....	....	....
1972-73	Los Angeles Sharks	WHA	1	1	0	0	60	2	0	2.00	....	....	....	....	....	....	....	....	....	....	....	....	....	....	....	....	....
1973-74	Greensboro Generals	SHL	16	....	....	....	930	62	0	4.01	....	....	....	....	....	....	....	....	....	....	....	....	....	....	....	....	....
	NHL Totals		**31**	**8**	**16**	**7**	**1827**	**103**	**3**	**3.38**	....	....	....	....	....	....	....	....	....	....	....	....	....	....	....	....	....
	Other Major League Totals		1	1	0	0	60	2	0	2.00	....	....	....	....	....	....	....	....	....	....	....	....	....	....	....	....	....

QJHL First All-Star Team (1950, 1951) • QHL First All-Star Team (1955) • Won Vezina Memorial Trophy (Top Goaltender - QHL) (1955) • QHL Second All-Star Team (1956) • AHL Second All-Star Team (1958, 1959, 1962, 1968) • Won Harry "Hap" Holmes Memorial Award (fewest goals against - AHL) (1959, 1968) • Shared James Norris Memorial Trophy (fewest goals against - IHL) with Gaye Cooley (1970)

Signed as a free agent by **Providence** (AHL), May 30, 1951. Traded to **Montreal** by **Providence** (AHL) for George McAvoy and cash, June 11, 1953. Promoted to **Montreal** from **Shawinigan** (QHL) to replace injured Jacques Plante in games from December 17 through 28, 1955. • Recorded a shutout (5-0) in NHL debut vs. Chicago, December 17, 1955. Claimed by **Detroit** (Hershey-AHL) from **Montreal** (Shawinigan-QHL) in Inter-League Draft, June 4, 1957. Promoted to **Detroit** from **Hershey** (AHL) to replace injured Terry Sawchuk in games from January 21 through 25, 1959. Traded to **Boston** by **Detroit** (Hershey-AHL) for Ed Chadwick and Barry Ashbee, June, 1962. Traded to **San Francisco** (WHL) by **Boston** for $25,000, June 4, 1963. Claimed by **Toronto** (Victoria-WHL) by **Boston** in Reverse Draft, June 9, 1965. Rights transferred to **Vancouver** (WHL) after WHL club purchased **Rochester** (AHL) franchise, August 13, 1968. Selected by **LA Sharks** (WHA) in 1972 WHA General Player Draft, February 12, 1972.

Season	Club	League	REGULAR SEASON GP	W	L	T	Mins	GA	SO	Avg	AAvg	Eff	SA	S%	SAPG	PLAYOFFS GP	W	L	T	Mins	GA	SO	Avg	Eff	SA	S%	SAPG

● PETTIE, Jim

James "Seaweed" G – L. 6', 195 lbs. b: Toronto, Ont., 10/24/1953. Boston's 10th, 142nd overall in 1973.

Season	Club	League	GP	W	L	T	Mins	GA	SO	Avg	AAvg	Eff	SA	S%	SAPG	GP	W	L	T	Mins	GA	SO	Avg	Eff	SA	S%	SAPG
1972-73	St. Catharines Black Hawks	OMJHL	31	....	....	....	1089	152	1	5.04	....	....	....	....	....	....	....	....	....	....	....	....	....	....	....	....	....
1973-74	Dayton Gems	IHL	40	....	....	....	2092	96	1	*2.75	....	....	....	....	....	4	1	3	0	197	15	0	4.57	....	....	....	....
1974-75	Dayton Gems	IHL	27	....	....	....	1310	73	0	3.34	....	....	....	....	....	13	6	7	0	197	30	0	*2.82	....	....	....	....
1975-76	Binghamton Dusters	NAHL	5	....	....	....	260	16	1	3.69	....	....	....	....	....	....	....	....	....	....	....	....	....	....	....	....	....
	Dayton Gems	IHL	51	....	....	....	2178	104	*5	2.86	....	....	....	....	....	15	12	3	0	921	43	1	2.80	....	....	....	....
1976-77	**Boston Bruins**	**NHL**	**1**	**1**	**0**	**0**	**60**	**3**	**0**	**3.00**	**2.79**	....	....	....	....	....	....	....	....	....	....	....	....	....	....	....	....
	Rochester Americans	AHL	43	26	15	1	2462	131	2	3.19	....	....	....	....	....	*11	6	5	0	*660	36	0	3.27	....	....	....	....
1977-78	**Boston Bruins**	**NHL**	**1**	**0**	**1**	**0**	**60**	**6**	**0**	**6.00**	**5.63**	....	....	....	....	....	....	....	....	....	....	....	....	....	....	....	....
	Rochester Americans	AHL	32	16	12	4	1897	107	2	3.38	....	....	....	....	....	3	0	3	0	188	8	0	2.55	....	....	....	....
1978-79	**Boston Bruins**	**NHL**	**19**	**8**	**6**	**2**	**1037**	**62**	**1**	**3.59**	**3.18**	....	....	....	....	....	....	....	....	....	....	....	....	....	....	....	....
	Rochester Americans	AHL	9	0	7	1	451	39	0	5.19	....	....	....	....	....	....	....	....	....	....	....	....	....	....	....	....	....
1979-80	New Haven Nighthawks	AHL	33	16	13	3	1975	131	2	4.00	....	....	....	....	....	2	1	1	0	120	11	0	5.00	....	....	....	....
1980-81	Birmingham Bulls	CHL	21	....	....	....	1189	109	0	5.50	....	....	....	....	....	....	....	....	....	....	....	....	....	....	....	....	....
	Richmond Rifles	EHL	1	0	1	0	62	7	0	6.77	....	....	....	....	....	....	....	....	....	....	....	....	....	....	....	....	....
	NHL Totals		**21**	**9**	**7**	**2**	**1157**	**71**	**1**	**3.68**	....	....	....	....	....	....	....	....	....	....	....	....	....	....	....	....	....

IHL Second All-Star Team (1976)

● PIETRANGELO, Frank

"Saint Peter" G – L. 5'10", 185 lbs. b: Niagara Falls, Ont., 12/17/1964. Pittsburgh's 4th, 64th overall in 1983.

Season	Club	League	GP	W	L	T	Mins	GA	SO	Avg	AAvg	Eff	SA	S%	SAPG	GP	W	L	T	Mins	GA	SO	Avg	Eff	SA	S%	SAPG
1979-80	Niagara Falls Canucks	OJHL-B	12	....	....	....	452	40	0	5.31	....	....	....	....	....	....	....	....	....	....	....	....	....	....	....	....	....
1980-81	Brampton Chevies	OJHL	28	....	....	....	1650	159	0	5.78	....	....	....	....	....	....	....	....	....	....	....	....	....	....	....	....	....
1981-82	Niagara Falls Canucks	OJHL-B	STATISTICS NOT AVAILABLE																								
1982-83	University of Minnesota	WCHA	25	15	6	1	1348	80	1	3.56	....	....	....	....	....	....	....	....	....	....	....	....	....	....	....	....	....
1983-84	University of Minnesota	WCHA	20	13	7	0	1141	66	0	3.47	....	....	....	....	....	....	....	....	....	....	....	....	....	....	....	....	....
1984-85	University of Minnesota	WCHA	17	8	3	3	912	52	0	3.42	....	....	....	....	....	....	....	....	....	....	....	....	....	....	....	....	....
1985-86	University of Minnesota	WCHA	23	15	7	0	1284	76	0	3.55	....	....	....	....	....	....	....	....	....	....	....	....	....	....	....	....	....
1986-87	Muskegon Lumberjacks	IHL	35	23	11	0	2090	119	2	3.42	....	....	....	....	....	15	10	4	0	923	46	0	2.99	....	....	....	....
1987-88	**Pittsburgh Penguins**	**NHL**	**21**	**9**	**11**	**0**	**1207**	**80**	**1**	**3.98**	**3.32**	**5.31**	**600**	**.867**	**29.8**	....	....	....	....	....	....	....	....	....	....	....	....
	Muskegon Lumberjacks	IHL	15	11	3	1	868	43	2	2.97	....	....	....	....	....	....	....	....	....	....	....	....	....	....	....	....	....
1988-89	**Pittsburgh Penguins**	**NHL**	**15**	**5**	**3**	**0**	**669**	**45**	**0**	**4.04**	**3.36**	**4.44**	**409**	**.890**	**36.7**	....	....	....	....	....	....	....	....	....	....	....	....
	Muskegon Lumberjacks	IHL	13	10	1	0	760	38	1	3.00	....	....	....	....	....	9	*8	1	0	566	29	0	3.07	....	....	....	....
1989-90	**Pittsburgh Penguins**	**NHL**	**21**	**8**	**6**	**2**	**1066**	**77**	**0**	**4.33**	**3.68**	**5.75**	**580**	**.867**	**32.6**	....	....	....	....	....	....	....	....	....	....	....	....
	Muskegon Lumberjacks	IHL	12	9	2	1	691	38	0	3.30	....	....	....	....	....	....	....	....	....	....	....	....	....	....	....	....	....
1990-91 ♦	**Pittsburgh Penguins**	**NHL**	**25**	**10**	**11**	**1**	**1311**	**86**	**0**	**3.94**	**3.55**	**4.75**	**714**	**.880**	**32.7**	**5**	**4**	**1**	....	**288**	**15**	***1**	**3.13**	**3.17**	**148**	**.899**	**30.8**
1991-92	**Pittsburgh Penguins**	**NHL**	**5**	**2**	**1**	**0**	**225**	**20**	**0**	**5.33**	**4.78**	**8.20**	**130**	**.846**	**34.7**	....	....	....	....	....	....	....	....	....	....	....	....
	Hartford Whalers	**NHL**	**5**	**3**	**1**	**1**	**306**	**12**	**0**	**2.35**	**2.10**	**1.81**	**156**	**.923**	**30.6**	**7**	**3**	**4**	....	**425**	**19**	**0**	**2.68**	**2.09**	**244**	**.922**	**34.4**
1992-93	**Hartford Whalers**	**NHL**	**30**	**4**	**15**	**1**	**1373**	**111**	**0**	**4.85**	**4.17**	**6.88**	**783**	**.858**	**34.2**	....	....	....	....	....	....	....	....	....	....	....	....
1993-94	**Hartford Whalers**	**NHL**	**19**	**5**	**11**	**1**	**984**	**59**	**0**	**3.60**	**3.46**	**4.49**	**473**	**.875**	**28.8**	....	....	....	....	....	....	....	....	....	....	....	....
	Springfield Indians	AHL	23	9	10	2	1314	73	0	3.33	....	....	....	....	....	6	2	4	0	324	23	0	4.26	....	....	....	....
1994-95	Minnesota Moose	IHL	15	3	8	1	756	52	0	4.12	....	....	....	....	....	....	....	....	....	....	....	....	....	....	....	....	....
1995-96	HC Asiago	Italy	-	STATISTICS NOT AVAILABLE																							
1996-97	HC Bolzano	Alpenliga	39	....	....	....	2340	145	0	3.73	....	....	....	....	....	....	....	....	....	....	....	....	....	....	....	....	....
1997-98	KAC Kaufburen	Germany-2	14	....	....	....	840	45	0	3.21	....	....	....	....	....	....	....	....	....	....	....	....	....	....	....	....	....
1998-99	Manchester Storm	Britain	63	....	....	....	3796	136	6	2.14	....	....	....	....	....	....	....	....	....	....	....	....	....	....	....	....	....
	Manchester Storm	EuroHL	6	2	3	1	374	20	0	3.21	....	....	....	....	....	....	....	....	....	....	....	....	....	....	....	....	....
99-2000	Manchester Storm	BH-Cup	9	....	....	....	555	18	1	1.95	....	....	....	....	....	....	....	....	....	....	....	....	....	....	....	....	....
	Manchester Storm	Britain	19	....	....	....	910	59	1	3.89	....	....	....	....	....	....	....	....	....	....	....	....	....	....	....	....	....
	Manchester Storm	EuroHL	5	0	5	0	252	15	0	3.58	....	....	....	....	....	....	....	....	....	....	....	....	....	....	....	....	....
	NHL Totals		**141**	**46**	**59**	**6**	**7141**	**490**	**1**	**4.12**	....	....	**3845**	**.873**	**32.3**	**12**	**7**	**5**	....	**713**	**34**	**1**	**2.86**	....	**392**	**.913**	**33.0**

Traded to **Hartford** by **Pittsburgh** for Hartford's 3rd (Sven Butenschon) and 7th (Serge Aubin) round choices in 1994 Entry Draft, March 10, 1992. Signed as a free agent by **NY Islanders**, July 28, 1994.

● PLANTE, Jacques

Joseph Jacques Omer "Jake the Snake" G – L. 6', 175 lbs. b: Shawinigan Falls, Que., 1/17/1929 d: 2/27/1986. **HHOF**

Season	Club	League	GP	W	L	T	Mins	GA	SO	Avg	AAvg	Eff	SA	S%	SAPG	GP	W	L	T	Mins	GA	SO	Avg	Eff	SA	S%	SAPG
1947-48	Quebec Citadelle	QJHL	31	18	11	1	1840	87	2	2.84	....	....	....	....	....	9	4	5	0	545	28	2	3.08	....	....	....	....
	Montreal Jr. Canadiens	QJHL	2	0	0	2	120	5	0	2.50	....	....	....	....	....	....	....	....	....	....	....	....	....	....	....	....	....
1948-49	Quebec Citadelle	QJHL	47	35	8	4	2860	95	8	1.99	....	....	....	....	....	13	7	6	0	790	43	0	3.27	....	....	....	....
1949-50	Montreal Royals	QSHL	58	27	22	9	3590	180	0	3.01	....	....	....	....	....	6	2	4	0	400	20	0	3.00	....	....	....	....
1950-51	Montreal Royals	QMHL	60	28	29	3	3670	201	4	3.29	....	....	....	....	....	7	2	5	0	420	26	1	3.71	....	....	....	....
1951-52	Montreal Royals	QMHL	60	30	24	6	3560	201	4	3.39	....	....	....	....	....	7	3	4	0	420	21	1	3.00	....	....	....	....
1952-53	Montreal Royals	QMHL	29	20	8	1	1760	61	4	2.08	....	....	....	....	....	....	....	....	....	....	....	....	....	....	....	....	....
♦	**Montreal Canadiens**	**NHL**	**3**	**2**	**0**	**1**	**180**	**4**	**0**	**1.33**	**1.69**	....	....	....	....	**4**	**3**	**1**	....	**240**	**7**	**1**	***1.75**	....	....	....	....
	Buffalo Bisons	AHL	33	13	19	1	2000	114	2	3.42	....	....	....	....	....	....	....	....	....	....	....	....	....	....	....	....	....
1953-54	**Montreal Canadiens**	**NHL**	**17**	**7**	**5**	**5**	**1020**	**27**	**5**	**1.59**	**1.99**	....	....	....	....	**8**	**5**	**3**	....	**480**	**15**	***2**	**1.88**	....	....	....	....
	Buffalo Bisons	AHL	55	32	17	6	3370	148	3	*2.64	....	....	....	....	....	....	....	....	....	....	....	....	....	....	....	....	....
1954-55	**Montreal Canadiens**	**NHL**	**52**	**31**	**13**	**7**	**3040**	**110**	**5**	**2.17**	**2.57**	....	....	....	....	***12**	**6**	**3**	....	**639**	**30**	**0**	**2.82**	....	....	....	....
1955-56 ♦	**Montreal Canadiens**	**NHL**	**64**	***42**	**12**	**10**	**3840**	**119**	**7**	***1.86**	**2.18**	....	....	....	....	***10**	***8**	**2**	....	**600**	**18**	***2**	***1.80**	....	....	....	....
1956-57 ♦	**Montreal Canadiens**	**NHL**	**61**	**31**	**18**	**12**	**3660**	**122**	***9**	***2.00**	**2.21**	....	....	....	....	***10**	***8**	**2**	....	***616**	**17**	**1**	***1.66**	....	....	....	....
1957-58 ♦	**Montreal Canadiens**	**NHL**	**57**	***34**	**14**	**8**	**3386**	**119**	***9**	***2.11**	**2.23**	....	....	....	....	**10**	***8**	**2**	....	**618**	**20**	***1**	***1.94**	....	....	....	....
1958-59 ♦	**Montreal Canadiens**	**NHL**	**67**	***38**	**16**	**13**	**4000**	**144**	***9**	***2.16**	**2.19**	....	....	....	....	**11**	***8**	**3**	....	**670**	**26**	**0**	***2.33**	....	....	....	....
1959-60 ♦	**Montreal Canadiens**	**NHL**	**69**	***40**	**17**	**12**	**4140**	**175**	**3**	***2.54**	**2.59**	....	....	....	....	**8**	***8**	**0**	....	**489**	**11**	***3**	***1.35**	....	....	....	....
1960-61	**Montreal Canadiens**	**NHL**	**40**	**23**	**11**	**6**	**2400**	**112**	**2**	**2.80**	**2.87**	....	....	....	....	**6**	**2**	**4**	....	**412**	**16**	**0**	**2.33**	....	....	....	....
	Montreal Royals	EPHL	8	3	4	1	480	24	0	3.00	....	....	....	....	....	....	....	....	....	....	....	....	....	....	....	....	....
1961-62	**Montreal Canadiens**	**NHL**	***70**	***42**	**14**	**14**	***4200**	**166**	**4**	***2.37**	**2.33**	....	....	....	....	**6**	**2**	**4**	....	**360**	**19**	**0**	**3.17**	....	....	....	....
1962-63	**Montreal Canadiens**	**NHL**	**56**	**22**	**14**	**19**	**3320**	**138**	***5**	***2.49**	**2.53**	....	....	....	....	**5**	**1**	**4**	....	**300**	**14**	**0**	**2.80**	....	....	....	....
1963-64	**New York Rangers**	**NHL**	**65**	**22**	**36**	**7**	**3900**	**220**	**3**	**3.38**	**3.92**	....	....	....	....	....	....	....	....	....	....	....	....	....	....	....	....
1964-65	**New York Rangers**	**NHL**	**33**	**10**	**17**	**5**	**1938**	**109**	**2**	**3.37**	**3.67**	....	....	....	....	....	....	....	....	....	....	....	....	....	....	....	....
	Baltimore Clippers	AHL	17	6	9	1	1018	51	1	3.01	....	....	....	....	....	5	2	3	0	315	14	1	2.67	....	....	....	....
1965-1968			OUT OF HOCKEY – RETIRED																								
1968-69	**St. Louis Blues**	**NHL**	**37**	**18**	**12**	**6**	**2139**	**70**	**5**	***1.96**	**2.00**	....	....	....	....	***10**	***8**	**2**	....	***589**	**14**	***3**	**1.43**	....	....	....	....
1969-70	**St. Louis Blues**	**NHL**	**32**	**18**	**9**	**5**	**1839**	**67**	**5**	**2.19**	**2.30**	....	....	....	....	**6**	**4**	**1**	....	**324**	**8**	***1**	***1.48**	....	....	....	....
1970-71	**Toronto Maple Leafs**	**NHL**	**40**	**24**	**11**	**4**	**2329**	**73**	**4**	***1.88**	**1.83**	....	....	....	....	**3**	**0**	**2**	....	**134**	**7**	**0**	**3.13**	....	....	....	....
1971-72	**Toronto Maple Leafs**	**NHL**	**34**	**16**	**13**	**5**	**1965**	**86**	**2**	**2.63**	**2.65**	....	....	....	....	**1**	**0**	**1**	....	**60**	**5**	**0**	**5.00**	....	....	....	....
1972-73	**Toronto Maple Leafs**	**NHL**	**32**	**8**	**14**	**6**	**1717**	**87**	**1**	**3.04**	**2.86**	....	....	....	....	....	....	....	....	....	....	....	....	....	....	....	....
	Boston Bruins	**NHL**	**8**	**7**	**1**	**0**	**480**	**16**	**2**	**2.00**	**1.88**	....	....	....	....	**2**	**0**	**2**	....	**120**	**10**	**0**	**5.00**	....	....	....	....
1973-74	Quebec Nordiques	WHA	DID NOT PLAY – GENERAL MANAGER																								
1974-75	Edmonton Oilers	WHA	31	15	14	1	1592	88	1	3.32	....	....	....	....	....	....	....	....	....	....	....	....	....	....	....	....	....
	NHL Totals		**837**	**435**	**247**	**145**	**49493**	**1964**	**82**	**2.38**	....	....	....	....	....	**112**	**71**	**36**	....	**6651**	**237**	**14**	**2.14**	....	....	....	....
	Other Major League Totals		31	15	14	1	1592	88	1	3.32	....	....	....	....	....	....	....	....	....	....	....	....	....	....	....	....	....

QJHL First All-Star Team (1948, 1949) • Won Vezina Memorial Trophy (Top Goaltender - QMHL) (1953) • NHL First All-Star Team (1956, 1959, 1962) • Won Vezina Trophy (1956, 1957, 1958, 1959, 1960, 1962) • NHL Second All-Star Team (1957, 1958, 1960, 1971) • Won Hart Trophy (1962) • Shared Vezina Trophy with Glenn Hall (1969) • Played in NHL All-Star Game (1956, 1957, 1958, 1959, 1960, 1962, 1969, 1970)

Signed to a three-game amateur tryout contract by **Montreal** and replaced injured Gerry McNeil in games from November 1 through 6, 1952. Signed as a free agent by **Montreal** (Buffalo-AHL), December 29, 1952. • Recorded a shutout (3-0) in NHL playoff debut at Chicago, April 4, 1953. Traded to **NY Rangers** by **Montreal** with Don Marshall and Phil Goyette for Gump Worsley, Dave Balon, Leon Rochefort and Len Ronson, June 4, 1963. • Signed to try-out contract by **California**, September, 1967. • Ordered to leave training camp when it was confirmed his rights were still property of **NY Rangers**, September, 1967. Claimed by **St. Louis** from **NY Rangers** in Intra-League Draft, June 12, 1968. Traded to **Toronto** by **St. Louis** for cash, May 18, 1970. Selected by **Miami-Philadelphia** (WHA) in 1972 WHA General Player Draft, February 12, 1972. Traded to **Boston** by **Toronto** with Toronto's 3rd round choice (Doug Gibson) in 1973 Amateur Draft for Boston's 1st round choice (Ian Turnbull) in 1973 Amateur Draft and future considerations (Eddie Johnston, May 22, 1973), March 3, 1973. Selected by **Edmonton** (WHA) in 1973 WHA Professional Player Draft, June, 1973.

• PLASSE, Michel

Michel Pierre G – L. 5'11", 172 lbs. b: Montreal, Que., 6/1/1948. Montreal's 1st, 1st overall in 1968.

			REGULAR SEASON													PLAYOFFS											
Season	Club	League	GP	W	L	T	Mins	GA	SO	Avg	AAvg	Eff	SA	S%	SAPG	GP	W	L	T	Mins	GA	SO	Avg	Eff	SA	S%	SAPG
1965-1967	Drummondville Rangers	QJHL	STATISTICS NOT AVAILABLE																								
1967-68	Drummondville Rangers	QJHL	30	....	....	....	1800	63	3	*2.10	....	....	....	....	....	10	8	2	0	600	32	1	3.20	....	....	....	....
	Drummondville Rangers	Mem-Cup	4	1	3	0	250	19	0	4.56	....	....	....	....	....	....	....	....	....	....	....	....	....	....	....	....	....
1968-69	Cleveland Barons	AHL	7	2	4	0	320	27	0	5.06	....	....	....	....	....	....	....	....	....	....	....	....	....	....	....	....	....
1969-70	Jacksonville Rockets	EHL	61	....	....	....	3660	297	0	4.87	....	....	....	....	....	4	0	4	0	240	35	0	8.75	....	....	....	....
1970-71	Kansas City Blues	CHL	16	....	....	....	960	42	0	2.63	....	....	....	....	....	....	....	....	....	....	....	....	....	....	....	....	....
	St. Louis Blues	**NHL**	**1**	**1**	**0**	**0**	**60**	**3**	**0**	**3.00**	**2.97**	....	....	....	....	....	....	....	....	....	....	....	....	....	....	....	....
1971-72	Nova Scotia Voyageurs	AHL	36	17	13	4	2036	94	1	2.77	....	....	....	....	....	15	*12	3	0	912	19	*3	*1.25	....	....	....	....
1972-73♦	**Montreal Canadiens**	**NHL**	**17**	**11**	**2**	**3**	**932**	**40**	**0**	**2.58**	**2.43**	....	....	....	....	....	....	....	....	....	....	....	....	....	....	....	....
1973-74	**Montreal Canadiens**	**NHL**	**15**	**7**	**4**	**2**	**839**	**57**	**0**	**4.08**	**3.96**	....	....	....	....	....	....	....	....	....	....	....	....	....	....	....	....
1974-75	**Kansas City Scouts**	**NHL**	**24**	**4**	**16**	**3**	**1420**	**96**	**0**	**4.06**	**3.68**	....	....	....	....	....	....	....	....	....	....	....	....	....	....	....	....
	Pittsburgh Penguins	**NHL**	**20**	**9**	**5**	**4**	**1094**	**73**	**0**	**4.00**	**3.62**	....	....	....	....	....	....	....	....	....	....	....	....	....	....	....	....
1975-76	**Pittsburgh Penguins**	**NHL**	**55**	**24**	**19**	**10**	**3096**	**178**	**2**	**3.45**	**3.13**	....	....	....	....	**3**	**1**	**2**	....	**180**	**8**	**1**	**2.67**	....	....	....	....
	Hershey Bears	AHL	5	0	4	0	278	25	0	5.40	....	....	....	....	....	....	....	....	....	....	....	....	....	....	....	....	....
1976-77	**Colorado Rockies**	**NHL**	**54**	**12**	**29**	**10**	**2986**	**190**	**0**	**3.82**	**3.57**	....	....	....	....	....	....	....	....	....	....	....	....	....	....	....	....
1977-78	**Colorado Rockies**	**NHL**	**25**	**3**	**12**	**8**	**1383**	**90**	**0**	**3.90**	**3.67**	....	....	....	....	....	....	....	....	....	....	....	....	....	....	....	....
	Hampton Gulls	AHL	2	0	1	1	124	5	0	2.42	....	....	....	....	....	....	....	....	....	....	....	....	....	....	....	....	....
1978-79	Philadelphia Firebirds	AHL	7	0	6	1	423	31	0	4.39	....	....	....	....	....	....	....	....	....	....	....	....	....	....	....	....	....
	Colorado Rockies	**NHL**	**41**	**9**	**29**	**2**	**2302**	**152**	**0**	**3.96**	**3.52**	....	....	....	....	....	....	....	....	....	....	....	....	....	....	....	....
1979-80	**Colorado Rockies**	**NHL**	**6**	**0**	**3**	**2**	**327**	**26**	**0**	**4.77**	**4.22**	....	....	....	....	....	....	....	....	....	....	....	....	....	....	....	....
	Fort Worth Texans	CHL	32	9	13	3	1632	113	0	4.15	....	....	....	....	....	*14	*8	5	0	*827	41	*1	2.97	....	....	....	....
1980-81	**Quebec Nordiques**	**NHL**	**33**	**10**	**14**	**9**	**1933**	**118**	**0**	**3.66**	**2.96**	....	....	....	....	**1**	**0**	**0**	....	**15**	**1**	**0**	**4.00**	....	....	....	....
1981-82	**Quebec Nordiques**	**NHL**	**8**	**2**	**3**	**1**	**388**	**35**	**0**	**5.41**	**4.18**	....	....	....	....	....	....	....	....	....	....	....	....	....	....	....	....
	Binghamton Whalers	AHL	8	3	3	1	444	32	0	4.32	....	....	....	....	....	....	....	....	....	....	....	....	....	....	....	....	....
	NHL Totals		**299**	**92**	**136**	**54**	**16760**	**1058**	**2**	**3.79**	....	....	....	....	....	**4**	**1**	**2**	....	**195**	**9**	**1**	**2.77**	....	....	....	....

QJHL Second All-Star Team (1968) • Scored a goal while with Kansas City (CHL), February 21, 1971.

Loaned to **Kansas City** (CHL) by **Montreal**, October 1, 1970. Traded to **St. Louis** by **Montreal** for cash, December 11, 1970. Traded to **Montreal** by **St. Louis** for cash, August 23, 1971. Claimed by **Kansas City** from **Montreal** in Expansion Draft, June 12, 1974. Traded to **Pittsburgh** by **Kansas City** for Denis Herron and Jean-Guy Lagace, January 10, 1975. Transferred to **Colorado** from **Pittsburgh** with Simon Nolet and the loan of Colin Campbell for the 1976-77 season (September 1, 1976) as compensation for Pittsburgh's signing of free agent Denis Herron, August 7, 1976. Signed as a free agent by **Quebec**, September 14, 1980. Traded to **Hartford** by **Quebec** with Quebec's 4th round choice (Ron Chyzowski) in 1983 Entry Draft for John Garrett, January 12, 1982.

• PLAXTON, Hugh

Hugh John G. 5'10", 184 lbs. b: Barrie, Ont., 5/16/1904 Deceased.

Season	Club	League	GP	W	L	T	Mins	GA	SO	Avg	AAvg	Eff	SA	S%	SAPG	GP	W	L	T	Mins	GA	SO	Avg	Eff	SA	S%	SAPG
1932-33	**Montreal Maroons**	**NHL**	**1**	**0**	**1**	**0**	**57**	**5**	**0**	**5.26**	**7.06**	....	....	....	....	....	....	....	....	....	....	....	....	....	....	....	....
	NHL Totals		**1**	**0**	**1**	**0**	**57**	**5**	**0**	**5.26**	....	....	....	....	....	....	....	....	....	....	....	....	....	....	....	....	....

• **Montreal Maroons'** left winger replaced injured Flat Walsh in 1st period, November 22, 1932. (NY Americans 5, Montreal Maroons 2)

• POTVIN, Felix

"The Cat" G – L. 6'1", 190 lbs. b: Anjou, Que., 6/23/1971. Toronto's 2nd, 31st overall in 1990.

Season	Club	League	GP	W	L	T	Mins	GA	SO	Avg	AAvg	Eff	SA	S%	SAPG	GP	W	L	T	Mins	GA	SO	Avg	Eff	SA	S%	SAPG
1987-88	Montreal-Bourassa Canadiens	QAAA	27	15	7	3	1585	103	3	3.90	....	....	....	....	....	6	2	4	0	341	20	0	3.51	....	....	....	....
1988-89	Chicoutimi Sagueneens	QMJHL	*65	25	31	1	*3489	271	*2	4.66	....	....	....	....	....	....	....	....	....	....	....	....	....	....	....	....	....
1989-90	Chicoutimi Sagueneens	QMJHL	*62	*31	26	2	*3478	231	*2	3.99	....	....	....	....	....	....	....	....	....	....	....	....	....	....	....	....	....
1990-91	Chicoutimi Sagueneens	QMJHL	54	33	15	4	3216	145	*6	*2.70	....	....	....	....	....	*16	*11	5	....	*992	46	0	*2.78	....	....	....	....
	Canada	WJC-A	2	....	....	....	80	3	....	2.25	....	....	....	....	....	....	....	....	....	....	....	....	....	....	....	....	....
	Chicoutimi Sagueneens	Mem-Cup	3	1	2	0	174	8	0	2.76	....	....	....	....	....	....	....	....	....	....	....	....	....	....	....	....	....
1991-92	**Toronto Maple Leafs**	**NHL**	**4**	**0**	**2**	**1**	**210**	**8**	**0**	**2.29**	**2.05**	**1.53**	**120**	**.933**	**34.3**	....	....	....	....	....	....	....	....	....	....	....	....
	St. John's Maple Leafs	AHL	35	18	10	6	2070	101	2	2.93	....	....	....	....	....	11	7	4	....	642	41	0	3.83	....	....	....	....
1992-93	**Toronto Maple Leafs**	**NHL**	**48**	**25**	**15**	**7**	**2781**	**116**	**2**	***2.50**	**2.13**	**2.26**	**1286**	**.910**	**27.7**	***21**	**11**	**10**	....	***1308**	**62**	**1**	**2.84**	**2.77**	**636**	**.903**	**29.2**
	St. John's Maple Leafs	AHL	5	3	0	2	309	18	0	3.50	....	....	....	....	....	....	....	....	....	....	....	....	....	....	....	....	....
1993-94	**Toronto Maple Leafs**	**NHL**	**66**	**34**	**22**	**9**	**3883**	**187**	**3**	**2.89**	**2.77**	**2.69**	**2010**	**.907**	**31.1**	**18**	**9**	**9**	....	**1124**	**46**	**3**	**2.46**	**2.18**	**520**	**.912**	**27.8**
1994-95	**Toronto Maple Leafs**	**NHL**	**36**	**15**	**13**	**7**	**2144**	**104**	**0**	**2.91**	**3.05**	**2.70**	**1120**	**.907**	**31.3**	**7**	**3**	**4**	....	**424**	**20**	**1**	**2.83**	**2.24**	**253**	**.921**	**35.8**
1995-96	**Toronto Maple Leafs**	**NHL**	**69**	**30**	**26**	**11**	**4009**	**192**	**2**	**2.87**	**2.85**	**2.58**	**2135**	**.910**	**32.0**	**6**	**2**	**4**	....	**350**	**19**	**0**	**3.26**	**3.13**	**198**	**.904**	**33.9**
1996-97	**Toronto Maple Leafs**	**NHL**	***74**	**27**	**36**	**7**	***4271**	**224**	**0**	**3.15**	**3.40**	**2.89**	**2438**	**.908**	**34.2**	....	....	....	....	....	....	....	....	....	....	....	....
1997-98	**Toronto Maple Leafs**	**NHL**	**67**	**26**	**33**	**7**	**3864**	**176**	**5**	**2.73**	**3.26**	**2.55**	**1882**	**.906**	**29.2**	....	....	....	....	....	....	....	....	....	....	....	....
	Canada	WC-A	4	3	0	1	240	8	0	2.00	....	....	....	....	....	....	....	....	....	....	....	....	....	....	....	....	....
1998-99	**Toronto Maple Leafs**	**NHL**	**5**	**3**	**2**	**0**	**299**	**19**	**0**	**3.81**	**4.53**	**5.10**	**142**	**.866**	**28.5**	....	....	....	....	....	....	....	....	....	....	....	....
	New York Islanders	**NHL**	**11**	**2**	**7**	**1**	**606**	**37**	**0**	**3.66**	**4.36**	**3.93**	**345**	**.893**	**34.2**	....	....	....	....	....	....	....	....	....	....	....	....
99-2000	**New York Islanders**	**NHL**	**22**	**5**	**14**	**3**	**1273**	**68**	**1**	**3.21**	**3.67**	**3.45**	**632**	**.892**	**29.8**	....	....	....	....	....	....	....	....	....	....	....	....
	Vancouver Canucks	**NHL**	**34**	**12**	**13**	**7**	**1966**	**85**	**0**	**2.59**	**2.96**	**2.43**	**906**	**.906**	**27.7**	....	....	....	....	....	....	....	....	....	....	....	....
	NHL Totals		**436**	**179**	**183**	**60**	**25306**	**1216**	**13**	**2.88**	....	....	**13016**	**.907**	**30.9**	**52**	**25**	**27**	....	**3206**	**147**	**5**	**2.75**	....	**1607**	**.909**	**30.1**

QMJHL Second All-Star Team (1990) • QMJHL First All-Star Team (1991) • Canadian Major Junior Goaltender of the Year (1991) • Memorial Cup All-Star Team (1991) • Won Hap Emms Memorial Trophy (Memorial Cup Tournament Top Goaltender) (1991) • AHL First All-Star Team (1992) • Won Dudley "Red" Garrett Memorial Trophy (Top Rookie - AHL) (1992) • Won Baz Bastien Memorial Trophy (Top Goaltender - AHL) (1992) • NHL All-Rookie Team (1993) • Played in NHL All-Star Game (1994, 1996)

Traded to **NY Islanders** by **Toronto** with Toronto's 6th round choice (later traded to Tampa Bay - Tampa Bay selected Fedor Fedorov) in 1999 Entry Draft for Bryan Berard and NY Islanders' 6th round choice (Jan Sochor) in 1999 Entry Draft, January 9, 1999. Traded to **Vancouver** by **NY Islanders** with NY Islanders' compensatory 2nd (later traded to New Jersey - New Jersey selected Teemu Laine) and 3rd (Thatcher Bell) round choices in 2000 Entry Draft for Kevin Weekes, Dave Scatchard and Bill Muckalt, December 19, 1999.

• PRONOVOST, Claude

G – L. 5'9", 190 lbs. b: Shawinigan Falls, Que., 7/22/1935.

Season	Club	League	GP	W	L	T	Mins	GA	SO	Avg	AAvg	Eff	SA	S%	SAPG	GP	W	L	T	Mins	GA	SO	Avg	Eff	SA	S%	SAPG
1952-53	Shawinigan Cataracts	QMHL	2	0	2	0	120	5	0	2.50	....	....	....	....	....	....	....	....	....	....	....	....	....	....	....	....	....
1953-54	Montreal Royals	QJHL	21	....	....	....	1260	80	1	3.81	....	....	....	....	....	....	....	....	....	....	....	....	....	....	....	....	....
	Kitchener Greenshirts	OHA-Jr.	33	....	....	....	1980	122	2	3.70	....	....	....	....	....	....	....	....	....	....	....	....	....	....	....	....	....
1954-55	Montreal Jr. Canadiens	QJHL	46	24	21	1	2760	143	2	3.10	....	....	....	....	....	5	1	4	0	315	23	0	4.38	....	....	....	....
	Chicoutimi Sagueneens	QHL	3	1	2	0	180	10	0	3.33	....	....	....	....	....	....	....	....	....	....	....	....	....	....	....	....	....
1955-56	Montreal Royals	QHL	9	4	5	0	540	31	0	3.44	....	....	....	....	....	....	....	....	....	....	....	....	....	....	....	....	....
	Boston Bruins	**NHL**	**1**	**1**	**0**	**0**	**60**	**0**	**1**	**0.00**	**0.00**	....	....	....	....	....	....	....	....	....	....	....	....	....	....	....	....
	Chicoutimi Sagueneens	QHL	2	0	2	0	108	7	0	3.89	....	....	....	....	....	....	....	....	....	....	....	....	....	....	....	....	....
1956-57	Chicoutimi Sagueneens	QHL	1	1	0	0	60	1	0	1.00	....	....	....	....	....	....	....	....	....	....	....	....	....	....	....	....	....
	Montreal Royals	QHL	9	2	6	1	554	36	0	3.90	....	....	....	....	....	....	....	....	....	....	....	....	....	....	....	....	....
	Shawinigan Cataracts	QHL	11	4	7	0	662	37	1	3.35	....	....	....	....	....	....	....	....	....	....	....	....	....	....	....	....	....
	Edmonton Flyers	WHL	3	1	2	0	190	10	0	3.16	....	....	....	....	....	....	....	....	....	....	....	....	....	....	....	....	....
1957-58	Montreal Royals	QHL	16	6	9	1	960	66	1	4.13	....	....	....	....	....	1	1	0	0	46	1	0	1.30	....	....	....	....
	Shawinigan Cataracts	QHL	1	0	1	0	60	5	0	5.00	....	....	....	....	....	....	....	....	....	....	....	....	....	....	....	....	....
1958-59	Montreal Royals	QHL	37	18	14	5	2220	91	2	*2.46	....	....	....	....	....	6	*3	3	0	364	15	*1	*2.47	....	....	....	....
	Montreal Canadiens	**NHL**	**2**	**0**	**1**	**0**	**60**	**7**	**0**	**7.00**	**7.47**	....	....	....	....	....	....	....	....	....	....	....	....	....	....	....	....
1959-60	Calgary Stampeders	WHL	37	15	21	1	2220	125	0	3.37	....	....	....	....	....	....	....	....	....	....	....	....	....	....	....	....	....
1960-61	Montreal Royals	EPHL	27	....	....	....	1620	85	1	3.15	....	....	....	....	....	....	....	....	....	....	....	....	....	....	....	....	....
1961-62	North Bay Trappers	EPHL	4	1	3	0	240	16	0	4.00	....	....	....	....	....	....	....	....	....	....	....	....	....	....	....	....	....
1962-63	Hull-Ottawa Canadiens	EPHL	1	0	1	0	60	5	0	5.00	....	....	....	....	....	....	....	....	....	....	....	....	....	....	....	....	....
	NHL Totals		**3**	**1**	**1**	**0**	**120**	**7**	**1**	**3.50**	....	....	....	....	....	....	....	....	....	....	....	....	....	....	....	....	....

• Brother of Marcel and Jean • QHL First All-Star Team (1959) • Won Vezina Memorial Trophy (Top Goaltender - QHL) (1959)

Loaned to **Boston** by **Montreal** (Montreal Royals-QHL) to replace John Henderson, January 14, 1956. • Recorded shutout (2-0) in NHL debut vs. Montreal, January 14, 1956. Traded to **Chicago** by **Montreal** for cash, September 10, 1959.

			REGULAR SEASON													PLAYOFFS											
Season	Club	League	GP	W	L	T	Mins	GA	SO	Avg	AAvg	Eff	SA	S%	SAPG	GP	W	L	T	Mins	GA	SO	Avg	Eff	SA	S%	SAPG

• PUPPA, Daren

Daren James G – R. 6'4", 205 lbs. b: Kirkland Lake, Ont., 3/23/1965. Buffalo's 6th, 76th overall in 1983.

Season	Club	League	GP	W	L	T	Mins	GA	SO	Avg	AAvg	Eff	SA	S%	SAPG	GP	W	L	T	Mins	GA	SO	Avg	Eff	SA	S%	SAPG
1982-83	Kirkland Lake Intermediates	NOIHA	STATISTICS NOT AVAILABLE																								
1983-84	RPI Engineers	ECAC	32	24	6	0	1816	89	0	2.94	....	....	....	....	....	....	....	....	....	....	....	....	....	....	....	....	....
1984-85	RPI Engineers	ECAC	32	31	1	0	1830	78	0	2.56	....	....	....	....	....	....	....	....	....	....	....	....	....	....	....	....	....
1985-86	**Buffalo Sabres**	**NHL**	**7**	**3**	**4**	**0**	**401**	**21**	**1**	**3.14**	**2.45**	**3.58**	**184**	**.886**	**27.5**	....	....	....	....	....	....	....	....	....	....	....	....
	Rochester Americans	AHL	20	8	11	0	1092	79	0	4.34	....	....	....	....	....	....	....	....	....	....	....	....	....	....	....	....	....
1986-87	**Buffalo Sabres**	**NHL**	**3**	**0**	**2**	**1**	**185**	**13**	**0**	**4.22**	**3.57**	**6.86**	**80**	**.838**	**25.9**	....	....	....	....	....	....	....	....	....	....	....	....
	Rochester Americans	AHL	57	*33	14	0	3129	146	1	2.80	....	....	....	....	....	*16	*10	6	....	*944	48	*1	3.05	....	....	....	....
1987-88	**Buffalo Sabres**	**NHL**	**17**	**8**	**6**	**1**	**874**	**61**	**0**	**4.19**	**3.49**	**5.45**	**469**	**.870**	**32.2**	**3**	**1**	**1**	....	**142**	**11**	**0**	**4.65**	**7.63**	**67**	**.836**	**28.3**
	Rochester Americans	AHL	26	14	8	2	1415	65	2	2.76	....	....	....	....	....	2	0	1	....	108	5	0	2.78	....	....	....	....
1988-89	**Buffalo Sabres**	**NHL**	**37**	**17**	**10**	**6**	**1908**	**107**	**1**	**3.36**	**2.79**	**3.74**	**961**	**.889**	**30.2**	....	....	....	....	....	....	....	....	....	....	....	....
1989-90	**Buffalo Sabres**	**NHL**	**56**	***31**	**16**	**6**	**3241**	**156**	**1**	**2.89**	**2.43**	**2.80**	**1610**	**.903**	**29.8**	**6**	**2**	**4**	....	**370**	**15**	**0**	**2.43**	**1.90**	**192**	**.922**	**31.1**
1990-91	**Buffalo Sabres**	**NHL**	**38**	**15**	**11**	**6**	**2092**	**118**	**2**	**3.38**	**3.04**	**3.88**	**1029**	**.885**	**29.5**	**2**	**0**	**1**	....	**81**	**10**	**0**	**7.41**	**16.11**	**46**	**.783**	**34.1**
1991-92	**Buffalo Sabres**	**NHL**	**33**	**11**	**14**	**4**	**1757**	**114**	**0**	**3.89**	**3.49**	**4.76**	**932**	**.878**	**31.8**	....	....	....	....	....	....	....	....	....	....	....	....
	Rochester Americans	AHL	2	0	2	0	119	9	0	4.54	....	....	....	....	....	....	....	....	....	....	....	....	....	....	....	....	....
1992-93	**Buffalo Sabres**	**NHL**	**24**	**11**	**5**	**4**	**1306**	**78**	**0**	**3.58**	**3.07**	**3.96**	**706**	**.890**	**32.4**	....	....	....	....	....	....	....	....	....	....	....	....
	Toronto Maple Leafs	**NHL**	**8**	**6**	**2**	**0**	**479**	**18**	**2**	**2.25**	**1.92**	**1.75**	**232**	**.922**	**29.1**	**1**	**0**	**0**	....	**20**	**1**	**0**	**3.00**	**4.29**	**7**	**.857**	**21.0**
1993-94	**Tampa Bay Lightning**	**NHL**	**63**	**22**	**33**	**6**	**3653**	**165**	**4**	**2.71**	**2.59**	**2.73**	**1637**	**.899**	**26.9**	....	....	....	....	....	....	....	....	....	....	....	....
1994-95	**Tampa Bay Lightning**	**NHL**	**36**	**14**	**19**	**2**	**2013**	**90**	**1**	**2.68**	**2.80**	**2.55**	**946**	**.905**	**28.2**	....	....	....	....	....	....	....	....	....	....	....	....
1995-96	**Tampa Bay Lightning**	**NHL**	**57**	**29**	**16**	**9**	**3189**	**131**	**5**	**2.46**	**2.43**	**2.01**	**1605**	**.918**	**30.2**	**4**	**1**	**3**	....	**173**	**14**	**0**	**4.86**	**7.91**	**86**	**.837**	**29.8**
1996-97	**Tampa Bay Lightning**	**NHL**	**6**	**1**	**1**	**2**	**325**	**14**	**0**	**2.58**	**2.78**	**2.41**	**150**	**.907**	**27.7**	....	....	....	....	....	....	....	....	....	....	....	....
	Adirondack Red Wings	AHL	1	1	0	0	62	3	0	2.90	....	....	....	....	....	....	....	....	....	....	....	....	....	....	....	....	....
1997-98	**Tampa Bay Lightning**	**NHL**	**26**	**5**	**14**	**6**	**1456**	**66**	**0**	**2.72**	**3.25**	**2.72**	**660**	**.900**	**27.2**	....	....	....	....	....	....	....	....	....	....	....	....
1998-99	**Tampa Bay Lightning**	**NHL**	**13**	**5**	**6**	**1**	**691**	**33**	**2**	**2.87**	**3.41**	**2.71**	**350**	**.906**	**30.4**	....	....	....	....	....	....	....	....	....	....	....	....
99-2000	**Tampa Bay Lightning**	**NHL**	**5**	**1**	**2**	**0**	**249**	**19**	**0**	**4.58**	**5.24**	**6.75**	**129**	**.853**	**31.1**	....	....	....	....	....	....	....	....	....	....	....	....
	NHL Totals		**429**	**179**	**161**	**54**	**23819**	**1204**	**19**	**3.03**	....	....	**11680**	**.897**	**29.4**	**16**	**4**	**9**	....	**786**	**51**	**0**	**3.89**	....	**398**	**.872**	**30.4**

AHL First All-Star Team (1987) • NHL Second All-Star Team (1990) • Played in NHL All-Star Game (1990)

• Recorded shutout (2-0) in NHL debut vs. Edmonton, November 1, 1985. Traded to **Toronto** by **Buffalo** with Dave Andreychuk and Buffalo's 1st round choice (Kenny Jonsson) in 1993 Entry Draft for Grant Fuhr and Toronto's 5th round choice (Kevin Popp) in 1995 Entry Draft, February 2, 1993. Claimed by **Florida** from **Toronto** in Expansion Draft, June 24, 1993. Claimed by **Tampa Bay** from **Florida** in Phase II of Expansion Draft, June 25, 1993. • Missed majority of 1996-97 season recovering from groin injury suffered in training camp, September, 1997. • Missed majority of 1997-98 and 1998-99 seasons recovering from back injury suffered in game vs. Boston on December 27, 1997.

• PUSEY, Chris

G – L. 6', 180 lbs. b: Brantford, Ont., 6/30/1965. Detroit's 7th, 109th overall in 1983.

Season	Club	League	GP	W	L	T	Mins	GA	SO	Avg	AAvg	Eff	SA	S%	SAPG	GP	W	L	T	Mins	GA	SO	Avg	Eff	SA	S%	SAPG
1981-82	Orillia Terriers	OJHL	33	....	....	....	1617	179	0	6.44	....	....	....	....	....	....	....	....	....	....	....	....	....	....	....	....	....
1982-83	London Knights	OHL	1	0	1	0	60	7	0	7.00	....	....	....	....	....	....	....	....	....	....	....	....	....	....	....	....	....
	Brantford Alexanders	OHL	20	5	11	0	991	85	0	5.15	....	....	....	....	....	....	....	....	....	....	....	....	....	....	....	....	....
1983-84	Brantford Alexanders	OHL	50	26	18	2	2858	158	2	3.32	....	....	....	....	....	5	0	1	0	300	17	0	3.40	....	....	....	....
1984-85	Hamilton Steelhawks	OHL	49	17	19	2	2450	179	1	4.38	....	....	....	....	....	15	7	6	0	824	73	0	5.32	....	....	....	....
1985-86	**Detroit Red Wings**	**NHL**	**1**	**0**	**0**	**0**	**40**	**3**	**0**	**4.50**	**3.51**	**11.25**	**12**	**.750**	**18.0**	....	....	....	....	....	....	....	....	....	....	....	....
	Adirondack Red Wings	AHL	22	7	12	1	1171	76	1	3.89	....	....	....	....	....	1	0	0	0	27	4	0	8.89	....	....	....	....
1986-87	Adirondack Red Wings	AHL	11	4	5	0	617	40	0	3.89	....	....	....	....	....	....	....	....	....	....	....	....	....	....	....	....	....
	Indianapolis Checkers	IHL	6	1	4	0	330	36	0	6.55	....	....	....	....	....	....	....	....	....	....	....	....	....	....	....	....	....
	Carolina Thunderbirds	ACHL	4	....	....	....	238	20	0	5.04	....	....	....	....	....	....	....	....	....	....	....	....	....	....	....	....	....
1987-88	Dundas Real McCoys	OHA-Sr.	STATISTICS NOT AVAILABLE																								
1988-89	Saint John Vitos	NBSHL	18	....	....	....	824	48	*1	*3.49	....	....	....	....	....	5	....	....	....	320	20	0	3.75	....	....	....	....
1989-90	Winston-Salem Thunderbirds	ECHL	3	2	1	0	180	13	0	4.33	....	....	....	....	....	....	....	....	....	....	....	....	....	....	....	....	....
1990-91			DID NOT PLAY																								
1991-92	Brantford Smoke	ColHL	2	0	2	0	100	11	0	6.60	....	....	....	....	....	....	....	....	....	....	....	....	....	....	....	....	....
	NHL Totals		**1**	**0**	**0**	**0**	**40**	**3**	**0**	**4.50**	....	....	**12**	**.750**	**18.0**	....	....	....	....	....	....	....	....	....	....	....	....

OHL Second All-Star Team (1984)

• RACICOT, Andre

"Red Light" G – L. 5'11", 165 lbs. b: Rouyn-Noranda, Que., 6/9/1969. Montreal's 6th, 83rd overall in 1989.

Season	Club	League	GP	W	L	T	Mins	GA	SO	Avg	AAvg	Eff	SA	S%	SAPG	GP	W	L	T	Mins	GA	SO	Avg	Eff	SA	S%	SAPG
1985-86	Rouyn Aces	NOJHA	16	....	....	....	924	62	0	4.03	....	....	....	....	....	....	....	....	....	....	....	....	....	....	....	....	....
1986-87	Longueuil Chevaliers	QMJHL	3	1	2	0	180	19	0	6.33	....	....	....	....	....	....	....	....	....	....	....	....	....	....	....	....	....
1987-88	Victoriaville Tigers	QMJHL	8	....	....	....	469	28	1	3.44	....	....	....	....	....	....	....	....	....	....	....	....	....	....	....	....	....
	Hull Olympiques	QMJHL	14	....	....	....	668	43	0	3.86	....	....	....	....	....	....	....	....	....	....	....	....	....	....	....	....	....
	Granby Bisons	QMJHL	8	....	....	....	390	34	0	5.23	....	....	....	....	....	5	1	4	....	298	23	0	4.63	....	....	....	....
1988-89	Granby Bisons	QMJHL	54	22	24	3	2944	198	0	4.04	....	....	....	....	....	4	0	4	....	218	18	0	4.95	....	....	....	....
1989-90	**Montreal Canadiens**	**NHL**	**1**	**0**	**0**	**0**	**13**	**3**	**0**	**13.85**	**11.74**	**69.25**	**6**	**.500**	**27.7**	....	....	....	....	....	....	....	....	....	....	....	....
	Sherbrooke Canadiens	AHL	33	19	11	2	1948	97	1	2.99	....	....	....	....	....	5	0	4	....	227	18	0	4.76	....	....	....	....
1990-91	Montreal Canadiens	Fr-Tour	2	0	1	0	56	5	0	5.35	....	....	....	....	....	....	....	....	....	....	....	....	....	....	....	....	....
	Montreal Canadiens	**NHL**	**21**	**7**	**9**	**2**	**975**	**52**	**1**	**3.20**	**2.87**	**3.47**	**479**	**.891**	**29.5**	**2**	**0**	**1**	....	**12**	**2**	**0**	**10.00**	**14.29**	**14**	**.857**	**70.0**
	Fredericton Canadiens	AHL	22	13	8	1	1252	60	1	2.88	....	....	....	....	....	....	....	....	....	....	....	....	....	....	....	....	....
1991-92	**Montreal Canadiens**	**NHL**	**9**	**0**	**3**	**3**	**436**	**23**	**0**	**3.17**	**2.84**	**3.33**	**219**	**.895**	**30.1**	**1**	**0**	**0**	....	**1**	**0**	**0**	**0.00**	**0.00**	**1**	**1.000**	**60.0**
	Fredericton Canadiens	AHL	28	14	8	5	1666	86	0	3.10	....	....	....	....	....	....	....	....	....	....	....	....	....	....	....	....	....
1992-93♦	**Montreal Canadiens**	**NHL**	**26**	**17**	**5**	**1**	**1433**	**81**	**1**	**3.39**	**2.90**	**4.03**	**682**	**.881**	**28.6**	**1**	**0**	**0**	....	**18**	**2**	**0**	**6.67**	**14.82**	**9**	**.778**	**30.0**
1993-94	**Montreal Canadiens**	**NHL**	**11**	**2**	**6**	**2**	**500**	**37**	**0**	**4.44**	**4.27**	**6.68**	**246**	**.850**	**29.5**	....	....	....	....	....	....	....	....	....	....	....	....
	Fredericton Canadiens	AHL	6	1	4	0	292	16	0	3.28	....	....	....	....	....	....	....	....	....	....	....	....	....	....	....	....	....
1994-95	Portland Pirates	AHL	19	10	7	0	1080	53	1	2.94	....	....	....	....	....	....	....	....	....	....	....	....	....	....	....	....	....
	Phoenix Roadrunners	IHL	3	1	0	0	132	8	0	3.62	....	....	....	....	....	2	0	0	....	20	0	0	0.00	....	....	....	....
1995-96	Albany River Rats	AHL	2	2	0	0	120	4	0	2.00	....	....	....	....	....	....	....	....	....	....	....	....	....	....	....	....	....
	Columbus Chill	ECHL	1	1	0	0	60	2	0	2.00	....	....	....	....	....	....	....	....	....	....	....	....	....	....	....	....	....
	Indianapolis Ice	IHL	11	3	6	0	547	43	0	4.71	....	....	....	....	....	....	....	....	....	....	....	....	....	....	....	....	....
	Peoria Rivermen	IHL	4	2	1	1	240	14	0	3.50	....	....	....	....	....	11	6	5	....	654	34	1	3.12	....	....	....	....
1996-97	Indianapolis Ice	IHL	2	1	0	1	120	3	1	1.50	....	....	....	....	....	....	....	....	....	....	....	....	....	....	....	....	....
	Kansas City Blades	IHL	6	1	4	0	273	21	0	4.60	....	....	....	....	....	....	....	....	....	....	....	....	....	....	....	....	....
	Las Vegas Thunder	IHL	13	6	5	1	759	40	1	3.16	....	....	....	....	....	....	....	....	....	....	....	....	....	....	....	....	....
1997-98	Monroe Moccasins	WPHL	31	16	12	2	1789	80	1	*2.68	....	....	....	....	....	....	....	....	....	....	....	....	....	....	....	....	....
	Basingstoke Bison	Britain	3	....	....	....	186	11	....	3.55	....	....	....	....	....	5	0	5	0	303	21	0	4.16	....	....	....	....
1998-99	Monroe Moccasins	WPHL	48	25	18	5	2806	148	1	3.16	....	....	....	....	....	6	2	4	....	380	21	*1	3.32	....	....	....	....
99-2000	Neftekhimik Nizhnekamsk	Russia	20	....	....	....	1133	49	1	2.59	....	....	....	....	....	4	....	....	....	240	16	0	4.00	....	....	....	....
	NHL Totals		**68**	**26**	**23**	**8**	**3357**	**196**	**2**	**3.50**	....	....	**1632**	**.880**	**29.2**	**4**	**0**	**1**	....	**31**	**4**	**0**	**7.74**	....	**24**	**.833**	**46.5**

QMJHL Second All-Star Team (1989) • Shared Harry "Hap" Holmes Trophy (fewest goals against - AHL) with J.C. Bergeron (1990)

Signed as a free agent by **Los Angeles**, September 22, 1994. Signed as a free agent by **Chicago**, August 25, 1995.

• RACINE, Bruce

Bruce M. G – L. 6', 170 lbs. b: Cornwall, Ont., 8/9/1966. Pittsburgh's 3rd, 58th overall in 1985.

Season	Club	League	GP	W	L	T	Mins	GA	SO	Avg	AAvg	Eff	SA	S%	SAPG	GP	W	L	T	Mins	GA	SO	Avg	Eff	SA	S%	SAPG
1983-84	Hawkesbury Hawks	OJHL	30	....	....	....	1543	121	0	4.70	....	....	....	....	....	....	....	....	....	....	....	....	....	....	....	....	....
1984-85	Northeastern University	H-East	26	11	14	1	1615	103	1	3.83	....	....	....	....	....	....	....	....	....	....	....	....	....	....	....	....	....
1985-86	Northeastern University	H-East	32	17	14	1	1920	147	0	4.56	....	....	....	....	....	....	....	....	....	....	....	....	....	....	....	....	....
1986-87	Northeastern University	H-East	33	12	18	3	1966	133	0	4.06	....	....	....	....	....	....	....	....	....	....	....	....	....	....	....	....	....
1987-88	Northeastern University	H-East	30	15	11	4	1808	108	1	3.58	....	....	....	....	....	....	....	....	....	....	....	....	....	....	....	....	....
1988-89	Muskegon Lumberjacks	IHL	51	*37	11	0	*3039	184	*3	3.63	....	....	....	....	....	5	4	1	....	300	15	0	3.00	....	....	....	....
1989-90	Muskegon Lumberjacks	IHL	49	29	15	4	2911	182	1	3.75	....	....	....	....	....	9	5	4	....	566	32	1	3.34	....	....	....	....
1990-91	Albany Choppers	IHL	29	7	18	1	1567	104	0	3.98	....	....	....	....	....	....	....	....	....	....	....	....	....	....	....	....	....
	Muskegon Lumberjacks	IHL	9	4	4	1	516	40	0	4.65	....	....	....	....	....	....	....	....	....	....	....	....	....	....	....	....	....
1991-92	Muskegon Lumberjacks	IHL	27	13	10	3	1559	91	1	3.50	....	....	....	....	....	1	0	1	....	60	6	0	6.00	....	....	....	....
1992-93	Cleveland Lumberjacks	IHL	35	13	16	6	1949	140	1	4.31	....	....	....	....	....	2	0	0	....	37	2	0	3.24	....	....	....	....
1993-94	St. John's Maple Leafs	AHL	37	20	9	2	1875	116	0	3.71	....	....	....	....	....	1	0	0	....	20	1	0	0.00	....	....	....	....

Season	Club	League	GP	W	L	T	Mins	GA	SO	Avg	AAvg	Eff	SA	S%	SAPG	GP	W	L	T	Mins	GA	SO	Avg	Eff	SA	S%	SAPG
			REGULAR SEASON													PLAYOFFS											
1994-95	St. John's Maple Leafs	AHL	27	11	10	4	1492	85	1	3.42						2	1	1		119	3	0	1.51				
1995-96	**St. Louis Blues**	**NHL**	**11**	**0**	**3**	**0**	**230**	**12**	**0**	**3.13**	**3.11**	**3.72**	**101**	**.881**	**26.3**	**1**	**0**	**0**		**1**	**0**	**0**	**0.00**	**0.00**	**0**	**.000**	**0.0**
	Peoria Rivermen	IHL	22	11	10	1	1228	69	1	3.37						1	0	1		59	3	0	3.05				
1996-97	San Antonio Dragons	IHL	44	25	14	2	2426	122	6	3.02						6	3	2		325	17	0	3.13				
1997-98	San Antonio Dragons	IHL	*15	*4	9	1	*836	51	0	3.66																	
	Fort Wayne Komets	IHL	*45	*30	10	4	*2605	109	1	2.51						3	1	2		152	10	0	3.95				
1998-99	Fort Wayne Komets	IHL	53	21	18	11	3024	154	1	3.06						1	0	1		60	5	0	5.00				
99-2000	Kansas City Blades	IHL	33	12	17	1	1765	84	1	2.86																	
	NHL Totals		**11**	**0**	**3**	**0**	**230**	**12**	**0**	**3.13**			**101**	**.881**	**26.3**	**1**	**0**	**0**		**1**	**0**	**0**	**0.00**		**0**		**0.0**

Hockey East Second All-Star Team (1985) • Hockey East First All-Star Team (1987) • NCAA East First All-American Team (1987, 1988) • IHL First All-Star Team (1998)

Signed as a free agent by **Toronto**, August 11, 1993. Signed as a free agent by **St. Louis**, August 10, 1995. Signed as a free agent by **San Jose**, September 8, 1998. Signed as a free agent by **Kansas City** (IHL), July 13, 1999.

• RAM, Jamie

G – L. 5'11", 175 lbs. b: Scarborough, Ont., 1/18/1971. NY Rangers' 9th, 213th overall in 1991.

Season	Club	League	GP	W	L	T	Mins	GA	SO	Avg	AAvg	Eff	SA	S%	SAPG	GP	W	L	T	Mins	GA	SO	Avg	Eff	SA	S%	SAPG
1988-89	Henry Carr Crusaders	OJHL-B	24	11	8	2	1200	82	*1	4.10																	
1989-90	Henry Carr Crusaders	OJHL-B	23	14	5	2	1302	63	1	2.90																	
1990-91	Michigan Tech Huskies	WCHA	14	5	9	0	826	57	0	4.14																	
1991-92	Michigan Tech Huskies	WCHA	23	9	9	1	1144	83	0	4.35																	
1992-93	Michigan Tech Huskies	WCHA	*36	16	14	5	*2078	115	0	3.32																	
1993-94	Michigan Tech Huskies	WCHA	39	12	20	5	2192	117	*1	3.20																	
1994-95	Binghamton Rangers	AHL	26	12	10	2	1472	81	1	3.30						11	6	5		663	29	1	2.62				
1995-96	**New York Rangers**	**NHL**	**1**	**0**	**0**	**0**	**27**	**0**	**0**	**0.00**	**0.00**	**0.00**	**9**	**1.000**	**20.0**												
	Binghamton Rangers	AHL	40	18	16	3	2262	151	1	4.01						1	0	0		34	1	0	1.75				
1996-97	Kentucky Thoroughblades	AHL	50	25	19	5	2937	161	4	3.29						1	0	1		60	3	0	3.00				
1997-98	Kentucky Thoroughblades	AHL	44	17	18	5	2553	124	3	2.91																	
	Utah Grizzlies	IHL	7	3	4	0	398	24	0	3.61						1	0	1		59	3	0	3.04				
1998-99	Cincinnati Mighty Ducks	AHL	35	14	19	1	1916	109	2	3.41																	
99-2000	Canada	Nat-Team	32	14	12	4	1759	80	0	2.73																	
	Canada	WC-A	DID NOT PLAY – SPARE GOALTENDER																								
	NHL Totals		**1**	**0**	**0**	**0**	**27**	**0**	**0**	**0.00**			**9**	**1.000**	**20.0**												

WCHA First All-Star Team (1993, 1994) • NCAA West First All-American Team (1993, 1994)

Signed as a free agent by **San Jose**, August 19, 1997. Signed as a free agent by **Anaheim**, July 30, 1998.

• RANFORD, Bill

William Edward G – L. 5'11", 185 lbs. b: Brandon, Man., 12/14/1966. Boston's 2nd, 52nd overall in 1985.

Season	Club	League	GP	W	L	T	Mins	GA	SO	Avg	AAvg	Eff	SA	S%	SAPG	GP	W	L	T	Mins	GA	SO	Avg	Eff	SA	S%	SAPG
1982-83	Red Deer Chiefs	AAHA	STATISTICS NOT AVAILABLE																								
1983-84	New Westminster Bruins	WHL	27	10	14	0	1450	130	0	5.38						1	0	0		27	2	0	4.44				
1984-85	New Westminster Bruins	WHL	38	19	17	0	2034	142	0	4.19						7	2	3		309	26	0	5.05				
1985-86	New Westminster Bruins	WHL	53	17	29	1	2791	225	1	4.84																	
	Boston Bruins	**NHL**	**4**	**3**	**1**	**0**	**240**	**10**	**0**	**2.50**	**1.95**	**2.36**	**106**	**.906**	**26.5**	**2**	**0**	**2**		**120**	**7**	**0**	**3.50**	**5.57**	**44**	**.841**	**22.0**
1986-87	**Boston Bruins**	**NHL**	**41**	**16**	**20**	**2**	**2234**	**124**	**3**	**3.33**	**2.81**	**3.63**	**1137**	**.891**	**30.5**	**2**	**0**	**2**		**123**	**8**	**0**	**3.90**	**5.67**	**55**	**.855**	**26.8**
	Moncton Golden Flames	AHL	3	3	0	0	180	6	0	2.00																	
1987-88	Maine Mariners	AHL	51	27	16	6	2856	165	1	3.47																	
♦	**Edmonton Oilers**	**NHL**	**6**	**3**	**0**	**2**	**325**	**16**	**0**	**2.95**	**2.46**	**2.97**	**159**	**.899**	**29.4**												
1988-89	**Edmonton Oilers**	**NHL**	**29**	**15**	**8**	**2**	**1509**	**88**	**1**	**3.50**	**2.91**	**4.29**	**718**	**.877**	**28.5**												
1989-90♦	**Edmonton Oilers**	**NHL**	**56**	**24**	**16**	**9**	**3107**	**165**	**1**	**3.19**	**2.69**	**3.60**	**1463**	**.887**	**28.3**	***22**	***16**	**6**		***1401**	**59**	**1**	**2.53**	**2.22**	**672**	**.912**	**28.8**
1990-91	**Edmonton Oilers**	**NHL**	**60**	**27**	**27**	**3**	**3415**	**182**	**0**	**3.20**	**2.87**	**3.42**	**1705**	**.893**	**30.0**	**3**	**1**	**2**		**135**	**8**	**0**	**3.56**	**3.65**	**78**	**.897**	**34.7**
1991-92	Canada	Can-Cup	8	6	0	2	480	14		2.00																	
	Edmonton Oilers	**NHL**	**67**	**27**	**26**	**10**	**3822**	**228**	**1**	**3.58**	**3.21**	**4.14**	**1971**	**.884**	**30.9**	**16**	**8**	**8**		**909**	**51**	***2**	**3.37**	**3.55**	**484**	**.895**	**31.9**
1992-93	**Edmonton Oilers**	**NHL**	**67**	**17**	**38**	**6**	**3753**	**240**	**1**	**3.84**	**3.30**	**4.46**	**2065**	**.884**	**33.0**												
	Canada	WC-A	6	5	1	0	354	11	*2	1.86																	
1993-94	**Edmonton Oilers**	**NHL**	**71**	**22**	**34**	**11**	**4070**	**236**	**1**	**3.48**	**3.35**	**3.53**	**2325**	**.898**	**34.3**												
	Canada	WC-A	6	*6	0	0	360	7	1	1.17																	
1994-95	**Edmonton Oilers**	**NHL**	**40**	**15**	**20**	**3**	**2203**	**133**	**2**	**3.62**	**3.82**	**4.25**	**1134**	**.883**	**30.9**												
1995-96	**Edmonton Oilers**	**NHL**	**37**	**13**	**18**	**5**	**2015**	**128**	**1**	**3.81**	**3.80**	**4.76**	**1024**	**.875**	**30.5**												
	Boston Bruins	**NHL**	**40**	**21**	**12**	**4**	**2307**	**109**	**1**	**2.83**	**2.81**	**2.99**	**1030**	**.894**	**26.8**	**4**	**1**	**3**		**239**	**16**	**0**	**4.02**	**5.74**	**112**	**.857**	**28.1**
1996-97	Canada	W-Cup	DID NOT PLAY – SPARE GOALTENDER																								
	Boston Bruins	**NHL**	**37**	**12**	**16**	**8**	**2147**	**125**	**2**	**3.49**	**3.77**	**3.96**	**1102**	**.887**	**30.8**												
	Washington Capitals	**NHL**	**18**	**8**	**7**	**2**	**1009**	**46**	**0**	**2.74**	**2.95**	**3.06**	**412**	**.888**	**24.5**												
1997-98	**Washington Capitals**	**NHL**	**22**	**7**	**12**	**2**	**1183**	**55**	**0**	**2.79**	**3.33**	**2.76**	**555**	**.901**	**28.1**												
1998-99	**Tampa Bay Lightning**	**NHL**	**32**	**3**	**18**	**3**	**1568**	**102**	**1**	**3.90**	**4.67**	**4.64**	**858**	**.881**	**32.8**												
	Detroit Red Wings	**NHL**	**4**	**3**	**0**	**1**	**244**	**8**	**0**	**1.97**	**2.34**	**1.61**	**98**	**.918**	**24.1**	**4**	**2**	**2**		**183**	**10**	**1**	**3.28**	**3.12**	**105**	**.905**	**34.4**
99-2000	**Edmonton Oilers**	**NHL**	**16**	**4**	**6**	**3**	**785**	**47**	**0**	**3.59**	**4.11**	**4.15**	**407**	**.885**	**31.1**												
	NHL Totals		**647**	**240**	**279**	**76**	**35936**	**2042**	**15**	**3.41**			**18269**	**.888**	**30.5**	**53**	**28**	**25**		**3110**	**159**	**4**	**3.07**		**1550**	**.897**	**29.9**

WHL West Second All-Star Team (1986) • Won Conn Smythe Trophy (1990) • Canada Cup All-Star Team (1991) • WC-A All-Star Team (1994) • Named Best Goaltender at WC-A (1994) • Played in NHL All-Star Game (1991)

Traded to **Edmonton** by **Boston** with Geoff Courtnall and Boston's 2nd round choice (Petro Koivunen) in 1988 Entry Draft for Andy Moog, March 8, 1988. Traded to **Boston** by **Edmonton** for Mariusz Czerkawski, Sean Brown and Boston's 1st round choice (Matthieu Descoteaux) in 1996 Entry Draft, January 11, 1996. Traded to **Washington** by **Boston** with Adam Oates and Rick Tocchet for Jim Carey, Anson Carter, Jason Allison and Washington's 3rd round choice (Lee Goren) in 1997 Entry Draft, March 1, 1997. Traded to **Tampa Bay** by **Washington** for Tampa Bay's 3rd round choice (Todd Hornung) in 1998 Entry Draft and 2nd round choice (Michal Sivek) in 1999 Entry Draft, June 18, 1998. Traded to **Detroit** by **Tampa Bay** for future considerations, March 23, 1999. Signed as a free agent by **Edmonton**, August 4, 1999.

• RAYMOND, Alain

G – L. 5'10", 180 lbs. b: Rimouski, Que., 6/24/1965. Washington's 7th, 224th overall in 1983.

Season	Club	League	GP	W	L	T	Mins	GA	SO	Avg	AAvg	Eff	SA	S%	SAPG	GP	W	L	T	Mins	GA	SO	Avg	Eff	SA	S%	SAPG
1980-81	Montreal L'est Cantonniers	QAAA	16	7	7	2	960	83	0	5.16																	
1981-82	Montreal L'est Cantonniers	QAAA	19	13	4	2	1140	97	0	5.14						8				365	21	0	3.45				
1982-83	Hull Olympiques	QMJHL	17	....	....	....	809	80	0	5.93																	
	Trois Rivieres Draveurs	QMJHL	22	....	....	....	1176	124	0	6.33						2				120	12	0	6.00				
1983-84	Trois Rivieres Draveurs	QMJHL	53	18	25	0	2725	223	*2	4.91																	
1984-85	Trois Rivieres Draveurs	QMJHL	58	29	26	1	3295	220	*2	4.01						7	3	4	0	438	32	0	4.38				
1985-86	Canada	Nat-Team	46	25	18	3	2571	151	4	3.52																	
1986-87	Fort Wayne Komets	IHL	45	23	16	0	2433	134	1	*3.30						6	2	3	0	320	23	0	4.31				
1987-88	**Washington Capitals**	**NHL**	**1**	**0**	**1**	**0**	**40**	**2**	**0**	**3.00**	**2.50**	**3.00**	**20**	**.900**	**30.0**												
	Fort Wayne Komets	IHL	40	20	15	3	2271	142	2	3.75						2	0	1	0	67	7	0	6.27				
1988-89	Baltimore Skipjacks	AHL	41	14	22	2	2301	162	0	4.22																	
1989-90	Baltimore Skipjacks	AHL	11	4	5	2	612	34	0	3.33																	
	Hampton Roads Admirals	ECHL	31	17	12	1	2048	123	0	3.60						5	2	3	0	302	24	0	4.77				
1990-91	Peoria Rivermen	IHL	5	1	3	1	304	22	0	4.34																	
	Nashville Knights	ECHL	43	21	18	3	2508	189	1	4.52																	
1991-92	Peoria Rivermen	IHL	6	1	3	2	370	27	0	4.38																	
	NHL Totals		**1**	**0**	**1**	**0**	**40**	**2**	**0**	**3.00**			**20**	**.900**	**30.0**												

QMJHL First All-Star Team (1984) • QMJHL Second All-Star Team (1985) • Shared James Norris Memorial Trophy (fewest goals against - IHL) with Michel Dufour (1987) • ECHL First All-Star Team (1990)

Signed as a free agent by **St. Louis**, September 12, 1990.

• RAYNER, Chuck
Claude Earl "Bonnie Prince Charlie" G – L. 5'11", 190 lbs. b: Sutherland, Sask., 8/11/1920. **HHOF**

			REGULAR SEASON													PLAYOFFS											
Season	Club	League	GP	W	L	T	Mins	GA	SO	Avg	AAvg	Eff	SA	S%	SAPG	GP	W	L	T	Mins	GA	SO	Avg	Eff	SA	S%	SAPG
1936-37	Saskatoon Wesleys	N-SJHL	....	....	....	....	....	....	....	....	....	....	....	....	....	3	*3	0	0	180	4	0	*1.33	....	....	....	....
	Saskatoon Wesleys	Mem-Cup	9	7	2	0	550	20	2	2.18	....	....	....	....	....	....	....	....	....	....	....	....	....	....	....	....	....
1937-38	Kenora Thistles	MJHL	22	....	....	....	1350	103	0	4.58	....	....	....	....	....	....	....	....	....	....	....	....	....	....	....	....	....
1938-39	Kenora Thistles	MJHL	22	....	....	....	1350	64	0	2.84	....	....	....	....	....	....	....	....	....	....	....	....	....	....	....	....	....
1939-40	Kenora Thistles	MJHL	24	*15	5	4	1480	66	*1	2.68	....	....	....	....	....	9	....	....	....	540	18	0	*2.00	....	....	....	....
1940-41	**New York Americans**	**NHL**	**12**	**2**	**7**	**3**	**773**	**44**	**0**	**3.42**	**3.93**	....	....	....	....	....	....	....	....	....	....	....	....	....	....	....	....
	Springfield Indians	AHL	37	17	13	6	2280	87	*6	*2.29	....	....	....	....	....	....	....	....	....	....	....	....	....	....	....	....	....
1941-42	**Brooklyn Americans**	**NHL**	**36**	**13**	**21**	**2**	**2230**	**129**	**1**	**3.47**	**3.44**	....	....	....	....	....	....	....	....	....	....	....	....	....	....	....	....
	Springfield Indians	AHL	1	1	0	0	60	4	0	4.00	....	....	....	....	....	....	....	....	....	....	....	....	....	....	....	....	....
1942-43	Victoria Navy	NNDHL	12	....	....	....	720	39	*1	*3.25	....	....	....	....	....	6	2	4	0	370	29	0	4.70	....	....	....	....
1943-44	Victoria Navy	PCHL	18	....	....	....	1080	52	*1	*2.89	....	....	....	....	....	2	1	1	0	130	6	0	2.77	....	....	....	....
	Halifax RCAF	HCHL	STATISTICS NOT AVAILABLE																								
	Halifax RCAF	Al-Cup	2	1	1	0	130	6	0	2.77	....	....	....	....	....	....	....	....	....	....	....	....	....	....	....	....	....
1944-45			MILITARY SERVICE																								
1945-46	**New York Rangers**	**NHL**	**40**	**12**	**21**	**7**	**2377**	**149**	**1**	**3.76**	**3.49**	....	....	....	....	....	....	....	....	....	....	....	....	....	....	....	....
1946-47	**New York Rangers**	**NHL**	**58**	**22**	**30**	**6**	**3480**	**177**	***5**	**3.05**	**2.92**	....	....	....	....	....	....	....	....	....	....	....	....	....	....	....	....
1947-48	**New York Rangers**	**NHL**	**12**	**4**	**7**	**0**	**691**	**42**	**0**	**3.65**	**3.83**	....	....	....	....	**6**	**2**	**4**	....	**360**	**17**	**0**	**2.83**	....	....	....	....
	New Haven Ramblers	AHL	15	7	6	2	900	40	0	2.67	....	....	....	....	....	....	....	....	....	....	....	....	....	....	....	....	....
1948-49	**New York Rangers**	**NHL**	**58**	**16**	**31**	**11**	**3480**	**168**	**7**	**2.90**	**3.29**	....	....	....	....	....	....	....	....	....	....	....	....	....	....	....	....
1949-50	**New York Rangers**	**NHL**	**69**	**28**	**30**	**11**	**4140**	**181**	**6**	**2.62**	**2.90**	....	....	....	....	**12**	**7**	**5**	....	**775**	**29**	**1**	**2.25**	....	....	....	....
1950-51	**New York Rangers**	**NHL**	**66**	**19**	**28**	**19**	**3940**	**187**	**2**	**2.85**	**3.23**	....	....	....	....	....	....	....	....	....	....	....	....	....	....	....	....
1951-52	**New York Rangers**	**NHL**	**53**	**18**	**25**	**10**	**3180**	**159**	**2**	**3.00**	**3.60**	....	....	....	....	....	....	....	....	....	....	....	....	....	....	....	....
1952-53	**New York Rangers**	**NHL**	**20**	**4**	**8**	**8**	**1200**	**58**	**1**	**2.90**	**3.73**	....	....	....	....	....	....	....	....	....	....	....	....	....	....	....	....
1953-54	Saskatoon Quakers	WHL	68	31	28	9	4045	204	6	3.03	....	....	....	....	....	6	2	4	0	360	23	1	3.83	....	....	....	....
1954-55	Nelson Maple Leafs	WIHL	2	....	....	....	120	4	0	2.00	....	....	....	....	....	1	1	0	0	60	2	0	2.00	....	....	....	....
1955-56	Nelson Maple Leafs	WIHL	6	....	....	....	360	18	0	3.00	....	....	....	....	....	....	....	....	....	....	....	....	....	....	....	....	....
	NHL Totals		**424**	**138**	**208**	**77**	**25491**	**1294**	**25**	**3.05**	....	....	....	....	....	**18**	**9**	**9**	....	**1135**	**46**	**1**	**2.43**	....	....	....	....

AHL Second All-Star Team (1941) • NHL Second All-Star Team (1949, 1950, 1951) • Won Hart Trophy (1950) • Played in NHL All-Star Game (1949, 1950, 1951)

Signed as a free agent by **NY Americans**, October 11, 1939. Signed as a free agent by **NY Rangers** after **Brooklyn** franchise folded, 1945. Signed as a free agent by **Saskatoon** (WHL), September 25, 1953.

• REAUGH, Daryl
Daryl K. G – L. 6'4", 200 lbs. b: Prince George, B.C., 2/13/1965. Edmonton's 2nd, 42nd overall in 1984.

Season	Club	League	GP	W	L	T	Mins	GA	SO	Avg	AAvg	Eff	SA	S%	SAPG	GP	W	L	T	Mins	GA	SO	Avg	Eff	SA	S%	SAPG
1982-83	Cowichan Valley Capitals	BCJHL	32	....	....	....	1673	191	0	5.96	....	....	....	....	....	....	....	....	....	....	....	....	....	....	....	....	....
1983-84	Kamloops Jr. Oilers	WHL	55	....	....	....	2748	199	1	4.34	....	....	....	....	....	17	*14	3	0	972	57	0	*3.52	....	....	....	....
	Kamloops Jr. Oilers	Mem-Cup	4	1	2	0	190	19	0	6.00	....	....	....	....	....	....	....	....	....	....	....	....	....	....	....	....	....
1984-85	Kamloops Blazers	WHL	49	*36	8	1	2749	170	2	3.71	....	....	....	....	....	*14	....	....	....	*787	56	0	4.27	....	....	....	....
	Edmonton Oilers	**NHL**	**1**	**0**	**1**	**0**	**60**	**5**	**0**	**5.00**	**3.99**	**7.14**	**35**	**.857**	**35.0**	....	....	....	....	....	....	....	....	....	....	....	....
1985-86	Nova Scotia Oilers	AHL	38	15	18	4	2205	156	0	4.24	....	....	....	....	....	....	....	....	....	....	....	....	....	....	....	....	....
1986-87	Nova Scotia Oilers	AHL	46	19	22	0	2637	163	1	3.71	....	....	....	....	....	2	0	2	0	120	13	0	6.50	....	....	....	....
1987-88	**Edmonton Oilers**	**NHL**	**6**	**1**	**1**	**0**	**176**	**14**	**0**	**4.77**	**3.98**	**5.86**	**114**	**.877**	**38.9**	....	....	....	....	....	....	....	....	....	....	....	....
	Nova Scotia Oilers	AHL	8	2	5	0	443	33	0	4.47	....	....	....	....	....	....	....	....	....	....	....	....	....	....	....	....	....
	Milwaukee Admirals	IHL	9	0	8	0	493	44	0	5.35	....	....	....	....	....	....	....	....	....	....	....	....	....	....	....	....	....
1988-89	Cape Breton Oilers	AHL	13	3	10	0	778	72	0	5.55	....	....	....	....	....	....	....	....	....	....	....	....	....	....	....	....	....
	Karpat Oulu	Finland	13	7	5	1	756	46	2	3.65	....	....	....	....	....	....	....	....	....	....	....	....	....	....	....	....	....
1989-90	Binghamton Whalers	AHL	52	8	31	6	2375	192	0	4.21	....	....	....	....	....	....	....	....	....	....	....	....	....	....	....	....	....
1990-91	**Hartford Whalers**	**NHL**	**20**	**7**	**7**	**1**	**1010**	**53**	**1**	**3.15**	**2.83**	**3.49**	**479**	**.889**	**28.5**	....	....	....	....	....	....	....	....	....	....	....	....
	Springfield Indians	AHL	16	7	6	3	912	55	0	3.62	....	....	....	....	....	....	....	....	....	....	....	....	....	....	....	....	....
1991-92	Springfield Indians	AHL	22	3	12	2	1005	63	0	3.76	....	....	....	....	....	1	0	0	0	39	1	0	1.54	....	....	....	....
1992-93	Hershey Bears	AHL	1	0	0	0	22	1	0	2.73	....	....	....	....	....	....	....	....	....	....	....	....	....	....	....	....	....
1993-94	Dayton Bombers	ECHL	4	1	3	0	160	17	0	6.38	....	....	....	....	....	....	....	....	....	....	....	....	....	....	....	....	....
	NHL Totals		**27**	**8**	**9**	**1**	**1246**	**72**	**1**	**3.47**	....	....	**628**	**.885**	**30.2**	....	....	....	....	....	....	....	....	....	....	....	....

WHL West First All-Star Team (1985)

Signed as a free agent by **Hartford**, October 9, 1989.

• REDDICK, Pokey
Eldon Wade G – L. 5'8", 170 lbs. b: Halifax, N.S., 10/6/1964.

Season	Club	League	GP	W	L	T	Mins	GA	SO	Avg	AAvg	Eff	SA	S%	SAPG	GP	W	L	T	Mins	GA	SO	Avg	Eff	SA	S%	SAPG
1981-82	Swift Current Broncos	SJHL	STATISTICS NOT AVAILABLE																								
	Billings Bighorns	WHL	1	0	1	0	60	7	0	7.00	....	....	....	....	....	....	....	....	....	....	....	....	....	....	....	....	....
1982-83	Nanaimo Islanders	WHL	*66	19	38	1	*3549	383	0	6.46	....	....	....	....	....	....	....	....	....	....	....	....	....	....	....	....	....
1983-84	New Westminster Bruins	WHL	50	24	22	2	2930	215	0	4.40	....	....	....	....	....	9	4	5	....	542	53	0	5.87	....	....	....	....
1984-85	Brandon Wheat Kings	WHL	47	14	30	1	2585	243	0	5.64	....	....	....	....	....	....	....	....	....	....	....	....	....	....	....	....	....
1985-86	Fort Wayne Komets	IHL	29	15	11	0	1674	86	*3	3.00	....	....	....	....	....	....	....	....	....	....	....	....	....	....	....	....	....
1986-87	**Winnipeg Jets**	**NHL**	**48**	**21**	**21**	**4**	**2762**	**149**	**0**	**3.24**	**2.74**	**3.84**	**1256**	**.881**	**27.3**	**3**	**0**	**2**	....	**166**	**10**	**0**	**3.61**	**4.88**	**74**	**.865**	**26.7**
1987-88	**Winnipeg Jets**	**NHL**	**28**	**9**	**13**	**3**	**1487**	**102**	**0**	**4.12**	**3.44**	**5.90**	**712**	**.857**	**28.7**	....	....	....	....	....	....	....	....	....	....	....	....
	Moncton Hawks	AHL	9	2	6	1	545	26	0	2.86	....	....	....	....	....	....	....	....	....	....	....	....	....	....	....	....	....
1988-89	**Winnipeg Jets**	**NHL**	**41**	**11**	**17**	**7**	**2109**	**144**	**0**	**4.10**	**3.42**	**5.22**	**1132**	**.873**	**32.2**	....	....	....	....	....	....	....	....	....	....	....	....
1989-90♦	**Edmonton Oilers**	**NHL**	**11**	**5**	**4**	**2**	**604**	**31**	**0**	**3.08**	**2.61**	**3.37**	**283**	**.890**	**28.1**	**1**	**0**	**0**	....	**2**	**0**	**0**	**0.00**	**0.00**	**1**	**1.000**	**30.0**
	Cape Breton Oilers	AHL	15	9	4	1	821	54	0	3.95	....	....	....	....	....	....	....	....	....	....	....	....	....	....	....	....	....
	Phoenix Roadrunners	IHL	3	2	1	0	185	7	0	2.27	....	....	....	....	....	....	....	....	....	....	....	....	....	....	....	....	....
1990-91	**Edmonton Oilers**	**NHL**	**2**	**0**	**2**	**0**	**120**	**9**	**0**	**4.50**	**4.05**	**6.86**	**59**	**.847**	**29.5**	....	....	....	....	....	....	....	....	....	....	....	....
	Cape Breton Oilers	AHL	31	19	10	0	1673	97	2	3.48	....	....	....	....	....	2	0	2	....	124	10	0	4.84	....	....	....	....
1991-92	Cape Breton Oilers	AHL	16	5	3	3	765	45	0	3.53	....	....	....	....	....	....	....	....	....	....	....	....	....	....	....	....	....
	Fort Wayne Komets	IHL	14	6	5	2	787	40	1	3.05	....	....	....	....	....	7	3	4	....	369	18	0	2.93	....	....	....	....
1992-93	Fort Wayne Komets	IHL	54	33	16	4	3043	156	3	3.08	....	....	....	....	....	*12	*12	0	....	723	18	0	*1.49	....	....	....	....
1993-94	**Florida Panthers**	**NHL**	**2**	**0**	**1**	**0**	**80**	**8**	**0**	**6.00**	**5.77**	**10.67**	**45**	**.822**	**33.8**	....	....	....	....	....	....	....	....	....	....	....	....
	Cincinnati Cyclones	IHL	54	31	12	6	2894	147	*2	3.05	....	....	....	....	....	10	6	2	....	498	21	*1	2.53	....	....	....	....
1994-95	Las Vegas Thunder	IHL	40	23	13	1	2075	104	*3	3.01	....	....	....	....	....	10	4	6	....	592	31	0	3.14	....	....	....	....
1995-96	Las Vegas Thunder	IHL	47	27	12	4	2636	129	1	2.94	....	....	....	....	....	15	8	6	....	770	43	0	3.35	....	....	....	....
1996-97	Grand Rapids Griffins	IHL	61	30	14	10	3244	134	6	2.48	....	....	....	....	....	5	2	3	....	335	13	0	2.32	....	....	....	....
1997-98	Grand Rapids Griffens	IHL	10	5	5	0	575	33	0	3.44	....	....	....	....	....	....	....	....	....	....	....	....	....	....	....	....	....
	San Antonio Dragons	IHL	16	5	9	1	861	45	1	3.13	....	....	....	....	....	....	....	....	....	....	....	....	....	....	....	....	....
	Kansas City Blades	IHL	22	10	7	3	1255	55	1	2.63	....	....	....	....	....	4	2	1	....	203	14	0	4.14	....	....	....	....
1998-99	Fort Wayne Komets	IHL	33	12	15	5	1874	102	1	3.27	....	....	....	....	....	1	0	1	....	60	4	0	4.00	....	....	....	....
99-2000	Frankfurt Lions	Germany	52	....	....	....	2943	144	1	2.94	....	....	....	....	....	5	....	....	....	317	16	0	3.03	....	....	....	....
	NHL Totals		**132**	**46**	**58**	**16**	**7162**	**443**	**0**	**3.71**	....	....	**3487**	**.873**	**29.2**	**4**	**0**	**2**	....	**168**	**10**	**0**	**3.57**	....	**75**	**.867**	**26.8**

WHL West First All-Star Team (1984) • Shared James Norris Memorial Trophy (fewest goals against - IHL) with Rick St. Croix (1986) • Won "Bud" Poile Trophy (Playoff MVP - IHL) (1993)

Signed as a free agent by **Winnipeg**, September 27, 1985. Traded to **Edmonton** by **Winnipeg** for future considerations, September 28, 1989. Signed as a free agent by **Florida**, July 12, 1993.

• REDDING, George
G – L. 5'7", 145 lbs. b: Peterborough, Ont., 3/6/1903 Deceased.

Season	Club	League	GP	W	L	T	Mins	GA	SO	Avg	AAvg	Eff	SA	S%	SAPG	GP	W	L	T	Mins	GA	SO	Avg	Eff	SA	S%	SAPG
1924-25	**Boston Bruins**	**NHL**	**1**	**0**	**0**	**0**	**11**	**1**	**0**	**5.45**	**6.65**	....	....	....	....	....	....	....	....	....	....	....	....	....	....	....	....
	NHL Totals		**1**	**0**	**0**	**0**	**11**	**1**	**0**	**5.45**	....	....	....	....	....	....	....	....	....	....	....	....	....	....	....	....	....

• **Boston** defenseman replaced Hec Fowler, December 22, 1924. (Toronto 10, Boston 1)

• REDQUEST, Greg

G – L. 5'10", 190 lbs. b: Toronto, Ont., 7/30/1956. Pittsburgh's 5th, 65th overall in 1976.

			REGULAR SEASON													PLAYOFFS											
Season	Club	League	GP	W	L	T	Mins	GA	SO	Avg	AAvg	Eff	SA	S%	SAPG	GP	W	L	T	Mins	GA	SO	Avg	Eff	SA	S%	SAPG
1973-74	Hamilton Red Wings	OMJHL	64	....	....	....	1226	111	1	5.43	....	....	....	....	....	....	....	....	....	....	....	....	....	....	....	....	....
1974-75	Hamilton Fincups	OMJHL	32	....	....	....	1920	123	1	3.82	....	....	....	....	....	8	....	....	....	470	27	1	3.45	....	....	....	....
1975-76	Hamilton Fincups	OMJHL	1	0	1	0	60	5	0	5.00	....	....	....	....	....	....	....	....	....	....	....	....	....	....	....	....	....
	Oshawa Generals	OMJHL	55	....	....	....	3053	217	0	4.26	....	....	....	....	....	5	2	3	0	274	25	0	5.48	....	....	....	....
1976-77	Columbus Owls	IHL	31	....	....	....	1596	105	1	3.95	....	....	....	....	....	3	....	....	....	95	6	0	3.79	....	....	....	....
1977-78	**Pittsburgh Penguins**	**NHL**	**1**	**0**	**0**	**0**	**13**	**3**	**0**	**13.85**	**12.99**	....	....	....	....	....	....	....	....	....	....	....	....	....	....	....	....
	New Jersey Devils	NYSHL	STATISTICS NOT AVAILABLE																								
	Flint Generals	IHL	1	1	0	0	60	3	0	3.00	....	....	....	....	....	....	....	....	....	....	....	....	....	....	....	....	....
1978-79	New Jersey-Hampton Aces	NEHL	22	....	....	....	1150	90	0	4.70	....	....	....	....	....	....	....	....	....	....	....	....	....	....	....	....	....
	NHL Totals		**1**	**0**	**0**	**0**	**13**	**3**	**0**	**13.85**	....	....	....	....	....	....	....	....	....	....	....	....	....	....	....	....	....

OMJHL Second All-Star Team (1976)

• REECE, Dave

David Barrett G – R. 6'1", 190 lbs. b: Troy, NY, 9/13/1948.

			REGULAR SEASON													PLAYOFFS											
Season	Club	League	GP	W	L	T	Mins	GA	SO	Avg	AAvg	Eff	SA	S%	SAPG	GP	W	L	T	Mins	GA	SO	Avg	Eff	SA	S%	SAPG
1968-69	University of Vermont	ECAC-2	25	13	12	0	1500	84	3	3.36	....	....	....	....	....	....	....	....	....	....	....	....	....	....	....	....	....
1969-70	University of Vermont	ECAC-2	24	16	8	0	1440	65	*4	*2.71	....	....	....	....	....	....	....	....	....	....	....	....	....	....	....	....	....
1970-71	University of Vermont	ECAC-2	26	17	9	0	1560	75	3	2.88	....	....	....	....	....	....	....	....	....	....	....	....	....	....	....	....	....
1971-72	Dayton Gems	EHL	DID NOT PLAY – SPARE GOALTENDER																								
1972-73	Boston Braves	AHL	41	....	....	....	2183	112	3	3.07	....	....	....	....	....	....	....	....	....	....	....	....	....	....	....	....	....
1973-74	Boston Braves	AHL	*57	18	28	11	*3241	189	1	3.49	....	....	....	....	....	....	....	....	....	....	....	....	....	....	....	....	....
1974-75	Rochester Americans	AHL	42	19	16	7	2478	121	1	2.92	....	....	....	....	....	11	6	5	0	680	34	0	3.00	....	....	....	....
1975-76	**Boston Bruins**	**NHL**	**14**	**7**	**5**	**2**	**777**	**43**	**2**	**3.32**	**3.01**	....	....	....	....	....	....	....	....	....	....	....	....	....	....	....	....
	Springfield Indians	AHL	20	13	7	0	1202	78	0	3.89	....	....	....	....	....	....	....	....	....	....	....	....	....	....	....	....	....
1976-77	Rochester Americans	AHL	32	....	....	....	1891	111	1	3.52	....	....	....	....	....	....	....	....	....	....	....	....	....	....	....	....	....
	Rhode Island Reds	AHL	11	....	....	....	634	51	0	4.82	....	....	....	....	....	....	....	....	....	....	....	....	....	....	....	....	....
	United States	WEC-A	5	....	....	....	299	16	0	3.21	....	....	....	....	....	....	....	....	....	....	....	....	....	....	....	....	....
	NHL Totals		**14**	**7**	**5**	**2**	**777**	**43**	**2**	**3.32**	....	....	....	....	....	....	....	....	....	....	....	....	....	....	....	....	....

NCAA (College Div.) East All-American Team (1970, 1971) • AHL Second All-Star Team (1975)

Signed as a free agent by **Boston** (Boston-AHL), November 24, 1972.

• REESE, Jeff

Jeffrey K. "Pieces" G – L. 5'9", 180 lbs. b: Brantford, Ont., 3/24/1966. Toronto's 3rd, 67th overall in 1984.

			REGULAR SEASON													PLAYOFFS											
Season	Club	League	GP	W	L	T	Mins	GA	SO	Avg	AAvg	Eff	SA	S%	SAPG	GP	W	L	T	Mins	GA	SO	Avg	Eff	SA	S%	SAPG
1982-83	Hamilton Kilty Bees	OJHL-B	40	....	....	....	2380	176	0	4.44	....	....	....	....	....	....	....	....	....	....	....	....	....	....	....	....	....
1983-84	London Knights	OHL	43	18	19	1	2308	173	0	4.50	....	....	....	....	....	6	3	3	....	327	27	0	4.95	....	....	....	....
1984-85	London Knights	OHL	50	31	15	1	2878	186	1	3.88	....	....	....	....	....	8	5	2	....	440	20	1	2.73	....	....	....	....
1985-86	London Knights	OHL	*57	25	26	3	*3281	215	0	3.93	....	....	....	....	....	5	0	4	....	299	25	0	5.02	....	....	....	....
1986-87	Newmarket Saints	AHL	50	11	29	0	2822	193	1	4.10	....	....	....	....	....	....	....	....	....	....	....	....	....	....	....	....	....
1987-88	**Toronto Maple Leafs**	**NHL**	**5**	**1**	**2**	**1**	**249**	**17**	**0**	**4.10**	**3.42**	**5.45**	**128**	**.867**	**30.8**	....	....	....	....	....	....	....	....	....	....	....	....
	Newmarket Saints	AHL	28	10	14	3	1587	103	0	3.89	....	....	....	....	....	....	....	....	....	....	....	....	....	....	....	....	....
1988-89	**Toronto Maple Leafs**	**NHL**	**10**	**2**	**6**	**1**	**486**	**40**	**0**	**4.94**	**4.12**	**6.91**	**286**	**.860**	**35.3**	....	....	....	....	....	....	....	....	....	....	....	....
	Newmarket Saints	AHL	37	17	14	3	2072	132	0	3.82	....	....	....	....	....	....	....	....	....	....	....	....	....	....	....	....	....
1989-90	**Toronto Maple Leafs**	**NHL**	**21**	**9**	**6**	**3**	**1101**	**81**	**0**	**4.41**	**3.74**	**5.67**	**630**	**.871**	**34.3**	**2**	**1**	**1**	....	**108**	**6**	**0**	**3.33**	**4.00**	**50**	**.880**	**27.8**
	Newmarket Saints	AHL	7	3	2	2	431	29	0	4.04	....	....	....	....	....	....	....	....	....	....	....	....	....	....	....	....	....
1990-91	**Toronto Maple Leafs**	**NHL**	**30**	**6**	**13**	**3**	**1430**	**92**	**1**	**3.86**	**3.48**	**5.11**	**695**	**.868**	**29.2**	....	....	....	....	....	....	....	....	....	....	....	....
	Newmarket Saints	AHL	3	2	1	0	180	7	0	2.33	....	....	....	....	....	....	....	....	....	....	....	....	....	....	....	....	....
1991-92	**Toronto Maple Leafs**	**NHL**	**8**	**1**	**5**	**1**	**413**	**20**	**1**	**2.91**	**2.60**	**2.77**	**210**	**.905**	**30.5**	....	....	....	....	....	....	....	....	....	....	....	....
	Calgary Flames	**NHL**	**12**	**3**	**2**	**2**	**587**	**37**	**0**	**3.78**	**3.39**	**4.82**	**290**	**.872**	**29.6**	....	....	....	....	....	....	....	....	....	....	....	....
1992-93	**Calgary Flames**	**NHL**	**26**	**14**	**4**	**1**	**1311**	**70**	**1**	**3.20**	**2.74**	**3.56**	**629**	**.889**	**28.8**	**4**	**1**	**3**	....	**209**	**17**	**0**	**4.88**	**9.12**	**91**	**.813**	**26.1**
1993-94	**Calgary Flames**	**NHL**	**1**	**0**	**0**	**0**	**13**	**1**	**0**	**4.62**	**4.44**	**9.24**	**5**	**.800**	**23.1**	....	....	....	....	....	....	....	....	....	....	....	....
	Hartford Whalers	**NHL**	**19**	**5**	**9**	**3**	**1086**	**56**	**1**	**3.09**	**2.97**	**3.30**	**524**	**.893**	**29.0**	....	....	....	....	....	....	....	....	....	....	....	....
1994-95	**Hartford Whalers**	**NHL**	**11**	**2**	**5**	**1**	**477**	**26**	**0**	**3.27**	**3.43**	**3.63**	**234**	**.889**	**29.4**	....	....	....	....	....	....	....	....	....	....	....	....
1995-96	**Hartford Whalers**	**NHL**	**7**	**2**	**3**	**0**	**275**	**14**	**1**	**3.05**	**3.03**	**2.51**	**170**	**.918**	**37.1**	....	....	....	....	....	....	....	....	....	....	....	....
	Tampa Bay Lightning	**NHL**	**19**	**7**	**7**	**1**	**994**	**54**	**0**	**3.26**	**3.24**	**3.79**	**464**	**.884**	**28.0**	**5**	**1**	**1**	....	**198**	**12**	**0**	**3.64**	**4.37**	**100**	**.880**	**30.3**
1996-97	**New Jersey Devils**	**NHL**	**3**	**0**	**2**	**0**	**139**	**13**	**0**	**5.61**	**6.04**	**11.22**	**65**	**.800**	**28.1**	....	....	....	....	....	....	....	....	....	....	....	....
	Detroit Vipers	IHL	32	23	4	3	1763	55	4	*1.87	....	....	....	....	....	11	7	3	....	518	22	0	2.55	....	....	....	....
1997-98	Detroit Vipers	IHL	46	27	9	8	2570	95	4	2.22	....	....	....	....	....	*22	*13	9	....	*1276	52	*2	2.44	....	....	....	....
1998-99	St. John's Maple Leafs	AHL	27	17	7	3	1555	66	1	2.55	....	....	....	....	....	3	1	1	....	142	8	0	3.39	....	....	....	....
	Toronto Maple Leafs	**NHL**	**2**	**1**	**1**	**0**	**106**	**8**	**0**	**4.53**	**5.39**	**7.11**	**51**	**.843**	**28.9**	....	....	....	....	....	....	....	....	....	....	....	....
99-2000	**Tampa Bay Lightning**	**NHL**	DID NOT PLAY – ASSISTANT COACH																								
	NHL Totals		**174**	**53**	**65**	**17**	**8667**	**529**	**5**	**3.66**	....	....	**4381**	**.879**	**30.3**	**11**	**3**	**5**	....	**515**	**35**	**0**	**4.08**	....	**241**	**.855**	**28.1**

IHL Second All-Star Team (1997, 1998) • Shared James Norris Memorial Trophy (fewest goals against — IHL) with Rich Parent (1997)

Traded to **Calgary** by **Toronto** with Craig Berube, Alexander Godynyuk, Gary Leeman and Michel Petit for Doug Gilmour, Jamie Macoun, Ric Nattress, Rick Wamsley and Kent Manderville, January 2, 1992. Traded to **Hartford** by **Calgary** for Dan Keczmer, November 19, 1993. Traded to **Tampa Bay** by **Hartford** for Tampa Bay's 9th round choice (Ashhat Rakhmatullin) in 1996 Entry Draft, December 1, 1995. Traded to **New Jersey** by **Tampa Bay** with Chicago's 2nd round choice (previously acquired, New Jersey selected Pierre Dagenais) in 1996 Entry Draft and Tampa Bay's 8th round choice (Jason Bertsch) in 1996 Entry Draft for Corey Schwab, June 22, 1996. Signed as a free agent by **Toronto**, January 5, 1999. Traded to **Tampa Bay** by **Toronto** with Toronto's 9th round choice (later traded to Philadelphia - Philadelphia selected Milan Kopecky) in 2000 Entry Draft for Tampa Bay's 9th round choice (Jean-Phillipe Cote) in 2000 Entry Draft, August 6, 1999.

• RESCH, Chico

Glenn Allan G – L. 5'9", 165 lbs. b: Moose Jaw, Sask., 7/10/1948.

			REGULAR SEASON													PLAYOFFS											
Season	Club	League	GP	W	L	T	Mins	GA	SO	Avg	AAvg	Eff	SA	S%	SAPG	GP	W	L	T	Mins	GA	SO	Avg	Eff	SA	S%	SAPG
1966-67	Regina Pats	SJHL	5	....	....	....	300	17	0	3.40	....	....	....	....	....	6	2	4	0	360	26	0	4.33	....	....	....	....
1967-68	University of Minnesota-Duluth	WCHA	DID NOT PLAY – FRESHMAN																								
1968-69	University of Minnesota-Duluth	WCHA	24	5	19	0	1424	117	0	4.93	....	....	....	....	....	....	....	....	....	....	....	....	....	....	....	....	....
1969-70	University of Minnesota-Duluth	WCHA	25	12	12	1	1500	97	1	3.88	....	....	....	....	....	....	....	....	....	....	....	....	....	....	....	....	....
1970-71	University of Minnesota-Duluth	WCHA	26	11	14	1	1518	107	0	4.23	....	....	....	....	....	....	....	....	....	....	....	....	....	....	....	....	....
1971-72	Muskegon Mohawks	IHL	59	....	....	....	3488	180	*4	*3.09	....	....	....	....	....	11	....	....	....	617	29	0	2.82	....	....	....	....
1972-73	New Haven Nighthawks	AHL	43	....	....	....	2408	166	0	4.13	....	....	....	....	....	....	....	....	....	....	....	....	....	....	....	....	....
1973-74	**New York Islanders**	**NHL**	**2**	**1**	**1**	**0**	**120**	**6**	**0**	**3.00**	**2.90**	....	....	....	....	....	....	....	....	....	....	....	....	....	....	....	....
	Fort Worth Wings	CHL	55	24	20	11	3300	175	2	3.18	....	....	....	....	....	5	1	4	0	300	21	0	3.60	....	....	....	....
1974-75	**New York Islanders**	**NHL**	**25**	**12**	**7**	**5**	**1432**	**59**	**3**	**2.47**	**2.22**	....	....	....	....	**12**	**8**	**4**	....	**692**	**25**	**1**	**2.17**	....	....	....	....
1975-76	**New York Islanders**	**NHL**	**44**	**23**	**11**	**8**	**2546**	**88**	**7**	**2.07**	**1.85**	....	....	....	....	**7**	**3**	**3**	....	**357**	**18**	**0**	**3.03**	....	....	....	....
1976-77	Canada	Can-Cup	DID NOT PLAY – SPARE GOALTENDER																								
	New York Islanders	**NHL**	**46**	**26**	**13**	**6**	**2711**	**103**	**4**	**2.28**	**2.10**	....	....	....	....	**3**	**1**	**1**	....	**144**	**5**	**0**	**2.08**	....	....	....	....
1977-78	**New York Islanders**	**NHL**	**45**	**28**	**9**	**7**	**2637**	**112**	**3**	**2.55**	**2.37**	....	....	....	....	**7**	**3**	**4**	....	**388**	**15**	**0**	**2.32**	....	....	....	....
1978-79	**New York Islanders**	**NHL**	**43**	**26**	**7**	**10**	**2539**	**106**	**2**	**2.50**	**2.19**	....	....	....	....	**5**	**2**	**3**	....	**300**	**11**	***1**	**2.20**	....	....	....	....
1979-80♦	**New York Islanders**	**NHL**	**45**	**23**	**14**	**6**	**2606**	**132**	**3**	**3.04**	**2.68**	....	....	....	....	**4**	**0**	**2**	....	**120**	**9**	**0**	**4.50**	....	....	....	....
1980-81	**New York Islanders**	**NHL**	**32**	**18**	**7**	**5**	**1817**	**93**	***3**	**3.07**	**2.47**	....	....	....	....	....	....	....	....	....	....	....	....	....	....	....	....
	Colorado Rockies	**NHL**	**8**	**2**	**4**	**2**	**449**	**28**	**0**	**3.74**	**3.02**	....	....	....	....	....	....	....	....	....	....	....	....	....	....	....	....
1981-82	**Colorado Rockies**	**NHL**	**61**	**16**	**31**	**11**	**3424**	**230**	**0**	**4.03**	**3.11**	....	....	....	....	....	....	....	....	....	....	....	....	....	....	....	....
	United States	WEC-A	4	0	4	0	239	21	0	5.27	....	....	....	....	....	....	....	....	....	....	....	....	....	....	....	....	....
1982-83	**New Jersey Devils**	**NHL**	**65**	**15**	**35**	**12**	**3650**	**242**	**0**	**3.98**	**3.20**	**4.98**	**1933**	**.875**	**31.8**	....	....	....	....	....	....	....	....	....	....	....	....
1983-84	**New Jersey Devils**	**NHL**	**51**	**9**	**31**	**3**	**2641**	**184**	**1**	**4.18**	**3.30**	**5.39**	**1426**	**.871**	**32.4**	....	....	....	....	....	....	....	....	....	....	....	....
1984-85	United States	Can-Cup	2	0	1	1	108	9	0	5.00	....	....	....	....	....	....	....	....	....	....	....	....	....	....	....	....	....
	New Jersey Devils	**NHL**	**51**	**15**	**27**	**5**	**2884**	**200**	**0**	**4.16**	**3.32**	**5.94**	**1401**	**.857**	**29.1**	....	....	....	....	....	....	....	....	....	....	....	....

Season	Club	League	REGULAR SEASON GP	W	L	T	Mins	GA	SO	Avg	AAvg	Eff	SA	S%	SAPG	PLAYOFFS GP	W	L	T	Mins	GA	SO	Avg	Eff	SA	S%	SAPG
1985-86	New Jersey Devils	NHL	31	10	20	0	1769	126	0	4.27	3.34	6.08	885	.858	30.0	....	....	....	....	....	....	....	....	....	....	....	....
	Philadelphia Flyers	NHL	5	1	2	0	187	10	0	3.21	2.51	3.82	84	.881	27.0	1	0	0	....	7	1	0	8.57	85.70	1	.000	8.6
1986-87	Philadelphia Flyers	NHL	17	6	5	2	867	42	0	2.91	2.46	2.80	436	.904	30.2	2	0	0	....	36	1	0	1.67	1.39	12	.917	20.0
	NHL Totals		571	231	224	82	32279	1761	26	3.27	....	....	....	....	....	41	17	17	....	2044	85	2	2.50	....	....	....	....

WCHA Second All-Star Team (1971) • IHL First All-Star Team (1972) • Won James Norris Memorial Trophy (fewest goals against - IHL) (1972) • Won Garry F. Longman Memorial Trophy (Top Rookie - IHL) (1972) • CHL First All-Star Team (1974) • Won Tommy Ivan Trophy (MVP - CHL) (1974) • NHL Second All-Star Team (1976, 1979) • Won Bill Masterton Trophy (1982) • Played in NHL All-Star Game (1976, 1977, 1984)

Traded to **NY Islanders** by **Montreal** with Denis Dejordy, Germain Gagnon, Tony Featherstone, Murray Anderson and Alex Campbell for cash, June 26, 1972. Traded to **Colorado** by **NY Islanders** with Steve Tambellini for Mike McEwen and Jari Kaarela, March 10, 1981. Transferred to **New Jersey** after **Colorado** franchise relocated, June 30, 1982. Traded to **Philadelphia** by **New Jersey** for Philadelphia's 3rd round choice (Marc Laniel) in 1986 Entry Draft, March 11, 1986.

• RHEAUME, Herb Herbert Elbert G – L. 6′, 200 lbs. b: Mason, Que., 1/12/1900 d: 1/1/1955.

Season	Club	League	GP	W	L	T	Mins	GA	SO	Avg	AAvg	Eff	SA	S%	SAPG	GP	W	L	T	Mins	GA	SO	Avg	Eff	SA	S%	SAPG
1915-16	Ottawa Grand Trunk	OCHL	3	2	1	0	180	9	1	3.00	....	....	....	....	....	....	....	....	....	....	....	....	....	....	....	....	....
1916-17	Ottawa Grand Trunk	OCHL	8	2	5	1	480	22	1	2.75	....	....	....	....	....	....	....	....	....	....	....	....	....	....	....	....	....
1917-18	Hull Canadians	OCHL	4	0	4	0	240	11	0	2.75	....	....	....	....	....	....	....	....	....	....	....	....	....	....	....	....	....
	Hull Canadiens	HOHL	5	....	....	....	300	10	0	2.00	....	....	....	....	....	....	....	....	....	....	....	....	....	....	....	....	....
1918-19	Hamilton Tigers	OHA-Sr.	8	*6	2	0	480	35	0	4.38	....	....	....	....	....	4	2	2	0	240	13	0	3.25	....	....	....	....
	Hamilton Tigers	Al-Cup	2	1	1	0	130	6	0	2.77	....	....	....	....	....	....	....	....	....	....	....	....	....	....	....	....	....
1919-20	Hamilton Tigers	OHA-Sr.	6	*5	1	0	360	17	0	*2.83	....	....	....	....	....	2	1	1	0	120	6	0	3.00	....	....	....	....
1920-21	Hamilton Tigers	OHA-Sr.	9	3	6	0	540	39	0	4.33	....	....	....	....	....	....	....	....	....	....	....	....	....	....	....	....	....
1921-22	Boston Westminsters	USAHA	STATISTICS NOT AVAILABLE																								
1922-23	New Haven Westminsters	USAHA	STATISTICS NOT AVAILABLE																								
1923-24	Trois-Rivieres Renards	ECHA	2	1	1	0	120	1	1	0.50																	
1924-25	Quebec Sons of Ireland	ECHA	8	4	4	0	480	23	0	2.88	....	....	....	....	....	....	....	....	....	....	....	....	....	....	....	....	....
1925-26	Montreal Canadiens	NHL	31	10	20	1	1889	92	0	2.92	4.01	....	....	....	....	....	....	....	....	....	....	....	....	....	....	....	....
1926-27	Boston Tigers	Can-Am	32	14	15	3	1980	46	5	*1.39	....	....	....	....	....	....	....	....	....	....	....	....	....	....	....	....	....
1927-28	Boston Tigers	Can-Am	40	21	14	5	2500	71	6	1.70	....	....	....	....	....	2	2	0	0	120	4	0	2.00	....	....	....	....
1928-29	Boston Tigers	Can-Am	40	*21	15	4	2474	56	*11	1.36	....	....	....	....	....	4	4	0	0	240	*4	*1	*1.00	....	....	....	....
1929-30	Boston Tigers	Can-Am	40	17	18	5	2471	129	1	3.13	....	....	....	....	....	3	2	1	0	180	7	1	2.33	....	....	....	....
1930-31	St. Louis Flyers	AHA	34	10	21	3	2043	101	3	2.97	....	....	....	....	....	....	....	....	....	....	....	....	....	....	....	....	....
1931-32	St. Louis Flyers	AHA	35	13	14	8	2159	62	7	1.70	....	....	....	....	....	....	....	....	....	....	....	....	....	....	....	....	....
1932-33	Regina-Vancouver Maroons	WCHL	30	15	13	2	1800	102	0	3.40	....	....	....	....	....	2	0	1	0	120	8	0	4.00	....	....	....	....
1933-34	Portland Buckaroos	NWHL	34	....	....	....	2040	118	1	3.47	....	....	....	....	....	....	....	....	....	....	....	....	....	....	....	....	....
1934-35	Edmonton Eskimos	NWHL	21	....	....	....	1260	79	1	3.76	....	....	....	....	....	....	....	....	....	....	....	....	....	....	....	....	....
1935-36	Vancouver Lions	NWHL	10	7	1	2	630	20	2	1.91	....	....	....	....	....	7	*3	4	0	430	19	*1	2.65	....	....	....	....
	NHL Totals		31	10	20	1	1889	92	0	2.92	....	....	....	....	....	....	....	....	....	....	....	....	....	....	....	....	....

Signed as a free agent by **Montreal Canadiens**, December 13, 1925.

• RHODES, Damian "Dusty" G – L. 6′, 190 lbs. b: St. Paul, MN, 5/28/1969. Toronto's 6th, 112th overall in 1987.

Season	Club	League	GP	W	L	T	Mins	GA	SO	Avg	AAvg	Eff	SA	S%	SAPG	GP	W	L	T	Mins	GA	SO	Avg	Eff	SA	S%	SAPG
1985-86	Richfield Spartans	Hi-School	16	....	....	....	720	56	0	3.50	....	....	....	....	....	....	....	....	....	....	....	....	....	....	....	....	....
1986-87	Richfield Spartans	Hi-School	19	....	....	....	673	51	1	4.55	....	....	....	....	....	....	....	....	....	....	....	....	....	....	....	....	....
1987-88	Michigan Tech Huskies	WCHA	29	16	10	1	1625	114	0	4.20	....	....	....	....	....	....	....	....	....	....	....	....	....	....	....	....	....
	United States	WJC-A	5	....	....	....	204	20	....	5.88	....	....	....	....	....	....	....	....	....	....	....	....	....	....	....	....	....
1988-89	Michigan Tech Huskies	WCHA	37	15	22	0	2216	163	0	4.41	....	....	....	....	....	....	....	....	....	....	....	....	....	....	....	....	....
1989-90	Michigan Tech Huskies	WCHA	25	6	17	0	1358	119	0	6.26	....	....	....	....	....	....	....	....	....	....	....	....	....	....	....	....	....
1990-91	Toronto Maple Leafs	NHL	1	1	0	0	60	1	0	1.00	0.90	0.38	26	.962	26.0	....	....	....	....	....	....	....	....	....	....	....	....
	Newmarket Saints	AHL	38	8	24	3	2154	144	1	4.01	....	....	....	....	....	....	....	....	....	....	....	....	....	....	....	....	....
	United States	WEC-A	DID NOT PLAY – SPARE GOALTENDER																								
1991-92	St. John's Maple Leafs	AHL	43	20	16	5	2454	148	0	3.62	....	....	....	....	....	6	4	1	....	331	16	0	2.90	....	....	....	....
1992-93	St. John's Maple Leafs	AHL	*52	27	16	8	*3074	184	1	3.59	....	....	....	....	....	9	4	5	....	538	37	0	4.13	....	....	....	....
1993-94	Toronto Maple Leafs	NHL	22	9	7	3	1213	53	0	2.62	2.51	2.57	541	.902	26.8	1	0	0	....	1	0	0	0.00	0.00	0	.000	0.0
1994-95	Toronto Maple Leafs	NHL	13	6	6	1	760	34	0	2.68	2.80	2.26	404	.916	31.9	....	....	....	....	....	....	....	....	....	....	....	....
1995-96	Toronto Maple Leafs	NHL	11	4	5	1	624	29	0	2.79	2.77	2.69	301	.904	28.9	....	....	....	....	....	....	....	....	....	....	....	....
	Ottawa Senators	NHL	36	10	22	4	2123	98	2	2.77	2.75	2.61	1041	.906	29.4	....	....	....	....	....	....	....	....	....	....	....	....
1996-97	Ottawa Senators	NHL	50	14	20	14	2934	133	1	2.72	2.92	2.98	1213	.890	24.8	....	....	....	....	....	....	....	....	....	....	....	....
1997-98	Ottawa Senators	NHL	50	19	19	7	2743	107	5	2.34	2.78	2.18	1148	.907	25.1	10	5	5	....	590	21	0	2.14	1.90	236	.911	24.0
1998-99	Ottawa Senators	NHL	45	22	13	7	2480	101	3	2.44	2.90	2.32	1060	.905	25.6	2	0	2	....	150	6	0	2.40	2.22	65	.908	26.0
99-2000	Atlanta Thrashers	NHL	28	5	19	3	1561	101	1	3.88	4.46	4.88	803	.874	30.9	....	....	....	....	....	....	....	....	....	....	....	....
	United States	WC-A	5	3	1	1	300	12	1	2.40	....	....	....	....	....	....	....	....	....	....	....	....	....	....	....	....	....
	NHL Totals		256	90	111	40	14498	657	12	2.72	....	....	6537	.899	27.1	13	5	7	....	741	27	0	2.19	....	301	.910	24.4

• Credited with scoring a goal while with Michigan Tech (WCHA), January 21, 1989. • Credited with scoring a goal vs. New Jersey, January 2, 1999.

• Played 10 seconds of playoff game vs. San Jose, May 6, 1994. Traded to **NY Islanders** by **Toronto** with Ken Belanger for future considerations (Kirk Muller and Don Beaupre, January 23, 1996), January 23, 1996. Traded to **Ottawa** by **NY Islanders** with Wade Redden for Don Beaupre, Martin Straka and Bryan Berard, January 23, 1996. Traded to **Atlanta** by **Ottawa** for future considerations, June 18, 1999.

• RICCI, Nick Nicholas Joseph G – L. 5′10″, 160 lbs. b: Niagara Falls, Ont., 6/3/1959. Pittsburgh's 4th, 94th overall in 1979.

Season	Club	League	GP	W	L	T	Mins	GA	SO	Avg	AAvg	Eff	SA	S%	SAPG	GP	W	L	T	Mins	GA	SO	Avg	Eff	SA	S%	SAPG
1976-77	Toronto Red Wings	OHA-B	STATISTICS NOT AVAILABLE																								
	Niagara Falls Flyers	OMJHL	7	....	....	....	309	32	0	6.21	....	....	....	....	....	....	....	....	....	....	....	....	....	....	....	....	....
1977-78	Toronto Red Wings	OHA-B	STATISTICS NOT AVAILABLE																								
1978-79	Niagara Falls Flyers	OMJHL	52	....	....	....	3129	183	3	3.49	....	....	....	....	....	20	....	....	....	1172	54	1	2.66	....	....	....	....
1979-80	Pittsburgh Penguins	NHL	4	2	2	0	240	14	0	3.50	3.09	....	....	....	....	....	....	....	....	....	....	....	....	....	....	....	....
	Grand Rapids Owls	IHL	29	....	....	....	1585	113	1	4.28	....	....	....	....	....	....	....	....	....	....	....	....	....	....	....	....	....
1980-81	Pittsburgh Penguins	NHL	9	4	5	0	540	35	0	3.89	3.14	....	....	....	....	....	....	....	....	....	....	....	....	....	....	....	....
	Binghamton Whalers	AHL	8	2	4	0	359	34	0	5.68	....	....	....	....	....	....	....	....	....	....	....	....	....	....	....	....	....
1981-82	Pittsburgh Penguins	NHL	3	0	3	0	160	14	0	5.25	4.06	....	....	....	....	....	....	....	....	....	....	....	....	....	....	....	....
	Erie Blades	AHL	40	16	19	4	2254	175	0	4.66	....	....	....	....	....	....	....	....	....	....	....	....	....	....	....	....	....
1982-83	Pittsburgh Penguins	NHL	3	1	2	0	147	16	0	6.53	5.25	13.57	77	.792	31.4	....	....	....	....	....	....	....	....	....	....	....	....
	Baltimore Skipjacks	AHL	9	3	3	2	486	41	0	5.06	....	....	....	....	....	....	....	....	....	....	....	....	....	....	....	....	....
1983-84	St. Catharines Saints	AHL	15	3	4	1	597	47	0	4.72	....	....	....	....	....	....	....	....	....	....	....	....	....	....	....	....	....
	Muskegon Mohawks	IHL	13	1	11	1	764	59	0	4.63	....	....	....	....	....	....	....	....	....	....	....	....	....	....	....	....	....
1984-85	Peoria Rivermen	IHL	7	4	3	0	423	30	0	4.26	....	....	....	....	....	....	....	....	....	....	....	....	....	....	....	....	....
	NHL Totals		19	7	12	0	1087	79	0	4.36	....	....	....	....	....	....	....	....	....	....	....	....	....	....	....	....	....

Traded to **Toronto** by **Pittsburgh** with Pat Graham for Vincent Tremblay and Rocky Saganiuk, August 15, 1983.

• RICHARDSON, Terry Terrance Paul G – R. 6′1″, 190 lbs. b: Powell River, B.C., 5/7/1953. Detroit's 1st, 11th overall in 1973.

Season	Club	League	GP	W	L	T	Mins	GA	SO	Avg	AAvg	Eff	SA	S%	SAPG	GP	W	L	T	Mins	GA	SO	Avg	Eff	SA	S%	SAPG
1970-71	New Westminster Royals	BCJHL	STATISTICS NOT AVAILABLE																								
1971-72	New Westminster Bruins	WCJHL	49	....	....	....	2737	140	3	3.07	....	....	....	....	....	5	1	4	0	300	19	0	3.80	....	....	....	....
1972-73	New Westminster Bruins	WCJHL	*68	31	22	15	3800	239	0	3.77	....	....	....	....	....	5	....	....	....	300	32	0	6.40	....	....	....	....
1973-74	Detroit Red Wings	NHL	9	1	4	0	315	28	0	5.33	5.17	....	....	....	....	....	....	....	....	....	....	....	....	....	....	....	....
	Virginia Wings	AHL	14	5	7	2	744	44	0	3.54	....	....	....	....	....	....	....	....	....	....	....	....	....	....	....	....	....
	London Lions	Britain	14	....	....	....	710	37	0	3.12	....	....	....	....	....	....	....	....	....	....	....	....	....	....	....	....	....
1974-75	Detroit Red Wings	NHL	4	1	2	0	202	23	0	6.83	6.19	....	....	....	....	....	....	....	....	....	....	....	....	....	....	....	....
	Virginia Wings	AHL	30	10	13	3	1612	96	1	3.57	....	....	....	....	....	2	0	2	0	119	7	0	3.52	....	....	....	....
1975-76	Springfield Indians	AHL	20	6	10	1	1080	77	0	4.28	....	....	....	....	....	....	....	....	....	....	....	....	....	....	....	....	....
	Detroit Red Wings	NHL	1	0	1	0	60	7	0	7.00	6.34	....	....	....	....	....	....	....	....	....	....	....	....	....	....	....	....
	New Haven Nighthawks	AHL	4	1	2	1	243	14	0	3.46	....	....	....	....	....	2	0	2	0	126	6	0	2.86	....	....	....	....

			REGULAR SEASON													PLAYOFFS											
Season	Club	League	GP	W	L	T	Mins	GA	SO	Avg	AAvg	Eff	SA	S%	SAPG	GP	W	L	T	Mins	GA	SO	Avg	Eff	SA	S%	SAPG
1976-77	**Detroit Red Wings**	**NHL**	**5**	**1**	**3**	**0**	**269**	**18**	**0**	**4.01**	**3.73**	....	....	....	....	....	....	....	....	....	....	....	....	....	....	....	....
	Kalamazoo Wings	IHL	65	....	....	....	3612	218	0	3.62	....	....	....	....	....	10	5	5	0	585	30	0	3.08	....	....	....	....
1977-78	Kansas City Red Wings	CHL	*63	*27	32	2	*3766	199	1	3.17	....	....	....	....	....	....	....	....	....	....	....	....	....	....	....	....	....
1978-79	**St. Louis Blues**	**NHL**	**1**	**0**	**1**	**0**	**60**	**9**	**0**	**9.00**	**7.97**	....	....	....	....	....	....	....	....	....	....	....	....	....	....	....	....
	Salt Lake Golden Eagles	CHL	40	30	7	3	2422	102	*5	*2.53	....	....	....	....	....	7	....	....	....	398	21	0	3.17	....	....	....	....
1979-80	Springfield Indians	AHL	46	15	22	7	2661	162	0	3.65	....	....	....	....	....	....	....	....	....	....	....	....	....	....	....	....	....
	NHL Totals		**20**	**3**	**11**	**0**	**906**	**85**	**0**	**5.63**	....	....	....	....	....	....	....	....	....	....	....	....	....	....	....	....	....

IHL Second All-Star Team (1977) • Won James Norris Memorial Trophy (fewest goals against - IHL) (1977) • CHL Second All-Star Team (1978, 1979) • Shared Terry Sawchuk Trophy (fewest goals against - CHL) with Doug Grant (1979)

Signed as a free agent by **St. Louis**, July 26, 1978. Traded to **NY Islanders** by **St. Louis** with Barry Gibbs for future considerations, June 9, 1979. Traded to **Hartford** by **NY Islanders** for Ralph Klassen, June 14, 1979.

• RICHTER, Mike

G – L. 5'11", 187 lbs. b: Abington, PA, 9/22/1966. NY Rangers' 2nd, 28th overall in 1985.

Season	Club	League	GP	W	L	T	Mins	GA	SO	Avg	AAvg	Eff	SA	S%	SAPG	GP	W	L	T	Mins	GA	SO	Avg	Eff	SA	S%	SAPG
1983-84	Philadelphia Jr. Flyers	NEJHL	36	23	10	3	2160	94	0	2.61	....	....	....	....	....	....	....	....	....	....	....	....	....	....	....	....	....
1984-85	Northwood Huskies	Hi-School	24	....	....	....	1374	52	2	2.27	....	....	....	....	....	....	....	....	....	....	....	....	....	....	....	....	....
	United States	WJC-A	3	....	....	....	43	6	0	8.37	....	....	....	....	....	....	....	....	....	....	....	....	....	....	....	....	....
1985-86	University of Wisconsin	WCHA	24	14	9	0	1394	92	1	3.96	....	....	....	....	....	....	....	....	....	....	....	....	....	....	....	....	....
	United States	WJC-A	4	3	1	0	208	9	0	2.60	....	....	....	....	....	....	....	....	....	....	....	....	....	....	....	....	....
	United States	WEC-A	1	0	0	0	53	5	0	5.66	....	....	....	....	....	....	....	....	....	....	....	....	....	....	....	....	....
1986-87	University of Wisconsin	WCHA	36	19	16	1	2136	126	0	3.54	....	....	....	....	....	....	....	....	....	....	....	....	....	....	....	....	....
	United States	WEC-A	2	0	2	0	80	8	0	6.00	....	....	....	....	....	....	....	....	....	....	....	....	....	....	....	....	....
1987-88	United States	Nat-Team	29	17	7	2	1559	86	0	3.31	....	....	....	....	....	....	....	....	....	....	....	....	....	....	....	....	....
	United States	Olympics	4	....	....	....	230	15	0	3.91	....	....	....	....	....	....	....	....	....	....	....	....	....	....	....	....	....
	Colorado Rangers	IHL	22	16	5	0	1298	68	1	3.14	....	....	....	....	....	10	5	3	....	536	35	0	3.92	....	....	....	....
1988-89	Denver Rangers	IHL	*57	23	26	0	3031	217	1	4.30	....	....	....	....	....	4	0	4	....	210	21	0	6.00	....	....	....	....
	New York Rangers	**NHL**	....	....	....	....	....	....	....	....	....	....	....	....	....	**1**	**0**	**1**	....	**58**	**4**	**0**	**4.14**	**5.52**	**30**	**.867**	**31.0**
1989-90	**New York Rangers**	**NHL**	**23**	**12**	**5**	**5**	**1320**	**66**	**0**	**3.00**	**2.54**	**2.89**	**686**	**.904**	**31.2**	**6**	**3**	**2**	....	**330**	**19**	**0**	**3.45**	**3.60**	**182**	**.896**	**33.1**
	Flint Spirits	IHL	13	7	4	2	782	49	0	3.76	....	....	....	....	....	....	....	....	....	....	....	....	....	....	....	....	....
1990-91	**New York Rangers**	**NHL**	**45**	**21**	**13**	**7**	**2596**	**135**	**0**	**3.12**	**2.80**	**3.03**	**1392**	**.903**	**32.2**	**6**	**2**	**4**	....	**313**	**14**	***1**	**2.68**	**2.06**	**182**	**.923**	**34.9**
1991-92	United States	Can-Cup	7	4	3	0	420	22	0	3.00	....	....	....	....	....	....	....	....	....	....	....	....	....	....	....	....	....
	New York Rangers	**NHL**	**41**	**23**	**12**	**2**	**2298**	**119**	**3**	**3.11**	**2.78**	**3.07**	**1205**	**.901**	**31.5**	**7**	**4**	**2**	....	**412**	**24**	**1**	**3.50**	**3.72**	**226**	**.894**	**32.9**
1992-93	**New York Rangers**	**NHL**	**38**	**13**	**19**	**3**	**2105**	**134**	**1**	**3.82**	**3.28**	**4.34**	**1180**	**.886**	**33.6**	....	....	....	....	....	....	....	....	....	....	....	....
	Binghamton Rangers	AHL	5	4	0	1	305	6	0	1.18	....	....	....	....	....	....	....	....	....	....	....	....	....	....	....	....	....
	United States	WC-A	4	1	1	2	237	13	0	3.29	....	....	....	....	....	....	....	....	....	....	....	....	....	....	....	....	....
1993-94♦	**New York Rangers**	**NHL**	**68**	***42**	**12**	**6**	**3710**	**159**	**5**	**2.57**	**2.46**	**2.32**	**1758**	**.910**	**28.4**	**23**	***16**	**7**	....	**1417**	**49**	***4**	**2.07**	**1.63**	**623**	**.921**	**26.4**
1994-95	**New York Rangers**	**NHL**	**35**	**14**	**17**	**2**	**1993**	**97**	**2**	**2.92**	**3.06**	**3.20**	**884**	**.890**	**26.6**	**7**	**2**	**5**	....	**384**	**23**	**0**	**3.59**	**4.37**	**189**	**.878**	**29.5**
1995-96	**New York Rangers**	**NHL**	**41**	**24**	**13**	**3**	**2396**	**107**	**3**	**2.68**	**2.66**	**2.35**	**1221**	**.912**	**30.6**	**11**	**5**	**6**	....	**661**	**36**	**0**	**3.27**	**3.82**	**308**	**.883**	**28.0**
1996-97	United States	W-Cup	6	4	2	0	370	15	0	2.00	....	....	....	....	....	....	....	....	....	....	....	....	....	....	....	....	....
	New York Rangers	**NHL**	**61**	**33**	**22**	**6**	**3598**	**161**	**4**	**2.68**	**2.88**	**2.22**	**1945**	**.917**	**32.4**	**15**	**9**	**6**	....	**939**	**33**	***3**	**2.11**	**1.43**	**488**	**.932**	**31.2**
1997-98	**New York Rangers**	**NHL**	***72**	**21**	**31**	**15**	**4143**	**184**	**0**	**2.66**	**3.18**	**2.59**	**1888**	**.903**	**27.3**	....	....	....	....	....	....	....	....	....	....	....	....
	United States	Olympics	4	1	3	0	237	14	0	3.55	....	....	....	....	....	....	....	....	....	....	....	....	....	....	....	....	....
1998-99	**New York Rangers**	**NHL**	**68**	**27**	**30**	**8**	**3878**	**170**	**4**	**2.63**	**3.13**	**2.36**	**1898**	**.910**	**29.4**	....	....	....	....	....	....	....	....	....	....	....	....
99-2000	**New York Rangers**	**NHL**	**61**	**22**	**31**	**8**	**3622**	**173**	**0**	**2.87**	**3.29**	**2.74**	**1815**	**.905**	**30.1**	....	....	....	....	....	....	....	....	....	....	....	....
	NHL Totals		**553**	**252**	**205**	**65**	**31659**	**1505**	**22**	**2.85**	....	....	**15872**	**.905**	**30.1**	**76**	**41**	**33**	....	**4514**	**202**	**9**	**2.68**	....	**2228**	**.909**	**29.6**

WCHA Second All-Star Team (1987) • World Cup All-Star Team (1996) • Named World Cup MVP (1996) • Played in NHL All-Star Game (1992, 1994, 2000)

Claimed by **Nashville** from **NY Rangers** in Expansion Draft, June 26, 1998. Signed as a free agent by **NY Rangers**, July 15, 1998.

• RIDLEY, Curt

Charles Curtis G – L. 6', 190 lbs. b: Minnedosa, Man., 9/24/1951. Boston's 3rd, 28th overall in 1971.

Season	Club	League	GP	W	L	T	Mins	GA	SO	Avg	AAvg	Eff	SA	S%	SAPG	GP	W	L	T	Mins	GA	SO	Avg	Eff	SA	S%	SAPG
1968-69	Portage Terriers	MJHL	STATISTICS NOT AVAILABLE																								
1969-70	Portage Terriers	MJHL	23	....	....	....	....	90	0	3.86	....	....	....	....	....	....	....	....	....	....	....	....	....	....	....	....	....
1970-71	Portage Terriers	MJHL	45	....	....	....	2685	148	*5	*3.31	....	....	....	....	....	....	....	....	....	....	....	....	....	....	....	....	....
	Brandon Wheat Kings	WCJHL	5	....	....	....	299	14	0	2.81	....	....	....	....	....	....	....	....	....	....	....	....	....	....	....	....	....
1971-72	Oklahoma City Blazers	CHL	41	12	18	4	1869	127	1	4.07	....	....	....	....	....	1	0	1	0	42	5	0	7.14	....	....	....	....
1972-73	Dayton Gems	IHL	56	....	....	....	3217	145	2	*2.70	....	....	....	....	....	6	3	3	0	360	19	0	3.17	....	....	....	....
	Boston Braves	AHL	....	....	....	....	....	....	....	....	....	....	....	....	....	4	0	3	0	192	17	0	5.31	....	....	....	....
1973-74	Providence Reds	AHL	39	19	11	6	2234	107	1	2.87	....	....	....	....	....	1	1	0	0	60	4	0	4.00	....	....	....	....
1974-75	**New York Rangers**	**NHL**	**2**	**1**	**1**	**0**	**81**	**7**	**0**	**5.19**	**4.69**	....	....	....	....	....	....	....	....	....	....	....	....	....	....	....	....
	Providence Reds	AHL	*57	*32	14	9	*3311	181	1	3.27	....	....	....	....	....	6	2	4	0	373	24	0	3.86	....	....	....	....
1975-76	Tulsa Oilers	CHL	30	15	10	5	1779	79	2	*2.66	....	....	....	....	....	....	....	....	....	....	....	....	....	....	....	....	....
	Vancouver Canucks	**NHL**	**9**	**6**	**0**	**2**	**500**	**19**	**1**	**2.28**	**2.06**	....	....	....	....	**2**	**0**	**2**	....	**120**	**8**	**0**	**4.00**	....	....	....	....
1976-77	**Vancouver Canucks**	**NHL**	**37**	**8**	**21**	**4**	**2074**	**134**	**0**	**3.88**	**3.62**	....	....	....	....	....	....	....	....	....	....	....	....	....	....	....	....
1977-78	**Vancouver Canucks**	**NHL**	**40**	**9**	**17**	**8**	**2010**	**136**	**0**	**4.06**	**3.83**	....	....	....	....	....	....	....	....	....	....	....	....	....	....	....	....
1978-79	Dallas Black Hawks	CHL	33	22	10	0	1871	115	1	3.69	....	....	....	....	....	*9	*8	1	0	*520	26	0	*3.00	....	....	....	....
1979-80	**Vancouver Canucks**	**NHL**	**10**	**2**	**6**	**2**	**599**	**39**	**0**	**3.91**	**3.46**	....	....	....	....	....	....	....	....	....	....	....	....	....	....	....	....
	Toronto Maple Leafs	**NHL**	**3**	**0**	**1**	**0**	**110**	**8**	**0**	**4.36**	**3.85**	....	....	....	....	....	....	....	....	....	....	....	....	....	....	....	....
	Dallas Black Hawks	CHL	4	0	4	0	218	21	0	5.78	....	....	....	....	....	....	....	....	....	....	....	....	....	....	....	....	....
1980-81	**Toronto Maple Leafs**	**NHL**	**3**	**1**	**1**	**0**	**124**	**12**	**0**	**5.81**	**4.70**	....	....	....	....	....	....	....	....	....	....	....	....	....	....	....	....
	New Brunswick Hawks	AHL	2	1	1	0	120	7	0	3.50	....	....	....	....	....	....	....	....	....	....	....	....	....	....	....	....	....
1981-82	Cincinnati Tigers	CHL	22	10	6	1	1043	73	0	4.20	....	....	....	....	....	1	0	1	0	63	3	0	2.86	....	....	....	....
	NHL Totals		**104**	**27**	**47**	**16**	**5498**	**355**	**1**	**3.87**	....	....	....	....	....	**2**	**0**	**2**	....	**120**	**8**	**0**	**4.00**	....	....	....	....

MJHL First All-Star Team (1971) • Won Terry Sawchuk Trophy (fewest goals against - CHL) (1976)

Claimed by **NY Rangers** (Providence-AHL) from **Boston** in Reverse Draft, June 13, 1973. Traded to **Atlanta** by **NY Rangers** for Jerry Byers, September 9, 1975. Traded to **Vancouver** by **Atlanta** for Vancouver's 1st round choice (Dave Shand) in 1976 Amateur Draft, January 20, 1976. Traded to **Toronto** by **Vancouver** for cash, February 10, 1980.

• RIENDEAU, Vincent

G – L. 5'10", 185 lbs. b: St-Hyacinthe, Que., 4/20/1966.

Season	Club	League	GP	W	L	T	Mins	GA	SO	Avg	AAvg	Eff	SA	S%	SAPG	GP	W	L	T	Mins	GA	SO	Avg	Eff	SA	S%	SAPG
1983-84	Des Moines Buccaneers	USHL	15	....	....	....	753	63	0	5.02	....	....	....	....	....	....	....	....	....	....	....	....	....	....	....	....	....
	Verdun Juniors	QMJHL	41	22	13	2	2133	147	2	4.14	....	....	....	....	....	....	....	....	....	....	....	....	....	....	....	....	....
1984-85	Sherbrooke College	CEGEP	STATISTICS NOT AVAILABLE																								
1985-86	Drummondville Voltigeurs	QMJHL	57	33	20	3	3336	215	2	3.87	....	....	....	....	....	23	10	13	....	1271	106	1	5.00	....	....	....	....
1986-87	Sherbrooke Canadiens	AHL	41	25	14	0	2363	114	2	2.89	....	....	....	....	....	13	8	5	....	742	47	0	3.80	....	....	....	....
1987-88	**Montreal Canadiens**	**NHL**	**1**	**0**	**0**	**0**	**36**	**5**	**0**	**8.33**	**6.94**	**18.93**	**22**	**.773**	**36.7**	....	....	....	....	....	....	....	....	....	....	....	....
	Sherbrooke Canadiens	AHL	44	27	13	3	2521	112	*4	*2.67	....	....	....	....	....	2	0	2	....	127	7	0	3.31	....	....	....	....
1988-89	**St. Louis Blues**	**NHL**	**32**	**11**	**15**	**5**	**1842**	**108**	**0**	**3.52**	**2.93**	**4.55**	**836**	**.871**	**27.2**	....	....	....	....	....	....	....	....	....	....	....	....
1989-90	**St. Louis Blues**	**NHL**	**43**	**17**	**19**	**5**	**2551**	**149**	**1**	**3.50**	**2.96**	**4.10**	**1271**	**.883**	**29.9**	**8**	**3**	**4**	....	**397**	**24**	**0**	**3.63**	**3.91**	**223**	**.892**	**33.7**
1990-91	**St. Louis Blues**	**NHL**	**44**	**29**	**9**	**6**	**2671**	**134**	**3**	**3.01**	**2.70**	**3.25**	**1241**	**.892**	**27.9**	**13**	**6**	**7**	....	**687**	**35**	***1**	**3.06**	**3.64**	**294**	**.881**	**25.7**
1991-92	**St. Louis Blues**	**NHL**	**3**	**1**	**2**	**0**	**157**	**11**	**0**	**4.20**	**3.76**	**4.81**	**96**	**.885**	**36.7**	....	....	....	....	....	....	....	....	....	....	....	....
	Detroit Red Wings	**NHL**	**2**	**2**	**0**	**0**	**87**	**2**	**0**	**1.38**	**1.24**	**0.89**	**31**	**.935**	**21.4**	**2**	**1**	**0**	....	**73**	**4**	**0**	**3.29**	**4.39**	**30**	**.867**	**24.7**
	Adirondack Red Wings	AHL	3	2	1	0	179	8	0	2.68	....	....	....	....	....	....	....	....	....	....	....	....	....	....	....	....	....
1992-93	**Detroit Red Wings**	**NHL**	**22**	**13**	**4**	**2**	**1193**	**64**	**0**	**3.22**	**2.76**	**3.95**	**522**	**.877**	**26.3**	....	....	....	....	....	....	....	....	....	....	....	....
1993-94	**Detroit Red Wings**	**NHL**	**8**	**2**	**4**	**0**	**345**	**23**	**0**	**4.00**	**3.85**	**7.02**	**131**	**.824**	**22.8**	....	....	....	....	....	....	....	....	....	....	....	....
	Adirondack Red Wings	AHL	10	6	3	0	582	30	0	3.09	....	....	....	....	....	....	....	....	....	....	....	....	....	....	....	....	....
	Boston Bruins	**NHL**	**18**	**7**	**6**	**1**	**976**	**50**	**1**	**3.07**	**2.95**	**3.70**	**415**	**.880**	**25.5**	**2**	**1**	**1**	....	**120**	**8**	**0**	**4.00**	**7.62**	**42**	**.810**	**21.0**
1994-95	**Boston Bruins**	**NHL**	**11**	**3**	**6**	**1**	**565**	**27**	**0**	**2.87**	**3.01**	**3.51**	**221**	**.878**	**23.5**	....	....	....	....	....	....	....	....	....	....	....	....
	Providence Bruins	AHL	0	0	0	0	0	0	0	0.00	....	....	....	....	....	1	1	0	....	60	3	0	3.00	....	....	....	....
1995-96	SC Riessersee	Germany	47	....	....	....	2776	184	....	4.00	....	....	....	....	....	3	....	....	....	189	20	0	6.35	....	....	....	....
1996-97	Manitoba Moose	IHL	41	10	18	5	1941	113	0	3.49	....	....	....	....	....	....	....	....	....	....	....	....	....	....	....	....	....
1997-98	Revier Lowen	Germany	14	....	....	....	750	38	0	3.04	....	....	....	....	....	....	....	....	....	....	....	....	....	....	....	....	....
	HC Lugano	Switz.	1	0	0	1	65	2	0	1.85	....	....	....	....	....	....	....	....	....	....	....	....	....	....	....	....	....

			REGULAR SEASON													PLAYOFFS											
Season	Club	League	GP	W	L	T	Mins	GA	SO	Avg	AAvg	Eff	SA	S%	SAPG	GP	W	L	T	Mins	GA	SO	Avg	Eff	SA	S%	SAPG
1998-99	Ayr Scottish Eagles	BH-Cup	9	5	2	2	531	23	1	2.60	....	....	....	....	....	....	....	....	....	....	....	....	....	....	....	....	....
	Ayr Scottish Eagles	Britain	18	8	7	3	1120	58	0	3.11	....	....	....	....	....	....	....	....	....	....	....	....	....	....	....	....	....
	Ayr Scottish Eagles	EuroHL	5	2	3	0	309	20	0	3.88	....	....	....	....	....	....	....	....	....	....	....	....	....	....	....	....	....
	Lada Togliatti	Russia	5	....	....	....	235	6	0	1.53	....	....	....	....	....	7	....	....	....	407	14	1	2.06	....	....	....	....
99-2000	Lada Togliatti	Russia	16	....	....	....	722	26	4	2.16	....	....	....	....	....	1	0	1	0	14	2	0	8.57	....	....	....	....
	NHL Totals		**184**	**85**	**65**	**20**	**10423**	**573**	**5**	**3.30**	....	....	**4786**	**.880**	**27.6**	**25**	**11**	**12**		**1277**	**71**	**1**	**3.34**	....	**589**	**.879**	**27.7**

QMJHL Second All-Star Team (1986) • Won Harry "Hap" Holmes Memorial Trophy (fewest goals-against - AHL) (1987) • AHL Second All-Star Team (1988) • Shared Harry "Hap" Holmes Memorial Trophy (fewest goals-against - AHL) with Jocelyn Perreault (1988)

Signed as a free agent by **Montreal**, October 9, 1985. Traded to **St. Louis** by **Montreal** with Sergio Momesso for Jocelyn Lemieux, Darrell May and St. Louis' 2nd round choice (Patrice Brisebois) in 1989 Entry Draft, August 9, 1988. Traded to **Detroit** by **St. Louis** for Rick Zombo, October 18, 1991. Traded to **Boston** by **Detroit** for Boston's 5th round choice (Chad Wilchynski) in 1995 Entry Draft, January 17, 1994.

• RIGGIN, Dennis

Dennis Melville G – L. 5'11", 156 lbs. b: Kincardine, Ont., 4/11/1936.

Season	Club	League	GP	W	L	T	Mins	GA	SO	Avg	AAvg	Eff	SA	S%	SAPG	GP	W	L	T	Mins	GA	SO	Avg	Eff	SA	S%	SAPG
1951-52	Windsor Spitfires	OHA-Jr.	25	....	....	....	1480	163	0	6.61	....	....	....	....	....	....	....	....	....	....	....	....	....	....	....	....	....
1952-53	Windsor Spitfires	OHA-Jr.	55	....	....	....	3300	177	4	3.21	....	....	....	....	....	....	....	....	....	....	....	....	....	....	....	....	....
1953-54	Hamilton Cubs	OHA-Jr.	53	30	20	3	3180	176	3	*3.32	....	....	....	....	....	7	....	....	....	420	23	0	3.39	....	....	....	....
	Hamilton Tigers	OHA-Sr.	1	1	0	0	60	1	0	1.00	....	....	....	....	....	....	....	....	....	....	....	....	....	....	....	....	....
1954-55	Hamilton Tiger Cubs	OHA-Jr.	49	21	23	5	2940	173	0	3.45	....	....	....	....	....	12	....	....	....	720	42	*2	3.50	....	....	....	....
1955-56	Hamilton Tiger Cubs	OHA-Jr.	47	13	29	5	2820	244	0	5.19	....	....	....	....	....	....	....	....	....	....	....	....	....	....	....	....	....
	Edmonton Flyers	WHL	8	3	5	0	480	29	0	3.63	....	....	....	....	....	3	0	3	0	188	13	0	4.15	....	....	....	....
1956-57	Edmonton Flyers	WHL	67	38	25	4	4085	200	1	2.94	....	....	....	....	....	8	3	5	0	480	21	0	2.62	....	....	....	....
1957-58	Edmonton Flyers	WHL	69	37	28	4	4190	222	5	3.18	....	....	....	....	....	5	2	3	0	300	13	*1	2.60	....	....	....	....
	Calgary Stampeders	WHL	1	0	1	0	60	4	0	4.00	....	....	....	....	....	....	....	....	....	....	....	....	....	....	....	....	....
1958-59	Edmonton Flyers	WHL	13	7	5	1	800	27	3	2.03	....	....	....	....	....	....	....	....	....	....	....	....	....	....	....	....	....
1959-60	**Detroit Red Wings**	**NHL**	**9**	**2**	**6**	**1**	**540**	**30**	**1**	**3.33**	**3.49**	....	....	....	....	....	....	....	....	....	....	....	....	....	....	....	....
	Edmonton Flyers	WHL	59	30	25	4	3580	200	3	3.35	....	....	....	....	....	4	0	4	0	274	13	0	2.85	....	....	....	....
1960-61	Edmonton Flyers	WHL	69	26	*43	0	4140	289	0	4.19	....	....	....	....	....	....	....	....	....	....	....	....	....	....	....	....	....
1961-62	Edmonton Flyers	WHL	10	9	1	0	602	18	1	1.79	....	....	....	....	....	....	....	....	....	....	....	....	....	....	....	....	....
1962-63	**Detroit Red Wings**	**NHL**	**9**	**5**	**3**	**1**	**459**	**22**	**0**	**2.88**	**3.00**	....	....	....	....	....	....	....	....	....	....	....	....	....	....	....	....
	Pittsburgh Hornets	AHL	19	1	16	1	1140	112	0	5.89	....	....	....	....	....	....	....	....	....	....	....	....	....	....	....	....	....
	Edmonton Flyers	WHL	8	3	4	1	480	34	0	4.25	....	....	....	....	....	....	....	....	....	....	....	....	....	....	....	....	....
	NHL Totals		**18**	**7**	**9**	**2**	**999**	**52**	**1**	**3.12**	....	....	....	....	....	....	....	....	....	....	....	....	....	....	....	....	....

• Father of Pat • WHL Prairie Division Second All-Star Team (1957) • Won WHL Prairie Division Rookie of the Year Award (1957) • WHL Prairie Division First All-Star Team (1958) • WHL Second All-Star Team (1960)

• Suffered eventual career-ending eye injury in game vs. Seatlle (WHL), November 10, 1961.

• RIGGIN, Pat

Patrick Michael G – R. 5'9", 170 lbs. b: Kincardine, Ont., 5/26/1959. Atlanta's 3rd, 33rd overall in 1979.

Season	Club	League	GP	W	L	T	Mins	GA	SO	Avg	AAvg	Eff	SA	S%	SAPG	GP	W	L	T	Mins	GA	SO	Avg	Eff	SA	S%	SAPG
1975-76	London Knights	OMJHL	29	....	....	....	1385	86	0	3.68	....	....	....	....	....	1	0	1	0	60	6	0	6.00	....	....	....	....
1976-77	London Knights	OMJHL	48	....	....	....	2809	138	*2	*2.95	....	....	....	....	....	20	10	8	2	1197	66	2	3.20	....	....	....	....
	Ottawa 67's	Mem-Cup	4	*3	1	0	244	12	0	2.98	....	....	....	....	....	....	....	....	....	....	....	....	....	....	....	....	....
1977-78	London Knights	OMJHL	38	....	....	....	2266	140	0	3.65	....	....	....	....	....	9	6	2	1	536	27	0	3.03	....	....	....	....
1978-79	Birmingham Bulls	WHA	46	16	22	5	2511	158	1	3.78	....	....	....	....	....	....	....	....	....	....	....	....	....	....	....	....	....
1979-80	**Atlanta Flames**	**NHL**	**25**	**11**	**9**	**2**	**1368**	**73**	**2**	**3.20**	**2.83**	....	....	....	....	....	....	....	....	....	....	....	....	....	....	....	....
	Birmingham Bulls	CHL	12	8	2	2	746	32	0	2.57	....	....	....	....	....	....	....	....	....	....	....	....	....	....	....	....	....
1980-81	**Calgary Flames**	**NHL**	**42**	**21**	**16**	**4**	**2411**	**154**	**0**	**3.83**	**3.10**	....	....	....	....	**11**	**6**	**4**	....	**629**	**37**	**0**	**3.53**	....	....	....	....
1981-82	**Calgary Flames**	**NHL**	**52**	**19**	**19**	**11**	**2934**	**207**	**2**	**4.23**	**3.27**	....	....	....	....	**3**	**0**	**3**	....	**194**	**10**	**0**	**3.09**	....	....	....	....
1982-83	**Washington Capitals**	**NHL**	**38**	**16**	**9**	**9**	**2161**	**121**	**0**	**3.36**	**2.69**	**4.01**	**1015**	**.881**	**28.2**	**3**	**0**	**1**	....	**101**	**8**	**0**	**4.75**	....	....	....	....
1983-84	Hershey Bears	AHL	3	2	0	1	185	7	0	2.27	....	....	....	....	....	....	....	....	....	....	....	....	....	....	....	....	....
	Washington Capitals	**NHL**	**41**	**21**	**14**	**2**	**2299**	**102**	***4**	***2.66**	**2.08**	**2.94**	**924**	**.890**	**24.1**	**5**	**1**	**3**	....	**230**	**9**	**0**	**2.35**	**2.61**	**81**	**.889**	**21.1**
1984-85	**Washington Capitals**	**NHL**	**57**	**28**	**20**	**7**	**3388**	**168**	**2**	**2.98**	**2.36**	**3.39**	**1478**	**.886**	**26.2**	**2**	**1**	**1**	....	**122**	**5**	**0**	**2.46**	**3.15**	**39**	**.872**	**19.2**
	Canada	WEC-A	4	2	1	0	213	11	0	3.10	....	....	....	....	....	....	....	....	....	....	....	....	....	....	....	....	....
1985-86	**Washington Capitals**	**NHL**	**7**	**2**	**3**	**1**	**369**	**23**	**0**	**3.74**	**2.92**	**6.47**	**133**	**.827**	**21.6**	....	....	....	....	....	....	....	....	....	....	....	....
	Boston Bruins	**NHL**	**39**	**17**	**11**	**8**	**2272**	**127**	**1**	**3.35**	**2.61**	**4.37**	**973**	**.869**	**25.7**	**1**	**0**	**1**	....	**60**	**3**	**0**	**3.00**	**3.91**	**23**	**.870**	**23.0**
1986-87	**Boston Bruins**	**NHL**	**10**	**3**	**5**	**1**	**513**	**29**	**0**	**3.39**	**2.87**	**4.17**	**236**	**.877**	**27.6**	....	....	....	....	....	....	....	....	....	....	....	....
	Moncton Golden Flames	AHL	14	6	5	0	798	34	1	2.56	....	....	....	....	....	....	....	....	....	....	....	....	....	....	....	....	....
	Pittsburgh Penguins	**NHL**	**17**	**8**	**6**	**3**	**988**	**55**	**0**	**3.34**	**2.83**	**3.95**	**465**	**.882**	**28.2**	....	....	....	....	....	....	....	....	....	....	....	....
	Canada	WEC-A	DID NOT PLAY – SPARE GOALTENDER																								
1987-88	**Pittsburgh Penguins**	**NHL**	**22**	**7**	**8**	**4**	**1169**	**76**	**0**	**3.90**	**3.25**	**5.11**	**580**	**.869**	**29.8**	....	....	....	....	....	....	....	....	....	....	....	....
	Muskegon Lumberjacks	IHL	18	13	2	0	956	43	0	2.70	....	....	....	....	....	2	1	1	....	110	12	0	6.55	....	....	....	....
	NHL Totals		**350**	**153**	**120**	**52**	**19872**	**1135**	**11**	**3.43**	....	....	....	....	....	**25**	**8**	**13**	....	**1336**	**72**	**0**	**3.23**	....	....	....	....
	Other Major League Totals		46	16	22	5	2511	158	1	3.78	....	....	....	....	....	....	....	....	....	....	....	....	....	....	....	....	....

• Son of Dennis • OMJHL First All-Star Team (1977) • Memorial Cup All-Star Team (1977) • Won Hap Emms Memorial Trophy (Memorial Cup Tournament Top Goaltender) (1977) • OMJHL Second All-Star Team (1978) • NHL Second All-Star Team (1984) • Shared William M. Jennings Trophy with Al Jensen (1984)

Loaned to **Ottawa** (OHL) by **London** (OHL) for Memorial Cup Tournament, May 6, 1977. Signed as a free agent by **Birmingham** (WHA), July, 1978. Transferred to **Calgary** after **Atlanta** franchise relocated, June 24, 1980. Traded to **Washington** by **Calgary** with Ken Houston for Howard Walker, George White, Washington's 6th round choice (Mats Kihlstron) in 1982 Entry Draft, 3rd round choice (Perry Berezan) in 1983 Entry Draft and 2nd round choice (Paul Ranheim) in 1984 Entry Draft, June 9, 1982. Traded to **Boston** by **Washington** for Pete Peeters, November 14, 1985. Traded to **Pittsburgh** by **Boston** for Roberto Romano, February 6, 1987.

• RING, Bob

G – L. 5'10", 170 lbs. b: Winchester, MA, 10/6/1946.

Season	Club	League	GP	W	L	T	Mins	GA	SO	Avg	AAvg	Eff	SA	S%	SAPG	GP	W	L	T	Mins	GA	SO	Avg	Eff	SA	S%	SAPG
1964-65	Niagara Falls Flyers	OHA-Jr.	1	0	0	0	40	3	0	4.50	....	....	....	....	....	....	....	....	....	....	....	....	....	....	....	....	....
1965-66	Niagara Falls Flyers	OHA-Jr.	22	....	....	....	1320	74	1	3.24	....	....	....	....	....	....	....	....	....	....	....	....	....	....	....	....	....
	Boston Bruins	**NHL**	**1**	**0**	**0**	**0**	**33**	**4**	**0**	**7.27**	**7.36**	....	....	....	....	....	....	....	....	....	....	....	....	....	....	....	....
	Springfield Indians	AHL	1	0	0	0	20	3	0	9.00	....	....	....	....	....	....	....	....	....	....	....	....	....	....	....	....	....
1966-67	Acadia University	AUAA	STATISTICS NOT AVAILABLE																								
1967-68	Acadia University	AUAA	16	10	5	1	940	62	0	3.96	....	....	....	....	....	....	....	....	....	....	....	....	....	....	....	....	....
1968-69	Acadia University	AUAA	18	12	5	1	1080	56	0	3.11	....	....	....	....	....	....	....	....	....	....	....	....	....	....	....	....	....
1969-70	Acadia University	AUAA	10	....	....	....	600	43	0	4.30	....	....	....	....	....	....	....	....	....	....	....	....	....	....	....	....	....
1970-71			OUT OF HOCKEY – RETIRED																								
1971-72	Concord Eastern Olympics	NESHL	STATISTICS NOT AVAILABLE																								
	NHL Totals		**1**	**0**	**0**	**0**	**33**	**4**	**0**	**7.27**	....	....	....	....	....	....	....	....	....	....	....	....	....	....	....	....	....

OHA-Jr. Second All-Star Team (1966) • AUAA First All-Star Team (1968)

• **Boston's** spare goaltender replaced injured Ed Johnston in 2nd period, October 30, 1965. (NY Rangers 8, Boston 2)

• RIVARD, Fern

Fernand Joseph G – L. 5'9", 160 lbs. b: Grand'Mere, Que., 1/18/1946.

Season	Club	League	GP	W	L	T	Mins	GA	SO	Avg	AAvg	Eff	SA	S%	SAPG	GP	W	L	T	Mins	GA	SO	Avg	Eff	SA	S%	SAPG
1961-62	Quebec Citadelle	QJHL	6	....	....	....	360	22	0	3.67	....	....	....	....	....	....	....	....	....	....	....	....	....	....	....	....	....
1962-63	Quebec Citadelle	QJHL	STATISTICS NOT AVAILABLE																								
1963-64	Quebec Citadelle	QJHL	....	....	....	....	....	....	....	....	....	....	....	....	....	7	3	4	0	420	40	0	5.71	....	....	....	....
	Quebec Aces	AHL	1	1	0	0	60	2	0	2.00	....	....	....	....	....	....	....	....	....	....	....	....	....	....	....	....	....
1964-65	Thetford Mines Eperviers	QJHL	19	12	7	0	1140	69	1	3.63	....	....	....	....	....	....	....	....	....	....	....	....	....	....	....	....	....
	Montreal Jr. Canadiens	OHA-Jr.	26	....	....	....	1560	92	1	3.54	....	....	....	....	....	7	....	....	....	400	30	0	4.50	....	....	....	....
1965-66	Peterborough Petes	OHA-Jr.	15	....	....	....	880	61	0	4.16	....	....	....	....	....	1	0	1	0	60	7	0	7.00	....	....	....	....
1966-67	Muskegon Mohawks	IHL	68	....	....	....	4080	265	1	3.91	....	....	....	....	....	....	....	....	....	....	....	....	....	....	....	....	....
1967-68	Quebec Aces	AHL	46	19	16	7	2529	132	0	3.13	....	....	....	....	....	*11	....	....	....	*614	36	0	3.52	....	....	....	....
1968-69	**Minnesota North Stars**	**NHL**	**13**	**0**	**6**	**4**	**657**	**48**	**0**	**4.38**	**4.56**	....	....	....	....	....	....	....	....	....	....	....	....	....	....	....	....
	Memphis South Stars	CHL	29	....	....	....	1682	101	2	3.53	....	....	....	....	....	....	....	....	....	....	....	....	....	....	....	....	....
1969-70	**Minnesota North Stars**	**NHL**	**14**	**3**	**5**	**5**	**800**	**42**	**1**	**3.15**	**3.35**	....	....	....	....	....	....	....	....	....	....	....	....	....	....	....	....
	Iowa Stars	CHL	18	9	5	4	1050	61	1	3.49	....	....	....	....	....	7	3	4	0	415	24	*1	3.47	....	....	....	....

Season	Club	League	GP	W	L	T	Mins	GA	SO	Avg	AAvg	Eff	SA	S%	SAPG	GP	W	L	T	Mins	GA	SO	Avg	Eff	SA	S%	SAPG
			REGULAR SEASON													PLAYOFFS											
1970-71	Cleveland Barons	AHL	36	15	14	4	2047	102	2	2.98	....	....	....	....	....	1	0	1	0	60	6	0	6.00	....	....	....	....
1971-72	Cleveland Barons	AHL	40	12	19	5	2199	118	1	3.21	....	....	....	....	....	4	1	2	0	173	11	0	3.82	....	....	....	....
1972-73	Jacksonville Barons	AHL	*65	....	....	....	*3643	250	2	4.11	....	....	....	....	....	....	....	....	....	....	....	....	....	....	....	....	....
1973-74	**Minnesota North Stars**	**NHL**	**13**	**3**	**6**	**2**	**701**	**50**	**1**	**4.28**	**4.15**	....	....	....	....	....	....	....	....	....	....	....	....	....	....	....	....
	New Haven Nighthawks	AHL	12	7	3	2	700	41	2	3.51	....	....	....	....	....	....	....	....	....	....	....	....	....	....	....	....	....
1974-75	**Minnesota North Stars**	**NHL**	**15**	**3**	**9**	**0**	**707**	**50**	**0**	**4.24**	**3.84**	....	....	....	....	....	....	....	....	....	....	....	....	....	....	....	....
	New Haven Nighthawks	AHL	7	1	4	1	404	26	0	3.86	....	....	....	....	....	....	....	....	....	....	....	....	....	....	....	....	....
	NHL Totals		**55**	**9**	**26**	**11**	**2865**	**190**	**2**	**3.98**	....	....	....	....	....	....	....	....	....	....	....	....	....	....	....	....	....

QJHL First All-Star Team (1963, 1964)

• Regular season totals for **Quebec** (QJHL) in 1963-64 season unavailable. Rights transferred to **Philadelphia** after NHL club purchased **Quebec** (AHL) franchise, May 8, 1967. Claimed by **Minnesota** from **Philadelphia** in Intra-League Draft, June 12, 1968.

• ROACH, John Ross

"Little Napolean" G – L. 5'5", 130 lbs. b: Port Perry, Ont., 6/23/1900 d: 7/9/1973.

Season	Club	League	GP	W	L	T	Mins	GA	SO	Avg	AAvg	Eff	SA	S%	SAPG	GP	W	L	T	Mins	GA	SO	Avg	Eff	SA	S%	SAPG
1919-20	Toronto Aura Lee	OHA-Jr.	6	4	2	0	360	31	0	5.17	....	....	....	....	....	....	....	....	....	....	....	....	....	....	....	....	....
1920-21	Toronto Granites	OHA-Sr.	10	*8	2	0	566	12	3	*1.27	....	....	....	....	....	2	1	1	0	120	7	0	3.50	....	....	....	....
1921-22	**Toronto St. Pats**	**NHL**	**22**	**11**	**10**	**1**	**1340**	**91**	**0**	**4.07**	**3.16**	....	....	....	....	**2**	**1**	**0**	**1**	**120**	**4**	**1**	**2.00**	....	....	....	....
♦	Toronto St. Pats	St-Cup	5	3	2	0	305	9	1	1.77	....	....	....	....	....	....	....	....	....	....	....	....	....	....	....	....	....
1922-23	**Toronto St. Pats**	**NHL**	***24**	**13**	**10**	**1**	**1469**	**88**	**1**	**3.59**	**3.48**	....	....	....	....	....	....	....	....	....	....	....	....	....	....	....	....
1923-24	**Toronto St. Pats**	**NHL**	**23**	**10**	**13**	**0**	**1380**	**80**	**1**	**3.48**	**4.42**	....	....	....	....	....	....	....	....	....	....	....	....	....	....	....	....
1924-25	**Toronto St. Pats**	**NHL**	***30**	***19**	**11**	**0**	**1800**	**84**	**1**	**2.80**	**3.50**	....	....	....	....	**2**	**0**	**2**	**0**	**120**	**5**	**0**	***2.50**	....	....	....	....
1925-26	**Toronto St. Pats**	**NHL**	***36**	**12**	**21**	**3**	**2231**	**114**	**2**	**3.07**	**4.30**	....	....	....	....	....	....	....	....	....	....	....	....	....	....	....	....
1926-27	**Toronto St. Pats/Leafs**	**NHL**	***44**	**15**	**24**	**5**	**2764**	**94**	**4**	**2.04**	**3.12**	....	....	....	....	....	....	....	....	....	....	....	....	....	....	....	....
1927-28	**Toronto Maple Leafs**	**NHL**	**43**	**18**	**18**	**7**	**2690**	**88**	**4**	**1.96**	**3.16**	....	....	....	....	....	....	....	....	....	....	....	....	....	....	....	....
1928-29	**New York Rangers**	**NHL**	***44**	**21**	**13**	**10**	**2760**	**65**	**13**	**1.41**	**2.93**	....	....	....	....	***6**	**3**	**2**	**1**	***392**	**5**	***3**	**0.77**	....	....	....	....
1929-30	**New York Rangers**	**NHL**	***44**	**17**	**17**	**10**	**2770**	**143**	**1**	**3.10**	**3.21**	....	....	....	....	**4**	**1**	**2**	**1**	**309**	**7**	**0**	**1.36**	....	....	....	....
1930-31	**New York Rangers**	**NHL**	***44**	**19**	**16**	**9**	***2760**	**87**	**7**	**1.89**	**2.35**	....	....	....	....	**4**	**2**	**2**	**0**	**240**	**4**	**1**	***1.00**	....	....	....	....
1931-32	**New York Rangers**	**NHL**	***48**	**23**	**17**	**8**	**3020**	**112**	***9**	**2.23**	**2.68**	....	....	....	....	***7**	**3**	**4**	**0**	***480**	**27**	***1**	**3.38**	....	....	....	....
	Springfield Indians	IHL	1	1	0	0	60	1	0	1.00	....	....	....	....	....	....	....	....	....	....	....	....	....	....	....	....	....
1932-33	**Detroit Red Wings**	**NHL**	***48**	***25**	**15**	**8**	**2970**	**93**	**10**	**1.88**	**2.46**	....	....	....	....	**4**	**2**	**2**	**0**	**240**	**8**	**1**	**2.00**	....	....	....	....
1933-34	**Detroit Red Wings**	**NHL**	**19**	**9**	**8**	**1**	**1030**	**45**	**1**	**2.62**	**3.33**	....	....	....	....	....	....	....	....	....	....	....	....	....	....	....	....
	Syracuse Stars	IHL	13	....	....	....	780	36	2	2.77	....	....	....	....	....	6	....	....	....	360	19	0	3.17	....	....	....	....
1934-35	**Detroit Red Wings**	**NHL**	**23**	**7**	**11**	**5**	**1460**	**62**	**4**	**2.55**	**3.09**	....	....	....	....	....	....	....	....	....	....	....	....	....	....	....	....
	Detroit Olympics	IHL	9	4	4	1	560	15	1	1.61	....	....	....	....	....	....	....	....	....	....	....	....	....	....	....	....	....
	NHL Totals		**492**	**219**	**204**	**68**	**30444**	**1246**	**58**	**2.46**	....	....	....	....	....	**29**	**12**	**14**	**3**	**1901**	**60**	**7**	**1.89**	....	....	....	....

NHL First All-Star Team (1933)

Signed as a free agent by **Toronto**, December 5, 1921. Traded to **NY Rangers** by **Toronto** for Lorne Chabot and $10,000, October 18, 1928. Traded to **Detroit** by **NY Rangers** for cash, October 25, 1932.

• ROBERTS, Moe

G – R. 5'9", 165 lbs. b: Waterbury, CT, 12/13/1905 d: 2/7/1975.

Season	Club	League	GP	W	L	T	Mins	GA	SO	Avg	AAvg	Eff	SA	S%	SAPG	GP	W	L	T	Mins	GA	SO	Avg	Eff	SA	S%	SAPG
1923-24	Somerville High School	Hi-School	STATISTICS NOT AVAILABLE																								
1924-25	Boston AA Unicorn	USAHA	....	....	....	....	....	....	....	....	....	....	....	....	....	1	0	0	0	30	1	0	1.50	....	....	....	....
1925-26	**Boston Bruins**	**NHL**	**2**	**1**	**1**	**0**	**85**	**5**	**0**	**3.53**	**4.68**	....	....	....	....	....	....	....	....	....	....	....	....	....	....	....	....
1926-27	New Haven Eagles	Can-Am	32	*18	14	0	1980	66	1	2.00	....	....	....	....	....	4	1	2	1	240	9	0	2.25	....	....	....	....
1927-28	New Haven Eagles	Can-Am	40	16	*20	4	2450	90	4	2.20	....	....	....	....	....	....	....	....	....	....	....	....	....	....	....	....	....
1928-29	Philadelphia Arrows	Can-Am	40	12	*21	7	2490	73	5	1.76	....	....	....	....	....	....	....	....	....	....	....	....	....	....	....	....	....
1929-30	Philadelphia Arrows	Can-Am	40	20	18	2	2470	121	3	2.94	....	....	....	....	....	1	....	....	....	120	5	0	2.50	....	....	....	....
1930-31	Philadelphia Arrows	Can-Am	40	12	22	6	2460	108	3	2.63	....	....	....	....	....	....	....	....	....	....	....	....	....	....	....	....	....
1931-32	New Haven Eagles	Can-Am	22	12	10	0	1370	48	2	2.10	....	....	....	....	....	2	0	2	0	120	8	0	4.00	....	....	....	....
	New York Americans	**NHL**	**1**	**1**	**0**	**0**	**60**	**1**	**0**	**1.00**	**1.22**	....	....	....	....	....	....	....	....	....	....	....	....	....	....	....	....
1932-33	New Haven Eagles	Can-Am	44	16	23	5	2680	123	*4	2.75	....	....	....	....	....	....	....	....	....	....	....	....	....	....	....	....	....
1933-34	**New York Americans**	**NHL**	**6**	**1**	**4**	**0**	**336**	**25**	**0**	**4.46**	**5.70**	....	....	....	....	....	....	....	....	....	....	....	....	....	....	....	....
	Cleveland Falcons	IHL	35	....	....	....	2100	98	3	2.80	....	....	....	....	....	....	....	....	....	....	....	....	....	....	....	....	....
1934-35	Cleveland Falcons	IHL	44	*20	*23	1	2670	132	4	2.97	....	....	....	....	....	2	0	2	0	140	6	0	2.57	....	....	....	....
1935-36	Cleveland Falcons	IHL	13	8	3	2	810	28	2	2.07	....	....	....	....	....	2	1	1	0	120	3	*1	1.50	....	....	....	....
	Syracuse Stars	IHL	1	1	0	0	60	0	1	0.00	....	....	....	....	....	....	....	....	....	....	....	....	....	....	....	....	....
	Rochester Cardinals	IHL	15	8	5	2	930	31	2	2.00	....	....	....	....	....	....	....	....	....	....	....	....	....	....	....	....	....
1936-37	Cleveland Barons	IAHL	45	13	24	8	2840	134	3	2.83	....	....	....	....	....	....	....	....	....	....	....	....	....	....	....	....	....
1937-38	Cleveland Barons	IAHL	45	24	11	9	2810	103	5	2.20	....	....	....	....	....	2	0	2	0	183	9	0	2.95	....	....	....	....
1938-39	Cleveland Barons	IAHL	*54	23	22	9	*3410	138	4	2.43	....	....	....	....	....	*9	*7	2	0	*635	12	*4	*1.13	....	....	....	....
1939-40	Cleveland Barons	IAHL	*56	24	24	8	*3482	130	5	*2.24	....	....	....	....	....	....	....	....	....	....	....	....	....	....	....	....	....
1940-41	Cleveland Barons	AHL	43	20	15	7	2640	122	3	2.77	....	....	....	....	....	4	2	1	0	239	10	0	2.51	....	....	....	....
1941-42	Cleveland Barons	AHL	27	17	7	2	1560	79	2	3.04	....	....	....	....	....	....	....	....	....	....	....	....	....	....	....	....	....
	Pittsburgh Hornets	AHL	3	1	2	0	180	14	0	4.67	....	....	....	....	....	....	....	....	....	....	....	....	....	....	....	....	....
1942-1945			MILITARY SERVICE																								
1945-46	Washington Lions	EAHL	24	....	....	....	1440	97	2	4.04	....	....	....	....	....	6	....	....	....	360	22	*1	3.67	....	....	....	....
1946-1951			DID NOT PLAY																								
1951-52	**Chicago Black Hawks**	**NHL**	**1**	**0**	**0**	**0**	**20**	**0**	**0**	**0.00**	**0.00**	....	....	....	....	....	....	....	....	....	....	....	....	....	....	....	....
	NHL Totals		**10**	**3**	**5**	**0**	**501**	**31**	**0**	**3.71**	....	....	....	....	....	....	....	....	....	....	....	....	....	....	....	....	....

IAHL Second All-Star Team (1938) • IAHL First All-Star Team (1940)

Signed as a free agent by **Boston**, December 8, 1925. Signed as a free agent by **NY Americans**, October 18, 1931. Promoted to **NY Americans** from **New Haven** (Can-Am) to replace injured Roy Worters, March 10, 1932. (NY Americans 5, NY Rangers 1). Loaned to **Rochester** (IHL) by **Cleveland** (IHL) for cash, January 3, 1936. Returned to **Cleveland** (IHL) by **Rochester** (IHL) for Bill Taugher, February 16, 1936. • Served as arena manager for USHL's Milwaukee Sea Gulls 1950-51. • **Chicago's** assistant trainer replaced injured Harry Lumley in game vs. Detroit, November 25, 1951. (Detroit 5, Chicago 2)

• ROBERTSON, Earl

Earl Cooper G – L. 5'10", 165 lbs. b: Bengough, Sask., 11/24/1910 d: 1/19/1979.

Season	Club	League	GP	W	L	T	Mins	GA	SO	Avg	AAvg	Eff	SA	S%	SAPG	GP	W	L	T	Mins	GA	SO	Avg	Eff	SA	S%	SAPG
1925-26	Regina Falcons	S-SJHL	8	*4	3	1	500	22	0	*2.64	....	....	....	....	....	2	0	2	0	120	9	0	4.50	....	....	....	....
	Regina Falcons	Mem-Cup	2	0	2	0	120	9	0	4.50	....	....	....	....	....	....	....	....	....	....	....	....	....	....	....	....	....
1926-27	Regina Falcons	S-SJHL	6	4	2	0	370	11	0	1.76	....	....	....	....	....	1	0	1	0	60	3	0	3.00	....	....	....	....
1927-28	Vancouver Monarchs	VCAHL	8	4	2	2	500	18	0	2.16	....	....	....	....	....	....	....	....	....	....	....	....	....	....	....	....	....
	Vancouver Monarchs	Al-Cup	4	1	2	1	240	11	0	2.75	....	....	....	....	....	....	....	....	....	....	....	....	....	....	....	....	....
1928-29	Victoria Cubs	PCHL	34	7	*21	6	2130	86	1	2.42	....	....	....	....	....	....	....	....	....	....	....	....	....	....	....	....	....
1929-30	Victoria Cubs	PCHL	32	....	....	....	1920	112	1	3.50	....	....	....	....	....	....	....	....	....	....	....	....	....	....	....	....	....
1930-31	Tacoma Tigers	PCHL	10	....	....	....	600	24	2	2.40	....	....	....	....	....	....	....	....	....	....	....	....	....	....	....	....	....
	Oakland Sheiks	Cal-Pro	1	1	0	0	60	1	0	1.00	....	....	....	....	....	....	....	....	....	....	....	....	....	....	....	....	....
1931-32	Hollywood Stars	Cal-Pro	31	*20	7	4	1860	86	....	*2.77	....	....	....	....	....	7	*4	3	0	420	20	*1	*2.86	....	....	....	....
1932-33	Edmonton Eskimos	WCHL	27	....	....	....	1620	73	*6	2.70	....	....	....	....	....	8	....	....	....	480	15	*1	1.88	....	....	....	....
1933-34	Edmonton Eskimos	WCHL	33	....	....	....	1960	89	4	2.70	....	....	....	....	....	2	0	2	0	120	7	0	3.50	....	....	....	....
1934-35	Windsor Bulldogs	IHL	40	14	19	7	2490	100	*6	2.41	....	....	....	....	....	....	....	....	....	....	....	....	....	....	....	....	....
1935-36	Windsor Bulldogs	IHL	48	18	19	11	2998	120	4	2.40	....	....	....	....	....	8	3	4	1	505	18	*2	2.14	....	....	....	....
	Rochester Cardinals	IHL	2	0	2	0	120	7	0	3.50	....	....	....	....	....	....	....	....	....	....	....	....	....	....	....	....	....
1936-37	Pittsburgh Hornets	IAHL	29	14	15	0	1820	74	5	2.44	....	....	....	....	....	4	1	3	0	240	12	0	3.00	....	....	....	....
♦	**Detroit Red Wings**	**NHL**	....	....	....	....	....	....	....	....	....	....	....	....	....	**6**	**3**	**2**	....	**340**	**8**	**2**	**1.41**	....	....	....	....
1937-38	**New York Americans**	**NHL**	***48**	**19**	**18**	**11**	***3000**	**111**	**6**	**2.22**	**2.62**	....	....	....	....	**6**	**3**	**3**	....	**475**	**12**	**0**	***1.52**	....	....	....	....
1938-39	**New York Americans**	**NHL**	**46**	**17**	**18**	**10**	**2850**	**136**	**3**	**2.86**	**3.52**	....	....	....	....	....	....	....	....	....	....	....	....	....	....	....	....
1939-40	**New York Americans**	**NHL**	***48**	**15**	**29**	**4**	**2960**	**140**	**6**	**2.84**	**3.55**	....	....	....	....	**3**	**1**	**2**	....	**180**	**9**	**0**	**3.00**	....	....	....	....
1940-41	**New York Americans**	**NHL**	**36**	**6**	**22**	**8**	**2260**	**142**	**1**	**3.77**	**4.52**	....	....	....	....	....	....	....	....	....	....	....	....	....	....	....	....
	Springfield Indians	AHL	11	4	5	2	680	37	0	3.26	....	....	....	....	....	3	1	2	0	236	5	0	*1.27	....	....	....	....

Season	Club	League	GP	W	L	T	Mins	GA	SO	Avg	AAvg	Eff	SA	S%	SAPG	GP	W	L	T	Mins	GA	SO	Avg	Eff	SA	S%	SAPG
			REGULAR SEASON													PLAYOFFS											
1941-42	Brooklyn Americans	NHL	12	3	8	1	750	46	0	3.68	3.62	....	....	....	....	....	....	....	....	....	....	....	....	....	....	....	....
	Springfield Indians	AHL	41	24	14	3	2460	125	2	3.05	....	....	....	....	....	3	2	1	0	160	15	0	5.63	....	....	....	....
1942-43				MILITARY SERVICE																							
1943-44	Edmonton Vics	X-Games		STATISTICS NOT AVAILABLE																							
	Edmonton Vics	Al-Cup	3	0	3	0	180	26	0	8.67	....	....	....	....	....	....	....	....	....	....	....	....	....	....	....	....	....
	NHL Totals		**190**	**60**	**95**	**34**	**11820**	**575**	**16**	**2.92**	....	....	....	....	....	**15**	**7**	**7**	....	**995**	**29**	**2**	**1.75**	....	....	....	....

IAHL Second All-Star Team (1936) • NHL Second All-Star Team (1939)

Traded to **Detroit** by **Windsor** (IAHL) for $1,500, October 21, 1936. Traded to **NY Americans** by **Detroit** for John Doran and $7,500, May 9, 1937. • Recorded a shutout (3-0) in NHL regular season debut vs. Chicago, November 4, 1937.

• ROLLINS, Al

Elwin Ira G – L. 6'2", 175 lbs. b: Vanguard, Sask., 10/9/1926 d: 7/27/1996.

Season	Club	League	GP	W	L	T	Mins	GA	SO	Avg	AAvg	Eff	SA	S%	SAPG	GP	W	L	T	Mins	GA	SO	Avg	Eff	SA	S%	SAPG
1942-43	Moose Jaw Canucks	S-SJHL	15	6	7	2	900	51	0	3.40	....	....	....	....	....	2	0	2	0	120	7	0	3.50	....	....	....	....
1943-44	New York Rovers	EAHL	22	....	....	....	1290	120	0	5.58	....	....	....	....	....	....	....	....	....	....	....	....	....	....	....	....	....
1944-45	Seattle Ironmen	PCHL	27	20	6	1	1620	84	....	3.11	....	....	....	....	....	....	....	....	....	....	....	....	....	....	....	....	....
1945-46	Seattle Ironmen	PCHL	55	....	....	....	3300	210	*2	*3.65	....	....	....	....	....	3	....	....	....	180	12	0	4.00	....	....	....	....
1946-47	Vancouver Canucks	PCHL	54	27	26	1	3240	253	0	4.59	....	....	....	....	....	4	1	3	0	240	17	0	4.25	....	....	....	....
1947-48	Edmonton Flyers	WCSHL	46	24	20	2	2800	167	1	3.20	....	....	....	....	....	10	*8	1	1	600	32	0	3.20	....	....	....	....
	Edmonton Flyers	Al-Cup	14	*12	2	0	840	27	*4	*1.93	....	....	....	....	....	....	....	....	....	....	....	....	....	....	....	....	....
1948-49	Kansas City Pla-Mors	USHL	60	29	21	10	3600	189	1	3.16	....	....	....	....	....	2	0	2	0	120	6	0	3.00	....	....	....	....
1949-50	Cleveland Barons	AHL	6	4	0	2	360	17	0	2.83	....	....	....	....	....	....	....	....	....	....	....	....	....	....	....	....	....
	Toronto Maple Leafs	**NHL**	**2**	**1**	**1**	**0**	**100**	**4**	**1**	**2.40**	**2.67**	....	....	....	....	....	....	....	....	....	....	....	....	....	....	....	....
	Pittsburgh Hornets	AHL	20	9	7	4	1200	43	3	2.15	....	....	....	....	....	....	....	....	....	....	....	....	....	....	....	....	....
1950-51 ♦	**Toronto Maple Leafs**	**NHL**	**40**	***27**	**5**	**8**	**2373**	**70**	**5**	***1.77**	**1.92**	....	....	....	....	**4**	**3**	**1**	....	**210**	**6**	**0**	**1.71**	....	....	....	....
1951-52	**Toronto Maple Leafs**	**NHL**	***70**	**29**	**24**	**16**	**4170**	**154**	**5**	**2.22**	**2.53**	....	....	....	....	**2**	**0**	**2**	....	**120**	**6**	**0**	**3.00**	....	....	....	....
1952-53	**Chicago Black Hawks**	**NHL**	***70**	**27**	**28**	**15**	***4200**	**175**	**6**	**2.50**	**3.21**	....	....	....	....	**7**	**3**	**4**	....	**425**	**18**	**0**	**2.54**	....	....	....	....
1953-54	**Chicago Black Hawks**	**NHL**	**66**	**12**	**47**	**7**	**3960**	**213**	**5**	**3.23**	**4.38**	....	....	....	....	....	....	....	....	....	....	....	....	....	....	....	....
1954-55	**Chicago Black Hawks**	**NHL**	**44**	**9**	**27**	**8**	**2640**	**150**	**0**	**3.41**	**4.30**	....	....	....	....	....	....	....	....	....	....	....	....	....	....	....	....
1955-56	**Chicago Black Hawks**	**NHL**	**58**	**17**	**30**	**11**	**3480**	**171**	**3**	**2.95**	**3.72**	....	....	....	....	....	....	....	....	....	....	....	....	....	....	....	....
	Buffalo Bisons	AHL	6	2	3	1	360	25	1	4.17	....	....	....	....	....	....	....	....	....	....	....	....	....	....	....	....	....
1956-57	**Chicago Black Hawks**	**NHL**	***70**	**16**	**39**	**15**	***4200**	**224**	**3**	**3.20**	**3.83**	....	....	....	....	....	....	....	....	....	....	....	....	....	....	....	....
1957-58	Calgary Stampeders	WHL	68	30	33	5	4130	214	3	3.11	....	....	....	....	....	*14	6	*8	0	*880	47	0	3.20	....	....	....	....
1958-59	Winnipeg Warriors	WHL	31	17	14	0	1860	99	3	3.19	....	....	....	....	....	7	3	4	0	420	22	0	3.14	....	....	....	....
1959-60	Winnipeg Warriors	WHL	55	22	31	2	3300	193	2	3.51	....	....	....	....	....	....	....	....	....	....	....	....	....	....	....	....	....
	New York Rangers	**NHL**	**10**	**3**	**4**	**3**	**600**	**31**	**0**	**3.10**	**3.24**	....	....	....	....	....	....	....	....	....	....	....	....	....	....	....	....
1960-61				OUT OF HOCKEY – RETIRED																							
1961-62	Portland Buckaroos	WHL	8	5	3	0	480	18	1	2.25	....	....	....	....	....	7	3	4	0	432	18	0	*2.49	....	....	....	....
1962-1965	Drumheller Miners	ASHL		DID NOT PLAY – COACHING																							
1965-66	Drumheller Miners	ASHL	....	....	....	....	....	....	....	....	....	....	....	....	....	2	2	0	0	120	3	0	1.50	....	....	....	....
	Drumheller Miners	Al-Cup	15	*12	3	0	911	32	*3	*2.11	....	....	....	....	....	....	....	....	....	....	....	....	....	....	....	....	....
	NHL Totals		**430**	**141**	**205**	**83**	**25723**	**1192**	**28**	**2.78**	....	....	....	....	....	**13**	**6**	**7**	....	**755**	**30**	**0**	**2.38**	....	....	....	....

Won Vezina Trophy (1951) • Won Hart Trophy (1954) • Played in NHL All-Star Game (1954)

Traded to **Cleveland** (AHL) by **Chicago** (Kansas City-USHL) for Doug Baldwin and Bus Wycherley, September 13, 1949. Traded to **Toronto** by **Cleveland** (AHL) for Bobby Dawes, $40,000 and future considerations (Phil Samis, Eric Pogue and the rights to Bob Shropshire, April 6, 1950), November 29, 1949. Traded to **Chicago** by **Toronto** with Gus Mortson, Cal Gardner and Ray Hannigan for Harry Lumley, September 11, 1952. Loaned to **NY Rangers** by **Chicago** (Winnipeg-WHL) for the loan of Ray Mikulan, future considerations and cash, February 20, 1960. • Regular season totals for **Drumheller** (ASHL) during 1965-66 deason unavailable.

• ROLOSON, Dwayne

Albert Dwayne G – L. 6'1", 190 lbs. b: Simcoe, Ont., 10/12/1969.

Season	Club	League	GP	W	L	T	Mins	GA	SO	Avg	AAvg	Eff	SA	S%	SAPG	GP	W	L	T	Mins	GA	SO	Avg	Eff	SA	S%	SAPG
1984-85	Simcoe Penguins	OJHL-C	3	....	....	....	100	21	0	12.60	....	....	....	....	....	....	....	....	....	....	....	....	....	....	....	....	....
1985-86	Simcoe Rams	OJHL-C	1	....	....	....	60	6	0	6.00	....	....	....	....	....	....	....	....	....	....	....	....	....	....	....	....	....
1986-87	Norwich Merchants	OJHL-C	19	....	....	....	1091	55	0	*3.03	....	....	....	....	....	....	....	....	....	....	....	....	....	....	....	....	....
1987-88	Belleville Bobcats	OJHL-B	21	9	6	1	1070	60	*2	3.36	....	....	....	....	....	....	....	....	....	....	....	....	....	....	....	....	....
1988-89	Thorold Black Hawks	OJHL-B	27	15	6	4	1490	82	0	3.30	....	....	....	....	....	....	....	....	....	....	....	....	....	....	....	....	....
1989-90	Thorold Black Hawks	OJHL-B	30	18	8	1	1683	108	0	3.85	....	....	....	....	....	....	....	....	....	....	....	....	....	....	....	....	....
1990-91	U. of Massachusetts-Lowell	H-East	15	5	9	0	823	63	0	4.59	....	....	....	....	....	....	....	....	....	....	....	....	....	....	....	....	....
1991-92	U. of Massachusetts-Lowell	H-East	12	3	8	0	660	52	0	4.73	....	....	....	....	....	....	....	....	....	....	....	....	....	....	....	....	....
1992-93	U. of Massachusetts-Lowell	H-East	*39	20	17	2	*2342	150	0	3.84	....	....	....	....	....	....	....	....	....	....	....	....	....	....	....	....	....
1993-94	U. of Massachusetts-Lowell	H-East	*40	*23	10	7	*2305	106	0	2.76	....	....	....	....	....	....	....	....	....	....	....	....	....	....	....	....	....
1994-95	Saint John Flames	AHL	46	16	21	8	2734	156	1	3.42	....	....	....	....	....	5	1	4	....	298	13	0	2.61	....	....	....	....
	Canada	WC-A		DID NOT PLAY – SPARE GOALTENDER																							
1995-96	Saint John Flames	AHL	67	*33	22	11	4026	190	1	2.83	....	....	....	....	....	16	10	6	....	1027	49	1	2.86	....	....	....	....
1996-97	**Calgary Flames**	**NHL**	**31**	**9**	**14**	**3**	**1618**	**78**	**1**	**2.89**	**3.11**	**2.97**	**760**	**.897**	**28.2**	....	....	....	....	....	....	....	....	....	....	....	....
	Saint John Flames	AHL	8	6	2	0	481	22	1	2.75	....	....	....	....	....	....	....	....	....	....	....	....	....	....	....	....	....
1997-98	**Calgary Flames**	**NHL**	**39**	**11**	**16**	**8**	**2205**	**110**	**0**	**2.99**	**3.58**	**3.30**	**997**	**.890**	**27.1**	....	....	....	....	....	....	....	....	....	....	....	....
	Saint John Flames	AHL	4	3	0	1	245	8	0	1.96	....	....	....	....	....	....	....	....	....	....	....	....	....	....	....	....	....
1998-99	**Buffalo Sabres**	**NHL**	**18**	**6**	**8**	**2**	**911**	**42**	**1**	**2.77**	**3.29**	**2.53**	**460**	**.909**	**30.3**	**4**	**1**	**1**	....	**139**	**10**	**0**	**4.32**	**6.45**	**67**	**.851**	**28.9**
	Rochester Americans	AHL	2	2	0	0	120	4	0	2.00	....	....	....	....	....	....	....	....	....	....	....	....	....	....	....	....	....
99-2000	**Buffalo Sabres**	**NHL**	**14**	**1**	**7**	**3**	**677**	**32**	**0**	**2.84**	**3.25**	**3.28**	**277**	**.884**	**24.5**	....	....	....	....	....	....	....	....	....	....	....	....
	NHL Totals		**102**	**27**	**45**	**16**	**5411**	**262**	**2**	**2.91**	....	....	**2494**	**.895**	**27.7**	**4**	**1**	**1**	....	**139**	**10**	**0**	**4.32**	....	**67**	**.851**	**28.9**

Hockey East First All-Star Team (1994) • NCAA East First All-American Team (1994)

Signed as a free agent by **Calgary**, July 4, 1994. Signed as a free agent by **Buffalo**, July 15, 1998. Selected by **Columbus** from **Buffalo** in Expansion Draft, June 23, 2000.

• ROMANO, Roberto

G – L. 5'6", 170 lbs. b: Montreal, Que., 10/10/1962.

Season	Club	League	GP	W	L	T	Mins	GA	SO	Avg	AAvg	Eff	SA	S%	SAPG	GP	W	L	T	Mins	GA	SO	Avg	Eff	SA	S%	SAPG
1979-80	Quebec Remparts	QMJHL	52	21	17	3	2411	183	0	4.55	....	....	....	....	....	3	1	1	0	150	12	0	4.80	....	....	....	....
1980-81	Quebec Remparts	QMJHL	59	24	26	2	3174	233	0	4.40	....	....	....	....	....	4	1	2	0	164	18	0	6.59	....	....	....	....
1981-82	Quebec Remparts	QMJHL	1	....	....	....	60	4	0	4.00	....	....	....	....	....	....	....	....	....	....	....	....	....	....	....	....	....
	Hull Olympiques	QMJHL	56	....	....	....	3090	194	*1	3.77	....	....	....	....	....	13	....	....	....	760	50	0	3.95	....	....	....	....
1982-83	Baltimore Skipjacks	AHL	38	19	14	3	2163	146	0	4.05	....	....	....	....	....	....	....	....	....	....	....	....	....	....	....	....	....
	Pittsburgh Penguins	**NHL**	**3**	**0**	**3**	**0**	**155**	**18**	**0**	**6.97**	**5.60**	**13.07**	**96**	**.813**	**37.2**	....	....	....	....	....	....	....	....	....	....	....	....
1983-84	**Pittsburgh Penguins**	**NHL**	**18**	**6**	**11**	**0**	**1020**	**78**	**1**	**4.59**	**3.62**	**5.69**	**629**	**.876**	**37.0**	....	....	....	....	....	....	....	....	....	....	....	....
	Baltimore Skipjacks	AHL	31	23	6	1	1759	106	0	3.62	....	....	....	....	....	9	5	3	0	544	36	0	3.97	....	....	....	....
1984-85	**Pittsburgh Penguins**	**NHL**	**31**	**9**	**17**	**2**	**1629**	**120**	**1**	**4.42**	**3.53**	**5.45**	**974**	**.877**	**35.9**	....	....	....	....	....	....	....	....	....	....	....	....
	Baltimore Skipjacks	AHL	12	2	8	2	719	44	0	3.67	....	....	....	....	....	....	....	....	....	....	....	....	....	....	....	....	....
1985-86	**Pittsburgh Penguins**	**NHL**	**46**	**21**	**20**	**3**	**2684**	**159**	**2**	**3.55**	**2.77**	**4.05**	**1394**	**.886**	**31.2**	....	....	....	....	....	....	....	....	....	....	....	....
1986-87	**Pittsburgh Penguins**	**NHL**	**25**	**9**	**11**	**2**	**1438**	**87**	**0**	**3.63**	**3.07**	**4.43**	**713**	**.878**	**29.7**	....	....	....	....	....	....	....	....	....	....	....	....
	Baltimore Skipjacks	AHL	5	0	3	0	274	18	0	3.94	....	....	....	....	....	....	....	....	....	....	....	....	....	....	....	....	....
	Boston Bruins	**NHL**	**1**	**0**	**1**	**0**	**60**	**6**	**0**	**6.00**	**5.08**	**10.59**	**34**	**.824**	**34.0**	....	....	....	....	....	....	....	....	....	....	....	....
	Moncton Golden Flames	AHL	1	0	0	0	65	3	0	2.77	....	....	....	....	....	....	....	....	....	....	....	....	....	....	....	....	....
1987-88	Maine Mariners	AHL	16	5	8	1	875	52	0	3.57	....	....	....	....	....	....	....	....	....	....	....	....	....	....	....	....	....
1988-89	HC Merano	Italy		STATISTICS NOT AVAILABLE																							
1989-90	HC Bolzano	Italy	32	....	....	....	1778	105	0	3.54	....	....	....	....	....	....	....	....	....	....	....	....	....	....	....	....	....
1990-91	HC Milano	Italy	10	....	....	....	538	31	0	3.45	....	....	....	....	....	....	....	....	....	....	....	....	....	....	....	....	....
1991-92	HC Milano	Alpenliga	29	....	....	....	1704	78	2	2.74	....	....	....	....	....	....	....	....	....	....	....	....	....	....	....	....	....
	HC Milano	Italy	17	....	....	....	973	42	1	2.58	....	....	....	....	....	2	....	....	....	120	2	1	1.00	....	....	....	....
	Italy	WC-A	3	....	....	....	151	11	0	4.37	....	....	....	....	....	....	....	....	....	....	....	....	....	....	....	....	....

			REGULAR SEASON													PLAYOFFS											
Season	Club	League	GP	W	L	T	Mins	GA	SO	Avg	AAvg	Eff	SA	S%	SAPG	GP	W	L	T	Mins	GA	SO	Avg	Eff	SA	S%	SAPG
1992-93	HC Milano	Alpenliga	28	....	....	....	1549	73	0	2.82	....	....	....	....	....	....	....	....	....	....	....	....	....	....	....	....	....
1993-94	**Pittsburgh Penguins**	**NHL**	**2**	**1**	**0**	**1**	**125**	**3**	**0**	**1.44**	**1.38**	**0.77**	**56**	**.946**	**26.9**	....	....	....	....	....	....	....	....	....	....	....	....
	Cleveland Lumberjacks	IHL	11	2	7	2	642	45	1	4.20	....	....	....	....	....	....	....	....	....	....	....	....	....	....	....	....	....
	NHL Totals		**126**	**46**	**63**	**8**	**7111**	**471**	**4**	**3.97**	....	....	**3896**	**.879**	**32.9**	....	....	....	....	....	....	....	....	....	....	....	....

QMJHL First All-Star Team (1982)

Signed as a free agent by **Pittsburgh**, December 6, 1982. Traded to **Boston** by **Pittsburgh** for Pat Riggin, February 6, 1987. Signed as a free agent by **Pittsburgh**, October 7, 1993.

• ROSATI, Mike

G – L. 5'10", 170 lbs. b: Toronto, Ont., 1/7/1968. NY Rangers' 6th, 131st overall in 1988.

Season	Club	League	GP	W	L	T	Mins	GA	SO	Avg	AAvg	Eff	SA	S%	SAPG	GP	W	L	T	Mins	GA	SO	Avg	Eff	SA	S%	SAPG
1984-85	St. Michael's Buzzers	OJHL-B	19	....	....	....	1027	93	0	5.13	....	....	....	....	....	....	....	....	....	....	....	....	....	....	....	....	....
1985-86	St. Michael's Buzzers	OJHL-B	20	8	11	1	1100	95	0	5.18	....	....	....	....	....	34	....	....	....	1648	119	0	4.33	....	....	....	....
	Hamilton Steelhawks	OHL	1	0	0	1	70	5	0	4.29	....	....	....	....	....	....	....	....	....	....	....	....	....	....	....	....	....
1986-87	Hamilton Steelhawks	OHL	26	....	....	....	1334	85	1	3.82	....	....	....	....	....	....	....	....	....	....	....	....	....	....	....	....	....
1987-88	Hamilton Steelhawks	OHL	62	29	25	3	3468	233	1	4.03	....	....	....	....	....	14	8	6	0	833	66	0	4.75	....	....	....	....
1988-89	Niagara Falls Thunder	OHL	52	*28	15	2	2339	174	1	4.46	....	....	....	....	....	16	10	4	....	861	62	0	4.32	....	....	....	....
1989-90	Erie Panthers	ECHL	18	12	5	0	1056	73	0	4.14	....	....	....	....	....	....	....	....	....	....	....	....	....	....	....	....	....
1990-91	HC Bolzano	Italy	46	....	....	....	2700	212	0	4.71	....	....	....	....	....	....	....	....	....	....	....	....	....	....	....	....	....
1991-92	HC Bolzano	Italy	18	11	6	1	1022	58	2	3.22	....	....	....	....	....	7	5	2	....	409	30	0	4.28	....	....	....	....
1992-93	HC Bolzano	Italy	26	....	....	....	1525	78	1	3.07	....	....	....	....	....	....	....	....	....	....	....	....	....	....	....	....	....
1993-94	HC Bolzano	Italy	29	....	....	....	1683	104	0	3.71	....	....	....	....	....	....	....	....	....	....	....	....	....	....	....	....	....
1994-95	HC Bolzano	Italy	47	....	....	....	2705	149	1	3.30	....	....	....	....	....	....	....	....	....	....	....	....	....	....	....	....	....
	Italy	WC-A	3	2	0	0	133	3	0	1.35	....	....	....	....	....	....	....	....	....	....	....	....	....	....	....	....	....
1995-96	HC Bolzano	Italy	45	36	5	3	2465	137	3	3.33	....	....	....	....	....	....	....	....	....	....	....	....	....	....	....	....	....
1996-97	Adler Mannheim	Germany	44	....	....	....	2625	104	6	2.38	....	....	....	....	....	9	....	....	....	514	24	0	2.80	....	....	....	....
1997-98	Adler Mannheim	Germany	43	....	....	....	2567	116	2	2.71	....	....	....	....	....	*10	*9	1	....	569	17	*1	*2.00	....	....	....	....
	Adler Mannheim	EuroHL	2	2	0	0	118	5	1	0.87	....	....	....	....	....	....	....	....	....	....	....	....	....	....	....	....	....
1998-99	**Washington Capitals**	**NHL**	**1**	**1**	**0**	**0**	**28**	**0**	**0**	**0.00**	**0.00**	**0.00**	**12**	**1.000**	**25.7**	....	....	....	....	....	....	....	....	....	....	....	....
	Portland Pirates	AHL	32	9	23	0	1783	111	1	3.74	....	....	....	....	....	....	....	....	....	....	....	....	....	....	....	....	....
	Manitoba Moose	IHL	8	5	1	2	479	16	1	2.00	....	....	....	....	....	5	2	3	....	314	18	0	3.44	....	....	....	....
99-2000	Adler Mannheim	Germany	55	....	....	....	3245	170	3	3.14	....	....	....	....	....	5	....	....	....	280	15	2	3.21	....	....	....	....
	Adler Mannheim	EuroHL	1	0	0	0	20	1	0	3.00	....	....	....	....	....	....	....	....	....	....	....	....	....	....	....	....	....
	Italy	WC-A	3	1	2	0	150	12	1	4.79	....	....	....	....	....	....	....	....	....	....	....	....	....	....	....	....	....
	NHL Totals		**1**	**1**	**0**	**0**	**28**	**0**	**0**	**0.00**	....	....	**12**	**1.000**	**25.7**	....	....	....	....	....	....	....	....	....	....	....	....

Signed as a free agent by **Washington**, July 15, 1998.

• ROUSSEL, Dominic

G – L. 6'1", 191 lbs. b: Hull, Que., 2/22/1970. Philadelphia's 4th, 63rd overall in 1988.

Season	Club	League	GP	W	L	T	Mins	GA	SO	Avg	AAvg	Eff	SA	S%	SAPG	GP	W	L	T	Mins	GA	SO	Avg	Eff	SA	S%	SAPG
1986-87	Lac St-Louis Lions	QAAA	24	8	12	0	1334	85	1	3.69	....	....	....	....	....	....	....	....	....	....	....	....	....	....	....	....	....
1987-88	Trois Rivieres Draveurs	QMJHL	51	18	25	4	2905	251	0	5.18	....	....	....	....	....	....	....	....	....	....	....	....	....	....	....	....	....
1988-89	Shawinigan Cataracts	QMJHL	46	24	15	2	2555	171	0	4.02	....	....	....	....	....	10	6	4	....	638	36	0	3.39	....	....	....	....
1989-90	Shawinigan Cataracts	QMJHL	37	20	14	1	1985	133	0	4.02	....	....	....	....	....	2	1	1	....	120	12	0	6.00	....	....	....	....
1990-91	Hershey Bears	AHL	45	20	14	7	2507	151	1	3.61	....	....	....	....	....	7	3	4	....	366	21	0	3.44	....	....	....	....
1991-92	**Philadelphia Flyers**	**NHL**	**17**	**7**	**8**	**2**	**922**	**40**	**1**	**2.60**	**2.32**	**2.38**	**437**	**.908**	**28.4**	....	....	....	....	....	....	....	....	....	....	....	....
	Hershey Bears	AHL	35	15	11	6	2040	121	1	3.56	....	....	....	....	....	....	....	....	....	....	....	....	....	....	....	....	....
1992-93	**Philadelphia Flyers**	**NHL**	**34**	**13**	**11**	**5**	**1769**	**111**	**1**	**3.76**	**3.22**	**4.47**	**933**	**.881**	**31.6**	....	....	....	....	....	....	....	....	....	....	....	....
	Hershey Bears	AHL	6	0	3	3	372	23	0	3.71	....	....	....	....	....	....	....	....	....	....	....	....	....	....	....	....	....
1993-94	**Philadelphia Flyers**	**NHL**	**60**	**29**	**20**	**5**	**3285**	**183**	**1**	**3.34**	**3.21**	**3.47**	**1762**	**.896**	**32.2**	....	....	....	....	....	....	....	....	....	....	....	....
1994-95	**Philadelphia Flyers**	**NHL**	**19**	**11**	**7**	**0**	**1075**	**42**	**1**	**2.34**	**2.44**	**2.02**	**486**	**.914**	**27.1**	**1**	**0**	**0**	....	**23**	**0**	**0**	**0.00**	**0.00**	**8**	**1.000**	**20.9**
	Hershey Bears	AHL	1	0	1	0	59	5	0	5.07	....	....	....	....	....	....	....	....	....	....	....	....	....	....	....	....	....
1995-96	**Philadelphia Flyers**	**NHL**	**9**	**2**	**3**	**2**	**456**	**22**	**1**	**2.89**	**2.87**	**3.57**	**178**	**.876**	**23.4**	....	....	....	....	....	....	....	....	....	....	....	....
	Hershey Bears	AHL	12	4	4	3	690	32	0	2.78	....	....	....	....	....	....	....	....	....	....	....	....	....	....	....	....	....
	Winnipeg Jets	**NHL**	**7**	**2**	**2**	**0**	**285**	**16**	**0**	**3.37**	**3.35**	**4.02**	**134**	**.881**	**28.2**	....	....	....	....	....	....	....	....	....	....	....	....
1996-97	Philadelphia Phantoms	AHL	36	18	9	3	1852	82	2	2.66	....	....	....	....	....	1	0	0	....	26	3	0	6.93	....	....	....	....
1997-98	Canada	Nat-Team	41	25	12	1	2307	86	5	2.24	....	....	....	....	....	....	....	....	....	....	....	....	....	....	....	....	....
	Star Bulls Rosenheim	Germany	2	....	....	....	120	12	0	6.00	....	....	....	....	....	....	....	....	....	....	....	....	....	....	....	....	....
1998-99	**Mighty Ducks of Anaheim**	**NHL**	**18**	**4**	**5**	**4**	**884**	**37**	**1**	**2.51**	**2.98**	**1.94**	**478**	**.923**	**32.4**	....	....	....	....	....	....	....	....	....	....	....	....
99-2000	**Mighty Ducks of Anaheim**	**NHL**	**20**	**6**	**5**	**3**	**988**	**52**	**1**	**3.16**	**3.62**	**3.69**	**445**	**.883**	**27.0**	....	....	....	....	....	....	....	....	....	....	....	....
	NHL Totals		**184**	**74**	**61**	**21**	**9664**	**503**	**7**	**3.12**	....	....	**4853**	**.896**	**30.1**	**1**	**0**	**0**	....	**23**	**0**	**0**	**0.00**	....	**8**	**1.000**	**20.9**

Traded to **Winnipeg** by **Philadelphia** for Tim Cheveldae and Winnipeg's 3rd round choice (Chester Gallant) in 1996 Entry Draft, February 27, 1996. Signed as a free agent by **Philadelphia**, July 3, 1996. Traded to **Nashville** by **Philadelphia** with Jeff Staples for Nashville's 7th round choice (Cam Ondrik) in 1998 Entry Draft, June 26, 1998. Traded to **Anaheim** by **Nashville** for Chris Mason and Marc Moro, October 5, 1998.

• ROY, Patrick

G – L. 6', 192 lbs. b: Quebec City, Que., 10/5/1965. Montreal's 4th, 51st overall in 1984.

Season	Club	League	GP	W	L	T	Mins	GA	SO	Avg	AAvg	Eff	SA	S%	SAPG	GP	W	L	T	Mins	GA	SO	Avg	Eff	SA	S%	SAPG
1981-82	Ste-Foy Gouverneurs	QAAA	40	27	3	10	2400	156	0	2.63	....	....	....	....	....	....	....	....	....	....	....	....	....	....	....	....	....
1982-83	Granby Bisons	QMJHL	54	13	35	1	2808	293	0	6.26	....	....	....	....	....	....	....	....	....	....	....	....	....	....	....	....	....
1983-84	Granby Bisons	QMJHL	61	29	29	1	3585	265	0	4.44	....	....	....	....	....	4	0	4	....	244	22	0	5.41	....	....	....	....
1984-85	Granby Bisons	QMJHL	44	16	25	1	2463	228	0	5.55	....	....	....	....	....	....	....	....	....	....	....	....	....	....	....	....	....
	Montreal Canadiens	**NHL**	**1**	**1**	**0**	**0**	**20**	**0**	**0**	**0.00**	**0.00**	**0.00**	**2**	**1.000**	**6.0**	....	....	....	....	....	....	....	....	....	....	....	....
	Sherbrooke Canadiens	AHL	1	1	0	0	60	4	0	4.00	....	....	....	....	....	13	10	3	....	*769	37	0	*2.89	....	....	....	....
1985-86 ♦	**Montreal Canadiens**	**NHL**	**47**	**23**	**18**	**3**	**2651**	**148**	**1**	**3.35**	**2.61**	**4.18**	**1185**	**.875**	**26.8**	**20**	***15**	**5**	....	**1218**	**39**	***1**	**1.92**	**1.48**	**506**	**.923**	**24.9**
1986-87	**Montreal Canadiens**	**NHL**	**46**	**22**	**16**	**6**	**2686**	**131**	**1**	**2.93**	**2.47**	**3.17**	**1210**	**.892**	**27.0**	**6**	**4**	**2**	....	**330**	**22**	**0**	**4.00**	**5.09**	**173**	**.873**	**31.5**
1987-88	**Montreal Canadiens**	**NHL**	**45**	**23**	**12**	**9**	**2586**	**125**	**3**	**2.90**	**2.40**	**2.90**	**1248**	**.900**	**29.0**	**8**	**3**	**4**	....	**430**	**24**	**0**	**3.35**	**3.69**	**218**	**.890**	**30.4**
1988-89	**Montreal Canadiens**	**NHL**	**48**	**33**	**5**	**6**	**2744**	**113**	**4**	***2.47**	**2.04**	**2.27**	**1228**	**.908**	**26.9**	**19**	**13**	**6**	....	**1206**	**42**	**2**	***2.09**	**1.66**	**528**	**.920**	**26.3**
1989-90	**Montreal Canadiens**	**NHL**	**54**	***31**	**16**	**5**	**3173**	**134**	**3**	**2.53**	**2.12**	**2.22**	**1524**	**.912**	**28.8**	**11**	**5**	**6**	....	**641**	**26**	**1**	**2.43**	**2.16**	**292**	**.911**	**27.3**
1990-91	Montreal Canadiens	Fr-Tour	2	....	....	....	62	3	0	2.90	....	....	....	....	....	....	....	....	....	....	....	....	....	....	....	....	....
	Montreal Canadiens	**NHL**	**48**	**25**	**15**	**6**	**2835**	**128**	**1**	**2.71**	**2.42**	**2.55**	**1362**	**.906**	**28.8**	**13**	**7**	**5**	....	**785**	**40**	**0**	**3.06**	**3.11**	**394**	**.898**	**30.1**
1991-92	**Montreal Canadiens**	**NHL**	**67**	**36**	**22**	**8**	**3935**	**155**	***5**	***2.36**	**2.09**	**2.03**	**1806**	**.914**	**27.5**	**11**	**4**	**7**	....	**686**	**30**	**1**	**2.62**	**2.52**	**312**	**.904**	**27.3**
1992-93 ♦	**Montreal Canadiens**	**NHL**	**62**	**31**	**25**	**5**	**3595**	**192**	**2**	**3.20**	**2.73**	**3.39**	**1814**	**.894**	**30.3**	**20**	***16**	**4**	....	**1293**	**46**	**0**	***2.13**	**1.51**	**647**	**.929**	**30.0**
1993-94	**Montreal Canadiens**	**NHL**	**68**	**35**	**17**	**11**	**3867**	**161**	***7**	**2.50**	**2.39**	**2.06**	**1956**	**.918**	**30.3**	**6**	**3**	**3**	....	**375**	**16**	**0**	**2.56**	**1.80**	**228**	**.930**	**36.5**
1994-95	**Montreal Canadiens**	**NHL**	**43**	**17**	**20**	**6**	**2566**	**127**	**1**	**2.97**	**3.11**	**2.78**	**1357**	**.906**	**31.7**	....	....	....	....	....	....	....	....	....	....	....	....
1995-96	**Montreal Canadiens**	**NHL**	**22**	**12**	**9**	**1**	**1260**	**62**	**1**	**2.95**	**2.93**	**2.74**	**667**	**.907**	**31.8**	....	....	....	....	....	....	....	....	....	....	....	....
♦	**Colorado Avalanche**	**NHL**	**39**	**22**	**15**	**1**	**2305**	**103**	**1**	**2.68**	**2.66**	**2.44**	**1130**	**.909**	**29.4**	***22**	***16**	**6**	....	***1454**	**51**	***3**	**2.10**	**1.65**	**649**	**.921**	**26.8**
1996-97	**Colorado Avalanche**	**NHL**	**62**	***38**	**15**	**7**	**3698**	**143**	**7**	**2.32**	**2.48**	**1.78**	**1861**	**.923**	**30.2**	**17**	**10**	**7**	....	**1034**	**38**	***3**	**2.21**	**1.50**	**559**	**.932**	**32.4**
1997-98	**Colorado Avalanche**	**NHL**	**65**	**31**	**19**	**13**	**3835**	**153**	**4**	**2.39**	**2.84**	**2.00**	**1825**	**.916**	**28.6**	**7**	**3**	**4**	....	**430**	**18**	**0**	**2.51**	**2.37**	**191**	**.906**	**26.7**
	Canada	Olympics	6	4	2	0	*369	9	1	1.46	....	....	....	....	....	....	....	....	....	....	....	....	....	....	....	....	....
1998-99	**Colorado Avalanche**	**NHL**	**61**	**32**	**19**	**8**	**3648**	**139**	**5**	**2.29**	**2.71**	**1.90**	**1673**	**.917**	**27.5**	**19**	**11**	**8**	....	**1173**	**52**	**1**	**2.66**	**2.13**	**650**	**.920**	**33.2**
99-2000	**Colorado Avalanche**	**NHL**	**63**	**32**	**21**	**8**	**3704**	**141**	**2**	**2.28**	**2.59**	**1.96**	**1640**	**.914**	**26.6**	**17**	**11**	**6**	....	**1039**	**31**	**3**	**1.79**	**1.29**	**431**	**.928**	**24.9**
	NHL Totals		**841**	**444**	**264**	**103**	**49108**	**2155**	**48**	**2.63**	....	....	**23488**	**.908**	**28.7**	***196**	**121**	**73**	....	***12094**	**475**	***15**	**2.36**	....	**5778**	**.918**	**28.7**

• Brother of Stephane • NHL All-Rookie Team (1986) • Won Conn Smythe Trophy (1986, 1993) • Shared William Jennings Trophy with Brian Hayward (1987, 1988, 1989) • NHL Second All-Star Team (1988, 1991) • NHL First All-Star Team (1989, 1990, 1992) • Won Trico Goaltending Award (1989, 1990) • Won Vezina Trophy (1989, 1990, 1992) • Won William M. Jennings Trophy (1992) • Played in NHL All-Star Game (1988, 1990, 1991, 1992, 1993, 1994, 1997, 1998)

Traded to **Colorado** by **Montreal** with Mike Keane for Andrei Kovalenko, Martin Rucinsky and Jocelyn Thibault, December 6, 1995.

• RUPP, Pat

Patrick Lloyd G – L. 5'11", 180 lbs. b: Detroit, MI, 8/12/1942.

			REGULAR SEASON													PLAYOFFS											
Season	Club	League	GP	W	L	T	Mins	GA	SO	Avg	AAvg	Eff	SA	S%	SAPG	GP	W	L	T	Mins	GA	SO	Avg	Eff	SA	S%	SAPG
1961-62	Flin Flon Bombers	SJHL	51	....	....	....	3060	178	2	3.49	....	....	....	....	....	....	....	....	....	....	....	....	....	....	....	....	....
1962-63	Flin Flon Bombers	SJHL	52	....	....	....	3120	226	2	4.34	....	....	....	....	....	6	....	....	....	360	28	0	4.67	....	....	....	....
1963-64	Philadelphia Ramblers	EHL	38	....	....	....	2280	191	0	5.03	....	....	....	....	....	....	....	....	....	....	....	....	....	....	....	....	....
	United States	Nat-Team	STATISTICS NOT AVAILABLE																								
	United States	Olympics	6	2	3	0	329	22	0	4.01	....	....	....	....	....	....	....	....	....	....	....	....	....	....	....	....	....
	Detroit Red Wings	**NHL**	**1**	**0**	**1**	**0**	**60**	**4**	**0**	**4.00**	**4.45**	....	....	....	....	....	....	....	....	....	....	....	....	....	....	....	....
1964-65	Dayton Gems	IHL	28	....	....	....	1680	160	0	5.75	....	....	....	....	....	....	....	....	....	....	....	....	....	....	....	....	....
	New Jersey Devils	EHL	41	....	....	....	2460	188	1	4.59	....	....	....	....	....	....	....	....	....	....	....	....	....	....	....	....	....
1965-66	Dayton Gems	IHL	69	33	34	2	4140	316	2	4.58	....	....	....	....	....	11	5	6	0	660	45	0	4.09	....	....	....	....
1966-67	Dayton Gems	IHL	71	44	24	3	4260	277	0	3.85	....	....	....	....	....	4	0	4	0	240	19	0	4.75	....	....	....	....
1967-68	United States	Nat-Team	STATISTICS NOT AVAILABLE																								
	United States	Olympics	7	2	4	1	380	18	0	2.84	....	....	....	....	....	....	....	....	....	....	....	....	....	....	....	....	....
1968-69	Dayton Gems	IHL	41	....	....	....	2420	136	4	3.37	....	....	....	....	....	3	....	....	....	185	6	0	1.94	....	....	....	....
1969-70	Dayton Gems	IHL	28	....	....	....	1320	90	1	4.09	....	....	....	....	....	1	0	0	0	37	2	0	3.24	....	....	....	....
1970-71	Dayton Gems	IHL	27	....	....	....	1509	95	1	3.78	....	....	....	....	....	6	....	....	....	333	14	*1	*2.52	....	....	....	....
1971-72	Dayton Gems	IHL	49	....	....	....	2949	161	0	3.28	....	....	....	....	....	5	1	4	0	271	22	0	4.87	....	....	....	....
1972-1975			DID NOT PLAY																								
1975-76	Buffalo Norsemen	NAHL	4	....	....	....	148	13	0	5.25	....	....	....	....	....	....	....	....	....	....	....	....	....	....	....	....	....
1976-1979			OUT OF HOCKEY – RETIRED																								
1979-80	Dayton Gems	IHL	1	0	0	0	20	1	0	3.00	....	....	....	....	....	....	....	....	....	....	....	....	....	....	....	....	....
	NHL Totals		**1**	**0**	**1**	**0**	**60**	**4**	**0**	**4.00**	....	....	....	....	....	....	....	....	....	....	....	....	....	....	....	....	....

Shared James Norris Memorial Trophy (fewest goals against - IHL) with John Adams (1969)

Loaned to **Detroit** by **Philadelphia** (EHL) to replace injured Terry Sawchuk, March 22, 1964. (Toronto 4, Detroit 1)

• RUTHERFORD, Jim

James Earl G – L. 5'8", 168 lbs. b: Beeton, Ont., 2/17/1949. Detroit's 1st, 10th overall in 1969.

Season	Club	League	GP	W	L	T	Mins	GA	SO	Avg	AAvg	Eff	SA	S%	SAPG	GP	W	L	T	Mins	GA	SO	Avg	Eff	SA	S%	SAPG
1966-67	Aurora Tigers	OHA-C	30	....	....	....	1800	63	2	2.10	....	....	....	....	....	....	....	....	....	....	....	....	....	....	....	....	....
1967-68	Aurora Tigers	OHA-B	STATISTICS NOT AVAILABLE																								
	Hamilton Red Wings	OHA-Jr.	9	....	....	....	510	19	0	2.24	....	....	....	....	....	1	0	0	0	20	0	0	0.00	....	....	....	....
1968-69	Hamilton Red Wings	OHA-Jr.	45	....	....	....	2730	153	*3	3.36	....	....	....	....	....	5	....	....	....	300	27	0	5.40	....	....	....	....
	Montreal Jr. Canadiens	Mem-Cup	6	6	0	0	366	20	0	3.28	....	....	....	....	....	....	....	....	....	....	....	....	....	....	....	....	....
1969-70	Fort Worth Wings	CHL	35	12	14	8	2060	92	1	2.68	....	....	....	....	....	4	3	1	0	244	12	0	2.95	....	....	....	....
1970-71	**Detroit Red Wings**	**NHL**	**29**	**7**	**15**	**3**	**1498**	**94**	**1**	**3.77**	**3.75**	....	....	....	....	....	....	....	....	....	....	....	....	....	....	....	....
	Fort Worth Wings	CHL	3	....	....	....	180	11	0	3.66	....	....	....	....	....	....	....	....	....	....	....	....	....	....	....	....	....
1971-72	**Pittsburgh Penguins**	**NHL**	**40**	**17**	**15**	**5**	**2160**	**116**	**1**	**3.22**	**3.26**	....	....	....	....	**4**	**0**	**4**	....	**240**	**14**	**0**	**3.50**	....	....	....	....
	Hershey Bears	AHL	3	3	0	0	180	7	0	2.33	....	....	....	....	....	....	....	....	....	....	....	....	....	....	....	....	....
1972-73	**Pittsburgh Penguins**	**NHL**	**49**	**20**	**22**	**5**	**2660**	**129**	**3**	**2.91**	**2.73**	....	....	....	....	....	....	....	....	....	....	....	....	....	....	....	....
1973-74	**Pittsburgh Penguins**	**NHL**	**26**	**7**	**12**	**4**	**1432**	**82**	**0**	**3.44**	**3.33**	....	....	....	....	....	....	....	....	....	....	....	....	....	....	....	....
	Detroit Red Wings	**NHL**	**25**	**9**	**11**	**4**	**1420**	**86**	**0**	**3.63**	**3.52**	....	....	....	....	....	....	....	....	....	....	....	....	....	....	....	....
1974-75	**Detroit Red Wings**	**NHL**	**59**	**20**	**29**	**10**	**3478**	**217**	**2**	**3.74**	**3.39**	....	....	....	....	....	....	....	....	....	....	....	....	....	....	....	....
1975-76	**Detroit Red Wings**	**NHL**	**44**	**13**	**25**	**6**	**2640**	**158**	**4**	**3.59**	**3.26**	....	....	....	....	....	....	....	....	....	....	....	....	....	....	....	....
1976-77	**Detroit Red Wings**	**NHL**	**48**	**7**	**34**	**6**	**2740**	**180**	**0**	**3.94**	**3.69**	....	....	....	....	....	....	....	....	....	....	....	....	....	....	....	....
	Canada	WEC-A	2	1	0	0	89	7	0	4.72	....	....	....	....	....	....	....	....	....	....	....	....	....	....	....	....	....
1977-78	**Detroit Red Wings**	**NHL**	**43**	**20**	**17**	**4**	**2468**	**134**	**1**	**3.26**	**3.06**	....	....	....	....	**3**	**2**	**1**	....	**180**	**12**	**0**	**4.00**	....	....	....	....
1978-79	**Detroit Red Wings**	**NHL**	**32**	**13**	**14**	**5**	**1892**	**103**	**1**	**3.27**	**2.89**	....	....	....	....	....	....	....	....	....	....	....	....	....	....	....	....
	Canada	WEC-A	6	1	5	0	320	24	0	4.50	....	....	....	....	....	....	....	....	....	....	....	....	....	....	....	....	....
1979-80	**Detroit Red Wings**	**NHL**	**23**	**6**	**13**	**3**	**1326**	**92**	**1**	**4.16**	**3.69**	....	....	....	....	....	....	....	....	....	....	....	....	....	....	....	....
1980-81	**Detroit Red Wings**	**NHL**	**10**	**2**	**6**	**2**	**600**	**43**	**0**	**4.30**	**3.48**	....	....	....	....	....	....	....	....	....	....	....	....	....	....	....	....
	Toronto Maple Leafs	**NHL**	**18**	**4**	**10**	**2**	**961**	**82**	**0**	**5.12**	**4.15**	....	....	....	....	....	....	....	....	....	....	....	....	....	....	....	....
	Los Angeles Kings	**NHL**	**3**	**3**	**0**	**0**	**180**	**10**	**0**	**3.33**	**2.69**	....	....	....	....	**1**	**0**	**0**	....	**20**	**2**	**0**	**6.00**	....	....	....	....
1981-82	**Los Angeles Kings**	**NHL**	**7**	**3**	**3**	**0**	**380**	**43**	**0**	**6.79**	**5.26**	....	....	....	....	....	....	....	....	....	....	....	....	....	....	....	....
	New Haven Nighthawks	AHL	29	12	11	4	1614	90	0	3.35	....	....	....	....	....	2	0	2	0	144	8	0	3.33	....	....	....	....
1982-83	**Detroit Red Wings**	**NHL**	**1**	**0**	**1**	**0**	**60**	**7**	**0**	**7.00**	**5.62**	**12.56**	**39**	**.821**	**39.0**	....	....	....	....	....	....	....	....	....	....	....	....
	Adirondack Red Wings	AHL	12	3	7	1	591	44	0	4.47	....	....	....	....	....	....	....	....	....	....	....	....	....	....	....	....	....
	NHL Totals		**457**	**151**	**227**	**59**	**25895**	**1576**	**14**	**3.65**	....	....	....	....	....	**8**	**2**	**5**	....	**440**	**28**	**0**	**3.82**	....	....	....	....

OHA-Jr. First All-Star Team (1969)

Claimed by **Pittsburgh** from **Detroit** in Intra-League Draft, June 8, 1971. Traded to **Detroit** by **Pittsburgh** with Jack Lynch for Ron Stackhouse, January 17, 1974. Traded to **Toronto** by **Detroit** for Mark Kirton, December 4, 1980. Traded to **LA Kings** by **Toronto** for LA Kings' 5th round choice (Barry Brigley) in 1981 Entry Draft, March 10, 1981. Signed as a free agent by **Detroit**, September 13, 1982.

• RUTLEDGE, Wayne

Wayne Alvin G – L. 6'2", 200 lbs. b: Barrie, Ont., 1/5/1942.

Season	Club	League	GP	W	L	T	Mins	GA	SO	Avg	AAvg	Eff	SA	S%	SAPG	GP	W	L	T	Mins	GA	SO	Avg	Eff	SA	S%	SAPG
1958-59	Newmarket Flyers	OHA-C	STATISTICS NOT AVAILABLE																								
1959-60	Barrie Flyers	OHA-Jr.	48	24	18	6	2840	168	3	3.55	....	....	....	....	....	6	....	....	....	300	30	0	5.00	....	....	....	....
1960-61	Niagara Falls Flyers	OHA-Jr.	47	22	20	5	2790	159	2	3.42	....	....	....	....	....	6	....	....	....	300	37	0	6.17	....	....	....	....
1961-62	Niagara Falls Flyers	OHA-Jr.	43	....	....	....	2580	163	2	3.79	....	....	....	....	....	10	....	....	....	600	36	0	3.60	....	....	....	....
1962-63	Windsor Bulldogs	OHA-Sr.	30	....	....	....	1800	95	2	3.17	....	....	....	....	....	11	....	....	....	660	22	*3	*2.00	....	....	....	....
	Clinton Comets	EHL	5	....	....	....	300	20	1	4.00	....	....	....	....	....	....	....	....	....	....	....	....	....	....	....	....	....
	Kingston Frontenacs	EPHL	4	3	1	0	240	9	0	2.25	....	....	....	....	....	....	....	....	....	....	....	....	....	....	....	....	....
	Windsor Bulldogs	Al-Cup	13	*11	2	0	790	34	1	*2.58	....	....	....	....	....	....	....	....	....	....	....	....	....	....	....	....	....
1963-64	Windsor Bulldogs	IHL	65	....	....	....	3900	243	0	3.74	....	....	....	....	....	6	2	4	0	360	20	0	3.33	....	....	....	....
1964-65	St. Paul Rangers	CPHL	39	22	16	1	2320	134	2	3.47	....	....	....	....	....	....	....	....	....	....	....	....	....	....	....	....	....
1965-66	Minnesota Rangers	CPHL	*70	*34	25	11	*4200	197	*7	2.81	....	....	....	....	....	7	3	4	0	454	19	*1	2.51	....	....	....	....
1966-67	Omaha Knights	CPHL	*70	*36	24	10	*4200	203	2	2.90	....	....	....	....	....	*12	5	7	0	*742	36	*1	2.91	....	....	....	....
1967-68	**Los Angeles Kings**	**NHL**	**45**	**20**	**18**	**4**	**2444**	**117**	**2**	**2.87**	**3.19**	....	....	....	....	**3**	**1**	**1**	....	**149**	**8**	**0**	**3.22**	....	....	....	....
1968-69	**Los Angeles Kings**	**NHL**	**17**	**6**	**7**	**4**	**921**	**56**	**0**	**3.65**	**3.79**	....	....	....	....	**5**	**1**	**3**	....	**229**	**12**	**0**	**3.14**	....	....	....	....
1969-70	**Los Angeles Kings**	**NHL**	**20**	**2**	**12**	**1**	**960**	**68**	**0**	**4.25**	**4.55**	....	....	....	....	....	....	....	....	....	....	....	....	....	....	....	....
	Springfield Kings	AHL	6	....	....	....	340	23	0	4.06	....	....	....	....	....	....	....	....	....	....	....	....	....	....	....	....	....
	Long Island Ducks	EHL	3	....	....	....	180	21	0	7.00	....	....	....	....	....	....	....	....	....	....	....	....	....	....	....	....	....
1970-71	Denver Spurs	WHL	47	15	18	12	2648	142	3	3.22	....	....	....	....	....	3	1	2	0	198	13	0	3.94	....	....	....	....
1971-72	Salt Lake Golden Eagles	WHL	*60	24	27	8	*3517	206	1	3.51	....	....	....	....	....	....	....	....	....	....	....	....	....	....	....	....	....
1972-73	Houston Aeros	WHA	36	20	14	2	2163	110	0	3.05	....	....	....	....	....	7	4	3	0	422	20	0	2.84	....	....	....	....
1973-74	Houston Aeros	WHA	25	12	12	1	1509	84	0	3.34	....	....	....	....	....	....	....	....	....	....	....	....	....	....	....	....	....
1974-75	Houston Aeros	WHA	35	20	15	0	2098	113	2	3.23	....	....	....	....	....	....	....	....	....	....	....	....	....	....	....	....	....
1975-76	Houston Aeros	WHA	25	14	10	0	1456	77	1	3.17	....	....	....	....	....	4	1	2	0	200	10	0	3.00	....	....	....	....
1976-77	Houston Aeros	WHA	42	23	14	4	2512	132	3	3.15	....	....	....	....	....	2	2	0	0	120	4	0	2.00	....	....	....	....
1977-78	Houston Aeros	WHA	12	4	7	0	634	47	0	4.45	....	....	....	....	....	3	1	2	0	131	8	0	3.66	....	....	....	....
1978-79	Orillia Terriers	OIHA	17	....	....	....	1020	119	0	7.00	....	....	....	....	....	....	....	....	....	....	....	....	....	....	....	....	....
	NHL Totals		**82**	**28**	**37**	**9**	**4325**	**241**	**2**	**3.34**	....	....	....	....	....	**8**	**2**	**4**	....	**378**	**20**	**0**	**3.17**	....	....	....	....
	Other Major League Totals		175	93	72	7	10372	563	6	3.26	....	....	....	....	....	16	8	7	....	873	42	0	2.89	....	....	....	....

CPHL Second All-Star Team (1966) • Won Terry Sawchuk Trophy (fewest goals against - CPHL) (1966) • CPHL First All-Star Team (1967) • WHL Second All-Star Team (1972)

Claimed by **LA Kings** from **NY Rangers** in Expansion Draft, June 6, 1967. Claimed by **Salt Lake** (WHL) from **LA Kings** in Reverse Draft, June, 1971. Selected by **Houston** (WHA) in 1972 WHA General Player Draft, February 12, 1972.

• ST. CROIX, Rick

Richard V. G – L. 5'10", 160 lbs. b: Kenora, Ont., 1/3/1955. Philadelphia's 3rd, 72nd overall in 1975.

Season	Club	League	GP	W	L	T	Mins	GA	SO	Avg	AAvg	Eff	SA	S%	SAPG	GP	W	L	T	Mins	GA	SO	Avg	Eff	SA	S%	SAPG
1970-71	Kenora Muskies	MJHL	23	....	....	....	1265	71	0	3.37	....	....	....	....	....	....	....	....	....	....	....	....	....	....	....	....	....
1971-72	Kenora Muskies	MJHL	43	....	....	....	2402	172	0	4.30	....	....	....	....	....	....	....	....	....	....	....	....	....	....	....	....	....
	Winnipeg Jets	WCJHL	3	....	....	....	160	13	0	4.88	....	....	....	....	....	....	....	....	....	....	....	....	....	....	....	....	....
1972-73	Oshawa Generals	OMJHL	52	....	....	....	3176	247	0	4.67	....	....	....	....	....	....	....	....	....	....	....	....	....	....	....	....	....

			REGULAR SEASON													PLAYOFFS											
Season	Club	League	GP	W	L	T	Mins	GA	SO	Avg	AAvg	Eff	SA	S%	SAPG	GP	W	L	T	Mins	GA	SO	Avg	Eff	SA	S%	SAPG
1973-74	Oshawa Generals	OMJHL	33	....	....	....	1932	130	1	4.04	....	....	....	....	....	....	....	....	....	....	....	....	....	....	....	....	....
1974-75	Oshawa Generals	OMJHL	32	....	....	....	1965	131	1	4.00	....	....	....	....	....	1	0	1	0	60	9	0	9.00	....	....	....	....
1975-76	Flint Generals	IHL	42	....	....	....	2201	118	0	3.22	....	....	....	....	....	....	....	....	....	....	....	....	....	....	....	....	....
1976-77	Springfield Indians	AHL	1	1	0	0	60	3	0	3.00	....	....	....	....	....	....	....	....	....	....	....	....	....	....	....	....	....
	Flint Generals	IHL	53	....	....	....	2956	179	3	3.63	....	....	....	....	....	5	1	4	0	337	30	0	5.34	....	....	....	....
1977-78	**Philadelphia Flyers**	**NHL**	**7**	**2**	**4**	**1**	**395**	**20**	**0**	**3.04**	**2.85**	....	....	....	....	....	....	....	....	....	....	....	....	....	....	....	....
	Maine Mariners	AHL	40	22	14	2	2266	116	2	3.07	....	....	....	....	....	4	1	3	0	174	18	0	6.21	....	....	....	....
1978-79	**Philadelphia Flyers**	**NHL**	**2**	**0**	**1**	**1**	**117**	**6**	**0**	**3.08**	**2.72**	....	....	....	....	....	....	....	....	....	....	....	....	....	....	....	....
	Philadelphia Firebirds	AHL	9	4	4	1	484	22	0	2.73	....	....	....	....	....	....	....	....	....	....	....	....	....	....	....	....	....
	Maine Mariners	AHL	22	10	9	3	1312	63	0	2.88	....	....	....	....	....	....	....	....	....	....	....	....	....	....	....	....	....
1979-80	**Philadelphia Flyers**	**NHL**	**1**	**1**	**0**	**0**	**60**	**2**	**0**	**2.00**	**1.77**	....	....	....	....	....	....	....	....	....	....	....	....	....	....	....	....
	Maine Mariners	AHL	46	25	14	7	2729	132	1	*2.90	....	....	....	....	....	5	1	4	0	311	16	0	3.09	....	....	....	....
1980-81	**Philadelphia Flyers**	**NHL**	**27**	**13**	**7**	**6**	**1567**	**65**	**2**	**2.49**	**2.00**	....	....	....	....	**9**	**4**	**5**	....	**541**	**27**	***1**	**2.99**	....	....	....	....
1981-82	**Philadelphia Flyers**	**NHL**	**29**	**13**	**9**	**6**	**1729**	**112**	**0**	**3.89**	**3.00**	....	....	....	....	**1**	**0**	**1**	....	**20**	**1**	**0**	**3.00**	....	....	....	....
1982-83	**Philadelphia Flyers**	**NHL**	**16**	**9**	**5**	**2**	**940**	**54**	**0**	**3.45**	**2.77**	**4.31**	**432**	**.875**	**27.6**	....	....	....	....	....	....	....	....	....	....	....	....
	Toronto Maple Leafs	**NHL**	**17**	**4**	**9**	**2**	**920**	**58**	**0**	**3.78**	**3.03**	**4.32**	**508**	**.886**	**33.1**	**1**	**0**	**0**	....	**1**	**1**	**0**	**60.00**	....	....	....	....
1983-84	**Toronto Maple Leafs**	**NHL**	**20**	**5**	**10**	**0**	**939**	**80**	**0**	**5.11**	**4.04**	**7.70**	**531**	**.849**	**33.9**	....	....	....	....	....	....	....	....	....	....	....	....
	St. Catharines Saints	AHL	8	7	1	0	482	29	0	3.61	....	....	....	....	....	3	1	1	0	133	10	0	4.50	....	....	....	....
1984-85	**Toronto Maple Leafs**	**NHL**	**11**	**2**	**9**	**0**	**628**	**54**	**0**	**5.16**	**4.12**	**8.87**	**314**	**.828**	**30.0**	....	....	....	....	....	....	....	....	....	....	....	....
	St. Catharines Saints	AHL	18	6	10	1	1076	92	0	5.13	....	....	....	....	....	....	....	....	....	....	....	....	....	....	....	....	....
1985-86	Fort Wayne Komets	IHL	42	25	13	0	2474	132	2	3.20	....	....	....	....	....	8	3	4	0	411	30	0	4.38	....	....	....	....
	NHL Totals		**130**	**49**	**54**	**18**	**7295**	**451**	**2**	**3.71**	....	....	....	....	....	**11**	**4**	**6**	....	**562**	**29**	**1**	**3.10**	....	....	....	....

OMJHL Second All-Star Team (1973) • AHL First All-Star Team (1980) • Shared Harry "Hap" Holmes Memorial Award (fewest goals against - AHL) with Robbie Moore (1980) • IHL Second All-Star Team (1986) • Shared James Norris Memorial Trophy (fewest goals against - IHL) with Pokey Reddick (1986)

Traded to **Toronto** by **Philadelphia** for Michel Larocque, January 11, 1983.

• ST. LAURENT, Sam

G – L: 5'10", 190 lbs. b: Arvida, Que., 2/16/1959.

Season	Club	League	GP	W	L	T	Mins	GA	SO	Avg	AAvg	Eff	SA	S%	SAPG	GP	W	L	T	Mins	GA	SO	Avg	Eff	SA	S%	SAPG
1975-76	Chicoutimi Sagueneens	QMJHL	17	....	....	....	889	81	0	5.47	....	....	....	....	....	1	....	....	....	40	9	0	13.50	....	....	....	....
1976-77	Chicoutimi Sagueneens	QMJHL	21	....	....	....	901	81	0	5.39	....	....	....	....	....	4	....	....	....	200	19	0	5.70	....	....	....	....
1977-78	Chicoutimi Sagueneens	QMJHL	60	....	....	....	3251	351	0	6.48	....	....	....	....	....	....	....	....	....	....	....	....	....	....	....	....	....
1978-79	Chicoutimi Sagueneens	QMJHL	70	....	....	....	3806	290	0	4.57	....	....	....	....	....	1	....	....	....	47	8	0	10.21	....	....	....	....
1979-80	Maine Mariners	AHL	5	2	1	0	229	17	0	4.45	....	....	....	....	....	....	....	....	....	....	....	....	....	....	....	....	....
	Toledo Goaldiggers	IHL	38	....	....	....	2143	138	2	3.86	....	....	....	....	....	4	0	4	0	239	24	0	6.03	....	....	....	....
1980-81	Maine Mariners	AHL	7	3	3	0	363	28	0	4.63	....	....	....	....	....	....	....	....	....	....	....	....	....	....	....	....	....
	Toledo Goaldiggers	IHL	30	....	....	....	1614	113	1	4.20	....	....	....	....	....	....	....	....	....	....	....	....	....	....	....	....	....
1981-82	Toledo Goaldiggers	IHL	4	....	....	....	248	11	0	2.66	....	....	....	....	....	....	....	....	....	....	....	....	....	....	....	....	....
	Maine Mariners	AHL	25	15	7	1	1396	76	0	3.27	....	....	....	....	....	4	1	3	0	240	18	0	4.50	....	....	....	....
1982-83	Toledo Goaldiggers	IHL	13	....	....	....	785	52	0	3.97	....	....	....	....	....	....	....	....	....	....	....	....	....	....	....	....	....
	Maine Mariners	AHL	30	12	12	4	1739	109	0	3.76	....	....	....	....	....	*17	8	9	0	*1012	54	0	3.20	....	....	....	....
1983-84	Maine Mariners	AHL	38	14	18	4	2158	145	0	4.03	....	....	....	....	....	12	9	2	0	708	32	*1	*2.71	....	....	....	....
1984-85	Maine Mariners	AHL	55	26	22	7	3245	168	4	3.11	....	....	....	....	....	10	5	5	0	656	45	0	4.12	....	....	....	....
1985-86	**New Jersey Devils**	**NHL**	**4**	**2**	**1**	**0**	**188**	**13**	**1**	**4.15**	**3.24**	**4.86**	**111**	**.883**	**35.4**	....	....	....	....	....	....	....	....	....	....	....	....
	Maine Mariners	AHL	50	24	20	4	2862	161	1	3.38	....	....	....	....	....	....	....	....	....	....	....	....	....	....	....	....	....
1986-87	**Detroit Red Wings**	**NHL**	**6**	**1**	**2**	**2**	**342**	**16**	**0**	**2.81**	**2.38**	**3.33**	**135**	**.881**	**23.7**	....	....	....	....	....	....	....	....	....	....	....	....
	Adirondack Red Wings	AHL	25	7	13	0	1397	98	1	4.21	....	....	....	....	....	3	0	2	0	105	10	0	5.71	....	....	....	....
1987-88	**Detroit Red Wings**	**NHL**	**6**	**2**	**2**	**0**	**294**	**16**	**0**	**3.27**	**2.72**	**3.54**	**148**	**.892**	**30.2**	**1**	**0**	**0**	....	**10**	**1**	**0**	**6.00**	**8.57**	**7**	**.857**	**42.0**
	Adirondack Red Wings	AHL	32	12	14	4	1826	104	2	3.42	....	....	....	....	....	1	0	1	0	59	6	0	6.10	....	....	....	....
1988-89	**Detroit Red Wings**	**NHL**	**4**	**0**	**1**	**1**	**141**	**9**	**0**	**3.83**	**3.19**	**3.79**	**91**	**.901**	**38.7**	....	....	....	....	....	....	....	....	....	....	....	....
	Adirondack Red Wings	AHL	34	20	11	3	2054	113	0	3.30	....	....	....	....	....	16	*11	5	0	956	47	*2	*2.95	....	....	....	....
1989-90	**Detroit Red Wings**	**NHL**	**14**	**2**	**6**	**1**	**607**	**38**	**0**	**3.76**	**3.19**	**4.40**	**325**	**.883**	**32.1**	....	....	....	....	....	....	....	....	....	....	....	....
	Adirondack Red Wings	AHL	13	10	2	1	785	40	0	3.06	....	....	....	....	....	....	....	....	....	....	....	....	....	....	....	....	....
1990-91	Binghamton Rangers	AHL	45	19	16	4	2379	138	1	3.48	....	....	....	....	....	3	1	2	0	160	11	0	4.13	....	....	....	....
1991-92	Canada	Nat-Team	1	0	1	0	60	3	0	3.00	....	....	....	....	....	....	....	....	....	....	....	....	....	....	....	....	....
	Canada	Olympics	DID NOT PLAY – SPARE GOALTENDER																								
	Binghamton Rangers	AHL	1	0	0	0	20	2	0	6.00	....	....	....	....	....	....	....	....	....	....	....	....	....	....	....	....	....
	NHL Totals		**34**	**7**	**12**	**4**	**1572**	**92**	**1**	**3.51**	....	....	**810**	**.886**	**30.9**	**1**	**0**	**0**	....	**10**	**1**	**0**	**6.00**	....	**7**	**.857**	**42.0**

AHL Second All-Star Team (1985, 1986) • Shared Harry "Hap" Holmes Memorial Award (fewest goals against - AHL) with Karl Friesen (1986) • Won Aldege "Baz" Bastien Memorial Award (Top Goaltender - AHL) (1986) • Won Jack A. Butterfield Trophy (Playoff MVP - AHL) (1989)

Signed as a free agent by **Philadelphia**, October 10, 1979. Traded to **New Jersey** by **Philadelphia** for future considerations, September 27, 1984. Traded to **Detroit** by **New Jersey** for Steve Richmond, August 18, 1986. Traded to **NY Rangers** by **Detroit** for cash, June 26, 1990.

• SALO, Tommy

Tomas Mikael G – L. 5'11", 173 lbs. b: Surahammar, Sweden, 2/1/1971. NY Islanders' 5th, 118th overall in 1993.

Season	Club	League	GP	W	L	T	Mins	GA	SO	Avg	AAvg	Eff	SA	S%	SAPG	GP	W	L	T	Mins	GA	SO	Avg	Eff	SA	S%	SAPG
1990-91	Vasteras IK	Sweden	2	....	....	....	100	11	0	6.60	....	....	....	....	....	....	....	....	....	....	....	....	....	....	....	....	....
	Sweden	WJC-A	6	3	3	0	343	19	*1	3.32	....	....	....	....	....	....	....	....	....	....	....	....	....	....	....	....	....
1991-92	Vasteras IK	Swede-Jr.	STATISTICS NOT AVAILABLE																								
1992-93	Vasteras IK	Sweden	24	....	....	....	1431	59	2	2.47	....	....	....	....	....	2	....	....	....	120	6	0	3.00	....	....	....	....
1993-94	Vasteras IK	Sweden	32	....	....	....	1896	106	0	3.35	....	....	....	....	....	....	....	....	....	....	....	....	....	....	....	....	....
	Sweden	Olympics	6	5	1	0	370	13	1	2.11	....	....	....	....	....	....	....	....	....	....	....	....	....	....	....	....	....
	Sweden	WC-A	3	1	1	1	180	10	....	3.33	....	....	....	....	....	....	....	....	....	....	....	....	....	....	....	....	....
1994-95	Denver Grizzlies	IHL	*65	*45	14	4	*3810	165	*3	*2.60	....	....	....	....	....	8	7	0	....	390	20	0	3.07	....	....	....	....
	New York Islanders	**NHL**	**6**	**1**	**5**	**0**	**358**	**18**	**0**	**3.02**	**3.16**	**2.88**	**189**	**.905**	**31.7**	....	....	....	....	....	....	....	....	....	....	....	....
1995-96	**New York Islanders**	**NHL**	**10**	**1**	**7**	**1**	**523**	**35**	**0**	**4.02**	**4.00**	**5.63**	**250**	**.860**	**28.7**	....	....	....	....	....	....	....	....	....	....	....	....
	Utah Grizzlies	IHL	45	28	15	2	2695	119	*4	2.65	....	....	....	....	....	22	*15	7	....	1342	51	*3	2.28	....	....	....	....
1996-97	Sweden	W-Cup	2	1	1	0	160	4	0	2.00	....	....	....	....	....	....	....	....	....	....	....	....	....	....	....	....	....
	New York Islanders	**NHL**	**58**	**20**	**27**	**8**	**3208**	**151**	**5**	**2.82**	**3.03**	**2.70**	**1576**	**.904**	**29.5**	....	....	....	....	....	....	....	....	....	....	....	....
	Sweden	WC-A	10	6	3	1	597	20	1	2.01	....	....	....	....	....	....	....	....	....	....	....	....	....	....	....	....	....
1997-98	**New York Islanders**	**NHL**	**62**	**23**	**29**	**5**	**3461**	**152**	**4**	**2.64**	**3.15**	**2.48**	**1617**	**.906**	**28.0**	....	....	....	....	....	....	....	....	....	....	....	....
	Sweden	Olympics	4	2	2	0	238	9	0	2.27	....	....	....	....	....	....	....	....	....	....	....	....	....	....	....	....	....
	Sweden	WC-A	9	*9	0	0	540	7	3	0.78	....	....	....	....	....	....	....	....	....	....	....	....	....	....	....	....	....
1998-99	**New York Islanders**	**NHL**	**51**	**17**	**26**	**7**	**3018**	**132**	**5**	**2.62**	**3.12**	**2.53**	**1368**	**.904**	**27.2**	....	....	....	....	....	....	....	....	....	....	....	....
	Edmonton Oilers	**NHL**	**13**	**8**	**2**	**2**	**700**	**27**	**0**	**2.31**	**2.74**	**2.24**	**279**	**.903**	**23.9**	**4**	**0**	**4**	....	**296**	**11**	**0**	**2.23**	**1.65**	**149**	**.926**	**30.2**
	Sweden	WC-A	8	....	....	....	424	13	....	1.84	....	....	....	....	....	....	....	....	....	....	....	....	....	....	....	....	....
99-2000	**Edmonton Oilers**	**NHL**	**70**	**27**	**28**	**13**	**4164**	**162**	**2**	**2.33**	**2.65**	**2.01**	**1875**	**.914**	**27.0**	**5**	**1**	**4**	....	**297**	**14**	**0**	**2.83**	**2.98**	**133**	**.895**	**26.9**
	Sweden	WC-A	6	3	3	0	359	10	1	1.68	....	....	....	....	....	....	....	....	....	....	....	....	....	....	....	....	....
	NHL Totals		**270**	**97**	**124**	**36**	**15432**	**677**	**16**	**2.63**	....	....	**7154**	**.905**	**27.8**	**9**	**1**	**8**	....	**593**	**25**	**0**	**2.53**	....	**282**	**.911**	**28.5**

IHL First All-Star Team (1995) • Won Garry F. Longman Memorial Trophy (Top Rookie - IHL) (1995) • Won James Norris Memorial Trophy (Fewest goals against - IHL) (1995) • Won James Gatschene Memorial Trophy (MVP - IHL) (1995) • Shared James Norris Memorial Trophy (fewest goals against — IHL) with Mark McArthur (1996) • Won "Bud" Poile Trophy (Playoff MVP - IHL) (1996) • WC-A All-Star Team (1997, 1998, 1999) • Named Best Goaltender at WC-A (1997, 1999) • Played in NHL All-Star Game (2000)

Traded to **Edmonton** by **NY Islanders** for Mats Lindgren and Edmonton's 8th round choice (Radek Martinek) in 1999 Entry Draft, March 20, 1999.

• SANDS, Charlie

G. 5'9", 160 lbs. b: Fort William, Ont., 3/23/1911 Deceased.

Season	Club	League	GP	W	L	T	Mins	GA	SO	Avg	AAvg	Eff	SA	S%	SAPG	GP	W	L	T	Mins	GA	SO	Avg	Eff	SA	S%	SAPG
1939-40	**Montreal Canadiens**	**NHL**	**1**	**0**	**0**	**0**	**25**	**5**	**0**	**12.00**	**14.71**	....	....	....	....	....	....	....	....	....	....	....	....	....	....	....	....
	NHL Totals		**1**	**0**	**0**	**0**	**25**	**5**	**0**	**12.00**	....	....	....	....	....	....	....	....	....	....	....	....	....	....	....	....	....

• **Montreal** center replaced injured Wilf Cude in 2nd period, February 22, 1940. (Chicago 10, Montreal 1)

			REGULAR SEASON													PLAYOFFS											
Season	Club	League	GP	W	L	T	Mins	GA	SO	Avg	AAvg	Eff	SA	S%	SAPG	GP	W	L	T	Mins	GA	SO	Avg	Eff	SA	S%	SAPG

• SANDS, Mike

G – L. 5'9", 170 lbs. b: Mississauga, Ont., 4/6/1963. Minnesota's 3rd, 31st overall in 1981.

Season	Club	League	GP	W	L	T	Mins	GA	SO	Avg	AAvg	Eff	SA	S%	SAPG	GP	W	L	T	Mins	GA	SO	Avg	Eff	SA	S%	SAPG
1979-80	Streetsville Derbys	OJHL-B	20	....	....	....	1049	57	0	3.26	....	....	....	....	....	....	....	....	....	....	....	....	....	....	....	....	....
	Dixie Beehives	OJHL	4	2	1	....	220	12	1	3.55	....	....	....	....	....	....	....	....	....	....	....	....	....	....	....	....	....
1980-81	Sudbury Wolves	OMJHL	50	15	28	2	2789	236	0	5.08	....	....	....	....	....	....	....	....	....	....	....	....	....	....	....	....	....
1981-82	Sudbury Wolves	OHL	53	13	33	1	2854	265	1	5.57	....	....	....	....	....	....	....	....	....	....	....	....	....	....	....	....	....
	Nashville South Stars	CHL	7	3	3	1	380	26	0	4.11	....	....	....	....	....	....	....	....	....	....	....	....	....	....	....	....	....
1982-83	Sudbury Wolves	OHL	43	11	27	0	2320	204	1	5.28	....	....	....	....	....	....	....	....	....	....	....	....	....	....	....	....	....
	Canada	WJC-A	5	....	....	....	240	13	....	3.25	....	....	....	....	....	....	....	....	....	....	....	....	....	....	....	....	....
	Birmingham South Stars	CHL	4	0	4	0	169	14	0	4.97	....	....	....	....	....	....	....	....	....	....	....	....	....	....	....	....	....
1983-84	Salt Lake Golden Eagles	CHL	23	7	12	1	1145	93	0	4.87	....	....	....	....	....	....	....	....	....	....	....	....	....	....	....	....	....
1984-85	**Minnesota North Stars**	**NHL**	**3**	**0**	**3**	**0**	**139**	**14**	**0**	**6.04**	**4.82**	**9.61**	**88**	**.841**	**38.0**	....	....	....	....	....	....	....	....	....	....	....	....
	Springfield Indians	AHL	46	23	17	3	2589	140	2	3.24	....	....	....	....	....	3	0	3	0	130	15	0	6.92	....	....	....	....
1985-86	Springfield Indians	AHL	27	8	15	1	1490	94	0	3.79	....	....	....	....	....	....	....	....	....	....	....	....	....	....	....	....	....
1986-87	**Minnesota North Stars**	**NHL**	**3**	**0**	**2**	**0**	**163**	**12**	**0**	**4.42**	**3.74**	**5.10**	**104**	**.885**	**38.3**	....	....	....	....	....	....	....	....	....	....	....	....
	Springfield Indians	AHL	19	4	10	0	1048	77	0	4.41	....	....	....	....	....	....	....	....	....	....	....	....	....	....	....	....	....
1987-88	Kalamazoo Wings	IHL	3	0	2	1	184	16	0	5.22	....	....	....	....	....	....	....	....	....	....	....	....	....	....	....	....	....
	Baltimore Skipjacks	AHL	4	0	4	0	185	22	0	7.14	....	....	....	....	....	....	....	....	....	....	....	....	....	....	....	....	....
1988-89	Canada	Nat-Team	21	6	13	1	1012	75	0	4.45	....	....	....	....	....	....	....	....	....	....	....	....	....	....	....	....	....
	NHL Totals		**6**	**0**	**5**	**0**	**302**	**26**	**0**	**5.17**	....	....	**192**	**.865**	**38.1**	....	....	....	....	....	....	....	....	....	....	....	....

• Suspended for remainder of 1987-88 season by **Minnesota** for leaving **Baltimore** (AHL) without permission, October, 1987. Signed as a free agent by **Kalamazoo** (IHL) after release by Minnesota, March, 1988.

• SARJEANT, Geoff

Geoffrey I. G – L. 5'9", 180 lbs. b: Newmarket, Ont., 11/30/1969. St. Louis' 1st, 17th overall in 1990 Supplemental Draft.

Season	Club	League	GP	W	L	T	Mins	GA	SO	Avg	AAvg	Eff	SA	S%	SAPG	GP	W	L	T	Mins	GA	SO	Avg	Eff	SA	S%	SAPG
1985-86	Newmarket Royals	OMHA	STATISTICS NOT AVAILABLE																								
	Newmarket Flyers	OJHL	DID NOT PLAY – SPARE GOALTENDER																								
1986-87	Aurora Eagles	OJHL	28	14	8	3	1624	130	0	4.80	....	....	....	....	....	....	....	....	....	....	....	....	....	....	....	....	....
1987-88	Aurora Eagles	OJHL-B	*33	....	....	....	*1878	136	0	4.35	....	....	....	....	....	....	....	....	....	....	....	....	....	....	....	....	....
1988-89	Michigan Tech Huskies	WCHA	6	0	3	2	329	22	0	4.01	....	....	....	....	....	....	....	....	....	....	....	....	....	....	....	....	....
1989-90	Michigan Tech Huskies	WCHA	19	4	13	0	1043	94	0	5.41	....	....	....	....	....	....	....	....	....	....	....	....	....	....	....	....	....
1990-91	Michigan Tech Huskies	WCHA	23	5	15	3	1540	97	0	3.78	....	....	....	....	....	....	....	....	....	....	....	....	....	....	....	....	....
1991-92	Michigan Tech Huskies	WCHA	23	7	13	0	1201	90	1	4.50	....	....	....	....	....	....	....	....	....	....	....	....	....	....	....	....	....
1992-93	Peoria Rivermen	IHL	41	22	14	3	2356	130	0	3.31	....	....	....	....	....	3	0	3	....	179	13	0	4.36	....	....	....	....
1993-94	Peoria Rivermen	IHL	41	25	9	2	2275	93	*2	*2.45	....	....	....	....	....	4	2	2	....	211	13	0	3.69	....	....	....	....
1994-95	Peoria Rivermen	IHL	55	32	12	8	3146	158	0	3.01	....	....	....	....	....	4	0	3	....	206	20	0	5.81	....	....	....	....
	St. Louis Blues	**NHL**	**4**	**1**	**0**	**0**	**120**	**6**	**0**	**3.00**	**3.14**	**3.46**	**52**	**.885**	**26.0**	....	....	....	....	....	....	....	....	....	....	....	....
1995-96	**San Jose Sharks**	**NHL**	**4**	**0**	**2**	**1**	**171**	**14**	**0**	**4.91**	**4.88**	**7.90**	**87**	**.839**	**30.5**	....	....	....	....	....	....	....	....	....	....	....	....
	Kansas City Blades	IHL	41	18	18	1	2167	140	1	3.88	....	....	....	....	....	2	0	1	....	99	3	0	1.82	....	....	....	....
1996-97	Cincinnati Cyclones	IHL	59	32	20	5	3287	157	1	2.87	....	....	....	....	....	3	0	3	....	158	12	0	4.55	....	....	....	....
1997-98	Cincinnati Cyclones	IHL	54	25	19	9	3118	142	5	2.73	....	....	....	....	....	5	4	1	....	353	14	0	2.38	....	....	....	....
1998-99	Cincinnati Cyclones	IHL	14	6	5	1	733	42	1	3.44	....	....	....	....	....	....	....	....	....	....	....	....	....	....	....	....	....
	Flint Generals	UHL	3	0	2	1	179	11	0	3.69	....	....	....	....	....	....	....	....	....	....	....	....	....	....	....	....	....
	Detroit Vipers	IHL	8	1	5	1	421	26	0	3.71	....	....	....	....	....	....	....	....	....	....	....	....	....	....	....	....	....
	Long Beach Ice Dogs	IHL	1	1	0	0	60	1	0	1.00	....	....	....	....	....	....	....	....	....	....	....	....	....	....	....	....	....
	Indianapolis Ice	IHL	23	13	7	2	1354	57	2	2.53	....	....	....	....	....	3	0	1	....	115	10	0	5.22	....	....	....	....
99-2000	Ayr Scottish Eagles	BH-Cup	8	5	3	0	480	22	1	2.75	....	....	....	....	....	....	....	....	....	....	....	....	....	....	....	....	....
	Ayr Scottish Eagles	Britain	23	9	10	4	1396	62	0	2.97	....	....	....	....	....	6	2	4	0	359	13	0	2.17	....	....	....	....
	NHL Totals		**8**	**1**	**2**	**1**	**291**	**20**	**0**	**4.12**	....	....	**139**	**.856**	**28.7**	....	....	....	....	....	....	....	....	....	....	....	....

IHL First All-Star Team (1994)

Signed as a free agent by **San Jose**, September 23, 1995. Signed as a free agent by **Cincinnati** (IHL), August 30, 1996.

• SAUVE, Bob

Robert F. G – L. 5'8", 175 lbs. b: Ste. Genevieve, Que., 6/17/1955. Buffalo's 1st, 17th overall in 1975.

Season	Club	League	GP	W	L	T	Mins	GA	SO	Avg	AAvg	Eff	SA	S%	SAPG	GP	W	L	T	Mins	GA	SO	Avg	Eff	SA	S%	SAPG
1971-72	Verdun Maple Leafs	QMJHL	34	....	....	....	2020	202	0	6.00	....	....	....	....	....	2	0	2	0	120	12	0	6.00	....	....	....	....
1972-73	Laval Titan	QMJHL	35	....	....	....	2100	224	0	6.40	....	....	....	....	....	3	....	....	....	160	20	0	7.50	....	....	....	....
1973-74	Laval Titan	QMJHL	61	....	....	....	3620	341	0	5.65	....	....	....	....	....	11	....	....	....	660	60	0	5.45	....	....	....	....
1974-75	Laval Titan	QMJHL	57	....	....	....	3403	287	0	5.06	....	....	....	....	....	16	....	....	....	960	81	0	5.06	....	....	....	....
1975-76	Providence Reds	AHL	14	5	8	1	848	44	0	3.11	....	....	....	....	....	....	....	....	....	....	....	....	....	....	....	....	....
	Charlotte Checkers	SHL	17	....	....	....	979	36	2	2.21	....	....	....	....	....	7	....	....	....	420	10	*2	*1.43	....	....	....	....
1976-77	**Buffalo Sabres**	**NHL**	**4**	**1**	**2**	**0**	**184**	**11**	**0**	**3.59**	**3.34**	....	....	....	....	....	....	....	....	....	....	....	....	....	....	....	....
	Rhode Island Reds	AHL	25	....	....	....	1346	94	0	4.14	....	....	....	....	....	....	....	....	....	....	....	....	....	....	....	....	....
	Hershey Bears	AHL	9	....	....	....	539	38	0	4.23	....	....	....	....	....	....	....	....	....	....	....	....	....	....	....	....	....
1977-78	**Buffalo Sabres**	**NHL**	**11**	**6**	**2**	**0**	**480**	**20**	**0**	**2.50**	**2.34**	....	....	....	....	....	....	....	....	....	....	....	....	....	....	....	....
	Hershey Bears	AHL	16	4	6	3	872	59	0	4.05	....	....	....	....	....	....	....	....	....	....	....	....	....	....	....	....	....
1978-79	**Buffalo Sabres**	**NHL**	**29**	**10**	**10**	**7**	**1610**	**100**	**0**	**3.73**	**3.30**	....	....	....	....	**3**	**1**	**2**	....	**181**	**9**	**0**	**2.98**	....	....	....	....
	Hershey Bears	AHL	5	3	2	0	278	14	0	3.02	....	....	....	....	....	....	....	....	....	....	....	....	....	....	....	....	....
1979-80	**Buffalo Sabres**	**NHL**	**32**	**20**	**8**	**4**	**1880**	**74**	**4**	***2.36**	**2.07**	....	....	....	....	**8**	**6**	**2**	....	**501**	**17**	***2**	***2.04**	....	....	....	....
1980-81	**Buffalo Sabres**	**NHL**	**35**	**16**	**10**	**9**	**2100**	**111**	**2**	**3.17**	**2.55**	....	....	....	....	....	....	....	....	....	....	....	....	....	....	....	....
1981-82	**Buffalo Sabres**	**NHL**	**14**	**6**	**1**	**5**	**760**	**35**	**0**	**2.76**	**2.13**	....	....	....	....	....	....	....	....	....	....	....	....	....	....	....	....
	Detroit Red Wings	**NHL**	**41**	**11**	**25**	**4**	**2365**	**165**	**0**	**4.19**	**3.24**	....	....	....	....	....	....	....	....	....	....	....	....	....	....	....	....
1982-83	**Buffalo Sabres**	**NHL**	**54**	**25**	**20**	**7**	**3110**	**179**	**1**	**3.45**	**2.76**	**4.43**	**1393**	**.872**	**26.9**	**10**	**6**	**4**	....	**545**	**28**	***2**	**3.08**	....	....	....	....
1983-84	**Buffalo Sabres**	**NHL**	**40**	**22**	**13**	**4**	**2375**	**138**	**0**	**3.49**	**2.74**	**4.59**	**1050**	**.869**	**26.5**	**2**	**0**	**1**	....	**41**	**5**	**0**	**7.32**	**26.14**	**14**	**.643**	**20.5**
1984-85	**Buffalo Sabres**	**NHL**	**27**	**13**	**10**	**3**	**1564**	**84**	**0**	**3.22**	**2.56**	**4.66**	**581**	**.855**	**22.3**	....	....	....	....	....	....	....	....	....	....	....	....
1985-86	**Chicago Black Hawks**	**NHL**	**38**	**19**	**13**	**2**	**2099**	**138**	**0**	**3.94**	**3.08**	**4.49**	**1210**	**.886**	**34.6**	**2**	**0**	**2**	....	**99**	**8**	**0**	**4.85**	**6.36**	**61**	**.869**	**37.0**
1986-87	**Chicago Blackhawks**	**NHL**	**46**	**19**	**19**	**5**	**2660**	**159**	**1**	**3.59**	**3.04**	**3.81**	**1497**	**.894**	**33.8**	**4**	**0**	**4**	....	**245**	**15**	**0**	**3.67**	**4.05**	**136**	**.890**	**33.3**
1987-88	**New Jersey Devils**	**NHL**	**34**	**10**	**16**	**3**	**1804**	**107**	**0**	**3.56**	**2.96**	**4.63**	**823**	**.870**	**27.4**	**5**	**2**	**1**	....	**238**	**13**	**0**	**3.28**	**3.61**	**118**	**.890**	**29.7**
1988-89	**New Jersey Devils**	**NHL**	**15**	**4**	**5**	**1**	**720**	**56**	**0**	**4.67**	**3.89**	**7.85**	**333**	**.832**	**27.8**	....	....	....	....	....	....	....	....	....	....	....	....
	NHL Totals		**420**	**182**	**154**	**54**	**23711**	**1377**	**8**	**3.48**	....	....	....	....	....	**34**	**15**	**16**	....	**1850**	**95**	**4**	**3.08**	....	....	....	....

• Brother of Jean-Francois • QMJHL First All-Star Team (1974) • Shared Vezina Trophy with Don Edwards (1980) • Shared William M. Jennings Trophy with Tom Barrasso (1985)

Traded to **Detroit** by **Buffalo** for future considerations, December 2, 1981. Signed as a free agent by **Buffalo**, June 1, 1982. Traded to **Chicago** by **Buffalo** for Chicago's 3rd round choice (Kevin Kerr) in 1986 Entry Draft, October 15, 1985. Signed as a free agent by **New Jersey**, July 10, 1987.

• SAWCHUK, Terry

Terrance Gordon "Ukey" G – L. 5'11", 195 lbs. b: Winnipeg, Man., 12/28/1929 d: 5/31/1970. **HHOF**

Season	Club	League	GP	W	L	T	Mins	GA	SO	Avg	AAvg	Eff	SA	S%	SAPG	GP	W	L	T	Mins	GA	SO	Avg	Eff	SA	S%	SAPG
1945-46	Winnipeg Monarchs	MJHL	10	....	....	....	600	58	0	5.80	....	....	....	....	....	2	0	2	0	120	12	0	6.00	....	....	....	....
1946-47	Galt Red Wings	OHA-Jr.	30	....	....	....	1800	94	4	3.13	....	....	....	....	....	2	0	2	0	125	9	0	4.32	....	....	....	....
1947-48	Windsor Spitfires	OHA-Jr.	4	....	....	....	240	11	0	2.75	....	....	....	....	....	....	....	....	....	....	....	....	....	....	....	....	....
	Windsor Spitfires	IHL	3	3	0	0	180	5	0	1.67	....	....	....	....	....	....	....	....	....	....	....	....	....	....	....	....	....
	Omaha Knights	USHL	54	30	18	5	3248	174	*4	3.21	....	....	....	....	....	3	1	2	0	180	9	0	3.00	....	....	....	....
1948-49	Indianapolis Capitols	AHL	67	38	17	2	4020	205	2	3.06	....	....	....	....	....	2	0	2	0	120	9	0	4.50	....	....	....	....
1949-50	Indianapolis Capitols	AHL	61	31	20	10	3660	188	3	3.08	....	....	....	....	....	8	*8	0	0	480	12	0	*1.50	....	....	....	....
	Detroit Red Wings	**NHL**	**7**	**4**	**3**	**0**	**420**	**16**	**1**	**2.29**	**2.55**	....	....	....	....	....	....	....	....	....	....	....	....	....	....	....	....
1950-51	**Detroit Red Wings**	**NHL**	***70**	***44**	**13**	**13**	***4200**	**139**	***11**	**1.99**	**2.12**	....	....	....	....	**6**	**2**	**4**	....	**463**	**13**	**1**	**1.68**	....	....	....	....
1951-52♦	**Detroit Red Wings**	**NHL**	***70**	***44**	**14**	**12**	***4200**	**133**	***12**	***1.90**	**2.12**	....	....	....	....	***8**	***8**	**0**	....	**480**	**5**	***4**	***0.63**	....	....	....	....
1952-53	**Detroit Red Wings**	**NHL**	**63**	***32**	**15**	**16**	**3780**	**120**	**9**	***1.90**	**2.33**	....	....	....	....	**6**	**2**	**4**	....	**372**	**21**	**1**	**3.39**	....	....	....	....
1953-54♦	**Detroit Red Wings**	**NHL**	**67**	***35**	**19**	**13**	**4004**	**129**	**12**	**1.93**	**2.36**	....	....	....	....	***12**	***8**	**4**	....	***751**	**20**	***2**	***1.60**	....	....	....	....
1954-55♦	**Detroit Red Wings**	**NHL**	**68**	***40**	**17**	**11**	**4040**	**132**	***12**	**1.96**	**2.27**	....	....	....	....	**11**	***8**	**3**	....	***660**	**26**	***1**	***2.36**	....	....	....	....
1955-56	**Boston Bruins**	**NHL**	**68**	**22**	**33**	**13**	**4080**	**177**	**9**	**2.60**	**3.21**	....	....	....	....	....	....	....	....	....	....	....	....	....	....	....	....
1956-57	**Boston Bruins**	**NHL**	**34**	**18**	**10**	**6**	**2040**	**81**	**2**	**2.38**	**2.71**	....	....	....	....	....	....	....	....	....	....	....	....	....	....	....	....
1957-58	**Detroit Red Wings**	**NHL**	***70**	**29**	**29**	**12**	***4200**	**206**	**3**	**2.94**	**3.26**	....	....	....	....	**4**	**0**	**4**	....	**252**	**19**	**0**	**4.52**	....	....	....	....
1958-59	**Detroit Red Wings**	**NHL**	**67**	**23**	**36**	**8**	**4020**	**207**	**5**	**3.09**	**3.33**	....	....	....	....	....	....	....	....	....	....	....	....	....	....	....	....

Season	Club	League	GP	W	L	T	Mins	GA	SO	Avg	AAvg	Eff	SA	S%	SAPG	GP	W	L	T	Mins	GA	SO	Avg	Eff	SA	S%	SAPG
			REGULAR SEASON													PLAYOFFS											
1959-60	**Detroit Red Wings**	**NHL**	**58**	**24**	**20**	**14**	**3480**	**155**	**5**	**2.67**	**2.75**	....	....	....	....	**6**	**2**	**4**	....	**405**	**20**	**0**	**2.96**	....	....	....	....
1960-61	**Detroit Red Wings**	**NHL**	**38**	**12**	**17**	**7**	**2210**	**114**	**2**	**3.10**	**3.21**	....	....	....	....	**8**	**5**	**3**	....	**465**	**18**	**1**	**2.32**	....	....	....	....
1961-62	**Detroit Red Wings**	**NHL**	**43**	**14**	**21**	**8**	**2580**	**141**	**5**	**3.28**	**3.40**	....	....	....	....	....	....	....	....	....	....	....	....	....	....	....	....
1962-63	**Detroit Red Wings**	**NHL**	**48**	**21**	**17**	**7**	**2781**	**118**	**3**	**2.55**	**2.61**	....	....	....	....	***11**	**5**	**6**	....	***660**	**35**	**0**	**3.18**	....	....	....	....
1963-64	**Detroit Red Wings**	**NHL**	**53**	**25**	**20**	**7**	**3140**	**138**	**5**	**2.64**	**2.91**	....	....	....	....	**13**	**6**	**5**	....	**677**	**31**	**1**	**2.75**	....	....	....	....
1964-65	**Toronto Maple Leafs**	**NHL**	**36**	**17**	**13**	**6**	**2160**	**92**	**1**	**2.56**	**2.72**	....	....	....	....	**1**	**0**	**1**	....	**60**	**3**	**0**	**3.00**	....	....	....	....
1965-66	**Toronto Maple Leafs**	**NHL**	**27**	**10**	**11**	**3**	**1521**	**80**	**1**	**3.16**	**3.20**	....	....	....	....	**2**	**0**	**2**	....	**120**	**6**	**0**	**3.00**	....	....	....	....
1966-67♦	**Toronto Maple Leafs**	**NHL**	**28**	**15**	**5**	**4**	**1409**	**66**	**2**	**2.81**	**2.89**	....	....	....	....	***10**	***6**	**4**	....	***565**	**25**	**0**	**2.65**	....	....	....	....
1967-68	**Los Angeles Kings**	**NHL**	**36**	**11**	**14**	**6**	**1936**	**99**	**2**	**3.07**	**3.42**	....	....	....	....	**5**	**2**	**3**	....	**280**	**18**	***1**	**3.86**	....	....	....	....
1968-69	**Detroit Red Wings**	**NHL**	**13**	**3**	**4**	**3**	**641**	**28**	**0**	**2.62**	**2.71**	....	....	....	....	....	....	....	....	....	....	....	....	....	....	....	....
1969-70	**New York Rangers**	**NHL**	**8**	**3**	**1**	**2**	**412**	**20**	**1**	**2.91**	**3.09**	....	....	....	....	**3**	**0**	**1**	....	**80**	**6**	**0**	**4.50**	....	....	....	....
	NHL Totals		***972**	***446**	**332**	**171**	***57254**	**2391**	***103**	**2.51**	....	....	....	....	....	**106**	**54**	**48**	....	**6290**	**266**	**12**	**2.54**	....	....	....	....

USHL Second All-Star Team (1948) • Won Outstanding Rookie Cup (Top Rookie - USHL) (1948) • Won Dudley "Red" Garrett Memorial Award (Top Rookie - AHL) (1949) • AHL First All-Star Team (1950) • NHL First All-Star Team (1951, 1952, 1953) • Won Calder Memorial Trophy (1951) • Won Vezina Trophy (1952, 1953, 1955) • NHL Second All-Star Team (1954, 1955, 1959, 1963) • Shared Vezina Trophy with Johnny Bower (1965) • Won Lester Patrick Trophy (1971) • Played in NHL All-Star Game (1950, 1951, 1952, 1953, 1954, 1955, 1956, 1959, 1963, 1964, 1968)

Traded to **Boston** by **Detroit** with Marcel Bonin, Lorne Davis and Vic Stasiuk for Gilles Boisvert, Real Chevrefils, Norm Corcoran, Warren Godfrey and Ed Sandford, June 3, 1955. • Missed remainder of 1956-57 season recovering from nervous exhaustion, January 16, 1957. Traded to **Detroit** by **Boston** for John Bucyk, July 10, 1957. Claimed by **Toronto** from **Detroit** in Intra-League Draft, June 10, 1964. Claimed by **LA Kings** from **Toronto** in Expansion Draft, June 6, 1967. Traded to **Detroit** by **LA Kings** for Jimmy Peters, October 10, 1968. Traded to **NY Rangers** by **Detroit** with Sandy Snow for Larry Jeffrey, June 17, 1969.

• SCHAEFER, Joe

G – L. 5'8", 165 lbs. b: Long Island, NY, 12/21/1924.

Season	Club	League	GP	W	L	T	Mins	GA	SO	Avg	AAvg	Eff	SA	S%	SAPG	GP	W	L	T	Mins	GA	SO	Avg	Eff	SA	S%	SAPG
1955-56	New Haven Blades	EHL	1	....	....	....	60	3	0	3.00	....	....	....	....	....	....	....	....	....	....	....	....	....	....	....	....	....
1956-57	Philadelphia Ramblers	EHL	2	....	....	....	120	9	0	4.50	....	....	....	....	....	....	....	....	....	....	....	....	....	....	....	....	....
1957-58	Buffalo Bisons	AHL	1	0	1	0	60	12	0	12.00	....	....	....	....	....	....	....	....	....	....	....	....	....	....	....	....	....
	Philadelphia Ramblers	EHL	1	....	....	....	60	5	0	5.00	....	....	....	....	....	....	....	....	....	....	....	....	....	....	....	....	....
1958-59	Johnstown Jets	EHL	1	0	1	0	60	11	0	11.00	....	....	....	....	....	....	....	....	....	....	....	....	....	....	....	....	....
1959-60	**New York Rangers**	**NHL**	**1**	**0**	**1**	**0**	**39**	**5**	**0**	**7.69**	**8.06**	....	....	....	....	....	....	....	....	....	....	....	....	....	....	....	....
1960-61	**New York Rangers**	**NHL**	**1**	**0**	**1**	**0**	**47**	**3**	**0**	**3.83**	**3.95**	....	....	....	....	....	....	....	....	....	....	....	....	....	....	....	....
	NHL Totals		**2**	**0**	**2**	**0**	**86**	**8**	**0**	**5.58**	....	....	....	....	....	....	....	....	....	....	....	....	....	....	....	....	....

• **NY Rangers'** assistant trainer/practice goaltender replaced injured Gump Worsley in 2nd period, February 17, 1960. (Chicago 5, NY Rangers 1). • **NY Rangers'** assistant trainer/practice goaltender replaced injured Gump Worsley in 1st period, March 8, 1961. (Chicago 4, NY Rangers 3)

• SCHAFER, Paxton

G – L. 5'9", 164 lbs. b: Medicine Hat, Alta., 2/26/1976. Boston's 3rd, 47th overall in 1995.

Season	Club	League	GP	W	L	T	Mins	GA	SO	Avg	AAvg	Eff	SA	S%	SAPG	GP	W	L	T	Mins	GA	SO	Avg	Eff	SA	S%	SAPG
1992-93	Medicine Hat Midget Tigers	AAHA	27	....	....	....	1601	95	1	3.56	....	....	....	....	....	....	....	....	....	....	....	....	....	....	....	....	....
1993-94	Medicine Hat Tigers	WHL	19	6	9	1	909	67	0	4.42	....	....	....	....	....	....	....	....	....	....	....	....	....	....	....	....	....
1994-95	Medicine Hat Tigers	WHL	61	32	26	2	3519	185	0	3.15	....	....	....	....	....	5	1	4	....	339	18	0	3.19	....	....	....	....
1995-96	Medicine Hat Tigers	WHL	60	24	30	3	3256	200	1	3.69	....	....	....	....	....	5	1	4	....	251	25	0	5.98	....	....	....	....
1996-97	**Boston Bruins**	**NHL**	**3**	**0**	**0**	**0**	**77**	**6**	**0**	**4.68**	**5.04**	**11.23**	**25**	**.760**	**19.5**	....	....	....	....	....	....	....	....	....	....	....	....
	Providence Bruins	AHL	22	9	10	0	1206	75	1	3.73	....	....	....	....	....	....	....	....	....	....	....	....	....	....	....	....	....
	Charlotte Checkers	ECHL	4	3	1	0	239	7	0	1.75	....	....	....	....	....	....	....	....	....	....	....	....	....	....	....	....	....
1997-98	Providence Bruins	AHL	3	1	1	0	158	11	0	4.16	....	....	....	....	....	....	....	....	....	....	....	....	....	....	....	....	....
	Charlotte Checkers	ECHL	44	21	17	5	2538	131	1	3.10	....	....	....	....	....	7	3	4	....	428	21	0	2.94	....	....	....	....
1998-99	Greenville Growl	ECHL	40	17	16	7	2326	115	2	2.97	....	....	....	....	....	....	....	....	....	....	....	....	....	....	....	....	....
	Providence Bruins	AHL	1	1	0	0	61	3	0	2.94	....	....	....	....	....	....	....	....	....	....	....	....	....	....	....	....	....
99-2000	Pee Dee Pride	ECHL	41	26	10	2	2331	94	2	2.42	....	....	....	....	....	2	0	1	....	98	8	0	4.91	....	....	....	....
	NHL Totals		**3**	**0**	**0**	**0**	**77**	**6**	**0**	**4.68**	....	....	**25**	**.760**	**19.5**	....	....	....	....	....	....	....	....	....	....	....	....

WHL East First All-Star Team (1995)

• SCHWAB, Corey

G – L. 6', 180 lbs. b: North Battleford, Sask., 11/4/1970. New Jersey's 12th, 200th overall in 1990.

Season	Club	League	GP	W	L	T	Mins	GA	SO	Avg	AAvg	Eff	SA	S%	SAPG	GP	W	L	T	Mins	GA	SO	Avg	Eff	SA	S%	SAPG
1988-89	North Battleford North Stars	SJHL	STATISTICS NOT AVAILABLE																								
	Seattle Thunderbirds	WHL	10	2	2	0	386	31	0	4.82	....	....	....	....	....	....	....	....	....	....	....	....	....	....	....	....	....
1989-90	Seattle Thunderbirds	WHL	27	15	2	1	1150	69	1	3.60	....	....	....	....	....	3	0	0	....	49	2	0	2.45	....	....	....	....
1990-91	Seattle Thunderbirds	WHL	*58	32	18	3	*3289	224	0	4.09	....	....	....	....	....	6	1	5	....	382	25	0	3.93	....	....	....	....
1991-92	Utica Devils	AHL	24	9	12	1	1322	95	0	4.31	....	....	....	....	....	....	....	....	....	....	....	....	....	....	....	....	....
	Cincinnati Cyclones	ECHL	8	6	0	1	450	31	0	4.13	....	....	....	....	....	9	6	3	....	540	29	0	3.22	....	....	....	....
1992-93	Utica Devils	AHL	40	18	16	5	2387	169	*2	4.25	....	....	....	....	....	1	0	1	....	59	6	0	6.10	....	....	....	....
	Cincinnati Cyclones	IHL	3	1	2	0	185	17	0	5.51	....	....	....	....	....	....	....	....	....	....	....	....	....	....	....	....	....
1993-94	Albany River Rats	AHL	51	27	21	3	3058	184	0	3.61	....	....	....	....	....	5	1	4	....	298	20	0	4.02	....	....	....	....
1994-95	Albany River Rats	AHL	45	25	10	9	2711	117	3	*2.59	....	....	....	....	....	7	6	1	....	425	19	0	2.68	....	....	....	....
1995-96	**New Jersey Devils**	**NHL**	**10**	**0**	**3**	**0**	**331**	**12**	**0**	**2.18**	**2.17**	**2.20**	**119**	**.899**	**21.6**	....	....	....	....	....	....	....	....	....	....	....	....
	Albany River Rats	AHL	5	3	2	0	299	13	0	2.61	....	....	....	....	....	....	....	....	....	....	....	....	....	....	....	....	....
1996-97	**Tampa Bay Lightning**	**NHL**	**31**	**11**	**12**	**1**	**1462**	**74**	**2**	**3.04**	**3.27**	**3.13**	**719**	**.897**	**29.5**	....	....	....	....	....	....	....	....	....	....	....	....
1997-98	**Tampa Bay Lightning**	**NHL**	**16**	**2**	**9**	**1**	**821**	**40**	**1**	**2.92**	**3.48**	**3.16**	**370**	**.892**	**27.0**	....	....	....	....	....	....	....	....	....	....	....	....
1998-99	**Tampa Bay Lightning**	**NHL**	**40**	**8**	**25**	**3**	**2146**	**126**	**0**	**3.52**	**4.21**	**3.85**	**1153**	**.891**	**32.2**	....	....	....	....	....	....	....	....	....	....	....	....
	Cleveland Lumberjacks	IHL	8	1	6	1	477	31	0	3.90	....	....	....	....	....	....	....	....	....	....	....	....	....	....	....	....	....
99-2000	Orlando Solar Bears	IHL	16	9	4	2	868	31	1	2.14	....	....	....	....	....	....	....	....	....	....	....	....	....	....	....	....	....
	Vancouver Canucks	**NHL**	**6**	**2**	**1**	**1**	**269**	**16**	**0**	**3.57**	**4.08**	**4.97**	**115**	**.861**	**25.7**	....	....	....	....	....	....	....	....	....	....	....	....
	Syracuse Crunch	AHL	12	7	5	0	720	42	0	3.50	....	....	....	....	....	4	1	3	....	246	11	1	2.69	....	....	....	....
	NHL Totals		**103**	**23**	**50**	**6**	**5029**	**268**	**3**	**3.20**	....	....	**2476**	**.892**	**29.5**	....	....	....	....	....	....	....	....	....	....	....	....

AHL Second All-Star Team (1995) • Shared Harry "Hap" Holmes Memorial Trophy (fewest goals against - AHL) with Mike Dunham (1995) • Shared Jack A. Butterfield Trophy (Playoff MVP - AHL) with Mike Dunham (1995)

Traded to **Tampa Bay** by **New Jersey** for Jeff Reese, Chicago's 2nd round choice (previously acquired, New Jersey selected Pierre Dagenais) in 1996 Entry Draft and Tampa Bay's 8th round choice (Jason Bertsch) in 1996 Entry Draft, June 22, 1996. Claimed by **Atlanta** from **Tampa Bay** in Expansion Draft, June 25, 1999. Traded to **Vancouver** by **Atlanta** for Vancouver's 4th round choice (Carl Mallette) in 2000 Entry Draft, October 29, 1999.

• SCOTT, Ron

G – L. 5'8", 155 lbs. b: Guelph, Ont., 7/21/1960.

Season	Club	League	GP	W	L	T	Mins	GA	SO	Avg	AAvg	Eff	SA	S%	SAPG	GP	W	L	T	Mins	GA	SO	Avg	Eff	SA	S%	SAPG
1978-79	Cornwall Royals	QMJHL	56	....	....	....	2827	248	1	5.26	....	....	....	....	....	7	....	....	....	394	29	1	4.42	....	....	....	....
1979-80	Cornwall Royals	QMJHL	41	....	....	....	2086	165	0	4.75	....	....	....	....	....	16	....	....	....	904	55	1	3.65	....	....	....	....
	Cornwall Royals	Mem-Cup	5	*3	2	0	301	28	0	5.57	....	....	....	....	....	....	....	....	....	....	....	....	....	....	....	....	....
1980-81	Michigan State Spartans	CCHA	33	11	21	1	1899	123	2	3.89	....	....	....	....	....	....	....	....	....	....	....	....	....	....	....	....	....
1981-82	Michigan State Spartans	CCHA	39	24	13	1	2298	109	2	2.85	....	....	....	....	....	....	....	....	....	....	....	....	....	....	....	....	....
1982-83	Michigan State Spartans	CCHA	40	29	9	1	2273	100	2	2.64	....	....	....	....	....	....	....	....	....	....	....	....	....	....	....	....	....
1983-84	**New York Rangers**	**NHL**	**9**	**2**	**3**	**3**	**485**	**29**	**0**	**3.59**	**2.83**	**4.10**	**254**	**.886**	**31.4**	....	....	....	....	....	....	....	....	....	....	....	....
	Tulsa Oilers	CHL	29	13	13	3	1717	109	0	3.81	....	....	....	....	....	5	....	....	....	280	20	0	4.28	....	....	....	....
1984-85	New Haven Nighthawks	AHL	36	13	18	4	2047	130	0	3.81	....	....	....	....	....	....	....	....	....	....	....	....	....	....	....	....	....
1985-86	**New York Rangers**	**NHL**	**4**	**0**	**3**	**0**	**156**	**11**	**0**	**4.23**	**3.30**	**8.31**	**56**	**.804**	**21.5**	....	....	....	....	....	....	....	....	....	....	....	....
	New Haven Nighthawks	AHL	19	8	8	1	1069	66	1	3.70	....	....	....	....	....	2	1	1	0	143	8	0	3.36	....	....	....	....
1986-87	**New York Rangers**	**NHL**	**1**	**0**	**0**	**1**	**65**	**5**	**0**	**4.62**	**3.91**	**6.60**	**35**	**.857**	**32.3**	....	....	....	....	....	....	....	....	....	....	....	....
	New Haven Nighthawks	AHL	29	16	7	0	1744	107	2	3.68	....	....	....	....	....	....	....	....	....	....	....	....	....	....	....	....	....
1987-88	**New York Rangers**	**NHL**	**2**	**1**	**1**	**0**	**90**	**6**	**0**	**4.00**	**3.33**	**5.85**	**41**	**.854**	**27.3**	....	....	....	....	....	....	....	....	....	....	....	....
	New Haven Nighthawks	AHL	17	8	7	1	963	49	0	3.05	....	....	....	....	....	....	....	....	....	....	....	....	....	....	....	....	....
	Colorado Rangers	IHL	8	3	4	0	395	33	0	5.01	....	....	....	....	....	5	1	4	0	259	16	....	3.71	....	....	....	....

			REGULAR SEASON													PLAYOFFS											
Season	Club	League	GP	W	L	T	Mins	GA	SO	Avg	AAvg	Eff	SA	S%	SAPG	GP	W	L	T	Mins	GA	SO	Avg	Eff	SA	S%	SAPG
1988-89	Denver Rangers	IHL	18	7	11	0	990	79	0	4.79	....	....	....	....	....	....	....	....	....	....	....	....	....	....	....	....	....
1989-90	**Los Angeles Kings**	**NHL**	**12**	**5**	**6**	**0**	**654**	**40**	**0**	**3.67**	**3.11**	**4.57**	**321**	**.875**	**29.4**	**1**	**0**	**0**	....	**32**	**4**	**0**	**7.50**	**30.00**	**10**	**.600**	**18.8**
	New Haven Nighthawks	AHL	22	8	11	1	1224	79	1	3.87	....	....	....	....	....	....	....	....	....	....	....	....	....	....	....	....	....
1990-91	New Haven Nighthawks	AHL	29	5	15	4	1540	104	0	4.05	....	....	....	....	....	....	....	....	....	....	....	....	....	....	....	....	....
	NHL Totals		**28**	**8**	**13**	**4**	**1450**	**91**	**0**	**3.77**	....	....	**707**	**.871**	**29.3**	**1**	**0**	**0**	....	**32**	**4**	**0**	**7.50**	....	**10**	**.600**	**18.8**

WCHA First All-Star Team (1981) • CCHA First All-Star Team (1982, 1983) • NCAA West First All-American Team (1982, 1983) • Shared Terry Sawchuk Trophy (fewest goals against - CHL) with John Vanbiesbrouck (1984)

Signed as a free agent by **NY Rangers**, May 25, 1983. Signed as a free agent by **LA Kings**, January 12, 1990.

• SEVIGNY, Richard

Richard F. G – L. 5'8", 172 lbs. b: Montreal, Que., 4/11/1957. Montreal's 11th, 124th overall in 1977.

Season	Club	League	GP	W	L	T	Mins	GA	SO	Avg	AAvg	Eff	SA	S%	SAPG	GP	W	L	T	Mins	GA	SO	Avg	Eff	SA	S%	SAPG
1974-75	Granby Vics	QJHL	50	....	....	....	2966	240	*2	4.85	....	....	....	....	....	....	....	....	....	....	....	....	....	....	....	....	....
	Sherbrooke Castors	QMJHL	2	....	....	....	62	4	0	3.87	....	....	....	....	....	....	....	....	....	....	....	....	....	....	....	....	....
1975-76	Sherbrooke Castors	QMJHL	55	....	....	....	3058	196	2	3.85	....	....	....	....	....	15	....	....	....	797	56	0	4.22	....	....	....	....
	Canada	WJC	4	....	....	....	226	23	....	6.10	....	....	....	....	....	....	....	....	....	....	....	....	....	....	....	....	....
1976-77	Sherbrooke Castors	QMJHL	65	....	....	....	3656	248	*2	4.07	....	....	....	....	....	18	....	....	....	1058	60	2	3.40	....	....	....	....
	Sherbrooke Castors	Mem-Cup	4	0	*4	0	240	19	0	4.75	....	....	....	....	....	....	....	....	....	....	....	....	....	....	....	....	....
1977-78	Kalamazoo Wings	IHL	35	....	....	....	1897	95	1	3.01	....	....	....	....	....	7	....	....	....	296	12	0	*2.43	....	....	....	....
1978-79	Springfield Indians	AHL	22	6	12	3	1302	77	0	3.55	....	....	....	....	....	....	....	....	....	....	....	....	....	....	....	....	....
	Nova Scotia Voyageurs	AHL	20	12	6	1	1169	57	1	2.93	....	....	....	....	....	10	5	5	0	607	37	0	3.66	....	....	....	....
1979-80	**Montreal Canadiens**	**NHL**	**11**	**5**	**4**	**2**	**632**	**31**	**0**	**2.94**	**2.60**	....	....	....	....	....	....	....	....	....	....	....	....	....	....	....	....
	Nova Scotia Voyageurs	AHL	35	17	12	4	2104	114	*3	3.25	....	....	....	....	....	4	1	3	0	239	15	0	3.77	....	....	....	....
1980-81	**Montreal Canadiens**	**NHL**	**33**	**20**	**4**	**3**	**1777**	**71**	**2**	***2.40**	**1.93**	....	....	....	....	**3**	**0**	**3**	....	**180**	**13**	**0**	**4.33**	....	....	....	....
1981-82	**Montreal Canadiens**	**NHL**	**19**	**11**	**4**	**2**	**1027**	**53**	**0**	**3.10**	**2.39**	....	....	....	....	....	....	....	....	....	....	....	....	....	....	....	....
1982-83	**Montreal Canadiens**	**NHL**	**38**	**15**	**11**	**8**	**2130**	**122**	**1**	**3.44**	**2.75**	**4.02**	**1045**	**.883**	**29.4**	**1**	**0**	**0**	....	**28**	**0**	**0**	**0.00**	....	....	....	....
1983-84	**Montreal Canadiens**	**NHL**	**40**	**16**	**18**	**2**	**2203**	**124**	**1**	**3.38**	**2.65**	**4.43**	**946**	**.869**	**25.8**	....	....	....	....	....	....	....	....	....	....	....	....
1984-85	**Quebec Nordiques**	**NHL**	**20**	**10**	**6**	**2**	**1104**	**62**	**1**	**3.37**	**2.68**	**4.26**	**491**	**.874**	**26.7**	....	....	....	....	....	....	....	....	....	....	....	....
1985-86	**Quebec Nordiques**	**NHL**	**11**	**3**	**5**	**1**	**468**	**33**	**0**	**4.23**	**3.30**	**5.77**	**242**	**.864**	**31.0**	....	....	....	....	....	....	....	....	....	....	....	....
	Fredericton Express	AHL	6	3	3	0	362	21	0	3.48	....	....	....	....	....	....	....	....	....	....	....	....	....	....	....	....	....
1986-87	**Quebec Nordiques**	**NHL**	**4**	**0**	**2**	**0**	**144**	**11**	**0**	**4.58**	**3.88**	**9.00**	**56**	**.804**	**23.3**	....	....	....	....	....	....	....	....	....	....	....	....
	Fredericton Express	AHL	16	4	10	0	884	62	0	4.21	....	....	....	....	....	....	....	....	....	....	....	....	....	....	....	....	....
1987-88	Fredericton Express	AHL	1	0	0	0	16	2	0	7.50	....	....	....	....	....	....	....	....	....	....	....	....	....	....	....	....	....
1988-89			OUT OF HOCKEY – RETIRED																								
1989-90	HC Chamonix	France-2	DID NOT PLAY – COACHING																								
1990-91	HC Briancon	France	DID NOT PLAY – COACHING																								
	NHL Totals		**176**	**80**	**54**	**20**	**9485**	**507**	**5**	**3.21**	....	....	....	....	....	**4**	**0**	**3**	....	**208**	**13**	**0**	**3.75**	....	....	....	....

QMJHL West First All-Star Team (1976) • IHL Second All-Star Team (1978) • Shared Vezina Trophy with Denis Herron and Michel Larocque (1981)

Signed as a free agent by **Quebec**, July 4, 1984.

• SHARPLES, Scott

Warren Scott G – L. 6', 180 lbs. b: Montreal, Que., 3/1/1968. Calgary's 8th, 184th overall in 1986.

Season	Club	League	GP	W	L	T	Mins	GA	SO	Avg	AAvg	Eff	SA	S%	SAPG	GP	W	L	T	Mins	GA	SO	Avg	Eff	SA	S%	SAPG
1985-86	Penticton Broncos	BCJHL	28	20	6	0	1522	94	0	*3.71	....	....	....	....	....	....	....	....	....	....	....	....	....	....	....	....	....
1986-87	University of Michigan	CCHA	32	12	16	1	1728	148	1	5.14	....	....	....	....	....	....	....	....	....	....	....	....	....	....	....	....	....
1987-88	University of Michigan	CCHA	33	18	15	0	1930	132	0	4.10	....	....	....	....	....	....	....	....	....	....	....	....	....	....	....	....	....
1988-89	University of Michigan	CCHA	33	17	11	2	1887	116	0	3.69	....	....	....	....	....	....	....	....	....	....	....	....	....	....	....	....	....
1989-90	University of Michigan	CCHA	*39	20	10	6	*2165	117	0	3.24	....	....	....	....	....	....	....	....	....	....	....	....	....	....	....	....	....
	Salt Lake Golden Eagles	IHL	3	0	3	0	178	13	0	4.38	....	....	....	....	....	....	....	....	....	....	....	....	....	....	....	....	....
1990-91	Salt Lake Golden Eagles	IHL	37	21	11	1	2097	124	2	3.55	....	....	....	....	....	4	0	3	0	188	14	0	4.47	....	....	....	....
1991-92	**Calgary Flames**	**NHL**	**1**	**0**	**0**	**1**	**65**	**4**	**0**	**3.69**	**3.30**	**3.69**	**40**	**.900**	**36.9**	....	....	....	....	....	....	....	....	....	....	....	....
	Salt Lake Golden Eagles	IHL	35	9	18	4	1936	121	0	3.75	....	....	....	....	....	1	0	1	0	60	7	0	7.00	....	....	....	....
1992-93	St. John's Maple Leafs	AHL	25	9	8	3	1168	80	0	4.11	....	....	....	....	....	1	0	0	0	7	0	0	0.00	....	....	....	....
	Brantford Smoke	ColHL	7	5	1	0	400	27	0	4.05	....	....	....	....	....	....	....	....	....	....	....	....	....	....	....	....	....
	NHL Totals		**1**	**0**	**0**	**1**	**65**	**4**	**0**	**3.69**	....	....	**40**	**.900**	**36.9**	....	....	....	....	....	....	....	....	....	....	....	....

• SHIELDS, Al

G. 6', 188 lbs. b: Ottawa, Ont., 5/10/1907 d: 9/24/1975.

Season	Club	League	GP	W	L	T	Mins	GA	SO	Avg	AAvg	Eff	SA	S%	SAPG	GP	W	L	T	Mins	GA	SO	Avg	Eff	SA	S%	SAPG
1931-32	**New York Americans**	**NHL**	**2**	**0**	**0**	**0**	**41**	**9**	**0**	**13.17**	**16.23**	....	....	....	....	....	....	....	....	....	....	....	....	....	....	....	....
	NHL Totals		**2**	**0**	**0**	**0**	**41**	**9**	**0**	**13.17**	....	....	....	....	....	....	....	....	....	....	....	....	....	....	....	....	....

• **NY Americans'** defenseman replaced injured Roy Worters in 3rd period, November 17, 1931. (NY Rangers 3, NY Americans 0) • Replaced injured Roy Worters in 2nd period, January 19, 1932. (Toronto 11, NY Americans 3)

• SHIELDS, Steve

Stephen Charles G – L. 6'3", 215 lbs. b: Toronto, Ont., 7/19/1972. Buffalo's 5th, 101st overall in 1991.

Season	Club	League	GP	W	L	T	Mins	GA	SO	Avg	AAvg	Eff	SA	S%	SAPG	GP	W	L	T	Mins	GA	SO	Avg	Eff	SA	S%	SAPG
1988-89	North Bay Trappers	NOJHA	STATISTICS NOT AVAILABLE																								
1989-90	St. Mary's Lincolns	OJHL-B	26	....	....	....	1512	121	0	4.80	....	....	....	....	....	....	....	....	....	....	....	....	....	....	....	....	....
1990-91	University of Michigan	CCHA	37	26	6	3	1963	106	0	3.24	....	....	....	....	....	....	....	....	....	....	....	....	....	....	....	....	....
1991-92	University of Michigan	CCHA	*37	*27	7	2	*2090	99	1	2.84	....	....	....	....	....	....	....	....	....	....	....	....	....	....	....	....	....
1992-93	University of Michigan	CCHA	*39	*30	6	2	2027	75	2	*2.22	....	....	....	....	....	....	....	....	....	....	....	....	....	....	....	....	....
1993-94	University of Michigan	CCHA	36	*28	6	1	1961	87	0	2.66	....	....	....	....	....	....	....	....	....	....	....	....	....	....	....	....	....
1994-95	Rochester Americans	AHL	13	3	8	0	673	53	0	4.72	....	....	....	....	....	1	0	0	....	20	3	0	9.00	....	....	....	....
	South Carolina Stingrays	ECHL	21	11	5	2	1158	52	2	2.69	....	....	....	....	....	3	0	2	....	144	11	0	4.58	....	....	....	....
1995-96	**Buffalo Sabres**	**NHL**	**2**	**1**	**0**	**0**	**75**	**4**	**0**	**3.20**	**3.18**	**4.00**	**32**	**.875**	**25.6**	....	....	....	....	....	....	....	....	....	....	....	....
	Rochester Americans	AHL	43	20	17	2	2357	140	1	3.56	....	....	....	....	....	*19	*15	3	....	*1127	47	1	2.50	....	....	....	....
1996-97	**Buffalo Sabres**	**NHL**	**13**	**3**	**8**	**2**	**789**	**39**	**0**	**2.97**	**3.20**	**2.59**	**447**	**.913**	**34.0**	**10**	**4**	**6**	....	**570**	**26**	**1**	**2.74**	**2.13**	**334**	**.922**	**35.2**
	Rochester Americans	AHL	23	14	6	2	1331	60	1	2.70	....	....	....	....	....	....	....	....	....	....	....	....	....	....	....	....	....
1997-98	**Buffalo Sabres**	**NHL**	**16**	**3**	**6**	**4**	**785**	**37**	**0**	**2.83**	**3.38**	**2.57**	**408**	**.909**	**31.2**	....	....	....	....	....	....	....	....	....	....	....	....
	Rochester Americans	AHL	1	0	1	0	59	3	0	3.04	....	....	....	....	....	....	....	....	....	....	....	....	....	....	....	....	....
1998-99	**San Jose Sharks**	**NHL**	**37**	**15**	**11**	**8**	**2162**	**80**	**4**	**2.22**	**2.63**	**1.76**	**1011**	**.921**	**28.1**	**1**	**0**	**1**	....	**60**	**6**	**0**	**6.00**	**10.00**	**36**	**.833**	**36.0**
99-2000	**San Jose Sharks**	**NHL**	**67**	**27**	**30**	**8**	**3797**	**162**	**4**	**2.56**	**2.92**	**2.27**	**1826**	**.911**	**28.9**	**12**	**5**	**7**	....	**696**	**36**	**0**	**3.10**	**3.46**	**323**	**.889**	**27.8**
	NHL Totals		**135**	**49**	**55**	**22**	**7608**	**322**	**8**	**2.54**	....	....	**3724**	**.914**	**29.4**	**23**	**9**	**14**	....	**1326**	**68**	**1**	**3.08**	....	**693**	**.902**	**31.4**

CCHA First All-Star Team (1993, 1994) • NCAA West Second All-American Team (1993, 1994)

Traded to **San Jose** by **Buffalo** with Buffalo's 4th round choice (Miroskav Zalesak) in 1998 Entry Draft for Kay Whitmore, Colorado's 2nd round choice (previously acquired, Buffalo selected Jaroslav Kristek) in 1998 Entry Draft and San Jose's 5th round choice (later traded to Columbus - Columbus selected Tyler Kolarik) in 2000 Entry Draft, June 18, 1998.

• SHTALENKOV, Mikhail

Mikhail A. G – L. 6'2", 185 lbs. b: Moscow, USSR, 10/20/1965. Anaheim's 5th, 108th overall in 1993.

Season	Club	League	GP	W	L	T	Mins	GA	SO	Avg	AAvg	Eff	SA	S%	SAPG	GP	W	L	T	Mins	GA	SO	Avg	Eff	SA	S%	SAPG
1986-87	Dynamo Moscow	USSR	17	....	....	....	893	36	1	2.41	....	....	....	....	....	....	....	....	....	....	....	....	....	....	....	....	....
1987-88	Dynamo Moscow	USSR	25	....	....	....	1302	72	1	3.31	....	....	....	....	....	....	....	....	....	....	....	....	....	....	....	....	....
1988-89	Dynamo Moscow	USSR	4	....	....	....	80	3	0	2.25	....	....	....	....	....	....	....	....	....	....	....	....	....	....	....	....	....
1989-90	Dynamo Moscow	Fr-Tour	1	0	0	0	2	0	0	0.00	....	....	....	....	....	....	....	....	....	....	....	....	....	....	....	....	....
	Dynamo Moscow	USSR	6	....	....	....	20	1	0	3.00	....	....	....	....	....	....	....	....	....	....	....	....	....	....	....	....	....
1990-91	Dynamo Moscow	Fr-Tour	1	1	0	0	60	1	0	1.00	....	....	....	....	....	....	....	....	....	....	....	....	....	....	....	....	....
	Dynamo Moscow	USSR	31	....	....	....	1568	56	2	2.14	....	....	....	....	....	....	....	....	....	....	....	....	....	....	....	....	....
	Dynamo Moscow	Super-S	3	....	....	....	160	11	....	4.13	....	....	....	....	....	....	....	....	....	....	....	....	....	....	....	....	....
1991-92	Soviet Union	Can-Cup	5	1	2	1	276	11	....	2.00	....	....	....	....	....	....	....	....	....	....	....	....	....	....	....	....	....
	Dynamo Moscow	CIS	27	....	....	....	1268	45	1	2.12	....	....	....	....	....	....	....	....	....	....	....	....	....	....	....	....	....
	Russia	Olympics	8	*7	1	0	440	12	1	1.64	....	....	....	....	....	....	....	....	....	....	....	....	....	....	....	....	....
	Russia	WC-A	6	3	1	1	293	10	1	2.05	....	....	....	....	....	....	....	....	....	....	....	....	....	....	....	....	....

Season	Club	League	GP	W	L	T	Mins	GA	SO	Avg	AAvg	Eff	SA	S%	SAPG	GP	W	L	T	Mins	GA	SO	Avg	Eff	SA	S%	SAPG
			REGULAR SEASON													PLAYOFFS											
1992-93	Milwaukee Admirals	IHL	47	26	14	5	2669	135	2	3.03	....	....	....	....	....	3	1	2	....	209	11	0	3.16	....	....	....	....
1993-94	**Mighty Ducks of Anaheim**	**NHL**	**10**	**3**	**4**	**1**	**543**	**24**	**0**	**2.65**	**2.54**	**2.40**	**265**	**.909**	**29.3**	....	....	....	....	....	....	....	....	....	....	....	....
	San Diego Gulls	IHL	28	15	11	2	1616	93	0	3.45	....	....	....	....	....	....	....	....	....	....	....	....	....	....	....	....	....
	Russia	WC-A	6	3	1	0	296	5	*2	1.01	....	....	....	....	....	....	....	....	....	....	....	....	....	....	....	....	....
1994-95	**Mighty Ducks of Anaheim**	**NHL**	**18**	**4**	**7**	**1**	**810**	**49**	**0**	**3.63**	**3.81**	**3.97**	**448**	**.891**	**33.2**	....	....	....	....	....	....	....	....	....	....	....	....
1995-96	**Mighty Ducks of Anaheim**	**NHL**	**30**	**7**	**16**	**3**	**1637**	**85**	**0**	**3.12**	**3.10**	**3.26**	**814**	**.896**	**29.8**	....	....	....	....	....	....	....	....	....	....	....	....
	Russia	WC-A	3	2	1	0	185	10	....	3.24	....	....	....	....	....	....	....	....	....	....	....	....	....	....	....	....	....
1996-97	Russia	W-Cup	DID NOT PLAY – SPARE GOALTENDER																								
	Mighty Ducks of Anaheim	**NHL**	**24**	**7**	**8**	**1**	**1079**	**52**	**2**	**2.89**	**3.11**	**2.79**	**539**	**.904**	**30.0**	**4**	**0**	**3**	....	**211**	**10**	**0**	**2.84**	**1.75**	**162**	**.938**	**46.1**
1997-98	**Mighty Ducks of Anaheim**	**NHL**	**40**	**13**	**18**	**5**	**2049**	**110**	**1**	**3.22**	**3.86**	**3.44**	**1031**	**.893**	**30.2**	....	....	....	....	....	....	....	....	....	....	....	....
	Russia	Olympics	5	4	1	0	290	8	0	1.65	....	....	....	....	....	....	....	....	....	....	....	....	....	....	....	....	....
1998-99	**Edmonton Oilers**	**NHL**	**34**	**12**	**17**	**3**	**1819**	**81**	**3**	**2.67**	**3.18**	**2.77**	**782**	**.896**	**25.8**	....	....	....	....	....	....	....	....	....	....	....	....
	Phoenix Coyotes	**NHL**	**4**	**1**	**2**	**1**	**243**	**9**	**0**	**2.22**	**2.64**	**1.92**	**104**	**.913**	**25.7**	....	....	....	....	....	....	....	....	....	....	....	....
99-2000	**Phoenix Coyotes**	**NHL**	**15**	**7**	**6**	**2**	**904**	**36**	**2**	**2.39**	**2.73**	**2.33**	**370**	**.903**	**24.6**	....	....	....	....	....	....	....	....	....	....	....	....
	Florida Panthers	**NHL**	**15**	**8**	**4**	**2**	**882**	**34**	**0**	**2.31**	**2.64**	**2.13**	**369**	**.908**	**25.1**	....	....	....	....	....	....	....	....	....	....	....	....
	NHL Totals		**190**	**62**	**82**	**19**	**9966**	**480**	**8**	**2.89**	....	....	**4722**	**.898**	**28.4**	**4**	**0**	**3**	....	**211**	**10**	**0**	**2.84**	....	**162**	**.938**	**46.1**

USSR Rookie of the Year (1987) • Won Garry F. Longman Memorial Trophy (Top Rookie - IHL) (1993)

Claimed by **Nashville** from **Anaheim** in Expansion Draft, June 26, 1998. Traded to **Edmonton** by **Nashville** with Jim Dowd for Eric Fichaud, Drake Berehowsky and Greg de Vries, October 1, 1998. Traded to **Phoenix** by **Edmonton** for Phoenix's 5th round choice (later traded to Nashville - Nashville selected Matt Koalska) in 2000 Entry Draft, March 11, 1999. Traded to **Florida** by **Phoenix** with Phoenix's 4th round choice (Chris Eade) in 2000 Entry Draft for Sean Burke and Florida's 5th round choice (Nate Kiser) in 2000 Entry Draft, November 18, 1999.

• SHULMISTRA, Richard

G – R. 6'2", 185 lbs. b: Sudbury, Ont., 4/1/1971. Quebec's 1st, 4th overall in 1992 Supplemental Draft.

Season	Club	League	GP	W	L	T	Mins	GA	SO	Avg	AAvg	Eff	SA	S%	SAPG	GP	W	L	T	Mins	GA	SO	Avg	Eff	SA	S%	SAPG
1988-89	St. Michael's Buzzers	OJHL-B	12	10	2	0	715	29	*1	2.43	....	....	....	....	....	....	....	....	....	....	....	....	....	....	....	....	....
1989-90	Thunder Bay Flyers	TBJHL	37	....	....	....	2090	131	0	3.76	....	....	....	....	....	....	....	....	....	....	....	....	....	....	....	....	....
1990-91	University of Miami-Ohio	CCHA	20	2	12	2	920	80	0	5.21	....	....	....	....	....	....	....	....	....	....	....	....	....	....	....	....	....
1991-92	University of Miami-Ohio	CCHA	19	3	5	2	850	67	0	4.72	....	....	....	....	....	....	....	....	....	....	....	....	....	....	....	....	....
1992-93	University of Miami-Ohio	CCHA	33	22	6	4	1949	88	1	2.71	....	....	....	....	....	....	....	....	....	....	....	....	....	....	....	....	....
1993-94	University of Miami-Ohio	CCHA	27	13	12	1	1521	74	0	2.92	....	....	....	....	....	....	....	....	....	....	....	....	....	....	....	....	....
1994-95	Cornwall Aces	AHL	20	4	9	2	937	58	0	3.71	....	....	....	....	....	8	4	3	....	446	22	0	2.95	....	....	....	....
1995-96	Cornwall Aces	AHL	36	9	18	2	1844	100	0	3.25	....	....	....	....	....	1	0	0	....	9	1	0	6.76	....	....	....	....
1996-97	Albany River Rats	AHL	23	5	9	2	1062	43	2	2.43	....	....	....	....	....	2	1	0	....	77	2	0	1.56	....	....	....	....
1997-98	Fort Wayne Komets	IHL	11	3	8	0	656	34	1	3.11	....	....	....	....	....	....	....	....	....	....	....	....	....	....	....	....	....
	New Jersey Devils	**NHL**	**1**	**0**	**1**	**0**	**62**	**2**	**0**	**1.94**	**2.31**	**1.29**	**30**	**.933**	**29.0**	....	....	....	....	....	....	....	....	....	....	....	....
	Albany River Rats	AHL	35	20	8	4	2022	78	2	*2.31	....	....	....	....	....	13	8	3	....	696	32	1	2.76	....	....	....	....
1998-99	Manitoba Moose	IHL	44	25	11	7	2469	117	2	2.84	....	....	....	....	....	....	....	....	....	....	....	....	....	....	....	....	....
	Albany River Rats	AHL	12	6	4	0	596	34	0	3.42	....	....	....	....	....	2	0	2	....	64	3	0	2.82	....	....	....	....
99-2000	**Florida Panthers**	**NHL**	**1**	**1**	**0**	**0**	**60**	**1**	**0**	**1.00**	**1.14**	**0.48**	**21**	**.952**	**21.0**	....	....	....	....	....	....	....	....	....	....	....	....
	Louisville Panthers	AHL	27	12	11	2	1447	80	2	3.32	....	....	....	....	....	....	....	....	....	....	....	....	....	....	....	....	....
	Orlando Solar Bears	IHL	9	5	1	3	520	16	1	1.85	....	....	....	....	....	1	0	1	....	30	3	0	5.90	....	....	....	....
	NHL Totals		**2**	**1**	**1**	**0**	**122**	**3**	**0**	**1.48**	....	....	**51**	**.941**	**25.1**	....	....	....	....	....	....	....	....	....	....	....	....

CCHA Second All-Star Team (1993) • AHL Second All-Star Team (1998)

Transferred to **Colorado** after **Quebec** franchise relocated, June 21, 1995. Signed as a free agent by **New Jersey**, December 31, 1997. Signed as a free agent by **Florida**, July 27, 1999.

• SIDORKIEWICZ, Peter

G – L. 5'9", 180 lbs. b: Dabrowa Bialostocka, Pol., 6/29/1963. Washington's 5th, 91st overall in 1981.

Season	Club	League	GP	W	L	T	Mins	GA	SO	Avg	AAvg	Eff	SA	S%	SAPG	GP	W	L	T	Mins	GA	SO	Avg	Eff	SA	S%	SAPG
1980-81	Oshawa Legionaires	OHA-B	22	....	....	....	1300	70	1	3.23	....	....	....	....	....	....	....	....	....	....	....	....	....	....	....	....	....
	Oshawa Generals	OMJHL	7	3	3	0	308	24	0	4.68	....	....	....	....	....	5	2	2	....	266	20	0	4.52	....	....	....	....
1981-82	Oshawa Generals	OHL	29	14	11	1	1553	123	*2	4.75	....	....	....	....	....	1	0	0	....	13	1	0	4.62	....	....	....	....
1982-83	Oshawa Generals	OHL	60	36	20	3	3536	213	0	3.61	....	....	....	....	....	17	15	1	....	1020	60	0	3.53	....	....	....	....
	Oshawa Generals	Mem-Cup	5	*3	2	0	293	25	0	5.12	....	....	....	....	....	....	....	....	....	....	....	....	....	....	....	....	....
1983-84	Oshawa Generals	OHL	52	28	21	1	2966	250	1	4.15	....	....	....	....	....	7	3	4	....	420	27	*1	3.86	....	....	....	....
1984-85	Binghamton Whalers	AHL	45	31	9	5	2691	137	3	3.05	....	....	....	....	....	8	4	4	....	481	31	0	3.87	....	....	....	....
	Fort Wayne Komets	IHL	10	4	4	2	590	43	0	4.37	....	....	....	....	....	....	....	....	....	....	....	....	....	....	....	....	....
1985-86	Binghamton Whalers	AHL	49	21	22	3	2819	150	2	*3.19	....	....	....	....	....	4	1	3	....	235	12	0	3.06	....	....	....	....
1986-87	Binghamton Whalers	AHL	57	23	16	0	3304	161	4	2.92	....	....	....	....	....	13	6	7	....	794	36	0	*2.72	....	....	....	....
1987-88	**Hartford Whalers**	**NHL**	**1**	**0**	**1**	**0**	**60**	**6**	**0**	**6.00**	**5.00**	**10.00**	**36**	**.833**	**36.0**	....	....	....	....	....	....	....	....	....	....	....	....
	Binghamton Whalers	AHL	42	19	17	3	2345	144	0	3.68	....	....	....	....	....	3	0	2	....	147	8	0	3.27	....	....	....	....
1988-89	**Hartford Whalers**	**NHL**	**44**	**22**	**18**	**4**	**2635**	**133**	**4**	**3.03**	**2.51**	**3.34**	**1207**	**.890**	**27.5**	**2**	**0**	**2**	....	**124**	**8**	**0**	**3.87**	**6.88**	**45**	**.822**	**21.8**
	Canada	WEC-A	1	0	0	0	25	0	0	0.00	....	....	....	....	....	....	....	....	....	....	....	....	....	....	....	....	....
1989-90	**Hartford Whalers**	**NHL**	**46**	**19**	**19**	**7**	**2703**	**161**	**1**	**3.57**	**3.02**	**4.78**	**1203**	**.866**	**26.7**	**7**	**3**	**4**	....	**429**	**23**	**0**	**3.22**	**3.84**	**193**	**.881**	**27.0**
1990-91	**Hartford Whalers**	**NHL**	**52**	**21**	**22**	**7**	**2953**	**164**	**1**	**3.33**	**2.99**	**4.25**	**1284**	**.872**	**26.1**	**6**	**2**	**4**	....	**359**	**24**	**0**	**4.01**	**5.53**	**174**	**.862**	**29.1**
1991-92	**Hartford Whalers**	**NHL**	**35**	**9**	**19**	**6**	**1995**	**111**	**2**	**3.34**	**2.99**	**3.94**	**940**	**.882**	**28.3**	....	....	....	....	....	....	....	....	....	....	....	....
1992-93	**Ottawa Senators**	**NHL**	**64**	**8**	**46**	**3**	**3388**	**250**	**0**	**4.43**	**3.82**	**6.38**	**1737**	**.856**	**30.8**	....	....	....	....	....	....	....	....	....	....	....	....
1993-94	**New Jersey Devils**	**NHL**	**3**	**0**	**3**	**0**	**130**	**6**	**0**	**2.77**	**2.66**	**3.02**	**55**	**.891**	**25.4**	....	....	....	....	....	....	....	....	....	....	....	....
	Albany River Rats	AHL	15	6	7	2	907	60	0	3.97	....	....	....	....	....	....	....	....	....	....	....	....	....	....	....	....	....
	Fort Wayne Komets	IHL	11	6	3	0	591	27	*2	2.74	....	....	....	....	....	*18	10	8	....	*1054	59	*1	3.36	....	....	....	....
1994-95	Fort Wayne Komets	IHL	16	8	6	1	941	58	1	3.70	....	....	....	....	....	3	1	2	....	144	12	0	5.00	....	....	....	....
1995-96	Albany River Rats	AHL	32	19	7	5	1809	89	3	2.95	....	....	....	....	....	1	0	1	....	59	3	0	3.06	....	....	....	....
1996-97	Albany River Rats	AHL	62	31	23	6	3539	171	2	2.90	....	....	....	....	....	16	7	8	....	920	48	0	3.13	....	....	....	....
1997-98	**New Jersey Devils**	**NHL**	**1**	**0**	**0**	**0**	**20**	**1**	**0**	**3.00**	**3.58**	**3.75**	**8**	**.875**	**24.0**	....	....	....	....	....	....	....	....	....	....	....	....
	Albany River Rats	AHL	43	21	15	5	2422	115	3	2.85	....	....	....	....	....	2	1	1	....	89	6	0	4.01	....	....	....	....
1998-2000	Erie Otters	OHL	DID NOT PLAY – ASSISTANT COACH																								
	NHL Totals		**246**	**79**	**128**	**27**	**13884**	**832**	**8**	**3.60**	....	....	**6470**	**.871**	**28.0**	**15**	**5**	**10**	....	**912**	**55**	**0**	**3.62**	....	**412**	**.867**	**27.1**

AHL Second All-Star Team (1987) • NHL All-Rookie Team (1989) • Played in NHL All-Star Game (1993)

Traded to **Hartford** by **Washington** with Dean Evason for David Jensen, March 12, 1985. Claimed by **Ottawa** from **Hartford** in Expansion Draft, June 18, 1992. Traded to **New Jersey** by **Ottawa** with future considerations (Mike Peluso, June 26, 1993) for Craig Billington, Troy Mallette and New Jersey's 4th round choice (Cosmo Dupaul) in 1993 Entry Draft, June 20, 1993.

• SIMMONS, Don

Donald William "Dippy" G – R. 5'10", 150 lbs. b: Port Colborne, Ont., 9/13/1931.

Season	Club	League	GP	W	L	T	Mins	GA	SO	Avg	AAvg	Eff	SA	S%	SAPG	GP	W	L	T	Mins	GA	SO	Avg	Eff	SA	S%	SAPG
1948-49	Galt Rockets	OHA-Jr.	12	....	....	....	720	73	0	6.08	....	....	....	....	....	....	....	....	....	....	....	....	....	....	....	....	....
1949-50	Port Colbourne Sailors	OHA-B	STATISTICS NOT AVAILABLE																								
1950-51	St. Catharines Teepees	OHA-Jr.	53	....	....	....	3180	181	3	3.41	....	....	....	....	....	6	....	....	....	360	19	1	3.17	....	....	....	....
1951-52	Springfield Indians	EAHL	37	18	18	1	2270	121	0	3.20	....	....	....	....	....	3	0	3	0	180	19	0	6.33	....	....	....	....
1952-53	Springfield Indians	EAHL	44	*31	11	2	2680	168	0	3.76	....	....	....	....	....	....	....	....	....	....	....	....	....	....	....	....	....
1953-54	Johnstown Jets	IHL	24	....	....	....	1440	66	2	2.75	....	....	....	....	....	10	6	4	0	600	21	1	2.10	....	....	....	....
1954-55	Springfield Indians	AHL	54	30	21	3	3240	185	2	3.43	....	....	....	....	....	4	1	3	0	258	16	0	3.72	....	....	....	....
1955-56	Springfield Indians	AHL	52	13	37	2	3120	233	0	4.48	....	....	....	....	....	....	....	....	....	....	....	....	....	....	....	....	....
1956-57	Springfield Indians	AHL	25	10	12	3	1300	84	0	3.36	....	....	....	....	....	....	....	....	....	....	....	....	....	....	....	....	....
	Boston Bruins	**NHL**	**26**	**13**	**9**	**4**	**1560**	**63**	**4**	**2.42**	**2.76**	....	....	....	....	***10**	**5**	**5**	....	**600**	**29**	***2**	**2.90**	....	....	....	....
1957-58	**Boston Bruins**	**NHL**	**39**	**15**	**14**	**9**	**2288**	**92**	**5**	**2.41**	**2.61**	....	....	....	....	***11**	**6**	**5**	....	***671**	**25**	***1**	**2.24**	....	....	....	....
1958-59	**Boston Bruins**	**NHL**	**58**	**24**	**26**	**8**	**3480**	**183**	**3**	**3.16**	**3.41**	....	....	....	....	....	....	....	....	....	....	....	....	....	....	....	....
1959-60	**Boston Bruins**	**NHL**	**28**	**12**	**13**	**3**	**1680**	**91**	**2**	**3.25**	**3.42**	....	....	....	....	....	....	....	....	....	....	....	....	....	....	....	....
1960-61	**Boston Bruins**	**NHL**	**18**	**3**	**9**	**6**	**1079**	**58**	**1**	**3.23**	**3.34**	....	....	....	....	....	....	....	....	....	....	....	....	....	....	....	....
	Providence Reds	AHL	10	3	7	0	590	51	0	5.19	....	....	....	....	....	....	....	....	....	....	....	....	....	....	....	....	....
1961-62	Rochester Americans	AHL	51	24	22	5	3060	169	0	3.31	....	....	....	....	....	....	....	....	....	....	....	....	....	....	....	....	....
♦	**Toronto Maple Leafs**	**NHL**	**9**	**5**	**3**	**1**	**540**	**21**	**1**	**2.33**	**2.37**	....	....	....	....	**3**	**2**	**1**	....	**165**	**8**	**0**	**2.91**	....	....	....	....
1962-63♦	**Toronto Maple Leafs**	**NHL**	**28**	**15**	**8**	**5**	**1680**	**69**	**1**	**2.46**	**2.53**	....	....	....	....	....	....	....	....	....	....	....	....	....	....	....	....
	Rochester Americans	AHL	9	4	5	0	540	27	1	3.00	....	....	....	....	....	....	....	....	....	....	....	....	....	....	....	....	....
1963-64♦	**Toronto Maple Leafs**	**NHL**	**21**	**9**	**9**	**1**	**1191**	**63**	**3**	**3.17**	**3.55**	....	....	....	....	....	....	....	....	....	....	....	....	....	....	....	....
1964-65	Tulsa Oilers	CPHL	*69	*35	26	8	*3540	219	3	3.17	....	....	....	....	....	*12	6	6	0	*720	38	*1	3.17	....	....	....	....

			REGULAR SEASON													PLAYOFFS											
Season	**Club**	**League**	**GP**	**W**	**L**	**T**	**Mins**	**GA**	**SO**	**Avg**	**AAvg**	**Eff**	**SA**	**S%**	**SAPG**	**GP**	**W**	**L**	**T**	**Mins**	**GA**	**SO**	**Avg**	**Eff**	**SA**	**S%**	**SAPG**
1965-66	Baltimore Clippers	AHL	13	4	6	2	750	42	0	3.36	....	....	....	....	....	....	....	....	....	....	....	....	....	....	....	....	....
	New York Rangers	**NHL**	**11**	**1**	**6**	**1**	**491**	**37**	**0**	**4.52**	**4.62**	....	....	....	....	....	....	....	....	....	....	....	....	....	....	....	....
1966-67	Vancouver Canucks	WHL	*72	*38	32	2	*4326	213	*7	2.95	....	....	....	....	....	3	2	0	0	140	3	0	1.29	....	....	....	....
1967-68	**New York Rangers**	**NHL**	**5**	**2**	**1**	**2**	**300**	**13**	**0**	**2.60**	**2.88**	....	....	....	....	....	....	....	....	....	....	....	....	....	....	....	....
	Buffalo Bisons	AHL	22	9	7	5	1279	74	0	3.47	....	....	....	....	....	....	....	....	....	....	....	....	....	....	....	....	....
1968-69	**New York Rangers**	**NHL**	**5**	**2**	**2**	**1**	**206**	**8**	**0**	**2.33**	**2.41**	....	....	....	....	....	....	....	....	....	....	....	....	....	....	....	....
	Buffalo Bisons	AHL	5	2	3	0	259	14	1	3.24	....	....	....	....	....	....	....	....	....	....	....	....	....	....	....	....	....
	NHL Totals		**248**	**101**	**100**	**41**	**14495**	**698**	**20**	**2.89**	....	....	....	....	....	**24**	**13**	**11**	....	**1436**	**62**	**3**	**2.59**	....	....	....	....

EAHL Second All-Star Team (1952, 1953) • AHL Second All-Star Team (1955) • WHL First All-Star Team (1967) • Played in NHL All-Star Game (1963)

Traded to **Boston** by **Springfield** (AHL) for Norm Defelice, future considerations (Floyd Smith, June, 1957) and the loan of Jack Bionda, January 22, 1957. Traded to **Toronto** by **Boston** for Ed Chadwick, January 31, 1961. Claimed by **NY Rangers** from **Toronto** (Tulsa - CHL) in Inter-League Draft, June 8, 1965. Traded to **Buffalo** (AHL) by **NY Rangers** for cash, June 10, 1969.

• SIMMONS, Gary

Gary Byrne "The Cobra" G – L. 6'2", 200 lbs. b: Charlottetown, P.E.I., 7/19/1944.

Season	**Club**	**League**	**GP**	**W**	**L**	**T**	**Mins**	**GA**	**SO**	**Avg**	**AAvg**	**Eff**	**SA**	**S%**	**SAPG**	**GP**	**W**	**L**	**T**	**Mins**	**GA**	**SO**	**Avg**	**Eff**	**SA**	**S%**	**SAPG**
1963-64	Edmonton Oil Kings	CAHL	STATISTICS NOT AVAILABLE																								
1964-65	Edmonton Oil Kings	CAHL	....	....	....	....	....	....	....	....	....	....	....	....	....	1	0	1	0	60	8	0	8.00	....	....	....	....
	Edmonton Oil Kings	Mem-Cup	13	9	4	0	790	43	0	3.27	....	....	....	....	....	....	....	....	....	....	....	....	....	....	....	....	....
1965-66	Port Huron–Des Moines	IHL	20	....	....	....	1200	93	0	4.65	....	....	....	....	....	....	....	....	....	....	....	....	....	....	....	....	....
	Toledo Blades	IHL	1	0	1	0	60	9	0	9.00	....	....	....	....	....	....	....	....	....	....	....	....	....	....	....	....	....
1966-67	Conception Bay Ceebees	Nfld-Sr.	37	23	14	0	2265	147	0	3.97	....	....	....	....	....	13	*9	4	0	780	52	0	4.00	....	....	....	....
1967-68	Conception Bay Ceebees	Nfld-Sr.	40	20	17	3	2400	180	*2	4.50	....	....	....	....	....	6	2	4	0	360	36	0	6.00	....	....	....	....
1968-69	Conception Bay Ceebees	Nfld-Sr.	40	8	27	5	2400	233	0	5.83	....	....	....	....	....	....	....	....	....	....	....	....	....	....	....	....	....
1969-70	Calgary Stampeders	ASHL	*38	*30	8	0	*2280	113	0	*2.97	....	....	....	....	....	....	....	....	....	....	....	....	....	....	....	....	....
1970-71	San Diego Gulls	WHL	14	5	6	0	717	41	0	3.43	....	....	....	....	....	....	....	....	....	....	....	....	....	....	....	....	....
1971-72	Calgary Stampeders	ASHL	21	....	....	....	1260	66	*2	*2.90	....	....	....	....	....	....	....	....	....	....	....	....	....	....	....	....	....
1972-73	Phoenix Roadrunners	WHL	36	18	15	2	2078	119	3	3.44	....	....	....	....	....	3	1	1	0	166	10	0	3.61	....	....	....	....
1973-74	Tulsa Oilers	CHL	1	0	1	0	60	7	0	7.00	....	....	....	....	....	....	....	....	....	....	....	....	....	....	....	....	....
	Phoenix Roadrunners	WHL	49	28	17	2	2861	143	0	3.00	....	....	....	....	....	*9	*8	1	0	*566	22	*2	2.33	....	....	....	....
1974-75	**California Golden Seals**	**NHL**	**34**	**10**	**21**	**3**	**2029**	**124**	**2**	**3.67**	**3.32**	....	....	....	....	....	....	....	....	....	....	....	....	....	....	....	....
1975-76	**California Golden Seals**	**NHL**	**40**	**15**	**19**	**5**	**2360**	**131**	**2**	**3.33**	**3.01**	....	....	....	....	....	....	....	....	....	....	....	....	....	....	....	....
1976-77	**Cleveland Barons**	**NHL**	**15**	**2**	**8**	**4**	**840**	**51**	**1**	**3.64**	**3.39**	....	....	....	....	....	....	....	....	....	....	....	....	....	....	....	....
	Los Angeles Kings	**NHL**	**4**	**1**	**2**	**1**	**240**	**16**	**0**	**4.00**	**3.72**	....	....	....	....	**1**	**0**	**0**	....	**20**	**1**	**0**	**3.00**	....	....	....	....
1977-78	**Los Angeles Kings**	**NHL**	**14**	**2**	**7**	**2**	**693**	**44**	**0**	**3.81**	**3.58**	....	....	....	....	....	....	....	....	....	....	....	....	....	....	....	....
1978-79	Springfield Indians	AHL	5	2	2	1	306	13	0	2.55	....	....	....	....	....	....	....	....	....	....	....	....	....	....	....	....	....
	NHL Totals		**107**	**30**	**57**	**15**	**6162**	**366**	**5**	**3.56**	....	....	....	....	....	**1**	**0**	**0**	....	**20**	**1**	**0**	**3.00**	....	....	....	....

Nfld.-Sr. Second All-Star Team (1967) • ASHL First All-Star Team (1970) • ASHL MVP (1970)

• Regular season totals for **Edmonton** (CAHL) in 1964-65 season unavailable. Rights transferred to **Phoenix** (WHA) after owners of **Phoenix** (WHL) franchise granted WHA expansion team, September 14, 1973. Traded to **California** by **Phoenix** (WHA) for cash, October 1, 1974. • Recorded shutout (3-0) in NHL debut vs. Atlanta, October 11, 1974. Transferred to **Cleveland** after **California** franchise relocated, August 26, 1976. Traded to **LA Kings** by **Cleveland** with Jim Moxey for Gary Edwards and Juha Widing, January 22, 1977.

• SKIDMORE, Paul

G – L. 6', 180 lbs. b: Smithtown, NY, 7/22/1956. St. Louis' 6th, 61st overall in 1976.

Season	**Club**	**League**	**GP**	**W**	**L**	**T**	**Mins**	**GA**	**SO**	**Avg**	**AAvg**	**Eff**	**SA**	**S%**	**SAPG**	**GP**	**W**	**L**	**T**	**Mins**	**GA**	**SO**	**Avg**	**Eff**	**SA**	**S%**	**SAPG**
1970-71	Long Island Ducklings	NYJHL	STATISTICS NOT AVAILABLE																								
1971-72	Suffolk Ducks	NYJHL	30	....	....	....	1800	134	1	4.47	....	....	....	....	....	....	....	....	....	....	....	....	....	....	....	....	....
1972-73	Suffolk Ducks	NYJHL	37	....	....	....	2179	142	2	3.91	....	....	....	....	....	....	....	....	....	....	....	....	....	....	....	....	....
1973-74	Suffolk Ducks	NYJHL	12	....	....	....	819	46	3	3.37	....	....	....	....	....	....	....	....	....	....	....	....	....	....	....	....	....
1974-75	Suffolk Ducks	NYJHL	11	....	....	....	660	36	0	3.27	....	....	....	....	....	....	....	....	....	....	....	....	....	....	....	....	....
1975-76	Boston College	ECAC	27	13	10	1	1500	105	0	4.20	....	....	....	....	....	....	....	....	....	....	....	....	....	....	....	....	....
1976-77	Boston College	ECAC	25	15	9	1	1510	105	1	4.17	....	....	....	....	....	....	....	....	....	....	....	....	....	....	....	....	....
1977-78	Boston College	ECAC	25	18	7	0	1417	88	2	3.73	....	....	....	....	....	....	....	....	....	....	....	....	....	....	....	....	....
1978-79	Boston College	ECAC	18	8	9	0	1039	95	0	5.49	....	....	....	....	....	....	....	....	....	....	....	....	....	....	....	....	....
1979-80	Port Huron Flags	IHL	36	....	....	....	2138	131	2	3.68	....	....	....	....	....	1	0	0	0	31	5	0	9.62	....	....	....	....
1980-81	Salt Lake Golden Eagles	CHL	40	24	14	2	2414	150	1	3.73	....	....	....	....	....	4	1	2	0	179	15	0	5.03	....	....	....	....
1981-82	**St. Louis Blues**	**NHL**	**2**	**1**	**1**	**0**	**120**	**6**	**0**	**3.00**	**2.32**	....	....	....	....	....	....	....	....	....	....	....	....	....	....	....	....
	Salt Lake Golden Eagles	CHL	50	21	27	1	2996	192	*3	3.85	....	....	....	....	....	10	5	5	0	640	46	0	4.31	....	....	....	....
1982-83	Salt Lake Golden Eagles	CHL	40	21	19	0	2414	155	3	3.85	....	....	....	....	....	3	0	1	0	120	14	0	7.00	....	....	....	....
1983-84	Montana Magic	CHL	1	0	1	0	60	8	0	8.00	....	....	....	....	....	....	....	....	....	....	....	....	....	....	....	....	....
	Carolina Thunderbirds	ACHL	29	....	....	....	1621	112	0	4.15	....	....	....	....	....	....	....	....	....	....	....	....	....	....	....	....	....
1984-85	Salt Lake Golden Eagles	IHL	1	0	1	0	40	5	0	7.50	....	....	....	....	....	....	....	....	....	....	....	....	....	....	....	....	....
	NHL Totals		**2**	**1**	**1**	**0**	**120**	**6**	**0**	**3.00**	....	....	....	....	....	....	....	....	....	....	....	....	....	....	....	....	....

ECAC Second All-Star Team (1976, 1977) • NCAA Championship All-Tournament Team (1978) • Played w/ RHI's Utah Rollerbees in 1993 (7-0-3-0-221-50-0-10.86)

• SKORODENSKI, Warren

G – L. 5'8", 165 lbs. b: Winnipeg, Man., 3/22/1960.

Season	**Club**	**League**	**GP**	**W**	**L**	**T**	**Mins**	**GA**	**SO**	**Avg**	**AAvg**	**Eff**	**SA**	**S%**	**SAPG**	**GP**	**W**	**L**	**T**	**Mins**	**GA**	**SO**	**Avg**	**Eff**	**SA**	**S%**	**SAPG**
1976-77	West Kildonan North Stars	MJHL	22	....	....	....	1170	78	0	4.00	....	....	....	....	....	....	....	....	....	....	....	....	....	....	....	....	....
1977-78	Calgary Wranglers	WHL	53	8	22	10	2460	213	1	5.20	....	....	....	....	....	....	....	....	....	....	....	....	....	....	....	....	....
1978-79	Calgary Wranglers	WHL	*66	26	31	5	*3595	309	1	5.16	....	....	....	....	....	15	7	8	0	884	61	0	4.14	....	....	....	....
1979-80	Calgary Wranglers	WHL	66	39	23	2	3724	261	1	4.21	....	....	....	....	....	7	3	4	0	357	29	1	4.87	....	....	....	....
1980-81	New Brunswick Hawks	AHL	2	0	1	0	124	9	0	4.35	....	....	....	....	....	....	....	....	....	....	....	....	....	....	....	....	....
	Flint Generals	IHL	47	....	....	....	2602	189	2	4.36	....	....	....	....	....	6	2	4	0	301	18	0	3.58	....	....	....	....
1981-82	**Chicago Black Hawks**	**NHL**	**1**	**0**	**1**	**0**	**60**	**5**	**0**	**5.00**	**3.86**	....	....	....	....	....	....	....	....	....	....	....	....	....	....	....	....
	New Brunswick Hawks	AHL	28	16	8	4	1644	70	*3	*2.55	....	....	....	....	....	2	0	2	0	90	6	0	4.00	....	....	....	....
1982-83	Springfield Indians	AHL	13	3	6	0	592	49	0	4.97	....	....	....	....	....	....	....	....	....	....	....	....	....	....	....	....	....
	Birmingham South Stars	CHL	25	11	11	1	1450	81	1	3.35	....	....	....	....	....	5	0	4	0	195	19	0	5.85	....	....	....	....
1983-84	Sherbrooke Jets	AHL	19	5	10	2	1048	88	0	5.04	....	....	....	....	....	....	....	....	....	....	....	....	....	....	....	....	....
	Springfield Indians	AHL	14	3	11	0	756	67	0	5.32	....	....	....	....	....	2	0	2	0	124	3	0	6.28	....	....	....	....
1984-85	**Chicago Black Hawks**	**NHL**	**27**	**11**	**9**	**3**	**1396**	**75**	**2**	**3.22**	**2.56**	**3.12**	**775**	**.903**	**33.3**	**2**	**0**	**0**	....	**33**	**6**	**0**	**10.91**	**23.38**	**28**	**.786**	**50.9**
1985-86	**Chicago Black Hawks**	**NHL**	**1**	**0**	**1**	**0**	**60**	**6**	**0**	**6.00**	**4.69**	**8.00**	**45**	**.867**	**45.0**	....	....	....	....	....	....	....	....	....	....	....	....
	Nova Scotia Oilers	AHL	32	11	14	2	1716	109	0	3.81	....	....	....	....	....	....	....	....	....	....	....	....	....	....	....	....	....
1986-87	**Chicago Blackhawks**	**NHL**	**3**	**1**	**0**	**1**	**155**	**7**	**0**	**2.71**	**2.29**	**2.11**	**90**	**.922**	**34.8**	....	....	....	....	....	....	....	....	....	....	....	....
	Nova Scotia Oilers	AHL	32	10	15	0	1813	121	2	4.00	....	....	....	....	....	....	....	....	....	....	....	....	....	....	....	....	....
	Saginaw Generals	IHL	6	4	1	0	319	21	0	3.95	....	....	....	....	....	6	3	2	0	304	24	0	4.74	....	....	....	....
1987-88	**Edmonton Oilers**	**NHL**	**3**	**0**	**0**	**0**	**61**	**7**	**0**	**6.89**	**5.74**	**19.29**	**25**	**.720**	**24.6**	....	....	....	....	....	....	....	....	....	....	....	....
	Nova Scotia Oilers	AHL	46	25	15	5	2746	171	0	3.74	....	....	....	....	....	5	1	4	0	305	22	0	4.33	....	....	....	....
1988-89	Cape Breton Oilers	AHL	25	11	13	1	1497	111	0	4.45	....	....	....	....	....	....	....	....	....	....	....	....	....	....	....	....	....
	Canada	Nat-Team	22	8	9	1	1160	82	0	4.24	....	....	....	....	....	....	....	....	....	....	....	....	....	....	....	....	....
1989-90	Canada	Nat-Team	41	18	17	0	2182	140	0	3.85	....	....	....	....	....	....	....	....	....	....	....	....	....	....	....	....	....
1990-91	Canada	Nat-Team	2	2	0	0	120	5	0	2.50	....	....	....	....	....	....	....	....	....	....	....	....	....	....	....	....	....
	NHL Totals		**35**	**12**	**11**	**4**	**1732**	**100**	**2**	**3.46**	....	....	....	....	....	**2**	**0**	**0**	....	**33**	**6**	**0**	**10.91**	....	**28**	**.786**	**50.9**

Shared Harry "Hap" Holmes Memorial Award (fewest goals against - AHL) with Bob Janecyk (1982)

Signed as a free agent by **Chicago**, August 12, 1979. • Suspended 20 games by AHL for assaulting referee Dave Lynch during game vs. New Haven (AHL), November 20, 1983. Signed as a free agent by **Edmonton**, October 8, 1987.

• SKUDRA, Peter

G – L. 6'1", 185 lbs. b: Riga, USSR, 4/24/1973.

Season	**Club**	**League**	**GP**	**W**	**L**	**T**	**Mins**	**GA**	**SO**	**Avg**	**AAvg**	**Eff**	**SA**	**S%**	**SAPG**	**GP**	**W**	**L**	**T**	**Mins**	**GA**	**SO**	**Avg**	**Eff**	**SA**	**S%**	**SAPG**
1992-93	Pardaugava Riga	CIS	27	....	....	....	1498	74	....	2.96	....	....	....	....	....	1	....	....	....	60	5	0	5.00	....	....	....	....
	Latvia	WC-B	2	1	0	0	81	0	1	0.00	....	....	....	....	....	....	....	....	....	....	....	....	....	....	....	....	....
1993-94	Pardaugava Riga	CIS	14	....	....	....	783	42	....	3.22	....	....	....	....	....	1	....	....	....	55	4	0	4.36	....	....	....	....
	Latvia	WC-B	DID NOT PLAY – SPARE GOALTENDER																								
1994-95	Greensboro Monarchs	ECHL	33	13	9	5	1612	113	0	4.20	....	....	....	....	....	6	2	2	....	341	28	0	4.92	....	....	....	....
	Memphis River Kings	CHL	2	0	1	0	60	8	0	6.01	....	....	....	....	....	....	....	....	....	....	....	....	....	....	....	....	....

Season	Club	League	REGULAR SEASON													PLAYOFFS											
			GP	W	L	T	Mins	GA	SO	Avg	AAvg	Eff	SA	S%	SAPG	GP	W	L	T	Mins	GA	SO	Avg	Eff	SA	S%	SAPG
1995-96	Erie Panthers	ECHL	12	3	8	1	681	47	0	4.14	....	....	....	....	....	....	....	....	....	....	....	....	....	....	....	....	....
	Johnstown Chiefs	ECHL	30	12	11	4	1657	98	0	3.55	....	....	....	....	....	....	....	....	....	....	....	....	....	....	....	....	....
1996-97	Hamilton Bulldogs	AHL	32	8	16	2	1615	101	0	3.75	....	....	....	....	....	....	....	....	....	....	....	....	....	....	....	....	....
	Johnstown Chiefs	ECHL	4	2	1	1	200	11	0	3.30	....	....	....	....	....	....	....	....	....	....	....	....	....	....	....	....	....
	Latvia	WC-A	1	0	0	0	25	3	0	7.16	....	....	....	....	....	....	....	....	....	....	....	....	....	....	....	....	....
1997-98	**Pittsburgh Penguins**	**NHL**	**17**	**6**	**4**	**3**	**851**	**26**	**0**	**1.83**	**2.18**	**1.40**	**341**	**.924**	**24.0**	....	....	....	....	....	....	....	....	....	....	....	....
	Houston Aeros	IHL	9	5	3	1	499	23	0	2.77	....	....	....	....	....	....	....	....	....	....	....	....	....	....	....	....	....
	Kansas City Blades	IHL	13	10	3	0	775	37	0	2.86	....	....	....	....	....	8	4	4	....	512	20	1	*2.34	....	....	....	....
1998-99	**Pittsburgh Penguins**	**NHL**	**37**	**15**	**11**	**5**	**1914**	**89**	**3**	**2.79**	**3.32**	**3.02**	**822**	**.892**	**25.8**	....	....	....	....	....	....	....	....	....	....	....	....
99-2000	**Pittsburgh Penguins**	**NHL**	**20**	**5**	**7**	**3**	**922**	**48**	**1**	**3.12**	**3.57**	**4.00**	**374**	**.872**	**24.3**	**1**	**0**	**0**	....	**20**	**1**	**0**	**3.00**	**2.73**	**11**	**.909**	**33.0**
	NHL Totals		**74**	**26**	**22**	**11**	**3687**	**163**	**4**	**2.65**	....	....	**1537**	**.894**	**25.0**	**1**	**0**	**0**	....	**20**	**1**	**0**	**3.00**	....	**11**	**.909**	**33.0**

Signed as a free agent by **Pittsburgh**, September 25, 1997. • Played w/ RHI's Oklahoma Coyotes in 1996 (18-10-4-1-(1)-721-90-0-5.99).

• SMITH, Al

Allan Robert "The Bear" G – L. 6'1", 200 lbs. b: Toronto, Ont., 11/10/1945.

Season	Club	League	GP	W	L	T	Mins	GA	SO	Avg	AAvg	Eff	SA	S%	SAPG	GP	W	L	T	Mins	GA	SO	Avg	Eff	SA	S%	SAPG
1961-62	Toronto Midget Marlboros	MTHL	STATISTICS NOT AVAILABLE																								
	Toronto Marlboros	MTJHL	1	....	....	....	60	4	0	4.00	....	....	....	....	....	....	....	....	....	....	....	....	....	....	....	....	....
1962-63	Lakeshore Bruins	OHA-B	STATISTICS NOT AVAILABLE																								
1963-64	Lakeshore Bruins	OHA-B	STATISTICS NOT AVAILABLE																								
1964-65	Lakeshore Bruins	OHA-B	STATISTICS NOT AVAILABLE																								
	Toronto Marlboros	OHA-Jr.	3	....	....	....	180	20	0	6.67	....	....	....	....	....	....	....	....	....	....	....	....	....	....	....	....	....
1965-66	Toronto Marlboros	OHA-Jr.	22	....	....	....	1320	92	0	4.15	....	....	....	....	....	14	....	....	....	840	37	0	2.61	....	....	....	....
	Toronto Maple Leafs	**NHL**	**2**	**1**	**0**	**0**	**62**	**2**	**0**	**1.94**	**1.96**	....	....	....	....	....	....	....	....	....	....	....	....	....	....	....	....
1966-67	**Toronto Maple Leafs**	**NHL**	**1**	**0**	**1**	**0**	**60**	**5**	**0**	**5.00**	**5.16**	....	....	....	....	....	....	....	....	....	....	....	....	....	....	....	....
	Victoria Maple Leafs	WHL	56	24	26	5	3375	180	6	3.20	....	....	....	....	....	....	....	....	....	....	....	....	....	....	....	....	....
	Vancouver Canucks	WHL	....	....	....	....	....	....	....	....	....	....	....	....	....	6	1	4	0	345	15	*1	2.61	....	....	....	....
	California Seals	WHL	....	....	....	....	....	....	....	....	....	....	....	....	....	1	0	1	0	60	4	0	4.00	....	....	....	....
1967-68	Tulsa Oilers	CPHL	40	23	12	5	2278	126	0	3.32	....	....	....	....	....	4	2	2	0	240	11	0	2.75	....	....	....	....
1968-69	**Toronto Maple Leafs**	**NHL**	**7**	**2**	**2**	**1**	**335**	**16**	**0**	**2.87**	**2.97**	....	....	....	....	....	....	....	....	....	....	....	....	....	....	....	....
	Tulsa Oilers	CHL	8	....	....	....	480	22	0	2.87	....	....	....	....	....	....	....	....	....	....	....	....	....	....	....	....	....
	Rochester Americans	AHL	34	13	12	7	1979	114	2	3.46	....	....	....	....	....	....	....	....	....	....	....	....	....	....	....	....	....
1969-70	Baltimore Clippers	AHL	3	....	....	....	180	8	0	2.67	....	....	....	....	....	....	....	....	....	....	....	....	....	....	....	....	....
	Pittsburgh Penguins	**NHL**	**46**	**15**	**20**	**8**	**2555**	**129**	**2**	**3.03**	**3.22**	....	....	....	....	**3**	**1**	**2**	....	**180**	**10**	**0**	**3.33**	....	....	....	....
1970-71	**Pittsburgh Penguins**	**NHL**	**46**	**9**	**22**	**9**	**2472**	**128**	**2**	**3.11**	**3.08**	....	....	....	....	....	....	....	....	....	....	....	....	....	....	....	....
1971-72	**Detroit Red Wings**	**NHL**	**43**	**18**	**20**	**4**	**2500**	**135**	**4**	**3.24**	**3.28**	....	....	....	....	....	....	....	....	....	....	....	....	....	....	....	....
1972-73	New England Whalers	WHA	51	31	19	1	3059	162	3	3.18	....	....	....	....	....	*15	*12	3	0	*909	49	0	3.23	....	....	....	....
1973-74	New England Whalers	WHA	55	30	21	2	3194	164	2	3.08	....	....	....	....	....	7	3	4	0	399	21	*1	3.16	....	....	....	....
1974-75	New England Whalers	WHA	59	*33	21	4	3494	202	2	3.47	....	....	....	....	....	6	2	4	0	366	28	0	4.59	....	....	....	....
1975-76	**Buffalo Sabres**	**NHL**	**14**	**9**	**3**	**2**	**840**	**43**	**0**	**3.07**	**2.78**	....	....	....	....	**1**	**0**	**0**	....	**17**	**1**	**0**	**3.53**	....	....	....	....
1976-77	**Buffalo Sabres**	**NHL**	**7**	**0**	**3**	**0**	**265**	**19**	**0**	**4.30**	**4.00**	....	....	....	....	....	....	....	....	....	....	....	....	....	....	....	....
1977-78	New England Whalers	WHA	55	*30	20	3	3246	174	2	*3.22	....	....	....	....	....	3	0	2	0	120	14	0	7.00	....	....	....	....
1978-79	New England Whalers	WHA	40	17	17	5	2396	132	1	3.31	....	....	....	....	....	4	1	2	0	153	12	0	4.71	....	....	....	....
1979-80	Springfield Indians	AHL	2	1	1	0	120	6	0	3.00	....	....	....	....	....	....	....	....	....	....	....	....	....	....	....	....	....
	Hartford Whalers	**NHL**	**30**	**11**	**10**	**8**	**1754**	**107**	**2**	**3.66**	**3.24**	....	....	....	....	**2**	**0**	**2**	....	**120**	**10**	**0**	**5.00**	....	....	....	....
1980-81	**Colorado Rockies**	**NHL**	**37**	**9**	**18**	**4**	**1909**	**151**	**0**	**4.75**	**3.86**	....	....	....	....	....	....	....	....	....	....	....	....	....	....	....	....
	NHL Totals		**233**	**74**	**99**	**36**	**12752**	**735**	**10**	**3.46**	....	....	....	....	....	**6**	**1**	**4**	....	**317**	**21**	**0**	**3.97**	....	....	....	....
	Other Major League Totals		260	141	98	15	15389	834	10	3.25	....	....	....	....	....	35	18	15	....	1947	124	1	3.82	....	....	....	....

WHA First All-Star Team (1978) • Won Ben Hatskin Trophy (WHA Top Goaltender) (1978) • Played in NHL All-Star Game (1968)

Promoted to **Toronto** from **Toronto** (OHA-Jr.) and replaced Gary Smith in third period on February 20 (Detroit 4, Toronto 1) and in first period on February 23, 1966. (Toronto 3, Chicago 2). Claimed by **Pittsburgh** from **Toronto** in Intra-League Draft, June 11, 1969. Claimed by **Detroit** from **Pittsburgh** in Intra-League Draft, June 8, 1971. Selected by **New England** (WHA) in 1972 WHA General Player Draft, February 12, 1972. Traded to **Buffalo** by **Detroit** for future considerations, March 10, 1975. Signed as a free agent by **New England** (WHA), August 15, 1977. NHL rights retained by **Hartford** prior to Expansion Draft, June 9, 1979. Traded to **Colorado** by **Hartford** for cash, September 4, 1980.

• SMITH, Billy

William John "Hatchet Man" G – L. 5'10", 185 lbs. b: Perth, Ont., 12/12/1950. Los Angeles' 3rd, 59th overall in 1970. **HHOF**

Season	Club	League	GP	W	L	T	Mins	GA	SO	Avg	AAvg	Eff	SA	S%	SAPG	GP	W	L	T	Mins	GA	SO	Avg	Eff	SA	S%	SAPG
1968-69	Smiths Falls Bears	OHA-B	STATISTICS NOT AVAILABLE																								
1969-70	Cornwall Royals	QJHL	55	....	....	....	3300	249	1	4.53	....	....	....	....	....	6	....	....	....	360	14	1	2.33	....	....	....	....
1970-71	Springfield Kings	AHL	49	19	20	6	2728	160	2	3.51	....	....	....	....	....	11	*9	1	0	*682	29	*1	*2.56	....	....	....	....
1971-72	**Los Angeles Kings**	**NHL**	**5**	**1**	**3**	**1**	**300**	**23**	**0**	**4.60**	**4.66**	....	....	....	....	....	....	....	....	....	....	....	....	....	....	....	....
	Springfield Kings	AHL	28	13	10	5	1649	77	*4	2.80	....	....	....	....	....	4	1	2	0	192	13	0	4.06	....	....	....	....
1972-73	**New York Islanders**	**NHL**	**37**	**7**	**24**	**3**	**2122**	**147**	**0**	**4.16**	**3.96**	....	....	....	....	....	....	....	....	....	....	....	....	....	....	....	....
1973-74	**New York Islanders**	**NHL**	**46**	**9**	**23**	**12**	**2615**	**134**	**0**	**3.07**	**2.96**	....	....	....	....	....	....	....	....	....	....	....	....	....	....	....	....
1974-75	**New York Islanders**	**NHL**	**58**	**21**	**18**	**17**	**3368**	**156**	**3**	**2.78**	**2.49**	....	....	....	....	**6**	**1**	**4**	....	**333**	**23**	**0**	**4.14**	....	....	....	....
1975-76	**New York Islanders**	**NHL**	**39**	**19**	**10**	**9**	**2254**	**98**	**3**	**2.61**	**2.35**	....	....	....	....	**8**	**4**	**3**	....	**437**	**21**	**0**	**2.88**	....	....	....	....
1976-77	**New York Islanders**	**NHL**	**36**	**21**	**8**	**6**	**2089**	**87**	**2**	**2.50**	**2.31**	....	....	....	....	**10**	**7**	**3**	....	**580**	**27**	**0**	**2.79**	....	....	....	....
1977-78	**New York Islanders**	**NHL**	**38**	**20**	**8**	**8**	**2154**	**95**	**2**	**2.65**	**2.47**	....	....	....	....	**1**	**0**	**0**	....	**47**	**1**	**0**	**1.28**	....	....	....	....
1978-79	**New York Islanders**	**NHL**	**40**	**25**	**8**	**4**	**2261**	**108**	**1**	**2.87**	**2.53**	....	....	....	....	**5**	**4**	**1**	....	**315**	**10**	***1**	***1.90**	....	....	....	....
1979-80♦	**New York Islanders**	**NHL**	**38**	**15**	**14**	**7**	**2114**	**104**	**2**	**2.95**	**2.60**	....	....	....	....	***20**	***15**	**4**	....	***1198**	**56**	**1**	**2.80**	....	....	....	....
1980-81♦	**New York Islanders**	**NHL**	**41**	**22**	**10**	**8**	**2363**	**129**	**2**	**3.28**	**2.64**	....	....	....	....	***17**	***14**	**3**	....	***994**	**42**	**0**	***2.54**	....	....	....	....
1981-82	Canada	Can-Cup	DID NOT PLAY – SPARE GOALTENDER																								
♦	**New York Islanders**	**NHL**	**46**	***32**	**9**	**4**	**2685**	**133**	**0**	**2.97**	**2.28**	....	....	....	....	***18**	***15**	**3**	....	***1120**	**47**	***1**	**2.52**	....	....	....	....
1982-83♦	**New York Islanders**	**NHL**	**41**	**18**	**14**	**7**	**2340**	**112**	**1**	**2.87**	**2.29**	**2.69**	**1195**	**.906**	**30.6**	***17**	***13**	**3**	....	**962**	**43**	***2**	***2.68**	....	....	....	....
1983-84	**New York Islanders**	**NHL**	**42**	**23**	**13**	**2**	**2279**	**130**	**2**	**3.42**	**2.69**	**3.55**	**1252**	**.896**	**33.0**	***21**	***12**	**8**	....	***1190**	**54**	**0**	**2.72**	**2.59**	**567**	**.905**	**28.6**
1984-85	**New York Islanders**	**NHL**	**37**	**18**	**14**	**3**	**2090**	**133**	**0**	**3.82**	**3.04**	**4.62**	**1100**	**.879**	**31.6**	**6**	**3**	**3**	....	**342**	**19**	**0**	**3.33**	**3.48**	**182**	**.896**	**31.9**
1985-86	**New York Islanders**	**NHL**	**41**	**20**	**14**	**4**	**2308**	**143**	**1**	**3.72**	**2.90**	**4.42**	**1204**	**.881**	**31.3**	**1**	**0**	**1**	....	**60**	**4**	**0**	**4.00**	**4.71**	**34**	**.882**	**34.0**
1986-87	**New York Islanders**	**NHL**	**40**	**14**	**18**	**5**	**2252**	**132**	**1**	**3.52**	**2.98**	**4.61**	**1007**	**.869**	**26.8**	**2**	**0**	**0**	....	**67**	**1**	**0**	**0.90**	**0.41**	**22**	**.955**	**19.7**
1987-88	**New York Islanders**	**NHL**	**38**	**17**	**14**	**5**	**2107**	**113**	**2**	**3.22**	**2.68**	**3.43**	**1062**	**.894**	**30.2**	....	....	....	....	....	....	....	....	....	....	....	....
1988-89	**New York Islanders**	**NHL**	**17**	**3**	**11**	**0**	**730**	**54**	**0**	**4.44**	**3.70**	**6.59**	**364**	**.852**	**29.9**	....	....	....	....	....	....	....	....	....	....	....	....
1989-1993	**New York Islanders**	**NHL**	DID NOT PLAY – ASSISTANT COACH																								
1993-2000	**Florida Panthers**	**NHL**	DID NOT PLAY – ASSISTANT COACH																								
	NHL Totals		**680**	**305**	**233**	**105**	**38431**	**2031**	**22**	**3.17**	....	....	....	....	....	**132**	**88**	**36**	....	**7645**	**348**	**5**	**2.73**	....	....	....	....

• Brother of Gord • QJHL Second All-Star Team (1970) • NHL First All-Star Team (1982) • Won Vezina Trophy (1982) • Shared William M. Jennings Trophy with Roland Melanson (1983) • Won Conn Smythe Trophy (1983) • Played in NHL All-Star Game (1978) • Credited with scoring a goal vs. Colorado, November 28, 1979.

Claimed by **NY Islanders** from **LA Kings** in Expansion Draft, June 6, 1972.

• SMITH, Gary

Gary Edward "Suitcase" G – L. 6'4", 215 lbs. b: Ottawa, Ont., 2/4/1944.

Season	Club	League	GP	W	L	T	Mins	GA	SO	Avg	AAvg	Eff	SA	S%	SAPG	GP	W	L	T	Mins	GA	SO	Avg	Eff	SA	S%	SAPG
1961-62	St. Michael's Majors	MTJHL	31	*24	6	1	1860	83	*3	*2.68	....	....	....	....	....	12	....	....	....	720	36	0	*3.00	....	....	....	....
	St. Michael's Majors	Mem-Cup	4	0	3	0	182	20	0	6.59	....	....	....	....	....	....	....	....	....	....	....	....	....	....	....	....	....
1962-63	Neil McNeil Maroons	MTJHL	28	....	....	....	1660	65	*3	*2.35	....	....	....	....	....	10	....	....	....	600	40	0	*4.00	....	....	....	....
	Neil McNeil Maroons	Mem-Cup	6	2	4	0	360	27	0	4.50	....	....	....	....	....	....	....	....	....	....	....	....	....	....	....	....	....
1963-64	Toronto Marlboros	OHA-Jr.	55	*40	8	7	3270	186	3	3.41	....	....	....	....	....	9	....	....	....	540	26	1	2.89	....	....	....	....
	Toronto Marlboros	Mem-Cup	12	*11	1	0	720	38	0	3.17	....	....	....	....	....	....	....	....	....	....	....	....	....	....	....	....	....
1964-65	Rochester Americans	AHL	1	0	0	0	2	0	0	0.00	....	....	....	....	....	....	....	....	....	....	....	....	....	....	....	....	....
	Tulsa Oilers	CPHL	1	0	1	0	60	5	0	5.00	....	....	....	....	....	....	....	....	....	....	....	....	....	....	....	....	....
	Victoria Maple Leafs	WHL	8	1	5	0	411	30	0	4.38	....	....	....	....	....	....	....	....	....	....	....	....	....	....	....	....	....
1965-66	Rochester Americans	AHL	37	20	11	4	2038	97	2	2.86	....	....	....	....	....	4	2	2	0	188	12	0	3.83	....	....	....	....
	Toronto Maple Leafs	**NHL**	**3**	**0**	**2**	**0**	**118**	**7**	**0**	**3.56**	**3.60**	....	....	....	....	....	....	....	....	....	....	....	....	....	....	....	....
1966-67	Rochester Americans	AHL	17	6	5	4	871	38	1	2.62	....	....	....	....	....	....	....	....	....	....	....	....	....	....	....	....	....
	Victoria Maple Leafs	WHL	17	6	8	3	1029	51	2	2.97	....	....	....	....	....	....	....	....	....	....	....	....	....	....	....	....	....
	Toronto Maple Leafs	**NHL**	**2**	**0**	**2**	**0**	**115**	**7**	**0**	**3.65**	**3.77**	....	....	....	....	....	....	....	....	....	....	....	....	....	....	....	....
1967-68	**Oakland Seals**	**NHL**	**21**	**2**	**13**	**4**	**1129**	**60**	**1**	**3.19**	**3.55**	....	....	....	....	....	....	....	....	....	....	....	....	....	....	....	....

Season	Club	League	REGULAR SEASON GP	W	L	T	Mins	GA	SO	Avg	AAvg	Eff	SA	S%	SAPG	PLAYOFFS GP	W	L	T	Mins	GA	SO	Avg	Eff	SA	S%	SAPG
1968-69	**Oakland Seals**	**NHL**	**54**	**21**	**24**	**7**	**2993**	**148**	**4**	**2.97**	**3.07**	....	....	....	....	**7**	**3**	**4**	....	**420**	**23**	**0**	**3.29**	....	....	....	....
1969-70	**Oakland Seals**	**NHL**	**65**	**19**	**34**	**12**	**3762**	**195**	**2**	**3.11**	**3.32**	....	....	....	....	**4**	**0**	**4**	....	**248**	**13**	**0**	**3.15**	....	....	....	....
1970-71	**California Golden Seals**	**NHL**	***71**	**19**	**48**	**4**	***3975**	**256**	**2**	**3.86**	**3.88**	....	....	....	....	....	....	....	....	....	....	....	....	....	....	....	....
1971-72	**Chicago Black Hawks**	**NHL**	**28**	**14**	**5**	**6**	**1540**	**62**	**5**	**2.42**	**2.43**	....	....	....	....	**2**	**1**	**1**	....	**120**	**3**	**1**	**1.50**	....	....	....	....
1972-73	**Chicago Black Hawks**	**NHL**	**23**	**10**	**10**	**2**	**1340**	**79**	**0**	**3.54**	**3.34**	....	....	....	....	**2**	**0**	**1**	....	**65**	**5**	**0**	**4.62**	....	....	....	....
1973-74	**Vancouver Canucks**	**NHL**	**66**	**20**	**33**	**8**	**3632**	**208**	**3**	**3.44**	**3.34**	....	....	....	....	....	....	....	....	....	....	....	....	....	....	....	....
1974-75	**Vancouver Canucks**	**NHL**	***72**	**32**	**24**	**9**	**3828**	**197**	**6**	**3.09**	**2.78**	....	....	....	....	**4**	**1**	**3**	....	**257**	**14**	**0**	**3.27**	....	....	....	....
1975-76	**Vancouver Canucks**	**NHL**	**51**	**20**	**24**	**6**	**2864**	**167**	**2**	**3.50**	**3.17**	....	....	....	....	....	....	....	....	....	....	....	....	....	....	....	....
1976-77	**Minnesota North Stars**	**NHL**	**36**	**10**	**17**	**8**	**2090**	**139**	**1**	**3.99**	**3.73**	....	....	....	....	**1**	**0**	**0**	....	**43**	**4**	**0**	**5.58**	....	....	....	....
1977-78	**Washington Capitals**	**NHL**	**17**	**2**	**12**	**3**	**980**	**68**	**0**	**4.16**	**3.91**	....	....	....	....	....	....	....	....	....	....	....	....	....	....	....	....
	Hershey Bears	AHL	1	0	0	1	65	4	0	3.69	....	....	....	....	....	....	....	....	....	....	....	....	....	....	....	....	....
	Minnesota North Stars	**NHL**	**3**	**0**	**2**	**1**	**180**	**9**	**0**	**3.00**	**2.81**	....	....	....	....	....	....	....	....	....	....	....	....	....	....	....	....
	Fort Worth Texans	CHL	13	8	3	1	765	38	1	2.98	....	....	....	....	....	9	5	4	0	511	25	*1	2.94	....	....	....	....
1978-79	Indianapolis Racers	WHA	11	0	10	1	664	61	0	5.51	....	....	....	....	....	....	....	....	....	....	....	....	....	....	....	....	....
	Winnipeg Jets	WHA	11	7	3	0	626	31	0	2.97	....	....	....	....	....	10	*8	2	0	563	35	0	*3.73	....	....	....	....
1979-80	**Winnipeg Jets**	**NHL**	**20**	**4**	**11**	**4**	**1073**	**73**	**0**	**4.08**	**3.61**	....	....	....	....	....	....	....	....	....	....	....	....	....	....	....	....
	Tulsa Oilers	CHL	22	7	11	4	1324	73	0	3.31	....	....	....	....	....	1	0	1	0	60	6	0	6.00	....	....	....	....
	NHL Totals		**532**	**173**	**261**	**74**	**29619**	**1675**	**26**	**3.39**	....	....	....	....	....	**20**	**5**	**13**	....	**1153**	**62**	**1**	**3.23**	....	....	....	....
	Other Major League Totals		22	7	13	1	1290	92	0	4.28	....	....	....	....	....	10	8	2	....	563	35	0	3.73	....	....	....	....

• Son of Des • Brother of Brian • Shared Vezina Trophy with Tony Esposito (1972) • Played in NHL All-Star Game (1975)

Promoted to **Toronto** from **Rochester** (AHL) to replace injured Terry Sawchuk and played in games on February 19, 20, 23, 1966. Claimed by **California** from **Toronto** in Expansion Draft, June 6, 1967. Traded to **Chicago** by **California** for Kerry Bond, Gerry Pinder and Gerry Desjardins, September 9, 1971. Selected by **Chicago** (WHA) in 1972 WHA General Player Draft, February 12, 1972. Traded to **Vancouver** by **Chicago** with Jerry Korab for Dale Tallon, May 14, 1973. Traded to **Minnesota** by **Vancouver** for Cesare Maniago, August 23, 1976. Signed as a free agent by **Washington**, September 3, 1977. Traded to **Minnesota** by **Washington** for cash, February 19, 1978. Signed as a free agent by **Indianapolis** (WHA), September, 1978. Signed as a free agent by **Winnipeg** (WHA) after **Indianapolis** (WHA) franchise folded, December 17, 1978. NHL rights retained by **Winnipeg** prior to Expansion Draft, June 9, 1979.

• SMITH, Normie

Norman Eugene G – L. 5'7", 165 lbs. b: Toronto, Ont., 3/18/1908 d: 2/2/1988.

Season	Club	League	GP	W	L	T	Mins	GA	SO	Avg	AAvg	Eff	SA	S%	SAPG	GP	W	L	T	Mins	GA	SO	Avg	Eff	SA	S%	SAPG
1929-30	Toronto Willys-Overland	TMHL	9	3	4	2	560	19	1	2.04	....	....	....	....	....	....	....	....	....	....	....	....	....	....	....	....	....
1930-31	Montreal AAA	MCHL	STATISTICS NOT AVAILABLE																								
	Windsor Bulldogs	IHL	7	5	1	1	430	16	1	2.23	....	....	....	....	....	6	*4	1	1	390	11	0	1.69	....	....	....	....
1931-32	**Montreal Maroons**	**NHL**	**21**	**5**	**12**	**4**	**1267**	**62**	**0**	**2.94**	**3.63**	....	....	....	....	....	....	....	....	....	....	....	....	....	....	....	....
	Windsor Bulldogs	IHL	14	7	3	4	890	36	3	2.43	....	....	....	....	....	6	1	3	2	380	8	*3	*1.11	....	....	....	....
1932-33	Windsor Bulldogs	IHL	42	14	22	6	2520	120	2	2.86	....	....	....	....	....	6	2	4	0	360	18	0	3.00	....	....	....	....
1933-34	Quebec Castors	Can-Am	32	12	12	8	2009	64	3	*1.91	....	....	....	....	....	....	....	....	....	....	....	....	....	....	....	....	....
1934-35	**Detroit Red Wings**	**NHL**	**25**	**12**	**11**	**2**	**1550**	**52**	**2**	**2.01**	**2.40**	....	....	....	....	....	....	....	....	....	....	....	....	....	....	....	....
	Detroit Olympics	IHL	26	15	7	4	1630	53	4	*1.95	....	....	....	....	....	5	*5	0	0	300	5	0	*1.00	....	....	....	....
	Windsor Bulldogs	IHL	1	1	0	0	60	3	0	*3.00	....	....	....	....	....	2	0	2	2	130	9	0	4.15	....	....	....	....
	Detroit Olympics	L-W-S	5	3	2	0	320	15	*1	*2.81	....	....	....	....	....	....	....	....	....	....	....	....	....	....	....	....	....
1935-36♦	**Detroit Red Wings**	**NHL**	***48**	***24**	**16**	**8**	***3030**	**103**	**6**	**2.04**	**2.85**	....	....	....	....	**7**	***6**	**1**	**0**	**538**	**12**	***2**	**1.34**	....	....	....	....
1936-37♦	**Detroit Red Wings**	**NHL**	***48**	***25**	**14**	**9**	**2980**	**102**	***6**	***2.05**	**2.47**	....	....	....	....	**5**	**3**	**1**	....	**282**	**6**	**1**	**1.28**	....	....	....	....
1937-38	**Detroit Red Wings**	**NHL**	**47**	**11**	**25**	**11**	**2930**	**130**	**3**	**2.66**	**3.23**	....	....	....	....	....	....	....	....	....	....	....	....	....	....	....	....
1938-39	**Detroit Red Wings**	**NHL**	**4**	**0**	**4**	**0**	**240**	**12**	**0**	**3.00**	**3.62**	....	....	....	....	....	....	....	....	....	....	....	....	....	....	....	....
	Pittsburgh Hornets	IAHL	1	0	1	0	60	5	0	5.00	....	....	....	....	....	....	....	....	....	....	....	....	....	....	....	....	....
1939-1943			OUT OF HOCKEY – RETIRED																								
1943-44	**Detroit Red Wings**	**NHL**	**5**	**3**	**1**	**1**	**300**	**15**	**0**	**3.00**	**2.23**	....	....	....	....	....	....	....	....	....	....	....	....	....	....	....	....
1944-45	**Detroit Red Wings**	**NHL**	**1**	**1**	**0**	**0**	**60**	**3**	**0**	**3.00**	**2.48**	....	....	....	....	....	....	....	....	....	....	....	....	....	....	....	....
	NHL Totals		**199**	**81**	**83**	**35**	**12357**	**479**	**17**	**2.33**	....	....	....	....	....	**12**	**9**	**2**	**0**	**820**	**18**	**3**	**1.32**	....	....	....	....

NHL First All-Star Team (1937) • Won Vezina Trophy (1937)

Signed as a free agent by **Montreal Maroons**, July 29, 1930. Traded to **St. Louis** by **Montreal Maroons** with Vern Ayres to complete transaction that sent Al Shields to Montreal Maroons (September 20, 1934), October 22, 1934. Traded to **Detroit** by **St. Louis** for Burr Williams, October 22, 1934. • Suspended by **Detroit** for refusing to play following game vs. NY Rangers, November 15, 1938. Rights traded to **Boston** by **Detroit** with $15,000 for Tiny Thompson, November 28, 1938. • Officially announced retirement, November 29, 1938.

• SNEDDON, Bob

Robert Allan G – R. 6'2", 190 lbs. b: Montreal, Que., 5/31/1944.

Season	Club	League	GP	W	L	T	Mins	GA	SO	Avg	AAvg	Eff	SA	S%	SAPG	GP	W	L	T	Mins	GA	SO	Avg	Eff	SA	S%	SAPG
1963-64	St. Catharines Black Hawks	OHA-Jr.	52	29	16	7	3080	184	4	3.58	....	....	....	....	....	11	....	....	....	660	45	1	4.09	....	....	....	....
1964-65	Muskegon-Port Huron	IHL	45	....	....	....	2700	230	0	4.89	....	....	....	....	....	....	....	....	....	....	....	....	....	....	....	....	....
1965-66	Port Huron Flags	IHL	67	....	....	....	3980	254	*5	3.83	....	....	....	....	....	9	8	1	0	540	27	0	*3.00	....	....	....	....
1966-67	St. Louis Braves	CPHL	20	7	7	6	1200	66	1	3.30	....	....	....	....	....	....	....	....	....	....	....	....	....	....	....	....	....
1967-68	Dallas Black Hawks	CPHL	36	17	14	1	1777	119	3	4.02	....	....	....	....	....	5	2	3	0	300	11	*1	*2.20	....	....	....	....
1968-69	Portland Buckaroos	WHL	2	0	0	1	80	7	0	5.26	....	....	....	....	....	....	....	....	....	....	....	....	....	....	....	....	....
	Quebec Aces	AHL	13	5	4	1	626	37	0	3.55	....	....	....	....	....	....	....	....	....	....	....	....	....	....	....	....	....
1969-70	Springfield Kings	AHL	27	....	....	....	1493	108	0	4.34	....	....	....	....	....	8	....	....	....	481	30	0	3.74	....	....	....	....
1970-71	**California Golden Seals**	**NHL**	**5**	**0**	**2**	**0**	**225**	**21**	**0**	**5.60**	**5.56**	....	....	....	....	....	....	....	....	....	....	....	....	....	....	....	....
	Providence Reds	AHL	16	7	6	1	807	55	1	4.19	....	....	....	....	....	....	....	....	....	....	....	....	....	....	....	....	....
1971-72	Tidewater Wings	AHL	5	1	3	0	213	14	0	3.94	....	....	....	....	....	....	....	....	....	....	....	....	....	....	....	....	....
	Seattle Totems	WHL	23	3	13	2	1174	104	0	5.31	....	....	....	....	....	....	....	....	....	....	....	....	....	....	....	....	....
1972-73	Springfield Kings	AHL	36	....	....	....	1936	133	0	4.12	....	....	....	....	....	....	....	....	....	....	....	....	....	....	....	....	....
1973-74	Rochester Americans	AHL	31	15	9	6	1807	114	1	3.78	....	....	....	....	....	2	0	2	0	120	10	0	5.00	....	....	....	....
1974-75	Rochester Americans	AHL	35	22	7	2	1924	101	0	3.14	....	....	....	....	....	1	0	1	0	60	6	0	6.00	....	....	....	....
1975-76	Baltimore Clippers	AHL	19	3	13	1	1049	91	0	5.20	....	....	....	....	....	....	....	....	....	....	....	....	....	....	....	....	....
1976-77	Binghamton Dusters	NAHL	16	8	6	1	901	70	0	4.53	....	....	....	....	....	....	....	....	....	....	....	....	....	....	....	....	....
	Johnstown Jets	NAHL	16	....	....	....	913	77	0	4.93	....	....	....	....	....	....	....	....	....	....	....	....	....	....	....	....	....
1977-78	Brantford Alexanders	OHA-Sr.	24	....	....	....	1485	104	0	4.20	....	....	....	....	....	....	....	....	....	....	....	....	....	....	....	....	....
1978-79	Welland Cougars	OHA-I	34	....	....	....	2085	201	0	5.78	....	....	....	....	....	....	....	....	....	....	....	....	....	....	....	....	....
1979-80	Dundas Blues	OHA-I	20	....	....	....	1050	96	0	4.61	....	....	....	....	....	....	....	....	....	....	....	....	....	....	....	....	....
	NHL Totals		**5**	**0**	**2**	**0**	**225**	**21**	**0**	**5.60**	....	....	....	....	....	....	....	....	....	....	....	....	....	....	....	....	....

IHL First All-Star Team (1966) • Won James Norris Memorial Trophy (fewest goals against - IHL) (1966)

Traded to **Philadelphia** by **Chicago** for Brian Bradley, December, 1968. Claimed by **LA Kings** (Springfield-AHL) from **Philadelphia** in Reverse Draft, June 12, 1969. Claimed by **California** (Providence-AHL) from **Los Angeles** in Reverse Draft, June, 1970. Claimed by **Detroit** (Tidewater-AHL) from **California** (Cleveland-AHL) in Reverse Draft, June, 1971. Traded to **Seattle** (WHL) by **Detroit** for Art Stratton, November, 1971.

• SNOW, Garth

Garth E. G – L. 6'3", 200 lbs. b: Wrentham, MA, 7/28/1969. Quebec's 6th, 114th overall in 1987.

Season	Club	League	GP	W	L	T	Mins	GA	SO	Avg	AAvg	Eff	SA	S%	SAPG	GP	W	L	T	Mins	GA	SO	Avg	Eff	SA	S%	SAPG
1986-87	Mount St. Charles Mounties	Hi-School	30	....	....	....	1795	53	10	1.77	....	....	....	....	....	....	....	....	....	....	....	....	....	....	....	....	....
1987-88	Stratford Cullitons	OJHL-B	30	20	6	0	1642	93	2	3.40	....	....	....	....	....	....	....	....	....	....	....	....	....	....	....	....	....
1988-89	University of Maine	H-East	5	2	2	0	241	14	1	3.49	....	....	....	....	....	....	....	....	....	....	....	....	....	....	....	....	....
1989-90	University of Maine	H-East	DID NOT PLAY – ACADEMICALLY INELIGIBLE																								
1990-91	University of Maine	H-East	25	*18	4	0	1290	64	2	2.98	....	....	....	....	....	....	....	....	....	....	....	....	....	....	....	....	....
1991-92	University of Maine	H-East	31	*25	4	2	1792	73	*2	*2.44	....	....	....	....	....	....	....	....	....	....	....	....	....	....	....	....	....
1992-93	University of Maine	H-East	23	*21	0	1	1210	42	1	*2.08	....	....	....	....	....	....	....	....	....	....	....	....	....	....	....	....	....
1993-94	United States	Nat-Team	23	13	5	3	1324	71	1	3.22	....	....	....	....	....	....	....	....	....	....	....	....	....	....	....	....	....
	United States	Olympics	5	1	3	1	299	17	0	3.41	....	....	....	....	....	....	....	....	....	....	....	....	....	....	....	....	....
	Quebec Nordiques	**NHL**	**5**	**3**	**2**	**0**	**279**	**16**	**0**	**3.44**	**3.31**	**4.33**	**127**	**.874**	**27.3**	....	....	....	....	....	....	....	....	....	....	....	....
	Cornwall Aces	AHL	16	6	5	3	927	51	0	3.30	....	....	....	....	....	13	8	5	....	790	42	0	3.19	....	....	....	....
1994-95	Cornwall Aces	AHL	*62	*32	20	7	*3558	162	3	2.73	....	....	....	....	....	8	4	3	....	402	14	*2	*2.09	....	....	....	....
	Quebec Nordiques	**NHL**	**2**	**1**	**1**	**0**	**119**	**11**	**0**	**5.55**	**5.82**	**9.69**	**63**	**.825**	**31.8**	**1**	**0**	**0**	....	**9**	**1**	**0**	**6.67**	**22.23**	**3**	**.667**	**20.0**
1995-96	**Philadelphia Flyers**	**NHL**	**26**	**12**	**8**	**4**	**1437**	**69**	**0**	**2.88**	**2.86**	**3.07**	**648**	**.894**	**27.1**	**1**	**0**	**0**	....	**1**	**0**	**0**	**0.00**	**0.00**	**0**	**.000**	**0.0**
1996-97	**Philadelphia Flyers**	**NHL**	**35**	**14**	**8**	**8**	**1884**	**79**	**2**	**2.52**	**2.71**	**2.44**	**816**	**.903**	**26.0**	**12**	**8**	**4**	....	**699**	**33**	**0**	**2.83**	**3.06**	**305**	**.892**	**26.2**

Season	Club	League	GP	W	L	T	Mins	GA	SO	Avg	AAvg	Eff	SA	S%	SAPG	GP	W	L	T	Mins	GA	SO	Avg	Eff	SA	S%	SAPG
			REGULAR SEASON													PLAYOFFS											
1997-98	**Philadelphia Flyers**	**NHL**	**29**	**14**	**9**	**4**	**1651**	**67**	**1**	**2.43**	**2.90**	**2.39**	**682**	**.902**	**24.8**	....	....	....	....	....	....	....	....	....	....	....	....
	Vancouver Canucks	**NHL**	**12**	**3**	**6**	**0**	**504**	**26**	**0**	**3.10**	**3.70**	**3.08**	**262**	**.901**	**31.2**	....	....	....	....	....	....	....	....	....	....	....	....
	United States	WC-A	5	1	2	1	260	12	0	2.77	....	....	....	....	....	....	....	....	....	....	....	....	....	....	....	....	....
1998-99	**Vancouver Canucks**	**NHL**	**65**	**20**	**31**	**8**	**3501**	**171**	**6**	**2.93**	**3.50**	**2.92**	**1715**	**.900**	**29.4**	....	....	....	....	....	....	....	....	....	....	....	....
99-2000	**Vancouver Canucks**	**NHL**	**32**	**10**	**15**	**3**	**1712**	**76**	**0**	**2.66**	**3.04**	**2.61**	**775**	**.902**	**27.2**	....	....	....	....	....	....	....	....	....	....	....	....
	NHL Totals		**206**	**77**	**80**	**27**	**11087**	**515**	**9**	**2.79**	....	....	**5088**	**.899**	**27.5**	**14**	**8**	**4**	....	**709**	**34**	**0**	**2.88**	....	**308**	**.890**	**26.1**

Hockey East Second All-Star Team (1992, 1993) • NCAA Championship All-Tournament Team (1993)

Transferred to **Colorado** after **Quebec** franchise relocated, June 21, 1995. Traded to **Philadelphia** by **Colorado** for Philadelphia's 3rd (later traded to Washington — Washington selected Shawn McNeil) and 6th (Kai Fischer) round choices in 1996 Entry Draft, July 12, 1995. Traded to **Vancouver** by **Philadelphia** for Sean Burke, March 4, 1998.

• SODERSTROM, Tommy

G – L. 5'7", 157 lbs. b: Stockholm, Sweden, 7/17/1969. Philadelphia's 14th, 214th overall in 1990.

Season	Club	League	GP	W	L	T	Mins	GA	SO	Avg	AAvg	Eff	SA	S%	SAPG	GP	W	L	T	Mins	GA	SO	Avg	Eff	SA	S%	SAPG
1986-87	Djurgardens IF Stockholm	Sweden-Jr.	9	....	....	....	540	11	*3	1.22	....	....	....	....	....	....	....	....	....	....	....	....	....	....	....	....	....
	Sweden	EJC-A	5	....	....	....	300	4	....	0.80	....	....	....	....	....	....	....	....	....	....	....	....	....	....	....	....	....
1987-88	Djurgardens IF Stockholm	Sweden-Jr.	3	2	1	0	179	17	0	5.67	....	....	....	....	....	....	....	....	....	....	....	....	....	....	....	....	....
1988-89	Djurgardens IF Stockholm	Sweden-Jr.	7	....	....	....	420	22	0	3.14	....	....	....	....	....	....	....	....	....	....	....	....	....	....	....	....	....
	Sweden	WJC-A	3	....	....	....	180	7	....	2.33	....	....	....	....	....	....	....	....	....	....	....	....	....	....	....	....	....
1989-90	Djurgardens IF Stockholm	Sweden	4	....	....	....	240	14	0	3.50	....	....	....	....	....	....	....	....	....	....	....	....	....	....	....	....	....
	Viking AIK	Sweden-2	3	3	0	0	180	3	1	1.00	....	....	....	....	....	....	....	....	....	....	....	....	....	....	....	....	....
1990-91	Djurgardens IF Stockholm	Sweden	39	22	12	6	2340	104	3	2.67	....	....	....	....	....	7	....	....	....	423	10	2	1.42	....	....	....	....
	Sweden	WEC-A	1	0	0	1	60	3	0	3.00	....	....	....	....	....	....	....	....	....	....	....	....	....	....	....	....	....
1991-92	Sweden	Can-Cup	4	2	2	0	240	12	0	3.00	....	....	....	....	....	....	....	....	....	....	....	....	....	....	....	....	....
	Djurgardens IF Stockholm	Sweden	39	15	8	11	2340	109	4	2.79	....	....	....	....	....	10	....	....	....	635	28	0	2.65	....	....	....	....
	Sweden	Olympics	5	3	1	1	298	13	0	2.62	....	....	....	....	....	....	....	....	....	....	....	....	....	....	....	....	....
	Sweden	WC-A	5	4	1	0	299	7	*2	1.40	....	....	....	....	....	....	....	....	....	....	....	....	....	....	....	....	....
1992-93	**Philadelphia Flyers**	**NHL**	**44**	**20**	**17**	**6**	**2512**	**143**	**5**	**3.42**	**2.93**	**3.69**	**1327**	**.892**	**31.7**	....	....	....	....	....	....	....	....	....	....	....	....
	Hershey Bears	AHL	7	4	1	0	373	15	0	2.41	....	....	....	....	....	....	....	....	....	....	....	....	....	....	....	....	....
	Sweden	WC-A	7	4	3	0	386	20	0	3.10	....	....	....	....	....	....	....	....	....	....	....	....	....	....	....	....	....
1993-94	**Philadelphia Flyers**	**NHL**	**34**	**6**	**18**	**4**	**1736**	**116**	**2**	**4.01**	**3.87**	**5.47**	**851**	**.864**	**29.4**	....	....	....	....	....	....	....	....	....	....	....	....
	Hershey Bears	AHL	9	3	4	1	461	37	0	4.81	....	....	....	....	....	....	....	....	....	....	....	....	....	....	....	....	....
1994-95	**New York Islanders**	**NHL**	**26**	**8**	**12**	**3**	**1350**	**70**	**1**	**3.11**	**3.26**	**3.04**	**717**	**.902**	**31.9**	....	....	....	....	....	....	....	....	....	....	....	....
1995-96	**New York Islanders**	**NHL**	**51**	**11**	**22**	**6**	**2590**	**167**	**2**	**3.87**	**3.87**	**4.72**	**1370**	**.878**	**31.7**	....	....	....	....	....	....	....	....	....	....	....	....
1996-97	Sweden	W-Cup	2	2	0	0	120	2	1	1.00	....	....	....	....	....	....	....	....	....	....	....	....	....	....	....	....	....
	New York Islanders	**NHL**	**1**	**0**	**0**	**0**	**1**	**0**	**0**	**0.00**	**0.00**	**0.00**	**0**	**.000**	**0.0**	....	....	....	....	....	....	....	....	....	....	....	....
	Rochester Americans	AHL	2	2	0	0	120	8	0	4.00	....	....	....	....	....	....	....	....	....	....	....	....	....	....	....	....	....
	Utah Grizzlies	IHL	26	12	11	0	1463	76	0	3.12	....	....	....	....	....	....	....	....	....	....	....	....	....	....	....	....	....
1997-98	Djurgardens IF Stockholm	Sweden	*46	....	....	....	*2760	103	....	*2.24	....	....	....	....	....	*15	....	....	....	*936	34	....	2.18	....	....	....	....
	Sweden	Olympics	DID NOT PLAY – SPARE GOALTENDER																								
1998-99	Djurgardens IF Stockholm	Sweden	*48	....	....	....	2918	134	1	2.76	....	....	....	....	....	4	....	....	....	240	11	0	2.75	....	....	....	....
99-2000	Djurgardens IF Stockholm	Sweden	21	....	....	....	1248	59	1	2.84	....	....	....	....	....	....	....	....	....	....	....	....	....	....	....	....	....
	NHL Totals		**156**	**45**	**69**	**19**	**8189**	**496**	**10**	**3.63**	....	....	**4265**	**.884**	**31.2**	....	....	....	....	....	....	....	....	....	....	....	....

EJC-A All-Star Team (1987) • Named Best Goaltender at EJC-A (1987) • Swedish Rookie of the Year (1991) • Swedish World All-Star Team (1992) • Named Best Goaltender at WC-A (1992)

Traded to **NY Islanders** by **Philadelphia** for Ron Hextall and NY Islanders' 6th round choice (Dmitry Tertyshny) in 1995 Entry Draft, September 22, 1994. • Played 10 seconds in game on March 31, 1997.

• SOETAERT, Doug

Douglas Henry "Soapy" G – L. 6', 180 lbs. b: Edmonton, Alta., 4/21/1955. NY Rangers' 2nd, 30th overall in 1975.

Season	Club	League	GP	W	L	T	Mins	GA	SO	Avg	AAvg	Eff	SA	S%	SAPG	GP	W	L	T	Mins	GA	SO	Avg	Eff	SA	S%	SAPG
1970-71	Edmonton Canadians	AAHA	STATISTICS NOT AVAILABLE																								
	Edmonton Oil Kings	AJHL	3	....	....	....	180	21	0	7.00	....	....	....	....	....	....	....	....	....	....	....	....	....	....	....	....	....
1971-72	Edmonton Oil Kings	WCJHL	37	....	....	....	1738	105	3	3.62	....	....	....	....	....	6	....	....	....	267	13	0	2.92	....	....	....	....
1972-73	Edmonton Oil Kings	WCJHL	43	....	....	....	2111	129	1	3.67	....	....	....	....	....	6	....	....	....	339	33	0	5.84	....	....	....	....
1973-74	Edmonton Oil Kings	WCJHL	39	....	....	....	2190	163	1	4.47	....	....	....	....	....	3	....	....	....	141	9	0	3.83	....	....	....	....
1974-75	Edmonton Oil Kings	WCJHL	65	....	....	....	3706	273	1	4.42	....	....	....	....	....	....	....	....	....	....	....	....	....	....	....	....	....
	Canada	WJC-A	2	....	....	....	120	5	....	2.50	....	....	....	....	....	....	....	....	....	....	....	....	....	....	....	....	....
1975-76	**New York Rangers**	**NHL**	**8**	**2**	**2**	**0**	**273**	**24**	**0**	**5.27**	**4.78**	....	....	....	....	....	....	....	....	....	....	....	....	....	....	....	....
	Providence Reds	AHL	16	6	9	1	896	65	0	4.35	....	....	....	....	....	1	0	1	0	59	6	0	6.10	....	....	....	....
1976-77	**New York Rangers**	**NHL**	**12**	**3**	**4**	**1**	**570**	**28**	**1**	**2.95**	**2.74**	....	....	....	....	....	....	....	....	....	....	....	....	....	....	....	....
	New Haven Nighthawks	AHL	16	6	9	0	947	61	0	3.86	....	....	....	....	....	....	....	....	....	....	....	....	....	....	....	....	....
1977-78	**New York Rangers**	**NHL**	**6**	**2**	**2**	**2**	**360**	**20**	**0**	**3.33**	**3.12**	....	....	....	....	....	....	....	....	....	....	....	....	....	....	....	....
	New Haven Nighthawks	AHL	38	16	16	6	2252	141	0	3.75	....	....	....	....	....	*15	8	7	0	*916	53	0	3.47	....	....	....	....
1978-79	**New York Rangers**	**NHL**	**17**	**5**	**7**	**3**	**900**	**57**	**0**	**3.80**	**3.36**	....	....	....	....	....	....	....	....	....	....	....	....	....	....	....	....
	New Haven Nighthawks	AHL	3	2	1	0	180	11	1	3.67	....	....	....	....	....	....	....	....	....	....	....	....	....	....	....	....	....
1979-80	**New York Rangers**	**NHL**	**8**	**5**	**2**	**0**	**435**	**33**	**0**	**4.55**	**4.03**	....	....	....	....	....	....	....	....	....	....	....	....	....	....	....	....
	New Haven Nighthawks	AHL	32	17	18	5	1808	108	*3	3.58	....	....	....	....	....	8	5	3	0	478	24	0	3.01	....	....	....	....
1980-81	**New York Rangers**	**NHL**	**39**	**16**	**16**	**7**	**2320**	**152**	**0**	**3.93**	**3.18**	....	....	....	....	....	....	....	....	....	....	....	....	....	....	....	....
	New Haven Nighthawks	AHL	12	5	5	1	668	35	2	3.14	....	....	....	....	....	4	0	3	0	220	19	0	5.18	....	....	....	....
1981-82	**Winnipeg Jets**	**NHL**	**39**	**13**	**14**	**8**	**2157**	**155**	**2**	**4.31**	**3.34**	....	....	....	....	**2**	**1**	**1**	....	**120**	**8**	**0**	**4.00**	....	....	....	....
1982-83	**Winnipeg Jets**	**NHL**	**44**	**19**	**19**	**6**	**2533**	**174**	**0**	**4.12**	**3.31**	**5.40**	**1328**	**.869**	**31.5**	**1**	**0**	**0**	....	**20**	**0**	**0**	**0.00**	....	....	....	....
1983-84	**Winnipeg Jets**	**NHL**	**47**	**18**	**15**	**7**	**2539**	**182**	**0**	**4.30**	**3.39**	**5.65**	**1385**	**.869**	**32.7**	**1**	**0**	**1**	....	**20**	**5**	**0**	**15.00**	**39.47**	**19**	**.737**	**57.0**
1984-85	**Montreal Canadiens**	**NHL**	**28**	**14**	**9**	**4**	**1606**	**91**	**0**	**3.40**	**2.70**	**4.97**	**622**	**.854**	**23.2**	**1**	**0**	**0**	....	**20**	**1**	**0**	**3.00**	**3.33**	**9**	**.889**	**27.0**
1985-86♦	**Montreal Canadiens**	**NHL**	**23**	**11**	**7**	**2**	**1215**	**56**	**3**	**2.77**	**2.16**	**2.91**	**533**	**.895**	**26.3**	....	....	....	....	....	....	....	....	....	....	....	....
1986-87	**New York Rangers**	**NHL**	**13**	**2**	**7**	**2**	**675**	**58**	**0**	**5.16**	**4.38**	**8.13**	**368**	**.842**	**32.7**	....	....	....	....	....	....	....	....	....	....	....	....
	NHL Totals		**284**	**110**	**104**	**42**	**15583**	**1030**	**6**	**3.97**	....	....	....	....	....	**5**	**1**	**2**	....	**180**	**14**	**0**	**4.67**	....	....	....	....

Traded to **Winnipeg** by **NY Rangers** for Winnipeg's 3rd round choice (Vesa Salo) in 1983 Entry Draft, September 8, 1981. Traded to **Montreal** by **Winnipeg** for Mark Holden, October 9, 1984. Signed as a free agent by **NY Rangers**, July 24, 1986.

• SOUCY, Christian

Christian G. G – L. 5'11", 160 lbs. b: Gatineau, Que., 9/14/1970.

Season	Club	League	GP	W	L	T	Mins	GA	SO	Avg	AAvg	Eff	SA	S%	SAPG	GP	W	L	T	Mins	GA	SO	Avg	Eff	SA	S%	SAPG
1989-90	Pembroke Lumber Kings	OJHL	47	16	24	4	2721	212	1	4.67	....	....	....	....	....	....	....	....	....	....	....	....	....	....	....	....	....
1990-91	Pembroke Lumber Kings	OJHL	*54	*27	24	1	*3109	198	2	3.82	....	....	....	....	....	....	....	....	....	....	....	....	....	....	....	....	....
1991-92	University of Vermont	ECAC	30	15	11	3	*1783	81	0	2.83	....	....	....	....	....	....	....	....	....	....	....	....	....	....	....	....	....
1992-93	University of Vermont	ECAC	29	11	15	3	1708	90	1	3.16	....	....	....	....	....	....	....	....	....	....	....	....	....	....	....	....	....
1993-94	**Chicago Blackhawks**	**NHL**	**1**	**0**	**0**	**0**	**3**	**0**	**0**	**0.00**	**0.00**	**0.00**	**0**	**.000**	**0.0**	....	....	....	....	....	....	....	....	....	....	....	....
	Indianapolis Ice	IHL	46	14	25	1	2302	159	1	4.14	....	....	....	....	....	....	....	....	....	....	....	....	....	....	....	....	....
1994-95	Indianapolis Ice	IHL	42	15	17	5	2216	148	0	4.01	....	....	....	....	....	....	....	....	....	....	....	....	....	....	....	....	....
1995-96	Fort Worth Fire	CHL	5	3	2	0	300	19	0	3.80	....	....	....	....	....	....	....	....	....	....	....	....	....	....	....	....	....
	Jacksonville Lizard Kings	ECHL	3	2	1	0	179	11	0	3.68	....	....	....	....	....	....	....	....	....	....	....	....	....	....	....	....	....
	Indianapolis Ice	IHL	22	12	9	0	1198	62	0	3.11	....	....	....	....	....	....	....	....	....	....	....	....	....	....	....	....	....
1996-97	Kentucky Thoroughblades	AHL	3	0	2	0	138	11	0	4.77	....	....	....	....	....	....	....	....	....	....	....	....	....	....	....	....	....
	Baton Rouge Kingfish	ECHL	46	18	20	3	2421	128	3	3.17	....	....	....	....	....	....	....	....	....	....	....	....	....	....	....	....	....
1997-98	Austin Ice-Bats	WPHL	11	6	5	0	658	38	0	3.46	....	....	....	....	....	5	2	3	....	321	14	0	*2.61	....	....	....	....
	Houston Aeros	IHL	5	4	1	0	288	9	0	1.87	....	....	....	....	....	....	....	....	....	....	....	....	....	....	....	....	....
1998-99	Baton Rouge Kingfish	ECHL	25	9	9	4	1386	69	2	2.99	....	....	....	....	....	....	....	....	....	....	....	....	....	....	....	....	....
	Tucson Gila Monsters	WCHL	16	6	7	2	903	56	0	3.72	....	....	....	....	....	....	....	....	....	....	....	....	....	....	....	....	....
99-2000	Arkansas GlacierCats	WPHL	*65	31	20	9	*3652	225	1	3.70	....	....	....	....	....	6	3	3	....	372	31	1	5.00	....	....	....	....
	NHL Totals		**1**	**0**	**0**	**0**	**3**	**0**	**0**	**0.00**	....	....	**0**	**.000**	**0.0**	....	....	....	....	....	....	....	....	....	....	....	....

ECAC First All-Star Team (1992) • NCAA East Second All-American Team (1992) • ECAC Second All-Star Team (1993)

Signed as a free agent by **Chicago**, June 21, 1993.• Shares NHL record (w/ Robbie Irons) for having shortest career (three minutes) in league history.

• SPOONER, Red

Andrew George G – L. 5'8", 170 lbs. b: Port Arthur, Ont., 8/24/1910 d: 5/7/1984.

			REGULAR SEASON													PLAYOFFS											
Season	**Club**	**League**	**GP**	**W**	**L**	**T**	**Mins**	**GA**	**SO**	**Avg**	**AAvg**	**Eff**	**SA**	**S%**	**SAPG**	**GP**	**W**	**L**	**T**	**Mins**	**GA**	**SO**	**Avg**	**Eff**	**SA**	**S%**	**SAPG**
1926-27	Port Arthur Bruins	TBJHL	....	....	....	....	....	....	....	....	....	....	....	....	....	3	2	1	0	190	5	*1	*1.58	....	....	....	....
	Port Arthur Bearcats	TBSHL	1	....	....	....	60	2	0	2.00	....	....	....	....	....	....	....	....	....	....	....	....	....	....	....	....	....
	Port Arthur Bruins	Mem-Cup	6	3	3	0	370	19	0	3.08	....	....	....	....	....	....	....	....	....	....	....	....	....	....	....	....	....
1927-28	Port Arthur Bearcats	TBSHL	1	1	0	0	60	2	0	2.00	....	....	....	....	....	....	....	....	....	....	....	....	....	....	....	....	....
1928-29	Fort William Forts	TBSHL	STATISTICS NOT AVAILABLE																								
1929-30	Fort William Forts	TBSHL	STATISTICS NOT AVAILABLE																								
	Pittsburgh Pirates	**NHL**	**1**	**0**	**1**	**0**	**60**	**6**	**0**	**6.00**	**6.20**	....	....	....	....	....	....	....	....	....	....	....	....	....	....	....	....
1930-31	Port Arthur Ports	TBSHL	STATISTICS NOT AVAILABLE																								
1931-32	Port Arthur Ports	TBSHL	STATISTICS NOT AVAILABLE																								
1932-33	Port Arthur Ports	TBSHL	6	....	....	....	360	10	2	1.67	....	....	....	....	....	1	....	....	....	60	3	0	3.00	....	....	....	....
	NHL Totals		**1**	**0**	**1**	**0**	**60**	**6**	**0**	**6.00**	....	....	....	....	....	....	....	....	....	....	....	....	....	....	....	....	....

Loaned to **Pittsburgh** by **Fort William Forts** (TBSHL) to replace injured Joe Miller, January 18, 1930. (NY Rangers 6, Pittsburgh 5).

• SPRING, Jesse

G. 6', 185 lbs. b: Alba, PA, 1/18/1901 d: 3/25/1942.

Season	Club	League	GP	W	L	T	Mins	GA	SO	Avg	AAvg	Eff	SA	S%	SAPG	GP	W	L	T	Mins	GA	SO	Avg	Eff	SA	S%	SAPG
1924-25	**Hamilton Tigers**	**NHL**	**1**	**0**	**0**	**0**	**2**	**0**	**0**	**0.00**	**0.00**	....	....	....	....	....	....	....	....	....	....	....	....	....	....	....	....
	NHL Totals		**1**	**0**	**0**	**0**	**2**	**0**	**0**	**0.00**	....	....	....	....	....	....	....	....	....	....	....	....	....	....	....	....	....

• **Hamilton** defenseman replaced penalized Jake Forbes, February 14, 1925. (Toronto 3, Hamilton 1)

• STANIOWSKI, Ed

Edward Emile G – L. 5'9", 170 lbs. b: Moose Jaw, Sask., 7/7/1955. St. Louis' 1st, 27th overall in 1975.

Season	Club	League	GP	W	L	T	Mins	GA	SO	Avg	AAvg	Eff	SA	S%	SAPG	GP	W	L	T	Mins	GA	SO	Avg	Eff	SA	S%	SAPG
1970-71	Moose Jaw Canucks	SJHL	STATISTICS NOT AVAILABLE																								
1971-72	Regina Pat Blues	SJHL	STATISTICS NOT AVAILABLE																								
	Regina Pats	WCJHL	15	....	....	....	777	41	2	3.17	....	....	....	....	....	1	....	....	....	60	6	0	6.00	....	....	....	....
1972-73	Regina Pats	WCJHL	64	....	....	....	3768	236	0	3.76	....	....	....	....	....	4	....	....	....	240	17	0	4.25	....	....	....	....
1973-74	Regina Pats	WCJHL	62	*39	12	9	3629	185	2	3.06	....	....	....	....	....	16	....	....	....	965	47	1	2.92	....	....	....	....
	Regina Pats	Mem-Cup	3	*2	1	0	180	9	*1	*3.00	....	....	....	....	....	....	....	....	....	....	....	....	....	....	....	....	....
1974-75	Regina Pats	WCJHL	65	....	....	....	3898	255	2	3.95	....	....	....	....	....	11	....	....	....	673	39	0	3.48	....	....	....	....
	Canada	WJC-A	2	2	0	0	120	3	0	1.50	....	....	....	....	....	....	....	....	....	....	....	....	....	....	....	....	....
	New Westminster Bruins	Mem-Cup	DID NOT PLAY – SPARE GOALTENDER																								
1975-76	Providence Reds	AHL	29	15	11	1	1709	108	0	3.79	....	....	....	....	....	....	....	....	....	....	....	....	....	....	....	....	....
	St. Louis Blues	**NHL**	**11**	**5**	**3**	**2**	**620**	**33**	**0**	**3.19**	**2.89**	....	....	....	....	**3**	**1**	**2**	....	**206**	**7**	**0**	**2.04**	....	....	....	....
1976-77	Kansas City Blues	CHL	17	8	9	0	1008	59	2	3.51	....	....	....	....	....	....	....	....	....	....	....	....	....	....	....	....	....
	St. Louis Blues	**NHL**	**29**	**10**	**16**	**1**	**1589**	**108**	**0**	**4.08**	**3.81**	....	....	....	....	**3**	**0**	**2**	....	**102**	**9**	**0**	**5.29**	....	....	....	....
1977-78	**St. Louis Blues**	**NHL**	**17**	**1**	**10**	**2**	**886**	**57**	**0**	**3.86**	**3.63**	....	....	....	....	....	....	....	....	....	....	....	....	....	....	....	....
	Salt Lake Golden Eagles	CHL	31	18	13	0	1805	96	0	3.19	....	....	....	....	....	6	2	4	0	402	22	0	3.28	....	....	....	....
1978-79	**St. Louis Blues**	**NHL**	**39**	**9**	**25**	**3**	**2291**	**146**	**0**	**3.82**	**3.39**	....	....	....	....	....	....	....	....	....	....	....	....	....	....	....	....
	Salt Lake Golden Eagles	CHL	5	2	2	1	309	10	2	1.94	....	....	....	....	....	....	....	....	....	....	....	....	....	....	....	....	....
	Canada	WEC-A	3	1	1	0	160	19	0	7.12	....	....	....	....	....	....	....	....	....	....	....	....	....	....	....	....	....
1979-80	**St. Louis Blues**	**NHL**	**22**	**2**	**11**	**3**	**1108**	**80**	**0**	**4.33**	**3.84**	....	....	....	....	....	....	....	....	....	....	....	....	....	....	....	....
	Salt Lake Golden Eagles	CHL	4	3	1	0	239	6	0	1.51	....	....	....	....	....	....	....	....	....	....	....	....	....	....	....	....	....
1980-81	**St. Louis Blues**	**NHL**	**19**	**10**	**3**	**3**	**1010**	**72**	**0**	**4.28**	**3.46**	....	....	....	....	....	....	....	....	....	....	....	....	....	....	....	....
1981-82	**Winnipeg Jets**	**NHL**	**45**	**20**	**19**	**6**	**2643**	**174**	**1**	**3.95**	**3.05**	....	....	....	....	**2**	**0**	**2**	....	**120**	**12**	**0**	**6.00**	....	....	....	....
1982-83	**Winnipeg Jets**	**NHL**	**17**	**4**	**8**	**0**	**827**	**65**	**1**	**4.72**	**3.80**	**7.36**	**417**	**.844**	**30.3**	....	....	....	....	....	....	....	....	....	....	....	....
	Sherbrooke Jets	AHL	10	1	7	0	573	48	0	5.03	....	....	....	....	....	....	....	....	....	....	....	....	....	....	....	....	....
1983-84	**Winnipeg Jets**	**NHL**	**1**	**0**	**0**	**0**	**40**	**8**	**0**	**12.00**	**9.46**	**48.00**	**20**	**.600**	**30.0**	....	....	....	....	....	....	....	....	....	....	....	....
	Hartford Whalers	**NHL**	**18**	**6**	**9**	**1**	**1041**	**74**	**0**	**4.27**	**3.37**	**5.68**	**556**	**.867**	**32.0**	....	....	....	....	....	....	....	....	....	....	....	....
1984-85	**Hartford Whalers**	**NHL**	**1**	**0**	**0**	**0**	**20**	**1**	**0**	**3.00**	**2.39**	**3.00**	**10**	**.900**	**30.0**	....	....	....	....	....	....	....	....	....	....	....	....
	Binghamton Whalers	AHL	10	4	4	2	612	44	0	4.31	....	....	....	....	....	....	....	....	....	....	....	....	....	....	....	....	....
	Salt Lake Golden Eagles	IHL	9	4	5	0	538	33	0	3.68	....	....	....	....	....	5	1	4	0	265	17	0	3.85	....	....	....	....
	NHL Totals		**219**	**67**	**104**	**21**	**12075**	**818**	**2**	**4.06**	....	....	....	....	....	**8**	**1**	**6**	....	**428**	**28**	**0**	**3.93**	....	....	....	....

WCJHL First All-Star Team (1975) • Canadian Major Junior Player of the Year (1975) • Shared Terry Sawchuk Trophy (fewest goals against - CHL) with Doug Grant (1978)

Traded to **Winnipeg** by **St. Louis** with Bryan Maxwell and Paul MacLean for Scott Campbell and John Markell, July 3, 1981. Traded to **Hartford** by **Winnipeg** for Mike Veisor, November 10, 1983.

• STARR, Harold

Harold William "Twinkle" G. 5'11", 176 lbs. b: Ottawa, Ont., 7/6/1906 Deceased.

Season	Club	League	GP	W	L	T	Mins	GA	SO	Avg	AAvg	Eff	SA	S%	SAPG	GP	W	L	T	Mins	GA	SO	Avg	Eff	SA	S%	SAPG
1931-32	**Montreal Maroons**	**NHL**	**1**	**0**	**0**	**0**	**3**	**0**	**0**	**0.00**	**0.00**	....	....	....	....	....	....	....	....	....	....	....	....	....	....	....	....
	NHL Totals		**1**	**0**	**0**	**0**	**3**	**0**	**0**	**0.00**	....	....	....	....	....	....	....	....	....	....	....	....	....	....	....	....	....

• **Montreal Maroons'** defenseman replaced injured Norm Smith in 3rd period, January 2, 1933. (Montreal Canadiens 5, Montreal Maroons 1)

• STAUBER, Robb

Robert T. G – L. 5'11", 180 lbs. b: Duluth, MN, 11/25/1967. Los Angeles' 5th, 107th overall in 1986.

Season	Club	League	GP	W	L	T	Mins	GA	SO	Avg	AAvg	Eff	SA	S%	SAPG	GP	W	L	T	Mins	GA	SO	Avg	Eff	SA	S%	SAPG
1984-85	Duluth-Denfield Wildcats	Hi-School	22	....	....	....	990	27	0	1.70	....	....	....	....	....	....	....	....	....	....	....	....	....	....	....	....	....
1985-86	Duluth-Denfield Wildcats	Hi-School	27	....	....	....	1215	66	0	3.26	....	....	....	....	....	....	....	....	....	....	....	....	....	....	....	....	....
1986-87	University of Minnesota	WCHA	20	13	5	0	1072	63	0	3.53	....	....	....	....	....	....	....	....	....	....	....	....	....	....	....	....	....
	United States	WJC-A	4	....	....	....	220	17	....	4.64	....	....	....	....	....	....	....	....	....	....	....	....	....	....	....	....	....
1987-88	University of Minnesota	WCHA	44	34	10	0	2621	119	5	2.72	....	....	....	....	....	....	....	....	....	....	....	....	....	....	....	....	....
1988-89	University of Minnesota	WCHA	34	26	8	0	2024	82	0	2.43	....	....	....	....	....	....	....	....	....	....	....	....	....	....	....	....	....
	United States	WEC-A	6	3	3	0	313	19	0	3.64	....	....	....	....	....	....	....	....	....	....	....	....	....	....	....	....	....
1989-90	**Los Angeles Kings**	**NHL**	**2**	**0**	**1**	**0**	**83**	**11**	**0**	**7.95**	**6.74**	**20.34**	**43**	**.744**	**31.1**	....	....	....	....	....	....	....	....	....	....	....	....
	New Haven Nighthawks	AHL	14	6	6	2	851	43	0	3.03	....	....	....	....	....	5	2	3	....	302	24	0	4.77	....	....	....	....
1990-91	New Haven Nighthawks	AHL	33	13	16	4	1882	115	1	3.67	....	....	....	....	....	....	....	....	....	....	....	....	....	....	....	....	....
	Phoenix Roadrunners	IHL	4	1	2	0	160	11	0	4.13	....	....	....	....	....	....	....	....	....	....	....	....	....	....	....	....	....
1991-92	Phoenix Roadrunners	IHL	22	8	12	1	1242	80	0	3.86	....	....	....	....	....	....	....	....	....	....	....	....	....	....	....	....	....
1992-93	**Los Angeles Kings**	**NHL**	**31**	**15**	**8**	**4**	**1735**	**111**	**0**	**3.84**	**3.29**	**4.32**	**987**	**.888**	**34.1**	**4**	**3**	**1**	....	**240**	**16**	**0**	**4.00**	**4.08**	**157**	**.898**	**39.3**
1993-94	**Los Angeles Kings**	**NHL**	**22**	**4**	**11**	**5**	**1144**	**65**	**1**	**3.41**	**3.28**	**3.14**	**706**	**.908**	**37.0**	....	....	....	....	....	....	....	....	....	....	....	....
	Phoenix Roadrunners	IHL	3	1	1	0	121	13	0	6.42	....	....	....	....	....	....	....	....	....	....	....	....	....	....	....	....	....
1994-95	**Los Angeles Kings**	**NHL**	**1**	**0**	**0**	**0**	**16**	**2**	**0**	**7.50**	**7.86**	**25.00**	**6**	**.667**	**22.5**	....	....	....	....	....	....	....	....	....	....	....	....
	Buffalo Sabres	**NHL**	**6**	**2**	**3**	**0**	**317**	**20**	**0**	**3.79**	**3.97**	**5.05**	**150**	**.867**	**28.4**	....	....	....	....	....	....	....	....	....	....	....	....
1995-96	Rochester Americans	AHL	16	6	7	1	833	49	0	3.53	....	....	....	....	....	....	....	....	....	....	....	....	....	....	....	....	....
1996-97	Portland Pirates	AHL	30	13	13	2	1606	82	0	3.06	....	....	....	....	....	....	....	....	....	....	....	....	....	....	....	....	....
1997-98	Hartford Wolf Pack	AHL	39	20	10	6	2221	89	2	2.40	....	....	....	....	....	7	3	4	....	419	30	0	4.29	....	....	....	....
1998-99	Manitoba Moose	IHL	5	2	1	1	213	17	0	4.79	....	....	....	....	....	....	....	....	....	....	....	....	....	....	....	....	....
	NHL Totals		**62**	**21**	**23**	**9**	**3295**	**209**	**1**	**3.81**	....	....	**1892**	**.890**	**34.5**	**4**	**3**	**1**	....	**240**	**16**	**0**	**4.00**	....	**157**	**.898**	**39.3**

WCHA First All-Star Team (1988) • NCAA West First All-American Team (1988) • Won Hobey Baker Memorial Award (Top U.S. Collegiate Player) (1988) • WCHA Second All-Star Team (1989)

Traded to **Buffalo** by **Los Angeles** with Alexei Zhitnik, Charlie Huddy and Los Angeles' 5th round choice (Marian Menhart) in 1995 Entry Draft for Philippe Boucher, Denis Tsygurov and Grant Fuhr, February 14, 1995. Signed as a free agent by **Washington**, August 27, 1996. Signed as a free agent by **NY Rangers**, September 2, 1997. • Scored a goal while with Rochester (AHL), October 9, 1995.

• STEFAN, Greg

Gregory Steven G – L. 5'11", 180 lbs. b: Brantford, Ont., 2/11/1961. Detroit's 5th, 128th overall in 1981.

Season	Club	League	GP	W	L	T	Mins	GA	SO	Avg	AAvg	Eff	SA	S%	SAPG	GP	W	L	T	Mins	GA	SO	Avg	Eff	SA	S%	SAPG
1978-79	Oshawa Generals	OMJHL	33	....	....	....	1635	133	0	4.88	....	....	....	....	....	....	....	....	....	....	....	....	....	....	....	....	....
1979-80	Oshawa Generals	OMJHL	17	8	6	0	897	58	0	3.88	....	....	....	....	....	....	....	....	....	....	....	....	....	....	....	....	....
1980-81	Oshawa Generals	OMJHL	46	23	14	3	2407	174	0	4.34	....	....	....	....	....	6	2	3	0	298	20	0	4.02	....	....	....	....
1981-82	**Detroit Red Wings**	**NHL**	**2**	**0**	**2**	**0**	**120**	**10**	**0**	**5.00**	**3.86**	....	....	....	....	....	....	....	....	....	....	....	....	....	....	....	....
	Adirondack Red Wings	AHL	29	11	13	3	1571	99	2	3.78	....	....	....	....	....	1	0	0	0	20	0	0	0.00	....	....	....	....

Season	Club	League	REGULAR SEASON													PLAYOFFS											
			GP	W	L	T	Mins	GA	SO	Avg	AAvg	Eff	SA	S%	SAPG	GP	W	L	T	Mins	GA	SO	Avg	Eff	SA	S%	SAPG
1982-83	**Detroit Red Wings**	**NHL**	**35**	**6**	**16**	**9**	**1847**	**139**	**0**	**4.52**	**3.64**	**6.63**	**947**	**.853**	**30.8**	....	....	....	....	....	....	....	....	....	....	....	....
1983-84	**Detroit Red Wings**	**NHL**	**50**	**19**	**22**	**2**	**2600**	**152**	**2**	**3.51**	**2.76**	**4.36**	**1223**	**.876**	**28.2**	**3**	**1**	**2**	....	**210**	**8**	**0**	**2.29**	**2.13**	**86**	**.907**	**24.6**
1984-85	**Detroit Red Wings**	**NHL**	**46**	**21**	**19**	**3**	**2635**	**190**	**0**	**4.33**	**3.46**	**6.04**	**1361**	**.860**	**31.0**	**3**	**0**	**3**	....	**138**	**17**	**0**	**7.39**	**18.21**	**69**	**.754**	**30.0**
1985-86	**Detroit Red Wings**	**NHL**	**37**	**10**	**20**	**5**	**2068**	**155**	**1**	**4.50**	**3.53**	**6.46**	**1080**	**.856**	**31.3**	....	....	....	....	....	....	....	....	....	....	....	....
1986-87	**Detroit Red Wings**	**NHL**	**43**	**20**	**17**	**3**	**2351**	**135**	**1**	**3.45**	**2.92**	**4.30**	**1082**	**.875**	**27.6**	**9**	**4**	**5**	....	**508**	**24**	**0**	**2.83**	**2.70**	**252**	**.905**	**29.8**
1987-88	**Detroit Red Wings**	**NHL**	**33**	**17**	**9**	**5**	**1854**	**96**	**1**	**3.11**	**2.58**	**3.23**	**923**	**.896**	**29.9**	**10**	**5**	**4**	....	**531**	**32**	***1**	**3.62**	**4.91**	**236**	**.864**	**26.7**
1988-89	**Detroit Red Wings**	**NHL**	**46**	**21**	**17**	**3**	**2499**	**167**	**0**	**4.01**	**3.34**	**5.19**	**1290**	**.871**	**31.0**	**5**	**2**	**3**	....	**294**	**18**	**0**	**3.67**	**4.37**	**151**	**.881**	**30.8**
1989-90	**Detroit Red Wings**	**NHL**	**7**	**1**	**5**	**0**	**359**	**24**	**0**	**4.01**	**3.40**	**6.55**	**147**	**.837**	**24.6**	....	....	....	....	....	....	....	....	....	....	....	....
	Adirondack Red Wings	AHL	3	1	0	1	128	7	0	3.28	....	....	....	....	....	....	....	....	....	....	....	....	....	....	....	....	....
1990-91	Adirondack Red Wings	AHL	2	0	1	0	66	7	0	6.36	....	....	....	....	....	....	....	....	....	....	....	....	....	....	....	....	....
	NHL Totals		**299**	**115**	**127**	**30**	**16333**	**1068**	**5**	**3.92**	....	....	....	....	....	**30**	**12**	**17**	....	**1681**	**99**	**1**	**3.53**	....	**794**	**.875**	**28.3**

• Suffered eventual career-ending knee injury in game vs. Edmonton, November 25, 1989.

• STEIN, Phil

G – L. 5'11", b: Toronto, Ont., 9/13/1913.

Season	Club	League	GP	W	L	T	Mins	GA	SO	Avg	AAvg	Eff	SA	S%	SAPG	GP	W	L	T	Mins	GA	SO	Avg	Eff	SA	S%	SAPG
1930-31	Toronto Marlboros	OHA-Jr.	7	....	....	....	420	18	0	2.57	....	....	....	....	....	2	....	....	....	120	5	0	2.50	....	....	....	....
1931-32	Toronto Marlboros	OHA-Jr.	8	....	....	....	460	15	0	*1.96	....	....	....	....	....	4	....	....	....	240	4	1	1.00	....	....	....	....
1932-33	Toronto Marlboros	OHA-Jr.	9	....	....	....	540	6	*2	1.56	....	....	....	....	....	3	....	....	....	180	6	*1	2.00	....	....	....	....
1933-34	Syracuse Stars	IHL	23	....	....	....	1380	51	3	2.22	....	....	....	....	....	2	....	....	....	120	4	0	2.00	....	....	....	....
	Toronto Red Indians	TMHL	15	3	*11	1	920	68	0	4.34	....	....	....	....	....	....	....	....	....	....	....	....	....	....	....	....	....
1934-35	Syracuse Stars	IHL	36	15	17	4	2220	97	2	2.62	....	....	....	....	....	2	0	2	0	120	7	0	3.50	....	....	....	....
1935-36	Syracuse Stars	IHL	40	22	15	3	2480	105	3	2.54	....	....	....	....	....	3	0	3	0	180	8	0	2.67	....	....	....	....
1936-37	Syracuse Stars	IAHL	*50	*29	16	5	*3080	135	2	2.63	....	....	....	....	....	*9	*6	3	0	*540	15	*2	*1.66	....	....	....	....
1937-38	Syracuse Stars	IAHL	*48	21	20	7	*2970	122	3	2.46	....	....	....	....	....	*8	*5	3	0	612	23	0	2.25	....	....	....	....
1938-39	Syracuse Stars	IAHL	49	23	18	8	3030	109	6	2.16	....	....	....	....	....	3	1	2	0	180	6	0	2.00	....	....	....	....
1939-40	Omaha Knights	AHA	6	3	3	0	360	16	0	2.67	....	....	....	....	....	....	....	....	....	....	....	....	....	....	....	....	....
	Providence Reds	IAHL	19	10	5	4	1190	56	1	2.82	....	....	....	....	....	....	....	....	....	....	....	....	....	....	....	....	....
	Toronto Maple Leafs	**NHL**	**1**	**0**	**0**	**1**	**70**	**2**	**0**	**1.71**	**2.08**	....	....	....	....	....	....	....	....	....	....	....	....	....	....	....	....
1940-41	New Haven Eagles	AHL	53	26	21	6	3270	142	4	2.61	....	....	....	....	....	2	0	2	0	130	3	0	1.38	....	....	....	....
1941-42	New Haven Eagles	AHL	54	26	24	4	3330	204	2	3.68	....	....	....	....	....	2	0	2	0	120	4	0	2.00	....	....	....	....
1942-43	Toronto Research Colonels	TIHL	8	2	6	0	490	57	0	6.98	....	....	....	....	....	....	....	....	....	....	....	....	....	....	....	....	....
	Toronto Staffords	TMHL	7	4	2	1	420	19	0	2.71	....	....	....	....	....	5	0	4	1	320	22	0	4.13	....	....	....	....
	NHL Totals		**1**	**0**	**0**	**1**	**70**	**2**	**0**	**1.71**	....	....	....	....	....	....	....	....	....	....	....	....	....	....	....	....	....

Signed as a free agent by **Toronto**, October 30, 1934. Promoted to **Toronto** from **Providence** (IAHL) to replace injured Turk Broda, January 18, 1940. (NY Americans 2, Toronto 2). Traded to **New Haven** (AHL) by **Toronto** for cash, October 22, 1940.

• STEPHENSON, Wayne

Wayne Frederick G – L. 5'9", 175 lbs. b: Fort William, Ont., 1/29/1945.

Season	Club	League	GP	W	L	T	Mins	GA	SO	Avg	AAvg	Eff	SA	S%	SAPG	GP	W	L	T	Mins	GA	SO	Avg	Eff	SA	S%	SAPG
1963-64	Winnipeg Braves	MJHL	29	11	*15	3	1804	120	0	3.99	....	....	....	....	....	....	....	....	....	....	....	....	....	....	....	....	....
1964-65	Winnipeg Braves	MJHL	43	*26	12	5	2580	128	*2	*2.97	....	....	....	....	....	4	*4	0	0	240	12	0	3.00	....	....	....	....
	Edmonton Oil Kings	Mem-Cup	5	1	4	0	300	25	0	5.00	....	....	....	....	....	....	....	....	....	....	....	....	....	....	....	....	....
1965-66	Canada	Nat-Team	STATISTICS NOT AVAILABLE																								
1966-67	Canada	Nat-Team	STATISTICS NOT AVAILABLE																								
	Canada	WEC-A	1	1	0	0	60	1	0	1.00	....	....	....	....	....	....	....	....	....	....	....	....	....	....	....	....	....
1967-68	Winnipeg Nats	WCSHL	15	....	....	....	900	30	1	2.11	....	....	....	....	....	....	....	....	....	....	....	....	....	....	....	....	....
	Canada	Olympics	3	2	0	0	140	3	1	1.29	....	....	....	....	....	....	....	....	....	....	....	....	....	....	....	....	....
1968-69	Canada	Nat-Team	STATISTICS NOT AVAILABLE																								
	Canada	WEC-A	8	3	5	0	480	27	1	3.38	....	....	....	....	....	....	....	....	....	....	....	....	....	....	....	....	....
1969-70	Canada	Nat-Team	STATISTICS NOT AVAILABLE																								
1970-71	Canada	Nat-Team	STATISTICS NOT AVAILABLE																								
1971-72	Kansas City Blues	CHL	21	5	11	4	1210	80	0	3.93	....	....	....	....	....	....	....	....	....	....	....	....	....	....	....	....	....
	St. Louis Blues	**NHL**	**2**	**0**	**1**	**0**	**100**	**9**	**0**	**5.40**	**5.47**	....	....	....	....	....	....	....	....	....	....	....	....	....	....	....	....
1972-73	**St. Louis Blues**	**NHL**	**45**	**18**	**15**	**7**	**2535**	**128**	**1**	**3.03**	**2.85**	....	....	....	....	**3**	**1**	**2**	....	**160**	**14**	**0**	**5.25**	....	....	....	....
1973-74	**St. Louis Blues**	**NHL**	**40**	**13**	**21**	**5**	**2360**	**123**	**2**	**3.13**	**3.02**	....	....	....	....	....	....	....	....	....	....	....	....	....	....	....	....
1974-75♦	**Philadelphia Flyers**	**NHL**	**12**	**7**	**2**	**1**	**639**	**29**	**1**	**2.72**	**2.45**	....	....	....	....	**2**	**2**	**0**	....	**123**	**4**	**1**	**1.95**	....	....	....	....
1975-76	**Philadelphia Flyers**	**NHL**	**66**	**40**	**10**	**13**	**3819**	**164**	**1**	**2.58**	**2.31**	....	....	....	....	**8**	**4**	**4**	....	**494**	**22**	**0**	**2.67**	....	....	....	....
1976-77	**Philadelphia Flyers**	**NHL**	**21**	**12**	**3**	**2**	**1065**	**41**	**3**	**2.31**	**2.14**	....	....	....	....	**9**	**4**	**3**	....	**532**	**23**	**1**	**2.59**	....	....	....	....
1977-78	**Philadelphia Flyers**	**NHL**	**26**	**14**	**10**	**1**	**1482**	**68**	**3**	**2.75**	**2.57**	....	....	....	....	....	....	....	....	....	....	....	....	....	....	....	....
1978-79	**Philadelphia Flyers**	**NHL**	**40**	**20**	**10**	**5**	**2187**	**122**	**2**	**3.35**	**2.96**	....	....	....	....	**4**	**0**	**3**	....	**213**	**16**	**0**	**4.51**	....	....	....	....
1979-80	**Washington Capitals**	**NHL**	**56**	**18**	**24**	**10**	**3146**	**187**	**0**	**3.57**	**3.16**	....	....	....	....	....	....	....	....	....	....	....	....	....	....	....	....
1980-81	Washington Capitals	DN-Cup	2	1	0	0	89	2	0	1.34	....	....	....	....	....	....	....	....	....	....	....	....	....	....	....	....	....
	Washington Capitals	**NHL**	**20**	**4**	**7**	**5**	**1010**	**66**	**1**	**3.92**	**3.17**	....	....	....	....	....	....	....	....	....	....	....	....	....	....	....	....
	NHL Totals		**328**	**146**	**103**	**49**	**18343**	**937**	**14**	**3.06**	....	....	....	....	....	**26**	**11**	**12**	....	**1522**	**79**	**2**	**3.11**	....	....	....	....

Played in NHL All-Star Game (1976, 1978)

Signed as a free agent by **St. Louis**, January 2, 1972. Traded to **Philadelphia** by **St. Louis** for rights to Randy Andreachuk and Philadelphia's 2nd round choice (Jamie Masters) in 1975 Amateur Draft, September 16, 1974. Traded to **Washington** by **Philadelphia** for Washington's 3rd round choice (Barry Tabobondung) in 1981 Entry Draft, August 16, 1979.

• STEVENSON, Doug

G – L. 5'8", 170 lbs. b: Regina, Sask., 4/6/1924.

Season	Club	League	GP	W	L	T	Mins	GA	SO	Avg	AAvg	Eff	SA	S%	SAPG	GP	W	L	T	Mins	GA	SO	Avg	Eff	SA	S%	SAPG
1941-42	Edmonton Athletic Club	EJrHL	11	....	....	....	660	44	*1	4.00	....	....	....	....	....	....	....	....	....	....	....	....	....	....	....	....	....
	Edmonton Maple Leafs	Mem-Cup	3	1	2	0	150	20	1	8.00	....	....	....	....	....	....	....	....	....	....	....	....	....	....	....	....	....
1942-43	**Chicago Black Hawks**	**NHL**	DID NOT PLAY – SPARE GOALTENDER																								
1943-44	Kingston Frontenacs	OHA-Sr.	2	1	1	0	130	12	0	5.54	....	....	....	....	....	....	....	....	....	....	....	....	....	....	....	....	....
1944-45	**New York Rangers**	**NHL**	**4**	**0**	**4**	**0**	**240**	**20**	**0**	**5.00**	**4.16**	....	....	....	....	....	....	....	....	....	....	....	....	....	....	....	....
	New York Rovers	EAHL	20	....	....	....	1200	99	0	4.95	....	....	....	....	....	6	....	....	....	360	31	0	5.17	....	....	....	....
	Chicago Black Hawks	**NHL**	**2**	**1**	**1**	**0**	**120**	**7**	**0**	**3.50**	**2.90**	....	....	....	....	....	....	....	....	....	....	....	....	....	....	....	....
1945-46	**Chicago Black Hawks**	**NHL**	**2**	**1**	**1**	**0**	**120**	**12**	**0**	**6.00**	**5.50**	....	....	....	....	....	....	....	....	....	....	....	....	....	....	....	....
	Kansas City Pla-Mors	USHL	52	....	....	....	3120	169	2	3.25	....	....	....	....	....	....	....	....	....	....	....	....	....	....	....	....	....
	St. Paul Saints	USHL	4	....	....	....	240	13	0	3.25	....	....	....	....	....	....	....	....	....	....	....	....	....	....	....	....	....
1946-47	St. Paul Saints	USHL	28	....	....	....	1680	114	2	4.07	....	....	....	....	....	....	....	....	....	....	....	....	....	....	....	....	....
	New Haven Ramblers	AHL	1	0	0	0	20	1	0	3.00	....	....	....	....	....	....	....	....	....	....	....	....	....	....	....	....	....
1947-48	St. Paul Saints	USHL	3	1	2	0	180	9	0	3.00	....	....	....	....	....	....	....	....	....	....	....	....	....	....	....	....	....
	New Haven Ramblers	AHL	39	18	17	4	2340	154	0	3.95	....	....	....	....	....	4	2	2	0	240	11	0	2.75	....	....	....	....
1948-49	Tacoma Rockets	PCHL	59	27	27	5	3540	216	0	3.66	....	....	....	....	....	6	3	3	0	384	21	1	3.28	....	....	....	....
1949-50	Tacoma Rockets	PCHL	70	*34	27	9	4200	238	4	3.40	....	....	....	....	....	5	2	3	0	310	12	0	2.32	....	....	....	....
1950-51	Tacoma Rockets	PCHL	70	27	26	17	4200	219	4	3.12	....	....	....	....	....	6	2	4	0	366	16	1	2.62	....	....	....	....
1951-52	Tacoma Rockets	PCHL	70	34	25	11	4200	236	1	3.37	....	....	....	....	....	7	3	4	0	452	28	0	3.72	....	....	....	....
1952-53	Tacoma Rockets	WHL	68	27	29	12	4080	231	4	3.40	....	....	....	....	....	....	....	....	....	....	....	....	....	....	....	....	....
	Seattle Bombers	WHL	....	....	....	....	....	....	....	....	....	....	....	....	....	1	0	1	0	60	6	0	6.00	....	....	....	....
1953-54	Seattle Bombers	WHL	2	0	2	0	120	7	0	3.50	....	....	....	....	....	....	....	....	....	....	....	....	....	....	....	....	....
	Kelowna Packers	OSHL	26	....	....	....	1560	91	0	3.50	....	....	....	....	....	8	4	4	0	480	31	0	3.87	....	....	....	....
1954-55	Saskatoon Quakers	WHL	23	5	14	4	1380	85	2	3.70	....	....	....	....	....	....	....	....	....	....	....	....	....	....	....	....	....
	Kamloops Chiefs	OSHL	8	....	....	....	480	29	0	3.62	....	....	....	....	....	....	....	....	....	....	....	....	....	....	....	....	....
	Vancouver Canucks	WHL	1	1	0	0	60	3	0	3.00	....	....	....	....	....	....	....	....	....	....	....	....	....	....	....	....	....
	Calgary Stampeders	WHL	32	11	15	6	1920	121	0	3.78	....	....	....	....	....	9	4	5	0	546	25	*1	2.75	....	....	....	....

Season	Club	League	REGULAR SEASON GP	W	L	T	Mins	GA	SO	Avg	AAvg	Eff	SA	S%	SAPG	PLAYOFFS GP	W	L	T	Mins	GA	SO	Avg	Eff	SA	S%	SAPG
1955-56	Brandon Regals	WHL	2	0	2	0	128	8	0	3.75	....	....	....	....	....	....	....	....	....	....	....	....	....	....	....	....	....
	Saskatoon Quakers	WHL	2	0	2	0	120	10	0	5.00	....	....	....	....	....	....	....	....	....	....	....	....	....	....	....	....	....
	Edmonton Flyers	WHL	2	0	1	1	130	9	0	4.15	....	....	....	....	....	....	....	....	....	....	....	....	....	....	....	....	....
	Calgary Stampeders	WHL	10	6	4	0	603	39	1	3.88	....	....	....	....	....	....	....	....	....	....	....	....	....	....	....	....	....
	NHL Totals		**8**	**2**	**6**	**0**	**480**	**39**	**0**	**4.88**	....	....	....	....	....	....	....	....	....	....	....	....	....	....	....	....	....

PCHL Northern Second All-Star Team (1950) • PCHL Second All-Star Team (1951)

Signed as a free agent by **Chicago**, October, 1942. Loaned to **Chicago** by **NY Rangers** to replace injured Mike Karakas, March 17, 1945. (Montreal 4, Chicago 3)

• STEWART, Charles

Charles Elmer "Doc" G – L. 5'7", 140 lbs. b: Carleton Place, Ont., 11/13/1895.

Season	Club	League	GP	W	L	T	Mins	GA	SO	Avg	AAvg	Eff	SA	S%	SAPG	GP	W	L	T	Mins	GA	SO	Avg	Eff	SA	S%	SAPG
1912-13	Kingston Collegiate Institute	OHA-Jr.	STATISTICS NOT AVAILABLE																								
1913-14	Kingston Collegiate Institute	OHA-Jr.	6	4	2	0	360	40	0	6.67	....	....	....	....	....	....	....	....	....	....	....	....	....	....	....	....	....
1914-15	Kingston Frontenacs	OHA-Sr.	STATISTICS NOT AVAILABLE																								
1915-16	Toronto Argonauts	OHA-Sr.	3	2	1	0	180	8	0	2.67	....	....	....	....	....	2	0	1	1	112	7	0	3.75	....	....	....	....
1916-17	Toronto Dentals	OHA-Sr.	10	*7	2	1	620	26	*2	*2.52	....	....	....	....	....	4	*4	0	0	280	8	0	*1.71	....	....	....	....
1917-18	Toronto Dentals	OHA-Sr.	9	*9	0	0	540	35	0	*3.89	....	....	....	....	....	2	0	1	1	118	7	0	3.56	....	....	....	....
1918-19	Toronto Dentals	OHA-Sr.	7	5	2	0	420	27	0	*3.86	....	....	....	....	....	2	1	1	0	120	6	0	*3.00	....	....	....	....
1919-20	Toronto Dentals	OHA-Sr.	6	3	3	0	390	24	0	3.69	....	....	....	....	....	....	....	....	....	....	....	....	....	....	....	....	....
1920-21	Toronto Aura Lee	OHA-Sr.	9	3	5	0	529	22	1	2.50	....	....	....	....	....	....	....	....	....	....	....	....	....	....	....	....	....
1921-22	Hamilton Tigers	OHA-Sr.	9	4	4	1	570	34	0	3.56	....	....	....	....	....	....	....	....	....	....	....	....	....	....	....	....	....
1922-23	Hamilton Tigers	OHA-Sr.	12	*9	2	0	699	28	1	2.40	....	....	....	....	....	2	0	1	1	120	6	0	3.00	....	....	....	....
1923-24	Hamilton Tigers	OHA-Sr.	10	*9	1	0	620	26	0	*2.52	....	....	....	....	....	6	4	2	0	358	16	0	2.68	....	....	....	....
1924-25	**Boston Bruins**	**NHL**	**21**	**5**	**16**	**0**	**1266**	**65**	**2**	**3.08**	**3.87**	....	....	....	....	....	....	....	....	....	....	....	....	....	....	....	....
1925-26	**Boston Bruins**	**NHL**	**35**	**16**	**14**	**4**	**2173**	**80**	**6**	**2.21**	**2.90**	....	....	....	....	....	....	....	....	....	....	....	....	....	....	....	....
1926-27	**Boston Bruins**	**NHL**	**21**	**9**	**11**	**1**	**1303**	**49**	**2**	**2.26**	**3.47**	....	....	....	....	....	....	....	....	....	....	....	....	....	....	....	....
	Hamilton Tigers	Can-Pro	9	4	4	1	541	16	1	1.77	....	....	....	....	....	1	0	0	0	30	5	0	10.00	....	....	....	....
	NHL Totals		**77**	**30**	**41**	**5**	**4742**	**194**	**10**	**2.45**	....	....	....	....	....	....	....	....	....	....	....	....	....	....	....	....	....

OHA-Sr. Second All-Star Team (1918) • OHA-Sr. First All-Star Team (1919, 1922, 1923, 1924)

Signed as a free agent by **Boston**, December 25, 1924. Loaned to **Hamilton** (Can-Pro) by **Boston**, January 28, 1927.

• STEWART, Jim

G – L. 5'11", 170 lbs. b: Cambridge, MA, 4/23/1957.

Season	Club	League	GP	W	L	T	Mins	GA	SO	Avg	AAvg	Eff	SA	S%	SAPG	GP	W	L	T	Mins	GA	SO	Avg	Eff	SA	S%	SAPG
1976-77	South Shore Whalers	NEJHL	44	....	....	....	2336	156	1	4.01	....	....	....	....	....	....	....	....	....	....	....	....	....	....	....	....	....
1977-78	Holy Cross College	ECAC-2	15	10	5	0	905	51	....	3.37	....	....	....	....	....	....	....	....	....	....	....	....	....	....	....	....	....
	Cape Cod Freedoms	NEHL	1	0	1	0	60	6	0	6.00	....	....	....	....	....	....	....	....	....	....	....	....	....	....	....	....	....
1978-79	Holy Cross College	ECAC-2	5	1	4	0	316	22	....	4.19	....	....	....	....	....	....	....	....	....	....	....	....	....	....	....	....	....
1979-80	**Boston Bruins**	**NHL**	**1**	**0**	**1**	**0**	**20**	**5**	**0**	**15.00**	**13.27**	....	....	....	....	....	....	....	....	....	....	....	....	....	....	....	....
	Binghamton Dusters	AHL	13	4	6	2	690	46	0	4.00	....	....	....	....	....	....	....	....	....	....	....	....	....	....	....	....	....
	Utica Mohawks	EHL	30	....	....	....	1673	122	3	4.38	....	....	....	....	....	2	0	1	0	80	12	0	9.00	....	....	....	....
1980-81	Springfield Indians	AHL	3	0	3	0	180	14	0	4.67	....	....	....	....	....	....	....	....	....	....	....	....	....	....	....	....	....
	Indianapolis Checkers	CHL	3	1	1	0	140	11	1	4.71	....	....	....	....	....	....	....	....	....	....	....	....	....	....	....	....	....
	Salem Raiders	EHL	16	....	....	....	892	69	0	4.64	....	....	....	....	....	....	....	....	....	....	....	....	....	....	....	....	....
	Saginaw Gears	IHL	3	....	....	....	153	16	0	6.27	....	....	....	....	....	....	....	....	....	....	....	....	....	....	....	....	....
1981-82	Binghamton Whalers	AHL	4	1	3	0	240	17	0	4.25	....	....	....	....	....	1	0	0	0	9	1	0	6.67	....	....	....	....
	Nashville South Stars	CHL	3	1	1	0	110	8	0	4.37	....	....	....	....	....	....	....	....	....	....	....	....	....	....	....	....	....
	Cape Cod Buccaneers	ACHL	26	....	....	....	1410	98	0	4.17	....	....	....	....	....	....	....	....	....	....	....	....	....	....	....	....	....
	Baltimore Skipjacks	ACHL	7	....	....	....	370	16	0	2.59	....	....	....	....	....	7	....	....	....	392	36	0	5.51	....	....	....	....
	NHL Totals		**1**	**0**	**1**	**0**	**20**	**5**	**0**	**15.00**	....	....	....	....	....	....	....	....	....	....	....	....	....	....	....	....	....

NCAA (College Div.) East All-American Team (1978) • ACHL First All-Star Team (1982)

Signed as a free agent by **Boston**, September, 1979.

• STORR, Jamie

G – L. 6'2", 195 lbs. b: Brampton, Ont., 12/28/1975. Los Angeles' 1st, 7th overall in 1994.

Season	Club	League	GP	W	L	T	Mins	GA	SO	Avg	AAvg	Eff	SA	S%	SAPG	GP	W	L	T	Mins	GA	SO	Avg	Eff	SA	S%	SAPG
1990-91	Brampton Capitals	OJHL-B	24	....	....	....	1145	91	0	4.77	....	....	....	....	....	15	....	....	....	885	60	0	4.07	....	....	....	....
1991-92	Owen Sound Platers	OHL	34	11	16	1	1732	128	0	4.43	....	....	....	....	....	5	1	4	....	299	28	0	5.62	....	....	....	....
1992-93	Owen Sound Platers	OHL	41	20	17	3	2362	180	0	4.57	....	....	....	....	....	8	4	4	....	454	35	0	4.63	....	....	....	....
1993-94	Owen Sound Platers	OHL	35	21	11	1	2004	120	1	3.59	....	....	....	....	....	9	4	5	....	547	44	0	4.83	....	....	....	....
	Canada	WJC-A	4	....	....	....	240	10	....	2.50																	
	Canada	WC-A	DID NOT PLAY – SPARE GOALTENDER																								
1994-95	Owen Sound Platers	OHL	17	5	9	2	977	64	0	3.93	....	....	....	....	....	....	....	....	....	....	....	....	....	....	....	....	....
	Canada	WJC-A	4	....	....	....	240	14	....	3.50	....	....	....	....	....	....	....	....	....	....	....	....	....	....	....	....	....
	Los Angeles Kings	**NHL**	**5**	**1**	**3**	**1**	**263**	**17**	**0**	**3.88**	**4.07**	**4.34**	**152**	**.888**	**34.7**	....	....	....	....	....	....	....	....	....	....	....	....
	Windsor Spitfires	OHL	4	3	1	0	241	8	1	1.99	....	....	....	....	....	10	6	3	....	520	34	1	3.92	....	....	....	....
1995-96	**Los Angeles Kings**	**NHL**	**5**	**3**	**1**	**0**	**262**	**12**	**0**	**2.75**	**2.73**	**2.24**	**147**	**.918**	**33.7**	....	....	....	....	....	....	....	....	....	....	....	....
	Phoenix Roadrunners	IHL	48	22	20	4	2711	139	2	3.08	....	....	....	....	....	2	1	1	....	118	4	1	2.03	....	....	....	....
1996-97	**Los Angeles Kings**	**NHL**	**5**	**2**	**1**	**1**	**265**	**11**	**0**	**2.49**	**2.68**	**1.86**	**147**	**.925**	**33.3**	....	....	....	....	....	....	....	....	....	....	....	....
	Phoenix Roadrunners	IHL	44	16	22	4	2441	147	0	3.61	....	....	....	....	....	....	....	....	....	....	....	....	....	....	....	....	....
1997-98	**Los Angeles Kings**	**NHL**	**17**	**9**	**5**	**1**	**920**	**34**	**2**	**2.22**	**2.64**	**1.57**	**482**	**.929**	**31.4**	**3**	**0**	**2**	....	**145**	**9**	**0**	**3.72**	**4.35**	**77**	**.883**	**31.9**
	Long Beach Ice Dogs	IHL	11	7	2	1	629	31	0	2.96	....	....	....	....	....	....	....	....	....	....	....	....	....	....	....	....	....
1998-99	**Los Angeles Kings**	**NHL**	**28**	**12**	**12**	**2**	**1525**	**61**	**4**	**2.40**	**2.85**	**2.02**	**724**	**.916**	**28.5**	....	....	....	....	....	....	....	....	....	....	....	....
99-2000	**Los Angeles Kings**	**NHL**	**42**	**18**	**15**	**5**	**2206**	**93**	**1**	**2.53**	**2.89**	**2.33**	**1008**	**.908**	**27.4**	**1**	**0**	**1**	....	**36**	**2**	**0**	**3.33**	**2.66**	**25**	**.920**	**41.7**
	NHL Totals		**102**	**45**	**37**	**10**	**5441**	**228**	**7**	**2.51**	....	....	**2660**	**.914**	**29.3**	**4**	**0**	**3**	....	**181**	**11**	**0**	**3.65**	....	**102**	**.892**	**33.8**

Named Best Goaltender at WJC-A (1994) • OHL First All-Star Team (1994) • NHL All-Rookie Team (1998, 1999)

• STUART, Herb

Herbert Neville G – L. 5'6", 175 lbs. b: Brantford, Ont., 3/30/1899 Deceased.

Season	Club	League	GP	W	L	T	Mins	GA	SO	Avg	AAvg	Eff	SA	S%	SAPG	GP	W	L	T	Mins	GA	SO	Avg	Eff	SA	S%	SAPG
1916-17	Brantford Alexanders	OHA-Jr.	4	3	1	0	240	15	0	3.75	....	....	....	....	....	2	0	1	1	120	7	0	3.50	....	....	....	....
1917-18	Paris AAA	OHA-Jr.	5	*5	0	0	300	11	0	2.20	....	....	....	....	....	2	1	1	0	120	14	0	7.00	....	....	....	....
1918-19	Paris AAA	OHA-Jr.	STATISTICS NOT AVAILABLE																								
1919-20	Brandon Elks	MHL-Sr.	2	0	2	0	120	18	0	9.00	....	....	....	....	....	....	....	....	....	....	....	....	....	....	....	....	....
	Brandon Elks	Al-Cup	5	4	1	0	300	19	2	3.80	....	....	....	....	....	....	....	....	....	....	....	....	....	....	....	....	....
1920-21	Brandon Elks	MHL-Sr.	11	7	4	0	660	47	0	4.27	....	....	....	....	....	....	....	....	....	....	....	....	....	....	....	....	....
	Brandon Elks	Al-Cup	4	3	1	0	240	16	0	4.00	....	....	....	....	....	....	....	....	....	....	....	....	....	....	....	....	....
1921-22	Brandon Elks	MHL-Sr.	12	9	3	0	720	55	0	4.58	....	....	....	....	....	2	2	0	0	120	5	0	2.50	....	....	....	....
1922-23	Brandon Elks	MHL-Sr.	16	9	7	0	960	57	0	3.56	....	....	....	....	....	....	....	....	....	....	....	....	....	....	....	....	....
1923-24	Brandon Elks	MHL-Sr.	12	9	3	0	720	36	*1	3.00	....	....	....	....	....	4	1	2	1	240	7	1	1.75	....	....	....	....
1924-25	Edmonton Eskimos	WCHL	17	7	9	1	1060	68	1	3.85	....	....	....	....	....	....	....	....	....	....	....	....	....	....	....	....	....
1925-26	Edmonton Eskimos	WHL	*30	*19	11	0	1800	77	2	2.57	....	....	....	....	....	2	0	1	1	120	5	0	2.50	....	....	....	....
1926-27	**Detroit Cougars**	**NHL**	**3**	**1**	**2**	**0**	**180**	**5**	**0**	**1.67**	**2.54**	....	....	....	....	....	....	....	....	....	....	....	....	....	....	....	....
1927-28	Detroit Olympics	Can-Pro	41	24	13	4	2540	73	2	1.72	....	....	....	....	....	2	1	1	0	120	4	0	2.00	....	....	....	....
1928-29	Detroit Olympics	Can-Pro	42	*27	10	5	2750	67	*11	*1.56	....	....	....	....	....	7	4	3	0	420	14	2	1.83	....	....	....	....
1929-30	Detroit Olympics	IHL	42	....	....	....	2520	74	7	1.76	....	....	....	....	....	3	....	....	....	180	7	0	2.33	....	....	....	....
1930-31	London Tecumsehs	IHL	48	21	21	6	3010	83	12	1.65	....	....	....	....	....	....	....	....	....	....	....	....	....	....	....	....	....
1931-32	London Tecumsehs	IHL	48	21	15	12	2880	70	*13	*1.46	....	....	....	....	....	6	1	2	3	360	10	*3	1.67	....	....	....	....
1932-33	London Tecumsehs	IHL	44	*27	9	8	2640	66	*12	*1.46	....	....	....	....	....	6	2	3	1	360	11	1	1.83	....	....	....	....

			REGULAR SEASON													PLAYOFFS											
Season	Club	League	GP	W	L	T	Mins	GA	SO	Avg	AAvg	Eff	SA	S%	SAPG	GP	W	L	T	Mins	GA	SO	Avg	Eff	SA	S%	SAPG
1933-34	Syracuse Stars	IHL	2	....	....	....	120	4	0	2.00	....	....	....	....	....	....	....	....	....	....	....	....	....	....	....	....	....
	London Tecumsehs	IHL	44	18	17	9	2640	80	6	1.81	....	....	....	....	....	6	5	1	0	360	9	*1	*1.50	....	....	....	....
1934-35	London Tecumsehs	IHL	36	17	14	5	2230	90	4	2.42	....	....	....	....	....	....	....	....	....	....	....	....	....	....	....	....	....
1935-36	London Tecumsehs	IHL	48	23	22	3	2950	125	3	2.54	....	....	....	....	....	2	0	1	1	130	4	0	1.85	....	....	....	....
	NHL Totals		**3**	**1**	**2**	**0**	**180**	**5**	**0**	**1.67**	....	....	....	....	....	....	....	....	....	....	....	....	....	....	....	....	....
	Other Major League Totals		47	26	20	1	2860	145	3	3.04	....	....	....	....	....	2	0	1	....	120	5	0	2.50	....	....	....	....

IHL First All-Star Team (1930) • IHL Second All-Star Team (1935)

Signed as a free agent by **Edmonton** (WCHL), November 13, 1924. Traded to **Detroit** by **Edmonton** (WHL) for cash, October 5, 1926. Traded to **London** (IHL) by **Detroit** for cash, November 10, 1930.

• SYLVESTRI, Don

G – L. 6', 180 lbs. b: Sudbury, Ont., 6/2/1961. Boston's 8th, 182nd overall in 1981.

Season	Club	League	GP	W	L	T	Mins	GA	SO	Avg	AAvg	Eff	SA	S%	SAPG	GP	W	L	T	Mins	GA	SO	Avg	Eff	SA	S%	SAPG
1978-79	Nickel Centre Native Sons	NOJHA	30	....	....	....	1800	100	*2	2.99	....	....	....	....	....	....	....	....	....	....	....	....	....	....	....	....	....
1979-80	Nickel Centre Native Sons	NOJHA	5	....	....	....	250	22	0	5.28	....	....	....	....	....	....	....	....	....	....	....	....	....	....	....	....	....
	Oshawa Generals	OMJHL	16	5	4	0	621	49	0	4.73	....	....	....	....	....	....	....	....	....	....	....	....	....	....	....	....	....
1980-81	Clarkson College	ECAC	29	22	3	4	1740	84	1	2.90	....	....	....	....	....	....	....	....	....	....	....	....	....	....	....	....	....
1981-82	Clarkson College	ECAC	30	22	6	1	1800	87	2	2.90	....	....	....	....	....	....	....	....	....	....	....	....	....	....	....	....	....
1982-83	Clarkson College	ECAC	11	3	3	1	425	23	0	3.25	....	....	....	....	....	....	....	....	....	....	....	....	....	....	....	....	....
1983-84	Clarkson College	ECAC	16	5	4	0	611	31	1	3.04	....	....	....	....	....	....	....	....	....	....	....	....	....	....	....	....	....
1984-85	**Boston Bruins**	**NHL**	**3**	**0**	**0**	**2**	**102**	**6**	**0**	**3.53**	**2.81**	**4.07**	**52**	**.885**	**30.6**	....	....	....	....	....	....	....	....	....	....	....	....
	Indianapolis Checkers	IHL	14	5	7	0	676	57	0	5.06	....	....	....	....	....	....	....	....	....	....	....	....	....	....	....	....	....
	Pinebridge Bucks	ACHL	6	....	....	....	360	28	0	5.85	....	....	....	....	....	....	....	....	....	....	....	....	....	....	....	....	....
	NHL Totals		**3**	**0**	**0**	**2**	**102**	**6**	**0**	**3.53**	....	....	**52**	**.885**	**30.6**	....	....	....	....	....	....	....	....	....	....	....	....

ECAC First All-Star Team (1981) • NCAA East First All-American Team (1981)

• TABARACCI, Rick

G – L. 6'1", 190 lbs. b: Toronto, Ont., 1/2/1969. Pittsburgh's 2nd, 26th overall in 1987.

Season	Club	League	GP	W	L	T	Mins	GA	SO	Avg	AAvg	Eff	SA	S%	SAPG	GP	W	L	T	Mins	GA	SO	Avg	Eff	SA	S%	SAPG
1985-86	Markham Waxers	OJHL	40	19	11	6	2176	188	1	5.18	....	....	....	....	....	....	....	....	....	....	....	....	....	....	....	....	....
1986-87	Cornwall Royals	OHL	*59	23	32	3	*3347	290	1	5.20	....	....	....	....	....	5	1	4	....	303	26	0	3.17	....	....	....	....
1987-88	Cornwall Royals	OHL	58	*33	18	6	3448	200	*3	3.48	....	....	....	....	....	11	5	6	....	642	37	0	3.46	....	....	....	....
	Muskegon Lumberjacks	IHL	....	....	....	....	....	....	....	....	....	....	....	....	....	1	0	0	....	13	1	0	4.62	....	....	....	....
1988-89	**Pittsburgh Penguins**	**NHL**	**1**	**0**	**0**	**0**	**33**	**4**	**0**	**7.27**	**6.05**	**13.85**	**21**	**.810**	**38.2**	....	....	....	....	....	....	....	....	....	....	....	....
	Cornwall Royals	OHL	50	24	20	5	2974	210	1	4.24	....	....	....	....	....	18	10	8	....	1080	65	*1	3.61	....	....	....	....
1989-90	Moncton Hawks	AHL	27	10	15	2	1580	107	2	4.06	....	....	....	....	....	....	....	....	....	....	....	....	....	....	....	....	....
	Fort Wayne Komets	IHL	22	8	9	1	1064	73	0	4.12	....	....	....	....	....	3	1	2	....	159	19	0	7.17	....	....	....	....
1990-91	**Winnipeg Jets**	**NHL**	**24**	**4**	**9**	**4**	**1093**	**71**	**1**	**3.90**	**3.51**	**4.86**	**570**	**.875**	**31.3**	....	....	....	....	....	....	....	....	....	....	....	....
	Moncton Hawks	AHL	11	4	5	2	645	41	0	3.81	....	....	....	....	....	....	....	....	....	....	....	....	....	....	....	....	....
1991-92	**Winnipeg Jets**	**NHL**	**18**	**6**	**7**	**3**	**966**	**52**	**0**	**3.23**	**2.89**	**3.57**	**470**	**.889**	**29.2**	**7**	**3**	**4**	....	**387**	**26**	**0**	**4.03**	**4.94**	**212**	**.877**	**32.9**
	Moncton Hawks	AHL	23	10	11	1	1313	80	0	3.66	....	....	....	....	....	....	....	....	....	....	....	....	....	....	....	....	....
	Canada	WC-A	1	0	1	0	25	4	0	9.60	....	....	....	....	....	....	....	....	....	....	....	....	....	....	....	....	....
1992-93	**Winnipeg Jets**	**NHL**	**19**	**5**	**10**	**0**	**959**	**70**	**0**	**4.38**	**3.76**	**6.18**	**496**	**.859**	**31.0**	....	....	....	....	....	....	....	....	....	....	....	....
	Moncton Hawks	AHL	5	2	1	2	290	18	0	3.72	....	....	....	....	....	....	....	....	....	....	....	....	....	....	....	....	....
	Washington Capitals	**NHL**	**6**	**3**	**2**	**0**	**343**	**10**	**2**	**1.75**	**1.50**	**1.08**	**162**	**.938**	**28.3**	**4**	**1**	**3**	....	**304**	**14**	**0**	**2.76**	**2.42**	**160**	**.913**	**31.6**
1993-94	**Washington Capitals**	**NHL**	**32**	**13**	**14**	**2**	**1770**	**91**	**2**	**3.08**	**2.96**	**3.43**	**817**	**.889**	**27.7**	**2**	**0**	**2**	....	**111**	**6**	**0**	**3.24**	**3.89**	**50**	**.880**	**27.0**
	Portland Pirates	AHL	3	3	0	0	176	8	0	2.72	....	....	....	....	....	....	....	....	....	....	....	....	....	....	....	....	....
1994-95	**Washington Capitals**	**NHL**	**8**	**1**	**3**	**2**	**394**	**16**	**0**	**2.44**	**2.55**	**2.66**	**147**	**.891**	**22.4**	....	....	....	....	....	....	....	....	....	....	....	....
	Chicago Wolves	IHL	2	1	1	0	119	9	0	4.51	....	....	....	....	....	....	....	....	....	....	....	....	....	....	....	....	....
	Calgary Flames	**NHL**	**5**	**2**	**0**	**1**	**202**	**5**	**0**	**1.49**	**1.56**	**0.80**	**93**	**.946**	**27.6**	**1**	**0**	**0**	....	**19**	**0**	**0**	**0.00**	**0.00**	**9**	**1.000**	**28.4**
1995-96	**Calgary Flames**	**NHL**	**43**	**19**	**16**	**3**	**2391**	**117**	**3**	**2.94**	**2.92**	**3.16**	**1087**	**.892**	**27.3**	**3**	**0**	**3**	....	**204**	**7**	**0**	**2.06**	**1.72**	**84**	**.917**	**24.7**
1996-97	**Calgary Flames**	**NHL**	**7**	**2**	**4**	**0**	**361**	**14**	**1**	**2.33**	**2.51**	**2.10**	**155**	**.910**	**25.8**	....	....	....	....	....	....	....	....	....	....	....	....
	Tampa Bay Lightning	**NHL**	**55**	**20**	**25**	**6**	**3012**	**138**	**4**	**2.75**	**2.96**	**2.68**	**1415**	**.902**	**28.2**	....	....	....	....	....	....	....	....	....	....	....	....
	Canada	WC-A	3	0	0	0	50	0	0	0.00	....	....	....	....	....	....	....	....	....	....	....	....	....	....	....	....	....
1997-98	**Calgary Flames**	**NHL**	**42**	**13**	**22**	**6**	**2419**	**116**	**0**	**2.88**	**3.44**	**3.07**	**1087**	**.893**	**27.0**	....	....	....	....	....	....	....	....	....	....	....	....
1998-99	**Washington Capitals**	**NHL**	**23**	**4**	**12**	**3**	**1193**	**50**	**2**	**2.51**	**2.98**	**2.37**	**530**	**.906**	**26.7**	....	....	....	....	....	....	....	....	....	....	....	....
	Canada	WC-A	4	....	....	....	219	11	....	3.01	....	....	....	....	....	....	....	....	....	....	....	....	....	....	....	....	....
99-2000	Canada	Nat-Team	1	0	1	0	60	4	0	4.00	....	....	....	....	....	....	....	....	....	....	....	....	....	....	....	....	....
	Atlanta Thrashers	**NHL**	**1**	**0**	**1**	**0**	**59**	**4**	**0**	**4.07**	**4.65**	**5.09**	**32**	**.875**	**32.5**	....	....	....	....	....	....	....	....	....	....	....	....
	Cleveland Lumberjacks	IHL	10	5	5	0	568	28	0	2.96	....	....	....	....	....	....	....	....	....	....	....	....	....	....	....	....	....
	Orlando Solar Bears	IHL	21	11	6	4	1231	53	1	2.58	....	....	....	....	....	....	....	....	....	....	....	....	....	....	....	....	....
	Colorado Avalanche	**NHL**	**2**	**1**	**0**	**0**	**60**	**2**	**0**	**2.00**	**2.28**	**2.22**	**18**	**.889**	**18.0**	....	....	....	....	....	....	....	....	....	....	....	....
	Utah Grizzlies	IHL	11	4	4	3	626	24	1	2.30	....	....	....	....	....	3	1	2	....	179	7	0	2.34	....	....	....	....
	NHL Totals		**286**	**93**	**125**	**30**	**15255**	**760**	**15**	**2.99**	....	....	**7100**	**.893**	**27.9**	**17**	**4**	**12**	....	**1025**	**53**	**0**	**3.10**	....	**515**	**.897**	**30.1**

OHL First All-Star Team (1988) • OHL Second All-Star Team (1989)

Traded to **Winnipeg** by **Pittsburgh** with Randy Cunneyworth and Dave McLlwain for Jim Kyte, Andrew McBain and Randy Gilhen, June 17, 1989. Traded to **Washington** by **Winnipeg** for Jim Hrivnak and Washington's 2nd round choice (Alexei Budayev) in 1993 Entry Draft, March 22, 1993. Traded to **Calgary** by **Washington** for Calgary's 5th round choice (Joel Cort) in 1995 Entry Draft, April 7, 1995. Traded to **Tampa Bay** by **Calgary** for Aaron Gavey, November 19, 1996. Traded to **Calgary** by **Tampa Bay** for Calgary's 4th round choice (Eric Beaudoin) in 1998 Entry Draft, June 21, 1997. Traded to **Washington** by **Calgary** for future considerations, August 7, 1998. Signed as a free agent by **Atlanta**, September, 1999. Traded to **Colorado** by **Atlanta** for Shean Donovan, December 8, 1999. Selected by **Columbus** from **Colorado** in Expansion Draft, June 23, 2000. Signed as a free agent by **Dallas**, July 12, 2000.

• TAKKO, Kari

Kari M. G – L. 6'2", 189 lbs. b: Uusikaupunki, Finland, 6/23/1962. Minnesota's 5th, 97th overall in 1984.

Season	Club	League	GP	W	L	T	Mins	GA	SO	Avg	AAvg	Eff	SA	S%	SAPG	GP	W	L	T	Mins	GA	SO	Avg	Eff	SA	S%	SAPG
1978-79	HC Assat-Pori	Finland	2	....	....	....	120	2	0	1.00	....	....	....	....	....	....				....	....	....	....	....	....	....	....
	Finland	EJC-A	4	....	....	....	240	8	....	2.00	....	....	....	....	....	....				....	....	....	....	....	....	....	....
1979-80	HC Assat-Pori	Finland	2	....	....	....	120	8	....	4.00	....	....	....	....	....	....				....	....	....	....	....	....	....	....
1980-81	HC Assat-Pori	Finland	4	....	....	....	240	16	....	4.00	....	....	....	....	....	....				....	....	....	....	....	....	....	....
	Finland	WJC-A	4	2	1	1	240	12	0	3.00	....	....	....	....	....	....				....	....	....	....	....	....	....	....
1981-82	HC Assat-Pori	Finland	14	....	....	....	840	60	....	4.28	....	....	....	....	....	....				....	....	....	....	....	....	....	....
	Finland	WJC-A	7	5	2	0	420	29	0	4.14	....	....	....	....	....	....				....	....	....	....	....	....	....	....
1982-83	HC Assat-Pori	Finland	21	....	....	....	1260	77	0	3.66	....	....	....	....	....	....				....	....	....	....	....	....	....	....
	Finland	WEC-A	6	....	....	....	360	25	....	4.17	....	....	....	....	....	....				....	....	....	....	....	....	....	....
1983-84	HC Assat-Pori	Finland	32	....	....	....	1920	102	3	3.19	....	....	....	....	....	9				540	37	0	4.11	....	....	....	....
	Finland	Olympics	5	....	....	....	195	19	....	5.85	....	....	....	....	....	....				....	....	....	....	....	....	....	....
1984-85	HC Assat-Pori	Finland	35	....	....	....	2100	123	3	3.51	....	....	....	....	....	8				480	32	0	4.00	....	....	....	....
	Finland	WEC-A	7	....	....	....	420	23	....	3.28	....	....	....	....	....	....				....	....	....	....	....	....	....	....
1985-86	Springfield Indians	AHL	43	18	19	3	2286	161	1	4.05	....	....	....	....	....	....	....	....	....	....	....	....	....	....	....	....	....
	Minnesota North Stars	**NHL**	**1**	**0**	**1**	**0**	**60**	**3**	**0**	**3.00**	**2.34**	**2.65**	**34**	**.912**	**34.0**	....	....	....	....	....	....	....	....	....	....	....	....
1986-87	**Minnesota North Stars**	**NHL**	**38**	**13**	**18**	**4**	**2075**	**119**	**0**	**3.44**	**2.91**	**3.86**	**1061**	**.888**	**30.7**	....	....	....	....	....	....	....	....	....	....	....	....
	Springfield Indians	AHL	5	3	2	0	300	16	1	3.20	....	....	....	....	....	....	....	....	....	....	....	....	....	....	....	....	....
1987-88	Finland	Can-Cup	5	0	5	0	280	22	0	5.00	....	....	....	....	....	....	....	....	....	....	....	....	....	....	....	....	....
	Minnesota North Stars	**NHL**	**37**	**8**	**19**	**6**	**1919**	**143**	**1**	**4.47**	**3.74**	**5.97**	**1070**	**.866**	**33.5**	....	....	....	....	....	....	....	....	....	....	....	....
1988-89	**Minnesota North Stars**	**NHL**	**32**	**8**	**15**	**4**	**1603**	**93**	**0**	**3.48**	**2.89**	**3.51**	**922**	**.899**	**34.5**	**3**	**0**	**1**	....	**105**	**7**	**0**	**4.00**	**5.09**	**55**	**.873**	**31.4**
1989-90	**Minnesota North Stars**	**NHL**	**21**	**4**	**12**	**0**	**1012**	**68**	**0**	**4.03**	**3.42**	**5.69**	**482**	**.859**	**28.6**	**1**	**0**	**0**	....	**4**	**0**	**0**	**0.00**	**0.00**	**0**	**.000**	**0.0**
	Kalamazoo Wings	IHL	1	0	1	0	59	5	0	5.08	....	....	....	....	....	....	....	....	....	....	....	....	....	....	....	....	....
1990-91	Minnesota North Stars	Fr-Tour	2	....	....	....	49	4	0	4.89	....	....	....	....	....	....	....	....	....	....	....	....	....	....	....	....	....
	Minnesota North Stars	**NHL**	**2**	**0**	**2**	**0**	**119**	**12**	**0**	**6.05**	**5.44**	**9.81**	**74**	**.838**	**37.3**	....	....	....	....	....	....	....	....	....	....	....	....
	Kalamazoo Wings	IHL	5	4	1	0	300	10	1	2.00	....	....	....	....	....	....	....	....	....	....	....	....	....	....	....	....	....
	Edmonton Oilers	**NHL**	**11**	**4**	**4**	**0**	**529**	**37**	**0**	**4.20**	**3.78**	**5.57**	**279**	**.867**	**31.6**	....	....	....	....	....	....	....	....	....	....	....	....
	Finland	WEC-A	3	2	1	0	178	9	....	3.03	....	....	....	....	....	....	....	....	....	....	....	....	....	....	....	....	....
1991-92	HC Assat-Pori	Finland	28	....	....	....	1628	98	1	3.61	....	....	....	....	....	6				359	17	1	2.84	....	....	....	....
1992-93	HC Assat-Pori	Finland	45	....	....	....	2723	138	3	3.04	....	....	....	....	....	7				430	29	0	4.05	....	....	....	....
1993-94	HC Assat-Pori	Finland	48	....	....	....	1420	145	3	2.92	....	....	....	....	....	....				....	....	....	....	....	....	....	....
1994-95	HC Assat-Pori	Finland	49	....	....	....	2963	157	....	3.18	....	....	....	....	....	....				....	....	....	....	....	....	....	....

			REGULAR SEASON													PLAYOFFS											
Season	Club	League	GP	W	L	T	Mins	GA	SO	Avg	AAvg	Eff	SA	S%	SAPG	GP	W	L	T	Mins	GA	SO	Avg	Eff	SA	S%	SAPG
1995-96	HC Assat-Pori	Finland	42	....	....	....	2510	128	2	3.06	....	....	....	....	....	3	....	....	....	178	12	....	4.05	....	....	....	....
1996-97	Finland	W-Cup	2	1	1	0	119	7	0	3.53	....	....	....	....	....	....	....	....	....	....	....	....	....	....	....	....	....
	HC Assat-Pori	Finland	42	16	16	9	2492	139	1	3.35	....	....	....	....	....	4	1	3	0	217	15	0	4.14	....	....	....	....
1997-98	HV-71 Jonkoping	Sweden	38	....	....	....	2280	119	....	3.13	....	....	....	....	....	5	....	....	....	314	11	....	2.10	....	....	....	....
1998-99	HV-71 Jonkoping	Sweden	40	....	....	....	2475	107	5	2.59	....	....	....	....	....	....	....	....	....	....	....	....	....	....	....	....	....
99-2000	HV-71 Jonkoping	Sweden	38	....	....	....	2206	93	4	2.53	....	....	....	....	....	3	....	....	....	179	7	0	2.35	....	....	....	....
	NHL Totals		**142**	**37**	**71**	**14**	**7317**	**475**	**1**	**3.90**	....	....	**3922**	**.879**	**32.2**	**4**	**0**	**1**	....	**109**	**7**	**0**	**3.85**	....	**55**	**.873**	**30.3**

Finnish First All-Star Team (1985)

• Re-entered NHL draft. Originally Quebec's 8th choice, 200th overall, in 1981 Entry Draft. Traded to **Edmonton** by **Minnesota** for Bruce Bell, November 22, 1990.

• TALLAS, Robbie

Robert Wayne G – L. 6', 163 lbs. b: Edmonton, Alta., 3/20/1973.

Season	Club	League	GP	W	L	T	Mins	GA	SO	Avg	AAvg	Eff	SA	S%	SAPG	GP	W	L	T	Mins	GA	SO	Avg	Eff	SA	S%	SAPG
1989-90	South Surrey Eagles	BCJHL	STATISTICS NOT AVAILABLE																								
1990-91	Penticton Panthers	BCJHL	37	....	....	....	2055	196	0	5.72	....	....	....	....	....	....	....	....	....	....	....	....	....	....	....	....	....
1991-92	Seattle Thunderbirds	WHL	14	4	7	0	708	52	0	4.41	....	....	....	....	....	....	....	....	....	....	....	....	....	....	....	....	....
	Surrey Eagles	BCJHL	19	6	12	0	1043	112	1	6.44	....	....	....	....	....	....	....	....	....	....	....	....	....	....	....	....	....
1992-93	Seattle Thunderbirds	WHL	58	24	23	3	3151	194	2	3.69	....	....	....	....	....	5	1	4	....	333	18	0	3.24	....	....	....	....
1993-94	Seattle Thunderbirds	WHL	51	23	21	3	2849	188	0	3.96	....	....	....	....	....	9	5	4	....	567	40	0	4.23	....	....	....	....
1994-95	Charlotte Checkers	ECHL	36	21	9	3	2011	114	0	3.40	....	....	....	....	....	....	....	....	....	....	....	....	....	....	....	....	....
	Providence Bruins	AHL	2	1	0	0	82	4	1	2.90	....	....	....	....	....	....	....	....	....	....	....	....	....	....	....	....	....
1995-96	**Boston Bruins**	**NHL**	**1**	**1**	**0**	**0**	**60**	**3**	**0**	**3.00**	**2.98**	**3.10**	**29**	**.897**	**29.0**	....	....	....	....	....	....	....	....	....	....	....	....
	Providence Bruins	AHL	37	12	16	7	2136	117	1	3.29	....	....	....	....	....	2	0	2	....	135	9	0	4.01	....	....	....	....
1996-97	**Boston Bruins**	**NHL**	**28**	**8**	**12**	**1**	**1244**	**69**	**1**	**3.33**	**3.59**	**3.91**	**587**	**.882**	**28.3**	....	....	....	....	....	....	....	....	....	....	....	....
	Providence Bruins	AHL	24	9	14	1	1424	83	0	3.50	....	....	....	....	....	....	....	....	....	....	....	....	....	....	....	....	....
1997-98	**Boston Bruins**	**NHL**	**14**	**6**	**3**	**3**	**788**	**24**	**1**	**1.83**	**2.18**	**1.35**	**326**	**.926**	**24.8**	....	....	....	....	....	....	....	....	....	....	....	....
	Providence Bruins	AHL	10	1	8	1	575	39	0	4.07	....	....	....	....	....	....	....	....	....	....	....	....	....	....	....	....	....
1998-99	**Boston Bruins**	**NHL**	**17**	**7**	**7**	**2**	**987**	**43**	**1**	**2.61**	**3.10**	**2.67**	**421**	**.898**	**25.6**	....	....	....	....	....	....	....	....	....	....	....	....
99-2000	**Boston Bruins**	**NHL**	**27**	**4**	**13**	**4**	**1363**	**72**	**0**	**3.17**	**3.63**	**3.63**	**628**	**.885**	**27.6**	....	....	....	....	....	....	....	....	....	....	....	....
	NHL Totals		**87**	**26**	**35**	**10**	**4442**	**211**	**3**	**2.85**	....	....	**1991**	**.894**	**26.9**	....	....	....	....	....	....	....	....	....	....	....	....

Signed as a free agent by **Boston**, September 13, 1995.

• TANNER, John

John P. G – L. 6'3", 182 lbs. b: Cambridge, Ont., 3/17/1971. Quebec's 4th, 54th overall in 1989.

Season	Club	League	GP	W	L	T	Mins	GA	SO	Avg	AAvg	Eff	SA	S%	SAPG	GP	W	L	T	Mins	GA	SO	Avg	Eff	SA	S%	SAPG
1986-87	New Hamburg Spirit of '83	OJHL-C	15	....	....	....	889	83	0	5.60	....	....	....	....	....	....	....	....	....	....	....	....	....	....	....	....	....
1987-88	Peterborough Petes	OHL	26	18	4	3	1532	88	0	3.45	....	....	....	....	....	2	1	0	0	98	3	0	1.84	....	....	....	....
1988-89	Peterborough Petes	OHL	34	22	10	0	1923	107	2	*3.34	....	....	....	....	....	8	4	3	0	369	23	0	3.74	....	....	....	....
	Peterborough Petes	Mem-Cup	1	0	1	0	59	5	0	5.08	....	....	....	....	....	....	....	....	....	....	....	....	....	....	....	....	....
1989-90	**Quebec Nordiques**	**NHL**	**1**	**0**	**1**	**0**	**60**	**3**	**0**	**3.00**	**2.54**	**3.00**	**30**	**.900**	**30.0**	....	....	....	....	....	....	....	....	....	....	....	....
	Peterborough Petes	OHL	18	6	8	2	1037	70	0	4.05	....	....	....	....	....	....	....	....	....	....	....	....	....	....	....	....	....
	London Knights	OHL	19	12	5	1	1097	53	1	2.90	....	....	....	....	....	6	2	4	0	341	24	0	4.22	....	....	....	....
1990-91	**Quebec Nordiques**	**NHL**	**6**	**1**	**3**	**1**	**228**	**16**	**0**	**4.21**	**3.79**	**5.06**	**133**	**.880**	**35.0**	....	....	....	....	....	....	....	....	....	....	....	....
	London Knights	OHL	7	3	3	1	427	29	0	4.07	....	....	....	....	....	....	....	....	....	....	....	....	....	....	....	....	....
	Sudbury Wolves	OHL	19	10	8	0	1043	60	0	3.45	....	....	....	....	....	5	1	4	0	274	21	0	4.60	....	....	....	....
1991-92	**Quebec Nordiques**	**NHL**	**14**	**1**	**7**	**4**	**796**	**46**	**1**	**3.47**	**3.11**	**4.05**	**394**	**.883**	**29.7**	....	....	....	....	....	....	....	....	....	....	....	....
	New Haven Nighthawks	AHL	16	7	6	2	908	57	0	3.77	....	....	....	....	....	....	....	....	....	....	....	....	....	....	....	....	....
	Halifax Citadels	AHL	12	6	5	1	672	29	2	2.59	....	....	....	....	....	....	....	....	....	....	....	....	....	....	....	....	....
1992-93	Halifax Citadels	AHL	51	20	18	7	2852	199	0	4.19	....	....	....	....	....	....	....	....	....	....	....	....	....	....	....	....	....
1993-94	Cornwall Aces	AHL	38	14	15	4	2035	123	1	3.63	....	....	....	....	....	....	....	....	....	....	....	....	....	....	....	....	....
	San Diego Gulls	IHL	13	5	3	2	629	37	0	3.53	....	....	....	....	....	3	0	1	0	118	5	0	2.53	....	....	....	....
1994-95	Greensboro Monarchs	ECHL	6	0	4	1	342	27	0	4.73	....	....	....	....	....	....	....	....	....	....	....	....	....	....	....	....	....
	San Diego Gulls	IHL	8	1	3	1	344	28	0	4.87	....	....	....	....	....	....	....	....	....	....	....	....	....	....	....	....	....
1995-96	Detroit Falcons	ColHL	2	1	0	0	112	8	0	4.27	....	....	....	....	....	....	....	....	....	....	....	....	....	....	....	....	....
	Muskegon Fury	ColHL	2	0	2	0	89	8	0	5.38	....	....	....	....	....	....	....	....	....	....	....	....	....	....	....	....	....
	Rochester Americans	AHL	10	3	6	1	579	38	0	3.94	....	....	....	....	....	....	....	....	....	....	....	....	....	....	....	....	....
1996-97	Wheeling Nailers	ECHL	19	7	10	1	940	59	0	3.76	....	....	....	....	....	....	....	....	....	....	....	....	....	....	....	....	....
	NHL Totals		**21**	**2**	**11**	**5**	**1084**	**65**	**1**	**3.60**	....	....	**557**	**.883**	**30.8**	....	....	....	....	....	....	....	....	....	....	....	....

Traded to **Anaheim** by **Quebec** for Anaheim's 4th round choice (Tomi Kallio) in 1995 Entry Draft, February 20, 1994.

• TATARYN, Dave

David Nathan G – L. 5'9", 160 lbs. b: Sudbury, Ont., 7/17/1950. St. Louis' 8th, 104th overall in 1970.

Season	Club	League	GP	W	L	T	Mins	GA	SO	Avg	AAvg	Eff	SA	S%	SAPG	GP	W	L	T	Mins	GA	SO	Avg	Eff	SA	S%	SAPG
1967-68	Niagara Falls Flyers	OHA-Jr.	5	....	....	....	300	16	0	3.55	....	....	....	....	....	....	....	....	....	....	....	....	....	....	....	....	....
	Niagara Falls Flyers	Mem-Cup	1	0	0	0	2	0	0	0.00	....	....	....	....	....	....	....	....	....	....	....	....	....	....	....	....	....
1968-69	Niagara Falls Flyers	OHA-Jr.	49	....	....	....	2940	197	2	4.04	....	....	....	....	....	14	....	....	....	820	67	0	4.88	....	....	....	....
1969-70	Niagara Falls Flyers	OHA-Jr.	38	....	....	....	2280	223	0	5.87	....	....	....	....	....	....	....	....	....	....	....	....	....	....	....	....	....
1970-71			DID NOT PLAY																								
1971-72	University of Toronto	OUAA	12	....	....	....	7200	21	0	1.75	....	....	....	....	....	....	....	....	....	....	....	....	....	....	....	....	....
1972-73	Laurentian University	OUAA	16	....	....	....	960	63	0	3.94	....	....	....	....	....	....	....	....	....	....	....	....	....	....	....	....	....
1973-74	Laurentian University	OUAA	17	....	....	....	1020	66	0	3.88	....	....	....	....	....	....	....	....	....	....	....	....	....	....	....	....	....
1974-75	Laurentian University	OUAA	14	....	....	....	800	48	0	3.60	....	....	....	....	....	....	....	....	....	....	....	....	....	....	....	....	....
1975-76	Toronto Toros	WHA	23	7	12	1	1261	100	0	4.76	....	....	....	....	....	....	....	....	....	....	....	....	....	....	....	....	....
	Columbus Owls	IHL	4	....	....	....	183	14	0	4.59	....	....	....	....	....	....	....	....	....	....	....	....	....	....	....	....	....
	Buffalo Norsemen	NAHL	2	2	0	0	120	7	0	3.50	....	....	....	....	....	....	....	....	....	....	....	....	....	....	....	....	....
	Whitby Warriors	OHA-Sr.	2	2	0	0	120	4	0	2.00	....	....	....	....	....	....	....	....	....	....	....	....	....	....	....	....	....
1976-77	Charlotte Checkers	SHL	39	....	....	....	2284	114	1	2.99	....	....	....	....	....	....	....	....	....	....	....	....	....	....	....	....	....
	Mohawk Valley Comets	NAHL	1	0	1	0	60	7	0	7.00	....	....	....	....	....	....	....	....	....	....	....	....	....	....	....	....	....
	New York Rangers	**NHL**	**2**	**1**	**1**	**0**	**80**	**10**	**0**	**7.50**	**6.98**	....	....	....	....	....	....	....	....	....	....	....	....	....	....	....	....
	New Haven Nighthawks	AHL	3	2	1	0	179	11	0	3.69	....	....	....	....	....	....	....	....	....	....	....	....	....	....	....	....	....
1977-78	Cambridge Hornets	OHA-Sr.	20	....	....	....	1250	73	*1	*3.50	....	....	....	....	....	....	....	....	....	....	....	....	....	....	....	....	....
1978-79	Cambridge Hornets	CIHL	20	....	....	....	1240	81	0	3.92	....	....	....	....	....	....	....	....	....	....	....	....	....	....	....	....	....
1979-80	Cambridge Hornets	OHA-Sr.	28	....	....	....	1637	88	1	3.23	....	....	....	....	....	....	....	....	....	....	....	....	....	....	....	....	....
1980-81	Cambridge Hornets	OHA-Sr.	27	....	....	....	1598	94	1	*3.53	....	....	....	....	....	....	....	....	....	....	....	....	....	....	....	....	....
1981-1984	Cambridge Hornets	OHA-Sr.	STATISTICS NOT AVAILABLE																								
	NHL Totals		**2**	**1**	**1**	**0**	**80**	**10**	**0**	**7.50**	....	....	....	....	....	....	....	....	....	....	....	....	....	....	....	....	....
	Other Major League Totals		23	7	12	1	1261	100	0	4.76	....	....	....	....	....	....	....	....	....	....	....	....	....	....	....	....	....

OUAA First All-Star Team (1972, 1974) • OUAA Second All-Star Team (1973, 1975)

Signed as a free agent by **Toronto** (WHA), June, 1975. Signed as a free agent by **NY Rangers** (New Haven-AHL) after Southern Hockey League folded, January 30, 1977.

• TAYLOR, Bobby

Robert Ian G – L. 6'1", 180 lbs. b: Calgary, Alta., 1/24/1945.

Season	Club	League	GP	W	L	T	Mins	GA	SO	Avg	AAvg	Eff	SA	S%	SAPG	GP	W	L	T	Mins	GA	SO	Avg	Eff	SA	S%	SAPG
1962-63	Calgary Buffalos	CCJHL	STATISTICS NOT AVAILABLE																								
1963-64	Calgary Buffalos	CCJHL	STATISTICS NOT AVAILABLE																								
1964-65	St. Catharines Black Hawks	OHA-Jr.	18	....	....	....	1060	85	0	4.81	....	....	....	....	....	....	....	....	....	....	....	....	....	....	....	....	....
	Edmonton Oil Kings	CAHL	....	....	....	....	....	....	....	....	....	....	....	....	....	4	1	3	0	260	16	0	3.69	....	....	....	....
	Edmonton Oil Kings	Mem-Cup	3	2	1	0	180	14	0	4.67	....	....	....	....	....	....	....	....	....	....	....	....	....	....	....	....	....
1965-66	St. Louis Braves	CPHL	DID NOT PLAY – SPARE GOALTENDER																								
1966-67	Calgary Spurs	WCSHL	16	....	....	....	960	40	0	*2.50	....	....	....	....	....	4	....	....	....	240	15	0	3.75	....	....	....	....
	Calgary Spurs	Al-Cup	10	6	4	0	532	29	1	3.27	....	....	....	....	....	....	....	....	....	....	....	....	....	....	....	....	....
1967-68	Calgary Spurs	WCSHL	27	....	....	....	1620	133	0	5.02	....	....	....	....	....	3	1	2	0	140	13	0	5.69	....	....	....	....
	Canada	Nat-Team	STATISTICS NOT AVAILABLE																								
1968-69	New Jersey Devils	EHL	70	25	38	7	4200	285	1	4.07	....	....	....	....	....	....	....	....	....	....	....	....	....	....	....	....	....

			REGULAR SEASON													PLAYOFFS											
Season	**Club**	**League**	**GP**	**W**	**L**	**T**	**Mins**	**GA**	**SO**	**Avg**	**AAvg**	**Eff**	**SA**	**S%**	**SAPG**	**GP**	**W**	**L**	**T**	**Mins**	**GA**	**SO**	**Avg**	**Eff**	**SA**	**S%**	**SAPG**
1969-70	Seattle Totems	WHL	5	....	....	....	240	14	0	3.50	....	....	....	....	....	....	....	....	....	....	....	....	....	....	....	....	....
	Quebec Aces	AHL	14	....	....	....	759	53	0	4.18	....	....	....	....	....	2	1	1	0	123	5	0	2.44	....	....	....	....
	New Jersey Devils	EHL	8	....	....	....	480	55	1	6.88	....	....	....	....	....	....	....	....	....	....	....	....	....	....	....	....	....
1970-71	Quebec Aces	AHL	39	13	15	8	2154	122	*5	3.39	....	....	....	....	....	....	....	....	....	....	....	....	....	....	....	....	....
1971-72	**Philadelphia Flyers**	**NHL**	**6**	**1**	**2**	**2**	**320**	**16**	**0**	**3.00**	**3.03**	....	....	....	....	....	....	....	....	....	....	....	....	....	....	....	....
	Richmond Robins	AHL	26	7	14	4	1538	78	1	3.04	....	....	....	....	....	....	....	....	....	....	....	....	....	....	....	....	....
1972-73	**Philadelphia Flyers**	**NHL**	**23**	**8**	**8**	**4**	**1144**	**78**	**0**	**4.09**	**3.87**	....	....	....	....	....	....	....	....	....	....	....	....	....	....	....	....
	Richmond Robins	AHL	6	....	....	....	337	23	0	4.09	....	....	....	....	....	....	....	....	....	....	....	....	....	....	....	....	....
1973-74	Richmond Robins	AHL	11	4	4	3	659	38	0	3.45	....	....	....	....	....	....	....	....	....	....	....	....	....	....	....	....	....
♦	**Philadelphia Flyers**	**NHL**	**8**	**3**	**3**	**0**	**366**	**26**	**0**	**4.26**	**4.12**	....	....	....	....	....	....	....	....	....	....	....	....	....	....	....	....
1974-75	Richmond Robins	AHL	5	3	1	1	303	18	0	3.56	....	....	....	....	....	....	....	....	....	....	....	....	....	....	....	....	....
	Philadelphia Flyers	**NHL**	**3**	**0**	**2**	**0**	**120**	**13**	**0**	**6.50**	**5.88**	....	....	....	....	....	....	....	....	....	....	....	....	....	....	....	....
1975-76	**Philadelphia Flyers**	**NHL**	**4**	**3**	**1**	**0**	**240**	**15**	**0**	**3.75**	**3.40**	....	....	....	....	....	....	....	....	....	....	....	....	....	....	....	....
	Richmond Robins	AHL	4	0	2	1	204	18	0	5.29	....	....	....	....	....	....	....	....	....	....	....	....	....	....	....	....	....
	Pittsburgh Penguins	**NHL**	**2**	**0**	**1**	**0**	**78**	**7**	**0**	**5.38**	**4.87**	....	....	....	....	....	....	....	....	....	....	....	....	....	....	....	....
	Springfield Indians	AHL	23	7	14	0	1230	86	0	4.20	....	....	....	....	....	....	....	....	....	....	....	....	....	....	....	....	....
	NHL Totals		**46**	**15**	**17**	**6**	**2268**	**155**	**0**	**4.10**	....	....	....	....	....	....	....	....	....	....	....	....	....	....	....	....	....

• On active roster for entire 1965-66 season but did not play. Signed as a free agent by **Philadelphia**, September, 1968. Traded to **Pittsburgh** by **Philadelphia** with Ed Van Impe for Gary Inness and future considerations, March 9, 1976.

• TENO, Harvey

Harvey George G – L. 5'7", 175 lbs. b: Windsor, Ont., 2/15/1915 Deceased.

Season	Club	League	GP	W	L	T	Mins	GA	SO	Avg	AAvg	Eff	SA	S%	SAPG	GP	W	L	T	Mins	GA	SO	Avg	Eff	SA	S%	SAPG
1932-33	Windsor Wanderers	MOHL	16	....	....	....	1080	55	1	3.06	....	....	....	....	....	....	....	....	....	....	....	....	....	....	....	....	....
1933-34	St. Michael's Majors	OHA-Jr.	11	....	....	....	660	30	1	2.73	....	....	....	....	....	3	....	....	....	180	9	0	*3.00	....	....	....	....
	St. Michael's Majors	Mem-Cup	13	*13	0	0	780	27	*3	*2.08	....	....	....	....	....	....	....	....	....	....	....	....	....	....	....	....	....
1934-35	St. Michael's Majors	OHA-Jr.	11	....	....	....	660	34	1	3.09	....	....	....	....	....	3	....	....	....	180	8	*1	2.67	....	....	....	....
	Toronto Dominions	TIHL	15	....	....	....	900	54	0	3.60	....	....	....	....	....	3	....	....	....	180	23	0	7.67	....	....	....	....
1935-36	Oakville Villans	OHA-Sr.	17	....	....	....	1020	53	1	3.12	....	....	....	....	....	2	....	....	....	120	7	0	3.50	....	....	....	....
	Toronto McColl-Frontenacs	TIHL	14	....	....	....	840	43	*1	3.07	....	....	....	....	....	4	....	....	....	240	17	0	4.25	....	....	....	....
1936-37	Atlantic City Seagulls	EAHL	48	*27	19	2	2880	116	*4	2.43	....	....	....	....	....	4	1	3	0	240	10	0	2.40	....	....	....	....
1937-38	Atlantic City Seagulls	EAHL	57	28	26	3	3420	168	3	2.94	....	....	....	....	....	....	....	....	....	....	....	....	....	....	....	....	....
1938-39	Pittsburgh Hornets	IAHL	20	6	13	1	1200	58	0	2.90	....	....	....	....	....	....	....	....	....	....	....	....	....	....	....	....	....
	Detroit Red Wings	**NHL**	**5**	**2**	**3**	**0**	**300**	**15**	**0**	**3.00**	**3.62**	....	....	....	....	....	....	....	....	....	....	....	....	....	....	....	....
	Hershey Bears	IAHL	1	0	0	1	70	4	0	3.43	....	....	....	....	....	....	....	....	....	....	....	....	....	....	....	....	....
	Philadelphia Ramblers	IAHL	2	0	1	1	130	11	0	5.08	....	....	....	....	....	4	1	3	0	240	9	1	2.25	....	....	....	....
1939-40	Pittsburgh Hornets	IAHL	*56	*25	22	9	3480	133	4	2.29	....	....	....	....	....	*9	4	5	0	*563	24	1	2.56	....	....	....	....
1940-41	Pittsburgh Hornets	AHL	24	9	12	2	1408	63	2	2.68	....	....	....	....	....	6	3	3	0	426	12	0	*1.69	....	....	....	....
	Cleveland Barons	AHL	6	3	2	1	370	13	0	2.11	....	....	....	....	....	....	....	....	....	....	....	....	....	....	....	....	....
	Buffalo Bisons	AHL	1	0	0	1	70	3	0	2.57	....	....	....	....	....	....	....	....	....	....	....	....	....	....	....	....	....
1941-42	Pittsburgh Hornets	AHL	53	22	26	5	3280	209	0	3.82	....	....	....	....	....	....	....	....	....	....	....	....	....	....	....	....	....
1942-43	Pittsburgh Hornets	AHL	52	25	21	6	3220	184	2	3.43	....	....	....	....	....	2	0	2	0	130	10	0	4.62	....	....	....	....
1943-44	Pittsburgh Hornets	AHL	6	1	4	1	360	19	0	3.17	....	....	....	....	....	....	....	....	....	....	....	....	....	....	....	....	....
1944-45	Cleveland Barons	AHL	55	*31	15	9	3300	178	4	3.23	....	....	....	....	....	12	*8	4	0	730	39	0	3.21	....	....	....	....
1945-46	Cleveland Barons	AHL	21	10	9	2	1260	94	1	4.48	....	....	....	....	....	12	7	5	0	755	50	1	3.97	....	....	....	....
1946-47	Minneapolis Millers	USHL	13	7	6	0	780	41	2	3.15	....	....	....	....	....	....	....	....	....	....	....	....	....	....	....	....	....
1947-48	Hershey Bears	AHL	....	....	....	....	....	....	....	....	....	....	....	....	....	2	0	2	0	100	6	0	3.60	....	....	....	....
	NHL Totals		**5**	**2**	**3**	**0**	**300**	**15**	**0**	**3.00**	....	....	....	....	....	....	....	....	....	....	....	....	....	....	....	....	....

EAHL Second All-Star Team (1937, 1938)

Signed as a free agent by **Detroit**, October 21, 1938. Promoted to **Detroit** from **Pittsburgh** (IAHL) to replace suspended Normie Smith, November 17, 1938. Loaned to **Boston** by **Detroit** for remainder of 1938-39 season, December 28, 1938. Traded to **Pittsburgh** (IAHL) by **Detroit** for cash, October 5, 1939. Traded to **Cleveland** (AHL) by **Pittsburgh** (AHL) for cash, October 17, 1944.

• TERRERI, Chris

Christopher Arnold G – L. 5'9", 170 lbs. b: Providence, RI, 11/15/1964. New Jersey's 3rd, 87th overall in 1983.

Season	Club	League	GP	W	L	T	Mins	GA	SO	Avg	AAvg	Eff	SA	S%	SAPG	GP	W	L	T	Mins	GA	SO	Avg	Eff	SA	S%	SAPG
1981-82	West-Warwick Wizards	Hi-School	STATISTICS NOT AVAILABLE																								
1982-83	Providence College	ECAC	11	7	1	0	528	17	2	1.93	....	....	....	....	....	....	....	....	....	....	....	....	....	....	....	....	....
1983-84	Providence College	ECAC	10	4	2	0	391	20	0	3.07	....	....	....	....	....	....	....	....	....	....	....	....	....	....	....	....	....
1984-85	Providence College	H-East	33	15	13	5	1956	116	1	3.35	....	....	....	....	....	....	....	....	....	....	....	....	....	....	....	....	....
	United States	WEC-A	3	....	....	....	111	12	....	6.48	....	....	....	....	....	....	....	....	....	....	....	....	....	....	....	....	....
1985-86	Providence College	H-East	22	6	16	0	1320	84	0	3.74	....	....	....	....	....	....	....	....	....	....	....	....	....	....	....	....	....
	United States	WEC-A	5	....	....	....	286	20	1	4.20	....	....	....	....	....	....	....	....	....	....	....	....	....	....	....	....	....
1986-87	**New Jersey Devils**	**NHL**	**7**	**0**	**3**	**1**	**286**	**21**	**0**	**4.41**	**3.74**	**5.35**	**173**	**.879**	**36.3**	....	....	....	....	....	....	....	....	....	....	....	....
	Maine Mariners	AHL	14	4	9	1	765	57	0	4.47	....	....	....	....	....	....	....	....	....	....	....	....	....	....	....	....	....
	United States	WEC-A	2	....	....	....	100	12	....	7.20	....	....	....	....	....	....	....	....	....	....	....	....	....	....	....	....	....
1987-88	Utica Devils	AHL	7	5	1	0	399	18	0	2.71	....	....	....	....	....	....	....	....	....	....	....	....	....	....	....	....	....
	United States	Nat-Team	26	17	7	2	1430	81	0	3.40	....	....	....	....	....	....	....	....	....	....	....	....	....	....	....	....	....
	United States	Olympics	3	....	....	....	127	14	....	6.58	....	....	....	....	....	....	....	....	....	....	....	....	....	....	....	....	....
1988-89	**New Jersey Devils**	**NHL**	**8**	**0**	**4**	**2**	**402**	**18**	**0**	**2.69**	**2.24**	**2.85**	**170**	**.894**	**25.4**	....	....	....	....	....	....	....	....	....	....	....	....
	Utica Devils	AHL	39	20	15	3	2314	132	0	3.42	....	....	....	....	....	2	0	1	....	80	6	0	4.50	....	....	....	....
1989-90	**New Jersey Devils**	**NHL**	**35**	**15**	**12**	**3**	**1931**	**110**	**0**	**3.42**	**2.89**	**3.75**	**1004**	**.890**	**31.2**	**4**	**2**	**2**	....	**238**	**13**	**0**	**3.28**	**4.14**	**103**	**.874**	**26.0**
1990-91	**New Jersey Devils**	**NHL**	**53**	**24**	**21**	**7**	**2970**	**144**	**1**	**2.91**	**2.60**	**3.11**	**1348**	**.893**	**27.2**	**7**	**3**	**4**	....	**428**	**21**	**0**	**2.94**	**2.86**	**216**	**.903**	**30.3**
1991-92	**New Jersey Devils**	**NHL**	**54**	**22**	**22**	**10**	**3186**	**169**	**1**	**3.18**	**2.84**	**3.56**	**1511**	**.888**	**28.5**	**7**	**3**	**3**	....	**386**	**23**	**0**	**3.58**	**4.06**	**203**	**.887**	**31.6**
1992-93	**New Jersey Devils**	**NHL**	**48**	**19**	**21**	**3**	**2672**	**151**	**2**	**3.39**	**2.90**	**3.87**	**1324**	**.886**	**29.7**	**4**	**1**	**3**	....	**219**	**17**	**0**	**4.66**	**6.71**	**118**	**.856**	**32.3**
1993-94	**New Jersey Devils**	**NHL**	**44**	**20**	**11**	**4**	**2340**	**106**	**2**	**2.72**	**2.61**	**2.53**	**1141**	**.907**	**29.3**	**4**	**3**	**0**	....	**200**	**9**	**0**	**2.70**	**2.19**	**111**	**.919**	**33.3**
1994-95♦	**New Jersey Devils**	**NHL**	**15**	**3**	**7**	**2**	**734**	**31**	**0**	**2.53**	**2.65**	**2.54**	**309**	**.900**	**25.3**	**1**	**0**	**0**	....	**8**	**0**	**0**	**0.00**	**0.00**	**2**	**1.000**	**15.0**
1995-96	**New Jersey Devils**	**NHL**	**4**	**3**	**0**	**0**	**210**	**9**	**0**	**2.57**	**2.55**	**2.51**	**92**	**.902**	**26.3**	....	....	....	....	....	....	....	....	....	....	....	....
	San Jose Sharks	**NHL**	**46**	**13**	**29**	**1**	**2516**	**155**	**0**	**3.70**	**3.69**	**4.34**	**1322**	**.883**	**31.5**	....	....	....	....	....	....	....	....	....	....	....	....
1996-97	**San Jose Sharks**	**NHL**	**22**	**6**	**10**	**3**	**1200**	**55**	**0**	**2.75**	**2.96**	**2.74**	**553**	**.901**	**27.7**	....	....	....	....	....	....	....	....	....	....	....	....
	Chicago Blackhawks	**NHL**	**7**	**4**	**1**	**2**	**429**	**19**	**0**	**2.66**	**2.86**	**2.63**	**192**	**.901**	**26.9**	**2**	**0**	**0**	....	**44**	**3**	**0**	**4.09**	**4.38**	**28**	**.893**	**38.2**
	United States	WC-A	6	2	3	1	357	16	0	2.69	....	....	....	....	....	....	....	....	....	....	....	....	....	....	....	....	....
1997-98	**Chicago Blackhawks**	**NHL**	**21**	**8**	**10**	**2**	**1222**	**49**	**2**	**2.41**	**2.87**	**2.28**	**519**	**.906**	**25.5**	....	....	....	....	....	....	....	....	....	....	....	....
	Indianapolis Ice	IHL	3	2	0	1	180	3	1	1.00	....	....	....	....	....	....	....	....	....	....	....	....	....	....	....	....	....
1998-99	**New Jersey Devils**	**NHL**	**12**	**8**	**3**	**1**	**726**	**30**	**1**	**2.48**	**2.95**	**2.53**	**294**	**.898**	**24.3**	....	....	....	....	....	....	....	....	....	....	....	....
99-2000♦	**New Jersey Devils**	**NHL**	**12**	**2**	**9**	**0**	**649**	**37**	**0**	**3.42**	**3.91**	**4.23**	**299**	**.876**	**27.6**	....	....	....	....	....	....	....	....	....	....	....	....
	NHL Totals		**388**	**147**	**163**	**41**	**21473**	**1104**	**9**	**3.08**	....	....	**10251**	**.892**	**28.6**	**29**	**12**	**12**	....	**1523**	**86**	**0**	**3.39**	....	**781**	**.890**	**30.8**

Hockey East First All-Star Team (1985) • NCAA East First All-American Team (1985) • NCAA Championship All-Tournament Team (1985) • NCAA Championship Tournament MVP (1985)

Traded to **San Jose** by **New Jersey** for San Jose's 2nd round choice (later traded to Pittsburgh - Pittsburgh selected Pavel Skrbek) in 1996 Entry Draft, November 15, 1995. Traded to **Chicago** by **San Jose** with Ulf Dahlen and Michal Sykora for Ed Belfour, January 25, 1997. Traded to **New Jersey** by **Chicago** for New Jersey's 2nd round choice (Stepan Mokhov) in 1999 Entry Draft, August 25, 1998. Selected by **Minnesota** from **New Jersey** in Expansion Draft, June 23, 2000. Traded to **New Jersey** by **Minnesota** with Minnesota's 9th round choice (later traded to Tampa Bay - Tampa Bay selected Thomas Ziegler) in 2000 Entry Draft for Brad Bombardir, June 23, 2000.

• THEODORE, Jose

G – R. 5'10", 182 lbs. b: Laval, Que., 9/13/1976. Montreal's 2nd, 44th overall in 1994.

Season	Club	League	GP	W	L	T	Mins	GA	SO	Avg	AAvg	Eff	SA	S%	SAPG	GP	W	L	T	Mins	GA	SO	Avg	Eff	SA	S%	SAPG
1990-91	Richelieu Bantam Regents	QAAA	42	....	....	....	2520	80	0	1.90	....	....	....	....	....	....	....	....	....	....	....	....	....	....	....	....	....
1991-92	Richelieu Riverains	QAAA	24	9	13	2	1440	96	0	3.99	....	....	....	....	....	....	....	....	....	....	....	....	....	....	....	....	....
1992-93	St-Jean Lynx	QMJHL	34	12	16	2	1776	112	0	3.78	....	....	....	....	....	3	0	2	....	175	11	0	3.77	....	....	....	....
1993-94	St-Jean Lynx	QMJHL	57	20	29	6	3225	194	0	3.61	....	....	....	....	....	5	1	4	....	296	18	0	3.65	....	....	....	....
1994-95	Hull Olympiques	QMJHL	*58	*32	22	2	*3348	193	5	3.46	....	....	....	....	....	*21	*15	6	....	*1263	59	*1	2.80	....	....	....	....
	Fredericton Canadiens	AHL	....	....	....	....	....	....	....	....	....	....	....	....	....	1	0	1	....	60	3	0	3.00	....	....	....	....
	Hull Olympiques	Mem-Cup	3	0	3	0	150	13	0	5.20	....	....	....	....	....	....	....	....	....	....	....	....	....	....	....	....	....

			REGULAR SEASON													PLAYOFFS											
Season	Club	League	GP	W	L	T	Mins	GA	SO	Avg	AAvg	Eff	SA	S%	SAPG	GP	W	L	T	Mins	GA	SO	Avg	Eff	SA	S%	SAPG
1995-96	**Montreal Canadiens**	**NHL**	1	0	0	0	9	1	0	6.67	6.63	33.35	2	.500	13.3	....	....	....	....	....	....	....	....	....	....	....	....
	Hull Olympiques	QMJHL	48	33	11	2	2807	158	0	3.38	....	....	....	....	....	5	2	3	....	299	20	0	4.01	....	....	....	....
	Canada	WJC-A	4	4	0	0	240	6	0	1.50	....	....	....	....	....	....	....	....	....	....	....	....	....	....	....	....	....
1996-97	**Montreal Canadiens**	**NHL**	16	5	6	2	821	53	0	3.87	4.17	4.04	508	.896	37.1	2	1	1	....	168	7	0	2.50	1.62	108	.935	38.6
	Fredericton Canadiens	AHL	26	12	12	0	1469	87	0	3.55	....	....	....	....	....	....	....	....	....	....	....	....	....	....	....	....	....
1997-98	Fredericton Canadiens	AHL	53	20	23	8	3053	145	2	2.85	....	....	....	....	....	4	1	3	....	237	13	0	3.28	....	....	....	....
	Montreal Canadiens	**NHL**	....	....	....	....	....	....	....	....	....	....	....	....	....	3	0	1	....	120	1	0	0.50	0.14	35	.971	17.5
1998-99	**Montreal Canadiens**	**NHL**	18	4	12	0	913	50	1	3.29	3.92	4.05	406	.877	26.7	....	....	....	....	....	....	....	....	....	....	....	....
	Fredericton Canadiens	AHL	27	12	13	2	1609	77	2	2.87	....	....	....	....	....	13	8	5	....	694	35	1	3.03	....	....	....	....
99-2000	**Montreal Canadiens**	**NHL**	30	12	13	2	1655	58	5	2.10	2.39	1.70	717	.919	26.0	....	....	....	....	....	....	....	....	....	....	....	....
	Canada	WC-A	8	5	3	0	478	13	2	1.63	....	....	....	....	....	....	....	....	....	....	....	....	....	....	....	....	....
	NHL Totals		65	21	31	4	3398	162	6	2.86	....	....	1633	.901	28.8	5	1	2	....	288	8	0	1.67	....	143	.944	29.8

QMJHL Second All-Star Team (1995, 1996) • WJC-A All-Star Team (1996) • Named Best Goaltender at WJC-A (1996)

• THIBAULT, Jocelyn

G – L. 5'11", 170 lbs. b: Montreal, Que., 1/12/1975. Quebec's 1st, 10th overall in 1993.

Season	Club	League	GP	W	L	T	Mins	GA	SO	Avg	AAvg	Eff	SA	S%	SAPG	GP	W	L	T	Mins	GA	SO	Avg	Eff	SA	S%	SAPG
1990-91	Laval Regents	QAAA	20	14	5	0	1178	78	1	3.94	....	....	....	....	....	5	1	4	0	300	20	0	4.00	....	....	....	....
1991-92	Trois Rivieres Draveurs	QMJHL	30	14	7	1	1496	77	0	3.09	....	....	....	....	....	3	1	1	....	110	4	0	2.19	....	....	....	....
1992-93	Sherbrooke Faucons	QMJHL	56	34	14	5	3190	159	3	2.99	....	....	....	....	....	15	9	6	....	882	57	0	3.87	....	....	....	....
1993-94	**Quebec Nordiques**	**NHL**	29	8	13	3	1504	83	0	3.31	3.18	3.58	768	.892	30.6	....	....	....	....	....	....	....	....	....	....	....	....
	Cornwall Aces	AHL	4	4	0	0	240	9	1	2.25	....	....	....	....	....	....	....	....	....	....	....	....	....	....	....	....	....
1994-95	Sherbrooke Faucons	QMJHL	13	6	6	1	776	38	1	2.94	....	....	....	....	....	....	....	....	....	....	....	....	....	....	....	....	....
	Quebec Nordiques	**NHL**	18	12	2	2	898	35	1	2.34	2.45	1.94	423	.917	28.3	3	1	2	....	148	8	0	3.24	3.41	76	.895	30.8
1995-96	**Colorado Avalanche**	**NHL**	10	3	4	2	558	28	0	3.01	2.99	3.80	222	.874	23.9	....	....	....	....	....	....	....	....	....	....	....	....
	Montreal Canadiens	**NHL**	40	23	13	3	2334	110	3	2.83	2.81	2.47	1258	.913	32.3	6	2	4	....	311	18	0	3.47	3.32	188	.904	36.3
1996-97	**Montreal Canadiens**	**NHL**	61	22	24	11	3397	164	1	2.90	3.12	2.62	1815	.910	32.1	3	0	3	....	179	13	0	4.36	5.61	101	.871	33.9
1997-98	**Montreal Canadiens**	**NHL**	47	19	15	8	2652	109	2	2.47	2.94	2.43	1109	.902	25.1	2	0	0	....	43	4	0	5.58	13.95	16	.750	22.3
1998-99	**Montreal Canadiens**	**NHL**	10	3	4	2	529	23	1	2.61	3.10	2.40	250	.908	28.4	....	....	....	....	....	....	....	....	....	....	....	....
	Chicago Blackhawks	**NHL**	52	21	26	5	3014	136	4	2.71	3.23	2.57	1435	.905	28.6	....	....	....	....	....	....	....	....	....	....	....	....
99-2000	**Chicago Blackhawks**	**NHL**	60	25	26	7	3438	158	3	2.76	3.16	2.60	1679	.906	29.3	....	....	....	....	....	....	....	....	....	....	....	....
	NHL Totals		327	136	127	43	18324	846	15	2.77	....	....	8959	.906	29.3	14	3	9	....	681	43	0	3.79	....	381	.887	33.6

QMJHL First All-Star Team (1993) • Canadian Major Junior First All-Star Team (1993) • Canadian Major Junior Goaltender of the Year (1993)

Transferred to **Colorado** after **Quebec** franchise relocated, June 21, 1995. Traded to **Montreal** by **Colorado** with Andrei Kovalenko and Martin Rucinsky for Patrick Roy and Mike Keane, December 6, 1995. Traded to **Chicago** by **Montreal** with Dave Manson and Brad Brown for Jeff Hackett, Eric Weinrich, Alain Nasreddine and Tampa Bay's 4th round choice (previously acquired, Montreal selected Chris Dyment) in 1999 Entry Draft, November 16, 1998.

• THOMAS, Wayne

Robert Wayne G – L. 6'2", 195 lbs. b: Ottawa, Ont., 10/9/1947.

Season	Club	League	GP	W	L	T	Mins	GA	SO	Avg	AAvg	Eff	SA	S%	SAPG	GP	W	L	T	Mins	GA	SO	Avg	Eff	SA	S%	SAPG
1965-66	Ottawa Jr. Senators	OJHL	STATISTICS NOT AVAILABLE																								
1966-67	Ottawa Jr. Senators	OJHL	STATISTICS NOT AVAILABLE																								
	Morrisburg Combines	Al-Cup	3	0	2	0	127	13	0	6.14	....	....	....	....	....	....	....	....	....	....	....	....	....	....	....	....	....
1967-68	University of Wisconsin	WCHA	DID NOT PLAY – FRESHMAN																								
1968-69	University of Wisconsin	WCHA	16	9	6	1	943	44	2	2.80	....	....	....	....	....	....	....	....	....	....	....	....	....	....	....	....	....
1969-70	University of Wisconsin	WCHA	21	14	7	0	1250	60	1	2.88	....	....	....	....	....	4	3	1	0	240	10	0	2.50	....	....	....	....
1970-71	Montreal Voyageurs	AHL	33	8	17	6	1845	111	1	3.57	....	....	....	....	....	3	0	3	0	179	12	0	4.02	....	....	....	....
1971-72	Nova Scotia Voyageurs	AHL	41	22	8	10	2393	100	1	2.51	....	....	....	....	....	....	....	....	....	....	....	....	....	....	....	....	....
1972-73	Nova Scotia Voyageurs	AHL	6	....	....	....	300	8	1	1.60	....	....	....	....	....	....	....	....	....	....	....	....	....	....	....	....	....
	Montreal Canadiens	**NHL**	10	8	1	0	583	23	1	2.37	2.23	....	....	....	....	....	....	....	....	....	....	....	....	....	....	....	....
1973-74	**Montreal Canadiens**	**NHL**	42	23	12	5	2410	111	1	2.76	2.66	....	....	....	....	....	....	....	....	....	....	....	....	....	....	....	....
1974-75	**Montreal Canadiens**	**NHL**	DID NOT PLAY – SPARE GOALTENDER																								
1975-76	**Toronto Maple Leafs**	**NHL**	64	28	24	12	3684	196	2	3.19	2.88	....	....	....	....	10	5	5	....	587	34	1	3.48	....	....	....	....
1976-77	**Toronto Maple Leafs**	**NHL**	33	10	13	6	1803	116	1	3.86	3.60	....	....	....	....	4	1	2	....	202	12	0	3.56	....	....	....	....
1977-78	**New York Rangers**	**NHL**	41	12	20	7	2352	141	4	3.60	3.38	....	....	....	....	1	0	1	....	60	4	0	4.00	....	....	....	....
1978-79	**New York Rangers**	**NHL**	31	15	10	3	1668	101	1	3.63	3.21	....	....	....	....	....	....	....	....	....	....	....	....	....	....	....	....
1979-80	**New York Rangers**	**NHL**	12	4	7	0	668	44	0	3.95	3.49	....	....	....	....	....	....	....	....	....	....	....	....	....	....	....	....
	New Haven Nighthawks	AHL	5	5	0	0	280	11	0	2.36	....	....	....	....	....	....	....	....	....	....	....	....	....	....	....	....	....
1980-81	**New York Rangers**	**NHL**	10	3	6	1	600	34	0	3.40	2.75	....	....	....	....	....	....	....	....	....	....	....	....	....	....	....	....
	NHL Totals		243	103	93	34	13768	766	10	3.34	....	....	....	....	....	15	6	8	....	849	50	1	3.53	....	....	....	....

WCHA Second All-Star Team (1970) • Played in NHL All-Star Game (1976)

Traded to **LA Kings** by **Toronto** with Brian Murphy and Gary Croteau for Grant Moore and Lou Deveault, October 15, 1968. Traded to **Montreal** by **LA Kings** with Leon Rochefort and Gregg Boddy for Jack Norris, Larry Mickey and Lucien Grenier, May 22, 1970. • Recorded shutout (3-0) in NHL debut vs. Vancouver, January 14, 1973. • On active roster for entire 1974-75 season but did not play. Traded to **Toronto** by **Montreal** for Toronto's 1st round choice (Peter Lee) in 1976 Amateur Draft, June 17, 1975. Claimed by **NY Rangers** from **Toronto** in Waiver Draft, October 10, 1977.

• THOMPSON, Tiny

Cecil Ralph G – L. 5'10", 160 lbs. b: Sandon, B.C., 5/31/1905 d: 2/11/1981. **HHOF**

Season	Club	League	GP	W	L	T	Mins	GA	SO	Avg	AAvg	Eff	SA	S%	SAPG	GP	W	L	T	Mins	GA	SO	Avg	Eff	SA	S%	SAPG
1919-20	Calgary Monarchs	CCJHL	STATISTICS NOT AVAILABLE																								
	Calgary Monarchs	Mem-Cup	2	1	0	1	120	11	0	5.50	....	....	....	....	....	....	....	....	....	....	....	....	....	....	....	....	....
1920-21	Calgary Alberta Grain	CCSHL	STATISTICS NOT AVAILABLE																								
1921-22	Bellevue Colts	AJHL	STATISTICS NOT AVAILABLE																								
1922-23	Bellevue Bulldogs	ASHL	STATISTICS NOT AVAILABLE																								
1923-24	Bellevue Bulldogs	ASHL	STATISTICS NOT AVAILABLE																								
	Bellevue Bulldogs	Al-Cup	4	1	2	1	240	10	1	2.50	....	....	....	....	....	....	....	....	....	....	....	....	....	....	....	....	....
1924-25	Duluth Hornets	USAHA	40	17	20	3	1920	59	11	1.38	....	....	....	....	....	....	....	....	....	....	....	....	....	....	....	....	....
1925-26	Minneapolis Millers	CHL	36	....	....	....	2160	59	10	1.64	....	....	....	....	....	3	3	0	0	180	1	2	0.33	....	....	....	....
1926-27	Minneapolis Millers	AHA	38	17	11	10	2253	51	9	1.42	....	....	....	....	....	6	3	3	0	361	8	1	1.33	....	....	....	....
1927-28	Minneapolis Millers	AHA	40	*28	7	5	2475	51	12	1.23	....	....	....	....	....	8	*4	0	4	520	3	*5	0.38	....	....	....	....
1928-29♦	**Boston Bruins**	**NHL**	*44	*26	13	5	2710	52	12	1.15	2.35	....	....	....	....	5	*5	0	0	300	3	*3	*0.60	....	....	....	....
1929-30	**Boston Bruins**	**NHL**	*44	*38	5	1	2680	98	3	*2.19	2.19	....	....	....	....	*6	3	3	0	432	12	0	1.67	....	....	....	....
1930-31	**Boston Bruins**	**NHL**	*44	*28	10	6	2730	90	3	1.98	2.47	....	....	....	....	5	2	3	0	343	13	0	2.27	....	....	....	....
1931-32	**Boston Bruins**	**NHL**	43	13	19	11	2698	103	*9	2.29	2.77	....	....	....	....	....	....	....	....	....	....	....	....	....	....	....	....
1932-33	**Boston Bruins**	**NHL**	*48	*25	15	8	3000	88	*11	*1.76	2.29	....	....	....	....	5	2	3	0	438	9	0	*1.23	....	....	....	....
1933-34	**Boston Bruins**	**NHL**	*48	18	25	5	2980	130	5	2.62	3.35	....	....	....	....	....	....	....	....	....	....	....	....	....	....	....	....
1934-35	**Boston Bruins**	**NHL**	*48	26	16	6	2970	112	8	2.26	2.70	....	....	....	....	4	1	3	0	275	7	1	1.53	....	....	....	....
1935-36	**Boston Bruins**	**NHL**	*48	22	20	6	2930	82	*10	*1.68	2.29	....	....	....	....	2	1	1	0	120	8	1	4.00	....	....	....	....
1936-37	**Boston Bruins**	**NHL**	*48	23	18	7	2970	110	*6	2.22	2.71	....	....	....	....	3	1	2	....	180	8	1	2.67	....	....	....	....
1937-38	**Boston Bruins**	**NHL**	*48	*30	11	7	2970	89	7	*1.80	2.08	....	....	....	....	3	0	3	....	212	6	0	1.70	....	....	....	....
1938-39	**Boston Bruins**	**NHL**	5	3	1	1	310	8	0	1.55	1.85	....	....	....	....	....	....	....	....	....	....	....	....	....	....	....	....
	Detroit Red Wings	**NHL**	39	16	17	6	2397	101	4	2.53	3.04	....	....	....	....	6	3	3	....	374	15	1	2.41	....	....	....	....
1939-40	**Detroit Red Wings**	**NHL**	46	16	24	6	2830	120	3	2.54	3.11	....	....	....	....	5	2	3	....	300	12	0	2.40	....	....	....	....
1940-41	Buffalo Bisons	AHL	1	0	0	0	40	1	0	1.50	....	....	....	....	....	....	....	....	....	....	....	....	....	....	....	....	....
1941-42			DID NOT PLAY																								
1942-43	Calgary RCAF Mustangs	CNDHL	....	....	....	....	....	....	....	....	....	....	....	....	....	4	....	....	....	....	11	0	3.00	....	....	....	....
	NHL Totals		553	284	194	75	34175	1183	81	2.08	....	....	....	....	....	44	20	24	0	2974	93	7	1.88	....	....	....	....

• Brother of Paul • Won Vezina Trophy (1930, 1933, 1936, 1938) • NHL Second All-Star Team (1931, 1935) • NHL First All-Star Team (1936, 1938) • Played in NHL All-Star Game (1937)

Signed as a free agent by **Minneapolis** (AHA), June 8, 1926. Traded to **Boston** by **Minneapolis** (AHA) for cash, May 12, 1928. • Recorded shutout (1-0) in NHL debut vs. Pittsburgh, November 15, 1928. Traded to **Detroit** by **Boston** for the rights to Normie Smith and $15,000, November 28, 1938. • Named Head Coach of **Buffalo** (AHL), October 11, 1940.

			REGULAR SEASON													PLAYOFFS											
Season	Club	League	GP	W	L	T	Mins	GA	SO	Avg	AAvg	Eff	SA	S%	SAPG	GP	W	L	T	Mins	GA	SO	Avg	Eff	SA	S%	SAPG

• TOPPAZZINI, Jerry

Gerald J. "Topper" G. 6', 180 lbs. b: Copper Cliff, Ont., 7/29/1931.

Season	Club	League	GP	W	L	T	Mins	GA	SO	Avg	AAvg	Eff	SA	S%	SAPG	GP	W	L	T	Mins	GA	SO	Avg	Eff	SA	S%	SAPG
1960-61	**Boston Bruins**	**NHL**	**1**	**0**	**0**	**0**	**1**	**0**	**0**	**0.00**	**0.00**	....	....	....	....	....	....	....	....	....	....	....	....	....	....	....	....
	NHL Totals		**1**	**0**	**0**	**0**	**1**	**0**	**0**	**0.00**	....	....	....	....	....	....	....	....	....	....	....	....	....	....	....	....	....

• **Boston** right winger replaced injured Don Simmons in 3rd period, October 16, 1960. (Chicago 5, Boston 2)

• TORCHIA, Mike

G – L. 5'11", 215 lbs. b: Toronto, Ont., 2/23/1972. Minnesota's 2nd, 74th overall in 1991.

Season	Club	League	GP	W	L	T	Mins	GA	SO	Avg	AAvg	Eff	SA	S%	SAPG	GP	W	L	T	Mins	GA	SO	Avg	Eff	SA	S%	SAPG
1987-88	Toronto Red Wings	MTHL	40	....	....	....	1800	93	5	2.33	....	....	....	....	....	....	....	....	....	....	....	....	....	....	....	....	....
	Henry Carr Crusaders	OJHL-B	1	0	0	0	2	1	0	30.00	....	....	....	....	....	....	....	....	....	....	....	....	....	....	....	....	....
1988-89	Kitchener Rangers	OHL	30	14	9	4	1672	112	0	4.02	....	....	....	....	....	2	0	2	....	126	8	0	3.81	....	....	....	....
1989-90	Kitchener Rangers	OHL	40	25	11	2	2280	136	1	3.58	....	....	....	....	....	*17	*11	6	....	*1023	60	0	3.52	....	....	....	....
	Kitchener Rangers	Mem-Cup	5	*3	2	0	354	23	0	3.90	....	....	....	....	....	....	....	....	....	....	....	....	....	....	....	....	....
1990-91	Kitchener Rangers	OHL	57	25	24	7	*3317	219	0	3.96	....	....	....	....	....	6	2	4	....	382	30	0	4.71	....	....	....	....
1991-92	Kitchener Rangers	OHL	*55	25	24	3	*3042	203	1	4.00	....	....	....	....	....	14	7	7	....	900	47	0	3.13	....	....	....	....
1992-93	Canada	Nat-Team	5	5	0	0	300	11	1	2.20	....	....	....	....	....	....	....	....	....	....	....	....	....	....	....	....	....
	Kalamazoo Wings	IHL	48	19	17	9	2729	173	0	3.80	....	....	....	....	....	....	....	....	....	....	....	....	....	....	....	....	....
1993-94	Kalamazoo Wings	IHL	43	23	12	2	2168	133	0	3.68	....	....	....	....	....	4	1	3	....	221	14	*1	3.80	....	....	....	....
1994-95	Kalamazoo Wings	IHL	41	19	14	5	2140	106	*3	2.97	....	....	....	....	....	6	0	4	....	257	17	0	3.97	....	....	....	....
	Dallas Stars	**NHL**	**6**	**3**	**2**	**1**	**327**	**18**	**0**	**3.30**	**3.46**	**3.45**	**172**	**.895**	**31.6**	....	....	....	....	....	....	....	....	....	....	....	....
1995-96	Portland Pirates	AHL	12	2	6	2	577	46	0	4.79	....	....	....	....	....	....	....	....	....	....	....	....	....	....	....	....	....
	Hampton Roads Admirals	ECHL	5	2	2	0	260	17	0	3.92	....	....	....	....	....	....	....	....	....	....	....	....	....	....	....	....	....
	Michigan K-Wings	IHL	1	1	0	0	60	1	0	1.00	....	....	....	....	....	....	....	....	....	....	....	....	....	....	....	....	....
	Orlando Solar Bears	IHL	7	3	1	1	341	17	0	2.99	....	....	....	....	....	....	....	....	....	....	....	....	....	....	....	....	....
	Baltimore Bandits	AHL	5	2	1	1	256	18	0	4.21	....	....	....	....	....	1	0	0	....	40	0	0	0.00	....	....	....	....
1996-97	Fort Wayne Komets	IHL	57	20	31	3	2970	172	1	3.47	....	....	....	....	....	....	....	....	....	....	....	....	....	....	....	....	....
	Baltimore Bandits	AHL	....	....	....	....	....	....	....	....	....	....	....	....	....	1	0	0	....	40	4	0	6.00	....	....	....	....
1997-98	Milwaukee Admirals	IHL	34	13	14	1	1828	94	1	3.09	....	....	....	....	....	....	....	....	....	....	....	....	....	....	....	....	....
	San Antonio Dragons	IHL	2	0	2	0	118	12	0	6.07	....	....	....	....	....	....	....	....	....	....	....	....	....	....	....	....	....
	Peoria Rivermen	ECHL	5	4	1	0	299	16	0	3.21	....	....	....	....	....	1	0	1	....	60	7	0	7.00	....	....	....	....
1998-99	HC Asagio	Alpenliga	30	....	....	....	1800	131	0	4.39	....	....	....	....	....	....	....	....	....	....	....	....	....	....	....	....	....
	HC Asagio	Italy	13	....	....	....	776	53	0	4.10	....	....	....	....	....	....	....	....	....	....	....	....	....	....	....	....	....
99-2000	Birmingham Bulls	ECHL	14	4	10	0	705	52	0	4.43	....	....	....	....	....	....	....	....	....	....	....	....	....	....	....	....	....
	Mohawk Valley Prowlers	UHL	23	8	9	4	1248	80	0	3.85	....	....	....	....	....	....	....	....	....	....	....	....	....	....	....	....	....
	NHL Totals		**6**	**3**	**2**	**1**	**327**	**18**	**0**	**3.30**	....	....	**172**	**.895**	**31.6**	....	....	....	....	....	....	....	....	....	....	....	....

Memorial Cup All-Star Team (1990) • Won Hap Emms Memorial Trophy (Memorial Cup Tournament Top Goaltender) (1990) • OHL First All-Star Team (1991)

Transferred to **Dallas** after **Minnesota** franchise relocated, June 9, 1993. Traded to **Washington** by **Dallas** for cash, July 14, 1995. Traded to **Anaheim** by **Washington** for Todd Krygier, March 8, 1996. • Scored goal with Mohawk Valley (UHL) vs. Binghamton (UHL), October 22, 1999.

• TREFILOV, Andrei

G – L. 6', 190 lbs. b: Kirovo-Chepetsk, USSR, 8/31/1969. Calgary's 14th, 261st overall in 1991.

Season	Club	League	GP	W	L	T	Mins	GA	SO	Avg	AAvg	Eff	SA	S%	SAPG	GP	W	L	T	Mins	GA	SO	Avg	Eff	SA	S%	SAPG
1990-91	Dynamo Moscow	USSR	20	....	....	....	1070	36	0	2.01	....	....	....	....	....	....	....	....	....	....	....	....	....	....	....	....	....
	Dynamo Moscow	Super-S	5	....	....	....	270	6	....	1.33	....	....	....	....	....	....	....	....	....	....	....	....	....	....	....	....	....
	Soviet Union	WEC-A	8	5	1	2	400	18	0	2.70	....	....	....	....	....	....	....	....	....	....	....	....	....	....	....	....	....
1991-92	Soviet Union	Can-Cup	1	0	0	0	4	0	0	0.00	....	....	....	....	....	....	....	....	....	....	....	....	....	....	....	....	....
	Dynamo Moscow	CIS	28	....	....	....	1326	35	0	1.58	....	....	....	....	....	....	....	....	....	....	....	....	....	....	....	....	....
	Russia	Olympics	4	0	0	0	39	2	0	3.08	....	....	....	....	....	....	....	....	....	....	....	....	....	....	....	....	....
	Russia	WC-A	2	1	0	0	66	2	0	1.82	....	....	....	....	....	....	....	....	....	....	....	....	....	....	....	....	....
1992-93	**Calgary Flames**	**NHL**	**1**	**0**	**0**	**1**	**65**	**5**	**0**	**4.62**	**3.96**	**5.92**	**39**	**.872**	**36.0**	....	....	....	....	....	....	....	....	....	....	....	....
	Salt Lake Golden Eagles	IHL	44	23	17	3	2536	135	0	3.19	....	....	....	....	....	....	....	....	....	....	....	....	....	....	....	....	....
	Russia	WC-A	6	4	2	0	360	14	0	2.33	....	....	....	....	....	....	....	....	....	....	....	....	....	....	....	....	....
1993-94	**Calgary Flames**	**NHL**	**11**	**3**	**4**	**2**	**623**	**26**	**2**	**2.50**	**2.40**	**2.13**	**305**	**.915**	**29.4**	....	....	....	....	....	....	....	....	....	....	....	....
	Saint John Flames	AHL	28	10	10	7	1629	93	0	3.42	....	....	....	....	....	....	....	....	....	....	....	....	....	....	....	....	....
1994-95	**Calgary Flames**	**NHL**	**6**	**0**	**3**	**0**	**236**	**16**	**0**	**4.07**	**4.27**	**5.01**	**130**	**.877**	**33.1**	....	....	....	....	....	....	....	....	....	....	....	....
	Saint John Flames	AHL	7	1	5	1	383	20	0	3.13	....	....	....	....	....	....	....	....	....	....	....	....	....	....	....	....	....
1995-96	**Buffalo Sabres**	**NHL**	**22**	**8**	**8**	**1**	**1094**	**64**	**0**	**3.51**	**3.49**	**3.40**	**660**	**.903**	**36.2**	....	....	....	....	....	....	....	....	....	....	....	....
	Rochester Americans	AHL	5	4	1	0	299	13	0	2.61	....	....	....	....	....	....	....	....	....	....	....	....	....	....	....	....	....
	Russia	WC-A	5	4	1	0	310	7	0	1.35	....	....	....	....	....	....	....	....	....	....	....	....	....	....	....	....	....
1996-97	Russia	W-Cup	4	2	1	0	200	9	1	3.00	....	....	....	....	....	....	....	....	....	....	....	....	....	....	....	....	....
	Buffalo Sabres	**NHL**	**3**	**0**	**2**	**0**	**159**	**10**	**0**	**3.77**	**4.06**	**3.85**	**98**	**.898**	**37.0**	**1**	**0**	**0**	....	**5**	**0**	**0**	**0.00**	**0.00**	**4**	**1.000**	**48.0**
1997-98	Rochester Americans	AHL	3	1	0	1	138	6	0	2.60	....	....	....	....	....	....	....	....	....	....	....	....	....	....	....	....	....
	Chicago Blackhawks	**NHL**	**6**	**1**	**4**	**0**	**299**	**17**	**0**	**3.41**	**4.07**	**4.00**	**145**	**.883**	**29.1**	....	....	....	....	....	....	....	....	....	....	....	....
	Indianapolis Ice	IHL	1	0	1	0	59	3	0	3.03	....	....	....	....	....	....	....	....	....	....	....	....	....	....	....	....	....
	Russia	Olympics	2	1	0	0	69	4	0	3.45	....	....	....	....	....	....	....	....	....	....	....	....	....	....	....	....	....
1998-99	AK Bars Kazan	Russia	3	....	....	....	160	7	1	2.63	....	....	....	....	....	....	....	....	....	....	....	....	....	....	....	....	....
	Chicago Blackhawks	**NHL**	**1**	**0**	**1**	**0**	**25**	**4**	**0**	**9.60**	**11.42**	**19.20**	**20**	**.800**	**48.0**	....	....	....	....	....	....	....	....	....	....	....	....
	Indianapolis Ice	IHL	18	9	6	2	986	39	0	2.37	....	....	....	....	....	....	....	....	....	....	....	....	....	....	....	....	....
	Calgary Flames	**NHL**	**4**	**0**	**3**	**0**	**162**	**11**	**0**	**4.07**	**4.84**	**5.33**	**84**	**.869**	**31.1**	....	....	....	....	....	....	....	....	....	....	....	....
	Detroit Vipers	IHL	27	17	8	2	1613	53	3	1.97	....	....	....	....	....	10	6	4	....	647	22	0	2.04	....	....	....	....
99-2000	Chicago Wolves	IHL	37	21	9	3	2060	81	3	2.36	....	....	....	....	....	9	7	1	....	489	11	1	*1.35	....	....	....	....
	NHL Totals		**54**	**12**	**25**	**4**	**2663**	**153**	**2**	**3.45**	....	....	**1481**	**.897**	**33.4**	**1**	**0**	**0**	....	**5**	**0**	**0**	**0.00**	....	**4**	**1.000**	**48.0**

IHL Second All-Star Team (1999) • Shared James Norris Memorial Trophy (fewest goals against - IHL) with Kevin Weekes (1999) • Won "Bud" Poile Trophy (Playoff MVP - IHL) (2000)

Signed as a free agent by **Buffalo**, July 11, 1995. Traded to **Chicago** by **Buffalo** for future considerations, November 12, 1997. Traded to **Calgary** by **Chicago** for future considerations, December 29, 1998.

• TREMBLAY, Vincent

G – L. 6'1", 180 lbs. b: Quebec City, Que., 10/21/1959. Toronto's 3rd, 72nd overall in 1979.

Season	Club	League	GP	W	L	T	Mins	GA	SO	Avg	AAvg	Eff	SA	S%	SAPG	GP	W	L	T	Mins	GA	SO	Avg	Eff	SA	S%	SAPG
1977-78	Quebec Remparts	QMJHL	50	....	....	....	2664	201	0	4.53	....	....	....	....	....	3	0	3	0	157	18	0	6.88	....	....	....	....
1978-79	Quebec Remparts	QMJHL	66	....	....	....	3588	273	2	4.56	....	....	....	....	....	6	....	....	....	350	30	0	5.14	....	....	....	....
1979-80	**Toronto Maple Leafs**	**NHL**	**10**	**2**	**1**	**0**	**329**	**28**	**0**	**5.11**	**4.52**	....	....	....	....	....	....	....	....	....	....	....	....	....	....	....	....
	New Brunswick Hawks	AHL	13	4	3	0	510	35	0	4.12	....	....	....	....	....	1	0	1	0	42	4	0	5.71	....	....	....	....
1980-81	**Toronto Maple Leafs**	**NHL**	**3**	**0**	**3**	**0**	**143**	**16**	**0**	**6.71**	**5.43**	....	....	....	....	....	....	....	....	....	....	....	....	....	....	....	....
	New Brunswick Hawks	AHL	46	24	12	8	2613	141	2	*3.24	....	....	....	....	....	....	....	....	....	....	....	....	....	....	....	....	....
1981-82	**Toronto Maple Leafs**	**NHL**	**40**	**10**	**18**	**8**	**2033**	**153**	**1**	**4.52**	**3.50**	....	....	....	....	....	....	....	....	....	....	....	....	....	....	....	....
1982-83	**Toronto Maple Leafs**	**NHL**	**1**	**0**	**0**	**0**	**40**	**2**	**0**	**3.00**	**2.41**	**2.22**	**27**	**.926**	**40.5**	....	....	....	....	....	....	....	....	....	....	....	....
	St. Catharines Saints	AHL	34	....	....	....	1699	133	0	4.70	....	....	....	....	....	....	....	....	....	....	....	....	....	....	....	....	....
1983-84	**Pittsburgh Penguins**	**NHL**	**4**	**0**	**4**	**0**	**240**	**24**	**0**	**6.00**	**4.73**	**10.14**	**142**	**.831**	**35.5**	....	....	....	....	....	....	....	....	....	....	....	....
	Baltimore Skipjacks	AHL	28	10	8	7	1590	106	0	4.00	....	....	....	....	....	....	....	....	....	....	....	....	....	....	....	....	....
1984-85	Riverview Trappers	NBSHL	STATISTICS NOT AVAILABLE																								
	Rochester Americans	AHL	33	13	10	8	1811	115	0	3.81	....	....	....	....	....	3	1	1	0	121	46	0	5.45	....	....	....	....
	NHL Totals		**58**	**12**	**26**	**8**	**2785**	**223**	**1**	**4.80**																	

QMJHL Second All-Star Team (1979)

Traded to **Pittsburgh** by **Toronto** with Rocky Saganiuk for Nick Ricci and Pat Graham, August 15, 1983. Signed as a free agent by **Buffalo**, March 7, 1985.

• TUCKER, Ted

Edward William G – L. 5'11", 165 lbs. b: Fort William, Ont., 5/7/1949.

Season	Club	League	GP	W	L	T	Mins	GA	SO	Avg	AAvg	Eff	SA	S%	SAPG	GP	W	L	T	Mins	GA	SO	Avg	Eff	SA	S%	SAPG
1965-66	Fort William Canadiens	TBJHL	24	....	....	....	1486	67	0	*2.74	....	....	....	....	....	....	....	....	....	....	....	....	....	....	....	....	....
	Fort William Canadiens	Mem-Cup	1	0	1	0	40	6	0	9.00	....	....	....	....	....	....	....	....	....	....	....	....	....	....	....	....	....
1966-67	Fort William Canadiens	TBJHL	30	*23	4	*3	1800	88	*3	*2.93	....	....	....	....	....	....	....	....	....	....	....	....	....	....	....	....	....
1967-68	Montreal Jr. Canadiens	OHA-Jr.	5	....	....	....	250	16	0	3.84	....	....	....	....	....	1	1	0	0	30	1	0	2.00	....	....	....	....

			REGULAR SEASON													PLAYOFFS											
Season	**Club**	**League**	**GP**	**W**	**L**	**T**	**Mins**	**GA**	**SO**	**Avg**	**AAvg**	**Eff**	**SA**	**S%**	**SAPG**	**GP**	**W**	**L**	**T**	**Mins**	**GA**	**SO**	**Avg**	**Eff**	**SA**	**S%**	**SAPG**
1968-69	Montreal Jr. Canadiens	OHA-Jr.	27	....	....	....	1600	89	2	3.34	....	....	....	....	....	2	0	1	0	80	7	0	5.38	....	....	....	....
1969-70	Clinton Comets	EHL	69	....	....	....	4140	211	*6	3.06	....	....	....	....	....	*17	*12	5	0	....	47	2	2.77	....	....	....	....
1970-71	Clinton Comets	EHL	74	31	32	11	4440	231	4	3.12	....	....	....	....	....	5	1	4	0	300	20	0	4.00	....	....	....	....
	Syracuse Blazers	EHL	....	....	....	....	....	....	....	....	....	....	....	....	....	2	0	2	0	120	14	0	7.00	....	....	....	....
1971-72	Clinton Comets	EHL	43	....	....	....	2610	142	2	3.26	....	....	....	....	....	3	1	2	0	220	12	0	3.27	....	....	....	....
1972-73	Salt Lake Golden Eagles	WHL	33	14	7	10	1919	112	1	3.50	....	....	....	....	....	7	2	5	0	427	26	0	3.63	....	....	....	....
1973-74	**California Golden Seals**	**NHL**	**5**	**1**	**1**	**1**	**177**	**10**	**0**	**3.39**	**3.28**	....	....	....	....	....	....	....	....	....	....	....	....	....	....	....	....
	Salt Lake Golden Eagles	WHL	13	6	6	0	713	61	0	5.13	....	....	....	....	....	3	0	3	0	160	12	0	4.49	....	....	....	....
1974-75	Toledo Goaldiggers	IHL	39	....	....	....	2166	114	2	3.16	....	....	....	....	....	11	....	....	....	522	31	1	3.56	....	....	....	....
1975-76	Toledo Goaldiggers	IHL	24	....	....	....	1044	73	0	4.20	....	....	....	....	....	1	0	1	0	60	5	0	5.00	....	....	....	....
	Columbus Owls	IHL	STATISTICS NOT AVAILABLE																								
	Port Huron Flags	IHL	STATISTICS NOT AVAILABLE																								
1976-77	Toledo Goaldiggers	IHL	3	....	....	....	164	12	0	4.39	....	....	....	....	....	....	....	....	....	....	....	....	....	....	....	....	....
	Muskegon Mohawks	IHL	46	....	....	....	2478	154	2	3.73	....	....	....	....	....	3	....	....	....	179	10	0	3.35	....	....	....	....
1977-78	Toledo-Port Huron Flags	IHL	41	....	....	....	2121	142	0	4.02	....	....	....	....	....	1	0	0	0	17	2	0	7.06	....	....	....	....
1978-79			DID NOT PLAY																								
1979-80	Dayton Gems	IHL	23	....	....	....	1189	91	0	4.59	....	....	....	....	....	....	....	....	....	....	....	....	....	....	....	....	....
	Saginaw Gears	IHL	12	....	....	....	691	33	0	2.87	....	....	....	....	....	4	....	....	....	205	11	0	3.22	....	....	....	....
1980-81	Saginaw Gears	IHL	40	....	....	....	2068	126	1	3.66	....	....	....	....	....	....	....	....	....	....	....	....	....	....	....	....	....
	NHL Totals		**5**	**1**	**1**	**1**	**177**	**10**	**0**	**3.39**	....	....	....	....	....	....	....	....	....	....	....	....	....	....	....	....	....

EHL North First All-Star Team (1970, 1971) • EHL North Rookie of the Year (1970)

Traded to **Atlanta** by **Montreal** for cash, June, 1972. Traded to **California** by **Atlanta** for cash, June 10, 1973.

• TUGNUTT, Ron

Ronald F. G – L. 5′11″, 160 lbs. b: Scarborough, Ont., 10/22/1967. Quebec's 4th, 81st overall in 1986.

Season	Club	League	GP	W	L	T	Mins	GA	SO	Avg	AAvg	Eff	SA	S%	SAPG	GP	W	L	T	Mins	GA	SO	Avg	Eff	SA	S%	SAPG
1983-84	Toronto Young Nationals	MTHL	34	....	....	....	1690	91	3	2.67	....	....	....	....	....	....	....	....	....	....	....	....	....	....	....	....	....
	Weston Dukes	OJHL-B	1	0	0	0	20	2	0	6.00	....	....	....	....	....	....	....	....	....	....	....	....	....	....	....	....	....
1984-85	Peterborough Petes	OHL	18	7	4	2	938	59	0	3.77	....	....	....	....	....	....	....	....	....	....	....	....	....	....	....	....	....
1985-86	Peterborough Petes	OHL	26	18	7	0	1543	74	1	2.88	....	....	....	....	....	3	2	0	....	133	6	0	2.71	....	....	....	....
1986-87	Peterborough Petes	OHL	31	21	7	2	1891	88	2	*2.79	....	....	....	....	....	6	3	3	....	374	21	1	3.37	....	....	....	....
1987-88	**Quebec Nordiques**	**NHL**	**6**	**2**	**3**	**0**	**284**	**16**	**0**	**3.38**	**2.81**	**4.40**	**123**	**.870**	**26.0**	....	....	....	....	....	....	....	....	....	....	....	....
	Fredericton Express	AHL	34	20	9	4	1964	118	1	3.60	....	....	....	....	....	4	1	2	....	204	11	0	3.24	....	....	....	....
1988-89	**Quebec Nordiques**	**NHL**	**26**	**10**	**10**	**3**	**1367**	**82**	**0**	**3.60**	**2.99**	**3.90**	**756**	**.892**	**33.2**	....	....	....	....	....	....	....	....	....	....	....	....
	Halifax Citadels	AHL	24	14	7	2	1368	79	1	3.46	....	....	....	....	....	....	....	....	....	....	....	....	....	....	....	....	....
1989-90	**Quebec Nordiques**	**NHL**	**35**	**5**	**24**	**3**	**1978**	**152**	**0**	**4.61**	**3.93**	**6.49**	**1080**	**.859**	**32.8**	....	....	....	....	....	....	....	....	....	....	....	....
	Halifax Citadels	AHL	6	1	5	0	366	23	0	3.77	....	....	....	....	....	....	....	....	....	....	....	....	....	....	....	....	....
1990-91	**Quebec Nordiques**	**NHL**	**56**	**12**	**29**	**10**	**3144**	**212**	**0**	**4.05**	**3.66**	**4.64**	**1851**	**.885**	**35.3**	....	....	....	....	....	....	....	....	....	....	....	....
	Halifax Citadels	AHL	2	0	1	0	100	8	0	4.80	....	....	....	....	....	....	....	....	....	....	....	....	....	....	....	....	....
1991-92	**Quebec Nordiques**	**NHL**	**30**	**6**	**17**	**3**	**1583**	**106**	**1**	**4.02**	**3.61**	**5.45**	**782**	**.864**	**29.6**	....	....	....	....	....	....	....	....	....	....	....	....
	Halifax Citadels	AHL	8	3	3	1	447	30	0	4.03	....	....	....	....	....	....	....	....	....	....	....	....	....	....	....	....	....
	Edmonton Oilers	**NHL**	**3**	**1**	**1**	**0**	**124**	**10**	**0**	**4.84**	**4.34**	**6.63**	**73**	**.863**	**35.3**	**2**	**0**	**0**	....	**60**	**3**	**0**	**3.00**	**2.65**	**34**	**.912**	**34.0**
1992-93	**Edmonton Oilers**	**NHL**	**26**	**9**	**12**	**2**	**1338**	**93**	**0**	**4.17**	**3.58**	**5.06**	**767**	**.879**	**34.4**	....	....	....	....	....	....	....	....	....	....	....	....
	Canada	WC-A	4	....	....	....	125	6	....	2.87	....	....	....	....	....	....	....	....	....	....	....	....	....	....	....	....	....
1993-94	**Anaheim Mighty Ducks**	**NHL**	**28**	**10**	**15**	**1**	**1520**	**76**	**1**	**3.00**	**2.88**	**2.75**	**828**	**.908**	**32.7**	....	....	....	....	....	....	....	....	....	....	....	....
	Montreal Canadiens	**NHL**	**8**	**2**	**3**	**1**	**378**	**24**	**0**	**3.81**	**3.66**	**5.32**	**172**	**.860**	**27.3**	**1**	**0**	**1**	....	**59**	**5**	**0**	**5.08**	**10.16**	**25**	**.800**	**25.4**
1994-95	**Montreal Canadiens**	**NHL**	**7**	**1**	**3**	**1**	**346**	**18**	**0**	**3.12**	**3.27**	**3.27**	**172**	**.895**	**29.8**	....	....	....	....	....	....	....	....	....	....	....	....
1995-96	Portland Pirates	AHL	58	21	23	6	3068	171	2	3.34	....	....	....	....	....	13	7	6	....	782	36	1	2.76	....	....	....	....
1996-97	**Ottawa Senators**	**NHL**	**37**	**17**	**15**	**1**	**1991**	**93**	**3**	**2.80**	**3.01**	**2.95**	**882**	**.895**	**26.6**	**7**	**3**	**4**	....	**425**	**14**	**1**	**1.98**	**1.64**	**169**	**.917**	**23.9**
1997-98	**Ottawa Senators**	**NHL**	**42**	**15**	**14**	**8**	**2236**	**84**	**3**	**2.25**	**2.68**	**2.14**	**882**	**.905**	**23.7**	**2**	**0**	**1**	....	**74**	**6**	**0**	**4.86**	**11.66**	**25**	**.760**	**20.3**
1998-99	**Ottawa Senators**	**NHL**	**43**	**22**	**10**	**8**	**2508**	**75**	**3**	***1.79**	**2.12**	**1.34**	**1005**	**.925**	**24.0**	**2**	**0**	**2**	....	**118**	**6**	**0**	**3.05**	**4.46**	**41**	**.854**	**20.8**
	Canada	WC-A	7	....	....	....	328	11	....	2.01	....	....	....	....	....	....	....	....	....	....	....	....	....	....	....	....	....
99-2000	**Ottawa Senators**	**NHL**	**44**	**18**	**12**	**8**	**2435**	**103**	**4**	**2.54**	**2.90**	**2.56**	**1020**	**.899**	**25.1**	....	....	....	....	....	....	....	....	....	....	....	....
	Pittsburgh Penguins	**NHL**	**7**	**4**	**2**	**0**	**374**	**15**	**0**	**2.41**	**2.75**	**1.84**	**197**	**.924**	**31.6**	**11**	**6**	**5**	....	**746**	**22**	**2**	**1.77**	**0.98**	**398**	**.945**	**32.0**
	NHL Totals		**398**	**134**	**170**	**49**	**21606**	**1159**	**15**	**3.22**	....	....	**10590**	**.891**	**29.4**	**25**	**9**	**13**	....	**1482**	**56**	**3**	**2.27**	....	**692**	**.919**	**28.0**

OHL First All-Star Team (1987) • Played in NHL All-Star Game (1999)

Traded to **Edmonton** by **Quebec** with Brad Zavisha for Martin Rucinsky, March 10, 1992. Claimed by **Anaheim** from **Edmonton** in Expansion Draft, June 24, 1993. Traded to **Montreal** by **Anaheim** for Stephan Lebeau, February 20, 1994. Signed as a free agent by **Washington**, September 25, 1995. Signed as a free agent by **Ottawa**, August 14, 1996. Traded to **Pittsburgh** by **Ottawa** with Janne Laukkanen for Tom Barrasso, March 14, 2000. Signed as a free agent by **Columbus**, July 4, 2000.

• TUREK, Roman

G – R. 6′3″, 190 lbs. b: Pisek, Czech., 5/21/1970. Minnesota's 6th, 113th overall in 1990.

Season	Club	League	GP	W	L	T	Mins	GA	SO	Avg	AAvg	Eff	SA	S%	SAPG	GP	W	L	T	Mins	GA	SO	Avg	Eff	SA	S%	SAPG
1987-88	Motor Ceske Budejovice	Czech-Jr.	STATISTICS NOT AVAILABLE																								
	Czechoslovakia	EJC-A	5	....	....	....	273	9	....	1.98	....	....	....	....	....	....	....	....	....	....	....	....	....	....	....	....	....
1988-89	Motor Ceske Budejovice	Czech-Jr.	STATISTICS NOT AVAILABLE																								
	Czechoslovakia	WJC-A	7	4	1	1	390	16	0	2.46	....	....	....	....	....	....	....	....	....	....	....	....	....	....	....	....	....
1989-90	Motor Ceske Budejovice	Czech-Jr.	STATISTICS NOT AVAILABLE																								
	Czechoslovakia	WJC-A	6	4	2	0	326	14	0	2.57	....	....	....	....	....	....	....	....	....	....	....	....	....	....	....	....	....
1990-91	Motor Ceske Budejovice	Czech.	26	....	....	....	1244	98	0	4.70	....	....	....	....	....	....	....	....	....	....	....	....	....	....	....	....	....
1991-92	Motor Ceske Budejovice	Czech-2	STATISTICS NOT AVAILABLE																								
1992-93	Motor Ceske Budejovice	Czech.	43	....	....	....	2555	121	....	2.84	....	....	....	....	....	....	....	....	....	....	....	....	....	....	....	....	....
	Czech-Republic	WC-A	DID NOT PLAY – SPARE GOALTENDER																								
1993-94	HC Ceske Budejovice	Czech-Rep	44	....	....	....	2584	111	....	2.51	....	....	....	....	....	3	....	....	....	180	12	0	4.00	....	....	....	....
	Czech-Republic	Olympics	2	2	0	0	120	3	....	1.50	....	....	....	....	....	....	....	....	....	....	....	....	....	....	....	....	....
	Czech-Republic	WC-A	2	....	....	....	120	4	....	2.00	....	....	....	....	....	....	....	....	....	....	....	....	....	....	....	....	....
1994-95	HC Ceske Budejovice	Czech-Rep	44	....	....	....	2587	119	....	2.76	....	....	....	....	....	9	....	....	....	498	25	....	3.01	....	....	....	....
	Czech-Republic	WC-A	6	3	3	0	359	9	2	1.50	....	....	....	....	....	....	....	....	....	....	....	....	....	....	....	....	....
1995-96	Nurnberg Ice Tigers	Germany	48	....	....	....	2787	154	....	3.31	....	....	....	....	....	5	....	....	....	338	14	....	2.48	....	....	....	....
	Czech-Republic	WC-A	8	7	0	1	480	15	*1	1.88	....	....	....	....	....	....	....	....	....	....	....	....	....	....	....	....	....
1996-97	Czech-Republic	W-Cup	3	0	3	0	82	10	0	7.00	....	....	....	....	....	....	....	....	....	....	....	....	....	....	....	....	....
	Dallas Stars	**NHL**	**6**	**3**	**1**	**0**	**263**	**9**	**0**	**2.05**	**2.20**	**1.43**	**129**	**.930**	**29.4**	....	....	....	....	....	....	....	....	....	....	....	....
	Michigan K-Wings	IHL	29	8	13	4	1555	77	0	2.97	....	....	....	....	....	....	....	....	....	....	....	....	....	....	....	....	....
1997-98	**Dallas Stars**	**NHL**	**23**	**11**	**10**	**1**	**1324**	**49**	**1**	**2.22**	**2.64**	**2.19**	**496**	**.901**	**22.5**	....	....	....	....	....	....	....	....	....	....	....	....
	Michigan K-Wings	IHL	2	1	1	0	119	5	0	2.51	....	....	....	....	....	....	....	....	....	....	....	....	....	....	....	....	....
1998-99♦	**Dallas Stars**	**NHL**	**26**	**16**	**3**	**3**	**1382**	**48**	**1**	**2.08**	**2.47**	**1.78**	**562**	**.915**	**24.4**	....	....	....	....	....	....	....	....	....	....	....	....
99-2000	**St. Louis Blues**	**NHL**	**67**	**42**	**15**	**9**	**3960**	**129**	***7**	**1.95**	**2.21**	**1.71**	**1470**	**.912**	**22.3**	**7**	**3**	**4**	....	**415**	**19**	**0**	**2.75**	**3.25**	**161**	**.882**	**23.3**
	NHL Totals		**122**	**72**	**29**	**13**	**6929**	**235**	**9**	**2.03**	....	....	**2657**	**.912**	**23.0**	**7**	**3**	**4**	....	**415**	**19**	**0**	**2.75**	....	**161**	**.882**	**23.3**

EJC-A All-Star Team (1988) • Czech Republic Player of the Year (1994) • WC-A All-Star Team (1995, 1996) • Named Best Goaltender at WC-A (1996) • Shared William M. Jennings Trophy with Ed Belfour (1999) • NHL Second All-Star Team (2000) • Won William M. Jennings Trophy (2000) • Played in NHL All-Star Game (2000)

Transferred to **Dallas** after **Minnesota** franchise relocated, June 9, 1993. Traded to **St. Louis** by **Dallas** for St. Louis' compensatory 2nd round choice (Dan Jancevski) in 1999 Entry Draft, June 20, 1999.

• TURNER, Joe

G – L. 5′10″, 182 lbs. b: Windsor, Ont., 1919 d: 1/12/1945.

Season	Club	League	GP	W	L	T	Mins	GA	SO	Avg	AAvg	Eff	SA	S%	SAPG	GP	W	L	T	Mins	GA	SO	Avg	Eff	SA	S%	SAPG
1933-34	Toronto Canoe Club	OHA-Jr.	9	....	....	....	540	24	0	*2.72	....	....	....	....	....	2	....	....	....	120	13	0	6.50	....	....	....	....
1934-35	Windsor Motors	MOHL	3	....	....	....	180	13	0	4.33	....	....	....	....	....	....	....	....	....	....	....	....	....	....	....	....	....
1935-36	Windsor Motors	MOHL	STATISTICS NOT AVAILABLE																								
1936-37	Windsor Bulldogs	MOHL	26	....	....	....	1560	91	0	3.50	....	....	....	....	....	5	1	2	2	300	13	0	2.68	....	....	....	....
1937-38	Stratford Midgets	OHA-Jr.	14	....	....	....	840	33	0	*2.36	....	....	....	....	....	7	2	3	1	420	23	1	3.28	....	....	....	....
1938-39	Guelph Indians	OHA-Jr.	14	....	....	....	840	38	*2	2.71	....	....	....	....	....	2	....	....	....	120	7	0	3.50	....	....	....	....

Season	Club	League	REGULAR SEASON GP	W	L	T	Mins	GA	SO	Avg	AAvg	Eff	SA	S%	SAPG	PLAYOFFS GP	W	L	T	Mins	GA	SO	Avg	Eff	SA	S%	SAPG
1939-40	Detroit Holzbaugh	MOHL	36	27	3	6	1620	76	*6	*2.11	....	....	....	....	....	12	9	3	0	730	27	2	2.22	....	....	....	....
	Windsor Chryslers	MOHL	1	1	0	0	60	1	0	1.00	....	....	....	....	....	....	....	....	....	....	....	....	....	....	....	....	....
	London Mohawks	OHA-Sr.	1	1	0	0	60	1	0	1.00	....	....	....	....	....	....	....	....	....	....	....	....	....	....	....	....	....
1940-41	Detroit Holzbaugh	MOHL	27	13	10	4	1620	84	1	3.11	....	....	....	....	....	7	4	3	0	420	25	0	3.57	....	....	....	....
1941-42	Indianapolis Capitols	AHL	52	*34	10	7	3175	129	4	*2.44	....	....	....	....	....	10	*7	3	0	630	34	0	3.24	....	....	....	....
	Detroit Red Wings	**NHL**	**1**	**0**	**0**	**1**	**70**	**3**	**0**	**2.57**	**2.51**	....	....	....	....	....	....	....	....	....	....	....	....	....	....	....	....
1942-1945			MILITARY SERVICE																								
	NHL Totals		**1**	**0**	**0**	**1**	**70**	**3**	**0**	**2.57**	....	....	....	....	....	....	....	....	....	....	....	....	....	....	....	....	....

AHL First All-Star Team (1942)

Promoted to **Detroit** from **Indianapolis** (AHL) to replace injured Johnny Mowers, February 5, 1942. (Toronto 3, Detroit 3). • Killed in action in Holland while serving with U.S. Marine Corps., January 12, 1945.

• VACHON, Rogie

Rogatien Rosaire G – L. 5'7", 170 lbs. b: Palmarolle, Que., 9/8/1945.

Season	Club	League	GP	W	L	T	Mins	GA	SO	Avg	AAvg	Eff	SA	S%	SAPG	GP	W	L	T	Mins	GA	SO	Avg	Eff	SA	S%	SAPG
1963-64	Montreal NDG Monarchs	MMJHL	29	....	....	....	1740	71	*4	2.45	....	....	....	....	....	18	*12	6	0	1080	57	1	3.17	....	....	....	....
	Montreal Jr. Canadiens	OHA-Jr.	7	....	....	....	400	29	0	4.35	....	....	....	....	....	....	....	....	....	....	....	....	....	....	....	....	....
	Montreal NDG Monarchs	Mem-Cup	10	7	3	0	600	34	*4	3.40	....	....	....	....	....	....	....	....	....	....	....	....	....	....	....	....	....
1964-65	Thetford Mines Aces	QJHL	13	10	3	0	780	35	0	2.69	....	....	....	....	....	5	1	4	....	300	30	0	6.00	....	....	....	....
	Montreal Jr. Canadiens	OHA-Jr.	14	....	....	....	840	58	0	4.14	....	....	....	....	....	....	....	....	....	....	....	....	....	....	....	....	....
1965-66	Thetford Mines Aces	QJHL	39	*25	13	1	2340	117	*2	3.00	....	....	....	....	....	11	7	4	0	659	31	1	2.82	....	....	....	....
	Quebec Aces	AHL	10	6	4	0	601	30	0	3.00	....	....	....	....	....	....	....	....	....	....	....	....	....	....	....	....	....
1966-67	Houston Apollos	CPHL	34	17	12	5	2020	99	2	2.91	....	....	....	....	....	....	....	....	....	....	....	....	....	....	....	....	....
	Montreal Canadiens	**NHL**	**19**	**11**	**3**	**4**	**1137**	**47**	**1**	**2.48**	**2.54**	....	....	....	....	**9**	***6**	**3**	....	**555**	**22**	**0**	***2.38**	....	....	....	....
1967-68♦	**Montreal Canadiens**	**NHL**	**39**	**23**	**13**	**2**	**2227**	**92**	**4**	**2.48**	**2.74**	....	....	....	....	**2**	**1**	**1**	....	**113**	**4**	**0**	**2.12**	....	....	....	....
1968-69♦	**Montreal Canadiens**	**NHL**	**36**	**22**	**9**	**3**	**2051**	**98**	**2**	**2.87**	**2.96**	....	....	....	....	**8**	**7**	**1**	....	**507**	**12**	**1**	**1.42**	....	....	....	....
1969-70	**Montreal Canadiens**	**NHL**	**64**	**31**	**18**	**12**	**3697**	**162**	**4**	**2.63**	**2.77**	....	....	....	....	....	....	....	....	....	....	....	....	....	....	....	....
1970-71♦	**Montreal Canadiens**	**NHL**	**47**	**23**	**12**	**9**	**2676**	**118**	**2**	**2.65**	**2.61**	....	....	....	....	....	....	....	....	....	....	....	....	....	....	....	....
1971-72	**Montreal Canadiens**	**NHL**	**1**	**0**	**1**	**0**	**20**	**4**	**0**	**12.00**	**12.14**	....	....	....	....	....	....	....	....	....	....	....	....	....	....	....	....
	Los Angeles Kings	**NHL**	**28**	**6**	**18**	**3**	**1586**	**107**	**0**	**4.05**	**4.13**	....	....	....	....	....	....	....	....	....	....	....	....	....	....	....	....
1972-73	**Los Angeles Kings**	**NHL**	**53**	**22**	**20**	**10**	**3120**	**148**	**4**	**2.85**	**2.67**	....	....	....	....	....	....	....	....	....	....	....	....	....	....	....	....
1973-74	**Los Angeles Kings**	**NHL**	**65**	**28**	**26**	**10**	**3751**	**175**	**5**	**2.80**	**2.69**	....	....	....	....	**4**	**0**	**4**	....	**240**	**7**	**0**	**1.75**	....	....	....	....
1974-75	**Los Angeles Kings**	**NHL**	**54**	**27**	**14**	**13**	**3239**	**121**	**6**	**2.24**	**2.00**	....	....	....	....	**3**	**1**	**2**	....	**199**	**7**	**0**	**2.11**	....	....	....	....
1975-76	**Los Angeles Kings**	**NHL**	**51**	**26**	**20**	**5**	**3060**	**160**	**5**	**3.14**	**2.84**	....	....	....	....	**7**	**4**	**3**	....	**438**	**17**	**1**	**2.33**	....	....	....	....
1976-77	Canada	Can-Cup	7	6	1	0	432	10	2	1.39	....	....	....	....	....	....	....	....	....	....	....	....	....	....	....	....	....
	Los Angeles Kings	**NHL**	**68**	**33**	**23**	**12**	**4059**	**184**	**8**	**2.72**	**2.51**	....	....	....	....	**9**	**4**	**5**	....	**520**	**36**	**0**	**4.15**	....	....	....	....
1977-78	**Los Angeles Kings**	**NHL**	**70**	**29**	**27**	**13**	**4107**	**196**	**4**	**2.86**	**2.67**	....	....	....	....	**2**	**0**	**2**	....	**120**	**11**	**0**	**5.50**	....	....	....	....
1978-79	**Detroit Red Wings**	**NHL**	**50**	**10**	**27**	**11**	**2908**	**189**	**0**	**3.90**	**3.47**	....	....	....	....	....	....	....	....	....	....	....	....	....	....	....	....
1979-80	**Detroit Red Wings**	**NHL**	**59**	**20**	**30**	**8**	**3474**	**209**	**4**	**3.61**	**3.20**	....	....	....	....	....	....	....	....	....	....	....	....	....	....	....	....
1980-81	**Boston Bruins**	**NHL**	**53**	**25**	**19**	**6**	**3021**	**168**	**1**	**3.34**	**2.69**	....	....	....	....	**3**	**0**	**2**	....	**164**	**16**	**0**	**5.85**	....	....	....	....
1981-82	**Boston Bruins**	**NHL**	**38**	**19**	**11**	**6**	**2165**	**132**	**1**	**3.66**	**2.82**	....	....	....	....	**1**	**0**	**0**	....	**20**	**1**	**0**	**3.00**	....	....	....	....
	NHL Totals		**795**	**355**	**291**	**127**	**46298**	**2310**	**51**	**2.99**	....	....	....	....	....	**48**	**23**	**23**	....	**2876**	**133**	**2**	**2.77**	....	....	....	....

• Father of Nick • QJHL First Team All-Star (1966) • Shared Vezina Trophy with Gump Worsley (1968) • NHL Second All-Star Team (1975, 1977) • Canada Cup All-Star Team (1976) • Played in NHL All-Star Game (1973, 1975, 1978)

Traded to **LA Kings** by **Montreal** for Denis Dejordy, Dale Hoganson, Noel Price and Doug Robinson, November 4, 1971. Signed as a free agent by **Detroit**, August 8, 1978. Traded to **Boston** by **Detroit** for Gilles Gilbert, July 15, 1980.

• VALIQUETTE, Stephen

G – L. 6'5", 206 lbs. b: Etobicoke, Ont., 8/20/1977. Los Angeles' 8th, 190th overall in 1996.

Season	Club	League	GP	W	L	T	Mins	GA	SO	Avg	AAvg	Eff	SA	S%	SAPG	GP	W	L	T	Mins	GA	SO	Avg	Eff	SA	S%	SAPG
1993-94	Burlington Cougars	OJHL	30	....	....	....	1663	112	1	4.04	....	....	....	....	....	....	....	....	....	....	....	....	....	....	....	....	....
1994-95	Burlington Cougars	OJHL	STATISTICS NOT AVAILABLE																								
	Sudbury Wolves	OHL	4	2	0	0	138	6	0	2.61	....	....	....	....	....	....	....	....	....	....	....	....	....	....	....	....	....
1995-96	Sudbury Wolves	OHL	39	13	16	2	1887	123	0	3.91	....	....	....	....	....	....	....	....	....	....	....	....	....	....	....	....	....
1996-97	Sudbury Wolves	OHL	*61	21	29	7	3311	232	1	4.20	....	....	....	....	....	....	....	....	....	....	....	....	....	....	....	....	....
	Dayton Bombers	ECHL	3	1	0	0	89	6	0	4.03	....	....	....	....	....	2	1	1	....	118	5	0	2.54	....	....	....	....
1997-98	Sudbury Wolves	OHL	14	5	7	1	807	50	0	3.72	....	....	....	....	....	....	....	....	....	....	....	....	....	....	....	....	....
	Erie Otters	OHL	28	16	7	3	1525	65	3	2.56	....	....	....	....	....	7	3	4	....	467	15	1	1.93	....	....	....	....
1998-99	Hampton Roads Admirals	ECHL	31	18	7	3	1713	84	1	2.94	....	....	....	....	....	2	0	1	....	60	7	0	7.00	....	....	....	....
	Lowell Lock Monsters	AHL	1	0	1	0	59	3	0	3.05	....	....	....	....	....	....	....	....	....	....	....	....	....	....	....	....	....
99-2000	**New York Islanders**	**NHL**	**6**	**2**	**0**	**0**	**193**	**6**	**0**	**1.87**	**2.14**	**0.96**	**117**	**.949**	**36.4**	....	....	....	....	....	....	....	....	....	....	....	....
	Lowell Lock Monsters	AHL	14	8	5	0	727	36	0	2.97	....	....	....	....	....	....	....	....	....	....	....	....	....	....	....	....	....
	Providence Bruins	AHL	1	1	0	0	60	3	0	3.00	....	....	....	....	....	....	....	....	....	....	....	....	....	....	....	....	....
	Trenton Titans	ECHL	12	5	6	1	692	36	1	3.12	....	....	....	....	....	....	....	....	....	....	....	....	....	....	....	....	....
	NHL Totals		**6**	**2**	**0**	**0**	**193**	**6**	**0**	**1.87**	....	....	**117**	**.949**	**36.4**	....	....	....	....	....	....	....	....	....	....	....	....

Signed as a free agent by **NY Islanders**, August 18, 1998.

• VANBIESBROUCK, John

"Beezer" G – L. 5'8", 176 lbs. b: Detroit, MI, 9/4/1963. NY Rangers' 5th, 72nd overall in 1981.

Season	Club	League	GP	W	L	T	Mins	GA	SO	Avg	AAvg	Eff	SA	S%	SAPG	GP	W	L	T	Mins	GA	SO	Avg	Eff	SA	S%	SAPG
1980-81	Sault Ste. Marie Greyhounds	OMJHL	56	31	16	1	2941	203	0	4.14	....	....	....	....	....	11	3	3	....	457	24	1	3.15	....	....	....	....
1981-82	Sault Ste. Marie Greyhounds	OHL	31	12	12	2	1686	102	0	3.62	....	....	....	....	....	7	1	4	....	276	20	0	4.35	....	....	....	....
	New York Rangers	**NHL**	**1**	**1**	**0**	**0**	**60**	**1**	**0**	**1.00**	**0.77**	**0.33**	**30**	**.967**	**30.0**	....	....	....	....	....	....	....	....	....	....	....	....
	United States	WJC-A	5	1	3	0	200	19	0	5.70	....	....	....	....	....	....	....	....	....	....	....	....	....	....	....	....	....
1982-83	Sault Ste. Marie Greyhounds	OHL	*62	39	21	1	3471	209	0	3.61	....	....	....	....	....	16	7	6	....	944	56	*1	3.56	....	....	....	....
	United States	WJC-A	5	....	....	....	280	17	....	3.64	....	....	....	....	....	....	....	....	....	....	....	....	....	....	....	....	....
1983-84	**New York Rangers**	**NHL**	**3**	**2**	**1**	**0**	**180**	**10**	**0**	**3.33**	**2.62**	**3.92**	**85**	**.882**	**28.3**	**1**	**0**	**0**	....	**1**	**0**	**0**	**0.00**	**0.00**	**0**	**.000**	**0.0**
	Tulsa Oilers	CHL	37	20	13	2	2153	124	*3	3.46	....	....	....	....	....	4	4	0	....	240	10	0	*2.50	....	....	....	....
1984-85	**New York Rangers**	**NHL**	**42**	**12**	**24**	**3**	**2358**	**166**	**1**	**4.22**	**3.37**	**5.20**	**1346**	**.877**	**34.2**	**1**	**0**	**0**	....	**20**	**0**	**0**	**0.00**	**0.00**	**12**	**1.000**	**36.0**
	United States	WEC-A	9	6	3	0	492	46	0	5.64	....	....	....	....	....	....	....	....	....	....	....	....	....	....	....	....	....
1985-86	**New York Rangers**	**NHL**	**61**	***31**	**21**	**5**	**3326**	**184**	**3**	**3.32**	**2.58**	**3.76**	**1625**	**.887**	**29.3**	**16**	**8**	**8**	....	**899**	**49**	***1**	**3.27**	**3.36**	**477**	**.897**	**31.8**
1986-87	**New York Rangers**	**NHL**	**50**	**18**	**20**	**5**	**2656**	**161**	**0**	**3.64**	**3.08**	**4.28**	**1369**	**.882**	**30.9**	**4**	**1**	**3**	....	**195**	**11**	**1**	**3.38**	**3.38**	**110**	**.900**	**33.8**
	United States	WEC-A	7	2	5	0	419	28	0	4.01	....	....	....	....	....	....	....	....	....	....	....	....	....	....	....	....	....
1987-88	United States	Can-Cup	4	2	2	0	240	9	0	2.00	....	....	....	....	....	....	....	....	....	....	....	....	....	....	....	....	....
	New York Rangers	**NHL**	**56**	**27**	**22**	**7**	**3319**	**187**	**2**	**3.38**	**2.81**	**3.72**	**1700**	**.890**	**30.7**	....	....	....	....	....	....	....	....	....	....	....	....
1988-89	**New York Rangers**	**NHL**	**56**	**28**	**21**	**4**	**3207**	**197**	**0**	**3.69**	**3.07**	**4.36**	**1666**	**.882**	**31.2**	**2**	**0**	**1**	....	**107**	**6**	**0**	**3.36**	**3.67**	**55**	**.891**	**30.8**
	United States	WEC-A	5	1	2	1	....	20	0	4.53	....	....	....	....	....	....	....	....	....	....	....	....	....	....	....	....	....
1989-90	**New York Rangers**	**NHL**	**47**	**19**	**19**	**7**	**2734**	**154**	**1**	**3.38**	**2.86**	**3.82**	**1362**	**.887**	**29.9**	**6**	**2**	**3**	....	**298**	**15**	**0**	**3.02**	**2.96**	**153**	**.902**	**30.8**
1990-91	**New York Rangers**	**NHL**	**40**	**15**	**18**	**6**	**2257**	**126**	**3**	**3.35**	**3.01**	**3.66**	**1154**	**.891**	**30.7**	**1**	**0**	**0**	....	**52**	**1**	**0**	**1.15**	**0.52**	**22**	**.955**	**25.4**
	United States	WEC-A	10	3	4	2	526	41	0	4.67	....	....	....	....	....	....	....	....	....	....	....	....	....	....	....	....	....
1991-92	United States	Can-Cup	1	1	0	0	60	3	0	3.00	....	....	....	....	....	....	....	....	....	....	....	....	....	....	....	....	....
	New York Rangers	**NHL**	**45**	**27**	**13**	**3**	**2526**	**120**	**2**	**2.85**	**2.54**	**2.57**	**1331**	**.910**	**31.6**	**7**	**2**	**5**	....	**368**	**23**	**0**	**3.75**	**4.82**	**179**	**.872**	**29.2**
1992-93	**New York Rangers**	**NHL**	**48**	**20**	**18**	**7**	**2757**	**152**	**4**	**3.31**	**2.83**	**3.30**	**1525**	**.900**	**33.2**	....	....	....	....	....	....	....	....	....	....	....	....
1993-94	**Florida Panthers**	**NHL**	**57**	**21**	**25**	**11**	**3440**	**145**	**1**	**2.53**	**2.42**	**1.92**	**1912**	**.924**	**33.3**	....	....	....	....	....	....	....	....	....	....	....	....
1994-95	**Florida Panthers**	**NHL**	**37**	**14**	**15**	**4**	**2087**	**86**	**4**	**2.47**	**2.58**	**2.12**	**1000**	**.914**	**28.7**	....	....	....	....	....	....	....	....	....	....	....	....
1995-96	**Florida Panthers**	**NHL**	**57**	**26**	**20**	**7**	**3178**	**142**	**2**	**2.68**	**2.66**	**2.58**	**1473**	**.904**	**27.8**	***22**	**12**	**10**	....	**1332**	**50**	**1**	**2.25**	**1.53**	**735**	**.932**	**33.1**
1996-97	**Florida Panthers**	**NHL**	**57**	**27**	**19**	**10**	**3347**	**128**	**2**	**2.29**	**2.45**	**1.85**	**1582**	**.919**	**28.4**	**5**	**1**	**4**	....	**328**	**13**	**1**	**2.38**	**1.68**	**184**	**.929**	**33.7**

Season	Club	League	REGULAR SEASON													PLAYOFFS											
			GP	W	L	T	Mins	GA	SO	Avg	AAvg	Eff	SA	S%	SAPG	GP	W	L	T	Mins	GA	SO	Avg	Eff	SA	S%	SAPG
1997-98	**Florida Panthers**	**NHL**	60	18	29	11	3451	165	4	2.87	3.43	2.89	1638	.899	28.5	....	....	....	....	....	....	....	....	....	....	....	....
	United States	Olympics	1	0	0	0	1	0	0	0.00	....	....	....	....	....	....	....	....	....	....	....	....	....	....	....	....	....
1998-99	**Philadelphia Flyers**	**NHL**	62	27	18	15	3712	135	6	2.18	2.58	2.13	1380	.902	22.3	6	2	4	....	369	9	1	1.46	0.90	146	.938	23.7
99-2000	**Philadelphia Flyers**	**NHL**	50	25	15	9	2950	108	3	2.20	2.50	2.08	1143	.906	23.2	....	....	....	....	....	....	....	....	....	....	....	....
	NHL Totals		829	358	318	114	47545	2367	38	2.99	....	....	23321	.899	29.4	71	28	38	....	3969	177	5	2.68	....	2073	.915	31.3

OHL Second All-Star Team (1983) • CHL First All-Star Team (1984) • Shared Terry Sawchuk Trophy (fewest goals against - CHL) with Ron Scott (1984) • Shared Tommy Ivan Trophy (MVP - CHL) with Bruce Affleck (1984) • NHL First All-Star Team (1986) • Won Vezina Trophy (1986) • NHL Second All-Star Team (1994) • Played in NHL All-Star Game (1994, 1996, 1997)

Traded to **Vancouver** by **NY Rangers** for future considerations (Doug Lidster, June 25, 1993), June 20, 1993. Claimed by **Florida** from **Vancouver** in Expansion Draft, June 24, 1993. Signed as a free agent by **Philadelphia**, July 16, 1998. Traded to **NY Islanders** by **Philadelphia** for NY Islanders' 4th round choice in 2001 Entry Draft, June 25, 2000.

• VEISOR, Mike

Michael David G – L. 5'9", 160 lbs. b: Toronto, Ont., 8/25/1952. Chicago's 3rd, 45th overall in 1972.

Season	Club	League	GP	W	L	T	Mins	GA	SO	Avg	AAvg	Eff	SA	S%	SAPG	GP	W	L	T	Mins	GA	SO	Avg	Eff	SA	S%	SAPG
1969-70	Hamilton Red Wings	OHA-Jr.	43	....	....	....	2580	172	0	4.00	....	....	....	....	....	....	....	....	....	....	....	....	....	....	....	....	....
1970-71	Hamilton Red Wings	OHA-Jr.	53	....	....	....	3177	266	0	5.02	....	....	....	....	....	7	2	4	1	409	30	0	4.41	....	....	....	....
1971-72	Peterborough Petes	OMJHL	49	....	....	....	2920	203	1	4.17	....	....	....	....	....	15	*11	2	2	900	32	*2	*2.13	....	....	....	....
	Peterborough Petes	Mem-Cup	3	*2	1	0	180	8	0	2.66	....	....	....	....	....	....	....	....	....	....	....	....	....	....	....	....	....
1972-73	Dallas Black Hawks	CHL	39	....	....	....	2160	99	*4	*2.75	....	....	....	....	....	4	....	....	....	219	14	0	3.83	....	....	....	....
1973-74	**Chicago Black Hawks**	**NHL**	10	7	0	2	537	20	1	2.23	2.15	....	....	....	....	2	0	1	....	80	5	0	3.75	....	....	....	....
1974-75	**Chicago Black Hawks**	**NHL**	9	1	5	1	460	36	0	4.70	4.26	....	....	....	....	....	....	....	....	....	....	....	....	....	....	....	....
	Dallas Black Hawks	CHL	16	11	5	0	958	52	0	3.26	....	....	....	....	....	*10	6	4	0	*656	28	*2	*2.56	....	....	....	....
1975-76	Dallas Black Hawks	CHL	*62	*28	22	9	*3561	174	*5	2.93	....	....	....	....	....	*9	5	4	0	*540	22	*1	2.44	....	....	....	....
1976-77	**Chicago Black Hawks**	**NHL**	3	1	2	0	180	13	0	4.33	4.03	....	....	....	....	....	....	....	....	....	....	....	....	....	....	....	....
	Dallas Black Hawks	CHL	40	17	15	6	2279	116	2	3.05	....	....	....	....	....	2	0	2	0	119	6	0	3.03	....	....	....	....
1977-78	**Chicago Black Hawks**	**NHL**	12	3	4	5	720	31	2	2.58	2.41	....	....	....	....	....	....	....	....	....	....	....	....	....	....	....	....
1978-79	**Chicago Black Hawks**	**NHL**	17	5	8	4	1020	60	0	3.53	3.12	....	....	....	....	....	....	....	....	....	....	....	....	....	....	....	....
1979-80	**Chicago Black Hawks**	**NHL**	11	3	5	3	660	37	0	3.36	2.97	....	....	....	....	1	0	1	....	60	6	0	6.00	....	....	....	....
1980-81	**Hartford Whalers**	**NHL**	29	6	13	6	1588	118	1	4.46	3.62	....	....	....	....	....	....	....	....	....	....	....	....	....	....	....	....
1981-82	**Hartford Whalers**	**NHL**	13	5	5	2	701	53	0	4.54	3.51	....	....	....	....	....	....	....	....	....	....	....	....	....	....	....	....
	Binghamton Whalers	AHL	22	13	8	1	1299	67	1	3.09	....	....	....	....	....	....	....	....	....	....	....	....	....	....	....	....	....
1982-83	**Hartford Whalers**	**NHL**	23	5	16	1	1280	118	1	5.53	4.46	8.01	815	.855	38.2	....	....	....	....	....	....	....	....	....	....	....	....
	Canada	WEC-A	DID NOT PLAY – SPARE GOALTENDER																								
1983-84	**Hartford Whalers**	**NHL**	4	1	3	0	240	20	0	5.00	3.94	8.77	114	.825	28.5	....	....	....	....	....	....	....	....	....	....	....	....
	Sherbrooke Jets	AHL	5	1	4	0	259	24	0	5.56	....	....	....	....	....	....	....	....	....	....	....	....	....	....	....	....	....
	Winnipeg Jets	**NHL**	8	4	1	2	420	26	0	3.71	2.92	5.61	172	.849	24.6	1	0	0	....	40	4	0	6.00	8.28	29	.862	43.5
	NHL Totals		139	41	62	26	7806	532	5	4.09	....	....	....	....	....	4	0	2	....	180	15	0	5.00	....	....	....	....

CHL First All-Star Team (1973, 1975) • Won Terry Sawchuk Trophy (fewest goals against - CHL) (1973) • Won Ken McKenzie Trophy (CHL's Rookie of the Year) (1973)

Traded to **Hartford** by **Chicago** for Hartford's 2nd round choice (Kevin Griffin) in 1981 Entry Draft, June 19, 1980. Traded to **Winnipeg** by **Hartford** for Ed Staniowski, November 10, 1983.

• VERNON, Mike

G – L. 5'9", 180 lbs. b: Calgary, Alta., 2/24/1963. Calgary's 2nd, 56th overall in 1981.

Season	Club	League	GP	W	L	T	Mins	GA	SO	Avg	AAvg	Eff	SA	S%	SAPG	GP	W	L	T	Mins	GA	SO	Avg	Eff	SA	S%	SAPG
1979-80	Calgary Canucks	AJHL	31	21	7	0	1796	88	0	2.95	....	....	....	....	....	....	....	....	....	....	....	....	....	....	....	....	....
1980-81	Calgary Wranglers	WHL	59	33	17	1	3154	198	1	3.77	....	....	....	....	....	22	14	8	....	1271	82	1	3.87	....	....	....	....
1981-82	Calgary Wranglers	WHL	42	22	14	2	2329	143	3	3.68	....	....	....	....	....	9	5	4	....	527	30	0	3.42	....	....	....	....
	Oklahoma City Stars	CHL	....	....	....	....	....	....	....	....	....	....	....	....	....	1	0	1	....	70	4	0	3.43	....	....	....	....
	Portland Winter Hawks	Mem-Cup	3	1	2	0	171	16	0	5.61	....	....	....	....	....	....	....	....	....	....	....	....	....	....	....	....	....
1982-83	**Calgary Flames**	**NHL**	2	0	2	0	100	11	0	6.59	5.29	15.76	46	.761	27.6	....	....	....	....	....	....	....	....	....	....	....	....
	Calgary Wranglers	WHL	50	29	18	2	2856	155	*3	*3.26	....	....	....	....	....	16	9	7	....	925	60	0	3.89	....	....	....	....
	Canada	WJC-A	4	3	0	0	180	10	0	3.33	....	....	....	....	....	....	....	....	....	....	....	....	....	....	....	....	....
	Portland Winter Hawks	M-Cup	3	3	0	0	180	14	0	4.67	....	....	....	....	....	....	....	....	....	....	....	....	....	....	....	....	....
1983-84	**Calgary Flames**	**NHL**	1	0	1	0	11	4	0	22.22	17.50	148.13	6	.333	32.7	....	....	....	....	....	....	....	....	....	....	....	....
	Colorado Flames	CHL	46	30	13	2	2648	148	1	*3.35	....	....	....	....	....	6	2	4	....	347	21	0	3.63	....	....	....	....
1984-85	Moncton Golden Flames	AHL	41	10	20	4	2050	134	0	3.92	....	....	....	....	....	....	....	....	....	....	....	....	....	....	....	....	....
1985-86	**Calgary Flames**	**NHL**	18	9	3	3	921	52	1	3.39	2.64	4.23	417	.875	27.2	*21	12	*9	....	*1229	60	0	2.93	3.02	583	.897	28.5
	Moncton Golden Flames	AHL	6	3	1	2	374	21	0	3.37	....	....	....	....	....	....	....	....	....	....	....	....	....	....	....	....	....
	Salt Lake Golden Eagles	IHL	10	6	4	0	600	34	1	3.40	....	....	....	....	....	....	....	....	....	....	....	....	....	....	....	....	....
1986-87	**Calgary Flames**	**NHL**	54	30	21	1	2957	178	1	3.61	3.06	4.21	1528	.884	31.0	5	2	3	....	263	16	0	3.65	4.29	136	.882	31.0
1987-88	**Calgary Flames**	**NHL**	64	39	16	7	3565	210	1	3.53	2.94	4.34	1708	.877	28.7	9	4	4	....	515	34	0	3.96	6.41	210	.838	24.5
1988-89♦	**Calgary Flames**	**NHL**	52	*37	6	5	2938	130	0	2.65	2.19	2.73	1263	.897	25.8	*22	*16	5	....	*1381	52	*3	2.26	2.14	550	.905	23.9
1989-90	Calgary Flames	Fr-Tour	3	....	....	....	129	3	....	1.39	....	....	....	....	....	....	....	....	....	....	....	....	....	....	....	....	....
	Calgary Flames	**NHL**	47	23	14	9	2795	146	0	3.13	2.64	4.07	1122	.870	24.1	6	2	3	....	342	19	0	3.33	4.22	150	.873	26.3
1990-91	**Calgary Flames**	**NHL**	54	31	19	3	3121	172	1	3.31	2.97	4.05	1406	.878	27.0	7	3	4	....	427	21	0	2.95	3.04	204	.897	28.7
	Canada	WEC-A	2	0	1	0	73	6	0	4.93	....	....	....	....	....	....	....	....	....	....	....	....	....	....	....	....	....
1991-92	**Calgary Flames**	**NHL**	63	24	30	9	3640	217	0	3.58	3.21	4.19	1853	.883	30.5	....	....	....	....	....	....	....	....	....	....	....	....
1992-93	**Calgary Flames**	**NHL**	64	29	26	9	3732	203	2	3.26	2.78	3.67	1804	.887	29.0	4	1	1	....	150	15	0	6.00	11.11	81	.815	32.4
1993-94	**Calgary Flames**	**NHL**	48	26	17	5	2798	131	3	2.81	2.69	3.04	1209	.892	25.9	7	3	4	....	466	23	0	2.96	3.09	220	.895	28.3
1994-95	**Detroit Red Wings**	**NHL**	30	19	6	4	1807	76	1	2.52	2.63	2.70	710	.893	23.6	18	12	6	....	1063	41	1	2.31	2.56	370	.889	20.9
1995-96	**Detroit Red Wings**	**NHL**	32	21	7	2	1855	70	3	2.26	2.24	2.19	723	.903	23.4	4	2	2	....	243	11	0	2.72	3.69	81	.864	20.0
1996-97♦	**Detroit Red Wings**	**NHL**	33	13	11	8	1952	79	0	2.43	2.61	2.45	782	.899	24.0	*20	*16	4	....	*1229	36	1	1.76	1.28	494	.927	24.1
1997-98	**San Jose Sharks**	**NHL**	62	30	22	8	3564	146	5	2.46	2.93	2.56	1401	.896	23.6	6	2	4	....	348	14	1	2.41	2.44	138	.899	23.8
1998-99	**San Jose Sharks**	**NHL**	49	16	22	10	2831	107	4	2.27	2.69	2.02	1200	.911	25.4	5	2	3	....	321	13	0	2.43	1.84	172	.924	32.1
99-2000	**San Jose Sharks**	**NHL**	15	6	5	1	772	32	0	2.49	2.84	2.21	360	.911	28.0	....	....	....	....	....	....	....	....	....	....	....	....
	Florida Panthers	**NHL**	34	18	13	2	2019	83	1	2.47	2.82	2.01	1020	.919	30.3	4	0	4	....	237	12	0	3.04	2.68	136	.912	34.4
	NHL Totals		722	371	241	86	41378	2047	23	2.97	....	....	18558	.890	26.9	138	77	56	....	8214	367	6	2.68	....	3525	.896	25.7

WHL First All-Star Team (1982, 1983) • Won Hap Emms Memorial Trophy (Memorial Cup Tournament Top Goaltender) (1983) • CHL Second All-Star Team (1984) • NHL Second All-Star Team (1989) • Shared William M. Jennings Trophy with Chris Osgood (1996) • Won Conn Smythe Trophy (1997) • Played in NHL All-Star Game (1988, 1989, 1990, 1991, 1993)

Traded to **Detroit** by **Calgary** for Steve Chiasson, June 29, 1994. Traded to **San Jose** by **Detroit** with Detroit's 5th round choice (Andrei Maximenko) in 1999 Entry Draft for San Jose's 2nd round choice (later traded to St. Louis - St. Louis selected Maxim Linnik) in 1998 Entry Draft and San Jose's 2nd round choice (later traded to Tampa Bay - Tampa Bay selected Sheldon Keefe) in 1999 Entry Draft, August 18, 1997. Traded to **Florida** by **San Jose** with San Jose's 3rd round choice (Sean O'Connor) in 2000 Entry Draft and future considerations for Radek Dvorak, December 30, 1999. Selected by **Minnesota** from **Florida** in Expansion Draft, June 23, 2000. Traded to **Calgary** by **Minnesota** for the rights to Dan Cavanaugh and Calgary's 8th round choice in 2001 Entry Draft, June 23, 2000.

• VEZINA, Georges

"Chicoutimi Cucumber" G – L. 5'6", 185 lbs. b: Chicoutimi, Que., 1/21/1887 d: 3/27/1926. **HHOF**

Season	Club	League	GP	W	L	T	Mins	GA	SO	Avg	AAvg	Eff	SA	S%	SAPG	GP	W	L	T	Mins	GA	SO	Avg	Eff	SA	S%	SAPG
1909-10	Chicoutimi Sagueneens	MCHL	STATISTICS NOT AVAILABLE																								
1910-11	Montreal Canadiens	NHA	16	8	8	0	980	62	0	3.80	....	....	....	....	....	....	....	....	....	....	....	....	....	....	....	....	....
1911-12	Montreal Canadiens	NHA	18	8	10	0	1109	66	0	3.57	....	....	....	....	....	....	....	....	....	....	....	....	....	....	....	....	....
1912-13	Montreal Canadiens	NHA	20	11	9	0	1217	81	1	3.99	....	....	....	....	....	....	....	....	....	....	....	....	....	....	....	....	....
1913-14	Montreal Canadiens	NHA	20	*13	7	0	1222	64	*1	*3.14	....	....	....	....	....	2	1	1	0	120	6	1	3.00	....	....	....	....
1914-15	Montreal Canadiens	NHA	20	6	14	0	1257	81	0	3.86	....	....	....	....	....	....	....	....	....	....	....	....	....	....	....	....	....
1915-16♦	Montreal Canadiens	NHA	24	*16	7	1	1482	76	0	3.08	....	....	....	....	....	5	*3	2	0	300	13	0	2.60	....	....	....	....
1916-17	Montreal Canadiens	NHA	20	10	10	0	1217	80	0	3.94	....	....	....	....	....	6	2	4	0	240	29	0	4.80	....	....	....	....
1917-18	**Montreal Canadiens**	**NHL**	21	*12	9	0	1282	84	*1	*3.93	2.35	....	....	....	....	2	1	1	0	120	10	0	5.00	....	....	....	....
1918-19	**Montreal Canadiens**	**NHL**	*18	10	8	0	1117	78	1	4.19	3.12	....	....	....	....	*5	*4	1	1	*300	18	*0	*3.60	....	....	....	....
	Montreal Canadiens	St-Cup	5	2	2	1	356	19	1	2.74	....	....	....	....	....	....	....	....	....	....	....	....	....	....	....	....	....
1919-20	**Montreal Canadiens**	**NHL**	*24	13	11	0	*1456	113	0	4.66	2.94	....	....	....	....	....	....	....	....	....	....	....	....	....	....	....	....
1920-21	**Montreal Canadiens**	**NHL**	*24	13	11	0	1441	99	1	4.12	2.94	....	....	....	....	....	....	....	....	....	....	....	....	....	....	....	....
1921-22	**Montreal Canadiens**	**NHL**	*24	12	11	1	1469	94	0	3.84	2.93	....	....	....	....	....	....	....	....	....	....	....	....	....	....	....	....
1922-23	**Montreal Canadiens**	**NHL**	*24	13	9	2	1488	61	2	2.46	2.12	....	....	....	....	2	0	2	0	120	4	0	2.00	....	....	....	....

Season	Club	League	GP	W	L	T	Mins	GA	SO	Avg	AAvg	Eff	SA	S%	SAPG	GP	W	L	T	Mins	GA	SO	Avg	Eff	SA	S%	SAPG
			REGULAR SEASON													PLAYOFFS											
1923-24	**Montreal Canadiens**	**NHL**	*24	13	11	0	1459	48	*3	*1.97	2.08	....	....	....	....	2	2	0	0	120	2	1	1.00	....	....	....	....
♦	Montreal Canadiens	St-Cup	4	4	0	0	240	4	1	1.00	....	....	....	....	....	....	....	....	....	....	....	....	....	....	....	....	....
1924-25	**Montreal Canadiens**	**NHL**	*30	17	11	2	*1860	56	5	*1.81	2.09	....	....	....	....	2	2	0	0	120	2	1	1.00	....	....	....	....
	Montreal Canadiens	St-Cup	4	1	3	0	240	16	0	4.00	....	....	....	....	....	....	....	....	....	....	....	....	....	....	....	....	....
1925-26	**Montreal Canadiens**	**NHL**	1	0	0	0	20	0	0	0.00	0.00	....	....	....	....	....	....	....	....	....	....	....	....	....	....	....	....
	NHL Totals		190	103	81	5	11592	633	13	3.28	....	....	....	....	....	13	9	4	1	780	36	2	2.77	....	....	....	....
	Other Major League Totals		138	72	65	1	8484	510	2	3.61	....	....	....	....	....	13	6	7	....	660	48	1	4.36	....	....	....	....

Rights retained by **Montreal Canadiens** after NHA folded, November 26, 1917. • 1923-24 Stanley Cup totals includes series with Calgary (WCHL) and Vancouver (PCHA). • Forced to retire because of tuberculosis after appearing in 325 consecutive regular-season games for Montreal Canadiens, November 28, 1925.

• VILLEMURE, Gilles

G – R. 5'8", 185 lbs. b: Trois-Rivieres, Que., 5/30/1940.

Season	Club	League	GP	W	L	T	Mins	GA	SO	Avg	AAvg	Eff	SA	S%	SAPG	GP	W	L	T	Mins	GA	SO	Avg	Eff	SA	S%	SAPG
1958-59	Trois-Rivieres Reds	QJHL	STATISTICS NOT AVAILABLE																								
	Troy Bruins	IHL	3	1	2	0	180	18	0	6.00	....	....	....	....	....	....	....	....	....	....	....	....	....	....	....	....	....
1959-60	Guelph Biltmores	OHA-Jr.	35	....	....	....	1980	128	1	3.66	....	....	....	....	....	5	....	....	....	300	19	*1	3.80	....	....	....	....
1960-61	New York Rovers	EHL	51	16	34	1	3060	223	1	4.37	....	....	....	....	....	....	....	....	....	....	....	....	....	....	....	....	....
1961-62	Long Island Ducks	EHL	65	25	39	1	3900	242	3	3.72	....	....	....	....	....	....	....	....	....	....	....	....	....	....	....	....	....
	Charlotte Checkers	EHL	1	0	1	0	60	7	0	7.00	....	....	....	....	....	....	....	....	....	....	....	....	....	....	....	....	....
	Johnstown Jets	EHL	1	1	0	0	60	2	0	2.00	....	....	....	....	....	....	....	....	....	....	....	....	....	....	....	....	....
1962-63	Vancouver Canucks	WHL	*70	35	31	4	*4200	228	*5	3.26	....	....	....	....	....	7	3	4	0	429	27	1	3.78	....	....	....	....
1963-64	Baltimore Clippers	AHL	66	31	33	2	3960	192	3	2.91	....	....	....	....	....	....	....	....	....	....	....	....	....	....	....	....	....
	New York Rangers	**NHL**	5	0	2	3	300	18	0	3.60	4.01	....	....	....	....	....	....	....	....	....	....	....	....	....	....	....	....
1964-65	Vancouver Canucks	WHL	60	27	26	6	3676	212	2	3.46	....	....	....	....	....	5	1	4	0	309	17	0	3.30	....	....	....	....
1965-66	Vancouver Canucks	WHL	*69	*32	34	3	*4178	223	*5	3.20	....	....	....	....	....	7	3	4	0	420	27	0	3.86	....	....	....	....
1966-67	Baltimore Clippers	AHL	*70	34	27	9	4180	238	*4	3.42	....	....	....	....	....	9	4	5	0	569	39	0	4.11	....	....	....	....
1967-68	**New York Rangers**	**NHL**	4	1	2	0	200	8	1	2.40	2.66	....	....	....	....	....	....	....	....	....	....	....	....	....	....	....	....
	Buffalo Bisons	AHL	37	18	13	6	2160	89	3	*2.47	....	....	....	....	....	5	1	3	0	247	15	0	3.64	....	....	....	....
1968-69	**New York Rangers**	**NHL**	4	2	1	1	240	9	0	2.25	2.32	....	....	....	....	1	0	1	....	60	4	0	4.00	....	....	....	....
	Buffalo Bisons	AHL	62	36	12	14	3674	148	*6	*2.42	....	....	....	....	....	6	2	4	0	360	19	1	3.17	....	....	....	....
1969-70	Buffalo Bisons	AHL	*65	....	....	....	*3714	156	*8	*2.52	....	....	....	....	....	*14	*11	3	0	*875	31	*1	*2.13	....	....	....	....
1970-71	**New York Rangers**	**NHL**	34	22	8	4	2039	78	4	2.30	2.26	....	....	....	....	2	0	1	....	80	6	0	4.50	....	....	....	....
1971-72	**New York Rangers**	**NHL**	37	24	7	4	2129	74	3	2.09	2.09	....	....	....	....	6	4	2	....	360	14	0	2.33	....	....	....	....
1972-73	**New York Rangers**	**NHL**	34	20	12	2	2040	78	3	2.29	2.14	....	....	....	....	2	0	1	....	61	2	0	1.97	....	....	....	....
1973-74	**New York Rangers**	**NHL**	21	7	7	3	1054	62	0	3.53	3.42	....	....	....	....	1	0	0	....	1	0	0	0.00	....	....	....	....
1974-75	**New York Rangers**	**NHL**	45	22	14	6	2470	130	2	3.16	2.85	....	....	....	....	2	1	0	....	94	6	0	3.83	....	....	....	....
1975-76	**Chicago Black Hawks**	**NHL**	15	2	7	5	797	57	0	4.29	3.89	....	....	....	....	....	....	....	....	....	....	....	....	....	....	....	....
1976-77	**Chicago Black Hawks**	**NHL**	6	0	4	1	312	28	0	5.38	5.01	....	....	....	....	....	....	....	....	....	....	....	....	....	....	....	....
	NHL Totals		205	100	64	29	11581	542	13	2.81	....	....	....	....	....	14	5	5	....	656	32	0	2.93	....	....	....	....

WHL Second All-Star Team (1963) • Won WHL Rookie of the Year Award (1963) • WHL First All-Star Team (1966) • AHL Second All-Star Team (1967) • AHL First All-Star Team (1969, 1970) • Won Harry "Hap" Holmes Memorial Award (fewest goals against - AHL) (1969, 1970) • Won Les Cunningham Award (MVP - AHL) (1969, 1970) • Shared Vezina Trophy with Ed Giacomin (1971) • Played in NHL All-Star Game (1971, 1972, 1973)

Loaned to **Charlotte** (EHL) by **Long Island** (EHL) as emergency injury replacement, Januray 30, 1962. Loaned to **Johnstown** (EHL) by **Long Island** (EHL) as emergency injury replacement, Januray 31, 1962. Promoted to **NY Rangers** from **Baltimore** (AHL) to replace injured Jacques Plante, November 20, 1963. (Boston 1, NY Rangers 1). • Played 22 seconds in playoff game vs. Philadelphia, April 23, 1974. Traded to **Chicago** by **NY Rangers** for Doug Jarrett, October 28, 1975.

• VOKOUN, Tomas

G – R. 6', 195 lbs. b: Karlovy Vary, Czech., 7/2/1976. Montreal's 11th, 226th overall in 1994.

Season	Club	League	GP	W	L	T	Mins	GA	SO	Avg	AAvg	Eff	SA	S%	SAPG	GP	W	L	T	Mins	GA	SO	Avg	Eff	SA	S%	SAPG
1993-94	Poldi Kladno	Czech-Rep	1	0	0	0	20	2	0	6.01	....	....	....	....	....	....	....	....	....	....	....	....	....	....	....	....	....
	Czech-Republic	EJC-A	5	....	....	....	300	11	....	2.20	....	....	....	....	....	....	....	....	....	....	....	....	....	....	....	....	....
1994-95	Poldi Kladno	Czech-Rep	26	....	....	....	1368	70	....	3.07	....	....	....	....	....	5	....	....	....	240	19	....	4.75	....	....	....	....
1995-96	Wheeling Thunderbirds	ECHL	35	20	10	2	1912	117	0	3.67	....	....	....	....	....	7	4	3	....	436	19	0	2.61	....	....	....	....
	Czech-Republic	WJC-A	6	2	2	2	356	21	1	3.54	....	....	....	....	....	....	....	....	....	....	....	....	....	....	....	....	....
	Fredericton Canadiens	AHL	....	....	....	....	....	....	....	....	....	....	....	....	....	1	0	1	....	59	4	0	4.09	....	....	....	....
1996-97	**Montreal Canadiens**	**NHL**	1	0	0	0	20	4	0	12.00	12.92	34.29	14	.714	42.0	....	....	....	....	....	....	....	....	....	....	....	....
	Fredericton Canadiens	AHL	47	12	26	7	2645	154	2	3.49	....	....	....	....	....	....	....	....	....	....	....	....	....	....	....	....	....
1997-98	Fredericton Canadiens	AHL	31	13	13	2	1735	90	0	3.11	....	....	....	....	....	....	....	....	....	....	....	....	....	....	....	....	....
1998-99	**Nashville Predators**	**NHL**	37	12	18	4	1954	96	1	2.95	3.52	2.72	1041	.908	32.0	....	....	....	....	....	....	....	....	....	....	....	....
	Milwaukee Admirals	IHL	9	3	2	4	539	22	1	2.45	....	....	....	....	....	2	0	2	....	149	8	0	3.22	....	....	....	....
99-2000	**Nashville Predators**	**NHL**	33	9	20	1	1879	87	1	2.78	3.18	2.66	908	.904	29.0	....	....	....	....	....	....	....	....	....	....	....	....
	Milwaukee Admirals	IHL	7	5	2	0	364	17	0	2.80	....	....	....	....	....	....	....	....	....	....	....	....	....	....	....	....	....
	NHL Totals		71	21	38	5	3853	187	2	2.91	....	....	1963	.905	30.6	....	....	....	....	....	....	....	....	....	....	....	....

EJC-A All-Star Team (1994) • Named Best Goaltender at EJC-A (1994)

Claimed by **Nashville** from **Montreal** in Expansion Draft, June 26, 1998.

• WAITE, Jimmy

James Dean G – L. 6'1", 180 lbs. b: Sherbrooke, Que., 4/15/1969. Chicago's 1st, 8th overall in 1987.

Season	Club	League	GP	W	L	T	Mins	GA	SO	Avg	AAvg	Eff	SA	S%	SAPG	GP	W	L	T	Mins	GA	SO	Avg	Eff	SA	S%	SAPG
1984-85	L'estrie-Maurice Cantonniers	QAAA	10	6	4	0	598	52	0	5.22	....	....	....	....	....	....	....	....	....	....	....	....	....	....	....	....	....
1985-86	L'estrie-Maurice Cantonniers	QAAA	29	11	15	1	1643	143	0	5.22	....	....	....	....	....	....	....	....	....	....	....	....	....	....	....	....	....
1986-87	Chicoutimi Sagueneens	QMJHL	50	23	17	3	2569	209	2	4.48	....	....	....	....	....	11	4	6	....	576	54	1	5.63	....	....	....	....
	Canada	WJC-A	4	....	....	....	220	12	....	3.27	....	....	....	....	....	....	....	....	....	....	....	....	....	....	....	....	....
1987-88	Chicoutimi Sagueneens	QMJHL	36	17	16	1	2000	150	0	4.50	....	....	....	....	....	4	1	2	....	222	17	0	4.59	....	....	....	....
	Canada	WJC-A	7	*6	1	0	419	16	0	2.29	....	....	....	....	....	....	....	....	....	....	....	....	....	....	....	....	....
1988-89	**Chicago Blackhawks**	**NHL**	11	0	7	1	494	43	0	5.22	4.35	8.87	253	.830	30.7	....	....	....	....	....	....	....	....	....	....	....	....
	Saginaw Hawks	IHL	5	3	1	0	304	10	0	1.97	....	....	....	....	....	....	....	....	....	....	....	....	....	....	....	....	....
1989-90	**Chicago Blackhawks**	**NHL**	4	2	0	0	183	14	0	4.59	3.89	6.98	92	.848	30.2	....	....	....	....	....	....	....	....	....	....	....	....
	Indianapolis Ice	IHL	54	*34	14	5	*3207	135	*5	*2.53	....	....	....	....	....	*10	*9	1	....	*602	19	*1	*1.89	....	....	....	....
1990-91	**Chicago Blackhawks**	**NHL**	1	1	0	0	60	2	0	2.00	1.80	1.43	28	.929	28.0	....	....	....	....	....	....	....	....	....	....	....	....
	Indianapolis Ice	IHL	49	*26	18	4	2888	167	3	3.47	....	....	....	....	....	6	2	4	....	369	20	0	3.25	....	....	....	....
1991-92	**Chicago Blackhawks**	**NHL**	17	4	7	4	877	54	0	3.69	3.31	5.74	347	.844	23.7	....	....	....	....	....	....	....	....	....	....	....	....
	Indianapolis Ice	IHL	13	4	7	1	702	53	0	4.53	....	....	....	....	....	....	....	....	....	....	....	....	....	....	....	....	....
	Hershey Bears	AHL	11	6	4	1	631	44	0	4.18	....	....	....	....	....	6	2	4	....	360	19	0	3.17	....	....	....	....
1992-93	**Chicago Blackhawks**	**NHL**	20	6	7	1	996	49	2	2.95	2.52	3.52	411	.881	24.8	....	....	....	....	....	....	....	....	....	....	....	....
1993-94	**San Jose Sharks**	**NHL**	15	3	7	0	697	50	0	4.30	4.14	6.74	319	.843	27.5	2	0	0	....	40	3	0	4.50	7.94	17	.824	25.5
1994-95	**Chicago Blackhawks**	**NHL**	2	1	1	0	119	5	0	2.52	2.64	2.47	51	.902	25.7	....	....	....	....	....	....	....	....	....	....	....	....
	Indianapolis Ice	IHL	4	2	1	1	239	13	0	3.25	....	....	....	....	....	....	....	....	....	....	....	....	....	....	....	....	....
1995-96	**Chicago Blackhawks**	**NHL**	1	0	0	0	31	0	0	0.00	0.00	0.00	8	1.000	15.5	....	....	....	....	....	....	....	....	....	....	....	....
	Indianapolis Ice	IHL	56	28	18	6	3157	179	0	3.40	....	....	....	....	....	5	2	3	....	298	15	1	3.02	....	....	....	....
1996-97	**Chicago Blackhawks**	**NHL**	2	0	1	1	105	7	0	4.00	4.31	4.83	58	.879	33.1	....	....	....	....	....	....	....	....	....	....	....	....
	Indianapolis Ice	IHL	41	22	15	4	2450	112	4	2.74	....	....	....	....	....	4	1	3	....	222	13	0	3.51	....	....	....	....
1997-98	**Phoenix Coyotes**	**NHL**	17	5	6	1	793	28	1	2.12	2.53	1.84	322	.913	24.4	4	0	3	....	171	11	0	3.86	4.38	97	.887	34.0
1998-99	**Phoenix Coyotes**	**NHL**	16	6	5	4	898	41	1	2.74	3.26	2.88	390	.895	26.1	....	....	....	....	....	....	....	....	....	....	....	....
	Springfield Falcons	AHL	8	3	4	1	483	19	0	2.36	....	....	....	....	....	2	0	2	....	118	6	0	3.05	....	....	....	....
	Utah Grizzlies	IHL	11	6	3	2	622	30	0	2.89	....	....	....	....	....	....	....	....	....	....	....	....	....	....	....	....	....
99-2000	St. John's Maple Leafs	AHL	*62	20	37	4	*3461	176	6	3.05	....	....	....	....	....	....	....	....	....	....	....	....	....	....	....	....	....
	NHL Totals		106	28	41	12	5253	293	4	3.35	....	....	2279	.871	26.0	6	0	3	....	211	14	0	3.98	....	114	.877	32.4

QMJHL Second All-Star Team (1987) • WJC-A All-Star Team (1988) • Named Best Goaltender at WJC-A (1988) • IHL First All-Star Team (1990) • Won James Norris Memorial Trophy (fewest goals against - IHL) (1990)

Traded to **San Jose** by **Chicago** for future considerations (Neil Wilkinson, July 9, 1993), June 18, 1993. Traded to **Chicago** by **San Jose** for Chicago's 4th round choice (later traded to NY Rangers - NY Rangers selected Tomi Kallarsson) in 1997 Entry Draft, February 5, 1995. Claimed by **Phoenix** from **Chicago** in NHL Waiver Draft, September 28, 1997. Signed as a free agent by **Toronto**, August 19, 1999.

• WAKALUK, Darcy

Darcy W. G – L. 5'11", 180 lbs. b: Pincher Creek, Alta., 3/14/1966. Buffalo's 7th, 144th overall in 1984.

			REGULAR SEASON													PLAYOFFS											
Season	Club	League	GP	W	L	T	Mins	GA	SO	Avg	AAvg	Eff	SA	S%	SAPG	GP	W	L	T	Mins	GA	SO	Avg	Eff	SA	S%	SAPG
1982-83	Pincher Creek Oilers	AJHL	38	....	....	....	2280	116	0	3.05	....	....	....	....	....	....	....	....	....	....	....	....	....	....	....	....	....
1983-84	Kelowna Wings	WHL	31	2	22	0	1555	163	0	6.29	....	....	....	....	....	....	....	....	....	....	....	....	....	....	....	....	....
1984-85	Kelowna Wings	WHL	54	19	30	4	3094	244	0	4.73	....	....	....	....	....	5	1	4	....	282	22	0	4.68	....	....	....	....
1985-86	Spokane Chiefs	WHL	47	21	22	1	2562	224	1	5.25	....	....	....	....	....	7	3	4	....	419	37	0	5.30	....	....	....	....
1986-87	Rochester Americans	AHL	11	2	2	0	545	26	0	2.86	....	....	....	....	....	5	2	0	....	141	11	0	4.68	....	....	....	....
1987-88	Rochester Americans	AHL	55	27	16	3	2763	159	0	3.45	....	....	....	....	....	6	3	3	....	328	22	0	4.02	....	....	....	....
1988-89	**Buffalo Sabres**	**NHL**	**6**	**1**	**3**	**0**	**214**	**15**	**0**	**4.21**	**3.50**	**7.02**	**90**	**.833**	**25.2**	....	....	....	....	....	....	....	....	....	....	....	....
	Rochester Americans	AHL	33	11	14	0	1566	97	1	3.72	....	....	....	....	....	....	....	....	....	....	....	....	....	....	....	....	....
1989-90	Rochester Americans	AHL	56	31	16	4	3095	173	2	3.35	....	....	....	....	....	*17	*10	6	....	*1001	50	0	*3.01	....	....	....	....
1990-91	**Buffalo Sabres**	**NHL**	**16**	**4**	**5**	**3**	**630**	**35**	**0**	**3.33**	**2.99**	**3.99**	**292**	**.880**	**27.8**	**2**	**0**	**1**	....	**37**	**2**	**0**	**3.24**	**2.95**	**22**	**.909**	**35.7**
	Rochester Americans	AHL	26	10	10	3	1363	68	4	*2.99	....	....	....	....	....	9	6	3	....	544	30	0	3.31	....	....	....	....
1991-92	**Minnesota North Stars**	**NHL**	**36**	**13**	**19**	**1**	**1905**	**104**	**1**	**3.28**	**2.93**	**3.90**	**874**	**.881**	**27.5**	....	....	....	....	....	....	....	....	....	....	....	....
	Kalamazoo Wings	IHL	1	1	0	0	60	7	0	7.00	....	....	....	....	....	....	....	....	....	....	....	....	....	....	....	....	....
1992-93	**Minnesota North Stars**	**NHL**	**29**	**10**	**12**	**5**	**1596**	**97**	**1**	**3.65**	**3.13**	**4.41**	**803**	**.879**	**30.2**	....	....	....	....	....	....	....	....	....	....	....	....
1993-94	**Dallas Stars**	**NHL**	**36**	**18**	**9**	**6**	**2000**	**88**	**3**	**2.64**	**2.53**	**2.38**	**978**	**.910**	**29.3**	**5**	**4**	**1**	....	**307**	**15**	**0**	**2.93**	**2.62**	**168**	**.911**	**32.8**
1994-95	**Dallas Stars**	**NHL**	**15**	**4**	**8**	**0**	**754**	**40**	**2**	**3.18**	**3.33**	**3.73**	**341**	**.883**	**27.1**	**1**	**0**	**0**	....	**20**	**1**	**0**	**3.00**	**3.33**	**9**	**.889**	**27.0**
1995-96	**Dallas Stars**	**NHL**	**37**	**9**	**16**	**5**	**1875**	**106**	**1**	**3.39**	**3.38**	**3.69**	**975**	**.891**	**31.2**	....	....	....	....	....	....	....	....	....	....	....	....
1996-97	**Phoenix Coyotes**	**NHL**	**16**	**8**	**3**	**1**	**782**	**39**	**1**	**2.99**	**3.22**	**3.02**	**386**	**.899**	**29.6**	....	....	....	....	....	....	....	....	....	....	....	....
	NHL Totals		**191**	**67**	**75**	**21**	**9756**	**524**	**9**	**3.22**	....	....	**4739**	**.889**	**29.1**	**8**	**4**	**2**	....	**364**	**18**	**0**	**2.97**	....	**199**	**.910**	**32.8**

Shared Harry "Hap" Holmes Memorial Trophy (fewest goals against - AHL) with David Littman (1991) • Scored a goal while with Rochester (AHL), December 6, 1987.

Traded to **Minnesota** by **Buffalo** for Minnesota's 8th round choice (Jiri Kuntos) in 1991 Entry Draft and Minnesota's 5th round choice (later traded to Toronto — Toronto selected Chris Deruiter) in 1992 Entry Draft, May 26, 1991. Transferred to **Dallas** after **Minnesota** franchise relocated, June 9, 1993. Signed as a free agent by **Phoenix**, July 23, 1996. • Suffered career-ending knee injury in game vs. Washington, January 4, 1997.

• WAKELY, Ernie

Ernest Alfred Linton G – L. 5'11", 160 lbs. b: Flin Flon, Man., 11/27/1940.

Season	Club	League	GP	W	L	T	Mins	GA	SO	Avg	AAvg	Eff	SA	S%	SAPG	GP	W	L	T	Mins	GA	SO	Avg	Eff	SA	S%	SAPG
1957-58	Winnipeg Braves	MJHL	27	12	14	1	1640	121	*1	4.48	....	....	....	....	....	5	2	3	0	300	20	0	4.00	....	....	....	....
1958-59	Winnipeg Braves	MJHL	30	*22	7	1	1810	107	1	3.54	....	....	....	....	....	8	*7	1	0	490	22	*1	*2.69	....	....	....	....
	Winnipeg Braves	Mem-Cup	16	*12	4	0	960	45	1	2.81	....	....	....	....	....	....	....	....	....	....	....	....	....	....	....	....	....
1959-60	Winnipeg Braves	MJHL	27	15	11	1	1640	99	1	3.62	....	....	....	....	....	4	1	3	0	250	15	0	3.60	....	....	....	....
	Winnipeg Warriors	WHL	4	1	3	0	240	16	0	4.00	....	....	....	....	....	....	....	....	....	....	....	....	....	....	....	....	....
1960-61	Winnipeg Braves	MJHL	31	18	13	0	1860	111	*2	*3.57	....	....	....	....	....	3	0	3	0	210	14	0	4.00	....	....	....	....
	Winnipeg Warriors	WHL	9	4	5	0	540	43	0	4.77	....	....	....	....	....	....	....	....	....	....	....	....	....	....	....	....	....
1961-62	Hull-Ottawa Canadiens	EPHL	2	1	0	1	120	4	0	2.00	....	....	....	....	....	....	....	....	....	....	....	....	....	....	....	....	....
	Kingston Frontenacs	EPHL	3	2	1	0	180	10	0	3.33	....	....	....	....	....	....	....	....	....	....	....	....	....	....	....	....	....
	North Bay Trappers	EPHL	6	1	4	1	360	18	0	3.00	....	....	....	....	....	....	....	....	....	....	....	....	....	....	....	....	....
1962-63	**Montreal Canadiens**	**NHL**	**1**	**1**	**0**	**0**	**60**	**3**	**0**	**3.00**	**3.12**	....	....	....	....	....	....	....	....	....	....	....	....	....	....	....	....
	Hull-Ottawa Canadiens	EPHL	41	26	12	3	2460	122	*2	*2.97	....	....	....	....	....	....	....	....	....	....	....	....	....	....	....	....	....
	Spokane Comets	WHL	3	1	2	0	180	16	0	5.33	....	....	....	....	....	....	....	....	....	....	....	....	....	....	....	....	....
1963-64	Quebec Aces	AHL	8	3	5	0	480	33	0	4.12	....	....	....	....	....	....	....	....	....	....	....	....	....	....	....	....	....
	Omaha Knights	CPHL	59	*38	16	5	3540	173	2	*2.93	....	....	....	....	....	10	*8	2	0	600	19	*3	*1.90	....	....	....	....
1964-65	Omaha Knights	CPHL	15	11	3	1	900	40	0	2.67	....	....	....	....	....	....	....	....	....	....	....	....	....	....	....	....	....
	Cleveland Barons	AHL	10	2	8	0	600	49	0	4.90	....	....	....	....	....	....	....	....	....	....	....	....	....	....	....	....	....
	Quebec Aces	AHL	20	9	10	1	1228	77	1	3.76	....	....	....	....	....	4	1	3	0	240	17	0	4.25	....	....	....	....
1965-66	Cleveland Barons	AHL	1	0	0	0	20	1	0	3.00	....	....	....	....	....	....	....	....	....	....	....	....	....	....	....	....	....
	Quebec Aces	AHL	1	0	1	0	60	6	0	6.00	....	....	....	....	....	....	....	....	....	....	....	....	....	....	....	....	....
	Seattle Totems	WHL	27	12	14	1	1617	83	2	3.08	....	....	....	....	....	....	....	....	....	....	....	....	....	....	....	....	....
1966-67	Cleveland Barons	AHL	*70	*36	25	9	*4187	216	0	3.10	....	....	....	....	....	5	2	3	0	301	10	0	1.99	....	....	....	....
1967-68	Houston Apollos	CPHL	*57	24	21	10	*3312	163	1	2.95	....	....	....	....	....	....	....	....	....	....	....	....	....	....	....	....	....
1968-69	**Montreal Canadiens**	**NHL**	**1**	**0**	**1**	**0**	**60**	**4**	**0**	**4.00**	**4.14**	....	....	....	....	....	....	....	....	....	....	....	....	....	....	....	....
	Cleveland Barons	AHL	*65	25	28	11	*3852	210	1	3.27	....	....	....	....	....	5	2	3	0	304	20	0	3.95	....	....	....	....
1969-70	**St. Louis Blues**	**NHL**	**30**	**12**	**9**	**4**	**1651**	**58**	**4**	***2.11**	**2.22**	....	....	....	....	**4**	**0**	**4**	....	**216**	**17**	**0**	**4.72**	....	....	....	....
1970-71	**St. Louis Blues**	**NHL**	**51**	**20**	**14**	**11**	**2859**	**133**	**3**	**2.79**	**2.75**	....	....	....	....	**3**	**2**	**1**	....	**180**	**7**	**1**	**2.33**	....	....	....	....
1971-72	**St. Louis Blues**	**NHL**	**30**	**8**	**18**	**2**	**1614**	**92**	**1**	**3.42**	**3.47**	....	....	....	....	**3**	**0**	**1**	....	**113**	**13**	**0**	**6.90**	....	....	....	....
1972-73	Winnipeg Jets	WHA	49	26	19	3	2889	152	2	3.16	....	....	....	....	....	7	4	3	0	420	22	*2	3.14	....	....	....	....
1973-74	Winnipeg Jets	WHA	37	15	18	4	2254	123	3	3.27	....	....	....	....	....	....	....	....	....	....	....	....	....	....	....	....	....
1974-75	Winnipeg Jets	WHA	6	3	3	0	355	16	1	2.70	....	....	....	....	....	....	....	....	....	....	....	....	....	....	....	....	....
	San Diego Mariners	WHA	35	20	12	2	2062	115	2	3.35	....	....	....	....	....	10	4	6	0	520	39	0	4.50	....	....	....	....
1975-76	San Diego Mariners	WHA	67	35	27	4	3824	208	3	3.26	....	....	....	....	....	11	5	6	0	640	39	0	3.66	....	....	....	....
1976-77	San Diego Mariners	WHA	46	22	18	3	2506	129	3	3.09	....	....	....	....	....	3	2	1	0	160	9	0	3.38	....	....	....	....
1977-78	Cincinnati Stingers	WHA	6	0	5	0	*311	26	0	5.02	....	....	....	....	....	....	....	....	....	....	....	....	....	....	....	....	....
	Houston Aeros	WHA	51	28	18	4	*3070	166	2	3.24	....	....	....	....	....	....	....	....	....	....	....	....	....	....	....	....	....
1978-79	Birmingham Bulls	WHA	37	15	17	1	2060	129	0	3.76	....	....	....	....	....	....	....	....	....	....	....	....	....	....	....	....	....
	Phoenix Roadrunners	PHL	1	1	0	0	60	4	0	4.00	....	....	....	....	....	....	....	....	....	....	....	....	....	....	....	....	....
	NHL Totals		**113**	**41**	**42**	**17**	**6244**	**290**	**8**	**2.79**	....	....	....	....	....	**10**	**2**	**6**	....	**509**	**37**	**1**	**4.36**	....	....	....	....
	Other Major League Totals		334	164	137	21	19331	1064	16	3.30	....	....	....	....	....	31	15	16	....	1740	109	2	3.76	....	....	....	....

Won Terry Sawchuk Trophy (fewest goals against - CPHL) (1964) • CPHL Second All-Star Team (1968) • AHL Second All-Star Team (1969) • WHA Second All-Star Team (1978) • Played in NHL All-Star Game (1971)

Traded to **St. Louis** by **Montreal** for Norm Beaudin and Bob Schmautz, June 27, 1969. Selected by **Winnipeg** (WHA) in 1972 WHA General Player Draft, February 12, 1972. Traded to **San Diego** (WHA) by **Winnipeg** (WHA) for cash and future considerations, January, 1975. Claimed by **Cincinnati** (WHA) from **San Diego** (WHA) in WHA Dispersal Auction, August, 1977. Traded to **Houston** (WHA) by **Cincinnati** (WHA) for cash, November, 1977. Signed as a free agent by **Birmingham** (WHA) after **Houston** (WHA) franchise folded, July 6, 1978.

• WALSH, Flat

James Patrick G – L. 5'11", 180 lbs. b: Kingston, Ont., 3/23/1897 d: 12/2/1959.

Season	Club	League	GP	W	L	T	Mins	GA	SO	Avg	AAvg	Eff	SA	S%	SAPG	GP	W	L	T	Mins	GA	SO	Avg	Eff	SA	S%	SAPG
1914-15	Kingston Collegiate	OHA-Jr.	4	3	1	0	260	14	0	3.23	....	....	....	....	....	3	1	1	1	180	13	0	4.33	....	....	....	....
1915-16	Kingston Frontenacs	OHA-Jr.	1	0	1	0	60	7	0	7.00	....	....	....	....	....	....	....	....	....	....	....	....	....	....	....	....	....
	Kingston Frontenacs	OHA-Sr.	STATISTICS NOT AVAILABLE																								
1916-17	Kingston AAC	OHA-Jr.	3	3	0	0	180	8	0	2.67	....	....	....	....	....	4	3	1	0	240	14	0	3.50	....	....	....	....
1917-18	Kingston AAC	OHA-I	STATISTICS NOT AVAILABLE																								
1918-19	Kingston AAC	OHA-I	4	3	1	0	240	11	1	2.75	....	....	....	....	....	8	4	4	0	480	26	0	3.25	....	....	....	....
1919-20	S.S. Marie Greyhounds	NOHA	5	1	3	1	330	23	0	4.18	....	....	....	....	....	....	....	....	....	....	....	....	....	....	....	....	....
	S.S. Marie Greyhounds	NMHL	14	9	3	2	930	26	2	1.68	....	....	....	....	....	....	....	....	....	....	....	....	....	....	....	....	....
1920-21	S.S. Marie Greyhounds	NOHA	9	*7	1	1	570	14	*4	*1.47	....	....	....	....	....	5	3	2	0	300	24	0	4.80	....	....	....	....
	S.S. Marie Greyhounds	NMHL	16	13	3	0	970	26	6	1.61	....	....	....	....	....	....	....	....	....	....	....	....	....	....	....	....	....
1921-22	S.S. Marie Greyhounds	NOHA	8	*7	1	0	500	18	*1	*2.16	....	....	....	....	....	2	0	1	1	120	7	0	3.50	....	....	....	....
	S.S. Marie Greyhounds	NMHL	12	*11	1	0	720	16	1	*1.33	....	....	....	....	....	....	....	....	....	....	....	....	....	....	....	....	....
1922-23	S.S. Marie Greyhounds	NOHA	8	4	4	0	476	22	0	*2.77	....	....	....	....	....	2	1	0	1	120	4	0	*2.00	....	....	....	....
	S.S. Marie Greyhounds	Al-Cup	5	4	1	0	300	17	0	3.40	....	....	....	....	....	....	....	....	....	....	....	....	....	....	....	....	....
1923-24	S.S. Marie Greyhounds	NOHA	7	*6	1	0	400	19	0	*2.85	....	....	....	....	....	7	5	2	0	420	11	2	1.57	....	....	....	....
1924-25	S.S. Marie Greyhounds	NOHA	STATISTICS NOT AVAILABLE																								
1925-26	S.S. Marie Greyhounds	CHL	32	....	....	....	1920	100	1	3.13	....	....	....	....	....	....	....	....	....	....	....	....	....	....	....	....	....
1926-27	Detroit Greyhounds	AHA	6	0	6	0	360	23	0	3.83	....	....	....	....	....	....	....	....	....	....	....	....	....	....	....	....	....
	Montreal Maroons	**NHL**	**1**	**0**	**1**	**0**	**60**	**3**	**0**	**3.00**	**4.58**	....	....	....	....	....	....	....	....	....	....	....	....	....	....	....	....
1927-28	**Montreal Maroons**	**NHL**	**1**	**0**	**0**	**0**	**40**	**1**	**0**	**1.50**	**2.41**	....	....	....	....	....	....	....	....	....	....	....	....	....	....	....	....
1928-29	**New York Americans**	**NHL**	**4**	**2**	**0**	**2**	**260**	**1**	**3**	**0.23**	**0.48**	....	....	....	....	....	....	....	....	....	....	....	....	....	....	....	....
	Montreal Maroons	**NHL**	**7**	**1**	**4**	**2**	**450**	**8**	**1**	**1.07**	**2.22**	....	....	....	....	....	....	....	....	....	....	....	....	....	....	....	....
1929-30	**Montreal Maroons**	**NHL**	**30**	**16**	**10**	**4**	**1897**	**74**	**2**	**2.34**	**2.37**	....	....	....	....	**4**	**1**	**3**	**0**	**312**	**11**	**1**	**2.12**	....	....	....	....
1930-31	**Montreal Maroons**	**NHL**	**16**	**7**	**7**	**2**	**961**	**36**	**2**	**2.25**	**2.86**	....	....	....	....	....	....	....	....	....	....	....	....	....	....	....	....

Season	Club	League	GP	W	L	T	Mins	GA	SO	Avg	AAvg	Eff	SA	S%	SAPG	GP	W	L	T	Mins	GA	SO	Avg	Eff	SA	S%	SAPG
			REGULAR SEASON													PLAYOFFS											
1931-32	**Montreal Maroons**	**NHL**	**27**	**14**	**10**	**3**	**1670**	**77**	**2**	**2.77**	**3.42**	....	....	....	....	**4**	**1**	**1**	**2**	**258**	**5**	***1**	***1.16**	....	....	....	....
	New Haven Eagles	Can-Am	18	7	9	2	1110	27	*6	1.46	....	....	....	....	....	....	....	....	....	....	....	....	....	....	....	....	....
1932-33	**Montreal Maroons**	**NHL**	**22**	**8**	**11**	**3**	**1303**	**56**	**2**	**2.58**	**3.48**	....	....	....	....	....	....	....	....	....	....	....	....	....	....	....	....
	Quebec Castors	Can-Am	3	2	1	0	180	3	2	1.00	....	....	....	....	....	....	....	....	....	....	....	....	....	....	....	....	....
	NHL Totals		**108**	**48**	**43**	**16**	**6641**	**256**	**12**	**2.31**	....	....	....	....	....	**8**	**2**	**4**	**2**	**570**	**16**	**2**	**1.68**	....	....	....	....

Signed as a free agent by **Detroit** (AHA), June 23, 1926. Signed as a free agent by **Montreal Maroons** after **Detroit** (AHA) franchise folded, December, 1926. Loaned to **NY Americans** by **Montreal Maroons** until NHL and club resolved the status of Roy Worters' contract, November 15, 1928.

• WAMSLEY, Rick

Richard James G – L. 5'11", 185 lbs. b: Simcoe, Ont., 5/25/1959. Montreal's 5th, 58th overall in 1979.

Season	Club	League	GP	W	L	T	Mins	GA	SO	Avg	AAvg	Eff	SA	S%	SAPG	GP	W	L	T	Mins	GA	SO	Avg	Eff	SA	S%	SAPG
1976-77	Simcoe Jets	OHA-B	STATISTICS NOT AVAILABLE																								
	St. Catharines Fincups	OMJHL	12	....	....	....	647	36	0	3.34	....	....	....	....	....	3	0	1	0	132	10	0	4.52	....	....	....	....
1977-78	Hamilton Fincups	OMJHL	25	....	....	....	1495	74	2	*2.97	....	....	....	....	....	3	2	1	0	333	9	0	2.90	....	....	....	....
1978-79	Brantford Alexanders	OMJHL	24	....	....	....	1444	128	0	5.32	....	....	....	....	....	....	....	....	....	....	....	....	....	....	....	....	....
1979-80	Nova Scotia Voyageurs	AHL	40	19	16	2	2305	125	2	3.25	....	....	....	....	....	3	1	1	0	143	12	0	5.03	....	....	....	....
1980-81	**Montreal Canadiens**	**NHL**	**5**	**3**	**0**	**1**	**253**	**8**	**1**	**1.90**	**1.53**	....	....	....	....	....	....	....	....	....	....	....	....	....	....	....	....
	Nova Scotia Voyageurs	AHL	43	17	19	3	2372	155	0	3.92	....	....	....	....	....	4	2	1	0	199	6	*1	1.81	....	....	....	....
1981-82	**Montreal Canadiens**	**NHL**	**38**	**23**	**7**	**7**	**2206**	**101**	**2**	**2.75**	**2.11**	....	....	....	....	**5**	**2**	**3**	....	**300**	**11**	**0**	***2.20**	....	....	....	....
1982-83	**Montreal Canadiens**	**NHL**	**46**	**27**	**12**	**5**	**2583**	**151**	**0**	**3.51**	**2.81**	**4.27**	**1240**	**.878**	**28.8**	**3**	**0**	**3**	....	**152**	**7**	**0**	**2.76**	....	....	....	....
	Canada	WEC-A	10	6	4	0	600	30	1	3.00	....	....	....	....	....	....	....	....	....	....	....	....	....	....	....	....	....
1983-84	**Montreal Canadiens**	**NHL**	**42**	**19**	**17**	**3**	**2333**	**144**	**2**	**3.70**	**2.91**	**5.45**	**977**	**.853**	**25.1**	**1**	**0**	**0**	....	**32**	**0**	**0**	**0.00**	**0.00**	**12**	**1.000**	**22.5**
1984-85	**St. Louis Blues**	**NHL**	**40**	**23**	**12**	**5**	**2319**	**126**	**0**	**3.26**	**2.59**	**3.75**	**1094**	**.885**	**28.3**	**2**	**0**	**2**	....	**120**	**7**	**0**	**3.50**	**4.38**	**56**	**.875**	**28.0**
	Canada	WEC-A	2	1	1	0	120	11	0	5.50	....	....	....	....	....	....	....	....	....	....	....	....	....	....	....	....	....
1985-86	**St. Louis Blues**	**NHL**	**42**	**22**	**16**	**3**	**2517**	**144**	**1**	**3.43**	**2.67**	**3.65**	**1354**	**.894**	**32.3**	**10**	**4**	**6**	....	**569**	**37**	**0**	**3.90**	**4.70**	**307**	**.879**	**32.4**
1986-87	**St. Louis Blues**	**NHL**	**41**	**17**	**15**	**6**	**2410**	**142**	**0**	**3.54**	**3.00**	**4.15**	**1212**	**.883**	**30.2**	**2**	**1**	**1**	....	**120**	**5**	**0**	**2.50**	**2.31**	**54**	**.907**	**27.0**
1987-88	**St. Louis Blues**	**NHL**	**31**	**13**	**16**	**1**	**1818**	**103**	**2**	**3.40**	**2.83**	**3.80**	**922**	**.888**	**30.4**	....	....	....	....	....	....	....	....	....	....	....	....
	Calgary Flames	**NHL**	**2**	**1**	**0**	**0**	**73**	**5**	**0**	**4.11**	**3.42**	**5.71**	**36**	**.861**	**29.6**	**1**	**0**	**1**	....	**33**	**2**	**0**	**3.64**	**9.10**	**8**	**.750**	**14.5**
1988-89♦	**Calgary Flames**	**NHL**	**35**	**17**	**11**	**4**	**1927**	**95**	**2**	**2.96**	**2.45**	**3.53**	**796**	**.881**	**24.8**	**1**	**0**	**1**	....	**20**	**2**	**0**	**6.00**	**12.00**	**10**	**.800**	**30.0**
1989-90	Calgary Flames	Fr-Tour	3	....	....	....	92	5	0	3.26	....	....	....	....	....	....	....	....	....	....	....	....	....	....	....	....	....
	Calgary Flames	**NHL**	**36**	**18**	**8**	**6**	**1969**	**107**	**2**	**3.26**	**2.76**	**4.08**	**855**	**.875**	**26.1**	**1**	**0**	**1**	....	**49**	**9**	**0**	**11.02**	**43.12**	**23**	**.609**	**28.2**
1990-91	**Calgary Flames**	**NHL**	**29**	**14**	**7**	**5**	**1670**	**85**	**0**	**3.05**	**2.74**	**3.40**	**762**	**.888**	**27.4**	**1**	**0**	**0**	....	**2**	**1**	**0**	**30.00**	**150.00**	**2**	**.500**	**60.0**
1991-92	**Calgary Flames**	**NHL**	**9**	**3**	**4**	**0**	**457**	**34**	**0**	**4.46**	**4.00**	**6.71**	**226**	**.850**	**29.7**	....	....	....	....	....	....	....	....	....	....	....	....
	Toronto Maple Leafs	**NHL**	**8**	**4**	**3**	**0**	**428**	**27**	**0**	**3.79**	**3.40**	**4.69**	**218**	**.876**	**30.6**	....	....	....	....	....	....	....	....	....	....	....	....
1992-93	**Toronto Maple Leafs**	**NHL**	**3**	**0**	**3**	**0**	**160**	**15**	**0**	**5.63**	**4.83**	**9.28**	**91**	**.835**	**34.1**	....	....	....	....	....	....	....	....	....	....	....	....
	St. John's Maple Leafs	AHL	2	0	1	0	112	8	0	4.29	....	....	....	....	....	....	....	....	....	....	....	....	....	....	....	....	....
	NHL Totals		**407**	**204**	**131**	**46**	**23123**	**1287**	**12**	**3.34**	....	....	....	....	....	**27**	**7**	**18**	....	**1397**	**81**	**0**	**3.48**	....	....	....	....

Shared William M. Jennings Trophy with Denis Herron (1982)

Traded to **St. Louis** by **Montreal** with Hartford's 2nd round choice (previously acquired, St. Louis selected Brian Benning) in 1984 Entry Draft, Montreal's 2nd (Tony Hrkac) and 3rd (Robert Dirk) round choices in 1984 Entry Draft for St. Louis' 1st (Shayne Corson) and 2nd (Stephane Richer) round choices in 1984 Entry Draft, June 9, 1984. Traded to **Calgary** by **St. Louis** with Rob Ramage for Brett Hull and Steve Bozek, March 7, 1988. Traded to **Toronto** by **Calgary** with Doug Gilmour, Jamie Macoun, Kent Manderville and Ric Nattress for Gary Leeman, Alexander Godynyuk, Jeff Reese, Michel Petit and Craig Berube, January 2, 1992.

• WATT, Jim

James Magnus G – L. 5'11", 180 lbs. b: Duluth, MN, 5/11/1950.

Season	Club	League	GP	W	L	T	Mins	GA	SO	Avg	AAvg	Eff	SA	S%	SAPG	GP	W	L	T	Mins	GA	SO	Avg	Eff	SA	S%	SAPG
1969-70	Michigan State Spartans	WCHA	1	0	0	0	42	4	0	5.70	....	....	....	....	....	....	....	....	....	....	....	....	....	....	....	....	....
1970-71	Michigan State Spartans	WCHA	25	....	....	....	1480	101	0	4.09	....	....	....	....	....	....	....	....	....	....	....	....	....	....	....	....	....
1971-72	Michigan State Spartans	WCHA	36	20	16	0	2160	128	0	3.56	....	....	....	....	....	....	....	....	....	....	....	....	....	....	....	....	....
1972-73	Denver Spurs	WHL	15	4	8	0	791	53	0	4.02	....	....	....	....	....	....	....	....	....	....	....	....	....	....	....	....	....
	Fort Worth Wings	CHL	7	....	....	....	335	26	0	4.65	....	....	....	....	....	....	....	....	....	....	....	....	....	....	....	....	....
1973-74	**St. Louis Blues**	**NHL**	**1**	**0**	**0**	**0**	**20**	**2**	**0**	**6.00**	**5.80**	....	....	....	....	....	....	....	....	....	....	....	....	....	....	....	....
	Denver Spurs	WHL	31	14	15	0	1827	112	0	3.68	....	....	....	....	....	....	....	....	....	....	....	....	....	....	....	....	....
1974-75	Denver Spurs	CHL	30	10	10	9	1738	100	0	3.45	....	....	....	....	....	....	....	....	....	....	....	....	....	....	....	....	....
1975-76	Tidewater Sharks	SHL	55	19	23	11	3147	172	1	3.28	....	....	....	....	....	....	....	....	....	....	....	....	....	....	....	....	....
	Kalamazoo Wings	IHL	8	....	....	....	420	25	0	3.57	....	....	....	....	....	6	2	4	0	381	18	1	2.83	....	....	....	....
1976-77	Winston-Salem Polar Bears	SHL	3	....	....	....	149	16	0	6.44	....	....	....	....	....	....	....	....	....	....	....	....	....	....	....	....	....
	NHL Totals		**1**	**0**	**0**	**0**	**20**	**2**	**0**	**6.00**	....	....	....	....	....	....	....	....	....	....	....	....	....	....	....	....	....

WCHA First All-Star Team (1972) • NCAA West First All-American Team (1972)

Signed as a free agent by **St. Louis** (Fort Worth-CHL), October 1, 1972.

• WEEKES, Kevin

G – L. 6', 195 lbs. b: Toronto, Ont., 4/4/1975. Florida's 2nd, 41st overall in 1993.

Season	Club	League	GP	W	L	T	Mins	GA	SO	Avg	AAvg	Eff	SA	S%	SAPG	GP	W	L	T	Mins	GA	SO	Avg	Eff	SA	S%	SAPG
1990-91	Toronto Red Wings	MTHL	STATISTICS NOT AVAILABLE																								
	St. Michael's Buzzers	OJHL-B	1	0	0	0	41	1	0	1.46	....	....	....	....	....	....	....	....	....	....	....	....	....	....	....	....	....
1991-92	Toronto Red Wings	MTHL	2	....	....	....	127	11	0	5.20	....	....	....	....	....	....	....	....	....	....	....	....	....	....	....	....	....
	St. Michael's Buzzers	OJHL	35	....	....	....	1575	68	4	1.94	....	....	....	....	....	....	....	....	....	....	....	....	....	....	....	....	....
1992-93	Owen Sound Platers	OHL	29	9	12	5	1645	143	0	5.22	....	....	....	....	....	1	0	0	....	26	5	0	11.50	....	....	....	....
1993-94	Owen Sound Platers	OHL	34	13	19	1	1974	158	0	4.80	....	....	....	....	....	....	....	....	....	....	....	....	....	....	....	....	....
1994-95	Ottawa 67's	OHL	41	13	23	4	2266	153	1	4.05	....	....	....	....	....	....	....	....	....	....	....	....	....	....	....	....	....
1995-96	Carolina Monarchs	AHL	60	24	25	8	3404	229	2	4.04	....	....	....	....	....	....	....	....	....	....	....	....	....	....	....	....	....
1996-97	Carolina Monarchs	AHL	51	17	28	4	2899	172	1	3.56	....	....	....	....	....	....	....	....	....	....	....	....	....	....	....	....	....
1997-98	**Florida Panthers**	**NHL**	**11**	**0**	**5**	**1**	**485**	**32**	**0**	**3.96**	**4.73**	**5.13**	**247**	**.870**	**30.6**	....	....	....	....	....	....	....	....	....	....	....	....
	Fort Wayne Komets	IHL	12	9	2	1	719	34	1	2.84	....	....	....	....	....	....	....	....	....	....	....	....	....	....	....	....	....
1998-99	Detroit Vipers	IHL	33	19	5	7	1857	64	*4	*2.07	....	....	....	....	....	....	....	....	....	....	....	....	....	....	....	....	....
	Vancouver Canucks	**NHL**	**11**	**0**	**8**	**1**	**532**	**34**	**0**	**3.83**	**4.56**	**5.07**	**257**	**.868**	**29.0**	....	....	....	....	....	....	....	....	....	....	....	....
99-2000	**Vancouver Canucks**	**NHL**	**20**	**6**	**7**	**4**	**987**	**47**	**1**	**2.86**	**3.27**	**2.92**	**461**	**.898**	**28.0**	....	....	....	....	....	....	....	....	....	....	....	....
	New York Islanders	**NHL**	**36**	**10**	**20**	**4**	**2026**	**115**	**1**	**3.41**	**3.91**	**3.34**	**1173**	**.902**	**34.7**	....	....	....	....	....	....	....	....	....	....	....	....
	NHL Totals		**78**	**16**	**40**	**10**	**4030**	**228**	**2**	**3.39**	....	....	**2138**	**.893**	**31.8**	....	....	....	....	....	....	....	....	....	....	....	....

Shared James Norris Memorial Trophy (fewest goals against - IHL) with Andrei Trefilov (1999)

Traded to **Vancouver** by **Florida** with Ed Jovanovski, Dave Gagner, Mike Brown and Florida's 1st round choice (Nathan Smith) in 2000 Entry Draft for Pavel Bure, Bret Hedican, Brad Ference and Vancouver's 3rd round choice (Robert Fried) in 2000 Entry Draft, January 17, 1999. Traded to **NY Islanders** by **Vancouver** with Dave Scatchard and Bill Muckalt for Felix Potvin and NY Islanders' compensatory 2nd (later traded to New Jersey - New Jersey selected Teemu Laine) and 3rd (Thatcher Bell) round choices in 2000 Entry Draft, December 19, 1999. Traded to **Tampa Bay** by **NY Islanders** with the rights to Kristian Kudroc and NY Islanders' 2nd round choice in 2001 Entry Draft for Tampa Bay's 1st round choice (Raffi Torres) in 2000 Entry Draft, Calgary's 4th round choice (previously acquired, NY Islanders selected Vladimir Gorbunov) in 2000 Entry Draft and NY Islanders' 7th round choice (previously acquired, NY Islanders selected Ryan Caldwell) in 2000 Entry Draft, June 24, 2000.

• WEEKS, Steve

Stephen K. G – L. 5'11", 170 lbs. b: Scarborough, Ont., 6/30/1958. NY Rangers' 12th, 176th overall in 1978.

Season	Club	League	GP	W	L	T	Mins	GA	SO	Avg	AAvg	Eff	SA	S%	SAPG	GP	W	L	T	Mins	GA	SO	Avg	Eff	SA	S%	SAPG
1975-76	Toronto Marlboros	OMJHL	18	....	....	....	873	73	0	5.02	....	....	....	....	....	....	....	....	....	....	....	....	....	....	....	....	....
1976-77	Northern Michigan University	CCHA	16	7	7	0	811	58	0	4.29	....	....	....	....	....	1	0	1	0	60	6	0	6.00	....	....	....	....
1977-78	Northern Michigan University	CCHA	19	10	5	2	1015	56	1	3.31	....	....	....	....	....	....	....	....	....	....	....	....	....	....	....	....	....
1978-79	Northern Michigan University	CCHA	25	13	8	2	1437	82	0	3.42	....	....	....	....	....	2	0	1	0	151	10	0	3.97	....	....	....	....
1979-80	Northern Michigan University	CCHA	36	29	6	1	2133	105	1	*2.95	....	....	....	....	....	6	4	1	0	330	18	0	3.27	....	....	....	....
1980-81	New Haven Nighthawks	AHL	36	14	17	3	2065	142	1	4.04	....	....	....	....	....	....	....	....	....	....	....	....	....	....	....	....	....
	New York Rangers	**NHL**	**1**	**0**	**1**	**0**	**60**	**2**	**0**	**2.00**	**1.62**	....	....	....	....	**1**	**0**	**0**	....	**14**	**1**	**0**	**4.29**	....	....	....	....
1981-82	**New York Rangers**	**NHL**	**49**	**23**	**16**	**9**	**2852**	**179**	**1**	**3.77**	**2.91**	....	....	....	....	**4**	**1**	**2**	....	**127**	**9**	**0**	**4.25**	....	....	....	....
1982-83	**New York Rangers**	**NHL**	**18**	**9**	**5**	**3**	**1040**	**68**	**0**	**3.92**	**3.15**	**5.43**	**491**	**.862**	**28.3**	....	....	....	....	....	....	....	....	....	....	....	....
	Tulsa Oilers	CHL	19	8	10	0	1116	60	0	3.23	....	....	....	....	....	....	....	....	....	....	....	....	....	....	....	....	....
1983-84	**New York Rangers**	**NHL**	**26**	**10**	**11**	**2**	**1361**	**90**	**0**	**3.97**	**3.13**	**5.36**	**667**	**.865**	**29.4**	....	....	....	....	....	....	....	....	....	....	....	....
	Tulsa Oilers	CHL	3	3	0	0	180	7	0	2.33	....	....	....	....	....	....	....	....	....	....	....	....	....	....	....	....	....

			REGULAR SEASON													PLAYOFFS											
Season	**Club**	**League**	**GP**	**W**	**L**	**T**	**Mins**	**GA**	**SO**	**Avg**	**AAvg**	**Eff**	**SA**	**S%**	**SAPG**	**GP**	**W**	**L**	**T**	**Mins**	**GA**	**SO**	**Avg**	**Eff**	**SA**	**S%**	**SAPG**
1984-85	**Hartford Whalers**	**NHL**	23	9	12	2	1397	91	2	3.91	3.12	5.08	700	.870	30.1	....	....	....	....	....	....	....	....	....	....	....	....
	Binghamton Whalers	AHL	5	5	0	0	303	13	0	2.57	....	....	....	....	....	....	....	....	....	....	....	....	....	....	....	....	....
	Canada	WEC-A	5	3	1	1	265	9	*1	2.04	....	....	....	....	....	....	....	....	....	....	....	....	....	....	....	....	....
1985-86	**Hartford Whalers**	**NHL**	27	13	13	0	1544	99	1	3.85	3.01	5.27	723	.863	28.1	3	1	2	....	169	8	0	2.84	3.55	64	.875	22.7
1986-87	**Hartford Whalers**	**NHL**	25	12	8	2	1367	78	1	3.42	2.89	4.34	615	.873	27.0	1	0	0	....	36	1	0	1.67	0.76	22	.955	36.7
1987-88	**Hartford Whalers**	**NHL**	18	6	7	2	918	55	0	3.59	2.99	5.09	388	.858	25.4	....	....	....	....	....	....	....	....	....	....	....	....
	Vancouver Canucks	**NHL**	9	4	3	2	550	31	0	3.38	2.81	3.66	286	.892	31.2	....	....	....	....	....	....	....	....	....	....	....	....
1988-89	**Vancouver Canucks**	**NHL**	35	11	19	5	2056	102	0	2.98	2.47	3.19	953	.893	27.8	3	1	1	....	140	8	0	3.43	3.47	79	.899	33.9
1989-90	**Vancouver Canucks**	**NHL**	21	4	11	4	1142	79	0	4.15	3.52	5.26	623	.873	32.7	....	....	....	....	....	....	....	....	....	....	....	....
1990-91	**Vancouver Canucks**	**NHL**	1	0	1	0	59	6	0	6.10	5.49	12.62	29	.793	29.5	....	....	....	....	....	....	....	....	....	....	....	....
	Milwaukee Admirals	IHL	37	16	19	0	2014	127	0	3.78	....	....	....	....	....	3	1	2	0	210	13	0	3.71	....	....	....	....
1991-92	**New York Islanders**	**NHL**	23	9	4	2	1032	62	0	3.60	3.23	3.94	566	.890	32.9	....	....	....	....	....	....	....	....	....	....	....	....
	Los Angeles Kings	**NHL**	7	1	3	0	252	17	0	4.05	3.63	5.06	136	.875	32.4	....	....	....	....	....	....	....	....	....	....	....	....
1992-93	**Ottawa Senators**	**NHL**	7	0	5	0	249	30	0	7.23	6.21	15.06	144	.792	34.7	....	....	....	....	....	....	....	....	....	....	....	....
	New Haven Senators	AHL	6	0	6	0	323	32	0	5.94	....	....	....	....	....	....	....	....	....	....	....	....	....	....	....	....	....
	NHL Totals		**290**	**111**	**119**	**33**	**15879**	**989**	**5**	**3.74**	....	....	**6321**	**.844**	**23.9**	**12**	**3**	**5**	....	**486**	**27**	**0**	**3.33**	....	....	....	....

CCHA Second All-Star Team (1979) • CCHA First All-Star Team (1980) • NCAA Championship All-Tournament Team (1980)

Traded to **Hartford** by **NY Rangers** for future considerations, September 5, 1984. Traded to **Vancouver** by **Hartford** for Richard Brodeur, March 8, 1988. Traded to **Buffalo** by **Vancouver** for future considerations, March 5, 1991. Signed as a free agent by **NY Islanders**, September 16, 1991. Traded to **LA Kings** by **NY Islanders** for LA Kings' 7th round choice (Steve O'Rourke) in 1992 Entry Draft, February 18, 1992. Signed as a free agent by **Washington**, June 16, 1992. Traded to **Ottawa** by **Washington** for future considerations, August 13, 1992.

• WETZEL, Carl

Carl David G – L. 6'1", 170 lbs. b: Detroit, MI, 12/12/1938.

Season	Club	League	GP	W	L	T	Mins	GA	SO	Avg	AAvg	Eff	SA	S%	SAPG	GP	W	L	T	Mins	GA	SO	Avg	Eff	SA	S%	SAPG
1956-57	Hamilton Tiger Cubs	OHA-Jr.	48	24	22	2	2880	167	3	3.48	....	....	....	....	....	4	1	3	0	240	13	0	3.25	....	....	....	....
1957-58	Hamilton Tiger Cubs	OHA-Jr.	50	26	17	7	2980	172	1	3.46	....	....	....	....	....	15	8	6	1	900	59	0	3.93	....	....	....	....
1958-59	Hamilton Tiger Cubs	OHA-Jr.	25	....	....	....	1500	105	0	4.26	....	....	....	....	....	....	....	....	....	....	....	....	....	....	....	....	....
	Edmonton Flyers	WHL	1	0	1	0	60	7	0	7.00	....	....	....	....	....	....	....	....	....	....	....	....	....	....	....	....	....
1959-60	Omaha Knights	IHL	62	....	....	....	3720	271	1	4.37	....	....	....	....	....	....	....	....	....	....	....	....	....	....	....	....	....
1960-61	Spokane Comets	WHL	5	0	5	0	302	25	0	4.97	....	....	....	....	....	....	....	....	....	....	....	....	....	....	....	....	....
	Indianapolis Chiefs	IHL	52	....	....	....	3120	202	0	3.88	....	....	....	....	....	....	....	....	....	....	....	....	....	....	....	....	....
	Fort Wayne Komets	IHL	....	....	....	....	....	....	....	....	....	....	....	....	....	8	3	3	0	480	26	0	3.25	....	....	....	....
1961-62	Sudbury Wolves	EPHL	61	25	26	10	3660	228	0	3.74	....	....	....	....	....	5	1	4	0	300	30	0	6.00	....	....	....	....
1962-63			MILITARY SERVICE																								
1963-64	San Francisco Seals	WHL	DID NOT PLAY – SPARE GOALTENDER																								
1964-65	**Detroit Red Wings**	**NHL**	2	0	1	0	32	4	0	7.50	8.05	....	....	....	....	....	....	....	....	....	....	....	....	....	....	....	....
	Pittsburgh Hornets	AHL	4	1	3	0	241	21	0	5.23	....	....	....	....	....	....	....	....	....	....	....	....	....	....	....	....	....
1965-66	Houston Apollos	CPHL	51	21	24	6	3040	171	4	3.38	....	....	....	....	....	....	....	....	....	....	....	....	....	....	....	....	....
	Quebec Aces	AHL	1	0	1	0	60	6	0	6.00	....	....	....	....	....	....	....	....	....	....	....	....	....	....	....	....	....
1966-67	United States	Nat-Team	12	....	....	....	720	38	0	3.17	....	....	....	....	....	....	....	....	....	....	....	....	....	....	....	....	....
	United States	WEC-A	7	3	3	1	420	23	*2	3.29	....	....	....	....	....	....	....	....	....	....	....	....	....	....	....	....	....
1967-68	**Minnesota North Stars**	**NHL**	5	1	2	1	269	18	0	4.01	4.46	....	....	....	....	....	....	....	....	....	....	....	....	....	....	....	....
	Memphis South Stars	CPHL	20	8	9	2	1095	61	0	3.34	....	....	....	....	....	....	....	....	....	....	....	....	....	....	....	....	....
	Rochester Americans	AHL	10	3	3	1	495	28	1	3.39	....	....	....	....	....	4	2	1	0	164	6	0	2.20	....	....	....	....
1968-69	Cleveland Barons	AHL	2	1	0	0	80	3	1	2.25	....	....	....	....	....	....	....	....	....	....	....	....	....	....	....	....	....
	Memphis South Stars	CHL	39	....	....	....	2276	170	0	4.48	....	....	....	....	....	....	....	....	....	....	....	....	....	....	....	....	....
1969-70	United States	Nat-Team	17	....	....	....	930	30	0	1.94	....	....	....	....	....	....	....	....	....	....	....	....	....	....	....	....	....
	Rochester Mustangs	USHL	4	....	....	....	240	15	0	3.75	....	....	....	....	....	....	....	....	....	....	....	....	....	....	....	....	....
1970-71	United States	Nat-Team	STATISTICS NOT AVAILABLE																								
	United States	WEC-A	8	1	6	0	400	38	0	5.70	....	....	....	....	....	....	....	....	....	....	....	....	....	....	....	....	....
1971-72	KAC Kitzbuhel	Austria	44	....	....	....	2640	132	4	3.00	....	....	....	....	....	....	....	....	....	....	....	....	....	....	....	....	....
1972-73	Minnesota Fighting Saints	WHA	1	0	1	0	60	3	0	3.00	....	....	....	....	....	....	....	....	....	....	....	....	....	....	....	....	....
	NHL Totals		**7**	**1**	**3**	**1**	**301**	**22**	**0**	**4.39**	....	....	....	....	....	....	....	....	....	....	....	....	....	....	....	....	....
	Other Major League Totals		1	0	1	0	60	3	0	3.00	....	....	....	....	....	....	....	....	....	....	....	....	....	....	....	....	....

WEC-A All-Star Team (1967) • Named Best Goaltender at WEC-A (1967)

• Served as spare goaltender for **San Francisco** (WHL) while completing compulsory military service, 1963-64. Claimed by **Montreal** (Quebec-AHL) from **Detroit** in Reverse Draft, June 9, 1965. Traded to **Minnesota** by **Montreal** for cash, June 14, 1967. Loaned to **Toronto** (Rochester-AHL) by **Minnesota** with the trade of Murray Hall, Ted Taylor, Len Lunde, Don Johns and Duke Harris for Jean-Paul Parise and Milan Marcetta, December 23, 1967. Signed as a free agent by **Minnesota** (WHA), January 23, 1973.

• WHITMORE, Kay

Kay B. G – L. 5'11", 175 lbs. b: Sudbury, Ont., 4/10/1967. Hartford's 2nd, 26th overall in 1985.

Season	Club	League	GP	W	L	T	Mins	GA	SO	Avg	AAvg	Eff	SA	S%	SAPG	GP	W	L	T	Mins	GA	SO	Avg	Eff	SA	S%	SAPG
1982-83	Sudbury Legionaires	NOJHA	43	....	....	....	2580	108	4	2.51	....	....	....	....	....	....	....	....	....	....	....	....	....	....	....	....	....
1983-84	Peterborough Petes	OHL	29	17	8	0	1471	110	0	4.49	....	....	....	....	....	....	....	....	....	....	....	....	....	....	....	....	....
1984-85	Peterborough Petes	OHL	*53	*35	16	2	*3077	172	*2	3.35	....	....	....	....	....	17	10	4	....	1020	58	0	3.41	....	....	....	....
1985-86	Peterborough Petes	OHL	41	27	12	2	2467	114	*3	*2.77	....	....	....	....	....	14	8	5	....	837	40	0	2.87	....	....	....	....
1986-87	Peterborough Petes	OHL	36	14	17	5	2159	118	1	3.28	....	....	....	....	....	7	3	3	....	366	17	1	2.79	....	....	....	....
1987-88	Binghamton Whalers	AHL	38	17	15	4	2137	121	*3	3.40	....	....	....	....	....	2	0	2	....	118	10	0	5.08	....	....	....	....
1988-89	**Hartford Whalers**	**NHL**	3	2	1	0	180	10	0	3.33	2.77	3.47	96	.896	32.0	2	0	2	....	135	10	0	4.44	6.08	73	.863	32.4
	Binghamton Whalers	AHL	*56	21	29	4	*3200	241	1	4.52	....	....	....	....	....	....	....	....	....	....	....	....	....	....	....	....	....
1989-90	**Hartford Whalers**	**NHL**	9	4	2	1	442	26	0	3.53	2.99	5.02	183	.858	24.8	....	....	....	....	....	....	....	....	....	....	....	....
	Binghamton Whalers	AHL	24	3	19	2	1386	109	0	4.72	....	....	....	....	....	....	....	....	....	....	....	....	....	....	....	....	....
1990-91	**Hartford Whalers**	**NHL**	18	3	9	3	850	52	0	3.67	3.30	5.04	379	.863	26.8	....	....	....	....	....	....	....	....	....	....	....	....
	Springfield Indians	AHL	33	22	9	1	1916	98	1	3.07	....	....	....	....	....	*15	*11	4	....	*926	37	0	*2.40	....	....	....	....
1991-92	**Hartford Whalers**	**NHL**	45	14	21	6	2567	155	3	3.62	3.25	4.34	1292	.880	30.2	1	0	0	....	19	1	0	3.16	6.32	5	.800	15.8
1992-93	**Vancouver Canucks**	**NHL**	31	18	8	4	1817	94	1	3.10	2.65	3.40	858	.890	28.3	....	....	....	....	....	....	....	....	....	....	....	....
1993-94	**Vancouver Canucks**	**NHL**	32	18	14	0	1921	113	0	3.53	3.40	4.70	848	.867	26.5	....	....	....	....	....	....	....	....	....	....	....	....
1994-95	**Vancouver Canucks**	**NHL**	11	0	6	2	558	37	0	3.98	4.18	5.28	279	.867	30.0	1	0	0	....	20	2	0	6.00	6.67	18	.889	54.0
1995-96	Detroit Vipers	IHL	10	3	5	0	501	33	0	3.95	....	....	....	....	....	....	....	....	....	....	....	....	....	....	....	....	....
	Los Angeles Ice Dogs	IHL	30	10	9	7	1563	99	1	3.80	....	....	....	....	....	....	....	....	....	....	....	....	....	....	....	....	....
	Syracuse Crunch	AHL	11	6	4	1	663	37	0	3.35	....	....	....	....	....	....	....	....	....	....	....	....	....	....	....	....	....
	Binghamton Rangers	AHL	....	....	....	....	....	....	....	....	....	....	....	....	....	2	0	2	....	127	9	0	4.27	....	....	....	....
1996-97	Sodertalje SK	Sweden	25	....	....	....	1320	85	0	3.86	....	....	....	....	....	....	....	....	....	....	....	....	....	....	....	....	....
1997-98	Long Beach Ice Dogs	IHL	46	28	12	3	2516	109	3	2.60	....	....	....	....	....	14	9	5	....	838	43	0	3.08	....	....	....	....
1998-99	Milwaukee Admirals	IHL	23	10	6	4	1304	64	0	2.94	....	....	....	....	....	....	....	....	....	....	....	....	....	....	....	....	....
	Hartford Wolf Pack	AHL	18	8	8	2	1080	47	0	2.61	....	....	....	....	....	....	....	....	....	....	....	....	....	....	....	....	....
99-2000	Providence Bruins	AHL	43	17	19	3	2393	127	1	3.18	....	....	....	....	....	1	0	1	....	59	2	0	2.04	....	....	....	....
	NHL Totals		**149**	**59**	**61**	**16**	**8335**	**487**	**4**	**3.51**	....	....	**3935**	**.876**	**28.3**	**4**	**0**	**2**	....	**174**	**13**	**0**	**4.48**	....	**96**	**.865**	**33.1**

OHL First All-Star Team (1986) • Won Jack A. Butterfield Trophy (Playoff MVP - AHL) (1991) • Shared James Norris Memorial Trophy (fewest goals against - IHL) with Mike Buzak (1998)

Traded to **Vancouver** by **Hartford** for Corrie D'Alessio and cash, October 1, 1992. Traded to **NY Rangers** by **Vancouver** for Joe Kocur, March 20, 1996. Signed as a free agent by **San Jose**, September 10, 1997. Traded to **Buffalo** by **San Jose** with Colorado's 2nd round choice (previously acquired, Buffalo selected Jaroslav Kristek) in 1998 Entry Draft and San Jose's 5th round choice (later traded to Columbus - Columbus selected Tyler Kolarik) in 2000 Entry Draft for Steve Shields and Buffalo's 4th round choice (Miroslav Zalesak) in 1998 Entry Draft, June 18, 1998. Signed as a free agent by **NY Rangers**, August 17, 1998. Signed as a free agent by **Boston**, August 25, 1999. Traded to **Edmonton** by **Boston** for Mike Matteucci, December 28, 1999.

• WILKINSON, Derek

Derek K. G – L. 6', 170 lbs. b: Lasalle, Ont., 7/29/1974. Tampa Bay's 7th, 145th overall in 1992.

Season	Club	League	GP	W	L	T	Mins	GA	SO	Avg	AAvg	Eff	SA	S%	SAPG	GP	W	L	T	Mins	GA	SO	Avg	Eff	SA	S%	SAPG
1989-90	Windsor Bulldogs	OJHL-B	3	1	1	0	164	18	0	6.59	....	....	....	....	....	....	....	....	....	....	....	....	....	....	....	....	....
	Belle River Canadiens	OJHL-C	2	....	....	....	115	2	1	1.04	....	....	....	....	....	....	....	....	....	....	....	....	....	....	....	....	....
1990-91	Chatham Mic-Macs	OJHL-B	24	....	....	....	1429	86	0	3.61	....	....	....	....	....	....	....	....	....	....	....	....	....	....	....	....	....
1991-92	Detroit Ambassadors	OHL	38	16	17	1	1943	138	1	4.26	....	....	....	....	....	7	3	2	....	313	28	0	5.37	....	....	....	....
1992-93	Detroit Jr. Red Wings	OHL	*4	1	2	1	*245	18	0	4.41	....	....	....	....	....	....	....	....	....	....	....	....	....	....	....	....	....
	Belleville Bulls	OHL	*59	21	24	11	*3370	237	0	4.22	....	....	....	....	....	7	3	4	....	434	29	0	4.01	....	....	....	....
1993-94	Belleville Bulls	OHL	*56	24	16	4	2860	179	*2	3.76	....	....	....	....	....	12	6	6	....	700	39	*1	3.34	....	....	....	....

Season	Club	League	GP	W	L	T	Mins	GA	SO	Avg	AAvg	Eff	SA	S%	SAPG	GP	W	L	T	Mins	GA	SO	Avg	Eff	SA	S%	SAPG
			REGULAR SEASON													PLAYOFFS											
1994-95	Atlanta Knights	IHL	46	22	17	2	2414	121	1	3.01	....	....	....	....	....	4	2	1	....	197	8	0	2.43	....	....	....	....
1995-96	**Tampa Bay Lightning**	**NHL**	**4**	**0**	**3**	**0**	**200**	**15**	**0**	**4.50**	**4.48**	**6.43**	**105**	**.857**	**31.5**	....	....	....	....	....	....	....	....	....	....	....	....
	Atlanta Knights	IHL	28	11	11	2	1433	98	1	4.10	....	....	....	....	....	....	....	....	....	....	....	....	....	....	....	....	....
1996-97	**Tampa Bay Lightning**	**NHL**	**5**	**0**	**2**	**1**	**169**	**12**	**0**	**4.26**	**4.59**	**7.10**	**72**	**.833**	**25.6**	....	....	....	....	....	....	....	....	....	....	....	....
	Cleveland Lumberjacks	IHL	46	20	17	6	2595	138	1	3.19	....	....	....	....	....	14	8	6	....	893	44	0	2.95	....	....	....	....
1997-98	**Tampa Bay Lightning**	**NHL**	**8**	**2**	**4**	**1**	**311**	**17**	**0**	**3.28**	**3.91**	**3.77**	**148**	**.885**	**28.6**	....	....	....	....	....	....	....	....	....	....	....	....
	Cleveland Lumberjacks	IHL	25	9	12	2	1295	63	1	2.92	....	....	....	....	....	1	0	0	....	27	1	0	2.19	....	....	....	....
1998-99	**Tampa Bay Lightning**	**NHL**	**5**	**1**	**3**	**1**	**253**	**13**	**0**	**3.08**	**3.66**	**3.13**	**128**	**.898**	**30.4**	....	....	....	....	....	....	....	....	....	....	....	....
	Cleveland Lumberjacks	IHL	34	10	15	2	1760	108	1	3.68	....	....	....	....	....	....	....	....	....	....	....	....	....	....	....	....	....
99-2000	Charlotte Checkers	ECHL	31	11	13	2	1435	83	0	3.47	....	....	....	....	....	....	....	....	....	....	....	....	....	....	....	....	....
	Chicago Wolves	IHL	1	0	0	1	60	5	0	5.00	....	....	....	....	....	....	....	....	....	....	....	....	....	....	....	....	....
	NHL Totals		**22**	**3**	**12**	**3**	**933**	**57**	**0**	**3.67**	....	....	**453**	**.874**	**29.1**	....	....	....	....	....	....	....	....	....	....	....	....

• WILLIS, Jordan

G – L. 5'9", 155 lbs. b: Kincardine, Ont., 2/28/1975. Dallas' 8th, 243rd overall in 1993.

Season	Club	League	GP	W	L	T	Mins	GA	SO	Avg	AAvg	Eff	SA	S%	SAPG	GP	W	L	T	Mins	GA	SO	Avg	Eff	SA	S%	SAPG
1991-92	Hannover Barons	OJHL-C	17	11	1	2	906	37	0	2.45	....	....	....	....	....	....	....	....	....	....	....	....	....	....	....	....	....
1992-93	London Knights	OHL	26	13	6	3	1428	101	1	4.24	....	....	....	....	....	7	2	4	....	355	19	0	3.21	....	....	....	....
1993-94	London Knights	OHL	44	20	19	2	2428	158	1	3.90	....	....	....	....	....	1	0	0	....	8	1	0	7.50	....	....	....	....
1994-95	London Knights	OHL	53	16	29	3	2824	202	0	4.29	....	....	....	....	....	3	0	3	....	165	15	0	5.45	....	....	....	....
1995-96	**Dallas Stars**	**NHL**	**1**	**0**	**1**	**0**	**19**	**1**	**0**	**3.16**	**3.14**	**2.26**	**14**	**.929**	**44.2**	....	....	....	....	....	....	....	....	....	....	....	....
	Michigan K-Wings	IHL	38	17	9	9	2184	118	1	3.24	....	....	....	....	....	4	1	3	....	238	17	0	4.29	....	....	....	....
1996-97	Canada	Nat-Team	15	7	4	2	804	42	0	3.13	....	....	....	....	....	....	....	....	....	....	....	....	....	....	....	....	....
	Daytona Bombers	ECHL	8	4	4	0	429	25	0	3.50	....	....	....	....	....	....	....	....	....	....	....	....	....	....	....	....	....
	Michigan K-Wings	IHL	2	0	2	0	102	8	0	4.70	....	....	....	....	....	....	....	....	....	....	....	....	....	....	....	....	....
1997-98	Michigan K-Wings	IHL	31	8	18	2	1584	93	1	3.52	....	....	....	....	....	....	....	....	....	....	....	....	....	....	....	....	....
1998-99	Baton Rouge Kingfish	ECHL	47	19	20	5	2521	131	4	3.12	....	....	....	....	....	6	3	3	....	374	18	1	2.89	....	....	....	....
99-2000	Nottingham Panthers	BH-Cup	8	....	....	....	205	28	0	4.33	....	....	....	....	....	....	....	....	....	....	....	....	....	....	....	....	....
	Nottingham Panthers	Britain	40	....	....	....	2344	141	0	3.61	....	....	....	....	....	....	....	....	....	....	....	....	....	....	....	....	....
	NHL Totals		**1**	**0**	**1**	**0**	**19**	**1**	**0**	**3.16**	....	....	**14**	**.929**	**44.2**	....	....	....	....	....	....	....	....	....	....	....	....

• WILSON, Dunc

Duncan Shepherd G. 5'11", 175 lbs. b: Toronto, Ont., 3/22/1948.

Season	Club	League	GP	W	L	T	Mins	GA	SO	Avg	AAvg	Eff	SA	S%	SAPG	GP	W	L	T	Mins	GA	SO	Avg	Eff	SA	S%	SAPG
1964-65	Toronto Red Wings	MTHL	STATISTICS NOT AVAILABLE																								
	Oshawa Generals	OHA-Jr.	2	....	....	....	70	8	0	6.86	....	....	....	....	....	....	....	....	....	....	....	....	....	....	....	....	....
1965-66	Niagara Falls Flyers	OHA-Jr.	22	....	....	....	137	82	1	3.59	....	....	....	....	....	4	1	2	1	240	17	0	4.25	....	....	....	....
1966-67	Niagara Falls Flyers	OHA-Jr.	1	0	1	0	40	6	0	9.00	....	....	....	....	....	....	....	....	....	....	....	....	....	....	....	....	....
	Peterborough Petes	OHA-Jr.	14	....	....	....	840	56	0	4.42	....	....	....	....	....	....	....	....	....	....	....	....	....	....	....	....	....
1967-68	Oshawa Generals	OHA-Jr.	30	....	....	....	1800	159	1	5.30	....	....	....	....	....	....	....	....	....	....	....	....	....	....	....	....	....
1968-69	Quebec Aces	AHL	37	11	14	9	1814	98	0	3.24	....	....	....	....	....	15	7	8	0	*835	38	0	*2.73	....	....	....	....
1969-70	**Philadelphia Flyers**	**NHL**	**1**	**0**	**1**	**0**	**60**	**3**	**0**	**3.00**	**3.18**	....	....	....	....	....	....	....	....	....	....	....	....	....	....	....	....
	Quebec Aces	AHL	57	....	....	....	3288	191	2	3.49	....	....	....	....	....	4	2	2	0	272	10	0	2.21	....	....	....	....
1970-71	**Vancouver Canucks**	**NHL**	**35**	**3**	**25**	**2**	**1791**	**128**	**0**	**4.29**	**4.29**	....	....	....	....	....	....	....	....	....	....	....	....	....	....	....	....
1971-72	**Vancouver Canucks**	**NHL**	**53**	**16**	**30**	**3**	**2870**	**173**	**1**	**3.62**	**3.69**	....	....	....	....	....	....	....	....	....	....	....	....	....	....	....	....
1972-73	**Vancouver Canucks**	**NHL**	**43**	**13**	**21**	**5**	**2423**	**159**	**1**	**3.94**	**3.74**	....	....	....	....	....	....	....	....	....	....	....	....	....	....	....	....
1973-74	**Toronto Maple Leafs**	**NHL**	**24**	**9**	**11**	**3**	**1412**	**68**	**1**	**2.89**	**2.79**	....	....	....	....	....	....	....	....	....	....	....	....	....	....	....	....
1974-75	**Toronto Maple Leafs**	**NHL**	**25**	**8**	**11**	**4**	**1393**	**86**	**0**	**3.70**	**3.35**	....	....	....	....	....	....	....	....	....	....	....	....	....	....	....	....
	New York Rangers	**NHL**	**3**	**1**	**2**	**0**	**180**	**13**	**0**	**4.33**	**3.91**	....	....	....	....	....	....	....	....	....	....	....	....	....	....	....	....
1975-76	**New York Rangers**	**NHL**	**20**	**5**	**9**	**3**	**1080**	**76**	**0**	**4.22**	**3.83**	....	....	....	....	....	....	....	....	....	....	....	....	....	....	....	....
	Baltimore Clippers	AHL	6	3	2	0	325	15	1	2.77	....	....	....	....	....	....	....	....	....	....	....	....	....	....	....	....	....
1976-77	**Pittsburgh Penguins**	**NHL**	**45**	**18**	**19**	**8**	**2627**	**129**	**5**	**2.95**	**2.73**	....	....	....	....	....	....	....	....	....	....	....	....	....	....	....	....
1977-78	**Pittsburgh Penguins**	**NHL**	**21**	**5**	**11**	**3**	**1180**	**95**	**0**	**4.83**	**4.56**	....	....	....	....	....	....	....	....	....	....	....	....	....	....	....	....
1978-79	**Vancouver Canucks**	**NHL**	**17**	**2**	**10**	**2**	**835**	**58**	**0**	**4.17**	**3.70**	....	....	....	....	....	....	....	....	....	....	....	....	....	....	....	....
	Binghamton Dusters	AHL	3	0	2	0	109	11	0	6.06	....	....	....	....	....	....	....	....	....	....	....	....	....	....	....	....	....
	Dallas Black Hawks	CHL	3	2	1	0	180	11	0	3.67	....	....	....	....	....	....	....	....	....	....	....	....	....	....	....	....	....
	NHL Totals		**287**	**80**	**150**	**33**	**15851**	**988**	**8**	**3.74**																	

Claimed by **Philadelphia** from **Boston** (Oshawa/OHA-Jr.) in Special Internal Amateur Draft, June, 1968. Claimed by **Vancouver** from **Philadelphia** in Expansion Draft, June 10, 1970. Traded to **Toronto** by **Vancouver** for Larry McIntyre and Murray Heatley, May 29, 1973. Claimed on waivers by **NY Rangers** from **Toronto**, February 15, 1975. Traded to **Pittsburgh** by **NY Rangers** for Pittsburgh's 4th round choice (Dave Silk) in 1978 Amateur Draft, October 8, 1976. Traded to **Vancouver** by **Pittsburgh** for cash, November 17, 1978.

• WILSON, Lefty

Ross Ingram G – L. 5'11", 178 lbs. b: Toronto, Ont., 10/15/1919.

Season	Club	League	GP	W	L	T	Mins	GA	SO	Avg	AAvg	Eff	SA	S%	SAPG	GP	W	L	T	Mins	GA	SO	Avg	Eff	SA	S%	SAPG
1937-38	Toronto Lions	OHA-Jr.	11	....	....	....	660	72	0	6.55	....	....	....	....	....	....	....	....	....	....	....	....	....	....	....	....	....
1938-1943			DID NOT PLAY																								
1943-44	St. Catharines Intermediates	OIHA	STATISTICS NOT AVAILABLE																								
1944-45	Toronto Navy	TIHL	7	*5	2	0	430	33	0	*4.60	....	....	....	....	....	7	*4	3	0	420	47	0	6.71	....	....	....	....
	Toronto Uptown Tires	TMHL	8	4	4	0	480	41	0	5.13	....	....	....	....	....	1	0	1	0	60	7	0	7.00	....	....	....	....
1945-46	Omaha Knights	USHL	3	....	....	....	180	15	0	4.99	....	....	....	....	....	....	....	....	....	....	....	....	....	....	....	....	....
	St. Paul Saints	USHL	1	....	....	....	60	4	0	4.00	....	....	....	....	....	....	....	....	....	....	....	....	....	....	....	....	....
1946-47			DID NOT PLAY																								
1947-48	Indianapolis Capitols	AHL	2	0	1	0	80	7	0	5.25	....	....	....	....	....	....	....	....	....	....	....	....	....	....	....	....	....
1948-49	Indianapolis Capitols	AHL	2	1	0	0	80	4	0	3.00	....	....	....	....	....	....	....	....	....	....	....	....	....	....	....	....	....
1949-50	Indianapolis Capitols	AHL	3	2	1	0	180	12	0	4.00	....	....	....	....	....	....	....	....	....	....	....	....	....	....	....	....	....
1953-54	**Detroit Red Wings**	**NHL**	**1**	**0**	**0**	**0**	**16**	**0**	**0**	**0.00**	**0.00**	....	....	....	....	....	....	....	....	....	....	....	....	....	....	....	....
1955-56	**Toronto Maple Leafs**	**NHL**	**1**	**0**	**0**	**0**	**13**	**0**	**0**	**0.00**	**0.00**	....	....	....	....	....	....	....	....	....	....	....	....	....	....	....	....
1957-58	**Boston Bruins**	**NHL**	**1**	**0**	**0**	**1**	**52**	**1**	**0**	**1.15**	**1.26**	....	....	....	....	....	....	....	....	....	....	....	....	....	....	....	....
	NHL Totals		**3**	**0**	**0**	**1**	**81**	**1**	**0**	**0.74**		....	....	....	....	....	....	....	....	....	....	....	....	....	....	....	....

• **Detroit's** assistant trainer/practice goaltender replaced injured Terry Sawchuk in 3rd period, October 10, 1953. (Montreal 4, Detroit 1). Loaned to **Toronto** by **Detroit** to replace injured Harry Lumley in 3rd period, January 22, 1956. (Detroit 4, Toronto 1). Loaned to **Boston** by **Detroit** to replace injured Don Simmons in 1st period, December 29, 1957. (Boston 2, Detroit 2)

• WINKLER, Hal

Harold Lang G. 5'8", 150 lbs. b: Gretna, Man., 3/20/1892 d: 5/29/1956.

Season	Club	League	GP	W	L	T	Mins	GA	SO	Avg	AAvg	Eff	SA	S%	SAPG	GP	W	L	T	Mins	GA	SO	Avg	Eff	SA	S%	SAPG
1913-14	Winnipeg Winnipegs	MHL-Sr.	8	2	6	0	480	47	0	5.87	....	....	....	....	....	....	....	....	....	....	....	....	....	....	....	....	....
1914-15	Winnipeg Winnipegs	MHL-Sr.	6	....	....	....	300	51	0	8.50	....	....	....	....	....	....	....	....	....	....	....	....	....	....	....	....	....
1915-16	Winnipeg 61st Battalion	MHL-Sr.	1	1	0	0	60	4	0	4.00	....	....	....	....	....	....	....	....	....	....	....	....	....	....	....	....	....
1916-17	Winnipeg Monarchs	MHL-Sr.	8	3	5	0	480	46	0	5.75	....	....	....	....	....	....	....	....	....	....	....	....	....	....	....	....	....
1917-18	Winnipeg Ypres	MHL-Sr.	8	*6	2	0	480	29	0	*3.63	....	....	....	....	....	1	1	0	0	60	0	*1	*0.00	....	....	....	....
	Winnipeg Ypres	Al-Cup	4	3	1	0	240	9	1	2.25	....	....	....	....	....	....	....	....	....	....	....	....	....	....	....	....	....
1918-19	Brandon Elks	MHL-Sr.	9	5	4	0	540	49	0	5.41	....	....	....	....	....	....	....	....	....	....	....	....	....	....	....	....	....
1919-20	Moose Jaw Maple Leafs	S-SSHL	12	*9	3	0	730	40	0	3.29	....	....	....	....	....	2	*2	0	0	120	4	0	*2.00	....	....	....	....
	Moose Jaw Maple Leafs	Al-Cup	5	3	2	0	300	26	0	5.20	....	....	....	....	....	....	....	....	....	....	....	....	....	....	....	....	....
1920-21	Saskatoon Crescents	N-SSHL	16	*10	6	0	960	49	*2	3.06	....	....	....	....	....	4	2	2	0	240	14	0	3.50	....	....	....	....
1921-22	Edmonton Eskimos	WCHL	14	10	4	0	831	33	1	*2.38	....	....	....	....	....	2	0	1	1	120	3	0	1.50	....	....	....	....
1922-23	Edmonton Eskimos	WCHL	28	*17	10	1	*1738	87	1	3.00	....	....	....	....	....	2	1	1	0	151	3	1	1.19	....	....	....	....
	Edmonton Eskimos	St-Cup	2	0	2	0	123	3	0	1.46	....	....	....	....	....	....	....	....	....	....	....	....	....	....	....	....	....
1923-24	Edmonton Eskimos	WCHL	26	9	13	4	1655	69	1	2.50	....	....	....	....	....	....	....	....	....	....	....	....	....	....	....	....	....
1924-25	Calgary Tigers	WCHL	*28	*17	11	0	1680	80	2	2.86	....	....	....	....	....	2	0	1	1	120	3	0	1.50	....	....	....	....
1925-26	Calgary Tigers	WHL	*30	10	17	3	1874	80	*6	2.56	....	....	....	....	....	....	....	....	....	....	....	....	....	....	....	....	....
1926-27	**New York Rangers**	**NHL**	**8**	**3**	**4**	**1**	**514**	**16**	**2**	**1.87**	**2.85**	....	....	....	....	....	....	....	....	....	....	....	....	....	....	....	....
	Boston Bruins	**NHL**	**23**	**12**	**9**	**2**	**1445**	**40**	**4**	**1.66**	**2.51**	....	....	....	....	***8**	**2**	**2**	**4**	***520**	**13**	***2**	**1.50**	....	....	....	....
1927-28	**Boston Bruins**	**NHL**	***44**	**20**	**13**	**11**	***2780**	**70**	***15**	**1.51**	**2.36**	....	....	....	....	**2**	**0**	**1**	**1**	**120**	**5**	**0**	**2.50**	....	....	....	....

			REGULAR SEASON													PLAYOFFS											
Season	Club	League	GP	W	L	T	Mins	GA	SO	Avg	AAvg	Eff	SA	S%	SAPG	GP	W	L	T	Mins	GA	SO	Avg	Eff	SA	S%	SAPG
1928-29	Minneapolis Millers	AHA	34	17	7	10	2144	35	*14	*0.98						4	1	3	0	240	7	0	1.75				
1929-30	Seattle Eskimos	PCHL	36	15	13	8	2160	58	9	1.61																	
1930-31	Boston Tigers	Can-Am	10	3	7	0	610	32	0	3.15																	
	NHL Totals		**75**	**35**	**26**	**14**	**4739**	**126**	**21**	**1.60**						**10**	**2**	**3**	**5**	**640**	**18**	**2**	**1.69**				
	Other Major League Totals		126	63	55	8	7778	349	11	2.69						6	1	3		391	9	1	1.38				

WCHL All-Star Team (1923)

Signed as a free agent by **Saskatoon** (N-SSHL), November 8, 1920. Traded to **Edmonton** (WCHL) by **Saskatoon** (WCHL) for cash, January 13, 1922. Traded to **Calgary** (WCHL) by **Edmonton** (WCHL) with Emory Sparrow for cash, August 28, 1924. Traded to **NY Rangers** by **Calgary** (WHL) for cash, October 27, 1926. • Recorded shutout (1-0) in NHL debut vs. Montreal Maroons, November 16, 1926. Traded to **Boston** by **NY Rangers** for $5,000, January 17, 1927. Signed as a free agent by **Seattle** (PCHL), October 28, 1929. Traded to **Boston** (Can-Am) by **Seattle** (PCHL) for cash, October 10, 1930.

• WOLFE, Bernie

Bernard Ronald G – L. 5′9″, 165 lbs. b: Montreal, Que., 12/18/1951.

Season	Club	League	GP	W	L	T	Mins	GA	SO	Avg	AAvg	Eff	SA	S%	SAPG	GP	W	L	T	Mins	GA	SO	Avg	Eff	SA	S%	SAPG
1972-73	Sir George Williams	QUAA	STATISTICS NOT AVAILABLE																								
1973-74	Sir George Williams	QUAA	18	10	4	4	1080	74	0	4.11																	
1974-75	Maine Nordiques	NAHL	37	19	17	1	2156	150	1	4.17																	
	Richmond Robins	AHL	17	6	7	2	918	142	2	2.74						7	3	4	0	427	26	0	3.65				
1975-76	**Washington Capitals**	**NHL**	**40**	**5**	**23**	**7**	**2134**	**148**	**0**	**4.16**	**3.79**																
	Richmond Robins	AHL	3	2	0	0	147	6	0	2.44																	
1976-77	**Washington Capitals**	**NHL**	**37**	**7**	**15**	**9**	**1779**	**114**	**1**	**3.84**	**3.58**																
1977-78	**Washington Capitals**	**NHL**	**25**	**4**	**14**	**4**	**1328**	**94**	**0**	**4.25**	**4.00**																
	Hershey Bears	AHL	3	3	0	0	180	4	1	1.33																	
1978-79	**Washington Capitals**	**NHL**	**18**	**4**	**9**	**1**	**863**	**68**	**0**	**4.73**	**4.20**																
	NHL Totals		**120**	**20**	**61**	**21**	**6104**	**424**	**1**	**4.17**																	

QUAA First All-Star Team (1972, 1974) • CIAU First All-Star Team (1974)

Signed as a free agent by **Washington**, October 1, 1974.

• WOOD, Alex

Alexander Jerome G – L. 5′11″, 165 lbs. b: Falkirk, Scotland, 1/15/1911.

Season	Club	League	GP	W	L	T	Mins	GA	SO	Avg	AAvg	Eff	SA	S%	SAPG	GP	W	L	T	Mins	GA	SO	Avg	Eff	SA	S%	SAPG
1928-29	Regina Pats	S-SJHL	6	*6	0	0	310	8	*2	*1.55																	
	Regina Pats	Mem-Cup	6	3	1	2	360	14	0	2.33																	
1929-30	Ottawa New Edinburghs	OCHL	3	1	2	0	180	9	0	3.00																	
	Regina Aces	S-SJHL	18	*15	1	2	1190	21	*6	*1.06						2	0	2	0	120	4	0	2.00				
1930-31	Cleveland Indians	IHL	19	12	4	3	1120	44	1	2.36						2	2	0		130	6	0	2.77				
1931-32	Cleveland Indians	IHL	30	12	13	5	1870	76	0	2.44																	
1932-33	Boston Cubs	Can-Am	3	0	2	1	190	14	0	4.67																	
	Quebec Castors	Can-Am	1	0	1	0	60	8	0	8.00																	
1933-34	Philadelphia Arrows	Can-Am	41	18	16	7	2540	101	2	2.39						2	0	2	0	120	6	0	3.00				
1934-35	Philadelphia Arrows	Can-Am	13	4	7	2	800	40	2	3.00																	
	Providence Reds	Can-Am	3	0	2	1	190	13	0	4.11																	
1935-36	Rochester Cardinals	IHL	4	0	4	0	240	14	0	3.50																	
	Buffalo Bisons	IHL	48	22	20	6	2990	101	*13	2.04						5	1	4	0	310	7	*1	*1.36				
1936-37	Buffalo Bisons	IAHL	11	3	8	0	660	30	1	2.73																	
	Cleveland Barons	IAHL	3	0	3	0	180	18	0	6.00																	
	New Haven Eagles	IAHL	20	5	14	1	1210	70	0	3.47																	
	New York Americans	**NHL**	**1**	**0**	**1**	**0**	**70**	**3**	**0**	**2.57**	**3.18**																
1937-38	Minneapolis Millers	AHA	48	24	15	9	3065	100	9	1.96						7	3	4	0	425	9	1	1.27				
1938-39	Minneapolis Millers	AHA	48	31	17	0	2977	139	4	2.81						4	2	2	0	255	8	*1	*1.88				
1939-40	Minneapolis Millers	AHA	48	26	22	0	2931	140	3	2.87						3	0	3	0	180	14	0	4.67				
1940-41	St. Louis Flyers	AHA	47	*31	16	0	2905	98	*7	2.02						7	*6	1	0	474	14	*1	*1.77				
1941-42	St. Louis Flyers	AHA	50	*30	15	5	3060	103	*11	2.02						3	0	3	0	180	11	0	3.67				
1942-43	New Haven Eagles	AHL	21	5	11	5	1260	77	0	3.67																	
	Hull Volants	OCHL	4				240	24	0	6.00						4				240	19	0	4.75				
1943-44	Hull Volants	OCHL	14	*7	*6	1	840	58	0	4.14						8	6	2	0	480	29	1	3.63				
1944-45	Hull Volants	QSHL	24	5	18	1	1440	176	0	7.33						2				120	8	0	4.00				
	NHL Totals		**1**	**0**	**1**	**0**	**70**	**3**	**0**	**2.57**																	

IHL First All-Star Team (1936) • AHA First All-Star Team (1938, 1941) • AHA Second All-Star Team (1942)

Signed as a free agent by **Chicago**, June 27, 1930. Signed as a free agent by **Cleveland** (IAHL) after **Buffalo** (IAHL) folded, December 9, 1936. • Released by Cleveland (IAHL), December, 1936. Signed as a free agent by **NY Americans**, December 31, 1936. Promoted to **NY Americans** from **New Haven** (IAHL) to replace Alfie Moore, January 31, 1937. (Montreal Maroons 3, NY Americans 2). Traded to **Chicago** by **St. Louis** (AHA) with Leo Carbol for cash, October 9, 1942.

• WORSLEY, Gump

Lorne John G – L. 5′7″, 180 lbs. b: Montreal, Que., 5/14/1929. **HHOF**

Season	Club	League	GP	W	L	T	Mins	GA	SO	Avg	AAvg	Eff	SA	S%	SAPG	GP	W	L	T	Mins	GA	SO	Avg	Eff	SA	S%	SAPG
1946-47	Verdun Cyclones	QJHL	25	6	18	1	1500	138	3	5.52																	
1947-48	Verdun Cyclones	QJHL	29	13	11	5	1740	95	1	3.28						5	1	4	0	317	21	0	3.97				
1948-49	Montreal St-Francis Xavier	MMJHL	47	24	21	2	2840	122	7	2.58						5	2	3	0	310	16	0	3.10				
	New York Rovers	QSHL	2				120	5	0	2.50																	
1949-50	New York Rovers	EAHL	47	25	17	5	2830	133	*7	2.86						12	*8	2	0	720	27	*1	*2.25				
	New Haven Ramblers	AHL	2	2	0	0	120	4	0	2.00																	
1950-51	St. Paul Saints	USHL	64	33	26	5	*3920	184	*3	*2.82						4	1	3	0	247	9	0	*2.19				
1951-52	Saskatoon Quakers	PCHL	66	33	19	14	3960	206	*5	3.07						13	*10	3	0	818	31	*1	2.27				
1952-53	Saskatoon Quakers	WHL	13	5	7	1	780	50	0	3.84																	
	Edmonton Flyers	WHL	1	1	0	0	60	2	0	2.00																	
	New York Rangers	**NHL**	**50**	**13**	**29**	**8**	**3000**	**153**	**2**	**3.06**	**4.04**																
1953-54	Vancouver Canucks	WHL	70	*39	24	7	4200	168	4	*2.40						12	7	4	0	709	29	0	2.45				
1954-55	**New York Rangers**	**NHL**	**65**	**15**	**33**	**17**	**3900**	**197**	**4**	**3.03**	**3.80**																
1955-56	**New York Rangers**	**NHL**	***70**	**32**	**28**	**10**	***4200**	**198**	**4**	**2.83**	**3.56**					**3**	**0**	**3**		**180**	**14**	**0**	**4.67**				
1956-57	**New York Rangers**	**NHL**	**68**	**26**	**28**	**14**	**4080**	**216**	**3**	**3.18**	**3.80**					**5**	**1**	**4**		**316**	**21**	**0**	**3.99**				
1957-58	**New York Rangers**	**NHL**	**37**	**21**	**10**	**6**	**2220**	**86**	**4**	**2.32**	**2.50**					**6**	**2**	**4**		**365**	**28**	**0**	**4.60**				
	Providence Reds	AHL	25	12	11	2	1528	83	0	3.26																	
1958-59	**New York Rangers**	**NHL**	**67**	**26**	**30**	**11**	**4001**	**198**	**2**	**2.97**	**3.18**																
1959-60	**New York Rangers**	**NHL**	**39**	**7**	**23**	**8**	**2301**	**135**	**0**	**3.52**	**3.76**																
	Springfield Indians	AHL	15	11	3	1	900	33	3	2.20																	
1960-61	**New York Rangers**	**NHL**	**59**	**20**	**29**	**8**	**3473**	**190**	**1**	**3.28**	**3.44**																
1961-62	**New York Rangers**	**NHL**	**60**	**22**	**27**	**9**	**3531**	**172**	**2**	**2.92**	**2.98**					**6**	**2**	**4**		**384**	**21**	**0**	**3.28**				
1962-63	**New York Rangers**	**NHL**	***67**	**22**	**34**	**10**	***3980**	**217**	**2**	**3.27**	**3.48**																
1963-64	**Montreal Canadiens**	**NHL**	**8**	**3**	**2**	**2**	**444**	**22**	**1**	**2.97**	**3.30**																
	Quebec Aces	AHL	47	30	16	1	2820	128	5	2.72						*9	4	5	0	*543	29	0	3.20				
1964-65	Quebec Aces	AHL	37	24	12	1	2247	101	2	2.70																	
♦	**Montreal Canadiens**	**NHL**	**19**	**10**	**7**	**1**	**1020**	**50**	**1**	**2.94**	**3.15**					**8**	**5**	**3**		**501**	**14**	***2**	***1.68**				
1965-66♦	**Montreal Canadiens**	**NHL**	**51**	**29**	**14**	**6**	**2899**	**114**	**2**	**2.36**	**2.32**					**10**	***8**	**2**		**602**	**20**	***1**	***1.99**				
1966-67	**Montreal Canadiens**	**NHL**	**18**	**9**	**6**	**2**	**888**	**47**	**1**	**3.18**	**3.29**					**2**	**0**	**1**		**80**	**2**	**0**	**1.50**				
1967-68♦	**Montreal Canadiens**	**NHL**	**40**	**19**	**9**	**8**	**2213**	**73**	**6**	***1.98**	**2.17**					**12**	***11**	**0**		**672**	**21**	***1**	**1.88**				
1968-69♦	**Montreal Canadiens**	**NHL**	**30**	**19**	**5**	**4**	**1703**	**64**	**5**	**2.25**	**2.31**					**7**	**5**	**1**		**370**	**14**	**0**	**2.27**				
1969-70	**Montreal Canadiens**	**NHL**	**6**	**3**	**1**	**2**	**360**	**14**	**0**	**2.33**	**2.47**																
	Minnesota North Stars	**NHL**	**8**	**5**	**1**	**1**	**453**	**20**	**1**	**2.65**	**2.81**					**3**	**1**	**2**		**180**	**14**	**0**	**4.67**				
1970-71	**Minnesota North Stars**	**NHL**	**24**	**4**	**10**	**8**	**1369**	**57**	**0**	**2.50**	**2.46**					**4**	**3**	**1**		**240**	**13**	**0**	**3.25**				

Season	Club	League	REGULAR SEASON GP	W	L	T	Mins	GA	SO	Avg	AAvg	Eff	SA	S%	SAPG	PLAYOFFS GP	W	L	T	Mins	GA	SO	Avg	Eff	SA	S%	SAPG
1971-72	**Minnesota North Stars**	**NHL**	**34**	**16**	**10**	**7**	**1923**	**68**	**2**	**2.12**	**2.12**	....	....	....	....	**4**	**2**	**1**	....	**194**	**7**	**1**	**2.16**	....	....	....	....
1972-73	**Minnesota North Stars**	**NHL**	**12**	**6**	**2**	**3**	**624**	**30**	**0**	**2.88**	**2.71**	....	....	....	....	....	....	....	....	....	....	....	....	....	....	....	....
1973-74	**Minnesota North Stars**	**NHL**	**29**	**8**	**14**	**5**	**1601**	**86**	**0**	**3.22**	**3.11**	....	....	....	....	....	....	....	....	....	....	....	....	....	....	....	....
	NHL Totals		**861**	**335**	**352**	**150**	**50183**	**2407**	**43**	**2.88**		....	....	....	....	**70**	**40**	**26**	....	**4084**	**189**	**5**	**2.78**	....	....	....	....

QJHL First All-Star Team (1949) • EAHL First All-Star Team (1950) • USHL First All-Star Team (1951) • Won Outstanding Rookie Cup (Top Rookie - USHL) (1951) • Won Charles Gardiner Memorial Trophy (USHL - Top Goaltender) (1951) • PCHL Second All-Star Team (1952) • Won Calder Memorial Trophy (1953) • WHL First All-Star Team (1954) • Won WHL Leading Goaltender Award (1954) • Won Leader Cup (WHL - MVP) (1954) • AHL First All-Star Team (1964) • NHL Second All-Star Team (1966) • Shared Vezina Trophy with Charlie Hodge (1966) • NHL First All-Star Team (1968) • Shared Vezina Trophy with Rogie Vachon (1968) • Played in NHL All-Star Game (1961, 1962, 1965, 1972)

Traded to **Montreal** by **NY Rangers** with Dave Balon, Leon Rochefort and Len Ronson for Jacques Plante, Don Marshall and Phil Goyette, June 4, 1963. Traded to **Minnesota** by **Montreal** for cash, February 27, 1970.

• WORTERS, Roy

"Shrimp" G – L. 5'3", 135 lbs. b: Toronto, Ont., 10/19/1900 d: 11/7/1957. HHOF

Season	Club	League	GP	W	L	T	Mins	GA	SO	Avg	AAvg	Eff	SA	S%	SAPG	GP	W	L	T	Mins	GA	SO	Avg	Eff	SA	S%	SAPG
1918-19	Parkdale Canoe Club	OHA-Jr.	8	*7	1	0	480	22	0	2.75	....	....	....	....	....	2	1	1	0	120	6	0	3.00	....	....	....	....
1919-20	Parkdale Canoe Club	OHA-Jr.	3	3	0	0	180	14	0	4.67	....	....	....	....	....	4	*4	0	0	240	16	0	4.00	....	....	....	....
	Parkdale Canoe Club	Mem-Cup	3	3	0	0	180	9	0	3.00	....	....	....	....	....	....	....	....	....	....	....	....	....	....	....	....	....
1920-21	Porcupine Miners	GBHL	10	7	2	1	630	27	0	2.57	....	....	....	....	....	2	0	2	0	120	10	0	5.00	....	....	....	....
1921-22	Porcupine Miners	GBHL	DID NOT PLAY – SUSPENDED																								
1922-23	Toronto Argonauts	TIHL	10	....	....	....	558	37	0	3.98	....	....	....	....	....	....	....	....	....	....	....	....	....	....	....	....	....
1923-24	Pittsburgh Yellowjackets	USAHA	20	*15	5	0	1225	25	*7	*1.23	....	....	....	....	....	13	*9	3	1	840	12	*5	*0.86	....	....	....	....
1924-25	Pittsburgh Yellowjackets	USAHA	39	*25	10	4	1895	34	*17	*0.81	....	....	....	....	....	8	*6	1	1	400	8	1	*1.20	....	....	....	....
1925-26	**Pittsburgh Pirates**	**NHL**	**35**	**18**	**16**	**1**	**2145**	**68**	**7**	**1.90**	**2.44**	....	....	....	....	**2**	**0**	**1**	**1**	**120**	**6**	**0**	**3.00**	....	....	....	....
1926-27	**Pittsburgh Pirates**	**NHL**	***44**	**15**	**26**	**3**	**2711**	**108**	**4**	**2.39**	**3.73**	....	....	....	....	....	....	....	....	....	....	....	....	....	....	....	....
1927-28	**Pittsburgh Pirates**	**NHL**	***44**	**19**	**17**	**8**	**2740**	**76**	**11**	**1.66**	**2.62**	....	....	....	....	**2**	**1**	**1**	**0**	**120**	**6**	**0**	**3.00**	....	....	....	....
1928-29	**New York Americans**	**NHL**	**38**	**16**	**12**	**10**	**2390**	**46**	**13**	**1.15**	**2.35**	....	....	....	....	**2**	**0**	**1**	**1**	**150**	**1**	**1**	**0.40**	....	....	....	....
1929-30	**New York Americans**	**NHL**	**36**	**11**	**21**	**4**	**2270**	**135**	**2**	**3.57**	**3.75**	....	....	....	....	....	....	....	....	....	....	....	....	....	....	....	....
	Montreal Canadiens	**NHL**	**1**	**1**	**0**	**0**	**60**	**2**	**0**	**2.00**	**2.06**	....	....	....	....	....	....	....	....	....	....	....	....	....	....	....	....
1930-31	**New York Americans**	**NHL**	***44**	**18**	**16**	**10**	***2760**	**74**	**8**	***1.61**	**1.97**	....	....	....	....	....	....	....	....	....	....	....	....	....	....	....	....
1931-32	**New York Americans**	**NHL**	**40**	**12**	**20**	**8**	**2459**	**110**	**5**	**2.68**	**3.31**	....	....	....	....	....	....	....	....	....	....	....	....	....	....	....	....
1932-33	**New York Americans**	**NHL**	**47**	**15**	**22**	**10**	**2970**	**116**	**5**	**2.34**	**3.15**	....	....	....	....	....	....	....	....	....	....	....	....	....	....	....	....
	Quebec Castors	Can-Am	1	0	1	0	60	3	0	3.00	....	....	....	....	....	....	....	....	....	....	....	....	....	....	....	....	....
1933-34	**New York Americans**	**NHL**	**36**	**12**	**13**	**10**	**2240**	**75**	**4**	**2.01**	**2.50**	....	....	....	....	....	....	....	....	....	....	....	....	....	....	....	....
1934-35	**New York Americans**	**NHL**	***48**	**12**	**27**	**9**	***3000**	**142**	**3**	**2.84**	**3.50**	....	....	....	....	....	....	....	....	....	....	....	....	....	....	....	....
1935-36	**New York Americans**	**NHL**	***48**	**16**	**25**	**7**	**3000**	**122**	**3**	**2.44**	**3.50**	....	....	....	....	**5**	**2**	**3**	**0**	**300**	**11**	***2**	**2.20**	....	....	....	....
1936-37	**New York Americans**	**NHL**	**23**	**6**	**14**	**3**	**1430**	**69**	**2**	**2.90**	**3.63**	....	....	....	....	....	....	....	....	....	....	....	....	....	....	....	....
	NHL Totals		**484**	**171**	**229**	**83**	**30175**	**1143**	**67**	**2.27**		....	....	....	....	**11**	**3**	**6**	**2**	**690**	**24**	**3**	**2.09**	....	....	....	....

Won Hart Trophy (1929) • Won Vezina Trophy (1931) • NHL Second All-Star Team (1932, 1934)

• Suspended for the entire 1921-22 season by GBHL for a high-sticking incident in playoff game vs. Iroquois Falls, March, 1921. Signed as a free agent by **Pittsburgh**, September 26, 1925. Traded to **NY Americans** by **Pittsburgh** for Joe Miller and $20,000, November 1, 1928. • Suspended by NHL President Frank Calder for refusing to report to **NY Americans**, November 12, 1928. • Was re-instated at a special Board of Governors meeting in December, 1928. Loaned to **Montreal Canadiens** by **NY Americans** to replace George Hainsworth, February 27, 1930. (Montreal Canadiens 6, Toronto 2). • Missed remainder of 1936-37 season recovering from hernia surgery, January 25, 1937.

• WORTHY, Chris

Christopher John G – L. 6', 180 lbs. b: Bristol, England, 10/23/1947.

Season	Club	League	GP	W	L	T	Mins	GA	SO	Avg	AAvg	Eff	SA	S%	SAPG	GP	W	L	T	Mins	GA	SO	Avg	Eff	SA	S%	SAPG
1965-66	Flin Flon Bombers	SJHL	53	....	....	....	3129	397	0	7.61	....	....	....	....	....	....	....	....	....	....	....	....	....	....	....	....	....
1966-67	Flin Flon Bombers	CMJHL	44	*40	4	0	2640	120	3	*2.73	....	....	....	....	....	14	8	6	0	857	52	0	3.64	....	....	....	....
	Flin Flon Bombers	Mem-Cup	6	2	4	0	354	25	0	4.24	....	....	....	....	....	....	....	....	....	....	....	....	....	....	....	....	....
1967-68	Flin Flon Bombers	WCJHL	60	47	8	5	3240	129	*10	*2.39	....	....	....	....	....	14	8	6	0	880	37	1	2.52	....	....	....	....
1968-69	**Oakland Seals**	**NHL**	**14**	**4**	**6**	**3**	**786**	**54**	**0**	**4.12**	**4.28**	....	....	....	....	....	....	....	....	....	....	....	....	....	....	....	....
1969-70	**Oakland Seals**	**NHL**	**1**	**0**	**1**	**0**	**60**	**5**	**0**	**5.00**	**5.31**	....	....	....	....	....	....	....	....	....	....	....	....	....	....	....	....
	Seattle Totems	WHL	31	14	14	3	1836	110	0	3.59	....	....	....	....	....	2	0	1	0	100	10	0	5.98	....	....	....	....
	Providence Reds	AHL	3	....	....	....	140	12	0	5.14	....	....	....	....	....	....	....	....	....	....	....	....	....	....	....	....	....
1970-71	**California Golden Seals**	**NHL**	**11**	**1**	**3**	**1**	**480**	**39**	**0**	**4.88**	**4.85**	....	....	....	....	....	....	....	....	....	....	....	....	....	....	....	....
1971-72	Kansas City Blues	CHL	19	3	10	5	1069	73	0	4.09	....	....	....	....	....	....	....	....	....	....	....	....	....	....	....	....	....
1972-73	Denver Spurs	WHL	37	12	14	7	1929	131	0	4.07	....	....	....	....	....	1	0	1	0	59	5	0	5.10	....	....	....	....
1973-74	Edmonton Oilers	WHA	29	11	12	1	1452	92	0	3.80	....	....	....	....	....	3	1	1	0	146	8	0	3.29	....	....	....	....
1974-75	Edmonton Oilers	WHA	29	11	13	3	1660	99	1	3.58	....	....	....	....	....	....	....	....	....	....	....	....	....	....	....	....	....
1975-76	Edmonton Oilers	WHA	24	5	14	0	1256	98	1	4.68	....	....	....	....	....	1	0	1	0	60	7	0	7.00	....	....	....	....
	NHL Totals		**26**	**5**	**10**	**4**	**1326**	**98**	**0**	**4.43**		....	....	....	....	....	....	....	....	....	....	....	....	....	....	....	....
	Other Major League Totals		82	27	39	4	4368	289	2	3.97		....	....	....	....	4	1	2	....	206	15	0	4.37	....	....	....	....

WCJHL All-Star Team (1968)

Traded to **Oakland** by **Detroit** with Gary Jarrett, Howie Young and Doug Roberts for Bob Baun and Ron Harris, May 27, 1968. Selected by **Dayton-Houston** (WHA) in 1972 WHA General Player Draft, February 12, 1972. Claimed by **Denver** (WHL) from **California** in Reverse Draft, June, 1972. Claimed by **Edmonton** (WHA) in 1973 WHA Professional Player Draft, June, 1973.

• WREGGET, Ken

Ken G – L. 6'1", 201 lbs. b: Brandon, Man., 3/25/1964. Toronto's 4th, 45th overall in 1982.

Season	Club	League	GP	W	L	T	Mins	GA	SO	Avg	AAvg	Eff	SA	S%	SAPG	GP	W	L	T	Mins	GA	SO	Avg	Eff	SA	S%	SAPG
1980-81	Brandon Bobcats	MJHL	STATISTICS NOT AVAILABLE																								
1981-82	Lethbridge Broncos	WHL	36	19	12	0	1713	118	0	4.13	....	....	....	....	....	3	2	0	....	84	3	0	2.14	....	....	....	....
1982-83	Lethbridge Broncos	WHL	48	26	17	1	2696	157	1	3.49	....	....	....	....	....	*20	14	5	....	*1154	58	*1	*3.02	....	....	....	....
1983-84	**Toronto Maple Leafs**	**NHL**	**3**	**1**	**1**	**1**	**165**	**14**	**0**	**5.09**	**4.01**	**5.57**	**128**	**.891**	**46.5**	....	....	....	....	....	....	....	....	....	....	....	....
	Lethbridge Broncos	WHL	53	32	20	0	3053	161	0	*3.16	....	....	....	....	....	4	1	3	....	210	18	0	5.14	....	....	....	....
1984-85	**Toronto Maple Leafs**	**NHL**	**23**	**2**	**15**	**3**	**1278**	**103**	**0**	**4.84**	**3.87**	**6.63**	**752**	**.863**	**35.3**	....	....	....	....	....	....	....	....	....	....	....	....
	St. Catharines Saints	AHL	12	2	8	1	688	48	0	4.19	....	....	....	....	....	....	....	....	....	....	....	....	....	....	....	....	....
1985-86	**Toronto Maple Leafs**	**NHL**	**30**	**9**	**13**	**4**	**1566**	**113**	**0**	**4.33**	**3.39**	**5.43**	**901**	**.875**	**34.5**	**10**	**6**	**4**	....	**607**	**32**	***1**	**3.16**	**3.13**	**323**	**.901**	**31.9**
	St. Catharines Saints	AHL	18	8	9	0	1058	78	1	4.42	....	....	....	....	....	....	....	....	....	....	....	....	....	....	....	....	....
1986-87	**Toronto Maple Leafs**	**NHL**	**56**	**22**	**28**	**3**	**3026**	**200**	**0**	**3.97**	**3.37**	**4.97**	**1598**	**.875**	**31.7**	**13**	**7**	**6**	....	**761**	**29**	**1**	**2.29**	**1.80**	**368**	**.921**	**29.0**
1987-88	**Toronto Maple Leafs**	**NHL**	**56**	**12**	**35**	**4**	**3000**	**222**	**2**	**4.44**	**3.72**	**5.76**	**1712**	**.870**	**34.2**	**2**	**0**	**1**	....	**108**	**11**	**0**	**6.11**	**10.84**	**62**	**.823**	**34.4**
1988-89	**Toronto Maple Leafs**	**NHL**	**32**	**9**	**20**	**2**	**1888**	**139**	**0**	**4.42**	**3.69**	**5.92**	**1037**	**.866**	**33.0**	....	....	....	....	....	....	....	....	....	....	....	....
	Philadelphia Flyers	**NHL**	**3**	**1**	**1**	**0**	**130**	**13**	**0**	**6.00**	**5.00**	**10.68**	**73**	**.822**	**33.7**	**5**	**2**	**2**	....	**268**	**10**	**0**	**2.24**	**1.61**	**139**	**.928**	**31.1**
1989-90	**Philadelphia Flyers**	**NHL**	**51**	**22**	**24**	**3**	**2961**	**169**	**0**	**3.42**	**2.89**	**3.71**	**1560**	**.892**	**31.6**	....	....	....	....	....	....	....	....	....	....	....	....
	Canada	WEC-A	1	1	0	0	60	0	1	0.00	....	....	....	....	....	....	....	....	....	....	....	....	....	....	....	....	....
1990-91	**Philadelphia Flyers**	**NHL**	**30**	**10**	**14**	**3**	**1484**	**88**	**0**	**3.56**	**3.20**	**4.75**	**660**	**.867**	**26.7**	....	....	....	....	....	....	....	....	....	....	....	....
1991-92	**Philadelphia Flyers**	**NHL**	**23**	**9**	**8**	**3**	**1259**	**75**	**0**	**3.57**	**3.20**	**4.81**	**557**	**.865**	**26.5**	....	....	....	....	....	....	....	....	....	....	....	....
♦	**Pittsburgh Penguins**	**NHL**	**9**	**5**	**3**	**0**	**448**	**31**	**0**	**4.15**	**3.72**	**6.37**	**202**	**.847**	**27.1**	**1**	**0**	**0**	....	**40**	**4**	**0**	**6.00**	**15.00**	**16**	**.750**	**24.0**
1992-93	**Pittsburgh Penguins**	**NHL**	**25**	**13**	**7**	**2**	**1368**	**78**	**0**	**3.42**	**2.93**	**3.85**	**692**	**.887**	**30.4**	....	....	....	....	....	....	....	....	....	....	....	....
1993-94	**Pittsburgh Penguins**	**NHL**	**42**	**21**	**12**	**7**	**2456**	**138**	**1**	**3.37**	**3.24**	**3.60**	**1291**	**.893**	**31.5**	....	....	....	....	....	....	....	....	....	....	....	....
1994-95	**Pittsburgh Penguins**	**NHL**	**38**	***25**	**9**	**2**	**2208**	**118**	**0**	**3.21**	**3.37**	**3.11**	**1219**	**.903**	**33.1**	**11**	**5**	**6**	....	**661**	**33**	**1**	**3.00**	**2.84**	**349**	**.905**	**31.7**
1995-96	**Pittsburgh Penguins**	**NHL**	**37**	**20**	**13**	**2**	**2132**	**115**	**3**	**3.24**	**3.22**	**3.09**	**1205**	**.905**	**33.9**	**9**	**7**	**2**	....	**599**	**23**	**0**	**2.30**	**1.61**	**328**	**.930**	**32.9**
1996-97	**Pittsburgh Penguins**	**NHL**	**46**	**17**	**17**	**6**	**2514**	**136**	**2**	**3.25**	**3.51**	**3.20**	**1383**	**.902**	**33.0**	**5**	**1**	**4**	....	**297**	**18**	**0**	**3.64**	**3.11**	**211**	**.915**	**42.6**
1997-98	**Pittsburgh Penguins**	**NHL**	**15**	**3**	**6**	**2**	**611**	**28**	**0**	**2.75**	**3.28**	**2.63**	**293**	**.904**	**28.8**	....	....	....	....	....	....	....	....	....	....	....	....
1998-99	**Calgary Flames**	**NHL**	**27**	**10**	**12**	**4**	**1590**	**67**	**1**	**2.53**	**3.01**	**2.38**	**712**	**.906**	**26.9**	....	....	....	....	....	....	....	....	....	....	....	....
99-2000	**Detroit Red Wings**	**NHL**	**29**	**14**	**10**	**2**	**1579**	**70**	**0**	**2.66**	**3.04**	**2.66**	**700**	**.900**	**26.6**	....	....	....	....	....	....	....	....	....	....	....	....
	NHL Totals		**575**	**225**	**248**	**53**	**31663**	**1917**	**9**	**3.63**	....	....	**16675**	**.885**	**31.6**	**56**	**28**	**25**	....	**3341**	**160**	**3**	**2.87**	....	**1796**	**.911**	**32.3**

WHL East First All-Star Team (1984)

Traded to **Philadelphia** by **Toronto** for Philadelphia's 1st round choice (Rob Pearson) and Calgary's 1st round choice (previously acquired, Toronto selected Steve Bancroft) in 1989 Entry Draft, March 6, 1989. Traded to **Pittsburgh** by **Philadelphia** with Rick Tocchet, Kjell Samuelsson and Philadelphia's 3rd round choice (Dave Roche) in 1993 Entry Draft for Mark Recchi, Brian Benning and Los Angeles' 1st round choice (previously acquired, Philadelphia selected Jason Bowen) in 1992 Entry Draft, February 19, 1992. Traded to **Calgary** by **Pittsburgh** with Dave Roche for German Titov and Todd Hlushko, June 17, 1998. Signed as a free agent by **Detroit**, July 23, 1999.

Season	Club	League	REGULAR SEASON													PLAYOFFS											
			GP	W	L	T	Mins	GA	SO	Avg	AAvg	Eff	SA	S%	SAPG	GP	W	L	T	Mins	GA	SO	Avg	Eff	SA	S%	SAPG

• YOUNG, Doug

Douglas Gordon "The Gleichen Cowboy" G. 5'10", 190 lbs. b: Medicine Hat, Alta., 10/1/1908 d: 5/15/1990.

Season	Club	League	GP	W	L	T	Mins	GA	SO	Avg	AAvg	Eff	SA	S%	SAPG	GP	W	L	T	Mins	GA	SO	Avg	Eff	SA	S%	SAPG
1933-34	**Detroit Red Wings**	**NHL**	**1**	**0**	**0**	**0**	**21**	**1**	**0**	**2.86**	**3.62**	....	....	....	....	....	....	....	....	....	....	....	....	....	....	....	....
	NHL Totals		**1**	**0**	**0**	**0**	**21**	**1**	**0**	**2.86**	....	....	....	....	....	....	....	....	....	....	....	....	....	....	....	....	....

• **Detroit** defenseman replaced injured John Ross Roach in 2nd period, December 14, 1933. (Chicago 4, Detroit 0)

• YOUNG, Wendell

Wendell Edward G – L. 5'9", 181 lbs. b: Halifax, N.S., 8/1/1963. Vancouver's 3rd, 73rd overall in 1981.

Season	Club	League	GP	W	L	T	Mins	GA	SO	Avg	AAvg	Eff	SA	S%	SAPG	GP	W	L	T	Mins	GA	SO	Avg	Eff	SA	S%	SAPG
1979-80	Cole Harbour Colts	MJrHL	25	....	....	....	1446	94	0	3.90	....	....	....	....	....	....	....	....	....	....	....	....	....	....	....	....	....
1980-81	Kitchener Rangers	OMJHL	42	19	15	0	2215	164	1	4.44	....	....	....	....	....	14	9	1	....	800	42	*1	3.15	....	....	....	....
	Kitchener Rangers	Mem-Cup	4	2	2	0	189	14	0	4.44	....	....	....	....	....	....	....	....	....	....	....	....	....	....	....	....	....
1981-82	Kitchener Rangers	OHL	*60	*38	17	2	*3470	195	1	3.37	....	....	....	....	....	15	12	1	....	900	35	*1	*2.33	....	....	....	....
	Kitchener Rangers	Mem-Cup	5	*2	2	0	243	18	0	*4.44	....	....	....	....	....	....	....	....	....	....	....	....	....	....	....	....	....
1982-83	Kitchener Rangers	OHL	61	*41	19	0	*3611	231	1	3.84	....	....	....	....	....	12	6	5	....	720	43	0	3.58	....	....	....	....
1983-84	Fredericton Express	AHL	11	7	3	0	569	39	1	4.11	....	....	....	....	....	....	....	....	....	....	....	....	....	....	....	....	....
	Milwaukee Admirals	IHL	6	4	1	1	339	17	0	3.01	....	....	....	....	....	....	....	....	....	....	....	....	....	....	....	....	....
	Salt Lake Golden Eagles	CHL	20	11	6	0	1094	80	0	4.39	....	....	....	....	....	4	0	2	....	122	11	0	5.42	....	....	....	....
1984-85	Fredericton Express	AHL	22	7	11	3	1242	83	0	4.01	....	....	....	....	....	....	....	....	....	....	....	....	....	....	....	....	....
1985-86	**Vancouver Canucks**	**NHL**	**22**	**4**	**9**	**3**	**1023**	**61**	**0**	**3.58**	**2.79**	**4.07**	**536**	**.886**	**31.4**	**1**	**0**	**1**	....	**60**	**5**	**0**	**5.00**	**7.81**	**32**	**.844**	**32.0**
	Fredericton Express	AHL	24	12	8	4	1457	78	0	3.21	....	....	....	....	....	....	....	....	....	....	....	....	....	....	....	....	....
1986-87	**Vancouver Canucks**	**NHL**	**8**	**1**	**6**	**1**	**420**	**35**	**0**	**5.00**	**4.24**	**7.81**	**224**	**.844**	**32.0**	....	....	....	....	....	....	....	....	....	....	....	....
	Fredericton Express	AHL	30	11	16	0	1676	118	0	4.22	....	....	....	....	....	....	....	....	....	....	....	....	....	....	....	....	....
1987-88	**Philadelphia Flyers**	**NHL**	**6**	**3**	**2**	**0**	**320**	**20**	**0**	**3.75**	**3.12**	**5.03**	**149**	**.866**	**27.9**	....	....	....	....	....	....	....	....	....	....	....	....
	Hershey Bears	AHL	51	*33	15	1	2922	135	1	2.77	....	....	....	....	....	12	*12	0	....	*767	28	*1	*2.19	....	....	....	....
1988-89	**Pittsburgh Penguins**	**NHL**	**22**	**12**	**9**	**0**	**1150**	**92**	**0**	**4.80**	**4.01**	**6.56**	**673**	**.863**	**35.1**	**1**	**0**	**0**	....	**39**	**1**	**0**	**1.54**	**1.40**	**11**	**.909**	**16.9**
	Muskegon Lumberjacks	IHL	2	1	0	1	125	7	0	3.36	....	....	....	....	....	....	....	....	....	....	....	....	....	....	....	....	....
1989-90	**Pittsburgh Penguins**	**NHL**	**43**	**16**	**20**	**3**	**2318**	**161**	**1**	**4.17**	**3.55**	**5.30**	**1267**	**.873**	**32.8**	....	....	....	....	....	....	....	....	....	....	....	....
1990-91 ♦	**Pittsburgh Penguins**	**NHL**	**18**	**4**	**6**	**2**	**773**	**52**	**0**	**4.04**	**3.64**	**4.91**	**428**	**.879**	**33.2**	....	....	....	....	....	....	....	....	....	....	....	....
1991-92 ♦	**Pittsburgh Penguins**	**NHL**	**18**	**7**	**6**	**0**	**838**	**53**	**0**	**3.79**	**3.40**	**4.22**	**476**	**.889**	**34.1**	....	....	....	....	....	....	....	....	....	....	....	....
1992-93	**Tampa Bay Lightning**	**NHL**	**31**	**7**	**19**	**2**	**1591**	**97**	**0**	**3.66**	**3.14**	**4.68**	**758**	**.872**	**28.6**	....	....	....	....	....	....	....	....	....	....	....	....
	Atlanta Knights	IHL	3	3	0	0	183	8	0	2.62	....	....	....	....	....	....	....	....	....	....	....	....	....	....	....	....	....
1993-94	**Tampa Bay Lightning**	**NHL**	**9**	**2**	**3**	**1**	**480**	**20**	**1**	**2.50**	**2.40**	**2.37**	**211**	**.905**	**26.4**	....	....	....	....	....	....	....	....	....	....	....	....
	Atlanta Knights	IHL	2	2	0	0	120	6	0	3.00	....	....	....	....	....	....	....	....	....	....	....	....	....	....	....	....	....
1994-95	Chicago Wolves	IHL	37	14	11	7	1882	112	0	3.57	....	....	....	....	....	....	....	....	....	....	....	....	....	....	....	....	....
	Pittsburgh Penguins	**NHL**	**10**	**3**	**6**	**0**	**497**	**27**	**0**	**3.26**	**3.42**	**3.45**	**255**	**.894**	**30.8**	....	....	....	....	....	....	....	....	....	....	....	....
1995-96	Chicago Wolves	IHL	61	30	20	6	3285	199	1	3.63	....	....	....	....	....	9	4	5	....	540	30	0	3.33	....	....	....	....
1996-97	Chicago Wolves	IHL	52	25	21	4	2931	170	1	3.48	....	....	....	....	....	4	1	3	....	256	13	0	3.04	....	....	....	....
1997-98	Chicago Wolves	IHL	51	31	14	3	2912	149	2	3.07	....	....	....	....	....	9	5	3	....	515	24	1	2.79	....	....	....	....
1998-99	Chicago Wolves	IHL	35	20	10	4	2047	84	3	2.46	....	....	....	....	....	7	4	3	....	421	19	1	2.71	....	....	....	....
99-2000	Chicago Wolves	IHL	48	32	12	4	2781	128	6	2.76	....	....	....	....	....	9	5	3	....	488	27	0	3.32	....	....	....	....
	NHL Totals		**187**	**59**	**86**	**12**	**9410**	**618**	**2**	**3.94**	....	....	**4977**	**.876**	**31.7**	**2**	**0**	**1**	....	**99**	**6**	**0**	**3.64**	....	**43**	**.860**	**26.1**

AHL First All-Star Team (1988) • Won Baz Bastien Memorial Trophy (Top Goaltender - AHL) (1988) • Won Jack Butterfield Trophy (Playoff MVP - AHL) (1988)

Traded to **Philadelphia** by **Vancouver** with Vancouver's 3rd round choice (Kimbi Daniels) in 1990 Entry Draft for Darren Jensen and Daryl Stanley, August 31, 1987. Traded to **Pittsburgh** by **Philadelphia** with Philadelphia's 7th round choice (Mika Valila) in 1990 Entry Draft for Pittsburgh's 3rd round choice (Chris Therien) in 1990 Entry Draft, Steptember 1, 1988. Claimed by **Tampa Bay** from **Pittsburgh** in Expansion Draft, June 18, 1992. Traded to **Pittsburgh** by **Tampa Bay** for future considerations, February 16, 1995. • Only goaltender to win Memorial Cup (1982); Calder Cup (1988); Stanley Cup (1991, 1992) and Turner Cup (1998, 2000).

• ZANIER, Mike

G – L. 5'11", 183 lbs. b: Trail, B.C., 8/22/1962.

Season	Club	League	GP	W	L	T	Mins	GA	SO	Avg	AAvg	Eff	SA	S%	SAPG	GP	W	L	T	Mins	GA	SO	Avg	Eff	SA	S%	SAPG
1979-80	Abbottsford Flyers	BCJHL	STATISTICS NOT AVAILABLE																								
	New Westminster Bruins	WHL	1	0	0	0	20	3	0	9.00	....	....	....	....	....	....	....	....	....	....	....	....	....	....	....	....	....
1980-81	New Westminster Bruins	WHL	49	11	27	1	2494	275	0	6.62	....	....	....	....	....	....	....	....	....	....	....	....	....	....	....	....	....
1981-82	Spokane Flyers	WHL	9	1	7	0	476	55	0	6.93	....	....	....	....	....	....	....	....	....	....	....	....	....	....	....	....	....
	Billings Bighorns	WHL	11	1	8	0	495	64	0	7.76	....	....	....	....	....	....	....	....	....	....	....	....	....	....	....	....	....
	Medicine Hat Tigers	WHL	13	3	8	0	620	70	0	6.77	....	....	....	....	....	....	....	....	....	....	....	....	....	....	....	....	....
	Calgary Wranglers	WHL	11	5	5	0	526	28	1	3.19	....	....	....	....	....	1	0	0	0	25	1	0	2.40	....	....	....	....
1982-83	Trail Smoke Eaters	WIHL	30	....	....	....	1734	116	0	4.01	....	....	....	....	....	....	....	....	....	....	....	....	....	....	....	....	....
1983-84	Moncton Alpines	AHL	31	11	15	1	1743	96	0	3.30	....	....	....	....	....	....	....	....	....	....	....	....	....	....	....	....	....
1984-85	**Edmonton Oilers**	**NHL**	**3**	**1**	**1**	**1**	**185**	**12**	**0**	**3.89**	**3.10**	**4.67**	**100**	**.880**	**32.4**	....	....	....	....	....	....	....	....	....	....	....	....
	Nova Scotia Oilers	AHL	44	20	17	5	2484	143	1	3.45	....	....	....	....	....	....	....	....	....	....	....	....	....	....	....	....	....
1985-86	Indianapolis Checkers	IHL	47	21	10	0	2727	151	0	3.32	....	....	....	....	....	2	1	1	0	120	9	0	4.50	....	....	....	....
1986-87	HC Salzburg	Austria	STATISTICS NOT AVAILABLE																								
	Indianapolis Checkers	IHL	14	6	8	0	807	60	0	4.46	....	....	....	....	....	6	2	4	0	359	21	0	3.51	....	....	....	....
1987-88	HC Bolzano	Italy	STATISTICS NOT AVAILABLE																								
1988-89	HC Bolzano	Italy	32	....	....	....	1920	114	2	3.56	....	....	....	....	....												
	Italy	WC-B	2	2	0	0	120	4	0	2.00	....	....	....	....	....	....	....	....	....	....	....	....	....	....	....	....	....
1989-90	HC Asiago	Italy	STATISTICS NOT AVAILABLE																								
1990-91	HC Milano	Italy	45	....	....	....	2650	167	1	3.78	....	....	....	....	....	....	....	....	....	....	....	....	....	....	....	....	....
	Italy	WC-B	1	0	0	0	20	0	0	0.00	....	....	....	....	....	....	....	....	....	....	....	....	....	....	....	....	....
1991-92	HC Milano	Alpenliga	24	....	....	....	1399	80	0	3.43	....	....	....	....	....	....	....	....	....	....	....	....	....	....	....	....	....
	HC Milano	Italy	11	....	....	....	619	36	1	3.49	....	....	....	....	....	....	....	....	....	....	....	....	....	....	....	....	....
	Italy	Olympics	3	....	....	....	155	14	....	5.42	....	....	....	....	....	....	....	....	....	....	....	....	....	....	....	....	....
1992-93	Dallas Freeze	CHL	40	24	14	2	2384	150	1	3.78	....	....	....	....	....	7	2	4	0	424	33	0	4.67	....	....	....	....
1993-94	HC Milano	Alpenliga	27	....	....	....	1589	92	0	3.47	....	....	....	....	....	....	....	....	....	....	....	....	....	....	....	....	....
	HC Milano	Italy	20	....	....	....	1163	74	0	3.82	....	....	....	....	....	....	....	....	....	....	....	....	....	....	....	....	....
1994-95	HC Milano	Italy	31	....	....	....	1755	108	0	3.69	....	....	....	....	....	....	....	....	....	....	....	....	....	....	....	....	....
1995-96	HC Milano	Italy	25	....	....	....	1496	79	2	3.17	....	....	....	....	....	....	....	....	....	....	....	....	....	....	....	....	....
1996-97	HC Milano	Alpenliga	28	....	....	....	1601	97	1	3.64	....	....	....	....	....	....	....	....	....	....	....	....	....	....	....	....	....
	HC Milano	EuroHL	6	....	....	....	184	26	0	8.48	....	....	....	....	....	....	....	....	....	....	....	....	....	....	....	....	....
	HC Milano	Italy	16	....	....	....	925	46	0	2.98	....	....	....	....	....	....	....	....	....	....	....	....	....	....	....	....	....
1997-98	Hannover Turtles	Germany-2	30	....	....	....	1798	98	0	3.27	....	....	....	....	....	....	....	....	....	....	....	....	....	....	....	....	....
1998-99	Nottingham Panthers	BH-Cup	4	2	1	1	240	7	1	1.75	....	....	....	....	....	....	....	....	....	....	....	....	....	....	....	....	....
	Nottingham Panthers	Britain	20	....	....	....	1158	68	1	3.52	....	....	....	....	....	2	....	....	....	120	9	0	4.50	....	....	....	....
99-2000	Olafstroms IK	Sweden-3	31	....	....	....	1803	96	1	3.19	....	....	....	....	....	....	....	....	....	....	....	....	....	....	....	....	....
	NHL Totals		**3**	**1**	**1**	**1**	**185**	**12**	**0**	**3.89**	....	....	**100**	**.880**	**32.4**	....	....	....	....	....	....	....	....	....	....	....	....

Signed as a free agent by **Edmonton**, October 4, 1983.

CHAPTER 81

Researching the Coach Register

Observations About the Men Behind the Bench

Eric Zweig

The decision to include a Coach Register in the first volume of *Total Hockey* was made relatively late in the game. As a result, there was not much time for first-hand research. The list was compiled mainly from the existing record books and team media directories. We were disappointed to discover that NHL game sheets never have included a line to list the coach, but when difficulties came up in determining who should be credited as the coach, we imposed the current NHL standard which maintains that even if a coach is absent for such reasons as illness, suspension or family emergency, he is to be credited with his team's results until such time as he is formally replaced.

One nagging coaching question remained unresolved in the first volume of *Total Hockey*. All previous accounts had credited Herb Gardiner with 44 games as coach of the Chicago Black Hawks in 1928–29 even though his playing records show that he split that season between Chicago and the Montreal Canadiens. Once we were able to nail down the exact nature of the transaction, the picture became clear.

Gardiner was loaned to the Black Hawks by the Canadiens prior to the 1928–29 season. He served as the team's "manager" and later saw some action as a player as well after Chicago fell hopelessly out of contention. Meanwhile, the Canadiens were legitimate Stanley Cup contenders, and on February 12, 1929, they recalled Gardiner to Montreal. When reporting on this in the Montreal papers, it is made clear that the Black Hawks would appoint a new "manager" for the remaining 12 games of the season.

On February 21, 1929, the *Windsor Star* reported that "[Dick] Irvin is filling in as manager of the Chicago team for the balance of the season." Obviously, he would continue playing for the team, as well, because when reporting on that night's game the following day, the paper claimed, "Dick Irvin, new skipper of the Hawks, lined up at right wing." In this version of the Coach Register, we list Herb Gardiner with a 5–23–4 record in 32 games as coach of the Black Hawks in 1928–29. A line has been added to Irvin crediting him with a 2–6–4 record in 12 games. This move was made even though a series of articles supposedly written by Irvin during the 1930s claim that Bill Tobin took over as manager in 1928–29. When asked about these articles, Canadiens broadcaster Dick Irvin Jr. claimed they were no more in his father's words "than the man in the moon." What appears likely is that Tobin would have taken over Gardiner's front-office duties while Irvin attended to the team's on-ice performance.

Incidentally, five games previously credited to Irvin with Chicago in 1931–32 have been removed from his record because Dick Irvin (the broadcaster) was able to confirm that his father was never in Chicago that season. He was at home in Regina until being hired by Conn Smythe in Toronto. The five games previously credited to Irvin in Chicago that season have been given to Bill Tobin, who always has been listed as being the Black Hawks coach in just 43 of 48 games that season.

The fact that coaches were so frequently referred to as "manager" during the 1920s and 1930s creates such a gray area that of the many hundreds of letters and e-mails we got in response to *Total Hockey* only a very small percentage dealt with the Coach Register. Two in particular have resulted in further changes to the register at this time.

Bill Kingstone of Gilmour, Ontario, has done considerable research on Toronto's early NHL teams, and he maintains that a man named George O'Donoghue should be credited as coach of the St. Pats for their Stanley Cup season of 1921–22. His findings were first published in *The Hockey News* (April 4, 1997) and his article addresses the coach-manager issue:

> *In the various accounts of the day, O'Donoghue, [Charles] Querrie and player Reg Noble are all referred to as manager. The muddle can be cleared away by applying modern terms to their responsibilities. Left winger Noble was the team's on-ice leader .... His role as captain was mainly leadership by example. Querrie, part owner of the club, hired and fired, made player trades, and was not hesitant about expressing his opinion on the team's progress. He was general manager.*
>
> *Noble and Querrie may have had considerable strategical input, but from the afternoon in early December, 1921, when George O'Donoghue called the players together for the first practice, it was he who ran the club on a daily basis. He traveled with the team. He was behind the bench at each of the team's games. He dealt with the players' problems and complaints .... Manager may have been his title, but his duties matched those of the modern coach.*

Though some hockey researchers were skeptical, maintaining that Charles Querrie never would have let anyone run his hockey teams, close inspection of Toronto newspapers leaves no doubt that O'Donoghue was the man current fans would recognize as the St. Pats coach. In fact, he continued to coach the team through the first five games of the 1922–23 season before resigning on January 3, 1923. One day later, the *Toronto Telegram* ran a picture of him on page 16. The caption read: "George O'Donoghue, who yesterday relinquished his position as manager of the St. Patricks Hockey club of the NHL, owing to differences with the management." An article a few pages later states that the club owners and O'Donoghue had differed over the retention or releasing of a player.

The *Toronto Star* reports that Jack Adams coached the team for its next game on January 6 (a 2–1 loss at Ottawa), but the *Telegram* merely reports that Adams had been named captain. So who coached the team? "Charles Querrie will tell you there are only about six people in Toronto who care," wrote the *Telegram* on January 5. "The rest believe [Reg] Noble or [Babe] Dye is doing the managing now."

That same day, the *Ottawa Citizen* reported that "Jack Adams is the ice captain and Reg Noble is manager," but admitted "Charles Querrie still does most of the talking." Querrie traveled to Ottawa for the January 6 game and was on the bench, as he often was even when others ran the team. Toronto papers never refer to a new coach being hired, and Ottawa papers make further references to Querrie running the team throughout the season. As such, we have credited Querrie as the coach for the remaining 18 games of the 1922–23 season, as well as 1923–24. No new coach is mentioned specifically in newspaper accounts until Eddie Powers joins the team in 1924–25. (Powers has often been listed as coach of Toronto's 1922 Cup team, though he was coaching an amateur club in Boston that season.)

Powers coached the St. Pats for two seasons before being replaced by Mike Rodden in the fall of 1926. Previously, Rodden has been credited as the St. Pats coach until the team became the Maple Leafs in February, 1927, but Bill Kingstone's research indicates that Rodden was released after just two games.

The St. Pats opened the 1926–27 season with a 4–1 loss to the Black Hawks in Chicago, then returned home and were beaten, 5–1, by the New York Rangers. Game three resulted in a 2–2 tie with the Ottawa Senators in a contest that Toronto newspapers all agree should have been won by the St. Pats. In his *Toronto Star* column, famed sportswriter Lou Marsh wrote (in the politically incorrect terms of the day) that the change in the play of the home team was like "a bunch of hop-heads on a fresh supply of 'snow.'" The cause of the change? "Mike Rodden is out as coach." Apparently, the players felt the future Hall of Fame hockey referee and college football coach was too technical in his approach to the game, so Charles Querrie took over the team once again. After the St. Pats were sold to Conn Smythe's syndicate on February 14, Querrie coached them in their final appearance as the St. Pats one night later. Alex Romeril then coached the club's first game as the Maple Leafs on February 17. It is interesting to note that on December 9, 1926—long before there are any reports of Smythe's desire to buy the team—Charles Querrie is quoted in the *Toronto Star* as saying he would like to rename the St. Pats the Maple Leafs.

Bill Kingstone has corrected one final oversight in the coaching history of Toronto NHL hockey. The 1920–21 season, previously given to Dick Carroll, is now credited to his brother Frank.

Another letter that sparked several hours of library research was received from Corey Bryant of Shelby, Montana. Although his letter resulted in only one significant change, the research required in making it highlighted the difficulties in determining who was a coach and who was a manager in the early days of the NHL.

Bryant quotes former NHL player Frank Finnigan, who said in the book *Old Scores, New Goals: The Story of the Ottawa Senators* that "In my day P.D. Green [Pete Green] was coach when I first turned pro, then Alec Curry, then Newsy Lalonde, then Dave Gill..." Curry is not a name that ever has been listed as a Senators coach, but in reconstructing the seasons of the late 1920s Curry is the only man the Ottawa newspapers refer to in that position in 1925–26—a season previously credited to Pete Green, who had coached the team in the NHL since 1918–19. Apparently the beginning of the end for the long-time Senators coach occured on January 24, 1925, when Tommy Gorman sold his ownership share in the Ottawa club to his partner, Frank Ahearne. Within days, David Gill was brought in as the new "manager." Still, the newspapers continue to refer to the popular Green as coach throughout the remainder of the 1924–25 season. However, one can find sentences in the same newspaper articles that applaud Green for his handling of the Ottawa lineup while noting that "manager Gill will have to instruct his players in the fine art of shooting."

Gill himself did become coach of the team in 1926–27, after Curry's one season on the job, and he led the Senators to their final Stanley Cup title that year. He remained back of the bench for two more seasons before turning the coaching reins over to Newsy Lalonde in 1929–30.

Another issue raised by Corey Bryant's letter is the question of who coached the Montreal Maroons in their inaugural season of 1924–25. Clearly, former Canadiens director Cecil Hart resigned his position to become "manager" of the new Montreal team, but was he also the coach?

According to the *Montreal Gazette,* Hart hired former Ottawa Senators star Eddie Gerard to coach the team two days before the season was set to start on November 30, 1924. Gerard was to coach the team "for the next few weeks," but by December 17, the *Gazette* reported the Montreal club was trying to arrange a deal for Gerard's services for the remainder of the season. Still, for the next four weeks, the only name mentioned in association with the Montreal team is that of Cecil Hart. However, when Gerard's name appears in the paper again on January 20, 1925, no mention is made of any absence from the team. While it is possible that Hart may have replaced him for eight games, there is no way to know for sure, and—using the modern guidelines that state the coach is the coach even if he is absent for any reason—Gerard is credited with all 30 games that season. (Note: Hart was fired as manager, i.e., general manager, on February 7, 1925, and Gerard added those responsibilities to his coaching role.)

While the early days of the NHL provide us with most of the coaching conundrums, such peculiarities are not limited to this time period. For example, several letter writers wondered why *Total Hockey* did not credit King Clancy for his 10-game coaching stint with the 1966–67 Toronto Maple Leafs—as he often has been in the past. The reason is that Clancy was merely serving as a temporary coach while Punch Imlach was hospitalized with heart problems. There was never any indication that Imlach would be replaced, and indeed he returned to action as soon as he was able to do so. Clancy's stint behind the bench as a replacement for John McLellan in 1971–72 came under similar circumstances. So, too, did the coaching efforts of Craig Ramsay when Philadelphia's Roger Neilson battled bone marrow cancer during the 1999–2000 season. However, when Dave Lewis and Barry Smith filled in for Scotty Bowman to start the 1998–99 season, there was not yet any indication as to whether Bowman would receive medical clearance to return to coaching, or that he would want to even if he did. The Red Wings were committed to going with Lewis and Smith for the long run, but were only too happy to welcome Bowman back by the sixth game of the season. In this edition of *Total Hockey,* situations such as these are explained with a note under the records of the appropriate coaches.

CHAPTER 82

Coach Register

Complete NHL Coaching Records

THE COACHES REGISTER contains complete career NHL coaching records. Included are playing coaches such as Odie Cleghorn and Charlie Smith and interim coaches such as Mike Smith and Phil Esposito. If a coach has played in the NHL, the reader is directed to his career playing record in the Pre-Expansion Player, Modern Player or Goaltender registers.

Each coach's data panel includes his date of birth, place of birth and date of death. If only the birth year is known, it is included. If the death date is unknown, the coach is listed as Deceased. If the coach is a member of the Hockey Hall of Fame (**HHOF**) or the U.S. Hockey Hall of Fame (**USHOF**), this is noted here.

GC – games coached. **W–L–T** – a coach is credited with a result for every game his team wins, loses or ties while he is under contract as coach. If a coach is absent due to illness, suspension or family emergency, he is still credited with his team's results.

RT – Beginning in 1999-2000, regular-season games ending in a tie result in each team being awarded a point. A team scoring in overtime receives an additional point. The point awarded for a team losing in overtime is recorded as a Regulation Tie (RT).

W% — Winning percentage is the percentage of available points gained in games coached. It is calculated as follows:

(W + W + T + RT) divided by (GC + GC)

Because of the additional points awarded for a Regulation Tie, a coach can now have a better winning percentage than his won-loss record would appear to indicate. For example, Kevin Constantine has a lifetime record of 141 wins, 145 losses, 59 ties and four regulation ties, resulting in a .500 winning percentage (345 points gained in 345 games).

• ABEL, Sid — HHOF

b: Melville, Sask., 2/22/1918.
Played in NHL. See Pre-Expansion Player Register for career statistics.

			REGULAR SEASON						PLAYOFFS				
Season	Club	League	GC	W	L	T	RT	W%	GC	W	L	T	W%
1952-53	Chicago	NHL	70	27	28	15	....	.493	7	3	4	0	.429
1953-54	Chicago	NHL	70	12	51	7	....	.221	....	....	....	....	....
1957-58	Detroit	NHL	33	16	12	5	....	.561	4	0	4	0	.000
1958-59	Detroit	NHL	70	25	37	8	....	.414	....	....	....	....	....
1959-60	Detroit	NHL	70	26	29	15	....	.479	6	2	4	0	.333
1960-61	Detroit	NHL	70	25	29	16	....	.471	11	6	5	0	.545
1961-62	Detroit	NHL	70	23	33	14	....	.429	....	....	....	....	....
1962-63	Detroit	NHL	70	32	25	13	....	.550	14	7	7	0	.500
1963-64	Detroit	NHL	70	30	29	11	....	.507	11	5	6	0	.455
1964-65	Detroit	NHL	70	40	23	7	....	.621	7	3	4	0	.429
1965-66	Detroit	NHL	70	31	27	12	....	.529	12	6	6	0	.500
1966-67	Detroit	NHL	70	27	39	4	....	.414	....	....	....	....	....
1967-68	Detroit	NHL	74	27	35	12	....	.446	....	....	....	....	....
1969-70	Detroit	NHL	74	38	21	15	....	.615	4	0	4	0	.000
1971-72	St. Louis	NHL	10	3	6	1	....	.350	....	....	....	....	....
1975-76	Kansas City	NHL	3	0	3	0	....	.000	....	....	....	....	....
	NHL Totals		**964**	**382**	**427**	**155**	....	**.477**	**76**	**32**	**44**	**0**	**.421**

• ADAMS, Jack — HHOF

b: Fort William, Ont., 6/14/1895 d: 5/1/1968.
Played in NHL. See Pre-Expansion Player Register for career statistics.

			REGULAR SEASON						PLAYOFFS				
Season	Club	League	GC	W	L	T	RT	W%	GC	W	L	T	W%
1927-28	Detroit	NHL	44	19	19	6	....	.500	....	....	....	....	....
1928-29	Detroit	NHL	44	19	16	9	....	.534	2	0	2	0	.000
1929-30	Detroit	NHL	44	14	24	6	....	.386	....	....	....	....	....
1930-31	Detroit	NHL	44	16	21	7	....	.443	....	....	....	....	....
1931-32	Detroit	NHL	48	18	20	10	....	.479	2	0	1	1	.250
1932-33	Detroit	NHL	48	25	15	8	....	.604	4	2	2	0	.500
1933-34	Detroit	NHL	48	24	14	10	....	.604	9	4	5	0	.444
1934-35	Detroit	NHL	48	19	22	7	....	.469	....	....	....	....	....
♦1935-36	Detroit	NHL	48	24	16	8	....	.583	7	6	1	0	.857
♦1936-37	Detroit	NHL	48	25	14	9	....	.615	10	6	4	0	.600
1937-38	Detroit	NHL	48	12	25	11	....	.365	....	....	....	....	....
1938-39	Detroit	NHL	48	18	24	6	....	.438	6	3	3	0	.500
1939-40	Detroit	NHL	48	16	26	6	....	.396	5	2	3	0	.400
1940-41	Detroit	NHL	48	21	16	11	....	.552	9	4	5	0	.444
1941-42	Detroit	NHL	48	19	25	4	....	.438	12	7	5	0	.583
♦1942-43	Detroit	NHL	50	25	14	11	....	.610	10	8	2	0	.800
1943-44	Detroit	NHL	50	26	18	6	....	.580	5	1	4	0	.200
1944-45	Detroit	NHL	50	31	14	5	....	.670	14	7	7	0	.500
1945-46	Detroit	NHL	50	20	20	10	....	.500	5	1	4	0	.200
1946-47	Detroit	NHL	60	22	27	11	....	.458	5	1	4	0	.200
	NHL Totals		**964**	**413**	**390**	**161**	....	**.512**	**105**	**52**	**52**	**1**	**.500**

• ALLEN, Keith — HHOF

b: Saskatoon, Sask., 8/21/1923.
Played in NHL. See Pre-Expansion Player Register for career statistics.

			REGULAR SEASON						PLAYOFFS				
Season	Club	League	GC	W	L	T	RT	W%	GC	W	L	T	W%
1967-68	Philadelphia	NHL	74	31	32	11	....	.493	7	3	4	0	.429
1968-69	Philadelphia	NHL	76	20	35	21	....	.401	4	0	4	0	.000
	NHL Totals		**150**	**51**	**67**	**32**	....	**.447**	**11**	**3**	**8**	**0**	**.273**

• ALLISON, Dave

b: Fort Frances, Ont., 4/14/1959.
Played in NHL. See Modern Player Register for career statistics.

			REGULAR SEASON						PLAYOFFS				
Season	Club	League	GC	W	L	T	RT	W%	GC	W	L	T	W%
1995-96	Ottawa	NHL	25	2	22	1	....	.100	....	....	....	....	....
	NHL Totals		**25**	**2**	**22**	**1**	....	**.100**	....	....	....	....	....

• ANDERSON, Jim

b: Pembroke, Ont., 12/1/1930.
Played in NHL. See Modern Player Register for career statistics.

			REGULAR SEASON						PLAYOFFS				
Season	Club	League	GC	W	L	T	RT	W%	GC	W	L	T	W%
1974-75	Washington	NHL	54	4	45	5	....	.120	....	....	....	....	....
	NHL Totals		**54**	**4**	**45**	**5**	....	**.120**	....	....	....	....	....

• ANGOTTI, Lou

b: Toronto, Ont., 1/16/1938.
Played in NHL. See Modern Player Register for career statistics.

			REGULAR SEASON						PLAYOFFS				
Season	Club	League	GC	W	L	T	RT	W%	GC	W	L	T	W%
1973-74	St. Louis	NHL	23	4	15	4	....	.261	....	....	....	....	....
1974-75	St. Louis	NHL	9	2	5	2	....	.333	....	....	....	....	....
1983-84	Pittsburgh	NHL	80	16	58	6	....	.238	....	....	....	....	....
	NHL Totals		**112**	**22**	**78**	**12**	....	**.250**	....	....	....	....	....

• ARBOUR, Al — HHOF

b: Sudbury, Ont., 11/1/1932.
Played in NHL. See Modern Player Register for career statistics.

			REGULAR SEASON						PLAYOFFS				
Season	Club	League	GC	W	L	T	RT	W%	GC	W	L	T	W%
1970-71	St. Louis	NHL	50	21	15	14	....	.560	....	....	....	....	....
1971-72	St. Louis	NHL	44	19	19	6	....	.500	11	4	7	0	.364
1972-73	St. Louis	NHL	13	2	6	5	....	.346	....	....	....	....	....
1973-74	NY Islanders	NHL	78	19	41	18	....	.359	....	....	....	....	....
1974-75	NY Islanders	NHL	80	33	25	22	....	.550	17	9	8	0	.529
1975-76	NY Islanders	NHL	80	42	21	17	....	.631	13	7	6	0	.538
1976-77	NY Islanders	NHL	80	47	21	12	....	.663	12	8	4	0	.667
1977-78	NY Islanders	NHL	80	48	17	15	....	.694	7	3	4	0	.429
1978-79	NY Islanders	NHL	80	51	15	14	....	.725	10	6	4	0	.600
♦1979-80	NY Islanders	NHL	80	39	28	13	....	.569	21	15	6	0	.714
♦1980-81	NY Islanders	NHL	80	48	18	14	....	.688	18	15	3	0	.833
♦1981-82	NY Islanders	NHL	80	54	16	10	....	.738	19	15	4	0	.789
♦1982-83	NY Islanders	NHL	80	42	26	12	....	.600	20	15	5	0	.750
1983-84	NY Islanders	NHL	80	50	26	4	....	.650	21	12	9	0	.571
1984-85	NY Islanders	NHL	80	40	34	6	....	.538	10	4	6	0	.400
1985-86	NY Islanders	NHL	80	39	29	12	....	.563	3	0	3	0	.000
1988-89	NY Islanders	NHL	53	21	29	3	....	.425	....	....	....	....	....
1989-90	NY Islanders	NHL	80	31	38	11	....	.456	5	1	4	0	.200
1990-91	NY Islanders	NHL	80	25	45	10	....	.375	....	....	....	....	....
1991-92	NY Islanders	NHL	80	34	35	11	....	.494	....	....	....	....	....
1992-93	NY Islanders	NHL	84	40	37	7	....	.518	18	9	9	0	.500
1993-94	NY Islanders	NHL	84	36	36	12	....	.500	4	0	4	0	.000
	NHL Totals		**1606**	**781**	**577**	**248**	....	**.564**	**209**	**123**	**86**	**0**	**.589**

• Won Jack Adams Award (1979)

• ARMSTRONG, George — HHOF

b: Skead, Ontario, 7/6/1930.
Played in NHL. See Modern Player Register for career statistics.

			REGULAR SEASON						PLAYOFFS				
Season	Club	League	GC	W	L	T	RT	W%	GC	W	L	T	W%
1988-89	Toronto	NHL	47	17	26	4	....	.404	....	....	....	....	....
	NHL Totals		**47**	**17**	**26**	**4**	....	**.404**	....	....	....	....	....

• BARKLEY, Doug

b: Lethbridge, Alta., 1/6/1937.
Played in NHL. See Pre-Expansion Player Register for career statistics.

Season	Club	League	Regular Season GC	W	L	T	RT	W%	Playoffs GC	W	L	T	W%
1970-71	Detroit	NHL	40	10	23	7	....	.338	....	....	....	....	....
1971-72	Detroit	NHL	11	3	8	0	....	.273	....	....	....	....	....
1975-76	Detroit	NHL	26	7	15	4	....	.346	....	....	....	....	....
	NHL Totals		**77**	**20**	**46**	**11**	....	**.331**	....	....	....	....	....

• BEAULIEU, Andre

b: unknown.

Season	Club	League	Regular Season GC	W	L	T	RT	W%	Playoffs GC	W	L	T	W%
1977-78	Minnesota	NHL	32	6	23	3	....	.234	....	....	....	....	....
	NHL Totals		**32**	**6**	**23**	**3**	....	**.234**	....	....	....	....	....

• BELISLE, Danny

b: South Porcupine, Ont., 5/9/1937.
Played in NHL. See Pre-Expansion Player Register for career statistics.

Season	Club	League	Regular Season GC	W	L	T	RT	W%	Playoffs GC	W	L	T	W%
1978-79	Washington	NHL	80	24	41	15	....	.394	....	....	....	....	....
1979-80	Washington	NHL	16	4	10	2	....	.313	....	....	....	....	....
	NHL Totals		**96**	**28**	**51**	**17**	....	**.380**	....	....	....	....	....

• BERENSON, Red

b: Regina, Sask., 12/8/1939.
Played in NHL. See Modern Player Register for career statistics.

Season	Club	League	Regular Season GC	W	L	T	RT	W%	Playoffs GC	W	L	T	W%
1979-80	St. Louis	NHL	56	27	20	9	....	.563	3	0	3	0	.000
1980-81	St. Louis	NHL	80	45	18	17	....	.669	11	5	6	0	.455
1981-82	St. Louis	NHL	68	28	34	6	....	.456	....	....	....	....	....
	NHL Totals		**204**	**100**	**72**	**32**	....	**.569**	**14**	**5**	**9**	**0**	**.357**

• Won Jack Adams Award (1981)

• BERGERON, Michel

b: Montreal, Que., 6/12/1946.

Season	Club	League	Regular Season GC	W	L	T	RT	W%	Playoffs GC	W	L	T	W%
1980-81	Quebec	NHL	74	29	29	16	....	.500	5	2	3	0	.400
1981-82	Quebec	NHL	80	33	31	16	....	.513	16	7	9	0	.438
1982-83	Quebec	NHL	80	34	34	12	....	.500	4	1	3	0	.250
1983-84	Quebec	NHL	80	42	28	10	....	.588	9	5	4	0	.556
1984-85	Quebec	NHL	80	41	30	9	....	.569	18	9	9	0	.500
1985-86	Quebec	NHL	80	43	31	6	....	.575	3	0	3	0	.000
1986-87	Quebec	NHL	80	31	39	10	....	.450	13	7	6	0	.538
1987-88	NY Rangers	NHL	80	36	34	10	....	.513	....	....	....	....	....
1988-89	NY Rangers	NHL	78	37	33	8	....	.526	....	....	....	....	....
1989-90	Quebec	NHL	80	12	61	7	....	.194	....	....	....	....	....
	NHL Totals		**792**	**338**	**350**	**104**	....	**.492**	**68**	**31**	**37**	**0**	**.456**

• BERRY, Bob

b: Montreal, Que., 11/29/1943.
Played in NHL. See Modern Player Register for career statistics.

Season	Club	League	Regular Season GC	W	L	T	RT	W%	Playoffs GC	W	L	T	W%
1978-79	Los Angeles	NHL	80	34	34	12	....	.500	2	0	2	0	.000
1979-80	Los Angeles	NHL	80	30	36	14	....	.463	4	1	3	0	.250
1980-81	Los Angeles	NHL	80	43	24	13	....	.619	4	1	3	0	.250
1981-82	Montreal	NHL	80	46	17	17	....	.681	5	2	3	0	.400
1982-83	Montreal	NHL	80	42	24	14	....	.613	3	0	3	0	.000
1983-84	Montreal	NHL	63	28	30	5	....	.484	....	....	....	....	....
1984-85	Pittsburgh	NHL	80	24	51	5	....	.331	....	....	....	....	....
1985-86	Pittsburgh	NHL	80	34	38	8	....	.475	....	....	....	....	....
1986-87	Pittsburgh	NHL	80	30	38	12	....	.450	....	....	....	....	....
1992-93	St. Louis	NHL	73	33	30	10	....	.521	11	7	4	0	.636
1993-94	St. Louis	NHL	84	40	33	11	....	.542	4	0	4	0	.000
	NHL Totals		**860**	**384**	**355**	**121**	....	**.517**	**33**	**11**	**22**	**0**	**.333**

• BEVERLEY, Nick

b: Toronto, Ont., 4/21/1947.
Played in NHL. See Modern Player Register for career statistics.

Season	Club	League	Regular Season GC	W	L	T	RT	W%	Playoffs GC	W	L	T	W%
1995-96	Toronto	NHL	17	9	6	2	....	.588	6	2	4	0	.333
	NHL Totals		**17**	**9**	**6**	**2**	....	**.588**	**6**	**2**	**4**	**0**	**.333**

• BLACKBURN, Don

b: Kirkland Lake, Ont., 5/14/1938.
Played in NHL. See Modern Player Register for career statistics.

Season	Club	League	Regular Season GC	W	L	T	RT	W%	Playoffs GC	W	L	T	W%
1979-80	Hartford	NHL	80	27	34	19	....	.456	3	0	3	0	.000
1980-81	Hartford	NHL	60	15	29	16	....	.383	....	....	....	....	....
	NHL Totals		**140**	**42**	**63**	**35**	....	**.425**	**3**	**0**	**3**	**0**	**.000**

• BLAIR, Wren

b: Lindsay, Ont., 10/2/1925.

Season	Club	League	Regular Season GC	W	L	T	RT	W%	Playoffs GC	W	L	T	W%
1967-68	Minnesota	NHL	74	27	32	15	....	.466	14	7	7	0	.500
1968-69	Minnesota	NHL	41	12	20	9	....	.402	....	....	....	....	....
1969-70	Minnesota	NHL	32	9	13	10	....	.438	....	....	....	....	....
	NHL Totals		**147**	**48**	**65**	**34**	....	**.442**	**14**	**7**	**7**	**0**	**.500**

• BLAKE, Toe — HHOF

b: Victoria Mines, Ont., 8/21/1912 d: 5/17/1995.
Played in NHL. See Pre-Expansion Player Register for career statistics.

Season	Club	League	Regular Season GC	W	L	T	RT	W%	Playoffs GC	W	L	T	W%
♦1955-56	Montreal	NHL	70	45	15	10	....	.714	10	8	2	0	.800
♦1956-57	Montreal	NHL	70	35	23	12	....	.586	10	8	2	0	.800
♦1957-58	Montreal	NHL	70	43	17	10	....	.686	10	8	2	0	.800
♦1958-59	Montreal	NHL	70	39	18	13	....	.650	11	8	3	0	.727
♦1959-60	Montreal	NHL	70	40	18	12	....	.657	8	8	0	0	1.000
1960-61	Montreal	NHL	70	41	19	10	....	.657	6	2	4	0	.333
1961-62	Montreal	NHL	70	42	14	14	....	.700	6	2	4	0	.333
1962-63	Montreal	NHL	70	28	19	23	....	.564	7	3	4	0	.429
1963-64	Montreal	NHL	70	36	21	13	....	.607	5	1	4	0	.200
♦1964-65	Montreal	NHL	70	36	23	11	....	.593	13	8	5	0	.615
♦1965-66	Montreal	NHL	70	41	21	8	....	.643	10	8	2	0	.800
1966-67	Montreal	NHL	70	32	25	13	....	.550	10	6	4	0	.600
♦1967-68	Montreal	NHL	74	42	22	10	....	.635	13	12	1	0	.923
	NHL Totals		**914**	**500**	**255**	**159**	....	**.634**	**119**	**82**	**37**	**0**	**.689**

• BOILEAU, Marc

b: Pointe Claire, Que., 9/3/1932.
Played in NHL. See Pre-Expansion Player Register for career statistics.

Season	Club	League	Regular Season GC	W	L	T	RT	W%	Playoffs GC	W	L	T	W%
1973-74	Pittsburgh	NHL	28	14	10	4	....	.571	....	....	....	....	....
1974-75	Pittsburgh	NHL	80	37	28	15	....	.556	9	5	4	0	.556
1975-76	Pittsburgh	NHL	43	15	23	5	....	.407	....	....	....	....	....
	NHL Totals		**151**	**66**	**61**	**24**	....	**.517**	**9**	**5**	**4**	**0**	**.556**

• BOIVIN, Leo — HHOF

b: Prescott, Ont., 8/2/1932.
Played in NHL. See Modern Player Register for career statistics.

Season	Club	League	Regular Season GC	W	L	T	RT	W%	Playoffs GC	W	L	T	W%
1975-76	St. Louis	NHL	43	17	17	9	....	.500	3	1	2	0	.333
1977-78	St. Louis	NHL	54	11	36	7	....	.269	....	....	....	....	....
	NHL Totals		**97**	**28**	**53**	**16**	....	**.371**	**3**	**1**	**2**	**0**	**.333**

• BOUCHER, Frank — HHOF

b: Ottawa, Ont., 10/7/1901 d: 12/12/1977.
Played in NHL. See Pre-Expansion Player Register for career statistics.

Season	Club	League	Regular Season GC	W	L	T	RT	W%	Playoffs GC	W	L	T	W%
♦1939-40	NY Rangers	NHL	48	27	11	10	....	.667	12	8	4	0	.667
1940-41	NY Rangers	NHL	48	21	19	8	....	.521	3	1	2	0	.333
1941-42	NY Rangers	NHL	48	29	17	2	....	.625	6	2	4	0	.333
1942-43	NY Rangers	NHL	50	11	31	8	....	.300	....	....	....	....	....
1943-44	NY Rangers	NHL	50	6	39	5	....	.170	....	....	....	....	....
1944-45	NY Rangers	NHL	50	11	29	10	....	.320	....	....	....	....	....
1945-46	NY Rangers	NHL	50	13	28	9	....	.350	....	....	....	....	....
1946-47	NY Rangers	NHL	60	22	32	6	....	.417	....	....	....	....	....
1947-48	NY Rangers	NHL	60	21	26	13	....	.458	6	2	4	0	.333
1948-49	NY Rangers	NHL	23	6	11	6	....	.391	....	....	....	....	....
1953-54	NY Rangers	NHL	40	14	20	6	....	.425	....	....	....	....	....
	NHL Totals		**527**	**181**	**263**	**83**	....	**.422**	**27**	**13**	**14**	**0**	**.481**

• BOUCHER, George — HHOF

b: Ottawa, Ont., 8/19/1896 d: 10/17/1960.
Played in NHL. See Pre-Expansion Player Register for career statistics.

Season	Club	League	Regular Season GC	W	L	T	RT	W%	Playoffs GC	W	L	T	W%
1930-31	Mtl. Maroons	NHL	12	6	5	1	....	.542	2	0	2	0	.000
1933-34	Ottawa	NHL	48	13	29	6	....	.333	....	....	....	....	....
1934-35	St. Louis	NHL	35	9	20	6	....	.343	....	....	....	....	....
1949-50	Boston	NHL	70	22	32	16	....	.429	....	....	....	....	....
	NHL Totals		**165**	**50**	**86**	**29**	....	**.391**	**2**	**0**	**2**	**0**	**.000**

• BOWMAN, Scotty — HHOF

b: Montreal, Que., 9/18/1933.

Season	Club	League	Regular Season GC	W	L	T	RT	W%	Playoffs GC	W	L	T	W%
1967-68	St. Louis	NHL	58	23	21	14	....	.517	18	8	10	0	.444
1968-69	St. Louis	NHL	76	37	25	14	....	.579	12	8	4	0	.667
1969-70	St. Louis	NHL	76	37	27	12	....	.566	16	8	8	0	.500
1970-71	St. Louis	NHL	28	13	10	5	....	.554	6	2	4	0	.333
1971-72	Montreal	NHL	78	46	16	16	....	.692	6	2	4	0	.333
♦1972-73	Montreal	NHL	78	52	10	16	....	.769	17	12	5	0	.706
1973-74	Montreal	NHL	78	45	24	9	....	.635	6	2	4	0	.333
1974-75	Montreal	NHL	80	47	14	19	....	.706	11	6	5	0	.545
♦1975-76	Montreal	NHL	80	58	11	11	....	.794	13	12	1	0	.923
♦1976-77	Montreal	NHL	80	60	8	12	....	.825	14	12	2	0	.857
♦1977-78	Montreal	NHL	80	59	10	11	....	.806	15	12	3	0	.800
♦1978-79	Montreal	NHL	80	52	17	11	....	.719	16	12	4	0	.750
1979-80	Buffalo	NHL	80	47	17	16	....	.688	14	9	5	0	.643
1981-82	Buffalo	NHL	35	18	10	7	....	.614	4	1	3	0	.250
1982-83	Buffalo	NHL	80	38	29	13	....	.556	10	6	4	0	.600
1983-84	Buffalo	NHL	80	48	25	7	....	.644	3	0	3	0	.000
1984-85	Buffalo	NHL	80	38	28	14	....	.563	5	2	3	0	.400
1985-86	Buffalo	NHL	37	18	18	1	....	.500	....	....	....	....	....
1986-87	Buffalo	NHL	12	3	7	2	....	.333	....	....	....	....	....
♦1991-92	Pittsburgh	NHL	80	39	32	9	....	.544	21	16	5	0	.762
1992-93	Pittsburgh	NHL	84	56	21	7	....	.708	12	7	5	0	.583
1993-94	Detroit	NHL	84	46	30	8	....	.595	7	3	4	0	.429
1994-95	Detroit	NHL	48	33	11	4	....	.729	18	12	6	0	.667
1995-96	Detroit	NHL	82	62	13	7	....	.799	19	10	9	0	.526
♦1996-97	Detroit	NHL	82	38	26	18	....	.573	20	16	4	0	.800
♦1997-98	Detroit	NHL	82	44	23	15	....	.628	22	16	6	0	.727
1998-99	Detroit	NHL	77	39	32	6	....	.545	10	6	4	0	.600
99-2000	Detroit	NHL	82	48	24	10	2	.659	9	5	4	0	.556
	NHL Totals		**1977**	**1144**	**539**	**294**	**2**	**.654**	**324**	**205**	**119**	**0**	**.633**

• Won Jack Adams Award (1977, 1996)

Associate coaches Dave Lewis and Barry Smith shared a 4-1-0 record while combining as co-head coaches until Scotty Bowman received medical clearance and decided to return to coaching on October 23, 1998.

• BOWNESS, Rick

b: Moncton, N.B., 1/25/1955.
Played in NHL. See Modern Player Register for career statistics.

Season	Club	League	GC	W	L	T	RT	W%	GC	W	L	T	W%
1988-89	Winnipeg	NHL	28	8	17	3	....	.339	....	....	....	....	....
1991-92	Boston	NHL	80	36	32	12	....	.525	15	8	7	0	.533
1992-93	Ottawa	NHL	84	10	70	4	....	.143	....	....	....	....	....
1993-94	Ottawa	NHL	84	14	61	9	....	.220	....	....	....	....	....
1994-95	Ottawa	NHL	48	9	34	5	....	.240	....	....	....	....	....
1995-96	Ottawa	NHL	19	6	13	0	....	.316	....	....	....	....	....
1996-97	NY Islanders	NHL	37	16	18	3	....	.473	....	....	....	....	....
1997-98	NY Islanders	NHL	63	22	32	9	....	.421	....	....	....	....	....
	NHL Totals		**443**	**121**	**277**	**45**	....	**.324**	**15**	**8**	**7**	**0**	**.533**

• BROOKS, Herb

USHOF

b: St. Paul, MN, 8/5/1937.

Season	Club	League	GC	W	L	T	RT	W%	GC	W	L	T	W%
1981-82	NY Rangers	NHL	80	39	27	14	....	.575	10	5	5	0	.500
1982-83	NY Rangers	NHL	80	35	35	10	....	.500	9	5	4	0	.556
1983-84	NY Rangers	NHL	80	42	29	9	....	.581	5	2	3	0	.400
1984-85	NY Rangers	NHL	45	15	22	8	....	.422	....	....	....	....	....
1987-88	Minnesota	NHL	80	19	48	13	....	.319	....	....	....	....	....
1992-93	New Jersey	NHL	84	40	37	7	....	.518	5	1	4	0	.200
99-2000	Pittsburgh	NHL	58	29	24	5	2	.560	11	6	5	0	.545
	NHL Totals		**507**	**219**	**222**	**66**	**2**	**.499**	**40**	**19**	**21**	**0**	**.475**

• BROPHY, John

b: Antigonish, N.S., 1/20/1933.

Season	Club	League	GC	W	L	T	RT	W%	GC	W	L	T	W%
1986-87	Toronto	NHL	80	32	42	6	....	.438	13	7	6	0	.538
1987-88	Toronto	NHL	80	21	49	10	....	.325	6	2	4	0	.333
1988-89	Toronto	NHL	33	11	20	2	....	.364	....	....	....	....	....
	NHL Totals		**193**	**64**	**111**	**18**	....	**.378**	**19**	**9**	**10**	**0**	**.474**

• BURNETT, George

b: Port Perry, Ont., 3/25/1962.

Season	Club	League	GC	W	L	T	RT	W%	GC	W	L	T	W%
1994-95	Edmonton	NHL	35	12	20	3	....	.386	....	....	....	....	....
	NHL Totals		**35**	**12**	**20**	**3**	....	**.386**	....	....	....	....	....

• BURNS, Charlie

b: Detroit, MI, 2/14/1936.
Played in NHL. See Modern Player Register for career statistics.

Season	Club	League	GC	W	L	T	RT	W%	GC	W	L	T	W%
1969-70	Minnesota	NHL	44	10	22	12	....	.364	6	2	4	0	.333
1974-75	Minnesota	NHL	42	12	28	2	....	.310	....	....	....	....	....
	NHL Totals		**86**	**22**	**50**	**14**	....	**.337**	**6**	**2**	**4**	**0**	**.333**

• BURNS, Pat

b: St-Henri, Que., 4/4/1952.

Season	Club	League	GC	W	L	T	RT	W%	GC	W	L	T	W%
1988-89	Montreal	NHL	80	53	18	9	....	.719	21	14	7	0	.667
1989-90	Montreal	NHL	80	41	28	11	....	.581	11	5	6	0	.455
1990-91	Montreal	NHL	80	39	30	11	....	.556	13	7	6	0	.538
1991-92	Montreal	NHL	80	41	28	11	....	.581	11	4	7	0	.364
1992-93	Toronto	NHL	84	44	29	11	....	.589	21	11	10	0	.524
1993-94	Toronto	NHL	84	43	29	12	....	.583	18	9	9	0	.500
1994-95	Toronto	NHL	48	21	19	8	....	.521	7	3	4	0	.429
1995-96	Toronto	NHL	65	25	30	10	....	.462	....	....	....	....	....
1997-98	Boston	NHL	82	39	30	13	....	.555	6	2	4	0	.333
1998-99	Boston	NHL	82	39	30	13	....	.555	12	6	6	0	.500
99-2000	Boston	NHL	82	24	39	19	6	.445	....	....	....	....	....
	NHL Totals		**847**	**409**	**310**	**128**	**6**	**.562**	**120**	**61**	**59**	**0**	**.508**

• Won Jack Adams Award (1989, 1993, 1998)

• BUSH, Eddie

b: Collingwood, Ont., 7/11/1918 d: 5/31/1984.
Played in NHL. See Pre-Expansion Player Register for career statistics.

Season	Club	League	GC	W	L	T	RT	W%	GC	W	L	T	W%
1975-76	Kansas City	NHL	32	1	23	8	....	.156	....	....	....	....	....
	NHL Totals		**32**	**1**	**23**	**8**	....	**.156**	....	....	....	....	....

• CAMPBELL, Colin

b: London, Ont., 1/28/1953.
Played in NHL. See Modern Player Register for career statistics.

Season	Club	League	GC	W	L	T	RT	W%	GC	W	L	T	W%
1994-95	NY Rangers	NHL	48	22	23	3	....	.490	10	4	6	0	.400
1995-96	NY Rangers	NHL	82	41	27	14	....	.585	11	5	6	0	.455
1996-97	NY Rangers	NHL	82	38	34	10	....	.524	15	9	6	0	.600
1997-98	NY Rangers	NHL	57	17	24	16	....	.439	....	....	....	....	....
	NHL Totals		**269**	**118**	**108**	**43**	....	**.519**	**36**	**18**	**18**	**0**	**.500**

• CARPENTER, Doug

b: Cornwall, Ont., 7/1/1942.

Season	Club	League	GC	W	L	T	RT	W%	GC	W	L	T	W%
1984-85	New Jersey	NHL	80	22	48	10	....	.338	....	....	....	....	....
1985-86	New Jersey	NHL	80	28	49	3	....	.369	....	....	....	....	....
1986-87	New Jersey	NHL	80	29	45	6	....	.400	....	....	....	....	....
1987-88	New Jersey	NHL	50	21	24	5	....	.470	....	....	....	....	....
1989-90	Toronto	NHL	80	38	38	4	....	.500	5	1	4	0	.200
1990-91	Toronto	NHL	11	1	9	1	....	.136	....	....	....	....	....
	NHL Totals		**381**	**139**	**213**	**29**	....	**.403**	**5**	**1**	**4**	**0**	**.200**

• CARROLL, Dick

b: Guelph, Ont., 1888 d: 1/21/1952.

Season	Club	League	GC	W	L	T	RT	W%	GC	W	L	T	W%
♦1917-18	Toronto	NHL	22	13	9	0	....	.591	7	4	3	0	.571
1918-19	Toronto	NHL	18	5	13	0	....	.278	....	....	....	....	....
	NHL Totals		**40**	**18**	**22**	**0**	....	**.450**	**7**	**4**	**3**	**0**	**.571**

• CARROLL, Frank

b: unknown Deceased.

Season	Club	League	GC	W	L	T	RT	W%	GC	W	L	T	W%
1920-21	Toronto	NHL	24	15	9	0	....	.625	2	0	2	0	.000
	NHL Totals		**24**	**15**	**9**	**0**	....	**.625**	**2**	**0**	**2**	**0**	**.000**

• CASHMAN, Wayne

b: Kingston, Ont., 6/24/1945.
Played in NHL. See Modern Player Register for career statistics.

Season	Club	League	GC	W	L	T	RT	W%	GC	W	L	T	W%
1997-98	Philadelphia	NHL	61	32	20	9	....	.598	....	....	....	....	....
	NHL Totals		**61**	**32**	**20**	**9**	....	**.598**	....	....	....	....	....

Shared an 0-2-0 record as co-coach with Ed Giacomin when Tom Webster was ill, suffering a 4-3 loss to Minnesota at New York on December 15, 1986, and a 7-4 loss at Edmonton on January 23, 1987. All games are credited to Webster's coaching record.

• CHAMBERS, Dave

b: Leaside, Ont., 5/7/1940.

Season	Club	League	GC	W	L	T	RT	W%	GC	W	L	T	W%
1990-91	Quebec	NHL	80	16	50	14	....	.288	....	....	....	....	....
1991-92	Quebec	NHL	18	3	14	1	....	.194	....	....	....	....	....
	NHL Totals		**98**	**19**	**64**	**15**	....	**.270**	....	....	....	....	....

• CHARRON, Guy

b: Verdun, Que., 1/24/1949.
Played in NHL. See Modern Player Register for career statistics.

Season	Club	League	GC	W	L	T	RT	W%	GC	W	L	T	W%
1991-92	Calgary	NHL	16	6	7	3	....	.469	....	....	....	....	....
	NHL Totals		**16**	**6**	**7**	**3**	....	**.469**	....	....	....	....	....

• CHEEVERS, Gerry

HHOF

b: St. Catharines, Ont., 12/7/1940.
Played in NHL. See Goaltender Register for career statistics.

Season	Club	League	GC	W	L	T	RT	W%	GC	W	L	T	W%
1980-81	Boston	NHL	80	37	30	13	....	.544	3	0	3	0	.000
1981-82	Boston	NHL	80	43	27	10	....	.600	11	6	5	0	.545
1982-83	Boston	NHL	80	50	20	10	....	.688	17	9	8	0	.529
1983-84	Boston	NHL	80	49	25	6	....	.650	3	0	3	0	.000
1984-85	Boston	NHL	56	25	24	7	....	.509	....	....	....	....	....
	NHL Totals		**376**	**204**	**126**	**46**	....	**.604**	**34**	**15**	**19**	**0**	**.441**

• CHERRY, Don

b: Kingston, Ont., 2/5/1934.
Played in NHL. See Pre-Expansion Player Register for career statistics.

Season	Club	League	GC	W	L	T	RT	W%	GC	W	L	T	W%
1974-75	Boston	NHL	80	40	26	14	....	.588	3	1	2	0	.333
1975-76	Boston	NHL	80	48	15	17	....	.706	12	5	7	0	.417
1976-77	Boston	NHL	80	49	23	8	....	.663	14	8	6	0	.571
1977-78	Boston	NHL	80	51	18	11	....	.706	15	10	5	0	.667
1978-79	Boston	NHL	80	43	23	14	....	.625	11	7	4	0	.636
1979-80	Colorado	NHL	80	19	48	13	....	.319	....	....	....	....	....
	NHL Totals		**480**	**250**	**153**	**77**	....	**.601**	**55**	**31**	**24**	**0**	**.564**

• Won Jack Adams Award (1976)

• CLANCY, King

HHOF

b: Ottawa, Ont., 2/25/1903 d: 11/8/1986.
Played in NHL. See Pre-Expansion Player Register for career statistics.

Season	Club	League	GC	W	L	T	RT	W%	GC	W	L	T	W%
1937-38	Mtl. Maroons	NHL	18	6	11	1	....	.361	....	....	....	....	....
1953-54	Toronto	NHL	70	32	24	14	....	.557	5	1	4	0	.200
1954-55	Toronto	NHL	70	24	24	22	....	.500	4	0	4	0	.000
1955-56	Toronto	NHL	70	24	33	13	....	.436	5	1	4	0	.200
	NHL Totals		**228**	**86**	**92**	**50**	....	**.487**	**14**	**2**	**12**	**0**	**.143**

Posted a 7-1-2 record as replacement coach when Punch Imlach was sidelined with heart problems, February 18 to March 11, 1967. All games are credited to Imlach's coaching record. Posted a 6-2-3 record as replacement coach when John McLellan was sidelined with a duodenal ulcer, February 23 to March 22, 1972. Posted a 3-1-0 regular season record and a 1-4 playoff record as replacement coach when John McLellan was again sidelined with a duodenal ulcer, March 25 to April 11, 1972. All games are credited to McLellan's coaching record.

• CLAPPER, Dit

HHOF

b: Newmarket, Ont., 2/9/1907 d: 1/21/1978.
Played in NHL. See Pre-Expansion Player Register for career statistics.

Season	Club	League	GC	W	L	T	RT	W%	GC	W	L	T	W%
1945-46	Boston	NHL	50	24	18	8	....	.560	10	5	5	0	.500
1946-47	Boston	NHL	60	26	23	11	....	.525	5	1	4	0	.200
1947-48	Boston	NHL	60	23	24	13	....	.492	5	1	4	0	.200
1948-49	Boston	NHL	60	29	23	8	....	.550	5	1	4	0	.200
	NHL Totals		**230**	**102**	**88**	**40**	....	**.530**	**25**	**8**	**17**	**0**	**.320**

• CLEGHORN, Odie

b: Montreal, Que., 9/19/1891 d: 7/13/1956.
Played in NHL. See Pre-Expansion Player Register for career statistics.

Season	Club	League	GC	W	L	T	RT	W%	GC	W	L	T	W%
1925-26	Pittsburgh	NHL	36	19	16	1	....	.542	2	0	1	1	.250
1926-27	Pittsburgh	NHL	44	15	26	3	....	.375	....	....	....	....	....
1927-28	Pittsburgh	NHL	44	19	17	8	....	.523	2	1	1	0	.500
1928-29	Pittsburgh	NHL	44	9	27	8	....	.295	....	....	....	....	....
	NHL Totals		**168**	**62**	**86**	**20**	....	**.429**	**4**	**1**	**2**	**1**	**.375**

• CLEGHORN, Sprague

HHOF

b: Montreal, Que., 3/11/1890 d: 7/11/1956.
Played in NHL. See Pre-Expansion Player Register for career statistics.

Season	Club	League	GC	W	L	T	RT	W%	GC	W	L	T	W%
1931-32	Mtl. Maroons	NHL	48	19	22	7	....	.469	4	1	1	2	.500
	NHL Totals		**48**	**19**	**22**	**7**	....	**.469**	**4**	**1**	**1**	**2**	**.500**

• COLVILLE, Neil — HHOF
b: Edmonton, Alta., 8/4/1914 d: 12/26/1987.
Played in NHL. See Pre-Expansion Player Register for career statistics.

Season	Club	League	GC	W	L	T	RT	W%	GC	W	L	T	W%
			REGULAR SEASON						PLAYOFFS				
1950-51	NY Rangers	NHL	70	20	29	21	....	.436	....	....	....	....	....
1951-52	NY Rangers	NHL	23	6	12	5	....	.370	....	....	....	....	....
	NHL Totals		**93**	**26**	**41**	**26**	....	**.419**	....	....	....	....	....

• CONACHER, Charlie — HHOF
b: Toronto, Ont., 12/20/1910 d: 12/30/1967.
Played in NHL. See Pre-Expansion Player Register for career statistics.

Season	Club	League	GC	W	L	T	RT	W%	GC	W	L	T	W%
1947-48	Chicago	NHL	32	13	15	4	....	.469	....	....	....	....	....
1948-49	Chicago	NHL	60	21	31	8	....	.417	....	....	....	....	....
1949-50	Chicago	NHL	70	22	38	10	....	.386	....	....	....	....	....
	NHL Totals		**162**	**56**	**84**	**22**	....	**.414**	....	....	....	....	....

• CONACHER, Lionel — HHOF
b: Toronto, Ont., 5/24/1901 d: 5/26/1954.
Played in NHL. See Pre-Expansion Player Register for career statistics.

Season	Club	League	GC	W	L	T	RT	W%	GC	W	L	T	W%
1929-30	NY Americans	NHL	44	14	25	5	....	.375	....	....	....	....	....
	NHL Totals		**44**	**14**	**25**	**5**	....	**.375**	....	....	....	....	....

• CONSTANTINE, Kevin
b: International Falls, MN, 12/27/1958.

Season	Club	League	GC	W	L	T	RT	W%	GC	W	L	T	W%
1993-94	San Jose	NHL	84	33	35	16	....	.488	14	7	7	0	.500
1994-95	San Jose	NHL	48	19	25	4	....	.438	11	4	7	0	.364
1995-96	San Jose	NHL	25	3	18	4	....	.200	....	....	....	....	....
1997-98	Pittsburgh	NHL	82	40	24	18	....	.598	6	2	4	0	.333
1998-99	Pittsburgh	NHL	82	38	30	14	....	.549	13	6	7	0	.462
99-2000	Pittsburgh	NHL	24	8	13	3	4	.479	....	....	....	....	....
	NHL Totals		**345**	**141**	**145**	**59**	**4**	**.500**	**44**	**19**	**25**	**0**	**.432**

• COOK, Bill — HHOF
b: Brantford, Ont., 10/9/1896 d: 4/6/1986.
Played in NHL. See Pre-Expansion Player Register for career statistics.

Season	Club	League	GC	W	L	T	RT	W%	GC	W	L	T	W%
1951-52	NY Rangers	NHL	47	17	22	8	....	.447	....	....	....	....	....
1952-53	NY Rangers	NHL	70	17	37	16	....	.357	....	....	....	....	....
	NHL Totals		**117**	**34**	**59**	**24**	....	**.393**	....	....	....	....	....

• CRAWFORD, Marc
b: Belleville, Ont., 2/13/1961.
Played in NHL. See Modern Player Register for career statistics.

Season	Club	League	GC	W	L	T	RT	W%	GC	W	L	T	W%
1994-95	Quebec	NHL	48	30	13	5	....	.677	6	2	4	0	.333
♦1995-96	Colorado	NHL	82	47	25	10	....	.634	22	16	6	0	.727
1996-97	Colorado	NHL	82	49	24	9	....	.652	17	10	7	0	.588
1997-98	Colorado	NHL	82	39	26	17	....	.579	7	3	4	0	.429
1998-99	Vancouver	NHL	37	8	23	6	....	.297	....	....	....	....	....
99-2000	Vancouver	NHL	82	30	37	15	8	.506	....	....	....	....	....
	NHL Totals		**413**	**203**	**148**	**62**	**8**	**.576**	**52**	**31**	**21**	**0**	**.596**

Won Jack Adams Award (1995)

• CREAMER, Pierre
b: Chomedy, Que, 7/6/1944.

Season	Club	League	GC	W	L	T	RT	W%	GC	W	L	T	W%
1987-88	Pittsburgh	NHL	80	36	35	9	....	.506	....	....	....	....	....
	NHL Totals		**80**	**36**	**35**	**9**	....	**.506**	....	....	....	....	....

• CREIGHTON, Fred
b: Hamiota, Man., 7/14/1933.

Season	Club	League	GC	W	L	T	RT	W%	GC	W	L	T	W%
1974-75	Atlanta	NHL	28	12	11	5	....	.518	....	....	....	....	....
1975-76	Atlanta	NHL	80	35	33	12	....	.513	2	1	1	0	.500
1976-77	Atlanta	NHL	80	34	34	12	....	.500	3	1	2	0	.333
1977-78	Atlanta	NHL	80	34	27	19	....	.544	2	0	2	0	.000
1978-79	Atlanta	NHL	80	41	31	8	....	.563	2	0	2	0	.000
1979-80	Boston	NHL	73	40	20	13	....	.637	....	....	....	....	....
	NHL Totals		**421**	**196**	**156**	**69**	....	**.548**	**9**	**2**	**7**	**0**	**.222**

• CRISP, Terry
b: Parry Sound, Ont., 5/28/1943.
Played in NHL. See Modern Player Register for career statistics.

Season	Club	League	GC	W	L	T	RT	W%	GC	W	L	T	W%
1987-88	Calgary	NHL	80	48	23	9	....	.656	9	4	5	0	.444
♦1988-89	Calgary	NHL	80	54	17	9	....	.731	22	16	6	0	.727
1989-90	Calgary	NHL	80	42	23	15	....	.619	6	2	4	0	.333
1992-93	Tampa Bay	NHL	84	23	54	7	....	.315	....	....	....	....	....
1993-94	Tampa Bay	NHL	84	30	43	11	....	.423	....	....	....	....	....
1994-95	Tampa Bay	NHL	48	17	28	3	....	.385	....	....	....	....	....
1995-96	Tampa Bay	NHL	82	38	32	12	....	.537	6	2	4	0	.333
1996-97	Tampa Bay	NHL	82	32	40	10	....	.451	....	....	....	....	....
1997-98	Tampa Bay	NHL	11	2	7	2	....	.273	....	....	....	....	....
	NHL Totals		**631**	**286**	**267**	**78**	....	**.515**	**43**	**24**	**19**	**0**	**.558**

• CROZIER, Joe
b: Winnipeg, Man., 2/19/1929.
Played in NHL. See Pre-Expansion Player Register for career statistics.

Season	Club	League	GC	W	L	T	RT	W%	GC	W	L	T	W%
1971-72	Buffalo	NHL	36	8	19	9	....	.347	....	....	....	....	....
1972-73	Buffalo	NHL	78	37	27	14	....	.564	6	2	4	0	.333
1973-74	Buffalo	NHL	78	32	34	12	....	.487	....	....	....	....	....
1980-81	Toronto	NHL	40	13	22	5	....	.388	....	....	....	....	....
	NHL Totals		**232**	**90**	**102**	**40**	....	**.474**	**6**	**2**	**4**	**0**	**.333**

• CROZIER, Roger
b: Bracebridge, Ont., 3/16/1942 d: 1/11/1996.
Played in NHL. See Goaltender Register for career statistics.

Season	Club	League	GC	W	L	T	RT	W%	GC	W	L	T	W%
1981-82	Washington	NHL	1	0	1	0	....	.000	....	....	....	....	....
	NHL Totals		**1**	**0**	**1**	**0**	....	**.000**	....	....	....	....	....

• CUNNIFF, John
b: South Boston, MA, 7/9/1943.

Season	Club	League	GC	W	L	T	RT	W%	GC	W	L	T	W%
1982-83	Hartford	NHL	13	3	9	1	....	.269	....	....	....	....	....
1989-90	New Jersey	NHL	66	31	28	7	....	.523	6	2	4	0	.333
1990-91	New Jersey	NHL	67	28	28	11	....	.500	....	....	....	....	....
	NHL Totals		**146**	**62**	**65**	**19**	....	**.490**	**6**	**2**	**4**	**0**	**.333**

• CURRY, Alex
b: unknown Deceased.

Season	Club	League	GC	W	L	T	RT	W%	GC	W	L	T	W%
1925-26	Ottawa	NHL	36	24	8	4	....	.722	2	0	1	1	.250
	NHL Totals		**36**	**24**	**8**	**4**	....	**.722**	**2**	**0**	**1**	**1**	**.250**

• DANDURAND, Leo — HHOF
b: Bourbonnais, IL, 7/9/1889 d: 6/26/1964.

Season	Club	League	GC	W	L	T	RT	W%	GC	W	L	T	W%
1921-22	Montreal	NHL	17	10	6	1	....	.618	....	....	....	....	....
1922-23	Montreal	NHL	24	13	9	2	....	.583	2	1	1	0	.500
♦1923-24	Montreal	NHL	24	13	11	0	....	.542	6	6	0	0	1.000
1924-25	Montreal	NHL	30	17	11	2	....	.600	6	3	3	0	.500
1925-26	Montreal	NHL	36	11	24	1	....	.319	....	....	....	....	....
1934-35	Montreal	NHL	32	14	15	3	....	.484	2	0	2	0	.000
	NHL Totals		**163**	**78**	**76**	**9**	....	**.506**	**16**	**10**	**6**	**0**	**.625**

• DAY, Hap — HHOF
b: Owen Sound, Ont., 6/14/1901 d: 2/17/1990.
Played in NHL. See Pre-Expansion Player Register for career statistics.

Season	Club	League	GC	W	L	T	RT	W%	GC	W	L	T	W%
1940-41	Toronto	NHL	48	28	14	6	....	.646	7	3	4	0	.429
♦1941-42	Toronto	NHL	48	27	18	3	....	.594	13	8	5	0	.615
1942-43	Toronto	NHL	50	22	19	9	....	.530	6	2	4	0	.333
1943-44	Toronto	NHL	50	23	23	4	....	.500	5	1	4	0	.200
♦1944-45	Toronto	NHL	50	24	22	4	....	.520	13	8	5	0	.615
1945-46	Toronto	NHL	50	19	24	7	....	.450	....	....	....	....	....
♦1946-47	Toronto	NHL	60	31	19	10	....	.600	11	8	3	0	.727
♦1947-48	Toronto	NHL	60	32	15	13	....	.642	9	8	1	0	.889
♦1948-49	Toronto	NHL	60	22	25	13	....	.475	9	8	1	0	.889
1949-50	Toronto	NHL	70	31	27	12	....	.529	7	3	4	0	.429
	NHL Totals		**546**	**259**	**206**	**81**	....	**.549**	**80**	**49**	**31**	**0**	**.613**

• DEA, Billy
b: Edmonton, Alta., 4/3/1933.
Played in NHL. See Modern Player Register for career statistics.

Season	Club	League	GC	W	L	T	RT	W%	GC	W	L	T	W%
1981-82	Detroit	NHL	11	3	8	0	....	.273	....	....	....	....	....
	NHL Totals		**11**	**3**	**8**	**0**	....	**.273**	....	....	....	....	....

• DELVECCHIO, Alex — HHOF
b: Fort William, Ont., 12/4/1932.
Played in NHL. See Modern Player Register for career statistics.

Season	Club	League	GC	W	L	T	RT	W%	GC	W	L	T	W%
1973-74	Detroit	NHL	67	27	31	9	....	.470	....	....	....	....	....
1974-75	Detroit	NHL	80	23	45	12	....	.363	....	....	....	....	....
1975-76	Detroit	NHL	54	19	29	6	....	.407	....	....	....	....	....
1976-77	Detroit	NHL	44	13	26	5	....	.352	....	....	....	....	....
	NHL Totals		**245**	**82**	**131**	**32**	....	**.400**	....	....	....	....	....

• DEMERS, Jacques
b: Montreal, Que., 8/25/1944.

Season	Club	League	GC	W	L	T	RT	W%	GC	W	L	T	W%
1979-80	Quebec	NHL	80	25	44	11	....	.381	....	....	....	....	....
1983-84	St. Louis	NHL	80	32	41	7	....	.444	11	6	5	0	.545
1984-85	St. Louis	NHL	80	37	31	12	....	.538	3	0	3	0	.000
1985-86	St. Louis	NHL	80	37	34	9	....	.519	19	10	9	0	.526
1986-87	Detroit	NHL	80	34	36	10	....	.488	16	9	7	0	.563
1987-88	Detroit	NHL	80	41	28	11	....	.581	16	9	7	0	.563
1988-89	Detroit	NHL	80	34	34	12	....	.500	6	2	4	0	.333
1989-90	Detroit	NHL	80	28	38	14	....	.438	....	....	....	....	....
♦1992-93	Montreal	NHL	84	48	30	6	....	.607	20	16	4	0	.800
1993-94	Montreal	NHL	84	41	29	14	....	.571	7	3	4	0	.429
1994-95	Montreal	NHL	48	18	23	7	....	.448	....	....	....	....	....
1995-96	Montreal	NHL	5	0	5	0	....	.000	....	....	....	....	....
1997-98	Tampa Bay	NHL	63	15	40	8	....	.302	....	....	....	....	....
1998-99	Tampa Bay	NHL	82	19	54	9	....	.287	....	....	....	....	....
	NHL Totals		**1006**	**409**	**467**	**130**	....	**.471**	**98**	**55**	**43**	**0**	**.561**

• Won Jack Adams Award (1987, 1988)

• DENNENY, Cy — HHOF
b: Farrow's Point, Ont., 12/23/1891 d: 10/12/1970.
Played in NHL. See Pre-Expansion Player Register for career statistics.

Season	Club	League	GC	W	L	T	RT	W%	GC	W	L	T	W%
♦1928-29	Boston	NHL	44	26	13	5	....	.648	5	5	0	0	1.000
1932-33	Ottawa	NHL	48	11	27	10	....	.333	....	....	....	....	....
	NHL Totals		**92**	**37**	**40**	**15**	....	**.484**	**5**	**5**	**0**	**0**	**1.000**

• DINEEN, Bill
b: Arvida, Que., 9/18/1932.
Played in NHL. See Pre-Expansion Player Register for career statistics.

Season	Club	League	GC	W	L	T	RT	W%	GC	W	L	T	W%
1991-92	Philadelphia	NHL	56	24	23	9	....	.509	....	....	....	....	....
1992-93	Philadelphia	NHL	84	36	37	11	....	.494	....	....	....	....	....
	NHL Totals		**140**	**60**	**60**	**20**	....	**.500**	....	....	....	....	....

• DUDLEY, Rick
b: Toronto, Ont., 1/31/1949.
Played in NHL. See Modern Player Register for career statistics.

Season	Club	League	GC	W	L	T	RT	W%	GC	W	L	T	W%
			REGULAR SEASON						PLAYOFFS				
1989-90	Buffalo	NHL	80	45	27	8	....	.613	6	2	4	0	.333
1990-91	Buffalo	NHL	80	31	30	19	....	.506	6	2	4	0	.333
1991-92	Buffalo	NHL	28	9	15	4	....	.393	....	....	....	....	....
	NHL Totals		**188**	**85**	**72**	**31**	....	**.535**	**12**	**4**	**8**	**0**	**.333**

• DUFF, Dick
b: Kirkland Lake, Ont., 2/18/1936.
Played in NHL. See Modern Player Register for career statistics.

Season	Club	League	GC	W	L	T	RT	W%	GC	W	L	T	W%
1979-80	Toronto	NHL	2	0	2	0	....	.000	....	....	....	....	....
	NHL Totals		**2**	**0**	**2**	**0**	....	**.000**	....	....	....	....	....

• DUGAL, Jules
b: unknown Deceased.

Season	Club	League	GC	W	L	T	RT	W%	GC	W	L	T	W%
1938-39	Montreal	NHL	18	9	6	3	....	.583	3	1	2	0	.333
	NHL Totals		**18**	**9**	**6**	**3**	....	**.583**	**3**	**1**	**2**	**0**	**.333**

• DUNCAN, Art
b: Sault Ste. Marie, Ont., 7/4/1894 d: 4/13/1975.
Played in NHL. See Pre-Expansion Player Register for career statistics.

Season	Club	League	GC	W	L	T	RT	W%	GC	W	L	T	W%
1926-27	Detroit	NHL	33	10	21	2	....	.333	....	....	....	....	....
1930-31	Toronto	NHL	42	21	13	8	....	.595	2	0	1	1	.250
1931-32	Toronto	NHL	5	0	3	2	....	.200	....	....	....	....	....
	NHL Totals		**80**	**31**	**37**	**12**	....	**.463**	**2**	**0**	**1**	**1**	**.250**

• DUTTON, Red HHOF
b: Russell, Man., 7/23/1898 d: 3/15/1987.
Played in NHL. See Pre-Expansion Player Register for career statistics.

Season	Club	League	GC	W	L	T	RT	W%	GC	W	L	T	W%
1935-36	NY Americans	NHL	48	16	25	7	....	.406	5	2	3	0	.400
1936-37	NY Americans	NHL	48	15	29	4	....	.354	....	....	....	....	....
1937-38	NY Americans	NHL	48	19	18	11	....	.510	6	3	3	0	.500
1938-39	NY Americans	NHL	48	17	21	10	....	.458	2	0	2	0	.000
1939-40	NY Americans	NHL	48	15	29	4	....	.354	3	1	2	0	.333
1940-41	NY Americans	NHL	48	8	29	11	....	.281	....	....	....	....	....
1941-42	Brooklyn	NHL	48	16	29	3	....	.365	....	....	....	....	....
	NHL Totals		**336**	**106**	**180**	**50**	....	**.390**	**16**	**6**	**10**	**0**	**.375**

• EDDOLLS, Frank
b: Lachine, Que., 7/5/1921 d: 8/13/1961.
Played in NHL. See Pre-Expansion Player Register for career statistics.

Season	Club	League	GC	W	L	T	RT	W%	GC	W	L	T	W%
1954-55	Chicago	NHL	70	13	40	17	....	.307	....	....	....	....	....
	NHL Totals		**70**	**13**	**40**	**17**	....	**.307**	....	....	....	....	....

• ESPOSITO, Phil HHOF
b: Sault Ste. Marie, Ont., 2/20/1942.
Played in NHL. See Modern Player Register for career statistics.

Season	Club	League	GC	W	L	T	RT	W%	GC	W	L	T	W%
1986-87	NY Rangers	NHL	43	24	19	0	....	.558	6	2	4	0	.333
1988-89	NY Rangers	NHL	2	0	2	0	....	.000	4	0	4	0	.000
	NHL Totals		**45**	**24**	**21**	**0**	....	**.533**	**10**	**2**	**8**	**0**	**.200**

• EVANS, Jack
b: Morriston, South Wales, 4/21/1928 d: 11/10/1996.
Played in NHL. See Pre-Expansion Player Register for career statistics.

Season	Club	League	GC	W	L	T	RT	W%	GC	W	L	T	W%
1975-76	California	NHL	80	27	42	11	....	.406	....	....	....	....	....
1976-77	Cleveland	NHL	80	25	42	13	....	.394	....	....	....	....	....
1977-78	Cleveland	NHL	80	22	45	13	....	.356	....	....	....	....	....
1983-84	Hartford	NHL	80	28	42	10	....	.413	....	....	....	....	....
1984-85	Hartford	NHL	80	30	41	9	....	.431	....	....	....	....	....
1985-86	Hartford	NHL	80	40	36	4	....	.525	10	6	4	0	.600
1986-87	Hartford	NHL	80	43	30	7	....	.581	6	2	4	0	.333
1987-88	Hartford	NHL	54	22	25	7	....	.472	....	....	....	....	....
	NHL Totals		**614**	**237**	**303**	**74**	....	**.446**	**16**	**8**	**8**	**0**	**.500**

• FASHOWAY, Gordie
b: Portage La Prairie, Man., 6/16/1926.
Played in NHL. See Pre-Expansion Player Register for career statistics.

Season	Club	League	GC	W	L	T	RT	W%	GC	W	L	T	W%
1967-68	Oakland	NHL	10	4	5	1	....	.450	....	....	....	....	....
	NHL Totals		**10**	**4**	**5**	**1**	....	**.450**	....	....	....	....	....

• FERGUSON, John
b: Vancouver, B.C., 9/5/1938.
Played in NHL. See Modern Player Register for career statistics.

Season	Club	League	GC	W	L	T	RT	W%	GC	W	L	T	W%
1975-76	NY Rangers	NHL	41	14	22	5	....	.402	....	....	....	....	....
1976-77	NY Rangers	NHL	80	29	37	14	....	.450	....	....	....	....	....
1985-86	Winnipeg	NHL	14	7	6	1	....	.536	3	0	3	0	.000
	NHL Totals		**135**	**50**	**65**	**20**	....	**.444**	**3**	**0**	**3**	**0**	**.000**

• FILION, Maurice
b: Montreal, Que., 2/12/1932.

Season	Club	League	GC	W	L	T	RT	W%	GC	W	L	T	W%
1980-81	Quebec	NHL	6	1	3	2	....	.333	....	....	....	....	....
	NHL Totals		**6**	**1**	**3**	**2**	....	**.333**	....	....	....	....	....

• FRANCIS, Bob
b: North Battleford, Sask., 12/5/1958.
Played in NHL. See Modern Player Register for career statistics.

Season	Club	League	GC	W	L	T	RT	W%	GC	W	L	T	W%
99-2000	Phoenix	NHL	82	39	35	8	4	.549	5	1	4	0	.200
	NHL Totals		**82**	**39**	**35**	**8**	**4**	**.549**	**5**	**1**	**4**	**0**	**.200**

• FRANCIS, Emile HHOF
b: North Battleford, Sask., 9/13/1926.
Played in NHL. See Goaltender Register for career statistics.

Season	Club	League	GC	W	L	T	RT	W%	GC	W	L	T	W%
1965-66	NY Rangers	NHL	50	13	31	6	....	.320	....	....	....	....	....
1966-67	NY Rangers	NHL	70	30	28	12	....	.514	4	0	4	0	.000
1967-68	NY Rangers	NHL	74	39	23	12	....	.608	6	2	4	0	.333
1968-69	NY Rangers	NHL	33	19	8	6	....	.667	4	0	4	0	.000
1969-70	NY Rangers	NHL	76	38	22	16	....	.605	6	2	4	0	.333
1970-71	NY Rangers	NHL	78	49	18	11	....	.699	13	7	6	0	.538
1971-72	NY Rangers	NHL	78	48	17	13	....	.699	16	10	6	0	.625
1972-73	NY Rangers	NHL	78	47	23	8	....	.654	10	5	5	0	.500
1973-74	NY Rangers	NHL	37	22	10	5	....	.662	13	7	6	0	.538
1974-75	NY Rangers	NHL	80	37	29	14	....	.550	3	1	2	0	.333
1976-77	St. Louis	NHL	80	32	39	9	....	.456	4	0	4	0	.000
1981-82	St. Louis	NHL	12	4	6	2	....	.417	10	5	5	0	.500
1982-83	St. Louis	NHL	32	10	19	3	....	.359	....	....	....	....	....
	NHL Totals		**778**	**388**	**273**	**117**	....	**.574**	**89**	**39**	**50**	**0**	**.438**

• FRASER, Curt
b: Cincinnati, OH, 1/12/1958.
Played in NHL. See Modern Player Register for career statistics.

Season	Club	League	GC	W	L	T	RT	W%	GC	W	L	T	W%
99-2000	Atlanta	NHL	82	14	61	7	4	.238	....	....	....	....	....
	NHL Totals		**82**	**14**	**61**	**7**	**4**	**.238**	....	....	....	....	....

• FREDRICKSON, Frank HHOF
b: Winnipeg, Man., 6/11/1895 d: 5/28/1979.
Played in NHL. See Pre-Expansion Player Register for career statistics.

Season	Club	League	GC	W	L	T	RT	W%	GC	W	L	T	W%
1929-30	Pittsburgh	NHL	44	5	36	3	....	.148	....	....	....	....	....
	NHL Totals		**44**	**5**	**36**	**3**	....	**.148**	....	....	....	....	....

• FTOREK, Robbie USHOF
b: Needham, MA, 1/2/1952.
Played in NHL. See Modern Player Register for career statistics.

Season	Club	League	GC	W	L	T	RT	W%	GC	W	L	T	W%
1987-88	Los Angeles	NHL	52	23	25	4	....	.481	5	1	4	0	.200
1988-89	Los Angeles	NHL	80	42	31	7	....	.569	11	4	7	0	.364
1998-99	New Jersey	NHL	82	47	24	11	....	.640	7	3	4	0	.429
99-2000	New Jersey	NHL	74	41	25	8	5	.642	....	....	....	....	....
	NHL Totals		**288**	**153**	**105**	**30**	**5**	**.592**	**23**	**8**	**15**	**0**	**.348**

• GADSBY, Bill HHOF
b: Calgary, Alta., 8/8/1927.
Played in NHL. See Pre-Expansion Player Register for career statistics.

Season	Club	League	GC	W	L	T	RT	W%	GC	W	L	T	W%
1968-69	Detroit	NHL	76	33	31	12	....	.513	....	....	....	....	....
1969-70	Detroit	NHL	2	2	0	0	....	1.000	....	....	....	....	....
	NHL Totals		**78**	**35**	**31**	**12**	....	**.526**	....	....	....	....	....

• GAINEY, Bob HHOF
b: Peterborough, Ont., 12/13/1953.
Played in NHL. See Modern Player Register for career statistics.

Season	Club	League	GC	W	L	T	RT	W%	GC	W	L	T	W%
1990-91	Minnesota	NHL	80	27	39	14	....	.425	23	14	9	0	.609
1991-92	Minnesota	NHL	80	32	42	6	....	.438	7	3	4	0	.429
1992-93	Minnesota	NHL	84	36	38	10	....	.488	....	....	....	....	....
1993-94	Dallas	NHL	84	42	29	13	....	.577	9	5	4	0	.556
1994-95	Dallas	NHL	48	17	23	8	....	.438	5	1	4	0	.200
1995-96	Dallas	NHL	39	11	19	9	....	.397	....	....	....	....	....
	NHL Totals		**415**	**165**	**190**	**60**	....	**.470**	**44**	**23**	**21**	**0**	**.523**

• GARDINER, Herb HHOF
b: Winnipeg, Man., 5/8/1891 d: 1/11/1972.
Played in NHL. See Pre-Expansion Player Register for career statistics.

Season	Club	League	GC	W	L	T	RT	W%	GC	W	L	T	W%
1928-29	Chicago	NHL	32	5	23	4	....	.219	....	....	....	....	....
	NHL Totals		**32**	**5**	**23**	**4**	....	**.219**	....	....	....	....	....

• GARDNER, Jimmy HHOF
b: Montreal, Que., 11/18/1881 d: 11/7/1940.

Season	Club	League	GC	W	L	T	RT	W%	GC	W	L	T	W%
1924-25	Hamilton	NHL	30	19	10	1	....	.650	....	....	....	....	....
	NHL Totals		**30**	**19**	**10**	**1**	....	**.650**	....	....	....	....	....

• GARVIN, Ted
b: Sarnia, Ont., 8/20/1923.

Season	Club	League	GC	W	L	T	RT	W%	GC	W	L	T	W%
1973-74	Detroit	NHL	11	2	8	1	....	.227	....	....	....	....	....
	NHL Totals		**11**	**2**	**8**	**1**	....	**.227**	....	....	....	....	....

• GEOFFRION, Bernie HHOF
b: Montreal, Que., 2/14/1931.
Played in NHL. See Modern Player Register for career statistics.

Season	Club	League	GC	W	L	T	RT	W%	GC	W	L	T	W%
1968-69	NY Rangers	NHL	43	22	18	3	....	.547	....	....	....	....	....
1972-73	Atlanta	NHL	78	25	38	15	....	.417	....	....	....	....	....
1973-74	Atlanta	NHL	78	30	34	14	....	.474	4	0	4	0	.000
1974-75	Atlanta	NHL	52	22	20	10	....	.519	....	....	....	....	....
1979-80	Montreal	NHL	30	15	9	6	....	.600	....	....	....	....	....
	NHL Totals		**281**	**114**	**119**	**48**	....	**.491**	**4**	**0**	**4**	**0**	**.000**

● **GERARD, Eddie** HHOF
b: Ottawa, Ont., 2/22/1890 d: 12/7/1937.
Played in NHL. See Pre-Expansion Player Register for career statistics.

Season	Club	League	GC	W	L	T	RT	W%	GC	W	L	T	W%
			REGULAR SEASON						PLAYOFFS				
1917-18	Ottawa	NHL	22	9	13	0	....	.409	....	....	....	....	....
1924-25	Mtl. Maroons	NHL	30	9	19	2	....	.333	....	....	....	....	....
♦1925-26	Mtl. Maroons	NHL	36	20	11	5	....	.625	8	5	1	2	.750
1926-27	Mtl. Maroons	NHL	44	20	20	4	....	.500	2	0	1	1	.250
1927-28	Mtl. Maroons	NHL	44	24	14	6	....	.614	9	5	3	1	.611
1928-29	Mtl. Maroons	NHL	44	15	20	9	....	.443	....	....	....	....	....
1930-31	NY Americans	NHL	44	18	16	10	....	.523	....	....	....	....	....
1931-32	NY Americans	NHL	48	16	24	8	....	.417	....	....	....	....	....
1932-33	Mtl. Maroons	NHL	48	22	20	6	....	.521	2	0	2	0	.000
1933-34	Mtl. Maroons	NHL	48	19	18	11	....	.510	4	1	2	1	.375
1934-35	St. Louis	NHL	13	2	11	0	....	.154	....	....	....	....	....
	NHL Totals		**421**	**174**	**186**	**61**	....	**.486**	**25**	**11**	**9**	**5**	**.540**

● **GILL, David**
b: unknown Deceased.

Season	Club	League	GC	W	L	T	RT	W%	GC	W	L	T	W%
♦1926-27	Ottawa	NHL	44	30	10	4	....	.727	6	3	0	3	.750
1927-28	Ottawa	NHL	44	20	14	10	....	.568	2	0	2	0	.000
1928-29	Ottawa	NHL	44	14	17	13	....	.466	....	....	....	....	....
	NHL Totals		**132**	**64**	**41**	**27**	....	**.587**	**8**	**3**	**2**	**3**	**.563**

● **GLOVER, Fred**
b: Toronto, Ont., 1/5/1928.
Played in NHL. See Pre-Expansion Player Register for career statistics.

Season	Club	League	GC	W	L	T	RT	W%	GC	W	L	T	W%
1968-69	Oakland	NHL	76	29	36	11	....	.454	7	3	4	0	.429
1969-70	Oakland	NHL	76	22	40	14	....	.382	4	0	4	0	.000
1970-71	California	NHL	78	20	53	5	....	.288	....	....	....	....	....
1971-72	California	NHL	3	0	1	2	....	.333	....	....	....	....	....
	Los Angeles	NHL	68	18	42	8	....	.324	....	....	....	....	....
1972-73	California	NHL	66	14	39	13	....	.311	....	....	....	....	....
1973-74	California	NHL	57	11	38	8	....	.263	....	....	....	....	....
	NHL Totals		**424**	**114**	**249**	**61**	....	**.341**	**11**	**3**	**8**	**0**	**.273**

● **GOODFELLOW, Ebbie** HHOF
b: Ottawa, Ont., 4/9/1907 d: 9/10/1965.
Played in NHL. See Pre-Expansion Player Register for career statistics.

Season	Club	League	GC	W	L	T	RT	W%	GC	W	L	T	W%
1950-51	Chicago	NHL	70	13	47	10	....	.257	....	....	....	....	....
1951-52	Chicago	NHL	70	17	44	9	....	.307	....	....	....	....	....
	NHL Totals		**140**	**30**	**91**	**19**	....	**.282**	....	....	....	....	....

● **GORDON, Jackie**
b: Winnipeg, Man., 3/3/1928.
Played in NHL. See Pre-Expansion Player Register for career statistics.

Season	Club	League	GC	W	L	T	RT	W%	GC	W	L	T	W%
1970-71	Minnesota	NHL	78	28	34	16	....	.462	12	6	6	0	.500
1971-72	Minnesota	NHL	78	37	29	12	....	.551	7	3	4	0	.429
1972-73	Minnesota	NHL	78	37	30	11	....	.545	6	2	4	0	.333
1973-74	Minnesota	NHL	17	3	8	6	....	.353	....	....	....	....	....
1974-75	Minnesota	NHL	38	11	22	5	....	.355	....	....	....	....	....
	NHL Totals		**289**	**116**	**123**	**50**	....	**.488**	**25**	**11**	**14**	**0**	**.440**

● **GORING, Butch**
b: St. Boniface, Man., 10/22/1949.
Played in NHL. See Modern Player Register for career statistics.

Season	Club	League	GC	W	L	T	RT	W%	GC	W	L	T	W%
1985-86	Boston	NHL	80	37	31	12	....	.538	3	0	3	0	.000
1986-87	Boston	NHL	13	5	7	1	....	.423	....	....	....	....	....
99-2000	NY Islanders	NHL	82	24	49	9	1	.354	....	....	....	....	....
	NHL Totals		**175**	**66**	**87**	**22**	**1**	**.443**	**3**	**0**	**3**	**0**	**.000**

● **GORMAN, Tommy** HHOF
b: Ottawa, Ont., 6/9/1886 d: 5/15/1961.

Season	Club	League	GC	W	L	T	RT	W%	GC	W	L	T	W%
1925-26	NY Americans	NHL	36	12	20	4	....	.389	....	....	....	....	....
1928-29	NY Americans	NHL	44	19	13	12	....	.568	2	0	1	1	.250
1932-33	Chicago	NHL	25	8	11	6	....	.440	....	....	....	....	....
♦1933-34	Chicago	NHL	48	20	17	11	....	.531	8	6	1	1	.813
♦1934-35	Mtl. Maroons	NHL	48	24	19	5	....	.552	7	5	0	2	.857
1935-36	Mtl. Maroons	NHL	48	22	16	10	....	.563	3	0	3	0	.000
1936-37	Mtl. Maroons	NHL	48	22	17	9	....	.552	5	2	3	0	.400
1937-38	Mtl. Maroons	NHL	30	6	19	5	....	.283	....	....	....	....	....
	NHL Totals		**327**	**133**	**132**	**62**	....	**.502**	**25**	**13**	**8**	**4**	**.600**

● **GOTTSELIG, Johnny**
b: Odessa, Russia, 6/24/1905 d: 5/15/1986.
Played in NHL. See Pre-Expansion Player Register for career statistics.

Season	Club	League	GC	W	L	T	RT	W%	GC	W	L	T	W%
1944-45	Chicago	NHL	49	13	29	7	....	.337	....	....	....	....	....
1945-46	Chicago	NHL	50	23	20	7	....	.530	4	0	4	0	.000
1946-47	Chicago	NHL	60	19	37	4	....	.350	....	....	....	....	....
1947-48	Chicago	NHL	28	7	19	2	....	.286	....	....	....	....	....
	NHL Totals		**187**	**62**	**105**	**20**	....	**.385**	**4**	**0**	**4**	**0**	**.000**

● **GOYETTE, Phil**
b: Lachine, Que., 10/31/1933.
Played in NHL. See Modern Player Register for career statistics.

Season	Club	League	GC	W	L	T	RT	W%	GC	W	L	T	W%
1972-73	NY Islanders	NHL	48	6	38	4	....	.167	....	....	....	....	....
	NHL Totals		**48**	**6**	**38**	**4**	....	**.167**	....	....	....	....	....

● **GRAHAM, Dirk**
b: Regina, Sask., 7/29/1959.
Played in NHL. See Modern Player Register for career statistics.

Season	Club	League	GC	W	L	T	RT	W%	GC	W	L	T	W%
1998-99	Chicago	NHL	59	16	35	8	....	.339	....	....	....	....	....
	NHL Totals		**59**	**16**	**35**	**8**	....	**.339**	....	....	....	....	....

● **GREEN, Gary**
b: Tillsonburg, Ont., 8/23/1953.

Season	Club	League	GC	W	L	T	RT	W%	GC	W	L	T	W%
1979-80	Washington	NHL	64	23	30	11	....	.445	....	....	....	....	....
1980-81	Washington	NHL	80	26	36	18	....	.438	....	....	....	....	....
1981-82	Washington	NHL	13	1	12	0	....	.077	....	....	....	....	....
	NHL Totals		**157**	**50**	**78**	**29**	....	**.411**	....	....	....	....	....

● **GREEN, Pete**
b: unknown Deceased.

Season	Club	League	GC	W	L	T	RT	W%	GC	W	L	T	W%
♦1919-20	Ottawa	NHL	24	19	5	0	....	.792	5	3	2	0	.600
♦1920-21	Ottawa	NHL	24	14	10	0	....	.583	7	5	2	0	.714
1921-22	Ottawa	NHL	24	14	8	2	....	.625	2	0	1	1	.250
♦1922-23	Ottawa	NHL	24	14	9	1	....	.604	8	6	1	1	.813
1923-24	Ottawa	NHL	24	16	8	0	....	.667	2	0	2	0	.000
1924-25	Ottawa	NHL	30	17	12	1	....	.583	....	....	....	....	....
	NHL Totals		**150**	**94**	**52**	**4**	....	**.640**	**24**	**14**	**8**	**2**	**.625**

● **GREEN, Shorty** HHOF
b: Sudbury, Ont., 7/17/1896 d: 4/19/1960.
Played in NHL. See Pre-Expansion Player Register for career statistics.

Season	Club	League	GC	W	L	T	RT	W%	GC	W	L	T	W%
1927-28	NY Americans	NHL	44	11	27	6	....	.318	....	....	....	....	....
	NHL Totals		**44**	**11**	**27**	**6**	....	**.318**	....	....	....	....	....

● **GREEN, Ted**
b: Eriksdale, Man., 3/23/1940.
Played in NHL. See Modern Player Register for career statistics.

Season	Club	League	GC	W	L	T	RT	W%	GC	W	L	T	W%
1991-92	Edmonton	NHL	80	36	34	10	....	.513	16	8	8	0	.500
1992-93	Edmonton	NHL	84	26	50	8	....	.357	....	....	....	....	....
1993-94	Edmonton	NHL	24	3	18	3	....	.188	....	....	....	....	....
	NHL Totals		**188**	**65**	**102**	**21**	....	**.402**	**16**	**8**	**8**	**0**	**.500**

● **GUIDOLIN, Aldo**
b: Forks of Credit, Ont., 6/6/1932.
Played in NHL. See Pre-Expansion Player Register for career statistics.

Season	Club	League	GC	W	L	T	RT	W%	GC	W	L	T	W%
1978-79	Colorado	NHL	59	12	39	8	....	.271	....	....	....	....	....
	NHL Totals		**59**	**12**	**39**	**8**	....	**.271**	....	....	....	....	....

● **GUIDOLIN, Bep**
b: Thorold, Ont., 12/9/1925.
Played in NHL. See Pre-Expansion Player Register for career statistics.

Season	Club	League	GC	W	L	T	RT	W%	GC	W	L	T	W%
1972-73	Boston	NHL	26	20	6	0	....	.769	5	1	4	0	.200
1973-74	Boston	NHL	78	52	17	9	....	.724	16	10	6	0	.625
1974-75	Kansas City	NHL	80	15	54	11	....	.256	....	....	....	....	....
1975-76	Kansas City	NHL	45	11	30	4	....	.289	....	....	....	....	....
	NHL Totals		**229**	**98**	**107**	**24**	....	**.480**	**21**	**11**	**10**	**0**	**.524**

● **HARKNESS, Ned** USHOF
b: Ottawa, Ont., 9/19/1921.

Season	Club	League	GC	W	L	T	RT	W%	GC	W	L	T	W%
1970-71	Detroit	NHL	38	12	22	4	....	.368	....	....	....	....	....
	NHL Totals		**38**	**12**	**22**	**4**	....	**.368**	....	....	....	....	....

● **HARRIS, Ted**
b: Winnipeg, Man., 7/18/1936.
Played in NHL. See Modern Player Register for career statistics.

Season	Club	League	GC	W	L	T	RT	W%	GC	W	L	T	W%
1975-76	Minnesota	NHL	80	20	53	7	....	.294	....	....	....	....	....
1976-77	Minnesota	NHL	80	23	39	18	....	.400	2	0	2	0	.000
1977-78	Minnesota	NHL	19	5	12	2	....	.316	....	....	....	....	....
	NHL Totals		**179**	**48**	**104**	**27**	....	**.344**	**2**	**0**	**2**	**0**	**.000**

● **HART, Cecil**
b: 1883 d: 1940.

Season	Club	League	GC	W	L	T	RT	W%	GC	W	L	T	W%
1926-27	Montreal	NHL	44	28	14	2	....	.659	4	1	1	2	.500
1927-28	Montreal	NHL	44	26	11	7	....	.670	2	0	1	1	.250
1928-29	Montreal	NHL	44	22	7	15	....	.670	3	0	3	0	.000
♦1929-30	Montreal	NHL	44	21	14	9	....	.580	6	5	0	1	.917
♦1930-31	Montreal	NHL	44	26	10	8	....	.682	10	6	4	0	.600
1931-32	Montreal	NHL	48	25	16	7	....	.594	4	1	3	0	.250
1936-37	Montreal	NHL	48	24	18	6	....	.563	5	2	3	0	.400
1937-38	Montreal	NHL	48	18	17	13	....	.510	3	1	2	0	.333
1938-39	Montreal	NHL	30	6	18	6	....	.300	....	....	....	....	....
	NHL Totals		**394**	**196**	**125**	**73**	....	**.590**	**37**	**16**	**17**	**4**	**.486**

● **HARTLEY, Bob**
b: Hawkesbury, Ont., 9/9/1960.

Season	Club	League	GC	W	L	T	RT	W%	GC	W	L	T	W%
1998-99	Colorado	NHL	82	44	28	10	....	.598	19	11	8	0	.579
99-2000	Colorado	NHL	82	42	29	11	1	.585	17	11	6	0	.647
	NHL Totals		**164**	**86**	**57**	**21**	**1**	**.591**	**36**	**22**	**14**	**0**	**.611**

● **HARTSBURG, Craig**
b: Stratford, Ont., 6/29/1959.
Played in NHL. See Modern Player Register for career statistics.

Season	Club	League	GC	W	L	T	RT	W%	GC	W	L	T	W%
1995-96	Chicago	NHL	82	40	28	14	....	.573	10	6	4	0	.600
1996-97	Chicago	NHL	82	34	35	13	....	.494	6	2	4	0	.333
1997-98	Chicago	NHL	82	30	39	13	....	.445	....	....	....	....	....
1998-99	Anaheim	NHL	82	35	34	13	....	.506	4	0	4	0	.000
99-2000	Anaheim	NHL	82	34	36	12	3	.506	....	....	....	....	....
	NHL Totals		**410**	**173**	**172**	**65**	**3**	**.505**	**20**	**8**	**12**	**0**	**.400**

• HARVEY, Doug HHOF
b: Montreal, Que., 12/19/1924 d: 12/26/1989.
Played in NHL. See Modern Player Register for career statistics.

Season	Club	League	GC	W	L	T	RT	W%	GC	W	L	T	W%
			REGULAR SEASON						PLAYOFFS				
1961-62	NY Rangers	NHL	70	26	32	12	....	.457	6	2	4	0	.333
	NHL Totals		**70**	**26**	**32**	**12**	....	**.457**	**6**	**2**	**4**	**0**	**.333**

• HAY, Don
b: Kamloops, B.C., 2/13/1954.
Played in NHL. See Modern Player Register for career statistics.

Season	Club	League	GC	W	L	T	RT	W%	GC	W	L	T	W%
1996-97	Phoenix	NHL	82	38	37	7	....	.506	7	3	4	0	.429
	NHL Totals		**82**	**38**	**37**	**7**	....	**.506**	**7**	**3**	**4**	**0**	**.429**

• HEFFERNAN, Frank
b: Peterborough, Ont., Deceased.
Played in NHL. See Pre-Expansion Player Register for career statistics.

Season	Club	League	GC	W	L	T	RT	W%	GC	W	L	T	W%
1919-20	Toronto	NHL	12	5	7	0	....	.417	....	....	....	....	....
	NHL Totals		**12**	**5**	**7**	**0**	....	**.417**	....	....	....	....	....

• HENNING, Lorne
b: Melfort, Sask., 2/22/1952.
Played in NHL. See Modern Player Register for career statistics.

Season	Club	League	GC	W	L	T	RT	W%	GC	W	L	T	W%
1985-86	Minnesota	NHL	80	38	33	9	....	.531	5	2	3	0	.400
1986-87	Minnesota	NHL	78	30	39	9	....	.442	....	....	....	....	....
1994-95	NY Islanders	NHL	48	15	28	5	....	.365	....	....	....	....	....
	NHL Totals		**206**	**83**	**100**	**23**	....	**.459**	**5**	**2**	**3**	**0**	**.400**

• HITCHCOCK, Ken
b: Edmonton, Alta., 12/17/1951.

Season	Club	League	GC	W	L	T	RT	W%	GC	W	L	T	W%
1995-96	Dallas	NHL	43	15	23	5	....	.407	....	....	....	....	....
1996-97	Dallas	NHL	82	48	26	8	....	.634	7	3	4	0	.429
1997-98	Dallas	NHL	82	49	22	11	....	.665	17	10	7	0	.588
♦1998-99	Dallas	NHL	82	51	19	12	....	.695	23	16	7	0	.696
99-2000	Dallas	NHL	82	43	29	10	6	.622	23	14	9	0	.609
	NHL Totals		**371**	**206**	**119**	**46**	**6**	**.625**	**70**	**43**	**27**	**0**	**.614**

• HOLMGREN, Paul
b: St. Paul, MN, 12/2/1955.
Played in NHL. See Modern Player Register for career statistics.

Season	Club	League	GC	W	L	T	RT	W%	GC	W	L	T	W%
1988-89	Philadelphia	NHL	80	36	36	8	....	.500	19	10	9	0	.526
1989-90	Philadelphia	NHL	80	30	39	11	....	.444	....	....	....	....	....
1990-91	Philadelphia	NHL	80	33	37	10	....	.475	....	....	....	....	....
1991-92	Philadelphia	NHL	24	8	14	2	....	.375	....	....	....	....	....
1992-93	Hartford	NHL	84	26	52	6	....	.345	....	....	....	....	....
1993-94	Hartford	NHL	17	4	11	2	....	.294	....	....	....	....	....
1994-95	Hartford	NHL	48	19	24	5	....	.448	....	....	....	....	....
1995-96	Hartford	NHL	12	5	6	1	....	.458	....	....	....	....	....
	NHL Totals		**425**	**161**	**219**	**45**	....	**.432**	**19**	**10**	**9**	**0**	**.526**

• HOWELL, Harry HHOF
b: Hamilton, Ont., 12/28/1932.
Played in NHL. See Modern Player Register for career statistics.

Season	Club	League	GC	W	L	T	RT	W%	GC	W	L	T	W%
1978-79	Minnesota	NHL	11	3	6	2	....	.364	....	....	....	....	....
	NHL Totals		**11**	**3**	**6**	**2**	....	**.364**	....	....	....	....	....

• IMLACH, Punch HHOF
b: Toronto, Ont., 3/15/1918 d: 12/1/1987.

Season	Club	League	GC	W	L	T	RT	W%	GC	W	L	T	W%
1958-59	Toronto	NHL	50	22	20	8	....	.520	12	5	7	0	.417
1959-60	Toronto	NHL	70	35	26	9	....	.564	10	4	6	0	.400
1960-61	Toronto	NHL	70	39	19	12	....	.643	5	1	4	0	.200
♦1961-62	Toronto	NHL	70	37	22	11	....	.607	12	8	4	0	.667
♦1962-63	Toronto	NHL	70	35	23	12	....	.586	14	8	6	0	.571
♦1963-64	Toronto	NHL	70	33	25	12	....	.557	10	8	2	0	.800
1964-65	Toronto	NHL	70	30	26	14	....	.529	6	2	4	0	.333
1965-66	Toronto	NHL	70	34	25	11	....	.564	4	0	4	0	.000
♦1966-67	Toronto	NHL	70	32	27	11	....	.536	12	8	4	0	.667
1967-68	Toronto	NHL	74	33	31	10	....	.514	....	....	....	....	....
1968-69	Toronto	NHL	76	35	26	15	....	.559	4	0	4	0	.000
1970-71	Buffalo	NHL	78	24	39	15	....	.404	....	....	....	....	....
1971-72	Buffalo	NHL	41	8	23	10	....	.317	....	....	....	....	....
1979-80	Toronto	NHL	10	5	5	0	....	.500	3	0	3	0	.000
	NHL Totals		**889**	**402**	**337**	**150**	....	**.537**	**92**	**44**	**48**	**0**	**.478**

Assistant general manager King Clancy posted a 7-1-2 record as replacement coach when Punch Imlach was sidelined with heart problems, February 18 to March 11, 1967. All games are credited to Imlach's coaching record.

• INGARFIELD, Earl
b: Lethbridge, Alta., 10/25/1934.
Played in NHL. See Modern Player Register for career statistics.

Season	Club	League	GC	W	L	T	RT	W%	GC	W	L	T	W%
1972-73	NY Islanders	NHL	30	6	22	2	....	.233	....	....	....	....	....
	NHL Totals		**30**	**6**	**22**	**2**	....	**.233**	....	....	....	....	....

• INGLIS, Bill
b: Ottawa, Ont., 5/11/1943.
Played in NHL. See Modern Player Register for career statistics.

Season	Club	League	GC	W	L	T	RT	W%	GC	W	L	T	W%
1978-79	Buffalo	NHL	56	28	18	10	....	.589	3	1	2	0	.333
	NHL Totals		**56**	**28**	**18**	**10**	....	**.589**	**3**	**1**	**2**	**0**	**.333**

• IRVIN, Dick HHOF
b: Hamilton, Ont., 7/19/1892 d: 3/16/1957.
Played in NHL. See Pre-Expansion Player Register for career statistics.

Season	Club	League	GC	W	L	T	RT	W%	GC	W	L	T	W%
1928-29	Chicago	NHL	12	2	6	4	....	.333	....	....	....	....	....
1930-31	Chicago	NHL	44	24	17	3	....	.580	9	5	3	1	.611
♦1931-32	Toronto	NHL	43	23	15	5	....	.593	7	5	1	1	.786
1932-33	Toronto	NHL	48	24	18	6	....	.563	9	4	5	0	.444
1933-34	Toronto	NHL	48	26	13	9	....	.635	5	2	3	0	.400
1934-35	Toronto	NHL	48	30	14	4	....	.667	7	3	4	0	.429
1935-36	Toronto	NHL	48	23	19	6	....	.542	9	4	5	0	.444
1936-37	Toronto	NHL	48	22	21	5	....	.510	2	0	2	0	.000
1937-38	Toronto	NHL	48	24	15	9	....	.594	7	4	3	0	.571
1938-39	Toronto	NHL	48	19	20	9	....	.490	10	5	5	0	.500
1939-40	Toronto	NHL	48	25	17	6	....	.583	10	6	4	0	.600
1940-41	Montreal	NHL	48	16	26	6	....	.396	3	1	2	0	.333
1941-42	Montreal	NHL	48	18	27	3	....	.406	3	1	2	0	.333
1942-43	Montreal	NHL	50	19	19	12	....	.500	5	1	4	0	.200
♦1943-44	Montreal	NHL	50	38	5	7	....	.830	9	8	1	0	.889
1944-45	Montreal	NHL	50	38	8	4	....	.800	6	2	4	0	.333
♦1945-46	Montreal	NHL	50	28	17	5	....	.610	9	8	1	0	.889
1946-47	Montreal	NHL	60	34	16	10	....	.650	11	6	5	0	.545
1947-48	Montreal	NHL	60	20	29	11	....	.425	....	....	....	....	....
1948-49	Montreal	NHL	60	28	23	9	....	.542	7	3	4	0	.429
1949-50	Montreal	NHL	70	29	22	19	....	.550	5	1	4	0	.200
1950-51	Montreal	NHL	70	25	30	15	....	.464	11	5	6	0	.455
1951-52	Montreal	NHL	70	34	26	10	....	.557	11	4	7	0	.364
♦1952-53	Montreal	NHL	70	28	23	19	....	.536	12	8	4	0	.667
1953-54	Montreal	NHL	70	35	24	11	....	.579	11	7	4	0	.636
1954-55	Montreal	NHL	70	41	18	11	....	.664	12	7	5	0	.583
1955-56	Chicago	NHL	70	19	39	12	....	.357	....	....	....	....	....
	NHL Totals		**1449**	**692**	**527**	**230**	....	**.557**	**190**	**100**	**88**	**2**	**.532**

• IVAN, Tommy HHOF
b: Toronto, Ont., 1/31/1911 d: 6/25/1999.

Season	Club	League	GC	W	L	T	RT	W%	GC	W	L	T	W%
1947-48	Detroit	NHL	60	30	18	12	....	.600	10	4	6	0	.400
1948-49	Detroit	NHL	60	34	19	7	....	.625	11	4	7	0	.364
♦1949-50	Detroit	NHL	70	37	19	14	....	.629	14	8	6	0	.571
1950-51	Detroit	NHL	70	44	13	13	....	.721	6	2	4	0	.333
♦1951-52	Detroit	NHL	70	44	14	12	....	.714	8	8	0	0	1.000
1952-53	Detroit	NHL	70	36	16	18	....	.643	6	2	4	0	.333
♦1953-54	Detroit	NHL	70	37	19	14	....	.629	12	8	4	0	.667
1956-57	Chicago	NHL	70	16	39	15	....	.336	....	....	....	....	....
1957-58	Chicago	NHL	33	10	17	6	....	.394	....	....	....	....	....
	NHL Totals		**573**	**288**	**174**	**111**	....	**.599**	**67**	**36**	**31**	**0**	**.537**

• IVERSON, Emil
b: unknown Deceased.

Season	Club	League	GC	W	L	T	RT	W%	GC	W	L	T	W%
1932-33	Chicago	NHL	21	8	7	6	....	.524	....	....	....	....	....
	NHL Totals		**21**	**8**	**7**	**6**	....	**.524**	....	....	....	....	....

• JOHNSON, Bob USHOF HHOF
b: Farmington, MI, 11/12/1948 d: 11/26/1991.

Season	Club	League	GC	W	L	T	RT	W%	GC	W	L	T	W%
1982-83	Calgary	NHL	80	32	34	14	....	.488	9	4	5	0	.444
1983-84	Calgary	NHL	80	34	32	14	....	.513	11	6	5	0	.545
1984-85	Calgary	NHL	80	41	27	12	....	.588	4	1	3	0	.250
1985-86	Calgary	NHL	80	40	31	9	....	.556	22	12	10	0	.545
1986-87	Calgary	NHL	80	46	31	3	....	.594	6	2	4	0	.333
♦1990-91	Pittsburgh	NHL	80	41	33	6	....	.550	24	16	8	0	.667
	NHL Totals		**480**	**234**	**188**	**58**	....	**.548**	**76**	**41**	**35**	**0**	**.539**

• JOHNSON, Tom HHOF
b: Baldur, Man., 2/18/1928.
Played in NHL. See Pre-Expansion Player Register for career statistics.

Season	Club	League	GC	W	L	T	RT	W%	GC	W	L	T	W%
1970-71	Boston	NHL	78	57	14	7	....	.776	7	3	4	0	.429
♦1971-72	Boston	NHL	78	54	13	11	....	.763	15	12	3	0	.800
1972-73	Boston	NHL	52	31	16	5	....	.644	....	....	....	....	....
	NHL Totals		**208**	**142**	**43**	**23**	....	**.738**	**22**	**15**	**7**	**0**	**.682**

• JOHNSTON, Eddie
b: Montreal, Que., 11/24/1935.
Played in NHL. See Goaltender Register for career statistics.

Season	Club	League	GC	W	L	T	RT	W%	GC	W	L	T	W%
1979-80	Chicago	NHL	80	34	27	19	....	.544	7	3	4	0	.429
1980-81	Pittsburgh	NHL	80	30	37	13	....	.456	5	2	3	0	.400
1981-82	Pittsburgh	NHL	80	31	36	13	....	.469	5	2	3	0	.400
1982-83	Pittsburgh	NHL	80	18	53	9	....	.281	....	....	....	....	....
1993-94	Pittsburgh	NHL	84	44	27	13	....	.601	6	2	4	0	.333
1994-95	Pittsburgh	NHL	48	29	16	3	....	.635	12	5	7	0	.417
1995-96	Pittsburgh	NHL	82	49	29	4	....	.622	18	11	7	0	.611
1996-97	Pittsburgh	NHL	62	31	26	5	....	.540	....	....	....	....	....
	NHL Totals		**596**	**266**	**251**	**79**	....	**.513**	**53**	**25**	**28**	**0**	**.472**

• JOHNSTON, Marshall
b: Birch Hills, Sask., 6/6/1941.
Played in NHL. See Modern Player Register for career statistics.

Season	Club	League	GC	W	L	T	RT	W%	GC	W	L	T	W%
1973-74	California	NHL	21	2	17	2	....	.143	....	....	....	....	....
1974-75	California	NHL	48	11	28	9	....	.323	....	....	....	....	....
1981-82	Colorado	NHL	56	15	32	9	....	.348	....	....	....	....	....
	NHL Totals		**125**	**28**	**77**	**20**	....	**.304**	....	....	....	....	....

• KASPER, Steve
b: Montreal, Que., 9/28/1961.
Played in NHL. See Modern Player Register for career statistics.

Season	Club	League	GC	W	L	T	RT	W%	GC	W	L	T	W%
1995-96	Boston	NHL	82	40	31	11	....	.555	5	1	4	0	.200
1996-97	Boston	NHL	82	26	47	9	....	.372	....	....	....	....	....
	NHL Totals		**164**	**66**	**78**	**20**	....	**.463**	**5**	**1**	**4**	**0**	**.200**

• KEATS, Duke HHOF

b: Montreal, Que., 3/1/1895 d: 1/16/1971.
Played in NHL. See Pre-Expansion Player Register for career statistics.

Season	Club	League	GC	W	L	T	RT	W%	GC	W	L	T	W%
			REGULAR SEASON						PLAYOFFS				
1926-27	Detroit	NHL	11	2	7	2	....	.273	....	....	....	....	....
	NHL Totals		**11**	**2**	**7**	**2**	....	**.273**	....	....	....	....	....

• KEENAN, Mike

b: Toronto, Ont., 10/21/1949.

Season	Club	League	GC	W	L	T	RT	W%	GC	W	L	T	W%
1984-85	Philadelphia	NHL	80	53	20	7	....	.706	19	12	7	0	.632
1985-86	Philadelphia	NHL	80	53	23	4	....	.688	5	2	3	0	.400
1986-87	Philadelphia	NHL	80	46	26	8	....	.625	26	15	11	0	.577
1987-88	Philadelphia	NHL	80	38	33	9	....	.531	7	3	4	0	.429
1988-89	Chicago	NHL	80	27	41	12	....	.413	16	9	7	0	.563
1989-90	Chicago	NHL	80	41	33	6	....	.550	20	10	10	0	.500
1990-91	Chicago	NHL	80	49	23	8	....	.663	6	2	4	0	.333
1991-92	Chicago	NHL	80	36	29	15	....	.544	18	12	6	0	.667
♦1993-94	NY Rangers	NHL	84	52	24	8	....	.667	23	16	7	0	.696
1994-95	St. Louis	NHL	48	28	15	5	....	.635	7	3	4	0	.429
1995-96	St. Louis	NHL	82	32	34	16	....	.488	13	7	6	0	.538
1996-97	St. Louis	NHL	33	15	17	1	....	.470	....	....	....	....	....
1997-98	Vancouver	NHL	63	21	30	12	....	.429	....	....	....	....	....
1998-99	Vancouver	NHL	45	15	24	6	....	.400	....	....	....	....	....
	NHL Totals		**995**	**506**	**372**	**117**	....	**.567**	**160**	**91**	**69**	**0**	**.569**

• Won Jack Adams Award (1985)

• KELLY, Pat

b: Sioux Lookout, Ont., 9/8/1935.

Season	Club	League	GC	W	L	T	RT	W%	GC	W	L	T	W%
1977-78	Colorado	NHL	80	19	40	21	....	.369	2	0	2	0	.000
1978-79	Colorado	NHL	21	3	14	4	....	.238	....	....	....	....	....
	NHL Totals		**101**	**22**	**54**	**25**	....	**.342**	**2**	**0**	**2**	**0**	**.000**

• KELLY, Red HHOF

b: Simcoe, Ont., 7/9/1927.
Played in NHL. See Pre-Expansion Player Register for career statistics.

Season	Club	League	GC	W	L	T	RT	W%	GC	W	L	T	W%
1967-68	Los Angeles	NHL	74	31	33	10	....	.486	7	3	4	0	.429
1968-69	Los Angeles	NHL	76	24	42	10	....	.382	11	4	7	0	.364
1969-70	Pittsburgh	NHL	76	26	38	12	....	.421	10	6	4	0	.600
1970-71	Pittsburgh	NHL	78	21	37	20	....	.397	....	....	....	....	....
1971-72	Pittsburgh	NHL	78	26	38	14	....	.423	4	0	4	0	.000
1972-73	Pittsburgh	NHL	42	17	19	6	....	.476	....	....	....	....	....
1973-74	Toronto	NHL	78	35	27	16	....	.551	4	0	4	0	.000
1974-75	Toronto	NHL	80	31	33	16	....	.488	7	2	5	0	.286
1975-76	Toronto	NHL	80	34	31	15	....	.519	10	5	5	0	.500
1976-77	Toronto	NHL	80	33	32	15	....	.506	9	4	5	0	.444
	NHL Totals		**742**	**278**	**330**	**134**	....	**.465**	**62**	**24**	**38**	**0**	**.387**

• KING, Dave

b: Saskatoon, Sask., 12/22/1947.

Season	Club	League	GC	W	L	T	RT	W%	GC	W	L	T	W%
1992-93	Calgary	NHL	84	43	30	11	....	.577	6	2	4	0	.333
1993-94	Calgary	NHL	84	42	29	13	....	.577	7	3	4	0	.429
1994-95	Calgary	NHL	48	24	17	7	....	.573	7	3	4	0	.429
	NHL Totals		**216**	**109**	**76**	**31**	....	**.576**	**20**	**8**	**12**	**0**	**.400**

• KINGSTON, George

b: Biggar, Sask., 8/20/1939.

Season	Club	League	GC	W	L	T	RT	W%	GC	W	L	T	W%
1991-92	San Jose	NHL	80	17	58	5	....	.244	....	....	....	....	....
1992-93	San Jose	NHL	84	11	71	2	....	.143	....	....	....	....	....
	NHL Totals		**164**	**28**	**129**	**7**	....	**.192**	....	....	....	....	....

• KISH, Larry

b: Welland, Ont., 12/11/1941.

Season	Club	League	GC	W	L	T	RT	W%	GC	W	L	T	W%
1982-83	Hartford	NHL	49	12	32	5	....	.296	....	....	....	....	....
	NHL Totals		**49**	**12**	**32**	**5**	....	**.296**	....	....	....	....	....

• KROMM, Bobby

b: Calgary, Alta., 6/8/1928.

Season	Club	League	GC	W	L	T	RT	W%	GC	W	L	T	W%
1977-78	Detroit	NHL	80	32	34	14	....	.488	7	3	4	0	.429
1978-79	Detroit	NHL	80	23	41	16	....	.388	....	....	....	....	....
1979-80	Detroit	NHL	71	24	36	11	....	.415	....	....	....	....	....
	NHL Totals		**231**	**79**	**111**	**41**	....	**.431**	**7**	**3**	**4**	**0**	**.429**

• Won Jack Adams Award (1978)

• KURTENBACH, Orland

b: Cudworth, Sask., 9/7/1936.
Played in NHL. See Modern Player Register for career statistics.

Season	Club	League	GC	W	L	T	RT	W%	GC	W	L	T	W%
1976-77	Vancouver	NHL	45	16	19	10	....	.467	....	....	....	....	....
1977-78	Vancouver	NHL	80	20	43	17	....	.356	....	....	....	....	....
	NHL Totals		**125**	**36**	**62**	**27**	....	**.396**	....	....	....	....	....

• LAFORGE, Bill

b: Edmonton, Alta., 9/2/1951.

Season	Club	League	GC	W	L	T	RT	W%	GC	W	L	T	W%
1984-85	Vancouver	NHL	20	4	14	2	....	.250	....	....	....	....	....
	NHL Totals		**20**	**4**	**14**	**2**	....	**.250**	....	....	....	....	....

• LALONDE, Newsy HHOF

b: Cornwall, Ont., 10/31/1888 d: 11/21/1971.
Played in NHL. See Pre-Expansion Player Register for career statistics.

Season	Club	League	GC	W	L	T	RT	W%	GC	W	L	T	W%
1917-18	Montreal	NHL	22	13	9	0	....	.591	2	1	1	0	.500
1918-19	Montreal	NHL	18	10	8	0	....	.556	10	6	3	1	.650
1919-20	Montreal	NHL	24	13	11	0	....	.542	....	....	....	....	....
1920-21	Montreal	NHL	24	13	11	0	....	.542	....	....	....	....	....
1921-22	Montreal	NHL	7	2	5	0	....	.286	....	....	....	....	....
1926-27	NY Americans	NHL	44	17	25	2	....	.409	....	....	....	....	....
1929-30	Ottawa	NHL	44	21	15	8	....	.568	2	0	1	1	.250
1930-31	Ottawa	NHL	44	10	30	4	....	.273	....	....	....	....	....
1932-33	Montreal	NHL	48	18	25	5	....	.427	2	0	1	1	.250
1933-34	Montreal	NHL	48	22	20	6	....	.521	2	0	1	1	.250
1934-35	Montreal	NHL	16	5	8	3	....	.406	....	....	....	....	....
	NHL Totals		**339**	**144**	**167**	**28**	....	**.466**	**18**	**7**	**7**	**4**	**.500**

• LAPOINTE, Ron

b: Verdun, Que., 11/12/1949.

Season	Club	League	GC	W	L	T	RT	W%	GC	W	L	T	W%
1987-88	Quebec	NHL	56	22	30	4	....	.429	....	....	....	....	....
1988-89	Quebec	NHL	33	11	20	2	....	.364	....	....	....	....	....
	NHL Totals		**89**	**33**	**50**	**6**	....	**.404**	....	....	....	....	....

• LAYCOE, Hal

b: Sutherland, Sask., 6/23/1922 d: 4/29/1997.
Played in NHL. See Pre-Expansion Player Register for career statistics.

Season	Club	League	GC	W	L	T	RT	W%	GC	W	L	T	W%
1969-70	Los Angeles	NHL	24	5	18	1	....	.229	....	....	....	....	....
1970-71	Vancouver	NHL	78	24	46	8	....	.359	....	....	....	....	....
1971-72	Vancouver	NHL	78	20	50	8	....	.308	....	....	....	....	....
	NHL Totals		**180**	**49**	**114**	**17**	....	**.319**	....	....	....	....	....

• LEHMAN, Hugh HHOF

b: Pembroke, Ont., 10/27/1885 d: 4/8/1961.
Played in NHL. See Goaltender Register for career statistics.

Season	Club	League	GC	W	L	T	RT	W%	GC	W	L	T	W%
1927-28	Chicago	NHL	21	3	17	1	....	.167	....	....	....	....	....
	NHL Totals		**21**	**3**	**17**	**1**	....	**.167**	....	....	....	....	....

• LEMAIRE, Jacques HHOF

b: LaSalle, Que., 9/7/1945.
Played in NHL. See Modern Player Register for career statistics.

Season	Club	League	GC	W	L	T	RT	W%	GC	W	L	T	W%
1983-84	Montreal	NHL	17	7	10	0	....	.412	15	9	6	0	.600
1984-85	Montreal	NHL	80	41	27	12	....	.588	12	6	6	0	.500
1993-94	New Jersey	NHL	84	47	25	12	....	.631	20	11	9	0	.550
♦1994-95	New Jersey	NHL	48	22	18	8	....	.542	20	16	4	0	.800
1995-96	New Jersey	NHL	82	37	33	12	....	.524	....	....	....	....	....
1996-97	New Jersey	NHL	82	45	23	14	....	.634	10	5	5	0	.500
1997-98	New Jersey	NHL	82	48	23	11	....	.652	6	2	4	0	.333
	NHL Totals		**475**	**247**	**159**	**69**	....	**.593**	**83**	**49**	**34**	**0**	**.590**

• LEPINE, Pit

b: St. Anne de Bellevue, Que., 7/30/1901 d: 8/2/1955.
Played in NHL. See Pre-Expansion Player Register for career statistics.

Season	Club	League	GC	W	L	T	RT	W%	GC	W	L	T	W%
1939-40	Montreal	NHL	48	10	33	5	....	.260	....	....	....	....	....
	NHL Totals		**48**	**10**	**33**	**5**	....	**.260**	....	....	....	....	....

• LeSUEUR, Percy HHOF

b: Quebec City, Que., 11/18/1881 d: 1/27/1962.

Season	Club	League	GC	W	L	T	RT	W%	GC	W	L	T	W%
1923-24	Hamilton	NHL	10	3	7	0	....	.300	....	....	....	....	....
	NHL Totals		**10**	**3**	**7**	**0**	....	**.300**	....	....	....	....	....

• LEWIS, Dave

b: Kindersley, Sask., 7/3/1953.
Played in NHL. See Modern Player Register for career statistics.

Season	Club	League	GC	W	L	T	RT	W%	GC	W	L	T	W%
1998-99	Detroit	NHL	5	4	1	0	....	.800	....	....	....	....	....
	NHL Totals		**5**	**4**	**1**	**0**	....	**.800**	....	....	....	....	....

Shared a 4-1-0 record with associate coach Barry Smith while serving as co-head coaches until Scotty Bowman received medical clearance and decided to return to coaching on October 23, 1998.

• LEY, Rick

b: Orillia, Ont., 11/2/1948.
Played in NHL. See Modern Player Register for career statistics.

Season	Club	League	GC	W	L	T	RT	W%	GC	W	L	T	W%
1989-90	Hartford	NHL	80	38	33	9	....	.531	7	3	4	0	.429
1990-91	Hartford	NHL	80	31	38	11	....	.456	6	2	4	0	.333
1994-95	Vancouver	NHL	48	18	18	12	....	.500	11	4	7	0	.364
1995-96	Vancouver	NHL	76	29	32	15	....	.480	....	....	....	....	....
	NHL Totals		**284**	**116**	**121**	**47**	....	**.491**	**24**	**9**	**15**	**0**	**.375**

• LINDSAY, Ted HHOF

b: Renfrew, Ont., 7/29/1925.
Played in NHL. See Pre-Expansion Player Register for career statistics.

Season	Club	League	GC	W	L	T	RT	W%	GC	W	L	T	W%
1979-80	Detroit	NHL	9	2	7	0	....	.222	....	....	....	....	....
1980-81	Detroit	NHL	20	3	14	3	....	.225	....	....	....	....	....
	NHL Totals		**29**	**5**	**21**	**3**	....	**.224**	....	....	....	....	....

• LONG, Barry

b: Brantford, Ont., 1/3/1949.
Played in NHL. See Modern Player Register for career statistics.

Season	Club	League	GC	W	L	T	RT	W%	GC	W	L	T	W%
1983-84	Winnipeg	NHL	59	25	25	9	....	.500	3	0	3	0	.000
1984-85	Winnipeg	NHL	80	43	27	10	....	.600	8	3	5	0	.375
1985-86	Winnipeg	NHL	66	19	41	6	....	.333	....	....	....	....	....
	NHL Totals		**205**	**87**	**93**	**25**	....	**.485**	**11**	**3**	**8**	**0**	**.273**

• LOUGHLIN, Clem

b: Carroll, Man., 11/15/1894 Deceased.
Played in NHL. See Pre-Expansion Player Register for career statistics.

Season	Club	League	GC	W	L	T	RT	W%	GC	W	L	T	W%
			REGULAR SEASON						PLAYOFFS				
1934-35	Chicago	NHL	48	26	17	5	....	.594	2	0	1	1	.250
1935-36	Chicago	NHL	48	21	19	8	....	.521	2	1	1	0	.500
1936-37	Chicago	NHL	48	14	27	7	....	.365	....	....	....	....	....
	NHL Totals		**144**	**61**	**63**	**20**	....	**.493**	**4**	**1**	**2**	**1**	**.375**

• LOW, Ron

b: Birtle, Man., 6/21/1950.
Played in NHL. See Goaltender Register for career statistics.

Season	Club	League	GC	W	L	T	RT	W%	GC	W	L	T	W%
1994-95	Edmonton	NHL	13	5	7	1	....	.423	....	....	....	....	....
1995-96	Edmonton	NHL	82	30	44	8	....	.415	....	....	....	....	....
1996-97	Edmonton	NHL	82	36	37	9	....	.494	12	5	7	0	.417
1997-98	Edmonton	NHL	82	35	37	10	....	.488	12	5	7	0	.417
1998-99	Edmonton	NHL	82	33	37	12	....	.476	4	0	4	0	.000
	NHL Totals		**341**	**139**	**162**	**40**	....	**.466**	**28**	**10**	**18**	**0**	**.357**

• LOWE, Kevin

b: Lachute, Que., 4/15/1959.
Played in NHL. See Modern Player Register for career statistics.

Season	Club	League	GC	W	L	T	RT	W%	GC	W	L	T	W%
99-2000	Edmonton	NHL	82	32	34	16	8	.537	5	1	4	0	.200
	NHL Totals		**82**	**32**	**34**	**16**	**8**	**.537**	**5**	**1**	**4**	**0**	**.200**

• LUDZIK, Steve

b: Toronto, Ont., 4/3/1962.
Played in NHL. See Modern Player Register for career statistics.

Season	Club	League	GC	W	L	T	RT	W%	GC	W	L	T	W%
99-2000	Tampa Bay	NHL	82	19	54	9	7	.329	....	....	....	....	....
	NHL Totals		**82**	**19**	**54**	**9**	**7**	**.329**	....	....	....	....	....

• MacDONALD, Parker

b: Sydney, N.S., 6/14/1933.
Played in NHL. See Modern Player Register for career statistics.

Season	Club	League	GC	W	L	T	RT	W%	GC	W	L	T	W%
1973-74	Minnesota	NHL	61	20	30	11	....	.418	....	....	....	....	....
1981-82	Los Angeles	NHL	42	13	24	5	....	.369	....	....	....	....	....
	NHL Totals		**103**	**33**	**54**	**16**	....	**.398**	....	....	....	....	....

• MacLEAN, Doug

b: Summerside, PEI, 4/12/1954.

Season	Club	League	GC	W	L	T	RT	W%	GC	W	L	T	W%
1995-96	Florida	NHL	82	41	31	10	....	.561	22	12	10	0	.545
1996-97	Florida	NHL	82	35	28	19	....	.543	5	1	4	0	.200
1997-98	Florida	NHL	23	7	12	4	....	.391	....	....	....	....	....
	NHL Totals		**187**	**83**	**71**	**33**	....	**.532**	**27**	**13**	**14**	**0**	**.481**

• MacMILLAN, Bill

b: Charlottetown, P.E.I., 3/7/1943.
Played in NHL. See Modern Player Register for career statistics.

Season	Club	League	GC	W	L	T	RT	W%	GC	W	L	T	W%
1980-81	Colorado	NHL	80	22	45	13	....	.356	....	....	....	....	....
1982-83	New Jersey	NHL	80	17	49	14	....	.300	....	....	....	....	....
1983-84	New Jersey	NHL	20	2	18	0	....	.100	....	....	....	....	....
	NHL Totals		**180**	**41**	**112**	**27**	....	**.303**	....	....	....	....	....

• MacNEIL, Al

b: Sydney, N.S., 9/27/1935.
Played in NHL. See Modern Player Register for career statistics.

Season	Club	League	GC	W	L	T	RT	W%	GC	W	L	T	W%
♦1970-71	Montreal	NHL	55	31	15	9	....	.645	20	12	8	0	.600
1979-80	Atlanta	NHL	80	35	32	13	....	.519	4	1	3	0	.250
1980-81	Calgary	NHL	80	39	27	14	....	.575	16	9	7	0	.563
1981-82	Calgary	NHL	80	29	34	17	....	.469	3	0	3	0	.000
	NHL Totals		**295**	**134**	**108**	**53**	....	**.544**	**43**	**22**	**21**	**0**	**.512**

• MAGNUSON, Keith

b: Saskatoon, Sask., 4/27/1947.
Played in NHL. See Modern Player Register for career statistics.

Season	Club	League	GC	W	L	T	RT	W%	GC	W	L	T	W%
1980-81	Chicago	NHL	80	31	33	16	....	.488	3	0	3	0	.000
1981-82	Chicago	NHL	52	18	24	10	....	.442	....	....	....	....	....
	NHL Totals		**132**	**49**	**57**	**26**	....	**.470**	**3**	**0**	**3**	**0**	**.000**

• MAHONEY, Bill

b: Peterborough, Ont., 6/23/1939.

Season	Club	League	GC	W	L	T	RT	W%	GC	W	L	T	W%
1983-84	Minnesota	NHL	80	39	31	10	....	.550	16	7	9	0	.438
1984-85	Minnesota	NHL	13	3	8	2	....	.308	....	....	....	....	....
	NHL Totals		**93**	**42**	**39**	**12**	....	**.516**	**16**	**7**	**9**	**0**	**.438**

• MALONEY, Dan

b: Barrie, Ont., 9/24/1950.
Played in NHL. See Modern Player Register for career statistics.

Season	Club	League	GC	W	L	T	RT	W%	GC	W	L	T	W%
1984-85	Toronto	NHL	80	20	52	8	....	.300	....	....	....	....	....
1985-86	Toronto	NHL	80	25	48	7	....	.356	10	6	4	0	.600
1986-87	Winnipeg	NHL	80	40	32	8	....	.550	10	4	6	0	.400
1987-88	Winnipeg	NHL	80	33	36	11	....	.481	5	1	4	0	.200
1988-89	Winnipeg	NHL	52	18	25	9	....	.433	....	....	....	....	....
	NHL Totals		**372**	**136**	**193**	**43**	....	**.423**	**25**	**11**	**14**	**0**	**.440**

• MALONEY, Phil

b: Ottawa, Ont., 10/6/1927.
Played in NHL. See Pre-Expansion Player Register for career statistics.

Season	Club	League	GC	W	L	T	RT	W%	GC	W	L	T	W%
1973-74	Vancouver	NHL	37	15	18	4	....	.459	....	....	....	....	....
1974-75	Vancouver	NHL	80	38	32	10	....	.538	5	1	4	0	.200
1975-76	Vancouver	NHL	80	33	32	15	....	.506	2	0	2	0	.000
1976-77	Vancouver	NHL	35	9	23	3	....	.300	....	....	....	....	....
	NHL Totals		**232**	**95**	**105**	**32**	....	**.478**	**7**	**1**	**6**	**0**	**.143**

• MANTHA, Sylvio HHOF

b: Montreal, Que., 4/14/1902 d: 8/7/1974.
Played in NHL. See Pre-Expansion Player Register for career statistics.

Season	Club	League	GC	W	L	T	RT	W%	GC	W	L	T	W%
1935-36	Montreal	NHL	48	11	26	11	....	.344	....	....	....	....	....
	NHL Totals		**48**	**11**	**26**	**11**	....	**.344**	....	....	....	....	....

• MARSHALL, Bert

b: Kamloops, B.C., 11/22/1943.
Played in NHL. See Modern Player Register for career statistics.

Season	Club	League	GC	W	L	T	RT	W%	GC	W	L	T	W%
1981-82	Colorado	NHL	24	3	17	4	....	.208	....	....	....	....	....
	NHL Totals		**24**	**3**	**17**	**4**	....	**.208**	....	....	....	....	....

• MARTIN, Jacques

b: St. Pascal, Ont., 10/1/1952.

Season	Club	League	GC	W	L	T	RT	W%	GC	W	L	T	W%
1986-87	St. Louis	NHL	80	32	33	15	....	.494	6	2	4	0	.333
1987-88	St. Louis	NHL	80	34	38	8	....	.475	10	5	5	0	.500
1995-96	Ottawa	NHL	38	10	24	4	....	.316	....	....	....	....	....
1996-97	Ottawa	NHL	82	31	36	15	....	.470	7	3	4	0	.429
1997-98	Ottawa	NHL	82	34	33	15	....	.506	11	5	6	0	.455
1998-99	Ottawa	NHL	82	44	23	15	....	.628	4	0	4	0	.000
99-2000	Ottawa	NHL	82	41	30	11	2	.579	6	2	4	0	.333
	NHL Totals		**526**	**226**	**217**	**83**	**2**	**.510**	**44**	**17**	**27**	**0**	**.386**

• Won Jack Adams Award (1999)

• MATHESON, Godfrey

b: unknown.

Season	Club	League	GC	W	L	T	RT	W%	GC	W	L	T	W%
1932-33	Chicago	NHL	2	0	2	0	....	.000	....	....	....	....	....
	NHL Totals		**2**	**0**	**2**	**0**	....	**.000**	....	....	....	....	....

• MAURICE, Paul

b: Sault Ste. Marie, Ont., 1/30/1967.

Season	Club	League	GC	W	L	T	RT	W%	GC	W	L	T	W%
1995-96	Hartford	NHL	70	29	33	8	....	.471	....	....	....	....	....
1996-97	Hartford	NHL	82	32	39	11	....	.457	....	....	....	....	....
1997-98	Carolina	NHL	82	33	41	8	....	.451	....	....	....	....	....
1998-99	Carolina	NHL	82	34	30	18	....	.524	6	2	4	0	.333
99-2000	Carolina	NHL	82	37	35	10	0	.512	....	....	....	....	....
	NHL Totals		**398**	**165**	**178**	**55**	**0**	**.484**	**6**	**2**	**4**	**0**	**.333**

• MAXNER, Wayne

b: Halifax, N.S., 9/27/1942.
Played in NHL. See Pre-Expansion Player Register for career statistics.

Season	Club	League	GC	W	L	T	RT	W%	GC	W	L	T	W%
1980-81	Detroit	NHL	60	16	29	15	....	.392	....	....	....	....	....
1981-82	Detroit	NHL	69	18	39	12	....	.348	....	....	....	....	....
	NHL Totals		**129**	**34**	**68**	**27**	....	**.368**	....	....	....	....	....

• McCAMMON, Bob

b: Kenora, Ont., 4/14/1941.

Season	Club	League	GC	W	L	T	RT	W%	GC	W	L	T	W%
1978-79	Philadelphia	NHL	50	22	17	11	....	.550	....	....	....	....	....
1981-82	Philadelphia	NHL	8	4	2	2	....	.625	4	1	3	0	.250
1982-83	Philadelphia	NHL	80	49	23	8	....	.663	3	0	3	0	.000
1983-84	Philadelphia	NHL	80	44	26	10	....	.613	3	0	3	0	.000
1987-88	Vancouver	NHL	80	25	46	9	....	.369	....	....	....	....	....
1988-89	Vancouver	NHL	80	33	39	8	....	.463	7	3	4	0	.429
1989-90	Vancouver	NHL	80	25	41	14	....	.400	....	....	....	....	....
1990-91	Vancouver	NHL	54	19	30	5	....	.398	....	....	....	....	....
	NHL Totals		**512**	**221**	**224**	**67**	....	**.497**	**17**	**4**	**13**	**0**	**.235**

• McCREARY, Bill

b: Sundridge, Ont., 12/2/1934.
Played in NHL. See Modern Player Register for career statistics.

Season	Club	League	GC	W	L	T	RT	W%	GC	W	L	T	W%
1971-72	St. Louis	NHL	24	6	14	4	....	.333	....	....	....	....	....
1973-74	Vancouver	NHL	41	9	25	7	....	.305	....	....	....	....	....
1974-75	California	NHL	32	8	20	4	....	.313	....	....	....	....	....
	NHL Totals		**97**	**23**	**59**	**15**	....	**.314**	....	....	....	....	....

• McGUIRE, Pierre

b: unknown.

Season	Club	League	GC	W	L	T	RT	W%	GC	W	L	T	W%
1993-94	Hartford	NHL	67	23	37	7	....	.396	....	....	....	....	....
	NHL Totals		**67**	**23**	**37**	**7**	....	**.396**	....	....	....	....	....

• McLELLAN, John

b: South Porcupine, Ont., 8/6/1928 d: 10/27/1979.
Played in NHL. See Pre-Expansion Player Register for career statistics.

Season	Club	League	GC	W	L	T	RT	W%	GC	W	L	T	W%
1969-70	Toronto	NHL	76	29	34	13	....	.467	....	....	....	....	....
1970-71	Toronto	NHL	78	37	33	8	....	.526	6	2	4	0	.333
1971-72	Toronto	NHL	78	33	31	14	....	.513	5	1	4	0	.200
1972-73	Toronto	NHL	78	27	41	10	....	.410	....	....	....	....	....
	NHL Totals		**310**	**126**	**139**	**45**	....	**.479**	**11**	**3**	**8**	**0**	**.273**

Assistant general manager King Clancy posted a 6-2-3 record as replacement coach when John McLellan was sidelined with a duodenal ulcer, February 23 to March 22, 1972. King Clancy posted a 3-1-0 record and a 1-4 playoff record as replacement coach when John McLellan was again sidelined with a duodenal ulcer, March 25 to April 11, 1972. All games are credited to McLellan's coaching record.

• McVIE, Tom
b: Trail, B.C., 6/6/1935.

Season	Club	League	GC	W	L	T	RT	W%	GC	W	L	T	W%
			REGULAR SEASON						PLAYOFFS				
1975-76	Washington	NHL	44	8	31	5	....	.239	....	....	....	....	....
1976-77	Washington	NHL	80	24	42	14	....	.388	....	....	....	....	....
1977-78	Washington	NHL	80	17	49	14	....	.300	....	....	....	....	....
1979-80	Winnipeg	NHL	77	19	47	11	....	.318	....	....	....	....	....
1980-81	Winnipeg	NHL	28	1	20	7	....	.161	....	....	....	....	....
1983-84	New Jersey	NHL	60	15	38	7	....	.308	....	....	....	....	....
1990-91	New Jersey	NHL	13	4	5	4	....	.462	7	3	4	0	.429
1991-92	New Jersey	NHL	80	38	31	11	....	.544	7	3	4	0	.429
	NHL Totals		**462**	**126**	**263**	**73**	....	**.352**	**14**	**6**	**8**	**0**	**.429**

• MEEKER, Howie
b: Kitchener, Ont., 11/4/1924.
Played in NHL. See Pre-Expansion Player Register for career statistics.

Season	Club	League	GC	W	L	T	RT	W%	GC	W	L	T	W%
1956-57	Toronto	NHL	70	21	34	15	....	.407	....	....	....	....	....
	NHL Totals		**70**	**21**	**34**	**15**	....	**.407**	....	....	....	....	....

• MELROSE, Barry
b: Kelvington, Sask., 7/15/1956.
Played in NHL. See Modern Player Register for career statistics.

Season	Club	League	GC	W	L	T	RT	W%	GC	W	L	T	W%
1992-93	Los Angeles	NHL	84	39	35	10	....	.524	24	13	11	0	.542
1993-94	Los Angeles	NHL	84	27	45	12	....	.393	....	....	....	....	....
1994-95	Los Angeles	NHL	41	13	21	7	....	.402	....	....	....	....	....
	NHL Totals		**209**	**79**	**101**	**29**	....	**.447**	**24**	**13**	**11**	**0**	**.542**

• MILBURY, Mike
b: Brighton, MA, 6/17/1952.
Played in NHL. See Modern Player Register for career statistics.

Season	Club	League	GC	W	L	T	RT	W%	GC	W	L	T	W%
1989-90	Boston	NHL	80	46	25	9	....	.631	21	13	8	0	.619
1990-91	Boston	NHL	80	44	24	12	....	.625	19	10	9	0	.526
1995-96	NY Islanders	NHL	82	22	50	10	....	.329	....	....	....	....	....
1996-97	NY Islanders	NHL	45	13	23	9	....	.389	....	....	....	....	....
1997-98	NY Islanders	NHL	19	8	9	2	....	.474	....	....	....	....	....
1998-99	NY Islanders	NHL	45	13	29	3	....	.322	....	....	....	....	....
	NHL Totals		**351**	**146**	**160**	**45**	....	**.480**	**40**	**23**	**17**	**0**	**.575**

• MOLLEKEN, Lorne
b: Regina, Sask., 6/11/1956.

Season	Club	League	GC	W	L	T	RT	W%	GC	W	L	T	W%
1998-99	Chicago	NHL	23	13	6	4	....	.652	....	....	....	....	....
99-2000	Chicago	NHL	24	5	15	4	2	.333	....	....	....	....	....
	NHL Totals		**47**	**18**	**21**	**8**	**2**	**.489**	....	....	....	....	....

• MUCKLER, John
b: Midland, Ont., 4/3/1934.

Season	Club	League	GC	W	L	T	RT	W%	GC	W	L	T	W%
1968-69	Minnesota	NHL	35	6	23	6	....	.257	....	....	....	....	....
♦1989-90	Edmonton	NHL	80	38	28	14	....	.563	22	16	6	0	.727
1990-91	Edmonton	NHL	80	37	37	6	....	.500	18	9	9	0	.500
1991-92	Buffalo	NHL	52	22	22	8	....	.500	7	3	4	0	.429
1992-93	Buffalo	NHL	84	38	36	10	....	.512	8	4	4	0	.500
1993-94	Buffalo	NHL	84	43	32	9	....	.565	7	3	4	0	.429
1994-95	Buffalo	NHL	48	22	19	7	....	.531	5	1	4	0	.200
1997-98	NY Rangers	NHL	25	8	15	2	....	.360	....	....	....	....	....
1998-99	NY Rangers	NHL	82	33	38	11	....	.470	....	....	....	....	....
99-2000	NY Rangers	NHL	78	29	38	11	3	.462	....	....	....	....	....
	NHL Totals		**648**	**276**	**288**	**84**	**3**	**.493**	**67**	**36**	**31**	**0**	**.537**

• MULDOON, Pete
b: St. Mary, Ont., 1881 d: 3/13/1929.

Season	Club	League	GC	W	L	T	RT	W%	GC	W	L	T	W%
1926-27	Chicago	NHL	44	19	22	3	....	.466	2	0	1	1	.250
	NHL Totals		**44**	**19**	**22**	**3**	....	**.466**	**2**	**0**	**1**	**1**	**.250**

• MUNRO, Dunc
b: Moray, Scotland, 1/19/1901 d: 1/3/1958.
Played in NHL. See Pre-Expansion Player Register for career statistics.

Season	Club	League	GC	W	L	T	RT	W%	GC	W	L	T	W%
1929-30	Mtl. Maroons	NHL	44	23	16	5	....	.580	4	1	3	0	.250
1930-31	Mtl. Maroons	NHL	32	14	13	5	....	.516	....	....	....	....	....
	NHL Totals		**76**	**37**	**29**	**10**	....	**.553**	**4**	**1**	**3**	**0**	**.250**

• MURDOCH, Bob
b: Kirkland Lake, Ont., 11/20/1946.
Played in NHL. See Modern Player Register for career statistics.

Season	Club	League	GC	W	L	T	RT	W%	GC	W	L	T	W%
1987-88	Chicago	NHL	80	30	41	9	....	.431	5	1	4	0	.200
1989-90	Winnipeg	NHL	80	37	32	11	....	.531	7	3	4	0	.429
1990-91	Winnipeg	NHL	80	26	43	11	....	.394	....	....	....	....	....
	NHL Totals		**240**	**93**	**116**	**31**	....	**.452**	**12**	**4**	**8**	**0**	**.333**

• Won Jack Adams Award (1990)

• MURPHY, Mike
b: Toronto, Ont., 9/12/1950.
Played in NHL. See Modern Player Register for career statistics.

Season	Club	League	GC	W	L	T	RT	W%	GC	W	L	T	W%
1986-87	Los Angeles	NHL	38	13	21	4	....	.395	5	1	4	0	.200
1987-88	Los Angeles	NHL	27	7	16	4	....	.333	....	....	....	....	....
1996-97	Toronto	NHL	82	30	44	8	....	.415	....	....	....	....	....
1997-98	Toronto	NHL	82	30	43	9	....	.421	....	....	....	....	....
	NHL Totals		**229**	**80**	**124**	**25**	....	**.404**	**5**	**1**	**4**	**0**	**.200**

• MURRAY, Andy
b: Gladstone, Man., 3/3/1951.

Season	Club	League	GC	W	L	T	RT	W%	GC	W	L	T	W%
99-2000	Los Angeles	NHL	82	39	31	12	4	.573	4	0	4	0	.000
	NHL Totals		**82**	**39**	**31**	**12**	**4**	**.573**	**4**	**0**	**4**	**0**	**.000**

• MURRAY, Bryan
b: Shawville, Que., 12/5/1942.

Season	Club	League	GC	W	L	T	RT	W%	GC	W	L	T	W%
			REGULAR SEASON						PLAYOFFS				
1981-82	Washington	NHL	66	25	28	13	....	.477	....	....	....	....	....
1982-83	Washington	NHL	80	39	25	16	....	.588	4	1	3	0	.250
1983-84	Washington	NHL	80	48	27	5	....	.631	8	4	4	0	.500
1984-85	Washington	NHL	80	46	25	9	....	.631	5	2	3	0	.400
1985-86	Washington	NHL	80	50	23	7	....	.669	9	5	4	0	.556
1986-87	Washington	NHL	80	38	32	10	....	.538	7	3	4	0	.429
1987-88	Washington	NHL	80	38	33	9	....	.531	14	7	7	0	.500
1988-89	Washington	NHL	80	41	29	10	....	.575	6	2	4	0	.333
1989-90	Washington	NHL	46	18	24	4	....	.435	....	....	....	....	....
1990-91	Detroit	NHL	80	34	38	8	....	.475	7	3	4	0	.429
1991-92	Detroit	NHL	80	43	25	12	....	.613	11	4	7	0	.364
1992-93	Detroit	NHL	84	47	28	9	....	.613	7	3	4	0	.429
1997-98	Florida	NHL	59	17	31	11	....	.381	....	....	....	....	....
	NHL Totals		**975**	**484**	**368**	**123**	....	**.559**	**78**	**34**	**44**	**0**	**.436**

• Won Jack Adams Award (1984)

• MURRAY, Terry
b: Shawville, Que., 7/20/1950.
Played in NHL. See Modern Player Register for career statistics.

Season	Club	League	GC	W	L	T	RT	W%	GC	W	L	T	W%
1989-90	Washington	NHL	34	18	14	2	....	.559	15	8	7	0	.533
1990-91	Washington	NHL	80	37	36	7	....	.506	11	5	6	0	.455
1991-92	Washington	NHL	80	45	27	8	....	.613	7	3	4	0	.429
1992-93	Washington	NHL	84	43	34	7	....	.554	6	2	4	0	.333
1993-94	Washington	NHL	47	20	23	4	....	.468	....	....	....	....	....
1994-95	Philadelphia	NHL	48	28	16	4	....	.625	15	10	5	0	.667
1995-96	Philadelphia	NHL	82	45	24	13	....	.628	12	6	6	0	.500
1996-97	Philadelphia	NHL	82	45	24	13	....	.628	19	12	7	0	.632
1998-99	Florida	NHL	82	30	34	18	....	.476	....	....	....	....	....
99-2000	Florida	NHL	82	43	33	6	6	.598	4	0	4	0	.000
	NHL Totals		**701**	**354**	**265**	**82**	**6**	**.568**	**89**	**46**	**43**	**0**	**.517**

• NANNE, Lou
USHOF

b: Sault Ste. Marie, Ont., 6/2/1941.
Played in NHL. See Modern Player Register for career statistics.

Season	Club	League	GC	W	L	T	RT	W%	GC	W	L	T	W%
1977-78	Minnesota	NHL	29	7	18	4	....	.310	....	....	....	....	....
	NHL Totals		**29**	**7**	**18**	**4**	....	**.310**	....	....	....	....	....

• NEALE, Harry
b: Sarnia, Ont., 3/9/1937.

Season	Club	League	GC	W	L	T	RT	W%	GC	W	L	T	W%
1978-79	Vancouver	NHL	80	25	42	13	....	.394	3	1	2	0	.333
1979-80	Vancouver	NHL	80	27	37	16	....	.438	4	1	3	0	.250
1980-81	Vancouver	NHL	80	28	32	20	....	.475	3	0	3	0	.000
1981-82	Vancouver	NHL	75	26	33	16	....	.453	....	....	....	....	....
1983-84	Vancouver	NHL	32	15	13	4	....	.531	4	1	3	0	.250
1984-85	Vancouver	NHL	60	21	32	7	....	.408	....	....	....	....	....
1985-86	Detroit	NHL	35	8	23	4	....	.286	....	....	....	....	....
	NHL Totals		**442**	**150**	**212**	**80**	....	**.430**	**14**	**3**	**11**	**0**	**.214**

• NEILSON, Roger
b: Toronto, Ont., 6/16/1934.

Season	Club	League	GC	W	L	T	RT	W%	GC	W	L	T	W%
1977-78	Toronto	NHL	80	41	29	10	....	.575	13	6	7	0	.462
1978-79	Toronto	NHL	80	34	33	13	....	.506	6	2	4	0	.333
1980-81	Buffalo	NHL	80	39	20	21	....	.619	8	4	4	0	.500
1981-82	Vancouver	NHL	5	4	0	1	....	.900	17	11	6	0	.647
1982-83	Vancouver	NHL	80	30	35	15	....	.469	4	1	3	0	.250
1983-84	Vancouver	NHL	48	17	26	5	....	.406	....	....	....	....	....
	Los Angeles	NHL	28	8	17	3	....	.339	....	....	....	....	....
1989-90	NY Rangers	NHL	80	36	31	13	....	.531	10	5	5	0	.500
1990-91	NY Rangers	NHL	80	36	31	13	....	.531	6	2	4	0	.333
1991-92	NY Rangers	NHL	80	50	25	5	....	.656	13	6	7	0	.462
1992-93	NY Rangers	NHL	40	19	17	4	....	.525	....	....	....	....	....
1993-94	Florida	NHL	84	33	34	17	....	.494	....	....	....	....	....
1994-95	Florida	NHL	48	20	22	6	....	.479	....	....	....	....	....
1997-98	Philadelphia	NHL	21	10	9	2	....	.524	5	1	4	0	.200
1998-99	Philadelphia	NHL	82	37	26	19	....	.567	6	2	4	0	.333
99-2000	Philadelphia	NHL	82	45	25	12	3	.640	18	11	7	0	.611
	NHL Totals		**998**	**459**	**380**	**159**	**3**	**.541**	**106**	**51**	**55**	**0**	**.481**

Assistant coach Craig Ramsay posted a 16-8-1-2 regular-season record and an 11-7 playoff record as interim coach after Roger Neilson was sidelined for treatment of bone marrow cancer on February 20, 2000. All games are credited to Neilson's coaching record.

• NOLAN, Ted
b: Sault Ste. Marie, Ont., 4/7/1958.
Played in NHL. See Modern Player Register for career statistics.

Season	Club	League	GC	W	L	T	RT	W%	GC	W	L	T	W%
1995-96	Buffalo	NHL	82	33	42	7	....	.445	....	....	....	....	....
1996-97	Buffalo	NHL	82	40	30	12	....	.561	12	5	7	0	.417
	NHL Totals		**164**	**73**	**72**	**19**	....	**.503**	**12**	**5**	**7**	**0**	**.417**

• Won Jack Adams Award (1997)

• NYKOLUK, Mike
b: Toronto, Ont., 12/11/1934.
Played in NHL. See Pre-Expansion Player Register for career statistics.

Season	Club	League	GC	W	L	T	RT	W%	GC	W	L	T	W%
1980-81	Toronto	NHL	40	15	15	10	....	.500	3	0	3	0	.000
1981-82	Toronto	NHL	80	20	44	16	....	.350	....	....	....	....	....
1982-83	Toronto	NHL	80	28	40	12	....	.425	4	1	3	0	.250
1983-84	Toronto	NHL	80	26	45	9	....	.381	....	....	....	....	....
	NHL Totals		**280**	**89**	**144**	**47**	....	**.402**	**7**	**1**	**6**	**0**	**.143**

● O'REILLY, Terry
b: Niagara Falls, Ont., 6/7/1951.
Played in NHL. See Modern Player Register for career statistics.

Season	Club	League	GC	W	L	T	RT	W%	GC	W	L	T	W%
			REGULAR SEASON						PLAYOFFS				
1986-87	Boston	NHL	67	34	27	6	....	.552	4	0	4	0	.000
1987-88	Boston	NHL	80	44	30	6	....	.588	23	12	10	1	.543
1988-89	Boston	NHL	80	37	29	14	....	.550	10	5	5	0	.500
	NHL Totals		**227**	**115**	**86**	**26**	....	**.564**	**37**	**17**	**19**	**1**	**.473**

● O'DONOGHUE, George
b: unknown Deceased.

Season	Club	League	GC	W	L	T	RT	W%	GC	W	L	T	W%
♦1921-22	Toronto	NHL	24	13	10	1	....	.563	7	4	2	1	.643
1922-23	Toronto	NHL	5	2	3	0	....	.400	....	....	....	....	....
	NHL Totals		**29**	**15**	**13**	**1**	....	**.534**	**7**	**4**	**2**	**1**	**.643**

● OLIVER, Murray
b: Hamilton, Ont., 11/14/1937.
Played in NHL. See Modern Player Register for career statistics.

Season	Club	League	GC	W	L	T	RT	W%	GC	W	L	T	W%
1981-82	Minnesota	NHL	4	3	0	1	....	.875	4	1	3	0	.250
1982-83	Minnesota	NHL	37	18	12	7	....	.581	9	4	5	0	.444
	NHL Totals		**41**	**21**	**12**	**8**	....	**.610**	**13**	**5**	**8**	**0**	**.385**

● OLMSTEAD, Bert HHOF
b: Sceptre, Sask., 9/4/1926.
Played in NHL. See Pre-Expansion Player Register for career statistics.

Season	Club	League	GC	W	L	T	RT	W%	GC	W	L	T	W%
1967-68	Oakland	NHL	64	11	37	16	....	.297	....	....	....	....	....
	NHL Totals		**64**	**11**	**37**	**16**	....	**.297**	....	....	....	....	....

● PADDOCK, John
b: Brandon, Man., 6/9/1954.
Played in NHL. See Modern Player Register for career statistics.

Season	Club	League	GC	W	L	T	RT	W%	GC	W	L	T	W%
1991-92	Winnipeg	NHL	80	33	32	15	....	.506	7	3	4	0	.429
1992-93	Winnipeg	NHL	84	40	37	7	....	.518	6	2	4	0	.333
1993-94	Winnipeg	NHL	84	24	51	9	....	.339	....	....	....	....	....
1994-95	Winnipeg	NHL	33	9	18	6	....	.364	....	....	....	....	....
	NHL Totals		**281**	**106**	**138**	**37**	....	**.443**	**13**	**5**	**8**	**0**	**.385**

● PAGE, Pierre
b: St-Hermas, Que., 4/30/1948.

Season	Club	League	GC	W	L	T	RT	W%	GC	W	L	T	W%
1988-89	Minnesota	NHL	80	27	37	16	....	.438	5	1	4	0	.200
1989-90	Minnesota	NHL	80	36	40	4	....	.475	7	3	4	0	.429
1991-92	Quebec	NHL	62	17	34	11	....	.363	....	....	....	....	....
1992-93	Quebec	NHL	84	47	27	10	....	.619	6	2	4	0	.333
1993-94	Quebec	NHL	84	34	42	8	....	.452	....	....	....	....	....
1995-96	Calgary	NHL	82	34	37	11	....	.482	4	0	4	0	.000
1996-97	Calgary	NHL	82	32	41	9	....	.445	....	....	....	....	....
1997-98	Anaheim	NHL	82	26	43	13	....	.396	....	....	....	....	....
	NHL Totals		**636**	**253**	**301**	**82**	....	**.462**	**22**	**6**	**16**	**0**	**.273**

● PARK, Brad HHOF
b: Toronto, Ont., 7/6/1948.
Played in NHL. See Modern Player Register for career statistics.

Season	Club	League	GC	W	L	T	RT	W%	GC	W	L	T	W%
1985-86	Detroit	NHL	45	9	34	2	....	.222	....	....	....	....	....
	NHL Totals		**45**	**9**	**34**	**2**	....	**.222**	....	....	....	....	....

● PATERSON, Rick
b: Kingston, Ont., 2/10/1958.
Played in NHL. See Modern Player Register for career statistics.

Season	Club	League	GC	W	L	T	RT	W%	GC	W	L	T	W%
1997-98	Tampa Bay	NHL	8	0	8	0	....	.000	....	....	....	....	....
	NHL Totals		**8**	**0**	**8**	**0**	....	**.000**	....	....	....	....	....

● PATRICK, Craig USHOF
b: Detroit, MI, 5/20/1946.
Played in NHL. See Modern Player Register for career statistics.

Season	Club	League	GC	W	L	T	RT	W%	GC	W	L	T	W%
1980-81	NY Rangers	NHL	60	26	23	11	....	.525	14	7	7	0	.500
1984-85	NY Rangers	NHL	35	11	22	2	....	.343	3	0	3	0	.000
1989-90	Pittsburgh	NHL	54	22	26	6	....	.463	....	....	....	....	....
1996-97	Pittsburgh	NHL	20	7	10	3	....	.425	5	1	4	0	.200
	NHL Totals		**169**	**66**	**81**	**22**	....	**.456**	**22**	**8**	**14**	**0**	**.364**

● PATRICK, Frank HHOF
b: Ottawa, Ont., 12/21/1885 d: 6/29/1960.

Season	Club	League	GC	W	L	T	RT	W%	GC	W	L	T	W%
1934-35	Boston	NHL	48	26	16	6	....	.604	4	1	3	0	.250
1935-36	Boston	NHL	48	22	20	6	....	.521	2	1	1	0	.500
	NHL Totals		**96**	**48**	**36**	**12**	....	**.563**	**6**	**2**	**4**	**0**	**.333**

● PATRICK, Lester HHOF
b: Drummondville, Que., 12/30/1883 d: 6/1/1960.
Played in NHL. See Pre-Expansion Player Register for career statistics.

Season	Club	League	GC	W	L	T	RT	W%	GC	W	L	T	W%
1926-27	NY Rangers	NHL	44	25	13	6	....	.636	2	0	1	1	.250
♦1927-28	NY Rangers	NHL	44	19	16	9	....	.534	9	5	3	1	.611
1928-29	NY Rangers	NHL	44	21	13	10	....	.591	6	3	2	1	.583
1929-30	NY Rangers	NHL	44	17	17	10	....	.500	4	1	2	1	.375
1930-31	NY Rangers	NHL	44	19	16	9	....	.534	4	2	2	0	.500
1931-32	NY Rangers	NHL	48	23	17	8	....	.563	7	3	4	0	.429
♦1932-33	NY Rangers	NHL	48	23	17	8	....	.563	8	6	1	1	.813
1933-34	NY Rangers	NHL	48	21	19	8	....	.521	2	0	1	1	.250
1934-35	NY Rangers	NHL	48	22	20	6	....	.521	4	2	1	1	.625
1935-36	NY Rangers	NHL	48	19	17	12	....	.521	....	....	....	....	....
1936-37	NY Rangers	NHL	48	19	20	9	....	.490	9	6	3	0	.667
1937-38	NY Rangers	NHL	48	27	15	6	....	.625	3	1	2	0	.333
1938-39	NY Rangers	NHL	48	26	16	6	....	.604	7	3	4	0	.429
	NHL Totals		**604**	**281**	**216**	**107**	....	**.554**	**65**	**32**	**26**	**7**	**.546**

● PATRICK, Lynn HHOF
b: Victoria, B.C., 2/3/1912 d: 1/26/1980.
Played in NHL. See Pre-Expansion Player Register for career statistics.

Season	Club	League	GC	W	L	T	RT	W%	GC	W	L	T	W%
1948-49	NY Rangers	NHL	37	12	20	5	....	.392	....	....	....	....	....
1949-50	NY Rangers	NHL	70	28	31	11	....	.479	12	7	5	0	.583
1950-51	Boston	NHL	70	22	30	18	....	.443	6	1	4	1	.250
1951-52	Boston	NHL	70	25	29	16	....	.471	7	3	4	0	.429
1952-53	Boston	NHL	70	28	29	13	....	.493	11	5	6	0	.455
1953-54	Boston	NHL	70	32	28	10	....	.529	4	0	4	0	.000
1954-55	Boston	NHL	30	10	14	6	....	.433	....	....	....	....	....
1967-68	St. Louis	NHL	16	4	10	2	....	.313	....	....	....	....	....
1974-75	St. Louis	NHL	2	1	0	1	....	.750	....	....	....	....	....
1975-76	St. Louis	NHL	8	3	5	0	....	.375	....	....	....	....	....
	NHL Totals		**443**	**165**	**196**	**82**	....	**.465**	**40**	**16**	**23**	**1**	**.413**

● PATRICK, Muzz
b: Victoria, B.C., 6/28/1915 d: 7/23/1998.
Played in NHL. See Pre-Expansion Player Register for career statistics.

Season	Club	League	GC	W	L	T	RT	W%	GC	W	L	T	W%
1953-54	NY Rangers	NHL	30	15	11	4	....	.567	....	....	....	....	....
1954-55	NY Rangers	NHL	70	17	35	18	....	.371	....	....	....	....	....
1959-60	NY Rangers	NHL	2	0	1	1	....	.250	....	....	....	....	....
1962-63	NY Rangers	NHL	34	11	19	4	....	.382	....	....	....	....	....
	NHL Totals		**136**	**43**	**66**	**27**	....	**.415**	....	....	....	....	....

● PERRON, Jean
b: St-Isidore d'Auckland, Que., 10/5/1946.

Season	Club	League	GC	W	L	T	RT	W%	GC	W	L	T	W%
♦1985-86	Montreal	NHL	80	40	33	7	....	.544	20	15	5	0	.750
1986-87	Montreal	NHL	80	41	29	10	....	.575	17	10	7	0	.588
1987-88	Montreal	NHL	80	45	22	13	....	.644	11	5	6	0	.455
1988-89	Quebec	NHL	47	16	26	5	....	.394	....	....	....	....	....
	NHL Totals		**287**	**142**	**110**	**35**	....	**.556**	**48**	**30**	**18**	**0**	**.625**

● PERRY, Don
b: Edmonton, Alta., 3/16/1930.

Season	Club	League	GC	W	L	T	RT	W%	GC	W	L	T	W%
1981-82	Los Angeles	NHL	38	11	17	10	....	.421	10	4	6	0	.400
1982-83	Los Angeles	NHL	80	27	41	12	....	.413	....	....	....	....	....
1983-84	Los Angeles	NHL	50	14	27	9	....	.370	....	....	....	....	....
	NHL Totals		**168**	**52**	**85**	**31**	....	**.402**	**10**	**4**	**6**	**0**	**.400**

● PIKE, Alf
b: Winnipeg, Man., 9/15/1917.
Played in NHL. See Pre-Expansion Player Register for career statistics.

Season	Club	League	GC	W	L	T	RT	W%	GC	W	L	T	W%
1959-60	NY Rangers	NHL	53	14	28	11	....	.368	....	....	....	....	....
1960-61	NY Rangers	NHL	70	22	38	10	....	.386	....	....	....	....	....
	NHL Totals		**123**	**36**	**66**	**21**	....	**.378**	....	....	....	....	....

● PILOUS, Rudy
b: Winnipeg, Man., 8/11/1914 d: 12/11/1994.

Season	Club	League	GC	W	L	T	RT	W%	GC	W	L	T	W%
1957-58	Chicago	NHL	37	14	22	1	....	.392	....	....	....	....	....
1958-59	Chicago	NHL	70	28	29	13	....	.493	6	2	4	0	.333
1959-60	Chicago	NHL	70	28	29	13	....	.493	4	0	4	0	.000
♦1960-61	Chicago	NHL	70	29	24	17	....	.536	12	8	4	0	.667
1961-62	Chicago	NHL	70	31	26	13	....	.536	12	6	6	0	.500
1962-63	Chicago	NHL	70	32	21	17	....	.579	7	3	4	0	.429
	NHL Totals		**387**	**162**	**151**	**74**	....	**.514**	**41**	**19**	**22**	**0**	**.463**

● PLAGER, Barclay
b: Kirkland Lake, Ont., 3/26/1941 d: 2/6/1988.
Played in NHL. See Modern Player Register for career statistics.

Season	Club	League	GC	W	L	T	RT	W%	GC	W	L	T	W%
1977-78	St. Louis	NHL	26	9	11	6	....	.462	....	....	....	....	....
1978-79	St. Louis	NHL	80	18	50	12	....	.300	....	....	....	....	....
1979-80	St. Louis	NHL	24	7	14	3	....	.354	....	....	....	....	....
1982-83	St. Louis	NHL	48	15	21	12	....	.438	4	1	3	0	.250
	NHL Totals		**178**	**49**	**96**	**33**	....	**.368**	**4**	**1**	**3**	**0**	**.250**

● PLAGER, Bob
b: Kirkland Lake, Ont., 3/11/1943.
Played in NHL. See Modern Player Register for career statistics.

Season	Club	League	GC	W	L	T	RT	W%	GC	W	L	T	W%
1992-93	St. Louis	NHL	11	4	6	1	....	.409	....	....	....	....	....
	NHL Totals		**11**	**4**	**6**	**1**	....	**.409**	....	....	....	....	....

● PLEAU, Larry
b: Lynn, MA, 1/29/1947.
Played in NHL. See Modern Player Register for career statistics.

Season	Club	League	GC	W	L	T	RT	W%	GC	W	L	T	W%
1980-81	Hartford	NHL	20	6	12	2	....	.350	....	....	....	....	....
1981-82	Hartford	NHL	80	21	41	18	....	.375	....	....	....	....	....
1982-83	Hartford	NHL	18	4	13	1	....	.250	....	....	....	....	....
1987-88	Hartford	NHL	26	13	13	0	....	.500	6	2	4	0	.333
1988-89	Hartford	NHL	80	37	38	5	....	.494	4	0	4	0	.000
	NHL Totals		**224**	**81**	**117**	**26**	....	**.420**	**10**	**2**	**8**	**0**	**.200**

● POLANO, Nick
b: Sudbury, Ont., 3/25/1941.

Season	Club	League	GC	W	L	T	RT	W%	GC	W	L	T	W%
1982-83	Detroit	NHL	80	21	44	15	....	.356	....	....	....	....	....
1983-84	Detroit	NHL	80	31	42	7	....	.431	4	1	3	0	.250
1984-85	Detroit	NHL	80	27	41	12	....	.413	3	0	3	0	.000
	NHL Totals		**240**	**79**	**127**	**34**	....	**.400**	**7**	**1**	**6**	**0**	**.143**

● POPEIN, Larry
b: Yorkton, Sask., 8/11/1930.
Played in NHL. See Modern Player Register for career statistics.

Season	Club	League	GC	W	L	T	RT	W%	GC	W	L	T	W%
1973-74	NY Rangers	NHL	41	18	14	9	....	.549	....	....	....	....	....
	NHL Totals		**41**	**18**	**14**	**9**	....	**.549**	....	....	....	....	....

• POWERS, Eddie

b: Toronto, Ont., d: 1/18/1943.

Season	Club	League	GC	W	L	T	RT	W%	GC	W	L	T	W%
			REGULAR SEASON						PLAYOFFS				
1924-25	Toronto	NHL	30	19	11	0	....	.633	2	0	2	0	.000
1925-26	Toronto	NHL	36	12	21	3	....	.375	....	....	....	....	....
	NHL Totals		**66**	**31**	**32**	**3**	....	**.492**	**2**	**0**	**2**	**0**	**.000**

• PRIMEAU, Joe — HHOF

b: Lindsay, Ont., 1/29/1906 d: 5/14/1989.
Played in NHL. See Pre-Expansion Player Register for career statistics.

Season	Club	League	GC	W	L	T	RT	W%	GC	W	L	T	W%
♦1950-51	Toronto	NHL	70	41	16	13	....	.679	11	8	2	1	.773
1951-52	Toronto	NHL	70	29	25	16	....	.529	4	0	4	0	.000
1952-53	Toronto	NHL	70	27	30	13	....	.479	....	....	....	....	....
	NHL Totals		**210**	**97**	**71**	**42**	....	**.562**	**15**	**8**	**6**	**1**	**.567**

• PRONOVOST, Marcel — HHOF

b: Shawinigan Falls, Que., 6/15/1930.
Played in NHL. See Modern Player Register for career statistics.

Season	Club	League	GC	W	L	T	RT	W%	GC	W	L	T	W%
1977-78	Buffalo	NHL	80	44	19	17	....	.656	8	3	5	0	.375
1978-79	Buffalo	NHL	24	8	10	6	....	.458	....	....	....	....	....
	NHL Totals		**104**	**52**	**29**	**23**	....	**.611**	**8**	**3**	**5**	**0**	**.375**

• PULFORD, Bob — HHOF

b: Newton Robinson, Ont., 3/31/1936.
Played in NHL. See Modern Player Register for career statistics.

Season	Club	League	GC	W	L	T	RT	W%	GC	W	L	T	W%
1972-73	Los Angeles	NHL	78	31	36	11	....	.468	....	....	....	....	....
1973-74	Los Angeles	NHL	78	33	33	12	....	.500	5	1	4	0	.200
1974-75	Los Angeles	NHL	80	42	17	21	....	.656	3	1	2	0	.333
1975-76	Los Angeles	NHL	80	38	33	9	....	.531	9	4	5	0	.444
1976-77	Los Angeles	NHL	80	34	31	15	....	.519	9	4	5	0	.444
1977-78	Chicago	NHL	80	32	29	19	....	.519	4	0	4	0	.000
1978-79	Chicago	NHL	80	29	36	15	....	.456	4	0	4	0	.000
1981-82	Chicago	NHL	28	12	14	2	....	.464	15	8	7	0	.533
1984-85	Chicago	NHL	27	16	7	4	....	.667	15	9	6	0	.600
1985-86	Chicago	NHL	80	39	33	8	....	.538	3	0	3	0	.000
1986-87	Chicago	NHL	80	29	37	14	....	.450	4	0	4	0	.000
99-2000	Chicago	NHL	58	28	24	6	0	.534	....	....	....	....	....
	NHL Totals		**829**	**363**	**330**	**136**	**0**	**.520**	**71**	**27**	**44**	**0**	**.380**

• Won Jack Adams Award (1975)

• QUENNEVILLE, Joel

b: Windsor, Ont., 9/15/1958.
Played in NHL. See Modern Player Register for career statistics.

Season	Club	League	GC	W	L	T	RT	W%	GC	W	L	T	W%
1996-97	St. Louis	NHL	40	18	15	7	....	.538	6	2	4	0	.333
1997-98	St. Louis	NHL	82	45	29	8	....	.598	10	6	4	0	.600
1998-99	St. Louis	NHL	82	37	32	13	....	.530	13	6	7	0	.462
99-2000	St. Louis	NHL	82	51	20	11	1	.695	7	3	4	0	.429
	NHL Totals		**286**	**151**	**96**	**39**	**1**	**.598**	**36**	**17**	**19**	**0**	**.472**

• Won Jack Adams Award (2000)

• QUERRIE, Charles

b: unknown Deceased.

Season	Club	League	GC	W	L	T	RT	W%	GC	W	L	T	W%
1922-23	Toronto	NHL	19	11	7	1	....	.605	....	....	....	....	....
1923-24	Toronto	NHL	24	10	14	0	....	.417	....	....	....	....	....
1926-27	Toronto	NHL	29	8	17	4	....	.345	....	....	....	....	....
	NHL Totals		**72**	**29**	**38**	**5**	....	**.438**	....	....	....	....	....

• QUINN, Mike

b: unknown Deceased.

Season	Club	League	GC	W	L	T	RT	W%	GC	W	L	T	W%
1919-20	Quebec	NHL	24	4	20	0	....	.167	....	....	....	....	....
	NHL Totals		**24**	**4**	**20**	**0**	....	**.167**	....	....	....	....	....

• QUINN, Pat

b: Hamilton, Ont., 1/29/1943.
Played in NHL. See Modern Player Register for career statistics.

Season	Club	League	GC	W	L	T	RT	W%	GC	W	L	T	W%
1978-79	Philadelphia	NHL	30	18	8	4	....	.667	8	3	5	0	.375
1979-80	Philadelphia	NHL	80	48	12	20	....	.725	19	13	6	0	.684
1980-81	Philadelphia	NHL	80	41	24	15	....	.606	12	6	6	0	.500
1981-82	Philadelphia	NHL	72	34	29	9	....	.535	....	....	....	....	....
1984-85	Los Angeles	NHL	80	34	32	14	....	.513	3	0	3	0	.000
1985-86	Los Angeles	NHL	80	23	49	8	....	.338	....	....	....	....	....
1986-87	Los Angeles	NHL	42	18	20	4	....	.476	....	....	....	....	....
1990-91	Vancouver	NHL	26	9	13	4	....	.423	6	2	4	0	.333
1991-92	Vancouver	NHL	80	42	26	12	....	.600	13	6	7	0	.462
1992-93	Vancouver	NHL	84	46	29	9	....	.601	12	6	6	0	.500
1993-94	Vancouver	NHL	84	41	40	3	....	.506	24	15	9	0	.625
1995-96	Vancouver	NHL	6	3	3	0	....	.500	6	2	4	0	.333
1998-99	Toronto	NHL	82	45	30	7	....	.591	17	9	8	0	.529
99-2000	Toronto	NHL	82	45	30	7	3	.610	12	6	6	0	.500
	NHL Totals		**908**	**447**	**345**	**116**	**3**	**.558**	**132**	**68**	**64**	**0**	**.515**

• Won Jack Adams Award (1980, 1992)

• RAMSAY, Craig

b: Weston, Ont., 3/17/1951.
Played in NHL. See Modern Player Register for career statistics.

Season	Club	League	GC	W	L	T	RT	W%	GC	W	L	T	W%
1986-87	Buffalo	NHL	21	4	15	2	....	.238	....	....	....	....	....
	NHL Totals		**21**	**4**	**15**	**2**	....	**.238**	....	....	....	....	....

Posted a 16-8-1-2 regular-season record and an 11-7 playoff record as interim coach when Roger Neilson was sidelined for treatment of bone-marrow cancer after February 20, 2000. All games are credited to Neilson's coaching record.

• RANDALL, Ken

b: Kingston, Ont., Deceased.
Played in NHL. See Pre-Expansion Player Register for career statistics.

Season	Club	League	GC	W	L	T	RT	W%	GC	W	L	T	W%
1923-24	Hamilton	NHL	14	6	8	0	....	.429	....	....	....	....	....
	NHL Totals		**14**	**6**	**8**	**0**	....	**.429**	....	....	....	....	....

• REAY, Billy

b: Winnipeg, Man., 8/21/1918.
Played in NHL. See Pre-Expansion Player Register for career statistics.

Season	Club	League	GC	W	L	T	RT	W%	GC	W	L	T	W%
1957-58	Toronto	NHL	70	21	38	11	....	.379	....	....	....	....	....
1958-59	Toronto	NHL	20	5	12	3	....	.325	....	....	....	....	....
1963-64	Chicago	NHL	70	36	22	12	....	.600	6	2	4	0	.333
1964-65	Chicago	NHL	70	34	28	8	....	.543	14	7	7	0	.500
1965-66	Chicago	NHL	70	37	25	8	....	.586	6	2	4	0	.333
1966-67	Chicago	NHL	70	41	17	12	....	.671	6	2	4	0	.333
1967-68	Chicago	NHL	74	32	26	16	....	.541	11	5	6	0	.455
1968-69	Chicago	NHL	76	34	33	9	....	.507	....	....	....	....	....
1969-70	Chicago	NHL	76	45	22	9	....	.651	8	4	4	0	.500
1970-71	Chicago	NHL	78	49	20	9	....	.686	18	11	7	0	.611
1971-72	Chicago	NHL	78	46	17	15	....	.686	8	4	4	0	.500
1972-73	Chicago	NHL	78	42	27	9	....	.596	16	10	6	0	.625
1973-74	Chicago	NHL	78	41	14	23	....	.673	11	6	5	0	.545
1974-75	Chicago	NHL	80	37	35	8	....	.513	8	3	5	0	.375
1975-76	Chicago	NHL	80	32	30	18	....	.513	4	0	4	0	.000
1976-77	Chicago	NHL	34	10	19	5	....	.368	....	....	....	....	....
	NHL Totals		**1102**	**542**	**385**	**175**	....	**.571**	**116**	**56**	**60**	**0**	**.483**

• REGAN, Larry

b: North Bay, Ont., 8/9/1930.
Played in NHL. See Pre-Expansion Player Register for career statistics.

Season	Club	League	GC	W	L	T	RT	W%	GC	W	L	T	W%
1970-71	Los Angeles	NHL	78	25	40	13	....	.404	....	....	....	....	....
1971-72	Los Angeles	NHL	10	2	7	1	....	.250	....	....	....	....	....
	NHL Totals		**88**	**27**	**47**	**14**	....	**.386**	....	....	....	....	....

• RENNEY, Tom

b: Cranbrooke, B.C., 3/1/1955.

Season	Club	League	GC	W	L	T	RT	W%	GC	W	L	T	W%
1996-97	Vancouver	NHL	82	35	40	7	....	.470	....	....	....	....	....
1997-98	Vancouver	NHL	19	4	13	2	....	.263	....	....	....	....	....
	NHL Totals		**101**	**39**	**53**	**9**	....	**.431**	....	....	....	....	....

• RISEBROUGH, Doug

b: Guelph, Ont., 1/29/1954.
Played in NHL. See Modern Player Register for career statistics.

Season	Club	League	GC	W	L	T	RT	W%	GC	W	L	T	W%
1990-91	Calgary	NHL	80	46	26	8	....	.625	7	3	4	0	.429
1991-92	Calgary	NHL	64	25	30	9	....	.461	....	....	....	....	....
	NHL Totals		**144**	**71**	**56**	**17**	....	**.552**	**7**	**3**	**4**	**0**	**.429**

• ROBERTS, Jim

b: Toronto, Ont., 4/9/1940.
Played in NHL. See Modern Player Register for career statistics.

Season	Club	League	GC	W	L	T	RT	W%	GC	W	L	T	W%
1981-82	Buffalo	NHL	45	21	16	8	....	.556	....	....	....	....	....
1991-92	Hartford	NHL	80	26	41	13	....	.406	7	3	4	0	.429
1996-97	St. Louis	NHL	9	3	3	3	....	.500	....	....	....	....	....
	NHL Totals		**134**	**50**	**60**	**24**	....	**.463**	**7**	**3**	**4**	**0**	**.429**

• ROBINSON, Larry — HHOF

b: Winchester, Ont., 6/2/1951.
Played in NHL. See Modern Player Register for career statistics.

Season	Club	League	GC	W	L	T	RT	W%	GC	W	L	T	W%
1995-96	Los Angeles	NHL	82	24	40	18	....	.402	....	....	....	....	....
1996-97	Los Angeles	NHL	82	28	43	11	....	.409	....	....	....	....	....
1997-98	Los Angeles	NHL	82	38	33	11	....	.530	4	0	4	0	.000
1998-99	Los Angeles	NHL	82	32	45	5	....	.421	....	....	....	....	....
♦99-2000	New Jersey	NHL	8	4	4	0	0	.500	23	16	7	0	.696
	NHL Totals		**336**	**126**	**165**	**45**	**0**	**.442**	**27**	**16**	**11**	**0**	**.593**

• RODDEN, Mike — HHOF

b: 4/24/1891 d: 1/11/1978.

Season	Club	League	GC	W	L	T	RT	W%	GC	W	L	T	W%
1926-27	Toronto	NHL	2	0	2	0	....	.000	....	....	....	....	....
	NHL Totals		**2**	**0**	**2**	**0**	....	**.000**	....	....	....	....	....

• ROMERIL, Alex

b: unknown.

Season	Club	League	GC	W	L	T	RT	W%	GC	W	L	T	W%
1926-27	Toronto	NHL	13	7	5	1	....	.577	....	....	....	....	....
	NHL Totals		**13**	**7**	**5**	**1**	....	**.577**	....	....	....	....	....

● **ROSS, Art** HHOF
b: Naughton, Ont., 1/13/1886 d: 8/5/1964.
Played in NHL. See Pre-Expansion Player Register for career statistics.

Season	Club	League	REGULAR SEASON GC	W	L	T	RT	W%	PLAYOFFS GC	W	L	T	W%
1917-18	Mtl. Wanderers...	NHL	6	1	5	0	....	.167	....	....	....	....	....
1922-23	Hamilton	NHL	24	6	18	0	....	.250	....	....	....	....	....
1924-25	Boston	NHL	30	6	24	0	....	.200	....	....	....	....	....
1925-26	Boston	NHL	36	17	15	4	....	.528	....	....	....	....	....
1926-27	Boston	NHL	44	21	20	3	....	.511	8	2	2	4	.500
1927-28	Boston	NHL	44	20	13	11	....	.580	2	0	1	1	.250
1929-30	Boston	NHL	44	38	5	1	....	.875	6	3	3	0	.500
1930-31	Boston	NHL	44	28	10	6	....	.705	5	2	3	0	.400
1931-32	Boston	NHL	48	15	21	12	....	.438	....	....	....	....	....
1932-33	Boston	NHL	48	25	15	8	....	.604	5	2	3	0	.400
1933-34	Boston	NHL	48	18	25	5	....	.427	....	....	....	....	....
1936-37	Boston	NHL	48	23	18	7	....	.552	3	1	2	0	.333
1937-38	Boston	NHL	48	30	11	7	....	.698	3	0	3	0	.000
♦1938-39	Boston	NHL	48	36	10	2	....	.771	12	8	4	0	.667
1941-42	Boston	NHL	48	25	17	6	....	.583	5	2	3	0	.400
1942-43	Boston	NHL	50	24	17	9	....	.570	9	4	5	0	.444
1943-44	Boston	NHL	50	19	26	5	....	.430	....	....	....	....	....
1944-45	Boston	NHL	50	16	30	4	....	.360	7	3	4	0	.429
	NHL Totals		**758**	**368**	**300**	**90**	....	**.545**	**65**	**27**	**33**	**5**	**.454**

● **RUEL, Claude**
b: Sherbrooke, Que., 9/12/1938.

Season	Club	League	REGULAR SEASON GC	W	L	T	RT	W%	PLAYOFFS GC	W	L	T	W%
♦1968-69	Montreal	NHL	76	46	19	11	....	.678	14	12	2	0	.857
1969-70	Montreal	NHL	76	38	22	16	....	.605	....	....	....	....	....
1970-71	Montreal	NHL	23	11	8	4	....	.565	....	....	....	....	....
1979-80	Montreal	NHL	50	32	11	7	....	.710	10	6	4	0	.600
1980-81	Montreal	NHL	80	45	22	13	....	.644	3	0	3	0	.000
	NHL Totals		**305**	**172**	**82**	**51**	....	**.648**	**27**	**18**	**9**	**0**	**.667**

● **RUFF, Lindy**
b: Warburg, Alta., 2/17/1960.
Played in NHL. See Modern Player Register for career statistics.

Season	Club	League	REGULAR SEASON GC	W	L	T	RT	W%	PLAYOFFS GC	W	L	T	W%
1997-98	Buffalo	NHL	82	36	29	17	....	.543	15	10	5	0	.667
1998-99	Buffalo	NHL	82	37	28	17	....	.555	21	14	7	0	.667
99-2000	Buffalo	NHL	82	35	36	11	4	.518	5	1	4	0	.200
	NHL Totals		**246**	**108**	**93**	**45**	**4**	**.539**	**41**	**25**	**16**	**0**	**.610**

● **SATHER, Glen** HHOF
b: High River, Alta., 9/2/1943.
Played in NHL. See Modern Player Register for career statistics.

Season	Club	League	REGULAR SEASON GC	W	L	T	RT	W%	PLAYOFFS GC	W	L	T	W%
1979-80	Edmonton	NHL	80	28	39	13	....	.431	3	0	3	0	.000
1980-81	Edmonton	NHL	62	25	26	11	....	.492	9	5	4	0	.556
1981-82	Edmonton	NHL	80	48	17	15	....	.694	5	2	3	0	.400
1982-83	Edmonton	NHL	80	47	21	12	....	.663	16	11	5	0	.688
♦1983-84	Edmonton	NHL	80	57	18	5	....	.744	19	15	4	0	.789
♦1984-85	Edmonton	NHL	80	49	20	11	....	.681	18	15	3	0	.833
1985-86	Edmonton	NHL	80	56	17	7	....	.744	10	6	4	0	.600
♦1986-87	Edmonton	NHL	80	50	24	6	....	.663	21	16	5	0	.762
♦1987-88	Edmonton	NHL	80	44	25	11	....	.619	19	16	2	1	.868
1988-89	Edmonton	NHL	80	38	34	8	....	.525	7	3	4	0	.429
1993-94	Edmonton	NHL	60	22	27	11	....	.458	....	....	....	....	....
	NHL Totals		**842**	**464**	**268**	**110**	....	**.616**	**127**	**89**	**37**	**1**	**.705**

• Won Jack Adams Award (1986)

● **SATOR, Ted**
b: Utica, NY, 11/18/1949.

Season	Club	League	REGULAR SEASON GC	W	L	T	RT	W%	PLAYOFFS GC	W	L	T	W%
1985-86	NY Rangers	NHL	80	36	38	6	....	.488	16	8	8	0	.500
1986-87	NY Rangers	NHL	19	5	10	4	....	.368	....	....	....	....	....
	Buffalo	NHL	47	21	22	4	....	.489	....	....	....	....	....
1987-88	Buffalo	NHL	80	37	32	11	....	.531	6	2	4	0	.333
1988-89	Buffalo	NHL	80	38	35	7	....	.519	5	1	4	0	.200
	NHL Totals		**306**	**137**	**137**	**32**	....	**.500**	**27**	**11**	**16**	**0**	**.407**

● **SAVARD, Andre**
b: Temiscamingue, Que., 2/9/1953.
Played in NHL. See Modern Player Register for career statistics.

Season	Club	League	REGULAR SEASON GC	W	L	T	RT	W%	PLAYOFFS GC	W	L	T	W%
1987-88	Quebec	NHL	24	10	13	1	....	.438	....	....	....	....	....
	NHL Totals		**24**	**10**	**13**	**1**	....	**.438**	....	....	....	....	....

● **SCHINKEL, Ken**
b: Jansen, Sask., 11/27/1932.
Played in NHL. See Modern Player Register for career statistics.

Season	Club	League	REGULAR SEASON GC	W	L	T	RT	W%	PLAYOFFS GC	W	L	T	W%
1972-73	Pittsburgh	NHL	36	15	18	3	....	.458	....	....	....	....	....
1973-74	Pittsburgh	NHL	50	14	31	5	....	.330	....	....	....	....	....
1975-76	Pittsburgh	NHL	37	20	10	7	....	.635	3	1	2	0	.333
1976-77	Pittsburgh	NHL	80	34	33	13	....	.506	3	1	2	0	.333
	NHL Totals		**203**	**83**	**92**	**28**	....	**.478**	**6**	**2**	**4**	**0**	**.333**

● **SCHMIDT, Milt** HHOF
b: Kitchener, Ont., 3/5/1918.
Played in NHL. See Pre-Expansion Player Register for career statistics.

Season	Club	League	REGULAR SEASON GC	W	L	T	RT	W%	PLAYOFFS GC	W	L	T	W%
1954-55	Boston	NHL	40	13	12	15	....	.513	5	1	4	0	.200
1955-56	Boston	NHL	70	23	34	13	....	.421	....	....	....	....	....
1956-57	Boston	NHL	70	34	24	12	....	.571	10	5	5	0	.500
1957-58	Boston	NHL	70	27	28	15	....	.493	12	6	6	0	.500
1958-59	Boston	NHL	70	32	29	9	....	.521	7	3	4	0	.429
1959-60	Boston	NHL	70	28	34	8	....	.457	....	....	....	....	....
1960-61	Boston	NHL	70	15	42	13	....	.307	....	....	....	....	....
1962-63	Boston	NHL	56	13	31	12	....	.339	....	....	....	....	....
1963-64	Boston	NHL	70	18	40	12	....	.343	....	....	....	....	....
1964-65	Boston	NHL	70	21	43	6	....	.343	....	....	....	....	....
1965-66	Boston	NHL	70	21	43	6	....	.343	....	....	....	....	....
1974-75	Washington	NHL	8	2	6	0	....	.250	....	....	....	....	....
1975-76	Washington	NHL	36	3	28	5	....	.153	....	....	....	....	....
	NHL Totals		**770**	**250**	**394**	**126**	....	**.406**	**34**	**15**	**19**	**0**	**.441**

● **SCHOENFELD, Jim**
b: Galt, Ont., 9/4/1952.
Played in NHL. See Modern Player Register for career statistics.

Season	Club	League	REGULAR SEASON GC	W	L	T	RT	W%	PLAYOFFS GC	W	L	T	W%
1985-86	Buffalo	NHL	43	19	19	5	....	.500	....	....	....	....	....
1987-88	New Jersey	NHL	30	17	12	1	....	.583	20	11	9	0	.550
1988-89	New Jersey	NHL	80	27	41	12	....	.413	....	....	....	....	....
1989-90	New Jersey	NHL	14	6	6	2	....	.500	....	....	....	....	....
1993-94	Washington	NHL	37	19	12	6	....	.595	11	5	6	0	.455
1994-95	Washington	NHL	48	22	18	8	....	.542	7	3	4	0	.429
1995-96	Washington	NHL	82	39	32	11	....	.543	6	2	4	0	.333
1996-97	Washington	NHL	82	33	40	9	....	.457	....	....	....	....	....
1997-98	Phoenix	NHL	82	35	35	12	....	.500	6	2	4	0	.333
1998-99	Phoenix	NHL	82	39	31	12	....	.549	7	3	4	0	.429
	NHL Totals		**580**	**256**	**246**	**78**	....	**.509**	**57**	**26**	**31**	**0**	**.456**

● **SHAUGHNESSY, Tom**
b: unknown Deceased.

Season	Club	League	REGULAR SEASON GC	W	L	T	RT	W%	PLAYOFFS GC	W	L	T	W%
1929-30	Chicago	NHL	21	10	8	3	....	.548	....	....	....	....	....
	NHL Totals		**21**	**10**	**8**	**3**	....	**.548**	....	....	....	....	....

● **SHERO, Fred**
b: Winnipeg, Man., 10/23/1925 d: 11/24/1990.
Played in NHL. See Pre-Expansion Player Register for career statistics.

Season	Club	League	REGULAR SEASON GC	W	L	T	RT	W%	PLAYOFFS GC	W	L	T	W%
1971-72	Philadelphia	NHL	78	26	38	14	....	.423	....	....	....	....	....
1972-73	Philadelphia	NHL	78	37	30	11	....	.545	11	5	6	0	.455
♦1973-74	Philadelphia	NHL	78	50	16	12	....	.718	17	12	5	0	.706
♦1974-75	Philadelphia	NHL	80	51	18	11	....	.706	17	12	5	0	.706
1975-76	Philadelphia	NHL	80	51	13	16	....	.738	16	8	8	0	.500
1976-77	Philadelphia	NHL	80	48	16	16	....	.700	10	4	6	0	.400
1977-78	Philadelphia	NHL	80	45	20	15	....	.656	12	7	5	0	.583
1978-79	NY Rangers	NHL	80	40	29	11	....	.569	18	11	7	0	.611
1979-80	NY Rangers	NHL	80	38	32	10	....	.538	9	4	5	0	.444
1980-81	NY Rangers	NHL	20	4	13	3	....	.275	....	....	....	....	....
	NHL Totals		**734**	**390**	**225**	**119**	....	**.612**	**110**	**63**	**47**	**0**	**.573**

• Won Jack Adams Award (1974)

● **SIMPSON, Joe** HHOF
b: Selkirk, Man., 8/13/1893 d: 12/25/1973.
Played in NHL. See Pre-Expansion Player Register for career statistics.

Season	Club	League	REGULAR SEASON GC	W	L	T	RT	W%	PLAYOFFS GC	W	L	T	W%
1932-33	NY Americans	NHL	48	15	22	11	....	.427	....	....	....	....	....
1933-34	NY Americans	NHL	48	15	23	10	....	.417	....	....	....	....	....
1934-35	NY Americans	NHL	48	12	27	9	....	.344	....	....	....	....	....
	NHL Totals		**144**	**42**	**72**	**30**	....	**.396**	....	....	....	....	....

● **SIMPSON, Terry**
b: Brantford, Ont., 8/30/1943.

Season	Club	League	REGULAR SEASON GC	W	L	T	RT	W%	PLAYOFFS GC	W	L	T	W%
1986-87	NY Islanders	NHL	80	35	33	12	....	.513	14	7	7	0	.500
1987-88	NY Islanders	NHL	80	39	31	10	....	.550	6	2	4	0	.333
1988-89	NY Islanders	NHL	27	7	18	2	....	.296	....	....	....	....	....
1993-94	Philadelphia	NHL	84	35	39	10	....	.476	....	....	....	....	....
1994-95	Winnipeg	NHL	15	7	7	1	....	.500	....	....	....	....	....
1995-96	Winnipeg	NHL	82	36	40	6	....	.476	6	2	4	0	.333
	NHL Totals		**368**	**159**	**168**	**41**	....	**.488**	**26**	**11**	**15**	**0**	**.423**

● **SIMS, Al**
b: Toronto, Ont., 4/18/1953.
Played in NHL. See Modern Player Register for career statistics.

Season	Club	League	REGULAR SEASON GC	W	L	T	RT	W%	PLAYOFFS GC	W	L	T	W%
1996-97	San Jose	NHL	82	27	47	8	....	.378	....	....	....	....	....
	NHL Totals		**82**	**27**	**47**	**8**	....	**.378**	....	....	....	....	....

● **SINDEN, Harry** HHOF
b: Collins Bay, Ont., 9/14/1932.

Season	Club	League	REGULAR SEASON GC	W	L	T	RT	W%	PLAYOFFS GC	W	L	T	W%
1966-67	Boston	NHL	70	17	43	10	....	.314	....	....	....	....	....
1967-68	Boston	NHL	74	37	27	10	....	.568	4	0	4	0	.000
1968-69	Boston	NHL	76	42	18	16	....	.658	10	6	4	0	.600
♦1969-70	Boston	NHL	76	40	17	19	....	.651	14	12	2	0	.857
1979-80	Boston	NHL	7	6	1	0	....	.857	10	4	6	0	.400
1984-85	Boston	NHL	24	11	10	3	....	.521	5	2	3	0	.400
	NHL Totals		**327**	**153**	**116**	**58**	....	**.557**	**43**	**24**	**19**	**0**	**.558**

• SKINNER, Jimmy
b: Selkirk, Man., 1/12/1918.

Season	Club	League	GC	W	L	T	RT	W%	GC	W	L	T	W%
			REGULAR SEASON						PLAYOFFS				
♦1954-55	Detroit	NHL	70	42	17	11	....	.679	11	8	3	0	.727
1955-56	Detroit	NHL	70	30	24	16	....	.543	10	5	5	0	.500
1956-57	Detroit	NHL	70	38	20	12	....	.629	5	1	4	0	.200
1957-58	Detroit	NHL	37	13	17	7	....	.446	....	....	....	....	....
	NHL Totals		**247**	**123**	**78**	**46**	....	**.591**	**26**	**14**	**12**	**0**	**.538**

• SMEATON, Cooper HHOF
b: Carleton Place, Ont., 7/22/1890 d: 10/3/1978.

Season	Club	League	GC	W	L	T	RT	W%	GC	W	L	T	W%
1930-31	Philadelphia	NHL	44	4	36	4	....	.136	....	....	....	....	....
	NHL Totals		**44**	**4**	**36**	**4**	....	**.136**	....	....	....	....	....

• SMITH, Alf HHOF
b: Ottawa, Ont., 6/3/1873 d: 8/21/1953.

Season	Club	League	GC	W	L	T	RT	W%	GC	W	L	T	W%
1918-19	Ottawa	NHL	18	12	6	0	....	.667	5	1	4	0	.200
	NHL Totals		**18**	**12**	**6**	**0**	....	**.667**	**5**	**1**	**4**	**0**	**.200**

• SMITH, Barry
b: Buffalo, NY, 8/21/1950.

Season	Club	League	GC	W	L	T	RT	W%	GC	W	L	T	W%
1998-99	Detroit	NHL	5	4	1	0	....	.800	....	....	....	....	....
	NHL Totals		**5**	**4**	**1**	**0**	....	**.800**	....	....	....	....	....

Shared a 4-1-0 record with associate coach Dave Lewis while serving as co-head coaches until Scotty Bowman received medical clearance and decided to return to coaching on October 23, 1998.

• SMITH, Floyd
b: Perth, Ont., 5/16/1935.
Played in NHL. See Modern Player Register for career statistics.

Season	Club	League	GC	W	L	T	RT	W%	GC	W	L	T	W%
1971-72	Buffalo	NHL	1	0	1	0	....	.000	....	....	....	....	....
1974-75	Buffalo	NHL	80	49	16	15	....	.706	17	10	7	0	.588
1975-76	Buffalo	NHL	80	46	21	13	....	.656	9	4	5	0	.444
1976-77	Buffalo	NHL	80	48	24	8	....	.650	6	2	4	0	.333
1979-80	Toronto	NHL	68	30	33	5	....	.478	....	....	....	....	....
	NHL Totals		**309**	**173**	**95**	**41**	....	**.626**	**32**	**16**	**16**	**0**	**.500**

• SMITH, Mike
b: Potsdam, NY, 8/31/1945.

Season	Club	League	GC	W	L	T	RT	W%	GC	W	L	T	W%
1980-81	Winnipeg	NHL	23	2	17	4	....	.174	....	....	....	....	....
	NHL Totals		**23**	**2**	**17**	**4**	....	**.174**	....	....	....	....	....

• SMITH, Ron
b: Port Hope, Ont., 11/19/1952.
Played in NHL. See Modern Player Register for career statistics.

Season	Club	League	GC	W	L	T	RT	W%	GC	W	L	T	W%
1992-93	NY Rangers	NHL	44	15	22	7	....	.420	....	....	....	....	....
	NHL Totals		**44**	**15**	**22**	**7**	....	**.420**	....	....	....	....	....

• SMYTHE, Conn HHOF
b: Toronto, Ont., 2/1/1895 d: 11/18/1980.

Season	Club	League	GC	W	L	T	RT	W%	GC	W	L	T	W%
1927-28	Toronto	NHL	44	18	18	8	....	.500	....	....	....	....	....
1928-29	Toronto	NHL	44	21	18	5	....	.534	4	2	2	0	.500
1929-30	Toronto	NHL	44	17	21	6	....	.455	....	....	....	....	....
1930-31	Toronto	NHL	2	1	0	1	....	.750	....	....	....	....	....
	NHL Totals		**134**	**57**	**57**	**20**	....	**.500**	**4**	**2**	**2**	**0**	**.500**

• SONMOR, Glen
b: Moose Jaw, Sask., 4/22/1929.
Played in NHL. See Pre-Expansion Player Register for career statistics.

Season	Club	League	GC	W	L	T	RT	W%	GC	W	L	T	W%
1978-79	Minnesota	NHL	69	25	34	10	....	.435	....	....	....	....	....
1979-80	Minnesota	NHL	80	36	28	16	....	.550	15	8	7	0	.533
1980-81	Minnesota	NHL	80	35	28	17	....	.544	19	12	7	0	.632
1981-82	Minnesota	NHL	76	34	23	19	....	.572	....	....	....	....	....
1982-83	Minnesota	NHL	43	22	12	9	....	.616	....	....	....	....	....
1984-85	Minnesota	NHL	67	22	35	10	....	.403	9	5	4	0	.556
1986-87	Minnesota	NHL	2	0	1	1	....	.250	....	....	....	....	....
	NHL Totals		**417**	**174**	**161**	**82**	....	**.516**	**43**	**25**	**18**	**0**	**.581**

• SPROULE, Harvey
b: unknown Deceased.

Season	Club	League	GC	W	L	T	RT	W%	GC	W	L	T	W%
1919-20	Toronto	NHL	12	7	5	0	....	.583	....	....	....	....	....
	NHL Totals		**12**	**7**	**5**	**0**	....	**.583**	....	....	....	....	....

• STANLEY, Barney HHOF
b: Paisley, Ont., 1/1/1893 d: 5/14/1971.
Played in NHL. See Pre-Expansion Player Register for career statistics.

Season	Club	League	GC	W	L	T	RT	W%	GC	W	L	T	W%
1927-28	Chicago	NHL	23	4	17	2	....	.217	....	....	....	....	....
	NHL Totals		**23**	**4**	**17**	**2**	....	**.217**	....	....	....	....	....

• STASIUK, Vic
b: Lethbridge, Alta., 5/23/1929.
Played in NHL. See Pre-Expansion Player Register for career statistics.

Season	Club	League	GC	W	L	T	RT	W%	GC	W	L	T	W%
1969-70	Philadelphia	NHL	76	17	35	24	....	.382	....	....	....	....	....
1970-71	Philadelphia	NHL	78	28	33	17	....	.468	4	0	4	0	.000
1971-72	California	NHL	75	21	38	16	....	.387	....	....	....	....	....
1972-73	Vancouver	NHL	78	22	47	9	....	.340	....	....	....	....	....
	NHL Totals		**307**	**88**	**153**	**66**	....	**.394**	**4**	**0**	**4**	**0**	**.000**

• STEWART, Bill
b: Toronto, Ont., 10/6/1957.
Played in NHL. See Modern Player Register for career statistics.

Season	Club	League	GC	W	L	T	RT	W%	GC	W	L	T	W%
1998-99	NY Islanders	NHL	37	11	19	7	....	.392	....	....	....	....	....
	NHL Totals		**37**	**11**	**19**	**7**	....	**.392**	....	....	....	....	....

• STEWART, Bill USHOF
b: Fitchburg, MA, 9/26/1894 d: 2/14/1964.

Season	Club	League	GC	W	L	T	RT	W%	GC	W	L	T	W%
♦1937-38	Chicago	NHL	48	14	25	9	....	.385	10	7	3	0	.700
1938-39	Chicago	NHL	21	8	10	3	....	.452	....	....	....	....	....
	NHL Totals		**69**	**22**	**35**	**12**	....	**.406**	**10**	**7**	**3**	**0**	**.700**

• STEWART, Ron
b: Calgary, Alta., 7/11/1932.
Played in NHL. See Modern Player Register for career statistics.

Season	Club	League	GC	W	L	T	RT	W%	GC	W	L	T	W%
1975-76	NY Rangers	NHL	39	15	20	4	....	.436	....	....	....	....	....
1977-78	Los Angeles	NHL	80	31	34	15	....	.481	2	0	2	0	.000
	NHL Totals		**119**	**46**	**54**	**19**	....	**.466**	**2**	**0**	**2**	**0**	**.000**

• SULLIVAN, Red
b: Peterborough, Ont., 12/24/1929.
Played in NHL. See Pre-Expansion Player Register for career statistics.

Season	Club	League	GC	W	L	T	RT	W%	GC	W	L	T	W%
1962-63	NY Rangers	NHL	36	11	17	8	....	.417	....	....	....	....	....
1963-64	NY Rangers	NHL	70	22	38	10	....	.386	....	....	....	....	....
1964-65	NY Rangers	NHL	70	20	38	12	....	.371	....	....	....	....	....
1965-66	NY Rangers	NHL	20	5	10	5	....	.375	....	....	....	....	....
1967-68	Pittsburgh	NHL	74	27	34	13	....	.453	....	....	....	....	....
1968-69	Pittsburgh	NHL	76	20	45	11	....	.336	....	....	....	....	....
1974-75	Washington	NHL	18	2	16	0	....	.111	....	....	....	....	....
	NHL Totals		**364**	**107**	**198**	**59**	....	**.375**	....	....	....	....	....

• SUTHERLAND, Bill
b: Regina, Sask., 11/10/1934.
Played in NHL. See Modern Player Register for career statistics.

Season	Club	League	GC	W	L	T	RT	W%	GC	W	L	T	W%
1979-80	Winnipeg	NHL	3	1	2	0	....	.333	....	....	....	....	....
1980-81	Winnipeg	NHL	29	6	20	3	....	.259	....	....	....	....	....
	NHL Totals		**32**	**7**	**22**	**3**	....	**.266**	....	....	....	....	....

• SUTTER, Brian
b: Viking, Alta., 10/7/1956.
Played in NHL. See Modern Player Register for career statistics.

Season	Club	League	GC	W	L	T	RT	W%	GC	W	L	T	W%
1988-89	St. Louis	NHL	80	33	35	12	....	.488	10	5	5	0	.500
1989-90	St. Louis	NHL	80	37	34	9	....	.519	12	7	5	0	.583
1990-91	St. Louis	NHL	80	47	22	11	....	.656	13	6	7	0	.462
1991-92	St. Louis	NHL	80	36	33	11	....	.519	6	2	4	0	.333
1992-93	Boston	NHL	84	51	26	7	....	.649	4	0	4	0	.000
1993-94	Boston	NHL	84	42	29	13	....	.577	13	6	7	0	.462
1994-95	Boston	NHL	48	27	18	3	....	.594	5	1	4	0	.200
1997-98	Calgary	NHL	82	26	41	15	....	.409	....	....	....	....	....
1998-99	Calgary	NHL	82	30	40	12	....	.439	....	....	....	....	....
99-2000	Calgary	NHL	82	31	41	10	5	.470	....	....	....	....	....
	NHL Totals		**782**	**360**	**319**	**103**	**5**	**.529**	**63**	**27**	**36**	**0**	**.429**

• Won Jack Adams Award (1991)

• SUTTER, Darryl
b: Viking, Alta., 8/19/1958.
Played in NHL. See Modern Player Register for career statistics.

Season	Club	League	GC	W	L	T	RT	W%	GC	W	L	T	W%
1992-93	Chicago	NHL	84	47	25	12	....	.631	4	0	4	0	.000
1993-94	Chicago	NHL	84	39	36	9	....	.518	6	2	4	0	.333
1994-95	Chicago	NHL	48	24	19	5	....	.552	16	9	7	0	.563
1997-98	San Jose	NHL	82	34	38	10	....	.476	6	2	4	0	.333
1998-99	San Jose	NHL	82	31	33	18	....	.488	6	2	4	0	.333
99-2000	San Jose	NHL	82	35	37	10	7	.530	12	5	7	0	.417
	NHL Totals		**462**	**210**	**188**	**64**	**7**	**.531**	**50**	**20**	**30**	**0**	**.400**

• TALBOT, Jean-Guy
b: Cap de La Madeliene, Que., 7/11/1932.
Played in NHL. See Modern Player Register for career statistics.

Season	Club	League	GC	W	L	T	RT	W%	GC	W	L	T	W%
1972-73	St. Louis	NHL	65	30	28	7	....	.515	5	1	4	0	.200
1973-74	St. Louis	NHL	55	22	25	8	....	.473	....	....	....	....	....
1977-78	NY Rangers	NHL	80	30	37	13	....	.456	3	1	2	0	.333
	NHL Totals		**200**	**82**	**90**	**28**	....	**.480**	**8**	**2**	**6**	**0**	**.250**

• TESSIER, Orval
b: Cornwall, Ont., 6/30/1933.
Played in NHL. See Pre-Expansion Player Register for career statistics.

Season	Club	League	GC	W	L	T	RT	W%	GC	W	L	T	W%
1982-83	Chicago	NHL	80	47	23	10	....	.650	13	7	6	0	.538
1983-84	Chicago	NHL	80	30	42	8	....	.425	5	2	3	0	.400
1984-85	Chicago	NHL	53	22	28	3	....	.443	....	....	....	....	....
	NHL Totals		**213**	**99**	**93**	**21**	....	**.514**	**18**	**9**	**9**	**0**	**.500**

• Won Jack Adams Award (1983)

• THOMPSON, Paul
b: Calgary, Alta., 11/2/1906 Deceased.
Played in NHL. See Pre-Expansion Player Register for career statistics.

Season	Club	League	GC	W	L	T	RT	W%	GC	W	L	T	W%
			REGULAR SEASON						PLAYOFFS				
1938-39	Chicago	NHL	27	4	18	5	....	.241	....	....	....	....	....
1939-40	Chicago	NHL	48	23	19	6	....	.542	2	0	2	0	.000
1940-41	Chicago	NHL	48	16	25	7	....	.406	5	2	3	0	.400
1941-42	Chicago	NHL	48	22	23	3	....	.490	3	1	2	0	.333
1942-43	Chicago	NHL	50	17	18	15	....	.490	....	....	....	....	....
1943-44	Chicago	NHL	50	22	23	5	....	.490	9	4	5	0	.444
1944-45	Chicago	NHL	1	0	1	0	....	.000	....	....	....	....	....
	NHL Totals		**272**	**104**	**127**	**41**	....	**.458**	**19**	**7**	**12**	**0**	**.368**

• THOMPSON, Percy
b: unknown Deceased.

Season	Club	League	GC	W	L	T	RT	W%	GC	W	L	T	W%
1920-21	Hamilton	NHL	24	6	18	0	....	.250	....	....	....	....	....
1921-22	Hamilton	NHL	24	7	17	0	....	.292	....	....	....	....	....
	NHL Totals		**48**	**13**	**35**	**0**	....	**.271**	....	....	....	....	....

• TOBIN, Bill
b: Ottawa, Ont., 5/20/1895 d: 5/8/1963.

Season	Club	League	GC	W	L	T	RT	W%	GC	W	L	T	W%
1929-30	Chicago	NHL	23	11	10	2	....	.522	2	0	1	1	.250
1931-32	Chicago	NHL	48	18	19	11	....	.490	2	1	1	0	.500
	NHL Totals		**71**	**29**	**29**	**13**	....	**.500**	**4**	**1**	**2**	**1**	**.375**

• TORTORELLA, John
b: Boston, MA, 6/24/1958.

Season	Club	League	GC	W	L	T	RT	W%	GC	W	L	T	W%
99-2000	NY Rangers		4	0	3	1	0	.125	....	....	....	....	....
	NHL Totals		**4**	**0**	**3**	**1**	**0**	**.125**	....	....	....	....	....

• TREMBLAY, Mario
b: Montreal, Que., 2/9/1956.
Played in NHL. See Modern Player Register for career statistics.

Season	Club	League	GC	W	L	T	RT	W%	GC	W	L	T	W%
1995-96	Montreal	NHL	77	40	27	10	....	.584	6	2	4	0	.333
1996-97	Montreal	NHL	82	31	36	15	....	.470	5	1	4	0	.200
	NHL Totals		**159**	**71**	**63**	**25**	....	**.525**	**11**	**3**	**8**	**0**	**.273**

• TROTZ, Barry
b: Winnipeg, Man., 7/15/1962.

Season	Club	League	GC	W	L	T	RT	W%	GC	W	L	T	W%
1998-99	Nashville	NHL	82	28	47	7	....	.384	....	....	....	....	....
99-2000	Nashville	NHL	82	28	47	7	7	.427	....	....	....	....	....
	NHL Totals		**164**	**56**	**94**	**14**	**7**	**.405**	....	....	....	....	....

• UBRIACO, Gene
b: Sault Ste. Marie, Ont., 12/26/1937.
Played in NHL. See Modern Player Register for career statistics.

Season	Club	League	GC	W	L	T	RT	W%	GC	W	L	T	W%
1988-89	Pittsburgh	NHL	80	40	33	7	....	.544	11	7	4	0	.636
1989-90	Pittsburgh	NHL	26	10	14	2	....	.423	....	....	....	....	....
	NHL Totals		**106**	**50**	**47**	**9**	....	**.514**	**11**	**7**	**4**	**0**	**.636**

• VACHON, Rogie
b: Palmarolle, Que., 9/8/1945.
Played in NHL. See Goaltender Register for career statistics.

Season	Club	League	GC	W	L	T	RT	W%	GC	W	L	T	W%
1983-84	Los Angeles	NHL	2	1	0	1	....	.750	....	....	....	....	....
1987-88	Los Angeles	NHL	1	0	1	0	....	.000	....	....	....	....	....
1994-95	Los Angeles	NHL	7	3	2	2	....	.571	....	....	....	....	....
	NHL Totals		**10**	**4**	**3**	**3**	....	**.550**	....	....	....	....	....

• VIGNEAULT, Alain
b: Quebec City, Que., 5/14/1961.
Played in NHL. See Modern Player Register for career statistics.

Season	Club	League	GC	W	L	T	RT	W%	GC	W	L	T	W%
1997-98	Montreal	NHL	82	37	32	13	....	.530	10	4	6	0	.400
1998-99	Montreal	NHL	82	32	39	11	....	.457	....	....	....	....	....
99-2000	Montreal	NHL	82	35	38	9	4	.506	....	....	....	....	....
	NHL Totals		**246**	**104**	**109**	**33**	**4**	**.498**	**10**	**4**	**6**	**0**	**.400**

• WATSON, Bryan
b: Bancroft, Ont., 11/14/1942.
Played in NHL. See Modern Player Register for career statistics.

Season	Club	League	GC	W	L	T	RT	W%	GC	W	L	T	W%
1980-81	Edmonton	NHL	18	4	9	5	....	.361	....	....	....	....	....
	NHL Totals		**18**	**4**	**9**	**5**	....	**.361**	....	....	....	....	....

• WATSON, Phil
b: Montreal, Que., 4/24/1914 Deceased.
Played in NHL. See Pre-Expansion Player Register for career statistics.

Season	Club	League	GC	W	L	T	RT	W%	GC	W	L	T	W%
1955-56	NY Rangers	NHL	70	32	28	10	....	.529	5	1	4	0	.200
1956-57	NY Rangers	NHL	70	26	30	14	....	.471	5	1	4	0	.200
1957-58	NY Rangers	NHL	70	32	25	13	....	.550	6	2	4	0	.333
1958-59	NY Rangers	NHL	70	26	32	12	....	.457	....	....	....	....	....
1959-60	NY Rangers	NHL	15	3	9	3	....	.300	....	....	....	....	....
1961-62	Boston	NHL	70	15	47	8	....	.271	....	....	....	....	....
1962-63	Boston	NHL	14	1	8	5	....	.250	....	....	....	....	....
	NHL Totals		**379**	**135**	**179**	**65**	....	**.442**	**16**	**4**	**12**	**0**	**.250**

• WATT, Tom
b: Toronto, Ont., 6/17/1935.

Season	Club	League	GC	W	L	T	RT	W%	GC	W	L	T	W%
1981-82	Winnipeg	NHL	80	33	33	14	....	.500	4	1	3	0	.250
1982-83	Winnipeg	NHL	80	33	39	8	....	.463	3	0	3	0	.000
1983-84	Winnipeg	NHL	21	6	13	2	....	.333	....	....	....	....	....
1985-86	Vancouver	NHL	80	23	44	13	....	.369	3	0	3	0	.000
1986-87	Vancouver	NHL	80	29	43	8	....	.413	....	....	....	....	....
1990-91	Toronto	NHL	69	22	37	10	....	.391	....	....	....	....	....
1991-92	Toronto	NHL	80	30	43	7	....	.419	....	....	....	....	....
	NHL Totals		**490**	**176**	**252**	**62**	....	**.422**	**10**	**1**	**9**	**0**	**.100**

• Won Jack Adams Award (1982)

• WEBSTER, Tom
b: Kirkland Lake, Ont., 10/4/1948.
Played in NHL. See Modern Player Register for career statistics.

Season	Club	League	GC	W	L	T	RT	W%	GC	W	L	T	W%
1986-87	NY Rangers	NHL	18	5	9	4	....	.389	....	....	....	....	....
1989-90	Los Angeles	NHL	80	34	39	7	....	.469	10	4	6	0	.400
1990-91	Los Angeles	NHL	80	46	24	10	....	.638	12	6	6	0	.500
1991-92	Los Angeles	NHL	80	35	31	14	....	.525	6	2	4	0	.333
	NHL Totals		**258**	**120**	**103**	**35**	....	**.533**	**28**	**12**	**16**	**0**	**.429**

Assistant coaches Wayne Cashman and Ed Giacomin posted 0-2-0 record when Tom Webster was ill, a 4-3 loss to Minnesota at New York on December 15, 1986, and a 7-4 loss at Edmonton on January 23, 1987. All games are credited to Webster's coaching record.

• WEILAND, Cooney HHOF
b: Seaforth (Edmondville), Ont., 11/5/1904 d: 7/3/1985.
Played in NHL. See Pre-Expansion Player Register for career statistics.

Season	Club	League	GC	W	L	T	RT	W%	GC	W	L	T	W%
1939-40	Boston	NHL	48	31	12	5	....	.698	6	2	4	0	.333
♦1940-41	Boston	NHL	48	27	8	13	....	.698	11	8	3	0	.727
	NHL Totals		**96**	**58**	**20**	**18**	....	**.698**	**17**	**10**	**7**	**0**	**.588**

• WHITE, Bill
b: Toronto, Ont., 8/26/1939.
Played in NHL. See Modern Player Register for career statistics.

Season	Club	League	GC	W	L	T	RT	W%	GC	W	L	T	W%
1976-77	Chicago	NHL	46	16	24	6	....	.413	2	0	2	0	.000
	NHL Totals		**46**	**16**	**24**	**6**	....	**.413**	**2**	**0**	**2**	**0**	**.000**

• WILEY, Jim
b: Sault Ste. Marie, Ont., 4/28/1950.
Played in NHL. See Modern Player Register for career statistics.

Season	Club	League	GC	W	L	T	RT	W%	GC	W	L	T	W%
1995-96	San Jose	NHL	57	17	37	3	....	.325	....	....	....	....	....
	NHL Totals		**57**	**17**	**37**	**3**	....	**.325**	....	....	....	....	....

• WILSON, Johnny
b: Kincardine, Ont., 6/14/1929.
Played in NHL. See Pre-Expansion Player Register for career statistics.

Season	Club	League	GC	W	L	T	RT	W%	GC	W	L	T	W%
1969-70	Los Angeles	NHL	52	9	34	9	....	.260	....	....	....	....	....
1971-72	Detroit	NHL	67	30	27	10	....	.522	....	....	....	....	....
1972-73	Detroit	NHL	78	37	29	12	....	.551	....	....	....	....	....
1976-77	Colorado	NHL	80	20	46	14	....	.338	....	....	....	....	....
1977-78	Pittsburgh	NHL	80	25	37	18	....	.425	....	....	....	....	....
1978-79	Pittsburgh	NHL	80	36	31	13	....	.531	7	2	5	0	.286
1979-80	Pittsburgh	NHL	80	30	37	13	....	.456	5	2	3	0	.400
	NHL Totals		**517**	**187**	**241**	**89**	....	**.448**	**12**	**4**	**8**	**0**	**.333**

• WILSON, Larry
b: Kincardine, Ont., 10/23/1930 d: 8/16/1979.
Played in NHL. See Pre-Expansion Player Register for career statistics.

Season	Club	League	GC	W	L	T	RT	W%	GC	W	L	T	W%
1976-77	Detroit	NHL	36	3	29	4	....	.139	....	....	....	....	....
	NHL Totals		**36**	**3**	**29**	**4**	....	**.139**	....	....	....	....	....

• WILSON, Ron
b: Toronto, Ont., 5/13/1956.
Played in NHL. See Modern Player Register for career statistics.

Season	Club	League	GC	W	L	T	RT	W%	GC	W	L	T	W%
1993-94	Anaheim	NHL	84	33	46	5	....	.423	....	....	....	....	....
1994-95	Anaheim	NHL	48	16	27	5	....	.385	....	....	....	....	....
1995-96	Anaheim	NHL	82	35	39	8	....	.476	....	....	....	....	....
1996-97	Anaheim	NHL	82	36	33	13	....	.518	11	4	7	0	.364
1997-98	Washington	NHL	82	40	30	12	....	.561	21	12	9	0	.571
1998-99	Washington	NHL	82	31	45	6	....	.415	....	....	....	....	....
99-2000	Washington	NHL	82	44	26	12	2	.622	5	1	4	0	.200
	NHL Totals		**542**	**235**	**246**	**61**	**2**	**.492**	**37**	**17**	**20**	**0**	**.459**

• YOUNG, Garry
b: Toronto, Ont., 1/2/1936.

Season	Club	League	GC	W	L	T	RT	W%	GC	W	L	T	W%
1972-73	California	NHL	12	2	7	3	....	.292	....	....	....	....	....
1974-75	St. Louis	NHL	69	32	26	11	....	.543	2	0	2	0	.000
1975-76	St. Louis	NHL	29	9	15	5	....	.397	....	....	....	....	....
	NHL Totals		**110**	**43**	**48**	**19**	....	**.477**	**2**	**0**	**2**	**0**	**.000**

CHAPTER 82

Selected Biographies

Noteworthy Active and Retired Players, Coaches and Builders

Eric Zweig

SID ABEL was the center of the Detroit Red Wings' famed Production Line in the late 1940s and early 1950s. He made his NHL debut in 1938–39 and became a regular in 1940–41. Abel earned a berth on the Second All-Star Team in 1941–42 and was team captain when Detroit won the Stanley Cup in 1943.

Abel was first teamed with Gordie Howe and Ted Lindsay during the 1946–47 season, but it was not until 1948–49 that the threesome was dubbed the Production Line. Abel won the Hart Trophy that year after leading the first-place Red Wings in scoring. Lindsay, Abel and Howe finished 1–2–3 respectively in the league scoring race in 1949–50, and Abel established career highs with 34 goals and 69 points. The Red Wings won the Stanley Cup that season, and again in 1952, before Abel was sold to Chicago where he became a playing coach with the Black Hawks. He gave up playing to concentrate solely on coaching in 1953–54, then returned to Detroit as a commentator on Red Wings television broadcasts. Midway through the 1957–58 season, Abel returned to coaching when the Wings' Jimmy Skinner was forced to resign due to illness.

Abel continued to coach the Red Wings until the 1967–68 season, and then again in 1969–70, and also served as general manager from 1962–63 until being replaced in 1970–71. His teams reached the Stanley Cup finals in 1961, 1963, 1964 and 1966 and had the best record in the NHL in 1964–65. Abel was inducted into the Hockey Hall of Fame in 1969.

CHARLES ADAMS worked his way up from grocery store clerk to the head of a major United States chain. In 1924, he purchased the rights to the first American team in the NHL, hiring Art Ross to run his new Boston franchise. The name Bruins was chosen from the many selections offered by fans, the news media and club employees, and the team was clad in the brown and yellow colors of Adams's grocery store chain.

The Bruins struggled in their first two years until Adams made some key player purchases for the 1926–27 season from the recently defunct Western Hockey League. The most prominent new player was Eddie Shore, who helped the Bruins establish themselves as an NHL power. The following season, Adams guaranteed a sum of $500,000 over a five-year span to help fund construction of Boston Garden. He was elected to the Hockey Hall of Fame as a builder in 1960. Later, the NHL's Adams Division was named in his honor. Son Weston, who succeeded him as Bruins president in 1936, was elected to the Hall of Fame in 1972.

JACK ADAMS had a Hall of Fame career as a player before becoming one of hockey's most famous coaches and executives over a long association with the Detroit Red Wings. He entered the NHL as a player during its first season of 1917–18 and was on a Stanley Cup winner that first year in Toronto. However, he did not emerge as a scoring star until entering the Pacific Coast Hockey Association with the Vancouver Millionaires in 1919–20. Adams had six goals in the Stanley Cup finals of 1922, though Vancouver lost to the Toronto St. Pats. He then returned to the NHL with the St. Pats the following season. His playing career ended in 1926–27 when he helped the Ottawa Senators win the Stanley Cup.

Joining a team then known as the Cougars, Adams signed on with Detroit for the new franchise's second season of 1927–28. As the club's coach and general manager, Adams sold hockey in Detroit by developing a strong farm system and building winning teams. The Red Wings won 12 regular-season championships under Adams, including seven in a row from 1948–49 to 1954–55, and seven Stanley Cup titles. In his 35 years with the Red Wings, Detroit missed the playoffs only seven times.

Adams was inducted into the Hockey Hall of Fame in 1959 and remained with the Red Wings until the end of the 1961–62 season. When the New York Rangers presented the Lester Patrick Trophy to the NHL in 1966 to recognize outstanding service to hockey in the United States, Adams was named the first winner. He had become president of the Central Hockey League following his departure from Detroit and died while at his desk on May 1, 1968. The NHL's coach of the year award is named in Adams's honor.

SIR H. MONTAGU ALLAN was a member of a prominent Montreal family that made its fortune in shipping and railroads. In 1908 he donated a trophy that would symbolize amateur hockey supremacy in Canada. William Northey, president of the Montreal Amateur Athletic Association, prevailed upon Allan to donate such a trophy because the Stanley Cup increasingly was becoming available only to professional teams. For many years, the Allan Cup rivaled the Stanley Cup in terms of its importance as a hockey trophy in Canada. In 1945, Sir H. Montagu Allan was among the original inductees into the Hockey Hall of Fame, along with Lord Stanley of Preston and 10 players.

In addition to the family shipping business, Allan was the last president of the Merchants Bank of Canada, which was amalgamated into the Bank of Montreal in 1922. He was president of the Montreal Jockey Club and owned horses that won the Queen's Plate. Allan was also honorary lieutenant-colonel of the Black Watch (a Royal Highland regiment) and he lost a son to military action during World War I. Two of Allan's daughters were killed in the 1915 sinking of the Lusitania.

TONY AMONTE starred at Boston University and signed his first professional contract with the New York Rangers on April 2, 1991—two days after BU lost the NCAA championship to Michigan in triple overtime. He made his NHL debut in game five of the Patrick Division semifinals that year and became a regular with the Rangers the following season.

Amonte scored 35 goals as a rookie in 1991–92 and was a finalist for the Calder Trophy which went to Pavel Bure that year. His offensive production declined during his third season and he was traded to the Chicago Blackhawks. One month later, on April 23, 1994, Amonte became just the second Blackhawks player (Denis Savard was the first) to score four goals in one playoff game. He has been a top offensive threat for Chicago ever since.

In international play, Amonte scored the series-winning goal in game three as the United States beat Canada in the 1996 World Cup of Hockey.

SYL APPS was the inspirational leader of the Toronto Maple Leafs in the late 1930s and 1940s, serving as team captain from 1940–41 to 1942–43, and again from 1945–46 until he retired after the 1947–48 season. In addition to his great hockey talent, Apps was an excellent football player at McMaster University in Hamilton. He also won the Canadian and British Empire championship in the pole vault in 1934 and finished sixth at the 1936 Berlin Olympics.

Apps entered the NHL with the Maple Leafs in 1936–37 and was named rookie of the year after finishing second in the league with 45 points. He was runner-up to linemate Gordie Drillon in the 1937–38 NHL scoring race and was rewarded with his first of three selections to the Second All-Star Team at center. Apps earned First Team honors in 1938–39 and 1941–42. He also won the Lady Byng Trophy in 1941–42 and played on his first Stanley Cup champion that year.

After a two-year absence from hockey while he served in the Canadian army, Apps returned to the Maple Leafs in 1945–46. He set new career highs in goals with 24, 25 and 26 over each of the next three seasons and helped the Leafs win the Stanley Cup again in 1947 and 1948 before he retired. In 1961, Apps was elected to the Hockey Hall of Fame.

AL ARBOUR ranks among the greatest coaches in NHL history, trailing only Scotty Bowman for most games and most wins in both regular-season and playoff history. His four Stanley Cup championships with the New York Islanders are surpassed only by Toe Blake, Bowman and Hap Day. Arbour was also on three Stanley Cup winners as a player.

A defenseman who wore glasses on the ice, Arbour broke into the NHL with the Detroit Red Wings in 1953–54. He joined the Chicago Black Hawks in 1958–59 and helped them to win their first Stanley Cup title in 23 years in 1961. The following year, he won another Stanley Cup championship as a member of the Toronto Maple Leafs.

Arbour was selected by the St. Louis Blues in the 1967 Expansion Draft. He began his coaching career with the Blues in 1970–71, but resigned during the season to continue playing. The following year, he became coach again. He joined the Islanders in their second season of 1973–74 and quickly developed the sad-sack expansion team into a powerhouse. Under Arbour, the Islanders had more than 100 points four years in a row between 1975–76 and 1978–79, then won four consecutive Stanley Cup titles from 1980 until 1983.

Following the 1985–86 season, Arbour retired from coaching to become a vice president with the Islanders, but was back behind the bench in 1988. He guided the team again until 1994, then returned to a position in the club's front office. He was elected to the Hockey Hall of Fame as a builder in 1996.

ACE BAILEY had his hockey career cut short tragically on December 12, 1933, when he was hit from behind by Eddie Shore of the Boston Bruins, suffering a fractured skull. In the seven-plus seasons in which he played in the NHL, Bailey had established himself first as a top scorer and then as a great defensive forward.

Irvine "Ace" Bailey began his pro career with the Toronto St. Pats in 1926–27. The team was renamed the Maple Leafs after being purchased by Conn Smythe later that season, and Bailey and Hap Day became cornerstones of the new club. Bailey led the NHL in both goals and points in 1928–29, and he was the Leafs' top scorer until the arrival of Charlie Conacher the following season. When the Kid Line of Conacher, Joe Primeau and Busher Jackson became the Leafs' top offensive unit, Bailey developed into a defensive specialist who helped Toronto win the Stanley Cup in 1932.

The NHL's first All-Star Game on February 14, 1934, was played to benefit Ace Bailey and his family. After recovering from his near-fatal accident, Bailey got into coaching and later joined the staff of off-ice officials at Maple Leaf Gardens, where he remained for many years. He was elected to the Hockey Hall of Fame in 1975.

HOBEY BAKER is a legend in United States hockey history, where the Hobey Baker Award has been presented annually since 1981 to the outstanding player in the NCAA. Baker was the greatest player in American hockey before, during and after the three years he spent at Princeton University from 1910 to 1913.

Hobart Amery Hare Baker first came to prominence in hockey with the St. Paul's School in Concord, New Hampshire. He was a rover during the era of the seven-man game, and he was an exceptional skater and stickhandler. In addition to his hockey skills, Baker was also prominent in football, golf, track, swimming and gymnastics, captaining the football team for a year at Princeton in addition to his two years as hockey captain.

After leaving Princeton, Baker continued to play hockey with the St. Nicholas Club in New York until 1916. In 1917 the United States entered World War I, and in 1918 Baker became a pilot with the 103rd Squadron—a unit that had been known as the Lafayette Esquadrille until it was transferred from the French to the U.S. Army. Baker later became commander of the 141st Squadron, a unit that incorporated Princeton's Tiger logo into its insignia. Baker survived the war, but he was killed in a tragic air accident shortly after the armistice was signed. He was one of the first 12 men selected to the Hockey Hall of Fame in 1945, and he later became an original inductee into the United States Hockey Hall of Fame in 1973.

BILL BARILKO was not known for his offensive talent, yet he scored one of the most famous goals in NHL history. On April 21, 1951, Barilko lifted a shot past Gerry McNeil of the Montreal Canadiens for a goal at 2:53 of overtime that won the Stanley Cup for the Toronto Maple Leafs. In the offseason, Barilko was killed in a plane crash while on a fishing trip in Northern Ontario. It was 11 years before his body was found and 11 years before the Maple Leafs won the Stanley Cup again.

Barilko was thought to be on the verge of stardom at the time of his death. A sturdy defenseman and solid checker, he had been summoned from Hollywood of the Pacific Coast Hockey League late in the 1946–47 season and helped the Leafs win the Stanley Cup in each of his first three seasons. Barilko's goal in 1951 capped a Stanley Cup finals in which each of the five games was decided in overtime.

ANDY BATHGATE was a strong skater, slick stickhandler, powerful shooter and skilled playmaker. He suffered a serious knee injury while playing in Guelph of the Ontario Hockey Association, but overcame the handicap of wearing a special brace to become a star in the NHL.

Bathgate won the Memorial Cup with Guelph in 1952 and joined the New York Rangers the following season. He became a regular in 1954–55, then led the Rangers in points each of the next eight seasons. Bathgate established career highs with 40 goals and 88 points in 1958–59 and won the Hart Trophy as the NHL's most valuable player. In 1961–62, Bathgate tied Bobby Hull for the NHL scoring lead with 84 points, but Hull was awarded the Art Ross Trophy because he had 54 goals to Bathgate's 28.

On February 22, 1964, New York traded Bathgate to the Toronto Maple Leafs as part of a seven-player swap. He won his only Stanley Cup championship with the Maple Leafs in the spring of 1964, but problems with his knee the following season limited him to just 55 games, and on May 20, 1965, he was dealt to the Detroit Red Wings. In 1967, he was acquired by the Pittsburgh Penguins in the Expansion Draft. He later spent two years with Vancouver of the Western Hockey League before playing his final NHL season with the Penguins in 1970–71.

After a coaching stint in Switzerland, Bathgate returned to Vancouver in 1973–74 as a coach with the Blazers of the World Hockey Association. He made a brief comeback as a player when he took part in 11 games with Vancouver the following year. Bathgate was elected to the Hockey Hall of Fame in 1978.

FATHER DAVID BAUER was a member of a prominent sports family. His brother Bobby Bauer was part of the Boston Bruins' famous Kraut Line as the right wing alongside Milt Schmidt and Woody Dumart during the 1930s and 1940s. David Bauer played left wing at St. Michael's College in Toronto and was loaned to the Oshawa Generals, along with teammates Ted Lindsay and Gus Mortson, for a playoff run that saw them win the 1944 Memorial Cup. While Lindsay and Mortson went on to pursue NHL careers, Bauer became a Basilian priest.

Following his ordination in 1953, Father Bauer joined the teaching staff at St. Michael's College in Toronto and coached the school's Junior A team to a Memorial Cup victory in 1961. St. Mike's discontinued its hockey program after that season and in June, 1962 the Canadian Amateur Hockey Association granted permission for Father Bauer to pursue a plan to develop an amateur Canadian national team to take part in international tournaments.

Father Bauer's national team first represented Canada abroad at the 1964 Winter Olympics in Innsbruck, Austria, where a last-minute change in the tie-breaking procedure robbed the team of a bronze medal. With Jackie McLeod as the new player-coach and Father Bauer as general manager, bronze medals were achieved at the 1966 and 1967 World Championships and at the 1968 Winter Olympics in Grenoble, France, but the program was discontinued after 1969. The national team concept was reborn when Canada returned to Olympic competition in 1980, and Father Bauer served as the managing director of the Canadian team at Lake Placid. In 1989, Father David Bauer was inducted into the Hockey Hall of Fame as a builder.

ED BELFOUR had previous experience with the Blackhawks, but was technically still a rookie when he became the top goalie in Chicago in 1990–91. He led the league with 74 games played, 43 wins and a 2.47 goals-against average that year, breaking Tony Esposito's club records for games and wins in a single season. Belfour also joined Esposito, Frank Brimsek and Tom Barrasso as the only goaltenders to be awarded the Vezina and Calder trophies in the same season. "The Eagle," as he is known, also won the Jennings Trophy for the fewest goals allowed by a team.

Over his first five full NHL seasons, Belfour led the NHL in shutouts four times, won the Jennings Trophy three times, the Vezina Trophy twice, and helped Chicago reach the Stanley Cup finals in 1992. His 41 wins in 1992–93 made Belfour just the fifth goalie in history to win 40-plus games more than once. However, his play began to decline after 1994–95, and the Blackhawks dealt Belfour to San Jose for three players during the 1996–97 campaign. He signed with the Dallas Stars in the offseason and recaptured his previous form in 1997–98 when he led the NHL with a 1.88 goals-against average and posted nine shutouts. In 1999, Belfour led the Stars to the franchise's first Stanley Cup title. He won his 300th regular-season game on February 13, 2000.

JEAN BELIVEAU was a rare blend of grace and power with a long, sweeping stride that gave him deceptive speed. At 6'3" and 205 pounds, he was difficult to check, but he was always a gentleman both on the ice and off.

Beliveau became a star in Victoriaville and Quebec City prior to joining the Montreal Canadiens. He made two brief NHL appearances before finally signing with the Canadiens amid much fanfare in 1953. Injuries plagued Beliveau during his rookie season of 1953–54, as they would throughout his career, but he blossomed into an NHL star during 1954–55. That year, Beliveau finished third in league scoring with 73 points, one behind teammate Maurice Richard and two back of Bernie Geoffrion. Beliveau was named to the First All-Star Team at center that year and would go on to be an all-star nine more times. In 1955–56, Beliveau led the NHL in scoring with a career-high 47 goals and 88 points. He won the Hart Trophy in addition to the Art Ross Trophy that year, and played on his first of 10 Stanley Cup champions.

Beliveau was named captain of the Canadiens in 1961–62, and in 1963–64 he won his second Hart Trophy. In 1965, he was the first recipient of the Conn Smythe Trophy as most valuable player in the playoffs. On March 3, 1968, Beliveau joined Gordie Howe as the only players to that point in NHL history to reach 1,000 career points. On February 11, 1971, he became just the fourth player in history to score 500 goals. Beliveau retired after the Canadiens upset the Chicago Black Hawks to win the Stanley Cup that spring. At the time, his 507 goals were the most ever scored by a center in the NHL. The traditional three-year waiting period was waived and Beliveau was elected to the Hockey Hall of Fame in 1972.

After his playing days, Beliveau moved into a front-office job with Montreal. He was a part of seven more Stanley Cup teams as an executive with the Canadiens before he retired in 1994. The Jean Beliveau Trophy is awarded annually to the Quebec Major Junior Hockey League player with the highest number of points in regular-season play.

DOUG BENTLEY was the first of three Bentley brothers to play in the NHL, breaking in with the Chicago Black Hawks in 1939–40. He possessed speed, stickhandling skill and scoring power in abundance, though he stood just 5'8" and weighed only 145 pounds.

Bentley advanced quickly through the amateur ranks in his home province of Saskatchewan before moving on to Drumheller, Alberta, for the 1938–39 season. The Drumheller team featured four Bentley brothers. When Doug and Max Bentley later joined forces in Chicago, both became stars. Doug led the NHL in goals and points in 1942–43 when his 73 points tied the NHL single-season record. He had 77 points in 1943–44, but lost the scoring title to the Boston Bruins' Herb Cain, who set a new single-season record with 82.

The 1945–46 season saw Max and Doug Bentley teamed with Bill Mosienko on the Pony Line. The trio was among the best in the NHL, as Max Bentley won the scoring title two years in a row and Doug was a First Team All-Star in 1946–47. The line was broken up the following year when Max was traded to the Toronto Maple Leafs, but Doug remained among the best scorers in the NHL over the next three seasons. In 1948–49, he finished second to linemate Roy Conacher in the NHL scoring race. In 1950, Bentley was named the greatest player in Black Hawks history.

By 1950–51, Doug Bentley was slowing down. He spent the better part of the next two seasons in the minors, but made a brief comeback when he joined Max with the New York Rangers in 1953–54. He remained active as a player, coach and scout after leaving the NHL. In 1964, Doug Bentley was inducted into the Hockey Hall of Fame. Brother Max was elected two years later.

MAX BENTLEY was known as "the Dipsy-Doodle Dandy from Delisle" for his skating and stickhandling skill (and his hometown in Saskatchewan). He only weighed 155 pounds, but he was one of the top players in the NHL during the 1940s and early 1950s.

Max joined his brother Doug with the Chicago Black Hawks during the 1940–41 season and by 1942–43, the Bentleys were among the most dangerous scorers in the NHL. Doug led the league in both goals and points that year, while Max finished third in scoring and won the Lady Byng Trophy. Max Bentley missed the next two seasons because of military service in World War II, but was back with the Black Hawks in 1945–46. The Bentleys were teamed with Bill Mosienko that year, and the Pony Line became the most effective trio in the NHL. Max was the league's leading scorer in 1945–46 and 1946–47, but on November 2, 1947, the struggling Black Hawks traded him to the Toronto Maple Leafs as the centerpiece in a seven-player swap.

Bentley helped Toronto repeat as Stanley Cup champions in 1948. He was with Stanley Cup winners in Toronto again in 1949 and in 1951, which proved to be his last great season. Injuries and a scoring slump saw Bentley return home to Saskatchewan during the 1952–53 season, and he was signed by the New York Rangers in 1953–54. Briefly reunited with Doug in New York, it would prove to be his last NHL season, though he would continue to play and, later, coach in Saskatoon for several years. Max Bentley was inducted into the Hockey Hall of Fame in 1966, two years after his brother Doug.

GARY BETTMAN was unanimously elected commissioner of the National Hockey League by the NHL Board of Governors on December 11, 1992. A graduate of Cornell University (1974) and New York University of Law (1977), he practiced law in Manhattan before joining the National Basketball Association in 1981 as assistant general counsel. In 1984, he became the NBA's senior vice president and general counsel.

Since Bettman assumed office as NHL commissioner on February 1, 1993, the league has achieved its first national network television contracts in the United States since the early 1970s and has expanded its presence on national cable outlets. The league has also successfully launched franchises in non-traditional hockey markets such as Florida, Dallas, Anaheim, Nashville, Columbus and Carolina, and has returned to Denver, Atlanta and Minnesota.

Under Bettman's leadership, the NHL reached a landmark agreement with the International Ice Hockey Federation in the summer of 1995 that resulted in the first World Cup of Hockey in 1996 and the NHL's participation in the Winter Olympics in 1998. The NHL will be returning to the Olympic Games at Salt Lake City in 2002.

In January, 1995, Bettman concluded the negotiation of a new Collective Bargaining Agreement with the NHL Players' Association. Twice extended, this agreement remains in effect until September 15, 2004.

ROB BLAKE is considered one of the top defensemen in the game. He joined the Los Angeles Kings late in 1989–90 and was named to the All-Rookie Team in 1990–91 after leading all rookie defensemen in scoring. Blake was chosen as the Kings' best defenseman in each of his first four full seasons before injuries began to limit his play.

Finally healthy again in 1997–98, Blake led all blueliners with 23 goals and won the Norris Trophy as the NHL's best defenseman as well as a selection to the First All-Star Team. He was also named the best defenseman at the 1998 Nagano Olympics, despite Canada's fourth-place finish. Blake's previous international experience includes winning a silver medal for Canada at the World Championships in 1991 and gold medals in 1994 and 1997.

Los Angeles slumped in 1998–99 when injuries once again cut Blake's season short, but both he and the Kings rebounded for fine seasons in 1999–2000. Blake was nominated for the Norris Trophy for the second time that season.

TOE BLAKE was a star player with the Montreal Canadiens during the 1930s and 1940s who later coached the team with great success during the 1950s and 1960s. Known as "the Lamplighter" for his scoring skill, Blake first came to prominence as a hockey player in Sudbury, Ontario, where he led the Cub Wolves to the Memorial Cup in 1932.

Blake played briefly with the Stanley Cup champion Montreal Maroons in 1934–35. He was traded to the Montreal Canadiens in 1936, and became a regular with the club in 1936–37. By 1938–39, he led the NHL in scoring, won the Hart Trophy as league MVP, and was named a First Team All-Star. Blake was the leading scorer on a weak club in three of the next four seasons and was named captain in 1940–41. In 1943–44, he was teamed with Maurice Richard and Elmer Lach and the Punch Line was born. The Canadiens cruised to first place that season and won their first Stanley Cup title in 13 years.

In 1944–45, Lach, Richard and Blake finished 1–2–3 in league scoring and were all named to the First All-Star Team. Blake was a Second Team All-Star and won the Lady Byng Trophy in 1945–46, when the Canadiens won another Stanley Cup championship. His NHL playing career came to an end when he broke his leg in a game against the New York Rangers on January 11, 1948. Blake finished the year as coach of the Houston Huskies in the United States Hockey League and led the team to the championship.

Blake was playing again in 1948–49 as a member of the Buffalo Bisons in the American Hockey League and took over as coach midway through the season. On February 10, 1950, he became the head coach while playing with the Valleyfield Braves of the Quebec Senior Hockey League. Blake remained the coach there until 1953–54. He was hired to coach the Montreal Canadiens for the 1955–56 season in the hope he would be able to harness the temper of his former linemate Maurice Richard. The Canadiens were Stanley Cup champions in Blake's first season as head coach and went on to win the Cup a record five years in a row.

Blake's teams continued to top the regular-season standings three times in four years between 1960–61 and 1963–64, then won the Stanley Cup again in 1965 and 1966. He retired after coaching his eighth Stanley Cup champion in 1968. Hector "Toe" Blake had been elected to the Hockey Hall of Fame as a player two years before.

PETER BONDRA joined the Washington Capitals in 1990–91 and led all club rookies with 12 goals and 28 points that year. By the 1992–93 season, he was the team's leading scorer with 37 goals and 85 points. On February 5, 1994, Bondra became just the second player in Washington history (Bengt Gustafsson was the first) to score five goals in a single game. In 1994–95, he became the first Capitals player to lead the NHL in goals when he scored 34 times in 47 games during the lockout-shortened, 48-game season. His 52 goals in 1997–98 tied Teemu Selanne for the league lead. Washington reached the Stanley Cup finals that year, but failed to reach the playoffs the next season. The Capitals rebounded to win the Southeast Division in 1999–2000, but injuries limited Bondra to just 21 goals.

Bondra was born in the Ukraine but raised in Czechoslovakia. He has held Slovakian citizenship since 1995. He helped the Slovakian national team qualify for the 1994 Winter Olympics and was the country's leading scorer at the World Cup of Hockey in 1996. Bondra was also a member of the Slovakian team that competed at the Nagano Olympics in 1998. He is known as one of the fastest skaters in the NHL.

MIKE BOSSY was a high-scoring junior with Laval of the Quebec Junior Hockey League, but was not selected in the 1977 Amateur Draft until the New York Islanders claimed him with the 15th choice. He would win the Calder Trophy in 1977–78 after setting a rookie scoring record with 53 goals, and went on to top 50 goals for a record nine consecutive seasons. Bossy fell short only in his final season of 1986–87 when injuries limited him to 38 goals in 63 games. He was the first Islanders player to reach 500 goals and 1,000 points.

Bossy scored 60 goals or more five times in his career (a mark equaled only by Wayne Gretzky), and led the league in 1978–79 and 1980–81. In the latter year, he equaled Maurice Richard's legendary achievement of 50 goals in 50 games. His career goals-per-game ratio of .792 (573 goals in 752 games) trails only Mario Lemieux's mark of .823 among the all-time scoring leaders and his 85 playoff goals rank fifth in NHL history. Bossy played a key role in all four Islanders Stanley Cup victories between 1980 and 1983, scoring the Cup-winning goal in 1982 and 1983. He won the Conn Smythe Trophy in 1982.

For the first eight seasons of his career, Bossy was selected as an NHL all-star at right wing, earning five berths on the First Team. He played for Team Canada at the Canada Cup in 1981 and 1984, winning in 1984 after scoring in overtime to eliminate the Soviet Union in the semifinals. A chronic back ailment forced Bossy to retire after the 1986–87 season. He was inducted into the Hockey Hall of Fame in 1991.

BRIAN BOUCHER was the Philadelphia Flyers' first choice in the 1995 NHL Entry Draft. Sharing netminding duties with John Vanbiesbrouck in his rookie season of 1999–2000, Boucher posted an NHL-best 1.91 goals-against average. He was the first rookie netminder to post an average below 2.00 since Terry Sawchuk and Al Rollins in 1950–51. He had taken over as the team's top netminder by the end of the season and helped the Flyers make a late rush to first-place overall in the Eastern Conference. In the playoffs, he helped Philadelphia reach the Eastern Conference final.

After an outstanding high school career at Mount St. Charles, Boucher went on to play junior hockey with the Tri-City Americans of the Western Hockey League and to twice represent the United States at the World Junior Championships. He spent two seasons with the Flyers' American Hockey League farm club prior to making his NHL debut.

FRANK BOUCHER was considered the best playmaker in hockey and the game's most sportsmanlike player during his days with the New York Rangers. He won the Lady Byng Trophy seven times in eight years between 1927–28 and 1934–35, and he was given permanent possession of the original trophy.

Boucher was a member of a prominent hockey-playing family in Ottawa. He and his brother George are both members of the Hall of Fame, while brothers Bob and Billy also spent time in the NHL. Frank made his NHL debut playing with his brother George on the Ottawa Senators in 1921–22, then spent four years with the Vancouver Maroons before returning to the NHL with the New York Rangers for their inaugural season of 1926–27.

With the Rangers, Frank Boucher centered a line with brothers Bill and Bun Cook that was the most productive unit in the NHL. With his precise passing, he ranked consistently among the NHL scoring leaders, leading the league in assists three times while helping the Rangers win the Stanley Cup in 1928 and 1933. He also earned selections to the First or Second All-Star Team on four occasions.

Boucher retired as a player to take over from Lester Patrick as coach of the Rangers in 1938–39. He led the team to a Stanley Cup victory the following year. He remained as coach until 1948–49 (including a brief comeback as a player in 1943–44), and he also succeeded Lester Patrick as general manager in 1946–47, staying with that job until 1954–55. In 1958, Frank Boucher was elected to the Hockey Hall of Fame.

RAYMOND BOURQUE is the only position player to win the Calder Trophy and earn a berth on the First All-Star Team as a rookie. From this auspicious start with the Boston Bruins in 1979–80, he went on to earn selections to either the First or Second All-Star Teams in each of his first 17 seasons, breaking Gordie Howe's record for consecutive all-star berths. Overall, he has been an all-star 18 times. As a five-time winner of the Norris Trophy, Bourque trails only Bobby Orr (eight) and Doug Harvey (seven) in the number of times he has been named the NHL's best defenseman.

Until late in the 1999–2000 season, Bourque had spent his entire professional career in Boston and is the club's all-time leader in assists and points. He surpassed Bobby Orr as the Bruins' all-time goal-scoring leader among defensemen with his 265th on January 22, 1992, and became the third defenseman in history (after Denis Potvin and Paul Coffey) to top 300 career goals. He became the first defenseman to top 400 goals on March 18, 2000.

Bourque led the Bruins in scoring five times and has ranked consistently among the top-scoring defensemen in the league. He ranks high among the NHL's all-time leaders in both assists and points, and when he collected his 1,000th assist on March 27, 1997, he became just the fifth player to reach that milestone, joining Wayne Gretzky, Gordie Howe, Marcel Dionne and Paul Coffey. He currently ranks third all-time in NHL history behind Gordie Howe and Larry Murphy in games played. Hoping to play for a Stanley Cup winner before he retires, Bourque asked the Bruins to trade him to a contender, and was dealt to the Colorado Avalanche on March 6, 2000.

Bourque had served as captain of the Bruins since 1988–89. He switched his uniform number from seven to 77 that season when the Bruins honored Phil Esposito by retiring his number on December 3, 1988.

SCOTTY BOWMAN has coached and won more games in both the regular season and playoffs than any man in NHL history. His eighth Stanley Cup coaching victory in 1998 tied him with the legendary Toe Blake for the most Cup championships ever. He had already been inducted into the Hall of Fame as a builder in 1991.

William Scott Bowman was a protege of Sam Pollock and became a coach with junior teams in the Montreal Canadiens organization after a head injury on March 7, 1952, forced him to cut short his playing career two years later. He also scouted for the Canadiens before making his NHL debut as coach of the St. Louis Blues in 1967–68. He was named general manager the following year and guided the Blues to the Stanley Cup finals in each of the team's first three seasons in the NHL.

In 1971–72, Pollock persuaded Bowman to return to Montreal. He won his first Stanley Cup title the following year and soon was coaching one of the greatest dynasties in NHL history. The Canadiens won the Stanley Cup four years in a row from 1976 until 1979 while posting some of the best regular-season win totals in NHL history. Bowman's Canadiens were 60–8–12 in 1976–77, setting a record for wins and points with 132.

Bowman left the Canadiens following the 1978–79 season to become coach, general manager and director of hockey operations with the Buffalo Sabres. He won a division title his first year in Buffalo and spent seven seasons with the Sabres. He was fired during the 1986–87 campaign and became a television analyst with Hockey Night in Canada the following season. He left that position in June, 1990 to become director of player development with the Pittsburgh Penguins. Bowman helped to assemble the Penguins team that won the Stanley Cup in 1991, then took over as coach during the illness of Bob Johnson and won another Stanley Cup title in 1992.

Bowman left the Penguins to become coach of the Red Wings in 1992–93. In his first three years in Detroit, his teams had excellent regular-season records, only to come up short in the playoffs. Bowman's Red Wings set a record with 62 wins (62–13–7) in 1995–96, but it was not until the following season that Detroit won its first Stanley Cup title since 1955. The Red Wings then made it two in a row with another Stanley Cup victory in 1998.

TURK BRODA never appeared to let the rigors of goaltending affect his cheerful personality. Always able to maintain his cool, Broda posted a lifetime 2.53 goals-against average, but was at his best in the postseason where his average was an incredible 1.98. He helped the Toronto Maple Leafs win the Stanley Cup five times and his 13 postseason shutouts were a modern NHL record until surpassed by Jacques Plante in 1970.

Broda had been playing in the Detroit Red Wings organization when Conn Smythe purchased him for $8,000 to replace aging veteran George Hainsworth in 1936–37. With Broda in goal, Toronto reached the Stanley Cup finals three years in a row from 1938 to 1940. In 1940–41, Broda won the Vezina Trophy for the first time. The following season, the Maple Leafs won the Stanley Cup.

The 1942–43 campaign was Broda's last before a two-year hitch in the military. He announced his retirement from hockey after the war, but was back with the Maple Leafs for the final 15 games of 1945–46. With Broda in goal full-time by 1946–47, the Leafs embarked on the most successful run in team history, winning the Stanley Cup three years in a row from 1947 to 1949, and adding a fourth championship in 1951. By that season, Broda was sharing the Maple Leafs goaltending job with Al Rollins. He played just one game during the 1951–52 season and retired after the playoffs.

Broda got into coaching after his playing career and guided the Toronto Marlboros to consecutive Memorial Cup championships in 1955 and 1956. Walter "Turk" Broda was inducted into the Hockey Hall of Fame in 1967.

MARTIN BRODEUR made his NHL debut with the New Jersey Devils as an emergency injury replacement late in the 1991–92 schedule. He won the Calder Trophy as rookie of the year after his first full season in 1993–94, and led the Devils to the first Stanley Cup title in franchise history the following year. All three of Brodeur's playoff shutouts in 1995 came in the second round against the Boston Bruins, making him just the fifth goalie in history (Dave Kerr, 1940; Frank McCool, 1945; Turk Broda, 1950; Felix Potvin, 1994) to record three shutouts in one playoff series.

Brodeur set an NHL record for minutes played with 4,433 in 1995–96, but the defending Stanley Cup champion Devils missed the playoffs. In 1996–97, Brodeur led the NHL with 10 shutouts and a 1.88 goals-against average. He was the first goalie to reach double digits in shutouts since Ken Dryden in 1976–77, and his goals-against average was the lowest since Tony Esposito's 1.77 mark in 1971–72, but he finished second behind Dominik Hasek in voting for the Vezina Trophy. Brodeur was the runner-up behind Hasek in Vezina voting again in 1997–98 despite leading the league with 43 wins. Brodeur did win the Jennings Trophy that season, after having shared the award with Devils teammate Mike Dunham in 1996–97. He led the league in wins again in 1998–99 and 1999–2000 and sparkled in the playoffs when the Devils won the Stanley Cup again in 2000.

Brodeur is a product of an athletic family. His brother Claude was a pitcher in the Montreal Expos system before an arm injury ended his career, and his father Denis (a long-time photographer for the Montreal Canadiens and Montreal Expos) won a bronze medal as a goalie with Canada on the 1956 Olympic team. Martin was a member of the Canadian Olympic team at Nagano in 1998.

PAVEL BURE was selected 113th overall by the Vancouver Canucks in the 1989 NHL Entry Draft. He then was declared draft-ineligible by NHL president John Ziegler on May 21, 1990, but the decision was reversed on June 14 and Bure was reinstated as Canucks property. Known as "The Russian Rocket," he made his debut in Vancouver in 1991–92 and set a club rookie record with 34 goals. Bure became the first Canucks player to receive a major NHL award when he won the Calder Trophy as rookie of the year.

In 1992–93, Bure became the first Vancouver player to top 50 goals and 100 points in a season when he scored 60 times and added 50 assists. He led the league when he scored 60 goals again in 1993–94, then led all playoff scorers with 16 goals as the Canucks reached the Stanley Cup finals before losing to the New York Rangers in seven games. He was the Canucks' scoring leader for the third year in a row in 1994–95, but injuries limited his play over the next two seasons. Healthy again in 1997–98, Bure returned to his position among the top scorers in the game. He was traded to the Florida Panthers on January 17, 1999, and won the Maurice Richard Trophy when he led the NHL with 58 goals in 1999–2000. Bure was also nominated for the Hart Trophy as most valuable player that year.

Bure had established himself as a star in the Soviet Union before his arrival in the NHL. He made the Central Red Army team as a 17-year-old in 1988–89 and starred on a line with Sergei Fedorov and Alexander Mogilny on the Soviet team that won the World Junior Championships that season. Bure was selected as the tournament's top forward. He has continued to represent Russia throughout his career and was named the best forward at the 1998 Nagano Olympics after topping the tournament with nine goals and leading his team to a silver medal.

CLARENCE CAMPBELL served as president of the National Hockey League from 1946 until 1977. A Rhodes Scholar at Oxford, Campbell had distinguished himself as a lawyer, then as a Canadian military officer in World War II. He commanded the 4th Canadian Armed Division headquarters throughout operations in Europe and joined the Canadian War Crimes Unit in 1945. He was again practicing law in Montreal when he was chosen to succeed Red Dutton as NHL president. Campbell had worked as a sports administrator and had been a referee in lacrosse and in the NHL prior to the war.

Campbell governed the NHL through much of the six-team era and successfully guided the league through expansion in 1967. By the time he retired in 1977, the NHL had grown to 18 teams. He also had helped pioneer the NHL Pension Society in 1946. In 1966, Campbell was elected to the Hockey Hall of Fame as a builder. The playoff champion in the NHL's Western Conference is presented with the Clarence Campbell Bowl.

CHRIS CHELIOS became the first American-born defenseman to win the Norris Trophy when he received the award as a member of the Montreal Canadiens in 1988–89. Chelios was also the Norris Trophy winner with the Chicago Blackhawks in 1992–93 and 1995–96. The 1995–96 season also saw him become the first blueliner in Blackhawks history to lead the team in scoring.

A native of Chicago, Chelios entered the NHL with the Canadiens in 1983–84 and was named to the All-Rookie Team in 1984–85. He was a member of Montreal's Stanley Cup-winning team of 1986 and played four more years with the club before being traded for Denis Savard on June 29, 1990. Combining both good offensive skills and an aggressive defensive game, Chelios firmly established his reputation as one of the best players at his position during his eight-plus seasons in Chicago. He was named team captain in 1995–96 and retained the honor until he was dealt to the Detroit Red Wings at the 1998–99 trade deadline. Chelios recorded a career-high +48 in his first full season with Detroit in 1999–2000, ranking second in the league behind Chris Pronger.

Internationally, Chelios has represented the United States at numerous tournaments. He was a key contributor to the U.S. team that beat Canada at the World Cup of Hockey in 1996, and also played for the U.S. Olympic team in Nagano in 1998.

BILL CHRISTIAN belongs to one of the most prominent families in U.S. hockey history. His father, Ed Christian, helped build the arena that housed the famed Warroad Lakers in Warroad, Minnesota. Bill and his brother, Roger, were both long-time stars of the team and members of the gold medal-winning 1960 U.S. Olympic hockey team. Bill's son Dave played for the 1980 "Miracle on Ice" gold medal team and went on to a long career in the NHL.

Bill Christian first got attention in hockey when he led his Warroad team to the finals of the second-ever Minnesota state youth tournament in 1952. Warroad was beaten by Eveleth, but Christian was named the tournament's most valuable player. The next year, he led Warroad High School to the finals of the state high school tournament.

After high school, Christian played one year for the University of Minnesota under coach John Mariucci before joining the 1957–58 U.S. national team that became the first American athletic club ever to play in the Soviet Union. He also played for the U.S. national team in 1960, 1962, 1964 and 1965 and is best remembered for his contributions in 1960, when he scored two goals in a 3–2 win over the Soviet Union that all but clinched the gold medal at the Squaw Valley Olympic Games.

In addition to his international experience, Bill Christian was a long-time member of the Warroad Lakers and played for 23 years before retiring after the 1979–80 season. The team never had a losing record during that time, winning the Canadian intermediate title in 1964 and 1974 and the Manitoba senior hockey title in 1969 and 1970. With the Lakers, Bill played with his brother, Roger, and also with sons Dave and Eddie. In 1964, he and other members of the dynasty helped start a hockey stick company, Christian Brothers Inc. He was also a successful coach in youth hockey in Warroad.

Bill Christian was enshrined in the United States Hockey Hall of Fame in 1984. Roger Christian was inducted five years later.

ROGER CHRISTIAN had a lengthy career with the Warroad Lakers and represented his country in international hockey, as did his younger brother and fellow U.S. Hockey Hall of Fame member Bill Christian. Roger started playing high school hockey in Warroad, Minnesota, in 1950, led the team in scoring in 1952, and helped it reach the finals of the state tournament in 1953. He was named all-Region twice during his high school career and to the all-State team once. Both he and Bill played with the 1958 U.S. national team that was the first American club ever to play in the Soviet Union; both were members of the gold medal-winning U.S. Olympic team in Squaw Valley, California, in 1960; and both played again with U.S. national teams in 1962, 1964 and 1965. Roger also played 18 years with the Warroad Lakers, who retired his uniform number (7) in 1974. He was elected to the U.S. Hockey Hall of Fame in 1989, five years after Bill.

KING CLANCY entered the NHL as an 18-year-old in 1921–22, and he remained a part of the game until his death on November 8, 1986. His father also had been an outstanding athlete, and it was from him that Francis Michael Clancy inherited his regal nickname. He was inducted as a member of the Hockey Hall of Fame in 1958.

Clancy played amateur hockey in his hometown of Ottawa before signing with the Senators in 1921–22. He and Frank Boucher were little-used spare players that season, but while Boucher left for Vancouver the following year, Clancy stayed in Ottawa to become a regular on defense after Eddie Gerard's retirement in 1923. He was among the smallest defensemen ever to play in the NHL, but he never backed down from his larger opponents.

Clancy helped Ottawa win the Stanley Cup in 1923 and in 1927, but the Senators played in the NHL's smallest market and the team was hit hard by the Depression. Many star players had to be sold after 1927, and the sale of King Clancy to the Toronto Maple Leafs for $35,000 (and players Art Smith and Eric Pettinger) before the 1930–31 season was then considered the biggest deal in hockey history. Conn Smythe expected Clancy to be the spark Toronto needed to achieve greatness, and he was right. Clancy helped the Maple Leafs win the Stanley Cup in just his second season. The club won three Canadian Division titles and was on its way to a fourth when Clancy retired early in 1936–37. He had been a First or Second Team All-Star four years in a row from 1930–31 to 1933–34, and he consistently ranked among the top-scoring defensemen in the NHL.

After leaving Toronto, Clancy coached the Montreal Maroons for the first half of the 1937–38 season and made his final appearance as a player during the all-star benefit for Howie Morenz. After being fired by the Maroons, Clancy then became a referee. He returned to the Maple Leafs to coach the team from 1953 to 1956, then worked as an assistant general manager under Punch Imlach. Clancy also served emergency stints behind the Leafs bench in 1966–67 and 1972–73 before settling into a role as the club's goodwill ambassador until the time of his death in 1986.

DIT CLAPPER was the first man to play 20 seasons in the NHL, spending them all with the Boston Bruins between 1927–28 and 1946–47. He was one of the top-scoring right wings in the game during his first 10 years, then one of the league's best defensemen over the final 10. He and Neil Colville are the only players in NHL history to be named to the All-Star Team as a forward and a defenseman.

Aubrey "Dit" Clapper was only 13 years old when he played junior hockey in Oshawa, and just 20 when he joined the Bruins. At 6'2" and almost 200 pounds, he was one of the biggest men of his era. He played on a line with Cooney Weiland and Dutch Gainor that quickly became Boston's best scoring unit, helping the Bruins to win the Stanley Cup in 1929. The trio then helped the team to rewrite the NHL record book when Boston went 38–5–1 in 1929–30, establishing the best single-season winning percentage in history. Clapper enjoyed his most productive season that year with 41 goals and 20 assists. Weiland topped the NHL with 43 goals and 30 assists.

By the 1937–38 season, the Bruins had added star forwards like Bill Cowley, Milt Schmidt, Bobby Bauer and Woody Dumart to the roster, so coach Art Ross converted Clapper to defense. Paired with the great Eddie Shore, both players were chosen to the First All-Star Team in 1938–39 after the Bruins won the Stanley Cup. Clapper was teamed with Flash Hollett the following year and helped the Bruins win another Stanley Cup in 1941. He earned his sixth and final all-star berth in 1943–44, then became a playing coach with the Bruins the following year.

On February 12, 1947, Dit Clapper retired as a player and was inducted immediately into the Hockey Hall of Fame. He continued to coach the Bruins until 1949. Clapper returned to hockey from business life to coach the Buffalo Bisons of the American Hockey League in 1959–60.

BOBBY CLARKE was diagnosed with diabetes at age 15, but despite the condition he became a junior hockey star in his hometown of Flin Flon, Manitoba, and went on to a 15-year NHL playing career as the heart and soul of the Philadelphia Flyers. Clarke was captain of the Flyers' Stanley Cup-winning teams of 1974 and 1975 and won the Hart Trophy as NHL MVP three times. He was elected to the Hockey Hall of Fame in 1987. The trophy awarded to the leading scorer in the Western Hockey League is named in his honor.

After a stellar junior career with the Flin Flon Bombers, Clarke was selected by the Flyers in the second round of the 1969 NHL Amateur Draft. His point totals increased steadily over his first three seasons, and in his fourth year he became the first player from an NHL expansion team to top 100 points, finishing second in the league with 104 points. He was also named captain in Philadelphia that season. Clarke remained among the top scorers in the NHL over the next five years, establishing a career high with 119 points in 1975–76 when he was runner-up to Guy Lafleur for the Art Ross Trophy. Clarke's 89 assists in both 1974–75 and 1975–76 were a single-season record for a center until being broken by Wayne Gretzky. In addition to his offensive talent, Clarke was one of the NHL's best face-off men and won the Selke Trophy as the NHL's best defensive forward in 1982–83.

Clarke retired as a player after the 1983–84 season as the leading scorer in Flyers history. He was immediately named general manager in Philadelphia and oversaw teams that reached the Stanley Cup finals in 1985 and 1987. He then left to become g.m. and vice president of the Minnesota North Stars in 1990. In 1993–94, Clarke served as g.m. and vice president of the expansion Florida Panthers. He returned to Philadelphia as president and general manager on June 15, 1994. Clarke served as one of four general managers for Canada's victorious Canada Cup team in 1987 and was head g.m. of Canada's Olympic team in 1998.

BILL CLEARY played on the silver medal-winning American Olympic team in 1956 and also represented the U.S. at the 1959 World Championships, then culminated his international career as the leading scorer on the gold medal-winning U.S. Olympic hockey team in 1960. He collected 14 points on seven goals and seven assists and scored the first goal in a key 3–2 win over the Soviet Union in the second-last game that all but clinched the surprising gold medal victory in the tournament.

Cleary was a native of Cambridge, Massachusetts, who gained hockey stardom during a standout career at Harvard. In his best season (1954–55), he set an NCAA single-season scoring record with 89 points and a Harvard record with 42 goals. He also set a school record with eight assists in a game and tied a record with a six-goal game. Cleary led Harvard to a 17–3–1 record that year, as the Crimson team won both the Beanpot Tournament (a Boston area event involving Boston University, Boston College, Northeastern and Harvard) and the Ivy League championship. Harvard finished third at the NCAA hockey tournament that year. Cleary earned all-Ivy League, all-East and all-American honors that same season, won the John Tudor Cup as Harvard's most valuable player, and was also named MVP in New England.

Cleary succeeded Cooney Weiland as head coach of the Harvard hockey team in March, 1971—having handled the freshmen since 1968 and acting as Weiland's assistant in 1970. He kept the position for the next 19 years, retiring after the 1989–90 season with a record of 324–201–22. During his tenure, Harvard reached the final four of the NCAA tournament seven times and played in the championship game three times, winning it all in 1988–89. Cleary also guided Harvard to 11 Ivy League crowns, four Beanpot championships and the Eastern Collegiate Athletic Conference tournament title in 1982–83 and 1986–87.

Bill Cleary was inducted into the United States Hockey Hall of Fame in 1976 and was joined by his brother Bob five years later.

BOB CLEARY played prep school hockey at Belmont Hill before going on to a stellar career at Harvard as his older brother Bill had done.

Bob Cleary led Belmont Hill to three consecutive Massachusetts private school championships while at the same time playing on the National junior champion Cusick team in the Amateur Hockey Association of the United States in 1952–53 and 1953–54. When his Harvard career began, he set a freshman record with 77 points, then went on to the varsity team in 1955–56 and amassed 100 goals and 102 assists over three seasons, topping the nation in scoring in both 1956–57 and 1957–58. In his senior year, Cleary served as team captain, led Harvard to a fourth-place finish at the NCAA hockey tournament for the second straight year, won his second consecutive Walter Brown Trophy as the outstanding player at an Eastern college, and was selected as an all-American.

In 1959, Cleary played for the U.S. national team at the World Championships and in 1960 he was a late addition to the U.S. Olympic team. Cleary teamed with his brother Bill and former Harvard teammate Bob McVey to form a high-scoring line that helped the Americans win a surprising gold medal. Bob Cleary was inducted into the U.S. Hockey Hall of Fame in 1981, five years after his brother.

PAUL COFFEY made his NHL debut in 1980–81 and helped the Edmonton Oilers become the greatest offensive team in hockey history. Coffey's own scoring totals increased every year over his first four seasons, and when Edmonton scored a record 446 goals in 1983–84, Coffey finished second to Wayne Gretzky in the NHL with 126 points. The Oilers won their first Stanley Cup title that season. Coffey won the Norris Trophy as the league's best defenseman for the first time the following year. In 1985–86, Coffey had a career-high 138 points (one short of Bobby Orr's record for defensemen), including 48 goals, which surpassed Orr's total of 46 from 1974–75. On March 14, 1986, Coffey tied Tom Bladon's record for defensemen with eight points in a single game (two goals, six assists).

In 1987, Coffey won his third Stanley Cup title with the Oilers, but on November 24, 1987, he was dealt to Pittsburgh. Now teamed with Mario Lemieux instead of Wayne Gretzky, Coffey maintained his status as the NHL's most gifted offensive defenseman. In 1991, he helped the Penguins to win their first Stanley Cup championship, but was traded to the Los Angeles Kings on February 19, 1992. Coffey was dealt to the Detroit Red Wings less than a year later. In 1994–95, he won the Norris Trophy for the third time, after becoming the first defenseman in Red Wings history to lead the team in scoring.

On the move again several times late in his career, Coffey became just the fourth player in NHL history to record 1,000 career assists. He led all defensemen in lifetime goals, assists and points until being surpassed as a goal scorer by Raymond Bourque during the 1999–2000 season. Coffey collected his 1,500th career point on December 23, 1999.

CHARLIE CONACHER was the best hockey player in one of Canada's greatest athletic families. Brothers Lionel, Charlie and Roy Conacher are all members of the Hockey Hall of Fame, while Charlie's son Pete and Lionel's son Brian also played in the NHL.

A member of the Toronto Marlboros Memorial Cup-winning team of 1929, Charlie Conacher entered the NHL with the Toronto Maple Leafs the following season. Playing on the famed Kid Line with Busher Jackson and Joe Primeau, Conacher quickly developed into the NHL's best right wing. He helped the Maple Leafs win the Stanley Cup in 1932, led the league in points twice, and led or tied for the NHL lead in goal-scoring five times. In his nine seasons with Toronto, the Leafs won four Canadian Division titles and reached the Stanley Cup finals five times.

Known as "the Big Bomber," Conacher stood 6'1" and weighed 195 pounds in his prime. He was as adept at making shifty moves around the net as he was at blasting a powerful wrist shot. He played a physical game, and injuries took their toll on him in his final years in Toronto. Conacher scored his 200th career goal with the Maple Leafs in 1937–38, but was sold to Detroit prior to the 1938–39 season and played out his career with the Red Wings and New York Americans. Conacher turned to coaching after his playing days, and guided the Oshawa Generals to the Memorial Cup in 1944. He returned to the NHL as coach of the Chicago Black Hawks in 1947–48, but he retired to the business world after the 1949–50 season. Charlie Conacher was elected to the Hockey Hall of Fame in 1961.

LEO DANDURAND was one of the top sports entrepreneurs of his day. In addition to owning the Montreal Canadiens, he owned racehorses; he was a director of the Montreal Royals baseball team; he founded the Montreal Alouettes football team; and he owned restaurants, laundries, dry cleaners and a soft drink company.

Dandurand was born in Bourbonnais, Illinois, but he came to Canada in 1905, later serving as a referee in the National Hockey Association. He met Joseph Cattarinich during a real estate venture, and in 1921, Dandurand, Cattarinich and Louis Letourneau (the Three Musketeers of Sport) purchased the Montreal Canadiens for $11,000. Dandurand invited politicians, judges and business leaders to join the team's board of directors while building an NHL powerhouse that boasted such stars as Aurel Joliat and Howie Morenz, the greatest player in the game.

Dandurand was a hands-on owner who coached the team from 1921–22 to 1925–26 and again in 1934–35. The Canadiens won the Stanley Cup in 1924, 1930 and 1931, and when economic pressures during the Great Depression forced the sale of the team in 1935, the price had reached $165,000. Dandurand was elected to the Hockey Hall of Fame as a builder in 1963.

HAP DAY had a 33-year association with the National Hockey League as a player, coach, referee and general manager. His given name was Clarence but his outgoing personality and provocative sense of humor earned him the nickname Happy or Hap.

Day played junior hockey in Midland, Ontario, and senior hockey with the Hamilton Tigers before attending the University of Toronto to study pharmacy. Charles Querrie convinced him to play pro hockey while still in school and he signed with the Toronto St. Pats on December 9, 1924. During his first two seasons in the NHL, Day played left wing on a line with Jack Adams and Babe Dye. He was later converted into a defenseman. On November 19, 1929, Day tied an NHL record for defensemen when he scored four goals in one game.

Day and Ace Bailey were the two players Conn Smythe built his franchise around after purchasing the St. Pats during the 1926–27 season and turning them into the Toronto Maple Leafs. Day was named the team's first captain, and held that position until he left Toronto after the 1936–37 season. During his time with the Maple Leafs, Day anchored the defense with King Clancy and Red Horner. The team won its first Stanley Cup title in 1932, and it reached the finals three other times over the next four years while winning three Canadian Division titles. He coached the West Toronto Nationals to the Memorial Cup while playing with the Leafs during the 1935–36 season.

Day played his final NHL season with the New York Americans in 1937–38. He spent the next two years as a referee before returning to Toronto as a highly successful coach. He guided the Leafs from 1940–41 to 1949–50, winning the Stanley Cup five times. He became assistant general manager to Conn Smythe in 1950, and he was responsible for running the team until 1957, when he retired to enter business life. Day was elected to the Hockey Hall of Fame in 1961.

PAVOL DEMITRA, a native of Slovakia, left home in 1993 to join the Ottawa Senators, who had made him a late-round selection in that year's Entry Draft. He spent the majority of his time in the minors over three years with Ottawa, as he did again in 1996–97 after his trade to St. Louis. Demitra emerged as the offensive leader of the Blues in 1998–99 after Brett Hull left the team for the Dallas Stars. He led the team in goals, assists, points and power-play goals that season, and ranked second in the NHL behind Hull with 10 game-winning goals. Demitra was the Blues scoring leader again in 1999–2000 when the club set team records with 51 wins and 114 points to lead the NHL. He also won the Lady Byng Trophy that year.

CY DENNENY was short and stocky and not a fast skater, but he possessed a hard, accurate shot. He scored more goals than any player in Ottawa Senators history, and only Newsy Lalonde and Joe Malone scored more among all players of his era. Denneny scored a career-high 36 goals in just 20 games for the Senators during the first NHL season of 1917–18, finishing second to Joe Malone, who had 44 goals that year. It was the first of five times over a nine-year span that Denneny would be the runner-up in the NHL scoring race. He led the league in scoring in 1923–24. Denneny scored goals in 12 consecutive games during the 1917–18 season, and had six in one game on March 7, 1921.

Denneny and his brother Corb began their pro careers with the Toronto Shamrocks in 1914–15 before joining the Toronto Blueshirts the following year. Centered by Duke Keats, the trio formed the top-scoring line in the National Hockey Association. Denneny and Joe Malone battled all year to win the scoring title before both were beaten by Newsy Lalonde in a close race.

Prior to the 1916–17 season, Denneny was purchased by the Senators. He was with Ottawa when the NHL was formed the following year. Denneny helped the team win the Stanley Cup in 1920, 1921, 1923 and 1927, before leaving to become a player-coach in Boston. He earned a fifth Stanley Cup championship with the Bruins in 1929, then spent the next season as a referee. He later coached junior and senior amateur teams in Ottawa in 1931–32 and the Senators in 1932–33. Cy Denneny was elected to the Hockey Hall of Fame in 1959.

ERIC DESJARDINS became the first defenseman in NHL history to record a hat trick in the Stanley Cup finals on June 2, 1993, as the Montreal Canadiens defeated the Los Angeles Kings, 3–2, in the second game of the 1993 series. Montreal went on to win the Stanley Cup in five games. Desjardins had made his NHL debut with Montreal in 1988–89 after a pair of excellent junior seasons and quickly established himself as a top defenseman in the NHL. He had earned a spot on Team Canada at the 1991 Canada Cup.

After six seasons with the Canadiens, Desjardins was traded to the Flyers with John LeClair on February 9, 1995. In Philadelphia, he has continued to rank among the league's best defensemen, representing Canada at the World Cup of Hockey in 1996 and at the Nagano Olympics in 1998. Earlier in his career, Desjardins won a gold medal at the 1989 World Junior Championships. He was named captain of the Flyers on March 27, 2000.

MARCEL DIONNE never played on a Stanley Cup winner in 18 seasons, but he ranks as one of the top players in NHL history. At the time of his retirement in 1989, Dionne's 731 goals trailed only Gordie Howe and his 1,040 assists ranked behind only Howe and Wayne Gretzky. His total of 1,771 points trails only Gretzky and Howe in NHL history.

Dionne had an outstanding junior career with St. Catharines of the Ontario Hockey Association and was selected by the Detroit Red Wings in 1971 as the second pick in the Amateur Draft behind Guy Lafleur. Dionne set a rookie record with 77 points in 1971–72, but trailed both Ken Dryden and Richard Martin in voting for the Calder Trophy. By 1974–75, Dionne had emerged as one of the game's top scorers, recording 121 points to rank third in the NHL behind Bobby Orr and Phil Esposito.

Dionne was acquired as a free agent by Los Angeles in 1975–76. He was the first player in NHL history to leave his team in this manner, and the league stepped in to force the Kings to trade several players to Detroit as compensation. He went on to star with the Kings for 12 seasons, ranking among the NHL's top-10 scorers seven times. Dionne centered the Triple Crown Line with Dave Taylor and Charlie Simmer in Los Angeles, and it was with this unit that he won his only scoring title in 1979–80. Dionne had 137 points that year to tie rookie Wayne Gretzky, but was awarded the Art Ross Trophy because he had 53 goals to Gretzky's 51. Dionne also edged Gretzky for the selection as center on the NHL's First All-Star Team.

On March 10, 1987, Dionne was traded by Los Angeles to the New York Rangers, where he finished his career in 1988–89. He was elected to the Hockey Hall of Fame in 1992 and remains the Kings' all-time leader in goals (550), assists (757) and points (1,307).

KEN DRYDEN was selected originally by the Boston Bruins in the 1964 Amateur Draft, but opted to attend Cornell University instead. He also played for the Canadian national team before joining the Montreal Canadiens organization in 1970–71. Dryden played only six games in goal for the Canadiens after joining the team late in the season, but then went on to star in the playoffs. He took part in all 20 postseason games, and won the Conn Smythe Trophy after leading Montreal to a surprising Stanley Cup victory. Dryden was still considered a rookie the following season, which enabled him to win the Calder Trophy. In September, 1972, Dryden shared goaltending duties with Tony Esposito on victorious Team Canada in the Summit Series against the Soviet Union. He then played on another Stanley Cup winner in 1973, and won the Vezina Trophy for the first of five times.

While at the peak of his game, Dryden sat out the 1973–74 season in a contract dispute with the Canadiens, working as a legal clerk in order to obtain his law degree from McGill University. He returned to the Canadiens in 1974–75 and from 1976 until 1979 the Canadiens won four consecutive championships. Although he was only 31, and had played just seven-plus seasons, Dryden retired in 1979. He had posted a record of 258–57–74 for a .758 winning percentage that is easily the best in NHL goaltending history.

It was expected that Dryden would enter law or politics, but instead he took his family to England and wrote a best-selling book called *The Game* based on his hockey experience. After returning to Canada in 1982, Dryden settled in Toronto where he served as Ontario Youth Commissioner from 1984 to 1986. He also continued to write, and hosted an acclaimed series of documentary television programs about hockey's role in Canadian culture.

On May 30, 1997, Dryden returned to active involvement in hockey when he was named president of the Toronto Maple Leafs. He has been a member of the Hockey Hall of Fame since 1983.

BILL DURNAN played only seven years in the NHL, but won the Vezina Trophy and was selected as the goaltender on the First All-Star Team six times. Durnan was ambidextrous, able to use his stick or catch the puck equally well with either hand, but the pressure of the game's most difficult position forced his retirement in 1950. His six Vezina Trophy wins were the most in NHL history until Jacques Plante earned his seventh such honor in 1968–69.

Durnan was born in Toronto, but first attracted attention playing goal with the Sudbury team that reached the all-Ontario junior finals in 1933. In 1940, he was a member of the Kirkland Lake Blue Devils when they won the Allan Cup. After three seasons with the Montreal Royals, Durnan finally entered the NHL as a 27-year-old rookie with the Montreal Canadiens in 1943–44. The Canadiens featured the high-scoring Punch Line of Elmer Lach, Maurice Richard and Toe Blake that season, but much of the credit for Montreal winning its first Stanley Cup title in 13 years went to Durnan. He helped the Canadiens win the Cup again in 1946.

Turk Broda broke off Durnan's four-year Vezina Trophy winning streak in 1947–48, but the Canadiens netminder was better than ever during the 1948–49 campaign. That year, he posted a career-best 2.10 goals-against average with 10 shutouts and set a modern NHL record when he went unscored upon for 309 minutes and 21 seconds, including four consecutive shutouts. Durnan's numbers were almost as impressive in 1949–50, but he retired after that season. In 1964, he was elected to the Hockey Hall of Fame.

PHIL ESPOSITO's size and strength made it difficult for defensemen to clear him out of the slot. The stocky center established himself as an effective scorer and playmaker over four seasons with the Chicago Black Hawks, and on May 15, 1967, he was the central figure in a six-player trade between the Black Hawks and the Bruins. In Boston, he combined with Bobby Orr to rewrite the NHL record book.

After finishing the 1967–68 season as the runner-up behind former Chicago teammate Stan Mikita for the NHL scoring title, Esposito became the first player in NHL history to reach 100 points in a season on March 2, 1969. He finished the 1968–69 season with 126 points and won the Art Ross Trophy for the first time. He also won the Hart Trophy as most valuable player. In 1970, Esposito helped Boston to win its first Stanley Cup title in 29 years. The Bruins set an NHL record in 1970–71 with 57 wins and 121 points, and Esposito led the way by smashing Bobby Hull's single-season record of 58 goals with 76. He also collected 76 assists for 152 points and another new record that would last until being surpassed by Wayne Gretzky. Boston was upset in the quarterfinals by the Montreal Canadiens in 1971, but the Bruins recaptured the Stanley Cup in 1972. In September, 1972, Esposito was the top scorer and inspirational leader of Team Canada in their hard-fought victory over the Soviet national team. By 1973–74, Esposito had won the Art Ross

Trophy for the fifth time and was again rewarded with the Hart as MVP.

On November 7, 1975, Phil Esposito was again the central figure in a multi-player deal when the Bruins surprised the hockey world by trading him to the New York Rangers. His best days were behind him now, but Esposito still led the Rangers in scoring four years in a row and helped them reach the Stanley Cup finals in 1979. When he retired in 1981, Esposito's 717 goals and 1,590 points trailed only Gordie Howe's totals of 801 and 1,850 among the NHL's all-time leaders. His 873 assists were third all-time. He was elected to the Hockey Hall of Fame in 1984.

Esposito served as Rangers general manager (and briefly as coach) between 1986–87 and 1988–89. He helped to land an NHL expansion team in Tampa Bay and became the first general manager of the Lightning, who began play in the NHL in 1992–93. He held the position until being fired at the start of the 1998–99 season.

TONY ESPOSITO was often referred to as Phil's kid brother when he broke into the NHL with the Stanley Cup champion Montreal Canadiens in 1968–69. His skill as a goaltender very quickly earned him recognition in his own right. Tony was claimed by the Chicago Black Hawks in the Intra-League Draft in June, 1969, and in 1969–70 he set a modern NHL record with 15 shutouts. He won both the Calder and Vezina trophies that season and was selected to the First All-Star Team.

Esposito helped the Black Hawks reach the Stanley Cup finals in 1971, and in September, 1972 he shared netminding duties with Ken Dryden on Team Canada. He led the Black Hawks to the Stanley Cup finals again in 1973, and in 1973–74 he tied Bernie Parent of the Philadelphia Flyers for the Vezina Trophy—the only time in history goaltenders with two different teams shared the award. Esposito remained the top goaltender in Chicago until 1982–83, and when he retired after the 1983–84 season, his 423 victories trailed only Terry Sawchuk (446) and Jacques Plante (435) among the NHL's all-time leaders. His 76 shutouts rank seventh in history. He was elected to the Hockey Hall of Fame in 1988.

After his playing days, Tony Esposito worked for the NHL Players' Association before becoming vice president and general manager of the Pittsburgh Penguins on April 14, 1988. Pittsburgh made the playoffs for the first time in seven years in 1988–89, but Esposito was fired in December, 1989. He joined brother Phil in the front office of the Tampa Bay Lightning when the franchise was granted officially in December, 1991, serving in several capacities until being fired early in the 1998–99 season.

VIACHESLAV FETISOV was recognized as one of the best defensemen in the world long before he made his NHL debut with the New Jersey Devils. The long-time captain of the Central Red Army team in Moscow had been an international star for years as a member of the Soviet national team.

Fetisov joined the Red Army in 1975–76 and got his first international exposure that year when the Soviets won gold at the European Junior Championships. In 1977–78, he was a member of the gold medal-winning team at the World Junior Championships and was named to the tournament all-star team along with future NHLers Wayne Gretzky, Anton Stastny, Mats Naslund and Risto Siltanen. Fetisov also won his first World Championship that year as a member of the Soviet national team. He went on to play in 10 more World Championships and won six more gold medals. He was named the top defenseman at the tournament five times and was chosen for the all-star team on nine occasions. He also won gold medals at the Olympics in 1984 and 1988, and a silver medal in 1980 when the Russians lost the gold to the United States. Fetisov was named the Soviet player of the year in 1981–82 and 1985–86 and was the top-scoring defenseman in the Soviet League in 1983–84 and from 1985–86 to 1987–88. He has received the Soviet Master of Sport award, a state honor comparable to induction into the Hockey Hall of Fame.

Fetisov was drafted by New Jersey back in 1983, but was not allowed to leave the Soviet Union for another six years. He made his NHL debut on October 5, 1989, and played five-plus seasons in New Jersey before being traded to the Detroit Red Wings. In 1997, Fetisov and former Red Army teammates Igor Larionov, Sergei Fedorov and Vladimir Konstantinov, plus fellow Russian Slava Kozlov, were part of the Detroit team that won the Stanley Cup for the first time since 1955. Fetisov organized the Stanley Cup's first visit to Russia that summer. The Red Wings repeated as champions in 1998. Fetisov became an assistant coach with the Devils in 1998–99 and helped them win the Stanley Cup in 2000.

THEOREN FLEURY was selected by the Calgary Flames with the 166th pick in the 1987 Entry Draft. He topped 100 points in each of his last three seasons in junior hockey, leading the Western Hockey League in scoring in 1987–88, but at just 5'6" and 160 pounds, he was thought to be too small to play in the NHL. He proved his critics wrong with his offensive skill and competitive spirit.

Fleury helped the Salt Lake Golden Eagles win the Turner Cup as International Hockey League champions in 1988, then joined the Flames midway through the 1988–89 season and helped Calgary to win the Stanley Cup. In 1990–91, he became just the fifth player in Flames history to top 50 goals and 100 points in a single season.

Fleury was the Flames' leading scorer six times in the seasons between 1990–91 and 1998–99, and often ranked among the league leaders as well. When he scored his 315th career goal during the 1997–98 season, he passed Joe Nieuwendyk as the all-time leading goal scorer in Flames history. In 1998-99, Fleury became the Flames' career points leader, but on February 28, 1999, he was traded to the Colorado Avalanche. Fleury finished the year among the NHL leaders in goals and points. After the season, he signed as a free agent with the New York Rangers.

In addition to his success in the NHL, Fleury has starred in the international arena. He was captain of the Canadian team that won the World Junior Championship in 1988 and earned a spot on the tournament's all-star team. He won a silver medal at the 1991 World Championships and represented Canada at the 1998 Nagano Olympics.

PETER FORSBERG was selected sixth overall by the Philadelphia Flyers in the first round of the 1991 NHL Entry Draft, but was sent to the Quebec Nordiques on June 30, 1992, as part of the deal that brought Eric Lindros to Philadelphia. Forsberg remained in his native Sweden until making his NHL debut in 1994–95. He set a tournament record with 31 points at the World Junior Championships in 1993, and scored the winning goal in a shootout when Sweden beat Canada for the gold medal at the 1994 Lillehammer Olympics.

Forsberg led all NHL rookies with 35 assists and 50 points in 1994–95 and won the Calder Trophy as rookie of the year. In 1995–96, the Nordiques moved to Denver, and the Colorado Avalanche became the first NHL club to win the Stanley Cup in its first year in a new city. Forsberg led the Avs with 86 assists that season and ranked fifth in the NHL with 115 points. He has continued to rank among the league's best players since then, though injuries slowed him down in both 1996–97 and 1999–2000.

A national hero in his homeland, Forsberg was depicted on a Swedish postage stamp commemorating his Olympic gold medal-winning goal. His father coached the Swedish national team from 1995 to 1998.

RON FRANCIS made his NHL debut on November 14, 1981, and has quietly become one of the NHL's all-time leaders in assists and points. In 10 seasons with the Hartford Whalers, Francis led the club in scoring on five occasions and in assists nine times. He was a four-time team MVP, and is the franchise's all-time leader in virtually every offensive category. Francis became captain of the Whalers in 1984–85 and continued to wear the "C" until the time of his trade to the Pittsburgh Penguins on March 4, 1991. The acquisition of Francis, along with Grant Jennings and Ulf Samuelsson, helped the Penguins to win their first Stanley Cup title. Francis led all playoff performers with 19 assists when Pittsburgh repeated as champions in 1992.

Surrounded by such offensive talents at Mario Lemieux and Jaromir Jagr, Francis finally earned recognition as one of the game's top players. He led the NHL in assists in 1994–95 and won both the Selke Trophy as best defensive forward and the Lady Byng Trophy for sportsmanlike conduct. In 1995–96, Francis established career highs when he tied Lemieux for the NHL lead with 92 assists and registered 119 points. Following the season, he returned to his original franchise when he signed as a free agent with the Carolina Hurricanes. He recorded his 1,500th career point on November 5, 1999.

GRANT FUHR finished second in the voting for the Vezina Trophy behind Billy Smith after his rookie season of 1981–82. He also received serious consideration for the Calder Trophy, which went to Dale Hawerchuk. He has gone on to become one of the winningest goaltenders in NHL history.

Fuhr's arrival in the NHL coincided with Edmonton's rise to power in the league and the Oilers' great scoring ability allowed him to set a record for goaltenders with 14 assists in 1983–84. Though his goals-against averages were often high behind such an offensive-minded team, Fuhr earned a reputation as a goalie who would not surrender the big goal. He was at his best in the playoffs, helping the Oilers to win the Stanley Cup in 1984, 1985, 1987 and 1988.

Fuhr missed the first 55 games of the 1990–91 season after being suspended by the NHL and was dealt to the Toronto Maple Leafs in a multi-player trade prior to the next season. With the emergence of Felix Potvin as a star in Toronto in 1992–93, Fuhr was dealt to the Buffalo Sabres in a deal that made Dave Andreychuk a Maple Leaf. The development of Dominik Hasek into the league's best goalie saw the Sabres send Fuhr to Los Angeles. His poor play with the Kings had many thinking his career was over, but Fuhr was signed by the Blues on July 14, 1995, and his career was revived.

The 1995–96 season saw Fuhr set an NHL record by playing in 79 games, including 76 in a row. He suffered a serious knee injury during the playoffs that year, and once again it was thought his career might be over, but Fuhr returned to play 73 games in 1996–97. He was picked up by the Calgary Flames in 1999–2000, but suffered through what proved to be an injury-plagued final season. He did, however, become just the sixth goalie in NHL history to win 400 regular-season games on October 22, 1999.

CHARLIE GARDINER is rated by most as the greatest goaltender of his day, and by many as the greatest of all time. He was at the height of his career when tragedy cut his life short at the age of 29. Just two months prior to his death on June 13, 1934, he had posted a 1–0 shutout in overtime that had given the Chicago Black Hawks their first Stanley Cup victory.

Born in Scotland, but raised in Winnipeg, Gardiner became a goaltender because he was a poor skater. He moved up quickly through the amateur ranks in Manitoba and turned pro with the Winnipeg Maroons of the American Hockey Association for the 1926–27 season. The following year, he replaced veteran Hugh Lehman in goal for the Black Hawks.

Chicago was last in its division in each of Gardiner's first two years, and the club's weak offense set a record for futility with just 33 goals in 44 games in 1928–29. The offense would show only minimal improvement over the years, but Gardiner made the team successful. He was at his finest in 1933–34, posting a career-best 1.63 goals-against average and leading the league with 10 shutouts. He won the Vezina Trophy for the second time and played for the NHL All-Stars in the Ace Bailey benefit game on February 14, 1934. He had been named captain of the Black Hawks that year, and his brilliant goaltending led the weak offensive team to second place in the American Division. Though plagued by headaches throughout the season, Gardiner played all 48 regular-season games.

Playoff victories over the Montreal Canadiens and Montreal Maroons put the Black Hawks in the finals against the Detroit Red Wings, but Gardiner's headaches became so bad that he would slump over the crossbar to rest when the play was in the other end. Still, he made 40 saves in the 1–0 Stanley Cup-winning victory on April 10, 1934. Two months later, while at home in Winnipeg, Gardiner collapsed and died of a brain hemorrhage. In 1945, Charles "Chuck" Gardiner became one of the original inductees into the Hockey Hall of Fame.

MIKE GARTNER was a junior hockey all-star who made his professional debut at age 19 with the Cincinnati Stingers in the final World Hockey Association season of 1978–79. One year later, he entered the NHL with the Washington Capitals.

Gartner established himself as one of the most consistent scorers in hockey history and on December 14, 1997, he became only the fifth player ever to score 700 career goals. Previously, he had become just the sixth player in history to top 600 goals and 600 assists. He was one of the fastest skaters in the game. Though he scored 50 goals just once in his career (1984–85), Gartner topped 30 more than any player in history, and established a record by scoring 30 goals for 15 consecutive years between 1979–80 and 1993–94.

Gartner spent his first 10 seasons with the Capitals, leading the team in goals on five occasions and in points four times. He was dealt to Minnesota at the NHL trade deadline in 1989, but did not even spend a full year with the North Stars before being sent to the New York Rangers at the trade deadline in 1990. Gartner led the Rangers in goals during each of his three full seasons with the club, but was traded to the Toronto Maple Leafs at the 1994 trade deadline. His consecutive 30-goal streak ended in Toronto during the lockout-shortened 1994–95 season, but he rebounded to lead the Maple Leafs with 35 goals in 1995–96.

Traded to the Phoenix Coyotes, Gartner went on to top 30 goals for the 17th time in 1996–97. Though he never played on a Stanley Cup winner, Gartner was a member of Team Canada for Canada Cup victories in 1984 and 1987. Always active in the NHL Players' Association, Gartner now serves as the NHLPA's director of business relations.

BERNIE GEOFFRION joined the Montreal Canadiens during the 1950–51 season and went on to become one of the top stars in the NHL. He had the misfortune of being a right wing in an era that boasted both Gordie Howe and Maurice Richard, and so was only named to three all-star teams, but his 393 career goals at the time of his retirement in 1968 then ranked fifth in NHL history. He was elected to the Hockey Hall of Fame in 1972.

"Boom Boom" Geoffrion played his first full season in Montreal in 1951–52 and led the Canadiens with 30 goals to win the Calder Trophy as rookie of the year. The following year, he played on his first Stanley Cup winner. In 1954–55, the late-season suspension of Rocket Richard allowed Geoffrion to win his first NHL scoring title. Over the next five years, Geoffrion was a key contributor to the Montreal teams that won the Stanley Cup five consecutive times. He enjoyed his greatest year in 1960–61 when he became just the second player in NHL history to score 50 goals in a season. He also collected 45 assists for a career-high 95 points (one short of the NHL record at the time) and won both the Art Ross and Hart trophies.

Geoffrion retired after the 1963–64 season and became coach of the Quebec Aces, Montreal's farm club in the American Hockey League. He quit after two first-place seasons because the Canadiens did not hire him as coach, and then returned to the NHL as a player with the New York Rangers in 1966–67. He took over as coach of the Rangers in 1968–69, but had to give up the job for health reasons. Geoffrion was a scout with the Rangers over the next three years before returning to coaching with the expansion Atlanta Flames in 1972–73. He had good success in Atlanta over three seasons, but stepped down in 1974–75. He finally got his chance to coach the Canadiens in 1979–80, but was replaced after just 30 games because of health concerns.

DOUG GILMOUR helped the Cornwall Royals to win their second straight Memorial Cup championship in 1981, and was the leading scorer in the Ontario Hockey League in 1982–83. Yet despite his impressive credentials, Gilmour was considered a defensive specialist during his early years with the St. Louis Blues.

In his fourth season of 1986–87, Gilmour scored a career-high 42 goals and placed fifth in the NHL with 105 points. He was traded to Calgary prior to the 1988–89 campaign and helped the Flames to win the Stanley Cup that season. He was named a co-captain in Calgary in 1990–91, but was dealt to Toronto on January 2, 1992. With the Maple Leafs, Gilmour emerged as one of the top stars in the game. He established career highs and Toronto single-season records with 95 assists and 127 points in 1992–93, and led the Maple Leafs to the Campbell Conference finals. Gilmour also won the Selke Trophy as the game's best defensive forward that year and finished runner-up to Mario Lemieux in voting for the Hart Trophy. In 1993–94, Gilmour ranked fourth in the league with 111 points and he again led the Maple Leafs to the conference finals.

Gilmour was named captain in Toronto for the 1994–95 season, but the team's fortunes began to sag. With the Maple Leafs slumping toward the bottom of the NHL standings in 1996–97, Gilmour was traded to New Jersey. He signed with the Chicago Blackhawks after the 1997–98 season, but was dealt to the Buffalo Sabres at the March, 2000 trade deadline.

SCOTT GOMEZ was born to a Mexican father and a Colombian-American mother in Anchorage, Alaska, on December 23, 1979. When he made the New Jersey Devils as a 19-year-old in 1999–2000, he became the first Hispanic to play in the NHL. His 70 points that year ranked second on the Devils and first among all rookie scorers. In the playoffs, he helped the Devils win the Stanley Cup. Just a few days later, he was named the winner of the Calder Trophy as rookie of the year. Previously, Gomez was chosen Alaskan high school player of the year in 1995 and 1996.

Gomez attended his first training camp with the Devils in 1998–99 and was one of the team's last cuts. He returned to the Tri-City Americans of the Western Hockey League, where his 78 assists led the league and his 108 points ranked fifth. He also represented the United States at the World Junior Championships for the second straight season. Gomez continued his high-scoring ways as an NHL rookie. His first career hat trick on December 26, 1999, made him just the second first-year player in Devils history to score three goals in a game and the first since Uli Hiemer managed the feat in 1984. Just three days past his 20th birthday, Gomez was also the youngest Devils player to record a hat trick.

WAYNE GRETZKY learned to play hockey on a backyard rink built by his father Walter in his hometown of Brantford, Ontario. He grew up to become the most prolific scorer in the history of the NHL. He held or shared 61 league records at the time of his retirement.

Gretzky was marked for stardom almost from the time he began to play organized hockey, particularly after the 1971–72 season when he collected 378 goals and 139 assists as an 11-year-old. He made his junior hockey debut in 1976–77 at age 15, and was a second team all-star as a 16-year-old with Sault Ste. Marie of the Ontario Hockey Association in 1977–78. It was in the Soo that season that Gretzky began to wear number 99.

Gretzky turned pro with the Indianapolis Racers of the World Hockey Association in 1978–79, but financial troubles saw him sent to the Edmonton Oilers after just eight games. Gretzky finished third in the WHA behind Real Cloutier and Robbie Ftorek with 110 points (46 goals, 64 assists) that season, but few expected he would match those totals when he entered the NHL as an 18-year-old in 1979–80. Gretzky proved his critics wrong when he led the league with 86 assists and tied Marcel Dionne with 137 points, though Dionne received the Art Ross Trophy because his 53 goals were two more than Gretzky's 51. Gretzky did receive the Hart Trophy as most valuable player for the first of eight consecutive times that season.

Great as he was as a rookie, it was his second season of 1980–81 when Gretzky began to rewrite the NHL record book. His 109 assists that season broke Bobby Orr's record of 102, and his record 164 points broke Phil Esposito's record of 152 and brought him the first of seven consecutive Art Ross Trophy wins. The next year, Gretzky shattered Esposito's record of 76 goals when he scored 92 times, including 50 goals in the first 39 games of the season. With 120 assists and 212 points that year, Gretzky surpassed his own records. He would up those marks to 163 assists and 215 points in 1985–86. In addition to his record-setting performances, Gretzky made the Oilers the best team in hockey, winning the Stanley Cup in 1984, 1985, 1987 and 1988.

On August 9, 1988, a stunned hockey public learned that Wayne Gretzky had been traded to the Los Angeles Kings. His arrival finally made hockey a hit in Southern California, and helped to promote the game all across the United States. It was with the Kings against Edmonton on October 15, 1989, that Gretzky surpassed his childhood hero Gordie Howe as the NHL's all-time leading scorer with 1,851 points. On March 23, 1994, Gretzky topped Howe with his 802nd goal.

With the Kings slumping, Gretzky was traded to the St. Louis Blues on February 27, 1996. Following that season, he signed with the New York Rangers. Though his production had tailed dramatically by this point, Gretzky tied for the NHL lead in assists during his first two years in New York. With his 1,851st career assist on October 26, 1997, Gretzky's assist total exceeded the point total of every other player in league history.

Wayne Gretzky announced his retirement from hockey on April 16, 1999, and played his final game two days later. He finished his career with 894 goals, and 1,963 assists for 2,857 points. The final goal of his career came on March 29, 1999, and gave him 1,072 for his total career (NHL and WHA, regular season and playoffs)—one more than Gordie Howe. Gretzky was inducted into the Hockey Hall of Fame in 1999, becoming the tenth, and final player, to have the traditional three-year waiting period waived. He was also named Canada's male athlete of the 20th century. He did not stay away from hockey for long, becoming part of a group negotiating to buy the Phoenix Coyotes in June, 2000.

In addition to his record-breaking performances in the NHL, Gretzky was a top star on the international stage. In 1978, he led the tournament in scoring as Team Canada won a bronze medal at the World Junior Championships. Gretzky was also the scoring leader at the 1982 World Championships, and at the 1981, 1984, 1987 and 1991 Canada Cup tournaments. His final two international appearances for Canada came at the World Cup of Hockey in 1996 and at the 1998 Nagano Olympics

GEORGE HAINSWORTH established an NHL record not likely to be broken when he recorded 22 shutouts during the 1928–29 season. He allowed only 43 goals while playing in all of the Montreal Canadiens' 44 games that year, posting a 0.92 goals-against average. His career goals-against average of 1.93 ranks second to Alex Connell for the lowest mark in NHL history.

Hainsworth was born in Toronto, but played most of his amateur hockey in Berlin, Ontario (which later became Kitchener). He played on championship teams at the junior, intermediate and senior levels, including an Allan Cup winner in 1918, before finally turning professional with the Saskatoon Crescents of the Western Canada Hockey League in 1923–24. He spent three seasons out west, then joined the Montreal Canadiens in 1926–27 after Newsy Lalonde suggested him as a replacement for the late Georges Vezina.

Hainsworth proved an immediate success in Montreal, posting outstanding numbers and winning the Vezina Trophy in each of his first three seasons. Forward passing rules were modernized after the 1928–29 season, making it impossible for Hainsworth to achieve such stellar numbers again. Still, he helped the Canadiens win consecutive Stanley Cup championships in 1930 and 1931.

Before the 1933–34 season, Hainsworth was traded to Toronto for Lorne Chabot. He helped the Maple Leafs win two Canadian Division titles and reach the Stanley Cup finals twice in the next three years. He was replaced by Turk Broda early in the 1936–37 season, and returned to the Canadiens briefly before retiring. His 94 career shutouts were an NHL record until Terry Sawchuk surpassed the total in 1963–64. When his 10 shutouts in Saskatoon are included, his total of 104 shutouts is actually one more than Sawchuk's 103. Hainsworth was elected to the Hockey Hall of Fame in 1961.

GLENN HALL was known as "Mr. Goalie" and was one of the greatest netminders in NHL history, though the stress of NHL puckstopping often made him ill before games. Still, he set an incredible endurance record by playing 502 consecutive games from 1955 until a back injury sidelined him on November 7, 1962. With 84 career shutouts, he is third on the NHL all-time list, trailing only Terry Sawchuk and George Hainsworth. He led the NHL in shutouts six times, including a career-high 12 in his rookie season.

Hall made two brief appearances with the Red Wings before replacing Terry Sawchuk as Detroit's goaltender in 1955–56. He won the Calder Trophy as rookie of the year, and was selected to the Second All-Star Team for the first of four times. He was a First Team All-Star for the first of seven times in 1956–57, but Detroit then traded him to the Chicago Black Hawks, along with Ted Lindsay, for four players. In 1961, Hall helped Chicago win its first Stanley Cup title since 1938. He starred for 10 years with the Black Hawks before becoming the first player selected by the St. Louis Blues in the 1967 Expansion Draft. He helped lead the Blues to the Stanley Cup finals in their first season of 1967–68, and won the Conn Smythe Trophy as playoff MVP despite losing to the Montreal Canadiens.

The following year, Hall wore a mask for the first time after Jacques Plante was brought out of retirement to team with him in the Blues net. The two veteran goalies shared the Vezina Trophy in 1968–69 as St. Louis again reached the Stanley Cup finals before losing to Montreal. Hall remained with St. Louis until retiring after the 1970–71 season. In 1975, he was inducted into the Hockey Hall of Fame.

DOUG HARVEY was the best defenseman in hockey during his heyday, and ranks with Bobby Orr and Eddie Shore among the greatest of all time. He could check, block shots, rush the puck, stickhandle and pass, but what made him truly unique was the way he could combine his skills to control the pace of the game. In addition to his hockey talent, Harvey played football and was good enough in baseball to be offered a pro contract by the old Boston Braves.

After a lengthy amateur career in his hometown of Montreal, Harvey entered the NHL with the Canadiens in 1947–48. By his fifth season, it was apparent he was among the best in the game. He earned his first all-star selection in 1951–52 and would be chosen for 11 straight years. In 10 of those 11 years, Harvey was selected as a First Team All-Star. He also won the Norris Trophy seven times in eight years between 1954–55 and 1961–62, missing out in 1958–59 when the award went to teammate Tom Johnson. Harvey played on Stanley Cup winners in Montreal in 1953 and in every year from 1956 to 1960. In 1960–61, he was named to succeed the retired Maurice Richard as captain of the Canadiens, but it would be his final season in Montreal, as he became player-coach with the New York Rangers in 1961–62. Harvey guided the Rangers into the playoffs, but gave up his coaching role after one season. He played with the Rangers for two more years, though much of his 1963–64 campaign was spent in the minors.

Harvey spent most of the next three years playing minor-league hockey. After expansion, he signed with St. Louis in time for the 1968 playoffs. He spent the 1968–69 season with the Blues before retiring. Harvey then returned to coaching with the junior Laval Saints. He was later an assistant coach with the Los Angeles Kings and with the Houston Aeros of the World Hockey Association. Harvey was elected to the Hockey Hall of Fame in 1973.

DOMINIK HASEK joined Roy Worters, Charlie Rayner, Al Rollins and Jacques Plante in 1996–97 as just the fifth goalie in NHL history to win the Hart Trophy. A year later, he became the first goalie to win consecutive MVP awards. In 1999, Hasek helped the Buffalo Sabres reach the Stanley Cup finals for just the second time in franchise history. Though he seemed to be at the height of his fame, Hasek announced that 1999–2000 would be his final NHL season. After injuries forced him out of the lineup from late October to early February, he decided to remain in Buffalo for one more year.

Hasek began his NHL career with the Chicago Blackhawks, but saw most of his action with Indianapolis of the International Hockey League before being traded to Buffalo on August 7, 1992. By his second season with the Sabres, "The Dominator" had established himself as a star in the NHL. His 1.95 goals-against average was the first below 2.00 since Bernie Parent's 1.89 mark in 1973–74, and he won the Vezina Trophy for the first of five times over the next six years. He also led the league in save percentage for the first of six straight years. After just five seasons in Buffalo, Hasek had established himself as the Sabres' all-time leader in shutouts. His 13 shutouts in 1997–98 represent the second highest total in the NHL since modern passing rules began to be introduced in 1929–30.

Before his arrival in North America in 1990–91, Hasek had been a star in his native Czechoslovakia, where he earned numerous individual awards. He has also starred on the international stage, most notably at the 1998 Winter Olympics in Nagano, where he was named the best goaltender after leading the Czech Republic to a surprising gold medal victory. Hasek has played more games in the NHL than any other European-born goaltender.

PAUL HENDERSON scored one of the most famous goals in hockey history when he poked a rebound past Vladislav Tretiak with 34 seconds left in the final game to give Team Canada a victory over the Soviet Union in the 1972 Summit Series. Henderson scored the deciding goal in each of the last three games as Canada rallied to win the eight-game series 4–3–1.

Henderson was a graduate of the Red Wings' junior farm club in Hamilton, Ontario. He earned regular NHL duty with Detroit in 1964–65, and topped 20 goals in each of the next two seasons before being traded to the Toronto Maple Leafs as part of the blockbuster deal that sent Frank Mahovlich to Detroit. Henderson was a solid performer in Toronto, establishing a career high with 38 goals in 1971–72.

Unable to live up to the high expectations created by his national celebrity status, Henderson slumped during a 1972–73 season that was dogged by injury. Unhappy playing under owner Harold Ballard, he left the Maple Leafs and joined the Toronto Toros of the World Hockey Association for the 1974–75 season. He remained with the team when it moved to Birmingham in 1976. When four WHA teams entered the NHL in 1979–80, Henderson returned to the league for a final season as a member of the Atlanta Flames.

FOSTER HEWITT's radio broadcasts from Maple Leaf Gardens helped make the Toronto team a national institution in Canada, and they made him as famous as the many superstars whose exploits he chronicled. Hewitt was a reporter with the *Toronto Star* when he broadcast his first hockey game from Toronto's Mutual Street Arena on March 22, 1923. He was hired by Conn Smythe to broadcast Maple Leaf games shortly after Smythe bought the team in February, 1927. His contribution to hockey as its pioneer of the airwaves was so great that Hewitt was inducted into the Hockey Hall of Fame as a builder in 1965. His father is also a Hall of Fame builder.

Over his career, Hewitt called thousands of hockey games, first on radio and later on television. His trademark greeting of "Hello, Canada" and his excited call "He shoots, he scores!" became a regular feature of the game. In addition to NHL hockey, Hewitt covered World and Olympic championships, as well as the action in many other sports, for listeners and viewers across Canada and the northeast United States. He became a successful businessman over the course of his broadcasting career, and he owned his own radio station in Toronto until he retired in 1981. His last great play-by-play assignment had been to call the action of the 1972 Canada-Russia Summit Series for Canadian television viewers.

TIM HORTON was a product of the Maple Leafs farm system who went on to play 18 full years in Toronto and 24 seasons in the NHL. During much of that time, he was recognized as the strongest player in the game and one of the league's best defensemen. He could rush the puck effectively and had a powerful slapshot. He earned a reputation as a peacemaker over the course of his career, deterring opposition fighters with a grasp known as the "Horton Bear Hug."

Horton, a graduate of the Maple Leafs junior team at St. Michael's College, spent the better part of three seasons with Toronto's Pittsburgh farm club in the American Hockey League before making the NHL to stay in 1952–53. He was a Second Team All-Star in his second season, but injuries hampered his effectiveness with a weak Toronto club over the next few years. In 1958–59, Horton was teamed with Allan Stanley and, along with Bob Baun and Carl Brewer, provided the solid defense that helped the Maple Leafs win the Stanley Cup in 1962, 1963, 1964 and 1967. Though the Maple Leafs declined rapidly after expansion, Horton was a First Team All-Star in both 1967–68 and 1968–69.

By 1969–70, Horton was 16 years older than any other Maple Leafs defenseman, and his $80,000 salary made him the most expensive player on Toronto's roster. With the team struggling in last place, Horton was dealt to the New York Rangers on March 5, 1970. He spent the entire 1970–71 season with the Rangers, then played a year with the Pittsburgh Penguins. He was in his second season with the Buffalo Sabres when a tragic single-car accident ended his life on February 21, 1974. He was inducted into the Hockey Hall of Fame in 1977.

GORDIE HOWE broke into the NHL with the Detroit Red Wings in 1946–47 and went on to star for 25 years, setting records that, at the time, seemed unbreakable. He had an effortless skating style and deceptive speed, combined with tremendous strength and a powerful shot. Howe retired after the 1970–71 season, but was back in the game two years later when he signed to play with sons Mark and Marty with the Houston Aeros of the World Hockey Association. After six years in the WHA, Howe returned to the NHL for a final season with the Hartford Whalers. When he finally retired after the 1979–80 campaign, he had 801 goals and 1,049 assists for 1,850 points in the NHL. Though those records have been broken, his 1,767 games over 26 NHL seasons are not likely to be surpassed.

Howe attended his first NHL training camp with the New York Rangers as a 15-year-old in 1943, but left the workouts in Winnipeg because he was homesick. The following year, he was invited to try out for the Red Wings, and by 1946 he was in the NHL. Howe was teamed on a line with Sid Abel and Ted Lindsay. The high-scoring trio was dubbed the Production Line in 1948–49, and in 1949–50 Howe made his first appearance among the league scoring leaders when Lindsay, Abel and Howe finished 1–2–3 in the NHL. The Red Wings went on to win the Stanley Cup that year, though Howe was badly injured in the very first game of the playoffs. He recovered, and won his first scoring title in 1950–51. Howe would win the scoring title again in each of the next three years and eventually claimed the Art Ross Trophy six times. He also won the Hart Trophy on six occasions. While those totals have been surpassed, his record of 21 selections to the NHL All-Star Team has not been beaten. Howe was picked to the First Team 12 times. He established a career high with 49 goals in 70 games in 1952–53, when the NHL was a tight defensive league. When offenses exploded following expansion in 1967, the 41-year-old Howe had 103 points in 1968–69. He cracked the top 10 in scoring for the 21st consecutive year in 1969–70, but retired after injuries limited his effectiveness in 1970–71. He was inducted into the Hockey Hall of Fame in 1972.

Though he had not played in two years and was now 45, Howe was an instant success when he joined the WHA, scoring 100 points in 1973–74 and helping Houston win the Avco Cup, which they won again the following year. In six seasons in the WHA with Houston and the New England Whalers, Howe collected 174 goals and 334 assists for 508 points to rank sixth in all-time WHA scoring. He returned to the NHL for a final season at age 51 and played all 80 games. For excellence and durability, his career will not be matched.

BOBBY HULL began earning accolades as a sure NHL prospect as early as age 10. He progressed rapidly through the ranks in minor hockey, and joined the Chicago Black Hawks as an 18-year-old in 1957–58. At the time of Hull's arrival, the Black Hawks had missed the playoffs four years in a row and in 11 of the last 12 seasons. Attendance was dismal and the franchise had been in danger of folding. Soon, Hull's scoring exploits were attracting huge crowds to Chicago Stadium. By 1961, the Black Hawks were Stanley Cup champions. The team would continue to dominate the regular-season standings into the 1970s.

Hull had an impressive body build, with a muscular torso and powerful legs. His booming slapshot was powerful and accurate, and he was the fastest skater in the game. Combining those facts with his blonde, good looks, Hull was nicknamed "The Golden Jet." In 16 NHL seasons, he led the league in goals on seven occasions and won the Art Ross Trophy three times. In 1961–62, he joined Maurice Richard and Bernie Geoffrion as the third player in league history to score 50 goals in a season. In 1965–66, he set a pre-expansion record with 54 goals and 97 points. He established a new NHL scoring record with 58 goals in 1968–69. That season, Phil Esposito, Hull and Gordie Howe were the first players in NHL history to top 100 points.

By the end of 1971–72, Bobby Hull's 604 goals ranked second only to Gordie Howe in NHL history, and he had been an All-Star on 12 occasions. But in June, 1972, Hull shocked the NHL establishment by signing a 10-year deal worth $2.75 million with the Winnipeg Jets of the World Hockey Association. Though his signing led to his ban from Team Canada when it played the USSR later that year, it gave instant credibility to the fledgling league. Hull continued his high-scoring ways in the WHA, and in 1974–75 he established what was then a single-season professional hockey record with 77 goals. In his seven seasons in the WHA, Hull collected 303 goals and 335 assists for 638 points, totals that rank second, sixth and third respectively among the league's all-time leaders. He also played on Avco Cup champions in 1976, 1978 and 1979.

When Winnipeg became one of four WHA teams to enter the NHL in 1979–80, Hull returned to the league with the Jets. He ended his career playing with Gordie Howe on the Hartford Whalers later that season. In 1983, Hull was elected to the Hockey Hall of Fame. His brother Dennis and son Brett have also starred in the NHL.

BRETT HULL is the son of Hockey Hall of Famer Bobby Hull, and has followed in his famous father's footsteps by becoming one of the greatest goal scorers in the NHL. His 86 goals in 1990–91 rank as the third-highest single-season total in history behind Wayne Gretzky's 92- and 87-goal seasons. Hull scored his 500th career goal on December 22, 1996, to make him and Bobby the only father-son combination ever to reach the milestone. Through 1999–2000, both Hulls have scored 610 regular season NHL goals.

Though he had good success in junior, university and minor league hockey, Brett Hull's poor work ethic meant he was not seen as a future star. He finally got a chance to see regular duty with the Calgary Flames in 1987–88, but on March 7, 1988, he was traded to the St. Louis Blues. Teamed with Adam Oates in 1989–90, Hull scored 72 times to emerge as the top goal scorer in the NHL. With 86 goals and 45 assists in 1990–91, Hull's 131 points trailed only Wayne Gretzky, and he was rewarded with the Hart Trophy as most valuable player. In 1991–92, Hull led the league for the third straight year with 70 goals and earned a third consecutive selection to the First All-Star Team. He topped 50 goals in each of the next two seasons as he surpassed Bernie Federko's total of 352 goals to become the leading goal scorer in Blues history. He upped his total to 527 goals in St. Louis before signing as a free agent with the Dallas Stars after the 1997–98 campaign. In 1999, Hull scored the winning goal in triple overtime as the Stars won the first Stanley Cup title in franchise history. He led the playoffs in both goals and points when Dallas reached the Stanley Cup finals again in 2000.

Though he was born in Belleville, Ontario, Brett Hull holds dual Canadian and U.S. citizenship, and has represented the United States several times. He was the tournament's top scorer when the Americans won the World Cup of Hockey in 1996, and was a member of the U.S. Olympic team at the 1998 Nagano Winter Games.

JAROMIR JAGR was the first player born and raised in Europe to win the Art Ross Trophy. His 70 points during the abbreviated 48-game 1994–95 season actually tied Eric Lindros for the league lead, but Jagr won the Art Ross because he had more goals (32 to 29) than Lindros.

Jagr entered the NHL in 1990–91 and helped the Pittsburgh Penguins win the Stanley Cup in each of his first two seasons in the league. Jagr's offensive numbers improved during each of his first four years, and he established career highs with 62 goals, 87 assists and 149 points in 1995–96. His goals and points ranked second in the NHL behind Penguins teammate Mario Lemieux that season, while his assists and points broke Mike Bossy's NHL records for a right wing. Jagr won the Art Ross Trophy outright in 1997–98 when his 35 goals and 67 assists made him the only player in the NHL to top 100 points. Jagr added the Hart Trophy to his Art Ross honors in 1998–99 after leading the league again with 127 points. Injuries limited him to just 63 games in 1999–2000, but he still led the league in scoring with 96 points and finished as the runner-up to Chris Pronger in the closest Hart Trophy vote in history. In the first game of the playoffs, Jagr set a Pittsburgh record with four assists as the Penguins trounced the Washington Capitals 7–0.

Jagr played in his hometown of Kladno, Czechoslovakia, before entering the NHL. His international experience includes winning a bronze medal with the Czechoslovakian team at the 1990 World Junior Championships and being named to the tournament all-star team. He earned another bronze medal at the World Championships that year, and later was a member of the Czech Republic team that was a surprising gold medal winner at the 1998 Nagano Olympics.

BOB JOHNSON began skating as a four-year-old, and played amateur hockey in his hometown of Minneapolis, Minnesota. He was captain of the team at Minneapolis Central High School in his senior year, then played college hockey at North Dakota and Minnesota.

In 1956, Johnson became head coach of Warroad High School in Warroad, Minnesota. After one season, he moved to Roosevelt High and won four city championships in six years. In 1963, Johnson took a position with Colorado College, then moved on to the University of Wisconsin in 1966. Johnson coached the Badgers for 15 years, winning NCAA titles in 1973, 1977 and 1981, and earning coach of the year honors in 1977. He also coached the U.S. national team from 1973 to 1976, and again in 1981. "Badger Bob" took time off from Wisconsin in 1975–76 to coach the U.S. Olympic hockey team.

Johnson entered the NHL in 1982 as head coach of the Calgary Flames. He spent five seasons with the club, leading Calgary to the Stanley Cup finals for the first time in 1986. He was executive director of USA Hockey over the next three years, supervising an unprecedented growth of amateur hockey in the United States. In 1990–91, Johnson returned to the NHL with the Pittsburgh Penguins and became just the second American-born coach to lead his team to the Stanley Cup (the first being Bill Stewart with the Chicago Black Hawks in 1938).

In September, 1991, Johnson was to coach the U.S. team at the Canada Cup, as he had in 1981 and 1984, but he was forced to relinquish the job because of ill health. He died on November 26, 1991. His gift for inspiring his players and everyone associated with him was recognized when he was named to the United States Hockey Hall of Fame in the coaches category in 1991 and inducted into the Hockey Hall of Fame as a builder in 1992.

AUREL JOLIAT was known as "The Mighty Atom" or "The Little Giant" because of his diminutive size and determined play. Joliat stood just 5'7" and weighed less than 140 pounds during most of his 16-year NHL career. His stature and great skating skill made him difficult for opponents to check, and Joliat earned a reputation as the greatest left wing in hockey.

A football star until a broken leg led him to concentrate on hockey, Joliat's early ice experience came in his hometown of Ottawa and with Iroquois Falls of the Northern Ontario Hockey Association. He went west to Saskatchewan, and was expected to join the Saskatoon Sheiks of the Western Canada Hockey League in 1922–23, but was instead sent to the Montreal Canadiens after Saskatoon bought Newsy Lalonde from the NHL team. Joliat was an instant success in Montreal, and when the Canadiens signed Howie Morenz for the 1923–24 season, the two became a terrific tandem that led Montreal to a Stanley Cup title that year.

Morenz and Joliat were first teamed on a line with Billy Boucher, and later Art Gagne, but the two were at their best when playing alongside Johnny Gagnon. This high-scoring combination led the Canadiens to back-to-back Stanley Cup victories in 1930 and 1931. Joliat led the Canadiens in goal-scoring four years in a row between 1932–33 and 1935–36, and won the Hart Trophy in 1933–34. His 270 career goals equaled Morenz as the most scored by any NHL player during their era.

Though he was small, Joliat played an aggressive game and suffered numerous injuries throughout his career. He began seeing less ice time by the 1936–37 season, and retired after the 1937–38 campaign. Joliat was elected to the Hockey Hall of Fame in 1947.

CURTIS JOSEPH was not selected in the NHL Entry Draft, but signed as a free agent with the St. Louis Blues on June 16, 1989, after an all-star season with the University of Wisconsin. He made his NHL debut on January 2, 1990, and went on to record 100 victories faster than any other goalie in Blues history (209 games).

Three times in his six seasons in St. Louis, Joseph finished among the leaders in voting for the Vezina Trophy. He finished as high as third in 1992–93 behind Tom Barrasso and winner Ed Belfour. On August 4, 1995, Joseph was traded to the Edmonton Oilers. After a contract holdout which saw him join Las Vegas of the International Hockey League, the Oilers traded Bill Ranford in order to make "Cujo" their number-one goaltender. In 1996–97, he helped the Oilers to reach the playoffs for the first time in five years. After spending three seasons with Edmonton, Joseph signed a lucrative four-year contract with Toronto. In 1998–99, he set a Maple Leafs record with 35 wins and finished as the runner-up to Dominik Hasek for the Vezina Trophy. He recorded 36 victories in 1999–2000 as the Leafs reached the 100-point plateau for the first time in franchise history and won the Northeast Division. Joseph was again a finalist for the Vezina Trophy and won the King Clancy Trophy for his humanitarian efforts.

In international hockey, Joseph won a silver medal with Team Canada at the 1996 World Championships and was named to the tournament's second all-star team. That experience helped him land one of the three goaltending positions for Canada at the 1996 World Cup of Hockey and at the 1998 Nagano Olympics.

PAUL KARIYA made his debut with the Mighty Ducks of Anaheim in 1994–95, and finished third behind Peter Forsberg and Jim Carey in voting for the Calder Trophy. He had 50 goals in 1995–96, and made his first appearance among the NHL scoring leaders with 108 points, earning a selection to the First All-Star Team at left wing and winning the Lady Byng Trophy. Kariya received both honors again in 1996–97, and also finished as the runner-up to Dominik Hasek for the Hart Trophy after leading Anaheim to the playoffs for the first time in franchise history. Kariya missed most of the 1997–98 season because of injuries, but is still one of the league's top talents.

A fast skater with an excellent shot, Kariya was already a star before reaching the NHL. He was twice named the most valuable player in the British Columbia Junior Hockey League, adding Canadian Junior A player of the year honors in 1991–92. In 1992–93, he set several school and conference records at the University of Maine while leading the school to the NCAA championships and becoming the first freshman to win the Hobey Baker Award as the outstanding U.S. college player. He also won a gold medal at the 1993 World Junior Championships, and was a tournament all-star.

Kariya was selected fourth overall by Anaheim at the 1993 NHL Entry Draft, but chose to spend the 1993–94 season with the Canadian national team. He was the team's top scorer when Canada won a silver medal at the 1994 Lillehammer Olympics, then led the team in scoring again when Canada earned gold at the World Championships. The victory represented Canada's first world title since 1961.

RED KELLY was a member of eight Stanley Cup winners. He is the only NHL player with that many titles who did not skate for the Montreal Canadiens. Kelly won four Stanley Cup titles (1950, 1952, 1954 and 1955) with the Detroit Red Wings and four more (1962, 1963, 1964 and 1967) with the Toronto Maple Leafs. He was inducted into the Hockey Hall of Fame in 1969.

Leonard Patrick "Red" Kelly played junior hockey with the St. Michael's Majors in Toronto, and entered the NHL with the Detroit Red Wings in 1947–48. In Kelly's second year, Detroit finished first in the NHL for the first of seven straight seasons. By his third season of 1949–50, the Red Wings were Stanley Cup champions. Kelly was named to the Second All-Star Team on defense that year, and would be an all-star for eight consecutive years. He also won the Lady Byng Trophy three times, and was the first recipient of the Norris Trophy as the NHL's best defenseman in 1953–54. Kelly was team captain in 1956–57 and 1957–58. He was an excellent checker who could rush the puck effectively, and was occasionally used as a forward by the Red Wings.

On February 5, 1960, it was announced that the Red Wings had traded Kelly to the Rangers, but the deal fell through when he refused to report. A few days later, he was sent to the Maple Leafs. Punch Imlach moved Kelly up to center in Toronto, where he continued to excel for seven seasons. Kelly played with Frank Mahovlich on his left wing and in 1960–61 he helped "The Big M" set what was then a Maple Leafs record with 48 goals. Kelly himself won the Lady Byng Trophy for a fourth time that season. In 1962, Kelly was convinced to enter politics. He served three years as a Liberal member of the House of Commons in Ottawa, while still playing hockey with the Maple Leafs.

After Toronto won its fourth Stanley Cup championship of the decade in 1967, Kelly gave up playing to become coach of the expansion Los Angeles Kings. He led the team into the playoffs for two straight years, but had less success over the next three years as coach of the Pittsburgh Penguins. In 1973, Kelly returned to Toronto as coach of the Maple Leafs. He guided the team to four consecutive quarterfinal appearances, including three memorable matchups with the Philadelphia Flyers.

TEEDER KENNEDY was one of the greatest stars in the greatest era of the Toronto Maple Leafs. He played on Toronto teams that won the Stanley Cup five times in seven years between 1945 and 1951, and is to date the last Maple Leafs player to win the Hart Trophy, being chosen as MVP in his final full season of 1954–55. Kennedy had a scrambling skating style and a fierce competitive spirit that made him a fan favorite at Maple Leaf Gardens, where shouts of "Come o-n-n-n-n, Teeder!" became the battle cry.

Ted Kennedy was originally property of the Montreal Canadiens, and attended their training camp as a 16-year-old in September, 1942. The Maple Leafs acquired his rights the following September, and he became a regular in Toronto in 1943–44. He led the team in both goals and points in 1944–45, and starred in the playoffs when the Maple Leafs upset the Canadiens and Detroit Red Wings to win the Stanley Cup. Kennedy was again Toronto's leading scorer in 1946–47, and led the Maple Leafs past Montreal for the Stanley Cup. After another Stanley Cup victory in 1948, Kennedy succeeded Syl Apps as Maple Leafs captain in 1948–49 and led Toronto to a third consecutive Stanley Cup title.

Individual honors finally began coming to Kennedy in 1949–50, when he was named to the Second All-Star Team. He was a Second Team All-Star again in 1950–51 when the Maple Leafs won yet another Stanley Cup title. Kennedy retired after his Hart Trophy-winning season of 1954–55, but made a comeback two years later to help bolster an injury-riddled Toronto lineup. He was elected to the Hockey Hall of Fame in 1966.

OLAF KOLZIG emerged as a top goaltender during the 1997–98 season when he ranked among the leaders in most statistical categories. "Ollie the Goalie" then emerged as a star during the 1998 playoffs, leading the Washington Capitals to the Stanley Cup finals for the first time in franchise history.

Kolzig made his NHL debut with the Capitals in 1989–90, but spent most of his first seven seasons with the organization playing in the minor leagues. In 1994 he won the Jack Butterfield Trophy as the MVP of the Calder Cup playoffs for leading Portland to the American Hockey League championship. He finally got his chance to see regular duty in Washington in 1996–97 and earned the number-one job in 1997–98. After a disappointing season in 1998–99, Kolzig again ranked among the NHL's best netminders in 1999–2000. He led the Capitals to first place in the Southeast Division and won the Vezina Trophy. He was also named to the First All-Star Team.

Born to German parents in Johannesburg, South Africa, Kolzig was raised in many different locales but grew up mostly in Toronto and Halifax. He represented Germany at the World Cup of Hockey in 1996 and played two games for the German team at the Nagano Olympics in 1998.

JARI KURRI surpassed Peter Stastny as the highest-scoring European player in the NHL on December 8, 1993. Four years later, on December 23, 1997, Kurri became just the eighth player in NHL history to score 600 career goals. Yet, even with his impressive offensive credentials, Kurri was known as one of the league's best defensive forwards during his career.

Kurri joined the Edmonton Oilers in 1980–81 after representing Finland at the Lake Placid Olympics the season before. Teamed on a line at right wing with Wayne Gretzky, Kurri quickly developed into one of the league's best scorers. He cracked the top 10 for the first time in 1982–83, and led all playoff performers with 14 goals when the Oilers won their first Stanley Cup title in 1984. He scored 71 goals in 1984–85, then tied a postseason record with 19 goals as the Oilers repeated as Stanley Cup champions. Kurri led the NHL with 68 goals in 1985–86, and was the top playoff goal scorer again in 1987 and 1988 when the Oilers won two more titles. He picked up his fifth Stanley Cup ring in 1990. Kurri then left the NHL after 10 seasons and played in Italy in 1990–91. That spring, he represented Finland at the World Championships in Helsinki, and though the Finns failed to reach the medal round, Kurri tied Mats Sundin for the tournament lead in scoring and was named to the all-star team.

On May 30, 1991, Kurri's rights were traded to the Los Angeles Kings in a three-way deal with Edmonton and the Philadelphia Flyers, and he returned to the NHL for the 1991–92 season. Paired again with Wayne Gretzky, Kurri helped to lead Los Angeles to the Stanley Cup finals in 1993. He was traded to the New York Rangers on March 14, 1996, then spent his final two seasons with the Mighty Ducks of Anaheim and the Colorado Avalanche. In 1998, he once again represented Finland at the Olympics in Nagano and helped to win a bronze medal.

GUY LAFLEUR had a combination of speed, style and scoring skill that made him the most exciting player in the NHL during his prime with the Montreal Canadiens. His six consecutive 50-goal seasons from 1974–75 to 1979–80 were a record at the time, and he played on five Stanley Cup champions in Montreal, including four in a row between 1976 and 1979. He won the Conn Smythe Trophy as playoff MVP in 1977.

Lafleur idolized Jean Beliveau growing up, and wore number 4 while starring with the Quebec Remparts. He capped his brilliant junior career with 130 goals and 79 assists and a Memorial Cup title with Quebec in 1970–71, then was selected first overall by the Canadiens in the 1971 NHL Amateur Draft. Though his first-year statistics of 29 goals and 64 assists were impressive for a rookie, more had been expected of Lafleur, but "the Flower" did not truly blossom until 1974–75, his fourth season, when he had 53 goals and 66 assists. He won his first of three consecutive NHL scoring titles the following season, and went on to become the youngest player in NHL history to score 400 goals and the youngest to reach 1,000 points. When he retired during the 1984–85 season, Lafleur's 518 goals ranked second in Canadiens history behind Maurice Richard. With a club record 728 assists, Lafleur's 1,246 points make him the leading scorer in the history of the storied franchise.

Lafleur was elected to the Hockey Hall of Fame in 1988, but decided to make a comeback for the 1988–89 season. He joined the New York Rangers that year, and on his first trip back to the Forum on February 4, 1988, he scored two goals. Lafleur spent the next two years with the Quebec Nordiques before retiring for good after the 1990–91 season. At the time, his 560 goals ranked seventh in NHL history, and his 1,353 points were eighth. The Guy Lafleur Trophy is awarded annually to the playoff MVP in the Quebec Major Junior Hockey League.

NEWSY LALONDE was the greatest scorer of his era. Equally skilled as a fighter, Lalonde was a tough customer who would not back down from any opponent, sometimes even clashing with teammates. Also a lacrosse star, Lalonde was named Canada's outstanding player of the half-century in that sport in 1950, the same year he was inducted into the Hockey Hall of Fame.

Edouard Charles "Newsy" Lalonde earned his nickname when he worked in a newsprint plant as a boy in his hometown of Cornwall, Ontario. His hockey career also began in that city in 1904–05. Two years later, he was playing in hockey's first professional league as a member of the Sault Ste. Marie, Ontario, team in the International (Pro) Hockey League. When the Ontario Professional Hockey League was formed in 1907–08, Lalonde joined the Toronto team and won his first scoring title. Toronto won the OPHL championship that year, but they lost a one-game Stanley Cup challenge to the Montreal Wanderers.

After a second season in the OPHL, Lalonde joined *les Canadiens* when the French-Canadian team was formed in Montreal for the inaugural campaign of the National Hockey Association. He was traded to the Renfrew Millionaires during the season, and ended the year as the league scoring leader. His nine goals for Renfrew on March 11, 1910, would remain a single-game high throughout the eight-year history of the NHA (though the mark was equaled by Tommy Smith).

After returning to the Canadiens, Lalonde joined former Renfrew teammate Frank Patrick out west when he signed with the Vancouver Millionaires for 1911–12 in the new Pacific Coast Hockey Association. After leading the PCHA with 27 goals that year, he returned to Montreal again, winning another goal-scoring title in 1915–16 as the Canadiens won their first Stanley Cup championship. He remained with the team through its entry into the NHL in 1917–18, and he went on to win a pair of NHL scoring titles. He scored six goals in a single game on January 10, 1920. Lalonde also served as coach of the Canadiens during much of this time.

Lalonde remained with Montreal until after the 1921–22 season, when he fell out of favor with owner Leo Dandurand, who sent him to the Saskatoon Sheiks of the Western Canada Hockey League in return for Aurel Joliat. Lalonde promptly led the WCHL with 30 goals as a player-coach in 1922–23. He returned to the NHL as a coach with the New York Americans in 1926–27, and he later coached the Ottawa Senators and Montreal Canadiens before retiring in 1935. He remained a lifelong fan of the Canadiens, continuing to attend games at the Forum until his death in 1971.

JOHN LeCLAIR scored 51 goals in 1997–98 to become the first American-born player to have three consecutive 50-goal seasons. He has ranked among the top performers in the NHL since joining the Philadelphia Flyers in a trade on February 9, 1995.

LeClair was drafted out of high school by the Montreal Canadiens in 1987, but spent the next four years at the University of Vermont before making his NHL debut on March 9, 1991. He was the first Vermont native ever to reach the NHL. He became a regular with the Canadiens in 1992–93, and helped Montreal to win the Stanley Cup that season, but it was not until his arrival in Philadelphia that he became one of the NHL's top scorers.

Playing left wing alongside Eric Lindros and Mikael Renberg on the Legion of Doom line, LeClair and his linemates all cracked the top 10 in scoring in 1994–95. The following season, LeClair scored 50 goals for the first time. He was either a First or Second Team All-Star for five straight seasons beginning in 1995, and was named to the all-star team at the World Cup of Hockey in 1996 after his six goals and 10 points ranked second in the tournament behind Brett Hull. He was also a member of the U.S. Olympic team in Nagano in 1998.

BRIAN LEETCH was a two-time high school hockey all-star who became an all-American at Boston College in 1986–87. He was also the first freshman ever nominated for the Hobey Baker Award, the top individual honor in U.S. college hockey. Leetch left the school after one season to join the U.S. national team. He made his NHL debut with the New York Rangers on February 29, 1988, after serving as captain of the U.S. team at the Calgary Olympics.

Leetch played his first full NHL season in 1988–89, and quickly established himself among the league's best defensemen. He led all rookies in assists and points that season, and won the Calder Trophy. His 71 points represented the second-highest total for a rookie defenseman behind Larry Murphy's 76 in 1980–81. Leetch established a Rangers record with 72 assists in 1990–91, and also set a team record for defensemen with 88 points. He broke both records with 80 assists and 102 points in 1991–92, and won the Norris Trophy as best defenseman.

Injuries kept Leetch out for most of the 1992–93 season, but he returned to star in 1993–94, particularly in the playoffs when he topped all scorers and won the Conn Smythe Trophy as the Rangers won the Cup for the first time since 1940. On December 27, 1996, Leetch surpassed Ron Greschner as the highest-scoring defenseman in Rangers history with his 611th point. Through 1999–2000, he trails only Rod Gilbert and Jean Ratelle among the Rangers' all-time scoring leaders.

In addition to his Olympic experience in 1988, Leetch's international experience includes winning a bronze medal at the 1986 World Junior Championships. In 1996, he was captain of the American team that beat Canada to win the World Cup of Hockey. In 1998, he returned to the Olympics as a member of the U.S. team in Nagano.

MARIO LEMIEUX was one of the most prolific and creative scorers in NHL history despite battling chronic back problems and Hodgkin's disease during the 12 years he played. He was described by Bobby Orr as being the most skilled player he had ever seen, but like Orr, Lemieux's physical ailments shortened his career. When he decided to retire after the 1996–97 season, the traditional three-year waiting period was waived and Lemieux was elected immediately to the Hockey Hall of Fame. Having been credited with saving the Pittsburgh franchise with his play, Lemieux put together a group that bought the club and saved it from bankruptcy in 1999.

Lemieux was a star from childhood who attracted great attention during the 1983–84 season when he set Quebec Major Junior Hockey League records with 133 goals and 282 points in 70 games. He led Laval to the Memorial Cup tournament that year, and was named the Canadian major junior player of the year. He then was picked by the Pittsburgh Penguins with the first choice in the 1984 NHL Entry Draft. At the time, the Penguins were struggling at the gate and on the ice, but Lemieux would emerge as Pittsburgh's hockey savior.

Lemieux scored his first NHL goal on his first shift in a game against the Boston Bruins on October 11, 1984. He went on to become just the third rookie in NHL history to score 100 points (Peter Stastny and Dale Hawerchuk were the others) and won the Calder Trophy. He ranked among the NHL scoring leaders in both his second and third seasons, but it was not until after playing alongside Wayne Gretzky and scoring the series-winning goal at the Canada Cup in 1987 that Lemieux finally emerged as a true superstar. He won both the Art Ross and Hart trophies after Wayne Gretzky was injured in 1987–88, but then beat Gretzky outright for the scoring title in 1988–89 when he established career highs with 85 goals, 114 assists and 199 points.

Back injuries first sidelined Lemieux during the 1989–90 season, but he returned late in the 1990–91 campaign and led Pittsburgh to its first Stanley Cup title. He won the Conn Smythe Trophy as playoff MVP that year, as he would again when Pittsburgh made it two in a row in 1992. During the 1992–93 season, Lemieux was diagnosed with Hodgkin's disease (a form of cancer). Radiation treatments lasted from February 1 to March 2, when Lemieux immediately returned to the lineup. He went on to win the Art Ross Trophy for the fourth time and again was awarded the Hart Trophy.

Because of his injuries and illness, Lemieux took the entire season off in 1994–95. He returned the following year and again won both the Hart and Art Ross trophies. He won his sixth scoring title during his final season of 1996–97. With 613 career goals and 1,494 points in just 745 games, Lemieux's average of .823 goals-per-game and 2.005 points are the best in NHL history.

NICKLAS LIDSTROM played three seasons in the Swedish Elite League before joining the Detroit Red Wings for the 1991–92 season. He led all rookies in assists (49) and plus-minus (+36) that year, and finished as the runner-up behind Pavel Bure in voting for the Calder Trophy. Lidstrom has gone on to become one of the top defensemen in the NHL, and was a key contributor when Detroit won its first Stanley Cup title in 42 years in 1997. He helped the Red Wings repeat as champions the following year, and was nominated for the Norris Trophy as the NHL's best defenseman for the first time in 1997–98 after leading all blueliners with 59 points. Lidstrom considered returning to his homeland after another fine season in 1998–99, but was re-signed by the Red Wings. He established career highs with 20 goals and 53 assists in 1999–2000 and earned his third straight nomination for the Norris Trophy. He was also nominated for the Lady Byng Trophy for the second straight year.

Lidstrom got his first international experience when he represented Sweden at the European Junior Championships in 1989. Since then he has played at numerous other international events, including the 1998 Nagano Olympics.

ERIC LINDROS stands 6'4" and weighs 236 pounds, which made him the biggest player in hockey when he entered the NHL. He boasts a combination of strength and skill that has seen him become a superstar—as had been projected for him since childhood. However, his physical style of play has made him very susceptible to injuries.

After starring in Junior B hockey with St. Michael's in Toronto, Lindros was drafted by the Sault Ste. Marie Greyhounds of the Ontario Hockey League in 1989, but refused to report. He played instead with Compuware in Detroit until the Greyhounds traded his rights to the Oshawa Generals. Lindros finished the 1989–90 season in Oshawa and helped the team to win the Memorial Cup. He also played on Canada's gold medal-winning team at the World Junior Championships that year. In 1990–91, he led the OHL with 71 goals and 149 points, won another world junior title, led the tournament in scoring, and was named the Canadian major junior player of the year.

Lindros was selected first overall by the Quebec Nordiques in the 1991 NHL Entry Draft, but refused to sign with the team he had asked not to choose him. Even though he was not under contract to an NHL club, the 18-year-old Lindros was asked to join Team Canada for the 1991 Canada Cup. He then spent the 1991–92 season with the Canadian national team, and helped Canada to win a silver medal at the Albertville Olympics.

On June 30, 1992, the Philadelphia Flyers sent six players, two first-round draft choices and cash to Quebec to obtain the rights to Lindros, though it took the ruling of an arbitrator to determine that Quebec had not dealt Lindros's rights to the New York Rangers first. He finally made his NHL debut in 1992–93 and set a Flyers rookie record with 41 goals that season. His offensive production increased in 1993–94, and in 1994–95 he tied Jaromir Jagr for the NHL lead with 70 points in an abbreviated 48-game season. Jagr received the Art Ross Trophy because he had scored more goals, but Lindros earned the Hart Trophy as MVP. He established a career high with 115 points in 1995–96, then led all playoff scorers with 26 points in 1997 as the Flyers reached the Stanley Cup finals before losing to the Detroit Red Wings. In 1998, Lindros was Canada's captain at the Nagano Olympics. His brother Brett played briefly with the New York Islanders before an injury ended his career.

TED LINDSAY was one of the toughest players in NHL history. Although small in stature at 5'8" and 163 pounds, "Terrible Ted" never was afraid to take on all comers, and thus became one of the most dangerous fighters, as well as a top offensive threat, in the NHL. He was named as an all-star at left wing nine times in his career, including eight selections to the First Team.

The son of former goaltender Bert Lindsay, Ted Lindsay became a star in junior hockey. He was a member of the St. Michael's College team that lost the Ontario junior finals to Oshawa in 1943–44, but then was added to the Generals roster in their successful bid to win the Memorial Cup. Lindsay turned pro with the Detroit Red Wings the following year, and began his NHL career on a line with veterans Mud Bruneteau and Syd Howe. He was first teamed with Gordie Howe and Sid Abel during the 1946–47 season. The following year, Lindsay cracked the top 10 in scoring for the first time. It was during the 1948–49 season that the Abel-Lindsay-Howe combination was dubbed the Production Line, and that year the trio led the Red Wings to the first of seven consecutive first-place finishes. Lindsay led the NHL in scoring in 1949–50, and played on his first Stanley Cup winner that year. Detroit won the Cup again in 1952. Lindsay succeeded Abel as team captain in 1952–53, and led the Red Wings to Stanley Cup victories in 1954 and 1955.

On July 23, 1957, Lindsay was traded to the Chicago Black Hawks as punishment for his attempts to form a strong players' union. Chicago had missed the playoffs four years in a row, and in 10 of the last 11 seasons, but Lindsay helped to revitalize the franchise. He retired after the 1959–60 campaign, yet made a remarkable comeback with Detroit in 1964–65, and helped the Red Wings finish in first place. He retired for good after that season, and was elected to the Hockey Hall of Fame in 1966. Lindsay later served as Red Wings general manager from 1976–77 to 1979–80, and also coached the team for the final nine games of the 1979–80 season and the first 20 games of 1980–81.

AL MacINNIS was a junior star who helped the Kitchener Rangers win the Memorial Cup in 1982 while being brought along slowly by the Calgary Flames. Although drafted in 1981, MacInnis did not spend his first full season in the NHL until 1984–85. With his booming slapshot, he quickly became one of the top defensemen in the NHL. MacInnis helped Calgary reach the Stanley Cup finals in 1986 and win it all in 1989. He topped the playoff scoring list with 24 assists and 31 points, and won the Conn Smythe Trophy, as the Flames won the Stanley Cup for the first time in franchise history.

MacInnis was named to the First All-Star Team in 1989–90, and again in 1990–91 when he became just the fourth defenseman in NHL history (behind Bobby Orr, Denis Potvin and Paul Coffey) to top 100 points in a season. He was a Second Team All-Star in 1993–94, but on July 4, 1994, MacInnis was traded to the St. Louis Blues for Phil Housley. He left Calgary as the Flames' all-time leader with 609 assists and 822 points. He won the Norris Trophy as the NHL's best defenseman for the first time in 1998–99 and helped the Blues post the best record in the NHL with a franchise record 51 wins and 114 points in 1999–2000.

In 1996, MacInnis was a member of Team Canada at the World Cup of Hockey, and in 1998 he played for the Olympic team at Nagano.

FRANK MAHOVLICH was hailed as a superstar while playing junior hockey, and he went on to record 533 goals and 570 assists during his NHL career. He was also named to the all-star team on nine occasions, yet "The Big M" was constantly criticized for not living up to expectations.

Mahovlich played his junior hockey at St. Michael's College and won the Red Tilson Memorial Trophy as the most valuable player in the Ontario Hockey Association in 1956–57. The following year, he joined the Toronto Maple Leafs and beat out Bobby Hull to win the Calder Trophy as rookie of the year. In 1960–61, Mahovlich established himself as one of the greatest goal scorers in hockey. He battled Bernie Geoffrion that season in a race to join Maurice Richard as the only 50-goal scorers to that point in NHL history. Mahovlich eventually fell two goals short, but his total of 48 was a Maple Leafs record until Rick Vaive scored 54 goals in 1981–82. Mahovlich led the Maple Leafs in goal-scoring every season from 1960–61 to 1965–66, and also led the team in points every year during that span except 1963–64. He was the main offensive weapon on Toronto teams that won the Stanley Cup in 1962, 1963, 1964 and 1967, yet Mahovlich did not get along with coach Punch Imlach, who traded him to the Detroit Red Wings on March 3, 1968.

In Detroit, Mahovlich joined a roster that featured his brother Peter and was teamed on a line with Gordie Howe and Alex Delvecchio. He established a career high with 49 goals in 1968–69, and helped the 41-year-old Howe become just the third player in NHL history (behind Phil Esposito and Bobby Hull) to record 100 points in a season. Mahovlich was traded to the Canadiens on January 13, 1971 (where he rejoined his brother), and the moody superstar went on to enjoy the happiest times of his career.

Mahovlich was transformed into a top playmaker in Montreal. He helped the Canadiens win the Stanley Cup in 1971, and was a member of Team Canada in the 1972 Summit Series. During the 1972–73 season, Mahovlich became the eighth player in NHL history to record 1,000 points (February 17, 1973), and the fifth player to score 500 goals (March 21, 1973). He also played for his sixth Stanley Cup winner that season.

In 1974–75, Mahovlich returned to Toronto as a member of the Toros in the World Hockey Association. He spent two years with the Toros and two more with the Birmingham Bulls before retiring in 1978. Mahovlich was elected to the Hockey Hall of Fame in 1981. In 1998, he was appointed to the Canadian Senate by Prime Minister Jean Chretien.

JOE MALONE was one of the most prolific players in hockey history, and second only to Newsy Lalonde among the goal scorers of his day. He led the NHL in scoring in its first season of 1917–18 with the astounding total of 44 goals in just 20 games played, and his seven goals on January 31, 1920, remain an NHL single-game record. Nicknamed "Phantom," Joe Malone was a slick stickhandler, deceptive skater and a sportsmanlike player in an era noted for its rough play.

Malone made his professional debut with the Quebec Bulldogs in 1908–09, but he spent the next season with Waterloo of the Ontario Professional Hockey League after Quebec was excluded from the National Hockey Association. When the Bulldogs entered the NHA in 1910–11, Malone returned to Quebec, though he had yet to show much scoring promise. The breakthrough came the following season when he led the team with 21 goals as the Bulldogs won the NHA title and the Stanley Cup. In 1912–13, he led the NHA with 43 goals and scored nine in one game on March 8, 1913, during a Stanley Cup challenge series against Sydney, Nova Scotia. Malone earned another NHA scoring title in 1916–17 when he tied Frank Nighbor for the league lead with 41 goals.

When the NHL was formed in 1917–18, Quebec chose not to operate its team and Malone joined the Montreal Canadiens. When the Bulldogs did enter the NHL in 1919–20, Malone returned to Quebec and won a second NHL scoring title with 39 goals and 10 assists, even though his team was 4–20–0. He moved with the franchise to Hamilton for the next two years, but he returned to Montreal as a substitute player in 1922–23 and 1923–24 before retiring. Malone was elected to the Hockey Hall of Fame in 1950.

JOHN MARIUCCI played hockey in high school in his native Eveleth, Minnesota, before going on to star in both hockey and football at the University of Minnesota. He was an all-American on the Golden Gophers hockey team that went undefeated in 1939–40. Mariucci turned pro the following season, playing first with Providence of the American Hockey League before being called up to the Chicago Black Hawks.

Mariucci was with the Black Hawks for two seasons before his career was interrupted by military service. He returned to Chicago in 1945–46, and was named captain of the Black Hawks, a position he held again in his final NHL season of 1947–48. After four years of minor-league hockey, Mariucci returned to his alma mater as the hockey coach at the University of Minnesota beginning in 1952–53.

As "The Godfather of Hockey in Minnesota," Mariucci encouraged the game at the high school level, and recruited American players for his university team (which previously had been stocked mainly with Canadians). In his second season with the Gophers, he led the team to the NCAA finals. He remained coach at Minnesota until 1966–67, producing one dozen all-Americans and leading the United States Olympic hockey team to a silver medal in 1956.

After leaving the University of Minnesota, Mariucci returned to the NHL as an assistant general manager with the Minnesota North Stars from 1967 until 1974. He spent the next season as a scout with the North Stars before taking over the U.S. national team, which he coached from 1975–76 to 1977–78. He later returned to the North Stars as assistant g.m. from 1982 until his death on March 23, 1987.

Mariucci was a firm believer that Americans could be as successful in hockey as Canadians. He was a charter member of the United States Hockey Hall of Fame in 1973, won the Lester Patrick Trophy for his contributions to hockey in the United States in 1977, and was elected to the Hockey Hall of Fame as a builder in 1985.

FRANK McGEE remains a legendary name in hockey more than 90 years after he last played his game, and over 80 years since he was killed in action while serving in France during World War I. The scoring star with the Ottawa Silver Seven is remembered best for pouring in 14 goals during a single Stanley Cup playoff game as Ottawa defeated a team from Dawson City 23–2.

Though he had lost the sight in one eye prior to joining the Silver Seven, McGee helped Ottawa win the Stanley Cup for the first time in 1903 and successfully defend its title against 10 different challengers before losing to the Montreal Wanderers in 1906. He won the only scoring title of his brief career during the 1904–05 season, when he tied Jack Marshall for first place in the Federal Amateur Hockey League with 17 goals in six games, but his best scoring season was 1905–06 when he potted 28 goals in just seven games to finish third in scoring in the Eastern Canada Amateur Hockey Association behind teammate Harry Smith and his great scoring rival Russell Bowie. It would be the final year of McGee's career.

In addition to his 14-goal game against Dawson City on January 16, 1905, McGee scored eight goals in a regular-season game against the Montreal Wanderers on March 3, 1906, and he had five goals in a game on seven occasions. He scored 71 goals in 23 regular-season games over four years, and another 63 goals in 22 playoff contests. McGee was inducted into the Hall of Fame as one of its 12 original members in 1945.

MARK MESSIER's combination of power, speed and skill have made him one of the great leaders in the NHL. He is a six-time Stanley Cup champion, and has played more playoff games than anyone in NHL history. Messier also ranks fourth all-time in NHL scoring behind only Wayne Gretzky, Gordie Howe and Marcel Dionne. He has represented Canada at several international tournaments, and the decision to leave him off the 1998 Olympic team was very controversial.

After one season in the World Hockey Association, Messier was the Edmonton Oilers' second choice in the Entry Draft when they joined the NHL for the 1979–80 season. By his third NHL season he was a star, scoring 50 goals and being named to the First All-Star Team at left wing. When the Oilers won their first Stanley Cup title in 1984, Messier earned the Conn Smythe Trophy as playoff MVP. Now playing center on a second line behind Wayne Gretzky, Messier was in the shadow of "The Great One" on three more Oilers championships. When Gretzky was traded to the Los Angeles Kings on August 9, 1988, Messier responded to the challenge of becoming captain. He established career highs with 84 assists and 129 points in 1989–90, won the Hart Trophy as NHL MVP, and led the Oilers to a fifth Stanley Cup title.

After an injury-plagued 1990–91 campaign, Messier was traded to the New York Rangers, who hoped his talent and leadership would end a Stanley Cup drought that dated back to 1940. Messier won the Hart Trophy again after leading the Rangers to a first-place finish in 1991–92, and a Stanley Cup championship came two years later. Messier's inspirational words and play in the Eastern Conference finals against the New Jersey Devils that spring went a long way toward bringing the Stanley Cup back to New York for the first time in 54 years.

Messier remained with the Rangers until 1996–97, when he was reunited with Wayne Gretzky. He then signed as a free agent with the Vancouver Canucks before the 1997–98 season. He returned to New York after a three-year absence on July 13, 2000, and was immediately named captain once again. Since Gretzky retired after the 1998–99 season, Messier is the NHL's active scoring leader.

STAN MIKITA came to Canada from Czechoslovakia as a boy with his aunt and uncle in 1948, and settled in St. Catharines, Ontario. He later became a star junior player in his adopted hometown, and went on to become one of the greatest players in NHL history over a 22-year career with the Chicago Black Hawks. Mikita and Bobby Hull helped change the Black Hawks from perennial losers into an NHL powerhouse. When he retired after the 1979–80 season, Mikita ranked second all-time behind Gordie Howe with 926 assists, sixth in goals with 541, and third in points with 1,467. His 1,394 games were the fifth-most in NHL history.

Mikita joined the Black Hawks for a three-game trial in 1958–59, and became a regular the following season. In 1961, he helped Chicago win its first Stanley Cup title in 23 years. Though he was just 5'9" and weighed only 169 pounds, Mikita was prone to taking penalties early in his career, but was also an effective scorer, leading the NHL in points in both 1963–64 and 1964–65. As he gained more experience, Mikita's penalty totals dropped. In 1966–67, he became the first player in history to win the Hart Trophy, the Art Ross Trophy and the Lady Byng Trophy in the same season. His 97 points that year tied the single-season record for the pre-expansion era set by Bobby Hull just one year before. Mikita remained the top scorer in the NHL after expansion, recording a career-high 40 goals in 1967–68 and again winning the Hart, Art Ross and Lady Byng trophies. He continued to be an effective scorer into the mid-1970s before his totals finally began to decline.

Mikita's contributions to hockey in the United States were recognized in 1976 when he was awarded the Lester Patrick Trophy. He established the American Impaired Hearing Association in 1972–73, and continues to work for the children's charity. Mikita was elected to the Hockey Hall of Fame in 1983.

MIKE MODANO was just the second American-born player to be selected first overall in the NHL Entry Draft when he was picked by the Minnesota North Stars in 1988. Five years earlier, the North Stars had made American Brian Lawton the number-one pick.

Modano was a high-scoring junior with the Prince Albert Raiders of the Western Hockey League and an all-star in his final season of 1988–89, despite missing 25 games with a broken wrist. He made his NHL debut when he played two playoff games for the North Stars that season, and became a regular in Minnesota in 1989–90. His 75 points ranked second behind Sergei Makarov in rookie scoring, and Modano finished as the runner-up behind Makarov in voting for the Calder Trophy. The following year, he helped the North Stars to reach the Stanley Cup finals.

Modano led the North Stars in points in 1991–92 and in 1992–93. The team moved to Dallas in 1993–94, and Modano scored 50 goals that season to join Brian Bellows and Dino Ciccarelli as the only players in franchise history to score 50 in a season. Since then, he has continued to rank as the Stars' top scorer, but has also developed into a solid defensive player. In 1999 he helped the Stars win the Stanley Cup for the first time in franchise history. In 1999–2000 he finished among the NHL's top-10 scorers for the first time in his career and helped Dallas return to the Stanley Cup finals.

Modano has represented the United States at numerous international events, including the 1989 World Junior Championships, where he finished second behind fellow American Jeremy Roenick in scoring. He was also a member of the American team that beat Canada at the World Cup of Hockey in 1996, and played for the U.S. Olympic team in Nagano in 1998.

DICKIE MOORE played on Memorial Cup champions with the Montreal Royals in 1948–49 and the Montreal Junior Canadiens in 1949–50 before joining the Montreal Canadiens midway through the 1951–52 NHL season. He saw part-time duty for three years before becoming a regular with the Canadiens in 1954–55. An excellent stickhandler and skater with a hard, accurate shot, Moore became one of the NHL's top offensive stars. He was also handy with his elbows and fists, and his aggressive play earned him the nickname "Digging Dicker."

Although plagued by injuries throughout his career, Moore managed to lead the NHL in scoring twice. He won his first title in 1957–58 despite playing the final three months of the season with a cast on his broken left wrist. In 1958–59, he established career highs with 41 goals and 55 assists, breaking Gordie Howe's single-season record of 95 points set six years before. Moore's 96 points would prove to be the second-highest total of the pre-expansion era. (Both Bobby Hull and Stan Mikita would later total 97.) Moore played on Stanley Cup champions in Montreal in 1953, and for five years in a row from 1956 to 1960.

Moore retired after the 1962–63 season, but made a comeback with the Toronto Maple Leafs in 1964–65. He retired again after that year, but returned to the NHL for a final appearance when he played 27 games with the St. Louis Blues in their first season of 1967–68. Moore was inducted into the Hockey Hall of Fame in 1974.

HOWIE MORENZ was voted Canada's outstanding hockey player of the half-century in 1950. He was considered the biggest star in the game during the colorful days of the 1920s and 1930s, and his great skill helped sell the sport in the United States, where he was often called "The Babe Ruth of Hockey" because of his box office appeal. His many other nicknames came from his fabulous skating speed, as the Montreal star was often tagged with labels like "The Canadien Comet," "The Hurtling Habitant," "The Mitchell Meteor" and "The Stratford Streak."

Morenz was born in Mitchell, Ontario, but first attracted attention as a hockey star in nearby Stratford. Leo Dandurand signed him to his first professional contract for the 1923–24 season, and Morenz immediately led the Montreal Canadiens to the Stanley Cup. In 1924–25 he had 28 goals in just 30 games and finished second on the team in scoring behind linemate Aurel Joliat. Over the next seven seasons, no other player would lead the Canadiens in either goals or points (though Joliat tied Morenz for the points lead in 1925–26). In both 1927–28 and 1930–31, Morenz was also the NHL's top scorer. He led the Canadiens to consecutive Stanley Cup championships in 1930 and 1931, and was a three-time winner of the Hart Trophy as the player most valuable to his team. When NHL All-Stars were selected for the first time in 1930–31, he was named to the First Team at center, and repeated the honor the following year.

An aggressive player throughout his career, injuries began to catch up with Morenz, and by 1933–34 his production had tailed off. He was traded to the Chicago Black Hawks prior to the 1934–35 season, and dealt again to the New York Rangers during the 1935–36 campaign. With the Canadiens slumping both on the ice and at the box office, Morenz was brought back to Montreal for the 1936–37 season. Though no longer the star he had once been, the fans again flocked to see him, and the Canadiens were leading the league when Morenz suffered a broken leg during a game on January 28, 1937. He died on March 8, 1937, while still in hospital. Over 10,000 fans attended a service at the Montreal Forum where his body lay in state, while thousands more lined the route of his funeral cortege. The NHL played its second All-Star Game to benefit the Morenz family on November 2, 1937. In 1945, he was one of the first 12 men inducted into the Hockey Hall of Fame.

BERNIE MORRIS entered the Pacific Coast Hockey Association with the Victoria Aristocrats in 1914–15, but was sent to Seattle when that city was granted a PCHA franchise the following year. He promptly led the league with 23 goals in 18 games. He scored a career-high 37 goals when the Mets won the league title in 1916–17, and his 17 assists gave him the league lead in points, though he had to settle for second place in the goal-scoring race behind Gordon Roberts who set a PCHA record with 43 goals that year.

Seattle's PCHA championship entitled them to host the Montreal Canadiens for the Stanley Cup in April, 1917. Morris scored three goals in an 8–4 loss in game one, then beat Georges Vezina twice more in a 6–1 Seattle victory in game two. He had another hat trick in game three, then poured in six goals as the Metropolitans romped to a 9–1 victory in game four and became the first American-based team to win the Stanley Cup. When Seattle won the PCHA championship again in 1919, Morris was not able to play in the Stanley Cup finals that year because he was embroiled in a legal dispute with the United States army over his alleged failure to report for military duty during World War I. He was eventually cleared of any wrongdoing, though not until he had missed the entire 1919–20 PCHA season. He returned in time to play for Seattle in the 1920 Stanley Cup finals against the Ottawa Senators.

Bernie Morris was traded to Calgary in 1923, and helped the Tigers win the Western Canada Hockey League title in 1923–24. He was acquired by Boston the following season to try and help the floundering NHL expansion team, but spent just six games with the Bruins. Morris finished the season with the Regina Capitals of the WCHL, then played minor-league hockey until retiring after the 1929–30 season. He ranks fourth all-time in goals (174) and third all-time in points (259) in the history of the Pacific Coast Hockey Association.

BILL MOSIENKO of the Chicago Black Hawks set an NHL record when he scored three goals in 21 seconds on March 23, 1952, in a 7–6 victory over the New York Rangers on the final night of the season. Mosienko was a productive scorer and sportsmanlike player throughout his career, winning the Lady Byng Trophy in 1944–45. He also was named to the Second All-Star Team in 1944–45 and 1945–46. Mosienko may well have earned more all-star selections had he not played right wing during the heyday of Rocket Richard and Gordie Howe.

Mosienko made his NHL debut with Chicago in 1941–42, and was a top-10 scorer one season later. In 1945–46, Black Hawks coach Johnny Gottselig put Mosienko together with brothers Max and Doug Bentley and the Pony Line was born. Though Mosienko was hurt for much of the 1945–46 season, the line combined for 179 points and was the NHL's top-scoring trio in 1946–47. Max Bentley led the NHL in scoring both seasons the line played together, but the combination was broken up in 1947–48 when Mosienko broke his ankle in the All-Star Game and Bentley was traded to the Toronto Maple Leafs. After the break up of the Pony Line, Mosienko played in combinations with Doug Bentley, Roy Conacher, Gus Bodnar, Gaye Stewart and Pete Babando.

Mosienko remained with the Black Hawks for his entire 14-year NHL career, and though the team was dismal during much of his time there, he was one of only a few players to score more than 250 goals during this era. Following his departure from the NHL after the 1954–55 season, Mosienko helped establish the Winnipeg Warriors in his hometown. He promptly led the team to the Western Hockey League title in its first season of 1955–56, and then to the Edinburgh Cup with a victory over the champions of the Quebec Hockey League. Mosienko played with the Warriors until 1958–59, and coached the team in 1959–60. He was inducted into the Hockey Hall of Fame in 1965.

LARRY MURPHY and Raymond Bourque both surpassed Tim Horton's record of 1,446 games played by an NHL defenseman during the 1998–99 season. One year later, Murphy moved past Alex Delvecchio into second place behind Gordie Howe among the NHL's all-time games played leaders.

Murphy's career began in 1980–81 when he set a record for rookie defensemen with 60 assists and 76 points, and was runner-up to Peter Stastny for the Calder Trophy. He is now one of the highest-scoring defenseman in NHL history, becoming the fourth blueliner to record 1,000 career points (after Denis Potvin, Paul Coffey and Bourque) when he reached the milestone on March 27, 1996.

A graduate of the Peterborough Petes, with whom he won the Memorial Cup in 1979, Larry Murphy played three full seasons with the Kings before a trade to the Washington Capitals in 1983. He continued to rank among the best defensemen in the NHL during his time in Washington, setting a career high with 23 goals in 1986–87. The Capitals traded him to Minnesota on March 7, 1989, but he played only one full season as a North Star before being sent to the Pittsburgh Penguins. Murphy was a key contributor to the success of the Penguins during his time in Pittsburgh, helping the team win the Stanley Cup in 1991 and 1992.

Murphy was traded to the Toronto Maple Leafs in 1995, but with the team slumping and his offensive numbers in decline by 1996–97, Toronto fans were critical of the veteran defenseman and he was dealt to Detroit. With the Red Wings, he became an important part of a team that won the Stanley Cup for the first time since 1955. He helped Detroit repeat as champions in 1998.

JOE NIEUWENDYK joined Mike Bossy as just the second rookie in NHL history to score 50 goals when he had 51 in 1987–88. He joined Bossy and Wayne Gretzky as the third player to score 50 goals in his first two NHL seasons after scoring another 51 in 1988–89.

Nieuwendyk was drafted by the Calgary Flames in 1985, but played two more seasons with Cornell in the NCAA before making a brief NHL debut in 1986–87. He went on to become the Flames' career leader with 314 goals (since surpassed by Theoren Fleury) before he was traded to the Dallas Stars on December 19, 1995. He also served as captain in Calgary from 1991–92 to 1994–95. Despite a serious knee injury suffered in 1998, Nieuwendyk has continued to be an effective scorer in Dallas, and led all playoff performers with 11 goals when the Stars won the Stanley Cup in 1999.

Nieuwendyk won a silver medal with the Canadian team at the World Junior Championships in 1986, and played at the World Championships in 1990. He was named to Team Canada for the 1991 Canada Cup but was injured during training camp. In 1998, he was a member of the Canadian Olympic team that competed at Nagano.

FRANK NIGHBOR was the first recipient of two of the NHL's oldest individual honors, winning the Hart Trophy in 1923–24 and the Lady Byng Trophy the following year. The stylish center was a great goal scorer and an excellent playmaker, as well as an early exponent of the poke check. Fans of his day often would debate whether he was more valuable offensively or defensively.

"The Flying Dutchman" or "the Pembroke Peach," as Nighbor was known, began his pro career with the Toronto Blueshirts of the National Hockey Association in 1912–13. He scored six goals in a game on February 15, 1913, finishing the season fourth in the league with 25 goals in 19 games. The following year, Nighbor joined the Vancouver Millionaires of the Pacific Coast Hockey Association. In 1914–15, he played left wing on a line with Mickey MacKay and Cyclone Taylor as the high-scoring trio led Vancouver to a Stanley Cup victory over the Ottawa Senators. Nighbor was named the all-star left wing in the PCHA that season, but he returned to the NHA with the Senators in 1915–16. He remained in Ottawa for 15 years.

Nighbor tied Joe Malone for the scoring lead with 41 goals in the NHA's final season of 1916–17, but he slumped during the NHL's inaugural campaign of 1917–18 before finishing among the league scoring leaders each of the next three years. The Senators became the best team in the NHL during the 1920s, winning the Stanley Cup in 1920, 1921, 1923 and 1927. Despite the success, the small-market team was losing money, and Nighbor was traded to the Toronto Maple Leafs during the 1929–30 season. It would be his last year in the NHL. He was elected to the Hockey Hall of Fame in 1947.

OWEN NOLAN rebounded from two off years to establish himself among the NHL's best scorers in 1999–2000. The former first-overall draft choice (1990) ranked second in the league behind Pavel Bure with 44 goals. His 84 points were also a career high and tied him for sixth in the NHL. The year before, he had become the fifth captain in San Jose Sharks history.

Nolan burst upon the NHL scene during his first full season of 1991–92 when he scored 42 goals for the Quebec Nordiques. He had at least 30 goals in four of the next five seasons, missing only in 1993–94 when injuries limited him to just six games. His 30 goals during the 48-game 1994–95 season ranked third in the league. Nolan was still with Quebec when the club moved to Colorado in 1995–96, but the Avalanche traded him to San Jose for Sandis Ozolonish early in the season. On December 19, 1995, Nolan set six Sharks records (some of which have since been equaled) when he collected four goals and an assist against the Mighty Ducks of Anaheim. Previously, Nolan had enjoyed a six-point night (one goal, five assists) on March 5, 1992, as a member of the Nordiques. In 1997, he helped Canada win a gold medal at the World Championships.

WILLIE O'REE became the first black player in NHL history when he joined the Boston Bruins for two games on January 18 and 19, 1958. He also played 43 games with the Bruins in 1960–61. Though his NHL career was brief, O'Ree had a lengthy professional career that stretched from 1956 to 1979. From 1962 to 1974, he was one of the best, and most popular, players in the Western Hockey League. Unbeknownst to anyone, O'Ree had suffered an injury in 1954 that had left him legally blind in his right eye.

In February, 1998, Willie O'Ree was named Director of Youth Development for the NHL and USA Hockey Diversity Task Force. He had begun staging the Willie O'Ree All-Star Game for underprivileged children in 1995. O'Ree continues to travel across Canada and the United States, working with these organizations, as well as the NHL Breakout in-line skate program. He goes into inner cities to try and get young boys and girls interested in playing hockey, and to teach them to set and attain life goals.

BOBBY ORR was not the first defenseman to rush the puck, but his immense skill at doing so changed the way hockey was played. Before Orr, defensemen rarely journeyed into the offensive zone, but he proved that defensemen could play a prominent role at both ends of the ice. Orr's stickhandling and skating skill was unmatched, and his shot was amazingly accurate.

Orr won the Calder Trophy after his rookie season of 1966–67, and was named to the Second All-Star Team. Unfortunately, he also suffered a knee injury that would bother him for the rest of his career. Still, Orr won the Norris Trophy and was selected to the First All-Star Team for each of the next eight years. He set a record for defensemen when he scored 21 goals in 1968–69, then smashed it with 33 goals the following year when he also became the first defenseman to top 100 points and win the NHL scoring title. In the playoffs, Orr scored the Stanley Cup-winning goal in overtime as the Bruins became NHL champions for the first time since 1941. He won both the Hart Trophy as the NHL MVP and the Conn Smythe Trophy as playoff MVP that year, and went on to become the first player in NHL history to win the Hart Trophy three years in a row. He won the Conn Smythe Trophy again after Boston won the Stanley Cup in 1972.

In 1970–71, Orr set a new NHL record with 102 assists. His 139 points that year remain a record for defensemen. He won a second scoring title with 135 points in 1974–75, and his mark of 46 goals by a defenseman that season has been topped only by Paul Coffey. Sadly, Orr never played another full season after that year. Injuries limited him to just 10 games in 1975–76, and the Bruins allowed him to sign with the Chicago Black Hawks after the season. Orr recovered in time to star for Team Canada at the inaugural Canada Cup event in September, 1976, but the tournament proved to be his swan song. Continued problems with his knees forced him to retire in November, 1978 at the age of 30. The traditional three-year waiting period was waived, and Bobby Orr was elected to the Hockey Hall of Fame in 1979.

FRANK PATRICK was a star player in his own right both before and after he and brother Lester Patrick formed the Pacific Coast Hockey Association in 1911–12. Both brothers served as players, coaches, managers and owners of PCHA franchises (Frank in Vancouver, Lester in Victoria) while Frank also served as league president. He was responsible for more than 20 changes to the way hockey was played that later became part of the NHL rule book.

Frank Patrick's hockey career began in Montreal, where he played with the Victorias, Westmount and McGill University, while his brother Lester starred with the Montreal Wanderers. The family later moved west to Nelson, British Columbia, where the brothers continued to play hockey. They returned east to join the Renfrew Millionaires when the National Hockey Association was formed in 1909–10. Frank played defense with Cyclone Taylor at Renfrew when the position was known as point and cover point, and the Patrick brothers formed a friendship with the star player that would last a lifetime. This led to his signing with Frank's Vancouver Millionaires in the PCHA's second season of 1912–13. Taylor's signing gave the fledgling league a major boost.

In order to form the Pacific Coast Hockey Association, the Patrick brothers used money from the sale of the family lumber business to build Canada's first artificial ice rinks in Vancouver and Victoria. They remained innovators throughout the history of the PCHA, adding blue lines to the ice, allowing forward passing, adopting assists as an official statistic, and refining the modern playoff format. Meanwhile, Frank continued to star on the ice. His six goals in a game on March 6, 1912, is a record unmatched by any NHL defenseman, and he helped his Vancouver team to win the Stanley Cup in 1915.

In later years, Patrick was forced to concentrate more on his duties as league president than as a player, and when the PCHA was reduced to two teams after the 1923–24 season, Frank's and Lester's Vancouver and Victoria franchises joined the Western Canada Hockey League. When pro hockey finally collapsed in the west after the 1925–26 season, Frank Patrick looked after the job of selling its players to NHL interests. He later served as managing director of the NHL (1933–34), as a coach with the Boston Bruins (1934–35, 1935–36) and as business manager of the Montreal Canadiens (1941–42). He was elected to the Hockey Hall of Fame as a builder in 1958.

LESTER PATRICK enjoyed one of the longest careers in hockey history, beginning as a player in 1903–04 and continuing as a coach, g.m., owner and NHL governor until his association with the New York Rangers ended in 1947, the same year he was inducted into the Hockey Hall of Fame. After leaving New York, he ran the minor-league Victoria Cougars of the Pacific Coast Hockey League until 1954.

Patrick learned to play hockey while growing up in Montreal, but he first came to prominence in 1903–04 as a rushing defenseman with a team from Brandon, Manitoba, that unsuccessfully challenged the Ottawa Silver Seven for the Stanley Cup. After a season with Westmount in Montreal, Patrick joined the Montreal Wanderers in 1905–06, helping that team dethrone Ottawa as Stanley Cup champions. He played on another championship team with the Wanderers the following season before moving west to Nelson, British Columbia, to work in the family lumber business. He continued to play hockey in Nelson on a team with his brother Frank, and he joined Edmonton in an unsuccessful Stanley Cup challenge against the Wanderers in December, 1908.

When the National Hockey Association was formed for the 1909–10 season, the Patrick brothers returned east as members of the Renfrew Millionaires. The brothers headed out west again after that season, and in 1911–12 they established the Pacific Coast Hockey Association. In order to form their league, the Patricks used money from the sale of the family lumber business to build Canada's first artificial ice rinks in Vancouver and Victoria. Both brothers served as players, coaches, managers and owners, Frank in Vancouver and Lester in Victoria. Lester remained active as a player until 1921–22, when he was forced to play two games in goal as an emergency replacement. He concentrated on his off-ice duties over the next three years, but he returned to play a complete season with Victoria in 1925–26. Hockey in the west collapsed after that season, and the Patricks sold the league's players to teams in the NHL.

Lester Patrick joined the New York Rangers as coach and general manager during the club's first season of 1926–27, and he generally is credited with making pro hockey a success in the northeastern United States. He guided the Rangers to a Stanley Cup victory in 1928 (which included his famous emergency stint in goal) and again in 1933, and he was named to the NHL First All-Star Team as a coach six times in seven years between 1930–31 and 1937–38. He gave up coaching in 1939, but continued as Rangers general manager until 1946. The Lester Patrick Trophy honoring contributions to hockey in the United States has been presented annually since 1966.

JACQUES PLANTE was one of the most influential goaltenders in NHL history. He was one of the first netminders to roam from his crease, playing the puck for his defensemen and stopping dump-ins behind the net. More importantly, he was the first goalie to popularize the use of the mask as a standard piece of equipment. Plante was plagued with asthma throughout his career and missed 13 games during the 1957–58 season because of a sinus operation. He then began using a mask in practice. Canadiens management was opposed to him wearing it in games, but relented after Plante was badly cut by a shot from Andy Bathgate on November 1, 1959. The Canadiens went undefeated over the next 10 games, and Plante was permitted to wear his mask full-time.

A product of the Montreal Canadiens farm system, Plante made brief but spectacular appearances with the Canadiens in 1952–53 and 1953–54 before becoming the club's regular goaltender in 1954–55. From 1955–56 until 1959–60, he won the Vezina Trophy five years in a row while Montreal won the Stanley Cup five consecutive times. In 1961–62, Plante won the Vezina Trophy for the sixth time while becoming the fourth goalie in NHL history (after Roy Worters, Chuck Rayner and Al Rollins) to win the Hart Trophy.

Plante remained with Montreal through the 1962–63 season, but was traded to the New York Rangers for Gump Worsley in a multi-player deal on June 4, 1963. He retired after two seasons in New York, but was lured back to the game by the St. Louis Blues to share goaltending duties with Glenn Hall in 1968–69. The veteran duo shared the Vezina Trophy that year, allowing Plante to surpass Bill Durnan with his record seventh Vezina victory. In 1970–71, Plante was traded to the Toronto Maple Leafs, where he was named to the Second All-Star Team after producing a 1.88 goals-against average. Plante helped to groom Bernie Parent for stardom during his time in Toronto, but ended his NHL career with the Boston Bruins after a late-season trade in 1972–73. He then served as coach and general manager of the Quebec Nordiques of the World Hockey Association in 1973–74, before making another comeback to play a final season in goal with the Edmonton Oilers.

Jacques Plante was elected to the Hockey Hall of Fame in 1978. His lifetime NHL totals of 435 wins and 82 shutouts are among the best in hockey history, and his 14 shutouts in the playoffs are topped only by Clint Benedict and Patrick Roy. The Quebec Major Junior Hockey League rewards its top goaltender with the Jacques Plante Trophy.

DENIS POTVIN was selected first overall by the New York Islanders in the 1973 Amateur Draft, and was expected to become the foundation for their developing team. By the time he retired after the 1987–88 season, Potvin had played for four Stanley Cup champions, been named to the All-Star Team seven times, and was the NHL's all-time leader in goals, assists and points by a defenseman. His number 5 was the first number ever retired by the Islanders.

Potvin was an Ottawa native who starred with the hometown 67's of the Ontario Hockey Association, setting a record for scoring by a defenseman with 123 points in his final junior year of 1972–73; the record lasted until 1988–89. He won the Calder Trophy as rookie of the year for the Islanders in 1973–74, and was the runner-up behind Bobby Orr in Norris Trophy voting in 1974–75. He won the Norris Trophy after just his third season, and was named the NHL's top defenseman again two more times.

In 1979–80, Potvin became captain of the Islanders and wore the "C" as his team won the Stanley Cup four years in a row. He continued to rank among the top players at his position, both offensively and defensively, after the Islanders Stanley Cup dynasty ended, and on April 4, 1987, Potvin became the first defenseman in NHL history to reach 1,000 career points. He was elected to the Hockey Hall of Fame in 1991.

Potvin has worked as a television analyst since the end of his playing career, and joined the broadcast crew of the Florida Panthers when the team entered the NHL in 1993–94. His brother Jean played in the NHL between 1970–71 and 1980–81.

CHRIS PRONGER was the Ontario Hockey League's top-scoring defenseman in 1991–92, and helped the Peterborough Petes to reach the Memorial Cup finals in 1993. He was then selected second overall, behind Alexander Daigle, by the Hartford Whalers in the 1993 NHL Entry Draft, and went on to be named Hartford's most valuable defenseman in 1993–94.

Much was expected of the 6'6", 220-pound defenseman, but Pronger struggled during his second year in Hartford and was considered a disappointment in St. Louis in 1995–96 after the Blues acquired him in a trade for Brendan Shanahan. However, Pronger led the Blues in plus-minus in 1996–97, and was named team captain in 1997–98. He responded by earning a nomination for the Norris Trophy as the NHL's best defenseman. Pronger helped the Blues finish atop the NHL standings with a team-record 51 wins and 114 points in 1999–2000. Not only did he win the Norris Trophy that year, he became the first defenseman since Bobby Orr in 1972 to win the Hart Trophy as the NHL's most valuable player.

Pronger was a member of the Canadian Olympic team in Nagano in 1998, and had previously represented his country at the World Junior Championships in 1993, where he won a gold medal.

MARK RECCHI made his NHL debut during the 1988–89 season but spent most of the year with Muskegon of the International Hockey League, where he helped the club to win the Turner Cup championship. He began the 1989–90 season in Muskegon but was recalled by Pittsburgh on October 18, 1989, and went on to rank second among NHL rookies with 30 goals. Recchi led the Penguins, and was fourth in the NHL, with 113 points in 1990–91, and his 34 points in the postseason ranked second behind Mario Lemieux as Pittsburgh won its first Stanley Cup championship.

The Penguins traded Recchi to the Philadelphia Flyers on February 19, 1992, and he finished the year with a combined 43 goals to earn a spot on the Second All-Star Team at right wing. In 1992–93, Recchi established career highs with 53 goals and 123 points to rank tenth in the NHL. He finished seventh with 107 points the following season.

On February 9, 1995, the Flyers traded Recchi to the Montreal Canadiens in a deal that brought them John LeClair and Eric Desjardins. Recchi led the Canadiens in goals and points during the 1994–95 season and continued to rank among the team's top scorers until he was traded back to Philadelphia late in 1998–99 season. His 91 points in 1999–2000 trailed only Jaromir Jagr and Pavel Bure among the NHL scoring leaders and his 63 assists were tops in the league.

Internationally, Recchi won a gold medal with Team Canada at the World Junior Championships in 1988 and at the World Championships in 1997. He was a late addition to the Olympic team in Nagano in 1998.

HENRI RICHARD did not possess the fiery temper of his famous older brother Maurice, but he proved to be an aggressive player who could not be intimidated despite his small size. Standing just 5'7" and weighing only 160 pounds, many predicted Richard was too small to stay in the league, but he lasted 20 years and played for a record 11 Stanley Cup champions. He is the Canadiens all-time leader in games played, ranking eighth in goals and third in both assists and points behind Guy Lafleur and Jean Beliveau.

Richard joined the Montreal Canadiens in 1955–56 when his brother Maurice was at the peak of his fame. Though he could not match the Rocket's brilliant goal-scoring ability, Henri proved to be a smoother skater and much better playmaker. "The Pocket Rocket" quickly became a fan favorite. Henri played for Stanley Cup winners in each of his first five seasons, and had established himself among the league's best offensive talents by his second year. In his third year, 1957–58, Richard led the NHL in assists and finished second overall in scoring behind teammate Dickie Moore.

Richard continued to star with the Canadiens throughout the 1960s, winning the Stanley Cup again in 1965, 1966, 1968 and 1969. A tenth Stanley Cup title came in 1971 when he scored the winning goal in the seventh game against the Chicago Black Hawks. In 1971–72, Richard was named to succeed Jean Beliveau as Canadiens captain, and he led the Canadiens to another Stanley Cup victory in 1973. He retired two years later and was inducted into the Hockey Hall of Fame in 1979.

MAURICE RICHARD was the heart and soul of the Montreal Canadiens during his 18 seasons in the NHL, and the idol of hockey fans throughout Quebec. The outpouring of emotion after his death on May 27, 2000, was proof that his legend had lived on long after his playing career. An estimated 115,000 people filed past his coffin at Montreal's Molson Centre. Thousands more crowded the sidewalks outside his state funeral at Notre-Dame Basilica.

Nicknamed "The Rocket" by sportswriter Baz O'Meara because of his blazing speed, Richard was the first player in NHL history to score 50 goals in a season and the first to score 500 in his career. The Rocket was named to the NHL All-Star Team 14 years in a row from 1943–44 until 1956–57, with eight of those selections to the First Team. He played on eight Stanley Cup champions, including five in a row from 1956 to 1960, and though he never led the league in points, he was the NHL's top goal scorer five times. Richard played the game with a burning desire, and his fiery temper often got him into trouble. After Richard was suspended for punching a linseman during a game, a riot broke out in Montreal four days later on March 17, 1955, that caused $500,000 worth of damage.

Richard was a native of Montreal who came up through the Canadiens system and broke into the NHL in 1942–43. He scored five goals in 16 games as a rookie in a season cut short by a broken ankle. Injuries would plague the Rocket throughout his career, but it would be years before they finally slowed him down. In 1943–44 he was teamed with Toe Blake and Elmer Lach on the Punch Line and led the Canadiens to the Stanley Cup. In 1944–45, Richard scored 50 goals in 50 games to establish a single-season record that would last until Bobby Hull scored 54 goals in a 70-game season in 1965–66. Not until Wayne Gretzky scored 50 goals in 39 games in 1980–81 was Richard's goal-a-game pace surpassed. On December 28, 1944, Richard had five goals and three assists for a record eight points in one game. That mark stood until Darryl Sittler recorded 10 points in a game on February 7, 1976.

On November 8, 1952, Rocket Richard became the NHL's all-time leading goal scorer when he surpassed Nels Stewart with his 325th career goal. He scored his 500th goal on October 19, 1957. Injuries kept Richard out of a lot of action over his final three years and he retired after the 1959–60 season with 544 goals. Gordie Howe soon surpassed Rocket's total, as have many players since, but his 544 goals still remain the highest in Canadiens history. Richard had 26 games in his career when he scored three goals or more, more than any player in the six-team era. He was also the most prolific playoff scorer of his day with 82 goals in the postseason, and though that record has been surpassed, his six playoff overtime goals remain the most in NHL history. Rocket Richard was inducted into the Hockey Hall of Fame in 1961. Since 1998–99, the NHL has awarded the Maurice Richard trophy to the league-leading goal scorer during the regular season.

LARRY ROBINSON's defensive prowess, combined with his ability to move the puck, made him one of the best defensemen in NHL history. He was part of "The Big Three" on the Montreal defense with Guy Lapointe and Serge Savard, helping the Canadiens win the Stanley Cup six times between 1973 and 1986. By the time he retired after the 1991–92 season, Robinson had set a record by playing in the playoffs for 20 consecutive years, and his 227 games played in the postseason were an NHL record, since surpassed only by Mark Messier.

Known as "Big Bird," the 6'4", 225-pound Robinson was a forward in junior hockey, but was converted to defense in the minors. He played on his first Stanley Cup-winning team as a rookie in 1973, and went on to win the Norris Trophy twice. He was also an NHL all-star five years in a row between 1976–77 and 1980–81. Robinson helped the Canadiens win the Stanley Cup four years in a row from 1976 to 1979, and again in 1986.

On July 26, 1989, Robinson signed with Los Angeles and spent his final three NHL seasons as a member of the Kings. He took a year off from the game after his retirement before joining the New Jersey Devils in 1993–94 as an assistant coach under former Canadiens teammate Jacques Lemaire. Robinson's influence made the Devils one of the NHL's best defensive teams and helped New Jersey to win the Stanley Cup in 1995. On July 26, 1995, Robinson was hired as the head coach in Los Angeles. He was inducted into the Hockey Hall of Fame the same year. Robinson guided the Kings back to the playoffs for the first time in five years in 1997–98, and finished as the runner-up to Pat Burns of the Boston Bruins for the Jack Adams Award as coach of the year, but was fired after the 1998–99 season. He returned to New Jersey as an assistant coach in 1999–2000 and replaced Robbie Ftorek as head coach with eight games left in the regular season. Robinson became the 14th man to have both played and coached a Stanley Cup winner when the Devils captured the 2000 title.

LUC ROBITAILLE was selected by the Los Angeles Kings with the 171st pick in the 1984 NHL Entry Draft, and went on to win the Calder Trophy as rookie of the year in 1986–87. His 45 goals and 84 points topped all first-year players that season, and made him the first rookie to lead the Kings in scoring. Robitaille earned a place on the All-Rookie Team with fellow Kings Jimmy Carson and Steve Duchesne.

Robitaille set an NHL record for left wings (and established the third-longest streak in NHL history) by topping 40 goals eight years in a row. He first reached 50 in his second season of 1987–88, and established career highs with 63 goals and 125 points in 1992–93. Those marks also established NHL records for left wings. Robitaille served as Kings captain in place of the injured Wayne Gretzky for the first 39 games of the 1992–93 season, and helped Los Angeles to reach the Stanley Cup finals for the first time in team history that year. The Kings missed the playoffs in 1994, and Robitaille was selected captain of the team that represented Canada at the IIHF World Championships, where his winning goal in a shootout gave Canada its first world title since the Trail Smoke Eaters won in 1961.

Robitaille was traded to Pittsburgh in 1994, but struggled during three years with the Penguins and New York Rangers before returning to L.A. in 1997. With the Kings he has regained his position among the NHL's best scorers.

ART ROSS was a defenseman who scored just one goal in three NHL games. It is ironic that he is remembered best today for donating the trophy awarded to the NHL scoring leader, but Ross was an important player, coach, manager, inventor and strategist throughout a lifetime of service to hockey.

Ross learned to play the game while growing up in Montreal with childhood friends Frank and Lester Patrick. Like Lester, Ross was one of hockey's first rushing defensemen. He headed out west to Brandon, Manitoba, in 1905–06, and he was on loan to the Kenora Thistles when they defeated the Montreal Wanderers to win the Stanley Cup in January, 1907. A year later, Ross was a member of the Wanderers, playing for another Stanley Cup champion. While with the Wanderers in 1907–08 and 1908–09, he would show up occasionally on the roster of other teams as a "ringer" paid to play in important games.

In 1909–10, Ross was managing a new team called All-Montreal in the Canadian Hockey Association, but when the league lost a power struggle with the National Hockey Association, he joined the NHA team in Haileybury. The following year, Ross was back with the Wanderers. He criticized the salary cap imposed by owners in 1910–11, and he and Bruce Stuart were at the forefront of a plan to form a new players' league that never materialized. Ross fought for players' rights again in 1914 and in 1915, and his attempts to form another new league nearly brought him a suspension from all of organized hockey.

After two seasons with the Ottawa Senators, Ross was back with the Wanderers in 1916–17. The team joined the NHL the following season, but it withdrew after a fire destroyed the Montreal Arena on January 2, 1918, and Ross retired as a player. He returned to the NHL as coach of the Hamilton Tigers in 1922–23. Next, he was hired as the coach and general manager of the Boston Bruins for their first season of 1924–25. Ross quickly built the team into a powerhouse, winning 10 division titles and the Stanley Cup three times by 1941. He coached the team on and off into the 1940s and served as the Bruins general manager until 1955. He also improved the design of the pucks and goal nets used in the NHL. The Art Ross net was in use until 1984, and his puck design has not been replaced. Ross was inducted into the Hockey Hall of Fame as one of its 12 original members in 1945.

PATRICK ROY made his NHL debut with the Montreal Canadiens on February 23, 1985, and became a regular during the 1985–86 season. He was good enough during his first full season to earn a spot on the NHL All-Rookie Team, but it was during the playoffs that Roy first displayed how great he could be when he led the Canadiens to a surprising Stanley Cup victory. Roy was rewarded with the Conn Smythe Trophy as playoff MVP.

Over the next six seasons, Roy established himself among the top goaltenders in the game. In 1992–93, Roy slumped to his highest goals-against average since his rookie season, but he avenged himself in the playoffs when he was absolutely brilliant in leading the Canadiens to another Stanley Cup title. His 16–4 postseason record included 10 consecutive overtime victories as he once again received the Conn Smythe Trophy.

Roy suffered through his first losing record when the Canadiens failed to make the playoffs in 1995, and after Mario Tremblay was brought in to coach the Canadiens early in the 1995–96 season, a clash between the two resulted in the star goaltender being dealt to the Colorado Avalanche on December 6, 1995. On February 19, 1996, Roy recorded the 300th victory of his career to become just the 12th player in history to win 300 games and the second-youngest behind Terry Sawchuk. In the playoffs that year, Roy helped Colorado to win the Stanley Cup. He stopped 63 shots when the Avalanche capped a Stanley Cup sweep with a 1–0 triple-overtime victory over the Florida Panthers. He became just the fifth goalie in NHL history to reach the 400-win plateau in 1998–99, and his 444 wins through the 1999–2000 season leave him just two short of Terry Sawchuk's all-time record. His 121 playoff victories are the most in NHL history.

Though he consistently has been among the best in the game, Roy never was selected to play for his country in the Canada Cup, and was overlooked again at the World Cup of Hockey in September, 1996. He finally was chosen to represent Canada at the 1998 Nagano Olympics.

BORJE SALMING was the first European player to become a star in the NHL. Signed by Toronto after the 1973 World Championships, the native of Kiruna, Sweden, was forced to endure taunts and physical abuse from opponents after breaking into the NHL with the Maple Leafs in 1973–74, but went on to become one of the top defensemen in the league over 17 seasons. He was elected to the Hockey Hall of Fame in 1996.

Salming excelled at blocking shots, and was a strong skater who could rush the puck effectively and set up plays. He established a Maple Leafs record by being named to the NHL All-Star Team for six straight seasons from 1974–75 to 1979–80, and was the runner up to Larry Robinson in Norris Trophy voting in 1976–77 and 1979–80. In his early years in Toronto, the Maple Leafs were an improving team that seemed on the verge of becoming one of the NHL's best, but during the 1980s Salming was the star attraction on a dismal club. When he left Toronto after the 1988–89 season, he was the Maple Leafs' all-time leader in goals, assists and points by a defenseman. He ranks first overall in franchise history with 620 assists, and trails only Darryl Sittler and Dave

Keon with 768 points. Salming played his final NHL season in 1989–90 as a member of the Detroit Red Wings.

Salming spent three years in the Swedish Elite league on either side of his NHL career. He also represented Sweden internationally before, during and after his 17 years in the NHL.

JOE SAKIC was selected by the Quebec Nordiques with the 15th choice in the 1988 NHL Entry Draft after they had chosen Bryan Fogarty with the ninth pick. Though the Nordiques only made the playoffs twice in Sakic's seven seasons in Quebec, he was able to establish himself as a star. He first cracked the top 10 in scoring with 102 points in his second season of 1989–90, and shared the Nordiques captaincy in 1990–91. Sakic assumed the role outright in 1992–93, and led Quebec into the playoffs for the first time in six years. The Nordiques missed the playoffs again in 1994, but had an excellent season in 1994–95 when they finished the abbreviated 48-game season with the best record in the Eastern Conference. Sakic was fourth in scoring in the NHL that year.

The Nordiques moved to Denver and became the Colorado Avalanche in 1995–96. Sakic finished third in the NHL in scoring that season by establishing career highs with 51 goals, 69 assists and 120 points. He then led all playoff performers in goals and points to win the Conn Smythe Trophy as the Avalanche became the first team to win the Stanley Cup during its first year in a city. Injuries slowed him down over the next few seasons but, when healthy, Sakic has remained one of the league's best offensive players. He ranked among the top-10 scorers again in both 1998–99 and 1999–2000 and reached the 1,000-point plateau on December 27, 1999.

In addition to his NHL success, Sakic has done well in the international arena. In 1988, he won a gold medal with Canada's team at the World Junior Championships, and in 1991 he was the team's leading scorer when Canada earned a silver medal at the World Championships. In 1994, Sakic helped Canada win its first World Championship since 1961. He was also a member of the Canadian team at the Nagano Olympics in 1998.

GLEN SATHER began his tenure with the Edmonton Oilers as a player in the World Hockey Association in 1976–77. On March 3, 1977, he assumed coaching duties, and on June 15, 1979 (after the team entered the NHL), Sather was named president and general manager. He was coach and g.m. for the Oilers' first 10 NHL seasons, and the architect of Edmonton's five Stanley Cup champions between 1984 and 1990. Sather remained with the Oilers through the 1999–2000 season before leaving to become president and general manager of the New York Rangers on June 1, 2000.

In 842 regular-season games as coach of the Oilers, Sather's teams had a 464–268–110 record for a .616 winning percentage, and he was honored in 1985–86 with the Jack Adams Award as coach of the year. In the playoffs, Sather's Oilers won 89 of 127 games for a .705 winning percentage that is the best in NHL history. He coached the Oilers' first four Stanley Cup winners. Internationally, Sather coached Team Canada to victory in the 1984 Canada Cup, and was part of the management team for the 1987 Canada Cup champions. He was also coach and general manager of the Canadian team that lost the World Cup of Hockey finals to the United States in 1996. Sather was elected to the Hockey Hall of Fame as a builder in 1997.

As a player, Sather was a member of the Edmonton Oil Kings in junior hockey and made his NHL debut with the Boston Bruins in 1966–67. Sather also played with the Penguins, Rangers, Blues, Canadiens and North Stars over 10 years in the NHL.

DENIS SAVARD was a high-scoring junior star in Montreal who was passed over by the Canadiens for Doug Wickenheiser as the top choice in the 1980 Entry Draft. Savard was selected third overall by Chicago, and went on to become one of the top offensive stars in the NHL. He was elected to the Hockey Hall of Fame in 2000.

Savard was among the top 10 in scoring five times in his career, finishing as high as third on two occasions including 1987–88 when he had a career-high 131 points. An exceptionally agile skater, he was one of the league's best playmakers, but also had three straight years with more than 40 goals. Still, Savard earned only one All-Star selection, being named to the Second Team in 1982–83. As a center, he was overshadowed throughout his career by Wayne Gretzky, Mario Lemieux, Bryan Trottier and Dale Hawerchuk.

After 10 seasons with the Blackhawks, Savard was traded to Montreal for Chris Chelios on June 29, 1990. Under the Canadiens' tight defensive system, he no longer produced points as he had in Chicago but he earned a Stanley Cup ring in 1993. The following season, Savard signed with the Tampa Bay Lightning, but was traded back to Chicago on April 6, 1995.

Savard's career ended with the Blackhawks after the 1996–97 season. He retired with 473 goals and 865 assists for 1,338 points, totals that rank him among the all-time leaders in NHL history.

SERGE SAVARD was a key member of teams that won eight Stanley Cup championships during the 15 seasons he played for the Montreal Canadiens. Savard was voted rookie of the year with Montreal's Central Hockey League farm club in Houston in 1966–67, and joined the Canadiens to stay in 1967–68, playing for his first Stanley Cup winner that year. He then became the first defenseman to win the Conn Smythe Trophy as playoff MVP when Montreal repeated as champions in 1969.

Savard suffered a badly broken leg during both the 1970–71 and 1971–72 seasons, but recovered sufficiently to play with Team Canada against the Soviet Union in September, 1972 and contribute to another Stanley Cup winner in Montreal in 1973. Later, he was a key member of Montreal's "Big Three" on defense with Guy Lapointe and Larry Robinson as Montreal won the Stanley Cup four times in a row from 1976 until 1979. In 1979, Savard also won the Bill Masterton Trophy for perseverance and dedication to hockey.

Savard retired after the 1980–81 season, but was persuaded to join the Winnipeg Jets for the 1981–82 campaign. The club had missed the playoffs in each of its first two seasons in the NHL, but with Savard in the lineup the Jets showed a record 36-point improvement and qualified for the postseason for the first time. He retired for good after playing one more year, then returned to Montreal when he was named managing director of the Canadiens on April 28, 1983. He was elected to the Hockey Hall of Fame in 1986.

During his time in the executive suite in Montreal, Savard built teams that won the Adams Division title on four occasions and reached the Stanley Cup finals three times, winning in 1986 and 1993. He was fired early in 1995–96 after the Canadiens had failed to make the playoffs the previous season.

TERRY SAWCHUK played more games, recorded more wins and posted more shutouts than any goalie in NHL history (though Patrick Roy is just two behind Sawchuk's 446 career wins through the 1999–2000 season). Sawchuk was an acrobatic netminder with lightning-fast reflexes who played out of a deep crouch, but his nervous temperament left him vulnerable to the stresses of hockey's most difficult position.

Sawchuk was rookie of the year in both the United States Hockey League (1947–48) and American Hockey League (1948–49) before arriving in the NHL for full-time duty with the Detroit Red Wings in 1950–51. He promptly earned the Calder Trophy as rookie of the year in the NHL, as well as a selection to the First All-Star Team. Sawchuk was an all-star again in each of the next four seasons, and won the Vezina Trophy three times. He also played on Stanley Cup champions in 1952, 1954 and 1955. In the 1952 playoffs, Sawchuk helped Detroit win the Stanley Cup with eight straight victories in two playoff series, while recording four shutouts and a 0.63 goals-against average—a modern record.

After his first five full seasons in Detroit, Sawchuk had recorded 57 shutouts and had a goals-against average of less than 2.00, yet he was traded to the Boston Bruins by Jack Adams after winning the Stanley Cup in 1955 in order to make room for Glenn Hall. Sawchuk battled illness during his second year in Boston, and by mid-January was overcome with stress-related depression. He left the team to recuperate, and was traded back to Detroit in 1957. The Red Wings were no longer the powerhouse they had been, but Sawchuk continued to play well and in 1963–64 he surpassed George Hainsworth's all-time NHL record when he recorded his 95th career shutout. Sawchuk was claimed by the Toronto Maple Leafs in the Intra-League Draft on June 10, 1964, and he teamed with Johnny Bower to form an excellent goaltending tandem. The two shared the Vezina Trophy for fewest goals against in 1964–65, and helped Toronto win the Stanley Cup in 1967. Sawchuk also recorded his 100th shutout that season.

In the Expansion Draft on June 6, 1967, Sawchuk was selected by the Los Angeles Kings. After a season in L.A., he was traded back to Detroit but saw limited action before being dealt to the New York Rangers the following season. Sawchuk was used sparingly by the Rangers in 1969–70 and died in a household accident after the season. The traditional three-year waiting period was waived and he was inducted into the Hockey Hall of Fame in 1971.

MILT SCHMIDT was the center and top scorer with the Boston Bruins' famed Kraut Line of the 1930s and 1940s. Tough as well as talented, Schmidt was a strong skater and clever stickhandler. He was always dangerous around the net, and would not give up the puck without a fight. Except for three years lost to military service in World War II, Schmidt was a Bruin as a player, coach, general manager and executive from midway through the 1936–37 season until 1973. He was elected to the Hockey Hall of Fame in 1961.

Schmidt played on his first Stanley Cup winner with Boston in 1939, then was a First Team All-Star and scoring champion in 1939–40 when he and linemates Woody Dumart and Bobby Bauer finished 1–2–3 in the league. Another Stanley Cup title followed in 1941 before military service took all three Bruins teammates away from the NHL during the 1941–42 season. Schmidt, Dumart and Bauer finished out the 1941–42 campaign with the Allan Cup-winning Ottawa RCAF team, and later saw active service with the Royal Canadian Air Force. Schmidt's play was not quite what it had been when he returned to Boston in 1945–46, but by 1946–47 he had regained his status as a First Team All-Star. He was named captain of the Bruins in 1950–51, and responded by winning the Hart Trophy.

On Christmas Day in 1954, Schmidt retired as a player and immediately took over as coach of the Bruins. He remained on the job until 1960–61, leading the Bruins to the Stanley Cup finals in 1957 and 1958. Phil Watson took over in 1961–62, but Schmidt replaced Watson during the 1962–63 season and remained the team's coach until 1965–66. He became general manager in 1967, and remained in that position through the 1971–72 season. Schmidt was given an executive position in 1972–73, but left Boston after that year when the team refused to grant his request for a four-year contract.

After leaving Boston, Schmidt became the first general manager of the Washington Capitals. He also coached the team during parts of its first two seasons, 1974–75 and 1975–76.

TEEMU SELANNE was drafted by the Winnipeg Jets tenth overall in 1988, but did not enter the NHL until 1992–93. "The Finnish Flash" was an immediate sensation, scoring 76 goals to obliterate Mike Bossy's rookie record of 53, and also shattering Peter Stastny's NHL rookie mark of 109 points with 132. Selanne's 76 goals equaled the fifth best total in NHL history and tied Alexander Mogilny for the league lead that season. Selanne easily won the Calder Trophy as rookie of the year, and was named to the First All-Star Team. An achilles tendon injury limited Selanne to just 51 games in 1993–94, but he still became the second-fastest player in NHL history to score 100 career goals when he reached the milestone in his 130th game. Mike Bossy had scored 100 goals in 129 games.

Selanne was traded to the Mighty Ducks of Anaheim in a multi-player deal on February 7, 1996, and teamed with Paul Kariya to form an explosive offensive duo for the Ducks. Selanne was second in the NHL with 51 goals and 109 points in 1996–97, and helped Anaheim to reach the playoffs for the first time in just the team's fourth season. In 1997–98, he tied Peter Bondra of the Washington Capitals for the NHL lead with 52 goals. He led the league outright with 47 goals in 1998–99, and was the first recipient of the Maurice "Rocket" Richard Trophy. He earned his fifth straight nomination for the Lady Byng Trophy in 1999–2000

Prior to his arrival in the NHL, Selanne had been a star in his native Finland. He was a Finnish all-star in both the 1990–91 and 1991–92 seasons, and led the Finnish league with 39 goals in 44 games in 1991–92. Internationally, he has represented his homeland on several occasions, including the 1998 Nagano Olympics, where he was the tournament's top scorer and helped Finland win a bronze medal.

BRENDAN SHANAHAN is one of the premier power forwards in the NHL, combining goal-scoring skill and toughness with strong leadership qualities. He was selected second overall by the New Jersey Devils behind Pierre Turgeon in the 1987 Entry Draft. Used mostly at center during his junior career with the London Knights, the Devils employed Shanahan at right wing during his rookie season of 1987–88. He struggled that year, but began to live up to expectations during the second half of the 1988–89 season and reached the 30-goal plateau for the first time in 1989–90.

Shanahan signed with the St. Louis Blues as a free agent in 1991, and scored 51 goals in 1992–93. The following year, he had 52 goals and led the Blues with 102 points to earn a spot on the NHL's First All-Star Team. Shanahan was second on St. Louis in scoring in 1994–95, but in 1995, he was traded to the Hartford Whalers for Chris Pronger. Shanahan was captain of the Whalers in 1995–96, and led the team with 44 goals and 78 points, but he was unhappy in Hartford and requested a trade. On October 9, 1996, he was dealt to the Detroit Red Wings.

Shanahan proved to be the spark a talented Detroit team needed to finally reach the top. He led the Red Wings with 46 goals and 87 points during the 1996–97 regular season, and had a team-leading nine goals in the playoffs as Detroit won the Stanley Cup for the first time since 1955. His gritty play despite a back injury in the 1998 playoffs helped the Red Wings repeat as Stanley Cup champions. He ranked among the league leaders, and topped the 40-goal plateau for the fifth time, in 1999–2000.

Shanahan first represented Canada in international hockey at the World Junior Championships in 1987 when he played for the team that was disqualified because of a brawl with the Soviet team. In 1994, he helped Canada to win its first gold medal at the World Championships since 1961. Shanahan also played for the Canadian team at the 1998 Nagano Olympics.

EDDIE SHORE is rivaled only by Doug Harvey and Bobby Orr as the greatest defenseman in hockey history, but he actually began his professional career as a forward with the Regina Caps of the Western Canada Hockey League in 1924–25. He was converted to defense by the Edmonton Eskimos the following year, and entered the NHL with the Boston Bruins in 1926–27 after the collapse of pro hockey in the west.

Shore came to personify the rough and tumble game of hockey in the late 1920s and 1930s. A supremely talented player with a temper to match, he excelled at rushing the puck end-to-end and literally would knock down players who got in his way. His style resulted in high point totals and even higher penalty minutes, as he outscored all fellow defensemen during his era and trailed only Red Horner in terms of penalties.

When the NHL began selecting an All-Star Team in 1930–31, Shore was named eight times in the first nine years, missing out only in 1936–37 when he suffered a broken bone in his back. Seven of his eight selections were to the First All-Star Team. He is also the only defenseman in NHL history to win the Hart Trophy four times. Shore anchored the defense on Stanley Cup-winning teams in Boston in 1929 and 1939, and helped the Bruins finish first in the American Division eight times.

Anticipating retirement, Shore bought the Springfield Indians of the American Hockey League in 1939–40, and acted as a playing owner that season. The Bruins arranged for him to play home games only, but soon traded him to the New York Americans where his NHL career ended that season. Shore owned and operated his Springfield team until 1967. He also served as coach and general manager of the Buffalo Bisons of the AHL during World War II and owned teams in Fort Worth (in the United States Hockey League) and Oakland (in the Pacific Coast Hockey League). He briefly operated a team in New Haven. Shore was elected to the Hockey Hall of Fame in 1947.

DARRYL SITTLER is the Toronto Maple Leafs' all-time career leader with 389 goals and 916 points, and was the first player in Maple Leafs history to score 100 points in a season. Sittler set an NHL single-game record with 10 points on six goals and four assists on February 7, 1976, and tied an NHL record on April 22 of that year when he scored five goals in one playoff game. In September, 1976, Sittler scored the winning goal in overtime in the final game against Czechoslovakia to give Team Canada a victory at the first Canada Cup tournament.

After a successful junior career, Sittler's numbers were unimpressive during his first two NHL seasons, but by 1973–74 he had emerged as one of the top offensive players in the game. Sittler succeeded Dave Keon as captain of the Maple Leafs in 1975–76 and Toronto's fortunes rose over the next three seasons, culminating in a trip to the semifinals in 1978. Sittler established career highs with 45 goals and 72 assists in 1977–78, and his 117 points that season were a Maple Leafs record until Doug Gilmour had 127 in 1992–93.

The return of Punch Imlach as Maple Leafs general manager in 1979–80 led to dissension in the dressing room and resulted in Lanny McDonald being traded to the Colorado Rockies on December 29, 1979. Sittler resigned as captain in protest, and though he resumed the captaincy for the start of the 1980–81 season, he demanded a trade the following season and was dealt to the Philadelphia Flyers on January 20, 1982. Sittler remained with the Flyers through the 1983–84 season and spent his final year with the Detroit Red Wings in 1984–85. At the time of his retirement, Sittler's 1,121 points ranked 15th in NHL history. He was elected to the Hockey Hall of Fame in 1989.

Sittler returned to the Maple Leafs as an assistant to club president Cliff Fletcher on August 8, 1991. He continues to work with the team in community and alumni relations.

CONN SMYTHE purchased the Toronto St. Patricks on February 14, 1927, and renamed the team the Toronto Maple Leafs. He chose the Maple Leaf name and emblem as a patriotic gesture because it had been the symbol of Canadian soldiers during World War I. It was also the emblem he wore during his days with the University of Toronto.

Smythe first came to prominence in hockey as the captain of the University of Toronto varsity team that won the Ontario junior championship in 1915. Later, he and most of his teammates enlisted for military service. Smythe returned to the University of Toronto after World War I, and graduated in 1920. He then operated a sand and gravel company, but continued his involvement in hockey at U of T. Smythe coached the Varsity seniors to the Allan Cup in 1927, but was not on hand when the team won the gold medal at the Olympics in 1928.

While coaching in Toronto, Smythe was hired by John Hammond in 1926 to assemble a team in New York after the Rangers were admitted into the NHL. Smythe signed relative unknowns like Lorne Chabot, Ching Johnson and Frank Boucher, among others, but was fired when he refused to acquire star Babe Dye, whom he did not think would fit in with his team approach. The team he did build in New York won the Stanley Cup under Lester Patrick in 1928, while Smythe used the money he was paid to leave New York to help finance his purchase of the St. Pats.

Once established in Toronto, Smythe quickly went about building the Maple Leafs into a winner by adding such players as King Clancy, Joe Primeau, Charlie Conacher and Red Horner. He also hired Foster Hewitt to broadcast games, and by 1931 had built Maple Leaf Gardens during the height of the Depression. The new arena brought respectability to pro hockey in Toronto, and the Leafs won their first Stanley Cup championship that season.

Toronto was the best team in hockey during the 1930s, but after World War II began, Smythe took a leave of absence from the Maple Leafs board and recruited a Sportsmen's Battery. He took it overseas, insisted on seeing combat duty himself and was badly wounded in July, 1944. He recovered, and was running the Maple Leafs again by 1945.

Smythe remained in charge of the Maple Leafs until retiring in 1961. He already had been inducted into the Hockey Hall of Fame as a builder in 1958, and in 1964, Maple Leaf Gardens Limited donated the Conn Smythe Trophy to reward the most valuable player in the playoffs. Smythe also owned a successful horse-racing stable, winning the Queen's Plate in 1953 and 1967, and was very active in children's charities in Toronto.

LORD STANLEY OF PRESTON was the son of a three-time Prime Minister of England and was himself a British Member of Parliament. He sat in the House of Lords, and he served a short stint as the Secretary of State for the British colonies. Publicly shy and politically careful, Lord Stanley was an advocate of closer ties between Britain and its colonies.

In 1888, Frederick Arthur, Lord Stanley of Preston, was appointed Governor-General of Canada. He enjoyed the winter sports he discovered during his posting, and his sons became accomplished hockey players with Ottawa's Rideau Rebels. During his final year in office (1893), Lord Stanley donated the Dominion Hockey Challenge Cup to recognize Canada's hockey champion. The original bowl was purchased in London at a cost of 10 guineas, about the equivalent of $50. It quickly became known as the Stanley Cup.

Originally an amateur trophy, the Dominion Hockey Challenge Cup did not belong to any one league; it was available by challenge to any team in Canada. By 1906, professional teams had begun to compete for it, and by 1910 the Stanley Cup had become the symbol of professional hockey supremacy in Canada. American teams first became eligible to compete for the Cup in 1914. The challenge aspect of the trophy ended after 1914, when a formalized playoff system was adopted by the National Hockey Association, the Pacific Coast Hockey Association and the Stanley Cup trustees. This system was continued by the NHL, the PCHA and later the Western Canada Hockey League. After pro hockey collapsed in the west in 1926, the NHL became the only league to play for hockey's most prized trophy.

Lord Stanley and Sir H. Montagu Allan, who donated the Allan Cup, were elected to the Hockey Hall of Fame as builders in 1945 as part of the Hall's first inductions.

PETER STASTNY and his brothers Anton and Marian were star players in their homeland during the 1970s and members of the Czechoslovakian Olympic team that competed at Lake Placid in 1980. Anton was drafted by the Quebec Nordiques in 1979, and Peter was signed as a free agent after the two defected to North America. Both made their debuts with the Nordiques in 1980–81, with Marian joining them the following year.

All three Stastny brothers made an impact in Quebec as the Nordiques improved steadily, but only Peter emerged as an NHL superstar. He had been player of the year in Czechoslovakia in 1979–80 and followed up by winning the Calder Trophy as rookie of the year in the NHL. His 70 assists and 109 points in 1980–81 established rookie scoring records. Stastny had 100 points or more seven times in his career, and was in the top-10 in scoring on six occasions, finishing second behind Wayne Gretzky in 1982–83. He played in six All-Star games, but in an era dominated by centers like Gretzky and Mario Lemieux, Stastny never earned a postseason all-star selection.

On March 6, 1990, Stastny was traded to the New Jersey Devils, but he was no longer the same offensive threat. In 1993, he returned to Bratislava, which was now recognized as part of Slovakia, and played for the Slovakian Olympic team at Lillehammer in 1994. He returned to the NHL with the St. Louis Blues as a free agent late in the 1993–94 season, and ended his playing days the following season. Stastny was the all-time leading scorer among Europeans in the NHL until being surpassed by Jari Kurri on December 8, 1993, and continues to rank highly among the all-time leaders in NHL history. He was elected to the Hockey Hall of Fame in 1998.

NELS STEWART was the most prolific scorer of his day. His 324 career goals stood as an NHL record from the time of his retirement in 1940 until Maurice Richard scored his 325th on November 8, 1952. Stewart was an awkward skater who appeared slow-footed, but the deadly accuracy of his shot earned him the nickname "Old Poison."

Stewart was born in Montreal but raised in Toronto and played his amateur hockey there before joining Cleveland of the United States Amateur Hockey Association in 1920–21. After leading the league in scoring four times in five seasons, he and Babe Siebert were signed by the Montreal Maroons for the team's second season of 1925–26 . This infusion of youthful talent helped the team win the Stanley Cup that year. Stewart led the NHL in scoring and was rewarded with the Hart Trophy.

Having already played together briefly, Stewart, Siebert and Hooley Smith were teamed in 1929–30 to form the powerful S-Line. Stewart responded with a career-high 39 goals in 44 games and earned his second Hart Trophy win that year. During the next season, he set an NHL record that still stands when he scored two goals in four seconds on January 3, 1931. (The record was equaled by Deron Quint of the Winnipeg Jets on December 15, 1995.)

The S-Line was one of the best in the NHL over three seasons, with Stewart providing most of the offense while Siebert and Smith took care of the backchecking. All three could be dangerous when the game got physical. The line was broken up when Stewart was dealt to the Boston Bruins prior to the 1932–33 season, but he continued to rank among the league's best scorers over the next four years. He was traded to the New York Americans in 1935–36 and, except for a brief return to Boston, remained there until his retirement. Stewart was elected to the Hockey Hall of Fame in 1962.

SCOTT STEVENS earned a spot on the NHL's All-Rookie Team after the 1982–83 season, and was third behind Dale Hawerchuk and Barry Pederson in voting for the Calder Trophy. He has gone on to rank as one of the top defensemen in hockey.

Stevens spent eight years with the Washington Capitals, earning his first of four all-star honors in 1987–88 in a season that saw him finish as runner-up to Raymond Bourque for the Norris Trophy. He signed as a free agent with the St. Louis Blues on July 16, 1990, and was named team captain for the 1990–91 season, but on September 3, 1991, he was awarded to the New Jersey Devils as compensation when St. Louis signed Devils free agent Brendan Shanahan. Stevens was named captain of the Devils in 1992–93, and finished second behind Bourque again in an exceedingly close vote for the Norris Trophy in 1993–94. In 1995, Stevens and the Devils were Stanley Cup champions. Since then, he has continued to anchor one of the best defenses in the NHL. In 2000 he won the Conn Smythe Trophy after leading the Devils to another Stanley Cup victory.

In addition to his Stanley Cup victories, Stevens won the Memorial Cup with the Kitchener Rangers in 1982, and won a Canada Cup title with Team Canada in 1991. He has also represented Canada at the World Championships, winning a bronze medal in 1983 and silver medals in 1987 and 1989. In 1998, he was a member of the Canadian Olympic team at Nagano.

MATS SUNDIN was the first European player ever selected number one in the NHL Entry Draft when the Quebec Nordiques chose him in 1989. He made his NHL debut in 1990–91, scoring his first goal in his first NHL game on October 4, 1990. He went on to be one of the top-scoring rookies in the league.

Sundin improved his offensive numbers in 1991–92, and in 1992–93 he led the Nordiques with 67 assists and 114 points as Quebec reached the playoffs for the first time in six years. Sundin had the longest scoring streak in the NHL that season when he recorded points in each of the Nordiques' first 30 games. After his statistics dipped in 1993–94, he was traded to the Toronto Maple Leafs in a multi-player deal. Sundin replaced Doug Gilmour as the top offensive player in Toronto, and after Gilmour was traded during the 1996–97 season, he replaced him as team captain in 1997–98. Sundin has been Toronto's top scorer every season he has played with the club, and he and Curtis Joseph have led the club's return to the upper echelons of the NHL since 1998–99—including the Maple Leafs' first 100-point season in 1999–2000.

Internationally, Sundin helped Sweden win the World Championships in 1991 and 1992. He also led the tournament in scoring when Sweden earned a bronze medal in 1994. Sundin represented Sweden at the Canada Cup in 1991 and at the World Cup of Hockey in 1996. He was named to the first all-star team in each of those tournaments. In 1998, he was a member of the Swedish team at the Nagano Olympics.

ANATOLI TARASOV is generally regarded as the architect of Soviet domination of international amateur hockey. He and Arkady Chernyshev coached the Soviet Union to nine straight World and Olympic Championships between 1963 and 1972, including three straight Olympic gold medals, before Tarasov retired after the 1972 Games in Sapporo, Japan. He was inducted into the Hockey Hall of Fame as a builder in 1974.

Tarasov himself was a product of the Soviet hockey system, playing for teams in the late 1940s and early 1950s that paved the way for the first World Championship win by the USSR in 1954. After retiring as a player, he first coached the Soviet national team at the World Championships in 1958. Tarasov was a strong believer in conditioning, and wrote many books on hockey. He also supervised the Soviet Golden Puck tournament for boys, in which more than one million youngsters were registered. In 1987, he served as a coaching consultant to the NHL's Vancouver Canucks.

CYCLONE TAYLOR earned his nickname for his matchless speed as a skater and the furious rushes he led from the defense during his time with the Ottawa Senators. Fredrick Wellington "Cyclone" Taylor was the greatest star of his day, and he helped give instant credibility to the new National Hockey Association in 1909–10. His decision to join the Pacific Coast Hockey Association did the same for that fledgling league in 1912–13.

Taylor grew up in Listowel, Ontario, and began his hockey career there. After refusing to join the Toronto Marlboros, he was banned from the Ontario Hockey Association, so he left home to play hockey in Portage la Prairie, Manitoba, in 1905. Before the end of the 1905–06 season, he had signed a professional contract with the International (Pro) Hockey League team in Houghton, Michigan, becoming a star with the Portage Lakers in the game's first professional league. When the league collapsed, he signed with the Ottawa Senators for the 1907–08 season.

A forward until this point in his career, Taylor was moved to defense in Ottawa because his new linemates could not keep up with him. Playing a position then known as cover point, Taylor was free to use his blazing speed to lead individual rushes up the ice, knowing he could get back in time to help out in his own end. In 1909, he helped Ottawa to win the Stanley Cup. In the offseason that followed, Taylor was at the center of a fierce bidding war for his services that eventually led to his signing with the Renfrew Millionaires. His contract was reported to pay him $5,250 for the 12-game NHA season, and it was said to be the richest deal in North American sports. (Ty Cobb was making $6,500 with baseball's Detroit Tigers, but he had to play 154 games.)

When Renfrew dropped out of professional hockey after the 1910–11 season, Taylor sat out a year while the Senators and Montreal Wanderers fought over his rights. He then spurned both teams when he signed with former Renfrew teammate Frank Patrick's Vancouver Millionaires. Taylor became a forward again, playing center and rover, and the former defenseman developed into a scoring star who led the PCHA in goals three times and points five times. Though he played fewer games than anyone else ranked among the PCHA's all-time top-10 scorers, Taylor is the league's career leader in assists with 104. He ranks fifth overall with 159 goals and is second behind long-time teammate Mickey MacKay with 263 points. He also had seven goals in three playoff games in 1915 when Vancouver became the first team from the PCHA to win the Stanley Cup. Cyclone Taylor was elected to the Hockey Hall of Fame in 1947.

KEITH TKACHUK was the first American-born player to lead the NHL in goals when he scored 52 in 1996–97. He was also the first player in the history of the Winnipeg Jets/Phoenix Coyotes franchise to have consecutive 50 goal seasons, and he joined John LeClair, Kevin Stevens and Jeremy Roenick as the only Americans to score 50 goals two years in a row. He also joined Stevens, Brendan Shanahan and Gary Roberts as the only players to top 50 goals and 200 penalty minutes in the same season.

Tkachuk was drafted directly out of high school, but then played one year at Boston University where he was named to the Hockey East all-freshman team and helped BU to reach the NCAA finals. He spent the 1991–92 season with the U.S. national team, then joined the Jets after competing at the Albertville Olympics. Tkachuk quickly became a star in Winnipeg, and was named team captain after the club moved to Phoenix in 1996. That same year, he was a leader of the American team that beat Canada at the World Cup of Hockey. In 1998 he returned to the Olympics with the U.S. team at Nagano.

VLADISLAV TRETIAK was the greatest goaltender ever produced by the Soviet Union, and one of the very best netminders in hockey history. He first played the game at the age of 11, and by 15 was practicing with Moscow's Central Red Army team. He joined the Red Army roster at 17 in 1968–69, and was a member of 13 Soviet League champions over the next 15 years. Tretiak was named as the goaltender on the first all-star team 14 straight seasons between 1970–71 and 1983–84.

Tretiak came to the attention of fans in North America with his brilliant play during the 1972 Summit Series between Team Canada and the Soviets. On New Year's Eve in 1975, he helped his Red Army Team earn a 3–3 tie with the Montreal Canadiens despite being outshot 38–13 in one of the greatest games ever played. He was named MVP when the Soviets won the Canada Cup in 1981, and won the Golden Stick award as the outstanding player in Europe three years in a row from 1981 to 1983. By the time he retired after the 1983–84 season, Tretiak had played for 10 World Champions with the Soviet national team and won Olympic gold medals in 1972, 1976 and 1984. In 98 World Championship games, he boasted a goals-against average of 1.92. He had a 1.74 mark in 19 Olympic games.

In 1989, Vladislav Tretiak was honored as the first Soviet-trained player elected to the Hockey Hall of Fame. He became the goaltender coach with the Chicago Blackhawks in 1990–91, and has remained a great ambassador for Russian hockey.

BRYAN TROTTIER was a member of six Stanley Cup champions during 18 seasons as a player in the NHL, winning four in a row with the New York Islanders between 1980 and 1983, and two straight with the Pittsburgh Penguins in 1991 and 1992. Trottier ended his career in 1993–94 as one of the highest-scoring players in hockey history, and as one of the best two-way centers ever to play the game. He was elected to the Hockey Hall of Fame in 1997.

Trottier was selected by the New York Islanders in the second round of the 1974 Amateur Draft, and entered the NHL in 1975–76. He promptly set an NHL rookie scoring record with 95 points and won the Calder Trophy. In 1977–78, he led the league with 77 assists and finished second behind Guy Lafleur in the NHL scoring race. Trottier won the Art Ross Trophy the following season, and also won the Hart Trophy as most valuable player. In 1980, he earned the Conn Smythe Trophy as playoff MVP when the Islanders won their first Stanley Cup championship. In addition to his four Stanley Cup titles, Trottier recorded over 100 points six times in 13 years with the Islanders.

On July 20, 1990, Trottier left the Islanders to sign as a free agent with Pittsburgh, where his leadership skills were credited with helping the talented Penguins develop into Stanley Cup champions. He retired after Pittsburgh's second Stanley Cup victory in 1992 and returned to the Islanders in a front-office job. Still feeling the desire to play, he went back to Pittsburgh for a final season in 1993–94, where he also acted as an assistant coach. Trottier joined the Colorado Avalanche as an assistant coach in 1998–99 and was in the running for the head coaching job with the expansion Columbus Blue Jackets in the summer of 2000.

At the time of his retirement, Trottier ranked 15th all-time in NHL history with 524 goals, sixth in assists with 901, and sixth in points with 1,425.

GEORGES VEZINA played most of his career in an era when goaltenders were required to remain standing at all times. As a result, his statistics are not as impressive as many goaltenders of a later day, but he often is ranked among the greatest goalies of all-time. His legend is perpetuated by the Vezina Trophy, awarded annually to the top goaltender in the NHL.

Vezina began playing hockey in his hometown of Chicoutimi, Quebec, and he became known as "The Chicoutimi Cucumber" for his ability to remain cool under pressure. He joined the Montreal Canadiens in 1910–11, never missing a regular-season or playoff game over the next 15 years. His 367-game streak ended on November 28, 1925, when chest pains forced him out of action. He never played again, and he died of tuberculosis on March 26, 1926. The ownership of the Montreal Canadiens donated the Vezina Trophy to honor his memory.

Over the course of his career, Vezina helped the Canadiens win either the National Hockey Association or NHL title on five occasions, and the Stanley Cup in 1916 and 1924. He led the NHL in goals-against average in its first season of 1917–18, and he saw his numbers improve dramatically after 1922 when defensive hockey began to dominate. In 1945, Vezina was one of the original 12 men elected to the Hockey Hall of Fame.

COONEY WEILAND played 11 years in the NHL, winning the Stanley Cup in his first season of 1928–29 and in his last season of 1938–39. Standing just 5'7" and weighing only 150 pounds, Weiland was a slick stickhandler skilled at outmaneuvering opposition players.

Ralph "Cooney" Weiland won the Memorial Cup with the Owen Sound Grays in 1924, then played the next four years in Minnesota before he and Tiny Thompson joined the Boston Bruins directly from the roster of the Minneapolis Millers in 1928–29. The Bruins won their first Stanley Cup title that season. Weiland centered the Dynamite Line with wings Dutch Gainor and Dit Clapper, and the high-scoring trio helped Boston rewrite the NHL record book after forward passing rules were modernized for the 1929–30 season. The Bruins went 38–5–1 that year, while Weiland obliterated Howie Morenz's mark of 51 points in a single season with 73.

The Dynamite Line was broken up in 1932–33 when Weiland was traded to Ottawa. He promptly led the last-place club in scoring, but the cash-strapped Senators sold him to Detroit the following year. Weiland played on another great line with the Red Wings, centering Herbie Lewis and Larry Aurie. He returned to Boston in 1935, where he spent four more seasons before retiring as a player after winning the Stanley Cup in 1939. He was immediately named coach of the Bruins, and led them to another Stanley Cup title in 1941.

Weiland spent the next four seasons as coach of the American Hockey League's Hershey Bears, then guided the New Haven Ramblers in 1945–46. He became the head coach at Harvard University in 1950–51, and remained on the job for 21 years before retiring in 1971. That same year, Weiland was inducted into the Hockey Hall of Fame.

STEVE YZERMAN made his NHL debut as an 18-year-old in 1983–84. He went on to play in the All-Star Game that year, and set Red Wings records for goals (39) and points (87) by a rookie. Yzerman finished runner-up behind Tom Barrasso in voting for the Calder Trophy.

Yzerman became the youngest captain in Red Wings history when he was named to the position as a 21-year-old in 1986–87. He went on to lead the team in scoring for seven straight seasons. In 1988–89, he established career highs and Red Wings single-season records with 65 goals, 90 assists and 155 points. He finished third in the NHL in scoring behind Mario Lemieux and Wayne Gretzky, and was also third in voting for the Hart Trophy that season. Yzerman did receive the Lester B. Pearson Award as the most outstanding player in voting by fellow NHLers. On February 24, 1993, Yzerman joined Gordie Howe and Alex Delvecchio as the only players in Red Wings history to record 1,000 career points. His 500th career goal came on January 17, 1996.

One of the NHL's most respected players, and the longest-serving captain in league history, Yzerman finally got a chance to raise the Stanley Cup in 1997 when the Red Wings won for the first time since 1955. He was a unanimous choice for the Conn Smythe Trophy as the most valuable player in the playoffs when Detroit made it two in a row in 1998. During the 1999–2000 season, Yzerman became the fifth player in NHL history to top both 600 goals and 900 assists. He led the Red Wings in scoring for the 11th time, won the Selke Trophy as the NHL's best defensive forward and was named to the First All-Star Team for the first time in his long career.

In addition to his success in the NHL, Yzerman has also starred in the international arena. He won a bronze medal as a member of the Canadian team at the World Junior Championships in 1983, and earned a silver medal with Team Canada at the World Championships in 1985 and 1989. He led all players in scoring at the 1990 World Championships. He also took part in the Nagano Olympics in 1998.

HOCKEY HALL OF FAME AND UNITED STATES HOCKEY HALL OF FAME MEMBERS

HOCKEY HALL OF FAME

PLAYERS

* Abel, Sid
* Adams, Jack
* Apps, Syl
Armstrong, George
* Bailey, Ace
* Bain, Dan
* Baker, Hobey
Barber,Bill
* Barry, Marty
Bathgate, Andy
* Bauer, Bobby
Beliveau, Jean
* Benedict, Clint
* Bentley, Doug
* Bentley, Max
* Blake, Hector "Toe"
Boivin, Leo
* Boon, Dickie
Bossy, Mike
Bouchard, Emile "Butch"
* Boucher, Frank
* Boucher, George
Bower, Johnny
* Bowie, Russell
* Brimsek, Frank
* Broadbent, Harry "Punch"
* Broda, Walter "Turk"
Bucyk, John
* Burch, Billy
* Cameron, Harry
Cheevers, Gerry
* Clancy, Francis "King"
* Clapper, Aubrey "Dit"
Clarke, Bobby
* Cleghorn, Sprague
* Colville, Neil
* Conacher, Charlie
* Conacher, Lionel
* Conacher, Roy
* Connell, Alex
* Cook, Fred "Bun"
* Cook, Bill
Coulter, Art
Cournoyer, Yvan
* Cowley, Bill
* Crawford, Rusty
* Darragh, Jack
* Davidson, Scotty
* Day, Clarence "Hap"
Delvecchio, Alex
* Denneny, Cy
Dionne, Marcel
* Drillon, Gordie
* Drinkwater, Charles Graham
Dryden, Ken
Dumart, Woody
* Dunderdale, Thomas
* Durnan, Bill
* Dutton, Mervyn "Red"
* Dye, Cecil "Babe"
Esposito, Tony
Esposito, Phil
* Farrell, Arthur
Flaman, Fern
* Foyston, Frank
* Fredrickson, Frank
Gadsby, Bill
Gainey, Bob
* Gardiner, Charlie
* Gardiner, Herb
* Gardner, Jimmy
Geoffrion, Bernie "Boom Boom"
* Gerard, Eddie
Giacomin, Eddie
Gilbert, Rod
* Gilmour, Billy
* Goheen, Frank X. "Moose"
* Goodfellow, Ebbie
Goulet, Michel
* Grant, Mike
* Green, Wilfred "Shorty"
Gretzky, Wayne
* Griffis, Si
* Hainsworth, George
Hall, Glenn
* Hall, Joe
* Harvey, Doug
* Hay, George
* Hern, Riley
* Hextall, Bryan Sr.
* Holmes, Harry "Hap"
* Hooper, Tom
Horner, Reginald "Red"
* Horton, Tim
Howe, Gordie
* Howe, Syd
Howell, Harry
Hull, Bobby
* Hutton, Bouse
* Hyland, Harry
* Irvin, Dick
* Jackson, Harvey "Busher"
* Johnson, Ernie "Moose"
* Johnson, Ivan "Ching"
Johnson, Tom
* Joliat, Aurel
* Keats, Gordon "Duke"
Kelly, Leonard "Red"
Kennedy, Teeder
Keon, Dave
Lach, Elmer
Lafleur, Guy
* Lalonde, Edouard "Newsy"
Laperriere, Jacques
Lapointe, Guy
Laprade, Edgar
* Laviolette, Jack
* Lehman, Hugh
Lemaire, Jacques
Lemieux, Mario
* LeSueur, Percy
* Lewis, Herbie
Lindsay, Ted
* Lumley, Harry
* MacKay, Duncan "Mickey"
Mahovlich, Frank
* Malone, Joe
* Mantha, Sylvio
* Marshall, Jack
* Maxwell, Fred "Steamer"
McDonald, Lanny
* McGee, Frank
* McGimsie, Billy
* McNamara, George
Mikita, Stan
Moore, Dickie
* Moran, Paddy
* Morenz, Howie
* Mosienko, Billy
Mullen, Joe
* Nighbor, Frank
* Noble, Reg
* O'Connor, Herbert "Buddy"
* Oliver, Harry
Olmstead, Bert
Orr, Bobby
Parent, Bernie
Park, Brad
* Patrick, Lynn
* Patrick, Lester
Perreault, Gilbert
* Phillips, Tommy
Pilote, Pierre
* Pitre, Didier
* Plante, Jacques
Potvin, Denis
* Pratt, Walter "Babe"
* Primeau, Joe
Pronovost, Marcel
Pulford, Bob
* Pulford, Harvey
* Quackenbush, Bill
* Rankin, Frank
Ratelle, Jean
Rayner, Chuck
Reardon, Kenny
Richard, Henri
* Richard, Maurice "Rocket"
* Richardson, George
* Roberts, Gordon
Robinson, Larry
* Ross, Art
* Russel, Blair
* Russell, Ernie
* Ruttan, Jack
Salming, Borje
Savard, Denis
Savard, Serge
* Sawchuk, Terry
* Scanlan, Fred
Schmidt, Milt
* Schriner, David "Sweeney"
* Seibert, Earl
* Seibert, Oliver
* Shore, Eddie
Shutt, Steve
* Siebert, Albert "Babe"
* Simpson, Harold "Bullet Joe"
Sittler, Darryl
* Smith, Alf
Smith, Clint
* Smith, Reginald "Hooley"
* Smith, Tommy
Smith, Billy
Stanley, Allan
* Stanley, Barney
Stastny, Peter
* Stewart, John "Black Jack"
* Stewart, Nels
* Stuart, Bruce
* Stuart, Hod
* Taylor, Fred "Cyclone"
* Thompson, Cecil "Tiny"
Tretiak, Vladislav
Trottier, Bryan
* Trihey, Harry
Ullman, Norm
* Vezina, Georges
* Walker, Jack
* Walsh, Marty
* Watson, Harry E.
Watson, Harry
* Weiland, Ralph "Cooney"
* Westwick, Harry
* Whitcroft, Fred
* Wilson, Gordon "Phat"
Worsley, Lorne "Gump"
* Worters, Roy

BUILDERS

* Adams, Charles
* Adams, Weston W.
* Ahearn, Frank
* Ahearne, J.F. "Bunny"
* Allan, Sir Montagu
Allen, Keith
Arbour, Al
* Ballard, Harold
* Bauer, Father David
* Bickell, John Paris
Bowman, Scott
* Brown, George V.
* Brown, Walter A.
* Buckland, Frank
Bush, Walter
Butterfield, Jack
* Calder, Frank
* Campbell, Angus
* Campbell, Clarence
* Cattarinich, Joseph
* Dandurand, J.V. "Leo"
* Dilio, Frank
* Dudley, George
* Dunn, Jimmy
Francis, Emile
* Gibson, J.L. "Doc"
* Gorman, Tommy
* Griffiths, Frank A.
* Hanley, William
* Hay, Charles
* Hendy, Jim
* Hewitt, Foster
* Hewitt, W.A.
* Hume, Fred
* Imlach, George "Punch"
* Ivan, Tommy
* Jennings, Bill
* Johnson, Bob
* Juckes, Gordon
* Kilpatrick, Gen. John Reed
* Knox, Seymour III
* Leader, Al
* LeBel, Robert
* Lockhart, Thomas
* Loicq, Paul
* Mariucci, John
Mathers, Frank
* McLaughlin, Major Frederic
* Milford, Jake
Molson, Hon. Hartland
Morrison, Ian "Scotty"
* Murray, Msgr. Athol
* Nelson, Francis
* Norris, Bruce A.
* Norris, James Sr.
* Norris, James
* Northey, William
* O'Brien, Ambrose
O'Neill, Brian
* Page, Fred
* Patrick, Frank
* Pickard, Allan
* Pilous, Rudy
Poile, Norman "Bud"
Pollock, Sam
* Raymond, Sen. Donat
* Robertson, John Ross
* Robinson, Claude
* Ross, Philip D.
Sabetzki, Gunther
Sather, Glen
* Selke, Frank J.
Sinden, Harry
* Smith, Frank
* Smythe, Conn
Snider, Ed
* Stanley of Preston, Lord
* Sutherland, James T.
* Tarasov, Anatoli
Torrey, Bill
* Turner, Lloyd
* Tutt, William Thayer
* Voss, Carl
* Waghorn, Fred
* Wirtz, Arthur
Wirtz, Bill
Ziegler, John A. Jr.

REFEREES/LINESMEN

Armstrong, Neil
Ashley, John
Chadwick, Bill
D'Amico, John
* Elliott, Chaucer
* Hayes, George
* Hewitson, Bobby
* Ion, Mickey
Pavelich, Matt
* Rodden, Mike
* Smeaton, Cooper
Storey, Roy "Red"
Udvari, Frank
Van Hellemond, Andy

UNITED STATES HOCKEY HALL OF FAME

PLAYERS

* Abel, Clarence Taffy
* Baker, Hobey
Bartholome, Earl
* Bessone, Peter
Blake, Bob
Boucha, Henry
* Brimsek, Frank
Cavanagh, Joe
* Chaisson, Ray
* Chase, John
Christian, Roger
Christian, Bill
Cleary, Bob
Cleary, Bill
* Conroy, Tony
Curran, Mike
Dahlstrom, Carl "Cully"
* Desjardins, Victor
* Desmond, Richard
* Dill, Bob
* Everett, Doug
Ftorek, Robbie
* Garrison, John
Garrity, Jack
* Goheen, Frank X. "Moose"
Grant, Wally
* Harding, Austie
* Iglehart, Stewart
* Johnson, Virgil
* Karakas, Mike
Kirrane, Jack
* Lane, Myles
Langevin, Dave
Langway, Rod
Larson, Reed
* Linder, Joseph
* LoPresti, Sam
* Mariucci, John
Matchefts, John
Mather, Bruce
Mayasich, John
McCartan, Jack
* Moe, Billy
Morrow, Ken
* Moseley, Fred
Mullen, Joe
* Murray, Muzz
* Nelson, Hub
* Nyrop, Bill
* Olson , Eddie
* Owen, Jr., George
* Palmer, Winthrop "Ding"
Paradise, Robert
Purpur, Clifford "Fido"
Riley, Bill
Roberts, Gordie
* Romnes, Elwin "Doc"
Rondeau, Dick
Sheehy, Tim
* Williams, Tommy
* Winters, Coddy
* Yackel, Ken

COACHES

* Almquist, Oscar
Bessone, Amo
Brooks, Herb
Ceglarski, Len
* Fullerton, James
Gambucci, Sergio
* Gordon, Malcolm
Harkness, Ned
Heyliger, Vic
Holt, Charlie
Ikola, Willard
* Jeremiah, Eddie
* Johnson, Bob
* Kelley, John "Snooks"
Kelley, Jack
Patrick, Craig
Pleban, Connie
Riley, Jack
* Ross, Larry
* Thompson, Cliff
* Stewart, Bill
Watson, Sid
* Winsor, Ralph

ADMINISTRATORS

* Brown, George V.
* Brown, Walter A.
Bush, Walter
* Clark, Donald
Claypool, James
* Gibson, J.C. "Doc"
* Jennings, Bill
* Kahler, Nick
* Lockhart, Tommy
Marvin, Cal
Ridder, Bob
* Schulz, Charles M.
Trumble, Hal
* Tutt, William Thayer
Wirtz, Bill
* Wright, Lyle

PLAYER/ADMINISTRATOR

Nanne, Lou

REFEREE

Chadwick, Bill

** Deceased*

Notes on Contributors and Acknowledgments

Contributors

Alan Adams is a national hockey writer for the *National Post* newspaper. He has been covering hockey at virtually every level of the game since 1984.

Kevin Allen has been *USA Today*'s hockey beat writer since 1986. He is the author of *USA Hockey: A Celebration of a Great Tradition* and *Shootin' and Smilin'*, a biography of Brett Hull. He is a member of the Professional Hockey Writers' Association and the Hockey Hall of Fame Selection Committee.

Fred Addis is a freelance writer specializing in both shipping and hockey history. Having lived in Port Colborne, Ontario, for 20 years, the careers of hometown hockey greats Teeder Kennedy, Don Gallinger, Don Simmons and the Horvath brothers: Bronco and Johnny, have been a lifelong interest. Addis now makes his home in Toronto.

Kerry Banks is a Vancouver-based freelance writer who writes about sports for the *Georgia Straight* and has written biographies about Pavel Bure, Teemu Selanne and Mats Sundin.

Ted Barris is the author of *Playing Overtime: A Celebration of Oldtimers' Hockey*.

Pavel Barta is a noted hockey journalist in the Czech Republic. For the last decade he has covered hockey for *Gol* magazine, the largest sports weekly in the Czech Republic.

Heiko Behrens (contributing historian) is a 30-year old farmer from the small German village of Bartelsdorf who contributed more than 50 pages of corrections, suggestions and updates to this edition. His main sporting interests include ice hockey, soccer and tennis.

Dave Bidini is a member of the Rheostatics whose book *On a Cold Road* describes rock and roll life in Canada. He has written about life and hockey for several publications. In March 1999, Bidini set off to explore the state of the game in places outside the traditional hockey hotbeds. He laced up the blades in such exotic ports of call as Hong Kong, Harbin, Dubai, Al Ain, Transylvania, Dublin and Belfast.

Mike Board covers the Calgary Flames for the *Calgary Herald*.

Ron Boileau is president of the British Columbia Hockey League. He is also an historian and statistician with a special interest in the Pacific Coast Hockey Association. Boileau is a member of the Society for International Hockey Research.

Paul Bontje (assistant editor) is a member of the editorial team that produces the *NHL Official Guide and Record Book* and *Total Stanley Cup*.

Mark Brender is a former staff writer with *The Hockey News* now working as a freelance writer and editor in Toronto.

Mike Brophy has been senior writer at *The Hockey News* for eight years after having covered the Peterborough Petes for 14 seasons. He won the Benjamin Franklin Award (best new voice) for his book *Curtis Joseph: The Acrobat*.

Frank Brown (senior editorial consultant) is vice president, media relations for the National Hockey League. He covered the New York Rangers for the *New York Daily News*.

Paul Bruno (contributing editor) specializes in the analysis of sports statistics. He is president of the Hockey Library and treasurer of the Society for International Hockey Research.

Ken Campbell covers the Toronto Maple Leafs and the NHL for the *Toronto Star*. He lives in Toronto with his wife and two young sons.

Tim Campbell covers hockey and other sports for the *Winnipeg Free Press*. He covered the Winnipeg Jets when that franchise was located in Manitoba.

David Candy (contributing historian) is a hockey historian whose love of the game encouraged him to compile the *International Ice Hockey Almanac*, an exhaustive compilation of leagues and league standings from around the world. A resident of Vancouver, he has donated his work to the Hockey Hall of Fame and the Vancouver Public Library.

James Carr (contributing editor) has been a season ticket holder for the Winnipeg Jets (WHA and NHL) and the Manitoba Moose (IHL).

Rich Chere covers the New Jersey Devils for the *Newark Star-Ledger*.

Steve Cherwonak has been involved in sports as a player, coach and administrator nearly all of his adult life. A former football player at the University of British Columbia, he has been directory of scheduling and media relations for the Western Professional Hockey League since its inception in 1996.

Dave Clamen has been collecting junior and senior hockey statistics and stories for the past 20 years. A native of Montreal, he now resides in Toronto.

Cammy Clark is a hockey columnist who covers the Mighty Ducks of Anaheim and the Los Angeles Kings for the *Orange County Register*.

Glenn Cole is a native of Montreal who has been involved in NHL hockey for more than 25 years as a writer and broadcaster. He is with the *Toronto Sun* and is the Puckmaster on SLAM! Sports, Sun Media's national Web site.

Stephen Cole is the author of *The Last Hurrah*, a chronicle of the 1966–67 NHL season. He writes for the *National Post*.

Pat Conway (contributing statistician) provided much of the biographical information used in *Total Hockey*. Mr Conway collected telephone books from numerous communities in Canada and the United States and painstakingly phoned or wrote to all the former players he could find. He passed away in 1994.

Norman de Mesquita is an Honorary Life Member of the British Ice Hockey Writers' Association, having been its chairman for 14 years. He first watched hockey at Wembley in London in 1946; stood outside the London rinks for several years selling *Ice Hockey World*, a weekly paper, refereed for 14 years in the 1950s and 1960s and covered the British scene for *The Times* for 12 years. He writes about the NHL for the British hockey magazine *Ice Hockey News Review*.

Dan Diamond (editor) designed the *NHL Official Guide & Record Book* in 1984 and has edited numerous books about the sport including the *Official NHL 75th Anniversary Book*. He has asked Gordie Howe for his autograph in five different decades,

Ralph Dinger (managing editor) is an experienced researcher and editor who has specialized in goaltending records. He is managing editor of the *NHL Official Guide & Record Book*.

Bruce Dowbiggin is a columnist with the *Calgary Herald*. He has worked as a broadcaster and has written several books about hockey, including *Of Ice and Men* and *The Defense Never Rests*.

Gregg Drinnan has covered the Western Hockey League for almost 30 years at the *Brandon Sun*, *Winnipeg Tribune*, *Regina Leader-Post* and *Kamloops Daily News*. He was the sports editor of the *Leader-Post* for almost 12 years and is now the sports editor of the *Daily News*. Drinnan received the CHL Media Award at the 1998 Memorial Cup.

Ken Dryden was a Hockey Hall of Fame netminder with the Montreal Canadiens who is currently the president of the Toronto Maple Leafs. He is the author of several books including *The Game* and *In School*.

Alex Dubiel (contributing statistician) is a musician and data base manager who has developed computer programs vital to updating *Total Hockey*'s statistical data.

Bob Duff is a hockey historian whose detailed statistical research has uncovered much information about the early years of the NHL. He covers the Detroit Red Wings for the *Windsor Star* and was the research editor for *The Hockey Encyclopedia* in 1983. He is a member of the Society for International Hockey Research.

Milt Dunnell is one of Canada's most distinguished sports editors and writers, having covered hockey and a wide range of sporting topics for the *Toronto Star* for more than half a century. He is a recipient of the Hockey Hall of Fame's Elmer Ferguson Memorial Award for writing.

James Duplacey (managing editor) is a former curator of the Hockey Hall of Fame. He is the author of the Hockey Superstars series of children's books and frequently consulted on matters of hockey history by broadcasters and journalists.

Jack Falla is an Adjunct Professor at Boston University's College of Communication where he teaches a course in Sports Journalism, a course Rene Cliche has not taken.

Ivan Filippov lives and works in Vancouver and Prague. His company, Bynamics Corporation, exports North American hockey-related products in the Czech Republic.

Stan and Shirley Fischler operate the Fischler Hockey Service in New York. Stan has authored some 70 books about hockey, many in collaboration with Shirley, including *The Hockey Encyclopedia* in 1983. He also works as a commentator on telecasts of New York Islanders and New Jersey Devils games and is a contributor to *The Hockey News*.

Bill Fitsell is a freelance writer and founding president of the Society for International Hockey Research. He has been a longtime contributor to the *Kingston Whig-Standard* in his home town of Kingston, Ontario.

Ernie Fitzsimmons (consulting statistician) is one of hockey's leading statistical historians. He has worked as the statistician for the Fredericton Canadiens of the American Hockey League. He is president of the Society for International Hockey Research.

Bruce Garrioch covers the Ottawa Senators hockey club for the *Ottawa Sun*.

Roger A. Godin was director of the United States Hockey Hall of Fame, 1971–83, 1985–87. His hockey speciality is American players at the collegiate and professional level. He is a vice president of the Society for International Hockey Research and lives in St. Paul, Minnesota.

Glen R. Goodhand is an ordained minister with an avid interest in hockey history. He has contributed columns to newspapers in the Beaverton, Ontario area and is a founding member of the Society for International Hockey Research.

Jeff Gordon has covered hockey for the *St. Louis Post-Dispatch* since 1986. His work has appeared in *The Hockey News*, *The Sporting News*, *Inside Sports*, *Hockey Digest*, *Rinkside*, *Power Play* and *Hockey Stars*.

Chrys Goyens co-wrote *Lions in Winter*, a history of the Montreal Canadiens, and *My Life in Hockey* with Jean Beliveau. He is also the author of children's books about the Toronto Maple Leafs and Montreal Canadiens. He was part of the editorial team that produced *The Montreal Forum: 1924–1996*.

Jay Greenberg has covered the NHL since 1972. He wrote for several Philadelphia newspapers while covering the Flyers for 14 years and has also written for *Sports Illustrated*, the *Toronto Sun* and *The Hockey News*. He is currently with the *New York Post*.

Bob Grove has written for numerous hockey publications. He is the author of *Pittsburgh Penguins: The Official History of the First 30 Years*. He has been covering the team since 1981 and his work has appeared in every Penguins game program since 1986.

Tu Thanh Ha is a correspondent with the Montreal bureau of the *Globe and Mail*. He came to Canada from Vietnam in 1975 and grew up watching the Guy Lafleur-era Canadiens.

Stu Hackel is lead hockey producer for FOXSports.com and formerly was director of broadcasting, video and publishing for the National Hockey League. He is the first and only president of the Gump Worsley fan club.

Martin Harris (contributing statistician) is Britain's foremost hockey historian. He is a former council member of the British Ice Hockey Association and a member of the Society for International Hockey Research.

Tom Hoffarth has covered the media (radio, television, computers etc.) for the *Los Angeles Daily News* for the past six years. He has written for several different Los Angeles-area newspapers over the past 20 years.

Patrick Houda is a freelance hockey writer and researcher who is fluent in five languages. He was *Total Hockey*'s most dedicated contributor, researching more than 10,000 new lines of statistics for both European and North American players. He is a regular contributor to the European NHL magazine "Pro Hockey." Along with North American researcher Joe Pelletier, he is putting the final touches on a history of the six Canada Cup and World Cup Tournaments, told from the perspective of fans on both sides of the Atlantic.

Douglas Hunter is a freelance writer, editor and graphic designer. He is the author of two books about yacht racing as well as the hockey books *War Games*, *Open Ice: The Tim Horton Story* and *A Breed Apart: An Illustrated History of Goaltending*.

Dick Irvin is a longtime Montreal-based broadcaster whose first book, the biographical *Now Back to You Dick*, was released in 1988. The son of legendary coach Dick Irvin Sr., he has also written about coaches, goaltenders and referees.

Ulf Jansson has been working as a professional ice hockey journalist since 1955 and has attended 43 World Championships and 10 Olympic Winter Games, as well as the 1972 Canada-Russia Summit Series. A close friend of Anatoli Tarasov, he became the NHL's first European scout when he was hired by Muzz Patrick of the New York Rangers in 1963. Jansson later worked for the St Louis Blues and the Hartford Whalers.

Marina Joukova (contributing statistician) worked for the Soviet Hockey Federation as a statistician in the late 1980s. She was responsible for one of the first projects that computerized Soviet hockey statistics.

Michael Kaiser is a web site producer who has played pickup hockey in Toronto since 1975 and plans to do so for another 25 years.

Sidney Katz was a *Maclean's* staff editor and writer from 1950 to 1965. He wrote widely on health and behavioral issues and was the first writer in North America to explain from personal experience the effects of taking LSD.

David Keon Jr. works for the National Hockey League in Toronto as manager, public relations. He also has worked as an NHL goal judge and off-ice official.

Paul Kitchen is a longtime member of the Society for International Hockey Research who served several terms as the organization's president.

Jeff Z. Klein is a staff editor with *The New York Times Magazine*. From 1990 through 1995 he was a sports editor at *The Village Voice*. He has written several books about hockey, many in collaboration with Karl-Eric Reif. His short story entitled "Now I Can Die in Peace" appeared in the fiction anthology *Original Six*.

Lenard Kotylo is a lawyer in Toronto. Has been a member of the Society for International Hockey Research since the early 1990s and has served as secretary of the organization since 1998.

Steve Knowles is the information coordinator for the public relations department of the Edmonton Oilers. He is also the chairman of the Canadian Interuniversity Athletic Union men's hockey top ten committee and has served as the statistician for Canada West Hockey since 1984–85.

Igor Kuperman (international editor) began compiling hockey statistics in his native Moscow. He worked as a sports journalist in the Soviet Union before coming to North America in 1991. He works in the hockey operations department of the Phoenix Coyotes.

Jim Leitner is the sports editor of the *Telegraph Herald* in Dubuque, Iowa, where he has covered the Fighting Saints of the Junior A United States Hockey League for the past 12 years. Leitner, who plays over-30 hockey twice a week, sits on the editorial board for *American Hockey Magazine*, the official publication of USA Hockey.

Patrick Lethert is an attorney, author and left winger who resides in St. Paul, Minnesota. He is currently working on an encyclopedia treatment of college hockey.

Donald G. MacEachern (contributing historian) A retired Associate Professor at the University of Minnesota, Mr. MacEachern specializes in researching the early history of hockey in his home state. His contributions included a series of meticulously indexed binders of corrections and additions. He promises to continue the hunt for future editions.

Al Mason (contributing statistician) played Junior A hockey and later coached in the Metropolitan Toronto Hockey League. Since 1985, he has scouted for Ontario Hockey League teams. He is a longtime collector of hockey and baseball statistical books.

Gary Mason is the sports editor and a columnist with the Vancouver Sun. He covers the Vancouver Canucks.

John McCauley is a freelance sports journalist who has always had an interest in hockey. He has a bachelor of arts degree from Carleton University and a journalism degree from Algonquin College.

Brian McFarlane has worked as a commentator on "Hockey Night in Canada," NBC and CBS. He is a recipient of the Foster Hewitt Memorial Award for broadcasting and has written more than 30 books about hockey. He is a member of the Society for International Hockey Research and has operated his own hockey museum.

Pierre McGuire is a former head coach in the NCAA and the NHL. He won the Stanley Cup as an assistant coach with the Pittsburgh Penguins in 1991. He is currently a radio broadcaster with the Montreal Canadiens.

Ross McKeon covers the San Jose Sharks for the *San Francisco Examiner*.

Gary Meagher (senior contributing editor) has worked with the National Hockey League since 1981. He is currently vice president, public relations and media services.

Howard "Howdie" Mickoski is the author of *Hockeyology: Digging Up Hockey's Past* and researches pre-1917 hockey history. He holds an HBA in history from Wilfrid Laurier University. Howard is also a banquet speaker and he impersonates famous hockey announcers. He is a new member of the Society for International Hockey Research.

Harry Neale was a member of the 1956 Memorial Cup champion Toronto Marlboros. He later became a coach in the World Hockey Association and a coach and general manager in the NHL before turning to broadcasting. Currently, he is the lead analyst for Toronto Maple Leafs and CBC telecasts.

Roger Neilson has been a head coach with seven NHL teams. He led the Vancouver Canucks to the Stanley Cup finals in 1982 and the New York Rangers to the Presidents' Trophy in 1992.

Brian O'Byrne played junior hockey in Peterborough (Ontario) and Montreal. In 1974 he was hired as technical directory by the Canadian Amateur Hockey Association. Today, he manages Hockey Canada's Ontario Centre of Excellence from an office located in Maple Leaf Gardens.

Aidan O'Hara has done extensive research and writing on the roots of hockey in greater Boston and its relationship to various communities. He received his Bachelor of Arts in history from The American University in Washington, D.C., and has since moved back to the Boston area where he also specializes in Theater Education.

Gerald Owen is acting Discovery editor for the *National Post* newspaper. He is a former editor of *The Idler* and *Books in Canada*.

Mark Paddock was a contributing writer and copy editor for the first edition of *Total Hockey*. He co-edited *Coolest Game on the Road: A Travel Guide to the NHL*, and has served as assistant editor of the *NHL Official Guide and Record Book*.

John Pasternak (data management) developed the data base of player and goaltender statistics for *Total Hockey* and the *NHL Official Guide & Record Book*. He lives and works in Hillsburgh, Ontario.

John Paton (contributing statistician) is a retired banker who has traveled extensively across Canada and the northern United States since the mid 1950s researching and compiling detailed statistical histories of the top senior and junior leagues for the 50 years following World War I.

Paul Patskou is a researcher and video archivist. He has been a member of the Society for International Hockey Research since 1998.

Joe Pelletier (contributing historian) is a researcher and author who founded the founder of the excellent Internet research site "Hockey over Time," where one can find updated information on the heroes of the game from all eras.

Ingrid Peritz grew up in Montreal listening to stories of the Maroons. She worked for the *Montreal Gazette* before joining the Montreal bureau of the *Globe and Mail* in 1998.

Glynis Peters is Senior Program Officer with Sports Canada. From 1990 to 1998 she was Program Manager of women's hockey with the Canadian Hockey Association. Peters won the Canadian Association for the Advancement of Women and Sports "Breakthrough Award" in 1998 for her work with girls and women's hockey.

Jim Proudfoot began to cover the NHL for the *Toronto Star* in 1954. He served as sports editor from 1970 to 1977 and wrote a daily column until 1998. He is a recipient of the Elmer Ferguson Memorial Award for writing and is a member of the Hockey Hall of Fame's Selection Committee.

Tom Ratschunas is the leading hockey statistician in Europe. He edited the *IIHF International Hockey Guide* during the 1970s and 1980s. He provides statistical services to many European hockey leagues and IIHF competitions.

Don Reddick is a novelist whose books include *Dawson City Seven*, *Killing Frank McGee* and *Victory Faust*. He lives in Walpole, Massachusetts, with his wife and three children.

Stuart Reid (contributing editor) is president of SQRA Corporation, a statistical software company. Beginning with hockey, they have expanded into 25 sports and recently licensed soccer, baseball and golf in Japan.

Karl-Eric Reif has worked for 15 years as a sportswriter, columnist and cartoonist for *The Village Voice*, *The American*, *The Hockey News* and other publications. He has co-authored several books about hockey with Jeff Z. Klein.

Stewart Roberts is a freelance journalist specializing in hockey. He has been editor/publisher of the British hockey yearbook *The Ice Hockey Annual* since 1976 and is a former publicity officer of the British Ice Hockey Association.

Jari Sarkka was born in Finland and came to Canada as a boy in 1957. He is an air pilot, a minor hockey coach and a teacher with the Lakehead School Board in Thunder Bay, Ontario, where he lives with his wife and two sons.

Howard Shubert is associate curator of Prints and Drawings at the Canadian Centre for Architecture, Montreal. He is presently at work on a history of skating rinks and hockey arenas in North America.

Ralph Slate (contributing statistician) has developed the most comprehensive statistical hockey database on the Internet, which features statistics for every player who has ever appeared in a professional hockey game. The site also offers complete histories of the NHL and WHA's Amateur, Entry and Supplemental Drafts, as well as an outstanding archives of trading card data and club logos. You can (and should) visit him at www.hockeydb.com

David Spaner has worked as a feature writer, reporter and editor for numerous publications. He is currently employed at the *Vancouver Province*.

Janne Stark is the editor of the Swedish hockey annual *Årets Ishockey*. He has covered the game since 1973 and is one of the founding members of the Swedish Professional Icehockey Writers Association, as well as the Swedish Icehockey Historical and Statistical Society.

Brian Stein has been associated with CCAA hockey for two decades—most recently as editor of both the *ACAC Hockey Information Guide* and the *Viking Cup Magazine*. He runs his own communications/information technology firm in Alberta.

Scott Surgent is a lecturer in mathematics at Arizona State University. He published *The Complete Historical and Statistical Reference to the World Hockey Association* in 1995.

Chris Tredree works with the National Hockey League in Toronto as manager, public relations.

Gordon Wade (contributing statistician) has been Britain's senior hockey statistician since 1982. He is the statistician for Britain's ice hockey Superleague and for Rupert Murdoch's British cable TV channel SkySport.

Jenny Wiedeke works for the National Team Development Program in Ann Arbor, Michigan. She earned a degree in journalism from the University of Kansas and earned her masters degree in sport administration from the University of North Carolina.

Ron Wight is a high school teacher at Guelph Collegiate whose hobby is hockey history. He has done fact-checking work for 25 to 30 hockey publications.

Charles Wilkins (contributing editor) has written extensively about hockey and other subjects. He recently wrote about Maurice Richard in *Saturday Night* magazine. He lives in Thunder Bay, Ontario.

John Jason Wilson is a member of the reggae band Tabarruk. He has done extensive research into the role of Irish Canadians in hockey around the time of the First World War. A member of the Society for International Hockey Research, Wilson also contributed to Don Reddick's piece on Frank McGee as it appears in this edition of *Total Hockey*.

Peter Wilton is a Toronto-based journalist who specializes in medical issues and Canadian history. In addition to his published work, he is a guest correspondent for CBC radio.

Herbert Warren Wind is best known for his writing about golf. He is the co-author of *Ben Hogan's Five Lessons: The Modern Fundamentals of Golf* and was a frequent contributor to *Sports Illustrated* and *The New Yorker*.

Philip Wolf is a longtime sportswriter for the *Nanaimo Daily News* and a longtime follower of the British Columbia Hockey League, where he played as a junior.

Martin Wright became a fan of the defending Stanley Cup champion Toronto Maple Leafs as a seven-year-old in the fall of 1967. He lives in Brampton with his wife and daughter and is a serious collector of Maple Leafs memorabilia.

Earl Zukerman is the Quebec vice president of the Society for International Hockey Research. He works for McGill University Athletics.

Eric Zweig (managing editor) is the author of the historical novel *Hockey Night in the Dominion of Canada* and three non-fiction books for children. He has written about sports history for several Canadian media outlets including *The Beaver* and CBC Radio.

ACKNOWLEDGMENTS

Thanks to the following contributors:

Copy Editors

W.D. Lighthall, Patricia MacDonald, Sheila Paterson

For the National Hockey League

Gary Bettman, Bill Daly, Bernadette Mansur, Pat Armstrong, Frank Bonello, Bill Daly, Glenn Horine, Brian Jennings

For the Hockey Hall of Fame

Craig Campbell, Jeff Denomme, Peter Jagla, Phil Pritchard, Pearl Rajwanth, Marilyn Robbins, Isaac Westgate, Tyler Wolosewich

For Total Sports

John Thorn, Donna Harris, Mikhail Horowitz, Sean Lahman, Chad Lawrence, Joe Nardone, Connie Newhouser, George Pattison, Jenna Risely, Dianne Robinson, Matt Silverman, David Stone, Ann Sullivan, Jed Thorn, Dave Weiner.

For Pubishers Group West

Charlie Winton, Mark Ouimet, Sarah Maclachlan

Contributing Statisticians

Bob Borgen, Anthony Buccongello, Wil Curry, Mokke Eronen, Mel Foster and Roger Leblond

Special Thanks

Maidie Oliveau, Arthur Gelgoot

Contributors

Juha Aaltonen, Jarvis Abela, Timo Alenan, Mike Altieri (Los Angeles Kings), Dale Amyotte, Don Andrews, Peter Anson, Kyle Arsenault, Paul Augustine, Mark Babiak, Stephen Bannen, Eric Barlow, David Barr, Patricia Barry, Kenneth Belbin, Art Berglund, Kevin Bixby, Stephen M. Black, Aaron Blackburn, Stephan Blatz, Curt Blood, Stephan Booker, Peter Borkowski, Paul Bouchard, Jeff Brasok, Rick Braunstein, Mike Briscoe, Rick Browrde, Corey Bryant, Mike Buchmann, W. Jack Burr, David J. Candy, James Carr, Paul R. Carroll, Steve Chartrand, Doug Ciceri, Ray Clow, Paul Cohen, Willy Cole, Matthew Condlin, David Cooper, Paul J. Costinett, Bill Crawford, Bryan J. Crider, Gino Cundari, Milan Cupka, Maryann Curry, Paul de Montigny, Vince Demarco, Paul Demers, Jennifer and Mike Denomme, Jacques Des Poelberch, Michel Desrochers, Gaeten Desserault, Mark DeWitt, Ralf Dreschmann, Francois Dupuis, John F. Dyer, Horst Eckert, Thomas Eden, Markku Eronen, Amina Essop, Jason R. Farris, Bruce Fein, Agnes Fisher, Marlene Fitzsimmons, Benjamin H. Foster, Marc Foster, Jamey Foster, Thomas R. Foster, Brad Freedman, Greg Garbutt, John P. Gedwill, Bill Giokas, Dan Gognavic, Gordon Goldbach, Miguel Gomes, John Goodwill, Peter Hanlon (Calgary Flames), Oli Helm, Leslie Hendy, Joachim Herfort, Stephan Herr, Laurie Hershey, Bill Hickey, Bob Hickey, Morey Holzman, Dave Homer, Joseph Houk, Stefan Hulak, Larry Huras, Gregg Inkpen, Gord Jennings, Heather Jessop, Steve Kanehl, James Karkoski, Roger Katz, Scott Kelly, Pat Kennedy, Stanley Kennedy, Pat Kenny, Steve Keough (Ottawa Senators), Bill Kingstone, Rick Kirik, Robert Kirk, Jeff Knott, Hal Knudsen, James Kochicas, Martin Kogler, Peter Kornemark, Ed Kozak, Dave Krause, Richard Kronish, Brad Kurtzberg, Serge Lagace, Richard Laporte, Aulis Lassila, Eric Leblanc, Steve Lederer, Paul Ledoux, Yrjo Leino, Kenneth Lepiez, Steve Leung, Ted E. Lotocki, Darren Lowe, Yuri Lukashin, Mike Machnik, John Mahoney, Claudio Mancini, Alan Mann, John Martin, William Martin, Paul Massop, Doug Mathieson, Pablo Maurelia, Christopher T. McDonald, Charlie McDougall, Penny McEwen, Mark J. Momorella, Gord Montgomery, Paul Montgomery, Herb Morell, Chris Mottola, Kevin S. Mullane, Ross Munro, Mary Murphy, NHL Players' Association, Greg Nesteroff, Michael W. Nicholson, Birger Nordmark, Craig Northey, Michael Orlosky,

Gregg Overguard, Eda Paltanen, Stephan Pang, Stephan Panuto, Pat Park (Toronto Maple Leafs), Joe Pascucci, Kevin J. Patriquin, Jeff Payne, Eric Phaneuf, Curt Phillips, Christine Pickard, Kenneth and Victoria Pietrusiewicz, John Powell, Armando Prato, Tom Prohaska, Ingmar Probst, Robert J. Reid, Tom Rheaume, Valentina Riazanova, Jeff Riddolls, Barry Roberts, Brent Robinson, Michael Rosenthal, Noam Rotenberg, Wille Runquist, Mayer Schiller, Brian Schmella, Robert Schultz, David W. Shepard, Tomi Silvennoinen, Rand Simon, Christine Simpson, George G. Sims, Cheryl Smith, Albert Speisman, Mark Stedman, Donald D. Stewart, A.D. Suehsdorf, Dave Talbot, Natalia Taran, Zhenya Taran, Brett A. Thompson, Rich Topp, Michal Travnicek, Daryl Turner, Jussi Uotila, Peter Vasoff, Linda Verigan, Guy Villeneuve, Randall W. Whatley, Torsten Weiss, W.A. Wheaton, Drew White, Jonas Wiederkehr, Steve Wodz, Jeff Wood, Klaus Zaugg, Anthony Zumpano.

Many persons over many years have contributed to the compilation and maintenance of the historical records of the National Hockey League. Our thanks to these current and former NHL employees and executives for their best efforts:

Susan Aglietti, Ron Andrews, Mark Atcheson, Rhonda Barber, Frank Brown, Mario Carangi, Jocelyne Comeau, Luc Coulombe, Linda Delisi, Lise Desjardins, Susan Elliott, Benny Ercolani, Jane Freer, Gail Glenister, Jim Gregory, Mike Griffin, Dave Griffiths, John Halligan, Gerry Helper, Greg Inglis, Norm Jewison, David Keon, Dan Leary, Roger Leblond, Belinda Lerner, Bryan Lewis, Duane Lewis, Garry Lovegrove, Preston Lovegrove, Ken McKenzie, Gary Meagher, NHL Central Registry, Joel Nixon, Brian O'Neill, Steve Pellegrini, Arthur Pincus, Carol Randall, Jackie Rinaldi, Carole Robertson, Michelle Romanin, Kelley Rossett, Madeline Supino, Chris Tredree, Hilda Turrif, Julie Young.

REFERENCES

Books: (Author/editor names follow book titles where appropriate) *NHL Entry Draft Book, NHL Official Guide & Record Book, NHL Guide, NHL Playoff Fact Guide, NHL Official Rule Book, NHL Year in Review, The Hockey News, Total Stanley Cup, The Hockey Encyclopedia* (Stan and Shirley Fischler with Bob Duff), *The Sporting News,* media guides from NHL teams, minor pro and junior leagues, *The Trail of the Stanley Cup* (Charles Coleman), *College Hockey Guide, Junior Hockey Guide and Prep School Guide* (Athletic Guide Publishing), *Eishockey Almanach* (Horst Eckert), *The Ice Hockey Annual* (Stewart Roberts), *Eishockey News, Eishockey* (Klaus Zaugg), *Jääkiekkokirja* (Arne Honkavaara), *Canada's Olympic Hockey Teams: The Complete History 1920-1998* (Andrew Podnieks), *Canada on Ice* (Robert Kirk), *Canadian Hockey Magazine, The (Annotated) Rules of Hockey* (James Duplacey), *USA Hockey* (Kevin Allen) *United States Hockey Hall of Fame* souvenir book, *Hockey Night in Hollywood* (Willie Runquist), *World Hockey Association 1972–1979* (Scott Surgent) and *Mackie's Hockey Atlas* (Roy W. Mackie).

Web sites:

www.hockeydb.com
www.eurohockey.com
www.eurohockey.net
www.iihf.com/index.htm
www.hockeyresearch.com/stats
www.lhspq.qc.ca
www.ptialaska.net/~carlsonj/uafhockey/ehockey.html
www.cyberbeach.net/~pelland/index.html
jimcarroll.forbin.com/blackhawks/preplinks/prepmain.htm
www.lhjaaaq.qc.ca/
cjahl.com/
www.weihenstephan.org/~michpohl/transdel_vor.html
www.minorhockey.net/dir1.html

LEAGUE AND INTERNATIONAL EVENT ABBREVIATIONS

LEAGUES

AAHA	Alberta Amateur Hockey Association
AAHL	All-American Hockey League (1987-88)
AAHL	Alaska Amateur Hockey League
AIHA	Alberta Intermediate Hockey Association (pre-1967)
ABCHL	Alberta-British Columbia Hockey League (1941-1947)
ACHL	Atlantic Coast Hockey League (1981-1987)
ACSHL	Atlantic Coast Senior Hockey League
AHA	American Hockey Association
AHAC	Amateur Hockey Association of Canada
AHL	American Hockey League (1940 to date)
AIAA	Atlantic Intercollegiate Athletic Association
AJHL	Alberta Junior Hockey Leagues
Alpenliga	Alpenliga (Austria, Italy, Slovenia 1994-1999)
AmAHL	American Amateur Hockey League
AMHL	Alberta Midget Hockey League
ASHL	Alberta Senior Hockey Leagues
AUAA	Atlantic University Athletic Association
Austria	Osterreichischer Eishockeyverband (OEHV)
BCAHA	British Columbia Amateur Hockey Association
BCBHL	British Columbia Boundary Hockey League
BCHA-I	British Columbia Hockey Association – Intermediate (aka BCIHA)
BCIHA	British Columbia Intermediate Hockey Association (pre-1967)
BCJHL	British Columbia Junior Hockey League
BCNDL	British Columbia National Defense League (aka Northern National Defense Hockey League)
Belgium	Belgium Elite Isjhockey Liga
BFCHL	Bishops Falls City Hockey League
BHL	Boundary Hockey League (aka BDHL, WKHL)
Big-4	Alberta Big-4 Hockey League (1919-20)
Big-4	Maritime Senior Big-4 League (1946-1951)
Big-6	Manitoba Big-6 Hockey League
Britain	British Premier/Super League
Britain-2	British National League
BSrHL	Boston Senior Hockey League (aka MBSHL)
CAHA	Canadian Amateur Hockey Association
CAHL	Canadian Amateur Hockey League
CAHL	Central Alberta Hockey League (1955-1964)
Cal-Pro	California Professional Hockey League (1925-1933)
Can-Am	Canadian-American Hockey League
Can-Pro	Canadian Professional Hockey League
CASH	Canadian-American Senior Hockey League (1980-1991)
CBMHL	Cape Breton Major Hockey League (1950-51)
CBSHL	Cape Breton Senior Hockey Leagues
CCAU	Canadian Colleges Athletic Union
CCHA	Central Collegiate Hockey Association
CCJHL	Calgary City Junior Hockey Leagues
CCPHL	City of Chicago Professional Hockey League
CCSHL	Calgary City Senior Hockey Leagues
CCSHL	Central Canada Senior Hockey League (1977-78)
CEGEP	Quebec College Prep
CHA	Canadian Hockey Association
CHL	Central Hockey League (1925-1941)
CHL	Central Hockey League (1968-1985)
CHL	Central Hockey League (1992 to date)
CIAU	Canadian Interuniversity Athletic Union
CIHU	Canadian Intercollegiate Hockey Union
CIS	Commonwealth of Independent States
CMJHL	Canadian Major Junior Hockey League (1966-67)
CNDHL	Calgary National Defense Hockey League (1941-1945)
CoMHL	Cobalt Mines Hockey League
ColHL	Colonial Hockey League (1991-1997)
CPHL	Central Professional Hockey League (1963-1968)
CWUAA	Canadian Western University Athletic Association
Czech.	Czechoslovakian Elite League (1922-1983)
Czech-Rep	Czech Republic Hokeje Extraliga (1983 to date)
Denmark	Denmarks Ishockey Union
EAHL	Eastern Amateur Hockey League (1933-1948, 1949-1953)
ECAC	Eastern College Athletic Conference
ECAHA	* Eastern Canada Amateur Hockey Association
ECHA	Eastern Canada Hockey Association
ECHA	Eastern Collegiate Hockey Association (1991 to date)
ECHL	Eastern Canada Professional Hockey League (1914-15)
ECHL	East Coast Hockey League (1988 to date)
ECSHL	Eastern Canada Senior Hockey League
EJrHL	Edmonton Junior Hockey Leagues
ESrHL	Edmonton Senior Hockey Leagues
EHL	Eastern Hockey League (1954-1973)
EHL	Eastern Hockey League (1979-1981)
EmJHL	Empire State Junior Hockey League
EOHL	Eastern Ontario Senior Hockey League
EPHL	Eastern Professional Hockey League (1959-1963)
ETSHL	Eastern Townships Senior Hockey League
EuroHL	European Hockey League (1995-2000)
X-Games	Exhibition Games, Series or Season
FAHL	Federal Amateur Hockey League
Finland	Suomien Jääkiekkoliitto SM Liiga (1975 to date)
Finland-Q	Finland Ice Hockey League Qualification Round
France	French National Hockey Association
Germany	Bundesliga/Deutsche Eishockey Liga
Germany-Q	Bundesliga/Deutsche Eishockey Liga Qualification Round
GBHL	Gold Belt Hockey League (1935-1945)
GBSHL	Georgian Bay Senior Hockey League (1978-1980)
GPAC	Great Plains Athletic Conference
HCHL	Halifax City Hockey League
H-East	Hockey East (1984 to date)
Hi-School	High School (post-1967)
HOHL	Hull-Ottawa Hockey League
Holland	Nederlandse Ijshockey Super Liga
H.S.	High School (Pre-1967)
IAHL	International-American Hockey League (1936 - 1940)
IEL	Internationale Eishockey Liga (1999-2000)
IJHL	Interstate Junior Hockey League
IHL	* International Professional Hockey League (1904 - 1907)
IHL	International Hockey League (1929-1936)
IHL	International Hockey League (1945 to date)
IIHL	International Intercollegiate Hockey League
IPAHU	Inter-Provincial Hockey Union
Italy	Italian National Hockey Association
Ivy	Ivy League Collegiate Hockey Division
Japan	Japanese Ice Hockey Federation (1966 to date)
KCHL	Kingston City Hockey League
KNDHL	Kingston National Defense Hockey League
LOHA	Lower Ottawa Hockey Association
LSJHL	Lower St. Lawrence Junior Hockey League
LSLHL	Lower St. Lawrence Hockey League
L-W-S	Little World Series (1935)
Man-Pro	* Manitoba Professional Hockey League (1907-1909)
MAHA	Manitoba Amateur Hockey Association
MIHA	Manitoba Intermediate Hockey Association (pre-1967)
MASHL	Mass-Amateur Senior Hockey League
MBAHA	Metropolitan Boston Amateur Hockey Association
MBHL	Montreal Banking Hockey League
MBSHL	Metropolitan Boston Senior Hockey League
MCBHL	Montreal City Bank Hockey League
MCHL	Montreal City Hockey League
MCJHL	Moncton City-Junior Hockey League
MCSHL	Moncton City-Senior Hockey League
MCIHL	Moncton City-Industrial Hockey League
MHA-I	Manitoba Hockey Association – Intermediate (post-1967)
MHL-Sr.	Manitoba Senior Hockey Leagues (1909 to date)
MIAA	Maritime Intercollegiate Athletic Union
MIAU	Michigan Intercollegiate Athletic Union
MIHL	Maritime Independent Hockey League
MIPHL	Manitoba Inter-Provincial Hockey League
MISSHL	Moncton Inter-Scholastic Hockey League
MJHL	Manitoba Junior Hockey League
MJJHL	Moose Jaw Junior Hockey League
MMHL	Maritime Major Hockey League
MNDHL	Moncton National Defense Hockey League
MOHL	Michigan-Ontario Hockey League
MPHL	* Maritime Professional Hockey League
MSHL	Maritime Senior Hockey League
MTBHL	Manitoba-Thunder Bay Hockey League
MTHL	Metro Toronto Hockey League
MTJHL	Metro Toronto Junior Hockey League (1961-1963)
MNHL	Michigan National Hockey League (Midget AAA)
MMJHL	Metropolitan Montreal Junior Hockey League
MMRHL	Montreal Mount Royal Hockey League
MRTHL	Montreal Radio-Telegraph Hockey League
MWJHL	Mid-West Junior Hockey League
NBAHA	New Brunswick Amateur Hockey Association
NFAHA	Newfoundland Amateur Hockey Association
NAHL	North American Hockey League
Nat-Team	National Teams
NBAHA	New Brunswick Amateur Hockey Association
NBHA-I	New Brunswick Intermediate Hockey League
NBHL	Nickel Belt Hockey League (1935-1945)
NBJHL	New Brunswick Junior Hockey Leagues
NBNDL	New Brunswick National Defense League
NBPEI	New Brunswick-Prince Edward Island Leagues
NBSHL	New Brunswick Senior Hockey Leagues
NCAA	National Collegiate Athletic Association
NCHA	Northern Collegiate Hockey Association
NDHL	National Defense Hockey League (1940-1946)
NEHL	North East Hockey League

LEAGUE AND INTERNATIONAL EVENT ABBREVIATIONS *continued*

NESHL New England Senior Hockey League
Nfld-Jr. Newfoundland Junior Hockey League
Nfld-Sr. Newfoundland Senior Hockey League
NHA * National Hockey Association (1909-1917)
NHL * National Hockey League (1917 to date)
NMHL Northern Michigan Hockey League
NNBSL Northern New Brunswick Senior Hockey League (1920-1999)
NNDHL Northern National Defense Hockey League (1940-1946)
NOHA Northern Ontario Hockey Association
NOJHA Northern Ontario Junior Hockey Association
NOHL Northern Ontario Hockey League
NOIHA Northern Ontario Intermediate Hockey Association
Norway Norges Ishockey Forbund Elite League
N-SJHL Northern Saskatchewan Junior Hockey League (1918-1945)
N-SSHL Northern Saskatchewan Senior Hockey League (1918-1945)
NSAHA Nova Scotia Amateur Hockey Association
NSAPC Nova Scotia-Annapolis-Pictou County Hockey League
NSNDL Nova Scotia National Defense League (1940-46)
NSSHL Nova Scotia Senior Hockey League
Nt-Team National Team (Pre-1967)
NWHL North West Hockey League
NWIHL North West International Hockey League (1936-1944)
NYHL New York Hockey League (aka NYSHL)
NYJHL New York Junior Hockey Leagues
NYOHL New York-Ontario Senior Hockey League
NYSHL New York Senior Hockey League (aka NYHL)
OHA Ontario Hockey Association (1893 to 1967)
OHA-I Ontario Hockey Association – Intermediate (post-1967)
OHA-Jr. Ontario Hockey Association Junior "A" Hockey League (1909 - 1971)
OHA-Sr. Ontario Hockey Association Senior "A" Hockey League (1909 - 1988)
OHL Ontario Hockey League (1981 to date)
OIHA Ontario Intermediate Hockey Association (pre-1967)
OJHL Ontario Junior "A" Hockey Leagues
OMHA Ontario Minor Hockey Association (1971 to date)
OMHL Ontario Major Hockey League (1950-51)
OMJHL Ontario Major Junior Hockey League (1971-1981)
OPHL * Ontario Professional Hockey League (1909-1911)
OPHL Ontario Professional Hockey League (1930–31)
OCJHL Ottawa City Junior Hockey League (1890-1990)
OCSHL Ottawa City Senior Hockey League (1890-1990)
ONDHL Ottawa National Defense Hockey League (aka OCHL 1940-1947)
OKML Okanagan Mainline Hockey League
OQAA Ontario-Quebec Athletic Association (1960-1971)
OSHL Okanogan Senior Hockey League
OSBHL Ontario Senior "B" Hockey Leagues (pre-1967)
OSrBL Ontario Senior "B" Hockey Leagues (aka OSrB)
OUAA Ontario University Athletic Association (1971 to date)
OVHL Ottawa Valley Hockey League (aka OVSHL)
OVJHL Ottawa Valley Junior Hockey League
OVSHL Ottawa Valley Senior Hockey League (aka OVHL)
PCHA * Pacific Coast Hockey Association (1911-1924)
PCHL Pacific Coast Hockey League
PEIHA Prince Edward Island Amateur Hockey Association
PEI-Jr. Prince Edward Island Junior Hockey League
PEI-Sr. Prince Edward Island Senior Hockey League
PHL Pacific Hockey League (1977-1979)
PIJHL Pacific International Junior Hockey League
PrHL Prairie Hockey League
PYHL Pembroke Youth House League
QAAA Quebec Amateur Athletic Association
QAHA-I Quebec Amateur Athletic Association - Intermediate (post-1967)
QIHA Quebec Intermediate Hockey Association (pre-1967)
QCHL Quebec City Hockey League
QCSHL Quebec Central Senior Hockey League (1996 to date)
QHL Quebec Hockey League (1953-1959)
QIPHL Quebec Interprovincial Hockey League (aka QPHL)
QJHL Quebec Junior Hockey Leagues (1893 to date)
QMHL Quebec Major Hockey League (1950-1953)
QMJHL Quebec Major Junior Hockey League
QPHL Quebec Provincial Hockey League
QSPHL Quebec Semi-Pro Hockey League (1996 to date)
QSHL Quebec Senior Hockey League (1920-1950, 1959-1994)
QUAA Quebec University Athletic Association (1971 to date)
RCJHL Regina City Junior Hockey League
RHI Roller Hockey International (1990-1997, 1998-2000)
RMJHL Rocky Mountain Junior Hockey League
RMSHL Rocky Mountain Senior Hockey League
RNDHL Regina National Defense Hockey League (1941-1945)
RSrHL Regina City Senior Hockey League
SAHA Saskatchewan Amateur Hockey Association
SAHA-I Amateur Hockey Association - Intermediate (post-1967)
SCJHL Saskatoon City Junior Hockey League
Scotland Scottish National Hockey Association (1930-1960)
SCSHL Southern California Senior Hockey League (1992-1994)
SHL Southern Hockey League (1973 - 1976)
SHL Southern Hockey League (1995 - 1997)
SIHA Saskatchewan Intermediate Hockey Association (pre-1967)
SJCHL St. John's City Hockey League
SJHL Saskatchewan Junior Hockey League
SJSHL St. John's Senior Hockey League
Slovakia Slovakia Republic Extraleague
Slovenia Slovenian Elite League
SLSHL St. Lawrence Senior Hockey League
SLVHL St. Lawrence Valley Hockey League
SNBHL Southern New Brunswick Hockey League
Spain Hielo Espanola Nationale Liga
SPHL Saskatchewan Professional Hockey League (aka Ssk-Pro)
S-SJHL Southern Saskatchewan Junior Hockey League (1918-1945)
S-SSHL Southern Saskatchewan Senior Hockey League (1918-1945)
SSHL Saskatchewan Senior Hockey League (1942-1980)
SunHL Sunshine Hockey League (1992-1995)
Sweden Svenska Ishockeyförbundet Elitserien
Sweden-Q Swedish Elitserien Qualification Round
Switz. Schweizerischer Eishockeyverband
TBIHA Thunder Bay Intermediate Hockey Association
TBJHL Thunder Bay Junior Hockey League
TBSHL Thunder Bay Senior Hockey League
TIHL Toronto Independent Hockey League
TJrHL Toronto Junior Hockey League
TMHL Toronto Mercantile Hockey League
TNDHL Toronto National Defense Hockey League (1942-1945)
TPHL Temiskaming Professional Hockey League
TSrHL Toronto Senior Hockey Leagues
Tri-State Tri-State Senior Hockey League (1932-33)
UHL United Hockey League (1998 to date)
USAHA United States Amateur Hockey Association
USHL United States (Pro) Hockey League (1945-1951)
USHL United States (Sr.) Hockey League (1960-1979)
USHL United States (Jr.) Hockey League (1979 to date)
USNHL United States National Hockey League (1916-17)
USSR Union of Soviet Socialist Republics (1946-1992)
VCAHL Vancouver City Amateur Hockey League (1925-1930)
WCHA Western Collegiate Hockey Association
WCHL * Western Canada Hockey League (1921-1925)
WCHL West Coast Hockey League (1995 to date)
WCIAA Western Canada Intercollegiate Athletic Association
WGHL Wild Goose (Saskatchewan) Hockey League
WJrHL Winnipeg Junior Hockey League
WKHL Western Kootenay Hockey League (1933-1946)
WKJHL Western Kootenay Junior Hockey League (1933-1946)
WNDHL Winnipeg National Defense Hockey League
WSrHL Winnipeg Senior Hockey League
WCIAU Western Canada Intercollegiate Athletic Union
WCJHL Western Canadian Junior Hockey League (1968 to date)
WCSHL Western Canada Senior Hockey League
WHA * World Hockey Association
WHL * Western Hockey League (1925–26)
WHL Western Hockey League (1951 to 1975)
WHL Western Canada Major Junior Hockey League (1977 to date)
WIHA Western Intercollegiate Hockey Association USA
WCMHL Western Canada Major Hockey League (1951-52)
WIHL Western International Hockey League (1947-1987)
WOHL Western Ontario Senior Hockey League
WPHL Western Pennsylvania Hockey League (1903, 1907-08)
WPHL Western Professional Hockey League (1995 to date)
WRMHL Western Rocky Mountain Hockey League
YCHL York County (New Brunswick) Hockey League

NOTES:

- Second, third and fourth division leagues in Europe are indicated by country name and division number (e.g. Germany-2, Austria-3, Italy -4).
- Junior B, C, and D leagues in Canada and the USA are indicated by the league name and letter (e.g. OHA-B, SJHL-C).
- European Junior leagues are indicated by country name plus "-Jr." (e.g. Finland-Jr.) European Junior B and C teams are indicated by team name followed by "-B," "-C" etc. (e.g. MoDo AIK-B).
- European clubs that operate additional teams in lower divisions are indicated by the team name followed by "-2" or "-3."
- An asterisk (*) indicates a major league. See Chapter 68, page 611, Introduction to the Player Registers.

INTERNATIONAL EVENTS

Can-Cup Canada Cup 1976, 1981, 1984, 1987, 1991
Chal-Cup NHL–Soviet Challenge Cup 1979
DN-Cup NHL–Sweden Dagens Nyheter Cup (1981, 1982)
EJC-A IIHF European Junior Championships, Pool A
Fr-Tour NHL–Soviet Friendship Tour
Olympics Winter Olympic Games 1924 to 1998
RV-87 Rendez-Vouz '87
Summit-72 Canada (NHL) Soviet Summit Series 1972
Summit-74 Canada (WHA) Soviet Summit Series 1974
Super-S NHL-Soviet Super Series
W-Cup World Cup of Hockey 1996
WC-A IIHF World Championships, Pool A
WC-B IIHF World Championships, Pool B
WC-C IIHF World Championships, Pool C
WC-C1 IIHF World Championships, Pool C, Group 1
WC-C2 IIHF World Championships, Pool C, Group 2
WC-D IIHF World Championships, Pool D
WEC IIHF World and European Championships
WEC-A IIHF World and European Championships, Pool A
WEC-B IIHF World and European Championships, Pool B
WEC-C IIHF World and European Championships, Pool C
WEC-D IIHF World and European Championships, Pool D
WJC-A IIHF World Junior Championships, Pool A
WJC-B IIHF World Junior Championships, Pool B
WJC-C IIHF World Junior Championships, Pool C
WJC-C1 IIHF World Junior Championships, Pool C, Group 1
WJC-C2 IIHF World Junior Championships, Pool C, Group 2
WJC-D IIHF World Junior Championships, Pool D

SPECIALTY CUP EVENTS

Al-Cup Allan Cup (Canadian Senior Hockey Championships 1909 to date)
Alx-Cup Alexander Cup (Canadian Major Senior Hockey Championships 1950-1953)
A-Cup Autumn Cup (Britain1930-1960)
Aut-Cup Autumn Trophy (Britain 1980-1990)
BH-Cup Benson & Hedges Cup (Britain 1991 to date)
Cen-Cup Centennial Cup (Canadian Junior "A" Championships 1971-1996)
Ed-Cup Edinburgh Trophy (WHL/QHL Challenge Series 1953-1956)
Ln-Cup London Cup (Britain Pre-Season Tournament 1930-1960)
M-Cup Memorial Cup (Canadian Junior Hockey Championships (1919-1967)
Mem-Cup Memorial Cup (Canadian Major Junior Hockey Championships (1968 to date)
Nat-Tmt Britain National Hockey Challenge Tournament
St-Cup Stanley Cup Challenge Series (1893-1926)

ACCURACY AND COMPREHENSIVENESS

remain *Total Hockey*'s top priorities.
We appreciate clarification and comments from our readers.
Please direct these to:

Total Hockey
194 Dovercourt Road
Toronto, Ontario
Canada M6J 3C8

To contact us by e-mail:
For comments regarding statistics:
jj.nhl@sympatico.ca
For comments regarding features:
dda.nhl@sympatico.ca

Readers who correct errors or contribute in other ways will be acknowledged in future editions.

Your involvement makes a better book.